usw.	und so weiter
v.	von
V.	Verb
verächtl.	verächtlich
veralt.	veraltet; veraltend
Verhaltensf.	Verhaltensforschung
verhüll.	verhüllend
Verkehrsw.	Verkehrswesen
Vermessungsw.	Vermessungswesen
Versicherungsw.	Versicherungswesen
vgl.	vergleiche
Vkl.	Verkleinerungsform
Völkerk.	Völkerkunde
Völkerr.	Völkerrecht
Volksk.	Volkskunde
volkst.	volkstümlich
vulg.	vulgär
Werbespr.	Werbesprache
westd.	westdeutsch
westfäl.	westfälisch
Wiederholungsz.	Wiederholungszahlwort
wiener.	wienerisch
Winzerspr.	Winzersprache
Wirtsch.	Wirtschaft
Wissensch.	Wissenschaft
Wz.	Warenzeichen
Zahnmed.	Zahnmedizin
z. B.	zum Beispiel
Zeitungsw.	Zeitungswesen
Zollw.	Zollwesen
Zool.	Zoologie
Zus.	Zusammensetzung
Zusschr.	Zusammenschreibung
*****	alte Schreibung

English abbreviations used in this dictionary

Im Wörterverzeichnis verwendete englische Abkürzungen

abbr(s).	abbreviation(s)
abs.	absolute
adj(s).	adjective(s)
Admin.	Administration, Administrative
adv.	adverb
Aeronaut.	Aeronautics
Agric.	Agriculture
Alch.	Alchemy
Amer.	American, America
Anat.	Anatomy
Anglican Ch.	Anglican Church
Anglo-Ind.	Anglo-Indian
Ant.	Antiquity
Anthrop.	Anthropology
arch.	archaic
Archaeol.	Archaeology
Archit.	Architecture
art.	article
Astrol.	Astrology
Astron.	Astronomy
Astronaut.	Astronautics
attrib.	attributive
Austral.	Australian, Australia
Bacteriol.	Bacteriology
Bibl.	Biblical
Bibliog.	Bibliography
Biochem.	Biochemistry
Biol.	Biology
Bookk.	Bookkeeping
Bot.	Botany
Brit.	British, Britain
Can.	Canadian, Canada
Chem.	Chemistry
Cinemat.	Cinematography
coll.	colloquial
collect.	collective
comb.	combination
Commerc.	Commerce, Commercial
Communication Res.	Communication Research
compar.	comparative
condit.	conditional
conj.	conjunction
Constr.	Construction
constr.	construed
contr.	contracted form
def.	definite
Dent.	Dentistry
derog.	derogatory
dial.	dialect
Diplom.	Diplomacy
Dressm.	Dressmaking
Eccl.	Ecclesiastical
Ecol.	Ecology
Econ.	Economics
Educ.	Education
Electr.	Electricity
ellipt.	elliptical
emphat.	emphatic
esp.	especially
Ethnol.	Ethnology
Ethol.	Ethology
euphem.	euphemistic
excl.	exclamation, exclamatory
expr.	expressing
fem.	feminine
fig.	figurative
Footb.	Football
Gastr.	Gastronomy
Geneal.	Genealogy
Geog.	Geography
Geol.	Geology
Geom.	Geometry
Graph. Arts	Graphic Arts
Her.	Heraldry
Hist.	History, Historical
Horol.	Horology
Hort.	Horticulture
Hydraulic Engin.	Hydraulic Engineering
imper.	imperative
impers.	impersonal
incl.	including
Ind.	Indian, India
indef.	indefinite
Information Sci.	Information Science
int.	interjection
interrog.	interrogative
Int. Law	International Law
Ir.	Irish, Ireland
iron.	ironical
joc.	jocular
Journ.	Journalism
lang.	language
Ling.	Linguistics
Lit.	Literature
lit.	literal
Magn.	Magnetism
Managem.	Management
masc.	masculine
Math.	Mathematics
Mech.	Mechanics
Mech. Engin.	Mechanical Engineering
Med.	Medicine
Metalw.	Metalwork
Metaph.	Metaphysics
Meteorol.	Meteorology
Mil.	Military
Min.	Mineralogy
Motor Veh.	Motor Vehicles
Mount.	Mountaineering
Mus.	Music
Mythol.	Mythology
n.	noun
Nat. Sci.	Natural Science
Naut.	Nautical
neg.	negative
N. Engl.	Northern English
ns.	nouns
Nucl. Engin.	Nuclear Engineering
Nucl. Phys.	Nuclear Physics
Num.	Numismatics
N.Z.	New Zealand
obj.	object
Oceanog.	Oceanography
Ornith.	Ornithology
Palaeont.	Palaeontology
Parapsych.	Parapsychology
Parl.	Parliament
pass.	passive
Pharm.	Pharmacy
Philat.	Philately
Philos.	Philosophy
Phonet.	Phonetics
Photog.	Photography
phr(s).	phrase(s)
Phys.	Physics
Physiol.	Physiology
pl.	plural
poet.	poetical
Polit.	Politics
poss.	possessive
postpos.	postpositive
p.p.	past participle
pred.	predicative
pref.	prefix
Prehist.	Prehistory
prep.	preposition
pres.	present
pres. p.	present participle
pr. n.	proper noun
pron.	pronoun
Pros.	Prosody
prov.	proverbial
Psych.	Psychology
p.t.	past tense
®	registered trade mark
Railw.	Railways
RC Ch.	Roman Catholic Church
refl.	reflexive
rel.	relative
Relig.	Religion
Res.	Research
Rhet.	Rhetoric
rhet.	rhetorical
S. Afr.	South African, South Africa
sb.	somebody
Sch.	School
Sci.	Science
Scot.	Scottish, Scotland
Shipb.	Shipbuilding
sing.	singular
sl.	slang
Sociol.	Sociology
Soc. Serv.	Social Services
Soil Sci.	Soil Science
St. Exch.	Stock Exchange
sth.	something
subord.	subordinate
suf.	suffix
superl.	superlative
Surv.	Surveying
symb.	symbol
tech.	technical
Teleph.	Telephony
Telev.	Television
Theol.	Theology
Univ.	University
usu.	usually
v. aux.	auxiliary verb
Vet. Med.	Veterinary Medicine
v. i.	intransitive verb
voc.	vocative
v. refl.	reflexive verb
v. t.	transitive verb
v. t. & i.	transitive and intransitive verb
W. Ind.	West Indian, West Indies
Woodw.	Woodwork
Zool.	Zoology

Oxford German Dictionary

Oxford German Dictionary

Third Edition

German–English • English–German

Chief Editors

W. Scholze-Stubenrecht • J. B. Sykes

Third Edition edited by

M. Clark • O. Thyen

OXFORD
UNIVERSITY PRESS

Great Clarendon Street, Oxford OX2 6DP

Oxford University Press is a department of the University of Oxford. It furthers the University's objective of excellence in research, scholarship, and education by publishing worldwide in

Oxford New York
Auckland Cape Town Dar es Salaam Hong Kong Karachi
Kuala Lumpur Madrid Melbourne Mexico City Nairobi
New Delhi Shanghai Taipei Toronto
With offices in

Argentina Austria Brazil Chile Czech Republic France Greece
Guatemala Hungary Italy Japan Poland Portugal Singapore
South Korea Switzerland Thailand Turkey Ukraine Vietnam

Oxford is a registered trade mark of Oxford University Press in the UK and in certain other countries

Published in the United States
by Oxford University Press Inc., New York

First published 1990
Reprinted in enlarged format 1994
Revised edition 1997
Second edition 1999
Reissue 2001
Third edition 2005, Reissue 2008

British Library Cataloguing in Publication Data
Data available

Library of Congress Cataloging in Publication Data
Data available

ISBN 978-0-19-954568-1

Typeset in Swift, Arial and Meta
by Interactive Sciences Ltd, Gloucester
Printed in China
via C&C Offset Ltd

5497551859844998

Preface

For this edition of the *Oxford German Dictionary* the design has been transformed by the use of colour and a new visual presentation, making it even more accessible and easy to use. Coverage has been increased and updated to take account of new vocabulary and recent developments in German and English. Thousands of additional words and phrases, selected using the unparalleled databases maintained and continually expanded for the 5 celebrated native-speaker dictionaries such as the *Concise Oxford Dictionary of English* and *Das große Wörterbuch der deutschen Sprache*, reflect scientific and technological innovations, particularly in the field of information technology, as well as changes in politics, culture, and society.

Notes on the life and culture of the German- and English-speaking countries of the world, new to this third edition, greatly extend the range of information provided in the text of the dictionary. Detailed usage boxes are also included to help with important areas of grammar and vocabulary. They highlight differences between German and English which may create difficulty for the learner and translator, explaining them in detail, and provide clear illustrative examples. Other boxes give the user key facts about types of words that behave alike, for example, names of towns and cities, languages, numbers, and days of the week. They provide ways of discussing topics such as age, dates, time, and measurements and offer essential practical information on asking the way, formulating greetings, apologizing, and letter-writing. Cross-references to the boxes are given at all the relevant entries, making them easily accessible points of reference for students and valuable aids to teaching. This new edition also includes a correspondence section giving models for communicating by letter in a wide range of situations, and guidance on using the telephone and on SMS messaging.

The editors are confident that the new features and expanded, up-to-date coverage will enhance the reputation of the *Oxford German Dictionary* as the leading and most authoritative reference tool for school, college, and university students, business people, and all those who require the fullest possible information on German and English in a single volume.

MICHAEL CLARK
Oxford University Press

Als Markenzeichen geschützte Wörter / Note on Proprietary Status

Editors and Contributors

Third Edition

Michael Clark
Olaf Thyen
Robin Sawers
Werner Scholze-Stubenrecht
Bernadette Mohan
Eva Vennebusch
Magdalena Seubel
Brigitte Alsleben
Neil Morris
Roswitha Morris

Data Input

Susan Wilkin
Anne McConnell

First Edition

John Sykes
Werner Scholze-Stubenrecht
Michael Clark
Roland Breitsprecher
Olaf Thyen
Robin Sawers
Brigitte Alsleben
Vineeta Gupta
Bernadette Mohan
Eckhard Böhle
Maria Dose
Gabriele Gassen
Colin Hope
Maurice Waite
John Pheby
Eva Vennebusch
Clare Rütsch
Wolfgang Eckey
Eva Krampe
Judith Cunningham
Susanne Lücking
Marion Trunk-Nußbaumer
Valerie Langrish
Christopher Burton
Timothy Connell

Inhalt / Contents

Erläuterungen zum deutsch–englischen Text / Key to German–English Entries

1 Stichwort und Aussprache / Headword and pronunciation

Stichwort. Alle Einträge sind streng alphabetisch angeordnet
Headword. All entries are listed in strict alphabetical order

bịndend *Adj.* binding (**für** on); definite ‹*answer*›

Bịnder *der;* **~s, ~** [1] (Krawatte) tie [2] (Bindemittel) binder [3] (Landw.) [reaper-]binder [4] (Bauw.: Stein) header [5] (Bauw.: Dachbalken) [roof] truss

Binderei *die;* **~, ~en** [1] (Blumen~) wreath and bouquet department [2] (Buch~) bindery

Bịnde-: ~strich *der* hyphen; **~wort** *das; Pl.* **~wörter** (Sprachw.) conjunction

Kompositablock. Eine Tilde ersetzt jeweils den gemeinsamen ersten Bestandteil der Komposita
Compound block with a swung dash representing the first element of each compound

Bịnd·faden *der* string; **ein [Stück] ~:** a piece of string; **es regnet Bindfäden** (ugs.) it's raining cats and dogs (coll.)

Die Ausspracheangaben (in IPA-Lautschrift) stehen unmittelbar hinter dem Stichwort (s. S. xviii). Die Aussprache eines Kompositums ohne Ausspracheangabe lässt sich von derjenigen seiner Bestandteile herleiten
Pronunciation is shown in IPA immediately after the headword (see p. xviii).The pronunciation of a compound where none is given can be derived from the pronunciations of its elements

Bischof /ˈbɪʃɔf/ *der;* **~s, Bischöfe** /ˈbɪʃœfə/, **Bịschöfin** *die;* **~, ~nen** bishop

Bremse[1] /ˈbrɛmzə/ *die;* **~, ~n** brake; **auf die ~ treten** put on the brakes

Brẹmse[2] *die;* **~, ~n** (Insekt) horsefly

Mehrere gleich geschriebene, aber nicht bedeutungsgleiche Wörter erscheinen als separate Stichwörter und sind mit hochgestellten Ziffern nummeriert
Headwords spelt the same but with different meanings are entered separately with a raised number

Buxtehude /bʊkstəˈhuːdə/ *in* **in/aus/nach ~** (fig. ugs.) at/from/to the back of beyond

Buy-out /ˈbaj̯aut/ *das;* **~s, ~s** (Wirtsch.) buyout

Buzzer /ˈbazɐ/ *der;* **~s, ~:** buzzer

BV *Abk.* (schweiz.) = **Bundesversammlung**

BVG *Abk.* [1] = **Bundesverwaltungsgericht** [2] = **Bundesverfassungsgericht** [3] = **Betriebsverfassungsgesetz**

b.w. *Abk.* = **bitte wenden** P.T.O.

BWL *Abk.* ▸**Betriebswirtschaftslehre**

Bypass /ˈbaipas/ *der;* **~es, Bypässe** (Med.) bypass

Auch Abkürzungen und Akronyme sind streng alphabetisch eingeordnet
Abbreviations and acronyms follow the same strict alphabetical order as other headwords

Ein senkrechter Strich nach dem ersten Bestandteil eines zusammengesetzten Verbs zeigt an, dass es sich um eine unfeste Zusammensetzung handelt
A vertical bar indicates that a compound verb is separable

dar|bieten (geh.)
[A] *unr. tr. V.* [1] (anbieten) offer; serve ‹*drinks, food*›; **die dargebotene Hand ausschlagen** (fig.) reject the proffered hand [of friendship] (fig.) [2] (aufführen, vortragen) perform; **es wurden Gedichte und Lieder dargeboten** a recital of poems and songs was presented

dar|legen *tr. V.* explain; set forth ‹*reasons, facts*›; expound ‹*theory*›; **jmdm. etw. ~:** explain sth. to sb.; **etw. schriftlich ~:** set sth. out in writing

Ein unter einen Vokal gesetzter waagerechter Strich zeigt die Länge des Vokals und in mehrsilbigen Wörtern zugleich die Betonung der betreffenden Silbe an
An underline indicates a long vowel, stressed in words of more than one syllable

Ein hochgestellter Stern vor einem Stichwort zeigt an, dass es sich um eine alte, künftig nicht mehr gültige Schreibung handelt. (Siehe die Hinweise zur Rechtschreibreform des Deutschen auf S. 1727)
Asterisk indicating old spelling. (See note on the revision of German spelling on p. 1727)

dass, *daß /das/ *Konj.* [1] that; **entschuldigen Sie bitte, ~ ich mich verspätet habe** please forgive me for being late; please forgive my being late; **ich weiß, ~ du Recht hast** I know [that] you are right; **ich verstehe nicht, ~ sie ihn geheiratet hat** I don't understand why she married him;

Erläuterungen zum deutsch–englischen Text

Ein in mittlerer Höhe auf der Zeile stehender Punkt im Stichwort markiert die Kompositionsfuge eines Kompositums
A dot marks the juncture of the elements of a compound

Degenerations·erscheinung *die* sign of degeneration

eggen *tr. V.* (Landw.) harrow

Ein unter einen Vokal gesetzter Punkt zeigt die Kürze des Vokals und in mehrsilbigen Wörtern zugleich die Betonung der betreffenden Silbe an
An underdot indicates a short vowel, stressed in words of more than one syllable

2 Grammatische Angaben / Grammatical information

Grammatische Gliederungspunkte und Wortartangaben
Grammatical categories and parts of speech

ehrenhaft
A *Adj.* honourable ‹*intentions, person*›; **ein ~er Mann** an honourable man; a man of honour
B *adv.* ‹*act*› honourably

Die Formen des Genitivs und des Plurals eines Substantivs
Genitive and plural forms of a noun

Entwickler *der;* **~s, ~** (Fot.) developer

erröten *itr. V.; mit sein* blush (**vor** with); **jmdn. zum Erröten bringen** make sb. blush

Der Hinweis *mit sein* zeigt an, dass das betreffende Verb die Perfekttempora mit dem Hilfsverb *sein* bildet
mit sein indicates that a verb is conjugated with the auxiliary verb *sein* in its perfect tenses

Unregelmäßige Steigerungsformen eines Adjektivs
Irregular comparative and superlative forms of an adjective

fromm /frɔm/, **frommer** *od.* **frömmer** /ˈfrœmɐ/, **frommst...** *od.* **frömmst...**
A *Adj.* 1 pious, devout ‹*person*›; devout ‹*Christian*›

3 Semantische Gliederungspunkte und Angaben zu Stil, Sachbereich, regionaler Zuordnung / Sense categories and labels

Semantische Gliederungspunkte
Sense categories

Geheim·nummer *die* 1 (Bankw.) personal identification number; PIN 2 (Telefonnummer) ex-directory number; unlisted number (Amer.)

gehören
A *itr. V.* 1 (Eigentum sein) **jmdm. ~:** belong to sb.; **das Haus gehört uns nicht** the house doesn't belong to us; we don't own the house; **der Jugend gehört die Zukunft** the future belongs to the young; **dir will ich ~** (dichter.) I want to be yours; **ihr Herz gehört einem anderen** (geh.) her heart belongs to another 2 (Teil eines Ganzen sein) **zu jmds. Freunden ~:** be one of sb.'s friends;

Bedeutungsindikatoren
Sense indicators

Stilistische Kennzeichnungen
Style labels

Geier /ˈgai̯ɐ/ *der;* **~s, ~:** vulture; **hol dich/hols der ~** (ugs.) to hell with you/it (coll.); **weiß der ~** (salopp) God only knows (coll.); Christ knows (sl.)

Genom /geˈnoːm/ *das;* **~s, ~e** (Biol.) genome

Gurtstraffer *der;* **~s, ~** (Kfz.-W.) [seat-]belt tensioner

Bereichsangaben
Subject labels

Angaben zur regionalen Zuordnung
Regional labels

Holler /ˈhɔlɐ/ *der;* **~s, ~** (bes. südd., österr.) ▸**Holunder**

Karre /ˈkarə/ *die;* **~, ~n** (bes. nordd.) 1 ▸**Karren** 2 (abwertend: Fahrzeug) [old] heap (coll.)

4 Übersetzungen / Translations

Übersetzungen
Translations

Kollokatoren (Wörter, mit denen zusammen das Stichwort häufig vorkommt) als Hilfe zur Auswahl der für den jeweiligen Kontext passenden Übersetzung
Collocates—words often used with the headword, shown to help select the correct translation for each context

Das Zeichen ≈ signalisiert eine nur annähernde Entsprechung
The sign ≈ is used to indicate approximate equivalence

Kle̲be·pflaster *das* adhesive plaster; sticking plaster

klein /klain/
A *Adj.* 1 ▸ℹ **S. 374** little; small; small ‹*format, letter*›; little ‹*finger, toe*›; **das Kleid ist mir zu ~:**

klirren /ˈklɪrən/ *itr. V.* ‹*glasses, ice cubes*› clink; ‹*weapons in fight*› clash; ‹*window pane*› rattle; ‹*chains, spurs*› clank, rattle; ‹*harness*› jingle;

kö̲niglich
A *Adj.* 1 royal 2 (vornehm) regal 3 (reichlich) princely ‹*gift, salary, wage*›; lavish ‹*hospitality*› 4 (ugs.: außerordentlich) tremendous (coll.) ‹*fun*›
B *adv.* 1 (reichlich) ‹*entertain*› lavishly; ‹*pay*› handsomely;

konzipieren /kɔntsiˈpiːrən/
A *tr. V.* draft ‹*speech, essay*›; draw up, draft ‹*plan, policy, etc.*›; design ‹*device, car, etc.*›
B *itr. V.* (Med.) conceive

Malte̲ser-: ~hilfsdienst *der* ≈ St John Ambulance Brigade; **~kreuz** *das* (auch Technik) Maltese cross; **~orden** *der* Order of the Knights of St John; **~ritter** *der* Knight of St John

Durch Adjektive attribuierte Substantive
Nouns modified by an adjective

Als Subjekte zu Verben auftretende Wörter
Subjects of a verb

Durch Adverbien attribuierte Verben oder Adjektive
Verbs or adjectives modified by an adverb

Als Objekte zu Verben auftretende Wörter
Objects of a verb

5 Anwendungsbeispiele / Phrases

Beispiele (jeweils mit einer Tilde an Stelle des Stichworts)
Examples (with a swung dash representing the headword)

Teile von Anwendungsbeispielen, zwischen denen ein kursiv gesetztes *od.* steht, sind synonym und gegeneinander austauschbar
Parts of a phrase separated by *od.* are synonymous and interchangeable

ragen /ˈraːgn̩/ *itr. V.* 1 (vertikal) rise [up]; ‹*mountains*› tower up; **aus dem Wasser ~:** stick *or* jut right out of the water; **in die Höhe** *od.* **in den Himmel ~:** tower *or* soar into the sky;

Regi̲erung *die*; **~, ~en** 1 (Herrschaft) rule; (eines Monarchen) reign; **die ~ übernehmen** *od.* **antreten** take over; come to power 2 (eines Staates) government

Ruf /ruːf/ *der*; **~[e]s, ~e** 1 call; (Schrei) shout; cry; (Tierlaut) call 2 (fig.: Aufforderung, Forderung) call (**nach** for); **der ~ zu den Waffen** (geh.) the call to arms; **dem ~ des Herzens/Gewissens/der Natur folgen** *od.* **gehorchen** follow one's heart/listen to the voice of conscience/nature;

Teile von Anwendungsbeispielen, zwischen denen ein Schrägstrich steht, sind syntaktisch gegeneinander austauschbar, aber nicht bedeutungsgleich
Parts of a phrase separated by a slash are syntactically interchangeable but have different meanings

6 Verweise / Cross references

Ein Pfeil verweist auf ein bedeutungsgleiches anderes Stichwort
An arrow directs the user to another headword with the same meaning

Das Symbol ▸ℹ mit einer Zahl verweist auf eine Buchseite, auf der sich in einem Informationskasten zusätzliche Informationen finden
The symbol ▸ℹ and a page-number cross reference direct the user to a usage box containing additional information

Stra̲mpler *der*; **~s, ~** ▸**Strampelhöschen**

töten /ˈtøːtn̩/ *tr., itr. V.* kill; deaden ‹*nerve etc.*›; **einen kranken Hund ~ lassen** have a sick dog put down; *s. auch* **Blick 1**; **Nerv 1**

tsche̲chisch ▸ℹ **S. 520**, ▸ℹ **S. 670**
A *Adj.* Czech
B *adv.* **~ sprechend** Czech-speaking; *s. auch* **deutsch**; **Deutsch**; **Deutsche**[2]

Mit *s. auch* wird auf ein Stichwort verwiesen, unter dem noch zusätzliche Informationen zu finden sind
s. auch directs the user to another headword where additional information can be found

Key to English–German Entries / Erläuterungen zum englisch–deutschen Text

1 Headword and pronunciation / Stichwort und Aussprache

Headword. All entries are listed in strict alphabetical order, except for *phrasal* verbs
Stichwort. Alle Einträge – mit Ausnahme der *Phrasal Verbs* – sind streng alphabetisch angeordnet

Compound block with a swung dash representing the first element of each compound
Kompositablock. Eine Tilde ersetzt jeweils den gemeinsamen ersten Bestandteil der Komposita

Each phrasal verb is entered on a new line immediately following the entry for the first element
Die *Phrasal Verbs* folgen, jedes auf einer neuen Zeile, direkt auf den Eintrag zu ihrem Grundverb

Pronunciation is shown in IPA immediately after the headword (see p. xviii).
Die Ausspracheangaben (in IPA-Lautschrift) stehen unmittelbar hinter dem Stichwort (s. S. xviii)

Stress mark, showing stress on the following syllable. If no stress is shown in a compound block, it falls on the first element
Betonungszeichen vor der betonten Silbe. Wo in Kompositablöcken keine Betonung angegeben ist, liegt der Ton auf dem ersten Bestandteil

Headwords spelt the same but with different meanings are entered separately with a raised number
Mehrere gleich geschriebene, aber nicht bedeutungsgleiche Wörter erscheinen als separate Stichwörter und sind mit hochgestellten Ziffern nummeriert.

Abbreviations and acronyms follow the same strict alphabetical order as other headwords
Auch Abkürzungen und Akronyme sind streng alphabetisch eingeordnet

batch /bætʃ/ *n.* 1 (of loaves) Schub, *der* 2 (of people) Gruppe, *die;* Schwung, *der* (ugs.); (of letters, books, files, papers) Stapel, *der;* Schwung, *der* (ugs.); (of rules, regulations) Bündel, *das*

batch: ~ file *n.* (Computing) Stapeldatei, *die;* **~ 'processing** *n.* (Computing) Schub-, Stapelverarbeitung, *die;* **~ production** *n.* Stapelfertigung, *die*

bate *n.* (Brit. coll. dated) Rage, *die* (ugs.); **be in a [terrible] ~:** [schrecklich] in Rage sein; **get/fly into a ~:** in Rage geraten

bated /ˈbeɪtɪd/ *adj.* **with ~ breath** mit angehaltenem *od.* (geh.) verhaltenem Atem

bath /bɑːθ/
A *n., pl.* **~s** /bɑːðz/ 1 Bad, *das;* **have** *or* **take a ~:** ein Bad nehmen 2 (vessel) **~[tub]** Badewanne, *die;* **room with ~:** Zimmer mit Bad…

bear[2]
A *v.t.*, **bore** /bɔː(r)/, **borne** /bɔːn/ …
- **~ a'way** *v.t.* wegtragen; davontragen ‹*Preis usw.*›; **be borne away** fort- *od.* davongetragen werden
- **~ 'down**
A *v.t.* niederdrücken; überwältigen ‹*Feind*›; **be borne down by the weight of …:** von der Last (+ *Gen.*) gebeugt sein
- **~ 'off** ▸ **~ away**
- **~ on** ▸ **~ upon**
- **~ 'out** *v.t.* 1 hinaustragen 2 (fig.) bestätigen ‹*Bericht, Erklärung*›; **~ sb. out** jmdm. Recht geben; **~ sb. out in sth.** jmdn. in etw. (*Dat.*) bestätigen

beastly /ˈbiːstlɪ/ *adj., adv.* (coll.) scheußlich

'beat-up *adj.* (coll.) ramponiert (ugs.)

bluff[1] /blʌf/
A *n.* (act) Täuschungsmanöver, *das;* Bluff, *der* (ugs.); **it's nothing but a ~:** das ist bloß [ein] Bluff; *see also* **call B 3**
B *v.i. & t.* bluffen (ugs.)

bluff[2]
A *n.* (headland) Kliff, *das;* Steilküste, *die;* (inland) Steilhang, *der*
B *adj.* 1 (abrupt, blunt, frank, hearty) raubeinig (ugs.) 2 (perpendicular) steil; schroff ‹*Felswand, Abhang, Küste*›; breit ‹*Schiffsbug*›

bryony /ˈbraɪənɪ/ *n.* (Bot.) Zaunrübe, *die*

BS *abbr.* 1 **= British Standard** Britische Norm 2 **= Bachelor of Surgery** „Bachelor" der Chirurgie; *see also* **BSc** 3 (Amer.) **= Bachelor of Science;** *see also* **BSc**

BSc /biːesˈsiː/ *abbr.* **= Bachelor of Science** Bakkalaureus der Naturwissenschaften; **John Clarke ~:** John Clarke, Bakkalaureus der Naturwissenschaften; **he is a** *or* **has a ~** ≈ er hat ein Diplom in Naturwissenschaften; …

BSE *abbr.* **= bovine spongiform encephalopathy** BSE

BSI *abbr.* **= British Standards Institution** Britischer Normenausschuss

BST *abbr.* **= British Summer Time** Britische Sommerzeit

Bt. *abbr.* **= baronet**

bubble /ˈbʌbl/
A *n.* 1 Blase, *die;* (small) …

2 Grammatical information / Grammatische Angaben

Grammatical categories and parts of speech
Grammatische Gliederungspunkte und Wortartangaben

capsize /kæp'saɪz/
A *v.t.* zum Kentern bringen
B *v.i.* kentern

catalysis /kə'tælɪsɪs/ *n., pl.* **catalyses** /kə'tælɪsiːz/ (Chem.) Katalyse, *die*

Irregular plural of a noun
Unregelmäßige Pluralform eines Substantivs

Irregular tenses of a verb (see also table on pp. 1746–1747)
Unregelmäßige Verbformen (siehe auch die Liste auf S. 1746–1747)

choose /tʃuːz/
A *v.t.*, **chose** /tʃəʊz/

chug /tʃʌg/
A *v.i.*, **-gg-** ‹*Motor:*› tuckern
B *n.* Tuckern, *das*

Doubling of a final consonant of a verb before -ed or -ing
Verdoppelung des Endkonsonanten eines Verbs vor -ed oder -ing

Irregular comparative and superlative forms of an adjective
Unregelmäßige Steigerungsformen eines Adjektivs

dry /draɪ/
A *adj.*, **drier** /'draɪə(r)/, **driest** /'draɪɪst/ 1 trocken; trocken, (very dry) herb ‹*Wein*›; ausgetrocknet ‹*Fluss, Flussbett*›

3 Sense categories and labels / Semantische Gliederungspunkte und Angaben zu Stil, Sachbereich, regionaler Zuordnung

Sense categories
Semantische Gliederungspunkte

extremity /ɪk'stremɪtɪ/ *n.* 1 (of branch, path, road) äußerstes Ende; (of region) Rand, *der;* **the southernmost ~ of a continent** die Südspitze eines Kontinents 2 *in pl.* (hands and feet) Extremitäten *Pl.*

facet /'fæsɪt/ *n.* 1 (of many-sided body, esp. of cut stone) Facette, *die* 2 (aspect) Seite, *die;* **every ~:** alle Seiten *od.* (geh.) Facetten

Sense indicators
Bedeutungsindikatoren

Subject labels
Bereichsangaben

fax: **~ machine** *n.* Faxgerät, *das;* **~ modem** *n.* (Computing) Faxmodem, *das;* **~ number** *n.* Faxnummer, *die*

genome /'dʒiːnəʊm/ *n.* (Biol.) Genom, *das*

goalie /'gəʊlɪ/ *n.* (coll.) Tormann, *der;* Schlussmann, *der* (ugs.)

Style labels
Stilistische Kennzeichnungen

gob[1] /gɒb/ *n.* (sl.) Gosche, *die* (landsch. derb); Schnauze, *die* (derb abwertend); Maul, *das* (derb abwertend); **shut your ~!** halts Maul! (derb); halt die Schnauze! (derb)

gob[2] *v.i.* (sl.: spit) rotzen (derb)

Regional labels
Angaben zur regionalen Zuordnung

hobo /'həʊbəʊ/ *n., pl.* **~es** (Amer.) Landstreicher, *der*/-streicherin, *die*

Hogmanay /'hɒgməneɪ/ *n.* (Scot., N. Engl.) Silvester, *der od. das*

4 Translations / Übersetzungen

Translations
Übersetzungen

ignore /ɪg'nɔː(r)/ *v.t.* ignorieren; nicht beachten; nicht befolgen ‹*Befehl, Rat*›; übergehen, überhören ‹*Frage, Bemerkung*›; **he ~d me in the street** er ist [auf der Straße] einfach an mir vorbeigegangen; **I shall ~ that remark!** ich habe das nicht gehört!

keg /keg/ *n.* 1 (barrel) [kleines] Fass; Fässchen, *das* 2 *attrib.* **~ beer** *aus luftdichten Metallbehältern gezapftes, mit Kohlensäure versetztes Bier;* ≈ Fassbier, *das*

The sign ≈ is used to indicate approximate equivalence
Das Zeichen ≈ signalisiert eine nur annähernde Entsprechung

insert
A /ɪn'sɜːt/ *v.t.* 1 einlegen ‹*Film*›; einwerfen ‹*Münze*›; einsetzen ‹*Herzschrittmacher*›; einstechen ‹*Nadel*›

Objects of a verb
Als Objekte zu Verben auftretende Wörter

intense /ɪn'tens/ *adj.*, **~r** /ɪn'tensə(r)/, **~st** /ɪn'tensɪst/ 1 intensiv; groß ‹*Hitze, Belastung*›; stark ‹*Schmerzen*›; kräftig, intensiv ‹*Farbe*›; äußerst groß ‹*Aufregung*›; ungeheuer ‹*Kälte, Helligkeit*›; **the day before the play opens is a period of ~ activity** am Tag vor der Premiere herrscht große Geschäftigkeit 2 (eager, ardent) eifrig, lebhaft ‹*Diskussion*›; stark, ausgeprägt ‹*Interesse*›

Nouns modified by an adjective
Durch Adjektive attribuierte Substantive

Collocates—words often used with the headword, shown to help select the correct translation for each context.
Kollokatoren (Wörter, mit denen zusammen das Stichwort häufig vorkommt) als Hilfe zur Auswahl der für den jeweiligen Kontext passenden Übersetzung

intensify /ɪn'tensɪfaɪ/
A *v.t.* intensivieren
B *v.i.* zunehmen; ‹*Hitze, Schmerzen*:› stärker werden; ‹*Kampf*:› sich verschärfen

Subjects of a verb
Als Subjekte zu Verben auftretende Wörter

keenly /'kiːnlɪ/ *adv.* 1 (sharply) scharf ‹*geschliffen*› 2 (coldly) scharf 3 (eagerly) eifrig ‹*arbeiten*›; brennend ‹*interessiert sein*›; **look forward ~ to sth.** auf etw. (*Akk.*) sehr gespannt sein 4 (piercingly) scharf ‹*ansehen*›

Verbs or adjectives modified by an adverb
Durch Adverbien attribuierte Verben oder Adjektive

5 Phrases / Anwendungsbeispiele

Examples (with a swung dash representing the headword)
Beispiele (jeweils mit einer Tilde an Stelle des Stichworts)

quandary /'kwɒndərɪ/ *n.* Dilemma, *das;* **this demand put him in a ~:** diese Forderung brachte ihn in eine verzwickte Lage; **he was in a ~ about what to do next** er wusste nicht, was er als Nächstes tun sollte

question /'kwestʃn/
A *n.* 1 Frage, *die;* **ask sb. a ~:** jmdm. eine Frage stellen; **put a ~ to sb.** an jmdn. eine Frage richten; **don't ask so many ~s!** frag nicht so viel!; **ask ~s** Fragen stellen; **beyond all** *or* **without ~:** zweifellos; ohne Frage *od.* Zweifel; **be beyond all** *or* **be without ~:** außer allem Zweifel stehen; außer Frage sein *od.* stehen;

Parts of a phrase separated by *or* are synonymous and interchangeable
Teile von Anwendungsbeispielen, zwischen denen ein kursiv gesetztes *or* steht, sind synonym und gegeneinander austauschbar

relapse /rɪ'læps/
A *v.i.* ‹*Kranker*:› einen Rückfall bekommen; **~ into** zurückfallen in (+ *Akk.*) ‹*Götzendienst, Barbarei*›; **~ into drug-taking/shoplifting** rückfällig werden [und wieder Drogen nehmen/Ladendiebstähle begehen]; **~ into silence/lethargy** wieder in Schweigen/Lethargie verfallen
B *n.* Rückfall, *der* (**into** in + *Akk.*)

Parts of a phrase separated by a slash are syntactically interchangeable but have different meanings
Teile von Anwendungsbeispielen, zwischen denen ein Schrägstrich steht, sind syntaktisch gegeneinander austauschbar, aber nicht bedeutungsgleich

6 Cross references / Verweise

An arrow directs the user to another headword with the same meaning
Ein Pfeil verweist auf ein bedeutungsgleiches anderes Stichwort

satiate /'seɪʃɪeɪt/ ▸ **sate**

silver /'sɪlvə(r)/
A *n.* 1 *no pl., no indef. art.* Silber, *das;* **the price of ~:** der Silberpreis 2 (colour) Silber, *das*
B *attrib. adj.* silbern; Silber‹*pokal, -münze*›; **have a ~ tongue** zungenfertig sein; *see also* **spoon**[1] **A 1; standard A 8**

***see also* directs the user to another headword where additional information can be found**
Mit *see also* wird auf ein Stichwort verwiesen, unter dem noch zusätzliche Informationen zu finden sind

The symbol ▸ⓘ and a page-number cross reference direct the user to a usage box containing additional information
Das Symbol ▸ⓘ mit einer Zahl verweist auf eine Buchseite, auf der sich in einem Informationskasten zusätzliche Informationen finden

solicitor /sə'lɪsɪtə(r)/ *n.* ▸ⓘ **p. 1260** 1 (Brit.: lawyer) Rechtsanwalt, *der*/-anwältin, *die* (der/die nicht vor höheren Gerichten auftritt) 2 (Amer.: canvasser) Werber, *der*

Guide to the use of the Dictionary / Hinweise für die Benutzung des Wörterbuchs

1 Order of entries

1 Anordnung der Artikel

A Headwords

A Alphabetische Ordnung der Stichwörter

Headwords (with the exception of phrasal verbs – see below) are entered in strict alphabetical order, ignoring hyphens, apostrophes, and spaces.

Die Stichwörter sind (mit Ausnahme der *Phrasal verbs* im englisch-deutschen Teil; s. u.) streng alphabetisch angeordnet, wobei Bindestriche, Apostrophe und Wortzwischenräume keine Rolle spielen.

Examples/Beispiele: **libellous**
liberal
liberal 'arts
liberalism

Pinte
Pin-up
Pin-up-Girl
Pinzette

Abbreviations are also entered in alphabetical order in the main Dictionary.

Abkürzungen sind ebenfalls an ihrer entsprechenden Stelle im Alphabet zu finden.

Examples/Beispiele: **clutter**
cm. *abbr.*
CND *abbr.*

Nockerl
NOK ... *Abk.*
nölen

Headwords spelt the same but with unrelated meanings (homographs) are entered separately with a raised number following each.

Zwei oder mehr Stichwörter mit gleicher Schreibung (Homographe) werden mit hochgestellten Ziffern (jeweils hinter dem letzten Buchstaben) nummeriert und dieser Nummerierung entsprechend eingeordnet.

Examples/Beispiele: **dam¹** ... [Stau]damm, *der*
dam² ... Muttertier, *das*

Bank¹ ... bench
Bank² ... bank

Each English phrasal verb is entered on a new line immediately following the entry for its first element, which is indicated by a swung dash.

Im englisch-deutschen Teil werden die Phrasal verbs auf einer neuen Zeile unmittelbar an das Grundwort angeschlossen, wobei dieses durch eine Tilde repräsentiert wird.

Examples/Beispiele: **plump¹**
~ 'out
~ 'up
plump²

B Compounds

All German compounds are entered in their alphabetical place in the Dictionary, as are English compounds if they are regarded as having independent status in the language, e.g. **love affair**. Those not so regarded are given as phrases in the entry for their first word, so for example **love game** is given as **~ game** under **love**.

Where two or more compounds with the same first element occur consecutively, they are given in paragraph-like blocks. The first element is given only once at the beginning of the block and is thereafter represented by a swung dash (~).

In the English–German section, a compound in a block is spelt with the same initial letter—capital or small—as the first element at the beginning of the block, unless the opposite is shown.

B Einordnung von Komposita

Im deutsch–englischen Teil des Wörterbuchs sind alle Komposita streng alphabetisch eingeordnet. Die im Englischen häufig getrennt geschriebenen Komposita werden als selbstständige Stichwörter behandelt, wenn sie als eigenständige Wörter gelten können; z. B. wird **love affair** als Stichwort an der entsprechenden Stelle im Alphabet aufgeführt. Wenn ein Kompositum als weniger eigenständig oder nur als Anwendungsbeispiel betrachtet wird, erscheint es unter dem Stichwort, das den ersten Bestandteil bildet, z. B. findet sich unter dem Stichwort **love** als Anwendungsbeispiel **love game**.

Mehrere aufeinander folgende als Stichwörter aufgeführte Komposita mit gemeinsamem erstem Element sind im Wörterbuch zu Absätzen zusammengefasst. Dabei steht das erste Element nur am Anfang des Absatzes; es wird innerhalb des Absatzes durch eine Tilde repräsentiert.

Wenn im englisch–deutschen Teil in einem Kompositablock sowohl groß- als auch kleingeschriebene Stichwörter vorkommen, so erscheint das erste Element zu Beginn des Absatzes entweder in Groß- oder in Kleinschreibung. Bei davon abweichender Schreibung im selben Block steht dann vor der Tilde der zu verwendende Buchstabe.

Examples/Beispiele: **grand: ~niece** ... **G~ Prix**
Great: ~ 'Bear ... **g~coat**

In the German–English section, the first element of a block of compounds has a capital letter if the block contains only nouns, and a small letter if it contains no nouns. If the block contains nouns and other parts of speech, both forms of the first element are given.

Wenn im deutsch–englischen Teil das erste Element sowohl in Groß- als auch in Kleinschreibung gezeigt wird, gilt die Großschreibung für alle Substantive und die Kleinschreibung für die anderen Wortarten.

Examples/Beispiele: **Stẹch-: ~fliege** ... **~zirkel**
kụrz-: ~treten ... **~um**
ẹnglisch-, Ẹnglisch-: ~họrn ... **~sprachig**

C Phrases

Idioms, fixed phrases, proverbs, and quotations are usually entered under only one word, and cross references, starting with *see also* or *s. auch*, are given at other words under which the user might look. At **ask B**, for example, there is the cross reference *see also* **trouble A 1**, because the expressions **you are asking for trouble** and **that's asking for trouble** are entered under **trouble**, and at **Stamm 1** there is the cross reference *s. auch* **Apfel 1**, because the expression **der Apfel fällt nicht weit vom Stamm** is entered under **Apfel**.

C Einordnung von festen Wendungen

Aus mehreren Wörtern bestehende feste Wendungen, idiomatische Ausdrücke, Sprichwörter, Zitate und dergleichen sind gewöhnlich nur unter einem Stichwort verzeichnet. Das Wörterbuch gibt, wo es den Bearbeitern nützlich erschien, Verweise auf Fundstellen. Solche Verweise haben die Form *see also* ... bzw. *s. auch* ... und stehen am Schluss eines Artikels bzw. eines Gliederungspunkts. So findet sich etwa unter **ask B** der Hinweis *see also* **trouble A 1**, weil unter dem Stichwort **trouble** die Beispiele **you are asking for trouble** und **that's asking for trouble** zu finden sind, und unter **Stamm 1** der Hinweis *s. auch* **Apfel 1**, weil unter **Apfel** die Redensart **der Apfel fällt nicht weit vom Stamm** behandelt ist.

2 Division of entries

2 Untergliederung der Artikel

A Letter categories

A Untergliederung durch Buchstaben

When a word can be used as different parts of speech, these are each given a separate upper-case letter.

Wenn ein Stichwort mehreren Wortarten angehören kann, steht vor jeder Wortartangabe ein Buchstabe.

> Examples/Beispiele: **blame** … **A** *v.t.* … **B** *n.*
> **entgegen** **A** *Adv.* … **B** *Präp. mit Dat.*

In verb entries, transitive, intransitive, and reflexive uses are also each given an upper-case letter.

Bei Verben unterscheiden die Buchstaben außerdem den transitiven, intransitiven und reflexiven Gebrauch des Verbs.

> Examples/Beispiele: **freeze** … **A** *v.i.* … **B** *v.t.*
> **beschäftigen** **A** *refl. V.* … **B** *tr. V.*

Entries for German prepositions are divided into letter sections if they can take more than one case.

Bei deutschen Präpositionen dienen die Buchstaben zur Untergliederung nach den Kasus, mit denen die Präposition stehen kann.

> Example/Beispiel: **an** … **A** *Präp. mit Dat.* … **B** *Präp. mit Akk.*

B Number categories

B Untergliederung durch Ziffern

When a word has more than one sense (as a particular part of speech) the different senses are distinguished by numbers.

Wenn ein Stichwort mehrere Bedeutungen haben kann, werden diese mit Ziffern unterschieden.

> Examples/Beispiele: **alien** …
> **A** *adj.* … **1** (strange) … **2** (foreign) … **3** (different) … **4** (repugnant) … **5** (contrary) …
>
> **gemütlich**
> **A** *Adj.* **1** (behaglich) … **2** (ungezwungen) … **3** (umgänglich) … **4** (gemächlich) …

3 The headword

3 Das Stichwort

A Form of the headword

A Form des Stichworts

The headword appears at the beginning of the entry.

Verbs are given as infinitives (without *to* in English).

Nouns are given in the nominative singular, but those which occur only in the plural are given in the nominative plural.

Das Stichwort erscheint am Anfang des Artikels.

Verben erscheinen im Infinitiv. (Im Englischen ohne *to*.)

Substantive erscheinen im Nominativ Singular. Substantive, die nur als Plural vorkommen, erscheinen im Nominativ Plural.

> Examples/Beispiele: **trousers** … *n. pl.*
> **Kosten** *Pl.*

German adjectives (and pronouns declined like adjectives) are given without endings, and adjectives which strictly speaking have no undeclined form are given with an ellipsis instead of any ending.

Deutsche Adjektive (und Pronomen, die wie Adjektive dekliniert werden) erscheinen in endungsloser Form. Auch Adjektive, die eigentlich keine endungslose Form haben, erscheinen ohne Endung, mit Auslassungspunkten.

> Example/Beispiel: **äußer**…

Separate entries are given for all forms of the German definite article and of German pronouns which are not declined like adjectives. So, for example, **der**, **den**, **dem**, **die**, etc., **euch**, and **ihr** are all entered as headwords. In the same way, all forms of English pronouns are headwords – **her**, for example, as well as **she**.

Deutsche Pronomen, die nicht wie Adjektive dekliniert werden, und die bestimmten Artikel erscheinen in allen Formen als selbstständige Stichwörter. Es erscheint also z. B. nicht nur **der**, sondern auch **des**, **dem**, **den** usw. als Stichwort, und die Form **euch** wird nicht unter **ihr** abgehandelt, sondern ist selbst Stichwort. Ebenso werden englische Pronomen in allen Formen als Stichwörter aufgeführt, also erscheint z. B. nicht nur **she**, sondern auch **her** als Stichwort.

German demonstrative pronouns are treated under the masculine nominative singular, e.g. **derjenige**.

Deutsche Demonstrativpronomen werden an der alphabetischen Stelle der maskulinen Form behandelt, also erscheinen z. B. **diejenige** und **dasjenige** unter dem Stichwort **derjenige**.

Inflected forms are entered as headwords with cross references to their root forms if these are not easily identifiable.

Als Stichwörter erscheinen auch bestimmte Flexionsformen, die sich nicht ohne weiteres auf ihre Grundform zurückführen lassen. Ein Verweis führt zur Grundform.

Examples/Beispiele: **did** ▸**do**[1]
apices *pl. of* **apex**
höher... ▸**hoch**
dasjenige ▸**derjenige**
zog *1. u. 3. Pers. Sg. Prät. v.* **ziehen**

B Symbols used with headwords

B Zeichen am Stichwort

With English headwords:

ˈ shows stress on the following syllable (for more information see 4).

Am englischen Stichwort kann das folgende Zeichen auftreten:

ˈ Betonungszeichen vor der zu betonenden Silbe. (Näheres siehe unter 4.)

With German headwords:

_ indicates a long vowel or a diphthong, stressed in words of more than one syllable.

Am deutschen Stichwort können die folgenden Zeichen auftreten:

_ Betonungszeichen in Form eines Strichs unter betonten langen Vokalen.

Examples/Beispiele: **Hieb**, **Blau**, **Hörer**, **amtieren**

. indicates a short vowel, stressed in words of more than one syllable.

. Betonungszeichen in Form eines Punktes unter betonten kurzen Vokalen.

Examples/Beispiele: **Recht**, **bitter**

· shows the juncture of elements forming a word.

· Punkt, der bei zusammengesetzten Wörtern die Kompositionsfuge markiert.

Examples/Beispiele: **Kern·kraft**, **um·branden**

| shows the juncture of elements forming a compound verb and indicates that the verb is separable (for more information see 'Outline of German grammatical forms' on pp. 1728–1733).

| senkrechter Strich, der bei zusammengesetzten Verben die Kompositionsfuge markiert und gleichzeitig anzeigt, dass das Verb unfest zusammengesetzt ist.

Examples/Beispiele: **vor|haben**, **um|werfen**

* preceding a German headword or compound indicates that the form is an 'old' spelling of the word, no longer valid according to the recently introduced reform of German spellings. See 'The revision of German spellings' on p. 1727.

Das Zeichen * vor einem deutschen Stichwort kennzeichnet die betreffende Form als „alte" (d.h. aufgrund der Rechtschreibreform nicht mehr gültige) Schreibung.

Examples/Beispiele: **bewusst·los**, ***bewußt·los**
***einbleuen** ▸**einbläuen**

Guide to the use of the Dictionary/Hinweise für die Benutzung des Wörterbuchs

4 Pronunciation

4 Angaben zur Aussprache

The pronunciation of a headword is given between forward slashes immediately after it, in the International Phonetic Alphabet (IPA), which is explained on pages xxxii–xxxiii. German pronunciations are based on the DUDEN-Aussprachewörterbuch, while English pronunciations are those common in educated Southern British English.

Die Aussprache des Stichworts ist in Lautschrift zwischen Schrägstrichen unmittelbar nach dem Stichwort angegeben. Die Ausspracheangaben für das Deutsche richten sich nach dem DUDEN-Aussprachewörterbuch, für das Englische nach der in Südengland als Standard geltenden Aussprache. Die dabei verwendeten Zeichen der internationalen Lautschrift der *International Phonetic Association* (IPA) sind auf Seite xxxii–xxxiii verzeichnet und erklärt.

A *simple headword* without a pronunciation given is pronounced in the same way as the headword immediately before it.

Bei mehreren *gleich lautenden Stichwörtern* ist die Aussprache nur beim ersten Stichwort zu finden.

The pronunciation of a *German derivative* with none given can be deduced from that of its root word. The stress, however, is always shown by _ or ̣ (see 3 B).

Bei deutschen *Ableitungen* ohne Ausspracheangabe kann die Aussprache vom Grundwort abgeleitet werden. Bei ihnen wird daher nur die Betonung angegeben, und zwar durch Zeichen am Stichwort selbst (s. 3 B).

Abbreviations without pronunciations given are pronounced as their full forms, except for English ones consisting of two or more capital letters, which are pronounced as individual letters, with the stress on the last, e.g. **BBC** is pronounced /bi:bi:'si:/.

Abkürzungen ohne Ausspracheangabe werden wie ihre vollen Formen ausgesprochen. Dies gilt jedoch nicht für die aus mindestens zwei Großbuchstaben bestehenden englischen Abkürzungen, die wie die einzelnen Buchstaben mit Betonung des letzten gesprochen werden (**BBC** also z.B. wie /bi:bi:'si:/).

The pronunciation of a *compound* with none given can be derived from the pronunciations of its elements, and, unless the compound is in a block, the stress is always shown by the symbol ', _, or ̣ (see 3 B), e.g. **'doughnut** is pronounced as **dough + nut**, with the stress on **dough**, and **bau·sparen** is pronounced as **Bau + sparen**, with the stress on **bau**. With German compounds, juncture between elements is shown either by · in the headword (as in 3 B) or, within a block of compounds, by the point where the compound is divided (as in 1 B).

Bei *Komposita* ohne Ausspracheangabe ergibt sich die Aussprache aus der der einzelnen Bestandteile. Bei ihnen ist daher nur die Betonung angegeben, und zwar durch Zeichen am Stichwort selbst (s. 3 B): **'doughnut** wird wie **dough + nut** ausgesprochen, die Betonung liegt auf **dough**, **bau·sparen** wird wie **Bau + sparen** ausgesprochen, die Betonung liegt auf **bau**. Bei deutschen Komposita wird die Kompositionsfuge entweder durch einen in das Stichwort gesetzten Punkt (siehe auch 3 B) oder durch die Eingliederung des Stichworts in einen Block von Komposita (siehe auch 1 B) deutlich.

If part of a German compound is not in the Dictionary as a headword, then just that part is given a pronunciation, with a hyphen standing for the rest.

Ist ein Bestandteil eines deutschen Kompositums nicht im Wörterbuch als Stichwort verzeichnet, wird die Aussprache nur für diesen Teil in Lautschrift angegeben, wobei für den anderen Teil ein Bindestrich steht.

> Example/Beispiel: **Schausteller** /-ʃtɛlɐ/

If stress alone needs to be shown, each syllable is represented by a hyphen.

Wenn nur die Betonung angegeben werden soll, steht für jede Silbe ein waagerechter Strich.

> Example/Beispiel: **come to** A /'--/ *v.t.* ... B /-'-/ *v.i.*

In blocks of compounds, stress is given as follows:

In Kompositablöcken ist die Betonung folgendermaßen angegeben:

In the English–German section:

Im englisch–deutschen Teil:

If no stress is shown (by the IPA stress mark), it falls on the first element.

Das erste Element ist normalerweise das betonte Element und nicht weiter gekennzeichnet. Ist ein anderes als das erste Element betont, so wird dies durch das IPA-Betonungszeichen gezeigt.

> Example/Beispiel: **country: ~ folk** ... **~ 'gentleman**

In the German–English section:

Im deutsch–englischen Teil:

When the first element at the beginning of the block has a stress mark, this stress applies to all compounds in the block.

Wenn das erste Element zu Beginn des Blocks durch einen untergesetzten Punkt oder Strich als betont markiert ist, gilt dies für alle Komposita im Block.

> Example/Beispiel: **Vanille-: ~eis** ... **~geschmack** ... **~pudding**

Exceptions are given (between forward slashes) with a hyphen standing for each syllable.

Ausnahmen davon werden (zwischen Schrägstrichen) angegeben, wobei für jede Silbe ein waagerechter Strich steht.

> Example/Beispiel: **drei-, Drei-:** ... **~käse·hoch** /-'---/

When no stress is shown for the first element at the beginning of a block, the stress of each compound is given individually.

Wenn das erste Element zu Beginn des Blocks nicht als betont markiert ist, wird bei jedem Kompositum im Block die Betonung angegeben.

Example/Beispiel: **nord-, Nord-: ~seite** /'--/ ... **~stern** /'--/ ... **~-Süd-Dialog** ... **~-Süd-Gefälle** ... **~südlich**

5 Grammatical information

5 Grammatische Angaben

Grammatical information on a headword immediately follows the headword or its pronunciation. The part of speech comes first; if the word can be more than one part of speech, each is listed in a separate letter section (see also 2 A).

Unmittelbar nach dem Stichwort bzw. der Ausspracheangabe folgen die grammatischen Angaben zum Stichwort. Die Wortart wird an erster Stelle angegeben. Wenn das Stichwort mehreren Wortarten angehören kann, steht vor jeder Wortartangabe ein Buchstabe (siehe auch 2 A).

The following grammatical information is given:

Die folgenden grammatischen Angaben werden gemacht:

A Nouns

A Bei Substantiven

In the English–German section, nouns are labelled with the abbreviation *n.* and proper nouns with *pr. n.* Irregular plurals are always given.

Im englisch–deutschen Teil werden Substantive durch die Angabe *n.* gekennzeichnet. Eigennamen werden mit *pr. n.* gekennzeichnet; unregelmäßige Pluralformen werden angegeben.

Examples/Beispiele: **boy** ... *n.*
Australia ... *pr. n.*
bijou ... *n., pl.* **~x**
mouse ... *n., pl.* **mice**
haddock ... *n., pl. same*

In the German–English section, nouns are denoted by the inclusion of a definite article.

Im deutsch–englischen Teil werden Substantive durch die Angabe des bestimmten Artikels gekennzeichnet.

Example/Beispiel: **Tante** ... *die;*

If this article is in parentheses, the word is a proper noun and the article is used only in certain circumstances.

Steht der Artikel in runden Klammern, handelt es sich bei dem Substantiv um einen Eigennamen, der nur unter gewissen Umständen mit dem bestimmten Artikel gebraucht wird.

Examples/Beispiele: **Belgien** ... *(das);*
Karl ... *(der)*

The definite article is followed by the genitive and plural endings for the noun with the headword represented by a swung dash.

Auf den Artikel folgen die Genitiv- und die Pluralendung des Substantivs. Dabei steht für das Stichwort die Tilde.

Example/Beispiel: **Tante** ... *die;* **~, ~n**

If only one ending is given, it is the genitive, and the word has no plural.

Wird nur eine Endung angegeben, so handelt es sich um die Genitivendung, das Stichwort hat in diesem Fall keinen Plural.

Example/Beispiel: **Schlaf** ... *der;* **~[e]s**

The label *n. pl.* or *Pl.* indicates that the noun exists only in the plural.

Die Angabe *n. pl.* im Englischen bzw. *Pl.* im Deutschen weist darauf hin, dass das Wort nur im Plural vorkommt.

Examples/Beispiele: **pants** ... *n. pl.*
police ... *n. pl.*
Ferien ... *Pl.*
Nieder·lande *Pl.*

B Verbs

Verbs are labelled as transitive, intransitive, or reflexive.

B Bei Verben

Verben werden als transitive, intransitive oder reflexive Verben gekennzeichnet.

Examples/Beispiele: **engrave** ... *v.t.*
creep ... *v.i.*
behave ... *v. refl.*
ehren *tr. V.*
leuchten *itr. V.*
freuen ... *refl. V.*

In the English–German section the following additional information is given:

The entries for irregular verbs give their past tense, past participle, and any other forms necessary. Identical forms are given only once.

Im englisch–deutschen Teil werden darüber hinaus folgende Angaben gemacht:

Bei unregelmäßigen Verben werden die Stammformen (Präteritum und 2. Partizip) und, wenn nötig, bestimmte andere Formen angegeben, wobei gleich lautende Formen nur einmal genannt werden.

Examples/Beispiele: **hide**[1] ... **hid** ... **hidden**
die[2] ... **dying**
make ... **made**

The doubling of a final consonant before **-ed** or **-ing** is also shown.

Wenn der Endkonsonant eines Verbs bei der Bildung einer Form auf **-ed** oder **-ing** verdoppelt wird, wird das ebenfalls angegeben.

Example/Beispiel: **bat**[4] *v. t.*, **-tt-:**

In the German–English section, the following additional information is given:

Irregular verbs are labelled *unr.*, and their parts (present, preterite, and past participle) are given on pp. 1742–1745.

Im deutsch–englischen Teil werden darüber hinaus folgende Angaben gemacht:

Unregelmäßige Verben werden mit *unr.* bezeichnet, ihre Stammformen (Präsens, Präteritum und 2. Partizip) können auf S. 1742–1745 nachgeschlagen werden.

Examples/Beispiele: **klingen** *unr. itr. V.*
leihen ... *unr. tr. V.*

Verbs which are always or sometimes conjugated with *sein* rather than *haben* are labelled accordingly.

Verben, die nicht oder nicht immer mit *haben* konjugiert werden, sind mit einem entsprechenden Hinweis versehen.

Examples/Beispiele: **sterben** ... *mit sein*
robben ... *meist, mit Richtungsangabe nur, mit sein*

Separable compound verbs are indicated by a vertical line at the point where the word is split.

Bei unfest zusammengesetzten Verben zeigt ein ins Wort hineingesetzter senkrechter Strich, wo das Verb gegebenenfalls getrennt wird.

Example/Beispiel: **auf|stehen**

C Adjectives and adverbs

Irregular and, in the German–English section, umlauted comparative and superlative forms are given.

C Bei Adjektiven und Adverbien

Zu Adjektiven und Adverbien werden unregelmäßige und—im deutsch–englischen Teil—umlautende Steigerungsformen angegeben:

Examples/Beispiele: **bad** ... **worse** ... **worst**
gut ... **besser** ... **best...**
kalt ... **kälter** ... **kältest...**

D Prepositions

The entry for each German preposition indicates with which case or cases it is used.

Examples/Beispiele: **um** ... *Präp. mit Akk.*
vor ... **A** *Präp. mit Dat.* ... **B** *Präp. mit Akk.*

Contractions of a preposition and a definite article are shown thus:

Example/Beispiel: **vom** ... *Präp. + Art.*

D Bei Präpositionen

Für jede deutsche Präposition wird der Kasus angegeben, mit dem die Präposition steht.

Präpositionen, die mit dem bestimmten Artikel zusammengezogen sind, werden so gekennzeichnet:

E Compounds

Compounds are always labelled with their part of speech or gender, but any further grammatical information is given at the entry for the second element.

Examples/Beispiele: **half** ... **~-life** *n.*
life ... *n., pl.* **lives**
Radau·bruder *der*
Bruder ... *der;* **~s, Brüder**

E Bei Komposita

Bei Komposita wird stets die Wortart angegeben. Wenn keine weiteren grammatischen Angaben gemacht werden, können diese dem Eintrag für das zweite Element des Kompositums entnommen werden.

6 Labels

After the grammatical information comes any necessary information on the style, usage, regional restrictions, or subject fields of a word, printed in italics within parentheses. Many labels are abbreviations, which are explained on the endpapers.

A label placed at the start of an entry or of a letter or number category applies to the whole of that entry or category.

6 Kennzeichnungen

Im Anschluss an die grammatischen Angaben wird der Benutzer auf die stilistische, zeitliche, regionale und fachliche Zuordnung des Stichworts hingewiesen. Diese Angaben stehen in Kursivschrift in runden Klammern. Sie sind häufig abgekürzt, eine Liste der verwendeten Abkürzungen befindet sich auf den Umschlaginnenseiten.

Wenn eine derartige Angabe am Anfang eines Artikels oder eines Gliederungspunktes steht, gilt sie für den ganzen Artikel oder Gliederungspunkt.

A Style and usage labels

Labels are used to mark all words and expressions which are not neutral in style. Both headwords and their translations are labelled to help the user to understand the headwords and to use the translations correctly in context.

The following style and usage labels are used to describe English:

(poet.) poetic (e.g. **beauteous**, **the deep**)

(literary) literary or elevated (e.g. **bed of sickness**, **countenance**, **valorous**)

(rhet.) used for deliberate impressive or persuasive effect (e.g. **bounteous**, **plenteous**)

A Angaben zur stilistischen Bewertung

Wörter und Wendungen, die nicht der normalsprachlichen Stilschicht angehören, werden sowohl in der Ausgangs- als auch in der Zielsprache mit Angaben zu ihrer stilistischen und zeitlichen Einordnung versehen. Der Benutzer kann somit die Stichwörter richtig verstehen und die Übersetzungen im korrekten Zusammenhang verwenden.

Für das Englische werden zur stilistischen Bewertung und zeitlichen Zuordnung die folgenden Angaben verwendet:

(poet.) in dichterischer, poetischer Sprache verwendet (z.B. **beauteous**, **the deep**)

(literary) für einen gehobenen, literarischen Stil charakteristisch (z.B. **bed of sickness**, **countenance**, **valorous**)

(rhet.) bewusst dazu eingesetzt, andere zu beeindrucken oder zu überzeugen (z.B. **bounteous**, **plenteous**)

(formal)	used only in formal speeches and writing (e.g. **hereafter, partake**)	(formal)	bei offiziellen und formellen Gelegenheiten unter Menschen, die sich nicht gut kennen, verwendet (z.B. **hereafter, partake**)
(coll.)	everyday, conversational language; not generally written, but would not cause offence or ridicule (e.g. **Aussie, cropper, loo**)	(coll.)	gesprochene Alltagssprache, die in schriftlichen Texten im Allgemeinen nicht verwendet wird (z.B. **Aussie, cropper, loo**)
(child lang.)	used only by or to small children (e.g. **bow-wow, choo-choo**)	(child lang.)	nur von kleinen Kindern oder im Umgang mit ihnen verwendet (z.B. **bow-wow, choo-choo**)
(sl.)	especially colloquial and expressive; often used only by particular groups (e.g. **crud, gob, shoot one's mouth off**)	(sl.)	besonders umgangssprachlich, oft nur von bestimmten Personengruppen verwendet (z.B. **crud, gob, shoot one's mouth off**)
(coarse)	coarse and offensive (e.g. **bollocks, fuck, piss**)	(coarse)	im Allgemeinen als anstößig empfunden (z.B. **bollocks, fuck, piss**)
(dated)	somewhat old-fashioned; used particularly by older people (e.g. **by Jove, ripping, top-hole**)	(dated)	zwar noch gelegentlich von älteren Leuten verwendet, aber altmodisch klingend (z.B. **by Jove, ripping, top-hole**)
(arch.)	found only in literature but still used jocularly, ironically, or for a deliberately old-fashioned effect (e.g. **forsooth, peradventure**)	(arch.)	heute nur noch gelegentlich in scherzhafter oder altertümelnder Weise verwendet (z.B. **forsooth, peradventure**)
(Hist.)	current term for an obsolete thing (e.g. **ducking stool, oubliette**)	(Hist.)	bedeutet, dass die bezeichnete Sache, Einrichtung usw. heute nicht mehr existiert; das so gekennzeichnete Wort ist aber nicht veraltet (z.B. **ducking stool, oubliette**)

The following style and usage labels are used to describe German:

Für das Deutsche werden zur stilistischen Bewertung und zeitlichen Zuordnung die folgenden Angaben verwendet:

(dichter.)	poetic (e.g. **Aar, Odem**)	(dichter.)	in dichterischer, poetischer Sprache verwendet (z.B. **Aar, Odem**)
(geh.)	formal, cultivated, or elevated; sometimes considered solemn or affected (e.g. **Antlitz, signifikant, dergestalt**)	(geh.)	für einen feierlichen, gehobenen oder gewählten Stil charakteristisch (z.B. **Antlitz, signifikant, dergestalt**)
(Papierdt.)	formal and stilted; mainly written (e.g. **seitens, in Wegfall kommen**)	(Papierdt.)	für einen unlebendigen, formellen und gespreizten Stil charakteristisch (z.B. **seitens, in Wegfall kommen**)
(ugs.)	everyday, conversational language; not generally written, but would not cause offence or ridicule (e.g. **Stunk, jmdm. über den Kopf wachsen**)	(ugs.)	gesprochene Alltagssprache, die in schriftlichen Texten im Allgemeinen nicht verwendet wird (z.B. **Stunk, jmdm. über den Kopf wachsen**)
(fam.)	used only between people on very familiar terms; otherwise considered silly or ridiculous (e.g. **Popo, Beißerchen**)	(fam.)	nur unter miteinander sehr vertrauten Menschen gebräuchlich; kann sonst als albern empfunden werden (z.B. **Popo, Beißerchen**)
(Kinderspr.)	used only by and to small children (e.g. **Wauwau, heia**)	(Kinderspr.)	nur von kleinen Kindern oder im Umgang mit ihnen verwendet (z.B. **Wauwau, heia**)
(salopp)	especially colloquial and expressive; often used only by particular groups (e.g. **Sauferei, ins Gras beißen müssen**)	(salopp)	besonders umgangssprachlich, oft nur von bestimmten Personengruppen verwendet (z.B. **Sauferei, ins Gras beißen müssen**)
(derb)	coarse and offensive (e.g. **Fresse, abkratzen**)	(derb)	im Allgemeinen als grob und anstößig empfunden (z.B. **Fresse, abkratzen**)
(vulg.)	especially coarse and offensive, mainly sexual terms (e.g. **ficken, Fotze**)	(vulg.)	als besonders anstößig und vulgär empfunden; vor allem aus dem Bereich der Sexualität (z.B. **ficken, Fotze**)
(volkst.)	avoided by specialists as potentially misleading or insufficiently scientific; mainly names of plants, animals, and illnesses (e.g. **Karfunkel, Schusterpalme**)	(volkst.)	von Fachleuten meist vermieden, weil missverständlich oder zu unspezifisch, vor allem Bezeichnungen für Pflanzen, Tiere und Krankheiten (z.B. **Karfunkel, Schusterpalme**)
(veralt.)	either dated or found only in literature but still used jocularly, ironically, or for a deliberately old-fashioned effect (e.g. **Schwindsucht, Spezerei**)	(veralt.)	heute nicht mehr oder kaum noch gebraucht, aber in älterer Literatur zu finden oder heute noch in scherzhafter, ironischer oder altertümelnder Weise verwendet (z.B. **Schwindsucht, Spezerei**)

B Regional labels

Words and expressions restricted to particular areas of the English- and German-speaking worlds are labelled accordingly. For English, the most common labels are (Brit.), (Amer.), (Austral.), and (Scot.). German items may be labelled, (österr.), (schweiz.), (nordd.), (südd.), (berlin.), etc.

The label (dial.) or (landsch.) indicates that a word is used in a number of regions or dialects.

B Angaben zur regionalen Zuordnung

Wörter und Wendungen, die nicht im gesamten englischen bzw. deutschen Sprachraum üblich sind, werden entsprechend gekennzeichnet. Für englische Stichwörter werden vor allem die Angaben (Brit.), (Amer.), (Austral.), (Scot.) gemacht. Deutsche Stichwörter können mit (österr.), (schweiz.), (nordd.), (südd.), (berlin.) usw. markiert sein.

Die Angabe (dial.) bzw. (landsch.) weist darauf hin, dass ein Wort in mehreren Regionen oder Mundarten gebräuchlich ist.

C Subject-field labels

Terms used in specialist or technical fields are labelled accordingly.

C Bereichsangaben

Wörter, die bestimmten Sachgebieten, Fachbereichen, Fach- oder Sondersprachen zuzuordnen sind, werden ebenfalls gekennzeichnet.

Examples/Beispiele: **colonnade** ... (Archit.)
entr'acte ... (Theatre)
Gelbfieber ... (Med.)
Hirschfänger ... (Jägerspr.)

German terms used in a number of fields but requiring only one translation are often simply labelled (fachspr.).

Deutsche Stichwörter, die mehreren Fachbereichen zugehören, aber nur eine Übersetzung haben, werden gelegentlich nur mit (fachspr.) gekennzeichnet.

Example/Beispiel: **binär** ... (fachspr.) binary

D Further usage labels

Figurative, derogatory, euphemistic, etc. use is indicated with appropriate labels.

D Weitere Kennzeichnungen

Bildlicher, abwertender, verhüllender usw. Gebrauch wird durch entsprechende Angaben markiert.

Examples/Beispiele: **assail** ... (fig.)
intimate ... (euphem. ...)
hochkarätig ... (fig.)
Quatsch ... (abwertend)

E Combinations of labels

Labels combined within parentheses, with no separating punctuation, apply simultaneously: (südd. ugs.) means that the word is used in southern Germany and is colloquial; (fig. coll.) means that in the sense or context in question the word is used figuratively and is colloquial.

Labels separated by commas or slashes cannot apply simultaneously: (Phys., Biol.) means that the word occurs in the fields of both physics and biology; (arch./joc.) means that the word occurs either in older texts or in jocular use.

E Kombination von mehreren Kennzeichnungen

Stehen in einer Klammer mehrere Kennzeichnungen nebeneinander, so gelten sie gleichermaßen: (südd. ugs.) bedeutet, dass das Wort in Süddeutschland gebräuchlich und umgangssprachlich ist; (fig. coll.) bedeutet, dass das Wort hier bildlich gebraucht wird und umgangssprachlich ist.

Werden die Kennzeichnungen durch Komma oder Schrägstrich getrennt, dann gelten sie unabhängig voneinander: (Phys., Biol.) bedeutet, dass das Wort zu den Fachbereichen Physik und Biologie gehört; (arch./joc.) bedeutet, dass das Wort entweder veraltet ist oder scherzhaft gebraucht wird.

7 Indicators

Indicators, given in parentheses before translations, distinguish between the various senses of a headword and, together with subject-field labels, tell the user which sense is being translated.

7 Indikatoren

Indikatoren sind kurze Hinweise, die angeben, zu welcher Bedeutung des Stichworts eine Übersetzung gehört. Sie stehen in runden Klammern vor der Übersetzung.

Examples/Beispiele:
flapjack … (oatcake) … (pancake) …
below … (position) … (direction) … (later in text) …
Kanadier … (Einwohner Kanadas) … (Boot) …
Luke … (Dach~) … (bei Schiffen) …

8 Translations and collocates

A Translations

Normally, one general translation is given for each word or sense of a word. If two or more are given, separated by semi-colons, they are synonymous and interchangeable.

8 Übersetzungen und Kollokatoren

A Die Übersetzung

Im Normalfall wird für jedes Stichwort bzw. jede Bedeutung eines Stichworts zuerst eine allgemeine Übersetzung gegeben; selten auch zwei oder mehrere gleichwertige und gegeneinander austauschbare Übersetzungen, die mit Semikolons aneinander gereiht sind.

Examples/Beispiele:
engrossing … fesselnd
anchovy … An[s]chovis, *die;* Sardelle, *die*
entzụ̈ckt … delighted
Elitedenken … élitist thinking; élitism

Unless qualified by labels, indicators, or collocates, a translation can be regarded as adequate in practically all contexts. Where necessary, a translation is labelled for style, region, etc. in a similar way to headwords.

Die angegebene Übersetzung, sofern sie nicht durch Zusätze (Kennzeichnungen, Indikatoren, Kollokatoren) eingeschränkt ist, kann als adäquate Übersetzung für nahezu alle Kontexte angesehen werden. Die Übersetzungen werden ähnlich wie die Stichwörter nötigenfalls mit Kennzeichnungen zur stilistischen Bewertung, zur regionalen Zuordnung usw. versehen.

Examples/Beispiele:
alongside … längsseits (Seemannsspr.)
grub … Fressen, *das* (salopp)
hợpp|nehmen … nab (coll.)
Hornhautentzündung … keratitis (Med.)

Specialist terms are often given two translations: a general or popular one and a specialist one, which is labelled (fachspr.) or (as tech. term).

Für Fachausdrücke werden oft zwei Übersetzungen gegeben, eine allgemeinsprachliche und eine fachsprachliche; die fachsprachliche Übersetzung ist dann mit (fachspr.) bzw. (as tech. term) gekennzeichnet.

Examples/Beispiele:
bilingual … zweisprachig; bilingual (fachspr.)
Schote … pod; siliqua (as tech. term)

English nouns which can signify a person of either sex are generally given a translation for each.

Bei englischen Substantiven, die Menschen beiderlei Geschlechts bezeichnen können, wird als Übersetzung im Allgemeinen sowohl die männliche als auch die weibliche Form angegeben.

Examples/Beispiele:
European … Europäer, *der*/Europäerin, *die*
buyer … Käufer, *der*/Käuferin, *die*
client … Auftraggeber, *der*/-geberin, *die*

Words which are untranslatable because they have no equivalent in the other language (mainly the names of institutions, customs, foods, etc.) are given a short explanation (gloss) in italic type.

Stichwörter, die nicht übersetzt werden können, weil sie in der Zielsprache kein Äquivalent haben (meist Bezeichnungen für Institutionen, Bräuche, Esswaren u. a.), sind mit einer kurzen Erklärung (Glosse) in Kursivschrift versehen.

> Examples/Beispiele: **gerrymander** … *willkürlich in Wahlbezirke aufteilen, um einer politischen Partei Vorteile zu verschaffen*
>
> **Christmas stocking** … *von den Kindern am Heiligabend aufgehängter Strumpf, den der Weihnachtsmann mit Geschenken füllen soll*
>
> **Einwohner·meldeamt** … *local government office for registration of residents*
>
> **Schützenfest** … *shooting competition with fair*

A gloss is occasionally added to a translation to aid understanding of the headword.

Glossen dieser Art werden gelegentlich auch zusätzlich zu einer Übersetzung gegeben, um die Bedeutung des Stichworts zu erläutern.

> Examples/Beispiele: **'clambake** *n.* (Amer.) Picknick, *das* (*bes. am Strand, bei dem Muscheln und Fisch auf heißen Steinen gebacken werden*)
>
> **Best·arbeiter** *der*, **Best·arbeiterin**, *die* (DDR) best worker (*worker receiving an award as being the most efficient in the department, factory, etc.*)

The symbol ≈ indicates that the translation given is to be taken only as an approximate equivalent.

Das Symbol ≈ zeigt an, daß die vorgeschlagene Übersetzung nur als ungefähres Äquivalent des Stichworts zu verstehen ist.

> Examples/Beispiele: **A level** … ≈ Abitur, *das*
>
> **Finanzamt** … ≈ Inland Revenue

A cross reference of the form ► indicates that a translation can be found under the entry referred to (see also **10**).

Ein Verweis mit ► auf ein anderes Stichwort zeigt, dass die Übersetzung dort nachgeschlagen werden kann (siehe auch **10**).

B Collocates

B Kollokatoren

As the choice of the correct translation often depends on the context in which it is to be used, collocates (words with which a translation typically occurs) are frequently supplied for translations of verbs, adjectives, adverbs, and combining forms. They are printed in italic type in angle brackets.

Oft hängt die Wahl der richtigen Übersetzung davon ab, mit welchen anderen Wörtern die Übersetzung im Satz verbunden werden soll. Zu vielen Übersetzungen von Verben, Adjektiven, Adverbien und Wortbildungselementen sind deshalb einige typischerweise mit der Übersetzung verbundene Wörter, so genannte Kollokatoren, angegeben. Sie stehen in Kursivschrift in Winkelklammern.

> Examples/Beispiele: **acquire** … erwerben ‹*Land, Besitz, Wohlstand, Kenntnisse*›; sammeln ‹*Erfahrungen*›; ernten ‹*Lob*›
>
> **flink** … nimble ‹*fingers*›; sharp ‹*eyes*›; quick ‹*hands*›

If a collocate goes with more than one translation, the translations concerned are separated by commas instead of semi-colons.

Wenn Kollokatoren sich auf mehrere gleichwertige Übersetzungen beziehen, sind diese Übersetzungen mit Kommas statt mit Semikolons aneinander gereiht.

> Examples/Beispiele: **achieve** … herstellen, herbeiführen ‹*Frieden, Harmonie*›
>
> **kürzen** … shorten, take up ‹*garment*›; … shorten, abridge ‹*article, book*›; … reduce, cut ‹*pension, budget, etc.*›

With verbs, typical subjects and objects are given as collocates. Subjects are placed before the translation.

Kollokatoren zu Verben sind Substantive, die typischerweise entweder als Subjekte oder als Objekte des Verbs fungieren. Ist der Kollokator das Subjekt des Verbs, steht er vor der Übersetzung.

> Examples/Beispiele: **hiss** … ‹*Katze, Lokomotive:*› fauchen
>
> **schwenken** … ‹*marching column*› swing, wheel; ‹*camera*› pan; ‹*path, road, car*› swing;

Objects are placed after the translation.

Ist der Kollokator das Objekt des Verbs, steht er hinter der Übersetzung.

Examples/Beispiele: **comb** ... kämmen ‹*Haare, Flachs, Wolle*› ... striegeln ‹*Pferd*› ... durchkämmen ‹*Gelände, Wald*›

herunterreißen ... pull off ‹*plaster, wallpaper*›; tear down ‹*poster*›

With English translations consisting of more than one word, collocates are placed at the appropriate point.

Bei mehrteiligen englischen Übersetzungen steht der Kollokator an der Stelle, wo er auch im Satz stehen müsste.

Example/Beispiel: **verheizen** ... use ‹*troops*› as cannon fodder; ... run ‹*employee, subordinate, etc.*› into the ground

With adjectives, collocates are nouns which the translations typically qualify. They are normally placed after the translation.

Kollokatoren zu Adjektiven sind Substantive, mit denen das Adjektiv typischerweise verwendet wird. Sie stehen normalerweise nach der Übersetzung.

Examples/Beispiele: **coated** ... gestrichen ‹*Papier*›; belegt ‹*Zunge*›; imprägniert ‹*Stoff*›; getönt ‹*Glas, Linsen*›

grimmig ... furious ‹*person*›; grim ‹*face, expression*›; fierce, ferocious ‹*enemy, lion, etc.*›

Where a collocate for an adjective is placed before the translation, the translation is postpositive—it must be used after the noun it qualifies.

Wenn ein Kollokator zu einem Adjektiv vor der Übersetzung steht, bedeutet dies, dass die Übersetzung nachgestellt werden muss.

Examples/Beispiele: **flowery** ... ‹*Wiese*› voller Blumen

eisenhaltig ... ‹*food*› containing iron

With a translation that is used in compounds, other elements with which it typically combines are given as collocates.

Bei Übersetzungen, die ein Wortbildungselement darstellen, werden als Kollokatoren solche Elemente angeführt, mit denen die Übersetzung typischerweise kombiniert wird.

Examples/Beispiele: **marine** ... See‹*versicherung, -recht, -schifffahrt*›

-süchtig ... ‹*drug-, heroin-, morphine-, etc.*›addicted

(Thus, **marine law** is translated as **Seerecht**, and **drogensüchtig** as **drug-addicted**. / Die Verbindung **marine law** wird also mit **Seerecht** übersetzt, **drogensüchtig** mit **drug-addicted**.)

With adverbs, collocates are verbs and adjectives which the translations typically qualify. Verbs are shown before the translation in the German–English section, but after it in the English–German, while adjectives and participles are always placed after, as in connected language.

Kollokatoren zu Adverbien sind Verben oder Adjektive oder adjektivisch gebrauchte Partizipien, mit denen das Adverb typischerweise verbunden wird. Dabei stehen im deutsch-englischen Teil Verben vor der Übersetzung, im englisch-deutschen Teil dahinter; Adjektive und Partizipien stehen immer hinter der Übersetzung, entsprechend ihrer Stellung im Satz.

Examples/Beispiele: **excessively** ... unmäßig ‹*essen, trinken*›

flimsily ... hastig ‹*errichtet*›; schlecht ‹*gebunden, verpackt*›

probeweise ... ‹*employ*› on a trial basis;

schwer ... seriously ‹*injured, wounded*›; greatly, deeply ‹*disappointed*›; ‹*punish*› severely, heavily

◼ Translation of abbreviations

◼ Die Übersetzung von Abkürzungen

Abbreviations are normally translated by the corresponding abbreviation in the other language.

Abkürzungen erhalten normalerweise die entsprechende Abkürzung in der Zielsprache als Übersetzung.

Examples/Beispiele: **e.g.** /iːˈdʒiː/ *abbr.* **= for example** z. B.

GDR ... DDR, *die*

WEZ ... GMT

usw. ... etc.

Where an abbreviation is best translated by one or more complete words, then they are given.

Wenn die gebräuchlichste zielsprachliche Entsprechung einer ausgangssprachlichen Abkürzung jedoch keine Abkürzung ist, wird als Übersetzung statt einer zielsprachlichen Abkürzung diese Entsprechung angegeben.

Examples/Beispiele: **s.a.e.** ... adressierter Freiumschlag
GPO ... Post, *die*
Pkw ... [private] car
WC ... toilet

If there is no corresponding abbreviation in the other language, the full form is translated or explained if not itself entered in the Dictionary.

Gibt es zu einer Abkürzung keine entsprechende Abkürzung in der Zielsprache, wird die volle Form angegeben und mit einer Übersetzung oder Erklärung versehen, sofern diese Vollform nicht selbst im Wörterverzeichnis zu finden ist.

Examples/Beispiele: **GCSE** ... **= General Certificate of Secondary Education**
FA ... **= Football Association** (*Britischer Fußballverband*)
MA ... **= Mittelalter**
ZDF ... **= Zweites Deutsches Fernsehen** Second German Television Channel

D Further information given with translations

D Zusätzliche Angaben bei Übersetzungen

Where necessary, translations are accompanied by information on usage, word order, etc.

The prepositions typically following verbs are given and translated.

Wo es nötig ist, sind die Übersetzungen mit Hinweisen zu ihrer Gebrauchsweise, ihrer Stellung im Satz usw. versehen.

Bei Verben wird der präpositionale Anschluss des Stichworts angegeben und übersetzt.

Examples/Beispiele: **conceal** ... verbergen (**from** vor + *Dat.*)
sinnieren ... ponder (**über** + *Akk.* over); muse (**über** + *Akk.* [up]on)

Where a German verb takes a case other than the accusative, this is shown, together with any English preposition used to 'translate' it.

Ebenso wird bei deutschen Verben der zum Anschluss an das Stichwort verwendete Kasus samt der entsprechenden englischen Präposition angegeben, sofern es sich nicht um den bei transitiven Verben stets erforderlichen Akkusativ handelt.

Example/Beispiel: **verdächtigen** ... suspect (*Gen.* of)

The indication *nachgestellt* or *postpos.* means that a translation of an adjective always follows its noun. (This is not shown when the fact is clear from the position of a collocator, as described in **8 B**.)

Bei Übersetzungen von Adjektiven besagt der Hinweis *nachgestellt* bzw. *postpos.*, dass die angegebene Übersetzung dem Substantiv nachgestellt werden muss. (Dieser Hinweis entfällt, wenn die Stellung eines Kollokators dies schon, wie unter **8 B** beschrieben, zeigt.)

Examples/Beispiele: **friendless** ... ohne Freund[e] *nachgestellt*
stahlhart ... as hard as steel *postpos.*

English translations marked *postpos.* can also be used predicatively, e.g. **she is as hard as steel**.

The indication *attr.* or *attrib.* means that a translation can be used attributively and not predicatively.

Mit *postpos.* markierte englische Übersetzungen können auch prädikativ gebraucht werden (also: **she is as hard as steel**).

Die Angabe *attr.* bzw. *attrib.* weist darauf hin, dass die angegebene Übersetzung nur als Attribut und nicht als Prädikatsteil verwendet werden darf.

Examples/Beispiele: **preferable** ... vorzuziehend *attr.*
achtseitig ... eight-page *attrib.*

The indication *präd.* or *pred.* means that a translation can be used predicatively and not attributively.

Die Angabe *präd.* bzw. *pred.* weist umgekehrt darauf hin, dass die angegebene Übersetzung nur als Prädikatsteil und nicht als Attribut verwendet werden darf.

Examples/Beispiele: **preferable** ... vorzuziehen *präd.*
irreparabel ... beyond repair *pred.*

The indication *Pl.* or *pl.* means that a translation of a noun exists only in the plural (in that sense).

Bei Übersetzungen von Substantiven bedeutet der Hinweis *Pl.* bzw. *pl.*, dass die angegebene Übersetzung ein Pluraletantum ist.

Examples/Beispiele: **measles** ... Masern *Pl.*
cost ... Kosten *Pl.*
Brille ... glasses *pl.*
Polizei ... police *pl.*

In the English–German section, German nouns are given the appropriate definite article. If this is in parentheses, the noun is a proper noun which is used with the article only in certain circumstances.

Im englisch–deutschen Teil erhalten als Übersetzungen angegebene deutsche Substantive den bestimmten Artikel. Steht der Artikel in runden Klammern, handelt es sich bei dem Substantiv um einen Eigennamen, der nur unter gewissen Umständen mit dem Artikel verbunden wird.

Examples/Beispiele: **cow**[1] ... Kuh, *die*
table ... Tisch, *der*
Italy ... Italien (*das*)
Eve ... Eva (*die*)

The indication *no art.* means that an English noun translation cannot be used with an article; *no def. art.* and *no indef. art.* mean that it cannot be used with a definite article and an indefinite article respectively.

Wenn Übersetzungen von deutschen Substantiven mit dem Hinweis *no art.* versehen sind, können sie nicht mit dem Artikel verbunden werden. Oft wird weiter differenziert zwischen *no def. art.* und *no indef. art.*

Example/Beispiel: **Ostermontag** ... Easter Monday *no def. art.*

Attributive use of an English noun is indicated by *attrib.* when it needs a separate translation.

Für den attributiven Gebrauch von englischen Substantiven wird oft eine eigene Übersetzung angegeben. Vor dieser Übersetzung steht dann der Hinweis *attrib.*

Examples/Beispiele: **marble** ... *attrib.* Marmor-
mountain ... *attrib.* Gebirgs-

9 Phrases

Following the general translation(s) of a headword are phrases in which the general translation(s) cannot be used. These include typical uses, fixed phrases, idioms, and proverbs. All are printed in bold type and are translated in their entirety. A swung dash is used to represent the headword.

9 Anwendungsbeispiele

Im Anschluss an die allgemeine[n] Übersetzung[en] des Stichworts werden Anwendungsbeispiele für Fälle gegeben, in denen die allgemeine Übersetzung nicht verwendbar ist. Außerdem werden typische Verwendungen des Stichworts, feste Wendungen, Redensarten und Sprichwörter gezeigt. Die Anwendungsbeispiele sind in halbfetter Schrift gedruckt und werden immer als Ganzes übersetzt. Innerhalb der Beispiele repräsentiert die Tilde das Stichwort.

Examples/Beispiele: **giggle** ... **have a ~ about sth.** ... **[a fit of] the ~s**
knistern ... **mit etw. ~** ... **eine ~de Atmosphäre**

In blocks of compounds, the swung dash in a phrase represents only the first element of the compound.

In Kompositablöcken steht auch in den Anwendungsbeispielen die Tilde immer nur für den ersten Bestandteil des Kompositums.

Examples/Beispiele: **apple:** ... **~ cart** ... **upset the ~ cart**
selbst-, Selbst-: ... **~bedienung** ... **hier ist ~bedienung**

Phrases and their translations can be given any of the labels mentioned in 6.

Die Anwendungsbeispiele und deren Übersetzungen werden gegebenenfalls mit den unter 6 erläuterten Kennzeichnungen versehen.

Examples/Beispiele: **corner** ... **cut ~s** (fig.)
edge ... **have/get the ~ [on sb./sth.]** (coll.)
Strang ... **über die Stränge schlagen** (ugs.)
Kapitel ... **das ist ein ~ für sich** (fig.)

In addition, any label attaching to a headword also applies to all phrases in that entry.

Außerdem gelten bereits für das Stichwort angegebene Kennzeichnungen auch für das Beispiel.

Examples/Beispiele: **beddy-byes** ... (child lang.) ... **off to ~**
Schmäh ... (österr. ugs.) ... **einen ~ führen**

To save space, phrases may be combined.

Aus Platzgründen werden oft mehrere Beispiele zusammengefasst.

- Two complete phrases separated by a comma are synonymous and share a translation.

- Wenn zwei vollständige Beispiele mit Komma aneinander gereiht sind, sind sie synonym und haben eine gemeinsame Übersetzung.

Examples/Beispiele: **cash** ... **pay [in] ~, pay ~ down** bar zahlen
aus|rasten ... **er rastete aus, es rastete bei ihm aus** ... something snapped in him

- Where portions of a phrase or translation are separated by *or* or *od.*, they are synonymous and interchangeable.

- Wenn Teile eines Beispiels oder einer Übersetzung mit *or* bzw. *od.* aneinander gereiht sind, haben sie die gleiche Bedeutung und sind beliebig austauschbar.

Examples/Beispiele: **decision** ... **come to** *or* **arrive at** *or* **reach a ~**: zu einer Entscheidung kommen
Bankrott ... **seinen ~ anmelden** *od.* **ansagen** *od.* **erklären** declare oneself bankrupt;

- Where portions of a phrase or translation are separated by a slash, they are syntactically interchangeable but have different meanings.

- Wenn Teile eines Beispiels bzw. einer Übersetzung mit Schrägstrich aneinander gereiht sind, sind sie zwar syntaktisch austauschbar, haben aber nicht dieselbe Bedeutung.

Examples/Beispiele: **beginning** ... **at the ~ of February/the month** Anfang Februar/des Monats;
durchschaubar ... **leicht ~** ‹*lie, plan, intention*› that is easy to see through *or* is easily seen through

- Portions of a phrase and its translation in square brackets may be omitted, but always together, i.e. both phrase and translation are to be read either with or without the bracketed portions.

- Wenn Teile eines Beispiels und Teile seiner Übersetzung in eckigen Klammern stehen, stellen sie einen auslassbaren Zusatz zu dem Beispiel dar. Beispiel und Übersetzung müssen also beide entweder mit oder ohne den eingeklammerten Teil gelesen werden.

Examples/Beispiele: **clear** ... **make it ~ [to sb.] that ...**: [jmdm.] klar und deutlich sagen, dass ...
verpflichten ... **sich verpflichtet fühlen[, etw. zu tun]** feel obliged [to do sth.]

NB: Square brackets are also used generally to enclose optional elements of words and phrases, e.g. **choos[e]y**; **cost sb. dear[ly]**; **Wach[t]·turm**; **er vermochte [es] nicht, mich zu überzeugen**.

In phrases and their translations, *jmd., jmds., jmdm., jmdn., sb.* and *sb.'s* stand for any noun or pronoun indicating one or more persons, and *etw., einer Sache* (genitive or dative), *sth.*, or *sth.'s* stand for any noun or pronoun indicating one or more things.

NB: Eckige Klammern werden außerdem generell dazu verwendet, beliebig auslassbare Teile von Wörtern und Sätzen einzuklammern, z.B. **choos[e]y**; **cost sb. dear[ly]**; **Wach[t]·turm**; **er vermochte [es] nicht, mich zu überzeugen**.

In den Anwendungsbeispielen und ihren Übersetzungen werden Substantive und Pronomen, die Personen im weitesten Sinne bezeichnen, durch die Abkürzungen *jmd., jmds., jmdm., jmdn.* auf der deutschen und *sb., sb.'s* auf der englischen Seite vertreten. Substantive und Pronomen, die Sachen im weitesten Sinne bezeichnen, werden durch die Abkürzungen *etw.* (oder auch *einer Sache* im Genitiv und Dativ) auf der deutschen und *sth., sth.'s* auf der englischen Seite vertreten.

Example/Beispiel: **Ohr** ... **jmdm. etw. ins ~ flüstern** whisper sth. in sb.'s ear

In German phrases and translations, the reflexive pronoun *sich* is accusative unless it is marked (*Dat.*) (= dative) or could only be dative, e.g. **etw. von sich geben; jmdm./sich Kühlung zufächeln**.

In phrases and their translations, stress which is unusual or affects meaning is shown using the symbols explained in **4**.

In deutschen Anwendungsbeispielen und Übersetzungen ist das Wort *sich* ein Akkusativ, wenn es nicht mit (*Dat.*) gekennzeichnet ist oder aufgrund des Kontextes eindeutig Dativ ist (wie etwa in **etw. von sich geben; jmdm./sich Kühlung zufächeln**).

Ungewöhnliche oder bedeutungsverändernde Betonungen werden bei Anwendungsbeispielen und deren Übersetzungen mithilfe der unter **4** erklärten Betonungszeichen angegeben.

Examples/Beispiele: **that** ... **he is 'like ~**

so·mit ... **und somit kommen wir zu Punkt 3**

In English phrases, *you, your, yourself*, etc. are generally translated as the 'familiar' *du, dich, dein*, etc. The more formal *Sie, Ihnen, Ihr*, etc. are used only when they are more appropriate for a given example. Similarly, the English colloquial contractions *can't, won't*, etc. are frequently used. In all cases it is up to the user to decide which forms are required by the context being translated.

Bei der Übersetzung von englischen Beispielsätzen ins Deutsche werden die Anrede *you* und ihre Formen im Allgemeinen durch das vertraulichere *du* und seine Formen wiedergegeben. Das förmlichere *Sie* wird nur verwendet, wenn das jeweilige Beispiel dies nahelegt. Ähnlich wird im Englischen häufig die umgangssprachliche Kurzform (z. B. *can't, won't, hasn't*) verwendet. Grundsätzlich bleibt es dem Benutzer überlassen, die Form dem Zweck und Kontext entsprechend zu wählen, für den die Übersetzung benötigt wird.

10 Cross references

Cross references beginning with ▸ which take the place of a translation refer to a headword at which the translation is to be found. This kind of cross reference occurs mainly in the following circumstances:

- with synonyms

Examples/Beispiele: **false 'move ▸false step**

fortbringen *unr. tr. V.:* **▸wegbringen**

- with variant spellings

Examples/Beispiele: **beduin ▸bedouin**

winklig *Adj.* **▸winkelig**

- with masculine and feminine forms of a German noun which have the same translation.

Example/Beispiel: **Primanerin** *die;* **~, ~nen ▸Primaner**

Cross references beginning with ▸ which are followed by a colon and a list of translations occasionally occur at derivatives, such as nouns and adverbs derived from adjectives. They refer the user to the entry containing the indicators and collocates necessary for distinguishing the translations.

10 Verweise

Verweise mit ▸ anstelle einer Übersetzung weisen auf ein anderes Stichwort, unter dem die Übersetzung zu finden ist. Diese Art von Verweis findet sich vor allem in den folgenden Fällen:

- bei Synonymen
- bei Wörtern mit mehreren Schreibweisen
- bei weiblichen und männlichen Formen eines deutschen Substantivs, die im Englischen die gleiche Übersetzung haben.

Verweise mit ▸, die vor einer Reihe von Übersetzungen stehen, treten gelegentlich bei Ableitungen auf, z. B. bei Substantiven oder Adverbien, die von einem Adjektiv abgeleitet sind. Sie zeigen, wo die Indikatoren und Kollokatoren, die zur Unterscheidung der Übersetzungen nötig sind, zu finden sind.

Examples/Beispiele: **cogent** ... *adj.* (convincing) überzeugend ‹*Argument, Grund*›; zwingend ‹*Grund*›; (valid) stichhaltig ‹*Kritik, Analyse*›

cogently ... *adv.* **▸cogent:** überzeugend; zwingend; stichhaltig

verbreiten

A *tr. V.* **1▸** (bekannt machen) spread ‹*rumour, lies, etc.*›; ... **2▸** (weitertragen) spread ‹*disease, illness, etc.*›; disperse ‹*seeds, spores, etc.*›; **3▸** (erwecken) radiate ‹*optimism, happiness, calm, etc.*›; spread ‹*fear*›

Verbreitung *die;* **~, ~en 1▸ ▸verbreiten**

A 1, 2, 3: spreading; ... dispersal; radiation

Cross references beginning with *see also* or *s. auch* refer to headwords at which further information may be found. They either help the user to find a phrase or idiom (see also **1 C**) or refer to an entry which serves as a model for a set of words because it is treated more comprehensively.

Verweise mit *see also* bzw. *s. auch* weisen auf ein Stichwort hin, unter dem zusätzliche Informationen gefunden werden können. Diese Art von Verweis dient entweder zum Auffinden von festen Wendungen usw. (vgl. **1 C**) oder weist auf ein Stichwort hin, das als Muster für einen bestimmten Typ besonders ausführlich behandelt wurde.

Examples/Beispiele: **Taurus** ... *see also* **Aries**
Französisch ... *s. auch* **Deutsch**

Cross references consisting of ►ⓘ and a page number direct the user to usage boxes which contain additional help and information, for example highlighting differences between German and English which may create difficulty for the learner and translator, or giving key facts about sets of words which behave alike, such as numbers or names of countries.

Verweise der Form ►ⓘ + Seitenzahl weisen auf Info-Boxen hin, in denen weitere Informationen und Hilfen zu finden sind. Dort werden z. B. Fälle behandelt, in denen strukturelle Unterschiede zwischen dem Deutschen und dem Englischen Schwierigkeiten bereiten können, oder es finden sich grundlegende Informationen zum Gebrauch bestimmter Wortkategorien, deren Vertreter alle im Wesentlichen gleich „funktionieren", wie etwa die Zahlen oder die Ländernamen.

Examples/Beispiele: **French** ... **►ⓘ p. 1277, ►ⓘ p. 1345**
eins ... **►ⓘ S. 29, ►ⓘ S. 729, ►ⓘ S. 826**

Die für das Deutsche verwendeten Zeichen der Lautschrift / Phonetic symbols used in transcriptions of German words

a	hat	hat
aː	Bahn	baːn
ɐ	Ober	'oːbɐ
ɐ̯	Uhr	uːɐ̯
ã	Grand Prix	grã'priː
ãː	Abonnement	abɔnə'mãː
ai̯	weit	vai̯t
au̯	Haut	hau̯t
b	Ball	bal
ç	ich	ɪç
d	dann	dan
d͜ʒ	Gin	d͜ʒɪn
e	Methan	me'taːn
eː	Beet	beːt
ɛ	mästen	'mɛstn̩
ɛː	wählen	'vɛːlən
ɛ̃	Ragoût fin	ragu'fɛ̃
ɛ̃ː	Timbre	'tɛ̃ːbr(ə)
eɪ	Skater	'skeɪtɐ
ə	Nase	'naːzə
əː	Surfer	'səːfɐ
f	Fass	fas
g	Gast	gast
h	hat	hat
i	vital	vi'taːl
iː	viel	fiːl
i̯	Studie	'ʃtuːdi̯ə
ɪ	Birke	'bɪrkə
j	ja	jaː
k	kalt	kalt
l	Last	last
l̩	Nabel	'naːbl̩
m	Mast	mast
m̩	Rhythm and Blues	'rɪðm̩ ɛnt 'bluːs
n	Naht	naːt
n̩	baden	'baːdn̩
ŋ	lang	laŋ
o	Moral	mo'raːl
oː	Boot	boːt
o̯	loyal	lo̯a'jaːl
õ	Fondue	fõ'dyː
õː	Fond	fõː
ɔ	Post	pɔst
ɔː	Skateboarder	'skeɪtbɔːdɐ
ø	Ökonom	øko'noːm
øː	Öl	øːl
œ	göttlich	'gœtlɪç
œ̃ː	Parfum	par'fœ̃ː
oʊ	Show	ʃoʊ
ɔy̯	Heu	hɔy̯
p	Pakt	pakt
p͜f	Pfahl	p͜faːl
r	Rast	rast
s	Hast	hast
ʃ	schal	ʃaːl
t	Tal	taːl
t͜s	Zahl	t͜saːl
t͜ʃ	Matsch	mat͜ʃ
θ	Thriller	'θrɪlɐ
ð	Rhythm and Blues	'rɪðm̩ ɛnt 'bluːs
u	kulant	ku'lant
uː	Hut	huːt
u̯	aktuell	ak'tu̯ɛl
ʊ	Pult	pʊlt
v	was	vas
w	Software	'sɔftwɛə
x	Bach	bax
y	Physik	fy'ziːk
yː	Rübe	'ryːbə
y̆	Nuance	'ny̆ãːsə
ʏ	Fülle	'fʏlə
z	Hase	'haːzə
ʒ	Genie	ʒe'niː

|	Glottal stop, e.g. Aa /a'|a/.	Stimmritzenverschlusslaut („Knacklaut"), z. B. Aa /a'|a/.
ː	Length sign, indicating that the preceding vowel is long, e.g. Chrom /kroːm/.	Längezeichen, bezeichnet Länge des unmittelbar davor stehenden Vokals, z. B. Chrom /kroːm/.
˜	Indicates a nasal vowel, e.g. Fond /fõː/.	Zeichen für nasale Vokale, z. B. Fond /fõː/.
'	Stress mark, immediately preceding a stressed syllable, e.g. Ballon /ba'lɔŋ/.	Betonung, steht unmittelbar vor einer betonten Silbe, z. B. Ballon /ba'lɔŋ/.
̩	Sign placed below a syllabic consonant, e.g. Büschel /'bʏʃl̩/.	Zeichen für silbischen Konsonanten, steht unmittelbar unter dem Konsonanten, z. B. Büschel /'bʏʃl̩/.
ˆ	Placed above or below a symbol indicates a non-syllabic vowel, e.g. Milieu /mi'li̯øː/.	Halbkreis, untergesetzt oder übergesetzt, bezeichnet unsilbischen Vokal, z. B. Milieu /mi'li̯øː/.

Die für das Englische verwendeten Zeichen der Lautschrift / Phonetic symbols used in transcriptions of English words

ɑ:	bah	bɑ:	m	mat	mæt
ɑ̃	ensemble	ɑ̃'sɑ̃mbl	n	not	nɒt
æ	fat	fæt	ŋ	sing	sɪŋ
æ̃	lingerie	'læ̃ʒərɪ	ɒ	got	gɒt
aɪ	fine	faɪn	ɔ:	paw	pɔ:
aʊ	now	naʊ	ɔ̃	Lyons	'li:ɔ̃
b	bat	bæt	ɔɪ	boil	bɔɪl
d	dog	dɒg	p	pet	pet
dʒ	jam	dʒæm	r	rat	ræt
e	met	met	s	sip	sɪp
eɪ	fate	feɪt	ʃ	ship	ʃɪp
eə	fairy	'feərɪ	t	tip	tɪp
əʊ	goat	gəʊt	tʃ	chin	tʃɪn
ə	ago	ə'gəʊ	θ	thin	θɪn
ɜ:	fur	fɜ:(r)	ð	the	ðə
f	fat	fæt	u:	boot	bu:t
g	good	gʊd	ʊ	book	bʊk
h	hat	hæt	ʊə	tourist	'tʊərɪst
ɪ	bit, lately	bɪt, 'leɪtlɪ	ʌ	dug	dʌg
ɪə	nearly	'nɪəlɪ	v	van	væn
i:	meet	mi:t	w	win	wɪn
j	yet	jet	x	loch	lɒx
k	kit	kɪt	z	zip	zɪp
l	lot	lɒt	ʒ	vision	'vɪʒn

:	Length sign, indicating that the preceding vowel is long, e.g. boot /bu:t/.	Längezeichen, bezeichnet Länge des unmittelbar davor stehenden Vokals, z. B. boot /bu:t/.
'	Stress mark, immediately preceding a stressed syllable, e.g. ago /ə'gəʊ/.	Betonung, steht unmittelbar vor einer betonten Silbe, z. B. ago /ə'gəʊ/.
(r)	An 'r' in parentheses is pronounced only when immediately followed by a vowel sound, e.g. pare /peə(r)/; pare away /peər ə'weɪ/.	Ein „r" in runden Klammern wird nur gesprochen, wenn im Textzusammenhang ein Vokal unmittelbar folgt, z. B. pare /peə(r)/; pare away /peər ə'weɪ/.

Festtags-, Feiertags- und Brauchtumskalender

January

1 8 15 22 29
2 9 16 23 30
3 10 17 24 31
4 11 18 25
5 12 19 26
6 13 20 27
7 14 21 28

1. Jan. – **New Year's Day** Neujahr. *Feiertag in England, Wales, Schottland, der Republik Irland und den USA.*
2. Jan. – *Feiertag in Schottland*

February

1 8 15 22
2 9 16 23
3 10 17 24
4 11 18 25
5 12 19 26
6 13 20 27
7 **14** 21 28

2. Feb. – **Groundhog Day**. *An diesem Tag soll das Murmeltier aus dem Winterschlaf erwachen und aus seiner Höhle kommen. Wenn es dann seinen Schatten sieht – das heißt, die Sonne scheint – so soll dies sechs weitere Wochen winterliches Wetter bedeuten.*
14. Feb. – **St Valentine's Day** Valentinstag

March

1 8 15 22 29
2 9 16 23 30
3 10 **17** 24 31
4 11 18 **25**
5 12 19 26
6 13 20 27
7 14 21 28

1. März – **St David's Day** Davidstag. *Schutzheiliger von Wales. Viele Waliser tragen an diesem Tag zu seinen Ehren eine Narzisse am Revers.*
17. März – **St Patrick's Day** Patrickstag. *Schutzheiliger Irlands. Feiertag in Irland und Nordirland. Der Tag wird auch in den USA begangen. In New York finden Umzüge statt.*
25. März – **Annunciation** Mariä Verkündigung

Bewegliche Feste im Jan./Feb./März:

Martin Luther King's Birthday Martin Luther Kings Geburtstag. *Feiertag in den USA.*
Chinese New Year Chinesisches Neujahrsfest
Washington's Birthday/Presidents' Day Washingtons Geburtstag. *Feiertag in den USA.*

Shrove Tuesday/Pancake Day Fastnachtsdienstag. *Traditionelles Fest vor dem Beginn der Fastenzeit. Man isst Pfannkuchen mit Zitronensaft und Zucker. Mancherorts werden „Pfannkuchenrennen" veranstaltet, bei denen es darum geht, einen Pfannkuchen im Laufen aus einer Pfanne herauszuschleudern und wieder aufzufangen.*

Ash Wednesday Aschermittwoch
Mother's Day (UK – auch **Mothering Sunday**) Muttertag. (*Der Muttertag wird in Großbritannien und Irland gewöhnlich im März, im deutschsprachigen Raum dagegen im Mai gefeiert.*)

April

1 8 15 22 29
2 9 16 **23** 30
3 10 17 24
4 11 18 25
5 12 19 26
6 13 20 27
7 14 21 28

1. Apr. – **April Fool's Day** Erster April
23. Apr. – **St George's Day** Georgstag. *Schutzheiliger Englands.*

May

1 8 15 22 29
2 9 16 23 30
3 10 17 24 31
4 11 18 25
5 12 19 26
6 13 20 27
7 14 21 28

1. Mai – **May Day** Erster Mai. *Traditionelles Frühlingsfest.*

June

1 8 15 22 29
2 9 16 23 30
3 10 17 **24**
4 11 18 25
5 12 19 26
6 13 20 27
7 14 21 28

24. Juni – **St John the Baptist's Day** Johannistag, Johanni

Bewegliche Feste im Apr./Mai/Juni:

Palm Sunday Palmsonntag
Maundy Thursday Gründonnerstag
First Day of Passover Beginn des Passahfestes
Good Friday Karfreitag
Easter Ostern, Ostersonntag
Easter Monday Ostermontag

Early Spring Bank Holiday* *Feiertag in England und Wales am ersten Montag im Mai.*
Late Spring Bank Holiday* *Feiertag in England und Wales am letzten Montag im Mai.*
Memorial Day *Feiertag in den USA, an dem der in den Kriegen Gefallenen gedacht wird.*

Mother's Day (US, Canada) Muttertag
Ascension Day Christi Himmelfahrt, Auffahrt
Shavuot Schawuot, Wochenfest
Whit Sunday Pfingsten, Pfingstsonntag
Whit Monday Pfingstmontag
Father's Day Vatertag

* **Bank Holiday**: Tag, an dem die Banken geschlossen sind (in England und Wales gewöhnlich gesetzlicher Feiertag).

July

1	8	15	22	29
2	9	16	23	30
3	10	17	24	31
[4]	11	18	25	
5	12	19	26	
6	13	20	27	
7	14	21	28	

4. Juli – **Independence Day** Unabhängigkeitstag. *Nationalfeiertag in den USA zur Feier der Unabhängigkeitserklärung des Jahres 1776. Traditionell mit Feuerwerken gefeiert.*

August

1	8	[15]	22	29
2	9	16	23	30
3	10	17	24	31
4	11	18	25	
5	12	19	26	
6	13	20	27	
7	14	21	28	

15. Aug. – **Assumption** Mariä Himmelfahrt

September

1	8	15	22	29
2	9	16	23	30
3	10	17	24	
4	11	18	25	
5	12	19	26	
6	13	20	27	
7	14	21	28	

Bewegliche Feste im Juli/Aug./Sept.:

Summer Bank Holiday* *Feiertag in England und Wales am letzten Montag im August.*

Labor Day Tag der Arbeit. *Feiertag in den USA zu Ehren der arbeitenden Menschen.*

October

1	8	15	22	29
2	9	16	23	30
3	10	17	24	[31]
4	11	18	25	
5	12	19	26	
6	13	20	27	
7	14	21	28	

31. Okt. – **Halloween** Halloween. *Ursprünglich im Mittelalter ein religiöses Fest, das an Allerheiligen begangen wurde. Es wurden zur Vertreibung böser Geister und zum Geleit der Seelen der Toten, die an diesem Tag in ihre Häuser zurückkehren sollten, Feuer entzündet. Heute ein weltliches Fest, bei dem man sich – als Hexe, Geist usw. – verkleidet und maskiert. Aus ausgehöhlten Kürbissen, in die Löcher geschnitten sind, die Gesichtszüge andeuten sollen, stellt man Laternen her. Kinder spielen „Trick-or-Treat" – ein Brauch, bei dem Kinder an den Haustüren klingeln und böse Streiche androhen für den Fall, dass man ihnen nicht eine kleine Gabe mit auf den Weg gibt.*

November

[1]	8	15	22	29
[2]	9	16	23	[30]
3	10	17	24	
4	[11]	18	25	
[5]	12	19	26	
6	13	20	27	
7	14	21	28	

1. Nov. – **All Saints' Day** Allerheiligen
2. Nov. – **All Souls' Day** Allerseelen
5. Nov. – **Guy Fawkes/Bonfire Night** *Jahrestag des geplanten Sprengstoffanschlags auf das Parlament von 1605. Traditionell wird an diesem Tag ein Bildnis, nach Guy Fawkes, der damals festgenommen und aufgrund seiner Beteiligung an der Verschwörung hingerichtet wurde, „Guy" genannt, verbrannt. Es werden Feuerwerke abgebrannt und Freudenfeuer entzündet. Penny for the guy: Kinder stellen sich mit einem selbst gebastelten „Guy" auf und bitten Passanten um eine Geldgabe, indem sie rufen: „Penny for the guy!".*
11. Nov. – **Veteran's Day**. *Feiertag in den USA, der am Jahrestag des Endes des Ersten Weltkriegs zu Ehren der amerikanischen Veteranen und Opfer aller Kriege begangen wird.*
30. Nov. – **St Andrew's Day** Andreastag. *Schutzheiliger Schottlands.*

December

1	8	15	22	29
2	9	16	23	30
3	10	17	[24]	[31]
4	11	18	[25]	
5	12	19	[26]	
6	13	20	27	
7	14	21	28	

24. Dez. – **Christmas Eve** Heiligabend, Heiliger Abend
25. Dez. – **Christmas Day** Weihnachten, erster Weihnachtstag. *Feiertag in England, Wales, Schottland, Nordirland, der Republik Irland und den USA.*
26. Dez. – **Boxing Day** Zweiter Weihnachtstag. *Feiertag in England, Nordirland und Schottland. So genannt nach dem Brauch, an diesem Tage Lieferanten ein Weihnachtspäckchen zu schenken.*
– **St Stephen's Day** Stephanstag. *Feiertag in der Republik Irland zu Ehren des christlichen Märtyrers, der der Blasphemie beschuldigt und gesteinigt wurde.*
31. Dez. – **New Year's Eve** Silvester *In Schottland nennt man Silvester „Hogmanay". Nach der Hogmanay-Tradition bringt ein dunkelhaariger Mann, der um Mitternacht die Schwelle überschreitet, Glück.*

Bewegliche Feste im Okt./Nov./Dez.:

Columbus Day Kolumbustag. *Feiertag in den USA zur Erinnerung an die Entdeckung der Neuen Welt durch Christoph Kolumbus 1492.*

Public Holiday in Republic of Ireland Feiertag in der Republik Irland

Remembrance Sunday Remembrance Sunday. *Der dem 11. November (dem Jahrestag des Waffenstillstands vom 11. November 1918) am nächsten gelegene Sonntag, an dem der Toten beider Weltkriege und späterer Konflikte gedacht wird. Auch als* **Poppy Day** *bekannt, da man traditionell rote Mohnblumen trägt und mit roten Mohnblumen gewundene Kränze auf Grabmalen niedergelegt, um die Toten zu ehren.*

Thanksgiving Erntedankfest. *Ein Nationalfeiertag in den USA. Kennzeichen sind religiöse Riten sowie ein traditionelles Truthahnessen. Der Feiertag erinnert an ein Erntefest, das die Pilgerväter 1621 gefeiert haben, und wird am vierten Donnerstag im November begangen.*

First Sunday in Advent Erster Advent

Von den Mondphasen abhängige bewegliche Daten:

Eid-ul-Fitr Id al-Fitr, Kleiner Bairam, „Zuckerfest"

Eid-ul-Adha Id al-Adha, Großer Bairam

Islamic New Year Islamisches Neujahrsfest

Jewish New Year (or **Rosh Hashanah**) Jüdisches Neujahrsfest (oder Rosch ha-Schana)

Day of Atonement (or **Yom Kippur**) Versöhnungstag (oder Jom Kippur)

First Day of Tabernacles (or **Succoth**) Erster Tag des Laubhüttenfestes (Sukkot)

First Day of Ramadan Erster Tag des Ramadan

Calendar of traditions, festivals, and holidays

Januar

1	8	15	22	29
2	9	16	23	30
3	10	17	24	31
4	11	18	25	
5	12	19	26	
6	13	20	27	
7	14	21	28	

1 Jan – **Neujahr** New Year's Day

6 Jan – **Heilige Drei Könige, Epiphanias** Epiphany. *Public holiday in Austria and in parts of Germany.*

Februar

1	8	15	22
2	9	16	23
3	10	17	24
4	11	18	25
5	12	19	26
6	13	20	27
7	14	21	28

2 Feb – **Mariä Lichtmess, Lichtmess** Candlemas. *In the Catholic Church, a festival marked by the blessing of candles and by candlelight processions. According to weather lore, if the bear sees its shadow when emerging from hibernation on this day – i.e. if the weather is sunny – it will creep back into its den, indicating six more weeks of wintry weather.*

14 Feb – **Valentinstag** St Valentine's Day

März

1	8	15	22	29
2	9	16	23	30
3	10	17	24	31
4	11	18	25	
5	12	19	26	
6	13	20	27	
7	14	21	28	

19 March – **Josephstag** St Joseph's Day. *Holiday in parts of Switzerland.*

25 March – **Mariä Verkündigung** Annunciation

Movable dates in Jan/Feb/Mar:

Chinesisches Neujahrsfest Chinese New Year

Schmutziger Donnerstag, Weiberfastnacht *Last Thursday of Carnival, when it is the custom in some areas for women to snip off men's ties.*

Rosenmontag *Day before Shrove Tuesday, when Carnival processions take place, particularly in the Rheinland.*

Fastnachtsdienstag Shrove Tuesday. *Traditional festival preceding Lent – the high point of the Carnival festivities, with parties, fancy-dress parades, masked balls, and processions.*

Aschermittwoch Ash Wednesday

April

1	8	15	22	29
2	9	16	23	30
3	10	17	24	
4	11	18	25	
5	12	19	26	
6	13	20	27	
7	14	21	28	

1 Apr – **Erster April** April Fool's Day

Mai

1	8	15	22	29
2	9	16	23	30
3	10	17	24	31
4	11	18	25	
5	12	19	26	
6	13	20	27	
7	14	21	28	

1 May – **Erster Mai** May Day. *Public holiday in Germany ('Maifeiertag'), Austria ('Staatsfeiertag'), and Switzerland ('Tag der Arbeit'); celebrated by trade unions as 'Kampftag der Arbeit' ('worker's day of action') and marked by demonstrations and rallies.*

Juni

1	8	15	22	29
2	9	16	23	30
3	10	17	24	
4	11	18	25	
5	12	19	26	
6	13	20	27	
7	14	21	28	

24 June – **Johannistag, Johanni** St John the Baptist's Day. *Feast of St John the Baptist, celebrated by some by the lighting of St John's fires in the evening.*

27 June – **Siebenschläfer.** *According to weather lore, if it rains on this day it will rain for the next seven weeks.*

Movable dates in Apr/May/June:

Palmsonntag Palm Sunday

Beginn des Passahfestes First Day of Passover

Karfreitag Good Friday

Ostern, Ostersonntag Easter Day, Easter Sunday. *At Easter, children traditionally hunt for Easter eggs which have supposedly been hidden by the Easter hare.*

Ostermontag Easter Monday

Weißer Sonntag Low Sunday. *The Sunday after Easter. In the Catholic Church, first communion is taken on this Sunday.*

Muttertag Mother's Day. *The second Sunday in May, on which mothers are particularly honoured by their children with gifts, visits, or written greetings. [Note that Mother's Day is usually in March in the UK and Republic of Ireland, and in May in the USA, Canada and German-speaking countries.]*

Christi Himmelfahrt, Auffahrt Ascension Day. *Public holiday in Germany, Austria, and Switzerland.*

Vatertag Father's Day. *On Ascension Day, groups of men, particularly fathers of families, often go off for the day on a walk or another excursion. A prominent feature of the day out is always a visit to one or more pubs, often resulting in excess alcohol consumption.*

Schawuot, Wochenfest Shavuot

Pfingsten, Pfingstsonntag Whitsun, Whit Sunday

Pfingstmontag Whit Monday. *Public holiday in Germany, Austria, and Switzerland.*

Fronleichnam Corpus Christi. *Public holiday in Austria and in parts of Germany and Switzerland.*

Juli

1	8	15	22	29
2	9	16	23	30
3	10	17	24	31
4	11	18	25	
5	12	19	26	
6	13	20	27	
7	14	21	28	

August

1	8	[15]	22	29
2	9	16	23	30
3	10	17	24	31
4	11	18	25	
5	12	19	26	
6	13	20	27	
7	14	21	28	

15 Aug – **Mariä Himmelfahrt** Assumption

September

1	8	15	22	29
2	9	16	23	30
3	10	17	24	
4	11	18	25	
5	12	19	26	
6	13	20	27	
7	14	21	28	

Oktober

1	8	15	22	29
2	9	16	23	30
[3]	10	17	24	[31]
4	11	18	25	
5	12	19	[26]	
6	13	20	27	
7	14	21	28	

3 Oct – **Tag der deutschen Einheit** Day of German Unity. *Public holiday in Germany, commemorating the reunification of Germany on 3 October 1990.*

26 Oct – **Nationalfeiertag** *National holiday in Austria.*

31 Oct – **Reformationsfest** Reformation Day. *Public holiday in some parts of Germany, commemorating the Reformation.*

November

[1]	8	15	22	29
[2]	9	16	23	30
3	10	17	24	
4	[11]	18	25	
5	12	19	26	
6	13	20	27	
7	14	21	28	

1 Nov – **Allerheiligen** All Saints' Day

2 Nov – **Allerseelen** All Souls' Day

11 Nov – **Martinstag, Martini** St Martin's Day, Martinmas. *This day is often celebrated with a traditional meal of roast goose ('Martinsgans'). On the evening before, children take part in lantern-light processions.*

– **Beginn der Fastnachtszeit** Beginning of Carnival. *At 11 a.m., a toast of sparkling wine is drunk to mark the beginning of the so-called 'fifth season'.*

Dezember

1	[8]	15	22	29
2	9	16	23	30
3	10	17	[24]	[31]
4	11	18	[25]	
5	12	19	[26]	
[6]	13	20	27	
7	14	21	28	

6 Dec – **Nikolaustag** St Nicholas' Day. *Children are given presents to mark St Nicholas' Day. They put their shoes outside the door on the evening before for St Nicholas to leave their presents in.*

8 Dec – **Mariä Empfängnis** Feast of the Immaculate Conception

24 Dec – **Heiligabend, Heiliger Abend** Christmas Eve. *On Christmas Eve in the evening, children are given their Christmas presents, Christmas trees are put up and decorated, and candles are lit on the Christmas trees to burn during the giving of the presents. A crib is often placed under the tree.*

25 Dec – **Weihnachten, erster Weihnachtstag, Christtag** Christmas Day

26 Dec – (in Germany) **Zweiter Weihnachtstag**, (in Austria and Switzerland) **Stephanstag** St Stephen's Day. *Public holiday.*

31 Dec – **Silvester** New Year's Eve. *The turn of the year is usually celebrated with lively parties till late in the night. At midnight the New Year is greeted with a toast of sparkling wine and with fireworks.*

Movable dates in Oct/Nov/Dec:

Volkstrauertag *On the Sunday two weeks before the first Sunday in Advent, there is a national day of mourning in Germany to commemorate the dead of both World Wars and the victims of National Socialism.*

Buß- und Bettag Day of Prayer and Repentance. *The Wednesday eleven days before the first Sunday in Advent is a public holiday in some parts of Germany.*

Erster Advent First Sunday in Advent

Movable dates related to lunar activity:

Id al-Fitr, Kleiner Bairam, 'Zuckerfest' Eid-ul-Fitr

Id al-Adha, Großer Bairam Eid-ul-Adha

Islamisches Neujahrsfest Islamic New Year

Jüdisches Neujahrsfest, Rosch ha-Schana Jewish New Year, Rosh Hashanah

Versöhnungstag, Jom Kippur Day of Atonement, Yom Kippur

Erster Tag des Laubhüttenfestes (Sukkot) First Day of Tabernacles (Succoth)

Erster Tag des Ramadans First Day of Ramadan

Deutsch–englisches Wörterverzeichnis
German–English Dictionary

a, A /aː/ *das;* ~, ~ **1** (Buchstabe) a/A; **kleines a** small a; **großes A** capital A; **das A und O** (fig.) the essential thing/things (*Gen.* for); **von A bis Z** (fig. ugs.) from beginning to end; **wer A sagt, muss auch B sagen** (fig.) if one starts a thing, one must go through with it **2** (Musik) [key of] A

ä, Ä /ɛː/ *das;* ~, ~: a umlaut

a *Abk.* = **Ar, Are**

à /a/ *Präp. mit Nom., Akk.* (Kaufmannsspr.) **zehn Marken à 50 Cent** ten stamps at 50 cents each; **zehn Kisten à zwölf Flaschen** ten cases of twelve bottles each

A *Abk.* **1** = **Autobahn** ≈ M **2** (Phys.) = **Ampere** A

Aa /aˈ|a/ *das;* ~ (Kinderspr.) poo[-poo] (child lang.); **Aa machen** do poo-poo *or* big jobs (child lang.); do a big job (Amer. child lang.)

AA[1] *Abk.* = **Anonyme Alkoholiker** AA

AA[2] *Abk.* = **Auswärtiges Amt**

Aachen /ˈaːxn/ *(das);* ~**s** Aix-la-Chapelle; Aachen

Aal /aːl/ *der;* ~**[e]s,** ~**e** eel; ~ **grün** (Kochk.) green eels; stewed eels; ~ **blau** (Kochk.) blue eel; **glatt wie ein** ~ **sein** be as slippery as an eel; **sich [drehen und] winden** *od.* **krümmen wie ein** ~: twist and turn like an eel

aalen *refl. V.* (ugs.) stretch out; **sich in der Sonne/auf der Wiese** *usw.* ~: lie stretched out in the sun/in the meadow *etc.*

aal-, Aal-: ~**glatt** (abwertend) **A** *Adj.* slippery; ~**glatt sein** be as slippery as an eel; **B** *adv.* smoothly; **sich** ~**glatt herausreden** glibly talk one's way out; ~**kasten** *der* eel trap; ~**suppe** *die* eel soup

a. a. O. *Abk.* = **am angegebenen Ort** loc. cit.

Aar /aːɐ̯/ *der;* ~**[e]s,** ~**e** (dichter. veralt.) eagle

Aas /aːs/ *das;* ~**es,** ~**e** *od.* **Äser** /ˈɛːzɐ/ **1** *Pl.* ~**e** (Kadaver) carrion *no pl., no indef. art.;* rotten carcass; ~ **fressen** eat carrion **2** *Pl.* **Äser** (salopp) (abwertend) swine; (mit Anerkennung) devil; **ein raffiniertes/kleines** ~: a cunning/little devil; **kein** ~: not one damned person

Aas·blume *die* (Bot.) carrion flower

aasen *itr. V.* (ugs., bes. nordd.) **mit etw.** ~: be wasteful with sth.; **mit dem Geld** ~: throw [one's] money around

aas-, Aas-: ~**fliege** *die* (Zool.) (Calliphorinae) blowfly; (Sarcophaginae) flesh fly; ~**fresser** *der* (Zool.) carrion-eater; scavenger; ~**geier** *der* vulture; **wie [die]** ~**geier** (abwertend) like vultures

aasig

A *Adv.* (ugs.) ~ **frieren** be absolutely frozen; ~ **kalt** damned cold; **es tut** ~ **weh** it hurts like mad (coll.)

B *Adj.* malicious; mean

Aas-: ~**käfer** *der* carrion beetle; ~**seite** *die* (Gerberei) flesh side

ab /ap/

A *Präp. mit Dat.* **1** (zeitlich) from; **ab 1980** as from 1980; **Jugendliche ab 16 Jahren** young people over the age of 16; **ab [dem] 3. April** from the 3rd of April; **ab wann?** from when?; from what time? **2** (bes. Kaufmannsspr.: räumlich) ex; **ab Werk** ex works; **ab [unserem] Lager** ex store; ex warehouse (Amer.); **ab Frankfurt fliegen** fly from Frankfurt; **ab Köln führt der Zug einen Speisewagen** from Cologne onwards the train has a dining car **3** ([Rang]folge) from … on[wards]; **ab der nächsten Ausgabe** from the next edition onwards; **ab zweitausend Stück aufwärts** from two thousand items onwards; **ab 20 Euro** from 20 euros [upwards]

B *Adv.* **1** (weg) off; away; **nicht weit ab vom Weg** not far [away] from the path; **an der Kreuzung links ab** turn off left at the junction; **[an etw.** (*Dat.*)**] ab sein** (ugs.: sich [von etw.] gelöst haben) have come off [sth.] **2** (ugs.: Aufforderung) off; away; **ab nach Hause** get off home; **ab die Post** (fig.) off you/we *etc.* go; **ab nach Kassel** (fig.) it's off and away; **X ab/X und Y ab** (Theater) exit X/exeunt X and Y; **Film/Ton ab!** (Film) camera!/sound!; **Film ab!** (im Vorführraum) film, please! **3** (milit. Kommando) **Gewehr ab!** order arms!; *s. auch* **Helm**[1] **1** **4** **ab und zu** *od.* (nordd.) **an** now and then; from time to time; *s. auch* **auf C 5, 6; von A 1, 2**

Abakus /ˈa(ː)bakʊs/ *der;* ~, ~: abacus

abänderbar, abänderlich *Adj.* alterable

ab|ändern

A *tr. V.* alter; change; amend ‹*text*›

B *itr. V.* (Biol.) mutate

Ab·änderung *die* alteration; (eines Paragraphen) amendment

Abänderungs-: ~**antrag** *der* ▸**Änderungsantrag;** ~**klage** *die* (Rechtsw.) application for a variation (*of periodical payments*)

Abandon /abãˈdõː/ *der;* ~**s,** ~**s** (Rechtsw.) abandonment

abandonnieren /abãdɔˈniːrən/ *tr., itr. V.* (Rechtsw.) abandon

ab|arbeiten

A *tr. V.* **1** (abgelten) work for ‹*meal*›; work off ‹*debt, amount*›; **seine Überfahrt** ~: work one's passage **2** (abnutzen) wear out [with work]; **abgearbeitete Hände** work-worn hands **3** (beseitigen) remove; (abfeilen) file off

B *refl. V.* slave [away]; work like a slave

Ab·art *die* variety

ab·artig *Adj.* deviant; abnormal

Ab·artigkeit *die* **1** (Eigenschaft) abnormality; deviancy **2** (Handlung) abnormal act

ab|äsen *tr. V.* (Jägerspr.) crop

ab|asten *refl. V.* (ugs.) slave [away]; **sich mit etw.** ~: heave sth. around; **sich** (*Dat.*) **[mit etw.] einen** ~ (salopp) slave away [heaving sth. around]

ab|ätzen *tr. V.* **1** (reinigen) clean [with corrosive] **2** (entfernen) remove [with corrosive]; (Med.) cauterize

Abb. *Abk.* = **Abbildung** Fig.

ab|backen *unr. itr. V.; mit sein* (Kochk.) ‹*dough etc.*› come away

ab|baken /ˈapbaːkn̩/ *tr. V.* (Seew.) mark [with buoys]; buoy

ab|balgen *tr. V.* (Jägerspr.) skin ‹*animal*›

Ab·bau *der* **1** (Zerlegung) dismantling; (von Zelten, Lagern) striking **2** (Senkung) reduction **3** ▸**abbauen A 4**: cutback (*Gen.* in); pruning; **der** ~ **von Beamten** the cutback in civil service jobs; **der** ~ **von Vorurteilen** the breaking down of prejudices **4** (Chemie, Biol.) breakdown **5** (Bergbau) mining; (im Steinbruch) quarrying; (von Flözen) working

ab|bauen

A *tr. V.* **1** (zerlegen) dismantle; strike ‹*tent, camp*›; dismantle, take down ‹*scaffolding*› **2** (senken) reduce ‹*wages*› **3** (beseitigen) gradually remove; break down ‹*prejudices, inhibitions*›; **etw. planmäßig** ~: phase sth. out **4** (verringern) cut back ‹*staff*›; prune ‹*jobs*› **5** (Chemie, Biol.) break down ‹*carbohydrates, alcohol*› **6** (Bergbau) mine ‹*coal, gold*›; quarry ‹*stone*›; work ‹*seam*›

B *itr. V.* **1** (nachlassen) fade; slow down; **kurz vor dem Ziel baute er stark ab** he faded badly just before the finish; **körperlich** ~: decay physically **2** (Landw.) ‹*crop variety*› decline in yield

Abbau·produkt *das* (Chemie) decomposition product; (Biol.) product of catabolism

abbau·würdig *Adj.* (Bergbau) workable

ab|bedingen *unr. tr. V.* (Rechtsspr.) waive

ab|beißen

A *unr. tr. V.* bite off; **eine Zigarre** ~: bite the end off a cigar

B *unr. itr. V.* have a bite; **lass deinen Bruder [von der Banane]** ~**!** let your brother have a bite [of the banana]!

ab|beizen *tr. V.* (Handw.) strip ‹*wooden object*›; **die alte Farbe [von etw.]** ~: strip the old paint off [sth.]

ab|bekommen *unr. tr. V.* **1** (bekommen) get; **sie hat keinen Mann** ~ (ugs.) she didn't catch herself a husband **2** (hinnehmen müssen) **einen Schlag/ein paar Kratzer** ~: get hit/get a few scratches; **den ganzen Segen** ~ (ugs. iron.) get the full benefit (iron.); **etwas** ~ (getroffen werden) get *or* be hit; (verletzt werden) get *or* be hurt; **er hat im Krieg etwas** ~ (ugs.) he was injured in the war; **der Wagen hat nichts** ~: the car wasn't damaged **3** (entfernen können) get ‹*paint, lid, chain*› off

ab|berufen *unr. tr. V.* recall ‹*ambassador, envoy*› **(aus, von** from); **Gott hat ihn aus diesem Leben** ~ (verhüll.) God has taken him from us

Ab·berufung *die* recall

ab|bestellen *tr. V.* cancel ‹*newspaper, hotel room, plumber, etc.*›; ask to have ‹*telephone*› disconnected; **jmdn.** ~: cancel sb.'s appointment

Ab·bestellung *die* cancellation

ab|betteln *tr. V.* (ugs.) **jmdm. etw.** ~: beg sth. from sb.

ab|bezahlen *tr. V.* pay off ‹*debts, television set, etc.*›

ab|biegen

A *unr. itr. V.;* ▸**i S. 800** *mit sein* turn off; **links/rechts/an der Kreuzung** ~: turn [off] left/right/at the junction

B *unr. tr. V.* **1** bend ‹*rod, metal sheet, etc.*› **2** (ugs.: abwenden) get out of (coll.) ‹*obligation*›; head off (coll.) ‹*row*›; **sie hat die Sache noch einmal abgebogen** she just managed to stop things going too far

Abbieger *der;* ~**s,** ~, **Abbiegerin** *die;* ~, ~**nen** (Verkehrsw.) motorist/cyclist/car *etc.* turning off

Abbiege·spur *die* turning lane

Ab·biegung *die* bend

Ab·bild *das* (eines Menschen) likeness; (eines Gegenstandes) copy; (im Spiegel) reflection; (fig.) portrayal

ab|bilden *tr. V.* copy; reproduce ‹*object, picture*›; portray, depict ‹*person*›; depict ‹*landscape*›; (fig.) portray; depict; **auf dem Foto ist ein Haus abgebildet** the photograph shows a

a

house; jmdn./einen Gegenstand/die Landschaft naturgetreu ~: depict sb./copy *or* reproduce an object/depict the scenery faithfully

Ab·bildung *die* [1] (Bild) illustration; (Schaubild) diagram; die ~ einer unbekleideten Dame a/the picture of a nude woman [2] (das Abbilden) reproduction; (fig.) portrayal

Abbildungs·fehler *der* (Optik) aberration; image defect

ab|bimsen *tr., itr. V.* (ugs.) crib ‹*exercises*›

ab|binden
[A] *unr. tr. V.* [1] (losbinden) untie; undo; die Schürze/Krawatte ~: undo *or* untie one's apron/tie; eine Schnur ~: untie a piece of string [2] (abschnüren) put a tourniquet on ‹*artery, arm, leg, etc.*›; tie ‹*umbilical cord*› [3] (Kochk.) thicken ‹*sauce, gravy*›; bind ‹*rissole etc.*› [4] (Zimmerei) make trial assembly of [5] (Landw.) wean ‹*calf*›
[B] *unr. itr. V.* (Bauw.) ‹*concrete*› set

Ab·bitte *die* (geh.) jmdm. ~ leisten *od.* tun ask sb.'s pardon

ab|bitten *unr. tr. V.* (geh.) jmdm. etwas/vieles abzubitten haben have something/a lot to apologize to sb. for

ab|blasen *unr. tr. V.* [1] (ugs.: absagen) call off ‹*enterprise, party*› [2] (Technik) discharge ‹*fumes*› [3] (Milit.) das Manöver/den Angriff/das Gefecht ~: sound the retreat [4] (Jägerspr.) die Jagd ~: call off the hounds/beaters *etc.*

ab|blassen *itr. V.; mit sein* fade

ab|blättern *itr. V.; mit sein* flake off

ab|bleiben *unr. itr. V.; mit sein* (ugs., bes. nordd.) wo ist er/es nur abgeblieben? where has he/it got to (Brit.) *or* (Amer.) gone?; where can he/it be?

abblendbar *Adj.* ~er Innenspiegel *od.* Rückspiegel anti-dazzle rear-view mirror

Ab·blende *die* (Film) fade[-out]

ab|blenden
[A] *tr., itr. V.* black out ‹*window, lights*›; dip (Brit.), dim (Amer.) ‹*headlights*›; bei Gegenverkehr frühzeitig ~: dip *or* (Amer.) dim headlights promptly when there is oncoming traffic
[B] *itr. V.* [1] (Film) fade [out] [2] (Fot.) stop down

Abblend-: ~licht *das* dipped (Brit.) *or* (Amer.) dimmed beam; mit ~licht fahren drive on dipped *or* dimmed headlights; ~schalter *der* dip switch (Brit.); dimmer switch (Amer.)

ab|blitzen *itr. V.; mit sein* (ugs.) sie ließ alle Verehrer ~: she gave all her admirers the brush-off; bei jmdm. [mit etw.] ~: fail to get anywhere [with sth.] with sb. (coll.)

ab|blocken *tr. V.* (Sport; auch fig.) block

ab|blühen *itr. V.; mit haben od. sein* (auch fig.) fade

ab|bohren *tr. V.* (Bergbau) drill out

Ab·brand *der* [1] (Kerntechnik) burn-up [2] (Metall.) melting loss

ab|brausen
[A] *tr. V.* ▸ abduschen
[B] *itr. V.; mit sein* (ugs.) roar off

ab|brechen
[A] *unr. tr. V.* [1] (abtrennen) break off; break ‹*needle, pencil*›; sich (*Dat.*) einen Fingernagel/Zahn ~: break a fingernail/a tooth [2] (zerlegen) strike ‹*tent, camp*› [3] (abreißen) demolish, pull down ‹*building, tower*› [4] (beenden) break off ‹*negotiations, [diplomatic] relations, discussion, conversation, connection, activity, training*›; call off ‹*strike*›; (vorzeitig, wider Erwarten) cut short ‹*conversation, studies, holiday, activity*›; den Kampf ~ (Boxen) stop the fight; ein abgebrochenes Studium an unfinished course of studies; abgebrochene Sätze fragmentary sentences; *s. auch* abgebrochen B
[B] *unr. itr. V.* [1] *mit sein* (entzweigehen) break [off]; die Armlehne von dem Sessel ist mir abgebrochen, als ich ... the arm broke off the armchair when I ... [2] (aufhören) break off [3] *mit sein* (beendet werden) die Verbindung brach ab the connection was cut off [4] *mit sein* (steil abfallen) fall away [steeply]
[C] *unr. refl. V.* sich (*Dat.*) einen/keinen ~ (salopp) put/not put oneself out

ab|bremsen
[A] *tr. V.* [1] brake; vor der Kurve den Wagen ~: slow the car down before the bend [2] retard ‹*motion*›; break ‹*fall*›; (fig.) curb ‹*zeal*›
[B] *itr. V.* brake; apply the brakes; stark/auf 40 ~: brake hard/to 40

ab|brennen
[A] *unr. itr. V.; mit sein* [1] (zerstört werden) be burned down; ‹*farm*› be burned out; das Haus ist abgebrannt the house has burned down; wir sind schon zweimal abgebrannt we've been burned out twice already; dreimal umgezogen ist [so gut wie] einmal abgebrannt (Spr.) you can lose just as much moving [house] three times as you can if your house burns down; *s. auch* abgebrannt B; Grundmauer [2] (sich aufbrauchen) ‹*fuse*› burn away; ‹*candle*› burn down; abgebrannte Streichhölzer used *or* burnt matches
[B] *unr. tr. V.* [1] let off ‹*firework*› [2] (zerstören) burn down ‹*building*›

Abbreviatur /abrevi̯a'tu:ɐ̯/ *die;* ~, ~en (Druckw., Mus.) abbreviation

ab|bringen *unr. tr. V.* [1] jmdn. von etw. ~: make sb. give up sth.; jmdn. vom Kurs ~: make sb. change course; jmdn. von der Fährte ~: throw sb. off the scent; jmdn. davon ~, etw. zu tun stop sb. doing sth.; (abraten) dissuade sb. from doing sth.; er lässt sich von seinem Plan nicht ~: he can't be persuaded to give up *or* drop his plan; jmdn. vom Thema ~: get sb. away from the subject [2] (ugs.: lösen) etw. [von etw.] ~: get sth. off [sth.]

ab|bröckeln *itr. V.; mit sein* (auch fig.) crumble away; (Börsenw.) ‹*price, exchange rate*› decline gradually

Ab·bruch *der* [1] demolition; pulling down; etw. auf ~ verkaufen sell sth. at demolition value [2] (Beendigung) breaking-off; (Sport) abandonment; (Boxen) stopping; Sieger durch ~ (Boxen) winner when the fight was stopped [3] einer Sache (*Dat.*) [keinen] ~ tun do [no] harm to sth.; das tut der Liebe keinen ~ (ugs. scherzh.) never mind (coll.) [4] (eines Zelts, Lagers) striking

abbruch-, Abbruch-: ~arbeit *die* demolition work; ~firma *die* demolition firm; ~haus *das* condemned house; ~reif *Adj.* ripe for demolition *postpos.*; ~sieg *der* (Boxen) win when the fight was stopped; ~unternehmen *das* demolition firm

ab|brühen *tr. V.* (Kochk.) blanch; *s. auch* abgebrüht B

ab|brummen *tr. V.* (ugs.) do (coll.); er muss noch drei Jahre ~: he has got another three years to do

ab|buchen *tr. V.* ‹*bank*› debit (von to); ‹*creditor*› claim by direct debit (von to); (fig.: als verloren betrachten) write off; etw. ~ lassen (durch die Bank) pay sth. by standing order; (durch Gläubiger) pay sth. by direct debit

Ab·buchung *die* debiting; ~ per Dauerauftrag payment by standing order/direct debit

ab|bügeln *tr. V.* (ugs.) reject, brush aside ‹*warning, question, criticism*›; rebuff ‹*person*›; (zurückweisen) dismiss

ab|bummeln *tr. V.* (ugs.) take time off in lieu for

ab|bürsten *tr. V.* [1] brush off; jmdm. die Haare/den Schmutz ~: brush the hairs/the dirt off sb.; die Haare/den Schmutz von etw. ~: brush the hairs/the dirt off sth. [2] (säubern) brush ‹*garment*› [3] (ugs.: zurechtweisen) jmdn. ~: give sb. a dressing down

ab|busseln *tr. V.* (österr.) ▸ abküssen

ab|büßen *tr. V.* [1] serve [out] ‹*prison sentence*› [2] (Rel.) atone for; do penance for

Abbüßung *die;* ~: nach ~ seiner Strafe after serving [out] his sentence

Abc /a(:)be(:)'tse:/ *das;* ~ [1] ABC; nach dem ~ ordnen arrange alphabetically [2] (fig.: Grundlagen) ABC; fundamentals *pl.*

Abc-Buch *das* (veralt.) ▸ Fibel 1

ab|checken *tr. V.* check; check through ‹*list*›; check off ‹*names etc.*›

Abc-Schütze *der,* **Abc-Schützin** *die* child just starting school

ABC-: ~-Staaten *Pl.* die ~-Staaten Argentina, Brazil, and Chile; ~-Waffen *Pl.* NBC weapons; ABC weapons

ab|dachen /'apdaxn̩/ *refl. V.* (Geogr.) slope down

Abdachung *die;* ~, ~en (Geogr.) downward slope *or* incline

ab|dämmen *tr. V.* [1] dam up ‹*river, pond, lake*›; dam off ‹*meadow, land*› [2] (isolieren) insulate

Abdämmung *die;* ~, ~en [1] dam; (am Ufer) dyke; (Verfahren) damming [2] (Isolierung) insulation

Ab·dampf *der* (Technik) exhaust steam

ab|dampfen
[A] *itr. V.; mit sein* steam away; (ugs.: abfahren) set off
[B] *tr. V.* (Chemie) evaporate

ab|dämpfen *tr. V.* damp, muffle ‹*sound*›; dim ‹*light*›

Abdampf-: ~heizung *die* exhaust-steam heating; ~rück·stand *der* residue from evaporation; ~turbine *die* exhaust-steam turbine

ab|danken *itr. V.* ‹*ruler*› abdicate; ‹*government, minister*› resign; *s. auch* abgedankt B

Abdankung *die;* ~, ~en [1] (eines Herrschers) abdication; (eines Ministers, einer Regierung) resignation [2] (veralt.: Entlassung) retirement [3] (bes. schweiz.: Trauerfeier) funeral service

ab|darben *refl. V.* sich (*Dat.*) etw. [vom Munde] ~ (geh.) stint oneself to save sth.

Abdeck·band *das; Pl.* ~bänder masking tape

ab|decken
[A] *tr. V.* [1] open up; uncover ‹*container*›; der Orkan hat viele Häuser abgedeckt the hurricane blew the roofs off many houses; das Bett ~: pull back the bedspread/bedclothes [2] (herunternehmen, -reißen) take off; remove; Bretter von einer Grube ~: take planks off a trench; der Sturm deckte das Dach ab the storm blew the roof off [3] (abräumen) clear ‹*table*›; clear away ‹*dishes*› [4] (zudecken) cover [up] ‹*trench, grave*›; etw. mit Plastikfolie ~: cover sth. [up] with plastic film [5] (schützen) cover ‹*person*›; (Schach) defend [6] (Sport) mark ‹*player*› [7] (bezahlen, ausgleichen, berücksichtigen) cover; meet ‹*need, demand*›; deal with ‹*problem*› [8] (veralt.: abhäuten) skin; flay
[B] *itr. V.* (den Tisch ~) clear the table

Abdecker *der;* ~s, ~ ▸❶ S. 113 (veralt.) knacker (Brit.); (der Tiere abhäutet) skinner

Abdeckerei *die;* ~, ~en (veralt.) knacker's yard; (wo Tiere abgehäutet werden) skinnery (arch.)

Abdeck-: ~plane *die* canvas; tarpaulin; ~platte *die* (Bauw.) coping stone

Ab·deckung *die* [1] (Bedeckung) covering [2] (Ausgleich, Bezahlung, Berücksichtigung) covering; (von Bedürfnissen, Forderungen) meeting; zur ~ des Risikos to cover the risk

ab|dichten *tr. V.* seal, stop up ‹*hole, crack, gap*›; seal ‹*pipe, container*›; plug ‹*leak*›; das Fenster/die Tür ~: draughtproof the window/the door

Ab·dichtung *die* [1] seal; (von Fenstern, Türen) draughtproofing [2] (Vorgang) sealing/draughtproofing

ab|dienen *tr. V.* serve [out]

abdingbar *Adj.* (Rechtsspr.) alterable by mutual consent

ab|dorren *itr. V.; mit sein* (geh.) dry up and wither away

ab|drängen *tr. V.* push away; force away; drive ‹*animal*› away; jmdn. von etw. ~: push sb. away from sth.; einen Spieler vom Ball ~ (Fußball) force a player off the ball; das Auto wurde von der Straße abgedrängt the car was forced off the road; ein Schiff vom Kurs ~: force a ship off course

ab|drehen
[A] *tr. V.* [1] (ausschalten) turn off; turn *or* switch off ‹*light, lamp, electricity, fire, radio*›; den Hahn ~ (fig.) turn off the supply [2] (Film) finish shooting ‹*scene, film*› [3] (abtrennen) twist off; einem Huhn den Hals *od.* Kopf ~: wring a chicken's

neck; *s. auch* **Gurgel** 4 (abschrauben) screw off ‹*lid, top*›

B *itr. V.; meist mit sein* (die Richtung ändern) turn off; **nach Süden ~:** turn [off] southwards

Ab·drift *die* (Seew.) leeway

ab|driften *itr. V.; mit sein* 1 (Seew.) be blown; make leeway (Naut.); **nach rechts/links/ins Drogenmilieu ~** (fig.) drift to the Right/Left/ into the world of drug addicts

ab|drosseln *tr. V.* (Technik) reduce ‹*fuel or power supply*›; throttle back ‹*motor, engine*›; (stoppen) cut ‹*motor, engine*›; (fig.: verringern) cut back; curb

Ab·druck[1] *der; Pl.* **Abdrücke** mark; imprint; (Finger~) fingermark; (Fuß~) footprint; footmark; (Wachs~) impression; (Gips~) cast; **einen ~ nehmen** *od.* **machen** make a cast/impression

Ab·druck[2] *der; Pl.* **~e** 1 (Vorgang) printing; (Wieder~) reprinting; **vor dem ~:** before printing 2 (Ergebnis) (einer Grafik) print; (eines Buchs, Artikels) [printed] text

ab|drucken *tr. V.* print; (veröffentlichen) publish

ab|drücken

A *itr. V.* (schießen) pull the trigger; shoot; **auf jmdn./etw. ~:** shoot *or* fire at sb./sth.

B *tr. V.* 1 (abfeuern) fire ‹*revolver, gun*› 2 (zudrücken) constrict 3 **jmdm. die Luft ~:** stop sb. breathing 4 **jmdm. das Herz ~:** burden sb.'s heart 5 (ugs.: umarmen) hug

C *refl. V.* 1 **sich [in etw.** (*Dat.*)**] ~:** make marks [in sth.]; ‹*track*› be imprinted [in sth.] 2 **sich [mit dem Fuß] ~:** push oneself away with one's foot

ab|ducken *tr., itr. V.* (Boxen) duck ‹*punch*›

ab|dunkeln *tr. V.* 1 (verdunkeln) darken ‹*room*›; dim ‹*light*› 2 (abtönen) tone down

ab|duschen *tr. V.* 1 **sich/jmdn. [kalt/warm] ~:** take/give sb. a [cold/hot] shower; **sich/jmdm. den Rücken ~:** shower one's/sb.'s back 2 (entfernen) shower off

ab|düsen *itr. V.; mit sein* (ugs.) zoom off; **nach Rom ~:** take off for Rome

ab|ebben *itr. V.; mit sein* recede; abate

-abend ▸ **Abend 1**

Abend /ˈaːbn̩t/ *der;* **~s, ~e** 1 ▸ⓘ **S. 331** evening; **es wird ~:** evening is drawing in; **als es ~ wurde** when evening came; **diesen ~:** that evening *or* night; (heute) this evening; tonight; **guten ~!** good evening; **des ~s** (geh.) of an evening; in the evenings; **eines [schönen] ~s** one evening; **am [frühen/späten] ~:** [early/late] in the evening; **am ~ vorher** *od.* **zuvor** the evening *or* (coll.) night before; the previous evening; **bis zum [späten] ~:** until [late in the] evening; (als Frist) by [late] evening; **am selben/nächsten ~:** the same/following evening *or* (coll.) night; **am ~ des 1. Mai** on the evening *or* (coll.) night of 1 May; **~ für ~, jeden ~:** every [single] evening *or* (coll.) night; **gegen ~:** towards evening; **während des ~s** during the evening; **während des ganzen ~s** throughout the [entire] evening; **zu ~ essen** have dinner; (allgemeiner) have one's evening meal; **was essen wir zu ~?** what are we having this evening?; what is there for dinner/ supper?; **was machen wir jetzt mit dem angebrochenen ~?** (ugs.) what shall we do with the rest of the evening?; **je später der ~, desto schöner die Gäste** (scherzh.) we're the happier to see you now you 'have come; **du kannst mich [mal] am ~ besuchen** (ugs. verhüll.) you know what 'you can do (coll.); **heute/ morgen/gestern ~:** this/tomorrow/yesterday evening; tonight/tomorrow night/last night (coll.); **was gibt es heute ~ [zu essen]?** what's for dinner/supper?; *s. auch* **heilig 2**; **Tag 1** 2 (Geselligkeit) evening; (Kultur~) soirée; **ein bunter ~:** a social [evening] *or* (coll.) night 3 (veralt.: Westen) the Occident (literary); **gen ~:** to the west *or* (literary) Occident 4 (geh.: Ende) evening

Abend-: ~abitur *das* 'Abitur' through evening classes; **~akademie** *die* evening school; **~andacht** *die* evening service; **~an·zug** *der* dinner dress; evening suit; **~aus·gabe** *die* evening edition; **~blatt** *das* evening [news]paper; **~brot** *das* evening meal; supper; **~brot essen** have one's evening meal; have supper; **wann gibt es ~brot?** when's supper?; **was gibt es zum ~brot?** what's for supper?; **~dämmerung** *die* [evening] twilight

> **Abendbrot, Abendessen**
>
> For most Germans, **Mittagessen** is still the main meal of the day. *Abendbrot* or *Abendessen* normally consists of bread, cheese, meats, perhaps a salad, and a hot drink. It is eaten by the whole family at about 6 or 7 p.m. *Abendessen* can also refer to a cooked meal, especially for people who are out at work all day.

abende·lang

A *Adj.* lasting whole evenings *postpos., not pred*

B *adv.* for whole evenings

abend-, Abend-: ~essen *das* dinner; **das ~essen einnehmen** (geh.) have dinner; **nach dem ~essen** after dinner; **was gibt es zum ~essen?** what's for dinner?; **~füllend** *Adj.* occupying a whole evening *postpos., not pred.;* **ein ~füllendes Programm** a full evening's programme; **~gage** *die* evening's fee; **~gebet** *das* evening prayers *pl.;* (von Kindern) bedtime prayers *pl.;* **das ~gebet sprechen** say one's evening/bedtime prayers; **~gottes·dienst** *der* evening service; (kath. Rel.) evening mass; **~gymnasium** *das* night school, evening classes *pl.* (leading to the 'Abitur'); **~himmel** *der* sunset sky; **~karte** *die* (Gastron.) evening menu; **~kasse** *die* box office (*open on the evening of the performance*); **~kleid** *das* evening dress *or* gown; **~kurs[us]** *der* evening class *or* course; **etw. in ~en lernen** learn sth. at night school

Abendland *das;* **~[e]s** West; Occident (literary)

abendländisch /-lɛndɪʃ/ *Adj.* Western; Occidental (literary)

abendlich

A *Adj.* evening ‹*quiet, coolness*› of the evening; **die ~en Straßen der Stadt** the streets of the town at evening

B *adv.* **es war ~ still geworden** the stillness of evening had descended; **der Himmel ist ~ gerötet** the sky is showing the red colours of evening

Abend·mahl *das* 1 (im Gottesdienst) Communion; **das ~ nehmen** receive Communion 2 (N. T.) Last Supper 3 (bes. südd.) ▸ **Abendessen**

Abendmahls-: ~gottes·dienst *der* Communion service; **~kelch** *der* Communion cup; **~wein** *der* Communion wine

Abend-: ~mahl·zeit *die* dinner; evening meal; **die ~mahlzeit einnehmen** (geh.) have dinner *or* one's evening meal; **~messe** *die* (kath. Rel.) evening mass; **~nachrichten** *Pl.* evening news *sing.;* **~programm** *das* evening programmes *pl.;* **was gibts im ~programm?** what's on this evening?; **damit ist das heutige ~programm beendet** that is the end of our programmes for today; **~rot** *das:* **ein/das ~rot** the redness of the sunset sky; **gestern war ~rot** there was a red sunset last night; **~röte** *die* (geh.) ▸ **Abendrot**

abends *Adv.* ▸ⓘ **S. 729** in the evenings; **um sechs Uhr ~:** at six o'clock in the evening; **Montag** *od.* **montags ~:** [on] Monday evenings; **von morgens bis ~:** from morning to night

Abend-: ~schule *die* night school; evening classes *pl.;* **~schüler** *der* student at evening classes; **~sonne** *die* evening sun; **~stern** *der* evening star; **~stille** *die* evening stillness; **die ländliche ~stille** the evening stillness of the countryside; **~studium** *das* (DDR) *course of evening classes leading to a degree or diploma;* **~stunde** *die* evening hour; **in den frühen/späten ~stunden** early/late in the evening; **bis in die späten ~stunden** till late in the evening; **~toilette** *die* evening dress; **in großer ~toilette** (geh.) in full evening dress; **~vorstellung** *die* evening performance; **~wind** *der* evening breeze; **~zeit** *die:* **zur ~zeit** in the evening; **~zeitung** *die* ▸ **~blatt**; **~zug** *der* evening train

Abenteuer /ˈaːbn̩tɔyɐ/ *das;* **~s, ~** 1 (auch fig.) adventure; **auf ~ ausgehen** go off in search of adventure 2 (Unternehmen) venture 3 (Liebesaffäre) affair

Abenteuer-: ~buch *das* adventure book; **~geschichte** *die* adventure story

abenteuerlich

A *Adj.* 1 (riskant) risky; hazardous 2 (bizarr) bizarre

B *adv.* (bizarr) bizarrely; bizarrely, fantastically ‹*dressed*›

Abenteuerlichkeit *die;* **~** 1 (Gewagtheit) riskiness; hazardousness 2 (Bizarrheit) bizarreness

abenteuer-, Abenteuer-: ~lust *die* thirst for adventure; **~lustig** *Adj.* adventurous; **~lustig sein** have a thirst for adventure; **~roman** *der* adventure novel; **~spielplatz** *der* adventure playground; **~urlaub** *der* adventure holiday; **sie bieten ~urlaub an** they organize adventure holidays

Abenteurer /ˈaːbn̩tɔyrɐ/ *der;* **~s, ~:** adventurer

Abenteurerin *die;* **~, ~nen** adventuress

Abenteurer-: ~leben *das* adventurer's life; **~natur** *die* 1 (Neigung) adventurous nature; 2 (Mensch) adventurous person

aber /ˈaːbɐ/

A *Konj.* 1 (jedoch) but; **wir ~ …** we, however, …; **~ trotzdem** but in spite of that; **da er das ~ nicht wusste** but *or* however, since he didn't know that; **oder ~ [auch]** or else 2 (Einwand) but; **~ warum denn?** but why?; **das stimmt ~ nicht** but that's not right 3 (veralt.: Anknüpfung) but; **als er ~ nicht kam …** but when he didn't come …

B *Adv.* (veralt.: wieder) **~ und abermals** again and again; time and again; *s. auch* **aberhundert; abertausend**

C *Partikel* **das ist ~ schön!** that's really nice!; **~ ja/nein!** why, yes/no! **~ natürlich!** but of course!; **alles, ~ auch alles** everything, but everything; **~ immer!** (ugs.) why, certainly!; **das hat ~ geschmeckt** that really tasted good; **das ist ~ auch zu dumm** it's just 'too stupid *or* (Amer.) dumb; **das dauert ~** (ugs.) what a time it's taking!; **du bist ~ groß!** aren't you tall!; **hat der ~ eine große Nase!** hasn't he got a big nose!; **Sie kommen ~ spät heute** you 'are late today; **~, ~, meine Herrschaften!** now, now, [ladies and] gentlemen

Aber *das;* **~s, ~: ich dulde kein ~:** it's no use your objecting; *s. auch* **Wenn**

Aber·glaube[n] *der* 1 (Irrglaube) superstition 2 (Vorurteil) myth

aber·gläubig (veralt.), **aber·gläubisch** /-glɔybɪʃ/ *Adj.* superstitious

aber·hundert *unbest. Zahlw.* (geh.) hundreds [upon hundreds] of

Aber·hunderte *Pl.* (geh.) hundreds [upon hundreds]

ab|erkennen *unr. tr. V.* **jmdm. ein Recht ~:** revoke sb.'s right (**auf** + *Akk.* to); (Sport) **jmdm. den Sieg/Titel ~:** disallow sb.'s victory/strip sb. of his/her title

Aberkennung *die;* **~, ~en** revocation; (Sport) **die ~ ihres Sieges/Titels** disallowing her victory/stripping her of her title

abermalig *Adj.* (wiederholt) repeated; (nochmalig) renewed

abermals /ˈaːbɐmaːls/ *Adv.* once again; once more

ab|ernten *tr. V.* finish the harvesting of; finish harvesting *or* picking ‹*fruit*›; **das Getreide ist abgeerntet** the corn is all in; **die Apfelbäume waren fast abgeerntet** nearly all the fruit had been picked from the apple trees; **abgeerntete Felder** empty fields

Aberration /apl̩ɛraˈt͜si̯oːn/ *die;* **~, ~en** (Astron., Optik) aberration

aber·tausend *unbest. Zahlw.* (geh.) thousands [upon thousands] of

Aber·tausende *Pl.* (geh.) thousands [upon thousands]

Aber·witz *der* (geh.) lunacy; **ein ~:** a piece of lunacy

aber·witzig *Adj.* crazy

ab|essen *unr. tr. V.* **1** (wegessen) **etw. [von etw.] ~:** eat sth. off [sth.] **2** (leer essen) clear ‹*plate, table*›; **abgegessene Teller** empty plates; **abgegessenes Geschirr** dirty dishes

Abessinien /abɛˈsiːni̯ən/ (*das*); **~s** (veralt.) **1** Abyssinia **2** (scherzh.: FKK-Strand) nudist beach

Abessinier *der;* **~s, ~, Abessinierin,** *die;* **~, ~nen** (veralt.) Abyssinian

Abf. *Abk.* **= Abfahrt** dep.

ab|fackeln *tr. V.* (Technik) flare [off]

abfahr·bereit *Adj.* ready to go *or* leave *pred.*; **die ~en Fahrzeuge** the vehicles which are/were ready to leave

ab|fahren

A *unr. itr. V.; mit sein* **1** (wegfahren) leave; depart; **wo fährt der Zug nach Paris ab?** where does the Paris train leave from? **2** (hinunterfahren) drive down; (Skisport) ski *or* go down **3** (salopp: sich begeistern) **auf jmdn./etw. [voll] ~:** be mad about sb./sth. **4** (salopp: abgewiesen werden) **jmdn. ~ lassen** tell sb. where he/she can go (sl.); **bei jmdm. ganz schön ~:** get absolutely nowhere with sb. (coll.)

B *unr. tr. V.* **1** (abtransportieren) take away **2** (abnutzen) wear out; **abgefahrene Reifen** worn tyres **3** *auch mit sein* (entlangfahren) drive the whole length of ‹*street, route*›; drive through ‹*district*› **4** (ugs.: abtrennen) **jmdm. ein Bein ~:** run over sb. and sever his/her leg **5** (Film, Ferns.) start

C *unr. refl. V.* (sich abnutzen) wear out

Ab·fahrt *die* **1** departure **2** (Skisport) descent; (Strecke) run; *s. auch* **Abfahrtslauf** **3** (Autobahn~) ▸ **Ausfahrt 1**

abfahrt·bereit ▸ **abfahrbereit**

Abfahrts-: ~lauf *der* (Skisport) downhill [racing]; **~läufer** *der*, **~läuferin** *die* (Skisport) downhill racer; **~rennen** *das* (Skisport) downhill [racing]

Abfahrt[s]·zeit *die* time of departure; departure time

Ab·fall *der* **1** (Küchen~ o. Ä.) rubbish, (Amer.) garbage *or* trash *no indef. art., no pl.*; (Fleisch~) offal *no indef. art., no pl.*; (Industrie~) waste *no indef. art.*; (auf der Straße) litter *no indef. art., no pl.*; **den ~ runtertragen** (ugs.) empty the rubbish **2** (Rückgang) drop (*Gen.*, **in** + *Dat.* in) **3** (*Abtrünnigkeit*) (vom Glauben) apostasy; (eines Landes) secession (**von** from)

Abfall-: ~beseitigung *die* refuse disposal; (industriell) waste disposal; **~eimer** *der* rubbish *or* waste bin; trash *or* garbage can (Amer.); (auf der Straße) litter bin; trash *or* litter basket *or* can (Amer.)

ab|fallen *unr. itr. V.; mit sein* **1** (ugs.: herausspringen) **wie viel fällt für jeden ab?** what will each person's share be?; **für dich wird auch eine Kleinigkeit ~:** you'll get something out of it too; **dabei fällt nicht viel ab** not much will come out of it **2** (übrig bleiben) be left [over] **3** (herunterfallen) fall off **4** (verschwinden) **von jmdm. ~:** leave sb.; **alle Unsicherheit fiel von ihm ab** he shed all his diffidence **5** (sich lossagen) ‹*country*› secede; **vom Glauben ~:** desert the faith; **seine Anhänger fielen von ihm ab** his followers deserted him **6** (nachlassen) drop **7** (bes. Sport: zurückfallen) drop *or* fall back **8** (sich senken) ‹*land, hillside, road*› drop away; slope **9** (im Vergleich) **gegenüber jmdm./etw.** *od.* **gegen jmdn./etw. stark ~:** be markedly inferior to sb./sth. **10** (Seemannsspr.) cast

Abfall·haufen *der* rubbish heap; (in einer Werkstatt usw.) waste pile

ab·fällig

A *Adj.* disparaging; derogatory

B *adv.* **sich ~ über jmdn. äußern** make disparaging *or* derogatory remarks about sb.

Abfall-: ~produkt *das* (auch fig.) by-product; (Sekundärstoff) secondary product; **~verwertung** *die* recycling of waste

ab|fälschen *tr. V.* (Ballspiele) deflect

ab|fangen *unr. tr. V.* **1** intercept ‹*agent, message, aircraft*› **2** (auf-, anhalten) catch **3** (Sport: einholen) **jmdn. ~:** catch sb. up; catch up with sb. **4** (abwehren) repel ‹*charge, assault*›; ward off ‹*blow, attack*›; (fig.) stop ‹*development*›; cushion ‹*impact*› **5** (Bauw.) shore up **6** (unter Kontrolle bringen) get ‹*vehicle, aircraft*› under control

Abfang·jäger *der* (Luftwaffe) interceptor

ab|färben *itr. V.* **1** ‹*colour, garment, etc.*› run; ‹*wet paint etc.*› leave marks **2** (beeinflussen) **auf jmdn./etw. ~:** rub off on sb./sth.

ab|fasen *tr. V.* (Technik) bevel ‹*edge*›

ab|fassen *tr. V.* write ‹*report, letter, etc.*›; draw up ‹*will*›

Ab·fassung *die* writing; (eines Testaments) drawing up

ab|faulen *itr. V.; mit sein* rot off

ab|federn

A *tr. V.* **1** (federnd abfangen) absorb **2** (Technik) spring ‹*axle etc.*›

B *itr. V.* bend at the knees on landing [to absorb the shock]; (beim Absprung) push off

ab|fegen *tr. V.* ▸ **abkehren**[2]

ab|feiern *tr. V.* use up ‹*excess hours worked*› (*by taking time off*)

ab|feilen *tr. V.* **1** (entfernen) file off; **etw. von etw. ~:** file sth. off sth. **2** (verkürzen, glätten) file down

ab|fertigen *tr. V.* **1** handle, dispatch ‹*mail*›; deal with ‹*applicant, application*›; deal with, handle ‹*passengers*›; serve ‹*customer*›; clear ‹*ship*› for sailing; clear ‹*aircraft*› for take-off; clear ‹*lorry*› for departure; (vorbereiten) prepare ‹*ship etc.*› for departure; prepare ‹*mail*› for dispatch; (kontrollieren) clear; check; **der Zoll hat zügig abgefertigt** customs clearance was quick **2** (ugs.: unfreundlich behandeln) **jmdn. [grob/barsch] ~:** [roughly/rudely] turn sb. away; **er hat mich ganz kurz abgefertigt** he was very short with me **3** (Sport) trounce; **der Gegner wurde [mit] 5:1 abgefertigt** the opponent was trounced 5:1

Ab·fertigung *die* **1** ▸ **abfertigen 1**: handling; dispatching; serving; clearing for sailing/take-off/departure; preparing for departure/dispatch; (Kontrolle) clearance; checking; **die unfreundliche ~ am Flughafen/im Laden** the unfriendly service at the airport/in the shop **2** (Abteilung) dispatch office **3** (österr.) ▸ **Abfindung**

Abfertigungs·schalter *der* (am Flughafen) check-in desk; (beim Zoll) customs desk

ab|feuern *tr. V.* fire; **Schüsse/eine Kanone [auf jmdn./etw.] ~:** fire shots/a cannon [at sb./sth.]; **das ganze Magazin ~:** fire off the whole magazine

ab|filtern, ab|filtrieren *tr. V.* (fachspr.) filter out

ab|finden

A *unr. tr. V.* (entschädigen) **jmdn. mit etw. ~:** compensate sb. with sth.; **seine Gläubiger ~:** settle with one's creditors; **er wurde großzügig abgefunden** he received a generous settlement

B *unr. refl. V.* **sich ~:** resign oneself; **sich ~ mit** come to terms with; learn to live with ‹*noise, heat*›; **sich damit ~, dass ...** come to terms with the fact that ...

Abfindung *die;* **~, ~en** **1** (Summe) settlement; **eine ~ in Höhe von ... zahlen** make a settlement of ... **2** (Vorgang) (Entschädigung) compensation; (von Gläubigern) paying off

Abfindungs·summe *die* ▸ **Abfindung 1**

ab|fischen *tr. V.* fish out

ab|flachen /ˈapflaxn̩/

A *tr. V.* (flacher machen) flatten [out]

B *refl. V.* **1** (flacher werden) flatten out; become flatter **2** (nachlassen) drop off

Abflachung *die;* **~, ~en** **1** flattening **2** (Nachlassen) dropping off

ab|flauen *itr. V.; mit sein* die down; subside; ‹*interest, conversation*› flag; ‹*business*› become slack; ‹*noise*› abate; **die Konjunktur flaut ab** the economy is running down

ab|flexen *tr. V.* grind off; (abschneiden) cut off with an angle grinder

ab|fliegen

A *unr. itr. V.; mit sein* ‹*person*› leave [by aeroplane]; ‹*aircraft*› take off; ‹*bird*› fly off *or* away; **die Maschine nach Brüssel fliegt um 13[30] Uhr ab** the plane for Brussels leaves at 13.30

B *unr. tr. V.* **1** (wegbringen) fly out (**aus** of) **2** (kontrollieren) fly over ‹*district*›; fly along ‹*road*›

ab|fließen *unr. itr. V.; mit sein* **1** flow off; (wegfließen) flow away; **aus etw. ~:** drain away from sth.; **von etw. ~:** run off sth.; **sämtliche Gewinne fließen ins Ausland ab** (fig.) all profits are siphoned off abroad **2** (sich leeren) **die Wanne fließt nicht ab** the bath won't empty

Ab·flug *der* departure

Abflug-: ~hafen *der* (Flugw.) airport of departure; **die Maschine kehrte zum ~hafen zurück** the aircraft returned to the airport it had started from; **~zeit** *die* departure time

Ab·fluss, *Ab·fluß *der* **1** drain; (von Gewässern) outlet; (Rohr) drainpipe; (für Abwasser) waste pipe **2** (das Abfließen) draining away; **der ~ von Kapital ins Ausland** (fig.) the flow of capital abroad

Abfluss-, *Abfluß-: ~graben *der* drainage ditch; **~rohr** *das* outlet pipe

Ab·folge *die* sequence; **die ~ der Jahreszeiten** the cycle of the seasons

ab|fordern *tr. V.* **jmdm. etw. ~:** demand sth. of sb.

ab|fotografieren *tr. V.* take pictures of

ab|fragen *tr. V.* **1** test; **jmdn.** *od.* **jmdm. die Vokabeln ~:** test sb. on his/her vocabulary **2** (DV) retrieve, read out ‹*data*›; interrogate ‹*measuring instrument, store*›

ab|fressen *unr. tr. V.* **1** (wegfressen) **etw. [von etw.] ~:** eat sth. off [sth.] **2** (leer fressen) strip ‹*tree, stem, etc.*› bare

ab|frieren

A *unr. itr. V.; mit sein* **die Ohren froren ihm ab** he lost his ears through frostbite

B *unr. refl. V.* **sich** (*Dat.*) **etw. ~:** lose sth. by frostbite; **sich** (*Dat.*) **einen ~** (ugs.) freeze to death (coll.)

ab|frottieren *tr. V.* rub down [thoroughly]

ab|frühstücken *tr. V.;* (ugs.) **1** (abspeisen) **jmdn. ~:** fob sb. off (**mit** with); **billig abgefrühstückt werden** be given short measure **2** (erledigen) deal with; **abgefrühstückt sein** ‹*subject*› be done to death; ‹*person*› be a spent force

ab|fühlen *tr. V.* feel; palpate (Med.)

Abfuhr *die;* **~, ~en** **1** (Abtransport) removal **2** (Zurückweisung) **jmdm. eine ~ erteilen** rebuff sb.; turn sb. down; **sich eine ~ holen** be rebuffed *or* turned down; **die Mannschaft holte sich eine deutliche ~:** the team was soundly trounced

ab|führen

A *tr. V.* **1** (nach Festnahme) take away **2** (zahlen) pay out; **Steuern ans Finanzamt ~:** pay taxes to the Inland Revenue **3** *auch itr.* (abbringen) take away; **jmdn. vom Thema ~:** take sb. away from the subject

B *itr. V.* **1** (für Stuhlgang sorgen) be a laxative; have a laxative effect; **ein ~des Mittel** a laxative; **ein stark ~des Mittel** a purgative **2** (den Darm leeren) move one's bowels **3** (abzweigen) ‹*road*› branch off

Abführ-: ~mittel *das* laxative; (stärker) purgative; **~pille** *die* laxative pill

Abfüll-: ~an·lage *die* bottling/canning plant; **~datum** *das* bottling/canning date

ab|füllen *tr. V.* fill ‹*sack, bottle, barrel*›; **Wein in Flaschen ~:** bottle wine; **Bier in Dosen ~:** can beer

ab|füttern[1] *tr., itr. V.* feed ‹*animals*›

ab|füttern[2] *tr. V.* line ‹*coat, jacket*›

Ab·gabe *die* **1** handing in; (eines Briefes, Pakets, Telegramms) delivery; (eines Gesuchs, Antrags) submission; **gegen ~ des Coupons erhalten Sie ...** on handing in *or* producing the coupon you will receive ... **2** (Steuer, Gebühr) tax; (auf Produkte) duty; (Gemeinde~) rate; (Beitrag) contribution **3** (Ausstrahlung) release; emission; **eine ~ von 60 Watt** an output of 60 watts **4** (Sport: Abspiel) pass **5** (das Abfeuern) firing **6** (das Äußern) (von Erklärungen) giving; (von Urteilen, Aussagen) making; (Stimm~) casting **7** (Verlust) loss; (Sport: von Punkten) dropping **8** (Verkauf) selling; **„~ nur in Kisten"** 'sold only by the crate'

abgaben·frei

A *Adj.* ‹*business, trade, product*› free from tax; (zollfrei) duty-free

B *adv.* without paying taxes

Abgaben·ordnung *die* (Finanzw.) tax law

abgabe[n]·pflichtig *Adj.* ‹*person, business, trade*› liable to tax; ‹*product*› subject to duty

Abgabe·zug *der* (Schach) sealed move

Ab·gang *der* **1** (das Weggehen) leaving; departure; (eines Zuges, Schiffes) departure (Theater) exit; (fig.) departure; **sich einen guten ~ verschaffen** (fig.) make a good exit **2** (jmd., der ausscheidet) departure; (Schule) leaver **3** (bes. Amtsspr.: Todesfall) death; **den ~ machen** (salopp) kick the bucket (sl.); croak (sl.) **4** (Turnen) dismount **5** (Ausscheidung) passing; (von Eiter, Würmern) discharge; **durch [einen] natürlichen ~:** by being passed naturally **6** ▸ⓘ **S. 439** (Med.: Fehlgeburt) miscarriage **7** (Absendung) dispatch; **nach ~ des Briefes** after posting off *or* sending the letter **8** (Kaufmannsspr.) **die Ware findet reißenden ~:** the product is a best seller

ab·gängig *Adj.* (bes. österr.) missing

Abgängigkeits·anzeige *die* (österr.) ▸**Vermisstenanzeige**

Abgangs·zeugnis *das* (Schulw.) ≈ leaving certificate

Ab·gas *das* exhaust; (in geschlossenem Raum) exhaust fumes *pl.*; **~e** exhaust fumes; **industrielle ~e** waste gases

abgas-, Abgas-: ~entgiftung *die* (Kfz-W.) emission control; **~frei** **A** *Adj.* exhaust-free ‹*engine*›; **B** *adv.* **das Auto fährt ~frei** the car produces no exhaust fumes; **~katalysator** *der* (Kfz-W.) catalytic converter; **~test**, **~untersuchung** *die* (Kfz-W.) exhaust emissions test; **~turbine** *die* (Technik) exhaust-driven turbine; **~verwertung** *die* (Technik) utilization of exhaust-gas heat; **~wolke** *die* cloud of exhaust fumes

ab|gaunern *tr. V.* (ugs.) **jmdm. etw. ~:** con sb. out of sth. (coll.)

abgearbeitet ▸**abarbeiten 2**

ab|geben

A *unr. tr. V.* **1** (aushändigen) hand over; deliver ‹*letter, parcel, telegram*›; hand in, submit ‹*application*›; hand in ‹*school work*›; **etw. bei jmdm. ~:** deliver sth. *or* hand sth. over to sb.; **etw. für jmdn. ~:** leave sth. for sb.; **den Mantel in der Garderobe ~:** leave one's coat in the cloakroom **2** (abtreten) **jmdm. [etwas] von etw. ~:** let sb. have some of sth.; **den Vorsitz/die Spitze ~:** give up the chair/the leadership; **einen Punkt/Satz/eine Runde ~** (Sport) drop a point/set/round **3** (abfeuern) fire; **einen Schuss [auf jmdn./etw.] ~:** fire a shot [at sb./sth.] **4** (ausstrahlen) emit ‹*radiation*›; radiate ‹*heat*›; give off ‹*gas*›; transmit ‹*radio message*› **5** (äußern) make ‹*judgement, statement*›; cast ‹*vote*›; **seine Stimme für jmdn. ~:** cast one's vote in favour of sb.; vote for sb. **6** (fungieren als) make; **eine traurige Figur ~:** cut a sorry figure **7** (verkaufen) sell; (zu niedrigem Preis) sell off; **gebrauchte Skier billig abzugeben** second-hand skis for sale cheap **8** *auch itr.* (Sport: abspielen) pass

B *unr. refl. V.* (sich befassen) **sich mit jmdm./etw. ~:** spend time on sb./sth.; (geringschätzig) waste one's time on sb./sth

ab·gebrannt

A *2. Part. v.* **abbrennen**

B *Adj.* (ugs.) broke (coll.)

ab·gebrochen

A *2. Part. v.* **abbrechen**

B *Adj.* (ugs. scherzh.) **1** **ein ~er Mediziner** *usw.*: *a former medical etc. student who never completed his training* **2** **ein ~er Riese** a midget

abgebrüht

A *2. Part. v.* **abbrühen**

B *Adj.* (ugs.) hardened

abgedankt

A *2. Part. v.* **abdanken**

B *Adj.* retired

ab·gedroschen *Adj.* (ugs.) hackneyed; well-worn; trite

Abgedroschenheit *die*; **~** (ugs.) triteness; hackneyedness

abgefeimt /ˈapgəfaimt/ *Adj.* infernally cunning ‹*villain, rogue*›; villainous ‹*scheme*›

Abgefeimtheit *die*; **~, ~en** (Handlung) piece of villainy; (Charakter) infernal cunning; **seine ~en** his villainy *sing.*

ab·gegriffen

A *2. Part. v.* **abgreifen**

B *Adj.* **1** (abgenutzt) battered **2** (fig.: abgedroschen) hackneyed; well-worn

abgehackt

A *2. Part. v.* **abhacken**

B *Adj.* broken ‹*voice*›; clipped ‹*speech*›; fragmentary ‹*sentence*›

C *adv.* in short bursts

ab·gehangen

A *2. Part. v.* **abhängen**[1]

B *Adj.* hung; **ein gut ~es Steak** a well-hung steak

abgehärmt

A *2. Part. v.* **abhärmen**

B *Adj.* careworn; haggard

abgehärtet

A *2. Part. v.* **abhärten**

B *Adj.* (körperlich) tough; (seelisch) callous

ab|gehen

A *unr. itr. V.*; *mit sein* **1** (sich entfernen) leave; go away *or* off; (Theater) exit; go off; **von der Bühne ~:** leave the stage; **nach hinten ~:** go out at the back **2** (ausscheiden) leave; **von der Schule ~:** leave school **3** (abfahren) ‹*train, ship, bus*› leave, depart **4** (abgeschickt werden) ‹*message, letter*› be sent [off] **5** (abzweigen) branch off; (in andere Richtung) turn off **6** (sich lösen) come off; ‹*spot, stain*› come out; ‹*avalanche*› come down **7** (Turnen) dismount **8** (abgerechnet werden) **von etw. [an jmdn.] ~:** have to be deducted from sth. [and paid to sb.] **9** (fehlen) **jmdm. geht etw. [völlig] ab** sb. is [totally] lacking in sth.; **mir geht jedes Interesse daran ab** it does not interest me in the slightest; **sich** (*Dat.*) **nichts ~ lassen** never stint oneself **10** (ausgehen) go off **11** (ausgeschieden werden) ‹*pus, worms*› be discharged; (mit normalen Ausscheidungen) be passed; **jmdm. geht Kot ab** sb. has a motion *or* (Amer.) movement; **eine Blähung ~ lassen** break wind; **ihm ging einer ab** (derb) he shot his load (coarse) **12** (aufgeben) **~ von** abandon ‹*demand, agreement, principle*›; give up ‹*habit*›

B *unr. tr. V.*; *auch mit sein* walk all along; go over ‹*area*› on foot

abgehetzt

A *2. Part. v.* **abhetzen**

B *Adj.* exhausted; (außer Atem) breathless

abgekämpft *Adj.* worn out; exhausted; combat-weary ‹*troops*›

abgekartet *Adj.* (ugs.) pre-arranged; **von vornherein ~:** set up in advance; **eine ~e Sache, ein ~es Spiel sein** be rigged in advance

abgeklappert

A *2. Part. v.* **abklappern**

B *Adj.* (abwertend) beat-up, (Brit. sl.) clapped-out ‹*machine, bicycle, horse, etc.*›; hackneyed, well-worn, trite ‹*expression*›

abgeklärt

A *2. Part. v.* **abklären**

B *Adj.* serene

Abgeklärtheit *die*; **~:** serenity

abgelagert

A *2. Part. v.* **ablagern**

B *Adj.* mature ‹*wine*›; seasoned ‹*timber, tobacco*›; **gut ~es Holz** well-seasoned timber

abgelebt

A *2. Part. v.* **ableben**

B *Adj.* [old and] weary ‹*person*›; worn ‹*face*›

ab·gelegen *Adj.* remote; (einsam) isolated; out-of-the-way ‹*district*›; (abgeschieden) secluded; (fig.) recondite

Ab·gelegenheit *die*; **~:** remoteness; (einsame Lage) isolation

ab|gelten *unr. tr. V.* satisfy, settle ‹*claim*›; pay ‹*overtime*›; **die Mehrarbeit in Freizeit ~:** give time off in lieu of overtime pay; **diese Leistung war bereits mit der Jahresgebühr abgegolten** payment for this service was already coverered in the annual fee; **jmdm. seine Treue gut ~:** reward sb. well for his/her loyalty; **eine Geldstrafe durch gemeinnützige Arbeit ~:** do community service in lieu of paying a fine; **die Gefängnisstrafe war bereits durch die Untersuchungshaft abgegolten** the prison sentence had already been served on remand

Ab·geltung *die*; **~, ~en** settlement

abgemagert

A *2. Part. v.* **abmagern**

B *Adj.* emaciated; wasted

ab·gemessen

A *2. Part. v.* **abmessen**

B *Adj.* (geh.) measured

C *adv.* (geh.) in a measured fashion

ab·geneigt *Adj.* **einer Sache** (*Dat.*) **~ sein** be averse to sth.; **ein stiller, jeder Publicity ~er Mensch** a quiet person averse to public notice; **die jeder Reform ~en Politiker** the politicians opposed to any reform; **jmdm. ~ sein** be ill-disposed towards sb.; **[nicht] ~ sein, etw. zu tun** [not] be averse to doing sth.

abgenutzt

A *2. Part. v.* **abnutzen**

B *Adj.* worn ‹*tyre, chair, handle*›; well-used ‹*implement*›; well-worn ‹*phrase*›

Abgeordnete *der/die*; *adj. Dekl.* member [of parliament]; (in Berlin, Frankreich) deputy; **Herr ~r [Schmidt]/Frau ~ [Müller]** (im Parlament) the honourable Member; **der [Herr] ~ Meier** Mr Meier

Abgeordneten·haus *das* parliament; (in Berlin, Frankreich) Chamber of Deputies

ab|geraten *unr. itr. V.*; *mit sein* (veralt.) **vom Weg ~:** lose one's way; stray from one's path

ab·gerissen

A *2. Part. v.* **abreißen**

B *Adj.* **1** (zerlumpt) ragged **2** (zusammenhanglos) disconnected; fragmentary

Ab·gesandte *der/die* (veralt.) ambassador; (fig.) emissary

Ab·gesang *der* **1** (Abschied) **ein ~ auf etw.** (*Akk.*) a farewell to sth. **2** (geh.: letztes Werk) swan song **3** (Verslehre) abgesang (final part of Minnesang strophe)

abgeschabt

A *2. Part. v.* **abschaben**

B *Adj.* shabby; worn

ab·geschieden

A *2. Part. v.* **abscheiden**

B *Adj.* **1** secluded; (abgelegen) isolated **2** (geh.: tot) departed

C *adv.* ‹*live*› in seclusion

Abgeschiedenheit *die*; **~:** seclusion; (Abgelegenheit) isolation

ab·geschlagen

A *2. Part. v.* **abschlagen**

B *Adj.* **1** (Sport) [well] beaten; **~ auf dem neunten Tabellenplatz** in lowly ninth place **2** (erschöpft) exhausted; tired out

ab·geschlossen

A *2. Part. v.* **abschließen**

B *Adj.* **1** (abgesondert) secluded; solitary **2** (in sich geschlossen) enclosed; self-contained ‹*flat*›

C *adv.* ‹*live*› in seclusion

Ab·geschlossenheit *die*; **~:** seclusion; (Abgelegenheit) isolation

abgeschmackt /ˈapgəʃmakt/ *Adj.* tasteless

ab·geschnitten

A *2. Part. v.* **abschneiden**

B *Adj.* isolated; **von der Außenwelt ~:** cut off from the outside world

ab·gesehen

A *2. Part. v.* **absehen**

B *Adv.* **~ von jmdm./etw.** apart from sb./sth.; **~ davon, dass ...** apart from the fact that ...

ab·gesessen

A *2. Part. v.* **absitzen**

B *Adj.* worn

ab·gespannt

A *2. Part. v.* **abspannen**

B *Adj.* weary; exhausted

Ab·gespanntheit *die*; **~:** weariness; exhaustion

abgespielt

A *2. Part. v.* **abspielen**

B *Adj.* ‹*record etc.*› worn out with repeated playing

ab·gestanden

A *2. Part. v.* **abstehen**

a

B *Adj.* 1 (schal) flat; (fig.) trite 2 (verbraucht) stale

ab·gestorben
A *2. Part. v.* **absterben**
B *Adj.* dead ‹*branch, tree*›; numb ‹*fingers, legs, etc.*›

abgestumpft
A *2. Part. v.* **abstumpfen**
B *Adj.* apathetic and insensitive ‹*person*›; deadened ‹*conscience, perception*›; **gegenüber einer Sache ~ sein** be hardened to sth.

Abgestumpftheit *die;* **~:** apathy and insensitivity

abgetakelt
A *2. Part. v.* **abtakeln**
B *Adj.* (salopp: heruntergekommen) faded

ab·getragen
A *2. Part. v.* **abtragen**
B *Adj.* well-worn

ab·getreten
A *2. Part. v.* **abtreten**
B *Adj.* worn down

abgewetzt
A *2. Part. v.* **abwetzen**
B *Adj.* well-worn; battered ‹*case etc.*›

ab|gewinnen *unr. tr. V.* 1 (beim Spiel) **jmdm. Geld ~:** win money from sb. 2 (erlangen von) **jmdm. etw. ~:** get sth. out of sb.; win sth. from sb.; **einer Sache** (*Dat.*) **etw. ~:** win *or* gain sth. from sth. 3 (fig.) **ich kann ihm/dem nichts ~:** he/it does not do anything for me (coll.); *s. auch* **Geschmack 1**

abgewirtschaftet
A *2. Part. v.* **abwirtschaften**
B *Adj.* run down

ab·gewogen
A *2. Part. v.* **abwägen, abwiegen**
B *Adj.* carefully weighed; balanced ‹*judgement*›; carefully considered ‹*account*›

ab|gewöhnen *tr. V.:* **jmdm. etw. ~:** make sb. give up *or* stop sth.; **sich** (*Dat.*) **etw. ~:** give up *or* stop sth.; **noch einen zum Abgewöhnen trinken/eine zum Abgewöhnen rauchen** (ugs.) have just one more (coll.); **zum Abgewöhnen [sein]** (ugs.) [be] awful

abgewrackt
A *2. Part. v.* **abwracken**
B *Adj.* (abwertend) superannuated

abgezehrt *Adj.* emaciated

abgezirkelt
A *2. Part. v.* **abzirkeln**
B *Adj.* measured out ‹*flower beds*›; carefully weighed ‹*words*›; **ein exakt ~er Pass** (Sport) a precisely calculated pass
C *adv.* with calculated precision

ab|gießen *unr. tr. V.* 1 pour away ‹*liquid*›; drain ‹*potatoes*›; **den Eimer ~:** pour some water *etc.* out of the bucket 2 (bild. Kunst; Gießerei) **etw. [in Bronze] ~:** cast sth. [in bronze]

Ab·glanz *der* 1 (Reflex) reflection 2 (Nachklang) distant echo; pale reflection

ab|gleichen *unr. tr. V.* (Funkw., Elektronik) balance

ab|gleiten *unr. itr. V.; mit sein* (geh.) 1 (abrutschen) slide *or* slip off; **von/an etw.** (*Dat.*) **~:** slip *or* slide off sth. 2 (absinken) **in etw.** (*Akk.*) **~:** slip down into sth.

Ab·gott *der* idol

Abgötterei /apgœtəˈraj/ *die;* **~:** idolatry

Ab·göttin *die* idol

abgöttisch /ˈapgœtɪʃ/
A *Adj.* idolatrous
B *adv.* **jmdn. ~ verehren/lieben** idolize sb.

ab|graben *unr. tr. V.* dig out; *s. auch* **Wasser 1**

ab|grasen *tr. V.* 1 graze away ‹*pasture*› 2 (ugs.: absuchen) **etw. nach etw. ~:** comb *or* scour sth. for sth.

ab|greifen *unr. tr. V.* 1 measure (*with one's hand*); **eine Strecke mit dem Zirkel ~:** measure a distance with compasses; *s. auch* **abgegriffen B** 2 (Elektrot.) pick up

ab|grenzen *tr. V.* 1 bound; **etw. nach allen Seiten ~:** enclose sth.; **etw. gegen** *od.* **von etw. ~:** separate sth. from sth. 2 (unterscheiden) differentiate; distinguish; (festlegen) demarcate; **zwei Theorien gegeneinander** *od.* **voneinander ~:** differentiate between two theories; **sich von jmdm. ~:** differentiate oneself from sb.

Abgrenzung *die;* **~, ~en** 1 boundary; **~ nach allen Seiten** enclosure 2 (Unterscheidung) differentiation; (Festlegung) demarcation; **Politik der ~:** policy of demarcation

Ab·grund *der* 1 (Schlucht) abyss; chasm; (Abhang) precipice 2 (fig. geh.) dark abyss; **die Abgründe der menschlichen Seele** the depths of the human soul; **ein ~ von Verzweiflung** an abyss of despair

abgründig /ˈapgrʏndɪç/ (geh.)
A *Adj.* 1 (rätselhaft) inscrutable ‹*smile*›; hidden ‹*meaning*›; dark ‹*secret*› 2 (unermesslich) unbounded
B *adv.* 1 (rätselhaft) ‹*smile*› inscrutably 2 (sehr) thoroughly

abgrund·tief *Adj.* out and out

Ab·gruppierung *die* salary downgrading

ab|gucken (ugs.)
A *tr. V.* 1 **[bei** *od.* **von] jmdm. etw. ~:** learn sth. by watching sb. 2 **ich guck dir nichts ab!** (fam.) you needn't be self-conscious just because I'm watching you
B *itr. V.* (abschreiben) **[bei jmdm.] ~:** copy [from sb.]; copy [sb. else's] work

Ab·guss, *Ab·guß *der* (bild. Kunst, Gießerei) (Verfahren) casting; (Ergebnis) cast; **ein ~ in Bronze** a bronze [cast]

ab|haben *unr. tr. V.* (ugs.) 1 *auch itr.* (erhalten) **etwas/ein Stück** *usw.* **[von etw.] ~:** have some/a piece *etc.* [of sth.]. **du kannst gerne davon ~:** you're welcome to have some 2 (abgenommen haben) have off; **du hast die Mütze ja schon wieder ab!** why, you've got your cap off again! 3 (entfernt haben) have got off

ab|hacken *tr. V.* chop off; **jmdm. die Hand** *usw.* **~:** chop sb.'s hand *etc.* off; *s. auch* **abgehackt B, C**

ab|haken *tr. V.* 1 (mit Haken versehen) tick off; check off (Amer.); (fig.: erledigen) deal with 2 (vom Haken abnehmen) unclip

ab|halftern *tr. V.* 1 (ugs.: entlassen) sack (coll.) 2 (das Halfter abnehmen von) **ein Pferd ~:** take the halter off a horse

ab|halten *unr. tr. V.* 1 (fernhalten) **[von jmdm./etw.] ~:** keep ‹*person, wind, cold, flies, etc.*› off [sb./sth.]; keep ‹*trouble*› away [from sb.] 2 (hindern) **jmdn. davon ~, etw. zu tun** stop sb. doing sth.; prevent sb. from doing sth. 3 (durchführen) hold ‹*elections, meeting, referendum*› 4 (bei der Notdurft) hold ‹*child*› out 5 (weghalten) hold away; **etw. ein Stück von sich ~:** hold sth. away from oneself

Ab·haltung *die* 1 (Verhinderung) **eine [dringende] ~ haben** be [unavoidably] held up 2 (Durchführung) holding

ab|handeln *tr. V.* 1 (abkaufen) **jmdm. etw. ~:** do a deal with sb. for sth. 2 (herunterhandeln) **jmdm. zehn Euro ~:** beat sb. down by ten euros; (fig.) **sich** (*Dat.*) **von etw. nichts ~ lassen** not be persuaded to part with any of sth. 3 (darstellen) treat; deal with

abhanden /apˈhandn̩/ *Adv.* **~ kommen** get lost; go astray; **etw. kommt jmdm. ~:** sb. mislays *or* loses sth.

Ab·handlung *die* 1 (Aufsatz) treatise (**über** + *Akk.* on) 2 (das Abhandeln) treatment

Ab·hang *der* slope; incline

ab|hängen[1] *unr. itr. V.* 1 (abhängig sein) **[ganz allein] von jmdm./etw. ~:** depend [entirely] on sb./sth.; **davon hängt sehr viel für mich ab** a lot depends on it for me; **von jmdm./etw. ~** (angewiesen sein) be dependent on sb./sth. 2 (hängen) hang; *s. auch* **abgehangen B** 3 (ugs.: sich entspannen, faulenzen) chill out (coll.)

ab|hängen[2]
A *tr. V.* 1 (abnehmen) take down; **ein Bild von der Wand ~:** take a picture [down] off the wall 2 (Eisenb.: abkuppeln) uncouple 3 (ugs.: abschütteln) shake off ‹*pursuer, competitor*›
B *itr. V.* (den Hörer auflegen) hang up

abhängig /ˈaphɛŋɪç/ *Adj.* 1 **von jmdm./etw. ~ sein** (bedingt) depend on sb./sth.; (angewiesen) be dependent on sb./sth.; **von einer Droge ~ sein** be addicted to *or* dependent on a drug; **etw. von etw. ~ machen** make sth. conditional upon sth. 2 (Sprachw.) indirect *or* reported ‹*speech*›; subordinate ‹*clause*›; oblique ‹*case*›

-abhängig *Adj.* dependent on …

Abhängige *der/die; adj. Dekl.* (Rechtsspr.) dependant; (Untergebene) subordinate

-abhängigkeit *die* dependence on …

Abhängigkeit *die;* **~, ~en** dependence; **~ von Drogen** addiction to *or* dependence on drugs; **in ~ von jmdm./etw. geraten** become dependent on sb./sth.

Abhängigkeits·verhältnis *das* relationship of dependence (**zu** on)

ab|härmen *refl. V.* **sich [um jmdn.] ~:** pine away with grief [over sb.]; *s. auch* **abgehärmt B**

ab|härten *tr. V.* harden; **sich/seinen Körper durch Sport ~:** harden oneself/one's body with sporting activity; *s. auch* **abgehärtet B**

Ab·härtung *die;* **~:** hardening; **zur ~:** to harden oneself

ab|haspeln *tr. V.* 1 (abwickeln) unwind; (von einer Spule) unreel 2 (hastig vortragen) reel off

ab|hauen
A *unr. tr. V.* 1 (abtrennen) chop off; **jmdm. den Arm** *usw.* **~:** cut sb.'s arm *etc.* off. 2 *Prät. nur* **haute ab** (abschlagen) knock off
B *unr. itr. V.; mit sein; Prät. nur* **haute ab** (salopp: verschwinden) beat it (coll.); **hau ab!** get lost! (coll.)

ab|häuten *tr. V.* skin

ab|heben
A *unr. tr. V.* 1 lift off ‹*lid, cover, etc.*›; **[den Hörer] ~:** answer [the telephone] 2 (Kartenspiel) (in zwei Hälften teilen) cut [the pack]; (nehmen) draw ‹*card*› 3 (von einem Konto) withdraw ‹*money*›; **ich möchte gern [Geld] ~:** I would like to make a withdrawal
B *unr. itr. V.* 1 (in die Luft) ‹*balloon*› rise; ‹*aircraft, bird*› take off; ‹*rocket*› lift off; **nachdem das Flugzeug abgehoben hatte** after take-off 2 **auf etw.** (*Akk.*) **~:** lay emphasis on sth.; stress sth. 3 (ugs.: unrealistisch werden) lose touch with the real world; **der hat abgehoben** (ist verrückt geworden) he's cracked (coll.)
C *unr. refl. V.* (sich abzeichnen) stand out; contrast; **sich von** *od.* **gegen etw./von jmdm. ~:** stand out against *or* contrast with sth./sb.

Ab·hebung *die* withdrawal

ab|heften *tr. V.* file; **etw. in einem** *od.* **einen Ordner ~:** file sth.

ab|heilen *itr. V.; mit sein* heal up

ab|helfen *unr. itr. V.* **einem Bedürfnis ~:** meet a need; **einem Missstand ~:** put an end to an abuse; **einem Übelstand ~:** remedy an evil; **dem ist leicht abzuhelfen** that is easily remedied

ab|hetzen
A *tr. V.* ride ‹*horse etc.*› to exhaustion
B *refl. V.* rush *or* dash [around]; **hetz dich doch nicht so ab!** don't rush around so much!; *s. auch* **abgehetzt B**

ab|heuern /ˈaphɔyɐn/ (Seemannsspr.)
A *tr. V.* pay off
B *itr. V.* be paid off

Ab·hilfe *die* action to improve matters; **~ schaffen** find a remedy; put things right; **baldige/schnellste ~:** speedy/immediate action

ab|hobeln *tr. V.* 1 plane down 2 (entfernen) plane off

abhol·bereit *Adj.* ready for collection *post-pos.*

ab·hold *Adj.* **einer Sache** (*Dat.*) **~ sein** (geh.) be averse to sth.

ab|holen *tr. V.* 1 collect, pick up ‹*parcel, book, tickets, etc.*›; pick up, fetch ‹*person*›; **ein Paket auf der Post ~:** collect a parcel at the post office; **ich hole Sie am Bahnhof ab** I'll pick you up at the station; **jmdn. zum Essen ~:** call for sb. and go for a meal 2 (ugs. verhüll.: verhaften) take away

Abholer *der;* **~s, ~, Abholerin** *die;* **~, ~nen** (Postw.) *addressee who collects mail from the*

post office instead of having it delivered

Abhol·markt *der (retail)* cash and carry [store]

Abholung *die;* ~, ~en collection

ab|holzen *tr. V.* fell ‹*trees*›; clear ‹*area*› [of trees]

Abhör·anlage *die* listening *or* (coll.) bugging system

ab|horchen *tr. V.* listen to; **sich ~ lassen** (beim Arzt) have one's lungs/chest sounded

ab|hören *tr. V.* [1] (abfragen) **jmdm.** *od.* **jmdn. Vokabeln ~:** test sb.'s vocabulary [orally]; **das Einmaleins ~:** ask questions on the multiplication table [2] (anhören, heimlich hören) listen to [3] (überwachen) tap ‹*telephone, telephone conversation*›; bug (coll.) ‹*conversation, premises*›; **jmdn. ~:** tap sb.'s telephone [4] ▸ **abhorchen**

Abhör·gerät *das* listening device; bug (coll.)

abhör·sicher *Adj.* bug-proof (coll.); tap-proof ‹*telephone*›

ab|hotten *itr. V.* (salopp) rave it up (coll.)

ab|hungern *tr. V.* [1] (verlieren) take off, lose ‹*weight*› [2] (sparen) **sich** (*Dat.*) **das Geld für die Reise ~:** go *or* (Amer.) do without to save the money for the trip

Abi /'abi/ *das;* **~s, ~s** (Schülerspr.) ▸ **Abitur**

ab|irren *itr. V.; mit sein* (geh.) stray; **vom Weg ~:** stray from one's path; (fig.) stray; err

ab|isolieren *tr. V.* (Elektrot.) strip the insulation off

Abisolier·zange *die* wire strippers *pl.*

Abitur /abi'tu:ɐ̯/ *das;* **~s, ~e** ▸ℹ **S. 331** Abitur; ≈ A levels (Brit.); **sein** *od.* **das ~ machen** do *or* take one's Abitur; **haben Sie ~?** have you got your Abitur?

> **Abitur**
>
> The *Abitur*, or *Matura* in Austria, is the final exam taken by pupils at a **Gymnasium**, usually when they are aged about 19. The final result is based on continuous assessment during the last two years before the *Abitur*, plus examinations in four subjects. On passing the *Abitur*, a *Zeugnis der allgemeinen Hochschulreife* is issued. This certificate is the obligatory qualification for university entrance.

Abiturient /abitu'ri̯ɛnt/ *der;* **~en, ~en** *sb. who is taking/has passed the 'Abitur'*

Abiturienten·klasse *die: class of pupils in last year at grammar school;* ≈ upper sixth *or* A-level class (Brit.)

Abiturientin *die;* **~, ~nen** ▸ **Abiturient**

Abitur·zeugnis *das* Abitur certificate

ab|jagen
A *tr. V.* (abnehmen) **jmdm. etw. ~:** finally get sth. away from sb.
B *refl. V.* ▸ **abhetzen B**

Abk. *Abk.* **= Abkürzung** abbr.

ab|kacken *itr. V.; mit sein* (derb) ‹*person*› mess up completely; ‹*thing*› pack up (coll.)

ab|kämmen *tr. V.* [1] (entfernen) comb out [2] (absuchen) comb, scour (**nach** for)

ab|kanten *tr. V.* (Technik) fold (near the edge)

ab|kanzeln *tr. V.* (ugs.) **jmdn. ~:** give sb. a dressing down; reprimand sb.

ab|kapiteln *tr. V.* (veralt.) **jmdn. ~:** read sb. a lesson; chide sb. (dated)

ab|kapseln *tr. V.* encapsulate; **sich gegen die Umwelt ~** (fig.) isolate oneself from one's surroundings

ab|karten *tr. V.* ▸ **abgekartet**

ab|kassieren
A *itr. V.* [1] **bei jmdm. ~** (im Restaurant) give sb. his/her bill; (ohne Rechnung) settle up with sb. [2] (ugs. abwertend) rake it in (coll.); **bei jmdm. ~:** fleece sb. [3] (ugs.) ▸ **kassieren B 2**
B [1] **jmdn. ~** (im Restaurant) give sb. his/her bill; (ohne Rechnung) settle up with sb.; **die Fahrgäste ~:** take the fares [2] (ugs. abwertend) fleece ‹*person*›; rake in (coll.) ‹*money*›

ab|kauen *tr. V.* chew ‹*pencil*›; bite ‹*fingernails*›

ab|kaufen *tr. V.* [1] **jmdm. etw. ~:** buy sth. from sb. [2] (ugs.: glauben) **das kaufe ich dir nicht ab** I'm not buying that story (coll.)

Abkehr *die;* **~: eine ~ von alten Traditionen** a rejection of *or* turning away from ancient traditions

ab|kehren¹ *tr. V.* (abwenden) turn away; **sein Gesicht ~:** turn one's face away; **sich [von jmdm./etw.] ~:** turn away [from sb./sth.]; **sich von der Welt ~** (fig.) turn one's back on the world; **die uns abgekehrte Seite des Mondes/des Schiffes** the far side of the moon/the ship

ab|kehren² *tr. V.* [1] (entfernen) brush off; **den Schmutz von etw. ~:** brush the dirt off sth. [2] (säubern) **etw. ~:** brush sth. clean

ab|ketteln, ab|ketten *tr.* (*auch itr.*) *V.* (Handarb.) cast off

ab|kippen
A *tr.* (*auch itr.*) *V.* (abladen) tip out; dump ‹*refuse*›
B *itr. V.; mit sein* (herunterfallen) tip over

ab|klappern *tr. V.* (ugs.) trudge round ‹*town, district*›; **alle Läden nach etw. ~:** do the rounds of all the shops looking for sth.; *s. auch* **abgeklappert B**

ab|klären *tr. V.* clear up; sort out (coll.); *s. auch* **abgeklärt B**

Ab·klatsch *der* (abwertend) pale imitation; poor copy

ab|klatschen *tr. V.* [1] (beim Tanzen) **jmdn. ~** (*clap one's hands and*) cut in to dance with sb.; **beim nächsten Tanz darf abgeklatscht werden** an excuse-me dance comes next [2] (Ballspiele) palm away ‹*ball, shot*›

ab|klemmen *tr. V.* [1] (zusammenpressen) clamp [2] (lösen) disconnect [3] (abtrennen) sever

ab|klingen *unr. itr. V.; mit sein* [1] (leiser werden) grow fainter [2] (nachlassen) subside; die away

ab|klopfen
A *tr. V.* [1] (entfernen) knock *or* tap off; **jmdm. etw. [von der Jacke] ~:** tap sth. off sb.['s jacket] [2] (säubern) knock/tap the dirt/snow/crumbs *etc.* off; **sich** (*Dat.*) **die Hände ~:** clap one's hands together to knock the flour/powder *etc.* off [3] (untersuchen) tap; **etw. auf seine Zuverlässigkeit hin ~** (fig.) check the reliability of sth.
B *itr., tr. V.* (Musik) tap one's baton to stop

ab|knabbern *tr. V.* nibble off; gnaw off

ab|knallen *tr. V.* (salopp) shoot down; gun down

ab|knapsen *tr. V.* (ugs.) [1] (wegnehmen) pinch (coll.); **jmdm. etwas/ein Drittel von seinem Lohn ~:** take some/a third of sb.'s wages [2] ▸ **abzwacken 1**

ab|kneifen *unr. tr. V.* nip off; pinch off

ab|knicken
A *tr. V.* [1] (abbrechen) snap *or* break off [2] (knicken) bend
B *itr. V.; mit sein* [1] (abbrechen) snap; break [2] (einknicken) bend over; **in der Hüfte ~:** bend at the hips [3] (Verkehrsw.) **~de Vorfahrt** priority for traffic turning right/left

ab|knipsen *tr. V.* (ugs.) snip off

ab|knöpfen *tr. V.* [1] unbutton [2] (salopp) **jmdm. Geld ~:** get money out of sb.

ab|knutschen *tr. V.* (ugs.) [1] kiss and fondle [2] (sexuell) **jmdn. ~/sich mit jmdm. ~:** smooch (coll.) *or* (coll.) neck with sb.; **sich ~:** smooch (coll.); neck (coll.)

ab|kochen
A *tr. V.* [1] (keimfrei machen) boil [2] (salopp: schröpfen) rip off (coll.); fleece (coll.)
B *itr. V.* (im Freien kochen) cook in the open air

ab|kommandieren *tr. V.* detail; (fig.) detail; send; **jmdn. zum Dienst/zu einer Einheit ~:** detail sb. for duty/to a unit; **jmdn. an die Front ~:** send sb. to the front

Abkomme *der;* **~n, ~n** (geh.) ▸ **Nachkomme**

ab|kommen *unr. itr. V.; mit sein* [1] (abweichen) **vom Weg ~:** lose one's way; **immer mehr vom Weg ~:** go further and further astray; **vom Kurs ~:** go off course; **von der Fahrbahn ~:** leave the road; **vom rechten Weg ~** (fig. geh.) stray from the straight and narrow [2] (abschweifen) digress; **vom Thema ~:** stray from the topic; digress [3] (aufgeben) **von einem Plan ~:** abandon *or* give up a plan [4] (Sport) **der Läufer ist gut/schlecht abgekommen** the runner got a good/bad start; **der Springer ist gut/schlecht abgekommen** the jumper made a good/bad take-off [5] (Schießen) aim

Ab·kommen *das;* **~s, ~:** agreement; **ein ~ [über etw.** (*Akk.*)**] treffen** *od.* **schließen** come to an agreement [on sth.]

abkömmlich /'apkœmlɪç/ *Adj.* free; available

Abkömmling /'apkœmlɪŋ/ *der;* **~s, ~e** [1] (Nachkomme) descendant [2] (Chemie) derivative

ab|können *unr. tr. V.* [1] (nordd.: mögen) stand; (vertragen) take [2] (ugs.: abgemacht werden dürfen) **das Bild kann ab** that picture can go

ab|konterfeien *tr. V.* (veralt.) **jmdn. ~** (zeichnen) draw a good likeness of sb.; (fotografieren) take sb.'s photograph

ab|koppeln *tr. V.* uncouple; (fig.) separate; dissociate

ab|kratzen
A *tr. V.* [1] (entfernen) (mit den Fingern) scratch off; (mit einem Werkzeug) scrape off [2] (säubern) scrape [clean]
B *itr. V.; mit sein* (derb) croak (sl.); snuff it (sl.)

ab|kriegen *tr. V.* (ugs.) ▸ **abbekommen**

ab|kucken *tr., itr. V.* (nordd.) ▸ **abgucken**

ab|kühlen
A *tr. V.* (kühlen) cool down; **jmds. Eifer ~** (fig.) dampen sb.'s ardour; **jmdn. ~** (fig.) cool sb. off
B *itr. V.; meist mit sein* (kühler werden) cool down; get cooler; **es hat stark abgekühlt** it has become a lot cooler; **die Begeisterung kühlte ab** (fig.) enthusiasm waned
C *refl. V.* (kühler werden) cool down; get cooler

Ab·kühlung *die* cooling; (fig.) cooling [off]

Abkunft /'apkʊnft/ *die;* **~** (geh.) descent; **ein Mädchen bürgerlicher ~:** a girl of bourgeois family

ab|kupfern *tr. V.* (ugs.) copy mechanically (**bei** from)

ab|kuppeln *tr. V.* ▸ **abkoppeln**

ab|kürzen *tr., itr. V.* [1] (räumlich); **eine Strecke um 5 km ~:** shorten a distance by 5 km; **den Weg ~:** take a shorter route; **wir haben abgekürzt, indem wir durch die Gärten gegangen sind** we took a short cut through the gardens [2] (zeitlich) cut short [3] (kürzer schreiben) abbreviate (**mit** to); **sich [mit] H. S. ~:** have the initials H. S.

Ab·kürzung *die* [1] (Weg) short cut [2] (Wort) abbreviation [3] (das Abkürzen) cutting short; **zur ~ des Verfahrens** to shorten the procedure

Abkürzungs-: **~liste** *die* ▸ **~verzeichnis**; **~punkt** *der* (Schriftw.) full stop; **~verzeichnis** *das* list of abbreviations

ab|küssen *tr. V.* cover with kisses

Abl. *Abk.* **= Ableitung**

ab|lachen *itr. V.* (salopp) laugh

ab|laden *unr. tr., itr. V.* [1] unload, offload ‹*case, sack, barrel, goods, vehicle*›; dump, unload ‹*gravel, sand, rubble*›; **seine Sorgen bei jmdm. ~** (fig.) unburden oneself to sb. [2] (Seew.: beladen) load ‹*ship*›

Ablader *der;* **~s, ~, Abladerin** *die;* **~, ~nen** (Seew.) shipping agent

Ab·lage *die* [1] (Vorrichtung) storage place [2] (Raum) storage room [3] (Büro) filing [4] (von Eiern) laying [5] (schweiz.) ▸ **Annahmestelle, Zweigstelle**

ab|lagern
A *tr. V.* [1] (absetzen) deposit [2] (deponieren) dump
B *refl. V.* be deposited
C *itr. V.; meist mit sein* (reifen) season; *s. auch* **abgelagert B**

Ab·lagerung *die* [1] deposit [2] (das Absetzen) deposition; **bei der ~ von Mineralien** when minerals have been deposited [3] (das Deponieren) dumping [4] (das Reifen) seasoning

ablandig *Adj.* (Seemannsspr.) offshore

Ablass, *Ablaß /'aplas/ *der;* **Ablasses, Ablässe** (kath. Rel.) indulgence

Ablass·brief, *Ablaß·brief *der* (hist.) letter of indulgence

a

ab|lassen
A *unr. tr. V.* **1** (ablaufen lassen) let out (**aus** of); **sein Wasser ~:** pass water **2** (ausströmen lassen) let off ‹*steam*›; let out ‹*air*›; **eine Blähung ~:** break wind **3** (leeren) empty **4** (abgeben) **jmdm. etw. ~:** let sb. have sth. **5** (nachlassen) **[jmdm.] vom Preis 20% ~:** give [sb.] a 20% discount **6** (ugs.: nicht anziehen, befestigen) leave ‹*tie, hat, badge, etc.*› off **7** (salopp: äußern) come out with
B *unr. itr. V.* **1** (aufgeben) **von etw. ~:** give sth. up **2** (sich nicht mehr befassen) **von jmdm./etw. ~:** leave sb./sth. alone

Ablass-, *Ablaß-: ~prediger *der* (hist.) pardoner; **~ventil** *das* (Technik) outlet valve

Ablativ /'ablati:f/ *der;* **~s, ~e** (Sprachw.) ablative

Ab·lauf *der* **1** (Verlauf) course; **der ~ der Ereignisse** the course of events; **der ~ des Überfalls/des Programms/der Handlung** the sequence of events during the raid/the order of events on the programme/the development of the plot **2** (das Stattfinden) passing *or* going off; **für den reibungslosen ~ einer Veranstaltung sorgen** ensure that an event passes *or* goes off smoothly **3** (Prozess) process **4** (Ende) **nach ~ eines Jahres** after a year; **nach ~ einer Frist** at the end of a period of time; **mit ~ des Kalenderjahres** at the end of one calendar year **5** (Abfluss) outlet

ab|laufen
A *unr. itr. V.; mit sein* **1** (abfließen) flow away; (aus einem Behälter) run *or* flow out; (sich leeren) empty; **das Badewasser ~ lassen** let the bathwater out **2** (herabfließen) run down; **von/an etw.** (*Dat.*) **~:** run off sth.; **an ihm läuft alles ab** (fig.) it's like water off a duck's back [with him]; **jmdn. ~ lassen** (ugs.) send sb. packing; **das Geschirr ~ lassen** let the dishes drain **3** (verlaufen) pass *or* go off; **gut/glimpflich abgelaufen sein** have gone *or* passed off well/smoothly **4** (stehen geblieben sein) ‹*alarm clock*› run down; ‹*parking meter*› expire **5** (aufhören, ungültig werden) ‹*period, contract, passport*› expire **6** (abspulen) **~ lassen** play ‹*tape*›; run ‹*film*› through **7** (abrollen) run out ‹*rope etc.*› **8** (Seemannsspr.) be launched
B *unr. tr. V.* **1** *auch mit sein* (entlanglaufen) walk all along; go over ‹*area*› on foot; (schnell) run all along **2** (abnutzen) wear down; *s. auch* **Bein 1**; **Fuß 2**; **Schuhsohle**

ab|lauschen *tr. V.* (geh.) **jmdm. etw. ~:** learn sth. by listening to sb.

Ab·laut *der* (Sprachw.) ablaut

ab|lauten *itr. V.* (Sprachw.) undergo ablaut; **das sind ~de Verben** these verbs undergo ablaut

ab|läuten *itr. V.* **1** ring the bell [to start] **2** (veralt.: beim Telefon) ring off

ab|leben *itr. V.; mit sein* (geh.) pass away; *s. auch* **abgelebt B**

Ab·leben *das* (geh.) decease; demise

ab|lecken *tr. V.* **1** (entfernen) lick off **2** (säubern) lick clean; **sich** (*Dat.*) **die Finger ~:** lick one's fingers

ab|ledern *tr. V.* leather down

ab|legen
A *tr. V.* **1** (niederlegen) lay *or* put down; lay ‹*egg*› **2** (Bürow.) file **3** (nicht mehr tragen) stop wearing; **abgelegte Kleidung** old clothes *pl.*; cast-offs *pl.* **4** (aufgeben) give up ‹*habit*›; lose ‹*shyness*›; put aside ‹*arrogance*› **5** (machen, leisten) swear ‹*oath*›; sit ‹*examination*›; give ‹*account*›; make ‹*confession*›; *s. auch* **Bekenntnis 1** **6** (geh.: beabsichtigen) **es auf etw.** (*Akk.*) **~:** want sth.
B *tr., itr. V.* **1** (ausziehen) take off; **möchten Sie ~?** would you like to take your coat off? **2** (Kartenspiel) (abwerfen) discard; (auflegen) put down
C *itr. V.* (Seemannsspr.: losfahren) **[vom Kai] ~:** cast off

Ableger *der;* **~s, ~** **1** (Bot.) layer **2** (Steckling) cutting; (fig. ugs.: Sohn) offspring; (fig.: Filiale) offshoot

ab|lehnen
A *tr. V.* **1** (zurückweisen) decline; decline, turn down ‹*money, invitation, position*›; reject ‹*suggestion, applicant*› **2** (nicht genehmigen) turn down; reject; reject, throw out ‹*bill*› **3** (verweigern) **es ~, etw. zu tun** refuse to do sth. **4** (missbilligen) disapprove of; reject
B *itr. V.* decline; **sie haben ohne Begründung abgelehnt** (nicht genehmigt) they rejected it/them without giving any reason

ablehnend
A *Adj.* negative ‹*reply, attitude*›; **ein ~er Bescheid** a rejection
B *adv.* **einer Sache** (*Dat.*) **~ gegenüberstehen** take a negative view of sth.; **sich ~ zu etw. äußern** voice one's opposition to sth.

Ablehnung *die;* **~, ~en** **1** (Zurückweisung) rejection; **auf ~ stoßen** meet with opposition **2** (Missbilligung) disapproval; **auf ~ stoßen** meet with disapproval **3** (Weigerung) refusal

ab|leisten *tr. V.* serve out

ab|leiten
A *tr. V.* **1** divert **2** (herleiten; auch Sprachw., Math.) **etw. aus/von etw. ~:** derive sth. from sth.; **das Wort ist aus dem Spanischen abgeleitet** the word is derived from Spanish **3** (Math.: differenzieren) differentiate ‹*function*›
B *refl. V.* (sich herleiten) **sich aus/von etw. ~:** derive *or* be derived from sth.

Ab·leitung *die* **1** (das Ableiten; auch Math., Sprachw.) derivation **2** (Sprachw.: Wort; Math.: Ergebnis des Differenzierens) derivative

Ableitungs·silbe *die* (Sprachw.) affix

ab|lenken
A *tr. V.* **1** (Richtung ändern) deflect; **einen Verdacht von sich ~** (fig.) divert suspicion from oneself **2** *auch itr.* (abbringen) **jmdn. von etw. ~:** distract sb. from sth.; **alles, was ablenkt** everything that is distracting **3** *auch itr.* (zerstreuen) divert; **sich ~:** amuse *or* divert oneself; **das lenkt dich davon ab** that'll take your mind off it; **das lenkt ab** it's amusing *or* diverting
B *itr. V.* (ausweichen) **[vom Thema] ~:** change the subject

Ab·lenkung *die* **1** (Richtungsänderung) deflection **2** (Störung) distraction **3** (Zerstreuung) diversion

Ablenkungs·manöver *das* diversion[ary tactic]

ablesbar *Adj.* **~ sein** ‹*scale, dial*› be readable; **an etw.** (*Dat.*) **~ sein** (fig.) be detectable from sth.

ab|lesen[1] *unr. tr. V.* **1** (wegnehmen) pick off **2** (säubern) pick clean; groom ‹*coat*›

ab|lesen[2]
A *unr. tr., itr. V.* **1** read ‹*speech, lecture*›; **werden Sie frei sprechen oder ~?** will you be talking from notes or reading your speech? **2** (feststellen, prüfen) check ‹*time, speed, temperature*›; **[das Gas/den Strom] ~:** read the gas/electricity meter; **die Temperatur auf dem** *od.* **am Thermometer ~:** read off the temperature on the thermometer; **das Thermometer/den Tacho ~:** read the thermometer/speedo
B *unr. tr. V.* (erkennen) see; gauge ‹*significance*›; **etw. an etw.** (*Dat.*) **~:** see sth. from sth.; **jmdm. jeden Wunsch von den Augen ~:** read sb.'s every wish in his/her eyes

ab|leuchten *tr. V.* shine a light all over

ab|leugnen *tr., itr. V.* deny ‹*involvement, guilt*›; deny any involvement in ‹*crime*›; **sie leugnet stur ab** she flatly denies it

ab|lichten *tr. V.* **1** (fotokopieren) photocopy **2** (fotografieren) take a photograph of

Ab·lichtung *die* **1** (das Fotografieren) photographing; (das Fotokopieren) photocopying; **er ist mit der ~ der Beweisstücke fertig** he has finished photographing/photocopying the evidence **2** (Fotokopie) photocopy

ab|liefern *tr., itr. V.* deliver ‹*goods*›; hand in ‹*manuscript, examination paper, weapon, etc.*›; (fig. ugs.) take/bring ‹*person*› (**in/auf** + *Dat.*, **bei** to); **er hat pünktlich abgeliefert** he delivered it/handed it in on time

Ab·lieferung *die* (von Waren) delivery; (von Manuskripten usw.) handing in

ab|liegen *unr. itr. V.* be out of the way; *s. auch* **abgelegen**

ab|listen /'aplɪstn̩/ *tr. V.* **jmdm. etw. ~** (durch Betrug) swindle sb. out of sth.; (durch Charme) cajole sb. into giving sth.

ab|locken *tr. V.* **jmdm. etw. ~:** coax sth. out of sb.

ablösbar *Adj.* **1** removable **2** (Finanzw.) redeemable

ab|löschen
A *tr. V.* **1** (trocknen) blot ‹*ink, letter, etc.*› **2** (abwischen) wipe ‹*blackboard*›; wipe out ‹*writing*› **3** (Kochk.) **etw. mit Rotwein** *usw.* **~:** add red wine *etc.* to sth. **4** (löschen) extinguish; put out
B *itr. V.* **1** (trocknen) blot it/them **2** (abwischen) wipe [the blackboard] **3** (Kochk.) **mit Rotwein** *usw.* **~:** add red wine *etc.*

Ablöse *die;* **~, ~n** **1** ▸ **Ablösesumme** **2** (österr.) *single payment made by tenant at start of tenancy*

ab|lösen
A *tr. V.* **1** (lösen) **etw. [von etw.] ~:** get sth. off [sth.]; remove sth. [from sth.] **2** (abwechseln) relieve; take over from; (fig.: ersetzen) replace; **sich** *od.* **einander ~:** take turns **3** (verhüll.: entlassen) remove from office **4** (Finanzw.: tilgen) redeem
B *refl. V.* (sich lösen) ‹*retina*› become detached; **sich von etw. ~:** come off sth.

Ablöse·summe *die* (Sport) transfer fee

Ab·lösung *die* **1** (eines Postens) changing; (fig.: Verdrängung, Ersetzung) replacement; **ich schicke Ihnen jemanden zur ~:** I'll send someone to relieve you **2** (Ersatz) relief **3** (das Ablösen) detaching; (der Netzhaut) detachment **4** (verhüll.: Entlassung) removal **5** (Finanzw.: Tilgung) redemption **6** (Psych.) dissolution of an emotional tie/emotional ties; **die ~ von seinen Eltern** breaking away emotionally from his parents

ab|luchsen /'aplʊksn̩/ *tr. V.* (salopp) **jmdm. etw. ~:** get *or* (sl.) wangle sth. out of sb.

Ab·luft *die* (Technik) vitiated air

ab|lutschen *tr. V.* **1** suck off; (säubern) suck clean; **die Marmelade von den Fingern ~:** suck the jam off one's fingers; **ein abgelutschter Bonbon** a half-sucked sweet **2** (vulg.) **jmdm. einen ~:** suck sb. off (coarse)

ABM *Abk.* = **Arbeitsbeschaffungsmaßnahme**

ab|machen *tr. V.* **1** (ugs.: entfernen) take off; take down ‹*sign, rope*›; **etw. von etw. ~:** take sth. off sth. **2** (vereinbaren) agree; arrange; **abgemacht, wir kommen mit!** all right, we'll come **3** (klären) sort out; **das muss er mit sich selbst ~:** that's something he'll have to sort out by himself

Abmachung *die;* **~, ~en** agreement; arrangement; **eine ~ [mit jmdm.] treffen** come to an agreement *or* arrangement [with sb.]

ab|magern
A *itr. V.; mit sein* become thin; (absichtlich) slim; **bis auf die Knochen ~:** become a mere skeleton; *s. auch* **abgemagert B**
B *tr. V.* **1** (Technik) **das Gemisch ~:** make the mixture leaner **2** (verringern) cut back on; (leichter machen) make lighter

Abmagerung *die;* **~, ~en** (Vorgang) weight loss; (Zustand) emaciation

Abmagerungs·kur *die* reducing diet; **eine ~ machen** go on a diet; **er macht gerade eine ~:** he's dieting at the moment

ab|mähen *tr. V.* mow

ab|mahnen *tr. V.* ▸ **verwarnen**

Ab·mahnung *die* ▸ **Verwarnung**

ab|malen *tr. V.* paint a picture of (**aus, von** from)

Ab·marsch *der* departure; **im ~ sein** be marching off; **~!** forward march!

abmarsch·bereit *Adj.* ready to depart; (Milit.) ready to march

ab|marschieren *itr. V.; mit sein* depart; (Milit.) march off

ab|matten /'apmatn̩/ *tr. V.* (geh.) fatigue

ab|meißeln *tr. V.* chisel *or* carve off

Abmelde·bestätigung *die: document confirming that one has notified the authorities of one's intention to move from an address*

ab|melden *tr. V.* 1) (das Weggehen melden) **sich/jmdn. ~:** report that one/sb. is leaving; **sich [bei jmdm.] vom Dienst ~:** report absent from duty [to sb.] 2) (Umzug melden) *notify the authorities that one is moving from an address;* **abgemeldet sein** have given notice of moving away 3) **ein Auto ~:** cancel a car's registration; **ein abgemeldetes Auto** a car of which the registration has been cancelled; **sein Telefon ~:** have one's phone disconnected; **seinen Fernseher ~:** cancel one's TV licence 4) (Sportjargon: beherrschen) **jmdn. ~:** shut sb. out of the game/race *etc.*; **abgemeldet sein** be kept out of the game/race *etc.* 5) (ugs.) **[bei jmdm.] abgemeldet sein** no longer be of interest [to sb.]; **er ist jetzt bei mir abgemeldet** I want nothing more to do with him

Ab·meldung *die* 1) (beim Weggehen) report that one is leaving 2) (beim Umzug) *registration of a move with the authorities at one's old address* 3) (des Telefons) disconnection 4) **~ eines Autos/eines Fernsehers** cancellation of a car's registration/a television licence 5) **▸Abmeldebestätigung**

ab|messen *unr. tr. V.* 1) measure; (fig.) measure; assess 2) (abteilen) measure off; *s. auch* **abgemessen B, C**

Ab·messung *die* 1) (Dimension) dimension; measurement 2) (das Abmessen) measuring

ab|mildern *tr. V.* 1) (dämpfen) break, cushion ‹*fall, impact*› 2) (abschwächen) tone down; take the edge off

ab|mischen *tr. V.* (Film, Rundf., Ferns.) mix; **neu ~:** remix

Ab·moderation *die* 1) (das Abmoderieren) signing-off; **sie ist gerade bei der ~:** she is just signing off 2) (Text, Wortlaut) sign-off; **sie hat sich** (*Dat.*) **eine witzige ~ einfallen lassen** she found something witty to sign off with

ab|moderieren *tr. V.* sign off at the end of ‹*programme, show*›

ab|montieren
A *tr. V.* (entfernen) take off, remove ‹*part, wheel*›; dismantle ‹*machine, equipment*›
B *itr. V.* (Fliegerspr.: sich lösen) come off

ab|mühen *refl. V.* **sich [mit jmdm./etw.] ~:** toil [for sb.'s benefit/with sth.]; **sie mühte sich mit dem schweren Koffer ab** she struggled with the heavy suitcase

ab|murksen *tr. V.* (salopp) do in (sl.)

ab|müssen *unr. itr. V.* (ugs.) **das muss ab** it will have to come off; **der Baum/das Plakat muss ab** the tree/poster will have to come down

ab|mustern (Seemannsspr.)
A *tr. V.* (entlassen) discharge
B *itr. V.* sign off; **von einem Schiff ~:** leave a ship

ab|nabeln *tr. V.* **ein Kind ~:** cut a child's cord; **sich vom Elternhaus ~** (fig.) break away from the parental home

ab|nagen *tr. V.* gnaw off; **etw. von etw. ~:** gnaw sth. off sth.; **ein abgenagter Knochen** a gnawed bone

ab|nähen *tr. V.* take in ‹*skirt, jacket, etc.*›

Abnäher /ˈapnɛːɐ/ *der;* **~s, ~:** tuck

Abnahme /ˈapnaːmə/ *die;* **~, ~n** 1) (das Entfernen) removal; **vor/bei/nach der ~ des Verbandes** before/when/after the bandage was/is removed 2) (Verminderung) decrease; decline 3) (Kauf) purchasing; **bei ~ größerer Mengen** when large quantities are purchased 4) (Prüfung) (eines Gebäudes, einer Strecke) inspection and approval; (eines Fahrzeugs) testing and passing; (Freigabe) passing 5) (Entgegennahme) (eines Eides) administration; (eines Versprechens) extraction; (einer Parade) taking the salute (*Gen.* at)

Abnahme·garantie *die* guaranteed purchase; firm order

abnehmbar *Adj.* detachable; removable

ab|nehmen
A *unr. tr. V.* 1) (entfernen) take off; remove; take down ‹*picture, curtain, lamp*›; **jmdm. das Bein ~:** take sb.'s leg off; **sich** (*Dat.*) **den Bart ~:** shave one's beard off 2) (übernehmen) take; **jmdm. den Koffer ~:** take sb.'s suitcase [from him/her]; **kann/darf ich Ihnen etwas ~?** can/may I carry something for you?; **jmdm. einen Weg/eine Arbeit ~:** save sb. a journey/a job; **jmdm. seine Sorgen ~:** relieve sb. of his/her worries 3) (entgegennehmen) **jmdm. ein Versprechen/einen Eid ~:** make sb. give a promise/swear an oath; **jmdm. die Beichte ~:** hear sb.'s confession; **eine Parade ~:** take the salute at a parade; **eine Prüfung ~:** conduct an examination 4) (prüfen) inspect and approve; test and pass ‹*vehicle*› 5) (stehlen) take; (beschlagnahmen) take away ‹*driving licence, passport*›; (abgewinnen) **jmdm. etw. ~:** take sth. off sb.; **jmdm. ein paar Meter ~:** gain a few metres over sb. 6) (abverlangen) **jmdm. etw. ~:** charge sb. sth. 7) (abkaufen) **jmdm. etw. ~:** buy sth. from sb. 8) (ugs.: glauben) buy (coll.); **diese Geschichte nehme ich dir nicht ab** I'm not buying that story (coll.) 9) (übertragen) take ‹*fingerprint*›
B *unr. itr. V.* 1) *auch tr.* (beim Telefon) answer; **den Hörer ~:** pick up the receiver 2) *auch tr.* (Handarb.) decrease 3) ▸❶ **S. 315** (Gewicht verlieren) lose weight; **sechs Kilo ~:** lose six kilos 4) (sich verringern) decrease; drop; ‹*attention, interest*› flag; ‹*brightness*› diminish; **die Tage nehmen ab** the days are getting shorter; **wir haben ~den Mond** there is a waning moon

Abnehmer *der;* **~s, ~, Abnehmerin** *die;* **~, ~nen** buyer

Ab·neigung *die* dislike (**gegen** for); aversion (**gegen** to)

ab|nicken *tr. V.* (ugs.) **etw. ~:** nod sth. through; let sth. through on the nod

abnorm /apˈnɔrm/
A *Adj.* abnormal; (ungewöhnlich) exceptional
B *adv.* abnormally; (ungewöhnlich) unusually

ab·normal *Adj., adv.* (bes. österr. u. schweiz.) **▸anormal**

Abnormität /apnɔrmiˈtɛːt/ *die;* **~, ~en** 1) (Missbildung) deformity 2) (Missgeburt) freak

ab|nötigen *tr. V.* (geh.) **jmdm. Respekt ~:** compel sb.'s respect; **jmdm. ein Geständnis/die Zustimmung ~:** extract a confession/agreement from sb.

ab|nutzen, (landsch.:) **ab|nützen**
A *tr. V.* wear out
B *refl. V.* wear out; become worn; ‹*expressions, arguments*› become hackneyed; **das Material nutzt sich rasch ab** the material wears very quickly; *s. auch* **abgenutzt B**

Ab·nutzung, (landsch.:) **Ab·nützung** *die* wear [and tear] *no indef. art.*

Abnutzungs·erscheinung *die* sign of wear and tear; (fig.) sign of disenchantment

Abonnement /abɔnəˈmãː/ *das;* **~s, ~s** subscription (+ *Gen.* to); (Theater, Oper) subscription ticket; **eine Zeitschrift im ~ beziehen** subscribe to *or* have a subscription to a magazine

Abonnement[s]-: ~karte *die* subscription ticket; **~konzert** *das* subscription concert

Abonnent /abɔˈnɛnt/ *der;* **~en, ~en, Abonnentin** *die;* **~, ~nen** subscriber (+ *Gen.* to); (Theater, Oper) season ticket holder

abonnieren /abɔˈniːrən/
A *tr. V.* subscribe to; have a subscription to; (Theater, Oper) have a season ticket for
B *itr. V.* (bes. schweiz.) **abonniert sein auf** (+ *Akk.*) have a subscription to ‹*newspaper, magazine, concerts*›; (Theater, Oper) have a season ticket for; (fig.) get as a matter of course

ab|ordnen *tr. V.* send; **jmdn. als Delegierten ~:** delegate sb.; **jmdn. zu einer Konferenz ~:** delegate sb. to a conference; **jmdn. nach Wien ~:** send sb. to Vienna

Ab·ordnung *die* delegation

Aboriginal /ɛbəˈrɪdʒinəl/ *der;* **~s, ~s** Aboriginal

Aborigine /ɛbəˈrɪdʒiniː/*der;* **~s, ~s** Aborigine

Abort[1] /aˈbɔrt/ *der;* **~[e]s, ~e** (veralt., noch fachspr.) lavatory

Abort[2] *der;* **~s, ~e** (Med.) 1) ▸❶ **S. 439** (Fehlgeburt) miscarriage 2) (Abtreibung) abortion

Abort·grube *die* cesspool

ab|packen *tr. V.* pack; wrap ‹*bread*›; **abgepacktes Obst/abgepackte Fleischportionen** packaged fruit/pieces of meat

ab|passen *tr. V.* 1) (abwarten) wait for 2) (aufhalten) catch

ab|pausen *tr., itr. V.* trace

ab|pellen *tr. V.* (nordd.) peel; peel the skin off ‹*sausage*›

ab|perlen *itr. V.*; *mit sein* **von etw. ~:** roll off sth.

ab|pfeifen (Sport)
A *itr. V.* blow the whistle; **der Schiedsrichter hatte abgepfiffen** the whistle had gone
B *tr. V.* 1) (unterbrechen) [blow the whistle to] stop 2) (beenden) blow the whistle for the end of ‹*match, game, half*›

Ab·pfiff *der* (Sport) final whistle; (Halbzeit~) half-time whistle

ab|pflücken *tr. V.* 1) pick; **sich** (*Dat.*) **etw. ~:** pick oneself sth. 2) (leer pflücken) pick clean

ab|placken (ugs.), **ab|plagen** *refl. V.* slave away; flog oneself to death (coll.); **sich mit etw./jmdm. ~** *od.* **abplagen** slave away at sth./for sb.'s benefit; **sich mit einem Problem ~** *od.* **abplagen** wrestle with a problem

ab|platten /ˈaplatn̩/ *tr. V.* flatten [out]

ab|platzen *itr. V.*; *mit sein* ‹*lacquer, enamel, plaster*› flake off; ‹*button*› fly off

ab|prägen
A *refl. V.* **sich in etw.** (*Dat.*) **~:** leave an impression in sth.; (fig.) leave its/their mark on sth.
B *tr. V.* (Technik) take ‹*cast*›; make ‹*mould*›

ab|prallen *itr. V.*; *mit sein* rebound; bounce off; ‹*missile*› ricochet; **an** *od.* **von etw.** (*Dat.*) **~:** rebound/ricochet off sth.; **an jmdm. ~** (fig.) bounce off sb.

Abpraller *der;* **~s, ~** (Sport) rebound; (ugs.: eines Geschosses) ricochet

ab|pressen *tr. V.* 1) (abnötigen) **jmdm. etw. ~:** extort sth. from sb. 2) (abschnüren) **das presste uns den Atem ab** it took our breath away

Ab·produkt *das* waste product

ab|protzen
A *tr. V.* (Milit.) unlimber
B *itr. V.* (derb) have *or* (Amer.) take a crap (coarse); crap (coarse)

ab|puffern *tr. V.* offset; offset, cushion ‹*effect*›

ab|pumpen *tr. V.* pump out; extract ‹*milk*› by breast pump

ab|putzen *tr. V.* (ugs.) 1) wipe; **jmdm./sich das Gesicht** *usw.* **~:** clean sb.'s/one's face *etc.* 2) (entfernen) **etw. von jmdm./etw. ~:** wipe sth. off sb./sth.

ab|quälen *refl. V.* **sich [mit etw.] ~:** struggle [with sth.]; **sich** (*Dat.*) **einen Brief ~:** force oneself to write a letter; **da hat er sich was abgequält** he must have had a struggle to get that out

ab|qualifizieren *tr. V.* denigrate; **jmdn./etw. als etw. ~:** dismiss sb./sth. as sth.; **sich selbst ~:** show oneself up

ab|quetschen
A *tr. V.* **jmdm. einen Arm/ein Bein ~:** crush sb.'s arm/leg
B *refl. V.* (ugs.: hervorbringen) **sich** (*Dat.*) **etw. ~:** force out ‹*words, smile*›; **sich** (*Dat.*) **ein paar Tränen ~:** squeeze out a few tears

ab|rackern *refl. V.* (ugs.) slave [away]; flog oneself to death (coll.); **sich mit etw. ~:** slave away at sth.

Abraham /ˈaːbraham/ (*der*) 1) Abraham 2) *in* **[sicher] wie in ~s Schoß** (ugs.) as safe as houses (coll.)

Abrakadabra /aːbrakaˈdaːbra/ *das;* **~s** 1) (Zauberwort) abracadabra 2) (unsinniges Gerede) blitherings *pl.*

ab|rasieren *tr. V.* shave off; **jmdm./sich den Bart ~:** shave off sb.'s/one's beard

ab|raten *unr. itr., tr. V.* **jmdm. von etw. ~:** advise sb. against sth.; **jmdm. [davon] ~, etw. zu tun** advise sb. not to do sth. *or* against doing sth.; **da kann ich nur abraten** I can only advise you against it

Ab·raum *der* (Bergbau) overburden

ab|räumen
A *tr. V.* 1) clear away 2) (leer machen) clear ‹*table*› 3) (Bergbau) remove ‹*overburden*›

a

B *itr. V.* **1** clear away **2** (vom Tisch) clear the table **3** (Bergbau) remove the overburden

ab|rauschen *itr. V.; mit sein* (*ugs.*) (schnell) rush off; (auffällig) sweep off

ab|reagieren
A *tr. V.* work off; **seine Wut an jmdm. ~:** take one's anger out on sb.
B *refl. V.* work off one's feelings

ab|rechnen
A *itr. V.* **1** cash up **2** (fig.) **mit jmdm. ~:** call sb. to account
B *tr. V.* **1** **die Kasse ~:** reckon up the till; total the cash *or* register (Amer.); **seine Einnahmen ~:** agree one's takings; **seine Spesen ~:** claim one's expenses **2** (abziehen) deduct

Ab·rechnung *die* **1** (Schlussrechnung) cashing up *no art.*; **die Kellnerin machte die ~:** the waitress was cashing up **2** (Aufstellung) statement; (Kaufmannsspr.: Bilanz) balance; (Dokument) balance sheet; **der Tag der ~:** the day of reckoning **3** (Vergeltung) reckoning **4** (Abzug) deduction; **nach ~ der Unkosten** after deducting expenses; **etw. in ~ bringen** (Amtsspr.) deduct sth.; **in ~ kommen** (Amtsspr.) be deducted

Abrechnungs-: ~stelle *die* (Finanzw.) clearing house; **~verkehr** *der* (Finanzw.) clearing

Ab·rede *die* **1** arrangement; agreement **2** **etw. in ~ stellen** deny sth.

ab|regeln *tr. V.* (fachspr.) **einen Wagen [bei 250 km/h] ~:** to limit the (top) speed of a car [to 250 kph]; **bei 7000 Touren wird abgeregelt** the speed limiter cuts in at 7000 revs; **eine [elektronisch] abgeregelte Höchstgeschwindigkeit** a top speed set [electronically] by the speed limiter

ab|regen *refl. V.* (ugs.) calm down; **reg dich ab!** cool it! (coll.); calm down!

ab|reiben *unr. tr. V.* **1** (entfernen) rub off; (Kochk.) grate; **etw. von etw. ~:** rub/grate sth. off sth.; **abgeriebene Zitronenschale** grated lemon peel **2** (säubern) rub; **[sich (*Dat.*)] die Hände an der Hose ~:** rub one's hands on one's trousers **3** (frottieren) rub down; **jmds. Hände mit Schnee ~:** rub sb.'s hands with snow

Ab·reibung *die* **1** (ugs.: Prügel) hiding (coll.); licking (Amer. coll.); **jmdm. eine ~ verpassen** give sb. a good hiding **2** (Med.) rubbing

Ab·reise *die* departure (**nach** for); **bei meiner ~:** when I left/leave

ab|reisen *itr. V.; mit sein* leave (**nach** for)

Abreiß·block *der; Pl.* **~s** *od.* **Abreißblöcke** tear-off notebook

ab|reißen
A *unr. tr. V.* **1** (entfernen) tear off; tear down ‹*poster, notice*›; pull off ‹*button*›; break off ‹*thread*›; *s. auch* **Kopf 1** **2** (niederreißen) demolish, pull down ‹*building*›; demolish ‹*area*› **3** (salopp: ableisten) get through; stick out (coll.); *s. auch* **abgerissen B**
B *unr. itr. V.; mit sein* **1** (sich lösen) fly off; ‹*shoelace*› break off **2** (aufhören) come to an end; ‹*connection, contact*› be broken off; **in nicht ~der Folge** in a never-ending procession

Abreiß·kalender *der* tear-off calendar

ab|reiten
A *unr. itr. V.; mit sein* (wegreiten) ride off *or* away
B *unr. tr. V.* **1** *mit sein od. haben* (entlangreiten) ride the whole length of; ride over ‹*district*› **2** (Pferdesport: vorbereiten) supple **3** (müde reiten) ride to exhaustion **4** (Seemannsspr.) ride out ‹*storm*›

Abreite·platz, Abreit·platz *der* (Pferdesport) warming-up arena

ab|richten *tr. V.* train

Ab·richter *der*, **Ab·richterin** *die* trainer

Ab·richtung *die;* **~:** training

ab|riegeln *tr., itr. V.* **1** (zusperren) **[die Tür] ~:** bolt the door **2** (absperren) seal *or* cordon off ‹*area*›

Abrieg[e]lung *die;* **~, ~en** sealing *or* cordoning off

ab|ringen *unr. tr. V.* **1** (abnötigen) **jmdm. etw. ~:** extract sth. from sb.; **sich (*Dat.*) ein Lächeln ~:** force a smile **2** (entreißen) **jmdm./einer Sache etw. ~:** wrest sth. from sb./sth.

ab|rippen *tr. V.* (salopp) **1** (berauben) rob; (mit Gewaltanwendung) mug (coll.) **2** (übervorteilen) rip off (coll.)

Ab·riss, *Ab·riß *der* **1** ▸**abreißen A 2**: demolition; pulling down; **auf ~ stehen** (ugs.) be scheduled for demolition **2** (von Eintrittskarten) tear-off section **3** (knappe Darstellung) outline

Abriss-, *Abriß-: ~arbeiten *Pl.* ▸**Abbrucharbeit**; **~birne** *die* demolition ball; wrecker's ball; **die ~birne kommt im Herbst** they're going to start demolition in autumn; **das Haus ist längst der ~birne zum Opfer gefallen** they pulled the building down ages ago

ab|rollen
A *tr. V.* unwind; **sich ~:** unwind [itself]
B *itr. V.; mit sein* **1** unwind [itself] **2** (vonstatten gehen) go off; ‹*events*› unfold; **sein Leben rollte vor seinen Augen ab** his life passed before his eyes **3** (Sport) roll over (**über** + *Akk.* on to)

ab|rubbeln *tr. V.* (bes. nordd.) **jmdn./sich ~:** dry sb./oneself by rubbing; rub sb./oneself down; **jmdm./sich den Rücken ~:** dry sb.'s/one's back by rubbing

ab|rücken
A *tr. V.* (wegschicken) move away
B *itr. V.; mit sein* **1** move away; **von jmdm./etw. ~:** move away from sb./sth. **2** (Milit.) (abmarschieren) move out; (zurückmarschieren) march back **3** (ugs.: sich entfernen) clear out (coll.)

Ab·ruf *der* **1** **auf ~:** on call; (DV) in retrievable form; **sich auf ~ bereithalten** be on call **2** (Kaufmannsspr.) request for delivery; **etw. auf ~ kaufen** buy sth. on call purchase

abrufbar *Adj.* **1** (DV) retrievable **2** (Finanzw.) withdrawable

abruf·bereit *Adj.* **1** on call *postpos.* **2** (Kaufmannsspr.) ready for delivery on demand *postpos.*

ab|rufen *unr. tr. V.* **1** summon, call ‹*person*›; **er wurde ins Jenseits/aus diesem Leben abgerufen** (geh. verhüll.) he was taken from us **2** (DV) retrieve **3** (Kaufmannsspr.) **etw. ~:** ask for sth. to be delivered **4** (Finanzw.) withdraw

ab|runden *tr. V.* **1** round off; **abgerundete Ecken** rounded corners **2** (auf eine runde Zahl bringen) round up/down (**auf** + *Akk.* to); **etw. nach oben/unten ~:** round sth. up/down; **ein Betrag von abgerundet 60 Euro** a rounded [up/down] sum of 60 euros **3** (vervollkommnen) round off; complete

Ab·rundung *die* **1** rounding off **2** (von Zahlen) rounding up/down **3** (Vervollkommnung) rounding off; **zur ~ des Geschmacks** to round off the taste

ab|rupfen *tr. V.* pull off

abrupt /ap'rʊpt/
A *Adj.* abrupt
B *adv.* abruptly

ab|rüsten *itr., tr. V.* disarm

Ab·rüstung *die;* **~:** disarmament

Abrüstungs-: ~konferenz *die* disarmament conference; **~verhandlungen** *Pl.* disarmament negotiations

ab|rutschen *itr. V.; mit sein* **1** (abgleiten) slip; **von etw. ~:** slip off sth.; **das Pferd rutschte mit den Hinterbeinen ab** the horse's hind feet slipped; **sie ist mit dem Messer abgerutscht** her knife slipped **2** (nach unten rutschen) slide down; ‹*earth*› subside; ‹*snow*› give way; ‹*aircraft*› side-slip; (fig.) ‹*pupil, competitor, etc.*› slip (**auf** + *Akk.* to) **3** (moralisch absinken) go downhill

Abs. *Abk.* **1** **= Absender** **2** **= Absatz**

ABS *Abk.* **= Antiblockiersystem**

ab|säbeln *tr. V.* (ugs.) hack off

ab·sacken[1] *itr. V.; mit sein* (ugs.) **1** (nach unten sinken) fall; ‹*ground*› subside; ‹*aircraft*› lose altitude **2** (moralisch absinken) go downhill

ab|sacken[2] *tr. V.* sack ‹*grain, sugar, etc.*›

Ab·sage *die* **1** (auf eine Einladung) refusal; (auf eine Bewerbung) rejection; **jmdm. eine ~ erteilen** reject sb.; **eine ~ an jede Form totalitärer Politik** a rejection of all forms of totalitarian politics **2** (Rundf.) closing announcement

ab|sagen
A *tr. V.* cancel; withdraw ‹*participation, cooperation*›
B *itr. V.* **1** cry off; **jmdm. ~:** tell sb. one cannot come; put sb. off (coll.); **telefonisch ~:** ring to say one cannot come; **ich muss Ihnen für Donnerstag ~:** I must cancel our meeting/visit/appointment *etc.* on Thursday **2** **dem Bewerber wurde abgesagt** the applicant was rejected **3** (Rundf.) make the closing announcement

ab|sägen *tr. V.* **1** saw off **2** (ugs.) **jmdn. ~:** get rid of sb.

ab|sahnen
A *itr. V.* (ugs.) make a killing (coll.).
B *tr. V.* **1** (ugs.) **100 000 Euro ~:** pocket 100,000 euros **2** (Rahm entfernen von) cream ‹*milk*›

ab|satteln *tr., itr. V.* unsaddle

Ab·satz *der* **1** (am Schuh) heel; **auf dem ~ kehrtmachen, sich auf dem ~ herumdrehen** turn on one's heel **2** (Textunterbrechung) break; **einen ~ machen** make a break; start a new line **3** (Abschnitt) paragraph **4** (Kauf-mannsspr.) sales *pl.*; **guten/keinen ~ finden** sell well/not sell at all; *s. auch* **reißend** **5** (einer Innentreppe) landing; (zwischen Geschossen) half landing; (Mauer~) ledge

absatz-, Absatz-: ~chance *die* (Kaufmannsspr.) sales prospect; **~flaute** *die* (Kaufmannsspr.) drop in sales; **~förderung** *die* (Kaufmannsspr.) sales promotion; **~gebiet** *das* (Kaufmannsspr.) sales territory; (von Produkten) market area; **~kick** *der* (Fußball) back-heel; **~markt** *der* (Kaufmannsspr.) market; **~schwierigkeiten** *Pl.* (Kaufmannsspr.) sales problems; (beim Vertrieb) marketing difficulties; **~steigerung** *die* (Kaufmannsspr.) increase in sales; **~trick** *der* (Fußball) clever back-heel; **~weise** *Adv.* paragraph by paragraph

ab|saufen *unr. itr. V.; mit sein* **1** (salopp: untergehen) go to the bottom **2** (derb: ertrinken) drown **3** (ugs.) ‹*engine, car*› flood **4** (salopp: sich mit Wasser füllen) flood; **abgesoffen sein** be under water; be flooded

ab|saugen *tr. V.* **1** (entfernen) suck away; **etw. aus/von etw. ~:** suck sth. out of/off sth. **2** (säubern) hoover (Brit. coll.); vacuum

ab|schaben *tr. V.* **1** (entfernen) scrape off; **sich (*Dat.*) den Bart ~** (scherzh.) have a shave **2** (säubern) scrape [clean]; *s. auch* **abgeschabt B**

ab|schaffen
A *tr. V.* **1** (beseitigen) abolish ‹*capital punishment, regulation, customs duty, institution*›; repeal ‹*law*›; put an end to ‹*injustice, abuse*›; **er möchte alle Flugzeuge ~:** he'd like to do away with aeroplanes completely **2** (aufgeben) get rid of
B *refl. V.* (südd., schweiz.) (sich abarbeiten) slave away; work oneself hard; (sich anstrengen) go at it

Ab·schaffung *die* **1** abolition; (von Gesetzen) repeal; (von Unrecht, Missstand) ending **2** (Aufgabe) **er sah sich zur ~ seines Autos/Hundes gezwungen** he was forced to get rid of *or* give up his car/dog

ab|schälen
A *tr. V.* **1** (lösen) peel off; **etw. von etw. ~:** peel sth. off sth. **2** (befreien von) bark ‹*tree*›
B *refl. V.* (sich lösen) peel off; **die Haut schält sich ab** the skin is peeling

abschaltbar *Adj.* which can be switched off *postpos., not pred.*; **das ist ~:** it can be switched off

ab|schalten
A *tr., itr. V.* (ausschalten) switch off; turn off; shut down ‹*power station*›
B *itr. V.* (ugs.: nicht zuhören; Abstand gewinnen) switch off

Ab·schaltung *die* switching off; (eines Kraftwerks) shutdown

Abschattung /'apʃatʊŋ/ *die;* **~, ~en** shade; hue; (fig.) shade; nuance

ab|schätzen *tr. V.* estimate; size up ‹*person, possibilities*›; **jmdn. ~d betrachten** look at sb. appraisingly

abschätzig /'apʃɛtsɪç/
A *Adj.* derogatory; disparaging
B *adv.* derogatorily; disparagingly

a

Abschätzigkeit *die* derogatoriness; disparagement

ab|schauen ▸**abgucken**

Ab·schaum *der* (abwertend) scum; dregs *pl.*

ab|scheiden *unr. tr. V.* 1 (Chemie) precipitate; (Physiol.) secrete 2 (geh.: abtrennen) separate; (fig.) isolate; *s. auch* **abgeschieden B**

Abscheider *der;* **~s,** ~ (Technik) separator

ab|scheren[1] *unr. tr. V.* shear off ‹*hair, wool*›; shear ‹*sheep, head*›

ab|scheren[2] (Technik)

A *tr. V.* (abtrennen) shear

B *itr. V.* (sich lösen) shear off

Ab·scheu *der;* **~s,** (selten:) *die;* **~:** detestation; abhorrence; **einen ~ vor jmdm./etw. haben** detest *or* abhor sb./sth.; **jmds. ~ erregen** arouse repugnance in sb.; repel sb.

ab|scheuern *tr. V.* 1 (entfernen) scrub off; **etw. von etw. ~:** scrub sth. off sth. 2 (säubern) scrub 3 (beschädigen) graze ‹*skin*›; wear away ‹*cloth*›; **ein abgescheuerter Kragen** a badly worn collar

abscheu·erregend *Adj.* ▸**abscheulich A 2**

abscheulich /apˈʃɔylɪç/

A *Adj.* 1 (widerwärtig) disgusting, awful ‹*smell, taste*›; repulsive, awful ‹*sight*› 2 (verwerflich, schändlich) disgraceful ‹*behaviour*›; abominable ‹*crime*›

B *adv.* 1 disgracefully; abominably 2 (ugs.: sehr) **~ frieren** freeze [half] to death (coll.); **das schmerzt ganz ~:** it hurts like hell (coll.); **~ kalt/scharf** terribly cold/sharp (coll.)

Abscheulichkeit *die;* **~, ~en** ▸**abscheulich A:** disgustingness; awfulness; repulsiveness; disgracefulness; abominableness

ab|schicken *tr. V.* send [off], post ‹*letter, parcel*›; dispatch, send [off], post ‹*goods, money*›; send ‹*messenger*›

ab|schieben

A *unr. tr. V.* 1 push *or* shove away; **das Bett von der Wand ~:** push *or* shove the bed away from the wall 2 (abwälzen) shift; **die Verantwortung/Schuld auf jmdn. ~:** shift [the] responsibility/the blame on to sb. 3 (Rechtsw.: ausweisen) deport; **jmdn. über die Grenze ~:** put sb. over the border 4 (ugs.: entfernen) get rid of; **jmdn. in ein Heim ~:** shove sb. into a home (coll.)

B *unr. itr. V.; mit sein* (salopp: weggehen) push off (coll.); shove off (coll.)

Ab·schiebung *die* (Rechtsw.) deportation

Abschiebungs·haft *die* (Rechtsw.) detention prior to deportation

Abschied /ˈapʃiːt/ *der;* **~[e]s, ~e** 1 (Trennung) parting (**von** from); farewell (**von** to); **[von jmdm./etw.] ~ nehmen** say goodbye [to sb./sth.]; take one's leave [of sb./sth.]; **von einer Gewohnheit ~ nehmen** give up a habit; **beim ~:** at parting; when saying goodbye; **sich zum ~ die Hände schütteln** shake hands on parting; **zum ~ Blumen schenken** give flowers as a parting gift; **jmdm. zum ~ zuwinken** wave goodbye to sb. 2 (geh.: Entlassung) resignation; **seinen ~ nehmen** resign; ‹*officer*› resign one's commission; **den ~ erhalten** (veralt.) be discharged

Abschieds-: ~besuch *der* farewell visit; **~brief** *der* farewell letter; **~essen** *das* farewell dinner; **~feier** *die* (Zeremonie) farewell ceremony; (Party) farewell *or* leaving party; **~geschenk** *das* farewell *or* parting gift; (einer Firma usw.) leaving present; **~gesuch** *das* (geh.) letter of resignation; **sein ~gesuch einreichen** tender one's resignation; ‹*officer*› resign one's commission; **~gruß** *der* goodbye; farewell; **~kuss** *der* goodbye *or* parting kiss; **~rede** *die* farewell speech; **~schmerz** *der* sorrow at parting; **~spiel** *das* (Fußball) farewell appearance; **~szene** *die* scene of sentimental farewells; **~vorstellung** *die* farewell performance

ab|schießen *unr. tr. V.* 1 loose, fire ‹*arrow*›; fire ‹*rifle, pistol, rocket, cannon*›; launch ‹*spacecraft*› 2 (töten) take; (salopp) shoot down ‹*person*› 3 (ugs.: entfernen) kick *or* throw ‹*person*› out 4 (von sich geben) fire off ‹*question*›; shoot ‹*glance*› 5 (zerstören) shoot down ‹*aeroplane*›; put ‹*tank*› out of action 6 (wegreißen) shoot off ‹*arm, leg, etc.*›

ab|schilfern *itr. V.; mit sein* peel

ab|schinden *unr. refl. V.* **sich ~:** work *or* (Brit. coll.) flog oneself to death; **sich mit etw. ~:** struggle along with sth.

Abschirm·dienst *der* (Milit.) counter-espionage service

ab|schirmen *tr. V.* 1 (schützen) shield; **jmdn./sich von der** *od.* **gegen die Umwelt ~:** screen sb./oneself off from the outside world 2 (abdecken) cover ‹*lamp*›; screen off ‹*light, radiation, radio station*›

Abschirmung *die;* **~, ~en** 1 (Schutz) shielding; (von der Umwelt usw.) screening off 2 (von Licht, Strahlung) screening off

ab|schirren *tr. V.* unharness ‹*horse*›; unyoke ‹*cattle*›

ab|schlachten *tr. V.* slaughter

ab|schlaffen /ˈapʃlafn̩/ (ugs.)

A *tr., itr. V.* (schlaff machen) take it out of; **das schlafft ab** it takes it out of you; **ein abgeschlaffter Typ** a lackadaisical fellow; **er saß abgeschlafft im Sessel** he sat limply in his chair

B *itr. V.; mit sein* (schlaff werden) wilt; sag; **geistig ~:** lose one's intellectual vigour

Ab·schlag *der* 1 (Kaufmannsspr.) reduction; discount 2 (Teilzahlung) interim payment; (Vorschuss) advance 3 (Fußball) goalkeeper's kick out 4 (Hockey) ▸**Bully** 5 (Golf) tee; (Schlag) drive 6 (Finanzw.) ▸**Disagio**

ab|schlagen

A *unr. tr. V.* 1 knock off; (mit dem Beil, Schwert usw.) chop off; **jmdm. den Kopf ~:** chop off sb.'s head 2 (ablehnen) refuse; **jmdm. etw. ~:** refuse *or* deny sb. sth. 3 (abwehren) beat *or* fend off 4 (zerlegen) dismantle; strike ‹*tent*› 5 (Seemannsspr.) unbend

B *unr. itr. V.* 1 *auch tr.* (Fußball) **[den Ball] ~:** kick the ball out 2 (Hockey) take a 15-metre hit

C *unr. refl. V.* (kondensieren) **sich an etw.** (*Dat.*) **~:** condense on sth.; *s. auch* **abgeschlagen B; Wasser 5**

abschlägig /ˈapʃlɛːgɪç/ (Amtsspr.)

A *Adj.* negative; **ein ~er Bescheid** a refusal *or* rejection

B *adv.* **jmdn. ~ bescheiden** refuse sb.; **jmds. Gesuch** (*Akk.*) **~ bescheiden** reject sb.'s application

Abschlag[s]·zahlung *die* ▸**Abschlag 2**

ab|schlecken *tr. V.* (österr., südd.) ▸**ablecken**

ab|schleifen

A *unr. tr. V.* 1 (entfernen) (von Holz) sand off; (von Metall, Glas usw.) grind off 2 (glätten) sand down ‹*wood*›; grind down ‹*metal, glass, etc.*›; smooth down ‹*broken tooth*›

B *unr. refl. V.* (sich abnutzen) wear away; **das schleift sich noch ab** (fig.) that will wear off in time

Abschlepp·dienst *der* (Kfz-W.) breakdown recovery service; tow[ing] service (Amer.)

ab|schleppen

A *tr. V.* 1 tow away; take ‹*ship*› in tow; **ein Auto zur Werkstatt ~:** tow a car to the garage 2 (salopp: mitnehmen) **jmdn. ~:** drag sb. off

B *refl. V.* (ugs.: schwer tragen) **sich mit/an etw.** (*Dat.*) **~:** break one's back carrying sth. (fig.)

Abschlepp-: ~seil *das* tow rope; (aus Draht) towing cable; **~stange** *die* tow bar; **~wagen** *der* breakdown vehicle; tow truck (Amer.); (der Polizei) tow-away vehicle

abschließbar *Adj.* lockable; **es ist nicht ~:** it cannot be locked

ab|schließen

A *unr. tr. V.* 1 *auch itr.* (zuschließen) lock ‹*door, gate, cupboard*›; lock [up] ‹*house, flat, room, park*›; **vergiss nicht, abzuschließen!** don't forget to lock up! 2 (absondern, trennen) **etw. luftdicht ~:** seal sth. hermetically; **sich ganz [von der Welt] ~:** cut oneself off [from the world] completely 3 (begrenzen) border 4 (zum Abschluss bringen) bring to an end; conclude; **die Bücher ~:** balance the books; **sein Studium ~:** finish one's studies; **Bewerber mit abgeschlossenem Universitätsstudium** applicants with a degree 5 (vereinbaren) strike ‹*bargain, deal*›; make ‹*purchase*›; enter into ‹*agreement*›; **Geschäfte ~:** conclude deals; (im Handel) do business; *s. auch* **abgeschlossen B; Versicherung 2; Wette**

B *unr. itr. V.* 1 (begrenzt sein) be bordered (**mit** by) 2 (aufhören, enden) end; **~d sagte er ...** in conclusion he said ...; **seine ~den Worte waren ...** his concluding words were ...; **mit [einem] Gewinn/Verlust ~** (Kaufmannsspr.) show a profit/deficit 3 **mit jmdm./etw. abgeschlossen haben** have finished with sb./sth. 4 (Kaufmannsspr.) **die Vertragspartner wollen morgen ~:** the parties [to the contract] want to close tomorrow

Ab·schluss, *Ab·schluß *der* 1 (Verschluss) seal; **ein luftdichter ~:** an airtight seal 2 (abschließender Teil) edge 3 (Beendigung) conclusion; end; **vor ~ der Arbeiten** before the completion of the work; **zum ~ noch eine Frage** one final question; **sich dem ~ nähern** be drawing to a conclusion; **kurz vor dem ~ stehen** be nearly finished *or* at an end; **etw. zum ~ bringen** finish sth.; bring sth. to an end *or* a conclusion; **zum ~ kommen** *od.* **gelangen** be completed; **wir müssen mit unseren Verhandlungen zum ~ kommen** we must bring our negotiations to a close; **zum ~ unseres Programms** to end our programme 4 (ugs.: ~zeugnis) **einen/keinen ~ haben** (Hochschulw.) ≈ have a/have no degree *or* (Amer.) diploma; (Schulw.) ≈ have some/no GCSE passes (Brit.); (Lehre) have/not have finished one's apprenticeship; **ohne ~:** without gaining a degree *or* (Amer.) diploma/any GCSE passes (Brit.)/finishing one's apprenticeship 5 (Kaufmannsspr.: Schlussrechnung) balancing 6 (Kaufmannsspr.: geschäftliche Vereinbarung) business deal; **einen ~ über 2 Millionen Tonnen Getreide tätigen** make a deal for 2 million tons of grain 7 (eines Geschäfts, Vertrags) conclusion; **durch den ~ einer Versicherung** by taking out an insurance policy 8 (Fußball) finishing move

Abschluss-, *Abschluß-: ~ball *der* final dance; **~examen** *das* final examination; **~feier** *die* (Schulw.) leaving party; **~klasse** *die* (Schulw.) final year; **~kundgebung** *die* final rally; **~prüfung** *die* 1 (Schulw.) leaving *or* (Amer.) final examination; (Hochschulw.) final examination; finals *pl.*; 2 (Wirtsch.) audit; **~veranstaltung** *die* final event; **~zeugnis** *das* (Schulw.) ≈ leaving certificate (Brit.); ≈ diploma (Amer.)

ab|schmatzen *tr. V.* (ugs.) **jmdn. ~:** kiss sb. noisily

ab|schmecken *tr. V.* 1 (kosten) taste; try 2 (würzen) season

ab|schmeicheln *tr. V.* **jmdm. etw. ~:** wheedle sth. out of sb.

ab|schmelzen

A *unr. itr. V.; mit sein* melt away

B *unr. tr. V.* melt; (fig.: verringern) reduce [the size of] ‹*assets, reserves*›

ab|schmettern *tr. V.* (ugs.) throw out; **jmdn. ~:** turn a deaf ear to sb.

ab|schmieren

A *tr. V.* 1 (Technik) grease 2 (ugs.: abschreiben) scribble down; (unerlaubt) copy; ‹*child in school*› crib (**von, bei** from)

B *itr. V.* 1 (ugs.) crib (**von, bei** from) 2 (Fliegerspr.) side-slip

Abschmier·presse *die* (Kfz-W.) grease gun

ab|schminken *tr. V.* 1 **jmdn./sich ~:** remove sb.'s/one's make-up; **sich** (*Dat.*) **das Gesicht/die Augen ~:** remove the make-up from one's face/eyes; **als ich sie abgeschminkt sah** when I saw her without her make-up 2 (salopp) **sich** (*Dat.*) **etw. ~:** get sth. out of one's head

ab|schmirgeln *tr. V.;* 1 (polieren) rub down with emery; (mit Sandpapier) sand down 2 (entfernen) rub off with emery; (mit Sandpapier) sand off

ab|schmücken *tr. V.* take the decorations off ‹*Christmas tree*›

ab|schnacken *tr. V.* (nordd.) ▸**abschwatzen**

a

ab|schnallen
A *tr. V.* 1 (abnehmen) unfasten; **[sich** (*Dat.*)**] den Tornister/das Holzbein ~:** take off one's knapsack/wooden leg 2 (losschnallen) unfasten; **sich ~:** unfasten one's seat belt
B *itr. V.* (salopp) 1 (nicht mehr folgen können) switch off 2 (fassungslos sein) be flabbergasted; **da schnallst du [echt] ab** you'll be flabbergasted

ab|schneiden
A *unr. tr. V.* 1 (abtrennen) cut off; cut down ‹*sth. hanging*›; **etw. von etw. ~:** cut sth. off sth.; **sich** (*Dat.*) **den Finger ~:** cut one's finger off; **sich** (*Dat.*) **eine Scheibe Brot/Fleisch ~:** cut oneself a slice of bread/meat; *s. auch* **Scheibe 2** 2 (kürzer schneiden) cut; **jmdm./sich die Haare/Fingernägel ~:** cut sb.'s/one's hair/fingernails; **ein Kleid/einen Rock [ein Stück] ~:** cut [a piece] off a dress/a skirt; **eine Zigarre ~:** cut the end off a cigar 3 **jmdm. den Weg ~:** take a short cut to get ahead of sb. 4 (trennen, isolieren) cut off; **die Truppen vom Nachschub ~:** cut off troops from reinforcements; *s. auch* **abgeschnitten B** 5 (unterbinden) **einen Einwurf/Einwand ~:** cut short an interjection/a protest
B *unr. itr. V.* 1 (ver-, abkürzen) ‹*path, road*› be a short cut; ‹*pedestrian, driver*› take a short cut 2 **bei etw. gut/schlecht ~:** do well/badly in sth.

ab|schnellen *refl. V.* **sich [vom Boden] ~:** take off

ab|schnippeln *tr. V.* (ugs.) **Stückchen von etw. ~:** cut little bits off sth.; (mit der Schere) snip bits off sth.

Ab·schnitt *der* 1 (Kapitel) section 2 (Milit.: Gebiet, Gelände) sector; (DDR: Wohnbereich) district; (DDR: Handelsbereich) section (*comprising ten retail shops belonging to a manufacturing cooperative*) 3 (Zeitspanne) phase 4 (Kontroll~) [detachable] portion; (eines Schecks) stub, counterfoil; **die Lebensmittelkarte hatte ~e für Butter, Brot, Zucker usw.** the ration card had coupons for butter, bread, sugar, etc. 5 (Math.: eines Kreises) segment

Abschnitts·bevollmächtigte *der* (DDR) ≈ community policeman

abschnitt[s]·weise
A *Adv.* in sections; **etw. ~ lesen** read sth. section by section
B *adj.* sectionalized

ab|schnüren *tr. V.* 1 apply a tourniquet to; **jmdm. die Luft/das Blut ~:** stop sb. from breathing/restrict sb.'s circulation; **einem Konkurrenten die Luft ~** (fig.) ruin a competitor 2 (blockieren) seal off

ab|schöpfen *tr. V.* skim off; (fig.) **den Rahm ~** (am meisten bekommen) take the lion's share; (das Beste bekommen) cream off the best; **den Gewinn** *od.* **Profit ~:** siphon off the profits; **überschüssige Kaufkraft ~:** absorb excess spending power

ab|schotten *tr. V.* 1 (Schiffbau) separate by a bulkhead/bulkheads 2 (fig.) **etw. [von etw.] ~:** seal sth. off [from sth.]; **sich jmdm. gegenüber ~:** seal oneself off from sb.

ab|schrägen *tr. V.* **einen Balken/ein Brett ~:** bevel a beam/the edges of a plank

ab|schrammen
A *tr. V.* (abschürfen) graze; **sich** (*Dat.*) **das Knie/die Haut ~:** graze one's knee/one's skin
B *itr. V.* 1 (nordd. salopp: weggehen) push off (coll.) 2 (salopp: sterben) croak (sl.); snuff it (sl.)

abschraubbar *Adj.* unscrewable

ab|schrauben *tr. V.* unscrew [and remove]; **etw. lässt sich ~:** sth. can be unscrewed

ab|schrecken
A *tr. V.* 1 (abhalten) deter; **sein Aussehen schreckt viele ab** many people are put off by his appearance 2 (fernhalten) scare off 3 (Metall.) quench 4 (Kochk.) pour cold water over; put ‹*boiled eggs*› into cold water
B *itr. V.* (eine ~de Wirkung haben) act as a deterrent; **das schreckt eher ab** it's more likely to put people off

abschreckend
A *Adj.* 1 (warnend) deterrent; **ein ~es Beispiel für alle Raucher** a warning to all smokers 2 (abstoßend) repulsive
B *adv.* **~ wirken** have a deterrent effect; **~ hässlich** repulsively ugly

Abschreckung *die;* ~, ~en 1 deterrence; **der ~** (*Dat.*) **dienen** serve as a deterrent 2 (Mittel zur ~) deterrent

Abschreckungs-: ~politik *die* policy of deterrence; **~potenzial** *das* deterrent potential; **~theorie** *die* (Rechtsw.) theory of the deterrent value of punishment; **~waffe** *die* deterrent [weapon]

ab|schreiben
A *unr. tr. V.* 1 (kopieren) copy out; **sich** (*Dat.*) **etw. ~:** copy sth. down; (aus einem Buch, einer Zeitung usw.) copy sth. out 2 **etw. von jmdm. ~** (in der Schule) copy sth. from *or* off sb.; (als Plagiator) plagiarize sth. from sb. 3 (Wirtsch.) amortize, write down (**mit** by) 4 (ugs.: verloren geben) write off; **jmdn. abgeschrieben haben** have written sb. off 5 (abnutzen) use up ‹*pencil, crayon, ballpoint or felt pen*›; wear out ‹*pen nib*›
B *unr. itr. V.* 1 **bei** *od.* **von jmdm. ~** (in der Schule) copy off sb.; (als Plagiator) copy from sb. 2 (brieflich absagen) **jmdm. ~:** write to sb. and say one cannot come

Ab·schreibung *die* (Wirtsch.) 1 (das Abschreiben) amortization 2 (Betrag) depreciation provision

Abschreibungs-: ~gesellschaft *die* (Wirtsch.) tax-loss company; **~möglichkeit** *die* (Wirtsch.) *possibility of setting off items against taxable income;* **~ruine** *die* (salopp) *building erected not for occupation, but for purposes of offsetting depreciation against tax*

ab|schreiten *unr. tr. V.* (geh.) 1 *mit sein od. haben* (entlanggehen an) inspect ‹*troops*›; pace ‹*distance*› 2 (schreitend abmessen) pace out

Ab·schrift *die* copy

ab|schrubben *tr. V.* (ugs.) 1 scrub; **sich/jmdm. den Rücken ~:** scrub one's/sb.'s back [down]; **sich/jmdn. ~:** scrub oneself/sb. [down] 2 (schrubbend entfernen) scrub away *or* off; **sich/jmdm. den Schmutz ~:** scrub the dirt off oneself/sb.

ab|schuften *refl. V.* (ugs.) work like a slave; **sosehr man sich auch abschuftet** however hard you slave *or* (Brit. coll.) graft

ab|schuppen
A *tr. V.* scale
B *refl. V.* **die Haut schuppt sich ab** the skin flakes off

ab|schürfen *tr. V.* **sich** (*Dat.*) **die Knie/die Ellenbogen ~:** graze one's knees/one's elbows; **sich** (*Dat.*) **die Haut ~:** chafe the skin

Ab·schürfung *die* 1 (das Abschürfen) grazing 2 (Schürfwunde) graze

Ab·schuss, *Ab·schuß *der* 1 (eines Flugzeugs) shooting down; (eines Panzers) putting out of action; **der Pilot hatte 50 Abschüsse** the pilot had 50 kills 2 (von Wild) shooting; (fig. salopp: Eroberung) lay (coll.); **Tiere zum ~ freigeben** permit the shooting of animals; **jmdn. zum ~ freigeben** (fig. ugs.) throw sb. to the wolves (fig.) 3 (das Abfeuern) (von Geschossen, Torpedos) firing; (von Raketen in den Weltraum) launching

Abschuss·basis, *Abschuß·basis *die* launch[ing] site

abschüssig /ˈapʃʏsɪç/ *Adj.* downward sloping ‹*land*›; **die Straße ist ~:** the road goes steeply downhill

Abschuss-, *Abschuß-: ~liste *die* (fig. ugs.) **er steht auf meiner ~liste** I've got it in for him (coll.); **auf der/jmds. ~liste stehen** be on the/sb.'s blacklist; **~prämie** *die* bounty (*for shot animals*); **~rampe** *die* launch[ing] pad

ab|schütteln *tr. V.* 1 (herunterschütteln) shake down ‹*fruit*›; **[sich** (*Dat.*)**] den Staub/den Schnee [vom Mantel] ~:** shake off the dust/the snow [from one's coat]; *s. auch* **Joch 1** 2 **ein Tischtuch ~:** shake [out] a tablecloth 3 (fig.: überwinden, loswerden) shake off

ab|schütten *tr. V.* ▸ **abgießen 1**

ab|schwächen
A *tr. V.* 1 (mildern) tone down, moderate ‹*statement, criticism*› 2 (verringern) lessen ‹*effect, impression*›; cushion ‹*blow, impact*› 3 (Fot.) reduce
B *refl. V.* (nachlassen) ‹*interest, demand*› wane; ‹*noise, storm*› abate; **das Tief/Hoch schwächt sich ab** (Met.) the low/high-pressure area is weakening; **der Preisauftrieb schwächt sich ab** price increases are slowing down

Ab·schwächung *die;* ~, ~en 1 (Milderung) toning down, moderation; (abgemilderte Form) attenuation 2 (eines Aufpralls, Stoßes usw.) cushioning 3 (Fot.) reduction 4 (das Nachlassen) waning; (eines Hochs, Tiefs) weakening; (zahlenmäßig) drop (*Gen.* in)

ab|schwatzen, (bes. südd.) **ab|schwätzen** *tr. V.* **jmdm. etw. ~:** talk sb. into giving one sth.; **sich** (*Dat.*) **etw. von jmdm. ~ lassen** let oneself be talked into giving sb. sth.

ab|schweifen *itr. V.; mit sein;* 1 digress; **ihr Blick schweifte ab** her gaze wandered 2 (geh.: vom Weg abgehen) stray

Abschweifung *die;* ~, ~en digression

ab|schwellen *unr. itr. V.; mit sein* 1 go down 2 (geh.: zurückgehen) ‹*flood*› subside; ‹*noise*› die away; ‹*music*› fade [away]

ab|schwemmen *tr. V.* 1 wash away 2 (durch Schwemmen reinigen) wash down

Abschwemmung *die;* ~, ~en washout

ab|schwenken
A *itr. V.; mit sein* turn aside; **links/rechts ~** (abbiegen) turn left/right; (die Richtung allmählich ändern) bear to the left/right
B *tr. V.* **die Tropfen vom Glas ~:** shake the drops off the glass; **die Gläser ~:** rinse the glasses and shake the drops off them

ab|schwindeln *tr. V.* **jmdm. etw. ~:** trick sb. out of sth.

ab|schwirren *itr. V.; mit sein* 1 ‹*bird, dragonfly*› whirr away; ‹*bee, beetle, fly, wasp*› buzz away 2 (ugs.: weggehen) buzz off (coll.)

ab|schwitzen *tr. V.* sweat off

ab|schwören *unr. itr. V.* **dem Teufel/seinem Glauben ~:** renounce the Devil/one's faith; **dem Alkohol/Laster ~:** forswear *or* swear off alcohol/vice

Ab·schwung *der* 1 (Turnen) dismount; **beim ~:** when dismounting 2 (Wirtsch.: Rezession) downward trend; **ein ~ der Konjunktur** a recession

ab|segeln
A *itr. V.* 1 *mit sein* (lossegeln) sail away; **von Kiel ~:** sail from Kiel 2 (die Saison beenden) have the last sail of the season
B *tr. V.* **die Küste ~:** sail along the coast

ab|segnen *tr. V.* (ugs. scherzh.) sanction

absehbar *Adj.* foreseeable; **in ~er Zeit** within the foreseeable future; **etw. ist noch gar nicht ~:** sth. cannot yet be predicted; **auf** *od.* **für ~e Zeit** for the foreseeable future; **nicht ~:** unforeseeable

ab|sehen
A *unr. tr. V.* 1 (voraussehen) predict; foresee ‹*event*› 2 (abzielen) **er hat es darauf abgesehen, uns zu ärgern** he's out to annoy us 3 (haben wollen) **es auf etw.** (*Akk.*) **abgesehen haben** be after sth.; **sie hat es bloß auf sein Geld abgesehen** she's only after his money; **er hat es auf sie abgesehen** he's got his eye on her 4 (schikanieren) **der Chef hat es auf ihn abgesehen** the boss has got it in for him 5 ▸ **abgucken A**
B *unr. itr. V.* 1 (nicht beachten) **von etw. ~:** leave aside *or* ignore sth.; *s. auch* **abgesehen B** 2 (verzichten) **von etw. ~:** refrain from sth.; **von einer Anzeige/Klage ~:** not report sth./not press charges 3 ▸ **abgucken B**

ab|seifen *tr. V.* wash down [with soap]; **jmdn./sich ~:** soap sb./oneself down

ab|seilen
A *tr. V.* lower [with a rope]
B *refl. V.* 1 (Bergsteigen) abseil 2 (salopp: sich davonmachen) push *or* buzz off (coll.)

Abseil·haken *der* (Bergsteigen) abseil piton

***ab|sein** ▸ **ab B1**

Ab·seite *die* (Textilw.) wrong side

abseitig *Adj.* 1 (geh.: abseits gelegen) remote 2 (ausgefallen, abwegig) esoteric 3 ▸ **abartig**

abseits /ˈapzaits/
A *Präp. mit Gen.* away from
B *Adv.* **1** (entfernt) far away; **etwas ~:** a little way away **2** (Ballspiele) **~ sein** *od.* **stehen** be offside

Abseits *das; ~, ~* **1** (Sport) **das war ein klares ~:** that was clearly offside; **im ~ stehen** be offside; **der Spieler lief ins ~:** the player put himself offside **2** (fig.) **im ~ stehen** have been pushed out into the cold; **ins ~ geraten** be pushed out into the cold

abseits-, Abseits-: ~falle *die* (Sport) offside trap; **~position** *die,* **~stellung** *die* (Sport) offside position; **sich in ~stellung befinden** be in an offside position; **~tor** (Sport) *das* offside goal; **~verdächtig** *Adj.* (Sport) which may have been offside *postpos.*; **[stark] ~verdächtig sein** look [very much] like offside

ab|senden *unr. od. regelm. tr. V.* dispatch

Ab·sender *der,* **Ab·senderin,** *die; ~, ~nen* ▸ ℹ **S. 143** sender; (~angabe) sender's address

Ab·sendung *die* dispatch

ab|sengen *tr. V.* singe off; singe ‹*poultry*›

ab|senken
A *refl. V.* **sich [zum See/Fluss hin] ~:** slope [down to the lake/river]
B *tr. V.* **1** (Tiefbau) lower **2** (versenken) sink **3** (Gartenbau) **Erdbeeren/Weinstöcke ~:** set strawberries/vines

Absenker *der; ~s, ~* (Gartenbau) runner; set

absentieren /apzɛnˈtiːrən/ *refl. V.* (geh., veralt.) withdraw

Absenz /apˈzɛnts/ *die; ~, ~en* **1** absence [of mind] **2** (bes. österr., schweiz.) absence (*from school*)

ab|servieren
A *itr. V.* clear away
B *tr. V.* **1** **ein Gedeck/den Tisch ~:** clear away a cover/clear the table **2** (salopp: absetzen, kaltstellen) throw out **3** (salopp: töten) **jmdn. ~:** bump sb. off (coll.)

absetzbar *Adj.* **1** (Steuerw.) **[steuerlich] ~:** [tax-]deductible **2** (verkäuflich) saleable **3** ▸ **absetzen A 4: er ist nicht ~:** he cannot be dismissed/be removed from office

ab|setzen
A *tr. V.* **1** (abnehmen) take off **2** (hinstellen) put down ‹*glass, bag, suitcase*› **3** (aussteigen lassen) **jmdn. ~** (im öffentlichen Verkehr) put sb. down; let sb. out (Amer.); (im privaten Verkehr) drop sb. [off] **4** (entlassen) dismiss ‹*minister, official*›; remove ‹*chancellor, judge*› from office; depose ‹*king, emperor*› **5** (ablagern) deposit **6** (absagen) drop; call off ‹*strike, football match*›; **einen Punkt von der Tagesordnung ~:** delete an item from the agenda **7** (nicht mehr anwenden) discontinue ‹*treatment, therapy*›; stop taking ‹*medicine, drug*› **8** (von den Lippen nehmen) take ‹*glass, trumpet*› from one's lips; (nicht mehr schreiben mit) lift ‹*pen*› from the paper **9** (verkaufen) sell **10** (Steuerw.) **etw. [von der Steuer] ~:** deduct sth. [from tax] **11** (abwerfen) throw ‹*rider*› **12** (Druckw.: als neue Zeile beginnen) start ‹*section*› on a new line; **die folgenden Zeilen ~:** treat the subsequent lines as a new paragraph **13** (Druckw.: setzen) compose; **einen Text/ein Manuskript ~:** set [up] a text/manuscript **14** (Seemannsspr.) **ein Boot [vom Ufer] ~:** push a boat off [from the shore] **15** (hervorheben) **farblich abgesetzt** of contrasting colour *postpos.*; **wir wollen den Saum farblich ~:** we want to use a contrasting colour for the hem; **den Saum mit Samt ~:** trim the hem with velvet
B *refl. V.* **1** (sich ablagern) be deposited; ‹*dust*› settle; ‹*particles in suspension*› settle out **2** (sich distanzieren) **sich von etw. ~:** distance oneself from sth. **3** (sich unterscheiden) ▸ **abheben D** **4** (ugs.: sich davonmachen) get away **5** (Milit.) withdraw

Absetzung *die; ~, ~en* **1** ▸ **absetzen A 4:** dismissal; removal from office; deposition **2** (Steuerw.) deduction **3** (Absage) cancellation; (eines Streiks, Fußballspiels usw.) calling off **4** (Abbruch) discontinuation

ab|sichern
A *tr. V.* **1** make safe **2** (fig.) substantiate ‹*argument, conclusions*›; validate ‹*result*›; **etw. rechtlich/vertraglich ~:** protect sth. legally/by contract; **tariflich abgesichert** protected by agreement *postpos.*
B *refl. V.* safeguard oneself; **sich vertraglich ~:** protect oneself by contract; **sich gegenseitig ~:** keep each other safe; **er will sich ~ für den Fall, dass ...** he wants to cover himself against the possibility that ...; **sich nach allen Seiten ~:** guard against all eventualities; (gegen Einwände) forestall criticism

Ab·sicherung *die* **1** (das Sichermachen) making safe; **die Polizei ist für die ~ des Geländes verantwortlich** the police are responsible for making the site safe **2** (fig.) substantiation; (von Ergebnissen) validation; **zur rechtlichen/vertraglichen ~ einer Sache** (*Gen.*) to protect sth. legally/by contract

Ab·sicht *die;* **1** intention; **die ~ haben, etw. zu tun** plan *or* intend to do sth.; **etw. mit** *od.* **aus ~ tun** do sth. intentionally *or* deliberately; **etw. ohne** *od.* **nicht mit ~ tun** do sth. unintentionally; **das ist ~:** that's intentional; **in der besten ~:** with the best of intentions; **aus** *od.* **in politischer/therapeutischer ~:** with a political/therapeutic purpose **2** (Rechtsw.) intent; **in betrügerischer ~ handeln** act with intent to deceive

ab·sichtlich
A *Adj.* intentional; deliberate
B *adv.* intentionally; deliberately

Absichts·erklärung *die* declaration of intent

absichtslos
A *Adj.* unintentional
B *adv.* unintentionally

Ab·siedlung *die* (Med.) dissemination

ab|singen *unr. tr. V.* **1** *auch itr.* **[etw.] vom Blatt ~:** sing [sth.] at sight **2** **unter Absingen der Nationalhymne/schmutziger Lieder** singing the national anthem/dirty songs

ab|sinken *unr. itr. V.; mit sein* **1** sink; (fig.: im Niveau) decline **2** ‹*temperature, blood pressure*› drop; ‹*interest, performance*› decline; **in seinen Leistungen ~:** do *or* perform less well

Absinth /apˈzɪnt/ *der; ~[e]s, ~e* absinth[e]

ab|sitzen
A *unr. tr. V.* **1** (hinter sich bringen) sit through; sit out ‹*hours of duty etc.*›; (im Gefängnis) serve; **zehn Jahre ~:** serve *or* (coll.) do ten years; **seine Jahre ~:** serve one's full sentence **2** ▸ **abgesessen B**
B *unr. itr. V. mit sein* **[vom Pferd] ~:** dismount [from one's horse]

absolut /apzoˈluːt/
A *Adj.* (auch Chemie, Physik) absolute; pure ‹*lyricism, art*›; **der ~e Knüller** (ugs.) the high spot; **der ~e Nullpunkt** (Physik) absolute zero; **der ~e Ablativ** (Sprachw.) the ablative absolute; **die ~e Mehrheit** (Pol.) an absolute majority
B *adv.* absolutely

Absolutheit *die; ~, ~en* absoluteness

Absolution /apzoluˈtsjoːn/ *die; ~, ~en* (kath. Rel.) absolution; **jmdm. die ~ erteilen** give sb. absolution

Absolutismus *der; ~* (hist.) absolutism *no art.*

absolutistisch
A *Adj.* absolutist
B *adv.* in an absolutist manner

Absolvent /apzɔlˈvɛnt/ *der; ~en, ~en,* **Absolventin** *die; ~, ~nen* (einer Schule) one who has taken the leaving *or* (Amer.) final examination; (einer Akademie) graduate; **die ~en der Handelsschule/eines Lehrgangs** those who have/had attended a commercial college/completed a course of training; **er ist ~ einer Abendschule** he has attended an evening school; *s. auch* **-in**

absolvieren /apzɔlˈviːrən/ *tr. V.* **1** complete; **das Gymnasium ~:** complete a grammar-school education **2** (erledigen, verrichten) put in ‹*hours*›; do ‹*performance, route, task*›; make ‹*visit*›; do (coll.) ‹*sights*› **3** (kath. Rel.) absolve

Absolvierung *die; ~:* completion; **nach [der] ~ einiger Besuche/seines Studiums** having paid some visits/finished one's studies

ab·sonderlich *Adj.* strange; odd

Absonderlichkeit *die; ~, ~en* strangeness; oddness

ab|sondern
A *tr. V.* **1** isolate ‹*patient*›; separate ‹*prisoner*› **2** (Biol., Physiol.) secrete; exude ‹*resin*›; discharge ‹*pus*›; (fig. abwertend) emit
B *refl. V.* **sich [von anderen] ~:** isolate oneself [from others]

Absonderung *die; ~, ~en* **1** isolation **2** (Biol., Med.) secretion **3** (österr.: Einzelhaft) solitary confinement

Absorbens /apˈzɔrbɛns/ *das; ~,* **Absorbenzien** *od.* **Absorbentia** (Chemie, Physik) absorbent

Absorber *der; ~s, ~* **1** ▸ **Absorbens** **2** (bei Kältemaschinen usw.) absorber

absorbieren *tr. V.* **1** (Chemie, Physik, Physiol.) absorb; **~d** absorbent **2** (fig.) absorb, engage ‹*attention*›

Absorption /apzɔrpˈtsjoːn/ *die; ~* (Chemie, Physik, Physiol.) absorption

Absorptions·vermögen *das* (Chemie, Physik, Physiol.) absorbency

ab|spalten
A *unr. od. regelm. tr. V.* **1** (abschlagen, fig.: trennen) split off **2** (Chemie) release
B *unr. od. regelm. refl. V.* split off *or* away (**aus** from); **sich von jmdm./etw. ~:** split with sb./sth.

Ab·spaltung *die* **1** (das Abschlagen, fig.: Trennung) splitting-off **2** (Chemie) separation

Ab·spann *der* (Ferns.) final credits

ab|spannen *tr. V.* **1** (ausspannen) unhitch ‹*wagon*›; unharness ‹*horse*›; unyoke ‹*oxen*› **2** (Technik: mit Seilen) anchor ‹*pole, mast*›; *s. auch* **abgespannt B**

Abspann·seil *das* (Brückenbau) inclined tension cable

Abspannung *die; ~, ~en* **1** (Ermüdung) weariness; fatigue **2** (Technik) anchoring; (Abspannseil) anchoring cable

ab|sparen *refl. V.* **sich** (*Dat.*) **etw. von seinem Lohn/Taschengeld ~:** save for sth. out of one's wages/pocket money; **er hatte sich** (*Dat.*) **ein paar Euro abgespart** he had managed to save a few euros; *s. auch* **Mund**

ab|specken (salopp)
A *tr. V.* shed
B *itr. V.* **1** (Gewicht verlieren) lose weight; slim [down] **2** (fig.: schrumpfen) slim down

ab|speichern *tr. V.* (DV) store

ab|speisen *tr. V.* **1** (vertrösten) **jmdn. mit etw. ~:** fob sb. off with sth. **2** (oft abwertend: beköstigen) feed

abspenstig /ˈapʃpɛnstɪç/ *Adj.* **jmdm. etw. ~ machen** get sb. to part with sth.; **jmdm. die Kunden/die Patienten/das Personal ~ machen** lure away sb.'s customers/patients/staff; **jmdm. den Freund/die Freundin ~ machen** steal sb.'s boyfriend/girlfriend

ab|sperren
A *tr. V.* **1** (blockieren) seal off; close off **2** **jmdm. das Gas/das Wasser/den Strom ~:** cut off sb.'s gas/water/electricity **3** (österr., südd.: abschließen) lock ‹*door*›
B *itr. V.* (österr., südd.) lock up

Absperr-: ~gitter *das* barrier; **~hahn** *der; Pl.* **~hähne,** (fachspr.) **~~en** (Technik) stopcock; **~kette** *die* cordon

Ab·sperrung *die* **1** (Blockierung) sealing off; closing off **2** (Sperre) barrier

Absperr·ventil *das* (Technik) stop valve

Ab·spiel *das* (Ballspiele) **1** (das Abspielen) passing **2** (Schuss) pass

ab|spielen
A *tr. V.* **1** (ablaufen lassen) **etw. ~:** play sth. through **2** **die Nationalhymne/Internationale ~:** play the national anthem/Internationale; **ein Musikstück vom Blatt ~:** play a piece of music at sight **3** (Ballspiele) pass; *s. auch* **abgespielt B**
B *refl. V.* **1** (stattfinden) take place **2** (sich ereignen) happen; take place; ‹*course of events*› proceed; ‹*war*› be waged; **da spielt sich [bei mir/ihm] nichts ab!** (salopp) nothing doing [as far as I'm/he's concerned] (coll.)

C *itr. V.* (Ballspiele) pass; **an jmdn. ~:** pass [the ball] to sb.

ab|splittern
A *itr. V.; mit sein* ‹*wood*› splinter off; ‹*lacquer, paint*› flake off
B *refl. V.* (fig.) **sich von einer Gruppe/Partei ~:** split away from a group/party

Ab·sprache *die* agreement; arrangement; **eine ~ mit jmdm. treffen** come to an agreement *or* make an arrangement with sb.; **nach ~ mit** by arrangement with; **nach vorheriger/ohne vorherige ~:** after/without prior consultation

absprache·gemäß *Adv.* as arranged *or* agreed

ab|sprechen
A *unr. tr. V.* **1** (aberkennen) **jmdm. etw. ~:** deprive sb. of sth. **2** (ableugnen) **jmdm. etw. ~:** deny that sb. has sth.; **jmdm. das Recht auf etw.** (*Akk.*) **~:** deny sb.'s right to sth.; **jmdm. das Recht ~, etw. zu tun** deny sb. the right to do sth. **3** (vereinbaren) arrange; **etw. miteinander ~:** arrange sth. together
B *unr. refl. V.* (sich einigen) **sich [mit jmdm.] [über etw.** (*Akk.*)**] ~:** come to *or* reach an agreement [with sb.] [about sth.]

ab|spreizen *tr. V.* stretch out ‹*arm, leg*› sideways; splay out ‹*fingers, toes*›; spread out ‹*hands*›; extend ‹*finger*›

ab|sprengen *tr. V.* **1** (lossprengen) split off; (Raumf.) jettison ‹*stage*› **2** (fig.) separate ‹*troops*›; **abgesprengte Truppenteile** isolated detachments of troops

ab|springen *unr. itr. V.; mit sein* **1** (losspringen) jump off; **[mit dem rechten/linken Bein] ~** ‹*jumper*› take off [on the right/left leg] **2** (herunterspringen) jump down; **vom Fahrrad/Pferd ~:** jump off one's bicycle/horse; **aus dem Flugzeug ~:** jump out of the aeroplane; **mit dem Fallschirm ~:** jump [with a parachute]; (bei Gefahr) bail out; **„Abspringen während der Fahrt verboten"** 'do not alight while the vehicle is in motion' **3** (abplatzen) come off; ‹*paint*› flake off; ‹*enamel*› splinter off **4** (sich lösen) fly off; ‹*bicycle chain*› jump off **5** (abprallen) rebound **6** (ugs.: sich zurückziehen) drop out; (von einem Abkommen) back out; **Kunden/Leser springen uns ab** we are losing customers/readers

ab|spritzen
A *tr. V.* **1** (reinigen) spray [down] **2** (entfernen) spray off; **einer Kuh** (*Dat.*) **den Kot ~:** spray the muck off a cow **3** (ns. verhüll.: ermorden) **jmdn. ~:** give sb. a lethal injection
B *itr. V.* **1** (vulgär: ejakulieren) come (coarse) **2** *mit sein* (veralt.: weggehen) race off **3** *mit sein* (spritzend abprallen) ‹*liquid*› splash off; ‹*mud, mortar, etc.*› splatter off

Ab·sprung *der* **1** (das Losspringen) take-off **2** (das Herunterspringen) jump **3** (fig.) break; **den ~ wagen** risk making the break; **den ~ schaffen** make the break; **den ~ verpassen** miss the boat

Absprung·balken *der* (Leichtathletik) take-off board

ab|spulen *tr. V.* **1** (abwickeln) unwind; **sich ~:** come unwound **2** (filmen) shoot **3** (vorführen) show **4** (salopp: herunterleiern) reel off **5** (salopp: fahren) cover

ab|spülen
A *tr. V.* **1** (wegspülen) wash off ‹*dirt, dust*› **2** (reinigen) rinse off; **sich** (*Dat.*) **die Hände** *usw.* **~:** rinse one's hands *etc.* **3** (bes. südd.) **das Geschirr ~:** wash the dishes
B *itr. V.* (bes. südd.) wash up

ab|stammen *itr. V.* **von jmdm./vom Affen ~:** be descended from sb./the apes

Abstammung *die;* **~, ~en** ▸ **❶ S. 520** descent; **seiner ~ nach ist er Deutscher** he is German by descent

Abstammungs·lehre *die* theory of evolution

Ab·stand *der* **1** (Zwischenraum) distance; **in 20 Meter ~:** at a distance of 20 metres; **im ~ von 10 Metern** 10 metres apart; **~ halten** keep one's distance **2** (Punktunterschied) gap; difference; (Rangunterschied) social distinction; **mit ~:** by far; far and away **3** (Zeitspanne) interval; (kürzer) gap; **in Abständen von 20 Minuten** at 20-minute intervals; **[von etw.] ~ gewinnen** (fig.) have time to recover [from sth.]; **mir fehlt noch der innere ~ zu den Geschehnissen** these events are still too close to me **4** (Zurückhaltung, Distanz) **~ halten** keep one's distance; **den [gebührenden/nötigen] ~ wahren** keep the proper/necessary distance **5** (geh.: Verzicht) **von etw. ~ nehmen** refrain from sth.; **von einer Intervention ~ nehmen** refrain from intervening; **davon ~ nehmen, etw. zu tun** refrain from doing sth.; **von einer Idee ~ nehmen** abandon an idea **6** (Entschädigung) compensation; (bei Übernahme einer Wohnung) *payment for furniture and fittings left by previous tenant*

Abstands·summe *die* ▸ **Abstand 6**

ab|statten /ˈapʃtatn̩/ *tr. V.* (geh.) **jmdm. einen Besuch ~:** pay sb. a visit; **jmdm. Bericht ~:** present one's *or* a report to sb.; **jmdm. seinen Dank ~:** convey one's thanks *or* express one's gratitude to sb.

ab|stauben *tr., itr. V.* **1** dust **2** (ugs.) (stehlen) **etw. ~:** pinch (coll.) *or* nick (Brit. coll.) *or* (Amer. coll.) lift sth.; (schnorren) **etw. bei jmdm. ~:** sponge sth. from sb.; **sie haben ordentlich abgestaubt** they've been pinching things left, right, and centre (coll.)/sponging from all over the place **3** (Fußballjargon) **ein Tor ~:** steal a goal

Abstauber *der;* **~s, ~** **1** ▸ **Abstaubertor** **2** (Fußballjargon) goal-hanger

Abstauberin *die;* **~, ~en** (Fußballjargon) goal-hanger

Abstauber·tor *das* (Fußballjargon) opportunist goal

ab|stechen
A *unr. tr. V.* **1** slaughter ‹*animal*› (*by cutting its throat*); **jmdn. ~** (derb) slit sb.'s throat; *s. auch* **Kalb 1** **2** (ab-, herauslösen) slice off; cut edge of ‹*lawn*›; cut ‹*peat*›; **Teig/Klöße [mit dem Löffel] ~:** cut up dough/cut out dumplings [with a spoon] **3** (ablaufen lassen) tap ‹*beer, wine*›; **einen Hochofen ~:** tap a blast furnace
B *unr. itr. V.* **von etw./jmdm. ~:** contrast with sth./sb.; **gegen etw. ~:** stand out against sth.

Abstecher *der;* **~s, ~:** side trip; (fig.: Abschweifung) digression

ab|stecken *tr. V.* **1** (abgrenzen) mark out; (fig.) define; **ein Gelände mit Pfählen/Pflöcken/Fähnchen ~:** mark out an area with stakes/pegs/flags **2** (Schneiderei) pin up ‹*hem*›; **ein Kleid ~:** fit a dress [by pinning]

ab|stehen *unr. itr. V.* **1** (nicht anliegen) ‹*hair*› stand up, stick out; ‹*pigtail[s]*› stick out; ‹*beard*› grow out; **~de Ohren** protruding ears **2** (wegstehen) **40 cm/zu weit von etw. ~:** be 40 cm. away/too far away from sth. **3** (geh.: Abstand nehmen) **von einem Plan ~:** abandon a plan; **davon ~, etw. zu tun** refrain from doing sth. **4** **Wasser ~ lassen** let water stand; *s. auch* **abgestanden B**; **Bein 1**

Ab·steige *die;* **~, ~n** (ugs. abwertend) cheap and crummy hotel (sl.); (Stundenhotel) sleazy hotel

ab|steigen *unr. itr. V.; mit sein* **1** (heruntersteigen) **[vom Pferd/Fahrrad] ~:** get off [one's horse/bicycle]; **vom Karren ~:** get down from the cart; **„Radfahrer ~"** 'cyclists dismount' **2** (abwärts gehen) go down; descend; **~d** descending ‹*pipe, branch*›; **vom Gipfel/ins Tal ~:** climb down *or* descend from the summit/into the valley; **gesellschaftlich ~** (fig.) decline in social status; **die ~de Linie** (Geneal.) the line of descent; *s. auch* **Ast 1** **3** (Sport) be relegated **4** (übernachten, wohnen) **in einem Hotel ~:** put up at a hotel

Absteige·quartier *das* **1** (veralt.) stopping place **2** (ugs. abwertend) ▸ **Absteige**

Ab·steiger *der* **1** **ein [gesellschaftlicher] ~:** one who has declined in social status **2** (Sport) (vor dem Abstieg stehend) team threatened with *or* facing relegation; (abgestiegen) relegated team

Ab·steigerin *die* ▸ **Absteiger 1**

Abstell·bahn·hof *der* [rail] sidings *pl.*

ab|stellen
A *tr. V.* **1** (absetzen) put down **2** (unterbringen, hinstellen) put; (parken) park **3** (ausschalten, abdrehen); turn *or* switch off; turn off ‹*gas, water*›; **jmdm. das Gas/den Strom ~:** cut sb.'s gas/electricity off; **jmdm. das Telefon ~:** disconnect sb.'s telephone **4** (unterbinden) put a stop to **5** (sein lassen) stop; (aufgeben) give up **6** (beordern) assign; detail [off] ‹*soldiers*› **7** **etw. [weiter] von etw. ~** (abrücken) move sth. [further] away from sth.; (entfernt stellen) put sth. at a [greater] distance from sth. **8** (ausrichten) **etw. auf etw.** (*Akk.*) **~:** gear sth. to sth.
B *itr. V.* **auf etw.** (*Akk.*) **~:** take account of sth.; take sth. into account; **darauf ~, dass ...** take account of *or* take into account the fact that ...

Abstell-: ~gleis *das* siding; **jmdn. aufs ~gleis schieben** (fig. ugs.) put sb. out of harm's way; **~kammer** *die* lumber room; **~raum** *der* storeroom

Abstellung *die;* **~, ~en** **1** (Unterbrechung, Außerbetriebsetzung) (von Zufuhr) disconnection; (von Maschine) shutting down; (auf immer) decommissioning **2** (Unterbindung, Behebung) ending; (von Mängeln) remedying **3** (Abkommandierung) secondment; [temporary] transfer

ab|stemmen
A *tr. V.* (abmeißeln) chisel off
B *refl. V.* push with one's feet; **sich mit den Armen vom Boden ~:** push oneself up from the floor with one's arms

ab|stempeln *tr. V.* **1** frank ‹*letter*›; cancel ‹*stamp*›; **der Brief war in Hamburg abgestempelt** the letter had a Hamburg postmark **2** (fig.) **jmdn. als** *od.* **zum Verbrecher/als geisteskrank ~:** label *or* brand sb. as a criminal/as insane

ab|steppen *tr. V.* backstitch

ab|sterben *unr. itr. V.; mit sein* **1** (eingehen, verfallen) [gradually] die; *s. auch* **abgestorben B** **2** (gefühllos werden) go numb; **mir sind die Finger abgestorben** my fingers have gone numb **3** (verschwinden) ‹*custom, tradition*› die out; ‹*state, social order*› wither away **4** (ugs.: ausgehen) ‹*engine*› die

Ab·stich *der* **1** (das Abstechen) cutting **2** (Metall.) tapping

Abstich-: ~loch *das* (Metall.) tapping hole; **~rinne** *die* (Metall.) tapping spout

Ab·stieg *der;* **~[e]s, ~e** **1** descent **2** (Niedergang) decline; **[sozialer** *od.* **gesellschaftlicher] ~:** fall *or* drop in [social] status **3** (Sport) relegation **4** (Weg abwärts) way down

abstiegs·gefährdet *Adj.* (Sport) threatened with *or* facing relegation *postpos.*

Abstiegs·kandidat *der* (Sportjargon) candidate for relegation

ab|stillen
A *tr. V.* wean
B *itr. V.* stop breastfeeding

ab|stimmen
A *itr. V.* vote; **es wird abgestimmt** a vote is taken; **geheim/namentlich/durch Handzeichen/durch Akklamation ~:** vote by secret ballot/by roll-call/by a show of hands/by acclamation; **über etw.** (*Akk.*) **~:** vote on sth.; **über etw.** (*Akk.*) **~ lassen** put sth. to the vote
B *tr. V.* **1** (vereinbaren); **etw. [miteinander] ~:** discuss and agree on sth. [with each other]; **etw. mit jmdm. ~:** discuss and agree sth. with sb. **2** (harmonisieren) **etw. auf etw.** (*Akk.*) **~:** suit sth. to sth.; (Mode) match sth. to sth.; **etw. auf jmdn. ~:** pitch sth. at sb.'s level; **eine fein abgestimmte Mischung** a finely balanced blend; **zwei/mehrere Dinge aufeinander ~:** make two/several things consistent with each other; **Zeitpläne/Programme aufeinander ~:** coordinate timetables/programmes **3** (Rundf., Ferns.: einstellen) tune **4** (Kfz-W.) tune [up]; adjust ‹*carburettor*›
C *refl. V.* **sich über etw.** (*Akk.*) **~:** discuss and agree on sth.

Ab·stimmung *die* **1** (Stimmabgabe) vote; ballot; **eine geheime ~:** a secret ballot; **zur ~ schreiten** (geh.) *od.* **kommen** come to the vote; **eine ~ [über etw.** (*Akk.*)**] durchführen** take a vote [on sth.]; **bei der ~:** in the vote; (während der ~) during the voting **2** (Absprache) agreement **3** (Harmonisierung) coordination

4 (Rundf., Ferns.) tuning

Abstimmungs-: ~ergebnis *das* result of a/the vote; **~nieder·lage** *die* defeat [in a/the vote]; **~sieg** *der* victory [in a/the vote]

abstinent /apsti'nɛnt/ *Adj.* **1** teetotal; **~ sein** be a non-drinker *or* teetotaller **2** **sexuell ~**: sexually abstinent; continent; **politisch ~ sein** (fig.) abstain from politics

Abstinenz /apsti'nɛnts/ *die;* **~** **1** teetotalism; **~ üben** be teetotal **2** **sexuelle ~**: sexual abstinence; continence; **politische ~** (fig.) political abstinence

Abstinenzler *der;* **~s, ~**, **Abstinenzlerin** *die;* **~, ~nen** teetotaller; non-drinker

Abstinenzlertum *das;* **~s** temperance

ab|stoppen

A *tr. V.* **1** (zum Stillstand bringen) halt; stop; check ‹*advance*›; stop ‹*machine*› **2** (mit der Stoppuhr) **einen Läufer ~**: time a runner with a stopwatch; **die Zeit ~**: measure the time with a stopwatch

B *itr. V.* come to a halt; ‹*person*› stop

Ab·stoß *der* **1** (Fußball) goal kick; **den ~ ausführen** take the goal kick **2** (Sport: beim Springen) take-off

ab|stoßen

A *unr. tr. V.* **1** (wegstoßen) push off *or* away; **das Boot [vom Ufer] ~**: push the boat out [from the bank] **2** (beschädigen) chip ‹*crockery, paintwork, stucco, plaster*›; batter ‹*furniture*›; scuff ‹*shoes*›; *s. auch* **Horn** **3** (verkaufen) sell off **4** (zurückweisen) reject **5** (Physik) repel **6** (anwidern) repel; put off; **sich von jmdm./etw. abgestoßen fühlen** find sb./sth. repulsive

B *unr. itr. V.* **1** *mit sein od. haben* (sich entfernen) be pushed off **2** (anwidern) be repulsive

C *refl. V.* **sich [vom Boden] ~**: push oneself off; (beim Sprung) take off

abstoßend *Adj.* repulsive

Abstoßung *die;* **~, ~en** **1** (Physik, auch fig.) repulsion **2** (Verkauf) sale **3** (Med., Physiol.) rejection

ab|stottern *tr. V.* (ugs.) pay for in instalments; pay off ‹*debt*› by instalments; **er muss jeden Monat 400 Euro ~**: he has to pay out 400 euros in instalments every month

ab|strafen *tr. V.* punish

Abstrafung *die;* **~, ~en** punishment

abstrahieren /apstra'hi:rən/

A *itr. V.* (absehen) **von etw. ~**: ignore sth.; leave sth. out of account

B *tr., itr. V.* (verallgemeinern) abstract (**aus** from)

ab|strahlen

A *tr. V.* (Physik) radiate; (Funkw., Elektrot.) emit ‹*wave, frequency*›

B *itr. V.* (fig.) **auf jmdn./etw. ~**: influence *or* affect sb./sth.

Ab·strahlung *die* (Physik) radiation; (Funkw., Elektrot.) emission

abstrakt /ap'strakt/

A *Adj.* abstract

B *adv.* abstractly; **~ denken** think in the abstract

Abstraktheit *die;* **~**: abstractness

Abstraktion /apstrak'tsi̯o:n/ *die;* **~, ~en** abstraction

Abstraktions·vermögen *das* capacity for abstraction

Abstraktum /ap'straktʊm/ *das;* **~s, Abstrakta** **1** (Philos.) abstract[ion] **2** (Sprachw.) abstract noun

ab|strampeln *refl. V.* (ugs.) **1** (beim Radfahren) pedal; **sich** (*Dat.*) **einige Pfunde ~**: pedal off a few pounds **2** ▸**abplacken**

ab|streichen

A *unr. tr. V.* **1** (abstreifen) wipe; (durch Streichen entfernen) wipe off **2** (ausstreichen) cross off **3** (abziehen) knock off; **davon muss man die Hälfte ~** (fig.) you have to take it with a pinch *or* grain of salt **4** (absuchen) sweep ‹*horizon*›; comb ‹*terrain*›

B *unr. itr. V.; mit sein* (Jägerspr.) fly away

Ab·streicher *der* ▸**Abtreter**

ab|streifen *tr. V.* **1** pull off; strip off ‹*berries*›; **sich** (*Dat.*) **die Handschuhe/den Ring ~**: take off *or* remove one's gloves/ring; **sich/jmdm. die Kleidung ~**: take off one's/sb.'s clothes; **die Asche [von der Zigarette/Zigarre] ~**: remove the ash [from one's cigarette/cigar] **2** (abwischen) wipe; (durch Streifen entfernen) wipe off; **seine** *od.* **sich** (*Dat.*) **die Schuhe/Sohlen ~**: wipe one's feet **3** (absuchen) comb (**nach** for)

Abstreifer *der;* **~s, ~** ▸**Abtreter**

Abstreif·gitter *das* grille (*for removing excess paint from paint roller*)

ab|streiten *unr. tr. V.* deny; **~, etw. getan zu haben** deny that one has done sth.; **das lässt sich nicht ~**: there's no denying that; that cannot be denied; **das kann ihm keiner ~**: you cannot deny him that

Ab·strich *der* **1** (Med.) taking of a swab; **einen ~ machen** take a swab **2** (Streichung, Kürzung) cut; **~e [an etw.** (*Dat.*)**] machen** make cuts [in sth.]; (Einschränkungen machen) make concessions [as regards sth.] **3** (Musik) downstroke

ab|strömen *itr. V.; mit sein* ‹*water*› flow away; ‹*air mass*› move away

abstrus /ap'stru:s/ *Adj.* (geh.) abstruse; (absurd) absurd

ab|stufen *tr. V.* **1** (in Stufen anlegen) terrace ‹*slope, hill*›; layer ‹*hair*› **2** (staffeln) grade; **abgestufte Abschreckung** (Milit.) graduated deterrence **3** (nuancieren) differentiate; (Kunstwiss.) nuance

Ab·stufung *die;* **~, ~en** **1** (im Gelände) terrace **2** (Staffelung) gradation; **die soziale ~**: the social hierarchy **3** (Nuance) shade; (Nuancierung) variety

ab|stumpfen

A *tr. V.* (gefühllos machen) deaden; *s. auch* **abgestumpft B**

B *itr. V.; mit sein* (gefühllos werden) **man stumpft ab** one's mind becomes deadened; **gegen etw. ~**: become dead to sth.; **der Gerechtigkeitssinn stumpft ab** one's sense of justice becomes blunted

Ab·sturz *der* **1** fall **2** (eines Flugzeugs) crash; **ein Flugzeug zum ~ bringen** cause a plane to crash **3** (Steilhang) precipice

ab|stürzen *itr. V.; mit sein* **1** fall; ‹*aircraft, pilot, passenger*› crash; **tödlich ~**: fall/crash to one's death **2** (geh.: abfallen) ‹*cliff*› plunge

Absturz·stelle *die* site of the [aircraft] crash

Absturz·ursache *die* cause of the crash

ab|stützen

A *refl. V.* support oneself (**mit** on, **an** + *Dat.* against); **sich von etw. ~**: push oneself away from sth.

B *tr. V.* support; (Bauw.: gegen Einsturz) shore up; (fig.: untermauern) support; back up

Ab·stützung *die* (Bauw.) shores *pl.*

ab|suchen *tr. V.* **1** search (**nach** for); (durchkämmen) comb (**nach** for); drag ‹*pond, river, etc.*› (**nach** for); **den Himmel/Horizont ~**: scan the sky/horizon (**nach** for) **2** (absammeln) **etw. von etw. ~**: pick sth. off sth.; **jmdm. die Läuse ~**: look for lice on sb.

Ab·sud /'apzu:t/ *der;* **~[e]s, ~e** (veralt.) decoction

absurd /ap'zʊrt/ *Adj.* absurd; **~es Theater** Theatre of the Absurd

absurderweise *Adv.* absurdly enough

Absurdität /apzʊrdi'tɛ:t/ *die;* **~, ~en** absurdity; (Ungereimtheit) inconsistency

Abszess, *Abszeß /aps'tsɛs/ *der* (*österr. auch: das*); **Abszesses, Abszesse** ▸❶ **S. 439** **1** (Med.) abscess **2** (Geschwür) ulcer

Abszisse /aps'tsɪsə/ *die;* **~, ~en** (Math.) abscissa

Abszissen·achse *die* (Math.) axis of abscissae

Abt /apt/ *der;* **~[e]s, Äbte** /'ɛptə/ abbot

Abt. *Abk.* **= Abteilung**

ab|takeln /'apta:kl̩n/ *tr. V.* (Seemannsspr.) unrig ‹*ship*›; *s. auch* **abgetakelt B**

ab|tanzen *itr. V.* (salopp) dance

ab|tasten *tr. V.* **etw. ~**: feel sth. all over; **jmdn. auf Waffen** (*Akk.*) **~**: frisk sb. for weapons

Abtast·nadel *die*, **Abtast·stift** *der* stylus

Abtau·automatik *die* (Elektrot.) automatic defrost

ab|tauchen *itr. V.* **1** (Seemannsspr.) submerge **2** (ugs.) **[in die Illegalität** *od.* **in den Untergrund] ~**: go underground

ab|tauen

A *itr. V.; mit sein* (wegschmelzen) melt away; (eis-/schneefrei werden) become clear of ice/snow; ‹*refrigerator*› defrost

B *tr. V.* (schnee-/eisfrei machen) melt; thaw; de-ice ‹*vehicle windows*›; **den Schnee/das Eis von etw. ~**: melt the snow/ice off sth.; **einen Kühlschrank ~**: defrost a refrigerator

Ab·tausch *der* **1** (Schach) exchange **2** ▸**Schlagabtausch** **3** (schweiz.) ▸**Tausch**

ab|tauschen *tr. V.* **1** (Schach) exchange **2** **jmdm. etw. ~**: get sth. from sb. by swapping **3** (schweiz.) ▸**tauschen**

Abtei /ap'tai̯/ *die;* **~, ~en** abbey

Abtei·kirche *die* abbey [church]

Abteil *das;* **~[e]s, ~e** compartment; (eines Regals) shelf; **ein ~ erster/zweiter Klasse** a first/second-class compartment

ab|teilen *tr. V.* **1** (aufteilen) divide [up] **2** (abtrennen) divide off

Abteil-: ~fenster *das* compartment window; **~tür** *die* compartment door

-abteilung *die* … department

Ab·teilung¹ *die* dividing off

Ab·teilung² *die* **1** department; (einer Behörde) department; section; **die ~ für Vor- und Frühgeschichte** the department of prehistory and early history **2** (Zool.) phylum; (Bot.) division **3** (Milit.) unit **4** (veralt.: Teil) part

Abteilungs·leiter *der*, **Abteilungs·leiterin** *die* head of department/section; departmental manager

ab|telefonieren *itr. V.* **[jmdm.] ~**: phone [sb.] to say one cannot come

ab|telegrafieren *itr. V.* **[jmdm.] ~**: send [sb.] a telegram to say one cannot come

ab|teufen *tr. V.* (Bergbau) sink

ab|tippen *tr. V.* (ugs.) type out

Äbtissin /ɛp'tɪsɪn/ *die;* **~, ~nen** abbess

ab|tönen *tr. V.* tint; (Sprachw.) shift

Abtön·farbe *die* tinting colour

Ab·tönung *die* **1** (das Abtönen) tinting; (Sprachw.) vowel shift **2** (Farbton) tone; shade

Abtönungs·partikel *die* (Sprachw.) modal particle

ab|töten *tr. V.* destroy ‹*parasites, germs*›; deaden ‹*nerve, feeling*›; mortify ‹*desire*›

Ab·tötung *die;* **~** ▸**abtöten**: destruction; deadening; mortification

ab|traben *itr. V.; mit sein* trot off *or* away

Abtrag /'aptra:k/ *der;* **~[e]s** (geh., veralt.) **einer Sache** (*Dat.*) **~ tun** be detrimental to sth.

ab|tragen *unr. tr. V.* **1** (abnutzen) wear out; *s. auch* **abgetragen B** **2** (geh.: abräumen) clear away **3** (einebnen) level; (Geol.) erode **4** (abbauen) demolish; (zum Wiederaufbau) take down **5** (geh.: abbezahlen) discharge ‹*debt*›; pay off ‹*loan*› **6** (Med.) (entfernen) remove; (abbauen) disperse

abträgig /'aptrɛ:gɪç/ (schweiz.), **abträglich** /'aptrɛ:klɪç/ *Adj.* (geh.) detrimental; harmful; (nachteilig) unfavourable; **einer Sache** (*Dat.*) **~ sein** be detrimental *or* harmful to sth.; **~e Kritik** unfavourable criticism

Abtragung *die;* **~, ~en** **1** (das Einebnen) levelling; (Geol.) erosion **2** (das Abbauen) demolition **3** (zum Wiederaufbau) taking down **4** (geh.: das Abbezahlen) discharge **5** (Med.: Entfernung) removal; (Abbau) dispersal

ab|trainieren

A *itr. V.* gradually reduce one's training schedule

B *tr. V.* **Fett/Pfunde ~**: get rid of fat/pounds

Ab·transport *der* ▸**abtransportieren**: taking away; removal; dispatch

ab|transportieren *tr. V.* take away; remove ‹*dead, injured*›; (befördern) dispatch ‹*goods*›

a

ab|treiben
A *unr. tr. V.* **1** (wegtreiben) carry away; **jmdn./ein Schiff vom Kurs ~:** drive *or* carry sb./a ship off course; **der Wind hat den Ballon nach Westen abgetrieben** the wind carried the balloon westwards **2** abort ‹*fetus*›; **ein Kind ~ lassen** have an abortion **3** (zu Tal treiben) bring down **4** (Med.: abgehen lassen) expel **5** (österr. Kochk.: rühren) beat
B *unr. itr. V.* **1** *mit sein* (weggetrieben werden) be carried away; ‹*ship*› be carried off course **2** (einen Abort vornehmen lassen) have an abortion; (Aborte vornehmen) carry out *or* perform abortions

Abtreibung *die;* ~, ~**en** abortion

Abtreibungs-: ~**klinik** *die* (ugs.) abortion clinic; ~**paragraph** *der* abortion law *Section 218 of the German criminal code;* ≈ Abortion Act; ~**tourismus** *der* abortion tourism; *travelling to another country or state in order to obtain an abortion;* ~**verbot** *das* ban on abortion; ~**versuch** *der* attempted abortion

ab|trennen *tr. V.* **1** detach; sever ‹*arm, leg, etc.*›; cut off ‹*button, collar, etc.*›; detach, tear off ‹*paper, voucher*› **2** (abteilen, absondern) divide off **3** (Rechtsw.) **ein Verfahren ~:** decide to handle a prosecution separately

abtretbar *Adj.* (Rechtsw.) transferable; cedable ‹*territory*›

ab|treten
A *unr. tr. V.* **1** **sich** (*Dat.*) **die Füße/Schuhe ~:** wipe one's feet; **sich** (*Dat.*) **den Schnee/den Schmutz von den Schuhen ~:** wipe the snow/dirt off one's feet **2** (überlassen) **jmdm. etw. ~:** let sb. have sth. **3** (Rechtsw.) transfer; cede ‹*territory*› **4** (abnutzen) wear down
B *unr. itr. V.; mit sein* **1** (Milit.) dismiss **2** (Theater, auch fig.) exit; make one's exit; **XY tritt ab/die Arbeiter treten ab** exit XY/exeunt workers; **von der Bühne ~** (fig.) step down; leave the arena **3** (zurücktreten) step down; ‹*monarch*› abdicate **4** (verhüll.: sterben) make one's exit
C *unr. refl. V.* (sich abnutzen) become worn; **sich leicht/schnell ~:** wear [out] easily/quickly

Abtreter *der;* ~**s,** ~: doormat

Abtretung *die;* ~, ~**en** (Rechtsw.) transfer; (eines Staatsgebiets) cession; **Deutschland wurde zur ~ Westpreußens gezwungen** Germany was forced to cede West Prussia

Ab·trieb *der* **1** (Vieh~) bringing down of cattle; **beim ~:** when bringing the cattle down **2** (österr. Kochk.) mixture

Ab·trift *die;* ~, ~**en** ▸ **Abdrift**

ab|trinken
A *unr. tr. V.* drink off; **einen Schluck ~:** take a sip (*from a full glass*)
B *unr. itr. V.* take a sip (*from a full glass*)

Ab·tritt *der* **1** (Theater) exit **2** (Rücktritt) resignation **3** (veralt.: Toilette) privy (arch.)

Abtrocken·tuch *das; Pl.* **Abtrockentücher** tea towel

ab|trocknen
A *tr. V.* dry; **das Geschirr ~:** dry the dishes; **sich** (*Dat.*) **die Hände/das Gesicht/die Tränen ~:** dry one's hands/face/tears; **ich muss noch [das Geschirr] ~:** I still have to dry the dishes
B *itr. V.; mit sein* (trocken werden) dry off

Abtropf·brett *das* draining board (Brit.); drainboard (Amer.)

ab|tropfen *itr. V.; mit sein* drip off; ‹*lettuce, dishes*› drain; ‹*clothing*› drip-dry; **von etw. ~:** drip off sth.

ab|trotzen *tr. V.* **jmdm. etw. ~:** wrest sth. from sb.

ab|trudeln *itr. V.* **1** (Fliegerspr.) go down in a spin **2** (ugs.: weggehen) push off *or* along (coll.)

abtrünnig *Adj.* (einer Partei) renegade; (einer Religion, Sekte) apostate; **ein ~er Vasall** a disloyal vassal; **der Kirche/dem Glauben ~ werden** desert the Church/the faith

Abtrünnige *der/die; adj. Dekl.* (einer Partei) renegade; deserter; (einer Religion, Sekte) apostate; turncoat

Abtrünnigkeit *die;* ~: apostasy; (Treulosigkeit) disloyalty (**von** to)

ab|tun *unr. tr. V.* **1** (beiseite schieben) dismiss; **etw. mit einer Handbewegung ~:** wave sth. aside **2** (erledigen) **damit ist die Sache abgetan** that's the end of the matter

ab|tupfen *tr. V.* dab away; **sich/jmdm. die Tränen ~:** dab away one's/sb.'s tears; **sich** (*Dat.*) **die Stirn/Mundwinkel ~:** dab one's brow/the corners of one's mouth

ab|urteilen *tr. V.* pass judgement on; (fig.) condemn

Aburteilung *die;* ~, ~**en** passing of judgement (+ *Gen.* on); condemnation; (fig.) condemnation

ABV /a:be:ˈfau̯/ *der;* ~**[s],** ~**[s]** (DDR) ▸ **Abschnittsbevollmächtigte**

Ab·verkauf *der* (österr., südd.) sale

ab|verkaufen *tr. V.* (österr., südd.) sell off

ab|verlangen *tr. V.* **jmdm. etw. ~:** demand sth. of sb.; **jmdm. Geld ~:** demand money from sb.; **es wird Ihnen einige Mühe ~:** it will cost you some effort

ab|wägen *unr. od. regelm. tr., itr. V.* **1** weigh up; **zwei Dinge gegeneinander ~:** weigh two things against each other; **die Vor- und Nachteile gegeneinander ~:** weigh the advantages and disadvantages; **lange ~:** weigh things/the problem *etc.* up for a long time; *s. auch* **abgewogen B** **2** (veralt.) ▸ **abwiegen**

abwägend
A *Adj.* appraising
B *adv.* appraisingly; **er sah mich kritisch~ an** he looked at me, sizing me up critically

Ab·wahl *die* voting out; **seit seiner ~:** since he was voted out

abwählbar *Adj.* **er/dieses Fach ist [nicht] ~:** he can[not] be voted out/this subject can[not] be dropped

ab|wählen *tr. V.* vote out; drop ‹*school subject*›; **sechs Leute wurden aus dem Ausschuss abgewählt** six members of the committee were not re-elected

ab|wälzen *tr. V.* pass on (**auf** + *Akk.* to); shift ‹*blame, responsibility*› (**auf** + *Akk.* on to)

abwandelbar *Adj.* **1** (variierbar) modifiable; **ein unendlich ~es Motiv/Thema** a motif/theme capable of infinite variation **2** (Sprachw. veralt.) ▸ **flektierbar**

ab|wandeln *tr. V.* **1** (variieren) adapt; modify **2** (Sprachw. veralt.) ▸ **flektieren**

ab|wandern
A *itr. V.; mit sein* **1** migrate (**aus** from, **in** + *Akk.* to); (in ein anderes Land) emigrate (**aus** from, **in** + *Akk.* to) **2** (fig.) move over; ‹*capital*› be transferred; **in einen anderen Beruf ~:** move into a different job; **viele Spieler wandern aus der Liga ab** many players are leaving the league **3** (Met.) move away
B *tr. V.; mit sein od. haben* (wandernd zurücklegen) walk *or* hike over; walk ‹*route*›

Ab·wanderung *die* **1** migration (**aus** from, **in** + *Akk.* to); (in ein anderes Land) emigration (**aus** from, **in** + *Akk.* to) **2** (fig.) moving over; **~ in einen anderen Beruf** movement into a different job; **~ des Kapitals** transfer of capital; **die ~ der Spieler aus der Liga** the departure of players from the league

Abwanderungs·verlust *der* (Soziol.) population drain

Ab·wandlung *die* adaptation; modification; (Variante) variation; **in ~ eines Wortes von Goethe** adapting a saying of Goethe's

Ab·wärme *die* (Technik) waste heat

Ab·wart *der;* ~**s,** ~**e** (schweiz.) caretaker

ab|warten
A *itr. V.* wait; **sie warteten ab** they awaited events; **warte ab!** wait and see; (als Drohung) just you wait!; **warten wir [erst mal] ab** let's wait and see; **sich ~d verhalten** adopt an attitude of 'wait and see'; **eine ~de Haltung einnehmen** decide to await events; **~ und Tee trinken** (ugs. scherzh.) wait and see what happens
B *tr. V.* **1** (warten auf) wait for; **wir müssen die Entwicklung der Dinge ~:** we must wait and see how things develop; **das bleibt [noch] abzuwarten** only time will tell **2** (warten auf das Ende von) **etw. ~:** wait for sth. to end

Abwartin *die;* ~, ~**nen** ▸ **Abwart**

abwärts /ˈapvɛrts/ *Adv.* downwards; (den Berg hinunter) downhill; (den Fluss hinunter) downstream; **der Fahrstuhl fährt ~:** the lift is going down; **„~"** 'going down'; **vom Major [an] ~:** from the major down; **mit ihm/dem Land/ihrer Gesundheit geht es ~** (fig.) he/the country is going downhill/her health is deteriorating; **seit damals ging es eigentlich immer nur ~** (fig.) from that time on things really only got worse

-abwärts *Adv.* ▸ **ⓘ S. 267 [weiter] rhein~/mosel~:** further down the Rhine/Mosel; **rhein~/mosel~ segeln** sail down the Rhine/Mosel

abwärts-, Abwärts-: ~**entwicklung** *die* deterioration; **die anhaltende ~entwicklung** the downward slide; ***~|gehen** ▸ **abwärts;** ~**trend** *der* downward trend

Abwasch¹ /ˈapvaʃ/ *der;* ~**[e]s** **1** (das Geschirrspülen) washing-up (Brit.); washing dishes (Amer.); **den ~ machen** do the washing-up/wash the dishes; **wir erledigen das gleichzeitig, das ist dann ein ~** (ugs.) we'll deal with that at the same time, and so kill two birds with one stone **2** (schmutziges Geschirr) dirty dishes *pl.*

Abwasch² *die;* ~, ~**en** (österr.) sink

abwaschbar *Adj.* washable

Abwasch·becken *das* sink

ab|waschen
A *unr. tr. V.* wash off; wash [up] ‹*dishes*›; wash down ‹*surface*›; **etw. von etw. ~:** wash sth. off sth.; **sich** (*Dat.*) **den Schmutz/das Blut ~:** wash the dirt/blood off oneself; **sich** (*Dat.*) **die Hände/sein Gesicht ~:** wash one's hands/face; **eine Schmach ~** (fig.) wipe out a disgrace
B *unr. itr. V.* wash up, do the washing-up (Brit.); wash the dishes (Amer.)

Abwasch-: ~**lappen** *der* dishcloth; ~**mittel** *das* ▸ **Spülmittel;** ~**tuch** *das; Pl.* ~**tücher** ▸ ~**lappen;** ~**wasser** *das* ▸ **Spülwasser 2**

Ab·wasser *das; Pl.* **Abwässer** sewage; **industrielle Abwässer** industrial effluent *sing.*

Abwasser-: ~**auf·bereitung** *die* sewage treatment; ~**beseitigung** *die* disposal of sewage; ~**kanal** *der* sewer; ~**reinigung** *die* sewage purification

ab|watschen *tr. V.* (ugs.) lambaste (coll.)

ab|wechseln *refl., itr. V.* alternate; **die beiden wechselten sich ab** the two of them took turns; **ich wechsle mich mit ihr beim Geschirrspülen ab** she and I take it in turns to do the dishes; **Regen und Sonne wechselten miteinander ab** it rained and was sunny by turns

abwechselnd *Adv.* alternately

Abwechslung *die;* ~, ~**en** (Wechsel) change; (Zerstreuung) **etwas/wenig ~:** some/not much variety; **zur ~:** for a change; **die ~ lieben** (verhüll.) like a bit of variety

abwechslungs-: ~**arm** **A** *Adj.* monotonous; **B** *adv.* monotonously; ~**halber** *Adv.* for a change; ~**los** **A** *Adj.* unvaried; **~los sein** lack variety. **B** *adv.* monotonously; ~**reich** **A** *Adj.* varied; **B** *adv.* **der Urlaub verlief sehr ~reich** the holiday *or* (Amer.) vacation was full of variety; **sich ~reich ernähren** eat a varied diet; **nicht sonderlich ~reich** without much variety; ~**weise** *Adv.* ▸ **abwechselnd**

Ab·weg *der* error; **auf ~e kommen** *od.* **geraten** go astray; **jmdn. auf ~e führen** lead sb. astray

abwegig *Adj.* (irrig, unzutreffend) erroneous; false ‹*suspicion*›; (falsch, abzulehnen) mistaken; wrong; (ungewöhnlich) outlandish; exceptional ‹*case*›

Abwegigkeit *die;* ~, ~**en** ▸ **abwegig:** erroneousness; falseness; mistakenness; wrongness; outlandishness; exceptionalness

Ab·wehr *die;* ~ **1** (Ablehnung) hostility **2** (Zurückweisung) repulsion; (von Schlägen) fending off **3** (Widerstand) resistance **4** (Milit.: Geheimdienst) counter-intelligence; **er ist bei der ~:** he is in counter-intelligence **5** (Sport) (Hintermannschaft) defence; (~aktion) clearance; clearing (Amer.)

abwehr-, Abwehr-: ~bereit *Adj.* ready to take defensive action *postpos.*; **~bereitschaft** *die* readiness to take defensive action; **~dienst** *der* counter-intelligence service

ab|wehren
A *tr. V.* 1 (zurückschlagen) repulse; fend off, parry ‹*blow*›; (Sport) clear ‹*ball, shot*›; save ‹*match point*› 2 (abwenden) avert ‹*danger, consequences*› 3 (von sich weisen) avert ‹*suspicion*›; deny ‹*rumour*›; decline ‹*thanks*› 4 (fernhalten) deter; **um die Blicke Neugieriger abzuwehren** [in order] to give protection from the stares of inquisitive people
B *itr. V.* 1 (Sport) clear; **zur Ecke ~:** clear the ball and give away *or* concede a corner 2 (ablehnend reagieren) demur; **eine ~de Geste** *od.* **Handbewegung** a deprecatory gesture

Abwehr-: ~kampf *der* defensive action; (über längere Zeit) defence; **~kraft** *die* power of resistance; **~mechanismus** *der* (Psychoanalyse, Physiol.) defence mechanism; **~reaktion** *die* (Physiol., fig.) defensive reaction; **~spieler** *der*, **~spielerin** *die* (Sport) defender

ab|weichen[1] *unr. itr. V.*; *mit sein* 1 deviate 2 (sich unterscheiden) differ; **voneinander ~:** differ from each other; **~des Verhalten** (Soziol.) deviant behaviour

ab|weichen[2]
A *itr. V.*; *mit sein* soften and come off
B *tr. V.* soak off

Abweichler /ˈapvaiçlɐ/ *der;* **~s, ~, Abweichlerin** *die;* **~, ~nen** (Politik) deviationist

abweichlerisch *Adj.* (Politik) deviationist

Abweichlertum *das;* **~s** (Politik) deviationism *no art.*

Abweichung *die;* **~, ~en** 1 deviation; **~en von der Geschäftsordnung** departures from the standing orders; **in ~** (*Dat.*) **von** in contrast with; **die ~ der Magnetnadel** the variation of the compass needle 2 (Unterschied) difference

ab|weiden *tr. V.* crop; browse ‹*twigs, leaves*›; (abgrasen) graze

ab|weisen *unr. tr. V.* 1 turn away; turn down ‹*applicant, suitor*› 2 (ablehnen) reject; dismiss ‹*action, case, complaint*›; disallow ‹*claim*›

abweisend
A *Adj.* cold ‹*look, tone of voice*›; negative ‹*reply*›; **in ~em Ton** coldly
B *adv.* coldly

Ab·weisung *die;* **~, ~en** ▸**abweisen**: turning away; turning down; rejection; dismissal; disallowance

ab|wenden
A *unr. od. regelm. tr. V.* 1 (wegwenden) turn away; **den Blick ~:** look away; avert one's gaze; **die Augen von etw. nicht ~ können** not be able to take one's eyes off sth.; **mit abgewendetem Kopf** with his/her head turned away 2 *nur regelm.* (verhindern) avert; **etw. von jmdm. ~:** protect sb. from sth.
B *unr. od. regelm. refl. V.* 1 turn away 2 (fig.) **sich von jmdm. ~:** turn one's back on sb.; (sich jmdm. allmählich entfremden) become estranged from sb.

Ab·wendung *die* 1 (Abkehr) **seit seiner ~ vom Sozialismus** since he turned away from socialism; **die ~ von der bisherigen Politik** turning away from previous policy 2 (Verhinderung) **zur ~ einer Sache** (*Gen.*) in order to avert sth.

ab|werben *unr. tr. V.* lure away; entice away; **jmdn. jmdm. ~:** lure *or* entice sb. away from sb.

Abwerber *der;* **~s, ~, Abwerberin** *die;* **~, ~nen** recruiter (enticing people away from their existing employment)

Ab·werbung *die* enticement (**bei** from)

ab|werfen
A *unr. tr. V.* 1 (herunterwerfen) drop; ‹*tree*› shed ‹*leaves, needles*›; ‹*stag*› shed ‹*antlers*›; throw off ‹*clothing*›; jettison ‹*ballast*›; throw ‹*rider*›; (Kartenspiel) discard; **das Joch der Knechtschaft/Tyrannei** *usw.* **~** (fig. geh.) throw *or* cast off the yoke of bondage/tyranny *etc.*; *s. auch* **Maske 1** 2 (herunterstoßen) knock down 3 (ins Spielfeld werfen) throw out ‹*ball*› 4 (einbringen) bring in; **Profit ~:** make a profit; **viel/wenig ~:** show a big/only a small profit
B *unr. itr. V.* (Sport) throw the ball out

ab|werten
A *tr., itr. V.* devalue
B *tr. V.* (fig.: herabwürdigen) run down; belittle

abwertend
A *Adj.* derogatory
B *adv.* derogatorily; in a derogatory way

Ab·wertung *die* 1 devaluation 2 (fig.: Herabwürdigung) reduction in status; (eines Begriffs) debasement; **eine ~ erfahren** lose status; **das soll keine ~ sein** that wasn't meant in any derogatory sense

abwesend
A *Adj.* 1 (nicht zugegen) absent 2 (zerstreut) absent-minded
B *adv.* absent-mindedly

Abwesende *der/die; adj. Dekl.* absentee

Abwesenheit *die;* **~** 1 (Fehlen) absence; **in ~** (Rechtsw.) in his/her/their absence; **durch ~ glänzen** (iron.) be conspicuous by one's absence 2 (fig.: Zerstreutheit) absent-mindedness

Ab·wetter *Pl.* (Bergbau) foul air

ab|wettern *tr. V.* (Seemannsspr., auch fig.) weather

ab|wetzen
A *tr. V., refl. V.* wear away; *s. auch* **abgewetzt B**
B *itr. V.*; *mit sein* (ugs.: weglaufen) bolt; scarper (Brit. coll.)

ab|wichsen *tr. V.* (derb) **sich** (*Dat.*) **einen ~:** wank (Brit. coarse); jerk [oneself] off (coarse); **jmdm. einen ~:** jerk sb. off (coarse); wank sb. (Brit. coarse)

ab|wickeln
A *tr. V.* 1 (herunterwickeln) unwind 2 (erledigen) deal with ‹*case*›; do ‹*business*›; (im Auftrag) handle ‹*correspondence*›; conduct, handle ‹*transaction, negotiations*› 3 (organisieren) stage 4 (Wirtsch.) wind up
B *refl. V.* 1 (sich abspulen) unwind [itself] 2 (durchgeführt werden) take place; (mit Erfolg) go off

Abwicklung *die;* **~, ~en** 1 ▸**abwickeln A 2**: dealing (*Gen.* with); doing; handling; conducting 2 (Organisation) staging; **für eine reibungslose ~ der Veranstaltung sorgen** see to it that the function goes off smoothly 3 (Kaufmannsspr., Rechtsw.: Liquidation) liquidation

ab|wiegeln
A *tr. V.* 1 pacify; calm down ‹*crowd*› 2 (abwertend) appease
B *itr. V.* 1 calm things down 2 (etw. herunterspielen) play down the issue

ab|wiegen *unr. tr. V.* weigh out; weigh ‹*single item*›

Abwiegler *der;* **~s, ~, Abwieglerin** *die;* **~, ~nen** 1 peacemaker 2 (abwertend) appeaser

Abwieglung *die;* **~, ~en** 1 conciliation 2 (abwertend) appeasement

ab|wimmeln *tr. V.* (ugs.) get rid of ‹*person*›; get out of ‹*duty, responsibility, etc.*›

Ab·wind *der* 1 (Met.) katabatic wind 2 (Flugw.) downwash

ab|winkeln *unr. tr. V.* bend; **mit abgewinkelten** (in die Hüfte gestützten) **Armen** with arms akimbo

ab|winken
A *itr. V.* (2. Part. landsch. od. scherzh.: abgewunken) **apathisch/uninteressiert ~:** wave it/them aside apathetically/uninterestedly
B *tr. V.* (Motorsport) **ein Rennen ~:** wave the chequered flag; (bei einer Unterbrechung) stop a race; **einen Fahrer ~:** wave *or* flag down a driver

ab|wirtschaften *itr. V.* **endgültig abgewirtschaftet haben** have gone to the wall; be finished for good; *s. auch* **abgewirtschaftet B**

ab|wischen *tr. V.* 1 (wegwischen) wipe away; **sich/jmdm. etw. ~:** wipe sth. off oneself/sb.; **sich/jmdm. den Schweiß von der Stirn ~:** wipe off the sweat from one's/sb.'s forehead; **Staub von den Regalen ~:** wipe off dust from the shelves; **sich/jmdm. die Tränen ~:** dry one's/sb.'s tears 2 (säubern) wipe; **sich/jmdm. die Nase/die Hände** *usw.* **~:** wipe one's/sb.'s nose/hands *etc.* (**an** + *Dat.* on); **damit können Sie sich den Hintern** *od.* **den Arsch ~** (derb) you know where you can stick that (sl.); (es ist wertlos) you might as well wipe your arse (Brit.) *or* (Amer.) ass with it (coarse)

ab|wohnen *tr. V.* 1 wear out ‹*furniture*›; make ‹*flat, house, room*› shabby; **abgewohnt** shabby 2 use up ‹*rent*›

ab|wracken /ˈapvrakn̩/ *tr. V.* scrap; *s. auch* **abgewrackt B**

Ab·wurf *der* 1 dropping; (von Ballast) jettisoning; **nach zwei Abwürfen wollte er nicht mehr reiten** after being thrown twice he didn't want to do any more riding 2 (Fußball) **beim ~ stolperte der Torwart** the goalkeeper stumbled as he threw the ball out 3 (Handball, Wasserball) goal throw 4 (Speer-, Diskus-, Hammerwurf) delivery 5 (Hochsprung) failure 6 (Springreiten) fault

ab|würgen *tr. V.* (ugs.) stifle; choke off; squash ‹*proposal*›; stall ‹*car, engine*›

ab|zahlen *tr. V.* pay off ‹*debt, loan*›; pay for ‹*home, car, etc.*›

ab|zählen
A *tr. V.* count; **„bitte das Fahrgeld abgezählt bereithalten!"** 'please tender exact fare'
B *itr. V.* 1 (Sport, Milit.) number off; **zu zweien/vieren ~:** number off in twos/fours 2 (mit Abzählreim) count out

Abzähl·reim *der* counting-out rhyme

Ab·zahlung *die;* **~, ~en** paying off; repayment; **etw. auf ~ kaufen/verkaufen** buy/sell sth. on easy terms *or* (Brit.) on HP

Abzahlungs-: ~kauf *der* credit *or* hire purchase; **~rate** *die* repayment; instalment

Abzähl·vers *der* ▸**Abzählreim**

ab|zapfen *tr. V.* tap ‹*beer, wine*›; let, draw off ‹*blood*›; draw off ‹*petrol*›; **Strom ~:** tap the electricity supply; **jmdm. Geld ~** (ugs.) touch sb. for some money (coll.)

ab|zappeln *refl. V.* (fig. ugs.) flog oneself; slave away

ab|zäumen *tr. V.* unbridle

ab|zäunen *tr. V.* fence off

Abzäunung *die;* **~, ~en** 1 fencing off 2 (Zaun) fencing

Abzehrung *die;* **~, ~en** (veralt.) wasting away; cachexia (Med.); **er starb an ~:** he wasted away and died

Ab·zeichen *das* 1 (Kennzeichen) emblem; (fig.) badge; **militärische ~:** military insignia 2 (Anstecknadel, Plakette) badge

ab|zeichnen
A *tr. V.* 1 (nachzeichnen, kopieren) copy 2 (signieren) initial
B *refl. V.* stand out; (fig.) begin to emerge; (drohend) loom

Abzieh·bild *das* transfer

ab|ziehen
A *unr. tr. V.* 1 pull off; peel off ‹*skin*›; strip ‹*bed*›; **ein Laken/das Bettzeug ~:** pull off a sheet/the bedclothes 2 (Fot.) make a print/prints of; **zweimal ~:** make two prints of 3 (Druckw.) run off; **etw. 50-mal ~:** run off 50 copies of sth. 4 (Milit., auch fig.) withdraw 5 (subtrahieren) subtract; take away (abrechnen) deduct; (kassieren) charge for; **jmdm. zu viel ~:** overcharge sb.; **davon kannst du die Hälfte/das meiste ~** (ugs.) you have to take it with a pinch of salt 6 (ugs.: abnehmen, ausziehen) take off 7 (schälen) peel ‹*peach, almond, tomato*›; string ‹*runner bean*› 8 (häuten) skin 9 **eine Handgranate ~:** pull the pin of a hand grenade 10 (herausziehen) take out ‹*key*› 11 (abfüllen) **Wein auf Flaschen ~:** bottle wine 12 (glätten) **Parkett ~:** sand [down] parquet flooring; **ein Messer/Rasiermesser ~:** sharpen a knife/razor 13 (Kochk.) thicken 14 (salopp: veranstalten) throw ‹*party*›; crack ‹*joke*›; *s. auch* **Schau 2**
B *unr. itr. V.* 1 *mit sein* (sich verflüchtigen) escape; (Met.) move away 2 *mit sein* (Milit.) withdraw 3 *mit sein* (ugs.: weggehen) push off (coll.); go away 4 *mit sein* (ugs.: beschleunigen) **der Wagen**

zieht vielleicht ab! the car really takes off [5] (abdrücken) fire

Ạbzieher *der;* ~**s,** ~, **Ạbzieherin** *die;* ~, ~**nen** (Druckw.) proof-puller

Ạbzieh·presse *die* (Druckw.) proof[ing] press

ạb|zielen *itr. V.* **auf etw.** (*Akk.*) ~: be aimed at *or* directed towards sth.

ạb|zinsen *tr. V.* (Finanzw.) reduce to the original value (by discounting interest); discount ‹*sum*›; **auf die Gegenwart** ~: reduce to current value; **abgezinst 800 Mill. Euro** 800 million euros discounting interest

ạb|zirkeln *tr. V.* measure off ‹*area, section*›; (fig.) delineate; measure ‹*words*›; *s. auch* **abgezirkelt B, C**

ạb|zischen *itr. V.; mit sein* (salopp) shoot off; **zisch ab!** (verschwinde!) beat it! (coll.); push off! (coll.)

ạb|zittern *itr. V.; mit sein* (salopp) beat it (coll.); push off (coll.)

Ạbzocke *die;* ~, ~**n** (salopp) rip-off (coll.)

ạb|zocken (salopp abwertend)

[A] *itr. V.* rake it in (coll.)

[B] *tr. V.* fleece ‹*person*›; rake in (coll.) ‹*money*›; **jmdm. 20 000 Euro** ~: fleece sb. of 20,000 euros

Ạbzocker *der;* ~**s,** ~ (salopp) rip-off merchant (coll.)

Abzockerei *die;* ~, ~**en** (salopp) profiteering *no pl.*; **das ist reine** ~: that's a complete rip-off (coll.)

Ạbzockerin *die;* ~, ~**nen** ▸**Abzocker**

ạb|zotteln *itr. V.; mit sein* (ugs.) trot off *or* away

Ạb·zug *der* [1] (an einer Schusswaffe) trigger; **die Hand** *od.* **den Finger am** ~ **haben** (auch fig.) have one's finger on the trigger [2] (Fot.) print [3] (Druckw.) proof [4] (Verminderung, Abgabe) deduction; **etw. in** ~ **bringen** deduct sth. [5] (Abmarsch, auch fig.) withdrawal; **jmdm. freien** ~ **gewähren** give sb. free passage [6] (Öffnung für Rauch usw.) vent [7] (von Rauch usw.) escape

abzüglich /ˈaptsy:klɪç/ *Präp. mit Gen.* (Kaufmannsspr.) less; ~ **3% Rabatt** *od.* **Rabatt von 3%** less 3% discount

ạbzugs-, Ạbzugs-: ~**fähig** *Adj.* (Steuerw.) [tax-]deductible; ~**frei** *Adj.* (Steuerw.) tax-free; ~**graben** *der* drainage ditch; ~**rohr** *das* flue; ~**schach** *das* (Schach) discovered check

ạb|zupfen *tr. V.* pluck off

ạb|zwacken *tr. V.* (ugs.) [1] **[sich** (*Dat.*)**] das Geld/die Zeit** ~: scrape the money together/spare the time [2] ▸**abzwicken**

Ạb·zweig *der* (Verkehrsw.) turn-off

Ạbzweig·dose *die* (Elektrot.) junction box

ạb|zweigen

[A] *itr. V.; mit sein* branch off

[B] *tr. V.* [1] (bereitstellen) set *or* put aside; **Geld für einen Plattenspieler** ~: put aside *or* put by money to buy a record player [2] (verhüll.: sich heimlich aneignen) appropriate

Ạbzweigung *die;* ~, ~**en** [1] turn-off; (einer Pipeline) branch; (Gabelung) fork; **die rechte** ~ **fahren** take the right fork [2] (Nebenlinie) branch line

ạb|zwicken *tr. V.* pinch *or* nip off

ạb|zwingen *unr. tr. V.* **jmdm. ein Geständnis** ~: force a confession out of sb.; **sich** (*Dat.*) **ein Lächeln** ~: force oneself to smile

ạb|zwitschern *itr. V.; mit sein* (ugs.) clear off (coll.); push off (coll.)

a cappella /a kaˈpɛla/ *Adv.* a cappella

Accent aigu /aksãtɛˈgy/ *der;* ~ ~, ~**s** ~**s** /aksãzɛˈgy/ acute [accent]

Accent circonflexe /aksãsirkõˈflɛks/ *der;* ~ ~, ~**s** ~**s** circumflex [accent]

Accent grave /aksãˈgraːv/ *der;* ~ ~, ~**s** ~**s** /aksãˈgraːv/ grave [accent]

Accessoire /aksɛˈsoa:ɐ̯/ *das;* ~**s,** ~**s** (geh.) accessory

Account /əˈkaʊnt/ *der;* ~**s,** ~**s** (DV) account

Acetat /atseˈta:t/ *das;* ~**s,** ~**e** (Chemie) acetate

Aceton *das;* ~**s** (Chemie) acetone

Acetylen /atsetyˈle:n/ *das;* ~**s** (Chemie) acetylene

Acetylen-: ~**brenner** *der* oxyacetylene torch; ~**gas** *das* acetylene

Acetylsalicyl·säure /atsetylzaliˈtsy:l-/ *die;* ~ acetylsalicylic acid

ach /ax/

[A] *Interj.* [1] (betroffen, mitleidig) oh [dear]; ~ **Gott** o dear [2] (bedauernd, unwirsch) oh [3] (klagend) ah; alas (dated); **Ach und Weh schreien** scream blue *or* (Amer.) bloody murder [4] (erstaunt) oh; ~**, wirklich?** no, really?; ~**, der!** oh, him!; ~**, ist das schön!** oh, how lovely! [5] ~ **so!** oh, I see; ~ **nein** no, no; ~ **was** *od.* **wo!** of course not

[B] *Adv.* (meist iron.) **unser** ~ **so edler Held** our oh-so-noble hero

Ach *das;* ~**s** *in:* **mit** ~ **und Krach** (ugs.) by the skin of one's teeth; **mit** ~ **und Weh** with a lot of weeping and wailing

Achat /aˈxa:t/ *der;* ~**[e]s,** ~**e** (Min.) agate

achaten *Adj.* agate

Achill /aˈxɪl/, **Achilles** /aˈxɪlɛs/ *(der)* Achilles

Achilles-: ~**ferse** *die* Achilles' heel; ~**sehne** *die* ▸**❶ S. 435** (Anat.) Achilles tendon

Achilleus /aˈxɪlɔys/ *(der)* ▸**Achill**

Ạch·laut, Ạch-Laut *der* velar fricative; ach-laut

achromatisch *Adj.* (Optik) achromatic

Ạchs-: ~**abstand** *der* ▸**Radstand**; ~**bruch** *der* ▸**Achsenbruch**

Achse /ˈaksə/ *die;* ~, ~**n** [1] (Rad~) axle; **auf [der]** ~ **sein** (ugs.) be on the road *or* move [2] (Dreh~, Astron.) axis; **sich um die** *od.* **um seine eigene** ~ **drehen** turn on one's/its own axis [3] (Math.) axis [4] **die** ~ **Berlin-Rom** (hist.) the Berlin-Rome axis

Achsel /ˈaksl̩/ *die;* ~, ~**n** (Schulter) shoulder; (~höhle) armpit; **jmdn. über die** ~ **ansehen** look down on sb.; look down one's nose at sb.; **die** *od.* **mit den** ~**n zucken** shrug one's shoulders; **jmdn. unter den** ~ **packen** seize sb. under the arms; **etw. unter die** ~ **klemmen** tuck sth. under one's arm

ạchsel-, Ạchsel-: ~**griff** *der* [1] (Rettungsgriff) underarm grip; [2] (Ringen) nelson; ~**grube** *die* ▸~**höhle**; ~**haare** *Pl.* hair *sing.* under one's arms; armpit hair *sing.*; ~**höhle** *die* armpit; ~**klappe** *die* epaulette; ~**schnur** *die* (Milit.) aiguillette; ~**schweiß** *der* underarm perspiration; ~**stück** *das* (Milit.) ▸~**klappe**; ~**zucken** *das;* ~~**s** shrug [of the shoulders]; **sein dauerndes** ~**zucken** his continual shoulder-shrugging; ~**zuckend** *Adj.* shrugging; **er ging** ~**zuckend hinaus** he went out with a shrug [of the shoulders]

ạchsen-, Ạchsen-: ~**ab·stand** *der* ▸**Radstand**; ~**bruch** *der* broken axle; ~**kreuz** *das* (Math.) axes *pl.* of coordinates; ~**mächte** *Pl.* (hist.) Axis Powers; ~**symmetrisch** *Adj.* (Math.) ~**symmetrisch sein** have axial symmetry; **eine** ~**symmetrische Kurve** a curve with axial symmetry; an axially symmetric curve

-achser *der;* ~**s,** ~ **ein Drei-/Sechs~**: a three-/six-axle vehicle *etc.*

-achsig *Adj.* **drei-/sechs~**: three-/six-axle

Ạchs-: ~**lager** *das* axle bearing; ~**last** *die* (Technik) axle weight; ~**schenkel** *der* (Kfz-W.) stub axle; ~**stand** *der* ▸**Radstand**; ~**welle** *die* (Technik) axle shaft

acht[1] /axt/ *Kardinalz.* ▸**❶ S. 29,** ▸**❶ S. 729,** ▸**❶ S. 826** eight; ~ **mal** ~ **ist 64** eight eights are *or* eight times eight makes 64; **wir waren** ~ *od.* (geh.) **unser** ~: we were eight; **je** ~ **bildeten eine Gruppe** they formed into groups of eight; **die ersten/letzten** ~: the first/last eight; **er ist** ~ **[Jahre]** he is eight [years old]; **mit** ~ **[Jahren]** as an eight-year-old; at eight years of age; **es ist** ~ **Uhr** it is eight o'clock; **um** ~ **Uhr zehn** at ten past eight; **um** ~ **[Uhr]** at eight [o'clock]; **um** ~ **herum, gegen** ~: [at] around *or* about eight [o'clock]; **um halb** ~: at half past seven; ~ **Minuten vor/nach halb** ~: twenty-two minutes past seven/twenty-two minutes to eight; **drei viertel** ~**, Viertel vor** ~: [a] quarter to eight; **in** ~ **Tagen** in a week's time; a week from now; **Freitag/morgen in** ~ **Tagen** a week on Friday/a week tomorrow; **[heute] vor** ~ **Tagen** a week ago [today]; **gestern vor** ~ **Tagen** a week ago yesterday; **im Jahre** ~ **nach/vor Christi Geburt** in the year AD 8/8 BC; **die Linie** ~ **[des Busses/der Straßenbahn]** the number eight [bus/tram]; **es steht** ~ **zu** ~**/**~ **zu 2** (Sport) the score is eight all/eight to two; **ein Vater von** ~ **Kindern** a father of eight; *s. auch* **Acht**[1]

ạcht[2] *in* **wir waren zu** ~: there were eight of us; **wir rückten ihm zu** ~ **auf die Bude** (ugs.) eight of us dropped in on him; **wir haben zu** ~ **ein Haus gemietet** the eight of us rented a house; **sie kamen zu** ~: eight of them came; **stellt euch zu** ~ **auf** make lines of eight

-ạcht *die* (Kartenspiel) eight of ...

ạcht... *Ordinalz.* ▸**❶ S. 165,** ▸**❶ S. 826** eighth; **der** ~**e** *od.* **8. September** the eighth of September; (im Brief auch) 8 September; **am** ~**en** *od.* **8. September** on the eighth of September; (im Brief auch) 8 September; **München, [den] 8. Mai 1984** Munich, 8 May 1984; **das** ~**e Kapitel/der** ~**e Abschnitt** chapter/section eight; **sie ging als Achte durchs Ziel** she came [in] *or* finished eighth; **jede** ~**e [Person/Kiste** *usw.***]** one out of every eight [persons/crates *etc.*]; one [person/crate *etc.*] in eight; **jeder Achte** one out of every eight; one in eight

Ạcht[1] *die;* ~, ~**en** [1] (Zahl) eight; **eine arabische/römische** ~: an arabic/Roman eight; **die** ~ **ist seine Glückszahl** eight is his lucky number [2] (Figur) figure eight [3] (Verbiegung) buckle; **mein Rad hat eine** ~: my wheel is buckled [4] (Spielkarte) eight [5] (ugs.: Bus-, Bahnlinie) [number] eight [6] (ugs.: Handschellen) cuffs *pl.* (coll.) [7] (auf der Speise-, Weinkarte) **ich nehme die** ~: I'll have number eight

Ạcht[2] *die;* ~ (hist.) outlawry; **über jmdn. die** ~ **verhängen, jmdn. mit der** ~ **belegen** outlaw sb.; **jmdn. in** ~ **und Bann tun** (kirchlich) anathematize *or* put the ban on sb.; (fig.) ostracize sb.

Ạcht[3] *die;* ~ *in* **etw. außer [aller]** ~ **lassen** disregard *or* ignore sth.; **sich in** ~ **nehmen** take care; be careful; **sich vor jmdm./etw. in** ~ **nehmen** be wary of sb./sth.; ~ **geben** *od.* (veralt.) **haben** be careful; watch out; **gib** *od.* (veralt.) **hab** ~**!** look out!; watch out!; **auf jmdn./etw.** ~ **geben** *od.* (veralt.) **haben** mind *or* take care of sb./sth.; **[auf jmds. Worte]** ~ **geben** *od.* (veralt.) **haben** pay attention [to what sb. says]; ~ **geben** *od.* (veralt.) **haben müssen, dass ...** have to be careful that ...; **er gab** *od.* (veralt.) **hatte nicht sonderlich** ~ **darauf** he did not pay any particular attention to it; **in der Schule besser** ~ **geben** *od.* (veralt.) **haben** pay more attention at school; **auf sich** (*Akk.*) ~ **geben** *od.* (veralt.) **haben** be careful

ạcht-, Ạcht-: ~**ad[e]rig** *Adj.* (Elektrot.) eight-core; ~**armig** *Adj.* eight-armed; ~**armig sein** have eight arms; ~**bänder** /-bɛndɐ/ *der;* ~~**s,** ~~ (Verlagsw.) eight-volume set; ~**bändig** *Adj.* eight-volume; ~**bändig sein/**~**bändig herausgebracht werden** be in/be published in eight volumes

ạchtbar *Adj.* (geh.) respectable; upright ‹*principles*›; **eine** ~**e Leistung** a creditable performance

Ạchtbarkeit *die;* ~ (geh.) respectability; (einer Gesinnung) uprightness

ạcht·beinig *Adj.* eight-legged; ~ **sein** have eight legs

Ạchte *der/die; adj. Dekl.* eighth; **er war [in der Leistung] der** ~: he came eighth; **der** ~ **[des Monats]** the eighth [of the month]; **Heinrich der** ~: Henry the Eighth

ạcht-, Ạcht-: ~**eck** *das* octagon; ~**eckig** *Adj.* octagonal; **ein Würfel ist** ~**eckig** a cube has eight corners; **ein Gebäude** ~**eckig bauen** make a building octagonal; **ein** ~**eckiger Hut** an eight-sided hat; ~**einhalb** *Bruchz.* ▸**❶ S. 826** eight and a half

achtel /ˈaxtl̩/ *Bruchz.* ▸❶ **S. 826** eighth; **ein ~ Kilo** an eighth of a kilo; **drei ~ Liter** three eighths of a litre

Achtel¹ *das, schweiz. meist der;* **~s, ~** ▸❶ **S. 826** 1) eighth 2) (ugs.: ~pfund) eighth of a pound; ≈ two ounces 3) (ugs.: ~liter) eighth of a litre (*of wine*)

Achtel² *die;* **~, ~** (Musik) ▸**Achtelnote**

Achtel-: **~finale** *das* (Sport) last sixteen; **~final·spiel** *das* (Sport) *match in the round before the quarter-finals;* **~liter** *der* eighth of a litre; **~los** *das* lottery ticket which has one eighth of the value of a whole ticket

achteln *tr. V.* **etw. ~:** divide/cut sth. up into eight pieces

Achtel-: **~note** *die* (Musik) quaver; eighth note (Amer.); **~pause** *die* (Musik) quaver rest; eighth rest (Amer.); **~pfund** *das* eighth of a pound

***achte·mal** ▸**Mal¹**

achten

A *tr. V.* respect; observe, respect ‹*laws, commandments*›; **jmdn./etw. hoch ~:** respect sb./sth. greatly; have a high regard for sb./sth.

B *itr. V.* 1) **auf etw.** (*Akk.*) **[nicht] ~** ([nicht] auf etw. aufpassen) [not] mind *or* look after sth.; (von etw. [keine] Notiz nehmen) pay [no] attention *or* heed to sth.; **es ist [besonders] darauf zu ~, dass ...** your attention is [particularly] drawn to the fact that ...; **auf jmdn. ~:** look out for sb.; (aufpassen) look after *or* keep an eye on sb. 2) (geh., veralt.) ▸**erachten**

ächten /ˈɛxtn̩/ *tr. V.* 1) (hist.: die Acht verhängen über) outlaw; (kirchlich) anathematize 2) (gesellschaftlich) ostracize; **sich geächtet fühlen** feel like an outcast 3) (verdammen) ban ‹*war, torture*›

Acht·ender *der;* **~s, ~** (Jägerspr.) eight-pointer

***achten·mal** ▸**Mal¹**

achtens /ˈaxtn̩s/ *Adv.* eighthly

achtens·wert *Adj.* respectable ‹*person*›; worthy, commendable ‹*motive*›

Achter /ˈaxtɐ/ *der;* **~s, ~** 1) (Rudern) eight 2) ▸**Acht¹ 1, 2, 3** 3) (ugs.: Autobus) number eight 4) (ugs.: Schraube, Dübel usw.) [number] eight

achter-, Achter-: **~aus** *Adv.* (Seemannsspr.) astern; **~bahn** *die* roller coaster; **~bahn fahren** go *or* ride on the roller coaster; **~deck** *das* (Seemannsspr.) afterdeck; **~gruppe** *die* group of eight; **~lastig** /-lastɪç/ *Adj.* (Seemannsspr.) stern-heavy

achterlei *indekl. Gattungsz.* 1) *attr.* eight kinds *or* sorts of; eight different ‹*sorts, kinds, sizes, possibilities*› 2) *subst.* eight [different] things

achterlich *Adj.* (Seemannsspr.) stern *attrib.;* **~ sein** be astern

achtern *Adv.* (Seemannsspr.) astern; aft; **nach ~ gehen** go astern; **nach ~ drehen** ‹*wind*› move astern; **von ~:** from astern

Achter-: **~reihe** *die* row *or* line of eight; **~rennen** *das* (Rudern) eights race; **~schiff** *das* (Seemannsspr.) stern; **~steven** *der* (Seemannsspr.) sternpost

acht-, Acht-: **~fach** *Vervielfältigungsz.* eightfold; **die ~fache Menge** eight times the quantity; **die ~- bis zehnfache Dosis** eight to ten times the [correct] dose; **etw. in ~facher Ausfertigung schicken** send eight copies of sth.; **~fach vergrößert/verkleinert, in ~facher Vergrößerung/Verkleinerung** magnified *or* enlarged/reduced eight times; **das Produkt ist ~fach geprüft worden** the product went through eight tests; **~fache** *das; adj. Dekl.* **das ~fache von 4 ist 32** eight fours are *or* eight times four makes 32; **er verdient das ~fache von mir** he earns eight times as much as I do; **um das ~fache steigen/steigern** increase ninefold *or* nine times; **~fältig** (veralt.) ▸**~fach**; **~flach** *das;* **~~s, ~~e, ~flächner** /-flɛçnɐ/ *der;* **~~s, ~~:** octahedron; **~füßer** *der;* **~~s, ~~** (Biol.) octopod; **~füßig** *Adj.* eight-footed; (Verslehre) eight-foot ‹*line*›; **~füßig sein** have eight feet

***acht|geben** ▸**Acht³**

acht-, Acht-: **~geschossig** *Adj.* ▸**~stöckig**; **~gliedrig** *Adj.* eight-membered; **~groschen·junge** *der* (abwertend) 1) (Denunziant, Spitzel) informer; nark (Brit. sl.); 2) (käufliches Subjekt) hireling

***acht|haben** ▸**Acht³**

acht-, Acht-: **~hebig** *Adj.* (Verslehre) ▸**~füßig**; **~hundert** *Kardinalz.* ▸❶ **S. 826** eight hundred; **~hundertjahr·feier** *die* octocentenary [celebrations *pl.*]; **~hundertst...** *Ordinalz.* eight hundredth; **~hunderttausend** *Kardinalz.* eight hundred thousand; **~jährig** *Adj.* (8 Jahre alt) eight-year-old *attrib.*; eight years old *pred.*; (8 Jahre dauernd) eight-year *attrib.*; **nach ~jährigem Studium** after eight years of study; **~jährig sterben** die at [the age of] eight; **seine ~jährige Tätigkeit an dem Institut** his eight years at the institute; **mit ~jähriger Verspätung** with a delay of eight years; eight years late; **~jährige** *der/die; adj. Dekl.* eight-year-old; **als ~jähriger** when one *etc.* is/was *etc.* eight years old; **~jährlich** A *Adj.* eight-yearly; **in ~jährlichem Turnus** in an eight-year cycle; B *adv.* every eight years; **~kampf** *der* (Turnen) eight-exercise gymnastic competition; **~kantig** A *Adj.* (Technik) eight-sided; B *adv.* (salopp) **~kantig rausfliegen** get kicked *or* (sl.) booted out; **jmdn. ~kantig rausschmeißen** throw sb. out on his/her ear (coll.); **~klassig** *Adj.* with eight classes; **~köpfig** *Adj.* eight-headed ‹*monster*›; ‹*family, committee*› of eight

Achtling /ˈaxtlɪŋ/ *der;* **~s, ~e** octuplet

acht·los

A *Adj.* heedless

B *adv.* heedlessly

Achtlosigkeit *die;* **~:** heedlessness

acht-, Acht-: **~mal** *Adv.* eight times; **~mal so groß/so viel/so viele** eight times as big/as much/as many; **~malig** *Adj.* **nach ~maliger Wiederholung bestand er die Prüfung** he passed the test at the ninth attempt; **nach ~maliger Aufforderung** at the eighth request; after being asked eight times; **trotz ~maligen Klingelns** in spite of ringing eight times; ***~millionen·mal** ▸**Mal¹**; **~minuten·takt** /-ˈ---/ *der* (Fernspr.): *system whereby telephone calls are charged at so much per eight minutes or part thereof;* **~minütig** *Adj.* eight-minute *attrib.*; lasting eight minutes *pred.*; **mit ~minütiger Verspätung** eight minutes late; **nach ~minütiger Sonnenbestrahlung** after eight minutes' exposure to the sun; **~monatig** *Adj.* (8 Monate alt) eight-month-old *attrib.*; eight months old *pred.*; (8 Monate dauernd) eight-month *attrib.*; lasting eight months *postpos.*; *s. auch* **~jährig**; **~monatlich** A *Adj.* eight-monthly; **im ~monatlichen Turnus** rotating every eight months; B *adv.* every eight months; **~monats·kind** *das* child born a month prematurely; **~pfünder** /-pfʏndɐ/ *der;* **~~s, ~~:** eight-pounder; **~pfündig** *Adj.* eight-pound; **~polig** *Adj.* (Elektrot.) eight-pin; eight-core ‹*cable*›; **~punkt·schrift** *die* (Druckw.) eight-point type; **~prozentig** *Adj.* eight per cent; **~räd[e]rig** *Adj.* eight-wheeled; **~räd[e]rig sein** have eight wheels

achtsam

A *Adj.* (geh.) attentive

B *adv.* (sorgsam) carefully; with care; **mit etw. [äußerst] ~ umgehen** handle sth. with [extreme] care

Achtsamkeit *die;* **~:** attentiveness; (Sorgsamkeit) care

acht-, Acht-: **~seitig** *Adj.* eight-page *attrib.* ‹*letter, article*›; **ein ~seitiges Vieleck** an eight-sided polygon; **~silber** *der;* **~~s, ~~** ▸**~silbler**; **~silbig** *Adj.* eight-syllable *attrib.*; octosyllabic; **~silbler** *der;* **~~s, ~~** (Verslehre) octosyllabic verse *or* line; **~sitzer** *der;* **~~s, ~~:** eight-seater; **~sitzig** *Adj.* eight-seater *attrib.*; **~sitzig sein** have eight seats; **~spaltig** (Druckw.) A *Adj.* **~spaltiger Artikel** eight-column article; **~spaltig sein** have eight columns; B *adv.* **~spaltig setzen** print in eight columns; **~spänner** *der;* **~~s, ~~:** eight-in-hand; **~spännig** *Adj.* eight-horse; *s. auch* **vierspännig**; **~sprachig** *Adj.* in eight languages *postpos.*; *s. auch* **zweisprachig**; **~sprossig** *Adj.* ‹*ladder*› with eight rungs; **~sprossig sein** have eight rungs; **~spurig** *Adj.* eight-lane ‹*road, motorway*›; eight-track ‹*cassette*›; **~stellig** *Adj.* eight-figure *attrib.*; **~stellig sein** have eight figures *or* digits; **~stimmig** A *Adj.* for eight-part; B *adv.* in eight parts; **~stöckig** A *Adj.* eight-storey *attrib.*; **~stöckig sein** have eight storeys *or* floors; be eight storeys high; B *adv.* **~stöckig bauen** build to eight storeys; **~strophig** /-ʃtro:fɪç/ *Adj.* with eight verses *postpos., not pred.*; **~strophig sein** have eight verses; **~stufig** *Adj.* with eight steps *postpos., not pred.*; **~stufig sein** have eight steps; **~stunden·rhythmus** /-ˈ----/ *der* eight-hour rhythm; **~stunden·tag** /-ˈ---/ *der* eight-hour day; **~stündig** *Adj.* eight-hour *attrib.*; lasting eight hours *postpos., not pred.*; **mit ~stündiger Verspätung** eight hours late; **nach ~stündigem Warten** after waiting for eight hours; **~stündlich** A *Adj.* eight-hourly; B *adv.* every eight hours; **~tägig** *Adj.* (8 Tage alt) eight-day-old *attrib.*; (8 Tage dauernd) eight-day[-long] *attrib.*; **mit ~tägiger Verspätung** eight days late; **nach ~tägiger Dauer** after lasting for eight days; **sie sind meist ~tägig** they mostly last eight days; **~täglich** A *Adj.* **in ~täglichem Wechsel** on an eight-day rota; B *adv.* every eight days; **~tausend** *Kardinalz.* ▸❶ **S. 826** eight thousand; **~tausender** *der: mountain over eight thousand metres high;* **~teiler** *der* (Rundf., Ferns.) eight-part series/serial; **~teilig** *Adj.* eight-piece ‹*tea service, tool set, etc.*›; eight-part ‹*series, serial*›; **~teilig sein** have eight pieces; (Rundf., Ferns.) be in eight parts; **~tonner** *der;* **~~s, ~~:** eight-tonner

Acht·uhr-: eight o'clock ‹*news, train, performance, etc.*›

acht-, Acht-: **~und·ein·halb** *Bruchz.* eight and a half; **~und·sechziger** *der;* **~~s, ~~, ~und·sechzigerin** *die;* **~~, ~~nen** member of the 1968 generation; **~und·vierziger** /--ˈ---/ *der,* **~und·vierzigerin** /--ˈ----/ *die* (hist.) forty-eighter (*one who took part in or sympathized with the 1848 revolution*); **~und·vierzig·stunden·woche** *die* forty-eight-hour week; **~und·zwanzig** *Kardinalz.* twenty-eight

Achtung *die;* **~** 1) (Wertschätzung) respect (**vor** + *Dat.* for); **gegenseitige ~:** mutual respect; **~ vor sich** (*Dat.*) **selbst** self-respect; **alle ~!** well done! 2) (Respektierung) respect (*Gen.* for) 3) (Aufmerksamkeit) attention; **~!** watch out!; **~! Stillgestanden!** (Milit.) attention!; **~, ~!** your attention, please!; **„~, Stufe!"** 'mind the step'; **„~, Hochspannung"** 'danger high voltage'; **~, fertig, los!** on your marks, get set, go!

Ächtung *die;* **~, ~en** 1) (hist.) outlawing; (kirchlich) anathematization 2) (gesellschaftliche ~) ostracism 3) (Verdammung) banning

achtung·gebietend *Adj.* (geh.) awe-inspiring

achtungs-, Achtungs-: **~applaus** *der* polite applause; **~erfolg** *der* reasonable success; **~voll** A *Adj.* respectful; B *adv.* respectfully

acht-: **~wöchentlich** A *Adj.* eight-weekly; **im ~wöchentlichen Turnus/Wechsel** every eight weeks; B *adv.* every eight weeks; **~wöchig** *Adj.* (8 Wochen alt) eight-week-old *attrib.*; (8 Wochen dauernd) eight-week[-long] *attrib.*; *s. auch* **~jährig**; **~zackig** *Adj.* eight-pointed

acht·zehn *Kardinalz.* ▸❶ **S. 29**, ▸❶ **S. 729**, ▸❶ **S. 826** eighteen; **mit ~ [Jahren] wird man volljährig** one reaches the age of majority at eighteen; **18 Uhr** 6 p.m.; (auf der 24-Stunden-Uhr) eighteen hundred hours; 1800; **18 Uhr 33** 6.33 p.m.; (auf der 24-Stunden-Uhr) 1833

achtzehn-, Achtzehn-: **~ender** *der;* **~~s, ~~** (Jägerspr.) eighteen-pointer; **~hundert** *Kardinalz.* ▸❶ **S. 826** eighteen hundred; **das war [im Jahre] ~hundert** *od.* **1800** that was in [the year] eighteen hundred *or* 1800; **~hundert** *od.* **1800 Euro pro Hektoliter** eighteen hundred *or* 1,800 euros per hectolitre;

a

~jährig *Adj.* (18 Jahre alt) eighteen-year-old *attrib.*; eighteen years old *pred.*; (18 Jahre dauernd) eighteen-year *attrib.*; *s. auch* **achtjährig**; **~jährige** *der/die; adj. Dekl.* eighteen-year-old; **als ~jähriger** when one *etc.* is/was *etc.* eighteen years old

ạchtzehnt... *Ordinalz.* ▸❶ **S. 165**, ▸❶ **S. 826** eighteenth; *s. auch* **acht...**

Ạcht·zehntel *das* eighteenth

ạcht·zeilig *Adj.* eight-line *attrib.*; **~ sein** have eight lines

achtzig /ˈaxtsɪç/ *Kardinalz.* ▸❶ **S. 29**, ▸❶ **S. 826** eighty; **[mit] ~ [km/h] fahren** drive at *or* (coll.) do eighty [k.p.h.]; **über/etwa ~ [Jahre alt] sein** be over/about eighty [years old]; **Mitte [der] ~ sein** be in one's mid-eighties; **in die ~ kommen** reach one's eighties; **mit ~ [Jahren]** at eighty [years of age]; **im Jahre ~ vor/nach Christi Geburt** in the year 80 BC/AD 80; **auf ~ sein** (fig. ugs.) be hopping mad (coll.)

Ạchtzig *die*; ~, **~en** eighty; *s. auch* **Acht**[1] **5**

ạchtziger *indekl. Adj.* **ein ~ Jahrgang** an '80 vintage; **die ~ Jahre** the eighties

Ạchtziger[1] *der*; **~s**, **~** [1] (80-Jähriger) eighty-year-old [man]; octogenarian [2] (ugs.: Autobus) number eighty [3] (Wein) '80 vintage

Ạchtziger[2] *die*; ~, ~ (ugs.: Briefmarke): eighty-cent/centime *etc.* stamp

Ạchtziger[3] *Pl.* eighties; **in den ~n sein** be in one's eighties

Ạchtzigerin *die*; ~, **~nen** eighty-year-old [woman]; octogenarian

Ạchtziger·jahre *Pl.* ▸❶ **S. 29**, ▸❶ **S. 165** eighties *pl.*

ạchtzig-, Ạchtzig-: ~jährig *Adj.* (80 Jahre alt) eighty-year-old *attrib.*; eighty years old *pred.*; (80 Jahre dauernd) eighty-year *attrib.*; *s. auch* **achtjährig**; **~jährige** *der/die; adj. Dekl.* eighty-year-old

achtzigst... /ˈaxtsɪçst/ *Ordinalz.* ▸❶ **S. 826** eightieth; **zum Achtzigsten herzlichen Glückwunsch** best wishes on your eightieth birthday; *s. auch* **acht...**

Ạchtzigstel *das*; **~s**, ~ ▸❶ **S. 826** eightieth

ạcht-, Ạcht-: ~zimmer·wohnung *die* eight-roomed flat; **~zöllig** *Adj.* eight-inch[-long] *attrib.*; eight-inch *attrib.* ‹*pipe*›; **~zöllig sein** be eight inches long; ‹*pipe*› be eight inches in diameter; **~zylinder** *der* (ugs.) eight-cylinder [engine/car]; **~zylinder·motor** *der* eight-cylinder engine; **~zylindrig** *Adj.* eight-cylinder *attrib.*; **~zylindrig sein** have eight cylinders

ächzen /ˈɛçtsn̩/ *itr. V.* [1] (schwer stöhnen) groan; **~ und stöhnen** grunt and groan [2] (knarren) creak

Ạ̈chzer *der*; **~s**, ~ (ugs.) groan

Ạcker /ˈakɐ/ *der*; **~s**, **Äcker** /ˈɛkɐ/ [1] field; **auf dem ~**: in the field; (bei der Feldarbeit) in the fields; **den ~ bestellen** till the field [2] *Pl.* ~ (altes Feldmaß) ≈ half acre (*usually about 2,500 sq.m.*); **vier ~ Land/Wald** ≈ two acres of land/woodland

ạcker-, Ạcker-: ~bau *der* agriculture *no indef. art.*; farming *no indef. art.*; **~bau treiben** farm; **~bau treibend** farming; **~bau und Viehzucht** farming and stockbreeding; **~bauer** *der*; **~~n**, **~~n**, **~bäuerin** *die* farmer; **~bau·treibend** ▸**Ackerbau**; **~boden** *der* soil [for cultivation]; **~bürger** *der*, **~bürgerin** *die* (hist.) *citizen who farmed land within the city area*; **~furche** *die* furrow; **~gaul** *der* (ugs. abwertend) carthorse; old nag (derog.); **aus einem ~gaul kann man kein Rennpferd machen** (Spr.) you can't make a silk purse out of a sow's ear (prov.); **~gerät** *das* farm implement; **~krume** *die* topsoil; **~land** *das* farmland

ạckern *itr. V.* (salopp) [1] (schwer arbeiten) slog one's guts out (coll.) [2] (sich anstrengen) put one's back into it (coll.); work like hell (coll.) [3] (veralt.: pflügen) plough

Ạcker-: ~schädling *der* field pest; **~scholle** *die* clod [of earth]

Ạcker·winde *die* (Bot.) field bindweed

a conto /a ˈkɔnto/ (Bankw.) on account

Acquis /aˈkiː/*der*; ~ /aˈkiːs/, **Acquis communautaire** /aˈkiː kɔmynoˈtɛːr/ *der*; ~ ~ (EU) acquis [communautaire]

Acrylamid *das*; **~s** acrylamide

Acryl-: ~farbe *die* acrylic paint; acrylic; **~faser** *die* acrylic fibre; acrylic; **~harz** *das* acrylic resin

Act /ɛkt/ *der*; **~s**, **~s** (Jargon) act

Action /ˈɛkʃən/ *die*; **~**: action

a. D. /aːˈdeː/ *Abk.* = **außer Dienst** retd.

A. D. *Abk.* = **Anno Domini** AD

Adabei *der*; **~s**, **~s** (österr. ugs.) hanger-on

ad absurdum /at apˈzʊrdʊm/ *in* **etw. ~ ~ führen** demonstrate the absurdity of sth.

ADAC *Abk.* = **Allgemeiner Deutscher Automobil-Club** *German automobile association*

> **ADAC — Allgemeiner Deutscher Automobil-Club**
>
> Europe's largest motoring organization, based in Munich, the *ADAC* acts as a powerful lobby for the German motorist. The *ADAC-Straßenwacht* provides free breakdown assistance for *ADAC* members.

ad acta /at ˈakta/ *in* **etw. ~ ~ legen** shelve sth.

Adagio /aˈdaːdʒo/ *das*; **~s**, **~s** (Musik) adagio

Adam[1] /ˈaːdam/ (*der*) Adam; **seit ~s Zeiten** since the beginning of time; **bei ~ und Eva anfangen** (ugs.) begin from the beginning; **der alte ~**: the old Adam

Adam[2] *der*; **~s**, **~s** (ugs. scherzh.: Mann) the male of the species

Adam Riese *in* **das macht nach ~ ~ 4,50 Euro** (ugs. scherzh.) my arithmetic makes it 4.50 euros (coll.)

Adams-: ~apfel *der* (ugs. scherzh.) Adam's apple; **~kostüm** *das* (ugs. scherzh.) **im ~kostüm** in one's birthday suit

Adaptation /adaptaˈtsi̯oːn/ *die*; ~, **~en** adaptation

adaptieren /adapˈtiːrən/ *tr. V.* [1] adapt; **für den Bildschirm/Film ~**: adapt for television/the screen [2] (österr.: herrichten) fit out

Adaptierung *die*; ~, **~en** [1] ▸**Adaptation** [2] (österr.: Herrichtung) fitting-out

Adaption /adapˈtsi̯oːn/ *die*; ~, **~en** ▸**Adaptation**

adaptiv /adapˈtiːf/ *Adj.* adaptive

adäquat /atɛˈkvaːt/

A *Adj.* (passend) appropriate (*Dat.* to); suitable (*Dat.* for); (angemessen) adequate ‹*reward, payment*›; appropriate, suitable ‹*measures, means*›

B *adv.* (passend) suitably; appropriately; (angemessen) adequately

addieren /aˈdiːrən/

A *tr. V.* add [up]

B *itr. V.* add

C *refl. V.* add up

Addier·maschine *die* adding machine

Addition /adiˈtsi̯oːn/ *die*; ~, **~en** addition

Additionalität /aditsi̯onaliˈtɛːt/ *die*; ~ (EU) additionality

additiv /adiˈtiːf/ *Adj.* additive

Additiv *das*; **~s**, **~e** (Chemie) additive

ade /aˈdeː/ *Adv.* (veralt.) farewell; **jmdm. ~** *od.* **Ade sagen** bid farewell to sb.; take one's leave of sb.; **einer Sache** (*Dat.*) **~** *od.* **Ade sagen** (fig.) bid farewell to sth.

Adebar /ˈaːdəbar/ *der*; **~s**, **~e** (scherzh., bes. nordd.) stork

Adel /ˈaːdl̩/ *der*; **~s** [1] nobility; **der niedere ~**: the lesser nobility *or* nobles; **der hohe ~**: the higher nobility; the aristocracy; **von ~ sein** be of noble blood; **~ verpflichtet** noblesse oblige; **er stammt aus altem ~**: he belongs to an old noble family [2] (Titel) **der erbliche/persönliche ~**: a hereditary/non-hereditary title; (hoher ~) a hereditary/life peerage [3] (geh.: edle Gesinnung) nobility

adelig ▸**adlig**

Adelige ▸**Adlige**

adeln

A *tr. V.* **jmdn. ~**: give sb. a title; (in den hohen Adel erheben) raise sb. to the peerage; (fig.) ennoble sb.

B *itr. V.* (geh.) ennoble

Adels-: ~brief *der* patent of nobility; **~familie** *die*, **~geschlecht** *das* noble family; **~haus** *das* noble family; **~krone** *die*: *coronet of the untitled lowest rank of nobility*; **~prädikat** *das* title of nobility; **~stand** *der* nobility; (hoher Adel) nobility; peerage; **jmdn. in den ~stand erheben** give sb. a title/raise sb. to the peerage; **~titel** *der* title of nobility

Adelung *die*; ~, **~en** conferral of a title; (in den hohen Adel) ennoblement

Adept /aˈdɛpt/ *der*; **~en**, **~en**, **Adeptin** *die*; ~, **~nen** [1] (hist.) initiate [2] (scherzh.) adherent; disciple

Ader /ˈaːdɐ/ *die*; ~, **~n** [1] ▸❶ **S. 435** (Anat., Zool.) blood vessel; vein; (Schlagader) artery; **in seinen ~n fließt Bauernblut** there is peasant blood in his veins; **sich** (*Dat.*) **die ~n öffnen** (geh.) slash one's wrists; **jmdn. zur ~ lassen** (veralt.) bleed sb.; (fig.) milk sb.; *s. auch* **Blut** [2] (Anlage, Begabung) streak [3] (Bot., Geol.) vein [4] (Elektrot.) core

Äderchen /ˈɛːdɐçən/ *das*; **~s**, **~**: small blood vessel *or* vein; (Bot.) small vein

Aderlass, ***Aderlaß** /ˈaːdɐlas/ *der*; **Aderlasses**, **Aderlässe** /-lɛsə/ [1] (Med.: Blutentnahme) bleeding [2] (fig.) drain; (finanziell) squeeze

Aderung /ˈaːdərʊŋ/ *die*; ~, **~en**, **Äderung** /ˈɛːdərʊŋ/ *die*; ~, **~en** veining

Adhäsion /athɛˈzi̯oːn/ *die*; ~, **~en** (Phys., Med., Bot.) adhesion

Adhäsions-: ~kraft *die* (Physik) power of adhesion; **~verschluss**, ***~verschluß** *der* resealable closure

ad hoc /at ˈhɔk/ *Adv.* [1] (zu diesem Zweck) ad hoc [2] (spontan) on the spur of the moment

Ad-hoc-: ~-Bildung *die* ▸**~-Prägung**; **~-Maßnahme** *die* ad hoc measure; **~-Prägung** *die* ad hoc coinage *or* formulation

adieu /aˈdi̯øː/ *Adv.* (veralt.) adieu; farewell; **jmdm. ~** *od.* **Adieu sagen** bid sb. adieu *or* farewell

Adieu *das*; **~s**, **~s** (veralt.) adieu

adipös /adiˈpøːs/ *Adj.* (Med.) [1] (fetthaltig) adipose ‹*tissue, abdomen*› [2] (fettleibig) obese ‹*child, adult*›

Adjektiv /ˈatjɛktiːf/ *das*; **~s**, **~e** (Sprachw.) adjective

adjektivisch /ˈatjɛktiːvɪʃ/ (Sprachw.)

A *Adj.* adjectival

B *Adv.* adjectivally

Adjunkt /atˈjʊnkt/ *der*; **~en**, **~en**, **Adjunktin** *die*; ~, **~nen** (veralt.) low-grade civil servant

adjustieren /atjʊsˈtiːrən/ *tr. V.* [1] (Technik) ▸**justieren 1** [2] (österr. Amtsspr.) provide with a uniform; kit out (Brit.)

Adjustierung *die*; ~, **~en** [1] ▸**Justierung 1** [2] (österr. Amtsspr.) uniform

Adjutant /atjuˈtant/ *der*; **~en**, **~en**, **Adjutantin** *die*; ~, **~nen** adjutant; aide-de-camp

Adjutum /atˈjuːtʊm/ *das*; **~s**, **Adjuten** (österr. Amtsspr.) grant

Adlatus /atˈlaːtʊs/ *der*; ~, **Adlaten** *od.* **Adlati** (scherzh.) loyal assistant

Adler /ˈaːdlɐ/ *der*; **~s**, **~**: eagle; **der ~** (Astron.) Aquila; the Eagle

adler-, Adler-: ~auge *das* (fig.) eagle eye; **~äugig** *Adj.* (fig.) eagle-eyed; **~blick** *der* eagle eye; **~farn** *der* (Bot.) eagle fern; bracken; **~horst** *der* eyrie; **~nase** *die* aquiline nose

adlig /ˈaːdlɪç/ *Adj.* noble; **~ sein** be a noble [man/woman]

Adlige *der/die; adj. Dekl.* noble [man/woman]

Administration /atmɪnɪstraˈtsi̯oːn/ *die*; ~, **~en** administration

administrativ /atmɪnɪstraˈtiːf/

A *Adj.* administrative

B *adv.* administratively

Administrator /atminɪsˈtraːtɔr/ *der;* ~**s**, ~**en** /-traˈtoːrən/, **Administratorin** *die;* ~, ~**nen** ▸❶ **S. 113** administrator

administrieren *itr. V.* administer

Admiral /atmiˈraːl/ *der;* ~**s**, ~**e** *od.* **Admiräle** /atmiˈrɛːlə/ 1) ▸❶ **S. 44** admiral 2) (Schmetterling) red admiral

Admiralität /atmiraliˈtɛːt/ *die;* ~, ~**en** admirals *pl.;* (Marineführung) admiralty

Admirals·rang *der* rank of admiral; **im ~ stehen** hold the rank of admiral

ADN *Abk.* (DDR) = **Allgemeiner Deutscher Nachrichtendienst** *GDR press agency*

Adoleszenz /adolesˈtsɛnts/ *die;* ~ (bes. Med., Psych.) adolescence

Adonis /aˈdoːnɪs/ *der;* ~, ~**se** Adonis

Adonis·röschen *das* (Bot.) adonis; (Adonis annua) pheasant's eye

adoptieren /adɔpˈtiːrən/ *tr. V.* adopt

Adoption /adɔpˈtsi̯oːn/ *die;* ~, ~**en** adoption

Adoptiv- /adɔpˈtiːf-/ **:** ~**bruder** *der* adoptive brother; brother by adoption; ~**eltern** *Pl.* adoptive parents; ~**kind** *das* adoptive *or* adopted child; ~**mutter** *die; Pl.* ~**mütter** adoptive mother; ~**schwester** *die* adoptive sister; sister by adoption; ~**sohn** *der* adoptive *or* adopted son; ~**tochter** *die* adoptive *or* adopted daughter; ~**vater** *der* adoptive father

Adrenalin /adrenaˈliːn/ *das;* ~**s** (Physiol., Med.) adrenalin

Adrenalin·stoß *der* (Med.) adrenalin shot; shot of adrenalin; (fig.: kräftige Hilfeleistung) shot in the arm

Adress·änderung, ***Adreß·änderung** *die* (schweiz.) change of address

Adressat /adrɛˈsaːt/ *der;* ~**en**, ~**en**, **Adressatin** *die;* ~, ~**nen** addressee; (einer Rede) hearer; (eines Buches) reader; (einer Sendung) listener/viewer; (nicht direkt angesprochen) implied target

Adress·buch, ***Adreß·buch** *das:* ~ **[der Stadt]** [town/city] directory

Adresse /aˈdrɛsə/ *die;* ~, ~**n** 1) ▸❶ **S. 143** (auch DV) address; (fig.: Unternehmen) establishment; **unter folgender ~:** at the following address; **eine Warnung an jmds. ~** *(Akk.)* **richten** (fig.) address a warning to sb.; **sich an die richtige ~ wenden** go to the right quarters (fig.); **bei jmdm. an die falsche ~ kommen** *od.* **geraten** (ugs.) come to the wrong address (fig.); **bei jmdm. an der falschen ~ sein** (ugs.) have come to the wrong place (fig.) 2) (geh.: Botschaft) message; (Meinungsäußerung) address

Adressen-: ~**änderung** *die* change of address; ~**büro** *das* mailing list broker; ~**handel** *der* mailing list business; ~**händler** *der,* ~**händlerin** *die* person running a mailing list business; ~**liste** *die* address list; ~**verzeichnis** *das* directory of addresses

adressieren *tr. V.* address

Adressier·maschine *die* addressing machine; Addressograph ®

adrett /aˈdrɛt/
A *Adj.* smart
B *adv.* smartly

Adria /ˈaːdri̯a/ *die;* ~**:** Adriatic

adriatisch /adriˈaːtɪʃ/ *Adj.* **das Adriatische Meer** the Adriatic [Sea]

adrig, ädrig *Adj.* ▸**aderig**, **äderig**

ADS *Abk.* = **Aufmerksamkeitsdefizit-Syndrom** ADD

Adsorbens /atˈzɔrbɛns/ *das;* ~, **Adsorbenzien** *od.* **Adsorbentia** (Chemie, Physik) adsorbent

adsorbieren *tr. V.* (Chemie, Physik) adsorb

Adsorption /atzɔrpˈtsi̯oːn/ *die;* ~, ~**en** (Chemie, Physik) adsorption

adult /aˈdʊlt/ *Adj.* (Biol., Genetik) adult

A-Dur *das* (Musik) A major; **Sonate/Etüde in ~:** sonata/study in A major; **die ~-Etüde** the A major study

Advent /atˈvɛnt/ *der;* ~**s** 1) Advent 2) (Adventssonntag) Sunday in Advent

Adventist *der;* ~**en**, ~**en** (Rel.) Adventist

adventlich
A *Adj.* Advent ‹*customs, music*›; pre-Christmas ‹*atmosphere*›
B *adv.* ~ **geschmückt** decorated for Advent; with Advent decorations; ~ **gestimmt** in a pre-Christmas mood; **etw. ~ verzaubern** cast an Advent spell on sth.

Advents-: ~**kalender** *der* Advent calendar; ~**kranz** *der: garland of fir sprigs with four candles for the Sundays in Advent;* ~**sonntag** *der* Sunday in Advent

Adventskranz

A garland made of fir sprigs, decorated with ribbons and four candles for the Sundays in Advent. Traditionally red ribbons and candles are used, and the wreath is either suspended from the ceiling or put on a table. On the first Sunday in Advent one candle is lit, two are lit on the next Sunday, three on the third, and all four are lit on the fourth Sunday in Advent.

Adverb /atˈvɛrp/ *das;* ~**s**, ~**ien** (Sprachw.) adverb

adverbial /atvɛrˈbi̯aːl/ (Sprachw.)
A *Adj.* adverbial; ~**e Bestimmung** adverbial qualification
B *adv.* adverbially; as an adverb

Adverbial·satz *der* adverbial clause

adversativ /atvɛrzaˈtiːf/ (Sprachw.)
A *Adj.* adversative
B *adv.* adversatively

Advocatus Diaboli /atvoˈkaːtʊs diˈaːboli/ *der;* ~ ~, **Advocati** ~ (kath. Kirche, fig.) devil's advocate

Advokat /atvoˈkaːt/ *der;* ~**en**, ~**en**, **Advokatin** *die;* ~, ~**nen** ▸❶ **S. 113** (österr., schweiz., sonst veralt.) lawyer; advocate (arch.); (fig.: Fürsprecher) advocate

Advokatur /atvokaˈtuːɐ̯/ *die;* ~, ~**en** legal profession; (Anwaltsbüro) legal practice

Advokatur·büro *das* (schweiz.), **Advokaturs·kanzlei** *die* (österr.) legal practice

aerob /aeˈroːp/ *Adj.* (Biol.) aerobic

Aerobic /ɛˈroːbɪk/ *das;* ~**s** aerobics *sing.*

aero-, Aero- /aero- *od.* ɛːro-/ **:** ~**dynamik** *die* aerodynamics *sing.;* ~**dynamisch** *Adj.* aerodynamic; ~**gramm** *das* air[mail] letter; ~**sol** /-ˈzoːl/ *das;* ~**s**, ~**e** aerosol

Affaire (veralt., österr.), **Affäre** /aˈfɛːrə/ *die;* ~, ~**n** affair; (Angelegenheit) affair; business; **die ~ Dreyfus** the Dreyfus affair; **sich aus der ~ ziehen** (ugs.) get out of it; **eine ~ von ein paar Stunden/Euro** (ugs.) a matter of a few hours/euros

Äffchen /ˈɛfçən/ *das;* ~**s**, ~**:** little ape/monkey

Affe /ˈafə/ *der;* ~**n**, ~**n** 1) monkey; (Menschen~) ape; (fig.) **du bist wohl vom wilden ~n gebissen!** (salopp) you're off your head (coll.) *or* (coll.) rocker!; **seinem ~n Zucker geben** (ugs.) really let oneself go; **jmdn. zum ~n machen** (ugs.) make a monkey out of sb. (coll.); *s. auch* **lausen**; **Schleifstein** 2) (derb: dummer Kerl) oaf; clot (Brit. coll.) 3) (derb: Geck) dandy; **ein eingebildeter ~:** a conceited so-and-so (coll.) 4) (Milit. ugs.) knapsack 5) (salopp: Rausch) **einen ~n [sitzen] haben** be plastered (sl.)

Affekt /aˈfɛkt/ *der;* ~**[e]s**, ~**e** 1) (Gemütsbewegung) feeling; emotion; affect (Psych.); **im ~:** in the heat of the moment 2) *Pl.* (Leidenschaften) passions

affekt·geladen *Adj.* emotive

Affekt·handlung *die* emotive act

affektiert /afɛkˈtiːɐ̯t/ (abwertend)
A *Adj.* affected
B *adv.* affectedly

Affektiertheit *die;* ~, ~**en** affectedness; affectation

affektiv /afɛkˈtiːf/ (Psych.)
A *Adj.* affective
B *adv.* affectively

Affekt·stauung *die* (Psych.) emotional block

affen-, Affen-: ~**arsch** *der* (derb) stupid bugger (coarse); **das sind doch alles ~ärsche** they are a stupid lot of buggers (coarse); ~**artig** *Adj.* (wie Menschenaffen) apelike; **mit ~artiger Geschwindigkeit** (ugs.) like a bat out of hell (coll.); ~**brot·baum** *der* (Bot.) baobab *or* monkey-bread tree; ~**haus** *das* monkey house; ~**hitze** *die* (salopp) blazing heat; **es herrschte gestern eine ~hitze** yesterday was a real scorcher; ~**jacke** *die,* ~**jäckchen** *das* (Soldatenspr. scherzh.) monkey jacket; ~**käfig** *der* monkey cage; ~**liebe** *die* (ugs.) infatuation **(zu** with); ~**mensch** *der* apeman; ~**pinscher** *der* affenpinscher; ~**schande** *die* (salopp) **es ist eine ~schande** it's monstrous; ~**schaukel** *die* (ugs. scherzh.) 1) (Milit.) aiguillette; 2) (Zopf) looped plait; ~**stall** *der* (salopp) dump (coll.); hole (coll.); **hier stinkt es wie in einem ~stall** (derb) this place smells like a pigsty (sl.); ~**tanz** *der* (salopp) ▸~**theater**; ~**tempo** *das* (salopp) **mit einem ~tempo** like mad (coll.); like the clappers (Brit. coll.); **ein ~tempo anschlagen** move like hell (coll.); ~**theater** *das* (salopp) farce; ~**weibchen** *das* female ape; ~**zahn** *der* (salopp) ▸~**tempo**; ~**zirkus** *der* (salopp) ▸~**theater**

affig (ugs. abwertend)
A *Adj.* dandyish; (lächerlich) ludicrous; (affektiert) affected
B *adv.* ~ **gekleidet** dressed in a dandyish/ludicrous/affected way

Affigkeit *die;* ~ (ugs. abwertend) ▸**affig**: dandyishness; ludicrousness; affectation

Äffin /ˈɛfɪn/ *die;* ~, ~**nen** female ape

Affinität /afiniˈtɛːt/ *die;* ~, ~**en** affinity **(zu** for)

Affirmation /afɪrmaˈtsi̯oːn/ *die;* ~, ~**en** (geh.) affirmation

affirmativ /afɪrmaˈtiːf/ *Adj.* affirmative

affizieren /afiˈtsiːrən/ *tr. V.* (geh.) influence; affect

Affront /aˈfrõː/ *der;* ~**s**, ~**s** affront

Afghane /afˈgaːnə/ *der;* ~**n**, ~**n** ▸❶ **S. 520** 1) Afghan 2) (Hund) Afghan hound

Afghanin *die;* ~, ~**nen** ▸❶ **S. 520** Afghan; *s. auch* **-in**

afghanisch *Adj.* ▸❶ **S. 520**, ▸❶ **S. 670** Afghan

Afghanistan /afˈgaːnɪstaːn/ *(das);* ~**s** Afghanistan

Afrika /ˈaːfrika/ *(das);* ~**s** Africa

Afrikaans /afriˈkaːns/ *das;* ~ ▸❶ **S. 670** Afrikaans

Afrika·forscher *der,* **Afrika·forscherin** *die* African explorer

Afrikaner /afriˈkaːnɐ/ *der;* ~**s**, ~, **Afrikanerin** *die;* ~, ~**nen** African; *s. auch* **-in**

afrikanisch *Adj.* African

Afrikanistik *die;* ~**:** African studies *pl., no art.*

afro-, Afro-: ~**amerikaner** *der,* ~**amerikanerin** *die* Afro-American; ~**amerikanisch** *Adj.* Afro-American; ~**asiatisch** *Adj.* Afro-Asian; ~**kubanisch** *Adj.* Afro-Cuban; ~**look** *der* Afro look

After /ˈaftɐ/ *der;* ~**s**, ~ ▸❶ **S. 435** anus

After-: ~**furche** *die* (Anat.) ▸❶ **S. 435** anal cleft; ~**mieter** *der,* ~**mieterin** *die* (veralt.) subtenant; ~**wissenschaft** *die* (veralt. abwertend) pseudoscience

After-Work-Party /ɑːftəˈwəːk-/ *die* after-work party

AG *die;* ~, ~**s** *Abk.* 1) = **Aktiengesellschaft** PLC (Brit.); Ltd. (private company) (Brit.); Inc. (Amer.) 2) = **Arbeitsgemeinschaft**

Ägäis /ɛˈgɛːɪs/ *die;* ~**:** Aegean

ägäisch *Adj.* Aegean

Agave /aˈgaːvə/ *die;* ~, ~**n** (Bot.) agave

Agende /aˈgɛndə/ *die;* ~, ~**n** (ev. Kirche) liturgy

Agens /ˈaːgɛns/ *das;* ~, **Agenzien** /aˈgɛntsi̯ən/ driving force; (Philos., Sprachw.) agent

Agent /aˈgɛnt/ *der;* ~**en**, ~**en** agent

Agenten-: ~**aus·tausch** *der* exchange of [captured] agents; ~**netz** *das* network of agents; **~ring** *der* spy ring; **~tätigkeit** *die* activity as a spy

Agentin *die;* ~, ~**nen** [female] agent

Agent provocateur /aˈʒã: provokaˈtø:ɐ̯/ *der;* ~ ~, ~**s** ~**s** agent provocateur

Agentur /agɛnˈtu:ɐ̯/ *die;* ~, ~**en** agency

Agentur·bericht *der,* **Agentur·meldung** *die* agency report

Agglomerat /aglomeˈra:t/ *das;* ~**[e]s,** ~**e** 1▸ (geh.: Anhäufung) conglomeration 2▸ (Geol.) agglomerate

Agglomeration /aglomeraˈtsi̯o:n/ *die;* ~, ~**en** (Soziol.) agglomeration

Agglutination /aglutinaˈtsi̯o:n/ *die;* ~, ~**en** (Sprachw.) agglutination

agglutinierend /aglutiˈni:rənt/ *Adj.* (Sprachw.) agglutinative

Aggregat /agreˈga:t/ *das;* ~**[e]s,** ~**e** (Technik) unit; (Elektrot.) set

Aggregat·zustand *der* (Chemie) state

Aggression /agrɛˈsi̯o:n/ *die;* ~, ~**en** aggression; **starke** ~**en haben** have strong feelings of aggression

Aggressions-: ~**krieg** *der* war of aggression; ~**politik** *die* policy of aggression; ~**trieb** *der* aggressive drive

aggressiv /agrɛˈsi:f/

A *Adj.* aggressive

B *adv.* aggressively

Aggressivität *die;* ~: aggressiveness

Aggressor /aˈgrɛsɔr/ *der;* ~**s,** ~**en** /-ˈso:rən/, **Aggressorin** *die;* ~, ~**nen** aggressor

Ägide /ɛˈgi:də/ (geh.) *in* **unter jmds.** ~ (*Dat.*) under sb.'s aegis

agieren /aˈgi:rən/ *itr. V.* (auch Theater, fig.) act; **als jmd.** ~: play sb.

agil /aˈgi:l/ *Adj.* (beweglich) agile; (geistig rege) mentally alert

Agilität /agiliˈtɛ:t/ *die;* ~: agility; (geistige Regsamkeit) mental alertness

Agitation /agitaˈtsi̯o:n/ *die;* ~ (Politik) agitation; ~ **betreiben** agitate

Agitator /agiˈta:tɔr/ *der;* ~**s,** ~**en** /-taˈto:rən/, **Agitatorin** *die;* ~, ~**nen** agitator

agitatorisch

A *Adj.* agitative; inflammatory ‹*speech*›

B *adv.* for purposes of agitation

agitieren

A *itr. V.* agitate

B *tr. V.* stir up

Agitprop /agɪtˈprɔp/ *die;* ~ (Politik) agitprop

Agnostiker /aˈgnɔstikɐ/ *der;* ~**s,** ~, **Agnostikerin** *die;* ~, ~**nen** (Philos.) agnostic

Agnostizismus /agnɔstiˈtsɪsmʊs/ *der;* ~ (Philos.) agnosticism *no art.*

Agonie /agoˈni:/ *die;* ~, ~**n: [die]** ~: the throes *pl.* of death; **in** ~ **liegen** be in the throes of death

Agrar- /aˈgra:ɐ̯-/ **:** ~**erzeugnis** *das* agricultural *or* farm product; ~**erzeugnisse** agricultural *or* farm produce *or* products; ~**fabrik** *die* (abwertend) factory farm; ~**gesellschaft** *die* agrarian society

Agrarier /aˈgra:ri̯ɐ/ *der;* ~**s,** ~, **Agrarierin** *die;* ~, ~**nen** (veralt.) landowner

agrarisch *Adj.* agrarian; agricultural

Agrar-: ~**land** *das* agrarian country; ~**markt** *der* agrarian *or* agricultural products market; ~**politik** *die* agricultural policy; ~**produkt** *das* ▸ ~**erzeugnis**; ~**wissenschaft** *die* ▸ **Agronomie**; ~**zoll** *der* import tariff (*on agricultural produce*)

Agrément /agreˈmã:/ *das;* ~**s,** ~**s** (Diplomatie) **jmdm. das** ~ **erteilen/verweigern** accord/refuse an agrément to sb.

Agri·kultur /agri-/ *die* (geh.) agriculture *no art.*

Agrikultur·chemie *die,* **Agro·chemie** /ˈa:gro-/ *die* (DDR) agricultural chemistry *no art.*

Agronom /agroˈno:m/ *der;* ~**en,** ~**en** agronomist

Agronomie /agronoˈmi:/ *die;* ~: agronomy *no art.*

Agro·technik *die* (DDR) agricultural technology *no art.*

Ägypten /ɛˈgʏptn̩/ (*das*); ~**s** Egypt; **die Flucht nach** ~: the flight into Egypt

Ägypter *der;* ~**s,** ~, **Ägypterin** *die;* ~, ~**nen** ▸❶ **S. 520** Egyptian

ägyptisch *Adj.* ▸❶ **S. 520,** ▸❶ **S. 670** Egyptian; *s. auch* **Finsternis 1**

Ägyptologe /ɛgʏptoˈlo:gə/ *der;* ~**n,** ~**n** Egyptologist

Ägyptologie /ɛgʏptoloˈgi:/ *die;* ~: Egyptology *no art.*

Ägyptologin *die;* ~, ~**nen** Egyptologist

ah /a:/ *Interj.* (verwundert) oh; (freudig, genießerisch) ah; (verstehend) oh; ah

äh /ɛ(:)/ *Interj.* 1▸ (angeekelt) ugh 2▸ (stotternd) er; hum

aha /aˈha(:)/ *Interj.* (verstehend) oh[, I see]; (triumphierend) aha

Aha-Erlebnis *das* (Psych.) aha experience

ahd. *Abk.* = **althochdeutsch** OHG

ahistorisch

A *Adj.* ahistorical

B *adv.* ahistorically

Ahle /ˈa:lə/ *die;* ~, ~**n** awl; (des Schriftsetzers) bodkin

ähm /ɛ:m/ *Interj.* er; erm

Ahn /a:n/ *der;* ~**[e]s** *od.* ~**en,** ~**en** (geh.) forebear; ancestor; (fig.) father

ahnden /ˈa:ndn̩/ *tr. V.* (geh.) punish

Ahndung *die;* ~: punishment

Ahne[1] *der;* ~**n,** ~**n** ▸**Ahn**

Ahne[2] *die;* ~, ~**n** (geh.) ancestress; forebear; (fig.) spiritual forebear

ähneln /ˈɛ:nl̩n/ *itr. V.* **jmdm.** ~: resemble *or* be like sb.; bear a resemblance to sb.; **jmdm. sehr/wenig** ~: strongly resemble *or* be very like sb./bear little resemblance to sb.; **das Mädchen ähnelt seiner Mutter** the girl takes after her mother; **jmdm. frappierend** ~: bear a striking resemblance to sb.; **einer Sache** (*Dat.*) ~: be similar to sth.; be like sth.; **sich** *od.* (geh.) **einander** ~: resemble one another; be alike; **sich sehr/wenig** ~: resemble each other very strongly *or* be very much alike/bear little resemblance to each other

ahnen /ˈa:nən/

A *tr. V.* 1▸ (im Voraus fühlen) have a presentiment *or* premonition of; **etw. dumpf** *od.* **dunkel** ~: have a vague presentiment *or* premonition of sth.; sense sth. dimly 2▸ (vermuten) suspect; (erraten) guess; **wer soll denn** ~, **dass ...** who would know that ...; how are you supposed to know that ...; **das konnte ich doch nicht** ~: I had no way of knowing that; **du ahnst es nicht, wen/wo/wie ...** you'll never guess whom/where/how ...; **ach, du ahnst es nicht!** (salopp) oh heck (coll.); oh Lord (coll.); **davon haben wir überhaupt nichts geahnt** we didn't suspect it for one moment; **nichts Böses** ~: be unsuspecting; **ohne es zu** ~: without suspecting *or* realizing [it] 3▸ (vage erkennen) just make out; **die Wagen waren in der Dunkelheit mehr zu** ~ **als zu sehen** one could sense the cars in the darkness, rather than see them

B *itr. V.* (geh.) **mir ahnt nichts Gutes** I fear the worst; **es ahnte mir, dass ...** I suspected that ...; **ihm ahnte Schreckliches** he was filled with *or* had a dreadful [sense of] foreboding

Ahnen-: ~**bild** *das* 1▸ (~porträt) ancestral portrait; 2▸ (Völkerk.) ▸ ~**figur;** ~**figur** *die* (Völkerk.) figure *or* effigy of an ancestor; ~**forschung** *die* genealogy; ~**galerie** *die* gallery of ancestral portraits; ~**kult** *der* ancestor worship; **ein javanischer** ~**kult** a Javanese ancestor cult; ~**pass,** *~**paß** *der* (ns.) proof of ancestry (proving Aryan descent); ~**tafel** *die* genealogical table; ~**verehrung** *die* ancestor worship

Ahn-: ~**frau** *die* (geh. veralt.) [first] ancestress; (fig.) spiritual forebear; ~**herr** *der* (geh. veralt.) [first] ancestor; (fig.) father; ~**herrin** *die* (geh. veralt.) [first] ancestor

Ahnin *die;* ~, ~**nen** ▸**Ahne**[2]

ähnlich /ˈɛ:nlɪç/

A *Adj.* similar; **jmdm.** ~ **sein** be similar to *or* be like sb.; (~ aussehen) resemble sb.; be like sb.; **das Kind ist seinem Vater** ~: the child takes after his father; **sich** (*Dat.*) *od.* (geh.) **einander** ~ **sein** be similar to one another; be alike; (~ aussehen) resemble one another; be alike; ~ **wie er/wir** like him/us; ~ **wie etw. aussehen/klingen** look/sound like sth.; **ein einer Ratte** ~**es Tier** an animal similar to a rat; **das sieht dir/ihm** ~! (ugs.) that's you/him all over; that's just like you/him; **[etwas] Ähnliches** something similar

B *adv.* similarly; ‹*answer, react*› in a similar way *or* manner; ~ **dumm/naiv** *usw.* **argumentieren** argue in a similarly stupid/naive *etc.* way *or* manner; ~ **dumm/naiv sein** be similarly stupid/naive; **uns geht es** ~: it is/will be much the same for us; (wir denken, fühlen ~) we feel much the same

C *Präp. mit Dat.* like

Ähnlichkeit *die;* ~, ~**en** similarity; (ähnliches Aussehen) similarity; resemblance; **mit jmdm.** ~ **haben** be similar to *or* be like sb.; (ähnlich aussehen) bear a resemblance to *or* be like sb.; **mit etw.** ~ **haben** bear a similarity to sth.

Ahnung *die;* ~, ~**en** 1▸ (Vorgefühl) presentiment; premonition; **eine** ~ **haben, dass ...** have a feeling *or* hunch that ... 2▸ (Befürchtung) foreboding 3▸ (ugs.: Kenntnisse) knowledge; **von etw. [viel]** ~ **haben** know [a lot] about sth.; **keine** ~! [I've] no idea; [I] haven't a clue; **du hast doch keine** ~: you don't know the first thing about it; **nicht die geringste** *od.* **keine blasse** ~ **[von etw.] haben** not have the faintest idea [about sth.]; **haben Sie eine** ~, **wer/wie ...?** have you any idea who/how ...?; **von Tuten und Blasen keine** ~ **haben, keine** ~ **von Ackerbau und Viehzucht haben** (salopp) not know the first thing about it; **hast du 'ne** ~! (ugs.) that's what you think!

ahnungs·los

A *Adj.* (nichts ahnend) unsuspecting; (naiv, unschuldig) naive; innocent; (unwissend) naive; **sich** ~ **stellen** play the innocent

B *adv.* (nichts ahnend) unsuspectingly; all unawares; (naiv, unschuldig) naively; innocently; (unwissend) naively

Ahnungslosigkeit *die;* ~ (Naivität, Unschuld) naivety; innocence; (Unwissenheit) naivety

ahnungs·voll *Adj.* (geh.) full of presentiment *postpos.*; (geheimnisvoll) mysterious; (Böses ahnend) full of foreboding *postpos.*

ahoi /aˈhɔy/ *Interj.* 1▸ (Seemannsspr.) **Boot/Schiff** *usw.* ~! boat/ship *etc.* ahoy! 2▸ ▸**helau**

Ahorn /ˈa:hɔrn/ *der;* ~**s,** ~**e** maple

Ahorn-: ~**blatt** *das* maple leaf; ~**sirup** *der* maple syrup

Ähre /ˈɛ:rə/ *die;* ~, ~**n** (von Getreide) ear; head; (von Gräsern) head; (Bot.: von Blüten) spike; ~**n lesen** glean

Ähren-: ~**feld** *das* (geh.) field of [ripening/ripe] corn; ~**kranz** *der* wreath of wheat ears; ~**lese** *die* gleaning

Aids /e:ts/ *das;* ~ ▸❶ **S. 439** AIDS

Aids-: ~**kranke** *der/die* person suffering from AIDS; ~**test** *der* AIDS test

Air /ɛ:ɐ̯/ *das;* ~**s,** ~**s** 1▸ air; aura 2▸ (Musik) air

Airbag /ˈɛ:ɐ̯bɛk/ *der;* ~**s,** ~**s** (Kfz.-W.) air bag

Air·bus /ˈɛ:ɐ̯-/ *der* (Flugw.) airbus

Airedale /ˈɛ:ɐ̯de:l/ *der;* ~**s,** ~**s** Airedale

Airedale·terrier *der* Airedale terrier

ais, Ais /ˈa:ɪs/ *das;* ~, ~ (Mus.) A sharp

Akademie /akadeˈmi:/ *die;* ~, ~**n** 1▸ academy 2▸ (Fachhochschule) academy; (Bergbau, Forst~, Bau~) school; college 3▸ (österr.: künstlerische Veranstaltung) cultural function

Akademie·mitglied *das* member of the/an academy; academician

Akademiker /akaˈde:mikɐ/ *der;* ~**s,** ~, **Akademikerin** *die;* ~, ~**nen** 1▸ (Hochschulabsolvent) [university/college] graduate 2▸ ▸**Akademiemitglied**

akademisch

A *Adj.* academic; ~**er Rat** [university] lecturer; ~**er Oberrat** senior [university] lecturer; **der** ~**e Mittelbau** *the non-professional teaching staff*; **das** ~**e Proletariat** *the mass of jobless graduates and graduates working in jobs for which they are*

overqualified; ~**er Lehrer** university teacher; **das** ~**e Viertel** *the 15 minutes' grace between the announced start and actual beginning of a lecture*
B *adv.* academically; ~ **[aus]gebildet sein** have [had] a university education; be university-educated; **dieses Problem stellt sich rein** ~**:** this problem is purely academic

Akademisierung *die;* ~**: die** ~ **des Bundestages schreitet weiter fort** the Bundestag is becoming increasingly peopled with [university] graduates

Akanthus /a'kantʊs/ *der;* ~, ~ (Bot., Kunstwiss.) acanthus

akausal (Philos.)
A *Adj.* acausal
B *adv.* acausally

Akazie /a'ka:tsiə/ *die;* ~, ~**n** (auch volkst.: Robinie) acacia

Akelei /akə'lai/ *die;* ~, ~**en** aquilegia; columbine

Akklamation /aklama'tsi̯o:n/ *die;* ~, ~**en** **1** (Abstimmung durch Zuruf) acclamation; **durch** *od.* **per** ~**:** by acclamation **2** (selten: Beifall) acclamation *no pl.*; acclaim *no pl.*

akklamieren /akla'mi:rən/ (geh.)
A *itr. V.* (zustimmen) applaud
B *tr. V.* (durch Beifall) acclaim

Akklimatisation /aklimatiza'tsi̯o:n/ *die;* ~, ~**en** acclimatization

akklimatisieren *refl. V.* become *or* get acclimatized

Akklimatisierung *die;* ~, ~**en** ▸**Akklimatisation**

Akkolade /ako'la:də/ *die;* ~, ~**n** **1** (Hist., Musik) accolade **2** (Druckw.) brace

Akkord /a'kɔrt/ *der;* ~**[e]s**, ~**e** **1** (Musik) chord **2** (Wirtsch.) (~arbeit) piecework; (~lohn) piecework pay *no indef. art., no pl.*; (~satz) piece rate; **im** ~ **sein** *od.* **arbeiten** be on piecework; **etw. im** ~ **tun** do sth. piecework; **im** ~ **hergestellt werden** be manufactured by pieceworkers **3** (geh.: Übereinstimmung) accord **4** (Rechtsspr.: Einigung) settlement

Akkord-: ~**arbeit** *die* piecework; **in** ~**arbeit hergestellt werden** be manufactured by pieceworkers; ~**arbeiter** *der,* ~**arbeiterin** *die* pieceworker

Akkordeon /a'kɔrdeɔn/ *das;* ~**s**, ~**s** accordion

Akkordeonist *der;* ~**en**, ~**en**, **Akkordeonistin** *die;* ~, ~**nen**, **Akkordeonspieler** *der,* **Akkordeon·spielerin** *die* accordionist

Akkord-: ~**lohn** *der* (Wirtsch.) piecework pay *no indef. art., no pl.*; ~**satz** *der* (Wirtsch.) piece rate; ~**zuschlag** *der* (Wirtsch.) piece-rate bonus

akkreditieren /akredi'ti:rən/ *tr. V.* **1** (bes. Dipl.) accredit (**bei** to) **2** (Finanzw.) **jmdn.** ~**:** grant sb. credit facilities; **akkreditiert sein** have credit facilities

Akkreditierung *die;* ~, ~**en** **1** (bes. Dipl.) accreditation (**bei** to) **2** (Finanzw.) **meine** ~ **bei der Bank** my credit facilities *pl. or* credit arrangement at the bank; **eine** ~ **von Euro 10 000** provision of 10,000 euros of credit

Akkreditiv /akredi'ti:f/ *das;* ~**s**, ~**e** **1** (Dipl.) credentials *pl.* **2** (Finanzw.) letter of credit

Akku /'aku/ *der;* ~**s**, ~**s** (ugs.) ▸**Akkumulator 1**

Akkulturation /akʊltura'tsi̯o:n/ *die;* ~, ~**en** (Völkerk., Sozialpsych.) acculturation

akkulturieren *tr. V.* (Völkerk., Sozialpsych.) acculturate

Akkumulation /akumula'tsi̯o:n/ *die;* ~, ~**en** (geh., Wirtsch.) accumulation

Akkumulator /akumu'la:tɔr/ *der;* ~**s**, ~**en** /-la'to:rən/ (Technik) **1** (Stromspeicher) accumulator (Brit.); storage battery *or* cell **2** (Druckspeicher, DV) accumulator

akkumulieren *tr., itr., refl. V.* (geh., Wirtsch., Soziol.) accumulate

akkurat /aku'ra:t/
A *Adj.* **1** (sorgfältig) meticulous; (sauber) neat **2** (exakt, genau) precise; exact
B *adv.* **1** (sorgfältig) meticulously; (sauber) neatly **2** (exakt, genau) precisely; exactly

Akkuratesse /akura'tɛsə/ *die;* ~ **1** (Sorgfalt) meticulousness; (Sauberkeit) neatness **2** (Exaktheit, Genauigkeit) precision

Akkusativ /'akuzati:f/ *der;* ~**s**, ~**e** (Sprachw.) accusative [case]; (Wort im ~) accusative [form]; **im/mit dem** ~ **stehen** be in/take the accusative [case]

Akkusativ·objekt *das* (Sprachw.) accusative *or* direct object

Akku·schrauber *der* cordless screwdriver

Akne /'aknə/ *die;* ~, ~**n** ▸❶ **S. 439** (Med.) acne

Akonto /a'kɔnto/ *das;* ~**s**, ~**s** *od.* **Akonten** (österr.), **Akonto·zahlung** *die* ▸**Anzahlung**

AKP-Staaten *Pl.* ACP States

akquirieren /akvi'ri:rən/ *itr. V.* (Wirtsch.) canvass [new] business

Akquirierung *die;* ~, ~**en** canvassing (**von** for); ~ **von Fachkräften** recruiting of specialist staff

Akquise /a'kvi:zə/ *die;* ~, ~**n** (ugs.) canvassing (**von** for); (als Freelancer) canvassing for work

Akquisiteur /akvizi'tø:ɐ̯/ *der;* ~**s**, ~**e**, **Akquisiteurin** *die;* ~, ~**nen** (Wirtsch.) canvasser

Akquisition /akvizi'tsi̯o:n/ *die;* ~, ~**en** (Wirtsch.) canvassing *no art.* for [new] business

Akquisitor /akvi'zi:tɔr/ *der;* ~**s**, ~**en** /-zi'to:rən/, **Akquisitorin** *die;* ~, ~**nen** (österr.) canvasser

Akribie /akri'bi:/ *die;* ~ (geh.) meticulousness; meticulous precision

akribisch /a'kri:bɪʃ/
A *Adj.* meticulous; meticulously precise
B *adv.* meticulously; with meticulous precision; ~ **genau** meticulously accurate

Akrobat /akro'ba:t/ *der;* ~**en**, ~**en** ▸❶ **S. 113** acrobat

Akrobaten·truppe *die* troupe of acrobats

Akrobatik *die;* ~ **1** (Körperbeherrschung) acrobatic skill **2** (akrobatische Übungen) acrobatics *pl.*

Akrobatin *die;* ~, ~**nen** ▸❶ **S. 113** acrobat

akrobatisch
A *Adj.* acrobatic
B *adv.* acrobatically

Akronym /akro'ny:m/ *das;* ~**s**, ~**e** (Sprachw.) acronym

Akt¹ /akt/ *der;* ~**[e]s**, ~**e** **1** (auch Theater, Zirkus~, Varietee~) act **2** (Zeremonie) ceremony; ceremonial act **3** (Geschlechts~) sexual act **4** (~bild) nude **5** (Amtshandlung) action

Akt² *der;* ~**[e]s**, ~**en** (bes. südd., österr.) ▸**Akte**

Akt-: ~**aufnahme** *die* nude photograph; ~**bild** *das* nude [picture]

Akte *die;* ~, ~**n** file; **die** ~ **Schulze** the Schulze file; **das kommt in die** ~**n** it goes on file; ~**n über jmdn./etw. führen** keep a file on sb./sth.; **etw. zu den** ~**n legen** file sth. away; (fig.) lay sth. to rest; **über etw.** (*Akk.*) **die** ~**n schließen** close the file on sth.

akten-, Akten-: ~**berg** *der* (ugs.) mountain of files; ~**deckel** *der* folder; ~**einsicht** *die* (Amtsspr.) ~**einsicht nehmen** examine the files; **jmdm.** ~**einsicht gewähren** allow sb. to examine the files; ~**koffer** *der,* (iron.) ~**köfferchen** *das* attaché case; ~**kundig** *Adj.* on record; ~**kundig werden** go on file; be recorded; ~**mappe** *die* **1** (~tasche) briefcase; **2** (~deckel) folder; ~**notiz** *die* **1** note [for the files]; **sich** (*Dat.*) **eine kurze** ~**notiz von etw. machen** make a brief note of sth. [for the files]; **2** (längeres Schreiben) memorandum; ~**ordner** *der* file; ~**schrank** *der* filing cabinet; ~**stoß** *der* stack *or* pile of files; ~**tasche** *die* briefcase; ~**vermerk** *der* ▸~**notiz 1**; ~**wolf** *der* [paper] shredder; ~**zeichen** *das* reference

Akteur /ak'tø:ɐ̯/ *der;* ~**s**, ~**e**, **Akteurin** *die;* ~, ~**nen** person involved; (Theater) member of the cast; (Varietee) performer; (Sportjargon) player; (Boxen, Ringen) contestant

Akt-: ~**foto** *das* nude photo; ~**fotografie** *die* **1** nude photography *no art.*; **2** (Bild) nude photograph; ~**gemälde** *das* nude [painting]

Aktie /'aktsi̯ə/ *die;* ~, ~**n** (Wirtsch.) share; ~**n** shares (Brit.); stock (Amer.); **sein Geld in** ~**n anlegen** invest one's money in shares (Brit.) *or* (Amer.) stocks; **die** ~**n fallen/steigen** share *or* stock prices are falling/rising; **junge** ~**n** new-issue shares *or* stocks; **wie stehen die** ~**n?** (ugs. scherzh.) (wie gehts) how are things?; (wie sind die Chancen) what are the prospects?; **seine/meine** *usw.* ~**n steigen** (fig. ugs.) his/my *etc.* prospects are improving

Aktien-: ~**besitz** *der* shareholdings *pl.*; ~**besitzer** *der,* ~**besitzerin** *die* shareholder; ~**fonds** *der* (Wirtsch.) share investment fund; ~**gesellschaft** *die* joint-stock company; ~**index** *der* share index; ~**kapital** *das* share capital; ~**kurs** *der* share price (Brit.); stock price (Amer.); ~**markt** *der* stock market; ~**mehrheit** *die* majority shareholding (*Gen.* in); ~**option** *die* (Finanzw.) share option (Brit.); stock option (Amer.); ~**paket** *das* block of shares; ~**urkunde** *die* share certificate (Brit.); stock certificate (Amer.)

Aktion /ak'tsi̯o:n/ *die;* ~, ~**en** **1** (Unternehmung) action *no indef. art.*; (militärisch) operation; **revolutionäre/politische** ~**en** revolutionary/political action *sing.* **2** (Kampagne) campaign; ~ **saubere Umwelt** campaign to clean up the environment; *s. auch* **konzertiert** **3** (das Handeln) action; **in** ~ **treten** go into action; ‹*safety device*› come into action **4** (Kaufmannsspr.: Verkauf zu Sonderpreisen) sale

Aktionär /aktsi̯o'nɛ:ɐ̯/ *der;* ~**s**, ~**e**, **Aktionärin** *die;* ~, ~**nen** shareholder

Aktionärs·versammlung *die* shareholders' meeting

Aktionismus *der;* ~**:** actionism *no art.*

Aktionist *der;* ~**en**, ~**en**, **Aktionistin** *die;* ~, ~**nen** actionist

aktionistisch
A *Adj.* actionist[ic]
B *adv.* actionistically

aktions-, Aktions-: ~**art** *die* (Sprachw.) aspect; ~**ausschuss**, *~**ausschuß** *der* action committee; ~**bereich** *der* ▸~**radius**; ~**einheit** *die* united action *no art.* (*Gen.* by); ~**fähig** *Adj.* capable of action *postpos.*; ~**fähigkeit** *die* ability to act; ~**gemeinschaft** *die:* **eine** ~**gemeinschaft herstellen/fordern** bring about/demand united action (**von** by); ~**gruppe** *die* action group; ~**komitee** *das* action committee; ~**preis** *der* (Kaufmannsspr.) sale price; **zum** ~**preis** at sale price; ~**programm** *das* programme for action; ~**radius** *der* **1** (Luftwaffe, Seew.) radius of action; **2** (Wirkungsbereich) range of activity; ~**unfähig** *Adj.* incapable of action *postpos.*; ~**zentrum** *das* **1** (Mittelpunkt) centre *or* focus for action; **2** (Met.) centre of action

aktiv /ak'ti:f/
A *Adj.* **1** (auch Chemie) active **2** (Milit.) serving *attrib.* ‹*officer, soldier*›; **er ist Soldat im** ~**en Dienst** he is a serving soldier; **er war in Vietnam** ~**:** he served in Vietnam **3** ~**e Bestechung** offering of a bribe/bribes to an official; ~**e Handelsbilanz** favourable balance of trade; ~**er Wortschatz** active vocabulary
B *adv.* actively; **sich** ~ **verhalten** be active

-aktiv¹ *Adj.* (Werbespr.) **saug**~**:** extra-absorbent; **wasch**~**e Substanzen** substances with a strong cleansing action; **atmungs**~**es Gewebe** fabric which allows the skin to breathe

-aktiv² *das;* ~**s**, ~**e** *od.* ~**s** (bes. DDR) **Verkehrssicherheits**~ / **Bezirks**~ / **Eltern**~ *usw.* traffic safety/district/parents *etc.* committee

Aktiv¹ /'akti:f/ *das;* ~**s**, ~**e** (Sprachw.) active; **im** ~ **stehen** be in the active

Aktiv² /ak'ti:f/ *das;* ~**s**, ~**e** *od.* ~**s** (bes. DDR) committee

Aktiva /ak'ti:va/ *Pl.* (Wirtsch.) assets

Aktiv-bürger *der,* **Aktiv-bürgerin** *die* (schweiz.) *citizen with full political and civil rights*

Aktive¹ /ak'ti:və/ *der/die; adj. Dekl.* (Sport) participant; (eines Vereins, einer Gewerkschaft) active member; (der Feuerwehr) regular

Aktive² *die;* **~n, ~n** (salopp) (nicht selbst gedrehte Zigarette) real fag (Brit. sl.); store-bought cigarette (Amer.); (filterlose Zigarette) plain fag (sl.); non-filter

Aktiven *Pl.:* ▸**Aktiva**

Aktiv·geschäft *das* (Finanzw.) lending and investment business

aktivierbar *Adj.* **er ist/sie sind** *usw.* **[politisch] ~:** he/they *etc.* can be [politically] mobilized

aktivieren *tr. V.* [1] mobilize ‹*party members, group, class, etc.*›; intensify, step up ‹*work, campaign*›; **den Kreislauf ~:** stimulate the circulation; **alte Freundschaften ~:** revive old friendships; **Beziehungen ~:** reactivate connections [2] (Chemie) activate [3] (Finanzw.) **etw. ~:** enter sth. on the assets side

Aktivierung *die;* **~, ~en** [1] (von Parteimitgliedern, einer Gruppe, Klasse) mobilization; (einer Arbeit, Kampagne) intensification; (von Beziehungen) reactivation; **die ~ des Kreislaufs/alter Freundschaften** stimulation of the circulation/reviving old friendships [2] (Chemie) activation [3] (Finanzw.) entry on the assets side; **die ~ von etw.** entering sth. on the assets side

aktivisch (Sprachw.)
[A] *Adj.* active
[B] *adv.* actively; in the active form

Aktivismus *der;* **~** (Politik) activism *no art.*

Aktivist *der;* **~en, ~en, Aktivistin** *die;* **~, ~nen** activist

aktivistisch *Adj.* (Politik) activist

Aktivität /aktivi'tɛ:t/ *die;* **~, ~en** (auch Chemie, Radio~) activity

Aktiv-: ~kohle *die* activated carbon *or* charcoal; **~kohle·filter** *der,* (fachspr. meist) *das* activated-carbon *or* activated-charcoal filter; **~posten** *der* (Kaufmannsspr., fig.) asset; **~saldo** *der* (Kaufmannsspr.) credit balance; **~seite** *die* (Kaufmannsspr.) assets side; **~urlaub** *der* (Werbespr.) activity holiday; **~vermögen** *das* (Kaufmannsspr.) realizable assets *pl.*; **~zinsen** *Pl.* (Kaufmannsspr.) interest *sing.* receivable

Akt-: ~malerei *die* nude painting *no art.*; **~modell** *das* nude model

Aktrice /ak'tri:sə/ *die;* **~, ~n** actress

Akt·studie *die* nude study

aktualisieren /aktu̯ali'zi:rən/
[A] *tr. V.* update
[B] *refl. V.* (sich manifestieren) be evident *or* clearly visible

Aktualisierung *die;* **~, ~en** updating; **er sorgte für die ~ des Themas** he ensured that the subject was made topical

Aktualität /aktu̯ali'tɛ:t/ *die;* **~, ~en** [1] (Gegenwartsbezug) relevance [to the present] [2] (von Nachrichten usw.) topicality [3] (Mode, Werbespr.) up-to-the-minute style

Aktuar /ak'tu̯a:ɐ̯/ *der;* **~s, ~e, Aktuarin** *die;* **~, ~nen** ▸❶ **S. 113** [1] (schweiz.: Schriftführer) secretary [2] (veralt.) ▸**Gerichtsschreiber**

aktuell /ak'tu̯ɛl/
[A] *Adj.* [1] (gegenwartsbezogen) topical; (gegenwärtig) current; **von ~er Bedeutung** of relevance to the present *or* current situation; **dieses Problem ist nicht mehr ~:** this is no longer a problem [2] (neu) up-to-the-minute; **das Aktuellste von den Olympischen Spielen** the latest from the Olympics; **eine ~e Sendung** (Ferns., Rundf.) a [news and] current affairs programme [3] (geh.: real) real [4] (Mode, Werbespr.) fashionable; **in den ~en Farben** in the latest colours
[B] *adv.* currently

Akt-: ~zeichnen *das* nude drawing *no art.*; **~zeichnung** *die* nude drawing

Akupressur /akuprɛ'su:ɐ̯/ *die;* **~, ~en** (Med.) acupressure

Akupunkteur /akupʊŋk'tø:ɐ̯/ *der;* **~s, ~e, Akupunkteurin** *die;* **~, ~nen** (Med.) acupuncturist

akupunktieren (Med.)
[A] *tr. V.* perform acupuncture on; **sich ~ lassen** have acupuncture
[B] *itr. V.* perform acupuncture

Akupunktur /akupʊŋk'tu:ɐ̯/ *die;* **~, ~en** (Med.) acupuncture

Akustik /a'kʊstɪk/ *die;* **~** [1] (Lehre vom Schall) acoustics *sing., no art.* [2] (Schallverhältnisse) acoustics *pl.*

akustisch
[A] *Adj.* acoustic
[B] *adv.* acoustically; **ich habe Sie ~ nicht verstanden** I didn't hear *or* catch what you said

akut /a'ku:t/
[A] *Adj.* [1] (vordringlich) acute; pressing, urgent ‹*question, issue*› [2] (Med.) acute
[B] *adv.* (Med.) in an acute form; **~ auftretende Asthmaanfälle** acute attacks of asthma

Akut *der;* **~[e]s, ~e** (Schriftw.) acute [accent]

AKW *Abk.* **= Atomkraftwerk**

Akzeleration /aktselera'tsi̯o:n/ *die;* **~, ~en** (Anthrop., Astron.) acceleration

Akzelerator /aktsele'ra:tɔr/ *der;* **~s, ~en** /-ra'to:rən/ (Kerntechnik) accelerator

Akzent /ak'tsɛnt/ *der;* **~[e]s, ~e** [1] (Sprachw.) (Betonung) accent; stress; (Betonungszeichen) accent [2] ▸❶ **S. 670** (Sprachmelodie, Aussprache) accent; **mit starkem koreanischem ~:** with a strong Korean accent [3] (Nachdruck, Gewicht) emphasis; stress; (in der Mode) accent; **den ~ [besonders] auf etw.** (*Akk.*) **legen** lay *or* put [particular] emphasis *or* stress on sth.; **die ~e werden verschoben** the emphasis *or* stress is shifted; **neue ~e setzen** set new directions; **diesen Herbst liegen die [modischen] ~e bei ...** this autumn the accent is on ...; **1969 hat neue ~e gesetzt** 1969 saw the beginning of new trends

akzent·frei
[A] *Adj.* without an *or* any accent *postpos.*
[B] *adv.* without an *or* any accent

akzentuieren /aktsentu'i:rən/ *tr. V.* [1] (deutlich aussprechen) enunciate; articulate; (betonen) accentuate; stress [2] (fig.: hervorheben, auch Mode) accentuate

Akzent·verschiebung *die* [1] (Sprachw.) stress shift [2] (fig.) shift of emphasis

Akzept /ak'tsɛpt/ *das;* **~[e]s, ~e** (Finanzw.) acceptance

akzeptabel /aktsɛp'ta:bl̩/
[A] *Adj.* acceptable
[B] *adv.* acceptably

Akzeptanz /aktsɛp'tants/ *die* (bes. Werbespr.) acceptance

akzeptieren *tr. V.* accept

Akzidens /'aktsidɛns/ *das;* **~, Akzidenzien** [1] (Philos.) accident; accidental property [2] (Musik) accidental

akzidentell /aktsidɛn'tɛl/, **akzidentiell** /-'tsi̯ɛl/ *Adj.* [1] (Philos., geh.) accidental (*Dat.* to) [2] (Med.) accidental

Akzidenz /aktsi'dɛnts/ *die;* **~, ~en** (Druckw.) job; **~en** job-work *sing.*; job printing *sing.*

à la /a la/ (Gastr., ugs.: im Stile von) à la

alaaf /a'la:f/ *Interj.* (rhein.) hurrah; hurray; **Kölle ~!** hurrah, Cologne!

Alabaster /ala'bastɐ/ *der;* **~s, ~:** alabaster

alabastern *Adj.* (geh.) alabaster

à la carte /ala'kart/ (Gastr.) à la carte

Alarm /a'larm/ *der;* **~[e]s, ~e** [1] (Warnung) alarm; (Flieger~) air-raid warning; **~ geben** raise *or* sound *or* give the alarm; **blinder ~:** false alarm; **~ schlagen** (ugs.) raise *or* sound the alarm; **bei ~:** if there is an alarm [2] (~zustand) alert; **da war ständig ~:** there was a permanent state of alert

alarm-, Alarm-: ~anlage *die* alarm system; **~bereit** *Adj.* on alert *postpos.*; ‹*fire crew, police*› on standby *postpos.*, standing by *pred.*; **~bereitschaft** *die* ▸**~bereit**: alert; **in [ständiger] ~bereitschaft** on [permanent] alert/standby; **jmdn./etw. in ~bereitschaft versetzen** place *or* put sb./sth. on alert/standby; **~fall** *der* alert; **im ~fall** in case of alert; in the event of an alert; **~glocke** *die* alarm bell

alarmieren *tr. V.* [1] (zu Hilfe rufen) call [out] ‹*doctor, police, fire brigade, etc.*› [2] (warnen) alarm; **~d** alarming; **nichts Alarmierendes** nothing alarming

Alarmierung *die;* **~: bei rechtzeitiger ~ der Bergwacht** *usw.* if the mountain rescue service *etc.* is/had been called [out] in time; **eine sofortige ~ der Feuerwehr wäre geboten gewesen** the fire service *or* (Amer.) department should have been called [out] immediately; **zur ~ aller Demokraten führen** cause alarm on the part of all democrats

Alarm-: ~klingel *die* alarm bell; **~pikett** *das* (schweiz.) ▸**Überfallkommando**; **~ruf** *der* (fig.) warning cry; **~signal** *das* (auch fig.) warning signal; **~sirene** *die* alarm *or* warning siren; **~stufe** *die* alert stage; **höchste ~stufe** maximum alert; **~stufe eins/zwei/drei** stage one/two/three alert; **~übung** *die* practice drill; (Milit.) practice alert; **~vorrichtung** *die* alarm [device]; **~zeichen** *das* (fig.) warning signal; **~zustand** *der* state of alert; **sich im ~zustand befinden** ‹*troops*› be on alert; ‹*fire service, police*› be on standby; ‹*country, province*› be on a state of alert; **in den ~zustand versetzen** put ‹*troops*› on alert; place *or* put ‹*fire service, police*› on standby; place *or* put ‹*country, province*› on a state of alert

Alaska /a'laska/ *(das);* **~s** Alaska

Alaun /a'lau̯n/ *der;* **~s, ~e** alum

Alaun·stift *der* styptic pencil

a-Laut *der* A-sound

Alb¹ /alp/ *der;* **~[e]s, ~en** (Myth.) elf

Alb² *der;* **~[e]s, ~e** (veralt.: Kobold) *goblin believed to give sleeping people nightmares by sitting on their chests at night;* ≈ incubus; **wie ein ~ auf der Brust lasten** (geh.) lie *or* weigh heavily on sb.; **ein ~ plagte ihn** he had nightmares

Albaner /al'ba:nɐ/ *der;* **~s, ~, Albanerin** *die;* **~, ~nen** ▸❶ **S. 520** Albanian

Albanien /al'ba:ni̯ən/ *(das);* **~s** Albania

albanisch *Adj.* ▸❶ **S. 520,** ▸❶ **S. 670** Albanian; *s. auch* **deutsch**

Albanisch *das;* **~s** ▸❶ **S. 670** Albanian; *s. auch* **Deutsch**

Albatros /'albatrɔs/ *der;* **~, ~se** (Zool.) albatross

Alb-: ~druck *der* nightmare; **~drücken** *das;* **~s** nightmares *pl*

Albe /'albə/ *die;* **~, ~n** (christl. Kirchen) alb

Albedo /al'be:do/ *die;* **~, ~s** (Astron.) albedo

Alben ▸**Alb, Albe, Album**

Alberei *die;* **~, ~en** ▸**Albernheit 2**

albern¹ *itr. V.* fool about *or* around

albern² *Adj.* [1] (kindisch, töricht) silly; foolish; **~es Zeug reden** talk silly *or* foolish nonsense; **stell dich nicht so ~ an** don't be so silly; **sich ~ benehmen** act silly; **sich** (*Dat.*) **~ vorkommen** feel silly; feel a fool [2] (ugs.: nebensächlich) silly; stupid

Albernheit *die;* **~, ~en** [1] (albernes Verhalten) silliness; foolishness [2] (alberne Handlung) silliness; (alberne Bemerkung/alberner Witz) silly remark/joke; **diese ~en** this silliness *sing.*

Albinismus /albi'nɪsmʊs/ *der;* **~:** albinism

Albino /al'bi:no/ *der;* **~s, ~s** albino

Alb·traum *der* nightmare

Album /'albʊm/ *das;* **~s, Alben** album

Albumin /albu'mi:n/ *das;* **~s, ~e** (Biol.) albumin

Alchemie /alçe'mi:/ *die;* **~** (bes. österr.), **Alchimie** /alçi'mi:/ *die;* **~:** alchemy *no art.*

Alchemist *der;* **~en, ~en** (bes. österr.), **Alchemistin** *die;* **~, ~nen** (bes. österr.), **Alchimist** *der;* **~en, ~en, Alchimistin** *die;* **~, ~nen** alchemist

Alchimisten·küche *die* alchemist's laboratory

alchimistisch
[A] *Adj.* alchemical; alchemistic
[B] *adv.* alchemistically; **~ beeinflusst** influenced by alchemy

Alcopop /'alkopɔp/ *der od. das;* **~s, ~s** alcopop

Aldehyd /alde'hy:t/ *der;* **~s, ~e** (Chem.) aldehyde

Alemanne /alə'manə/ *der;* **~n, ~n, Alemannin** *die;* ~, **~nen** Alemannian; **die ~n** Alemannians; (Hist.) the Alemanni

alemannisch *Adj.* Alemannic

alert /a'lɛrt/ *Adj.* (ugs.) dynamic

Aleuten /ale'u:tn̩/ *Pl.* **die ~:** the Aleutian Islands; the Aleutians

Alexandriner /alɛksan'dri:nɐ/ *der;* **~s,** ~ (Verslehre) alexandrine

Alfa·gras /'alfa-/ *das* alfa grass

Alge /'algə/ *die;* ~, **~n** alga

Algebra /'algebra, *österr.:* al'ge:bra/ *die;* ~, (fachspr.) **Algebren** algebra

Algebraiker *der;* **~s,** ~, **Algebraikerin** *die;* ~, **~nen** algebraist

algebraisch
A *Adj.* algebraic
B *adv.* algebraically

Algen-: **~pest** *die* seaweed plague; **~pilz** *der* comycete

Algerien /al'ge:riən/ *(das);* **~s** Algeria

Algerier *der;* **~s,** ~, **Algerierin** *die;* ~, **~nen ▸❶ S. 520** Algerian

algerisch *Adj.* **▸❶ S. 520** Algerian

Algier /'alʒi:ɐ̯/ *(das);* **~s ▸❶ S. 675** Algiers

Algorithmus /algo'rɪtmus/ *der;* ~, **Algorithmen** (Math., DV) algorithm

alias /'a:li̯as/ *Adv.* alias

Alibi /'a:libi/ *das;* **~s, ~s** **1** (Rechtsw.) alibi **2** (Ausrede) alibi (coll.); excuse

Alibi-: **~frau** *die* token woman; **~funktion** *die* use as an alibi (coll.) *or* excuse; **~funktion haben** serve as an alibi (coll.) *or* excuse

Alimente /ali'mɛntə/ *Pl.* (veralt., noch ugs.) maintenance *sing. (esp. for illegitimate child)*; **jmdn. auf ~ verklagen** sue sb. for maintenance

Alk[1] /alk/ *der;* **~[e]s, ~en** (Zool.) auk

Alk[2] *der;* **~s** (ugs.) alcohol; booze (coll.); **hast du auch was ohne ~?** have you got anything non-alcoholic?

alkäisch /al'kɛ:ɪʃ/ *Adj.* (Verslehre) alcaic

Alkali /al'ka:li/ *das;* **~s, Alkalien** alkali

alkali·frei *Adj.* (Werbespr.) non-alkaline

alkalisch *Adj.* (Chemie) alkaline

Alkaloid /alkalo'i:t/ *das;* **~[e]s, ~e** (Chemie) alkaloid

Alki /'alki/ *der;* **~s, ~s** (salopp) wino (coll.)

Alkohol /'alkoho:l/ *der;* **~s, ~e** alcohol; **unter ~ stehen** (ugs.) be under the influence (coll.); **jmdn. unter ~ setzen** (ugs.) get sb. drunk; *s. auch* **ertränken**

alkohol-, Alkohol-: **~abhängig** *Adj.* dependent on alcohol *postpos.;* **~abhängigkeit** *die* dependence on alcohol; alcohol dependence; **~arm** *Adj.* low in alcohol *pred.;* **~ausschank** *der* sale of alcohol[ic drinks]; **Kiosken ist der ~ausschank verboten** kiosks are forbidden to sell alcohol; **„kein ~ausschank an Jugendliche"** 'no alcohol may be sold to persons under 18'; **~einfluss,** ***~ein·fluß** *der,* **~ein·wirkung** *die* influence of alcohol *or* drink; **unter ~einfluss** *od.* **~einwirkung [stehen]** [be] under the influence of alcohol *or* drink; **~fahne** *die* smell of alcohol [on one's breath]; **eine ~fahne haben** smell of alcohol; **jmds. ~fahne riechen** smell the alcohol on sb.'s breath; **~frei** *Adj.* **1** (ohne ~gehalt) non-alcoholic; **~freie Getränke** soft *or* non-alcoholic drinks; **2** (ohne ~ausschank) dry ‹*country, state, etc.*›; **3** (ohne ~genuss) ‹*day, week, etc.*› without alcohol; **einen ~freien Tag einlegen** spend a day without drinking alcohol; **~gegner** *der,* **~gegnerin** *die* opponent of alcohol; **~gehalt** *der* alcohol content; **~genuss,** ***~genuß** *der* consumption of alcohol; **infolge ~genusses** as a result of consuming alcohol; **~haltig** *Adj.* containing alcohol *postpos., not pred.;* **~haltige Getränke** alcoholic drinks; **wenig/stark ~haltig sein** have a low/high alcohol content

Alkoholika /alko'ho:lika/ *Pl.* alcoholic drinks

Alkoholiker *der;* **~s,** ~, **Alkoholikerin** *die;* ~, **~nen** alcoholic

alkoholisch *Adj.* alcoholic

alkoholisieren *tr. V.* **1** (mit Alkohol versetzen) alcoholize **2** (scherzh.: betrunken machen) **jmdn. ~:** get sb. drunk

alkoholisiert *Adj.* inebriated; **in ~em Zustand** in a state of inebriation

Alkoholismus *der;* **~:** alcoholism *no art.*

alkohol-, Alkohol-: **~konsum** *der* consumption of alcohol; **er hat in letzter Zeit einen beträchtlichen ~konsum** (ugs.) he has recently been hitting the bottle (coll.); **~krank** *Adj.* (Med.) alcoholic; **~missbrauch,** ***~mißbrauch** *der* alcohol abuse; **~pegel** *der* (scherzh.) level of alcohol in one's blood; **sein ~pegel war schon ganz beträchtlich** he was already well primed (coll.); **~reich** *Adj.* ‹*drink, wine, etc.*› with a high alcohol content; **~reich sein** have a high alcohol content; **~schmuggler** *der,* **~schmugglerin** *die* bootlegger; **~spiegel** *der* level of alcohol in one's blood; **~steuer** *die* duty *or* tax on alcohol; **~sucht** *die* alcohol addiction; alcoholism; **~süchtig** *Adj.* addicted to alcohol *postpos.;* alcoholic; **~süchtige** *der/die; adj. Dekl.* alcoholic; **~sünder** *der,* **~sünderin** *die* (ugs.) drunk[en] driver; **~verbot** *das* ban on alcohol; **es herrschte ~verbot** alcohol was banned; **~vergiftung** *die* alcohol[ic] poisoning

Alkoven /al'ko:vn̩/ *der;* **~s, ~:** alcove; (Bettnische) bed recess

all /al/ *Indefinitpron. u. unbest. Zahlw.*

A *attr.* (ganz, gesamt...) all; **in ~er Deutlichkeit** in all clarity; **~e Freude, die sie empfunden hat** all the joy she felt; **~es Geld, das ich noch habe** all the money I have left; **~er Eifer nützte ihm nichts** all his zeal was to no avail; **ich kann diese Leute ~e nicht leiden** I can't stand any of these people; **ich will euch ~e nicht mehr sehen** I don't want to see any of you again; **die Ärzte verdienen ~e sehr viel** doctors all earn a great deal; **~es Geld spendete sie dem Roten Kreuz** she donated all her money to the Red Cross; **~es Leid der Welt** all the suffering in the world; **~ unser/mein** *usw.* **...** all our/my *etc.* ...; **~es andere/Weitere/Übrige** everything else; **~es Übrige hat sich nicht geändert** nothing else has changed; **~es Schöne/Neue/Fremde** everything *or* all that is beautiful/new/strange; **~es Gute!** all the best!; **~e Fenster schließen** close all the windows; **sie gaben ~e Waffen ab** they handed in all their weapons; **wir/ihr/sie ~e** all of us/you/them; we/you/they all; **das sagen sie ~e** (ugs.) that's what they all say; **~e Beteiligten/Anwesenden** all those involved/present; **trotz ~er Vorbehalte werde ich ...** in spite of all my reservations I shall ...; **~e beide/~e zehn** both of them/all ten of them; **~e Männer/Frauen/Kinder** all men/women/children; **~e Mädchen über zwölf Jahre** all girls over twelve; **~e Mädchen in der Schule** all the girls in the school; **~e Bewohner der Stadt** all the inhabitants of the town; **ohne ~en Anlass** for no reason [at all]; without any reason [at all]; **gegen ~e Erwartungen** contrary to all expectations; **~e Jahre wieder** every year; **~e fünf Minuten/Meter** every five minutes/metres; **Bücher ~er Art** books of all kinds; all kinds of books; **in ~er Eile** with all haste; **in ~er Ruhe** in peace and quiet; **trotz ~er Versuche/Anstrengungen** despite all [his/her/their/*etc.*] attempts/efforts

B *allein stehend* **1** (gesamt..., sämtlich) everything; **~es geht vorüber** everything passes [in time]; **~es für die Braut/den Bastler** everything for the bride/handicraft enthusiast; **das ~es** all that; **ich weiß nicht, was das ~es soll** I don't know what all that is supposed to mean; **das ist ~es Unsinn** that is all nonsense; **von ~em etwas verstehen/wissen** understand/know a bit about everything; **wer ~es war** *od.* **wer war ~es dort** who was there?; **wen ~es habt ihr getroffen?** who did you meet?; **das sind ~es Gauner** they're all scoundrels; **was gab es dort ~es zu sehen?** what was there to see?; **was es nicht ~es gibt!** well, would you believe it!; well, I never!; **~[es] und jedes** everything; (wahllos) anything and everything; **trotz ~em** in spite of *or* despite everything; **sie liebt ihren Hund über ~es** she loves her dog more than anything else; **zu ~em fähig sein** (fig.) be capable of anything; **~es schon mal da gewesen** (ugs.) it's all happened before; **das kenne ich ~es schon** I've heard it all before; **~es in ~em** all in all; **vor ~em** above all; **~es klar** *od.* **in Ordnung** (ugs.) everything's fine *or* (coll.) OK; **~es klar?** everything all right *or* (coll.) OK?; **dann treffen wir uns um 5 Uhr, ~es klar?** we'll meet at 5 o'clock then, all right *or* (coll.) OK?; **das ist ~es** that's all *or* (coll.) it; **ist das ~es?** is that all *or* (coll.) it?; **nach ~em, was man hört/weiß** to judge from everything *or* all one hears/knows **2** (jeder einzelne) everyone; **~e miteinander** all together; **ihr seid/wir sind/sie sind ..., ~e miteinander** you/we/they are ..., all of you/us/them; **~e auf einmal** all at once; **sprecht nicht ~e auf einmal!** don't all speak at once; **am besten, wir gehen ~e auf einmal zum Chef** the best thing would be for us all to go and see the boss together; **~e, die ...** all those who ...; **der Kampf ~er gegen ~e** unfettered competition; **in ~em einverstanden sein** agree *or* be agreed on everything; **von ~em etwas nehmen** take a bit of everything; **er ist bei ~em, was er tut, sehr genau** he is very precise in everything he does; **sie ist in ~em sehr empfindlich** she is very sensitive about everything
3 (Neutr. Sg.: ~e Beteiligten) **~es mal herhören!** (ugs.) listen everybody!; (stärker befehlend) everybody listen!; **~es war nach Hause gegangen** (ugs.) everyone *or* everybody had gone home; **~es aussteigen!** (ugs.) everyone *or* all out!; (vom Schaffner gesagt) all change!

All *das;* **~s** space *no art.;* (Universum) universe

all-: **~abendlich** **A** *Adj.* regular evening; **B** *adv.* every evening; **~bekannt** *Adj.* (geh.) universally known; **~da** *Adv.* (veralt.) there; **~dem ▸alledem; ~dieweil[en]** **A** *Konj.* (veralt.) since; because; **B** *Adv.* all the while

alle *Adj.* **1** (ugs.: verbraucht, verkauft usw.) **~ sein** be all gone; **~ werden** run out; **etw. ~ machen** finish sth. off **2** (salopp: erschöpft) all in *pred.* **3** **jmdn. ~ machen** (salopp) do sb. in (sl.)

alle·dem *Pron.: in* **trotz ~:** in spite of *or* despite all that; **von ~ wusste er nichts** he knew nothing about all that; **an ~ ist nichts wahr** there's no truth in any of it; **nichts von ~:** nothing of the sort *or* kind; **bei ~:** for all that; **zu ~:** in addition to *or* on top of all that

Allee /a'le:/ *die;* ~, **~n** avenue

Allee·baum *der* avenue tree

Allegorie /alego'ri:/ *die;* ~, **~n** allegory

Allegorik /ale'go:rɪk/ *die;* **~:** allegory

allegorisch
A *Adj.* allegorical
B *adv.* allegorically

Allegretto /ale'grɛto/ *das;* **~s, ~s** *od.* **Allegretti** allegretto

Allegro /a'le:gro/ *das;* **~s, ~s** *od.* **Allegri** allegro

allein /a'lain/

A *Adj.* **1** (ohne andere, für sich) alone; on one's/its own; by oneself/itself; **sie waren ~ im Zimmer** they were alone in the room; **ganz ~:** all on one's/its own; **jmdn. ~ lassen** leave sb. alone *or* on his/her own; **~ über den Atlantik segeln** sail alone across the Atlantic **2** (einsam) alone

B *adv.* (ohne Hilfe) by oneself/itself; on one's/its own; **sie kann ~ schwimmen** she can swim by herself *or* on her own; **etw. ~ machen** (herstellen) make sth. oneself; (tun) do sth. oneself; **von ~** (ugs.) by oneself/itself; **das müsstet ihr von ~ wissen** you shouldn't have to be told [that]

C *Adv.* **1** (geh.: ausschließlich) alone; **er ~ trägt die Verantwortung** he alone bears responsibility; it is his responsibility alone; **sie denkt ~ an sich** she thinks solely *or* only of herself; **~ durch den Glauben** by faith alone; only by faith; **nicht ~ ..., sondern auch ...** not only ..., but also ... **2** (von allem anderen abgesehen)

[schon] ~ der Gedanke/[schon] der Gedanke ~: the mere *or* very thought [of it]; **~ die Nebenkosten** the additional costs alone
D *Konj.* (veralt.) however; but; **~, es war zu spät** however, it was too late; it was too late, however

Allein-: ~besitz *der* sole *or* exclusive property; **im ~besitz von jmdm./in jmds. ~besitz sein** be sb.'s sole *or* exclusive property; **~besitzer** *der*, **~besitzerin** *die* sole owner

alleine (ugs.) ▸**allein**

allein-, Allein-: ~erbe *der*, **~erbin** *die* sole heir; **~erziehend** *Adj.* single ‹*mother, father, parent*›; **~erziehende** *der/die; adj. Dekl.* single parent; **~flug** *der* (Flugw.) solo flight; **~gang** *der* **1** (fig.: Tat) independent initiative; **etw. im ~gang tun** do sth. off one's own bat; **2** (Sport) solo run; (Radfahren) solo ride; **die Etappe praktisch im ~gang fahren** be out on one's own for practically the whole stage; **ein Tor im ~gang erzielen** score a goal from a solo run; **3** (Alpinistik) solo ascent *or* climb; **~gesellschafter** *der*, **~gesellschafterin** *die* (Rechtsw.) sole proprietor; **~herrschaft** *die* autocratic rule; (Diktatur) dictatorship; **~herrscher** *der*, **~herrscherin** *die* (auch fig.) autocrat; (Diktator, auch fig.) dictator

alleinig *Adj.* sole; sole, exclusive ‹*distribution rights*›

allein-, Allein-: ~inhaber *der*, **~inhaberin** *die* (Wirtsch.) sole owner; **~lage** *die* isolated situation; **in ~lage** set on its own; (Häuser) on separate plots; **~reisende** *der/die* person travelling alone; **~schuld** *die* sole blame *or* responsibility *no indef. art.*; **~sein** *das* **1** (das Verlassensein) loneliness; **2** (das Ungestörtsein) privacy; **~stehend** *Adj.* ‹*person*› living on his/her own *or* alone; (ledig) single ‹*person*›; **ich bin ~stehend** I live on my own *or* alone/am single; **~stehende** *der/die; adj. Dekl.* person living on his/her own *or* alone; (Ledige[r]) single person; **ich als ~stehender ...** living on my own I .../as a single person I ...; **~unterhalter** *der*, **~unterhalterin** *die* solo entertainer; **~verdiener** *der*, **~verdienerin** *die* sole earner; **~verschulden** *das* ▸**~schuld**; **~vertretung** *die* (Wirtsch.) sole agency; (Politik) sole representation; **~vertretungsanspruch** *der* (Politik) claim to be the sole legitimate representative; **~vertrieb** *der*: **den ~vertrieb von etw. haben/übernehmen** be/become the sole *or* exclusive distributor of sth.; have acquired sole *or* exclusive distribution rights to sth.

alle·mal *Adv.* (ugs.) any time (coll.); **was der kann, das kann ich doch ~:** anything he can do, I can do too; *s. auch* **ein[1] A**

allen·falls *Adv.* **1** (höchstens) at [the] most; at the outside; **~ 40 Leute** 40 people at most *or* at the outside; at most 40 people **2** (nötigenfalls) if need be; if necessary **3** (bestenfalls) at best

allenthalben /'alənt'halbn̩/ *Adv.* (geh.) everywhere

aller-: ~art *indekl. unbest. Gattungsz.*; (veralt.) all kinds *or* sorts of; **~äußerst...** *Adj.* **1** (entferntest) farthest; **2** (größt...) extreme; utmost; **mit ~äußerster Vorsicht** with extreme *or* [the] utmost caution; **3** (schlimmst...) worst; **im ~äußersten Fall** if the worst comes/came to the worst; **~best... A** *Adj.* very best; **~besten Dank** thank you very much indeed; **der/die/das Allerbeste sein** be the best of all; **es wäre das Allerbeste, wenn du ihn selbst fragst** the best thing [of all] would be for you to ask him yourself; **das ist das Allerbeste, was du tun kannst** that's the best thing you can do; **jmdm. das Allerbeste wünschen** wish sb. all the [very] best; **du bist mein Allerbester** you are my darling; **B** *adv.* **am ~besten** best of all; **am ~besten wäre es, wenn ...** the best thing [of all] would be if ...; **~dings A** *Adv.* **1** (einschränkend) though; **es stimmt ~dings, dass ...** it's true though that ...; **2** (zustimmend) [yes,] certainly; **Habe ich dich geweckt? — Allerdings!** Did I wake you up? — You certainly did!; **B** *Partikel* (Anteil nehmend) to be sure; **das war ~dings Pech** that was bad luck, to be sure; **~erst...** *Adj.* **1** (verstärkend: erst...) very first; **der/die/das ~erste** the very first; **als ~erste[r] etw. tun** be the very first to do sth.; **das ~erste, was ich tun muss** the very first thing I must do; **2** (best...) very best; **~frühest... A** *Adj.* very earliest; **B** *adv.* **am ~frühesten** earliest of all; **~frühestens** *Adv.* at the very earliest

allergen (Med.)
A *Adj.* allergenic
B *adv.* **~ wirken** have an allergenic effect

Allergen /alɛr'ge:n/ *das;* **~s, ~e** (Med.) allergen

Allergie /alɛr'gi:/ *die;* **~, ~n** ▸ⓘ **S. 439** (Med.) allergy

Allergiker /a'lɛrgikɐ/ *der;* **~s, ~, Allergikerin** *die;* **~, ~nen** (Med.) allergy sufferer

allergisch
A *Adj.* (Med.) allergic; **eine ~e Reaktion auf etw.** (*Akk.*) (auch fig.) an allergic reaction to sth.; **gegen etw. ~ sein** (auch fig.) be allergic to sth.
B *adv.* **auf etw.** (*Akk.*) **~ reagieren** have an allergic reaction to sth.; **~ auf jmdn./etw. reagieren** (fig.) be allergic to sb./sth.

aller-, Aller-: ~größt... *Adj.* utmost ‹*trouble, care, etc.*›; biggest *or* largest ‹*car, house, town, etc.*› of all; tallest ‹*person*› of all; **am ~größten sein** be [the] biggest *or* largest/tallest of all; **~hand** *indekl. unbest. Gattungsz.* (ugs.) **1** *attr.* all kinds *or* sorts of; **2** *allein stehend* all kinds *or* sorts of things; **das ist ~hand!** (viel) that's a lot; (sehr gut) that's quite something; **das ist ja** *od.* **doch ~hand!** that's just not on (Brit. coll.); that really is the limit (coll.); **~heiligen** *das;* **~~s** (bes. kath. Kirche) All Saints' Day; All Hallows; **~heiligste** *das;* **~~n** **1** (Tempelinneres) inner sanctum; (jüdisch, orth.) holy of holies; (fig.) holy of holies; inner sanctum; **2** (kath. Rel.) Blessed Sacrament; **~herzlichst A** *Adj.* warmest ‹*thanks, greetings, congratulations*›; most cordial ‹*reception, welcome, invitation*›; **B** *adv.* ‹*thank, greet, congratulate*› most warmly; ‹*welcome*› most warmly *or* cordially; **Sie sind ~herzlichst eingeladen ...** you are most cordially invited ...; **~höchst... A** *Adj.* highest ... of all; **der ~höchste Gipfel** the highest peak of all; the topmost peak; **der ~höchste Berg der Welt** the highest mountain in the world; **es ist ~höchste Zeit, dass ...** it really is high time that ...; **am ~höchsten sein** be the highest of all; **die ~höchsten Kreise** the very highest circles; **auf ~höchste Anordnung** on orders from the very top; **der ~höchste** (dichter.) the Most High; **B** *adv.* **am ~höchsten** ‹*fly, jump, etc.*› the highest of all; **~höchstens** *Adv.* at the very most

> **Allerheiligen**
>
> All Saints' Day (1 November), a festival in honour of Christian saints, is a public holiday in Catholic parts of Germany and Austria.

allerlei *indekl. unbest. Gattungsz.* all kinds *or* sorts of; *allein stehend* all kinds *or* sorts of things

Allerlei *das;* **~s, ~s** (Gemisch) potpourri; (Durcheinander) jumble; **Leipziger ~:** 'Leipzig-style' mixed vegetables (*carrots, green beans, peas, celery, kohlrabi, and asparagus*)

aller-, Aller-: ~letzt... *Adj.* **1** (verstärkend) very last; **der/die/das ~letzte** the very last [one]; **2** (drückt Ablehnung aus) most dreadful *or* awful (coll.); **das ist [ja** *od.* **wirklich] das Allerletzte** (ugs.) that [really] is the absolute limit; **3** (~neuest...) very latest; **~liebst** *Adj.* **1** (verstärkend) most favourite; **am ~liebsten besuchte er die Großmutter** best of all he liked to go and see his grandmother; **es wäre mir das Allerliebste** *od.* **am ~liebsten, wenn ...** I should like it best of all if ...; **das Allerliebste, was ich habe** my most favourite *or* treasured possession; **ihr Allerliebster/seine Allerliebste** her/his beloved; **2** (reizend) enchanting; delightful; **~meist** *Adv.* mostly; for the most part; **~meist... A** *Indefinitpron. u. unbest. Zahlw.* **1** (die größte Menge) by far the most *attrib.*; **das ~meiste/am ~meisten** most of all/by far the most; **2** (der größte Teil) **die ~meisten Gäste** the vast majority of the guests; **die ~meiste Zeit** by far the greatest part of the time; **die ~meisten [der Arbeiter** *usw.*] the vast majority [of the workers *etc.*]; **B** *Adv.* **am ~meisten** most of all; **die am ~meisten befahrene Straße** by far the most travelled road; **~mindest...** *Adj.* slightest; least; **das Allermindeste** the very least; **nicht das Allermindeste** absolutely nothing; **nicht im Allermindesten** not in the least *or* slightest; **zum Allermindesten** at the very least; **~nächst... A** *Adj.* very nearest *attrib.*; (räumliche od. zeitliche Reihenfolge ausdrückend) very next *attrib.*; very closest ‹*relatives*›; **in ~nächster Zeit** in the very near future; **am ~nächsten sein** be the nearest of all; **B** *adv.* **am ~nächsten** nearest of all; **~neu[e]st...** *Adj.* very latest *attrib.*; **das Allerneu[e]ste** the very latest; **~nötigst..., ~notwendigst... A** *Adj.* absolutely necessary; **ich habe nur die ~nötigsten** *od.* **~notwendigsten Kleider gepackt** I only packed the clothes that are/were absolutely necessary; **am ~nötigsten** *od.* **~notwendigsten hätte ich ...** what I'm most badly in need of is/are ...; **es am ~nötigsten** *od.* **~notwendigsten haben, etw. zu tun** be most in need of doing sth.; **der hat es am ~nötigsten** *od.* **~notwendigsten!** (ugs.) he's a fine one to talk; **das Allernötigste** what is/was absolutely necessary; **B** *adv.* **am ~nötigsten** ‹*need etc.*› most badly; **~orten** (veralt.), **~orts** *Adv.* (geh.) everywhere; **~schlimmst... A** *Adj.* very worst *attrib.*; **der/die/das Allerschlimmste** *od.* **am ~schlimmsten sein** be the worst of all; **das Allerschlimmste** the worst of all; **sich auf das Allerschlimmste gefasst machen** prepare oneself for the very worst; **B** *adv.* **am ~schlimmsten** worst of all; **~schönst... A** *Adj.* most beautiful *attrib.*; loveliest *attrib.*; (angenehmst...) very nicest *attrib.*; **in ~schönster Harmonie** in perfect harmony; **das Allerschönste, was ich je gesehen habe** the loveliest thing I have ever seen; **das wäre ja noch das Allerschönste** that would beat everything; **B** *adv.* **am ~schönsten war, dass ...** the best thing of all was that ...; **da werden alle Vorurteile aufs Allerschönste bestärkt** (iron.) that's the best possible way of reinforcing everyone's prejudices; **~seelen** *das;* **~~s** (kath. Kirche) All Souls' Day; **~seits** *Adv.* **1** (alle zusammen) **guten Morgen ~seits!** good morning everyone *or* everybody; **2** (überall) on all sides; on every side; **~seits sehr geschätzt sein** be highly regarded by everyone; **~spätestens** *Adv.* at the very latest

> **Allerseelen**
>
> All Souls' Day (2 November) is the day when Catholics remember their dead by visiting cemeteries to pray and place wreaths, flowers and lighted candles on graves. This is often done on the previous day as *Allerseelen* is not a public holiday.

Allerwelts-: ~gesicht/~wort/~mittel nondescript face/hackneyed word/cure-all

Allerwelts·kerl *der* Jack of all trades

Allerwelts·name *der* (ugs.) common or garden name

aller-, Aller-: ~wenigst... A *Adj.* least ... of all; *Pl.* fewest ... of all; **er hat von allen das ~wenigste Geld** *od.* **am ~wenigsten Geld** he has the least money of all; **die ~wenigsten [Menschen] wissen das** very few [people] know that; **das Allerwenigste, was er hätte tun können** the very least he could have done; **B** *adv.* **am ~wenigsten abbekommen/arbeiten** get/work [the] least of all; **das hätte ich von ihm am ~wenigsten erwartet** he's the very last person I would have expected that of; **das am ~wenigsten!** anything but that!; **~wenigstens** *Adv.* at the very least; **~werteste** *der; adj. Dekl.* (ugs. scherzh.) posterior

alles ▸**all**

alle·samt *Indefinitpron. u. unbest. Zahlw.* (ugs.) all [of you/us/them]; **wir ~:** all of us; we all

Alles-: **~brenner** *der* multi-fuel stove; **~fresser** *der* omnivore; **~kleber** *der* all-purpose adhesive *or* glue; **~könner** *der*, **~könnerin** *die* all-rounder; **~wisser** *der*; **~~s**, **~~**; **~wisserin** *die*; **~~**, **~~nen** (abwertend) know-all

alle·zeit *Adv.* (veralt.) ▸**allzeit**

all-, All-: **~fällig** (bes. österr., schweiz.) **A** *Adj.* possible; **~fällige Verluste** any losses which may occur; **Allfälliges** miscellaneous; (Tagesordnungspunkt) any other business; **B** *adv.* **~fällig anfallende Portokosten/~fällig vorkommende Ausnahmen** any postal charges/exceptions which may arise; **~gegenwart** *die* (christl. Theol., fig.) omnipresence; **~gegenwärtig** *Adj.* (christl. Theol., fig.) omnipresent

all·gemein

A *Adj.* general; universal ‹*conscription, suffrage*›; universally applicable ‹*law, rule*›; **auf ~en Wunsch** by popular *or* general request; **zur ~en Überraschung** to everyone's *or* everybody's surprise; **das ~e Wohl** the common good; **im ~en Interesse** in the common interest; in everybody's interest; **~e Redensarten** common expressions; **vom Allgemeinen auf das Besondere schließen** infer the particular from the general; **im Allgemeinen** in general; generally

B *adv.* [1] (überall, allerseits, von allen) generally; (generell, ausnahmslos) universally; **es ist ~ üblich, das zu tun** it is [the] common practice to do it; **~ verbreitet** widespread; **es ist ~ bekannt, dass ...** it is common knowledge that ...; **~ gängig** common; **~ zugänglich** open to all *or* everybody; **~ gültige Regeln** universally *or* generally applicable rules; **eine ~ gültige Definition/These** a universally *or* generally valid definition/thesis; **etw. ~ gültig formulieren** formulate sth. in universally *or* generally applicable terms; **~ verbindlich** universally binding; **~ verständlich** comprehensible *or* intelligible to all *postpos.*; readily comprehensible *or* intelligible; **es wird ~ diskutiert** it is being discussed by people at large; **wird das ~ gewünscht?** is that the general wish? [2] (nicht speziell, oft abwertend: unverbindlich) ‹*write, talk, discuss, examine, be worded*› in general terms; **eine ~ gehaltene Einführung** a general introduction; **das kann man nicht so ~ behaupten** one cannot generalize like that [3] (umfassend); **~ belesen/beschlagen sein** be well read/be knowledgeable about a wide range of subjects; **~ interessiert sein** have a wide range of interests

allgemein-, Allgemein-: **~befinden** *das* (Med.) general state of health; general condition; **~begriff** *der* (Philos., Sprachw.) general concept; **~besitz** *der* (auch fig.) common property; **~bildend** *Adj.* ‹*school, course, etc.*› providing a general *or* an all-round *or* (Amer.) all-around education; **das Zeitunglesen für ~bildend halten** hold that reading newspapers is of general educational value; **~bildung** *die* general *or* all-round *or* (Amer.) all-around education; ***~gültig** ▸**allgemein B1**; **~gültigkeit** *die* universal *or* general applicability/validity; **~gut** *das* (fig.) common knowledge

Allgemeinheit *die*; **~**, **~en** [1] (Öffentlichkeit) general public; public at large [2] (Unverbindlichkeit) generality [3] *Pl.* (Äußerungen) generalities

allgemein-, Allgemein-: **~interesse** *das* public interest; **~medizin** *die* general medicine; **~mediziner** *der*, **~medizinerin** *die* general practitioner; GP; **~platz** *der* platitude; commonplace; ***~verbindlich**, ***~verständlich** ▸**allgemein B1**; **~wissen** *das* general knowledge; **~wohl** *das* public welfare *or* good

all-, All-: **~gewalt** *die* (geh.) omnipotence; **~gewaltig** *Adj.* (geh.) omnipotent; all-powerful; **der Allgewaltige** the Almighty; **~gütig** *Adj.* all-gracious; **~heil·mittel** *das* (auch fig.) cure-all; panacea; universal remedy

Allianz /a'li̯ants/ *die*; **~**, **~en** alliance

Alligator /ali'ga:tɔr/ *der*; **~s**, **~en** /ga'to:rən/ alligator

alliieren /ali'i:rən/ *refl. V.* form an alliance; **sich mit jmdm. ~**: ally oneself with sb.

alliiert *Adj.* allied

Alliierte *der*; *adj. Dekl.* ally; **die ~n** the Allies

Alliteration /alıtera'tsi̯o:n/ *die*; **~**, **~en** (Verslehre) alliteration

all-, All-: **~jährlich** **A** *Adj.* annual; yearly; **B** *adv.* annually; every year; **~macht** *die* (geh.) omnipotence; **~mächtig** *Adj.* omnipotent; all-powerful; **der ~mächtige Gott** Almighty God; **~mächtiger Gott!** (ugs.) good God!; heavens above!; **~mächtige** *der*; *adj. Dekl.* **der ~mächtige** Almighty God; the Almighty; **~mächtiger!** good God!; heavens above!

all·mählich

A *Adv.* gradually; **es wird ~ Zeit** it's about time; **ich werde ~ müde** I'm beginning to get tired; **wir sollten ~ gehen** it's time we got going

B *adj.* gradual

Allmende /al'mɛndə/ *die*; **~**, **~n** common land

all-: **~monatlich** **A** *Adj.* monthly; **B** *adv.* monthly; every month; **~morgendlich** **A** *Adj.* regular morning; **B** *adv.* every morning; **~nächtlich** **A** *Adj.* nightly; **B** *adv.* nightly; every night

Allonge·perücke /a'lõ:ʒə-/ *die* full-bottomed wig

allo-, Allo-: **~path** /-'pa:t/ *der*; **~~en**, **~~en** allopath; **~pathie** /-pa'ti:/ *die*; **~~**: allopathy; **~pathin** *die*; **~~**, **~~nen** allopath; **~pathisch** **A** *Adj.* allopathic; **B** *adv.* allopathically; **~phon** *das*; **~~s**, **~~e** (Sprachw.) allophone

Allotria /a'lo:tria/ *das*; **~s** *od. Pl.* skylarking; **~ treiben** skylark; lark about (coll.)

All-: **~parteien·regierung** *die* all-party government; **~rad·antrieb** *der* (Kfz-W.) all-wheel drive; **~rad·fahrzeug** *das* four-by-four

Allround- /'ɔ:l'raʊnd-/ all-round; all-around (Amer.)

Allround·man /ɔ:l'raʊndmən/ *der*; **~s**, **Allroundmen** /'ɔ:l'raʊndmən/ all-rounder

all-, All-: **~seitig** **A** *Adj.* [1] (allgemein) general; all-round, (Amer.) all-around *attrib.*; **zur ~seitigen Zufriedenheit** to the satisfaction of all *or* everyone; [2] (umfassend) comprehensive; **eine ~seitige Ausbildung** an all-round *or* (Amer.) all-around education; **B** *adv.* [1] (allgemein) generally; **man war ~seitig einverstanden** there was agreement on all sides *or* general agreement; **~seitig geachtet** highly regarded by everyone; [2] (umfassend) comprehensively; **~seitig gebildet sein** have had an all-round *or* (Amer.) all-around education; **~seitig begabt/interessiert sein** have all-round *or* (Amer.) all-around talents/interests; **~seits** *Adv.* everywhere; on all sides; (in jeder Hinsicht) in all respects; in every respect; **~seits geschätzt** highly regarded by everyone; **~strom·gerät** *das* (Elektrot.) AC/DC appliance; **~stündlich** **A** *Adj.* hourly; **B** *adv.* hourly; every hour

All·tag *der* [1] (Werktag) weekday; **ein Mantel für den ~**: a coat for everyday wear; **zum ~ gehören** (fig.) be part of everyday life [2] (Einerlei) daily routine; **der graue ~**: the dull routine of everyday life; **der ~ der Ehe** the day-to-day realities of married life; **morgen geht der graue ~ wieder los** it's back to the daily grind tomorrow

all·täglich

A *Adj.* [1] /-'--/ (gewöhnlich) ordinary ‹*face, person, appearance, etc.*›; everyday ‹*topic, event, sight*›; commonplace ‹*remark*›; **ein nicht ~er Anblick** a sight one doesn't see every day; **etw. Alltägliches sein** be an everyday occurrence; **es ist nichts Alltägliches, wenn ...** it's not every day that ...; it doesn't happen every day that ... [2] (werktäglich) everyday, workaday *attrib.* ‹*clothes*› [3] /'-'--/ (täglich) daily

B *adv.* [1] (werktäglich) [on] weekdays [2] /'-'--/ (täglich) daily; every day

Alltäglichkeit *die*; **~**, **~en** [1] (das Alltäglichsein) ordinariness [2] (Gewohnheit) **eine ~ sein/zur ~ werden** be/become routine *or* commonplace [3] (alltäglicher Vorgang) everyday occurrence

all·tags *Adv.* [on] weekdays

Alltags- everyday *attrib.*; of everyday life *postpos., not pred.*; **~pflicht** daily duty

alltags, Alltags-: **~kleidung** *die* everyday *or* workaday clothes *pl.*; **~kultur** *die* everyday culture; **~mensch** *der* ordinary person; **~sprache** *die* (Sprachw.) everyday language; **~tauglich** *Adj.* suitable for everyday use *postpos.*; **~trott** *der* (abwertend) daily round *or* grind; **jetzt geht der ~trott wieder los** now it's back to the daily grind

all·um·fassend

A *Adj.* all-embracing; encyclopedic ‹*knowledge*›

B *adv.* ‹*plan, inform*› in comprehensive detail; **~ gebildet sein** have had an all-round *or* (Amer.) all-around education

Allüren /a'ly:rən/ *Pl.* (meist abwertend) behaviour *sing.*; (geziertes Benehmen) affectations; airs and graces

Alluvium /a'lu:vi̯ʊm/ *das*; **~s** (Geol.) Holocene epoch

all-, All-: **~wetter·straße** *die* all-weather road; **~wissend** *Adj.* omniscient; **er tut, als wäre er ~wissend** he acts as if he knew everything; **~wissenheit** *die*; **~~**: omniscience; **~wöchentlich** **A** *Adj.* weekly; **B** *adv.* weekly; every week; **~zeit** *Adv.* (veralt.) always; **~zeit bereit!** be prepared!

Allzeit-: **~hoch** *das* (Wirtsch.) all-time high; **auf ~hoch** at an all-time high; **~tief** *das* (Wirtsch.) all-time low; **auf ~tief** at an all-time low

all·zu *Adv.* all too; **er war nicht ~ begeistert** he was not too *or* not all that enthusiastic; **nicht ~ viele** not all that many (coll.); not too many; **kein ~ großes Gewicht** not too heavy a weight; **~ viele Fehler** far too many mistakes; **~ bald** all too soon; **~ früh** all too early; (**~** bald) all too soon; **nicht ~ früh** not too early; **etw. ~ gern mögen** like sth. only too much; **etw. ~ gern tun** do sth. only too willingly; **ich möchte es doch ~ gern machen** I would be only too pleased *or* delighted to do it; **ich esse zwar Fisch, aber nicht ~ gern** I'll eat fish but I'm not all that fond (coll.) *or* not overfond of it; **~ lange** too long; **~ oft** too often; **nicht ~ oft** not too often; not all that often (coll.); **~ sehr** too much; **~ sehr enttäuscht/begeistert** only too disappointed/enthusiastic; **nicht ~ sehr** not too much; not all that much (coll.); **etw. ~ sehr/nicht ~ sehr mögen** like sth. all too much/not like sth. too much *or* (coll.) all that much; **nicht ~ sehr interessiert** not too *or* (coll.) not all that interested; **ich habe mich ~ sehr/nicht ~ sehr bemüht** I tried only too hard/did not try too hard; **~ viel** too much; **~ viel ist ungesund** one should never overdo things; you can have too much of a good thing

All·zweck- multi-purpose

All·zweck-: **~halle** *die* multi-purpose hall; **~tuch** *das*; *Pl.* **~tücher** multi-purpose *or* all-purpose cloth; **~waffe** *die* (ugs.) universal secret weapon

Alm /alm/ *die*; **~**, **~en** mountain pasture; Alpine pasture

Alm·ab·trieb *der*: *driving of the cattle down from the mountain pastures in autumn*

Almanach /'almanax/ *der*; **~s**, **~e** (Buchw.) (hist.) almanac; (eines Verlages) yearbook (*containing a selection from the firm's publications during the year*)

Alm-: **~auf·trieb** *der*: *driving of the cattle up to the mountain pastures in spring*; **~hütte** *die* Alpine hut

Almosen /'almo:zn̩/ *das*; **~s**, **~** [1] (veralt.: Spende) alms *pl.*; **von ~ leben** live on charity [2] (abwertend: dürftiges Entgelt) pittance

Alm-: **~rausch** *der* (österr., südd.) Alpine rose; alpenrose; **~wirtschaft** *die* Alpine farming *no art.*

Aloe /'a:loe/ *die*; **~**, **~n** aloe

Aloe vera /'a:loe 've:ra/ *die*; **~~**, **~~s** aloe vera

a

Alp[1] /alp/ *die;* ~, ~**en** (bes. schweiz.) ▸**Alm**

*__Alp__[2] ▸**Alb**[2]

Alpaka[1] /al'paka/ *das;* ~**s**, ~**s** (Lama, Wolle) alpaca

Alpaka[2] *der;* ~**s** (Gewebe) alpaca

Alpaka[3] *das;* ~**s** (veralt.: Neusilber) German silver; nickel silver

Alpaka·wolle *die* alpaca wool

Alp-: ~**druck** ▸**Albdruck**; ~**drücken** ▸**Albdrücken**

Alpen *Pl.* **die** ~: the Alps

Alpen- Alpine

alpen-, Alpen-: ~**dollar** *der* (scherzh.) [Austrian] schilling; ~**glühen** *das;* ~~**s** alpenglow; ~**jäger** *Pl.* (Milit.) Alpine Troops; ~**land** *das* Alpine country *or* region; ~**ländisch** /-lɛndɪʃ/ *Adj.* ‹*music, customs, dances*› of the Alpine region; ‹*goods*› from the Alpine region; ~**pass**, *~**paß** *der* Alpine pass; ~**republik** *die* (ugs.) Alpine Republic (Austria or Switzerland); ~**rose** *die* rhododendron; Alpine rose; ~**veilchen** *das* cyclamen; ~**vorland** *das* foothills *pl.* of the Alps

Alpha /'alfa/ *das;* ~**[s]**, ~**[s]** alpha

Alphabet /alfa'be:t/ *das;* ~**[e]s**, ~**e** alphabet

alphabetisch
[A] *Adj.* alphabetical
[B] *adv.* alphabetically; **etw. ~ ordnen** arrange sth. in alphabetical order *or* alphabetically

alphabetisieren *tr. V.* [1] (ordnen) arrange in alphabetical order *or* alphabetically; alphabetize [2] (lesen u. schreiben lehren) **jmdn. ~:** teach sb. to read and write

Alphabetisierung *die;* ~ [1] (das Ordnen) alphabetization [2] (das Lehren) teaching literacy skills; **eine Kampagne zur ~ der Bevölkerung** a campaign against illiteracy in the population

alpha·numerisch (DV)
[A] *Adj.* alphanumeric
[B] *adv.* alphanumerically

Alpha-: ~**strahlen** *Pl.* (Kernphysik) alpha rays; ~**teilchen** *das* (Kernphysik) alpha particle; ~**tier** *das* (Verhaltensf.) alpha male; (fig.) top dog

Alp·horn *das* alpenhorn

alpin /al'pi:n/ *Adj.* [1] Alpine; ~**e Kombination** (Ski) Alpine combined [event] [2] (Bergsteigen) mountaineering

Alpinismus *der;* ~: Alpinism *no art.*

Alpinist *der;* ~**en**, ~**en** Alpinist

Alpinistik *die;* ~: Alpinism *no art.*

Alpinistin *die;* ~, ~**nen** Alpinist

alpinistisch *Adj.* mountaineering *attrib.*

Älpler /'ɛlplɐ/ *der;* ~**s**, ~, **Älplerin** *die;* ~, ~**nen** inhabitant of the Alps

Alp·traum ▸**Albtraum**

Alraune /al'raunə/ *die;* ~, ~**n** mandrake

als[1] *Konj.* [1] (zeitlich) when; (während) as; ~ **wir zu Hause ankamen, [da] fing es an zu regnen** when *or* after we had arrived home, it started to rain; **gleich ~:** as soon as; **damals, ~:** [in the days] when; **gerade ~:** just as; **gerade ~ Tante Ida hier war** just when Aunt Ida was here [2] (nach Komp.) than; **mehr/weniger ~:** more/less than; **mehr ~ arbeiten kann ich nicht** I can't do more than work [3] (bei Vergleichen) **niemand/nirgends anders ~:** nobody/nowhere but; **mir fehlt nichts weiter, ~ dass ...** there is nothing wrong with me other than that ...; **sie arbeiten mit anderen Methoden ~ wir** they work with different methods from ours; **alles andere ~:** anything but; **kein anderer** *od.* **niemand anderes ~ Karl** none other than Karl; **anders ~ wir sein/leben** be different/live differently from us; **so viel/so weit ~ möglich** as much/as far as possible; **so bald/schnell ~ möglich** as soon/as quickly as possible; *s. auch* **sowohl** [4] (bei Modalsätzen) as if; as though; ~ **ob** *od.* **wenn** as if; as though; ~ **ob ich das nicht wüsste!** as if I didn't know; ~ **ob das neu wäre!** as if that were something new [5] (in der Eigenschaft) as; ~ **Rentner/Arzt** as a pensioner/a doctor; **sich ~ Held fühlen** feel oneself [to be] a hero; **sich ~ wahr/falsch erweisen** prove [to be] true/false; **in seiner/ihrer Eigenschaft ~ ...** in his/her capacity as ... [6] (eine Folge ausdrückend) **die Kinder sind zu klein, ~ dass sie das verstehen könnten** the children are too young to understand that; **die Zeit war zu kurz, ~ dass wir ...** time was too short for us to ... [7] (einen Grund ausdrückend) **umso ..., ~ ...** all the more ... since *or* in that ... [8] (veralt.: vor Aufzählungen) ~ **[da sind]** to wit; namely; *s. auch* **insofern**

als[2] *Adv.* (westmd.) [1] (immer) ~ **etw. tun** keep on doing sth.; **gehen Sie ~ geradeaus** keep going straight on *or* ahead [2] (manchmal) sometimes

als-: ~**bald** *Adv.* (geh. veralt.) (sogleich) immediately; at once; (kurz danach) soon; ~**baldig** *Adj.* (Papierdt.) immediate; **„zum ~baldigen Verbrauch bestimmt"** 'for immediate consumption'; ~**dann** *Adv.* (geh. veralt.) then

also /'alzo/
[A] *Adv.* [1] (folglich) so; therefore; ~ **kommst du mit?** so you're coming too?; you're coming too, then? [2] (veralt.: so) thus
[B] *Partikel* [1] (das heißt) that is [2] (nach Unterbrechung) well [then]; ~, **wie ich schon sagte** well [then], as I was saying [3] (verstärkend): ~, **kommst du jetzt oder nicht?** well, are you coming now or not?; **na ~!** there you are[, you see]; ~ **schön** well all right then; ~ **so was/nun!** well, I don't know; well, really; ~, **so eine Frechheit** well, what a cheek; ~, **gute Nacht** goodnight then; ~ **dann** right then

Als-ob *das;* ~ (Philos.) **die Philosophie des ~:** the philosophy of 'as-if'

alt /alt/, **älter** /'ɛltɐ/, **ältest...** /'ɛltəst.../ *Adj.* [1] ▸❶ **S. 29** old; **Alt und Jung** old and young; **seine ~en Eltern** his aged parents; **hier werde ich nicht ~** (fig. ugs.) I won't be staying here long; **das Alte Testament** the Old Testament; **die Alte Welt** the Old World; ~ **aussehen** (fig. salopp) be in the cart (sl.); **eine drei Jahre ~e Tochter** a three-year-old daughter; **wie ~ bist du?** how old are you?; **man ist so ~, wie man sich fühlt** you're only as old as you feel; **aus Alt mach Neu** give your coat/furniture *etc.* a new lease of life; **immer die ~e Platte** *od.* **Leier** it's always the same old story; *s. auch* **Dame**; **Eisen**; **Hase**; **Herr** [2] (nicht mehr frisch) old; ~**es Brot** stale bread [3] (vom letzten Jahr) old; ~**e Äpfel/Kartoffeln** last year's apples/potatoes; **im ~en Jahr** (dieses Jahr) this year; (letztes Jahr) last year [4] (seit langem bestehend) ancient; old; **ein ~es Volk/ein ~er Brauch** an ancient people/an ancient *or* old custom; **eine ~e Freundschaft** a long-standing friendship; **in ~er Freundschaft, dein ...** yours, as ever, ... [5] (langjährig) long-standing ‹*acquaintance*›; long-serving ‹*employee*› [6] (antik, klassisch) ancient [7] (vertraut) old familiar ‹*streets, sights, etc.*›; **ganz der/die Alte sein** be just the same; **es bleibt alles beim Alten** things will stay as they were; **das ist nicht das ~e Prag** it's not the old Prague I/we *etc.* knew; **alles geht seinen ~en Gang** everything goes on just as before [8] (ugs.) (vertraulich) ~**er Freund/~es Haus!** old friend/pal (coll.); (bewundernd) **ein ~er Fuchs/Gauner** an old fox/rascal; (verstärkend) **die ~e Hexe/der ~e Geizkragen** the old witch/skinflint

Alt[1] *der;* ~**s**, ~**e** (Musik) [1] (Stimmlage) alto; (Frauenstimme) contralto; alto [2] (im Chor) altos *pl.*; contraltos *pl.* [3] (Sängerin) contralto; alto

Alt[2] *das;* ~**[s]**, ~: *top fermented, dark beer*

Alt·achtundsechziger *der,* **Alt·achtundsechzigerin** *die* former 1968 rebel

Altan /al'ta:n/ *der;* ~**[e]s**, ~**e** (Archit.) balcony

Altar /al'ta:ɐ̯/ *der;* ~**[e]s**, **Altäre** /al'tɛ:rə/ altar; **eine Frau zum ~ führen** (geh.) lead a woman to the altar; **jmdn./etw. auf dem ~ des Vaterlands opfern** (fig.) sacrifice sb./sth. for one's country

Altar-: ~**bild** *das* altarpiece; ~**gerät** *das* altar furniture; ~**raum** *der* chancel

alt-, Alt-: ~**backen** *Adj.* [1] (trocken) stale ‹*bread, roll, etc.*›; [2] (abwertend: altmodisch) outdated ‹*ideas, views, policies*›; old-fashioned ‹*clothes*›; ~**bau** *der; Pl.* ~~**ten** old building; ~**bauer** *der;* ~~**n**, ~~**n** old farmer; ~**bäuerin** *die* old farmer's wife; ~**bau·wohnung** *die* flat (esp. Brit.) *or* (esp. Amer.) apartment in an old building; old flat (esp. Brit.) *or* (esp. Amer.) apartment; ~**bekannt** *Adj.* well-known; ~**bewährt** *Adj.* well-tried; long-standing ‹*tradition, acquaintanceship*›; ~**bier** *das: top fermented, dark beer;* ~**bundes·kanzler** *der* former Federal Chancellor; ~**bundes·präsident** *der* former Federal President; ~**christlich** *Adj.* early Christian; ~**deutsch** *Adj.* old German; German Renaissance ‹*painting, art, etc.*›

Alte[1] *der; adj. Dekl.* [1] (alter Mann) old man; **komischer ~r** (Theater) comic old man [2] (salopp) (Vater, Ehemann) old man (coll.); (Chef) governor (coll.); boss (coll.) [3] (österr.: Wein) *fully fermented wine*

Alte[2] *die; adj. Dekl.* [1] (alte Frau) old woman; **komische ~** (Theater) comic old woman [2] (salopp) (Mutter) old woman (coll.); (Ehefrau) missis (coll.); old woman (coll.); (Chefin) boss (coll.)

Alte[3] *das; adj. Dekl.* **am ~n hängen** cling to the past; ~**s und Neues** the old and the new; **er kann nichts ~s wegwerfen** he cannot throw anything old away

Alte[4] *Pl.; adj. Dekl.* [1] (alte Menschen) old people [2] **die ~n** (salopp: Eltern) my/his *etc.* old man and old woman (coll.); (Zool.: Tiereltern) the parents; (geh.: Menschen der Antike) the ancients

alt-, Alt-: ~**ehrwürdig** *Adj.* (geh.) venerable; time-honoured ‹*customs*›; ~**eingeführt** *Adj.* old-established; ~**eingesessen** *Adj.* old-established; ~**eingesessene** *der/die; adj. Dekl.* old-established inhabitant; ~**eisen** *das* scrap iron; ~**englisch** *Adj.* Old English

Alten-: ~**heim** *das* old people's home; old-age home (Amer.); ~**pfleger** *der,* ~**pflegerin** *die* ▸❶ **S. 113** geriatric nurse; ~**residenz** *die* old people's home; ~**tages·stätte** *die* old people's day centre; ~**teil** *das: portion of farm property and certain rights retained by a farmer on handing over to his successor;* **sich aufs ~teil zurückziehen** (fig.) retire; **jmdn. aufs ~teil setzen** (fig.) send sb. into retirement; ~**wohnheim** *das* old people's home

älter /'ɛltɐ/
[A] ▸**alt**
[B] *Adj.* (nicht mehr jung) elderly; **eine Melodie für unsere ~en Hörer** a tune for our older listeners; *s. auch* **Mitbürger**

Alter *das;* ~**s**, ~ ▸❶ **S. 29** [1] age; (hohes ~) old age; **im ~:** in one's old age; **mit dem ~:** with age; **er ist in meinem ~:** he is my age; **in meinem ~ wirst du sehen, dass ...** when you are my age you will see that ...; **im ~ von** at the age of; **eine Frau mittleren ~s** a middle-aged woman; **Kinder in diesem ~:** children of this age; ~ **schützt vor Torheit nicht** (Spr.) there's no fool like an old fool (prov.) [2] (alte Menschen) old people *no art.* [3] (Menschen einer Altersstufe) age group

Alterchen *das;* ~**s**, ~ (ugs.) grandad (coll.)

Ältere *der/die; adj. Dekl.* [1] (älterer Mensch) older person/man/woman; **für uns ~:** for us older people [2] (bei Namen) elder; **Hans Holbein der ~:** Hans Holbein the Elder

Alter Ego /'altɐ 'e:go/ *das;* ~ ~ (Psych.; geh.: Freund) alter ego

altern
[A] *itr. V.; mit sein* [1] (älter werden) age [2] (reifen) mature
[B] *tr. V.* (alt machen) age, mature ‹*wine, spirits*›

alternativ /altɛrna'ti:f/
[A] *Adj.* (auch: Industriekultur usw. ablehnend) alternative
[B] *adv.* [1] (die Wahl lassend) alternatively [2] (Industriekultur ablehnend) ‹*work, farm*› using alternative methods; ~ **leben/einkaufen** adopt an alternative life style/do one's shopping in alternative shops

Alternativ·bewegung *die* alternative movement

Alternative[1] *die;* ~, ~**n** alternative; **jmdn. vor die ~ stellen, mehr Miete zu zahlen oder auszuziehen** give sb. the alternative of either paying more rent or moving out

ℹ Altersangaben

Wie alt?

Wie alt ist sie?
= How old is she?, What age is she?
Sie ist vierzig [Jahre alt]
= She is forty [years old] *od.* (*formeller*) forty years of age
Er ist gerade sechzig geworden
= He has just turned sixty
im Alter von zwanzig Jahren, mit zwanzig
= at the age of twenty, at twenty
ein Fünfzigjähriger
= a fifty-year-old [man], a man of fifty
eine Fünfzigjährige
= a fifty-year-old [woman], a woman of fifty
ein zehnjähriges Mädchen
= a ten-year-old girl
ein achtzigjähriger Rentner
= an eighty-year-old pensioner

Älter oder jünger?

Ich bin älter als du
= I'm older than you [are]
Sie ist viel jünger als er
= She's much younger than him *od.* than he is
Er ist vier Jahre älter als ich
= He's four years older than me *od.* (*formeller*) four years my senior
Du bist zwanzig Jahre jünger als sie
= You're twenty years younger than her *od.* (*formeller*) twenty years her junior
Sie sind gleich alt od. gleichaltrig
= They are the same age
Sie ist [genau] so alt wie Martin
= She is [just] the same age as Martin

Ungefähres Alter

Er ist um die fünfzig
= He's about fifty
Sie ist etwas über sechzig
= She's just over *od.* a little over sixty
Er wird bald vierzig
= He'll soon be forty, He's nearly forty
Sie geht auf die siebzig zu
= She's getting on for seventy
Sie sind in den Sechzigern
= They're in their sixties
Er ist Ende/Anfang/Mitte dreißig
= He's in his late thirties/early thirties/mid-thirties
Er ist noch ein Teenager
= He is still a teenager *od.* in his teens
Er ist gerade zehn geworden
= He's just ten
Das Kind ist noch keine zehn Jahre alt
= The child is barely ten years old
für Kinder unter zwölf [Jahren]
= for the under-twelves *od.* under-12s
für alle über sechzig
= for the over-sixties *od.* over-60s
Sie fühlt sich/sieht aus wie zwanzig
= She feels/looks like twenty

Alternative² *der/die; adj. Dekl.* supporter of the alternative society

Alternativ-: ~energie *die* alternative energy; **~kultur** *die* alternative culture

alternieren *itr. V.* alternate

alt·erprobt *Adj.* well-tried

alters *in* **seit ~, von ~ her** (geh.) from time immemorial

alters-, Alters-: ~ab·stand *der* age difference; **~angabe** *die* details *pl.* of one's age; **[nicht] zur ~angabe verpflichtet sein** [not] be obliged to give one's age; **~armut** *die* old-age poverty; **~aufbau** *der* age structure; **~bedingt** **A** *Adj.* occurring at a particular age *postpos., not pred.*; (im hohen Alter) due to *or* caused by old age *postpos.*; **B** *adv.* in relation to [one's/its] age; (durch hohes Alter) as a result of old age; **~beschwerden** *Pl.* complaints of old age; **~demenz** *die;* ▸ℹ **S. 439** **~~, ~~en** (Med.) senile dementia; **~erscheinung** *die* sign of old age; **~fleck** *der* age spot; liver spot; **~gemäß** **A** *Adj.* ‹*behaviour, education, etc.*› appropriate to one's/its age; **B** *adv.* in a manner appropriate to one's/its age; **das Kind entwickelt sich/spielt ~gemäß** the child is developing/playing as it should at its age; **~genosse** *der,* **~genossin** *die* contemporary; person/child of the same age; **meine ~genossen** my contemporaries; people of my age; **er ist ein ~genosse von mir** he is the same age as I am; he is my age; **~grenze** *die* age limit; (für Rente) retirement age; **~gründe** *Pl.* reasons of age; **~gruppe** *die* age group; **~heim** *das* old people's home; old-age home (Amer.); **~herz** *das* ▸ℹ **S. 439** (Med.) *heart which has undergone physiological changes due to old age;* **~jahr** *das* (schweiz.) ▸**Lebensjahr**; **~klasse** *die* (bes. Sport) age group; **~leiden** *das* complaint of old age; **~los** *Adj.* ageless; **~mäßig** **A** *Adj.* according to age *postpos., not pred.*; **B** *adv.* (dem Alter nach) according to age; (in Bezug auf das Alter) as far as age is concerned; **~präsident** *der,* **~präsidentin** *die* president by seniority; **der ~präsident des Bundestages** the oldest member of the Bundestag, acting as president; **~rente** *die* old-age pension; **~ruhegeld** *das* retirement pension; **~schwach** *Adj.* old and infirm ‹*person*›; old and weak ‹*animal*›; [old and] decrepit ‹*object*›; **~schwäche** *die* (bei Menschen) [old] age and infirmity; (bei Tieren) [old] age and weakness; (von Dingen) [age and] decrepitude; **~sicherung** *die* provision for one's old age; **~sichtig** *Adj.* presbyopic (Med.); **~sichtigkeit** *die* ▸ℹ **S. 439** presbyopia (Med.); **~sitz** *der* retirement home; **er wählte Genf als seinen ~sitz** he chose to spend his retirement in Geneva; **~starrsinn** *der* obstinacy of old age; **~stil** *der* later style; **~stufe** *die* age; **~unterschied** *der* age difference; **~versorgung** *die* provision for one's old age; **gibt es hier eine betriebliche ~versorgung?** do you have a pension scheme here?; **~verwirrt** *Adj.* suffering from senile dementia *postpos.*; **~vorsorge** *die* pension provision; **eine betriebliche ~vorsorge** a company pension scheme; **eine private ~vorsorge** a personal pension plan; **~werk** *das* later work; (Gesamtheit) later works *pl.*

Altertum *das;* **~s, Altertümer** /-ty:mɐ/ **1** antiquity *no art.*; **das deutsche ~:** early German history **2** *Pl.* (antike Kunstgegenstände) antiquities

Altertümelei *die;* **~, ~en** archaism

altertümeln /ˈaltɐty:mḷn/ *itr. V.* archaize

altertümlich
A *Adj.* ancient ‹*building, monument, etc.*›; old-fashioned ‹*dress, handwriting, etc.*›; antiquated, old-fashioned ‹*appliance, device, vehicle, etc.*›
B *adv.* ‹*dress, furnish, decorate*› in an old-fashioned style; ‹*work, function, etc.*› in an antiquated manner

Altertümlichkeit *die;* **~** ▸**altertümlich**: ancientness; old-fashionedness; antiquatedness

Altertums-: ~forscher *der,* **~forscherin** *die* archaeologist; **~forschung** *die,* **~kunde** *die* archaeology *no art.*; **~wert** *der: in* **~wert haben** have antique value

Alterung *die;* **~, ~en** **1** (das Altwerden) ageing **2** (von Werkstoffen) ageing; (von Legierungen) ageing; age-hardening **3** (von Wein usw.) ageing; maturing

Alterungs-prozess, ***Alterungs·prozeß** *der* ageing process

Älteste /ˈɛltəstə/ *der/die; adj. Dekl.* **1** (Dorf~, Vereins~, Kirchen~ usw.) elder **2** (Sohn, Tochter) eldest

Ältesten·rat *der* **1** (Bundesrepublik Deutschland) *all-party parliamentary committee, which assists the Bundestag President in carrying out his duties and in regulating parliamentary business* **2** (Völkerk.) council of elders

alt-, Alt-: ~flöte *die* (Querflöte) alto *or* bass flute; (Blockflöte) alto *or* treble recorder; **~fränkisch** (ugs. scherzh.) **A** *Adj.* old-fashioned; **B** *adv.* in an old-fashioned way; **~französisch** *das* Old French; **~gedient** *Adj.* long-serving; **~glas** *das* waste glass; (Flaschen) empty bottles; **zum ~glas kommen** go to the bottle bank; **~glas·behälter** *der* bottle bank; **~glas·container** *der* bottle bank; **~gold** *das* old gold; **~griechisch** *Adj.* ancient Greek; (Ling.) classical *or* ancient Greek; *s. auch* **deutsch, Deutsch, Deutsche**²; **~griechisch** *das* classical *or* ancient Greek; **~handel** *der* second-hand trade; **~hergebracht** *Adj.* traditional; **~herren·mannschaft** *die* (Sport): *team of players over thirty-two;* ≈ over-thirties' team; **~hochdeutsch** *Adj.* Old High German; **~hochdeutsch** *das* Old High German

Altist *der;* **~en, ~en** (Musik) alto

Altistin *die;* **~, ~nen** (Musik) alto; contralto

alt-, Alt-: ~jüngferlich /-jʏŋfɐlɪç/ **A** *Adj.* old-maidish; **B** *adv.* like an old maid/old maids; **~kanzler** *der* former Chancellor; ex-Chancellor; **~katholik** *der,* **~katholikin** *die* Old Catholic; **~katholisch** *Adj.* Old Catholic; **~kleider·sammlung** *die* collection of old clothes; **~klug; ~kluger, ~klugst...** **A** *Adj.* precocious; **B** *adv.* precociously; **~klugheit** *die* precociousness; **~lage** *die* (Musik) alto range; **in der ~lage singen** be an alto; **~last** **1** (Ökologie) old, improperly disposed of harmful waste *no indef. art.*; **2** (fig.) inherited problem; **eine ~last aus den 60er-Jahren** a hangover from the sixties

ältlich /ˈɛltlɪç/ *Adj.* rather elderly; oldish

alt-, Alt-: ~material *das* scrap; **~meister** *der* **1** (Vorbild) doyen; **2** (Sport) ex-champion; former champion; **~meisterin** *die* **1** (Vorbild) doyenne; **2** (Sport) ex-champion; former champion; **~metall** *das* scrap metal; **~modisch** **A** *Adj.* old-fashioned; **B** *adv.* in an old-fashioned way; **~öl** *das* used oil; **~papier** *das* waste paper; **~partie** *die* (Musik) alto part; **~philologe** *der* classical scholar; **~philologie** *die* classical studies *pl., no art.*; **~philologin** *die* classical scholar; **~philologisch** *Adj.* classical; **~römisch** *Adj.* ancient Roman; **~rosa** *Adj.* old rose

Altruismus /altruˈɪsmʊs/ *der;* **~** (geh.) altruism

Altruist *der;* **~en, ~en, Altruistin** *die;* **~, ~nen** (geh.) altruist

altruistisch (geh.)
A *Adj.* altruistic
B *adv.* altruistically

alt-, Alt-: ~sänger *der* alto; **~sängerin** *die* alto; contralto; **~saxophon** *das* alto saxophone; **~schlüssel** *der* (Musik) alto clef; **~schnee** *der* old snow; **~schneedecke** *die* layer *or* covering of old snow; **~silber** *das* **1** (veralt.: bereits verarbeitet) old silver; **2** (Silberart) oxidized silver; **~sprachler** /-ʃpra:xlɐ/ *der;* **~~s, ~~,** **~sprachlerin** *die;* **~~, ~~nen** classicist; **~sprachlich** *Adj.* classical; **~sprachliches Gymnasium** *grammar school concentrating on classical rather than modern languages;* **~stadt** *die* old [part of the] town; **die Düsseldorfer ~stadt** the old part of Düsseldorf; **~stadt·sanierung** *die* renovation of the old part of a/the town; **~stein·zeit** *die* Old Stone Age; Palaeolithic Age; **~stein·zeitlich** *Adj.* Palaeolithic; **~stimme** *die* alto voice; (von Frau) alto *or* contralto voice; **~testamentarisch**, **~testament·lich** *Adj.* Old Testament *attrib.*; **~überlie·fert** *Adj.* traditional; **~väterisch** /-fɛːtərɪʃ/ A *Adj.* old-fashioned; B *adv.* in an old-fashioned way; **~vertraut** *Adj.* old familiar *attrib.*; **~vordern** /-fɔrdɐn/ *Pl.* (veralt.) forbears; forefathers; ancestors; **~waren·händler** *der* second-hand dealer; **~wasser** *das*; *Pl.* **~~**: dead arm of a/the river; **~weiber·geschwätz**, **~wei·ber·gewäsch** *das* (abwertend) empty chatter; **~weiber·sommer** *der* 1) Indian summer; 2) (Spinnfäden) gossamer

Alu¹ /ˈaːlu/ *das*; **~s** (ugs.) aluminium (Brit.); aluminum (Amer.)

Alu² *die*; **~** *Abk.* (ugs.) = **Arbeitslosenunterstützung** dole [money] (Brit.); unemployment pay

Alu·folie *die* aluminium (Brit.) *or* (Amer.) aluminum foil

Aluminium /aluˈmiːni̯um/ *das*; **~s** aluminium (Brit.); aluminum (Amer.)

Aluminium·folie *die* aluminium foil

Alumna /aˈlʊmna/ *die*; **~**, **Alumnae** /...nɛ/ alumna

Alumnat /alʊmˈnaːt/ *das*; **~[e]s, ~e** boarding school

Alumnus /aˈlʊmnʊs/ *der*; **~**, **Alumni** /...ni/ alumnus

Alveolar /alveoˈlaːɐ̯/ *der*; **~s, ~e** (Sprachw.) alveolar [consonant]

Alweg·bahn /ˈalveːk-/ *die: type of overhead, high-speed monorail system*

Alzheimer /ˈaltshaimɐ/ *der*; **~s** (ugs.), **Alzheimer** *die*; **~** (ugs.) Alzheimer's

Alzheimer·krankheit *die* ▸ ⓘ **S. 439** Alzheimer's disease

Alzheimer·patient *der*, **Alzheimer·patientin** *die* patient with Alzheimer's

am /am/ *Präp. + Art.* 1) = **an dem** 2) (räumlich) **am Boden** on the floor; **Frankfurt am Main** Frankfurt on [the] Main; **am Rande** on the edge; **am Institut für ...** at the Institute for ...; **am Marktplatz** on the market square *or* place; **am Baum lehnen** lean against the tree; **am Meer/Fluss** by the sea/on *or* by the river; **am Atlantik** on the Atlantic; **am Anfang/Ende** at the beginning/end; **es am Herzen haben** (ugs.) have heart trouble; **sich am Kopf stoßen** bang one's head 3) (österr.: auf dem) on the 4) ▸ ⓘ **S. 816** (zeitlich) on; **am Freitag** on Friday; **am 19. November** on 19 November; **am Anfang/Ende** at the beginning/end; **am letzten Freitag** last Friday; **am Morgen/Nachmittag** in the morning/afternoon 5) (zur Bildung des Superlativs) **das rote gefällt mir am besten** I like the red one [the] best; **am gescheitesten/schönsten sein** be the cleverest/most beautiful; **am schnellsten laufen** run [the] fastest; **das machen wir am besten nachher** it's best if we do it afterwards 6) (nach bestimmten Verben) **am Gelingen eines Planes** *usw.* **zweifeln** have doubts about *or* doubt the success of a plan *etc.*; **schuld am Scheitern eines Planes** *usw.* **sein** be to blame for the failure of a plan *etc.*; **am Wettbewerb teilnehmen** take part in the contest 7) (zur Bildung der Verlaufsform) **am Verwelken/Verfallen sein** be wilting/decaying 8) (ugs.: bes. westf., rhein.) **ich bin gerade am Kochen** I'm right in the middle of cooking; **er ist sein Auto am Putzen** he's cleaning his car

Amalgam /amalˈgaːm/ *das*; **~s, ~e** (Chemie, auch fig.) amalgam

Amalgam·füllung *die* (Zahnmed.) amalgam filling

amalgamieren *tr., refl. V.* (Technik) (auch fig.) amalgamate

Amalgamierung *die*; **~, ~en** (auch fig.) amalgamation

Amaryllis /amaˈrʏlɪs/ *die*; **~**, **Amaryllen** amaryllis

-amateur *der* amateur ...

Amateur /amaˈtøːɐ̯/ *der*; **~s, ~e** (auch abwertend) amateur

Amateur- amateur

Amateur-: ~funk *der* amateur radio operating; **~funker** *der*, **~funkerin** *die* amateur radio operator

amateurhaft
A *Adj.* amateurish
B *adv.* amateurishly

Amateurin *die*; **~, ~nen** ▸ **Amateur**

Amateur-: ~status *der* (Sport) amateur status; **~theater** *das* amateur theatre

Amazonas /amaˈtso̯ːnas/ *der*; **~** ▸ ⓘ **S. 267** Amazon

Amazone /amaˈtso̯ːnə/ *die*; **~, ~n** 1) (Myth.) Amazon 2) (Reiterin) woman rider; equestrienne 3) (Fahrerin) [woman] racing driver 4) (veralt.: männlich wirkende Frau) amazon

Amazonen·springen *das* (Reiten) women's showjumping; (Veranstaltung) women's showjumping competition

Amazonien /amaˈtso̯ːni̯ən/ *(das)*; **~s** Amazonia

Amber /ˈambɐ/ *der*; **~s, ~[n]** ambergris

Ambiente /amˈbi̯ɛntə/ *das*; **~s** (geh.) ambience

Ambition /ambiˈtsi̯oːn/ *die*; **~, ~en** (geh.) ambition; **~en auf etw.** (*Akk.*) **haben** have ambitions of getting sth.

ambitioniert /ambitsi̯oˈniːɐ̯t/ *Adj.* (geh.) ambitious

ambivalent /ambivaˈlɛnt/ (geh.)
A *Adj.* ambivalent
B *adv.* ambivalently

Ambivalenz /ambivaˈlɛnts/ (geh.) *die*; **~, ~en** ambivalence

Amboss, ***Amboß** /ˈambɔs/ *der*; **Ambosses, Ambosse** 1) anvil 2) (Anat.) ▸ ⓘ **S. 435** anvil; incus

Ambra /ˈambra/ *die*; **~, ~s** ambergris

Ambrosia /amˈbroːzi̯a/ *die*; **~** (Myth.) ambrosia

ambrosisch *Adj.* (veralt., geh.) ambrosial

ambulant /ambuˈlant/
A *Adj.* 1) (Med.) outpatient *attrib.* ‹*treatment, therapy, etc.*›; **ein ~er Patient** an outpatient 2) (umherziehend) itinerant
B *adv.* 1) (Med.) **jmdn. ~ behandeln/versorgen** treat sb. as an outpatient *or* give sb. outpatient treatment/look after sb. as an outpatient 2) (umherziehend) **~ mit etw. handeln** travel around selling sth.

Ambulanz /ambuˈlants/ *die*; **~, ~en** 1) (Feldlazarett) field hospital 2) (in Kliniken) outpatient[s'] department 3) (in Betrieben) first-aid station 4) (Krankenwagen) ambulance

Ambulatorium /ambulaˈtoːri̯um/ *das*; **~s, Ambulatorien** (bes. DDR) outpatient[s'] department

Ameise /ˈaːmai̯zə/ *die*; **~, ~n** ant

Ameisen·bär *der* anteater

Ameisen-: ~haufen *der* anthill; **~pfad** *der* (Zool.) ant run; **~säure** *die* formic acid; **~staat** *der* ant colony

amen /ˈaːmɛn/ *Adv.* (christl. Rel.) amen; **zu allem ja und Amen** *od.* **~ sagen** (ugs.) agree to anything

Amen *das*; **~s, ~**: Amen; **das ist so sicher wie das ~ in der Kirche** (ugs.) you can bet your bottom dollar on it (coll.); **sein ~ zu etw. geben** (fig.) give one's blessing to sth.

American Football /ɛˈmɛrikn̩ ˈfutbɔːl/ *der*; **~ ~[s]** American Football

Amerika /aˈmeːrika/ *(das)*; **~s** America

> **Amerikahaus**
>
> In Germany and Austria, *Amerikahäuser* are US information centres with a cultural function. They have reference libraries and offer language courses and lectures.

Amerikaner /ameriˈkaːnɐ/ *der*; **~s, ~** 1) ▸ ⓘ **S. 520** American 2) (Gebäck) *small, flat iced cake*

Amerikanerin *die*; **~, ~nen** ▸ ⓘ **S. 520** American

amerikanisch *Adj.* ▸ ⓘ **S. 520** American *s. auch* **deutsch, Deutsch, Deutsche²**

amerikanisieren *tr. V.* Americanize

Amerikanisierung *die*; **~**: Americanization

Amerikanismus *der*; **~, Amerikanismen** Americanism

Amerikanist *der*; **~en, ~en** specialist in American studies *pl.*

Amerikanistik *die*; **~**: American studies *pl., no art.*

Amerikanistin *die*; **~, ~nen** ▸ **Amerikanist**

amerikanistisch *Adj.* American ‹*studies*›

Amethyst /ameˈtʏst/ *der*; **~[e]s, ~e** amethyst

Ami /ˈami/ *der*; **~[s], ~[s]** (ugs.) Yank (coll.)

Amigo *der*; **~s, ~s** (Jargon) buddy (coll.)

Amino·säure /aˈmiːno-/ *die* (Chemie) amino acid

Amischen /ˈaːmɪʃn̩/ *Pl.*; *adj. Dekl.* **die ~**: the Amish

Ammann /ˈaman/ *der*; **~[e]s, Ammänner** (schweiz.) (Gemeinde~, Bezirks~) ≈ mayor; (Land~) cantonal president

Amme /ˈamə/ *die*; **~, ~n** (Mensch) wet nurse; (Tier) foster-mother

Ammen·märchen *das* fairy tale *or* story

Ammer /ˈamɐ/ *die*; **~, ~n** bunting

Ammoniak /amoˈni̯ak/ *das*; **~s** (Chemie) ammonia

Ammonit /amoˈniːt/ *der*; **~en, ~en** (Paläont.) ammonite

Amnesie /amneˈziː/ *die*; **~, ~n** ▸ ⓘ **S. 439** (Med., Psych.) amnesia

Amnestie /amnɛsˈtiː/ *die*; **~, ~n** amnesty

amnestieren *tr. V.* grant an amnesty to; amnesty

Amnestierung *die*; **~, ~en**: **eine ~ politischer Gefangener** an amnesty for political prisoners

Amöbe /aˈmøːbə/ *die*; **~, ~n** (Biol.) amoeba

Amöben·ruhr *die* ▸ ⓘ **S. 439** (Med.) amoebic dysentery

Amok /ˈaːmɔk/ *der*; **~s** *in* **~ laufen** run amok; (ugs.: wütend werden) go wild (coll.); **~ fahren** go berserk at the wheel

Amok-: ~fahrer *der*, **~fahrerin** *die* berserk driver; **~fahrt** *die* crazed drive; **~lauf** *der* crazed rampage; **~läufer** *der* madman/madwoman; **der ~läufer, der mehrere Menschen erschossen hatte** the man who had gone berserk and shot several people; **~läuferin** *die* madwoman; **~schütze** *der*, **~schützin** *die* crazed gunman/gunwoman

a-Moll *das* A minor; **Sonate/Etüde in ~**: sonata/étude in A minor

a-Moll-: ~-Drei·klang *der* A minor triad; **~-Etüde** *die* study *or* étude in A minor; **~-Sonate** *die* sonata in A minor; **~-Ton·leiter** *die* scale of A minor

Amor /ˈaːmɔr/ *(der)* Cupid; **~s Pfeil** (dichter.) Cupid's arrow *or* dart

amoralisch (geh.)
A *Adj.* immoral
B *adv.* immorally

Amoralität *die*; **~** (geh.) immorality

Amorette /amoˈrɛtə/ *die*; **~, ~n** (Kunstwiss.) amoretto; [little] cupid

amorph /aˈmɔrf/ *Adj.* (geh.) amorphous

Amortisation /amɔrtizaˈtsi̯oːn/ *die*; **~, ~en** (Wirtsch.) 1) (Schuldentilgung) amortization 2) (Kostendeckung) **die Berechnung der ~ der Maschine** calculating how long the machine will take to pay for itself

amortisieren (Wirtsch.)
A *tr. V.* 1) (tilgen) amortize; pay off 2) (einbringen) repay ‹*initial investment, acquisition costs*›
B *refl. V.* (sich bezahlt machen) pay for itself

Amouren /aˈmuːrən/ *Pl.* (veralt., noch scherzh.) amours

amourös /amuˈrøːs/ *Adj.* amorous

Ampel /ˈampl̩/ *die*; **~, ~n** ▸ ⓘ **S. 800** 1) (Verkehrs~) traffic lights *pl.*; **die ~ sprang auf Rot**

the traffic lights turned to red; **halten Sie an der nächsten ~:** stop at the next set of traffic lights; **eine ~ umfahren** knock over a traffic light [2] (Hängelampe) hanging lamp [3] (für Pflanzen) hanging flowerpot

Ampel·anlage *die* set of traffic lights

> **Ampelkoalition**
>
> A term describing any coalition between the **SPD** (the party colour is red), the **FDP** (yellow) and the Green Party. This type of coalition has become increasingly common in local government over the last ten years, with some **Länder** ruled in this way.

Ampere /amˈpɛːɐ̯/ *das;* **~[s], ~:** ampere; amp (coll.)

Ampere-: **~meter** *das* ammeter; **~stunde** *die* ampere-hour

Ampfer /ˈampfɐ/ *der;* **~s, ~** (Bot.) dock

Amphibie /amˈfiːbi̯ə/ *die;* **~, ~n** (Zool.) amphibian

Amphibien·fahrzeug *das* amphibious vehicle

amphibisch (Zool., Milit.)
[A] *Adj.* amphibious
[B] *adv.* amphibiously

Amphi·theater /amˈfiː-/ *das* amphitheatre

Amphore /amˈfoːrə/ *die;* **~, ~n** amphora

Amplitude /ampliˈtuːdə/ *die;* **~, ~n** (Math., Physik) amplitude

Ampulle /amˈpʊlə/ *die;* **~, ~n** (Med.) ampoule

Amputation /amputaˈtsi̯oːn/ *die;* **~, ~en** (Med.) amputation

amputieren *tr.* (*auch itr.*) *V.* amputate; **amputiert werden** ‹*person*› have an amputation; **jmdm. das Bein/den Arm ~:** amputate sb.'s leg/arm

Amputierte *der/die; adj. Dekl.* amputee

Amsel /ˈamzl̩/ *die;* **~, ~n** blackbird

Amt /amt/ *das;* **~[e]s, Ämter** /ˈɛmtɐ/ [1] (Stellung) post; position; (hohes politisches od. kirchliches ~) office; **sein ~ antreten** take up one's post/take up office; **im ~ sein** be in office; **in ~ und Würden sein** be a man/woman of position and authority; **jmdn. aus dem ~ entfernen** remove sb. from his/her post/from office; **für ein ~ kandidieren** be a candidate for a post *or* position/an office; **von ~s wegen** because of one's profession *or* job; **kraft seines ~es** (geh.) by virtue of one's office [2] (Aufgabe) task; job; (Obliegenheit) duty; **seines ~es walten** (geh.) discharge the duties of one's office; **Scharfrichter, walte deines ~es!** executioner, do your duty! [3] (Behörde) (Pass~, Finanz~, ~ für Statistik) office; (Sozial~, Fürsorge~, ~ für Denkmalpflege, Vermessungswesen) department; **jmdn. dem zuständigen ~ melden** report sb. to the appropriate authorities; **von ~s wegen** by order of the authorities; *s. auch* **auswärtig 3** [4] (Gebäude usw.) office [5] (Fernsprechvermittlung) exchange; **das Fräulein vom ~** (veralt.) the operator; **vom ~ vermittelt werden** be put through by the operator [6] (kath. Rel.) [sung] mass

Ämtchen /ˈɛmtçən/ *das;* **~s, ~** (abwertend) petty little job

Ämter·patronage *die* [political] patronage in the distribution of posts/offices

Amt·frau *die* ▸**Amtmann**

amtieren *itr. V.* [1] hold office; **der ~de Generalsekretär** the incumbent Secretary General; **der seit zwei Jahren ~de Generalsekretär** the Secretary-General who has been in *or* has held office for two years; **als Bürgermeister ~:** hold the office of mayor [2] (vorübergehend) act (**als** as)

amtlich
[A] *Adj.* official; **~es Kennzeichen** registration number; (ugs.: sicher) definite; certain
[B] *adv.* officially

amtlicher·seits *Adv.* officially

Amt·mann *der; Pl.* **Amtmänner** *od.* **Amtleute, Amt·männin** /-mɛnɪn/ *die;* **~, ~nen** *senior civil servant*

amts-, Amts-: **~anmaßung** *die* (Rechtsw.) unauthorized assumption of authority; **~antritt** *der* assumption of office; **bei ~antritt** on assuming office; **~anwalt** *der: public prosecutor at a local court;* **~apparat** *der* machinery of officialdom; **~arzt** *der,* **~ärztin** *die* medical officer; **~ärztlich** [A] *Adj.* **~ärztliche Gesundheits-/Impfbescheinigung** certificate of health/vaccination issued by the medical officer; **~ärztliche Untersuchung** examination by the medical officer; [B] *adv.* ‹*authorized, certified*› by the medical officer; **sich ~ärztlich untersuchen lassen** have an official medical examination; **~blatt** *das* official gazette; (der EU) Official Journal; **~bonus** *der* advantage of being in office; **~bruder** *der* fellow clergyman; **~deutsch** *das* (abwertend) officialese; **~eid** *der* oath of office; **~einsetzung** *die* installation; **~enthebung** *die,* (bes. österr. u. schweiz.) **~entsetzung** *die* removal *or* dismissal from office; **~führung** *die* discharge of one's office; **~geheimnis** *das* [1] (Schweigepflicht) official secrecy *no art.*; **dem ~geheimnis unterliegen** be bound by official secrecy; [2] (geheime Sache) official secret; **~gericht** *das* [1] (Instanz) local *or* district court; [2] (Gebäude) local *or* district court building; **~geschäfte** *Pl.* official duties; **~handlung** *die* official act *or* duty; **~hilfe** *die* official assistance (*given by one authority to another*); **~kette** *die* chain of office; **~leitung** *die* exchange line; **~miene** *die* (meist iron.) official air; **~missbrauch,** ***~mißbrauch** *der* abuse of authority *or* one's position; **~müde** *Adj.* tired of office *postpos.*; **~nachfolger** *der,* **~nachfolgerin** *die* successor in office; **~person** *die* official; **~pflicht** *die* official duty; duty of one's office; **~richter** *der,* **~richterin** *die* (veralt.) local *or* district court judge; **~schimmel** *der* (scherzh.) officialism; bureaucracy; **der ~schimmel wiehert** that's bureaucracy for you; **~schwester** *die* fellow clergywoman; **~siegel** *das* official seal; (Dienststempel) official stamp; **~sitz** *der* [1] (Ort) [official] seat; [2] (Gebäude) official residence; **~sprache** *die* [1] (~deutsch) official language; officialese (derog.); **in der ~sprache** in official language/officialese; [2] (eines Landes, einer Organisation) official language; **~stube** *die* (veralt.) office; **~stunden** *Pl.* office hours; **~tracht** *die* robes *pl.* of office; official dress; (eines Geistlichen) vestments *pl.*; **~verweser** *der;* **~~s, ~, ~verweserin** *die;* **~~, ~~nen** (geh.) deputy; (eines Herrschers) regent; **~vorsteher** *der,* **~vorsteherin** *die* head *or* chief [of a/the department]; **~vorsteher der Passstelle/des Zollamtes** head of the passport/customs office; **~zeit** *die* period *or* term of office; **~zimmer** *das* office

> **Amtsgericht**
>
> *Amtsgerichte* (local or district courts), similar to the US municipal or county courts, are the lowest level of ordinary courts in Germany. They work in a two-tier system with the *Landgerichte* (regional courts) and deal with minor cases. There are four levels of ordinary courts hearing both civil and criminal cases: the *Amtsgericht* (Local Court), *Landgericht* (Regional Court), *Oberlandesgericht* (Higher Regional Court) and the *Bundesgerichtshof* (Federal Supreme Court). Most legal proceedings at the local court are handled by magistrates. The regional courts handle more serious cases and deal with local court appeals; a panel of lay judges sits with a professional judge in a regional court.

Amulett /amuˈlɛt/ *das;* **~[e]s, ~e** amulet; charm

amüsant /amyˈzant/
[A] *Adj.* amusing; entertaining
[B] *adv.* in an amusing *or* entertaining way

Amuse-Gueule /amyːsˈgœl/ *das;* **~[s], ~[s]** appetizer

Amüsement /amyzəˈmãː/ *das;* **~s, ~s** amusement

Amüsier·betrieb *der* (oft abwertend) nightclub; (Spielhalle) amusement arcade; arcade room (Amer.)

amüsieren
[A] *refl. V.* [1] (sich vergnügen) enjoy oneself; have a good time; **amüsier dich gut!** enjoy yourself!; have a good time!; **sich mit etw. ~** (auch iron.) have fun with sth.; **sich mit jmdm. ~:** have fun *or* a good time with sb. [2] (sich lustig machen) be amused; **sich über jmdn./etw. ~:** find sb./sth. funny; (über jmdn./etw. lachen) laugh at sb./sth.; (jmdn. verspotten) make fun of sb./sth.
[B] *tr. V.* amuse; **amüsiert zusehen** look on with amusement; **was amüsiert dich denn so?** what do you find so amusing *or* funny?

Amüsier·viertel *das* nightclub district

amusisch *Adj.* (geh.) with no feeling for art *postpos., not pred.*; **[völlig] ~ sein** have no feeling [at all] for art

an /an/
[A] *Präp. mit Dat.* [1] (räumlich) at; (auf) on; **an einem Ort** at a place; **an der Tür/Wand** on the door/wall; **an der Wand stehen** stand by *or* against the wall; **eine Blase an der Ferse haben** have a blister on one's heel; **an der Mosel/Donau liegen** be [situated] on the Moselle/Danube; **Frankfurt an der Oder** Frankfurt on [the] Oder; **ein Lehrer an dieser Schule** a teacher at this school; **an etw. lehnen** lean against sth.; **nah an etw. stehen** stand close to sth.; **jmdn. an der Hand nehmen** take sb. by the hand; **Tür an Tür** next door to one another; **Laden an Laden** shop after shop; one shop after the other; **an jmdm. vorbeigehen/vorbeisehen** go/look past sb.; **an etw. vorbeiplanen/vorbeibauen** plan/build without regard for sth.; *s. auch* **Bord²; Land 1** [2] ▸**❶ S. 165,** ▸**❶ S. 816** (zeitlich) on; **an jedem Sonntag** every Sunday; **an dem Abend, als er ...** [on] the evening he ...; **das war an dem Tag, als er ...** that was the day he ...; **an Ostern** (bes. südd.) at Easter [3] (nach bestimmten Substantiven, Adjektiven und Verben) in; **acht an der Zahl** eight in number; **arm/reich an Vitaminen** low/rich in vitamins; **jung an Jahren** young in years; **jmdn. an etw. erkennen** recognize sb. by sth.; **das Beste an etw.** the best thing about sth.; **ein Mangel an etw.** a shortage of sth.; **an etw. arbeiten** be working on sth.; **an etw. leiden** suffer from sth.; **was haben Sie an Zeitungen?** what newspapers have you got?; **es an der Leber bekommen/haben** get/have liver trouble; **an einer Krankheit sterben** die of a disease; **was mir an der Sache nicht gefällt** what I don't like about it; **es ist an ihm, das zu tun** it is up to him to do it; **er/sie hat etwas an sich** there is something about him/her; **was er an Rente bekam** what he received by way of a pension; **an [und für] sich** actually; **die Idee ist an [und für] sich ausgezeichnet** the idea is excellent in itself
[B] *Präp. mit Akk.* [1] to; (auf, gegen) on; **etw. an jmdn. schicken** send sth. to sb.; **etw. an etw. hängen** hang sth. on sth.; **an die Tafel schreiben** write on the blackboard; **etw. an etw. lehnen** lean sth. against sth.; **[bis] an die Decke reichen** reach [up] to the ceiling; *s. auch* **bis; Bord²; Land** [2] (nach bestimmten Substantiven, Adjektiven und Verben) **an etw./jmdn. glauben** believe in sth./sb.; **an etw. denken** think of sth.; **sich an etw. erinnern** remember *or* recall sth.; **an die Arbeit gehen** get down to work; **eine Bitte/Frage an jmdn. haben** have a request to make of sb./a question to ask sb.; **an etw. appellieren** appeal to sth.; **einen Gruß an jmdn. ausrichten lassen** send greetings to sb.; **ich konnte kaum an mich halten vor Lachen/Ärger** I could hardly contain myself for laughing/hardly contain my anger
[C] *Adv.* [1] (Verkehrsw.) **Köln an: 9.15** arriving Cologne 09.15 [2] (ugs.: in Betrieb) on; **die Waschmaschine/der Fernseher/das Licht/das Gas ist an** the washing machine/television/light/gas is on; **Scheinwerfer an!** spotlights on! [3] (ugs.: ungefähr) around; about; **an [die] 20 000 Euro** around *or* about 20,000 euros [4] *in* **ohne [et]was an** (ugs.) with nothing on; without anything on; *s. auch* **ab B 4; von A 1, 2**

Anabolikum /anaˈboːlikʊm/ *das;* **~s, Anabolika** (Med.) anabolic steroid

Anachronismus /anakroˈnɪsmʊs/ *der;* **~, Anachronismen** anachronism

a

ℹ an

Räumlich: Wo?

Zur Beschreibung der Lage verwendet man meist **on:**

eine Verletzung am Knie
= a wound on the knee
die Bilder an der Wand
= the pictures on the wall
eine Stadt an der Mosel
= a town on the Moselle
ein Haus am Fluss
= a house on *od.* by the river

Hier wird **by** verwendet, um die Nähe zum Fluss auszudrücken. Ebenso:

Er stand am Fenster
= He stood by *od.* at the window

Wenn es um die Lage an einem Ort oder Gebäude geht, heißt es **at:**

am Tatort
= at the scene of the crime
am Haupteingang
= at the main entrance
an der Vorderseite
= at the front
am Ende der Straße
= at the end of the road
am Theater/Kino/Bahnhof
= at the theatre/cinema/station

Räumlich: Wohin?

Wenn *an* sich auf eine Bewegung in eine bestimmte Richtung bezieht, wird es meist mit **on** übersetzt:

Lehne es an den Baum
= Lean it on *od.* against the tree
Hänge es an die Wand
= Hang it on the wall
Schreibe es an die Tafel
= Write it on the blackboard
Sie legte ihren Kopf an seine Schulter
= She laid her head on his shoulder

Beim Wechsel von einer Person zur anderen bzw. von einem Ort zum anderen heißt es **to:**

Schicke es an deinen Bruder
= Send it to your brother
die Übergabe an den neuen Besitzer
= the transfer to the new owner
Sie wurde an eine andere Schule versetzt
= She was moved to another school

Zeitlich: Wann?

In Verbindung mit einem bestimmten Tag, Datum oder Wochentag wird *an* bzw. *am* mit **on** (ohne *the*) übersetzt:

am 6. Juli
= on July 6th (*gesprochen:* on July the sixth, *in den USA auch:* July sixth)
am Mittwoch
= on Wednesday
an seinem Geburtstag
= on his birthday
an einem schönen Frühlingstag
= on a fine spring day

Ausnahmen (mit *the*) sind Daten ohne Angabe des Monats oder bestimmte Tage im Monat:

am 6.
= on the sixth
am ersten/letzten Sonntag im Monat
= on the first/last Sunday in the month

Bei vorangehenden oder folgenden Tagen steht meist nur *the*, d.h. *an* wird nicht übersetzt:

Am Tag/Mittwoch davor waren wir in London gewesen
= The day before/The previous Wednesday we had been in London
Am nächsten Tag fuhr er zurück
= The next day he went back
Am übernächsten Dienstag sind wir in Rom
= The Tuesday after next we'll be in Rome

In Verbindung mit Tageszeiten heißt es **in,** oder, wenn sie näher beschrieben werden, **on:**

am Morgen/Nachmittag/Abend
= in the morning/afternoon/evening
am ersten Morgen seines Besuchs
= on the first morning of his visit
an einem kalten Winterabend
= on a cold winter evening

Eine Ausnahme ist wieder:

am nächsten Morgen
= the next morning

In Verbindung mit Festen (süddeutscher Wortgebrauch) heißt es **at:**

an Ostern/Weihnachten
=at Easter/Christmas

Im Gegensatz zu *aus*

In der Bedeutung 'in Betrieb' wird *an* mit **on** übersetzt:

Das Licht/Die Spülmaschine ist an
= The light/The dishwasher is on

Im Gegensatz zu *ab*

Auf Fahrplänen (zur Angabe der Ankunftszeit) heißt es im Englischen **arriving** (Abkürzung **arr.**):

Köln an 17.30
= arriving *od.* arr. Cologne 17.30
an 12.30 – ab 12.35
= arr. 12.30 – dep. 12.35

---

anachronistisch
A *Adj.* anachronistic
B *adv.* anachronistically

anaerob /an|ae'ro:p/ *Adj.* (Biol.) anaerobic

Anagramm /ana'gram/ *das;* ~s, ~e anagram

Anakoluth /anako'lu:t/ *das od. der;* ~s, ~e (Sprachw.) anacoluthon

Anakonda /ana'kɔnda/ *die;* ~, ~s anaconda

Anakreontik /anakre'ɔntɪk/ *die;* ~ (Literaturw.) anacreontic verse

anal /a'na:l/ (Anat., Psych.)
A *Adj.* anal
B *adv.* anally; ~ **verkehren** have anal intercourse

Analeptikum /ana'lɛptikʊm/ *das;* ~s, **Analeptika** (Med.) analeptic

Anal·erotik *die;* ~: anal eroticism

Analgetikum /anal'ge:tikʊm/ *das;* ~s, **Analgetika** (Med.) analgesic

analog /ana'lo:k/
A *Adj.* **1** (gleichartig) analogous; ~ **[zu] diesem Fall** analogous to this case **2** (Technik, DV) analogue
B *adv.* **1** (gleichartig) analogously **2** (Technik, DV) ‹*display, reproduce*› in analogue form; ~ **arbeitende Geräte** analogue devices

Analogie *die;* ~, ~n (Entsprechung, auch Rechtsw., Biol., Sprachw.) analogy; **in ~ zu etw.** in analogy to sth.

Analog-: ~**rechner** *der* (DV) analogue computer; ~**uhr** *die* analogue clock; (Armbanduhr) analogue watch

An·alphabet *der;* ~en, ~en **1** illiterate [person]; ~ **sein** be illiterate **2** (fig. abwertend) ignoramus; **ein politischer ~ sein** be politically illiterate

Analphabetentum *das;* ~s illiteracy

Analphabetin *die;* ~, ~nen ▸**Analphabet**

Analphabetismus *der;* ~: illiteracy

Anal·verkehr *der* anal intercourse

Analysand /analy'zant/ *der;* ~en, ~en, **Analysandin** *die;* ~, ~nen (Psychoanalyse) analysand

Analyse /ana'ly:zə/ *die;* ~, ~n (auch: Psycho~) analysis

analysieren *tr. V.* analyse

Analysis /a'na:lyzɪs/ *die;* ~ (Math.) analysis

Analyst /ana'lʏst/ *der;* ~en, ~en, **Analystin** *die;* ~, ~nen ▸ℹ **S. 113** (Börsenw.) analyst

Analytiker *der;* ~s, ~, **Analytikerin** *die* analyst

analytisch
A *Adj.* analytical; ~**e Geometrie** analytical geometry
B *adv.* analytically

Anämie /anɛ'mi:/ *die;* ~, ~n ▸ℹ **S. 439** (Med.) anaemia

anämisch /a'nɛ:mɪʃ/ *Adj.* (Med., auch fig. abwertend) anaemic

Anamnese /anam'ne:zə/ *die;* ~, ~n (Med.) anamnesis

Ananas /'ananas/ *die;* ~, ~ *od.* ~se pineapple

Anapäst /ana'pɛ:st/ *der;* ~[e]s, ~e (Verslehre) anapaest

Anapher /a'nafɐ/ *die;* ~, ~n (Stilk.) anaphora

Anarchie /anar'çi:/ *die;* ~, ~n anarchy

anarchisch *Adj.* anarchic

Anarchismus *der;* ~: anarchism

Anarchist *der;* ~en, ~en, **Anarchistin** *die;* ~, ~nen anarchist

anarchistisch *Adj.* anarchistic

Anarcho·szene *die* (ugs.) anarchist scene

Anästhesie /an|ɛste'zi:/ *die;* ~, ~n (Med.) anaesthesia

anästhesieren *tr. V.* (Med.) anaesthetize

Anästhesist *der;* ~en, ~en, **Anästhesistin** *die;* ~, ~nen ▸ℹ **S. 113** (Med.) anaesthetist

Anatolien /ana'to:li̯ən/ *(das);* ~s Anatolia

Anatom /ana'to:m/ *der;* ~en, ~en (Med.) anatomist

Anatomie /anato'mi:/ *die;* ~, ~n (Med.) **1** anatomy **2** (Institut) anatomical institute

Anatomie·saal *der* (Med.) anatomy lecture theatre

anatomisch /ana'to:mɪʃ/ (Med.)
A *Adj.* anatomical
B *adv.* anatomically

an|backen[1]
A *unr. tr. V.* **etw. [kurz] ~:** bake sth. for a short time
B *unr. itr. V.; mit sein* (festbacken) become baked on (**an** + *Dat.* to); stick (**an** + *Dat.* on to)

an|backen[2] *itr. V.; mit sein* (nordd.: sich festsetzen) stick (**an** + *Dat.* to)

an|baggern *tr. V.* (salopp) make advances to

an|bahnen
A *tr. V.* initiate ‹*negotiations, talks, process, etc.*›; develop ‹*relationship, connection*›
B *refl. V.* ‹*development*› be in the offing; ‹*friendship, relationship*› start to develop; **zwischen den**

beiden bahnt sich etwas an there is something going on between those two

Anbahnung *die;* ~, ~**en** ►**anbahnen A**: initiation; development

an|bandeln /ˈanbandl̩n/ (südd., österr.), **an|bändeln** /ˈanbɛndl̩n/ *itr. V.* (ugs.) **mit jmdm.** ~ *od.* **anbändeln** (flirten) get off with sb. (Brit. coll.); pick sb. up; (Streit anfangen) pick a quarrel with sb.

-anbau *der:* **Flachs~/Hopfen~/Futter~:** cultivation of flax/hop/fodder plants

An·bau *der; Pl.* ~**ten** [1] building; **die Genehmigung für den ~ einer Garage an ein Haus bekommen** receive permission to build a garage on to a house [2] (Gebäude) extension [3] (das Anpflanzen) cultivation; growing

an|bauen

A *tr. V.* [1] build on; add; **eine Garage ans Haus ~**: build a garage on to the house [2] (anpflanzen) cultivate; grow

B *itr. V.* (das Haus vergrößern) build an extension; (~ lassen) have an extension built

Anbau-: ~**fläche** *die* area of arable land; (bebaute Fläche) area under cultivation; ~**gebiet** *das:* **die besten ~gebiete für Getreide** the best cereal-growing *or* grain-growing areas; **die wichtigsten ~gebiete für Rotwein** the principal red-wine-growing areas *or* areas for red wine; ~**küche** *die* fitted kitchen; unit kitchen (Amer.); ~**möbel** *das* piece of unit furniture; **teure ~möbel** expensive unit furniture *sing.;* ~**schrank** *der* cupboard unit

an|befehlen *unr. tr. V.* (geh.) [1] (befehlen) **jmdm. etw. ~**: urge sth. on sb. [2] (anvertrauen) **jmdm. etw. ~**: commend sth. to sb.; **jmdm. ein Kind ~**: commend a child to sb.'s care

An·beginn *der* (geh.) beginning; **von ~ [an]** right from the beginning

an|behalten *unr. tr. V.* (ugs.) **etw. ~**: keep sth. on

an·bei *Adv.* (Amtsspr.) herewith; **Rückporto ~:** return postage enclosed

an|beißen

A *unr. tr. V.* bite into; take a bite of; **er hat die Banane nur angebissen** he only took one bite of the banana; **zum Anbeißen sein** *od.* **aussehen** (ugs.) look good enough to eat

B *unr. itr. V.* (auch fig. ugs.) bite; **bei ihr hat noch keiner angebissen** (fig. ugs.) she hasn't managed to hook anybody yet

an|bekommen *unr. tr. V.* (ugs.) [1] (anziehen können) **etw. ~**: manage to get sth. on [2] (anzünden od. starten können) **ein Feuer/Streichholz ~**: manage to get a fire going/a match to light; **einen Motor ~**: manage to get an engine going *or* to start

an|belangen *tr. V. in* **was mich/diese Sache** *usw.* **anbelangt** as far as I am/this matter is *etc.* concerned

an|bellen *tr. V.* bark at

an|bequemen *refl. V.* (geh.) **sich einer Sache** (*Dat.*) **~:** adapt [oneself] to sth.

an|beraumen /ˈanbəraumən/ *tr. V.* (Amtsspr.) arrange, fix ‹*meeting*›; arrange, set, fix ‹*date*›

Anberaumung *die;* ~, ~**en** (Amtsspr.) ►**anberaumen**: arrangement; fixing; setting; **wir bitten um ~ eines neuen Termins** we should like a new date to be arranged *or* set

an|beten *tr. V.* (auch fig.) worship

Anbeter *der;* ~**s**, ~, **Anbeterin** *die;* ~, ~**nen** (auch fig.) worshipper; (fig.: Verehrer) admirer

An·betracht *der: in* **in ~ einer Sache** (*Gen.*) in consideration *or* view of sth.; **in ~ dessen, dass …** in view of the fact that …

an|betreffen *unr. tr. V. in* **was mich/diese Sache** *usw.* **anbetrifft** as far as I am/this matter *etc.* is concerned

an|betteln *tr. V.* **jmdn. ~:** beg from sb.; **jmdn. um etw. ~:** beg sb. for sth.; **[auf der Straße] angebettelt werden** be stopped [in the street] by a beggar and asked for money

Anbetung *die;* ~, ~**en** (auch fig.) worship; (fig.: Verehrung) adoration

anbetungs·würdig *Adj.* adorable

an|bezahlen *tr. V.* make a down payment on; pay a deposit on

an|biedern /ˈanbiːdɐn/ *refl. V.* (abwertend) **sich [bei jmdm.] ~:** curry favour [with sb.]

Anbiederung *die;* ~, ~**en** (abwertend) currying favour (**an** + *Akk.* with)

Anbiederungs·versuch *der* (abwertend) attempt to curry favour

an|bieten

A *unr. tr. V.* offer; offer, tender ‹*resignation*›; **jmdm. etw. ~**: offer sb. sth.; **jmdm. seine Begleitung ~**: offer to accompany sb.; **jmdm. ~, etw. zu tun** offer to do sth. for sb.; **ich habe dir immer wieder angeboten, dir zu helfen** I offered time and again to help you; **Verhandlungen ~**: offer to negotiate; **ich habe nichts anzubieten** *od.* **zum Anbieten** I have nothing to offer you/them; **sich auf der Straße ~**: offer oneself on the streets; **jmdm. Schläge ~** (iron.) threaten to hit sb.

B *unr. refl. V.* [1] offer one's services (**als** as); **sich ~, etw. zu tun** offer to do sth.; **sich fürs** *od.* **zum Geschirrspülen** *usw.* **~**: offer to do the dishes [2] (nahe liegen) ‹*opportunity*› present itself; ‹*possibility, solution*› suggest *or* present itself; **es bietet sich an, das zu tun** it would seem to be the thing to do [3] (geeignet sein) **sich für etw. ~**: be suitable for sth.; **dieses Tal bietet sich für die Einrichtung eines Sanatoriums geradezu an** this valley is an obvious place to build a sanatorium

An·bieter *der,* **An·bieterin** *die* (Wirtsch.) supplier

an|binden

A *unr. tr. V.* [1] (befestigen) tie [up] (**an** + *Dat. od. Akk.* to); tie up, moor ‹*boat*› (**an** + *Dat. od. Akk.* to); tether ‹*animal*› (**an** + *Dat. od. Akk.* to); **er lässt sich nicht ~** (fig.) he won't be tied down; **man kann Kinder nicht ~** (fig.) you can't keep children on a lead; *s. auch* **angebunden B** [2] (verbinden, anschließen) link (**an** + *Akk.* to) [3] (Landw.) rear

B *unr. itr. V.* (geh.) **mit jmdm. ~** (Streit anfangen) pick a quarrel with sb.; (flirten) flirt with sb.

An·bindung *die* linking (**an** + *Akk.* to); (psychische ~) involvement (**an** + *Akk.* in)

an|blaffen *tr. V.* (ugs., auch fig.) bark at

an|blasen *unr. tr. V.* [1] blow at; **jmdn. mit Rauch ~**: blow smoke at sb. [2] (anfachen) blow on; **einen Hochofen ~** (Technik) blow in a blast furnace [3] (salopp: zurechtweisen) **jmdn. ~:** bawl sb. out (coll.) [4] **die Jagd ~:** sound the horn for the start of the hunt [5] (Musik) sound ‹*note*›; blow ‹*instrument*›

an|blecken *tr. V.* bare its/their teeth at; (fig.) bare his/her/their *etc.* teeth at

an|bleiben *unr. itr. V.; mit sein* (ugs.) stay on

an|blenden *tr. V.* flash [at]; **jmdn. mit einer Taschenlampe ~:** flash a torch at sb. (Brit.); shine a flashlight at sb. (Amer.)

An·blick *der* sight; **einen erfreulichen/traurigen ~ bieten** be a welcome/sad sight; **ihm wurde beim bloßen ~ schon schlecht** the mere sight of it made him sick; **beim ~ der Pyramiden** at the sight of the Pyramids; **es war ein ~ für Götter, als du …** you looked a [real] sight when you …

an|blicken *tr. V.* look at; **jmdn. mit großen Augen ~:** look at sb. wide-eyed; **jmdn. flüchtig/starr ~:** glance/stare at sb.

an|blinken *tr. V.* ►**anblenden**

an|blinzeln *tr. V.* [1] blink at [2] (zuzwinkern) wink at

an|bohren *tr. V.* [1] bore into; (mit der Bohrmaschine) bore *or* drill into; **Saboteure hatten sämtliche Benzinfässer angebohrt** saboteurs had drilled holes in all the petrol drums [2] (erschließen) tap [by drilling]; (fig. ugs.: befragen) pump

an|branden *itr. V.; mit sein* (auch fig.) surge

an|brassen *tr. V.* (Seemannsspr.) brace up

an|braten *unr. tr. V.* (Kochk.) brown; **scharf ~:** sear

an|brauchen *tr. V.* (ugs.) start [using]; **eine angebrauchte Tube Senf** a half-used tube of mustard

an|bräunen

A *tr. V.* (Kochk.) brown [lightly]

B *itr. V.; mit sein* (ugs.: von der Sonne braun werden) tan [lightly]

an|brausen *itr. V.; mit sein* roar up; **angebraust kommen** come roaring along; (auf einen zu) come roaring up

an|brechen

A *unr. tr. V.* [1] crack; **sich** (*Dat.*) **einen Knochen ~:** crack a bone [2] (öffnen) open; start; **eine angebrochene Flasche** an opened bottle [3] (zu verbrauchen beginnen) break into ‹*supplies, reserves*›; **einen Hundertmarkschein ~:** break into *or* (Amer.) break a hundred mark note; **was machen wir mit dem angebrochenen Abend?** (fig. ugs.) what shall we do for the rest of the evening?

B *unr. itr. V.; mit sein* (geh.: beginnen) ‹*dawn*› break; ‹*day*› dawn, break; ‹*darkness, night*› come down, fall; ‹*age, epoch*› dawn; ‹*autumn, winter*› set in; ‹*spring, summer*› begin

an|brennen

A *unr. tr. V.* (anzünden) light

B *unr. itr. V.; mit sein* [1] burn; **jmdm. ist das Essen angebrannt** sb. has burnt the food; **nichts ~ lassen** (fig. ugs.) not miss out on anything; **der Torwart ließ nichts ~** (Sportjargon) the goalkeeper kept a clean sheet [2] (zu brennen beginnen) ‹*wood, coal, etc.*› catch

an|bringen *unr. tr. V.* [1] (befestigen) put up ‹*sign, aerial, curtain, plaque*› (**an** + *Dat.* on); fix ‹*lamp, camera*› (**an** + *Dat.* [on] to); **an etw.** (*Dat.*) **angebracht sein** be fixed [on] to sth. [2] (äußern) make ‹*request, complaint, comment, reference*› [3] (zeigen) display, demonstrate ‹*knowledge, experience*› [4] (ugs.: herbeibringen) bring; (nach Hause) bring home [5] (ugs.: verkaufen) sell; move

Anbringung *die;* ~ ►**anbringen 1**: putting up; fixing

An·bruch *der* [1] (geh.: Beginn) dawn[ing]; **der ~ des Tages** dawn; daybreak; **vor/nach/bei** *od.* **mit ~ der Nacht** before/after/at nightfall; **vor ~ der Dunkelheit** before darkness closes in [2] (Bergbau) lode; vein

an·brüchig *Adj.* (Jägerspr.) rotting

an|brühen *tr. V.* brew, make ‹*tea, coffee*›; blanch ‹*tomatoes, almonds, etc.*›

an|brüllen

A *tr. V.* [1] ‹*tiger, lion, etc.*› roar at; ‹*cow, bull, etc.*› bellow at [2] (ugs.: anschreien) bellow *or* bawl at

B *itr. V.* (ugs.: zu übertönen versuchen) **gegen etw. ~:** try to shout above [the noise of] sth.

an|brummen

A *tr. V.* (auch ugs.: unfreundlich anreden) growl at

B *itr. V.; mit sein* **angebrummt kommen** come roaring along; (auf einen zu) come roaring up

an|brüten *tr. V.* begin to sit on ‹*eggs*›; **angebrütete Eier** eggs that have been sat on

Anchovis ►**Anschovis**

Anciennitäts·prinzip /ãsiɛniˈtɛːts-/ *das* principle of seniority; **nach dem ~:** according to [the principle of] seniority

Andacht /ˈandaxt/ *die;* ~, ~**en** [1] (Sammlung im Gebet) silent prayer *or* worship; **in tiefer ~:** in deep devotion; **in ~ versunken** sunk in silent prayer *or* worship *or* in one's devotions [2] (innere Sammlung) rapt attention; **mit großer ~:** with rapt attention [3] (Gottesdienst) prayers *pl.*; **eine ~ halten** hold a [short] service; **zur ~ gehen** go to prayers *or* to the service

andächtig /ˈandɛçtɪç/

A *Adj.* [1] (ins Gebet versunken) devout; reverent [2] (innerlich gesammelt) rapt [3] (feierlich) reverent

B *adv.* [1] (ins Gebet versunken) devoutly; reverently [2] (innerlich gesammelt) with rapt attention; raptly

Andachts·bild *das* (Kunst, Rel.) devotional picture

andachts·voll (geh.) ►**andächtig**

Andalusien /andaˈluːzi̯ən/ *(das);* ~**s** Andalusia

an|dampfen *itr. V.; mit sein* **angedampft kommen** (ugs.) come steaming along; (auf einen zu) come steaming up; (fig. scherzh.) come charging along, puffing and blowing; (auf einen zu) come charging up, puffing and blowing

Andante /an'dantə/ *das;* **~s, ~s** (Musik) andante

an|dauen /'andauən/ *tr. V.* (Med.) **angedaute Nahrung** partially digested food

An·dauer *die* continuance; **bei längerer ~ des Fiebers/des schlechten Wetters** if the fever continues *or* persists/the bad weather lasts for a long time

an|dauern *itr. V.* ‹*negotiations*› continue, go on; ‹*weather, rain*› last, continue

andauernd
A ▸**andauern**
B *Adj.* continual; constant
C *adv.* continually; constantly; **warum fragst du denn ~ dasselbe?** why do you keep on asking the same thing?

Anden /'andn̩/ *Pl.* **die ~:** the Andes

an|denken *unr. tr. V.* start thinking about

An·denken *das;* **~s, ~** **[1]** memory; **jmds. ~ bewahren/in Ehren halten** keep/honour sb.'s memory; **jmdm. ein liebevolles ~ bewahren** keep fond memories of sb.; **zum ~ an jmdn./etw.** to remind you/us *etc.* of sb./sth.; **das schenke ich dir zum ~:** I'll give you that to remember me/us by **[2]** (Erinnerungsstück) memento, souvenir (**an** + *Akk.* of); (Reise~) souvenir (**an** + *Akk.* of)

Andenken·jäger *der,* **Andenken·jägerin** *die* souvenir hunter

Anden·staat *der* Andean country

ander... /'andɐ.../ *Indefinitpron.*
A *attr.* **[1]** (zweit..., weiter...) other; **ein ~er Mann/eine ~e Frau/ein ~es Haus** another man/woman/house; **zum ~n Mal** (veralt.) [for] a second time; **eine ~e Frage** another *or* a further question; **~e Fragen** other *or* further questions; **das Kleid gefällt mir nicht, haben Sie noch ~e/ein ~es?** I don't like that dress, do you have any others/another?
[2] **am/bis zum ~[e]n Tag** [on] the/by the next *or* following day; **von einem Tag zum ~n** from one day to the next
[3] (verschieden) different; **wir ~n** the rest of us; **~er Meinung sein** be of a different opinion; take a different view; **das ~e Geschlecht** the opposite sex; **bei ~er Gelegenheit** another time; **statt dieses Wagens hätte ich gern einen ~en** instead of that car I would like a different one; *s. auch* **Land**; **Städtchen**
[4] (neu) **einen ~en Arbeitsplatz finden** find another job; **er ist ein ~er Mensch geworden** he is a changed man
B *allein stehend* **[1]** (Person) **ein ~er/eine ~e** another [one]; **die ~n** the others; **alle ~n** all the others; everyone else; **jeder/jede ~e** anyone *or* anybody else; **kein ~er/keine ~e** nobody *or* no one else; **was ist mit den ~n?** what about the others *or* the rest?; **ich will weder den einen noch den ~en heiraten** I don't want to marry either of them; **niemand ~er als ...** nobody *or* no one but ...; **da muss ein ~er kommen** (fig.) it will take more than you/him *etc.*; **einen ~[e]n/eine ~e haben** (fig. ugs.) have found somebody *or* someone else; **auf ~e hören** listen to others; **eine war schöner als die ~e** one was more beautiful than the other; **einer hinter dem ~[e]n** one after another *or* the other; **nicht drängeln, einer nach dem ~n** don't push, one after the other; **der eine oder [der] ~e** one or two *or* a few people; **wenn der eine oder [der] ~e von Ihnen etwas Genaueres wissen möchte** if any of you would like further details; *s. auch* **recht 3**
[2] (Sache) **ein ~er/eine ~e/ein ~es** another [one]; **alles ~e** everything else; **ein[e]s nach dem ~[e]n** first things first; **das ~e schaffen wir schon allein** we can manage the rest on our own; **wir haben noch zwei ~e** we have two others; **es bleibt uns nichts ~es übrig** there's nothing else we can do; **sich eines ~n besinnen** change one's mind; **ich will weder das eine noch das ~e** I don't want either; (will beides nicht tun) I don't want to do either; **Möchtest du Tee oder Kaffee? — Weder das eine noch das ~e** Would you like tea or coffee? — Neither; **und ~es/vieles ~e mehr** and more/much more besides; **unter ~[e]m** among[st] other things; **so kam eins zum ~[e]n** what with one thing on top of the other; **das ist etwas [ganz] ~es** that's [something quite] different; **von etwas ~em sprechen** talk about something else; (um das bisherige Thema zu vermeiden) change the subject; **das bedeutet doch nichts ~es, als dass wir noch einmal ganz von vorn anfangen müssen** that means only one thing, that we must start all over again from the beginning; **ich habe nichts ~es erwartet** I didn't expect anything else; **dem hätte ich etwas ~es erzählt** (fig. ugs.) I would have given him a piece of my mind; **alles ~e als ...** anything but ...; **das ist alles ~e als das, was ich mir vorgestellt hatte** it's not at all what I had imagined; **~es zu tun haben** have other things to do

änderbar *Adj.* alterable

anderen·falls *Adv.* otherwise

anderen·orts *Adv.* (geh.) elsewhere

anderen·tags *Adv.* (geh.) [on] the next *or* following day

anderen·teils *Adv.* ▸**einesteils**

anderer·seits *Adv.* on the other hand

Ander·konto *das* (Finanzw.) trust account; client account

ander·mal *Adv.*: **ein ~:** another time

andern- ▸**anderen-**

ändern /'ɛndɐn/
A *tr. V.* change; alter; alter ‹*garment*›; change ‹*person*›; **etw. an etw.** (*Dat.*) **~:** change *or* alter sth. in sth.; **wenn ich an dem Kleid etwas ~ würde** if I was going to change anything about the dress; **daran kann man nichts ~:** nothing can be done *or* there's nothing you/we *etc.* can do about it; **das alles ändert nichts an der Tatsache, dass ...** none of that alters the fact that ...
B *refl. V.* change; alter; ‹*person, weather*› change; **daran hat sich nichts geändert** nothing about it has changed *or* altered

ander·orts ▸**anderenorts**

anders /'andɐs/ *Adv.* **[1]** (verschieden) ‹*think, act, feel, do*› differently (**als** from *or esp. Brit.* to); ‹*be, look, sound, taste*› different (**als** from *or esp. Brit.* to); **es war alles ganz ~:** it was all quite different; **er ist irgendwie ~:** there is something different about him; he has changed somehow; **wie könnte es ~ sein!** (iron.) surprise, surprise! (iron.); **mir wird ganz ~** (ugs.) I feel weak at the knees; **es wäre alles ~ gekommen** it would all have been different *or* would have turned out differently; **es kommt immer ~, als man denkt** things never turn out the way you think they will; **es kam ~, als wir dachten** things didn't turn out the way we expected; **wir haben es uns ~ überlegt** we've changed our minds; **ich kann auch ~** (ugs.) you'd/he'd *etc.* better watch it (coll.); **das hört sich schon ~ an** (ugs.) that's more like it; **so und nicht ~:** this way and no other; exactly like that; **das kennt er nicht ~:** he's never known any different; **das kennen wir gar nicht ~ von ihm** we wouldn't expect anything else from him; **ich konnte nicht ~:** I couldn't help it; (ich wurde gezwungen) I had no choice; **das habe ich nicht ~ erwartet** I didn't expect anything else; that was just what I expected; **wie nicht ~ zu erwarten** as [was to be] expected; **wenn es nicht ~ geht** if there is no other way; **~ geartet** different; of a different nature *postpos*; **~ denkend** dissident; dissenting; **~ lautend** to the contrary *postpos.*
[2] (sonst) else; **irgendwo/nirgendwo ~:** somewhere/nowhere else; **niemand ~:** nobody else; **jemand ~:** someone else; (verneint, in Fragen) anyone else **[3]** (ugs.: andernfalls) otherwise; or else

anders-, Anders-: ~artig *Adj.* different; **~artigkeit** *die* different nature; **das Bewusstsein seiner ~artigkeit** his consciousness that he was different; **~denkend** ▸**anders 1**; **~denkende** *der/die; adj. Dekl.* dissident; dissenter

anderseits ▸**andererseits**

anders-, Anders-: ~farbig **A** *Adj.* different-coloured *attrib.*; of a different colour *postpos.*; **B** *adv.* ‹*decorated*› in a different colour; **~farbig bezogen** covered in material of a different colour; **~farbige** *der/die* person of a different colour; **~geartet** ▸**anders 1**; **~geschlechtlich** *Adj.* of the opposite sex *postpos.*; **~gesinnte** /-gəˈzɪntə/ *der/die; adj. Dekl.* person of a different opinion; **die ~gesinnten** those with *or* of different opinions; **~gläubig** *Adj.* of a different faith *or* religion *postpos.*; **~gläubige** *der/die* person of a different faith *or* religion; **die ~gläubigen** those of different faiths *or* religions; **~herum** **A** *Adv.* the other way round *or* (Amer.) around; **etw. ~herum drehen** turn sth. the other way; **~herum gehen/fahren** go/drive round *or* (Amer.) around the other way; **B** *Adj.* ▸**~rum B**; **~lautend** ▸**anders 1**; **~rum** (ugs.) **A** *Adv.* ▸**~herum A**; **B** *Adj.* **~rum sein** be a poof (Brit. coll.) *or* a fairy (sl. derog.); be queer (sl.); **~sein** *das* (geh.) **sein ~sein akzeptieren** accept that one is different; **~wie** *Adv.* (ugs.) some other way; **~wo** *Adv.* (ugs.) elsewhere; **mach das doch ~wo** do it somewhere else *or* elsewhere; **weder dort noch ~wo** neither there nor anywhere else; **~woher** *Adv.* (ugs.) from elsewhere; from somewhere else; **kann man das ~woher beziehen?** can you get that [from] anywhere else?; **~wohin** *Adv.* (ugs.) elsewhere; somewhere else; **warum fahren wir nie ~wohin?** why do we never go somewhere else?; **wir fahren immer in die Berge, nie ~wohin** we always go up into the mountains, never anywhere else

anderthalb /'andɐt'halp/ *Bruchz.* ▸❶ **S. 826** one and a half; **~ Pfund Mehl** a pound and a half of flour; **~ Stunden** an hour and a half; **~ Jahre [alt] sein** be eighteen months [old]

anderthalb·fach *Vervielfältigungsz.* one and a half times; **einen ~en Salto machen** do a one-and-a-half somersault; **den ~en Preis verlangen** demand half as much again

anderthalb·mal *Adv.* one and a half times; **~ so viel Geld** half as much money again; **~ so viele Besucher** half as many visitors again; **~ so groß wie ...** half as big again as ...

Änderung *die;* **~, ~en** change (+ *Gen.* in); alteration (+ *Gen.* to); (an einem Kleidungsstück) alteration (**an** + *Dat.* to); (in einem Menschen) change (**in** + *Dat.* in); **eine ~ vornehmen** make a change *or* an alteration; **eine ~ zum Besseren** a change for the better; **eine ~ des Programms** a change of programme; **das hat uns zu einer ~ des Programms veranlasst** it has caused us to change *or* alter the programme; **„~en vorbehalten"** 'subject to alteration'

Änderungs-: ~antrag *der* (Politik) amendment; **~kündigung** *die* (Arbeitswelt): *notice of intention to terminate agreement on terms and conditions of employment if changes to the agreement are not accepted;* **~schneiderei** *die* tailor's [that does alterations]; **~vor·schlag** *der* suggested amendment *or* change; **~wunsch** *der* request for changes *or* alterations; **haben Sie irgendwelche ~wünsche?** are there any changes *or* alterations you would like to see?

anderwärts /-vɛrts/ *Adv.* (geh.) elsewhere

anderweitig /-vaitɪç/
A *Adj.* (sonstig) other
B *adv.* **[1]** (auf andere Weise) in another way; **~ beschäftigt sein** be otherwise engaged **[2]** (an jmd. anderen) to somebody else

an|deuten
A *tr. V.* **[1]** (zu verstehen geben) intimate; hint; **jmdm. etw. ~:** intimate *or* hint sth. to sb. **[2]** (nicht ausführen) outline; (kurz erwähnen) indicate
B *refl. V.* (sich abzeichnen) be indicated; **sobald sich die ersten wärmeren Sommertage andeuteten** as soon as there was a suggestion of the first warm days of summer

An·deutung *die* **[1]** (Anspielung) hint; **eine ~ machen** give *or* drop a hint (**über** + *Akk.* about); **in ~en sprechen** talk in hints **[2]** (schwaches Anzeichen) suggestion; hint

andeutungs·weise *Adv.* in the form of a hint *or* suggestion/hints *or* suggestions; **davon war nur ~ die Rede** it was only hinted at

a

an|dichten *tr. V.* **jmdm. etw. ~:** impute sth. to sb.; **man hatte ihm Wunderkräfte angedichtet** he had been credited with miraculous powers; **sie hatten ihm eine Affäre mit seiner Sekretärin angedichtet** they claimed that he'd had an affair with his secretary

an|dicken /'andıkn̩/ *tr. V.* (Kochk.) thicken

an|dienen
A *tr. V.* **jmdm. etw. ~:** offer sth. to sb.; (aufdringlich) press sth. on sb.
B *refl. V.* **sich jmdm. ~:** offer oneself *or* one's services to sb.; (aufdringlich) press oneself *or* one's services on sb.

an|diskutieren *tr. V.* [begin to] discuss briefly

an|docken *tr., itr. V.* (Raumf.) **an etw.** (*Dat.*) **~:** dock with sth.

an|donnern *itr. V.* (ugs.) **angedonnert kommen** come roaring *or* thundering along; (auf einen zu) come roaring *or* thundering up

An·drang *der* 1 crowd; (Gedränge) crush; **es herrschte großer ~:** there was a large crowd/great crush 2 (von Blut, Milch) rush; (von Wasser) surge

an|drängen *itr. V.; mit sein* surge (**gegen** against); ‹*crowd*› surge forward; ‹*army*› push forward; **gegen das Tor ~** (Sport) surge towards goal; **die ~de Flut/Menschenmenge** the surging tide/crowd

andre... ▸**ander...**

Andreas /an'dre:as/ (*der*) Andrew

Andreas·kreuz *das* 1 St Andrew's cross 2 (Verkehrsw.) diagonal cross

an|drehen *tr. V.* 1 (einschalten) turn on 2 (ugs.: verkaufen) **jmdm. etw. ~:** palm sb. off with sth.; palm sth. off on sb.; **lass dir bloß keinen von diesen Äpfeln ~:** don't let yourself be palmed off with any of those apples 3 (befestigen) screw ‹*nut*› on; screw ‹*screw*› in 4 (salopp) **jmdm. ein Kind ~:** knock sb. up (sl.); put sb. in the club (Brit. sl.)

andrerseits ▸**andererseits**

an|dressieren *tr. V.* 1 **einem Tier ein Kunststück/artfremdes Verhalten ~:** train an animal to perform a trick/to exhibit behaviour [patterns] foreign to the species; **andressiertes Verhalten** behaviour that is the result of training 2 (fig. abwertend) train; drill

an|dringen *unr. itr. V.; mit sein* (geh.) surge (**gegen** against); **der ~de Feind** the enemy surging forward

Androgen /andro'ge:n/ *das;* **~s, ~e** (Med.) androgen

androgyn /andro'gy:n/ *Adj.* (Psych., Bot.) androgynous

an|drohen *tr. V.* **jmdm. etw. ~:** threaten sb. with sth.; **er hat mir Prügel angedroht** he threatened to beat me

An·drohung *die* threat; **unter ~ von Gewalt** with the *or* under threat of violence; **durch die ~ seines Rücktritts** by threatening to resign

Android /andro'i:t/ *der;* **~en, ~en, Androide** /andro'i:də/ *der;* **~n, ~n** android

Androloge /andro'lo:gə/ *der;* **~n, ~n, Andrologin** *die;* **~, ~nen** (Med.) andrologist

An·druck *der;* **~[e]s, ~e** (Druckw.) 1 (Probe) proof; **bereit für den ~:** ready for proofing 2 (Beginn) going to press; **lange vor dem ~:** long before going to press

an|drucken (Druckw.)
A *tr. V.* 1 (beginnen) start printing 2 (zur Probe) proof; pull proofs of
B *itr. V.* 1 (beginnen) start printing; go to press; **wir können ~ lassen** we can go to press 2 (zur Probe) pull proofs

an|drücken *tr. V.* 1 press down; **den Bleistift leicht ~:** press lightly with the pencil 2 (einschalten) switch on

Andruck·exemplar *das* (Druckw.) 1 printed copy 2 (Probe) proof copy

an|dudeln *tr. V.* **in sich** (*Dat.*) **einen ~** (salopp) get plastered (sl.)

an|dünsten *tr. V.* (Kochk.) braise lightly

Äneas /ɛ'ne:as/ (*der*) Aeneas

an|ecken *itr. V.; mit sein* 1 (anstoßen) **an etw.** (*Dat.*) **~:** hit sth. 2 (ugs.: Ärger erregen) **bei jmdm. ~:** rub sb. [up (Brit.)] the wrong way

an|eifern *tr. V.* (südd., österr.) spur on

an|eignen *refl. V.* 1 (nehmen) appropriate; **sich** (*Dat.*) **etw. widerrechtlich ~:** misappropriate sth. 2 (lernen) acquire; learn 3 (angewöhnen) acquire; pick up

An·eignung *die* 1 appropriation; **widerrechtliche ~:** misappropriation 2 (Lernen) acquisition; learning 3 (Rechtsw.) acquisition of title (*Gen.* to)

an·einander *Adv.* (zusammen) together; (nebeneinander) next to each other; next to one another; (gegeneinander) against each other; against one another; **Häuser ~ bauen** build houses on to each other; **dicht ~ gebaut** built very close together; **Raumschiffe ~ koppeln** link up spacecraft; **sich ~ klammern** cling together *or* to each other; **sich ~ kuscheln** snuggle *or* cuddle up [together *or* to each other *or* to one another]; **sie lagen ~ gekuschelt** they lay snuggled *or* cuddled up [together]; **Perlen auf einer Schnur ~ reihen** thread pearls/beads on a string; **~ grenzen** ‹*properties, rooms, etc.*› adjoin [each other *or* one another]; ‹*countries*› border on each other *or* one another; **~ liegen** lie next to each other; ‹*properties*› adjoin [each other *or* one another]; **~ prallen** collide; **~ rücken** move [up] closer together; **~ schlagen** strike each other *or* one another; **sich ~ schmiegen** snuggle *or* cuddle up [together *or* to each other *or* to one another]; **stellt euch mal mit dem Rücken ~:** stand back to back; **~ stoßen** strike each other; ‹*heads, vehicles*› collide; **sie stießen mit den Köpfen ~:** their heads collided; **mit jmdm. ~ geraten** (sich prügeln) come to blows with sb.; (sich streiten) quarrel with sb; **~ denken** think of each other *or* one another; **~ vorbeigehen** pass each other *or* one another; go past each other *or* one another; **sich ~ gewöhnen** get used to each other *or* one another; **~ vorbeireden** talk at cross purposes; **sich ~ festhalten** hold each other *or* one another

aneinander-, Aneinander-: ***~|bauen** *usw.* ▸**aneinander**; **~reihung** *die* stringing together; **eine bloße ~reihung von Tatsachen** a series of facts just strung together; ***~|rücken** *usw.* ▸**aneinander**

Äneis /ɛ'ne:ıs/ *die;* **~:** Aeneid

Anekdote /anɛk'do:tə/ *die;* **~, ~n** anecdote

anekdoten·haft
A *Adj.* anecdotal
B *adv.* ‹*relate*› in anecdotes

anekdotisch
A *Adj.* anecdotal
B *adv.* **ein ~ gewürzter Vortrag** a lecture enlivened with anecdotes

an|ekeln *tr. V.* disgust; nauseate; **du ekelst mich an** you make me sick; **sich angeekelt abwenden** turn away in disgust

Anemo·meter /anemo-/ *das* (Met.) anemometer

Anemone /ane'mo:nə/ *die;* **~, ~n** anemone

an|empfehlen *unr. tr. V.* (geh.) recommend (*Dat.* to)

an|erbieten *unr. refl. V.* (geh.) offer one's services; **sich ~, etw. zu tun** offer to do sth.

Anerbieten *das;* **~s, ~** (geh.) offer

anerkannt *Adj.* recognized; recognized, acknowledged ‹*authority, expert*›; recognized, accepted, established ‹*fact*›

anerkanntermaßen *Adv.* **er gehört ~ zu den besten Spielern** he is generally recognized *or* acknowledged to be one of the best players

anerkennen *unr. tr. V.;* **ich erkenne an** (*od. seltener:* **anerkenne), anerkannt, anzuerkennen** 1 recognize ‹*country, record, verdict, qualification, document*›; acknowledge ‹*debt*›; accept ‹*demand, bill, conditions, rules*›; allow ‹*claim, goal*›; **ein Kind ~:** acknowledge a child as one's own; **jmdn. als gleichberechtigten Partner ~:** accept sb. as an equal partner 2 (nicht leugnen) acknowledge 3 (würdigen) acknowledge, appreciate ‹*achievement, efforts*›; appreciate ‹*person*›; respect ‹*viewpoint, opinion*›; **ein ~der Blick** an appreciative look; **~d nicken** nod appreciatively; **einige ~de Worte** a few words of appreciation

anerkennens·wert *Adj.* commendable

anerkennenswerter·weise *Adv.* commendably

An·erkenntnis *das;* **~ses, ~se** acknowledgement

Anerkennung *die;* **~, ~en** 1 ▸**anerkennen 1**: recognition; acknowledgement; acceptance; allowance 2 (Zugeständnis) acknowledgement 3 (Würdigung) ▸**anerkennen 3**: acknowledgement; appreciation; respect (*Gen.* for)

an|erziehen *unr. tr. V.* **jmdm. etw. ~:** instil sth. into sb.; **Kindern Pünktlichkeit ~:** bring children up to be punctual

an|essen *unr. refl. V.* **in sich** (*Dat.*) **einen Bauch ~:** develop a paunch

an|fachen *tr. V.* fan; (fig.) arouse ‹*anger, curiosity, enthusiasm*›; arouse, inflame ‹*passion*›; inspire, stir up ‹*hatred*›; inspire ‹*hope*›; ferment ‹*discord, war*›

an|fahren
A *unr. tr. V.* 1 run into; hit 2 (herbeifahren) deliver 3 (ansteuern) stop *or* call at ‹*village etc.*›; ‹*ship*› put in at ‹*port*›; **das Schiff fährt die Insel einmal wöchentlich an** the boat calls at the island once a week 4 (zurechtweisen) shout at 5 (in Betrieb nehmen) commission ‹*powerstation, blast furnace*›
B *unr. itr. V.; mit sein* 1 (starten) start off; **das Anfahren am Berg** hill-starting 2 (heranfahren) drive up; (mit dem Fahrrad, Motorrad) ride up; **angefahren kommen** come driving/riding up

An·fahrt *die* 1 (das Anfahren) journey; (als Autofahrer) drive; (Ankunft) arrival 2 (Weg) approach; (Einfahrt) entrance

Anfahrts-: ~weg *der* journey; (als Autofahrer) drive; **~zeit** *die* travelling time; **~zeiten als Arbeitszeit berechnen** count travelling time *sing.* as working time

An·fall *der* 1 (Attacke) attack; (epileptischer ~, fig.) fit; **einen ~ bekommen** *od.* (ugs.) **kriegen** have an attack/a fit; **in einem ~ von ...** (fig.) in a fit of ... 2 (Anfallendes) amount (**an** + *Dat.* of); (Ertrag) yield (**an** + *Dat.* of)

anfall·artig
A *Adj.* **~es Husten** fits *pl.* of coughing; coughing fits *pl.*; **~e Schmerzen** spasms *pl.* of pain
B *adv.* **plötzlich und ~ auftretende Zuckungen/Schmerzen** a sudden fit/sudden fits of twitching/a sudden spasm/sudden spasms of pain; **die Schmerzen kommen ~:** the pain comes in spasms

an·fallen
A *unr. tr. V.* 1 (angreifen) attack 2 (geh.: befallen) **Zweifel/Angst fiel mich an** I was assailed by doubt/fear; **Heimweh/Wut/Entsetzen fiel mich an** I was filled with homesickness/rage/horror; **Müdigkeit fiel mich an** I was overcome with tiredness
B *unr. itr. V.; mit sein* ‹*costs*› arise, be incurred; ‹*interest*› accrue; ‹*work*› come up; ‹*parcels etc.*› accumulate; **als Nebenprodukt/Nebenkosten ~:** be obtained as a by-product/be costs incurred; **alle ~den Reparaturen** any repairs that become necessary

an·fällig *Adj.* delicate ‹*child*›; temperamental ‹*engine*›; **gegen** *od.* **für etw. ~ sein** be susceptible to sth.; **für eine Krankheit ~ sein** be prone to an illness

An·fälligkeit *die;* **~, ~en** (eines Kindes usw.) delicateness; (eines Motors usw.) temperamental nature; **~ gegen** *od.* **für etw.** susceptibility to sth.; **~ für eine Krankheit** proneness to an illness

anfalls·weise *Adv.* **die Schmerzen kommen ~:** the pain comes in spasms

An·fang *der* ▸**❶ S. 29**, ▸**❶ S. 165** beginning; start; (erster Abschnitt) beginning; **ohne ~ und Ende** without a beginning *or* an end; **[ganz] am ~ der Straße** [right] at the start of the street; **von den Anfängen** from the beginnings; **am** *od.* **zu ~:** at first; to begin with; **am ~ schuf Gott ...** in the beginning God created ...; **du hättest ihm gleich zu ~ sagen sollen,**

a

dass ... you should have told him right at the beginning or outset that ...; von ~ an from the beginning or outset; ~ 1984/der Achtzigerjahre/Mai/der Woche usw. at the beginning of 1984/the eighties/May/the week etc.; von ~ bis Ende from beginning to end or start to finish; der ~ vom Ende the beginning of the end; im ~ war das Wort (bibl.) in the beginning was the Word; einen ~ machen make a start; ein ~ ist gemacht it's a start; we've/they've etc. made a start; den ~ machen make a start; start; (nach einem Zerwürfnis o. Ä.) make the first move; einen/keinen ~ finden know/not know how to begin or start; einen neuen ~ machen make a new or fresh start; aller ~ ist schwer (Spr.) it's always difficult at the beginning; seinen ~ nehmen (geh.) begin; start; in den od. seinen Anfängen stecken be in its infancy; wehret den Anfängen! these things must be stopped at the outset; aus bescheidenen Anfängen from small or humble beginnings

an·fangen

A unr. itr. V. **1** begin; start; das fängt ja gut an! (ugs. iron.) that's a good start! (iron.); mit dreißig fängt das Leben erst an life begins at thirty; der Monat fing mit einem Donnerstag an the first day of the month was a Thursday; wer fängt an? who is going to start?; habt ihr schon angefangen? have you already started?; fangt doch bitte schon an do please start; er hat ganz klein/als ganz kleiner Angestellter angefangen he started small/started [out] as a minor employee; mit etw. ~: start [on] sth.; fang nicht wieder damit an! don't start [all] that again!; ~, etw. zu tun start to do sth.; es fängt an zu schneien od. zu schneien an it's starting or beginning to snow; fang doch nicht gleich an zu weinen don't start crying; angefangen bei od. mit od. von ... starting or beginning with ...; Weiß fängt an white starts; er hat angefangen (mit dem Streit o. Ä.) he started it; [noch mal] von vorne ~: start [again] from the beginning; start all over again **2** (zu sprechen ~) begin; von etw. ~: start on about sth. **3** (eine Stelle antreten) start; bei einer Firma ~: start working for a firm; start with a firm

B unr. tr. V. **1** begin; start; (anbrechen) start; das Rauchen ~: start smoking; ich glaube, er will mit seiner Sekretärin was ~ (ugs.) I think he's trying to start something with his secretary; auf seinem Schreibtisch lag ein angefangener Brief on his desk lay a letter which he had started to write **2** (machen) do; damit kann ich nichts/nicht viel ~: that's no/not much good to me; (das verstehe ich nicht/kaum) that doesn't mean anything/much to me; kannst du noch etwas damit ~? is it any good or use to you?; mit ihm ist heute nichts anzufangen he is just not with it today; mit ihm kann ich wenig ~: he isn't my type of person; er weiß nichts mit sich anzufangen he doesn't know what to do with himself; wie hast du das nun wieder angefangen? how did you manage that?; du musst etwas Solides ~: you must get yourself a proper job/training etc.; du hättest es ganz anders ~ müssen you should have gone about it quite differently

An·fänger der; ~s, ~, **An·fängerin** die; ~, ~nen beginner; (abwertend: Stümper) amateur; (am Heck eines Autos) „~" 'learner'

Anfänger·kurs der beginners' course; course for beginners

anfänglich /ˈanfɛŋlɪç/

A Adj. initial

B adv. at first; initially

anfangs Adv. at first; initially; gleich ~: right at the beginning or outset

Anfangs-: ~buchstabe der initial [letter]; first letter; ~drittel das (Eishockey) first period; ~erfolg der initial success; ~gehalt das starting salary; ~geschwindigkeit die (Physik) initial velocity; ~gründe Pl. rudiments; ~kapital das starting capital; ~phase die first or initial phase; ~reim der initial or beginning rhyme; ~schwierigkeit die initial difficulty; ~silbe die first or initial syllable; ~stadium das initial stage; im ~stadium sein be in its/their initial stages pl.; ~unterricht der elementary instruction; ein Englischbuch für den ~unterricht an elementary-level English book; ~zeit die starting time

an|fassen

A tr. V. **1** (fassen, halten) take hold of; die Kinder fassen jeden Dreck an the children will pick up any bit of dirt **2** (berühren) touch; fass mal meine Stirn an feel my forehead; nicht ~! don't touch!; Geschichte zum Anfassen (fig.) history brought to life; ich fasse nie wieder eine Spielkarte an I'll never touch a pack of cards again **3** (bei der Hand nehmen) jmdn. ~: take sb.'s hand; fasst euch an take each other's hand **4** (angehen) approach, tackle ‹problem, task, etc.› **5** (behandeln) treat ‹person› **6** (geh.: befallen) Ekel/Sehnsucht/Mitleid fasste mich an I was seized with revulsion/filled with longing/pity

B itr. V. (mithelfen) [mit] ~: lend a hand

C refl. V. (sich anfühlen) feel; das fasst sich wie Wolle an it feels like wool

an|fauchen tr. V. **1** ‹cat› spit at **2** (fig.) snap at

an|faulen itr. V.; mit sein ‹fruit› start to go bad; ‹wood› start to rot; ein angefaulter Apfel/Balken a bad apple/rotting beam

anfechtbar Adj. **1** (bes. Rechtsw.) contestable **2** (kritisierbar, bestreitbar) disputable ‹statement, decision›; ‹book› open to criticism

Anfechtbarkeit die; ~ ▸anfechtbar: **1** contestable nature **2** disputable nature

an|fechten unr. tr. V. **1** (bes. Rechtsw.) challenge, dispute ‹validity, authenticity, statement›; contest ‹will›; contest, challenge ‹decision›; dispute ‹contract›; challenge ‹law, opinion› **2** (beunruhigen) trouble; bother; was ficht dich an? (geh.) what is wrong or the matter with you?

Anfechtung die; ~, ~en **1** (bes. Rechtsw.) ▸anfechten 1: challenging; disputing; contesting **2** (geh.: Versuchung) temptation

Anfechtungs·klage die (Rechtsw.) action for nullification

an|fegen itr. V.; mit sein angefegt kommen (ugs.) come belting along (coll.); (auf einen zu) come belting up (coll.)

an|feinden tr. V. treat with hostility

Anfeindung die; ~, ~en hostility; trotz aller ~en despite all the hostility sing. shown towards him/her etc.; ~en ausgesetzt sein be exposed to hostility sing.

an|fertigen tr. V. make; do ‹homework, translation›; make up ‹medicament, preparation›; prepare, draw up ‹report›; cut, make ‹key›; Kleider/einen Schlüssel ~ lassen have clothes made/a key cut

An·fertigung die **1** ▸anfertigen: making; doing; making up; preparing; drawing up; cutting **2** (Erzeugnis) das Regal ist eine eigene ~ [von mir] I made the shelves myself; eine spezielle ~ sein be specially made

an|feuchten tr. V. moisten ‹lips, stamp›; dampen, wet ‹ironing, cloth, etc.›

an|feuern tr. V. spur on; ~de Rufe/Gesten shouts of encouragement/rousing gestures

An·feuerung die spurring on; ~ und Beifall cheers and applause

Anfeuerungs·ruf der cheer

an|finden unr. refl. V. be found [again]; turn up

an|flachsen tr. V. (ugs.) tease; kid (sl.)

an|flanschen /ˈanflanʃn̩/ tr. V. (Technik) flange sth. on (an + Dat. od. Akk. to)

an|flattern itr. V.; mit sein angeflattert kommen come fluttering along; (auf einen zu) come fluttering up

an|flehen tr. V. beseech; implore; jmdn. um etw. ~: beg sb. for sth.

an|fliegen

A unr. itr. V.; mit sein ‹aircraft› fly in; (beim Landen) approach; come in to land; ‹bird etc.› fly in; angeflogen kommen come flying in; (auf einen zu) ‹bird› come flying up; gegen den Wind ~: fly into the wind

B unr. tr. V. **1** fly to ‹city, country, airport›; (beim Landen) approach ‹airport›; land on ‹runway etc.› **2** (ansteuern) ‹aircraft› approach; ‹bird› fly towards, approach

an|flitzen itr. V.; mit sein angeflitzt kommen (ugs.) come racing along; (auf einen zu) come racing up

An·flug der **1** approach; die Maschine befindet sich im ~ auf Berlin the plane is now approaching Berlin **2** (Hauch) hint; trace; ein humoristischer ~: a hint or trace of humour **3** (Anwandlung) fit; in einem ~ von Großzügigkeit in a fit of generosity **4** (Weg, Strecke) flight

an|flunkern tr. V. (ugs.) tell fibs to

an|fordern tr. V. request, ask for ‹help›; ask for ‹catalogue›; order ‹goods, materials›; send for ‹ambulance›

An·forderung die **1** (das Anfordern) request (Gen. for); die ~ von Waren/Materialien ordering goods/materials **2** (Anspruch) demand; große/hohe ~en an jmdn./etw. stellen make great demands on sb./sth.; den ~en nicht gewachsen sein not be up to the demands

An·frage die inquiry; (Parl.) question; große/kleine ~ (Parl.) oral/written question

an|fragen

A itr. V. inquire; ask; bei jmdm. um etw. ~: ask sb. for sth.

B tr. V. (schweiz.) ask

an|fressen

A unr. tr. V. **1** nibble [at]; ‹bird› peck [at] **2** (zersetzen) eat away [at]; ein von Rost angefressenes altes Auto a rusty old car

B unr. refl. V. sich (Dat.) einen Bauch ~ (salopp) develop a paunch; die Tiere fressen sich einen Winterspeck an the animals [eat to] put on winter fat

an|freunden refl. V. **1** make or become friends; sich mit jmdm./miteinander ~: make or become friends with sb./become friends **2** (fig.) sich mit einer Sache ~: get to like sth.

an|frieren unr. itr. V.; mit sein an etw. (Dat.) ~: freeze to sth.

an|fügen tr. V. add

An·fügung die addition

an|fühlen

A refl. V. feel; sich hart/weich ~: feel hard/soft; be hard/soft to the touch

B tr. V. (befühlen) feel

Anfuhr die; ~, ~en transport[ation]

an|führen tr. V. **1** lead; lead, head ‹procession›; unsere Mannschaft führt die Tabelle an our team heads the table or is [at the] top of the table **2** (zitieren) quote **3** (nennen) quote, give, offer ‹example›; give, offer ‹reason, details, proof›; zu meiner Entschuldigung möchte ich auch noch ~, dass ... I should also like to mention in my defence that ... **4** (benennen) name; cite **5** (ugs.: hereinlegen) have on (Brit. coll.); dupe; lass dich doch von ihm nicht ~: don't be had on (Brit.) or taken in by him (coll.) **6** (Druckw.: mit Anführungszeichen versehen) mark with opening quotation marks or (Brit.) inverted commas; Buchtitel werden an- und abgeführt book titles are put in quotation marks or (Brit.) inverted commas

An·führer der, **An·führerin** die **1** (Führer) leader **2** (Rädelsführer) ringleader

An·führung die **1** leadership; unter [der] ~ (+ Gen.) under the leadership of **2** (das Zitieren, Zitat) quotation **3** (Nennung) ▸anführen 3: quotation; giving; offering; ich beschränke mich auf die ~ einiger Beispiele I will confine myself to quoting or giving or offering just a few examples **4** (Benennung) naming; citing **5** (Druckw.: Anführungszeichen) opening quotation mark

Anführungs-: ~strich der, ~zeichen das quotation mark; inverted comma (Brit.); ein Wort mit ~strichen od. ~zeichen versehen put a word in quotation marks or (Brit.) inverted commas; ~striche od. ~zeichen unten/oben (beim Diktieren o. Ä.) quote/unquote; halbe ~striche od. ~zeichen single quotation marks or (coll.) quotes

an|füllen
A tr. V. fill [up]; **mit etw. angefüllt sein** be filled *or* full with sth.
B *refl. V.* fill [up]

an|funkeln *tr. V.* flash one's eyes at

an|futtern *refl. V. in* **sich** (*Dat.*) **einen Bauch/ein Bäuchlein ~** (ugs.) develop a paunch/(coll.) a bit of a tummy

An·gabe *die* 1 (das Mitteilen) giving; **ohne ~ von Gründen** without giving [any] reasons; **zur ~ dieser Daten bist du verpflichtet** you are obliged to give this information 2 (Auskunft, Aussage) **~n** information *sing.*; **jede einzelne ~ wurde überprüft** every piece of information has been checked 3 (Anweisung) instruction 4 (Prahlerei) boasting; bragging; (angeberisches Benehmen) showing-off; **das ist doch nur ~!** he is/they are *etc.* only boasting 5 (Ballspiele) service; serve; **[eine] ~ machen** serve; **ich habe [die] ~:** it's my serve

an|gaffen *tr. V.* (abwertend) gape at

an|gähnen *tr. V.* yawn at

an|galoppieren *itr. V.; mit sein* **angaloppiert kommen** come galloping along; (auf einen zu) come galloping up

an·gängig *Adj.* permissible

an|geben
A *unr. tr. V.* 1 give ‹*reason*›; declare ‹*income, dutiable goods*›; name, cite ‹*witness*›; **welche Haarfarbe er hatte, kann ich nicht [genau] ~:** I cannot say *or* state [exactly] what colour hair he had; **zur angegebenen Zeit** at the appointed time; **wie oben angegeben** as stated *or* mentioned above; **der Zeuge gab an, er habe drei Schüsse gehört** the witness stated *or* maintained that he heard three shots 2 (bestimmen) set ‹*course, direction*›; **den Takt ~:** keep time 3 (veralt.: anzeigen, melden) report ‹*theft etc.*›; give away ‹*accomplice etc.*›; **jmdn./einen Diebstahl bei der Polizei ~:** report sb./a theft to the police; **das geb ich an!** I'm going to report that!
B *unr. itr. V.* 1 (prahlen) boast; brag; (sich angeberisch benehmen) show off; **er gibt vor den Mädchen damit an, dass ...** he boasts to all the girls that ...; **Väter geben mit ihren Kindern an** fathers boast *or* brag about their children; **~ wie eine Tüte [voll] Mücken** (ugs.) be just a big show-off (coll.) 2 (Ballspiele) serve; **wer gibt an?** whose serve is it?; whose turn is it to serve?

Angeber *der;* **~s, ~** 1 (Prahler) boaster; braggart; (sich angeberisch Benehmender) show-off 2 (veralt.: Denunziant) informer

Angeberei *die;* **~, ~en** 1 (das Angeben) boasting; bragging; (angeberisches Benehmen) showing-off; **das ist doch nichts als ~:** he's/they are *etc.* only boasting/showing off 2 (Handlung) piece of showing-off; (Äußerung) boast; **mit seinen dummen ~en** with his stupid showing off/boasting

Angeberin *die;* **~, ~nen** 1 (Prahlerin) boaster; braggart; (sich angeberisch Benehmende) show-off 2 (veralt.: Denunziantin) informer

angeberisch (ugs.)
A *Adj.* boastful ‹*person*›; pretentious, showy ‹*glasses, car, jacket*›; (im Benehmen) ‹*person*› given to showing off; **~es Getue** *od.* **Verhalten** showing-off
B *adv.* boastfully

Angebetete *der/die; adj. Dekl.* (meist scherzh.) beloved; (Idol) idol

An·gebinde *das* (geh. veralt.) gift; present

angeblich
A *Adj.* alleged
B *adv.* supposedly; allegedly; **er ist ~ krank** he is supposed to be ill; (er sagt, er sei krank) he says he's ill

an·geboren *Adj.* innate ‹*characteristic*›; congenital ‹*disease*›; **die Schüchternheit ist ihm ~:** he is shy by nature *or* naturally shy

An·gebot *das* 1 offer 2 (Wirtsch.: Waren~) range; **das ~ an** *od.* **von Gemüse ist immer saisonabhängig** the selection of vegetables available always depends on the season; **das Verhältnis von ~ und Nachfrage** the relationship between supply and demand 3 (Kaufmannsspr.: Sonder~) [special] offer; **im ~:** on [special] offer; **~ der Woche** bargain of the week

an·gebracht
A *2. Part. v.* **anbringen**
B *Adj.* appropriate

an·gebunden
A *2. Part. v.* **anbinden**
B *Adj.* 1 tied down 2 *in* **kurz ~** (ugs.) short; abrupt

an·gedeihen *unr. itr. V. in* **jmdm. etw. ~ lassen** (geh.) provide sb. with sth.; grant sb. sth.

An·gedenken *das* remembrance; **jmdm. ein treues ~ bewahren** keep sb. in fond remembrance; **mein Großvater seligen ~s** (geh.) my grandfather of blessed memory; **eine Zeit unseligen ~s** (geh.) a notorious period

an·gegangen
A *2. Part. v.* **angehen**
B *Adj.* (bes. ostmd.) ‹*food*› that has gone off; **~ sein** have gone off

angegilbt /ˈangəgɪlpt/ *Adj.* yellowing; slightly yellowed

an·gegossen *Adj. in* **wie ~ sitzen/passen** (ugs.) fit like a glove

angegraut /ˈangəgraut/ *Adj.* greying

an·gegriffen
A *2. Part. v.* **angreifen**
B *Adj.* weakened ‹*health, stomach*›; strained ‹*nerves, voice*›; (erschöpft) exhausted; (nervlich) strained

angehaucht
A *2. Part. v.* **anhauchen**
B *Adj.* **links/rechts/sozialistisch** *usw.* **~ sein** have left-wing/right-wing/socialist *etc.* leanings

an·geheiratet *Adj.* **ein ~er Onkel/Vetter** *usw.* an uncle/a cousin *etc.* by marriage; **~ sein** be related by marriage

angeheitert /ˈangəhaitɐt/ *Adj.* tipsy; merry (coll.)

an|gehen
A *unr. itr. V.; mit sein* 1 (sich einschalten, entzünden) ‹*radio, light, heating*› come on; ‹*fire*› catch, start burning 2 (sich einschalten, entzünden lassen) ‹*radio, light*› go on; ‹*fire*› light, catch 3 (ugs.: beginnen) start 4 (anwachsen, wachsen) ‹*plant*› take root; ‹*vaccination*› take; ‹*bacteria*› grow 5 (geschehen dürfen) **es mag noch ~:** it's [just about] acceptable; **es geht nicht an, dass radikale Elemente die Partei unterwandern** radical elements must not be allowed to infiltrate the party 6 (bes. nordd.: wahr sein) **das kann doch wohl nicht ~!** that can't be true!; **das kann [wohl] ~:** that could be true 7 **gegen etw./jmdn. ~:** fight sth./sb.
B *unr. tr. V.* 1 (angreifen) attack; (Sport) tackle; challenge 2 (in Angriff nehmen) tackle ‹*problem, difficulty*›; take ‹*fence, bend*› 3 (bitten) ask; **jmdn. um etw. ~:** ask sb. for sth. 4 (betreffen) concern; **was geht dich das an?** what's it got to do with you?; **das geht dich nichts an** it's none of your business; **was das/mich angeht, [so] ...** as far as that is/I am concerned ...

angehend *Adj.* budding ‹*actor, artist, etc.*›; prospective ‹*teacher, husband, etc.*›

an|gehören *itr. V.* **jmdm./einer Sache ~:** belong to sb./sth.; **der Regierung/einer Familie/Kommission ~:** be a member of the government/a family/committee; **einander ~** (geh.) belong to each other; **einer Nation ~:** be a national of a country

an·gehörig *Adj.* belonging (*Dat.* to); **dem Bündnis ~e Staaten** states belonging to the alliance

Angehörige *der/die; adj. Dekl.* 1 (Verwandte) relative; relation; **der nächste ~:** the next of kin 2 (Mitglied) member

Angeklagte /ˈangəkla:ktə/ *der/die; adj. Dekl.* accused; defendant

angeknackst (ugs.)
A *2. Part. v.* **anknacksen**
B *Adj.* weakened ‹*trust, confidence*›; weakened ‹*health*›; **ihre Gesundheit ist ~:** she's not in the best of health *or* (coll.) not all that great

angekränkelt /ˈangəkrɛŋklt/ *Adj.* sickly; **von Eitelkeit ~:** afflicted with vanity

Angel /ˈaŋl/ *die;* **~, ~n** 1 fishing rod; rod and line; **die ~ auswerfen/einziehen** cast/pull in the line 2 (Tür~, Fenster~ usw.) hinge; **etw. aus den ~n heben** lift sth. off its hinges; (fig.) turn sth. upside down

an·gelegen
A *2. Part. v.* **anliegen**
B *Adj. in* **sich** (*Dat.*) **etw. ~ sein lassen** concern oneself with sth.

An·gelegenheit *die* matter; (Aufgabe, Problem) affair; concern; **öffentliche/kulturelle ~en** public/cultural affairs; **das ist meine/nicht meine ~:** that is my affair *or* business/not my concern *or* business; **kümmere dich um deine eigenen ~en!** mind your own business; **sich in jmds. ~en mischen** meddle in sb.'s affairs; **in welcher ~?** in what connection?; **in eigener/in einer privaten ~:** on a personal/private matter

an·gelegentlich (geh.)
A *Adj.* pressing ‹*question, request*›; earnest ‹*conversation, warning*›
B *adv.* ‹*look*› very closely, thoroughly; ‹*ask, inquire*› particularly; **sich mit einer Sache ~ beschäftigen** be intensively occupied with sth.; **jmdm. ~ empfehlen, nicht mehr zu rauchen** earnestly recommend sb. to give up smoking

angelegt
A *2. Part. v.* **anlegen**
B *Adj.* **auf Verteidigung/Entspannung** (*Akk.*) **~ sein** be intended for defence/be intended to promote détente

Angel-: ~gerät *das* 1 fishing rod; rod and line; 2 fishing tackle; **~haken** *der* fish hook; **~leine** *die* fishing line

angeln
A *tr. V.* (zu fangen suchen) fish for; (fangen) catch; **er angelt sich immer die Fleischstücke aus der Suppe** (fig.) he always fishes the pieces of meat out of the soup; **sie hat sich einen reichen Mann geangelt** (fig.) she has hooked a rich husband
B *itr. V.* angle; fish; **auf Hechte ~:** fish for pike; **nach etw. ~** (fig.) fish for sth.

an|geloben *tr. V.* (österr.) ▸ **vereidigen**

Angel-: ~punkt *der* crucial point; (eines Problems) crux; (zentrales Thema) central issue; **~rute** *die* fishing rod; **~sachse** *der* 1 (hist.) Anglo-Saxon; 2 (Engländer) Englishman; **die ~sachsen** the English; (Engländer u. Amerikaner) the Anglo-Saxons; **~sächsin** *die* 1 (hist.) Anglo-Saxon; 2 (Engländerin) English woman/English girl; **~sächsisch** *Adj.* 1 (hist.) Anglo-Saxon; 2 (englisch) English; **die ~sächsischen Länder** the Anglo-Saxon countries; **~schein** *der* fishing permit *or* licence; **~schnur** *die* fishing line; **~sport** *der* angling *no art.*

an·gemessen
A *2. Part. v.* **anmessen**
B *Adj.* appropriate; reasonable, fair ‹*price, fee*›; **den Umständen ~ sein** be appropriate to the circumstances
C *adv.* ‹*behave*› appropriately; ‹*reward*› adequately; ‹*recompense*› reasonably, fairly

an·genehm
A *Adj.* pleasant; agreeable; **ist Ihnen die Temperatur/ist es so ~?** is the temperature all right for you/is it all right like that?; **es ist mir gar nicht ~, dass ...** I don't at all like it that ...; **wenn Ihnen das ~er ist** if you [would] prefer; **~e Reise/Ruhe!** [have a] pleasant journey/have a good rest; **[sehr] ~!** delighted to meet you; **das Angenehme mit dem Nützlichen verbinden** combine business with pleasure
B *adv.* pleasantly; agreeably

angepasst, *angepaßt
A *2. Part. v.* **anpassen**
B *Adj.* conformist

Angepasstheit, *Angepaßtheit *die;* **~:** conformism

Anger /ˈaŋɐ/ *der;* **~s, ~:** [village] green

angeregt
A *2. Part. v.* **anregen**
B *Adj.* lively; animated
C *adv.* **sich ~ unterhalten/~ diskutieren** have a lively *or* an animated conversation/discussion

a

angesagt *Adj.* ~ **sein** (gefragt sein) be in vogue; (anstehen) be in order

angesäuselt (ugs.)
A *2. Part. v.* **ansäuseln**
B *Adj.* tipsy; merry (coll.)

angeschickert *Adj.* (ugs.) tipsy (**von** with)

an·geschlagen
A *2. Part. v.* **anschlagen**
B *Adj.* groggy; poor, weakened ‹*health*›

angeschmutzt /ˈangəʃmʊtst/ *Adj.* slightly soiled

Angeschuldigte *der/die; adj. Dekl.* suspect

angesehen
A *2. Part. v.* **ansehen**
B *Adj.* respected

An·gesicht *das;* ~**[e]s,** ~**er,** *österr. auch* ~**e** (geh.) **1** (Gesicht) face; **von** ~ **zu** ~**:** face to face; **jmdm. von** ~ **zu** ~ **gegenüberstehen** stand facing sb. *or* face to face with sb.; **jmdn. von** ~ **kennen** know sb. by sight **2** *in* **im** ~ (+ *Gen.*) ▸**angesichts 1**

angesichts *Präp. mit Gen.* (geh.) **1** ~ **des Feindes/der Gefahr/des Todes/der Stadt/der Küste** in the face of the enemy/of danger/death/in sight of the town/coast **2** (fig.: in Anbetracht) in view of

an·gespannt
A *2. Part. v.* **anspannen**
B *Adj.* **1** (angestrengt) close ‹*attention*›; taut ‹*nerves*› **2** (kritisch) tense ‹*situation*›; tight ‹*market, economic situation*›
C *adv.* ‹*work*› concentratedly; ‹*listen*› with concentrated attention

Angespanntheit *die;* ~ **1** (Angestrengtheit) attentiveness **2** (kritischer Zustand) ▸**angespannt 2**: tenseness; tightness

angestammt /ˈangəʃtamt/ *Adj.* hereditary ‹*right*›; inherited ‹*property*›; (scherzh.: altgewohnt) usual ‹*seat, place*›

angestaubt
A *2. Part. v.* **anstauben**
B *Adj.* outdated

angestellt
A *2. Part. v.* **anstellen**
B *Adj.* **bei jmdm.** ~ **sein** be employed by sb.; work for sb.; **fest** ~ **sein** have a permanent position

Angestellte *der/die; adj. Dekl.* ▸**ℹ S. 113** [salaried] employee; **die** ~**n des öffentlichen Dienstes** salaried public employees; **Arbeiter und** ~**:** workers and salaried staff; blue- and white-collar workers; **die leitenden** ~**n** the managerial staff; the managers; **sie ist** ~ **bei der Stadt** she works for the town council; (im Gegensatz zur Beamtin/Arbeiterin) she has a salaried position with the town council

Angestellten-: ~**gewerkschaft** *die* white-collar union; ~**verhältnis** *das* employment *no indef. art.* on a [monthly] salary; **im** ~**verhältnis stehen** be a salaried employee; (kein Beamter sein) not have guaranteed employment for life; ~**versicherung** *die* [salaried] employees' insurance

angestrengt
A *2. Part. v.* **anstrengen**
B *Adj.* close ‹*attention*›; concentrated ‹*work, study, thought*›; forced ‹*joke*›
C *adv.* ‹*work, think, search*› concentratedly

Angestrengtheit *die;* ~ ▸**angestrengt B**: closeness; concentratedness; forcedness

an·getan
A *2. Part. v.* **antun**
B *Adj. in* **von jmdm./etw.** ~ **sein** be taken with sb./sth.; **dazu** *od.* **danach** ~ **sein, etw. zu tun** (geh.) be suitable for doing sth.

Angetraute /ˈangətrautə/ *der/die; adj. Dekl.* (scherzh.) better half (joc.)

an·getrunken
A *2. Part. v.* **antrinken**
B *Adj.* [slightly] drunk

an·gewandt
A *2. Part. v.* **anwenden**
B *Adj.* applied

an·gewiesen
A *2. Part. v.* **anweisen**
B *Adj.: in* **auf etw.** (*Akk.*) ~ **sein** have to rely on sth.; **auf jmdn./jmds. Unterstützung** ~ **sein** be dependent on *or* have to rely on sb./sb.'s support; **auf sich selbst** ~ **sein** be thrown back upon one's own resources; **ich war auf jeden Cent** ~**:** I needed every cent

an|gewöhnen *tr. V.* **jmdm. etw.** ~**:** get sb. used to sth.; accustom sb. to sth.; **jmdm.** ~**, etw. zu tun** get sb. used to *or* accustom sb. to doing sth.; **sich** (*Dat.*) **etw.** ~**:** get into the habit of sth.; **sich** (*Dat.*) **schlechte Manieren** ~**:** become ill-mannered; **[es] sich** (*Dat.*) ~**, etw. zu tun** get into the habit of doing sth.; **sich** (*Dat.*) **das Rauchen** ~**:** take up smoking

An·gewohnheit *die* habit

angezeigt
A *2. Part. v.* **anzeigen**
B *Adj.* (geh.) advisable

an|giften /ˈangɪftn̩/ *tr. V.* (ugs.) lay into (coll.); let fly at

Angina /aŋˈgiːna/ *die;* ~**, Anginen** ▸**ℹ S. 439** tonsillitis

Angina pectoris /- ˈpɛktorɪs/ *die;* ~ ~ ▸**ℹ S. 439** (Med.) angina [pectoris]

an|gleichen
A *unr. tr. V.* **etw. einer Sache** (*Dat.*) *od.* **an etw.** (*Akk.*) ~**:** bring sth. into line with sth.; **Systeme einander** ~**:** bring systems into line with each other
B *unr. refl. V.* **sich jmdm./etw.** ~ *od.* **sich an jmdn./etw.** ~**:** become like sb./sth.; **sich [einander** *od.* **aneinander]** ~**:** become like each other *or* alike

An·gleichung *die:* **die** ~ **der Löhne an die Preise** bringing wages into line with prices

Angler *der;* ~**s,** ~**, Anglerin** *die;* ~**,** ~**nen** angler

Anglikaner /aŋgliˈkaːnɐ/ *der;* ~**s,** ~**, Anglikanerin** *die;* ~**,** ~**nen** Anglican

anglikanisch
A *Adj.* Anglican
B *adv.* ~ **beeinflusst sein** be influenced by Anglicanism

Anglikanismus *der;* ~**:** Anglicanism *no art.*

anglisieren *tr. V.* Anglicize

Anglist *der;* ~**en,** ~**en** English specialist *or* scholar; Anglicist; (Student) English student

Anglistik *die;* ~**:** Anglistics *sing.;* English [language and literature]; English studies *pl., no art.*

Anglistin *die;* ~**,** ~**nen** ▸**Anglist**

anglistisch *Adj.* Anglistics *attrib.,* English studies *attrib.* ‹*seminar, journal*›

Anglizismus *der;* ~**, Anglizismen** Anglicism

Anglo·amerikaner /aŋglo|ameriˈkaːnɐ/ *der,* **Anglo·amerikanerin** *die* **1** Anglo-American **2** (Angelsachse/Angelsächsin) Anglo-Saxon; **die Angloamerikaner** the British and the Americans

anglophil /aŋgloˈfiːl/ *Adj.* Anglophile

an|glotzen *tr. V.* (ugs.) gawp at (coll.)

Angola /aŋˈgoːla/ *(das);* ~**s** Angola

Angolaner *der;* ~**s,** ~**, Angolanerin** *die;* ~**,** ~**nen** Angolan

Angora- /aŋˈgoːra/: ~**kaninchen** *das* angora rabbit; ~**katze** *die* angora cat; ~**wolle** *die* angora [wool]; ~**ziege** *die* angora goat

angreifbar *Adj.* contestable

an|greifen
A *unr. tr. V.* **1** (attackieren; auch fig.) attack **2** (schwächen) weaken, affect ‹*health, heart*›; affect ‹*stomach, intestine, voice*›; weaken ‹*person*›; **die Nerven** ~**:** be a strain on the nerves; **die Fahrt hat mich sehr angegriffen** I was exhausted by the journey **3** ([be]schädigen) attack ‹*metal*›; harm ‹*hands*› **4** (anbrechen) break into ‹*supplies, savings, etc.*› **5** (ugs.: anfassen) touch
B *unr. itr. V.* (einen Angriff machen; auch fig.) attack

An·greifer *der,* **An·greiferin** *die* (auch fig.) attacker

an|grenzen *itr. V.* **an etw.** (*Akk.*) ~**:** border on *or* adjoin sth.; **die** ~**den Grundstücke** the adjoining properties

An·griff *der* attack; **einen** ~ **fliegen** make *or* carry out an attack *or* an air raid; **zum** ~ **übergehen** go over to the attack; take the offensive; **zum** ~ **blasen** (auch fig.) sound the charge *or* attack; **etw. in** ~ **nehmen** set about *or* tackle sth.; ~ **ist die beste Verteidigung** (Spr.) attack is the best form of defence

angriffs-, Angriffs-: ~**drittel** *das* (Eishockey) attacking zone; ~**fläche** *die:* **das Segel bot dem Wind eine große** ~**fläche** the sail presented a large area to the wind; **seinem Gegner eine** ~**fläche bieten** (fig.) leave oneself open to attack by one's opponent; ~**fuß·ball** *der* attacking football; ~**krieg** *der* war of aggression; ~**lust** *die* aggression; aggressiveness; ~**lustig** **A** *Adj.* aggressive; **B** *adv.* aggressively; ~**punkt** *der* target; ~**spieler** *der,* ~**spielerin** *die* (Sport) **1** (offensiver Spieler) attacking player; **2** (Stürmer) forward; ~**waffe** *die* offensive weapon

an|grinsen *tr. V.* grin at

angst /aŋst/ *Adj. in* **jmdm. ist/wird [es]** ~ **[und bange]** sb. is/becomes afraid *or* frightened; (jmd. sorgt sich) sb. is/becomes very worried *or* anxious

Angst *die;* ~**, Ängste** /ˈɛŋstə/ **1** (Furcht) fear; (Psych.) anxiety; ~ **bekommen** *od.* (ugs.) **kriegen** become *or* get frightened *or* scared; ~ **[vor jmdm./etw.] haben** be afraid *or* frightened [of sb./sth.]; **eine existenzielle** ~**:** existential fear; angst; **jmdn. in** ~ **und Schrecken versetzen** worry and frighten sb.; **es mit der** ~ **[zu tun] bekommen** *od.* (ugs.) **kriegen** become *or* get frightened *or* scared; **jmdm.** ~ **einflößen/einjagen/machen** frighten *or* scare sb.; **jmdm.** ~ **[und Bange] machen** frighten *or* scare sb.; (jmdn. unruhig machen) make sb. very worried *or* anxious; **keine** ~**!** don't be afraid; **aus** ~ **[vor etw./jmdm.] sich verstecken** hide in fear [of sth./sb.]; **aus** ~**, sich zu verraten, sagte er kein einziges Wort** he didn't say a word for fear of betraying himself; **in ständiger** ~ **vor etw.** (*Dat.*) **leben** live in constant fear of sth.; **er hat mehr** ~ **als Vaterlandsliebe** (ugs. scherzh.) he's a scaredy-cat (coll.); he's chicken (sl.); ~ **vor der eigenen Courage haben/bekommen** have got/get cold feet (fig.) **2** (Sorge) worry; anxiety; ~ **[um jmdn./etw.] haben** be worried *or* anxious [about sb./sth.]; **sie hat** ~**, ihn zu verletzen/enttäuschen** she is worried about hurting/disappointing him; **keine** ~**, ich vergesse es schon nicht!** don't worry, I won't forget [it]!; **keine** ~**, die Rechnung wird schon noch kommen!** the bill will come all right, don't [you] worry!; **in tausend Ängsten schweben** be terribly worried

Angst·beißer *der* dog that bites when frightened

angst-, Angst-: ~**erfüllt** *Adj.* (geh.) frightened; terrified; ~**frei** **A** *Adj.* anxiety-free ‹*atmosphere*›; ‹*school*› with an anxiety-free atmosphere; ‹*learning*› without tears; **B** *adv.* ‹*live*› without anxiety; ‹*learn*› without tears; ~**gefühl** *das* feeling of anxiety; ~**gegner** *der,* ~**gegnerin** *die* (Sport) bogy opponent; (Mannschaft) bogy team; ~**hase** *der* (ugs. abwertend) scaredy-cat (coll.)

ängstigen /ˈɛŋstɪgn̩/
A *tr. V.* frighten; scare; (beunruhigen) worry
B *refl. V.* be frightened *or* afraid; (sich sorgen) worry; **sich vor etw.** (*Dat.*)**/um jmdn.** ~**:** be frightened *or* afraid of sth./worried about sb.

ängstlich /ˈɛŋstlɪç/
A *Adj.* **1** (verängstigt) anxious; apprehensive **2** (furchtsam, schüchtern) timorous; timid **3** (übertrieben) **mit** ~**er Genauigkeit** with painful meticulousness **4** (besorgt) worried; anxious; **mit** ~**er Spannung** anxiously
B *adv.* **1** (verängstigt) anxiously; apprehensively **2** (besorgt) anxiously; ~ **gespannt** anxiously **3** (übermäßig genau) meticulously; ~ **bemüht** *od.* **darauf bedacht sein, etw. zu tun** be at great pains to do sth.

Ängstlichkeit *die;* ~ **1** (Furchtsamkeit) timorousness; timidity **2** (Schüchternheit) timidity **3** (übertriebene Genauigkeit) **die** ~**, mit der er**

die Vorschriften befolgt the painful meticulousness with which he follows regulations 4 (Besorgnis) anxiety

angst-, Angst-: ~neurose *die* anxiety neurosis; **~psychose** *die* anxiety psychosis; **~röhre** *die* (ugs. scherzh.) topper (coll.); top hat; **~schrei** *der* cry of fear; terrified cry; **~schweiß** *der* cold sweat; **der ~schweiß brach ihm aus** he broke out in a cold sweat; **~traum** *der* nightmare; **~verzerrt** *Adj.* ‹face› twisted in fear; **~voll** A *Adj.* anxious; apprehensive; B *adv.* anxiously; apprehensively; **~zustand** *der* [state of] panic; **~zustände haben/bekommen** *od.* (ugs.) **kriegen** be in a/get into a [state of] panic

an|gucken *tr. V.* (ugs.) look at; **sich** (*Dat.*) **etw./jmdn. ~:** look *or* have a look at sth./sb.; **guck dir das/den an!** [just] look at that/him!

an|gurten *tr. V.* strap in; **sich ~:** put on one's seat belt; (im Flugzeug) fasten one's seat belt

Angus·rind *das* 1 (Tier) Aberdeen Angus; **20 ~er** 20 Aberdeen Angus [cattle] 2 (Fleisch) Aberdeen Angus beef

Anh. *Abk.* **= Anhang** app.

an|haben *unr. tr. V.* 1 (ugs.: am Körper tragen) have on 2 **jmdm./einer Sache etwas ~ können** be able to harm sb./harm *or* damage sth.; **er sorgte dafür, dass niemand ihm etwas ~ konnte** he made sure that no one could touch him 3 (ugs.: in Betrieb haben) have on

an|haften *itr. V.* (geh.) **ein Nachteil/Risiko haftet einer Sache** (*Dat.*) **an** there is a disadvantage/risk in *or* attached to sth.; **die Schmach haftet ihr noch heute an** the disgrace remains with her even today

an|häkeln *tr. V.* crochet on (**an** + *Akk.* to)

An·halt *der* clue (**für** to); (für eine Vermutung) grounds *pl.* (**für** for)

an|halten
A *unr. tr. V.* 1 stop; **den Atem ~:** hold one's breath 2 (auffordern) urge 3 (an etw. halten) **etw. an etw.** (*Akk.*) **~:** hold sth. up against sth.; **jmdm./sich ein Kleidungsstück ~:** hold a garment up against sb./oneself
B *unr. itr. V.* 1 stop 2 (andauern) go on; last 3 **er hat [bei ihren Eltern] um sie** *od.* **um ihre Hand angehalten** he asked [her parents] for her hand [in marriage]

anhaltend
A *Adj.* constant; continuous
B *adv.* constantly; continuously

An·halter *der* hitch-hiker; **per ~ fahren** hitch[-hike]

An·halterin *die* hitch-hiker

Anhalte·weg *der* (Kfz-W.) [overall] stopping distance

Anhalts·punkt *der* clue (**für** to); (für eine Vermutung) grounds *pl.* (**für** for)

an·hand
A *Präp. mit Gen.* with the help of; on the basis of ‹current developments›
B *Adv.* **~ von** with the help of; on the basis of ‹current developments›

An·hang *der* 1 (eines Buches) appendix 2 (Anhängerschaft) following; **der Minister und sein ~:** the minister and his followers; **hoffentlich bringt er nicht seinen ganzen ~ mit** let's hope he doesn't bring his whole gang along 3 (Verwandtschaft) family; (in Heiratsanzeigen) **Witwe ohne ~:** widow, no family *or* dependants

an|hängen¹ *unr. itr. V.* (geh.) 1 (verbunden sein mit) be attached to 2 (glauben an) subscribe to ‹belief, idea, theory, etc.›; **einer Sekte ~:** be an adherent *or* follower of a sect 3 (verehren) be devoted to

an|hängen²
A *tr. V.* 1 hang up (**an** + *Akk.* on) 2 (ankuppeln) couple on (**an** + *Akk.* to); hitch up ‹trailer› (**an** + *Akk.* to) 3 (anfügen) add (**an** + *Akk.* to) 4 (ugs.: zuschreiben, anlasten) **jmdm. etw. ~:** blame sb. for sth.; blame sth. on sb.; **er will mir nur was ~:** he just wants to pin something on me 5 (ugs.: geben) **jmdm. etw. ~:** give sb. sth.; **jmdm. einen Prozess ~:** bring an action against sb.; take sb. to court; **lass dir keine vergammelten Tomaten ~!** don't let yourself be palmed off with bad tomatoes
B *refl. V.* 1 hang on (**an** + *Akk.* to) 2 (ugs.: sich anschließen) **sich [an jmdn.** *od.* **bei jmdm.] ~:** tag along [with sb.] (coll.)

An·hänger *der* 1 (Mensch) supporter; (einer Sekte) adherent; follower 2 (Wagen) trailer; **eine Straßenbahn mit zwei ~n** a tram (Brit.) *or* (Amer.) trolley with two extra cars 3 (Schmuckstück) pendant 4 (Schildchen) label; tag

Anhängerin *die;* **~, ~nen** ▸**Anhänger 1**

Anhänger·kupplung *die* tow bar

Anhängerschaft *die;* **~, ~en** supporters *pl.*; (einer Sekte) followers *pl.*; adherents *pl.*; **eine breite ~ gewinnen** gain a wide following

anhängig *Adj.* (Rechtsw.) pending ‹action›; **etw. ~ machen** start legal proceedings over sth.

anhänglich *Adj.* devoted ‹dog, friend›; devoted, affectionate ‹child›

Anhänglichkeit *die;* **~:** devotion (**an** + *Akk.* to); **aus alter ~** (Nostalgie) out of old affection

Anhängsel /ˈanhɛŋzl/ *das;* **~s, ~** 1 (Überflüssiges) appendage (*Gen.* to) 2 (veralt.: Anhänger) pendant; (am Armband) charm

An·hauch *der* (geh., auch fig.) breath; (Anflug) trace; touch

an|hauchen *tr. V.* breathe on ‹mirror, glasses›; blow on ‹fingers, hands›

an|hauen *tr. V.* (salopp) accost; **jmdn. um 50 Euro ~:** touch (coll.) *or* tap sb. for 50 euros

an|häufen
A *tr. V.* accumulate; amass; (hamstern) hoard
B *refl. V.* accumulate; pile up

An·häufung *die* 1 (das Anhäufen) accumulation; amassing; (das Hamstern) hoarding 2 (Haufen) accumulation; (von Hütten) cluster

an|heben¹ *unr. tr. V.* 1 (hochheben) lift [up] ‹cupboard, carpet›; raise ‹glass› 2 (erhöhen) raise ‹prices, wages, etc.›

an|heben² *unr. itr. V.* (geh.) commence; begin; **zu weinen/sprechen ~:** start *or* begin to cry/speak; start *or* begin crying/speaking

An·hebung *die* increase (*Gen.* in); raising (*Gen.* of)

an|heften *tr. V.* tack [on] ‹hem, sleeve, etc.›; attach ‹label, list›; put up ‹sign, notice›; **etw. mit Büroklammern/Reißnägeln/Heftklammern ~:** [paper] clip/pin/staple sth. (**an** + *Akk.* to); **jmdm. einen Orden ~:** pin a medal on sb.

anheim (geh.) *in* **jmdm./dem Staate ~ fallen** ‹wealth, property› pass to sb./the state; **der Vergessenheit/der Zerstörung/einem Betrug ~ fallen** sink into oblivion/fall prey to destruction/fall victim to a fraud; (geh.) **etw. den Flammen/dem Feuer ~ geben** commit sth. to the flames/fire; **jmds. Obhut ~ gegeben werden** be entrusted to sb.'s care; **sich jmdm./einer Sache ~ geben** entrust oneself to sb./sth.; **sich Gott ~ geben** put one's trust in God; **[es] jmdm. ~ stellen, etw. zu tun** leave it to sb. to do sth.; **es bleibt/ist dir ~ gestellt, dich zu beschweren** it is up to you to complain

anheimelnd *Adj.* homely; cosy

anheischig /ˈanhaiʃɪç/ *Adj.* (geh.) *in* **sich ~ machen, etw. zu tun** undertake to do sth.; **jetzt macht er sich auch noch ~, mich über meine Pflichten zu belehren** now he even takes it upon himself to tell me what my duties are

an|heizen
A *tr. V.* 1 fire up ‹stove, boiler, etc.› 2 (fig. ugs.) stimulate ‹interest›
B *itr. V.* put the heating on; (bei einer Lokomotive) fire up

an|herrschen *tr. V.* (geh.) bark at

an|hetzen *itr. V.; mit sein* **angehetzt kommen** (ugs.) come rushing *or* tearing along; (auf einen zu) come rushing *or* tearing up

an|heuern /ˈanhɔyɐn/
A *tr. V.* 1 (Seemannsspr.) sign on 2 (fig. ugs.: einstellen) sign on *or* up; (um Hilfe bitten) rope in
B *itr. V.* (Seemannsspr.) sign on

An·hieb *der:* **auf [den ersten] ~** (ugs.) straight off; first go

an|himmeln *tr. V.* (ugs.) 1 (verehren) idolize; worship 2 (ansehen) gaze adoringly at

An·höhe *die* rise; elevation; (Hügel) hill

an|hören
A *tr. V.* 1 listen to; **etw. [zufällig] mit ~:** overhear sth.; **er wurde verurteilt, ohne vorher auch nur angehört worden zu sein** he was sentenced without even being given a hearing; **sich** (*Dat.*) **jmdn./etw. ~:** listen to sb./sth.; **ich kann das nicht länger** *od.* **mehr mit ~!** I can't listen to that any longer 2 (anmerken) **man hörte ihr die Verzweiflung an** one could hear the despair in her voice
B *refl. V.* sound; **[das] hört sich nicht schlecht an** (ugs.) [that] doesn't sound bad

Anhörung *die;* **~, ~en** hearing

Anhörungs·verfahren *das* hearing

an|hupen *tr. V.* hoot at

an|husten *tr. V.* cough over; **jmdn. ~:** cough over sb. *or* in sb.'s face

Anhydrid /anhyˈdriːt/ *das;* **~s, ~e** (Chemie) anhydride

Änigma /ɛˈnɪgma/ *das;* **~s, ~ta** *u.* **Änigmen** (geh.) enigma

änigmatisch *Adj.* (geh.) enigmatic

Anilin /aniˈliːn/ *das;* **~s** (Chemie) aniline

Anilin·leder *das* aniline leather

animalisch /aniˈmaːlɪʃ/ *Adj.* 1 animal 2 (abwertend: triebhaft) animal; bestial

Animateur /animaˈtøːɐ̯/ *der;* **~s, ~e** ▸ⓘ **S. 113** host

Animateurin *die;* **~, ~nen** ▸ⓘ **S. 113** hostess

Animation /animaˈtsi̯oːn/ *die;* **~, ~en** animation

Animier·dame *die* hostess

animieren /aniˈmiːrən/ *tr.* (*auch itr.*) *V.* 1 encourage; **das soll zum Kaufen ~:** that's to encourage people to buy; **er fühlte sich [durch mein Beispiel] animiert** he felt prompted [by my example] 2 (Film) animate

Animier-: ~lokal *das* hostess bar; (Nachtklub) hostess nightclub; **~mädchen** *das* hostess

Animismus *der;* **~** animism

Animist *der;* **~en, ~en, Animistin** *die;* **~, ~nen** animist

animistisch *Adj.* animistic

Animosität /animoziˈtɛːt/ *die;* **~, ~en** 1 animosity 2 (Äußerung) hostile remark

Animus /ˈaːnimus/ *der;* **~** 1 (Psych.) animus 2 (ugs.: Ahnung) **ich habe so einen ~, dass ...** I have a feeling *or* hunch that ...

An·ion *das* (Chemie) anion

Anis /aˈniːs/ *der;* **~[es], ~e** 1 (Pflanze) anise 2 (Gewürz) aniseed 3 (Branntwein) aniseed brandy

Anisette /aniˈzɛt/ *der;* **~s, ~s** anisette

Anis-: ~likör *der* aniseed liqueur; **~plätzchen** *das* aniseed biscuit; **~schnaps** *der* aniseed brandy

Ank. *Abk.* **= Ankunft** arr.

an|kämpfen *itr. V.* **gegen jmdn./etw. ~:** fight [against] sb./sth.; **gegen den Strom/Wind/die Elemente ~:** battle against the current/the wind/the elements

an|karren *tr. V.* (ugs.) cart along; bring along ‹supporters, followers›

An·kathete *die* (Geom.) adjacent side

An·kauf *der* purchase; **„Heinrich Meyer, An- und Verkauf"** 'Heinrich Meyer, second-hand dealer'; **„An- und Verkauf von ..."** 'we buy and sell ...'; **durch den ~ einer Sache** (*Gen.*) by purchasing *or* buying sth.; by the purchase of sth.

an|kaufen *tr. V.* purchase; buy

an|keifen *tr. V.* scream at

Anker /ˈaŋkɐ/ *der;* **~s, ~** 1 (eines Schiffs) anchor; (fig.) support; **vor ~ gehen/liegen** *od.* **treiben** drop anchor/lie at anchor; **~ werfen** drop anchor 2 (Elektrot.) armature 3 (Uhrmacherei) anchor

Anker-: ~boje *die* anchor buoy; **~kette** *die* anchor cable; **~klüse** *die;* **~, ~n** hawse hole; (Rohr) hawsepipe; **~mast** *der* (Luftf.) mooring mast

a

ankern *itr. V.* ① (vor Anker gehen) anchor; drop anchor ② (vor Anker liegen) be anchored; lie at anchor

Anker-: ∼platz *der* anchorage; **∼wicklung** *die* (Elektrot.) armature winding; **∼winde** *die* windlass

an|ketten *tr. V.* chain up (*Dat.*, **an** + *Akk.* to)

an|kläffen *tr. V.* yap at

An·klage *die* ① charge; **der Staatsanwalt hat ∼ [wegen Mordes gegen ihn] erhoben** the public prosecutor brought a charge [of murder against him]; **unter ∼ stehen** have been charged (**wegen** with); **jmdn. unter ∼ stellen** charge sb. (**wegen** with) ② (∼vertretung) prosecution; **der Vertreter der ∼:** counsel for the prosecution; prosecuting counsel ③ (geh.: Vorwurf) accusation

Anklage-: ∼bank *die; Pl.* **∼bänke** dock; **auf der ∼bank sitzen** (auch fig.) be in the dock; **∼erhebung** *die* preferral of charges; **für eine ∼erhebung hinreichend sein** be sufficient to justify preferring charges

an|klagen
A *tr. V.* ① (Rechtsw.) charge; accuse; **jmdn. einer Sache** (*Gen.*) *od.* **wegen etw. ∼:** charge sb. with *or* accuse sb. of sth. ② (geh.: beschuldigen) accuse; **jmdn./sich einer Sache** (*Gen.*) **∼:** accuse sb./oneself of sth.; **jmdn./sich ∼, etw. zu tun** accuse sb./oneself of doing sth.; **sich als etw.** (Nom. od. Akk.) **∼:** accuse oneself of being sth.
B *itr. V.* cry out in accusation; **ein ∼des Buch** a book that cries out in accusation; **jmdn. ∼d ansehen** look at sb. accusingly

An·kläger *der*, **An·klägerin** *die* prosecutor

Anklage-: ∼schrift *die* indictment; **∼vertreter** *der*, **∼vertreterin** *die* prosecuting counsel; counsel for the prosecution; **∼vertretung** *die* (Vorgang, Partei) prosecution

an|klammern
A *tr. V.* peg (Brit.), pin (Amer.) ‹*clothes, washing*› up (**an** + *Akk.* to); clip ‹*copy, sheet, etc.*› (**an** + *Akk.* to); (mit Heftklammern) staple ‹*copy, sheet, etc.*› (**an** + *Akk.* on)
B *refl. V.* **sich an jmdn./etw. ∼:** cling to *or* hang on to sb./sth.

An·klang *der* ① *in* **[bei jmdm.] ∼ finden** meet with [sb.'s] approval; find favour [with sb.]; **mit dem Vorschlag wirst du keinen großen ∼ finden** you won't find any great support for that proposal; **wenig/keinen/großen ∼ finden** be poorly/badly/well received (**bei** by) ② (Ähnlichkeit) echo (**an** + *Akk.* of); **Anklänge an etw.** (*Akk.*) **enthalten** be reminiscent of sth.

an|klatschen *tr. V.* (ugs.) slap ‹*poster, wallpaper, etc.*› up *or* on (**an** + *Akk.* to); plaster ‹*hair*› down

an|kleben
A *tr.* (*auch itr.*) *V.* stick up ‹*poster, etc.*› (**an** + *Akk.* on); **„Ankleben verboten"** 'stick (Brit.) *or* post no bills'; 'bill-posting prohibited'; **sich** (*Dat.*) **einen falschen Bart ∼:** stick on a false beard
B *itr. V.; mit sein* stick (**an** + *Dat.* to)

an|kleckern *itr. V.; mit sein* **angekleckert kommen** (ugs.) (immer wieder kommen) come trotting along (coll.); (auf einen zu) come trotting up (coll.); (nach und nach eintreffen) come drifting along *or* in

Ankleide·kabine *die* changing cubicle

an|kleiden *tr. V.* (geh.) dress; **sich ∼:** get dressed; dress [oneself]

Ankleide·raum *der* dressing room

an|klicken *tr. V.* (DV) click on

an|klingeln *tr., itr. V.* (ugs.) **jmdn.** *od.* **bei jmdm. ∼:** ring *or* call sb. [up]

an|klingen *unr. itr. V.* ① (erinnern) be reminiscent (**an** + *Akk.* of) ② *auch mit sein* (wahrnehmbar sein) be discernible; **ein Thema ∼ lassen** touch on a theme

an|klopfen *itr. V.* knock (**an** + *Akk. od. Dat.* at *or* on); **bei jmdm. um etw. ∼** (ugs.) try to touch (coll.) *or* tap sb. for sth.

an|knabbern *tr. V.* (ugs.) nibble [at]; **der Staat muss seine Goldreserven ∼** (fig.) the state is having to dig into its gold reserves; **zum Anknabbern aussehen** (fig.) look good enough to eat

an|knacksen *tr. V.* (ugs.) crack ‹*bone, rib*›; (fig.) injure ‹*pride*›; badly affect ‹*health*›; *s. auch* **angeknackst B**

an|knipsen *tr. V.* (ugs.) switch *or* put on

an|knüpfen
A *tr. V.* ① tie on (**an** + *Akk.* to) ② (beginnen) start up ‹*conversation*›; open, start ‹*negotiations*›; establish ‹*relations, business links*›; form ‹*relationship*›; **eine Bekanntschaft mit jmdm. ∼:** strike up an acquaintance with sb.
B *itr. V.* **an etw.** (*Akk.*) **∼:** take sth. up; **ich knüpfe dort an, wo wir vorige Woche aufgehört haben** I'll pick up where we left off last week

Anknüpfung *die;* **∼, ∼en** ① ▸ **anknüpfen 2**: starting up; opening; starting; establishment; forming ② **die ∼ an etw.** (*Akk.*) taking sth. up; **unter [bewusster] ∼ an etw.** (*Akk.*) with [conscious] reference to sth.

Anknüpfungs·punkt *der* starting point [for a/the conversation]

an|knurren *tr. V.* growl at; **sich [gegenseitig] ∼** (auch fig.) growl at one another

an|kohlen *tr. V.* (ugs.) kid (coll.)

an|kommen
A *unr. itr. V.; mit sein* ① (eintreffen) arrive; ‹*letter, parcel*› come, arrive; ‹*bus, train, plane*› arrive, get in; **seid ihr gut angekommen?** did you arrive safely *or* get there all right?; **ich bin beim 6. Kapitel angekommen** I have reached *or* got to the sixth chapter; **wann sollen die Zwillinge denn ∼?** (ugs.: geboren werden) when are the twins due [to arrive]?; **bei ihr ist kürzlich das vierte Kind angekommen** (ugs.: geboren worden) she has just had her fourth child ② (ugs.: Anklang finden) **[bei jmdm.] [gut] ∼:** go down [very] well [with sb.]; **damit kommt er bei mir nicht an** he won't get anywhere with me with that; **er ist ein Typ, der bei den Frauen ankommt** he is the sort who is a success with women ③ **gegen jmdn./etw. ∼:** be able to cope *or* deal with sb./fight sth. ④ (unpers.: abhängen) **auf uns/auf das Wetter kommt es dabei nicht an** it doesn't depend on us/the weather; **es kommt [ganz] darauf an, ob …** it [all] depends whether …; **es kommt [ganz] darauf** *od.* **drauf an** (ugs.) it [all] depends; **es darauf** *od.* **drauf ∼ lassen** (ugs.) take a chance; chance it; **es auf etw.** (*Akk.*) **∼ lassen** [be prepared to] risk sth.; **man könnte es ja mal auf einen Versuch ∼ lassen** one could at least give it a try ⑤ (unpers.: entscheidend, wichtig sein) **es kommt auf etw.** (*Akk.*) **an** sth. matters; **auf die paar Euro/Minuten kommt es [mir] nicht an/soll es mir nicht ∼:** a few euros/minutes don't matter [to me]; **es kommt auf jede Minute/jeden Cent an** every minute/cent counts; **es käme auf einen Versuch an** it's *or* it would be worth a try; **da kommt es auf drei Leute mehr auch nicht mehr an** three more people won't make any difference; **es kommt nicht darauf an, was er sagt** it's not what he says that matters; **darauf kommt es mir nicht so sehr an** that doesn't matter so much to me ⑥ (herankommen) come along; **mit etw. ∼** (ugs.: etw. dauernd betonen) harp on about sth. ⑦ (ugs.: Erfolg haben) **er ist mit seinem Manuskript bisher noch bei keinem Verlag angekommen** up to now he hasn't had any success with publishers with his manuscript; **ohne Beziehungen kommt man heute nirgends mehr an** you won't *or* don't get anywhere these days without connections
B *tr. V.* (geh.) ① (überkommen) ‹*fear, desire, etc.*› come over ② **jmdn. hart/schwer** *usw.* **∼:** be hard/difficult *etc.* for sb.

Ankömmling /ˈankœmlɪŋ/ *der;* **∼s, ∼e** newcomer; (ugs.: Neugeborenes) new arrival

an|können *unr. itr. V.* ① **gegen jmdn./etw. ∼:** be able to fight sb./sth. ② (ugs.: an sein dürfen) **das Licht/Radio/die Heizung kann jetzt wieder an** you/he *etc.* can put the light/radio/heating on again now

an|koppeln
A *tr. V.* couple ‹*carriage*› up (**an** + *Akk.* to); hitch ‹*trailer*› up (**an** + *Akk.* to); dock ‹*spacecraft*› (**an** + *Akk.* with)
B *itr. V.* ‹*spacecraft*› dock (**an** + *Akk.* with)

an|kotzen *tr. V.* (salopp) ① throw up over; puke over (coarse) ② (fig.: anwidern) **jmdn. ∼:** make sb. sick

an|krallen *refl. V.* cling (**an** + *Akk. od. Dat.* at)

an|kratzen *tr. V.* scratch; (fig. ugs.) dent

an|kreiden *tr. V.* (ugs.) **jmdm. etw. ∼:** hold sth. against sb.; **man kreidet ihm sein Verhalten als Schwäche an** his behaviour is seen *or* regarded as weakness; **das muss man ihm dick ∼:** you've really got to hold that against him

An·kreis *der* (Geom.) escribed circle; excircle

an|kreuzen
A *tr. V.* mark with a cross; put a cross beside
B *itr. V.; meist mit sein* **gegen den Wind ∼** (Segeln) sail against *or* into the wind

an|kriechen *unr. itr. V.; mit sein* **angekrochen kommen** come creeping *or* crawling along; (auf einen zu) come creeping *or* crawling up

an|kucken (nordd.) ▸ **angucken**

an|kündigen
A *tr. V.* announce; **kündige dich bitte vorher an** please let me/us *etc.* know in advance that you are coming *or* give me/us *etc.* advance notice; **ein Gewitter ∼:** herald a storm; **eine angekündigte/nicht angekündigte Klassenarbeit** a class test announced in advance/a surprise test
B *refl. V.* ‹*spring, storm*› announce itself; ‹*illness*› show itself

An·kündigung *die* announcement; **er besuchte uns ohne vorherige ∼:** he visited us without letting us know in advance *or* with no advance notice

Ankunft /ˈankʊnft/ *die;* **∼, Ankünfte** arrival; **„∼"**: 'arrivals'

Ankunfts-: ∼halle *die* (Flugw.) arrival[s] hall; **∼tafel** *die* arrivals board

an|kuppeln *tr. V.* ▸ **ankoppeln A**

an|kurbeln *tr. V.* ① crank [up] ② (fig.) boost ‹*economy, production, etc.*›

Ankurb[e]lung *die;* **∼, ∼en** boosting; **Maßnahmen zur ∼ der Wirtschaft** measures to boost the economy

an|kuscheln *refl. V.* **sich an jmdn.** *od.* **bei jmdm./an etw.** (*Akk.*) **∼:** snuggle *or* cuddle up to sb./sth.

Anl. *Abk.* **= Anlage** encl.

an|lächeln *tr. V.* smile at; **jmdn. freundlich ∼:** give a friendly smile to sb.

an|lachen
A *tr. V.* smile at; **ich habe dich angelacht, nicht ausgelacht** I was laughing with you, not at you
B *refl. V.* **sich** (*Dat.*) **jmdn. ∼** (ugs.) get off with sb. (Brit. coll.); pick sb. up

An·lage *die* ① (das Anlegen) (einer Kartei) establishment; (eines Parks, Gartens usw.) laying out; construction; (eines Parkplatzes, Stausees) construction ② (Grün∼) park; (um ein Schloss, einen Palast usw. herum) grounds *pl.*; **die öffentlichen/städtischen ∼n** public/municipal parks and gardens ③ (Angelegtes, Komplex) complex ④ (Einrichtung) facilities *pl.*; **sanitäre/militärische ∼n** sanitary facilities/military installations; **die elektrische ∼:** the electrical equipment ⑤ (Werk) plant ⑥ (Musik∼, Lautsprecher∼ usw.) equipment; system ⑦ (Geld∼) investment ⑧ (Konzeption) conception; (Struktur) structure ⑨ (Veranlagung) aptitude, gift, talent (**zu** for); (Neigung) tendency, predisposition (**zu** to) ⑩ ▸ ❶ **S. 143** (Beilage zu einem Brief) enclosure; **als ∼ sende ich Ihnen/erhalten Sie ein ärztliches Attest** please find enclosed *or* I enclose a medical certificate

anlage-, Anlage-: ∼bedingt A *Adj.* constitutional; **B** *adv.* constitutionally; **∼berater** *der*, **∼beraterin** *die* ▸ ❶ **S. 113** investment advisor; **∼kapital** *das* investment capital

an|lagern (Chemie)
A *tr. V.* take up
B *refl. V.* be taken up (**an** + *Akk.* by)

Anlage·vermögen *das* fixed assets *pl. or* capital

an|landen *tr. V.* land

an|langen
A *itr. V.; mit sein* arrive; **bei/auf/an etw.** (*Dat.*) **~:** arrive at *or* reach sth.; **bei Kapitel 3 ~:** reach *or* get to chapter 3
B *tr. V.* 1 (südd.: anfassen) touch 2 ▸**anbelangen**

Anlass, *Anlaß /ˈanlas/ *der;* **Anlasses, Anlässe** /ˈanlɛsə/ 1 (Ausgangspunkt, Grund) cause (**zu** for); **der ~ des Streites** the cause of the dispute; **etw. zum ~ nehmen, etw. zu tun** use *or* take sth. as an opportunity to do sth.; **ich möchte aus gegebenem ~ darauf hinweisen, dass ...** I would like to take this opportunity to point out that ...; **aus ~ seines Geburtstags** on the occasion of *or* to celebrate his birthday; **jmdm. ~ zu Beschwerden geben** give sb. cause for complaint; **~ zur Sorge/Beunruhigung/Klage geben** give cause for concern/unease/complaint; **beim geringsten/kleinsten ~:** for the slightest reason; **aus aktuellem ~:** because of current events 2 (Gelegenheit) occasion; **bei festlichen Anlässen** on festive occasions

an|lassen
A *unr. tr. V.* 1 (in Betrieb lassen) leave ‹*light, radio, heating, etc.*› on; leave ‹*engine, tap*› on *or* running; leave ‹*candle*› burning 2 (anbehalten) keep ‹*coat, gloves, etc.*› on 3 (in Gang setzen) start [up]
B *unr. refl. V.* **sich gut/schlecht ~:** make a *or* get off to a good/bad *or* poor start; **wie lässt sich der neue Mitarbeiter denn an?** how is your new colleague getting on?

Anlasser *der;* **~s, ~** (Kfz-W.) starter

an·lässlich, *an·läßlich *Präp. mit Gen.* on the occasion of

an|lasten *tr. V.* **jmdm. ein Verbrechen ~:** accuse sb. of a crime; **jmdm. die Schuld an etw.** (*Dat.*) **~:** blame sb. for sth.; **jmdm. etw. als Versagen ~:** regard sth. as a failure on sb.'s part

an|latschen *itr. V.; mit sein* (ugs.) **angelatscht kommen** come trudging along; (auf einen zu) come trudging up; (schlurfend) come slouching along/up

An·lauf *der* 1 run-up; **[mehr] ~ nehmen** take [more of] a run-up; **mit/ohne ~:** with/without a run-up; **er sprang mit/ohne ~:** he did a running/standing jump; **ein Sprung mit/ohne ~:** a running/standing jump 2 (Versuch) attempt; **beim** *od.* **im ersten/dritten ~:** at the first/third attempt *or* (coll.) go; **einen [neuen] ~ nehmen** make another attempt; have another go (coll.) 3 (Sport) (Bahn) runway; (Strecke) run-up

Anlauf·adresse *die* ▸**Anlaufstelle**

an|laufen
A *unr. itr. V.; mit sein* 1 **angelaufen kommen** come running along; (auf einen zu) come running up 2 **gegen jmdn./etw. ~:** run at sb./sth.; **gegen etw. ~** (fig.) fight against sth. 3 (Anlauf nehmen) take a run-up 4 (zu laufen beginnen) ‹*engine*› start [up]; (fig.) ‹*film*› open; ‹*production, campaign, search*› start 5 (sich färben) turn; go 6 (beschlagen) mist *or* steam up
B *unr. tr. V.* put in at ‹*port*›

Anlauf-: ~schwierigkeiten *Pl.;* teething troubles *pl.;* **~stelle** *die* [place of] refuge; place to go; **die ~stelle für solche Reiserufe** the place to which to send such SOS messages; **~zeit** *die;* **der Motor braucht einige Minuten ~zeit** the engine needs a few minutes to warm up; **morgens braucht sie immer eine gewisse ~zeit** it always takes her a certain amount of time to get going in the mornings

An·laut *der* (Sprachw.) initial sound; **der Konsonant wird im ~ stimmhaft gesprochen** the consonant is voiced when in initial position

an|lauten *itr. V.* (Sprachw.) begin (**mit** with); **der ~de Vokal** the initial vowel

an|läuten *tr., itr. V.* (bes. südd.) ▸**anrufen A 3, B 1**

an|legen
A *tr. V.* 1 (an etw. legen) put *or* lay ‹*domino, card*› [down] (**an** + *Akk.* next to); place, position ‹*ruler, protractor*› (**an** + *Akk.* on); put ‹*ladder*› up (**an** + *Akk.* against); **ein Gewehr auf jmdn./etw. ~:** level a gun at sb./sth.; **sie legte das Baby an** she put the baby to her breast; **einen strengen Maßstab [an etw.** (*Akk.*)**] ~:** apply strict standards [to sth.] 2 (an den Körper legen) **die Flügel/Ohren ~:** close its wings/lay its ears back; **die Arme ~:** put one's arms to one's sides 3 (geh.: anziehen, umlegen) don; put on 4 (schaffen, erstellen) lay out ‹*town, garden, plantation, street*›; start ‹*file, album*›; compile ‹*statistics, index*› 5 (gestalten, entwerfen) structure ‹*story, novel*› 6 (investieren) invest 7 (ausgeben) spend (**für** on) 8 **er legt es auf einen Streit an** he is determined to have a fight; **es darauf ~, etw. zu tun** be determined to do sth. 9 (nachlegen) put on
B *itr. V.* 1 (festmachen, landen) moor; (am Liegeplatz) berth 2 (Kartenspiel) lay a card/cards; **bei jmdm. ~:** lay a card/cards on sb.'s hand; **ich kann nirgends/nicht ~:** I can't go 3 (Domino) play [a domino/dominoes] 4 (das Gewehr anlegen) aim (**auf** + *Akk.* at)
C *refl. V.* **sich mit jmdm. ~:** pick an argument *or* a quarrel with sb.

Anlege·platz *der* berth

Anleger *der;* **~s, ~** 1 (Schifffahrt) jetty; landing pier 2 (Investor) investor

Anlegerin *die;* **~, ~nen** investor

Anlege-: ~steg *der* jetty; landing stage; **~stelle** *die* mooring

an|lehnen
A *tr. V.* 1 (an etw. lehnen) lean (**an** + *Akk. od. Dat.* against) 2 leave ‹*door*› slightly open *or* ajar; leave ‹*window*› slightly open; **die Tür war angelehnt** the door was [left] slightly open *or* ajar
B *refl. V.* **sich [an jmdn.** *od.* **jmdm./etw.] ~:** lean [on sb./against sth.]; **er lehnte sich mit dem Rücken/der Schulter an die** *od.* **der Wand an** he leaned back *or* leaned his back/leaned [with] his shoulder against the wall; **sich an ein Vorbild ~** (fig.) follow an example

Anlehnung *die;* **~, ~en** 1 dependence (**an** + *Akk.* on); (Halt, Stütze) support; **~ an jmdn./etw. suchen/finden** look for/find support from sb./sth. 2 (Nachahmung) **in ~ an jmdn./etw.** following *or* in imitation of sb./sth.

Anlehnungs·bedürfnis *das* need for love and affection

anlehnungs·bedürftig *Adj.* in need of love and affection *postpos.;* **je mehr sie trank, desto ~er wurde sie** (scherzh.) the more she drank, the more amorous and affectionate she became

Anleihe *die;* **~, ~n** 1 (Darlehen) loan 2 (fig.) borrowing; **eine ~ bei Goethe/Picasso machen** borrow from Goethe/Picasso

an|leimen *tr. V.* stick *or* glue on (**an** + *Akk. od. Dat.* to)

an|leinen *tr. V.* put ‹*dog*› on the lead; **Hunde sind anzuleinen** dogs must be kept on a lead; **der Hund war nicht angeleint** the dog was not on a lead

an|leiten *tr. V.* 1 (unterweisen) instruct; teach; **jmdn. bei der Arbeit ~:** instruct sb. in the work; teach sb. the work 2 (anhalten, erziehen) teach; **die Kinder zur Selbstständigkeit/Pünktlichkeit ~:** teach the children to be independent/punctual

An·leitung *die* instructions *pl.*

Anlern·beruf *der* semi-skilled occupation *or* job

an|lernen
A *tr. V.* train; **ein angelernter Arbeiter** a semi-skilled worker
B *refl. V.* **sich** (*Dat.*) **etw. ~:** learn sth. up; **eine bloß angelernte Bildung** a superficially acquired education

Anlernling /ˈanlɛrnlɪŋ/ *der;* **~s, ~e** (veralt.) trainee; **~ sein** be a trainee

an|lesen
A *unr. tr. V.* begin *or* start reading *or* to read
B *unr. refl. V.* **sich** (*Dat.*) **etw. ~:** learn sth. by reading *or* from books; **eine nur angelesene Kenntnis** knowledge which comes straight out of books

an|leuchten *tr. V.* **jmdn./etw. ~:** shine a light on sb./light sth. up; **den Dieb mit der Taschenlampe ~:** shine a torch (Brit.) *or* (Amer.) flashlight on the thief

an|liefern *tr. V.* deliver

An·lieferung *die* delivery

an|liegen *unr. itr. V.* 1 (an etw. liegen) ‹*pullover etc.*› fit tightly *or* closely; ‹*hair, ears*› lie flat; **ein eng ~der Pullover** a tight- *or* close-fitting pullover 2 (ugs.: vorliegen) be on; (zu erledigen sein) to be done; **was liegt an?** (was kann ich für dich tun?) what's up? (coll.)

An·liegen *das;* **~s, ~** (Bitte) request; (Angelegenheit) matter; **etw. zu seinem persönlichen ~ machen** take a personal interest in sth.

anliegend *Adj.* 1 (angrenzend) adjacent 2 (beiliegend) enclosed

Anlieger *der;* **~s, ~, Anliegerin** *die;* **~, ~nen** resident; **„Anlieger frei", „frei für Anlieger"** 'access only'

Anlieger-: ~staat *der:* **die ~staaten des Mittelmeers** *usw.* the countries bordering the Mediterranean *etc.;* **~verkehr** *der* residents' vehicles *pl.;* **die Straße ist nur noch für den ~verkehr frei** the street is only open to residents; **„~verkehr frei"** 'residents only'

an|locken *tr. V.* attract ‹*customers, tourists, etc.*›; lure ‹*bird, animal*›

an|löten *tr. V.* solder on (**an** + *Akk. od. Dat.* to)

an|lügen *tr. V.* lie to

Anm. *Abk.* **= Anmerkung**

an|machen *tr. V.* 1 (anschalten, -zünden usw.) put *or* turn ‹*light, radio, heating*› on; light ‹*fire*› 2 (bereiten) mix ‹*cement, plaster, paint, etc.*›; dress ‹*salad*› 3 (ugs.: anbringen) put ‹*curtain, sign*› up; **ein Schild an der Tür ~:** put a sign up on the door; **dem Hund das Halsband ~:** put the collar on the dog 4 (ugs.: ansprechen) ‹*woman, girl*› give ‹*man, boy*› the come-on (coll.); ‹*man, boy*› chat ‹*woman, girl*› up (Brit. coll.) 5 (ugs.: begeistern, erregen) get ‹*audience etc.*› going; **das macht mich ungeheuer/nicht an** it really turns me on (coll.)/does nothing for me (coll.) 6 (provozieren) **mach mich nicht an!** leave me alone!

an|mahnen *tr. V.* send a reminder about; **er hat den angemahnten Betrag sofort überwiesen** he paid the outstanding amount as soon as he received a reminder

An·mahnung *die* reminder; **trotz mehrfacher ~:** despite repeated reminders *pl.*

an|malen *tr. V.* 1 (ugs.: bemalen) paint; **etw. rot ~:** paint sth. red 2 (ugs.: schminken) paint; **sich ~:** paint one's face 3 (auf etw. malen) paint (**an** + *Akk.* on); (auf etw. zeichnen) draw (**an** + *Akk.* on); **jmdm./sich einen Bart ~:** paint *or* draw a beard on sb.'s/one's face *or* on sb./oneself

An·marsch *der* 1 (das Anmarschieren) advance; **im ~ sein** (anrücken) be advancing; (ugs. scherzh.: unterwegs sein) be on one's way 2 (ugs.: Weg) walk

an|marschieren *itr. V.; mit sein* advance; **anmarschiert kommen** (ugs.) come marching along; (auf einen zu) come marching up

Anmarsch·weg *der* walk

an|maßen *refl. V.* **sich** (*Dat.*) **etw. ~:** claim sth. [for oneself]; arrogate sth. to oneself; **was maßt du dir an?** who do you think you are?; what do you think you are doing?; **sich ~, etw. zu tun** presume to do sth.; **darüber kannst du dir gar kein Urteil ~:** you have no right *or* it's not your place to pass judgement on that

an·maßend
A *Adj.* presumptuous; (arrogant) arrogant
B *adv.* presumptuously; (arrogant) arrogantly

Anmaßung *die;* **~, ~en** presumptuousness; presumption; (Arroganz) arrogance; **so eine [freche] ~!** what presumptuousness *or* presumption/arrogance!; **es ist eine ~ zu behaupten, dass ...** it is presumptuous to assert that ...

an|meckern *tr. V.* (ugs.) **jmdn. ~:** have a go at sb.

Anmelde·formular *das* 1 application form 2 (einer Meldebehörde) registration form

an|melden *tr. V.* 1 (als Teilnehmer) enrol; **jmdn./sich zu einem Kursus/in** *od.* **bei einer**

a

Schule ~: enrol sb./enrol for a course/at a school; **sich schriftlich ~:** register [in writing]; **jmdn. zu einer Impfung ~:** make an appointment for sb. to be vaccinated [2] (melden, anzeigen) license, get a licence for ‹*television, radio*›; apply for ‹*patent*›; register ‹*domicile, change of address, car, trade mark*›; **die Demonstration war nicht angemeldet** no notification had been given of the demonstration; **sich/seinen neuen Wohnsitz ~:** register one's new address; **jmdn./sich polizeilich** *od.* **bei der Polizei ~:** register sb./register with the police; *s. auch* **Konkurs** [3] (ankündigen) announce; (einen Termin vereinbaren) **sind Sie angemeldet?** do you have an appointment?; **sich beim Arzt ~:** make an appointment to see the doctor [4] (geltend machen) express, make known ‹*reservation, doubt, wish*›; put forward ‹*demand*›; assert ‹*right*› [5] (Kartenspiele: ansagen) bid [6] (Fernspr.) book; **ein Gespräch nach Übersee ~:** book an overseas call

Anmelde·pflicht *die* (für den Wohnsitz) obligation to register one's address; (für Fernsehen, Radio) obligation to obtain a licence; (für das Auto) obligation to register a/the vehicle; **für Demonstrationen besteht ~:** it is mandatory to notify the police in advance of demonstrations

anmelde·pflichtig *Adj.* **~ sein** ‹*television, radio*› need a licence; ‹*car*› have to be registered; ‹*demonstration*› have to be notified; **jeder Wohnungswechsel ist ~:** every change of address must be registered

An·meldung *die* [1] (zur Teilnahme) enrolment [2] ▸**anmelden 2**: licensing; registration; notification; **die ~ eines Patents** the application for a patent [3] (Ankündigung) announcement; (beim Arzt, Rechtsanwalt usw.) making an appointment [4] ▸**anmelden 4**: expression; putting forward; assertion [5] (Fernspr.) booking; **die ~ eines Gesprächs** booking a call [6] (Formular, Schreiben) registration [form] [7] (Büro, Schalter usw.) reception; **sie müssen zuerst zur/in die ~ [gehen]** you must go to reception first

an|merken *tr. V.* [1] **jmdm. seinen Ärger/seine Verlegenheit** *usw.* **~:** notice that sb. is annoyed/embarrassed *etc.*; notice sb.'s annoyance/embarrassment *etc.*; **man merkt ihm [nicht] an, dass er krank ist** you can[not] tell that he is ill; **sich nichts ~ lassen** not let it show [2] (geh.: bemerken) note [3] (geh.: anstreichen) mark

Anmerkung *die; ~, ~en* [1] (Fußnote) note [2] (geh.: Bemerkung) comment; remark; **wenn ich dazu eine ~ machen darf** if I may comment on that

an|mieten *tr. V.* rent; hire, rent ‹*car, van*›

an·mit *Adv.* (schweiz. Papierdt.) herewith

An·moderation *die* [1] (das Anmoderieren) introducing; **sie ist noch bei der ~ der Sendung** she is still introducing the programme [2] (Text, Wortlaut) introduction; **sie hat sich eine witzige ~ einfallen lassen** she thought of a witty way to introduce the programme

an·moderieren *tr. V.* introduce

an|montieren *tr. V.* fix on (**an** + *Akk. od. Dat.* to)

an|motzen *tr. V.* (ugs.) swear at

an|müssen *unr. itr. V.* have to be put on

an|mustern *tr., itr. V.* (Seemannsspr.) sign on

An·mut *die; ~* (geh.) grace; (Liebreiz, auch fig.: einer Landschaft usw.) charm; (fig.: eines Ausdrucks) elegance; gracefulness; **mit ~:** gracefully

an|muten *tr.* (*auch itr.*) *V.* (geh.) **etw. mutet [jmdn.] fremd** *usw.* **an** sth. seems strange *etc.* [to sb.]; **alles mutete ihn wie ein Traum an** everything seemed like a dream to him; **ein seltsam ~der Anblick** a sight that seems strange to me/him *etc.*

an·mutig (geh.)
A *Adj.* graceful ‹*girl, gesture, movement, dance*›; charming, delightful ‹*girl, smile, picture, landscape*›
B *adv.* ‹*move, dance*› gracefully; ‹*smile, greet*› charmingly, delightfully

anmuts·voll (geh.) ▸**anmutig**

an|nageln *tr. V.* nail on (**an** + *Akk. od. Dat.* to); nail up ‹*notice, picture*› (**an** + *Akk. od. Dat.* on); **wie angenagelt dastehen** (ugs.) stand [there] rooted to the spot

an|nagen *tr. V.* gnaw [at]; (fig. geh.) gnaw *or* nibble away at

an|nähen *tr. V.* sew on (**an** + *Akk.* to)

an|nähern
A *refl. V.* [1] approach; **die Straße nähert sich der Küste allmählich immer weiter an** the road gradually gets closer and closer to the coast; **sich einem Grenzwert ~** (Math.) converge towards a limit [2] (fig.: [menschlich] näher kommen) **sich jmdm. ~:** come *or* get closer to sb. [3] (sich angleichen) **sich einer Sache** (*Dat.*) **~:** come *or* get closer to sth.
B *tr. V.* (angleichen) bring closer (*Dat.* to); **verschiedene Standpunkte einander ~:** bring differing points of view closer together; **etw. einem Vorbild ~:** make sth. more like a model

annähernd
A *Adv.* (ungefähr) approximately; roughly; (fast) almost; nearly; **nicht ~ so teuer** not nearly as *or* nowhere near as expensive
B *adj.* approximate; rough; **mit ~er Sicherheit** with a rough degree of certainty

Annäherung *die; ~, ~en* [1] (das Sichannähern) approach (**an** + *Akk.* to); **bei ~ des Zuges** as the train approaches/approached [2] (fig.) **es kam zu einer ~ der beiden Parteien** the two parties came *or* moved closer together; **eine ~ zwischen zwei Staaten herbeiführen** bring two states closer together [3] (Angleichung) **eine ~ der gegenseitigen Standpunkte** bringing the points of view on each side closer together

annäherungs-, Annäherungs-: ~versuch *der* advance; (im politischen Bereich) attempted rapprochement; **immer wieder plumpe ~versuche machen** keep making [very] obvious advances; **~weise** *Adv.* approximately; roughly; **~wert** *der* ▸**Näherungswert**

Annahme /ˈannaːmə/ *die; ~, ~n* [1] (das Annehmen) acceptance; **die ~ eines Pakets verweigern** refuse to accept [delivery of] a parcel [2] (Vermutung) assumption; **ich war der ~, dass ...** I assumed that ...; **in der ~, dass ...** on the assumption that ...; **gehe ich recht in der ~, dass ...?** am I right in assuming that ...?; **ich gehe einmal von der ~ aus, dass ...** I am working *or* going on the assumption that ... [3] ▸**Annahmestelle** [4] (Billigung) approval; (einer Dissertation) acceptance [5] (einer Gewohnheit) adoption; (eines Namens) adoption; assumption [6] (Aufnahme) taking on; **über jmds. ~ entscheiden** decide if sb. should be taken on; **~ an Kindes statt** (veralt.) adoption

Annahme-: ~schluss, ***~schluß** *der* deadline [for acceptance]; **wann ist ~schluss?** when is the deadline [for acceptance]?; **freitags ist für Lottoscheine ~schluss** Friday is the last day of the week for lottery coupons; **~stelle** *die* (für Lotto/Wetten usw.) place where coupons/bets are accepted; (einer Reinigung) branch; (für Reparaturen) repairs counter/department; (für Telegramme, Pakete usw.) telegrams/parcels counter; (für Lieferungen) delivery point

Annalen /aˈnaːlən/ *Pl.* annals; **in die ~ der Firma eingehen** go down in the annals of the firm

annehmbar
A *Adj.* [1] (akzeptabel) acceptable [2] (recht gut) reasonable
B *adv.* reasonably [well]

an|nehmen
A *unr. tr. V.* [1] accept; take; accept ‹*alms, invitation, condition, help*›; take ‹*food, telephone call*›; accept, take [on] ‹*task, job, repairs*›; accept, take up ‹*offer, invitation, challenge*›; **die** *od.* **seine Wahl ~:** accept one's election [2] (Sport) take; **er nahm den Ball mit dem Kopf an** he headed the ball down [3] (billigen) approve; accept ‹*dissertation*›; pass ‹*law*›; approve, adopt ‹*resolution*› [4] (aufnehmen) take on ‹*worker, patient, pupil*› [5] (hinnehmen) accept ‹*fate, verdict, punishment*› [6] (adoptieren) adopt; **jmdn. an Kindes statt ~** (veralt.) adopt sb. [7] (haften lassen) take ‹*dye, ink*›; **kein Wasser ~:** repel water; be water-repellent; **Feuchtigkeit gut ~:** absorb moisture easily [8] (sich aneignen) adopt ‹*habit, mannerism*›; adopt, assume ‹*name, attitude*›; put on ‹*airs and graces*› [9] (bekommen) take on ‹*look, appearance, form, tone, dimension*› [10] (vermuten) assume; presume; **ich nehme es an/nicht an** I assume *or* presume so/not; **das ist/ist nicht anzunehmen** that can/cannot be assumed [11] (voraussetzen) assume; **etw. als gegeben** *od.* **Tatsache ~:** take sth. for granted *or* as read; **nehmen wir an, dass ...** let us assume that ...; **angenommen, [dass] ...** assuming [that] ...; **das kannst du ~!** (ugs.) you bet! (coll.) [12] (Jägerspr.: angreifen) attack; go for [13] (Jägerspr.: aufnehmen) **eine/die Fährte ~:** take up a/the scent
B *unr. refl. V.* (geh.) **sich jmds./einer Sache ~:** look after sb./sth.

Annehmlichkeit *die; ~, ~en* comfort; (Vorteil) advantage

annektieren /anɛkˈtiːrən/ *tr. V.* annex

Annektierung *die; ~, ~en*, **Annexion** /anɛˈksi̯oːn/ *die; ~, ~en* annexation

an|niesen *tr. V.* sneeze over

an|nieten *tr. V.* rivet on (**an** + *Akk. od. Dat.* to)

anno, Anno /ˈano/ *in* **~ 1910** *usw.* (veralt.) in [the year] 1910 *etc.*; **ein Auto von ~ 1932** (veralt.) a 1932 car; **~ dazumal** *od.* **dunnemals** *od.* **Tobak** (ugs. scherzh.) the year dot (Brit. coll.); long ago; **~ Domini 1656** (veralt.) in the year of our Lord 1656

Annonce /aˈnõːsə/ *die; ~, ~n* advertisement; ad (coll.); advert (Brit. coll.)

Annoncen·teil *der* advertisement section

annoncieren
A *itr. V.* advertise
B *tr. V.* (ankündigen) announce

annullieren /anʊˈliːrən/ *tr. V.* annul

Annullierung *die; ~, ~en* annulment

Anode /aˈnoːdə/ *die; ~, ~n* (Physik) anode

an|öden *tr. V.* (ugs.) bore stiff (coll.) *or* to death (coll.)

anomal /ˈanomaːl/
A *Adj.* anomalous; abnormal
B *adv.* anomalously; abnormally

Anomalie *die; ~, ~n* ▸❶ **S. 439** [1] anomaly; abnormality [2] (Med.: Missbildung) abnormality

anonym /anoˈnyːm/
A *Adj.* anonymous; **die Anonymen Alkoholiker** Alcoholics Anonymous
B *adv.* anonymously

Anonymität /anonymiˈtɛːt/ *die; ~:* anonymity

Anonymus /aˈnoːnymʊs/ *der; ~,* **Anonymi** (geh.) anonymous writer/composer/artist *etc.*

Anopheles /aˈnoːfelɛs/ *die; ~, ~* (Zool.) anopheles

Anorak /ˈanorak/ *der; ~s, ~s* anorak

an|ordnen *tr. V.* [1] (arrangieren) arrange [2] (befehlen) order

An·ordnung *die* [1] (Ordnung, Aufstellung) arrangement; **in alphabetischer ~:** in alphabetical order [2] (Weisung) order; **haben Sie die nötigen ~en getroffen?** have you given all the necessary orders?; **auf meine ~/auf ~ des Arztes** on my/doctor's orders *pl.*

anorektisch /an|oˈrɛktɪʃ/ *Adj.* anorexic

Anorexie /an|orɛˈksiː/ *die; ~* (Med.) anorexia

an·organisch *Adj.* inorganic

anormal
A *Adj.* abnormal
B *adv.* abnormally

an|packen
A *tr. V.* [1] (ugs.: greifen, anfassen) grab hold of; **jmdn. am Arm ~:** grab [hold of] sb. by the arm; **musst du das Buch mit deinen Dreckpfoten ~?** must you touch the book with your dirty hands? [2] (beginnen, angehen) tackle; **packen wir's an!** let's get down to it [3] (ugs.: behandeln) treat
B *itr. V.* (ugs.: mithelfen) **[mit] ~:** lend a hand

an|pappen (ugs.)
A *tr. V.* **etw. ~:** stick sth. on (**an** + *Dat.* to)
B *itr. V.*; *mit sein* stick (**an** + *Dat.* to)

a

an|passen
A *tr. V.* [1] (passend machen) fit; **jmdm. einen Anzug ~:** fit sb. for a suit; **Bauteile einander ~:** fit components together [2] (abstimmen) suit (*Dat.* to); **die Renten wurden am 1. Januar angepasst** pensions were adjusted on 1 January
B *refl. V.* adapt [oneself] (*Dat.* to); ‹*animal*› adapt; (gesellschaftlich) conform; **die am besten angepassten Arten** the species which have adapted best; *s. auch* **angepasst B**

Anpassung *die;* **~, ~en** adaptation (**an** + *Akk.* to); (der Renten, Löhne usw.) adjustment (**an** + *Akk.* to); (an die Gesellschaft) conformity

anpassungs·fähig *Adj.* adaptable

Anpassungs-: ~fähigkeit *die* adaptability (**an** + *Akk.* to); **~schwierigkeiten** *Pl.* difficulties in adapting (**an** + *Akk.* to)

an|peilen *tr. V.* [1] (Funkw.) take a bearing on [2] (fig. ugs.: anstreben) aim at [3] (anvisieren) take a sight on

an|peitschen *tr. V.* drive on

an|pesen *itr. V.; mit sein* (nordd. ugs.) **angepest kommen** come tearing *or* (coll.) belting along; (auf einen zu) come tearing *or* (coll.) belting up

an|pfeifen
A *unr. tr. V.* [1] **das Spiel/die zweite Halbzeit ~:** blow the whistle to start the game/the second half [2] (salopp: zurechtweisen) bawl out (coll.)
B *unr. itr. V.* blow the whistle

An·pfiff *der* [1] (Sport) whistle for the start of play; **der ~ zur zweiten Halbzeit** the whistle for the start of the second half [2] (salopp: Zurechtweisung) bawling-out (coll.)

an|pflanzen *tr. V.* [1] (pflanzen, bepflanzen) plant [2] (anbauen) grow; cultivate

An·pflanzung *die* [1] planting [2] (bepflanzte Fläche) cultivated area; **eine ~ anlegen** lay out an area for cultivation

an|pflaumen *tr. V.* (ugs.) [1] tease; take the mickey out of (Brit. sl.) [2] ▸ **anmeckern**

Anpflaumerei *die;* **~, ~en** (ugs.) teasing; mickey-taking (Brit. sl.); **lass doch deine ~en** stop teasing *or* (Brit. sl.) taking the mickey

an|pflocken *tr. V.* tie ‹*boat*› up; tether ‹*animal*›

an|picken[1] *tr. V.* peck at

an|picken[2] (österr. ugs.)
A *tr. V.* stick on
B *itr. V.; mit sein* be stuck on

an|pinkeln *tr. V.* (ugs.) pee on (coll.)

an|pinnen *tr. V.* (nordd.) pin up (**an** + *Akk.* on)

an|pinseln *tr. V.* (ugs.) [1] (anstreichen) paint [2] (an etw. pinseln) paint (**an** + *Akk.* on)

an|pirschen *refl. V.* creep up (**an** + *Akk.* on)

an|pissen *tr. V.* (derb) piss on (coarse)

An·pöbelei *die* (ugs.) abuse; **~en** abuse *sing.*

an|pöbeln *tr. V.* (ugs.) abuse

an|pochen *itr. V.* (südd.) ▸ **anklopfen**

An·prall *der;* **~[e]s** impact (**auf, an** + *Akk.* with, **gegen** against)

an|prallen *itr. V.; mit sein* crash; **gegen** *od.* **an etw. ~:** crash into sb./against sth.

an|prangern *tr. V.* denounce (**als** as)

an|preisen *unr. tr. V.* extol; **etw. als etw. ~:** extol sth. as being sth.; **jmdn./etw. jmdm. ~:** extol the virtues of sb./sth. to sb.; recommend sb./sth. highly to sb.

an|preschen *itr. V.; mit sein* **angeprescht kommen** (ugs.) come racing along; (auf einen zu) come racing up

an|pressen *tr. V.* press on (**an** + *Akk.* to)

An·probe *die* [1] fitting; **zur ~ kommen** come for a fitting [2] (Raum) (beim Schneider) fitting room; (im Kaufhaus) changing room (Brit.); dressing room (Amer.)

an|probieren
A *tr. V.* try on; **jmdm. etw. ~:** try sth. on sb.
B *itr. V.* **~ kommen** (ugs.) come for a fitting

an|pumpen *tr. V.* (ugs.) borrow money from; **jmdn. um 20 Euro ~:** touch (coll.) *or* tap sb. for 20 euros

an|pusten *tr. V.* (ugs.) blow on

an|quasseln *tr. V.* (salopp), **an|quatschen** *tr. V.* (salopp) speak to

Anrainer /'anraine/ *der;* **~s, ~** [1] (Nachbar) neighbour; **als ~ des Sees habe ich ...** as I live on *or* by the lake, I have ... [2] (bes. österr.: Anlieger) resident [3] ▸ **Anrainerstaat**

Anrainer·grundstück *das* neighbouring property; **die ~e des Sees** the properties on *or* by the lake

Anrainerin *die;* **~, ~nen** ▸ **Anrainer 1, 2**

Anrainer·staat *der* **die ~en des Bodensees** the countries bordering on Lake Constance

an|ranzen *tr. V.* (salopp) bawl out (coll.)

Anranzer *der;* **~s, ~** (salopp) bawling-out (coll.)

an|rasen *itr. V.; mit sein* (ugs.) race up; **gegen etw. ~:** crash into sth.; **angerast kommen** come racing along; (auf einen zu) come racing up

an|raten *unr. tr. V.* **jmdm. etw. ~:** recommend sth. to sb.; **jmdm. Vorsicht ~:** advise sb. to be careful; **auf Anraten des Arztes** on the *or* one's doctor's advice

an|rattern *itr. V.; mit sein* (ugs.) **angerattert kommen** come rattling along; (auf einen zu) come rattling up

an|rauchen *tr. V.* light up; **jmdm. eine Zigarette ~:** light up a cigarette for sb.; **eine angerauchte Zigarre** a partly smoked *or* half-smoked cigar

an|räuchern *tr. V.* lightly smoke

an|rauen, *an|rauhen *tr. V.* roughen

an|raunzen *tr. V.* (salopp) ▸ **anranzen**

Anraunzer *der;* **~s, ~** (salopp) ▸ **Anranzer**

an|rauschen *itr. V.; mit sein* (ugs.) **angerauscht kommen** come sweeping along; (auf einen zu) come sweeping up; ‹*vehicle*› come roaring along; (auf einen zu) come roaring up

anrechenbar *Adj.* **[auf etw. (*Akk.*)] ~ sein** count [towards sth.]

an|rechnen *tr. V.* [1] (gutschreiben, verbuchen) count; take into account; **jmdm. einen Betrag/seine Überstunden ~:** credit sb. with an amount/his/her overtime; **die Untersuchungshaft kann auf die Gefängnisstrafe angerechnet werden** time spent in custody can be counted as part of *or* taken into account in the prison sentence; **er bekam einen Pluspunkt angerechnet** he was given an extra mark; **jmdm. etw. als Verdienst/Fehler ~:** count sth. to sb.'s credit/as sb.'s mistake; **sich (*Dat.*) etw. zur Ehre ~** (geh.) consider sth. an honour; **jmdm. etw. hoch ~:** think highly of sb. for sth. [2] (in Rechnung stellen) **jmdm. etw. ~:** charge sb. for sth.; **das Porto wird dem Kunden angerechnet** postage is charged to the customer; **jmdm. zu viel ~:** overcharge sb.

An·rechnung *die* [1] **unter ~ der Untersuchungshaft** counting *or* taking into account time spent in custody; **eine ~ der Untersuchungshaft/des Praktikums ist nicht möglich** it is not possible to take time spent in custody/practical work into account [2] (Berechnung) charge; **eine ~ der Transportkosten erfolgt nicht** transport costs (Brit.) *or* (Amer.) transportation costs are not charged; **etw. in ~ bringen** (Papierdt.) charge for sth.

anrechnungs·fähig *Adj.* (Papierdt.) ▸ **anrechenbar**

An·recht *das* [1] right; **ein ~ auf etw. (*Akk.*) haben** *od.* **besitzen** have a right to *or* be entitled to sth. [2] (Abonnement) subscription

An·rede *die* ▸❶ **S. 44,** ▸❶ **S. 143** form of address; (Brief~) form of address; salutation; **wie ist die ~ eines Kardinals** *od.* **für einen Kardinal?** what is the correct form of address for a cardinal?

Anrede-: ~fall *der* ▸ **~kasus; ~für·wort** *das* ▸ **~pronomen; ~kasus** *der* vocative [case]

an|reden *tr. V.* [1] address; **jmdn. mit „du" ~:** address sb. as 'du'; use 'du' to sb.; **jmdn. mit dem Vornamen ~:** address *or* call sb. by his/her Christian name [2] **gegen den Lärm ~:** talk above the noise; **gegen etw. ~** (widersprechen) argue [against sth.]

Anrede·pronomen *das* personal pronoun used as form of address

an|regen
A *tr. V.* [1] (ermuntern) prompt; **jmdn. zum Nachdenken ~:** make sb. think [2] (vorschlagen) propose; suggest; raise ‹*question*›; **~, etw. zu tun** propose *or* suggest doing sth. [3] (Physik) excite
B *tr.* (*auch itr.*) *V.* stimulate ‹*imagination, digestion*›; sharpen, whet, stimulate ‹*appetite*›; **Kaffee regt an** coffee acts as a stimulant; *s. auch* **angeregt B**

anregend *Adj.* stimulating; **ein ~es Mittel** a stimulant; **Kaffee wirkt/ist ~:** coffee acts as a stimulant

An·regung *die* [1] (das Anregen) ▸ **anregen B:** stimulation; whetting; sharpening; **zur ~ der Verdauung/des Appetits** to stimulate the digestion/whet *etc.* the appetite [2] (Denkanstoß, Idee) stimulus [3] (Vorschlag) proposal; suggestion [4] (Physik) excitation

Anregungs·mittel *das* stimulant

an|reichen ▸ **zureichen**

an|reichern /'anraiçen/
A *tr. V.* [1] (gehaltvoller machen) enrich; **Trinkwasser mit Fluor ~:** add fluoride to drinking water [2] (akkumulieren) accumulate [3] (Kerntechnik) enrich
B *refl. V.* [1] (sich ansammeln) accumulate [2] (seinen Gehalt an etw. erhöhen) be enriched

Anreicherung *die;* **~, ~en** [1] enrichment; **die ~ von Trinkwasser mit Fluor** the addition of fluoride to drinking water [2] (Akkumulation) accumulation [3] (Kerntechnik) enrichment

an|reihen
A *tr. V.* add (**an** + *Akk.* to)
B *refl. V.* **sich hinten [an die Schlange] ~:** join the end of the queue (Brit.); get on the end of the line (Amer.)

An·reise *die* [1] journey [there/here]; **die ~ dauert 10 Stunden** the journey there/here takes ten hours; it takes 10 hours to get there/here [2] (Ankunft) arrival

an|reisen *itr. V.; mit sein* [1] travel there/here; **mit der Bahn ~:** go/come by train; travel there/here by train; **die aus dem ganzen Land anreisenden Besucher** the visitors travelling there/here from all over the country; **angereist kommen** come [2] (ankommen) arrive

Anreise·tag *der* day of arrival; **für den An- und den Abreisetag bekommen Sie Spesen** your expenses will be paid for the days of the journey there and the journey back

an|reißen *unr. tr. V.* [1] (durchzureißen beginnen) partly tear [2] (in Gang setzen) start [up] [3] (anzünden) strike ‹*match*› [4] (Technik) mark [out] [5] (kurz ansprechen) touch on [6] (ugs.: anbrechen) start; open [7] (ugs. abwertend: anlocken) lure

An·reißer *der* [1] (ugs. abwertend: Werber) tout [2] (ugs.: Ware) big attraction [3] (Berufsbez.) marker-out

Anreißerin *die;* **~, ~nen** ▸ **Anreißer 1, 3**

an·reißerisch (ugs. abwertend)
A *Adj.* flashily commercial; gimmicky (coll.) ‹*advertisement*›
B *adv.* **das Buch/die Reklame ist mir zu ~ aufgemacht** the book is too flashily commercial/the ad is too gimmicky for my liking (coll.)

an|reiten *unr. itr. V.; mit sein* [1] **angeritten kommen** come riding along; (auf einen zu) come riding up; **gegen den Feind ~:** charge the enemy [2] (ansteuern) ride at ‹*obstacle*› [3] (zureiten) break in ‹*horse*›

An·reiz *der* incentive; **ein ~ zum Sparen** an incentive to save

an|reizen *tr.* (*auch itr.*) *V.* [1] (anspornen) stimulate; encourage; **Steuerermäßigungen sollen zum Sparen ~:** tax reductions are supposed to stimulate *or* act as an incentive to saving [2] (anregen, erregen) stimulate

an|rempeln *tr. V.* barge into; (absichtlich) jostle

an|rennen
A *unr. itr. V.; mit sein* [1] **angerannt kommen** come running along; (auf einen zu) come running up; **er kommt wegen jeder Kleinigkeit**

ℹ Anreden und Titel

Die vier grundlegenden Anreden im Englischen sind:
Mr (= Herr) für Männer
Mrs (= Frau) für verheiratete Frauen
Miss (= Fräulein bzw. Frau) für Mädchen und (auch ältere) unverheiratete Frauen
Ms (= Frau) für (meist jüngere) Frauen

Im modernen Sprachgebrauch wird **Ms** oft statt **Miss** oder **Mrs** verwendet, es hat sich allerdings nicht so durchgesetzt wie im Deutschen die Anrede **Frau** für alle Frauen. Alle vier Anreden können entweder mit oder ohne den Vornamen stehen. Die nachgestellte Bezeichnung **Esq.** (*Esquire* = Herr) wird meist in höheren britischen gesellschaftlichen Kreisen auf Briefen statt **Mr** verwendet, gilt aber heute als etwas altmodisch. Ebenfalls nachgestellt wird in den USA die Abkürzung **Jr** (= Junior) für den Sohn eines gleichnamigen Vaters. Weitere Hinweise hinsichtlich der Form der Anschrift finden Sie unter **Briefeschreiben**.

Wie man jemanden anredet

Im Allgemeinen ist der Gebrauch im englischen Sprachraum weniger formell als in Deutschland, Österreich und der Schweiz. Für die Anrede mit "Sie" gibt es im Englischen keine Entsprechung, es wird immer **you** verwendet. Unter Kollegen, Nachbarn, in Gruppen und Vereinen spricht man sich generell mit Vornamen an. Vor allem in den USA redet man praktisch jeden, den man kennen lernt, sofort mit Vornamen an.

Beachten Sie, dass die Anreden **Mr, Mrs, Miss** und **Ms** nicht allein stehen dürfen (Ausnahme: Lehrerinnen werden noch von Schulkindern mit "miss" angeredet) und auch nicht in Kombination mit Titeln verwendet werden können:

Guten Morgen, Herr Professor
= Good morning, professor
Guten Abend, Frau Doktor
= Good evening, doctor
Auf Wiedersehen, Herr Oberst
= Goodbye, colonel
Jawohl, Herr Minister
= Yes, minister

In solchen Fällen wird oft der Name des bzw. der Angesprochenen hinzugefügt: "Good morning, Professor Evans" usw. Generell wird im englischen Sprachraum weniger Gebrauch von Titeln gemacht, so dass es etwa für "Herr Direktor" keine Entsprechung gibt, man sagt also einfach **Mr** und den Namen.

Vorgesetzte beim Militär werden nicht mit dem Namen, sondern meist einfach mit **sir** oder der Rangbezeichnung angeredet, während in der Schule Lehrer und Lehrerinnen meist von den jüngeren Schülern mit **sir** bzw. **miss** angeredet werden.

Kunden in Geschäften, Restaurants usw. werden oft noch mit **sir** bzw. **madam** (im Plural **gentlemen** bzw. **ladies**) angeredet:

Was darf es sein?
= Can I help you, sir/madam?
Was wünscht der Herr/die gnädige Frau zum Trinken?
= What would you like to drink, sir/madam?
Was wünschen die Damen/Herren?
= What would you like, ladies/gentlemen?

Anreden bei Würdenträgern und Adeligen

Ihre Majestät
= Your Majesty
Eure Hoheit
= Your Highness
Euer Gnaden
= Your Grace
Eure Eminenz
= Your Eminence
Eure Heiligkeit
= Your Holiness

Wenn man von jemandem spricht

Beachten Sie auch hier, dass im englischen Sprachraum weniger Gebrauch von Titeln gemacht wird. Die Bezeichnung *Herr* bzw. *Frau* wird in Kombinationen wie "Herr Doktor Reiter", "Frau Professor Elisabeth Meinhardt" nicht übersetzt, da **Mr, Mrs, Ms** und **Miss** nicht mit Titeln kombiniert werden dürfen:

Herr Doktor Dietrich Reiter
= Dr Dietrich Reiter
Frau Professor Elisabeth Meinhardt
= Professor Elisabeth Meinhardt
Herr Kapitän Richard Müller
= Captain Richard Müller
Herr Minister Baumann
= [the minister] Mr Baumann
Frau Direktorin Dr Stahlmeyer
= [the director/head teacher] Dr Stahlmeyer
Herr Kammersänger Eberhard Wächter
= Kammersänger Eberhard Wächter

Im letzten Beispiel gibt es keine Übersetzung, am besten lässt man den Titel also in der deutschen Originalform.

Adelstitel und Kirchentitel werden im Englischen ähnlich wie im Deutschen behandelt:

König Ludwig XIV. von Frankreich
= King Louis XIV of France (*gesprochen* Louis the Fourteenth)
Papst Johannes Paul II.
= Pope John Paul II (*gesprochen* John Paul the Second)
Prinzessin Ingeborg zu Schleswig-Holstein
= Princess Ingeborg of Schleswig-Holstein

---

bei mir angerannt he comes running to me about every little thing **2** **gegen den Sturm/feindliche Stellungen ∼:** run into *or* against the storm/storm enemy positions; **gegen jmdn./etw. ∼** (fig.) fight against sb./sth.
B *unr. refl. V.* (ugs.) **sich** (*Dat.*) **das Knie/den Kopf an etw.** (*Dat.*) **∼:** bump one's knee/head on sth.

Anrichte *die;* **∼, ∼n** **1** (Möbel) sideboard **2** (Raum) pantry

an|richten *tr. V.* **1** (auch itr.) arrange ‹*food*›; (servieren) serve; **es ist angerichtet** (geh.) dinner is served **2** cause ‹*disaster, confusion, devastation, etc.*›; **was hast du wieder alles angerichtet!** what have you gone and done now? (coll.)

an|ritzen *tr. V.* scratch

an|rollen
A *itr. V.; mit sein* **1** (zu rollen beginnen) ‹*vehicle, column, etc.*› start moving; (fig.) ‹*campaign, search operation*› start **2** (heranrollen) roll up; ‹*aircraft*› taxi up; **angerollt kommen** come rolling along; (auf einen zu) come rolling up **3** **die Wellen rollten gegen den Deich an** the waves rolled in against the dyke
B *tr. V.* roll up ‹*barrel*›; (auf einem Wagen o. Ä.) wheel up

an|rosten *itr. V.; mit sein* start to rust; get [a bit] rusty; **ein angerostetes Messer** a rusting knife; a knife that has started to rust

an|rösten *tr. V.* roast lightly; toast ‹*bread*› lightly

anrüchig /ˈanrʏçɪç/ *Adj.* **1** (berüchtigt) disreputable **2** (unanständig) indecent; (obszön) offensive

Anrüchigkeit *die;* **∼** **1** (schlechter Ruf) disreputableness **2** (Unanständigkeit) indecency; (Obszönität) offensiveness

an|rücken
A *itr. V.; mit sein* ‹*troops*› advance; move forward; ‹*firemen, police*› move in; **morgen rücken meine Verwandten an** (ugs. scherzh.) my relatives are descending on me/us tomorrow
B *tr. V.* push (**an** + *Akk.* against); (ziehen) pull (**an** + *Akk.* against)

An·ruf *der* **1** (telefonischer ∼) call; **danke für den ∼:** thanks for ringing (Brit.) *or* calling **2** (Zuruf) call; (eines Wachtpostens) challenge; **auf ∼:** when called/challenged; **ohne ∼ schießen** shoot without warning

Anruf·beantworter *der;* **∼s, ∼:** [telephone-]answering machine

an|rufen
A *unr. tr. V.* **1** call *or* shout to ‹*friend, passer-by*›; call ‹*sleeping person*›; hail ‹*ship*›; ‹*sentry*› challenge **2** (geh.: angehen, bitten) appeal to ‹*person, court*› (**um** for); call upon ‹*God*›; **Gott um Gnade ∼:** implore God's mercy **3** (telefonisch ∼) ring (Brit.); call **4** (geh.: begehren) implore, beg ‹*sb.'s mercy, help, protection, etc.*›
B *unr. itr. V.* **1** (antelefonieren) ring (Brit.); call; **bei jmdm. ∼:** ring (Brit.) *or* call sb.; **ruf doch mal in Köln an** ring (Brit.) *or* call Cologne; **im Büro ∼:** ring (Brit.) *or* call the office **2** (ugs., bes. südd.: telefonieren) make a phone call; **ich muss nur mal kurz ∼:** I must just make a quick phone call; **kann ich bei Ihnen/in Ihrem Büro mal ∼?** can I just use your telephone *or* phone/telephone from your office *or* use your office telephone?

Anrufer *der;* **∼s, ∼, Anruferin** *die;* **∼, ∼nen** caller

Anrufung *die;* **∼, ∼en** **1** (einer Gottheit o. Ä.) invocation **2** (eines Gerichts) appeal (*Gen.* to)

an|rühren *tr. V.* **1** touch; **keine Zigaretten/kein Buch ∼:** never touch cigarettes/never pick up a book **2** (bereiten) mix **3** (geh.: beeindrucken) move; touch

ans *Präp. + Art.* **1** = **an das** **2** (mit subst. Inf.) **sich ∼ Arbeiten machen** set to work; **wenn es ∼ Bezahlen geht** when it comes to paying

an|säen *tr. V.* sow ‹*grass, grain*›

An·sage *die* **1** (Ankündigung) announcement **2** (Kartenspiel) bid; **du hast die ∼:** it's your bid

an|sagen
A *tr. V.* **1** (ankündigen) announce; *s. auch* **Bankrott 1**; **Kampf 4** **2** (Kartenspiel) bid; *s. auch* **Schneider 3** **3** (Bürow.: diktieren) dictate **4** (veralt.: mitteilen) **sagt an, was …** pray tell me/us what … (arch.)
B *refl. V.* say that one is coming; **sich zum nächsten Wochenende/für Dienstagabend/bei jmdm. ∼:** say that one is coming next weekend/Tuesday evening/to see sb.

an|sägen *tr. V.* make a saw cut in; start to saw through

Ansager *der;* **∼s, ∼, Ansagerin** *die;* **∼, ∼nen** ▸ℹ S. 113 **1** (Radio, Fernsehen) announcer **2** (im Kabarett usw.) master of ceremonies; (Brit.) compère

an|sammeln
A *tr. V.* (anhäufen) accumulate; amass ‹*riches, treasure*›
B *refl. V.* **1** (zusammenströmen) gather **2** (sich anhäufen) accumulate; (fig.) ‹*anger, excitement*› build up

An·sammlung *die* 1 (von Gegenständen) collection; (Haufen) pile, heap; (von Wasser) pool 2 (Auflauf) crowd

ansässig /ˈanzɛsɪç/ *Adj.* resident; **eine in London ~e Firma** a firm with its registered office in London; **sich in Bayern ~ machen** settle in Bavaria

An·satz *der* 1 (erstes Zeichen, Beginn) beginnings *pl.*; **einen ~ zum Bauch haben** have the beginnings of a paunch; **Ansätze zur Besserung zeigen** show the first signs of improvement; **etw. im ~ unterdrücken** nip sth. in the bud; **die ersten Ansätze** the initial stages; **gute Ansätze zeigen** make a good start; **im ~** (ansatzweise) to some extent 2 (eines Körperteils) base 3 (Musik) (Lippenstellung) embouchure; (Tonerzeugung) attack 4 (Math.) statement 5 (bes. Philos.: Lösungsversuch) approach 6 (von Rost, Kalk usw.) formation; (Schicht) coating 7 (Wirtsch.: Voranschlag) estimate; (im Staatsbudget) amount budgeted; appropriation; **etw. für etw. in ~ bringen** (Amtsspr.) earmark sth. for sth.; **außer ~ bleiben** (Amtsspr.) be left out of account; be excluded 8 (Chemie: eines Versuchs) setting up 9 (Technik) (Verlängerungsstück) extension; (Nahtstelle) join

ansatz-, Ansatz-: ~punkt *der* starting point; point of departure; **~stück** *das* (Technik) extension; **~weise** *Adv.* to some extent

an|saufen *unr. refl. V.* (salopp) **sich** (*Dat.*) **einen [Rausch] ~:** get plastered (sl.); **sich** (*Dat.*) **einen Bierbauch ~:** get a beer belly

an|saugen
A *tr. V.* (geh. auch unr.) suck in *or* up
B *refl. V.* (geh. auch unr.) (sich festsetzen) ‹*leech etc.*› attach itself (*by suction*)

Ansaug·rohr *das* (Kfz-W.) intake manifold; (beim Einzylindermotor) inlet pipe

an|säuseln *refl. V.* **sich** (*Dat.*) **einen ~** (ugs.) get tipsy; *s. auch* **angesäuselt B**

Anschaffe /ˈanʃafə/ *die;* ~ (salopp) **auf [die] ~ gehen** (sich prostituieren) go on the game (Brit. sl.); walk the streets (Amer.); (stehlen) go out thieving

an|schaffen
A *tr. V.* 1 (kaufen) **[sich** (*Dat.*)**] etw. ~** (auch fig. ugs.) get [oneself] sth.; **sich** (*Dat.*) **Kinder ~** (fig. ugs.) have children *or* (coll.) kids 2 (südd., österr.: befehlen) **jmdm. ~, dass er etw. tut** order sb. to do sth. 3 (salopp: stehlen) pinch (coll.)
B *itr. V.* 1 (salopp: Prostitution betreiben) **~ [gehen]** be on the game (Brit. coll.); be walking the streets (Amer.); **für jmdn. ~:** work as a prostitute for sb. 2 (südd., österr.: befehlen) **[jmdm.] ~:** give [sb.] orders

An·schaffung *die* purchase; **~en machen** make purchases; **sich zur ~ eines Autos entschließen** decide to get *or* buy a car

Anschaffungs-: ~kosten *Pl.* original *or* initial cost *sing.*; acquisition cost *sing.*; **~wert** *der* value at the time of purchase

an|schalten *tr. V.* switch on

an|schauen (bes. südd., österr., schweiz.) ▸**ansehen**

anschaulich
A *Adj.* (deutlich) clear; (bildhaft, lebendig) vivid, graphic ‹*style, description*›; **etw. ~ machen** make sth. vivid; bring sth. to life; **etw. durch Beispiele ~ machen** illustrate sth. by examples; **ein ~er Unterricht** teaching that makes the subject come alive
B *adv.* (deutlich) clearly; (bildhaft, lebendig) vividly; ‹*describe*› vividly, graphically

Anschaulichkeit *die;* ~ ▸**anschaulich**: clarity; vividness; graphicness

Anschauung *die;* ~, **~en** 1 (Auffassung) view; (bestimmte Meinung) opinion 2 (Eindruck, Erfahrung) experience; **aus eigener ~:** from personal *or* one's own experience 3 (das Betrachten) contemplation

Anschauungs-: ~material *das* illustrative material; (für den Unterricht) visual aids *pl.*; **~unterricht** *der* visual instruction; (fig.) object lesson; **~weise** *die* view

An·schein *der* appearance; **allem** *od.* **dem ~ nach** to all appearances; **es hat den ~, als ob ...** it appears *or* looks as if ...; **sich** (*Dat.*) **den ~ geben, als ob man etw. glaubt** pretend to believe sth.; **den ~ erwecken, etw. zu sein** give the impression of being sth.

an·scheinend *Adv.* apparently; seemingly

an|scheißen (derb)
A *unr. tr. V.* 1 (betrügen) con (coll.); diddle (coll.) 2 (zurechtweisen) **jmdn. ~:** give sb. a bollocking (Brit. coarse); bawl sb. out (coll.)
B *unr. itr. V.; mit sein* **da kommt er schon wieder angeschissen** there he is, come to make a bloody nuisance of himself again (Brit. sl.)

an|schesen *itr. V.; mit sein* (nordd.) **angeschest kommen** come rushing along; (auf einen zu) come rushing up

an|schicken *refl. V.* (geh.) **sich ~, etw. zu tun** (sich bereit machen) get ready *or* prepare to do sth.; (anfangen, im Begriff sein) be about to do sth.; be on the point of doing sth.

an|schieben *unr. tr. V.* push ‹*vehicle*›; **könnt ihr mich mal ~?** could you give me a push?

an|schießen
A *unr. tr. V.* 1 (durch Schuss verletzen) shoot and wound; **das Reh war nicht tot, nur angeschossen** the deer was not dead, only wounded 2 (bes. Fußball) kick the ball against ‹*player*›; shoot straight at ‹*goalkeeper*› 3 (ugs.: kritisieren); **jmdn. ~:** give sb. some stick (sl.) 4 (Milit., Jagdw.: prüfen) test
B *unr. itr. V.; mit sein* **angeschossen kommen** come tearing *or* racing along; (auf einen zu) come tearing *or* racing up

an|schimmeln *itr. V.; mit sein* start to go mouldy; **angeschimmeltes Brot** bread that has started to go mouldy

an|schirren *tr. V.* harness ‹*horse*›

An·schiss, *An·schiß *der* (salopp) bollocking (Brit. coarse); bawling-out (coll.); **einen ~ kriegen** get a bollocking (Brit. coarse); get bawled out (coll.)

An·schlag *der* 1 (Bekanntmachung) notice; (Plakat) poster; **einen ~ machen** put up a notice/poster 2 (Attentat) assassination attempt; (auf ein Gebäude, einen Zug o. Ä.) attack; **einen ~ auf jmdn. verüben** make an attempt on sb.'s life; **einem ~ zum Opfer fallen** be assassinated 3 (Texterfassung) keystroke; **200 Anschläge pro Minute [schreiben]** ≈ [have a typing speed of] 40 words a minute 4 (Musik) touch 5 (Technik) stop; **etw. bis zum ~ niederdrücken/aufdrehen** push sth. right down/turn sth. on as far as it will go 6 (Häkeln, Stricken) first line of stitches; (Vorgang) casting on; **„~ 50 Maschen"** 'cast on 50 stitches' 7 (Milit., Jagdw.) aiming position; **mit dem Gewehr im ~:** with rifle/rifles levelled; **in ~ bringen** level ‹*gun*› 8 (Kaufmannsspr.) estimate; **etw. in ~ bringen** take sth. into account *or* consideration

Anschlag·brett *das* noticeboard (Brit.); bulletin board (Amer.)

an|schlagen
A *unr. tr. V.* 1 (aushängen) put up, post ‹*notice, announcement, message*› (**an** + *Akk.* on) 2 (Häkeln, Stricken) cast on 3 (beim Versteckspiel) tag 4 (beschädigen) chip 5 (bei Musikinstrumenten) strike ‹*string, key, etc.*›; strike, sound ‹*gong*› 6 (erklingen lassen) play ‹*note, melody, etc.*›; **einen anderen/ernsthaften Ton ~** (fig.) adopt a different/serious tone 7 (beginnen) **ein rascheres Tempo/eine schnellere Gangart ~:** increase one's pace; speed up 8 (befestigen) fix on (**an** + *Akk.* to); (mit Nägeln) nail on (**an** + *Akk.* to) 9 (beim Maschinenschreiben) press, hit ‹*key*› 10 (Seemannsspr.: festbinden) bend (**an** + *Dat.* to) 11 (markieren) **einen Baum ~:** mark a tree with a notch 12 (Milit., Jagdw. veralt.) level ‹*gun*› 13 (österr.: anstechen) tap ‹*barrel*›
B *unr. itr. V.* 1 *mit sein* (anstoßen) **an etw.** (*Akk.*) **~:** knock against sth.; **mit dem Knie/Kopf an etw.** (*Akk.*) **~:** knock one's knee/head on sth. 2 (Schwimmen) touch 3 (Tasten niederdrücken) press *or* hit the keys 4 (wirken) work 5 (ugs.: dick machen) be fattening; **bei jmdm. ~:** make sb. put on weight 6 (bellen) bark
C *unr. refl. V.* (stoßen) **sich** (*Dat.*) **das Knie** *usw.* **~:** knock one's knee *etc.* (**an** + *Dat.* on)

Anschlag·säule *die* advertising column

an|schleichen
A *unr. itr. V.; mit sein* creep up; **angeschlichen kommen** come creeping along; (auf einen zu) come creeping up
B *unr. refl. V.* **sich an jmdn./etw. ~:** creep up on sb./sth.

an|schleifen¹ *unr. tr. V.* grind; cut ‹*precious stone*›

an|schleifen² *tr. V.* (ugs.) drag along

an|schlendern *itr. V.; mit sein* **angeschlendert kommen** come strolling along; (auf einen zu) come strolling up

an|schleppen *tr. V.* 1 (herbeibringen) drag along 2 (zum Starten) tow-start

an|schließen
A *unr. tr. V.* 1 (befestigen) lock, secure (**an** + *Akk. od. Dat.* to) 2 (verbinden) connect (**an** + *Akk. od. Dat.* to); connect up ‹*electrical device*›; (mit Stecker und Steckdose) plug in; **angeschlossene Sender** (Rundf., Ferns.) linked stations 3 (anfügen) add
B *unr. refl. V.* 1 (sich beteiligen); **sich jmdm./einer Sache ~:** join sb./sth. 2 **sich an etw.** (*Akk.*) *od.* **sich einer Sache** (*Dat.*) **~** (zeitlich) follow sth.; (angrenzen an) adjoin sth.; **an den Vortrag schloss sich eine Diskussion an** the lecture was followed by a discussion; **an das Haus schließen sich Stallungen an** stables adjoin the house 3 (beipflichten) endorse; **ich schließe mich meinem Vorredner voll und ganz an** I endorse completely the remarks of the previous speaker 4 (sich zuwenden) follow ‹*example*›; grow close to ‹*person*›; **sich leicht/schwer an andere ~:** make/not make friends easily
C *unr. itr. V.* **an etw.** (*Akk.*) **~** ▸**B 2**

anschließend
A *Adv.* afterwards; **~ an etw.** (*Akk.*) after sth.
B *adj.* subsequent; **ein Vortrag mit ~em Theaterbesuch** a lecture followed by a visit to the theatre

An·schluss, *An·schluß *der* 1 (Netz~) connection; (Kabel) cable; **~ an etw.** (*Akk.*) **erhalten/haben** be connected [up] to sth.; **elektrischen ~ erhalten/haben** be connected up to the mains 2 (telefonische Verbindung) connection; **[keinen] ~ bekommen** [not] get through; **auf den ~ warten** wait to be connected 3 (Verkehrs~) connection; (Flugw.) connecting flight; **Sie haben ~ nach ...** there is a connection to ...; **den ~ verpasst haben** have missed one's connection; (fig. ugs.) (keinen Ehepartner gefunden haben) have got left on the shelf; (nicht Schritt gehalten haben) have got left behind 4 (Telefon) telephone; **kein ~ unter dieser Nummer** number unobtainable 5 (Kontakt); **~ finden** make friends; **~ suchen** want to meet and get to know people 6 (Verbindung nach vorn) contact (**an** + *Akk.* with); **den ~ verlieren** lose contact (**an** + *Akk.* with); **im ~ an** following; after; **im ~ an unseren Brief vom ...** further to our letter of ... 7 (Sport) ▸**~tor** 8 (Politik) (Vereinigung) union (**an** + *Akk.* with); (verhüll.: Annexion) anschluss (**an** + *Akk.* with)

Anschluss-, *Anschluß-: ~kabel *das* connecting cable *or* (esp. Brit.) lead; (zur Verlängerung) extension cable *or* (esp. Brit.) lead; **~tor** *das,* **~treffer** *der* (Sport) goal which leaves/left the side only one down; **ihm gelang das ~tor** he pulled one back to leave the side only a goal down; **~zug** *der* connecting train; **den ~zug verpassen** miss one's connection

an|schmachten *tr. V.* eye adoringly; **sich ~:** gaze adoringly at one another

an|schmieden *tr. V.* forge on (**an** + *Akk.* to); **jmdn. an etw. ~** (anketten) chain sb. to sth.

an|schmiegen
A *tr. V.* nestle (**an** + *Akk.* against)
B *refl. V.* nestle up, snuggle up (**an** + *Akk.* to, against); **sich an den Körper ~** (fig.) ‹*fabric, material*› cling to the body

an·schmiegsam *Adj.* affectionate ‹*child*›; soft and smooth ‹*material*›

an|schmieren *tr. V.* 1 (ugs.: täuschen) con (coll.); diddle (coll.) 2 (beschmutzen) smear; **jmdn./sich/etw. mit etw. ~:** get *or* smear sth. all over sb./oneself/sth.

an|schnallen *tr. V.* strap on ‹*rucksack*›; put on ‹*skis, skates*›; **jmdn. ~** (im Auto) strap sb. in; **sich ~** (im Auto) put on one's seat belt; (im Flugzeug) fasten one's seat belt; **„bitte ~!"** 'fasten your seat belts, please'

Anschnall-: ~gurt *der* seat belt; **~pflicht** *die* compulsory wearing of seat belts

an|schnauzen *tr. V.* (ugs.) shout at

An·schnauzer *der* (ugs.) **einen ~ [ab]kriegen** get shouted at

an|schneiden *unr. tr. V.* [1] cut [the first slice of]; **einen frischen Laib ~:** start a fresh loaf [2] (ansprechen) raise; broach; (gesprächsweise berühren) touch on [3] trim ‹*flower*› [4] (Schneiderei) **etw. an etw.** (*Akk.*) **~:** cut sth. in one piece with sth.; **angeschnittene Ärmel** sleeves cut in one piece with the garment [5] (Verkehrsw., Motorsport) cut ‹*corner*›

An·schnitt *der* [1] (Schnittfläche) cut end [2] (erstes Stück) first slice; end piece

an|schnorren *tr. V.* (salopp) **jmdn. [um etw.] ~:** tap sb. [for sth.] (coll.)

Anschovis /anˈʃoːvɪs/ *die;* **~, ~:** anchovy

an|schrauben *tr. V.* screw on (**an** + *Akk.* to)

an|schreiben

A *unr. tr. V.* [1] (hinschreiben) write up (**an** + *Akk.* on); (mit Kreide) chalk up; **angeschrieben stehen** be written/chalked up [2] (ugs.: stunden) **[jmdm.] etw. ~:** chalk sth. up [to sb.'s account]; **bei jmdm. gut/schlecht angeschrieben sein** (ugs.) be in sb.'s good/bad books; be on sb.'s good/black list (Amer.) [3] (schriftlich benachrichtigen) write to; **vierzig Prozent der angeschriebenen Studenten** forty per cent of the students written to

B *unr. itr. V.* (ugs.: Kredit geben) give credit; **er lässt immer ~:** he always buys on tick (coll.)

An·schreiben *das* covering letter

an|schreien *unr. tr. V.* shout at

An·schrift *die* ▸ⓘ **S. 143** address

An·schub *der;* **~[e]s, ~e** impetus, stimulus (**zu** for)

Anschub·finanzierung *die* (Wirtsch.) start-up financing

an|schuldigen /ˈanʃʊldɪgn̩/ *tr. V.* (geh.) accuse (*Gen.*, **wegen** of); **der Angeschuldigte/die Angeschuldigten** the accused

Anschuldigung *die;* **~, ~en** accusation

an|schwärmen

A *itr. V.; mit sein* ‹*bees*› swarm in

B *tr. V.* (verehren) idolize; adore

an|schwärzen *tr. V.* (ugs.) **jmdn. ~** (in Misskredit bringen) blacken sb.'s name; (schlecht machen) run sb. down (**bei** to); (denunzieren) inform *or* (Brit. sl.) grass on sb. (**bei** to)

an|schweigen *unr. tr. V.* **sich [gegenseitig]/jmdn. ~:** not speak *or* talk to each other/sb.

an|schweißen *tr. V.* (Technik) weld on (**an** + *Akk. od. Dat.* to)

an|schwellen *unr. itr. V.; mit sein* [1] (dicker werden) swell [up]; **stark angeschwollen** very swollen [2] (lauter werden) grow louder; ‹*noise*› rise [3] (zunehmen; auch fig.) swell, grow; ‹*water, river*› rise

An·schwellung *die* swelling

an|schwemmen *tr. V.* wash up *or* ashore

an|schwimmen *unr. itr. V.; mit sein* **angeschwommen kommen** come swimming along; (auf einen zu) come swimming up; **gegen die Strömung/Flut ~:** swim against the current/tide

an|schwindeln *tr. V.* (ugs.) **jmdn. ~:** tell sb. fibs

an|schwirren *itr. V.; mit sein* (heranfliegen) **angeschwirrt kommen** come whirring *or* buzzing along; (fig. ugs.) come buzzing along; (auf einen zu) come buzzing up

an|schwitzen *tr. V.* (Kochk.) brown lightly (in hot fat)

an|segeln

A *itr. V.* [1] *mit sein* **angesegelt kommen** come sailing along; (auf einen zu) come sailing up [2] (Saison eröffnen) open the sailing season

B *tr. V.* make *or* head for

an|sehen

A *unr. tr. V.* [1] (anblicken) look at; **jmdn. groß/böse ~:** stare at sb./give sb. an angry look; **hübsch** *usw.* **anzusehen sein** be pretty *etc.* to look at [2] (betrachten) look at; view, look at ‹*flat, house*›; watch ‹*television programme*›; see ‹*play, film*›; **sieh [mal] [einer] an!** (ugs.) well, I never! (coll.) [3] (erkennen) **man sieht ihm sein Alter nicht an** he does not look his age; **man sieht ihr die Strapazen an** she's showing the strain; **man sieht ihr nicht an, dass sie krank ist** there is nothing to show that she is ill; **das sah man ihm nicht an** one would not have thought so to look at him; *s. auch* **Nasenspitze** [4] (zusehen) **etw. [mit] ~:** watch sth.; **das kann man doch nicht [mit] ~:** I/you can't just stand by and watch that; **das habe ich lange genug angesehen** I've had *or* seen enough of that; **ich kann das nicht länger [mit] ~:** I can't stand this any longer [5] (beurteilen) see [6] (auffassen) regard; consider; **jmdn. als seinen Freund/als Betrüger ~:** regard sb. as a friend/a cheat; consider sb. [to be] a friend/a cheat; **etw. als/für seine Pflicht ~:** consider sth. one's duty

B *unr. refl. V.* [1] **sich** (*Dat.*) **etw. ~:** look at sth.; **sich** (*Dat.*) **ein Haus/Fernsehprogramm/Schauspiel/einen Film ~:** look at *or* view a house/watch a television programme/see a play/film; **das sehe sich einer an!** (ugs.) just look at that! [2] **das sieht sich hübsch/furchtbar** *usw.* **an** it looks pretty/terrible *etc.*

Ansehen *das;* **~s** [1] (Wertschätzung) [high] standing *or* reputation; **hohes ~ genießen** enjoy high standing *or* a good reputation; **[bei jmdm.] in hohem ~ stehen** be held in high esteem *or* high regard [by sb.] [2] (geh.: Aussehen) appearance; **[nur] von** *od.* **vom ~:** [only] by sight; **von** *od.* **vom ~ über jmdn. urteilen** judge sb. by appearances; **ohne ~ der Person** (Rechtsw.) without respect of persons

an·sehnlich *Adj.* [1] (beträchtlich) considerable [2] (gut aussehend, stattlich) handsome; **er hat sich** (*Dat.*) **einen ~en Bauch angefuttert** he's developed quite a stomach

an|seilen *tr. V.* rope [up]; **sich ~:** rope up

***an|sein** ▸**an C 2**

an|sengen *tr. V.* singe [slightly]; **es riecht angesengt** there's a smell of something singeing

an|setzen

A *tr. V.* [1] (in die richtige Stellung bringen) position ‹*ladder, jack, drill, saw*›; **die Feder/das Glas ~:** put pen to paper/the glass to one's lips; **den Geigenbogen/die Trompete ~:** put *or* place the violin bow in the bowing position/put the trumpet to one's lips; *s. auch* **Hebel** [2] (anfügen) attach, put on (**an** + *Akk. od. Dat.* to); fit (**an** + *Akk. od. Dat.* on to) [3] (festlegen) fix ‹*meeting etc.*› (**für, auf** + *Akk.* for); fix, set ‹*deadline, date, price*› [4] (veranschlagen) estimate; **die Kosten mit drei Millionen ~:** estimate the cost at three million; **etw. zu niedrig/hoch ~:** underestimate/overestimate sth. [5] (anrühren) mix; prepare [6] (ausbilden) **Rost/Grünspan ~:** go rusty/become covered with verdigris; **Fett ~:** put on weight; **Knospen/Früchte ~:** form buds/set fruit [7] (einsetzen) **jmdn. auf einen Erpresser** *usw.*/**ein Projekt** *usw.* **~:** set *or* put sb. on to a blackmailer *etc.*/put sb. on [to] a project; **Hunde [auf eine Spur]/auf jmdn. ~:** set dogs on sb.'s/an animal's trail/on sb.

B *itr. V.* [1] (beginnen) **zum Reden/Trinken ~:** open one's mouth to speak/raise the glass *etc.* to one's lips; **er setzte mehrmals [zum Sprechen] an, aber ...** he kept opening his mouth to speak, but ...; **zur Landung ~:** come in to land; **zum Sprung/Überholen ~:** get ready *or* prepare to jump/overtake; **hier muss die Diskussion/Kritik ~:** this is where the discussion/criticism must start [2] ‹*nose, tail, hair, etc.*› start [3] (sich festsetzen) stick

An·sicht *die* [1] (Meinung) opinion; view; **meiner ~ nach** in my opinion *or* view; **nach [der] ~ der Fachleute** in the opinion of the experts; **anderer/der gleichen ~ sein** be of a different/the same opinion; **der ~ sein, dass ...** be of the opinion that ...; **ich bin ganz Ihrer ~:** I entirely agree with you; **da bin ich anderer ~:** I disagree with you there; **die ~en sind geteilt** opinion is divided [2] (Bild) view; **Ludwigshafen in alten ~en** old views of Ludwigshafen [3] (Kaufmannsspr.) **zur ~:** on approval

ansichtig *Adj.* **jmds./einer Sache ~ werden** (geh.) catch sight of sb./sth.

Ansichts-: ~karte *die,* **~post·karte** *die* picture postcard; **~sache** *die:* *in* **~sache sein** be a matter of opinion; **~sendung** *die* article/articles [sent] on approval

an|siedeln

A *refl. V.* (ansässig werden) settle; ‹*industry, bacteria*› become established; **auf dieser Insel haben sich seltene Vogelarten angesiedelt** rare species of birds have colonized this island

B *tr. V.* (ansässig machen) settle ‹*immigrant, refugee, etc.*›; establish ‹*industry, species, variety, bacteria*›; **die Attentäter sind rechts anzusiedeln** (fig.) it can be assumed that the assassins are rightists; **etw. in einem exotischen Milieu ~** (fig.) give sth. an exotic setting

Ansiedelung ▸**Ansiedlung**

An·siedler *der,* **An·siedlerin** *die* settler

An·siedlung *die* [1] (das Ansiedeln) ▸**ansiedeln B**: settlement; establishment [2] (Ort) settlement

An·sinnen *das;* **~s, ~:** [unreasonable] request; **ein freches/seltsames** *usw.* **~:** an impudent/a strange *etc.* request

An·sitz *der* [1] (Jägerspr.) hide (Brit.); blind (Amer.); (Hochsitz) raised hide (Brit.) *or* (Amer.) blind [2] (österr.: Haus) residence

an·sonst *Konj.* (österr., schweiz.) otherwise

ansonsten *Adv.* (ugs.) [1] (außerdem) **der Verlag produziert ... und ~ noch Kinderbücher** the publishing house produces ... and, in addition, children's books; **aber ~ ist nichts Besonderes passiert** but apart from that *or* otherwise nothing particular has happened [2] (andernfalls) otherwise

an|spannen

A *tr. V.* [1] (einspannen) harness, hitch up ‹*horse etc.*› (**an** + *Akk.* to); hitch up, yoke up ‹*oxen*› (**an** + *Akk.* to); hitch up ‹*carriage, cart, etc.*› (**an** + *Akk.* to) [2] (anstrengen) strain; **seine ganze Kraft ~:** exert all one's energies

B *itr. V.* hitch up; **~ lassen** have the carriage made ready

An·spannung *die* strain; **unter ~ aller seiner Kräfte/Gedanken** by exerting all one's energies/by intense mental effort

an|spazieren *itr. V.; mit sein* (ugs.) **anspaziert kommen** come strolling along; (auf einen zu) come strolling up

An·spiel *das* [1] (Sport: Zuspiel) pass [2] (Spielbeginn) (Schach) **das ~ haben** make the first move; (Kartenspiel) **ich habe das ~:** it's my lead; (Fußball) ▸**Anstoß 3**

an|spielen

A *itr. V.* [1] (hinweisen) **auf jmdn./etw. ~:** allude to sb./sth.; **worauf wollen Sie ~?** what are you hinting at? [2] (Spiel beginnen) start; (Fußball) kick off; (Kartenspiel) lead; (Schach) make the first move

B *tr. V.* [1] (Sport: zuspielen) **jmdn. ~:** pass to sb. [2] (Kartenspiel: ins Spiel bringen) lead

Anspielung *die;* **~, ~en** allusion (**auf** + *Akk.* to); (verächtlich, böse) insinuation (**auf** + *Akk.* about)

an|spinnen

A *unr. tr. V.* (beginnen) [gradually] start ‹*conversation*›; start having ‹*affair*›; start hatching ‹*intrigue, plot*›

B *unr. refl. V.* develop; **zwischen den beiden spinnt sich etwas an** there's something going on between those two

an|spitzen *tr. V.* [1] (spitz machen) sharpen ‹*pencil*›; shape ‹*stake, post*› to a point [2] (ugs.: antreiben) **jmdn. ~:** give sb. a prod; **jmdn. ~, etw. zu tun** *od.* **dass er etw. tut** prod sb. into doing sth.

An·sporn *der* incentive

an|spornen *tr. V.* [1] (anfeuern) spur on; encourage [2] (die Sporen geben) spur ‹*horse*›

An·sprache *die* [1] (Rede) speech; address; **eine ~ halten** make a speech; give an address [2] (Kontakt) **~ suchen/haben** look for/have sb. to talk to

ansprechbar *Adj.* ① **ich bin jetzt beschäftigt und daher nicht ~:** you can't talk to me now, I'm too busy; **sie ist vor Müdigkeit nicht ~:** she's too tired to listen to anyone ② (zugänglich) amenable ③ (fähig zu reagieren) responsive

an|sprechen
A *unr. tr. V.* ① speak to; (zudringlich) accost; **jmdn. mit „Herr Doktor" ~:** address sb. as 'doctor'; **jmdn. mit seinem Vornamen ~:** use sb.'s first name; **jmdn. auf etw./jmdn./um etw. ~:** speak to sb. about sth./sb./approach *or* ask sb. for sth. ② (gefallen) appeal to ③ (zur Sprache bringen) mention; (kurz, oberflächlich) touch on ④ (Jagdw., Milit.) identify
B *unr. itr. V.* ① (gefallen) **[gut] ~:** go down well (**bei** with); be well received (**bei** by) ② (reagieren) ‹*patient, brake, clutch, etc.*› respond (**auf** + *Akk.* to) ③ (wirken) work; **bei jmdn. gut/nicht ~:** have/not have the desired effect on sb. ④ (Musik) **gut** *od.* **leicht ~** ‹*instrument*› be easy to play

ansprechend
A *Adj.* attractive; attractive, appealing ‹*personality*›
B *adv.* attractively

Ansprech·partner *der,* **Ansprech·partnerin** *die* contact

an|springen
A *unr. itr. V.; mit sein* ① (in Gang kommen) start ② (sich nähern) **angesprungen kommen** come bounding along; (auf einen zu) come bounding up ③ (ugs.) **auf ein Angebot/Geschäft ~:** take up an offer/agree to a deal; **sofort auf etw.** (*Akk.*) **~:** jump at sth. [straight away]
B *unr. tr. V.* ① (anfallen) pounce on ② (an jmdn. hochspringen) jump up at ③ (Turnen) mount ‹*box, horse, beam*› with a jump

an|spritzen
A *tr. V.* splash; (mit Gartenschlauch, Zerstäuber, Wasserpistole) spray
B *itr. V.; mit sein* (ugs.: sich nähern) **angespritzt kommen** come rushing along; (auf einen zu) come rushing up

An·spruch *der* ① claim; (Forderung) demand; **hohe Ansprüche [an jmdn.] haben** *od.* **stellen** demand a great deal [of sb.]; **~ auf etw.** (*Akk.*) **erheben** lay claim to sth.; **[keine] Ansprüche stellen** make [no] demands; **in ~ nehmen** (Gebrauch machen von) take up, take advantage of ‹*offer*›; exercise ‹*right*›; (beanspruchen) take up ‹*time*›; **jmds. Zeit/Hilfe in ~ nehmen** make demands on sb.'s time/enlist sb.'s aid; **jmdn. [stark] in ~ nehmen** make [heavy] demands on sb.; **jmdn. völlig in ~ nehmen** take up all [of] sb.'s time ② (bes. Rechtsspr.: Anrecht) claim; **[einen] ~/keinen ~ auf etw.** (*Akk.*) **haben** be/not be entitled to sth.; **auf etw.** (*Akk.*) **~ erheben** assert one's entitlement to sth.

an·spruchs-, An·spruchs-: ~denken *das* (abwertend): *attitude that everything one wants should be provided by the State;* **~los A** *Adj.* ① (genügsam) undemanding; ② (schlicht) unpretentious; simple; **B** *adv.* ① (genügsam) undemandingly; ‹*live*› modestly, simply; ② (schlicht) unpretentiously; simply; **~losigkeit** *die;* **~** ▸ **~los A:** undemanding nature; unpretentiousness; simplicity; **~voll A** *Adj.* ① (wählerisch); demanding, discriminating ‹*reader, audience, gourmet*›; (hohe Anforderungen stellend) demanding; ambitious ‹*subject*›; ② (Werbespr.) exquisite; **eine ~volle Zigarette/ein ~voller Sekt** a cigarette for the discriminating smoker/champagne for the discriminating drinker; **die Cremeseife für Anspruchsvolle** the cream soap for people with discriminating taste; **B** *adv.* (Werbespr.) exquisitely

an|spucken *tr. V.* spit at

an|spülen *tr. V.* wash up *or* ashore

an|stacheln *tr. V.* spur on (**zu** to); **jmds. Ehrgeiz/Eifer ~:** fire sb.'s ambition/enthusiasm

Anstalt /ˈanʃtalt/ *die;* **~, ~en** (auch verhüll.) institution; **eine ~ des öffentlichen Rechts** a public institution

Anstalten *Pl.* preparations; **[keine] ~ machen** *od.* (geh.) **treffen** make [no] preparations (**für** for); **~ machen/keine ~ machen, etw. zu tun** make a move/make no move to do sth.

Anstalts-: ~geistliche *der/die* [resident] chaplain; **~kleidung** *die* institutional clothing; **~leiter** *der,* **~leiterin** *die* (einer Schule) head; (eines Erziehungsheims) superintendent

An·stand[1] *der* (Jägerspr.) ▸ **Ansitz 1**

An·stand[2] *der* ① (Schicklichkeit) decency; **keinen ~ haben** have no sense of decency; **gegen jeden/den ~ verstoßen** offend against common decency; **sich mit ~ aus der Affäre ziehen** emerge from the affair with no damage to one's reputation ② (veralt.: Benehmen) good manners *pl.;* **dir werde ich ~ beibringen** I'll give you a lesson in manners ③ (südd., österr.: Ärger) trouble; **[keinen] ~ an etw.** (*Dat.*) **nehmen** [not] object to sth.; **keinen ~ nehmen[, etw. zu tun]** (nicht zögern) not hesitate [to do sth.]

an·ständig
A *Adj.* ① (sittlich einwandfrei, rücksichtsvoll) decent; decent, clean ‹*joke*›; (ehrbar) respectable; (gut angesehen) decent, respectable ‹*job*›; **bleib ~!** (auch scherzh.) behave yourself!; be good! ② (ugs.: zufrieden stellend) decent; respectable ‹*result, marks*› ③ (ugs.: beträchtlich) sizeable ‹*sum, amount, debts*›; **eine ~e Tracht Prügel** a good hiding (coll.); **ein ~es Stück gefahren sein** have come a tidy old (coll.) *or* pretty long way (coll.)
B *adv.* ① (sittlich einwandfrei) decently; (ordentlich) properly ② (ugs.: zufrieden stellend) **jmdn. ~ bezahlen** pay sb. pretty well; **ganz ~ abschneiden** do quite well; **~ arbeiten** do good work ③ (ugs.: ziemlich) **~ ausschlafen** have a decent sleep; **es regnet ganz ~:** it's raining pretty hard; **jmdn. ~ eine knallen** really belt sb. one (coll.)

anständigerweise *Adv.* out of decency

Anständigkeit *die;* **~:** decency

anstands-, Anstands-: ~besuch *der* formal courtesy call (**bei** on); formal courtesy visit (**bei** to); **~dame** *die* (veralt.) chaperone; **~halber** *Adv.* out of politeness; for the sake of politeness; **~happen** *der* (ugs.) **einen ~happen übrig lassen** leave the last piece out of politeness; **~los** *Adv.* (ohne Bedenken) readily; without [any] hesitation; (ohne Schwierigkeiten zu machen) without [any] objection; **~unterricht** *der* lessons *pl.* in deportment *or* manners; **~wau·wau** *der* (ugs. scherzh.) chaperone

an|stänkern *tr. V.* (salopp) **jmdn. ~:** lay into sb. (coll.)

an|starren *tr. V.* stare at

an·statt
A *Konj.* **~ zu arbeiten/~ dass er arbeitet** instead of working
B *Präp. mit Gen.* instead of

an|stauben *itr. V.; mit sein* get dusty; **leicht angestaubte Ware** slightly shopworn *or* (Brit.) shop-soiled goods *pl.*

an|stauen
A *tr. V.* dam up; (fig.) bottle up ‹*feelings*›
B *refl. V.* ‹*water*› accumulate; (fig.) ‹*feelings*› build up

an|staunen *tr. V.* **jmdn./etw. ~:** gaze *or* stare in wonder at sb./sth.; **jmdn./etw. mit offenem Mund ~:** gape at sb./sth. in wonder

an|stechen
A *unr. tr. V.* ① prick; puncture ‹*tyre*›; **wie ein angestochenes Schwein, wie angestochen** (derb) like a wild thing ② (anzapfen) tap ‹*barrel*›
B *unr. itr. V.* (anzapfen) tap a/the barrel

an|stecken
A *tr. V.* ① (feststecken) pin on ‹*badge, brooch*›; (am Finger) put *or* slip ‹*ring*›; **jmdm. eine Brosche/einen Ring ~:** pin a brooch on sb./put *or* slip a ring on sb.'s finger ② (infizieren, auch fig.) infect; **ich will dich nicht ~:** I don't want to give you my cold/germs *etc.* ③ (bes. nordd., mitteld.: anzünden) light; (in Brand setzen) set fire to
B *itr. V.* (sich übertragen) be infectious *or* catching; (durch Berührung) be contagious; (fig.) be infectious *or* contagious

ansteckend *Adj.* infectious; (durch Berührung) contagious; (fig.) infectious; contagious

Ansteck·nadel *die* (Brosche) pin; (Plakette) badge

Ansteckung *die;* **~, ~en** infection; (durch Berührung) contagion

Ansteckungs-: ~gefahr *die* risk or danger of infection; **~herd** *der* source of [the/an] infection

an|stehen *unr. itr. V.* ① (warten) queue [up], (Amer.) stand in line (**nach** for) ② *südd. mit sein* (geh.: sich ziemen) **jmdm. [wohl/übel] ~:** [well/ill] become sb. ③ (zu erledigen sein) be waiting to be dealt with; (zur Beratung ~) be on the agenda; **die ~den Probleme** the problems to be dealt with; **etw. ~ lassen** defer sth. ④ (Rechtsspr.: festgesetzt sein) be fixed *or* set (**auf** + *Akk.* for) ⑤ *in* **nicht ~, etw. zu tun** (geh.) have no hesitation in doing sth.; not hesitate to do sth. ⑥ (Geol.) outcrop; crop out

an|steigen *unr. itr. V.; mit sein* ① (bergan führen) ‹*hill*› rise; ‹*person, road, path*› climb, ascend; ‹*garden, ground*› slope up, rise ② (höher werden) ‹*water level, temperature, etc.*› rise; (fig.) ‹*price, cost, rent, etc.*› rise, go up, increase

an·stelle
A *Präp. mit Gen.* instead of
B *Adv.* **~ von** instead of; *s. auch* **Stelle 1**

an|stellen
A *refl. V.* ① (warten) queue [up], (Amer.) stand in line (**nach** for) ② (ugs.: sich verhalten) act; behave; **sich dumm/ungeschickt ~:** act *or* behave stupidly/be clumsy; **sich dumm/ungeschickt bei etw. ~:** go about sth. stupidly/clumsily; **sich geschickt ~:** go about it well; **stell dich nicht [so] an!** don't make [such] a fuss!
B *tr. V.* ① (aufdrehen) turn on ② (einschalten) switch on; turn on, switch on ‹*radio, television*›; start ‹*engine*› ③ (einstellen) employ (**als** as); **bei jmdm. angestellt sein** be employed by sb. ④ (ugs.: beschäftigen) **jmdn. zum Kartoffelschälen** *usw.* **~:** get sb. to peel the potatoes *etc.* ⑤ (anlehnen) **etw. an etw.** (*Akk.*) **~:** put *or* place sth. against sth. ⑥ (anrichten) **etwas/Unfug ~:** get up to something/to mischief; **was hast du nun wieder angestellt?** what have you been up to this time?; **sieh, was du angestellt hast** see what you've done ⑦ (ugs.: fertig bringen) manage; **wie soll ich es ~, dass er nichts merkt/dass ich rechtzeitig hinkomme?** how do I stop him noticing anything?/make sure of getting there in time? ⑧ (ugs.: versuchen) try ⑨ (vornehmen) do ‹*calculation*›; draw, make ‹*comparison*›; carry out ‹*experiment, investigation*›; make ‹*assumption*›; **Überlegungen ~, wie …** consider how …

anstellig *Adj.* clever; skilful

Anstelligkeit *die;* **~:** ability; skill

An·stellung *die* ① (das Einstellen) employment ② (Stellung) job; **ohne ~:** without a job; unemployed

Anstellungs-: ~verhältnis *das* employment *no indef. art.;* **~verhältnis auf Zeit** temporary employment; **~vertrag** *der* contract of employment

an|steuern *tr. V.* (auch fig.) head *or* make for; **ein Thema ~** (fig.) steer the conversation towards a subject

An·stich *der* ① (das Anstechen) tapping; broaching; **nach dem ~:** after tapping *or* broaching the barrel ② (Getränk) **[frischer] ~:** newly tapped beer/wine

an|stiefeln *itr. V.; mit sein* **angestiefelt kommen** come marching along; (auf einen zu) come marching up

Anstieg *der;* **~[e]s, ~e** ① (Zunahme, Erhöhung) rise, increase (+ *Gen.* in) ② (Steigung) gradient ③ (Aufstieg) climb; ascent; (Weg) way up; (für Bergsteiger) ascent route

an|stieren *tr. V.* (ugs.) stare at

an|stiften *tr. V.* ① (in Gang setzen) instigate; (verursachen) cause, bring about ‹*disaster, confusion*› ② (verleiten) **jmdn. [dazu] ~, etw. zu tun** incite sb. to do sth.; **jmdn. zum Betrug/Mord/zu einem Verbrechen ~:** incite sb. to deception/to murder/to commit a crime; **jmdn. zu dummen Streichen ~:** put sb. up to silly tricks

An·stifter *der,* **An·stifterin** *die* instigator

An·stiftung *die* incitement (**zu** to); **~ zu einer Straftat** incitement to commit a serious offence

an|stimmen *tr. V.* **1** (Musik) start singing ‹*song*›; start playing ‹*waltz, march, etc.*›; play ‹*note*›; ‹*band*› strike up ‹*waltz, march, etc.*› **2** (ausbrechen in) **Proteste/ein Geschrei ~:** start protesting/shouting; **ein Freudengeheul ~:** burst into shouts of joy

an|stinken (ugs.)
A *unr. tr. V.* (anwidern) **jmdn. ~:** make sb. sick
B *unr. itr. V.: in* **gegen jmdn./etw. nicht ~ können** be powerless against sb./sth.

an|stolzieren *itr. V.; mit sein* **anstolziert kommen** come strutting along; (auf einen zu) come strutting up

An·stoß *der* **1** (Impuls) stimulus (**zu** for); **den [ersten] ~ zu etw. geben** initiate sth.; **der ~ ging von ihr aus** she was the one who initiated things *or* [first] got things going; **es bedurfte eines neuen ~es** a fresh impetus was needed **2** **~ erregen** cause *or* give offence (**bei** to); **[keinen] ~ an etw.** (*Dat.*) **nehmen** [not] object to sth.; (sich [nicht] beleidigt fühlen) [not] take offence at sth.; *s. auch* **Stein 2** **3** (Fußball) kick-off; **den ~ ausführen** kick off; **welche Mannschaft hat ~?** which side will kick off? **4** (Aufprall) impact

an|stoßen
A *unr. itr. V.* **1** *mit sein* **an etw.** (*Akk.*) **~:** bump into sth.; **mit dem Kopf ~:** knock *or* bump one's head; **mit dem Koffer dauernd/überall ~:** keep bumping the case against things **2** (auf etw. trinken) **[mit den Gläsern] ~:** clink glasses; **auf jmdn./etw. ~:** drink to sb./sth. **3** (Fußball) kick off **4** *auch mit sein* (lispeln) **[mit der Zunge] ~:** lisp **5** *mit sein* (Anstoß erregen) give *or* cause offence (**bei** to); **man stößt leicht bei ihm an** he easily takes offence **6** (angrenzen) **an etw.** (*Akk.*) **~:** adjoin sth.
B *unr. tr. V.* **1** (einen Stoß geben) **jmdn./etw. ~:** give sb./sth. a push; **jmdn. aus Versehen ~:** knock into sb. inadvertently; **jmdn. mit dem Ellenbogen/Fuß ~** (als Zeichen) nudge/kick sb.; **sich** (*Dat.*) **den Kopf/die Zehe ~:** knock *or* bang one's head/stub one's toe **2** **eine Diskussion ~:** provoke a discussion

anstößig /ˈanʃtøːsɪç/
A *Adj.* offensive; offensive, objectionable ‹*behaviour*›
B *adv.* offensively; ‹*behave*› offensively, objectionably

Anstößigkeit *die;* **~, ~en** **1** offensiveness; (einer Handlung) offensiveness, objectionableness **2** (Handlung) piece of offensive *or* objectionable behaviour; **~en** offensive *or* objectionable behaviour *sing.*

an|strahlen *tr. V.* **1** illuminate; (mit Scheinwerfer) floodlight; (im Theater) spotlight; **ein Gebäude rot ~:** illuminate a building with red light **2** (anblicken) beam at; **ihre Augen strahlten ihn an** she beamed at him

an|streben *tr. V.* (geh.) aspire to; (mit großer Anstrengung) strive for

anstrebens·wert *Adj.* ▸**anstreben**: worth aspiring to/striving for *postpos.*

an|streichen *unr. tr. V.* **1** (mit Farbe) paint; (mit Tünche) whitewash **2** (hervorheben) mark (**als** as); **etw. rot ~:** mark sth. in red **3** (anzünden) strike, light ‹*match*›

An·streicher *der,* **An·streicherin** *die* (ugs.) [house] painter

an|strengen
A *refl. V.* (sich einsetzen) make an effort; exert oneself; (körperlich) exert oneself; **sich ~, etw. zu tun** make an effort to do sth.; **sich mehr/sehr ~:** make more of an effort/a great effort; **sich übermäßig** *od.* **zu sehr ~:** overexert oneself; **da hat er sich aber angestrengt** he has made a special effort *or* gone to a lot of trouble [there]
B *tr. V.* **1** (anspannen) strain ‹*eyes, ears, voice*›; **alle seine Kräfte ~:** make every effort; (körperlich) use all one's strength; **seinen Verstand ~:** think hard; **seine Fantasie ~:** exercise one's imagination **2** (strapazieren) strain, put a strain on ‹*eyes*›; be a strain on ‹*person*›; **jmdn. zu sehr ~:** be too much of a strain on sb. **3** (Rechtsw.: einleiten) **eine Klage/einen Prozess ~:** lay a charge/start proceedings (**gegen** against)

anstrengend *Adj.* (körperlich) strenuous; (geistig) demanding; **~ zu lesen/für die Augen sein** be a strain to read/on the eyes; **Nachtfahrten finde ich ~:** I find travelling at night a strain; **es war ~, dem Vortrag zu folgen** following the lecture was a strain

Anstrengung *die;* **~, ~en** **1** (Einsatz) effort; **~en machen** *od.* (geh.) **unternehmen** make an effort; **große ~en machen, etw. zu tun** make every effort to do sth.; **mit letzter/äußerster ~:** with one last/a supreme effort **2** (Strapaze) strain

An·strich *der* **1** (das Anstreichen) painting; (mit Tünche) whitewashing **2** (Farbe) paint; (Tünche) whitewash; **der erste/zweite ~:** the first/second coat **3** (Note) touch; (Aussehen) air; **einer Sache** (*Dat.*) **einen bestimmten ~ geben** lend sth. a certain air **4** (beim Schreiben) upstroke

an|stricken *tr. V.* **etw. an etw.** (*Akk.*) **~:** knit sth. on to sth.

an|strömen *itr. V.; mit sein* **1** (heranfließen) ‹*water*› flow in; ‹*air*› stream in; **von Westen ~de Kaltluft** a stream of cold air from the west **2** (herbeikommen) pour *or* stream in; **angeströmt kommen** come pouring *or* streaming in

an|stückeln, an|stücken *tr. V.* add a piece to ‹*carpet etc.*›; **ein Kleid/Hemd ~:** lengthen a dress/shirt [by adding a piece on]; **etw. an etw.** (*Akk.*) **~:** attach sth. to sth.

An·sturm *der* **1** (das Anstürmen) onslaught **2** (Andrang) (auf Kaufhäuser, Schwimmbäder) rush (**auf** + *Akk.* to); (auf Banken, Waren) run (**auf** + *Akk.* on)

an|stürmen *itr. V.; mit sein* **1** (gegen etw. drängen) **gegen etw. ~** ‹*waves, wind*› pound sth.; (Milit.) storm sth. **2** **angestürmt kommen** come charging *or* rushing along; (auf einen zu) come charging *or* rushing up

an|stürzen *itr. V.; mit sein* **angestürzt kommen** come tearing *or* dashing along; (auf einen zu) come tearing *or* dashing up

an|suchen *itr. V.* (österr., sonst veralt.) **[bei jmdm.] um etw. ~** (beantragen) apply [to sb.] for sth.; (bitten) ask [sb.] for sth.

Ansuchen *das;* **~s, ~** (österr., sonst veralt.) (Gesuch) application (**auf** + *Akk.* for); (Bitte) request (**auf** + *Akk.* for); **auf jmds. ~** (*Akk.*) at sb.'s request

an|sülzen *tr. V.* (salopp) blether at

Antagonismus /antagoˈnɪsmʊs/ *der;* **~, Antagonismen** antagonism (*Gen.,* **zwischen** between)

Antagonist *der;* **~en, ~en, Antagonistin** *die;* **~, ~nen** antagonist

antagonistisch
A *Adj.* antagonistic
B *adv.* antagonistically

an|tanzen *itr. V.; mit sein* (ugs.) show up (coll.); **angetanzt kommen** turn up

Antarktis /antˈlarktɪs/ *die;* **~** (Geogr.) **die ~:** the Antarctic

antarktisch *Adj.* Antarctic

an|tasten *tr. V.* **1** (verbrauchen) break into ‹*savings, provisions*›; **das Geld taste ich nicht an** I shall not touch the money **2** (beeinträchtigen) infringe, encroach on ‹*right, freedom, privilege*›; encroach on ‹*property, private life*›; **jmds. Ehre ~:** cast a slur on *or* impugn sb.'s honour **3** (berühren) touch; (fig.) touch on ‹*subject*›

an|tauchen *itr. V.* (österr.) **1** (anschieben) push **2** (sich mehr anstrengen) make more effort; try harder

an|tauen
A *itr. V.; mit sein* (zu tauen beginnen) ‹*ice, snow*› begin to melt *or* thaw; ‹*foodstuff*› begin to thaw
B *tr. V.* (tauen lassen) **etw. ~:** allow sth. to thaw slightly

an|täuschen
A *tr. V.* (Boxen) **einen linken Haken ~ und mit der Rechten zuschlagen** feint with the left and throw a right
B *itr. V.* (Fußball, Rugby) **[links/rechts] ~:** dummy (Brit.) *or* (Amer.) fake [to the left/right]

An·teil *der* **1** (jmdm. zustehender Teil) share (**an** + *Dat.* of); **~ an etw.** (*Dat.*) **haben** share in sth.; (zu etw. beitragen) play *or* have a part in sth. **2** (Wirtsch.) share **3** (Interesse) interest (**an** + *Dat.* in); **~ an jmdm./etw. nehmen** *od.* (geh.) **bekunden** take/show an interest in sb./sth.; **an jmds. Leid/Freude ~ nehmen** sympathize with sb. in his/her suffering/share in sb.'s joy; **viele Menschen nahmen ~ am Tod seiner Frau** many people felt for him when his wife died

anteilig, anteil·mäßig
A *Adj.* proportional; proportionate
B *adv.* proportionally; proportionately

Anteilnahme *die;* **~** **1** (Beteiligung) participation; **unter reger ~ der Bevölkerung** with the active participation of the public **2** (Interesse) interest (**an** + *Dat.* in) **3** (Mitgefühl) sympathy (**an** + *Dat.* with); **mit ~ zuhören** listen sympathetically

Anteil·schein *der* (Wirtsch.) share certificate

Anteils·eigner *der,* **Anteils·eignerin** *die* (Wirtsch.) shareholder

an|telefonieren *tr. V.* (ugs.) phone; call; ring (Brit.)

Antenne *die;* **~, ~n** **1** aerial; antenna (Amer.); **eine/keine ~ für etw. haben** (fig. ugs.) have a/no feeling for sth. **2** (Zool.) antenna

Anthologie /antoloˈgiː/ *die;* **~, ~n** anthology

Anthrax /ˈantraks/ *der;* **~** (Med.) anthrax

anthrazit /antraˈtsiːt/ *Adj.* anthracite[-grey]

Anthrazit *der;* **~s, ~e** anthracite

anthrazit-: ~farben, ~farbig *Adj.* anthracite[-coloured]; **~grau** *Adj.* anthracite-grey

Anthropologe /antropoˈloːgə/ *der;* **~n, ~n** ▸**❶ S. 113** anthropologist

Anthropologie *die;* **~, ~n** anthropology *no art.*

Anthropologin *die;* **~, ~nen** ▸**❶ S. 113** anthropologist; *s. auch* **-in**

anthropologisch
A *Adj.* anthropological
B *adv.* anthropologically

anthropomorph /antropoˈmɔrf/ *Adj.* anthropomorphic

Anthropomorphismus *der;* **~, Anthropomorphismen** **1** (Übertragung) anthropomorphism **2** (Eigenschaft) anthropomorphic feature

Anthroposoph /antropoˈzoːf/ *der;* **~en, ~en** anthroposophist

Anthroposophie *die;* **~:** anthroposophy *no art.*

Anthroposophin *die;* **~, ~nen** anthroposophist; *s. auch* **-in**

anthroposophisch *Adj.* anthroposophical

anthropozentrisch /antropoˈtsɛntrɪʃ/
A *Adj.* anthropocentric
B *adv.* anthropocentrically

anti-, Anti- /anti-:/ anti-

anti-, Anti-: ~alkoholiker *der,* **~alkoholikerin** *die* teetotaller; **~autoritär** **A** *Adj.* anti-authoritarian; **B** *adv.* in an anti-authoritarian manner; **~autoritär eingestellt sein** take an anti-authoritarian view; **~baby·pille** *die* (ugs.) contraceptive pill; **~bakteriell** **A** *Adj.* antibacterial; **B** *adv.* **~bakteriell wirken** have an antibacterial action

Antibiotikum /antiˈbi̯oːtikʊm/ *das;* **~s, Antibiotika** (Med.) antibiotic

anti-, Anti-: ~blockier·system *das* (Kfz-W.) anti-lock braking system; **~christ**[1] /ˈ---/ *der;* **~[s]** Antichrist; **~christ**[2] /ˈ---/ *der;* **~en, ~en, ~christin** *die* anti-christian; **~christlich** /ˈ----/ **A** *Adj.* anti-christian; **B** *adv.* **~christlich eingestellt/gesinnt sein** be anti-christian [in one's views]; **~demokratisch** **A** *Adj.* anti-democratic; **B** *adv.* **~demokratisch eingestellt/gesinnt sein** be anti-democratic [in one's views]; **~faschismus** *der* anti-fascism *no art.;* **~faschist** *der,* **~faschistin** *die* anti-fascist;

~faschistisch A *Adj.* anti-fascist; B *adv.* **~faschistisch eingestellt/gesinnt sein** be anti-fascist [in one's views]; **~gen** *das* (Med., Biol.) antigen; **~haft·beschichtung** *die* non-stick coating; **~held** /'---/ *der* anti-hero; **~heldin** /'----/ *die* anti-heroine

antichambrieren /antiʃam'bri:rən/ *itr. V.* 1 (veralt.: warten) wait in the antechamber 2 (geh. abwertend: dienern) bow and scrape (**bei** to)

antik /an'ti:k/

A *Adj.* 1 (des klassischen Altertums) classical 2 (altertümelnd) antique-style ‹*furniture, fittings, etc.*› 3 (aus vergangenen Zeiten) antique

B *adv.* (altertümelnd) ‹*make, furnish, etc.*› in antique style

Antike /an'ti:kə/ *die;* ~, ~n 1 (Epoche) classical antiquity *no art.* 2 (Kunstwerk) classical work of art

antikisieren *itr. V.* imitate classical forms

anti-, Anti-: ~klerikal A *Adj.* anticlerical; B *adv.* **~klerikal gesinnt/eingestellt sein** be anticlerical [in one's view]; **~klerikal denken/handeln** think/act anticlerically; **~klerikalismus** *der* anticlericalism; **~klopf·mittel** *das* (Kfz-W.) antiknock [agent]; **~kommunismus** *der* anti-communism; **~kommunist** *der,* **~kommunistin** *die* anti-communist; **~kommunistisch** A *Adj.* anti-communist; B *adv.* **~kommunistisch eingestellt/gesinnt sein** be anti-communist [in one's views]; **~körper** /'----/ *der* (Med.) antibody

Antillen /an'tɪlən/ *Pl.;* **die [Großen/Kleinen] ~:** the [Greater/Lesser] Antilles

Antilope /anti'lo:pə/ *die;* ~, ~n antelope

anti-, Anti-: ~militarismus *der* antimilitarism; **~militarist** *der,* **~militaristin** *die* antimilitarist; **~militaristisch** A *Adj.* antimilitaristic; B *adv.* ‹*argue*› along antimilitaristic lines; **~militaristisch gesinnt/eingestellt sein** be antimilitaristic [in one's views]

Antimon /anti'mo:n/ *das;* ~s (Chem.) antimony

Antinomie /antino'mi:/ *die;* ~, ~n (Philos., Rechtsspr.) antinomy

Antipathie /antipa'ti:/ *die;* ~, ~n antipathy; **eine ~ gegen jmdn./etw. haben** have an antipathy to sb./sth.

Antipode /anti'po:də/ *der;* ~n, ~n, **Antipodin** *die;* ~, ~nen 1 (Geogr.) antipodean 2 (geh.) antipode; exact opposite

an|tippen *tr. V.* (berühren) give ‹*person, thing*› a [light] tap; touch ‹*accelerator, brake, etc.*›; (fig.) touch on ‹*point, question*›

Antiqua /an'ti:kva/ *die;* ~ (Druckw.) roman [type]

Antiquar /anti'kva:ɐ̯/ *der;* ~s, ~e ▸❶ S. 113 antiquarian bookseller; (mit neueren gebrauchten Büchern) second-hand bookseller

Antiquariat /antikva'ri̯a:t/ 1 (Handel) antiquarian book trade; (mit neueren gebrauchten Büchern) second-hand book trade 2 (Laden/Abteilung) antiquarian bookshop/department; (mit neueren gebrauchten Büchern) second-hand bookshop/department; **modernes ~:** *shop/department selling remainders, defective copies, cheap editions, reprints, etc.*

Antiquarin *die;* ~, ~nen ▸**Antiquar**

antiquarisch

A *Adj.* antique; (Buchw.) antiquarian; (von neueren gebrauchten Büchern) second-hand

B *adv.* **ein Buch ~ kaufen** buy a book second-hand

Anti-quark *das* (Physik) antiquark

antiquiert /anti'kvi:ɐ̯t/ (abwertend)

A *Adj.* antiquated

B *adv.* in an antiquated way

Antiquität *die;* ~, ~en antique

Antiquitäten-: ~händler *der,* **~händlerin** *die* ▸❶ S. 113 antique dealer; **~laden** *der; Pl.* **~läden** antique shop; **~sammler** *der,* **~sammlerin** *die* collector of antiques; **~sammlung** *die* collection of antiques

anti-, Anti-: ~rakete /'-----/, **~raketen·rakete** *die* anti-missile missile; **~semit** *der,* **~semitin** *die* anti-Semite; **~semitisch** A *Adj.* anti-Semitic; anti-Semite; B *adv.* anti-Semitically; **~semitisch eingestellt/gesinnt sein** be anti-Semitic [in one's views]; **~semitismus** *der;* ~~, **~semitismen** anti-Semitism; **~septisch** *Adj.* (Med.) antiseptic; **~statisch** A *Adj.* (Physik) antistatic; B *adv.* **~statisch wirken** have an antistatic action; **~teilchen** /'----/ *das* (Kernphysik) antiparticle; **~these** /'----/ *die* antithesis

antithetisch

A *Adj.* antithetical

B *adv.* antithetically

Antiviren-: ~programm *das* (DV) antivirus program; **~software** *die* (DV) antivirus software

Antizipation /antitsipa'tsi̯o:n/ *die;* ~, ~en (geh.) anticipation

antizipieren *tr. V.* (geh.) anticipate

anti-zyklisch

A *Adj.* 1 (in unregelmäßiger Folge) irregular 2 (Wirtsch.) counter-cyclical

B *adv.* 1 (unregelmäßig) irregularly; at irregular intervals 2 (Wirtsch.) in a counter-cyclical way

Antlitz /'antlɪts/ *das;* ~es, ~e (dichter., geh.) countenance (literary); face

Antonym /anto'ny:m/ *das;* ~s, ~e (Sprachw.) antonym

an|törnen /'antœrnən/ ▸**anturnen¹**

an|traben *itr. V.* 1 *mit sein* (sich nähern) come trotting along; **angetrabt kommen** come trotting along; (auf einen zu) come trotting up; **jmdn. ~ lassen** (ugs.: kommen lassen) get sb. to come along promptly 2 start trotting; break into a trot; (aus dem Stillstand) set off at a trot

Antrag /'antra:k/ *der;* ~[e]s, **Anträge** 1 (Gesuch) application, request (**auf** + *Akk.* for); (Rechtsw.: schriftlich) petition; **einen ~ auf etw.** (*Akk.*) **stellen** make an application for sth.; apply for sth.; (Rechtsw.: schriftlich) enter a petition for sth.; **einem ~ stattgeben** grant an application/a petition; **auf jmds. ~:** at sb.'s request; (Rechtsw.: schriftlich) in response to sb.'s petition 2 (Formular) application form 3 (Heirats~) proposal of marriage; **jmdm. einen ~ machen** propose to sb. 4 (Parl.) motion; **einen ~ auf etw.** (*Akk.*) **stellen** *od.* **einbringen** table *or* put forward a motion for sth. 5 **jmdm. unzüchtige Anträge machen** make improper suggestions to sb.

an|tragen *unr. tr. V.* (geh.) offer; **jmdm. ~, etw. zu tun** put it to sb. that he/she should do sth.

Antrags·formular *das* application form

antrags·gemäß *adv.* in accordance with the/your/his *etc.* request

Antrag·steller *der;* ~s, ~, **Antrag·stellerin** *die;* ~, ~nen applicant

an|trainieren *tr. V.* **jmdm./sich Muskeln ~:** develop sb.'s/one's muscles; **Pünktlichkeit lässt sich ~:** you can train yourself to be punctual

an|trauen *tr. V.* (veralt.) **jmdn. jmdm. ~:** marry sb. to sb.; **meine [mir] angetraute Gattin** my wedded wife

an|treffen *unr. tr. V.* find; (zufällig) come across; **er trifft mich nie zu Hause an** he never catches me in

an|treiben

A *unr. tr. V.* 1 (vorwärts treiben) drive ‹*animals, column of prisoners*› on *or* along; (fig.) urge; **jmdn. zur Eile/zu immer besseren Leistungen ~** (fig.) urge sb. to hurry up/urge *or* drive sb. on to better and better performances 2 (in Bewegung setzen) drive; power ‹*ship, aircraft*› 3 (veranlassen) drive; **jmdn. [dazu] ~, etw. zu tun** drive sb. to do sth. 4 (anschwemmen) **etw. ~:** wash sth. up (**an** + *Akk.* on to); **etw. an den Strand ~:** wash sth. ashore *or* up 5 (Gartenbau) force

B *unr. itr. V.; mit sein* (herantreiben) drift *or* float ashore

An·treiber *der,* **An·treiberin** *die* (abwertend) slave driver

an|treten

A *unr. itr. V.; mit sein* 1 (sich aufstellen) form up; (in Linie) line up; (Milit.) fall in; **in Reih und Glied ~:** form up in rank and file; fall in 2 (sich stellen) meet one's opponent; (als Mannschaft) line up; **~ gegen** meet; (als Mannschaft) line up against; **zum Rückspiel ~:** line up for the return match 3 (sich einfinden) report (**bei** to); **zum Dienst/zur Arbeit ~:** report for duty/work

B *unr. tr. V.* 1 start ‹*job, apprenticeship*›; take up ‹*position, appointment*›; start, set out on ‹*journey*›; begin ‹*prison sentence*›; come into ‹*inheritance*›; **jmds. Nachfolge ~:** succeed sb.; **den Urlaub ~:** go on holiday 2 (festtreten) tread down ‹*soil*›

An·trieb *der* 1 (Triebkraft) drive; **ein Fahrzeug mit elektrischem ~:** an electrically powered *or* driven vehicle 2 (Anreiz) impulse; (Psych.) drive; impulse; **jmdm. neuen ~ geben** give sb. fresh impetus; **aus eigenem** *od.* **freiem** *od.* **persönlichem ~:** of one's own accord; on one's own initiative

Antriebs-: ~achse *die* (Technik) driving axle; **~kraft** *die* (Technik) motive *or* driving power; **~rad** *das* (Technik) drive wheel; **~welle** *die* (Technik) drive shaft

an|trinken

A *unr. refl. V.* **sich** (*Dat.*) **einen Rausch/Schwips ~:** get drunk/tipsy; **sich** (*Dat.*) **einen ~** (ugs.) get sloshed (coll.); **sich** (*Dat.*) **Mut ~:** give oneself Dutch courage

B *unr. tr. V.* start drinking ‹*wine, coffee, etc.*›; start drinking from ‹*glass*›; start drinking out of ‹*bottle*›; **eine schon angetrunkene Flasche Wein** a bottle of wine that has/had already been started

An·tritt *der* 1 beginning; **bei ~ seiner Stellung** on taking up his post; **vor ~ Ihres Urlaubs** before you go *or* before going on holiday (Brit.) *or* (Amer.) vacation; **vor ~ der Reise** before setting out on the journey; **bei ~ des Erbes/Amtes** on coming into the inheritance/taking up office 2 (Sport) acceleration *no indef. art.*

Antritts-: ~besuch *der* [formal] first visit; **seinen ~besuch bei jmdm. machen** pay one's [formal] first visit to sb.; **~rede** *die* inaugural speech; **~vor·lesung** *die* inaugural lecture

an|trocknen *itr. V.; mit sein* 1 (festkleben) **an etw.** (*Dat.*) **~:** dry and stick to sth. 2 (ein wenig trocknen) start *or* begin to dry

an|tuckern *itr. V.; mit sein* (ugs.) **angetuckert kommen** come chugging along; (auf einen zu) come chugging up

an|tun *unr. tr. V.* 1 **sich** (*Dat.*) **etw. Gutes ~:** give oneself a treat; treat oneself; **jmdm. ein Leid ~:** hurt sb.; **jmdm. etwas Böses/ein Unrecht ~:** do sb. harm/an injustice; **tu mir das nicht an!** don't do that to me!; **tu dir keinen Zwang an!** (ugs.) don't stand on ceremony!; **sich** (*Dat.*) **etw. ~** (ugs. verhüll.) do away with oneself 2 **das/er** *usw.* **hat es ihr angetan** she was taken with it/him *etc.*; *s. auch* **angetan B** 3 (geh.: anziehen) **[sich** (*Dat.*)**] etw. ~:** put sth. on; don sth.

an|turnen¹ /'antœrnən/ (ugs.)

A *tr. V.* **jmdn. ~** ‹*drugs, music, etc.*› turn sb. on (coll.)

B *itr. V.* turn people on (coll.)

an|turnen² *itr. V.; mit sein* (ugs.) **angeturnt kommen** come romping along; (auf einen zu) come romping up

Antwerpen /ant'vɛrpn̩/ *(das);* ~s ▸❶ S. 675 Antwerp

Antwort /'antvɔrt/ *die;* ~, ~en 1 (Erwiderung) answer; reply; (bei Examen usw.) answer; **er gab mir keine ~:** he didn't answer [me] *or* reply; he made no answer *or* reply; **er gab mir keine ~ auf meine Frage** he did not reply to *or* answer my question; **wer viel fragt, bekommt viel Antwort[en]** (Spr.) you'll have to make up your own mind; **keine ~ ist auch eine ~:** your/her *etc.* silence speaks for itself; **in ~ auf etw.** (*Akk.*) (Amtsspr.) in reply to sth.; **um ~ wird gebeten** (auf Einladungskarten) RSVP 2 (Reaktion) response; **als ~ auf etw.** (*Akk.*) in response to sth.

a

antworten *itr. V.* **1** (erwidern) answer; reply; **auf etw.** (*Akk.*) **~:** answer sth.; reply to sth.; **jmdm. ~:** answer sb.; reply to sb.; **jmdm. auf seine Frage ~:** reply to *or* answer sb.'s question; **wie/was soll ich ihm ~?** what answer shall I give him?/what shall I tell him?; **mit Ja/Nein ~:** answer yes/no **2** (reagieren) respond (**auf** + *Akk.* to)

Antwort-: ~karte *die*, **~postkarte** *die* (Postw.) reply card; **~schein** *der*: **internationaler ~schein** (Postw.) international reply coupon; **~schreiben** *das* reply (**auf** + *Akk.* to)

an|vertrauen
A *tr. V.* **1** (übergeben) **jmdm. etw. ~:** entrust sth. to sb.; entrust sb. with sth.; **sein Kind jmdm. ~:** entrust one's child to sb.'s care **2** (mitteilen) **jmdm./seinem Tagebuch etw. ~:** confide sth. to sb./one's diary
B *refl. V.* **1** (sich mitteilen) **sich jmdm. ~:** confide in sb. **2** (sich schützen lassen) **sich jmdm./einer Sache ~:** put one's trust in sb./sth.

an·verwandt *Adj.* (geh.) related

An·verwandte *der/die* (geh.) relation

an|visieren *tr. V.* **1** (Milit.) align the *or* one's sights on **2** (anstreben) aim at

an|wachsen *unr. itr. V.; mit sein* **1** (festwachsen) grow on; **wieder ~** ‹*finger, toe*› grow back on; **die transplantierte Haut ist angewachsen** the skin graft has/skin grafts have taken; **angewachsene Ohrläppchen** earlobes attached to the sides of one's head **2** (Wurzeln schlagen) take root; **steh nicht da wie angewachsen** (ugs.) don't just stand there like a stuffed dummy **3** (zunehmen) increase; grow

an|wackeln *itr. V.; mit sein* (ugs.) **angewackelt kommen** come waddling along; (auf einen zu) come waddling up

an|wählen *tr. V.* dial; **jmdn. ~:** dial sb.'s number

Anwalt /ˈanvalt/ *der;* **~[e]s, Anwälte** /ˈanvɛltə/, **Anwältin** *die;* **~, ~nen** ▸ⓘ **S. 113** **1** (Rechts~) lawyer; solicitor (Brit.); attorney (Amer.); (vor Gericht) barrister (Brit.); attorney[-at-law] (Amer.); advocate (Scot.); **einen ~ nehmen** get a lawyer *or* (Amer.) an attorney **2** (Fürsprecher) advocate; champion

Anwalts·büro *das* **1** (Räume) lawyer's office; solicitor's office (Brit.) **2** (Sozietät) firm of solicitors (Brit.); law firm (Amer.)

Anwaltschaft *die;* **~, ~en** **1** (Gesamtheit der Anwälte) legal profession **2** (Amt) ▸**Anwalt 1**: profession of lawyer/solicitor/attorney/barrister/advocate **3** (Vertretung) **die ~ in einer Sache übernehmen/ablehnen** take on/refuse to take on a case

Anwalts-: ~kammer *die* (Rechtsw.) *professional association of lawyers;* **~kanzlei** *die* ▸**~büro**

an|wandeln *tr. V.* (geh.) come over

An·wandelung, An·wandlung *die* (Laune) mood; (leichter Anfall) fit; **in einer ~ von Großzügigkeit** *usw.* in a fit of generosity *etc.;* **dann bekommt er wieder seine ~en** then he gets one of his moods again; **eine ~ von Furcht/Schwermütigkeit** a sudden feeling of fear/a fit of melancholy

an|wärmen *tr. V.* warm up; warm ‹*hands, feet*›

An·wärter *der* **1** candidate (**auf** + *Akk.* for); (Sport) contender (**auf** + *Akk.* for) **2** (auf den Thron) claimant; (Thronerbe) heir (**auf** + *Akk.* to)

An·wärterin *die* **1** ▸**Anwärter 1** **2** (auf den Thron) claimant; (Thronerbin) heiress (**auf** + *Akk.* to)

Anwartschaft *die;* **~, ~en** candidacy, candidature (**auf** + *Akk.* for); (Sport) being in contention (**auf** + *Akk.* for); (auf den Thron, einen Titel) claim (**auf** + *Akk.* to)

an|watscheln *itr. V.; mit sein* (ugs.) **angewatschelt kommen** come waddling along; (auf einen zu) come waddling up

an|wehen
A *tr. V.* **1** (geh.: gegen jmdn. wehen) ‹*wind, breeze*› blow [up]on **2** (anhäufen) drift ‹*snow, sand, etc.*›
B *itr. V.; mit sein* (sich anhäufen) drift

an|weisen *unr. tr. V.* **1** (beauftragen) **jmdn. ~:** give sb. instructions; **jmdn. ~, etw. zu tun** instruct *or* direct sb. to do sth. **2** (zuweisen) **jmdm. etw. ~:** allocate sth. to sb. **3** (anleiten) instruct **4** (überweisen) remit; (die Auszahlung veranlassen) order the payment of; *s. auch* **angewiesen B**

An·weisung *die* **1** (Anordnung) instruction; **~ haben, etw. zu tun** have instructions to do sth.; **auf ~ der Behörde** by order of *or* on instructions *pl.* from the authorities **2** (das Zuteilen) allocation **3** (Gebrauchs~) instructions *pl.* **4** (Überweisung) remittance; (Anordnung zur Auszahlung) **die ~ erfolgt demnächst** payment will be ordered shortly **5** (Bankw.: Formular) payment order

anwendbar *Adj.* applicable (**auf** + *Akk.* to); **schwer ~:** difficult to apply; **die Regel ist hier nicht ~:** the rule doesn't apply here

Anwendbarkeit *die;* **~:** applicability (**auf** + *Akk.* to)

an|wenden *unr.* (*auch regelm.*) *tr. V.* use, employ ‹*process, trick, method, violence, force*›; use ‹*medicine, money, time*›; take ‹*care, trouble*› (**auf** + *Akk.* over); apply ‹*rule, paragraph, proverb, etc.*› (**auf** + *Akk.* to); **sich auf etw.** (*Akk.*) **~ lassen** be applicable to sth.; apply to sth.

Anwender *der;* **~s, ~, Anwenderin** *die;* **~, ~nen** (DV) user

An·wendung *die* **1** ▸**anwenden**: use; employment; taking; application; **etw. in ~** (*Akk.*) *od.* **zur ~ bringen** (Amtsspr.) apply sth.; **zur ~ kommen** *od.* **gelangen, ~ finden** (Amtsspr.) ‹*rule, paragraph, etc.*› apply, be applicable **2** (DV, Med.) application

Anwendungs-: ~bereich *der,* **~gebiet** *das* range of application; (eines Gesetzes, einer Regel) scope; **~möglichkeit** *die* possible use *or* application

an|werben *unr. tr. V.* recruit (**für** to); (Milit.) enlist, recruit; **sich ~ lassen** be recruited; (Milit.) enlist (**für** in)

An·werbung *die* ▸**anwerben**: recruitment (**für** to); enrolment (**für** in)

an|werfen *unr. tr. V.* **1** (ugs.: in Gang bringen) start [up] ‹*machine, engine, vehicle*›; swing ‹*propeller*›; put *or* switch on ‹*electrical device*› **2** (an etw. werfen) **Kalk/Mörtel** *usw.* **an eine Wand ~:** roughcast a wall [with lime/plaster *etc.*]

An·wesen *das* property

anwesend *Adj.* present; **die nicht ~en Mitglieder** the members [who are/were] not present; **bei etw. ~ sein** be present at sth.; **ich war nicht ganz ~** (fig. ugs. scherzh.) I wasn't quite with it (coll.)

Anwesende *der/die; adj. Dekl.* **die ~n** those present; **jeder ~/einige ~/alle ~n** everyone/some of those/all those present; **~ natürlich ausgenommen** present company excepted, of course

Anwesenheit *die;* **~:** presence; **in ~:** in the presence (*Gen. od.* **von** of)

Anwesenheits·liste *die* attendance list

an|wetzen *itr. V.; mit sein* (ugs.) **angewetzt kommen** come rushing *or* tearing along; (auf einen zu) come rushing *or* tearing up

an|widern /ˈanviːdɐn/ *tr. V.* nauseate

an|winkeln *tr. V.* bend ‹*knee, arm, etc.*›

an|winseln *tr. V.* whimper at; **jmdn. um Hilfe ~:** come whining to sb. for help

Anwohner /ˈanvoːnɐ/ *der;* **~s, ~, Anwohnerin** *die;* **~, ~nen** resident; **Parken nur für ~:** residents-only parking

Anwohner·parken *das;* **~s** residents' parking; residents-only parking

Anwohnerschaft *die* residents *pl.*

An·wurf *der* **1** (Vorwurf) (esp. unjustified) reproach; (Beschuldigung) (esp. false) accusation **2** (Handball) throw-off; (Korbball) centre pass

an|wurzeln *itr. V.; mit sein* take root; **wie angewurzelt [da] stehen/stehen bleiben** stand rooted to the spot

An·zahl *die* number; **eine ganze ~:** a whole lot

an|zahlen *tr. V.* put down *or* pay a deposit on; (bei Ratenzahlung) make a down payment on; **50 Euro ~:** put down 50 euros as a deposit/make a down payment of 50 euros

an|zählen *tr. V.* (Boxen) **jmdn. ~:** start to give sb. the count

An·zahlung *die* deposit; (bei Ratenzahlung) down payment; **eine ~ auf etw.** (*Akk.*) **machen** *od.* **leisten** put down *or* pay a deposit on sth./make a down payment on sth.

an|zapfen
A *tr. V.* **1** tap ‹*barrel, tree*› **2** (ugs.: zum Abhören) tap ‹*telephone line, wire*› **3** (ugs.) ▸**anpumpen**
B *itr. V.* tap a/the barrel; **frisch ~:** tap a/the new barrel

An·zeichen *das* sign; indication; (Med.) symptom; **alle ~ deuten darauf hin, dass ...** all the signs *or* indications are that ...

an|zeichnen *tr. V.* **1** (an etw. zeichnen) draw (**an** + *Akk.* on) **2** (markieren) mark

Anzeige /ˈantsaigə/ *die;* **~, ~n** **1** (Straf~) report; **gegen jmdn. [eine] ~ [wegen etw.] erstatten** report sb. to the police/the authorities [for sth.]; **jmdn./etw. zur ~ bringen** (Amtsspr.) report sb./sth. to the police/the authorities **2** (Inserat) advertisement; **eine ~ in einer Zeitung aufgeben** place an advertisement in a newspaper **3** (Bekanntmachung) announcement **4** (ablesbarer Stand) display; (eines Messinstruments) reading **5** (Gerät) display unit

an|zeigen *tr. V.* **1** (Strafanzeige erstatten) **jmdn./etw. ~:** report sb./sth. to the police/the authorities; **sich selbst ~:** voluntarily admit an/the offence **2** (zeigen) show; indicate; show ‹*time, date*› **3** (bekannt geben) announce **4** (wissen lassen, geh.: ankündigen) **jmdm. etw. ~:** inform *or* notify sb. of sth.; **jmdm. ~, dass ...** inform *or* notify sb. [of the fact] that ...

Anzeigen-: ~akquise *die* canvassing for advertisers; selling advertising space; **~blatt** *das* advertiser; **~teil** *der* advertisement section *or* pages *pl.;* **~werbung** *die* newspaper and magazine advertising

Anzeige·pflicht *die* **1** statutory obligation to report a/the birth/death/[criminal] offence *etc.* **2** ▸**Meldepflicht 1**

An·zeiger *der* **1** indicator **2** (Zeitung) advertiser

Anzeige·tafel *die* (Sport) scoreboard

an|zetteln *tr. V.* (abwertend) hatch ‹*plot, intrigue*›; instigate ‹*revolt*›; foment ‹*war*›

an|ziehen
A *unr. tr. V.* **1** (an sich ziehen) draw up ‹*knees, feet, etc.*› **2** (anlocken) attract; draw; (durch Schönheit, freundliches Betragen usw.) attract; **sich von jmdm. angezogen fühlen** feel attracted to sb. **3** (anspannen) tighten, pull tight ‹*rope, wire, chain*›; tighten ‹*guitar string*› **4** (festziehen) tighten ‹*screw, knot, belt, etc.*›; put on, pull on ‹*handbrake*› **5** (Kleidung anlegen) dress; **sich ~:** get dressed **6** put on ‹*clothes*›; **sich** (*Dat.*) **etw. ~:** put sth. on; **jmdm. etw. ~:** put sth. on sb.; (als Hilfeleistung) put sth. on for sb. **7** (aufnehmen) absorb ‹*moisture*›; take on ‹*taste, smell*› **8** (Physik) ‹*magnet, body, etc.*› attract
B *unr. itr. V.* **1** (Tempo beschleunigen) accelerate **2** (sich in Bewegung setzen) ‹*car, train*› pull away, move off; ‹*horse*› move off **3** (Brettspiel) make the first move; move *or* go first **4** (Börsenw., Kaufmannsspr.) ‹*prices, costs*› rise, increase; ‹*shares, securities, commodities*› advance, move ahead

anziehend *Adj.* attractive; engaging ‹*manner, smile*›

An·ziehung *die* attraction

Anziehungs·kraft *die* **1** (Physik) attractive force; force of attraction **2** (Reiz) attraction

an|zischen
A *tr. V.* **1** hiss at **2** (ugs.: anfahren) snarl at
B *itr. V.; mit sein* (ugs.: sich nähern) **angezischt kommen** come whizzing along; (auf einen zu) come whizzing up

an|zockeln *itr. V.; mit sein* (ugs.) **angezockelt kommen** come jogging along; (auf einen zu) come jogging up; ‹*cart*› come trundling along/up

An·zug *der* **1** (Herren~) suit; **jmdn. aus dem ~ stoßen** *od.* **boxen** (salopp) beat *or* knock the living daylights (coll.) *or* the hell (coll.) out of sb. **2** **im ~ sein** ‹*danger*› be imminent; ‹*storm*› be approaching; ‹*fever, illness*› be coming on; ‹*enemy*› be advancing **3** (Beschleunigung) acceleration **4** (Brettspiele) first move; **~ haben** have the first move

anzüglich /ˈantsyːklɪç/
A *Adj.* **1** insinuating ‹*remark, question*›; **werde bloß nicht ~!** just don't start making insinuating remarks **2** (anstößig) offensive ‹*joke, remark*›
B *adv.* **1** in an insinuating way **2** (anstößig) offensively

Anzüglichkeit *die* ▸ **anzüglich 1, 2**: **1** (Art) insinuating nature; offensiveness **2** (Bemerkung) insinuating remark; offensive remark/joke

Anzug·stoff *der* suiting

Anzugs·vermögen *das* acceleration

Anzug·träger *der* man in a suit; men in suits *pl.*

an|zünden *tr. V.* light; **ein Gebäude** *usw.* **~:** set fire to a building *etc.*; set a building *etc.* on fire

An·zünder *der* (Gas~) gas lighter; (Feuer~) firelighter (Brit.)

an|zweifeln *tr. V.* doubt; question

an|zwinkern *tr. V.* wink at

an|zwitschern *refl. V.* (ugs.) *in* **sich** (*Dat.*) **einen ~:** get sloshed (coll.)

AOK *Abk.* **= Allgemeine Ortskrankenkasse**

> **AOK — Allgemeine Ortskrankenkasse**
>
> The largest health insurance organization in Germany. Foreign visitors to Germany who need medical assistance can get the necessary forms at the local *AOK* office.

Äols·harfe /ˈɛːɔls-/ *die* aeolian harp

Äon /ɛˈoːn/ *der;* **~s, ~en** (geh.) aeon

Aorta /aˈɔrta/ *die;* **~, Aorten** ▸❶ **S. 435** (Med.) aorta

Apanage /apaˈnaːʒə/ *die;* **~, ~n** apanage; (fig.) subsidy

apart /aˈpart/
A *Adj.* individual *attrib.*; **~ sein** be individual in style
B *adv.* **1** in an individual style **2** (Buchhandel: einzeln) individually

Apartheid /aˈpaːɐ̯thaɪ̯t/ *die;* **~:** apartheid *no art.*

Apartheid·politik *die* policy of apartheid

Apartheit *die;* **~:** individuality

Apartment /aˈpartmənt/ *das;* **~s, ~s** studio flat (esp. Brit.); flatlet (esp. Brit.); small flat (esp. Brit.); studio apartment (esp. Amer.)

Apartment·haus *das* block of studio flats (esp. Brit.) *or* (esp. Amer.) studio apartments

Apathie /apaˈtiː/ *die;* **~, ~n** apathy

apathisch /aˈpaːtɪʃ/
A *Adj.* apathetic
B *adv.* apathetically

Apenninen /apɛˈniːnən/ *Pl.* **die ~:** the Apennines

Apennin[en]·halbinsel *die* Apennine peninsula

aper /ˈaːpɐ/ *Adj.* (südd., österr., schweiz.) snowless; bare of snow *pred.*; ‹*street*› clear of snow *pred.*

Aperçu /apɛrˈsyː/ *das;* **~s, ~s** (geh.) bon mot

Aperitif /aperiˈtiːf/ *der;* **~s, ~s** aperitif

apern /ˈaːpɐn/ *itr. V.* (südd., österr., schweiz.) **es apert** the snow is going; **die Hänge/Straßen ~:** the snow on the slopes is going/the streets are becoming clear of snow

Apex /ˈaːpɛks/ *der;* **~, Apizes** /ˈaːpitseːs/ **1** (Astron.) apex **2** (Sprachw.) (Längezeichen) length mark; (Betonungszeichen) stress mark

Apfel /ˈapfl̩/ *der;* **~s, Äpfel** /ˈɛpfl̩/ **1** apple; **der ~ fällt nicht weit vom Stamm** *od.* (ugs. scherzh.) **Pferd** (Spr.) it's in the blood; **~ im Schlafrock** (Kochk.) apple dumpling; **Äpfel und Birnen zusammenzählen, Äpfel mit Birnen addieren** (ugs.) lump together totally different things; **[etw.] für einen ~ und ein Ei [kaufen]** [buy sth.] for a song; **in den sauren ~ beißen [und etw. tun]** (ugs.) grasp the nettle [and do sth.] **2** (~baum) apple tree

Apfel-: ~baum *der* apple tree; **~blüte** *die* **1** apple blossom; **2** (das Blühen) blossoming of the apple trees; **während der ~blüte** while the apple trees are/were in blossom

Äpfelchen *das;* **~s, ~:** little apple

apfel-, Apfel-: ~essig *der* apple vinegar; **~grün** apple-green; **~korn** *der* apple-flavoured schnapps; **~kuchen** *der* apple cake; (mit Äpfeln belegt) apple flan; **gedeckter ~kuchen** apple pie; **~most** *der* **1** (~saft) apple juice; **2** (südd.: gegorener ~saft) cider; **~mus** *das* apple purée; (zu Fleisch) apple sauce; **~saft** *der* apple juice; **~saftschorle** *die* apple juice with mineral water; **~schimmel** *der* dapple-grey [horse]; **~schorle** *die* ▸ **Apfelsaftschorle**

Apfelsine /apfl̩ˈziːnə/ *die;* **~, ~n** **1** orange **2** (Baum) orange tree

Apfel-: ~strudel *der* apfelstrudel; **~tasche** *die* apple turnover *or* puff; **~wein** *der* cider; **~wickler** *der* (Zool.) codling moth

Aphorismus /afoˈrɪsmʊs/ *der;* **~, Aphorismen** (geh.) aphorism

aphoristisch (geh.)
A *Adj.* aphoristic
B *adv.* aphoristically

Aphrodisiakum /afrodiˈziːakʊm/ *das;* **~s, Aphrodisiaka** (Med.) aphrodisiac

Aplomb /aˈplõː/ *der;* **~s** (geh.) aplomb

Apnoe /aˈpnoːə/ *die;* **~, ~n** (Med.) apnoea

Apnoiker /aˈpnoːikɐ/ *der;* **~s, ~, Apnoikerin** *die;* **~, ~nen** (Med.) apnoeic subject

APO, Apo /ˈaːpo/ *die;* **~:** *Abk.* **= außerparlamentarische Opposition**

apodiktisch /apoˈdɪktɪʃ/ *Adj.* (Philos., geh.) apodictic

Apokalypse /apokaˈlʏpsə/ *die;* **~, ~n** apocalypse

apokalyptisch /apokaˈlʏptɪʃ/ (Rel., fig.)
A *Adj.* apocalyptic; **die Apokalyptischen Reiter** the Four Horsemen of the Apocalypse
B *adv.* apocalyptically

apokryph /apoˈkryːf/ *Adj.* (Rel., fig.) apocryphal; **die Apokryphen** the Apocrypha *sing.*

apolitisch
A *Adj.* apolitical
B *adv.* apolitically

Apoll /aˈpɔl/ *der;* **~s, ~s** (geh.) Apollo

apollinisch /apɔˈliːnɪʃ/ *Adj.* (bes. Philos.) apollonian

Apollo /aˈpɔlo/ *der;* **~s, ~s** (Myth., geh.) Apollo

Apologet /apoloˈgeːt/ *der;* **~en, ~en** apologist

Apologetik /apoloˈgeːtɪk/ *die;* **~, ~en** **1** (geh.: Rechtfertigung) apologia (*Gen.* for) **2** (Theol.) apologetics *sing.*

Apologetin *die;* **~, ~nen** apologist

Apologie /apoloˈgiː/ *die;* **~, ~n** (geh.) apologia (*Gen.* for)

Aporie /apoˈriː/ *die;* **~, ~n** (Philos., geh.) aporia

-apostel *der* (meist iron.) apostle of ‹*economic growth, world peace, etc.*›; **ein Frischluft~/Gesundheits~:** a fresh air/health fanatic; **ein Spar~/Abnehm~:** an enthusiastic advocate of saving/slimming

Apostel /aˈpɔstl̩/ *der;* **~s, ~:** apostle; **die zwölf ~:** the twelve Apostles

Apostel-: ~brief *der* epistle; **~geschichte** *die* **1** (apokryphe Geschichte) Apocryphal New Testament story; **2** (Buch des N. T.) Acts of the Apostles *constr. as sing.*

a posteriori /aː posteˈrioːri/ (Philos.) a posteriori

aposteriorisch *Adj., adv.* (Philos.) a posteriori

apostolisch /apɔsˈtoːlɪʃ/ *Adj.* (Theol.) **1** apostolic; **das Apostolische Glaubensbekenntnis** the Apostles' Creed **2** (päpstlich) apostolic; **~er Segen** apostolic blessing; **Apostolischer Nuntius** Apostolic Nuncio; **Apostolischer Stuhl** Holy See

Apostroph /apoˈstroːf/ *der;* **~s, ~e** (Sprachw.) apostrophe

apostrophieren *tr. V.* **1** (Sprachw.: mit Apostroph versehen) apostrophize **2** **jmdn./etw. als etw. ~:** refer to sb./sth. as sth.; describe sb./sth. as sth.

Apotheke /apoˈteːkə/ *die;* **~, ~n** **1** chemist's [shop] (Brit.); drugstore (Amer.); (im Krankenhaus) dispensary **2** (Haus~) medicine cabinet; (Reise~, Bord~) first-aid kit **3** (ugs. abwertend: teures Geschäft) expensive shop; **das ist eine richtige ~:** they charge an arm and a leg there (coll.)

apotheken·pflichtig *Adj.* obtainable only at a chemist's [shop] (Brit.) *or* (Amer.) drugstore *postpos.*

Apotheker *der;* **~s, ~, Apothekerin** *die;* **~, ~nen** ▸❶ **S. 113** [dispensing] chemist (Brit.); druggist

Apotheker·preise *Pl.* (fig. ugs.) fancy prices (coll.)

Apotheose /apoteˈoːzə/ *die;* **~, ~n** (geh.) apotheosis

App. *Abk.* **1** **= Apparat** ext. **2** **= Appartement** Apt.

Apparat /apaˈraːt/ *der;* **~[e]s, ~e** **1** (Technik) apparatus *no pl.*; (Haushaltsgerät) appliance; (kleiner) gadget **2** (Radio~) radio; (Fernseh~) television; (Rasier~) razor; (elektrisch) shaver; (Foto~) camera; **wir haben einen neuen Fernseher gekauft, der alte ~ war 15 Jahre alt** we've bought a new television — our old set was fifteen years old **3** (Telefon) telephone; (Nebenstelle) extension; **am ~ verlangt werden** be wanted on the telephone; **am ~!** speaking!; **bleiben Sie am ~!** hold the line; **wer war am ~?** who answered?, who did you speak to? **4** (Personen und Hilfsmittel) organization; (Verwaltungs~) system **5** (ugs.: etwas Ausgefallenes, Riesiges) whopper (coll.); (dicker Mensch) heavyweight **6** (Hochschulw.: Bücher) *reference collection of books for a particular course* **7** (Lesarten) apparatus; **[text]kritischer ~:** apparatus criticus; critical apparatus

Apparate·bau *der* (Technik) design and manufacture of apparatus

Apparate·medizin *die* (oft abwertend) high-technology medicine

apparativ /aparaˈtiːf/
A *Adj.* **1** (Technik) **~e Einrichtungen** technical equipment *sing.*; **~e Lehrmittel** machine aids in the classroom; **~e Diagnostik** machine-aided diagnosis **2** (Verwaltung) **der ~e Ausbau der Organisation** the expansion of the organization's administrative system
B *adv.* **1** (Technik) with the aid of machines *or* technical equipment; **~ am Leben erhalten werden** be kept alive by life support systems **2** (Verwaltung) organizationally

Apparatschik /apaˈratʃɪk/ *der;* **~s, ~s** (abwertend) apparatchik

Apparatur /aparaˈtuːɐ̯/ *die;* **~, ~en** apparatus *no pl.*; equipment *no indef. art., no pl.*; (fig.) apparatus *no pl*; **~en** (Kontrollinstrumente usw.) instruments and controls

Apparillo /apaˈrɪlo/ *der;* **~s, ~s** (ugs. scherzh.) contraption (coll.); **Der Karpfen wiegt 6 Kilo. — Mann, ist das ein ~!** The carp weighs 6 kilos — That's 'some 'fish!

Appartement /apartəˈmãː,* schweiz. *auch:* -ˈmɛnt/ *das;* **~s, ~s** (*schweiz. auch:* **~e**) **1** ▸ **Apartment** **2** (Hotelsuite) suite

Appeal /əˈpiːl/ *der;* **~s** appeal

Appeasement /əˈpiːzmənt/ *das;* **~s** (Politik, meist abwertend) appeasement

Appell /aˈpɛl/ *der;* **~s, ~e** **1** (Mahnung) appeal (**zu** for, **an** + *Akk.* to); **einen ~ an jmdn. richten** make an appeal to sb.; appeal to sb. **2** (Milit.) muster; (Anwesenheits~) roll-call; (Besichtigung) inspection; **zum ~ antreten** fall in for roll-call inspection **3** (Jagdw.) obedience; **~/keinen ~ haben** be/not be obedient

Appellation /apɛlaˈtsi̯oːn/ *die;* **~, ~en** (Rechtsw., schweiz. sonst veralt.) appeal

Appellativ /apɛlaˈtiːf/ *das;* **~s, ~e, Appellativum** /apɛlaˈtiːvʊm/ *das;* **~s, Appellativa** (Sprachw.) appellative; common noun

appellieren *itr. V.* appeal (**an** + *Akk.* to)

a

Appendix¹ /a'pɛndɪks/ *der;* ~, **Appendizes** /-dɪtse:s/ *od.* ~**es,** ~**e** 1 (geh.: Anhängsel) appendage 2 (Buchw.) appendix

Appendix² *der od.* (fachspr.:) *die;* ~, **Appendizes** ▸ℹ **S. 435** (Anat.) appendix

Apperzeption /apɛrtsɛp'tsio:n/ *die;* ~, ~**en** (Philos., Psych.) apperception

Appetit /ape'ti:t/ *der;* ~**[e]s,** ~**e** (auch fig.) appetite (**auf** + *Akk.* for); ~ **auf etw. haben/bekommen** fancy sth.; **ich hätte so richtig** ~ **auf ...** I could just fancy *or* eat ...; I could really go for ... (Amer.); **guten** ~**!** enjoy your meal!; **jmdm. den** ~ **verderben** spoil sb.'s appetite; **das verschlug uns/ihnen** *usw.* **den** ~**:** that took away our/their *etc.* appetite; **mit** ~ **essen** enjoy one's food; **der** ~ **kommt beim** *od.* **mit dem Essen** appetite comes with eating (prov.)

appetit·anregend *Adj.* 1 (appetitlich) appetizing 2 (den Appetit fördernd) ‹*medicine etc.*› that stimulates the appetite; ~ **wirken** stimulate the appetite; **ein** ~**es Mittel** an appetite stimulant

Appetit-: ~**happen** *der* canapé; ~**hemmer** *der;* ~**s,** ~ ▸ ~**zügler**

appetitlich
A *Adj.* 1 (appetitanregend) appetizing 2 (sauber, ansprechend) attractive and hygienic 3 (adrett) attractive
B *adv.* 1 (appetitanregend) appetizingly 2 (sauber, ansprechend) attractively and hygienically ‹*packed*›; **ein** ~ **gedeckter Tisch** an attractively laid table

appetit-, Appetit-: ~**los** A *Adj.* without any appetite *postpos.;* ~**los sein** have lost one's appetite; **immer noch** ~**los sein** still have no appetite; B *adv.* without any appetite; ~**losigkeit** *die;* ~~: lack of appetite; ~**macher** *der* appetizer (also fig.); ~**zügler** *der* appetite suppressant

Appetizer /'ɛpɪtaɪzə/ *der;* ~**s,** ~ (Pharm.) appetite stimulant

applanieren *tr. V.* (österr.) smooth over; settle

applaudieren /aplau'di:rən/ *itr.* (*veralt. auch tr.*) *V.* applaud; **jmdm./einer Sache** ~**:** applaud sb./sth.

Applaus /a'plaus/ *der;* ~**es,** ~**e** applause

Applet /'ɛplɪt/ *das;* ~**s,** ~**s** (DV) applet

applikabel /apli'ka:bl/ *Adj.* (geh.) applicable

Applikation /aplika'tsio:n/ *die;* ~, ~**en** 1 (DV) application 2 (Med.: Verabreichung) administration; (äußerlich) application 3 (Textilw.) appliqué

applizieren /apli'tsi:rən/ *tr. V.* 1 (Med.) administer; (äußerlich) apply 2 (Textilw.) appliqué

apportieren /apɔr'ti:rən/ *tr.* (*auch itr.*) *V.* (Jägerspr.) retrieve; fetch

Apportier-hund *der* retriever

Apposition *die* (Sprachw.) apposition

appretieren /apre'ti:rən/ *tr. V.* (bes. Textilind.) dress, finish ‹*fabric, linen*›

Appretur /apre'tu:ɐ/ *die;* ~, ~**en** (bes. Textilind.) dressing; finishing

Approbation /aproba'tsio:n/ *die;* ~, ~**en** licence to practise (*as a doctor, dentist, chemist*)

approbieren /apro'bi:rən/ *tr. V.* (österr., sonst veralt.) approve

approbiert *Adj.* registered ‹*doctor, dentist, chemist*›

Apr. *Abk.* = **April** Apr.

Après-Ski /aprɛ'ʃi:/ *das;* ~**s** 1 (Kleidung) après-ski outfit 2 (Unterhaltung) après-ski [entertainment]

Aprikose /apri'ko:zə/ *die;* ~, ~**n** 1 (Frucht) apricot 2 (Baum) apricot tree

Aprikosen·marmelade *die* apricot jam

April /a'prɪl/ *der;* ~**[s],** ~**e** ▸ℹ **S. 165** April; **der** ~**:** April; ~, ~**!** April fool!; **der 1.** ~**:** the first of April; (in Bezug auf Aprilscherze) April Fool's *or* All Fools' Day; **jmdn. in den** ~ **schicken** make an April fool of sb.

April-: ~**scherz** *der* April fool trick; **das ist doch wohl ein** ~**scherz!** (fig.) you/they *etc.* can't be serious!; you/they *etc.* must be joking!; ~**wetter** *das* April weather

a priori /a:pri'o:ri/ (Philos.) a priori

apriorisch *Adj., adv.* (Philos.) a priori

apropos /apro'po:/ *Adv.* apropos; by the way; incidentally

Aquädukt /akvɛ'dʊkt/ *der od. das;* ~**[e]s,** ~**e** aqueduct

Aqua-jogging /'a:kva-/ *das;* ~**s** aquajogging

aquamarin /akvama'ri:n/ ▸ ~**blau**

Aquamarin *der;* ~**s,** ~**e** aquamarine

aquamarin-blau *Adj.* aquamarine

Aquanaut /akva'naut/ *der;* ~**en,** ~**en,** **Aquanautin** *die;* ~, ~**nen** aquanaut

Aquaplaning /akva'pla:nɪŋ/ *das;* ~**s** aquaplaning

Aquarell /akva'rɛl/ *das;* ~**s,** ~**e** (Malerei) watercolour [painting]

Aquarell-farbe *die* watercolour

aquarellieren *itr. V.* paint in watercolours

Aquarell-: ~**maler** *der,* ~**malerin** *die;* watercolour painter; watercolourist; ~**malerei** *die* 1 (Maltechnik) watercolour painting; **in** ~**malerei** in watercolour; 2 (Bild) watercolour

Aquarien /a'kva:riən/ ▸ **Aquarium**

Aquarien-: ~**fisch** *der* aquarium fish; ~**haus** *das* aquarium

Aquarium /a'kva:riʊm/ *das;* ~**s,** **Aquarien** aquarium

Aquatinta /akva'tɪnta/ *die;* ~, **Aquatinten** (bild. Kunst) aquatint

Äquator /ɛ'kva:tɔr/ *der;* ~**s;** ~**en** /-'to:rən/ (Erd~, Math.) equator

äquatorial /ɛkvato'ria:l/ *Adj.* equatorial

Äquator-taufe *die* crossing-the-line ceremony

Aquavit /akva'vi:t/ *der;* ~**s,** ~**e** aquavit

Äquilibrist /ɛkvili'brɪst/ *der;* ~**en,** ~**en,** **Äquilibristin** *die;* ~, ~**nen** equilibrist

Äquinoktium /ɛkvi'nɔktsiʊm/ *das;* ~**s,** **Äquinoktien** (Geogr.) equinox

äquivalent /ɛkviva'lɛnt/ *Adj.* equivalent

Äquivalent *das;* ~**[e]s,** ~**e** equivalent; (Ersatz) appropriate replacement; (Entschädigung) appropriate compensation

Äquivalenz /ɛkviva'lɛnts/ *die;* ~, ~**en** (auch Math., Logik) equivalence

Ar /a:ɐ/ *das od. der;* ~**s,** ~**e** ▸ℹ **S. 262** are

Ära /'ɛ:ra/ *die;* ~, **Ären** era; **die** ~ **Kreisky** the Kreisky era

Araber /'a:rabɐ/ *der;* ~**s,** ~ ▸ℹ **S. 520** (auch Pferd) Arab; Arabian

Araberin *die;* ~, ~**nen** ▸ℹ **S. 520** Arab; Arabian

Arabeske /ara'bɛskə/ *die;* ~, ~**n** (bild. Kunst, Musik) arabesque

Arabien /a'ra:biən/ *(das);* ~**s** Arabia

arabisch *Adj.* ▸ℹ **S. 520,** ▸ℹ **S. 670** Arabian; Arab; Arabic ‹*language, numeral, dialect, alphabet, literature*›; **die Arabische Halbinsel** the Arabian Peninsula; **das Arabische** Arabic; *s. auch* **deutsch, Deutsche²**

Arabisch *das;* ~**[s]** ▸ℹ **S. 670** Arabic *s. auch* **Deutsch**

Arabistik /ara'bɪstɪk/ *die;* ~**:** Arabic studies *pl., no art.*

Aralie /a'ra:liə/ *die;* ~, ~**n** (Bot.) aralia

aramäisch /ara'mɛ:ɪʃ/ *Adj.* Aramaic; **das Aramäische** Aramaic; *s. auch* **deutsch, Deutsch, Deutsche²**

Arancini /aran'tʃi:ni/, **Aranzini** /aran'tsi:ni/ *Pl.* (bes. österr.) *sugar- or chocolate-coated candied orange peel*

Aräo·meter /areo-/ *das* (Physik) hydrometer

Arbeit /'arbait/ *die;* ~, ~**en** 1 (auch Sport, Jagdw., Physik) work *no indef. art.;* (Politik, Soziol.: Arbeitskraft) labour *no indef. art.;* **die** ~**[en] am Staudamm** [the] work on the dam; **an die** ~ **gehen, sich an die** ~ **machen** get down to work; **die** ~ **mit Asbest ist gesundheitsschädigend** working with asbestos is injurious to health; **eine widerliche** ~ **sein** be a revolting job *or* task; **die** ~ **läuft uns nicht davon** (scherzh.) the work can wait; **ganze** *od.* **gründliche** ~ **leisten** *od.* **tun** *od.* **machen** (auch fig. iron.) make a good job of it; **nur halbe** ~ **machen** leave the job half-done; only half do the job; **Tag der** ~**:** Labour Day; **an** *od.* **bei der** ~ **sein** be at work; **jmdm. bei der** ~ **zusehen** watch sb. working *or* at work; **mit der** ~ **beginnen** start work; **bei der** ~ **mit Chemikalien** when working with chemicals; **viel** ~ **haben** have a lot of work [to do]; **seine** ~ **tun** *od.* **machen** do one's job; **gute** ~ **leisten** do good work; work well; **[wieder] an die** ~**!** [back] to work!; **die** ~ **niederlegen** stop work; (bei manueller ~) down tools; **der/die hat die** ~ **nicht erfunden** (scherzh.) he/she is not the world's hardest worker; **etw. in** ~ **geben** have sth. made; **jmdm. etw. in** ~ **geben** get sb. to make sth.; **etw. in** ~ **haben** be working on sth.; ~ **schändet nicht** work's no disgrace; **erst die** ~, **dann das Vergnügen** business before pleasure 2 (Mühe) trouble; ~ **machen** cause bother *or* trouble; **jmdm.** ~ **machen** make work for sb.; **machen Sie sich keine** ~**!** don't go to *or* put yourself to any trouble; **sich** (*Dat.*) ~ **[mit etw.] machen** take trouble [over sth.]; **viel** ~ **machen** *od.* **kosten** cost a lot of effort *or* hard work; **das war eine** ~**!** what a job that was! 3 (~splatz, ~sstätte) work *no indef. art.;* (Stellung) job; **eine** ~ **suchen/finden** look for/find work *or* a job; **die** ~ **Suchenden** those looking for work; **eine** ~ **als ...** work *or* a job as ...; **zur** *od.* (ugs.) **auf** ~ **gehen** go to work; **auf** ~ **sein** (ugs.) be at work; **auf** ~ **gehen** (ugs.: berufstätig sein) work; have a job; **ohne** ~ **sein** be out of work; be unemployed; **bei jmdm. in** ~ **stehen** *od.* **sein** work for sb.; be employed by sb.; **vor/nach der** ~ (ugs.) before/after work 4 (Aufträge) work *no indef. art.* 5 (Produkt, Ausführung) work; (handwerkliche ~) piece of work; (kurze schriftliche ~) article; (Dissertation) dissertation 6 (Klassen~) test; **eine** ~ **schreiben/schreiben lassen** do/set a test

arbeiten
A *itr. V.* 1 (Arbeit leisten) work; **zu** ~ **haben** have work to do; ~ **wie ein Pferd**/(ugs.) **ein Wilder** work like a slave *or* a Trojan/(coll.) like mad; **er arbeitet für zwei** he does the work of two; **an etw.** (*Dat.*) ~**:** work on sth.; **an sich** (*Dat.*) ~**:** work to improve one's abilities; **mit Silber/Akrylfarben** ~**:** work in silver/acrylic paints; **mit Behinderten/Taubstummen** ~**:** work with the disabled/the deaf and dumb; **sein Geld** ~ **lassen** (fig.) make one's money work for one 2 (beruflich tätig sein) work; **seine Frau arbeitet** his wife has a job *or* works; **40 Stunden in der Woche** ~**:** work 40 hours a week *or* a 40-hour week; **das Büro arbeitet freitags nur bis 14⁰⁰** (fig.) the office closes at 2 p.m. on Fridays; **bei der Bahn/einer Firma** ~**:** work on the railways (Brit.) *or* (Amer.) at the railroad/for a firm 3 **über jmdn./etw.** ~ (sich befassen mit) work on sb./sth. 4 (wirksam sein) **für/gegen jmdn./etw.** ~**:** work for/against sb./sth.; **die Zeit arbeitet für/gegen uns** time is on our side/against us; **an jmds. Untergang** (*Dat.*) ~**:** work to bring about sb.'s downfall 5 (funktionieren) ‹*heart, lungs, etc.*› work, function; ‹*machine*› work, operate; **mit Gas/Sonnenenergie** ~**:** run on gas/solar energy; **automatisch** ~**:** be automatic; **in meinem Magen arbeitet es** (fig.) my stomach is grumbling 6 (ankämpfen) work hard (**gegen** against) 7 (sich verändern) ‹*wood*› warp; ‹*must*› ferment; ‹*dough*› rise 8 (Sport) work (**mit** with) 9 (schneidern) **wo/bei wem lassen Sie** ~**?** where do you have *or* get your clothes made?; who makes your clothes?
B *tr. V.* 1 (herstellen) make; (in Ton, Silber, usw.) work; make; fashion 2 (tun) do; **was** ~ **Sie?** what are you doing?; (beruflich) what do you do for a living?; what's your job?
C *refl. V.* 1 **sich müde/krank** ~**:** tire oneself out/make oneself ill with work; **sich zu Tode** ~**:** work oneself to death 2 (Strecke zurücklegen); **sich durch etw./in etw.** (*Akk.*) ~**:** work one's way through/into sth.; **sich nach oben** ~ (fig.) work one's way up 3 **sich** (*Dat.*) **die Hände wund** ~**:** work one's fingers to the bone 4 *unpers.* **hier arbeitet es sich gut** this is a good place to work; **mit dieser Maschine arbeitet es sich gut/schneller** this machine is easy to work with/the work goes faster with

this machine; **mit ihm arbeitet es sich angenehm** it's nice working with him; he's pleasant to work with

Arbeiter *der;* ~s, ~ ▸❶ **S. 113** worker; (Bau~, Land~) labourer; (beim Straßenbau) workman; **der ~ Karl Müller** the factory worker/labourer/workman Karl Müller; **wir suchen ~ und Arbeiterinnen für folgende Bereiche** we are looking for men and women to work in the following areas; **~ und Arbeiterinnen werden oft ...** male and female workers are often ...; **die ~** (als Klasse) the workers

arbeiter-, Arbeiter-: **~auf·stand** *der* workers' rebellion *or* revolt; **~bewegung** *die* (Politik) labour movement; **~biene** *die* (Zool.) worker [bee]; **~denkmal** *das* [1] workers' monument; monument to the working classes; [2] (ugs. scherzh.) monument to inactivity (joc.); **~dichter** *der,* **~dichterin** *die* poet of the working class; **~familie** *die* working-class family; **~feindlich** *Adj.* anti-working-class; **~freundlich** *Adj.* favouring the workers *postpos.;* **~führer** *der,* **~führerin** *die* workers' leader; **~gewerkschaft** *die* trade union (Brit.); labor union (Amer.)

Arbeiterin *die;* ~, **~nen** ▸❶ **S. 113** (auch Zool.) worker; *s. auch* **Arbeiter**

Arbeiter-: **~jugend** *die* young working people; (Organisation) labour youth movement *or* organization; **~kampf·lied** *das* workers' [rallying] song; **~kind** *das* working-class child; **~klasse** *die* working class[es *pl.*]; **~kontrolle** *die* (bes. DDR) worker control; **~lied** *das* workers' song; **~massen** *Pl.* working masses; **~milieu** *das* working-class environment; **aus dem ~milieu stammen** come from a working-class environment *or* background; **~organisation** *die* labour organization; **~partei** *die* workers' party; **~priester** *der,* **~priesterin** *die* worker-priest; **~rat** *der* workers' council

Arbeiterschaft *die;* ~: workers *pl.;* **aus der ~:** from among the workers

Arbeiter-: **~schriftsteller** *der,* **~schriftstellerin** *die* worker-writer; working-class writer; **~selbstverwaltung** *die* workers' control *no indef. art.;* (Gremium) workers' management committee; **in ~selbstverwaltung arbeiten** be under workers' control; **~siedlung** *die* workers' housing estate (Brit.) *or* (Amer.) housing development; **~stadt** *die* workers' town; (ugs.: Industriestadt, in der viele Arbeiter leben) working-class town; **~student** *der* (DDR) worker-student; **~-und-Bauern-Fakultät** *die* (DDR) workers and farmers' faculty (preparing young workers for university study); **~-und-Bauern-Inspektion** *die* (DDR) *body charged with monitoring the implementation of party and Government policy in economic and social affairs;* **~-und-Bauern-Staat** *der* (DDR) workers' and farmers' state; **~-und-Soldaten-Rat** *der* (hist.) workers' and soldiers' council; **~unruhen** *Pl.* unrest *sing.* among the workers; **~verein** *der* workers' association; **~verräter** *der,* **~verräterin** *die* (Politik abwertend) traitor to the working class; **~viertel** *das* working-class district *or* area; **~wohl·fahrt** *die* workers' welfare association

Arbeit·geber *der* employer

Arbeitgeber·anteil *der* employer's contribution

Arbeitgeberin *die;* ~, **~nen** [female] employer; *s. auch* **-in**

Arbeitgeber-: **~seite** *die* employers' side; **~verband** *der* employers' association *or* organization

Arbeitnehmer *der;* ~s, ~: employee

Arbeitnehmer·anteil *der* employee's contribution

Arbeitnehmerin *die;* ~, **~nen** [female] employee; *s. auch* **-in**

Arbeitnehmer-: **~organisation** *die* workers' organization; **~seite** *die* employees' side

Arbeits·ab·lauf *der* programme of work

> **Arbeitsagentur**
>
> The local employment office to be found in every German town (formerly called *Arbeitsamt*). It provides career guidance, helps the unemployed find new jobs, and processes all claims for **Arbeitslosengeld I** and related benefits. Unemployed people have to report to the *Arbeitsamt* once every three months to prove that they are still looking for work.

Arbeits·alltag *der* typical workday

arbeitsam *Adj.* (geh. veralt.) [1] (fleißig) industrious; hard-working [2] (von Arbeit erfüllt) **ein ~es Leben** a life of hard work; **ein paar ~e Monate vor sich haben** have a few months of hard work ahead of one

arbeits-, Arbeits-: **~amt** *das* job centre (Brit.); employment exchange; labour exchange (Brit. dated); **~anfall** *der* volume of work; **~anfang** *der* starting time [at work]; **~anfang ist um 6 Uhr** work starts at 6 a.m.; **~anleitung** *die* instructions *pl.;* **~antritt** *die* **vor ~antritt** before starting work *or* the/a job; **bei ~antritt** when you start/he starts *etc.* work; **~anzug** *der* working clothes *pl.;* **blauer ~anzug** blue overalls *pl.;* **~atmosphäre** *die* working atmosphere; **~auffassung** *die* attitude to one's work; **~aufwand** *der:* **mit großem ~aufwand** with a great deal of work; **das wäre mir zu viel ~aufwand** it would be *or* involve too much work [for me]; **~aufwendig** **A** *Adj.* requiring a great deal of work *postpos., not pred.;* **[sehr] ~aufwendig sein** require a great deal of work; **B** *adv.* in a way that requires/required a great deal of work; **~ausfall** *der* loss of working hours; **ein ~ausfall von einigen Wochen** a loss of several working weeks; **~bedingungen** *Pl.* working conditions; **~beginn** *der* ▸ **~anfang**; **~belastung** *die* workload; **~bereich** *der* [1] (Tätigkeit) area of work; (~gebiet) field of work; **das gehört nicht in meinen ~bereich** that's not part of my job; [2] (im Raum) working area; [3] (eines Krans) working radius; **~beschaffung** *die* job creation; creation of employment; **~beschaffungs·maßnahme** *die* job-creation measure; **~beschaffungs·programm** *das* job-creation programme; **~bescheinigung** *die* certificate of employment (issued to employee on leaving job, and listing responsibilities, length of service, etc.); **~biene** *die* [1] (Zool.) worker bee; [2] (ugs.: emsige Frau) busy bee; **~dienst** *der* [1] (Arbeit) (low-paid) community-service work; [2] (Organisation) community service agency; [3] ▸ **Reichsarbeitsdienst**; **~direktor** *der,* **~direktorin** *die* ▸❶ **S. 113** personnel director (*with special responsibility for safeguarding the interests of the employees within the framework of co-determination*); **~disziplin** *die* discipline in one's approach to work; **~eifer** *der* enthusiasm for one's work; **~einsatz** *der* [1] (Arbeitsdienst) working experience; (statt Geldstrafe) community service *no indef. art.;* **flexiblerer ~einsatz** more flexible working; [2] (Engagement) **ein beträchtlicher/enormer ~einsatz** a considerable/enormous amount of work; **~elefant** *der* working elephant; **~ende** *das* finishing time [at work]; **nach/bei ~ende** after work/when it's time to go; **um fünf Uhr haben wir** *od.* **ist bei uns ~ende** we finish work at five o'clock; **~erlaubnis** *die* work permit; **~erleichternd** **A** *Adj.* labour-saving; **B** *adv.* in a labour-saving way; **~erleichterung** *die* saving of labour; **eine große ~erleichterung für jmdn. sein** make sb.'s work a great deal easier; save sb. a great deal of work; **~essen** *das* (bes. Politik) working lunch/dinner; **~ethos** *das* work ethic; **~fähig** *Adj.* fit for work *postpos.;* (grundsätzlich) able to work *postpos.;* viable ‹*government*›; **~fähigkeit** *die* fitness for work; (grundsätzlich) ability to work; **~feld** *das* (geh.) field of work; **~frei** *Adj.* **ein paar Tage/eine Woche ~frei** a few days/a week off; **Montag ist/haben wir ~frei** we've got Monday off; **~freude** *die* enthusiasm for one's work; **~friede** (geh.), **~frieden** *der* industrial peace; peaceful labour *or* industrial relations *pl.;* **~frühstück** *das* working breakfast; **~gang** *der* [1] (einzelne Operation) operation; [2] (Ablauf) process; **~gebiet** *das* field of work; **~gemeinschaft** *die* team; (Hochschulw.) study group; **~genehmigung** *die* work permit; **~gerät** *das* [1] (Gegenstand) tool; [2] (Gesamtheit) tools *pl.;* equipment *no indef. art., no pl.;* **~gericht** *das* industrial tribunal; **~gruppe** *die* study group; **~haus** *das* (hist.) *correctional institution for minor offenders where prisoners are required to work;* workhouse (Amer.); **~hypothese** *die* working hypothesis; **~intensiv** (Wirtsch.) **A** *Adj.* labour-intensive; **B** *adv.* labour-intensively; **~kampf** *der* industrial action; **~kampf·maßnahme** *die* form of industrial action; **~kleidung** *die* work clothes *pl.;* **~klima** *das* working atmosphere; **~kollege** *der,* **~kollegin** *die* (bei Arbeitern) workmate (Brit.); fellow worker; (bei Angestellten, Beamten) colleague; **~kraft** *die* [1] (Vermögen zu arbeiten) capacity for work; **seine ~kraft verkaufen** sell one's labour; **die menschliche ~kraft wird durch Roboter ersetzt** human labour is being replaced by robots; [2] (Mensch) worker; **~kreis** *der* study group; **~lager** *das* labour camp; **~last** *die* burden of work; **~leben** *das* [1] (Berufstätigkeit) working life; [2] (Arbeitswelt) world of work; working life *no art.;* **~leistung** *die* rate of output; **~lohn** *der* wage; wages *pl.;* (auf einer Rechnung) labour [costs *pl.*]; **~los** *Adj.* [1] unemployed; out of work *postpos.;* [2] *in* **~loses Einkommen** unearned income

> **Arbeitsgericht**
>
> Industrial tribunals are held at administrative courts (local, higher and federal), which handle all proceedings under administrative law. They deal with disputes between employers and employees, between employers and trade unions, and matters connected with the *Betriebsverfassungsgesetz* (industrial relations law).

Arbeitslose *der/die; adj. Dekl.* unemployed person/man/woman *etc.;* **die ~n** the unemployed *or* jobless; **es gab 2 Mio. ~:** there were 2 million [people] unemployed *or* out of work; **viele ~:** many unemployed people; many people who are/were unemployed *or* out of work

Arbeitslosen-: **~geld** *das* (full-rate) earnings-related unemployment benefit; **~heer** *das* army of unemployed; **~hilfe** *die* [1] (Geld) reduced-rate unemployment benefit; [2] (Institution) reduced-rate unemployment benefit system; **~unterstützung** *die* (volkst.) unemployment benefit *or* pay; **~versicherung** *die* unemployment insurance; **~zahl** *die* number of unemployed; jobless total; **~ziffer** *die* unemployment figures *pl.*

> **Arbeitslosengeld I**
>
> This is the benefit paid to all unemployed people who are looking for a new job and have already made a minimum contribution to the **Arbeitslosenversicherung**. The benefit is a proportion of the person's previous pay, and is higher for people supporting children. It is generally paid for up to one year. People who are not entitled to *Arbeitslosengeld I* can apply for the so-called *Arbeitslosengeld II*, which has replaced *Arbeitslosenhilfe*.

> **Arbeitslosenversicherung**
>
> This is the compulsory state-run insurance against unemployment. All *Arbeiter* and *Angestellte* have to pay into this scheme and in return are entitled to **Arbeitslosengeld I** and related benefits. Employees and employers each pay half of the unemployment insurance contributions. This area has been subject to wide-ranging reforms in recent years.

arbeits-, Arbeits-: **~losigkeit** *die;* ~~: unemployment *no indef. art.;* **eine ~losigkeit von 0,5%** a level of unemployment of 0.5%; **~mangel** *der* lack of work; **~markt** *der* labour market; **~material** *das* materials *pl.;*

(einschließlich Werkzeugen) materials [and equipment *or* tools]; (für den Unterricht) teaching aids *pl.*; **~medizin** *die* occupational medicine and health care; **~methode** *die* working method; method of working; **~minister** *der*, **~ministerin** *die* minister for employment; Secretary for Employment (Brit.); Secretary of Labor (Amer.); **~ministerium** *das* ministry for employment; Department of Employment (Brit.); Department of Labor (Amer.); **~mittel** *das* material; (Werkzeug, Wörterbuch usw.) tool; **~mittel** *Pl.* materials/tools; (Schreibzeug) materials; **~moral** *die* morale of the workers/staff; **~nachweis** *der* 1 (das Nachweisen) information *no indef. art.* about situations vacant; 2 (Stelle) employment office; **~niederlegung** *die* walkout; **mit ~niederlegungen drohen** threaten walkouts; **~ordnung** *die* 1 (Einteilung) organization of the work; 2 (Regelung des Betriebsablaufs) [office/factory/shop] regulations *pl.*; **~organisation** *die* organization of the/one's work; **~ort** *der* place of work; **~papier** *das* 1 (Thesenblatt) working paper; 2 *Pl.* (das Arbeitsverhältnis betreffende Papiere) employment papers

arbeit·sparend
A *Adj.* labour-saving
B *adv.* in a labour-saving way

Arbeits-: ~pause *die* break; **eine ~pause machen** take a break; **~pensum** *das* work quota; **~pferd** *das* (auch fig.) workhorse; **~plan** *der* work plan *or* schedule; **~platz** *der* 1 (Platz im Betrieb) workplace; **am ~platz** at one's workplace; 2 (~stätte) place of work; **den ~platz wechseln** change one's place of work; 3 (~verhältnis) job; **~platz·abbau** *der* reduction in the number of jobs; **~platz·garantie** *die* guarantee of employment; **~platz·sicherung** *die* safeguarding of jobs; **zur ~platzsicherung** to safeguard jobs; **~platz·studie** *die* job study; **~platz·wechsel** *der* change of job; **~probe** *die* sample of one's work; **~prozess**, *~prozeß** *der* 1 (Berufstätigkeit) **im ~prozess stehen** be in employment; have a job; **jmdn. wieder in den ~prozess eingliedern** get sb. back to work; 2 (~ablauf) work process; **~raum** *der* 1 workroom; (Büroraum) office; 2 ► **Arbeitszimmer**; **~recht** *das* labour law; **~rechtlich** *Adj.* **~rechtliche Fragen/Literatur** issues relating to/literature on labour law; **ein ~rechtlicher Streitfall** a dispute concerning labour law; **~reich** *Adj.* ‹*life, week, etc.*› full of hard work; **~richter** *der*, **~richterin** *die*: *judge on an industrial tribunal*; **~ruhe** *die* break [from work]; **gestern herrschte in ganz Italien ~ruhe** commerce and industry was at a standstill throughout Italy yesterday; **~sache** *die* 1 *Pl.* work things; 2 *Pl.* (Kleidung) work[ing] things *or* clothes; 3 (Rechtsw.) labour law dispute; **~scheu** *Adj.* work-shy; **~schluss**, *~schluß** *der* ► **~ende**; **~schutz** *der* protection of health and safety standards at work; **~schutz·bestimmung** *die* regulation concerning [the protection of] health and safety at work; **~sitzung** *die* working session; **~sklave** *der* slave labourer; **als ~sklaven verkauft werden** be sold as slave labour; **~soziologie** *die* occupational sociology; **~speicher** *der* (DV) main memory; **~stätte** *die* 1 (geh.) **das war Beethovens/Schillers ~stätte** this is [the place] where Beethoven/Schiller worked *or* did his work; 2 (Stätte beruflicher Tätigkeit) place of work; **~stelle** *die* 1 ► **Arbeitsstätte 2**; 2 (Job) ► **Stelle 7**; 3 (Abteilung) department; **~stil** *der* style of working; **~studie** *die* work study; **~stunde** *die* hour of work; **2 ~stunden** (bei Reparaturen usw.) two hours' labour; **die Herstellung erfordert 2 000 ~stunden** manufacture takes 2,000 man-hours; **~suche** *die* search for a job *or* for work; **auf ~suche sein** be looking for a job; **~süchtig** *Adj.* **~süchtig sein** be a compulsive worker *or* (coll.) a workaholic; **~tag** *der* working day; **mein erster ~tag nach dem Urlaub** my first day back at work after the holiday (Brit.) *or* (Amer.) vacation; **das war ein harter ~tag** that was a hard day's work; **~tagung** *die* conference; **~takt** *der* (Technik) power stroke; **~team** *das* team; **~technik** *die* work[ing] technique; **~teilig** A *Adj.* ‹*society, mode of production, etc.*› based on the division of labour; B *adv.* **die Produktion ~teilig gestalten** base production on the principle of the division of labour; **~teilung** *die* division of labour; **~tempo** *das* rate of work; work rate; **~therapie** *die* occupational therapy; **~tier** *das* 1 work animal; 2 (Arbeitssüchtiger) compulsive worker; workaholic (coll.); **~tisch** *der* work table; (für Schreibarbeiten) desk; (für technische Arbeiten) [work]bench; **~titel** *der* working title; **~überlastung** *die* overwork; **er klagt über ~überlastung** he complains that he's overworked

Arbeit-: ~suche *die* ► **Arbeitssuche**; **~suchende** *der/die; adj. Dekl.* person/man/woman looking for work; **die ~suchenden** those looking for work

arbeits-, Arbeits-: ~unfähig *Adj.* unable to work *postpos.*; (krankheitsbedingt) unfit for work *postpos.*; **die Arbeitsunfähigen** those unable to work/unfit for work; **~unfähigkeit** *die* ► **~unfähig**: inability to work; unfitness for work; **~un·fall** *der* industrial accident; **er hatte einen ~unfall** he had an accident at work; **~un·lust** *die* disinclination to work; **~unter·lage** *die* work paper; **das benutzt er als ~unterlage** he works from that; **~un·willig** *Adj.* unwilling to work *postpos.*; **~verfahren** *das* work process; **~verhältnis** *das* 1 *contractual relationship between employer and employee*; **ein ~verhältnis eingehen** enter employment; **in einem ~verhältnis stehen** be in employment; 2 *Pl.* working conditions; conditions of work; **~vermittlung** *die* 1 (Tätigkeit) arranging employment; 2 (Stelle) employment exchange; job centre (Brit.); (Firma) employment agency; **~verteilung** *die* allocation of [the] work; **~vertrag** *der* contract of employment; **~verweigerung** *die* refusal to work; **~vor·gang** *der* work process; **~vor·lage** *die*: **eine Skizze als ~vorlage benutzen** work from a sketch; **dieses Buch hat ihm als ~vorlage gedient** he worked from that book; **~weise** *die* 1 way *or* method of working; 2 (Funktionsweise) mode of operation; **~welt** *die* world of work; **~willig** *Adj.* **~willig sein** be willing to work; **~willige Kollegen** fellow employees who are willing to work; **~wissenschaft** *die* ergonomics *sing.*; **~woche** *die* 1 week's work; **während seiner ersten ~woche** during his first week at work; 2 (wöchentliche ~zeit) working week; **~wut** *die* fit of work-mania; **~wütig** *Adj.* **~wütig sein** suffer from work-mania; **~zeit** *die* 1 working hours *pl.*; **während der ~zeit** during working hours; **die ~zeit beginnt um 8 Uhr** work starts at 8 o'clock; 2 working time; **die tägliche/wöchentliche ~zeit** the working day/week; 3 (als Ware) labour time; **2 Stunden ~zeit** two hours' labour; **wir berechnen keine ~zeit** we don't charge for labour; **ich lasse mir die ~zeit bezahlen** I charge for my time; **~zeit·verkürzung** *die* reduction in working hours; **~zeug** *das* 1 work things *pl.*; 2 (Kleidung) work[ing] things *pl. or* clothes *pl.*; **~zeugnis** *das* reference [from one's employer]; **~zimmer** *das* study

arbiträr /arbiˈtrɛːɐ̯/ (geh.)
A *Adj.* arbitrary
B *adv.* in an arbitrary way; arbitrarily

archaisch /arˈçaːɪʃ/
A *Adj.* archaic
B *adv.* in an archaic way; archaically

archaisieren *itr. V.* (geh.) archaize; **eine ~de Sprache verwenden** use *or* employ an archaistic *or* a deliberately archaic style

Archaismus *der;* **~, Archaismen** (Sprachw., Stilk., Kunstw.) archaism

Archäologe /arçeoˈloːgə/ *der;* **~n, ~n** ► S. 113 archaeologist

Archäologie *die;* **~**: archaeology *no art.*

Archäologin *die;* **~, ~nen** ► S. 113 archaeologist

archäologisch
A *Adj.* archaeological
B *adv.* archaeologically

Arche /ˈarçə/ *die;* **~, ~n** ark; **die ~ Noah** Noah's Ark

Arche·typ *der* (Psych., Philos.) archetype

arche·typisch (Psych., Philos.)
A *Adj.* archetypal
B *adv.* archetypally

Arche·typus *der* ► **Archetyp**

Archimedes /arçiˈmeːdɛs/ (*der*) Archimedes

archimedisch *Adj.* Archimedean; **das ~e Prinzip** Archimedes' Principle

Archipel /arçiˈpeːl/ *der;* **~s, ~e** archipelago; **„der ~ Gulag"** 'the Gulag archipelago'

Architekt /arçiˈtɛkt/ *der;* **~en, ~en** ► S. 113 architect

Architekten·büro *das* 1 architect's office 2 (Firma) firm of architects

Architektin *die;* **~, ~nen** ► S. 113 architect

Architektonik /arçitɛkˈtoːnɪk/ *die;* **~, ~en** architectonics *sing., no art.*

architektonisch
A *Adj.* architectonic
B *adv.* architectonically

Architektur /arçitɛkˈtuːɐ̯/ *die;* **~, ~en** 1 architecture 2 (Bauwerk) edifice

Archiv /arˈçiːf/ *das;* **~s, ~e** archives *pl.*; archive

Archivalien /arçiˈvaːli̯ən/ *Pl.* papers and documents in/from the archives

Archivar /arçiˈvaːɐ̯/ *der;* **~s, ~e, Archivarin** *die;* **~, ~nen** ► S. 113 archivist

Archiv·bild *das* archive picture *or* photograph

archivieren *tr. V.* **etw. ~**: archive sth.; put sth. in the archives

Archivierung *die;* **~, ~en** archiving

ARD *Abk.* = **Arbeitsgemeinschaft der öffentlich-rechtlichen Rundfunkanstalten der Bundesrepublik Deutschland** *national radio and television network in Germany*

> **ARD — Arbeitsgemeinschaft der öffentlich-rechtlichen Rundfunkanstalten der Bundesrepublik Deutschland**
>
> An umbrella organization for the regional broadcasting stations of the various German **Länder**, financed by licence fees plus a certain amount of advertising. The *ARD* broadcasts **Das Erste**.

Ardennen /arˈdɛnən/ *Pl.* **die ~**: the Ardennes

Ardennen·offensive *die* (hist.) Ardennes offensive

Are /ˈaːrə/ *die;* **~, ~n** (schweiz.) ► **Ar**

Areal /areˈaːl/ *das;* **~s, ~e** 1 area 2 (Grundstück) grounds *pl.* 3 (Biol.) range

areligiös *Adj.* areligious

Aren ► **Ära**

Arena /aˈreːna/ *die;* **~, Arenen** 1 (hist., Sport, fig.) arena 2 (Stierkampf~) bullring 3 (Manege) [circus] ring

Areopag /areoˈpaːk/ *der;* **~s** (hist.) Areopagus

arg /ark/, **ärger** /ˈɛrgɐ/, **ärgst...** /ˈɛrgst .../
A *Adj.* 1 (geh., landsch.: schlimm) bad ‹*weather, condition, state*›; serious ‹*situation, wound*›; hard ‹*times*›; extremely hackneyed ‹*cliché*›; **etw. noch ärger machen** make sth. worse; **an nichts Arges denken** be completely unsuspecting; **das Ärgste befürchten** fear the worst; **wenn es zum Ärgsten kommt** if the worst comes to the worst; **im ~en liegen** be in a sorry state 2 (geh. veralt.: böse) wicked; evil; **es ist nichts Arges an ihm** there is no malice in him 3 (geh., landsch.: unangenehm groß, stark) severe ‹*pain, hunger, shock*›; severe, bitter ‹*disappointment*›; serious ‹*dilemma, error*›; extreme, (coll.) terrible ‹*embarrassment*›; gross ‹*exaggeration, injustice*›; heavy ‹*drinker*›; **in ~er Bedrängnis/Not sein** be in desperate straits; **mein ärgster Feind** my worst enemy *or* arch-enemy; **unser ärgster Konkurrent** our most dangerous competitor; **es herrschte ein ~es Gedränge** there was a dreadful crush (coll.)

a

B *adv.* (geh., landsch.) extremely, (coll.) awfully, (coll.) terribly ‹*painful, cold, steep, expensive, heavy, etc.*›; severely, bitterly ‹*disappointed*›; extremely, (coll.) terribly ‹*embarassed*›; ‹*suffer, weaken*› severely; ‹*offend*› deeply; ‹*deceive*› badly; ‹*rain, pull, punch*› hard; ‹*hurt*› a great deal; **der Garten ist ~ verwahrlost** the garden is badly neglected; **sich ~ blamieren** make a complete fool of oneself; **ihr treibt es gar zu ~!** you're going too far!; **etwas ~ laut** a bit too loud; **ich hab ihn ~ gern** I like him very much *or* (coll.) an awful lot; **hast du es ~ eilig?** are you in a great *or* (coll.) terrible hurry?; **es geht ihm ~ schlecht/gut** things are going really badly/well for him; **Schmeckt dir das Bier? — Nicht so ~:** Do you like the beer? — Not that much

Arg *das;* **~s** (geh. veralt.) malice; **kein ~ an der Sache finden** see no harm in it

Argentinien /argɛnˈtiːni̯ən/ (*das*); **~s** Argentina; the Argentine

Argentinier *der;* **~s, ~, Argentinierin** *die;* **~, ~nen** ▸ⓘ **S. 520** Argentinian; Argentine; *s. auch* **-in**

argentinisch *Adj.* ▸ⓘ **S. 520** Argentinian; Argentine

ärger ▸**arg**

Ärger /ˈɛrgɐ/ *der;* **~s** [1] annoyance; (Zorn) anger; **etw. erregt jmds. ~:** sth. annoys sb.; **seinem ~ Luft machen** vent one's anger; **seinen ~ an jmdm. auslassen** vent one's anger on sb. [2] (Unannehmlichkeiten) trouble; **häuslicher/beruflicher ~:** domestic problems *pl.*/problems *pl.* at work; **[jmdm.] ~ machen** cause [sb.] trouble; make trouble [for sb.]; **so ein ~!** how annoying!; **~ bekommen** get into trouble; **sonst gibt es ~:** otherwise there'll be trouble!

ärgerlich
A *Adj.* [1] annoyed; (zornig) angry; **ein ~es Gesicht machen** look annoyed/angry; **~ über jmdn. sein** be annoyed at/angry with sb.; **~ über etw.** (*Akk.*) **sein** be annoyed/angry about sth.; **~ über sich selbst** annoyed/angry at oneself; **~ werden** get angry/annoyed [2] (Ärger erregend) annoying; irritating; **wie ~!** how annoying!
B *adv.* [1] with annoyance; (zornig) angrily [2] (Ärger erregend) annoyingly; irritatingly

Ärgerlichkeit *die;* **~** [1] annoyance; (Zorn) anger [2] (einer Sache) troublesomeness; **bei aller ~ war es doch von Vorteil** even though it was annoying, it was still an advantage

ärgern
A *tr. V.* [1] **jmdn. ~:** annoy sb.; (zornig machen) make sb. angry; **so was ärgert einen natürlich** that sort of thing is annoying, of course [2] (reizen, necken) tease
B *refl. V.* get annoyed; (zornig werden) get angry; (verärgert sein) be annoyed/angry; **sich über jmdn. ~:** get annoyed/angry at sb.; **sich zu Tode ~** (fig.) be annoyed/angry to the point of distraction; **sich schwarz** *od.* **grün und blau ~:** fret and fume; **nicht ~, nur wundern!** (ugs.) there's no point in getting worked *or* (coll.) het up about it

Ärgernis *das;* **~ses, ~se** [1] offence; **Erregung öffentlichen ~ses** (Rechtsspr.) creating a public nuisance [2] (etw. Ärgerliches) annoyance; irritation; **häusliche/berufliche ~se** minor domestic troubles/irritations and annoyances at work [3] (etw. Anstößiges) nuisance; (etw. Skandalöses) scandal; outrage

arg-, Arg-: ~list *die* (geh.) (Hinterlist) guile; deceit; (Heimtücke, Rechtsw.) malice; **~listig** **A** *Adj.* (hinterlistig) guileful; deceitful; deceitful ‹*plan*›; (heimtückisch) malicious; crafty ‹*smile*›; **~listige Täuschung** (Rechtsspr.) malicious deception; **B** *adv.* (hinterlistig) guilefully; deceitfully; (heimtückisch) maliciously; ‹*smile*› craftily; **~listigkeit** *die;* **~~, ~~en** [1] (Hinterlistigkeit) guilefulness; deceitfulness; (eines Plans, einer Absicht) deceitfulness; (Heimtücke) malice; [2] (arglistige Handlung) ▸**arglistig 1**: guileful *or* deceitful/malicious act; **~los** **A** *Adj.* [1] guileless ‹*person*›; guileless, innocent ‹*question, remark*›; [2] (ohne Argwohn) unsuspecting; **~los, wie ich war …** all unsuspecting as I was …; **wie kannst du nur so ~los sein?** how can you be so naive?; **B** *adv.* [1] guilelessly; innocently; [2] (ohne Argwohn) unsuspectingly; **~losigkeit** *die;* **~** [1] (eines Menschen) guilelessness; (einer Äußerung, Absicht) innocence; **ich bin von seiner ~losigkeit überzeugt** I'm convinced he is not being deceitful/malicious; [2] (Vertrauensseligkeit) unsuspecting nature

Argon /ˈargɔn/ *das;* **~s** (Chemie) argon

ärgst… ▸**arg**

Argument /arguˈmɛnt/ *das;* **~[e]s, ~e** (auch Math.) argument

Argumentation /argumɛntaˈtsi̯oːn/ *die;* **~, ~en** argumentation

argumentativ /argumɛntaˈtiːf/
A *Adj.* **ein ~er Wahlkampf** an election campaign marked by reasoned argument; **eine rein ~e Auseinandersetzung** a conflict based solely on reasoned argument
B *adv.* by [reasoned] argument; **er ist ihr ~ überlegen** he is superior to her in argument

argumentieren *itr. V.* argue; **damit kannst du nicht ~!** you can't use that as an argument

Argus·augen /ˈargʊs-/ *Pl.* (geh.) eagle eye *sing.*; **jmdn. mit ~ beobachten** watch sb. like a hawk

Argwohn /ˈarkvoːn/ *der;* **~[e]s** suspicion; **jmds. ~ erregen/zerstreuen** arouse/allay sb.'s suspicions *pl.*; **~ gegen jmdn. hegen** be suspicious of sb.; *s. auch* **schöpfen A 3**

argwöhnen /ˈarkvøːnən/ *tr. V.* (geh.) suspect; **sie argwöhnten einen Verräter in ihm** they suspected him of being a traitor

argwöhnisch (geh.)
A *Adj.* suspicious
B *adv.* suspiciously

Aridität /aridiˈtɛːt/ *die;* **~** (Geogr.) aridity

Arie /ˈaːri̯ə/ *die;* **~, ~n** aria

Arier /ˈaːri̯ɐ/ *der;* **~s, ~, Arierin** *die;* **~, ~nen** (Völkerk., Sprachw., ns.) Aryan

arisch *Adj.* (Völkerk., Sprachw., ns.) Aryan

arisieren *tr. V.* (ns.) Aryanize

Aristokrat /arɪstoˈkraːt/ *der;* **~en, ~en** aristocrat

Aristokratie /arɪstokraˈtiː/ *die;* **~, ~n** aristocracy

Aristokratin *die;* **~, ~nen** aristocrat

aristokratisch
A *Adj.* aristocratic
B *adv.* aristocratically

Aristoteles /arɪsˈtoːtelɛs/ (*der*) Aristotle

Aristoteliker /arɪstoˈteːlikɐ/ *der;* **~s, ~, Aristotelikerin** *die;* **~, ~nen** Aristotelian

aristotelisch *Adj.* Aristotelian

Arithmetik /arɪtˈmeːtɪk/ *die;* **~, ~en** [1] arithmetic *no art.* [2] (Buch) textbook on arithmetic

arithmetisch
A *Adj.* arithmetical
B *adv.* arithmetically

Arkade /arˈkaːdə/ *die;* **~, ~n** [1] arch; **in** *od.* **unter den ~n** under the arcade [2] (Bogenreihe, Gang) arcade

arkadisch *Adj.* (dichter.) Arcadian

Arktis /ˈarktɪs/ *die;* **~** (Geogr.) **die ~:** the Arctic

arktisch
A *Adj.* (auch fig.) arctic
B *adv.* **das Klima ist ~ beeinflusst** the climate is influenced by the Arctic

Arkus /ˈarkʊs/ *der;* **~, ~** /ˈarkuːs/ (Geom.) arc

arm /arm/, **ärmer** /ˈɛrmɐ/, **ärmst…** /ˈɛrmst…/ *Adj.* (auch fig.) poor; **wir sind um 100 Euro ärmer** we are 100 euros worse off *or* [the] poorer; **Arm und Reich** (veralt.) rich and poor [alike]; **die Gegensätze zwischen Arm und Reich** the differences between rich and poor; **selig sind, die da geistlich ~ sind** (bibl.) blessed are the poor in spirit; **um etw. ärmer sein/werden** have lost/lose sth.; **~ an Bodenschätzen/Nährstoffen** poor in mineral resources/nutrients; **das Gebiet ist ~ an Wasser** the area is short of water; **~ an Vitaminen sein** ‹*food*› be lacking in *or* low in vitamins; **der/die Ärmste** *od.* **Arme** the poor man/boy/woman/girl; **ach, du Armer** *od.* **Ärmster!** (meist iron.) oh, you poor thing!; **ich Armer!** (dichter. veralt.) woe is me!; *s. auch* **dran 2**

Arm *der;* **~[e]s, ~e** [1] ▸ⓘ **S. 435** arm; **jmdn. am ~ führen** lead sb. by the arm; **er nahm** *od.* (geh.) **schloss sie in die ~e** he took her in his arms; **jmdm. in die ~e fallen** *od.* (geh.) **sinken** fall *or* sink into sb.'s arms; **nimm mich auf den ~!** carry me!; **etw. unter den ~ nehmen** put sth. under one's arm; **einen Mantel über dem ~ tragen** carry a coat over one's arm; **jmds. ~ nehmen** take sb.'s arm; take sb. by the arm; **jmdm. den ~ bieten** (geh.) offer sb. one's arm; **jmdn. im ~ halten** embrace sb.; **sich** (*Dat.*) **in den ~en liegen** lie in each other's *or* one another's arms; **sich aus jmds. ~en lösen** (geh.) free oneself from sb.'s embrace; **er hat einen langen ~** (fig.) his power and influence extend a long way; **den längeren ~ haben** (fig. ugs.) have more clout (coll.); **jmds. verlängerter ~ sein** (fig.) be sb.'s tool *or* instrument; **jmdn. auf den ~ nehmen** (fig. ugs.) have sb. on (Brit. coll.); pull sb.'s leg; **jmdm. in den ~ fallen** (fig.) stay sb.'s hand; **jmdm. in die ~e laufen** bump *or* run into sb.; **er ist mir in die ~e gelaufen** I bumped *or* ran into him; **jmdn. jmdm. in die ~e treiben** drive sb. into sb.'s arms; **jmdn. dem Alkoholismus/Terrorismus in die ~e treiben** drive sb. to alcoholism/to adopt terrorist tactics; **sich jmdm. in die ~e werfen** throw oneself into sb.'s arms; **jmdn. mit offenen ~en aufnehmen** *od.* **empfangen** welcome sb. with open arms; **jmdm. [mit etw.] unter die ~e greifen** help sb. out [with sth.]; **jmdn. am steifen ~ verhungern lassen** (salopp) put the screws (coll.) *or* (coll.) squeeze on sb.; **ein ~/zwei ~e voll Reisig** an armful/two armfuls of brushwood; *s. auch* **Bein 1** [2] (armartiger Teil) arm; (einer Waage) beam [3] (Ärmel) arm; sleeve; **ein Hemd/eine Bluse mit halbem ~:** a short-sleeved shirt/blouse

Armada /arˈmaːda/ *die;* **~, Armaden** *u.* **~s** (auch fig.) armada

arm·amputiert *Adj.* ‹*person*› with an *or* one arm/both [his/her] arms amputated; **er ist ~:** he has had an arm/both [his] arms amputated

Armatur /armaˈtuːɐ̯/ *die;* **~, ~en** (Technik) [1] fitting [2] (im Kfz) instrument

Armaturen·brett *das* instrument panel; (im Kfz) dashboard

Arm-: ~band *das; Pl.* **~bänder** bracelet; (Uhr~) strap; **~band·uhr** *die* wristwatch; **~beuge** *die* ▸ⓘ **S. 435** [1] inside of the/one's elbow; crook of the/one's arm; [2] (Turnen) press-up (Brit.); push-up; **~bewegung** *die* arm movement; **~binde** *die* [1] armband; [2] (Med.) sling; **~bruch** *der* fracture of the arm; **er wurde mit einem ~bruch ins Krankenhaus gebracht** he was taken to hospital with a fractured arm; **~brust** *die* crossbow

Ärmchen /ˈɛrmçən/ *das;* **~s, ~:** [little] arm

Arme *der/die; adj. Dekl.* poor man/woman; pauper; **die ~n** the poor *pl*; *s. auch* **arm**

Armee /arˈmeː/ *die;* **~, ~n** [1] (Streitkräfte) armed forces *pl.* [2] (Landstreitkräfte, Verband, fig.) army

Armee-: ~fahrzeug *das* army vehicle; **~korps** *das* army corps

Ärmel /ˈɛrml̩/ *der;* **~s, ~:** sleeve; **die ~ hochkrempeln** (fig. ugs.) roll up one's sleeves; **[sich** (*Dat.*)**] etw. aus dem ~ schütteln** (ugs.) produce sth. just like that; **leck mich am ~!** (salopp verhüll.) get stuffed (Brit. sl.)

Ärmel·auf·schlag *der* cuff

Armeleute-: ~essen *das* poor man's food; **~geruch** *der* smell of poverty; **~viertel** *das* poor district

Ärmel·halter *der* sleeve band

Ärmel·kanal *der* (Geogr.) **der ~:** the [English] Channel

Ärmel·schoner *der;* **~s, ~, Ärmel·schützer** *der;* **~s, ~:** oversleeve

Armen-: ~haus *das* (hist., fig.) poorhouse; **Irland war das ~haus Europas** (fig.) Ireland was the poor man of Europe; **~häusler** *der;*

a

~~s, ~~, ~häuslerin *die;* ~~, ~~nen (hist.) inmate of the poorhouse

Armenien /ar'me:niən/ *(das);* ~s Armenia

Armenier *der;* ~s, ~, **Armenierin** *die;* ~, ~nen ▸ⓘ S. 520 Armenian

armenisch *Adj.* ▸ⓘ S. 520, ▸ⓘ S. 670 Armenian; *s. auch* **deutsch, Deutsch**

Armen-: **~kasse** *die* poor-relief fund; **~recht** *das* (Rechtsw.) right to legal aid; **~viertel** *das* poor district

Armensünder- (österr.) ▸**Armsünder-**

ärmer ▸**arm**

Arme·sünder, Arme·sünderin ▸**Sünder**

Armesünder·glocke *die* ▸**Armsünderglocke**

armieren *tr. V.* 1 (Milit. veralt.) arm 2 (Technik) reinforce ‹*concrete*›; armour, sheathe ‹*cable*›

-armig *adj.* -armed; **sieben~:** seven-armed ‹*candelabrum*›; **dick~** ‹*person*› with fat arms

Arm-: **~länge** *die* arm length; (Abstand) arm's length; **ein Stück von ~länge** a piece the length of an *or* one's arm; **~lehne** *die* armrest; **~leuchter** *der* 1 candelabra; 2 (ugs. verhüll.) berk (Brit. coll.); jerk (coll.)

ärmlich /'ɛrmlɪç/

A *Adj.* cheap ‹*clothing*›; shabby ‹*flat, office*›; meagre ‹*meal*›; **in ~en Verhältnissen leben** live in impoverished circumstances; **aus ~en Verhältnissen** from a poor family

B *adv.* cheaply ‹*dressed, furnished*›; **~ leben/wohnen** live in impoverished circumstances

Ärmlichkeit *die;* ~ 1 ▸**ärmlich 1:** cheapness; shabbiness; meagreness 2 (Armut) poverty

Ärmling /'ɛrmlɪŋ/ *der;* ~s, ~e oversleeve

Arm-: **~loch** *das* 1 armhole; 2 (salopp verhüll.) berk (Brit. coll.); jerk (coll.); **~muskel** *der* ▸ⓘ S. 435 arm muscle; **~prothese** *die* artificial arm; arm prosthesis (Med.); **~reif** *der* armlet; **~schiene** *die* 1 (hist.) (für den Oberarm) brassard; (für den Unterarm) vambrace; 2 (Med.) arm splint

arm·selig

A *Adj.* 1 (sehr arm, dürftig, unbefriedigend) miserable; miserable, wretched ‹*dwelling*›; pathetic ‹*result, figure*›; meagre ‹*meal, food*›; paltry ‹*return, salary, sum, fee*›; **~e 10 Euro** a paltry 10 euros 2 (abwertend: erbärmlich) miserable, wretched ‹*swindler, quack*›; pathetic, miserable, wretched ‹*coward*›; pathetic, miserable ‹*amateur, bungler*›

B *adv.* **~ leben** lead *or* live a miserable life; **~ eingerichtet** miserably *or* wretchedly furnished

Armseligkeit *die;* ~ ▸**armselig A:** miserableness; wretchedness; patheticness; meagreness; paltriness

Arm·sessel *der* armchair

ärmst... ▸**arm**

Arm-: **~stuhl** *der* armchair; **~stumpf** *der* stump of the/one's arm

Armsünder-: **~glocke** *die* (hist.) *bell tolled during an execution;* **~miene** *die* (scherzh.) expression of misery and remorse

Armut /'armu:t/ *die;* ~ (auch fig.) poverty; **die ~ des Landes an Rohstoffen** (fig.) the country's lack of raw materials; **geistige ~** (fig.) lack of culture; cultural poverty

Armuts-: **~falle** *die* poverty trap; **~grenze** *die* (Soziol.) poverty line; **~risiko** *das* (Soziol.) risk of poverty; **~zeugnis** *das:* **in ein ~ zeugnis sein** be a sign of inadequacy; **jmdm. ein ~ zeugnis ausstellen** expose sb.'s inadequacy

***Armvoll** *der;* ~, ~: armful; **zwei ~ Reisig** two armfuls of brushwood

Arnika /'arnika/ *die;* ~, ~s arnica

Arom /a'ro:m/ *das;* ~s, ~e (dichter.) ▸**Aroma 1**

Aroma /a'ro:ma/ *das;* ~s, **Aromen** *od.* (veralt.) **Aromata** 1 (Duft) aroma; (Geschmack) flavour; taste 2 (Substanz, Essenz) flavouring

aromatisch /aro'ma:tɪʃ/ *Adj.* 1 (duftend) aromatic; **~ duften** give off an aromatic fragrance 2 (wohlschmeckend) distinctive ‹*taste*›; **sehr ~ schmecken** have a very distinctive taste

aromatisieren *tr. V.* (wohlriechend machen) aromatize; (wohlschmeckend machen) flavour ‹*tea, ice cream, chewing gum, etc.*›

Aron[s]·stab /'a:rɔn(s)-/ *der* arum; **Gefleckter ~:** cuckoo-pint; lords-and-ladies

Arrak /'arak/ *der;* ~s, ~e *od.* ~s arrack

Arrangement /arãʒə'mã:/ *das;* ~s, ~s (geh., Mus.) arrangement; **ein ~ treffen** come to an arrangement; **~: Gil Evans** arranger: Gil Evans

Arrangeur /arã'ʒø:ɐ̯/ *der;* ~s, ~e, **Arrangeurin** *die;* ~, ~nen (Musik) arranger

arrangieren /arã'ʒi:rən/

A *tr. V.* (geh., Musik) arrange

B *itr. V.* (Musik) **er kann gut ~:** he's a good arranger

C *refl. V.* **sich ~:** adapt, adjust; **sich mit jmdm. ~:** come to an accommodation with sb.; **sich mit etw. ~:** come to terms with sth.

Arrest /a'rɛst/ *der;* ~[e]s, ~e 1 (Milit., Rechtsw., Schule) detention; **einen Schüler mit ~ bestrafen** (veralt.) punish a pupil by putting him in detention 2 (Zivilrecht) **persönlicher ~:** attachment; **dinglicher ~:** attachment; distraint; **etw. unter ~ stellen** *od.* **mit ~ belegen** attach sth.

Arrestant /arɛs'tant/ *der;* ~en, ~en, **Arrestantin** *die* ~, ~nen detainee

Arrest·zelle *die* detention cell

arretieren /are'ti:rən/ *tr. V.* 1 *auch itr.* lock 2 (veralt.: festnehmen) detain; arrest

Arretierung *die;* ~, ~en 1 locking 2 (Vorrichtung) latch 3 (veralt.: Festnahme) detention; arrest

Arrhythmie /aryt'mi:/ *die;* ~, ~n ▸ⓘ S. 439 (Med.) arrhythmia

arrivieren /ari'vi:rən/ *itr. V.; mit sein* (geh.) arrive; **zum Superstar/zum Staatsfeind Nummer eins ~:** achieve superstar status/ become public enemy number one; **ein arrivierter Schriftsteller** a successful writer; (abwertend) a parvenu writer

Arrivierte *der/die; adj. Dekl.* (geh.) man/woman who has/had arrived; (abwertend: Emporkömmling) parvenu

arrogant /aro'gant/ (abwertend)

A *Adj.* arrogant

B *adv.* arrogantly

Arroganz /aro'gants/ *die;* ~ (abwertend) arrogance

arrondieren /arɔn'di:rən/ *tr. V.* (geh.) round off ‹*property, territory, etc.*›

Arsch /arʃ/ *der;* ~[e]s, **Ärsche** /'ɛrʃə/ (derb) 1 arse (Brit. coarse); bum (Brit. coll.); ass (Amer. coarse); **den ~ voll kriegen** get a bloody good hiding (Brit. sl.); **der ~ der Welt** (fig.) the back of beyond; **ihm geht der ~ mit Grundeis** (fig.) he is scared shitless (coarse); he is shitting himself (coarse); **den ~ offen haben** (fig.) be round the bloody twist (Brit. sl.); be crazy; **den ~ zukneifen** (fig.) kick the bucket (sl.); croak (sl.); **jmdm. den ~ aufreißen** (fig.) make sb. sweat blood; **jmdn. am ~ haben** (fig.) have sb. by the short and curlies (Brit. sl.); have sb. by the balls (coarse); **leck mich am ~!** (fig.) piss off (sl.); get stuffed (Brit. sl.); (verflucht noch mal!; na, so was!) bugger me! (coarse); **er kann mich [mal] am ~ lecken** (fig.) he can piss off (sl.); he can kiss my arse (Brit. coarse) *or* ass (Amer. sl.); **auf den ~ fallen** (fig.) come unstuck (coll.); **sich auf den ~ setzen** (fig.) (fleißig arbeiten) get *or* pull one's finger out (coll.); (perplex sein) freak (coll.); **jmdm. in den ~ kriechen** (fig.) kiss sb.'s arse (Brit. coarse) *or* ass (Amer. sl.); **das kannst du dir in den ~ stecken** (fig.) you can shove it up your arse (Brit. coarse) *or* ass (Amer. sl.); **ich könnte mir in den ~ beißen** I could kick myself; **jmdn. in den ~ treten** kick sb. *or* give sb. a kick up the arse (Brit. coarse) *or* kick in the ass (Amer. sl.); (fig.) give sb. a kick up the backside; **im ~ sein** (fig.) be buggered (coarse); **ein [ganzer] ~ voll** (fig.) a hell of a lot 2 (widerlicher Mensch) arsehole (Brit. coarse); asshole (Amer. sl.); **~ mit Ohren** arsehole (Brit. coarse); asshole (Amer. sl.) 3 (nichts geltender Mensch) piece of dirt; **wir sind die Ärsche hier** we are just so much dirt here

arsch-, Arsch-: **~backe** *die* (derb) cheek (coll.) [of the/one's arse (Brit. coarse) *or* bum (Brit. coll.) *or* ass (Amer. sl.)]; **~ficker** *der;* ~~s, ~~ (vulg.) arse-fucker (Brit. coarse); bum-fucker (Brit. coarse); butt-fucker (Amer. coarse); **~geige** *die* (derb abwertend) arsehole (Brit. coarse); **~karte** *die* (derb.) **die ~karte ziehen/haben** get the dirty end of the stick (coll.); **~klar** *Adj.* (derb) bloody (Brit. sl.) *or* damned obvious; **Ich mache mit. Ist doch ~klar** I'm game. 'Course I bloody am (Brit. sl.); **~kriecher** *der,* **~kriecherin** *die* (derb abwertend) arse-licker (Brit. coarse); ass-licker (Amer. sl.); **~kriecherei** *die* (derb abwertend) arse-licking (Brit. coarse); ass-licking (Amer. sl.); **~loch** *das* (derb) 1 (widerlicher Mensch) arsehole (Brit. coarse); asshole (Amer. sl.); **Mensch, ich bin doch ein ~loch** what a stupid arse (Brit. coarse) *or* (Amer. sl.) ass I am; 2 (bedauernswerter Mensch) poor bloody sod (Brit. sl.); poor bastard; **~-und-Titten-Presse** *die* (salopp) tit-and-bum press (Brit. sl.); tit-and-ass press (Amer. sl.); **~wisch** *der* (derb abwertend) useless piece of paper

Arsen /ar'ze:n/ *das;* ~s arsenic

Arsenal /arze'na:l/ *das;* ~s, ~e arsenal

arsen·haltig *Adj.* containing arsenic *postpos., not pred.;* arsenical; **~/stark ~ sein** contain arsenic/have a high arsenic content

Arsenik /ar'ze:nɪk/ *das;* ~s arsenic; arsenic trioxide

Art /a:ɐ̯t/ *die;* ~, ~en 1 (Sorte) kind; sort; (Biol.: Spezies) species; **Tische/Bücher aller ~:** tables/books of all kinds *or* sorts; all kinds *or* sorts of tables/books; **einzig in seiner ~:** unique of its kind; **ein Verbrecher übelster ~:** the worst sort *or* kind of criminal; **jede ~ von Gewalt ablehnen** reject all forms of violence; **diese ~ [von] Menschen** that kind *or* sort of person; people like that; **[so] eine ~ ...** a sort *or* kind of ...; **aus der ~ schlagen** not be true to type; (in einer Familie) be different from all the rest of the family; **in der ~ eines Gorillas** like a gorilla 2 (Wesen) nature; (Verhaltensweise) manner; way; **es liegt nicht in ihrer ~** *od.* **ist nicht ihre ~, das zu tun** it's not [in] her nature to do that; **das entspricht nicht seiner ~:** it's not [in] his nature; that's not his way 3 (gutes Benehmen) behaviour; **das ist doch keine ~!** that's no way to behave!; **was ist denn das für eine ~?** what sort of behaviour is that?; **die feine englische ~** (ugs.) the proper way to behave 4 (Weise) way; **auf diese ~:** in this way; **auf verschiedene ~en** in various ways; **auf welche ~?** in what way?; **auf grausamste ~:** in the cruellest way; **in einer ~:** in a way; **die richtige ~, darauf zu reagieren** the right way to react to it; **auf die eine oder andere ~:** in one way or another; **~ und Weise** way; **seine ~ und Weise zu arbeiten** his way of working; **Schweinesteak nach ~ des Hauses** (Kochk.) pork steak à la maison; **nach Schweizer** *od.* **auf schweizerische ~** (Kochk.) Swiss style; **dass es eine ~ hat/hatte** (veralt.) with a vengeance

Art·angabe *die* (Sprachw.) adverb of manner; (Phrase) adverbial phrase of manner

Artefakt /arte'fakt/ *das;* ~[e]s, ~e (geh.) artefact

art·eigen *Adj.* (Biol.) species-specific

arten-, Arten-: **~barriere** *die,* **~grenze** *die* (Biol.) species barrier; **~reich** *Adj.* (Biol.) species-rich; **~reichtum** *der* (Biol.) species-richness; **~schranke** *die* (Biol.) species barrier; **~schutz** *der* protection of species; species protection; **~vielfalt** *die* (Biol.) biodiversity

art·erhaltend *Adj.* (Biol., Verhaltensf.) species-preserving

Art·erhaltung *die* (Biol., Verhaltensf.) preservation of the species

Arterie /ar'te:ri̯ə/ *die;* ~, ~n ▸ⓘ S. 435 artery

arteriell /arte'ri̯ɛl/ *Adj.* (Anat.) arterial

Arterien·verkalkung *die* ▸ⓘ S. 439 hardening of the arteries; arteriosclerosis (Med.)

Arterio·sklerose /arteri̯o-/ *die* ▸ⓘ S. 439 (Med.) arteriosclerosis

artesisch /ar'te:zɪʃ/ *Adj.* *in* **~er Brunnen** artesian well

art-, Art-: ~fremd *Adj.* (Biol.) foreign [to a/the species]; **~genosse** *der,* **~genossin** *die* conspecific; creature of the same species; **~gerecht** **A** *Adj.* appropriate for *or* to the species *postpos.*; **B** *adv.* in a way appropriate for *or* to the species **~gleich** *Adj.* (Biol.) ‹*animal, individual*› of the same species

Arthritis /ar'tri:tɪs/ *die;* **~, Arthritiden** ▸ⓘ **S. 439** (Med.) arthritis

arthritisch *Adj.* (Med.) arthritic

Arthrose /ar'tro:zə/ *die;* **~, ~n** ▸ⓘ **S. 439** (Med.) arthrosis

artifiziell /artifi'tsi̯ɛl/ (geh.)
A *Adj.* artificial
B *adv.* artificially

artig
A *Adj.* [1] well-behaved; good; **sei ~:** be good; be a good boy/girl/dog *etc.* [2] (geh. veralt.: höflich) courteous [3] (veralt.: nett) charming
B *adv.* [1] **sich ~ benehmen** be good; behave well [2] (geh. veralt.: höflich) courteously [3] (veralt.: nett) charmingly

-artig
A *Adj.* **marmor~/gold~:** marble-like/gold-like
B *adv.* **sich explosions~ vermehren** increase explosively; **sich kegel~ verjüngen** taper like a cone

Artigkeit *die;* **~, ~en** [1] (geh. veralt.) courteousness [2] (Redensart) pleasantry; (Kompliment) compliment; **jmdm. ~en sagen** say nice things to sb./pay sb. compliments

Artikel /ar'ti:kl̩/ *der;* **~s, ~** [1] article [2] (Ware) article; item

Artikulation /artikula'tsi̯o:n/ *die;* **~, ~en** articulation

artikulieren
A *tr., itr. V.* articulate; enunciate; (Sprachw., geh.: zum Ausdruck bringen) articulate
B *refl. V.* [1] (sich ausdrücken) express oneself [2] (zum Ausdruck kommen) express itself; be expressed

Artillerie /artɪlə'ri:/ *die;* **~, ~n** artillery

Artillerie·beschuss, ***Artilleriebeschuß** *der* artillery fire

Artillerist *der;* **~en, ~en** artilleryman

artilleristisch (Milit.)
A *Adj.* **~e Unterstützung** artillery support
B *adv.* **~ unterstützt werden** have artillery support

Artischocke /arti'ʃɔkə/ *die;* **~, ~n** artichoke

Artischocken·boden *der* artichoke bottom

Artist /ar'tɪst/ *der;* **~en, ~en** ▸ⓘ **S. 113** [1] [variety/circus] artiste *or* performer [2] (geh.: Virtuose) artist

Artistik *die;* **~** [1] circus/variety performance *no art.* [2] (Geschicklichkeit) skill [3] (geh.: formale Könnerschaft) artistry

Artistin *die;* **~, ~nen** ▸ⓘ **S. 113** ▸**Artist**

artistisch
A *Adj.* [1] **eine ~e Glanzleistung** a superb circus/variety performance; **sein ~es Können** his skill as a [circus/variety] artiste [2] (geschickt) masterly [3] (geh.: technisch perfekt) virtuoso *attrib.*
B *adv.* [1] **eine ~ anspruchsvolle Nummer** a circus/variety act of great virtuosity [2] (geschickt) in a masterly way *or* fashion [3] (geh.: technisch perfekt) with great artistry *or* virtuosity

Artothek /arto'te:k/ *die;* **~, ~en** art lending library

Artus /'artʊs/ *(der)* [King] Arthur

art·verwandt *Adj.* related

Arznei /a:ɐ̯ts'nai̯/ *die;* **~, ~en** (veralt.) medicine; medicament; (zur äußeren Anwendung) medicament; **eine bittere/heilsame ~ für jmdn. sein** (fig. ugs.) be a painful/salutary lesson for sb.

Arznei-: ~buch *das* pharmacopoeia; **~kunde** *die,* **~lehre** *die* pharmacology; **~mittel** *das* medicine; medicament; (zur äußeren Anwendung) medicament; **~mittel·budget** *das* (Politik) medicines budget; drugs budget; **~mittel·gesetz** *das: law relating to the manufacture and distribution of medicines;* **~mittel·missbrauch,** ***~mittel·mißbrauch** *der* abuse of medicines; **~mittel·sucht** *die* addiction to medicines; pharmacomania (Med.); **~schränkchen** *das* medicine cabinet

Arzt /a:ɐ̯tst/ *der;* **~es, Ärzte** ▸ⓘ **S. 113** /'ɛ:ɐ̯tstə/ doctor; physician (arch./formal); **zum ~ gehen** go to the doctor['s]; **Sie sollten mal zum ~ gehen** you ought to see a/the doctor; **praktischer ~,** (fachspr.) **~ für Allgemeinmedizin** general practitioner; GP; **..., wie vom ~ verordnet** ... as directed by a physician; **ein ~ für Kinder-/Frauenkrankheiten** a paediatrician/gynaecologist

Arzt·beruf *der* job of doctor; **in den ~ drängen** crowd into the medical profession; **den ~ ergreifen** become a doctor

Ärzte-: ~kammer *die: professional body of doctors;* ≈ General Medical Council (Brit.); **~muster** *das* medical sample

Ärzteschaft *die;* **~:** medical profession

Arzt-: ~frau *die* doctor's wife; **~helferin** *die* ▸ⓘ **S. 113** doctor's receptionist

Ärztin /'ɛ:ɐ̯tstɪn/ *die;* **~, ~nen** ▸ⓘ **S. 113** doctor; physician (formal); *s. auch* **Arzt; -in**

ärztlich /'ɛ:ɐ̯tstlɪç/
A *Adj.* medical; **auf ~e Verordnung** on doctor's orders; **alle ~e Kunst** all the doctor's/doctors' skill
B *adv.* **sich ~ behandeln lassen** have medical treatment; **„~ empfohlen"** 'recommended by doctors'

Arzt-: ~praxis *die* doctor's surgery (Brit.) *or* practice; **~rechnung** *die* doctor's bill; **~wahl** *die:* **das Recht der freien ~wahl** the right to choose one's doctor

as, As¹ /as/ *das;* **~, ~** (Musik) [key of] A flat

***As²** ▸**Ass¹**

A-Saite *die* (Musik) A-string

Asbest /as'bɛst/ *der;* **~[e]s, ~e** asbestos

Asbest-: ~anzug *der* asbestos suit; **~platte** *die* (für Töpfe) asbestos mat; (für Bügeleisen) asbestos stand

Asch·becher *der* ▸**Aschenbecher**

asch·blond *Adj.* ash blond

Asche /'aʃə/ *die;* **~, ~n** ash[es *pl.*]; (sterbliche Reste) ashes *pl.*; **in ~ liegen/legen** (fig. geh.) lie/lay in ashes; **sich ~ aufs Haupt streuen** (fig. geh.) wear sackcloth and ashes

Asch·eimer *der* (nordd.) rubbish *or* waste bin

Aschen-: ~bahn *die* (Sport) cinder track; **~becher** *der* ashtray

Aschen·brödel /-brø:dl̩/ *das;* **~s, ~** (auch fig.) Cinderella

Aschen-: ~eimer *der* (nordd.) ▸**Mülleimer**; **~platz** *der* (Tennis) cinder court

Aschen·puttel /-pʊtl̩/ *das;* **~s, ~** ▸**Aschenbrödel**

Aschen·regen *der* rain of ash

Ascher *der;* **~s, ~** (ugs.) ashtray

Ascher·mittwoch *der* Ash Wednesday

asch-: ~fahl *Adj.* ashen; **~grau** *Adj.* ash-grey; (**~fahl**) ashen

Ascorbin·säure /askɔr'bi:n-/ *die* ascorbic acid

As-Dur *das* (Musik) A flat major; *s. auch* **A-Dur**

Ase /'a:zə/ *der;* **~n, ~n** (germ. Myth.) one of the Aesir; **die ~n** the Aesir

äsen /ɛ:zn̩/ *itr. V.* (Jägerspr.) browse; (weiden) graze

aseptisch (Med.)
A *Adj.* aseptic
B *adv.* aseptically

Äser ▸**Aas**

asexuell
A *Adj.* asexual
B *adv.* asexually

Asiat /a'zi̯a:t/ *der;* **~en, ~en, Asiatin** *die;* **~, ~nen** Asian

asiatisch *Adj.* Asian; (ost**~**) Asian; oriental; **~ aussehen** have an Asiatic look about one

Asien /'a:zi̯ən/ *(das);* **~s** Asia

Askese /as'ke:zə/ *die;* **~:** asceticism

Asket /as'ke:t/ *der;* **~en, ~en, Asketin** *die;* **~, ~nen** ascetic

asketisch
A *Adj.* ascetic
B *adv.* ascetically

Äskulap·stab /ɛsku'la:p-/ *der* staff of Aesculapius

as-Moll *das* (Musik) A flat minor

Äsop /ɛ'zo:p/ *(der)* Aesop

asozial
A *Adj.* asocial; (gegen die Gesellschaft gerichtet) antisocial; **ein ~er Mensch** a social misfit
B *adv.* asocially; antisocially

Asoziale *der/die; adj. Dekl.* social misfit

Asparagus /as'pa:ragʊs/ *der;* **~** [1] (Bot.) asparagus [2] (Grün) asparagus fern

Aspekt /as'pɛkt/ *der;* **~[e]s, ~e** aspect

Asphalt /as'falt/ *der;* **~[e]s, ~e** asphalt

Asphalt·decke *die* (Straßenbau) asphalt surface

asphaltieren *tr. V.* asphalt

Asphalt-: ~literat *der* (ns. abwertend): *writer associated with urban rootlessness and decadence;* **~straße** *die* asphalt road

Aspik /as'pi:k/ *der* (österr. *auch* **das**); **~s, ~e** aspic

Aspirant /aspi'rant/ *der;* **~en, ~en, Aspirantin** *die;* **~, ~nen** [1] (Anwärter) candidate [2] (DDR: Wissenschaftler) research student (*with some teaching responsibilities*)

Aspiration /aspira'tsi̯o:n/ *die;* **~, ~en** (Sprachw.) aspiration

aspirieren
A *tr. V.* (Sprachw.) aspirate
B *itr. V.* (österr. geh.) **auf etw.** (*Akk.*) **~:** be a candidate for sth.

aß /a:s/ *1. u. 3. Pers. Sg. Prät. v.* **essen**

Ass¹, *Aß /as/ *das;* **Asses, Asse** ace

Ass², *Aß *das;* **Asses, Asse** (österr. ugs.: Abszess) boil

assanieren /asa'ni:rən/ *tr. V.* (österr.) clean up

äße /'ɛ:sə/ *1. u. 3. Pers. Sg. Konjunktiv II v.* **essen**

Assekuranz /aseku'rants/ *die;* **~, ~en** (Wirtsch.) assurance (Brit.); insurance

Assel /'asl̩/ *die;* **~, ~n** [1] (Zool.) isopod [2] (Keller**~**, Mauer**~**) woodlouse

Asservat /asɛr'va:t/ *das;* **~[e]s, ~e** (Rechtw.) exhibit

Assessor /a'sɛsɔr/ *der;* **~s, ~en** /asɛ'so:rən/, **Assessorin** *die;* **~, ~nen** ▸ⓘ **S. 113** *holder of a higher civil service post, e.g. teacher or lawyer, who has passed the necessary examinations but has not yet completed his/her probationary period; s. auch* **-in**

Assimilation /asimila'tsi̯o:n/ *die;* **~, ~en** (auch fachspr.) assimilation (**an** + *Akk.* to)

assimilieren (auch fachspr.)
A *tr. V.* assimilate
B *refl. V.* assimilate (**an** + *Akk.* to)

Assistent /asɪs'tɛnt/ *der;* **~en, ~en, Assistentin** *die;* **~, ~nen** ▸ⓘ **S. 113** assistant; *s. auch* **wissenschaftlich**; **-in**

Assistenz /asɪs'tɛnts/ *die;* **~, ~en** assistance

Assistenz-: ~arzt *der,* **~ärztin** *die* junior doctor; **~professor** *der,* **~professorin** *die* assistant professor; reader (Brit.)

assistieren *itr. V.* **[jmdm.] ~:** assist [sb.] (**bei** at)

Assonanz /aso'nants/ *die;* **~, ~en** (Verslehre) assonance

Assoziation /asotsi̯a'tsi̯o:n/ *die;* **~, ~en** association

Assoziations·freiheit *die* (Rechtsw.) freedom of association

assoziativ /asotsi̯a'ti:f/
A *Adj.* associative
B *adv.* associatively

assoziieren
A *tr. V.* (bes. Psych., geh.) associate; **bei einem Namen** *usw.* **etw. ~:** associate sth. with a name *etc.*
B *itr. V.* make associations; **frei ~:** free-associate

C *refl. V.* (sich an-, zusammenschließen) form an association; **der Sudan ist der EG assoziiert** the Sudan is associated with the EC

Assoziierungs·abkommen *das;* **~s, ~:** (EU) association agreement

Ast /ast/ *der;* **~[e]s, Äste** /'ɛstə/ **1** branch; bough; **den ~ absägen, auf dem man sitzt** (fig. ugs.) saw off the branch one is sitting on; **auf dem absteigenden ~ sein** (fig. ugs.) be going downhill **2** (in Holz) knot **3** (landsch.) (Rücken) back; (Buckel) hunchback; humpback; **sich** (*Dat.*) **einen ~ lachen** (ugs.) split one's sides [with laughter]

AStA /'asta/ *der;* **~[s], ~[s]** *od.* **Asten** *Abk.* **= Allgemeiner Studentenausschuss** ≈ Students' Union

AStA – Allgemeiner Studentenausschuss

A students' union which consists of 12 student boards elected by a student parliament that is voted in annually. AStA deals with all student issues, including financial, cultural and social concerns, offering advice and support.

Ästchen /'ɛstçən/ *das;* **~s, ~:** [small] branch

Aster /'astɐ/ *die;* **~, ~n** aster; (Herbst~) Michaelmas daisy

Ast·gabel *die* (zwischen Stamm und Ast) fork of a/the tree; (zwischen Ast und Zweig) fork of a/the branch

Ästhet /ɛs'te:t/ *der;* **~en, ~en, Ästhetin** *die;* **~, ~nen** aesthete

Ästhetik /ɛs'te:tɪk/ *die;* **~, ~en** **1** aesthetics *sing.* **2** (Buch) [book on] aesthetics **3** (das Ästhetische) aesthetics *pl;* (Schönheitssinn) aesthetic sense; **er hat keinen Sinn für ~:** he has no aesthetic sense

ästhetisch
A *Adj.* aesthetic
B *adv.* aesthetically

ästhetisieren *tr.* (*auch itr.*) *V.* (geh.) aestheticize

Ästhetizismus *der;* **~** (geh.) aestheticism

ästhetizistisch *Adj.* (geh.) aestheticist; aestheticizing *attrib.*

Asthma /'astma/ *das;* **~s ▸❶ S. 439** asthma

Asthmatiker /ast'ma:tikɐ/ *der;* **~s, ~, Asthmatikerin** *die;* **~, ~nen** asthmatic

asthmatisch
A *Adj.* asthmatic
B *adv.* asthmatically; **~ bedingte Beschwerden** complaints linked to asthma

astig *Adj.* knotty

Ast·loch *das* knothole

astral /as'tra:l/ *Adj.* astral

Astral·leib *der* astral body

ast·rein
A *Adj.* (ugs.) (in Ordnung) on the level (coll.); (echt) genuine; (salopp: prima, toll) fantastic (coll.); great (coll.)
B *adv.* (salopp: prima) fantastically (coll.)

Astrologe /astro'lo:gə/ *der;* **~n, ~n ▸❶ S. 113** astrologer; (fig.) forecaster; pundit; **Kreml-~** (fig.) Kremlin-watcher *or* Kremlinologist

Astrologie *die;* **~:** astrology *no art.*

Astrologin *die;* **~, ~nen ▸❶ S. 113 ▸Astrologe**

astrologisch
A *Adj.* astrological
B *adv.* astrologically; **sich ~ beraten lassen** consult an astrologer

Astronaut /astro'naut/ *der;* **~en, ~en ▸❶ S. 113** astronaut

Astronautik /astro'nautɪk/ *die;* **~:** astronautics *sing., no art.*

Astronautin *die;* **~, ~nen** astronaut; *s. auch* **-in**

astronautisch
A *Adj.* astronautical
B *adv.* astronautically; **~ interessiert** interested in astronautics; **jmdn. ~ ausbilden** train sb. in astronautics

Astronom /astro'no:m/ *der;* **~en, ~en ▸❶ S. 113** astronomer

Astronomie *die;* **~:** astronomy *no art.*

Astronomin *die;* **~, ~nen ▸❶ S. 113** astronomer

astronomisch *Adj.* astronomical

astro-, Astro- /astro-/: **~physik** *die* astrophysics *sing., no art.;* **~physikalisch** **A** *Adj.* astrophysical; **B** *adv.* astrophysically; **~physiker** *der,* **~physikerin** *die* **▸❶ S. 113** astrophysicist

AStV *Abk.* (EU) **= Ausschuss der Ständigen Vertreter** Coreper

Ast·werk *das;* **~[e]s** branches *pl.*

Äsung *die;* **~, ~en** (Jägerspr.) grazing

Asyl /a'zy:l/ *das;* **~s, ~e** **1** [political] asylum; **jmdm. ~ gewähren** grant sb. asylum **2** (Obdachlosen~) hostel [for the homeless]

Asylant /azy'lant/ *der;* **~en, ~en, Asylantin** *die;* **~, ~nen** person granted [political] asylum; (Asylbewerber) person seeking [political] asylum

Asylanten·heim *das* asylum seekers' hostel

Asyl-: ~bewerber *der,* **~bewerberin** *die* person seeking [political] asylum; **~missbrauch** *der* abuse of [the right of] asylum; **~recht** *das* (Rechtsw.) **1** right of [political] asylum; **2** (eines Staates) right to grant [political] asylum; **~werber** *der;* **~~s, ~~, ~werberin** *die;* **~~, ~~nen** (österr.) **▸~bewerber**

Asymmetrie *die;* **~, ~n** asymmetry

asymmetrisch
A *Adj.* asymmetrical
B *adv.* asymmetrically

asynchron
A *Adj.* asynchronous; **Bild und Ton sind ~:** sound and picture are out of synchronization
B *adv.* asynchronously

Aszendent /astsɛn'dɛnt/ *der;* **~en, ~en** (Astron., Astrol., Genealogie) ascendant

A. T. *Abk.* **= Altes Testament** OT

ata /'ata/ *in* **~ [~] gehen** (Kinderspr.) go walkies (child lang., coll.)

Atavismus /ata'vɪsmʊs/ *der;* **~, Atavismen** (Biol., Psych.) atavism

atavistisch (Biol., Psych.)
A *Adj.* atavistic
B *adv.* atavistically

Atelier /atə'lie:/ *das;* **~s, ~s** studio

Atelier-: ~aufnahme *die* (Film, Fot.) studio shot; **~fest** *das* studio party; **~wohnung** *die* studio flat (esp. Brit.) *or* (esp. Amer.) apartment

Atem /'a:təm/ *der;* **~s** breath; **sein ~ wurde schneller** his breathing became faster; **einen kurzen ~ haben** be short of breath; (fig.) not have much staying power; **einen langen/den längeren ~ haben** (fig.) have great/the greater staying power; **jmdn. in ~ halten** (in Spannung halten) keep sb. in suspense; (pausenlos beschäftigen) keep sb. busy *or* at it; **den ~ anhalten** hold one's breath; **jmdm. den ~ verschlagen** take sb.'s breath away; **~ holen** *od.* (geh.) **schöpfen** (auch fig.) get one's breath back; **außer ~ sein/geraten** *od.* **kommen** be/get out of breath; **[wieder] zu ~ kommen** get one's breath back; **nach ~ ringen** (geh.) gasp for air; *s. auch* **ausgehen A 2**

atem-, Atem-: ~beklemmung *die* shortness of breath; **~beraubend** **A** *Adj.* breathtaking; **B** *adv.* breathtakingly; **~beschwerden** *Pl.* trouble *sing.* with one's breathing; **~holen** *das;* **~~s** breathing; **der Taucher kam zum ~holen an die Oberfläche** the diver came up to the surface for air; **~los** **A** *Adj.* breathless; **B** *adv.* breathlessly; **~losigkeit** *die;* **~~:** breathlessness; **~luft** *die* the air one breathes; **~maske** *die* (Med.) breathing mask; **~not** *die* difficulty in breathing; **~pause** *die* breathing space; **~technik** *die* breathing technique; **~übung** *die* breathing exercise; **~wege** *Pl.* respiratory tract *sing. or* passages; **~wegs·erkrankung** *die* respiratory disease; **~zug** *der* breath; **bis zum letzten ~zug** (geh.) to the last breath; **in einem** *od.* **im selben ~zug** in the same breath

Atheismus /ate'ɪsmʊs/ *der;* **~:** atheism *no art.*

Atheist *der;* **~en, ~en, Atheistin** *die;* **~, ~nen** atheist

atheistisch
A *Adj.* atheistic
B *adv.* atheistically; **er ist ~ erzogen worden** he had an atheistic upbringing

Athen /a'te:n/ *(das);* **~s ▸❶ S. 675** Athens

Athener ▸❶ S. 675
A *indekl. Adj.* Athens *attrib.;* of Athens *postpos.*
B *der;* **~s, ~:** Athenian; *s. auch* **Kölner**

Athenerin *die;* **~, ~nen** Athenian

athenisch *Adj.* Athenian

Äther /'ɛ:tɐ/ *der;* **~s, ~** (Chemie, Physik, geh.) ether

ätherisch /ɛ'te:rɪʃ/ *Adj.* (Chemie, dichter.) ethereal

Äther-: ~narkose *die* (Med.) ether anaesthesia; **~wellen** *Pl.* (veralt.) waves in the ether

Äthiopien /ɛ'tio:piən/ *(das);* **~s** Ethiopia

Äthiopier *der;* **~s, ~, Äthiopierin** *die;* **~, ~nen** Ethiopian; *s. auch* **-in**

Athlet /at'le:t/ *der;* **~en, ~en** **1** (Sportler) athlete **2** (ugs.: kräftiger Mann) muscleman

Athletik /at'le:tɪk/ *die;* **~:** athletics *sing., no art.*

Athletin *die;* **~, ~nen** athlete; *s. auch* **-in**

athletisch *Adj.* athletic

Äthyl·alkohol *der* (Chemie) ethyl alcohol; ethanol

Äthylen /ɛty'le:n/ *das;* **~s** (Chemie) ethylene

Atlant /at'lant/ *der;* **~en, ~en** (Archit.) telamon; atlas

Atlanten ▸Atlas¹, Atlant

Atlantik /at'lantɪk/ *der;* **~s** Atlantic

Atlantik·küste *die* Atlantic coast

atlantisch *Adj.* (Geogr.) Atlantic; **der Atlantische Ozean** the Atlantic Ocean

Atlas¹ /'atlas/ *der;* **~** *od.* **~ses, Atlanten** *od.* **~se** atlas

Atlas² *der;* **~** *od.* **~ses, ~se** (Textilw.) atlas

atmen /'a:tmən/
A *itr. V.* breathe; (Physiol., Bot.) respire
B *tr. V.* (geh., auch fig.: erfüllt sein von) breathe

Atmo /'atmo/ *die;* **~** (Jargon) atmosphere

Atmosphäre /atmo'sfɛ:rə/ *die;* **~, ~n** (auch fig.) atmosphere

atmosphärisch
A *Adj.* atmospheric; *s. auch* **Störung 2**
B *adv.* atmospherically

Atmung *die;* **~:** breathing; (Physiol., Bot.) respiration

Atmungs-: ~apparat *der* (Med.) respirator; **~organ** *das* respiratory organ

Ätna /'ɛtna/ *der;* **~[s]** Mount Etna

Atoll /a'tɔl/ *das;* **~s, ~e** atoll

Atom /a'to:m/ *das;* **~s, ~e** atom

atomar /ato'ma:ɐ̯/
A *Adj.* atomic; (Atomwaffen betreffend) nuclear; nuclear, atomic ‹*age, weapons*›
B *adv.* **~ angetrieben** nuclear-powered; atomic-powered; **~ aufrüsten** build up nuclear arms

Atom-, atom-: ~ausstieg *der* abandonment of nuclear energy; **~bombe** *die* nuclear bomb; atom bomb; **~bomben·sicher** *Adj.* nuclear-bomb-proof; **~bomben·versuch** *der* nuclear [weapons] test; **~bunker** *der* fallout shelter; **~energie** *die* nuclear *or* atomic energy *no indef. art.;* **~explosion** *die* nuclear *or* atomic explosion; **~gewicht** *das* atomic weight

atomisieren *tr. V.* **1** (vernichten) **etw. ~:** smash sth. to atoms **2** (zerstäuben) atomize ‹*liquid*› **3** (abwertend: zerstückelnd behandeln) atomize

Atomismus *der;* **~** (Philos.) atomism *no art.*

atom-, Atom-: ~kern *der* atomic nucleus; **~klub** *der* (Politik ugs.) nuclear club; **~kraft** *die* nuclear *or* atomic power *no indef. art.;* **~kraftwerk** *das* nuclear *or* atomic power station; **~krieg** *der* nuclear war; **~macht** *die* nuclear power; **~meiler** *der* atomic pile; **~modell** *das* (Physik) model of the/an atom; **~müll** *der* nuclear *or* atomic waste;

~**physik** *die* nuclear *or* atomic physics *sing., no art.*; ~**physiker** *der*, ~**physikerin** *die* ▸❶ S. 113 nuclear *or* atomic physicist; ~**pilz** *der* mushroom cloud; ~**programm** *das* nuclear programme; ~**rakete** *die* nuclear *or* atomic missile; ~**reaktor** *der* nuclear reactor; ~**sprengkopf** *der* nuclear warhead; ~**stopp** *der* nuclear freeze; ~**streitmacht** *die* nuclear force; ~**strom** *der* (ugs.) electricity generated by nuclear power; ~**test** *der* nuclear test; ~**test·stopp·abkommen** *das* (Politik) nuclear test ban treaty; ~**tod** *der* death in a nuclear war/accident; **„Kampf dem ~tod!"** 'ban the bomb'; ~**-U-Boot** *das* nuclear[-powered] submarine; ~**uhr** *die* atomic clock; ~**unterseeboot** *das* ▸~**-U-Boot**; ~**versuch** *der* nuclear test; ~**waffe** *die* nuclear *or* atomic weapon; ~**waffen·frei** *Adj.* nuclear-free; ~**waffen·sperr·vertrag** *der* (Politik) Nuclear Non-proliferation Treaty; ~**waffen·test** *der* nuclear test; ~**zeichen** *das* (Chemie) [chemical] symbol; ~**zeitalter** *das* nuclear *or* atomic age; ~**zerfall** *der* (Physik) radioactive decay; ~**zertrümmerung** *die* (Physik) splitting of the atom

atonal *Adj.* (Musik) atonal

Atonalität *die;* ~ (Musik) atonality

atoxisch *Adj.* (bes. Biol., Med.) non-toxic

Atrium /'a:triʊm/ *das;* ~**s**, **Atrien** atrium

Atrium·haus *das* (Archit.) house with an atrium

ätsch /ɛ:tʃ/ *Interj.* (Kinderspr.) ha ha

Attaché /ata'ʃe:/ *der;* ~**s**, ~**s** attaché

Attacke /a'takə/ *die;* ~, ~**n** 1) ▸❶ S. 439 (auch Med.) attack (**auf** + *Akk.* on) 2) (Reiter~) [cavalry] charge; **eine ~ [gegen jmdn./etw.] reiten** charge [sb./sth.]; (fig.) make an attack [on sb./sth.]

attackieren *tr. V.* 1) attack 2) (Milit.: zu Pferde) charge

Attentat /'atnta:t/ *das;* ~**[e]s**, ~**e** assassination attempt; (erfolgreiches) assassination; **ein ~ auf jmdn. verüben** make an attempt on sb.'s life/assassinate sb.; **ein ~ [auf jmdn.] vorhaben** (fig. ugs. scherzh.) want to ask a favour [of sb.]

Attentäter /'atntɛ:tɐ/ *der;* ~**s**, ~, **Attentäterin** *die;* ~, ~**nen** would-be assassin; (bei erfolgreichem Attentat) assassin

Attentismus /atɛn'tɪsmʊs/ *der;* ~ 1) wait-and-see attitude 2) (Wirtsch.) lack of activity [due to fear of a downturn]

attentistisch *Adj.* wait-and-see *attrib.*; ~ **sein** adopt a wait-and-see attitude

Attest /a'tɛst/ *das;* ~**[e]s**, ~**e** medical certificate; doctor's certificate

attestieren *tr. V.* certify; **jmdm. seine Unzurechnungsfähigkeit ~:** certify sb. as not responsible for his/her own actions

Attika /'atika/ *(das);* ~**s** Attica

attisch /'atɪʃ/ *Adj.* Attic

Attitüde /ati'ty:də/ *die;* ~, ~**n** (geh.) posture

Attraktion /atrak'tsi̯o:n/ *die;* ~, ~**en** attraction

attraktiv /atrak'ti:f/
A *Adj.* attractive
B *adv.* attractively

Attraktivität /atraktivi'tɛ:t/ *die;* ~: attractiveness

Attrappe /a'trapə/ *die;* ~, ~**n** dummy; **die ~ eines Fernsehgeräts/einer Flasche** a dummy television set/bottle

Attribut /atri'bu:t/ *das;* ~**[e]s**, ~**e** attribute

attributiv /atribu'ti:f/ (Sprachw.)
A *Adj.* attributive
B *adv.* attributively

Attribut-satz *der* (Sprachw.) attributive clause

atü /a'ty:/ *Abk.* (veralt.) = **Atmosphärenüberdruck; 1 ~:** 2 atm.; **3 ~:** 4 atm.

atypisch (geh.)
A *Adj.* atypical
B *adv.* atypically

At-Zeichen /'ɛt-/ *das* (DV) at sign

atzen /'atsn/ *tr. V.* (Jägerspr.) feed

ätzen /'ɛtsn/
A *tr. V.* 1) etch 2) (Med.) cauterize ‹*wound*›
B *itr. V.* corrode

ätzend
A *Adj.* 1) corrosive; (fig.) caustic ‹*wit, remark, criticism*›; pungent ‹*smell*›; acrid ‹*smoke*› 2) (Jugendspr.) (gut) great (coll.); ace (sl.); (schlecht) grotty (Brit. coll.); grot (Brit. coll.)
B *adv.* caustically ‹*ironic, critical*›

Ätz-natron *das* (Chemie) caustic soda

Atzung *die;* ~, ~**en** (Jägerspr.) 1) (Fütterung) feeding 2) (Nahrung) food; (fig. scherzh.) fodder

Ätzung *die;* ~, ~**en** 1) etching 2) (Med.) cauterization

au /au̯/ *Interj.* 1) (bei Schmerz) ow; ouch 2) (bei Überraschung, Begeisterung) oh

Au *die;* ~, ~**en** (südd., österr.) ▸**Aue 1**

aua /'au̯a/ *Interj.* (ugs.; Kinderspr.) ow; ouch

Aubergine /obɛr'ʒi:nə/ *die;* ~, ~**n** aubergine (Brit.); eggplant

auch /aux/
A *Adv.* 1) (ebenso, ebenfalls) as well; too; also; **Klaus war ~ dabei** Klaus was there as well *or* too; Klaus was also there; **Ich gehe jetzt. — Ich ~:** I'm going now — So am I; **Mir ist warm. — Mir ~:** I feel warm — So do I; **... — Ja, das ~:** ... — Yes, that too; **~ gut!** that's all right too; **das kann ich ~!** I can do that too; **was er verspricht, tut er ~:** what he promises to do, he does; **wenn er sagt, er kommt, dann kommt er ~:** if he says he's going to come, then he'll come; **nicht nur ..., sondern ~ ...** not only ..., but also ...; **grüß deine Frau und ~ die Kinder** give my regards to your wife and the children too; **sehr gut, aber ~ teuer** very good but expensive too; **~ das noch!** that's all I/we *etc.* need!; **oder ~:** or; **oder ~ nicht** or not, as the case may be; **das weiß ich ~ nicht** I don't know either; **ich weiß ~ das nicht** I don't know that either; **ich habe ~ keine Lust/kein Geld** I don't feel like it either/don't have any money either; **das hat ~ nichts genützt** that did not help either; **wir waren unter anderem ~ in Florenz** we were in Florence, among other places; *s. auch* **sowohl** 2) (sogar, selbst) even; **~ wenn** even if; **wenn ~:** even if *or* though; **ohne ~ nur zu fragen/eine Sekunde zu zögern** without even asking/hesitating for a second 3) (außerdem, im Übrigen) besides; **und ich sehe ~ gar nicht ein, warum ...** nor do I see why ...; and besides, I don't see why ...
B *Partikel* 1) *not translated* **etwas anderes habe ich ~ nicht erwartet** I never expected anything else; **du bist aber ~ ein Trottel** (ugs.) you're a real idiot[, you are] (coll.); **so schlimm ist es ~ [wieder] nicht** it's not as bad as all that; **den Teufel ~:** damn it [all]!; **nun hör aber ~ zu!** now listen!; **wozu [denn] ~?** what's the point? why should I/you *etc.?* 2) (zweifelnd) **bist du dir ~ im Klaren, was das bedeutet?** are you sure you understand what that means?; **bist du ~ glücklich?** are you truly happy?; **lügst du ~ nicht?** you're not lying, are you? 3) (mit Interrogativpron.) **wo .../wer .../wann .../was ...** *usw.* **~:** wherever/whoever/whenever/whatever *etc.* ...; **wie dem ~ sei** however that may be 4) (konzessiv) **mag er ~ noch so klug sein** however clever he may be; no matter how clever he is; **so oft ich ~ anrief** however often I rang; no matter how often I rang; **so gern ich es ~ täte, ...** much as I should like to [do it]; **so sehr er sich ~ bemühte** much as he tried; **wenn ~!** never mind

Audienz /au̯'di̯ɛnts/ *die;* ~, ~**en** audience

Audimax /au̯di'maks/ *das;* ~ (Studentenspr.) main lecture hall

Audiostream /'au̯di̯ostri:m/ *der;* ~**[s]**, ~**s** audio stream

audiovisuell /au̯di̯ovi'zu̯ɛl/
A *Adj.* audio-visual
B *adv.* audio-visually

auditiv /au̯di'ti:f/
A *Adj.* auditory
B *adv.* auditorily

Auditorium /au̯di'to:ri̯ʊm/ *das;* ~**s**, **Auditorien** 1) (Hörsaal) auditorium; ~ **maximum** (Hochschulw.) main lecture hall 2) (Zuhörerschaft) audience

Aue /'au̯ə/ *die;* ~, ~**n** 1) (dichter.) mead (poet.); meadow 2) (Geogr.) water meadow

Auen-wald *der* riverside forest

Auer- /'au̯ɐ-/: ~**hahn** *der; Pl.* ~**hähne** [cock] capercaillie; ~**henne** *die* [female *or* hen] capercaillie; ~**huhn** *das* capercaillie; ~**ochse** *der* aurochs

auf /au̯f/
A *Präp. mit Dat.* 1) on; **~ See** at sea; **~ dem Baum** in the tree; **~ der Erde** on earth; **~ der Welt** in the world; **~ der Straße** in the street; **~ dem Platz** in the square; **~ meinem Konto** in my account; **~ den Hebriden/Skye** in the Hebrides/on Skye; **~ Meereshöhe** at sea level; **~ beiden Augen blind** blind in both eyes; **das Thermometer steht ~ 15°** the thermometer stands at *or* says *or* reads 15° 2) (bei Räumen, Gebäuden, Institutionen) at ‹*post office, town, hall, police station*›; **~ seinem Zimmer** (ugs.) in his room; **Geld ~ der Bank haben** have money in the bank; **~ der Polizei** (ugs.) at the police station; **~ der Schule/Uni** at school/university 3) (bei Veranstaltungen usw.) at ‹*party, wedding*›; on ‹*course, trip, walk, holiday, tour*› 4) **was hat es damit ~ sich?** what's it all about?; **damit hat es nichts/etwas ~ sich** there is nothing/something in it
B *Präp. mit Akk.* 1) on; on to; **sich ~ einen Stuhl setzen** sit down on a chair; **sich ~ das Bett legen** lie down on the bed; **er nahm den Rucksack ~ den Rücken** he lifted the rucksack up on to his back; **~ einen Berg steigen** climb up a mountain; **sich** *(Dat.)* **einen Hut ~ den Kopf setzen** put a hat on [one's head]; **~ den Mond fliegen** fly to the moon; **~ die See hinausfahren** go out to sea; **jmdm. ~ den Fuß treten** step on sb.'s foot; **~ die Straße gehen** go [out] into the street; **~ den Grund des Meeres sinken** sink to the bottom of the sea; **jmdn. ~ den Rücken legen** lay sb. on his/her back; **jmdn. ~ den Rücken drehen** turn sb. on to his/her back; **~ die Hebriden** to the Hebrides; **~ die andere Seite der Schranke gehen** go over to the other side of the barrier; **etw. ~ ein Konto überweisen** transfer sth. to an account; **das Thermometer ist ~ 0° gefallen** the thermometer has fallen to 0°; **~ ihn!** (ugs.) get him! 2) (bei Institutionen, Veranstaltungen) to; **~ die Schule/Uni gehen** go to school/university; **~ einen Lehrgang gehen** go on a course; **~ Reisen/Urlaub/Tournee gehen** go travelling/on holiday/on tour 3) (bei Entfernungen) **~ 10 km [Entfernung]** for [a distance of] 10 km; **wir näherten uns der Hütte [bis] ~ 30 m** we approached to within 30 m of the hut 4) (zeitlich) for; **~ Jahre [hinaus]** for years [to come]; **etw. ~ nächsten Mittwoch festlegen/verschieben** arrange sth. for/postpone sth. until next Wednesday; **die Nacht von Sonntag ~ Montag** Sunday night; **das fällt ~ einen Montag** it falls on a Monday; **wir verschieben es ~ den 3. Mai** we'll postpone it to the 3 May; **sich ~ morgen vertagen** adjourn until tomorrow; **komm doch mal ~ eine Tasse Tee herüber** come round for a cup of tea some time 5) (zur Angabe der Art und Weise) **~ diese Art und Weise** in this way; **~ die Tour erreichst du bei mir nichts** (ugs.) you won't get anywhere with me like that; **komm mir bloß nicht ~ die Sentimentale!** (salopp) don't try *or* come the old sentimental bit with me! (coll.); **auf die Billige** (salopp) on the cheap; **~ Deutsch** in German; **~ das Sorgfältigste/Herzlichste** (geh.) most carefully/warmly; **~ a enden** end in a; **Wörter ~ a** words ending in a 6) (aufgrund) **~ Wunsch** on request; **~ vielfachen Wunsch/wiederholte Aufforderung [hin]** in response to numerous requests/repeated demands; **~ meine Bitte** at my request; **~ seine Initiative** on his initiative; **~ Befehl** on command; **~ meinen Vorschlag [hin]** at my suggestion; **erst ~ meinen Brief [hin]** only as a result of my letter 7) (sonstige Verwendungen) **ein Teelöffel ~ einen**

Liter Wasser one teaspoon to one litre of water; **das Bier geht ~ mich** (ugs.) the beer's on 'me (coll.); **~ wen geht die Cola?** who's paying for the Coke?; **Welle ~ Welle brandete ans Ufer** wave upon wave broke on the shore; **einen Text ~ orthographische Fehler [hin] durchsehen** examine a text for orthographical errors; **jmdn. ~ Tb untersuchen** examine sb. for TB; **jmdn. ~ seine Eignung prüfen** test sb.'s suitability; **~ die Sekunde/den Millimeter [genau]** [precise] to the second/millimetre; **ein Kabel ~ 1,50 m kürzen/abschneiden** shorten a cable to 1.50 m; **~ ein gutes Gelingen** to our/your success; **~ deine Gesundheit** your health; **~ bald/morgen!** (bes. südd.) see you soon/tomorrow; **~ 10 zählen** (bes. südd.) count [up] to 10; *s. auch* **einmal A 1; machen C 6**

C *Adv.* **1** (aufgerichtet, aufgestanden) up; **~!** up you get!; (zu einem Hund) up!; **Sprung ~! Marsch, marsch!** (Milit.) Up! At the double!

2 **sie waren längst ~ und davon** they had made off long before; **jetzt heißts ~ und davon** it's time to be off; *s. auch* **aufmachen, davonmachen**

3 (bes. südd.: los) come on; **~ gehts** off we go; let's go

4 (Aufforderung, sich aufzumachen) **~ ins Schwimmbad!/nach Schifferstadt!** come on, off to the swimming pool!/to Schifferstadt!

5 **~ und ab** *od.* (geh.) **nieder** up and down; **das Auf und Ab** the up-and-down movement; **das Auf und Ab des Lebens** (fig.) the ups and downs of life

6 **~ und ab** (hin und her) up and down; to and fro

7 (Aufforderung, sich etw. aufzusetzen) **Helm/Hut/Brille ~!** helmet/hat/glasses on!

8 (ugs.: geöffnet, offen) open; **Fenster/Türen/Mund ~!** open the window/doors/your mouth!

D **~ dass** *Konj.* (veralt.) so that; **~ dass er sich nicht erkälte[te]** lest he should catch [a] cold

auf|arbeiten *tr. V.* **1** (erledigen) catch up with ‹*correspondence etc.*› **2** (studieren, analysieren) review ‹*literature, material*›; look back on and reappraise ‹*one's past, childhood*› **3** (restaurieren, überholen) refurbish

Aufarbeitung *die;* **~, ~en** **1** (Erledigung) **die ~ der Post** catching up with the post (Brit.) *or* mail **2** (das Studieren, Analysieren) **die ~ der Literatur/Kindheit** reviewing the literature/looking back on and reappraising one's childhood **3** (Restaurierung) refurbishing

auf|atmen *itr. V.* **1** (fig.: erleichtert sein) breathe a sigh of relief; **ein Aufatmen** a sigh of relief **2** (tief atmen) breathe deeply

auf|backen *regelm.* (*auch unr.*) *tr. V.* crisp up ‹*bread, rolls, etc.*›

auf|bahren *tr. V.* lay out ‹*body, corpse*›; **jmdn./einen Toten ~:** lay out sb.'s body; **aufgebahrt sein** ‹*king, president, etc.*› lie in state

Auf·bau *der;* **~[e]s, ~ten** **1** (das Aufbauen) construction; building; (das Wiederaufbauen) reconstruction; rebuilding **2** (von Staat, Ökonomie, gesellschaftlicher Ordnung) building; **den wirtschaftlichen ~ beschleunigen** speed up economic development **3** (Biol.) synthesis **4** (Struktur) structure **5** *Pl.* (Schiffbau) superstructure *sing.* **6** (Bauw.) superstructure; **einen zweistöckigen ~ genehmigen** approve the addition of two extra storeys **7** (Kfz-W.) body

Aufbau·arbeit *die* construction work; (bei Wiederaufbau) reconstruction work

auf|bauen

A *tr. V.* **1** *auch itr.* (errichten, aufstellen) erect ‹*hut, kiosk, podium*›; set up ‹*equipment, train set*›; build ‹*house, bridge*›; put up ‹*tent*›; (wieder aufbauen) rebuild ‹*house, bridge*›; **ein Haus neu ~:** rebuild a house **2** (hinstellen, arrangieren) lay *or* set out ‹*food, presents, etc.*› **3** (fig.: schaffen) build ‹*state, economy, social order, life, political party, etc.*›; build up ‹*business, organization, army, spy network*›; **sich** (*Dat.*) **ein neues Leben ~:** build a new life [for oneself] **4** (fig.: strukturieren) structure **5** (fig.: fördern) **jmdn./etw. zu etw. ~:** build sb./sth. up into sth.; **jmdn. als etw. ~:** build sb. up as sth. **6** (gründen) **etw. auf etw.** (*Dat.*) **~:** base sth. upon sth. **7** (Biol.) synthesize

B *itr. V.* **auf etw.** (*Dat.*) **~:** be based on sth.

C *refl. V.* **1** (ugs.: sich hinstellen) plant oneself (**vor** + *Dat.* in front of) **2** (sich zusammensetzen) be composed (**aus** of) **3** (sich auftürmen, sich bilden) ‹*clouds, pressure, tension, etc.*› build up

aufbauend *Adj.* constructive ‹*criticism, geological process*›; restorative ‹*medicine*›; nutrient ‹*substance*›

auf|bäumen /ˈaufbɔymən/ *refl. V.* rear up; **sich gegen jmdn./etw. ~** (fig.) rise up against sb./sth.

Aufbau·prinzip *das* structural principle

auf|bauschen

A *tr. V.* **1** (aufblähen) billow; billow, belly [out] ‹*sail*› **2** (fig.: hochspielen) blow up (coll.); exaggerate

B *refl. V.* (fig.: sich auswachsen) **sich [zu etw.] ~:** blow up [into sth.] (coll.)

Aufbauten ▸ **Aufbau**

auf|begehren *itr. V.* (geh.) rebel

auf|behalten *unr. tr. V.* **etw. ~:** keep sth. on

auf|beißen *unr. tr. V.* **etw. ~:** bite sth. open; **sich** (*Dat.*) **die Lippe ~:** bite one's lip [and make it bleed]

auf|bekommen *unr. tr. V.* **1** (öffnen können) **etw. ~:** get sth. open **2** (aufessen können) manage to eat **3** (aufsetzen können) **etw. ~:** get sth. on **4** (aufgegeben bekommen) be given

auf|bereiten *tr. V.* **1** (Hüttenw., Bergbau) dress, prepare ‹*ore, coal*›; **Erz magnetisch ~:** separate ore magnetically **2** (Wasserwirtsch.) purify; treat **3** (Kerntechnik) reprocess **4** (Statistik) process **5** (geh.) (bearbeiten) adapt; (erschließen) reconstruct; **etw. literarisch/dramatisch ~:** put sth. into literary/dramatic form

Auf·bereitung *die* ▸ **aufbereiten 1-5**: dressing; preparation; purification; treatment; reprocessing; processing; adaptation; reconstruction

Aufbereitungs·anlage *die* (Hüttenw.) preparation plant; (Wasserwirtsch.) purification works *sing.*; treatment plant; (Kerntechnik) reprocessing plant

auf|bessern *tr. V.* improve; increase ‹*pension, wages, etc.*›

Auf·besserung *die* improvement (*Gen.* in); (bei Renten, Löhnen, Gehältern) increase (*Gen.* in); **zur ~ seines Taschengeldes/seiner Sprachkenntnisse** to increase his pocket money/to improve his linguistic proficiency

auf|bewahren *tr. V.* keep; store, keep ‹*medicines, food, provisions*›; (fig.: bewahren, erhalten) preserve ‹*memory, name, writings*›; **die Fahrkarte/das Testament musst du gut ~:** you must keep your ticket safe/keep the will in a safe place; **etw. kühl ~:** store sth. in a cool place

Auf·bewahrung *die* **1** ▸ **aufbewahren**: keeping; storage; **jmdm. etw. zur ~ geben/anvertrauen** give sth. to sb. for safe keeping/entrust sb. with the care of sth.; **bei ~ im Kühlschrank** if kept in a refrigerator **2** (Verkehrsw.) left-luggage office (Brit.); baggage check room (Amer.)

Aufbewahrungs-: ~ort *der:* **das ist kein geeigneter ~ort für Dokumente/Lebensmittel** that is not a suitable place to keep documents/keep *or* store food; **~schein** *der* (Verkehrsw.) left-luggage ticket (Brit.); baggage check *or* ticket (Amer.)

auf|biegen

A *unr. tr. V.* **1** **etw. ~:** bend sth. open **2** (hochbiegen) bend up[wards]

B *unr. refl. V.* **1** bend open **2** (sich hochbiegen) bend up[wards]

auf|bieten *unr. tr. V.* **1** (aufwenden) exert ‹*strength, energy, will power, influence, authority*›; call on ‹*skill, wit, powers of persuasion or eloquence*› **2** (einsetzen) call in ‹*police, troops*› **3** (Milit. veralt.: ausheben) call up ‹*troops*›; raise ‹*army*› **4** (zur Eheschließung) **ein Brautpaar ~:** read *or* call the banns of a couple to be married **5** (bei Versteigerung) **etw. [mit 400 Euro] ~:** put sth. up for auction [at a starting price of 400 euros]

Aufbietung *die;* **~** **1** **unter ~ aller Kräfte/seiner ganzen Überredungskunst** summoning up all one's strength/calling on all one's persuasive skills **2** (Milit. veralt.) calling up; (einer Armee) raising

auf|binden *unr. tr. V.* **1** (öffnen, lösen) untie; undo; **sich/jmdm. die Schuhe ~:** undo one's/sb.'s shoes **2** (hochbinden) tie *or* put up ‹*hair*›; tie ‹*plant*› up straight; **jmdm./sich die Haare ~:** tie *or* put up sb.'s/one's hair **3** (auf den Rücken binden) **jmdm./einem Tier eine Last ~:** tie a burden on to sb.'s/an animal's back **4** (ugs.: weismachen) **wer hat dir das aufgebunden?** who spun you that yarn?; **jmdm. ein Märchen/eine Fabel ~:** spin sb. a yarn; *s. auch* **Bär** **5** (binden auf) **etw. auf etw.** (*Akk.*) **~:** tie sth. on to sth. **6** (Buchw.: binden) bind

auf|blähen

A *tr. V.* distend ‹*body, stomach*›; puff out ‹*cheeks, feathers*›; flare ‹*nostrils*›; billow, fill, belly [out] ‹*sail*›; billow ‹*washing, clothing*›; (fig.: vergrößern) over-inflate; **ein aufgeblähter Beamtenapparat** (fig.) an overblown bureaucracy

B *refl. V.* **1** ‹*sail*› billow *or* belly out; ‹*balloon, lungs, chest*› expand; ‹*stomach*› swell up, become swollen *or* distended **2** (abwertend: sich aufspielen) puff oneself up

Auf·blähung *die* (fig.) overexpansion

aufblasbar *Adj.* inflatable

auf|blasen

A *unr. tr. V.* blow up; inflate; **die Backen ~:** puff out one's cheeks; **etw. zu etw. ~** (fig.) blow sth. up into sth.

B *unr. refl. V.* (ugs. abwertend: sich aufspielen); **sich ~ [wie ein Frosch]** puff oneself up (**mit** about); *s. auch* **aufgeblasen B**

auf|bleiben *unr. itr. V.; mit sein* **1** (geöffnet bleiben) stay open **2** (nicht zu Bett gehen) stay up

auf|blenden

A *tr. V.* (Kfz-W.) **die Scheinwerfer ~:** switch one's headlights to full beam; **mit aufgeblendeten Scheinwerfern fahren** drive with headlights on full beam

B *itr. V.* **1** (Kfz-W.) switch to full beam **2** (Fot., Film) open up the lens; increase the [lens] aperture

auf|blicken *itr. V.* **1** look up; (kurz) glance up; **von etw. ~:** look/glance up from sth. **2** (verehrend) **zu jmdm. ~:** look up to sb.

auf|blinken *itr. V.* **1** ‹*light*› flash; ‹*metal*› glint; ‹*star*› blink **2** (ugs.: kurz aufblenden) flash one's headlights

auf|blitzen *itr. V.* flash; ‹*wave, white caps*› sparkle

auf|blühen *itr. V.; mit sein* **1** bloom; come into bloom; ‹*bud*› open; **eine halb/voll aufgeblühte Tulpe** a half-open tulip/a tulip in full bloom **2** (fig.: aufleben) blossom [out] **3** (fig.: einen Aufschwung nehmen) ‹*trade, business, town, industry*› flourish and expand; ‹*cultural life, science*› blossom and flourish

auf|bocken *tr. V.* **etw. ~:** jack sth. up

auf|bohren *tr. V.* **etw. ~:** drill a hole in sth.; drill ‹*tooth*›; bore out ‹*cylinder, engine*›

auf|branden *itr. V.; mit sein* (geh.) **die Wellen brandeten an den Felsen auf** the waves broke against the rock with a roar; **Beifall/Jubel brandete auf** (fig.) thunderous applause/cheering burst out

auf|braten *unr. tr. V.* **etw. ~:** fry sth. up [again]

auf|brauchen *tr. V.* use up

auf|brausen *itr. V.; mit sein* **1** (zornig werden) flare up; **schnell/leicht ~:** be quick-tempered *or* hot-tempered; have a quick temper **2** (zu brausen beginnen) ‹*sea, surf, wave*› surge [up]; ‹*liquid*› seethe, boil up; ‹*wind*› rise to a roar; **Beifall/Jubel brauste auf** there was a sudden roar of applause/a thunderous cheer went up

aufbrausend *Adj.* quick-tempered; hot-tempered; **ein ~es Temperament haben** be quick-tempered *or* hot-tempered; have a quick temper

auf|brechen

A *unr. tr. V.* **1** (öffnen) break open ‹*lock, safe, box, crate, etc.*›; break into ‹*car*›; force [open] ‹*door*›; break up ‹*ground, surface*›; (geh.: aufreißen) tear open ‹*letter, telegram*›; (fig.) break down ‹[*social*] structures›; break ‹system› **2** (Jägerspr.: ausnehmen) gut

B unr. itr. V.; mit sein **1** (sich öffnen) ‹bud› open [up], burst [open]; ‹ice [sheet], surface, ground› break up; ‹wound› open; **alte Wunden brechen auf** (fig.) old wounds are opening [again] **2** (sich auf den Weg machen) set off, start out (**zu** on) **3** (geh.: spürbar werden) become evident; emerge

auf|brennen unr. tr. V. **einem Tier ein Zeichen/ein Mal ~:** brand an animal; **jmdm. eins ~** (salopp: auf jmdn. schießen) let sb. have it

auf|brezeln refl. V. (ugs.) get dolled up (coll.)

auf|bringen unr. tr. V. **1** (beschaffen) find; raise, find ‹money›; (fig.) find, summon [up] ‹strength, energy, courage›; find ‹patience› **2** (kreieren) introduce, start ‹fashion, custom›; introduce ‹slogan, theory›; start, put about ‹rumour› **3** (in Wut bringen) **jmdn. ~:** make sb. angry; infuriate sb. **4** (aufwiegeln) **jmdn. gegen jmdn./etw. ~:** set sb. against sb./sth. **5** (auftragen) put on, apply ‹paint, ointment, varnish, etc.› **6** (Seew.) seize; (in den Hafen bringen) bring in **7** (bes. südd.) ▸**aufbekommen 1, 2, 3**

Auf·bruch der **1** departure; (fig. geh.) awakening; **im ~ begriffen sein** be on the point of departure or of setting off; (fig. geh.) experience an awakening; **das Zeichen zum ~ geben** give the signal to set off or leave; **zum ~ rüsten** get ready to set off or leave **2** (aufgebrochene Stelle) crack

Aufbruchs·stimmung die: **es herrschte allgemeine ~:** everybody was getting ready to go; **bist du schon in ~?** are you all ready to go?

auf|brühen tr. V. brew [up]

auf|brüllen itr. V. let out or give a roar; ‹animal› bellow

auf|brummen tr. V. (ugs.) **jmdm. etw. ~:** slap sth. on sb. (coll.); **einem Schüler viele Hausaufgaben ~:** lumber (Brit.) or burden a pupil with a lot of homework; **jmdm. die Kosten für etw. ~:** land sb. with the costs for sth.

auf|bügeln tr. V. iron; **etw. [auf etw.** (Akk.)**] ~:** iron sth. on [to sth.]; **Flicken zum Aufbügeln** iron-on patches

auf|bürden tr. V. (geh.) **jmdm./einem Tier etw. ~:** load sth. on to sb./an animal; **jmdm./sich etw. ~** (fig.) burden sb./oneself with sth.; **jmdm. die Schuld ~:** put the blame on sb.

auf|bürsten tr. V. **etw. ~:** brush sth. up; give sth. a brush-up

auf|decken

A tr. V. **1** uncover; **das Bett ~:** pull back the covers; **sich im Schlaf ~:** throw off one's covers **2** (Kartenspiele) show; **die od. seine Karten ~** (fig.) lay one's cards on the table (fig.) **3** (enthüllen) expose ‹corruption, error, weakness, misdeeds, crime, plot, abuse, etc.›; (erkennen und bewusst machen) reveal, uncover ‹connections, motive, processes, cause, error, weakness, contradiction, etc.› **4** (für eine Mahlzeit) **etw. ~:** put sth. on the table

B itr. V. lay the table

Auf·deckung die ▸**aufdecken A 3**: exposure; revelation; uncovering

auf|donnern refl. V. (ugs. abwertend) tart (Brit.) or doll oneself up (coll.); get tarted (Brit.) or dolled up (coll.)

auf|drängen

A tr. V. **jmdm. etw. ~:** force sth. on sb.; **jmdm. seine Ansichten ~:** force or impose one's views on sb.

B refl. V. **1** **sich jmdm. ~:** force one's company or oneself on sb.; **ich will mich aber nicht ~:** I don't want to impose **2** (fig.: in den Sinn kommen) **mir drängte sich der Verdacht auf, dass ...** I couldn't help suspecting that ...; **dieser Gedanke drängt sich [einem] förmlich auf** one simply can't help but think so; the thought is unavoidable

auf|drehen

A tr. V. **1** (öffnen) unscrew ‹bottle cap, nut›; undo ‹screw›; turn on ‹tap, gas, water›; open ‹valve, bottle, vice› **2** (ugs.: laut stellen) turn up ‹radio, record player, etc.› **3** (ugs.: aufziehen) wind up ‹musical box, watch, toy, etc.› **4** (zu Locken drehen) turn up, twist up ‹moustache›; **sich/jmdm. die Haare ~:** put one's/sb.'s hair in curlers

B itr. V. (ugs.) **1** (das Tempo steigern) **[voll] ~:** put one's foot [right] down (coll.); step on the gas (Amer.); (fig.) step the pace [right] up **2** (in Schwung kommen) get into the mood; get going

auf·dringlich

A Adj. importunate, (coll.) pushy ‹person›; insistent ‹music, advertisement, questioning›; pestering attrib. ‹journalist›; pungent ‹perfume, smell›; loud, gaudy ‹colour, wallpaper›; **~e Vertraulichkeit** overfamiliarity; **~e Freundlichkeit** overfriendliness; **sei nicht so ~!** don't pester so!; **~ riechen** have a pungent smell; be pungent

B adv. ‹behave› importunately, (coll.) pushily; ‹ask› insistently

Aufdringlichkeit die; ~, **~en** **1** ▸**aufdringlich**: insistent manner; insistence; importunity; pushiness (coll.); pungency **2** (Äußerung, Handlung) piece of overfamiliarity; **die ~en der Männer** the overfamiliarity sing. of the men

auf|dröseln /ˈaufdrøːzl̩n/ tr. V. (ugs., auch fig.) unravel; unpick ‹piece of knitting›

Auf·druck der; **~[e]s, ~e** **1** imprint **2** (Philat.) ▸**Überdruck**[2]

auf|drucken tr. V. **etw. auf etw.** (Akk.) **~:** print sth. on sth.; **Briefumschläge mit aufgedruckter Adresse** envelopes with the address printed on them

auf|drücken tr. V. **1** (öffnen) push open **2** (aufplatzen lassen) squeeze ‹pimple, boil› **3** (aufstempeln, aufprägen) **etw. auf etw.** (Akk.) **~:** stamp sth. on sth.; **jmdm. einen Kuss ~:** plant a kiss on sb.; **einer Sache** (Dat.) **sein Gepräge ~** (fig.) leave one's mark or stamp on sth.; s. auch **Stempel 1** **4** (auf etw. drücken) **etw. auf etw.** (Akk.) **~:** press sth. on to sth.; **drück den Bleistift nicht so fest auf** don't press so hard with your pencil

auf·einander Adv. on top of one another or each other; (zusammen) together; (gegeneinander) against each other; against one another; **die Bücher sollen ~ liegen** the books should lie one on top of the other; **zwei Autos waren ~ gefahren** two cars had collided with each other or one another; **~ warten** wait for each other or one another; **~ zugehen** walk towards or approach one another or each other; **die Zähne ~ beißen** clench one's teeth; **~ folgen** follow each other or one another; **~ folgend** successive; **an mehreren ~ folgenden Tagen** several days running; on several successive days; **wenn es regnet, hängt man den ganzen Tag im Hotel ~** (ugs.) when it rains, people hang around on top of each other all day in the hotel; **die Hunde ~ hetzen** set the dogs on each other or one another; **~ prallen** crash into each other or one another; collide; ‹armies› clash; (fig.) ‹opinions› clash; **etw. ~ schichten** stack sth. up; **Kisten ~ türmen** stack crates [up] one on top of the other; **wo die Linien ~ stoßen** where the lines meet; **~ treffen** ‹teams, enemies, opponents, streets› meet; ‹missiles› collide, hit each other; hit one another

***aufeinander|beißen** usw. ▸**aufeinander**

Aufeinander·folge die; **~:** sequence; **in rascher ~:** in rapid or quick succession

***aufeinander|folgen** usw. ▸**aufeinander**

-aufenthalt der: **Frankreich~/Italien~:** stay in France/Italy

Aufenthalt /ˈaufǀɛnthalt/ der; **~[e]s, ~e** **1** stay; **der ~ im Depot ist verboten** personnel/the public etc. are not permitted to remain within the depot; **~ nehmen** (geh.) reside **2** (Fahrtunterbrechung) stop; **der Zug hatte dort [10 Minuten] ~:** the train stopped there [for 10 minutes]; **ohne ~ durchfahren** travel through non-stop or without stopping **3** (geh.: Ort) residence

Aufenthalts-: **~bewilligung** die ▸**~erlaubnis**; **~dauer** die length of stay; **bei einer ~dauer von weniger als sechs Monaten** for a stay of less than six months; **~erlaubnis** die residence permit; **~genehmigung** die ▸**~erlaubnis**; **~ort** der [place of] residence; **jmds. ~ort ermitteln** establish sb.'s whereabouts pl.; **~raum** der (in einer Schule o. Ä.) common room (Brit.); (in einer Jugendherberge) day room; (in einem Betrieb o. Ä.) recreation room; (in einem Hotel o. Ä.) lounge

auf|erlegen, auf·erlegen tr. V. (geh.) **jmdm. etw. ~:** impose sth. on sb.; **du solltest dir etwas Zurückhaltung ~:** you should exercise some restraint; **die Kosten wurden dem Kläger auferlegt** costs were awarded against the plaintiff; **jmdm. eine schwere Prüfung ~:** subject sb. to or put sb. through a severe test

auf|erstehen unr. itr. V.; mit sein rise [again]; **von den Toten ~:** rise from the dead; **Christus ist auferstanden** Christ is risen

Auferstehung die; **~, ~en** resurrection

auf·erwecken tr. V. **jmdn. ~:** bring sb. back to life; raise sb. from the dead; **jmdn. von den Toten ~:** raise sb. from the dead; **der Lärm hätte einen Toten ~ können** (fig.) the noise was enough to waken the dead

Auf·erweckung die: **die ~ eines Toten** raising someone from the dead

auf|essen unr. tr. (auch itr.) V. eat up

auf|fächern

A tr. V. fan [out]; (fig.) set out

B refl. V. fan out; **sich in Einzeldisziplinen ~:** develop into separate disciplines

auf|fädeln tr. V. **etw. [auf etw.** (Akk.)**] ~:** thread sth. on to sth.

auf|fahren

A unr. itr. V.; mit sein **1** (aufprallen) **auf ein anderes Fahrzeug ~:** drive or run into the back of another vehicle; **auf etw./jmdn. ~:** drive or run into sth./sb.; **das Schiff ist auf ein Riff aufgefahren** the ship has run aground on a reef **2** (aufschließen) **auf den Vordermann zu dicht ~:** drive too close to the car in front; tailgate; **fahr doch nicht so dicht od. nah auf!** don't drive so close!; **zu dichtes Auffahren** driving too close to the vehicle in front; tailgating **3** (vorfahren) drive up **4** (in Stellung gehen) move up [into position] **5** (Bergmannsspr.) go/come up; **aufgefahren kommen** come up **6** (gen Himmel fahren) ascend **7** (aufschrecken) start; **aus dem Schlaf ~:** awake with a start **8** (aufbrausen) flare up

B unr. tr. V. **1** (in Stellung bringen) bring or move up **2** (ugs.: auftischen) serve up

auf·fahrend Adj. quick-tempered; hot-tempered

Auf·fahrt die **1** (das Hinauffahren) climb; drive up; **die ~ zum Gipfel** the drive up to the summit **2** (zu Gebäuden) drive **3** (zur Autobahn) slip road (Brit.); access road (Amer.) **4** (schweiz.) (Himmelfahrt) Ascension; (Himmelfahrtstag) Ascension [Day]

Auffahrts·fest das (schweiz.) feast of the Ascension

Auffahr·unfall der rear-end collision

auf|fallen unr. itr. V.; mit sein **1** (auffällig sein) stand out; **diese Fettflecken/Druckfehler fallen kaum auf** these grease marks/printing errors are hardly noticeable; **tu das so, dass es nicht auffällt** do it so that it doesn't attract attention or so that nobody notices; **er fällt durch seine abstehenden Ohren auf** the fact that his ears stick out makes him conspicuous; **seine Abwesenheit fiel nicht auf** his absence was not noticed; **um nicht aufzufallen** so as not to attract attention; **sie will nur ~:** she just wants to attract attention; **jmdm. fällt etw. auf** sb. notices sth.; sth. strikes sb.; **fällt dir an diesem Satz etwas auf?** does anything strike you about that sentence?; **er ist mir angenehm/unangenehm aufgefallen** he made a good/bad impression on me; **ist Ihnen nichts aufgefallen?** did you not notice anything?; did nothing strike you?; **so etwas fällt sofort/nie auf** that sort of thing will be noticed right away/will never be noticed; **es fiel allgemein auf, dass ...** it was generally noticed that ... **2** (auftreffen) fall (**auf** + Akk. on [to]); strike (**auf** + Akk. sth.); **das ~de Licht** the light falling on [to] or striking the surface etc.; (Optik) the incident light

a

auffallend
A *Adj.* (auffällig) conspicuous; (eindrucksvoll, bemerkenswert) striking ‹*contrast, figure, appearance, beauty, similarity*›; **das Auffallendste an ihr** the most striking thing about her
B *adv.* (auffällig) conspicuously; (eindrucksvoll, bemerkenswert) ‹*contrast, differ*› strikingly; **stimmt ~!** (scherzh.) you're so right!

auf·fällig
A *Adj.* conspicuous; garish, loud ‹*colour*›; **eine recht ~e Erscheinung sein** have a most striking appearance
B *adv.* conspicuously; **sich ~ kleiden** dress showily; **~er hätte er es nicht machen können** he couldn't have made it more obvious [if he had tried]

Auf·fälligkeit *die* **1** conspicuousness; (Grellheit) garishness; loudness **2** (etw. Auffälliges) distinctive feature

auf|falten
A *tr. V.* fold open; unfold
B *refl. V.* (Geol.) fold upward

auf|fangen *unr. tr. V.* **1** (fangen) catch; (fig.) regain control of ‹*aircraft*› **2** (aufnehmen, sammeln) collect; collect, catch ‹*liquid*›; (fig.) receive ‹*refugees*› **3** (wahrnehmen) catch ‹*words, conversation*›; (Funkw.: empfangen) pick up **4** (absorbieren) absorb **5** (Milit.: aufhalten) hold ‹*attack, advance*› **6** (Handarb.) pick up ‹*stitch*› **7** (ausgleichen) offset ‹*price increase etc.*›

Auffang·lager *das* reception camp

auf|fassen *tr. V.* **1** (ansehen als) **etw. als etw. ~:** see *or* regard sth. as sth.; **etw. als Scherz/Kompliment/Beleidigung/Kritik ~:** take sth. as a joke/compliment/insult/criticism; **etw. persönlich/falsch ~:** take sth. personally/misunderstand sth. **2** (begreifen) grasp; comprehend

Auf·fassung *die* **1** (Meinung, Ansicht) view; (Begriff) conception; **nach meiner ~:** in my view; **der ~ sein, dass ...** take the view that ...; be of the opinion that ...; **eine andere ~ von etw. haben** take a different view of sth. **2** ▸ **Auffassungsgabe**

Auffassungs-: ~gabe *die* powers *pl.* of comprehension; **eine leichte/schnelle ~gabe haben** be quick on the uptake; **~sache** *die:* in **~sache sein** depend on one's point of view; **~vermögen** *das* ▸ **~gabe**

auf|fegen *tr. (auch itr.) V.* (bes. nordd.) sweep up

auffindbar *Adj.* findable; **der Schlüssel muss doch ~ sein!** we must be able to find the key somewhere!; **es ist nirgends/nicht ~:** it's nowhere to be found/it can't be *or* isn't to be found; **schwer/leicht ~ sein** be hard/easy to find

auf|finden *unr. tr. V.* find

auf|fischen *tr. V.* (ugs.) fish out (coll.)

auf|flackern *itr. V.; mit sein* flicker up; (fig.) ‹*hope*› flicker up; ‹*revolt, unrest, passion, anger*› flare up

auf|flammen *itr. V.; mit sein* (auch fig.) flare up; **in seinen Augen flammte Zorn auf** (fig.) his eyes flashed with anger

auf|flexen *tr. V.* cut open with an angle grinder; cut ‹*lock*› with an angle grinder

auf|fliegen *unr. itr. V.; mit sein* **1** (hochfliegen) fly up **2** (sich öffnen) fly open **3** (ugs.: scheitern) ‹*illegal organization, drug ring*› be *or* get busted (coll.); **den Parteitag/einen Schmugglerring ~ lassen** ruin *or* (Brit. sl.) scupper the party conference/bust a smuggling ring (coll.)

auf|fordern *tr. V.* **1** *auch itr.* **jmdn. ~, etw. zu tun** call upon *or* ask sb. to do sth.; **jmdn. zur Teilnahme/Zahlung ~:** call upon *or* ask sb. to take part/ask sb. for payment; **ich fordere Sie zum letzten Mal auf, ...** I am asking you for the last time ...; **jmdn. dringend ~, etw. zu tun** urgently request sb. to do sth. **2** (einladen, ermuntern) **jmdn. ~, etw. zu tun** invite *or* ask sb. to do sth.; **jmdn. zu einem Spaziergang/zum Mitspielen/Sitzen ~:** invite sb. for a walk/invite *or* ask sb. to join in/sit down; **jmdn. [zum Tanz] ~:** ask sb. to dance

auffordernd
A *Adj.* **mit einer ~en Geste** with a gesture of invitation; **mit ~em Blick** with a look of encouragement
B *adv.* encouragingly

Auf·forderung *die* **1** request; (nachdrücklicher) demand; **nach dreimaliger/mehrmaliger ~:** after three/repeated requests **2** (Einladung, Ermunterung) invitation

Aufforderungs·satz *der* (Sprachw.) *clause/sentence expressing a wish, desire, or command*

auf|forsten
A *tr. V.* afforest; (wieder ~) reforest; **einen Wald ~:** restock a forest
B *itr. V.* establish woods; (wieder ~) re-establish the woods

Aufforstung *die; ~, ~en* afforestation; (Wieder~) reforestation; **die ~ der Wälder** restocking the forests

auf|fressen
A *unr. tr. V.* **1** eat up; (fig.) swallow up ‹*small business*›; eat up ‹*savings, money, etc.*›; **er wird dich [deswegen] nicht [gleich]** ~ (ugs.) he won't *or* isn't going to bite your head off [for that] **2** (fig. ugs.: krank machen) **jmdn. ~:** eat sb. up **3** (fig.: auflösen) **etw. ~** ‹*acid etc.*› eat sth.
B *unr. itr. V.* ‹*animal*› eat [all] its food up; (salopp) ‹*person*› eat [everything] up

auf|frischen
A *tr. V.* **1** (wieder frisch machen) freshen up; brighten up ‹*colour, paintwork*›; renovate ‹*polish, furniture*›; (restaurieren) restore ‹*tapestry, fresco, etc.*›; (fig.) revive ‹*old memories*›; renew ‹*acquaintance, friendship*›; **seine Englischkenntnisse ~:** brush up one's [knowledge of] English **2** (auffüllen) stock up on ‹*supplies*›
B *itr. V.; auch mit sein* ‹*wind*› freshen

Auffrischung *die; ~, ~en* ▸ **auffrischen**: **1** freshening up; brightening up; renovation; restoration; renewal; **zur ~ meiner Englischkenntnisse** to brush up my [knowledge of] English **2** **die ~ der Biervorräte** *usw.* stocking up on beer [supplies] *etc.*

aufführbar *Adj.* stageable ‹*play, ballet, opera*›; performable ‹*piece of music*›

auf|führen
A *tr. V.* **1** put on, stage ‹*play, ballet, opera*›; screen, put on ‹*film*›; perform ‹*piece of music*›; put on ‹*concert*›; **führ doch nicht so ein Theater auf!** don't make such a fuss! **2** (nennen) cite, quote, adduce ‹*example, reason, fact*›; cite ‹*witness*›; **Waren/Preise in einem Verzeichnis ~:** list goods/prices
B *refl. V.* behave; **er hat sich wieder einmal aufgeführt** he made another fuss

Auf·führung *die* **1** performance; **zur ~ bringen** (Papierdt.) put on, stage ‹*play, ballet, opera*›; screen, put on ‹*film*›; perform ‹*piece of music*›; put on ‹*concert*›; **zur ~ gelangen** *od.* **kommen** (Papierdt.) ‹*play, ballet, opera*› be staged; ‹*film*› be screened; ‹*piece of music, composer*› be performed; ‹*concert*› be put on **2** (Nennung) ▸ **aufführen A 2**: citation; quotation; listing

Aufführungs·recht *das* performing rights *pl.*

auf|füllen
A *tr. V.* **1** (voll füllen, füllen) fill up; fill in ‹*hole, gap, crack*› **2** (fig.: ergänzen) replenish ‹*stocks*›; bring ‹*team, battalion, etc.*› up to full strength **3** (ugs.: nachfüllen) **Wasser/Öl/Benzin ~:** top up (Brit.) *or* (Amer.) fill up with water/oil/fill up with petrol (Brit.) *or* (Amer.) gasoline
B *refl. V.* (Met.) ‹*low-pressure area*› fill

auf|futtern *tr. (auch itr.) V.* (fam.) eat up

auf|füttern *tr. V.* rear ‹*animal*› (**mit** on)

Auf·gabe *die* **1** (zu Bewältigendes) task; **sich** (*Dat.*) **zur ~ machen, etw. zu tun** make it one's task *or* job to do sth.; **sich** (*Dat.*) **etw. zur ~ machen** make sth. one's task *or* job **2** (Pflicht) task; responsibility; duty **3** (fig.: Zweck, Funktion) function **4** (Schulw.) (Übung) exercise; (Prüfungs~) question **5** (Schulw.: Haus~) piece of homework; **~n** homework *sing.*; **ich muss noch ~n machen** I still have homework to do **6** (Rechen~, Mathematik~) problem **7** (Beendigung) abandonment **8** (Kapitulation) retirement; (im Schach) resignation; **jmdn. zur ~ zwingen** force sb. to retire/resign **9** (Verzicht) giving up; (eines Plans, einer Forderung) giving up; abandonment; dropping; (eines Berufs, Versuchs) giving up; abandonment **10** (einer Postsendung) posting (Brit.); mailing (Amer.); (eines Telegramms) handing in; (einer Bestellung, einer Annonce) placing **11** (von Gepäck) depositing; (am Flughafen) checking in **12** (bes. Volleyball) service

auf|gabeln *tr. V.* (salopp) pick up; **wo hat die Firma bloß diesen Analphabeten aufgegabelt?** where on earth did the firm get hold of this illiterate?

Aufgaben-: ~bereich *der,* **~gebiet** *das* area of responsibility; **~stellung** *die* nature of the task; **sich mit der neuen ~stellung vertraut machen** (bei Ressortwechsel) familiarize oneself with one's new duties *or* responsibilities; **~verteilung** *die* **1** (das Verteilen) allocation of duties *or* responsibilities; **2** (das Verteiltsein) distribution of responsibilities

Aufgabe-: ~ort *der* (Postw.) place of posting (Brit.) *or* (Amer.) mailing; **~stempel** *der* (Postw.) postmark [showing time and place of posting (Brit.) *or* (Amer.) mailing]

Auf·gang *der* **1** (Sonnen~, Mond~ usw.) rising **2** (Treppe) stairs *pl.*; staircase; stairway; (in einem Bahnhof, zu einer Galerie, einer Tribüne) steps *pl.* **3** (Weg) **der ~ zur Burgruine** the path up to the ruined castle **4** (Turnen) mount (**auf** + *Akk.* on to)

auf|geben
A *unr. tr. V.* **1** (beenden) give up; **gibs auf!** (ugs.) you might as well give up!; why don't you give up! **2** (sich trennen von) give up ‹*habit, job, flat, business, practice, etc.*›; give up, abandon, drop ‹*plans, demand*›; give up, abandon ‹*profession, attempt*›; give up, stop ‹*smoking, drinking*› **3** (verloren geben) give up ‹*patient*›; give up hope on *or* with ‹*wayward son, daughter, etc.*›; give up, abandon ‹*chessman*›; **sich selbst ~:** give oneself up for lost **4** (nicht länger zu gewinnen versuchen) give up ‹*struggle*›; retire from ‹*race, competition*›; **eine Partie ~:** concede a game **5** (übergeben, übermitteln) post (Brit.), mail ‹*letter, parcel*›; hand in, (telefonisch) phone in ‹*telegram*›; place ‹*advertisement, order*›; check ‹*luggage*› in; (am Flughafen) check ‹*baggage*› in; (zur Aufbewahrung im Bahnhof) deposit ‹*luggage*› **6** (Schulw.: als Hausaufgabe) set (Brit.); assign (Amer.); **viel/nichts ~:** set (Brit.) *or* (Amer.) assign a lot of/no homework **7** (zur Lösung vorlegen) **jmdm. ein Rätsel/eine Frage ~:** set (Brit.) *or* (Amer.) assign sb. a puzzle/pose sb. a question **8** (geh. veralt.: auftragen, auferlegen) **jmdm. ~, etw. zu tun** charge sb. with doing sth.; **es war ihr aufgegeben, schweigend zu dulden** it was her lot to suffer in silence **9** (landsch.: auf den Teller geben) serve [up]; **jmdm. etw. ~:** serve sb. [up] sth.
B *unr. itr. V.* **1** give up; (im Sport) retire; (Schach) resign **2** ▸ **aufschlagen A 4** **3** (landsch.: Essen auf den Teller geben) dish up; **jmdm. ~:** serve sb.; **jmdm. zum zweiten Mal ~:** give sb. a second helping

auf·geblasen
A *2. Part. v.* **aufblasen**
B *Adj.* puffed up

Aufgeblasenheit *die; ~:* self-importance

Auf·gebot *das* **1** (aufgebotene Menge) contingent; (Sport: Mannschaft) contingent; squad; (an Arbeitern) squad; **ein gewaltiges ~ an Polizisten/Fahrzeugen/Material** a huge force of police/array of vehicles/materials **2** (zur Heirat) notice of an/the intended marriage; (kirchlich) banns *pl.*; **das ~ bestellen** give notice of an/the intended marriage; (kirchlich) put up the banns

auf·gedreht
A *2. Part. v.* **aufdrehen**
B *Adj.* (ugs.) in high spirits *pred.*; **er war unheimlich ~:** he was in tremendously high spirits

auf·gedunsen *Adj.* bloated

auf|gehen *unr. itr. V.; mit sein* **1** (am Horizont erscheinen) rise **2** (sich öffnen [lassen]) ‹*door, parachute, wound*› open; ‹*stage curtain*› go up, rise; ‹*knot, button, zip, bandage, shoelace, stitching*› come undone; ‹*boil, pimple, blister*› burst; ‹*flower, bud*› open [up]; **das Weckglas ist wieder aufgegangen** the top has come off the preserving jar [3] (keimen) come up [4] (aufgetrieben werden) ‹dough, cake› rise [5] (Math.) ‹calculation› work out, come out; ‹equation› come out; **3 geht in 12 auf** 3 goes into 12; 12 is divisible by 3; **12 durch 3 geht glatt** *od.* **genau auf** 3 goes into 12 without a remainder; **7 durch 3 geht nicht auf** threes into seven won't go; **seine Rechnung ging nicht auf** (fig.) he had miscalculated; **die Patience geht auf** (fig.) the game of patience comes out [6] (klar werden) **etw. geht jmdm. auf** sb. realizes sth.; **der Sinn dieses Satzes ist mir noch nicht ganz aufgegangen** I don't quite grasp the meaning of this sentence [7] (einbezogen werden) **in etw.** (*Dat.*) **~:** become absorbed into sth.; *s. auch* **Flamme** [8] (Erfüllung finden) **in etw.** (*Dat.*) **~:** be completely absorbed in sth.; **er geht ganz in seiner Familie auf** his whole life revolves around his family [9] (Jagdw.: beginnen) **die Jagd geht im August auf** the hunting season *or* open season starts in August

auf|geilen *tr. V.* (salopp) **jmdn. [mit/durch etw.] ~:** get sb. randy [with sth.]; **sich [an etw.** (*Dat.*)**] ~:** get randy [with sth.]; (fig.) get worked up [about sth.]

aufgeklärt
A *2. Part. v.* **aufklären**
B *Adj.* enlightened; (sexualkundlich) **~ sein/werden** know/be taught the facts of life; *s. auch* **Absolutismus**

Aufgeklärtheit *die;* **~:** enlightened views *pl.*; **bei aller ~:** although he is/they are *etc.* so enlightened

aufgekratzt
A *2. Part. v.* **aufkratzen**
B *Adj.* (ugs.) in high spirits *pred.*; **in ~er Stimmung** in high spirits

Auf·geld *das* (landsch.) ▸ **Aufschlag 2**

auf·gelegt
A *2. Part. v.* **auflegen**
B *Adj.* [1] (gelaunt) **gut/schlecht/heiter** *usw.* **~ sein** be in a good/bad/cheerful *etc.* mood; **zu etw. ~ sein** be in the mood for sth.; **dazu ~ sein, etw. zu tun** be in the mood to do sth. [2] (offensichtlich) **ein ~er Schwindel** a blatant swindle

auf·gelöst
A *2. Part. v.* **auflösen**
B *Adj.* distraught; **vor Schmerz/Trauer/Freude ~ sein** be beside oneself with pain/grief/joy; *s. auch* **Träne**

aufgeräumt
A *2. Part. v.* **aufräumen**
B *Adj.* jovial

aufgeregt
A *2. Part. v.* **aufregen**
B *Adj.* (erregt) excited; (nervös, beunruhigt) agitated
C *adv.* (erregt) excitedly; (nervös, beunruhigt) agitatedly

Aufgeregtheit *die;* **~:** excitement; agitation; (Nervosität) agitation

auf·geschlossen
A *2. Part. v.* **aufschließen**
B *Adj.* open-minded (**gegenüber** as regards, about); (interessiert, empfänglich) receptive, open (+ *Dat.*, **für** to); (mitteilsam) communicative; (zugänglich) approachable; **einer Sache** (*Dat.*) **~ gegenüberstehen** be open-minded about sth.

Auf·geschlossenheit *die* ▸ **aufschließen B**: open-mindedness; receptiveness; openness; communicativeness; approachableness

auf·geschmissen *Adj.* (ugs.) *in* **[ganz] [schön] ~ sein** be [right] up the creek (sl.); be in a [real] fix

auf·geschossen *2. Part. v.* **aufschießen**

aufgesetzt
A *2. Part. v.* **aufsetzen**
B *Adj.* put on

aufgestellt
A *2. Part. v.* **aufstellen**
B *Adj.* (schweiz.) ▸ **aufgeschlossen**

aufgeweckt
A *2. Part. v.* **aufwecken**
B *Adj.* bright; sharp

Aufgewecktheit *die;* **~:** brightness; sharpness

auf|gießen *unr. tr. V.* [1] (aufbrühen) make, brew [up] ‹tea›; make ‹coffee› [2] (gießen auf, darauf gießen) **etw. [auf etw.** (*Akk.*)**] ~:** pour sth. on [to sth.] [3] (übergießen) **etw. mit Milch/Wasser** *usw.* **~:** pour milk/water *etc.* on [to] sth.

auf|gliedern *tr. V.* subdivide, break down, split up (**in** + *Akk.* into); structure ‹essay›; (nach Kategorien) categorize; **aufgegliedert nach Berufen/Einkommen** broken down by occupation/income

Auf·gliederung *die* ▸ **aufgliedern**: subdivision; breakdown; structuring; categorization

auf|glimmen *unr.* (*auch regelm.*) *itr. V.; mit sein* [begin to] glimmer; (fig.) ‹hope, suspicion› flicker up

auf|glühen *itr. V.; mit sein* [begin to] glow; (fig.) ‹passion› begin to burn; **eine Hoffnung glühte in ihm auf** he felt a gleam of hope

auf|graben *unr. tr. V.* (umgraben) dig over; (freilegen) dig up

auf|greifen *unr. tr. V.* [1] (festnehmen) pick up [2] (sich befassen mit) take *or* pick up ‹subject, suggestion› [3] (fortsetzen) take up again; continue

auf Grund, aufgrund ▸ **Grund 3**

Auf·guss, ***Auf·guß** *der* infusion; (fig.) rehash

Aufguss·beutel, ***Aufguß·beutel** *der;* (Teebeutel) tea bag; (für Kräutertee) herb sachet

auf|haben (ugs.)
A *unr. tr. V.* [1] (aufgesetzt haben) have on; wear; **sie hat ihre Brille nicht aufgehabt** she didn't have her glasses on; she wasn't wearing her glasses [2] (geöffnet haben) have ‹zip› undone; have ‹door, window, jacket, blouse› open; **die Augen ~:** have one's eyes open; **seinen Laden/sein Büro ~:** have one's shop/office open; be open [3] (aufbekommen haben) have got ‹cupboard, case, safe, etc.› open; have got ‹knot, zip› undone [4] (für die Schule) **etw. ~:** have sth. as homework; **viel/wenig ~:** have a lot of/not have much homework; **haben wir etwas in** *od.* **für Englisch auf?** have we got any English homework? [5] (aufgegessen haben) have eaten up *or* finished
B *unr. itr. V.* ‹shop, office› be open; **wir haben bis 17.30 auf** we are open until 5.30 p.m.

auf|hacken *tr. V.* (mit einer Hacke) break up; (mit dem Schnabel) peck *or* break open

auf|halsen /ˈaufhalzn̩/ *tr. V.* (ugs.) **jmdm./sich etw. ~:** saddle sb./oneself with sth.; **sich** (*Dat.*) **etw. ~ lassen** get oneself saddled with sth.

auf|halten
A *unr. tr. V.* [1] (anhalten) halt; halt, check ‹inflation, advance, rise in unemployment›; **jmdn. an der Grenze ~:** hold sb. up at the border [2] (stören) hold up [3] (ugs.: geöffnet halten) hold ‹sack, door, etc.› open; **die Augen [und Ohren] ~:** keep one's eyes [and ears] open; **die Hand ~** (auch fig.) hold out one's hand
B *unr. refl. V.* [1] (sich befassen) **sich mit jmdm./etw. ~:** spend [a long] time on sb./sth.; **sich zu lange mit jmdm./etw. ~:** spend too long on sb./sth.; **sich bei etw. ~:** linger over sth. [2] (verweilen) stay; **tagsüber hielt er sich im Museum auf** he spent the day in the museum; **sich im Winter in der Küche ~:** live in the kitchen in the winter; **der Gesuchte soll sich in Frankreich ~:** the wanted man is thought to be in France

aufhältig *Adj.* (Amtsspr.) resident

aufhältlich *Adj.* (Amtsspr.) resident

auf|hängen
A *tr. V.* [1] (auf etw. hängen) hang up; hang ‹picture, curtains›; **die Wäsche ~:** hang up the washing *or* (Amer.) wash; (draußen) hang out the washing; **den Hörer ~:** hang up [2] (erhängen) hang; **jmdn. an etw.** (*Dat.*) **~:** hang sb. from sth. [3] (ugs.) **jmdm. etw. ~** (andrehen) palm sth. off on sb.; (glauben machen) talk sb. into believing sth.; (aufbürden) saddle sb. with sth. [4] **etw. an einer Frage/einem bestimmten Fall** *usw.* **~:** use a question/a specific case *etc.* as a peg to hang sth. on
B *refl. V.* (sich erhängen) hang oneself; **wo kann ich mich ~?** (ugs. scherzh.) where can I hang up my things?

Aufhänger *der;* **~s, ~** [1] (Schlaufe) loop [2] (fig.: aktuelles Ereignis) peg; **ein guter ~ für etw.** a good peg to hang sth. on

Aufhängung *die;* **~** (Technik) suspension

auf|hauen *unr.* (*ugs. auch regelm.*) *tr. V.* [1] (öffnen) knock a hole in ‹ice, wall›; crack open ‹nut, coconut› [2] (ugs.: verletzen) **sich** (*Dat.*) **das Knie/die Stirn usw. ~:** gash one's knee/forehead *etc.*

auf|häufen
A *tr. V.* pile up; (fig.) amass ‹treasure, riches›
B *refl. V.* (auch fig.) pile up; accumulate

auf|hebeln *tr. V.* lever open; force open ‹jaws›; (aufbrechen) break open

auf|heben *unr. tr. V.* [1] (hochheben) pick up; pick *or* lift up ‹heavy object, burden›; lift [off] ‹lid, cover› [2] (aufbewahren) keep; preserve; **gut/schlecht aufgehoben sein** be/not be in good hands (**bei** with); **dein Geheimnis ist bei mir sicher aufgehoben** your secret is quite safe with me [3] (abschaffen) abolish; repeal ‹law›; rescind, revoke ‹order, instruction›; cancel ‹contract›; lift ‹ban, prohibition›; **das neue Gesetz hebt die alte Regelung auf** the new law supersedes the old regulation; *s. auch* **aufschieben 1** [4] (ausgleichen) cancel out; neutralize, cancel ‹effect›; **sich [gegenseitig] ~:** cancel each other out [5] (beenden) close ‹meeting›; lift ‹blockade, siege, martial law›; **die Tafel ~** (geh.) bring the meal to a close [6] (erheben) **die Hand/den Kopf ~:** raise one's hand/head

Aufheben *das;* **~s** *in* **viel ~[s]/kein ~ von jmdm./etw. machen** make a great fuss/not make any fuss about sb./sth.; **ohne jedes/großes ~:** without any/a great deal of *or* much fuss

Auf·hebung *die* [1] (Abschaffung) ▸ **aufheben 3**: abolition; repeal; rescindment; revocation; cancellation; lifting [2] (Beendigung) ▸ **aufheben 5**: closure; lifting

Aufhebungs·vertrag *der* agreement to terminate a/the contract

auf|heitern
A *tr. V.* (heiterer stimmen) cheer up; brighten up ‹life›
B *refl. V.* [1] (froher werden) ‹mood, face, expression› brighten [2] (heller werden) ‹weather› clear *or* brighten up; ‹sky› brighten
C *itr. V.* **es heitert auf** it is clearing up; **zeitweilig ~d** [some] bright periods

Aufheiterung *die;* **~, ~en** [1] (des Wetters) bright period [2] (Erheiterung) cheering up; **zur allgemeinen ~:** to cheer everyone up

auf|heizen (bes. Physik, Technik)
A *tr. V.* heat [up]; (fig.) inflame ‹tensions, conflict›; fuel ‹mistrust›
B *refl. V.* heat up

auf|helfen *unr. itr. V.* [1] (beim Aufstehen helfen) **jmdm. ~:** help sb. up; (fig.) help sb. [to get] back on his/her feet again [2] (aufbessern) boost ‹self-confidence, income›

auf|hellen
A *tr. V.* [1] (heller machen) brighten; lighten ‹hair, shadow, darkness›; (fig.) brighten [up] ‹mood, life› [2] (klären) shed *or* cast *or* throw light on
B *refl. V.* [1] (hell werden) ‹sky› brighten; ‹hair› turn *or* go lighter; ‹day, weather› brighten [up]; **sein Gesicht/seine Miene hellte sich auf** his face/expression brightened; **es hat sich aufgehellt** it's brightened up [2] (durchschaubar werden) ‹sense, meaning› become clear

Aufheller *der;* **~s, ~** [1] (Fot.) fill-in photoflood [2] (in Waschmitteln) colour-intensifier; brightener [3] (ugs.: Medikament) pep pill (coll.)

auf|hetzen *tr. V.* incite; **jmdn. zur Meuterei/zu Gewalttaten ~:** incite sb. to mutiny/violence

Aufhetzung *die;* **~, ~en** incitement

auf|heulen *itr. V.* [1] (heulen) ‹siren› wail; ‹animal› howl; ‹engine, crowd› give a roar [2] (ugs.: weinen) howl

auf|holen
A *tr. V.* make up ‹time, delay›; make up, pull back ‹lead›; catch up on ‹studies, neglected work›; **ein paar Sekunden/Meter ~:** make up *or* pull back a few seconds/metres
B *itr. V.* [1] catch up; ‹train› make up time; ‹ath-

lete, competitor› make up ground; (Zeit ~) make up time 2 (Börsenw.) ‹*shares*› rise

auf|horchen *itr. V.* prick up one's ears; **die Öffentlichkeit ~ lassen** (fig.) make the public [sit up and] take notice

auf|hören *itr. V.* stop; ‹*friendship*› end; (ugs.: das Arbeitsverhältnis aufgeben) finish; **das muss ~!** this has got to stop!; **da hört [sich] doch alles auf!** (ugs.) that really is the limit! (coll.); **die Musik hörte auf** the music ended *or* came to an end; (wurde abgebrochen) the music stopped; **es hat aufgehört zu schneien** it's stopped snowing; **[damit] ~, etw. zu tun** stop doing sth.; **nicht [damit] ~, etw. zu tun** keep on doing sth.; **hört mit dem Lärm/Unsinn auf** stop that noise/nonsense; **ich habe mit dem Buch aufgehört und ein anderes angefangen** I've stopped reading that book and started another; **mit dem Fußboden kannst du jetzt aufhören, der ist sauber genug** you can leave the floor now, it's clean enough; **ich höre hier bald auf** I'm just about to finish; (kündige bald) I'm giving up this job soon; **ohne aufzuhören** without stopping; *s. auch* **Spaß 2**

auf|hübschen *tr. V.* smarten up; improve ‹*complexion*›; spruce up ‹*image*›; **sich ~ lassen** have a makeover

auf|jagen *tr. V.* start ‹*game, animals*› from cover; put up ‹*birds*›; **jmdn. aus dem Schlaf ~** (fig.) rouse sb. [violently] from his/her sleep

auf|jauchzen *itr. V.*; **[vor Freude/Entzücken** *usw.***] ~:** shout for joy/with delight *etc.*

auf|jaulen *itr. V.* howl; give a howl

Auf·kauf *der* buying up; **durch Aufkäufe kleiner Firmen** by buying up smaller firms

auf|kaufen *tr. V.* buy up

Auf·käufer *der*, **Auf·käuferin** *die* buyer

auf|kehren *tr.* (*auch itr.*) *V.* (bes. südd.) sweep up

auf|keimen *itr. V.*; *mit sein* sprout; (fig.) ‹*suspicion, doubt, fear, longing, reluctance*› begin to grow; ‹*hope, passion, love, sympathy*› burgeon

auf|klaffen *itr. V.*; *mit sein* open wide; gape (also fig.)

aufklappbar *Adj.* ‹*chair, table*› which folds open; folding *attrib.* ‹*chair, table*›; fold-back ‹*car hood*›; opening *attrib.* ‹*window*›; hinged ‹*flap, lid*›; **eine zu einem Doppelbett ~e Couch** a settee which converts into a double bed

auf|klappen
A *tr. V.* open, fold open ‹*chair, table*›; open [up] ‹*suitcase, trunk*›; fold back ‹*car hood*›; open ‹*window, door, book, knife*›
B *itr. V.*; *mit sein* ‹*shutters, door*› open, swing open

auf|klaren *itr. V.* (Met.) ‹*sky*› clear; ‹*weather*› clear up; **örtlich ~d** clearing locally

auf|klären
A *tr. V.* 1 (klären) clear up ‹*matter, mystery, question, misunderstanding, error, confusion*›; solve ‹*crime, problem*›; elucidate, explain ‹*event, incident, cause*›; resolve ‹*contradiction, disagreement*› 2 (unterrichten) enlighten; (informieren) inform; **jmdn. über jmdn./etw. ~:** enlighten/inform sb. about sb./sth.; **jmdn. [darüber] ~, wie .../was ...** enlighten/inform sb. how .../what ... 3 (sexualkundlich) **ein Kind ~:** tell a child the facts of life; educate a child in sexual matters 4 (Milit.) reconnoitre
B *refl. V.* 1 (sich klären) ‹*misunderstanding, mystery*› be cleared up 2 (sich aufhellen) ‹*weather*› clear up; brighten [up]; ‹*sky*› clear, brighten

Aufklärer *der;* **~s, ~** 1 (hist.) philosopher of the Enlightenment 2 (Luftwaffe: Flugzeug) reconnaissance plane *or* aircraft 3 (Milit.: Soldat, Spion) scout

Aufklärerin *die;* **~, ~nen** ▸ **Aufklärer 1, 3**

aufklärerisch
A *Adj.* ‹*mission, intention*› to instruct and inform, to combat ignorance
B *adv.* **~ wirken** instruct and inform; combat ignorance

Auf·klärung *die* 1 ▸ **aufklären A 1**: clearing up; solution; elucidation; explanation; resolution; **ihm gelang die ~ des Verbrechens** he succeeded in solving the crime 2 (Information) information; **jmdm. einige ~en geben** give sb. some information *sing.* 3 (Belehrung) enlightenment; (von offizieller Stelle) informing; **um ~ darüber bitten, was vorgefallen ist** ask to be told what has happened 4 (über Sexualität) education in sexual matters; **die ~ der Kinder** telling the children the facts of life 5 (hist.) **die ~:** the Enlightenment 6 (Milit.) reconnaissance

Aufklärungs-: ~arbeit *die* educational work; **politische ~arbeit** political education; **~buch** *das* sex education book; **~film** *der* sex education film; **~flug** *der* (Luftwaffe) reconnaissance flight *or* mission; **~flug·zeug** *das* (Luftwaffe) reconnaissance plane *or* aircraft; **~kampagne** *die* information campaign; **~schrift** *die* information pamphlet; **~ziel** *das* (Milit.) reconnaissance objective

auf|klauben *tr. V.* (landsch., auch fig.) pick up

auf|kleben *tr. V.* stick on; (mit Kleister) paste on; (mit Klebstoff, Leim) stick *or* glue on

Auf·kleber *der* sticker; adhesive label

auf|klinken *tr. V.* open ‹*door*› by the handle

auf|klopfen *tr. V.* 1 (öffnen) crack open 2 (aufschütteln) plump up ‹*cushion etc.*›

auf|knacken *tr. V.* 1 crack [open] ‹*nut, cherry stone, etc.*› 2 (ugs.: aufbrechen) break into ‹*car, desk, drawer*›; break down ‹*door*›; crack ‹*safe*›

auf|knien
A *itr. V.*; *auch mit sein* (Turnen) kneel (**auf** + *Akk. od. Dat.* on)
B *refl. V.* kneel (**auf** + *Akk./Dat.* on)

auf|knöpfen *tr. V.* 1 unbutton; undo 2 **etw. auf etw.** (*Akk.*) **~:** button sth. on to sth.

auf|knoten *tr. V.* untie, undo ‹*parcel, bundle, etc.*›; unknot ‹*string, rope*›

auf|knüpfen (ugs.)
A *tr. V.* 1 (erhängen) string up (coll.), hang (**an** + *Dat.* from) 2 (aufknoten) undo, untie ‹*knot, parcel, bundle*›; unknot ‹*string, rope*›
B *refl. V.* hang oneself

auf|kochen
A *tr. V.* 1 (zum Kochen bringen) bring to the boil 2 (noch einmal kochen) reboil
B *itr. V.* 1 *mit sein* (zu kochen beginnen) come to the boil; **etw. ~ lassen** bring sth. to the boil 2 (südd., österr.: üppig kochen) prepare a magnificent spread

auf|kommen *unr. itr. V.*; *mit sein* 1 (entstehen) ‹*wind*› spring up; ‹*storm, gale*› blow up; ‹*fog*› come down; ‹*rumour*› start; ‹*suspicion, doubt, feeling*› arise; ‹*fashion, style, invention*› come in; ‹*boredom*› set in; ‹*mood, atmosphere*› develop; **etw. ~ lassen** give rise to sth. 2 **~ für** (bezahlen) bear, pay ‹*costs*›; pay for ‹*damage*›; pay, defray ‹*expenses*›; be liable for ‹*debts*›; stand ‹*loss*›; **für jmdn. ~:** pay for sb.'s upkeep 3 **~ für** (Verantwortung tragen für) be responsible for 4 **er lässt niemanden neben sich** (*Dat.*) **~:** he won't let anybody become a rival; he brooks no rivals (literary) 5 (auftreffen) land (**auf** + *Akk.* on) 6 (Sport: aufholen) (beim Wettlauf) close the gap; (Fußball, Boxen) come back 7 (sich behaupten) **gegen jmdn./etw. ~:** prevail against sb./sth. 8 (bes. südd.: entdeckt werden) be discovered; **wenn das aufkommt, ...** if it comes out, ... 9 (Seemannsspr.: in Sicht kommen) approach

Aufkommen *das;* **~s, ~** (Wirtsch.) revenue (**aus** from)

auf|kratzen *tr. V.* 1 (öffnen) scratch open ‹*wound, sore*› 2 (verletzen) scratch

auf|kreischen *itr. V.* ‹*person*› shriek, give a shriek; ‹*brake, saw*› screech

auf|krempeln *tr. V.* roll up ‹*sleeves, trousers*›; **jmdm./sich die Ärmel ~:** roll up sb.'s/one's sleeves

auf|kreuzen *itr. V.* 1 *mit sein* (ugs.: erscheinen) turn up 2 *auch mit sein* (Seemannsspr.) **gegen den Wind ~:** beat to windward

auf|kriegen (ugs.) ▸ **aufbekommen**

auf|künden (geh., schweiz.), **auf|kündigen** *tr. V.* terminate ‹*lease, contract*›; cancel ‹*subscription, membership*›; foreclose ‹*mortgage*›; **seinen Dienst ~:** hand in one's notice; **jmdm. die Freundschaft/den Gehorsam ~** (geh.) break off one's friendship with sb./refuse sb. further obedience

Auf·kündigung *die* ▸ **aufkündigen**: termination; cancellation; foreclosure; breaking off

Aufl. *Abk.* = **Auflage** ed.

auf|lachen *itr. V.* give a laugh; laugh; (schallend) burst out laughing

Auflade·karte *die* top-up card

auf|laden
A *unr. tr.* (*auch itr.*) *V.* 1 load (**auf** + *Akk.* on [to]) 2 (ugs.: tragen lassen) **jmdm. etw. ~:** load sb. with sth.; (fig.) saddle *or* load sb. with sth. 3 (Physik: elektrisch laden) charge [up] ‹*battery*›; put ‹*battery*› on charge; (nach Entladung auch) recharge; **emotional aufgeladen** (fig.) emotionally charged 4 (Kfz-W.) supercharge ‹*engine*›
B *unr. refl. V.* (Physik) ‹*battery*› charge, become charged; (nach Entladung) recharge; become recharged; **sich elektrostatisch ~:** become electrostatically charged

Auf·ladung *die* 1 (Kfz-W.) supercharging 2 (Physik) (das Aufladen) charging [up]; (nach Entladung) recharging

Auf·lage *die* 1 (Buchw.) edition; (gedruckte ~ einer Zeitung) print run; (verkaufte ~ einer Zeitung) circulation; **dieses Buch/diese Zeitung hat hohe ~n erreicht** large numbers of copies of this book have been sold/this newspaper has reached high circulation figures; **sieben ~n erleben** go through seven editions 2 (bes. Rechtsw.: Verpflichtung) condition; **mit der ~, etw. zu tun** with the condition that *or* on condition that one does sth.; **[es] jmdm. zur ~ machen, dass ...** impose on sb. the condition that ... 3 (DDR Wirtsch.) target 4 (auf Sitzmöbeln) cushion 5 (Metallüberzug) plating; **eine ~ aus Silber haben** be silver-plated 6 (Stütze) rest; support

Auflage·fläche *die* supporting surface

Auflagen·höhe *die* (Buchw.) number of copies printed; (einer Zeitung) circulation

auflagen·stark *Adj.* high-circulation ‹*newspaper, magazine*›; **~ sein** have a high *or* large circulation

Auf·lager *das* (Bauw.) support; bearer; (beweglich) bearing

auflandig (Seemannsspr.) onshore

auf|lassen *unr. tr. V.* 1 (ugs.: offen lassen) leave open 2 (ugs.: aufbehalten) keep on 3 (ugs.: aufbleiben lassen) let ‹*child*› stay up 4 (aufsteigen lassen) send up ‹*balloon, rocket, satellite*›; release ‹*carrier pigeon*› 5 (bes. südd., österr.: schließen; Bergbau: stilllegen) close *or* shut down; **eine aufgelassene Grube** a closed-down pit

Auflassung *die;* **~, ~en** (bes. südd., österr.: Schließung; Bergbau: Stilllegung) closing *or* shutting down

auf|lauern *itr. V.* **jmdm. ~:** lie in wait for sb.; (~ und angreifen) waylay sb.

Auf·lauf *der* 1 (Menschen~) crowd 2 (Speise) soufflé

auf|laufen *unr. itr. V.*; *mit sein* 1 (Seemannsspr.) run aground (**auf** + *Akk. od. Dat.* on) 2 (Sport) **zur Spitze/zu den Führenden ~:** move to the front/catch up with the leaders 3 (aufprallen) **auf jmdn./etw. ~:** run into sb./sth.; **jmdn. ~ lassen** (Fußball) body-check sb. 4 (sich ansammeln) accumulate; mount up

Auflauf·form *die* baking dish; (für Eierspeisen) soufflé dish

auf|leben *itr. V.*; *mit sein* revive; (fig.: wieder munter werden) come to life; liven up; **etw. ~ lassen** revive sth.

auf|lecken *tr. V.* lap up

auf|legen
A *tr. V.* 1 (auf etw. legen) put on ‹*record, coal, logs, tablecloth, adhesive plaster, saddle*›; **noch ein Gedeck ~:** set another place; **das Silber ~:** put out the silverware; **jmdm. das Fleisch ~:** serve sb. his/her meat; **jmdm. die Hand ~** ‹*faith healer*› lay one's hands on sb.; **den Hörer ~:** put down the receiver 2 (Buchw.) publish; **ein Buch neu** *od.* **wieder ~:** bring out a new edition of a book; (nachdrucken) reprint a book

3 (Finanzw.) issue, float ‹*shares*› **4** (Seemannsspr.) lay up ‹*ship*›
B **1** *itr. V.* (den Hörer ~) hang up; ring off (Brit.) **2** (salopp) deejay (coll.)

Auflegung *die* **1** (zur Einsichtnahme) laying open **2** (Finanzw.) issue **3** (Rel.) ~ **der Hände** laying on of hands

auf|lehnen
A *refl. V.* **sich gegen jmdn./etw. ~:** rebel *or* revolt against sb./sth.
B *tr. V.* (landsch.: aufstützen) **sich/die Arme auf etw.** (*Akk. od. Dat.*) **~:** lean on sth./lean *or* rest one's arms on sth.

Auflehnung *die;* **~, ~en** rebellion; revolt

auf|leimen *tr. V.* glue on (**auf** + *Akk.* to)

auf|lesen *unr. tr. V.* **1** (aufsammeln) pick up; gather [up]; (fig. ugs.: sich holen) pick up, catch ‹*germ, disease, illness*› **2** (ugs.: mitnehmen) pick up; **jmdn. von der Straße ~:** pick sb. up off the street

auf|leuchten *itr. V.; auch mit sein* light up; (für kurze Zeit) flash; ‹*brake light*› come on; ‹*star*› shine out; (fig.) ‹*eyes, face*› light up

auf|liegen
A *unr. itr. V.* **1** (auf etw. liegen) lie, rest (**auf** + *Dat.* on) **2** (Seemannsspr.) be laid up
B *unr. refl. V.* (ugs.: sich wundliegen) get bedsores

Auflieger *der;* **~s, ~:** trailer

auf|listen *tr. V.* list

Auflistung *die;* **~, ~en** **1** (das Auflisten) listing **2** (Liste) list

auf|lockern
A *tr. V.* **1** (locker machen) break up, loosen ‹*soil*›; loosen ‹*stuffing, hair*›; **die Muskeln ~:** loosen up one's muscles; **aufgelockerte Bewölkung** broken cloud **2** (abwechslungsreicher machen) introduce some variety into ‹*landscape, lesson, lecture*›; relieve, break up ‹*pattern, façade*› **3** (unbeschwerter machen) make ‹*mood, atmosphere, evening*› more relaxed
B *refl. V.* (seine Muskeln lockern) loosen up

Auf·lockerung *die* **1** (des Bodens) breaking up; loosening; (einer Füllung, des Haars) loosening; (der Muskeln) loosening up **2** (einer Fassade, eines Musters) relieving; breaking up; **zur ~ des Unterrichts/Vortrags** to introduce some variety into the lesson/lecture **3** **zur ~ der Stimmung/Atmosphäre/des Abends** to make the mood/atmosphere/evening more relaxed

auf|lodern *itr. V.; mit sein* (geh.) ‹*fire*› blaze *or* flare up; ‹*flames*› leap up; (fig.) ‹*jealousy, hatred, anger, passion*› flare up; **wie eine Fackel ~:** go up like a torch

auflösbar *Adj.* soluble; soluble, solvable ‹*equation, problem*›; dissoluble ‹*marriage*›

Auf·lösbarkeit *die;* ~ ▸**auflösbar**: solubility; solvability; dissolubility

auf|lösen
A *tr. V.* **1** dissolve; resolve ‹*difficulty, contradiction*›; solve ‹*puzzle, equation*›; break off ‹*engagement*›; terminate, cancel ‹*arrangement, contract, agreement*›; dissolve, disband ‹*organization*›; remove ‹*brackets*›; **etw. in seine Bestandteile ~:** resolve sth. into its constituent parts; *s. auch* **Haushalt** **2** (geh.: aufbinden) undo, untie ‹*knot, shoelace, plait*›; let down ‹*hair*›; (fig.) disentangle **3** (Musik) cancel ‹*accidental*›; resolve ‹*discord*› **4** (Optik, Fot.) resolve
B *refl. V.* **1** dissolve; ‹*parliament*› dissolve itself; ‹*crowd, demonstration*› break up; ‹*fog, mist*› disperse, lift; ‹*cloud*› break up; (fig.) ‹*resistance, vision*› dissolve; ‹*empire, kingdom, social order*› disintegrate; **sich in etw.** (*Akk.*)**/in nichts ~** (auch fig.) dissolve into sth./into nothing **2** (geh.: aufgehen) ‹*shoelace, hair, bow*› come undone **3** (sich aufklären) ‹*misunderstanding, difficulty, contradiction*› be resolved; ‹*puzzle, equation*› be solved; *s. auch* **aufgelöst B**

Auf·lösung *die* **1** ▸**auflösen A 1-4**: dissolving; resolution; solution; breaking off; termination; cancellation; dissolution; disbandment; removal; undoing; untying; disentanglement **2** ▸**auflösen B 1**: dissolving; dispersing; lifting; breaking up; (fig.) dissolving; disintegration **3** (Verstörtheit) distraction

Auflösungs-: **~erscheinung** *die* sign of disintegration; **~zeichen** *das* (Musik) natural

auflüpfisch /ˈaufl̩ʏpfɪʃ/ *Adj., adv.* (schweiz.) ▸**aufmüpfig**

aufm /ˈaufm̩/ (ugs.) = **auf dem**

auf|machen
A *tr. V.* **1** (öffnen) open; undo ‹*button, knot*›; open, undo ‹*parcel, packet*› **2** (ugs.: eröffnen) open [up] ‹*shop, theatre, business, etc.*› **3** (gestalten) get up; present; **das wurde von der Presse groß aufgemacht** the press gave it headline treatment
B *itr. V.* **1** (geöffnet werden) ‹*shop, office, etc.*› open **2** (ugs.: die Tür öffnen) open up; open the door; **jmdm. ~:** open the door to sb.; **mach auf!** open up! **3** (ugs.: eröffnet werden) ‹*shop, business*› open [up]
C *refl. V.* (aufbrechen) set out; start [out]

Auf·macher *der* (Zeitungsw.) (Schlagzeile) lead headline; (Bild) main front-page photograph

Aufmachung *die;* **~, ~en** **1** (Gestaltung) presentation; (Kleidung) get-up; **ein Buch in ansprechender ~:** an attractively presented book **2** (Zeitungsw.) **die Zeitungen haben darüber in großer ~ berichtet** it was splashed across the pages of the newspapers **3** ▸**Aufmacher**

auf|malen *tr. V.* paint on

Auf·marsch *der* **1** (Milit.: zum Kampf) deployment **2** (Parade) march past; parade **3** (schweiz.: Zulauf) attendance

Aufmarsch·gebiet *das* (Milit.) deployment area

auf|marschieren *itr. V.; mit sein* draw up; assemble; (heranmarschieren) march up; (vorbeimarschieren) march past; parade; ‹*demonstrators, delegations*› parade; **die Zeugen zur Vernehmung ~ lassen** (salopp) march the witnesses in for examination; **Truppen sind an der Grenze aufmarschiert** troops were deployed along the border

auf|meißeln *tr. V.* chisel open

auf|merken *itr. V.* **1** (aufhorchen) [sit up and] take notice **2** (geh.: aufpassen) pay attention (**auf** + *Akk.* to)

aufmerksam
A *Adj.* **1** (konzentriert) attentive ‹*pupil, reader, observer*›; keen, sharp ‹*eyes*›; **~e Nachbarn hatten bemerkt, dass ...** observant neighbours had noticed that ...; **jmdn. auf jmdn./etw. ~ machen** draw sb.'s attention to sb./sth.; bring sb./sth. to sb.'s notice; **jmdn. darauf ~ machen, dass ...** draw sb.'s attention to *or* bring to sb.'s notice the fact that ...; **auf jmdn./etw. ~ werden** become aware of *or* notice sb./sth.; **~ werden** notice **2** (höflich) attentive; **danke, sehr ~:** thank you, that's very *or* most kind of you
B *adv.* attentively

Aufmerksamkeit *die;* **~, ~en** **1** (Konzentration) attention; **jmds. ~** (*Dat.*) **entgehen** escape sb.'s attention **2** (Höflichkeit) attentiveness **3** (Geschenk) **eine [kleine] ~:** a small gift

Aufmerksamkeits-defizit-Syndrom *das* (Psych., Med.) attention deficit disorder

aufmischen *tr. V.* **1** liven up ‹*disco, meeting, city etc.*›; shake up ‹*organization, political party, etc.*›; **etw. richtig ~:** give sth. a good shake-up **2** (ugs.: verprügeln) beat up

auf|möbeln *tr. V.* (ugs.) **1** (verbessern) do up; **seinen Ruf/seine Deutschkenntnisse ~:** polish up one's reputation/knowledge of German **2** (beleben) pep *or* buck up (coll.); (aufmuntern) buck (coll.) *or* cheer up

auf|montieren *tr. V.* mount; fit [on]

auf|motzen *tr. V.* (ugs.) tart up (Brit. coll.); doll up (coll.); repackage ‹*edition, novel, record*›; (schneller machen) soup up (coll.) ‹*car, engine*›

auf|mucken, auf|mucksen *itr. V.* (ugs.) kick up *or* make a fuss; **gegen etw. ~:** balk at sth.

auf|muntern *tr. V.* **1** (aufheitern) cheer up **2** (beleben) liven up; pep up (coll.) **3** (ermutigen) encourage; **jmdn. zum Weitermachen/Widerstand/Kampf** *usw.* **~:** encourage sb. to carry on/resist/fight *etc.*

Aufmunterung *die;* **~, ~en** **1** (Aufheiterung) cheering up **2** (Belebung) livening up; pepping up (coll.); **eine Tasse Kaffee zur ~:** a cup of coffee to liven *or* (coll.) pep me/you *etc.* up **3** (Ermutigung) encouragement

aufmüpfig /ˈaufmʏpfɪç/ (ugs.)
A *Adj.* rebellious
B *adv.* rebelliously

Aufmüpfigkeit *die;* **~:** rebelliousness

aufn /ˈaufn̩/ (ugs.) = **auf den**

auf|nähen *tr. V.* sew on; **etw. auf etw.** (*Akk.*) **~:** sew sth. on [to] sth.

Aufnahme *die;* **~, ~n** **1** (Beginn) (von Verhandlungen, Gesprächen) opening; starting; (der Arbeit, einer Ermittlung, der Produktion) start; (von Beziehungen, Verbindungen) establishment; (von Studien, einer Tätigkeit) taking up; **vor ~ der Arbeit** before starting work **2** (Empfang) reception; (Beherbergung) accommodation; **jmds. ~ in ein Krankenhaus** sb.'s admission to hospital; **jmdm. eine herzliche ~ bereiten** give sb. a warm reception; **sie fanden ~ bei einer Familie** they were taken in [and looked after] by a family **3** (in einen Verein, eine Schule, Organisation) admission (**in** + *Akk.* into) **4** (von Hypotheken, Geld, Anleihen) raising **5** (Aufzeichnung) taking down; (von Personalien, eines Diktats) taking [down]; **die ~ des Protokolls der Sitzung** taking the minutes of the meeting **6** (das Fotografieren) photographing; (eines Bildes) taking; (das Filmen) shooting; filming; **bei der ~:** while taking the photograph/while shooting *or* filming **7** (Bild) picture; shot; photo[graph]; **eine ~ machen** take a picture *or* shot *or* photo[graph] **8** (das Aufnehmen auf Tonträger, das Aufgenommene) recording **9** (Anklang) reception; response (*Gen.* to) **10** (Einverleibung, Absorption) absorption **11** (das Einschließen, Verzeichnen) inclusion; **die ~ eines Wortes in den Wortschatz** the adoption of a word into the language **12** (~raum) reception (Brit.); reception office (Amer.); **in der ~ warten** wait in reception (Brit.) *or* (Amer.) the reception office

aufnahme-, Aufnahme-: **~antrag** *der* application for membership; **~bedingung** *die* **1** condition of admission; **~bedingungen** conditions *or* terms of admission; **2** *Pl.* (bei Tonaufnahme) recording conditions; (Fot., Film) shooting conditions; **~fähig** *Adj.* **1** (konzentriert) receptive (**für** to); **ich bin nicht mehr ~fähig** I can't take any more in; **2** (Wirtsch.) receptive ‹*market*›; **~fähigkeit** *die* **1** (Konzentration) receptivity (**für** to); ability to take things in; **2** (Wirtsch.) receptivity (**für** to); **~gebühr** *die* enrolment fee; **~land** *das* host country; **~leiter** *der,* **~leiterin** *die* (Film, Rundf., Ferns.) production manager; **~prüfung** *die* entrance examination; **~studio** *das* (Tonstudio) recording studio; (Filmstudio) film studio; **~wagen** *der* recording van

aufnahms-, Aufnahms- (österr.) ▸**aufnahme-, Aufnahme-**

auf|nehmen *unr. tr. V.* **1** (hochheben) pick up; lift up; (aufsammeln) pick up; (fig.) **es mit jmdm./etw. ~/nicht ~ können** be a/no match for sb./sth.; **an Intelligenz kann es keiner mit ihm ~:** nobody can compare with him for intelligence **2** (beginnen mit) open, start ‹*negotiations, talks*›; establish ‹*relations, contacts*›; take up ‹*studies, activity, occupation*›; start ‹*production, investigation*›; (fortsetzen) take up ‹*idea, theme*›; **den Kampf gegen etw. ~** (fig.) take up the fight against sth.; **etw. wieder ~:** resume sth.; **um ein Wort des Kanzlers aufzunehmen** to borrow an expression used by the chancellor **3** (empfangen) receive; (beherbergen) take in; (fig.: umhüllen) ‹*night, darkness, mist*› envelop; **in ein** *od.* **einem Krankenhaus aufgenommen werden** be admitted to hospital **4** (beitreten lassen) admit (**in** + *Akk.* to); **jmdn. als Mitglied in einen Verein** *usw.* **~:** admit sb. as a member of a club *etc.;* admit sb. to membership of a club *etc.;* **jmdn. als Teilhaber in sein Geschäft ~:** bring sb. into one's business as a partner **5** (einschließen, verzeichnen) include **6** (fassen) take; hold; absorb ‹*immigrants, goods, workers*› **7** (erfassen) take in, absorb ‹*impressions, information, etc.*›; **etw. ganz in sich ~:** take sth. in *or* absorb sth. completely **8** (absorbieren) absorb; **wieder Nahrung ~**

‹patient› take food again **9** (leihen) raise ‹mortgage, money, loan› **10** (reagieren auf) receive; **etw. positiv/mit Begeisterung ~:** give sth. a positive/an enthusiastic reception **11** (aufschreiben) take down; take [down] ‹dictation, particulars›; (Kartographie) survey and record ‹area, district› **12** (fotografieren) take ‹picture›; take a photograph of, photograph ‹scene, subject›; (filmen) film **13** (auf Tonträger) record **14** (Handarbeit) increase ‹stitch› **15** (bes. Fußball) take ‹ball›; ‹goalkeeper› take, gather ‹ball› **16** (nordd.: aufwischen) mop *or* wipe up **17** (österr.: einstellen) take on ‹staff, workers›

Aufnehmer *der;* **~s,** ~ (nordd.) cloth

äufnen /ˈɔyfnən/ *tr. V.* (schweiz.) accumulate ‹money, fortune›

auf|nesteln *tr. V.* undo

auf|norden *tr. V.* (ns.) nordicize

auf|nötigen *tr. V.* **jmdm. etw. ~:** force sth. on sb.; **die Lage nötigt uns Zurückhaltung auf** the situation forces us to be cautious

auf|oktroyieren /ˈaufǀɔktroaji:rən/ *tr. V.* **jmdm. etw. ~:** impose *or* force sth. on sb.

auf|opfern
A *tr. V.* (geh.: opfern) sacrifice (*Dat.* to)
B *refl. V.* (sich einsetzen) devote oneself sacrificingly (**für** to)

aufopfernd
A *Adj.* self-sacrificing ‹person, love, work›
B *adv.* self-sacrificingly

Auf·opferung *die* **1** (das Opfern) sacrifice **2** (das Sicheinsetzen) self-sacrifice

aufopferungs·voll ▸**aufopfernd**

auf|packen *tr. V.* **etw. ~:** load sth. on; **jmdm./einem Tier etw. ~:** load sth. on to sb./an animal; **sich** (*Dat.*) **etw. ~:** load oneself with sth.; **jmdm./sich etw. ~** (fig.) burden sb./oneself with sth.

auf|päppeln *tr. V.* feed up; (fig.) pep up

auf|passen *itr. V.* **1** look *or* watch out; (konzentriert sein) pay attention; **pass mal auf!** (ugs.) (du wirst sehen) you just watch!; (hör mal zu!) now listen; (sei aufmerksam!) pay attention!; **aufgepasst!** (ugs.) look *or* watch out!; **kannst du denn nicht ~?** can't you be more careful?; **wir haben immer aufgepasst, aber jetzt ist meine Frau doch schwanger** (ugs.) we've always been careful, but my wife's got pregnant all the same (coll.) **2** (beaufsichtigen) **auf jmdn./etw. ~:** keep an eye on sb./sth.

Aufpasser *der;* **~s,** ~ **1** (abwertend) spy **2** (Wärter, Bewacher) guard; (aus Gründen des Anstands) chaperone

Aufpasserin *die;* **~, ~nen 1** (abwertend) spy **2** (Wärterin) guard; (Anstandsdame) protector; chaperone

auf|peitschen *tr. V.* **1** (bewegen) whip up ‹sea, waves› **2** (erregen) inflame ‹passions, emotions, senses›; inflame, stir up ‹populace, crowd›

auf|peppen /ˈaufpɛpn̩/ *tr. V.* (salopp) pep up (coll.)

auf|pflanzen
A *tr. V.* **1** (aufstellen) set up **2** fix ‹bayonet›
B *refl. V.* **sich vor jmdm./etw. ~** (ugs.) plant oneself in front of sb./sth.

auf|pfropfen *tr. V.* (auch fig.) graft on (**auf** + *Akk.* to)

auf|picken *tr. V.* **1** (aufnehmen) ‹bird› peck up; (fig. ugs.) pick up ‹expression, idea, piece of information› **2** (öffnen) peck open **3** (österr.: aufkleben) stick on (**auf** + *Akk.* to)

auf|platzen *itr. V.; mit sein* burst open; ‹seam, cushion› split open; ‹wound› open up

auf|plustern
A *tr. V.* ruffle [up] ‹feathers›; puff up ‹cheeks›; (fig. ugs.: aufbauschen) blow up (**zu** into)
B *refl. V.* **1** ‹bird› ruffle [up] its feathers **2** (ugs. abwertend: sich wichtig tun) puff oneself up

auf|polieren *tr. V.* (auch fig.) polish up

auf|polstern *tr. V.* reupholster

auf|prägen *tr. V.* emboss; stamp; **jmdm./einer Sache einen Stempel ~** (fig.) leave one's/its mark on sb./sth.

Auf·prall *der;* **~[e]s, ~e** impact

auf|prallen *itr. V.; mit sein* **auf etw.** (*Akk.*, seltener *Dat.*) **~:** strike *or* hit sth.; (auf etw. auffahren) collide with *or* run into sth.

Auf·preis *der* extra *or* additional charge; **gegen ~:** for an extra *or* additional charge

auf|probieren *tr. V.* try on ‹hat, cap, spectacles›

auf|pulvern *tr.* (*auch itr.*) *V.* (ugs.) pep up (coll.); boost, lift ‹morale›; **Kaffee pulvert [einen] auf** coffee peps you up (coll.)

auf|pumpen
A *tr. V.* pump up, inflate ‹tyre›; inflate ‹air mattress, rubber boat›; pump up *or* inflate the tyres of *or* on ‹bicycle›
B *refl. V.* (ugs.) ‹bird› ruffle [up] its feathers

auf|putschen *tr. V.* (abwertend) **1** (stimulieren) stimulate; arouse ‹passions, urge›; **~de Mittel** stimulants; **jmdn./sich mit Kaffee ~:** give sb. coffee/drink coffee as a stimulant **2** (aufhetzen) incite; stir up (**gegen** against)

Aufputsch·mittel *das* stimulant

Auf·putz *der* get-up; **die Häuser standen in festlichem ~:** the houses were festively decorated

auf|putzen *tr. V.* **1** decorate ‹Christmas tree, building, etc.› **2** (fig. ugs.) **mit bürgerlichen Ideen aufgeputzter Sozialismus** socialism dressed up in bourgeois ideas

auf|quellen *unr. itr. V.; mit sein* **1** (größer werden) swell up; ‹dough› rise; **aufgequollene Augen/Wangen** swollen eyes/cheeks **2** (geh.: emporsteigen, auch fig.) well *or* rise up; ‹smoke› rise [up]

auf|raffen
A *tr. V.* (hochnehmen) gather up
B *refl. V.* **1** (sich erheben) pull oneself up [on to one's feet]; struggle to one's feet **2** (sich überwinden) pull oneself together; **sich dazu ~, etw. zu tun** bring oneself to do sth.; **sich zu einer Arbeit/Entscheidung ~:** bring oneself to do a piece of work/come to a decision

auf|ragen *itr. V.* tower [up]; ‹tower, mountain range› rise up

auf|rappeln *refl. V.* (ugs.) **1** ▸**aufraffen B 1, 2 2** (Schwäche überwinden) recover

auf|rauchen *tr. V.* finish [smoking] ‹cigarette, pipe, etc.›; **die ganze Schachtel/alle Zigaretten ~:** get through *or* smoke the whole packet/all the cigarettes

auf|rauen, *auf|rauhen *tr. V.* roughen [up]; nap ‹cloth›

Aufräum·arbeit *die* **1** clearing the way *no art.* **2** *Pl.* clearing-up operations

auf|räumen
A *tr. V.* **1** (in Ordnung bringen) tidy *or* clear up; (fig.) sort out **2** (wegräumen) clear *or* put away
B *itr. V.* **1** (Ordnung machen) tidy *or* clear up; (fig.) sort things out **2** (beseitigen) **mit jmdm./etw. ~:** eliminate sb./sth.

Aufräumungs·arbeiten *Pl.* clearance work *sing.*

auf|rechnen *tr. V.* **1** (berechnen) charge for **2** (verrechnen) **etw. gegen etw. ~:** set sth. off against sth.

auf·recht
A *Adj.* **1** (aufgerichtet) upright ‹position›; upright, erect ‹posture, bearing›; **der ~e Gang ist für den Menschen charakteristisch** human beings characteristically walk upright; **etw. ~ hinstellen** place sth. upright *or* in an upright position **2** (redlich) upright
B *adv.* (aufgerichtet) ‹walk, sit, hold oneself› straight, erect; **die Aussicht/Hoffnung hält ihn ~** (fig.) the prospect/hope keeps him going; **sich kaum noch ~ halten können** be hardly able to stand

aufrecht|erhalten *unr. tr. V.* maintain; maintain, keep up ‹deception, fiction, contact, custom›; keep to ‹decision›; **nur der Gedanke an ein kühles Bier erhielt ihn aufrecht** (fig.) it was only the thought of a cool beer that kept him going

Aufrecht·erhaltung *die* ▸**aufrechterhalten**: maintenance; keeping up; **zur ~ des Kontakts** in order to maintain contact

auf|regen
A *tr. V.* (erregen) excite; (ärgerlich machen) annoy; irritate; (beunruhigen) agitate; (ugs.: entrüsten) upset; **du regst mich auf** you're getting on my nerves
B *refl. V.* get worked up (**über** + *Akk.* about)

Auf·regung *die* (Erregung) excitement *no pl.*; (Beunruhigung) agitation *no pl.*; **jmdn. in ~ versetzen** make sb. excited/agitated; **nur keine ~!** don't get excited!; **alles war in heller ~:** everything was in utter confusion; **der Vorfall hat das ganze Land in ~ versetzt** the whole country is in an uproar over the case

auf|reiben
A *unr. tr. V.* **1** (zermürben) wear down **2** (vernichten) wipe out **3** (wund reiben) **sich** (*Dat.*) **die Hände/Fersen** *usw.* **~:** rub one's hands/heels *etc.* sore; **das Seil hatte ihm die Hände aufgerieben** the rope had chafed his hands
B *unr. refl. V.* wear oneself out

aufreibend
A *Adj.* wearing; trying ‹day, time›; (stärker) gruelling
B *adv.* tryingly, exasperatingly

auf|reihen
A *tr. V.* **1** thread ‹beads, pearls› **2** (aufstellen) line up; put in a row/rows
B *refl. V.* (sich aufstellen) line up

auf|reißen
A *unr. tr. V.* **1** (öffnen) tear *or* rip open; tear open ‹collar, shirt, etc.›; wrench open ‹drawer›; fling open ‹door, window›; **die Augen/den Mund ~:** open one's eyes/mouth wide **2** (beschädigen) tear *or* rip open; rip, tear ‹clothes›; break up ‹road, soil›; **sich** (*Dat.*) **die Haut/den Ellbogen/Ärmel ~:** gash one's skin/elbow/rip *or* tear one's sleeve **3** (bes. Fußballjargon) open up ‹defence› **4** (aufbrechen) tear up ‹road surface, pavement› **5** (Bautechnik) make a drawing of **6** (salopp: Kontakt finden mit) pick up (coll.) **7** (salopp: sich verschaffen) get hold of; get, land oneself ‹job›
B *itr. V.; mit sein* (auseinander reißen) ‹clothes› tear, rip; ‹seam› split; ‹wound› open; ‹clouds› break up

auf|reizen *tr. V.* **1** (erregen) excite ‹senses, imagination›; rouse ‹passions›; (wütend machen) provoke **2** (aufwiegeln) incite; **jmdn. zum Widerstand ~:** incite sb. to resist

auf·reizend
A *Adj.* provocative
B *adv.* provocatively

auf|ribbeln *tr. V.* (ugs.) unpick

Aufrichte *die;* **~, ~n** (schweiz.) topping-out ceremony

auf|richten
A *tr. V.* **1** (hochrichten) **den Kopf/Oberkörper ~:** raise one's head/upper body; **jmdn. ~** (auf die Beine stellen) help sb. up; **jmdn. im Bett ~:** sit sb. up in bed; **sich ~:** stand up [straight]; (aus gebückter Haltung) straighten up; (nach einem Sturz) get to one's feet; **sich im Bett ~:** sit up in bed; **sich zur vollen Länge ~:** draw oneself up to one's full height **2** (errichten) erect; put up; (fig.) build up ‹business, empire› **3** (trösten) **jmdn. [wieder] ~:** give fresh heart to sb. **4** (beleben) restore ‹pride, self-confidence›; **jmds. Mut ~:** give sb. new courage
B *refl. V.* (Mut schöpfen) take heart; **sich an jmdm./etw. [wieder] ~:** take heart from sb./sth.

auf·richtig
A *Adj.* honest, sincere ‹person, efforts›; sincere ‹regret, sympathy, affection›; genuine ‹pleasure, admiration›; **~ zu jmdm.** *od.* **gegen jmdn. sein** be honest *or* straightforward with sb.; **wenn ich ~ sein soll** to be honest *or* frank
B *adv.* sincerely; ‹speak› honestly, frankly

Auf·richtigkeit *die* sincerity; (eines Menschen) honesty; sincerity

Auf·riss, *Auf·riß *der* **1** (Bautechnik) elevation; **etw. im ~ darstellen** draw sth. in elevation **2** (Darstellung) outline

Aufriss·zeichnung, *Aufriß·zeichnung *die* (Bautechnik) elevation

auf|ritzen *tr. V.* **1** (öffnen) slit [open] **2** (verletzen) scratch; **sich** (*Dat.*) **die Haut/den Arm ~:** scratch oneself/one's arm

auf|rollen *tr. V.* **1** (zusammenrollen) roll up; coil *or* roll up ‹hose, cable›; (auf eine Rolle) roll up ‹hose, cable›; **sich** (*Dat.*) **die Haare ~** (ugs.) put one's hair up in rollers *or* curlers **2** (auseinander rollen) unroll; unfurl ‹*flag*› **3** (aufkrempeln) roll up ‹*sleeve, trouser leg*› **4** (erörtern) go into ‹*subject, question*›; **der Prozess musste noch einmal aufgerollt werden** the case had to be retried **5** (Milit.) **den Feind ~:** turn ‹*enemy, enemy position*›

auf|rücken *itr. V.; mit sein* **1** (aufschließen) move up; **dicht aufgerückt stehen** stand close [up] together **2** (befördert werden) move up; be promoted; **zum Major ~:** be promoted to major; **in eine leitende Stellung ~:** rise to a managerial position

Auf·ruf *der* **1** (das Aufrufen) call; **„Eintritt nur nach ~"** 'do not enter until called' **2** (Appell) appeal (**an** + *Akk.* to); **einen ~ an jmdn. richten** appeal to sb. **3** (DV) call **4** (Bankw.) calling-in

auf|rufen *unr. tr. V.* **1** *auch itr.* (auffordern) **jmdn. ~, etw. zu tun** call upon sb. to do sth.; **jmdn. zum Widerstand/zu Spenden ~:** call on sb. to resist/for donations; **zum [General]streik ~:** call a [general] strike **2** (namentlich) call ‹*name*›; **jmdn. ~:** call sb.; call sb.'s name; **einen Schüler ~:** call upon a pupil to answer **3** (Rechtsw.) appeal for ‹*witnesses*› [to come forward]; **etwaige Erben ~:** call on possible heirs to make themselves known **4** (DV) call

Aufruhr *der;* **~s, ~e** **1** (Widerstand) revolt; rebellion; **in ~ sein** be in revolt **2** (Erregung) turmoil; **jmdn./etw. in ~ versetzen** plunge *or* throw sb./sth. into [a state of] turmoil

auf|rühren *tr. V.* **1** stir up **2** (geh.: hervorrufen) stir up, rouse ‹*feelings*› **3** (in Erinnerung rufen) stir up ‹*memory*›; rake up ‹*scandal, story*› **4** (geh.: erregen) upset; disturb

Aufrührer *der;* **~s, ~, Aufrührerin** *die;* **~, ~nen** rabble-rouser

aufrührerisch

A *Adj.* **1** (aufwiegelnd) seditious; inflammatory **2** (in Aufruhr befindlich) rebellious

B *adv.* (aufwiegelnd) seditiously

auf|runden *tr. V.* round off (**auf** + *Akk.* to)

auf|rüsten *tr., itr. V.* arm; **wieder ~:** rearm

Auf·rüstung *die* armament

auf|rütteln *tr. V.* **jmdn. [aus dem Schlaf] ~:** shake sb. out of his/her sleep; **jmds. Gewissen ~** (fig.) stir sb.'s conscience; **jmdn. aus seiner Apathie/Lethargie** *usw.* **~** (fig.) shake sb. out of his/her apathy/lethargy *etc.*

aufs *Präp.* + *Art.* **1** = **auf das** **2** **~ Klo gehen** (ugs.) go to the loo (Brit. coll.) *or* (Amer. coll.) john; **sich ~ Bitten verlegen** resort to appeals

auf|sagen *tr. V.* **1** (sagen) recite **2** (geh.: aufkündigen) **[jmdm.] seinen Dienst ~:** give in one's notice [to sb.] (Brit.); give [one's] notice [to sb.] (Amer.); **jmdm. die Freundschaft ~:** break with sb.

auf|sammeln *tr. V.* **1** (aufheben) pick *or* gather up **2** (ugs.: aufgreifen) pick up

aufsässig /ˈaufzɛsɪç/

A *Adj.* **1** (trotzig) recalcitrant **2** (veralt.: rebellisch) rebellious

B *adv.* **1** (trotzig) recalcitrantly **2** (veralt.: rebellisch) rebelliously

Aufsässigkeit *die;* **~, ~en** **1** (Trotz) recalcitrance; (Rebellion) rebelliousness **2** (Handlung) piece of recalcitrance/rebelliousness

auf|satteln *tr. V.* saddle ‹*horse*›; hitch up ‹*trailer, sled*›

Auf·satz *der* **1** (Schul~, Abhandlung) essay; (in einer Zeitschrift) article **2** (Aufbau) top *or* upper part **3** (Orgelbau) resonator **4** (Tafel~) epergne

Aufsatz-: ~heft *das* essay book; **~thema** *das* essay subject

auf|saugen *unr.* (*auch regelm.*) *tr. V.* soak up; (fig.) absorb; (verschlucken) absorb; swallow up

auf|schauen (südd., österr., schweiz.) ▸ **aufblicken**

auf|schaukeln *refl. V.* **1** (Tech.) ‹*vehicle*› start rocking more and more violently **2** (ugs.: sich steigern) ‹*excitement etc.*› build up

auf|schäumen

A *itr. V.; meist mit sein* ‹*champagne, beer, etc.*› foam up; ‹*sea*› foam

B *tr. V.* (Technik) **etw. auf die Wand ~:** apply sth. to *or* spray sth. on to the wall as a foam

auf|scheinen *unr. itr. V.; mit sein* (auch fig., auch österr. Amtsspr.) appear

auf|scheuchen *tr. V.* **1** (aufjagen) put up ‹*birds, animals*› **2** (ugs.: in Unruhe versetzen) startle; **jmdn. aus seiner Gleichgültigkeit/Lethargie** *usw.* **~:** shake *or* jolt sb. out of his/her apathy/lethargy

auf|scheuern

A *tr. V.* (verletzen) chafe; **sich** (*Dat.*) **die Haut/die Fersen ~:** chafe one's skin/heels

B *refl. V.* (verletzt werden) become chafed *or* sore

auf|schichten *tr. V.* stack up; build [up] ‹*wall, mound, stack, pile*›; pile up ‹*straw*› [in layers]

auf|schieben *unr. tr. V.* **1** (verschieben) postpone; put off; **aufgeschoben ist nicht aufgehoben** there'll be another opportunity; there is always another time **2** slide open ‹*door, window*›; slide *or* draw back ‹*bolt*›

auf|schießen

A *unr. itr. V.; mit sein* **1** (nach oben schießen) shoot up; ‹*flames*› shoot *or* leap up **2** (schnell wachsen) shoot up; **ein lang aufgeschossener Junge** a tall gangling *or* gangly youth

B *unr. tr. V.* (Seemannsspr.) coil [up]

Auf·schlag *der* **1** (das Aufprallen) impact **2** (Preis~) extra charge; surcharge **3** (Ärmel~) cuff; (Hosen~) turn-up; (Revers) lapel **4** (Tennis usw.) serve; service; **jetzt habe ich ~:** now it's my serve

auf|schlagen

A *unr. itr. V.* **1** *mit sein* (aufprallen) **auf etw.** (*Dat. od. Akk.*) **~:** hit *or* strike sth.; **mit der Stirn/dem Kopf ~:** hit one's forehead/head on sth. **2** *auch mit sein* (teurer werden) ‹*price, rent, costs*› go up **3** (Tennis usw.) serve; **Sie schlagen auf!** it's your serve *or* service **4** (auflodern) ‹*flames*› leap up; ‹*fire*› leap *or* blaze up

B *unr. tr. V.* **1** (öffnen) crack ‹*nut, egg*› [open]; knock a hole in ‹*ice*›; **sich** (*Dat.*) **das Knie/den Kopf ~:** fall and cut one's knee/head **2** (aufblättern) open ‹*book, newspaper*›; (zurückschlagen) turn back ‹*bedclothes, blanket*›; **schlagt S. 15 auf!** turn to page 15 **3** **die Augen ~:** open one's eyes **4** (hoch-, umschlagen) turn up ‹*collar, sleeve, trouser leg*› **5** (aufbauen) set up ‹*camp*›; pitch, put up ‹*tent*›; put up ‹*bed, hut, scaffolding*› **6** (erhöhen) put up, raise, increase ‹*prices*›; **5% auf etw.** (*Akk.*) **~:** put 5% on sth. **7** (sich niederlassen) **seinen Wohnsitz in der Hauptstadt/einem Bauernhaus ~:** take up residence in the capital/a farmhouse **8** (Stricken) cast on

Auf·schläger *der,* **Auf·schlägerin** *die* (Tennis usw.) server

Aufschlag-: ~fehler *der* (Tennis usw.) [service] fault; **~zünder** *der* percussion fuse

auf|schlecken *tr. V.* lap up

auf|schließen

A *unr. tr. V.* **1** unlock; **jmdm. die Tür ~:** unlock the door for sb. **2** (Bergbau) develop **3** (Chemie, Biol.) break down **4** (Amtsspr.: erschließen) develop

B *unr. itr. V.* **1** **[jmdm.] ~:** unlock the door/gate *etc.* [for sb.] **2** (aufrücken) close up; (Milit.) close ranks; **die Autos fuhren dicht aufgeschlossen** the cars were bumper to bumper **3** (Sport) catch up (**zu** with)

auf|schlitzen *tr. V.* slit open; slash open ‹*stomach, dress*›

auf|schluchzen *itr. V.* give a sob; (stoßweise schluchzen) sob convulsively

Auf·schluss, ***Auf·schluß** *der* **1** (Auskunft) information *no pl.*; **über etw.** (*Akk.*) **~ geben** give *or* provide information about sth.; **jmdm. über etw.** (*Akk.*) **~ geben** inform sb. about sth.; **über etw.** (*Akk.*) **~ verlangen** demand an explanation of sth. **2** (Bergbau) development **3** (Chemie, Biol.) breaking up **4** (im Gefängnis) **um 7 Uhr ist ~:** the cells are unlocked at 7 o'clock

auf|schlüsseln *tr. V.* break down (**nach** according to)

Aufschlüsselung, Aufschlüsslung *die;* **~, ~en** breakdown

aufschluss·reich, ***aufschluß·reich** *Adj.* informative; (enthüllend) revealing

auf|schnallen *tr. V.* **1** (öffnen) unbuckle; unstrap; unbuckle, unfasten ‹*belt*› **2** (befestigen) strap on; **sich** (*Dat.*) **den Rucksack ~:** strap one's rucksack on [to] one's back

auf|schnappen

A *tr. V.* **1** (ugs.: hören) pick up **2** (auffangen) snap up

B *itr. V.; mit sein* (sich öffnen) snap *or* spring open

auf|schneiden

A *unr. tr. V.* **1** (öffnen) cut open; cut ‹*knot*›; lance ‹*abscess, boil*›; **sich** (*Dat.*) **den Finger ~:** cut one's finger [open]; **ein neues Buch ~:** cut the pages of a new book **2** (zerteilen) cut, slice ‹*bread, cake, cheese*›; carve, slice ‹*meat, poultry*›

B *unr. itr. V.* (ugs. abwertend: prahlen) boast, brag (**mit** about)

Auf·schneider *der,* **Auf·schneiderin** *die* (ugs. abwertend) boaster; braggart

Auf·schneiderei *die* (ugs. abwertend) boasting; bragging

auf|schnellen *itr. V.; mit sein* leap up

Auf·schnitt *der* [assorted] cold meats *pl.*/cheeses *pl.*; **kalter ~:** cold cuts *pl.*

auf|schnüren *tr. V.* undo, untie ‹*knot, parcel, string*›; unlace, undo ‹*shoe, boot, corset*›

auf|schrauben *tr. V.* **1** (öffnen, lösen) unscrew; unscrew the top of ‹*bottle, jar, etc.*› **2** (auf etw. schrauben, mit Schrauben befestigen) screw on (**auf** + *Akk.* to)

auf|schrecken

A *tr. V.* (erschrecken) startle; make ‹*person*› jump; **jmdn. aus dem Schlaf ~:** startle sb. from his/her sleep

B *itr. V.; im Präsens und Prät. auch unr.; mit sein* start [up]; **aus dem Schlaf ~:** awake with a start; start from one's sleep; **aus einem Traum/seinen Gedanken ~:** start from a dream/one's reflections

Auf·schrei *der* cry; (stärker) yell; (schriller) scream; **ein ~ der Empörung** *od.* **Entrüstung** (fig.) an outcry

auf|schreiben

A *unr. tr. V.* **1** write down; **[sich** (*Dat.*)**] etw. ~:** make a note of sth.; **er wurde von einem Polizisten aufgeschrieben** the policeman took his name and particulars **2** (ugs.: verordnen) prescribe ‹*medicine*›

B *unr. itr. V.* (bes. südd., österr.: anschreiben) give credit; **bei jmdm. ~ lassen** get credit from sb.

auf|schreien *unr. itr. V.* cry out; (stärker) yell out; (schrill) scream

Auf·schrift *die* **1** (Beschriftung) inscription; (Etikett) label **2** (Anschrift) address

Auf·schub *der* delay; (absichtliche Verschiebung) postponement; **die Sache duldet keinen ~:** the matter brooks no delay; **jmdm. ~ gewähren** (Zahlungs~) allow *or* grant sb. a period of grace; **ein ~ der Hinrichtung** a reprieve

auf|schürfen *tr. V.* **sich** (*Dat.*) **das Knie/die Haut ~:** graze one's knee/oneself

auf|schütteln *tr. V.* shake *or* plump up ‹*pillow, cushion*›

auf|schütten *tr. V.* **1** (auf etw. schütten) pour on ‹*liquid*›; **etw. auf etw.** (*Akk.*) **~:** pour sth. on *or* over sth.; **noch etwas Kohle [auf die Glut] ~:** put some more coal on [the fire] **2** (aufhäufen) pile up; pile *or* heap up ‹*sand, earth, straw*› **3** (errichten) build ‹*dam, embankment, pile*›; (erhöhen) raise ‹*road*›; (verbreitern) widen ‹*road*› **4** (Geol.) deposit

Aufschüttung *die;* **~, ~en** **1** (Erhöhung) earth bank **2** (Geol.) deposit

auf|schwatzen, (bes. südd.) **auf|schwätzen** *tr. V.* **jmdm. etw. ~:** talk sb. into having sth.; **sich** (*Dat.*) **etw. ~ lassen** be talked into having sth.

auf|schwellen

A *unr. itr. V.; mit sein* **1** (dick werden) swell up; **aufgeschwollene Leiber/Wangen** swollen bodies/cheeks **2** (laut werden) swell

B *tr. V.* (auch fig.) swell

auf|schwemmen *tr. V.* **jmdn./jmds. Gesicht ~:** make sb./sb.'s face bloated

auf|schwingen

A *unr. refl. V.* **1** (emporfliegen) ‹*bird*› soar up **2** (sich aufraffen) **sich ~, etw. zu tun** bring

oneself to do sth.; **sich zum Arbeiten/zu einem Entschluss/Brief ~:** bring oneself to get down to work/bring oneself to make a decision/write a letter 3 **sich zum Sittenrichter/Diktator** *usw.* **~:** set oneself up as a judge of morals/as a dictator *etc.*
B *unr. itr. V.* (Turnen) swing [oneself] up

Auf·schwung *der* 1 (Auftrieb) uplift; **das gab mir neuen ~:** that gave me a lift 2 (gute Entwicklung) upswing; upturn (*Gen.* in); **einen ~ erleben** experience an upswing *or* upturn 3 (Turnen) swing up

auf|sehen *unr. itr. V.* 1 look up 2 (bewundern) **zu jmdm. ~:** look up to sb.

Aufsehen *das;* **~s** stir; sensation; **[großes] ~ erregen** cause *or* create a [great] stir *or* sensation; **sich ohne großes ~ davonmachen** make off without causing a lot of fuss; **um jedes ~ zu vermeiden, reiste er inkognito** to avoid causing *or* creating a stir, he travelled incognito

aufsehen·erregend *Adj.* sensational

Auf·seher *der* (im Gefängnis) warder (Brit.); [prison] guard (Amer.); (im Park) park-keeper; (im Museum, auf dem Parkplatz) attendant; (bei Prüfungen) invigilator (Brit.); proctor (Amer.); (auf einem Gut, Sklaven~) overseer; (im Warenhaus) shopwalker (Brit.); floorwalker (Amer.)

Aufseherin *die;* **~, ~nen** (im Gefängnis) warder (Brit.); [prison] guard (Amer.); (im Museum) attendant; (bei Prüfungen) invigilator (Brit.); proctor (Amer.); (im Warenhaus) shopwalker (Brit.); floorwalker (Amer.)

***auf|sein** ▸ **auf C 1, 8**

aufseiten *Präp. + Gen.* **~ der Direktion** on the management side

auf|setzen
A *tr. V.* 1 put on ‹*hat, glasses, mask*›; **eine Miene/ein Lächeln ~** (fig.) put on an expression/a smile; **sich** (*Dat.*) **etw. ~:** put sth. on 2 (aufs Feuer setzen) put on; **Wasser [zum Kochen] ~:** put water on [to boil] 3 (entwerfen) draft; (verfassen) draw up ‹*minutes, contract, will*› 4 (aufrecht hinsetzen) **jmdn. ~:** sit sb. up; **sich ~:** sit up 5 (auf eine Unterlage) set down; lower ‹*record player arm*›; **den Fuß ~:** put one's foot on the ground *or* down 6 (aufschichten) stack [up] 7 (aufrecht hinstellen) set up ‹*skittles*› 8 (Seemannsspr.) beach 9 (Flugw.) land ‹*aircraft*›; set ‹*aircraft*› down
B *itr. V.* ‹*aircraft*› touch down, land; *s. auch* **aufgesetzt B**; **Horn 1**; **Dämpfer 2**

Auf·setzer *der* (Fußball, Handball) bouncer; bouncing ball

auf|seufzen *itr. V.* **[laut/tief] ~:** heave a [loud/deep] sigh

Auf·sicht *die* 1 (Überwachung) supervision; (bei Prüfungen) invigilation (Brit.); proctoring (Amer.); **[die] ~ haben** *od.* **führen** be in charge (**über +** *Akk.* of); (bei Prüfungen) invigilate (Brit.); proctor (Amer.); **eine ~ führende Person** a person in charge; **die ~ führende Behörde** the supervising authority; **der ~ führende Lehrer** the teacher in charge *or* on duty; **ohne ~:** unsupervised; without supervision; **unter [jmds.] ~** (*Dat.*) under [sb.'s] supervision; **unter ärztlicher/polizeilicher ~:** under medical/police supervision; **während der Pause auf dem Schulhof ~ haben** ‹*teacher*› be on duty during break 2 (Person) person in charge; (Lehrer) teacher in charge *or* on duty; (im Museum) attendant

aufsicht·führend ▸ **Aufsicht 1**

Aufsicht·führende *der/die; adj. Dekl.:* ▸ **Aufsicht 2**

Aufsichts-: ~beamte *der,* **~beamtin** *die* attendant; (im Bahnhof) supervisor; **~pflicht** *die* (Rechtsw.) legal responsibility *or* obligation to exercise proper supervision; **die elterliche ~pflicht** legal parental responsibility to keep children under proper supervision; **~rat** *der* (Wirtsch.) 1 (Gremium) board of directors; supervisory board; 2 (Mitglied) member of the board [of directors] *or* supervisory board; **~rätin** *die* ▸ **~rat 2**

auf|sitzen *unr. itr. V.* 1 *mit sein* (auf ein Reittier) mount; (auf ein Fahrzeug) get on; **auf ein Pferd ~:** mount a horse; **aufgesessen!** (Milit.) mount! 2 *mit sein* (Turnen) come to a sitting position 3 *mit sein* (hereinfallen) **jmdm./einer Sache ~:** be taken in by sb./sth. 4 (ugs.: aufrecht sitzen) sit up 5 (aufliegen) **auf etw.** (*Dat.*) **~** ‹*machine part, beam, etc.*› sit on sth. 6 (Seemannsspr.) be grounded *or* aground

Aufsitzer *der;* **~s, ~** (österr.) flop (coll.)

auf|spalten
A *unr.* (*auch regelm.*) *tr. V.* split; (fig.) split [up]
B *unr. refl. V.* split

Auf·spaltung *die* splitting; (fig.) splitting [up]

auf|spannen *tr. V.* 1 (öffnen) open, put up ‹*umbrella, parasol*›; stretch out ‹*net, jumping-sheet*›; put up ‹*tennis net, badminton net, etc.*› 2 (spannen) stretch, mount ‹*canvas*› (**auf +** *Akk.* on)

auf|sparen *tr. V.* (auch fig.) save [up]; keep

auf|speichern
A *tr. V.* (auch fig.) store up; **seine aufgespeicherte Wut/Energie** (fig.) his pent-up rage/energy
B *refl. V.* (auch fig.) build up

auf|sperren *tr. V.* 1 (ugs.: öffnen) **[weit] ~:** open wide 2 (bes. südd., österr.: aufschließen) unlock

auf|spielen
A *refl. V.* 1 (ugs. abwertend: angeben) put on airs; **sich vor jmdm. ~:** show off in front of sb. 2 (als etw. hinstellen) **sich als Held/Märtyrer ~:** act the hero/martyr; **sich als Kenner/als jmds. Anwalt ~:** set oneself up as an expert/as sb.'s lawyer
B *itr. V.* 1 (musizieren) play; **zum Tanz ~:** play dance music 2 (Sport) **groß/eindrucksvoll ~:** give a fine/impressive display

auf|spießen *tr. V.* 1 run ‹*animal, person*› through; skewer ‹*piece of meat*›; (mit der Gabel) take ‹*piece of meat*› on one's fork; (auf die Hörner nehmen) gore; **jmdn. mit seinen Blicken ~** (fig.) look daggers at sb. 2 (befestigen) pin ‹*butterfly, insect*›

auf|splittern
A *itr. V.; mit sein* ‹*wood*› splinter
B *tr. V.* (in Teile auflösen) split up ‹*party, group, country, etc.*›
C *refl. V.* ‹*party, group, country, etc.*› split up

Aufsplitterung *die;* **~, ~en** ▸ **aufsplittern**: splintering; splitting up

auf|sprengen *tr. V.* force [open]; break open; (mit Sprengstoff) blow open

auf|springen *unr. itr. V.; mit sein* 1 (hochspringen) jump *or* leap up 2 (auf ein Fahrzeug) jump on; **auf etw.** (*Akk.*) **~:** jump on [to] sth. 3 (rissig werden) crack; ‹*skin, lips*› crack, chap 4 (sich öffnen) ‹*door, window*› fly *or* burst open; ‹*bud, seed pod*› burst open 5 (auftreffen) bounce

auf|spriten /ˈaufʃprɪtn̩/ *tr. V.* fortify ‹*wine*›

auf|spritzen
A *itr. V.; mit sein* 1 (hochspritzen) ‹*blood*› spurt [up]; ‹*mud, spray, waves, sea, surf*› spray up 2 (ugs.: aufspringen) leap up; leap to one's feet
B *tr. V.* spray on; **etw. auf etw.** (*Akk.*) **~:** spray sth. on [to] sth.

auf|sprudeln *itr. V.; mit sein* ‹*spring, water*› bubble up

auf|sprühen
A *tr. V.* spray on; **etw. auf etw.** (*Akk.*) **~:** spray sth. on [to] sth.
B *itr. V.; mit sein* ‹*flames*› shoot up; ‹*sparks, spray*› fly up; ‹*water*› spray up

Auf·sprung *der* landing; (eines Balls) bounce

auf|spulen *tr. V.* wind ‹*cotton, ribbon, fishing line*› on to a/the reel *or* spool

auf|spüren *tr. V.* (auch fig.) track down

auf|stacheln *tr. V.* 1 (aufhetzen) incite; **jmdn. zur Revolte/zum Widerstand** *usw.* **~:** incite sb. to revolt/offer resistance *etc.* 2 (anspornen) spur on ‹*person, team*›; fire ‹*passion, jealousy, imagination, etc.*›

auf|stampfen *itr. V.* stamp; **mit dem Fuß ~:** stamp one's foot

Auf·stand *der* rebellion; revolt; **im ~:** in rebellion *or* revolt

auf·ständisch *Adj.* rebellious; rebel *attrib.*, insurgent ‹*army unit*›

Aufständische *der/die; adj. Dekl.* rebel; insurgent

auf|stapeln *tr. V.* stack up

auf|stauen
A *refl. V.* ‹*water*› pile up; (fig.) ‹*anger, aggression, bitterness, etc.*› build up; **aufgestaute Wut/Erbitterung** *usw.* (fig.) pent-up rage/bitterness *etc.*
B *tr. V.* dam [up]; **etw. in sich** (*Dat.*) **~** (fig.) bottle sth. up inside [one]

auf|stechen *unr. tr. V.* 1 lance, prick ‹*boil*›; prick ‹*blister*›; lance ‹*abscess*›; **jmdm./sich eine Blase ~:** prick sb.'s/one's blister 2 (ugs.: aufdecken) uncover; bring to light

Aufsteck·blitz *der* (Fot.) hot-shoe flash [unit]

auf|stecken
A *tr. V.* 1 put up ‹*curtains*›; turn up ‹*hem, dress, trousers*›; **sich** (*Dat.*) **das Haar/die Zöpfe ~:** pin *or* put one's hair/plaits up; **sie trug das Haar aufgesteckt** she wore her hair up; **Kerzen auf den Leuchter ~:** put candles on the candelabrum 2 (ugs.: aufgeben) **etw. ~:** give sth. up; pack sth. in (coll.); **einen Plan ~:** give up a plan
B *itr. V.* (bes. Sport: aufgeben) retire

auf|stehen *unr. itr. V.* 1 *mit sein* (vom Sitzplatz) stand up; (aus dem Liegen) get up; get to one's feet; (aus dem Bett) get up; (als Kranker) get up; get out of bed; **aus seinem Sessel ~:** get up from one's chair; **vom Tisch ~:** rise from the table; **für jmdn. im Bus ~:** get up for sb. in the bus; **da musst du früher** *od.* **eher ~!** (ugs.) you'll have to be a lot sharper than that!; *s. auch* **Huhn 1** 2 (offen stehen) ‹*door, window, etc.*› be open 3 *mit sein* (geh. veralt.: sich auflehnen) rise in revolt; **gegen jmdn./etw. ~:** rise [up] against sb./sth.

auf|steigen *unr. itr. V.; mit sein* 1 (auf ein Fahrrad, einen Wagen usw.) get *or* climb on; **auf etw.** (*Akk.*) **~:** get *or* climb on [to] sth.; **auf ein Pferd ~:** get on [to] *or* mount a horse 2 (bergan steigen) climb; **zum Gipfel ~:** climb [up] to the top *or* summit 3 (hochsteigen) ‹*smoke, mist, sap, air, moon, sun*› rise; ‹*storm*› gather; **eine ~de Linie** (fig.) an ascending line 4 (beruflich, gesellschaftlich) rise (**zu** to); **zum Direktor ~:** rise to the post of *or* to be manager; **zu Macht und Einfluss ~:** rise to power and influence 5 (hochfliegen) go up; ‹*bird*› soar up; **in** *od.* **mit einem Ballon ~:** go up in a balloon 6 **an die Oberfläche ~:** rise to the surface 7 (geh.: entstehen) **in jmdm. ~** ‹*hatred, revulsion, fear, etc.*› rise [up] in sb.; ‹*memory, thought*› come into sb.'s mind; ‹*doubt*› arise in sb.'s mind; ‹*tears*› well up inside sb. 8 (Sport) be promoted, go up (**in +** *Akk.* to) 9 (geh.: aufragen) rise up; tower

Auf·steiger *der* 1 **ein [sozialer] ~:** a social climber 2 (Sport) (aufsteigende Mannschaft) promotion team *or* side; (aufgestiegene Mannschaft) newly promoted side

Auf·steigerin *die* ▸ **Aufsteiger 1**

auf|stellen
A *tr. V.* 1 (hinstellen) put up (**auf +** *Akk.* on); set up ‹*skittles*›; (aufrecht hinstellen) stand up 2 (postieren) post; station 3 (auswählen) select, pick ‹*team, player*›; put together ‹*team of experts*›; raise ‹*army*›; **jmdn. für ein Spiel ~** (Sport) play sb. in a match; pick *or* select sb. for a match 4 (nominieren) nominate; put up; **jmdn. als Kandidaten ~:** nominate sb. *or* put sb. up as a candidate 5 (errichten) put up; put up, erect ‹*scaffolding, monument*›; put in, install ‹*machine*› 6 (hochstellen) erect ‹*spines*›; turn up ‹*collar*›; **die Ohren ~** ‹*animal*› prick up its ears 7 (ausarbeiten) work out ‹*programme, budget, plan*›; draw up ‹*contract, statute, balance sheet*›; make [out], draw up ‹*list*›; set up ‹*hypothesis*›; establish ‹*norm*›; prepare ‹*statistics*›; **eine Formel für etw. ~:** devise a formula for sth. 8 (erzielen) set up, establish ‹*record*› 9 (formulieren) put forward ‹*theory, conjecture, demand*› 10 (bes. südd.: aufsetzen) put on ‹*soup, potatoes, etc.*› 11 (nordd.) ▸ **anstellen 6**
B *refl. V.* 1 (postieren) position *or* place oneself; take up position; (in einer Reihe, zum Tanz) line up; **sich im Kreis ~:** form a circle; **sich in Reih und Glied ~** (Milit.) fall in 2 ‹*hairs, bristles*› rise

Auf·stellung *die* 1 ▸ **aufstellen A 1**: putting up; setting up; standing up 2 ▸ **aufstellen 5**: putting up; erection; installation

[3] (einer Mannschaft, eines Spielers) selection; picking; (einer Spezialeinheit) putting together; (eines Heeres) raising; (aufgestellte Mannschaft) [team] line-up [4] (Nominierung) nomination [5] (Milit.) ~ **nehmen** *od.* **beziehen** line up; **das Bataillon hatte vor dem Palast ~ genommen** *od.* **bezogen** the battalion was drawn up in front of the palace [6] ▸**aufstellen 7**: working out; drawing up; making out; setting up; establishment; preparation [7] (das Erzielen) setting up; establishment [8] (das Formulieren) putting forward [9] (Liste) list; (Tabelle) table

auf|stemmen *tr. V.* [1] (öffnen) force ‹*door*› open [with a crowbar]; force *or* prise ‹*box*› open [with a crowbar] [2] (aufstützen) **seinen Fuß/Arm ~:** brace one's foot/arm (**auf** + *Akk.* on)

auf|stieben *unr. itr. V.; mit sein* fly up

Aufstieg *der;* **~[e]s, ~e** [1] (das Hinaufsteigen) climb; ascent [2] (Aufwärtsentwicklung) rise; **den ~ zum Geschäftsleiter/in den Vorstand schaffen** succeed in rising to the position of manager/rising to become a member of the board of directors; **ein wirtschaftlicher/sozialer ~:** economic/social advancement [3] (Sport) promotion (**in** + *Akk.* to) [4] (Weg) way up; **ein gefährlicher ~ zum Gipfel** a dangerous route up *or* ascent to the summit

Aufstiegs-: ~chance *die* prospect of promotion; **~spiel** *das* (Sport) promotion decider

auf|stöbern *tr. V.* [1] (aufjagen) put up ‹*birds, animals*› [2] (entdecken) track down; run to earth

auf|stocken *tr. (auch itr.) V.* [1] **ein Gebäude ~:** add a storey to a building; **wir haben aufgestockt** we've added another storey [2] (vermehren, erweitern) increase ‹*capital, budget, funds, pensions*›; build up ‹*supplies*›; **die Gesellschaft stockt auf** the company is increasing its capital

auf|stöhnen *itr. V.* groan; **laut/erleichtert ~:** give *or* utter a loud groan/a sigh of relief

auf|stören *tr. V.* [1] (aufschrecken) put up ‹*bird, animal*›; disturb ‹*wasps' nest, anthill*› [2] (stören) disturb

auf|stoßen
[A] *unr. tr. V.* [1] (öffnen) push open; (mit einem Fußtritt) kick open [2] (heftig aufsetzen) **etw. auf etw.** (*Akk.*) **~:** bang sth. down on sth.; **den Stock auf den Boden ~:** thump one's stick on the ground [3] (verletzen) **sich** (*Dat.*) **den Ellbogen** *usw.* **~:** graze one's elbow *etc.*
[B] *unr. itr. V.* [1] (rülpsen) belch; burp (coll.); ‹*baby*› bring up wind, (coll.) burp [2] *auch mit sein* (Aufstoßen verursachen) **[jmdm.] ~:** repeat [on sb.]; **das könnte Ihnen übel ~** (fig.) you might have to pay dearly for that (fig.); you could live to regret that [3] *mit sein* (ugs.: auffallen) **jmdm. ~:** strike sb.

auf|streben *itr. V.* (geh.) tower [up]; **steil ~de Felswände** towering rock walls

aufstrebend *Adj.* rising ‹*talent, bourgeoisie, industry*›; ‹*nation, people*› striving for progress; **ein ~er junger Mann** an ambitious and up-and-coming young man

auf|streichen *unr. tr. V.* spread ‹*butter, jam, etc.*› (**auf** + *Akk.* on); put on, apply ‹*ointment, paint*› (**auf** + *Akk.* to)

auf|streuen *tr. V.* sprinkle on; **etw. auf etw.** (*Akk.*) **~:** sprinkle sth. on sth.; **den Tieren Stroh ~:** put down straw for the animals

Auf·strich *der* [1] (Brot~) spread [2] (Schriftw.) upstroke [3] (Musik) up-bow

auf|stülpen *tr. V.* [1] (stülpen auf) **etw. auf etw.** (*Akk.*) **~:** plonk sth. on sth. [2] (hochschlagen) turn *or* roll up ‹*sleeves, trousers*›; turn up ‹*collar*›; **die Lippen ~** (fig.) purse one's lips; (verführerisch) pout

auf|stützen
[A] *tr. V.* [1] (auf etw. stützen) **die Ellbogen/Arme auf etw.** (*Akk. od. Dat.*) **~:** rest one's elbows/arms on sth.; **mit aufgestütztem Kopf** with one's head resting on one's hands [2] (aufrichten) **jmdn./sich [im Bett] ~:** prop sb./oneself up [in bed]
[B] *refl. V.* support oneself

auf|stylen *tr. V.* (ugs.) do up ‹*person, thing*›; **sich ~:** do oneself up

auf|suchen *tr. V.* [1] (hingehen zu) call on, go and see ‹*friends, relatives*›; visit ‹*museum, grave, monument*›; **den Arzt ~:** go to the doctor; go and see the doctor; **die Toilette ~:** go to the toilet *or* lavatory [2] (in einem Buch usw.) look up

auf|summen, auf|summieren
[A] *tr. V.* (DV) sum
[B] *refl. V.* add *or* mount up

auf|takeln /ˈaufta:kl̩n/ *refl. V.* (ugs. abwertend) tart (Brit.) *or* doll oneself up (coll.); **aufgetakelt** tarted (Brit.) *or* dolled up (coll.)

Auf·takt *der* [1] prelude; (Beginn) start; **den ~ zu etw. bilden** form the prelude to sth./be the start of sth. [2] (Musik) upbeat; anacrusis [3] (Verslehre) anacrusis

auf|tanken
[A] *tr. V.* fill up; refuel ‹*aircraft*›; **2 000 Liter ~** ‹*aircraft*› take on 2,000 litres; **neue Kräfte ~** (fig.) recharge one's batteries (fig.)
[B] *itr. V.* fill up; ‹*aircraft*› refuel

auf|tauchen *itr. V.; mit sein* [1] (aus dem Wasser) surface; ‹*frogman, diver*› surface, come up [2] (sichtbar werden) appear; (aus dem Dunkel, dem Nebel) emerge; appear [3] (erscheinen, gefunden werden) turn up; (fig.) ‹*problem, question, difficulties*› crop up, arise

auf|tauen
[A] *tr. V.* thaw ‹*ice, frozen food*›; thaw [out] ‹*earth, ground*›; defrost ‹*windscreen*›; ‹*sun*› thaw the ice on ‹*windscreen*›
[B] *itr. V.; mit sein* (auch fig.) thaw; ‹*earth, ground*› thaw [out]; **der See ist wieder aufgetaut** the ice on the lake has melted

auf|teilen *tr. V.* [1] (verteilen) share out (**unter** + *Akk. od. Dat.* among) [2] (aufgliedern) divide [up] (**in** + *Akk.* into)

Auf·teilung *die* ▸**aufteilen 1, 2**: sharing out (**unter** + *Akk. od. Dat.* among); dividing [up] (**in** + *Akk.* into)

auf|tischen
[A] *tr. V.* [1] (servieren) serve [up]; **jmdm. etw. ~:** serve sb. with sth. [2] (ugs. abwertend: erzählen) serve up ‹*excuses, lies, etc.*›; **jmdm. etw. ~:** serve sb. up with sth.
[B] *itr. V.* **jmdm. reichlich ~:** serve sb. up a substantial meal

Auftrag *der;* **~[e]s, Aufträge** [1] (Anweisung) instructions *pl.*; (Aufgabe) task; job; **in jmds. ~** (*Dat.*) on sb.'s instructions; **Luigi, ich habe einen ~ für dich** I've got a job for you, Luigi; **im ~ des/der ...** (für jmdn.) on behalf of the ...; (auf jmds. Anweisung) on the instructions of the ...; **jmdm. den ~ geben** *od.* **erteilen, etw. zu tun** instruct sb. to do sth.; give sb. the job of doing sth.; **einen ~ ausführen** carry out an instruction *or* order; **den ~ haben, etw. zu tun** have been instructed to do sth. [2] (Bestellung) order; (bei Künstlern, Architekten usw.) commission; **ein ~ über** *od.* **auf etw.** (*Akk.*) an order/a commission for sth.; **etw. in ~ geben** (Kaufmannsspr.) order/commission sth. (**bei** from) [3] (Mission) task; mission [4] (das Auftragen [von Farbe]) application

auf|tragen
[A] *unr. tr. V.* [1] **jmdm. ~, etw. zu tun** instruct sb. to do sth.; **jmdm. eine Besorgung/eine Botschaft ~:** instruct sb. to get sth./to deliver a message; **er hat mir aufgetragen, dich zu grüßen** he asked me to pass on his regards [2] (aufstreichen) apply, put on ‹*paint, make-up, ointment, etc.*›; **etw. auf etw.** (*Akk. od. Dat.*) **~:** apply sth. to sth.; put sth. on sth. [3] (verschleißen) wear out ‹*clothes*› [4] (geh.: servieren) serve [up]
[B] *unr. itr. V.* [1] ‹*clothes*› be too bulky [2] (ugs.: übertreiben) **dick** *od.* **stark ~:** lay it on thick (coll.)

Auftrag-: ~geber *der,* **~geberin** *die* client; customer; (eines Künstlers, Architekten, Schriftstellers usw.) client; **~nehmer** *der;* **~~s, ~~, ~nehmerin** *die;* **~~, ~~nen** contractor

auftrags-, Auftrags-: ~buch *das* (Kaufmannsspr.) order book; **~gemäß** [A] *Adj.* in accordance with instructions *postpos.*; [B] *adv.* as instructed; as ordered; as per instructions; **~killer** *der,* **~killerin** *die* contract killer; **~lage** *die* (Kaufmannsspr.) situation as regards orders; **~rückgang** *der* (Kaufmannsspr.) falling-off of orders; **~werk** *das* commissioned work

auf|treffen *unr. itr. V.; mit sein* **auf etw.** (*Akk.*) **~:** strike *or* hit sth.; **mit der Stirn auf etw.** (*Akk.*) **~:** hit one's forehead on sth.

auf|treiben
[A] *unr. tr. V.* [1] (aufwirbeln) raise ‹*dust*›; blow up ‹*dry leaves, sand*› [2] (aufblähen) bloat; swell; make ‹*dough*› rise [3] (ugs.: ausfindig machen) get hold of; **ein Quartier ~:** find somewhere to stay [4] (auf den Markt) drive ‹*livestock*› to market; (auf die Almen) drive ‹*cattle, livestock*› up to [the] high pastures
[B] *unr. itr. V.; mit sein* ‹*body, corpse, face*› become bloated *or* swollen; ‹*dough*› rise

auf|trennen *tr. V.* unpick; undo; unpick ‹*garment*›

auf|treten
[A] *unr. itr. V.; mit sein* [1] tread; **er kann mit dem verletzten Bein nicht ~:** he can't walk on *or* put his weight on his injured leg [2] (sich benehmen) behave; **forsch/schüchtern ~:** have a forceful/shy manner; **mit Entschlossenheit ~:** act with firmness [3] (fungieren) appear; **als Zeuge/Kläger ~:** appear as a witness/a plaintiff; **als Vermittler/Sachverständiger ~:** act as mediator/be called in as an expert; **gegen jmdn./etw. ~:** speak out against sb./sth. [4] (als Künstler, Sänger usw.) appear; **sie ist seit Jahren nicht mehr aufgetreten** she hasn't given any public performances for years; **zum ersten Mal ~:** make one's first appearance [5] (die Bühne betreten) enter [6] (auftauchen) ‹*problem, question, difficulty*› crop up, arise; ‹*difference of opinion*› arise; (vorkommen) occur; ‹*pest, symptom, danger*› appear
[B] *unr. tr. V.* kick open ‹*door, gate*›

Auftreten *das;* **~s** [1] (Benehmen) manner [2] (das Fungieren) appearance [3] (das Vorkommen) occurrence; (von Schädlingen, Gefahren) appearance; **seit dem ~ von Aids** since the appearance of AIDS

Auf·trieb *der* [1] (Physik) buoyancy; (in der Luft) lift [2] (Elan, Aufschwung) impetus; **das hat ihm ~/neuen ~ gegeben** that has given him a lift/given him new impetus; **neuen ~ erhalten** ‹*industry, economy*› receive a boost [3] (von Vieh zum Markt) **der ~ an** *od.* **von Ferkeln** *usw.* the number of piglets *etc.* [brought] for sale [4] (auf Almen) **der ~ des Viehs** the driving of cattle up to [the] high pastures

Auftriebs·kraft *die* (Physik) buoyancy; (in der Luft) lift

Auf·tritt *der* [1] (als Künstler, Sänger usw.) appearance [2] (Theater: das Auftreten) entrance; (Szene) scene; **er hat erst im 3. Akt seinen ~:** he doesn't make his entrance until the third act [3] (Streit) row; **jmdm. einen ~ machen** go off the deep end at sb. (coll.)

auf|trumpfen *itr. V.* show one's superiority; show how good one is; **„Na siehst du", trumpfte sie auf** 'there you are', she crowed; **mit seinem Wissen/seinen Leistungen ~:** show off with one's knowledge/achievements

auf|tun
[A] *unr. refl. V.* (geh.: sich öffnen) open; (fig.) ‹*abyss, plain, street, new world, new horizons*› open up; **sich jmdm. ~:** open up before sb.
[B] *unr. tr. V.* [1] (ugs.: entdecken) find [2] (ugs.: servieren) **jmdn./sich etw. ~:** help sb./oneself to sth. [3] (geh.: öffnen) open ‹*door, window*›; **den Mund/die Augen ~:** open one's mouth/eyes [4] (landsch.: aufsetzen) put on ‹*hat, spectacles, etc.*›
[C] *unr. itr. V.* **jmdm./sich ~:** help sb./oneself (**von** to)

auf|türmen
[A] *tr. V.* pile up (**zu** into)
[B] *refl. V.* ‹*mountain range*› tower up; (fig.) ‹*work, problems, difficulties*› pile up

auf|wachen *itr. V.; mit sein* (auch fig.) wake up, awaken (**aus** from); **aus der Narkose/Ohnmacht ~:** come round from the anaesthetic/faint

auf|wachsen *unr. itr. V.; mit sein* grow up

auf|wallen *itr. V.; mit sein* boil up; **etw. ~ lassen** bring sth. to the boil; **in jmdm. ~** (fig. geh.) ‹*joy, tenderness, hatred, passion, etc.*› surge [up] within sb.

Auf·wallung *die;* ~, ~**en** (geh.) surge

Aufwand *der;* ~**[e]s** [1] expenditure (**an** + *Dat.* of); (das Aufgewendete) cost; expense; **mit einem ~ von 1,5 Mio. Euro** at a cost of 1.5 million euros; **ein unnützer ~ an Zeit** a waste of time; **der dazu nötige ~ an Zeit/Kraft** the time/energy needed [2] (Luxus) extravagance; **~ [mit etw.] treiben** be extravagant [with sth.]

aufwändig ▸ **aufwendig**

Aufwands·entschädigung *die* expense allowance

auf|wärmen
[A] *tr. V.* heat *or* warm up ‹*food*›; (fig. ugs.: wieder erwähnen) rake *or* drag up
[B] *refl. V.* [1] (sich wärmen) warm oneself up [2] (Sport) warm up

Aufwarte·frau *die* (bes. md.) cleaning woman; domestic help

auf|warten *itr. V.* [1] (geh.) **jmdm. mit etw. ~** (anbieten) offer sb. sth.; (vorsetzen) serve sb. [with] sth. [2] (zu bieten haben) **mit etw. ~:** come up with sth. [3] (veralt.: bedienen) **jmdm. ~:** wait *or* attend on sb.; **bei Tisch ~:** wait *or* serve at table

aufwärts *Adv.* upwards; (bergauf) upwards; uphill; **den Fluss ~:** upstream; **~!** (beim Fahrstuhl) going up!; **vom Major [an] ~:** from major up; **~ führen** (fig.) lead towards prosperity; **mit seiner Gesundheit/dem Land/Geschäft geht es ~:** his health is improving/the country/firm is doing better; **mit ihm geht es ~** (gesundheitlich) he's getting better; (finanziell, geschäftlich, beruflich, in der Schule) he's doing better

-aufwärts *Adv.* ▸ ❶ **S. 267 [weiter] rhein~/mosel~:** further up the Rhine/Mosel; **rhein~/mosel~ segeln** sail up the Rhine/Mosel

Aufwärts-: ~entwicklung *die* upward trend; **~haken** *der* (Boxen) uppercut; **~trend** *der* upward trend

Auf·wartung *die: in* **jmdm. seine ~ machen** (geh.) make *or* pay a courtesy call on sb.; pay sb. a courtesy visit

Aufwasch *der;* ~**[e]s** (bes. md.) ▸ **Abwasch**[1]

auf|waschen *unr. tr., itr. V.* (bes. md.) wash up; **das ist ein/geht in einem Aufwaschen** (ugs.) it can all be done in one go

auf|wecken *tr. V.* wake [up]; waken; (fig.) waken; *s. auch* **aufgeweckt**

auf|wehen
[A] *tr. V.* [1] (hochwehen) blow up; raise, blow up ‹*dust*› [2] (aufhäufen) pile up ‹*snow, leaves, etc.*› [3] (öffnen) blow open
[B] *itr. V.; mit sein* (emporwirbeln) blow up

auf|weichen
[A] *tr. V.* soften; (fig.) weaken ‹*system*›; **den Boden ~:** make the ground soft *or* sodden
[B] *itr. V.; mit sein* become soft; soften up; (fig.) weaken

auf|weisen *unr. tr. V.* [1] (zeigen) demonstrate; show [2] (erkennen lassen) show; exhibit; **der Ort hat viele Sehenswürdigkeiten aufzuweisen** the town has many sights to offer

auf|wenden *unr.* (*auch regelm.*) *tr. V.* use ‹*skill, influence*›; expend ‹*energy, resources*›; spend ‹*money, time*›; **viel Geld/seine ganze Freizeit für etw. ~:** spend a great deal of money/all one's spare time on sth.

auf·wendig
[A] *Adj.* lavish; (kostspielig) costly; expensive
[B] *adv.* lavishly; (kostspielig) expensively

Auf·wendung *die* [1] ▸ **aufwenden**: using; expenditure; spending; **unter ~ von etw.** by using/expending/spending sth. [2] *Pl.* (Kosten) expenditure *sing.*

auf|werfen
[A] *unr. tr. V.* [1] (aufhäufen) pile *or* heap up ‹*earth, snow, etc.*›; build, raise ‹*embankment, dam, etc.*› [2] (öffnen) fling open ‹*door, window*› [3] (ansprechen) raise ‹*problem, question*› [4] (hochwerfen) throw up; **den Kopf ~:** toss one's head [5] (schürzen) **die Lippen ~:** purse one's lips; **aufgeworfene Lippen** pursed lips
[B] *unr. refl. V.* (abwertend: sich aufspielen) **sich zu etw. ~:** set oneself up as sth.; **sich zum Richter ~:** set oneself up as judge

auf|werten *tr. V.* [1] *auch itr.* revalue [2] (fig.) enhance the status of; enhance ‹*standing, reputation, status*›

Auf·wertung *die* revaluation; **dieses Amt hat durch ihn eine ~ erfahren** he has enhanced the status of this office

auf|wickeln *tr. V.* [1] wind up; (ohne Rolle, Spule) roll *or* coil up [2] (auf Lockenwickler) **jmdm./sich die Haare ~:** put sb.'s/one's hair in curlers; **sich** (*Dat.*) **die Haare ~ lassen** have one's hair curled [3] (öffnen) unwrap, undo ‹*parcel, bundle*›

Aufwiegelei *die;* ~, ~**en** (abwertend) incitement [to revolt]

auf|wiegeln /ˈaufviːgl̩n/ *tr. V.* (abwertend) incite; stir up (**gegen** against); **jmdn. zum Aufstand/Streik ~:** incite sb. to rebel/strike

Aufwiegelung *die;* ~, ~**en** (abwertend) incitement; **die ~ der Massen zum Widerstand** inciting the masses to resist

auf|wiegen *unr. tr. V.* make up for; **die Vorteile wiegen die Nachteile auf** the advantages offset the disadvantages; *s. auch* **Gold**

Aufwiegler *der;* ~**s**, ~, **Aufwieglerin** *die;* ~, ~**nen** (abwertend) agitator

aufwieglerisch (abwertend)
[A] *Adj.* seditious; inflammatory, seditious ‹*speech, pamphlet*›
[B] *adv.* seditiously

Aufwieglung ▸ **Aufwiegelung**

Auf·wind *der* (Met.) anabatic wind; (Flugw.) up-current; **wieder ~ bekommen** (fig.) get new impetus (**durch** from)

auf|wirbeln
[A] *tr. V.* swirl up; swirl up, raise ‹*dust*›; *s. auch* **Staub**
[B] *itr. V.; mit sein* swirl up

auf|wischen *tr. V.* [1] (entfernen) wipe *or* mop up [2] (säubern) wipe ‹*floor*›; (mit Wasser) wash; **die Küche/das Badezimmer ~:** wipe/wash the kitchen/bathroom floor

auf|wogen *itr. V.; mit sein* (dichter.) ‹*sea*› surge

auf|wühlen *tr. V.* churn up ‹*water, sea, mud, soil*›; (fig.) stir ‹*person, emotions, passions*› deeply; (auf schmerzhafte Weise) upset ‹*person*› deeply; **ein ~des Erlebnis** (fig.) a deeply moving experience; **jmdn. bis ins Innerste ~:** move sb. to the depths of his/her soul

auf|zahlen (südd., österr.)
[A] *tr. V.* **20 Euro ~:** pay 20 euros on top; pay an extra 20 euros.
[B] *itr. V.* pay extra; make an additional payment

auf|zählen *tr. V.* enumerate; list; enumerate, give ‹*dates, names, facts*›

Auf·zahlung *die* (südd., österr.) additional payment

Auf·zählung *die* [1] (das Aufzählen) enumeration; listing [2] (Liste) list

auf|zäumen *tr. V.* bridle ‹*horse*›; **etw. verkehrt ~** (fig.) go about sth. the wrong way; *s. auch* **Pferd 1**

auf|zehren (geh.)
[A] *tr. V.* exhaust ‹*food, supplies, savings*›; (fig.) consume, sap ‹*energy, strength*›
[B] *refl. V.* wear oneself out; ‹*energy, supplies, money, etc.*› give out

auf|zeichnen *tr. V.* [1] (notieren) record [2] (zeichnen) draw

Auf·zeichnung *die* [1] (das Notieren) recording [2] (das Aufgezeichnete) record; (Film~, Magnetband~) recording; **~en** (Notizen) notes [3] (das Zeichnen) drawing

auf|zeigen *tr. V.* (nachweisen) demonstrate; show; (darlegen) expound; (hinweisen auf) point out; highlight

auf|ziehen
[A] *unr. tr. V.* [1] (öffnen) pull open ‹*drawer*›; open, draw [back] ‹*curtains*›; undo ‹*zip*›; undo, untie ‹*bow*› [2] (die Feder spannen von) wind up ‹*clock, watch, toy, etc.*› [3] (spannen, aufkleben) mount ‹*photograph, print, etc.*› (**auf** + *Akk.* on); stretch ‹*canvas*›; **Saiten/neue Saiten auf ein Instrument ~:** string/restring an instrument; **neue Saiten ~:** put new strings on; *s. auch* **Saite** [4] (großziehen) bring up, raise ‹*children*›; raise, rear ‹*animals*›; raise ‹*plants, vegetables*› [5] (ugs.: gründen) set up ‹*company, department, business, political party, organization, system*› [6] (ugs.: durchführen) organize, stage ‹*festival, event, campaign, rally*›; **wir haben das Ganze völlig falsch aufgezogen** we've gone about it completely the wrong way [7] (ugs.: verspotten) rib (coll.), tease (**mit, wegen** about); **sie hat ihn damit aufgezogen, dass er so große Ohren hat** she ribbed him (coll.) *or* poked fun at him because of his big ears [8] (nach oben ziehen) pull *or* draw up; haul up ‹*fishing nets, heavy load*›; hoist, run up ‹*flag*›; hoist ‹*sail*›; raise ‹*barrier, curtain, sluice gate, signal, drawbridge, etc.*› [9] (auftrennen) undo; unpick; unpick ‹*garment*› [10] (auf eine Spritze) draw up ‹*vaccine etc.*› [11] (füllen) fill ‹*hypodermic syringe*›
[B] *unr. itr. V.; mit sein* [1] (näher kommen) ‹*storm*› gather, come up; ‹*clouds*› gather; ‹*star, mist, haze*› come up [2] (sich aufstellen) take up position; (aufmarschieren) march up

Auf·zucht *die* raising; rearing

Aufzucht·station *die* animal rescue centre

Auf·zug *der* [1] (Lift) lift (Brit.); elevator (Amer.); (Lasten~, Bau~) hoist [2] (abwertend: Aufmachung) get-up [3] (Theater: Akt) act [4] (Aufmarsch) parade; (feierlicher Zug) procession; **der ~ der Garde** the mounting of the guard

Aufzugs·schacht *der* lift (Brit.) *or* (Amer.) elevator shaft

auf|zwingen
[A] *unr. tr. V.* **jmdm. etw. ~:** force sth. [up]on sb.; **jmdm. seinen Willen ~:** impose one's will [up]on sb.
[B] *unr. refl. V.* **sich jmdm. ~:** impose oneself *or* force one's company [up]on sb.; **der Gedanke zwingt sich [einem] ja förmlich auf** the idea positively forces itself upon you

Aug·apfel *der* eyeball; **er hütet das wie seinen ~:** it's his most treasured possession; **sie ist der ~ ihrer Großmutter** (fig.) she is the apple of her grandmother's eye

Auge /ˈaugə/ *das;* ~**s**, ~**n** [1] ▸ ❶ **S. 435** eye; **gute/schlechte ~n haben** have good/poor eyesight; **er hat so gute ~n, dass ...** his eyesight is so good that ...; **meine ~n sind schlechter geworden** my eyesight has deteriorated; **auf einem ~ blind sein** be blind in one eye; (fig.) have two different sets of standards; **ich konnte ihm nicht in die ~n sehen** (fig.) I could not look him in the eye; **etw. mit eigenen ~n gesehen haben** have seen sth. with one's own eyes; **die ~n schließen** *od.* **zumachen** close *or* shut one's eyes; **mit bloßem ~:** with the naked eye; **ihm fallen die ~n zu** his eyelids are drooping; **ganz kleine ~n haben** (fig.) be all sleepy; **~n links/rechts/geradeaus!** (Milit.) eyes left/right/front!; **mit verbundenen ~n** blindfold[ed]; **jmdn. aus großen ~n unschuldig ansehen** look at sb. all wide-eyed and innocent; **hast du keine ~n im Kopf?** haven't you got eyes in your head?; are you blind?; **etw. im ~ haben** have sth. in one's eye; (fig.: haben wollen) have one's eye on sth.; **das ~ des Gesetzes** (fig.: Polizist) the law (coll.); **so weit das ~ reicht** as far as the eye can see; **die ~n sind größer als der Magen** *od.* **Bauch** (fig. ugs.) your *etc.* eyes are bigger than your *etc.* belly; **ihr/ihm** *usw.* **gingen die ~n auf** (fig.) the scales fell from her/his *etc.* eyes; **ihm/ihr** *usw.* **werden die ~n noch aufgehen** (fig.) he/she *etc.* is in for a rude awakening; **da wird er ~n machen** (fig. ugs.) his eyes will pop out of his head; **ihnen fielen fast die ~n aus dem Kopf** their eyes nearly popped out of their heads; **ein ~ voll Schlaf nehmen** (fig. ugs.) have forty winks *or* a short nap; **da blieb kein ~ trocken** (fig. ugs.) everyone laughed till they cried *or* till the tears ran down their faces; (es blieb niemand verschont) no one was safe; **ich traute meinen [eigenen] ~n nicht** (ugs.) I couldn't believe my eyes; **~n wie ein Luchs haben** have eyes like a lynx; **ich habe doch hinten keine ~n** (ugs.) I haven't got eyes in the back of my head; **nur ~n für jmdn. haben** (fig.)

have eyes only for sb.; **ich kann doch meine ~n nicht überall haben!** I can't be looking everywhere at once; **sie hat ihre ~n überall** she doesn't miss a thing; **[große] ~n machen** (fig. ugs.) be wide-eyed; **jmdm. [schöne] ~n machen** (fig. veralt.) make eyes at sb.; **die ~n offen haben** *od.* **offen halten [ob, …]** (fig.) keep one's eyes open [and see whether …]; **die ~n vor etw.** (*Dat.*) **verschließen** (fig.) shut *or* close one's eyes to sth.; **sich** (*Dat.*) **nach jmdm./etw. die ~n ausgucken** *od.* **aus dem Kopf sehen** (fig. ugs.) look out eagerly *or* expectantly for sb./sth.; **ein ~** *od.* **beide ~n zudrücken** (fig.) turn a blind eye; **ein ~ auf jmdn./etw. geworfen haben** (fig.) have taken a liking to sb./have one's eye on sth.; **ein ~ auf jmdn./etw. haben** (Acht geben) keep an eye on sb./sth.; (Gefallen finden) have taken a fancy to sb./have one's eye on sth.; **ein ~/ein sicheres ~ für etw. haben** have an eye/a sure eye for sth.; **kein ~ von jmdm. lassen** (fig.) not take one's eyes off sb.; **ich habe ja schließlich ~n im Kopf** (ugs.) I'm not blind, you know; **jmdm. die ~n öffnen** (fig.) open sb.'s eyes; **sich** (*Dat.*) **die ~n ausweinen** *od.* **aus dem Kopf weinen** (fig.) cry one's eyes out; **jmdn./etw. nicht aus den ~n lassen** not take one's eyes off sb./sth.; not let sb./sth. out of one's sight; **jmdn./etw. aus dem ~** *od.* **den ~n verlieren** lose sight of sb./sth.; (fig.) lose contact *or* touch with sb./lose touch with sth.; **ich kann vor Arbeit/Müdigkeit nicht mehr aus den ~n gucken** (ugs.) I've got so much work I don't know whether I'm coming or going/I'm so tired I can't see straight; **aus den ~n, aus dem Sinn!** (Spr.) out of sight, out of mind; **geh mir aus den ~n!** get out of my sight!; **ein solches Ereignis muss auch etwas fürs ~ sein** such an event must also have visual appeal; **das ist mehr fürs ~**: it's only [there] for decoration; **jmdm./einander ~ in ~ gegenüberstehen** face sb./one another; **Aug in Aug** (veralt.) face to face; **jmdn./etw. im ~ behalten** (fig.) keep an eye on sb./bear *or* keep sth. in mind; **in jmds. ~n** (*Dat.*) (fig.) to sb.'s mind; in sb.'s opinion; **jmdm. ins ~** *od.* **in die ~n fallen** *od.* **springen** (fig.) hit sb. in the eye; **etw. ins ~ fassen** (fig.) consider sth.; think about sth.; **ins ~ fassen, etw. zu tun** (fig.) have it in mind to do sth.; contemplate doing sth.; **einer Sache** (*Dat.*) **ins ~ sehen** (fig.) face sth.; **der Wahrheit/Gefahr ins ~ sehen** (fig.) face up to the truth/danger; **ins ~ gehen** (fig. ugs.) (schlimm ausgehen) end in disaster; (erfolglos ausgehen) end in failure; **mit einem lachenden und einem weinenden ~** (fig.) with mixed feelings; **mit offenen ~n schlafen** (ugs.) be daydreaming; **mit offenen ~n durch die Welt gehen** (fig.) walk about with one's eyes open; **jmdn./etw. mit anderen** *od.* **neuen ~n betrachten** *od.* **ansehen** (fig.) see sb./sth. in a different *or* new light; **~ um ~, Zahn um Zahn** an eye for an eye, a tooth for a tooth; **unter vier ~n** (fig.) in private; **unter jmds. ~n** (*Dat.*) right in front of sb.; right under sb.'s nose; **komm mir nicht mehr unter die ~n!** never let me set eyes on you again!; **jmdm. jeden Wunsch von den ~n ablesen** (fig.) anticipate sb.'s every wish; **vor aller ~n** in front of everybody; **jmdm. etw. vor ~n führen** *od.* **halten** *od.* **stellen** (fig.) bring sth. home to sb.; **wenn man sich** (*Dat.*) **das mal vor ~n führt** (fig.) when you stop and think about it; **jmdn./etw. vor ~n haben** (fig.) see sb./sth. in one's mind's eye; *s. auch* **auskratzen A 1**; **beleidigen**; **blau**; **Null[1] 2**; **schließen A 1**; **schwarz A 1**; **schweben 1**; **zutun**

[2] (auf Würfeln, Spielkarten, Dominosteinen) pip; **drei ~n werfen** throw a three; **wie viele ~n hat er geworfen?** how many has he thrown?

[3] (Keim) eye; bud; (bei Kartoffeln) eye

[4] ▸ **Fettauge**

äugeln /ˈɔyɡl̩n/

A *itr. V.* (hinsehen) **nach jmdm./etw. ~**: cast secret glances at sb./sth.

B *tr. V.* (Gartenbau) bud

äugen /ˈɔyɡn̩/ *itr. V.* peer

Augen-: ~abstand *der* (Med.) interocular distance; **~arzt** *der*, **~ärztin** *die* ▸ⓘ **S. 113** eye specialist; **~aufschlag** *der* [upward] glance; **mit unschuldigem ~aufschlag** with wide-eyed innocence; **~binde** *die* blindfold; (Verband) eye bandage

Augen·blick /*auch:* --ˈ-/ *der* moment; **alle ~e** (ugs.) all the time; *s. auch* **Moment[1]**

augenblicklich /*auch:* --ˈ--/

A *Adj.* [1] (unverzüglich) immediate [2] (gegenwärtig) present; (vorübergehend) temporary; (einen Augenblick dauernd) momentary

B *adv.* [1] (sofort) immediately; at once [2] (zur Zeit) at the moment

augen·blicks *Adv.* immediately; at once

Augenblicks-: ~erfolg *der* short-lived success; **~sache** *die* matter of a moment

augen-, Augen-: ~braue *die* ▸ⓘ **S. 435** eyebrow; **~brauen·stift** *der* eyebrow pencil; **~deckel** *der* (ugs.) eyelid; **~fällig** **A** *Adj.* striking; (offensichtlich) obvious; **B** *adv.* strikingly; (offensichtlich) obviously; **~farbe** *die* colour of one's eyes; **~fehler** *der* eye defect; **~fleck** *der* (Biol.) eyespot; ocellus; **~glas** *das*; *Pl.* **~gläser** (österr., sonst Amtsspr.) (Monokel) monocle; (Zwicker) pince-nez; **~gläser** (Brille) spectacles; **~heilkunde** *die* ophthalmology; **~höhe** *die* eye level; **in/auf ~höhe** at/to eye level; **auf [gleicher] ~höhe** on an equal footing, on equal terms (**mit** with); **~höhle** *die* eye socket; **~klappe** *die* eyepatch; **~klinik** *die* eye hospital; **~kontakt** *der* eye contact; **jmds. ~kontakt suchen** try to catch sb.'s eye; **~krankheit** *die* eye disease; disease of the eye; **~lid** *das* ▸ⓘ **S. 435** eyelid; **~-Make-up** *das* eye make-up; **~maß** *das*: **ein gutes/schlechtes ~maß haben** have a good eye/no eye for distances; **jegliches ~maß verlieren** (fig.) lose all sense of proportion; **~mensch** *der* (ugs.) visual type *or* person; **~merk** *das*: **sein ~merk auf jmdn./etw. richten** *od.* **lenken** give one's attention to sb./sth.; **~optiker** *der*, **~optikerin** *die* ▸ⓘ **S. 113** ophthalmic optician; **~paar** *das* (geh.) pair of eyes; **~ränder** *Pl.* rims of one's/the eyes; **sie hatte gerötete ~ränder** the rims of her eyes were red; **~ringe** *Pl.* rings under the eyes; **~schatten** *Pl.* shadows under the eyes

Augen·schein *der* (geh.) [1] (Eindruck) appearance; **dem ~ nach** by all appearances; **dem ersten ~ nach** at first sight; **allem ~ zum Trotz** despite all appearances [2] (Betrachtung) inspection; **jmdn./etw. in ~ nehmen** have a close look at sb./sth.; give sb./sth. a close inspection

augen·scheinlich (geh.)

A *Adj.* (scheinbar) apparent; evident; (sichtbar) obvious; evident

B *adv.* (scheinbar) apparently; evidently; (sichtbar) obviously; evidently

augen-, Augen-: ~schmaus *der* (scherzh.) feast for the eyes; **~spiegel** *der* (Med.) ophthalmoscope; **~spiegelung** *die* (Med.) ophthalmoscopy; **~stern** *der* [1] (dichter.: Pupille) pupil; [2] (veralt.: Liebstes) apple of one's eye; **~trost** *der* (Bot.) eyebright; **~weide** *die* feast for the eyes; **~wimper** *die* eyelash; **~winkel** *der* corner of one's eye; **~wischerei** *die* eyewash; **~zahn** *der* eye tooth; **~zeuge** *der* eyewitness; **~zeuge sein** be an eyewitness; **~zeugen·bericht** *der* eyewitness report; **~zeugin** *die* ▸ **~zeuge**; **~zwinkern** *das*; **~~s**: **mit einem ~zwinkern** with a wink; **durch ~zwinkern** by winking; **~zwinkernd** **A** *Adj.* tacit ‹*agreement*›; **B** *adv.* with a wink

Augias·stall /auˈɡiːas-/ *der* (geh.) Augean stables; **den ~ ausmisten** *od.* **reinigen** create order out of chaos

-äugig /-|ɔyɡɪç/ *Adj.* ▸ⓘ **S. 435** -eyed; **ein~/blau~/groß~/hell~**: one-eyed/blue-eyed/big-eyed/bright-eyed

Augur /ˈauɡʊr/ *der*; **~s** *od.* **~en** /-ˈɡuːrən/, **~en** (geh., spött.) pundit

Auguren·lächeln *das* (geh.) knowing smile

August[1] /auˈɡʊst/ *der*; **~[e]s** *od.* **~**, **~e** ▸ⓘ **S. 165** August; *s. auch* **April**

August[2] /ˈaugʊst/ *in* **dummer ~**: clown

augusteisch /auɡʊsˈteːɪʃ/ *Adj. in* **~es Zeitalter** (geh.) Augustan age

Augustiner /auɡʊsˈtiːnɐ/ *der*; **~s**, **~**: Augustinian monk

Augustinerin *die*; **~**, **~nen** Augustinian nun

Augustinus /auɡʊsˈtiːnʊs/ (*der*) St Augustine

Auktion /aukˈtsi̯oːn/ *die*; **~**, **~en** auction

Auktionator /auktsi̯oˈnaːtɔr/ *der*; **~s**, **~en** /-naˈtoːrən/, **Auktionatorin** *die*; **~**, **~nen** ▸ⓘ **S. 113** auctioneer

Auktions·haus *das* auction house

Aula /ˈaula/ *die*; **~**, **Aulen** *od.* **~s** (einer Universität) [great] hall; (einer Schule) [assembly] hall

Aupair /oˈpɛːr/ *das*; **~s**, **~s** au pair

Aupair·mädchen, Au-pair-Mädchen /oˈpɛːr-/ *das* au pair [girl]

Aura /ˈaura/ *die*; **~**, **Auren** (geh.) aura

Aureole /aureˈoːlə/ *die*; **~**, **~n** [1] (Heiligenschein) aureole; halo [2] (Met.) aureole

aus /aus/

A *Präp. mit Dat.* [1] (räumlich: ~ dem Inneren von) out of; **~ dem Bett steigen** get out of bed; **~ der Flasche trinken** drink out of the bottle *or* from the bottle

[2] (Herkunft, Quelle, Ausgangspunkt angebend, auch zeitlich) from; **~ Spanien/Griechenland** *usw.* from Spain/Greece *etc.*; **er kommt** *od.* **stammt ~** *od.* **ist gebürtig ~ Hamburg** he comes from Hamburg; **~ der Ferne** from a distance; (von weitem) from far away; **jmdm. etw. ~ dem Urlaub mitbringen** bring sth. back from holiday *or* (Amer.) one's vacation for sb.; **~ guter Familie stammen** come from a good family; **~ dem Deutschen ins Englische** from German into English; **etw. ~ dem Zusammenhang reißen** take sth. out of [its] context

[3] (Veränderung eines Zustandes angebend) **~ der Mode/Übung sein** be out of fashion/training; **~ dem Gleichgewicht** out of balance; **~ tiefem Schlaf erwachen** awake from a deep sleep

[4] (Grund, Ursache angebend) out of; **etw. ~ Erfahrung wissen** know sth. from experience; **~ folgendem Grund** for the following reason; **~ Versehen** inadvertently; by mistake; **~ einer Laune heraus** on impulse; **~ Furcht vor** for fear of; **~ Spaß/Jux** (ugs.) for fun/a laugh; **ein Verbrechen ~ Leidenschaft** a crime of passion; **~ sich heraus** on one's own initiative; of one's own accord

[5] (hergestellt ~) made of; **eine Bank ~ Holz/Stein** a bench made of wood/stone; a wooden/stone bench; **etw. ~ Fertigteilen bauen** build sth. out of prefabricated components; **eine Figur ~ Holz schnitzen** carve a figure in wood; **~ etw. bestehen** consist of sth.

[6] (Entwicklung angebend) **~ ihm ist ein guter Arzt geworden** he made a good doctor; **~ der Sache wird nichts** nothing will come of it; **~ den Raupen entwickeln sich Schmetterlinge** caterpillars develop into butterflies; **einen Soldaten ~ jmdm. machen** make a soldier out of sb.; **etwas ~ sich machen** make something of oneself; **~ ihm ist nichts geworden** he never made anything of his life

[7] (österr.: in) in; **eine Prüfung ~ Biologie** an examination in biology

B *Adv.* [1] (vorbei, vorüber, zu Ende) **~ sein** ‹*play, film, war*› be over, have ended; **wann ist die Vorstellung ~?** what time does the performance end?; **die Schule ist ~**: school is out *or* has finished; **mit ihm ist es ~**: he's had it (coll.); he's finished; **es ist ~ mit dem schönen Leben/der Faulenzerei** the good life is over/[there'll be] no more lazing around; **zwischen uns ist es ~**: it's [all] over between us; **~ jetzt!** that's enough; **~, habe ich gesagt** that's enough, I said; **~ und vorbei** over and done with; *s. auch* **aushaben**

[2] (ausgeschaltet) off; **„~"** (an Lichtschaltern) 'out'; (an Geräten) 'off'; **Licht/Radio ~!** lights *pl.* out!/turn the radio off

[3] (erloschen) out

[4] (Sport: im Aus) out

[5] (außer Haus, ausgegangen) out

[6] (bes. Kinderspr.: ausgeschieden) out

[7] **vom Flugplatz/Fenster/obersten Stockwerk ~**: from the airport/window/top storey; **von hier/München ~**: from here/Munich; **von seinem Standpunkt ~**: from his point of

view; **von mir ~** (ugs.) if you like *or* want; **von sich** (*Dat.*) **~:** of one's own accord **8** **auf etw.** (*Akk.*) **~ sein** be after *or* interested in sth.; *s. auch* **ein²**

Aus *das;* **~ 1** **der Ball ging ins ~** (Tennis) the ball was out; (Fußball) the ball went out of play; **den Ball ins ~ schlagen** hit the ball out **2** (Sport: das Ausscheiden) exit; (fig.) end

aus|arbeiten
A *tr. V.* **1** (erstellen) work out, develop ‹*guidelines, system, method*›; prepare, draw up ‹*agenda, draft, regulations, contract*›; prepare ‹*leaflet*› **2** (vollenden) work out the details of ‹*plan, proposal, list, lecture, etc.*›; elaborate the details of ‹*picture, drawing*›
B *refl. V.* (durch Sport, körperliche Anstrengung) work out; have a workout

Ausarbeitung *die;* **~, ~en 1** ▸**ausarbeiten A 1**: working out; developing; preparation; drawing up **2** ▸**ausarbeiten A 2**: working out the details; elaboration of the details

aus|arten *itr. V.; mit sein* **1** degenerate (**in** + *Akk.*, **zu** into) **2** (sich schlecht benehmen) become unruly

aus|atmen *itr., tr. V.* breathe out; exhale

aus|backen *regelm.* (*auch unr.*) *tr. V.* (Kochk.) **1** (in Fett) fry **2** (fertigbacken) **etw. ~:** bake sth. until it is done

aus|baden *tr. V.* (ugs.) carry *or* take the can for (Brit. coll.); take the rap for (coll.)

aus|baggern *tr. V.* **1** excavate ‹*hole, basement, ditch, etc.*› **2** (säubern) dredge ‹*channel, river bed, etc.*› **3** (herausholen) dredge up ‹*mud, detritus, etc.*›

aus|balancieren
A *tr. V.* (auch fig.) balance
B *refl. V.* balance; (fig.) balance out

aus|baldowern *tr. V.* (ugs.) spy out

Aus·ball *der* (Ballspiele) **auf ~ entscheiden** decide that the ball was out; **bei ~:** when the ball goes out of play

Aus·bau *der* **1** (Erweiterung) extension; (einer Straße) improvement; **ein ~ des Hauses** an extension to the house; **der ~ der Beziehungen zwischen zwei Staaten/Organisationen** the building of closer relations between two states/organizations **2** (Ausgestaltung) conversion (**zu** into) **3** (Entfernung) removal (**aus** from)

aus|bauen *tr. V.* **1** (entfernen) remove (**aus** from) **2** (erweitern) extend; (fig.) build up, cultivate ‹*friendship, relationship*›; expand ‹*theory, knowledge, market*›; **eine Fachhochschule zu einer Universität ~:** expand *or* enlarge a college into a university; **eine Straße ~:** improve a road; **seinen Vorsprung weiter ~** (fig.) extend one's lead; **seine Position ~** (fig.) consolidate *or* strengthen one's position; **ein Gebäude zu einem** *od.* **als Theater ~:** convert a building into a theatre *or* for use as a theatre

ausbau·fähig *Adj.* ‹*building etc.*› suitable for extension; ‹*market*› that can be expanded; ‹*position, job*› with [good] prospects; **er hat ~e Englischkenntnisse** he has a good grounding in English

aus|bedingen *unr. refl. V.* **sich** (*Dat.*) **etw. ~** (etw. verlangen) insist on sth.; (etw. zur Bedingung machen) make sth. a condition; **sich** (*Dat.*) **das Recht/die Freiheit ~, etw. zu tun** reserve the right/freedom to do sth.

aus|beißen *unr. refl. V.* **sich** (*Dat.*) **einen Zahn ~:** break a tooth (**an** + *Dat.* on); **sich** (*Dat.*) **an einem Problem die Zähne ~** (fig.) sweat over a problem

aus|bekommen *unr. tr. V.* (ugs.) get off

aus|bessern *tr. V.* **1** (reparieren) repair; fix (Amer.); mend ‹*clothes*›; touch up ‹*paintwork*› **2** (beseitigen) mend; **einen Schaden an etw.** (*Dat.*) **~:** repair damage to sth.

Aus·besserung *die* repair

ausbesserungs-, Ausbesserungs-: ~arbeiten *Pl.* repairs; repair work *sing.*; **~bedürftig** *Adj.* in need of repair *postpos.*; **~werk** *das* (Eisenb.) repair shed

aus|beulen
A *tr. V.* **1** remove a/the dent/the dents in; (mit einem Hammer) beat out **2** (dehnen) make baggy; **ausgebeulte Knie** baggy knees
B *refl. V.* ‹*trousers*› go baggy; ‹*pocket*› bulge

Aus·beute *die* yield; (einer Untersuchung) results *pl.*; (eines Einkaufsbummels) spoils *pl.*; **unsere ganze ~ betrug drei Pilze** we ended up with only three mushrooms between us

aus|beuteln *tr. V.* (bes. österr.) shake out

aus|beuten *tr. V.* (auch abwertend) exploit

Ausbeuter *der;* **~s, ~, Ausbeuterin** *die;* **~, ~nen** (abwertend) exploiter

ausbeuterisch (abwertend)
A *Adj.* exploitative
B *adv.* exploitatively

Ausbeuter·klasse *die;* **~** (abwertend) exploiting class

Ausbeutung *die;* **~, ~en** exploitation

aus|bezahlen *tr. V.* **1** (auszahlen) pay [out]; **er bekommt 2 000 Euro ausbezahlt** his take-home pay is 2,000 euros **2** (entlohnen) pay; (entlohnen und entlassen) pay off **3** (abfinden) buy out ‹*shareholder, joint heir, etc.*›

Aus·bezahlung *die* ▸**ausbezahlen**: payment; paying; paying off; buying out

aus|bilden
A *tr. V.* **1** (schulen, unterrichten) train; **sich in etw.** (*Dat.*) **~ lassen** take a training in sth.; (studieren) study sth.; **sich als** *od.* **zu etw. ~ lassen** train to be sth.; (studieren) study to be sth.; **sich im Gesang/Zeichnen ~ lassen** take singing lessons/study drawing; **jmdn. an einem Instrument/einer Maschine ~:** teach sb. to play an instrument/train sb. on a machine *or* to use a machine **2** (fördern) cultivate, develop ‹*talent, skill, feeling, etc.*› **3** (entwickeln) develop; (gestalten) design; (formen) shape; form
B *refl. V.* **1** (sich schulen) **sich in etw.** (*Dat.*) **~:** take a training in sth.; (studieren) study sth. **2** (sich entwickeln) develop

Ausbilder *der;* **~s, ~, Ausbilderin** *die;* **~, ~nen** instructor

Ausbildner *der;* **~s, ~, Ausbildnerin** *die;* **~, ~nen** (österr.) instructor

Aus·bildung *die* **1** (Schulung) training; **sich noch in der ~ befinden** still be training; (an einer Lehranstalt) still be at college **2** (Entwicklung) development

Ausbildungs-: ~bei·hilfe *die* [education] grant; (für Berufsschüler, Lehrlinge) training grant; **~beruf** *der* trade requiring an apprenticeship; **~förderung** *die* provision of [education] grants; (für Berufsschüler, Lehrlinge) provision of training grants; **~gang** *der* training syllabus; **~platz** *der* trainee post; (für Lehrlinge) apprenticeship; **~stätte** *die* place of training; **~vertrag** *der* articles of apprenticeship

> **Ausbildungsplatz**
>
> Over 500,000 firms in all branches of the economy, including the independent professions and the public sector, provide trainee posts for **Azubis**. Young people can only apply for these in state-recognized occupations for which vocational training is required. Large firms have their own training workshops, but smaller firms train their apprentices on the job.

aus|bitten *unr. refl. V.* **1** (geh.: erbitten) **sich** (*Dat.*) **von jmdm. etw. ~:** request sth. from sb.; ask sb. for sth. **2** (verlangen) **sich** (*Dat.*) **etw. ~:** demand sth.; **ich bitte mir Ruhe/mehr Sorgfalt aus** I must insist on silence/that you take more care

aus|blasen *unr. tr. V.* **1** (löschen, ausatmen) blow out **2** (leer blasen) blow ‹*egg*›

aus|blassen *itr. V.; mit sein* (geh.) fade

aus|bleiben *unr. itr. V.; mit sein* **1** (nicht eintreten) ‹*effect, disaster, success, reward*› fail to materialize; ‹*symptom*› be absent, not appear; **es konnte nicht ~, dass ...** it was inevitable that ...; **das Ausbleiben einer Nachricht** the absence *or* lack of any news; **beim Ausbleiben der Regelblutung** if a period is missed **2** (fernbleiben) ‹*guests, visitors, customers*› stay away, fail to appear; ‹*order, commission, help, offer, support, rain*› fail to arrive; **wenn jahrelang der Regen ausbleibt** if the rains fail year after year; **sein Ausbleiben** his absence **3** (nicht heimkommen) stay out **4** (ugs.: ausgeschaltet bleiben) stay off **5** (stocken) ‹*pulse, breathing*› stop

aus|bleichen
A *unr. itr. V.; mit sein* fade; **ausgebleichte Gebeine/Haare** bleached bones/hair
B *tr. V.* bleach; ‹*light, sun*› fade ‹*material, curtains, etc.*›

aus|blenden
A *tr. V.* (Rundf., Ferns., Film) fade out; (fig.: nicht berücksichtigen) take no account of, leave out of account ‹*facts, information*›
B *refl. V.* (Rundf., Ferns.) **sich [aus einer Übertragung] ~:** fade oneself out of a transmission

Aus·blendung *die* (Film, Rundf., Ferns.) fade-out; **nach unserer ~ aus der Übertragung** after we leave this transmission

Aus·blick *der* **1** view (**auf** + *Akk.* of); **jmdm. den ~ versperren** block *or* obstruct sb.'s view; **ein Zimmer mit ~ aufs Meer/auf die Berge** a room overlooking the sea/with a view of the mountains **2** (Vorausschau) **jmdm. einen ~ auf etw.** (*Akk.*) **geben** give sb. a preview of sth.; **einen optimistischen ~ in die Zukunft gestatten** permit an optimistic view of the prospects for the future

aus|blicken *itr. V.* (geh.) **nach jmdm./etw. ~:** look out for sb./sth.

aus|bluten *itr. V.; mit sein* bleed to death; (fig.) bleed dry; **~ lassen** bleed ‹*animal*›

aus|bohren *tr. V.* **1** (bohren) bore; (mit Bohrgerät) drill; (erweitern) drill out **2** (entfernen) bore out; (mit Bohrgerät) drill out

aus|bomben *tr. V.* bomb out; *s. auch* **Ausgebombte**

aus|booten *tr. V.* **1** (ugs.: verdrängen) get rid of (**aus** from) **2** (Seew.: an Land bringen) disembark ‹*passengers*› by boat

aus|borgen *tr. V.* (ugs.) **1** (sich ausleihen) **[sich** (*Dat.*)**] etw. ~:** borrow sth. (**von, bei** from) **2** (überlassen) **jmdm. etw. ~:** lend sb. sth.; lend sth. to sb.

aus|braten
A *unr. itr. V.; mit sein* ‹*fat*› run out (**aus** of)
B *unr. tr. V.* (auslassen) fry the fat out of ‹*bacon*›

aus|brechen
A *unr. itr. V.; mit sein* **1** (entkommen, auch Milit.) break out (**aus** of); (fig.) break free (**aus** from) **2** (austreten) **jmdm. bricht der [kalte] Schweiß aus** sb. breaks into a [cold] sweat **3** ‹*volcano*› erupt **4** (beginnen) break out; ‹*crisis*› break; ‹*misery, despair*› set in; *s. auch* **Wohlstand 5** **in Gelächter/Weinen ~:** burst out laughing/crying; **in Beifall/Tränen ~:** burst into applause/tears; **in den Ruf ~ „..."** break into the cry, '...'; **in Schweiß ~:** break out into a sweat; **in Zorn/Wut ~:** explode with anger/rage **6** (sich lösen) ‹*hook, dowel, etc.*› come out; **ihm waren zwei Zähne ausgebrochen** he had broken two teeth **7** (Richtung ändern) ‹*car, horse*› swerve
B *unr. tr. V.* **1** take *or* knock down ‹*wall*›; **Steine aus einer Wand ~:** knock stones out of a wall; **sich** (*Dat.*) **einen Zahn ~:** break a tooth; **eine Tür/ein Fenster [in einer Mauer] ~:** put a doorway/window [in a wall] **2** (erbrechen) bring up; vomit [up]

Aus·brecher *der,* **Aus·brecherin** *die;* **~, ~nen** (ugs.) escaped prisoner *or* convict; (gewohnheitsmäßiger) jail-breaker

aus|breiten
A *tr. V.* **1** (entfalten) spread [out] ‹*map, cloth, sheet, etc.*›; open out ‹*fan, newspaper*›; (nebeneinander legen) spread out; **ein Tuch über etw.** (*Akk. od. Dat.*) **~:** spread *or* put a cloth over sth.; **seine Wünsche/Pläne/Ansichten/sein Leben vor jmdm. ~** (fig.) unfold one's desires/plans/views/life story to sb. **2** (ausstrecken) **die Arme/Flügel ~:** spread one's arms/its wings; **die Arme nach jmdm. ~:** stretch out one's arms to sb.
B *refl. V.* **1** (sich verbreiten) spread **2** (ugs.: sich breit machen) spread oneself out **3** (sich erstrecken) extend; stretch [out] **4** (abwertend: erörtern) **sich**

über etw. (*Akk.*) **~:** go on [at great length] about sth.

aus|brennen
A *unr. itr. V.; mit sein* **1** (zu Ende brennen) burn out; **ausgebrannte Kernbrennstäbe** (fig.) spent nuclear fuel rods **2** (zerstört werden) ‹*building, room*› be gutted, be burnt out; ‹*ship, aircraft, vehicle*› be burnt out; **ausgebrannt sein** be burnt out **3** (ugs.: seine Habe verlieren) be burnt out
B *unr. tr. V.* **1** (reinigen) cauterize ‹*wound*› **2** (entfernen) burn out; burn off ‹*weeds*›; *s. auch* **ausgebrannt B**

aus|bringen *unr. tr. V.* **1** (sprechen) propose; **einen Trinkspruch** *od.* **Toast auf jmdn./etw. ~:** propose a toast to sb./sth. **2** (Seemannsspr.) lower ‹*boat, anchor*›; lay, lower ‹*net*›; lay *or* run out ‹*mooring line*›

Aus·bruch *der* **1** (Flucht) escape; (lit. or fig.), breakout (also Mil.) (**aus** from); **an ~ denken** think of escape **2** (Beginn) outbreak; **vor/nach ~ des Krieges** before/after the outbreak of war; **zum ~ kommen** break out; ‹*crisis, storm*› break **3** (Gefühls~) outburst; (stärker) explosion; (von Wut, Zorn) eruption; explosion; **zum ~ kommen** explode; erupt **4** (eines Vulkans) eruption

Ausbruchs·versuch *der* attempted breakout *or* escape; (fig.) attempt to break free; (Milit.) attempted breakout

aus|brüten *tr. V.* **1** hatch out; (im Brutkasten) incubate **2** (ugs.: sich ausdenken) hatch [up] ‹*plot, scheme*› **3** **etwas/einen Infekt ~** (ugs.: krank werden) be going down with something/an infection

aus|buchen *tr. V.* (Kaufmannsspr., Bankw.) **etw. ~** (streichen) delete sth. from the accounts; (abschreiben) write sth. off; *s. auch* **ausgebucht B**

aus|buchten *tr. V.* bulge; widen ‹*road*› (*to form a parking area, passing point, etc.*)

Ausbuchtung *die;* **~, ~en** bulge

aus|buddeln *tr. V.* (ugs., auch fig.) dig up

aus|bügeln *tr. V.* **1** (ugs.: bereinigen) iron out ‹*differences, problem, misunderstanding, defect*›; make good ‹*loss, mistake*› **2** iron ‹*shirt, dress, etc.*›; press ‹*seam, suit, trousers*›; iron out ‹*crease, fold*›

aus|buhen *tr. V.* (ugs.) boo

Aus·bund *der* (oft iron.) **ein ~ an** *od.* **von Tugend** a paragon *or* model of virtue; **ein ~ an** *od.* **von Bosheit/Frechheit** malice/impudence itself *or* personified

aus|bürgern *tr. V.* **jmdn. ~:** deprive sb. of citizenship

Ausbürgerung *die;* **~, ~en** deprivation of citizenship

aus|bürsten *tr. V.* brush out ‹*dust, dirt*› (**aus** of); brush ‹*clothes, upholstery, etc.*›

aus|büxen /ˈausbʏksn̩/ *itr. V.; mit sein* (ugs.) skedaddle (coll.); scarper (Brit. coll.); **jmdm. ~:** run away from sb.; **vor jmdm./etw. ~:** run away from sb./sth.

aus|checken *tr. V.* check out

aus|chillen *itr. V.* (salopp) chill out (coll.)

Aus·dauer *die* staying power; stamina; (Beharrlichkeit) perseverance; (Hartnäckigkeit) persistence; **[beim Lernen, Lesen] ~/keine ~ haben** have/lack perseverance [when it comes to learning, reading]

aus·dauernd
A *Adj.* **1** ‹*runner, swimmer, etc.*› with stamina *or* staying power; (beharrlich) persevering; tenacious; (hartnäckig) persistent; unflagging ‹*diligence, enthusiasm, efforts*›; enduring ‹*love, sympathy*› **2** (Bot.) perennial
B *adv.* perseveringly; tenaciously; (hartnäckig) persistently

Ausdauer·training *das* stamina training

aus·dehnbar *Adj.* ‹*company, market*› capable of expansion; ‹*norm, application, etc.*› capable of extension *or* of being extended (**auf** + *Akk.* to); elastic ‹*material*›

aus|dehnen
A *tr. V.* **1** (räumlich) stretch ‹*clothes, piece of elastic*›; expand ‹*rail*›; (fig.) extend ‹*power, borders, trading links*›; expand, increase ‹*capacity*› **2** (einbeziehen) **etw. auf etw.** (*Akk.*) **~:** extend sth. to sth. **3** (zeitlich) prolong; **ein ausgedehntes Frühstück** a leisurely breakfast; **ausgedehnte Ausflüge/Spaziergänge** extended trips/walks
B *refl. V.* **1** (räumlich) ‹*metal, water, gas, etc.*› expand; ‹*fog, mist, fire, epidemic*› spread; (fig.) ‹*business, firm, trade*› expand **2** (zeitlich) go on (**bis** until) **3** (sich erstrecken) extend; **ein ausgedehnter Park** an extensive park; **sich bis zum Meer ~:** extend *or* stretch to the sea

Aus·dehnung *die* **1** (Zunahme an Volumen, Vergrößerung) expansion; (fig.: der Macht, von Beziehungen, Grenzen) extension **2** (zeitlich) prolongation; (von Öffnungszeiten) extension **3** (Ausmaß, Größe) extent

ausdehnungs-, Ausdehnungs-: ~fähig *Adj.* (bes. Physik) expansible; capable of expansion *postpos.*; **~fähigkeit** *die* (bes. Physik) expansibility; **~koeffizient** *der* (Physik) coefficient of expansion

aus|denken
A *unr. refl. V.* **sich** (*Dat.*) **etw. ~:** think of sth.; (erfinden) think sth. up; (sich vorstellen) imagine sth.; **sich** (*Dat.*) **etw. in allen Einzelheiten ~:** think sth. out in every detail; **da musst du dir schon etwas anderes ~!** you'll have to come up with *or* think of something better than that!
B *unr. tr. V.* (zu Ende denken) **etw. ~:** think sth. out *or* through [completely]; **[das ist] nicht auszudenken** it's impossible to imagine; (zu schrecklich) it does not bear thinking about

aus|deuten *tr. V.* interpret; **etw. falsch ~:** misinterpret sth.; **etw. dahin ~, dass …** interpret sth. to mean that …

aus|deutschen *tr. V.* (österr.) **jmdm. etw. ~:** explain sth. to sb. in words of one syllable

Aus·deutung *die* interpretation

aus|dienen *itr. V.* (Milit. veralt.) **ausgedient haben** have finished *or* completed one's military service; (fig. ugs.) have had it (coll.); *s. auch* **ausgedient B**

aus|diskutieren *tr. V.* **etw. ~:** discuss sth. fully *or* thoroughly

aus|dorren ▸ **ausdörren B**

aus|dörren
A *tr. V.* dry up; dry up, parch ‹*land, soil*›; parch ‹*throat, lips*›
B *itr. V.; mit sein* dry up; ‹*land, soil*› dry up, become parched; ‹*plant*› wither

aus|drehen *tr. V.* **1** (ausschalten) switch *or* turn off ‹*radio, light, engine*›; turn off ‹*gas*› **2** (Technik) drill [out] ‹*hole*›

Aus·druck[1] *der;* **~[e]s, Ausdrücke** **1** (Wort) expression; (Terminus) term; **du sollst nicht solche Ausdrücke gebrauchen** you mustn't use language like that; **Sie haben sich im ~ vergriffen** your choice of words is most unfortunate; **dumm/ärgerlich** *usw.* **ist gar kein ~:** stupid/angry *etc.* isn't the word for it **2** (Ausdrucksweise, Gesichts~) expression; **etw. zum ~ bringen** express sth.; give expression to sth.; **einer Sache** (*Dat.*) **~ geben** *od.* **verleihen** (geh.) express sth.; **mit dem ~ der Entrüstung/des Dankes** with an expression of indignation/thanks; **in etw.** (*Dat.*) **zum ~ kommen** be expressed *or* find expression in sth.

Aus·druck[2] *der;* **~[e]s, ~e** (Nachrichtenw., DV) printout

aus|drucken
A *tr. V.* **1** (Druckerspr.: fertig drucken) finish printing ‹*book etc.*› **2** (Nachrichtenw., DV) print out **3** (angeben, aufführen) **im Katalog [mit 400 Euro] ausgedruckt** listed in the catalogue [at 400 euros]; **in Abänderung unseres ausgedruckten Programms** in a change to our advertised programme
B *itr. V.* (Druckerspr.) **gut/schlecht ~:** print well/badly

aus|drücken
A *tr. V.* **1** (auspressen) squeeze ‹*juice*› out; squeeze [out] ‹*lemon, orange, grape, etc.*›; squeeze out ‹*sponge*›; squeeze ‹*boil, pimple*›; **den Saft aus einer Zitrone ~:** squeeze *or* press the juice out of *or* from a lemon **2** (auslöschen) stub out ‹*cigarette*›; pinch out ‹*candle*› **3** (formulieren, widerspiegeln) express; **anders ausgedrückt** to put it another way; **… und das ist noch milde ausgedrückt** …, and that's putting it mildly; **jmdm. seinen Dank ~:** express one's thanks to sb.; **etw. in** *od.* **mit Worten ~:** express sth. in *or* put sth. into words; **seine Miene drückte Zufriedenheit aus** his expression was one of contentment
B *refl. V.* **1** (sich äußern) express oneself; **um mich gelinde/höflich auszudrücken** to put it mildly/politely **2** (offenbar werden) be expressed

ausdrücklich /*od.* -ˈ--/
A *Adj.* express *attrib.* ‹*command, wish, etc.*›; explicit ‹*reservation*›; **gegen jmds. ~es Verbot** although sb. has/had expressly forbidden it
B *adv.* expressly; ‹*mention*› explicitly; **etw. ~ betonen** give sth. particular emphasis

ausdrucks-, Ausdrucks-: ~fähigkeit *die* expressiveness; (sprachliche Gewandtheit) articulateness; **~kraft** *die* expressive power; expressiveness; **~los** **A** *Adj.* **1** expressionless; **2** (ohne Ausdruckskraft) unexpressive ‹*style, delivery, etc.*›; **B** *adv.* **1** expressionlessly; **2** (ohne Ausdruckskraft) unexpressively; **~losigkeit** *die* **1** expressionlessness; **2** (Fehlen von Ausdruckskraft) lack of expressiveness; **~mittel** *das* means of expression; **~schwach** **A** *Adj.* unexpressive; **~schwach sein** be lacking in expression; **B** *adv.* unexpressively; **~stark** **A** *Adj.* expressive; forceful ‹*language*›; bold ‹*pattern, colour*›; **B** *adv.* expressively; **~tanz** *der* expressive dance; **~voll** **A** *Adj.* expressive; **B** *adv.* expressively; **~weise** *die* way of expressing oneself

aus|dünnen *tr. V.* thin out

aus|dünsten
A *tr. V.* (ausströmen) give off; ‹*factory*› emit ‹*fumes etc.*›
B *itr. V.* (Feuchtigkeit abgeben) transpire

Aus·dünstung *die* **1** (das Ausdünsten) transpiration **2** (Dampf) vapour; (Geruch) odour

aus·einander *Adv.* **1** (voneinander getrennt) apart; **etw. ~ schreiben** write sth. as separate words; **zwei Schüler ~ setzen** seat two pupils apart; **weit ~ stehen** be far apart; ‹*teeth*› be widely spaced; ‹*eyes, legs*› be wide apart; **weit ~ stehende Zähne** widely spaced teeth; **etw. ~ bekommen** *od.* (ugs.) **kriegen [können]** be able to get sth. apart; **~ brechen** break up; **etw. ~ brechen** break sth. up; **etw. ~ breiten** spread sth. out; **das hat die beiden ~ gebracht** this led to the two of them parting company; **nichts kann sie ~ bringen** nothing can part them; **sich ~ entwickeln** develop away; ‹*friends etc.*› grow apart [from each other *or* one another]; **~ falten** +*Akk.* unfold; open ‹*newspaper*›; **~ gehen** part; ‹*crowd*› disperse; ‹*views*› differ, diverge; ‹*streets*› diverge; ‹*relationship*› break up; (ugs.) ‹*person*› get round and podgy; **zwei Verbündete ~ zu dividieren suchen** seek to drive a wedge between two allies; **zwei Dinge ~ halten** distinguish between two things; **zwei Menschen ~ halten** tell two people apart; **~ klaffen** ‹*hole, wound*› gape; (fig.) ‹*views*› be poles apart; **etw. ~ klamüsern** (nordd. ugs.) unravel sth.; sort sth. out; **~ laufen** run off in different directions; ‹*crowd*› scatter; ‹*roads etc.*› diverge; ‹*paint etc.*› run; **sich ~ leben** grow apart (**mit** from); **etw. ~ nehmen** take sth. apart; **jmdn. ~ nehmen** (salopp.) take sb. apart (coll.); **etw. ~ reißen** tear sth. up; **eine Familie ~ reißen** tear a family apart; **Dinge ~ rücken** move things apart; **~ rücken** move apart; **etw. ~ schrauben** unscrew sth. and take it apart; **jmdm. etw. ~ setzen** explain sth. to sb.; **er hat sich mit diesem Problem seit Jahren ~ gesetzt** he's concerned himself with this problem for years; **sich mit den Dingen [ernsthaft] ~ setzen** give things serious thoughts; **sich mit jmdm. ~ setzen** have it out with sb.; argue the/a matter out with sb.; **sich mit seinen Gläubigern ~ setzen** battle with one's creditors; **etw. ~ sprengen** burst sth. [apart *or* open]; **~ stieben** scatter; **~ treiben** +*Akk.* scatter ‹*birds, animals*›; disperse ‹*crowd, clouds*›; ~

a

treiben drift apart; **den Tisch ~ ziehen** pull out the table leaf; **sich ~ ziehen** ‹*column, competitors in race*› string *or* spread out; **sie sind [im Alter] ein Jahr ~**: they are a year apart in age; **~!** get away from each other!; break it up!; **~ sein** (ugs.) (sich getrennt haben) have separated; have split up; (aufgelöst sein) ‹*engagement*› have been broken off; be off; ‹*marriage, relationship, friendship*› have broken up **2** (eines aus dem anderen) **Behauptungen/Formeln** *usw.* **~ ableiten** deduce propositions/formulae *etc.* one from another

***auseinander|bekommen** *usw.* ▸ **auseinander 1**

Auseinandersetzung *die;* **~, ~en** **1** (eingehende Beschäftigung) examination (**mit** of) **2** (Diskussion) debate, discussion (**über** + *Akk.* about, on) **3** (Streit) argument; (zwischen Arbeitgeber und Arbeitnehmer) dispute; **es kam wegen etw. zu einer ~**: an argument/a dispute developed over sth. **4** (Kampfhandlung) clash; **es kam zu ~en zwischen Polizisten und Demonstranten** there were clashes between police and demonstrators **5** (Rechtsw.) partition

***auseinander|sprengen** *usw.* ▸ **auseinander 1**

aus|erkiesen *unr. tr. V.* (geh., Präsensformen dicht. veralt.) choose; **zu etw. auserkoren sein** be chosen for sth.

Aus·erkorene *der/die; adj. Dekl.* (scherzh.) intended (coll.)

aus·erlesen
A *Adj.* (geh.) select ‹*company, audience*›; choice ‹*fruits, wines, etc.*›; exquisite ‹*taste*›; **von ~er Eleganz** of exquisite elegance
B *adv.* (überaus) exquisitely ‹*beautiful, fine, charming*›

aus|ersehen *unr. tr. V.* (geh.) choose

aus|erwählen *tr. V.* (geh.) choose; **zu etw. auserwählt sein** be chosen for sth.; **das auserwählte Volk** (jüd. Rel.) the chosen people

Aus·erwählte *der/die; adj. Dekl.* **1** (geh.) chosen one; **die ~n** the chosen **2** (scherzh.) (Freund[in]) beloved (joc.); (Verlobte[r]) intended (coll.)

aus·fahrbar *Adj.* telescopic ‹*aerial*›; retractable, pop-up ‹*headlights*›

aus|fahren
A *unr. tr. V.* **1** **jmdn. ~** (im Kinderwagen, Rollstuhl) take sb. out for a walk; (im Auto o. Ä.) take sb. out for a drive *or* ride **2** (ausliefern) deliver ‹*newspapers, parcels, laundry*› **3** (Technik: nach außen bringen) extend ‹*aerial, crane, landing flaps, telescope, etc.*›; lower ‹*undercarriage*›; raise ‹*periscope*› **4** (abnutzen) damage; **ausgefahrene Straßen** rutted and damaged roads; *s. auch* **Gleis 2** **5** *mit sein* **eine Kurve ~**: take a bend wide **6** (maximal beschleunigen) drive ‹*car*› flat out; run ‹*engine*› at full power **7** (die Kapazität ausnutzen) **etw. voll/zu 40% ~**: operate *or* run sth. at full capacity/40% of capacity **8** (Seemannsspr.: ausbringen) lay out, run out ‹*warp, cable*›; run out ‹*anchor*›; rig out, set ‹*boom*›
B *unr. itr. V.; mit sein* **1** (spazieren fahren) go out for a drive **2** (hinausfahren) ‹*boat, ship*› put to sea; ‹*train*› leave, pull out; ‹*car, lorry*› leave; **aus dem Hafen ~**: leave harbour; **der Zug fuhr aus dem Bahnhof aus** the train pulled out of *or* left the station **3** (Bergmannsspr.: aus dem Schacht fahren) come up **4** (Technik: hervorkommen) extend **5** (den Körper verlassen) **[von jmdm.] ~** ‹*evil spirit etc.*› leave sb.

Aus·fahrt *die* **1** (Stelle zum Hinausfahren, Autobahn~) exit (*Gen.* from); **die ~ Bremen-Ost** the Bremen-East exit; the exit for Bremen East **2** (das Hinausfahren) departure; (Bergmannsspr.: aus dem Schacht) ascent; **bei der ~ aus dem Bahnhof sahen wir ...** as the train pulled out of *or* left the station, we saw ...; **bei der ~ aus dem Hafen tutete das Schiff** as it left [the] harbour, the ship hooted; **der Zug hat keine ~**: the train has not been given the signal for departure **3** (Spazierfahrt) (mit dem Auto) drive; (mit dem Fahrrad, Motorrad) ride; **eine ~ machen** go for a drive/ride

Ausfahrt·signal *das* (Eisenb.) starting signal

Ausfahrts-: ~schild *das; Pl.* **~~er** exit sign; **~signal** *das* (Eisenb.) ▸ **Ausfahrtsignal**; **~straße** *die* exit [road]

Aus·fall *der* **1** (das Nichtstattfinden) cancellation; **ein hoher ~ an Unterrichtsstunden** a large number of cancelled lessons **2** (Einbuße, Verlust) loss; (an Einnahmen, Lohn) drop (*Gen.* in) **3** (Technik) (eines Motors) failure; (einer Maschine, eines Autos) breakdown; (fig.: eines Organs) failure; loss of function **4** (das Ausscheiden) retirement; (vor einem Rennen) withdrawal; (Abwesenheit) absence; **nach [dem] ~ von vier Läufern** after four runners had retired *or* dropped out **5** (das Herausfallen) **zum ~ der Haare/Zähne führen** cause hair loss/cause teeth to fall out **6** (Ergebnis) outcome; result **7** (beleidigende Äußerungen) attack (**gegen** on) **8** (Fechten) lunge; **im ~**: in the lunge position **9** (Gewichtheben) split; **in den ~ springen** split the legs **10** (Turnen) splits *pl.* **11** (Milit.: Ausbruch) rally; sortie

aus|fallen *unr. itr. V.; mit sein* **1** (herausfallen) fall out; **mir fallen die Haare aus** my hair is falling out **2** (nicht stattfinden) be cancelled; **etw. ~ lassen** cancel sth.; **der Unterricht/die Schule fällt morgen aus** lessons are cancelled/there is no school tomorrow **3** (ausscheiden) drop out; (während eines Rennens) retire; drop out; (fehlen) be absent; **wenn der Pilot ausfällt, muss der Kopilot das Steuer übernehmen** if the pilot becomes unable to fly the plane, the co-pilot must take over the controls **4** (nicht mehr funktionieren) ‹*engine, brakes, signal*› fail; ‹*machine, car*› break down; **der Strom fiel aus** there was a power failure **5** (ein bestimmtes Ergebnis zeigen) turn out; **gut/schlecht** *usw.* **~**: turn out well/badly *etc.*; **wie ist die Prüfung ausgefallen?** (für dich) how did you do in the examination?; (insgesamt) what were the examination results like?; **die Niederlage fiel sehr deutlich aus** the defeat turned out to be *or* was most decisive **6** (Milit.: einen Ausfall machen) make a sortie **7** (Chemie: sich abscheiden) be precipitated **8** (Sprachw.: wegfallen) be dropped; *s. auch* **ausgefallen B**

aus|fällen *tr. V.* (Chemie) precipitate

ausfallend *Adj.* **[gegen jmdn.] ~ sein/werden** be/become abusive [towards sb.]

aus·fällig *Adj.* ▸ **ausfallend**

Ausfalls·erscheinung *die* (Med.) deficiency symptom

Ausfall·straße *die* (Verkehrsw.) main road [leading] out of the/a town/city

Ausfall[s]·winkel *der* (Physik) angle of reflection

Ausfall·zeit *die* (Versicherungsw.) credited service period

aus|fasern *itr. V.; meist mit sein* fray

aus|fechten *unr. tr. V.* fight out

aus|fegen *tr.* (*auch itr.*) *V.* (bes. nordd.) sweep up ‹*dirt*›; sweep out ‹*room etc.*›; *s. auch* **eisern 3**

aus|feilen *tr. V.* file down ‹*key, cogwheel, etc.*›; file [out] ‹*hole*›; (fig.) polish ‹*speech, essay, poem, etc.*›

aus|fertigen *tr. V.* (Amtsspr.) **1** (ausstellen) draw up ‹*document, agreement, will, etc.*›; issue ‹*passport, certificate*›; make out ‹*bill, receipt*› **2** (unterzeichnen) sign

Aus·fertigung *die* (Amtsspr.) **1** ▸ **ausfertigen 1**: drawing up; issuing; making out **2** (Exemplar) copy; **in doppelter/dreifacher ~**: in duplicate/triplicate; **etw. in vier ~en einreichen** submit four copies of sth.

aus·findig *Adv.* **in jmdn./etw. ~ machen** find sb./sth.

aus|flicken *tr. V.* (ugs.) patch up

aus|fliegen
A *unr. itr. V.; mit sein* **1** (hinausfliegen) fly out; **die ganze Familie ist ausgeflogen** (ugs. fig.) the whole family has gone out [for a walk/drive etc.] **2** (flügge werden) leave the nest
B *unr. tr. V.* **jmdn./etw. ~**: fly sb./sth. out; (per Luftbrücke) airlift sb./sth.

aus|fließen *unr. itr. V.; mit sein* (herausfließen) flow *or* run out (**aus** of)

aus|flippen *itr. V.; mit sein* (salopp) **1** freak out (coll.); **ausgeflippt** (im Drogenrausch) freaked *or* spaced out (coll.); **eine ausgeflippte Idee** a freaky idea (coll.) **2** (überschnappen) flip one's lid *or* one's top (coll.)

Aus·flucht *die;* **~, Ausflüchte** /-flʏçtə/ excuse; **Ausflüchte machen** make excuses

Aus·flug *der* **1** outing; (vom Reisebüro o. Ä. organisiert) excursion; (Wanderung) ramble; walk; (fig.) excursion; **einen ~ machen** go on an outing/excursion; go for a ramble *or* walk **2** (das Ausschwärmen) flight [from the nest/hive] **3** (Imkerei: Flugloch) [hive] entrance

Ausflügler /ˈausfly:klɐ/ *der;* **~s, ~, Ausflüglerin** *die;* **~, ~nen** tripper (Brit.); day tripper; excursionist (Amer.)

Ausflugs-: ~dampfer *der* pleasure steamer; (allgemeiner) excursion boat; **~lokal** *das* restaurant/café catering for [day] trippers; **~ort** *der* resort for [day] trippers; **~verkehr** *der* (am Wochenende) weekend holiday traffic; (an Feiertagen) holiday traffic; **~ziel** *das* destination for [day] trippers; **unser ~ziel war ...** the destination of our excursion *or* outing was ...

Aus·fluss, *Aus·fluß *der* **1** (das Ausfließen) outflow; (von Gas) escape **2** ▸ **❶ S. 439** (Med.: Absonderung) discharge **3** (geh.: Auswirkung) product **4** (Abfluss) outlet **5** (Technik: ausfließende Menge) outflow

aus|folgen *tr. V.* (österr.) issue; release ‹*body*›

aus|formen *tr. V.* **1** (formen) shape (**zu** into) **2** (endgültig gestalten) give final shape to ‹*text, work of art*›

aus|formulieren *tr. V.* formulate ‹*ideas, questions*›; flesh out ‹*paper*› [from notes]

Aus·formung *die* **1** (das Ausformen) shaping **2** (Gestalt) form

aus|forschen *tr. V.* **1** (ausfragen) question (**nach** about) **2** (herausfinden) find out; (erforschen) investigate; (zu Spionagezwecken) gather information on **3** (österr. Amtsspr.: ausfindig machen) find

Aus·forschung *die* **1** (Befragung) questioning **2** (das Herausfinden) finding out; (das Erforschen) investigation; **zur ~ von militärischen Betrieben** to gather information about military establishments **3** (österr. Amtsspr.: Ermittlung) finding

aus|fragen *tr. V.* **jmdn. ~**: question sb., ask sb. questions (**nach, über** + *Akk.* about); (verhören) interrogate sb. (**nach, über** + *Akk.* about); **so fragt man die Leute aus** that would be telling

aus|fransen
A *itr. V.; mit sein* fray
B *tr. V.* fringe

aus|fressen *unr. tr. V.* **etw. ausgefressen haben** (ugs.) have been up to sth. (coll.)

Aus·fuhr *die;* **~, ~en** **1** (das Exportieren) export **2** (Export) exports *pl.*

ausführbar *Adj.* **1** (durchführbar) practicable; workable ‹*plan*› **2** (für die Ausfuhr geeignet) exportable

aus|führen *tr. V.* **1** (ausgehen mit) **jmdn. ~**: take sb. out **2** (spazieren führen) take ‹*person, animal*› for a walk; take *or* lead ‹*prisoners*› out for their exercise **3** (exportieren) export **4** (durchführen) carry out ‹*work, repairs, plan, threat*›; execute, carry out ‹*command, order, commission*›; execute, perform ‹*movement, dance step*›; put ‹*idea, suggestion*› into practice; perform ‹*operation*›; perform, carry out ‹*experiment, analysis*›; **die ~de Gewalt** (Politik) the executive power **5** (Fußball, Eishockey usw.) take ‹*penalty, free kick, corner*› **6** (ausarbeiten) **etw. ~**: work sth. out in detail *or* fully; **etw. näher ~**: work sth. out in more detail **7** (erläutern, darlegen) explain

Ausfuhr-: ~gut *das* article for export; **~güter** goods for export; **~hafen** *der* port of exportation; **~land** *das* (Wirtsch.) **1** (Land, das ausführt) exporting country; **2** (Land, in das ausgeführt wird) export market

ausführlich /*auch:* ·ˈ--/
A *Adj.* detailed, full ‹*account, description, report, discussion*›; thorough, detailed, full ‹*investigation, debate*›; detailed ‹*introduction, instruction, letter*›; **~ werden** go into detail
B *adv.* in detail; ‹*investigate*› thoroughly, fully;

etw. ∼er/sehr ∼ beschreiben describe sth. in more *or* greater/in great detail

Ausführlichkeit /*auch:* ˈ-ˈ---/ *die;* ∼ ▸**ausführlich A**: fullness; thoroughness; **mit großer ∼:** in great detail; (umständlich) at great length

Ausfuhr-: ∼prämie *die* (Wirtsch.) export premium; **∼sperre** *die* (Wirtsch.) ▸**∼verbot**

Aus·führung *die* **1** (das Durchführen) ▸**ausführen 4**: carrying out; execution; performing; implementation; playing; giving; **zur ∼ gelangen** *od.* **kommen** (Papierdt.) ‹*plan*› be carried out *or* put into effect **2** (Fußball, Eishockey) taking; **nach der ∼ des Freistoßes** after the free kick has/had been taken **3** (Art der Herstellung) (Version) version; (äußere ∼) finish; (Modell) model; (Stil) style; **in der gleichen ∼:** of the same design **4** (Darlegung) explanation; (Bemerkung) remark; observation **5** (Ausarbeitung) **der Entwurf war fertig, jetzt ging es an die ∼ des Romans/der Einzelheiten** the draft was ready, and the next task was to work the novel out in detail/to work out the details

Ausfuhr·verbot *das* (Wirtsch.) export embargo

aus|füllen *tr. V.* **1** (füllen) fill in ‹*trench, excavation, gravel pit*›; (zustopfen) fill ‹*hole, joint*› **2** (beanspruchen, einnehmen) take up ‹*space*›; ‹*person*› fill ‹*chair, doorway, etc.*›; **ihr Leben ist ganz mit Arbeit ausgefüllt** her life is completely taken up by work **3** (die erforderlichen Angaben eintragen in) fill in ‹*form, crossword puzzle*›; write *or* make out ‹*prescription, cheque*› **4** (verbringen) fill ‹*pause*›; **seine freie Zeit mit etw. ∼:** fill [up] one's free time with sth.; **er füllte die Wartezeit mit Lesen aus** he filled in the time [he had to wait] with reading **5** (in Anspruch nehmen) take up **6** (bekleiden, versehen) **seinen Posten gut/nicht ∼:** do one's job well/not do one's job **7** (innerlich befriedigen) **jmdn. ∼:** fulfil sb.; give sb. fulfilment; **ihr Beruf füllt sie ganz aus** she finds complete fulfilment in her work; **er lebt ein ausgefülltes Leben** he lives a full life

aus|füttern *tr. V.* line

Aus·gabe *die* **1** (das Austeilen) distribution; giving out; (von Essen) serving; **die ∼ des Essens erfolgt ab ...** lunch/dinner *etc.* is [served] from ... **2** (das Aushändigen) issuing; (von Meldungen, Nachrichten) release; **nach ∼ des Befehls** after the order was/had been issued **3** (Geld∼) item of expenditure; expense; **∼n** expenditure *sing.* (**für** on); **seine ∼n übersteigen seine Einnahmen** his outgoings exceeded his income **4** (Edition, Auflage) edition; (Nummer einer Zeitschrift; Finanzw., Postw.) issue; **∼ erster/letzter Hand** *first/last edition personally supervised by the author;* **die letzte ∼ der Tagesschau** (fig.) the late news bulletin **5** ▸**Ausgabestelle 6** (Ausführung, auch fig.) version **7** (DV) output

Ausgabe-: ∼gerät *das* (DV) output device; **∼kurs** *der* (Finanzw.) issue price

Ausgaben-: ∼buch *das* petty-cash book; **∼politik** *die* expenditure policy

Ausgabe·stelle *die* (Schalter) issuing counter; (Büro) issuing office

Aus·gang *der* **1** (Erlaubnis zum Ausgehen) time off; (von Soldaten) leave; **zwei Tage ∼ haben** ‹*servant*› have two days off; ‹*soldier*› have a two-day pass; **bis sechs Uhr ∼ haben** ‹*servant*› be free till six; ‹*soldier*› have a pass until six **2** (Tür ins Freie) exit (*Gen.* from) **3** (Endpunkt, Grenze) **am ∼ des Dorfes/der Allee/des Waldes** at the end of the village/avenue/on the edge of the forest **4** (Anat.: Öffnung eines Organs) outlet **5** (Ende) end; (eines Romans, Films usw.) ending **6** (Ergebnis) outcome; (eines Wettbewerbs) result; **ein Unfall mit tödlichem ∼:** an accident with fatal consequences; a fatal accident **7** (Ausgangspunkt) starting point; **seinen ∼ von etw. nehmen** take sth. as one's starting point; ‹*style, plan, suggestion*› originate with sth. **8** (Bürow.: Postversand) posting (Brit.); mailing **9** (Bürow.: abgehende Post) outgoing mail **10** (Spaziergang) walk; **das war der erste ∼ des Rekonvaleszenten** that was the convalescent's first time out **11** (Elektrot.) output

ausgangs

A *Adv.* **∼ von** on the outskirts of

B *Präp. mit Gen.* **1** (räumlich) coming out of **2** (zeitlich) at the end of; **ein Mann ∼ der Fünfziger** a man in his late fifties

Ausgangs-: ∼basis *die* starting point; **∼lage** *die* initial position *or* situation; **∼position** *die* initial position; starting position; (bei einem Rennen) starting position; **∼punkt** *der* starting point; **∼situation** *die* starting position; **∼sperre** *die* (bes. Milit.) (für Zivilisten) curfew; (für Soldaten) confinement to barracks; **[eine] ∼sperre verhängen** impose a curfew/confine the soldiers/regiment *etc.* to barracks; **∼sperre haben** be confined to barracks; **∼sprache** *die* (Sprachw.) source language; **∼stellung** *die* **1** (Sport) starting position; **2** (Milit.) initial position; **∼zeile** *die* (Druckw.) break line

aus|geben

A *unr. tr. V.* **1** (austeilen) distribute; give out; serve ‹*food, drinks*› **2** (aushändigen, erteilen; Finanzw., Postw.: herausgeben) issue; (fig.) put about ‹*story, rumour*› **3** (verbrauchen) spend ‹*money*› (**für** on) **4** (ugs.: spendieren) **einen ∼:** treat everybody; (eine Runde geben) stand a round of drinks (coll.); **ich gebe [dir] einen aus** I'll treat you **5** (fälschlich bezeichnen) **jmdn./etw. als** *od.* **für jmdn./etw. ∼:** pretend sb./sth. is sb./sth.; **sich als jmd./etw.** *od.* **für jmdn./etw. ∼:** pretend to be sb./sth. **6** (DV) output

B *unr. refl. V.* **sich [völlig** *od.* **vollständig] ∼:** push oneself right to the limit

ausgebeult *2. Part. v.* **ausbeulen**

ausgebombt *2. Part. v.* **ausbomben**

Ausgebombte *der/die; adj. Dekl.* person who has/had been bombed out; **die ∼n** those who have/had been bombed out

aus·gebrannt

A *2. Part. v.* **ausbrennen**

B *Adj.* (fig.) burnt out

ausgebucht

A *2. Part. v.* **ausbuchen**

B *Adj.* (ausverkauft, belegt, auch fig. ugs.) booked up

ausgebufft /ˈaʊ̯sgəbʊft/ *Adj.* (salopp) (clever) canny; (durchtrieben) crafty

Aus·geburt *die* (geh. abwertend) **1** (übles Erzeugnis) evil product; **eine ∼ der Hölle** the spawn of hell **2** (Inbegriff) epitome

aus·gedient

A *2. Part. v.* **ausdienen**

B *Adj.* (ugs.: unbrauchbar) worn out, (Brit. coll.) clapped out, (Amer. coll.) beat up ‹*vehicle, engine, etc.*›

ausgedörrt *2. Part. v.* **ausdörren**

aus·gefallen

A *2. Part. v.* **ausfallen**

B *Adj.* unusual

Ausgeflippte *der/die; adj. Dekl.* (salopp) drop-out (coll.)

ausgefranst *2. Part. v.* **ausfransen**

ausgefuchst *Adj.* (ugs.) wily; crafty; **∼e Spezialisten** experienced specialists

ausgeglichen

A *2. Part. v.* **ausgleichen**

B *Adj.* **1** (harmonisch) balanced, harmonious ‹*structure, façade, etc.*›; well-balanced ‹*person*›; **ein ∼es Wesen haben** have an even *or* well-balanced temperament **2** (stabil) stable; equable ‹*climate*› **3** (Sport) even

Ausgeglichenheit *die;* ∼ (einer Struktur, Fassade usw.) balance; harmony; **die ∼ ihres Wesens/ihre ∼:** the evenness of her temperament

aus·gegoren *Adj.* **[voll] ∼:** fully fermented; (fig.) fully worked out ‹*plan, idea*›

Ausgeh·anzug *der* best suit; (Milit.) walking-out uniform (Brit.)

aus|gehen

A *unr. itr. V.; mit sein* **1** (irgendwohin gehen) go out; **er geht selten aus** he doesn't go out much **2** (fast aufgebraucht sein; auch fig.) run out; **jmdm. geht etw. aus** sb. is running out of sth.; **ihr ging die Geduld/der Gesprächsstoff aus** (fig.) she ran out of patience/conversation; **ihm geht der Atem** *od.* **die Luft** *od.* (ugs.) **die Puste aus** (er gerät außer Atem) he is getting short *or* out of breath; he is running out of puff (Brit. coll.); (er verliert seine Kraft, Energie) he is running out of steam (fig.); (er ist finanziell am Ende) he is going broke (coll.) **3** (ausfallen) fall out; **mir gehen die Haare aus** I'm losing my hair; my hair is falling out **4** (aufhören zu brennen) go out **5** (enden) end; **unentschieden ∼:** end in a draw; **gut/schlecht ∼:** turn out well/badly; ‹*story, film*› end happily/unhappily; *s. auch* **leer 1; straffrei 6** (herrühren) **von jmdm./etw. ∼:** come from sb./sth. **7** **von etw. ∼** (etw. zugrunde legen) take sth. as one's starting point; **gehen wir davon aus, dass ...** let us assume that ...; let us start from the assumption that ...; **du gehst von falschen Voraussetzungen aus** you're starting from false assumptions **8** **auf Abenteuer ∼:** look for adventure; **auf Entdeckungen ∼:** be bent on making discoveries; **auf Eroberungen ∼** (scherzh.) set out *or* be aiming to make a few conquests **9** (seinen Ausgang nehmen) **vom Hauptplatz** *usw.* ∼ ‹*road*› lead off from the main square *etc.*; (strahlenförmig) radiate from the main square *etc.* **10** (ausgestrahlt werden) radiate; **von jmdm./etw. geht Ruhe/Sicherheit aus** sb./sth. radiates calm/confidence **11** (abgeschickt werden) be sent off; **die ∼de Post** the outgoing mail **12** (blasser werden) ‹*colour*› run; ‹*fabric*› fade

B *unr. refl. V.* (österr.: ausreichen) be enough; ‹*equation, calculation*› come out; **es geht sich aus** there's enough; (zeitlich) there's enough time

ausgehend *Adj.* **im ∼en Mittelalter** towards the end of the Middle Ages; **das ∼e 19. Jahrhundert** the end of *or* closing years of the 19th century

ausgehungert

A *2. Part. v.* **aushungern**

B *Adj.* **1** (sehr hungrig) starving; **nach etw. ∼ sein** (fig.) be starved of sth. **2** (abgezehrt) emaciated

Ausgeh-: ∼uniform *die* (Milit.) walking-out uniform (Brit.); **∼verbot** *das* curfew; (Milit.) confinement to barracks

ausgeklügelt *2. Part. v.* **ausklügeln**

ausgekocht

A *2. Part. v.* **auskochen**

B *Adj.* (ugs. abwertend: durchtrieben) crafty

aus·gelassen

A *2. Part. v.* **auslassen**

B *Adj.* exuberant ‹*mood, person*›; lively ‹*party, celebration*›; (wild) boisterous

C *adv.* exuberantly; (wild) boisterously; **nebenan wurde ∼ gefeiert** there was a lively party going on next door

Aus·gelassenheit *die* exuberance; (Wildheit) boisterousness

Ausgeliefertsein *das;* **∼s** helplessness

aus·gelitten *Adj.* in **er hat ∼** (geh.) he has been released from his suffering

aus·gemacht

A *2. Part. v.* **ausmachen**

B *Adj.* **1** (beschlossen) agreed; **es ist [eine] ∼e Sache, dass ...** it is an accepted fact that ... **2** (vollkommen) complete; complete, utter ‹*nonsense*›; **eine ∼e Dummheit** downright stupidity

C *adv.* (überaus) extremely; (ausgesprochen) decidedly

aus·genommen

A *2. Part. v.* **ausnehmen**

B *Konj.* (außer) except; apart from; **alle sind anwesend, ∼ er** *od.* **er ∼:** everyone is present apart from *or* except him; **er kommt bestimmt, ∼ es regnet** he's sure to come, unless it rains

ausgepicht /ˈaʊ̯sgəpɪçt/ *Adj.* (ugs.) crafty; **ein ∼er Bursche** a wily customer (coll.)

ausgeprägt

A *2. Part. v.* **ausprägen**

B *Adj.* (ausgesprochen, stark entwickelt) distinctive ‹*personality, character*›; marked ‹*inclination, tendency, disinclination*›; pronounced ‹*feature, tendency*›; **einen ∼en Sinn für etw. haben** have a highly developed sense of sth.

ausgepumpt

A *2. Part. v.* **auspumpen**

B *Adj.* (salopp: erschöpft) knackered (Brit. coll.); shattered (Brit. coll.); tuckered out (Amer. coll.)

ausgerechnet
A *2. Part. v.* **ausrechnen**
B *Adv.* (*ugs.: gerade*) ~ **heute/morgen** today/tomorrow of all days; ~ **hier** here of all places; ~ **Sie** you of all people; ~ **jetzt kommt er/muss er kommen** he would have to come [just] now [of all times]; ~ **ihm muss das passieren** it would have to happen to him of all people; ~ **das** that of all things

ausgereift
A *2. Part. v.* **ausreifen**
B *Adj.* mature; fully developed ‹*device, concept*›

aus·geschlafen
A *2. Part. v.* **ausschlafen**
B *Adj.* (ugs.: gewitzt) wide awake

aus·geschlossen
A *2. Part. v.* **ausschließen**
B *Adj.* **das ist ~:** that is out of the question; **es ist nicht ~, dass ...** one cannot rule out the possibility that ...; it is not impossible that ...; **jeder Irrtum ist ~:** there can be no possibility of a mistake

aus·geschnitten
A *2. Part. v.* **ausschneiden**
B *Adj.* low-cut ‹*dress, blouse, etc.*›; **ein tief/weit ~es Kleid** a dress with a plunging neckline; a very low-cut dress

ausgesorgt *Adj.* (ugs.) **[finanziell] ~ haben** be comfortably off

ausgespielt
A *2. Part. v.* **ausspielen**
B *Adj. in* ~ **haben** be finished; **bei mir hat er ~** (ugs.) he's had it as far as I'm concerned (coll.)

aus·gesprochen
A *2. Part. v.* **aussprechen**
B *Adj.* definite, marked ‹*preference, inclination, resemblance*›; pronounced ‹*dislike*›; marked ‹*contrast*›; **~es Pech/Glück haben** be decidedly unlucky/lucky; **ein ~es Talent für etw.** a definite talent for sth.; **ein ~er Gegner von etw. sein** be a strong opponent of sth.
C *adv.* (besonders) decidedly; downright ‹*stupid, ridiculous, ugly*›

aus|gestalten *tr. V.* **1** (in bestimmter Weise gestalten) arrange; (formulieren) formulate **2** (ausbauen) develop (**zu** into)

Aus·gestaltung *die* **1** ▸**ausgestalten 1, 2**: arrangement; development; formulation **2** (Form) form

ausgestellt
A *2. Part. v.* **ausstellen**
B *Adj.* flared ‹*skirts, trousers, etc.*›

aus·gestorben
A *2. Part. v.* **aussterben**
B *Adj.* **[wie] ~:** deserted; **die Stadt ist wie ~:** this is like a ghost town

Ausgestoßene *der/die; adj. Dekl.* outcast

aus·gesucht
A *2. Part. v.* **aussuchen**
B *Adj.* **1** (erlesen) choice; exquisite ‹*jewellery, clothes, furniture*›; select ‹*company*› **2** (besonders groß) exceptional; extreme **3** (wenig Auswahl bietend) **diese Sachen sind ziemlich ~:** there aren't many good things left
C *adv.* exceptionally; extremely

aus·gewachsen
A *2. Part. v.* **auswachsen**
B *Adj.* **1** fully-grown; adult ‹*man, woman*› **2** (fig. ugs.) (richtig) real ‹*storm, gale*›; (groß) full-blown ‹*scandal*›; utter, complete ‹*nonsense, fool, idiot*›

ausgewiesen
A *2. Part. v.* **ausweisen**
B *Adj.* (schweiz.) **1** (nachweislich) proven **2** (mit Zeugnissen versehen) **gut ~:** with good references *postpos.*

aus·gewogen
A *2. Part. v.* **auswiegen**
B *Adj.* (ausgeglichen) balanced; [well-]balanced ‹*personality*›
C *adv.* in a balanced way

Aus·gewogenheit *die;* **~:** balance

ausgezeichnet /*od.* '--'--/
A *2. Part. v.* **auszeichnen**
B *Adj.* excellent; outstanding ‹*expert*›
C *adv.* excellently; ~ **Tennis spielen können** be an excellent tennis player; **sie passt ~ zu ihm** she suits him very well indeed

ausgiebig /'ausgi:bɪç/
A *Adj.* **1** substantial, large ‹*meal*›; good long ‹*walk, sleep, rest, drive*›; extensive ‹*study*›; abundant ‹*credit*›; **ein ~er Regen** continuous heavy rain; **~en Gebrauch von etw. machen** make full use of sth. **2** (veralt.) ▸**ergiebig**
B *adv.* ‹*profit*› handsomely; ‹*read*› extensively; **von etw. ~ Gebrauch machen** make full use of sth.; **~ frühstücken** eat a substantial breakfast; **~ wandern** walk extensively; **etw. ~ betrachten** have a long close look at sth.; **sich ~ strecken** have a good stretch; **~ gähnen** have a good yawn

aus|gießen *unr. tr. V.* **1** (aus einem Gefäß gießen) pour out (**aus** of) **2** (leeren) empty **3** (geh.: über jmdn./etw. gießen) pour (**über** + *Akk.* over); **seinen Spott/seine Verachtung/seinen Zorn über jmdn. ~:** pour scorn/contempt on sb./vent one's rage on sb. **4** (Technik: ausfüllen) fill (**mit** with)

Ausgießung *die;* ~ *in* **die ~ des Heiligen Geistes** (christl. Rel.) the effusion of the Holy Spirit

Ausgleich *der;* **~[e]s, ~e** **1** (von Unregelmäßigkeiten) evening out; (von Spannungen) easing; (von Differenzen, Gegensätzen) reconciliation; (eines Konflikts) settlement; (Schadensersatz) compensation; (einer Rechnung, Schuld) settlement; (eines Kontos) balancing; **einen ~ der verschiedenen Interessen anstreben** strive to reconcile differing interests; **um ~ bemüht sein** be at pains to promote compromise; **als** *od.* **zum ~ für etw.** to make up *or* compensate for sth.; **im Büro hat er wenig Bewegung, deshalb spielt er Tennis zum ~:** he doesn't get much exercise in the office, so, to compensate, he plays tennis; **eine auf ~ und Zusammenarbeit gerichtete Politik** policies aimed at conciliation and cooperation; **zum ~ Ihrer Rechnung/Ihres Kontos** in settlement of your invoice/to balance your account; **einen ~ in etw.** (*Dat.*) **finden** be made up *or* compensated for by sth. **2** (Gleichgewicht) balance **3** (Sport) equalizer; **den ~ erzielen, zum ~ kommen** equalize; score the equalizer

aus|gleichen
A *unr. tr. V.* even out ‹*irregularities, differences in height*›; ease ‹*tensions*›; reconcile ‹*differences of opinions, contradictions*›; settle ‹*conflict*›; redress ‹*injustice*›; compensate for ‹*damage*›; equalize, balance ‹*forces, values*›; make up for, compensate for ‹*misfortune, lack*›; (Kaufmannsspr.) settle ‹*bill, debt*›; discharge ‹*obligation*›; make up ‹*loss*›; (Bankw.) balance ‹*account, budget*›; **etw. durch etw. ~:** compensate for sth. by sth.; make up for sth. with sth.; **~de Gerechtigkeit** poetic justice; *s. auch* **ausgeglichen B**
B *unr. refl. V.* **1** (sich nivellieren) balance out; (sich ganz aufheben) cancel each other out; **das gleicht sich wieder aus** one thing makes up for the other **2** (Kaufmannsspr., Bankw.) ‹*account, budget*› balance
C *unr. itr. V.* (Sport) equalize; **zum 3:3 ~:** level the scores at three all

Ausgleichs-: **~amt** *das: authority which administers system of compensation paid to individuals for damage and losses during and immediately after the Second World War;* **~getriebe** *das* (Technik) differential gear; **~sport** *der* sport for fitness; **~tor** *das,* **~treffer** *der* (Ballspiele) equalizer; **~zahlung** *die* compensation payment

aus|gleiten *unr. itr. V.; mit sein* (geh.) ▸**ausrutschen**

aus|gliedern *tr. V.* hive off; (fig.: ausklammern) exclude

aus|glühen *tr. V.* **1** (Med.) sterilize by heating **2** (Technik) anneal

aus|graben *unr. tr. V.* dig up; dig [out] ‹*trench, hole*›; dig out ‹*trapped person, avalanche victim, etc.*›; dig up, excavate ‹*archaeological object*›; excavate ‹*temple, settlement, etc.*›; dig, lift ‹*potatoes*›; (aus dem Grab) disinter, exhume ‹*body, corpse*›; (fig. ugs.) dig up; dig up, unearth ‹*old manuscripts, maps, etc.*›; **eine alte Geschichte wieder ~** (fig.) dig *or* rake up an old story; *s. auch* **Kriegsbeil**

Aus·grabung *die* (Archäol.) **1** excavation **2** (Fund) find

Ausgrabungs-: **~arbeit** *die* excavation work *no pl.;* **~arbeiten** excavation work *sing.;* **~stätte** *die* excavation site

aus|greifen *unr. itr. V.* step out; **~d** extended ‹*gallop*›; striding ‹*movement*›; long ‹*stride*›; **weit ~d** widely spreading ‹*branches*›; (fig.) wide-ranging ‹*speech*›; large-scale ‹*plans, objectives*›

aus|grenzen *tr. V.* mark off (**aus** from); mark out ‹*area*›; (ausklammern, isolieren) exclude (**aus** from)

Ausgrenzung *die;* **~:** marking off; (einer Fläche) marking out; (Ausklammerung, Isolierung) exclusion

aus|gründen *tr. V.* (Wirtsch.) hive off (**aus** from)

Ausguck *der;* **~[e]s, ~e** **1** (ugs., auch Seemannsspr.) lookout post; **~ halten** keep a lookout (**nach** for) **2** (Seemannsspr.: Matrose) lookout

aus|gucken *itr. V.* (ugs.) keep a lookout (**nach** for); *s. auch* **Auge 1**

Aus·guss, *Aus·guß *der* **1** (Becken) sink **2** (Abfluss) wastepipe **3** (landsch.: Tülle) spout

aus|haben (ugs.)
A *unr. tr. V.* **1** (ausgelesen haben) have finished **2** (ausgezogen haben) have taken off
B *unr. itr. V.* (Schule, Unterricht beendet haben) finish school

aus|hacken *tr. V.* **1** hoe ‹*weeds*›; lift ‹*potatoes, turnips, etc.*› using a hoe **2** (auspicken) **jmdm. die Augen ~:** peck out sb.'s eyes; *s. auch* **Krähe** **3** (österr.: zerlegen) cut up

aus|haken
A *tr. V.* unhook
B *refl. V.* come unhooked; ‹*zip fastener*› come undone
C *itr. V.* (unpers.) **es hakte bei ihr aus** (ugs.) (sie begriff es nicht) she just didn't get it; (ihre Geduld war zu Ende) she lost her patience

aus|halten
A *unr. tr. V.* **1** (ertragen) stand, bear, endure ‹*pain, suffering, hunger, blow, noise, misery, heat, etc.*›; withstand ‹*attack, pressure, load, test, wear and tear*›; stand up to ‹*strain, operation*›; **er konnte es zu Hause nicht mehr ~:** he couldn't stand it at home any more; **er hält es nirgends lange aus** he never stays in one place for long; (wechselt häufig die Stellung) he never stays in one job for long; **den Vergleich mit jmdm./etw. ~:** stand comparison with sb./sth.; **es lässt sich ~:** it's bearable; I can put up with it; **hier lässt es sich ~:** I could get to like this place; **er konnte es im Bett nicht ~:** he couldn't stand being in bed; **es ist nicht/nicht mehr zum Aushalten** it is/has become unbearable *or* more than anyone can bear; **es ist nicht mehr zum Aushalten mit dir** you've become unbearable; **das Material muss viel ~:** the material has to take a lot of wear [and tear] **2** (ugs. abwertend: jmds. Unterhalt bezahlen) keep; **er lässt sich von seiner Freundin ~:** he gets his girlfriend to keep him **3** (Musik: anhalten) hold
B *unr. itr. V.* (durchhalten) hold out

aus|handeln *tr. V.* negotiate

aus|händigen *tr. V.* hand over; issue ‹*passport, document, etc.*›; **jmdm. etw. ~:** hand sth. over to sb./issue sb. with sth.

Aushändigung *die;* **~:** handing over; (eines Passes, Dokuments usw.) issue

Aus·hang *der* notice; **einen ~ machen** put up a notice

Aushänge·bogen *der* (Druckw.) advance sheet

aus|hängen[1] *unr. itr. V.* ‹*notice, timetable, etc.*› have been put up; **am schwarzen Brett ~:** be up on the noticeboard (Brit.) *or* (Amer.) bulletin board

aus|hängen[2]
A *tr. V.* **1** (öffentlich anschlagen) put up ‹*notice, timetable, etc.*› **2** (herausheben) take ‹*door*› off its hinges; take ‹*window*› out; unhitch ‹*coupling*›
B *refl. V.* **1** (sich lösen) ‹*chain*› come undone *or* unfastened; ‹*shutter, door, etc.*› come off its hinges **2** (sich glätten) ‹*crease*› drop out

Aus·hänger *der* (Druckw.) ▸**Aushängebogen**

Aushänge·schild *das; Pl.* **~er** [advertising] sign; advertisement (lit. or fig.)

aus|harren *itr. V.* (geh.) hold out; **an jmds. Seite** *(Dat.)* **~:** remain at sb.'s side; **auf seinem Posten ~:** remain *or* wait at one's post

aus|härten *tr., itr. V.* (Technik) cure

aus|hauchen *tr. V.* (geh.) give off ‹*smell, fumes*›; exhale, give off ‹*perfume, scent*›; **seinen Geist** *od.* **sein Leben** *od.* **seine Seele ~** (geh. verhüll.) breathe one's last (literary)

aus|hauen *unr. tr. V.* **1** (hineinschlagen) hew out **2** (ausmeißeln) carve ‹*statue, inscription, etc.*› **3** (fällen) thin out ‹*trees*› **4** (roden) clear ‹*forest, vineyard, etc.*› **5** (auslichten) prune ‹*trees, bushes, etc.*›

aushäusig /ˈaushɔyzɪç/ *Adj.* out-of-house, (Amer.) independent ‹*worker, contractor*›; **[viel] ~ sein** be away from home [a great deal]

aus|heben *unr. tr. V.* **1** (ausschaufeln) dig out ‹*earth, sand, etc.*›; dig ‹*channel, trench, grave*› **2** ▸**aushängen² A 2** **3** (aus dem Nest nehmen) steal ‹*eggs, birds*›; (leeren) rob ‹*nest*›; (fig.: unschädlich machen) break up ‹*gang, ring, etc.*›; raid ‹*club, casino, hiding place, outpost*›; pick up, catch ‹*criminal, terrorist*› **4** (österr.) empty ‹*postbox*› **5** (veralt.: einziehen) levy, recruit ‹*troops, army*› **6** (Ringen) **jmdn. ~:** execute a pick-up on sb.

aus|hebern *tr. V.* (Med.) **jmdm. den Magen ~:** pump out sb.'s stomach

aus|hecken *tr. V.* (ugs.) hatch ‹*plan, intrigue*›; plan ‹*attack*›; **immer neue Streiche ~:** keep on thinking up new tricks

aus|heilen
A *itr. V.; mit sein* ‹*injury, organ*› heal [up]; ‹*patient, illness*› be cured
B *tr. V.* **bis er seine Verletzung ausgeheilt hatte** until his injury had healed

aus|helfen *unr. itr. V.* help out; **jmdm. [mit** *od.* **bei etw.] ~:** help sb. out [with sth.]

aus|heulen *refl. V.* (ugs.) **sich bei jmdm. ~:** cry one's heart out on sb.'s shoulder

Aus·hilfe *die* **1** (das Aushelfen) help; **sie arbeitet in der Kantine zur ~:** she helps out in the canteen **2** (Aushilfskraft) temporary worker; (in Läden, Gaststätten) temporary helper *or* assistant; (Sekretärin) temporary secretary; temp (coll.); **als ~ arbeiten** help out on a temporary basis

Aushilfs-, aushilfs-: ~arbeit *die* temporary work *no pl.*; **~arbeiten** temporary work *sing.*; temporary jobs; **~kraft** *die* temporary worker; (in Läden, Gaststätten) temporary helper *or* assistant; (Sekretärin) temporary secretary; temp (coll.); **~weise** *adv.* on a temporary basis

aus|höhlen *tr. V.* hollow out; erode ‹*rock, cliff, etc.*›; (fig.: untergraben) undermine; **ausgehöhlte Wangen** (fig.) hollow cheeks; **einen Begriff ~** (fig.) render a concept meaningless

Aushöhlung *die;* **~, ~en** **1** ▸**aushöhlen**: hollowing out; erosion; undermining **2** (ausgehöhlte Stelle) hollow

aus|holen
A *itr. V.* **1** (zu einer Bewegung ansetzen) **[mit dem Arm] ~:** draw back one's arm; (zum Schlag) raise one's arm; **er holte zum Schlag aus** he raised his fist/sword *etc.* to strike; **er holte zum Wurf aus** he drew back his arm ready to throw; **zum Gegenschlag ~** (fig.) prepare to counter-attack; **zu einem Coup ~** (fig.) prepare a coup **2** (ausgreifen) step out; **[weit] ~de Schritte** long strides **3** (weitschweifig sein) range far afield; (weit zurückgehen) go back a long way
B *tr. V.* (landsch.: ausfragen) **jmdn. über etw.** *(Akk.) od.* **nach etw. ~:** question *or* (coll.) quiz sb. about sth.

aus|holzen *tr. V.* **1** (lichten) thin out **2** (abholzen) clear

aus|horchen *tr. V.* **jmdn. über etw.** *(Akk.) od.* **nach etw. ~:** sound sb. out about sth.

Aus·hub *der* (Tiefbau) **1** excavation **2** (ausgehobene Erde) excavated material

aus|hungern *tr. V.* starve out ‹*city, fortress, garrison, etc.*›; *s. auch* **ausgehungert B**

aus|husten
A *tr. V.* cough up
B *itr., auch refl. V.* (zu Ende husten) finish coughing

aus|ixen *tr. V.* (ugs.) x out

aus|jäten *tr. V.* weed ‹*garden, flower bed*›; weed out ‹*dandelions etc.*›; **Unkraut ~:** weed

aus|kämmen *tr. V.* **1** (entfernen) comb out ‹*dust, dirt*›; **jmdm./sich etw. aus dem Haar ~:** comb sth. out of sb.'s/one's hair **2** (glätten, ordnen) comb out ‹*hair*›

aus|kegeln *tr. V.* **1** **einen Pokal** *usw.* **~:** bowl for a cup *etc.* **2** (südd., österr.: ausrenken) **sich/jmdm. den Arm ~:** put one's/sb.'s arm out [of joint]

aus|kehren *tr. (auch itr.) V.* (bes. südd.) ▸**ausfegen**

aus|keimen *itr. V.; auch mit sein* germinate; ‹*potatoes*› sprout

aus|kennen *unr. refl. V.* (in einer Stadt, an einem Ort usw.) know one's way around *or* about; (in einem Fach, einer Angelegenheit usw.) know what's what; **sie kennt sich in dieser Stadt aus** she knows her way around the town; **man kennt sich bei ihm nicht aus** you don't know where you are with him; **sich [gut] mit/in etw.** *(Dat.)* **~:** know [a lot] about sth.; **sich mit den Klassikern/jmds. Jargon ~:** be familiar with the classics/sb.'s jargon; **sich bei den Frauen ~:** know a lot about women

aus|kernen *tr. V.* stone

aus|kippen *tr. V.* **1** (entfernen aus) tip out **2** (leeren) empty

aus|klammern *tr. V.* **1** (Math.) place outside the brackets **2** (beiseite lassen) leave aside; (nicht zulassen) exclude

aus|klamüsern *tr. V.* (ugs.) figure *or* work out

Aus·klang *der* **1** (geh.; Abschluss) end; **zum ~ der Saison/des Festes** to end *or* close the season/festival **2** (Musik: Ende) final notes/chord/chorus *etc.*; **einen heiteren ~ haben** end brightly

ausklappbar /ˈausklapbaːɐ̯/ *Adj.* fold-out; **die Couch ist ~:** the couch folds out

aus|klarieren *tr. V.* (Zollw., Seew.) clear

aus|klauben *tr. V.* (südd., österr., schweiz.) pick out

aus|kleiden
A *tr. V.* **1** (geh.: entkleiden) undress **2** (überziehen mit) line
B *refl. V.* (geh.) undress; disrobe (formal)

Aus·kleidung *die* lining; (eines Schwimmbeckens, Gartenteichs) liner

aus|klingen *unr. itr. V.* **1** *mit sein* (ausgehen) end **2** *mit sein* (verklingen) ‹*song*› finish; ‹*music, final notes*› die away **3** ‹*bell*› cease *or* stop ringing

aus|klinken
A *tr. (auch itr.) V.* release
B *refl. V.* release itself/themselves; (fig.) opt out

aus|klopfen *tr. V.* **1** (entfernen) (mit einem Stock, Schläger) beat out (**aus** + *Dat.* of); (durch Anklopfen) knock *or* tap out (**aus** + *Dat.* of) **2** (säubern) beat ‹*carpet*›; knock *or* tap ‹*pipe*› out

Aus·klopfer *der;* **~s, ~:** carpet beater

aus|klügeln *tr. V.* think out; work out; **ein ausgeklügeltes System** a cleverly devised system

aus|kneifen *unr. itr. V.; mit sein* (ugs.) run away (**vor, aus** from)

aus|knipsen *tr. V.* (ugs.) switch *or* turn off

aus|knobeln *tr. V.* (ugs.) **1** (durch Knobeln entscheiden) **sie knobelten aus, wer anfangen sollte** they threw dice to decide who would start; **die nächste Runde Bier ~:** throw dice to decide who will stand the next round of beer **2** (austüfteln) work out

ausknöpfbar /ˈausknœpfbaːɐ̯/ *Adj.* removable, detachable ‹*lining*›

aus|kochen *tr. V.* **1** (kochen, säubern) boil **2** (keimfrei machen) sterilize ‹*instruments etc.*› [in boiling water] **3** (salopp abwertend: sich ausdenken) cook up, concoct; *s. auch* **ausgekocht B**

aus|kommen *unr. itr. V.; mit sein* **1** (ausreichend haben, zurechtkommen) **mit etw. ~:** manage on *or* (coll.) get by on sth.; **ohne jmdn./etw. ~:** manage without *or* (coll.) get by without sb./sth.; **der Motor kommt mit sechs Litern aus** the engine can run for a hundred kilometres on six litres **2** (sich verstehen) **mit jmdm. [gut] ~:** get along *or* on [well] with sb.; **mit ihm ist einfach nicht auszukommen** he's just impossible to get on with **3** (südd., österr.: entkommen) escape (**aus** + *Dat.* from) **4** (bes. schweiz.: bekannt werden) get out

Auskommen *das;* **~s** **1** (Lebensunterhalt) livelihood; **sein ~ haben** make a living **2** **mit ihm/ihr ist kein ~:** he/she is quite impossible [to get on with]

auskömmlich /ˈauskœmlɪç/
A *Adj.* adequate; **ein ~es Gehalt haben** earn enough to live on
B *adv.* adequately

aus|kosten *tr. V.* (geh.) **1** (genießen) **etw. ~:** enjoy sth. to the full **2** (erleiden) suffer

aus|kotzen (derb)
A *tr. V.* puke up (coarse)
B *refl. V.* puke (coarse); **sich bei jmdm. ~** (fig.) have a bloody good moan to sb. (Brit. sl.)

aus|kramen *tr. V.* (ugs.) dig out; (fig.) dig up ‹*memories, knowledge, story*›

aus|kratzen
A *tr. V.* **1** (entfernen) scrape out ‹*dirt, remains, deposit, etc.*› (**aus** from); scratch ‹*words, writing, inscription*› out; (reinigen) scrape [out] ‹*bowl, pan, etc.*›; **jmdm. am liebsten die Augen ~ mögen** (ugs.) want to scratch sb.'s eyes out **2** (Med.) ▸**ausschaben 2**
B *itr. V.; mit sein* (salopp) do a bunk (Brit. coll.); beat it (coll.); **vor jmdm. ~:** beat it to avoid sb.

Auskratzung *die;* **~, ~en** (Med.) ▸**Ausschabung**

aus|kreuzen *itr. V.* (Biol.) cross-pollinate (**auf** + *Akk.* with)

Aus·kreuzung *die* (Biol.) cross-pollination

aus|kriechen *unr. itr. V.; mit sein* hatch [out]

aus|kriegen *tr. V.* (ugs.) ▸**ausbekommen**

aus|kristallisieren
A *tr. V.* crystallize out
B *itr. V.; mit sein* crystallize out

aus|kugeln *tr. V.* **sich** *(Dat.)* **den Arm/die Schulter** *usw.* **~:** put one's arm/shoulder *etc.* out [of joint]; dislocate one's arm/shoulder *etc.*; **jmdm. den Arm/die Schulter ~:** dislocate sb.'s arm/shoulder *etc.*

aus|kühlen
A *tr. V.* chill ‹*person, body*› through
B *itr. V.; mit sein* cool down

Aus·kühlung *die* loss of body heat; exposure

auskultieren /auskʊlˈtiːrən/ *tr. V.* (Med.) auscultate

aus|kundschaften *tr. V.* find out; trace ‹*arrival, relative*›; find ‹*opportunity*›; track down ‹*refugee, criminal, enemy, etc.*›; sound out ‹*mood, attitude*›; spy out ‹*place*›

Auskunft *die;* **~, Auskünfte** **1** (Information) piece of information; **Auskünfte** information *sing.*; **[jmdm. über etw.** *(Akk.)***] ~ geben** *od.* **erteilen** give [sb.] information [about sth.]; **sie gab auf alle Fragen ~:** she answered all the questions; **können Sie mir bitte ~ geben, wann ...?** (geh.) can you please tell me when ...?; **~/Auskünfte über jmdn./etw. einholen** *od.* **einziehen** obtain information about sb./sth.; *s. auch* **näher 2** **2** (Stelle) information desk/counter/office/centre *etc.*; (Fernspr.) directory enquiries *no art.* (Brit.); directory information *no art.* (Amer.); **„~“** 'Information'; 'Enquiries' (Brit.)

Auskunftei *die;* **~, ~en** private detective agency; (Kredit**~**) credit reference agency

Auskunfts-: ~beamte *der,* **~beamtin** *die* enquiry office clerk (Brit.); information office clerk (Amer.); **~büro** *das* information office; enquiry office (Brit.); **~dienst** *der* (Fernspr.) directory enquiries *no art.* (Brit.); directory information *no art.* (Amer.); **~pflicht** *die* (Rechtsw.) obligation to provide information; **~schalter** *der* information counter; **~stelle** *die* information office

aus|kungeln *tr. V.* (ugs. abwertend) do a deal on the quiet on ‹*prices, an agreement*›

aus|kuppeln *itr. V.* disengage the clutch; declutch

a

aus|kurieren *tr. V.* heal ‹*wound*› [completely]; **jmdn. ~:** cure sb. [completely]; **der Spieler, der seit Wochen eine Oberschenkelzerrung auskuriert** the player, who has been recovering from a thigh strain for weeks

aus|lachen *tr. V.* **jmdn. ~:** laugh at sb.; **lass dich nicht ~:** don't be ridiculous

aus|laden[1] *unr. tr. V.* unload (**aus** from)

aus|laden[2] *unr. tr. V.* **jmdn. ~:** cancel one's invitation to sb.

ausladend *Adj.* prominent ‹*forehead*›; jutting ‹*chin*›; broad ‹*shoulders*›; extensive ‹*roots*›; widely spreading ‹*branches*›; (fig.) sweeping ‹*gestures, movements*›

Aus·lage *die* 1 *Pl.* (Unkosten) expenses; **unsere ~n für Strom/Heizung/Wasser** *usw.* our outlay *sing.* on electricity/heating/water *etc.* 2 (ausgestellte Ware) item *or* article on display; **~n** goods on display 3 (Schaufenster) shop window; window display; (Vitrine) display cabinet 4 (Boxen) stance; **in der linken/rechten ~ boxen** use the orthodox stance/be a southpaw (coll.) *or* left-hander 5 (Fechten) on-guard position 6 (Rudern) recovery; **in die ~ gehen** recover

Aus·land *das* foreign countries *pl.*; **im/ins ~:** abroad; **aus dem ~:** from abroad; **die Literatur/Intervention/Hilfe des ~s** foreign literature/intervention/aid; **die Meinung des ~s** opinion abroad; **das ~ hat zurückhaltend reagiert** foreign reaction *or* the reaction of other countries *pl.* was guarded

Ausländer *der;* **~s, ~:** foreigner; alien (Admin. lang., Law); **~ sein** be a foreigner

ausländer·feindlich *Adj.* hostile to foreigners *postpos.*; xenophobic

Ausländer·feindlichkeit *die* hostility to foreigners; xenophobia

Ausländerin *die;* **~, ~nen** ▸**Ausländer**; *s. auch* **-in**

ausländisch *Adj.* foreign; exotic ‹*plant, animal*›

Auslands-: ~anleihe *die* (Bankw.) foreign loan; **~aufenthalt** *der* stay abroad; **~beziehungen** *Pl.* foreign relations; **~deutsche** *der/die* expatriate German; German national living abroad; **~einsatz** *der* (Milit.) overseas deployment; **bei einem ~einsatz in Sierra Leone** while serving abroad in Sierra Leone; **~gespräch** *das* (Fernspr.) international call; **~korrespondent** *der* foreign correspondent; **~reise** *die* trip abroad; **~schule** *die: school run by one country on another's territory;* **~schutzbrief** *der* (Versicherungsw.) international travel cover documents *pl.;* **~tournee** *die* foreign tour; **~vertretung** *die* 1 (von Firmen usw.) foreign agency; 2 (diplomatische Vertretung) foreign mission

aus|langen *itr. V.* (landsch.) 1 (ausholen) **[mit dem Arm] ~:** draw back one's arm; (zum Schlag) raise one's hand; **nach jmdm. ~:** raise one's arm to hit sb. 2 (ausreichen) be enough

Auslass, *Auslaß *der;* **Auslasses, Auslässe** (Technik) outlet

aus|lassen

A *unr. tr. V.* 1 (weglassen) leave out; leave out, omit ‹*detail, passage, word, etc.*› 2 (versäumen) miss ‹*chance, opportunity, etc.*› 3 (abreagieren) vent (**an** + *Dat.* on); release ‹*tension*›; **seinen Ärger/Zorn/seine Wut an jmdm. ~:** vent one's anger on sb.; take one's anger out on sb. 4 (ugs.: nicht tragen, nicht einschalten) **etw. ~:** leave sth. off 5 (zerlassen) melt ‹*bacon fat*› down; melt ‹*butter*› 6 (länger machen) let down; (weiter machen) let out

B *unr. refl. V.* (abwertend: sich äußern) talk, speak (**über** + *Akk.* about); (schriftlich) write (**über** + *Akk.* about); (sich verbreiten) hold forth (**über** + *Akk.* about); **sich im Detail/näher ~:** go into detail/more detail; *s. auch* **ausgelassen B, C**

Auslassung *die;* **~, ~en** 1 (Weglassung) omission 2 (oft abwertend: Äußerung) remark

Auslassungs-: ~punkte *Pl.* omission marks; ellipsis *sing.;* **~zeichen** *das* (Sprachw.) apostrophe

aus|lasten *tr. V.* 1 (voll laden) fully load 2 (voll ausnutzen) **etw. ~:** use sth. to full capacity; **seine/ihre** *usw.* **Kapazität ~** ‹*mine, factory, etc.*› be working to full capacity; **ausgelastet sein** ‹*mine, factory, etc.*› be working to full capacity 3 (voll beanspruchen) fully occupy; (befriedigen) fulfil

aus|latschen *tr. V.* (ugs.) wear ‹*shoes etc.*› out of shape

Auslauf *der* 1 **keinen/zu wenig ~ haben** have no/too little chance to run around outside; **der Hund braucht viel ~:** the dog needs plenty of exercise 2 (Raum) space to run around in; (für Hühner, Enten usw.) run; (für Pferde) paddock 3 (Fechten) run-back; (Ski) outrun; run-out 4 (Abfluss) outlet

aus|laufen

A *unr. itr. V.; mit sein* 1 (herausfließen) run out (**aus** of); ‹*pus*› drain 2 (leer laufen) empty; ‹*eye*› drain; ‹*egg*› run out; (undicht sein) leak 3 (in See stechen) sail, set sail (**nach** for) 4 (erlöschen) ‹*contract, agreement, etc.*› run out 5 (nicht fortgesetzt werden) ‹*model, line*› be dropped *or* discontinued; **etw. ~ lassen** drop *or* discontinue sth. 6 (zum Stillstand kommen) come *or* roll to a stop 7 (auseinander laufen) ‹*colour, ink, etc.*› run 8 (Sport: abbremsen) slow down 9 (enden) ‹*path, road, etc.*› end, (allmählich) peter out 10 (übergehen) run (**in** + *Akk.* into); **spitz ~de Türme** towers tapering to a point 11 (einen bestimmten Ausgang nehmen) end

B *unr. refl. V.* **die Kinder konnten sich mal richtig ~:** the children could run about to their heart's content

Aus·läufer *der* 1 (Geogr.) foothill *usu. in pl.* 2 (Met.) (eines Hochs) ridge; (eines Tiefs) trough 3 (Bot.) runner 4 (schweiz.: Bote) delivery man/boy

Aus·läuferin *die* (schweiz.) delivery woman/girl

aus|laugen *tr. V.* leach ‹*soil*›; leach [out] ‹*salts etc.*› (**aus** from); (fig.) drain, exhaust, wear out ‹*person*›; exhaust ‹*economy*›

Aus·laut *der* (Sprachw.) final sound; auslaut; **im ~:** in final position

aus|lauten *itr. V.* (Sprachw.) **auf „d" ~:** have 'd' in final position; **ein ~der Konsonant** a final consonant

aus|läuten *tr. V.* 1 **das alte Jahr ~:** ring out the old year 2 (veralt.: bekannt machen) ring out; proclaim

aus|leben

A *refl. V.* 1 (das Leben genießen) live life to the full; **sich in seiner Arbeit ~:** find complete fulfilment in one's work 2 (sich entfalten) find *or* be given complete expression

B *tr. V.* (geh.: verwirklichen) give full expression to; realize ‹*talent*›

aus|lecken *tr.* (*auch itr.*) *V.* lick out (**aus** of)

aus|leeren *tr. V.* empty [out]; empty ‹*ashtray, dustbin, etc.*›; (austrinken) drain

aus|legen *tr. V.* 1 (zur Ansicht, Einsicht hinlegen) lay out; display ‹*goods, exhibits*› 2 (bedecken mit) **etw. mit Fliesen/Teppichboden ~:** tile/carpet sth.; **einen Schrank [mit Papier] ~:** line a cupboard [with paper] 3 (leihen) lend; **jmdm. etw.** *od.* **etw. für jmdn. ~:** lend sb. sth.; lend sth. to sb.; **ich habe das Porto für dich ausgelegt** I paid the postage for you 4 (interpretieren) interpret; **etw. falsch ~:** misinterpret sth.; **etw. als Furcht ~:** take sth. to be fear 5 (für Tiere) lay ‹*bait*›; put down ‹*poison*›; set ‹*trap, net*› 6 (Technik: verlegen) lay ‹*mine, cable, fuse, etc.*› 7 (Landw.) plant 8 (Technik: auf eine bestimmte Leistung hin) **etw. auf** *od.* **für etw. ~:** design sth. for sth.

Ausleger *der;* **~s, ~** 1 (eines Krans) jib; boom 2 (Bootsbau) outrigger

Auslege·ware *die* carpeting

Auslegung *die;* **~, ~en** interpretation

aus|leiern (ugs.)

A *itr. V.; mit sein* wear out; ‹*clothes*› go baggy; **ausgeleiert** worn out; baggy ‹*pullover, trousers, etc.*›

B *refl. V.* wear out; ‹*pullover, trousers*› go baggy; ‹*elastic band, material*› lose its stretch

C *tr. V.* wear out; make ‹*pullover, trousers, etc.*› go baggy; make ‹*rubber band*› lose its stretch

Ausleihe *die;* **~, ~n** 1 (das Ausleihen) lending 2 (Stelle) issue desk

aus|leihen *unr. tr. V.* 1 (leihen) borrow; **[sich** (*Dat.*)**] etw. von jmdm. ~:** borrow sth. from sb. 2 (verleihen) lend; **jmdm.** *od.* **an jmdn. etw. ~:** lend sb. sth.; lend sth. to sb.

aus|lernen *itr. V.* finish one's apprenticeship; **ein ausgelernter Schreiner** a trained carpenter; **man lernt nie aus** (Spr.) you learn something new every day

Aus·lese *die* 1 (Auswahl) selection; **eine ~ treffen** make a selection 2 (geh.: Elite) elite; cream 3 (Wein) *fine wine made with selected bunches of fully ripe grapes*

aus|lesen[1] *unr. tr. V.* 1 (aussondern) pick out (**aus** from) 2 (von Minderwertigem befreien) sort ‹*peas, lentils, etc.*›

aus|lesen[2] *unr. tr. V.* (ugs.) **etw. ~:** finish [reading] sth.; **etw. in einem Zug ~:** read sth. [from beginning to end] at one sitting

Auslese·verfahren *das* selection process

aus|leuchten *tr. V.* illuminate; (fig.) throw light on; (untersuchen) probe; **die Bühne ~:** floodlight the stage

aus|lichten *tr.* (*auch itr.*) *V.* prune ‹*bush, tree, etc.*›; thin ‹*wood, area, etc.*›

aus|liefern *tr. V.* 1 (übergeben) **jmdm. etw.** *od.* **etw. an jmdn. ~:** hand sth. over to sb.; **jmdn. an ein Land ~:** extradite sb. to a country; **jmdm./einer Sache ausgeliefert sein** (fig.) be at the mercy of sb./sth. 2 *auch itr.* (Kaufmannsspr.: liefern) deliver

Aus·lieferung *die* 1 (Übergabe) handing over; (an ein Land) extradition; **jmds. ~ fordern** demand that sb. be handed over/extradited 2 (Kaufmannsspr.: Lieferung) delivery

Auslieferungs-: ~abkommen *das* ▸**~vertrag**; **~antrag** *der* application for extradition; **~lager** *das* (Wirtsch.) distribution centre; **~vertrag** *der* extradition treaty

aus|liegen *unr. itr. V.* 1 (zur Ansicht, Einsicht) be displayed; ‹*newspapers, plans, etc.*› be laid out, be available 2 (zum Fang) ‹*trap*› be set

Aus·linie *die* (Ballspiele) touchline

aus|loben *tr. V.* **10 000 Euro ~:** offer a reward of 10,000 euros; (bei einem Wettbewerb) offer a prize of 10,000 euros

aus|löffeln *tr. V.* 1 (aufessen) **etw. ~:** spoon up [all of] sth.; **jetzt muss** *od.* **kann er die Suppe ~[, die er sich eingebrockt hat]** (fig.) he's made his [own] bed and now he must lie in it 2 (leer essen) spoon up everything out of ‹*plate, bowl, etc.*›

aus|loggen *refl. V.* (DV) log off *or* out

aus|löschen *tr. V.* 1 (löschen) extinguish, put out ‹*fire, lamp*›; snuff, put out, extinguish ‹*candle*›; (geh.) extinguish ‹*light*› 2 (beseitigen) rub out, erase ‹*drawing, writing*›; ‹*wind, rain*› obliterate ‹*tracks, writing*›; (fig.) obliterate, wipe out ‹*memory*›; extinguish ‹*life*›; wipe out ‹*people, population*›

aus|losen *tr. V.* **etw. ~:** draw lots for sth.; **es wurde ausgelost, wer beginnt** lots were drawn to decide who would start; **den Gewinner ~:** draw lots to decide the winner

aus|lösen

A *tr. V.* 1 (in Gang setzen) trigger ‹*mechanism, device, etc.*›; set off, trigger ‹*alarm*›; release ‹*camera shutter*› 2 (hervorrufen, herbeiführen) provoke ‹*discussion, anger, laughter, reaction, outrage, heart attack, sympathy*›; cause ‹*sorrow, horror, surprise, disappointment, panic, war*›; excite, arouse ‹*interest, enthusiasm*›; evoke ‹*memories*›; draw ‹*applause*›; trigger [off] ‹*crisis, chain of events, rebellion, strike*› 3 (veralt.: einlösen, freikaufen) redeem 4 (südd., österr.: lösen aus, von) remove, take out (**aus** from); shell ‹*peas, beans*›

B *refl. V.* ‹*alarm*› go off

Auslöser *der;* **~s, ~** (Fot.) shutter release; (fig., Psych., Verhaltensf.) trigger

Aus·losung *die* draw

Aus·lösung *die* 1 (Betätigung) (eines Mechanismus) triggering; (eines Alarms) setting off; triggering 2 (Hervorrufung, Herbeiführung) ▸**auslösen 2**: provocation; causing; exciting; arousal; evocation; drawing; triggering [off] 3 (veralt.: Einlösung, Freikauf) redemption

aus|loten *tr. V.* 1 (Seew.) sound the depth of; sound, plumb ‹*depth*›; (fig.) sound out ‹*intentions*›; **ein Problem ~** (fig.) try to get to the bottom of a problem 2 (Bauw.) plumb ‹*wall*›

aus|lüften
A *tr., itr. V.* air
B *refl. V.* (ugs. scherzh.) get some fresh air

aus|lutschen *tr. V.* (ugs.) suck out ‹*juice*›; suck the juice from ‹*orange, lemon, etc.*›

ausm, *aus'm /ˈausm̩/ (ugs.) = **aus dem**

aus|machen *tr. V.* 1 (ugs.: ausschalten, auslöschen) put out ‹*light, fire, cigarette, candle*›; turn *or* switch off ‹*television, radio, hi-fi*›; turn off ‹*gas*› 2 (vereinbaren) agree; **einen Termin/ein Honorar ~:** agree [on] a deadline/fee; **etw. mit jmdm. ~:** agree sth. with sb. 3 (auszeichnen, kennzeichnen) make up; constitute; **was einen großen Künstler ausmacht** what goes to make a great artist; **die Farben machen den Reiz seiner Bilder aus** it is the colours which make his pictures attractive 4 (ins Gewicht fallen) make a difference; **wenig/nichts/viel ~:** make little/no/a great *or* big difference 5 (stören) **das macht mir nichts aus** I don't mind [that]; **macht es Ihnen etwas aus, wenn ...?** would you mind if ...?; **würde es Ihnen etwas ~, den Platz zu wechseln?** would you mind swapping places? 6 (klären) settle; **etw. mit sich allein/mit seinem Gewissen ~:** sort sth. out for oneself/with one's conscience 7 (erkennen) make out; **es lässt sich nicht mit Sicherheit ~, ob ...** it cannot be determined with certainty whether ... 8 (betragen) come to; **der Zeitunterschied/die Entfernung macht ... aus** the time difference/distance is ...; *s. auch* **ausgemacht**

aus|malen
A *tr. V.* 1 (mit Farbe ausfüllen) colour in 2 (mit Malereien ausschmücken) **das Innere einer Kirche ~:** decorate the interior of a church with murals/frescoes *etc.* 3 (schildern) describe
B *refl. V.* **sich** (*Dat.*) **etw. ~:** picture sth. to oneself; imagine sth.; **das hatte ich mir so schön ausgemalt** I had pictured it as being so beautiful

aus|manövrieren *tr. V.* outmanoeuvre

aus|marschieren *itr. V.; mit sein* march out (**aus** of)

Aus·maß *das* 1 (Größe, Ausdehnung) size; dimensions *pl.*; **die ~e des Rumpfs/Kraters** *usw.* the size *sing. or* dimensions of the fuselage/crater *etc.*; **gewaltige ~e haben** be of huge *or* vast dimensions 2 (Umfang, Grad) extent; **bis zu einem gewissen ~:** to a certain extent; **erschreckende ~e annehmen** assume horrifying dimensions; **eine Katastrophe unvorstellbaren ~es** a disaster on an unimaginable scale

aus|mergeln /ˈausmɛrgl̩n/ *tr. V.* emaciate; **ausgemergelt** gaunt, emaciated ‹*face, body*›

aus|merzen /ˈausmɛrtsn̩/ *tr. V.* 1 (ausrotten) eradicate ‹*pests, insects, weeds, etc.*› 2 (beseitigen) eliminate ‹*errors, slips, etc.*›; eliminate, cut out ‹*offensive passages*› 3 (aussondern) cull ‹*animal*›

aus|messen *unr. tr. V.* measure up

aus|misten *tr.* (*auch itr.*) *V.* 1 (von Mist säubern) muck out 2 (ugs.: von Unbrauchbarem leeren, aussortieren) clear out

aus|mustern *tr. V.* 1 (Milit.: als untauglich erklären) **jmdn. ~:** reject sb. as unfit [for service] 2 (als unbrauchbar ausscheiden) take ‹*vehicle, machine*› out of service

Aus·nahme *die;* **~, ~n** exception; **mit ~ von Peter/des Pfarrers** with the exception of Peter/of the priest; **ohne ~:** without exception; **mit** *od.* **bei jmdm. eine ~ machen** make an exception in sb.'s case; **~n bestätigen die Regel, keine Regel ohne ~:** the exception proves the rule

Ausnahme-: ~erscheinung *die* exceptional phenomenon; **~fall** *der* exceptional case; **im ~fall** in exceptional cases; **~situation** *die* exceptional situation; **~zustand** *der* state of emergency

ausnahms-: ~los A *Adj.* unanimous ‹*approval, agreement*›; B *adv.* without exception; **~weise** *Adv.* by way of *or* as an exception; **Dürfen wir mitkommen? — Ausnahmsweise ja** May we come too? — Yes, just this once; **er hat es mir ~weise erlaubt** he gave me permission by way of an exception; **kann ich heute ~weise früher weg?** can I go earlier today, just as a special exception?; **wenn ich ~weise keinen Schirm bei mir habe** when, just for once, I don't have my umbrella with me

aus|nehmen
A *unr. tr. V.* 1 gut ‹*fish, rabbit, chicken*› 2 (ausschließen von) exclude; (gesondert behandeln) make an exception of; **jeder irrt sich einmal, ich nehme mich nicht aus** everyone makes mistakes once in a while, and I'm no exception; *s. auch* **ausgenommen B** 3 (die Eier herausnehmen aus) rob ‹*nest*› 4 (ugs. abwertend: neppen) **jmdn. ~:** fleece sb.
B *unr. refl. V.* (geh.: wirken) look; (sich anhören) sound

ausnehmend (geh.)
A *Adj.* exceptional
B *adv.* exceptionally

aus|nüchtern *tr., itr., refl. V.* sober up

Ausnüchterung *die;* **~, ~en** sobering up; **jmdn. zur ~ auf die Wache bringen** take sb. to the [police] station to sober up

Ausnüchterungs·zelle *die* drying-out cell

aus|nutzen, (bes. südd., österr.) **aus|nützen** *tr. V.* 1 (nutzen) **etw. [voll] ~:** take [full] advantage of sth.; make [full] use of sth.; **den Raum/seine Zeit für etw. ~:** use the space/one's time for sth. 2 (Vorteil ziehen aus) take advantage of; (ausbeuten) exploit

Aus·nutzung *die,* (bes. südd., österr.) **Ausnützung** *die;* **~:** use; (Ausbeutung) exploitation; **unter voller ~ einer Sache** (*Gen.*) making full use of sth.

aus|packen
A *tr., itr. V.* unpack (**aus** from); unwrap ‹*present*›; (fig. ugs.: erzählen) come out with
B *itr. V.* (ugs.) 1 (Geheimnisse verraten) talk (coll.); squeal (sl.) 2 (seine Meinung sagen) sound off

aus|peitschen *tr. V.* whip; (aufgrund eines Gerichtsurteils) flog

Auspeitschung *die;* **~, ~en** whipping; (aufgrund eines Gerichtsurteils) flogging

aus|pendeln *itr. V.; mit sein* commute; **die über die Grenze ~den Arbeitnehmer** those commuting to work over the border

Aus|pendler *der* commuter; **die Stadt hat mehr Einpendler als ~:** more people commute to the city than from it

aus|pennen (salopp)
A *itr., refl. V.* have a decent *or* good kip (Brit. coll.) *or* sleep-in
B *tr. V.* **seinen Rausch ~:** sleep it off

aus|pfeifen *unr. tr. V.* **jmdn./etw. ~:** give sb./sth. the bird

aus|pflanzen *tr. V.* plant out

Auspizium /ausˈpiːtsi̯ʊm/ *das;* **~s, Auspizien** (geh.) auspice; **unter jmds. Auspizien** (*Dat.*) under sb.'s auspices

aus|plaudern *tr. V.* let out; blab

aus|plündern *tr. V.* 1 (ausrauben) **jmdn./etw. ~:** rob sb./sth. [of everything] 2 (völlig plündern, auch fig.) plunder

aus|polstern *tr. V.* pad; pad ‹*jacket, coat, etc.*› [out]; **gut ausgepolstert sein** (fig. scherzh.) be well upholstered (joc.)

aus|posaunen *tr. V.* (ugs. abwertend) tell the whole world about (fig.)

aus|powern /-poːvɐn/ *tr. V.* (ugs. abwertend) bleed ‹*organization, country, nation*› dry *or* white; exploit ‹*workers, masses*›; (fig.) impoverish ‹*soil, fields, market*›

aus|prägen
A *refl. V.* 1 (offenbar werden) show itself; ‹*contradiction*› manifest itself 2 (sich herausbilden) develop; ‹*peculiarity*› become more pronounced; *s. auch* **ausgeprägt B**
B *tr. V.* (prägen) mint (**zu** into)

Aus·prägung *die* 1 (das Prägen) minting 2 (charakteristische Form) form 3 (das Sichherausbilden) development [in a more pronounced form]; (der Persönlichkeit) moulding

aus|pressen *tr. V.* press *or* squeeze out ‹*juice*›; squeeze ‹*orange, lemon*›; (mit einer Presse) press the juice from ‹*grapes etc.*›; press out ‹*juice, oil*›; (fig.: ausbeuten) squeeze ‹*country, population, etc.*› [dry]; (fig.: ausfragen) grill; (aus Neugier) pump; *s. auch* **Zitrone**

aus|probieren *tr. V.* try out

Aus·puff *der* exhaust

Auspuff-: ~gase *Pl.* exhaust fumes *pl.*; **~rohr** *das* exhaust pipe; **~topf** *der* silencer (Brit.); muffler (Amer.)

aus|pumpen *tr. V.* pump out; *s. auch* **ausgepumpt B**

aus|punkten *tr. V.* (Boxen) outpoint; beat on points; (fig.) outdo

aus|pusten *tr. V.* (ugs.) blow out; blow ‹*egg*›

aus|putzen
A *tr. V.* 1 (auslichten, beschneiden) prune 2 (bes. südd.: reinigen) clean out 3 (veralt.: schmücken) deck out
B *itr. V.* (Fußball) play as sweeper

Aus·putzer *der;* **~s, ~, Aus·putzerin** *die;* **~, ~nen** (Fußball) sweeper

aus|quartieren *tr. V.* move out; billet out ‹*troops*›

aus|quatschen (salopp)
A *tr. V.* let out; blab; **alles ~:** spill the beans (coll.)
B *refl. V.* **sich mit jmdm. ~:** have a really *or* (Amer.) real good chat with sb.; (sich aussprechen) have a heart-to-heart with sb. (coll.)

aus|quetschen *tr. V.* 1 squeeze out; squeeze ‹*orange, lemon, etc.*› 2 (ugs.: ausfragen) grill; (aus Neugier) pump; *s. auch* **Zitrone**

aus|radieren *tr. V.* rub out; erase; (fig.) annihilate, wipe out ‹*village, city, etc.*›; liquidate ‹*person*›

aus|rangieren *tr. V.* (ugs.) throw out; discard; scrap ‹*vehicle, machine*›; **ausrangierte Fahrzeuge** scrap vehicles

aus|rasieren *tr. V.* shave ‹*neck, leg, etc.*›; shave off ‹*hair*›; **jmdm./sich die Haare im Nacken/den Nacken ~:** shave sb.'s/one's neck

aus|rasten[1] *itr. V.; mit sein* (Technik) disengage; **er rastete aus, es rastete bei ihm aus** (fig. salopp) something snapped in him

aus|rasten[2] *itr., refl. V.* (südd., österr.) have a decent *or* good rest

aus|rauben *tr. V.* rob

aus|räubern *tr. V.* raid; rob; (scherzh.: plündern) raid; **jmdn. ~:** rob sb. [of everything]; (fig.) clean sb. out

aus|räuchern *tr. V.* (auch fig.) smoke out; fumigate ‹*room*›

aus|raufen *tr. V.* pull *or* tear out; **ich könnte mir die Haare ~** (fig.) I could kick myself

aus|räumen
A *tr. V.* 1 (herausnehmen) clear out (**aus** of); clear *or* move out ‹*furniture*› (**aus** of) 2 (leer räumen) clear out 3 (beseitigen) clear up; dispel ‹*prejudice, suspicion, misgivings*› 4 (ugs.: ausrauben) clear out (coll.) 5 (Med.) remove; (mit der Kürette) curette
B *itr. V.* clear everything out

aus|rechnen
A *tr. V.* 1 (lösen) work out 2 (errechnen) work out; calculate
B *refl. V.* **das kannst du dir leicht ~** (ugs.) you can easily work that out [for yourself]; **sich** (*Dat.*) **Vorteile/gute Chancen ~:** reckon that one has advantages/good prospects; *s. auch* **ausgerechnet B**

Aus·rede *die* excuse

aus|reden
A *itr. V.* (zu Ende reden) finish [speaking]
B *tr. V.* **jmdm. etw. ~:** talk sb. out of sth.; **sie versuchten, ihm das Mädchen auszureden** (ugs.) they tried to persuade him to give up the girl
C *refl. V.* (südd., österr.) ▸ **aussprechen B 3**

aus|regnen *itr., refl. V.* (unpers.) stop raining

aus|reiben *unr. tr. V.* 1 (entfernen aus) rub out ‹*stain etc.*› 2 (reinigen) rub ‹*pot, pan, etc.*› clean; wipe out ‹*glasses*›; **sich** (*Dat.*) **die Augen ~:** rub one's eyes 3 (österr.: scheuern) scrub

aus|reichen *itr. V.* [1] (genügen) be enough *or* sufficient (**zu** for); **die Zeit/der Platz reicht [nicht] aus** there's [not] enough *or* sufficient time/space [2] (ugs.: auskommen) get by (coll.), manage (**mit** on)

ausreichend
A *Adj.* sufficient; enough; (als Note) fair
B *adv.* sufficiently; **etw. ~ begründen/erklären** give an adequate justification for/explanation of sth.

aus|reifen *itr. V.; mit sein* ‹*fruit, cereal, etc.*› ripen fully; ‹*cheese, wine, etc.*› mature fully; (fig.) mature [fully]; *s. auch* **ausgereift**

Aus·reise *die:* **jmdm. die ~ verweigern** refuse sb. permission to leave [the/a country]; **vor/bei der ~:** before/when leaving the country

Ausreise-: ~erlaubnis *die,* **~genehmigung** *die* exit permit

aus|reisen *itr. V.; mit sein* leave [the country]; **aus einem Land/nach Österreich** *usw.* **~:** leave a country/go to Austria *etc.*

ausreise·willig *Adj.* wanting to leave the country *postpos.*

aus|reißen
A *unr. tr. V.* tear out; pull out ‹*plants, weeds*›; **jmdm. die Haare ~:** tear sb.'s hair out; **einer Fliege** (*Dat.*) **die Beine/Flügel ~:** pull a fly's legs/wings off
B *unr. itr. V.; mit sein* [1] (sich lösen) ‹*sleeve*› come off *or* away; ‹*button, handle*› come off; (einreißen) ‹*buttonhole*› tear; ‹*seam*› split, pull apart [2] (ugs.: weglaufen) run away (*Dat.* from); **von zu Hause ~:** run away from home [3] (Sport: Vorsprung gewinnen) break away (*Dat.* from)

Aus·reißer *der* [1] (ugs.) runaway [2] (Statistik) outlier [3] (Sport: Läufer/Radfahrer) runner/rider breaking away from the field [4] (Schießsport) stray bullet

Ausreißerin *die;* **~, ~nen ▸ Ausreißer 1, 3**

aus|reiten
A *unr. itr. V.; mit sein* [1] (wegreiten) ride out (**aus** of) [2] (einen Ausritt machen) go for a ride; go riding
B *unr. tr. V.* (Reitsport) [1] (bewegen) exercise [2] (die Höchstleistung abfordern) **ein Pferd ~:** ride a horse to its limit

aus|reizen *tr. V.* (Kartenspiel) **seine Karten ~:** bid the full value of one's cards

aus|renken *tr. V.* dislocate; **jmdm./sich den Arm ~:** dislocate sb.'s/one's arm; **sich [nach jmdm.] den Hals ~** (ugs.) crane one's neck [to look for sb.]

aus|richten
A *tr. V.* [1] (übermitteln) **jmdm. etw. ~:** tell sb. sth.; **ich werde es ~:** I'll pass the message on; **kann ich ihm etwas ~?** can I give him a message?; **richte ihr einen Gruß [von mir] aus** give her my regards; **jmdm. ~, dass ...** tell sb. that ... [2] (einheitlich anordnen) line up; **etw./sich in einer Linie ~:** line sth. up/line up [3] (Technik: in eine bestimmte Lage bringen) align, line up (**auf** + *Akk.* with) [4] (fig.) **etw. auf jmdn./etw. ~:** orientate sth. towards sb./sth.; **sein ganzes Denken und Handeln auf etw.** (*Akk.*) **~:** direct all one's thoughts and energies towards sth.; **etw. nach** *od.* **an jmdm./etw. ~:** gear sth. to sb./sth.; **seine Entscheidung an den Bedürfnissen der Menschen ~:** make one's decision to fit in with people's needs; **reformerisch/kommunistisch ausgerichtet sein** be oriented towards reform/be communist in one's/its orientations [5] (erwirken) accomplish; achieve; **bei jmdm. wenig/nichts ~ können** not be able to get very far/anywhere with sb.; **gegen jmdn./etw. etwas ~ können** be able to do something against sb./sth.; **gegen ihn wirst du nichts ~ können** you won't be able to do anything about him [6] (veranstalten) organize; **jmdm. die Hochzeit ~:** make the arrangements for sb.'s wedding [7] (schweiz.: zahlen) pay (**an** + *Akk.* to); make ‹*payment*›
B *refl. V.* [1] (Milit.) dress ranks; **sich nach seinem Vorder-/Hinter-/Nebenmann ~:** line [oneself] up with the person in front/behind/next to one [2] **sich an einem Vorbild ~:** follow an example

Aus·richtung *die* [1] (Technik: das Ausrichten) alignment [2] (Orientierung) orientation (**auf** + *Akk.* towards); (an Bedürfnissen, Interessen) gearing (**an** + *Dat.*, **nach** to) [3] (Veranstaltung) organization; **die ~ einer Hochzeit** making the arrangements for a wedding [4] (schweiz.: Zahlung) payment

aus|ringen *unr. tr. V.* (bes. ostmitteld.) **▸ auswringen**

aus|rinnen *unr. itr. V.; mit sein* (bes. südd., österr.) [1] (herausfließen) run out [2] (leer werden) empty

Aus·ritt *der* [1] (das Ausreiten) riding out [2] (Spazierritt) ride [out]

aus|roden *tr. V.* root *or* grub up ‹*tree, bush*›; clear ‹*forest*›

aus|rollen
A *tr. V.* roll out
B *itr. V.; mit sein* roll to a stop

aus|rotten *tr. V.* eradicate ‹*weeds, vermin, etc.*›; (fig.) wipe out ‹*family, enemy, etc.*›; eradicate, stamp out ‹*superstition, idea, evil, etc.*›; eliminate ‹*error*›

aus|rücken
A *itr. V.; mit sein* [1] (bes. Milit.: in den Einsatz gehen) move out; ‹*fire brigade, police*› turn out [2] (ugs.: weglaufen) make off; **seinen Bewachern ~:** give one's guards the slip; **von zu Hause ~:** run away from home
B *tr. V.* [1] (Druckw.) **etw. [nach links/rechts] ~:** set sth. out to the left/right [2] (Technik: auskuppeln) disengage

Aus·ruf *der* cry

aus|rufen *unr. tr. V.* [1] (äußern) call out; **„Schön!", rief er aus** 'Lovely', he exclaimed; **jmdn.** *od.* **jmds. Namen ~ lassen** have a call put out for sb.; (im Hotel) have sb. paged; **die Haltestellen ~:** call out [the names of] the stops [2] (offiziell verkünden) proclaim; declare ‹*state of emergency*›; call ‹*strike*›; **jmdn. zum König/als Präsidenten ~:** proclaim sb. king/president [3] (zum Kauf anbieten) **seine Waren ~:** cry one's wares

Ausrufe-: ~satz *der* (Sprachw.) exclamation; exclamatory clause; **~wort** *das; Pl.* **~wörter** (Sprachw.) interjection; **~zeichen** *das* exclamation mark

Ausrufung *die;* **~, ~en ▸ ausrufen 2:** proclamation; declaration; calling; **nach seiner ~ zum König/Präsidenten** after he had been proclaimed king/president

Ausrufungs·zeichen *das* (österr., schweiz.) exclamation mark

aus|ruhen
A *refl., itr. V.* (sich erholen) have a rest; **[sich] ein wenig/richtig ~:** rest a little/have a proper *or* good rest; **ausgeruht sein** be rested; *s. auch* **Lorbeer 3**
B *tr. V.* (ruhen lassen) rest

aus|rupfen *tr. V.* pluck out ‹*feathers, hair*›; pull up ‹*grass, weeds, flowers*›

aus|rüsten *tr. V.* [1] equip; equip, fit out ‹*ship*›; **ein Auto mit Sicherheitsgurten ~:** fit safety belts to a car; fit a car with safety belts [2] (Textilw.: veredeln) finish

Aus·rüstung *die* [1] (das Ausrüsten) equipping; (von Schiffen) equipping; fitting out; **die ~ des Autos mit Gurten** *usw.* the fitting of belts *etc.* to the car [2] (Ausrüstungsgegenstände, technische Einrichtung) equipment *no pl.*; **eine neue ~:** a new set of equipment; **technische ~en** technical equipment *sing.* [3] (Textilw.) finishing

Ausrüstungs·gegenstand *der* item of equipment

aus|rutschen *itr. V.; mit sein* slip; (fig.) put one's foot in it; **jmdm. rutscht das Beil/die Feder aus** sb.'s axe/pen slips

Ausrutscher *der;* **~s, ~** [1] (ugs., auch fig.) slip [2] (Sport: Niederlage) surprise defeat

Aus·saat *die* [1] sowing; **mit der ~ beginnen** begin sowing [2] (Saatgut) seed

aus|säen *tr.* (*auch itr.*) *V.* (auch fig.) sow

Aus·sage *die* [1] (Feststellung) statement; stated view; **nach ~ von Experten** according to what the experts say [2] (vor Gericht, bei der Polizei) statement; **eine ~ machen** make a statement; give evidence; **die ~ verweigern** refuse to make a statement; (vor Gericht) refuse to give evidence; **~ steht gegen ~:** it's one person's word against another's [3] (geistiger Gehalt) message; **dem Gemälde fehlt jede ~:** the painting conveys nothing

Aussage·kraft *die* meaningfulness; (Ausdruckskraft) expressiveness

aussage·kräftig *Adj.* meaningful; (ausdruckskräftig) expressive

aus|sagen
A *tr. V.* [1] (zum Ausdruck bringen) say; **damit wird ausgesagt, dass ...** this expresses the idea that ... [2] (eine bestimmte Aussagekraft haben) ‹*picture, novel, etc.*› express [3] (vor Gericht, vor der Polizei) **~, dass ...** state that ...; (unter Eid) testify that ...
B *itr. V.* make a statement; (unter Eid) testify

aus|sägen *tr. V.* saw out

Aussage-: ~satz *der* (Sprachw.) affirmative clause; **~verweigerung** *die* (Rechtsw.) refusal to give evidence

Aus·satz *der* **▸ ❶ S. 439** (Med. veralt., fig.) leprosy

aussätzig *Adj.* (Med. veralt., fig.) leprous

Aussätzige *der/die; adj. Dekl.* (Med. veralt., fig.) leper

aus|saufen *unr. tr.* (*auch itr.*) *V.* [1] ‹*animal*› drink [up] ‹*water etc.*› (**aus** out of); empty ‹*trough etc.*› [2] (derb) **den ganzen Schnaps/eine halbe Flasche [Schnaps] ~:** drink all the schnapps/half a bottle [of schnapps]; **ein Glas Bier in einem Zuge ~:** down a glass of beer in one (sl.)

aus|saugen *regelm.* (*geh. auch unr.*) *tr. V.* [1] suck out (**aus** of); (leer saugen) suck dry; **eine Wunde/Apfelsine ~:** suck the poison out of a wound/suck the juice from an orange [2] (fig.: ausbeuten) **jmdn./etw. ~:** bleed sb./sth. [white]; **jmdn. bis aufs Blut** *od.* **Mark ~:** bleed sb. white

aus|schaben *tr. V.* [1] scrape out [2] (Med.) remove; (mit der Kürette) curette

Ausschabung *die;* **~, ~en ▸ Kürettage**

aus|schachten *tr. V.* excavate; sink ‹*well, shaft*›

Ausschachtung *die;* **~, ~en** [1] (das Ausschachten) excavation; (eines Brunnens, Schachtes) sinking [2] (Grube, Schacht usw.) excavation

aus|schälen *tr. V.* (auch Med.) remove (**aus** from)

aus|schalten *tr. V.* [1] (abstellen) switch *or* turn off [2] (ausschließen) eliminate; exclude ‹*emotion, influence*›; dismiss ‹*doubt, objection*›; shut out ‹*feeling, thought*›

Aus·schaltung *die* [1] (das Abstellen) switching *or* turning off; **bei ~ des Geräts** when switching *or* turning off the apparatus [2] (Eliminierung) **▸ ausschalten 2:** elimination; exclusion; dismissal

Aus·schank *der;* **~[e]s, Ausschänke** /ˈausʃɛŋkə/ [1] serving; **„Heute kein ~"** 'closed today'; **„Kein ~ an Jugendliche unter 16 Jahren"** 'persons under sixteen will not be served with alcoholic drinks' [2] (Schanktisch) bar; counter [3] (Gaststätte) bar; pub (Brit.); bar (Amer.)

Aus·schau *in* **nach jmdm./etw. ~ halten** look out for *or* keep a lookout for sb./sth.

aus|schauen *itr. V.* [1] (Ausschau halten) **nach jmdm./etw. ~** (auch fig.) look out for *or* keep a lookout for sb./sth. [2] (südd., österr.) **▸ aussehen**

aus|schaufeln *tr. V.* dig out ‹*earth, rubble, buried person*›; dig ‹*trench, grave, hole, etc.*›

Ausscheid *der;* **~[e]s, ~e** (bes. DDR Sport) qualifier

aus|scheiden
A *unr. itr. V.; mit sein* [1] (eine Gemeinschaft verlassen) **aus etw. ~:** leave sth.; **aus dem Amt ~:** leave office [2] (Sport) be eliminated; (wegen Defekt, Verletzung) retire [3] (nicht in Betracht kommen) **diese Möglichkeit/dieser Kandidat scheidet aus** this possibility/candidate has to be ruled out
B *unr. tr. V.* [1] (absondern) (Physiol.) excrete ‹*waste*›;

eliminate, expel ‹*poison*›; exude ‹*sweat*›; (Chem.) precipitate **2** (aussondern) eliminate; rule out ‹*proposal, possibility*›

Aus·scheidung *die* **1** ▸**ausscheiden B 1**: excretion; elimination; expulsion; exudation; precipitation **2** *Pl.* (Physiol.) excreta **3** (Sport) qualifier

Ausscheidungs-: ~kampf *der* (Sport) qualifier; **~organ** *das* (Physiol.) excretory organ; **~runde** *die* (Sport) qualifying round; **~spiel** *das* (Sport) qualifying game *or* match

aus|schelten *unr. tr. V.* scold

aus|schenken

A *tr. V.* **1** (servieren) serve ‹*alcohol, drink*› **2** (eingießen) pour out; (verteilen) serve

B *itr. V.* serve drinks

aus|scheren *itr. V.; mit sein* **1** (eine Gruppe, Reihe usw. verlassen) ‹*car, driver*› pull out; ‹*ship*› break out of [the] line; ‹*aircraft*› peel off, break formation; (fig.) (aus einer Organisation) pull out (**aus** of) **2** (aus der Spur geraten) skid

aus|schicken *tr. V.* send out

aus|schießen *unr. tr. V.* **1** **jmdm. ein Auge ~:** shoot sb.'s eye out **2** (Druckw.) impose **3** (Schießsport) hold ‹*competition*›; shoot for ‹*prize*›; **den besten Schützen ~:** hold a competition to find the best marksman; **die Sache ~** (salopp) ‹*cowboys etc.*› shoot it out (coll.)

aus|schiffen *tr. V.* disembark ‹*passengers*›; unload ‹*cargo*›

aus|schildern *tr. V.* signpost

aus|schimpfen *tr. V.* **jmdn. ~:** give sb. a telling-off; tell sb. off

aus|schlachten *tr. V.* **1** (ugs.: brauchbare Teile ausbauen aus) cannibalize ‹*machine, vehicle*›; break ‹*vehicle*› for spares **2** (ugs. abwertend: ausnutzen) exploit; **etw. politisch ~:** make political capital out of sth. **3** eviscerate ‹*animal*›

aus|schlafen

A *unr. itr., refl. V.* have a good *or* proper sleep; **[hast du jetzt] ausgeschlafen?** have you had a long enough sleep?; **ich hatte** *od.* **war nicht ausgeschlafen** I hadn't had enough sleep

B *unr. tr. V.* **seinen Rausch ~:** sleep off the effects of alcohol

Aus·schlag *der* **1** (Haut~) rash; **[einen] ~ bekommen** break out *or* come out in a rash **2** (Abweichung) (einer Magnetnadel, Waage) deflection; (eines Pendels) swing; **den ~ geben** (fig.) turn *or* tip the scales (fig.); **das gab den ~ für seine Entscheidung** that was the crucial factor in his decision; that decided him

aus|schlagen

A *unr. tr. V.* **1** (herausschlagen) knock out; **jmdm. einen Zahn ~:** knock one of sb.'s teeth out **2** (ablehnen) turn down; reject; refuse ‹*inheritance*› **3** (löschen) beat out ‹*fire*› **4** (auskleiden) line ‹*room, walls*› **5** (Handw.: breit schlagen) beat out

B *unr. itr. V.* **1** (stoßen) ‹*horse*› kick **2** *auch mit sein* (schwingen) ‹*needle, pointer*› be deflected, swing; ‹*divining rod*› dip; ‹*scales*› turn; ‹*pendulum*› swing **3** *auch mit sein* (sprießen) come out [in bud] **4** (zu Ende schlagen) **ausgeschlagen haben** ‹*clock*› have stopped striking; (fig. geh.) ‹*heart*› have stopped [beating] **5** *mit sein* (sich entwickeln) turn out; **zu jmds. Nachteil ~:** turn out to sb.'s disadvantage

ausschlag·gebend *Adj.* decisive; **das war ~ für seine Entscheidung** that was the crucial factor in his decision; that decided him

aus|schlecken ▸**auslecken**

aus|schließen *unr. tr. V.* **1** (aus einer Gemeinschaft entfernen) expel (**aus** from) **2** (nicht teilnehmen lassen) exclude (**aus** from); **er schließt sich von allem aus** he won't join in anything **3** (ausnehmen) exclude; exclude, rule out ‹*possibility*›; **die zwei Behauptungen schließen einander aus** the two statements are mutually exclusive **4** (unmöglich machen) **jedes Missverständnis/jeden Irrtum** *usw.* **~:** rule out all possibility of misunderstanding/error *etc.*; **es ist nicht auszuschließen, dass ...** one cannot rule out the possibility that ... **5** (aussperren) lock out **6** (Druckw.) justify; *s. auch* **ausgeschlossen B**

aus·schließlich /*od.* '-'--, -'--/

A *Adj.* (alleinig) exclusive; exclusive, sole ‹*concern, right*›

B *Adv.* (nur) exclusively; **das ist ~ sein Verdienst** the credit is his alone

C *Präp. mit Gen.* (ohne, außer) excluding; exclusive of; **der Preis versteht sich ~ Porto** the price does not include postage

Ausschließlichkeit /*od.* '-'---/ *die; ~:* exclusiveness; **er widmet sich seinem Beruf mit einer ~, die ...** he devotes himself to his job with a single-mindedness which ...

Aus·schlupf *der* way out; (Möglichkeit zum Entkommen) means of escape

aus|schlüpfen *itr. V.; mit sein* hatch [out]; ‹*butterfly*› emerge

aus|schlürfen *tr. V.* sip ‹*drink*› noisily; suck ‹*oyster, egg*›; **sein Glas/seine Tasse ~:** empty one's glass/cup noisily

Aus·schluss, *Aus·schluß *der* **1** (das Ausschließen) exclusion (**von** from); (aus einer Gemeinschaft) expulsion (**aus** from); (aus einem Wettbewerb) disqualification (**aus** from); **unter ~ der Öffentlichkeit** with the public excluded; (Rechtsw.) in camera **2** (Druckw.) spaces *pl.*; spacing material

aus|schmücken *tr. V.* decorate; deck out; (fig.) embellish ‹*story, incident, report, etc.*›

Ausschmückung *die; ~, ~en* **1** ▸**ausschmücken**: decoration; decking out; embellishment **2** (etw. Ausschmückendes) decoration; (erfundene Einzelheit) embellishment

aus|schnaufen (österr., südd. ugs.) ▸**verschnaufen**

aus|schneiden *unr. tr. V.* **1** (herausschneiden) cut out **2** prune ‹*tree*›; **einen Apfel ~:** cut the rotten parts out of an apple; *s. auch* **ausgeschnitten B**

Aus·schnitt *der* **1** (Zeitungs~) cutting; clipping **2** (Hals~) neck; **ein tiefer ~:** a plunging neckline; **er versuchte, ihr in den ~ zu gucken** he tried to look down the front of her dress **3** (Teil, Auszug) part; (eines Textes) excerpt; (eines Films) clip; excerpt; (Bild~) detail; **etw. in ~en lesen/kennen lernen** read/show/get to know parts of sth. **4** (Kreis~) sector **5** (Loch) [cut-out] opening

ausschnitt·weise

A *Adj.* **die ~ Lektüre ist unbefriedigend** reading extracts is unsatisfactory; **die ~ Wiedergabe einer Rede/Vorführung eines Films** the reporting of parts of a speech/showing clips from a film

B *adv.* **etw. ~ zitieren/abdrucken** quote/print extracts from sth.; **einen Film ~ zeigen** show clips from a film

aus|schnitzen *tr. V.* **etw. ~:** carve sth. out

aus|schöpfen *tr. V.* **1** (herausschöpfen) scoop out (**aus** from); (mit dem Schöpflöffel) ladle out (**aus** of); **Wasser aus einem Boot ~:** bale water out of a boat **2** (leeren) bale ‹*boat*› out **3** (voll ausnutzen) exhaust; **alle Lebensgenüsse voll ~:** enjoy to the full all the pleasures life has to offer

aus|schrauben *tr. V.* screw out (**aus** of)

aus|schreiben *unr. tr. V.* **1** (nicht abgekürzt schreiben) **etw. ~:** write sth. out in full; **einen Betrag ~:** write an amount out in words **2** (ausstellen) write *or* make out ‹*cheque, invoice, receipt*› **3** (bekannt geben) announce, call ‹*election, meeting*›; impose ‹*tax*›; advertise ‹*flat, job*›; put ‹*supply order etc.*› out to tender

Aus·schreibung *die* **1** ▸**ausschreiben 3**: announcement; calling; imposition; advertisement; **die ~ von Lieferungen** the invitation of tenders for supplies **2** (Text) announcement; (bei Wahlen) election notice; (Steuerw.) schedule; (Anzeige, Inserat) advertisement; (Angebotseinholung) invitation to tender

aus|schreien

A *unr. tr. V.:* ▸**ausrufen 3**

B *unr. refl. V.* **sich** (*Dat.*) **die Kehle** *od.* **die Lunge ~:** shout *or* yell one's head off

aus|schreiten (geh.)

A *unr. itr. V.; mit sein* step out

B *unr. tr. V.* **eine Strecke ~:** pace out a distance

Ausschreitung *die; ~, ~en* **1** (Gewalttätigkeit) act of violence; **es kam zu ~en** violence broke out **2** (veralt.: Ausschweifung) excess

aus|schulen *tr. V.* **ausgeschult werden** leave school

Aus·schulung *die:* **nach der ~:** after leaving school

Aus·schuss, *Aus·schuß *der* **1** (Kommission) committee; **~ der Ständigen Vertreter** (EU) Committee of Permanent Representatives **2** (Waren) rejects *pl.*

Ausschuss-, ***Ausschuß-: ~mitglied** *das* committee member; **~quote** *die* reject rate; **~sitzung** *die* committee meeting; **~ware** *die* rejects *pl.*

aus|schütteln *tr. V.* shake ‹*dust, tablecloth, etc.*› out

aus|schütten *tr. V.* **1** tip out ‹*water, sand, coal, etc.*›; (ausleeren) empty ‹*bucket, bowl, container*›; (verschütten) spill; **jmdm. seinen Kummer ~** (fig.) recount one's woes *pl.* to sb.; **sich vor Lachen ~ [wollen]** (ugs.) split one's sides laughing; die laughing (coll.); *s. auch* **Herz 2** **2** (auszahlen) distribute ‹*dividends, prizes, etc.*›

Ausschüttung *die; ~, ~en* **1** distribution **2** (Börsenw.) dividend [paid]

aus|schwärmen *itr. V.; mit sein* (auch fig.) swarm out; ‹*soldiers*› deploy; (fächerartig) fan out

aus|schwefeln *tr. V.* **1** (desinfizieren) sulphur; fumigate with sulphur **2** (entfernen) smoke out ‹*insects, vermin*› with sulphur

aus|schweifen *itr. V.; mit sein* **1** ‹*imagination*› run riot **2** (in seiner Lebensweise) indulge in excess

ausschweifend

A *Adj.* wild ‹*imagination, emotion, hope, desire, orgy*›; extravagant ‹*idea*›; exaggerated ‹*account, portrayal*›; riotous, wild ‹*enjoyment*›; dissolute, dissipated ‹*life*›; dissolute ‹*person*›

B *adv.* **~ leben** lead a dissolute life

Ausschweifung *die; ~, ~en* (im Genießen) dissolution; dissipation; **nächtliche ~en** nightly excesses; (stärker) nightly orgies

aus|schweigen *unr. refl. V.* remain silent

aus|schwemmen *tr. V.* **1** wash out; wash *or* flush out ‹*impurities, poisons*› **2** (aushöhlen) erode ‹*rock*›; erode, wash away ‹*beach, river bank*›

aus|schwenken

A *tr. V.* **1** (nach außen schwenken) swing out **2** (reinigen) rinse out

B *itr. V.; mit sein* ‹*lorry, tram*› swing out; (Milit.) ‹*rearguard etc.*› wheel; **nach rechts/links ~!** left-wheel/right-wheel!

aus|schwitzen *tr. V.* **1** (ausscheiden) sweat out; **eine Erkältung ~** (fig.) sweat out a cold **2** (aussondern) ‹*wall, stone, etc.*› sweat ‹*moisture etc.*›; ‹*tree, plant*› exude ‹*sap etc.*› **3** (Kochk.) sweat ‹*onion, flour*›

aus|segnen *tr. V.* (christl. Kirchen) give the last blessing to ‹*dead person*›

aus|sehen *unr. itr. V.* look (**wie** like); **gut ~:** look good; (gesund) look well; (schön) be good-looking; **gut ~d** good-looking; **zum Fürchten ~:** look terrifying; **es sieht nach Regen aus** it looks like rain; **nach etwas/nichts ~** (ugs.) look something special/not look anything special; **wie sieht ein Okapi aus?** what does an okapi look like?; **wie siehts aus, kannst du mitkommen?** (ugs.) how are you fixed, can you come with us? (coll.); **na, wie siehts aus, wie weit seid ihr?** (ugs.) how is it going, how far have you got (Brit.) *or* (Amer.) are you?; **wie sieht der denn aus?!** what does he look like!; just look at him!; **ich habe [vielleicht] ausgesehen!** I looked a real sight!; **es sieht danach** *od.* **so aus, als ob ...** it looks as if ...; **Erfolgreicher junger Unternehmer! Der sieht [mir] gerade danach aus!** (iron.) A successful young executive! I bet!; **sehe ich so** *od.* **danach aus?** (ugs.) what do you take me for?; **so siehst du aus!** (ugs.) you've got another think coming (coll.); that's what you think!; **es sieht [nicht] gut mit ihm/damit aus** things [don't] look good for him/on that front; *s. auch* **danach 4**

Aussehen *das; ~s* appearance; **dem ~ nach** going *or* judging by appearances; **etw. nach dem ~ beurteilen** judge sth. by appearances

***aus|sein ▸ aus B**

außen /ˈausn̩/ *Adv.* [1] outside; **die Vase ist ~ bemalt** the vase is painted on the outside; **~ an der Windschutzscheibe** on the outside of the windscreen; **nach ~ hin** on the outside; outwardly; **das Fenster geht nach ~ auf** the window opens outwards; **von dem Skandal darf nichts nach ~ dringen** (fig.) nothing must get out about the scandal; **er ist nur auf Wirkung nach ~ [hin] bedacht** (fig.) he is only concerned with [outward] effect; **von ~:** from the outside; **Hilfe von ~ nötig haben** (fig.) need outside help; **er läuft/spielt ~** (Sport) he's running in the outside lane/playing on the wing; **~ vor bleiben** (ugs.) be ignored; **jmdn./etw. ~ vor lassen** (ugs.) ignore sb./sth.; **~ vor lassen, dass ...** (ugs.) ignore the fact that ... [2] (österr.: [hier] draußen) outside; out here; **hier ~:** out here

Außen *der;* **~,** **~** (Sport) wing; winger

Außen-: ~ansicht *die* exterior view; **~antenne** *die* outdoor aerial; **~arbeiten** *Pl.* outside work; **~aufnahme** *die* (Film) exterior [shot]; location shot; **~bahn** *die* (Sport) outside lane; **~bezirk** *der* outlying district

Außenborder /-bɔrdɐ/ *der;* **~s,** **~** (ugs.: Motor, Boot) outboard

Außenbord·motor *der* outboard motor

außenbords *Adv.* (Seemannsspr.) outboard; **das Schiff muss ~ gestrichen werden** the hull of the ship must be painted

aus|senden *unr.* (*auch regelm.*) *tr. V.* [1] (wegschicken) send out [2] (ausstrahlen) send out, emit ‹*rays, light, etc.*›; transmit ‹*news, radio programme, etc.*›

außen-, Außen-: ~dienst *der:* **im ~dienst sein** *od.* **arbeiten, ~dienst machen** *od.* **haben** be working out of the office; ‹*salesman*› be on the road; **~durchmesser** *der* external diameter; **~fläche** *die* outer surface; (der Hand) back [of the hand]; **~geleitet** *Adj.* (Soziol.) other-directed; **~handel** *der* foreign trade *no art.*; **~handels·bilanz** *die* balance of trade; **~haut** *die* [outer] skin; (aus Metallplatten) shell plating; **~kurve** *die* outside bend; **~läufer** *der,* **~läuferin** *die* (Ballspiele) wing half; **~linie** *die* (Ballspiele) touchline; **~minister** *der,* **~ministerin** *die* ▸ⓘ S. 113 Foreign Minister; Foreign Secretary (Brit.); Secretary of State (Amer.); **~ministerium** *das* Foreign Ministry; Foreign and Commonwealth Office (Brit.); Foreign Office (Brit. coll.); State Department (Amer.); **~netz** *das* (Ballspiele) outside of the net; **~pfosten** *der* (Ballspiele) outside of the post; **~politik** *die* foreign politics *sing.*; (bestimmte) foreign policy/policies *pl.*; **~politiker** *der,* **~politikerin** *die* politician concerned with foreign affairs; **~politisch** [A] *Adj.* foreign-policy *attrib.* ‹*debate*›; ‹*question*› relating to foreign policy; ‹*mistake*› in foreign policy; ‹*reporting*› of foreign affairs; ‹*experience*› in foreign affairs; ‹*speaker, expert*› on foreign affairs; **auf ~politischem Gebiet** in foreign affairs; [B] *adv.* as regards foreign policy; **~politisch gesehen** from the point of view of foreign policy; **~politisch unter Druck geraten** come under foreign pressure; **~posten** *der* outpost; **~rist** *der* (bes. Fußball) outside of the *or* one's foot; **~rolle** *die* flick-up; **~seite** *die* outside; (eines Stoffes) right side; (fig.: eines Menschen) exterior

Außenseiter *der;* **~s,** **~,** **Außenseiterin** *die;* **~,** **~nen** (Sport, fig.) outsider

Außen-: ~spiegel *der* exterior mirror; **~stände** *Pl.* outstanding debts *or* accounts

Außenstehende *der/die; adj. Dekl.* outsider

Außen-: ~stelle *die* branch; **~stürmer** *der,* **~stürmerin** *die* (Ballspiele) winger; outside forward; **~tasche** *die* outside pocket; **~temperatur** *die* outside temperature; (im Freien herrschende Temperatur) outdoor temperature; **bei 15° ~temperatur** when the temperature outdoors is 15°; **~wand** *die* external *or* outside wall; **~welt** *die* outside world; **~winkel** *der* exterior angle; **~wirtschaft** *die* foreign trade and investment

außer /ˈausɐ/
[A] *Präp. mit Dat.* [1] (abgesehen von) apart from; aside from (Amer.); (ausgenommen auch) except [for]; **alle ~ mir** all except [for] me [2] (außerhalb von) out of; **~ Atem** out of breath; **~ Haus[es]/Land[es] sein** be out of the house/country; **~ Landes gehen** leave the country; **~ Zweifel stehen** be beyond doubt; **~ sich sein** be beside oneself (**vor** with) [3] (zusätzlich zu) in addition to
[B] *Präp. mit Akk.* **etw. ~ jeden Zweifel stellen** make sth. very clear *or* clear beyond all doubt; **vor Wut/Dankbarkeit/Erleichterung ~ sich geraten** become beside oneself with rage/be overcome with gratitude/relief; *s. auch* **Acht**[3]; **Betrieb 2**; **Dienst 2**; **Frage 3**; **Gefecht 1**; **Kraft 7**; **Kurs 2**; **Zeit 2**; **Zweifel**
[C] *Konj.* (es sei denn) except; **ich komme, ~ es regnet** I'll come unless it rains; **~ dass ...** except that ...; **~ wenn ...** except when ...; **niemand ~ ich selbst** nobody but me

äußer... /ˈɔysɐ.../ *Adj.* [1] (sich außen befindend) outer ‹*layer, courtyard, ring road*›; outer, outside ‹*wall, door*›; external ‹*diameter*›; outside ‹*pocket*›; outlying ‹*district, area*›; external ‹*injury*›; **die ~e Seite** the outside [2] (von außen kommend) external ‹*cause, force, etc.*› [3] (von außen wahrnehmbar) outward ‹*appearance, similarity, effect, etc.*›; external ‹*form, circumstances*› [4] (auswärtig) foreign; **Minister des Äußeren** ▸ **Außenminister**

außer-, Außer-: ~acht·lassung /--ˈ---/ *die;* **~~:** disregard; **unter ~achtlassen** *od.* **~achtlassung der Vorschriften** disregarding *or* ignoring the regulations; **~beruflich** *Adj.* ‹*interests, pressures, etc.*› outside one's job; **~betriebnahme** *die;* **~~,** **~~n** decommissioning *no indef. art.*; **~börslich** [A] *Adj.* off-exchange, over-the-counter ‹*business, share purchase*›; [B] *adv.* off exchange; over the counter; **~dem** /*auch:* --ˈ-/ *Adv.* (dazu) as well; besides; (überdies) besides; anyway; **sie ist Ärztin, Politikerin und ~dem noch Mutter von drei Kindern** she is a doctor, a politician, and a mother of three children as well; **~dienstlich** [A] *Adj.* private; social, unofficial ‹*event*›; unofficial ‹*commitment, activity*›; [B] *adv.* out of working hours; **mit jmdm. ~dienstlich verkehren** meet with sb. on a social basis

Äußere *das;* **~n** [outward] appearance; **das ~ täuscht oft** appearances are often deceptive; **dem ~n nach zu urteilen** to judge by appearances; judging by appearances

außer-, Außer-: ~ehelich [A] *Adj.* extramarital ‹*relationship*›; illegitimate ‹*child, birth*›; [B] *adv.* outside marriage; **ein ~ehelich geborenes Kind** a child born out of wedlock; **~europäisch** *Adj.* non-European; **Reisen ins ~europäische Ausland** journeys to countries outside Europe; **~fahrplan·mäßig** /-ˈ----/ [A] *Adj.* unscheduled ‹*train, bus*›; [B] *adv.* **dieser Zug verkehrt ~fahrplanmäßig** this train is not a scheduled one; **~gerichtlich** (Rechtsw.) [A] *Adj.* out of court *attrib.* ‹*settlement, arrangement*›; ‹*settlement, arrangement*› arrived at *or* reached out of court; [B] *adv.* **sich ~gerichtlich einigen** arrive at *or* reach a settlement out of court; **~gewöhnlich** [A] *Adj.* [1] (vom Üblichen abweichend) unusual; **dies ist ein ganz ~gewöhnlicher Fall** this case is quite out of the ordinary; this is a most unusual case; [2] (das Gewohnte übertreffend) exceptional; [B] *adv.* [1] (unüblich) unusually; [2] (sehr) exceptionally; **~halb** [A] *Präp. mit Gen.* outside; **~halb der Legalität** (fig.) outside the law; **~halb der Sprechstunde/Dienstzeit** out of *or* outside consulting hours/working hours *or* office hours; [B] *Adv.* out of town; **~halb von Bremen wohnen** live outside Bremen; **nach/von ~halb** out of/from out of town; **~irdisch** [A] *Adj.* [1] (nicht auf der Erde) ‹*phenomenon, object*› in space; [2] (von einem anderen Planeten) extraterrestrial; (fig. dichter.) heavenly ‹*beauty etc.*›; [B] *adv.* [1] (nicht auf der Erde) ‹*stationed etc.*› in space; [2] (fig. dichter.: überirdisch) **~irdisch anmutende Musik** heavenly-sounding music; **~irdische** *der/die; adj. Dekl.* extraterrestrial; **er ist ein ~irdischer/sie ist eine ~irdische** (fig.) he/she is in a class of his/her own; **~kirchlich** [A] *Adj.* civil ‹*wedding*›; non-ecclesiastical ‹*organization*›; [B] *adv.* **sie sind ~kirchlich getraut** they had a civil wedding; they had a registry-office wedding (Brit.); **~kraft·setzung** /-ˈ---/ *die* repeal; (des Kriegsrechts) lifting

äußerlich
[A] *Adj.* [1] (an der Außenseite) external ‹*use, injury*›; **zur ~en Anwendung** for external use [2] (nach außen hin) outward ‹*appearance, calm, similarity, etc.*› [3] (oberflächlich) superficial; **einer Sache** (*Dat.*) **~ sein** (geh.) be extrinsic to sth.
[B] *adv.* [1] (an der Außenseite) externally [2] (nach außen hin) outwardly; **~ gesehen** on the face of it

Äußerlichkeit *die;* **~,** **~en** [1] (äußere Form) formality [2] (Unwesentliches) minor point [3] *Pl.* (Aussehen) appearances [4] *Pl.* (Philos., Rel.) externals

äußern
[A] *tr. V.* express, voice ‹*opinion, view, criticism, reservations, disapproval, doubt*›; express ‹*joy, happiness, wish*›; voice ‹*suspicion*›
[B] *refl. V.* [1] (Stellung nehmen) **sich über etw.** (*Akk.*) **~:** give one's view on sth.; **ich möchte mich dazu jetzt nicht ~:** I don't want to comment on that at present; **sich abfällig/begeistert über etw.** (*Akk.*) **~:** make disparaging remarks about sth./speak enthusiastically about sth.; **sich dahin gehend ~, dass ...** make a comment to the effect that ... [2] (in Erscheinung treten) ‹*illness*› manifest itself (**in** + *Dat.*, **durch** in); ‹*emotion*› show itself, be expressed (**in** + *Dat.* in, **durch** through)

außer-: ~ordentlich [A] *Adj.* [1] (ungewöhnlich) extraordinary; [2] (zusätzlich) extraordinary ‹*meeting*›; special ‹*court, conference*›; *s. auch* **Professor 1**; [3] (das Gewohnte übertreffend) exceptional; [B] *adv.* (sehr) exceptionally; ‹*value*› highly; extremely ‹*pleased, relieved*›; **~ordentlich viel Mühe** an enormous *or* exceptional amount of trouble; **~orts** *Adv.* (schweizer., österr.) out of town; **~parlamentarisch** [A] *Adj.* extra-parliamentary ‹*opposition, organization, etc.*›; [B] *adv.* outside parliament; **~planmäßig** *Adj.* [1] unscheduled; unbudgeted ‹*expenditure*›; *s. auch* **Professor 1**; [2] ▸ **~fahrplanmäßig**; **~schulisch** [A] *Adj.* ‹*topics, problems*› unconnected with school; out-of-school *attrib.* ‹*activities*›; ‹*interests*› outside school; [B] *adv.* outside school; **~sinnlich** (Parapsych.) [A] *Adj.* extrasensory ‹*perception, communication*›; [B] *adv.* **~sinnlich begabt** with extrasensory powers *postpos.*; **~sprachlich** *Adj.* extra-linguistic

äußerst *Adv.* extremely; extremely, exceedingly ‹*important*›; **~ knapp gewinnen/entkommen** *usw.* only just win/escape *etc.*

äußerst... *Adj.* [1] extreme; **mit ~er Umsicht/Behutsamkeit/Missbilligung** with extreme *or* the utmost circumspection/care/disapproval; **mit ~er Willenskraft** using all one's will power; **aufs Äußerste erschrocken/angestrengt/verwirrt** frightened in the extreme/strained to the utmost/utterly confused; **von ~er Wichtigkeit sein** be of extreme *or* the utmost importance; **im ~en Norden/Süden der Stadt/des Landes** in the northernmost/southernmost part of the town/in the far north/south of the country [2] (letztmöglich) latest possible, last possible ‹*date, deadline*›; (höchst...) highest ‹*price*›; (niedrigst...) lowest ‹*price*›; **das Äußerste wagen/versuchen** risk/try everything; **bis zum Äußersten gehen** go to the last extreme [3] (schlimmst...) worst; **im ~en Fall** if the worst comes/came to the worst; **auf das Äußerste gefasst sein** be prepared for the worst; *s. auch* **äußer... 1**

außer·stand /*auch:* ˈ---/, **außerstande** *Adv.* **~e sein, etw. zu tun** (nicht befähigt) be unable to do sth.; (nicht in der Lage) not be in a position to *or* not be able to do sth.; **jmdn. außerstand setzen, etw. zu tun** make it impossible for sb. to do sth.

äußersten·falls *Adv.* [1] at most; **~ bis 19 Uhr** until 7 p.m. at the outside [2] ▸ **schlimmstenfalls**

a

außertourlich /-tu:ɐ̯lɪç/ (österr.)
A *Adj.* additional ‹*bus, train*›; additional, special ‹*concert*›
B *adv.* in addition; **~ befördert werden** be promoted ahead of turn

Äußerung *die;* **~, ~en** **1** (Bemerkung) comment; remark; **eine amtliche ~:** an official comment *or* statement **2** (Ausdruck) expression

außeruniversitär *Adj.* non-university ‹*research, institute, experience, etc.*›

aus|setzen
A *tr. V.* **1** (verlassen) abandon ‹*baby, animal*›; (auf einer einsamen Insel) maroon; (ansiedeln) release ‹*animal*› [into the wild]; (ins Freiland bringen) plant out ‹*plants, seedlings*› **2** (auf See) launch, lower ‹*boat*›; get ‹*passengers*› into the boats; (an Land bringen) put ‹*passengers*› ashore **3** (der Einwirkung von etw. überlassen) expose (*Dat.* to); **jmdm. ausgesetzt sein** be at sb.'s mercy; **dem Spott/der Kritik/einer Gefahr** *usw.* **ausgesetzt sein** be exposed to ridicule/criticism/a danger *etc.*; **Belastungen/Missdeutungen ausgesetzt werden** be subject to strains/misinterpretations **4** *in* **an jmdm./etw./allem etwas auszusetzen haben** find fault with sb./sth./everything; **was hast du an ihm/daran auszusetzen?** what don't you like about him/it?; **daran war nichts auszusetzen** there was nothing wrong with that; **ich habe nur eines daran auszusetzen** I've only one objection to make about it **5** (zur Verfügung stellen) offer ‹*reward, prize, salary*›; bequeath, leave ‹*inheritance*›; **eine große Summe für etw. ~:** provide a large sum for sth.; **jmdm.** *od.* **für jmdn. eine Rente ~:** provide sb. with a pension; settle an annuity on sb. **6** (Kaufmannsspr.) prepare ‹*consignment*› [for packing] **7** (unterbrechen) interrupt **8** (Rechtsw.) suspend ‹*proceedings*›; defer ‹*judgement, imprisonment*›; *s. auch* **Bewährung 1**
B *itr. V.* **1** (aufhören) stop; ‹*engine, machine*› cut out, stop; ‹*heart*› stop [beating] **2** (eine Pause machen) ‹*player*› miss a turn; **mit etw. ~:** stop sth.; **mit der Arbeit/dem Training [ein paar Wochen] ~:** stop work/training [for a few weeks]; **mit seinem Studium ~:** interrupt one's studies; **mit den Tabletten ~:** stop taking the tablets

Aus·setzer *der,* **Aus·setzerin** *die* (Kaufmannsspr.) *employee who prepares consignments etc. for packing*

Aussetzung *die;* **~, ~en** **1** ▸**aussetzen A 1**: abandonment; marooning; release [into the wild]; planting out **2** ▸**aussetzen A 2**: launching; lowering **3** ▸**aussetzen A 5**: offering; bequesting; leaving **4** ▸**aussetzen A 8**: suspension; deferment

Aus·sicht *die* **1** (Blick) view (**auf** + *Akk.* of); **ein Zimmer mit ~ aufs Meer** a room overlooking the sea; **jmdm. die ~ nehmen/versperren** block *or* obstruct sb.'s view **2** (Perspektive) prospect (**auf** + *Akk.* of); **das sind ja vielleicht [heitere] ~en!** (iron.) that's a fine prospect! (iron.); **~ auf etw.** (*Akk.*) **haben** have the prospect of sth.; **sie hat nicht die geringste ~ auf Erfolg** she hasn't the slightest chance *or* prospect of success; **er hat gute ~en, gewählt zu werden** he stands a good chance of being elected; **etw. in ~ haben** have the prospect of sth.; have sth. in prospect; **jmdn./etw. für etw. in ~ nehmen** consider sb./sth. for sth.; **in ~ stehen** be in prospect; **jmdm. etw. in ~ stellen** hold out the prospect of sth. to sb.; **weitere ~en** (Met.) further outlook *sing.*

aussichts·los
A *Adj.* hopeless
B *adv.* hopelessly

Aussichtslosigkeit *die;* **~:** hopelessness

aussichts-, Aussichts-: ~punkt *der* vantage point; **~reich** *Adj.* **1** promising; **2** (österr.: mit schöner Aussicht) **in ~reicher Wohnlage** offering attractive views *postpos.*; **~turm** *der* lookout *or* observation tower; **~voll** *Adj.* promising; **~wagen** *der* observation car

Aussie /'ɔsi/ *der;* **~[s], ~s** Aussie

aus|sieben *tr. V.* sift out; screen ‹*coal*›; filter out ‹*frequencies*›; (fig.) select; pick out ‹*candidates etc.*›; weed out ‹*weak candidates etc.*›

aus|siedeln *tr. V.* move out and resettle; (evakuieren) evacuate

Aussiedelung *die;* **~, ~en** ▸**Aussiedlung**

Aus·siedler *der,* **Aus·siedlerin** *die* (Auswanderer) emigrant; (Evakuierter) evacuee; (Umsiedler) resettled person

Aussiedler·hof *der: farm, formerly part of a strip-farming system and with its buildings in the village, now resited away from the village on a single area of land*

Aus·siedlung *die* (Evakuierung) evacuation; (Umsiedlung) resettlement

aus|sinnen *unr. tr. V.* (geh.) think up; devise ‹*plan*›

aus|sitzen *unr. tr. V.* **etw. ~:** sit sth. out

aus|söhnen
A *refl. V.* **sich mit jmdm./** (fig.) **etw. ~:** become reconciled with sb./to sth.; **sie haben sich ausgesöhnt** they have become reconciled; they have made it up
B *tr.* (*auch itr.*) *V.* reconcile; **jmdn. mit jmdm./** (fig.) **etw. ~:** reconcile sb. with sb./to sth.

Aussöhnung *die;* **~, ~en** reconciliation

aus|sondern *tr. V.* **1** (ausscheiden) weed out; **ausgesonderte Ware** reject goods *pl.* **2** (auswählen) sort *or* pick out; select

Aussonderung *die;* **~, ~en** **1** weeding out **2** (das Auswählen) selection

aus|sortieren *tr. V.* sort out

aus|spähen
A *itr. V.* (ausschauen) keep a lookout (**nach** for)
B *tr. V.* (auskundschaften) spy out; spy on ‹*organization*›

aus|spannen
A *tr. V.* **1** unharness, unhitch ‹*horse, mule*›; unyoke ‹*oxen*› **2** (salopp: wegnehmen) **jmdm. etw. ~:** get sb. to part with sth.; **jmdm. den Freund/die Freundin ~:** pinch sb.'s boyfriend/girlfriend (coll.) **3** (lösen) unhitch ‹*cart, plough, etc.*›; take out ‹*sheet of paper*› (**aus** of) **4** (ausbreiten) spread out ‹*cloth, net*›; stretch ‹*rope, cable, line*›; **die Flügel ~:** spread its/their wings
B *itr. V.* **1** (ausruhen) take *or* have a break **2** (Pferde ~) unharness *or* unhitch the horses; (Ochsen ~) unyoke the oxen

Aus·spannung *die* relaxation

aus|sparen *tr. V.* leave ‹*line etc.*› blank; (fig.) leave out; omit; **eine ausgesparte Lücke** a gap left free

Aussparung *die;* **~, ~en** **1** (das Aussparen) leaving blank **2** (Stelle) gap; (im Text) blank space

aus|speien (geh.)
A *unr. tr. V.* **1** (ausspucken) spit out **2** (erbrechen) bring up; vomit [up]
B *unr. itr. V.* spit; **vor jmdm. ~:** spit at sb.'s feet

aus|sperren
A *tr. V.* **1** (ausschließen) lock out; shut ‹*animal*› out **2** (im Streik) lock out
B *itr. V.* organize a lockout; lock the workforce out

Aus·sperrung *die* lockout

aus|spielen
A *tr. V.* **1** (Kartenspiel) lead; **sein ganzes Wissen ~** (fig.) make use of all one's knowledge; bring all one's knowledge to bear; **einen/seinen letzten Trumpf ~** (fig.) play one's last trump card **2** (manipulieren) **jmdn./etw. gegen jmdn./etw. ~:** play sb./sth. off against sb./sth. **3** (Sport: spielen um) play for ‹*cup, title, etc.*› **4** (als Preis aussetzen) put up as ‹*prize money*› **5** (Sport) (deklassieren) outplay; (umspielen) beat; go round **6** (Theater) act out; *s. auch* **ausgespielt B**
B *itr. V.* (Kartenspiel) lead; **wer spielt aus?** whose lead is it?

aus|spinnen *unr. tr. V.* elaborate ‹*story, idea*›; develop, pursue ‹*train of thought*›

aus|spionieren *tr. V.* **1** (entdecken, herausbekommen) spy out; **die Zahlenkombination des Safes ~:** discover the combination of the safe by spying **2** (ugs.: aushorchen) pump

aus|spotten *tr. V.* (bes. österr., schweiz.) ▸**verspotten**

Aus·sprache *die* **1** (von Wörtern) pronunciation; (Art des Artikulierens) articulation; (Akzent) accent; *s. auch* **feucht 2** (Gespräch) discussion; (zwangloseres) talk; **eine offene ~ herbeiführen** bring things out into the open

Aussprache-: ~angabe *die,* **~bezeichnung** *die* phonetic transcription; **~angaben haben** show pronunciation; **~wörterbuch** *das* pronouncing dictionary; dictionary of pronunciation

aussprechbar *Adj.* pronounceable; **nicht ~:** unpronounceable; impossible to pronounce *postpos.*; unrepeatable ‹*thought, idea, wish*›

aus|sprechen
A *unr. tr. V.* **1** pronounce **2** (ausdrücken) express; voice ‹*suspicion, request*›; (verkünden) pronounce ‹*judgement, sentence, etc.*›; grant ‹*divorce*›; **~, dass ...** state that ...; **der Regierung sein Vertrauen ~:** pass a vote of confidence in the government
B *unr. refl. V.* **1** (sich sprechen lassen) be pronounced; **ihr Name spricht sich schwer aus** her name is difficult to pronounce **2** (äußern) speak; **sich lobend/missbilligend über jmdn./etw. ~:** speak highly/disapprovingly of sb./sth.; **er hat sich nicht näher darüber ausgesprochen** he did not say anything further about it; **sich für jmdn./etw. ~:** declare *or* pronounce oneself in favour of sb./sth.; **sich gegen jmdn./etw. ~:** declare *or* pronounce oneself against sb./sth. **3** (offen sprechen) say what's on one's mind; **sich über etw.** (*Akk.*) **mit** *od.* **bei jmdm. ~:** have a heart-to-heart talk with sb. about sth.; **na los, sprich dich aus!** (ugs.) come on, get it off your chest! **4** (Strittiges klären) have it out, talk things out (**mit** with); **wir haben uns über alles ausgesprochen** we had everything out
C *unr. itr. V.* (zu Ende sprechen) finish [speaking]; *s. auch* **ausgesprochen B, C**

aus|spritzen *tr. V.* **1** squirt out ‹*liquid, contents*›; **sein Gift gegen jmdn. ~** (fig.) spit venom at sb. **2** (reinigen) flush out; rinse out ‹*tooth*›; syringe ‹*ear*› **3** (löschen) put out ‹*fire*› [with a hose/hoses]

Aus·spruch *der* remark; (Sinnspruch) saying

aus|spucken
A *itr. V.* spit; **vor jmdm. ~:** spit at sb.'s feet
B *tr. V.* **1** spit out; (fig. ugs.) ‹*machine, factory, computer*› spew out; cough up (coll.) ‹*money*›; regurgitate ‹*facts, information, etc.*›; **nun los, spucks aus, sei nicht so schüchtern!** (ugs. fig.) come on, spit it out and don't be so shy! **2** (ugs.: erbrechen) sick up (Brit. coll.); throw up

aus|spülen *tr. V.* **1** (reinigen) rinse out; (Med.) irrigate; wash out; **sich** (*Dat.*) **den Mund ~:** rinse one's mouth out **2** (entfernen) flush *or* wash out; ‹*river, sea*› wash away, erode ‹*soil, rock*›

Aus·spülung *die* ▸**ausspülen 1, 2**: rinsing out; irrigation; washing out; flushing *or* washing out; washing away; erosion

aus|staffieren /'aʊsʃtafi:rən/ *tr. V.* kit *or* rig out; fit out, furnish ‹*room etc.*›; (verkleiden) dress up; **sie hat ihre Tochter sonntäglich ausstaffiert** she dressed her daughter up in her Sunday best

Aus·staffierung *die* outfit; get-up (coll.)

Aus·stand *der* strike; **im ~ sein** be on strike; **in den ~ treten** go on strike

aus·ständig *Adj.* (südd., österr.: ausstehend) outstanding

aus|stanzen *tr. V.* punch out

aus|statten /'aʊsʃtatn̩/ *tr. V.* provide (**mit** with); (mit Kleidung) provide; fit out; (mit Gerät) equip ‹*office, kitchen, hospital, school, etc.*›; (mit Möbeln, Teppichen, Gardinen usw.) furnish ‹*room, flat, office, etc.*›; **mit Rechten/Befugnissen ausgestattet sein** be vested with powers/authority *sing.*; have powers/authority *no pl.* vested in one; **mit Talent ausgestattet sein** be endowed with talent; **ein prächtig ausgestatteter Band** a splendidly produced volume

a

Ausstattung *die;* ~, ~en 1 (das Ausstatten) ▸**ausstatten**: provision; fitting out; equipping; furnishing; vesting; production 2 (Ausrüstung) equipment; (Innen~ eines Autos) trim 3 (Einrichtung) furnishings *pl.* 4 (Aufmachung) (eines Films, Theaterstücks) decor and costumes; (Verpackung) packaging; (eines Buchs) design and layout; (typographisch) design

Ausstattungs-: ~film *der* period film; **~stück** *das* spectacular [opera/play *etc.*]

aus|stechen *unr. tr. V.* 1 **jmdm. die Augen ~:** put *or* gouge sb.'s eyes out 2 (entfernen) dig up ‹*plants*›; cut ‹*turf*› 3 (herstellen) dig [out] ‹*trench, hole, etc.*›; (Kochk.) press *or* cut out ‹*biscuits*› 4 (übertreffen) outdo; **jmdn. bei jmdm. ~:** oust sb. in sb.'s affections/esteem/favour; **jmdn. in etw.** (*Dat.*) **~:** outshine sb. *or* put sb. in the shade in sth.

aus|stehen
A *unr. itr. V.* **noch ~** ‹*debt*› be outstanding; ‹*decision*› be still to be taken, have not yet been taken; ‹*book*› be still to appear; ‹*solution*› be still to be found; **ihre Entscheidung/Antwort steht noch aus** I am/we are *etc.* still awaiting their decision/reply; **eine offizielle Bestätigung steht noch aus** there has as yet been no official confirmation; **~de Forderungen** outstanding demands; **Geld ~ haben** (ugs.) have money owing [one]; **euer Besuch bei mir steht noch aus** you still owe me a visit
B *unr. tr. V.* (ertragen) endure ‹*pain, suffering*›; suffer ‹*worry, anxiety*›; (erdulden) put up with; **ausgestanden sein** be all over; **ich kann ihn/das nicht ~:** I can't stand *or* bear him/it

aus|steigen *unr. itr. V.; mit sein;* 1 (aus einem Auto, Boot) get out (**aus** of); (aus einem Zug, Bus) get off; alight (formal); (Fliegerspr.: abspringen) bale out; **aus einem Zug/Bus ~:** get off a train/bus; alight from a train/bus (formal); **alles ~!** all change! 2 (ugs.: sich nicht mehr beteiligen) **~ aus** opt out of; give up ‹*show business, job*›; leave ‹*project*› 3 (Sport: aus einem Rennen o. Ä.) drop out (**aus** of); retire (**aus** from) 4 (ugs.: der Gesellschaft den Rücken kehren) drop out

Aussteiger *der;* ~s, ~, **Aussteigerin** *die;* ~, ~nen (ugs.) dropout (coll.)

aus|stellen *tr. V.* 1 *auch itr.* (im Schaufenster) put on display; display; (im Museum, auf einer Messe) exhibit; **ausgestellt sein** ‹*goods*› be on display/be exhibited; ‹*painting*› be exhibited; **die Galerie wird Hans Meyer ~:** the gallery is going to put on a Hans Meyer exhibition; **bekannte Künstler/viele Betriebe stellen hier aus** famous artists/many firms exhibit here 2 (ausfertigen) make out, write [out] ‹*cheque, prescription, receipt*›; make out ‹*bill*›; issue ‹*visa, passport, certificate*›; **einen Scheck auf jmdn. ~:** make out a cheque to sb. 3 (ugs.: ausschalten) turn *or* switch off ‹*cooker, radio, heating, engine*› 4 (nach außen stellen) open out ‹*window*›; roll out ‹*blind*›; pull out ‹*aerial*› 5 (aufstellen) put up ‹*poster, sign*›; post ‹*sentry*›; set ‹*trap*›; *s. auch* **ausgestellt B**

Aussteller *der;* ~s, ~, **Ausstellerin** *die;* ~, ~nen 1 (auf Messen) exhibitor 2 (eines Dokuments) issuer; (Behörde) issuing authority; (eines Schecks) drawer

Aus·stellung *die* 1 (das Präsentieren) exhibiting 2 (das Ausfertigen) ▸**ausstellen 2**: making out; writing [out]; issuing; **Datum und Ort der ~:** date and place of issue 3 (Veranstaltung) exhibition 4 (das Aufstellen) ▸**ausstellen 5**: putting up; posting; setting

Ausstellungs-: ~datum *das* date of issue; **~fläche** *die* exhibition area; **~gelände** *das* exhibition site; **~halle** *die* exhibition hall; **~katalog** *der* exhibition catalogue; **~ort** *der* place of issue; **~raum** *der* 1 exhibition space; 2 (Zimmer) exhibition room; **~stand** *der* exhibition stand; **~stück** *das* (in Schaufenstern usw.) display item; (in Museen usw.) exhibit; (auf Messen) **dieses Fahrzeug ist ein ~stück** this vehicle is for display purposes only; **dein Auto ist ja nicht gerade ein ~stück!** (iron.) your car isn't exactly much to look at!

Aussterbe·etat *der* (ugs.) *in* **auf dem ~ sein** *od.* **stehen, sich auf dem ~ befinden** be on its last legs

aus|sterben *unr. itr. V.; mit sein* (auch fig.) die out; ‹*species*› die out, become extinct; **ein ~des Handwerk** (fig.) a dying craft; **die Dummen sterben nicht** *od.* **nie aus** there's one born every minute

Aus·steuer *die* trousseau (*consisting mainly of household linen*)

aus|steuern *tr. V.* 1 (Elektronik) modulate ‹*signal, wave*›; (bei der Aufnahme) control the recording level of; control the power level of ‹*amplifier*› 2 **ein Auto ~:** [use the steering wheel to] bring a car under control 3 (Versicherungsw.) **jmdn. ~:** end sb.'s entitlement to benefits

Ausstieg *der:* ~[e]s, ~e 1 (Ausgang) exit; (Tür) door[s]; (~luke) hatch 2 (das Aussteigen) climbing out (**aus** of); **„kein ~"** 'no exit'; **der ~ aus dem Bus/Zug** getting off the bus/train; alighting from the bus/train (formal); **der ~ aus der Höhle** the way up out of the cave 3 (fig.) **ein ~ aus dem heiklen Thema** a way of getting off the awkward subject

aus|stopfen *tr. V.* stuff ‹*cushion, animal, doll, etc.*›; fill ‹*crack*›

Aus·stoß *der* (Wirtsch.) output

aus|stoßen *unr. tr. V.* 1 (nach außen pressen) expel; give off, emit ‹*gas, fumes, smoke*›; fire ‹*torpedo*› 2 give ‹*cry, whistle, laugh, etc.*›; let out ‹*cry, scream, yell*›; heave, give ‹*sigh*›; utter ‹*curse, threat, accusation, etc.*› 3 **jmdm. ein Auge ~:** put sb.'s eye out; **sich** (*Dat.*) **einen Zahn ~:** knock a tooth out 4 (ausschließen) (aus einem Verein, einer Gesellschaft) expel (**aus** from); (aus der Armee) drum out (**aus** of); **sich ausgestoßen fühlen** feel an outcast; *s. auch* **Ausgestoßene** 5 (Wirtsch.) turn out; produce

aus|strahlen
A *tr. V.* 1 (verbreiten, auch fig.) radiate; radiate, give off ‹*heat*›; ‹*lamp*› give out ‹*light*› 2 (Rundf., Ferns.) broadcast; transmit 3 (ausleuchten) floodlight
B *itr. V.* 1 (ausgehen) radiate; ‹*heat*› radiate, be given off; ‹*light*› be given out; (fig.) ‹*pain*› spread, extend 2 (wirken) **auf jmdn./etw. ~:** communicate itself to sb./influence sth.

Aus·strahlung *die* 1 (Wirkung) radiation; (eines Menschen) charisma; **~ haben** ‹*person*› have charisma 2 (Rundf., Ferns.) transmission

aus|strecken
A *tr. V.* extend, stretch out ‹*arms, legs*›; stretch out ‹*hand*›; put out ‹*feelers*›; stick *or* put out ‹*tongue*›; **mit ausgestreckten Armen** with arms extended; with outstretched arms
B *refl. V.* stretch [oneself] out; **ausgestreckt am Boden liegen** lie stretched out on the floor

aus|streichen *unr. tr. V.* 1 (durchstreichen) cross *or* strike out; delete; (fig.) obliterate; **jmds. Namen auf einer Liste ~:** cross sb.'s name off a list 2 (verteilen) spread 3 (Kochk.) grease ‹*tin, pan, etc.*› 4 (füllen) fill, smooth over ‹*cracks*›

aus|streuen *tr. V.* 1 (verstreuen) scatter; distribute ‹*gifts, leaflets, money*›; spread, put about ‹*rumour, story, lies, etc.*›; **er ließ ~, dass …** he caused the rumour to be spread about that … 2 (bestreuen) **etw. mit etw. ~:** sprinkle sth. with sth.

Aus·strich *der* (Med., Biol.) smear

aus|strömen
A *tr. V.* radiate ‹*warmth*›; give off ‹*scent*›; (fig.) radiate ‹*optimism, confidence, etc.*›
B *itr. V.; mit sein* stream *or* pour out; ‹*gas, steam*› escape; **etw. strömt von jmdm./etw. aus** (fig.) sb./sth. radiates sth.

aus|suchen *tr. V.* choose; pick; **such dir was aus!** choose what you want; take your pick; **man kann es sich nicht immer ~:** there isn't always any choice in the matter; *s. auch* **ausgesucht B, C**

aus|sülzen *refl. V.* (salopp) (lange reden) go on [and on]; (zu Ende reden) finish spouting

aus|täfeln *tr. V.* panel

aus|tapezieren *tr. V.* paper

aus|tarieren *tr. V.* 1 (ins Gleichgewicht bringen) balance ‹*scales*› 2 (österr.: Tara feststellen von) determine the tare of

Aus·tausch *der* 1 exchange; **im ~ für** *od.* **gegen** in exchange for 2 (das Ersetzen) replacement (**gegen** with); (Sport) substitution (**gegen** by)

austauschbar *Adj.* interchangeable; (ersetzbar) replaceable ‹*parts etc.*›

aus|tauschen
A *tr. V.* 1 exchange (**gegen** for) 2 (ersetzen) replace (**gegen** with); (Sport) substitute (**gegen** by)
B *refl. V.* (über etw. sprechen) exchange views/experiences [with each other]

Austausch-: ~motor *der* (Kfz-W.) replacement engine; **~schüler** *der,* **~schülerin** *die* exchange pupil *or* student

aus|teilen *tr. V.* distribute (**unter** + *Dat.* among, **an** + *Akk.* to); (aushändigen) hand *or* give out ‹*books, post, etc.*› (**an** + *Akk.* to); issue, give ‹*orders*›; deal [out] ‹*cards*›; give out ‹*marks, grades*›; administer ‹*sacrament*›; (servieren) serve ‹*food etc.*›; (fig.) give ‹*blessing*›; **Prügel ~** (fig.) hand out beatings

Aus·teilung *die* ▸**austeilen**: distribution; handing *or* giving out; issuing; giving; dealing [out]; administering; serving

Auster /ˈaustɐ/ *die;* ~, ~n oyster

Austern-: ~bank *die; Pl.* **~bänke** oyster bed; oyster bank; **~fischer** *der* oystercatcher; **~park** *der* oyster farm; **~zucht** *die* oyster farming

austherapiert *Adj.* (Med. Jargon) ‹*patient*› on whom all possible therapies have been used; **Sie sind ~:** there is no further treatment we can give you

aus|tilgen *tr. V.* 1 (vernichten) exterminate ‹*pests, race*›; eradicate ‹*weeds*›; wipe out, eradicate ‹*disease*› 2 (streichen, auch fig.) obliterate

aus|toben
A *refl. V.* 1 (spielen) romp about; have a good romp 2 (sich amüsieren) indulge oneself; **die Jugend will sich ~:** youth must have its fling
B *tr. V.* (abreagieren) work off ‹*anger etc.*› (**an** + *Dat.* on)

aus|tollen *refl. V.* (ugs.) romp about; have a good romp

Austrag *der;* ~[e]s 1 (das Austragen) settlement; resolution 2 (Sport) holding 3 (österr.) ▸**Altenteil**

aus|tragen *unr. tr. V.* 1 (zustellen) deliver ‹*newspapers, post*› 2 (im Mutterleib) carry ‹*child*› to full term; (nicht abtreiben) have ‹*child*› 3 (ausfechten) settle; (bis zum Ende) carry on ‹*quarrel, hostilities*›; settle, resolve ‹*conflict, differences*›; fight out ‹*battle*›; **etw. vor Gericht ~:** take sth. to court; **einen Streit mit jmdm. ~:** have it out with sb. 4 (Sport) hold ‹*race, competition, etc.*› 5 (löschen) delete, take out ‹*data, figures*›; (aus einer Liste) cross ‹*person, name*› off

Aus·träger *der* delivery boy/man; (Zeitungsjunge) newspaper boy

Aus·trägerin *die* delivery woman/girl; (Zeitungsmädchen) newspaper girl

Austragung *die;* ~, ~en 1 carrying on; (bis zum Ende) (eines Streits) settlement 2 (Sport) holding

Austragungs-: ~modus *der* (bes. Sport) procedure; **~ort** *der* (Sport) venue

Australide /austraˈliːdə/ *der/die; adj. Dekl.* Australoid

Australien /ausˈtraːli̯ən/ (*das*); ~s Australia; **~ und Ozeanien** Australasia

Australier *der;* ~s, ~, **Australierin** *die;* ~, ~nen ▸❶ **S. 520** Australian; **er ist Australier/sie ist Australierin** he/she is [an] Australian

australisch *Adj.* ▸❶ **S. 520** Australian

aus|träumen *itr.* (*auch tr.*) *V.* finish dreaming; **der Traum [vom Glück] ist ausgeträumt** the dream [of happiness] is over

aus|treiben
A *unr. tr. V.* 1 (verbannen) exorcize, cast out ‹*evil spirit, demon*› 2 (abgewöhnen) **jmdm. etw. ~:** cure sb. of sth. 3 (geh.: vertreiben, auch fig.) drive out (**aus** from) 4 (auf die Weide) drive ‹*cattle, sheep*› out to pasture 5 (hervorbringen) put forth ‹*leaves, buds*›; produce ‹*blossom*›

B *unr. itr. V.* [1] (ausschlagen) sprout [2] (hervorkommen) ‹*shoot, bud*› appear

Austreibung *die;* ~, ~**en** expulsion (**aus** from); (von Dämonen) exorcism; casting out

aus|treten
A *unr. tr. V.* [1] tread out ‹*spark, cigarette end*›; trample out ‹*fire*› [2] (bahnen) tread out ‹*path*›; **ausgetretene Pfade** (fig.) well-trodden paths [3] (abnutzen) wear down; **eine ausgetretene Steintreppe** a stone staircase with worn-down steps [4] (weiten) wear out ‹*old shoes*›; break in ‹*new shoes*›
B *unr. itr. V.; mit sein* [1] (ugs.: zur Toilette gehen) pay a call (coll.); **der Schüler fragte, ob er ~ dürfe** the pupil asked to be excused [2] (ausscheiden) **aus etw. ~:** leave sth.; **aus einer Vereinigung ~:** resign from a society [3] (Jägerspr.) come out into the open; **aus der Deckung ~:** break cover [4] (nach außen gelangen) come out; (entweichen) escape; ‹*blood*› issue; ‹*pus*› be discharged

austriakisch /austri'akɪʃ/ (österr. geh.)
A *Adj.* Austrian
B *adv.* ~ **eingefärbt** with an Austrian flavour

Austriazismus /austria'tsɪsmus/ *der;* ~, **Austriazismen** Austrianism

aus|tricksen *tr. V.* (ugs.) trick

aus|trinken
A *tr. V.* finish, drink up ‹*wine, beer, coffee, etc.*›; finish, drain ‹*glass, bottle, etc.*›
B *itr. V.* drink up

Aus·tritt *der* [1] (das Ausscheiden) leaving; (aus einem Verband, einer Vereinigung) resignation (**aus** from); **seinen ~ aus der Partei/Kirche erklären** announce that one is leaving the party/church; **die Partei hatte viele ~e zu verzeichnen** the party recorded a large drop in membership [2] (das Hervorquellen) outflow; (das Entweichen) escape; (von Blut) issue; (von Eiter) discharge

Austritts·erklärung *die* [notice of] resignation

aus|trocknen
A *tr. V.* [1] (ausdörren) dry out; dry up ‹*river bed, marsh*›; parch ‹*throat*› [2] (trockenlegen) drain ‹*marsh, swamp*›
B *itr. V.; mit sein* dry out; ‹*river bed, pond, etc.*› dry up; ‹*skin, hair*› become dry; ‹*throat*› become parched

Austro·marxismus /austro-/ *der* Austro-Marxism

aus|trompeten *tr. V.* (ugs.) ▸**ausposaunen**

aus|trudeln
A *itr. V.* (ugs.) **etw. ~ lassen** let sth. fizzle out
B *tr. V.* (ugs.) ▸**auswürfeln**

aus|tüfteln *tr. V.* (ugs.) (ausarbeiten) work out; (ersinnen) think up

aus|üben *tr. V.* [1] (nachgehen) practise ‹*art, craft*›; follow ‹*profession*›; carry on ‹*trade*›; do ‹*job*›; **welche Tätigkeit üben Sie aus?** what is your occupation? [2] (innehaben) hold ‹*office*›; wield, exercise ‹*power*›; exercise ‹*control*›; (wahrnehmen) exercise ‹*right*›; (wirksam werden lassen) exert

Aus·übung *die* ▸**ausüben**: practising; following; carrying on; doing; holding; wielding; exercising

aus|ufern *itr. V.; mit sein* [1] (überhand nehmen) get out of hand [2] (selten: über die Ufer treten) burst *or* break its banks

Aus·verkauf *der* [clearance] sale; (wegen Geschäftsaufgabe) closing-down (Brit.) *or* (Amer.) liquidation sale; (fig.: Verrat) sell-out; **etw. im ~ kaufen** buy sth. at the sale[s]

aus|verkaufen *tr. V.* [1] (verkaufen) sell out of; **Mineralwasser ist ausverkauft** there is no mineral water left [in stock] [2] (räumen) sell off, clear ‹*stock*›; clear ‹*warehouse, shop*›

ausverkauft *Adj.* sold out; **vor ~em Haus spielen** play to a full house; **~e Ränge** (Sport) packed stands

aus|wachsen
A *unr. refl. V.* [1] (sich normalisieren) right *or* correct itself [2] (sich entwickeln) grow (**zu** into)
B *unr. itr. V.; mit sein* [1] (ugs.: verzweifeln) go round the bend (coll.); **zum Auswachsen sein** be enough to drive you up the wall (coll.) [2] (keimen) sprout prematurely

Aus·wahl *die* [1] (das Auswählen) choice; selection; **Sie haben die [freie] ~:** the choice is yours; you can choose whichever you like; **drei Sorten/Tee und Kaffee stehen zur ~:** there are three kinds to choose from/one can choose between tea and coffee; **bei uns stehen Ihnen mehr als 600 Wagen zur ~:** we offer you a choice of over 600 cars; **eine ~ treffen** make a selection [2] (Auslese) selection; (von Gedichten, Erzählungen) anthology; selection [3] (Sortiment) range; **viel/wenig ~ haben** have a wide/limited selection (**an** + *Dat.*, **von** of); **hier hat man keine ~:** there is no choice here; **Backwaren in reicher ~:** a wide selection of bread, cakes, and pastries [4] (Sport: Mannschaft) [selected] team

Auswahl·band *der* anthology

aus|wählen *tr. V.* choose, select (**aus** from, **unter** + *Dat.* from among); **sich** (*Dat.*) **etw. ~:** choose *or* select sth. [for oneself]

Auswahl-: **~mannschaft** *die* (Sport) [selected] team; **~möglichkeit** *die* choice; **~prinzip** *das* method of selection; **~spieler** *der,* **~spielerin** *die* (Sport) [selected] player

aus|walzen *tr. V.* roll out ‹*metal*›; (fig. ugs.) drag out ‹*subject*›; **eine Geschichte zu einem Roman ~:** spin a story out into a novel

Aus·wanderer *der,* **Aus·wanderin** *die* emigrant

aus|wandern *itr. V.; mit sein* emigrate (**nach,** **in** + *Akk.* to); ‹*tribe*› migrate

Aus·wanderung *die* emigration

auswärtig /'ausvɛrtɪç/ *Adj.* [1] (woanders befindlich) non-local; **eine ~e Filiale/Bank** a branch/bank in another area/town [2] (von woanders stammend) ‹*student, guest, etc.*› from out of town [3] (das Ausland betreffend) foreign; **der Minister des Auswärtigen** the Foreign Minister; the Foreign Secretary (Brit.); the Secretary of State (Amer.); **das Auswärtige Amt** the Foreign Ministry; the Foreign and Commonwealth Office (Brit.); the Foreign Office (Brit. coll.); the State Department (Amer.); **der ~e Dienst** the foreign service

auswärts *Adv.* [1] (nach außen) outwards [2] (nicht zu Hause) ‹*sleep, live*› away from home; **~ essen** eat out [3] (nicht am Ort) in another town; (Sport) away; **ich habe ~ zu tun** I have to do a few things out of town; **~ sprechen** (ugs. scherzh.) talk foreign (coll.)

Auswärts-: **~sieg** *der* (Sport) away win; **~spiel** *das* (Sport) away match *or* game

aus|waschen *unr. tr. V.* [1] wash out; (ausspülen) rinse out [2] (Geol.) erode

auswechselbar *Adj.* changeable; exchangeable; (untereinander) interchangeable; (ersetzbar) replaceable

aus|wechseln
A *tr. V.* [1] change (**gegen** + *Akk.* for) [2] (ersetzen) replace (**gegen** with); (Sport) substitute ‹*player*›; **A gegen B ~:** replace A by B; **sie war wie ausgewechselt** she was a different person
B *itr. V.* (Sport) bring on a substitute; make a substitution

Auswechsel·spieler *der,* **Auswechsel·spielerin** *die* (Sport) substitute

Auswechselung, Auswechslung *die;* ~, **~en** change; (Ersatz) replacement; (Sport) substitution; **die ~ von A gegen B** the replacement of A by B

Aus·weg *der* way out (**aus** of); **der letzte ~ für jmdn. sein** be a last resort for sb.

ausweg·los
A *Adj.* hopeless
B *adv.* hopelessly

Ausweglosigkeit *die;* ~: hopelessness

aus|weichen *unr. itr. V.; mit sein* [1] (Platz machen) make way (*Dat.* for); (wegen Gefahren, Hindernissen) get out of the way (*Dat.* of); **[nach] rechts/nach der Seite ~:** move to the right/move aside to make way/get out of the way [2] (entgehen wollen) get out of the way (*Dat.* of); **einem Schlag/Angriff ~:** dodge a blow/evade an attack [3] (meiden) **dem Feind ~:** avoid [contact with] the enemy; **jmdm./einem Kampf/Hindernis ~** (auch fig.) avoid sb./a fight/an obstacle; **einer Frage/Entscheidung/einem Zwang/Verbot ~:** evade a question/decision/obligation/ban; **~de Antworten** evasive answers; **der Beantwortung weiterer Fragen ~:** avoid answering any more questions [4] (zurückgreifen) **auf etw.** (*Akk.*) **~:** switch [over] to sth.

Ausweich·manöver *das* evasive manoeuvre; ~ *Pl.* evasive action *sing.*; **das sind doch nur ~** (fig.) these are just evasions

aus|weinen
A *refl. V.* have a good cry; **sie hat sich bei mir darüber ausgeweint** (ugs.) she had a cry on my shoulder about it
B *tr. V.* (geh.) **seinen Kummer/sein Elend ~:** find relief for one's sorrow/misery in tears; *s. auch* **Auge 1**
C *itr. V.* finish crying

Ausweis /'ausvais/ *der;* **~es, ~e** [1] card; (Personal~, Kennkarte) identity card; (Mitglieds~) membership card [2] (österr. veralt.: Zeugnis) certificate; (Schulzeugnis) report [3] *in* **nach ~** (Papierdt.) ▸**ausweislich**

aus|weisen
A *unr. tr. V.* [1] (aus dem Land) expel (**aus** from) [2] (erkennen lassen) **jmdn. als etw. ~:** show that sb. is/was sth.; **seine Papiere wiesen ihn als … aus** his papers proved *or* established his identity as … [3] (angeben) reveal [4] (zeigen) demonstrate ‹*ability, skill, etc.*›
B *unr. refl. V.* [1] (seinen Ausweis zeigen) prove *or* establish one's identity [by showing one's papers]; **können Sie sich ~?** do you have any means of identification? [2] (sich erweisen) **sich als etw. ~:** prove oneself to be sth.

ausweislich *Präp. mit Gen.* (Papierdt.) according to

Ausweis·papiere *Pl.* identity papers

Aus·weisung *die* expulsion (**aus** from)

aus|weiten
A *tr. V.* (dehnen) stretch; (fig.: erweitern) expand (**zu** into); extend ‹*jurisdiction, study*›
B *refl. V.* [1] (zu weit werden) stretch [2] (sich erweitern) expand; **sich zur Krise ~:** develop *or* grow into a crisis

Ausweitung *die;* ~, **~en** expansion; (des Studiums, der Gerichtsbarkeit) extension

aus·wendig *Adv.* **etw. ~ können/lernen** know/learn sth. [off] by heart; **etw. ~ spielen/aufsagen** play/recite sth. from memory; **das kenne ich ja schon ~** (ugs. abwertend fig.) I know it backwards; *s. auch* **inwendig**

Auswendig·lernen *das* learning by heart

aus|werfen *unr. tr. V.* [1] cast ‹*net, anchor, rope, line, etc.*› [2] (herausschleudern) throw out ‹*sparks*›; ‹*volcano*› eject, spew out ‹*lava, ash, etc.*›; eject ‹*cartridge case*› [3] (geh.: ausspucken) cough up ‹*blood, phlegm, etc.*› [4] (ausschaufeln) throw up ‹*earth, sand, etc.*› [5] (anlegen) dig [out] ‹*trench, pit, ditch, etc.*› [6] (zur Ausgabe bestimmen) allocate ‹*sum*›; pay [out] ‹*dividend, premium, etc.*› [7] (produzieren) produce; turn out [8] **jmdm. ein Auge ~:** put sb.'s eye out (*by throwing sth.*)

auswertbar *Adj.* [1] **leicht/schwer ~ sein** be easy/difficult to analyse and evaluate; **maschinell ~:** machine-analysable [2] (nutzbar) utilizable

aus|werten *tr. V.* [1] analyse and evaluate [2] (nutzbar machen) utilize

Aus·wertung *die* [1] analysis and evaluation; (das Nutzbarmachen) utilization [2] (Ergebnis) analysis

aus|wetzen *tr. V.:* ▸**Scharte 1**

aus|wickeln *tr. V.* [1] (Verpackung entfernen) unwrap (**aus** from) [2] unwind ‹*person*› (**aus** from)

aus|wiegen *unr. tr. V.* [1] (das Gewicht feststellen) weigh [2] (portionsweise) weigh out; *s. auch* **ausgewogen B, C**

aus|wildern *tr. V.* (bes. Jägerspr.) return ‹*animal*› to the wild

Auswilderung *die;* ~, **~en** return to the wild

aus|winden *unr. tr. V.* (südd., schweiz.) wring out

a

aus|wirken *refl. V.* have an effect (**auf** + *Akk.* on); **sich in etw.** (*Dat.*) **~:** result in sth.; **sich günstig/negativ** *usw.* **~:** have a favourable/an unfavourable *etc.* effect (**auf** + *Akk.* on); **sich zu jmds. Vorteil ~:** work to sb.'s advantage

Aus·wirkung *die* (Wirkung) effect (**auf** + *Akk.* on); (Folge) consequence (**auf** + *Akk.* for); (Rückwirkung) repercussion (**auf** + *Akk.* on)

aus|wischen
A *tr. V.* **1** (entfernen) wipe ‹*dirt etc.*› out (**aus** of) **2** (säubern) wipe [clean]; **sich** (*Dat.*) **die Augen ~:** wipe one's eyes **3** *in* **jmdm. eins ~** (ugs.) get one's own back on sb. (coll.)
B *itr. V.*; *mit sein* (ugs.) get away, escape (*Dat.* from)

aus|wringen *unr. tr. V.* (bes. nordd.) wring out

Aus·wuchs *der* **1** ▸ⓘ **S. 439** (Wucherung) growth; excrescence (Med., Bot.); (Missbildung) deformity **2** (fig.) unhealthy product; (Folge) harmful consequence; (Übersteigerung, Missstand) excess **3** (Landw.) premature sprouting of the kernel

aus|wuchten *tr. V.* (Technik) **die Räder ~:** balance the wheels

Aus·wurf *der* **1** (Med.) sputum; **~/blutigen ~ haben** be bringing up phlegm/coughing up blood **2** (das Auswerfen) ejection **3** (Lava, Geröll usw.) ejected material; ejecta *pl.* **4** (abwertend: Abschaum) scum

aus|würfeln *tr. V.* **eine Runde Bier** *usw.* **~:** throw dice to decide who will pay for a round of beer *etc.*

aus|zacken *tr. V.* serrate; (mit der Zickzackschere) pink ‹*fabric*›

aus|zahlen
A *tr. V.* **1** (aushändigen) pay out; **sich** (*Dat.*) **einen Scheck ~ lassen** cash a cheque; **ausgezahlt bekommt er 1 650 Euro** his net pay is 1,650 euros **2** (entlohnen) pay off; buy out ‹*business partner, shareholder, etc.*›
B *refl. V.* (sich lohnen) pay off; (einbringen) pay; **Verbrechen zahlen sich nicht aus** crime doesn't pay

aus|zählen *tr. V.* **1** (zählen) count [up] ‹*votes etc.*› **2** (Boxen) count out **3** *auch itr.* (aussondern) choose by counting; (bei Kinderspielen) count out

Aus·zahlung *die* **1** (das Aushändigen) paying out **2** (das Entlohnen) paying off; (eines Geschäftspartners) buying out

Aus·zählung *die* counting [up]; **mit der ~ wurde bereits begonnen** the count had already started

aus|zanken *tr. V.* (bes. ostmd.) **jmdn. ~:** give sb. a scolding *or* a telling off

aus|zehren *tr. V.* (geh.) exhaust ‹*person, soil*›; ‹*disease*› debilitate ‹*person*›; (abzehren) emaciate ‹*person*›

Auszehrung *die*; **~** **1** (Kräfteverfall) emaciation **2** (veralt.: Schwindsucht) consumption

aus|zeichnen
A *tr. V.* **1** (mit einem Preisschild) mark, price (**mit** at); **etw. mit einem Preisschild ~:** put a price tag on sth. **2** (ehren) honour; **jmdn. mit einem Orden ~:** decorate sb. [with a medal]; **jmdn./etw. mit einem Preis/Titel ~:** award a prize/title to sb./sth. **3** (Druckw.: hervorheben) display; **wichtige Stellen sind durch Kursivschrift ausgezeichnet** important sections are displayed in italics **4** (Druckw.: zum Satz fertig machen) mark up **5** (bevorzugt behandeln) single out for special favour; (ehren) single out for special honour; **jmdn. mit** *od.* **durch etw. ~** (bevorzugt behandeln) favour sb. with sth.; (ehren) honour sb. with sth. **6** (kennzeichnen) distinguish (**gegenüber, vor** + *Dat.* from); **Klugheit und Fleiß zeichneten ihn aus** he was distinguished by his intelligence and industriousness
B *refl. V.* (sich hervortun) (durch eine Eigenschaft) stand out (**durch** for); (durch Leistung) ‹*person*› distinguish oneself (**durch** by); **sich als Politiker/im Sport ~:** distinguish oneself as a politician/at sport; **der Stoff zeichnet sich durch seine Haltbarkeit aus** the outstanding feature of the material is its durability; *s. auch* **ausgezeichnet B, C**

Aus·zeichnung *die* **1** (von Waren) marking **2** (Schildchen) [price] ticket *or* tag **3** (Ehrung) honouring; (mit Orden) decoration; (Gunstbeweis) mark of favour; **die ~ mit dem „Oscar" war sein größter Erfolg** the award of the Oscar was his greatest success; **die ~ der Preisträger** the presentation of awards to the winners **4** (Orden) decoration; (Preis) award; prize **5** (Druckw.: das Hervorheben) displaying **6** (Druckw.: das Satzfertigmachen) marking up **7** (Druckw.: Zeichen im Manuskript) mark **8** *in* **mit ~:** with distinction

Aus·zeit *die* (Basketball, Volleyball, Schach) time-out

ausziehbar *Adj.* extendible; telescopic ‹*aerial*›; extending *attrib.* ‹*ladder*›; sliding-leaf *attrib.* ‹*table*›

Auszieh·couch *die* sofa bed

aus|ziehen
A *unr. tr. V.* **1** (vergrößern) pull out ‹*couch*›; extend ‹*table, tripod, etc.*› **2** (ablegen) take off, remove ‹*clothes*› **3** (entkleiden) undress; **sich ~:** undress; get undressed; **sich ganz/nackt ~:** strip off *or* undress completely; **jmdn. mit den Augen ~** (ugs.) undress sb. with one's eyes **4** (auszupfen) pull out ‹*hair etc.*› **5** (herausschreiben) extract ‹*words, passages, etc.*› **6** (nachzeichnen) draw in; **mit Tusche ~:** ink in; **ausgezogene und punktierte Linien** continuous and dotted lines
B *unr. itr. V.*; *mit sein* **1** (aus einer Wohnung usw.) move out (**aus** of) **2** (losgehen) set off; **auf Abenteuer/zur Jagd ~:** set off *or* out in search of adventure/for the hunt

Auszieh·tisch *der* extending table; sliding-leaf table

aus|zischen *tr. V.* hiss ‹*speaker, play, etc.*›

Auszubildende *der/die; adj. Dekl.* ▸ⓘ **S. 113** (bes. Amtsspr.) trainee; (im Handwerk) apprentice

Aus·zug *der* **1** (das Ausziehen) move **2** (Abschrift) extract; (Bankw.) statement **3** (Textstelle) extract; excerpt **4** (das Hinausgehen) departure; (feierlich) procession (**aus** out of); (als Protest) walk out; **der ~ der Kinder Israel** (bibl.) the Exodus **5** (Extrakt) extract **6** (schweiz.) *first age group of men liable for military service*

auszugs·weise *Adv.* in extracts *or* excerpts; **etw. ~ lesen** read extracts from sth.

aus|zupfen *tr. V.* pluck out; pull out ‹*weeds*›

autark /au̯'tark/ *Adj.* **1** (Wirtsch.) self-sufficient; autarkic *as tech. term* **2** (geh.: eigenständig, selbstgenügsam) independent; self-sufficient

Autarkie /au̯tar'ki:/ *die*; **~, ~n** **1** (Wirtsch.) self-sufficiency; autarky *as tech. term* **2** (geh.: Selbstgenügsamkeit) self-sufficiency; independence

authentisch /au̯'tɛntɪʃ/
A *Adj.* (echt) authentic; (zuverlässig) reliable ‹*report*›
B *adv.* authentically; ‹*prove*› reliably

Authentizität /au̯tɛntitsi'tɛ:t/ *die*; **~** (geh.) authenticity

Autismus /au̯'tɪsmʊs/ *der*; **~** ▸ⓘ **S. 439** (Med.) autism

Autist *der*; **~en, ~en, Autistin** *die*; **~, ~nen** autistic

autistisch (Med.)
A *Adj.* autistic
B *adv.* autistically

Auto /'au̯to/ *das*; **~s, ~s** car; automobile (Amer.); **~ fahren** drive [a car]; (mitfahren) go in the car; **mit dem ~ fahren** go by car; **er hat wie ein Auto geguckt** (ugs.) his eyes popped out of his head

Auto·atlas *der* road atlas

Auto·bahn *die* motorway (Brit.); expressway (Amer.); (mit Gebühren) turnpike (Amer.); (in Germany, Austria, Switzerland also) autobahn

Autobahn- motorway (Brit.), expressway (Amer.) ‹*exit, intersection, junction, service area, etc.*›

> **Autobahn**
>
> Germany's motorway network is very extensive and not subject to a general speed limit, other than a recommended limit of about 80 mph. But increasingly speed limits are in force on long stretches of the *Autobahn*. Many motorways have only two lanes. To ease congestion, lorries are not allowed to use the *Autobahn* on Sundays. German motorways are free for passenger traffic. Lorries over 12 tonnes pay **Autobahngebühren**. On Austrian and Swiss motorways all vehicles must display a **Vignette**.

Autobahn-: ~anschluss, ***~anschluß** *der* motorway (Brit.) *or* (Amer.) expressway access road; **~auffahrt** *die* motorway access road (Brit.); expressway entrance [ramp] (Amer.); **~ausfahrt** *die* motorway (Brit.) *or* (Amer.) expressway exit; **~brücke** *die* motorway (Brit.) *or* (Amer.) expressway bridge; **~dreieck** *das* motorway (Brit.) *or* (Amer.) expressway junction *or* merging point; **~gebühr** *die* motorway (Brit.) *or* (Amer.) expressway toll; **~kreuz** *das* motorway (Brit.) *or* (Amer.) expressway interchange; **~raststätte** *die* motorway (Brit.) *or* (Amer.) expressway service area; **~ring** *der* motorway (Brit.) *or* (Amer.) expressway ring road; **~vignette** *die* ▸**Gebührenvignette**; **~zubringer** *der* motorway (Brit.) *or* (Amer.) expressway approach road *or* feeder [road]

auto-, Auto-: ~biographie /-----'-/ *die* autobiography; **~biographisch** /----'--/ **A** *Adj.* autobiographical; **B** *adv.* autobiographically; **~bus** *der* bus; (Reisebus) coach; **~car** *der* (schweiz.) coach

Autodafé /au̯toda'fe:/ *das*; **~s, ~s** **1** (hist.: Ketzerverbrennung) auto-da-fé **2** (Bücherverbrennung) book-burning

Auto·didakt /-di'dakt/ *der*; **~en, ~en, Autodidaktin** *die*; **~, ~nen** autodidact; **~ sein** be an autodidact; be self-taught

auto·didaktisch
A *Adj.* self-study *attrib.*, self-teaching *attrib.* ‹*aids, materials*›; **~es Studium** self-study; self-instruction
B *adv.* **sich ~ weiterbilden** continue one's education by self-study

Auto·dieb *der*, **Auto·diebin** *die* car thief

Autodrom *das*; **~s, ~e** **1** ▸**Motodrom** **2** (österr.: für Skooter) dodgems *pl.*; bumper cars *pl.*

auto-, Auto-: ~elektrik *die* automotive electrics *pl.*; (Anlage) [car] electrical system; **~erotik** *die* auto-eroticism *no art.*; **~fähre** *die* car ferry; **~fahren** *das*; **~~s** driving; motoring; **~fahrer** *der* [car] driver; **~fahrer·gruß** *der* (ugs.) *driver's tapping of the forehead in response to stupid action by other driver, cyclist, pedestrian, etc.*; **~fahrerin** *die* [car] driver; **~fahrt** *die* ▸ⓘ **S. 224** drive; **~fokus** *der* autofocus; **~frei** *Adj.* ‹*day, time*› when no cars are/were allowed on the road; ‹*place*› where no cars are/were allowed; **X ist ~frei** no cars are allowed in X; **~friedhof** *der* (ugs.) car dump; **~gen** /-'ge:n/ **A** *Adj.* **1** (Technik) **~genes Schneiden/Schweißen** gas *or* oxyacetylene cutting/welding; **2** (Psych.) **~genes Training** autogenic training; autogenics; **B** *adv.* (Technik) **~gen schweißen/schneiden** weld/cut using an oxyacetylene flame; **~gramm** /--'-/ *das*; **~~s, ~~e** autograph; **~gramm·jäger** /-'---/ *der*, **~gramm·jägerin** *die* autograph hunter; **~händler** *der*, **~händlerin** *die* ▸ⓘ **S. 113** car dealer; **~hypnose** /---'--/ *die* (Psych.) autohypnosis; **~immunerkrankung** *die* autoimmune disease; **~karte** *die* road map; **~kino** *das* drive-in cinema; **~knacker** *der*, **~knackerin** *die*; **~~, ~~nen** (ugs.) car burglar; **~kolonne** *die* line of cars; **~krat** /au̯to'kra:t/ *der*; **~~en, ~~en** autocrat; **~kratie** /---'-/ *die*; **~~, ~~n** autocracy; **~kratin** *die*; **~~, ~~nen** ▸**Autokrat**; **~kratisch** /--'-/ **A** *Adj.* autocratic; **B** *adv.* autocratically; **~marder** *der* car burglar; **~marke** *die* make of car

Automat /au̯to'ma:t/ *der;* **~en, ~en** 1 (Verkaufs~) [slot] machine; vending machine; (Spiel~) slot machine; fruit machine; (Musik~) jukebox 2 (in der Produktion, auch fig.: Mensch) robot; automaton; **ich bin doch kein ~:** I'm not a machine 3 (Math., DV) automaton

Automaten-: ~knacker *der,* **~knackerin** *die;* **~~, ~~nen** (ugs.) thief who breaks into slot machines; **~restaurant** *das* vending machine restaurant; automat (Amer.)

Automatik *die;* **~, ~en** (Technik) 1 (Vorrichtung) automatic control mechanism; (Getriebe~) automatic transmission; **eine ~ haben** ‹*car*› have automatic transmission; ‹*camera*› have automatic exposure control 2 (Vorgang) automatic process

Automatik·gurt *der* (Kfz-W.) inertia-reel belt

Automation *die;* **~:** automation

automatisch (auch fig.)
A *Adj.* automatic
B *adv.* automatically

automatisieren *tr. V.* automate

Automatisierung *die;* **~, ~en** automation

Automatismus *der;* **~, Automatismen** 1 (Technik, fig.) automatic mechanism 2 (Med., Biol., Psych.) automatism *no art.*

Auto-: ~mechaniker *der,* **~mechanikerin** *die* motor mechanic; **~minute** *die:* ▸ℹ **S. 224 zehn ~minuten entfernt sein** be ten minutes [away] by car; be ten minutes' drive [away]; **~mobil** /---'-/ *das;* **~~s, ~~e** (geh.) motor car; automobile (Amer.)

Automobil-: ~aus·stellung *die* motor show (Brit.); automobile show (Amer.); **~bau** *der* car manufacture; **~industrie** *die* motor industry

auto-, Auto-: ~mobilist /----'-/ *der;* **~~en, ~~en, ~mobilistin** *die;* **~~, ~~nen** (bes. schweiz.) motorist; car driver; **~mobil·klub** /---'--/ *der* motoring organization; **~nom** /--'-/ A *Adj.* autonomous; autonomic ‹*nervous system*›; B *adv.* autonomously; **~nomie** /---'-/ *die;* **~~, ~~n** autonomy; **~nummer** *die* [car] registration number; **~papiere** *Pl.* car documents; **~pilot** *der* (Flugw.) autopilot

Autopsie /au̯tɔ'psi:/ *die;* **~, ~n** (Med.) autopsy; post-mortem [examination]

Autor /'au̯tɔr/ *der;* **~s, ~en** /-'to:rən/ ▸ℹ **S. 113** author

Auto-: ~radio *das* car radio; **~reifen** *der* car tyre; **~reise·zug** *der* Motorail train (Brit.); auto train (Amer.)

Autoren-: ~film *der* writer-director's film; **~kollektiv** *das* authors' collective; **~lesung** *die* author reading

Auto·rennen *das* (Sportart) motor (Brit.) *or* (Amer.) auto racing; (Veranstaltung) motor (Brit.) *or* (Amer.) auto race

Autoren·team *das* writing team

Auto·reparatur *die* car repair; repair to the/a car

Autorin *die;* **~, ~nen** authoress; author

Autorisation /au̯toriza'tsi̯o:n/ *die;* **~, ~en** authorization

autorisieren *tr. V.* authorize

autoritär /au̯tori'tɛ:ɐ̯/
A *Adj.* authoritarian
B *adv.* in an authoritarian manner

Autoritarismus /au̯torita'rɪsmʊs/ *der;* **~** authoritarianism

Autorität /au̯tori'tɛ:t/ *die;* **~, ~en** authority; **als ~ auf einem Gebiet gelten** be regarded as an authority in a field

autoritativ /au̯torita'ti:f/
A *Adj.* (geh.) authoritative
B *adv.* authoritatively

autoritäts·gläubig *Adj.* trusting in authority *pred.*

Autoritäts·gläubigkeit *die* trust in authority

Autor·korrektur *die* (Buchw.) author's correction; (Fahne) author's proof; (Korrekturlesen) author's reading of the proofs

Autorschaft *die;* **~:** authorship

auto-, Auto-: ~schalter *der* drive-in counter; **~schlange** *die* queue *or* line of cars; **~schlosser** *der,* **~schlosserin** *die* ▸**~mechaniker**; **~schlüssel** *der* car key; **~skooter** *der* dodgem; bumper car; **~stopp** *der* hitch-hiking; hitching (coll.); **per** *od.* **mit ~stopp fahren, ~stopp machen** hitch-hike; hitch (coll.); **~strich** *der* (ugs.) *area where prostitutes wait to be picked up by kerb-crawlers;* **~stunde** *die:* **zwei ~stunden entfernt sein** be two hours [away] by car; be two hours' drive [away]; **~suggestion** /----'-/ *die* (Psych.) auto-suggestion; **~telefon** *das* car telephone; **~test** *der* car test; **~tür** *die* car door; **~typie** /---'-/ *die;* **~~, ~~n** (Druckw.) half-tone photoengraving; **~unfall** *der* car accident; **~verkehr** *der* [motor] traffic; **~verladung** *die* loading of cars; (Ort, Einrichtung) car-loading facility; **~verleih** *der,* **~vermietung** *die* car hire (Brit.) *or* rental firm *or* service; **~verwerter** *der,* **~verwerterin** *die* ▸ℹ **S. 113** car breaker; **~verwertung** *die* car breaker's [yard]; **~werkstatt** *die* garage; car repair shop; **~zubehör** *das* car accessories *pl.*; **~zug** *der* ▸ **Autoreisezug**

autsch /au̯tʃ/ *Interj.* ouch; ow

Au·wald *der* ▸**Auenwald**

auweh /au̯'ve:/ *Interj.* oh dear; (Ausruf des Schmerzes) ouch

auwei[a] /au̯'vai̯(a)/ *Interj.* (ugs.) oh dear

Avance /a'vã:sə/ *die;* **~, ~n** in **jmdm. ~n machen** make approaches to sb.; (geh.: einen Flirt beginnen) make advances to sb.

avancieren /avã'si:rən/ *itr. V.; mit sein* (geh.) **zu etw. ~:** be promoted to sth. (also iron.); rise to sth.; **zum Bestseller ~** (fig.) become a best seller

Avantgarde /avã'gardə/ *die;* **~, ~n** avant-garde; (Politik) vanguard (fig.)

Avantgardismus *der;* **~:** avant-gardism

Avantgardist *der;* **~en, ~en, Avantgardistin** *die;* **~, ~nen** member of the avant-garde; avant-gardist

avantgardistisch
A *Adj.* avant-garde
B *adv.* ‹*paint etc.*› in an avant-garde style

AvD *Abk.* **= Automobilclub von Deutschland** Automobile Club of Germany

Ave-Maria /'a:vema'ri:a/ *das;* **~s, ~s** (kath. Kirche) Ave Maria; Hail Mary

Avers /a'vɛrs/ *der;* **~es, ~e** (Münzk.) obverse

Aversion /avɛr'zi̯o:n/ *die;* **~, ~en** aversion; **eine ~** *od.* **~en gegen jmdn./etw. haben** have an aversion to sb./sth.

Avis /a'vi:/ *der* **~** /a'vi:s/, **~** /a'vi:s/ 1 (Kaufmannsspr., Bankw.) advice; (schriftlich) advice note 2 (EU) avis

avisieren /avi'zi:rən/ *tr. V.* (bes. Wirtsch.) send notification of; advise *or* notify of

Aviso /a'vi:zo/ *das;* **~s, ~s** (österr.) ▸**Avis**

Avocado /avo'ka:do/ *die;* **~, ~s** avocado [pear]

Axel /'aksl/ *der;* **~s, ~** (Eis-, Rollkunstlauf) axel

axial /a'ksi̯a:l/ *Adj.* (Technik) axial

Axiom /a'ksi̯o:m/ *das;* **~s, ~e** axiom

Axiomatik /aksi̯o'ma:tɪk/ *die;* **~** 1 (Lehre) axiomatics *sing.; no art.;* study of axioms 2 (Verfahren) axiomatization

axiomatisch
A *Adj.* axiomatic
B *adv.* axiomatically

Axt /akst/ *die;* **~, Äxte** /'ɛkstə/ axe; **die ~ im Haus erspart den Zimmermann** (Spr.) it saves trouble if you don't have to get someone in; **sich benehmen wie die ~ im Walde** behave like a boor

Axt·hieb *der* blow of the/an axe

Azalee /at̮sa'le:ə/ *die;* **~, ~n, Azalie** /a'tsa:li̯ə/ *die;* **~, ~n** azalea

Azetat ▸**Acetat**

Azimut /at̮si'mu:t/ *das od. der;* **~s** (Astron.) azimuth

Azoren /a'tso:rən/ *Pl.* **die ~:** the Azores

Azteke /ats'te:kə/ *der;* **~n, ~n, Aztekin** *die;* **~, ~nen** Aztec

Azteken·reich *das* Aztec empire

Azubi /'a:tsubi/ *der;* **~s, ~s,** *die;* **~, ~s** (ugs.) ▸**Auszubildende**

Azubi

Trainees and apprentices are known as *Azubis* or *Auszubildende*. They are trained within the German dual system (*das duale Ausbildungssystem*), which combines practical on-the-job training in recognized occupations with theoretical instruction at a **Berufsschule**. During the training period *Azubis* receive a small wage from their employer. In order to gain professional qualifications *Azubis* take an examination at the end of their two- or three-year apprenticeship. The exam is conducted by a board of examiners such as the chamber of industry and commerce, the chamber of crafts, or representatives of employers and vocational school teachers.

Azubine /at̮su'bi:nə/ *die;* **~, ~n** (ugs.) female trainee; (im Handwerk) female apprentice

Azur /a'tsu:ɐ̯/ *der;* **~s** (dichter.) 1 (Farbe) azure 2 (Himmel) azure (literary)

azur·blau, azurn *Adj.* (geh.) azure[-blue]

azyklisch /'at̮sy:klɪʃ/ *Adj.* 1 (unregelmäßig) irregular 2 (Bot., Chemie) acyclic

Bb

b, B /be:/ *das;* ~, ~ **1** (Buchstabe) b/B **2** (Musik) [key of] B flat; *s. auch* **a, A**

B *Abk.* **= Bundesstraße** ≈ A (Brit.)

BA *Abk.* **= Bundesanstalt für Arbeit**

BAB *Abk.* **= Bundesautobahn** ≈ M (Brit.)

babbeln /ˈbabl̩n/ *itr., tr. V.* (landsch. ugs.) (auch abwertend) babble

Babel /ˈba:bl̩/
A *(das);* **~s** Babel; **der Turm zu ~:** the Tower of Babel
B *das;* **~s,** ~ **1** (Sünden~) hotbed of vice; sink of iniquity **2** (vielsprachiger Ort) babel

Baby /ˈbe:bi/ *das;* **~s, ~s** baby

baby-, Baby-: **~artikel** *Pl.* baby goods; **~ausstattung** *die* layette; **~bauch** *der* (ugs.) [baby] bump (coll.); **~blau** *Adj.* baby blue; **~klappe** *die* baby flap; **~korb** *der* Moses basket

Babylon /ˈba:bylɔn/
A *(das);* **~s** Babylon
B *das;* **~s, ~s** ▸ **Babel B**

Babylonien /babyˈlo:ni̯ən/ *(das);* **~s** Babylonia

Babylonier *der;* **~s,** ~, **Babylonierin** *die;* ~, **~nen** Babylonian

babylonisch *Adj.* Babylonian; **ein ~es Sprachgewirr** a babel of languages; **der Babylonische Turm** the Tower of Babel

baby-, Baby-: **~pause** *die* (period of) maternity leave; (des Vaters) (period of) paternity leave; **~puppe** *die* baby doll; **~rosa** *Adj.* baby pink; **~sitten** /-sɪtn̩/ *itr. V.; nur im Inf.* (ugs.) babysit; **~sitter** /-sɪtɐ/ *der;* **~~s,** **~~,** **~sitterin** *die;* **~~,** **~~nen** babysitter; **~sitting** /-sɪtɪŋ/ *das;* **~s** babysitting; **~speck** *der* (ugs.) puppy fat (Brit.); baby fat (Amer.); **~strich** *der* (ugs.) child prostitution; **~waage** *die* baby scales; **~wäsche** *die* baby clothes

bacchantisch /baˈxantɪʃ/ (geh.)
A *Adj.* Bacchanalian
B *adv.* in a Bacchanalian manner *or* fashion

Bach /bax/ *der;* **~[e]s, Bäche** /ˈbɛçə/ **1** stream; brook; **den ~ runtergehen** (ugs.) ‹*company*› go downhill **2** (Rinnsal) stream [of water]; *s. auch* **Bächlein**

bach·ab *Adv.* downstream

Bache /ˈbaxə/ (Jägerspr.) *die;* ~, **~n** wild sow

Bächelchen /ˈbɛçl̩çən/ *das;* **~s,** ~**:** rivulet

Bach·forelle *die* brown trout

Bächlein /ˈbɛçlai̯n/ *das;* **~s,** ~**:** rivulet; **ein ~ machen** (Kinderspr.) do a wee-wee (child lang.)

Bach·stelze *die* (Motacilla alba alba) white wagtail; (M.a. yarrellii) pied wagtail

Back /bak/ *die;* ~, **~en** (Seemannsspr.) **1** (Decksaufbau) forecastle; fo'c's'le **2** (Schüssel) wooden serving bowl (in which sailors' food is served) **3** (Tisch) mess table **4** (Tischgemeinschaft) mess

Back·blech *das* baking sheet

Back·bord *das* (Seew., Luftf.) port [side]; **über ~:** over the port side

backbord[s] /ˈbakbɔrt(s)/ *Adv.* (Seew., Luftf.) on the port side

Bäckchen /ˈbɛkçən/ *das;* **~s,** ~**:** [little] cheek

Backe /ˈbakə/ *die;* ~, **~n** **1** ▸❶ **S. 435** (Wange) cheek; **au ~!** (ugs.) oh heck (coll.); *s. auch* **voll A 1** **2** ▸❶ **S. 435** (ugs.: Gesäß~) buttock; cheek (sl.); *s. auch* **abreißen 3** **3** (Seitenteil) (eines Schraubstocks) jaw; cheek; (eines Gewehrs) cheekpiece; (Brems~) (eines Autos) shoe; (eines Fahrrads) block

backen¹ /ˈbakn̩/
A *unr. itr. V.* **1** bake; do the baking; **ich backe immer selbst** I do all my own baking **2** (garen) ‹*cake etc.*› bake; **der Kuchen muss noch 10 Minuten ~:** the cake has to stay in the oven for another 10 minutes **3** ‹*oven*› bake
B *unr. tr. V.* **1** bake ‹*cakes, bread, etc.*›; **ich backe vieles selbst** I do a lot of my own baking; (fig.) **das frisch gebackene Ehepaar** (ugs.) the newly-weds *pl.* (coll.); **eine frisch gebackene Ärztin** (ugs.) a newly-fledged doctor **2** (bes. südd.: braten) roast; (in der Bratpfanne) fry **3** (trocknen) dry ‹*fruit, mushrooms, etc.*›; bake ‹*brick*›

backen² (bes. nordd.)
A *itr. V.* ‹*snow, earth*› stick (**an** + *Dat.* to)
B *tr. V.* stick (**an** + *Akk.* on to)

Backen-: **~bart** *der* side whiskers *pl.;* sideboards *pl.* (sl.); **~bremse** *die* (Technik) (eines Autos) shoe brake; (eines Fahrrads) block brake; **~knochen** *der* ▸❶ **S. 435** cheekbone; **~streich** *der* (veralt.) slap in the face; **~tasche** *die* [cheek] pouch; **~zahn** *der* ▸❶ **S. 435** molar; **kleiner** *od.* **vorderer/großer** *od.* **hinterer ~zahn** premolar/back molar

Bäcker /ˈbɛkɐ/ *der;* **~s,** ~ ▸❶ **S. 113** **1** baker; **~ lernen** learn the baker's trade; learn to be a baker; **er will ~ werden/ist ~:** he wants to be/is a baker **2** (Geschäft) baker's [shop]; **zum ~ gehen** go to the baker's; **beim ~:** at the baker's

Back·erbsen *Pl.* (Kochk.) *small crisp round noodles added to soup*

Bäckerei *die;* ~, **~en** **1** (Bäckerladen) baker's [shop]; (Backstube) bakery **2** (das Backen) baking **3** (Handwerk) bakery trade **4** (südd., österr.) ▸ **Backwerk**

Bäcker-: **~geselle** *der,* **~gesellin** *die* journeyman baker; **~hand·werk** *das* bakery trade

Bäckerin *die;* ~, **~nen** ▸❶ **S. 113** baker

Bäcker-: **~innung** *die* bakers' guild; **~junge** *der* (Gehilfe) baker's boy *or* lad; (Lehrling) baker's apprentice; **~laden** *der; Pl.* **~läden** baker's shop; **~lehre** *die* baker's apprenticeship; **~lehrling** *der* baker's apprentice; **~meister** *der,* **~meisterin** *die* master baker

Bäckers·frau *die* baker's wife

back-, Back-: **~fertig** *Adj.* oven-ready; **~fisch** *der* **1** (Kochk.) fried fish (*in breadcrumbs*); **2** (veralt.: Mädchen) teenager; teenage girl; **~form** *die* baking tin (Brit.); baking pan (Amer.); (für Kuchen) cake tin (Brit.); cake pan (Amer.); (aus Ton) earthenware baking mould

Background /ˈbɛkgraunt/ *der;* **~s, ~s** background

Backhähnchen *das* fried chicken (in breadcrumbs)

Back-: **~hendl** *das* (österr.), **~huhn** *das* fried chicken (*in breadcrumbs*); **~mulde** *die* ▸ **~trog**; **~obst** *das* dried fruit; **~ofen** *der* oven; (beim Bäcker) [baker's] oven; **~pfeife** *die* (bes. nordd.) slap in the face; **~pfeifen·gesicht** *das* (salopp abwertend) ▸ **Ohrfeigengesicht**; **~pflaume** *die* prune; **~pulver** *das* baking powder; **~rohr** *das* (südd., österr.), **~röhre** *die* oven; **~stein** *der* brick; **~stein·bau** *der; Pl.* **~~ten** brick building; **~stein·gotik** *die* (Kunstwiss.) brick Gothic [architecture]; **~stein·mauer** *die* brick wall; **~stube** *die* bakery; bakehouse; **~trog** *der* kneading trough; dough tray *or* trough; **~waren** *Pl.* bread, cakes, and pastries; **~werk** *das* biscuits *or* (Amer.) cookies and pastries

Bad /ba:t/ *das;* **~[e]s, Bäder** /ˈbɛ:dɐ/ **1** (Wasser) bath; **[sich** *(Dat.)***] ein ~ einlaufen lassen** run [oneself] a bath **2** (das Baden) bath; (das Schwimmen) swim; (im Meer o. Ä.) bathe; **ein ~ nehmen** (geh.) have *or* take a bath; (schwimmen) go for a swim; (im Meer o. Ä.) bathe; **nach dem ~:** after bathing; **beim ~ im Meer/** (fig.) **in der Sonne** when bathing in the sea/when sunbathing; **jmdm. Bäder verordnen** (Med.) prescribe a course of baths for sb. **3** (Badezimmer) bathroom; **ein Zimmer mit ~:** a room with [private] bath **4** (Schwimm~) [swimming] pool; swimming bath **5** (Heil~) spa; (Seebad) [seaside] resort **6** (Technik, Chemie) bath

Bade-: **~anstalt** *die* swimming baths *pl.* (Brit.); public pool (Amer.); **~an·zug** *der* swimming *or* bathing costume; swimsuit; **~arzt** *der* spa doctor; **~gast** *der* **1** (im Schwimmbad) bather; swimmer; **2** (im Kurort) visitor to a/the spa; **~hose** *die* swimming *or* bathing trunks *pl;* **~kabine** *die* changing cubicle (Brit.); locker (Amer.); **~kappe** *die* swimming *or* bathing cap; **~kur** *die* course of treatment at a spa; **~mantel** *der* dressing gown; bathrobe; (Strandkleidung) beach robe; **~matte** *die* bath mat; **~meister** *der,* **~meisterin** *die* swimming pool attendant; **~mütze** *die* swimming *or* bathing cap

baden
A *itr. V.* **1** (in der Wanne) have *or* take a bath; bath; **warm/kalt ~:** have *or* take a hot/cold bath **2** (schwimmen) bathe; swim; **~ gehen** go for a bathe *or* a swim; go bathing *or* swimming; **[bei** *od.* **mit etw.] ~ gehen** (ugs.) come a cropper (coll.) [over sth.]
B *tr. V.* bath ‹*child, patient, etc.*›; bathe ‹*wound, face, eye, etc.*›; **in Schweiß gebadet** (fig.) bathed in sweat; **du bist wohl als Kind zu heiß gebadet worden!** (ugs. scherzh.) you must have been dropped on your head as a baby

Baden /ˈba:dn̩/ *(das);* **~s** Baden

Badener /ˈba:dənɐ/ *der;* **~s,** ~, **Badenerin** *die;* ~, **~nen,** (ugs.) **Badenser** /baˈdɛnzɐ/ *der;* **~s,** ~, **Badenserin** *die;* ~, **~nen** inhabitant of Baden; (von Geburt) native of Baden; *s. auch* **Kölner**

Baden-Württemberger
A *indekl. Adj.* Baden-Württemberg *attrib.*
B *der;* **~s,** ~**:** native of Baden-Württemberg; (Einwohner) inhabitant of Baden-Württemberg

Bade-: **~ofen** *der* bathwater heater; **~ort** *der* **1** (Seebad) [seaside] resort; **2** (Kurort) spa; **~platz** *der* bathing place

Bäder ▸ **Bad**

Bade-: **~sachen** *Pl.* bathing *or* swimming things; **~saison** *die* bathing *or* swimming season; (im Kurort) spa season; **~salz** *das* bath salts *pl.;* **~schwamm** *der* [bath] sponge; **~strand** *der* bathing beach; **~tuch** *das; Pl.* **~tücher** bath towel; **~wanne** *die* bath[tub]; **~wasser** *das* bath water; **~wetter** *das* bathing weather; weather warm enough *or* suitable for bathing *or* swimming; **~zeit** *die*

b

1 (bei Heilbehandlungen) immersion time; **2** (in ∼anstalten) swimming time; **die ∼zeit ist beendet** the pool is now closing; **3** ▸∼**saison**; ∼**zeug** *das* (ugs.) bathing *or* swimming things *pl.*; ∼**zimmer** *das* bathroom; ∼**zusatz** *der* (∼salz) bath salts; (Schaumbad) bubble bath

badisch *Adj.* of Baden *postpos.*; ‹*wine, produce, etc.*› from Baden; **die ∼e Mundart** the Baden dialect; **das Badische** (Sprachw.) the Baden dialect; (Region) Baden

Badminton /ˈbɛtmɪntən/ *das;* ∼**s** badminton

baff /baf/ *in* ∼ **sein** (ugs.) be flabbergasted

Bafög /ˈbaːfœk/ *das;* ∼**s** (ugs.) [state] grant; **[500 Euro]** ∼ **kriegen** get a [state] grant [of 500 euros]; *s. auch* **BAföG**

BAföG *Abk.* = **Bundesausbildungsförderungsgesetz**

> **BAföG – Bundesausbildungsförderungsgesetz**
>
> The financial assistance which about a quarter of German students receive from the state. Whether they are entitled to a *BAföG* grant or loan (federal education and training assistance), and how much they get, depends on the students' and their parents' financial circumstances. Half of this assistance is awarded in the form of a grant, and the rest as an interest-free loan which usually has to be repaid within five years of the end of the maximum entitlement period. The payments are made by the **Studentenwerke** (student welfare services).

Bagage /baˈgaːʒə/ *die;* ∼, ∼**n** (abwertend) (Familie) tribe (derog.); (Gesindel) rabble; crowd (coll.); **die ganze** ∼: the whole lot of them

Bagatell-: ∼**betrag** *der* trifling amount; ∼**delikt** *das* (Rechtsw.) petty *or* minor offence

Bagatelle /bagaˈtɛlə/ *die;* ∼, ∼**n** **1** (Kleinigkeit) trifle; bagatelle; **das ist keine** ∼: it's no mere trifle **2** (Musik) bagatelle

bagatellisieren
A *tr. V.* trivialize; minimize
B *itr. V.* trivialize matters

Bagatell-: ∼**leiden** *das* trifling *or* minor ailment; ∼**sache** *die* petty *or* minor case; ∼**schaden** *der* minor damage *no indef. art.*; ∼**schäden** minor damage *sing.*

Bagger /ˈbagɐ/ *der;* ∼**s**, ∼: excavator; digger; (Schwimmbagger) dredger

Bagger·führer *der,* **Bagger·führerin** *die* excavator driver; (eines Schwimmbaggers) dredger master

baggern
A *itr. V.* **1** excavate; (mit dem Schwimmbagger) dredge **2** (Volleyball) dig the ball
B *tr. V.* **1** excavate; (mit dem Schwimmbagger) dredge **2** (Volleyball) dig ‹*ball*›

Bagger·see *der* flooded gravel pit

Baguette /baˈgɛt/ *die;* ∼, ∼**n** baguette

bah /baː/ *Interj.* ugh

bäh /bɛː/ *Interj.* **1** (bei Ekel) ugh; (schadenfroh) heehee; tee-hee **2** (von Schafen) baa

Bahama·inseln /baˈhaːma-/, **Bahamas** *Pl.* **die** ∼: the Bahamas

bähen /ˈbɛːən/ *tr. V.* (südd., österr., schweiz.) toast ‹*bread, roll, etc.*›

Bahn /baːn/ *die;* ∼, ∼**en** **1** (Weg) path; way; (von Wasser) course; **sich** (*Dat.*) ∼ **brechen** ‹*invention, idea*› establish itself; **einer Sache** ∼ **brechen** pave *or* prepare the way for sth.; **jmdn. aus der** ∼ **werfen** *od.* **bringen** *od.* **schleudern** (fig.) knock sb. sideways (fig.); **auf die schiefe** ∼ **geraten** (fig.) go astray; *s. auch* **ebnen**; **tüchtig A 1** **2** (Strecke) path; (Umlauf∼) orbit; (einer Rakete) [flight] path; (eines Geschosses) trajectory; **sich in neuen** ∼**en bewegen** (fig.) break new *or* fresh ground (fig.); **etw. [wieder] in die richtige** ∼ **lenken** (fig.) get sth. [back] on the right track (fig.) **3** (Sport) track; (für Pferderennen) course (Brit.); track (Amer.); (für einzelne Teilnehmer) lane; (Kegel∼) alley; (Schlitten∼, Bob∼) run; (Bowling∼) lane; ∼ **frei!** make way!; get out of the way! **4** (Fahr∼) lane **5** (Eisen∼) train; (Bahnnetz) railways *pl.*; railroad *pl.* (Amer.); **jmdn. zur** ∼ **bringen/an der** ∼ **abholen** take sb. to/pick sb. up from the station; **mit der** *od.* **per** ∼: by train; ∼ **fahren** go by train **6** (Straßen∼) tram; streetcar (Amer.) **7** (Schienenweg) railway [track] **8** (Streifen) (Stoff∼) length; (Tapeten∼) strip; length; (eines Rocks) panel

bahn-, Bahn-: ∼**amtlich** *Adj.* (Amtsspr.) official railway; ∼**arbeiter** *der,* ∼**arbeiterin** *die* railway *or* (Amer.) railroad worker; ∼**beamte** *der,* ∼**beamtin** *die* railway *or* (Amer.) railroad official; ∼**brechend** *Adj.* pioneering; ∼**brechend für etw. sein** pave *or* prepare the way for sth.; ∼**brechendes geleistet haben** have done pioneering work; ∼**brecher** *der,* ∼**brecherin** *die;* ∼∼, ∼∼**nen** pioneer; ∼**bus** *der* railway bus

> **BahnCard**
>
> A rail pass for frequent rail travellers which entitles its holder to cheaper travel within Germany. *Bahncard* 25/50/100 entitle the holder to 25%, 50%, or 100% discount respectively. There are a number of other passes and saver tickets, such as the *InterRailCard* which offer reductions throughout Germany, Austria, Switzerland and neighbouring countries.

Bähnchen /ˈbɛːnçən/ *das;* ∼**s**, ∼: narrow-gauge railway; (in Vergnügungsparks usw.) miniature railway

Bahn·damm *der* railway *or* (Amer.) railroad embankment

bahnen *tr. V.* clear ‹*way, path*›; ‹*river etc.*› carve out ‹*channel, bed*›; **jmdm./einer Sache einen Weg** ∼: clear the *or* a way for sb./sth.; (fig.) pave *or* prepare the way for sb./sth.; **sich** (*Dat.*) **einen Weg durch etw.** ∼: force a *or* one's way through sth.

bahnen·weise *Adv.* in lengths; (bei Tapeten) in strips *or* lengths

bahn-, Bahn-: ∼**fahrt** *die* train *or* rail journey; ∼**frei** *Adj., adv.* (Kaufmannsspr.) free on rail; ∼**gleis** *das* railway *or* (Amer.) railroad track *or* line

Bahn·hof *der* [railway *or* (Amer.) railroad] station; ∼ **Käfertal** Käfertal station; **sich im/am** ∼ **treffen** meet at the station; **ich verstehe nur** ∼ (ugs.) it's [all] double Dutch to me; **[ein] großer** ∼ (ugs.) the red-carpet treatment; **jmdm. einen großen** ∼ **bereiten** (ugs.) roll *or* put out the red carpet for sb.

Bahnhofs-: ∼**buch·handlung** *die* station bookshop; (Bücherstand) station bookstall; ∼**gast·stätte** *die* station restaurant; ∼**halle** *die* station concourse; ∼**hotel** *das* station hotel; ∼**mission** *die* ≈ Travellers' Aid (*charitable organization for helping rail travellers in need of care or assistance*); ∼**platz** *der* square in front of the station; ∼**restaurant** *das* station restaurant; ∼**vor·platz** *der* station forecourt; ∼**vorstand** *der,* ∼**vorsteher** *der,* ∼**vorsteherin** *die* station manager; ∼**wirtschaft** *die* station buffet

bahn-, Bahn-: ∼**körper** *der* permanent way; ∼**lagernd** **A** *Adj.* to be collected from the station *postpos.*; **B** *adv.* **Waren** ∼**lagernd schicken** send goods to await collection at the station; ∼**linie** *die* railway *or* (Amer.) railroad line; ∼**meisterei** *die;* ∼∼, ∼∼**en** permanent way (Brit.) *or* (Amer.) railroad maintenance department; ∼**polizei** *die* railway *or* (Amer.) railroad police; ∼**post** *die* travelling *or* railway post office (Brit.); ∼**reise** *die* train *or* rail journey; (Pauschalreise) package holiday (Brit.) *or* (Amer.) vacation trip by train; ∼**reisende** *der/die* [rail] passenger; ∼**schranke** *die* level crossing (Brit.) *or* (Amer.) grade crossing barrier/gate; ∼**station** *die* [railway *or* (Amer.) railroad] halt (Brit.) *or* (Amer.) stop; ∼**steig** /-ʃtaik/ *der;* ∼**[e]s**, ∼**e** [station] platform; ∼**steig·karte** *die* platform ticket; ∼**überführung** *die* **1** underbridge; underline bridge; **2** (ugs.: Brücke über die Bahnlinie) bridge over the/a railway *or* (Amer.) railroad; ∼**über·gang** *der* level crossing (Brit.); grade *or* railroad crossing (Amer.); ∼**unterführung** *die* **1** overbridge; overline bridge; **2** (ugs.: Brücke für die Eisen∼) railway *or* (Amer.) railroad bridge; ∼**verbindung** *die* rail (Brit.) *or* train connection; ∼**wärter** *der* level crossing (Brit.) *or* (Amer.) grade crossing attendant; crossing keeper; (Streckenwärter) linesman (Brit.); trackman (Amer.); ∼**wärter·häuschen** *das* crossing keeper's hut

Bahre /ˈbaːrə/ *die;* ∼, ∼**n** **1** (Kranken∼) stretcher **2** (Toten∼) bier

Bahr·tuch *das; Pl.* **Bahrtücher** pall

Bai /bai/ *die;* ∼, ∼**en** bay

bairisch /ˈbairɪʃ/ *Adj.* Bavarian

Baiser /bɛˈzeː/ *das;* ∼**s**, ∼**s** meringue

Baisse /ˈbɛːsə/ *die;* ∼, ∼**n** (Börsenw.) fall; **auf** ∼ **spekulieren** speculate for a fall; bear

Baisse·spekulant *der;* ∼**en**, ∼**en**, **Baissier** /bɛˈsi̯eː/ *der;* ∼**s**, ∼**s** (Börsenw.) bear

Bajonett /bajoˈnɛt/ *das;* ∼**[e]s**, ∼**e** bayonet

Bajonett-: ∼**fassung** *die* (Elektrot.) bayonet socket; ∼**verschluss**, *∼**verschluß** *der* bayonet connection

Bajuware /bajuˈvaːrə/ *der;* ∼**n**, ∼**n**, **Bajuwarin** *die;* ∼, ∼**nen** (scherzh.) Bavarian

bajuwarisch *Adj.* (scherzh.) Bavarian

Bake /ˈbaːkə/ *die;* ∼, ∼**n** **1** (vor Eisenbahnübergängen, an Autobahnen) countdown marker **2** (zur Absperrung) [movable] barrier **3** (für Schiffe, Flugzeuge) beacon **4** (Vermessungsw.) ranging pole; range pole

Bakelit (Wz) /bakəˈliːt/ *das;* ∼**s** bakelite ®

Baken·tonne *die* (Seew.) marker buoy

Bakkarat /ˈbakara(t)/ *das;* ∼**s** baccarat

Bakken /ˈbakn̩/ *der;* ∼**s**, ∼ (Skispringen) [jumping] hill

Bakschisch /ˈbakʃɪʃ/ *das;* ∼**[e]s**, ∼**e** baksheesh

Bakterie /bakˈteːri̯ə/ *die;* ∼, ∼**n** bacterium; **voller** ∼**n** full of germs

bakteriell /bakteˈri̯ɛl/ (Med., Biol.)
A *Adj.* bacterial
B *adv.* ∼ **verursacht** caused by bacteria

Bakterien-: ∼**kultur** *die* bacterial culture; ∼**träger** *der,* ∼**trägerin** *die* carrier

Bakteriologe /bakteri̯oˈloːgə/ *der;* ∼**n**, ∼**n** bacteriologist

Bakteriologie *die;* ∼: bacteriology *no art.*

Bakteriologin *die;* ∼, ∼**nen** bacteriologist

bakteriologisch
A *Adj.* bacteriological
B *adv.* ‹*investigate, detect*› using bacteriological methods

bakterizid /bakteriˈt͜siːt/ (Med.)
A *Adj.* bactericidal
B *adv.* ∼ **wirken** act as a bactericide; have a bactericidal effect

Bakterizid *das;* ∼**s**, ∼**e** bactericide

Balalaika /balaˈlai̯ka/ *die;* ∼, ∼**s** *od.* **Balalaiken** balalaika

Balance /baˈlaŋsə/ *die;* ∼, ∼**n** balance; **die** ∼ **halten/verlieren** keep/lose one's balance; **die** ∼ **zwischen ... und ... halten** (fig.) keep a balance between ... and ...

Balance·akt *der* (auch fig.) balancing act

balancieren /balaŋˈsiːrən/
A *itr. V.; mit sein* (auch fig.) balance; **über etw.** (*Akk.*) ∼: pick one's way precariously across sth.
B *tr. V.* balance

Balancier·stange *die* balancing pole

balbieren /balˈbiːrən/ *tr. V.* ▸**Löffel 1**

bald /balt/ *Adv.* **1** **eher** /ˈeːɐ̯/, **am ehesten** /-ˈeːəstn̩/ (in kurzer Zeit) soon; (leicht, rasch) quickly; easily; ∼ **danach** *od.* **darauf** soon afterwards; **so** ∼ **als** *od.* **wie möglich** as soon as possible; **möglichst** ∼: as soon as possible; **so etwas kommt so** ∼ **nicht wieder vor** something like that won't happen again in a long while *or* (coll.) in a hurry; **bist du** ∼ **still?** will you just be quiet; **wirds** ∼**?** how much longer are you going to be?; get a move on, will you; **bis** *od.* **auf** ∼: see you soon; **seit** ∼ **zwei Jahren** for nearly two years **2** (ugs.: fast) almost; nearly; **das ist** ∼ **nicht mehr schön** that's getting beyond a joke (Brit.); that's not funny any more (Amer.) **3** (veralt.) *in* ∼ **...,** ∼ **...** now ..., now ...; ∼ **so,** ∼ **so** now this way, now that

b

Baldachin /ˈbaldaxiːn/ *der;* **~s, ~e** baldachin; (über dem Bett) canopy

Bälde /ˈbɛldə/ *in* **in ~** (Papierdt.) in the near future

baldig *Adj.* speedy; quick; **auf ~es Wiedersehen** (geh.) see you again soon

baldigst *Adv.* as soon as possible

bald·möglichst *adv.* (Papierdt.) as soon as possible

baldowern /balˈdoːvɐn/ (ugs.)

A *tr. V.* check out

B *itr. V.* check everything out

Baldrian /ˈbaldriaːn/ *der;* **~s, ~e** valerian

Baldrian·tropfen *Pl.* valerian drops

Balearen /baleˈaːrən/ *Pl.* **die ~:** the Balearic Islands

Balg¹ /balk/ *der;* **~[e]s, Bälge** /ˈbɛlgə/ **1** (von Tieren) pelt; skin; (eines Vogels) skin; **einem Tier den ~ abziehen** skin an animal **2** (salopp) (Bauch) belly; (Leib) body; *s. auch* **rücken B 1** **3** (Bot. od. südd.) (Haut) skin; (Hülle, Schote) pod **4** (Blase~; bei einer Kamera) bellows *pl.*

Balg² *das;* **~[e]s, Bälger** /ˈbɛlgɐ/ *od.* **Bälge** /ˈbɛlgə/ (ugs., oft abwertend) kid (sl.); brat (derog.)

balgen *refl. V.* (ugs.) scrap (coll.); **sich um etw. ~:** scrap (coll.) over sth.; (fig.) fight over sth.

Balgen *der;* **~s, ~** (Fot.) bellows *pl.*

Balgerei *die;* **~, ~en** (ugs.) scrap (coll.)

Balg·geschwulst *die* sebaceous cyst

Balkan /ˈbalkaːn/ *der;* **~s** **1** (Halbinsel) **der ~:** the Balkans; **auf dem ~:** in the Balkans **2** (Gebirge) Balkan Mountains

Balkan·halbinsel *die* Balkan Peninsula

balkanisieren *tr. V.* (auch fig.) Balkanize

Balkanisierung *die;* **~, ~en** (auch fig.) Balkanization

Balkan·staat *der* Balkan State

Balken /ˈbalkn̩/ *der;* **~s, ~** **1** (Holz~) beam; (aus Stahl) beam; girder; (Stütz~) prop; shore; **lügen, dass sich die ~ biegen** tell a [complete] pack of lies; *s. auch* **Splitter, Wasser 1** **2** (Her.) fess **3** (Schwebe~) beam **4** (Musik) cross-stroke **5** (Waage~) beam **6** (Leichtathletik) (beim Weitsprung) take-off board; (beim Kugelstoßen) stop board; toe board **7** (dicker Strich) thick stroke; (fette Linie) thick line

Balken-: **~decke** *die* ceiling with wooden beams; **~diagramm** *das* (DV) bar chart; **~konstruktion** *die* timber-frame structure; **~überschrift** *die* (Zeitungsw.) banner headline; **~waage** *die* beam-balance

Balkon /balˈkɔŋ, balˈkoːn/ *der;* **~s, ~s** /balˈkɔŋs/ *od.* **~e** /balˈkoːnə/ **1** balcony **2** (Theater) [dress] circle; (im Kino) circle; **~ sitzen** sit in the [dress] circle **3** (ugs.: Busen) big boobs *pl.* (coll.); big bust

Balkonien /balˈkoːni̯ən/ *(das);* **~s** (ugs. scherzh.) **nach ~ fahren** stay at home and relax on one's own balcony

Balkon-: **~pflanze** *die* balcony plant; **~tür** *die* balcony door; **~zimmer** *das* room with a balcony

Ball /bal/ *der;* **~[e]s, Bälle** /ˈbɛlə/ **1** ball; **~ spielen** play ball; **am ~ sein** have the ball; (fig. ugs.) be in touch; be on the ball (coll.); **am ~ bleiben** keep [possession of] the ball; (fig.) stick (coll.) *or* keep at it; **hart am ~ bleiben** (fig. ugs.) stay right with it (coll.); **jmdm./einander/sich [gegenseitig] die Bälle zuspielen** *od.* **zuwerfen** (fig.) feed sb./each other lines **2** (Sportjargon: Schuss, Wurf) ball; (aufs Tor) shot **3** (Fest) ball **4** (Punkt) (Tennis) point; (Baseball) ball **5** (fig.: Kugel) ball; **der glühende ~ der Sonne** (geh.) the fiery orb of the sun

ballaballa /balaˈbala/ *Adj.* (salopp) crackers (sl.); daft

Ballade /baˈlaːdə/ *die;* **~, ~n** ballad

balladenhaft, balladesk /balaˈdɛsk/ *Adj.* ballad-like

Ballast /baˈlast/ *der;* **~[e]s, ~e** ballast; (fig.: in Buch, Artikel usw.) padding; **~ abwerfen** *od.* **über Bord werfen** shed *or* jettison ballast; (fig.) rid oneself of unnecessary burdens; **jmdn./etw. als ~ empfinden** (fig.) find sb./sth. a burden *or* an encumbrance

Ballast-: **~stoffe** *Pl.* (Med.) roughage *sing.*; **~wasser** *das;* **~~s, ~~** ballast water

Bällchen /ˈbɛlçən/ *das;* **~s, ~:** [little] ball

ballen

A *tr. V.* clench ‹*fist*›; crumple ‹*paper*› into a ball; press ‹*snow etc.*› into a ball; *s. auch* **Faust; geballt B**

B *refl. V.* ‹*clouds*› gather, build up; ‹*crowd*› gather; ‹*traffic*› build up; ‹*fist*› clench; (fig.) ‹*problems, difficulties, etc.*› accumulate, mount up

Ballen *der;* **~s, ~** **1** (Packen) bale; **ein ~ Stroh/Stoff** a bale of straw/cloth **2** (Hand~, Fuß~) ball; (bei Tieren) pad **3** (Med.) bunion **4** (Wurzel~) [root] ball

ballen·weise *Adv.* by the bale

Ballerei *die;* **~, ~en** (ugs.) shoot-out

Ballerina /baləˈriːna/ *die;* **~, Ballerinen** ▸ **i** S. 113 ballerina; ballet dancer

Baller-: **~mann** *der* (ugs.) shooting iron (coll.); shooter (coll.) **~spiel** *das* (ugs.) shoot 'em up [game]; shooter game

ballern (ugs.)

A *itr. V.* **1** (schießen) fire [away]; bang away **2** (schlagen) bang, hammer (**gegen** on)

B *tr. V.* **1** (werfen) hurl **2** **jmdm. eine ~:** sock sb. one (sl.) **3** (Sportjargon) fire ‹*ball*›

Ballett /baˈlɛt/ *das;* **~[e]s, ~e** ballet; **beim ~ sein** (ugs.) be a dancer with the ballet; be a ballet dancer

Ballett·abend *der* evening ballet programme *or* performance

***Ballettänzer** *der,* ***Ballettänzerin** *die* ballet dancer

Balletteuse /balɛˈtøːzə/ *die;* **~, ~n** dancer

Ballett-: **~meister** *der* ballet master; **~meisterin** *die* ballet mistress; **~musik** *die* ballet music; **~ratte** *die* (ugs. scherzh.) ballet pupil; **~röckchen** *das* tutu; **~schuh** *der* ballet shoe; **~schule** *die* ballet school; **~tänzer** *der,* **~tänzerin** *die* ballet dancer; **~truppe** *die* ballet company; (im Gegensatz zu den Solotänzern) corps de ballet

ball-, Ball-: **~fertig** *Adj.* (Fußball) ‹*player*› with good ball skills; skilled on the ball *pred.*; **~fertigkeit** *die;* **~~** (Fußball) skill on the ball; ball skills *Pl.*; **~führung** *die* (Ballspiele) ball control; **~haus** *das* real-tennis court; (hist.) tennis court

Ballistik *die;* **~:** ballistics *sing., no art.*

Ballistiker *der;* **~s, ~, Ballistikerin** *die;* **~, ~nen** ballistics expert

ballistisch

A *Adj.* ballistic

B *adv.* ballistically

Ball-: **~junge** *der* ballboy; **~kleid** *das* ball dress *or* gown; **~königin** *die* belle of the ball; **~künstler** *der,* **~künstlerin** *die* (Fußballjargon) artist with the ball

Ballon /baˈlɔŋ/ *der;* **~s, ~s** **1** balloon **2** (salopp: Kopf) nut (coll.); **eins auf** *od.* **an den ~ kriegen** get hit on the nut (coll.); **[so] einen ~ kriegen** *od.* **bekommen** go as red as a beetroot **3** (Flasche) demijohn **4** (Chemie) carboy

Ballon-: **~mütze** *die* Mao cap; **~reifen** *der* balloon tyre

Ball-: **~saal** *der* ballroom; **~spiel** *das* ball game; **~spielen** *das;* **~~s** playing ball *no art.*; **~spielen verboten** no ball games; **~technik** *die* ball control

Ballung /ˈbalʊŋ/ *die;* **~, ~en** build-up; concentration; (fig.: von Problemen, Schwierigkeiten) accumulation

Ballungs-: **~gebiet** *das,* **~raum** *der* conurbation; **~zentrum** *das* centre of population; **ein ~zentrum der chemischen Industrie** a centre of the chemical industry

Ball·wechsel *der* (Tennis, Tischtennis, Badminton) rally

Balsam /ˈbalzaːm/ *der;* **~s, ~e** balsam; balm; (fig.) balm; **~ auf jmds. Wunden gießen** (fig.) pour balm on sb.'s wounds

Balsam·essig *der* balsamic vinegar

balsamieren ▸ **einbalsamieren**

balsamisch

A *Adj.* **1** (wohlriechend) balmy; fragrant; (lindernd) soothing ‹*cream, ointment, etc.*› **2** (Balsam enthaltend) balsamic

B *adv.* fragrantly ‹*scented*›; soothingly ‹*cooling*›

Balte /ˈbaltə/ *der;* **~n, ~n, Baltin** *die;* **~, ~nen** person *or* man/woman from the Baltic; Balt; **er ist Balte** he comes from the Baltic

Baltikum /ˈbaltikʊm/ *das;* **~s** Baltic States *pl.*

baltisch *Adj.* Baltic

Balustrade /balʊsˈtraːdə/ *die;* **~, ~n** balustrade

Balz /balts/ *die;* **~, ~en** **1** (Liebesspiel) courtship display **2** (Zeit) mating season

balzen *itr. V.* perform its/their courtship display

Balz-: **~flug** *der* (Zool.) mating flight; **~zeit** *die* mating season

Bambi /ˈbambi/ *das;* **~s, ~s** (Kinderspr.) little deer

Bambule /bamˈbuːlə/ *die;* **~, ~n** (salopp) shindy; **~ machen** go on the rampage

Bambus /ˈbambʊs/ *der;* **~** *od.* **~ses, ~se** bamboo

Bambus-: **~rohr** *das* bamboo [cane]; **~sprossen** *Pl.* bamboo shoots; **~vorhang** *der* (Politik) bamboo curtain

Bammel /ˈbaml̩/ *der;* **~s** (ugs.) **~ vor jmdm./etw. haben** be scared stiff of sb./sth. (coll.)

bammeln (bes. nordd.) ▸ **baumeln**

banal /baˈnaːl/

A *Adj.* **1** (abwertend: platt) banal; trite, banal ‹*speech, reply, response, excuse*› **2** (gewöhnlich) commonplace; ordinary

B *adv.* **1** (abwertend: platt) banally; tritely **2** (gewöhnlich) **~ gesagt** to put it plainly and simply

banalisieren *tr. V.* make ‹*idea*› seem trite; trivialize ‹*idea, feeling*›

Banalität *die;* **~, ~en** **1** (das Banalsein) ▸ **banal A 1, 2**: banality; triteness; commonplaceness; ordinariness **2** (Äußerung) banality

Banane /baˈnaːnə/ *die;* **~, ~n** banana

Bananen-: **~dampfer** *der* banana boat; **~flanke** *die* (Fußballjargon) curving cross; **~republik** *die* (abwertend) banana republic; **~schale** *die* banana skin; **~split** *das;* **~~s, ~~s** banana split; **~stecker** *der* (Elektrot.) banana plug

Banause /baˈnaʊ̯zə/ *der;* **~n, ~n** (abwertend) philistine

banausenhaft (abwertend)

A *Adj.* philistine

B *adv.* in a philistine way

Banausentum *das;* **~s** (abwertend) philistinism *no indef. art.*

Banausin *die;* **~, ~nen** ▸ **Banause**

banausisch ▸ **banausenhaft**

band /bant/ *1. u. 3. Pers. Sg. Prät. v.* **binden**

Band¹ *das;* **~[e]s, Bänder** /ˈbɛndɐ/ **1** (Schmuck~; auch fig.) ribbon; (Haar~, Hut~) band; (Schürzen~) string; (zum Zusammenhalten, Kleben) tape; (für Sicherheitsgurte usw.) webbing; **das Blaue ~:** the Blue Ribband *or* Ribbon; **das Bundesverdienstkreuz am ~e** the Federal Service Cross on a ribbon **2** (Mess~) tape measure; measuring tape; (Farb~) ribbon; (Ziel~, Isolier~) tape **3** (Ton~) [magnetic] tape; **etw. auf ~** (*Akk.*) **aufnehmen** tape[-record] sth.; **etw. auf ~** (*Akk.*) **sprechen/diktieren** record/dictate sth. on to tape **4** (Förder~) conveyor belt; (Fließ~) production line; **am ~ stehen** work on the production line; **vom ~ laufen** come off the production line; **etw. auf ~** (*Akk.*) **legen** put sth. into production; **am laufenden ~** (ugs.) nonstop; continuously **5** (Anat.) ligament **6** (Säge~) band **7** (Beschlag) hinge **8** (Metall~ um Ballen usw.) band; (Fass~) hoop **9** (Nachrichtenw.) [frequency] band

Band² *der;* **~[e]s, Bände** /ˈbɛndə/ volume; **etw. spricht Bände** (ugs.) sth. speaks volumes

Band³ /bɛnt/ *die;* **~, ~s** band; (Beat~, Rock~ usw.) band; group

Band⁴ *das;* **~[e]s, ~e** **1** (dichter. veralt.: Fessel) bond; fetter; shackle; **jmdn. in ~e schlagen** clap sb. in irons; **in ~en liegen** lie in chains **2** (fig.: Unfreiheit) **~e** shackles; **frei von allen**

~en free from all ties [3] (fig.: Bindung) **ein ~ der Liebe/Freundschaft** a bond of love/friendship; **die ~e des Bluts** the ties of blood; **verwandtschaftliche ~e** family ties; **zarte ~e knüpfen** (geh., scherzh.) start a romance

Bandage /ban'da:ʒə/ *die;* **~, ~n** bandage; **mit harten ~n kämpfen** (fig.) fight with the gloves off (fig.)

bandagieren /banda'ʒi:rən/ *tr. V.* bandage

Band-: ~aufnahme *die* tape recording; **~breite** *die* [1] (Nachrichtenw.) bandwidth; [2] (fig.: Bereich, Umfang) range

Bändchen¹ /'bɛntçən/ *das;* **~s, ~:** little ribbon

Bändchen² *das;* **~s, ~** (kleines Buch) little volume

Bande¹ /'bandə/ *die;* **~, ~n** [1] (Verbrecher~) gang [2] (ugs.: Gruppe) mob (coll.); crew

Bande² *die;* **~, ~n** [1] (Sport) [perimeter] barrier; (mit Reklame) billboards *pl.*; (Billard) cushion; (der Reitbahn) rail; (der Kegelbahn) side; edge; (im Zirkus) ring fence; (der Eisbahn) boards *pl.* [2] (Physik) band

Band·eisen *das* strip iron

Bandel /'bandl̩/ *das;* **~s, ~** (bayr., österr. ugs.), **Bändel** /'bɛndl̩/ *der od. das;* **~s, ~** (landsch.) ribbon; (Schuhband) shoelace; **jmdn. am ~ haben** (ugs.) have got sb. on a string

Banden-: ~bildung *die* formation of an armed gang; **~chef** *der,* **~chefin** *die* (ugs.), **~führer** *der,* **~führerin** *die* gang leader; **~krieg** *der* gang war; **~spektrum** *das* (Physik) band spectrum; **~unwesen** *das* ▸ **~wesen**; **~werbung** *die: advertising on hoardings around the perimeter of a football pitch etc.*; **~wesen** *das* gangsterism; activities of the criminal gangs

Bänder ▸ **Band¹**

Banderole /bandə'ro:lə/ *die;* **~, ~n** [1] (Steuer~) revenue stamp *or* seal [2] (Kunstwiss.) banderole

Bänder-: ~riss, *~riß *der* ▸ⓘ **S. 439** (Med.) torn ligament; **~zerrung** *die* ▸ⓘ **S. 439** (Med.) pulled ligament

Band-: ~förderer *der* (Technik) conveyor belt; **~geschwindigkeit** *die* tape speed

-bändig /-bɛndɪç/ *adj.* (Buchw.) -volume; **viel~/acht~:** multi-volume/eight-volume ‹*encyclopedia etc.*›; ‹*encyclopedia etc.*› in many/eight volumes

bändigen /'bɛndɪgn̩/ *tr. V.* tame ‹*animal*›; control ‹*person, anger, child, thoughts, voice*›; (fig.) control, master, overcome ‹*desire, urge, etc.*›; bring ‹*fire*› under control; keep ‹*floods, river, natural forces*› in check; overcome ‹*tiredness*›

Bändigung *die;* **~** ▸ **bändigen**: taming; controlling; mastering; overcoming; **die ~ von Naturgewalten** keeping natural forces in check

Bandit /ban'di:t/ *der;* **~en, ~en** bandit; brigand; (fam. scherzh.) rascal; (fig. abwertend) robber; **einarmiger ~** (ugs.) one-armed bandit (coll.)

Band·keramik *die* (Archäol.) [1] Bandkeramik; band ceramics; **~en** Bandkeramik pieces [2] (Epoche) Danubian I stage

Bandleader /'bɛntli:dɐ/ *der;* **~s, ~:** bandleader

Band-: ~maß *das* tape measure; measuring tape; **~nudeln** *Pl.* tagliatelle *sing.*; **~säge** *die* bandsaw; **~scheibe** *die* ▸ⓘ **S. 435** [intervertebral] disc; **~scheiben·schaden** *der* slipped disc; **~scheiben·vorfall** *der* ▸ⓘ **S. 439** (Med.) prolapsed intervertebral disc (Med.); slipped disc; **~stahl** *der* strip steel; steel strip; **~wurm** *der* tapeworm; **~wurm·satz** *der* (ugs.) interminable sentence

bang /baŋ/ ▸ **bange**

Bang·büx[e] *die* (nordd. ugs.) scaredy-cat (coll.); chicken (coll.)

bange; banger, bangst... *od.* **bänger** /bɛŋɐ/, **bängst...** /bɛŋst.../

A *Adj.* afraid; scared; (besorgt) anxious; worried; **mir ist/wurde ~ [zumute]** I am *or* feel/became scared *or* frightened; **das wirst du schon schaffen, da ist mir gar nicht ~:** you'll manage that all right, I'm sure of it; **jmdn. ~ machen** scare *or* frighten sb.; **ihm wurde ~ und bänger** he became more and more afraid *or* scared; **mir ist ~ vor ihm/davor** I'm afraid *or* frightened *or* scared of him/it; **Bangemachen gilt nicht** (ugs.); (gekniffen wird nicht) you can't chicken out now (coll.); (ich lasse mich nicht ängstigen) you can't put the wind up (coll.) *or* scare me

B *adv.* anxiously

Bange *die;* **~** (bes. nordd.) fear; **[nur] keine ~!** don't be afraid; (sei nicht besorgt) don't worry; **da habe ich keine ~:** I've no fears about that; **[große] ~ vor jmdm./etw. haben** be [very] scared *or* frightened of sb./sth; **jmdm. ~ machen** scare *or* frighten sb.; *s. auch* **bange A**

bangen *itr. V.* be anxious *or* worried; **um jmdn./etw. ~:** be anxious *or* worried about sb./sth.; worry about sb./sth.; **ihm bangt [es] vor dir/der Operation** he's afraid *or* frightened of you/the operation

Bangigkeit *die;* **~** (Furcht) fear; (Beklemmung) apprehension; (Besorgnis) anxiety

Bangladesch /baŋgla'dɛʃ/ *(das);* **~s** Bangladesh

bänglich /'bɛŋlɪç/

A *Adj.* nervous; timid

B *adv.* nervously; timidly

Bangnis *die;* **~, ~se** (geh.) (Furcht) fear; (Besorgnis) anxiety; (Beklommenheit) trepidation

Banjo /'banjo/ *das;* **~s, ~s** banjo

Bank¹ /baŋk/ *die;* **~, Bänke** /'bɛŋkə/ [1] (Sitz~, Parlaments~, Schul~; Sport: Ersatz~, Turngerät) bench; (mit Lehne) bench seat; (Kirchen~) pew; (Anklage~) dock; **setz dich in deine ~!** (Schul~) sit at your desk; **etw. auf die lange ~ schieben** (ugs.) put sth. off; **vor leeren Bänken spielen** play to an empty house; **durch die ~** (ugs.) every single one; the whole lot of them [2] (Werk~) workbench; (Dreh~) lathe [3] (Sand~) sandbank [4] (Austern~) bed; (Korallen~) [coral] reef [5] (Nebel~, Wolken~) bank [6] (Geol.) layer; bed [7] (Ringen) crouch [position]

Bank² *die;* **~, ~en** [1] bank; **Geld auf der ~ [liegen] haben** have money in the bank; **ein Konto bei einer ~ eröffnen** open an account with a bank; **bei einer ~ arbeiten** *od.* **sein** work in a bank; **Geld bei der ~ abheben** withdraw money from the bank [2] (Glücksspiel) bank; **die ~ sprengen** break the bank; **die ~ halten** be [the] banker; have the bank

Bank-: ~angestellte *der/die; adj. Dekl.,* (veralt.) **~beamte** *der,* **~beamtin** *die* ▸ⓘ **S. 113** bank employee

Bänkchen /'bɛŋkçən/ *das;* **~s, ~:** little *or* small bench; (mit Lehne) little *or* small seat

Bank-: ~direktor *der,* **~direktorin** *die* director of a/the bank; **~ein·bruch** *der* bank raid **~ein·zug** *der* direct debit

Bänkel- /'bɛŋkl̩-/: **~lied** *das* street ballad; **~sang** *der* performance of street ballads; **~sänger** *der,* **~sängerin** *die* singer of street ballads

Banker *der;* **~s, ~, Bankerin** *die;* **~, ~nen** (ugs.) banker

bankerott /baŋkə'rɔt/ ▸ **bankrott**

Bankert /'baŋkɐt/ *der;* **~s, ~e** (veralt. abwertend) bastard

Bankett¹ /baŋ'kɛt/ *das;* **~[e]s, ~e** banquet

Bankett² *das;* **~[e]s, ~e, Bankette** *die;* **~, ~n** [1] (an Straßen) shoulder; (unbefestigt) verge; **„~ nicht befahrbar"** 'soft verges' [2] (an Häusern) footing

Bank-: ~fach *das* [1] (Berufsgebiet) banking *no art.*; banking profession; [2] (Schließfach) safe-deposit box; **~filiale** *die* branch of a/the bank; **~gebäude** *das* bank; **~geheimnis** *das* (Wirtsch.) bankers' duty to maintain confidentiality; **~gut·haben** *das* bank balance; **~halter** *der,* **~halterin** *die* (Glücksspiel) banker; **~haus** *das* banking house

Bankier /baŋ'kie:/ *der;* **~s, ~s** banker

Bank-: ~kauffrau *die,* **~kaufmann** *der* [qualified] bank/building society/stock market clerk; **~konto** *das* bank account; **~kredit** *der* bank loan; **~lehre** *die* training as a bank clerk; **~leit·zahl** *die* [bank] sort code; **~nachbar** *der,* **~nachbarin** *die* (Schulw.) **er war mein ~nachbar** he sat next to me [at school]; **~note** *die* ▸ⓘ **S. 299** banknote; bill (Amer.); **~raub** *der* bank robbery; **~räuber** *der,* **~räuberin** *die* bank robber

bankrott /baŋ'krɔt/ *Adj.* [1] bankrupt; **jmdn./etw. ~ machen** bankrupt sb./sth.; **Bankrott** *od.* ***bankrott gehen** go bankrupt [2] (fig.) (moralisch) bankrupt; (politisch) discredited

Bankrott *der;* **~[e]s, ~e** [1] bankruptcy; **seinen ~ anmelden** *od.* **ansagen** *od.* **erklären** declare oneself bankrupt; **~ machen** go bankrupt; *s. auch* **bankrott** [2] (fig.) downfall; (moralisch) bankruptcy

Bankrott·erklärung *die* declaration of bankruptcy; (fig.) declaration of [one's own] failure

Bankrotteur /baŋkrɔ'tø:ɐ̯/ *der;* **~s, ~e, Bankrotteurin** *die;* **~, ~nen** bankrupt

Bank-: ~überfall *der* bank raid; **~üblich** *Adj.* **das ist ~üblich** that is normal banking practice; **~übliche Zinssätze** normal bank interest rates; **~verbindung** *die* particulars of one's bank account; **~verkehr** *der* bank transactions *pl.*; **~vollmacht** *die* third-party mandate; *(given by firm)* signing powers *pl.*; **~wesen** *das* banking system

Bann /ban/ *der;* **~[e]s** [1] (hist.) excommunication; **den ~ über jmdn. aussprechen** *od.* **verhängen, jmdn. mit dem ~ belegen, jmdn. in den ~ tun** excommunicate sb. [2] (geh.: Wirkung) spell; **in jmds. ~/im ~e einer Sache stehen** be under sb.'s spell/under the spell of sth.; **jmdn. in seinen ~ schlagen** *od.* **ziehen** cast one's/its spell over sb.

Bann·bulle *die* (hist.) bull of excommunication

bannen *tr. V.* [1] (festhalten) entrance; captivate; **[wie] gebannt** ‹*watch, listen, etc.*› spellbound; **ein Geschehen auf die Leinwand/auf Zelluloid ~** (fig.) capture an event on canvas/film; *s. auch* **Platte 1** [2] (vertreiben) exorcize ‹*spirit*›; avert, ward off ‹*danger*›; banish ‹*worries, poverty*›; (geh.) banish ‹*disease*› [3] (hist.: exkommunizieren) excommunicate

Banner *das;* **~s, ~:** banner; **das ~ der Freiheit/des Fortschritts hochhalten** (fig.) hold high the banner of freedom/progress

Banner·träger *der,* **~trägerin** *die* (auch fig.) standard-bearer

Bann·fluch *der* (hist.) excommunication; anathema; **den ~ gegen jmdn. schleudern** excommunicate *or* anathematize sb.

bannig *Adv.* (nordd. ugs.) extremely; terribly (coll.)

Bann-: ~kreis *der* (geh.) influence; **in jmds. ~kreis/in den ~kreis einer Sache geraten** fall under sb.'s influence/the influence of sth.; **~meile** *die: restricted area surrounding government buildings, where no public meetings or marches may be held;* **~spruch** *der* (hist.) excommunication; anathema

Bantam- /'bantam-/: **~gewicht** *das* (Schwerathletik) [1] bantamweight; *s. auch* **Fliegengewicht**; [2] (Sportler) ▸ **~gewichtler**; **~gewichtler** /-gəvɪçtlɐ/ *der;* **~s, ~:** bantamweight; **~huhn** *das* bantam

Bantu /'bantu/ *der;* **~s, ~[s]** Bantu

Bantu-: ~frau *die* Bantu woman; **~sprache** *die* Bantu language

Baptismus /bap'tɪsmʊs/ *der;* **~:** Baptist faith

Baptist *der;* **~en, ~en** Baptist

Baptisterium /baptɪs'te:ri̯ʊm/ *das;* **~s, Baptisterien** (christl. Rel., Kunstwiss.) [1] (Gebäude) baptistery [2] (Taufbecken) [baptismal] font; (in einer Baptistenkapelle) baptistery

Baptistin *die;* **~, ~nen** Baptist

baptistisch *Adj.* Baptist

bar /ba:ɐ̯/

A *Adj.* [1] ▸ⓘ **S. 299** cash; **~es Geld** cash; **in ~:** in cash; **etw. [in] ~ bezahlen** pay for sth. in cash; pay cash for sth.; **Verkauf/Reparaturen nur gegen ~:** cash sales only/repairs must be prepaid in cash; **gegen ~ verkauft/gekauft**

b

sold/bought for cash; *s. auch* **Münze 1** [2] (pur) pure; sheer; utter, pure, sheer ‹*nonsense*›; absolute ‹*reality*› [3] (veralt.: nackt) bare; **~en Hauptes** bareheaded; **einer Sache** (*Gen.*) **~ [sein]** (geh.) [be] devoid of *or* without sth.

B *adv.* ▸❶ **S. 299** in cash; **~ auf die Hand** (ugs.) *od.* (salopp) **Kralle** cash on the nail

Bar¹ *die;* **~, ~s** [1] (Nachtlokal) nightclub; bar [2] (Theke) bar

Bar² *das;* **~s, ~s** (Physik, Met.) bar; **2,5 ~:** 2.5 bar[s]

Bär¹ /bɛːɐ̯/ *der;* **~en, ~en** bear; **ein richtiger ~** (ugs.) a hulking great brute of a man (fig. coll.); **ich bin hungrig wie ein ~** (ugs.) I'm so hungry I could eat a horse (coll.); **er ist stark/schläft wie ein ~** (ugs.) he is as strong as an ox/sleeps like a log; **der Große/Kleine ~** (Astron.) the Great/Little Bear; Ursa Major/Minor; **jmdm. einen ~en aufbinden** have sb. on (coll.); pull sb.'s leg

Bär² *der;* **~s, ~en** (Technik) ram

Baracke /ba'rakə/ *die;* **~, ~n** hut; **eine elende ~:** a miserable shack

Baracken-: ~lager *das* hutted camp; **~siedlung** *die* shanty town

Barbar /bar'baːɐ̯/ *der;* **~en, ~en** (auch hist.) barbarian

Barbarei *die;* **~, ~en** [1] (Rohheit) barbarity [2] (Kulturlosigkeit) barbarism *no indef. art.*

Barbarin *die;* **~, ~nen** (auch hist.) barbarian

barbarisch

A *Adj.* [1] (roh) barbarous; savage; barbarous, brutal ‹*torture*› [2] (unzivilisiert) barbaric; barbaric, uncivilized ‹*person*› [3] (furchtbar) dreadful (coll.), terrible (coll.) ‹*noise, cold, etc.*› [4] (hist.) barbarian

B *adv.* [1] (roh) barbarously; ‹*torture*› barbarously, brutally [2] (unzivilisiert) barbarically; in an uncivilized manner [3] (sehr) dreadfully (coll.); terribly (coll.)

Barbarismus *der;* **~, Barbarismen** (Sprachw.) barbarism

Barbe /'barbə/ *die;* **~, ~n** (Zool.) barbel

bärbeißig /-baisɪç/

A *Adj.* gruff

B *adv.* gruffly

Bar-: ~bestand *der* (Buchf.) cash in hand; (Finanzw.) cash reserve; **~betrag** *der* cash sum; **ein ~betrag von 800 Euro** a sum of 800 euros in cash

Barbier /bar'biːɐ̯/ *der;* **~s, ~e, Barbierin** *die;* **~, ~nen** (veralt., noch scherzh.) barber

barbieren *tr. V.* (veralt.) **jmdn. ~:** shave sb.; (den Bart beschneiden) trim sb.'s beard

Barbiturat /barbitu'raːt/ *das;* **~s, ~e** (Pharm.) barbiturate

Barbitur·säure /barbi'tuːɐ̯-/ *die* (Chemie) barbituric acid

bar-: ~brüstig /-brʏstɪç/ *Adj.;* bare-breasted; **~busig** /-buːzɪç/ *Adj.* topless ‹*pin-up, waitress, etc.*›

Barchent /'barçn̩t/ *der;* **~[e]s, ~e** barchent

Bar·code *der* bar code

Bar·dame *die* barmaid; (verhüll.: Prostituierte) hostess

Barde /'bardə/ *der;* **~n, ~n** bard

bären-, Bären-: ~dienst *der: in* **jmdm. einen ~dienst erweisen** do sb. a disservice; **~dreck** *der* (südd., österr.) liquorice; **~fell** *das* bearskin; **~fell·mütze** *die* bearskin; **~führer** *der,* **~führerin** *die* [1] (veralt.) bear trainer; [2] (ugs. scherzh.: Fremdenführer) guide; **für jmdn. den ~führer abgeben/spielen** show *or* shepherd sb. around; **~haut** *die: in* **auf der ~haut liegen** (ugs.) lounge *or* laze about; **~hunger** *der* (ugs.) **einen ~hunger haben/kriegen** be famished (coll.) *or* starving (coll.)/get famished (coll.) *or* ravenous (coll.); **~kräfte** *Pl.* (ugs.) the strength *sing.* of an ox; **~kräfte haben** be as strong as an ox; **~markt** *der* (Börsenw.) bear market; **~natur** *die* (ugs.) very tough constitution; **eine ~natur haben** be very tough; **~ruhe** *die* (ugs.) complete unflappability (coll.); **eine ~ruhe haben** be completely unflappable (coll.); **~stark** *Adj.* as strong as an ox *postpos.*

Barett /ba'rɛt/ *das;* **~[e]s, ~e** (eines Geistlichen) biretta; (eines Richters, Professors) cap; (Baskenmütze) beret

Bar·frau *die* ▸❶ **S. 113** barmaid

bar-, Bar-: ~fuß *indekl. Adj.* barefooted; **~fuß herumlaufen/gehen** run about/go barefoot; **~fuß·arzt** *der* barefoot doctor; **~füßer** *der;* **~~s, ~~:** discalced *or* barefoot monk; **~füßerin** *die;* **~~, ~~nen** discalced nun; **~füßig** /-fyːsɪç/ *Adj.* (geh.) barefooted

barg /bark/ *1. u. 3. Pers. Sg. Prät. v.* **bergen**

bar-, Bar-: ~geld *das* ▸❶ **S. 299** cash; **~geld·los** **A** *Adj.* ▸❶ **S. 299** cashless; **B** *adv.* without using cash; **~geschäft** *das* (Kaufmannsspr.) cash transaction; **~häuptig** /-hɔyptɪç/ *Adj.* (geh.) bareheaded; **~hocker** *der* bar stool

Bärin /'bɛːrɪn/ *die;* **~, ~nen** she-bear

Bariton /'ba(ː)ritɔn/ *der;* **~s, ~e** [1] baritone [voice] [2] (im Chor) baritones *pl.* [3] (Partie) baritone part [4] (Sänger) baritone

Bariton·schlüssel *der* (Musik) baritone clef

Barium /'baːri̯ʊm/ *das;* **~s** (Chemie) barium

Bark /bark/ *die;* **~, ~en** barque

Barkarole /barka'roːlə/ *die;* **~, ~n** (Musik) barcarole

Barkasse /bar'kasə/ *die;* **~, ~n** launch

Bar·kauf *der* (Kaufmannsspr.) cash purchase; **3% Skonto bei ~ geben** give a 3% discount on cash purchases

Barke /'barkə/ *die;* **~, ~n** [small] rowing boat

Bar·keeper /'baːɐ̯kiːpɐ/ *der;* **~s, ~** ▸❶ **S. 113** barman; barkeeper (Amer.)

Bärlapp /'bɛːɐ̯lap/ *der;* **~s, ~e** (Bot.) lycopod

Bar-: ~mädchen *das* bar hostess; **~mann** *der* ▸❶ **S. 113** barman; barkeeper (Amer.)

barmen /'barmən/ *itr. V.* (nordd.) lament (literary)

barmherzig /barm'hɛrtsɪç/ (geh.)

A *Adj.* merciful; compassionate; (mildtätig) charitable; **selig sind die Barmherzigen** (bibl.) blessed are the merciful; **~er Gott/Himmel!** merciful God/Heaven!; **die Barmherzigen Brüder/Schwestern** the hospitallers/the Sisters of Mercy; *s. auch* **Samariter**

B *adv.* mercifully; compassionately; (mildtätig) charitably

Barmherzigkeit *die;* **~** (geh.) mercy; compassion; (Mildtätigkeit) charity; **gegen jmdn. ~ üben** show compassion/charity towards sb.

Bar·mittel *Pl.* cash resources

Bar-: ~mixer *der* barman; barkeeper (Amer.); **~mixerin** *die;* **~, ~nen** barmaid

barock /ba'rɔk/

A *Adj.* [1] baroque [2] (schwülstig) baroque, florid ‹*style etc.*›; (üppig) voluptuous ‹*figure*›

B *adv.* [1] ‹*conceived, designed, etc.*› in the baroque style [2] (schwülstig) floridly

Barock *das od. der;* **~[s]** [1] (Stil) baroque; **das Zeitalter des ~:** the baroque period *or* age [2] (Zeit) baroque period *or* age

Barock-: ~dichtung *die* baroque poetry; **~engel** *der* baroque angel; **~kirche** *die* baroque church; **~musik** *die* baroque music; **~zeit** *die* baroque period *or* age

Barometer /baro'meːtɐ/ *das* barometer; **das ~ steht auf Sturm** the barometer is pointing to 'Storm'; (fig.) the atmosphere is very strained

Barometer·stand *der* barometer reading

baro·metrisch *Adj.* barometric

Baron /ba'roːn/ *der;* **~s, ~e** ▸❶ **S. 44** baron; (als Anrede) **[Herr] ~:** ≈ my lord

Baroness, *Baroneß, Baronesse /baro'nɛs(ə)/ *die;* **~, Baronessen** baroness (*baron's daughter*); (als Anrede) **[verehrte] ~:** ≈ my lady

Baronin *die;* **~, ~nen** ▸❶ **S. 44** baroness (*baron's wife*); (als Anrede) **[Frau] ~:** ≈ my lady

Bar·pianist *der,* **Bar·pianistin** *die* bar pianist

Barrakuda /bara'kuːda/ *der;* **~s, ~s** (Zool.) barracuda

Barras /'baras/ *der;* **~** (Soldatenspr.) army; **beim ~:** in the army; **zum ~ müssen** have to go into the army

Barrel /'bɛrəl/ *das;* **~s, ~s** barrel; **10 ~[s] Öl** ten barrels of oil

Barren /'barən/ *der;* **~s, ~** [1] (Gold~, Silber~ usw.) bar [2] (Sport) parallel bars *pl.* [3] (südd., österr.: Trog) trough

Barriere /ba'ri̯eːrə/ *die;* **~, ~n** (auch fig.) barrier

Barrikade /bari'kaːdə/ *die;* **~, ~n** barricade; **auf die ~n gehen** *od.* **steigen** (ugs.) go on the warpath

Barrikaden·kampf *der* fight on the barricades; **Barrikadenkämpfe** fighting *sing.* on the barricades

Barrique /ba'rik/ *die;* **~, ~s** *od. das;* **~s, ~s** barrique; (Eichenfass) oak barrel

Bar·sänger *der,* **Bar·sängerin** *die* bar singer

barsch /barʃ/

A *Adj.* curt

B *adv.* curtly; **jmdn. ~ anfahren** snap at sb.

Barsch *der;* **~[e]s, ~e** (Zool.) perch

Barschaft *die;* **~, ~en** [ready] cash; **seine ganze ~ bestand aus 20 Euro** all he had was 20 euros

Bar·scheck *der* open *or* uncrossed cheque

Barschheit *die;* **~:** curtness

Barsoi /bar'zɔy/ *der;* **~s, ~s** borzoi

Bar·sortiment *das* (Buchhandel) book wholesaler's; book distribution centre

barst /barst/ *1. u. 3. Pers. Sg. Prät. v.* **bersten**

Bart /baːɐ̯t/ *der;* **~[e]s, Bärte** /'bɛːɐ̯tə/ [1] (Kinn~) beard; (Oberlippen~, Schnurr~) moustache; **er bekommt jetzt einen ~:** his beard is starting to grow; **sich** (*Dat.*) **einen ~ wachsen** *od.* **stehen lassen** grow a beard; **einen acht Tage alten ~ haben** have a week's growth on one's chin; (fig.) **der ~ ist ab** (ugs.) that's quite enough; **wenn er das noch mal macht, dann ist der ~ aber ab** if he does it once more, that'll be it (coll.); **der Witz hat [so] einen ~** (ugs.) that joke is as old as the hills; **beim ~e des Propheten** (scherzh.) cross my heart; **etw. in seinen ~ brummen** *od.* **murmeln** mumble sth.; **jmdm. um den ~ gehen** (abwertend) butter sb. up [2] (von Ziegen, Vögeln, Getreide, Muscheln) beard; (von Katzen, Mäusen, Robben) whiskers *pl.* [3] (am Schlüssel) bit

Bart·binde *die* moustache-trainer

Bärtchen /'bɛːɐ̯tçən/ *das;* **~s, ~:** [small] beard; (Schnurr~) [thin] moustache

Barteln /'bartl̩n/ *Pl.* (Zool.) barbels

Barten·wal *der* (Zool.) whalebone whale

Bart-: ~faden *der* (Zool.) barbel; **~flaum** *der* down; **~flechte** *die* [1] (an Bäumen) *lichen of the family Usneaceae;* (Usnea) old man's beard; [2] (beim Menschen) sycosis; **~geier** *der* (Zool.) bearded vulture; **~haar** *das* beard; (von Robben) whiskers *pl.*

Bar·theke *die* bar

Barthel /'bartl̩/ *in* **wissen, wo ~ [den] Most holt** (ugs.) know every trick in the book

bärtig /'bɛːɐ̯tɪç/ *Adj.* bearded; **Bärtige** men with beards

bart-, Bart-: ~los *Adj.* beardless; **~nelke** *die* sweet william; **~stoppel** *die* piece of stubble; **~stoppeln** stubble *sing.;* **~tracht** *die* style of beard; **~träger** *der* man with a beard; **~wuchs** *der* growth of beard; **starken ~wuchs haben** have a strong growth of beard; **~wuchs bei Frauen** women's facial hair

Bar·vermögen *das* cash resources *pl.*

Baryt /ba'ryːt/ *der;* **~[e]s, ~e** (Mineral.) barytes

Bar-: ~zahlung *die* cash payment; **bei ~zahlung** for cash payment; if payment is made in cash; **~zahlungs·rabatt** *der* cash discount

Basalt /ba'zalt/ *der;* **~[e]s, ~e** basalt

Basal·temperatur /ba'zaːl-/ *die* (Med.) basal body temperature

Basar /ba'za:ɐ̯/ *der;* ~**s,** ~**e** 1 (im Orient, Wohltätigkeits~) bazaar 2 (DDR) (Warenhaus) department store; (Ladenstraße) shopping precinct *or* (Amer.) mall

Base¹ /'ba:zə/ *die;* ~, ~**n** 1 (veralt.: Cousine) cousin 2 (schweiz.: Tante) aunt

Base² *die;* ~, ~**n** (Chemie) base

Baseball /'beɪsbɔ:l/ *der;* ~**s** baseball

Baseball·kappe *die* baseball cap

Basedow·krankheit /'ba:zədo-/ *die* ▸❶ S. 439 (Med.) exophthalmic goitre; Graves' disease

Basel /'ba:zl̩/ *(das);* ~**s** ▸❶ S. 675 Basle

Basen ▸**Basis, Base**

basieren *itr. V.* **auf etw.** *(Dat.)* ~: be based on sth.

Basilika /ba'zi:lika/ *die;* ~, **Basiliken** (Kunstwiss.) basilica

Basilikum /ba'zi:likʊm/ *das;* ~**s** basil

Basilisk /bazi'lɪsk/ *der;* ~**en,** ~**en** (Fabeltier, Leguan) basilisk

Basilisken·blick *der* basilisk stare

Basis /'ba:zɪs/ *die;* ~, **Basen** 1 (Grundlage) basis; **auf einer festen ~ ruhen** have a firm basis; **etw. auf eine feste ~ stellen** put sth. on a firm foundation (fig.) 2 (Math., Archit., Fläche, Zahl, Milit.) base 3 (marx.) base; **~ und Überbau** base and superstructure 4 (Politik) grass roots *pl.*; **an der ~ arbeiten** work at grass-roots level

Basis·arbeit *die* (Politik) work at grass-roots level

basisch (Chemie)
A *Adj.* basic
B *adv.* ‹*react*› as a base

Basis-: ~**demokratie** *die* (Politik) grass-roots democracy; ~**demokratisch** A *Adj.* based on grass-roots democracy *postpos.*; **~demokratische Wende** changeover to grass-roots democracy; **~demokratische Mitbestimmung** grass-roots participation [in decision-making]; B *adv.* democratically at grass-roots level; ~**gruppe** *die* (Politik) action group (*usually left-wing*); ~**lager** *das* base camp; ~**wissen** *das* basic knowledge; **jmdm. das nötige ~wissen in etw.** *(Dat.)* **vermitteln** give sb. a basic grounding in sth.

Baske /'baskə/ *der;* ~**n,** ~**n** ▸❶ S. 520 Basque

Baskenland *das;* ~**[e]s** Basque region

Baskenmütze *die* beret

Basket·ball /'ba(:)skətbal/ *der* basketball

Baskin *die;* ~, ~**nen** Basque

baskisch *Adj.* ▸❶ S. 520, ▸❶ S. 670 Basque

Basler /'ba:zlɐ/
A *indekl. Adj.* of Basle *postpos.*
B *der;* ~**s,** ~: native of Basle; (Einwohner) inhabitant of Basle; *s. auch* **Kölner**

Baslerin *die;* ~, ~**nen** ▸**Basler B**

Bas·relief /'ba-/ *das* (Kunstwiss.) bas-relief

bass, *baß /bas/ *Adv.* **in ~ erstaunt sein** (veralt.) be quite taken aback

Bass, *Baß *der;* **Basses, Bässe** /'bɛsə/ (Musik) 1 (Stimmlage) bass [voice] 2 (im Chor) basses *pl.*; bass section 3 (Partie) bass part 4 (Sänger) bass 5 (Instrument) double bass; bass (coll.) 6 (Lautsprecher) bass speaker; woofer

Bass·bariton, *Baß·bariton *der* bass-baritone

Basset /'bɛsɪt/ *der;* ~**s,** ~**s** basset [hound]

Bassett·horn /ba'sɛt-/ *das* basset horn

Bass·geige, *Baß·geige *die* (volkst.) double bass

Bassin /ba'sɛ̃:/ *das;* ~**s,** ~**s** (Schwimm~) pool; (im Garten) pond

Bassist *der;* ~**en,** ~**en** (Musik) 1 (Sänger) bass 2 (Instrumentalist) double bass player; bassist; (in einer Rockband) bass guitarist

Bassistin *die;* ~, ~**nen** ▸**Bassist 2**

Bass-, *Baß-: ~**klarinette** *die* bass clarinet; ~**lautsprecher** *der* bass loudspeaker; woofer; ~**saite** *die* bass string; ~**schlüssel** *der* (Musik) bass clef; ~**stimme** *die* bass voice

Bast /bast/ *der;* ~**[e]s,** ~**e** 1 bast; (Raffia~) raffia 2 (Jägerspr.) velvet

basta /'basta/ *Interj.* (ugs.) that's enough; **und damit ~!** and that's that

Bastard /'bastart/ *der;* ~**s,** ~**e** 1 (veralt.: uneheliches Kind) bastard 2 (Biol.) hybrid 3 (salopp) bastard

Bastard·schrift *die* (Druckw.) bastard type

Bastel-: ~**arbeit** *die* 1 (Gegenstand) piece of handicraft work; ~**arbeiten** handicraft work *sing.*; 2 handicraft work; ~**ecke** *die* (in einer Zeitung, Zeitschrift) handicraft corner *or* column

Bastelei *die;* ~, ~**en** 1 (Gegenstand) piece of handicraft work; ~**en** handicraft work *sing.* 2 (ugs.: das Basteln) handicraft work

basteln /'bastl̩n/
A *tr. V.* make; make, build ‹*model, device*›
B *itr. V.* (Bastelarbeiten herstellen) make things [with one's hands]; do handicraft work; **an etw.** *(Dat.)* ~: be working on sth.; (etw. herstellen) be making sth.; (etw. laienhaft bearbeiten) tinker with sth.; **sein Hobby ist Basteln** his hobby is making things [with his hands]; his hobby is handicraft work

Bast·faser *die* bast fibre

Bastille /bas'ti:jə/ *die;* ~: Bastille

Bastion /bas'ti̯o:n/ *die;* ~, ~**en** bastion

Bastler /'bastlɐ/ *der;* ~**s,** ~, **Bastlerin** *die;* ~, ~**nen** handicraft enthusiast; **ein guter/leidenschaftlicher ~ sein** be good *or* clever with one's hands/love making [and repairing] things

Bastonade /basto'na:də/ *die;* ~, ~**n** bastinado

Bast·rock *der* bast skirt; (aus Raffia) raffia skirt

bat /ba:t/ *1. u. 3. Pers. Sg. Prät. v.* **bitten**

BAT *Abk.* = **Bundesangestelltentarif**

Bataille /ba'taljə/ *die;* ~, ~**n** (veralt.) battle

Bataillon /batal'jo:n/ *das;* ~**s,** ~**e** (Milit.) battalion

Bataillons-: ~**führer** *der,* ~**kommandeur** *der* (Milit.) battalion commander

Bathy·sphäre /baty-/ *die* (Meereskunde) abyssal zone

Batik /'ba:tɪk/ *der;* ~**s,** ~**en** *od. die;* ~, ~**en** batik

batiken
A *tr. V.* **etw. ~:** decorate sth. with batik work
B *itr. V.* do batik work

Batist /ba'tɪst/ *der;* ~**[e]s,** ~**e** batiste

batisten *Adj.* batiste

Batterie /batə'ri:/ *die;* ~, ~**n** 1 (Milit., Elektrot., Technik) battery 2 (ugs.: große Anzahl) battery; (von Flaschen) rows *pl.*

batterie-, Batterie-: ~**betrieb** *der* battery operation; **auf ~betrieb laufen** run on batteries; ~**betrieben** *Adj.* battery-operated; ~**gerät** *das* battery[-operated] device; (Radio) battery set; ~**huhn** *das* battery chicken; (Henne) battery hen

Batzen /'batsn̩/ *der;* ~**s,** ~ 1 (ugs.: Klumpen) lump 2 (ugs.: Menge) pile (coll.); **ein [schöner** *od.* **ganzer] ~ Geld** a pile (coll.) [of money] 3 (MA.: Münze) batz

-bau *der;* ~**s** (Landw.) -growing

Bau¹ /bau̯/ *der;* ~**[e]s,** ~**ten** 1 (Errichtung) building; construction; **im ~ sein, sich im ~ befinden** be under construction; **mit dem ~ [von etw.] beginnen** start construction [of sth.]; start building [sth.] 2 (Gebäude) building 3 (Baustelle) building site; **auf dem ~ arbeiten** (Bauarbeiter sein) be in the building trade; **auf den** *od.* **zum ~ gehen** (Bauarbeiter werden) go into the building trade; **vom ~ sein** (fig. ugs.) be an expert 4 (Struktur) structure 5 (Körperbau) build; **von schmalem ~ sein** be slenderly built; have a slender physique 6 (Landw.: Anbau) growing

Bau² /bau̯/ *der;* ~**[e]s,** ~**e** 1 (Höhle) (Kaninchen~) burrow; hole; (Fuchs~) earth; (Wolfs~) lair; (Dachs~) sett; earth; (Biber~) lodge 2 (ugs.: Wohnung) **nicht aus dem ~ gehen/kommen** not stick *or* put one's nose outside the door (coll.) 3 (Soldatenspr.: Strafe) glasshouse (Mil. sl.); **er bekam sieben Tage ~:** he got seven days in the glasshouse 4 (Bergmannsspr.: Stollen) workings *pl.*

Bau-: ~**abschnitt** *der* phase *or* stage of building; ~**amt** *das* department of planning and building inspection; ~**arbeiten** *Pl.* building *or* construction work *sing.*; (Straßenarbeiten) roadworks; ~**arbeiter** *der,* ~**arbeiterin** *die* ▸❶ S. 113 building *or* construction worker; ~**art** *die* type of construction; **ein Haus in italienischer ~art** a house built in the Italian style; ~**aufsicht** *die* supervision of building *or* construction [work]; ~**beginn** *der* start of building *or* construction; ~**boom** *der* building boom; ~**bude** *die* site hut; ~**büro** *das* site office

Bauch /bau̯x/ *der;* ~**[e]s, Bäuche** /'bɔy̯çə/ 1 ▸❶ S. 435 stomach; belly; abdomen (Anat.); tummy (coll.); (fig.: von Schiffen, Flugzeugen) belly; **mir tut der ~ weh** I have [a] stomach ache *or* (coll.) tummy ache; **sich** *(Dat.)* **den ~ voll schlagen** (ugs.) stuff oneself (coll.); **jmdm. den ~ aufschneiden** (salopp) cut sb. open; **ein Kind im ~ haben** (ugs.) have a baby on the way; **er hat ihr einen dicken ~ gemacht** (salopp) he put her in the club (sl.); **ein voller ~ studiert nicht gern** (Spr.) you can't work hard on a full stomach; **ich habe nichts im ~** (ugs.) I haven't had anything to eat; **sich** *(Dat.)* **[vor Lachen] den ~ halten** (ugs.) split one's sides [with laughing]; (fig.) **auf den ~ fallen** (ugs.) come a cropper (sl.) **(mit** with); **vor jmdm. auf dem ~ liegen** *od.* **kriechen** (ugs. abwertend) crawl *or* grovel to sb.; **aus dem hohlen ~** (salopp) off the top of one's head (sl.) 2 (Wölbung) paunch; corporation (coll.); (fig.: eines Kruges usw.) belly 3 (Kochk.) (beim Schwein) belly; (beim Kalb) flank

Bauch-: ~**an·satz** *der* beginnings *pl.* of a paunch; ~**atmung** *die* abdominal respiration; ~**binde** *die* 1 woollen body belt; 2 (ugs.: bei Zigarren, Büchern) band; ~**decke** *die* ▸❶ S. 435 (Med.) abdominal wall; ~**fell** *das* ▸❶ S. 435 (Anat.) peritoneum; ~**fleisch** *das* (Kochk.) (vom Schwein) belly pork; (vom Rind) flank; ~**flosse** *die* (Zool.) ventral fin; ~**gegend** *die* stomach region; region of the stomach; ~**grimmen** *das* (veralt.) stomach ache *or* pains *pl.*; ~**höhle** *die* (Anat.) ▸❶ S. 435 abdominal cavity; ~**höhlen·schwangerschaft** *die* (Med.) abdominal pregnancy

bauchig *Adj.* bulbous

Bauch-: ~**klatscher** /-klatʃɐ/ *der;* ~~**s,** ~~ (ugs.) bellyflop (coll.); ~**kneifen** *das;* ~~**s** stomach ache *or* pains *pl.*; ~**laden** *der; Pl.* ~**läden** vendor's tray; ~**lage** *die* prone position; **in der ~lage schlafen** sleep on one's front; ~**landung** *die* (ugs.) belly landing

Bäuchlein /'bɔy̯çlai̯n/ *das;* ~**s,** ~: stomach; tummy (coll.)

bäuchlings /'bɔy̯çlɪŋs/ *Adv.* on one's stomach

bauch-, Bauch-: ~**muskel** *der* ▸❶ S. 435 stomach muscle; ~**nabel** *der* ▸❶ S. 435 (ugs.) belly button (coll.); tummy button (coll.); ~**nabel·gepierct** /-gəpi:ɐ̯st/ *Adj.* with pierced belly button(s) *postpos., not pred.*; ~**nabel·piercing** *das* belly button piercing; (Schmuck) belly button stud; navel stud; ~**pinseln** *tr. V.:* ▸**gebauchpinselt**; ~**reden** *itr. V.; nur Inf. gebr.* ventriloquize; ~**redner** *der,* ~**rednerin** *die* ventriloquist; ~**schmerz** *der* stomach pain; ~**schmerzen** stomach ache *sing.*; stomach pains; ~**schuss, *~schuß** *der* shot in the stomach; (Verwundung) stomach wound; ~**speck** *der* 1 (Kochk.) belly of pork; 2 (ugs.: Fettansatz) spare tyre (coll.); ~**speichel·drüse** *die* ▸❶ S. 435 pancreas; ~**tanz** *der* belly dance; ~**tanzen** *itr. V.; nur Inf. gebr.* belly dance; ~**tänzerin** *die* belly dancer

Bauchung *die;* ~, ~**en** bulge

Bauch-: ~**weh** *das* (ugs.) tummy ache (coll.); stomach ache; ~**welle** *die* (Turnen) hip-circle

Baude /'bau̯də/ *die;* ~, ~**n** (ostmd.) mountain hut; (Berggasthof) mountain inn

Bau-: ~**denkmal** *das* architectural monument; ~**element** *das* component

b

bauen
A *tr. V.* [1] build, construct ‹*house, road, bridge, etc.*›; build ‹*nest, lair*›; make ‹*burrow*›; **sich** (*Dat.*) **ein Haus ~:** have a house built; **sich** (*Dat.*) **sein Haus selbst ~:** build one's own house; *s. auch* **Bett 1** [2] (entwickeln, herstellen) build ‹*model, vehicle, aircraft, organ*›; make ‹*violin, piano*›; **sich** (*Dat.*) **einen Anzug ~ lassen** (ugs. scherzh.) have a suit made; **einen Satz ~** (Sprachw.) construct a sentence [3] (ugs.) **das Abitur/seinen Doktor ~:** do one's Abitur/Ph.D. [4] (ugs.: verursachen) **einen Unfall ~:** have an accident [5] (Landw.: an~) grow [6] (veralt.: bestellen) cultivate
B *itr. V.* [1] build; **wir wollen ~:** we want to build a house; (~ lassen) we want to have a house built; **zurzeit wird nicht viel gebaut** there's not much building going on at the moment; **solide/großzügig ~:** build solidly/on a lavish scale; **modern ~:** build in a modern style; **hoch ~:** put up high-rise buildings; **an etw.** (*Dat.*) **~:** do building work on sth. [2] (vertrauen) **auf jmdn./etw. ~:** rely on sb./sth.

-bauer *der;* **-~s, -~** (Bauw.) -constructor

Bauer[1] /ˈbauɐ/ *der;* **~n, ~n** [1] (Landwirt) farmer; (als Vertreter einer ärmlichen Klasse) peasant; (ugs. abwertend) peasant; **die dümmsten ~n haben die dicksten Kartoffeln** (abwertend) fortune favours fools (prov.); **was der ~ nicht kennt, das frisst er nicht** (abwertend) some people won't eat anything they've never seen before [2] (beim Schach) pawn [3] (in Kartenspielen) jack [4] (beim Kegeln) corner; copper

Bauer[2] *das od. der;* **~s, ~:** [bird]cage

Bäuerchen /ˈbɔyɐçən/ *das;* **~s, ~** [1] **[ein] ~ machen** (Kinderspr.) burp [2] ▸**Bäuerlein**

Bäuerin /ˈbɔyərɪn/ *die;* **~, ~nen** (Landwirtin) [lady] farmer; (Frau eines Landwirts) farmer's wife; (als Vertreterin einer ärmlichen Klasse) peasant [woman]

Bäuerlein /ˈbɔyɐlain/ *das;* **~s, ~:** [simple] peasant

bäuerlich /ˈbɔyɐlɪç/
A *Adj.* (landwirtschaftlich) farming *attrib.*; (ländlich) rural; **kleine ~e Betriebe** small farms
B *adv.* rurally

Bauern-: **~aufstand** *der* peasants' revolt; **~brot** *das* ▸**Landbrot**; **~bub** *der* (südd., österr., schweiz.) ▸**~junge**; **~bursche** *der* ▸**~junge**; **~dorf** *das* farming village; **~fang** *der: in* **auf ~fang ausgehen** (ugs. abwertend) set out to con people out of their money (coll.); **~fänger** *der* (ugs. abwertend) con man (coll.); con artist (coll.); **~fängerei** *die;* **~~** (ugs. abwertend) con tricks *pl.* (coll.); **das ist ~fängerei** it's a con (coll.); **~fängerin** *die* (ugs. abwertend) con artist (coll.); **~frühstück** *das: fried potatoes mixed with scrambled egg and bacon;* **~gut** *das* farm; **~haus** *das* farmhouse; **~hochzeit** *die* country wedding; **~hof** *der* farm; **~junge** *der* country lad; (~sohn) farmer's son; **~kalender** *der* farming calendar; **~krieg** *der* (hist.) peasants' revolt; **der Große ~krieg, die ~kriege** the Peasant[s'] War; **~legen** *das;* **~~s** driving out small farmers; **~lümmel** *der* (abwertend) loutish yokel; **~mädchen** *das* country girl; (~tochter) farmer's daughter; **~möbel** *das* piece of rustic-style furniture; **teure ~möbel** expensive rustic-style furniture *sing.*; **~opfer** *das* (Schach) sacrifice of a pawn; **~partei** *die* [1] Agrarian Party; [2] (DDR) Peasants' Party; **~regel** *die* country saying

Bauernschaft *die;* **~:** farmers *pl.*; farming community; (als ärmliche Klasse) peasantry; peasants *pl.*

bauern-, Bauern-: **~schlau** **A** *Adj.* cunning; sly; crafty; **B** *adv.* cunningly; slyly; craftily; **~schläue** *die* peasant cunning *or* slyness *or* craftiness; **~sohn** *der* farmer's son; **~stand** *der* farming community; **~stube** *die* room furnished in rustic style; **~tochter** *die* farmer's daughter; **~tölpel** *der* (abwertend) yokel; country bumpkin

Bauerntum *das;* **~s** (Bauernstand) farming community; (bäuerliches Wesen) character of the farming community

Bauern·verband *der* farmers' union

Bauers-: **~frau** *die* farmer's wife; (Landwirtin) [lady] farmer; (Frau vom Lande) countrywoman; **~leute** *Pl.* [1] (veralt.) country folk; [2] (Bauer und Bäuerin) **die [beiden] ~leute** the farmer and his wife; **~mann** *der; Pl.* **~leute** (veralt.) countryman

bau-, Bau-: **~erwartungs·land** *das* land shortly to be made available for building; **~fach** *das* building trade; **~fällig** *Adj.* ramshackle; badly dilapidated; unsafe ‹*roof, ceiling*›; **~fälligkeit** *die* bad state of dilapidation; badly dilapidated state; **~firma** *die* building *or* construction firm; **~flucht** *die,* **~fluchtlinie** *die* building line; **~gelände** *das* (~stelle) building site; (~land) building land; **~genehmigung** *die* planning permission and building regulations clearance; **~genossenschaft** *die: co-operative housing association which builds and maintains houses or flats for its members;* **~gerüst** *das* scaffolding; **~gewerbe** *das* building trade; **~gleich** *Adj.* of identical construction *postpos.*; identical in construction *pred.* (**mit** to); **~grube** *die* excavation; **~handwerk** *das* building trade; **~handwerker** *der,* **~handwerkerin** *die* skilled building worker; building craftsman/craftswoman; **~helfer** *der,* **~helferin** *die* builder's labourer; **~herr** *der,* **~herrin** *die* client (*for whom a house etc. is being built*); **„~herr: Stadt Mannheim"** 'under construction for the city of Mannheim'; **er ist ~herr** he is having a house built; **~holz** *das* building timber; **~hütte** *die* [1] site hut; [2] (MA.) stonemasons' lodge; **~ingenieur** *der,* **~ingenieurin** *die* ▸❶ **S. 113** building engineer; **~jahr** *das* year of construction; (bei Autos) year of manufacture; **für Modelle dieses ~jahres** for models manufactured in that year; **das ~jahr des Hauses** the year in which the house was built; **welches ~jahr ist dein Wagen?** what year is your car?; **mein Auto ist ~jahr 95** my car is a 1995 model; **~kasten** *der* construction set *or* kit; (mit Holzklötzen) box of bricks; **~kasten·system** *das* unit construction system; **~klotz** *der; Pl. ugs. auch* **~klötzer** building brick; **~klötze[r] staunen** (salopp) be staggered (coll.) *or* flabbergasted; **~klötzchen** *das* building brick; **~kolonne** *die* construction gang; **~kosten** *Pl.* building *or* construction costs; **~kosten·zuschuss**, *~kosten·zuschuß *der: contribution to cost of building, rebuilding, or renovation paid by tenant to landlord;* **~kran** *der* construction crane; **~kunst** *die* (geh.) architecture; **~land** *das* building land; **~leiter** *der,* **~leiterin** *die* clerk of the works; **~leitung** *die* engineers supervising the building *or* construction work; (~büro) site office; **~leute** *Pl.* building workers

> **Bauhaus**
>
> A school of architecture and the applied arts founded in 1919 in Weimar and later housed at Dessau. Under the leadership of Walter Gropius (1883-1969) and Ludwig Mies van der Rohe (1886-1969) it became the centre of modern design in the 1920s and played a key role in establishing a relationship between architecture, technology, and functionality. The *Bauhaus* was closed down by the Nazis in 1933.

baulich
A *Adj.*; structural ‹*alteration, condition, defect, etc.*›; architectural ‹*character, value*›; **~e Anlagen** buildings
B *adv.* **ein Gebäude ~ verbessern/verändern** carry out structural improvements/alterations to a building; **den Stadtkern ~ neu gestalten** redevelop the town centre

Baulichkeit *die;* **~, ~en** building

Bau-: **~los** *das* section; **~löwe** *der* (ugs. abwertend) building speculator; **~lücke** *die* vacant lot

Baum /baum/ *der;* **~[e]s, Bäume** /ˈbɔymə/ [1] tree; **auf einen ~ klettern** climb up [into] a tree; **er ist stark wie ein ~:** he's as strong as an ox; (fig.) **es ist dafür gesorgt, dass die Bäume nicht in den Himmel wachsen** nobody has everything his own way all of the time; **alte Bäume soll man nicht verpflanzen** old people are happiest left in their familiar surroundings; **Bäume ausreißen können** (ugs.) be *or* feel ready to tackle anything; **der ~ der Erkenntnis** (bibl.) the Tree of Knowledge; **vom ~ der Erkenntnis essen** learn by experience; find out for oneself; **zwischen ~ und Borke sitzen** *od.* **stecken** be on the horns of a dilemma; *s. auch* **Wald** [2] (ugs.: Weihnachtsbaum) [Christmas] tree; **den ~ anzünden** light the candles on the tree [3] (Seemannsspr.) boom

Baum·arbeiten *Pl.* tree work *sing.*

Bau·markt *der* [1] building *or* construction market [2] (Kaufhaus) DIY hypermarket

baum·arm *Adj.* very thinly wooded; **relativ ~:** relatively thinly wooded

Bau-: **~maschine** *die* piece of construction plant *or* machinery; **~maschinen** construction plant *sing. or* machinery; **~maßnahme** *die* (Amtsspr.) building project; **~material** *das* building material; (~materialien) building materials *pl.*

Baum-: **~bestand** *der* tree stock; **~bewohner** *der* tree-dweller; arboreal animal; **~blüte** *die* [1] blossoming of the trees; [2] (Zeitraum) **zur ~blüte/während der ~blüte** when/while the trees are in blossom

Bäumchen /ˈbɔymçən/ *das;* **~s, ~:** small tree; (junger Baum) sapling; young tree; **~, wechsle dich** (Kinderspiel) puss in the corner; (ugs. scherzh.: Partnerwechsel) partner-swapping

Bau·meister *der,* **Bau·meisterin** *die* [1] (hist.) [architect and] master builder [2] (Bautechniker, Bauhandwerker) master builder; (Bauunternehmer) building contractor (*with professional qualifications*)

baumeln /ˈbaumḷn/ *itr. V.* [1] (ugs.) dangle (**an** + *Dat.* from); **die Beine ~ lassen** dangle one's legs [2] (derb: gehängt werden) swing (sl.)

bäumen /ˈbɔymən/ *refl. V.:* ▸**aufbäumen**

baum-, Baum-: **~farn** *der* tree fern; **~frevel** *der* unlawful and malicious damaging of trees; **~grenze** *die* ▸❶ **S. 374** treeline; timberline; **~gruppe** *die* clump of trees; **~krone** *die* treetop; crown [of the/a tree]; **~kuchen** *der: tall cylindrical cake, hollow in the centre;* **~lang** *Adj.* (ugs.) tremendously tall (coll.); **~läufer** *der* (Zool.) treecreeper; **~los** *Adj.* treeless; **~reich** *Adj.* wooded; **~riese** *der* (geh.) giant tree; **~rinde** *die* bark [of trees]; **~schere** *die* tree pruner; **~schule** *die* tree nursery; **~stamm** *der* tree trunk; **~stark** *Adj.* as strong as an ox *postpos.*; **~sterben** *das;* **~~s, ~~:** dying-off of trees; **~strunk** *der* dead tree stump; **~stumpf** *der* tree stump; **~wachs** *das* grafting wax

Baum·wolle *die* cotton

baum·wollen *Adj.* cotton

Baumwoll-: **~ernte** *die* cotton harvest; **~pflücker** *der,* **~pflückerin** *die* cotton picker; **~plantage** *die* cotton plantation; **~spinnerei** *die* [1] cotton spinning; [2] (Betrieb) cotton mill

Baum·wurzel *die* tree root

bau-, Bau-: **~ordnung** *die* building regulations *pl.*; **~plan** *der* (Entwurf, Zeichnung) building plans *pl.*; (für eine Maschine) designs *pl.*; (fig.) structure; **~planung** *die* building design; **~platz** *der* site for building *or* construction; **~polizei** *die* building inspectorate; **~polizeilich** **A** *Adj.* building ‹*regulations*›; **eine ~polizeiliche Kontrolle** a visit from the building inspector/inspectors; **B** *adv.* ‹*detected, approved, etc.*› by the building inspectorate; **~preis** *der* building costs *pl.*; **~rat** *der* chief architect; **~recht** *das* planning laws and building regulations *pl.*; **~reif** *Adj.* **ein ~reifes Grundstück** a cleared building plot; **~reihe** *die* series; (bei Lokomotiven) class

Bäurin ▸**Bäuerin**

bäurisch /ˈbɔyrɪʃ/ (abwertend)
A *Adj.* boorish; oafish
B *adv.* boorishly; oafishly

Bau-: **~ruine** *die* (ugs.) building abandoned only half-finished; **~satz** *der* kit

Bausch /bauʃ/ *der;* **~[e]s, ~e** *od.* **Bäusche** /ˈbɔyʃə/ [1] (am Kleid, Ärmel) puff; **einen ~**

machen (ugs.) ‹dress› bulge [2] **ein ~ Watte** a wad of cotton wool [3] **etw. in ~ und Bogen verwerfen/verdammen** reject/condemn sth. wholesale

Bau·schaffende /-ʃafn̩də/ *der/die; adj. Dekl.* (DDR) building *or* construction worker

Bäuschchen /ˈbɔyʃçən/ *das;* **~s, ~:** [small] wad

bauschen

A *tr. V.* billow, fill ‹*sail, curtains, etc.*›; **gebauschte Ärmel** puffed *or* puff sleeves

B *refl. V.* ‹*dress, sleeve*› puff out; (ungewollt) bunch up; become bunched up; (im Wind) ‹*curtain, flag, etc.*› billow [out]

bauschig

A *Adj.* puffed ‹*dress*›; baggy ‹*trousers*›

B *adv.* **~ fallen** ‹*skirt*› be full

Bau-: ~schlosser *der,* **~schlosserin** *die* fitter [in the building trade]; **~schutt** *der* building rubble; **~soldat** *der,* **~soldatin** *die* (DDR): *conscript allowed to do non-military (esp. building) work*

bau·sparen *itr. V.; nur Inf. gebr.* save with a building society

> **Bausparen**
>
> German building societies expect people to have saved up a sizeable sum towards the purchase of a house before they will give them a mortgage. For this reason, many Germans have a *Bausparvertrag* (a tax-efficient savings contract for an agreed sum) with a building society, even if they are not planning to buy their Eigenheim for some time.

Bau·sparer *der,* **Bau·sparerin** *die* building-society investor

Bauspar-: ~kasse *die* ≈ building society; **~vertrag** *der* savings contract with a building society (*to save a specified sum which earns interest and is later used towards the purchase of a house*)

Bau-: ~stahl *der* structural steel; **~stein** *der* [1] building stone; [2] (Bestandteil) element; component; (Elektronik, DV) module; **die ~steine der Materie** the constituents of matter; [3] (~klötzchen) building brick; **~stelle** *die* building site; (beim Straßenbau) roadworks *pl.*; (bei der Eisenbahn) site of engineering works; **„Betreten der ~stelle verboten"** 'no entry *or* access for unauthorized persons'; **die Strecke war wegen einer ~stelle gesperrt** the road was closed because of roadworks/the line was closed because of engineering works; **~stil** *der* architectural style; **im italienischen ~stil** in the Italian style; **~stoff** *der* [1] building material; [2] (Biol.) nutrient; **~stopp** *der* suspension of building work (**für** on); **~substanz** *die* fabric [of the building/buildings]; (Bestand an Gebäuden) building stock; **~summe** *die* building costs *pl.*; **~tätigkeit** *die* building activity; **~teil** *das* component

Bauten *Pl.:* ▸ **Bau**

Bau-: ~tischler *der,* **~tischlerin** *die* [building] joiner; **~unternehmen** *das* building firm; **~unternehmer** *der,* **~unternehmerin** *die* ▸❶ **S. 113** building contractor; builder; **~vorhaben** *das* building project; **~weise** *die* [1] method of building *or* construction; [2] (~art) type of construction; **in geschlossener/offener ~weise errichtet** built as terrace houses/detached houses; **~werk** *das* building; (Brücke, Staudamm) structure; **~wirtschaft** *die* building *or* construction industry

Bauxit /bauˈksiːt/ *der;* **~s, ~e** bauxite

bauz /bau̯ts/ *Interj.* flop

Bau-: ~zaun *der* site fence; **~zeichnung** *die* construction drawing; **~zeit** *die* construction time

Bayer /ˈbai̯ɐ/ *der;* **~n, ~n, Bayerin** *die;* **~, ~nen** ▸❶ **S. 520** Bavarian

bay[e]risch ▸❶ **S. 520,** ▸❶ **S. 670**

A *Adj.* Bavarian; **der Bayerische Wald** the Bayerischer Wald; the Bavarian Forest

B *adv.* **~ sprechen** speak Bavarian dialect; (mit bayerischem Akzent) speak with a Bavarian accent; **~ gekleidet** dressed in Bavarian costume; *s. auch* **deutsch, badisch**

Bayern /ˈbai̯ɐn/ *(das);* **~s** Bavaria

> **Bayreuth**
>
> The Franconian city of Bayreuth in Bavaria is a magnet for opera fans. The German composer Richard Wagner (1813-83) lived there from 1872, and since 1876 the Richard Wagner Festival has been staged annually in the *Festspielhaus*. The Bayreuth festival theatre was built between 1872 and 1876 with funding by the Bavarian King Ludwig II, who was one of Wagner's greatest admirers.

Bazi /ˈbaːt͡si/ *der;* **~s, ~s** (südd., österr. abwertend) [1] (Faulpelz) lazy good-for-nothing [2] (Wichtigtuer) big-head (coll.)

Bazille /baˈt͡sɪlə/ *die;* **~, ~n** (ugs.) ▸ **Bazillus**

Bazillen·träger *der,* **Bazillen·trägerin** *die* carrier

Bazillus /baˈt͡sɪlʊs/ *der;* **~, Bazillen** [1] bacillus [2] (fig.) cancer; **der ~ der Korruption** the cancer of corruption

Bazooka /baˈzuːka/ *die;* **~, ~s** bazooka

Bd. *Abk.* **= Band** Vol.

Bde. *Abk.* **= Bände** Vols.

BDM *Abk.* **= Bund Deutscher Mädel** (ns.) *National Socialist organization for girls*

B-Dur /ˈbeː-/ *das* (Musik) B flat major; *s. auch* **A-Dur**

BE *Abk.* **= Broteinheit**

beabsichtigen /bəˈlapzɪçtɪgn̩/ *tr. V.* intend; **~, etw. zu tun** intend *or* mean to do sth.; **das war nicht beabsichtigt** it wasn't intentional *or* deliberate; **was hast du mit dieser Frage beabsichtigt?** what did you mean by your question?; **die beabsichtigte Wirkung** the intended *or* desired effect

beachten *tr. V.* [1] observe, follow ‹*rule, regulations*›; follow ‹*instruction*›; heed, follow ‹*advice*›; obey ‹*traffic signs*›; observe ‹*formalities*› [2] (berücksichtigen) **etw. ~:** take account of sth.; (Aufmerksamkeit schenken) pay attention to *or* take notice of sth.; **es ist zu ~, dass …** please note that … [3] (beobachten) notice; **jmdn. nicht ~:** ignore sb.

beachtens·wert *Adj.* remarkable; (erwähnenswert) noteworthy

beachtlich

A *Adj.* [1] (erheblich) considerable; marked, considerable ‹*improvement, increase, change, etc.*›; notable, considerable ‹*success*›; **er verdient jetzt ~e zehntausend Euro im Monat** he is now earning as much as ten thousand euros a month [2] (anerkennenswert) important ‹*job, post*›; **Beachtliches leisten** make one's mark [3] (Amtsspr.: zu berücksichtigen) **~ sein** have to be given due consideration

B *adv.* considerably; ‹*improve, increase, change*› markedly, considerably

Beachtung *die* [1] (Einhaltung) ▸ **beachten 1:** observance; following; heeding; obeying; **bei ~ der Regeln** if one observes *or* follows the rules [2] (Berücksichtigung) consideration; **unter ~ aller Umstände** taking all the circumstances into account [3] (Aufmerksamkeit) attention; **~/keinerlei ~ finden** receive attention/be ignored completely; **jmdm./einer Sache ~/keine ~ schenken** pay attention/no attention to sb./sth.; take notice/no notice of sb./sth.

Beach·volleyball /ˈbiːtʃ-/ *der* beach volleyball

beackern *tr. V.* [1] (ugs.: bearbeiten) go over ‹*subject*›; plough through ‹*literature, regulations*› [2] (ugs.: überreden) **jmdn. ~:** work on sb. (coll.) [3] (bebauen) cultivate

beamen /ˈbiːmən/ *tr. V.* [1] beam [2] (ausstrahlen) send ‹*message, information*›

Beamer /ˈbiːmɐ/ *der;* **~s, ~** digital projector

Beamte /bəˈlamtə/ *der; adj. Dekl.* ▸❶ **S. 113** official; (Staats~) [permanent] civil servant; (Kommunal~) [established] local government officer *or* official; (Polizei~) [police] officer; (Zoll~) [customs] officer *or* official; **ein typischer ~r** a typical civil servant; **ein kleiner ~r** (meist abwertend) a minor *or* (derog.) petty official

> **Beamte**
>
> This term covers civil servants and other officials, but also occupations like teachers and lecturers. *Beamte* are legally obliged to support the democratic system in Germany and are not allowed to go on strike. In return, they enjoy many privileges, such as total job security, private health insurance, and exemption from social security contributions.

Beamten-: ~apparat *der* bureaucracy; **~beleidigung** *die* insulting a public servant; **~bestechung** *die* bribery of a public servant/public servants; **~deutsch** *das* (abwertend) officialese (derog.); **~laufbahn** *die* career in the civil service *or* as a civil servant; **die ~laufbahn einschlagen** join *or* enter the civil service; become a civil servant; **~recht** *das* administrative law; **~seele** *die* (abwertend) petty official *or* bureaucrat; **~silo** *der* (ugs. scherzh.) huge impersonal office block full of bureaucrats

Beamtentum *das;* **~s** [1] civil service mentality [2] (Beamtenschaft) civil servants *pl.*; civil service; (in den Gemeinden) local government officers *or* officials *pl.*

Beamten·verhältnis *das:* **im ~ stehen** be a [permanent] civil servant; **ins ~ übernommen werden** attain permanent status

beamtet *Adj.* **~ sein** have permanent civil servant status; **ein ~er Lehrer** a teacher with permanent civil servant status

Beamtete *der/die; adj. Dekl.* (Amtsspr.) ▸ **Beamte, Beamtin**

Beamtin *die;* **~, ~nen** ▸❶ **S. 113** ▸ **Beamte;** (Polizei~) [woman] police officer

beängstigen *tr. V.* (veralt.) alarm

beängstigend

A *Adj.* worrying ‹*feeling*›; unsettling ‹*sign*›; eerie ‹*silence*›; alarming ‹*speed*›; **ein ~es Gedränge** a frightening crush of people; **sein Zustand ist ~:** his condition is giving cause for anxiety

B *adv.* alarmingly; **~ schnell** at an alarming speed

beanspruchen *tr. V.* [1] claim; **etw. ~ können** be entitled to expect sth. [2] (ausnutzen) make use of ‹*person, equipment*›; take advantage of ‹*hospitality, offer of help, services*›; **jmds. Geduld übermäßig ~:** try *or* strain sb.'s patience [3] (abverlangen) demand ‹*energy, attention, stamina*›; **das beansprucht ihn sehr/wenig** that demands a lot/doesn't demand much of him; **sein Beruf beansprucht ihn sehr/völlig** his job is very demanding/takes up all his time and energy [4] (benötigen) take up ‹*time, space, etc.*›

Beanspruchung *die;* **~, ~en** [1] demands *pl.* (*Gen.* on) [2] (Inanspruchnahme) **die ~ durch den Beruf** the demands of his/her job; **~en** (*Dat.*) **ausgesetzt werden** ‹*material, machine*› be subjected to stresses *or* strains

beanstanden, (österr. auch) **beanständen** *tr. V.* object to; take exception to; (sich beklagen über) complain about; **an der Arbeit ist nichts/allerlei zu ~:** there is nothing/there are all sorts of things wrong with the work; **die Waren wurden beanstandet** there were complaints about the goods; **~, dass …** complain that …

Beanstandung *die;* **~, ~en** complaint; **Anlass zu ~en geben** give cause for complaint *sing.*

beantragen *tr. V.* [1] apply for; **~, versetzt zu werden** apply to be transferred; apply for a transfer; **etw. bei den Behörden ~:** apply to the authorities for sth. [2] (fordern) call for; demand [3] (vorschlagen) propose; **~, etw. zu tun** propose doing sth.; **Schluss der Debatte ~:** move the closure

beantworten *tr. V.* answer; reply to, answer ‹*letter*›; respond to ‹*insult*›; return ‹*greeting*›; **jmdm. eine Frage ~:** answer a question for sb.; **bitte ~ Sie meine Frage mit Ja oder Nein** please answer yes or no to my question

b

Beantwortung *die;* ~, ~en **1** **die ~ einer Frage/eines Briefes** an answer to a question/ a reply *or* an answer to a letter; **in ~** (Amtsspr.) in reply (*Gen.* to); **zur ~ Ihrer Frage** in order to answer your question **2** (Reaktion) response; **die ~ seiner Beleidigung** the response to his insult

bearbeiten *tr. V.* **1** deal with; work on, handle ‹*case*› **2** (adaptieren) adapt (**für** for); **ein Buch völlig neu ~:** revise a book completely; **ein Stück für Klavier ~:** arrange a piece for the piano **3** (behandeln) treat (**mit** with); work ‹*wood, metal, leather, etc.*›; **etw. mit Politur/ einem Hammer/einer Feile** *usw.* **~:** polish/ hammer/file *etc.* sth.; **etw. mit einer Drahtbürste ~:** work on sth. with a wire brush **4** cultivate ‹*field, land*›; (fig. ugs.) hammer away on ‹*piano, organ*›; **den Boden ~:** work the soil **5** (ugs.: schlagen) beat [repeatedly]; **jmdn. mit den Fäusten ~:** pummel sb. **6** (untersuchen) treat, examine ‹*subject, aspect*› **7** (ugs.: überreden) work on; **jmdn. ~, dass er etw. macht** work on sb. to get him to do sth.

Bearbeiter *der,* **Bearbeiterin** *die* **1** **der zuständige Bearbeiter:** the person who is dealing/who dealt with the matter; **sie war nicht die Bearbeiterin des Antrags** she did not deal with the application **2** (eines Romans, Schauspiels) adapter; (eines Textes) reviser; (Herausgeber) editor; (eines Musikstücks) arranger

Bearbeitung *die;* ~, ~en **1** **die ~ eines Antrags/eines Falles** *usw.* dealing with an application/working on *or* handling a case *etc.*; **die ~ der Post ist ...** dealing with the mail is... **2** (Fassung, Veränderung) adaptation; (eines Musikstücks) arrangement; **die englische ~:** the English version **3** (Behandlung) treatment; (von Holz, Metall, Leder usw.) working; **die ~ des Metalls ist schwer** it is difficult to work the metal; **zur weiteren ~:** in order to be worked further/for further treatment **4** (Untersuchung) examination; (eines Themas) treatment

Bearbeitungs-: ~gebühr *die* administrative charge; (Bankw.) handling charge; **~methode** *die:* **~methoden für Stahl** *usw.* methods of working steel *etc.*; **~zeit** *die:* **die ~zeit für etw.** the time required to deal with sth.

beargwöhnen *tr. V.* **jmdn./etw. ~:** be suspicious of sb./sth.; regard sb./sth. with suspicion; **beargwöhnt werden** be regarded with suspicion

Beat /bi:t/ *der;* ~s, ~s **1** beat **2** (Musikrichtung) beat [music]

Beat-: ~band *die* beat group; **~club** *der:* ▸**~lokal**; **~fan** *der* beat fan; **~lokal** *das* beat club

beatmen *tr. V.* (Med.) **jmdn. [künstlich] ~:** administer artificial respiration to sb.; (während einer Operation) ventilate sb.

Beatmung *die;* ~, ~en: **[künstliche] ~:** artificial respiration; (während einer Operation) ventilation

Beatmungs·gerät *das* respirator

Beat·musik *die* beat music

Beatnik /'bi:tnɪk/ *der;* ~s, ~s beatnik

Beat·schuppen *der* (ugs.) beat club

Beau /bo:/ *der;* ~s, ~s dandy

Beaufort·skala /'bo:fɐt-/ *die* (Met.) Beaufort scale

beaufsichtigen *tr. V.* supervise; mind, look after ‹*child*›; **jmdn. bei der Arbeit ~:** supervise sb. while he/she is working

Beaufsichtigung *die;* ~, ~en supervision; **unter ~ stehen** be kept under supervision

beauftragen *tr. V.* **1** **jmdn./einen Ausschuss** *usw.* **mit etw. ~:** entrust sb./a committee *etc.* with sth.; charge sb./a committee *etc.* with sth.; **jmdn./einen Ausschuss** *usw.* **~, etw. zu tun** give sb./a committee *etc.* the job *or* task of doing sth.; **jmdn. ~, die Urkunden zu unterschreiben** authorize sb. to sign the documents; **man hat mich beauftragt, Sie darüber zu informieren** I have been asked to tell you about this; **einen Künstler/Architekten ~, etw. zu tun** commission an artist/ architect to do sth. **2** (beordern) **jmdn. ~, etw. zu tun** order sb. to do sth.

Beauftragte *der/die; adj. Dekl.* representative; **der ~ der DDR für Kirchenfragen** the GDR official responsible for church affairs

beaugapfeln *tr. V.* (scherzh.) **jmdn./etw. ~:** give sb./sth. the once-over (coll.)

beäugen *tr. V.* eye ‹*person*›; inspect ‹*thing*›

beaugenscheinigen /bə'laugn̩ʃaɪnɪgn̩/ *tr. V.* (Amtsspr., scherzh.) inspect

Beauté /bo'te:/ *die;* ~, ~s (geh.) beauty

bebändert /bə'bɛndɐt/ *Adj.* decorated with ribbons; beribboned

bebauen *tr. V.* **1** build on; develop; **ein Gelände mit Häusern ~:** build houses on a site; **mit etw. bebaut werden** have sth. built on it **2** cultivate ‹*land*›; **einen Acker mit Kartoffeln ~:** grow potatoes in a field

bebaut *Adj.* **ein [dicht] ~es Gebiet** a densely built-up area; **ein ~es Gelände** a developed site

Bebauung *die;* ~, ~en **1** (mit Gebäuden) development **2** (Gebäude) buildings *pl.*; **das Gebiet hat eine völlig uneinheitliche ~:** the buildings in this area lack any unity of style **3** (eines Ackers) cultivation

Bebauungs·plan *der* development plan

Bébé /be'be:/ *das;* ~s, ~s (schweiz.) baby

beben /'be:bn̩/ *itr. V.* **1** shake; tremble **2** (geh.: zittern) tremble, shake (**vor** + *Dat.* with); ‹*lips*› tremble; ‹*knees*› shake

Beben *das;* ~s, ~ **1** shaking; trembling **2** (Erd~) quake (coll.); earthquake **3** (geh.: Zittern) shaking; trembling; **das ~ seiner Stimme** the tremble in his voice

bebildern *tr. V.* illustrate

Bebilderung *die;* ~, ~en illustrations *pl.*

bebrillt /bə'brɪlt/ *Adj.* bespectacled

bebrüten *tr. V.* **1** brood; incubate **2** (Biol.) incubate

Béchamel·soße /beʃa'mɛl-/ *die* (Kochk.) béchamel [sauce]

Becher /'bɛçɐ/ *der;* ~s, ~ **1** (Glas~, Porzellan~) glass; tumbler; (Plastik~) beaker; cup; (Eis~) (aus Glas, Metall) sundae dish; (aus Pappe) tub; (Joghurt~) carton; **ein ~ Eis** a tub of ice cream **2** (bei Pflanzen) cupule; cup

Becher·glas *das* (Chemie) beaker

bechern *tr., itr. V.* (ugs. scherzh.) **[einen] ~:** have a few (coll.); **bis zum frühen Morgen ~:** booze into the small hours

Becher·werk *das* (Technik) bucket elevator

becircen /bə'tsɪrtsn̩/ *tr. V.* (ugs.) **1** bewitch ‹*man*› **2** (überreden) **jmdn. ~[, dass er etw. tut]** wrap sb. round one's little finger [and get him to do sth.]

Becken /'bɛkn̩/ *das;* ~s, ~ **1** (Wasch~) basin; (Abwasch~) sink; (Toiletten~) pan; bowl **2** (Anat.) ▸❶ **S. 435** pelvis **3** *Pl.* (Musik) cymbals **4** (Schwimm~) pool; (Plansch~) paddling pool; (eines Brunnens, einer Schleuse) basin; (Fisch~) pond **5** (Geol.) basin

Becken-: ~bruch *der* ▸❶ **S. 439** (Med.) pelvic fracture; fractured pelvis; **~end·lage** *die* (Med.) breech position; **~knochen** *der* ▸❶ **S. 435** hip bone; pelvic bone

Beckmesser /'bɛkmɛsɐ/ *der;* ~s, ~ (abwertend) caviller; carper

Beckmesserei *die;* ~, ~en (abwertend) cavilling; carping

Beckmesserin *die;* ~, ~nen ▸**Beckmesser**

beckmessern *itr. V.* (abwertend) cavil; carp

bedachen /bə'daxn̩/ *tr. V.* put the roof on ‹*house*›; **bedacht** roofed; covered ‹*bridge*›

bedacht

A *2. Part. v.* **bedenken; bedachen**

B *Adj.* **1** carefully considered; (umsichtig) circumspect **2** **auf etw.** (*Akk.*) **~ sein** be intent on sth.; **auf seinen eigenen Vorteil ~ sein** have an eye to one's own advantage; **darauf ~/sehr ~ sein, etw. zu tun** be intent on doing sth./be [most] anxious to do sth.; **[ängstlich] darauf ~ sein, dass etw. nicht geschieht** be [extremely] anxious to prevent sth. from happening; **er ist stets auf korrekte Kleidung ~:** he makes a point of being correctly dressed

C *adv.* in a carefully considered way; (umsichtig) circumspectly

Bedacht *der: in* **ohne ~:** rashly; without thinking *or* forethought; **mit ~:** in a carefully considered way; (umsichtig) circumspectly; **voll ~:** very carefully; **auf etw.** (*Akk.*) **~ nehmen** (geh.) pay regard to sth.

Bedachte *der/die; adj. Dekl.* (Rechtsw.) beneficiary; (eines Legats) legatee

bedächtig /bə'dɛçtɪç/

A *Adj.* **1** deliberate; measured ‹*steps, stride, speech*› **2** (besonnen) thoughtful; well-considered ‹*words*›; (vorsichtig) careful

B *adv.* **1** deliberately; **~ reden** speak in measured tones **2** (besonnen) thoughtfully; (vorsichtig) carefully

Bedächtigkeit *die;* ~ **1** deliberateness **2** (Besonnenheit) thoughtfulness; (Vorsichtigkeit) carefulness

bedachtsam (geh.)

A *Adj.* thoughtful; (vorsichtig) careful

B *adv.* thoughtfully; (vorsichtig) carefully

Bedachung *die;* ~, ~en **1** roofing **2** (Dach) roof

bedang /bə'daŋ/ *1. u. 3. Pers. Sg. Prät. v.* **bedingen²**

bedanken

A *refl. V.* say thank you; express one's thanks; **ich bedanke mich** thank you; (ugs. iron.: nein danke!) thank you 'very much; **sich bei jmdm. [für etw.] ~:** thank sb. *or* say thank you to sb. [for sth.]; **sich bei jmdm. ~, dass er/sie etw. getan hat** thank sb. for doing sth.; **dafür kannst du dich bei ihm ~** (ugs. iron.) you've got him to thank for that (iron.)

B *tr. V.* (geh.) **etw. ~:** express one's thanks for sth.; **Seien Sie herzlich bedankt** please accept my/our warmest thanks

-bedarf *der;* ~[e]s ... requirement

Bedarf /bə'darf/ *der;* ~[e]s **1** need (**an** + *Dat.* of); requirement (**an** + *Dat.* for); (Bedarfsmenge) needs *pl.*; requirements *pl.*; **Dinge des täglichen ~s** everyday necessities; **der persönliche ~:** one's personal needs *pl.*; **bei ~:** if and when the need arises; if required; **bei dringendem ~:** in cases of urgent need; **~ an etw.** (*Dat.*) **haben** (Kaufmannsspr.) require sth.; **je nach ~:** as required; **kein ~!** (salopp) I don't feel like it **2** (Nachfrage) demand (**an** + *Dat.* for); **dafür besteht kein ~:** there is no demand for it/them; **mein ~ an Überraschungen ist für heute gedeckt** (fig.) I've had enough surprises for 'one day

bedarfs-, Bedarfs-: ~ampel *die* (Verkehrsw.) pedestrian-controlled *or* -operated lights; **~deckung** *die* satisfaction of its/ one's needs *or* requirements; **~fall** *der: in* **im ~fall[e]** if required; if the need arises/arose; **~gerecht** **A** *Adj.* designed to meet requirements; tailor-made; **eine ~gerechte Versorgung der Bevölkerung** a supply system tailored to the needs of the people; **B** *adv.* in line with demand; **~güter** *Pl.* consumer goods; **~halte·stelle** *die* request stop; **~weckung** *die;* ~~: stimulation of demand

bedauerlich *Adj.* regrettable; unfortunate

bedauerlicher·weise *Adv.* regrettably; unfortunately

bedauern *tr., itr. V.* **1** feel sorry for; **sie hat es gern, bedauert zu werden** she likes people to feel sorry for her; **sie lässt sich gerne ~:** she likes being pitied **2** ▸❶ **S. 227** (schade finden) regret; **ich bedaure sehr, dass ...** I am very sorry that ...; **wir ~, Ihnen mitteilen zu müssen** we regret to [have to] inform you; **bedaure!** sorry!

Bedauern *das;* ~s **1** sympathy; **jmdm. sein ~ ausdrücken** offer one's sympathy to sb. **2** ▸❶ **S. 227** (Betrübnis) regret; **zu meinem ~:** to my regret; **ich habe zu meinem ~ gehört, dass ...** I was sorry to hear that ...; **zu unserem ~ müssen wir Ihnen mitteilen, dass ...** we regret to [have to] inform you that ...; it is with regret that we must inform you that ...; **mit ~:** with regret; **mit ~ habe ich festgestellt, dass ...** I have discovered to my regret that ...

bedauerns-: ~wert (geh.), **~würdig** *Adj.* unfortunate ⟨*person, coincidence*⟩; regrettable, unfortunate ⟨*incident*⟩

bedecken
[A] *tr. V.* [1] cover (**mit** with); **mit etw. bedeckt sein** be covered with sth.; **von Schlamm/Schmutz bedeckt sein** be covered in mud/dirt [2] (österr.: ausgleichen) meet ⟨*costs*⟩
[B] *refl. V.* cover oneself up

bedeckt *Adj.* overcast ⟨*sky*⟩; **bei ~em Himmel** when the sky is overcast; **sich ~ halten** (fig.) keep a low profile

Bedecktsamer /-za:mɐ/ *der;* **~s, ~** (Bot.) angiosperm

bedecktsamig /-za:mɪç/ *Adj.* (Bot.) angiospermous

Bedeckung *die* [1] covering [2] (Schutz) guard; **zehn Mann ~:** a ten-man bodyguard *sing.* [3] (das Bedeckende) covering [4] (österr.: Deckung) meeting

bedenken
[A] *unr. tr. V.* [1] consider; think about; **wenn ich es recht bedenke/wenn man es recht bedenkt** when I/you stop and think about it; **~, dass ...** consider *or* think that ... [2] (beachten) take into consideration; **du musst ~, dass ...** you should bear in mind that *or* take into consideration the fact that ...; **ich gebe [dir]/er gab [uns] zu ~, dass ...** I would ask you/he asked us to bear in mind that *or* take into consideration the fact that ... [3] (geh.: beschenken) **jmdn. reich ~:** shower sb. with gifts; **jmdn. mit etw. ~:** present sb. with sth.; **jmdn. großzügig mit Lob ~:** lavish praise on sb.
[B] *refl. V.* reflect; think; **ohne sich lange zu ~:** without stopping to reflect

Bedenken *das;* **~s, ~** [1] reflection; **nach kurzem/langem ~:** after a moment's/after much reflection *or* consideration; **ohne ~:** without hesitation [2] (Zweifel) doubt; reservation; **~ haben** *od.* **hegen** *od.* (geh.) **tragen** have doubts *or* reservations (**gegen** about); **aber jetzt kommen mir ~:** but now I'm having second thoughts

bedenken·los
[A] *Adj.* unconsidered; (ohne Zögern) unhesitating; prompt ⟨*intervention*⟩; (skrupellos) unscrupulous
[B] *adv.* without a moment's hesitation; without stopping to think; (ohne Zögern) without hesitation; ⟨*intervene*⟩ promptly; (skrupellos) unscrupulously

Bedenkenlosigkeit *die;* **~:** lack of consideration; (mangelndes Zögern) absence of any hesitation; (Skrupellosigkeit) unscrupulousness; lack of scruples

bedenkens·wert *Adj.* ⟨*argument, suggestion*⟩ worthy of consideration; **~ sein** be worth considering *or* worthy of consideration

bedenklich
[A] *Adj.* [1] dubious, questionable ⟨*methods, transactions, etc.*⟩ [2] (bedrohlich) alarming; disturbing; **~ sein/werden** be giving/be starting to give cause for concern [3] (besorgt) concerned; apprehensive; anxious; **ein ~es Gesicht machen** look concerned *etc.*; **das machte** *od.* **stimmte mich ~** (ließ mich nachdenken) that gave me food for thought; (machte mich ängstlich) that gave me cause for concern
[B] *adv.* [1] alarmingly; disturbingly [2] (besorgt) apprehensively; anxiously

Bedenklichkeit *die;* **~** [1] dubiousness; questionableness [2] (Bedrohlichkeit) alarming *or* disturbing nature

Bedenk·zeit *die* time for reflection; **um ~/einige Tage ~ bitten** ask for some time/a few days to think about it; **nach einer kurzen ~:** after a pause for thought; **ich gebe Ihnen vierundzwanzig Stunden ~:** I'll give you twenty-four hours to think about it

bedeppert /bə'dɛpɐt/ *Adj.* (salopp) (ratlos) confused and embarrassed; (töricht, dümmlich) gormless (coll.); (niedergeschlagen) crestfallen

bedeuten *tr. V.* [1] (bezeichnen, heißen) mean; **was bedeutet dieses Wort?** what does that word mean?; what is the meaning of that word?; **was soll das ~?** what does that mean?; **er weiß, was es bedeutet, krank zu sein** he knows what it means to be ill; **„Ph. D." bedeutet Doktor der Philosophie** 'Ph.D.' stands for Doctor of Philosophy; **was bedeutet diese Zeremonie?** what's the significance of this ceremony? [2] (sein) represent; **das bedeutet ein Wagnis** that is being really daring; **einen Eingriff in die Pressefreiheit ~:** amount to *or* represent an attack on press freedom [3] (hindeuten auf) mean; **das bedeutet nichts Gutes** that bodes ill; that's a bad sign; **schönes Wetter ~:** mean good weather; be a sign of good weather to come [4] (wichtig sein) mean; **Geld bedeutet ihm nichts** money means nothing to him; **das hat nichts zu ~:** that doesn't mean anything [5] (geh.: anraten) **jmdm. ~, etw. zu tun** intimate *or* indicate to sb. that he/she should do sth. [6] (veralt.: belehren) inform

bedeutend
[A] *Adj.* [1] (wichtig) significant, important ⟨*step, event, role, measure, etc.*⟩; important ⟨*city, port, artist, writer, etc.*⟩ [2] (groß) considerable; substantial; considerable ⟨*success*⟩; substantial ⟨*pension*⟩
[B] *adv.* considerably

bedeutsam
[A] *Adj.* [1] ▸ **bedeutend** [2] (viel sagend) meaningful; significant
[B] *adv.* meaningfully; significantly

Bedeutung *die;* **~, ~en** [1] meaning; significance; **einer Sache** (*Dat.*) **zu große ~ beimessen** attach too much significance to sth. [2] (Wort~) meaning [3] (Tragweite) significance; importance; **[an] ~ gewinnen** become more significant; **nichts von ~:** nothing important *or* significant; nothing of [any] importance *or* significance [4] (Berühmtheit) importance; **ein Mann von ~:** an important figure

bedeutungs-, Bedeutungs-: ~erweiterung *die* (Sprachw.) extension of meaning; **~gehalt** *der* semantic content (Ling.); meaning; **~lehre** *die* (Sprachw.) semantics; **~los** *Adj.* insignificant; unimportant; **~losigkeit** *die;* **~~:** insignificance; unimportance; **~schwer** *Adj.* (geh.) loaded with meaning; (folgenschwer) critical; momentous; **~unterschied** *der* (Sprachw.) difference in meaning; **~verengung** *die* (Sprachw.) restriction of meaning; **~verlust** *der* loss of importance; **~voll** [A] *Adj.* [1] significant; [2] (viel sagend) meaningful; meaning ⟨*look*⟩; [B] *adv.* meaningfully; significantly; **~wandel** *der* (Sprachw.) change in *or* of meaning; semantic change (Ling.); **~wörterbuch** *das* defining dictionary

Bedien·element *das* control unit

bedienen
[A] *tr. V.* [1] wait on; ⟨*waiter, waitress*⟩ wait on, serve; ⟨*sales assistant*⟩ serve; (salopp: sexuell) satisfy; **jmdn. vorn und hinten ~** (ugs.) wait on sb. hand and foot; **werden Sie schon bedient?** are you being served?; **aufmerksam bedient werden** receive attentive service [2] (handhaben) operate ⟨*machine*⟩ [3] *in* **[mit etw.] gut/schlecht bedient sein** (ugs.) be well-served/ill-served [by sth.]; **mit diesem Artikel sind Sie gut bedient** this article will give you good value for money; **bedient sein** (salopp) have had enough; have had all one can take [4] (Kartenspiel) play; **Kreuz/Trumpf ~:** play a club/trump; **eine Farbe ~:** follow suit [5] (Fußball) **jmdn. ~:** pass to sb.; **die Stürmer mit hervorragenden Pässen ~:** provide the forwards with excellent service [6] ⟨*means of transport*⟩ serve; operate on ⟨*route*⟩; maintain ⟨*network of routes*⟩
[B] *itr. V.* [1] (im Restaurant, Geschäft) serve; **wer bedient hier?** who is serving here? [2] (Kartenspiel) follow suit; **falsch ~:** revoke
[C] *refl. V.* [1] help oneself; **sich selbst ~** (im Geschäft, Restaurant usw.) serve oneself [2] (geh.) **sich einer Sache** (*Gen.*) **~:** make use of *or* use sth.

Bedienerin *die;* **~, ~nen** (österr.) cleaning woman

bedienstet /bə'di:nstət/ *Adj. in* **~ sein** (österr.) be employed (**bei** by)

Bedienstete *der/die; adj. Dekl.* [1] (Amtsspr.) employee [2] (veralt.: Diener) servant

Bediente /bə'di:ntə/ *der/die; adj. Dekl.* (veralt.) servant

Bedienung *die;* **~, ~en** [1] (das Bedienen) service; **~ inbegriffen** service included [2] (das Handhaben) operation; **für die ~ dieser Maschine bekommt er ...** for operating this machine he receives ... [3] (Person) (in einem Lokal) waiter/waitress; (in einem Geschäft) [sales] assistant; (gesamtes Personal) staff; **hallo, ~!** waiter/waitress! [4] (österr.) cleaning woman

Bedienungs-: ~anleitung *die* operating instructions *pl.*; (Heft) instruction book; **~aufschlag** *der,* **~geld** *das:* ▸ **Bedienungszuschlag**; **~komfort** *der* ease of operation; **~fehler** *der* operator's error; **~mannschaft** *die* operating crew; (am Geschütz) gun crew; **~zuschlag** *der* service charge

bedingen[1] /bə'dɪŋən/ *tr. V.* [1] cause [2] (erfordern) require; demand; (voraussetzen) presuppose [3] (abhängig sein von) **einander ~:** be interdependent *or* mutually dependent

bedingen[2] *unr. refl. V.* (veralt.) **sich** (*Dat.*) **etw. ~:** stipulate sth.; make sth. a condition

bedingt /bə'dɪŋt/
[A] *Adj.* [1] qualified ⟨*praise, acceptance, approval*⟩ [2] (von etw. abhängig) conditional; **~er Reflex** (Physiol.) conditioned reflex; **psychologisch ~ sein** have psychological causes
[B] *adv.* **~ richtig/gelten** partly/be partly true; **nur ~ tauglich** fit for certain duties only

-bedingt *Adj.* associated with *postpos.*; due to *postpos.*; **alters~:** associated with old age *postpos.*; **berufsbedingte Krankheiten** occupational illnesses; **witterungsbedingte Schäden** damage caused by the weather

Bedingtheit *die;* **~, ~en** [1] (Abhängigkeit) relative nature; (Begrenztheit) limited *or* restricted nature [2] (Bestimmtheit) **wechselseitige ~:** interdependence; mutual dependence

Bedingung *die;* **~, ~en** condition; **etw. zur ~ machen** make sth. a condition; **zu annehmbaren ~en** on acceptable terms; **unter diesen ~en** on these conditions; **unter keiner ~:** under no circumstances; **unter der ~, dass ...** on condition that ...; **~ ist, dass ...** it is a condition that ...

bedingungs-, Bedingungs-: ~form *die* (Sprachw.) conditional; **~los** [A] *Adj.* unconditional ⟨*surrender, acceptance, etc.*⟩; absolute, unquestioning ⟨*obedience, loyalty, devotion*⟩; [B] *adv.* ⟨*surrender, accept, etc.*⟩ unconditionally; ⟨*subordinate oneself*⟩ unquestioningly; **sich ~los für jmdn. einsetzen** give sb. one's unqualified support; **~satz** *der* (Sprachw.) conditional clause

bedrängen *tr. V.* [1] besiege ⟨*town, fortress, person*⟩; put ⟨*opposing player*⟩ under pressure; **vom Feind bedrängt sein** be hard pressed by the enemy; **mit Fragen bedrängt werden** be assailed with questions [2] (belästigen) pester [3] (belasten) distress; **von Zweifeln bedrängt** beset with doubts; **in einer bedrängten/sehr bedrängten Lage sein** be hard-pressed/be in a difficult/desperate situation *or* in dire straits *pl.*

Bedrängnis *die;* **~, ~se** (geh.) (innere Not) distress; (wirtschaftliche Not) [great] difficulties *pl.*; **in ~ geraten/sein** get into/be in great difficulties *pl.*; **in arger ~:** in dire straits *pl.*; **jmdn. in ~ bringen** cause sb. great difficulties/distress

bedripst /bə'drɪpst/ *Adj.* (nordd. ugs.) (ratlos) confused and embarrassed; (niedergeschlagen) crestfallen

bedrohen *tr. V.* [1] threaten [2] (gefährden) threaten; endanger; **den Frieden ~:** be a threat *or* danger to peace; **vom Feuer bedroht sein** be in danger of catching fire; **vom Aussterben bedroht sein** be threatened with extinction; **bedrohte Arten** endangered species

bedrohlich
[A] *Adj.* (drohend) threatening, menacing ⟨*gesture*⟩; (Unheil verkündend) ominous; (gefährlich) dangerous
[B] *adv.* (drohend) threateningly; menacingly; (Unheil verkündend) ominously; (gefährlich) dangerously; **~ nahe kommen** come ominously/dangerously near

Bedrohlichkeit *die;* **~:** dangerousness; (einer Krankheit usw.) dangerous nature

Bedrohung *die* threat (*Gen.* to); **in ständiger ~:** under a constant threat

bedröppelt /bə'drœpl̩t/ (nordd. ugs.)
A *Adj.* glum; gloomy ‹*face, mood*›; (kleinlaut) sheepish ‹*person, face*›
B *adv.* gloomily; (kleinlaut) sheepishly

bedrucken *tr. V.* print; **etw. mit einer Adresse ~:** print an address on sth.; **ein mit Blumen bedrucktes Kleid** a flower-print dress

bedrücken *tr. V.* **1** depress; **es bedrückt mich, dass ...** I feel depressed that ...; **bedrückt dich was?** is something weighing on your mind? **2** (veralt.: unterdrücken) oppress

bedrückend *Adj.* oppressive; depressing ‹*sight, thought, news*›

bedruckt *Adj.* printed; print *attrib.* ‹*dress etc.*›

bedrückt *Adj.* depressed; oppressed ‹*people*›

Bedrückung *die;* **~, ~en** depression; (eines Volkes) oppression

Beduine /bedu'i:nə/ *der;* **~n, ~n, Beduinin** *die;* **~, ~nen** Bed[o]uin

bedungen /bə'dʊŋən/ *2. Part. v.* **bedingen²**

bedürfen *unr. itr. V.* (geh.) **jmds./einer Sache ~:** require *or* need sb./sth.; **es bedarf einer Sache** there is need for sth.; **es bedarf nur eines Wortes von Ihnen** you need only say so; **es bedarf keines weiteren Wortes** no more need be said; **es bedarf einiger Mühe** (geh.) some effort is needed *or* required

Bedürfnis *das;* **~ses, ~se** need (**nach** for); **dafür besteht kein ~:** there is no necessity for that; **das ~ haben, etw. zu tun** feel a need to do sth.; **ein ~ nach etw. haben** be in need of sth.; **es war mir ein ~, das zu tun** I felt the need to do it

bedürfnis-, Bedürfnis-: ~anstalt *die* (Amtsspr.) public convenience; **~befriedigung** *die* satisfaction of one's needs; (polit. Ökonomie) satisfaction of needs; **~los A** *Adj.* ‹*person*› with few [material] needs; modest, simple ‹*life*›; **~los sein** have few [material] needs; **B** *adv.* **~los leben** have a [very] modest lifestyle; **~losigkeit** *die;* **~:** lack of [material] needs

bedürftig *Adj.* **1** needy; **die Bedürftigen** the needy; those in need **2** *in* **jmds./einer Sache ~ sein** (geh.) be in need of sb./sth.

Bedürftigkeit *die;* **~:** neediness; **die ~ einer Familie feststellen** means-test a family

beduseln *refl. V.* (ugs.) get merry (coll.); **ich war beduselt** (fig.) my head was spinning

Beef·steak /'bi:fste:k/ *das* [beef]steak; **deutsches ~:** ≈ beefburger

beehren (geh.)
A *tr. V.* **1** **jmdn. mit seinem Besuch/seiner Anwesenheit ~** (auch iron.) honour sb. with a visit/one's presence **2** (gespreizt: besuchen) **~ Sie uns bald wieder** (im Geschäft/privat) we hope to have the pleasure of your custom/company again
B *refl. V.* **sich ~, etw. zu tun** have the honour to do sth.

beeiden /bə'|aidn̩/ *tr. V.* **~, dass ...** swear [on oath] that ...; **eine Aussage ~:** swear to the truth of a statement

beeidigen /bə'|aidɪgn̩/ **1** (geh.) **▸ beeiden** **2** (veralt.: vereidigen) swear in; **ein beeidigter Zeuge** a sworn witness

beeilen *refl. V.* **1** hurry [up (coll.)]; **beeil dich!** hurry [up]; **sich bei einer Arbeit ~:** hurry over a task; **du musst dich aber mächtig beeilt haben** (ugs.) you must have really got a move on (coll.) **2** (nicht zögern) **sich ~, etw. zu tun** hasten to do sth.

Beeilung *Interj.* **[los], ~!** (ugs.), **~ bitte!** (ugs.) get a move on! (coll.); hurry up!

beeindrucken *tr. V.* impress; **sich von etw. ~ lassen** be impressed by sth.; **~d** impressive

beeinflussbar, *beeinflußbar *Adj.* **leicht/schwer ~ sein** ‹*person*› be easily influenced/hard *or* difficult to influence; **das ist nicht ~:** it cannot be influenced

beeinflussen /bə'|ainflʊsn̩/ *tr. V.* influence; influence, affect ‹*result, process, etc.*›; **jmdn./etw. positiv/nachhaltig ~:** have a positive/lasting influence on sb./sth.; **sich leicht ~ lassen** be easily influenced

Beeinflussung *die;* **~, ~en 1** (das Einflussnehmen) influencing; **seine ~ durch die Schule** the influence of the school on him **2** (Einfluss) influence

beeinträchtigen /bə'|aintrɛçtɪgn̩/ *tr. V.* restrict ‹*sights, freedom*›; detract from, spoil ‹*pleasure, enjoyment*›; spoil ‹*appetite, good humour*›; detract from, diminish ‹*value*›; diminish, impair ‹*quality*›; impair ‹*reactions, efficiency, vision, hearing*›; damage, harm ‹*sales, reputation*›; reduce ‹*production*›; **jmdn. in seiner Freiheit ~:** restrict sb.'s freedom; **sich beeinträchtigt fühlen** feel hampered

Beeinträchtigung *die;* **~, ~en ▸ beeinträchtigen:** restriction; detracting (+ *Gen.* from); spoiling; diminution; impairment; damage (*Gen.* to); harm (*Gen.* to); reduction; **eine ~ der Freiheit** a restriction on one's freedom

beelenden *tr. V.* (schweiz.) sadden

Beelzebub /'be:ltsə-/ (*der*) Beelzebub; **den Teufel mit** *od.* **durch ~ austreiben** (fig.) replace one evil by *or* with another

beenden, beendigen *tr. V.* end; finish ‹*piece of work, dissertation, etc.*›; end, conclude ‹*negotiations, letter, lecture*›; complete, finish ‹*studies*›; end, bring to an end ‹*meeting, relationship, dispute, strike*›; **das Fest wurde mit einem Feuerwerk beendet** the celebration ended with a firework display; **damit ~ wir unser heutiges Programm** that brings to an end our programmes for today

Beendigung *die;* **~, Beendung** *die;* **~** (Ende) end; (Fertigstellung) completion; **nach/vor ~ des Unterrichts** after/before school is/was over

beengen *tr. V.* hinder, restrict ‹*movements*›; (fig.) restrict ‹*freedom [of action]*›; **das Kleid/dieses Zimmer beengt mich** the dress hinders *or* restricts my movements/this room is too cramped for me; **beengt wohnen** live in cramped surroundings *or* conditions; **sich beengt fühlen** feel cramped; (fig.: durch Regeln usw.) feel constricted; **diese kleinbürgerliche Atmosphäre beengte ihn** (fig.) he found this petit bourgeois atmosphere stifling *or* restricting

Beengtheit *die;* **~** (von Räumen) crampedness; **ein Gefühl der ~:** a feeling of being cramped

beerben *tr. V.* **jmdn. ~:** inherit sb's estate

beerdigen /bə'|e:ɐ̯dɪgn̩/ *tr. V.* bury; **jmdn. kirchlich ~:** give sb. a Christian burial

Beerdigung *die;* **~, ~en** (Bestattung) burial; (Trauerfeier) funeral; **auf der falschen ~ sein** (salopp, scherzh.) have come to the wrong place

Beerdigungs·institut *das* [firm *sing.* of] undertakers *pl. or* funeral directors *pl.*

Beere /'be:rə/ *die;* **~, ~n** berry

Beeren-: ~auslese *die: wine made from selected overripe grapes;* **~obst** *das* soft fruit

Beet /be:t/ *das;* **~[e]s, ~e** (Blumen~) bed; (Gemüse~) plot

Beete ▸ Bete

befähigen /bə'fɛ:ɪgn̩/ *tr. V.* **jmdn. ~, etw. zu tun** enable sb. to do sth.; ‹*qualifications, training, etc.*› qualify sb. to do sth.

befähigt
A *2. Part. v.* **befähigen**
B *Adj.* **1** (qualifiziert) qualified **2** (begabt) gifted

Befähigung *die;* **~ 1** (Qualifikation) qualification; **die ~ zum Internisten/Hochschulstudium/Richteramt** the qualifications *pl.* for becoming an internist/studying at university/being a judge **2** (Können) ability; (Talent) talent; **seine ~ zum Schriftsteller** his talent as a writer *or* for writing

Befähigungs·nachweis *der* (Amtsspr.) proof of one's qualifications

befahl /bə'fa:l/ *1. u. 3. Pers. Sg. Prät. v.* **befehlen**

befahrbar *Adj.* passable; navigable ‹*canal, river*›; **nicht ~:** impassable/unnavigable

befahren¹ *unr. tr. V.* **1** drive on, use ‹*road*›; drive across, use ‹*bridge, pass*›; use ‹*railway line*›; **die Straße kann nur im Sommer ~ werden** this road is passable only in summer; **die Straße ist nur in einer Richtung zu ~:** traffic can only use the road in one direction; **„Seitenstreifen nicht ~!"** 'keep off verges'; **die Straße ist stark/wenig ~:** the road is heavily/little used; **eine stark ~e Straße** a busy road **2** sail ‹*sea*›; navigate, sail up/down ‹*river, canal*›; **eine stark ~e Wasserstraße** a busy waterway; **die Weltmeere ~:** sail the oceans **3** (Bergmannsspr.) **eine Grube ~:** go down a mine

befahren² *Adj.* **1** (Seemannsspr.) seasoned; experienced **2** (Jägerspr.) inhabited ‹*earth etc.*›

Befall *der;* **~[e]s ~** (Landw.) attack (*Gen.* on; **durch, von** by)

befallen *unr. tr. V.* **1** (überkommen) overcome; ‹*misfortune*› befall; **Fieber/eine Grippe befiel ihn** (geh.) he was stricken by fever/influenza; **von Panik/Angst/Heimweh** *usw.* **~ werden** be seized *or* overcome with *or* by panic/fear/homesickness *etc.*; **von einer Ohnmacht/Schwäche/von Resignation ~ werden** faint/feel faint/be overcome with a feeling of resignation **2** ‹*pests*› attack

befangen
A *Adj.* **1** (gehemmt) self-conscious, awkward ‹*person*›; **jmdn. ~ machen** make sb. self-conscious *or* awkward **2** (bes. Rechtsw.: voreingenommen) biased; **einen Richter als ~ ablehnen** challenge a judge on grounds of bias **3** **in einem Glauben/Irrtum ~ sein** (geh.) labour under a belief/misapprehension; **in Vorurteilen ~ sein** be prejudiced
B *adv.* self-consciously; awkwardly

Befangenheit *die;* **~ 1** self-consciousness; awkwardness **2** (bes. Rechtsw.: Voreingenommenheit) bias

Befangenheits·antrag *der* (Rechtsw.) challenge on grounds of bias

befassen
A *refl. V.* **sich mit etw. ~:** occupy oneself with sth.; (studieren) study sth.; ‹*article, book*› deal with sth.; **sich nicht mit Kleinigkeiten ~:** not concern *or* bother oneself with trivial details; **mit diesem Thema haben wir uns lange genug befasst** we've spent enough time on this subject; **sich mit jmdm./einem Fall/einer Angelegenheit ~:** deal with *or* attend to sb./a case/matter; **ich habe mich schon mit dieser Sache befasst** I've already been into this matter; **sich viel mit jmdm. ~:** give sb. a great deal of attention; spend a great deal of time with sb.; **sich mit jedem Kind einzeln ~** ‹*teacher*› give each child individual attention
B *tr. V.* (bes. Amtsspr.) **jmdn. mit etw. ~:** get *or* instruct sb. to deal with sth.; **die mit diesem Fall befasste Behörde** the authorities dealing *or* involved with this case

befehden /bə'fe:dn̩/ *tr. V.* **1** (hist.) feud with **2** (geh.) attack ‹*plan, proposal, etc.*›; **sich/einander ~:** feud [with each other]; attack each other

Befehl /bə'fe:l/ *der;* **~[e]s, ~e 1** order; command; **jmdm. den ~ geben, etw. zu tun** order *or* command sb. to do sth.; **den ~ haben, etw. zu tun** be under orders *or* have been ordered to do sth.; **auf jmds. ~** (*Akk.*) on sb.'s orders; **auf ~ handeln** act under orders; **~ ist ~:** orders are orders; **zu ~ [Herr Leutnant/Oberst/General/Kapitän]!** yes, sir!; aye, aye, sir! (Navy); **dein Wunsch ist** *od.* **sei mir ~** (ugs. scherzh.) your wish is my command **2** (Befehlsgewalt) command; **den ~ über jmdn./etw. haben** have command of *or* be in command of sb./sth.; **unter jmds. ~** (*Dat.*) **stehen** be under sb.'s command; **den ~ übernehmen** take command **3** (DV) instruction; command

befehlen
A *unr. tr., itr. V.* **1** order; (Milit.) order; command; (heißen) tell; **jmdm. Stillschweigen ~:** order sb. to keep silent; **man befahl ihm zu warten** he was told to wait; **er befahl die Räumung des Dorfes** he ordered the village to be cleared; **er befiehlt gern** he likes to order people about; **von Ihnen lasse ich mir nichts ~:** I don't take orders from you; **[ganz] wie**

Sie ~ (veralt.) [just] as you wish; **~ gnädige Frau sonst noch etwas?** (veralt.) is there anything else, ma'am? **2** (beordern) order; (zu sich) summon; **jmdn. zum Rapport ~:** order/summon sb. to report **3** (geh. veralt.) commend; **seine Seele Gott/in Gottes Hände ~** (bibl.) commend one's soul to God; **befiehl dem Herrn deine Wege!** (bibl.) commit thy ways unto the Lord
B *unr. itr. V.* have command; be in command; **über eine Armee ~:** have command of *or* be in command of an army

befehligen *tr. V.* have command of; be in command of; **von ... befehligt werden** be commanded by ...; be under the command of ...

befehls-, Befehls-: ~aus·gabe *die* (Milit.) issuing of orders; briefing; **~bereich** *der* [area of] command; **~empfänger** *der,* **~empfängerin** *die* recipient of an order/orders; **bloße ~empfänger [der Zentrale] sein** just follow *or* take orders [from headquarters]; **~form** *die* (Sprachw.) imperative [form]; **~gemäß A** *Adj.* **die ~gemäße Durchführung des Plans** *usw.* carrying out the plan *etc.* in accordance with orders *or* as ordered; **B** *adv.* in accordance with orders; as ordered; **~gewalt** *die* command (**über** + *Akk.* of); **jmds. ~gewalt** (*Dat.*) **unterstehen** be under sb.'s command; **~haber** /-ha:bɐ/ *der;* **~~s, ~~** (Milit.) commander; **~notstand** *der* (Rechtsw.) **unter ~notstand handeln** be acting under orders; **in einem ~notstand sein/sich in einem ~notstand befinden** have to obey orders; **~satz** *der* (Sprachw.) imperative sentence; **~stab** *der* (Eisenb.) station official's rod and signalling disc; ≈ guard's flag; **~ton** *der* peremptory tone; **~verweigerung** *die* refusal to obey an order/orders; **~widrig A** *Adj.* contrary to orders *postpos.;* **B** *adv.* contrary to orders

befeinden *tr. V.* be hostile to; **die Juden wurden dort befeindet** there was hostility to the Jews there

befestigen *tr. V.* **1** fix (**mit** with); **etw. mit Stecknadeln/Bindfaden ~:** fasten sth. with pins/string; **etw. mit Schrauben/Leim ~:** fasten *or* fix sth. with screws/fix *or* stick sth. with glue; **etw. an der Wand ~:** fix sth. to the wall; **einen Anhänger an einem Koffer ~:** attach *or* fasten a label to a case; **ein Boot an einem Pfosten ~:** tie up *or* moor a boat to a post **2** (haltbar machen) stabilize ‹*bank, embankment*›; make up ‹*road, path, etc.*› **3** (sichern) fortify ‹*town etc.*›; strengthen ‹*border*› **4** (festigen) consolidate ‹*reputation, authority*›; enhance ‹*standing*›; strengthen ‹*friendship, confidence*›

Befestigung *die;* **~, ~en 1** (Milit.) fortification **2** ▸ **befestigen 1**: fixing; fastening; attachment; tying up; mooring **3** (Haltbarmachung) (eines Ufers) stabilization; (eines Weges) making up **4** (Stärkung) ▸ **befestigen 4**: consolidation; enhancement; strengthening

Befestigungs-: ~an·lage *die* fortifications *pl.;* **~linie** *die* line of fortifications

befeuchten /bəˈfɔyçtn̩/ *tr. V.* moisten; damp ‹*hair, cloth*›; **von Tränen/Tau befeuchtet** moist *or* wet with tears/dew

befeuern *tr. V.* **1** (beheizen) fuel **2** (beschießen) shoot at; fire on **3** (ugs.: bewerfen) pelt (**mit** with) **4** (geh.: anfeuern) inspire **5** (Schifffahrt, Flugw.) mark ‹*coastline, runway, etc.*› with lights *or* beacons

Befeuerung *die* lights *pl.;* beacons *pl.*

Beffchen /ˈbɛfçən/ *das;* **~s, ~:** [collar *sing.* with] bands *pl.* (*worn esp. by Protestant clergymen*)

befiehlst /bəˈfi:lst/, **befiehlt** /bəˈfi:lt/ *2., 3. Pers. Sg. Präsens v.* **befehlen**

befinden
A *unr. refl. V.* be; **sich im Urlaub/auf Reisen ~:** be on holiday/be away on a trip; **unter ihnen befand sich jemand, der ...** among them there was somebody who ...; **sich wohl ~** (geh.) be well
B *unr. tr. V.* (geh.) **1** **etw. für gut/richtig ~:** find *or* consider sth. [to be] good/right; **jmdn. für tauglich ~:** declare sb. [to be] fit; **jmdn. für** *od.* **als schuldig ~:** find sb. guilty **2** (äußern) declare; assert
C *unr. itr. V.* **über etw.** (*Akk.*) **~:** decide [on] sth.; make a decision on sth.; **darüber habe ich nicht zu ~:** that's not for me to decide

Befinden *das;* **~s 1** health; (eines Patienten) condition; **sich nach jmds. ~ erkundigen** enquire after *or* about sb.'s health; **wie ist Ihr ~ heute?** (geh.) how are you today? **2** (geh.: Urteil) judgement; **etw. nach eigenem ~ entscheiden** use one's own judgement in deciding sth.; **nach seinem/ihrem [eigenen] ~:** in his/her [own] judgement *or* estimation

befindlich *Adj.* **1** (liegend) to be found *postpos.;* **das in der Kasse ~e Geld** the money in the till; **eine am Stadtrand ~e Siedlung** an estate [situated] on the edge of town **2** (in einem Zustand) **die im Bau ~en Häuser** the houses [which are/were] under construction

Befindlichkeit *die;* **~, ~en** (geh.) state

befingern *tr. V.* (salopp) finger

beflaggen *tr. V.* **etw. ~:** decorate *or* [be]deck sth. with flags; **ein Schiff ~:** dress a ship

Beflaggung *die;* **~:** decoration with flags; (eines Schiffes) dressing

beflecken *tr. V.* **1** stain; **sich mit Blut ~** (verhüll. geh.) stain one's hand with blood **2** (fig.) besmirch; stain; defile ‹*sanctity*›

Befleckung *die;* **~** (fig.) besmirching; staining; (eines Heiligtums) defilement

befleißigen *refl. V.* (geh.) **sich eines klaren Stils/höflicheren Tons** *usw.* **~:** make a great effort to cultivate a clear style/to adopt a more polite tone of voice *etc.;* **sich größter Zurückhaltung ~:** endeavour to exercise the greatest restraint

befliegen *unr. tr. V.* fly ‹*route*›; **eine stark beflogene Route** a route with heavy [air] traffic

beflissen /bəˈflɪsn̩/ (geh.)
A *Adj.* keen; eager; (emsig) assiduous; zealous; **~ sein/ängstlich ~ sein, etw. zu tun** be keen *or* eager/anxious to do sth.
B *adv.* keenly; eagerly; (emsig) assiduously; zealously

Beflissenheit *die;* **~:** keenness; eagerness; (Emsigkeit) assiduousness; zeal

beflissentlich *Adj.:* ▸ **geflissentlich**

beflügeln *tr. V.* (geh.) **1** **jmdn. ~:** inspire sb.; ‹*success, praise*› spur sb. on, inspire sb. **2** (schneller machen) **jmds. Schritte/Gang ~** ‹*fear, joy*› wing sb.'s steps; **jmdn. ~:** spur sb. on

befohlen /bəˈfo:lən/ *2. Part. v.* **befehlen**

befolgen *tr. V.* follow, obey ‹*instruction, grammatical rule*›; obey, comply with ‹*law, regulation*›; follow, take ‹*advice*›; follow ‹*suggestion*›

Befolgung *die;* **~** ▸ **befolgen**: following; obedience (*Gen.* to); compliance (*Gen.* with); **die ~ des Gesetzes** obedience to *or* compliance with the law

Beförderer *der,* **Beförderin** *die* carrier

befördern *tr. V.* **1** carry; transport; convey; **etw. mit der Post/per Schiff/Luftfracht ~** (schicken) send sth. by post/sea/air; **jmdn. ins Freie** *od.* **an die Luft ~** (ugs.) chuck (coll.) *or* throw sb. out; *s. auch* **Jenseits 2** (aufrücken lassen) promote; **zum Direktor befördert werden** be promoted to director

Beförderung *die* **1** (Waren~) carriage; transport; conveyance; (Personen~) transport; conveyance; **Schäden, die bei der ~ entstehen** damage in transit; **die ~ per Luft/zu Lande** carriage *or* transport by air/road; **Züge zur ~ der Urlaubsreisenden** trains to carry the holiday passengers **2** (das Aufrücken) promotion (**zu** to)

Beförderungs-: ~bedingungen *Pl.* conditions of carriage; **~kosten** *Pl.* cost *sing.* of transport *or* transportation; transport *or* transportation costs; **~mittel** *das* means of transport; **~pflicht** *die: obligation on bus companies, airlines, etc. to accept and convey passengers and goods;* **~stau** *der* lack of promotion opportunities

Befördrerin *die* carrier

befrachten *tr. V.* load (**mit** with); **mit Emotionen befrachtet** (fig.) ‹*discussion etc.*› charged with emotion; **mit Geschichte befrachtet** (fig.) ‹*castle, church, etc.*› steeped in history

Befrachter *der,* **Befrachterin** *die;* **~, ~nen** freighter

befrackt *Adj.* **ein ~er Herr** a gentleman wearing *or* in tails

befragen *tr. V.* **1** (ausfragen) question (**über** + *Akk.* about); **einen Zeugen ~:** question *or* examine a witness; **auf Befragen** when questioned **2** (fragen) ask; consult; **jmdn. nach seiner Meinung ~:** ask sb. for his/her opinion; **ein Orakel/die Karten ~:** consult an oracle/the cards

Befragte *der/die; adj. Dekl.* man/woman/person questioned; **20% der ~n** 20% of those questioned

Befragung *die;* **~, ~en 1** questioning; (vor Gericht) questioning; examination; **eine ~ aller Schüler vornehmen** question all the pupils **2** (Konsultation) consultation; **nach ~ des Arztes** after consulting the doctor **3** (Umfrage) opinion poll

befreien
A *tr. V.* **1** free ‹*prisoner*›; set ‹*animal*› free; **jmdn. aus den Händen seiner Entführer ~:** rescue sb. from the hands of his/her abductors **2** (frei machen) liberate ‹*country, people*› (**von** from) **3** (freistellen) exempt (**von** from); **jmdn. vom Turnunterricht/Wehrdienst/von einer Pflicht ~:** excuse sb. [from] physical education/exempt sb. from military service/release sb. from an obligation; **jmdn. von einer Aufgabe ~:** excuse sb. from *or* let sb. off a task **4** (erlösen) **jmdn. von Schmerzen ~:** free sb. of pain; **von seinen Leiden befreit werden** (durch den Tod) be released from one's sufferings; **jmdn. von Angst/einer Sorge ~:** remove sb.'s fear/free sb. of a worry; **ein ~des Lachen** a laugh which breaks/broke the tension **5** (reinigen) **die Straße von Schnee/Eis ~:** clear the road of snow/ice; **etw. von Läusen ~:** rid sth. of lice
B *refl. V.* free oneself (**von** from); **sich von Vorurteilen/traditionellen Denkweisen ~:** rid oneself of prejudice *sing.*/break away from traditional ways of thinking

Befreier *der,* **Befreierin** *die;* **~, ~nen** liberator

befreit
A *Adj.* relieved; **sich ~ fühlen** feel relieved
B *adv.* with relief; **~ aufatmen** heave a sigh of relief

Befreiung *die;* **~ 1** freeing; **eine ~ des Kindes aus den Händen der Entführer ...** rescuing the child from the hands of its abductors ... **2** (das Freiwerden) liberation; **die ~ der Frau** the emancipation of women **3** (Erlösung) **die ~ von Schmerzen** release from pain **4** (Erleichterung) relief **5** (Freistellung) exemption; **um ~ vom Sportunterricht/von einer Pflicht bitten** ask to be excused [from] sport/released from an obligation

Befreiungs-: ~armee *die* army of liberation; **~bewegung** *die* liberation movement; **~front** *die* liberation front; **~kampf** *der* liberation struggle; **~krieg** *der* **1** war of liberation; **2** *Pl.* (hist.) Wars of Liberation (*1813-1815*); **~versuch** *der* rescue bid *or* attempt; (Ausbruchsversuch) escape bid *or* attempt

befremden /bəˈfrɛmdn̩/
A *tr. V.* **jmdn. ~:** put sb. off; (erstaunen) take sb. aback; **es befremdete ihn, dass ...** he was taken aback [to find] that ...
B *itr. V.* be disturbing

Befremden *das;* **~s** surprise and displeasure

befremdlich (geh.)
A *Adj.* strange; odd
B *adv.* strangely

Befremdung *die;* **~** ▸ **Befremden**

befreunden /bəˈfrɔyndn̩/ *refl. V.* **1** make *or* become friends (**mit** with); **sich miteinander ~:** make *or* become friends **2** (gewöhnen) **sich mit etw. ~:** get used to sth.

befreundet *Adj.* **[gut** *od.* **eng] ~ sein** be [good *or* close] friends (**mit** with); **ein uns** (*Dat.*) **~es**

Ehepaar/~er Schauspieler a couple with whom we are friends/an actor who is a friend of ours; **~e Familien/Kinder** families which are friendly with each other/children who are friends; **das ~e Ausland** friendly [foreign] countries

befrieden *tr. V.* (geh.) bring peace to ‹*country*›; **das Land ist jetzt befriedet** (oft verhüll.) the country is now at peace

befriedigen /bəˈfriːdɪgn̩/ *tr.* (*auch itr.*) *V.* [1] satisfy; satisfy, meet ‹*demand, need*›; satisfy, fulfil ‹*wish*›; satisfy, gratify ‹*lust*›; **seine Gläubiger ~:** satisfy one's creditors; **das Ergebnis befriedigte mich** the result satisfied me *or* was satisfactory to me; **seine Leistung befriedigte [nicht]** his performance was [un]satisfactory; **leicht/schwer zu ~ sein** be easy/hard to satisfy; be easily/not easily satisfied [2] (ausfüllen) ‹*job, occupation, etc.*› fulfil [3] (sexuell) satisfy; **sich [selbst] ~:** masturbate

befriedigend
A *Adj.* [1] satisfactory; satisfactory, adequate ‹*reply, performance*›; **nicht ~ sein** be unsatisfactory/inadequate; **in Latein hat er „~" bekommen** ≈ he got a C in Latin [2] (erfüllend) ‹*job, occupation, etc.*› fulfilling
B *adv.* satisfactorily; ‹*answer*› satisfactorily, adequately

befriedigt
A *Adj.* satisfied
B *adv.* with satisfaction

Befriedigung *die;* ~ [1] ▸**befriedigen 1**: satisfaction; meeting; fulfilment; gratification; **sexuelle ~:** sexual satisfaction; **zur ~ deiner Neugier** to satisfy your curiosity [2] (Genugtuung) satisfaction; **~ darin finden, etw. zu tun** get satisfaction from doing sth.

Befriedung *die;* **~: ein Plan zur ~ des Landes** a plan to bring peace to the country

befristen *tr. V.* **etw. ~:** limit the duration of sth. (**auf** + *Akk.* to)

befristet *Adj.* temporary ‹*visa*›; fixed-term ‹*ban, contract*›; **ein auf zwei Jahre ~er Vertrag** a two-year fixed-term contract; **~ sein** ‹*visa, permit*› be valid for a limited period [only]; **auf ein Jahr ~ sein** ‹*visa, permit*› be valid for one year; **ein auf zwei Jahre ~es Abkommen** an agreement running for *or* lasting two years

Befristung *die;* ~, **~en** setting of a time limit/time limits; **mit einer ~ auf fünf Jahre gelten** have a time limit of five years

befruchten *tr. V.* [1] fertilize ‹*egg*›; pollinate ‹*flower*›; impregnate ‹*female*›; (fig. geh.) make ‹*fields, land*› fertile; **ein Tier künstlich ~:** artificially inseminate an animal [2] (geh.) **jmdn./etw. ~, einen ~den Einfluss auf jmdn./etw. haben** have *or* be a stimulating *or* inspiring influence [up]on sb./sth.

Befruchtung *die;* ~, **~en** [1] ▸**befruchten 1**: fertilization; pollination; impregnation; **künstliche ~:** artificial insemination [2] (geh.: Anregung) stimulation; inspiration

befugen *tr. V.* authorize; **dazu befugt sein, etw. zu tun** be authorized to do sth.; **befugte/nicht befugte Personen** authorized/unauthorized persons

Befugnis *die;* ~, **~se** authority; **seine ~se überschreiten** exceed one's authority *sing.*; **die ~ haben, etw. zu tun** have the authority to do sth.; be authorized to do sth.

befühlen *tr. V.* feel; (streicheln) run one's fingers over; fondle

befummeln *tr. V.* (ugs.) [1] paw (coll.) [2] (sexuell berühren) grope (coll.); feel up (coll.) [3] (regeln, erledigen) fix; take care of

Befund *der* (bes. Med.) result[s *pl.*]; **ohne ~:** negative

befürchten *tr. V.* fear; **ich befürchte, dass ...** I am afraid that ...; **das Schlimmste ~:** fear the worst; **das ist nicht zu ~:** there is no fear of that; **eine militärische Auseinandersetzung ~:** fear that there may be a military conflict

Befürchtung *die;* ~, **~en** fear; **die ~ haben** *od.* (geh.) **hegen, dass ...** be afraid that ...

befürworten /bəˈfyːɐ̯vɔrtn̩/ *tr. V.* support; (genehmigen) approve

Befürworter *der;* **~s**, ~, **Befürworterin** *die;* ~, **~nen** supporter

Befürwortung *die;* ~, **~en** support; (Genehmigung) approval

begaben *tr. V.* (geh.) endow

begabt /bəˈgaːpt/ *Adj.* talented; gifted; **hoch ~:** highly gifted *or* talented; **vielseitig ~ sein** be many-talented; have many talents; **für etw. ~ sein** have a gift *or* talent for sth.

Begabte *der/die; adj. Dekl.* gifted *or* talented person/man/woman *etc.*

Begabten·förderung *die* assistance to gifted pupils/students

Begabung *die;* ~, **~en** [1] (Talent) talent; gift; **eine ~ [für etw.] haben** have a gift *or* talent [for sth.]; **die ~ haben, etw. zu tun** (iron.) have a talent for *or* the knack of doing sth. (iron.) [2] (begabter Mensch) talented person/man/woman *etc.*; talent; **er war eine musikalische ~:** he had a talent for music

begaffen *tr. V.* (ugs. abwertend) gawp at (coll.); stare at

begann /bəˈgan/ *1. u. 3. Pers. Sg. Prät. v.* **beginnen**

begasen /bəˈgaːzn̩/ *tr. V.* (Landw.) gas

begatten /bəˈgatn̩/
A *tr. V.* mate with; ‹*man, husband*› copulate with; ‹*stallion, bull*› cover
B *refl. V.* mate; ‹*persons*› copulate

Begattung *die* mating; (bei Menschen) copulation

Begattungs·organe *Pl.* reproductive organs

begaunern *tr. V.* (ugs. abwertend) **jmdn. ~:** rip sb. off (coll.); swindle sb.

begeben *unr. refl. V.* (geh.) [1] proceed; make one's way; go; **sich nach Hause/ins Hotel ~:** proceed *or* make one's way *or* go home/into the hotel; **sich auf den Heimweg ~:** start for home; **sich zu Bett ~:** retire to bed; **sich in ärztliche Behandlung ~:** get medical treatment; go to a doctor for treatment; *s. auch* **Gefahr** [2] (beginnen) commence; **sich daran ~, etw. zu tun** commence doing sth.; **sich an die Arbeit ~:** commence work [3] (unpers.: geschehen) happen; occur; **es begab sich aber zu der Zeit, dass ...** (bibl.) and it came to pass in those days that ... [4] (verzichten auf) **sich einer Möglichkeit/eines Rechts** *usw.* **~:** forgo an opportunity/a right *etc.*

Begebenheit *die;* ~, **~en** (geh.) event; occurrence

begegnen /bəˈgeːgnən/ *itr. V.; mit sein* [1] **jmdm. ~:** meet sb.; **sich** (*Dat.*) *od.* **einander ~:** meet [each other]; **ihre Blicke begegneten sich** (*Dat.*) (geh.) their eyes met [2] (antreffen) **einer Sache** (*Dat.*) **~:** encounter sth.; come across sth.; **solche Ausdrücke ~ einem** one encounters such expressions [3] (geh.: widerfahren) **etw. begegnet jmdm.** sth. happens to sb. [4] (geh.: behandeln) **jmdm. freundlich/höflich** *usw.* **~:** behave in a friendly/polite *etc.* way towards sb.; treat sb. in a friendly/polite *etc.* way; **einem Vorschlag kühl ~:** treat a suggestion with coolness [5] (geh.: entgegentreten) counter ‹*accusation, attack*›; combat ‹*illness, disease, misuse of drugs, alcohol, etc.*›; meet ‹*difficulty, danger*›; deal with ‹*emergency*›

Begegnung *die;* ~, **~en** [1] meeting; (das Antreffen) encounter; **eine Stätte internationaler ~en** an international meeting place [2] (Sport) match; **die ~ Schweden gegen Italien** the match between Sweden and Italy

Begegnungs·stätte *die* (Amtsspr.) community centre

begehbar *Adj.* **der Weg ist nicht ~:** the path cannot be used *or* is impassable; **ein ~es Dach** a roof that is safe to walk on; **etw. besser ~ machen** make sth. easier to walk along

begehen *unr. tr. V.* [1] commit ‹*crime, adultery, indiscretion, sin, suicide, faux-pas, etc.*›; make ‹*mistake*›; **eine [furchtbare] Dummheit/Taktlosigkeit ~:** do something [really] stupid/tactless; **einen Mord an jmdm. ~:** murder sb.; **ein oft begangener Fehler** a frequent *or* common mistake; *s. auch* **Verrat** [2] (geh.: feiern) celebrate; **ein Fest würdig ~:** celebrate an occasion fittingly [3] (abgehen) inspect [on foot] [4] (gehen) walk along ‹*path*›; walk across ‹*bridge*›; (benutzen) use

Begehr /bəˈgeːɐ̯/ *der od. das;* **~s** (veralt.) wish; desire; **was ist euer ~?** what is it that you require?

begehren *tr. V.* [1] (haben wollen) desire; wish for; desire ‹*woman*›; **ein Mädchen zur Frau ~** (veralt.) ask for a girl's hand in marriage; **du sollst nicht ~ ...** (bibl.) thou shalt not covet ...; *s. auch* **Herz 2** [2] (veralt.: wollen) desire [3] (bitten um) ask for

Begehren *das;* **~s** (geh.) desire, wish (**nach** for); **jmdn. nach seinem ~ fragen** inquire *or* ask what sb. desires; **einem ~ entsprechen** grant sb.'s request

begehrens·wert *Adj.* desirable

begehrlich
A *Adj.* (gierig) greedy; (verlangend) longing
B *adv.* (gierig) greedily; (verlangend) longingly

Begehrlichkeit *die;* ~, **~en** (Gier) greed; (Verlangen) desire

begehrt *Adj.* much sought-after; **~ bei den Damen sein** be much in demand with the ladies

Begehung *die;* ~, **~en** [1] (Ausführung) **die ~ eines Verbrechens/eines Fehlers** committing a crime/making a mistake [2] (Feier) celebration [3] (das Abgehen) inspection [on foot]

begeifern *tr. V.* (abwertend: schmähen) run down; vilify

begeistern
A *tr. V.* **jmdn. [für etw.] ~:** fill *or* fire sb. with enthusiasm [for sth.]; **das Publikum ~:** fire the audience; **das kann mich nicht ~:** that leaves me cold
B *refl. V.* get *or* be enthusiastic (**für** about); **sich an der schönen Landschaft/für die Oper ~:** be very fond of the beautiful scenery/be keen on opera

begeisternd *Adj.* rousing

begeistert
A *Adj.* enthusiastic; **von jmdm./etw. ~ sein** be taken by *or* with sb./be enthusiastic about sth.
B *adv.* enthusiastically

Begeisterung *die;* **~:** enthusiasm; **etw. aus ~ tun** do sth. out of enthusiasm; **in ~ geraten** become *or* get enthusiastic

begeisterungs-, Begeisterungs-: ~fähig *Adj.* ‹*children, people, etc.*› who are able to get enthusiastic *or* are capable of enthusiasm; **~fähig sein** be able to get enthusiastic; **er ist sehr ~fähig** his enthusiasm is easily aroused; **~fähigkeit** *die* capacity for enthusiasm; **~sturm** *der* storm of enthusiastic applause

Begier *die;* ~ (geh.), **Begierde** /bəˈgiːɐ̯də/ *die;* **~de**, **~den** desire (**nach** for); **fleischliche ~den** (veralt.) desires of the flesh; carnal desires

begierig
A *Adj.* eager; (gierig) greedy; hungry; **ganz ~ auf jmds. Besuch** (*Akk.*) **sein** be eagerly looking forward to sb.'s visit; **~ sein, etw. zu tun** be [desperately] eager to do sth.; **mit ~en Blicken** with hungry *or* greedy glances
B *adv.* eagerly; (gierig) greedily; hungrily

begießen *unr. tr. V.* [1] water ‹*plants*›; baste ‹*meat*›; **jmdn./etw. mit Wasser ~:** pour water over sb./sth. [2] (ugs.) **etw. ~:** celebrate sth. with a drink; **das muss begossen werden** that calls for a drink; *s. auch* **Nase**

Beginn /bəˈgɪn/ *der;* **~[e]s** start; beginning; **[gleich] zu** *od.* **am ~:** [right] at the start *or* beginning; **mit ~ des Semesters** at the start of the semester

beginnen
A *unr. itr. V.* start; begin; **mit einer Arbeit/dem Studium ~:** start *or* begin a piece of work/one's studies; **mit dem Bau ~:** start *or* begin building; **dort beginnt der Wald** the forest starts there
B *unr. tr. V.* [1] start; begin; start ‹*argument*› [2] (unternehmen) go *or* set about; **~, etw. zu tun** go *or* set about doing sth.; **was hättet ihr nur**

ohne mich begonnen? what would you have done without me?; **nichts mit sich zu ~ wissen** not know what to do with oneself

Beginnen *das;* **~s** (geh.) enterprise

beginnend *Adj.* incipient; **mit der ~en Morgendämmerung** as dawn begins/began to break; **im ~en 19. Jahrhundert** at the beginning of the 19th century

beglaubigen /bəˈglaubɪgn̩/ *tr. V.* **1** certify; authenticate ‹*account, report, etc.*›; **eine beglaubigte Kopie** a certified copy; *s. auch* **notariell** **2** (akkreditieren) accredit (*Dat.*, **bei** to)

Beglaubigung *die;* **~, ~en** **1** certification; (eines Berichts) authentication; **zur ~:** for certification; to be certified **2** (Akkreditierung) accreditation

Beglaubigungs·schreiben *das* letter of accreditation

begleichen *unr. tr. V.* settle, pay ‹*bill, debt*›; pay ‹*sum*›; **mit jmdm. eine Rechnung zu ~ haben** (fig.) have a score to settle with sb.

Begleichung *die;* **~** (einer Rechnung, einer Schuld) settlement; payment; (einer Summe) payment; **ein Scheck zur ~ meiner Schulden** a cheque in payment of my debts

Begleit·brief *der* covering *or* accompanying letter

begleiten *tr. V.* **1** accompany; escort ‹*ship*›; **jmdn. zur Tür ~:** show sb. to the door; **jmdn. nach Hause ~:** see sb. home **2** (Musik) accompany (**an, auf** + *Dat.* on) **3** (fig.) accompany; **von Erfolg begleitet werden** be attended by success; **etw. mit einem Kommentar ~:** add a commentary to sth.

Begleiter *der;* **~s, ~, Begleiterin** *die;* **~, ~nen** **1** companion; (zum Schutz) escort; (Führer[in]) guide; **ihr ständiger ~/seine ständige ~in** (verhüll.) his/her constant companion **2** (Musik) accompanist

Begleit-: ~erscheinung *die* concomitant; (einer Krankheit) accompanying symptom; **das Alter und seine unangenehmen ~erscheinungen** old age and its attendant ills; **~hund** *der* escort dog; (für Behinderte) assistance dog; **~instrument** *das* accompanying instrument; **~musik** *die* background music; (fig.) accompaniment; **~papiere** *Pl.* accompanying documents; **~person** *die* escort; **Kinder haben nur mit einer ~person Zutritt** children must be accompanied by an adult; **~schein** *der* (Zollw.) [customs] bond note; **~schiff** *das* escort [vessel]; **~schreiben** *das* ▸**~brief**; **~text** *der* accompanying text; **~umstand** *der* attendant circumstance

Begleitung *die;* **~, ~en** **1** **er bot uns seine ~ an** he offered to accompany us; **in ~ einer Frau/eines Erwachsenen** in the company of *or* accompanied by a woman/an adult; **er ist in ~ hier** he's here with someone **2** (Musik) accompaniment; **ohne ~ singen/spielen** sing/play unaccompanied *or* without accompaniment; **die ~ übernehmen** take over as accompanist **3** (Person[en]) companion[s]; (zum Schutz) escort

beglotzen *tr. V.* (ugs.) gawp at (coll.)

beglücken *tr. V.* (geh.) **jmdn. ~:** make sb. happy; delight sb.; **jmdn. mit etw. ~** (oft iron.) favour sb. with sth.; **die Frauen/Männer ~:** gratify women/men; **ein ~des Erlebnis** a gladdening experience

Beglücker *der;* **~s, ~, Beglückerin** *die;* **~, ~nen** bringer of happiness (*Gen.* to)

beglückt
A *Adj.* happy; delighted
B *adv.* happily; delightedly

Beglückung *die;* **~, ~en** **1** **zur ~ der Menschheit beitragen** contribute to the sum of human happiness; **die ~ des Volkes** bringing Utopia to the people **2** (Glück) happiness; delight

beglück·wünschen *tr. V.* congratulate (**zu** on); **sich zu etw. ~:** congratulate oneself on sth.

begnaden /bəˈgnaːdn̩/ *tr. V.* (geh.) bless

begnadet *Adj.* (geh.) divinely gifted

begnadigen *tr. V.* pardon; reprieve; **einen zum Tode Verurteilten zu „lebenslänglich" ~:** commute the convicted prisoner's death sentence to life imprisonment

Begnadigung *die;* **~, ~en** reprieving; (Straferlass) pardon; reprieve

Begnadigungs-: ~gesuch *das* application for reprieve; **~recht** *das* right to grant reprieve

begnügen /bəˈgnyːgn̩/ *refl. V.* **sich mit etw. ~:** content oneself *or* make do with sth.; **sich damit ~, etw. zu tun** content oneself with doing sth.

Begonie /beˈgoːni̯ə/ *die;* **~, ~n** begonia

begonnen /bəˈgɔnən/ *2. Part. v.* **beginnen**

begraben *unr. tr. V.* **1** bury; **dort möchte ich nicht ~ sein** (ugs.) I wouldn't live there if you paid me (coll.) **2** (fig.: aufgeben) abandon ‹*hope, plan, etc.*›; **du kannst dich ~ lassen** (ugs.) you may as well give up; **du kannst dich mit diesem Plan ~ lassen** (ugs.) that plan won't get you anywhere

Begräbnis /bəˈgrɛːpnɪs/ *das;* **~ses, ~se** burial; (**~**feier) funeral

Begräbnis-: ~feier *die* funeral; **~kosten** *Pl.* funeral expenses; **~stätte** *die* (geh.) burial place

begradigen /bəˈgraːdɪgn̩/ *tr. V.* straighten

Begradigung *die;* **~, ~en** straightening

begrast /bəˈgraːst/ *Adj.* grass-covered

begreifbar *Adj.* comprehensible; understandable; **schwer ~ sein** be difficult to comprehend *or* understand

begreifen
A *unr. tr. V.* **1** understand; understand, grasp, comprehend ‹*connection, problem, meaning, necessity of sth., concept*›; **er konnte nicht ~, was geschehen war** he could not grasp what had happened; **kaum zu ~ sein** be almost incomprehensible; **hast du mich begriffen?** you understand? **2** (Verständnis zeigen für) understand; **das begreife, wer will** it's beyond me **3** (geh.: betrachten) regard, see (**als** as) **4** **etw. in sich ~** (veralt.) include sth. **5** (ugs.: befühlen) feel; (betasten) touch
B *itr. V.* understand; **schnell** *od.* **leicht/langsam** *od.* **schwer ~:** be quick/slow on the uptake; be quick/slow to grasp things

begreiflich *Adj.* understandable; **das ist mir nicht ~:** I can't understand it; **jmdm. etw. ~ machen** make sb. understand sth.

begreiflicher·weise *Adv.* understandably; **~ hat er das abgelehnt** understandably enough, he refused

begrenzen *tr. V.* **1** limit, restrict (**auf** + *Akk.* to) **2** (die Grenze bilden von) mark the boundary of; **durch etw. begrenzt sein** be bounded by sth.

begrenzt *Adj.* limited; restricted

Begrenztheit *die;* **~:** limitedness

Begrenzung *die;* **~, ~en** **1** (Grenze) boundary; (Zaun) boundary fence **2** (das Begrenzen) limiting; restriction; (der Geschwindigkeit) restriction

Begriff *der* **1** concept; (Terminus) term; **in ~en denken** think abstractly **2** (Auffassung) idea; **einen/keinen ~ von etw. haben** have an idea/no idea of sth.; **keinen ~ davon haben, wie ...** have no idea how ...; **sich** (*Dat.*) **keinen ~ von etw. machen können** not be able to imagine sth.; **nach menschlichen ~en** in human terms; **für meine ~e** in my estimation; **ein/kein ~ sein** be/not be well known; **jmdm. ein/kein ~ sein** mean something/nothing to sb.; **der ganzen Welt ein ~ sein** be known all over the world **3** **im ~ sein** *od.* **stehen, etw. zu tun** be about to do sth. **4** (Begreifen) **schwer** *od.* **langsam von ~ sein** (ugs. abwertend) be slow on the uptake

begriffen /bəˈgrɪfn̩/
A *2. Part. v.* **begreifen**
B *Adj.* in **im Aufbruch/Fallen ~ sein** be leaving/falling; **in der Entwicklung/im Bau ~ sein** be in [the] process of development/construction

begrifflich
A *Adj.* conceptual
B *adv.* conceptually; **~ denken** think abstractly

begriffs-, Begriffs-: ~bestimmung *die* definition [of the/a concept]; **~mäßig** *Adj., adv.:* ▸**begrifflich**; **~stutzig**, (österr.:) **~stützig** (abwertend) **A** *Adj.* obtuse; slow-witted; gormless (coll.); **B** *adv.* obtusely; slow-wittedly; gormlessly (coll.); **~stutzigkeit** *die;* **~~**, (österr.:) **~stützigkeit** *die;* **~~** (abwertend) obtuseness; slow-wittedness; gormlessness (coll.); **~vermögen** *das* comprehension; **über jmds. ~vermögen** (*Akk.*) **hinausgehen** be beyond sb.'s comprehension *or* grasp; **~verwirrung** *die* conceptual confusion

begründen
A *tr. V.* **1** substantiate ‹*statement, charge, claim*›; give reasons for ‹*decision, refusal, opinion*›; **womit** *od.* **wie begründet sie ihren Entschluss/ihr Verhalten?** what reasons does she give for her decision?/how does she account for her behaviour?; **etw. sachlich ~:** give objective reasons for sth.; **~, warum man etw. tut** give one's reason[s] for doing sth.; **er begründete seinen Meinungswechsel damit, dass ...** he gave as the reason for his change of opinion the fact that ...; **ein Urteil ~:** give the grounds for a judgement; *s. auch* **begründet** **2** (gründen) found; establish ‹*fame, reputation*›; start ‹*family*›; **einen Hausstand ~:** set up house
B *refl. V.* be based; **wie begründet sich das?** what is that based on?

Begründer *der,* **Begründerin** *die* founder

begründet *Adj.* well-founded; reasonable ‹*demand, objection, complaint*›; **sachlich ~:** objectively based; **nicht ~:** unfounded; **in etw.** (*Dat.*) **~ sein** be the result of sth.

Begründung *die;* **~, ~en** **1** reason[s]; **mit der ~, dass ...** on the grounds that ...; **seine ~ war ...** the reason/reasons he gave was/were ...; **für diese These fehlt eine ~:** there is no evidence to support this thesis; **etw. zur ~ einer Sache** (*Gen.*) **sagen** give sth. as the reason for sth.; **ohne jede ~:** without giving any reasons **2** (Gründung) founding; establishment; (eines Hausstands) setting up; (einer Familie) starting

begrünen *tr. V.* **etw. ~:** plant greenery in/on sth.; (mit Rasen) grass sth.; **etw. [mit Rasen/Bäumen/Sträuchern** *usw.***] ~:** plant sth. with grass/trees/shrubs *etc.*

begrüßen *tr. V.* **1** greet; ‹*host, hostess*› greet, welcome; **ich freue mich, Sie in meinem Hause ~ zu dürfen** (geh.) it's a pleasure to welcome you into my home; **ich begrüße Sie** how do you do?; **es würde uns freuen, wenn wir Sie Freitagabend bei uns ~ dürften** (geh.) we should be delighted to have the pleasure of your company on Friday evening **2** (gutheißen) welcome ‹*suggestion, proposal*›; **ich begrüße es, dass ...** I am glad that ...; **es wäre zu ~, wenn ...** it would be a welcome development if ... **3** (schweiz.) consult

begrüßens·wert *Adj.* welcome

Begrüßung *die;* **~, ~en** greeting; (von Gästen) welcoming; (Zeremonie) welcome (*Gen.* for); **jmdm. zur ~ einen Strauß Blumen überreichen** welcome sb. with a bouquet of flowers; **sich** *od.* (geh.) **einander zur ~ die Hand schütteln** shake hands by way of greeting

Begrüßungs-: ~an·sprache *die* speech of welcome; welcoming speech; **~kuss**, ***~kuß** *der* welcoming kiss; **~rede** *die* ▸**~ansprache**; **~wort** *das; Pl.* **~~e** word of welcome

begucken *tr. V.* (ugs.) look at; have *or* take a look at; **lass dich mal ~:** let's have *or* take a look at you

begünstigen /bəˈgʏnstɪgn̩/ *tr. V.* **1** favour; encourage ‹*exports, trade, growth*›; further ‹*plan*›; **vom Rückenwind begünstigt** assisted *or* helped by a following wind; **vom Schicksal begünstigt werden** be blessed by fate **2** (bevorzugen) favour; show favour to **3** (Rechtsw.) **jmdn. ~:** be an accessory of sb. after the fact

Begünstigte *der/die; adj. Dekl.* beneficiary

Begünstigung *die;* **~, ~en** **1** ▸**begünstigen 1**: favouring; encouragement; furthering **2** (Bevorzugung) preferential treatment **3** (Rechtsw.) being an accessory after the fact

b

begutachten *tr. V.* 1 examine and report on; **ein Gemälde/das Flugzeugwrack ~, um etw. festzustellen** examine a painting/the [aircraft] wreckage in order to establish sth.; **ein Gebäude ~:** carry out a survey of a building 2 (ugs.) look at; have *or* take a look at; **lass dich mal ~!** let's have *or* take a look at you

Begutachter *der;* **~s, ~, Begutachterin** *die;* **~, ~nen** ▸**Gutachter**

Begutachtung *die;* **~, ~en** examination; (von Gebäuden) survey; **eine schriftliche ~:** a written report

begütert /bəˈgyːtɐt/ *Adj.* 1 wealthy; affluent 2 (veralt.) landed *attrib.* ‹*gentry, nobility, etc.*›; **~ sein** own land

begütigen /bəˈgyːtɪgn̩/ *tr. V.* placate; mollify; pacify; **~d auf jmdn. einreden** speak soothingly to sb.

Begütigung *die;* **~, ~en** placating; mollifying; pacifying

behaart /bəˈhaːɐ̯t/ *Adj.* hairy; **grau/schwarz/stark ~ sein** be covered with grey/black hair/covered with hair; **stark ~e Beine** very hairy legs

Behaarung *die;* **~, ~en** covering of hair; (Haar) hair *no indef. art.*; **seine starke ~ auf dem Rücken** the thick hair on his back

behäbig /bəˈhɛːbɪç/
A *Adj.* 1 stolid and portly 2 (langsam und schwerfällig) slow and ponderous 3 (geruhsam und gemütlich) placid and easygoing 4 (ausladend) large and solid ‹*furniture, house*›
B *adv.* slowly and ponderously

Behäbigkeit *die;* **~** 1 portliness; stoutness 2 (Langsamkeit) slowness and ponderousness 3 (ausladende Form) size and solidity

behacken *tr. V.* 1 hoe ‹*plants*› 2 (hacken an) hack at

behaftet *Adj.* (geh.) **mit einem Makel/einer Krankheit ~ sein** be marked with a blemish/afflicted with a disease; **mit einem schlechten Ruf/einem Fehler/Laster ~ sein** have a bad name/a defect/be tainted with a vice; **mit Fehlern ~ sein** contain defects

behagen /bəˈhaːgn̩/ *itr. V.* please; **das behagt mir/behagt mir nicht** that pleases/does not please me; I like/do not like that; **er behagt mir gar nicht** I don't like him at all

Behagen *das;* **~s** (Zufriedenheit) contentment; (Vergnügen) pleasure; **mit [sichtlichem] ~:** with [obvious] contentment/pleasure; **etw. mit ~ essen** eat sth. with relish

behaglich
A *Adj.* 1 comfortable; comfortable, cosy ‹*atmosphere, room, home, etc.*›; **es jmdm./sich ~ machen** make sb./oneself comfortable 2 (genießerisch, zufrieden) contented
B *adv.* 1 comfortably, cosily ‹*warm, furnished*› 2 (genießerisch, zufrieden) contentedly

Behaglichkeit *die;* **~** ▸**behaglich A:** 1 comfortableness; cosiness 2 contentment

behalten *unr. tr. V.* 1 keep; keep on ‹*workers, employees*›; keep, retain ‹*value, expressive power, etc.*›; **den Hut auf dem Kopf ~:** keep one's hat on; **Nahrung bei sich ~:** keep food down; **jmdn. als Gast bei sich ~:** have sb. stay on as one's guest; **etw. für sich ~:** keep sth. to oneself; **die Nerven/die Ruhe ~:** keep one's nerve/keep calm; **ob wir das gute Wetter ~?** will the good weather hold? 2 (zurück~) be left with; **einen Herzschaden** *usw.* **~:** be left with a weak heart *etc.*; **sie behielt von dem Unfall ein steifes Knie** the accident left her with a stiff knee 3 (sich merken) remember ‹*number, date*›; **ich habe die Adresse nicht ~:** I've forgotten the address; **er kann Geschichtszahlen schlecht ~:** he has no memory for historical dates; **jmdn. in freundlicher Erinnerung ~:** have fond memories of sb.; *s. auch* **Recht 4**

Behälter /bəˈhɛltɐ/ *der;* **~s, ~** 1 container; (für Abfälle) receptacle 2 (Container) container

Behälter-: ~schiff *das* container ship; **~verkehr** *der* container traffic

Behältnis *das;* **~ses, ~se** (geh.) container

behämmern *tr. V.* hammer

behämmert *Adj.* (salopp) ▸**bekloppt**

behänd /bəˈhɛnt/, **behände**
A *Adj.* (geschickt) deft; adroit; (flink) nimble; agile
B *adv.*; *s. Adj.*: deftly; adroitly; nimbly; agilely

behandeln *tr. V.* 1 (umgehen mit) treat ‹*person*›; handle ‹*matter, machine, device*›; **jmdn. freundlich/herablassend/schlecht ~:** treat sb. in a friendly way/condescendingly/badly; **eine Maschine sachgemäß ~:** handle *or* use a machine correctly; **sie weiß, wie man Kinder/den Chef ~ muss** she knows how to handle children/the manager 2 (bearbeiten) treat (**mit** with) 3 (darstellen, analysieren) deal with, treat ‹*subject, question, theme*› 4 ▸ⓘ **S. 439** (ärztlich) treat ‹*patient, illness, symptom*› (**mit** with; **auf** + *Akk.*, **wegen** for); **jmdn. ambulant/stationär ~:** give sb. treatment as an outpatient/inpatient; **der ~de Arzt** the doctor treating the patient

Behändigkeit *die;* **~** ▸**behänd A**: deftness; adroitness; nimbleness; agility

Behandlung *die;* **~, ~en** ▸ⓘ **S. 439** 1 treatment; **eine solche ~ lasse ich mir nicht gefallen** I won't stand for being treated like that; **bessere ~ verdienen** deserve better treatment *or* to be treated better; **bei einem/diesem Arzt in ~ sein** be under medical treatment/this doctor 2 (Besprechung) discussion; (Analyse) treatment

behandlungs-, Behandlungs-: ~bedürftig *Adj.* **~bedürftig sein** require treatment; **~kosten** *Pl.* cost *sing.* of treatment; **~methode** *die* method of treatment; **~pflicht** *die: obligation on a doctor to respond to a call for medical assistance*; **~raum** *der* treatment room; **~stuhl** *der* chair for the patient; (beim Zahnarzt) [dentist's] chair; **~weise** *die* ▸**~methode**

behandschuht *Adj.* gloved

Behang *der;* **~[e]s, Behänge** 1 (Wand~) hanging 2 (am Baum) decoration; (Ertrag) crop 3 (Jägerspr.) (Ohr) lop-ear; (Ohren) lop ears *pl.*

behangen *Adj.* **ein mit Äpfeln ~er Baum** a tree laden with apples; **mit Schmuck ~:** festooned with jewellery

behängen *tr. V.* 1 **etw. mit etw. ~:** hang *or* decorate sth. with sth. 2 (ugs. abwertend) **jmdn./sich mit etw. ~:** festoon sb./oneself with sth.

beharken *tr. V.* 1 (Soldatenspr.) rake with gunfire 2 (salopp) pitch into (coll.); set about (coll.)

beharren *itr. V.* 1 **auf etw.** (*Dat.*) **~** (etw. nicht aufgeben) persist in sth.; (auf etw. bestehen) insist on sth.; **darauf ~, etw. zu tun** insist on doing sth. 2 (beharrlich behaupten) insist 3 (geh.: bleiben) (an einem Ort) remain; (in einem Zustand) persist

Beharren *das;* **~s** insistence

beharrlich
A *Adj.* dogged; persistent
B *adv.* doggedly; persistently; **~ bei seiner Meinung bleiben** stick doggedly to one's opinion

Beharrlichkeit *die;* **~:** doggedness; persistence

Beharrung *die;* **~:** persistence

Beharrungs·vermögen *das* (Physik) inertia

behauchen *tr. V.* 1 breathe on 2 (Phon.) aspirate; **behauchte Konsonanten** aspirates

behauen *unr. tr. V.* hew; **roh ~e Steine** rough-hewn stone blocks

behaupten /bəˈhaupt̩n/
A *tr. V.* 1 maintain; assert; **~, jmd. zu sein/etw. zu wissen** claim to be sb./know sth.; **das kann man nicht ~:** you cannot say that; **man behauptet** *od.* **es wird behauptet, dass …** it is said *or* claimed that …; *s. auch* **steif B 3** 2 (verteidigen) maintain ‹*position*›; retain ‹*record*›; *s. auch* **Feld 6**
B *refl. V.* 1 assert oneself; (nicht untergehen) hold one's ground; (dableiben) survive; **die Kirche/der Dollar konnte sich ~:** the church/the dollar was able to maintain its position 2 (Sport) win through

Behauptung *die;* **~, ~en** 1 claim; assertion 2 (Verteidigung) **für die ~ seiner Stellung kämpfen** fight to maintain one's position 3 (Durchsetzung) assertion

Behauptungs·wille *der* determination [to assert oneself]

behausen *tr. V.* (geh.) house; accommodate; accommodate, put up ‹*guest*›

Behausung *die;* **~, ~en** 1 (geh.: das Behausen) housing; accommodation 2 (oft abwertend: Wohnung) dwelling

Behaviorismus /bihevjəˈrɪsmʊs/ *der;* **~** (Verhaltensf.) behaviourism *no art.*

behavioristisch (Biol., Psych.)
A *Adj.* behaviourist
B *adv.* behaviouristically

beheben *unr. tr. V.* 1 remove ‹*doubt, danger, difficulty*›; repair ‹*damage*›; remedy ‹*abuse, defect*›; clear ‹*disturbance*› 2 (österr.: abheben) withdraw ‹*money*›

Behebung *die;* **~, ~en** 1 ▸**beheben 1**: removal; repair; remedying; clearing 2 (österr.: Abhebung) withdrawal

beheimaten *tr. V.* provide a home for ‹*person*›; **Tiere/Pflanzen in einer Gegend ~:** introduce animals/plants into an area

beheimatet *Adj.* 1 (heimisch) **an einem Ort/in einem Land ~ sein** ‹*plant, animal, tribe, race*› be native *or* indigenous to a place/country; ‹*person*› come from a place/country; **wo ist er ~?** where does he come from? 2 (ansässig) resident (**in** + *Dat.* in)

beheizbar *Adj.* heatable; **eine ~e Heckscheibe** a heated rear window

beheizen *tr. V.* heat

Beheizung *die;* **~:** heating

Behelf /bəˈhɛlf/ *der;* **~[e]s, ~e** (Notlösung) stopgap; makeshift; (Ersatz) substitute

behelfen *unr. refl. V.* 1 **sich mit etw. ~:** make do *or* manage with sth. 2 (zurechtkommen) get by; manage; **sich allein ~:** get by *or* manage on one's own

behelfs-, Behelfs-: ~aus·fahrt *die* (Verkehrsw.) temporary exit (*from a motorway*); **~heim** *das* makeshift *or* temporary home; **~mäßig** A *Adj.* makeshift; temporary; B *adv.* in a makeshift way *or* fashion; **~unterkunft** *die* temporary dwelling; **~weise** *Adv.* (vorübergehend) temporarily; (ersatzweise) as a substitute

behelligen /bəˈhɛlɪgn̩/ *tr. V.* (lästig werden für) bother; (zudringlich werden gegenüber) pester

Behelligung *die;* **~, ~en ich verbitte mir solche ~en** stop bothering *or* pestering me

behelmt /bəˈhɛlmt/ *Adj.* helmeted

***behend, *behende** ▸**behänd**

beherbergen *tr. V.* 1 accommodate, put up ‹*guest*› 2 (Raum bieten für) accommodate 3 (enthalten) contain

Beherbergung *die;* **~:** accommodation

Beherbergungs·gewerbe *das* hotel trade

beherrschen
A *tr. V.* 1 rule; **den Markt ~:** dominate *or* control the market; **von Hassgefühlen/Leidenschaften beherrscht sein** (geh.) be ruled by feelings of hatred/by passions 2 (meistern) control ‹*vehicle, animal*›; be in control of ‹*situation*› 3 (bestimmen, dominieren) dominate ‹*townscape, landscape, discussions, relationship*› 4 (zügeln) control ‹*feelings*›; control, curb ‹*impatience*›; **seine Zunge ~** (geh.) curb one's tongue 5 (gut können) have mastered ‹*instrument, trade*›; have a good command of ‹*language*›; **es kostet viele Jahre ständiger Übung, ein Instrument zu ~:** it takes many years of constant practice to master an instrument; **Englisch fast so gut wie Deutsch ~:** speak English almost as well as German
B *refl. V.* control oneself; **ich kann mich ~** (iron.) I can resist the temptation (iron.); **kannst du dich so wenig ~, dass …?** have you got so little self-control that …?

Beherrscher *der;* **~s, ~, Beherrscherin** *die;* **~, ~nen** ruler

beherrscht
A *Adj.* self-controlled
B *adv.* with self-control; **völlig ~:** with complete self-control

Beherrschtheit *die;* **~**: self-control

Beherrschung *die;* **~** [1] control; (Verwaltung) rule; (eines Markts) domination; control [2] (das Meistern) control [3] (Beherrschtheit) self-control; **seine** *od.* **die ~ verlieren** lose one's self-control [4] (das Können) mastery

beherzigen /bəˈhɛrtsɪgn̩/ *tr. V.* **etw. ~**: take sth. to heart; heed sth.

beherzigens·wert *Adj.* worth taking to heart *or* heeding *postpos.*

Beherzigung *die;* **~**: heeding; **dies zur ~!** I want you to heed *or* take good heed of this

beherzt
A *Adj.* spirited; **einige Beherzte** a few brave souls
B *adv.* spiritedly

Beherztheit *die;* **~**: spirit

behexen *tr. V.* bewitch

behilflich /bəˈhɪlflɪç/ *Adj.* **jmdm. [beim Aufräumen** *usw.***] ~ sein** help sb. [clear up *or* with the clearing-up *etc.*]; **kann ich [Ihnen] ~ sein?** can I help [you]?

behindern *tr. V.* [1] hinder; hamper, impede ‹*movement*›; hold up ‹*traffic*›; impede ‹*view*›; **jmdn. in etw.** (*Dat.*) **~**: hinder sb. in sth.; **ein behindertes Kind** a handicapped child [2] (Sport, Verkehrsw.) obstruct

Behinderte *der/die; adj. Dekl.* handicapped person; **die ~n** the handicapped; **WC für ~**: toilet for disabled persons

behinderten-, Behinderten-: ~gerecht A *Adj.* ‹*accommodation, toilet, bus, lift, etc.*› which caters for the needs of people with disabilities; B *adv.* **das Hotel ist ~gerecht ausgestattet** the hotel is equipped to cater for [the needs of] people with disabilities; **~sport** *der* disabled sport; **~sportler** *der* disabled sportsman; **~sportlerin** *die* disabled sportswoman

Behinderung *die;* **~, ~en** [1] **um ~en bei der Zollabfertigung zu vermeiden** to avoid hold-ups at customs; **zur ~ des Flugverkehrs beitragen** help to cause delays to air traffic; **~ der Sicht** obstruction to the view [2] (Sport, Verkehrsw.) obstruction; **Falschparken mit ~**: parking illegally and causing an obstruction [3] (Hindernis) hindrance [4] (Gebrechen) handicap

behobeln *tr. V.* plane

behorchen *tr. V.* [1] (ugs.) listen to [2] (belauschen) eavesdrop on

Behörde /bəˈhøːɐ̯də/ *die;* **~, ~n** [1] authority; (Amt, Abteilung) department; **die ~n** the authorities [2] (Gebäude) government offices *pl.*/[local] council offices *pl.*

Behörden-: ~apparat *der* administrative apparatus; (abwertend: Bürokratie) bureaucracy; **~deutsch** *das* (abwertend) officialese; **~gang** *der* visit to the authorities

behördlich
A *Adj.* official; **~e Genehmigung** permission from the authorities; official permission; **auf ~e Anordnung** by order of the authorities
B *adv.* officially; **das ist ~ genehmigt worden** it has been approved by the authorities

behördlicher·seits *Adv.* (durch die Behörde) by the authorities; (seitens der Behörde) on the part of the authorities

behost /bəˈhoːst/ *Adj.* (ugs.) in trousers *postpos.*

Behuf *der;* **~[e]s, ~e** *in* **zu diesem ~[e]** (veralt.) to this end

behufs *Präp. mit Gen.* (veralt.) with a view to

behuft /bəˈhuːft/ *Adj.* hoofed

behum[p]sen /bəˈhʊmpsn̩, bəˈhʊmzn̩/ *tr. V.* (ugs., bes. ostmd.) diddle (coll.)

behüten *tr. V.* (bewahren, beschützen) protect (**vor** + *Dat.* from); (sorgen für) take care of; (bewachen) guard; **ein Geheimnis ~**: keep a secret; **jmdn. vor einer Gefahr ~**: keep *or* safeguard sb. from a danger; **[Gott] behüte!** God *or* Heaven forbid!

Behüter *der;* **~s, ~, Behüterin** *die;* **~, ~nen** (geh.) protector

behütet *Adj.* sheltered ‹*upbringing, life*›

behutsam /bəˈhuːtzaːm/
A *Adj.* careful; cautious; cautious, discreet ‹*question*›; (zartfühlend) gentle
B *adv.* carefully; cautiously; (zartfühlend) gently

Behutsamkeit *die;* **~**: care; caution; (Zartgefühl) gentleness

bei /bai̯/ *Präp. mit Dat.* [1] (nahe) near; (dicht an, neben) by; **die Schlacht ~ Leipzig** the battle of Leipzig; **irgendwo ~ Stuttgart** somewhere near Stuttgart; **nahe ~m Bahnhof** near the station; **~m Gepäck/Auto** *usw.* **bleiben** stay with the luggage/car; **wer steht da ~ ihm?** who is standing there with him?; **sich ~ jmdm. entschuldigen/beklagen/erkundigen** apologize/complain to sb./ask sb.; **wir haben Physik ~ Herrn Meyer** we do physics with Mr Meyer; **der Wert liegt ~ 10 000 Euro** the value is around *or* about 10,000 euros; **~m Fenster herausschauen** (österr.) look out of the window
[2] (unter) among; **war heute ein Brief für mich ~ der Post?** was there a letter for me in the post today?
[3] (an) by; **jmdn. ~ der Hand nehmen** take sb. by the hand; **jmdn. ~ der Schulter packen** seize sb. by the shoulder; *s. auch* **beim 2**
[4] (im Wohnbereich) (längerfristig) with; (kurzfristig) at; **~ uns tut man das nicht** we don't do that; **~ mir [zu Hause]** at my house; **~ uns um die Ecke/gegenüber** round the corner from us/opposite us; **~ seinen Eltern leben** live with one's parents; **wir sind ~ ihr eingeladen** we have been invited to her house; **wir treffen uns ~ uns/Peter** we'll meet at our/Peter's place; **morgen schlafe ich ~ meinen Großeltern** I'm sleeping at my grandparents' tomorrow; **~ uns in Österreich** in Austria [where I/we come from/live]; **[hier/damals] ~ uns in Österreich** here in Austria/in Austria in those days; **wir haben ~ [den] Clarks gefeiert** we went to a party at the Clarks'; (im Geschäft) **~m Bäcker/Fleischer** *usw.* at the baker's/butcher's *etc.*; **~ uns in der Firma** in our company; **~ Schmidt** (auf Briefen) c/o Schmidt
[5] (im geistigen Bereich) with; **~ jmdm. Verständnis finden** get sympathy and understanding from sb.; **die Verantwortung liegt ~ Ihnen** responsibility lies with you
[6] (im Arbeitsbereich) **~ einer Firma sein** be with a company; **~ jmdm./einem Verlag arbeiten** work for sb./a publishing house; **~ der Bundeswehr/Luftwaffe sein** be in the forces/air force; *s. auch* **~ 1**
[7] (im Bereich eines Vorgangs) at; **~ einer Hochzeit/einem Empfang** *usw.* **sein** be at a wedding/reception *etc.*; **~ der Organisation von etw./~ einer Aufführung mitwirken** be involved in the organization of sth./appear in a production
[8] (im Werk von) **~ Goethe** in Goethe; **~ Schiller heißt es …** Schiller says *or* writes that …
[9] (im Falle von) in the case of; **wie ~ den Römern** as with the Romans; **hoffentlich geht es nicht wie ~ mir** I hope the same thing doesn't happen as happened in my case
[10] (im eigenen Bereich) with; **etw. ~ sich haben** have sth. with *or* on one; **~ sich [selbst] anfangen** start with oneself; **nicht [ganz] ~ sich sein** be not quite with it; **~ mir ist es zehn Uhr** I make it ten o'clock
[11] (Zeitpunkt) at ‹*beginning, end*›; **~ seiner Ankunft/seinem Eintritt** on his arrival/entry; **~ diesen Worten errötete er** at this he blushed
[12] (Zeitspanne) **~ Tag/Nacht** by day/night; **~ Sonnenaufgang/-untergang** at sunrise/sunset; **~ unserer Begegnung** at our meeting; **~ einem Unfall** in an accident; **~ einer Schlägerei** in a brawl; **~ Tisch sein** be at table; **~ der Arbeit** at work; *s. auch* **beim 2**
[13] (gleichzeitig mit) with; **~ zunehmendem Alter** with advancing age
[14] (modal) **~ Tag und Nacht** day and night; **~ Tageslicht** by daylight; **~ Nebel** in fog; **~ Kälte** when it's cold; **~ einem Glas Wein** over a glass of wine; **~ offenem Fenster schlafen** sleep with the window open
[15] (betreffs) with; **das gilt auch ~ …** this applies to … also; **~ so etwas ist er geschickt** he is skilled at things like that
[16] (im Falle von) **„~ Feuer Scheibe einschlagen"** 'in case of fire, break glass'; **„~ Regen Schleudergefahr"** 'slippery when wet'; **~ hohem Fieber** when sb. has a high temperature
[17] (aufgrund von) with; **~ dieser Hitze** in this heat; **~ diesem Sturm/Lärm** with this storm blowing/noise going on; **~ deinen guten Augen/ihrem Talent** with your good eyesight/her talent; **er erblasste ~ der Nachricht** he turned pale at the news
[18] (trotz) **~ all seinem Engagement/seinen Bemühungen** in spite of *or* despite *or* for all his commitment/efforts; **~ allem Verständnis, aber ich kann das nicht** much as I sympathize, I cannot do that
[19] (in Beteuerungsformeln) by; **~ Gott!** by God!; **~ meiner Ehre!** (veralt.) upon my honour!

bei|behalten *unr. tr. V.* keep, retain ‹*distinction, wording, penalty, measure, practice, laws*›; keep up ‹*custom, habit*›; continue, maintain ‹*way of life*›; keep to ‹*course, method*›; preserve, maintain ‹*attitude*›

Beibehaltung *die;* **~ ▸beibehalten**: keeping; retention; keeping up; continuance; maintenance; preservation

bei|biegen *unr. tr. V.* (ugs.) **jmdm. etw. ~**: get sb. to understand sth.

Bei·blatt *das* insert

Bei·boot *das* ship's boat

bei|bringen *unr. tr. V.* [1] **jmdm. etw. ~**: teach sb. sth.; **jmdm. Gehorsam ~**: teach sb. obedience; **ich werde dir ~, mich zu betrügen!** (ugs.) I'll teach you to cheat me! (coll.) [2] (ugs.: mitteilen) **jmdm. ~, dass …** break it to sb. that … [3] (zufügen) **jmdm./sich etw. ~**: inflict sth. on sb./oneself [4] (beschaffen) produce ‹*witness, evidence*›; provide, supply ‹*reference, proof*›; produce, furnish ‹*money*›

Beichte /ˈbai̯çtə/ *die;* **~, ~n** confession *no def. art.*; **zur ~ gehen** go to confession; **jmdm. die ~ abnehmen** hear sb.'s confession

beichten
A *itr. V.* go to confession; **~ gehen** go to confession
B *tr. V.* (fig.) confess

Beicht-: ~formel *die* form of confession; **~geheimnis** *das* seal of confession; **~gespräch** *das* (kath. Rel.) talk with the priest before confession; **~stuhl** *der* confessional; **~vater** *der* father confessor

beid-: ~armig A *Adj.* two-handed; (mit ~en Armen gleich geschickt) ambidextrous; B *adv.* with both hands; **~beinig** A *Adj.* two-legged; B *adv.* with both feet

beide /ˈbai̯də/ *Indefinitpron. u. Zahlw.* [1] *mit Art. od. Pron.* **die/seine ~n Brüder** the/his two brothers; (mit Nachdruck) both the/his brothers; **die ~n ersten Strophen** the first two verses; **kennst du die ~n?** do you know those two?; **alle ~**: both of us/you/them; **sie sind alle ~ sehr schön** they're both very nice; both of them are very nice; **sie sind ~ nicht hübsch** neither of them is pretty; **ihr/euch ~**: you two; **ihr/euch ~ nicht** neither of you; **wir/uns ~**: the two of us/both of us [2] *o. Art.* both; **er hat ~ Eltern verloren** he has lost both [his] parents; **mit ~n Händen** with both hands; **~ Male** both times; **ich habe ~ gekannt** I knew both of them; **~ haben hier gearbeitet** both [of them] worked here; **einer/eins von ~n** one of the two; **keiner/keins von ~n** neither [of them] [3] *Neutr. Sg.* both *pl.*; **~s ist möglich** either is possible; **ich glaube ~s/~s nicht** I believe both things/neither thing; **das ist ~s nicht richtig** neither of those is correct; **er hat sich in ~m geirrt** he was wrong on both counts; **er hatte von ~m wenig Ahnung** he had little idea of either

***beide·mal** ▸**Mal¹**

beiderlei /ˈbai̯dɐˈlai̯/ *Gattungsz., indekl.* **~ Geschlechts** of both sexes; **von ~ Art** of both kinds; **das Abendmahl in** *od.* **unter ~ Gestalt** (ev. Rel.) communion in both kinds

beider·seitig
A *Adj.* mutual ‹*decision, agreement*›; **~e Freude**

joy on both sides; **zur ∼en Überraschung** to the surprise of both of us/them; **in ∼em Einverständnis** by mutual agreement **B** *adv.* by both sides; **eine ∼ interessierende Frage** a question of interest to both sides **C** *Adv.* on both sides

beider·seits
A *Präp. mit Gen.* on both sides of
B *Adv.* on both sides

beid-: ∼füßig *Adj., adv.* with both feet; **∼händig** **A** *Adj.* **1** (mit ∼en Händen gleich geschickt) ambidextrous; **2** (mit ∼en Händen) two-handed; **B** *adv.* with two hands; **eine ∼händig geschlagene Rückhand** a two-handed backhand

bei|drehen *itr. V.* (Seemannsspr.) heave to

beid·seitig
A *Adj.* mutual
B *adv.* **1** (auf beiden Seiten) ‹*be printed etc.*› on both sides; **∼ gelähmt sein** be paralysed down both sides **2** (gegenseitig) ▸ **beiderseitig B**

beidseits (bes. schweiz.) ▸ **beiderseits**

bei·einander *Adv.* together; **etw. ∼ haben** have got sth. together; **er hat sie nicht alle ∼** (ugs.) he's not all there (coll.); **∼ sein** (ordentlich sein) be neat and tidy; **gut/schlecht ∼ sein** (ugs.) be in good/bad shape; **nicht ganz ∼ sein** (ugs.) be not quite all there (coll.) **∼ Trost suchen** seek comfort from each other

*__beieinander|haben__ *usw.* ▸ **beieinander**

Beieinander·sein *das* get-together

*__beieinander|sitzen__ *usw.* ▸ **beieinander**

Bei·fahrer *der*, **Bei·fahrerin** *die* **1** (im Kfz) [front-seat] passenger; (auf dem Motorrad) pillion passenger; (im Beiwagen) sidecar passenger **2** (berufsmäßig) co-driver; (auf einem LKW) driver's mate

Beifahrer·sitz *der* (im Kfz) passenger seat; (eines Motorrads) pillion

Bei·fall *der* **1** applause; (Zurufe) cheers *pl.*; cheering; (Händeklatschen) applause; clapping; **stürmischer** *od.* **tosender ∼:** a storm of applause; **∼ klatschen/spenden** applaud; **jmdn. ∼ heischend ansehen** look at sb. in the hope of getting applause **2** (Zustimmung) approval; **∼ finden** meet with approval; **jmdn. ∼ heischend ansehen** look at sb. in the hope of getting approval

beifall·heischend ▸ **Beifall**

bei·fällig
A *Adj.* approving; favourable ‹*judgement*›; **∼es Gemurmel** murmurs *pl.* of approval
B *adv.* approvingly; **∼ nicken** nod approvingly *or* in approval; **∼ aufgenommen werden** be received favourably *or* with approval

Beifall·klatschen *das* clapping; applause

Beifalls-: ∼äußerung *die* expression of approval; **∼bekundung** *die*, **∼bezeigung** *die* demonstration of approval; **∼kundgebung** *die* ovation; **∼kundgebungen** ovation *sing.*; **∼ruf** *der* shout of approval; cheer; **∼sturm** *der* storm of applause

Bei·fang *der* (Fischerei) by-catch

bei|fügen *tr. V.* **1** (dazulegen) **einer Bewerbung etw. ∼:** enclose sth. with an application; **einem Paket eine Zollerklärung ∼:** attach a customs declaration to a parcel; **einem Blumenstrauß eine Grußkarte ∼:** put a greetings card in with a bouquet **2** (hinzufügen) add; **dem Teig Zucker/Mehl ∼:** add sugar/flour to the mixture

Bei·fügung *die* **1** (Sprachw.) attribute **2** (Amtsspr.: das Beifügen) **unter ∼ eines Lebenslaufs/Schecks** enclosing a curriculum vitae/cheque

Bei·fuß *der* (Bot.) artemisia; (Artemisia vulgaris) mugwort

Bei·gabe *die* **1** (das Beigeben) **unter ∼** (*Dat.*) **von etw.** adding sth. **2** (Hinzugefügtes) addition; (Beilage) side dish

beige /be:ʃ/ *Adj.* beige; **ein ∼** *od.* (ugs.) **∼s Kleid** a beige dress

Beige *das;* **∼,** **∼** *od.* (ugs.) **∼s** beige

bei|geben
A *unr. tr. V.* **1** (hinzufügen) add (*Dat.* to) **2** (mitgeben) assign (*Dat.* to)
B *unr. itr. V. in* **klein ∼** (ugs.) give in

beige·farben *Adj.* beige[-coloured]

bei|gehen *unr. itr. V.; mit sein* (nordd.) ▸ **darangehen**

Beigeordnete *der/die; adj. Dekl.* ≈ town council official

Bei·geschmack *der* **einen bitteren** *usw.* **∼ haben** have a slightly bitter *etc.* taste [to it]; taste slightly bitter *etc.*; **dieses Wort hat einen negativen ∼** (fig.) this word has slightly negative overtones *pl.*; **einen ∼ von Petroleum haben** have a slight taste of paraffin (Brit.) *or* (Amer.) kerosene; taste slightly of petrol

bei|gesellen (geh.)
A *tr. V.* **jmdm. jmdn. ∼:** put sb. with sb.
B *refl. V.* **sich jmdm. ∼:** attach oneself to sb.

Bei·heft *das* (zum Lehrbuch) supplement; (einer Zeitschrift) supplementary number

bei|heften *tr. V.* **einer Sache** (*Dat.*) **etw. ∼:** attach sth. to sth.

Bei·hilfe *die* **1** (materielle Hilfe) aid; assistance; (Geldunterstützung) [financial] aid *or* assistance; (Zuschuss für Kleidung, Heizung, Miete, Kinderreiche, Studenten usw.) allowance; (Subvention) subsidy **2** (Rechtsw.: Mithilfe) aiding and abetting; **jmdn. wegen ∼ zum Mord anklagen** charge sb. with aiding and abetting a murder *or* with acting as accessory to a murder

Bei·klang *der* (geh.) [accompanying] sound; (fig.) overtone[s *pl.*]; underlying note

Bei·koch *der*, **Bei·köchin** *die* assistant chef

bei|kommen *unr. itr. V.; mit sein* **1** (gewachsen sein) **jmdm. ∼:** get the better of sb. **2** (bewältigen) **den Schwierigkeiten/der Unruhe/jmds. Sturheit ∼:** overcome the difficulties/deal with the unrest/cope with sb.'s obstinacy **3** (ugs.: herbeikommen) come **4** (ugs.: heranreichen) reach **5** *unpers.* (geh.) **es kommt jmdm. bei, etw. zu tun** sb. has the idea of doing sth.

Bei·kost *die* diet supplement; **vitaminreiche/nahrhafte ∼ bekommen** have a vitamin-rich/nutritious supplementary diet

Beil /bail/ *das;* **∼[e]s, ∼e** **1** axe; (kleiner) hatchet; (Fleischer∼) cleaver **2** (Fall∼) guillotine

bei|laden *unr. tr. V.* **1** (zuladen) add **2** (Rechtsw.) summon ‹*third party interested in the outcome of a case*›

Bei·ladung *die* additional load

Bei·lage *die* **1** (Zeitungs∼) supplement **2** (zu Speisen) side dish; (Gemüse∼) vegetables *pl.*; (Salat∼) side salad; **ein Fleischgericht mit diversen ∼n** a meat dish with a selection of trimmings **3** (das Beilegen) enclosure; **unter ∼ von ...** enclosing ...; **gegen ∼ von Rückporto** if return postage is enclosed **4** (österr.: Anlage) enclosure (**zu** with)

Bei·lager *das* **1** (geh. veralt.: Beischlaf) sexual intercourse **2** (hist.: Akt der Eheschließung) consummation of the marriage

bei·läufig
A *Adj.* **1** (nebensächlich) casual; casual, passing ‹*remark, mention*› **2** (österr.: ungefähr) approximate; rough
B *adv.* **1** (nebenbei) casually; **etw. ∼ erwähnen** *od.* **bemerken** mention sth. casually *or* in passing; **∼ bemerkt, ...** incidentally, ...; **etw. ∼ erfahren** learn sth. by chance; **jmdn. ∼ ausfragen** get information unobtrusively from sb. **2** (österr.: ungefähr) approximately; roughly

Beiläufigkeit *die;* **∼, ∼en** **1** (Nonchalance) casualness **2** (Nebensächlichkeit) triviality; **∼en** trivia

bei|legen *tr. V.* **1** (dazulegen) enclose; (einem Buch, einer Zeitschrift) insert (*Dat.* in); **einem Brief** *usw.* **etw. ∼:** enclose sth. with a letter *etc.* **2** (schlichten) settle ‹*dispute, controversy, etc.*› **3** (beimessen) attach; **einer Sache** (*Dat.*) **Gewicht/Bedeutung** *usw.* **∼:** attach weight/importance *etc.* to sth. **4** (geben, verleihen) **jmdm. einen Titel/Namen ∼:** bestow *or* confer a title/bestow a name on sb.; **sich** (*Dat.*) **einen Titel/Namen ∼:** assume *or* adopt a title/name

Beilegung *die;* **∼, ∼en** settlement

beileibe /bai'laibə/ *Adv.* **∼ nicht** certainly not; **er ist ∼ kein Genie** he is by no means a genius

Bei·leid *das* sympathy; **[mein] herzliches** *od.* **aufrichtiges ∼!** please accept my sincere condolences; **jmdm. sein [aufrichtiges] ∼ [zu etw.] aussprechen** offer one's [sincere] condolences *pl.* to sb. [on sth.]

Beileids-: ∼besuch *der* visit of condolence; visit to offer one's condolences; **∼bezeigung** *die;* **∼∼, ∼∼en, ∼bezeugung** *die* expression of sympathy; **∼karte** *die* condolence *or* sympathy card

Beil·hieb *der* blow with an/the axe

bei|liegen *unr. itr. V.* **1** (beigefügt sein) **einem Brief ∼:** be enclosed with a letter; **dem Buch liegt ein Prospekt bei** the book contains a catalogue as an insert **2** (geh. veralt.: Geschlechtsverkehr haben mit) **jmdm. ∼:** lie with sb. (arch.) **3** (Seemannsspr.) lie to

bei·liegend *Adj.* (Amtsspr.) enclosed; **∼ senden wir ...** please find enclosed ...

beim /baim/ *Präp. + Art.* **1** = **bei dem** **2** **jmdn. ∼ Ärmel zupfen** tug at sb.'s sleeve; **∼ Film sein** be in films **3** (zeitlich) **er will ∼ Arbeiten nicht gestört werden** he doesn't want to be disturbed when *or* while [he's] working; **∼ Essen spricht man nicht** you shouldn't talk while [you're] eating; **den Hund darf man ∼ Fressen nicht stören** you mustn't disturb the dog while it's eating; **∼ Verlassen des Gebäudes** when *or* on leaving the building; **∼ Fasching** at carnival time; **∼ Lesen/Essen/Duschen sein** be reading/be having breakfast/dinner *etc.*/be taking a shower

bei|mengen *tr. V.* add (*Dat.* to)

Beimengung *die;* **∼, ∼en** **1** (das Beimengen) addition **2** (Zusatz) admixture

bei|messen *unr. tr. V.* attach; **jmdm./einer Sache Bedeutung/Wert** *usw.* **∼:** attach importance/value *etc.* to sb./sth.

bei|mischen *tr. V.* (geh.) add (*Dat.* to); **meiner Bewunderung war Grauen beigemischt** (fig.) my admiration was tinged with horror

Bei·mischung *die* **1** (das Beimischen) addition **2** (Zusatz) admixture

Bein /bain/ *das;* **∼[e]s, ∼e** **1** ▸ ❶ **S. 435** leg; **jmdm. ∼e machen** (ugs.) make sb. get a move on (coll.); **du hast jüngere ∼e** (ugs.) your legs are younger than mine; **ein langes ∼ machen** (Fußballjargon) make a sliding tackle; **ein ∼ stehen lassen** (Fußballjargon) put *or* (coll.) stick one's foot out; **sich** (*Dat.*) **die ∼e nach etw. ablaufen** (fig.) chase round everywhere for sth.; **er hat sich** (*Dat.*) **kein ∼ ausgerissen** (ugs.) he didn't overexert himself; **jmdm. ein ∼ stellen** (zum Stolpern bringen) trip sb.; (fig.: hereinlegen) put *or* throw a spanner *or* (Amer.) a monkey wrench in sb.'s works; **jmdm. [einen] Knüppel** *od.* **Prügel zwischen die ∼e werfen** (fig.) put *or* throw a spanner *or* (Amer.) a monkey wrench in sb.'s works; **das hat ∼e gekriegt** (fig. ugs.) it seems to have [grown legs and] walked (coll.); **die ∼e in die Hand** *od.* **unter die Arme nehmen** (fig. ugs.) (sich beeilen) step on it (coll.); (weglaufen) take to one's heels; **die ∼e unter jmds. Tisch strecken** (fig. ugs.) live at sb.'s expense; **sich** (*Dat.*) **die ∼e in den Bauch stehen** (fig. ugs.) cool one's heels; **alles, was ∼e hat** (fig. ugs.) everyone who possibly can; **wieder auf den ∼en sein** be back on one's feet again; **[wieder] auf die ∼e kommen** (ugs.) get back on one's/its feet [again]; **jmdn./etw. [wieder] auf die ∼e bringen** (ugs.) put sb./sth. back on his/her/its feet again; **eine Firma/Expedition/ein Programm auf die ∼e stellen** (ugs.) start a business/mount an expedition/put together a programme; **jmdm. auf die ∼e helfen** help sb. to his/her feet; (fig. ugs.) help to get *or* put sb. back on his/her feet again; **ich kann mich nicht mehr/kaum noch auf den ∼en halten** I can't/can hardly stand up; **auf eigenen ∼en stehen** (fig.) stand on one's own two feet; support oneself; **auf schwachen ∼en stehen** (fig.) ‹*argument*› rest on shaky foundations; ‹*firm*› be in a precarious position; **das geht in die ∼e** (Alkohol) it makes you unsteady on your feet; (Musik) it makes you want to get up and dance; **mit beiden ~en im Leben** *od.* **[fest] auf der Erde stehen** have both feet [firmly] on the ground; **mit dem linken ~ zuerst aufgestanden sein** (ugs.) have got out of bed on the wrong side; **mit einem ~ im Gefängnis/Grab[e] stehen** (fig.) stand a good chance of ending up in prison/have one foot in the grave; **von einem ~ aufs andere treten** (ugs.) shift from one foot to the other; **auf einem ~ kann man nicht stehen** (scherzh.) one drink isn't enough to wet one's whistle; *s. auch* **Klotz 1**; **Kopf 5**; **vertreten B** **2** (Hosenbein, Teil eines Möbelstückes, Stativ) leg **3** (nordd.: Fuß) foot **4** (südd., österr., schweiz.: Knochen) bone; **jmdm. in die ~e fahren** go right through sb.; *s. auch* **Mark² 1**

bei·nah[e] /ˈbaina:(ə)/ *Adv.* almost; nearly; **wir wären ~ zu spät gekommen** we were nearly too late; **ich möchte ~ sagen, dass ...** I would almost say that ...

Beinahe·zusammenstoß *der* (Flugw.) airmiss

Bei·name *der* epithet

bein-, Bein-: ~amputation *die* leg amputation; **~amputiert** *Adj.* ‹*person*› with a *or* one leg/both [his/her] legs amputated; **sie ist ~amputiert** she has had a leg/both [her] legs amputated; **~arbeit** *die* (beim Boxen, Ringen, Tanzen) footwork; (beim Schwimmen) leg action; **~bruch** *der* broken leg; **das ist [doch] kein ~bruch!** (ugs.) it's not the end of the world (coll.)

beinern /ˈbainɐn/ *Adj.* **1** (knöchern) bone *attrib.*; made of bone *postpos.* **2** (aus Elfenbein) ivory *attrib.*; made of ivory *postpos.*

Bein-: ~fleisch *das* (österr.) beef cooked and served on the bone; **~freiheit** *die* legroom

beinhalten /bəˈɪnhaltn̩/ *tr. V.* (Papierdt.) involve

bein·hart (österr., südd.)
A *Adj.* rock-hard; tough ‹*movie*›; ‹*person*› as hard as nails
B *adv.* **~ gefroren** frozen hard; **~ spielen** (Sportjargon) be hard and physical

Bein·haus *das* (hist.) charnel house

-beinig *Adj.* ▸ⓘ **S. 435** -legged; **drei~/lang~:** three-legged/long-legged; **ein zwölf~es Insekt** an insect with twelve legs

Bein-: ~kleid *das* (veralt.) trousers *pl.*; **~leiden** *das* ▸ⓘ **S. 439** (Med.) leg condition

Beinling /ˈbainlɪŋ/ *der*; **~s, ~e** (veralt.) leg

Bein-: ~prothese *die* artificial leg; **~schere** *die* (Ringen) leg scissors *sing.*; **~schiene** *die* **1** (Sport) [long] shin pad; (Cricket, Hockey) pad; **2** (Teil der Rüstung) greave *usu. in pl.*; **~stumpf** *der* stump [of the leg]

bei|ordnen *tr. V.* **1** **jmdm. jmdn. ~:** assign sb. to assist sb. **2** (Rechtsw.) **als Pflichtverteidiger beigeordnet werden** be called in as duty solicitor (Brit.) *or* (Amer.) court-appointed lawyer **3** (Sprachw.) ▸**nebenordnen**

Bei·ordnung *die* **1** (Sprachw.) coordination **2** (Rechtsw.) assignment

Bei·pack *der* extra item [ordered]

bei|packen *tr. V.* **einer Warensendung etw. ~:** pack sth. in with a consignment of goods

Beipack·zettel *der* instruction leaflet

bei|pflichten /ˈbaipflɪçtn̩/ *itr. V.* **jmdm. [in einer Sache] ~:** agree with sb. [on sth.]; **einem Vorschlag** *usw.* **~:** agree with a proposal *etc.*; **Sie werden mir darin ~, dass ...** you will agree with me that ...

Bei·programm *das* supporting programme

Bei·rat *der* advisory committee *or* board

beirren *tr. V.* **sich durch nichts/von niemandem ~ lassen** not be put off *or* deterred by anything/anybody; not let anything/anybody put one off *or* deter one; **nichts konnte ihn in seinen Ansichten ~:** nothing could shake him in his views

Beirut /baiˈru:t/ *(das)*; **~s** Beirut

beisammen /baiˈzamən/ *Adv.* together; **[gut] ~ sein** (ugs.) be in good health *or* shape

beisammen-, Beisammen-: ~|haben *unr. tr. V.* **1** (gesammelt haben) have got together; **2** **er hat nicht alle ~** (ugs.) he's not all there (coll.); he's a bit soft in the head (coll.); **~|halten** *unr. tr. V.* keep together; hold on to ‹*money*›; ***~|sein** ▸**beisammen**; **~sein** *das* get-together; **~|sitzen** *unr. itr. V.* sit together

Bei·satz *der* (Sprachw.) appositive

Bei·schlaf *der* (geh., Rechtsw.) sexual intercourse

bei|schließen *unr. tr. V.* (österr.) **einem Brief** *usw.* **etw. ~:** enclose sth. with a letter *etc.*

Bei·schluss, *Bei·schluß *der* (österr.: Anlage) enclosure

Bei·segel *das* (Segeln) additional sail

Bei·sein *das*: *in* **im ~ von jmdm., in jmds. ~:** in the presence of sb. *or* in sb.'s presence; **ohne ~ von jmdm., ohne jmds. ~:** in the absence of sb. *or* in sb.'s absence

bei·seite *Adv.* **1** (auf die Seite) aside; **jmdn. ~ ziehen/schieben** draw/push sb. to one side *or* aside; **etw. ~ bringen** get sth. hidden away; hide sth. away; **etw. ~ lassen** (fig.) leave sth. aside; **etw. ~ legen** (sparen) put sth. by *or* aside; (Angefangenes weglegen) put *or* lay sth. aside; **jmdn./die Leiche ~ schaffen** (ugs.) get rid of sb./the body; **die Beute/das Geld ~ schaffen** (ugs.) stash (coll.) *or* hide the loot/money away; **jmdn./etw. ~ schieben** (fig.) push sb./sth. aside **2** (auf der Seite) on *or* to one side; **~ stehen** (fig.) take second place

Beis[e]l /ˈbaizl̩/ *das*; **~s, ~** *od.* **~n** (österr.) pub (Brit.); bar (Amer.)

bei|setzen *tr. V.* **1** (geh.: beerdigen) bury; inter; lay to rest; inter ‹*ashes*› **2** (Seemannsspr.) set, hoist ‹*sail*›

Bei·setzung *die*; **~, ~en** (geh.) funeral; burial

Beisetzungs·feierlichkeiten *Pl.* funeral [ceremony] *sing.*

Bei·sitz *der* assessorship; **den ~ haben** act as assessor

Bei·sitzer *der*; **~s, ~, Bei·sitzerin** *die*; **~, ~nen** assessor; (bei Ausschüssen) committee member

Bei·spiel *das* **1** example (**für** of); **zum ~:** for example *or* instance; **wie zum ~:** as for example; such as; **ohne ~ sein** be without parallel *or* unparalleled; (unerhört sein) be outrageous **2** (Vorbild) example; **ein warnendes ~:** a warning; **jmdm. ein ~ geben** set an example to sb.; **sich** *(Dat.)* **an jmdm./etw. ein ~ nehmen** follow sb.'s example/take sth. as one's example; **mit gutem ~ vorangehen** set a good example

beispiel·gebend *Adj.* exemplary; **~ für jmdn. sein** be an example to sb.

beispielhaft
A *Adj.* exemplary
B *adv.* in an exemplary fashion

beispiel-, Beispiel-: ~halber *Adv.* ▸**beispielshalber**, **~los** **A** *Adj.* unparalleled; (unerhört) outrageous; **B** *adv.* incomparably ‹*well, badly, etc.*›; **~los erfolgreich/grausam** with unparalleled success/cruelty; **~satz** *der* (Sprachw.) example sentence; illustrative sentence

beispiels-: ~halber *Adv.* for example *or* instance; **etw. ~halber anführen** offer *or* give sth. by way of example; **~weise** *Adv.* for example *or* instance

bei|springen *unr. itr. V.*; *mit sein* **jmdm. [in der Not] ~:** leap *or* rush to sb.'s aid *or* assistance [in an emergency]; **jmdm. mit Geld ~:** help sb. out with money

beißen /ˈbaisn̩/
A *unr. tr., itr. V.* **1** bite; **in etw.** *(Akk.)* **~:** bite into sth.; **auf etw.** *(Akk.)* **~:** bite on sth.; **an den Nägeln ~:** bite one's nails; **sich** *(Dat.)* **die Lippen wund ~:** bite one's lips till they bleed; **ich habe mich** *od.* **mir auf die Zunge/in die Lippe gebissen** I've bitten my tongue/lip; **der Hund hat mir** *od.* **mich ins Bein gebissen** the dog bit me in the leg; **nach jmdm./etw. ~:** snap at sb./sth.; **der Hund biss [wild] um sich** the dog snapped [wildly] in all directions **2** (bissig sein; auch fig.) bite **3** (ätzen) sting; **in die** *od.* **in den Augen ~:** sting one's eyes; make one's eyes sting; **auf der Zunge ~:** burn the tongue **4** (Angelsport: an~) bite **5** (kauen) **nicht mehr [richtig] ~ können** no longer be able to chew things [properly]; **nichts/nicht viel zu ~ haben** (fig.) have nothing/not have much to eat; **sich in den Arsch** (derb) *od.* **Hintern** (salopp) **~** (fig.) kick oneself
B *unr. refl. V.* (ugs.) ‹*colours, clothes*› clash

beißend *Adj.* biting ‹*cold*›; acrid ‹*smoke, fumes*›; sharp ‹*frost*›; biting, cutting ‹*wind*›; pungent, sharp ‹*smell, taste*›; (fig.) biting ‹*ridicule*›; cutting ‹*irony*›

Beißer *der*; **~s, ~** (bissiger Hund) biter

Beißerchen *das*; **~s, ~** (fam.) toothy-peg (child lang.)

Beißerei *die*; **~, ~en** fight

Beiß-: ~ring *der* teething ring; **~zange** *die* ▸**Kneifzange**

Bei·stand *der* **1** (geh.: Hilfe) aid; assistance; help; **jmdm. ~ leisten** give sb. aid *or* assistance; come to sb.'s aid *or* assistance **2** (Rechtsw.: Rechtshelfer) *lay person acting in support of a defendant*

Beistands-: ~abkommen *das* (Politik) treaty of mutual assistance; **~pakt** *der* (Politik) mutual assistance pact; **~vertrag** *der* (Politik) treaty of mutual assistance

bei|stehen *unr. itr. V.* **jmdm. ~:** aid *or* assist *or* help sb.; (zur Seite stehen) stand by sb.

bei|stellen *itr. V.* (österr.: bereitstellen) make available; provide

Beistell-: ~möbel *das* piece of occasional furniture; **teure ~möbel** expensive occasional furniture *sing.*; **~tisch** *der*, **~tischchen** *das* occasional table; (im Restaurant) side table

Bei·steuer *die* (südd.) contribution

bei|steuern *tr. V.* contribute; make ‹*contribution*›

bei|stimmen *itr. V.*: ▸**zustimmen**

Bei·strich *der* (veralt.) comma

Beitel /ˈbaitl̩/ *der*; **~s, ~:** chisel

Beitrag /ˈbaitra:k/ *der*; **~[e]s, Beiträge** /ˈbaitrɛ:gə/ **1** (Zahlung, Mitwirkung) contribution; (Versicherungs~) premium; (Mitglieds~) subscription; **einen ~ zu etw. leisten** make a contribution to sth. **2** (Aufsatz, Kommentar) article (**zu** on); (in einer Zeitschrift, einem Sammelband) article, contribution (**zu** on)

bei|tragen *unr. tr., itr. V.* contribute (**zu** to); **das Seine/viel zu etw. ~:** contribute one's share/a great deal to sth.

beitrags-, Beitrags-: ~finanziert *Adj.* funded from contributions *postpos.*; **~frei** *Adj.* non-contributory; ‹*person*› not liable to pay contributions; **~gruppe, ~klasse** *die* (Sozialw.) contribution class (Brit.); insurance group (Amer.); **~marke** *die* stamp; **~pflicht** *die* (Sozialw.) liability to pay contributions; **~pflichtig** *Adj.* (Sozialw.) ‹*employee*› liable to pay contributions; ‹*earnings*› on which contributions are payable; **~satz** *der* contribution rate; **~zahler** *der*; **~~s, ~~, ~zahlerin** *die*; **~~, ~~nen** contributor; **~zahlung** *die* contribution

bei|treiben *unr. tr. V.* (Rechtsw.) enforce payment of

Beitreibung *die*; **~, ~en** (Rechtsw.) enforcement of payment

bei|treten *unr. itr. V.*; *mit sein* **1** (Mitglied werden bei) join; **einem Verein** *usw.* **~:** join a club *etc.* **2** (sich anschließen an) **einem Abkommen/Pakt ~:** accede to an agreement/a pact **3** (Rechtsw.) **einem Verfahren/einer Verhandlung ~:** attend proceedings *pl.*/a hearing

Bei·tritt *der* **1** (Eintritt) joining; **seinen ~ erklären** affirm one's wish to become a member **2** (Rechtsw.) **jmds. ~ anordnen** *od.* **verfügen** order sb. to attend [the proceedings] **3** (zur EU) accession (**zu** to)

Beitritts-: ~erklärung *die* declaration (*affirming one's wish to become a member*); **~land** *das* accession country; **~verhandlungen** *Pl.* accession negotiations

Bei·wagen *der* **1** (Seitenwagen) sidecar **2** (veralt.: Anhänger) (einer U-Bahn) car; (einer Straßenbahn) trailer

Beiwagen-: ~fahrer *der,* **~fahrerin** *die* sidecar passenger; **~maschine** *die* motorcycle combination (Brit.); sidecar motorcycle (Amer.)

Bei·werk *das* accessories *pl.*; **in Opern ist die Handlung oft nur ~:** in opera the plot is often of only secondary importance

bei|willigen *itr. V.* (schweiz.) ▸**zustimmen**

bei|wohnen *itr. V.* 1 (geh.: anwesend sein) **einer Sache** (*Dat.*) **~:** be present at *or* attend sth. 2 (veralt. verhüll.) **jmdm. ~:** lie with sb. (arch.)

Bei·wort *das;* **~[e]s, Beiwörter** 1 ▸**Adjektiv** 2 (Epitheton) epithet

Beiz /baits/ *die;* **~, ~en** (schweiz.) ▸**Beize³**

Beize¹ /ˈbaitsə/ *die;* **~, ~n** 1 (Holzbearb.) [wood] stain 2 (Gerberei) bate 3 (Textilbearb.) mordant 4 (Metallbearb.) pickle 5 (Landw.) disinfectant; seed dressing 6 (Tabakind.) sauce 7 (Kochk.) marinade 8 (das Beizen) ▸**beizen¹**: staining; bating; mordanting; pickling; disinfecting; sauce casing; marinading

Beize² *die;* **~, ~n** (Jagdw.) hawking

Beize³ *die;* **~, ~n** (schweiz.) pub (Brit.); bar (Amer.)

beizeiten /baiˈtsaitn̩/ *Adv.* in good time

beizen¹ /ˈbaitsn̩/ *tr. V.* (mit Beize behandeln) 1 (Holzbearb.) stain 2 (Gerberei) bate 3 (Textilbearb.) mordant 4 (Landw.) disinfect, dress ‹*seed*› 5 (Metallbearb., Tabakind.) pickle 6 (Kochk.) marinate

beizen² *tr., itr. V.* (Jägerspr.) hawk

Beizer *der;* **~s, ~, Beizerin** *die* stainer

bei|ziehen *unr. tr. V.* (südd., österr., schweiz.) call in ‹*lawyer, psychologist, expert, etc.*›; bring in, enlist ‹*helpers*›; consult, make use of ‹*reference book etc.*›

Bei·ziehung *die* (südd., österr., schweiz.) calling in

Beiz-: ~jagd *die* ▸**Beize²**; **~vogel** *der* falcon; hawk

bejahen /bəˈjaːən/

A *tr. V.* 1 (mit Ja beantworten) **etw. ~:** give an affirmative answer to sth.; answer sth. in the affirmative 2 (gutheißen, befürworten) approve of; **das Leben ~:** have a positive *or* an affirmative attitude to life

B *itr. V.* answer in the affirmative; give an affirmative answer; **sie bejahte lebhaft** she replied with an animated 'yes'

bejahend

A *Adj.* affirmative; affirmative, positive ‹*attitude*›

B *adv.* ‹*answer*› in the affirmative; ‹*nod*› affirmatively

bejahrt /bəˈjaːɐ̯t/ *Adj.* (geh.) advanced in years

Bejahrtheit *die;* **~:** advanced age

Bejahung *die;* **~, ~en** 1 affirmative answer *or* reply; **ein Zeichen/eine Geste der ~:** an affirmative sign/gesture 2 (das Gutheißen) approval

bejammern *tr. V.* lament; **die Toten ~:** lament for the dead; **dazu neigen, sich selbst zu ~:** tend towards self-pity

bejammerns·wert *Adj.* pitiable ‹*person*›; wretched ‹*situation*›; lamentable, pitiable ‹*condition, state*›; pitiful ‹*sight*›

bejubeln *tr. V.* cheer; acclaim; **jmdn. als Helden** *usw.* **~:** acclaim sb. as a hero *etc.*

bekacken (vulg.)

A *tr. V.* shit (coarse) in ‹*nappy etc.*›; **bekackte Windeln** shitty nappies (Brit.) *or* (Amer.) diapers (coarse)

B *refl. V.* shit oneself (coarse)

bekakeln *tr. V.* (ugs.) talk over; discuss

bekämpfen *tr. V.* 1 fight against; **sich [gegenseitig] ~:** fight [one another *or* each other] 2 (einzudämmen versuchen) combat, fight ‹*disease, epidemic, pest*›; combat ‹*unemployment, crime, alcoholism*›; curb ‹*curiosity, prejudice*›

Bekämpfung *die;* **~** 1 fight (+ *Gen.* against); **zur ~ des Feindes aufrufen** call for battle against the enemy 2 ▸**bekämpfen 2**: combating; fighting; curbing; **zur ~ einer Krankheit beitragen** contribute to combating *or* fighting a disease; **unsere Aufgabe ist die ~ der Kriminalität/Arbeitslosigkeit** our task is to combat crime/unemployment

bekannt /bəˈkant/

A *2. Part. v.* **bekennen**

B *Adj.* 1 (von vielen gewusst) well-known; **es wurde ~, dass ...** it became known *or* public knowledge that ...; **für etw. ~ sein** be well known for sth.; **es ist nichts davon ~:** nothing is known concerning it; **wegen etw. ~ sein** be well-known on account of sth.; **etw. ~ machen** announce sth.; (der Öffentlichkeit) make sth. public; (veröffentlichen) publish sth.; **etw. ~ geben** announce sth. 2 (berühmt) well-known; famous; **~er sein** be better known; **international ~ sein** be internationally known *or* famous 3 (vertraut, bewusst) **die Aufgaben sind ihm ~:** he knows what his duties are; **sie ist mir ~:** I know her; **davon ist mir nichts ~:** I know nothing about that; **mit jmdm. ~ sein/werden** know *or* be acquainted with sb./get to know *or* become acquainted with sb.; **mit etw. ~ sein/werden** be/become familiar *or* acquainted with sth.; **jmdn./sich mit jmdm. ~ machen** introduce sb./oneself to sb.; **Darf ich ~ machen? Meine Eltern** may I introduce my parents?; **jmdn./sich mit etw. ~ machen** acquaint sb./oneself with sth.; **jmdm. ~ vorkommen** seem familiar to sb.; **der Witz kommt mir ~ vor** I think I've heard that joke somewhere before

Bekannte *der/die adj. Dekl.* 1 acquaintance 2 (verhüll.: Freund/Freundin) boyfriend/girl[friend]

Bekannten·kreis *der* circle of acquaintances; **jmds. engerer** *od.* **näherer ~:** sb.'s circle of close acquaintances

bekannter·maßen *Adv.* (Papierdt.) ▸**bekanntlich**

Bekannt·gabe *die;* **~:** announcement

***bekannt|geben** ▸**bekannt B 1**

Bekanntheit *die;* **~** 1 (Kenntnis) acquaintance, familiarity (*Gen.* with) 2 (Berühmtheit) fame

Bekanntheits·grad *der;* **~es einen großen ~ haben** be very well known

bekanntlich *Adv.* as is well known; **etw. ist ~ der Fall** it is known that sth. is the case; sth. is known to be the case; **der Walfisch ist ~ ein Säugetier** it is well known that the whale is a mammal; **~ sind Steuererhöhungen sehr unbeliebt** we all know that tax increases are highly unpopular

***bekannt|machen** ▸**bekannt B 1**

Bekannt·machung *die;* **~, ~en** 1 (das ~machen) announcement; (das Veröffentlichen) publication 2 (Mitteilung) announcement; notice

Bekanntschaft *die;* **~, ~en** 1 (Bekanntsein) acquaintance; **bei näherer ~:** on closer acquaintance; **jmds. ~ machen** make sb.'s acquaintance; **du wirst bald mit der Polizei ~ machen** (ugs.) you're going to get into trouble with the police soon; **dein Hosenboden wird gleich mit meiner Hand ~ machen** (ugs.) you'll feel my hand across your backside any minute 2 (Mensch, den man kennt) acquaintance; (Bekanntenkreis) circle of acquaintances

***bekannt|werden** ▸**bekannt B 1**

bekaufen *refl. V.* make a bad buy

bekehren

A *tr. V.* convert (**zu** to); **jmdn. zum Anhänger des Buddhismus / Nacktbadens / Monetarismus ~:** convert sb. to Buddhism/nude bathing/monetarism; **vom Alkohol bekehrt sein** have turned one's back on alcohol

B *refl. V.* become converted (**zu** to)

Bekehrer *der;* **~s, ~, Bekehrerin** *die;* **~, ~nen** converter; (Missionar) missionary

Bekehrte *der/die; adj. Dekl.* convert

Bekehrung *die;* **~, ~en** (auch fig.) conversion (**zu** to)

bekennen

A *unr. tr. V.* 1 (eingestehen) admit ‹*mistake, defeat*›; confess ‹*sin*›; admit, confess ‹*guilt, truth*› 2 (Rel.) profess; **die Bekennende Kirche** (hist.) the Confessional Church

B *refl. V.* **sich zu Buddha/Mohammed ~:** profess *or* declare one's faith in Buddha/Muhammad; **nur wenige seiner früheren Freunde bekannten sich zu ihm** only a few of his former friends stood by him; **sich zu seiner Vergangenheit ~:** acknowledge one's past; **sich zu seiner Schuld ~:** admit *or* confess one's guilt; **sich zum Sozialismus ~:** declare one's belief in socialism; **sich schuldig/nicht schuldig ~:** admit *or* confess/not admit *or* not confess one's guilt; (vor Gericht) plead guilty/not guilty; **sich zu einem Bombenanschlag ~:** claim responsibility for a bomb attack; **sich als jmd[n]. ~:** admit *or* confess that one is sb.; admit *or* confess to being sb.

Bekenner *der;* **~s, ~, Bekennerin** *die;* **~, ~nen** confessor

Bekenner-: ~brief *der* letter (*Gen.* from) claiming responsibility; **~geist** *der,* **~mut** *der* courage of one's convictions

Bekenntnis *das;* **~ses, ~se** 1 (Eingeständnis) confession; **ein ~ ablegen** make a confession 2 (Eintreten) **ein ~ für die Sache des Friedens/zum Frieden** a declaration of belief in the cause of peace/a declaration for peace; **ein ~ zum Christentum/zur Demokratie ablegen** profess one's faith in Christianity/declare one's belief in democracy 3 (Konfession) denomination 4 (formulierter Inhalt) confession; **das Augsburger ~:** the Confession of Augsburg

bekenntnis-, Bekenntnis-: ~freiheit *die* religious freedom; freedom of worship; **~kirche** *die* Confessional Church; **~los** *Adj.* not belonging to any denomination *postpos., not pred.*; **~los sein** not belong to any denomination; **~schule** *die* denominational school

bekieken *tr. V.* (nordd. ugs.) look at; have a look at

bekiffen *refl. V.* get stoned (sl.)

bekifft /bəˈkɪft/ *Adj.* (ugs.) stoned (sl.)

beklagen

A *tr. V.* (geh.) 1 (betrauern) mourn; **Menschenleben waren nicht zu ~:** there were no fatalities; there was no loss of life 2 (bedauern) lament; **sein/jmds. Los ~:** lament *or* bewail one's fate/deplore sb.'s fate; **wir haben einen großen Umsatzrückgang zu ~:** we have to note with regret a large drop in sales

B *refl. V.* complain; **sich über jmdn./etw. ~:** complain about sb./sth.; **ich kann mich nicht ~:** I can't complain; **du kannst dich nicht ~:** you've got nothing to complain about *or* no reason to complain

beklagens-: ~wert, ~würdig (geh.)

A *Adj.* pitiful ‹*sight, impression*›; pitiable ‹*person*›; lamentable, pitiable, deplorable ‹*condition, state*›; wretched ‹*situation*›; B *adv.* lamentably; deplorably

beklagt /bəˈklaːkt/ *Adj.* **die ~e Partei** the defendant; (bei Ehescheidungen) the respondent; **die ~en Personen** the defendants

Beklagte *der/die; adj. Dekl.* defendant; (bei Ehescheidungen) respondent

beklatschen *tr. V.* 1 clap; applaud 2 (ugs.: klatschen über) gossip about

beklauen *tr. V.* (salopp) rob; do (coll.)

bekleben *tr. V.* **eine Wand** *usw.* **mit etw. ~:** stick sth. all over a wall *etc.*; **mit etw. beklebt sein** have sth. stuck all over it

bekleckern (ugs.)

A *tr. V.* **seinen Schlips** *usw.* **mit Soße** *usw.* **~:** drop *or* spill sauce *etc.* down one's tie *etc.*; **mit Senf bekleckerte Teller** plates smeared with mustard

B *refl. V.* **ich habe mich bekleckert** I've dropped *or* spilled sth. down myself; **sich mit Soße** *usw.* **~:** drop *or* spill sauce *etc.* down oneself; *s. auch* **Ruhm**

beklecksen *tr. V.* spatter; **etw. mit Tinte** *usw.* **~:** spatter ink *etc.* on sth.

bekleiden *tr. V.* 1 clothe; **mit etw. bekleidet sein** be dressed in *or* be wearing sth. 2 (geh.: innehaben) occupy, hold ‹*office, position*› 3 (geh. veralt.: versehen) **jmdn. mit etw. ~:** bestow sth. on sb.

Bekleidung *die* clothing; clothes *pl.*; garments *pl.*; (Aufmachung) dress; attire

Bekleidungs-: ~gewerbe *das,* **~handwerk** *das* clothing trade; **~industrie** *die*

clothing industry; **~stück** *das* **▸Kleidungsstück**; **~vorschriften** *Pl.* dress regulations; regulations governing dress

bekleistern *tr. V.* (ugs.) **1** (mit Kleister bestreichen) apply paste to **2** (bekleben) **etw. mit Aufklebern** *usw.* **~**: plaster stickers *etc.* all over sth.

beklemmen *tr. V.* oppress; **jmdm. das Herz** *od.* **jmds. Herz ~** (geh.) weigh upon sb.'s heart

beklemmend
A *Adj.* oppressive
B *adv.* oppressively

Beklemmung *die;* **~**, **~en** oppressive feeling; (Angst) [feeling of] unease; (stärker) [feeling of] apprehension; **ich bekomme** *od.* **kriege ~en** I feel as if I'm being stifled

beklommen /bəˈklɔmən/
A *Adj.* uneasy; shaky ‹*voice*›; (stärker) apprehensive
B *adv.* uneasily; (stärker) apprehensively

Beklommenheit *die;* **~**: uneasiness; (stärker) apprehensiveness

beklönen *tr. V.* (nordd. ugs.) talk over

beklopfen *tr. V.* tap

bekloppt /bəˈklɔpt/ *Adj.* (salopp) barmy (Brit. coll.); loony (coll.); **dieser ~e Fahrer** this nutcase of a driver (Brit. coll.); this nutty driver (coll.); **ein Bekloppter** a nutcase (Brit. coll.); a nut (coll.)

beknackt *Adj.* (salopp) lousy (coll.); **ein ~er Typ** a berk (Brit. coll.); a jerk (coll.); **so was Beknacktes** what a load of rubbish! (coll.)

beknien *tr. V.* (ugs.) beg

bekochen *tr. V.* (ugs.) cook for

beködern *tr. V.* (Angeln) bait ‹*hook*›

bekommen
A *unr. tr. V.* **1** (erhalten) get; get, receive ‹*money, letter, reply, news, orders*›; **ich habe seit Monaten keinen Brief mehr von ihm ~**: I haven't had a letter from him for months; **Anschluss/eine Verbindung [zu einem Ort] ~**: get through [to a place]; **fünf Tage Urlaub ~**: get five days' holiday (Brit.) *or* (Amer.) vacation; **drei Monate Gefängnis ~**: get *or* receive three months in prison; **eine Flasche** *usw.* **an den Kopf ~**: get hit on the head with a bottle *etc.*; **was ~ Sie?** (im Geschäft) can I help you?; (im Lokal, Restaurant) what would you like?; (wie viel Geld?) how much is that?; (bei mehreren Sachen) how much does that come to?; **wir ~ Regen/besseres Wetter** we're going to get some rain/some better weather; there's rain/better weather on the way; **sie bekommt ein Kind** she's expecting a baby; **wann bekommt sie ihr Kind?** when is the baby due? **2** (finden, erlangen) get; obtain; catch ‹*train, bus, flight*›; **eine Vorstellung/einen Eindruck von etw. ~**: get some *or* an idea/impression of sth.; **seinen Willen ~**: get one's way **3** (ein bestimmtes Ziel erreichen) get; **etw. durch die Tür/in den Kofferraum ~**: get sth. through the door/into the boot (Brit.) *or* (Amer.) trunk; **etw. zu Papier ~**: get sth. down on paper; **jmdn. nicht aus dem Bett ~**: be unable to get sb. out of bed *or* up; **jmdn. zum Reden ~**: get sb. to talk; **jmdn. dazu ~, die Wahrheit zu sagen** get sb. to tell the truth; **etw. sauber/wohnlich ~**: get sth. clean/make sth. homely *or* comfortable **4** (entwickeln, erleiden) get ‹*goose pimples, measles, spots, diarrhoea, practice, experience, etc.*›; **Hunger/Durst ~**: get hungry/thirsty; **einen roten Kopf/eine Glatze ~**: go red/bald; **Mut/Angst ~**: take heart/become frightened; **Gestalt/Form ~**: take shape; **er bekommt einen Bart** he's growing a beard; **sie bekommt eine Brust** her breasts are developing; **Zähne ~** ‹*baby*› teethe; **er bekommt seine Weisheitszähne** his wisdom teeth are coming through **5** (+ *Inf.*) **etw. zu essen/trinken ~**: have sth. to eat/drink; **wo bekomme ich etwas zu essen/trinken?** where can I get something to eat/drink?; **etw./jmdn. zu fassen ~**: get hold of sth./lay one's hands on sb.; *s. auch* **hören, spüren 6** + *2. Part.* get; **etw. geschenkt ~**: get [given] sth. *or* be given sth. as a present; **etw. direkt vom Verlag geschickt ~**: get sth. direct from the publisher; **seine Arbeit von anderen gemacht ~**: get one's work done by other people **7** *in* **es nicht über sich** (*Akk.*) **~, etw. zu tun** be unable to bring oneself to do sth.
B *unr. itr. V.; mit sein* **jmdm. gut ~**: do sb. good; be good for sb.; **jmdm. [gut] ~** ‹*food, medicine*› agree with sb.; **jmdm. schlecht** *od.* **nicht ~**: not be good for sb.; not do sb. any good; ‹*food, medicine*› not agree with sb.; **wohl bekomms!** your [very good] health!

bekömmlich /bəˈkœmlɪç/ *Adj.* easily digestible; **leicht/schwer ~ sein** be easily digestible/difficult to digest

Bekömmlichkeit *die;* **~**: easy digestibility

beköstigen /bəˈkœstɪgn̩/ *tr. V.* cater for; **er wird von seiner Tante beköstigt** he gets his meals provided by his aunt

Beköstigung *die;* **~ 1** catering *no indef. art.* **2** (Kost) food *no indef. art.*

bekotzen *tr. V.* (derb) puke over (coarse)

bekräftigen *tr. V.* reinforce ‹*statement*›; reaffirm ‹*promise*›; confirm, strengthen ‹*suspicion, conviction*›; **eine Vereinbarung durch Handschlag ~**: seal an agreement with a handshake

Bekräftigung *die* confirmation

bekränzen /bəˈkrɛntsn̩/ *tr. V.* **jmdn./etw. ~**: crown sb. with a wreath/garland sth.

bekreuzen
A *tr. V.* (kath. Kirche) make the sign of the cross over
B *refl. V.* **▸bekreuzigen**

bekreuzigen *refl. V.* (kath. Kirche) cross oneself

bekriegen *tr. V.* wage war on; (fig.) fight; **bekriegt werden** be attacked; **sich ~**: be at war; (fig.) fight [each other *or* one another]

bekritteln *tr. V.* (abwertend) find fault with (*in a petty way*)

bekritzeln *tr. V.* scribble on; **die Wände waren von oben bis unten bekritzelt** the walls were covered with graffiti; **die Buchränder mit Anmerkungen ~**: scribble comments in the margins of the book

bekrönen *tr. V.* (auch fig., Archit.) crown

bekucken (nordd.) **▸begucken**

bekümmern *tr. V.* **jmdn. ~**: cause sb. worry; **das braucht dich nicht zu ~**: you needn't worry about that

Bekümmernis *die* (geh.) worry; trouble; (stärker) distress

bekümmert /bəˈkʏmɐt/
A *Adj.* worried; troubled; (stärker) distressed
B *adv.* **~ schweigen** maintain a worried silence

bekunden /bəˈkʊndn̩/
A *tr. V.* **1** (geh.: zeigen) express **2** (Rechtsw.: bezeugen) make ‹*statement*›; **er bekundete, dass ...** he testified that ...
B *refl. V.* (geh.: sich zeigen) manifest itself

Bekunden *das: in* **nach seinem/ihrem** *usw.* **eigenen ~**: according to his/her *etc.* own statement[s]

Bekundung *die;* **~**, **~en** expression; (Aussage) statement

belabern *tr. V.* (salopp abwertend) keep on [and on] at

belächeln *tr. V.* smile [pityingly/tolerantly *etc.*] at; **belächelt werden** meet with a pitying smile

belachen *tr. V.* laugh at

beladen[1] *unr. tr. V.* **1** (mit einer Ladung versehen) load ‹*ship*›; load [up] ‹*car, wagon*›; **Be- und Entladen gestattet/verboten** loading and unloading permitted/no loading or unloading **2** (zu tragen geben) load up ‹*horse, donkey*› **3** (reich bedecken) load ‹*table*›

beladen[2] *Adj.* loaded, laden (**mit** with); **hoch ~**: heavily laden; **mit etw. ~ sein** be laden with sth.; **sie war schwer mit Paketen ~**: she was loaded *or* laden down with parcels; **mit Sorgen/Schuld ~ sein** (fig.) ‹*person*› be burdened with cares/guilt; **mit einem Fluch ~ sein** be under a curse

Belag /bəˈlaːk/ *der;* **~[e]s, Beläge** /bəˈlɛːgə/ **1** (Schicht) coating; film; (Zungen~) fur *no indef. art.;* coating; (Zahn~) film; **Sie haben einen ~ auf der Zunge** your tongue is coated **2** (Fußboden~) covering; (Straßen~) surface; (Brems~) lining **3** (von Kuchen, Pizza, halben Brötchen) topping; (von Sandwiches) filling

Belagerer /bəˈlaːgərɐ/ *der;* **~s**, **~**: besieger

belagern *tr. V.* **1** (Milit.) besiege; lay siege to **2** (fig.: bedrängen) besiege

Belagerung *die;* **~**, **~en 1** (Milit.) siege **2** (fig.: Bedrängung) besieging

Belagerungs-: ~maschine *die* siege machine; **~ring** *der* (Milit.) ring of besieging forces; **~zustand** *der* state of siege; (Ausnahmezustand) state of emergency; **den ~zustand ausrufen** declare a state of siege/emergency; **über die Stadt wurde der ~zustand verhängt** the town was declared under siege/a state of emergency was declared in the town

belämmern /bəˈlɛmɐn/ *tr. V.* (nordd. ugs.) bother; (sehr aufdringlich) pester

belämmert *Adj.* (ugs.) **1** (niedergedrückt) miserable; **er stand [wie] ~ da** he stood there miserably **2** (scheußlich) awful (coll.); terrible (coll.); dreadful (coll.)

Belang /bəˈlaŋ/ *der;* **~[e]s**, **~e 1** (Bedeutung) **[für etw.] von/ohne ~ sein** be of importance/of no importance [for sth.]; **für jmdn. von/ohne ~ sein** be important/not be important to sb. **2** *Pl.* (Interessen) interests; **jmds. ~e wahrnehmen/vertreten** look after/represent sb.'s interests

belangen *tr. V.* **1** (Rechtsw.) sue; (strafrechtlich) prosecute; **jmdn. wegen etw. ~**: sue/prosecute sb. for sth. **2** (veralt. unpers.: betreffen) **was mich/ihn** *usw.* **belangt, so ...** as far as I am/he *etc.* is concerned, ...

belang-, Belang-: ~los *Adj.* (trivial) trivial; (unerheblich) of no importance (**für** for); **~losigkeit** *die;* **~~**, **~~en 1** (Trivialität) triviality; (Unerheblichkeit) unimportance; **2** (triviale Äußerung) triviality; **~voll** *Adj.* (geh.) important (**für** for)

belassen *unr. tr. V.* **1** (unverändert lassen) leave; **jmdn. in seinem Amt ~**: keep sb. in his/her post; **~ wir es dabei** let's leave it at that **2** (überlassen) **jmdm. etw. ~**: let sb. keep sth.

belastbar *Adj.* **1** (mit Last, Gewicht) tough, resilient ‹*material*›; ‹*material*› able to withstand stress *pred.*; **[nur] mit 3,5 t ~ sein** be able to take a load of [only] 3.5 t **2** (beanspruchbar) tough, resilient ‹*person*›; **seelisch/körperlich ~ sein** be emotionally/physically tough *or* resilient; be able to stand emotional/physical stress; **ein ~er Mitarbeiter** an employee who can work under pressure; **die Umwelt ist nicht weiter ~**: the pressures on the environment have become intolerable

Belastbarkeit *die;* **~**, **~n 1** (von Material) ability to withstand stress; (von Konstruktionen) load-bearing capacity **2** (von Menschen) toughness; resilience; (von Mitarbeitern) ability to work under pressure

belasten *tr. V.* **1** (beschweren) load ‹*vehicle etc.*›; put weight on ‹*ski*›; **der Fahrstuhl darf nur mit vier Personen belastet werden** the lift (Brit.) *or* (Amer.) elevator must not carry more than four persons **2** (beeinträchtigen) pollute ‹*atmosphere*›; put pressure on ‹*environment*› **3** (in Anspruch nehmen) burden (**mit** with) **4** (zu schaffen machen) **jmdn. ~** ‹*responsibility, guilt*› weigh upon sb.; ‹*thought*› weigh upon sb.'s mind; **Fett belastet den Magen** fat puts a strain on the stomach; **es belastet ihn seelisch schwer, dass ihn seine Frau verlassen hat** the fact that his wife has left him is causing him great emotional strain and distress **5** (Rechtsw.: schuldig erscheinen lassen) incriminate; **~des Material** incriminating evidence **6** (Geldw.) **jmds. Konto mit 100 Euro ~**: debit sb.'s account with 100 euros; **jmdn. mit zusätzlichen Steuern ~**: increase the tax burden on sb.; **den Staatshaushalt ~**: place a burden on the national budget; **das Haus ist mit einer Hypothek belastet** the house is encumbered with a mortgage

belästigen /bəˈlɛstɪgn̩/ *tr. V.* bother; (sehr aufdringlich) pester; (sexuell) molest; **sich von etw. belästigt fühlen** regard sth. as a nuisance

Belästigung *die;* **~**, **~en am schlimmsten empfanden wir die ~ durch die Reporter/Insekten** we found the worst thing was being pestered by reporters/bothered by insects; **etw. als ~ empfinden** regard sth. as a nuisance

Belastung /bəˈlastʊŋ/ *die;* ~, ~en [1] **die ~ der Atmosphäre/Umwelt durch Schadstoffe** the pollution of the atmosphere by harmful substances/the pressure on the environment caused by harmful substances [2] (Inanspruchnahme) strain; **für jmdn. eine ~ sein** put a strain on sb. [3] (Bürde, Sorge) burden; **das stellte eine schwere seelische ~ für sie dar** it was causing her great strain and distress [4] (Rechtsw.: Beschuldigung) incrimination [5] (Geldw.) charge; (steuerlich) burden; **außergewöhnliche ~en** extraordinary expenses (*partly deductible as a charge on one's income*); **eine weitere ~ meines Kontos kann ich mir nicht erlauben** I can't afford to draw any more money from my account [6] (Beschwerung) loading; **die maximale ~ der Brückenpfeiler** the safe maximum load for the bridge piers

belastungs-, Belastungs-: ~-EKG *das* (Med.) electrocardiogram after effort; **~fähig** *Adj.* ▸**belastbar**; **~grenze** *die* limit; (der Atmosphäre, des Wasserhaushalts) maximum tolerable level of pollution; **~material** *das* (Rechtsw.) incriminating evidence; **~probe** *die* (bei Menschen) endurance test; (bei Materialien) stress test; (bei Konstruktionen) load test; **~spitze** *die* (Elektrot.) peak load; **~zeuge** *der* (Rechtsw.) witness for the prosecution

belatschern /bəˈlaːtʃɐn/ *tr. V.* (berlin. salopp) [1] **jmdn. ~, dass er etw. macht** talk sb. into doing sth.; **er hat mich belatschert** he talked me into it [2] (ansprechen) accost

belauben *refl. V.* come into leaf; **belaubte Pappeln** poplars in leaf

Belaubung *die;* ~ [1] coming into leaf [2] (Laubwerk) foliage; leaves *pl.*

belauern *tr. V.* **jmdn. ~** (versteckt beobachten) watch sb. from hiding; (mit lauerndem Blick beobachten) eye *or* watch sb. carefully; keep a watchful eye on sb.

belaufen *unr. refl. V.* **sich auf ...** (*Akk.*) **~:** amount *or* come to ...; ‹*rent, price*› come to ..., be ...

belauschen *tr. V.* [1] eavesdrop on [2] (geh.: beobachten) observe

Belcanto /belˈkanto/ *der;* ~s (Musik) bel canto

beleben
A *tr. V.* [1] (in Schwung bringen) enliven; liven up (coll.); (wieder ~) put new life into; stimulate ‹*demand*› [2] (lebendig gestalten) enliven; brighten up [3] (lebendig machen) give life to [4] (bevölkern) inhabit; populate
B *refl. V.* [1] (lebhafter werden) ‹*eyes*› light up; ‹*face*› brighten [up]; ‹*market, economic activity*› revive, pick up [2] (lebendig, bevölkert werden) come to life; **sich neu belebt fühlen** feel revived

belebend
A *Adj.* stimulating; invigorating
B *adv.* **~ wirken** have a stimulating *or* invigorating effect

belebt *Adj.* [1] (lebhaft, bevölkert) busy ‹*street, crossing, town, etc.*› [2] (lebendig, auch fig.) living; **die ~e Natur** the living world of nature

Belebtheit *die;* **~:** bustle; bustling activity

Belebung *die;* ~, ~en revival; **eine ~ der Wirtschaft** a revival in the economy; **eine ~ des Absatzes** a stimulation of demand; **ein Getränk** *usw.* **zur ~:** a drink *etc.* to revive oneself

belecken *tr. V.* lick; **von Kultur/Geschichte nicht/wenig beleckt sein** (fig. ugs.) have no/not much trace of culture/knowledge of history

Beleg /bəˈleːk/ *der;* ~[e]s, ~e [1] (Beweisstück) piece of [supporting] documentary evidence; (Quittung) receipt; **~e** [supporting] documentary proof *sing.* or evidence *sing. no indef. art.*/receipts [2] (Beispiel) instance, example (**für** of); (Quellennachweis) reference; **als ~ für etw.** as evidence for sth.; **ein ~ für ein Wort** an example of the use of a word [3] (Archäol.: Fundstück) find

Beleg·arzt *der* doctor on duty (*who shares responsibility for hospital inpatients*)

belegbar *Adj.* verifiable

belegen
A *tr. V.* [1] (Milit.: beschießen) bombard; (mit Bomben) attack [2] (mit Belag versehen) cover ‹*floor*› (**mit** with); fill ‹*flan base, sandwich*›; top ‹*open sandwich*›; **eine Scheibe Brot mit Schinken/Käse ~:** put some ham/cheese on a slice of bread [3] (reservieren) reserve, book ‹*seat, table, room*›; (nutzen) occupy ‹*seat, room, etc.*›; (Hochschulw.) enrol for, register for ‹*seminar, lecture course*› [4] (Sport) **den ersten/letzten Platz ~:** come first *or* take first place/come last [5] (nachweisen) prove; give a reference for ‹*quotation*›; (fig.) substantiate ‹*demand*›; **etw. mit** *od.* **durch Quittungen ~:** support sth. with receipts [6] (versehen) **jmdn./etw. mit etw. ~:** impose sth. on sb./sth.; **jmdn. mit einem Spitznamen ~:** give sb. a nickname [7] **eine Schule mit Flüchtlingen ~:** accommodate refugees in a school
B *itr. V.* (Hochschulw.) enrol *or* register [for seminars/lectures] for the coming semester

Beleg-: ~exemplar *das* voucher copy; (für Autoren) author's copy; **~frist** *die* (Hochschulw.) enrolment period; **~leser** *der* (DV) document reader; **~material** *das* documentary evidence

Belegschaft *die;* ~, ~en staff; employees *pl.*

Belegschafts-: ~aktie *die* employees' share; **~mitglied** *das* employee; **~versammlung** *die* meeting of the staff

Beleg-: ~stelle *die* reference; **~stück** *das* ▸**~exemplar**

belegt
A *2. Part. v.* **belegen**
B *Adj.* [1] **ein ~es Brot** (offen) an open *or* (Amer.) open-face sandwich; (zugeklappt) a sandwich; **ein ~es Brötchen** (offen) a roll with topping; an open-face roll (Amer.); (zugeklappt) a filled roll; a sandwich roll (Amer.) [2] (mit Belag bedeckt) coated, furred ‹*tongue, tonsils*› [3] (heiser) husky ‹*voice*›; **eine ~e Stimme haben** be hoarse [4] (nicht mehr frei) ‹*room, flat*› occupied; ‹*hotel, hospital*› full

Belegung *die;* ~, ~en (Reservierung) reservation; booking; (Nutzung) occupying

belehnen *tr. V.* [1] (hist.) **jmdn. mit Land/einem Amt ~:** enfeoff sb. with land/in an office [2] (schweiz.) ▸**beleihen**

belehrbar *Adj.* teachable

belehren *tr. V.* [1] (lehren) teach; instruct; (aufklären) enlighten; (informieren) inform; advise; **jmdn. über etw.** (*Akk.*) **~:** inform sb. about sth.; **jmdn. über seine Rechte ~/die Bedeutung des Eides ~** (Rechtsw.) inform *or* advise sb. of his/her rights/caution *or* warn sb. about the meaning of the oath [2] (von einer irrigen Meinung abbringen) **sich ~ lassen** [be willing to] listen *or* take advice *or* be told; **ich bin belehrt** I've learnt something; **sich eines anderen ~ lassen müssen** learn otherwise; *s. auch* **besser**

belehrend *Adj.* didactic

Belehrung *die;* ~, ~en [1] (das Belehrtwerden) instruction [2] (Zurechtweisung) lecture [3] (Rechtsw.) caution; warning

beleibt /bəˈlaipt/ *Adj.* (geh.) stout; portly; corpulent

Beleibtheit *die;* ~ (geh.) stoutness; portliness; corpulence

beleidigen /bəˈlaidɪgn̩/ *tr. V.* insult; offend; **jmds. Ehre ~:** offend sb.'s honour; **~d** offensive; **~de Äußerungen** (Rechtsw.) (schriftlich) libellous statements; (mündlich) slanderous statements; **das beleidigt mein Ohr/mein Auge** (fig.) it offends my ear/eye

beleidigt *Adj.* insulted; offended; (gekränkt) offended; **ein ~es Gesicht machen** put on a hurt expression; **er ist schnell ~:** he easily takes offence; **jmdn. ~ ansehen** give sb. an offended look

Beleidigung *die;* ~, ~en insult; (Rechtsw.) (schriftlich) libel; (mündlich) slander; **etw. als ~ empfinden** regard sth. as an insult; **eine ~ für das Auge/Ohr** (fig.) an offence to the eye/ear

Beleidigungs-: ~klage *die* (Rechtsw.) (wegen schriftlicher Beleidigung) action for libel; libel action; (wegen mündlicher Beleidigung) action for slander; slander action; **eine ~klage gegen jmdn. erheben** sue sb. for libel/slander; bring an action for libel/slander against sb.; **~prozess**, ***~prozeß** *der* (Rechtsw.) (wegen schriftlicher Beleidigung) libel suit; (wegen mündlicher Beleidigung) slander suit

beleihen *unr. tr. V.* [1] (als Pfand nehmen) grant a loan on the security of; grant a mortgage on ‹*home, property*›; raise money on ‹*insurance, policy*›; **etw. ~ lassen** raise a loan/mortgage on sth.; **ihr Schmuck wurde mit 15 000 Euro beliehen** she raised a loan of 15,000 euros on her jewellery [2] (hist.) ▸**belehnen 1**

Beleihung *die;* ~, ~en **die ~ von etw.** raising a loan on sth.

***belemmern** ▸**belämmern**

***belemmert** ▸**belämmert**

belesen *Adj.* well-read

Belesenheit *die;* ~ **[große] ~:** [very] wide reading

Beletage /bɛleˈtaːʒə/ *die;* ~, ~n (veralt.) first floor (Brit.); second floor (Amer.)

beleuchten *tr. V.* [1] illuminate; light up; light ‹*stairs, room, street, etc.*›; **festlich beleuchtet** festively lit [2] (fig.: untersuchen) examine ‹*topic, problem*›

Beleuchter *der;* ~s, ~ (Theater, Film) lighting technician

Beleuchter·brücke *die* (Theater, Film) lighting bridge

Beleuchterin *die;* ~, ~nen (Theater, Film) lighting technician

Beleuchtung *die;* ~, ~en [1] (Licht) light; **die ~ in der Stadt fiel aus** all the lights *pl.* of the town went out [2] (das Beleuchten) lighting; (Anstrahlung) illumination [3] (fig.: Untersuchung) examination

Beleuchtungs-: ~an·lage *die* lighting installation; **~effekt** *der* lighting effect; **~technik** *die* lighting engineering

beleumdet /bəˈlɔymdət/, **beleumundet** /bəˈlɔymʊndət/ *Adj.* **übel/gut ~ sein** have a bad/good reputation

belfern /ˈbɛlfɐn/
A *itr. V.* (ugs.) bark; (fig.) ‹*cannon*› boom; ‹*rifle*› crack
B *tr. V.* bark; bark [out] ‹*order*›

Belgien /ˈbɛlgi̯ən/ (*das*); ~s Belgium

Belgier /ˈbɛlgi̯ɐ/ *der;* ~s, ~, **Belgierin** *die;* ~, ~nen ▸❶ **S. 520** Belgian; *s. auch* **-in**

belgisch *Adj.* ▸❶ **S. 520** Belgian; *s. auch* **deutsch; Deutsche²**

Belgrad /ˈbɛlgraːt/ (*das*); ~s ▸❶ **S. 675** Belgrade

belichten
A *tr. V.* [1] (Fot.) expose; **eine Aufnahme richtig/falsch ~:** give a shot the right/wrong exposure [2] (fachspr.: beleuchten) light
B *itr. V.* (Fot.) **richtig/falsch/kurz ~:** use the right/wrong exposure/a short exposure time

Belichtung *die* [1] (Fot.) exposure [2] (fachspr.: Licht) light

Belichtungs-: ~automatik *die* (Fot.) automatic exposure control; **~dauer** *die* (Fot.) ▸**~zeit**; **~messer** *der;* ~s, ~ (Fot.) exposure meter; **~tabelle** *die* (Fot.) exposure table; **~zeit** *die* (Fot.) exposure time

belieben *itr. V.* (unpers.) (geh.) **[ganz] wie es dir beliebt** [just] as you like; **was beliebt?** (veralt.) what can I do for you?; **wie beliebt?** (veralt.) I beg your pardon?; **~, etw. zu tun** like doing sth.; **Sie ~ zu scherzen** (iron.) you are joking, of course; **ihr könnt tun, was euch** (*Dat.*) **beliebt** you can do what you like

Belieben *das;* **~s es steht in deinem ~/es bleibt Ihrem ~ überlassen** it is up to you; **nach ~:** just as you/they *etc.* like

beliebig
A *Adj.* any; **du kannst ein ~es Beispiel/einen ~en Tag wählen** you can choose any example/day you like; **fünf ~e Personen** any five people; **in ~er Reihenfolge** in any order; **eine ~e Reihe von Beispielen** an arbitrary series of examples; **die Reihenfolge/Farbe ist ~:** any order/colour will do
B *adv.* as you like/he likes *etc.*; **~ lange/viele** as

long/many as you like/he likes *etc.*; **wähle eine ~ große Zahl** choose any number[, as high as] you like; **wir konnten ~ lange wegbleiben** we could stay out [for] as long as we liked; **diese beiden Begriffe sind nicht ~ austauschbar** these two terms are not interchangeable at will

beliebt *Adj.* popular; favourite *attrib.*; **sich [bei jmdm.] ~ machen** make oneself popular [with sb.]

Beliebtheit *die;* **~:** popularity; **sich großer ~** *(Gen.)* **erfreuen** (geh.) enjoy great popularity

beliefern *tr. V.* supply; **jmdn. mit etw. ~:** supply sb. with sth.

Belieferung *die* supply; **die ~ von jmdm. mit etw.** supplying sb. with sth.

Belladonna /bɛla'dɔna/ *die;* **~, Belladonnen** (Bot., Pharm.) belladonna

bellen /'bɛlən/
A *itr. V.* **1** ‹*dog, fox*› bark; ‹*hound*› bay; (fig.) ‹*cannon*› boom **2** (laut husten) have a hacking cough; **ein ~der Husten** a hacking cough
B *tr. V.* (abwertend) bark out ‹*orders*›

Belletristik /bɛle'trɪstɪk/ *die;* **~:** belles-lettres *pl.*

belletristisch
A *Adj.* belletristic ‹*literature*›; **ein ~er Verlag** a publishing house specializing in belletristic literature
B *adv.* **er hat seine Darstellung ~ aufgelockert** he made his account lighter and more entertaining

Bellizismus /bɛli'tsɪsmʊs/ *der;* **~:** warmongering; (bes. Politik) hawkish attitude

Bellizist *der;* **~en, ~en, Bellizistin** *die;* **~, ~nen** warmonger; (bes. Politik) hawk

bellizistisch
A *Adj.* belligerent; (bes. Politik) hawkish
B *adv.* **~ tönend** belligerent-sounding; (bes. Politik) hawkish-sounding

belobigen /bə'lo:bɪgn̩/ *tr. V.* commend

Belobigung *die;* **~, ~en** commendation; **jmdm. eine ~ aussprechen** commend sb.

Belobigungs·schreiben *das* letter of commendation

belohnen *tr. V.* **1** (beschenken) reward; **jmdn. mit/für etw. ~:** reward sb. with/for sth. **2** (vergelten) repay, reward ‹*patience, loyalty, trust*›

Belohnung *die;* **~, ~en** **1** (Lohn) reward; **eine ~ für etw. aussetzen** offer a reward for sth. **2** (das Belohnen) rewarding

Belt /bɛlt/ *der;* **~s** (Geogr.) **der Kleine/Große ~:** The Little/Great Belt

belüften *tr. V.* ventilate; (auslüften) air; **das Zimmer wurde nur durch eine kleine Luke in der Decke belüftet** the only means of ventilation in the room was a small skylight

Belüftung *die* ventilation

Belüftungs·anlage *die* ventilation system

Beluga[1] /be'lu:ga/ *die;* **~, ~s** (Zool.) beluga [sturgeon]; (Wal) white whale

Beluga[2] *der;* **~s** beluga caviare

belügen *unr. tr. V.* **jmdn. ~:** lie to *or* tell lies to sb.; **sich selbst ~:** deceive oneself; *s. auch* **Strich**

belustigen
A *tr. V.* **jmdn. ~:** amuse sb.; (zum Lachen bringen) make sb. laugh
B *refl. V.* **1** (geh.) **sich über jmdn./etw. ~:** make fun of *or* laugh at sb./sth. **2** (veralt.: sich vergnügen) amuse oneself

belustigt
A *Adj.* amused
B *adv.* in amusement

Belustigung *die;* **~, ~en** **1** (Fest, Vergnügen) entertainment **2** (Belustigtsein, Belustigtwerden) amusement; **der allgemeinen ~ dienen** serve to amuse everybody

bemächtigen /bə'mɛçtɪgn̩/ *refl. V.* (geh.) **1** (in seine Gewalt bringen) **sich einer Sache/eines Menschen ~:** seize sth./a person; **sich der Regierungsgewalt/des Thrones ~:** seize power/the throne **2** (überkommen) **Angst bemächtigte sich seiner** he was seized by fear; **Unruhe/Unsicherheit bemächtigte sich seiner** a feeling of unease/uncertainty came over him; **Entsetzen bemächtigte sich eines jeden** everyone was horrified

bemäkeln *tr. V.* (ugs.) find fault with

bemalen
A *tr. V.* **1** (bunt streichen) paint; (verzieren) decorate ‹*porcelain etc.*›; **mit etw. bemalt sein** be painted/decorated with sth. **2** (ugs.: stark schminken) paint
B *refl. V.* (ugs.) paint one's face; put on one's warpaint (coll.); **warum hast du dich so bemalt?** why have you put so much warpaint on? (coll.)

Bemalung *die;* **~, ~en** **1** (Bemalen) painting; (Verzierung) decorating **2** (Farbschicht) painting

bemängeln /bə'mɛŋl̩n/ *tr. V.* find fault with; **Bremsen/Reifen ~:** find the brakes/tyres to be faulty; **etw. an jmdm./etw. ~:** criticize sth. about sb./sth.

Bemäng[e]lung *die;* **~, ~en** criticism; **die häufige ~ von Fabrikationsfehlern** the frequent complaints about *or* of manufacturing defects

bemannen *tr. V.* man

Bemannung *die;* **~, ~en** **1** (das Bemannen) manning **2** (Mannschaft) crew

bemänteln /bə'mɛntl̩n/ *tr. V.* cover up

Bemänt[e]lung *die;* **~, ~en** covering up

Bembel /'bɛmbl̩/ *der;* **~s, ~** (hess.: Krug) mug; (zum Servieren) jug; pitcher

bemeistern (geh. veralt.)
A *tr. V.* master; control ‹*rage, excitement, etc.*›
B *refl. V.* control oneself

bemerkbar *Adj.* noticeable; perceptible; **sich ~ machen** (auf sich aufmerksam machen) attract attention [to oneself]; (eine Wirkung ausüben, sich zeigen) ‹*disadvantage*› become apparent; ‹*tiredness*› make itself felt; **mach dich ~, wenn du etwas brauchst** if you need anything, let me know

bemerken *tr. V.* **1** (wahrnehmen) notice; **ich wurde nicht bemerkt** I was unobserved; **sie bemerkte zu spät, dass ...** she realized too late that ... **2** (äußern) remark; **nebenbei bemerkt** by the way; incidentally

Bemerken *das;* **~s** (Amtsspr.) *in* **mit dem ~ ...** with the comment ...

bemerkenswert
A *Adj.* (beachtlich, bedeutend) remarkable; notable; (Aufmerksamkeit verdienend, auffallend) remarkable
B *adv.* remarkably

Bemerkung *die;* **~, ~en** **1** (Äußerung) remark; comment **2** (Notiz) note; (Anmerkung) comment

bemessen
A *unr. tr. V.* **etw. nach etw. ~:** measure sth. according to sth.; **die Zeit ist kurz/sehr knapp ~:** time is short *or* limited/very limited; **das Trinkgeld war reichlich ~:** the tips were generous
B *unr. refl. V.* (Amtsspr.) **sich ~ nach** be measured on the basis of; **die Vergütung bemisst sich nach ...** payment is calculated on the basis of ...

Bemessung *die* calculation; **die ~ der Strafe richtet sich nach der Schwere des Deliktes** the penalty is fixed in accordance with the seriousness of the offence

Bemessungs·grundlage *die* (Amtsspr.) basis for assessment

bemitleiden *tr. V.* pity; feel sorry for; **er ist zu ~:** he is to be pitied; **sich selbst ~:** feel sorry for oneself

bemitleidens·wert *Adj.* pitiable

Bemitleidung *die;* **~:** pity *no indef. art.* (+ *Gen.* for)

bemittelt *Adj.* (veralt.) well-to-do; well off

Bemme /'bɛmə/ *die;* **~, ~n** (ostmd.) open *or* (Amer.) open-face sandwich; (mit Butter bestrichen) slice of bread and butter; (zusammengeklappt) sandwich

bemogeln *tr. V.* (ugs.) cheat; diddle (coll.); con (sl.)

bemoost *Adj.* mossy; covered in moss *postpos.*; **ein ~es Haupt** (ugs., bes. Studentenspr.) a perpetual student

bemühen
A *refl. V.* **1** (sich anstrengen) try; make an effort; **sich sehr ~:** try hard; make a great effort; **sich ~, etw. zu tun** try *or* endeavour to do sth.; **bemüht sein, etw. zu tun** endeavour to do sth.; **bitte, ~ Sie sich nicht [weiter]!** please do not trouble yourself [any further] **2** (sich kümmern) **sich um jmdn./etw. ~:** seek to help sb./endeavour *or* strive to achieve sth.; **um das Wohl der Hotelgäste bemüht sein** make every effort to ensure the comfort and enjoyment of the hotel patrons **3** (zu erlangen suchen) **sich um etw. ~:** try *or* endeavour to obtain sth.; **sich um eine Stelle/Wohnung ~:** try to get a job/a flat (esp. Brit.) *or* (esp. Amer.) apartment; **sich um eine Dame ~:** pay every attention to a lady; **sich um einen Regisseur/Trainer/Wissenschaftler ~:** try *or* endeavour to obtain the services of a director/manager/scientist **4** (geh.: sich begeben) proceed (formal); **er hat sich sogar in meine Wohnung bemüht** he even took the trouble to go/come to my flat
B *tr. V.* (geh.) **1** (in Anspruch nehmen) trouble; call in, call upon the services of ‹*lawyer, architect, etc.*›; (als Beweis heranziehen) bring in a quotation/quotations from ‹*author, philosopher, etc.*› **2** (bitten, zu kommen) trouble sb. to come; **jmdn. ins oberste Stockwerk ~:** trouble sb. to come/go up to the top floor

Bemühen *das;* **~s** (geh.) effort; endeavour; **unser ~ um eine Sanierung dieses Stadtteils** our efforts *pl.* *or* endeavours *pl.* to redevelop this part of the town; **trotz jahrelangen ~s** despite years of effort

bemühend *Adj.* (schweiz.) [painfully] embarrassing; (unerfreulich) unpleasant

bemüht
A 2. *Part. v.* **bemühen**
B *Adj.* forced; forced, constrained ‹*cheerfulness*›; constrained ‹*person*›

Bemühung *die;* **~, ~en** **1** (Anstrengung) effort; endeavour; **alle ~en waren vergeblich** all efforts were in vain; **trotz aller ~en, allen ~en zum Trotz** in spite of *or* despite all our/his *etc.* efforts; **vielen Dank für Ihre ~en** thank you very much for your efforts *or* trouble; **niemand wollte ihn in seinen ~en unterstützen** no one wanted to support him in his endeavours **2** *Pl.* (Dienstleistung) services

bemüßigen *refl. V.* (geh.) **sich einer Sache** *(Gen.)* **~:** make use of sth.

bemüßigt /bə'my:sɪçt/ (geh. iron.) **in sich ~ sehen** *od.* **fühlen** *od.* **finden, etw. zu tun** feel obliged to do sth.; feel it incumbent on oneself to do sth.

bemuttern *tr. V.* mother

Bemutterung *die;* **~, ~en** mothering

benachbart *Adj.* neighbouring *attrib.*; **~e Fachgebiete** related fields of study; **ihre Häuser sind ~:** their houses are next door to each other

benachrichtigen /bə'na:xrɪçtɪgn̩/ *tr. V.* inform; notify; **jmdn. von etw. ~:** inform *or* notify sb. of *or* about sth.

Benachrichtigung *die;* **~, ~en** notification; **ich bitte um sofortige ~:** I wish to be informed *or* notified immediately; **warum habt ihr uns denn keine ~ geschickt?** why didn't you contact us *or* let us know?

benachteiligen *tr. V.* put at a disadvantage; ‹*disability*› handicap; (diskriminieren) discriminate against; **sich benachteiligt fühlen** feel at a disadvantage/feel discriminated against; **er fühlte sich von seinen Lehrern benachteiligt** he felt unfairly treated by his teachers; **ein wirtschaftlich benachteiligtes Gebiet** an economically deprived area; **die sozial benachteiligten Schichten** the underprivileged classes

Benachteiligte *der/die; adj. Dekl.* disadvantaged person; **die ~n** the disadvantaged; those at a disadvantage; **die sozial ~n** the underprivileged; the socially deprived

Benachteiligung *die;* **~, ~en** (Vorgang) discrimination *(Gen.* against); (Zustand) disadvantage *(Gen.* to); **der Firma wurde eine ~ der Frauen vorgeworfen** the firm was accused of discriminating against women

benagen *tr. V.* gnaw *or* nibble [at] ‹*bread, cheese, etc.*›; gnaw [at] ‹*tree, bark, etc.*›

benähen *tr. V.* **einen Rock** *usw.* **mit etw. ~:** sew sth. on to a skirt *etc.*

benässen *tr. V.* (geh.) wet

***Bendel** ▸ **Bändel**

benebeln *tr. V.* befuddle; **mit benebeltem Kopf aufwachen** wake up with a muzzy head

Benediktiner /benedɪk'ti:nɐ/ *der;* **~s, ~** 1 (Mönch) Benedictine [monk] 2 (Kräuterlikör) Benedictine

Benediktinerin *die;* **~, ~nen** Benedictine [nun]

Benediktiner·orden *der* Benedictine order; order of St. Benedict

Benefiz /bene'fi:ts/ *das;* **~es, ~e** 1 (veralt.: Vorstellung) benefit performance 2 (Wohltätigkeitsveranstaltung) charity performance/match, *etc.*

Benefiz-: ~konzert *das* charity concert; **~spiel** *das* charity game *or* match

benehmen

A *unr. refl. V.* behave (**wie** like); (in Bezug auf Umgangsformen) behave [oneself]; **sich schlecht ~:** behave badly; misbehave; **sie kann sich einfach nicht ~:** she simply does not know how to behave; **wenn du dich nicht ~ kannst, …** if you can't behave yourself, …

B *unr. tr. V.* (geh.: wegnehmen) **es benahm mir den Atem** it took my breath away

Benehmen *das;* **~s** 1 behaviour; **kein ~ haben** have no manners *pl.* 2 (Amtsspr.) *in* **sich mit jmdm. ins ~ setzen** make contact with sb.

beneiden *tr. V.* envy; be envious of; **jmdn. um etw. ~:** envy sb. sth.; **du bist [nicht] zu ~:** I [don't] envy you

beneidens·wert

A *Adj.* enviable

B *adv.* enviably

Benelux·staaten *Pl.* Benelux countries

benennen *unr. tr. V.* 1 (mit einem Namen versehen) name; **etw./jmdn. nach jmdm. ~:** name sth./name *or* call sb. after *or* (Amer.) for sb. 2 (namhaft machen) call ‹*witness*›; **jmdn. als Kandidaten ~:** nominate sb. as a candidate; **jmdn. als** *od.* **zum Zeugen ~:** call sb. as a witness

Benennung *die* 1 (Namengebung) naming 2 (das Namhaftmachen) **durch ~ zweier weiterer Zeugen** by calling two more witnesses 3 (Name) name; (Bezeichnung) designation

benetzen *tr. V.* (geh.) moisten; ‹*dew*› cover; **mit Tau/von Schweiß benetzt** covered *or* wet with dew/damp with perspiration

Bengale /bɛŋ'ga:lə/ *der;* **~n, ~n,** Bengali; Bengalese

Bengalen *(das);* **~s** Bengal

Bengali /bɛŋ'ga:li/ *das;* **~[s]** Bengali

Bengalin *die;* **~, ~nen** ▸ **Bengale**

bengalisch *Adj.* ▸ **i S. 670** Bengalese; Bengali, Bengalese ‹*people, language*›; **~e Beleuchtung, ~es Feuer** Bengal light *or* fire

Bengel /'bɛŋl/ *der;* **~s, ~** *od.* (nordd.) **~s** 1 (abwertend: junger Bursche) young rascal 2 (fam.: kleiner Junge) little lad *or* boy; **ein süßer ~:** a dear little lad *or* boy 3 (veralt.: Knüppel) stick

Benimm /bə'nɪm/ *der;* **~s** (ugs.) manners *pl.*; **jmdm. ~ beibringen** teach sb. some manners

Benimm-: ~buch *das* (ugs.) book of good manners; **~regel** *die* rule of good manners; **~regeln** *Pl.* [proper] etiquette *sing.*; **eine ~regel sein** be good manners

Benjamin /'bɛnjami:n/ *der;* **~s, ~e** (scherzh.) youngest boy; **er ist der ~ der Familie** he's the baby of the family

benommen /bə'nɔmən/

A *2. Part. v.* **benehmen**

B *Adj.* bemused; dazed; (durch Fieber, Medikamente, Alkohol) muzzy (**von** from)

Benommenheit *die;* **~:** bemused *or* dazed state; (durch Fieber, Medikamente, Alkohol) muzziness

benoten *tr. V.* mark (Brit.); grade (Amer.); **einen Test mit „gut" ~:** mark a test 'good' (Brit.); assign a grade of 'good' to a test (Amer.)

benötigen *tr. V.* need; require; **das benötigte Geld** the necessary money

Benotung *die;* **~, ~en** 1 (das Benoten) marking (Brit.); grading (Amer.); **sich um eine gerechte ~ bemühen** try *or* endeavour to mark (Brit.) *or* (Amer.) grade fairly 2 (Note) mark (Brit.); grade (Amer.)

benutzbar *Adj.* usable; **„Aufzug vorübergehend nicht ~"** 'lift temporarily out of service'; **schwer ~:** difficult to use

benutzen, (bes. südd.) **benützen** *tr. V.* use (**für** for); take, use ‹*car, lift*›; take ‹*train, taxi*›; use, consult ‹*reference book*›; **das benutzte Geschirr** the dirty dishes; **etw. als Vorwand/Alibi ~:** use sth. as an excuse/alibi; **wir benutzten den freien Tag zu einem Ausflug** we made use of *or* took advantage of the free day to go on an excursion

Benutzer, (bes. südd.) **Benützer** *der;* **~s, ~:** user; (eines entliehenen Buchs) borrower

benutzer·freundlich *Adj.* user-friendly

Benutzerin, (bes. südd.) **Benützerin** *die;* **~, ~nen** ▸ **Benutzer**

Benutzer-: ~kreis *der* users *pl.*; (von Büchereien) borrowers *pl.*; **ein großer ~kreis** a large number of users/borrowers; **~name** *der* (DV) user name

Benutzung *die;* **~,** (bes. südd.) **Benützung** *die;* **Benützung** use; **jmdm. etw. zur ~ überlassen** give sb. the use of sth.; allow sb. to use sth.; **in ~** (*Dat.*) **sein** be in use; **etw. in ~** (*Akk.*) **nehmen** bring sth. into use; **etw. zur ~ freigeben** open sth.; **unter ~ einer Sache** (*Gen.*) making use of sth.

Benutzungs-: ~gebühr *die* charge; (in Büchereien) borrowing charge; **die ~gebühr für etw.** the charge for using/borrowing sth.; **~ordnung** *die:* **die ~ordnung der Badeanstalt/Bibliothek** *usw.* the rules and conditions *pl.* for the use of the pool/library *etc.*

Benzin /bɛn'tsi:n/ *das;* **~s** petrol (Brit.); gasoline (Amer.); gas (Amer. coll.); (Wasch~) benzine; (Feuerzeug~) petrol (Brit.); gasoline (Amer.); lighter fuel

benzin-, Benzin-: ~betrieben *Adj.* with a petrol engine *postpos., not pred.*; petrol-engined; **~dunst** *der* petrol (Brit.) *or* (Amer.) gasoline fumes *pl.*; **~einspritzung** *die;* **~~** (Kfz-W.) fuel injection

Benziner *der;* **~s, ~** (ugs.) car that runs on petrol (Brit.) *or* (Amer.) gasoline; car with a petrol (Brit.) *or* (Amer.) gasoline engine; petrol-driven (Brit.) *or* (Amer.) gasoline-powered car

Benzin-: ~feuerzeug *das* petrol (Brit.) *or* (Amer.) gasoline lighter; **~gut·schein** *der* petrol (Brit.) *or* (Amer.) gasoline coupon; **~kanister** *der* petrol (Brit.) *or* (Amer.) gasoline can; **~leitung** *die* fuel pipe; **~motor** *der* petrol (Brit.) *or* (Amer.) gasoline engine; **~preis** *der* price of petrol (Brit.) *or* (Amer.) gasoline; **~pumpe** *die* petrol (Brit.) *or* (Amer.) gasoline pump; **~tank** *der* petrol (Brit.) *or* (Amer.) gasoline tank; **~uhr** *die* (Kfz-W.) fuel gauge; **~verbrauch** *der* fuel consumption

Benzoe /'bɛntsoe/ *die;* **~** (Chemie) [gum] benzoin

Benzoe·säure *die* (Chemie) benzoic acid

Benzol /bɛn'tso:l/ *das;* **~s, ~e** (Chemie) benzene

beobachtbar *Adj.* observable

beobachten /bə'|o:baxtn̩/ *tr. V.* 1 observe; watch; (als Zeuge) see; **er hat beobachtet, wie sie das Radio stahl** he watched her steal the radio; **jmdn. ~ lassen** put sb. under surveillance; have sb. watched 2 (bemerken) notice; observe; **etw. an jmdm. ~:** notice sth. about sb.; **eine Veränderung an jmdm. ~:** notice a change in sb. 3 (geh.: beachten) observe

Beobachter *der;* **~s, ~, Beobachterin** *die* observer

Beobachtung *die;* **~, ~en** 1 (das Beobachten, die Feststellung) observation; **~en anstellen** keep a watch; **zur ~:** for observation; **unter ~ stehen** be kept under surveillance 2 (geh.: Beachtung) observation

Beobachtungs-: ~ballon *der* observation balloon; **~gabe** *die* powers *pl.* of observation; **~posten** *der* observation post; **auf ~posten stehen** be on lookout duty; **~station** *die* 1 (im Krankenhaus) observation ward; 2 ▸ **Wetterstation**

beölen *refl. V.* (Jugendspr.) kill *or* (coarse) piss oneself laughing

beordern *tr. V.* order; **jmdn. nach Hause/ins Ausland ~:** order *or* summon sb. home/order sb. [to go] abroad

bepacken *tr. V.* load; **etw./jmdn./sich mit etw. ~:** load sth. up with/load sb./oneself with sth.

bepfanden *tr. V.* charge a deposit on ‹*bottle etc.*›

bepflanzen *tr. V.* plant (**mit** with)

Bepflanzung *die* 1 (das Bepflanzen) planting (**mit** with) 2 (Pflanzen) plants *pl.* (*Gen.* in)

bepflastern *tr. V.* 1 (ugs.) put a plaster on ‹*wound etc.*› 2 (mit Pflasterung versehen) pave; (fig.: mit Orden, Aufklebern usw.) plaster 3 (Soldatenspr.: bombardieren) plaster (coll.); bombard

bepinkeln (ugs.)

A *tr. V.* pee on (coll.)

B *refl. V.* wet oneself

bepinseln *tr. V.* 1 (ugs.: einpinseln) paint ‹*gums*›; brush ‹*dough, cake mixture*› 2 (ugs. abwertend: anstreichen) paint; **etw. mit Farbe ~:** paint sth.

bepissen *tr. V.* (derb) piss on (coarse)

beplanken *tr. V.* plank ‹*deck, hull*›; board ‹*wall, ceiling, etc.*›; (mit Platten usw.) panel; cover ‹*fuselage*›

Beplankung /bə'plaŋkʊŋ/ *die;* **~, ~en** (Boots~) planking; (Flugzeug~) skin

bepudern *tr. V.* powder

bequasseln *tr. V.* (salopp) ▸ **bequatschen 1**

bequatschen *tr. V.* (salopp) 1 (bereden) **etw. [ausführlich] ~:** have a [long] jaw about sth. (coll.) 2 (überreden) persuade; **jmdn. ~, dass er mitkommt** talk sb. into coming along

bequem /bə'kve:m/

A *Adj.* 1 (angenehm) comfortable; **es sich** (*Dat.*) **~ machen** make oneself comfortable; **machen Sie es sich ~:** make yourself at home 2 (mühelos) easy; **ein ~es Leben führen** have an easy *or* comfortable life 3 (abwertend: träge) lazy; idle

B *adv.* 1 (angenehm) comfortably; **liegen/sitzen Sie ~ so?** are you comfortable like that? 2 (leicht) easily; comfortably

bequemen *refl. V.* (geh.) 1 (abwertend) **sich dazu ~, etw. zu tun** (sich herablassen) condescend *or* deign to do sth.; (sich endlich entschließen) bring oneself to do sth 2 (veralt.: sich fügen) become adapted (*Dat.* to)

bequemlich *Adj.* (veralt.) ▸ **bequem**

Bequemlichkeit *die;* **~, ~en** 1 (Annehmlichkeit, Komfort) comfort 2 (Trägheit) laziness; idleness; **aus [reiner] ~:** out of [sheer] laziness *or* idleness

berappeln *refl. V.* (ugs.) recover

berappen /bə'rapn̩/ *tr., itr. V.* (ugs.) cough up (coll.), shell out (coll.), fork over (sl.) ‹*money*›

beraten

A *unr. tr. V.* 1 advise; **jmdn. gut/schlecht ~:** give sb. good/bad advice; **sich ~ lassen** take *or* get advice (**von** from); **du bist gut ~, wenn du …** you'd be well advised to … 2 (besprechen) discuss ‹*plan, matter*›

B *unr. itr. V.* **über etw.** (*Akk.*) **~:** discuss sth.; **sie berieten lange** they were a long time in discussion

C *unr. refl. V.* **sich mit jmdm. ~, ob …** discuss with sb. whether …; **sich mit seinem Anwalt ~:** consult one's lawyer

beratend *Adj.* advisory, consultative ‹*function, role, etc.*›

Berater *der;* **~s, ~, Beraterin** *die;* **~, ~nen** adviser

Berater-: ~stab *der* team of advisers; **~vertrag** *der* consultancy contract

beratschlagen /bəˈraːtʃlaːgn̩/
A *tr. V.* discuss
B *itr. V.* **über etw.** (*Akk.*) **~:** discuss sth.

Beratschlagung *die;* **~, ~en** discussion

Beratung *die;* **~, ~en** 1 advice *no indef. art.;* (durch Arzt, Rechtsanwalt) consultation; **ohne juristische ~:** without [taking] legal advice 2 (Besprechung) discussion; **Gegenstand der ~ war ...** the subject under discussion was ...; **sich zur ~ zurückziehen** withdraw for discussions *pl.* 3 ▸**Beratungsstelle**

Beratungs-: ~kosten *Pl.* consultation fees; **~stelle** *die* advice centre (Brit.); counseling center (Amer.); **~zimmer** *das* conference room

berauben *tr. V.* (auch fig.) rob; **jmdn. einer Sache** (*Gen.*) **~** (geh.) rob sb. of sth.; **jmdn. seiner Freiheit/Hoffnungen ~** (fig.) deprive sb. of his/her freedom/hopes

Beraubung *die;* **~, ~en** robbing *no indef. art.*

berauschen (geh.)
A *tr. V.* (auch fig.) intoxicate; ‹*alcohol*› intoxicate, inebriate; ‹*drug*› make euphoric; ‹*speed*› exhilarate; **der Erfolg/die Macht berauschte ihn** he was intoxicated *or* drunk with success/drunk with power
B *refl. V.* become intoxicated; **sich an etw.** (*Dat.*) **~:** become intoxicated with sth.; **sich an seinen eigenen Worten ~:** become carried away by one's own words

berauschend
A *Adj.* intoxicating; **~ auf jmdn. wirken** have an intoxicating effect on sb.; heady, intoxicating ‹*perfume, scent*›; **das ist nicht ~** (ugs.) it's nothing very special *or* (coll.) nothing to write home about
B *adv.* **~ schön** enchantingly beautiful; **der Abend war ~ schön** (iron.) the evening was just great (iron.)

Berber /ˈbɛrbɐ/ *der;* **~s, ~** 1 Berber 2 (Teppich) Berber carpet/rug 3 (Pferderasse) Barbary horse 4 (Nichtsesshafter) tramp

Berberin *die;* **~, ~nen** ▸**Berber 1, 4**

Berberitze /bɛrbəˈrɪtsə/ *die;* **~, ~n** (Bot.) common barberry

Berber·teppich *der* Berber carpet/rug

berechenbar /bəˈrɛçnbaːɐ̯/ *Adj.* calculable; predictable ‹*behaviour*›

Berechenbarkeit *die;* **~:** calculability; (des Verhaltens) predictability

berechnen *tr. V.* 1 (ermitteln) calculate ‹*quantity, cost, price, risk, etc.*›; predict ‹*behaviour, consequences*›; (fig.) calculate ‹*effect*› 2 (anrechnen) charge; **jmdm. etw. mit 10 Euro ~:** charge sb. 10 euros for sth.; **jmdm. etw. nicht ~:** not charge sb. for sth.; **für etw. nichts ~:** not charge for sth.; make no charge for sth.; **jmdm. zu viel ~:** overcharge sb.; charge sb. too much 3 (kalkulieren) calculate; (vorsehen) intend; **der Architekt berechnete die Bauzeit auf sieben Monate** the architect estimated that the construction time would be seven months; **für sechs Personen berechnet sein** ‹*recipe, buffet*› be for six people

berechnend *Adj.* calculating

Berechnung *die* 1 (das Berechnen) calculation; **nach meiner ~, meiner ~ nach** according to my calculations *pl.* 2 (abwertend: Eigennutz) [calculating] self-interest; **etw. aus ~ tun** do sth. from motives of self-interest 3 (Überlegung) deliberation; calculation; **mit kühler ~ vorgehen** act with cool deliberation

berechtigen /bəˈrɛçtɪgn̩/
A *tr. V.* entitle; **jmdn. ~, etw. zu tun** entitle sb. *or* give sb. the right to do sth.; **das berechtigt ihn zu dieser Kritik** it entitles him *or* gives him the right to criticize [in this way]
B *itr. V.* **die Karte berechtigt zum Eintritt** the ticket entitles the bearer to admission; **sein Talent berechtigt zu den schönsten Hoffnungen** his talent gives grounds for very great hopes indeed; **das berechtigt zu der Annahme, dass ...** it justifies the assumption that ...

berechtigt *Adj.* justified, legitimate ‹*demand, criticism, objection, doubt, complaint, hope*›; just ‹*accusation*›; **jmd. ist ~, etw. zu tun** sb. is authorized to do sth.

berechtigterweise *Adv.* (Papierdt.) legitimately; with justification

Berechtigung *die;* **~, ~en** 1 (Befugnis) entitlement; (Recht) right; **mit welcher ~ kritisiert er mich?** what right has he to criticize me? 2 (Rechtmäßigkeit) legitimacy; **seine/ihre ~ haben** be justified *or* legitimate

Berechtigungs·schein *der* authorization; (zum Zutritt, Einlass usw.) pass

bereden
A *tr. V.* 1 (besprechen) talk over; discuss 2 (überreden) **jmdn. ~, etw. zu tun** talk sb. into doing sth.; **sich ~ lassen, etw. zu tun** let oneself be talked into doing sth.
B *refl. V.* **sich [mit jmdm.] über etw.** (*Akk.*) **~:** talk sth. over *or* discuss sth. [with sb.]

beredsam /bəˈreːtzaːm/
A *Adj.* (beredt) eloquent; (iron.: redefreudig) **~ sein** have the gift of the gab (coll.)
B *adv.* (beredt) eloquently; (iron.: redefreudig) **~ für etw. werben** use one's gift of the gab to promote sth. (coll.)

Beredsamkeit *die;* **~** ▸**beredsam:** eloquence; gift of the gab (coll.)

beredt /bəˈreːt/
A *Adj.* (auch fig.) eloquent; **~es Zeugnis von etw. ablegen** bear eloquent witness to sth.; **es herrschte ein ~es Schweigen** there was a meaningful silence
B *adv.* eloquently

beregnen *tr. V.* water ‹*field*› using an overhead sprinkling system; water ‹*lawn*› using a sprinkler

Beregnung *die;* **~** ▸**beregnen:** watering using an overhead sprinkling system/a sprinkler

Beregnungs·anlage *die* overhead sprinkling system

Bereich *der;* **~[e]s, ~e** 1 (Gebiet) area; **im ~/außerhalb des ~s der Stadt** within/outside the town; **im nördlichen ~:** in northern areas *pl.* 2 (Sphäre) sphere; area; (Fachgebiet) field; area; **in jmds. ~** (*Akk.*) **fallen** be [within] sb.'s province; **im ~ des Möglichen liegen** be within the bounds *pl.* of possibility; **aus dem ~ der Kunst/Politik** from the sphere of art/politics 3 (Wirkungsfeld) **im privaten/staatlichen ~:** in the private/public sector; **sich im ~ eines Tiefs befinden** be under the influence of a low-pressure area

bereichern /bəˈraiçɐn/
A *refl. V.* get rich; **sich an jmdm./etw. ~:** make a great deal of money at sb.'s expense/out of sth.
B *tr. V.* enrich; enlarge, increase ‹*collection, knowledge*›; **diese Erfahrung hat mich bereichert** I gained a lot from the experience

Bereicherung *die;* **~, ~en** 1 (das Sichbereichern) moneymaking 2 (Nutzen) valuable acquisition; **eine wertvolle ~ der koreanischen Literatur** a valuable addition to Korean literature

bereifen[1] *tr. V.* put tyres on ‹*car*›; put a tyre on ‹*wheel*›; **neu ~:** put a new tyre/new tyres on; **gut bereift sein** ‹*car*› have good tyres

bereifen[2]
A *tr. V.* cover with hoar frost *or* rime
B *itr. V.* become covered with hoar frost *or* rime

Bereifung *die;* **~, ~en** [set *sing.* of] tyres *pl.*

bereinigen
A *tr. V.* 1 (klären) clear up ‹*misunderstanding*›; settle, resolve ‹*dispute*›; **mit jmdm. etw. zu ~ haben** have sth. to sort out with sb. 2 (verbessern) correct ‹*text*›; adjust, correct ‹*statistics*› (**um** for)
B *refl. V.* resolve itself; sort itself out

Bereinigung *die* (eines Missverständnisses) clearing up; (eines Streites) settlement; resolution; (eines Textes) correction; (einer Statistik) adjustment; correction

bereisen *tr. V.* travel around *or* about; travel through ‹*towns*›; (beruflich) ‹*representative etc.*› cover ‹*area*›; **fremde Länder ~:** travel in foreign countries; **ganz Afrika ~:** travel throughout Africa

bereit /bəˈrait/ *Adj.* 1 (fertig, gerüstet) ready; *s. auch* **bereithaben, bereithalten** 2 (gewillt) **~ sein, etw. zu tun** be willing *or* ready *or* prepared to do sth.; **sich ~ zeigen/finden, etw. zu tun** show oneself/be willing *or* ready *or* prepared to do sth.; **sich ~ erklären, etw. zu tun** declare oneself willing *or* ready to do sth.

bereiten
A *tr. V.* 1 (zu~) prepare; make ‹*tea, coffee*›; run ‹*bath*›; **jmdm.** od. **für jmdn. etw. ~:** prepare/make/run sth. for sb. 2 (zufügen) cause ‹*trouble, sorrow, frustration, difficulty, etc.*›; **jmdm. Freude/einen begeisterten Empfang ~:** give sb. great pleasure/an enthusiastic reception; **einer Sache** (*Dat.*) **ein Ende ~:** put an end to sth.
B *refl. V.* (geh.: sich vor~) prepare oneself; **sich zum Sterben ~:** prepare to die

bereit-: ~|haben *unr. tr. V.* have ready; **~|halten** A *unr. tr. V.* have ready; (für Notfälle) keep ready; B *unr. refl. V.* be ready; **der Arzt musste sich auf Abruf ~halten** the doctor was on call; **~|legen** *tr. V.* lay out ready; **jmdm.** od. **für jmdn. etw. ~legen** lay sth. out ready for sb.; **~|liegen** *unr. itr. V.* be ready; ‹*surgical instruments, tools, papers*› be laid out ready; **~|machen** A *tr. V.* get ready; make up ‹*bed*›; B *refl. V.* get ready

bereits *Adv.* already; **sie sind ~ gestern angekommen** they [in fact] arrived yesterday; **~ seit fünf Jahren** for [as long as] five years; **~ vor drei Stunden** three 'hours ago; **~ damals** even then *or* at that time; **~ im 17. Jh.** as early as the 17th century; **~ am nächsten Tag** by the very next day; **~ in zwei Wochen** in only two weeks' time

Bereitschaft *die;* **~; ~en** 1 willingness; readiness; preparedness; **etw. in ~ haben** have sth. ready 2 (ugs.: **~**sdienst) **~ haben** ‹*doctor, nurse*› be on call; ‹*policeman, fireman*› be on standby duty; ‹*chemist's*› be on rota duty (*for dispensing outside normal hours*) 3 (Einheit) unit

Bereitschafts-: ~arzt *der* doctor on call; **~dienst** *der:* **~dienst haben** ‹*doctor, nurse*› be on call; ‹*policeman, fireman*› be on standby duty; ‹*chemist's*› be on rota duty (*for dispensing outside normal hours*); **~polizei** *die* police; (bei Demonstrationen usw.) riot police

bereit-: ~|stehen *unr. itr. V.* be ready; ‹*car, train, aircraft*› be waiting; ‹*troops*› be standing by; **für uns steht ein Auto ~:** a car is/will be waiting for us; **etw. ~stehen haben** have sth. ready; **~|stellen** *tr. V.* place ready; get ready ‹*food, drinks*›; provide, make available ‹*money, funds*›; **die Getränke sind nebenan ~gestellt** the drinks are ready next door

Bereitung *die;* **~** (Papierdt.) preparation; (von Tee, Kaffee) making

bereit·willig
A *Adj.* willing
B *adv.* readily

Bereitwilligkeit *die;* **~:** willingness

berennen *unr. tr. V.* storm, attack ‹*castle, fortress*›; (Sport) storm, (Amer.) rush ‹*goal*›

berenten *tr. V.* (Amtsspr.) **jmdn. ~:** retire sb. on a pension; **sich ~ lassen** retire on a pension

bereuen
A *tr. V.* regret; **seine Sünden ~:** repent [of] one's sins; **ich bereue, dass ...** I'm sorry *or* I regret that ...; **nichts zu ~ haben** have no regrets
B *itr. V.* be sorry; (Rel.) repent

Berg /bɛrk/ *der;* **~[e]s, ~e** 1 ▸ⓘ **S. 374** hill; (im Hochgebirge) mountain; **über ~ und Tal** up hill and down dale; **~ Heil!** *greeting between mountaineers;* **wenn der ~ nicht zum Propheten kommt, muss der Prophet zum ~e kommen** (Spr.) if the mountain won't come to Muhammad, then Muhammad must go to the mountain (prov.); **jmdm. goldene ~e versprechen** (fig.) promise sb. the moon; **mit etw. hinter dem** od. **hinterm ~ halten** (fig.) keep sth. to oneself; keep quiet about sth.; **mit seiner Meinung nicht hinter dem** od. **hinterm ~ halten** (fig.) not keep one's views *pl.* to oneself; not hesitate to speak one's mind; **~e versetzen [können]** (fig.) [be able to] move mountains (fig.); **über den ~ sein** (ugs.) be out of the wood (Brit.) or (Amer.) woods; ‹patient› be on the mend, have turned the corner; [längst] über alle ~e sein (ugs.) be miles away 2 Pl. (Gebirge) mountains; in die ~e fahren go up into the mountains 3 (Haufen) enormous or huge pile; (von Akten, Abfall auch) mountain

berg-, Berg-: ~ab /-'-/ Adv. downhill; einen steilen Weg ~ab fahren go down a steep path; mit dem Patienten/der Firma geht es ~ab (fig. ugs) the patient's getting worse/the firm's going downhill; ~abwärts /-'--/ Adv. downhill; ~ahorn der sycamore [maple]; ~akademie die school of mining

Bergamotte /bɛrga'mɔtə/ die; ~, ~n 1 (Pomeranze) bergamot [orange] 2 (Birne) bergamot [pear]

berg-, Berg-: ~amt das [local] mining authority; ~an /-'-/ ▸ ~auf; ~arbeiter der, ~arbeiterin die miner; mineworker; ~auf /-'-/ Adv. uphill; es geht ~auf mit der Firma (fig. ugs.) things are looking up for the firm; mit dem Patienten gehts ~auf the patient's on the mend; ~aufwärts /-'--/ Adv. uphill; ~bahn die mountain railway; (Seilbahn) mountain cableway; ~bau der mining; ~bauer der; ~~n, ~~n, ~bäuerin die mountain farmer; ~dorf das mountain village

berge·hoch ▸ berghoch

Berge·lohn der salvage payment

bergen unr. tr. V. 1 (retten) rescue, save ‹person›; salvage ‹ship›; salvage, recover ‹cargo, belongings›; (einbringen) gather or get in ‹harvest›; jmdn. tot/lebend ~: recover sb.'s body/rescue sb. alive; sich geborgen fühlen feel safe; die Segel ~ (Seemannsspr.) take in or furl the sails 2 (geh.: enthalten) hold; Gefahren/Vorteile in sich (Dat.) ~ (fig.) hold dangers/have advantages 3 (geh.: ver~) hide; (vor Regen) shelter; (vor Sonne) protect; den Kopf in den Händen ~: bury one's head in one's hands

berg-, Berg-: ~fach das mining no art.; ~fahrt die 1 (Schifffahrt) passage upstream; 2 (Hochgebirgstour) mountaineering expedition; auf ~fahrt gehen go mountaineering; ~fest das (ugs.) party to celebrate reaching the halfway stage; ~fex /-fɛks/ der; ~~es, ~~e (ugs.) enthusiastic climber; mountaineering freak (coll.); ~fried /-fri:t/ der; ~~[e]s, ~~e keep; ~führer der, ~führerin die ▸ⓘ S. 113 mountain guide; ~geist der: legendary sorcerer, kobold, gnome, or giant living inside a mountain; ~gipfel der mountain peak or top; summit; ~grat der mountain ridge; ~hoch A Adj. as high as a mountain/as mountains; mountainous ‹waves, seas›; B adv. ~hoch aufsteigende Wellen mountainous waves or seas; ~hütte die mountain hut

bergig Adj. hilly; (mit hohen Bergen) mountainous

Berg-: ~ingenieur der, ~ingenieurin die [qualified] mining engineer; ~kessel der corrie; cirque; ~kette die range or chain of mountains; mountain range or chain; ~krankheit die mountain sickness; ~kristall der rock crystal; ~kuppe die [rounded] peak or mountain top; ~land das hilly country no indef. art; (mit hohen ~en) mountainous country no indef. art.; das spanische ~land the hill country of Spain; das Schottische ~land the Highlands of Scotland

Bergler /'bɛrklɐ/ der; ~s, ~, **Berglerin** die; ~, ~nen mountain-dweller

Berg·mann der; Pl. Bergleute ▸ⓘ S. 113 miner; mineworker

berg·männisch /-mɛnɪʃ/
A Adj. miner's attrib.
B adv. by miners

Bergmanns-: ~gruß der miner's greeting; ~sprache die mining terminology

berg-, Berg-: ~massiv das massif; ~not die: in ~not sein/geraten ‹climber› be/get into difficulties while climbing [in the mountains]; jmdn. aus ~not retten rescue sb. who has got into difficulties while climbing [in the mountains]; ~predigt die Sermon on the Mount; ~recht das laws relating to mining; ~rennen das (Motorsport) hill climbing; ein ~rennen a hill climb; ~rettungs·dienst der ▸ ~wacht; ~riese der giant of a mountain; ~rücken der mountain ridge; ~rutsch der landslide; landslip; ~sattel der saddle; col; ~schuh der mountaineering boot; ~see der mountain lake; ~spitze die [mountain] peak; mountain top; ~sport der mountaineering; mountain climbing; ~station die top station; ~steigen unr. itr. V.; mit haben od. sein; nur im Inf. und Part. go mountaineering or mountain climbing; ~steigen das; ~~s mountaineering no art.; mountain climbing no art.; ~steiger der, ~steigerin die; ~~, ~~nen ▸ⓘ S. 113 mountaineer; mountain climber; ~steigerisch A Adj. mountaineering; B adv. ~steigerisch [gesehen] from a mountaineering point of view; ~stock der 1 (Spazierstock) alpenstock; 2 ▸ Gebirgsstock; ~straße die 1 mountain road; 2 (Geogr.) die ~straße the Bergstraße (hilly wine-growing and orchard district between Darmstadt and Heidelberg); ~sturz der rock fall; ~tour die trip up into the mountains; (zu Fuß) mountain climb; (Wanderung) hike in the mountains; ~-und-Tal-Bahn die roller coaster; switch back (Brit.); big dipper (Brit.); ~-und-Tal-Fahrt die journey full of steep climbs and descents; das war die reinste ~-und-Tal-Fahrt it was just like going up and down on a roller coaster or (Brit.) switchback

Bergung die; ~, ~en 1 (erste Hilfe) rescue; saving 2 (von Schiffen, Gut) salvaging; salvage 3 (der Ernte) gathering in

Bergungs-: ~arbeiten Pl. rescue work sing.; ~kommando das rescue team; ~schiff das salvage vessel; ~versuch der rescue attempt; (Versuch, ein Schiff zu bergen) salvage attempt

Berg-: ~volk das mountain people; ~vorsprung der spur; (Absatz) ledge; ~wacht die mountain rescue service; ~wald der alpine forest; ~wand die mountain face; ~wandern itr. V.; mit sein ich ~wandere, ~gewandert, ~zuwandern go hill walking; das Bergwandern hill walking; ~wanderung die hike in the mountains; ~welt die (geh.) mountain landscape

Berg·werk das mine; im ~ arbeiten work down the mine

Bergwerks·gesellschaft die mining company

Berg-: ~wertung die (Radsport) mountain classification; ~wesen das (Bergbau) mining no art.; ~wiese die mountain pasture

Beriberi /beri'be:ri/ die; ~ ▸ⓘ S. 439 (Med.) beriberi

Bericht /bə'rɪçt/ der; ~[e]s, ~e report; einen ~ von etw. od. über etw. (Akk.) geben give a report on sth.; [jmdm.] [von etw.] ~ erstatten report or give a report [to sb.] [on sth.]

berichten tr., itr. V. report; jmdm. etw. ~: report sth. to sb.; über etw. (Akk.) od. von etw. ~: report on sth.; es wird berichtet, dass ... it is reported that ...; es wird soeben berichtet, dass ... reports are coming in that ...; mir ist berichtet worden, dass ... I have heard a report/reports that ...; wie uns berichtet wurde according to reports reaching us

Bericht-: ~erstatter /-ɛɐ̯ʃtatɐ/ der; ~~s, ~~, ~erstatterin die; ~~, ~~nen reporter; (Referent) rapporteur; unser ~erstatter aus Paris our Paris correspondent; ~erstattung die reporting no indef. art.; zur ~erstattung zurückgerufen werden ‹ambassador etc.› be recalled to make a report; die ~erstattung durch Presse und Rundfunk über diese Ereignisse press and radio coverage of these events; ~haus das (schweiz.) information centre

berichtigen tr. V. correct

Berichtigung die; ~, ~en correction; (berichtigte Fassung) corrected version; der Lehrer gab uns die Arbeiten zur ~ zurück the teacher gave the work back to us for the corrections to be done

Berichts-: ~heft das (Schulw.) (apprentice's/trainee's) record book; ~jahr das (bes. Wirtsch.) year [covered by the report]

beriechen unr. tr. V. 1 (riechen an) smell; sniff [at] 2 (ugs.: vorsichtig Kontakt aufnehmen mit) sich [gegenseitig] ~: size each other or one another up

berieseln tr. V. 1 (besprühen) water ‹field› using an overhead sprinkling system; water ‹lawn› using a sprinkler 2 (ugs. abwertend) mit Werbung/Musik berieselt werden be subjected to a constant [unobtrusive] stream of advertisements/to constant background music

Berieselung die 1 ▸ berieseln: watering using an overhead sprinkling system/a sprinkler 2 (ugs. abwertend) die ständige ~ mit Musik subjection to constant background music

Berieselungs·anlage die sprinkler system

beringen tr. V. put a ring on; ring ‹bird›

Bering·straße /'be:rɪŋ-/ die (Geogr.) Bering Strait

beringt Adj. beringed ‹finger, hand›; ‹hand› covered with rings

beritten 1 (reitend) mounted; on horseback postpos. 2 (mit Pferden ausgerüstet) mounted; gut ~ sein have good mounts or horses

Berittene der/die; adj. Dekl. rider; horseman/horsewoman

Berlin /bɛr'li:n/ (das); ~s ▸ⓘ S. 675 Berlin

> **Berlin**
>
> After Wiedervereinigung, Berlin took over from Bonn as the capital of Germany, but the German government did not start moving there until 1998. This vibrant city in the heart of Europe lies on the river Spree. It has about 3.5 million inhabitants and is a major cultural and commercial centre.

Berliner[1] ▸ⓘ S. 675
A indekl. Adj. Berlin; ~ Weiße [mit Schuss] light, very fizzy beer flavoured with a dash of raspberry juice or woodruff
B der; ~s, ~: Berliner; s. auch Kölner

Berliner[2] der; ~s, ~ (~ Pfannkuchen) [jam (Brit.) or (Amer.) jelly] doughnut

Berlinerin die; ~, ~nen Berliner; s. auch -in

berlinerisch Adj. (ugs.) ▸ berlinisch

berlinern itr. V. (ugs.) speak [in] Berlin dialect

berlinisch Adj. ▸ⓘ S. 675 Berlin attrib.; im Berlinischen (Sprachw.) in Berlin dialect; „Schrippe" ist ~: 'Schrippe' is Berlin dialect

Bermuda·inseln /bɛr'mu:da-/ Pl. Bermuda sing., no art.; Bermudas

Bermudas Pl. 1 Bermudas; Bermuda sing., no art. 2 ▸ Bermudashorts

Bermuda·shorts Pl. Bermuda shorts

Bern /bɛrn/ (das); ~s ▸ⓘ S. 675 Bern[e]

Berner indekl. ▸ⓘ S. 675
A Adj. Bernese; eine ~ Zeitung a Bern[e] newspaper; die ~ Konvention the Berne Convention; das ~ Oberland the Bernese Oberland
B der; ~s, ~: Bernese

Bernerin die; ~, ~nen Bernese

Bernhardiner /bɛrnhar'di:nɐ/ der; ~s, ~: St. Bernard [dog]

Bern·stein /'bɛrn-/ der amber

bernstein·farben Adj. amber[-coloured]

Berserker /bɛr'zɛrkɐ/ der; ~s, ~ 1 (hist.) berserker; berserk 2 wie ein ~ arbeiten work like mad (coll.); wie ein ~ auf jmdn. einschlagen go berserk and attack sb.

bersten /'bɛrstn̩/ unr. itr. V.; mit sein (geh.) ‹ice› break or crack up; ‹glass› shatter [into pieces]; ‹wall› crack up; [bis] zum B~ voll od. gefüllt sein be full to bursting point; vor Neugier/Ungeduld/Freude/Zorn ~ (fig.) be bursting with curiosity/impatience/joy/rage

berüchtigt /bə'rʏçtɪçt/ Adj. notorious (wegen for); (verrufen) disreputable; als Raufbold ~ sein be a notorious ruffian

berücken tr. V. (geh.) captivate; charm; enchant; ein ~der Anblick an enchanting or a bewitching sight

ℹ Berufe

Was machen Sie beruflich?, Was sind Sie von Beruf?
= What's your job?, What do you do for a living?
In welcher Branche sind Sie tätig?
= What's your field [of work]?, What's your line of business?
Ich arbeite bei einer Bank/in einer Buchhandlung/bei einem Verlag
= I work in *od.* for a bank/in a bookshop/at a publisher's *od.* for a publisher
Er ist in der Textilindustrie/Versicherungsbranche tätig
= He is in textiles/insurance
Ich arbeite bei einem kleinen Unternehmen/einem großen Konzern
= I am with *od.* work for a small company *od.* firm/a large combine *od.* group
Sie besitzt/leitet einen kleinen Betrieb
= She owns/runs a small business
Mein Mann ist bei der gleichen Firma angestellt
= My husband works for *od.* is employed by the same firm
Sie arbeitet ganztags od. hat eine Ganztagsstelle
= She works full time *od* has a full-time job
Er arbeitet halbtags od. hat eine Halbtagsstelle/ Teilzeitstelle
= He works part time *od.* has a part-time job

Ich arbeite freiberuflich/bin selbstständig
= I work freelance/am self-employed

Beachten Sie, dass bei der Angabe des Berufs im Englischen der unbestimmte Artikel **a/an** verwendet wird. Auch wird mit der Berufsbezeichnung keine Aussage über das Geschlecht gemacht; es gibt zwar ein paar Ausnahmen **(authoress, manageress)**, diese Formen werden aber meist als sexistisch vermieden:

Er ist [von Beruf] Bäcker
= He's a baker [by trade]
Sie ist Lehrerin [von Beruf]
= She's a teacher [by profession]
Michael will Systemanalytiker werden
= Michael wants to be a systems analyst
Bettina ist als Journalistin tätig
= Bettina works as a journalist

Wenn man ausdrücklich von einer Frau in einem bestimmten Beruf spricht, stellt man der Berufsbezeichnung das Wort **woman** oder **female** voran:

Sie möchte lieber von einer Ärztin behandelt werden
= She prefers to be treated by a woman doctor
Es gibt mehr und mehr Anwältinnen
= There are more and more women *od.* female lawyers

Aber:
Sie ist Ärztin/Anwältin
= She's a doctor/lawyer

Stellensuche

Ich suche eine Stelle als Sekretärin
= I am looking for a job as a secretary
Bei den Stellenanzeigen habe ich nichts Geeignetes gefunden
= I didn't find anything suitable in the situations vacant
Ich will mich um diese Stelle bewerben
= I want to apply for this job
Der Bewerbung sind ein Lebenslauf und ein Foto beizulegen
= A CV and a photograph should be sent with the application
Können Sie am 24. März zu einem Vorstellungsgespräch kommen?
= Could you come for an interview on March 24th?
Wann wäre Ihr frühestmöglicher Einstellungstermin?
= What is the earliest [date] you could start?

berücksichtigen /bəˈrʏkzɪçtɪgn̩/ *tr. V.* **1** (einbeziehen) take into account *or* consideration; **jmds. Alter ~:** make allowances for sb.'s age; **wir müssen auch ~, dass etwa 7 % der Arbeitszeit durch Krankheit entfallen** we also have to allow for the fact that about 7% of working time is lost through illness **2** (beachten) consider ‹*applicant, application, suggestion*›

Berücksichtigung *die;* ~ **1** (das Einbeziehen) **bei ~ aller Umstände** taking all the circumstances into account; **in** *od.* **unter ~ der Vor- und Nachteile** taking account of all the advantages and disadvantages **2** (Beachtung) consideration; **eine ~ Ihres Auftrags ist nicht möglich** we cannot consider your application

Beruf *der;* **~[e]s, ~e** ▸ℹ **S. 113** **1** occupation; (akademischer, wissenschaftlicher, medizinischer ~) profession; (handwerklicher ~) trade; (Stellung) job; (Laufbahn) career; **was sind Sie von ~?** what do you do for a living?; what is your occupation?; **er ist von ~ Bäcker/Lehrer** *od.* **Bäcker/Lehrer von ~:** he's a baker by trade/a teacher by profession; **20 Jahre im ~ stehen** have been in the profession/trade for 20 years; **von ~s wegen** because of one's job; **den ~ verfehlt haben** (scherzh.) have missed one's vocation; *s. auch* **ergreifen, frei 2** (geh. veralt.) ▸ **Berufung 2**

berufen[1]
A *unr. tr. V.* **1** (einsetzen) appoint; **jmdn. auf einen Lehrstuhl/in ein Amt ~:** appoint sb. to a chair/an office **2** (ugs.: beschreien) **berufe es nicht!** don't speak too soon!; **ich will es nicht ~, aber bisher hat die Sache immer geklappt** I don't want to tempt fate *or* providence, but until now it's worked every time **3** (veralt.: zusammenrufen) call, summon ‹*person*› **(zu** to); call a meeting of ‹*council, cabinet, etc.*›
B *unr. refl. V.* **sich auf etw.** (*Akk.*) **~:** refer to sth.; quote *or* cite sth.; **sich auf jmdn. als Zeugen ~:** appeal to sb. as a witness; **wenn Sie sich vorstellen, können Sie sich auf mich ~:** when you introduce yourself, you can mention my name

berufen[2] *Adj.* **1** competent; **aus ~em Munde** from somebody *or* one competent *or* qualified to speak **2** (prädestiniert) **sich dazu ~ fühlen, etw. zu tun** feel called to do sth.; feel one has a mission to do sth.; **sich zu großen Taten ~ fühlen** feel called to great things; **zum Dichter/zu Höherem ~ sein** have a vocation as a poet/be destined for greater things

beruflich
A *Adj.* occupational, vocational ‹*training etc.*›; (bei akademischen Berufen) professional ‹*training etc.*›; **seine ~e Tätigkeit** his occupation; **er hat ~e Probleme** he has problems at work *or* in his job; **aus ~en Gründen** because of one's job; (bei akademischen Berufen) for professional reasons
B *adv.* **meine Reise war ~ bedingt** my trip was business-related; **~ erfolgreich sein** be successful in one's career; **~ viel unterwegs sein** be away a lot on business; **sich ~ weiterbilden** undertake further job training; **~ verhindert sein** be detained by one's work

berufs-, Berufs-: ~akademie *die* vocational college; **~armee** *die* ▸ **~heer**; **~ausbildung** *die* occupational *or* vocational training; (als Lehrer, Wissenschaftler, Arzt) professional training; **eine [solide] ~ausbildung [als etw.] bekommen** receive [a thorough] training [as sth.]; **~aussichten** *Pl.* job prospects (*in a particular profession etc.*); **~beamte** *der* ≈ established civil servant; *s. auch* **Beamte**; **~beamtentum** *das* civil service with lifelong job security; **~beamtin** *die* ▸ **~beamte**; **~bedingt** *Adj.* occupational ‹*disease*›; ‹*expenses, difficulties*› connected with one's job; **~berater** *der,* **~beraterin** *die* ▸ℹ **S. 113** vocational adviser; **~beratung** *die* vocational guidance; **~bezeichnung** *die* job title; **~bezogen** *Adj.* vocationally orientated; **~bild** *das* outline of a/the profession/trade as a career; **~bildend** *Adj.* **~bildende Schule** vocational training school; **~boxer** *der,* **~boxerin** *die* ▸ℹ **S. 113** professional boxer; **~einsteiger** *der,* **~einsteigerin** *die* new recruit [to the/a profession]; **~erfahren** *Adj.* [professionally] experienced; with considerable [professional] experience *postpos., not pred.*; **~erfahrung** *die* [professional] experience; **~ethos** *das* (geh.) professional code of ethics; **~fachschule** *die* vocational college (providing full-time vocational training); **~fahrer** *der,* **~fahrerin** *die* [professional] driver; **~feuerwehr** *die* [professional] fire service; **~fremd** *Adj.* ‹*task, work, job*› unconnected with the profession/trade for which one has been trained; **„~fremde werden eingearbeitet"** '[on-the-job] training will be given where necessary'; **~geheimnis** *das* professional secret; (Schweigepflicht) professional secrecy; **~genossenschaft** *die: professional/trade association having liability for industrial safety and insurance;* **~gruppe** *die* occupational group; **~heer** *das* regular *or* professional army; **~jugendliche** *der/die; adj. Dekl.* (ugs., meist abwertend) man/woman trying to look and act eternally young; **~kleidung** *die* [prescribed] work[ing] clothes *pl.*; **~krankheit** *die* occupational disease; **~leben** *das* working life; **im ~leben stehen** be working; **ins ~leben treten** start one's working life; start in one's first job; **~mäßig** **A** *Adj.* professional; **B** *adv.* professionally; **~musiker** *der,* **~musikerin** *die* professional musician; **~offizier** *der,* **~offizierin** *die* regular officer; **~politiker** *der,* **~politikerin** *die* ▸ℹ **S. 113** professional politician; **~richter** *der,* **~richterin** *die* ▸ℹ **S. 113** full-time salaried judge; **~risiko** *das* occupational risk; **~schule** *die* vocational school; **~schüler** *der,* **~schülerin** *die* student at a vocational school; **~soldat** *der,* **~soldatin** *die* ▸ℹ **S. 113** regular *or* professional soldier; **~sportler** *der,* **~sportlerin** *die* professional sportsman; **~stand** *der* profession; (Gewerbe) trade; **~ständisch** *Adj.* professional;

> **Berufsfachschule**
>
> A full-time vocational college which offers preparation courses for a period of one to three years. Only pupils with a *Haupt-* or *Realschulabschluss* can attend a *Berufsfachschule*. The courses count as part of an apprenticeship or can even replace it.

> **Berufsschule**
>
> A college for young people who are doing a **Lehre**. They attend *Berufsschule* one or two days a week (or sometimes in blocks of several weeks) to continue their general education and receive formal training in their chosen type of job.

berufs-, Berufs-: ~tätig *Adj.* working *attrib.*; **es gibt mehr ~tätige Männer als Frauen** more men than women have a job *or*

b

are in paid employment; **[halbtags] ~tätig sein** work [part-time]; **~tätige** *der/die; adj. Dekl.* working person; **~tätige** *Pl.* working people; **~unfähigkeit** *die* incapacity *(to follow one's profession/trade)*; **~verband** *der* professional/trade association; **~verbot** *das: debarment from practising a particular profession or trade; (für den öffentlichen Dienst) official debarment, on political grounds, from all civil service professions;* **~verbrecher** *der,* **~verbrecherin** *die* professional criminal; **~verkehr** *der* rush hour traffic; **~wahl** *die* choice of career; **~wechsel** *der* change of career; **~wunsch** *der* preferred choice of career; **~zweig** *der* branch of the profession/trade

Berufung *die; ~, ~en* [1] (für ein Amt) offer of an appointment (**auf, in, an** + *Akk.* to); **seit seiner ~ nach ...** since he took up the appointment in ... [2] (innerer Auftrag) vocation; **die ~ zum Künstler in sich** (*Dat.*) **verspüren** feel one has a vocation as an artist [3] (das Sichberufen) **unter ~** (*Dat.*) **auf jmdn./etw.** referring *or* with reference to sb./sth. [4] (Rechtsw.: Einspruch) appeal; **~ einlegen** lodge an appeal; appeal; **in die ~ gehen** appeal [5] (veralt.: Einberufung) summoning

Berufungs-: ~frist *die* (Rechtsw.) period within which an appeal must be lodged; period allowed for an appeal; **~instanz** *die* (Rechtsw.) court of appeal; **~verfahren** *das* (Rechtsw.) appeal proceedings *pl.*

beruhen *itr. V.* **auf etw.** (*Dat.*) **~:** be based on sth.; **etw. auf sich** (*Dat.*) **~ lassen** let sth. rest; *s. auch* **Gegenseitigkeit**

beruhigen /bəˈruːɪɡn̩/

[A] *tr. V.* calm [down]; quieten, pacify ‹*child, baby*›; (trösten) soothe; (die Befürchtung nehmen) reassure; salve, soothe ‹*conscience*›; **die Nerven/den Magen ~:** calm one's nerves/settle the stomach; **beruhigt schlafen/nach Hause gehen können** be able to sleep/go home with one's mind set at ease

[B] *refl. V.* ‹*person*› calm down; ‹*wind*› drop, die down; ‹*sea*› become calm; ‹*storm*› abate, die down; ‹*struggle, traffic*› lessen; ‹*rush of people*› subside; ‹*prices, stock exchange, stomach*› settle down; **die Lage beruhigt sich** the situation is becoming more stable; **meine Nerven haben sich beruhigt** my nerves have steadied

Beruhigung *die; ~* [1] ▸**beruhigen A**: calming [down]; quietening; pacifying; soothing; salving; reassurance; **jmdm. etw. zur ~ geben** give sb. sth. to calm him/her [down] [2] (das Ruhigwerden); **eine ~ des Wetters ist vorauszusehen** the weather can be expected to become more settled; **zu Ihrer ~ kann ich sagen, ...** you'll be reassured to know that ...; **jmdm. ein Gefühl der ~ geben** reassure sb.; **eine ~ der politischen Lage ist nicht zu erwarten** we should not expect that the political situation will become more stable

Beruhigungs-: ~mittel *das* sedative; tranquillizer; **~pille** *die* sedative [pill]; tranquillizer; (fig.) sop; **~spritze** *die* sedative injection; **~zelle** *die* cooling-off cell; holding cell; **~zigarette** *die* calming cigarette; cigarette to calm one's nerves

berühmt /bəˈryːmt/ *Adj.* famous; **durch diesen Roman wurde er ~:** the novel made him famous; **wegen** *od.* **für etw. ~ sein** be famous for sth.; **das ist nicht gerade ~** (ugs. iron.) it's nothing to write home about (coll.) *or* no big deal (coll.)

berühmt-berüchtigt *Adj.* notorious

Berühmtheit *die; ~, ~en* [1] (Ruhm) fame; **~ erlangen/gewinnen** become famous/win fame; **zu trauriger ~ gelangen** become notorious [2] (Mensch) celebrity

berühren *tr. V.* [1] (anrühren) touch; **sich** *od.* (geh.) **einander ~:** touch; **„Bitte Waren nicht ~!“** 'please do not touch the merchandise' [2] (kurz erwähnen) touch on ‹*topic, issue, question*› [3] (beeindrucken) affect; **das berührte ihn seltsam/schmerzlich** he was strangely affected/painfully moved by it; **wir fühlten uns davon unangenehm/peinlich berührt** it made an unpleasant impression on us/made us feel embarrassed; **das berührt mich [überhaupt] nicht** it's a matter of [complete] indifference to me

Berührung *die; ~, ~en* [1] (das Berühren) touch; **mit etw. in ~** (*Akk.*) **kommen** come into contact with sth.; **jede ~ mit jmdm. vermeiden** avoid all physical contact with sb.; **bei der geringsten ~:** at the slightest touch [2] (Kontakt) contact; **mit jmdm./etw. in ~** (*Akk.*) **kommen** come into contact with sb./sth.; **jmdn. in ~** (*Akk.*) **mit jmdm./etw. bringen** bring sb. into contact with sb./sth. [3] (Erwähnung) mention

berührungs-, Berührungs-: ~angst *die* (Psych.) fear of contact; haptephobia (Psych.); **~empfindlich** *Adj.* [1] (Elektrot.) touch-sensitive; [2] (Med.) ‹*skin etc.*› that is sensitive to touch; **~los** (Physik, Technik) [A] *Adj.* contactless; non-contact; [B] *adv.* without direct contact; **~punkt** *der* [1] (Math.) point of contact *or* tangency; [2] (Gemeinsamkeit) point of contact; **politische ~punkte mit jmdm. besitzen** have the same views as sb. on a number of political issues

Beryll /beˈrʏl/ *der; ~s, ~e* (Mineral.) beryl

Beryllium /beˈrʏli̯ʊm/ *das; ~s* (Chemie) beryllium

besabbern *tr. V.* (salopp) slobber [on *or* over]

besäen *tr. V.* sow

besagen *tr. V.* say; (bedeuten) mean; **das besagt noch gar nichts/sehr viel** that doesn't mean anything/means a great deal

besagt *Adj.* (Amtsspr.) aforementioned

besamen /bəˈzaːmən/ *tr. V.* fertilize; (künstlich) inseminate

besammeln *refl. V.* (schweiz.) ▸**versammeln**

Besammlung *die; ~, ~en* (schweiz.) ▸**Versammlung**

Besamung *die; ~, ~en* fertilization; (künstlich) insemination

Besan /beˈzaːn/ *der; ~s, ~e* [1] (Segel) mizzen[sail] [2] (~mast) mizzenmast

besänftigen /bəˈzɛnftɪɡn̩/

[A] *tr. V.* calm [down]; pacify; calm, soothe ‹*temper*›

[B] *refl. V.* calm down; ‹*sea*› become calm

Besänftigung *die; ~:* calming [down]; pacifying; (von jmds. Zorn) calming; soothing

Besan-mast *der* mizzenmast

besät /bəˈzɛːt/ *Adj.* sown (**mit** with); (fig.) covered (**mit, von** with); **mit Blütenblättern/Sternen ~:** strewn with petals/studded with stars

Besatz *der* [1] (Mode: Borte) trimming *no indef. art.* [2] (Jagdw., Landw., Fischereiw.) stock

Besatzer /bəˈzat͡sɐ/ *der; ~s, ~,* **Besatzerin** *die; ~, ~nen* member of the occupying forces; **die Besatzer** the occupying forces

Besatzung *die* [1] (Mannschaft) crew [2] (Milit.: Verteidigungstruppe) garrison [3] (Milit.: Okkupationstruppen) occupying troops *pl. or* forces *pl.*

Besatzungs-: ~armee *die* occupying army; army of occupation; **~kind** *das: child of a [non-white] member of the occupying forces and a local woman;* **~macht** *die* occupying power; **~truppen** *Pl.* occupying troops *or* forces; **~zone** *die* occupied zone

besaufen *unr. refl. V.* (salopp) get boozed up (Brit. sl.) *or* canned (Brit. sl.) *or* bombed (Amer. sl.); *s. auch* **sinnlos B 3**

Besäufnis /bəˈzɔyfnɪs/ *die; ~, ~se od. das; ~ses, ~se* (salopp) booze-up (Brit. sl.); blast (Amer. sl.)

besäuseln *refl. V.* (ugs.) get merry (Brit. coll.) *or* tipsy; **besäuselt** merry (coll.); tipsy

beschädigen *tr. V.* damage

Beschädigte *der/die; adj. Dekl.* (veralt.) disabled person

Beschädigung *die* [1] (das Beschädigen) damaging [2] (Schaden) damage; **zahlreiche/mehrere ~en** a lot of/quite a lot of damage *sing.*

beschaffbar *Adj.* obtainable; **schwer/leicht ~:** difficult/easy to obtain

beschaffen[1] *tr. V.* obtain; get; get ‹*job*›; **ein Quartier ~:** find accommodation; **jmdm. etw. ~:** obtain/get sb. sth. *or* sth. for sb.; **sich** (*Dat.*) **Geld/die Genehmigung ~:** get [hold of] money/get *or* obtain the permit/licence

beschaffen[2] *Adj.* **so ~ sein, dass ...** ‹*goods, materials*› be made in such a way that ...; ‹*substance*› be such that ...

Beschaffenheit *die; ~:* composition; (von Menschen) make-up; **raue/glatte ~:** roughness/smoothness

Beschaffung *die* ▸**beschaffen**[1]: obtaining; getting; finding

Beschaffungs-: ~amt *das* (Milit.) ≈ Procurement Executive (Brit.) *or* (Amer.) Office; **~kosten** *Pl.* procurement cost *sing.*; cost *sing.* of acquisition; **~kriminalität** *die* crime in the pursuit of drug acquisition

beschäftigen /bəˈʃɛftɪɡn̩/

[A] *refl. V.* **sich mit etw. ~:** occupy *or* busy oneself with sth.; **sich viel mit Musik/den Kindern ~:** devote a great deal of one's time to music/the children; **sich mit den Schriften Hegels ~:** be engaged in a study of the writings of Hegel; **sich mit einem Fall ~:** deal with a case; **mit etw. beschäftigt sein** be [busy] working on sth.; **sehr beschäftigt sein** be very busy

[B] *tr. V.* [1] (geistig in Anspruch nehmen) **jmdn. ~:** be on sb.'s mind; preoccupy sb.; **was beschäftigt dich so?** what's on your mind?; **Märchen ~ die Fantasie der Kinder** fairy stories engage children's imaginations [2] (angestellt haben) employ ‹*workers, staff*›; **bei einer Firma beschäftigt sein** work for a firm [3] (zu tun geben) occupy; **jmdn. mit etw. ~:** give sb. sth. to occupy him/her; **du musst die Kinder ~:** you must keep the children occupied

Beschäftigte *der/die; adj. Dekl.* employee; **die Fabrik/das Kaufhaus hat 500 ~:** the factory has a workforce/the department store has a staff of 500

Beschäftigung *die; ~, ~en* [1] (Tätigkeit) activity; occupation; **bei dieser ~ solltest du ihn nicht stören** you shouldn't disturb him while he's occupied with that; **einer ~ nachgehen** pursue an activity [2] (berufliche Tätigkeit) job; **seiner ~ nachgehen** go about one's business; **er geht wieder seiner ~ nach** he's now back at work; **ohne ~ sein** not be working; (unfreiwillig) be unemployed [3] (mit einer Frage, einem Problem) consideration (**mit** of); (Untersuchung, Studium) study (**mit** of) [4] (das Angestelltwerden) employment [5] (das Beschäftigtsein) **die ~ in diesem Betrieb/im Staatsdienst** working for this firm/in the Civil Service

beschäftigungs-, Beschäftigungs-: ~grad *der* (Wirtsch.) level of employment; **~los** *Adj.* [1] (untätig) **~los sein** have nothing to do; [2] (ohne Arbeit) **~los sein** not be working; (unfreiwillig) be unemployed; **~programm** *das* employment programme; **~therapie** *die* (Med.) occupational therapy

beschälen *tr. V.* cover, serve ‹*mare*›

Beschäler *der; ~s, ~:* breeding stallion; stud horse

beschallen *tr. V.* [1] fill with sound [2] (Med.) treat with ultrasonic waves *or* ultrasound

beschämen *tr. V.* shame; **jmdn. durch seine Großmütigkeit ~:** make sb. ashamed by one's generosity

beschämend

[A] *Adj.* [1] (schändlich) shameful [2] (demütigend) humiliating; **für jmdn. ~ sein** be humiliating for sb.; bring humiliation upon sb.

[B] *adv.* shamefully

beschämt *Adj.* ashamed; abashed; **ein ~es Gesicht** a shamefaced expression; **sich ~ fühlen** be ashamed *or* abashed

Beschämung *die; ~:* shame; **zu meiner ~ muss ich gestehen, dass ...** to my shame I must confess that ...

beschatten *tr. V.* [1] (geh.) shade; (fig.) overshadow, cast a cloud over ‹*event*›; cloud ‹*face*› [2] (heimlich überwachen) shadow; **jmdn. ~ lassen** have sb. shadowed [3] (Fußball, Hockey) mark closely

Beschatter *der; ~s, ~,* **Beschatterin** *die; ~, ~nen* shadow

Beschattung *die; ~* (eines Verdächtigen) shadowing

Beschau *die* inspection

beschauen *tr. V.* (bes. md.) ▸**betrachten**

Beschauer *der;* **~s, ~, Beschauerin** *die;* **~, ~nen** viewer

beschaulich /bəˈʃaulɪç/

A *Adj.* 1 (behaglich) peaceful, tranquil ‹*life, manner, etc.*›; meditative, contemplative ‹*person, character*› 2 (kath. Rel.) **~e Orden** contemplative orders

B *adv.* peacefully; tranquilly

Beschaulichkeit *die;* **~:** peacefulness; tranquillity

Bescheid /bəˈʃait/ *der;* **~[e]s, ~e** 1 (Auskunft) information; (Antwort) answer; reply; **jmdm. ~ geben** *od.* **sagen[, ob ...]** let sb. know or tell sb. [whether ...]; **sage bitte im Restaurant ~, dass ...** please let the restaurant know *or* let them know in the restaurant that ...; **jmdm. ~ sagen** (ugs.: sich beschweren) give sb. a piece of one's mind (coll.); **[über etw.** (*Akk.*)**] ~ wissen** know [about sth.]; **in einer Stadt/mit Autos ~ wissen** know one's way around a town/know about cars; **jmdm. ~ stoßen** (ugs.) give sb. a dressing-down (coll.); **Entschuldigung, wissen Sie hier ~?** excuse me, do you know your way around here? 2 (Entscheidung) decision; **ein abschlägiger/günstiger ~:** a refusal/a positive reply

bescheiden[1]

A *unr. tr. V.* 1 (Amtsspr.: Mitteilung machen an) **jmdn./etw. abschlägig ~:** turn sb./sth. down; refuse sb./sth.; **jmdn. ~[, dass ...]** inform *or* notify sb. [that ...] 2 (geh.: zuteil werden lassen) **jmdm. etw. ~:** grant sb. sth.; **es war ihm nicht beschieden, den Erfolg seines Romans zu erleben** it was not granted to him to live to see the success of his novel

B *unr. refl. V.* (geh.) be content; **man muss sich ~ können** one has to be able to make do with less *or* moderate one's needs

bescheiden[2]

A *Adj.* 1 (unaufdringlich) modest; modest, unassuming ‹*person, behaviour*› 2 (einfach) modest; simple ‹*meal*›; **darf ich die ~e Frage stellen, wie ...?** (auch iron.) may I venture to ask how ...?; **aus ~en Anfängen** from modest *or* humble beginnings; **in ~en Verhältnissen aufwachsen** grow up in humble circumstances 3 (dürftig) modest ‹*salary, results, pension, etc.*› 4 (ugs. verhüll.: sehr schlecht) lousy (coll.); bloody awful (Brit. coll.)

B *adv.* modestly; **darf ich mal ganz ~ anfragen, wie ...?** (auch iron.) may I venture to ask how ...?

Bescheidenheit *die;* **~:** modesty; **keine falsche ~!** don't be shy!; **~ ist eine Zier, doch weiter kommt man ohne ihr** (scherzh.) modesty is a virtue, but it doesn't get you very far; **aus falscher ~:** out of false modesty

Bescheidung *die* (geh.) moderation in one's needs

bescheinen *unr. tr. V.* shine [up]on; **vom Mond/von der Sonne beschienen** moonlit/sunlit

bescheinigen /bəˈʃainɪgn̩/ *tr. V.* **etw. ~:** confirm sth. in writing; **den Tod [auf dem Totenschein] ~:** sign the death certificate; **jmdm. den Empfang des Geldes ~:** acknowledge receipt of the money; (durch Quittung) give sb. a receipt for the money; **sich** (*Dat.*) **~ lassen, dass man arbeitsunfähig ist/die Rechnung bezahlt hat** get oneself certified as unfit for work/get a receipt for the bill; **du wirst deinen Fehler noch bereuen, das kann ich dir ~** (fig.) you'll regret your mistake, I can guarantee you that

Bescheinigung *die;* **~, ~en** 1 (Schriftstück) written confirmation *no indef. art.*; (Schein) certificate; (Quittung) receipt; **eine ~ des Arztes** a doctor's certificate; a certificate from the doctor; a medical certificate 2 (das Bescheinigen) confirmation in writing

bescheißen *unr. tr. V.* (derb) **jmdn. ~:** rip sb. off (coll.); screw sb. (coarse); **jmdn. um etw. ~:** do sb. out of sth. (coll.)

beschenken *tr. V.* **jmdn. ~:** give sb. a present/presents; **jmdn. reich ~:** shower sb. with presents; **jmdn. mit etw. ~:** give sb. sth. as a present; **sich [gegenseitig] ~:** give each other presents

bescheren

A *tr. V.* 1 (schenken) **jmdn. [mit etw.] ~:** give sb. [sth. as] a Christmas present/Christmas presents; **jmdm. etw. ~:** give sb. sth. for Christmas 2 (zuteil werden lassen) **ihnen waren keine Kinder beschert** they were not blessed with children; **ich bin gespannt, was uns dieser Tag ~ wird** I wonder what today will bring; **ihm waren noch viele Jahre des Glücks beschert** he was granted many more happy years

B *itr. V.* **nach dem Abendessen wird beschert** the presents are given out after supper

Bescherung *die;* **~, ~en** 1 (zu Weihnachten) giving out of the Christmas presents; **die Kinder konnten die ~ kaum erwarten** the children could hardly wait for the presents to be given out 2 (ugs. iron.: unangenehme Überraschung) **das ist ja eine schöne ~:** this is a pretty kettle of fish; **jetzt haben wir die ~:** that's done it, I told you so; **nun guck dir die ~ an** just look at this mess

bescheuert *Adj.* (salopp) 1 (verrückt) barmy (Brit. coll.); nuts (coll.) 2 (unangenehm) stupid ‹*task, party, etc.*›; **jmdn./etw. ~ finden** find sb./sth. a real pain [in the neck] (coll.)

beschichten *tr. V.* (Technik) coat; **mit Kunststoff beschichtet** plastic-coated

Beschichtung *die;* **~, ~en** (Technik) coating

beschicken *tr. V.* 1 supply ‹*market, shop*›; send representatives to ‹*meeting, congress, etc.*›; send exhibits to ‹*art exhibition*› 2 (Technik: füllen) charge ‹*furnace*›

beschickert /bəˈʃɪkɐt/ *Adj.* (ugs.: angetrunken) tipsy; merry (Brit. coll.)

Beschickung *die;* **~, ~en** (Technik: eines Hochofens) (das Beschicken) charging; (Füllung) charge

beschießen *unr. tr. V.* 1 fire *or* shoot at; (mit Artillerie) bombard 2 (Kernphysik) bombard

Beschießung *die;* **~, ~en** ▸**beschießen:** 1 **die ~ der feindlichen Flugzeuge** firing *or* shooting at the enemy aircraft; **hält diese ~ weiter an, ...** if this firing *or* shooting/bombardment continues ... 2 **die ~ mit Neutronen/Alphateilchen** bombardment with neutrons/alpha particles

beschildern *tr. V.* label ‹*jar etc.*›; put up direction signs along ‹*road, path*›

Beschilderung *die* 1 labelling; **die ~ der Straße/des Wanderwegs** putting up direction signs along the road/footpath 2 (Schilder) direction signs

beschimpfen *tr. V.* abuse; swear at; **ich lasse mich von Ihnen nicht ~!** I won't stand for being sworn at *or* abused by you

Beschimpfung *die;* **~, ~en** 1 (das Beschimpfen) abuse *no indef. art.*; **die öffentliche ~ des Staatsoberhaupts** publicly insulting the head of state 2 (Äußerung) insult; **~en** abuse *sing.*; insults

beschirmen *tr. V.* (geh.) 1 (beschützen) protect (**vor** + *Dat.* from) 2 (vor Licht) shade

beschirmt *Adj.* (scherzh.) **~ sein** have an *or* one's umbrella [with one]

Beschiss, *Beschiß *der;* **Beschisses** (derb) rip-off (coll.); **das ist doch alles ~!** it's a rip-off (coll.) *or* swindle

beschissen /bəˈʃɪsn̩/ (derb)

A *Adj.* lousy (coll.); shitty (coarse)

B *adv.* ‹*behave*› in a bloody awful manner (Brit. coll.), shittily (coarse); **ihm geht es ~:** he's having a lousy *or* (Brit.) bloody awful time of it (sl.)

beschlafen *unr. tr. V.* (ugs.) 1 (den Beischlaf ausüben mit) lay (sl.); sleep with 2 (überdenken) sleep on

Beschlag *der* 1 (an Truhen) metal fitting; (an Fenstern, Türen, Möbelstücken, Sätteln) metal mount; (Scharnier) hinge; (Schließe) clasp 2 *in* **jmdn./etw. mit ~ belegen** *od.* **in ~ nehmen, jmdn./etw. in ~ halten** monopolize sb./sth. 3 (Hufeisen) horseshoe

beschlagen[1]

A *unr. tr. V.* shoe ‹*horse*›; **ein Fass mit Reifen ~:** hoop a barrel; **Schuhsohlen mit Nägeln ~:** stud the soles of shoes with [hob]nails

B *unr. itr. V.; mit sein* ‹*window*› mist up (Brit.), fog up (Amer.); (durch Dampf) steam up; **~e Scheiben** misted-up/fogged-up/steamed-up windows

C *unr. refl. V.* mist up (Brit.); fog up (Amer.); (durch Dampf) steam up

beschlagen[2] *Adj.* knowledgeable; **in etw.** (*Dat.*) **[gut] ~ sein** be knowledgeable about sth.; **auf einem Gebiet ~ sein** be knowledgeable about *or* well-versed in a subject

Beschlagenheit *die;* **~:** thorough *or* sound knowledge (**auf** + *Dat.* of)

Beschlag·nahme /-naːmə/ *die;* **~, ~n** seizure; confiscation

beschlagnahmen *tr. V.* 1 (konfiszieren) seize; confiscate 2 (scherzh.: in Anspruch nehmen) **jmdn. ~:** monopolize sb.

Beschlagnahmung *die;* **~, ~en** ▸**Beschlagnahme**

beschleichen *unr. tr. V.* 1 (heranschleichen an) creep up on *or* to; steal up to; ‹*hunter*› stalk ‹*game, prey*› 2 (geh.: überkommen) creep over

beschleunigen /bəˈʃlɔynɪgn̩/

A *tr. V.* speed up; increase ‹*speed*›; quicken ‹*pace, step[s], pulse*›; accelerate ‹*atomic particle*›; speed up, expedite ‹*work, delivery*›; hasten ‹*departure, collapse*›; accelerate, speed up, expedite ‹*process*›; **etw. beschleunigt erledigen** deal with sth. as a matter of priority

B *refl. V.* ‹*speed, heart rate*› increase; ‹*pulse*› quicken

C *itr. V.* ‹*car*› accelerate; ‹*engine*› speed up

Beschleuniger *der;* **~s, ~** (Kernphysik) accelerator

Beschleunigung *die;* **~, ~en** 1 ▸**beschleunigen A:** speeding up; increasing; quickening; acceleration; expedition; hastening; **eine ~ der Arbeit erreichen** speed up the work; **eine weitere ~ des Tempos** a further increase in speed 2 (ugs.: ~svermögen) acceleration; **eine gute ~ haben** have good acceleration 3 (Physik) acceleration

Beschleunigungs-: ~anlage *die* ▸**Beschleuniger**; **~vermögen** *das* (Technik) (eines Kfz) acceleration; (eines Motors) throttle response; **~wert** *der* (Technik) acceleration figure

beschließen

A *unr. tr. V.* 1 (entscheiden) **~, etw. zu tun** decide *or* resolve to do sth.; **das ist beschlossene Sache** it's settled 2 (einen Mehrheitsbeschluss fassen über) pass ‹*law*›; **~, etw. zu tun** resolve to do sth. 3 (beenden) end; end, conclude ‹*lecture*›; end, close ‹*letter*›; **seine Tage ~** (geh.) end one's days

B *unr. itr. V.* **über etw.** (*Akk.*) **~:** decide concerning sth.

beschlossen /bəˈʃlɔsn̩/

A *2. Part. v.* **beschließen**

B *in* **in etw.** (*Dat.*) **~ sein** *od.* **liegen** (geh.) be summed up in sth.

Beschluss, *Beschluß *der* 1 (Entscheidung) decision; (gemeinsam festgelegt) resolution; **einen ~ fassen** come to a decision/pass a resolution; **laut ~ des Gerichtes/der Direktion** in accordance with the decision of the court/management 2 (veralt.: Ende) end; **zum ~:** to end *or* conclude

beschluss-, *beschluß-, Beschluss-, *Beschluß-: ~fähig *Adj.* quorate; **~fähig sein** have a quorum; be quorate; **~fähigkeit** *die* presence of a quorum; **die ~fähigkeit herstellen** make a quorum; **~fassung** *die* (Amtsspr.) **einen Entwurf zur ~fassung vorlegen** submit a draft resolution; **~lage** *die* the state of the decision-making process; **~organ** *das* decision-making body; **~unfähig** *Adj.* inquorate; **~unfähig sein** not have a quorum; be inquorate

beschmeißen *unr. tr. V.* (salopp) **jmdn./sich [gegenseitig] mit etw. ~:** pelt sb./each other with sth.; **jmdn./etw. mit Schmutz** *od.* **Dreck ~** (fig.) fling mud at sb./sth.

beschmieren *tr. V.* 1 **etw./sich ~:** get sth./oneself in a mess; **sich** (*Dat.*) **die Kleidung/Hände mit etw. ~:** smear *or* get sth. [smeared] all over one's clothes/hands 2 (abwertend) (bemalen) daub paint all over; (bekritzeln) scrawl *or* scribble all over [3] (bestreichen) **sein Brot mit etw. ~:** spread sth. on one's bread; **das Brot mit Butter ~:** butter the bread; **etw. mit Fett/Salbe ~:** grease sth./smear ointment on sth. [4] (abwertend: voll schreiben) cover ‹*paper*›

beschmunzeln *tr. V.* smile at

beschmutzen *tr. V.* **etw. ~:** make sth. dirty; **ganz beschmutzt sein** be covered in dirt; **jmds. Namen/Gedenken ~** (fig.) besmirch sb.'s name/memory; **sich ~** (verhüll.) dirty oneself

beschneiden *unr. tr. V.* [1] (stutzen) cut, trim, clip ‹*hedge*›; prune, cut back ‹*bush*›; cut back ‹*tree*›; trim ‹*book block*›; **einem Vogel die Flügel ~:** clip a bird's wings [2] (Med., Rel.) circumcise; **ein Beschnittener** a circumcised boy/man [3] (einschränken) cut ‹*salary, income, wages*›; restrict ‹*rights*›; **jmdn. in seinen Rechten ~:** restrict sb.'s rights

Beschneidung *die*; ~, ~en [1] (das Stutzen) ▸**beschneiden 1**: trimming; cutting; clipping; pruning; cutting back [2] (Einschränkung) ▸**beschneiden 3**: cutting; restriction; **die ~ seines Einkommens in Kauf nehmen** accept a cut in [one's] income [3] (Med., Rel.) circumcision

beschneit *Adj.* snow-covered

beschnüffeln *tr. V.* [1] (beriechen) sniff at [2] (ugs.: prüfen) **jmdn./sich ~:** size sb./each other up [3] (ugs. abwertend: bespitzeln) spy on

beschnuppern *tr. V.*: ▸**beschnüffeln 1, 2**

beschönigen /bəˈʃøːnɪɡn̩/ *tr. V.* gloss over

Beschönigung *die*; ~, ~en glossing over; **das wäre eine ~:** that would be to gloss over the true situation

beschränken /bəˈʃrɛŋkn̩/

A *tr. V.* restrict; limit; **etw. auf etw.** (*Akk.*) **~:** restrict *or* limit sth. to sth.; **jmdn. in seinen Rechten ~:** restrict sb.'s rights; **die Mittel sind beschränkt** my/our *etc.* resources are limited; **beschränkte Verhältnisse** straitened circumstances

B *refl. V.* tighten one's belt (fig.); **sich auf etw.** (*Akk.*) **~:** restrict *or* confine oneself to sth.

beschrankt *Adj.* ‹*level crossing*› with barriers; **~ sein** have barriers

beschränkt

A *Adj.* [1] (abwertend: dumm) dull-witted [2] (engstirnig) ‹*person*› of restricted *or* limited outlook; narrow-minded ‹*person*›; narrow[-minded] ‹*views, outlook*›; **~ sein** have a restricted *or* limited outlook; be narrow-minded; **einen ~en Horizont haben** have limited horizons *pl.*

B *adv.* narrow-mindedly; in a narrow-minded way

Beschränktheit *die*; ~ [1] (Dummheit) lack of intelligence; **in ihrer ~:** with her limited intelligence [2] (das Begrenztsein) limitedness; restrictedness

Beschränkung *die*; ~, ~en [1] (das Beschränken) limitation; restriction [2] (das, was beschränkt) restriction; **jmdm./einer Sache ~en auferlegen** impose restrictions on sb./sth.

beschreiben *unr. tr. V.* [1] write on; (voll schreiben) write ‹*page, side, etc.*›; **eng beschriebene Seiten** closely written pages [2] (darstellen) describe; **ich kann dir [gar] nicht ~, wie ..., es ist [gar] nicht zu ~, wie ...** I [simply] can't tell you how ...; **ihre Leiden waren nicht zu ~:** her sufferings were indescribable *or* beyond description; **wer beschreibt seine Freude, als ...** who could describe his joy when ... [3] (durch Kreisbewegung herstellen) describe ‹*circle, orbit, curve, etc.*›

Beschreibung *die*; ~, ~en [1] description; **jeder ~ spotten** defy *or* be beyond description [2] (Gebrauchsanweisung) instructions *pl.*

beschreien *unr. tr. V.*: ▸**berufen¹ A 2**

beschreiten *unr. tr. V.* (geh.) walk along ‹*path etc.*›; **neue Wege ~** (fig.) tread new paths; ‹*medicine, technology, etc.*› pursue new methods; **den Rechtsweg ~:** have recourse to litigation

Beschrieb *der* (schweiz.) description

beschriften /bəˈʃrɪftn̩/ *tr. V.* label; address ‹*envelope, letter*›; inscribe ‹*stone*›; letter ‹*sign*›

Beschriftung *die*; ~, ~en [1] labelling; (eines Briefes) addressing; (eines Steines) inscribing; (eines Schildes) lettering [2] (Aufschrift) label; (eines Briefes) address; (eines Steines) inscription; (eines Schildes) lettering

beschuhen /bəˈʃuːən/ *tr. V.* (Technik) shoe; tip [with metal]

beschuht *Adj.* shod; **ein weiß ~er Fuß** a foot [shod] in a white shoe

beschuldigen /bəˈʃʊldɪɡn̩/ *tr. V.* accuse (+ *Gen.* of); **jmdn. des Mordes/des Mordes an seiner Frau ~:** accuse sb. of murder/of the murder of his wife; **jmdn. ~, etw. getan zu haben/etw. zu sein** accuse sb. of doing/being sth.

Beschuldigte *der/die; adj. Dekl.* accused

Beschuldigung *die*; ~, ~en accusation; **~en gegen jmdn. erheben** make accusations against sb.

beschummeln *tr. V.* (ugs.), **beschupsen** *tr. V.* (salopp) cheat; diddle (coll.); burn (Amer. sl.); **jmdn. um etw. ~** *od.* **beschupsen** diddle *or* do sb. out of sth. (coll.)

Beschuss, ***Beschuß** *der* [1] fire; (aus Kanonen) shelling; (mit Pfeilen) shooting; **unter ~ nehmen** fire at/shell/shoot at; (fig.: kritisieren) attack; **[heftig** *od.* **stark] unter ~ geraten/stehen** *od.* **liegen** (auch fig.) come/be under [heavy] fire [2] (Physik) **~ mit Neutronen** *usw.* bombardment with neutrons *etc.*

beschützen *tr. V.* protect (**vor** + *Dat.* from); **~d den Arm um jmdn. legen** put a protective arm around sb.; **~de Werkstätte** sheltered workshop

Beschützer *der*; ~s, ~, **Beschützerin** *die*; ~, ~nen protector (**vor** from)

Beschützer·instinkt *der* protective instinct

beschwatzen, (bes. südd.) **beschwätzen** *tr. V.* (ugs.) [1] **jmdn. ~:** talk sb. round; **jmdn. zu etw. ~:** talk sb. into sth.; **jmdn. ~, etw. zu tun** talk sb. into doing sth. [2] (bereden) chat about *or* over

Beschwerde /bəˈʃveːɐ̯də/ *die*; ~, ~n [1] complaint (**gegen, über** + *Akk.* about); **~ führen** (Amtsspr.) *od.* **einlegen** (Rechtsw.) lodge a complaint; (gegen einen Entscheid) lodge an appeal [2] ▸❶ **S. 439** *Pl.* (Schmerz) pain *sing.*; (Leiden) trouble *sing.*; **er fragte mich nach meinen ~n** he asked me what the trouble was; **jmdm. [ziemliche/große] ~n machen** give sb. [quite a lot of/considerable] pain; **~n [mit der Verdauung** *usw.***] haben** have trouble [with one's digestion *etc.*]; **die ~n des Alters** the aches and pains *or* infirmities of old age

beschwerde-, Beschwerde-: ~aus·schuss, ***~aus·schuß** *der* (DDR) appeal tribunal (*against actions of official bodies*); **~buch** *das* complaints book; **~frei A** *Adj.* trouble-free; (ohne Schmerzen) free from pain *postpos.*; **B** *adv.* without pain; **relativ ~frei leben** live a life relatively free from pain; **~frist** *die* (Rechtsw.) time limit for lodging an appeal; **~führer** *der*, **~führerin** *die* complainant; (gegen einen Entscheid) appellant; **~weg** *der*: *in* **auf dem ~weg** by appealing; by means of an appeal

beschweren /bəˈʃveːrən/

A *refl. V.* complain (**über** + *Akk.*, **wegen** about); **sich bei jmdm. ~:** complain to sb.

B *tr. V.* weight; (etw. Schweres auflegen) weight down; (fig.: belasten) burden ‹*person, memory*›

beschwerlich

A *Adj.* arduous; (ermüdend) exhausting; **jmdm. ~ fallen** (veralt., geh.) ‹*person, children*› be a burden to sb.; **jmdm. fällt etw. ~** (veralt. geh.) sb. finds sth. troublesome

B *adv.* laboriously; with an effort

Beschwerlichkeit *die*; ~, ~en [1] arduousness [2] *Pl.* (Anstrengungen) tribulations

Beschwernis *die*; ~, ~se (geh.) tribulation

Beschwerung *die*; ~, ~en [1] weighting; **zur ~:** in order to weight it [down] [2] (Gegenstand) weight; **etw. als ~ benutzen** use sth. as ballast

beschwichtigen /bəˈʃvɪçtɪɡn̩/ *tr. V.* pacify; calm ‹*excitement*›; placate, mollify ‹*anger etc.*›; **sein Gewissen ~:** ease one's conscience; **er versucht [uns] zu ~, wenn wir in Streit geraten** he tries to conciliate *or* placate us when we quarrel; **~de Worte** soothing words

Beschwichtigung *die*; ~, ~en pacification; (des Zorns, Hasses) mollification

Beschwichtigungs·politik *die* policy of appeasement

beschwindeln *tr. V.* (ugs.) **jmdn. ~:** tell sb. a fib/fibs; (betrügen) hoodwink sb.

beschwingt /bəˈʃvɪŋt/

A *Adj.* elated, lively ‹*mood*›; lively, lilting ‹*tune, melody*›; **~ sein/sich ~ fühlen** ‹*person*› be/feel elated; **~en Schrittes/Fußes** (geh.) with a spring in one's step

B *adv.* **~ gehen** walk with a spring in one's step; **~ tanzen** dance with great élan

Beschwingtheit *die*; ~: elation; (einer Melodie) liveliness; (des Ganges) springiness

beschwipst /bəˈʃvɪpst/ *Adj.* tipsy

beschwören *unr. tr. V.* [1] **~, dass ...** swear that ...; **etw. ~:** swear to sth.; **eine Aussage ~:** swear a statement on *or* under oath [2] charm ‹*snake*› [3] (erscheinen lassen) invoke, conjure up ‹*spirit*›; (fig.) evoke, conjure up ‹*pictures, memories, etc.*›; **ein Unheil ~:** make a disaster happen (*by thinking/talking about it*); **die Vergangenheit ~:** revive memories of the past [4] (bitten) beg; implore; **in ~dem Ton** in a beseeching *or* imploring tone; **mit ~dem Blick** with an imploring glance; **sie sah ihn ~d an** she looked at him imploringly [5] (veralt.: bannen) exorcize ‹*evil spirit*›

Beschwörung *die*; ~, ~en [1] (Zauberspruch) spell; incantation [2] (Bitte) entreaty [3] (das Erscheinenlassen) invoking; conjuring up

Beschwörungs·formel *die* incantation

beseelen /bəˈzeːlən/ *tr. V.* animate; **ein fester Glaube beseelte ihn** a steadfast faith was his inspiration

besehen *unr. tr. V.* have a look at; **sich** (*Dat.*) **etw. [genau] ~:** have a [close] look at sth.; inspect sth. [closely]; **er besah sich im Spiegel** he looked at himself in the mirror

beseitigen /bəˈzaitɪɡn̩/ *tr. V.* [1] (entfernen) remove; get rid of; eliminate ‹*error, difficulty*›; dispose of ‹*rubbish*›; clear ‹*snow*›; eradicate ‹*injustice, abuse*› [2] (verhüll.: ermorden) dispose of; eliminate

Beseitigung *die*; ~ [1] removal; (eines Fehlers, einer Schwierigkeit) elimination; (des Mülls) disposal; (eines Missstands) eradication [2] (verhüll.: Ermordung) elimination

beseligen /bəˈzeːlɪɡn̩/ *tr. V.* fill with delight *or* joy; **ein ~des Gefühl/ein ~der Gedanke** a delightful *or* blissful feeling/thought

Besen /ˈbeːzn̩/ *der*; ~s, ~ [1] broom; (Reisig~) besom; (Hand~) brush; **~ und Schaufel** dustpan and brush; **die Hexe auf ihrem ~:** the witch on her broomstick; **ich fress einen ~, wenn das stimmt** (salopp) I'll eat my hat if that's right (coll.); **neue ~ kehren gut** (Spr.) a new broom sweeps clean (prov.); **mit eisernem ~ [aus]kehren** (fig.) apply drastic remedies [2] (salopp abwertend: Frau) battleaxe (coll.)

besen-, Besen-: ~binder *der*, **~binderin** *die*; ~~, ~~nen broom-maker; (von Reisigbesen) besom-maker; **~ginster** *der* (Bot.) broom; **~kammer** *die* broom cupboard; broom closet (Amer.); **~macher** *der*, **~macherin** *die* broom-maker; **~rein** *Adj.* swept clean *postpos.*; **~schrank** *der* ▸**~kammer**; **~stiel** *der* broom handle; (eines Reisigbesens) broomstick; **er läuft herum, als habe er einen ~stiel verschluckt** (ugs.) he runs around as stiff as a ramrod

Besenwirtschaft

An inn set up temporarily by a local wine-grower for a few weeks after the new wine has been made. A blown-up pig's bladder is hung up outside the door to indicate that the new vintage may be sampled here. This is mainly found in Southern Germany and is similar to the Austrian **Heurige**. See also **Straußwirtschaft**.

besessen /bəˈzɛsn̩/
A *2. Part. v.* **besitzen**
B *Adj.* 1 possessed; **vom Teufel ~ sein** be possessed by *or* (dated) of the Devil; **wie ~:** like one possessed 2 (heftig ergriffen) obsessive ‹*gambler*›; fanatical ‹*racing driver, footballer, etc.*›; **von einer Idee** *usw.* **~ sein** be obsessed with an idea *etc.*

Besessene *der/die; adj. Dekl.* **ein ~r/eine ~:** one possessed; **zum/zur ~n werden** become like one possessed; become fanatical

Besessenheit *die;* **~** 1 (durch einen Dämon, Teufel) possession 2 (Ergriffenheit) obsessiveness; **mit wahrer ~:** in a truly obsessive manner; **zur ~ werden** become obsessive *or* an obsession

besetzen *tr. V.* 1 (mit Pelz, Spitzen) edge; trim; **mit Perlen/Edelsteinen besetzt** set with pearls/precious stones 2 (belegen; auch Milit.: erobern) occupy; (füllen) fill (**mit** with); (Jagdw., Fischereiw.) stock ‹*shoot, pond, etc.*›; (reservieren) keep, reserve ‹*seat, table, etc.*›; **der Bus kann mit 50 Personen besetzt werden** the bus can carry 50 people 3 (vergeben) fill ‹*post, position, role, etc.*›; cast ‹*role, play, etc.*›; **einen Ausschuss ~:** fill [the places on] a committee; **die frei werdenden Stellungen werden nicht mehr neu besetzt** no new appointments are being made to positions which become vacant

besetzt *Adj.* occupied; ‹*table, seat*› taken *pred.*; ‹*washing machine, drier, etc.*› in use *pred.*; (gefüllt) full; filled to capacity; **es** *od.* **die Leitung/die Nummer ist ~:** the line/number is engaged *or* (Amer.) busy; **er ist im Moment ~:** he is occupied *or* busy at the moment; **die amerikanisch ~e Zone** the American zone of occupation

Besetzt·zeichen *das* (Fernspr.) engaged tone (Brit.); busy signal (Amer.)

Besetzung *die;* **~, ~en** 1 (einer Stellung) filling; (einer Rolle) casting; (eines Ausschusses) composition; (Jagdw., Fischereiw.) stocking *no indef. art.* 2 (Mitwirkende) (Film, Theater usw.) cast; (einer Popgruppe) line-up; **das Stück in hervorragender ~ sehen** see the play with an outstanding cast; **in der besten/der neuen ~ antreten** (Sport) ‹*team*› field its best side/new line-up; **die erste/zweite ~** (Theater) the first/second cast 3 (Eroberung) occupation; **die ~ des Brückenkopfes** the taking of the bridgehead

besichtigen /bəˈzɪçtɪgn̩/ *tr. V.* see ‹*sights*›; see the sights of ‹*town*›; look round ‹*building*›; view ‹*house, flat*›; (prüfend) inspect ‹*troops, joc.: baby, girlfriend*›

Besichtigung *die;* **~, ~en** viewing; (Führung) tour; (Prüfung von Truppen) inspection; **etw. zur ~ freigeben** open sth. to visitors *or* to the public; **die ~ der Kirche ist zwischen 10 und 16 Uhr möglich** the church is open to visitors between 10 a.m. and 4 p.m.

Besichtigungs-: ~reise *die* sightseeing trip; **~zeit** *die* opening time

besiedeln *tr. V.* 1 settle (**mit** with); **neu ~:** resettle; **ein dicht/dünn besiedeltes Land** a densely/thinly populated country 2 (heimisch sein in) ‹*animal, plant*› inhabit, be found in

Besiedlung *die* settlement

Besiedlungs·dichte *die* population density

besiegeln *tr. V.* set the seal on; **sein Schicksal ist besiegelt** his fate is sealed

Besieg[e]lung *die;* **~, ~en** sealing; **die ~ von etw. sein** seal sth.; **zur ~ des Geschäftes/unserer Freundschaft** to seal the transaction/our friendship

besiegen *tr. V.* 1 defeat; **sich besiegt geben** admit defeat 2 (überwinden) overcome ‹*doubts, difficulties, curiosity, etc.*›

Besiegte *der/die; adj. Dekl.* loser

besingen *unr. tr. V.* 1 (geh.) celebrate in verse; (durch ein Lied) celebrate in song 2 **eine Platte ~:** make a record [of songs]

besinnen
A *unr. refl. V.* 1 think it *or* things over; **sich anders/eines Besseren ~:** change one's mind/think better of it 2 (sich erinnern) **sich [auf jmdn./etw.] ~:** remember *or* recall [sb./sth.]; **sich darauf ~, wann ...** recall when ...; **wenn ich mich recht besinne** if I remember correctly 3 (sich bewusst werden) **sich auf die Bedeutung von etw. ~:** become aware of the significance of sth.
B *unr. tr. V.* reflect on

besinnlich *Adj.* contemplative; thoughtful ‹*person*›; reflective ‹*story*›; **in einer ~en Stunde** in a quiet moment; when one has time to think; **ein ~er Abend** an evening of reflection

Besinnlichkeit *die;* **~:** contemplation; **Stunden der ~:** moments of reflection

Besinnung *die;* **~** 1 consciousness; **die ~ verlieren** (das Bewusstsein verlieren) lose consciousness; (ohnmächtig werden) faint; **ohne** *od.* **nicht bei ~:** unconscious; **[wieder] zur ~ kommen** come to; regain consciousness 2 (Nachdenken) reflection; **zur ~ kommen** stop and think things over; **ehe ich recht zur ~ kommen konnte** before I had time to think; **jmdn. zur ~ bringen** bring sb. to his/her senses

Besinnungs·aufsatz *der* reflective essay

besinnungs·los
A *Adj.* 1 (bewusstlos) unconscious 2 (fig.) mindless, blind ‹*rage, hatred*›; **~ vor Angst** out of one's mind with fear
B *adv.* mindlessly; **~ auf jmdn. einschlagen** hit out at sb. in a blind *or* uncontrollable rage

Besinnungslosigkeit *die;* **~:** unconsciousness *no art.*; **er betrank sich bis zur ~:** he drank himself into oblivion

Besitz *der* 1 property; **nur wenig ~ haben** have only a few possessions *pl.*; **jmdm. den rechtmäßigen ~ [einer Sache** (*Gen.*)**] streitig machen** dispute sb.'s legal title to his/her property [in sth.] 2 (das ~en) possession; **sich in jmds. ~** (*Dat.*) **befinden, in jmds. ~** (*Dat.*) **sein** be in sb.'s possession; **es befindet sich seit mehreren Generationen im ~ unserer Familie** it has been in our family for several generations; **sich in privatem ~ befinden** be privately owned; be in private ownership *or* hands; **in amerikanischem ~:** in American ownership; **in jmds. ~** (*Akk.*) **übergehen** *od.* **kommen** pass *or* come into sb.'s possession; **in den ~ eines Hauses** *usw.* **kommen** become the owner of a house *etc.*; (durch eigene Bemühungen) gain possession of a house *etc.*; **im ~ einer Sache** (*Gen.*)**/von etw. sein, etw. in ~ haben** be in possession of sth.; possess sth.; **im vollen ~ seiner geistigen Kräfte sein** be in full possession of one's faculties; **etw. in [seinen] ~ nehmen, von etw. ~ ergreifen** take possession of sth.; **von jmdm. ~ ergreifen** (geh.) take hold of sb. 3 (Landbesitz) estate

besitz-, Besitz-: ~anspruch *der* claim to ownership; **einen ~anspruch auf etw.** (*Akk.*) **anmelden** file a claim to ownership of sth.; **~anzeigend** *Adj.* (Sprachw.) possessive; **~bürgertum** *das* property-owning bourgeoisie

besitzen *unr. tr. V.* 1 own; have ‹*quality, talent, etc.*›; (nachdrücklicher) possess; **seit wann besitzt er ein Auto?** since when does he own a car?; how long has he had a car?; **alles, was er besaß** all he possessed; **keinen Pfennig/Cent ~** (ugs.) not have a penny to one's name; **er besaß die Frechheit/Unverschämtheit, zu ...** he had the cheek *or* nerve/impertinence to ...; **die ~de Klasse** the propertied class; **das Recht ~, zu ...** have the right to ... 2 (geh. verhüll.) **eine Frau ~:** possess a woman

Besitzer *der;* **~s, ~** 1 owner; (eines Betriebs usw.) proprietor (formal); **den ~ wechseln** change hands *pl.* 2 (österr.) property owner

besitz·ergreifend
A *Adj.* possessive
B *adv.* possessively

Besitz·ergreifung *die* seizure

Besitzerin *die;* **~, ~nen** ▸ **Besitzer**

Besitzer-: ~stolz *der* pride of ownership; **voller ~stolz** very much the proud owner; **~wechsel** *der* change of ownership

besitz-, Besitz-: ~gier *die* cupidity; acquisitiveness; **~los** *Adj.* destitute; **die ~lose Klasse** the propertyless class; **~nahme** *die;* **~~, ~~n** appropriation; (mit Gewalt) seizure; **~stand** *der* standard of living; **den ~stand wahren** maintain living standards; **~stands·denken** *das* preoccupation with living standards

Besitztum *das;* **~s, Besitztümer** /-tyːmɐ/ 1 possession 2 (Gut) estate

Besitzung *die;* **~, ~en** (geh.) estate

Besitz·verhältnisse *Pl.* matters relating to ownership; (marxistische Theorie) conditions of ownership

besoffen /bəˈzɔfn̩/
A *2. Part. v.* **besaufen**
B *Adj.* (salopp) boozed [up] (sl.); plastered (sl.); pissed *pred.* (sl.); **völlig ~:** completely stoned (sl.); blind drunk

Besoffene *der/die; adj. Dekl.* (salopp) drunk

besohlen *tr. V.* sole; **neu ~:** resole

Besohlung *die;* **~** 1 soling; **eine neue ~ der Schuhe** resoling the shoes 2 (Sohle) sole

besolden *tr. V.* pay ‹*soldier*›; pay ‹*civil servant*› his/her salary; **eine gut besoldete Stelle** a well-paid job

Besoldung /bəˈzɔldʊŋ/ *die;* **~, ~en** pay; (Gehalt) salary

Besoldungs-: ~gruppe *die* salary bracket; **~ordnung** *die* [tables of] pay scales *pl.* (*for civil servants*)

besonder... /bəˈzɔndɐ.../ *Adj.* special; (mehr als gewohnt) particular ‹*pleasure, enthusiasm, effort, etc.*›; (hervorragend) exceptional ‹*quality, beauty, etc.*›; **im Besonderen** in particular; **im Allgemeinen und im Besonderen** in general and in particular; **ein ~es Ereignis** an unusual *or* a special event; **keine ~en Vorkommnisse wurden gemeldet** no incidents of any particular note were reported; **~e Merkmale** (im Pass usw.) distinguishing marks; **~en Wert auf etw.** (*Akk.*) **legen** lay particular emphasis on sth.; **keine ~e Leistung** no great achievement; **einen ~en Geschmack haben** ‹*person*› have exceptional taste; ‹*dish*› have an unusual taste; **es ist mir eine [ganz] ~e Freude/Ehre** it is a particular pleasure/honour for me

Besondere *das; adj. Dekl.* 1 **etwas [ganz] ~s** something [really] special; **nichts ~s** nothing special; (nichts Interessantes) nothing of note *or* worth mentioning; **das ist doch nichts ~s** there's nothing special *or* unusual about that; **das ~ daran** the special thing about it 2 (Einzelerscheinung) **vom ~n zum Allgemeinen kommen** proceed from the particular to the general

Besonderheit *die;* **~, ~en** special *or* distinctive feature; (Eigenart) peculiarity; **dieser Fall stellt eine ~ dar** this is a special case

besonders *Adv.* 1 particularly; **~ du solltest das wissen** you of all people should know that; **~ bei schönem Wetter** especially in fine weather; **das hat ihn ~ gefreut** that gave him particular pleasure; **das braucht man wohl nicht ~ zu erwähnen** presumably one does not have to mention this specifically; **nicht ~ viel Geld haben** not be particularly well off 2 **nicht ~ sein** be nothing special; be nothing to write home about; **ich fand den Film nicht ~:** I didn't think the film was anything special *or* was up to much; **es geht ihm nicht ~:** he doesn't feel too well 3 (getrennt) separately

besonnen /bəˈzɔnən/
A *2. Part. v.* **besinnen**
B *Adj.* prudent; (umsichtig) circumspect; **ruhig und ~:** calm and collected; **~es Urteil** considered judgement
C *adv.* prudently; (umsichtig) circumspectly

Besonnenheit *die;* **~** ▸ **besonnen B**: prudence; circumspection

besonnt /bəˈzɔnt/ *Adj.* sunlit

besorgen *tr. V.* 1 get; (kaufen) buy; **jmdm. etw. ~:** get/buy sb. sth. *or* sth. for sb.; **ich will mir das Buch ~:** I want to get the book [for myself] 2 (ugs. verhüll.: stehlen) **sich** (*Dat.*) **etw. ~:** help oneself to sth. 3 (erledigen) take care of; deal with; prepare ‹*edition*›; **einen Brief ~:** post a letter; **er besorgte die Auswahl der Gedichte** he was responsible for the selection of poems; **was du heute kannst ~, das verschiebe nicht auf morgen** (Spr.) never put off to tomorrow what you can do today (prov.) 4 (betreuen) look after ‹*children, flowers, etc.*›; **jmdm. den Haushalt/die Wäsche ~:** keep house/do the washing for sb. 5 **es jmdm. ~** (ugs.: heimzahlen) get back at sb. (coll.); get one's own back on sb. (Brit. coll.); (derb: geschlechtlich befriedigen) give it to sb. (sl.)

Besorgnis *die;* ~, **~se** concern; **echte ~ [um jmdn./über etw.** (*Akk.*)**] empfinden** be genuinely concerned [about sb./sth.]; **jmds. ~ erregen** cause sb. concern; **jmds. ~se zerstreuen** put an end to sb.'s worries

besorgnis·erregend *Adj.* serious; **~ sein** give cause for concern

besorgt
A *Adj.* worried (**über** + *Akk.*, **um** about); concerned *usu. pred.* (**über** + *Akk.*, **um** about); **er macht einen sehr ~en Eindruck** he appears to be very concerned; **sie war rührend um das Wohl ihrer Gäste ~:** she showed a touching concern for the well-being of her guests; **er war ~, es könnte etwas passieren** he was concerned lest something should happen *or* worried that something might happen
B *adv.* with concern; (ängstlich) anxiously; **sich sehr ~ äußern** express one's great concern

Besorgtheit *die;* ~: concern

Besorgung *die;* ~, **~en** 1 purchase; **[einige] ~en machen** do some shopping; **kleinere ~en machen** do odd bits of shopping 2 (das Beschaffen) getting; (das Kaufen) buying 3 (das Betreuen) **die ~ des Haushalts** *usw.* looking after the household *etc.*

bespannen *tr. V.* 1 cover ‹*wall, chair, car, etc.*›; string ‹*racket, instrument*› 2 (mit Zugtieren) **einen Wagen mit einem Pferd ~:** harness a horse to a cart; **mit zwei Schimmeln bespannt** harnessed to *or* pulled by two white horses

Bespannung *die;* ~, **~en** covering; (eines Schlägers, eines Instruments) stringing

bespeien *unr. tr. V.* (geh.) spit at

bespiegeln *tr. V.* 1 **sein eigenes Ich** *od.* **sich selbst ~:** contemplate one's own ego 2 (darstellen) mirror; portray

bespielbar *Adj.* 1 **das Band ist nicht mehr ~:** one can no longer record on this tape 2 (Sport) playable ‹*ground, tennis court*›

bespielen *tr. V.* 1 make a recording on ‹*tape, cassette*›; **ein Band mit Liedern ~:** record songs on a tape; **die Kassette ist schon bespielt** the cassette already has a recording on it 2 (Theaterw.) **eine Bühne ~:** play a theatre

bespitzeln *tr. V.* spy on

Bespitz[e]lung *die;* ~, **~en** spying

bespötteln *tr. V.* mock; make fun of

besprechen
A *unr. tr. V.* 1 discuss; talk over; (rezensieren) review; **gut/schlecht besprochen werden** get a good/bad review; (mehrfach) get good/bad reviews 2 (aufnehmen) **eine Kassette ~:** make a [voice] recording on a cassette; (statt eines Briefes) record a message on a cassette; **eine Platte mit Gedichten ~:** make a record of poems 3 (beschwören) **etw. ~:** utter a magic incantation *or* spell over sth.
B *unr. refl. V.* confer (**über** + *Akk.* about); **sich [ausführlich] über etw.** (*Akk.*) **~:** discuss sth. [in detail]; **sich mit jmdm. ~:** have a talk with sb.; confer with sb. (formal)

Besprechung *die;* ~, **~en** 1 discussion; (Konferenz) meeting; **in einer ~ sein, [gerade] eine ~ haben** be in a meeting 2 (Rezension) review (*Gen.*, **von** of) 3 (das Beschwören) incantation

Besprechungs·exemplar *das* (Buchw.) review copy

besprengen *tr. V.* sprinkle

besprenkeln *tr. V.* spatter

bespringen *unr. tr. V.* ‹*stallion, bull, etc.*› cover, mount ‹*mare, cow, etc.*›

bespritzen *tr. V.* 1 splash; (mit einem Wasserstrahl) spray 2 (beschmutzen) bespatter

besprühen *tr. V.* spray

bespucken *tr. V.* **jmdn. [mit etw.] ~:** spit [sth.] at sb.

Bessemer·birne /ˈbɛsəmɐ-/ *die* (Metallbearb.) Bessemer converter

besser /ˈbɛsɐ/
A ▸ **gut**
B *Adj.* 1 better; **~ dran sein** be better off; **[auch] schon [mal] ~e Zeiten gesehen haben** (ugs.) have seen better days; **es wäre ~, du hieltest deinen Mund** it would be better if you kept your mouth shut; **~ werden** get better; ‹*work etc.*› improve; **umso ~:** so much the better; all the better; **es wurde noch ~** (iron.) there was more *or* better to come (iron.); that wasn't the best of it (iron.); **das wäre ja noch ~!** (iron.) that really is the limit!; **ich habe Besseres zu tun** I've got better things to do; **~ ist ~:** better safe than sorry; just to be on the safe side; **jmdn. eines Besseren belehren** (geh.) put sb. right; **schließlich hat er sich doch eines Besseren belehren lassen** in the end he accepted that he was wrong; *s. auch* **besinnen** 2 (sozial höher gestellt) superior; upper-class; **~e** *od.* **die ~en Kreise** more elevated circles; **es verkehren hier die ~en Leute** you get a better *or* superior class of people here; **eine ~e Gegend/Adresse** a smart[er] *or* [more] respectable area/address; **jmdn. [finanziell] ~ stellen** improve sb.'s [financial] position 3 (abwertend) glorified; **wir arbeiten in einer ~en Baracke** we work in a glorified hut
C *adv.* 1 **[immer] alles ~ wissen** always know better; **es ~ haben** be better off; (es leichter haben) have an easier time of it; **es kommt noch ~** (iron.) it gets even better (iron.); **~ gesagt** to be [more] precise; **sie war nicht ganz offen, oder ~ gesagt, sie hat uns belogen** she was not quite frank, or to put it bluntly, she lied to us; **es geht ihm ~:** he feels better; **kurze Zeit später ging es ihr schon wieder ~:** a short time later, she had already recovered 2 (lieber) **das lässt du ~ sein** *od.* (ugs.) **bleiben** you'd better not do that; **er ließe es ~ bleiben, sich einzumischen** he would be better advised not to interfere; **er täte ~ daran, zu ...** he would do better to ...; **geh ~ zum Arzt** you'd better go to the doctor

***besser|gehen** ▸ **besser C 1**

Bessergestellte /-gəʃtɛltə/ *Pl.; adj. Dekl.* **die ~n** the better off; the well-to-do

bessern
A *refl. V.* improve; ‹*person*› mend one's ways
B *tr. V.* improve; reform ‹*criminal*›

***besser|stellen** ▸ **besser B 2**

Besserung *die;* ~ 1 (Genesung) recovery; **[ich wünsche dir] gute ~:** [I hope you] get well soon; **sich auf dem Wege der ~ befinden** be on the road to recovery *or* on the mend 2 (Verbesserung) improvement (+ *Gen.* in); (eines Kriminellen) reform; **~ geloben** promise to mend one's ways

Besserungs·anstalt *die* (ugs. veralt.) reform school; reformatory (esp. Amer.)

besser-, Besser-: ~wissen *das* ▸ **~wisserei**; **~wisser** *der;* **~~s, ~~** (abwertend) know-all; smart aleck; **~wisserei** /----ˈ-/ *die;* **~~** (abwertend) superior attitude; **~wisserin** *die;* **~~, ~~nen** ▸ **~wisser**; **~wisserisch** *Adj.* (abwertend) superior; know-all; **sei nicht so ~wisserisch!** don't always pretend you know better

best... /ˈbɛst.../
A ▸ **gut**
B *Adj.* 1 *attr.* best; **aus ~em Hause sein** *od.* **stammen** come from one of the very best families; **bei ~er Gesundheit/Laune sein** be in the best of health/spirits *pl.*; **im ~en Falle** at best; **er wird im ~en Falle mit einer Geldstrafe davonkommen** the best he can hope for is to get off with a fine; **in den ~en Jahren, im ~en Alter** in one's prime; **~e** *od.* **die ~en Grüße an ...** (*Akk.*) best wishes to ...; **mit den ~en Grüßen** *od.* **Wünschen** with best wishes; (als Briefschluss) ≈ yours sincerely; **~en Dank** many thanks *pl.*; *s. auch* **Dank, Familie, Weg, Wille** 2 **es ist** *od.* **wäre das Beste, wenn ...** it would be best if ...; **es wäre das Beste, zu ...** it would be best to ...; **er hielt es für das Beste, sofort abzureisen** he thought it best to leave immediately; **am ~en** best; **am ~en fährst du mit dem Zug** it would be best for you to go by train; **du bleibst am ~en zu Hause** you had best stay at home; **alles aufs Beste regeln** *od.* **richten** arrange everything in the best way possible; **es steht nicht zum Besten mit etw.** things are not going too well for sth.; **mit seiner Gesundheit steht es nicht zum Besten** his health is none too good; **der/die/das nächste ~e ...** the first ... one comes across; **sie hat den ersten ~en Mann geheiratet, der ihr über den Weg lief** she married the first man who happened to cross her path; **eine Geschichte/einen Witz zum Besten geben** entertain [those present] with a story/a joke; **jmdn. zum Besten halten** *od.* **haben** pull sb.'s leg 3 *subst.* best; **der Beste in unserer Gruppe** the best person in our group; **der/die Beste der Klasse** the best [pupil/student] in the class; **das Beste vom Besten** the very best; **das Beste ist gerade gut genug** only the best is good enough; **sein Bestes tun** do one's best; **das Beste aus etw./daraus machen** make the best of sth./of it; **aufs** *od.* **auf das Beste hoffen** hope for the best; **ich will nur dein Bestes** I am doing this for your own good; **zu deinem Besten** for your benefit; in your best interests *pl.*

bestallen /bəˈʃtalən/ *tr. V.* (Amtsspr.) appoint (**zu, als** as)

Bestallung *die* (Amtsspr.) appointment (**zu, als** as)

Bestallungs·urkunde *die* (Amtsspr.) certificate of appointment

Bestand *der* 1 continued existence; survival; **keinen ~ haben, nicht von ~ sein** not last; not last long 2 (Vorrat) stock (**an** + *Dat.* of); *s. auch* **eisern A 4** 3 (Forstw.) **~ von Eichen und Buchen** [mixed] stand of oaks and beeches; **Bestände durchforsten** thin out standing timber 4 (österr.: Dauer des Bestehens) **nach 15-jährigem ~:** after 15 years of existence; after existing for 15 years 5 (südd., österr.: Pacht) **etw. in ~ haben/geben** lease sth./lease sth. [out]

bestanden /bəˈʃtandn̩/
A *2. Part. v.* **bestehen**
B *Adj.* 1 **von** *od.* **mit etw. ~ sein** have sth. growing on it; **mit Blumen ~e Wiesen** flower-covered meadows; meadows full of flowers; **mit Tannen ~e Hügel** fir-covered hills 2 **nach ~er Prüfung** after passing one's examination 3 (schweiz.: alt) elderly

beständig
A *Adj.* 1 (dauernd) constant 2 (gleich bleibend) constant; steadfast ‹*person*›; (zuverlässig) reliable; settled ‹*weather*›; (Chemie) stable ‹*compound*›; **seine Leistungen sind ~:** his work is consistent 3 (widerstandsfähig) resistant (**gegen, gegenüber** to)
B *adv.* 1 constantly; **sie klagt ~:** she is constantly *or* for ever complaining 2 (gleich bleibend) consistently

-beständig *adj.* **hitze~/wetter~/säure~:** heat-/weather-/acid-resistant

Beständigkeit *die;* ~ 1 constancy; steadfastness; (bei der Arbeit) consistency; (Zuverlässigkeit) reliability 2 (Widerstandsfähigkeit) resistance (**gegen, gegenüber** to)

Bestands·aufnahme *die* stocktaking; **[eine] ~ machen** do a stocktaking; take inventory (Amer.); (fig.) take stock

Bestand·teil *der* component; **ein notwendiger ~ unserer Nahrung** an essential part *or* element of our diet; **sich in seine ~e auflösen** fall apart; fall to pieces; **etw. in seine [sämtlichen] ~e zerlegen** dismantle sth. [completely]

Best·arbeiter *der,* **Best·arbeiterin** *die* (DDR) best worker (*worker receiving an award as being the most efficient in the department, factory, etc.*)

bestärken
A *tr. V.* confirm; **jmdn. in seinem Plan** *od.* **Vorsatz** *od.* **darin ~, etw. zu tun** strengthen sb.'s resolve *or* confirm sb. in his/her resolve to do sth.
B *refl. V.* grow

Bestärkung *die* confirmation

bestätigen /bəˈʃtɛːtɪgn̩/ **A** *tr. V.* confirm; endorse ‹*document*›; acknowledge ‹*receipt*›; **ein Urteil ~** (Rechtsw.) uphold a judgement; **jmdn. [in seinem Amt] als Schulleiter** *usw.* **~:** confirm sb.'s appointment as headmaster (Brit.) *or* (Amer.) principal *etc.*; **hiermit wird bestätigt, dass ...** (in Urkunden) this is to confirm *or* certify that ...; **jmdm. [schriftlich] ~, dass er ...** give sb. [written] confirmation that he ...; certify that sb. ...; **sich in seiner Meinung/in seinen Vorurteilen bestätigt fühlen** have one's opinion/prejudices reinforced; **einen Brief/eine Bestellung ~** (Kaufmannsspr.) acknowledge [receipt of] a letter/an order **B** *refl. V.* be confirmed; ‹*rumour*› prove to be true; **damit hat sich meine Vermutung bestätigt** this confirmed my supposition

Bestätigung *die*; **~, ~en** confirmation; (des Empfangs) acknowledgement; (schriftlich) letter of confirmation; **zur ~ seiner Aussage erbrachte er Beweise** he produced evidence to support *or* back up his statement; **die ~ [in seinem Amt] als ...** the confirmation of his appointment as ...

bestatten /bəˈʃtatn̩/ *tr. V.* (geh.) inter (formal); bury; **bestattet werden** be laid to rest

Bestatter *der*; **~s, ~, Bestatterin** *die*; **~, ~nen** ▸ⓘ **S. 113** undertaker; mortician (Amer.); (bei Firmennamen) funeral director

Bestattung *die*; **~, ~en** (geh.) interment (formal); burial; (Feierlichkeit) funeral; **„Meier und Schulze, ~en"** 'Meier and Schulze, Funeral Directors *or* (Amer.) Morticians'

Bestattungs-: ~institut *das*, **~unternehmen** *das* [firm of] undertakers *pl.* *or* funeral directors *pl.*; funeral parlor (Amer.)

bestäuben /bəˈʃtɔybn̩/ *tr. V.* [1] dust [2] (Biol.) pollinate

Bestäubung *die*; **~, ~en** (Biol.) pollination

bestaunen *tr. V.* marvel at; (bewundernd anstarren) gaze in wonder at; (bewundernd anerkennen) be lost in admiration for

best-bezahlt *Adj.* best-paid

beste ▸ **best...**

Beste *das*; **~n** ▸ **best... B 3**

bestechen **A** *unr. tr. V.* [1] bribe [2] (für sich einnehmen) win over, captivate ‹*audience etc.*› **B** *unr. itr. V.* win people over

bestechend *Adj.* attractive; captivating, winning ‹*smile, charm*›; persuasive ‹*argument, logic*›; tempting ‹*offer*›; **von ~er Logik** irresistibly logical; **in ~er Form** (Sport) in irresistible form

bestechlich *Adj.* corruptible; open to bribery *postpos.*

Bestechlichkeit *die*; **~:** corruptibility

Bestechung *die*; **~, ~en** bribery *no indef. art.*; **eine ~:** a case of bribery; **der ~ eines Beamten/der ~ schuldig sein** be guilty of bribing of an official/of bribery; **aktive ~** (Rechtsw.) giving bribes; **passive ~** (Rechtsw.) accepting bribes

Bestechungs-: ~geld *das* bribe; **~skandal** *der* bribery scandal; **~summe** *die* bribe; **~versuch** *der* attempted bribery

Besteck /bəˈʃtɛk/ *das*; **~[e]s, ~e** [1] cutlery setting; **noch ein ~ auflegen** lay another place; **~e putzen** polish cutlery [2] (ugs.: Gesamtheit der ~e) cutlery [3] (Med.) [set *sing.* of] instruments *pl.* [4] (Seemannsspr.) fix; (aus Kurs und Geschwindigkeit bestimmt) dead reckoning [position]

bestecken *tr. V.* **A mit B ~:** stick B in/on A; **der Adventskranz war mit Tannenzapfen besteckt** the Advent wreath had fir cones stuck in it

Besteck-: ~kasten *der* cutlery box; (größer) canteen; **~schublade** *die* cutlery drawer

bestehen **A** *unr. itr. V.* [1] exist; **die Schule besteht noch nicht sehr lange** the school has not been in existence *or* has not been going for very long; **es besteht [die] Aussicht/Gefahr, dass ...** there is a prospect/danger that ...; **darüber bestand noch immer keine Klarheit** it was still unclear; **es besteht noch** *od.* **noch besteht die Hoffnung, dass ...** there is still hope that ...; **~ bleiben** remain; ‹*doubt*› persist; ‹*regulation*› remain in force; **etw. ~ lassen** retain sth.; **einen Einwand ~ lassen** allow an objection to stand [2] (fortdauern) survive; last; (standhalten) hold one's own; **gegen diese Konkurrenz werden wir kaum ~ können** we shall hardly be able to survive *or* keep going in the face of this competition; **seine Arbeit kann vor jeder Kritik ~:** his work can stand up to any criticism; **in einer Gefahr** *usw.* **~:** prove oneself in a dangerous situation *etc.* [3] (zusammengesetzt sein) **aus etw. ~:** consist of sth.; (aus einem Material) be made of sth.; **in etw.** (*Dat.*) **~:** consist of *or* in sth.; **ihre Aufgabe besteht in der Aufstellung der Liste** her task is to draw up the list; **der Unterschied besteht darin, dass ...** the difference is that ...; **eine Möglichkeit besteht darin, zu beweisen ...** one possibility would be to prove ... [4] (beharren) **auf etw.** (*Dat.*) **~:** insist on sth.; **er bestand darauf, den Chef zu sprechen** he insisted on seeing the boss; **ich bestehe darauf, dass man mich darüber informiert** I insist that I be *or* on being informed about it [5] (die Prüfung ~) pass [the examination] **B** *unr. tr. V.* [1] pass ‹*test, examination*› [2] (ertragen) withstand ‹*blows of fate*›; face up to ‹*difficulties*›

Bestehen *das*; **~s** [1] existence; **die Firma feiert ihr 10-jähriges ~:** the firm is celebrating its tenth anniversary; **seit ~ der Bundesrepublik** since the Federal Republic came into existence; since the founding of the Federal Republic [2] (einer Prüfung) passing; **mit ~ der Prüfung** on passing the examination [3] (Beharren) insistence (**auf** + *Dat.* on)

***bestehen|bleiben** ▸ **bestehen A 1**

bestehend *Adj.* existing; current ‹*conditions*›; **das seit 5 Jahren ~e Gesetz** the law which has been in existence for five years

***bestehen|lassen** ▸ **bestehen A 1**

bestehlen *unr. tr. V.* **jmdn. [um etw.] ~:** rob sb. [of sth.]

besteigen *unr. tr. V.* [1] climb; mount ‹*horse, bicycle*›; climb into ‹*pulpit*›; ascend ‹*throne*› [2] (betreten) board ‹*ship, aircraft*›; get on ‹*bus, train*› [3] ▸ **bespringen**

Besteigung *die* ascent

Bestell-buch *das* order book

bestellen **A** *tr. V.* [1] order (**bei** from); **sich** (*Dat.*) **etw. ~:** order sth. [for oneself]; **würden Sie mir bitte ein Taxi ~?** would you order me a taxi? [2] (reservieren lassen) reserve ‹*table, tickets*› [3] (kommen lassen) **jmdn. [für 10 Uhr] zu sich ~:** ask sb. to go/come to see one [at 10 o'clock]; **jmdn. in ein Café ~:** ask sb. to meet one in a café; **beim** *od.* **zum Arzt bestellt sein** have an appointment with the doctor; **dastehen wie bestellt und nicht abgeholt** (ugs. scherzh.) stand there like a little boy/girl lost [4] (ausrichten) **jmdm. etw. ~:** pass on sth. to sb.; tell sb. sth.; **bestell deinem Mann schöne Grüße von mir** give your husband my regards; **würden Sie Ihrer Kollegin etwas von mir ~?** would you give your colleague a message from me?; **er lässt dir ~, dass ...** he left a message [for you] that ...; **nichts/nicht viel zu ~ haben** have no say/little *or* not much say [5] (ernennen) appoint (**zu, als** as) [6] (bearbeiten) cultivate, till ‹*field*›; keep, look after ‹*garden*› [7] **es ist um jmdn./etw.** *od.* **mit jmdm./etw. schlecht bestellt** sb./sth. is in a bad way; **mit seiner Gesundheit ist es schlecht bestellt** he is in poor health **B** *itr. V.* order

Besteller *der*; **~s, ~, Bestellerin** *die*; **~, ~nen** customer (*who has ordered sth.*)

***Bestelliste** ▸ **Bestellliste**

Bestell-: ~liste *die* checklist (*of goods for ordering*); **~nummer** *die* order number; **~schein** *der* order form

Bestellung *die* [1] order (**über, auf** + *Akk.* for); (das Bestellen) ordering *no indef. art.*; **bei ~ von/bei ~en über mehr als 1000 Stück** if more than 1,000 are ordered/for orders of more than 1,000; **auf ~:** to order; (im Lokal) **eine ~ aufgeben** give one's order; **jmds. ~/die ~en aufnehmen** take sb.'s/the orders [2] (Reservierung) reservation [3] (Nachricht) **eine ~ übermitteln** *od.* **ausrichten** pass on a message [4] (das Ernennen) appointment; (Wahl) selection [5] (das Bearbeiten) cultivation; tilling; **~ des Gartens** gardening; work on the garden

Bestell-zettel *der* order form

besten-falls *Adv.* at best

Besten-liste *die* (Sport) list of top athletes/sportsmen

bestens *Adv.* [1] excellently; extremely well; **sich ~ verstehen** get on splendidly; **sich ~ unterhalten** have a splendid time [2] (vielmals) **jmdn. ~ grüßen** give sb. one's best wishes; **wir danken Ihnen/bedanken uns ~:** we thank you very much

besteuern *tr. V.* tax; **besteuert sein** be subject to tax; **höher besteuert werden** be more heavily taxed; **etw. höher ~:** increase the tax on sth.

Besteuerung *die* taxation; **bei einer ~ des Einkommens von 45 %** where income is taxed at [a rate of] 45%

best-, Best-: ~form *die* (Sport) best form; **in ~form** in top form; **~gehasst**, ***~gehaßt** *Adj.* (ugs. iron.) most heartily disliked; **~gehütet** *Adj.* most closely guarded; best-kept ‹*secret*›; **~gekleidet** *Adj.* best-dressed

bestialisch /bɛsˈti̯aːlɪʃ/ **A** *Adj.* [1] (abwertend) bestial [2] (ugs.: schrecklich) ghastly (coll.); awful (coll.) **B** *adv.* [1] (abwertend) in a bestial manner; **~ schreien** scream like a wild beast [2] (ugs.: schrecklich) awfully (coll.); unbearably; **~ kalt** beastly cold

Bestialität /bɛsti̯aliˈtɛːt/ *die*; **~, ~en** [1] bestiality; **ein Verbrechen von solcher ~:** a crime of such a bestial nature *or* of such brutality [2] (Tat) brutality; atrocity

Bestiarium /bɛsˈti̯aːri̯ʊm/ *das*; **~s, Bestiarien** bestiary

besticken *tr. V.* embroider; **ein mit Perlen besticktes Kleid** a dress sewn with pearls

Bestie /ˈbɛsti̯ə/ *die*; **~, ~n** (auch fig. abwertend) beast

bestimmbar *Adj.* ascertainable; (identifizierbar) identifiable; **nicht [genau] ~ sein** be impossible to ascertain/identify [precisely]

bestimmen **A** *tr. V.* [1] (festsetzen) decide on; fix ‹*price, time, etc.*›; **das Gesetz bestimmt, dass ...** the law provides that ...; **nichts zu ~ haben** have no say; **jmdn. zum** *od.* **als Nachfolger ~:** decide on sb. as one's successor; (nennen) name sb. as one's successor [2] (vorsehen) destine; intend; set aside ‹*money*›; **das ist für dich bestimmt** that is meant for you; **er ist zu Höherem bestimmt** he is destined for higher things; **füreinander bestimmt sein** be meant for each other [3] (ermitteln, definieren) identify ‹*part of speech, find, plant, etc.*›; determine ‹*age, position*›; define ‹*meaning*› [4] (prägen) determine the character of; give ‹*landscape, townscape*› its character; **unser Leben ~:** play a dominant *or* decisive role in our lives [5] (veranlassen) **jmdn. zum Nachgeben/Bleiben ~:** induce sb. to give in/stay; **sich von jmdm. zu etw. ~ lassen** allow sb. to talk one into sth. **B** *itr. V.* [1] make the decisions; **hier bestimme ich** I'm in charge *or* the boss here; my word goes around here [2] (verfügen) **über jmdn. ~:** tell sb. what to do; **[frei] über etw.** (*Akk.*) **~:** do as one wishes with sth.

bestimmend **A** *Adj.* decisive; determining **B** *adv.* decisively

bestimmt **A** *Adj.* [1] (speziell) particular; (gewiss) certain; (genau) definite; **soll es ein ~es Buch sein?** have you a particular book in mind?; **es sind immer ganz ~e Leute, die so was tun** it is always a particular type of person who does something like that; **ich habe schon eine ~e Vorstellung davon, wie ...** I already have a clear *or* definite idea of how ...; **ich kann**

noch nichts Bestimmtes sagen I can say nothing definite *or* I cannot say anything definite yet; **ich habe nichts Bestimmtes vor** I am not doing anything in particular [2] (festgelegt) fixed; given ‹*quantity*› [3] (Sprachw.) definite ‹*article etc.*› [4] (entschieden) firm; **in sehr ~em Ton** very firmly; in a very firm voice; **~es Auftreten** resolute manner

[B] *adv.* [1] (deutlich) clearly; (genau) precisely [2] (entschieden) firmly; **sich ~ gegen etw. aussprechen** express one's firm opposition to sth.

[C] *Adv.* for certain; **du weißt es doch [ganz] ~ noch** I'm sure you must remember it; **ganz ~, ich komme** I'll definitely come; yes, certainly, I'll come; **Vergiss sie nicht wieder. — Nein, ~ nicht** Don't forget them again — Don't worry, I won't; **sie wird das ~ schaffen** she is certain *or* bound to manage it; **er hat es ~ vergessen** he is bound to have forgotten; **ich habe das ~ liegengelassen** I must have left it behind; **das ist ~ nicht richtig** that can't be right

Bestimmtheit *die;* ~ [1] firmness; (im Auftreten) decisiveness; **etw. mit aller ~ sagen/ablehnen** say sth. very firmly/reject sth. categorically [2] (Gewissheit) **mit ~:** for certain

Bestimmung *die* [1] (das Festsetzen) fixing [2] (Vorschrift) regulation; **gesetzliche ~en** legal requirements [3] (Zweck) purpose; **eine Brücke** *usw.* **ihrer ~ übergeben** [officially] open a bridge *etc.* [4] (das Ermitteln) identification; (eines Begriffs) definition; (des Alters, der Position) determination; (der Bedeutung) definition; **~ der Satzteile** distinguishing the parts of a sentence; parsing [5] (Sprachw.) modifier; **adverbiale ~:** adverbial qualification [6] (Schicksal) **das ist ~:** that is destiny *or* fate; **göttliche ~:** Divine Providence; **es war höhere ~, dass wir uns begegneten** it was ordained [by fate] that we should meet [7] (veralt.: ~sort) destination

bestimmungs-, Bestimmungs-: ~bahnhof *der* (Eisenb.) destination; **~gemäß** *Adv.* in accordance with the regulations *or* requirements [of the law]; **~hafen** *der* [port of] destination; **~ort** *der; Pl.* **~e** destination; **~wort** *das; Pl.* **~wörter** (Sprachw.) qualifying element (*of a compound*); modifier

best-, Best-: ~leistung *die* best performance; (absolute ~leistung) record; **persönliche ~leistung** personal best; **~mann** *der* (Seew.) mate (*of a coaster*); **~marke** *die* (Sport) record; **~möglich** [A] *Adj.* best possible; **das ~mögliche tun/getan haben** do the best one can/have done the best one could; [B] *adv.* as well as possible *or* as one possibly can

Best.-Nr. *Abk.* = **Bestellnummer** order no.

bestochen /bəˈʃtɔxn̩/ *2. Part. v.* **bestechen**

bestrafen *tr. V.* punish (**für, wegen** for); **es wird mit Gefängnis bestraft** it is punishable by imprisonment

Bestrafung *die;* ~, **~en** punishment; (Rechtsw.) penalty; (Geldstrafe) fine

bestrahlen *tr. V.* [1] (beleuchten) illuminate; floodlight ‹*building*›; (scheinen auf) ‹*sun etc.*› shine on; (erhellen) light up [2] (Med.) treat ‹*tumour, part of body*› using radiotherapy; (mit Höhensonne) use sunray *or* sunlamp treatment on ‹*part of body*›

Bestrahlung *die;* ~, **~en** [1] (Med.) radiation [treatment] *no indef. art.;* (bes. mit Röntgenstrahlen) radiotherapy *no art.;* (mit Höhensonne) sunray *or* sunlamp treatment [2] (das Beleuchten) illumination; (eines Gebäudes) floodlighting; (der Bühne) lighting; **eine intensive ~ durch die Sonne** concentrated exposure to the sun's rays

Bestrahlungs·lampe *die* radiation lamp; (Höhensonne) sun[ray] lamp

Bestreben *das* endeavour[s *pl.*]; **in seinem** *od.* **im ~, keine Schwächen zu zeigen** in his efforts *or* endeavours to show no weakness

bestrebt *Adj.* **~/sehr ~ sein, etw. zu tun** endeavour/take great pains *or* go to great trouble to do sth.

Bestrebung *die;* ~, **~en** effort; (Versuch) attempt

bestreichen *unr. tr. V.* **A mit B ~:** spread B on A; **sein Brot mit Butter ~:** spread butter on one's bread; butter one's bread; **den Braten/das Hähnchen mit Öl** *usw.* **~:** baste the roast/chicken with oil *etc.;* **die Plätzchen mit Eigelb ~:** brush *or* coat the biscuits (Brit.) *or* (Amer.) cookies with egg yolk

bestreiken *tr. V.* take strike action against; **diese Firma wird bestreikt** there is a strike [on] at this firm

bestreitbar *Adj.* disputable; questionable, dubious ‹*argument*›; **es ist nicht ~[, dass ...]** it is indisputable *or* cannot be denied [that ...]

bestreiten *unr. tr. V.* [1] dispute; contest; (leugnen) deny; **er bestreitet, dass ...** he denies that ...; **es lässt sich nicht/wohl kaum ~, dass ...** it cannot/can hardly be denied that ...; there is no disputing/it can hardly be disputed that ...; **jmdm. ein Recht auf etw.** (*Akk.*) **~:** dispute *or* challenge sb.'s right to sth. [2] (finanzieren) finance ‹*studies*›; pay for ‹*studies, sb.'s keep, etc.*›; meet ‹*costs, expenses*› [3] (gestalten) carry ‹*programme, conversation, etc.*› [4] (Sport) take part in ‹*game*›

Bestreitung *die;* ~ [1] financing [2] **eine ~ seiner Aussage liegt mir fern** I have no intention of disputing *or* challenging his statement

bestreuen *tr. V.* **etw. mit Zucker ~:** sprinkle sth. with sugar; **einen Weg mit Sand/Salz ~:** scatter sand on a path/salt a path

bestricken *tr. V.* [1] ensnare; captivate [2] (für andere stricken) knit things for

bestrumpft /bəˈʃtrʊmpft/ *Adj.* stockinged; **lila ~:** in mauve stockings

Bestseller /ˈbɛstzɛlɐ/ *der;* **~s, ~:** best seller

Bestseller-: ~autor *der,* **~autorin** *die* best-selling author; **~liste** *die* best-seller list; **~verdächtig** *Adj.* likely to become a best-seller *postpos.*; **ein ~verdächtiges Buch** a potential bestseller

bestücken *tr. V.* fit; equip; (mit Waffen) arm; (mit Waren) stock [up]

Bestückung *die;* ~, **~en** equipment; (mit Waffen) armament; (mit Waren) stocking; **eine ordnungsgemäße ~ des Lagers garantieren** ensure that the correct stock level is maintained at the warehouse

bestuhlen /bəˈʃtuːlən/ *tr. V.* provide with seats

Bestuhlung *die;* ~, **~en** [1] fitting of [the] seats (*Gen.* in) [2] (Stühle) seating

bestürmen *tr. V.* [1] storm; (Fußball) besiege ‹*goal*› [2] (bedrängen) besiege (**mit** with)

Bestürmung *die* storming; (Angriff) assault

bestürzen *tr. V.* dismay; (erschüttern) shake; (erschrecken) alarm; **es hat ihn sehr bestürzt zu hören, dass ...** he was deeply dismayed to hear that ...

bestürzend *Adj.* disturbing; (erschreckend) alarming

bestürzt

[A] *Adj.* dismayed (**über** + *Akk.* about); (erschrocken) alarmed (**über** + *Akk.* about); **sie machte ein [sehr] ~es Gesicht** her face fell [a mile (coll.)]; she looked [deeply] dismayed

[B] *adv.* with dismay *or* consternation; **jmdn. [ganz** *od.* **sehr] ~ ansehen** look at sb. in *or* with [great] consternation

Bestürzung *die;* **~:** dismay; consternation; **mit ~ feststellen, dass ...** find to one's consternation that ...

bestusst, *bestußt /bəˈʃtʊst/ *Adj.* (salopp) barmy (Brit. coll.); loopy (coll.)

Best-: ~wert *der* optimum result; (~leistung) maximum performance figure; (beim Wettbewerb) maximum mark; **~zeit** *die* (Sport) best time; **[persönliche] ~zeit** personal best [time]; **~zeit laufen/schwimmen** run/swim a best time/one's personal best *or* one's best time

-besuch *der:* **Deutschland~/England~/USA-Besuch:** visit to Germany/England/the USA; **Messe~:** visit to the/a fair

Besuch /bəˈzuːx/ *der;* **~[e]s, ~e** [1] visit; **ein ~ bei jmdm.** a visit to sb.; (kurz) a call on sb.; **~ eines Museums** *usw.* visit to a museum *etc.;* **bei seinem letzten ~:** on his last visit; **wir erwarten den ~ alter Freunde** we are expecting a visit from some old friends; **~ von jmdm. bekommen** receive a visit from sb.; **auf** *od.* **zu ~ kommen** come for a visit; (auf länger) come to stay; **er ist bei uns auf ~:** he is staying with us; **jmdm. einen ~ abstatten** pay sb. a visit [2] (das ~en) visiting; (Teilnahme) attendance; **der ~ der Schule/Vorlesungen/Gottesdienste** attendance at school/lectures/services; **die Konzerte erfreuen sich eines regen ~s** the concerts are well attended [3] (Gast) visitor; (Gäste) visitors *pl.;* **~ bekommen/erwarten** have/expect visitors/a visitor; **ich bekomme gleich ~:** I've got visitors/a visitor coming any minute

besuchen *tr. V.* [1] visit ‹*person*›; (weniger formell) go to see ‹*person*›; **gestern hat mich ein alter Bekannter besucht** yesterday an old friend came to see me *or* called on me [2] visit ‹*place*›; go to ‹*exhibition, theatre, museum, etc.*›; (zur Besichtigung) go to see ‹*church, exhibition, etc.*›; **die Schule/Universität ~:** go to *or* (formal) attend school/university; **hast du diese Ausstellung schon besucht?** have you been to [see] this exhibition yet?; **er hat sämtliche Lokale der Umgebung besucht** he patronized all the pubs (Brit.) *or* (Amer.) bars in the neighbourhood; *s. auch* **besucht**

-besucher *der:* **Berlin~:** visitor to Berlin; **Messe~:** visitor to the/a fair

Besucher *der* visitor; **~ eines Museums** *usw.* visitor to a museum *etc.;* **die ~ des Theaters** the theatre audience; the theatre goers; **er ist ständiger ~ der Oper/von Konzerten** he is a regular opera-goer/concert-goer; **alle ~ des Kurses/der Vorstellung/des Vortrags** all those attending the course/performance/lecture

Besucherin *die;* ~, **~nen** ▸ **Besucher**

Besucher-: ~strom *der* stream of visitors; **~zahl** *die* number of visitors

besuchs-, Besuchs-: ~erlaubnis *die* visiting permit; **~halber** *adv.* on a visit; **~ritze** *die* (ugs. scherzh.) join between the [twin] beds; **~tag** *der* visiting day; **~zeit** *die* visiting time *or* hours *pl.*; **es ist keine ~zeit** it is not visiting time

besucht *Adj.* **gut/schlecht ~:** well/poorly attended ‹*lecture, performance, etc.*›; much/little frequented ‹*restaurant etc.*›

besudeln *tr. V.* (geh. abwertend) besmirch; **jmds. Andenken/Namen ~** (fig.) cast a slur on sb.'s memory/name

Beta /ˈbeːta/ *das;* **~[s], ~s** beta

Beta·blocker /-blɔkɐ/ *der;* **~s, ~** (Med.) betablocker

betagt /bəˈtaːkt/ *Adj.* (geh.) elderly; (scherzh.) ancient ‹*car etc.*›; **noch als ~er Mann** even in his old age

Betagtheit *die;* ~ (geh.) old age

betanken *tr. V.* refuel

betasten *tr. V.* feel [with one's fingers]

Beta-: ~strahlen *Pl.* (Physik) beta rays; **~teilchen** *das* (Physik) beta particle

betätigen

[A] *refl. V.* busy *or* occupy oneself; **sich politisch/literarisch/körperlich ~:** engage in political/literary/physical activity; **sich als etw. ~:** act as sth.; **wenn du dich ~ willst, kannst du mir beim Spülen helfen** if you want to do something [useful], you can help me with the washing-up

[B] *tr. V.* operate ‹*lever, switch, flush, etc.*›; press ‹*button*›; apply ‹*brake*›

Betätigung *die;* ~, **~en** [1] activity; **ich werde schon eine ~ für dich finden** I'll find you something to do [2] (das Bedienen) operation; (einer Bremse) application; (eines Knopfes) pressing

Betätigungs-: ~drang *der* [compulsive] urge to be up and doing [something]; **~feld** *das* sphere of activity

betatschen *tr. V.* (salopp abwertend) finger; (sexuell) paw (coll.)

betäuben /bəˈtɔybn̩/ *tr. V.* [1] (Med.) anaesthetize; make numb, deaden ‹*nerve*›; **einen Patienten örtlich ~:** give a patient a local anaesthetic [2] (unterdrücken) ease, deaden ‹*pain*›; quell, still ‹*unease, fear*›; **seinen Kummer mit Alkohol ~** (fig.) drown one's sorrows [in drink] [3] (benommen machen) daze; (mit einem Schlag) stun; **ein ~der Duft** a heady *or* intoxicating scent; **ein ~der Lärm** a deafening noise

Betäubung *die; ~, ~en* [1] (Med.) anaesthetization; (Narkose) anaesthesia; **eine örtliche ~ vornehmen** administer a local anaesthetic; **zur ~ der Schmerzen** to deaden the pain [2] (Benommenheit) daze

Betäubungs·mittel *das* narcotic; (Med.) anaesthetic

Betäubungsmittel·gesetz *das* narcotics law (regulating the use of cocaine, morphine, cannabis, etc.)

betaut /bəˈtaut/ *Adj.* (geh.) covered in dew *postpos.*; bedewed (literary)

Bet·bruder /ˈbeːt-/ *der* (abwertend) over-pious type (coll.)

Bete /ˈbeːtə/ *die; ~, ~n in* **Rote ~**: beetroot (Brit.); [red] beet (Amer.)

beteilen *tr. V.* (österr.) provide (**mit** with)

beteiligen

[A] *refl. V.* **sich an etw.** (*Dat.*) **~**: participate *or* take part in sth.; **er hat sich kaum an der Diskussion beteiligt** he took hardly any part in the discussion; **sich an einem Geschäft ~**: take a share in *or* come in on a deal; **sich an etw. mit einer Million ~**: contribute a million to sth.

[B] *tr. V.* **jmdn. [mit 10 %] an etw.** (*Dat.*) **~**: give sb. a [10%] share of sth.

beteiligt *Adj.* [1] involved (**an** + *Dat.* in) [2] (finanziell) **an einem Unternehmen/am Gewinn ~ sein** have a share in a business/in the profit; **er ist mit 20 000 Euro ~**: he has a 20,000 euros share

Beteiligte *der/die; adj. Dekl.* person involved (**an** + *Dat.* in); (an einem Spiel, einer Sitzung usw.) participant (**an** + *Dat.* in); **die [meisten] an dem Unfall/der Affäre ~n** [most of] those involved in the accident/affair

Beteiligung *die; ~, ~en* [1] (Teilnahme) participation (**an** + *Dat.* in); (Zahl der Beteiligten) number of participants (**an** + *Dat.* in); (an einem Verbrechen) involvement (**an** + *Dat.* in); **unter ~ von** with the participation of [2] (Anteil) share (**an** + *Dat.* in); **eine ~ am Gewinn/Umsatz** a share in the profits/turnover

Beteiligungs·gesellschaft *die* (Wirtsch.) holding company; (mit weniger als 50% Beteiligung) associated company

Betel /ˈbeːtl̩/ *der; ~s* betel

Betel·nuss, *Betel·nuß *die* betel nut

beten /ˈbeːtn̩/

[A] *itr. V.* pray (**für, um** for); **zu Gott ~, dass etw. geschehen möge** pray to God that sth. should happen; **es wird gebetet** prayers are said

[B] *tr. V.* say ‹*prayer*›

Beter *der; ~s, ~,* **Beterin** *die; ~, ~nen* prayer (= *one who prays*)

beteuern /bəˈtɔyɐn/ *tr. V.* affirm; assert, protest ‹*one's innocence*›; **jmdm. seine Liebe ~**: avow one's love to sb.; **sie beteuerte, dass sie mit dieser Sache nichts zu tun habe** she protested that she had nothing to do with this business

Beteuerung *die; ~, ~en* ▸**beteuern**: affirmation; assertion; protestation

Bet·haus *das* synagogue

betiteln /bəˈtiːtl̩n/ *tr. V.* [1] (ugs. abwertend) **jmdn. [mit] X/mit einem Schimpfnamen ~**: call sb. X/a rude name [2] (mit Titel anreden) **jmdn. [mit] Doktor/Professor ~**: address sb. as *or* call sb. 'Doctor'/'Professor' [3] (mit Titel versehen) give ‹*book etc.*› a title

Beton /beˈtɔŋ, *bes. österr.*: beˈtoːn/ *der; ~s, ~s* /-ɔŋs/ *od.* **~e** /-oːnə/ concrete

Beton-: ~bau *der; Pl.* **~~ten** [1] concrete building; [2] (Bauweise) concrete construction *no art.*; **~bunker** *der* [1] concrete bunker; (Luftschutzbunker) concrete shelter; [2] (abwertend: ~bau) concrete box; **~burg** *die* (ugs., meist abwertend) concrete monstrosity (derog.)

betonen /bəˈtoːnən/ *tr. V.* [1] stress ‹*word, syllable*›; accent ‹*syllable, beat*›; **ein Wort falsch ~**: put the wrong stress on a word [2] (hervorheben) emphasize; **ich möchte ~, dass ...** I should like to emphasize *or* stress that ...; **warum betont er seine Herkunft so?** why does he lay such stress on his origins?; **die Taille ~**: accentuate the waist

betonieren /betoˈniːrən/ *tr. V.* [1] concrete; surface ‹*road etc.*› with concrete; lay a concrete floor in ‹*cellar etc.*›; **frisch betonierte Fläche** recently laid concrete [2] (festlegen) harden ‹*attitude*›; reinforce ‹*prejudice*›

Betonierung *die; ~, ~en* [1] concreting [2] (Betondecke) concrete surface

Beton-: ~klotz *der* [1] concrete block; [2] (abwertend: massiver ~bau) concrete monolith; **~kopf** *der* (abwertend) hardliner; **~mischer** *der,* **~misch·maschine** *die* concrete mixer

betont /bəˈtoːnt/

[A] *Adj.* [1] stressed; accented [2] (bewusst) pointed, studied; deliberate, studied ‹*simplicity, elegance*›

[B] *adv.* pointedly; deliberately; **sich ~ sportlich kleiden** wear clothes with a strong *or* pronounced sporting character; **sich ~ zurückhaltend verhalten** behave with studied reserve

Beton·träger *der* concrete beam

Betonung *die; ~, ~en* [1] stressing; accenting [2] (Akzent) stress; accent (esp. Mus.); (Intonation) intonation [3] (das Hervorheben) emphasis (*Gen.* on); (von Formen, Farben) accentuation; **ein Lernprogramm mit ~ des Musisch-Kreativen** a syllabus with the emphasis on artistic creativity

Betonungs·zeichen *das* stress mark

Beton·wüste *die* (ugs. abwertend) concrete desert

betören /bəˈtøːrən/ *tr. V.* (geh.) [1] captivate; bewitch [2] (verblenden) beguile, entice ‹*purchaser, consumer*›

Betörung *die; ~, ~en* (geh.) captivation; bewitching

betr. *Abk.* **= betreffs, betrifft** re

Betr. *Abk.* **= Betreff** re

Betracht /bəˈtraxt/ *in* **jmdn./etw. in ~ ziehen** consider sb./sth.; **jmdn./etw. außer ~ lassen** discount *or* disregard sb./sth.; **eine Frage außer ~ lassen** pass over a question; (zeitweilig) leave a question on one side; **er/sie kommt/kommt nicht in ~**: he/she can/cannot be considered; **das kommt nicht in ~**: that is not worth considering; that is out of the question; **außer ~ bleiben** be passed over; (zeitweilig) be left on one side

betrachten *tr. V.* [1] look at; (bei einer Tätigkeit) watch; observe; (fig.: studieren) observe, study ‹*history, development, etc.*›; **sich** (*Dat.*) **etw. [genau] ~**: take a [close] look at sth.; watch *or* observe sth. [closely]; **sich im Spiegel ~**: look at oneself in the mirror; (längere Zeit) contemplate oneself in the mirror; **jmdn. von oben bis unten ~**: look sb. up and down; **genau/bei Licht betrachtet** (fig.) upon closer consideration/seen in the light of day [2] (für etw. halten) **jmdn./etw. als ... ~**: regard sb./sth. as ...; **sich als jmds. Freund ~**: regard oneself as *or* consider oneself sb.'s friend [3] (beurteilen) consider; view; **objektiv betrachtet** viewed objectively; from an objective point of view; **so betrachtet** seen in this light *or* from this point of view

Betrachter *der; ~s, ~,* **Betrachterin** *die; ~, ~nen* observer

beträchtlich /bəˈtrɛçtlɪç/

[A] *Adj.* considerable; **um ein Beträchtliches** to a considerable degree

[B] *adv.* considerably

Betrachtung *die; ~, ~en* [1] contemplation; (Untersuchung) examination; **bei genauer[er] ~**: upon close[r] examination; (fig.) upon close[r] consideration; **bei nachträglicher ~**: [viewed] in retrospect [2] (Überlegung) observation; **~en über etw.** (*Akk.*) **anstellen** make observations *or* comments about sth.

Betrachtungs·weise *die* way of looking at things; (Standpunkt) point of view

Betrag /bəˈtraːk/ *der; ~[e]s,* **Beträge** /bəˈtrɛːɡə/ sum; amount; **ein Scheck über einen ~ von 1 000 Euro** a cheque for 1,000 euros; **~ dankend erhalten** (auf Quittungen) received *or* paid with thanks

betragen

[A] *unr. itr. V.* be; (bei Geldsummen) come to; amount to; **die Zeitdifferenz beträgt 3 Stunden** the time difference is three hours

[B] *unr. refl. V.* behave (**gegenüber, gegen** towards)

Betragen *das; ~s* behaviour; (in der Schule) conduct; **in ~ eine gute Note bekommen** get a good mark for conduct

Betragens·note *die* mark for conduct

betrauen *tr. V.* **jmdn. mit etw. ~**: entrust sb. with sth.; **jmdn. damit ~, etw. zu tun** entrust sb. with the task of doing sth.

betrauern *tr. V.* mourn ‹*death, loss*›; **jmdn. ~**: mourn for sb.

beträufeln *tr. V.* sprinkle (**mit** with drops of)

Betrauung *die; ~*: entrusting

Betreff /bəˈtrɛf/ *der; ~[e]s, ~e* (Amtsspr., Kaufmannsspr.) subject; matter; (~zeile) heading; reference line; **den ~ angeben** state the subject [of the letter]; (im Brief) **~: Ihr Schreiben vom 26. d. M.** re: your letter of the 26th inst.

betreffen *unr. tr. V.* [1] concern; ‹*new rule, change, etc.*› affect; **was mich betrifft, ...** as far as I'm concerned ...; **was mich betrifft, bin ich** *od.* **ich bin einverstanden** for my part I am in agreement; **was das betrifft, ...** as regards that; as far as that goes [2] (geh.: widerfahren) befall [3] (geh. veralt.: bestürzt machen) hurt; **es hat mich schmerzhaft betroffen zu hören, dass ...** it saddened me to hear that ... [4] (geh. veralt.: ertappen) apprehend

betreffend *Adj.* concerning; **der ~e Sachbearbeiter** the person concerned with *or* dealing with this matter; **in dem ~en Fall** in the case concerned *or* in question

Betreffende *der/die; adj. Dekl.* person concerned; **die ~n** the people concerned

betreffs *Präp. mit Gen.* (Amtsspr., Kaufmannsspr.) concerning

betreiben *unr. tr. V.* [1] tackle ‹*task*›; proceed with, (energisch) press ahead with ‹*task, case, etc.*›; pursue ‹*policy, studies*›; carry on ‹*trade*›; **auf jmds./sein Betreiben** (*Akk.*) **[hin]** at the instigation of sb./at his instigation; **das Tischlerhandwerk ~**: ply the carpenter's trade [2] (führen) run ‹*business, shop*›; **Radsport ~**: go in for cycling as a sport [3] (antreiben) drive (**mit** by); **etw. elektrisch ~**: drive sth. by electricity *or* electrically; **ein atomar/mit Dampf betriebenes Schiff** a nuclear-powered/steam-powered ship [4] (schweiz.: Rechtsw.) sue (*for payment of a debt*)

Betreiber *der,* **Betreiberin** *die* operator

Betreiberfirma *die* operating company; operator

Betreibung *die; ~, ~en* **die ~ eines Geschäfts/einer Anlage** running a business/driving a plant

betresst, *betreßt /bəˈtrɛst/ *Adj.* braided

betreten[1] *unr. tr. V.* (hineintreten in) enter; (treten auf) walk *or* step on to; (begehen) walk on ‹*carpet, grass, etc.*›; **er hat das Haus nicht mehr** *od.* **nie wieder ~**: he never set foot in the house again; **„Betreten verboten"** 'Keep off'; (kein Eintritt) 'Keep out'; **„Betreten der Baustelle verboten"** 'Building site. No entry *or* Keep out'; **den Rasen nicht ~**: keep off the grass; *s. auch* **Neuland**

betreten[2]

[A] *Adj.* embarrassed; **ein ~es Gesicht machen** look embarrassed

[B] *adv.* with embarrassment; **man schwieg ~**: there was an embarrassed silence

Betretenheit *die; ~*: embarrassment

betreuen /bəˈtrɔyən/ *tr. V.* look after; care for ‹*invalid*›; supervise ‹*youth group*›; see to the needs of ‹*tourists, sportsmen*›; look after, be in charge of ‹*department etc.*›

Betreuer *der; ~s, ~* (für Alte, Kranke, Behinderte) social worker; (für Kinder) minder; (für Entlassene aus Krankenhaus/Gefängnis) aftercare worker; (für Sportler, Künstler) manager; (für Touristen) courier; travel guide; (einer Delegation) secretary

Betreuerin *die;* ~, ~**nen** [1] (Kinder~) childminder; (ganztägig) nanny (Brit.); nursemaid (Amer.); (Krankenpflegerin) nurse [2] ▸**Betreuer**

Betreuung *die;* ~ [1] care *no indef. art.;* **die ~ der Gäste** taking care of the guests; **jmdn. zur ~ des Großvaters einstellen** take on sb. to look after *or* care for grandfather; **zwei Reiseleiter waren zu unserer ~ vorhanden** there were two couriers *or* travel guides to see to our needs [2] (Person) minder; (Krankenpfleger) nurse

Betrieb *der;* ~**[e]s,** ~**e** [1] business; (Firma) firm; **ein staatlicher ~:** a state-owned *or* nationalized concern; **ein landwirtschaftlicher ~:** an agricultural holding; **im ~ sein/bleiben/essen** be/stay/eat at work; *s. auch* **volkseigen** [2] (das In-Funktion-Sein) operation; (Arbeitsprozess) working process; operations *pl., no art.;* **in ~ sein** be running; be in operation; **außer ~ sein** be out of order; **in/außer ~ setzen** start up/stop ‹*machine etc.*›; (ein-/ausschalten) switch on/off; **in ~ nehmen** put into operation; put ‹*bus, train*› into service; **ein Kraftwerk wird in ~ genommen** a power plant is commissioned; **den ~ einstellen** close down *or* cease operations; (in einer Fabrik) stop work; (einer Buslinie o. Ä.) withdraw the service; **den [ganzen] ~ aufhalten** (ugs.) hold everybody up [3] (ugs.: Treiben) bustle; commotion; (Verkehr) traffic; **es herrscht großer ~, es ist viel ~:** it's very busy; **bei dem ~ kann man nicht arbeiten** one cannot work with all that [commotion] going on

betrieblich *Adj.* firm's; company; (inner~) internal; within the company *postpos.;* **aus ~en Gründen** for reasons to do with the state of the company

betriebsam
[A] *Adj.* busy; (ständig ~) constantly on the go *postpos.;* ~**e Naturen** hyperactive types; eager beavers (coll.); (Frauen) busy bees (coll.)
[B] *adv.* busily

Betriebsamkeit *die;* ~**:** [bustling] activity; **eine hektische ~ an den Tag legen** become frantically busy

betriebs-, Betriebs-: ~**angehörige** *der/die* employee; *Pl.* company staff; ~**anleitung** *die,* ~**anweisung** *die* operating instructions *pl.;* (Heft) instruction manual; ~**arzt** *der,* ~**ärztin** *die* company doctor; ~**ausflug** *der* staff outing; ~**bedingt** [A] *Adj.* operational ‹*reasons*›; ~**bedingte Kündigungen** dismissals for operational reasons; [B] *adv.* ‹*dismiss*› for operational reasons; ~**begehung** *die* factory *etc.* inspection tour; ~**bereit** *Adj.* ready to be put into operation *postpos.;* ~**bereit sein** be operational; ~**besichtigung** *die* visit to a firm; (Fabrikbesichtigung) factory visit; (eines landwirtschaftlichen Betriebs) farm visit; ~**blind** *Adj.* inured to the shortcomings of working methods *postpos.;* professionally blinkered; ~**blind werden** get into a rut *or* become blinkered in one's work; ~**blindheit** *die* blinkered attitude to one's work; ~**eigen** *Adj.* company-owned; ~**ergebnis** *das* trading result; ~**erlaubnis** *die* operating permit; ~**ferien** *Pl.* firm's annual close-down *sing.;* **das Geschäft hat ~ferien** the shop is closed for its annual holidays; **„Wegen ~ferien geschlossen"** 'closed for annual holidays'; ~**fertig** *Adj.:* ▸~**bereit**; ~**fest** *das* firm's party; ~**fremd** *Adj.* who are not company employees *postpos., not pred.;* outside; **„Zutritt ~fremden nicht gestattet"** 'Staff Only'; ~**frieden** *der* harmonious relationship between employer and employed (*which all parties are obliged to uphold*); industrial peace; ~**führer** *der,* ~**führerin** *die* ▸~**leiter**; ~**führung** *die* ▸~**leitung**; ~**geheimnis** *das* company secret; trade secret (also fig.); **das ~geheimnis verletzen** infringe the confidentiality of company matters; ~**gruppe** *die* trade union membership (*within one company*); ~**intern** [A] *Adj.* internal; internal company *attrib.;* [B] *adv.* internally; within the company; ~**kapital** *das* [1] working capital; [2] (Anfangskapital) initial capital; ~**kindergarten** *der* nursery school for employees' children; ~**klima** *das* working atmosphere; ~**kosten** *Pl.* running costs; (einer Firma) operating costs; ~**krankenkasse** *die* company sickness insurance scheme; ~**leiter** *der,* ~**leiterin** *die* manager; (einer Fabrik) works manager; ~**leitung** *die* management [of the firm]; ~**nudel** *die* (ugs.) [1] live wire in the office; (Komiker) office comedian; [2] (übergeschäftige Person) eager beaver (coll.); (Frau) busy bee (coll.); ~**obfrau** *die,* ~**obmann** *der,* ~**obmännin** *die;* ~~, ~~**nen** workers' representative (*in a small firm*); ~**prüfer** *der,* ~**prüferin** *die* ▸ⓘ **S. 113** auditor; ~**prüfung** *die* audit of a/the firm's accounts (*by the taxation authorities*); ~**rat** *der; Pl.:* ~**räte** [1] works committee; [2] (Person) member of a/the works committee; ~**rätin** *die* ▸~**rat 2**; ~**ratsmitglied** *das* member of a/the works committee; ~**rats·vorsitzende** *der/die* chairman of a/the works committee; ~**rente** *die* company pension; ~**ruhe** *die:* ~**ruhe haben** ‹*business, factory*› be closed; ~**schließung** *die* closure [of a/the firm]; ~**schluss**, *~**schluß** *der* (im Geschäft) end of business hours; (in der Fabrik) end of working hours; **kurz vor ~schluss** shortly before it was time to go home *or* (coll.) knocking-off time; **nach ~schluss geht er gleich nach Hause** after work he goes straight home; ~**sicher** *Adj.* [operationally] safe; ~**sicher sein** be safe to operate *or* run; ~**sicherheit** *die* [operational] safety; (in der Fabrik) safety at work; ~**stilllegung** *die* closure [of a/the firm]; (eines Werks) works closure; ~**störung** *die* malfunction; ~**system** *das* (DV) operating system; ~**treue** *die* loyalty to a/the company; **10-jährige ~treue** 10 years' service with a/the company; ~**unfall** *der* [1] (veralt.) industrial accident; [2] (ugs.: Ungeschicklichkeit) slip-up; little mishap; ~**vereinbarung** *die: agreement between 'Betriebsrat' and management;* ~**verfassung** *die* code of industrial relations (*covering worker participation and representation*); ~**verfassungs·gesetz** *das* industrial relations law (*for the private sector*); ~**versammlung** *die* meeting of the workforce; ~**wirt** *der,* ~**wirtin** *die* graduate in business management; ~**wirtschaft** *die* business management; ~**wirtschaftlich** [A] *Adj.* business management *attrib.;* [B] *adv.* from the business management standpoint; ~**wirtschafts·lehre** *die* [theory of] business management; (Fach) management studies *sing., no art.;* ~**wissenschaft** *die* ▸~**wirtschaftslehre**; ~**zeitung** *die* company newspaper

> **Betriebsrat**
>
> The staff in any German company with at least five employees are entitled to have a *Betriebsrat*. This is a committee elected by the workers to represent their interests as opposed to those of management. It allows workers to participate in decisions on pay and other benefits, redundancies, and even some business matters.

betrinken *unr. refl. V.* get drunk; **sich fürchterlich/sinnlos ~:** get terribly/blind drunk

betroffen /bəˈtrɔfn̩/
[A] *2. Part. v.* **betreffen**
[B] *Adj.* upset; (bestürzt) dismayed; **zutiefst** *od.* **im Innersten ~:** extremely upset; (gekränkt) deeply hurt
[C] *adv.* in dismay *or* consternation; **~ schweigen** be too upset/dismayed to say anything

Betroffene *der/die; adj. Dekl.* person affected; **die von ... ~n** those affected by ...

Betroffenheit *die;* ~**:** dismay; consternation

betrog /bəˈtroːk/ *1. u. 3. Pers. Sg. Prät. v.* **betrügen**

betrogen *2. Part. v.* **betrügen**

betrüben
[A] *tr. V.* sadden; **seine Eltern durch sein Verhalten ~:** cause one's parents distress through one's behaviour
[B] *refl. V.* (geh. veralt.) **sich über etw.** (*Akk.*) **~:** become dejected *or* depressed about sth.

betrüblich *Adj.* gloomy; (deprimierend) depressing; **ich muss Ihnen die ~e Mitteilung machen, dass ...** unfortunately I have to inform you that ...

betrüblicher·weise *Adv.* unfortunately; (traurigerweise) sadly

Betrübnis /bəˈtryːpnɪs/ *die;* ~, ~**se** (geh.) sadness

betrübt /bəˈtryːpt/
[A] *Adj.* (traurig) sad (**über** + *Akk.* about); (deprimiert) dismayed, depressed (**über** + *Akk.* about); gloomy ‹*face etc.*›; **~ aussehen** look gloomy; *s. auch* **Tod**
[B] *adv.* sadly; (schwermütig) gloomily

betrug /bəˈtruːk/ *1. u. 3. Pers. Sg. Prät. v.* **betragen**

Betrug *der;* ~**[e]s;** *Pl. schweiz.:* **Betrüge** deception; (Mogelei) cheating *no indef. art.;* (Delikt) fraud; **das ist [glatter] ~:** that's [plain] fraud/cheating; **mehrfacher** *od.* (Rechtsw.) **fortgesetzter ~:** repeated fraud; **ein frommer ~:** a well-meaning deception; (Selbsttäuschung) [a case of] self-deception

betrügen
[A] *unr. tr. V.* [1] deceive; be unfaithful to ‹*husband, wife*›; (Rechtsw.) defraud ‹*firm, customer, etc.*›; (beim Spielen) cheat; **sich [in etw.** (*Dat.*)**] betrogen sehen** be deceived [in sth.]; (in seinem Vertrauen) be betrayed [in sth.]; (enttäuscht) be let down [in sth.]; **er sah sich in all seinen Hoffnungen betrogen** all his hopes were dashed; he was disappointed in all his hopes; **sich selbst ~:** deceive oneself [2] (um etw. bringen) **jmdn. um 100 Euro ~:** cheat *or* (coll.) do sb. out of 100 euros; (arglistig) swindle sb. out of 100 euros; **um sein Recht betrogen werden** be cheated of one's rights
[B] *unr. itr. V.* cheat; (bei Geschäften) swindle people

Betrüger *der;* ~**s,** ~**:** swindler; (Hochstapler) con man (coll.); (beim Spielen) cheat; (der Ehefrau) deceiver

Betrügerei *die;* ~, ~**en** deception; (beim Spielen usw.) cheating; (bei Geschäften) swindling; **eine kleine ~:** a bit of a swindle *or* of swindling; a bit of cheating; **deine ~en** your swindling *sing.*/cheating *sing.*

Betrügerin *die;* ~, ~**nen** swindler; (beim Spielen) cheat; (des Ehemanns) deceiver

betrügerisch *Adj.* deceitful; (Rechtsw.) fraudulent; **in ~er Absicht** with intent to deceive

betrunken /bəˈtrʊŋkn̩/
[A] *2. Part. v.* **betrinken**
[B] *Adj.* drunken *attrib.;* drunk *pred.;* **ein total ~er Fahrer** a completely drunk and incapable driver
[C] *adv.* drunkenly

Betrunkene *der/die; adj. Dekl.* drunk; **eine ~:** a drunken woman

Bet-: ~**saal** *der* meeting hall; [primitive] chapel; ~**schwester** *die* (abwertend) over-pious type (coll.); ~**stuhl** *der* prayer stool

Bett /bɛt/ *das;* ~**[e]s,** ~**en** [1] bed; **das ~ machen** make the bed; **die ~en bauen** (ugs. scherzh.) make the beds; **jmdm. das Frühstück ans ~ bringen** bring sb. breakfast in bed; **sie ging an sein ~/saß an seinem ~:** she went to/sat at his bedside; **jmdn. aus dem ~ holen** (ugs.) get sb. out of bed; **er kommt nur schwer aus dem ~:** he doesn't like getting up; **im ~:** in bed; **[mit Fieber] im ~ liegen** be in bed [with a temperature]; **ins** *od.* **zu ~ gehen, sich ins** *od.* **zu ~ legen** go to bed; **ins ~ fallen** (ugs.) fall into bed; **die Kinder ins ~ bringen** put the children to bed; **das ~ hüten [müssen]** (fig.) [have to] stay in bed; **er hütet seit einer Woche das ~** (fig.) he has been in bed for a week; **das ~ mit jmdm. teilen** (fig. geh.) share bed and board with sb.; live together with sb.; **mit jmdm. ins ~ gehen** *od.* **steigen** (fig. ugs.) go to bed with sb.; **sich ins gemachte ~ legen** (fig.) have everything handed to one on a plate (fig.); *s. auch* **fesseln, klingeln** [2] (Feder~) duvet [3] (Fluss~) bed; **der Fluss hat sich ein neues ~ gesucht** the river has formed a new bed [4] (Technik) bed

Bet·tag *der* ▸**Buß- und Bettag**

Bett-: ~**an·zug** *der* (schweiz.), ~**bezug** *der* duvet cover; ~**couch** *die* bed settee; studio couch; **~decke** *die* **1** blanket; (gesteppt) quilt; **2** (Tagesdecke) bedspread

Bettel /ˈbɛtl̩/ *der;* **~s** **1** (ugs.) junk (coll.) **2** (veralt.: ~n) begging *no art.*

bettel-, Bettel-: ~arm *Adj.* destitute; penniless; **~brief** *der* begging letter

Bettelei *die;* **~, ~en** begging *no art.*

Bettel-: ~mann *der; Pl.:* **~leute** (veralt.) beggar; **~mönch** *der* mendicant friar

betteln /ˈbɛtl̩n/ *itr. V.* beg (**um** for); **~ gehen** go begging; **„B~ verboten!"** 'No begging'; **bei jmdm. um etw. ~:** beg sb. for sth.; **darum ~, aufbleiben zu dürfen** beg to be allowed to stay up

Bettel-: ~orden *der* mendicant order; **~stab** *der: in* **jmdn. an den ~stab bringen** reduce sb. to penury; **~weib** *das* (veralt.) beggar woman

betten (geh.)

A *tr. V.* **1** lay; **jmdn. flach ~:** lay sb. [down] flat; **jmdn. weich ~:** make a soft bed for sb. to lie on; **weich gebettet sein** (fig.) have an easy time of it; be feather-bedded **2** (ein~) **etw. in etw.** (*Akk.*) **~:** embed sth. in sth.

B *refl. V.* (fig.) **wie man sich bettet, so liegt man** as you make your bed, so you must lie on it; **sich weich ~:** feather one's nest

Betten-: ~burg *die* **1** (Hotel) giant hotel; **2** (Urlaubsort) overdeveloped resort; **~machen** *das;* **~~s** making the beds *no art.;* (allgemein) making beds *no art.;* **das tägliche ~machen** the daily making of beds; **~mangel** *der* shortage of beds

bett-, Bett-: ~feder *die* **1** bedspring; **2** *Pl.* (Füllung) [pillow/bed] feathers; **~flasche** *die* hot-water bottle; **~genosse** *der,* **~genossin** *die* bedfellow; **~geschichte** *die* (abwertend) **1** (Verhältnis) purely physical relationship; **seine ~geschichten schildern** describe one's bedroom experiences; **2** (Klatschgeschichte) bedroom saga; **~geschichten der Filmstars** gossip about film stars' love lives; **~gestell** *das* bedstead; **~häschen** *das,* **~hase** *der* (ugs. scherzh.) sex kitten; **~himmel** *der* bed canopy; **~hupferl** /-hʊpfɐl/ *das;* **~~s, ~~:** bedtime treat; **~jäckchen** *das,* **~jacke** *die* bed-jacket; **~kante** *die* edge of the bed; **~kasten** *der* bedding box (*under a bed*); **~lade** *die* (südd., österr.) ▸ **~gestell; ~lägerig** /-lɛːɡərɪç/ *Adj.* bedridden; **~laken** *das* sheet; **~lektüre** *die* bedtime reading *no indef. art.*

Bettler /ˈbɛtlɐ/ *der;* **~s, ~:** beggar

Bettlerin *die;* **~, ~nen** beggar [woman]

bett-, Bett-: ~nässen *das;* **~~s** bed-wetting *no art.;* **~nässer** *der;* **~~s, ~~, ~nässerin** *die;* **~~, ~~nen** bed-wetter; **~pfanne** *die* bedpan; **~reif** *Adj.* (ugs.) ready for bed *pred.;* **~ruhe** *die* bed rest; **zwei Wochen [absolute] ~ruhe** two weeks of [complete] bed rest; **~schwere** *die* **die nötige** *od.* **notwendige ~schwere haben** (ugs.) be ready for one's bed; **~statt** *die;* **~, ~stätten** /-ʃtɛtn̩/ (südd., österr.), **~stelle** *die* ▸ **Bettgestell; ~szene** *die* (Film) bedroom scene; **~tuch** *das; Pl.* **~tücher** sheet; **~über·zug** *der* duvet cover

***Bettuch** ▸ **Betttuch**

Bett·umrandung *die* bedside carpeting (*on three sides of the bed*)

Bettung *die;* **~, ~en** (Eisenb., Straßenbau) roadbed

Bett-: ~vorlage *die,* **~vorleger** *der* bedside rug; **~wäsche** *die* bedlinen; **~zeug** *das* (ugs.) bedclothes *pl.*

betucht /bəˈtuːxt/ *Adj.* (ugs.) **[gut] ~:** well-heeled (coll.); well-off

betulich /bəˈtuːlɪç/

A *Adj.* **1** fussy; (besorgt) worried; agitated **2** (gemächlich) leisurely; unhurried

B *adv.* **1** fussily **2** (gemächlich) in a calm unhurried way

Betulichkeit *die;* **~** **1** fussiness; (Besorgtheit) agitation **2** (Gemächlichkeit) calm unhurried manner

betun *unr. refl. V.* (ugs.) fuss around

betupfen *tr. V.* dab

betuppen /bəˈtʊpn̩/ *tr. V.* (nordwestd. ugs.) diddle (coll.); do (coll.)

betüteln /bəˈtyːtl̩n/ *tr. V.* ▸ **betütern**

betütern /bəˈtyːtɐn/ (nordd. ugs.)

A *tr. V.* mollycoddle

B *refl. V.* get merry *or* tipsy

betütert *Adj.* (nordd. ugs.) **1** (beschwipst) merry; tipsy **2** (verwirrt) not quite with it *pred.* (coll.)

beugbar *Adj.* (Sprachw.) declinable ‹*noun, adjective*›; conjugable ‹*verb*›

Beuge /ˈbɔyɡə/ *die;* **~, ~n** **1** (Turnen) bend; **eine ~ machen** bend over; (Knie~) **in die ~ gehen** do a knees-bend **2** (Biegung) bend **3** (Arm~/Bein~) crook of one's arm *or* elbow/knee

Beuge·haft *die* (Rechtsw.) coercive detention

Beugel /ˈbɔyɡl̩/ *das;* **~s, ~** (österr.) filled croissant

Beuge·muskel *der* ▸ ❶ **S. 435** (Anat.) flexor

beugen

A *tr. V.* **1** bend; bow ‹*head*›; **den Rumpf ~:** bend from the waist; **gebeugt gehen** walk with a stoop; **vom Alter/vom Kummer gebeugt** (geh.) bent *or* bowed with age *postpos.*/bowed down with grief *postpos.* **2** (geh.: brechen) **jmdn. ~:** break sb.'s resistance; **jmds. Starrsinn/Stolz ~:** break sb.'s stubborn/proud nature **3** (Sprachw.: flektieren) inflect ‹*word*›; decline ‹*noun, adjective*›; conjugate ‹*verb*›; **stark/schwach gebeugt werden** be strong/weak; have strong/weak endings; **ein stark/schwach gebeugtes Adjektiv** an adjective with strong/weak endings **4** (Rechtsw.) bend ‹*law*›; **das Recht ~:** pervert the course of justice **5** (Physik) diffract ‹*light ray etc.*›

B *refl. V.* **1** bend over; (sich bücken) stoop; **sich nach vorn/hinten ~:** bend forwards/bend over backwards; **sich aus dem Fenster ~:** lean out of the window; **sich über den Tisch/das Geländer** *usw.* **~:** lean over the table/the banisters *etc.*; **er beugte sich über ihre Hand** he bowed his head over her hand **2** (sich fügen) give way; give in; **sich dem Druck ~:** yield *or* give way to pressure; **sich der Mehrheit ~:** bow to the will of the majority

Beugung *die;* **~, ~en** **1** (das Biegen) bending; (Biegung) bend **2** (Sprachw.) inflexion; (eines Substantivs) declension; (eines Verbs) conjugation; **ein Adjektiv mit starker/schwacher ~:** an adjective with strong/weak endings *or* inflexion **3** (Rechtsw.: des Gesetzes) bending; **~ des Rechts** perversion of justice **4** (Physik) diffraction

Beugungs·endung *die* ▸ **Flexionsendung**

Beule /ˈbɔylə/ *die;* **~, ~n** **1** bump; swelling; (Furunkel) boil **2** (Vertiefung) dent (**an** + *Dat.* in); (Vorwölbung) bump; bulge

beulen *itr. V.* bulge; ‹*trousers*› be baggy

Beulen·pest *die* bubonic plague

beunruhigen /bəˈ|ʊnruːɪɡn̩/

A *tr. V.* worry; **es beunruhigte ihn sehr** it made him very worried; **über etw.** (*Akk.*) **beunruhigt sein** be worried about sth.; **bist du nicht beunruhigt darüber, dass ...?** aren't you worried that ...?

B *refl. V.* worry (**um, wegen** about)

Beunruhigung *die;* **~, ~en** worry; concern; **eine deutliche ~:** an obvious sense of concern

beurkunden /bəˈ|uːɐ̯kʊndn̩/ *tr. V.* record; (belegen) document, provide a record of

beurlauben /bəˈ|uːɐ̯laubn̩/

A *tr. V.* **1** **jmdn. [für zwei Tage] ~:** give sb. [two days'] leave of absence; **sich ~ lassen** obtain leave of absence; **beurlaubt sein** be on leave [of absence]; **Professor X ist in diesem Semester beurlaubt** Professor X is on sabbatical leave this term **2** (suspendieren) suspend

B *refl. V.* (veralt.) take one's leave

Beurlaubung *die;* **~, ~en** **1** leave of absence *no indef. art.;* **eine [einjährige] ~ beantragen** apply for [one year's] leave of absence; ‹*professor*› apply for a [one-year] sabbatical **2** (Suspendierung) suspension

beurteilen *tr. V.* judge; assess; **etw. falsch ~:** misjudge sth.; assess sth. wrongly; **sie ~ die Lage als kritisch** they judge the situation to be critical *or* see the situation as critical; **er kann doch nicht ~, was wirklich passiert ist** he cannot possibly tell *or* is in no position to say what really happened

Beurteilung *die;* **~, ~en** **1** judgement; (einer Lage usw.) assessment; **bei nüchterner ~ der Ereignisse muss man ...** if one views the events dispassionately, one has to ... **2** (Gutachten) assessment; (für eine Bewerbung) reference

Beurteilungs·maßstab *der* criterion of judgement/assessment

Beuschel /ˈbɔyʃl̩/ *das;* **~s, ~** **1** (österr., bayr.) *dish made of finely chopped lights usu. with heart and other offal* **2** (österr. salopp: Lunge) lung **3** (österr. salopp: Eingeweide) guts *pl.* (coll.)

Beute[1] /ˈbɔytə/ *die;* **~, ~n** **1** (Gestohlenes) haul; loot *no indef. art.;* (Kriegs~) booty; spoils *pl.;* **eine ~ in Millionenhöhe machen** make a haul worth millions; **fette ~ machen** get rich pickings *pl.* **2** (von Raubtieren) prey; (eines Jägers) bag; **[seine] ~ schlagen** catch one's prey; **leichte ~:** easy prey **3** (geh.: Opfer) prey (+ *Gen.* to); **eine ~ der Flammen werden** be consumed by the flames

Beute[2] *die;* **~, ~n** (Imkerspr.) hive

beute-, Beute-: ~gierig *Adj.* **1** rapacious; on the prowl *postpos.;* ravening ‹*wolf*›; **2** (auf Raub aus) greedy for loot *postpos.;* **~greifer** *der* predator

Beutel /ˈbɔytl̩/ *der;* **~s, ~** **1** bag; (kleiner, für Tabak usw.) pouch **2** (ugs.: Geld~) purse; **jmds. ~ ist leer** sb. is broke (coll.); **tief in den ~ greifen müssen** have to dig deep into one's pocket; **etw. reißt ein großes Loch in jmds. ~:** sth. makes a big hole in sb.'s pocket **3** (Zool.) pouch

beuteln

A *tr. V.* **1** (südd., österr.: schütteln) shake **2** (fig.: hart bedrängen) batter; **das Leben hat ihn gebeutelt** life has given him some hard knocks **3** (übervorteilen) **jmdn. ~:** take sb. for a ride (coll.)

B *itr. V.* bulge; ‹*trousers*› be baggy

Beutel-: ~ratte *die* opossum; **~schneider** *der,* **~schneiderin** *die* (veralt.) **1** cutpurse (arch.); (Gauner) crook; **2** (geh.: Nepper) shark; racketeer; **~tier** *das* marsupial

Beute·zug *der* thieving spree; raid

Beutler /ˈbɔytlɐ/ *der;* **~s, ~** (Zool.) marsupial

bevölkern /bəˈfœlkɐn/

A *tr. V.* populate; inhabit; (besiedeln) settle; (fig.) fill; invade; **ein stark/dünn** *od.* **wenig bevölkertes Land** a densely/thinly *or* sparsely populated country; **von Touristen bevölkert** (fig.) full of tourists

B *refl. V.* become populated; ‹*bar, restaurant, etc.*› fill up

Bevölkerung *die;* **~, ~en** **1** population; (Volk) people **2** (Besiedlung) settling

Bevölkerungs-: ~abnahme *die* decline in population; **~dichte** *die* population density; **~explosion** *die* population explosion; **~gruppe** *die* section of the population; **~schicht** *die* section *or* stratum of society; **~schwund** *der* ▸ **~abnahme; ~statistik** *die* demography *no art.;* **~zahl** *die* population; **~zunahme** *die,* **~zuwachs** *der* increase in population

bevollmächtigen /bəˈfɔlmɛçtɪɡn̩/ *tr. V.* **jmdn. [dazu] ~, etw. zu tun** authorize sb. to do sth.; (in Rechtshandlungen) give sb. power of attorney to do sth.

Bevollmächtigte *der/die; adj. Dekl.* authorized representative

Bevollmächtigung *die;* **~, ~en** authorization; (Rechtsw.) power of attorney

bevor /bəˈfoːɐ̯/ *Konj.* before; **noch ~ ich antworten konnte** before I could [even] reply; **~ du nicht unterschreibst/unterschrieben hast** until you sign/have signed

bevor·munden *tr. V.* **jmdn. ~:** impose one's will on sb.; **sie wollen sich nicht länger ~ lassen** they do not want to be dictated to any longer

Bevormundung *die;* ~, ~**en** imposing one's will (+ *Gen.* on); **wie kann sie sich diese ~ durch ihre Eltern gefallen lassen?** how can she put up with her parents telling her what to do?

bevor·raten *tr. V.* (Amtsspr.) lay in stocks of ‹*goods, materials*›; **gut bevorratet werden/sein** be kept/be well stocked *or* supplied

bevor|stehen *unr. itr. V.* be near; be about to happen; **[unmittelbar] ~:** be imminent; **jmdm. steht etw. bevor** sth. is in store for sb.; **mir steht etwas Schlimmes bevor** there's something unpleasant in store for me; **die schwerste Prüfung steht ihm noch bevor** he has still to face his severest test; his severest test is still to come

bevorstehend *Adj.* forthcoming; coming ‹*winter*›; **[unmittelbar] ~:** imminent; **die [dir/uns] ~en Probleme** the problems facing you/us

bevorzugen /bəˈfoːɐ̯tsuːɡn̩/ *tr. V.* 1▸ prefer (**vor** + *Dat.* to) 2▸ (begünstigen) favour; give preference *or* preferential treatment to (**vor** + *Dat.* over)

bevorzugt

A *Adj.* favoured; (privilegiert) privileged; preferential ‹*treatment*›

B *adv.* **jmdn. ~ behandeln** give sb. preferential treatment; **jmdn. ~ abfertigen/bedienen** give sb. priority *or* precedence/serve sb. first; **etw. ~ erledigen/bearbeiten** give sth. priority

Bevorzugung *die;* ~, ~**en** preferential treatment; preference (*Gen.*, **von** for)

bewachen *tr. V.* guard; (Ballspiele) mark; **die Gefangenen werden streng bewacht** a close watch is kept on the prisoners; the prisoners are closely guarded; **ihr Mann bewacht sie wie ein Schießhund** her husband watches over her like a guard dog; **bewachter Parkplatz** car park with an attendant

Bewacher *der;* ~**s**, ~, **Bewacherin** *die;* ~, ~**nen** guard; (Ballspiele) marker

bewachsen *unr. tr. V.* grow over; cover; **eine mit Efeu ~e Laube** a summer house overgrown with ivy; an ivy-covered summer house; **ein dicht ~es Tal/Blumenbeet** a valley full of dense vegetation/a border packed with flowers

Bewachung *die;* ~, ~**en** 1▸ guarding; (Ballspiele) marking; **zur ~ des Geländes** to guard the site; **unter scharfer ~:** closely guarded; **jmdn. unter ~ stellen** put sb. under guard; **sich der ~ entziehen** (Ballspiele) escape one's marker/markers 2▸ (Wachmannschaft) guard

bewaffnen /bəˈvafnən/

A *tr. V.* arm; **ein Heer [neu] ~:** supply an army with [new] weapons

B *refl. V.* (auch fig.) arm oneself (**mit** with)

bewaffnet *Adj.* armed; **bis an die Zähne ~:** armed to the teeth; **~er Raubüberfall/Widerstand** armed robbery/resistance; **mit Fotoapparaten ~** (fig.) armed with cameras

Bewaffnete *der/die; adj. Dekl.* armed man/woman/person; **~:** people bearing arms; armed men/women

Bewaffnung *die;* ~, ~**en** 1▸ arming 2▸ (Waffen) weapons *pl.*

bewahren *tr. V.* 1▸ **jmdn. vor etw.** (*Dat.*) **~:** protect *or* preserve sb. from sth.; **vor einer Enttäuschung bewahrt bleiben** be saved *or* spared a disappointment; **[Gott** *od.* **i] bewahre!** good Lord, no!; (Gott behüte) God forbid! 2▸ (erhalten) **seine Fassung** *od.* **Haltung ~:** keep *or* retain one's composure; **Stillschweigen/Treue ~:** remain silent/faithful; **sich** (*Dat.*) **etw. ~:** retain *or* preserve sth. 3▸ (geh.: auf~) keep; **etw. im Gedächtnis ~** (fig.) preserve the memory of sth.; **etw. im Herzen ~** (fig.) treasure sth. in one's heart

bewähren

A *refl. V.* prove oneself/itself; prove one's/its worth; **sich als [guter] Freund ~:** prove to be a [good] friend; **sich im Leben ~:** prove oneself in life; make something of one's life; **das Gerät hat sich doch noch bewährt** this gadget has turned out to be useful after all; **sich gut/schlecht ~:** prove/not prove to be worth while *or* a success; **sich am besten ~:** prove to be best; **unsere Freundschaft hat sich über all die Jahre bewährt** our friendship has stood the test of time over all these years

B *tr. V.* (veralt.) prove

bewahrheiten /bəˈvaːɐ̯haitn̩/ *refl. V.* prove to be true; **an ihm bewahrheitet sich der Spruch, dass ...** he demonstrates the truth of the saying that ...

bewährt *Adj.* proven ‹*method, design, etc.*›; well-tried, tried and tested ‹*recipe, cure*›; reliable ‹*worker*›

Bewahrung *die;* ~ 1▸ protection *no indef. art.* (**vor** + *Dat.* from) 2▸ (geh.: Auf~) keeping 3▸ (Beibehaltung) **zur ~ seines Andenkens** to preserve his memory

Bewährung *die;* ~, ~**en** 1▸ (Rechtsw.) probation; **3 Monate Gefängnis mit ~:** three months suspended sentence [with probation]; **eine Strafe zur ~ aussetzen** [conditionally] suspend a sentence on probation 2▸ (das Sichbewähren) proving; (das Testen) testing

Bewährungs-: ~auflage *die* (Rechtsw.): *obligation imposed as a condition of sentence being suspended;* **~frist** *die* (Rechtsw.) period of probation; **~helfer** *der,* **~helferin** *die* probation officer; **~hilfe** *die* (Rechtsw.) probation supervision; (Dienst) probation service; **~probe** *die* [crucial] test; trial [of one's/its worth]; **jmdn./jmds. Nerven auf eine [harte] ~probe stellen** subject sb. to a [severe] test/be a severe test of sb.'s nerves; **~strafe** *die* suspended sentence with probation; **~zeit** *die* (Rechtsw.) probation period

bewaldet /bəˈvaldət/ *Adj.* wooded

Bewaldung *die;* ~, ~**en** 1▸ tree cover; (Wälder) woodlands *pl.*; **eine spärliche ~:** a few trees *pl.* 2▸ (Aufforstung) afforestation *no indef. art.*

bewältigen /bəˈvɛltɪɡn̩/ *tr. V.* deal with; cope with; overcome ‹*difficulty, problem*›; cover ‹*distance*›; (innerlich verarbeiten) get over ‹*experience*›; **die Vergangenheit ~:** come to terms with the past

Bewältigung *die;* ~, ~**en** ▸**bewältigen**: coping with; overcoming; covering; getting over, coming to terms with; **zur ~ der Arbeit** *usw.* to deal *or* cope with the work *etc.*

bewandert /bəˈvandɐt/ *Adj.* well-versed; knowledgeable; **auf einem Gebiet/in etw.** (*Dat.*) **~ sein** be well-versed *or* well up in a subject/in sth.

Bewandtnis /bəˈvantnɪs/ *die;* ~, **~se mit etw. hat es [s]eine eigene/besondere ~:** there's a particular explanation for sth. *or* a [special] story behind sth.; **mit jmdm. hat es seine eigene/besondere ~:** there's a special story about sb.; sb. is a special case; **damit hat es folgende ~:** the story behind *or* reason for it is this

bewässern *tr. V.* irrigate; (begießen) water

Bewässerung *die;* ~, ~**en** irrigation; (das Begießen) watering

Bewässerungs-: ~an·lage *die* irrigation system; (für Grünflächen usw.) watering system; **~graben** *der* irrigation ditch; **~kanal** *der* irrigation channel; **~system** *das* irrigation system

bewegbar *Adj.* movable

bewegen[1] /bəˈveːɡn̩/

A *tr. V.* 1▸ move; **den Koffer von der Stelle ~:** move *or* shift the suitcase [from the spot]; **die Pferde/den Hund ~:** exercise the horses/the dog; **Erde ~:** shift *or* remove earth 2▸ (ergreifen) move; **eine ~de Rede** a moving speech; **niemand wusste, was ihn so bewegte** nobody knew what was affecting him so deeply 3▸ (innerlich beschäftigen) preoccupy; **das bewegt mich schon lange** I have been preoccupied with this *or* this has exercised my mind for a long time

B *refl. V.* 1▸ move; **die Blätter bewegten sich sanft** the leaves stirred gently; **der Hund bewegte sich nicht** the dog did not stir *or* was quite still 2▸ (ugs.: sich Bewegung verschaffen) **ich muss mich ein bisschen ~:** I must get some exercise; **du solltest/musst dich mehr ~:** you ought to/must take more exercise 3▸ (fig.) **seine Ausführungen ~ sich in der gleichen Richtung** his comments have the same drift *or* are on the same lines 4▸ (schwanken) vary; fluctuate; **der Preis bewegt sich zwischen 10 und 20 Euro** the price varies *or* fluctuates between 10 and 20 euros 5▸ (sich verhalten) behave; **sich mit großer Sicherheit ~:** bear oneself with great confidence

bewegen[2] *unr. tr. V.* **jmdn. dazu ~, etw. zu tun** ‹*thing*› make sb. do sth., induce sb. to do sth.; (überreden) ‹*person*› prevail upon *or* persuade sb. to do sth.; **jmdn. zu etw. ~:** talk sb. into sth.; **jmdn. zum Einlenken ~:** persuade sb. to give way

Beweg·grund *der* motive

beweglich

A *Adj.* 1▸ movable; mobile ‹*troops etc.*›; moving ‹*target*›; **die ~en Teile einer Maschine** the moving parts of a machine; **seine ~e Habe** one's goods and chattels *pl.*; one's personal effects *pl.*; **~e Feste** movable feasts; **etw. ist leicht/schwer ~:** sth. is easy/difficult to move 2▸ (rege) agile, active ‹*mind*›; (wendig) flexible ‹*policy*›; **geistig ~ sein** be nimble-minded; have an agile mind 3▸ (veralt.: rührend) moving

B *adv.* (veralt.) movingly

Beweglichkeit *die;* ~ 1▸ mobility 2▸ (Wendigkeit) agility; **taktische ~:** tactical flexibility

bewegt /bəˈveːkt/

A 2. *Part. v.* **bewegen**[1]

B *Adj.* 1▸ eventful; (unruhig) turbulent; **ein ~es Leben** an eventful/turbulent life; **sie hat eine ~e Vergangenheit** she has a colourful past 2▸ (gerührt) moved *pred.*; emotional ‹*words, voice*›; **mit tief ~en Worten/~er Stimme** in words/a voice heavy with emotion 3▸ (unruhig) **leicht/stark ~** ‹*sea*› slightly choppy/very rough

Bewegung *die;* ~, ~**en** 1▸ movement; (bes. Technik, Physik) motion; (von Erdmassen) moving; **in ~ sein** ‹*person*› be on the move; ‹*thing*› be in motion; **sie ist immer in ~:** she is never still; **jmdn. in ~ bringen/halten** get sb. moving *or* going/keep sb. on the go; **eine Maschine** *usw.* **in ~ setzen** start [up] a machine *etc.*; **sich in ~ setzen** ‹*train etc.*› start to move; ‹*procession*› move off; ‹*person*› get moving; *s. auch* **Hebel** 2▸ (körperliche ~) exercise 3▸ (Ergriffenheit) emotion; **große ~ auslösen** arouse strong emotions *pl. or* feelings *pl.* 4▸ (Bestreben, Gruppe) movement

bewegungs-, Bewegungs-: ~ablauf *der* sequence of movements; **~drang** *der* urge to be on the move; **~energie** *die* (Physik) kinetic energy; **~freiheit** *die* freedom of movement; **~krieg** *der* mobile warfare; **~los** A *Adj.* motionless; **vor Schreck ~los** paralysed with fright; B *adv.* without moving; **~los liegen/sitzen/stehen** lie/sit/stand motionless; **~losigkeit** *die;* ~~: motionlessness; immobility; **~mangel** *der* lack of exercise; **~studie** *die* time and motion study; **~therapie** *die* physical *or* exercise therapy; **~unfähig** *Adj.* unable to move *postpos.*; (gelähmt) paralysed; ‹*vehicle*› immobilized

bewehren *tr. V.* (veralt.) arm ‹*person*›; fortify ‹*castle*›

beweiden *tr. V.* (Landw.) 1▸ graze the grass in ‹*garden etc.*› 2▸ (als Weide nutzen) use ‹*meadow etc.*› as pasture

Beweidung *die;* ~ (Landw.) 1▸ grazing 2▸ (Nutzung als Weide) use as pasture

beweih·räuchern /bəˈvairɔyçɐn/ *tr. V.* surround with incense; (fig. abwertend) idolize; **sich selbst ~:** sing one's own praises; blow one's own trumpet

Beweih·räucherung *die* (fig. abwertend) idolization; adulation

beweinen *tr. V.* lament; (weinend) weep over; **jmdn./jmds. Tod ~:** mourn sb./sb.'s passing

Beweinung *die;* ~: **die ~ Christi** the mourning of Christ

Beweis /bəˈvais/ *der;* ~**es**, ~**e** proof (*Gen.*, **für** of); (Zeugnis) evidence; **belastende ~e** incriminating evidence; **einen ~/~e für etw. haben** have proof/evidence of sth.; **haben Sie einen**

~ **dafür, dass ...?** have you any proof/evidence that ...?; **als** *od.* **zum ~ seiner Aussage/Theorie** to substantiate *or* in support of his statement/theory; **bis zum ~ des Gegenteils** until there is proof/evidence to the contrary; **den ~ für etw. antreten** *od.* **erbringen** produce proof [in support] of sth.; **aus Mangel an ~en** owing to lack of evidence; **etw. unter ~ stellen** (Amtsspr.) provide proof of sth.; **sie lassen sich kaum unter ~ stellen** they are hardly susceptible of proof; **jmdm. einen ~ seines Vertrauens/seiner Hochachtung geben** give sb. a token of one's trust/esteem; **zahlreiche ~e der Anteilnahme** numerous expressions of sympathy

Beweis-: ~antrag *der* (Rechtsw.) application to produce evidence; **~aufnahme** *die* (Rechtsw.) hearing of [the] evidence

beweisbar *Adj.* provable; susceptible of proof *postpos.*; **das ist nicht ~:** it cannot be proved

beweisen

A *unr. tr. V.* **1** prove; **jmdm. seine Beteiligung an etw.** (*Dat.*) **~:** prove sb.'s participation in sth.; **dem Angeklagten konnte die Tat nicht bewiesen werden** it could not be proved that the accused committed the crime; **was [noch] zu ~ wäre** which has yet to be proved; **was zu ~ war** which was the point at issue *or* which needed clarifying **2** (zeigen) show; **damit beweist er seine mangelnde Einsicht** that shows his lack of understanding

B *unr. refl. V.* prove oneself *or* one's worth (**vor** + *Dat.* to)

beweis-, Beweis-: ~erhebung *die* ▸ **~aufnahme**; **~führung** *die* **1** (Rechtsw.) presentation of the evidence *or* case; **2** (Argumentation) reasoning; argumentation; **~gegenstand** *der* (Rechtsw.) issue; **~kraft** *die* value as evidence; (einer Argumentation) cogency; **~kräftig** *Adj.* of value as evidence *postpos.*; (Rechtsw.) of probative value *postpos.*; cogent ‹*reasoning*›; conclusive ‹*test result*›; **~last** *die* (Rechtsw.) **1** (~pflicht) burden of proof; **2** (Nachteil) *disadvantage due to one's inability to prove a fact material to one's case*; **~material** *das* evidence; (~stück) piece of evidence; **~mittel** *das* (Rechtsw.) form of evidence; **~not** *die* want of proof; lack of evidence; **sich in ~not befinden** lack evidence; be short of evidence; **~pflichtig** *Adj.* (Rechtsw.) **für etw. ~pflichtig sein** be obliged to furnish proof of sth.; **~stück** *das* piece of evidence; **~stücke [für etw.]** evidence *sing.* [of sth.]; **~umkehr** *die* (Rechtsw.) reversal of the burden of proof

bewenden *unr. V.: in* **es bei** *od.* **mit etw. ~ lassen** [have to] content oneself with sth.

Bewenden *das;* **~s damit hat es sein ~:** that is the end of the matter; **damit, dass sie entlassen wird, wird es keineswegs sein ~ haben** even if she is dismissed, the matter won't end there

bewerben

A *unr. refl. V.* apply (**um** for); **sich bei einer Firma** *usw.* **~:** apply to a company *etc.* [for a job]; **sich als Buchhalter** *usw.* **~:** apply for a job as a bookkeeper *etc.*; **die Firma bewarb sich um den Auftrag** the firm competed for the contract

B *unr. tr. V.* advertise; promote

Bewerber *der;* **~s, ~, Bewerberin** *die;* **~, ~nen** **1** applicant; (Sport: Titel~) contender **2** (veralt.: Freier) suitor; *s. auch* **-in**

Bewerbung *die* application (**um** for)

Bewerbungs-: ~bogen *der* application form; **~mappe** *die* job application portfolio; **~schreiben** *das* letter of application; **~unterlagen** *Pl.* documents in support of an/the application

bewerfen *unr. tr. V.* **1** **jmdn./etw. mit etw. ~:** throw sth. at sb./sth.; **jmdn. mit [faulen] Eiern ~:** pelt sb. with [rotten] eggs; **jmds. Namen mit Schmutz ~** (fig.) sling mud at sb. (fig.); drag sb.'s good name through the mud **2** (Bauw.) render ‹*wall*›; **mit Lehm beworfen** covered *or* faced with clay

bewerkstelligen /bəˈvɛrkʃtɛlɪgn̩/ *tr. V.* pull off, manage ‹*deal, sale, etc.*›; **es ~, etw. zu tun** contrive *or* manage to do sth.

Bewerkstelligung *die* managing

bewertbar *Adj.* assessable

bewerten *tr. V.* assess; rate; (dem Geldwert nach) value (**mit** at); (beurteilen) judge ‹*person*›; (Schulw., Sport) mark; grade (Amer.); **etw. als Heldentat ~:** rate sth. as a heroic deed; **etw. zu hoch/niedrig ~:** overrate/underrate sth.; (dem Geldwert nach) overvalue/undervalue sth.; **Arbeiten schlecht ~** (Schulw.) give work low marks *or* (Amer.) grades; **einen Aufsatz mit [der Note] „gut" ~:** mark *or* (Amer.) grade an essay 'good'; **eine Kür mit Noten zwischen 5,6 und 5,9 ~** (Eiskunstlauf, Turnen) give a programme marks between 5.6 and 5.9

Bewertung *die* **1** (das Bewerten) assessment; (des Geldwerts) valuation; (eines Menschen) judgement; (das Benoten einer Schularbeit) marking; grading (Amer.) **2** (Äußerung) assessment; (Note) mark; grade (Amer.)

Bewertungs·maß·stab *der* criterion of assessment

bewies /bəˈviːs/ *1. u. 3. Pers. Sg. Prät. v.* **beweisen**

bewiesen /bəˈviːzn̩/ *1. u. 3. Pers. Pl. Prät. u. 2. Part. v.* **beweisen**

bewiesenermaßen *Adv.* demonstrably; as can be proved

bewilligen /bəˈvɪlɪgn̩/ *tr. V.* grant; award ‹*salary, grant*›; (im Parlament usw.) approve ‹*sum, tax increase, etc.*›; **jmdm. eine Stundung/zwei Mitarbeiter** *usw.* **~:** allow sb. deferment/two assistants *etc.*

Bewilligung *die;* **~, ~en** granting; (Zustimmung) approval; (eines Gehalts, Stipendiums) award

bewimpert /bəˈvɪmpɐt/ *Adj.* lashed; (Zool.) ciliate

bewirken *tr. V.* bring about; cause; **~, dass etw. geschieht** cause sth. to happen; **damit/dadurch hast du nur bewirkt, dass ...** all you have achieved by this *or* the only effect of this is that ...; **nichts/das Gegenteil bei jmdm. ~:** have *or* produce no effect/the opposite effect on sb.; **durch gutes Zureden bewirkt man bei ihm nichts** you don't get anywhere with him by talking to him nicely

bewirten /bəˈvɪrtn̩/ *tr. V.* feed; **jmdn. mit etw. ~:** serve sth. to sb.; serve sb. sth.

bewirtschaften *tr. V.* **1** run, manage ‹*estate, farm, restaurant, business, etc.*› **2** (bestellen) farm ‹*fields, land*›; cultivate ‹*field*› **3** (staatlich lenken) ration; **den Wohnraum ~:** make living accommodation subject to government control; **Devisen ~:** operate currency controls

Bewirtschaftung *die;* **~, ~en** **1** running; management **2** (Bestellung) farming; cultivation **3** (staatliche Lenkung) government control

Bewirtung *die;* **~, ~en** provision of food and drink; (Gastfreundschaft) hospitality; **die ~ der Gäste** catering for the guests

bewitzeln *tr. V.* joke about; poke fun at

bewog /bəˈvoːk/ *1. u. 3. Pers. Sg. Prät. v.* **bewegen**[2]

bewogen *2. Part. v.* **bewegen**[2]

bewohnbar *Adj.* habitable

Bewohnbarkeit *die;* **~:** suitability *or* fitness for habitation

bewohnen *tr. V.* inhabit, live in ‹*house, area*›; live in ‹*room, flat*›; live on ‹*4th storey etc.*›; ‹*animal, plant*› be found in

Bewohner *der;* **~s, ~, Bewohnerin** *die;* **~, ~nen** (eines Hauses, einer Wohnung) occupant; (einer Stadt, eines Gebietes) inhabitant; **ein ~ der Steppe** (Mensch) a steppe-dweller; (Tier, Pflanze) a native of the steppes; **ein ~ des Waldes** a forest-dweller; (Tier) a woodland creature

Bewohner·parken *das;* **~s** ▸ **Anwohnerparken**

Bewohnerschaft *die;* **~, ~en** inhabitants *pl.*; (eines Wohnblocks) occupants *pl.*

bewohnt *Adj.* occupied ‹*house etc.*›; inhabited ‹*area*›; **ist das Haus noch ~?** is the house still lived in *or* occupied?

bewölken /bəˈvœlkn̩/ *refl. V.* cloud over; become overcast; **seine Stirn bewölkte sich** (fig.) his face darkened

bewölkt *Adj.* cloudy; overcast; **dicht** *od.* **stark ~:** heavily overcast; **der Himmel ist nur leicht ~:** there is only a light cloud cover

Bewölkung *die;* **~, ~en** **1** clouding over **2** (Wolkendecke) cloud [cover]; **wechselnde ~:** variable amounts *pl.* of cloud

Bewölkungs-: ~auf·lockerung *die* breaking up of the cloud cover; **~zunahme** *die* increase in the cloud cover

Bewuchs *der* plant cover; vegetation *no indef. art.*

Bewunderer *der;* **~s, ~, Bewunderin** *die;* **~, ~nen** admirer

bewundern *tr. V.* admire (**wegen, für** for); **ich kann sie nur ~:** I really admire her

bewunderns-: ~wert, ~würdig **A** *Adj.* admirable; worthy of admiration *postpos.*; **B** *adv.* admirably; in an admirable fashion

Bewunderung *die;* **~, ~en** admiration

bewunderungs·würdig ▸ **bewundernswert**

Bewurf *der* (Bauw.) rendering

bewusst, *bewußt /bəˈvʊst/

A *Adj.* **1** (im Bewusstsein vorhanden) conscious ‹*reaction, behaviour, etc.*›; (absichtlich) deliberate ‹*lie, deception, attack, etc.*›; **~e Ablehnung** conscious *or* deliberate rejection; **ein ~er Sozialist** a convinced socialist; **etw. ist/wird jmdm. ~:** sb. is/becomes aware of sth.; sb. realizes sth.; **mir war nicht recht ~, was ich tat** I was not really conscious of what I was doing; **jmdm. etw. ~ machen** make sb. realize sth.; **sich** (*Dat.*) **etw. ~ machen** realize sth. **2** (klar erkennend) **ein ~er Mensch** a thinking person; **sich** (*Dat.*) **einer Sache** (*Gen.*) **~ sein/werden** be/become aware *or* conscious of something **3** (bekannt) particular; (fraglich) in question *postpos.*

B *adv.* **1** (absichtlich) deliberately **2** (klar erkennend) consciously; **~er leben** live with greater awareness

Bewusstheit, *Bewußtheit *die;* **~:** deliberateness

bewusst·los, *bewußt·los *Adj.* unconscious; **~ zusammenbrechen** collapse unconscious; **der/die Bewusstlose** the unconscious man/woman

Bewusstlosigkeit, *Bewußtlosigkeit *die;* **~:** unconsciousness; **aus der ~ erwachen** regain consciousness; **bis zur ~** (ugs.) ad nauseam

***bewußt|machen** ▸ **bewusst A 1**

Bewusst·sein, *Bewußt·sein *das* **1** (deutliches Wissen) awareness; **im ~ seiner Kraft** [secure] in the knowledge *or* awareness of one's strength; **im ~, seine Pflicht getan zu haben** conscious of having done one's duty; **sich** (*Dat.*) **etw. ins ~ rufen** remember *or* recall sth.; **jmdm. etw. ins ~ bringen** remind sb. of sth.; **gewisse Themen in das allgemeine ~ bringen** make the general public aware of certain issues; bring certain issues to the notice of the general public; **etw. mit ~ erleben** be fully aware of sth. [one is experiencing]; **jmdm. zu[m] ~ kommen** become clear to sb.; **jetzt erst kam ihr zu ~, dass ...** only now did she realize that ... **2** (Psych., Politik, Philos. usw.) consciousness; **ein historisches ~:** a consciousness *or* awareness of history **3** (geistige Klarheit) consciousness; **das ~ verlieren** lose consciousness; **wieder zu ~ kommen, das ~ wieder erlangen** regain consciousness; **bei vollem ~ sein** be fully conscious; **bei vollem ~ operiert werden** be operated on while fully conscious

bewusstseins-, *bewußtseins-, Bewusstseins-, *Bewußtseins-: ~bildung *die* creation of [greater] awareness; **eine politische ~bildung** the creation of political consciousness *or* awareness; **~erweiternd** **A** *Adj.* mind-expanding; psychedelic; **B** *adv.* **~erweiternd wirken** have a mind-expanding effect; **~erweiterung** *die* expansion of consciousness; **~spaltung** *die*

(Med., Psych.) split consciousness; schizophrenia; **~störung** *die* disturbance of consciousness; **~trübung** *die* clouding *or* dimming of consciousness; **~verändernd** **A** *Adj.* mind-bending ‹*drug*›; **dieses Erlebnis war ~verändernd** this experience changed sb.'s outlook; **B** *adv.* **auf jmdn. ~verändernd wirken** change sb.'s awareness; **~veränderung** *die* change of awareness *or* outlook

Bewusstwerdung, ***Bewußtwerdung** *die;* **~:** development of awareness

bez. *Abk.* **= bezahlt** pd.

bezahlbar *Adj.* affordable; (wirtschaftlich vernünftig) economic; **diese Miete ist für ihn kaum ~:** he can hardly afford this rent

bezahlen ▸ⓘ **S. 299**
A *tr. V.* pay ‹*person, bill, taxes, rent, amount*›; pay for ‹*goods etc.*›; **etw. [in] bar ~:** pay [in] cash for sth.; **etw. mit [einem] Scheck ~:** pay for sth. by cheque; **jmdm. etw. ~:** pay for sth. for sb.; **bekommst du das Essen bezahlt?** do you get your meals paid for?; **[jmdm.] für etw. 10 Euro ~:** pay [sb.] 10 euros for sth.; **bezahlter Urlaub** paid leave; holiday[s] with pay; **er musste seinen Leichtsinn teuer ~** (fig.) he had to pay dearly for his carelessness; **das macht sich bezahlt** it pays off; **als ob ers bezahlt bekäme** *od.* **kriegte** (ugs.) for all he's worth (coll.); like a mad thing; **gut/schlecht bezahlt** well-paid/badly *or* poorly paid; **hoch ~:** highly paid
B *itr. V.* pay; **Herr Ober, ich möchte ~** *od.* **bitte ~:** waiter, the bill *or* (Amer.) check please; **heute bezahle ich** it's on me today (coll.)

Bezahlung *die* payment; (Lohn, Gehalt) pay; **die ~ der Waren** the payment for the goods; **gegen ~ arbeiten** work for payment *or* money

bezähmen
A *tr. V.* **1** contain, control ‹*wrath, curiosity, impatience*›; restrain ‹*desire*› **2** (veralt.: zähmen) tame
B *refl. V.* restrain oneself

bezaubern
A *tr. V.* enchant; **von etw. bezaubert** enchanted with *or* by sth.
B *itr. V.* enchant; be enchanting

bezaubernd
A *Adj.* enchanting; **es war ~ von euch, das Fest zu geben** it was wonderfully kind of you to give the party
B *adv.* enchantingly

bezecht /bəˈt͜sɛçt/ *Adj.* drunken *attrib.*; drunk *pred.*

bezeichnen *tr. V.* **1** **jmdn./sich/etw. als etw. ~:** call sb./oneself/sth. sth.; describe sb./oneself/sth. as sth.; **das muss man schon als anmaßend ~:** that can only be described as arrogant; **wie bezeichnet man das?** what is it called?; **mit dem Wort bezeichnet man eine Art Jacke** this word is used to denote *or* describe a kind of jacket; **jmdn. als Halunken** *od.* **mit dem Wort Halunke ~:** describe sb. as a scoundrel; call sb. a scoundrel; **jmdn. als Feigling ~:** call sb. a coward; **etw. als Verrat ~:** call sth. treachery; **so kann man das auch ~:** that's one way of describing it **2** (Name sein für) denote **3** (markieren) mark; (durch Zeichen angeben) indicate

bezeichnend *Adj.* characteristic, typical (*für* of); (bedeutsam) significant; **das ist ~ für ihn** that is typical *or* characteristic of him

bezeichnender·weise *Adv.* characteristically; typically; (als Zeichen dafür) significantly

Bezeichnung *die* **1** marking; (Angabe durch Zeichen) indication **2** (Name) name; **mir fällt die richtige ~ dafür nicht ein** I can't think of the right word for it/them

bezeigen (geh.)
A *tr. V.* show; give proof of ‹*courage*›; **jmdm. Ehrfurcht** *od.* **Respekt ~:** show sb. respect
B *refl. V.* **sich dankbar/erkenntlich ~:** show one's gratitude/appreciation

bezeugen *tr. V.* **1** testify to; **er/sie bezeugte, dass ...** he/she testified that ...; **der Ort ist schon im 8. Jh. [dokumentarisch] bezeugt** [the existence of] this place is documented as early as the 8th century **2** (bezeigen) show; **jmdm. sein Wohlwollen ~:** give sb. proof of one's goodwill

Bezeugung *die* **1** attestation; (das Bezeugen) testifying (*Gen.* to) **2** (das Bezeigen) showing; demonstration

bezichtigen /bəˈt͜sɪçtɪgn̩/ *tr. V.* accuse; **jmdn. des Verrats ~:** accuse sb. of treachery; **jmdn. ~, etw. getan zu haben** *od.* **er/sie habe etw. getan** accuse sb. of having done sth.

Bezichtigung *die;* **~, ~en** accusation

beziehbar *Adj.* **1** ready for occupation *postpos.* **2** (anwendbar) applicable (**auf** + *Akk.* to)

beziehen
A *unr. tr. V.* **1** cover, put a cover/covers on ‹*seat, cushion, umbrella, etc.*›; **die Betten frisch ~:** put clean sheets on the beds; **einen Schirm neu ~:** re-cover an umbrella; **das Sofa ist mit Leder bezogen** the sofa is upholstered in leather **2** (einziehen in) move into ‹*house, office*› **3** (Milit.) take up ‹*position, post*›; **einen klaren Standpunkt ~** (fig.) adopt a clear position; take a definite stand; *s. auch* **Stellung** **4** (regelmäßig erhalten) receive, obtain [one's supply of] ‹*goods*›; take ‹*newspaper*›; draw, receive ‹*pension, salary*›; **Prügel ~** (ugs.) get a hiding (coll.) **5** (in Beziehung setzen) apply (**auf** + *Akk.* to); **etw. auf sich ~:** take sth. personally; **seine Kritik auf etw.** (*Akk.*) **~:** direct one's criticism at sth.
B *unr. refl. V.* **1** **es/der Himmel bezieht sich** it/the sky is clouding over *or* becoming overcast **2** **sich auf jmdn./etw. ~** (sich berufen auf) ‹*person, letter, etc.*› refer to sb./sth.; (betreffen) ‹*question, statement, etc.*› relate to sb./sth.; **wir ~ uns auf Ihr Schreiben vom 28. 8./unser Telefongespräch** with reference to your letter of 28 August/our telephone conversation; **diese Kritik bezieht sich nicht auf dich** this criticism is not aimed at you

Bezieher *der;* **~s, ~, Bezieherin** *die;* **~, ~nen** (einer Zeitung) reader; subscriber (*Gen.*, **von** to); (einer Rente, eines Gehalts) recipient; *s. auch* **-in**

Beziehung *die* **1** (Verbindung) relations *pl.* (**zu** with); **gute ~en** *od.* **eine gute ~ zu jmdm./einer Firma haben** have good relations with sb./a firm; be on good terms with sb./a firm; **intime ~en zu jmdm. haben** have intimate relations with sb.; **diplomatische ~en aufnehmen/unterhalten/abbrechen** establish/maintain/break off diplomatic relations **2** *Pl.* (Verbindungen, die Vorteile verschaffen) connections (**zu** with); **etw. durch ~en bekommen** get sth. through connections; **seine ~en spielen lassen** pull some strings **3** (Verhältnis) relationship (**zwischen** between, **zu** with); (Verständnis) affinity (**zu** for); **zu jmdm. keine ~ haben** be unable to relate to sb.; **er hat keine ~ zur Kunst** he has a blind spot where the arts are concerned; the arts are a closed book to him **4** (Zusammenhang) connection (**zu** with); **zwischen A und B besteht keine/eine ~:** there is no/a connection between A and B; **A zu B in ~ setzen** relate A to B; see A in relation to B; **A und B in ~ zueinander setzen** relate A and B to each other; connect *or* link A and B; **das steht in keiner ~ dazu** that is not connected with *or* related to it; **in dieser/jeder ~:** in this/every respect; **in mancher ~:** in many respects; **mit ~ auf etw.** (*Akk.*) with reference to sth.

beziehungs-, Beziehungs-: ~kiste *die* (ugs.) relationship; **~los** **A** *Adj.* unconnected; unrelated; **B** *adv.* without any connection; **~reich** *Adj.* evocative; rich in associations *postpos.*; (vielseitig) many-faceted; **~weise** *Konj.* **1** (oder vielmehr) that is; or to be precise; **2** (und im anderen Fall) and ... respectively; (oder) or; **die beiden Münzen waren aus Kupfer ~weise aus Nickel** the two coins were made of copper and of nickel respectively; **sie sind in Schwarz ~weise in Weiß lieferbar** they are available in black or in white

beziffern /bəˈt͜sɪfɐn/
A *tr. V.* **1** (nummerieren) number; **bezifferter Bass** (Musik) figured bass **2** (angeben) estimate (**auf** + *Akk.* at); **den Schaden auf 3 000 Euro ~:** estimate the damage at 3,000 euros
B *refl. V.* **sich auf 10 Millionen** (*Akk.*) **Euro ~:** come *or* amount to 10 million euros

Bezifferung *die;* **~, ~en** **1** numbering **2** (Zahlen) numbers *pl.*

Bezirk /bəˈt͜sɪrk/ *der;* **~[e]s, ~e** **1** district; **Vertreter für den ~ Südhessen** representative for the South Hessen area **2** (Verwaltungs~) [administrative] district; (DDR) [administrative] area; (in West-Berlin) borough **3** (DDR: Behörde) local *or* area authority; **auf dem ~:** at the local *or* area authority offices *pl.*

bezirklich *Adj.* district *attrib.*; (DDR) area *attrib.*

Bezirks-: ~amt *das* district *or* (DDR) area authority; **~bürger·meister** *der*, **~bürger·meisterin** *die* Borough Mayor (in Berlin); **~gericht** *das* district *or* (DDR) area court; **~hauptfrau** *die*, **~hauptmann** *der; Pl.* **~hauptleute** (österr.) *chief officer of an administrative district;* **~hauptmannschaft** *die* (österr.) district authority; **auf der ~hauptmannschaft** at the district authority offices; **~klasse** *die* (Sport) district *or* (DDR) area league; **~leiter** *der*, **~leiterin** *die* **1** (DDR) head of the area administration; **2** (Kaufmannsspr.) area manager; **~regierung** *die* (BRD) district authority; **~stadt** *die* (DDR) chief town of the area; area capital; **~tag** *der* (DDR) area assembly; **~verordneten·versammlung** *die* borough assembly (in Berlin)

bezirzen /bəˈt͜sɪrt͜sn̩/ ▸ **becircen**

bezog /bəˈt͜soːk/ *1. u. 3. Pers. Sg. Prät. v.* **beziehen**

bezogen
A *2. Part. v.* **beziehen**
B *Adj.* **~ auf jmdn./etw.** [seen] in relation to sb./sth.

-bezogen *Adj.* -related

Bezogene *der/die; adj. Dekl.* drawee (*of cheque*)

***bezug** ▸ **Bezug 4**

Bezug *der* **1** (für Kissen usw.) cover; (für Polstermöbel) loose cover; slip cover (Amer.); (für Betten) duvet cover; (für Kopfkissen) pillowcase **2** (Erwerb) obtaining; (Kauf) purchase; **~ einer Zeitung** taking a newspaper; **bei ~ von mehr als 100 Stück** if more than 100 are ordered **3** *Pl.* (österr. auch Sg.) (Gehalt) salary *sing.*; **die Bezüge der Beamten** the salaries of the civil servants **4** (Verbindung) connection, link (**zu** with); **der Film vermeidet jeden ~ zur Gegenwart** this film avoids all allusion to the present; **mit** *od.* **unter ~ auf etw.** (*Akk.*) (Amtsspr., Kaufmannsspr.) with reference to sth.; **in ~ auf jmdn./etw.** concerning *or* regarding sb./sth.; **auf etw.** (*Akk.*) **~ nehmen** (Amtsspr., Kaufmannspr.) refer to sth.; **~ nehmend auf unser Telex** with reference to our telex

Bezüger /bəˈt͜syːgɐ/ *der;* **~s, ~, Bezügerin** *die;* **~, ~nen** (schweiz.) **1** ▸ **Bezieher** **2** (von Steuern) collector

bezüglich /bəˈt͜syːklɪç/
A *Präp. mit Gen.* concerning; regarding
B *Adj.* **auf etw.** (*Akk.*) **~:** relating to sth.; **die darauf ~en Paragraphen** the relevant paragraphs; **~es Fürwort** (Sprachw.) relative pronoun

Bezugnahme /bəˈt͜suːknaːmə/ *die;* **~, ~n** (Amtsspr.) reference; **unter ~ auf etw.** (*Akk.*) with reference to sth.

bezugs-, Bezugs-: ~aktie *die* (Wirtsch.) new share; **~berechtigt** *Adj.* entitled to receive goods/payment *postpos.*; **~berechtigt sind folgende** the following are entitled to benefit; **~fertig** *Adj.* ready to move into *pred.*; **eine ~fertige Wohnung** a flat (esp. Brit.) *or* (esp. Amer.) apartment that is ready to move into; **~person** *die* (Psych., Soziol.) **jedes Kind braucht eine ~person** every child needs someone it can relate to and take as an example; **~preis** *der* [subscription] price; **~punkt** *der* point of reference; **~quelle** *die* source of supply; (Firma) supplier; **~recht** *das* (Wirtsch.) preemptive *or* subscription right; **~satz** *der* (Sprachw.) relative clause; **~schein** *der* [ration] coupon; **auf ~schein** on coupons *pl.*; **~system** *das* **1** (Koordinatensystem) reference frame; **2** (System des Denkens usw.) terms *pl.* of reference

bezuschussen /bəˈtsuːʃʊsn̩/ *tr. V.* (Amtsspr.) subsidize

Bezuschussung *die;* ~, ~en [1] subsidization [2] (Betrag) subsidy

bezwecken /bəˈtsvɛkn̩/ *tr. V.* aim to achieve; aim at; **was willst du damit ~?** what do you expect to achieve by [doing] that?; **was soll das ~?** what is the point of that?; what is that supposed to achieve?

bezweifeln *tr. V.* doubt; question; **sie bezweifelt, dass** *od.* **ob ...** she doubts whether ...; **ich bezweifle nicht, dass ...** I do not doubt that ...; **das ist nicht zu ~:** there is no doubt about that; **das möchte ich doch ~:** I have my doubts about that

bezwingbar *Adj.* [1] (zu besiegen) conquerable; (fig.) controllable; **er/sie/es ist ~:** he/she/it can be beaten *or* overcome [2] (zu bewältigen) manageable; negotiable ‹*course, slope*›

bezwingen
[A] *unr. tr. V.* conquer ‹*enemy, mountain, pain, etc.*›; defeat ‹*opponent*›; take, capture ‹*fortress*›; master ‹*pain, hunger*›; **seinen Zorn/seine Neugier ~:** keep one's anger/curiosity under control; **er konnte diese Piste/diesen Pass nicht ~:** he was unable to negotiate this course/pass
[B] *unr. refl. V.* control *or* restrain oneself

bezwingend *Adj.* compelling; irresistible ‹*smile*›

Bezwinger *der,* **Bezwingerin** *die;* ~, ~nen conqueror

Bezwingung *die;* ~, ~en [1] defeat; (Sieg) victory (+ *Gen.* over); (fig.) control [2] (Bewältigung) conquest

BfA *Abk.* = **Bundesversicherungsanstalt für Angestellte**

BGB *Abk.* = **Bürgerliches Gesetzbuch**

BGH *Abk.* = **Bundesgerichtshof**

BGS *Abk.* = **Bundesgrenzschutz**

BH /beːˈhaː/ *der;* ~[s], ~[s] *Abk.* = **Büstenhalter** bra

bi /biː/ *indekl. Adj.* (salopp) bi (sl.)

Biathlon /ˈbiːatlɔn/ *das;* ~s, ~s (Sport) biathlon

bibbern /ˈbɪbɐn/ *itr. V.* (ugs.) (vor Kälte) shiver (**vor** with); (vor Angst) shake, tremble (**vor** with); **um jmdn./etw. ~:** fear *or* tremble for sb./sth.

Bibel /ˈbiːbl̩/ *die;* ~, ~n (auch fig.) Bible

bibel-, Bibel-: **~fest** *Adj.* well versed in the Bible *postpos.*; who knows his/her *etc.* Bible *postpos., not pred.*; **du bist ziemlich ~fest** you know your Bible pretty well; **~forscher** *der,* **~forscherin** *die* (veralt.) Jehovah's Witness; **~spruch** *der* biblical saying; **~stunde** *die: Bible reading with discussion and prayer;* **~vers** *der* verse from the Bible; **~wort** *das; Pl.* ~~e biblical saying

Biber[1] /ˈbiːbɐ/ *der;* ~s, ~: beaver; **Mantel aus ~:** beaver coat

Biber[2] *der od. das;* ~s (Stoff) flannelette

Biber-: **~geil** *das;* ~[e]s castor; **~pelz** *der* beaver [fur]; (einzelner Pelz) beaver pelt; **ein Mantel** *usw.* **aus ~pelz** a beaver coat *etc.*; **~schwanz** [1] beaver's tail; [2] (Ziegel) plain *or* plane tile (*with curved lower edge*)

Bibliograph /biblioˈgraːf/ *der;* ~en, ~en ▸ⓘ S. 113 bibliographer

Bibliographie *die;* ~, ~n bibliography

bibliographieren *tr. V.* [1] **Bücher/Titel ~:** list books/titles in a bibliography [2] (Daten feststellen) establish the bibliographical details of ‹*book, essay*›; identify ‹*book*›; identify the source of ‹*essay etc.*›

Bibliographin *die;* ~, ~nen ▸ⓘ S. 113 ▸**Bibliograph**

bibliographisch
[A] *Adj.* bibliographical
[B] *adv.* bibliographically; as a bibliography

biblioman /biblioˈmaːn/ *Adj.* bibliomaniac

Bibliomane /biblioˈmaːnə/ *der;* ~n, ~n bibliomaniac

Bibliomanie *die;* ~: bibliomania

Bibliomanin *die;* ~, ~nen ▸**Bibliomane**

bibliophil /biblioˈfiːl/ *Adj.* [1] bibliophilic ‹*interests etc.*›; bibliophile ‹*collector*› [2] (wertvoll) for the bibliophile *postpos.*; **~e Ausgabe** collector's edition

Bibliophile *der/die; adj. Dekl.* bibliophile; book lover

Bibliophilie *die;* ~: bibliophily (formal); love of books

Bibliothek /biblioˈteːk/ *die;* ~, ~en library; **bei** *od.* **an einer ~ angestellt sein** have a job in a library

Bibliothekar /biblioteˈkaːɐ̯/ *der;* ~s, ~e, **Bibliothekarin** *die;* ~, ~nen ▸ⓘ S. 113 librarian

Bibliotheks-: **~benutzer** *der,* **~benutzerin** *die* library user; **„die ~benutzer werden gebeten, ..."** 'readers are requested ...'; **~katalog** *der* library catalogue; **~wesen** *das* library system

biblisch /ˈbiːblɪʃ/ *Adj.* biblical; **ein ~es Alter** a grand old age

Bick·beere /ˈbɪk-/ *die* (nordd.) ▸**Heidelbeere**

Bidet /biˈdeː/ *das;* ~s, ~s bidet

bieder /ˈbiːdɐ/
[A] *Adj.* [1] unsophisticated; (langweilig) stolid; (treuherzig) trusting [2] (veralt.: rechtschaffen) upright
[B] *adv.* in an unsophisticated manner; **etw. brav und ~ ausführen** carry sth. out faithfully and unquestioningly

Biederkeit *die;* ~ [1] (Rechtschaffenheit) [bourgeois] probity; [stolid] uprightness [2] (Rückständigkeit) conventional attitudes *pl.*; (Einfältigkeit) lack of sophistication

Bieder·mann *der* [1] (veralt.) man of integrity *or* probity [2] (Spießer) petty bourgeois

biedermännisch /ˈbiːdɐmɛnɪʃ/ *Adj.* [1] (veralt.) stolidly upright [2] (spießig) stuffily correct; petty bourgeois

Biedermeier *das;* ~s Biedermeier [period/style]

Biedermeier-: **~stil** *der* Biedermeier style; **~sträußchen** *das: small bouquet wrapped in white lace-paper;* **~zeit** *die* Biedermeier period

Bieder·sinn *der* (geh.) [stolid] uprightness; moral rectitude

biegbar *Adj.* flexible; pliable ‹*material*›; **leicht ~:** easily bent

Biege /ˈbiːgə/ *die;* ~, ~n bend; **eine ~ drehen** (salopp) stretch one's legs; **eine ~ fahren/fliegen** (salopp) go for a spin [in the car/aircraft]

biegen /ˈbiːgn̩/
[A] *unr. tr. V.* [1] bend; incline ‹*head*›; **das Recht ~** (fig. veralt.) bend the law; **mit gebogenem Rücken sitzen** sit with one's back hunched [2] (österr., Sprachw.) ▸**beugen A 3**
[B] *unr. refl. V.* bend; (nachgeben) give; sag; **der Tisch bog sich unter der Last der Speisen** the table sagged *or* groaned under the weight of the food; **sich vor Lachen ~** (ugs.) double up with laughter; **ihre Augenbrauen ~/ihre Nase biegt sich nach oben** her eyebrows curve upward/her nose is turned up
[C] *unr. itr. V.; mit sein* [1] turn; **um die Ecke ~:** turn the corner; ‹*car*› take the corner [2] **auf Biegen oder** *od.* **und Brechen** (ugs.) at all costs; by hook or by crook; **es geht auf Biegen oder** *od.* **und Brechen** (ugs.) it has come to the crunch *or* (Amer.) showdown

biegsam *Adj.* flexible; pliable ‹*material*›; supple ‹*joints, person*›; **ein ~er Charakter** (fig.) a malleable personality

Biegsamkeit *die;* ~ ▸**biegsam**: flexibility; pliability; suppleness; (fig.) malleability

Biegung *die;* ~, ~en [1] bend; **eine [enge] ~ nach rechts machen** bend [sharply] to the right [2] (österr. Sprachw.) ▸**Beugung 2**

Biene /ˈbiːnə/ *die;* ~, ~n [1] bee [2] (ugs. veralt.: Mädchen) bird (Brit. sl.); dame (Amer. sl.); **eine flotte ~:** a smashing bird (Brit. sl.); a luscious piece (sl.)

Bienen-: **~fleiß** *der* unflagging industry; **mit wahrem ~fleiß ging er daran** he set about it industriously; **~haus** *das* apiary; **~honig** *der* bees' honey; **~kasten** *der* beehive; (as tech. term) frame hive; **~königin** *die* queen bee; **~korb** *der* straw hive; **~schwarm** *der* swarm of bees; **~sprache** *die* language of bees; **~staat** *der* bee colony; **~stich** *der* [1] bee sting; [2] (Kuchen) *cake with a topping of sugar and almonds (and sometimes a cream filling);* **~stock** *der* beehive; **~wachs** *das* beeswax; **~zucht** *die* bee-keeping; **~züchter** *der,* **~züchterin** *die* bee-keeper

Biennale /bieˈnaːlə/ *die;* ~, ~n biennial

Bier /biːɐ̯/ *das;* ~[e]s, (Sorten:) ~e beer; **ein kleines/großes ~:** a small/large [glass of] beer; **zwei ~:** two beers; two glasses of beer; **10 verschiedene ~e** ten different beers *or* types of beer; **das ist [nicht] mein ~** (ugs.) that is [not] my affair *or* business; **etw. wie sauer** *od.* **saures ~ anpreisen** praise sth. to the skies in an effort to get rid of it/them

> **Bier**
>
> Germany and Austria rank among the world's top beer consumers, with a vast range of beer varieties (*Bock, Alt, Dunkel, Export, Hell, Kölsch, Lager, Malzbier, Pils, Märzen, Weizenbier* or *Weißbier*, and *Berliner Weiße*) to choose from. Germans brew more than 5000 varieties, and each beer tastes different depending on the ratio of ingredients, brewing temperature and technique, alcoholic content, ageing time, and colour. Although there are now some big brewing conglomerates, the local brew from small independent breweries (there are about 1300 in Germany) is still the best and most popular. German beer is brewed according to the *Reinheitsgebot* (beer purity regulations) of 1516, which stipulates that no ingredients other than hops, malted barley, yeast and water can be used. Dortmund and Munich are among the top beer-producing cities in the world. Drinking beer is a vital part of everyday life for many people; they regularly meet up at their **Stammtisch** in a *Kneipe* (pub) or in a **Biergarten**.

Bier-: **~bar** *die* beer bar; **~bauch** *der* (ugs. spött.) beer belly; **~brauer** *der* [beer] brewer; **~brauerei** *die* [1] **die ~brauerei** the brewing of beer; brewing beer; [2] (Betrieb) brewery; **~brauerin** *die* ▸**~brauer**

Bierchen *das;* ~s, ~ (ugs.) [1] (gute Sorte) **so ein ~:** such a beer; a beer like that; **das ist ein ~!** that's quite some beer! (Brit.); great beer! (Amer.) [2] (Glas Bier) little [glass of] beer

bier-, Bier-: **~deckel** *der* beer mat; **~dose** *die* beer can; **~durst** *der:* **[schrecklichen] ~durst haben** be [badly] in need of a beer; **~ernst** (ugs.) [A] *Adj.* deadly serious; solemn; [B] *adv.* solemnly; **so ~ernst** with such deadly seriousness; **~ernst** *der* deadly seriousness; **~fass**, *~faß *das* beer barrel; **~filz** *der* beer mat; **~flasche** *die* beer bottle; (voll) bottle of beer; **~garten** *der* beer garden; **~glas** *das* beer glass; **~kasten** *der* beer crate; **~keller** *der* beer cellar; **~kneipe** *die* ≈ pub (Brit.); beerhouse (Amer.); **~krug** *der* beer mug; (aus Glas, Zinn) tankard; **~kutscher** *der,* **~kutscherin** *die* (ugs.) brewery delivery driver; **~laune** *die* (ugs.) **in einer ~laune, aus einer ~laune heraus** in an exuberant mood; **~leiche** *die* (ugs. scherzh.) drunk lying dead to the world; **~lokal** *das* pub (Brit.); beerhouse (Amer.); **~ruhe** *die* (ugs.) unruffled calm; unflappability (coll.); **~schinken** *der: slicing sausage containing pieces of ham;* **~schwemme** *die* beer hall; **~seidel** *das* beer mug; (aus Glas, Zinn) tankard; **~selig** (scherzh.) [A] *Adj.* beery ‹*mood*›; **~selig, wie er war** in his beerily happy state; [B] *adv.* in a beerily happy state; ‹*laugh*› in beery merriment; **~stube** *die* ≈ small pub (Brit.); beer bar (Amer.); **~suppe** *die: soup containing beer, sugar, and eggs or rye bread;* **~tisch** *der:* **am ~tisch** over a glass of beer; in the pub (Brit.) *or* (Amer.) bar; **~trinker** *der,* **~trinkerin** *die* beer drinker; **~verlag** *der,* **~vertrieb** *der* beer wholesaler's; **~wärmer** *der;* ~~s, ~~: beer warmer; **~wurst** *die: smoked slicing sausage containing beef, pork, bacon, and spices;* **~zeitung** *die* joke newspaper (*made up for a closed group*); **~zelt** *das* beer tent; **~zipfel** *der: tag worn* by member of a student corporation, bearing its colours

Biergarten

A rustic open-air pub, or beer garden, which is traditional in Bavaria and Austria but can now be found throughout Germany. It is usually set up for the summer in the yard of a pub or restaurant and serves beer and simple meals. In Munich beer gardens the drink comes in a litre-sized glass, called a *Maß*. The standard everyday pale beer most people order is a *Helles*, a dark beer is a *Dunkles*, and a wheat beer is a *Weißbier*.

Biese /'bi:zə/ *die;* ~, ~**n** 1 (bes. Milit.) trouser stripe; (Paspel) piping 2 (Fältchen) tuck

Biest /bi:st/ *das;* ~**[e]s,** ~**er** (ugs. abwertend) 1 (Tier, Gegenstand) wretched thing; (Bestie) creature; **ein riesiges ~ von einem Elefanten** a huge elephant 2 (Mensch) beast (derog.); wretch; **das freche ~:** the cheeky devil (coll.)

Biesterei *die;* ~, ~**en** (ugs. abwertend) (Gemeinheit) beastly trick (coll.); (etw. Ärgerliches) blasted nuisance (coll.)

biestig (ugs. abwertend)
A *Adj.* 1 beastly (coll.) (**zu** to); **ganz schön ~ werden** turn really nasty 2 (unangenehm) filthy, beastly (coll.) ‹weather›; frightful (coll.) ‹cold›
B *adv.* 1 (gemein) nastily; in a beastly way (coll.) 2 (sehr) horribly (coll.)

Biet /bi:t/ *das;* ~**[e]s,** ~**e** (schweiz.) area

bieten /'bi:tn̩/
A *unr. tr. V.* 1 offer; put on ‹*programme etc.*›; provide ‹*shelter, guarantee, etc.*›; (bei Auktionen, Kartenspielen) bid (**für, auf** + *Akk.* for); **jmdm. Geld/eine Chance ~:** offer sb. money/a chance; **wir ~ beim Pokern bis zu 5 Euro** we play poker for stakes of up to five euros; **was** *od.* **wie viel bietest du mir dafür?** what will you give me for it?; **jmdm. den Arm ~** (geh.) offer sb. one's arm; **jmdm. die Hand zur Versöhnung ~** (fig. geh.) hold out the olive branch to sb.; **für Jugendliche wird nichts geboten** there is nothing for young people to do; **eine hervorragende Leistung ~:** put up an outstanding performance; **das bietet keine Schwierigkeiten** that presents no difficulties; **das Stadion bietet Platz für 40 000 Personen** the stadium has room for *or* can hold 40,000 people 2 **ein schreckliches/gespenstisches** *usw.* **Bild ~:** present a terrible/eerie *etc.* picture; be a terrible/eerie *etc.* sight; **einen prächtigen Anblick ~:** look splendid; be a splendid sight 3 (zumuten) **das lasse ich mir nicht ~:** I won't put up with *or* stand for that
B *unr. refl. V.* **sich jmdm. ~:** present itself to sb.; **es bietet sich ...** there is ...; **hier bietet sich dir eine Chance** this is an opportunity for you; this offers you an opportunity; **ihnen bot sich ein Bild des Grauens** a horrific sight confronted them
C *unr. itr. V.* bid (**auf** + *Akk.* for); **jeder kann auf einer Auktion ~:** anyone can make a bid at an auction

Bieter *der;* ~**s,** ~, **Bieterin** *die;* ~, ~**nen** bidder

Bifido·bakterium /'bi:fido-/ *das* (Biol.) bifidobacterium

Bifokal·brille /bifo'ka:l-/ *die* bifocal spectacles *pl.*; bifocals *pl.*

Bigamie /biga'mi:/ *die;* ~, ~**n** bigamy *no def. art.*

Bigamist *der;* ~**en,** ~**en, Bigamistin** *die;* ~, ~**nen** bigamist

Bigband /'bɪg 'bend/ *die;* ~, ~**s** big band

Bigbusiness /'bɪg 'bɪznɪs/ *das;* ~**:** big business *no art.*; **zum ~ gehören** belong to the world of big business

bigott /bi'gɔt/ (abwertend)
A *Adj.* 1 religiose; over-devout 2 (scheinheilig) sanctimonious; holier-than-thou; (heuchlerisch) hypocritical; **~e Heuchler** sanctimonious hypocrites
B *adv.* sanctimoniously; (heuchlerisch) hypocritically

Bigotterie /bigɔtə'ri:/ *die;* ~ (abwertend) religious bigotry; religiosity; (Scheinheiligkeit) sanctimoniousness

Bijou /bi'ʒu:/ *das;* ~**s,** ~**s** (veralt., schweiz.) piece of jewellery; ~**s** jewellery *sing.*

Bijouterie /biʒutə'ri:/ *die;* ~, ~**n** (veralt., schweiz.) jeweller's shop

Bike /baik/ *das;* ~**s,** ~**s** (Jargon) bike

biken /baikn̩/ *itr. V.; mit sein* (Jargon) cycle

Biker /'baikɐ/ *der;* ~**s,** ~**s** (Jargon) biker

Bikerin *die;* ~, ~**nen** (Jargon) [female] cyclist

Bikini /bi'ki:ni/ *der;* ~**s,** ~**s** bikini; **im ~:** in a bikini/in bikinis

Bikini-: ~**höschen** *das* bikini bottom; ~**oberteil** *das* bikini top

bi·konkav *Adj.* (Optik) biconcave

bi·konvex *Adj.* (Optik) biconvex

bi·labial *Adj.* (Phon.) bilabial

Bilanz /bi'lants/ *die;* ~, ~**en** 1 (Kaufmannsspr., Wirtsch.) balance sheet; **die ~ des Jahres** the year's results *pl.*; **eine ~ aufstellen** make up the accounts *pl.*; draw up a balance sheet 2 (Ergebnis) outcome; (Endeffekt) net result; **erfreuliche ~:** happy outcome; **~ ziehen** take stock; sum things up; **[die] ~ aus etw. ziehen** draw conclusions *pl.* about sth.; (rückblickend) take stock of sth.

Bilanz-: ~**analyse** *die* (Wirtsch., Kaufmannsspr.) balance sheet analysis; ~**buchhalter** *der,* ~**buchhalterin** *die* (Wirtsch., Kaufmannsspr.) [stewardship] accountant

bilanziell
A *Adj.* on the balance sheet *postpos.*
B *adv.* as regards the balance sheet

bilanzieren (Wirtsch., Kaufmannsspr.)
A *itr. V.* balance; **mit ... Euro ~:** show a balance of ... euros
B *tr. V.* balance ‹*account*›; show ‹*turnover*› in the balance sheet; (fig.) sum up

Bilanz-: ~**prüfer** *der,* ~**prüferin** *die* (Wirtsch., Kaufmannsspr.) auditor; ~**summe** *die* (Wirtsch., Kaufmannsspr.) balance sheet total

bi·lateral (Politik)
A *Adj.* bilateral
B *adv.* bilaterally

Bild /bɪlt/ *das;* ~**[e]s,** ~**er** 1 picture; (in einem Buch usw.) illustration; (Spielkarte) picture *or* court card; **ein ~ [von jmdm./etw.] machen** take a picture [of sb./sth.]; **wie viele ~er hast du noch auf dem Film?** how many photos *or* exposures have you left on the film?; **ein ~ von einem Mann/einer Frau sein** be a fine specimen of a man/woman; be a fine-looking man/woman; **ein lebendes ~:** a tableau vivant 2 (Aussehen) appearance; (Anblick) sight; **das ~ der Stadt** the appearance of the town; the townscape; **ein ~ des Jammers sein** *od.* **bieten** be a pathetic sight; **ein ~ für [die] Götter [sein]** (scherzh.) [be] a sight for sore eyes 3 (Metapher) image; metaphor; **im ~ bleiben** extend *or* continue the metaphor 4 (Abbild) image; (Spiegel~) reflection; **er ist [ganz] das ~ seines Vaters** he is the [very] image of his father 5 (Vorstellung) image; **ein falsches/merkwürdiges ~ von etw. haben** have a wrong impression/curious idea of sth.; **sich** (*Dat.*) **ein ~ von jmdm./etw. machen** form an impression of sb./sth.; **jmdn. [über etw.** (*Akk.*)**] ins ~ setzen** put sb. in the picture [about sth.]; **[über etw.** (*Akk.*)**] im ~e sein** be in the picture [about sth.]; **ich bin im ~e** (als Reaktion: ich verstehe) I'm with you 6 (Theater) scene

Bild-: ~**archiv** *das* picture library; ~**ausfall** *der* loss of picture *or* vision; ~**ausschnitt** *der* section of a/the picture; (bes. Kunst) detail; ~**autor** *der,* ~**autorin** *die* photographer (*who takes the photographs for a book*); ~**band** *der* copiously illustrated book

bildbar *Adj.* formable (**aus** from); malleable ‹*personality, mind*›; **schwer ~e Laute** sounds which are difficult to form

Bild-: ~**bearbeitung** *die* (DV) image editing; ~**beilage** *die* pictorial *or* illustrated supplement; ~**bericht** *der* photo-reportage; ~**beschreibung** *die* picture description; ~**datei** *die* (DV) image file; ~**dokument** *das* pictorial document; (Film) pictorial record

bilden
A *tr. V.* 1 form (**aus** from); (modellieren) mould (**aus** from); **den Charakter ~:** form *or* mould sb.'s personality; **eine Gasse ~:** make a path *or* passage; **sich** (*Dat.*) **ein Urteil [über jmdn./etw.] ~:** form an opinion [of sb./sth.] 2 (ansammeln) build up ‹*fund, capital*› 3 (darstellen) be, represent ‹*exception etc.*›; constitute ‹*rule etc.*›; **den Höhepunkt des Abends bildete sein Auftritt** his appearance was the high spot of the evening 4 (erziehen) educate; **Reisen bildet den Geist** travel broadens the mind
B *refl. V.* 1 (entstehen) form; **eine starke Opposition bildete sich** a strong opposition developed *or* came into being 2 (lernen) educate oneself
C *itr. V.* **Lesen bildet** reading educates *or* cultivates the mind; **Reisen bildet** travel broadens the mind

bildend *Adj.* 1 **die ~e Kunst, die ~en Künste** the plastic arts *pl.* (*including painting and architecture*) 2 (belehrend) educational

Bilder·bogen *der* pictorial broadsheet

Bilder·buch *das* picture book (*for children*); **aussehen wie im** *od.* **aus dem ~:** look a picture

Bilderbuch-: perfect ‹*landing, weather*›; picture book ‹*weather, village*›; story book ‹*marriage, career*›; archetypal ‹*Catholic, proletarian, capitalist*›

Bilder-: ~**flut** *die* stream of images; ~**geschichte** *die* picture story; (Comic) strip cartoon; ~**kult** *der* idolatry; ~**rahmen** *der* picture frame; ~**rätsel** *das* picture puzzle; (Rebus) rebus; ~**schrift** *die* pictographic [system of] writing; (Hieroglyphen) hieroglyphics *pl.*; ~**sturm** *der* (hist.) iconoclasm; ~**stürmer** *der,* ~**stürmerin** *die* (hist.; auch fig.) iconoclast

bild-, Bild-: ~**fläche** *die:* **auf der ~fläche erscheinen** (ugs.) appear on the scene; (auftauchen) turn up; **von der ~fläche verschwinden** (ugs.) (rasch weggehen) make oneself scarce (coll.); (aus der Öffentlichkeit verschwinden) disappear from the scene; ~**folge** *die* 1 (im Film) sequence of shots; 2 [picture] sequence; ~**frequenz** *die* (Film, Ferns.) picture frequency; ~**gebend** *Adj.* (fachspr., bes. Med.) imaging *attrib.*; ~**gebung** *die;* ~~ (fachspr., bes. Med.) imaging; ~**geschichte** *die* ▸ **Bildergeschichte**; ~**haft** A *Adj.* graphic; pictorial, illustrative ‹*language, sense, etc.*›; vivid ‹*imagination, clarity, etc.*›; B *adv.* graphically; (lebhaft) vividly; ~**haftigkeit** *die;* ~~**:** vividness; graphic quality; (der Sprache) pictorial *or* illustrative quality; ~**hauer** *der* ▸ⓘ **S. 113** sculptor; ~**hauerei** /---'-/ *die;* ~~**:** sculpture *no def. art.*; ~**hauerin** *die;* ~~, ~~**nen** ▸ⓘ **S. 113** sculptress; ~**hauerisch** /-hauərɪʃ/ *Adj.* sculptural; ~**hauer·kunst** *die* ▸ **Bildhauerei**; ~**hübsch** *Adj.* really lovely; stunningly beautiful ‹*girl*›

bildlich
A *Adj.* pictorial; (übertragen) figurative; **~er Ausdruck, ~e Wendung** figure of speech; image
B *adv.* 1 pictorially; **sich etw. ~ vorstellen** picture sth. to oneself 2 figuratively; **~ gesprochen** metaphorically speaking

Bild-: ~**material** *das* pictures *pl.* (**über** + *Akk.* of); (Fotos/Film) photographic/film material (**über** + *Akk.* of); ~**mischer** *der,* ~**mischerin** *die;* ~~, ~~**nen** (Ferns.) vision mixer

bildnerisch
A *Adj.* artistic; creative ‹*abilities*›
B *adv.* artistically

Bildnis /'bɪltnɪs/ *das;* ~**ses,** ~**se** portrait; (Plastik) sculpture

Bild-: ~**platte** *die* video disc; ~**platten·spieler** *der* video disc player; ~**punkt** *der* (DV) picture element; pixel; ~**qualität** *die* picture quality; ~**rand** *der* edge of the picture; ~**redakteur** *der,* ~**redakteurin** *die* picture editor; ~**redaktion** *die* 1 picture department; 2 (Redakteure) picture editors *pl.*; ~**regie** *die* photographic direction; ~**reportage** *die* photo-reportage; ~**reporter** *der,* ~**reporterin** *die*

▸❶ **S. 113** photojournalist; **~röhre** *die* (Ferns.) picture tube

bildsam *Adj.* (geh.) malleable; impressionable

Bild·schärfe *die* (Fot., Ferns.) definition

Bild·schirm *der* (Ferns., Informationst.) screen; **am ~ arbeiten** work at *or* with a VDU; **einen Text am ~ korrigieren** correct a text on screen

bildschirm-, Bildschirm-: ~arbeit *die* VDU work *no art., no pl.*; **~gerät** *das* VDU; visual display unit; **~gerecht** *Adj.* in screen format *postpos.*; **~schoner** *der;* **~~s, ~~** (DV) screen saver; **~text** *der* viewdata; **~zeitung** *die* teletext

bild-, Bild-: ~schnitzer *der,* **~schnitzerin** *die* ▸❶ **S. 113** wood carver; wood sculptor; **~schön** *Adj.* really lovely; stunningly beautiful ‹*girl, woman*›; **~seite** *die* [1] (einer Münze) obverse; (beim Werfen) **die ~seite ist oben** it's heads; [2] (bei Büchern, Zeitungen) picture page; **zwei ~seiten** two pages of pictures; **~serie** *die* series *or* sequence of pictures; **~sprache** *die* pictorial language; **~stelle** *die* picture and film library; **~stock** *der* wayside shrine; **~störung** *die* interference *no def. art.* on vision; **~synchron** *Adj.* (Film, Ferns.) synchronized [with the picture]; **~telefon** *das* video telephone; **~teppich** *der* tapestry

Bildung *die;* **~, ~en** [1] (Erziehung) education; (Kultur) culture; **eine umfassende ~:** a broad educational and cultural background; **das gehört zur allgemeinen ~:** that is something every educated person should know; **[keine] ~ haben** be [un]educated; ([un]kultiviert sein) be [un]cultivated *or* [un]cultured [2] (das Formen, Schaffung) formation; **die ~ einer Untersuchungskommission** setting up a committee of investigation [3] (Form, Gestalt) form; shape; **die seltsamen ~en der Wolken/Eiskristalle** the strange formations of the clouds/ice crystals

bildungs-, Bildungs-: ~anstalt *die* (Amtsspr.) educational establishment; **~arbeit** *die* educational work *no art.*; **~auftrag** *der* educational remit; **~beflissen** *Adj.* keen on education *postpos.*; (sich bilden wollend) keen on self-improvement *postpos.*; **~bürger** *der,* **~bürgerin** *die* [traditionally educated] middle-class intellectual; **~bürgerlich** **A** *Adj.* educated middle class *attrib.* **B** *adv.* following educated middle class principles; **~chancen** *Pl.* educational opportunities; **~dünkel** *der* intellectual arrogance *or* snobbery; **~einrichtung** *die* ▸ **~anstalt**; **~erlebnis** *das* formative experience; **~fähig** *Adj.* fast-learning; receptive to teaching *postpos.*; **~feindlich** *Adj.* hostile to education *postpos.*; anti-education; **~gang** *der* educational career; **~grad** *der* level of education; **~gut** *das* material for one's general education; (Kulturgut) cultural heritage; **~hunger** *der* thirst for education; **~hungrig** *Adj.* eager to be educated *postpos.*; **~ideal** *das* educational ideal; **~lücke** *die* gap in one's education; **das ist eine ~lücke!** that's culpable ignorance!; **~minister** *der,* **~ministerin** *die* minister of education; ≈ Secretary of State for Education (Brit.); **~monopol** *das* monopoly of education; **~notstand** *der* state of emergency in education; **~politik** *die* educational policy; **~politisch** *Adj.* educational-policy *attrib.* ‹*measure, strategy*›; ‹*discussion*› concerning educational policy; **~reform** *die* educational reform; **~reise** *die* educational tour; **~roman** *der* (Literaturw.) novel of character development; Bildungsroman; **~stätte** *die* (geh.) educational establishment; (Universität) seat of learning; **~system** *das* education system; **~urlaub** *der* educational leave; **~weg** *der* educational course; **der zweite ~weg** the second chance to study; the alternative way of studying (*in adult classes*); **auf dem zweiten ~weg** using the second chance to study (*in adult classes*); **~wesen** *das* education system; **das ~wesen** education; **~ziel** *das* educational goal

Bild-: ~unter·schrift *die* caption; **~wand** *die* [projection] screen; **~werfer** *der* epidiascope; **~werk** *das* (geh.) sculpture; **~wörter·buch** *das* pictorial dictionary; (für Kinder) picture dictionary; **~zuschrift** *die* reply enclosing a photograph

> **Bild Zeitung**
>
> Germany's largest-selling daily newspaper, *Bild* is a typical tabloid with huge headlines, lots of photos, scandal stories, gossip and nude models. It is known for its right-wing views. *Bild* sells about 4.5 million copies every day, almost eight times more than any other newspaper in Germany. Its Sunday edition is called *Bild am Sonntag*.

Bilge /ˈbɪlgə/ *die;* **~, ~n** (Seemannsspr.) bilge

bilingual /bilɪŋˈgu̯aːl/ **A** *Adj.* bilingual **B** *adv.* bilingually

Billard /ˈbɪljart, *österr.:* biˈjaːɐ̯/ *das;* **~s, ~e,** *österr.:* **~s** billiards

Billard-: ~kugel *die* billiard ball; **~stock** *der* billiard cue; **~tisch** *der* billiard table

Billet /bɪlˈeː/ *das* **~s, ~s** (schweiz.), **Billett** /bɪlˈjɛt/ *das;* **~[e]s, ~e** *od.* **~s** [1] (schweiz., sonst veralt.) [entrance] ticket [2] (schweiz., sonst veralt.) [train/tram/bus] ticket [3] (österr., sonst veralt.) note [4] (österr.: Glückwunschkarte) greetings card (Brit.); greeting card (Amer.)

Billiarde /bɪˈli̯ardə/ *die;* **~, ~n** thousand million million; quadrillion (Amer.)

billig /ˈbɪlɪç/ **A** *Adj.* [1] cheap; **ein ~er Preis** (ugs.) a low price [2] (abwertend: primitiv) shabby, cheap ‹*trick*›; feeble ‹*excuse*›; **ist dir das nicht zu ~?** isn't that beneath you?; **ein ~er Trost** cold comfort [3] (veralt.: angemessen) reasonable; proper **B** *adv.* [1] cheaply; **~ einkaufen** shop cheaply; **~ abzugeben** (in Anzeigen) for sale cheap; **~ davonkommen** (fig. ugs.) get off lightly [2] (veralt.: angemessen) **nicht mehr als ~:** no more than is reasonable *or* proper; **jeder ~ denkende Mensch** any fair-minded person; *s. auch* **recht**

Billig·angebot *das* special *or* cut-price offer

billigen *tr. V.* approve; **~, dass jmd. etw. tut** approve of sb.'s doing sth.; **ich kann nicht ~, dass du dich daran beteiligst** I cannot approve of *or* condone your taking part; **etw. stillschweigend ~:** give sth. one's tacit approval; **etw. ~d in Kauf nehmen** regard sth. as an acceptable consequence

billigermaßen, billigerweise *Adv.* rightly; justifiably

Billig-: ~flagge *die* flag of convenience; **~flug** *der* cheap flight; **~fluglinie** *die* budget airline; low-cost airline

Billigkeit *die;* **~** [1] cheapness; low cost [2] (Rechtsw. od. geh.) fairness; equitableness

Billig-: ~laden *der; Pl.* **~läden** cut-price shop; **~lohn** *der* low wages *pl.*; **~lohnland** *das* low-wage country; **~preis** *der* low price; (verbilligter Preis) cut price; **~produkt** *das* cheap product; cheap and nasty product (Brit. derog.)

Billigung *die;* **~:** approval; **jmds. ~ finden** meet with *or* receive sb.'s approval

Billig·ware *die* cheap goods; **~n** cheap goods

Billion /bɪˈli̯oːn/ *die;* **~, ~en** ▸❶ **S. 826** trillion; million million

Bilsen·kraut /ˈbɪlzn̩-/ *das* henbane

Bilux·lampe /ˈbiːlʊks-/ *die* twin-filament bulb

bim /bɪm/ *Interj.* ding; **~, bam** ding dong

Bimbam *in* **[ach du] heiliger ~!** (ugs.) [oh] my sainted aunt! (sl.); glory be! (coll.)

Bi-metall *das* (Technik) bimetallic strip; **aus ~:** bimetallic

Bimmel /ˈbɪml̩/ *die;* **~, ~n** (ugs.) [ting-a-ling] bell

Bimmel·bahn *die* (ugs. scherzh.) narrow-gauge railway (*with a warning bell*)

Bimmelei *die;* **~** (ugs. abwertend) constant ringing; (lautmalend) ting-a-ling-a-ling

bimmeln *itr. V.* (ugs.) ring

Bimse /ˈbɪmzə/ *Pl.* (ugs.) **~ kriegen** get a walloping (coll.) *or* thrashing

bimsen *tr. V.* (ugs.) [1] (drillen) drill [2] (einexerzieren) practise [3] (Schülerspr.: pauken) mug up (sl.)

Bims·stein /ˈbɪms-/ *der* [1] pumice stone [2] (Gestein) pumice [3] (Baustein) pumice block

bin /bɪn/ *1. Pers. Sg. Präsens v.* **sein¹**

binar /biˈnaːɐ̯/, **binär** /biˈnɛːɐ̯/, **binarisch** /biˈnaːrɪʃ/ *Adj.* (fachspr.) binary

binaural /binau̯ˈraːl/ *Adj.* (Med., Technik) binaural

Binde /ˈbɪndə/ *die;* **~, ~n** [1] (Verband) bandage; (Augen~) blindfold [2] (Arm~) armband [3] (ugs.: Damen~) [sanitary] towel (Brit.) *or* (Amer.) napkin [4] (veralt.: Krawatte) tie; **sich** (*Dat.*) **einen hinter die ~ gießen** *od.* **kippen** (ugs.) have a drink or two

Binde-: ~gewebe *das* (Anat.) ▸❶ **S. 435** connective tissue; **~glied** *das* [connecting] link; **~haut** *die* (Anat.) ▸❶ **S. 435** conjunctiva; **~haut·entzündung** *die* ▸❶ **S. 439** (Med.) conjunctivitis *no art.*; **~mittel** *das* binder

binden **A** *unr. tr. V.* [1] (bündeln) tie; **etw. zu etw. ~:** tie sth. into sth. [2] (herstellen) make up ‹*wreath, bouquet*›; make ‹*broom*› [3] (fesseln) bind; **jmdn. an Händen und Füßen ~:** bind sb. hand and foot; *s. auch* **gebunden, Hand** [4] (verpflichten) bind; **ich bin zu jung, um mich schon zu ~:** I am too young to be tied down; **nicht mehr gebunden sein** be free of any ties [5] (befestigen, auch fig.) tie (**an** + *Dat.* to); **nicht an einen Ort gebunden sein** (fig.) not be tied to one place; **jmdn. an sich** (*Akk.*) **~** (fig.) make sb. dependent on one [6] (knüpfen) tie ‹*knot, bow, etc.*›; knot ‹*tie*› [7] (festhalten) bind ‹*soil, mixture, etc.*›; thicken ‹*sauce*›; **der Regen bindet den Staub** the rain lays the dust [8] (Buchw.) bind [9] (Musik) slur [10] (Verslehre) **Wörter durch Reime ~:** link words in rhyme; **in gebundener Rede/Sprache** in verse **B** *unr. itr. V.* (fest machen) bind

bindend *Adj.* binding (**für** on); definite ‹*answer*›

Binder *der;* **~s, ~** [1] (Krawatte) tie [2] (Bindemittel) binder [3] (Landw.) [reaper-]binder [4] (Bauw.: Stein) header [5] (Bauw.: Dachbalken) [roof] truss

Binderei *die;* **~, ~en** [1] (Blumen~) wreath and bouquet department [2] (Buch~) bindery

Binde-: ~strich *der* hyphen; **~wort** *das; Pl.* **~wörter** (Sprachw.) conjunction

Bind·faden *der* string; **ein [Stück] ~:** a piece of string; **es regnet Bindfäden** (ugs.) it's raining cats and dogs (coll.)

Bindung *die;* **~, ~en** [1] (Beziehung) relationship (**an** + *Akk.* to); **seine politische ~ an die Sozialdemokraten** his political commitment to *or* ties with the Social Democrats [2] (Verbundenheit) attachment (**an** + *Akk.* to) [3] (Ski~) binding [4] (Chemie) bond [5] (Weberei) weave

Bingo /ˈbɪŋgo/ *das;* **~[s]** bingo

binnen /ˈbɪnən/ *Präp. mit Dat. od.* (*geh.*) *Gen.* within; **~ Jahresfrist** within a year; **~ kurzem** *od.* **Kurzem** soon

binnen-, Binnen-: ~bords *Adv.* (Seemannsspr.) inboard; **~deich** *der* inner dyke; **~deutsch** **A** *Adj.* ‹*dialect*› spoken in Germany; ‹*word, expression, etc.*› used in Germany; **B** *adv.* in Germany; **~fischerei** *die* freshwater fishing; **~gewässer** *das* inland water; **~hafen** *der* inland port; **~handel** *der* domestic or home trade; **~land** *das* interior; **im ~land** inland; **~ländisch** *Adj.* inland; **~markt** *der* (Wirtsch.) domestic *or* home market; **europäischer ~markt** internal European market; **~meer** *das* inland sea; **~nachfrage** *die* (Wirtsch.) domestic demand; **~reim** *der* (Literaturw.) internal rhyme; **~schiffer** *der,* **~schifferin** *die* member of an inland ship's crew; (auf Schlepp-, Schubkahn) bargee (Brit.); bargeman/bargewoman (Amer.); **~schifffahrt** *die* inland navigation; **~see** *der* lake; **~staat** *der* land locked country *or* state; **~zoll** *der* internal duty *or* tariff

binokular /binokuˈlaːɐ̯/ *Adj.* binocular

Binom /biˈnoːm/ *das;* **~s, ~e** (Math.) binomial
binomisch *Adj.* (Math.) binomial
Binse /ˈbɪnzə/ *die;* **~, ~n** (Bot.) rush; **in die ~n gehen** (ugs.) (misslingen) fall through; (verloren gehen, entzweigehen) go for a burton (Brit. coll.); come to grief (Amer.); ‹*money*› go down the drain (coll.); ‹*vehicle, machine*› pack up (sl.); **die Prüfung ist in die ~n gegangen** the exam was a disaster
Binsen·weisheit *die* truism
Bio /ˈbiːo/ (Schülerspr.) biol (school sl.); biology
Bio- (ugs.) organic ‹*farmer, garden, vegetables, etc.*›
bio-, Bio-: ~abfall *der* biowaste, biological waste; **~aktiv** **A** *Adj.* biological ‹*washing powder*›; **B** *adv.* biologically; **~bauer** *der,* **~bäuerin** *die* organic farmer; **~chemie** *die* biochemistry; **~chemiker** *der,* **~chemikerin** *die* ▸ⓘ **S. 113** biochemist; **~chemisch** *Adj.* biochemical; **~diesel** *der;* **~~** biodiesel; **~dynamisch** **A** *Adj.* organic; **B** *adv.* organically; **~ethik** *die* bioethics *sing.*; **~ethisch** **A** *Adj.* bioethical; **B** *adv.* bioethically; **~gas** *das* (Ökologie) biogas; **~genese** *die* biogenesis; **~genetisch** *Adj.* biogenetic; **~graph** *der* biographer; **~graphie** *die* **[1]** (Beschreibung) biography; **[2]** (Lebenslauf) life [history]; **~graphin** *die;* **~~, ~~nen** biographer; **~graphisch** *Adj.* biographical; **~haus** *das* biohouse; **~informatik** *die* biocomputing; **~kraftstoff** *der* biofuel; **~laden** *der; Pl.* **~läden** (ugs.) health food shop; **~loge** *der;* **~~n, ~~n** ▸ⓘ **S. 113** biologist; **~logie** *die;* **~~:** biology *no art.*; **~login** *die;* **~~, ~~nen** ▸ⓘ **S. 113** biologist; *s. auch* **-in**; **~logisch** **A** *Adj.* **[1]** biological; **ein ~logisches Standardwerk** a standard work of biology; **[2]** (natürlich) natural ‹*medicine, cosmetic, etc.*›; **B** *adv.* **[1]** biologically; **[2]** (natürlich) naturally; **~masse** *die* biomass; **~metrisch** **A** *Adj.* biometric **B** *adv.* biometrically; **~müll** *der* organic waste

> **Bioladen**
>
> A health food shop which sells only organically grown products. Many health-conscious people buy their herbal teas, cosmetics, medicines, and health foods there.

Bionik /biˈoːnɪk/ *die;* **~:** bionics *sing., no art.*
Bio·physik *die* biophysics *sing., no art.*
bio·physikalisch *Adj.* biophysical
Biopsie /biɔˈpsiː/ *die;* **~, ~n** (Med.) biopsy
Bio-: ~rhythmus *der* biorhythm; **~sphäre** /-ˈ--/ *die* biosphere; **~techfirma** *die* biotech company; **~technik** *die* bioengineering; (Biotechnologie) biotechnology; **~technologie** *die* biotechnology; **~terrorismus** *der* bioterrorism; **~tonne** *die* biobin; green bin

> **Biotonne**
>
> ▸ Recycling.

Biotop /bioˈtoːp/ *der od. das;* **~s, ~e** (Biol.) biotope
Bio-: ~waffe *die* biological weapon; **~wissenschaften** *Pl.* life sciences
bi·polar *Adj.* (bes. Math., Physik) bipolar
bi·quadratisch *Adj.* (Math.) biquadratic
Bircher·mü[e]sli /ˈbɪrçɐmyː(ə)sli/ *das* muesli (*made with fresh fruit*)
Birke /ˈbɪrkə/ *die;* **~, ~n** **[1]** (Baum) birch [tree] **[2]** (Holz) birch[wood]
Birken-: ~holz *das* birch[wood]; **~wald** *der* birchwood; (größer) birch forest; **~wasser** *das; Pl.* **~wässer** hair lotion made from birch sap
Birk-: ~hahn *der; Pl.* **~hähne** blackcock; **~huhn** *das* black grouse
Birma /ˈbɪrma/ *(das);* **~s** Burma
Birmane /bɪrˈmaːnə/ *der;* **~n, ~n, Birmanin** *die;* **~, ~nen** Burmese; *s. auch* **-in**
Birn·baum *der* **[1]** pear tree **[2]** (Holz) pearwood
Birne /ˈbɪrnə/ *die;* **~, ~n** **[1]** pear **[2]** (Glüh~) [light]bulb **[3]** (salopp: Kopf) nut (coll.); **eine weiche ~ haben** (salopp) be soft in the head
Birnen·geist *der* pear brandy
bis /bɪs/ ▸ⓘ **S. 165**
A *Präp. mit Akk.* **[1]** (zeitlich) until; till; (die ganze Zeit über und ~ zu einem bestimmten Zeitpunkt) up to; up until; up till; (nicht später als) by; **ich muss ~ fünf Uhr warten** I have to wait until *or* till five o'clock; **~ [einschließlich] Freitag** by Friday; **von Dienstag ~ Donnerstag** from Tuesday to Thursday; Tuesday through Thursday (Amer.); **von sechs ~ sieben [Uhr]** from six until *or* till seven [o'clock]; **~ Ende März ist er zurück/verreist** he'll be back by/away until the end of March; **~ dann** *od.* **dahin will ich Ergebnisse sehen/muss ich mich noch gedulden** I want to see results by then/I must be patient until then; **~ wann dauert das Konzert?** till *or* until when does the concert go on?; how long does the concert last?; **~ jetzt ist nichts geschehen** up to now *or* so far nothing has happened; **~ dann/gleich/später/morgen/nachher!** see you then/in a while/later/tomorrow/later!; **~ spätestens Montag** *od.* **Montag spätestens** by Monday at the latest; **er ist [nur] ~ 17 Uhr hier** he is [only] here until *or* till 5 o'clock; **er ist [spätestens] ~ 17 Uhr hier** he will be here by 5 o'clock [at the latest]; *s. auch* **dato** **[2]** (räumlich) to; **dieser Zug fährt nur ~ Offenburg** this train only goes to *or* as far as Offenburg; **~ wohin fährt der Bus?** how far does the bus go?; **nur ~ Seite 100** only up to *or* as far as page 100; **~ 5 000 Euro** up to 5,000 euros; **von Anfang ~ Ende** from beginning to end; **~ dahin sind es 2 km** it's 2 km to there **[3]** *in* **~ auf** (einschließlich) down to; (mit Ausnahme von) except for; **~ auf weiteres** *od.* **Weiteres** for the time being **[4]** *in* **~ zu** up to; **Städte ~ zu 50 000 Einwohnern** towns of up to 50,000 inhabitants
B *Adv.* **~ zu 6 Personen** up to six people; **Kinder ~ 6 Jahre** children up to the age of six *or* up to six years of age; **die Feier dauerte ~ gegen 10 Uhr** the party went on until *or* till about 10 o'clock; **~ gegen 10 Uhr ist es fertig** it will be ready by about 10 o'clock; **~ nach Köln** to Cologne; **~ an die Decke** up to the ceiling; **~ ins Kleinste** *od.* **Letzte** down to the smallest *or* last detail
C *Konj.* **[1]** (nebenordnend) to; **vier ~ fünf** four to five; **heiter ~ wolkig** fair or cloudy **[2]** (bevor nicht) until; till; **~ dass der Tod euch scheidet** (geh.) until *or* till death do you part **[3]** (österr.: sobald) when; **gleich ~ er aufgewacht ist** as soon as he's woken up
Bisam /ˈbiːzam/ *der;* **~s, ~e** *od.* **~s** **[1]** ▸ **Moschus** **[2]** (Pelz) musquash
Bisam·ratte *die* muskrat
Bischof /ˈbɪʃɔf/ *der;* **~s, Bischöfe** /ˈbɪʃœfə/, **Bischöfin** *die;* **~, ~nen** bishop
bischöflich *Adj.* episcopal
Bischofs-: ~amt *das* episcopate; office of bishop; **~hut** *der* bishop's hat; **~konferenz** *die* conference of bishops; **~mütze** *die* [bishop's] mitre; **~sitz** *der* seat of a/the bishopric; **~stab** *der* [bishop's] crosier *or* crook; **~stadt** *die* ▸ **~sitz**
Bise /ˈbiːzə/ *die;* **~, ~n** (schweiz.): *north[-east] wind to the north of the Alps;* bise
Bi·sexualität *die* bisexuality
bi·sexuell
A *Adj.* bisexual
B *adv.* bisexually
bis·her *Adv.* up to now; (aber jetzt nicht mehr) until now; till now; **~ war alles in Ordnung** everything has been all right up to now/everything was all right until *or* till now; **er hat sich ~ nicht gemeldet** he hasn't been in touch up to now *or* as yet; **das wusste ich ~ nicht** I didn't know that till now *or* before; **ein ~ unbekanntes Buch** a hitherto *or* previously unknown book
bisherig *Adj.* (vorherig) previous; (momentan) present; **sie ziehen um, ihre ~e Wohnung wird zu klein** they are moving — their present flat is getting too small; **sie sind umgezogen, ihre ~e Wohnung wurde zu klein** they have moved — their previous flat became too small
Biskaya /bɪsˈkaːja/ *die;* **~: die ~/der Golf von ~:** the Bay of Biscay
Biskuit /bɪsˈkviːt/ *das od. der;* **~[e]s, ~s** *od.* **~e** **[1]** sponge biscuit **[2]** (~teig) sponge
Biskuit-: ~rolle *die* Swiss roll; **~teig** *der* sponge mixture
bis·lang *Adv.:* ▸ **bisher**
Bismarck·hering /ˈbɪsmark-/ *der* Bismarck herring
Bison /ˈbiːzɔn/ *der;* **~s, ~s** bison
Biss, *Biß /bɪs/ *der;* **Bisses, Bisse;** **[1]** bite **[2]** (ugs.: Engagement) punch
bisschen, *bißchen *indekl. Indefinitpron.* **[1]** (in der Funktion eines Adjektivs) **ein ~ Geld/Brot/Milch/Wasser** a bit of *or* a little money/bread/a drop of *or* a little milk/water; **ich würde ihm kein ~ Geld mehr leihen** I wouldn't lend him any more money at all; **das ~ Geld/Farbe** that [little] bit of money/[little] drop of paint; **ein/kein ~ Angst haben** be a bit/not a bit frightened **[2]** (in der Funktion eines Adverbs) **ein/kein ~:** a bit *or* a little/not a *or* one bit; **ich werde mich ein ~ aufs Ohr legen** I'm going to lie down for a bit; **er hat mir kein ~ geholfen** he didn't help me one [little] bit; **ein klein ~:** a little bit; **ein ~ zu viel/mehr** a bit too much/a bit more; **ein ~ sehr teuer sein** be getting rather expensive **[3]** (in der Funktion eines Substantivs) **ein ~:** a bit; a little; (bei Flüssigkeiten) a drop; a little; **von dem ~ werde ich nicht satt** that little bit/drop won't fill me up; **das/kein ~:** the little [bit]/not a *or* one bit; *s. auch* **lieb A 4**
bissel /ˈbɪsl̩/ (südd., österr. ugs.) ▸ **bisschen**
Bissen *der;* **~s, ~:** mouthful; **lass mich mal einen kleinen ~ davon probieren** let me try a small piece *or* a little bit; **sie brachte keinen ~ herunter** she couldn't eat a thing; **ich muss erst mal einen ~ essen** I must have a bite to eat first; **ein fetter ~** (fig.) a really good deal; **jmdm. die ~ in den Mund zählen** (fig.) watch how much sb. eats; **ihm blieb der ~ im Hals[e] stecken** (ugs.) the food stuck in his throat; **sich** (*Dat.*) **jeden** *od.* **den letzten ~ vom Munde absparen** scrimp [and save]
bisserl /ˈbɪsɐl/ ▸ **bissel**
bissig
A *Adj.* **[1]** **~ sein** ‹*dog*› bite; **ein ~er Hund** a dog that bites; **„Vorsicht, ~er Hund"** 'beware of the dog' **[2]** cutting, caustic ‹*remark, tone, etc.*›; **du brauchst doch nicht gleich so ~ zu werden** there's no need to bite my/his *etc.* head off **[3]** (Sportjargon) **ein ~er Spieler** a sharp, attacking player
B *adv.* (boshaft) ‹*say*› cuttingly, caustically; ‹*grin*› maliciously
Bissigkeit *die;* **~, ~en** **[1]** (von Hunden); **Kettenhunde neigen zur ~:** dogs that are chained up tend to bite **[2]** (Schärfe) **die ~ seiner Antwort zeigte nur, wie wütend er war** his cutting *or* caustic answer just showed how angry he was **[3]** (Bemerkung) cutting *or* caustic remark
Biss-, *Biß-: ~spur *die* bite mark; **~verletzung** *die* bite wound; **~wunde** *die* bite
bist /bɪst/ *2. Pers. Sg. Präsens v.* **sein**
biste (ugs.) = **bist du;** *s. auch* **haste**
Bistro /ˈbɪstro/ *das;* **~s, ~s** bistro
Bistum /ˈbɪstuːm/ *das;* **~s, Bistümer** /ˈbɪstyːmɐ/ bishopric; diocese; **das ~ Limburg** the diocese of Limburg
bis·weilen *Adv.* (geh.) from time to time; now and then
Bit /bɪt/ *das;* **~s, ~[s]** (DV) bit
Bitt·brief *der* letter of request; (Bittgesuch) petition
bitte /ˈbɪtə/ *Höflichkeitsformel* **[1]** (bittend) please; **können Sie mir ~ sagen ...?** could you please tell me ...?; **~ nicht!** no, please don't!; (ich möchte nicht) I'd rather not; **~ nach Ihnen** after you; **~, ~ machen** (Kindersprache) clap hands [to mean 'please'] **[2]** (auffordernd) please; **der Nächste ~!** next please!; **ja, ~?** (am Telefon) hello?; yes?; **nehmen Sie ~ Platz** please sit down; **~[, treten Sie ein]!** (geh.) come in!; **~ hier, hier ~!** over here, please!; **~ [schön]?**

(im Laden) can I help you?; (im Lokal) what would you like?; **Hast du mal ein Tempotuch für mich? — Bitte [schön** *od.* **sehr]!** Could you let me have a tissue? — There you are; **~, gern/selbstverständlich** certainly/of course; **Entschuldigung! — Bitte!** I'm sorry — That's all right; **~, nur zu** [go on,] help yourself **3** (bejahend) please; **aber ~!** yes, do; **~ ja!, ja ~!** yes please! **4** (Dank erwidernd) **~ [schön** *od.* **sehr]** not at all; you're welcome **5** (nachfragend) **[wie] ~?** sorry?; (iron.) what? **6** (missbilligend) all right; **aber ~, macht, was ihr wollt** just [go ahead and] do what you want; **na ~!** there you are!

Bitte *die;* **~, ~n** request; (inständig) plea; **eine große ~ [an jmdn.]/nur die eine ~ haben** have a [great] favour to ask [of sb.]/have [just] one request *or* just one thing to ask; **auf seine ~ hin** at his request; **jmdm. keine ~ abschlagen** *od.* **ausschlagen können** not be able to refuse sb. anything

bitten
A *unr. itr. V.* **1** **um etw. ~:** ask for *or* request sth.; (inständig) beg for sth.; **der Blinde bat um eine milde Gabe** the blind man begged for alms; **ich bitte einen Moment um Geduld/Ihre Aufmerksamkeit** I must ask you to be patient for a moment/may I ask for your attention for a moment; **darf ich [um den nächsten Tanz]?** may I have the pleasure [of the next dance]?; **[ich] bitte gehorsamst, gehen zu dürfen** (veralt., scherzh.) [I] respectfully beg permission to leave; **es half ihm kein Bitten** pleading was *or* pleas were of no avail; **~ und betteln** beg and plead **2** (einladen) ask; **ich lasse ~:** [please] ask him/her/them to come in; **der Herr Konsul lässt ~:** the consul will see you now; **darf ich zu Tisch ~?** may I ask you to come and sit down at the table? **3** (geh.: Fürsprache einlegen) plead; **bei jmdm. für jmdn. ~:** plead with sb. on sb.'s behalf
B *unr. tr. V.* **1** (sich höflich wenden an) **jmdn. um etw. ~:** ask sb. for sth.; **darf ich Sie um Feuer/ein Glas Wasser ~?** could I ask you for a light/a glass of water, please?; **darf ich die Herrschaften um Geduld/Ruhe ~?** could I ask you to be patient/silent?; **es wird gebeten, die Tiere nicht zu füttern** please do not feed the animals; **allmächtiger Gott, wir ~ dich, erhöre uns!** almighty God, we beseech Thee to hear us; **ich bitte dich um alles in der Welt** I beg [of] you; **[aber] ich bitte dich/Sie!** [please] don't mention it; **so, jetzt geht ihr ins Bett, aber ein bisschen plötzlich, wenn ich ~ darf** into bed with you, at once if you please; **darum möchte ich doch sehr gebeten haben!** (ugs.) I should hope so (coll.); **ich muss doch [sehr] ~!** really!; **er ließ sich nicht lange** *od.* **erst ~:** he didn't have to be asked twice; **er lässt sich gern ~:** he likes to be asked; **jmdn. zu sich ~:** ask sb. to come and see one **2** (einladen) ask, invite; **jmdn. zum Tee [zu sich] ~:** ask *or* invite sb. to tea; **jmdn. ins Haus/Zimmer ~:** ask *or* invite sb. [to come] in; **jmdn. zum Tanz ~:** ask sb. to dance; **er wurde für neun Uhr zur Direktion gebeten** he was asked to be at the manager's office at 9 o'clock; **jmdn. zu Tisch ~:** ask sb. to come and sit down at the table

bitter
A *Adj.* **1** bitter; plain ‹*chocolate*› **2** (schmerzlich) bitter ‹*experience, irony, contempt, disappointment, etc.*›; painful, hard ‹*loss*›; painful, bitter, hard ‹*truth*›; hard ‹*time, fate, etc.*›; **eine ~e Lehre** a hard lesson; **bis zum ~en Ende** to the bitter end; **das ist mein ~ster Ernst** I am deadly serious; **eine solche Erfahrung ist ~:** an experience like that is a bitter one **3** (verbittert) bitter; **ein ~es Gefühl** a feeling of bitterness; **er hatte einen ~en Zug um den Mund** he had a look of bitterness on his face; **jmdn. ~ machen** embitter sb.; make sb. bitter **4** (groß, schwer) bitter ‹*cold, tears, grief, remorse, regret*›; dire ‹*need*›; desperate ‹*poverty*›; grievous ‹*injustice, harm*›; **es herrschte [eine] ~e Kälte** it was bitterly cold **5** (verbittert) bitter ‹*enemy*›
B *adv.* **1** (verbittert) bitterly **2** (sehr stark) desperately; ‹*regret*› bitterly; **etw. ~ nötig haben** be in dire need of sth.; **das wird sich ~ rächen** you'll/he'll *etc.* pay dearly for that

bitter-: **~arm** *Adj.* wretchedly poor; **~böse** **A** *Adj.* furious; **B** *adv.* furiously; **~ernst** **A** *Adj.* deadly serious; **damit ist es mir ~ernst!** I am deadly serious; **B** *adv.* **ich meine das ~ernst** I mean it deadly seriously; **~kalt** *Adj.* bitterly cold

Bitterkeit *die;* **~** **1** (auch fig.) bitterness **2** (Verbitterung) bitterness

Bitterlemon /ˈbɪtɐˈlɛmən/ *das;* **~[s], ~,** *auch* **Bitter Lemon** *das;* **~ ~[s], ~ ~** bitter lemon

bitterlich
A *Adj.* slightly bitter ‹*taste*›; **etwas ~:** slightly bitter
B *adv.* (heftig) ‹*cry, complain, etc.*› bitterly

Bitter-: **~mandel** *die* bitter almond; **~mandel·öl** *das* bitter almond oil; oil of bitter almonds

Bitternis *die;* **~, ~se** (geh.) **1** (Geschmack) bitterness **2** (Gefühl) bitterness; (Leiden) suffering

Bitter-: **~salz** *das* Epsom salts *pl.*; **~stoff** *der* bitter principle; bitter ingredient (also fig.); **~süß, ~-süß** *Adj.* (auch fig.) bitter-sweet

Bitte·schön *das;* **~s mit einem höflichen ~ überreichte er das Geschenk** he said politely 'this is for you' as he presented the gift

Bitt-: **~gang** *der* **1** (zu jmdm.) **ein ~gang [nach einem Ort]** going [to a place] with a request; **einen ~gang zu jmdm. machen** go to sb. with a request; **2** (kath. Rel.: **~**prozession) Rogation procession; **~gebet** *das* (Rel.) prayer of supplication; **~gesuch** *das* petition; **~gottes·dienst** *der* (Rel.) Rogation service; **~prozession** *die* (kath. Rel.) Rogation procession

bitt·schön (ugs. Höflichkeitsformel) **~, der Herr** there we are, sir; **Vielen Dank. — Bittschön, gern geschehen** Thank you very much — My pleasure; *s. auch* **bitte 2**

Bitt-: **~schreiben** *das* petition; **~schrift** *die* petition; **~steller** /-ʃtɛlɐ/ *der;* **~~s, ~~,** **~stellerin** *die;* **~~, ~~nen** petitioner

Bitumen /biˈtuːmən/ *das;* **~s, ~** (auch:) **Bitumina** /-mina/ (Chemie) bitumen

bitzeln /ˈbɪtsl̩n/ *itr. V.* (südd., westd.) tingle; ‹*fabric, itching-powder, etc.*› prickle

bivalent /biveˈlɛnt/ *Adj.* (Chemie, Sprachw.) bivalent

Biwak /ˈbiːvak/ *das;* **~s, ~s** (bes. Milit., Bergsteigen) bivouac

biwakieren *itr. V.* (bes. Milit., Bergsteigen) bivouac

bizarr /biˈtsar/
A *Adj.* bizarre; fantastic, grotesque ‹*coral reef, tree, formation, etc.*›
B *adv.* bizarrely

Bizarrerie /bitsarəˈriː/ *die;* **~, ~n** bizarreness; (Handlung) bizarre action

Bizeps /ˈbiːtsɛps/ *der;* **~[es], ~e** biceps

BKA *Abk.* **= Bundeskriminalamt**

B-Klarinette /ˈbeː-/ *die* B-flat clarinet

Blabla /blaˈblaː/ *das;* **~[s]** (ugs.) blah[-blah] (coll.)

Blach·feld /ˈblax-/ *das* (dichter. veralt.) plain; champaign (literary)

Blackbox·methode /ˈblɛkbɔks-/ *die* (Kybernetik) black-box method

Black-out /ˈblɛkaut/ *das od. der;* **~s, ~s** blackout

bladen /ˈbleɪdn̩/ *itr. V.; mit sein* rollerblade

blaffen /ˈblafn̩/, **bläffen** /ˈblɛfn̩/ *itr. V.* **1** bark; give a short bark; (kläffen) yap **2** (schimpfen) snap

Bläh·bauch *der* (ugs.) bloated belly; **einen ~ kriegen/haben** get/be bloated

blähen /ˈblɛːən/
A *tr. V.* **1** swell, distend ‹*stomach*›; billow, fill, belly [out] ‹*sail*›; billow ‹*sheet, curtain, clothing*› **2** (aufblasen) flare ‹*nostrils*›; **mit vor Stolz geblähter Brust schritt er ...** his chest swollen with pride, he strode ...
B *refl. V.* **1** (rund werden) ‹*sail*› billow *or* belly out; ‹*nostrils*› dilate **2** (angeben) puff oneself up
C *itr. V.* (Blähungen verursachen) cause flatulence *or* wind; **~de Speisen** flatulent foods; **das bläht fürchterlich** it causes terrible flatulence

Blähung *die;* **~, ~en** flatulence *no art., no pl.*; wind *no art., no pl.*; **~en** flatulence *sing.*; wind *sing.*; **eine ~ abgehen lassen** break wind

blaken /ˈblaːkn̩/ *itr. V.* (nordd.) smoke

bläken /ˈblɛːkn̩/ *itr. V.* (ugs. abwertend) ‹*child*› yell; bawl; ‹*animal*› bellow

blakig *Adj.* (nordd.) smoky *pred.*

blamabel /blaˈmaːbl̩/
A *Adj.* shameful, disgraceful ‹*behaviour etc.*›; embarrassing ‹*situation*›
B *adv.* shamefully; disgracefully

Blamage /blaˈmaːʒə/ *die;* **~, ~n** disgrace

blamieren /blaˈmiːrən/
A *tr. V.* (bloßstellen) disgrace; (in Verlegenheit bringen) embarrass
B *refl. V.* (sich bloßstellen) disgrace oneself; (sich lächerlich machen) make a fool of oneself

blanchieren /blãˈʃiːrən/ *tr. V.* (Kochk.) blanch

blank /blaŋk/ *Adj.* **1** (glänzend) shiny; **etw. ~ reiben/polieren** rub/polish sth. till it shines; **die Gläser werden nicht ~:** the glasses won't polish to a shine; **~ polierte Schuhe** highly polished shoes **2** (ugs.: abgewetzt) shiny **3** (unbekleidet) bare; naked; **mit ~en Beinen kannst du nicht gehen** you can't go without any tights/stockings/socks on **4** (ugs.: mittellos) **~ sein** be broke (coll.) **5** (bloß) bare ‹*wood, plaster, earth, etc.*›; **er ist mit dem ~en Messer auf mich losgegangen** he came at me with his knife drawn **6** (rein) pure; sheer; utter ‹*mockery*› **7** (dichter.: hell) bright; **der Blanke Hans** (dichter. nordd.) the stormy North Sea **8** (österr.: ohne Mantel) coatless; without a coat

Blankett /blaŋˈkɛt/ *das;* **~s, ~e** **1** (Wirtsch.) blank [form]; (mit Blankounterschrift) signed blank [form] **2** (Technik) blank

blanko /ˈblaŋko/ *Adv.* **1** (bei Schriftstücken) blank; **ich schreibe dir mal ~ einen Scheck aus** I'll write you a blank cheque **2** (bei Papier) plain

Blanko-: **~scheck** *der* (Wirtsch., fig.) blank cheque; **~unter·schrift** *die* blank signature; **~voll·macht** *die* (Wirtsch., fig.) carte blanche

blank·poliert ▸ **blank 1**

Blank·vers *der* blank verse

Bläschen /ˈblɛːsçən/ *das;* **~s, ~** **1** [small] bubble **2** (in der Haut) [small] blister

Bläschen·aus·schlag *der* ▸❶ **S. 439** (Med.) herpes simplex

Blase /ˈblaːzə/ *die;* **~, ~n** **1** bubble; (im Farbenanstrich) blister; **~n werfen** *od.* **ziehen** ‹*paint*› blister; ‹*wallpaper*› bubble; **es regnet ~n** it's pelting [down] **2** (in der Haut) blister; **sich** (*Dat.*) **~n laufen** get blisters [from walking/running] **3** ▸❶ **S. 435** (Harn~) bladder; **eine erkältete ~ haben/sich** (*Dat.*) **die ~ erkälten** have/get a chill in the bladder; **eine schwache ~ haben** (ugs.) have a weak bladder **4** (salopp abwertend: Leute) mob (coll.)

Blase·balg *der; Pl.* **Blase·bälge** bellows *pl.*; pair of bellows

blasen
A *unr. itr. V.* **1** blow **2** (ein Blasinstrument spielen) play; **auf dem Kamm ~:** play the comb **3** **zum Angriff/Rückzug/Aufbruch ~:** sound the charge/retreat/departure **4** (wehen) ‹*wind*› blow **5** (bes. südd., österr.: kühlen) **in die Suppe/auf eine Brandwunde ~:** blow on one's soup/a burn
B *unr. tr. V.* **1** blow **2** (spielen) play ‹*musical instrument, tune, melody, etc.*› **3** (wehen) ‹*wind*› blow **4** (formen) blow ‹*bottle, glass, etc.*› **5** (derb) suck off (coarse); **jmdm. einen ~:** suck sb. off (coarse); give sb. a blow job (coarse)
C *unr. unpers. V.* **es bläst** it's windy *or* blowy

Blasen-: **~bildung** *die* blistering; **sonst kommt es zur ~bildung** or blisters will form; **~katarrh** *der* ▸❶ **S. 439** (Med.) cystitis *no indef. art.*; **~leiden** *das* bladder complaint; **ein ~leiden haben** have bladder trouble *or* a bladder complaint; **~schwäche** *die* bladder weakness; **~stein** *der* (Med.) bladder stone; vesical calculus (Med.); **~tee** *der:* herbal

b

b

tea taken for bladder complaints

Bläser /ˈblɛːzɐ/ *der;* **~s,** ~ **1** (Musik) wind player; **die ~:** the wind section *sing.* **2** (Bergmannsspr.) blower

Bläser·ensemble *das* wind ensemble

Bläserin *die;* **~, ~nen** (Musik) wind player

Bläser·quartett *das* wind quartet

blasiert /blaˈziːɐ̯t/ (abwertend)
A *Adj.* blasé
B *adv.* in a blasé way

Blasiertheit *die;* **~:** blasé attitude

blasig *Adj.* blistered ‹*paint, skin*›; bubbly ‹*liquid*›; [light and] frothy ‹*dough*›

Blas-: ~instrument *das* wind instrument; **~kapelle** *die* brass band; **~musik** *die* brass band music; (~kapelle) brass band; **~orchester** *das* brass band

Blasphemie /blasfeˈmiː/ *die;* **~, ~n** blasphemy

blasphemisch
A *Adj.* blasphemous
B *adv.* blasphemously

Blas·rohr *das* **1** (Waffe) blowpipe **2** (Technik) blast pipe

blass, *blaß /blas/
A *Adj.* **1** pale ‹*face, skin, colour, complexion*›; pale, wan ‹*light, glow*›; faint ‹*writing*›; (fig.) colourless ‹*account, portrayal, etc.*›; **~ werden** turn *or* go pale; (vor Angst, Schreck) pale; turn *or* go pale; **Rot macht dich ~:** red makes you look pale [in the face]; **~ wie eine Wand/wie der Tod** white as a sheet/deathly pale; **~ vor Neid sein/werden** (fig.) be/turn *or* go green with envy **2** (schwach) faint, dim ‹*recollection, suspicion*›; faint ‹*hope, similarity*›; only slight ‹*effect*› **3** **der ~e Neid** sheer *or* pure envy
B *adv.* (matt) palely

blass·blau, *blaß·blau *Adj.* pale blue

Blässe /ˈblɛsə/ *die;* **~** (der Haut) paleness; pallor; (der Farbe) paleness; (des Lichts) paleness; wanness

blass: ~gelb *Adj.* pale yellow; **~grün** *Adj.* pale green

Bläss·huhn, *Bläß·huhn /ˈblɛs-/ *das* coot

blässlich, *bläßlich
A *Adj.* **1** rather pale; palish **2** (unscheinbar, nichts sagend) colourless ‹*person, account, portrayal, etc.*›
B *adv.* (nichts sagend) colourlessly

blass·rosa, *blaß·rosa *indekl. Adj.* pale pink

Blatt /blat/ *das;* **~[e]s, Blätter** /ˈblɛtɐ/ **1** (von Pflanzen) leaf; **kein ~ vor den Mund nehmen** not mince one's words **2** (Papier) sheet; **ein ~ Papier** a sheet of paper; **fliegende Blätter** loose leaves *or* sheets; **[noch] ein unbeschriebenes ~ sein** (ugs.) (unerfahren sein) be inexperienced; (unbekannt sein) be an unknown quantity **3** (Buchseite usw.) page; leaf; **etw. vom ~ spielen** sight-read sth.; **auf einem anderen ~ stehen** (fig.) be [quite] another *or* a different matter **4** (Zeitung) paper **5** (Spielkarten) hand; **das ~ hat sich gewendet** (ugs.) things have changed **6** (am Werkzeug, Ruder) blade **7** (Grafik) print **8** (Jägerspr.) shoulder

Blatt·ader *die* leaf vein

Blättchen /ˈblɛtçən/ *das;* **~s,** ~ **1** (von Pflanzen) [small] leaf **2** (Papier) [small] sheet **3** (abwertend: Zeitung) rag (derog.)

Blätter·dach *das* leafy canopy

blatterig ▸ **blattrig**

blätterig ▸ **blättrig**

-blätterig ▸ **-blättrig**

blättern /ˈblɛtɐn/
A *itr. V.* **1** **in einem Buch ~:** leaf through a book **2** *mit sein* (zerfallen) flake **3** *mit sein* (sich ablösen) ‹*paint, plaster, etc.*› flake off
B *tr. V.* put down [one by one]; **er blätterte mir 50 Euro auf den Tisch** he counted me out fifty euros in notes on the table

Blattern *Pl.* ▸ **i S. 439** smallpox *sing.*

Blatter·narbe *die* pockmark

blatternarbig *Adj.* pockmarked

Blätter-: ~pilz *der* agaric; **~schmuck** *der* (geh.) foliage; **~teig** *der* puff pastry; **~teiggebäck** *das* puff pastries *pl.*; **~wald** *der* (scherzh.) press; **es rauscht im ~wald** there are murmurings *or* rumblings in the press; **~werk** *das* foliage

blatt-, Blatt-: ~feder *die* (Technik) leaf spring; **~gewächs** *das* (Bot.) foliage plant; **~gold** *das* gold leaf; **~grün** *das* chlorophyll; **~knospe** *die* leaf bud; **~laus** *die* aphid; greenfly; **~los** *Adj.* leafless; **~metall** *das* foil; **~pflanze** *die* foliage plant

blattrig *Adj.* pockmarked

blättrig *Adj.* **1** (von Pflanzen) leafy **2** (abblätternd) flaky

-blättrig *adj.* -leaved

blatt-, Blatt-: ~säge *die* wide-bladed [hand]saw; **~salat** *der* green salad; **~silber** *das* silver leaf; **~spinat** *der* leaf spinach; **~wanze** *die* lygus bug; **~weise** *Adv.* **1** (bei Pflanzen) leaf by leaf; **2** (bei Papier) sheet by sheet; **~werk** *das* (geh.) foliage

blau /blau̯/ *Adj.* blue; **ein ~es Auge [haben/** (ugs.) **kriegen]** [have/get] a black eye; **mit einem ~en Auge davonkommen** (fig. ugs.) get off fairly lightly; **jmdm. ein ~es Auge hauen** *od.* **schlagen** give sb. a black eye; **etw. nicht nur wegen jmds. schöner ~er Augen tun** not do sth. just out of the goodness of one's heart; **ein ~er Fleck** a bruise; **die ~en Jungs** (ugs.: die Marine) the boys in blue; **der Blaue Planet** Earth; **die ~e Stunde** (dichter.) the twilight hour; **die ~e Blume [der Romantik]** the Blue Flower [of the Romantics]; **ein ~er Brief** (ugs.) (Kündigung) one's cards *pl.*; (*Schulw.*) *letter informing parents that their child is in danger of having to repeat a year;* **Forelle ~** (Kochk.) blue trout; **einen ~en Montag einlegen** *od.* **machen** (ugs.) skip work on Monday; **sein ~es Wunder erleben** (ugs.) get a nasty surprise; **jmdm. ~en Dunst vormachen** (ugs.) pull the wool over sb.'s eyes; **~ sein** (fig. ugs.) be tight (coll.) *or* canned (sl.); **~ sein wie ein Veilchen** *od.* **wie eine [Strand]haubitze** *od.* **wie [zehn]tausend Mann** (salopp) be [completely] canned (sl.)

> **Blauer Brief**
>
> A letter sent by a school to inform parents that their son or daughter is in danger of having to repeat the year, a concept colloquially known as **sitzen bleiben.**

> **Blauer Engel**
>
> The Blue Angel is a round logo of a figure with spread arms within a wreath. The label shows consumers that the product on sale is environmentally friendly. Information as to what makes it an environmentally compatible product is given on the label.

Blau *das;* **~s,** ~ *od.* (ugs.:) **~s** blue

blau-, Blau-: ~alge *die* blue-green alga; **~äugig** *Adj.* **1** blue-eyed; **2** (naiv) naive; **~äugigkeit** /-lɔygɪçkai̯t/ *die;* **~** (fig.) naivety; **~bart** *der* Bluebeard; **~beere** *die* bilberry; whortleberry; **~blütig** *Adj.* (meist iron.) blue-blooded

Blaue /ˈblau̯ə/ *das;* **~n** blue; **das ~ vom Himmel [herunter]lügen** (ugs.) lie like anything; tell a pack of lies; **jmdm. das ~ vom Himmel [herunter] versprechen** (ugs.) promise sb. the earth *or* the moon; **wir wollen einfach ins ~ fahren** we'll just set off and see where we end up; *s. auch* **Fahrt 3**

Bläue /ˈblɔy̯ə/ *die;* **~** (geh.) blue; blueness; (des Himmels) blue

bläuen *tr. V.* **1** (färben) dye ‹*material, clothes, etc.*› blue; turn ‹*litmus paper*› blue **2** (aufhellen) blue

blau-, Blau-: ~färbung *die* blue colour; blueness; **~felchen** *das* Blaufelchen; whitefish; **~filter** *der od. das* (Fot.) blue filter; **~fuchs** *der* **1** (Tier) Arctic fox; blue fox; **2** (Fell) blue fox [fur]; **~grau** *Adj.* blue-grey; bluish grey; **~grün** *Adj.* blue-green; bluish green; **~hemd** *das* (DDR) **1** (Hemd) blue shirt [of the Free German Youth]; **2** (ugs.: Mitglied) member of the Free German Youth; **~holz** *das* logwood; **~kabis** *der* (schweiz.), **~kohl** *der* (bes. nordd.), **~kraut** *das* (südd., österr.) ▸ **Rotkohl**

bläulich *Adj.* bluish

Blau·licht *das; Pl.* **~er** flashing blue light; **ein Krankenwagen raste mit ~ vorbei** an ambulance raced past with [its] blue light flashing

blau-, Blau-: ~|machen (ugs.) **A** *itr. V.* skip work; **B** *tr. V.* **den Freitag ~machen** skip work on Friday; **~mann** *der* (ugs.) boiler suit; **~meise** *die* blue tit; **~papier** *das* [blue] carbon paper; **~pause** *die* blueprint; **~rot** *Adj.* purple; **~säure** *die* (Chemie) prussic acid; hydrocyanic acid; **~schimmel** *der* blue mould; **~schwarz** *Adj.* blue-black; **~stichig** /-ʃtɪçɪç/ *Adj.* (Fot.) with a blue cast *postpos., not pred.*; **~stichig sein** have a blue cast; **~stift** *der* blue pencil; **~strumpf** *der* (abwertend) bluestocking; **~tanne** *die* blue spruce; Colorado spruce; **~wal** *der* blue whale

Blazer /ˈbleːzɐ/ *der;* **~s, ~:** blazer

Blech /blɛç/ *das;* **~[e]s, ~e** **1** (Metall) sheet metal **2** (Platte) metal sheet; (Grob~) metal plate **3** (Back~) [baking] tray **4** (ugs.: Unsinn) rubbish; nonsense; tripe (coll.) **5** (ugs. abwertend: Orden) medals *pl.*; gongs *pl.* (coll.) **6** (Musik: ~bläser) brass

Blech-: ~bläser *der*, **~bläserin** *die* brass player; **die ~bläser** (im Orchester) the brass [section] *sing;* **~blas·instrument** *das* brass instrument; **~büchse** *die*, **~dose** *die* tin; **~eimer** *der* metal bucket

blechen *tr., itr. V.* (ugs.) cough up (coll.); fork out (coll.)

blechern /ˈblɛçɐn/
A *Adj.* **1** (aus Blech) metal **2** (metallisch klingend) tinny ‹*sound, voice*›
B *adv.* (metallisch) tinnily

Blech-: ~instrument *das* brass instrument; **~kiste** *die* (ugs. abwertend) crate (sl.); **~lawine** *die* (ugs. scherzh.) solid line of cars; **~musik** *die* (abwertend) brass band music; **~napf** *der* metal bowl

Blechner *der;* **~s, ~, Blechnerin** *die;* **~, ~nen** (südd.) ▸ **Klempner**

Blech-: ~schaden *der* (Kfz-W.) damage *no indef. art.* to the bodywork; **~schere** *die* metal shears *pl.;* **~schmied** *der*, **~schmiedin** *die* (nordwestd.) ▸ **Klempner**; **~trommel** *die* tin drum

blecken /ˈblɛkn̩/ *tr. V.* **die Zähne ~:** bare one's/its teeth

Blei[1] /blai̯/ *das;* **~[e]s, ~e** **1** lead; **~ gießen** *pour lead into cold water to tell one's fortune for the coming year;* **jmdm. wie ~ in den Gliedern** *od.* **Knochen liegen** ‹*tiredness, exhaustion, shock, etc.*› make sb.'s limbs feel like lead; **jmdm. wie ~ im Magen liegen** (schwer verdaulich sein) weigh heavily on sb.'s stomach; (jmdn. bedrücken) prey on sb.'s mind **2** (Lot) plumb [bob] **3** (veralt.) (Gewehrkugeln) lead

Blei[2] *der od. das;* **~[e]s, ~e** (~stift) pencil

Bleibe *die;* **~, ~n** place to stay; **keine ~ haben** have nowhere to stay

bleiben /ˈblai̯bn̩/ *unr. itr. V.; mit sein* **1** (an einem Ort) stay; remain; **~ Sie bitte am Apparat** hold the line please; **wo bleibt er so lange?** where has he got to?; **wo bleibst du denn so lange?** where have you been *or* what's been keeping you all this time?; **wo bleibt der Kaffee?** where has the coffee got to?; what has happened to the coffee?; **wo sind die Blumen geblieben?** what's happened to the flowers?; **wo ~ nur die Jahre?** how the years have flown!; **zum Abendessen ~:** stay for supper; **auf dem Weg ~:** keep to *or* stay on the path; **da ~ wir ganz unter** (*Dat.*) *od.* **für uns** there will just be us; **jmdm. in Erinnerung** *od.* **im Gedächtnis ~:** stay in sb.'s mind *or* memory; **von etw. ~** (ugs.) stay *or* keep away from sth.; **das bleibt unter uns** (*Dat.*) that's [just] between ourselves; **zusehen, wo man bleibt** (ugs.) have to fend for oneself; **ich kann sehen, wo ich bleibe** I'm left to shift for myself; **jmdn. zum Bleiben auffordern** ask sb. to stay; **hier ist meines Bleibens nicht länger** (veralt., scherzh.) I shall not stay here any longer; **bleibe im Lande und nähre dich redlich**

there's a good living to be had in your own country; *s. auch* **Rahmen 2**; **Sache 2** **2** (Zustand, Eigenschaft beibehalten) stay; remain; **der Kuchen bleibt mehrere Tage frisch** the cake will keep for several days; **bleib ruhig!** keep calm!; **das Geschäft bleibt heute geschlossen** the shop is closed today; **der Brief blieb unbeantwortet** the letter went *or* remained unanswered; **unbestraft/unbeachtet ~:** go unpunished/go unnoticed *or* escape notice; **dieser Tag wird uns** (*Dat.*) **immer unvergessen ~:** we shall always remember this day; **sitzen ~:** stay *or* remain sitting down *or* seated; **~ Sie doch bitte sitzen** please don't get up; **ich bleibe lieber stehen** I would rather stand; **Freunde ~:** remain friends; go on being friends **3** (übrig ~) be left; remain; **uns** (*Dat.*) **bleibt noch Zeit** we still have time; **bis zur Abreise bleibt uns weniger als eine Stunde** there is less than an hour before we leave; **es blieb ihm keine Hoffnung mehr** he had no hope left; **was bleibt mir dann noch?** what shall I have left?; *s. auch* **Wahl 4** (für die Zukunft) **es bleibt abzuwarten, ob ...** it remains to be seen whether ...; **es bleibt zu hoffen, dass ...** we can only hope that ...; **bei dem Wein ~ wir** we'll stick to *or* with *or* keep to this wine **5** (nicht ändern) **bei etw. ~:** keep *or* stick to sth.; **ich bleibe dabei, dass ...** I still say that ...; **dabei bleibt es!** that's that; that's the end of it **6** (verhüll.: sterben) **im Feld/im Krieg/auf See ~:** die *or* fall in action/die in the war/at sea **7** **etw. ~ lassen** give sth. a miss; forget sth.; **das wirst du mal schön ~ lassen** you can forget about that; **das Rauchen ~ lassen** give up *or* stop smoking

bleibend *Adj.* lasting; permanent ‹*damage*›

***bleiben|lassen** ▸ **bleiben 7**

Bleibe·recht *das* right of abode

bleich /blaiç/ *Adj.* **1** pale; **~ vor Angst/Wut sein** be white with fear/rage; **~ wie eine Wand/wie der Tod** white as a sheet/deathly pale; **~ werden** turn *or* go pale; (vor Angst, Schreck) pale; turn *or* go pale **2** (geh.: fahl) pale ‹*light, gleam*›

Bleiche *die*; **~, ~n** **1** (veralt.: für Wäsche) bleaching field; bleaching ground **2** (geh.: Blässe) paleness; (des Gesichts, der Haut) pallor; paleness

bleichen¹ *tr. V.* bleach

bleichen² *regelm.* (*veralt. auch unr.*) *itr. V.* become bleached; bleach; **in der Sonne ~:** be bleached by the sun

bleich-, Bleich-: ~gesicht *das*; *Pl.* **~er** **1** pale face; (ugs.: blasser Mensch) pale-faced *or* pasty-faced type (coll.); **2** (scherzh.: Weißer) paleface; **~gesichtig** *Adj.* (ugs.) pale-faced; pasty-faced; **~mittel** *das* bleach; bleaching agent; **~sucht** *die* (veralt.) chlorosis; greensickness; **~süchtig** *Adj.* (veralt.) chlorotic; greensick

bleiern /ˈblaiən/

A *Adj.* **1** (aus Blei) lead; **er schwimmt wie eine ~e Ente** (ugs. scherzh.) he can't swim for toffee (Brit. coll.) *or* swim a stroke **2** (geh.: bleifarben) leaden ‹*sky, grey*› **3** (schwer) heavy ‹*sleep, tiredness, etc.*›; leaden ‹*heaviness*›; **seine Füße waren ~:** his feet were like lead

B *adv.* (fig.: schwer) heavily; **es lag ihr ~ in den Gliedern** her limbs felt like lead *or* as heavy as lead

blei-, Blei-: ~erz *das* lead ore; **~farben, ~farbig** *Adj.* lead-coloured; lead-grey; leaden ‹*sky*›; **~frei** **A** *Adj.* unleaded ‹*fuel*›; **B** *adv.* **~frei fahren/tanken** drive on/use unleaded fuel; **~fuß** *der*: **in mit ~fuß fahren** (ugs. scherzh.) drive with one's foot down to the floor; **~gehalt** *der* lead content; **~gewicht** *das* (auch fig.) lead weight; **~gießen** *das*: *pouring lead into cold water to tell one's fortune for the coming year*; **~glanz** *der* (Mineral.) galena; **~glas** *das* lead glass; **~haltig** *Adj.* ‹*petrol, paint, etc.*› containing lead; plumbiferous, lead-bearing ‹*ore*›; **~haltig sein** ‹*petrol, paint, etc.*› contain lead; **die Luft hier ist ziemlich ~haltig** (salopp scherzh.) there's plenty of lead flying around; **~hütte** *die* lead works *sing.*; **~kristall** *das* lead crystal; **~kugel** *die* **1** (Geschoss) lead bullet; **2** (Kugel) lead ball; **~oxid, ~oxyd** *das* (Chemie) lead oxide; **~satz** *der* (Druckw.) hot-metal composition; **~schürze** *die* lead apron; **~schwer** **A** *Adj.* heavy as lead *postpos.*; **B** *adv.* heavily; like a heavy *or* lead weight; **~soldat** *der* lead soldier

Blei·stift *der* pencil; **mit ~:** in pencil

Bleistift-: ~absatz *der* stiletto heel; **~mine** *die* [pencil] lead; **~spitzer** *der* pencil sharpener; **~zeichnung** *die* pencil drawing

Blei-: ~vergiftung *die* lead poisoning; **~wüste** *die* (Jargon, abwertend) solid mass of print

Blend /blɛnt/ *der od. das*; **~s, ~s** blend

Blende *die*; **~, ~n** **1** (Lichtschutz) shade; (am Fenster) blind; (im Auto) [sun] visor **2** (Optik, Film, Fot.: Vorrichtung) diaphragm; **die ~ öffnen/schließen** open up the aperture/stop down **3** (Film, Fot.: ~nzahl) aperture setting; f-number; **mit** *od.* **bei ~ 8** at [an aperture setting of] f/8; **~ 11 einstellen** set the aperture to *or* at f/11 **4** (Film: Einstellung) fade; **einen Film mit einer ~ anfangen/enden lassen** start a film with a fade-in/end a film with a fade-out **5** (Stoffstreifen) trimming **6** (Archit.) blind window/arch/niche *etc.* **7** (Chemie) blende

blenden

A *tr. V.* **1** (auch beeindrucken, täuschen) dazzle **2** (blind machen) blind **3** (Kürschnerei) blend

B *itr. V.* **1** ‹*light*› be dazzling **2** (täuschen) dazzle people

Blenden·automatik *die* (Fot.) automatic aperture control

blendend

A *Adj.* splendid; brilliant ‹*musician, dancer, speech, achievement, etc.*›; **es geht mir ~:** I feel wonderfully well *or* wonderful

B *adv.* **wir haben uns ~ amüsiert** we had a wonderful *or* marvellous time

Blender *der*; **~s, ~, Blenderin** *die*; **~, ~nen** (ugs.) fraud; phoney (sl.)

blend·frei *Adj.* **1** (nicht blendend) non-dazzle **2** (nicht spiegelnd) non-dazzle; non-reflective

Blend·laterne *die* dark lantern

Blendung *die*; **~, ~en** **1** dazzling **2** (Täuschung) deception **3** (Strafe) blinding **4** (Kürschnerei) blending

Blend·werk *das* (geh. abwertend) deception; **ein ~ des Teufels** a trap set by the devil

Blesse /ˈblɛsə/ *die*; **~, ~n** **1** (Fleck) blaze **2** (Tier) horse/cow *etc.* with a/the blaze

Bless·huhn, *Bleß·huhn *das* ▸ **Blässhuhn**

blessiert /blɛsiːɐ̯t/ *Adj.* (geh., scherzh.) (verletzt) injured; (verwundet) wounded

Blessur /blɛˈsuːɐ̯/ *die*; **~, ~en** (veralt., scherzh.) (Verletzung) injury; (Wunde) wound

bleu /blø:/ *indekl. Adj.* light *or* pale blue

Bleu *das*; **~s, ~** *od.* (ugs.) **~s** light *or* pale blue

blich /blɪç/ *1. u. 3. Pers. Sg. Prät. v.* **bleichen²**

Blick /blɪk/ *der*; **~[e]s, ~e** **1** (das Anschauen) look; (flüchtig) glance; **jmdm. einen ~/sich ~e zuwerfen** give sb. a look/exchange glances; **einen kurzen ~ auf etw.** (*Akk.*) **werfen** take a quick look at *or* glance [briefly] at sth.; **einen ~ riskieren** (ugs.) venture a glance; **jmds. ~** (*Dat.*) **ausweichen** avoid sb.'s glance *or* eye; **jmds. ~** (*Akk.*) **erwidern** return sb.'s look *or* gaze; **ein ~ in die Vergangenheit/Zukunft** a look back [into the past]/a look into the future; **auf den ersten ~:** at first glance; **auf den zweiten ~:** looking at it again *or* a second time; **etw. mit einem ~ sehen** see sth. at a glance; **keinen ~ für jmdn./etw. haben** take no notice of sb./sth.; **jmdn./etw. im ~ haben** be looking at sb./sth.; **wenn ~e töten könnten!** if looks could kill; **einen ~ hinter die Kulissen werfen** *od.* **tun** take a look behind the scenes; **den ~ heben** (geh.) raise one's eyes; look up; **den ~ senken** (geh.) lower one's eyes; look down; **mein ~ fiel auf den Brief** my eye fell on the letter; the letter caught my eye; **er wendete keinen ~ von der attraktiven Frau** his eyes never left the attractive woman; **jmdn. mit seinen ~en verschlingen** devour sb. with one's eyes; **jmdn. mit ~en durchbohren** look piercingly at sb.; *s. auch* **Liebe 1**; **würdigen 2** **2** (Ausdruck) look in one's eyes; **mit misstrauischem ~:** with a suspicious look in one's eye; **mit zärtlichem ~:** with a tender look in one's eyes; *s. auch* **böse** **3** (Aussicht) view; **ein Zimmer mit ~ aufs Meer** a room with a sea view; **jmdn./etw. aus dem ~ verlieren** lose sight of sb./sth.; **etw. im ~ haben** be able to see sth. **4** (Urteil[skraft]) eye; **einen sicheren/geschulten ~ für etw. haben** have a sure/trained eye for sth.; **keinen ~ für etw. haben** have no eye for sth.; **seinen ~ für etw. schärfen** sharpen one's awareness of sth.

blicken

A *itr. V.* look; (flüchtig) glance; **jmdm. gerade in die Augen ~:** look sb. straight in the eye; **zur Seite ~:** look away; **auf das vergangene Jahr ~** (fig.) look back on the past year; **das lässt tief ~** (ugs.) that's very revealing

B *tr. V.* **sich ~ lassen** put in an appearance; **lass dich mal wieder ~:** come again some time; **er hat sich lange nicht mehr ~ lassen** he hasn't been seen for a long time; **sie wagt es nicht, sich ~ zu lassen** she dare not show her face; **er lässt sich ja nie ~:** he's never around (coll.)

Blick-: ~fang *der* eye-catcher; **als ~fang dienen** serve to catch the eye; **~feld** *das* field of vision *or* view; **er hat ein recht enges ~feld** (fig.) he has really narrow horizons *pl.*; **jmdn./etw. ins ~feld der Öffentlichkeit rücken** make sb./sth. the focus of public attention; **~kontakt** *der* eye contact; **~punkt** *der* view; field of vision; **im ~punkt der Öffentlichkeit stehen** (fig.) be in the public eye; **jmdn. in den ~punkt rücken** (fig.) single sb. out; **in den ~punkt treten** (fig.) become the focus of attention; enter the limelight; **~richtung** *die* **1** line of sight *or* vision; **in ~richtung [nach] rechts** to the *or* on your right; looking to your right; **2** (fig.) perspective; **~winkel** *der* **1** angle of vision; **2** (fig.) point of view; viewpoint; perspective

blieb /bli:p/ *1. u. 3. Pers. Sg. Prät. v.* **bleiben**

blies /bli:s/ *1. u. 3. Pers. Sg. Prät. v.* **blasen**

Blimp /blɪmp/ *der*; **~s, ~s** blimp

blind /blɪnt/

A *Adj.* **1** blind; **~ werden** go blind; **auf einem Auge ~ sein** be blind in one eye; **auf dem Auge ist sie ~** (fig. ugs.) she refuses to see that; **~ für etw. sein** be blind to sth.; **~ vor Tränen** (geh.) blinded by tears; *s. auch* **Huhn** **2** (maßlos) blind ‹*rage, hatred, fear, etc.*›; indiscriminate ‹*violence*›; **~ fliegen** fly blind; **~ schreiben** touch-type **3** (kritiklos) blind ‹*obedience, enthusiasm, belief, etc.*› ; **~er Eifer schadet nur** (Spr.) haste makes waste (prov.) **4** (trübe) clouded ‹*glass*›; dull, tarnished ‹*metal*› **5** (verdeckt) concealed; invisible ‹*seam*›; **ein ~er Passagier** a stowaway **6** **~er Alarm** a false alarm **7** (undurchschaubar) **der ~e Zufall** pure *or* sheer chance; **das ~e Walten des Schicksals** (geh.) the unfathomable workings *pl.* of fate **8** (vorgetäuscht) false ‹*pocket, buttonhole, etc.*›; blind ‹*window, arch, etc.*›

B *adv.* **1** (ohne hinzusehen) without looking; (wahllos) blindly; wildly **2** (unkritisch) ‹*trust*› implicitly; ‹*obey*› blindly **3** (verdeckt) **der Mantel wird ~ geknöpft** the coat has concealed buttons

Blind-: ~band *der*; *Pl.* **~bände** (Buchw.) dummy; **~bewerbung** *die* unsolicited application

Blind·darm *der* **1** ▸**i** **S. 435** (Anat.: Teil des Dickdarms) caecum **2** (volkst.: Wurmfortsatz) appendix

Blind·darm-: ~entzündung *die* ▸**i** **S. 439** (volkst.) appendicitis; **~operation** *die* (volkst.) appendix operation; **~reizung** *die* (volkst.) grumbling appendix

Blinde *der/die*; *adj. Dekl.* blind person; blind man/woman; **die ~n** the blind; **das sieht doch ein ~r [mit dem Krückstock]** (ugs.) anyone *or* any fool can see that; *s. auch* **einäugig**

Blinde·kuh *in* **~ spielen** play blind man's buff

b

Blinden-: ~**anstalt** *die* ▸ ~heim; ~**führer** *der*, ~**führerin** *die* blind person's guide; ~**heim** *das* home for the blind; ~**hund** *der* guide dog; ~**schrift** *die* Braille; ~**stock** *der* white stick

blind-, Blind-: ~**fenster** *das* (Bauw.) blind window; ~**fisch** *der* 1 (Zool.) blindfish; 2 (ugs.) clueless individual; ~|**fliegen** ▸ blind A1; ~**flug** *der* blind flight; (das ~fliegen) blind flying; **im ~flug** ‹*land, take off, etc.*› blind; ~**gänger** *der*; ~~s, ~~ 1 (Geschoss) unexploded shell; dud (sl.); 2 (salopp: Versager) dead loss (coll.)

Blindheit *die*; ~ (auch fig.) blindness; **[wie] mit ~ geschlagen sein** be [as if struck] blind

Blind·landung *die* (Flugw.) blind landing

blindlings /ˈblɪntlɪŋs/ *Adv.* blindly; ‹*trust*› implicitly

blind-, Blind-: ~**material** *das* (Druckw.) spacing material; ~**probe** *die* blind tasting; ~**schleiche** /-ʃlaiçə/ *die*; ~~, ~~n slow-worm; blindworm; ~|**schreiben** ▸ blind A1; ~**spiel** *das* (Schach) blindfold game; ~**verkostung** *die s.* **Blindprobe**; ~**versuch** *der* blind test; ~**wütig** A *Adj.* raging ‹*anger, hatred, fury, etc.*›; wild ‹*rage*›; **~wütige Schläge** furious blows; B *adv.* in a blind rage *or* fury; ~**wütigkeit** *die*; ~~: blind rage *or* fury

blinken /ˈblɪŋkn̩/

A *itr. V.* 1 (Verkehrsw.) indicate 2 (Signal geben) **mit Lampen ~:** flash lamps 3 (leuchten) ‹*light, glass, crystal*› flash; ‹*star*› twinkle; ‹*metal, fish*› gleam; ‹*water, wine*› sparkle; **das ganze Haus blinkte vor Sauberkeit** the whole house was sparkling clean

B *tr. V.* (Signal geben) flash; **SOS ~:** flash an SOS [signal]

Blinker *der*; ~s, ~ 1 (am Auto) indicator [light]; winker 2 (Angeln) spoon[-bait]

Blink-: ~**feuer** *das* (Seew.) flashing light; ~**gerät** *das* (Milit.) signalling apparatus; signal lamp; ~**leuchte** *die* (Kfz-W.) indicator [light]; winker; ~**licht** *das*; *Pl.* ~~er (Verkehrsw.) flashing light; ~**licht·anlage** *die* (Verkehrsw.) flashing lights *pl.*; ~**signal** *das*, ~**zeichen** *das* flashlight signal

blinzeln /ˈblɪntsl̩n/ *itr. V.* blink; (mit einem Auge, um ein Zeichen zu geben) wink

Blitz /blɪts/ *der*; ~es, ~e 1 (bei Gewitter) lightning *no indef. art.*; **ein ~:** a flash of lightning; **der ~ hat eingeschlagen** lightning has struck; **war das ein ~?** was that [a flash of] lightning?; **seine Augen schossen ~e** (fig.) his eyes flashed; **potz ~!** (veralt.) upon my soul!; good heavens!; **[schnell] wie der ~:** like lightning; as fast as lightning; **wie ein geölter ~** (ugs.) like greased lightning; **wie ein ~ aus heiterem Himmel** like a bolt from the blue; **wie ein ~ einschlagen** be a bombshell; **wie vom ~ getroffen** thunderstruck 2 (~licht) flash

blitz-, Blitz-: ~**ab·leiter** *der* lightning conductor; ~**aktion** *die* lightning operation; ~**angriff** *der* (Milit.) lightning attack; ~**artig** A *Adj.* lightning; B *adv.* like lightning; ‹*disappear*› in a flash; ~**blank** *Adj.* (ugs.) **~blank [geputzt]** sparkling clean; brightly polished ‹*shoes*›

blitzeblank ▸ blitzblank

Blitz·eis *das* sheet ice

blitzen

A *itr. V.* 1 *unpers.* (bei Gewitter) **es blitzte** (einmal) there was a flash of lightning; (mehrmals) there was lightning; there were flashes of lightning; **bei dir blitzt es** (ugs. scherzh.) your slip is showing; Charlie's dead (Brit. coll.); it's snowing down south (Brit. coll.) 2 (glänzen) ‹*light, glass, crystal*› flash; ‹*metal*› gleam; **sie hatte weiße, ~de Zähne** she had sparkling white teeth; **das Haus blitzte vor Sauberkeit** the house was sparkling clean; **Zorn blitzte aus ihren Augen** (fig.) her eyes flashed with anger 3 (nackt laufen) streak (coll.) 4 (ugs.: mit Blitzlicht) use [a] flash; **er fing wie wild an zu ~:** he started to flash away like mad (coll.)

B *tr. V.* (ugs.: mit Blitzlicht) take a flash photo of

Blitzer *der*; ~s, ~, **Blitzerin** *die*; ~, ~nen (ugs.) streaker (coll.)

Blitzes·schnelle *die*: in **in** *od.* **mit ~:** at lightning speed; ‹*disappear*› in a flash

blitz-, Blitz-: ~**gerät** *das* (Fot.) flash [unit]; flashgun; ~**gescheit** *Adj.* very bright; ~**gespräch** *das* priority call (*with tenfold call charge*); ~**krieg** *der* (Milit.) blitzkrieg; ~**licht** *das*; *Pl.* ~er flash[light]; **mit ~licht** by flash[light]; ~**licht·aufnahme** *die* flash[light] photograph; ~**licht·foto** *das* flash photo[graph]; ~**licht·gewitter** *das* (ugs.) explosion of flashlights; ~**reise** *die* flying visit; ~**sauber** *Adj.* **~sauber [geputzt]** sparkling clean; ~**schlag** *der* flash of lightning; **von einem ~schlag getroffen werden** be struck *or* hit by lightning; ~**schnell** A *Adj.* lightning *attrib.*; **~schnell sein** be like lightning; B *adv.* like lightning; ‹*disappear*› in a flash; **das alles geschah so ~schnell, dass ...** it all happened so quickly that ...; ~**sieg** *der* (Milit.) lightning victory; ~**start** *der* lightning start; ~**telegramm** *das* priority telegram (*with tenfold charge*); ~**um·frage** *die* lightning poll; ~**würfel** *der* (Fot.) flashcube

Blizzard /ˈblɪzɐt/ *der*; ~s, ~s blizzard

blochen /ˈblɔxn̩/ *tr., itr. V.* (bes. schweiz.) polish

Blocher *der*; ~s, ~ (schweiz.) floor polisher

Block /blɔk/ *der*; ~[e]s, **Blöcke** /ˈblœkə/ *od.* ~s 1 *Pl. nur* **Blöcke** (Brocken) block; (Fels~) boulder 2 (Wohn~) block 3 *Pl. nur* **Blöcke** (Gruppierung von politischen Kräften, Staaten) bloc 4 (Schreib~) pad 5 (Basketball) screen; (Volleyball) block 6 *Pl. nur* ~s (Eisenb.) block 7 (Philat.) block 8 (ns.: Organisationseinheit) block [of houses]

Blockade /blɔˈkaːdə/ *die*; ~, ~n 1 (Absperrung) blockade; **eine ~ brechen** run a blockade 2 (Druckw.) [space marked by] turned letter[s] (*indicating missing or illegible material*)

Blockade·brecher *der*, **Blockade·brecherin** *die*; ~, ~nen blockade-runner

Block-: ~**bildung** *die* formation *or* creation of a bloc/blocs; ~**buchstabe** *der* block capital *or* letter

blocken

A *tr. V.* 1 (südd.: bohnern) polish 2 (bes. Boxen: abfangen; Ballspiele: sperren) block

B *itr. V.* 1 (südd.: bohnern) polish 2 (bes. Boxen: abfangen; Ballspiele: sperren) block 3 (Jägerspr.) perch

block-, Block-: ~**flöte** *die* recorder; ~**frei** *Adj.* non-aligned ‹*country, state*›; ~**freie** *der*; *adj. Dekl.* non-aligned country *or* state; ~**haus** *das*, ~**hütte** *die* log cabin; ~**heiz·kraftwerk** *das* block heating and generating plant

blockieren

A *tr. V.* 1 (sperren) blockade ‹*country, port*›; block ‹*access road, border crossing point, etc.*› 2 (verstopfen) block; jam ‹*telephone line*› 3 (unterbrechen) block ‹*supply*›; stop, halt ‹*traffic*› 4 (anhalten) lock ‹*wheel, machine, etc.*› 5 (unterbinden) block ‹*negotiations, proposal, etc.*› 6 (Druckw.) mark with turned letter[s] *etc.* (*to indicate missing or illegible material*)

B *itr. V.* (stehen bleiben) ‹*wheels*› lock; ‹*gears*› jam

Blockierung *die*; ~, ~en ▸ blockieren: blockade; blocking; locking; jamming; stopping; halting

Block-: ~**partei** *die* (bes. DDR) bloc party; ~**politik** *die* (bes. DDR) bloc policy; ~**schokolade** *die* cooking chocolate; ~**schrift** *die* block capitals *pl. or* letters *pl.*; ~**staaten** *Pl.* aligned countries *or* states; **die ~staaten des Westens und des Ostens** the countries of the Western and Eastern blocs; ~**stunde** *die* (Schulw.) double period; ~**unterricht** *der* theme-work teaching *no art.*; teaching using the theme method *or* approach *no art.*; ~**wart** *der* (ns.) block warden

blöd[e] /ˈbløːt, ˈbløːdə/

A *Adj.* 1 (schwachsinnig) mentally deficient; imbecilic 2 (unsinnig, ugs.: dumm) stupid; idiotic (coll.) 3 (ugs.: unangenehm) stupid; **das Blöde ist nur, dass ...** the stupid thing is that ...

B *adv.* 1 (schwachsinnig) imbecilically 2 (unsinnig, ugs.: dumm) stupidly; idiotically (coll.); **er hat vielleicht ~ geguckt** a really stupid look came across his face; **frag doch nicht so ~:** don't ask such stupid *or* (coll.) idiotic questions 3 (ärgerlich) stupidly

Blödel /ˈbløːdl̩/ *der*; ~s, ~ ▸ **Blödian**

Blödelei *die*; ~, ~en 1 messing *or* fooling about *no indef. art.* 2 (Äußerung) silly joke

blödeln *itr. V.* 1 mess *or* fool about 2 (sich äußern) make silly jokes

blöder·weise *Adv.* (ugs.) stupidly

Blöd·hammel *der* (salopp abwertend) stupid fool *or* (coll.) idiot *or* (Brit. coll.) twit *or* (Amer. coll.) jerk

Blödheit *die*; ~, ~en 1 (Dummsein) stupidity 2 (dumme Äußerung) stupid remark; (dumme Tat) stupidity 3 (Schwachsinnigkeit) mental deficiency; imbecility

Blödian /ˈbløːdi̯aːn/ *der*; ~s, ~e (ugs. abwertend) idiot (coll.); fool

Blödler *der*; ~s, ~, **Blödlerin** *die* (ugs.) silly joker

Blödling *der*; ~s, ~e ▸ **Blödian**

blöd-, Blöd-: ~**mann** *der* (salopp) stupid idiot (coll.) *or* fool; ~**sinn** *der* (ugs. abwertend) nonsense; **jetzt habe ich ~sinn gemacht** now I've [gone and] messed it up; **mach doch keinen ~sinn!** don't be stupid; **was machst du denn da für einen ~sinn?** what are you messing about at?; **hör jetzt auf mit dem ~sinn** stop that nonsense; stop fooling *or* messing around; **höherer ~sinn** (iron.) high-flown nonsense; ~**sinnig** A *Adj.* 1 (ugs.: unsinnig) stupid; idiotic (coll.); 2 (schwachsinnig) mentally deficient; imbecilic; B *adv.* (ugs.) stupidly; idiotically (coll.); **frag doch nicht so ~sinnig** don't ask such stupid *or* (coll.) idiotic questions; ~**sinnigkeit** *die*; ~~ (ugs.) stupidity; idiocy (coll.)

blöken /ˈbløːkn̩/ *itr. V.* ‹*sheep*› bleat; ‹*cattle*› low

blond /blɔnt/ *Adj.* fair-haired, blond ‹*man, race*›; blonde, fair-haired ‹*woman*›; blond/blonde, fair ‹*hair*›; **ein ~es Gift** (ugs. scherzh.) a blonde bombshell; **~ gefärbt** dyed blond/blonde; **~ gelocktes Haar** fair curly hair; **ein ~ gelocktes Kind** a child with fair curly hair

Blond *das*; ~s blond; (von Frauenhaar) blonde; **ihr ~ ist aus der Tube** her blonde hair comes from a bottle

Blondchen *das*; ~s, ~ (ugs. abwertend) blonde bimbo (coll.)

Blonde[1] *der/die*; *adj. Dekl.* (blonder Mann) fair-haired *or* blond man; (blonde Frau) blonde

Blonde[2] *das od. die*; *adj. Dekl.* (ugs.: Bier) light beer; ≈ lager

blond·gefärbt, blond·gelockt ▸ blond

blondieren *tr. V.* bleach; (mit Färbemittel) dye blond/blonde; **sich ~ lassen** have one's hair bleached/dyed blond/blonde

Blondierung *die*; ~, ~en 1 ▸ blondieren: bleaching; dyeing blond/blonde 2 (blonde Farbe) blond colour

Blondine /blɔnˈdiːnə/ *die*; ~, ~n blonde

Blond-: ~**kopf** *der* 1 (Kopf) blond/blonde hair; fair hair; 2 (Kind) blond/blonde child; fair-haired child; ~**schopf** *der* (fam.) fair-haired lad

bloß /bloːs/

A *Adj.* 1 (nackt) bare; naked; **du kannst nicht mit ~en Beinen gehen** you can't go without tights/stockings/socks; **mit ~em Oberkörper** stripped to the waist; **den Pullover kann man nicht auf der ~en Haut tragen** you can't wear this pullover next to the skin *or* with nothing on underneath; **mit ~em Kopf** bareheaded; **mit ~en Füßen** barefoot; **mit ~en Händen** with one's bare hands; **auf der ~en Erde** on the ground 2 (nichts als) mere ‹*words, promises, triviality, suspicion, etc.*›; **der ~e Gedanke daran** the mere *or* very thought of it; **er kam mit dem ~en Schrecken davon** he escaped with no more than a fright; **nach dem ~en Augenschein beurteilen** judge simply by appearances; **ein ~er Zufall** mere *or* pure chance; **~es Gerede** mere gossip

B *Adv.* (ugs.: nur) only; **ich habe ~ noch zehn Euro** I only have ten euros left; **das ist alles ~ deine Schuld** it's all your fault; **ich habe**

das Buch, ~ weiß ich nicht mehr, wo ich es hingelegt habe I've got the book, but *or* only I don't know where I've put it

C *in* **nicht ~ ..., sondern auch ...** not only ..., but also ...; **er sagt das nicht ~, er glaubt es auch** he doesn't just say it, he believes it as well

D *Partikel* (verstärkend) **was hast du dir ~ dabei gedacht?** what on earth *or* whatever were you thinking of?; **sieh ~ zu, dass ...** just make sure that ...; **wie konnte das ~ geschehen?** how on earth did it happen?

Blöße /ˈbløːsə/ *die;* ~, ~n [1] (geh.: Nacktheit) nakedness [2] **sich** (*Dat.*) **eine/keine ~ geben** show a/not show any weakness; **er wollte sich** (*Dat.*) **nicht die ~ geben, das einzugestehen** he didn't want to show a weakness by admitting it; **jmdm. eine ~ bieten** reveal a weakness to sb. [3] (Gerberei) skin prepared for tanning [4] (im Wald) clearing [5] (Fechten) target; **eine ~ freigeben** *od.* **öffnen** present a target

bloß-, Bloß-: **~|legen** *tr. V.* uncover; expose; (fig.) (herausfinden) uncover; reveal; (enthüllen) expose; reveal ‹*error, defect, etc.*›; **~|liegen** *unr. itr. V.; mit sein* be uncovered *or* exposed; **~|stellen** *tr. V.* show up; unmask, expose ‹*swindler, criminal, etc.*›; **sich ~stellen** show oneself up; **~stellung** *die* ▸ **~stellen**: showing up; unmasking; exposure; **~|strampeln** *refl. V.* kick the *or* one's covers off

Blouson /bluˈzõː/ *das od. der;* ~s, ~s blouson; bomber jacket

blubbern /ˈblʊbɐn/ *itr. V.* (ugs.) [1] (Blasen bilden) bubble [2] (undeutlich reden) mutter; mumble

Blücher /ˈblʏçɐ/ *in* **er/sie geht ran wie ~** (ugs.) he/she really goes hard at it

Bluejeans /ˈbluːdʒiːns/ *Pl. od. die;* ~, ~: [blue] jeans *pl.;* denims *pl.;* **er trug ~/eine ~:** he wore [a pair of] jeans *or* denims

Blues /bluːs/ *der;* ~, ~ (Musik, Tanz) blues *pl.*

Bluff /blʊf/ *der;* ~s, ~s bluff

bluffen *tr., itr. V.* bluff

blühen /ˈblyːən/ *itr. V.* [1] ‹*plant*› flower, bloom, be in flower *or* bloom; ‹*flower*› bloom, be in bloom, be out; ‹*tree*› be in blossom; **~de Gärten/Wiesen** gardens/meadows full of flowers; **es blüht** there are flowers in bloom; **diese Rosensorte blüht rot** this type of rose has red flowers; **Azaleen zum Blühen bringen** get azaleas to flower [2] (florieren) flourish; thrive [3] (ugs.: bevorstehen) **jmdm. ~:** be in store for sb.; **das Gleiche blüht mir nächste Woche** I've got the same thing coming [to me] next week; **da blüht dir ja was Nettes** (iron.) that'll be nice for you (iron.); **das kann dir auch noch ~:** the same may *or* could happen to you; **sonst blüht dir was!** otherwise you'll catch it!

blühend *Adj.* [1] (frisch, gesund) glowing ‹*colour, complexion, etc.*›; radiant ‹*health*›; **ein ~es Geschäft** a flourishing trade; **er sieht ~ aus** he looks marvellous *or* the picture of health; **aussehen wie das ~e Leben** look the very picture of health; **sie starb im ~en Alter von 20 Jahren** she died at 20, in the full bloom of youth [2] (übertrieben) vivid, lively ‹*imagination*›; absolute, utter ‹*nonsense*›

Blühet *die;* ~ (schweiz.) blossom

Blümchen /ˈblyːmçən/ *das;* ~s, ~: [little] flower

Blümchen·kaffee *der* (ugs. scherzh.) [1] weak coffee [2] (Kaffee-Ersatz) coffee substitute

Blume /ˈbluːmə/ *die;* ~, ~n [1] (auch fig. dichter.) flower; **vielen Dank für die ~n** (iron.) thank you very much (iron.); thanks for nothing; **etw. durch die ~ sagen** say sth. in a roundabout way; **jmdm. etw. durch die ~ sagen** *od.* **zu verstehen geben** tell sb. sth. in a roundabout way [2] (des Weines) bouquet [3] (des Biers) head [4] (Jägerspr.: des Hasen, Kaninchens) tail; scut

blumen-, Blumen-: **~beet** *das* flower bed; **~bukett** *das* (geh.) bouquet [of flowers]; **~draht** *der* florist's wire; **~erde** *die* potting compost; **~fenster** *das* window full of flowers; (spezielles Fenster) flower window; **~flor** *der* (geh.) abundance of flowers; **~frau** *die* flower woman; **~fülle** *die* abundance of flowers; **~garten** *der* flower garden; **~geschäft** *das* florist's; flower shop; **~geschmückt** *Adj.* flower bedecked; adorned with flowers *postpos.;* **~gruß** *der* bouquet of flowers; **~händler** *der,* **~händlerin** *die* florist; **~kasten** *der* flower box; (vor einem Fenster) window box; **~kind** *das* flower child; **~kohl** *der* cauliflower; **~korb** *der* (für ~) flower basket; (mit ~) basket of flowers; **~kranz** *der* floral wreath; garland of flowers; **~laden** *der; Pl.* **~läden** ▸ **~geschäft**; **~mädchen** *das* flower girl; **~markt** *der* flower market; **~muster** *das* floral pattern; **~pracht** *die* magnificent display of flowers; **~rabatte** *die* flower border; herbaceous border; **~reich** **A** *Adj.* [1] (voller ~) full of flowers *postpos.;* flowery; [2] flowery ‹*language, style, etc.*›; **B** *adv.* ‹*speak*› in a flowery way; ‹*write*› in a flowery style; **~schale** *die* (Schale für ~) plant bowl; (Schale mit ~) bowl of plants; **~schmuck** *der* floral decoration; **~stand** *der* flower stall; **~stock** *der* [flowering] pot plant; **~strauß** *der; Pl.* **~sträuße** bunch of flowers; (Bukett) bouquet of flowers; **~teppich** *der* carpet of flowers; **~topf** *der* [1] (Topf für Pflanzen) flowerpot; [2] (ugs.: Topfpflanze) [flowering] pot plant; **damit kannst du keinen ~topf gewinnen** (ugs.) that won't get you anywhere; **~uhr** *die* floral clock; **~vase** *die* (Vase für ~) [flower] vase; (Vase mit ~) vase of flowers; **~zwiebel** *die* bulb

blümerant /blyməˈrant/ *Adj.* queasy; **mir ist ~:** I feel queasy

blumig

A *Adj.* flowery ‹*language, style, perfume, wine, etc.*›

B *adv.* ‹*speak*› in a flowery way; ‹*write*› in a flowery style

Blunze /ˈblʊntsə/ *die;* ~, ~n, **Blunzen** *die;* ~n, ~n (bayr., österr.) [1] black pudding [2] (ugs. abwertend: Frau) fat cow (sl. derog.)

Bluse /ˈbluːzə/ *die;* ~, ~n blouse; **ganz schön etwas in** *od.* **unter der ~ haben** (salopp) be well stacked (coll. joc.) *or* well endowed (joc.); **jmdm. an die ~ gehen** (salopp) try to grope sb.'s boobs *pl.* (coll.)

Blüse /ˈblyːzə/ *die;* ~, ~n (Seemannsspr.) light

blusig

A *Adj.* bloused

B *adv.* **~ geschnitten/fallend** bloused

Blust /bluːst/ *der od. das* (veralt., schweiz.) blossom

Blut /bluːt/ *das;* ~[e]s ▸ ℹ **S. 435** blood; **deine Stirn ist ja voller ~:** your forehead is covered in blood; **~ abgenommen bekommen** have a blood sample taken; **gleich ins ~ gehen** pass straight into the bloodstream; **jmdm. steigt das ~ in den Kopf** the blood rushes to sb.'s head; **es wurde viel ~ vergossen** there was a great deal of bloodshed; **er kann kein ~ sehen** he can't stand the sight of blood; **er lag in seinem ~:** he lay in a pool of blood; **~ und Boden** (ns.) blood and soil; **wenn sie so was sieht, kocht ihr das ~ in den Adern** (fig.) when she sees something like that, it makes her blood boil; **den Zuschauern gefror** *od.* **stockte** *od.* **gerann das ~ in den Adern** (fig.) the spectators' blood ran cold; **heißes/feuriges ~ haben** (fig.) be hot-blooded; **französisches/russisches ~ in den Adern haben** (fig.) have French/Russian blood in one *or* in one's veins (fig.); **~ ist dicker als Wasser** (fig.) blood is thicker than water (fig.); **ein junges ~** (fig. dichter.) a young thing (fig.); **an jmds. Händen klebt ~** (fig. geh.) there is blood on sb.'s hands (fig.); **blaues ~ in den Adern haben** (fig.) have blue blood in one's veins (fig.); **kaltes ~ bewahren** (fig.) remain cold and unmoved; **böses ~ machen** *od.* **schaffen** (fig.) cause *or* create bad blood; **~ und Wasser schwitzen** (fig. ugs.) sweat blood (fig. coll.); **~ geleckt haben** (fig. ugs.) have got a taste for it; **[nur/immer] ruhig ~!** (ugs.) keep your hair on! (Brit. coll.); keep your cool! (coll.); **jmdn. bis aufs ~ quälen** *od.* **peinigen** (fig.) torment sb. mercilessly; **jmdm. im ~ liegen** (fig.) be in sb.'s blood (fig.); **ins ~ gehen** get into one's blood; really get one going; **etw. mit seinem ~ besiegeln** (dichter.) lay down one's life for sth.; **nach [jmds.] ~ lechzen** *od.* **dürsten** (geh.) thirst for [sb.'s] blood (fig.)

blut-, Blut-: **~ader** *die* ▸ ℹ **S. 435** (Anat.) vein; **~alkohol** *der* blood alcohol level; **~andrang** *der* ▸ ℹ **S. 439** (Med.) congestion; hyperaemia (Med.); **~apfelsine** *die* ▸ **~orange**; **~arm** *Adj.* (Med.) anaemic; **~armut** *die* ▸ ℹ **S. 439** (Med.) anaemia; **~auffrischung** *die* (fig.) **die Firma braucht eine ~auffrischung** the company needs some new blood; **~aus·strich** *der* (Med.) blood smear; **~austausch** *der* (Med.) exchange transfusion; **~bad** *das* bloodbath; **~bahn** *die* bloodstream; **~bank** *die; Pl.* **~~en** (Med.) blood bank; **~befleckt** *Adj.* bloodstained; **seine Hände sind ~befleckt** (fig.) he has blood on his hands (fig.); **~beschmiert** *Adj.* smeared with blood *postpos.;* **~bild** *das* (Med.) blood picture; **~bildung** *die* (Med.) blood formation; **~blase** *die* blood blister; **~buche** *die* copper beech; **~druck** *der; Pl.* **~drücke** blood pressure; **~druck·messung** *die* blood-pressure test; **~druck·senkend** *Adj.* (Med.) antihypertensive; **~durchtränkt** *Adj.* blood-soaked; **~dürstig** *Adj.* (geh.) bloodthirsty

Blüte /ˈblyːtə/ *die;* ~, ~n [1] flower; bloom; (eines Baums) blossom; **die ~ der Jugend** (dichter.) the flower of the young men; **~n treiben** flower; bloom; ‹*tree*› blossom; **seltsame** *od.* **wunderliche ~n treiben** (fig.) produce strange effects; ‹*custom, fashion*› take strange forms; **seine Fantasie trieb üppige/die seltsamsten ~n** (fig.) his imagination produced extravagant/the strangest fancies [2] (das Blühen) flowering; blooming; (Baum~) blossoming; **die ~ der Tulpen/Obstbäume hat schon begonnen** the tulips have started to flower *or* bloom/the fruit trees have started to blossom; **in [voller] ~ stehen** be in [full] flower *or* bloom/blossom; **in der ~ seiner Jahre** (fig. geh.) in his prime; in the prime of his life [3] (geh.: Entwicklungsstand) **seine/ihre ~ erreichen** ‹*culture*› reach its full flowering; **die Renaissance war für die Kunst eine Zeit der ~:** art flourished during the Renaissance [4] (ugs.: falsche Banknote) dud note (sl.) [5] (ugs. abwertend: unfähiger Mensch) duffer

Blut·egel *der* leech

bluten *itr. V.* [1] (Blut verlieren) bleed (**aus** from); **mir blutet das Herz** (iron.) it makes my heart bleed (iron.); **~den Herzens, mit ~dem Herzen** with a heavy heart; **wie ein Schwein ~** (derb) bleed like a stuck pig [2] (ugs.: viel bezahlen) **[ganz schön] ~:** cough up (sl.) *or* fork out (coll.) a[n awful] lot of money (**für** for)

blüten-, Blüten-: **~blatt** *das* petal; **~flor** *der* (dichter.) abundance of flowers; **~honig** *der* blossom honey; **~hülle** *die* (Bot.) perianth; **~kelch** *der* (Bot.) calyx; **~knospe** *die* flower bud; **~lese** *die* (veralt.) florilegium (arch.); **~meer** *das* (geh.) sea of flowers; **~pflanze** *die* (Bot.) flowering plant; **~rein** *Adj.* spotless; perfectly clear ‹*conscience*›; **eine ~reine Weste haben** have a spotless record; **~stand** *der* (Bot.) inflorescence; **~staub** *der* (Bot.) pollen

Blut·entnahme *die* taking of a blood sample; **zur ~entnahme zum Arzt gehen** go to the doctor to have a blood sample taken

blüten-, Blüten-: **~traum** *der* wonderful display of blossom; (fig.: Wunschtraum) beautiful [day]dream; **nicht alle ~träume reifen** (geh.) not every beautiful dream comes true; **~weiß** *Adj.* sparkling white; **~zweig** *der* flowering branch; (kleiner) flowering twig

Bluter /ˈbluːtɐ/ *der;* ~s, ~ ▸ ℹ **S. 439** (Med.) haemophiliac

Blut·erguss, *Blut·erguß *der* ▸ ℹ **S. 439** haematoma; (blauer Fleck) bruise

Bluterin *die;* ~, ~nen ▸ **Bluter**

Bluter·krankheit *die* ▸ ℹ **S. 439** haemophilia *no art.*

Blüte·zeit *die* [1] **die ~ der Geranien ist von Mai bis Oktober** geraniums flower *or* are in flower from May to October; **während der ~**

der Obstbäume when the fruit trees are/were in blossom [2] (fig.) heyday; seine ~ erleben ‹culture, empire› be in its heyday; das frühe 17. Jahrhundert war eine ~ des Dramas drama flourished in the early 17th century

b

blut-, Blut-: ~farbstoff der (Physiol.) haemoglobin; ~fett das (Med.) blood fat; ~fett·spiegel der (Med.) blood fat level; ~fleck[en] der bloodstain; ~flüssigkeit die ►~plasma; ~gefäß das ►❶ S. 435 (Anat.) blood vessel; ~geld das (veralt.) blood money; ~gerinnsel das blood clot; ~gerinnung die (Physiol.) clotting of the blood; ~gerüst das (geh.) scaffold; ~getränkt Adj. blood-soaked; ~gier die (auch fig.) bloodlust; ~gierig Adj. (auch fig.) bloodthirsty; ~grätsche die (Fußball Jargon) vicious [sliding] tackle [from behind]; ~gruppe die (Med.) blood group; blood type; jmds. ~gruppe bestimmen od. feststellen blood type sb.; type sb.'s blood; er hatte ~gruppe 0 he was blood group 0; ~gruppen·bestimmung die (Med.) blood-typing; ~gruppen·untersuchung die (Med.) blood test; ~hund der bloodhound; (fig.) bloodthirsty murderer

blutig
[A] Adj. [1] bloody; jmdn. ~ schlagen beat sb. to a pulp; ~ geschlagen werden be left battered and bleeding [2] (fig. ugs.: total, völlig) absolute, complete ‹beginner, layman, etc.›; das ist mein ~er Ernst! I am deadly serious
[B] adv. bloodily; sich ~ rächen take bloody revenge

blut-, Blut-: ~jung Adj. very young; ~konserve die (Med.) container of stored blood; ~konserven stored blood; ~körperchen das; ~~s, ~~ ►❶ S. 435 (Anat.) blood corpuscle; rote/weiße ~körperchen red/white corpuscles; ~krebs der ►❶ S. 439 (Med.) leukaemia; ~kreis·lauf der (Physiol.) blood circulation; ~kuchen der (Med.) blood clot; clot of blood; ~lache die pool of blood; ~leer Adj. bloodless; ihr Gesicht wurde ganz ~leer the blood drained from her face; ~leere die restricted blood supply; ischaemia (Med.); ~mangel der [1] lack of blood; [2] (Anämie) anaemia; ~orange die blood orange; ~pfropf der (Physiol.) blood clot; clot of blood; ~plasma das (Physiol.) blood plasma; ~plättchen das (Physiol.) blood platelet; ~probe die (Med.) [1] (~entnahme, ~untersuchung) blood test; [2] (kleine ~menge) blood sample; ~rache die blood revenge; blood vengeance; ~rausch der (geh.) murderous frenzy; ~reinigend Adj. blood-cleansing; ~reinigung die purification of the blood; ~reinigungs·tee der blood-cleansing tea; ~rot Adj. blood-red; ~rünstig /-rʏnstɪç/ [A] Adj. bloodthirsty; [B] adv. bloodthirstily; ~sauger der, ~saugerin die; ~~, ~~nen [1] (Insekt, abwertend: Ausbeuter) bloodsucker; [2] (Vampir) vampire

Bluts-: ~bande Pl. blood ties; ~brüderschaft die blood brotherhood; ~brüderschaft schließen become blood brothers

blut-, Blut-: ~schande die incest; ~schänder der; ~~s, ~~, ~schänderin die; ~~, ~~nen incestuous person; ~schänderisch Adj. incestuous; ~schuld die (geh.) blood guilt; ~schwamm der ►❶ S. 439 (Med.) strawberry mark; ~senkung die (Med.) erythrocyte sedimentation test; zur ~senkung gehen (ugs.) go to have a sedimentation test; ~serum das (Physiol.) blood serum; ~spende die (das Spenden) giving no indef. art. of blood; donation of blood; (~menge) blood donation; ~spender der, ~spenderin die blood donor; ~spende·zentrale die blood donor centre; ~spucken das; ~~s ►❶ S. 439 spitting of blood; haemoptysis (Med.); ~spur die [1] trail of blood; [2] Pl. (auf Kleidung o. Ä.) traces of blood; ~stillend Adj. styptic; ~stillende Mittel styptics; ~strom der bloodstream

Bluts·tropfen der drop of blood

Blut·sturz der [1] (ugs.: aus Mund und Nase) er erlitt einen ~sturz he was bleeding from [his] nose and mouth [2] (Med.) haemorrhage

bluts-, Bluts-: ~verwandt Adj. related by blood postpos.; sie ist nicht ~verwandt mit ihm she is not related to him by blood; sie sind nicht ~verwandt they are not blood relations; ~verwandte der/die blood relation; ~verwandtschaft die blood relationship

blut-, Blut-: ~tat die (geh.) bloody deed; ~transfusion die blood transfusion; ~triefend Adj. dripping with blood pred.; ~überströmt Adj. streaming with blood pred.; covered in blood pred.; ~übertragung die blood transfusion

Blut-und-Boden-Dichtung die; ~ (abwertend) blood-and-soil literature

Blutung die; ~, ~en [1] bleeding no indef. art., no pl.; haemorrhage; innere/äußere ~en internal/external bleeding sing.; eine ~ im Gehirn a brain haemorrhage [2] (Regel~) period

blut-, Blut-: ~unterlaufen Adj. suffused with blood postpos.; bloodshot ‹eyes›; ~untersuchung die (Med.) blood test; ~vergießen das; ~~s bloodshed; ~vergiftung die ►❶ S. 439 blood poisoning no indef. art., no pl.; ~verklebt Adj. caked with blood postpos.; ‹hair, feathers› matted with blood postpos.; ~verlust der loss of blood; ~verschmiert Adj. bloodstained, smeared with blood pred.; ~wäsche die (Med.) purification of the blood; ~wert der (Med.) blood value; ~wurst die black pudding; ~zirkulation die blood circulation; ~zoll der (geh.) toll of lives; ~zucker der (Physiol.) blood sugar; ~zucker·spiegel der (Physiol.) blood-sugar level; ~zufuhr die blood supply

b-Moll /ˈbeːmɔl/ das B flat minor; s. auch a-Moll

BMX-Fahrrad, BMX-Rad /beɛmˈɪks.../ das BMX [bike]

BND Abk. = Bundesnachrichtendienst

Bö /bøː/ die; ~, ~en gust [of wind]; (mit Niederschlag) squall; in ~en orkanartig gusting to hurricane force

Boa /ˈboːa/ die; ~, ~s (Schlange, Feder~) boa

boarden /ˈbɔːdn̩/
[A] itr. V. [1] (Flugw.) board [2] mit sein (snowboarden) snowboard
[B] tr. V. [1] (an Bord nehmen) board ‹passengers›; [2] (Seew. Jargon) board [and inspect] ‹vessel›

Bob /bɔp/ der; ~, ~s bob[sleigh]

Bob·bahn die bob[sleigh] run

Bobbycar(Wz) /ˈbɔbikaːɐ̯/ das; ~s, ~s Bobby car; ride-on car

Bob-: ~fahrer der, ~fahrerin die bobber; ~mannschaft die bob[sleigh] team; ~rennen das bob[sleigh] racing; (einzelne Veranstaltung) bob[sleigh] race; ~sport der bobsleighing; ~tail /-teɪl/ der; ~~s, ~~s [Old English] sheepdog

Boccia /ˈbɔtʃa/ das; ~s boccie; boccia

Bock[1] /bɔk/ der; ~[e]s, Böcke /ˈbœkə/ [1] (Reh~, Kaninchen~) buck; (Ziegen~) billy goat; he-goat; (Schafs~) ram; ein steifer ~ od. steif wie ein ~ sein (ugs.) be as stiff as a board; stur wie ein ~ sein (ugs.) be as stubborn as a mule; stinken wie ein ~ (salopp) stink to high heaven (coll.); jmdn. stößt der ~ (ugs.) sb. is being contrary (coll.); etw. aus ~ tun (ugs.) do sth. just for the fun of it; einen ~ schießen (fig. ugs.) boob (Brit. coll.); make a booboo (Amer. coll.); (einen Fauxpas begehen) drop a clanger (coll.); den ~ zum Gärtner machen (ugs.) be asking for trouble; die Böcke von den Schafen trennen (fig.) separate the sheep from the goats; einen/keinen ~ auf etw. (Akk.) haben (ugs.) fancy/not fancy sth.; einen/keinen ~ haben, etw. zu tun (ugs.) fancy/not fancy doing sth. [2] (ugs.: Schimpfwort) der geile alte ~: the randy old goat; sturer ~! you stubborn git (sl. derog.) [3] (Gestell) trestle [4] (Turnen) buck [5] (Kutsch~) box

Bock[2] das; ~s (Bier) bock [beer]

bock-, Bock-: ~beinig (ugs.) [A] Adj. contrary (coll.); stubborn and awkward; [B] adv. contrarily (coll.); ~bier das bock [beer]

bockel·hart /ˈbɔkl̩-/
[A] Adj. rock-hard; ‹meat› as tough as old boots postpos.; (fig.) tough and uncompromising ‹negotiations›; rock-hard ‹defence›; da bin ich ~: I won't give an inch on that one
[B] adv. ‹negotiate› uncompromisingly

bocken itr. V. [1] (nicht weitergehen) refuse to go on; (vor einer Hürde) refuse; (sich aufbäumen) buck; rear; die alte Karre bockt mal wieder (salopp) the old heap is playing up again [2] (fam.: trotzig sein) be stubborn and awkward; play up [3] (Landw.: brünstig sein) be on heat [4] (derb: koitieren) have it away or off (sl.); have a screw (coarse)

bockig
[A] Adj. stubborn and awkward; contrary (coll.)
[B] adv. stubbornly [and awkwardly]; contrarily (coll.)

Bock-: ~kitz das (Jägerspr.) young buck; ~mist der (salopp) bilge no indef. art. (sl.); bullshit no indef. art. (coarse); einen ziemlichen ~mist verzapfen come out with a load of bilge; einen schönen ~mist machen make a real cock-up (Brit. sl.) or a holy mess

Bocks-: ~bart der [1] (bei der Ziege) [goat's] beard; (beim Mann) goatee [beard]; [2] (Bot.) goat's-beard; ~beutel der [1] (Flasche) bocksbeutel; wide, bulbous bottle for fine Franconian wines; [2] (Wein) bocksbeutel wine; Franconian wine sold in a bocksbeutel

Bock·schein der (salopp) (prostitute's) certificate of health

Bocks-: ~fuß der goat's foot; ~horn das sich [nicht] [von jmdm.] ins ~horn jagen lassen (ugs.) (sich [nicht] einschüchtern lassen) [not] let oneself be browbeaten [by sb.]; (sich [nicht] erschrecken und verwirren lassen) [not] let oneself get worked up into a state [by sb.]

Bock-: ~springen das (Turnen) vaulting [over the buck]; (ohne Gerät) leapfrog; ~sprung der [1] (Turnen) (Disziplin) vaulting [over the buck]; (einzelner Sprung) vault [over the buck]; [2] (ungelenker Sprung) [ungainly] jump or leap; ~sprünge machen jump or leap about; vor Freude ~sprünge machen jump for joy; ~wurst die bockwurst

Boden /ˈboːdn̩/ der; ~s, Böden /ˈbøːdn̩/ [1] (Erde) ground; soil; er wäre am liebsten im ~ versunken he wished the ground would open and swallow him up; den ~ für jmdn./etw. [vor]bereiten prepare the ground for sb./sth.; [bei jmdm.] auf fruchtbaren ~ fallen ‹advice, warning› have some effect [on sb.]; etw. [nicht] aus dem ~ stampfen können [not] be able to conjure sth. up [out of thin air]; wie aus dem ~ gestampft od. gewachsen as if by magic [2] (Fuß~) floor; bei ihr kann man vom ~ essen her floors are so clean that you could eat off them; zu ~ fallen/sich zu ~ fallen lassen fall/drop to the ground; der Boxer ging zu ~: the boxer went down; die Augen zu ~ schlagen look down; jmdn. zu ~ schlagen od. (geh.) strecken knock sb. down; floor sb.; (fig.) sich auf unsicherem ~ bewegen be on shaky ground (fig.); sich auf schwankenden ~ begeben get into a risky area (fig.); jmdm. wird der ~ unter den Füßen zu heiß od. brennt der ~ unter den Füßen (ugs.) things are getting too hot for sb. (fig.); festen ~ unter den Füßen haben be back on terra firma; (Tatsachen behaupten) be on firm ground; (wirtschaftlich gesichert sein) be firmly on one's feet; jmdm. den ~ unter den Füßen wegziehen cut the ground from under sb.'s feet; einem Gerücht/einer Theorie den ~ entziehen scotch a rumour/explode a theory; sie hatte das Gefühl, den ~ unter den Füßen zu verlieren she felt the ground fall from beneath her feet; er scheint völlig den ~ unter den Füßen verloren zu haben the bottom seems to have dropped out of his world; am ~ liegen be bankrupt; am ~ zerstört [sein] (ugs.) [be] shattered (coll.); jmdn. zu ~ drücken ‹cares, worries› get on top of sb. [3] (Grundlage) bleiben wir doch auf dem ~ der Tatsachen let's stick to the facts; hart auf den ~ der Wirklichkeit

b

zurückgeholt werden be brought back down to earth with a bump (fig.); **auf dem ∼ der Verfassung/des Gesetzes stehen** ‹person› be within the constitution/law [4] (Terrain) **heiliger ∼:** holy ground; **feindlicher ∼:** enemy territory; **auf französischem ∼:** on French soil; **∼ gutmachen** od. **wettmachen** (ugs.) make up ground; **[an] ∼ gewinnen/verlieren** gain/lose ground [5] (unterste Fläche) bottom; (Hosen∼) seat; (Torten∼) base; **auf dem ∼ des Meeres** at the bottom of the sea; on the seabed; s. auch **doppelt** [6] (Dach∼, Heu∼) loft; (Wäsche∼) drying room; **auf dem ∼:** in the loft/drying room

boden-, Boden-: ∼abwehr *die* (Milit.) ground defence; **∼bearbeitung** *die* cultivation of the land; tillage; **∼belag** *der* (Teppich, Linoleum) floor covering; (Fliesen, Parkett) flooring; **∼beschaffenheit** *die* [1] (der Erde) condition of the soil; [2] (des Fußbodens) condition of the ground; conditions *pl.* underfoot; **∼biologie** *die* soil biology; **∼-∼-Rakete** *die* (Milit.) surface-to-surface missile; **∼erosion** *die* soil erosion; **∼ertrag** *der* crop yield; **∼feuchtigkeit** *die* soil moisture; **∼fräse** *die* (Landw.) rotary cultivator; **∼freiheit** *die* (Technik) ground clearance; **∼frost** *der* ground frost; **∼gefecht** *das* (Milit.) ground battle; **∼haftung** *die* (Kfz-W.) roadholding *no indef. art.*; **∼haltung** *die* (Landw.) deep-litter system (*of poultry farming*); **∼heizung** *die* underfloor heating; **∼kammer** *die* attic; **∼kampf** *der* [1] (Judo, Ringen) groundwork; [2] (Milit.) ground battle; **∼krieg** *der* ground war; **∼kunde** *die* soil science; **∼lang** *Adj.* full-length ‹*skirt, dress, etc.*›; **∼los** *Adj.* [1] (tief) bottomless; **ins ∼lose fallen** fall into a bottomless abyss; [2] (ugs.: unerhört) incredible, unbelievable ‹*foolishness, meanness, etc.*›; **∼-Luft-Rakete** *die* (Milit.) surface-to-air missile; **∼nähe** *die* (Flugw.) **in ∼nähe** at a low level; **∼nebel** *der* ground mist; (dichter) ground fog; **∼nutzung** *die* agricultural land use; **∼personal** *das* (Flugw.) ground staff; **∼raum** *der* loft; **∼recht** *das* (Rechtsw.) land law; **∼reform** *die* land reform; **∼rente** *die* ground rent; **∼satz** *der* sediment; (von Kaffee) grounds *pl.*; (fig.) (Rest) residue; (Grundbestandteil) basic component *or* ingredient; **∼schätze** *Pl.* mineral resources

Bodensee *der;* **∼s** Lake Constance

> **Bodensee**
>
> This is the German name for Lake Constance, Germany's biggest lake, bordered by Germany, Switzerland, and Austria. The River Rhine flows through it. This popular recreation area enjoys a particularly mild climate, especially on the three islands Lindau, Mainau, and Reichenau.

boden-, Boden-: ∼sicht *die* (Flugw.) ground visibility; **∼spekulation** *die* land speculation; **∼ständig** *Adj.* indigenous, native ‹*culture, population, etc.*›; local ‹*custom, craft, cuisine, tradition*›; ‹*novel*› rooted in the soil; **∼ständigkeit** *die;* **∼:** **die ∼ständigkeit des echten Kölners geht so weit, dass ...** the roots of the genuine native of Cologne go so deep that ...; **die Schwarzwaldbauern verlieren ihre ∼ständigkeit** the farmers of the Black Forest are losing the close links with their native soil; **∼station** *die* (Raumf.) ground station; **∼streitkräfte** *Pl.:* ▸ **∼truppen**; **∼treppe** *die* attic stairs *pl.*; **∼truppen** *Pl.* ground forces *or* troops; **∼turnen** *das* floor exercises *pl.*; **∼vase** *die* large vase (*standing on the floor*); **∼verhältnisse** *Pl.* ground conditions; **∼welle** *die* [1] (Unebenheit) bump; [2] (Funkw.) ground wave; **∼wichse** *die* (schweiz.) floor polish

bodigen /ˈboːdɪgn̩/ *tr. V.* (schweiz.: besiegen) beat; defeat

Bodmerei /boːdməˈrai̯/ *die;* **∼, ∼en** (Seew.) bottomry

Bodybuilder /ˈbɔdibɪldɐ/ *der;* **∼s, ∼, Bodybuilderin** *die;* **∼, ∼nen** bodybuilder

Bodybuilding /ˈbɔdibɪldɪŋ/ *das;* **∼s** bodybuilding *no art.*; **∼ betreiben** do bodybuilding exercises

Bodycheck /ˈbɔditʃɛk/ *der;* **∼s, ∼s** (Eishockey) body-check

Böe /ˈbøːə/ *die;* **∼, ∼n** ▸ **Bö**

Bofist /ˈboːfɪst/ *der;* **∼[e]s, ∼e** puffball

bog /boːk/ *1. u. 3. Pers. Sg. Prät. v.* **biegen**

Bogen /ˈboːgn̩/ *der;* **∼s, ∼,** (südd., österr.:) **Bögen** /ˈbøːgn̩/ [1] (gebogene Linie) curve; (Math.) arc; (Skifahren) turn; (Schlittschuhlaufen) curve; **einen ∼ schlagen** move in a curve; **der Weg macht/beschreibt einen ∼:** the path bends/the path describes a curve; **immer, wenn ich sie auf der Straße sehe, mache ich einen großen ∼** (fig. ugs.) whenever I see her in the street I make a detour [round her]; **einen großen ∼ um jmdn./etw. machen** (fig. ugs.) give sb./sth. a wide berth; **das Wasser spritzte in hohem ∼ heraus** the water spurted out in a great arc; **in hohem ∼ hinausfliegen** (fig. ugs.) be chucked out (sl.); **große ∼ spucken** (ugs.) talk big; *s. auch* **heraushaben** [2] (Archit.) arch [3] (Waffe) bow; **den ∼ überspannen** (fig.) go too far [4] (Musik: Geigen∼ usw.) bow [5] (Papier∼) sheet; **ein ∼ Schreibpapier/Packpapier** a sheet of writing paper/wrapping paper; **ein A4-∼:** a sheet of A4 paper [6] (Musik: Zeichen) slur; (bei gleicher Notenhöhe) tie

bogen-, Bogen-: ∼brücke *die* arch bridge; **∼fenster** *das* arched window; **∼förmig** *Adj.* arched; **∼führung** *die* (Musik) bowing *no indef. art.*; **∼gang** *der* [1] (Arkaden) arcade; [2] (Anat.) semicircular canal; **∼lampe** *die* (Elektrot.) arc lamp; **∼pfeiler** *der* pillar *or* column of the/an arch; **∼säge** *die* coping saw; **∼schießen** *das* (Sport) archery *no art.*; **∼schütze** *der,* **∼schützin** *die* (Sport) archer

Bohei /boˈhai̯/ ▸ **Buhei**

Boheme /boˈeːm/ *die;* **∼:** bohemian world *or* society

Bohemien /boeˈmi̯ɛ̃ː/ *der;* **∼s, ∼s** bohemian

Bohle /ˈboːlə/ *die;* **∼, ∼n** [thick] plank

Bohlen·belag *der* planking *no indef. art.*

böhmakeln /ˈbøːmakl̩n/ *itr. V.* (österr. ugs. abwertend) speak with a dreadful Czech accent

Böhme /ˈbøːmə/ *der;* **∼n, ∼n** Bohemian

Böhmen /ˈbøːmən/ *(das);* **∼s** Bohemia

Böhmer·wald *der* Bohemian Forest

Böhmin *die;* **∼, ∼nen** Bohemian; *s. auch* **-in**

böhmisch *Adj.* Bohemian

Böhnchen /ˈbøːnçən/ *das;* **∼s, ∼:** [small] bean

Bohne /ˈboːnə/ *die;* **∼, ∼n** bean; **grüne ∼n** green beans; French beans (Brit.); **dicke/weiße ∼n** broad/haricot beans; **gebackene ∼n** casserole *sing.* of beans with pork; **blaue ∼n** (Soldatenspr. veralt., noch scherzh.) bullets; **nicht die ∼** (ugs.) not one little bit

Bohnen-: ∼ein·topf *der* bean stew; **∼kaffee** *der* [1] (∼) real coffee; **gemahlener ∼kaffee** ground coffee; [2] (Getränk) real coffee; **∼kraut** *das* savory; **∼salat** *der* bean salad; **∼stange** *die* (auch ugs.: Mensch) beanpole; **∼stroh** *das* **dumm wie ∼stroh** (ugs.) as thick as two short planks (coll.); **∼suppe** *die* bean soup

Bohner *der;* **∼s, ∼** ▸ **Bohnerbesen**

Bohner-: ∼besen *der* floor polisher; floor-polishing brush; **∼maschine** *die* floor polisher; floor-polishing machine

bohnern *tr., itr. V.* polish; **hier ist frisch gebohnert** this floor has/these stairs have *etc.* been freshly polished; **„Vorsicht, frisch gebohnert!"** 'freshly polished floor/stairs *etc.*'

Bohner·wachs *das* floor polish

bohren /ˈboːrən/

A *tr. V.* [1] bore; (mit Bohrer, Bohrmaschine) drill, bore ‹*hole*›; sink ‹*well, shaft*›; bore, drive ‹*tunnel*›; sink ‹*pole, post etc.*› (**in** + *Akk.* into) [2] (bearbeiten) drill ‹*wood, concrete, etc.*› [3] (drücken in) poke (**in** + *Akk.* in[to])

B *itr. V.* [1] (eine Bohrung vornehmen) drill; **in einem Zahn ∼:** drill a tooth; **in der Nase ∼:** pick one's nose; **nach Öl/Wasser** *usw.* **∼:** drill for oil/water *etc.* [2] (fig.: nagen) gnaw; **Zweifel bohrten in ihm** he had nagging doubts [3] (ugs.: drängen, fragen) keep on; **jetzt hört auf zu ∼:** now, don't keep on; **ich habe so lange gebohrt, bis ...** I kept on and on until ...

C *refl. V.* (eindringen) bore its way; **das Flugzeug hatte sich tief in die Erde gebohrt** the aircraft had buried itself deep in the ground

bohrend *Adj.* [1] gnawing ‹*pain, hunger, remorse*› [2] (hartnäckig) piercing ‹*look etc.*›; probing ‹*question*›

Bohrer *der;* **∼s, ∼** [1] (Gerät) drill; (zum Vorbohren) gimlet [2] (Arbeiter) driller

Bohrerin *die;* **∼, ∼nen** ▸ **Bohrer 2**

Bohr-: ∼hammer *der* hammer drill; **∼insel** *die* drilling rig; (für Öl) drilling rig; oil rig; **∼kern** *der* (Technik) drill core; **∼loch** *das* borehole; (in Metall, Holz) drill hole; (einer Ölquelle) well; **∼maschine** *die* drill; **∼meißel** *der* bit; **∼probe** *die* core [sample]; **∼schrauber** *der* power drill/screwdriver; **∼turm** *der* derrick

Bohrung *die;* **∼, ∼en** [1] ▸ **bohren A 1**: drilling; boring; sinking; driving [2] (Bohrloch) borehole; (in Holz, Metall) drill hole [3] (lichte Weite) **die ∼ des Zylinders** the bore of the cylinder

böig *Adj.* gusty; (mit Niederschlag) squally; **∼ auffrischend** freshening in gusts/squalls

Boiler /ˈbɔy̆lɐ/ *der;* **∼s, ∼:** boiler; (im Haushalt) water heater

Boje /ˈboːjə/ *die;* **∼, ∼n** buoy

Bolero /boˈleːro/ *der;* **∼s, ∼s** [1] (Tanz, Jacke) bolero [2] (Hut) bolero hat

Bolid /boˈliːt/ *der;* **∼s** od. **∼en, ∼e** od. **∼en** (Astron.) bolide

Bolivianer /boliˈvi̯aːnɐ/ *der;* **∼s, ∼, Bolivianerin** *die;* **∼, ∼nen** Bolivian; *s. auch* **-in**

bolivianisch *Adj.* Bolivian

Bolivien /boˈliːvi̯ən/ *(das);* **∼s** Bolivia

bölken /ˈbœlkn̩/ *itr. V.* (nordd., westd.) ‹*cow*› moo; ‹*sheep*› bleat; ‹*person*› bawl, shout

Bolle[1] /ˈbɔlə/ *die;* **∼, ∼n** (berlin.) [1] (Zwiebel) onion [2] (Loch in der Socke) hole

Bolle[2] *(der)* in **sich wie ∼ [auf dem Milchwagen] amüsieren** (berlin.) have a marvellous *or* (coll.) great time

Böller /ˈbœlɐ/ *der;* **∼s, ∼** [1] (Geschütz) [small] cannon (*used on ceremonial occasions*) [2] (Feuerwerkskörper) banger

bollern /ˈbɔlɐn/ *itr. V.;* *mit sein* (bes. nordd.) thud; **die Kinder bollerten die Treppe hinunter** the children clattered down the stairs

böllern *itr. V.* **es wurde 21-mal geböllert** there was a 21-gun salute

Böller·schuss, *Böller·schuß *der* gun salute; **der Admiral wurde mit fünf Böllerschüssen begrüßt** the admiral was greeted with a five-gun salute

Boller·wagen *der* (nordd.) handcart

Bollette /bɔˈlɛtə/ *die;* **∼, ∼n** (österr. Amtsspr.) customs declaration

Boll·werk *das* [1] (Befestigung) bulwark; (fig.) bulwark; bastion; stronghold [2] (Kai) quay

Bolschewik /bɔlʃeˈvɪk/ *der;* **∼en, ∼i,** (abwertend:) **∼en, Bolschewikin** *die;* **∼, ∼nen** [1] (hist.) Bolshevik [2] (abwertend: Kommunist) Bolshevik; Commie (coll. derog)

bolschewisieren /bɔlʃeviˈziːrən/ *tr. V.* Bolshevize

Bolschewismus /bɔlʃeˈvɪsmʊs/ *der;* **∼:** Bolshevism *no art.*

Bolschewist *der;* **∼en, ∼en, Bolschewistin** *die;* **∼, ∼nen** Bolshevist

bolschewistisch

A *Adj.* [1] Bolshevik; Bolshevist [2] (abwertend) Bolshevik; bolshy (sl)

B *adv.* [1] **∼ geführt** Bolshevik-led; led by the Bolsheviks [2] (abwertend) **∼ unterwandert sein** be Bolshevik-infiltrated; be infiltrated by the Bolsheviks

bolzen /ˈbɔltsn̩/ (ugs.)

A *itr. V.* (Fußball spielen) kick the ball about

B *tr. V.* (treten) slam, (coll.) belt ‹*ball*›; kick ‹*stone*›

Bolzen *der;* **∼s, ∼** [1] (Stift) pin; bolt; (mit Gewinde) bolt [2] (Geschoss) bolt

bolzen·gerade

A *Adj.* perfectly *or* absolutely straight ‹*back*›

B *adv.* ‹*sit, stand*› bolt upright

Bolzen·schneider *der* bolt cutters *pl.*

Bolzerei *die;* ~, ~**en** (ugs.) [aimless] kick-about

Bolz·platz *der* [children's] football area; **hier war in meiner Jugend der** ~: this is where we used to have kick-abouts (Brit.) when I was young

bömakeln ▸ **böhmakeln**

Bombardement /bɔmbardəˈmã:/ *das;* ~**s,** ~**s** 1 (Milit. veralt.: Artilleriebeschuss) bombardment 2 (Milit.: Bombenabwurf) bombing 3 (ugs.: Überhäufung) **ein** ~ **mit Briefen/von Fragen** a flood of letters/deluge of questions

bombardieren /bɔmbarˈdi:rən/ *tr. V.* 1 (Milit. veralt.: beschießen) bombard 2 (Milit.: Bomben abwerfen auf) bomb 3 (ugs.: bewerfen, überhäufen) bombard

Bombardierung *die;* ~, ~**en** 1 (Milit. veralt.: Beschuss) bombardment 2 (Milit.: Bombenabwurf) bombing 3 (ugs.: das Bewerfen) bombardment 4 (ugs.: Überhäufung) **die** ~ **mit Fragen/Bitten** the rush of questions/requests

Bombast /bɔmˈbast/ *der;* ~**[e]s** (abwertend) bombast *no indef. art.*

bombastisch (abwertend)
A *Adj.* bombastic ‹*speech, language, style, etc.*›; ostentatious ‹*architecture, production*›
B *adv.* ‹*speak, write*› bombastically; ostentatiously ‹*dressed*›

Bombe /ˈbɔmbə/ *die;* ~, ~**n** 1 (Sprengkörper) bomb; **die Nachricht schlug ein wie eine** ~: the news came as a bombshell; **die** ~ **ist geplatzt** (fig. ugs.) the balloon has gone up (fig.) 2 (ugs.: Atom~) **die** ~: the bomb (coll.) 3 (Sportjargon: Schuss) thunderbolt; tremendous shot (coll.) 4 (Geol.) bomb 5 (ugs.: Hut) bowler [hat]

bomben
A *tr. V.* (ugs.: bombardieren) bomb
B *itr. V.* (Sportjargon: schießen) slam; blast (coll.)

bomben-, Bomben-: ~**angriff** *der* bomb attack; bombing raid; **einen** ~**angriff fliegen** fly a bombing raid; ~**an·schlag** *der* bomb attack; ~**attentat** *das* bomb attack; ~**drohung** *die* bomb threat; ~**erfolg** *der* (ugs.) smash hit (sl.); ~**fest** *Adj.* 1 (unzerstörbar) bombproof; 2 /ˈ-ˈ-/ (ugs.: unveränderbar) dead certain; ~**fest stehen** be dead certain; be a dead cert (Brit. sl.); **mein Entschluss steht** ~**fest** my mind is completely made up; ~**flug·zeug** *das* bomber; ~**form** *die* (ugs.) top form; ~**gehalt** *das* (ugs.) tremendous salary (coll.); **er kriegt doch sicher ein** ~**gehalt** he must earn a fortune *or* (coll.) bomb; ~**geschäft** *das* (ugs.) **ein** ~**geschäft machen** do a roaring trade; **ein/kein** ~**geschäft sein** be/not be a gold mine (fig.); ~**geschwader** *das* bomber wing; bomber group (Amer.); ~**krater** *der* bomb crater; ~**nacht** *die* night of bombing; ~**rolle** *die* (ugs.) tremendous *or* terrific part (coll.); ~**schaden** *der* bomb damage *no indef. art.;* ~**schuss,** *~**schuß** *der* (Sportjargon) thunderbolt; tremendous shot (coll.); ~**sicher A** *Adj.* 1 (unzerstörbar) bombproof; 2 /ˈ-ˈ-/ (ugs.: gewiss) dead certain; **das ist eine** ~**sichere Sache** that's dead certain; that's a dead cert (Brit. sl.) *or* a sure thing (Amer.); **ein** ~**sicherer Tipp** a dead cert [tip] (Brit. sl.); a sure thing (Amer.); **B** *adv.* (ugs.: gewiss) as sure as eggs are eggs (coll.); ~**splitter** *der* bomb fragment *or* splinter; ~**stimmung** *die* (ugs.) tremendous *or* fantastic atmosphere (coll.); ~**teppich** *der:* **das Gebiet wurde mit einem** ~**teppich belegt** the area was carpet-bombed; ~**terror** *der* terrorist bombing; ~**trichter** *der* bomb crater

Bomber *der;* ~**s,** ~ 1 (ugs.: Flugzeug) bomber 2 (Sportjargon) **der** ~ **der Nation** the player with the fiercest shot in the country

Bomber·verband *der* bomber wing; bomber group (Amer.)

bombig (ugs.)
A *Adj.* super (coll.); smashing (coll.); terrific (coll.); fantastic (coll.)
B *adv.* **sich** ~ **schlagen** make a terrific *or* fantastic showing (coll.)

Bommel /ˈbɔml̩/ *die;* ~, ~**n** *od. der;* ~**s,** ~ (bes. nordd.) bobble; pompom

Bon /bɔŋ/ *der;* ~**s,** ~**s** 1 voucher; coupon 2 (Kassenzettel) receipt; sales slip

Bonbon /bɔŋˈbɔŋ/ *der od.* (österr. nur) *das;* ~**s,** ~**s** 1 sweet; candy (Amer.); (fig.) treat 2 (ugs. scherzh.; bes. ns.: Parteiabzeichen) [party] badge

bonbon-: ~**bunt A** *Adj.* jazzy; jazzily-coloured; **B** *adv.* in jazzy colours; ~**farben,** ~**farbig** *Adj.* (abwertend) candy-coloured

Bonbonniere /bɔŋbɔˈni̯e:rə/ *die;* ~, ~**n** 1 (Behälter) sweet jar (Brit.); candy jar (Amer.) 2 (Schachtel) box of chocolates

bonbon-, Bonbon-: ~**papier** *das* sweet wrapper; sweet paper; ~**rosa** *indekl. Adj.* candy pink; bright pink

bongen /ˈbɔŋən/ (ugs.)
A *tr. V.* ring up; **gebongt sein** (ugs.) be fine; **ist gebongt!** (ugs.) fine!
B *itr. V.* **ich habe falsch gebongt** I've rung up the wrong amount

Bongo /ˈbɔŋgo/ *das;* ~**s,** ~**s** *od. die;* ~, ~**s** bongo [drum]

Bongo·trommel *die* bongo drum

Bonhomie /bɔnoˈmi:/ *die;* ~, ~**n** (geh.) bonhomie

Bonifatius /boniˈfa:tsi̯ʊs/, **Bonifaz** /boniˈfa:ts/ (*der*) Boniface

Bonität /boniˈtɛ:t/ *die;* ~ (Kaufmannsspr.) creditworthiness; [good] credit rating

Bonmot /bõˈmo:/ *das;* ~**s,** ~**s** bon mot

Bonn (*das*); ~**s** ▸ **i** S. 675 Bonn

> **Bonn**
> Bonn was the capital of the Federal Republic of Germany from 1949 until **Berlin** was made the capital of reunified Germany, and it remains home to a number of government institutions. This relatively small, quiet city of about 300,000 inhabitants enjoys a picturesque location on the River Rhine.

Bonner ▸ **i** S. 675
A *indekl. Adj.* Bonn; **die** ~ **Regierung** the FRG Government
B *der;* ~**s,** ~: inhabitant of Bonn; (von Geburt) native of Bonn; *s. auch* **Kölner**

Bonnerin *die;* ~, ~**nen** ▸ **Bonner B**

Bonsai *der;* ~**s,** ~**s** bonsai [tree]

Bonus /ˈbo:nʊs/ *der;* ~ *od.* ~**ses,** ~ *od.* ~**se,** (auch:) **Boni** /ˈbo:ni/ 1 (Kaufmannsspr.) (Rabatt) discount; (Dividende) extra dividend; (Versicherungsw.) bonus 2 (Schadenfreiheitsrabatt) [no-claims] bonus 3 (Punktvorteil) bonus points *pl.*

Bonus-: ~**meile** *die* air mile; ~**track** *der* bonus track

Bon·vivant /bõviˈvã:/ *der;* ~**s,** ~**s** (geh.) bon vivant

Bonze /ˈbɔntsə/ *der;* ~**n,** ~**n** 1 (abwertend: Funktionär) bigwig (coll.); big noise (coll.); big wheel (Amer. coll.) 2 (Mönch) bonze

Boogie-Woogie /ˈbʊgiˈvʊgi/ *der;* ~**s,** ~**s** boogie-woogie

boolesch /ˈbu:lʃ/ *Adj.* (Math., DV) Boolean

Boom /bu:m/ *der;* ~**s,** ~**s** boom

Boot /bo:t/ *das;* ~**[e]s,** ~**e** boat; **wir sitzen alle in einem** *od.* **im selben** ~ (fig. ugs.) we're all in the same boat

Boot·diskette /ˈbu:t-/ *die* (DV) boot disk

booten /ˈbu:tn̩/ *tr. V.* (DV) boot [up]; **neu** ~: reboot

Boots-: ~**bau** *der* boatbuilding *no art.;* ~**fahrt** *die* boat trip; ~**haken** *der* boathook; ~**haus** *das* boathouse; ~**länge** *die* [boat's] length; ~**mann** *der Pl.* ~**leute** 1 (Handelsmarine) ≈ boatswain, bosun; 2 (Bundesmarine) ≈ petty officer; ~**steg** *der* landing stage; ~**verleih** *der* 1 (das Verleihen) boat hire; hiring of boats; 2 (Unternehmen) boat hire [business]

Bor /bo:ɐ̯/ *das;* ~**s** (Chemie) boron

Borax /ˈbo:raks/ *der;* ~**[es]** (Chemie) borax

Bord[1] /bɔrt/ *das;* ~**[e]s,** ~**e** 1 (Wandbrett) shelf 2 (veralt., noch schweiz.: Abhang) bank

Bord[2] *der;* ~**[e]s,** ~**e** (eines Schiffes) side; **an** ~: on board; **an** ~ **eines Schiffes/der „Baltic"** on board *or* aboard a ship/the 'Baltic'; **alle Mann an** ~**!** all aboard!; **über** ~: overboard; **über** ~ **gehen** go overboard; **Mann über** ~**!** man overboard!; **etw. über** ~ **werfen** (auch fig.) throw sth. overboard; **von** ~ **gehen** leave the ship; ‹*passengers at destination*› disembark, leave the ship; (aus dem Flugzeug) leave the aircraft

Bord-: ~**buch** *das* log[book]; ~**computer** *der* on-board computer

bordeaux *indekl. Adj.* ▸ **bordeauxrot**

Bordeaux /bɔrˈdo:/ *der;* ~ /bɔrˈdo:s/ ▸ **Bordeauxwein**

bordeaux·rot *Adj.* bordeaux-red; claret

Bordeaux·wein *der* Bordeaux [wine]; **roter** ~: claret

bord·eigen *Adj.* ships/plane's [own] *attrib.*

Bordell /bɔrˈdɛl/ *das;* ~**s,** ~**e** brothel; **in ein** ~ **gehen** visit a brothel

Bordell-: ~**besucher** *der* patron of a/the brothel; ~**gegend** *die* red-light district

Bord-: ~**flugzeug** *das* ship's aircraft; ~**funk** *der* [ship's/aircraft] radio; ~**funker** *der,* ~**funkerin** *die* radio operator; ~**kamera** *die* on-board camera; ~**mittel** *Pl.* (ugs.) one's own resources; **mit** ~**mitteln** with the means at one's disposal; ~**personal** *das* (Flugw.) cabin crew; ~**rechner** *der* ▸ ~**computer;** ~**stein** *der* kerb; ~**steinkante** *die* [edge of the] kerb

Bordüre /bɔrˈdy:rə/ *die;* ~, ~**n** edging

Bord-: ~**waffen** *Pl.* armament *sing.;* ~**wand** *die* /ship's/ side/side [of the/an aircraft]

Boreas /ˈbo:reas/ *der;* ~: north wind

Borg /bɔrk/ *in* **auf** ~ (veralt.) on credit; on tick (Brit. coll.); on the cuff (Amer. coll.)

borgen /ˈbɔrgn̩/ *tr., itr. V.* 1 (geben) lend; **jmdm. etw.** ~: lend sb. sth.; lend sth. to sb. 2 (erhalten) borrow; **[sich** (*Dat.*)**] etw. von jmdm.** ~: borrow sth. from sb.

Borgis /ˈbɔrgɪs/ *die;* ~ (Druckw.) 9-point type; bourgeois (Hist.)

Borke /ˈbɔrkə/ *die;* ~, ~**n** 1 (Rinde) bark 2 (ugs.: auf Wunden) scab

Borken-: ~**flechte** *die* ▸ **i** S. 439 ([Tier]med.) ringworm; ~**käfer** *der* bark beetle; ~**krepp** *der* bark crêpe; crépon; ~**schokolade** *die: thin-sheet chocolate made into rough-surfaced rolls;* chocolate bark

borkig *Adj.* 1 (rissig) cracked ‹*earth*›; chapped, cracked ‹*skin*› 2 (ugs.) ‹*knee, arm, etc.*› covered in scabs

Born /bɔrn/ *der;* ~**[e]s,** ~**e** (dichter.) spring; fount (poet./rhet.)

borniert /bɔrˈni:ɐ̯t/ (abwertend)
A *Adj.* narrow-minded; bigoted
B *adv.* in a narrow-minded *or* bigoted way

Borniertheit *die;* ~, ~**en** 1 (Eigenschaft) narrow-mindedness; bigotry 2 (Äußerung, Handlung) piece of narrow-mindedness *or* bigotry

Borretsch /ˈbɔrɛtʃ/ *der;* ~**[e]s** borage

Bor-: ~**salbe** *die* boric acid ointment; ~**säure** *die* (Chemie) boric acid (Chem.); boracic acid

Borsalino Ⓦⓩ /bɔrzaˈli:no/ *der;* ~**s,** ~**s** Borsalino ®

Börse /ˈbœrzə/ *die;* ~, ~**n** 1 (Aktienbörse) stock market; **an der** ~: on the stock market 2 (Gebäude) stock exchange 3 (geh. veralt.: Geld~) purse 4 (Boxen) purse

börsen-, Börsen-: ~**beginn** *der* opening of the [stock] market; **bei** ~**beginn** when the [stock] market opens/opened; ~**bericht** *der* stock market report; ~**fähig,** ~**gängig** *Adj.* (Wirtsch.) ‹*commodity, security, etc.*› negotiable on the stock market; ~**gang** *der* (Wirtsch.) [stock market] flotation; ~**geschäft** *das* stock market transaction; ~**krach** *der* stock market crash; collapse of the [stock] market; ~**kurs** *der* [stock] market price; ~**makler** *der,* ~**maklerin** *die* ▸ **i** S. 113 stockbroker; ~**notierung** *die* [stock exchange] quotation; ~**schluss,**

*∼**schluß** *der* close of the [stock] market; **bei ∼schluss** when the [stock] market closes/closed; ∼**spekulation** *die* speculation on the stock market; ∼**sturz** *der* ▸∼**krach**; ∼**tendenz** *die* [stock] market trend; ∼**tipp**, *∼**tip** *der* market tip

börsentäglich
A *Adj.* daily stock exchange *attrib.* ‹*turnover, trading times*›
B *Adv.* daily on the stock exchange

Börsianer *der;* ∼**s**, ∼, **Börsianerin** *die;* ∼, ∼**nen** (ugs.) [1] (Makler[in]) stockbroker [2] (Spekulant[in]) stock market speculator

börslich
A *Adj.* stock exchange *attrib.* ‹*trading, supervision, etc.*›.
B *adv.* on the stock exchange

Borste /ˈbɔrstə/ *die;* ∼, ∼**n** [1] bristle [2] *Pl.* (ugs.: beim Menschen) hair *sing.*; **seine ∼n aufstellen** (fig.) bristle

Borsten·vieh *das* (ugs.) (Schwein) pig; (Schweine) pigs *pl.*

borstig
A *Adj.* [1] (struppig) bristly [2] (grob) crusty ‹*person, manner, etc.*›
B *adv.* (grob) crustily

Borte /ˈbɔrtə/ *die;* ∼, ∼**n** braiding *no indef. art.*; trimming *no indef. art.*; edging *no indef. art.*

Bor·wasser *das* boric acid [eye] lotion

bös /bøːs/ ▸**böse A 3, 4, B**

bös·artig
A *Adj.* [1] (heimtückisch) malicious ‹*person, remark, etc.*›; vicious ‹*animal*› [2] (Med.) malignant
B *adv.* (heimtückisch) maliciously

Bös·artigkeit *die* [1] maliciousness; (von Tieren) viciousness [2] (Med.) malignancy

Böschung /ˈbœʃʊŋ/ *die;* ∼, ∼**en** (an der Straße) bank; embankment; (am Bahndamm) embankment; (am Fluss) bank

Böschungs·winkel *der* gradient

böse /ˈbøːzə/
A *Adj.* [1] (verwerflich) wicked; evil; **eine ∼ Zunge haben** have a wicked *or* malicious tongue; **Schneewittchen hatte eine ∼ Stiefmutter** Snow White had a wicked stepmother; **etw. aus ∼r Absicht/∼m Willen tun** do sth. with evil intent; **Böses mit Gutem vergelten** repay evil with good; **jmdm. Böses tun** (geh.) do sb. harm; **ich will dir doch nichts Böses** I don't mean you any harm; (bei Rat, Bemerkung) I don't mean it nastily [2] (übel) bad ‹*times, illness, dream, etc.*›; nasty ‹*experience, affair, situation, trick, surprise, etc.*›; **ein ∼s Ende nehmen** end in disaster; **eine ∼ Geschichte** a bad *or* nasty business; **nichts Böses ahnen** be unsuspecting; **nichts Böses ahnend** unsuspectingly; not suspecting anything is/was wrong; **den ∼n Blick haben** have the evil eye; **die ∼ Sieben** (fig.) the unlucky seven [3] ▸ⓘ **S. 227** (ugs.) (wütend) mad (coll.); (verärgert) cross; ∼ **mit jmdm.** *od.* **auf jmdn. werden** get mad at (coll.)/cross with sb.; ∼ **auf jmdn.** *od.* **mit jmdm. sein** be mad at (coll.)/cross with sb.; ∼ **über etw.** (*Akk.*) **sein** be mad at (coll.)/cross about sth.; **im Bösen auseinander gehen** part on bad terms; *s. auch* **Blut** [4] (fam.: ungezogen) naughty [5] (ugs.: entzündet) bad, sore ‹*knee, finger, etc.*› [6] (ugs.: arg) terrible (coll.) ‹*pain, fall, shock, disappointment, storm, etc.*›
B *adv.* [1] (übel) ‹*end*› badly; **mit ihm wird es noch ∼ enden** he'll come to a bad end; **das wird ∼ enden** it is bound to end in disaster; **es war doch nicht ∼ gemeint** I didn't mean it nastily [2] (ugs.) (wütend) angrily; (verärgert) crossly [3] (ugs.: arg) terribly (coll.); ‹*hurt*› badly; **er hat sich ∼ geirrt** he was badly wrong; **er ist ∼ gefallen** he had a nasty fall (coll.)

Böse[1] *der/die; adj. Dekl.* evil *or* wicked person; **er spielt den ∼n** he plays the villain *or* (coll.) baddy; **die ∼n kommen in die Hölle** the wicked go to hell

Böse[2] *der; adj. Dekl.* (veralt.: Teufel) the Evil One; the Devil

Böse·wicht *der; Pl.* ∼**er** [1] (ugs. scherzh.: Schlingel) rascal [2] (veralt., noch fig.: Schuft) villain; **jedes Mal bin ich der ∼** (fig.) I'm always the villain of the piece

boshaft /ˈboːshaft/
A *Adj.* malicious
B *adv.* maliciously

Boshaftigkeit *die;* ∼, ∼**en** [1] maliciousness [2] (Bemerkung) malicious remark; (Handlung) piece of maliciousness

Bosheit *die;* ∼, ∼**en** [1] (Art) malice; **mit konstanter ∼:** out of sheer spite [2] (Bemerkung) malicious remark; (Handlung) piece of maliciousness

Boskop /ˈbɔskɔp/ *der;* ∼**s**, ∼, **Boskoop** /ˈbɔskoːp/ *der;* ∼**s**, ∼ russet

Bosnien /ˈbɔsniən/ *(das);* ∼**s** Bosnia

Bosnien und Herzegowina /--hertseˈgoːvina/ *(das);* ∼**s** Bosnia-Herzegovina

Bosporus /ˈbɔsporʊs/ *der;* ∼**:** Bosporus

Boss, ***Boß** /bɔs/ *der;* **Bosses**, **Bosse** (ugs.) boss (coll.)

Bossa Nova /ˈbɔsaˈnoːva/ *der;* ∼, ∼**s** bossa nova

bosseln /ˈbɔsl̩n/ *tr., itr. V.* (ugs.) **etw./an etw.** (*Dat.*) ∼**:** beaver away (Brit.) *or* slave away making sth.; **er braucht immer was zu ∼:** he always needs to be working on *or* making something

bös-, **Bös-:** ∼**willig** **A** *Adj.* malicious; wilful ‹*desertion*›; **B** *adv.* maliciously; wilfully ‹*desert*›; ∼**willigkeit** *die;* ∼∼**:** malice; maliciousness

bot /boːt/ *1. u. 3. Pers. Sg. Prät. v.* **bieten**

Botanik /boˈtaːnɪk/ *die;* ∼ [1] botany *no art.* [2] (ugs.: Natur) nature

Botaniker *der;* ∼**s**, ∼, **Botanikerin** *die;* ∼, ∼**nen** ▸ⓘ **S. 113** botanist; *s. auch* **-in**

botanisch
A *Adj.* botanical
B *adv.* botanically

botanisieren *itr. V.* botanize

Botanisier·trommel *die* (veralt.) [botanist's] vasculum

Bötchen /ˈbøːtçən/ *das;* ∼**s**, ∼**:** little boat

Bote /ˈboːtə/ *der;* ∼**n**, ∼**n** [1] (Überbringer) messenger; (fig.) herald; harbinger [2] (Laufbursche) errand boy; messenger [boy]

Boten-: ∼**dienst** *der* job as a messenger/errand boy; **sie verdient sich ein Taschengeld durch ∼dienste** she earns pocket money as a messenger *or* by carrying messages/running errands; ∼**gang** *der* errand; ∼**gänge erledigen** run errands; ∼**lohn** *der* [messenger's/errand boy's] payment *or* tip; ∼**stoff** *der* (Med., Physiol.) messenger

Botin *die;* ∼, ∼**nen** ▸**Bote 1, 2:** messenger; errand girl

bot·mäßig (geh. veralt.)
A *Adj.* (gehorsam) obedient; (untertänig) submissive
B *adv.* (gehorsam) obediently; (untertänig) submissively

Botmäßigkeit *die;* ∼ (geh. veralt.) [1] (Herrschaft) dominion; sway [2] (Gehorsam) obedience; (Untertänigkeit) submissiveness

-botschaft *die:* **Friedens-/Kriegs-/Sieges∼:** news of peace/war/victory

Botschaft *die;* ∼, ∼**en** [1] (geh.: Nachricht) message; **die freudige ∼:** the good *or* happy news; **die Frohe ∼** (christl. Rel.) the Gospel [2] (Verlautbarung) message [3] (diplomatische Vertretung, auch Gebäude) embassy

Botschafter *der;* ∼**s**, ∼, **Botschafterin** *die;* ∼, ∼**nen** ▸ⓘ **S. 113** ambassador

Botschafts-: ∼**rat** *der* counsellor; ∼**sekretär** *der* [embassy] secretary

Böttcher /ˈbœtçɐ/ *der;* ∼**s**, ∼ ▸ⓘ **S. 113** cooper

Böttcherei *die;* ∼, ∼**en** [1] (Handwerk) cooper's trade; cooperage *no art.* [2] (Werkstatt) cooper's workshop; cooperage

Böttcherin *die;* ∼, ∼**nen** ▸ⓘ **S. 113** ▸**Böttcher**

Bottich /ˈbɔtɪç/ *der;* ∼**s**, ∼**e** tub

Bottnische Meer·busen /ˈbɔtnɪʃə/ *der* Gulf of Bothnia

Bouclé[1], **Buklee** /buˈkleː/ *das;* ∼**s**, ∼**s** bouclé [yarn]

Bouclé[2], **Buklee** *der;* ∼**s**, ∼**s** [1] (Stoff) bouclé [2] (Teppich) bouclé carpet

Boudoir /buˈdo̯aːɐ̯/ *das;* ∼**s**, ∼**s** (veralt.) boudoir

Bouillabaisse /bujaˈbɛːs/ *die;* ∼, ∼**s** /-ˈbɛːs/ (Kochk.) bouillabaisse

Bouillon /bulˈjɔŋ/ *die;* ∼, ∼**s** [1] (Brühe) bouillon; consommé [2] (Med.) bouillon; broth

Bouillon·würfel *der* bouillon cube

Boule /buːl/ *das;* ∼**s** boule[s *pl.*]

Boulette ▸**Bulette**

Boulevard /buləˈvaːɐ̯/ *der;* ∼**s**, ∼**s** boulevard

Boulevard-: ∼**blatt** *das* ▸∼**zeitung**; ∼**presse** *die* (abwertend) popular press; ∼**stück** *das* (Theater) boulevard drama; ∼**theater** *das* light theatre; ∼**zeitung** *die* (abwertend) popular rag (derog.); tabloid

Bouquet /buˈkeː/ *das;* ∼**s**, ∼**s** ▸**Bukett**

Bourbone /bʊrˈboːnə/ *der;* ∼**n**, ∼**n**, **Bourbonin** *die;* ∼, ∼**nen** (hist.) Bourbon

bourgeois /bʊrˈʒo̯a/ *Adj.* (abwertend, auch Soziol.) bourgeois

Bourgeois *der;* ∼, ∼ (abwertend, auch Soziol.) bourgeois

Bourgeoisie /bʊrʒo̯aˈziː/ *die;* ∼, ∼**n** (abwertend, auch Soziol.) bourgeoisie

Boutique /buˈtiːk/ *die;* ∼, ∼**s** *od.* ∼**n** boutique

Bovist ▸**Bofist**

Bowden·zug /ˈbaudn̩-/ *der* (Technik) Bowden cable

Bowle /ˈboːlə/ *die;* ∼, ∼**n** [1] punch (*made of wine, champagne, sugar, and fruit or spices*) [2] (Gefäß) punchbowl

bowlen /ˈboulən/ *itr. V.* (Sport) (auf der Bahn) bowl; (auf dem Rasen) play bowls

Bowlen·glas *das; Pl.* **Bowlengläser** punch glass

Bowler /ˈboulɐ/ *der;* ∼**s**, ∼**:** bowler [hat]

Bowling /ˈboulɪŋ/ *das;* ∼**s**, ∼**s** (auf der Bahn) [tenpin] bowling; (auf dem Rasen) bowls; ∼ **spielen gehen** go [tenpin] bowling/go to play bowls

Bowling·bahn *die* [tenpin] bowling alley

Box /bɔks/ *die;* ∼, ∼**en** [1] (Lautsprecher) speaker [2] (Pferde-) [loose] box [3] (für Autos) [partitioned off] [parking] space [4] (Kamera) box camera [5] (Behälter) box [6] (Montageplatz) pit; **an den ∼en** in the pits

Boxcalf ▸**Boxkalf**

boxen
A *itr. V.* box; **gegen jmdn. ∼:** fight sb.; box [against] sb.; **um die Weltmeisterschaft** *usw.* ∼**:** fight for the world championship *etc.*; **jmdm. in den Magen ∼:** punch sb. in the stomach
B *tr. V.* [1] (schlagen) punch [2] (Sportjargon: kämpfen gegen) fight
C *refl. V.* [1] (ugs.: Weg bahnen) fight one's way [2] (ugs.: sich prügeln) have a punch-up (coll.) *or* fight; **hört auf, euch zu ∼:** stop fighting

Boxen-: ∼**luder** *das* (Motorsport) pit babe (coll.); (in Formel 1 auch) F1 babe; ∼**stopp** *der* (Motorsport) pit stop

Boxer *der;* ∼**s**, ∼ ▸ⓘ **S. 113** [1] (Sportler, Hund) boxer [2] (ugs.: Schlag) punch

Boxer·aufstand *der* (hist.) Boxer Rebellion

Boxerin *die;* ∼, ∼**nen** ▸ⓘ **S. 113** boxer

boxerisch *Adj.* boxing ‹*skill, know-how, etc.*›

Boxer-: ∼**motor** *der* (Technik) horizontally opposed engine; ∼**nase** *die* boxer's nose; ∼**shorts** *Pl.* boxer shorts

Box·hand·schuh *der* boxing glove

Box·kalf /-kalf/ *das;* ∼**s**, ∼**s** boxcalf

Box-: ∼**kampf** *der* [1] (Kampf) boxing match; (im Streit) fist fight; **er hat 200 ∼kämpfe ausgetragen** he's had 200 fights *or* bouts; [2] (Disziplin) boxing *no art.*; ∼**ring** *der* boxing ring; ∼**sport** *der* boxing *no art.*; ∼**staffel** *die* boxing team

Boy /bɔy/ *der;* ∼**s**, ∼**s** [1] (Diener) servant; (im Hotel) pageboy [2] (Jugendspr.) (junger Mann) boy; (Freund) boyfriend

b

Boykott /bɔy'kɔt/ *der;* **~[e]s, ~s** boycott; **einem Land den ~ erklären** declare a boycott of a country

Boykott-: ~aufruf *der* boycott call; call for a boycott; **~hetze** *die* (DDR Amtspr., Rechtsw.) anti-state agitation

boykottieren *tr. V.* boycott

Boykott·maßnahme *die* boycott [action]; **sich zu weiteren ~n gegen ein Land entschließen** decide to tighten the boycott of a country

Bozen /'bo:tsn̩/ *(das);* **~s** Bolzano

BR *Abk.* **= Bayrischer Rundfunk** Bavarian Radio

brabbeln /'brabl̩n/ *tr., itr. V.* (ugs.) mutter; mumble; ‹*baby*› babble

Brabbel·wasser *das* (ugs. scherzh.) **1** schnapps **2** **~ getrunken haben** (ugs. scherzh.) have verbal diarrhoea (sl.)

brach[1] /bra:x/ *1. u. 3. Pers. Sg. Prät. v.* **brechen**

brach[2] *Adj.* (veralt.) fallow; (auf Dauer) uncultivated; waste

Brache *die;* **~, ~n** **1** (Feld) [piece of] fallow land; (auf Dauer) [piece of] uncultivated *or* waste land **2** (Zeit) fallow period

brachial /bra'xia:l/ *Adj.* **1** violent; **~e Gewalt** brute force **2** (Med.) brachial

Brachial·gewalt *die* brute force

Brachiosaurus /braxio'zaurus/ *der;* **~, Brachiosaurier** /...zaurie/ brachiosaurus

Brach·land *das* fallow [land]; (auf Dauer) uncultivated *or* waste land

brach|liegen *unr. itr. V.* (auch fig.) lie fallow; (auf Dauer) lie waste

brachte /'braxtə/ *1. u. 3. Pers. Sg. Prät. v.* **bringen**

Brach·vogel *der* curlew

brackig *Adj.* (niederd.) brackish

Brack·wasser *das* brackish water

Brahmane /bra'ma:nə/ *der;* **~n, ~n, Brahmanin** *die;* **~, ~nen** Brahmin

brahmanisch *Adj.* Brahminical

Brainstorming /'breɪnstɔ:mɪŋ/ *das;* **~s** brainstorming; **ein ~:** a brainstorming session

bramarbasieren /bramarba'zi:rən/ *itr. V.* (geh. abwertend) brag, boast (**von** about)

Bram·segel /'bra:m-/ *das* topgallant sail

Branche /'brã:ʃə/ *die;* **~, ~n** **1** [branch of] industry; **alle ~n der Bekleidungsindustrie** all branches of the clothing industry; **er kennt sich in der ~ am besten aus** he has the most knowledge of the industry **2** (Fachgebiet) field; **die ~ wechseln** move into a different field

branchen-, Branchen-: ~fremd *Adj.* new to the industry *postpos.;* ‹*person*› who knows nothing of the industry *postpos., not pred.;* **~führer** *der,* **~führerin** *die* (Wirtsch.) market[-sector] leader; (einer Industrie) industry leader; **~jargon** *der* trade jargon; **~kenntnisse** *Pl.* knowledge *sing.* of the industry; **~kundig** *Adj.* experienced in the industry *postpos.;* with knowledge of the industry *postpos., not pred.;* **~mix** *der* (Wirtsch.) mix of trades and industries; **~spezifisch** *Adj.* specific to an/the industry *postpos.;* **~üblich** *Adj.* usual in the industry *postpos.;* **im Baugewerbe ~üblich** usual in the building industry

Branchen·verzeichnis *das* classified directory; (Telefonbuch) Yellow Pages ® *pl.*

Brand /brant/ *der;* **~[e]s, Brände** /'brɛndə/ **1** fire **2** (Brennen) **beim ~ der Scheune** when the barn caught fire; **in ~ geraten** catch fire; **etw. in ~ setzen** *od.* **stecken** set fire to sth.; set sth. on fire **3** (ugs.: Durst) raging thirst; **einen fürchterlichen ~ haben** have a terrible thirst **4** ▸ⓘ **S. 439** (Med.) **[trockener/feuchter] ~:** [dry/moist] gangrene **5** (Bot.) blight

brand-, Brand-: ~aktuell *Adj.* very latest ‹*news*›; up-to-the-minute ‹*report*›; red-hot ‹*news item, issue*›; highly topical ‹*book*›; **~anschlag** *der* arson attack (**auf** + *Akk.* on); **~bekämpfung** *die* firefighting *no art.;* **~binde** *die* dressing [for burns]; **~blase** *die* [burn] blister; **~bombe** *die* fire bomb; incendiary bomb; **~direktor** *der* chief fire officer; fire chief (Amer.); **~eilig** *Adj.* (ugs.) extremely urgent

branden *itr. V.* (geh.) break; **~der Beifall** (fig.) thunderous applause

Branden·burg *(das);* **~s** Brandenburg

Brandenburger

A *indekl. Adj.* Brandenburg *attrib.;* **das ~ Tor** the Brandenburg Gate

B *der;* **~s, ~:** native of Brandenburg; (Einwohner) inhabitant of Brandenburg; **die ~:** the people of Brandenburg

brandenburgisch *Adj.* Brandenburg *attrib.*

brand-, Brand-: ~fackel *die* firebrand; flaming torch; **~fall** *der* fire; **im ~fall/für den ~fall** in case of fire; **~fleck** *der* burn mark; **~gefahr** *die* danger of fire; **bei ~gefahr** when there is danger of fire; **~gefährlich** *Adj.* perilous; highly dangerous; **~geruch** *der* smell of burning; **~herd** *der* source of the fire

brandig *Adj.* **1** ‹*smell*› of burning; burnt ‹*taste*›; **es riecht ~:** there is a smell of burning **2** (Med.) gangrenous **3** (Bot.) suffering from blight *postpos.*

brand-, Brand-: ~kasse *die* fire insurance company; **~katastrophe** *die* disastrous fire; **~leger** /-le:gɐ/ *der;* **~~s, ~~, ~legerin** *die;* **~~, ~~nen** (österr.) ▸ **~stifter; ~legung** *die;* **~~, ~~en** (österr.) ▸ **~stiftung; ~mal** *das* (geh.) burn mark; (fig.: Stigma) stigma; **~marken** *tr. V.* brand ‹*person*›; denounce ‹*thing*›; **jmdn. [als Verräter] ~marken** brand sb. [as a traitor]; **~markung** *die;* **~~, ~~en** branding; (Äußerung) denunciation; **~mauer** *die* fire wall; **~meister** *der* chief fire officer; fire chief (Amer.); **~neu** *Adj.* (ugs.) brand-new; **~opfer** *das* **1** (Rel.) burnt offering; **2** (Opfer eines **~es**) fire victim; victim of the/a fire; **~rede** *die* fiery tirade; **~rodung** *die* slash and burn; **~salbe** *die* ointment for burns; **~satz** *der* incendiary mixture; **~schaden** *der* fire damage *no pl., no indef. art.;* **die ~schäden in den Wäldern** the damage to forests caused by fire; **~schatzen** *tr. V.* (hist.) pillage and threaten to burn; **~schatzung** *die;* **~~, ~~en** (hist.) pillaging and threat of burning; **~schutz** *der* fire safety *no art.;* **~sohle** *die* insole; **~stelle** *die* **1** scene of the fire; **2** (verbrannte Stelle) burn; (größer) burnt patch; **~stifter** *der,* **~stifterin** *die* arsonist; **~stiftung** *die* arson; **eine ~stiftung** a case of arson; **~teig** *der* (Kochk.) choux pastry

Brandung *die;* **~, ~en** surf; breakers *pl.;* **die ~ donnerte gegen die Felsen** the breakers crashed against the rocks; **bei starker ~:** when the surf is high

Brandungs-: ~boot *das* surfboat; **~welle** *die* breaker

Brand-: ~versicherung *die* fire insurance; (Gesellschaft) fire-insurance company; **~wache** *die* **1** fire-watcher; (Mannschaft) fire-watchers *pl.;* **2** (Dienst) fire-watch; **~wunde** *die* burn; (Verbrühung) scald; **~zeichen** *das* brand

brannte /'brantə/ *1. u. 3. Pers. Sg. Prät. v.* **brennen**

Brannt·wein *der* spirits *pl.;* **Wodka ist ein ~:** vodka is a type of spirit

Branntwein-: ~brenner *der,* **~brennerin** *die;* **~~, ~~nen** distiller; **~monopol** *das* monopoly of spirits; liquor monopoly (Amer.); **~steuer** *die* tax on spirits; liquor tax (Amer.)

bräsig /'brɛ:zɪç/ (bes. nordd.)

A *Adj.* complacent

B *adv.* complacently

Bräsigkeit *die;* **~** (bes. nordd.) complacency

Brasil[1] /bra'zi:l/ *der;* **~s, ~e** *od.* **~s** Brazil[ian] tobacco

Brasil[2] *die;* **~, ~[s]** Brazil cigar

Brasil·holz *das* Brazil wood

Brasilianer /brazi'lia:nɐ/ *der;* **~s, ~, Brasilianerin** *die;* **~, ~nen** ▸ⓘ **S. 520** Brazilian; *s. auch* **-in**

brasilianisch *Adj.* ▸ⓘ **S. 520** Brazilian

Brasilien /bra'zi:liən/ *(das);* **~s** Brazil

Brasil-: ~tabak *der* Brazil[ian] tobacco; **~zigarre** *die* Brazil cigar

***Brass, Braß** *der;* **Brasses** (ugs.) **~ haben, in ~ sein** be mad (coll.) *or* angry; **in ~ kommen** get mad (coll.) *or* angry; **jmdn. in ~ bringen** make sb. mad (coll.) *or* angry

Brasse /'brasə/ *die;* **~, ~n** (Seemannsspr.) brace

Brasserie /brasə'ri:/ *die;* **~, ~n** brasserie

brät /brɛ:t/ *3. Pers. Sg. Präsens v.* **braten**

Brät *das;* **~s** *lean minced pork used esp. as filling for sausages*

Brat·apfel *der* baked apple

braten /'bra:tn̩/

A *unr. tr. V.* (auf dem Herd) fry; (im Backofen) (mit Fett, im eigenen Saft) roast; (ohne Fett) bake; **etw. braun ~:** fry sth. until it is brown; **etw. am Spieß ~:** roast sth. on a spit

B *unr. itr. V.* (auf dem Herd) fry; (im Backofen) (mit Fett, im eigenen Saft) roast; (ohne Fett) bake; **in der Sonne ~** (fig.) roast in the sun

Braten *der;* **~s, ~:** joint; (gebratene Portion) roast [meat] *no indef. art.;* **sonntags gab es bei uns immer ~:** we always had a roast *or* a joint on Sundays; **kalter ~:** cold meat; **den fetten ~ konnte er sich nicht entgehen lassen** (fig. ugs.) he couldn't miss the chance of making such a big killing (coll.); **den ~ riechen** (fig. ugs.) smell a rat

Braten-: ~fett *das* [meat] fat; [meat] juices *pl.;* **~rock** *der* (veralt. scherzh.) frock coat; **~saft** *der* meat juice[s *pl.*]; **~soße** *die* gravy; **~wender** *der* slice; turner

Brat-: ~fett *das* [cooking] fat; **~fisch** *der* fried fish; **~hähnchen** *das,* (südd., österr.) **~hendl** *das* **1** roast chicken; (gegrillt) broiled chicken; **2** (Hähnchen zum **~en**) roasting chicken; (zum Grillen) broiling chicken; **~hering** *der* fried herring; **~huhn** *das,* **~hühnchen** *das* ▸ **~hähnchen; ~kartoffeln** *Pl.* fried potatoes; home fries (Amer.); *s. auch* **daher 2; ~kartoffel·verhältnis** *das* (ugs. veralt.) **er hat ein ~kartoffelverhältnis mit ihr** he treats her as his meal ticket; **~ofen** *der* oven; **~pfanne** *die* frying pan; **~röhre** *die* ▸ **~ofen; ~rost** *der* grill

Bratsche /'bra:tʃə/ *die;* **~, ~n** (Musik) viola

Bratschen·schlüssel *der* (Musik) ▸ **Altschlüssel**

Bratschist *der;* **~en, ~en, Bratschistin** *die;* **~, ~nen** violist; viola player

Brat-: ~spieß *der* **1** spit; (kleiner) skewer; **2** (Gericht) kebab; **~wurst** *die* **1** [fried/grilled] sausage; **2** (Wurst zum **~en**) sausage [for frying/grilling]

Brauch /braux/ *der;* **~[e]s, Bräuche** /'brɔyçə/ custom; **so ist es ~, so will es der ~:** that's the custom; **das ist bei ihnen so ~:** that's their custom; **nach altem ~:** in accordance with an old custom

brauchbar

A *Adj.* useful; (benutzbar) usable; wearable ‹*clothes*›; (ordentlich) decent ‹*worker, pupil*›; **er ist ganz ~:** he is a decent worker/pupil *etc.*

B *adv.* **er schreibt/arbeitet ganz ~:** he's a useful writer/he does useful work

Brauchbarkeit *die;* **~:** usefulness; (Benutzbarkeit) usability

brauchen

A *tr. V.* **1** (benötigen) need; **alles, was man zum Leben braucht** everything one needs in order to live reasonably; **ich kann dich jetzt nicht ~** (fam.) I don't want you around just now; **deine guten Ratschläge kann ich nicht ~:** I can well do without your advice **2** (aufwenden müssen) **mit dem Fahrrad/Auto braucht er nur zehn Minuten** it only takes him ten minutes on his bicycle/by car; **er hat für die Arbeit Jahre gebraucht** the work took him years; **wie lange brauchst du dafür?** how long will it take you?; (im Allgemeinen) how long does it take you? **3** (benutzen, verwenden, ver**~**) use; **ich**

könnte es gut ~: I could do with it
B *itr. V.* (geh. veralt.: bedürfen) **es braucht keines weiteren Beweises** no further proof is needed *or* necessary
C *mit Inf. mit „zu", verneintes od. eingeschränktes Modalverb* need; **du brauchst nicht zu helfen** there is no need [for you] to help; you don't need to help; **du brauchst doch nicht gleich zu weinen** there's no need to start crying; **das hättest du nicht zu tun ~:** there was no need to do it; you needn't have done that; **das hätte nicht zu sein ~:** that needn't have happened; **es braucht nicht sofort zu sein** it doesn't need *or* have to be done immediately; **du brauchst es [mir] nur zu sagen** you only have to tell me; **du brauchst es nur zu sagen** you only have to say so

Brauchtum *das;* **~s, Brauchtümer** /-ty:mɐ/ custom; **zum ~ dieser Region gehört ...** one of the customs in this area is ...

Braue /ˈbraʊ̯ə/ *die;* **~, ~n** ▸ⓘ **S. 435** [eye]brow

brauen
A *tr. V.* 1 brew 2 (ugs.: aufbrühen, zubereiten) brew [up] ‹*tea, coffee*›; concoct ‹*potion etc.*›; mix ‹*cocktail*›
B *itr. V.* 1 (Bier ~) brew [beer] 2 (dichter.: wallen) ‹*mist, fog*› gather

Brauer *der;* **~s, ~:** brewer

Brauerei *die;* **~, ~en** 1 brewing 2 (Betrieb) brewery

Brauerin *die;* **~, ~nen** brewer

Brau-: ~haus *das* brewery; **~meister** *der,* **~meisterin** *die* master brewer

braun /braʊ̯n/ *Adj.* 1 brown; **~ werden** (sonnengebräunt) get brown; get a tan; **sich von der Sonne ~ brennen lassen** sit/lie in the sun and get a tan; **~ gebrannt** [sun]tanned 2 (abwertend: nationalsozialistisch) Nazi; **er war ~:** he was a Nazi

Braun *das;* **~s, ~,** (ugs.) **~s** brown

braun·äugig *Adj.* brown-eyed; **~ sein** have brown eyes

Braun·bär *der* brown bear

Braune *der; adj. Dekl.* 1 bay [horse] 2 (österr.: Kaffee) [cup of] white coffee (Brit.); [cup of] coffee with milk/cream

Bräune /ˈbrɔy̯nə/ *die;* **~:** [sun]tan

bräunen
A *tr. V.* 1 tan; **die Sonne hat sein Gesicht stark gebräunt** the sun has tanned his face a deep brown 2 (Kochk.) brown
B *itr. V.* 1 **die südliche Sonne bräunt stark** the Southern sun gives you a good tan 2 (Kochk.) ‹*meat*› brown; ‹*cake*› go golden brown; ‹*butter*› go brown

braun-, Braun-: ~gebrannt ▸**braun 1**; **~hemd** *das* (ns.) 1 brown shirt; 2 (Träger des ~hemds) Brownshirt; **~kohl** *der* ▸**Grünkohl**; **~kohle** *die* brown coal; lignite

bräunlich *Adj.* brownish

Braunschweig /ˈbraʊ̯nʃvai̯k/ *(das);* **~s** ▸ⓘ **S. 675** Braunschweig; Brunswick (Hist.)

braunschweigisch *Adj.* Braunschweig *attrib.; s. auch* **hannoversch**

Bräunung *die;* **~, ~en** browning; (durch die Sonne) [sun]tan

Bräunungs·studio *das* solarium

Braus /braʊ̯s/ ▸**Saus**

Brause /ˈbraʊ̯zə/ *die;* **~, ~n** 1 fizzy drink; (~pulver) sherbet 2 (veralt.: Dusche) shower; **sich unter die ~ stellen** take *or* have a shower 3 (Sprühteil) (einer Gießkanne) rose; (einer Dusche) shower head

Brause-: ~bad *das* (veralt.) 1 shower [bath]; 2 (Duschbad) shower; **ein ~bad nehmen** take *or* have a shower; **~kopf** *der* (veralt.) hothead; **~limonade** *die* fizzy lemonade

brausen
A *itr. V.* 1 ‹*wind, water, etc.*› roar; (fig.) ‹*organ, applause, etc.*› thunder; **hier braust der Verkehr bei Tag und Nacht** there is a constant roar of traffic here day and night 2 (duschen) [take *or* have a] shower 3 (sich schnell bewegen) race
B *tr. V.* put ‹*children etc.*› under the shower
C *refl. V.* [take *or* have a] shower

Brausen *das;* **~s** roar; **das ~ in meinen Ohren** the ringing *or* buzzing in my ears

Brause-: ~pulver *das* sherbet; **~tablette** *die* effervescent tablet

-braut *die* (ugs.) **Fußball~:** football player's/fan's girlfriend/wife; **Rocker~:** rocker's girl; (Mitglied der Bande) girl rocker

Braut /braʊ̯t/ *die;* **~, Bräute** /ˈbrɔy̯tə/ 1 bride 2 (Verlobte) fiancée; bride-to-be 3 (ugs.: Freundin) girl[friend]

Braut-: ~bett *das* (hist.) bridal bed; **~eltern** *Pl.* bride's parents

Bräutigam /ˈbrɔy̯tɪgam/ *der;* **~s, ~e** 1 [bride]groom 2 (veralt.: Verlobter) fiancé; husband-to-be

Braut-: ~jungfer *die* bridesmaid; **~kleid** *das* wedding dress; **~kranz** *der* bridal wreath; **~leute** *Pl.:* ▸**~paar**; **~mutter** *die; Pl.* **~mütter** bride's mother; **~nacht** *die* wedding night; **~paar** *das* bridal couple; bride and groom; **~schau** *die: in* **auf ~schau gehen, ~schau halten** (ugs. scherzh.) go *or* be looking for a wife; **~schleier** *der* bridal veil; **~vater** *der* bride's father

brav /bra:f/
A *Adj.* 1 (artig) good; **sei [schön] ~:** be good; **sei ein ~es Kind** be a good boy/girl 2 (redlich) honest; upright; **er soll ein ~es Mädchen heiraten** he should marry a good honest girl 3 (hausbacken) plain and conservative ‹*clothes*› 4 (veralt.: tapfer) brave
B *adv.* 1 **nun iss schön ~ deine Suppe** be a good boy/girl and eat up your soup; eat up your soup like a good boy/girl; **die Kinder spielten ~ in ihrem Zimmer** the children were being good and playing quietly in their room 2 (redlich) honestly 3 (bieder) **[recht] ~ spielen/schreiben** play/write quite nicely 4 (veralt.: tapfer) bravely

bravo /ˈbra:vo/ *Interj.* bravo

Bravo *das;* **~s, ~s** cheer; **das laute ~ der Zuschauer** the loud cheers *or* cheering of the audience; **ein ~ für ...** three cheers for ...

Bravo·ruf *der* cheer

Bravour /braˈvu:ɐ̯/ *die;* **~** 1 stylishness; **mit ~:** with style and élan 2 (Tapferkeit) daring and bravery

Bravour·leistung *die* brilliant performance

bravourös /bravuˈrø:s/
A *Adj.* 1 (rasant) **mit ~em Tempo** at magnificent speed 2 (meisterhaft) brilliant
B *adv.* 1 (rasant) with great dash 2 (meisterhaft) brilliantly

Bravour·stück *das* piece of bravura; brilliant performance

BRD *Abk.* **= Bundesrepublik Deutschland** FRG

Break /breɪk/ *das;* **~s, ~s** (Sport, Musik) break

Breakdance /ˈbreɪkdɛns/ *der;* **~[s]** breakdancing

brechbar *Adj.* 1 breakable; **nicht ~:** unbreakable 2 (ablenkbar) refrangible

Brech-: ~bohne *die* French bean (Brit.); green bean; **~durch·fall** *der* diarrhoea and vomiting *no indef. art.;* **~eisen** *das* ▸**~stange**

brechen /ˈbrɛçn̩/ ▸ⓘ **S. 439**
A *unr. tr. V.* 1 break; cut ‹*marble, slate, etc.*›; **Blumen ~** (dichter.) pluck flowers; **sich** (Dat.) **den Arm/das Genick ~:** break one's arm/neck; **nichts zu ~ und zu beißen haben** (geh.) not have anything at all to eat 2 (ablenken) break ‹*water etc.*›; refract ‹*light*› 3 (bezwingen) overcome ‹*resistance*›; break ‹*will, silence, record, blockade, etc.*› 4 (nicht einhalten) break ‹*agreement, contract, promise, the law, etc.*› 5 (ugs.: er~) bring up
B *unr. itr. V.* 1 *mit sein* break; ‹*leather*› crack; **mir bricht das Herz** (fig.) it breaks my heart; **~d voll sein** be full to bursting 2 (Beziehungen aufgeben) break; **er brach mit der Familientradition** he broke [away from] the family tradition; **mit einer Gewohnheit ~:** break a habit 3 *mit sein* (hervorkommen) break **(durch** through) 4 (ugs.: sich er~) throw up
C *unr. refl. V.* ‹*waves etc.*› break **(an** + *Dat.* on); ‹*rays etc.*› be refracted

Brecher *der;* **~s, ~** 1 (Welle) breaker 2 (Maschine) crusher

Brech-: ~mittel *das* emetic; **der Mann ist ein echtes ~mittel** (fig. ugs. abwertend) that man makes me sick (coll.) *or* (coarse) want to puke; **~reiz** *der* nausea; **~stange** *die* crowbar; **mit der ~stange vorgehen** (fig.) go about it with a sledgehammer; **ein Sieg mit der ~stange** (Sport) a victory by sheer force

brecht[i]sch /ˈbrɛçt(ɪ)ʃ/ *Adj.* Brechtian

Brechung *die;* **~, ~en** 1 (Physik) refraction 2 (Sprachw.) breaking

Brechungs·winkel *der* (Physik) angle of refraction

Bredouille /breˈdʊljə/ *die;* **~, ~n** (ugs.) **in der ~ sein** *od.* **sitzen** be in real trouble; **in die ~ kommen** get into real trouble

Bregen /ˈbre:gn̩/ *der;* **~s, ~** (nordd.) brains *pl.*

Brei /brai̯/ *der;* **~[e]s, ~e** (Hafer~) porridge (Brit.), oatmeal (Amer.) *no indef. art.;* (Reis~) rice pudding; (Grieß~) semolina *no indef. art.;* **etw. zu einem ~ verrühren** make sth. into a mash *or* purée; **um den [heißen] ~ herumreden** (ugs.) beat about the bush

breiig *Adj.* mushy; **eine ~e Masse** a thick paste

breit /brai̯t/
A *Adj.* 1 ▸ⓘ **S. 454** wide ‹*street, river, bridge, window, margin, etc.*›; broad, wide ‹*hips, face, shoulders, forehead, etc.*›; **etw. ~er machen** widen sth.; **einen ~en Buckel** *od.* **Rücken haben** (fig. ugs.) have broad shoulders (fig.); **die Beine ~ machen** (auch fig.) open one's legs; **die Schuhe ~ treten** stretch one's shoes out of shape; **ein ~es Lachen** a guffaw; **eine ~e Aussprache** a broad accent 2 (bei Maßangaben) wide; **ein 5 cm ~er Saum** a hem 5 cm wide; **einen Finger ~ sein** be the width of a finger *or* a finger's breadth 3 (groß) **die ~e Masse** the general public; most people *pl.;* **die ~e Öffentlichkeit** the general public; **~e Bevölkerungsschichten** large sections of the population; **ein ~es Interesse finden** arouse a great deal of interest 4 (ugs.: im Rausch) high (coll.); stoned (sl.) 5 **sich ~ machen** take up room; (sich ausbreiten) be spreading; (sich niederlassen) make oneself at home; **mach dich nicht so ~:** don't take up so much room
B *adv.* 1 **~ gebaut** sturdily *or* well built; **~ lachen** guffaw; **etw. ~ darstellen** (fig.) describe sth. in great detail 2 **der Stoff liegt doppelt ~:** the material is double width 3 **~ gefächert** wide ‹*range, choice*›

Breit-: ~band *das* (Elektrot.) broadband; **~band·anschluss** *der* (Elektrot.) broadband connection; **~band·antibiotikum** *das* (Med.) broad-spectrum antibiotic; **~band·kabel** *das* (Elektrot.) broadband cable

breit·beinig
A *Adj.* rolling ‹*gait*›
B *adv.* with one's legs apart; **er stand ~ vor uns** he stood squarely in front of us

Breite *die;* **~, ~n** 1 ▸ⓘ **S. 454** width; breadth; (bei Maßangaben) width; **etw. der ~ nach durchsägen** saw through sth. widthways *or* widthwise; **etw. in epischer ~ schildern** (fig.) describe sth. in great detail *or* down to the last detail; **in die ~ gehen** (ugs.) put on weight 2 (Geogr.) latitude; **auf/unter 50° nördlicher ~:** at/below latitude 50° north 3 *Pl.* (Gebiet) **in diesen ~n** in these latitudes

breiten *tr., refl. V.* (geh.) spread

Breiten-: ~grad *der* degree of latitude; **New York und Mailand liegen auf demselben ~grad** New York and Milan have the same latitude; **der 30. ~grad** the 30th parallel; **~kreis** *der* [line of] latitude; parallel; **~sport** *der* popular sport; **~wirkung** *die* widespread effect

breit-, Breit-: ~flächig *Adj.* wide; **~flächig gebaut** built over a wide area *postpos.;* **~gefächert** ▸**breit B3**; **~krempig** *Adj.* broad-brimmed; ***~|machen** ▸**breit A5**; **~randig** *Adj.* broad-brimmed; **~|schlagen** *unr. tr. V.* (ugs.) **sich zu etw. ~schlagen lassen** let oneself be talked into sth.; **er ließ**

sich ~schlagen he let himself be persuaded; **~schult[e]rig** *Adj.* broad-shouldered; **~schwanz** *der* karakul; broadtail; **~seite** *die* 1 (eines Tisches, Gebäudes, Zimmers usw.) long side; (eines Schiffes) side; 2 ([Abfeuern der] Geschütze) broadside; **~spur** *die* (Eisenb.) broad gauge; **~spurig** *Adj.* broad-gauge ‹*railway etc.*›; ‹*car etc.*› with a wide track; **~|treten** *unr. tr. V.* (ugs. abwertend) go on about; **das Thema ist ~getreten** this subject has been flogged to death; **~|walzen** *tr. V.* (ugs. abwertend) discuss at length; chew over; **~wand** *die* (Kino) wide *or* big screen; **~wand·film** *der* widescreen *or* big-screen film

b

Bremen *(das);* **~s** ▸ℹ **S. 675** Bremen

Bremer ▸ℹ **S. 675**

A *indekl. Adj.* Bremen; **der ~ Hafen** the Port of Bremen

B *der;* **~s, ~:** native/inhabitant of Bremen; *s. auch* **Kölner**

Bremerin *die;* **~, ~nen** ▸**Bremer B**

bremisch *Adj.* Bremen *attrib.*

Brems-: ~backe *die* (Kfz-W.) brake shoe; **~belag** *der* (Kfz-W.) brake lining

Bremse¹ /ˈbrɛmzə/ *die;* **~, ~n** brake; **auf die ~ treten** put on the brakes

Bremse² *die;* **~, ~n** (Insekt) horsefly

bremsen

A *itr. V.* brake; **der Dynamo bremst ganz erheblich** the dynamo has quite a considerable braking effect

B *tr. V.* 1 brake; (um zu halten) stop 2 (fig.) slow down ‹*rate, development, production, etc.*›; restrict ‹*imports etc.*›; **jmdn. ~** (ugs.) stop sb.; **er ist nicht [mehr] zu ~** (ugs.) there's no stopping him

C *refl. V.* (ugs.) stop oneself; hold oneself back

Bremser *der;* **~s, ~, Bremserin** *die;* **~, ~nen** (Eisenb., Bobsport) brakeman/brakewoman

Brems-: ~flüssigkeit *die* (Kfz-W.) brake fluid; **~hebel** *der* brake arm; **~klotz** *der* 1 (am Fahrrad) brake block; (am Wagen) brake pad; 2 (Klotz, der vor das Rad geschoben wird) [wheel] chock; 3 (fig.) obstacle to progress; **~kraft·verstärker** *der* (Kfz-W.) brake servo; **~leitung** *die* (Kfz-W.) brake pipe; **~leuchte** *die*, **~licht** *das; Pl.* **~~er** brake light; **~pedal** *das* brake pedal; **~probe** *die* brake test; **~scheibe** *die* (Kfz-W.) brake disc; **~spur** *die* skid mark; **~trommel** *die* (Kfz-W.) brake drum

Bremsung *die;* **~, ~en** braking

Brems-: ~weg *der* braking distance; **~zug** *der* brake cable; **~zylinder** *der* (Kfz-W.) brake cylinder

brenn-, Brenn-: ~bar *Adj.* [in]flammable; combustible; **leicht ~bar** highly [in]flammable *or* combustible; **~dauer** *die* 1 (einer Glühlampe) life; 2 (im **~ofen**) firing time; **~eisen** *das* 1 ▸**~schere**; 2 (für Brandzeichen) branding iron

brennen /ˈbrɛnən/

A *unr. itr. V.* 1 ‹*wood etc.*› burn; ‹*house etc.*› burn, be on fire; **schnell/leicht ~:** catch fire quickly/easily; **es brennt!** fire!; **in der Hotelbar hat es gebrannt** there was a fire in the hotel bar; **wo brennt's denn?** (fig. ugs.) what's the panic? 2 (glühen) be alight 3 (leuchten) be on; **in ihrem Zimmer brennt Licht** there is a light on in her room; **das Licht ~ lassen** leave the light on; **die Birne/Kerze brennt ganz schwach** the bulb is glowing very dimly/the candle is burning very low 4 (scheinen) **die Sonne brannte so stark** the sun was so strong; **die Sonne brannte** the sun was burning down 5 (schmerzen) ‹*wound etc.*› burn, sting; ‹*feet etc.*› hurt, be sore; **mir ~ die Augen** my eyes are stinging *or* smarting; **Pfeffer brennt auf der Zunge** pepper burns the tongue 6 (trachten) **darauf ~, etw. zu tun** be dying *or* longing to do sth.; **auf Rache ~:** be bent on *or* dying for revenge 7 (ungeduldig sein) **vor Neugier ~:** be dying to know; **er brannte vor Ehrgeiz** he was burning with ambition

B *unr. tr. V.* 1 burn ‹*hole, pattern, etc.*›; **einem Tier ein Zeichen ins Fell ~:** brand an animal; **gebranntes Kind scheut das Feuer** (Spr.) once bitten, twice shy (prov.) 2 (mit Hitze behandeln) fire ‹*porcelain etc.*›; distil ‹*spirits*›; **gebrannter Kalk** quicklime 3 (rösten) roast ‹*coffee beans, almonds, etc.*›; brown ‹*flour, sugar, etc.*›

brennend

A *Adj.* (auch fig.) burning; urgent ‹*topic, subject*›; lighted ‹*cigarette*›; raging ‹*thirst*›; violent ‹*homesickness*›

B *adv.* **ich würde ~ gern mal ein Wochenende dort verbringen** I should absolutely love to spend a weekend there; **ich wüsste ~ gern, ob …** I'm dying to know whether …; **es scheint dich ja ~ zu interessieren, was besprochen wurde** you seem to be dying to know what was discussed

Brenner *der;* **~s, ~:** burner

Brennerei *die;* **~, ~en** 1 distilling 2 (Betrieb) distillery

***Brennessel** ▸**Brennnessel**

Brenn-: ~glas *das* burning glass; **~holz** *das* firewood; **~material** *das* fuel; **wir benutzen alte Zeitungen als ~material** we use old newspapers to burn on the fire; **~nessel** *die* stinging nettle; **~ofen** *der* kiln; **~punkt** *der* (auch Mathematik, Optik) focus; **im ~punkt des Interesses stehen** be the focus of attention *or* interest; **in den ~punkt der Diskussion rücken** become the focal point of discussion; **~schere** *die* curling tongs *pl.* (Brit.); curling iron (Amer.); **~spiegel** *der* (Optik) burning mirror; **~spiritus** *der* methylated spirits; **~stab** *der* (Kerntechnik) fuel rod; **~stoff** *der* fuel; **~stoff·zelle** *die* fuel cell; **~weite** *die* (Optik) focal length; **~wert** *der* (Energietechnik, Physiol.) calorific value

brenzlig /ˈbrɛntslɪç/ *Adj.* 1 ‹*smell, taste, etc.*› of burning *not pred.*; **~ riechen/schmecken** smell of burning/taste burnt 2 (ugs.: bedenklich) dicey (coll.); **mir wird die Sache zu ~:** things are getting too hot for me

Bresche /ˈbrɛʃə/ *die;* **~, ~n** gap; breach; **[für jmdn.] in die ~ springen** stand in [for sb.]; **für jmdn./etw. eine ~ schlagen** give one's backing to sb./sth.

Bretagne /breˈtanjə/ *die;* **~:** Brittany

Bretone /breˈtoːnə/ *der;* **~n, ~n, Bretonin** *die;* **~, ~nen** Breton

Brett /brɛt/ *das;* **~[e]s, ~er** 1 board; (lang und dick) plank; (Diele) floorboard; **hier ist die Welt [wie] mit ~ern vernagelt** (ugs.) this place is like the end of the earth; **das schwarze ~:** the noticeboard; **ein ~ vor dem Kopf haben** (fig. ugs.) be thick; **ich habe heute einfach ein ~ vor dem Kopf** (fig. ugs.) I just can't think straight today; **das ~ bohren, wo es am dünnsten ist** (fig. ugs.) take the easy way out 2 (für Spiele) board 3 *Pl.* (Skisport) skis 4 *Pl.* (Bühne) stage *sing.*; boards; **auf den ~ern stehen** be on [the] stage *or* on the boards; **die ~er, die die Welt bedeuten** (geh.) the stage *sing.*; the boards 5 *Pl.* (Boxen) floor *sing.*; canvas *sing.*; **er schickte seinen Gegner auf die ~er** he put his opponent on the canvas; he floored his opponent

Brettchen *das;* **~s, ~** 1 *wooden board used for breakfast* 2 (zum Schneiden) board

Brettel /ˈbrɛtl̩/ *das;* **~s, ~[n]** (südd., österr.) 1 board 2 *Pl.* (Skisport) skis

Bretter-: ~boden *der* wooden floor; **~bude** *die* [wooden] hut, shack; **~verschlag** *der* [wooden] shed; **~wand** *die* wooden wall *or* partition; **~zaun** *der* wooden fence

bretthart

A *Adj.* 1 hard as a board *pred.*; rock-hard ‹*earth, bread, suspension*›; 2 (unnachgiebig) relentless; implacable ‹*opposition*›; (Sport) ‹*shot*› like a bullet *postpos.*.

B *adv.* **~ gefedert** (Kfz.-W.) with rock-hard suspension; **~ schießen** (Sport) send a in shot like a bullet

Brettspiel *das* board game

Brevier /breˈviːɐ̯/ *das;* **~s, ~e** 1 (kath. Rel.) breviary 2 (Leitfaden) guide (**für** to)

Brezel /ˈbreːtsl̩/ *die;* **~, ~n, Brezen** /ˈbreːtsn̩/ *der;* **~s, ~** *od. die;* **~, ~** (österr.) pretzel

Bridge /brɪtʃ/ *das;* **~:** bridge

Brief /briːf/ *der;* **~[e]s, ~e** ▸ℹ **S. 143** 1 letter; **offener ~** (fig.) open letter; **jmdm. ~ und Siegel [auf etw.** (Akk.)**] geben** (fig.) promise sb. faithfully *or* give sb. one's word [on sth.] 2 (Rauschgiftpäckchen) deck

Brief-: ~beschwerer *der;* **~s, ~:** paperweight; **~block** *der; Pl.* **~~s** *od.* **~blöcke** writing pad; letter pad; **~bogen** *der* sheet of writing paper *or* notepaper; **~bögen mit Kopf** letter-headed writing paper *sing. or* notepaper *sing.*; **~bombe** *die* letter bomb

Briefchen *das;* **~s, ~** 1 **ein ~ Nähnadeln/Streichhölzer** a packet of needles/book of matches 2 (kurzer Brief) note

Briefdruck·sache *die* (Postw.) printed paper (*sent as a letter*); **eine ~:** a piece of printed matter; **die Gebühren für ~n** the rates for printed matter *sing.*

briefen /ˈbriːfn̩/ *tr. V.* brief

Brief-: ~freund *der*, **~freundin** *die* penfriend; pen pal (coll.); **~geheimnis** *das* privacy of the post; secrecy of correspondence

Briefing /ˈbriːfɪŋ/ *das;* **~s, ~s** briefing

Brief-: ~karte *die* correspondence card; **~kasten** *der* 1 postbox; pillar box (Brit.); 2 (privat) letter box; **lebender/toter ~kasten** (Geheimdienstjargon) [live] letter box/letter box; 3 (in der Zeitung) agony column (coll.)

Briefkasten-: ~firma *die* accommodation address; **~tante** *die* (ugs. scherzh.) agony aunt (coll.)

Brief-: ~kopf *der* 1 letter-heading; 2 (aufgedruckt) letterhead; **~kurs** *der* (Börsenw.) offer price; **~kuvert** *das* (veralt.) ▸▸**~umschlag**

brieflich

A *Adj.* written

B *adv.* by letter

Brief·marke *die* [postage] stamp

Briefmarken-: ~album *das* stamp album; **~sammler** *der*, **~sammlerin** *die* stamp collector; philatelist; **~sammlung** *die* stamp collection; **wollen Sie sich meine ~sammlung ansehen?** (fig. verhüll.) come up and see my etchings (joc.)

Brief-: ~öffner *der* letter-opener; **~papier** *das* writing paper; notepaper; **~partner** *der*, **~partnerin** *die* penfriend; **~porto** *das* [letter] rate; **~post** *die* letter post; **~roman** *der* epistolary novel; **~schreiber** *der*, **~schreiberin** *die* [letter-]writer; **~sendung** *die* item sent by letter post; **~tasche** *die* wallet; **~taube** *die* carrier pigeon; **~träger** *der* ▸ℹ **S. 113** postman; letter-carrier (Amer.); **~trägerin** *die* ▸ℹ **S. 113** postwoman; female letter-carrier (Amer.); **~um·schlag** *der* envelope; **~waage** *die* letter scales *pl.*; **~wahl** *die* postal vote; **~wechsel** *der* 1 correspondence; **einen ~wechsel führen** have a *or* be in correspondence; **mit jmdm. in ~wechsel stehen** be in correspondence *or* correspond with sb.; 2 (gesammelte ~e) correspondence

Brie·käse /ˈbriː-/ *der* Brie

Bries /briːs/ *das;* **~es, ~e** thymus [gland] (*esp. of calf*); (Kochk.) sweetbreads *pl.*

briet /briːt/ *1. u. 3. Pers. Sg. Prät. v.* **braten**

Brigade /briˈgaːdə/ *die;* **~, ~n** 1 (Milit.) brigade 2 (DDR) work team; [work] brigade

Brigade·general *der* (Milit.) brigadier

Brigadier 1 /brigaˈdi̯eː/ *der;* **~s, ~s** (Milit.) brigadier 2 /brigaˈdi̯eː *od.* brigaˈdiːɐ̯/ *der;* **~s, ~s** *od.* **~e** (DDR) [work] team leader; brigade leader

Brigadierin *die;* **~, ~nen** (DDR) [work] team leader; brigade leader; *s. auch* **-in**

Brigg /brɪk/ *die;* **~, ~s** (Seew.) brig

Brikett /briˈkɛt/ *das;* **~s, ~s** briquette

brillant /brɪlˈjant/

A *Adj.* brilliant

B *adv.* brilliantly

Brillant¹ /brɪlˈjant/ *der;* **~en, ~en** brilliant

Brillant² *die;* **~** (Druckw.) 3-point type

Brillantine /brɪljanˈtiːnə/ *die;* **~, ~n** (veralt.) brilliantine

Brillant-: ~kollier *das* (brilliant-cut) diamond necklace; **~ring** *der* (brilliant-cut) diamond ring;

ℹ Briefeschreiben

Der Umschlag

Im Gegensatz zu deutschen Anschriften steht der Titel des Adressaten zusammen mit dem Namen auf der ersten Zeile. Vor allem in Großbritannien haben Häuser oft einen Namen anstelle einer oder zusätzlich zur (vor dem Straßennamen stehenden!) Hausnummer. In GB folgt dann die Stadt, aber bei einer kleineren Ortschaft oder einem Stadtteil steht diese(r) davor auf einer eigenen Zeile; nach der Stadt folgt meist die Grafschaft, es sei denn, es handelt sich um eine 'county town', die der Grafschaft ihren Namen gibt, oder eine Großstadt mit eigener Postleitzahl (**postcode**). Letztere steht dann allein auf der letzten Zeile. Britische Adressen können also leicht sieben oder sogar acht Zeilen einnehmen. In den USA dagegen werden die Adressen einfacher gehalten; hier steht auch die Postleitzahl (**Zip code**) an letzter Stelle, davor aber der Staat, auf zwei Buchstaben abgekürzt (CA = California, NJ = New Jersey usw.).

GB:
Mr James Bainbridge
oder: James Bainbridge Esq.
5 Avon Crescent
Kenilworth
Warwickshire
CV8 2PQ

Ms B. Gordon
Kirkbrae
10 Strathmore Road
Cults
Aberdeen
AB1 9TJ

Sir Alan and Lady Weston
Aberdare House
Llanyre
Llandrindod Wells
Powys
LD1 6DX

USA:
Robert J. Hale Jr.
1496 Pacific Boulevard
Monterey
CA 93940

Mrs Nancy Bright
PO Box 731
Milville
NJ 08332

Miss Abigail Schott
c/o Floyd
1100 North Street
Harrisburg
PA 17105

PO Box = *Postfach*, **c/o** (für **care of**) = *bei.* Zu den verschiedenen Anreden (Mr, Mrs, Miss, Ms usw.) siehe □ **Anreden und Titel.**

Bei Geschäftsbriefen kann der Name des Adressaten entweder vor oder nach der Firma bzw. Organisation stehen, im letzteren Fall oft mit **FAO (for the attention of)** oder **Attn. (attention)** davor. In den USA ist es üblich, nach dem Namen des Inhabers einer leitenden Position diese anzugeben. Partnerschaften und Firmen mit dem Zusatz "& Co." kann **Messrs.** = *Herren* vorangestellt werden.

Messrs. Gibbons & Prestwick
FAO Anita Dobby
45 Albright Way
London
W11 2BJ

John C. Wagner
President
Bix Corporation
222 Madison Avenue
New York
NY 10016

Der Absender steht, wenn er überhaupt genannt wird, links oben oder auf der Rückseite.

Der Brief selbst

Die Adresse des Absenders steht oben entweder rechts oder in der Mitte, darunter das Datum:

10 Copthall Avenue
West Drayton
Middlesex
UB7 2FL

24th September 2004

Anrede

Es gibt fast nur die eine Möglichkeit: **Dear** und der Name des Adressaten, und zwar der Vorname, bei Freunden und Verwandten oder wenn man weniger formell erscheinen will, sonst Titel und Familienname:

Dear Charles/Mary/Mr Churchill/Dr Watson/Professor Andrews

Bei Geschäftsbriefen schreibt man, wenn man den Namen des Adressaten nicht kennt, **Dear Sir or Madam**, und wenn man eine Firma oder andere Organisation anschreibt, **Dear Sirs.**

Zum Schluss

Informell:	Yours Charles	Love Mary	All our love Brian and Wendy
Etwas formeller:	With best wishes Kind regards		
Formeller Schluss:	Yours sincerely (*brit.*) Yours truly (*amerik.*)		
Sehr formell:	Yours faithfully (*brit.*) Yours very truly (*amerik.*)		

~schliff *der* brilliant cut; **~schmuck** *der* (brilliant-cut) diamond jewellery

Brillanz /brɪl'jants/ *die;* ~ **1▸** brilliance **2▸** (Akustik) clarity; sound quality

Brille /'brɪlə/ *die;* **~, ~n 1▸** glasses *pl.;* spectacles *pl.;* specs (coll.) *pl.;* **eine ~:** a pair of glasses *or* spectacles; **eine ~ tragen** wear glasses *or* spectacles; **etw. durch eine gefärbte ~ sehen** (fig.) look at sth. subjectively *or* from one's own point of view; **etw. durch eine rosa[rote] ~ sehen** *od.* **betrachten** (fig.) see sth. through rose-coloured *or* rose-tinted spectacles **2▸** (ugs.: Klosett~) [lavatory *or* toilet] seat

Brịllen-: ~etui *das,* **~futteral** *das* glasses case; spectacle case; **~gestell** *das* spectacle frame; [glasses] frame; **~glas** *das* [spectacle] lens; **~schlange** *die* **1▸** (Zool.) spectacled cobra; **2▸** (ugs. scherzh.) **in der Schule wurde ich oft ~schlange genannt** I was often called 'four-eyes' at school; **~träger** *der,* **~trägerin** *die* person who wears glasses; person with glasses

brillieren /brɪl'ji:rən/ *itr. V.* (geh.) be brilliant

Brimborium /brɪm'bo:ri̯ʊm/ *das;* **~s** (ugs. abwertend) hoo-ha (coll.)

bringen /'brɪŋən/ *unr. tr. V.* **1▸** (her~) bring; (hin~) take; **sie brachte mir/ich brachte ihr ein Geschenk** she brought me/I took her a present; **Unglück/Unheil [über jmdn.] ~:** bring misfortune/disaster [upon sb.]; **jmdm. Glück/Unglück ~:** bring sb. [good] luck/bad luck; **jmdm. eine Nachricht ~:** bring sb. news; **der letzte Winter brachte uns viel Schnee** (fig.) we had a lot of snow last winter **2▸** (begleiten) take; **jmdn. nach Hause/zum Bahnhof ~:** take sb. home/to the station; **das Auto in die Garage ~:** put the car in the garage; **die Kinder ins Bett** *od.* **zu Bett ~:** put the children to bed **3▸ es zu etwas/nichts ~:** get somewhere/get nowhere *or* not get anywhere; **er hat es zu nichts weiter gebracht als zum Redaktionsassistenten** he didn't get further than assistant editor; **es bis zum Direktor ~:** make it to director; **es zu hohem Ansehen ~:** acquire standing *or* a high reputation; **es weit ~:** get on *or* do very well; **es im Leben weit ~:** go far in life **4▸ jmdn. ins Gefängnis ~** ‹*crime, misdeed*› land sb. in prison *or* gaol; **eine Sache vor Gericht ~:** take a matter to court; **das Gespräch auf etw./ein anderes Thema ~:** bring the conversation round to sth./change the topic of conversation; **jmdn. wieder auf den rechten Weg ~** (fig.) get sb. back on the straight and narrow; **jmdn. zum Lachen/zur Verzweiflung ~:** make sb. laugh/drive sb. to despair; **jmdn. dazu ~, etw. zu tun** get sb. to do sth.; **du hast mich auf eine gute Idee gebracht** you have given me a good idea; **etw. hinter sich ~** (ugs.) get sth. over and done with; **es nicht über sich** (*Akk.*) **~ [können], etw. zu tun** not be able to bring oneself to do sth.; **etw. an sich** (*Akk.*) **~** (ugs.) collar sth. (sl.) **5▸** (*mit Präp.* **um**) **jmdn. um seinen Besitz ~:** do sb. out of his property (coll.); **jmdn. um den Schlaf/Verstand ~:** rob sb. of his/her sleep/drive sb. mad **6▸** (veröffentlichen) publish; **die Zeitschrift bringt jetzt eine Artikelserie über ...** the magazine is running a series of articles about ...; **was bringt denn die Zeitung heute darüber?** what does it say about it in today's paper?; **alle Zeitungen brachten Berichte über das Massaker** all the papers carried reports of the massacre **7▸** (senden) broadcast; **um 23.00 Uhr ~ wir die letzten Nachrichten** the late-night news will be at 11 o'clock; **das Fernsehen bringt eine Sondersendung** there is a special programme on television; **einen Film im Fernsehen ~:** show a film on television; **das Fernsehen hat nichts darüber gebracht** there was nothing about it on television **8▸** (dar~) **das/ein Opfer ~:** make the/a sacrifice; **eine Nummer/ein Ständchen ~:** perform a number/a serenade **9▸** (er~) **einen großen Gewinn/hohe Zinsen ~:** make a large profit/earn high interest; **das Gemälde brachte 50 000 Euro** the painting fetched 50,000 euros; **das bringt nichts** (ugs.) it's pointless **10▸ das bringt es mit sich, dass ...** that means that ...; **seine Krankheit bringt es mit sich, dass ...** it's because of *or* to do with his illness that ... **11▸** (verursachen) cause ‹*trouble, confusion*›; **es kann dir doch nur Vorteile ~:** it can only be to your advantage **12▸** (salopp: schaffen, erreichen) **das bringst du doch nicht** you'll never do it; **der Wagen/diese Kneipe bringts doch nicht** the car/this pub is no good; **der Wagen bringt 210 km/h** the car can *or* will do 210 km/h **13▸** (hinein~, heraus~, bewegen) get (**in** + *Akk.* into, **aus** out of); **der Schrank ist viel zu groß, als dass ich ihn allein von der Stelle ~ könnte** the cupboard is far too big for me to shift on my own; **den Wagen zum Laufen ~:** get the car to go; **ich bringe den Schlüssel nicht ins Schloss** (bes. südd.) I can't get the key into the lock

Brịng·schuld *die* (Rechtsw.): *debt to be paid at the creditor's domicile*

b

brisant /briˈzant/ *Adj.* explosive; **ein recht ~es Unternehmen** a highly risky undertaking; **~e Sprengstoffe** highly explosive materials

Brisanz /briˈzants/ *die;* **~, ~en** **1** explosiveness; explosive nature; **ein Thema von hoher politischer ~:** a highly explosive political subject **2** (Waffenkunde) explosive force

Brise /ˈbriːzə/ *die;* **~, ~n** breeze

Britannien /briˈtaniən/ *(das);* **~s** Britain; (hist.) Britannia

Brite /ˈbrɪtə/ *der;* **~n, ~n** ▸ **S. 520** Briton; **die ~n** the British; **er ist [kein] ~:** he is [not] British; **der ~ gewann eine Medaille** the British athlete/scholar *etc.* won a medal

Britin *die;* **~, ~nen** ▸ **S. 520** Briton; British girl/woman; **die ~nen** the British [girls/ women]; **sie ist [keine] ~:** she is [not] British; *s. auch* **-in**

britisch *Adj.* ▸ **S. 520** British; **die Britischen Inseln** the British Isles

Bröckchen /ˈbrœkçən/ *das;* **~s, ~:** bit; small piece

bröckchen·weise *Adv.* ▸ **brockenweise**

bröckelig *Adj.* crumbly

bröckeln /ˈbrœkl̩n/ *tr., itr. V.* **1** crumble **2** *mit sein* **von der Decke/Wand ~:** crumble away from the ceiling/wall

Brocken /ˈbrɔkn̩/ *der;* **~s, ~** **1** (von Brot) hunk, chunk; (von Fleisch) chunk; (von Lehm, Kohle, Erde) lump **2** (fig.) **ein paar ~ Englisch** a smattering of English; **ein paar ~ eines Gesprächs auffangen** catch a few snatches of a conversation; **jmdm. einen fetten ~ wegschnappen** (ugs.) snap up a real opportunity from under sb.'s nose; **das war ein harter ~** (ugs.) that was a tough *or* a hard nut to crack **3** (ugs.: dicke Person) lump; **ist das ein ~!** what a big fat lump he/she is!

brocken·weise *Adv.* (auch fig.) bit by bit

bröcklig ▸ **bröckelig**

brodeln /ˈbroːdl̩n/ *itr. V.* bubble; **es brodelt in der Masse/Bevölkerung** (fig.) there is seething unrest among the masses/in the population

Brodem /ˈbroːdəm/ (geh.) vapour (literary)

Broiler /ˈbrɔylɐ/ *der;* **~s, ~** (DDR) ▸ **Brathähnchen**

Brokat /broˈkaːt/ *der;* **~[e]s, ~e** brocade

Brokat-: **~kleid** *das* brocade dress; **~vorhang** *der* brocade curtain

Broker /ˈbroːkɐ/ *der;* **~s, ~** ▸ **S. 113** broker

Brokerin *die;* **~, ~nen** ▸ **S. 113** [female] broker

Brokkoli /ˈbrɔkoli/ *der;* **~s, ~[s]** broccoli

Brom /broːm/ *das;* **~s** (Chemie) bromine

Brom·beere /ˈbrɔm-/ *die* **1** bramble; blackberry bush **2** (Frucht) blackberry; **~n pflücken gehen** go blackberrying

Brombeer-: **~konfitüre** *die,* **~marmelade** *die* blackberry jam; **~strauch** *der* bramble; blackberry bush

Bronchial-: **~asthma** *das* ▸ **S. 439** (Med.) bronchial asthma; **~katarrh** *der* ▸ **S. 439** (Med.) ▸ **Bronchitis**; **~tee** *der* bronchial tea

Bronchie /ˈbrɔnçi̯ə/ *die;* **~, ~n** ▸ **S. 435** (Med.) bronchial tube; bronchus

Bronchitis /brɔnˈçiːtɪs/ *die;* **~, Bronchitiden** ▸ **S. 439** (Med.) bronchitis

Bronze /ˈbrõːsə/ *die;* **~:** bronze; **diese Leistung reichte gerade noch für ~** (Sportjargon) this performance was just enough to get a bronze; *s. auch* **Gold**

Bronze·medaille *die* bronze medal

bronzen /ˈbrõːsn̩/ *Adj.* bronze ‹object›; bronzed ‹skin›; **~ schimmern** glint like bronze

Bronze·zeit *die* Bronze Age

Brosame /ˈbroːzaːmə/ *die;* **~, ~n** (geh. veralt., auch fig.) crumb

Brosche /ˈbrɔʃə/ *die;* **~, ~n** brooch

broschiert /brɔˈʃiːrt/ *Adj.* paperback; **eine ~e Ausgabe** a paperback *or* soft-cover edition; **~e Heftchen** booklets

Broschüre /brɔˈʃyːrə/ *die;* **~, ~n** booklet; pamphlet; (Reiseprospekt) brochure

Brösel /ˈbrøːzl̩/ *der;* **~s, ~,** (österr.) *das;* **~s, ~:** breadcrumb

bröselig *Adj.* crumbly

bröseln
A *itr. V.* crumble
B *tr. V.* crumble

Brot /broːt/ *das;* **~[e]s, ~e** **1** bread *no pl., no indef. art.;* (Laib **~**) loaf [of bread]; **wes ~ ich ess, des Lied ich sing** (Spr.) he/she is not going to bite the hand that feeds him/her; **Bier ist flüssiges ~** (scherzh.) beer is full of nourishment; **der Mensch lebt nicht vom ~ allein** (Spr.) man shall not live by bread alone (bibl.); **~ und Arbeit finden** find a paid job **2** (Scheibe **~**) slice [of bread] **3** ▸ **Butter~** **4** (Lebensunterhalt) daily bread (fig.); **das ist ein hartes ~:** it's a hard way to earn a *or* your living

Brot-: **~aufstrich** *der* spread; **~belag** *der* topping; (im zusammengeklappten **~**) filling; **~beruf** *der* occupation that enables one to make a living; **~beutel** *der* satchel

Brötchen /ˈbrøːtçən/ *das;* **~s, ~:** roll; **kleinere ~ backen [müssen]** (fig. ugs.) [have to] lower one's sights; **seine/die ~ verdienen** (ugs.) earn one's/the daily bread

Brötchen·geber *der;* **~s, ~, Brötchengeberin** *die;* **~, ~nen** (scherzh.) employer

brot-, Brot-: **~einheit** *die* carbohydrate unit; **~erwerb** *der* way to earn a living; **~fabrik** *die* bakery (producing bread on a large scale); **~frucht·baum** *der* breadfruit tree; **~kanten** *der* [bread] crust; **~kasten** *der* bread bin; **~korb** *der* bread basket; **jmdm. den ~korb höher hängen** (ugs.) put sb. on short rations; (fig.) put the squeeze on sb. (coll.); **~krume** *die,* **~krümel** *der* breadcrumb; **~kruste** *die* [bread] crust; **~laib** *der* loaf [of bread]; **~los** *Adj.* unemployed; **jmdn. ~los machen** put sb. out of work; **das ist eine ~lose Kunst** there's no money in that; **~maschine** *die* bread slicer; **~messer** *das* bread knife; **~neid** *der* jealousy of sb.'s position/salary; **~rinde** *die* [bread] crust; **~scheibe** *die* slice of bread; **~schneide·maschine** *die* ▸ **~maschine**; **~studium** *das:* **für einen großen Teil der Studenten heute ist die Medizin ein reines ~studium** a lot of today's students choose medicine because it will get them a well-paid job; **~teig** *der* bread dough; **~trunk** *der* kvass; **~zeit** *die* (südd.) **1** (Pause) [tea/coffee/lunch] break; **2** (Vesper) snack; (Vesper**~**) sandwiches *pl.*

Browser /ˈbrauzɐ/ *der;* **~s, ~** (DV) browser

brr /brr/ *Interj.* **1** (bei Kälte) brr; (vor Ekel) ugh **2** (Zuruf an Zugtier) whoa

BRT *Abk.* **= Bruttoregistertonne** grt

Bruch[1] /brʊx/ *der;* **~[e]s, Brüche** /ˈbrʏçə/ **1** (das Brechen) break; **der ~ des Deiches/Dammes** the breaching (Brit.) *or* (Amer.) breaking of the dyke/dam; **das hätte ~ geben können** (ugs.) there could have been a crash; **~ machen** (ugs.) break things; (Fliegerspr.) crash; **in die Brüche gehen** (zerbrechen) break; get broken; (enden) break up; **zu ~ gehen** break; get broken; **etw. zu ~ fahren** smash sth. up **2** (**~**stelle) break; **die Brüche im Deich** the breaches (Brit.) *or* (Amer.) breaks in the dyke **3** ▸ **S. 439** (Med.: Knochen**~**) fracture; break **4** ▸ **S. 439** (Med.: Eingeweide**~**) hernia; rupture; **sich** *(Dat.)* **einen ~ heben** rupture oneself *or* give oneself a hernia [by lifting sth.] **5** (fig.) (eines Versprechens) breaking; (eines Abkommens, Gesetzes, einer Verfassung) break; violation; (mit der Vergangenheit, Tradition, Partei) break (**mit** with); (einer Freundschaft) break; (einer Ehe) break-up; **ein ~ des Waffenstillstandes** a violation of the ceasefire; **der ~ mit dem Elternhaus** the break with home; **es kam zum ~ zwischen ihnen** they broke up **6** ▸ **S. 826** (Math.) fraction **7** (Kaufmannsspr.: beschädigte Ware) **diese Schokolade ist ~:** this chocolate is broken **8** (Falte) crease; **nach dem ~ falten** fold along the crease/creases **9** (salopp: Einbruch) break-in; **einen ~ machen** do a break-in

Bruch[2] *der od. das;* **~[e]s, Brüche** (Sumpfland) marsh

bruch-, Bruch-: **~band** *das; Pl.* **~bänder** (Med.) truss; **~bude** *die* (ugs. abwertend) hovel; dump (coll.); **~fest** *Adj.* unbreakable

brüchig /ˈbrʏçɪç/ *Adj.* **1** brittle, crumbly ‹rock, brickwork›; **das Leder mit Creme einreiben, damit es nicht ~ wird** rub cream into the leather to keep it from cracking; **der Stoff ist ziemlich ~:** the material is splitting quite a bit **2** (fig.) crumbling ‹relationship, marriage, etc.› **3** (rau) rough; cracked

Brüchigkeit *die;* **~** **1** brittleness; crumbliness **2** **die ~ ihrer Beziehung/Ehe ist für alle offenbar** it is obvious to everyone that their relationship/marriage is breaking up **3** (Rauheit) roughness

bruch-, Bruch-: **~|landen** *itr. V.; mit sein; nur im Inf. u. 2. Part.* crash-land; make a crash-landing; **~landung** *die* crash-landing; **~los** *Adj.* without a break *postpos.;* **~operation** *die* hernia operation; **~pilot** *der* (ugs.) crash-happy pilot; **~rechnen** *itr. V.; nur im Inf.* do fractions; **~rechnen** *das* fractions *pl.;* **jmdm. [das] ~rechnen beibringen** teach sb. how to do fractions; **beim ~rechnen ...** when doing fractions ...; **~rechnung** *die* fractions *pl.;* **~schaden** *der* breakage; **~schokolade** *die* broken chocolate; **~sicher** *Adj.* unbreakable; **~stein** *der* undressed stone; **~stelle** *die* break; (von Knochen auch) fracture; **die ~stelle mit Klebstoff bestreichen** apply adhesive to the broken area; **~strich** *der* fraction line; **~stück** *das* fragment; (großes Stück) piece; (fig.) snatch; **~stückhaft** **A** *Adj.* fragmentary; **B** *adv.* in a fragmentary way; **~teil** *der* fraction; **im ~teil einer Sekunde** in a fraction of a second; in a split second; **er kam um den ~teil einer Sekunde zu spät** he came a split second too late; **~zahl** *die* ▸ **S. 826** fraction

Brücke /ˈbrʏkə/ *die;* **~, ~n** **1** (auch: Schiffs**~**, Zahnmed., Bodenturnen, Ringen) bridge; **die** *od.* **alle ~n hinter sich** *(Dat.)* **abbrechen** (fig.) burn one's bridges (fig.); **jmdm. eine [goldene] ~** *od.* **[goldene] ~n bauen** (fig.) make things easier for sb. **2** (Landungs**~**) landing stage **3** (Teppich) rug **4** (Anat.) pons [Varolii]

Brücken-: **~bau** *der; Pl.* **~~ten** **1** building *or* construction of a/the bridge; (allgemein) bridge-building; bridge construction; **2** (Brücke) bridge [structure]; **~bogen** *der* arch [of a/the bridge]; **~geländer** *das* parapet; railing; **~heilige** *der/die* sculptured saint [on a/the bridge]; **~kopf** *der* (Milit., auch fig.) bridgehead; **~pfeiler** *der* pier [of a/the bridge]; **~tag** *der* (ugs.) extra day [off] *(taken between a public holiday and a weekend or between two public holidays);* **~waage** *die* weighbridge; **~zoll** *der* [bridge] toll; **~zoll bezahlen** pay a [bridge] toll

Bruder /ˈbruːdɐ/ *der;* **~s, Brüder** /ˈbryːdɐ/ **1** (auch: Mitmensch, Mönch) brother; **die Brüder Müller** the Müller brothers; the brothers Müller; **~ Peter** Brother Peter; **und willst du nicht mein ~ sein, so schlag ich dir den Schädel ein** if you're not my friend, then I'll treat you as an enemy; **der große ~** (fig.) Big Brother; **der große/kleine ~** (fig. scherzh.) the larger/smaller edition; **unter Brüdern** (fig. ugs. scherzh.) between *or* amongst friends **2** (ugs. abwertend: Mann) guy (coll.); **ein ziemlich windiger ~:** a bit of a dodgy (Brit.) *or* shady character (coll.); **~ Lustig** *od.* **Leichtfuß** (veralt. scherzh.) light-hearted fellow; *s. auch* **warm A 3**

Bruder·bund *der* (geh., bes. DDR) comradeship; fraternal links *pl.*

Brüderchen /ˈbryːdɐçən/ *das;* **~s, ~:** little brother; **ein kleines ~:** a little brother

Bruder-: **~herz** *das* (veralt., noch scherzh.) dear brother; **hör mal, ~herz** listen, brother dear; **~krieg** *der* fratricidal war; **~kuss,** ***~kuß** *der* brotherly kiss; **~land** *das* (geh., bes. DDR) fraternal country

brüderlich
A *Adj.* brotherly; (im politischen Bereich) fraternal
B *adv.* in a brotherly way; (im politischen Bereich) fraternally; **etw. ~ [mit jmdm.] teilen** share sth. [with sb.] in a fair and generous way

Brüderlichkeit *die;* **~:** brotherliness; (im politischen Bereich) fraternity

Bruder-: **~liebe** *die* brotherly love; **~mord** *der* fratricide; **~mörder** *der*, **~mörderin** *die* fratricide

Bruder·partei *die* (bes. DDR) fraternal party

Bruderschaft *die;* ~, **~en** (Rel.) brotherhood

Brüderschaft *die: in* **[mit jmdm.] Brüderschaft trinken** drink to close friendship [with sb.] (*agreeing to use the familiar 'du' form*)

Bruder-: **~volk** *das* **1** (bes. DDR) sister people; **2** (veralt. geh.) kindred people; **~zwist** *der* feud between brothers; (im politischen Bereich) fraternal feud

Brühe /'bry:ə/ *die;* ~, **~n** **1** stock; (als Suppe) clear soup; broth **2** (ugs. abwertend: Getränk) muck; **eine abscheuliche ~** (fig.) a revolting concoction **3** (abwertend: verschmutztes Wasser) dirty *or* filthy water **4** (Kochk.: Kochwasser) water **5** (ugs.: Schweiß) sweat

brühen *tr. V.* **1** blanch **2** (auf~) brew, make ‹*tea*›; make ‹*coffee, soup*›

brüh-, Brüh-: **~warm** (ugs.) **A** *Adj.* hot ‹*news*›; very latest ‹*gossip etc.*›; **B** *adv.* **etw. ~warm weitererzählen** pass sth. on *or* spread sth. around straight away; **~würfel** *der* stock cube; **~wurst** *die* sausage (*which is heated in boiling water*)

Brüll·affe *der* (Zool.) howler [monkey]; howling monkey

brüllen /'brʏlən/
A *itr. V.* **1** ‹*bull, cow, etc.*› bellow; ‹*lion, tiger, etc.*› roar; ‹*elephant*› trumpet **2** (ugs.: schreien) roar; shout; **vor Schmerzen/Lachen ~:** roar with pain/laughter; **brüll nicht so!** there's no need to shout like that; **nach jmdm. ~:** shout to *or* for sb.; **~des Gelächter** roars *pl.* of laughter; **das ist [ja] zum Brüllen** (ugs.) it's a [real] scream; what a scream **3** (ugs.: weinen) howl; bawl; **er brüllte wie am Spieß** he bawled his head off
B *tr. V.* yell; shout

Brüller *der;* **~s,** ~ (ugs.) **1** (etw. sehr Komisches) scream (coll.); **der ~ sein** be a scream (coll.); **nicht gerade ein ~ sein** not be exactly a barrel of laughs (coll.); **2** (Erfolg) hit; **3** (abwertend: Schreier) bawler

Brüllerin *die* (abwertend) screamer; bawler

Brumm-: **~bär** *der* (ugs.) grouch (coll.); **~bass,** ***~baß** *der* **1** (ugs.) deep *or* bass voice; **2** ▸ **Kontrabass**

brummelig
A *Adj.* [rather] grumpy; (schmollend) sulky
B *adv.* [rather] grumpily; (schmollend) sulkily

brummeln /'brʊmḷn/ *tr., itr. V.* (ugs.) mumble; mutter

brummen /'brʊmən/ *tr., itr. V.* **1** ‹*insect*› buzz; ‹*bear*› growl; ‹*engine etc.*› drone; **mir brummt der Schädel** *od.* **Kopf** (ugs.) my head is buzzing **2** (sich ~d bewegen) ‹*fly etc.*› buzz; ‹*lorry etc.*› thunder; ‹*moped*› buzz **3** (unmelodisch singen) drone **4** (mürrisch sprechen) mumble; mutter **5** (ugs. veralt.: in Haft sein) do time (coll.); **zwei Jahre ~:** do two years **6** (ugs.: nachsitzen) stay behind

Brummer *der;* **~s,** ~ (ugs.) **1** (Fliege) bluebottle **2** (Lkw) heavy lorry (Brit.) *or* truck

Brummi *der;* **~s, ~s** (ugs.) lorry (Brit.); truck

brummig (ugs.)
A *Adj.* grumpy
B *adv.* grumpily

Brumm-: **~kreisel** *der* humming top; **~schädel** *der* (ugs.) thick head; **~ton** *der; Pl.* **~töne** humming noise

brunchen /'brantʃn̩/ *itr. V.* have brunch

brünett /bry'nɛt/ *Adj.* dark-haired ‹*person*›; dark ‹*hair*›; **sie ist ~:** she's [a] brunette

Brünette *die;* ~, **~n** brunette

Brunft /brʊnft/ *die;* ~, **Brünfte** /'brʏnftə/ (Jägerspr.) ▸ **Brunst**

brunften *itr. V.* (Jägerspr.) ▸ **brunsten**

Brunft·hirsch *der* (Jägerspr.) rutting stag

brunftig *Adj.* (Jägerspr.) rutting ‹*male animal*›; ‹*female animal*› in *or* on heat

Brunft-: **~schrei** *der* (Jägerspr.) bell; **~zeit** (Jägerspr.) ▸ **Brunstzeit**

Brunnen /'brʊnən/ *der;* **~s,** ~ **1** well; (fig. geh.) fountain (literary); **den ~ [erst] zudecken, wenn das Kind hineingefallen ist** lock the stable door after the horse has bolted (fig.) **2** (Spring~) fountain **3** (Wasser einer Heilquelle) spring water; **~ trinken** take the waters *pl.*

Brunnen-: **~becken** *das* basin [of a/the fountain]; **~figur** *die* figure on a/the fountain; **~haus** *das* pump room; **~kresse** *die* watercress; **~kur** *die* [spa] cure; **eine ~kur machen** take a cure/a course of treatment at a spa; **~putzer** *der: in* **schaffen wie ein ~putzer** (ugs., bes. südwestd.) slave away; work like a horse; **~vergifter** *der;* **~~s,** **~~,** **~vergifterin** *die;* **~~,** **~~nen** water poisoner; (fig. abwertend) troublemaker; **~vergiftung** *die* water poisoning; (fig. abwertend) troublemaking

Brünnlein /'brʏnlain/ *das;* **~s,** ~ **1** [little] well **2** (Springbrunnen) [little] fountain

Brunst /brʊnst/ *die;* ~, **Brünste** /'brʏnstə/ (von männlichen Tieren) rut; (von weiblichen Tieren) heat; **Männchen/Weibchen in der ~:** rutting males/females in *or* on heat

brunsten *itr. V.* ‹*male animal*› rut; ‹*female animal*› be in *or* on heat

brünstig /'brʏnstɪç/
A *Adj.* rutting ‹*male animal*›; ‹*female animal*› in *or* on heat
B *adv.* **~ röhren** bell

Brunst-: **~schrei** *der* bell; **~zeit** *die* (bei männlichen Tieren) rut; rutting season; (bei weiblichen Tieren) [season of] heat

brunzen /'brʊntsn̩/ *itr. V.* (landsch. derb) [have a] piss (coarse); take a leak (sl.)

brüsk /brʏsk/
A *Adj.* brusque; abrupt
B *adv.* brusquely; abruptly

brüskieren *tr. V.* offend; (stärker) insult; (schneiden) snub

Brüskierung *die;* ~, **~en** ▸ **brüskieren:** piece of offensive behaviour; insult; snub

Brüssel /'brʏsḷ/ *(das);* **~s** ▸ **i S. 675** Brussels

Brüsseler ▸ **i S. 675**
A *indekl. Adj.* Brussels; **~ Spitzen** Brussels lace *sing.*
B *der;* **~s,** **~:** inhabitant of Brussels; (von Geburt) native of Brussels; *s. auch* **Kölner**

Brüsselerin *die;* ~, **~nen** ▸ **Brüsseler B**

Brust /brʊst/ *die;* ~, **Brüste** /'brʏstə/ **1** ▸ **i S. 435** chest; (fig. geh.) breast; heart; **~ an ~:** face to face; **sich in die ~ werfen** puff oneself up; **mit geschwellter ~:** proudly; as proud as a peacock; **er sang aus voller ~:** he sang lustily; **einen zur ~ nehmen** (ugs.) have a drink or two; **schwach auf der ~ sein** (ugs.: anfällig sein) have a weak chest; (ugs.: wenig Geld haben) be short [of money] **2** ▸ **i S. 435** (der Frau) breast; **einem Kind die ~ geben** breast-feed a baby **3** (Hähnchen~) breast; (Rinder~) brisket **4** (Sport) breaststroke

Brust-: **~behaarung** *die* chest hair; **~bein** *das* ▸ **i S. 435** breastbone; **~beutel** *der* purse (*worn around the neck*); **~drüse** *die* ▸ **i S. 435** (Anat.) mammary gland

brüsten /'brʏstn̩/ *refl. V.* (abwertend) **sich mit etw. ~:** boast *or* brag about sth.

brust-, Brust-: **~fell·entzündung** *die* ▸ **i S. 439** (Med.) pleurisy; **~flosse** *die* (Zool.) (bei Fischen) pectoral fin; (beim Wal) flipper; **~haar** *das* hair on the chest; chest hair; **~harnisch** *der* (hist.) breastplate; **~hoch** *Adj.* chest-high; **~höhe** *die:* **in ~höhe** at chest height; **~höhle** *die* ▸ **i S. 435** (Anat.) thoracic cavity; **~kasten** (ugs.) ▸ **i S. 435** chest; **~kind** *das* (ugs.) breastfed baby; **~korb** *der* ▸ **i S. 435** (Anat.) thorax (Anat.); **~krebs** *der* breast cancer; cancer of the breast; **~schutz** *der* (Fechten) plastron; **~schwimmen** *itr. unr. V.; nur im Inf.* do [the] breaststroke; **~schwimmen** *das* breaststroke; **~stimme** *die* (Musik) chest-voice; **~stück** *das* (Kochk.) breast; (vom Rind) brisket; **~tasche** *die* breast pocket; (Innentasche) inside breast pocket; (an der Latzhose) front pocket; **~tee** *der* pectoral tea; **~ton** *der; Pl.* **~töne** (Musik) chest tone; **im ~ton der Überzeugung** (fig.) with utter conviction; **~tuch** *das; Pl.* **~tücher** neckerchief (*worn with traditional costume*); **~umfang** *der* chest measurement; (bei Frauen) bust measurement

Brüstung *die;* ~, **~en** **1** parapet; (Balkon~) balustrade; (Logen~) ledge **2** (Fenster~) breast

Brust-: **~warze** *die* ▸ **i S. 435** nipple; **~wickel** *der* (Med.) chest compress; **~wirbel** *der* ▸ **i S. 435** (Anat.) thoracic vertebra

Brut /bru:t/ *die;* ~, **~en** **1** (das Brüten) brooding **2** (Jungtiere, auch fig. scherzh.: Kinder) brood **3** (abwertend: Gesindel) mob

brutal /bru'ta:l/
A *Adj.* brutal; violent ‹*attack, programme, etc.*›; brute ‹*force, strength*›
B *adv.* brutally

brutalisieren *tr. V.* brutalize

Brutalisierung *die;* **~:** brutalization

Brutalität /brutali'tɛ:t/ *die;* ~, **~en** **1** brutality **2** (Handlung) act of brutality *or* violence

Brut·apparat *der* incubator

brüten /'bry:tn̩/
A *itr. V.* **1** brood **2** (geh.: lasten) hang heavily; **~de Hitze** stifling heat; **~d heiß** (ugs.) boiling *or* stifling hot **3** (grübeln) ponder (**über** + *Dat.* over); **über einem Plan ~:** work on a plan; **in dumpfes Brüten versinken** *od.* **verfallen** fall to brooding
B *tr. V.* (Kernphysik) breed

***brütend·heiß** ▸ **brüten A2**

Brüter *der;* **~s,** ~ (Kernphysik) breeder; **schneller ~:** fast breeder

Brut-: **~henne** *die* sitting hen; **~hitze** *die* (ugs.) stifling *or* sweltering heat; **~kasten** *der* incubator; **in ihrem Haus ist eine Hitze wie in einem ~kasten** it's like an oven in her house; **~pflege** *die* (Zool.) care of the brood; **~reaktor** *der* (Kernphysik) breeder reactor; **~stätte** *die* breeding ground; (fig.) breeding ground (*Gen.*, **für** for); hotbed (*Gen.*, **für** for)

brutto /'brʊto/ *Adv.* ▸ **i S. 315** gross; **~ 4 000 Euro, 4 000 Euro ~:** 4,000 euros gross; **~ 800 kg** 800 kilos gross

Brutto-: **~einkommen** *das* gross income; **~ertrag** *der* gross return; **~gehalt** *das* gross salary; **~gewicht** *das* gross weight; **~inlands·produkt** *das* (Wirtsch.) gross domestic product; **~lohn** *der* gross wage; **~preis** *der* full price; **~raum·zahl** *die* gross register tonnage; **~register·tonne** *die* (Seew.) gross register[ed] ton; **~sozial·produkt** *das* (Wirtsch.) gross national product

brutzeln /'brʊtsḷn/
A *itr. V.* sizzle; **die Kartoffeln müssen noch 10 Minuten ~:** the potatoes have to fry [gently] for another ten minutes
B *tr. V.* (ugs.) fry [up]; **sich** (*Dat.*) **etw. ~:** fry oneself sth.

Bruyère·holz /bry'jɛ:r-/ *das* brierwood

BSE /be:ɛs'e:/ *die* ▸ **i S. 439** BSE

BSE-: **~frei** *Adj.* BSE-free; free from BSE *post-pos.*; **~-Test** *der* BSE-test; test for BSE

Btx /be:te:'ɪks/ *Abk.* = **Bildschirmtext**

Bub /bu:p/ *der;* **~en, ~en** (südd., österr., schweiz.) boy; lad

Bübchen /'by:pçən/ *das;* **~s,** ~ (südd., österr., schweiz.) [little] boy; [little] lad

bübchenhaft
A *Adj.* little-boy-like; **~es Aussehen** little-boy looks
B *adv.* like a little boy/little boys

Bube /'bu:bə/ *der;* **~n, ~n** **1** (Kartenspiele) jack; knave **2** (veralt. abwertend) scoundrel; rogue; knave; **der böse ~:** the bad boy

Buben-: **~streich** *der* **1** childish prank; **2** (veralt.: Übeltat) knavish trick; **~stück** *das* (veralt.) knavish trick

Bubi /'bu:bi/ *der;* **~s, ~s** **1** [little] boy *or* lad *or* fellow **2** (salopp abwertend: Schnösel) young lad

Bubi-: **~kopf** *der* bobbed hair[cut]; bob; **sie hat sich** (*Dat.*) **einen ~kopf schneiden**

lassen she had her hair bobbed; **~kragen** *der* (veralt.) Peter Pan collar

Bübin *die;* ~, ~nen scoundrel

bübisch /ˈbyːbɪʃ/

A *Adj.* 1 mischievous 2 (veralt. abwertend: schurkisch) villainous

B *adv.;* ▸A: mischievously; villainously

Buch /buːx/ *das;* **~[e]s, Bücher** /ˈbyːçɐ/ 1 book; **über seinen Büchern sitzen** pore over one's books; **das Goldene ~ der Stadt** the visitors' book of the town; **sie ist ein aufgeschlagenes** *od.* **offenes ~ für mich** I can read her like an open book; **das ~ der Bücher** the Book of Books; **wie ein ~ reden** (ugs.) talk nineteen to the dozen; **ein Detektiv/ein Faulpelz, wie er im ~e steht** a classic [example of a] detective/a complete lazybones; **ein ~ mit sieben Siegeln** a closed book; a complete mystery; **sich [mit etw.] ins ~ der Geschichte eintragen** (geh.) go down in the annals *pl.* of history [for sth.]; **ein schlaues ~** (ugs.) a reference book/textbook; **die fünf Bücher Mose** the Pentateuch; **das erste/zweite/dritte/vierte/fünfte ~ Mose** Genesis/Exodus/Leviticus/Numbers/Deuteronomy 2 (Dreh~) script 3 (Geschäfts~) book; **er führt selbst die Bücher** he keeps his own books *or* accounts; **über etw.** (*Akk.*) **~ führen/genau ~ führen** keep a record of sth./keep an exact record of sth.; **zu ~[e] schlagen** (den Etat beeinflussen) be reflected in the budget; (ins Gewicht fallen) have a big influence; **es schlägt mit ca. 200 Euro zu ~[e]** it makes a difference of about 200 euros 4 (Wettliste) book; **~ machen** make a book

Buch-: ~besprechung *die* book review; **~binder** *der* ▸❶ S. 113 bookbinder; **~binderei** *die* 1 bookbinding; 2 (Betrieb) bindery; **~binderin** *die;* ~~, ~~nen ▸❶ S. 113 bookbinder; **~block** *der; Pl.* **~blöcke** *od.* **~~s** book block; **~deckel** *der* [book] cover (*front or back*); **~druck** *der* letterpress printing; **im ~druck** in letterpress; **~drucker** *der* ▸❶ S. 113 printer; **~druckerei** *die* 1 letterpress printing; 2 (Betrieb) printing works; **~druckerin** *die* ▸❶ S. 113 printer; **~drucker·kunst** *die* art of printing

Buche *die;* ~, ~n 1 beech [tree] 2 (Holz) beech[wood]

Buch-: ~ecker *die* beech nut; **~einband** *der* binding; [book] cover

buchen[1] *tr. V.* 1 enter; **etw. auf ein Konto ~:** enter sth. into an account; **etw. als Erfolg ~** (fig.) count sth. as a success; **einen Sieg für sich ~** (fig.) chalk up a victory 2 (vorbestellen) book ‹*holiday, trip, flight*›; book, reserve ‹*seat, berth, room*›

buchen[2] *Adj.* beech; of beech[wood] *postpos.*

Buchen-: ~hain *der* beech grove; **~holz** *das* beechwood; **~wald** *der* beech wood

Bücher-: ~bord *das* 1 ▸**~brett**; 2 ▸**~regal**; **~brett** *das* bookshelf; **~bus** *der* mobile library (*in a bus*); book bus

Bücherei *die;* ~, ~en library

Bücher-: ~freund *der,* **~freundin** *die* book lover; **~gestell** *das* bookshelves *pl.*; **~kiste** *die* book crate; (Kiste mit ~n) crate of books; **~narr** *der,* **~närrin** *die* book fiend; **sie ist eine wahre ~närrin** she's really mad on books; **~regal** *das* bookshelves *pl.*; **~schrank** *der* bookcase; **~sendung** *die:* **etw. als ~sendung aufgeben/schicken** send sth. at printed paper rate; **das ist eine ~sendung** this can be/has been sent at printed paper rate; **~stube** *die* bookshop; **~stütze** *die* bookend; **~verbot** *das* (kath. Kirche) ban on books; **~verbrennung** *die* burning of books; **~wand** *die* 1 bookshelf unit; 2 (Wand mit ~regal) wall of bookshelves; **~weisheit** *die* (abwertend) book learning; **~wurm** *der* (scherzh.) bookworm

Buch-: ~fink *der* chaffinch; **~form** *die: in* **in ~form** in book form; **~führung** *die* bookkeeping; **einfache/doppelte ~führung** single/double-entry bookkeeping; **~gemeinschaft** *die* book club; **~halter** *der,* **~halterin** *die* ▸❶ S. 113 bookkeeper

buchhalterisch

A *Adj.* bookkeeping *attrib.*

B *adv.* **~ gesehen** from a bookkeeping point of view

Buch-: ~haltung *die* 1 accountancy; 2 (Abteilung) accounts department; **~handel** *der* book trade; **im ~handel erhältlich** available from bookshops; **~händler** *der,* **~händlerin** *die* ▸❶ S. 113 bookseller; **~handlung** *die* bookshop; **„~handlung Franz Maier"** 'Franz Maier's Bookshop'; **~hülle** *die* [book] cover; **~illustration** *die* book illustration; **~klub** *der* book club; **~kritik** *die* book review; **~laden** *der; Pl.* **~läden** ▸**~handlung**

Büchlein *das;* ~s, ~: little book

Buch-: ~macher *der,* **~macherin** *die* ▸❶ S. 113 bookmaker; bookie (coll.); **~malerei** *die* illumination; **~markt** *der* book market; **~messe** *die* book fair; **~prüfer** *der,* **~prüferin** ▸❶ S. 113 *die* auditor; **~rücken** *der* spine

Buchs·baum /ˈbʊks-/ *der* box [tree]

Buchse /ˈbʊksə/ *die;* ~, ~n 1 (Elektrot.) socket 2 (Technik) bush; liner

Büchse /ˈbʏksə/ *die;* ~, ~n 1 tin; **die ~ der Pandora** Pandora's box 2 (ugs.: Sammel~) [collecting] box 3 (Gewehr) rifle; (Schrot~) shotgun; **jmdm. vor die ~ kommen** come into sb.'s sights *pl.*

Büchsen-: ~fleisch *das* tinned (Brit.) *or* (Amer.) canned meat; **~gemüse** *das* tinned (Brit.) *or* (Amer.) canned vegetables *pl.*; **~macher** *der,* **~macherin** *die* ▸❶ S. 113 gunsmith; **~milch** *die* tinned (Brit.) *or* (Amer.) canned milk; **~öffner** *der* tin-opener (Brit.); can opener (Amer.); **~spanner** *der* (Helfer) assistant; aide (esp. Polit.); (Handlanger) henchman; **~spannerin** *die;* ~~, ~~nen assistant; aide (esp. Polit.)

Buchstabe /ˈbuːxʃtaːbə/ *der;* **~ns, ~n** letter; (Druckw.) character; **ein großer/kleiner ~:** a capital [letter]/small letter; **nach dem ~n des Gesetzes** (fig.) according to the letter of the law; **sich auf seine vier ~n setzen** (ugs. scherzh.) sit [oneself] down

buchstaben-, Buchstaben-: ~getreu A *Adj.* literal; B *adv.* to the letter; **~rätsel** *das* word puzzle; **~rechnung** *die* simple algebra; **~schloss, *~schloß** *das* letter-lock; **~schrift** *die* alphabetic script; **~wort** *das; Pl.* **~wörter** acronym

buchstabieren *tr. V.* 1 spell 2 (mühsam lesen) spell out

buchstäblich /ˈbuːxʃtɛːplɪç/

A *Adv.* literally

B *Adj.* literal

Buch·stütze *die* ▸**Bücherstütze**

Bucht /bʊxt/ *die;* ~, ~en 1 bay 2 (für Schweine) sty; (für Pferde) stall

Buchtel /ˈbʊxtl̩/ *die;* ~, ~n (österr.) yeast pastry with jam or poppy-seed filling

Buch·titel *der* title

Buchung *die;* ~, ~en 1 entry 2 ▸**buchen**[1] **2**: booking; reservation

Buchungs·maschine *die* accounting machine

Buch-: ~weizen *der* buckwheat; **~wert** *der* (Finanzw.) book value; **~wesen** *das* book trade; (Studienfach) the book trade; **~wissen** *das* (abwertend) book learning; **das ist nur ~wissen** that is only knowledge gained from books; **~zeichen** *das* bookmark[er]

Bücke /ˈbʏkə/ *die;* ~, ~n (Turnen) stoop vault

Buckel /ˈbʊkl̩/ *der;* **~s,** ~ 1 (ugs.: Rücken) back; **den ~ voll kriegen** get a good hiding (coll.); **einen ~ machen** ‹*cat*› arch its back; ‹*person*› hunch one's shoulders; **rutsch mir den ~ runter!** (salopp) get lost! (coll.); **der kann** *od.* **soll mir mal den ~ runterrutschen** (salopp) he can get lost *or* take a running jump (coll.); **den ~ voll Schulden haben** be up to one's neck *or* ears in debt; **den ~ hinhalten** (fig.) take the blame; carry the can (Brit. coll.); **einen krummen ~ machen, den ~ krumm machen** (fig.) bow and scrape; kowtow; **genug/viel auf dem ~ haben** (fig.) have enough/a lot on one's plate (fig.); **schon 40 Jahre** *od.* **Jährchen auf dem ~ haben** be 40 already; **wenn du so viele Jahre auf dem ~ hast wie ich** when you are as old as I am; *s. auch* **breit A 1** 2 (Rückenverkrümmung) hunchback; hump 3 (ugs.: Hügel) hillock 4 (ugs.: gewölbte Stelle) bump

buckelig ▸**bucklig**

buckeln *itr. V.* (ugs.) 1 (abwertend) bow and scrape; kowtow; **vor jmdm. ~:** kowtow to sb.; **nach oben ~ und nach unten treten** bow to superiors and kick underlings 2 ‹*cat*› arch its back

Buckel-: ~piste 1 (Skipiste) mogul piste; 2 (Autoteststrecke) washboard track; **~rind** *das* zebu

bücken /ˈbʏkn̩/ *refl. V.* bend down; **sich nach etw. ~:** bend down to pick sth. up

bucklig *Adj.* 1 hunchbacked; humpbacked 2 (ugs.: uneben) bumpy

Bucklige *der/die; adj. Dekl.* hunchback; humpback

Bückling[1] /ˈbʏklɪŋ/ *der;* **~s, ~e** (ugs. scherzh.: Verbeugung) bow

Bückling[2] *der;* **~s, ~e** (Hering) smoked herring; bloater

Bück·ware *die* (ugs.) under-the-counter items

Büdchen /ˈbyːtçən/ *das;* **~s, ~:** little hut

Buddel /ˈbʊdl̩/ *die;* ~, ~n (nordd.) bottle

Buddelei /bʊdəˈlai̯/ *die;* ~, ~en (ugs. abwertend) digging *no pl.*; **eine ~:** a piece of digging

Buddel·kasten *der* sandpit

buddeln (ugs.)

A *itr. V.* dig; **die Kinder ~ im Garten/im Sand** the children are digging about in the garden/sand

B *tr. V.* 1 dig ‹*hole, tunnel*› 2 (ausgraben) dig up; **etw. aus der Erde ~:** dig sth. up out of the ground

Buddha /ˈbʊda/ *der;* **~s, ~s** Buddha

Buddhismus *der;* ~: Buddhism *no art.*

Buddhist *der;* **~en, ~en, Buddhistin** *die;* **~, ~nen** Buddhist

buddhistisch

A *Adj.* Buddhist *attrib.*

B *adv.* **~ beeinflusst** influenced by Buddhism

Bude /ˈbuːdə/ *die;* ~, ~n 1 kiosk; (Markt~) stall; (Jahrmarkts~) booth 2 (Bau~) hut 3 (ugs.: Haus) dump (coll.) 4 (ugs.: Zimmer) room; digs *pl.* (Brit. coll.); **Leben in die ~ bringen** liven the place up; **mir fällt die ~ auf den Kopf** I'm feeling *or* getting claustrophobic; **[jmdm.] die ~ auf den Kopf stellen** turn the *or* sb.'s place upside down; **jmdm. die ~ einrennen** pester *or* badger sb.; **jmdm. auf die ~ rücken** (mit einem Anliegen) go/come round to sb.'s place; (als Besuch) drop in on sb. 5 (ugs. abwertend: Laden, Lokal) outfit (coll.)

Budel /ˈbuːdl̩/ *die;* ~, ~n (bayr., österr.) counter

Buden-: ~besitzer *der,* **~besitzerin** *die* stallholder; stallkeeper; **~zauber** *der* (ugs. veralt.) **~zauber machen** have a rave-up (coll.)

Budget /bʏˈdʒeː/ *das;* **~s, ~s** budget

budgetär /bʏdʒeˈtɛːɐ̯/ *Adj.* budgetary

Budget-: ~beratung *die* budget discussion; **~entwurf** *der* draft budget

budgetieren /bʏdʒeˈtiːrən/ (Politik, Wirtsch.)

A *itr. V.* set a/the budget; budget; **neu/anders ~:** set a new/different budget

B *tr. V.* (bes. schweiz.) include ‹*amount*› in a budget; budget for ‹*possibility*›

Budgetierung *die;* ~, ~en (Politik, Wirtsch.) budget-setting; **~en** *Pl.* budget-setting *sing.*

Budike /buˈdiːkə/ *die;* ~, ~n (berl.) 1 little shop 2 (Lokal) pub (Brit.); bar

Budiker *der;* **~s,** ~ (berl.) landlord

Budikerin *die;* ~, ~nen (berl.) landlady

Budo /ˈbuːdo/ *das;* **~s** budo

Büfett /byˈfɛt/ *das;* **~[e]s, ~s** *od.* **~e** 1 sideboard 2 (Schanktisch) bar 3 (Verkaufstisch) counter 4 **kaltes ~:** cold buffet 5 (schweiz.: Bahnhofsrestaurant) station restaurant

Büfett·fräulein *das* barmaid (Brit.)

Büfettier /byfɛˈti̯eː/ *der;* **~s, ~s** barman

Büffel /ˈbʏfl/ *der;* **~s, ~:** buffalo

Büffelei *die* (ugs.) swotting *no pl.* (Brit. sl.)

Büffel-: ~herde *die* herd of buffalo; **~leder** *das* buffalo hide

büffeln (ugs.)
A *itr. V.* swot (Brit. sl.); cram
B *tr. V.* swot up (Brit. sl.); cram

Buffet /byˈfeː/ *das;* **~s, ~s,** (österr. auch:) **Büffet** /byˈfɛt/ *das;* **Büffets, Büffets** ▸ **Büfett**

Buffo /ˈbʊfo/ *der;* **~s, ~s** *od.* **Buffi** buffo

Bug /buːk/ *der;* **~[e]s, ~e** *u.* **Büge** /ˈbyːgə/ 1 *Pl.:* **~e** (Schiffs~) bow; (Flugzeug~) nose; **jmdm. eine vor den ~ knallen** (salopp) (einen Schlag versetzen) sock (coll.) *or* give sb. one; (einschüchtern) sock (coll.) *or* give it to sb.; *s. auch* **Schuss 1** 2 (Schulterstück) shoulder 3 *Pl.:* **Büge** (Technik) brace; strut

Bügel /ˈbyːgl̩/ *der;* **~s, ~** 1 hanger; **über einen/einem ~:** on a hanger 2 (Steig~) stirrup 3 (Brillen~) earpiece 4 (an einer Tasche, Geldbörse) frame 5 (Griff einer Handtasche) handle 6 (Stromabnehmer) bow; pantograph 7 (Säge~) frame 8 (Gewehr~) trigger guard

bügel-, Bügel-: ~automat *der* ▸ **~maschine; ~brett** *das* ironing board; **~eisen** *das* iron; **~falte** *die* [trouser] crease; **~frei** *Adj.* non-iron; **~maschine** *die* ironing machine

bügeln *tr., itr. V.* iron ‹*clothes*›; *s. auch* **gebügelt**

Bügel·säge *die* hacksaw

Buggy /ˈbagi/ *der;* **~s, ~s** buggy

Bügler *der;* **~s, ~, Büglerin** *die;* **~, ~nen** ironer

Bug-: ~rad *das* (Flugw.) nose wheel; **~see** *die* (Seemannsspr.) ▸ **~welle**

Bugsier·dampfer *der* (Seemannsspr.) tug [boat]

bugsieren /bʊˈksiːrən/ *tr. V.* 1 (ugs.) shift; manoeuvre; steer ‹*person*› 2 (Seemannsspr.) tow

Bug-: ~spriet *das od. der* (Seemannsspr.) bowsprit; **~welle** *die* (Seemannsspr.) bow wave

buh /buː/ *Interj.* boo; **~ rufen** boo

Buh *das;* **~s, ~s** (ugs.) boo; **die ~s** the boos *or* booing *sing.*

Buhei /buˈhai/ *das;* **~s** (bes. westd.) fuss

buhen *itr. V.* (ugs.) boo

Buh·frau *die* (ugs. abwertend) [female] scapegoat

Bühl /byːl/ *der;* **~[e]s, ~e** (südd., schweiz., österr.) hill

Buhle[1] /ˈbuːlə/ *der;* **~n, ~n** (dichter. veralt.) paramour

Buhle[2] *die;* **~, ~n** (dichter. veralt.) paramour; mistress

buhlen /ˈbuːlən/ *itr. V.* 1 (abwertend) **um jmds. Gunst ~:** court sb.'s favour; **um jmds. Anerkennung ~:** strive for recognition by sb.; **um jmdn. ~** (veralt.) court *or* woo sb. 2 (veralt.: eine Liebschaft haben) **mit jmdm. ~:** have a liaison with sb.

Buhler *der;* **~s, ~** 1 ▸ **Buhle**[1] 2 (geh. abwertend: Werber) wooer

Buhlerin *die;* **~, ~nen** ▸ **Buhle**[2]

buhlerisch (veralt. abwertend)
A *Adj.* 1 amorous 2 (werbend) ingratiating
B *adv.* 1 amorously 2 (werbend) ingratiatingly

Buh·mann *der* (ugs.) 1 whipping boy; scapegoat 2 (Schreckgestalt) bogyman

Buhne /ˈbuːnə/ *die;* **~, ~n** groyne

Bühne /ˈbyːnə/ *die;* **~, ~n** 1 stage; **es gab mehrmals Beifall auf offener ~:** there were several rounds of applause during the play; **ein Stück auf die ~ bringen** put on *or* stage a play; **seit Monaten steht er jeden Abend als Faust auf der ~:** he has been playing Faust [on the stage] every evening for months; **auf der politischen ~** (fig.) on the political scene; **über die ~ bringen** (ugs.) finish ‹*process*›; get ‹*event*› over; **über die ~ gehen** (ugs.) go off; **von der ~ des Lebens abtreten** (geh. verhüll.) depart this life; **von der ~ abtreten** disappear from *or* leave the scene 2 (Theater) theatre; **die Städtischen ~n Köln** the Cologne municipal theatres; **das Stück ging über alle ~n** the play was put on *or* staged in all the theatres; **an** *od.* **bei der ~ sein** be on the stage *or* in the theatre; **zur ~ gehen** go on the stage *or* into the theatre 3 (landsch.: Dachboden) attic; loft 4 (landsch.: Heuboden) [hay] loft 5 (Hebe~) lift; ramp

bühnen-, Bühnen-: ~anweisung *die* stage direction; **~arbeiter** *der,* **~arbeiterin** *die* ▸ **S. 113** stagehand; **~aussprache** *die* standard *or* received pronunciation; **~ausstattung** *die* stage set; **~autor** *der,* **~autorin** *die* playwright; **~bearbeitung** *die* stage adaptation; **~beleuchtung** *die* stage lighting; **~bild** *das* [stage] set; **~bildner** *der;* **~~s, ~~, ~bildnerin** *die;* **~~, ~~nen** stage *or* set designer; **~dekoration** *die* [stage] setting; stage decoration; **~dichtung** *die* drama; theatre; **~effekt** *der* stage effect; **~eingang** *der* stage door; **~erfahrung** *die* stage experience; **~erfolg** *der* 1 stage success; **das Stück hatte einen großen ~erfolg** the play was a big success; 2 (Theaterstück) stage hit; **ein großer ~erfolg am Broadway** a big Broadway hit; **~fassung** *die* ▸ **~bearbeitung; ~gerecht** *Adj.* ‹*form*› suitable for the stage; stage ‹*adaptation*›; **etw. ~gerecht bearbeiten** adapt sth. for the stage; **~himmel** *der* cyclorama; **~kunst** *die* ▸ **Schauspielkunst; ~maler** *der,* **~malerin** *die* scene-painter; **~manuskript** *das* script; **~musik** *die* incidental music; **~raum** *der* stage [and backstage]; **~reif** *Adj.* ‹*play etc.*› ready for the stage; ‹*imitation etc.*› worthy of the stage; dramatic ‹*entrance etc.*›; **~schaffende** *der/die; adj. Dekl.* dramatic artist; **~stück** *das* stage play; **~technik** *die* stage equipment *or* machinery; **~werk** *das* work for the stage; (im engeren Sinne: dramatisches Werk) dramatic work; **~wirksam** *Adj.* effective on the stage *pred.;* **~wirkung** *die* dramatic effectiveness

Buh·ruf *der* boo

buk /buːk/ *1. u. 3. Pers. Sg. Prät. v.* **backen**

Bukarest /ˈbuːkarɛst/ *(das);* **~s** ▸ **S. 675** Bucharest

Bukett /buˈkɛt/ *das;* **~s, ~s** *od.* **~e** 1 (geh.) bouquet; **ein ~ Rosen** a bouquet of roses 2 (bei Wein) bouquet

Bukolik /buˈkoːlɪk/ *die;* **~** (Literaturw.) bucolic *or* pastoral poetry

bukolisch *Adj.* 1 (Literaturw.) bucolic; pastoral; 2 (geh.: idyllisch) idyllic

Bulette /buˈlɛtə/ *die;* **~, ~n** (bes. berl.) rissole; **ran an die ~n!** (ugs.) go to it! (coll.)

Bulgare /bʊlˈgaːrə/ *der;* **~n, ~n** Bulgarian

Bulgarien /bʊlˈgaːri̯ən/ *(das);* **~s** Bulgaria

Bulgarin *die;* **~, ~nen** Bulgarian; *s. auch* **-in**

bulgarisch *Adj.* ▸ **S. 670** Bulgarian; *s. auch* **deutsch, Deutsch**

Bulk·ladung /ˈbalk-/ *die* (Seemannsspr.) bulk cargo

Bull- /bʊl-/: **~auge** *das* circular porthole; **~dogge** *die* bulldog

Bulldozer /ˈbʊldoːzɐ/ *der;* **~s, ~:** bulldozer

Bulle[1] /ˈbʊlə/ *der;* **~n, ~n** 1 bull 2 (ugs. abwertend: Mann) great ox; big bull 3 (salopp abwertend: Polizist) cop (coll.); **die ~n kommen!** here come the fuzz (sl.) *or* the cops (coll.)!

Bulle[2] *die;* **~, ~n** 1 (päpstlicher Erlass) bull; *s. auch* **golden** 2 (Urkundensiegel) bulla

bullen-, Bullen-: ~beißer *der;* **~~s, ~~** 1 ▸ **Bulldogge;** 2 (ugs. abwertend: Mensch) aggressive fellow; **~hitze** *die* (ugs.) sweltering *or* boiling heat; **~kalb** *das* bull calf; **~markt** *der* (Börsenw.) bull market; **~stark** *Adj.* (ugs.) as strong as an ox *pred.*

bullern /ˈbʊlɐn/ *itr. V.* (ugs.) ‹*water*› bubble [away]; ‹*fire etc.*› roar [away]

Bulletin /bylˈtɛ̃ː/ *das;* **~s, ~s** bulletin

bullig
A *Adj.* 1 beefy, stocky ‹*person, appearance, etc.*›; chunky, hefty ‹*car*› 2 (drückend) sweltering, boiling ‹*heat*›
B *adv.* swelteringly; **~ heiß** boiling hot

Bullshit /ˈbʊlʃɪt/ *der;* **~s** (derb abwertend) bullshit

Bull·terrier *der* bull terrier

Bully /ˈbʊli/ *das;* **~s, ~s** (Sport) bully; **das ~ ausführen** take a bully

bum /bʊm/ *Interj.* bang

Bumerang /ˈbuməraŋ/ *der;* **~s, ~e** *od.* **~s** boomerang; **es erwies sich als ~** (fig.) it boomeranged [on him/her/them]

Bumerang·effekt *der* boomerang effect

Bummel /ˈbʊml̩/ *der;* **~s, ~** 1 stroll (**durch** around); **einen ~ [durch den Park] machen** go for *or* take a stroll [in the park] 2 (durch Lokale) pub crawl (coll.)

Bummelant /bʊməˈlant/ *der;* **~en, ~en, Bummelantin** *die;* **~, ~nen** (ugs. abwertend) 1 slowcoach (Brit.); slowpoke (Amer.); dawdler 2 (Faulenzer) idler; loafer

Bummelei *die;* **~, ~en** (ugs. abwertend) 1 dawdling 2 (Faulenzerei) idling *or* loafing about

bummelig (ugs. abwertend)
A *Adj.* 1 slow 2 (nachlässig) slovenly; slipshod
B *adv.* 1 slowly 2 (nachlässig) in a slovenly *or* slipshod way

Bummel·liese *die* (ugs. abwertend) slowcoach; dawdler

bummeln *itr. V.* 1 *mit sein* (ugs.) stroll (**durch** around); **[im Park] ~ gehen** go for *or* take a stroll [in the park] 2 *mit sein* (ugs.: durch Lokale) go round the pubs (Brit. coll.); go on a pub crawl (Brit. coll.) 3 (ugs. abwertend: trödeln) dawdle; **bei den Schulaufgaben ~:** dawdle over one's homework 4 (ugs. abwertend: faulenzen) laze about; do nothing

Bummel-: ~streik *der* go-slow; (bei Beamten usw.) work to rule; **in einen ~streik treten** go on a go-slow; **~zug** *der* (ugs.) slow *or* stopping train

bummern /ˈbʊmɐn/ *itr. V.* (landsch.) bang; **gegen die Tür ~:** bang on the door

Bummler *der;* **~s, ~, Bummlerin** *die;* **~, ~nen** (ugs.) 1 (Spaziergänger) stroller 2 ▸ **Bummelant**

bummlig ▸ **bummelig**

bums /bʊms/ *Interj.* bang!; **es machte laut ~:** there was a loud bang *or* thud

Bums *der;* **~es, ~e** 1 (ugs.) bang; (dumpfer) thud; thump 2 (salopp abwertend: Lokal) dive (coll.) 3 (salopp abwertend: Tanzvergnügen) hop (coll.) 4 (Fußballjargon) **einen unerhörten ~ haben** have a tremendous shot

bumsen
A *itr. V.* (ugs.) 1 *unpers.* **es bumste ganz furchtbar** there was a terrible bang/thud *or* thump; **es bumste an der Tür** there was a bang/thump on the door; **an dieser Kreuzung bumst es mindestens einmal am Tag** (fig.) there's at least one smash *or* crash a day at this junction; **hör auf, oder es bumst [gleich]!** (fig.) stop it, or you'll catch it [in a minute]! (coll.) 2 (schlagen) bang; (dumpfer) thump; **gegen die Tür ~:** bang/thump on the door 3 *mit sein* (stoßen) bang; bash; **er ist mit dem Kopf gegen die Wand gebumst** he banged *or* bashed his head on the wall 4 (salopp: koitieren) have it off (sl.); screw (coarse)
B *tr. V.* 1 (Fußballjargon) thump 2 (salopp: koitieren mit) have it off with (sl.); screw (coarse); **gebumst werden** get laid (sl.); be screwed (coarse)

bums-, Bums-: ~lokal *das* (ugs. abwertend) dive (coll.); **~musik** *die* (ugs. abwertend) oompah music (coll.); **~voll** *Adj.* (salopp) full to bursting *pred.*

b

Bund¹ /bʊnt/ *der;* **~[e]s, Bünde** /ˈbʏndə/ **1▸** (Verband, Vereinigung) association; society; (Bündnis, Pakt) alliance; **der Dritte im ~e** (fig.) the third in the trio; **der Alte ~/der Neue ~** (Rel.) the Old/New Testament; **den ~ der Ehe eingehen, den ~ fürs Leben schließen** (geh.) enter into the bond of marriage; **mit jmdm. im ~e sein** *od.* **stehen** be in league with sb. **2▸** (föderativer Staat) federation; **der ~ und die Länder** the Federation *or* Federal Government and the Länder *or* States; (in Austria) the Federation *or* Federal Government and the provinces **3▸** (ugs.: ~eswehr) forces *pl;* **beim ~:** in the forces *pl.;* **zum ~ gehen** do one's military service; **er hat sich freiwillig zum ~ gemeldet** he joined up voluntarily **4▸** (an Röcken od. Hosen) waistband **5▸** (an Instrumenten) fret

Bund

This term refers to the federal state as the top level of government, as opposed to the individual *Länder* which make up the Federal Republic. *Bund* and *Länder* have different responsibilities, with the *Bund* in charge of foreign policy, defence, transport, health, employment, etc.

Bund² *das;* **~[e]s, ~e** bunch; **ein ~ Petersilie/Mohrrüben/Spargel** a bunch of parsley/carrots/asparagus

Bündchen /ˈbʏntçən/ *das;* **~s, ~** (am Hals) [neck]band; (am Ärmel) [sleeve] band; (an der Taille) [waist]band; (am Knöchel) [ankle] band

Bündel /ˈbʏndl̩/ *das;* **~s, ~ 1▸** bundle; **ein ~ von Fragen** (fig.) a set *or* cluster of questions; **ein hilfloses/schreiendes ~** (ugs.) a helpless/howling little bundle; **jeder hat sein ~ zu tragen** (fig.) everybody has his cross to bear; **sein ~ packen** *od.* **schnüren** pack one's bags *pl.* **2▸** (Zusammengebundenes) bundle; sheaf **3▸** (Geom.) sheaf

bündeln *tr. V.* bundle up ‹*newspapers, old clothes, rags, etc.*›; tie ‹*banknotes etc.*› into bundles/a bundle; tie ‹*flowers, radishes, carrots, etc.*› into bunches/a bunch; sheave ‹*straw, hay, etc.*›

Bündelung *die;* **~, ~en** (Konzentration) concentration; (Verbindung) combination

bündel·weise *Adv.* by the bundle; in bundles; (bei Blumen, Möhren, Radieschen usw.) by the bunch; in bunches

bundes-, Bundes-: ~adler *der* federal eagle; **~amt** *das* federal department (**für** of); (schweiz.) federal office (**für** of); **~angestellten·tarif** *der* [civil servants'] statutory salary scale; **~anleihe** *die* government bond; **~anstalt** *die* federal institute (**für** of); **~anwalt** *der* **1▸** Federal Prosecutor; **2▸** (beim ~verwaltungsgericht) prosecutor in the Supreme Administrative Court; **3▸** (schweiz.) public prosecutor; **~anwältin** *die* ▸ **~anwalt**; **~anwaltschaft** *die* **1▸** Federal Supreme Court prosecutors *pl.;* **2▸** (beim ~verwaltungsgericht) Supreme Administrative Court prosecutors *pl.;* **~anzeiger** *der* federal gazette; **~arbeitsgericht** *das* Federal Labour Court; **~ausbildungs·förderungsgesetz** *das* Federal Education and Training Assistance Act; **~auto·bahn** *die* federal motorway; **~bahn** *die* Federal Railway; **~bank** *die* federal bank; **die Deutsche ~bank** the German Federal Bank; **~beamte** *der,* **~beamtin** *die* federal civil servant; **~beauftragte** *der/die; adj. Dekl.* Federal Commissioner; **~behörde** *die* federal authority; **~bruder** *der* fellow member [of a/the students' association]; **~bürger** *der,* **~bürgerin** *die* German citizen; **~deutsch** *Adj.* German; **der ~deutsche Alltag** everyday life in West Germany; **~deutsche** *der/die; adj. Dekl.* West German; **~ebene** *die:* **auf ~ebene** at federal *or* national level; **~eigen** *Adj.* federal-owned; nationalized; **~gebiet** *das* federal territory; **das ~gebiet** (Deutschland) Germany; **~genosse** *der,* **~genossin** *die* ally; **~gericht** *das* Federal Court; **~gerichts·hof** *der* Federal Supreme Court; **~gesetz·blatt** *das* Federal Law Gazette; **~grenzschutz** *der* Federal Border Police; **~hauptstadt** *die* federal capital; **~haus** *das* Federal Parliament; (Gebäude) federal parliament [building]; **~haushalt** *der* federal *or* national budget; **~heer** *das* (österr., schweiz.) [federal] armed forces *pl.;* **~kabinett** *das* Federal Cabinet; **~kanzlei** *die* Federal Chancellery; **~kanzler** *der* **1▸** Federal Chancellor; **2▸** (schweiz.) Chancellor of the Confederation; **~kanzler·amt** *das* Federal Chancellery; **~kanzlerin** *die* ▸ **~kanzler**; **~kriminal·amt** *das* Federal Criminal Investigation Agency; **~lade** *die* (jüd. Rel.) Ark of the Covenant; **~land** *das* [federal] state; (österr.) province; **~liga** *die* national *or* federal division; **~ligist** /-lɪgɪst/ *der* **~~en, ~~en** team in the national *or* federal division; **~marine** *die* Federal Navy; German Navy; **~minister** *der,* **~ministerin** *die* Federal Minister; **~ministerium** *das* Federal Ministry; **~mittel** *Pl.* federal funds; **~nach·richtendienst** *der* Federal Intelligence Agency; **~politisch A▸** *Adj.* relating to Federal politics *postpos.;* ‹*key figure*› in Federal politics; **B▸** *adv.* in Federal politics; **~post** *die* Federal Post Office; **~präsident** *der,* **~präsidentin** *die* **1▸** [Federal] President; **2▸** (schweiz.) President of the Confederation; **~rat** *der* **1▸** [Federal] Upper House of Parliament; Bundesrat; **2▸** (österr., schweiz.) Federal Council; **~rechnungs·hof** *der* Federal Audit Office; **~recht** *das* federal law; **~regierung** *die* Federal Government; **~republik** *die* federal republic; **die ~republik Deutschland** The Federal Republic of Germany; **~republikanisch** *Adj.* German; **~richter** *der,* **~richterin** *die* federal judge; **~sieger** *der,* **~siegerin** *die* national winner; **~staat** *der* federal state; **~straße** *die* federal highway; ≈ A road (Brit.)

Bundesbank

Properly called the *Deutsche Bundesbank*, Germany's central bank is an autonomous non-governmental institution located in Frankfurt am Main. With the introduction of the euro in 1999, some of the bank's functions passed to the European Central Bank (also in Frankfurt).

Bundesheer

The *Bundesheer* is the Austrian federal army, which ensures the country's neutrality. All 18-year-old Austrian males must serve for a compulsory six months, plus two further months reserve duty at later dates. Conscientious objectors do public service. No foreign military bases are allowed on Austrian territory.

Bundeskanzler

The Chancellor is the head of government in Germany and Austria. The German chancellor is normally elected for four years by the MPs in the **Bundestag** after being proposed by the **Bundespräsident**. The *Bundeskanzler* chooses the ministers and decides on government policies.

Bundesland

▸ Land

Bundesliga

In soccer, the German *Bundesliga* is the top division and is made up of 18 teams. League games draw hundreds of thousands of people every week during the regular season.

Bundesminister

The Federal Government consists of the **Bundeskanzler** and the *Bundesminister* (Federal Ministers). The Chancellor appoints ministers and determines their number and responsibilities in the Cabinet. Ministers run their ministries independently but within the framework of the guidelines of the Chancellor's policy.

Bundespräsident

The President is the head of state in Germany and Austria. The German president is elected for five years by the MPs and delegates from the *Länder*. The *Bundespräsident* acts mainly as a figurehead, representing Germany abroad, and does not get involved in party politics, although he often takes a moral lead in major issues and can exercise personal authority through his neutral mediating function. The *Bundespräsident* can only be re-elected once.

Bundesrat

This is the upper house of the German parliamentary system, where the *Länder* are represented. The *Bundesrat* members are appointed by the *Länder* governments. The *Bundesrat* has to approve laws affecting the *Länder*, and also any changes to the **Grundgesetz**. Sometimes the opposition parties actually hold a majority in the *Bundesrat*, which allows them to influence German legislation.

Bundesrepublik

Short form of the official name of the German state, *Bundesrepublik Deutschland* (Federal Republic of Germany). Before reunification, the shortened form was used to distinguish the West German state from the East German GDR (German Democratic Republic), but it is now commonly used to refer to the reunified state.

Bundes·tag *der* [Federal] Lower House of Parliament; Bundestag

Bundestag

The lower house of the German parliament, which is elected every four years by the German people. The *Bundestag* is responsible for federal legislation, the federal budget, and electing the **Bundeskanzler**. Half of the MPs are elected directly and half by proportional representation, in a complicated voting system where each voter has two votes.

Bundestags-: ~abgeordnete *der/die* member of parliament; member of the Bundestag; **~fraktion** *die* parliamentary group; group in the Bundestag; **~präsident** *der,* **~präsidentin** *die* President of the Bundestag; **~wahl** *die* parliamentary *or* general election

bundes-, Bundes-: ~trainer *der,* **~trainerin** *die* national team manager; national coach; **~treue** *die* federal allegiance; **~verband** *der* federal association; **~verband der Deutschen Industrie** Federation of German Industries; **~verdienst·kreuz** *das* Order of Merit of the Federal Republic; **~verfassung** *die* federal constitution; **~verfassungs·gericht** *das* Federal Constitutional Court; **~versammlung** *die* Federal Assembly; **~versicherungs·anstalt** *die* federal insurance institution; **die ~versicherungsanstalt für Angestellte** the Federal Insurance Institution [for salaried employees]; **~verwaltungs·gericht** *das* Supreme Administrative Court; **~wehr** *die* [Federal] Armed Forces *pl.;* **~weit A▸** *Adj.* nationwide; national; **B▸** *adv.* nationwide; nationally; **~zwang** *der* federal obligation

Bundesverfassungsgericht

As the supreme court in Germany, the Federal Constitutional Court in Karlsruhe is the guardian of the **Grundgesetz** and the final arbiter in any German legal appeal. It passes judgement on constitutional complaints and has the power to order a party's dissolution if it is unconstitutional and possibly poses a threat to democracy. The Federal Government has to accept the judges' ruling, however controversial the case may be. The *Bundesverfassungsgericht* consists of two panels, each with eight judges who are elected for a single twelve-year term. Half of the panel is elected by the **Bundestag** and half by the **Bundesrat**.

Bundeswappen

The federal coat of arms is the eagle. This heraldic bird - the emblem of the Roman emperors - was adopted by Charlemagne and became the coat of arms of the German Empire when it was founded in 1871. The Weimar Republic used it in its present form in 1919, and since 1950 it has been the official coat of arms of the Federal Republic of Germany.

Bundeswehr

This is the name for the German armed forces, which come under the control of the defence minister. The *Bundeswehr* consists of professional soldiers and conscripts serving their **Wehrdienst**. Until 1994, the **Grundgesetz** did not allow German forces to be deployed abroad, but they now take part in certain operations, notably UN peacekeeping missions.

Bund-: ~falten *Pl.* pleats; **~falten·hose** *die* pleat[ed]-front trousers *pl.*; **~hose** *die* knee breeches

bündig /ˈbʏndɪç/
A *Adj.* 1 concise; succinct 2 (schlüssig) conclusive; *s. auch* **kurz A 2** 3 (Bauw.) flush; level
B *adv.* 1 concisely; succinctly; *s. auch* **kurz B 2** 2 (schlüssig) conclusively 3 (Bauw.) flush

Bündigkeit *die;* ~ 1 conciseness; succinctness 2 (Schlüssigkeit) conclusiveness

Bündnis /ˈbʏntnɪs/ *das;* **~ses, ~se** alliance

Bündnis 90/Die Grünen

This party came into being in 1993 as the result of a merger of the West German Green party and civil rights movements of the former GDR. It is an important force in the German parliament, committed to environmental and social issues.

bündnis-, Bündnis-: ~frei *Adj.* non-aligned; **~grüne** *der/die* (Politik) ▸**Grüne²**; **~partner** *der,* **~partnerin** *die* ally; **~politik** *die* 1 alliance policy; 2 (um ~se zu schließen) policy of alliance; **~system** *das* system of alliance; **das atlantische ~system** the Atlantic alliances *pl.*; **~treue** *die* loyalty to the alliance

Bund·weite *die* waist; (Maß) waist measurement

Bungalow /ˈbʊŋgalo/ *der;* **~s, ~s** bungalow

Bungee /ˈbandʒi-/: **~springen** *das;* **~~s** bungee jumping; **~springer** *der,* **~springerin** *die* bungee jumper; **~sprung** *der* bungee jump

Bunker /ˈbʊŋkɐ/ *der;* **~s,** ~ 1 (auch Behälter) bunker; (für Getreide) silo; (für Raketen) silo; bunker 2 (Luftschutz~) air-raid shelter 3 (salopp: Gefängnis) clink (sl.)

bunkern
A *tr. V.* 1 bunker ‹*coal*›; store ‹*grain etc.*› 2 (salopp: verstecken) stash away (coll.)
B *itr. V.* (Seemannsspr.) refuel

Bunsen·brenner /ˈbʊnzn̩-/ *der* Bunsen burner

bunt /bʊnt/
A *Adj.* 1 (farbig) coloured; (vielfarbig) colourful; **~e Farben/Kleidung** bright colours/brightly coloured *or* colourful clothes; **~e Luftballons** different coloured balloons; **zu ~e Kleidung** garish clothing 2 (fig.) colourful ‹*sight*›; varied ‹*programme etc.*›; **ein ~er Abend** a social [evening]; **ein ~er Teller [mit Äpfeln, Nüssen und Süßigkeiten]** a plate of assorted fruit, nuts, and sweets (Brit.) *or* (Amer.) candy; **Männer und Frauen bilden eine ~e Reihe** men and women alternate; **Buntes** (DDR ugs.) West German currency; *s. auch* **Hund 1** 3 (ungeordnet) confused ‹*muddle etc.*›; **ein ~es Treiben** a real hustle and bustle; **jetzt wird es mir zu ~** (ugs.) that's *or* it's too much
B *adv.* 1 colourfully; **die Vorhänge waren ~ geblümt** the curtains had a colourful floral pattern; **etw. ~ bemalen/streichen** paint sth. a bright colour/in bright colours; **~ schillernd** iridescent; **~ bemalte Eier** brightly *or* colourfully painted eggs; **~ gefärbte Federn** multicoloured feathers; **~ gefiederte Vögel** birds with colourful *or* brightly coloured feathers; **~ gekleidet sein** be colourfully dressed; have colourful clothes 2 (fig.) **ein ~ gemischtes Programm** a varied programme; **ein ~ gemischtes Publikum** a very mixed audience/(im Restaurant) clientele 3 (ungeordnet) **~ durcheinander liegen** be in a complete muddle; **es zu ~ treiben** (ugs.) go too far; overdo it

bunt-, Bunt-: ~bemalt ▸**bunt B1**; **~druck** *der; Pl.* **~~e** 1 (Verfahren) colour printing; 2 (Gedrucktes) colour print; **~film** *der* ▸**Farbfilm**; **~geblümt** ▸**bunt B 1**; **~gefärbt** ▸**bunt B 1**; **~gefiedert** ▸**bunt B 1**; **~metall** *das* non-ferrous metal; **~papier** *das* coloured paper; **~sandstein** *der* 1 red sandstone; 2 (Geol.) Bunter; **~scheckig** *Adj.* spotted; **~schillernd** ▸**bunt B 1**; **~specht** *der* spotted woodpecker; **~stift** *der* coloured pencil/crayon; **~wäsche** *die* coloureds *pl.*

Bürde /ˈbʏrdə/ *die;* **~, ~n** (geh.) weight; load; (fig.) burden; **jmdm. zur ~ werden** (fig.) become a burden to sb.

bürden *tr. V.* (geh. veralt.) **die Verantwortung für etw. auf jmds. Schultern** (*Akk.*) **~:** burden sb. with the responsibility for sth.

Bure /ˈbuːrə/ *der;* **~n, ~n** Boer

Buren·krieg *der* Boer War

Bürette /bʏˈrɛtə/ *die;* **~, ~n** (Chemie) burette

Burg *die;* **~, ~en** 1 castle 2 (Strand~) wall of sand 3 (Sand~) [sand]castle 4 (Jägerspr.) lodge

Burg-: ~anlage *die* castle buildings *pl.*; castle complex; **~berg** *der* castle hill; (aufgeschüttet) castle mound; **~bewohner** *der,* **~bewohnerin** *die* inhabitant of a/the castle; **die ~bewohner** those living in the castle

Bürge /ˈbʏrgə/ *der;* **~n, ~n** 1 guarantor; **einen ~n stellen** offer surety *or* a guarantor; **er muss zwei ~n stellen** he has to give the names of two guarantors 2 (fig.) guarantee

bürgen *itr. V.* 1 **für jmdn./etw. ~:** vouch for *or* act as guarantor for sb./vouch for or guarantee sth.; **wer bürgt mir dafür, dass ich das Geld zurückbekomme?** who can guarantee *or* what guarantee do I have that I'll get the money back? 2 (fig.) guarantee; **der Name bürgt für Qualität** the name is a guarantee of quality

Bürger *der;* **~s, ~** 1 (Staats~) citizen; **akademischer ~** (veralt.) [university] student; *s. auch* **Uniform** 2 (einer Gemeinde) citizen; resident; **die Bremer ~:** the citizens *or* people of Bremen; **die ~ von Calais** the burghers of Calais 3 (Bourgeois) bourgeois

Bürger-: ~aktion *die* public campaign; **~beauftragte** *der/die* ombudsman; **~begehren** *das* public petition; **~beteiligung** *die* public participation *or* involvement; **~entscheid** *der* local referendum; **~forum** *das* open forum; public debate; **~freundlich A** *Adj.* citizen-friendly; people-friendly; **B** *adv.* in a citizen-friendly *or* people-friendly way; **~geld** *das* (Sozialvers.) all-inclusive monthly benefit (*replacing social security, unemployment pay, pension, etc.*); **~haus** *das* [bourgeois] town house

Bürgerin *die;* **~, ~nen** 1 (Staats~) citizen 2 (einer Gemeinde) citizen; resident 3 (zur Bourgeoisie gehörend) bourgeois[e]

Bürger-: ~initiative *die* citizens' action group; **~krieg** *der* civil war; **der Spanische ~krieg** the Spanish Civil War

Bürgerinitiativen

Citizens' action groups have been operating since the early 1970s, getting together when there is a grievance they feel has been neglected by public authorities. The government usually claims to welcome and support groups that draw attention to social problems, and the *Bürgerinitiativen* often achieve their objectives.

bürgerlich
A *Adj.* 1 (staats~) civil ‹*rights, marriage, etc.*›; civic ‹*duties*›; **das Bürgerliche Gesetzbuch** the [German] Civil Code; **sein ~er Name** his real name 2 (dem Bürgertum zugehörig) middle class; **die ~e Küche** good plain cooking; good home cooking; **das ~e Trauerspiel** domestic tragedy 3 (Polit.) non-socialist; (nicht marxistisch) non-Marxist 4 (abwertend: spießerhaft) bourgeois
B *adv.* 1 ‹*think, etc.*› in a middle-class way; **~ leben** live a middle-class life; **gut ~ essen** have a good plain meal; (gewohnheitsmäßig) eat good plain food 2 (abwertend: spießerhaft) in a bourgeois way; **dieses ~ engstirnige Denken** this bourgeois, narrow-minded way of thinking

Bürgerliche *der/die; adj. Dekl.* 1 (Nichtadlige) commoner 2 (Polit.) non-socialist

Bürgerlichkeit *die;* **~:** middle-class *or* bourgeois way of life; **eine erdrückende Atmosphäre der ~:** a stifling middle-class *or* bourgeois atmosphere

bürger-, Bürger-: ~meister *der* ▸ⓘ **S. 44**, ▸ⓘ **S. 113** mayor; **~meisteramt** *das* 1 (Gemeindeverwaltung) local authority; 2 (Amt des ~meisters) office of mayor; 3 (Gebäude) local council offices *pl.*; **~meisterin** *die* ▸ⓘ **S. 44**, ▸ⓘ **S. 113** mayor; **~mut** *der* ▸**Zivilcourage**; **~nah** *Adj.* which/who reflects the general public's interests *postpos., not pred.*; **~nahe Politik** politics for the people; **~nähe** *die:* **~nähe in der Politik** politics for the people; **~nähe bewahren** keep a close relationship with the people; **~pflicht** *die* civic duty; duty as a citizen; *s. auch* **Ruhe 6**; **~recht** *das* one of the civil rights; **~rechte** civil rights; **~rechtler** *der;* **~~s, ~~,** **~rechtlerin** *die;* **~~, ~~nen** civil-rights campaigner; **~rechtsbewegung** *die* civil-rights movement; **~rechts·kämpfer** *der,* **~rechts·kämpferin** *die* ▸**~rechtler**

Bürgerschaft *die;* **~, ~en** 1 citizens *pl.*; **die ganze ~:** all the citizens 2 (in Hamburg u. Bremen) city parliament

Bürger·schreck *der* bogey of the middle classes

Bürgers-: ~frau *die* (veralt.) 1 middle-class woman; 2 (zur Bourgeoisie gehörend) bourgeoise; **~mann** *der; Pl.* **~leute** (veralt.) 1 middle-class man; 2 (zur Bourgeoisie gehörend) bourgeois

Bürger-: ~sohn *der* 1 son of a middle-class family; 2 (zur Bourgeoisie gehörend) son of a bourgeois family; **~stand** *der* (veralt.) 1 middle class; 2 (Großbürgertum) bourgeoisie; **~steig** *der* pavement (Brit.); sidewalk (Amer.); **~tochter** *die* 1 daughter of a middle-class family; 2 (zur Bourgeoisie gehörend) daughter of a bourgeois family

Bürgertum *das;* **~s** 1 middle class 2 (wohlhabender Bürgerstand) bourgeoisie

Bürger-: ~versicherung *die* (Sozialvers.) universal national insurance scheme (*based on income and personal circumstances*); **~wehr** *die* vigilante group

Burg-: ~fräulein *das* (hist.) daughter of the lord of the/a castle; **~fried** *der;* **~~[e]s, ~~e** ▸**Bergfried**; **~friede** *der* 1 truce; 2 (hist.: Schutz) castle precincts *pl.*; **~graben** *der* [castle] moat; **~graf** *der* (hist.) burgrave; **~gräfin** *die* (hist.) chatelaine; **~herr** *der* (hist.) lord of the/a castle; **~herrin** *die* (hist.) lady of the/a castle

Bürgin /ˈbʏrgɪn/ *die;* **~, ~nen** ▸**Bürge**

Burg·ruine *die* castle ruins *pl.*; ruined castle

Bürgschaft *die;* **~, ~en** 1 (Rechtsw.) guarantee; security; **die ~ für jmdn./etw. übernehmen** agree to act as sb.'s guarantor/to guarantee sth. 2 (Garantie) guarantee; **~ für etw. leisten** vouch for *or* guarantee sth. 3 (Betrag) penalty

Bürgschafts-: ~erklärung *die* guarantee; **~nehmer** *der;* **~~s, ~~,** **~nehmerin** *die;* **~~, ~~nen** creditor

Burgund /bʊrˈgʊnt/ (*das*); **~s** Burgundy

Burgunder *der;* **~s, ~** 1 (Einwohner, auch hist.) Burgundian 2 (Wein) burgundy

burgunder·farben *Adj.* burgundy [red]

Burgunderin *die;* **~, ~nen** ▸**Burgunder 1**

Burgunder·wein *der* burgundy

b

Burg-: **~verlies** *das* [castle] dungeon; **~vogt** *der* ▸ **~graf**

Burin *die;* ~, ~**nen** Boer; *s. auch* **-in**

Burka /'bʊrka/ *die;* ~, ~**s** burka

Burkina Faso /bʊr'ki:na 'fa:zo/ *(das)* Burkina

Burkiner *der;* ~**s**, ~, **Burkinerin** *die;* ~, ~**nen** Burkinan; *s. auch* **-in**

burkinisch *Adj.* Burkinan

burlesk /bʊr'lɛsk/ *Adj.* burlesque

Burleske *die;* ~, ~**n** (Theater, Musik) burlesque

Burma /'bʊrma/ ▸ **Birma**

Burnus /'bʊrnʊs/ *der;* ~**ses**, ~**se** burnous

Büro /by'ro/ *das;* ~**s**, ~**s** office

Büro-: **~angestellte** *der/die* ▸❶ **S. 113** office worker; **~arbeit** *die* office work *no pl.;* **alle ~arbeiten** all types of office work; **~artikel** *der* item of office equipment; **~artikel** *Pl.* office supplies *or* equipment; **~automation** *die* office automation; **~bedarf** *der* office supplies *pl.;* **~fläche** *die* office space; **~gebäude** *das* office building; **~gehilfe** *der* office boy; **~gehilfin** *die* office girl; **~haus** *das* office block; **~hengst** *der* (ugs. abwertend) office clerk; pen-pusher (coll.); **~kauffrau** *die,* **~kaufmann** *der* [qualified] office executive; **~klammer** *die* paper clip; **~kraft** *die* clerical worker

Bürokrat /byro'kra:t/ *der;* ~**en**, ~**en** (abwertend) bureaucrat

Bürokratie /byrokra'ti:/ *die;* ~, ~**n** bureaucracy

Bürokratin *die;* ~, ~**nen** bureaucrat

bürokratisch
[A] *Adj.* bureaucratic
[B] *adv.* bureaucratically

bürokratisieren *tr. V.* bureaucratize

Bürokratismus *der;* ~ (abwertend) bureaucracy

Büro-: **~maschine** *die* office machine; **~material** *das* ▸ **~bedarf**; **~mensch** *der* (ugs.) office clerk; **~schluss**, *~**schluß** *der* [office] closing time; **bei uns ist um 17 h ~schluss** our office closes at 5 o'clock; **nach ~schluss** after the office closes/the offices close; after office hours; **~stunden** *Pl.* office hours; **~tätigkeit** *die* **eine ~tätigkeit** office work; an office job; **Mädchen für leichte ~tätigkeit gesucht** girl required to carry out basic clerical duties; **~turm** *der* high-rise office building; office tower block; **~zeit** *die* office hours *pl.;* **während der ~zeit** during office hours

Bursch /bʊrʃ/ *der;* ~**en**, ~**en** [1] *member of a student fraternity* [2] ▸ **Bursche**

Bürschchen /'bʏrʃçən/ *das;* ~**s**, ~: little fellow; little chap; **ein freches ~:** a cheeky little devil; **sei vorsichtig, mein ~:** be careful, sonny *or* laddie

Bursche /'bʊrʃə/ *der;* ~**n**, ~**n** [1] boy; lad [2] (junger Mann) young man; **die jungen ~n aus dem Dorf** the village youths; **er hält sich für einen ganz tollen ~n** (ugs.) he thinks he's really something; **er ist ein toller ~** (ugs.) he's a reckless devil [3] (abwertend: Kerl) guy (coll.); character; **ein übler ~:** a nasty piece of work (coll.) [4] (ugs.: Prachtexemplar) specimen; **der Hecht, den er gefangen hat, ist ein prächtiger ~:** the pike he caught is a real whopper (coll.) [5] (Milit. hist.) batman; orderly [6] ▸ **Bursch 1**

Burschenschaft *die;* ~, ~**en** students' duelling society

> **Burschenschaft**
>
> A students' duelling society like a fraternity, which was founded in Jena in 1815 to strengthen their patriotic feeling. The tradition was abolished in 1935, but ten years later male students formed a new fraternity, the *Deutsche Burschenschaft*. Most of these generally right-wing social organisations for students are now called *studentische Verbindungen*. There are now also *Verbindungen* for women.

Burschenschafter *der;* ~**s**, ~: member of a/the students' duelling society

burschikos /bʊrʃi'ko:s/
[A] *Adj.* [1] sporty ‹*clothes, look*›; [tom]boyish ‹*behaviour, girl, haircut*› [2] (ungezwungen) casual ‹*comment, behaviour, etc.*›
[B] *adv.* [1] [tom]boyishly; **sich ~ benehmen** behave like a [tom]boy [2] (ungezwungen) in a colloquial way

Burschikosität /bʊrʃikozi'tɛ:t/ *die;* ~, ~**en** ▸ **burschikos A**: sportiness; [tom]boyishness; casualness

Burse /'bʊrzə/ *die;* ~, ~**n** (hist.) hostel (*for students and journeymen*)

Bürste /'bʏrstə/ *die;* ~, ~**n** [1] brush [2] (Haarschnitt) crew cut [3] (Elektrot.) brush

bürsten *tr. V.* [1] brush [2] (vulg.: koitieren) screw (coarse)

Bürsten-: **~abzug** *der* (Druckw.) brush proof; **~binder** *der:* in **trinken** (ugs.) *od.* (salopp) **saufen wie ein ~binder** drink like a fish; **~macher** *der,* **~macherin** *die* broom-and brushmaker; **~schnitt** *der* crew cut

Bürzel /'bʏrtsl̩/ *der;* ~**s**, ~ [1] (Zool.) rump [2] (Jägerspr.) tail

Bus /bʊs/ *der;* ~**ses**, ~**se** (auch DV) bus; (Privat- und Reisebus auch) coach

Bus·bahn·hof *der* bus station; (für Reisebusse auch) coach station

Busch /bʊʃ/ *der;* ~**[e]s**, **Büsche** /'bʏʃə/ [1] bush; (fig.) **auf den ~ klopfen** (ugs.) sound things out; **bei jmdm. auf den ~ klopfen** (ugs.) sound sb. out; **mit etw. hinterm ~ halten** (ugs.) keep sth. to oneself; **es ist etw. im ~** (ugs.) something's up; **sich [seitwärts] in die Büsche schlagen** (ugs.) slip away [2] (Geogr.) bush [3] (ugs.: Urwald) jungle; **aus dem ~ kommen** have come from the backwoods *pl.* [4] (Strauß) bunch [5] (Büschel) tuft; **ein ~ Haare/Federn** a tuft of hair/feathers

Busch·bohne *die* dwarf bean

Büschel /'bʏʃl̩/ *das;* ~**s**, ~ (von Haaren, Federn, Gras usw.) tuft; (von Heu, Stroh) handful; **ein ~ Federn** a tuft of feathers

büschel·weise *Adv.* ▸ **Büschel**: in tufts/in handfuls; **~ Unkraut** whole clumps of weeds

Buschen *der;* ~**s**, ~ (südd., österr. ugs.) **ein ~ [Blumen/Zweige]** a bunch [of flowers]/bundle [of twigs]; **einen ~ über die Tür hängen** hang a bundle of twigs above the door

Buschen·schenke *die* (österr.) ▸ **Strauß·wirtschaft**

buschig *Adj.* bushy; **~e Rosen** rose bushes

Busch-: **~mann** *der* Bushman; **~mann·frau** *die* Bushman woman; **~messer** *das* machete; **~werk** *das* bushes *pl.;* **~wind·röschen** *das* wood anemone

Busen /'bu:zn̩/ *der;* ~**s**, ~ [1] bust; **sie hat wenig ~** (ugs.) she has very little bosom; **in dem Film wurde viel ~ gezeigt** (ugs.) in this film there was plenty of bosom on display; **eine Schlange** *od.* **Natter an seinem ~ nähren** (veralt.) nourish a viper in one's bosom (literary) [2] (dichter. veralt.: Brust) bosom; breast; **am ~ der Natur** (fig. scherzh.) in the bosom of nature [3] (dichter. veralt.: Inneres) bosom; heart [4] (dichter. veralt.: Mieder) bodice; bosom

busen-, **Busen-:** **~frei** *Adj.* topless; **~freund** *der,* **~freundin** *die* (oft iron.) bosom friend; **~star** *der* (ugs.) sex symbol

Bus-: **~fahrer** *der,* **~fahrerin** *die* ▸❶ **S. 113** bus driver; (von Reisebussen auch) coach driver; **~halte·stelle** *die* bus stop; (von Reisebussen auch) coach stop

Business /'bɪznɪs/ *das;* ~ [1] (abwertend: vom Profitdenken bestimmtes Geschäft) business; (Handel) trade [2] (Geschäftsleben) business; [3] (Business-Class) business; **~ fliegen** fly business class

Business·plan *der* business plan

Bus·linie *die* bus route; **mein Haus liegt an der ~ 7** my house is on the number 7 bus route

Bussard /'bʊsart/ *der;* ~**s**, ~**e** (Zool.) buzzard

Buße /'bu:sə/ *die;* ~, ~**n** [1] (Rel.) penance *no art.;* **~ tun** (veralt.) do penance [2] (Reue) repentance [3] (Rechtsw.) damages *pl.* [4] (schweiz. Rechtsspr.: Geldstrafe) fine

Bussel /'bʊsl̩/ *das;* ~**s**, ~**[n]** ▸ **Busserl**

busseln ▸ **busserln**

büßen /'by:sn̩/
[A] *tr. V.* [1] (Rel.: sühnen) atone for; expiate [2] (bestraft werden für) atone for; **das sollst du mir ~:** you'll pay for that [3] (fig.: bezahlen) pay for
[B] *itr. V.* [1] (Rel.) **für etw. ~:** atone for *or* expiate sth. [2] (bestraft werden) suffer [3] (fig.: bezahlen) pay

Büßer *der;* ~**s**, ~ (Rel.) penitent

Büßer-: **~gewand** *das,* **~hemd** *das* penitential robe; **sich im ~hemd zeigen, im ~hemd erscheinen** (fig.) show repentance

Büßerin *die;* ~, ~**nen** (Rel.) penitent

Busserl /'bʊsɐl/ *das;* ~**s**, ~**[n]** (südd., österr. ugs.) kiss

busserln *tr., itr. V.* (südd., österr. ugs.) kiss

buß-, **Buß-:** **~feier** *die* (kath. Rel.) ▸ **~gottes·dienst**; **~fertig** (Rel.) [A] *Adj.* penitent; (fig.) repentant; [B] *adv.* penitently; **~fertigkeit** *die* (Rel.) penitence; (fig.) repentance; **~gang** *der* (geh.) **einen ~gang antreten** *od.* **machen** go to to beg for forgiveness; **~gebet** *das* (Rel.) prayer of repentance *or* penitence; **~geld** *das* (Rechtsw.) fine; **~geld·bescheid** *der* official demand for payment of a fine; **einen ~geldbescheid bekommen** be fined (**von** by); **~gesang** *der* (Rel.) hymn of repentance; **~gottes·dienst** *der* (kath. Rel.) service of confession and general absolution

Bussi /'bʊsi/ *das;* ~**s**, ~**s** (ugs.) kiss

Bussi-Bussi /'bʊsi'bʊsi/ *das;* ~**s**, ~**s** (ugs., bes. österr., südd.) kisses *pl.* on both cheeks

Bussole /bʊ'so:lə/ *die;* ~, ~**n** compass; (Elektrot.) galvanometer

Buß-: **~prediger** *der,* **~predigerin** *die* repentance preacher; **~predigt** *die* sermon calling to repentance; **~sakrament** *das* (Rel.) sacrament of penance; **~tag** *der* [1] (kath. Rel.) day of repentance; [2] ▸ **~- und Bettag**; **~- und Bettag** *der* (ev. Kirche) Wednesday eleven days before Advent (*as day of penance*)

Büsten·halter *der* bra; brassiere (formal)

Bus-: **~verbindung** *die* [1] (Linie) bus service; [2] (Anschluss) bus connection; (für Reisebusse auch) coach connection; **~verkehr** *der* bus service; (von Fernreisebussen auch) coach service

Butan /bu'ta:n/ *das;* ~**s**, ~**e** (Chemie) butane

Butan·gas *das* butane gas

Butt /bʊt/ *der;* ~**[e]s**, ~**e** flounder; butt

Bütt /bʏt/ *die;* ~, ~**en** speaker's platform; [carnival] soapbox; **in der ~ stehen** stand on the platform *or* soapbox; **in die ~ steigen** take the platform; get up on the soapbox

Butte *die;* ~, ~**n** [1] (südd., österr., schweiz.) ▸ **Bütte** [2] (Winzerspr.) dosser; pannier

Bütte *die;* ~, ~**n** [1] tub [2] (Papierherstellung) vat

Büttel /'bʏtl̩/ *der;* ~**s**, ~ [1] (abwertend) lackey [2] (veralt.: Häscher) bailiff [3] (geh. abwertend: Polizist) minion of the law

Bütten *das;* ~**s** ▸ **~papier**

Bütten-: **~papier** *das* handmade paper (*with deckle edge*); **~rand** *der* deckle edge; **~rede** *die* carnival speech; **~redner** *der,* **~rednerin** *die* carnival speaker

Butter /'bʊtɐ/ *die;* ~: butter; **gute ~** (veralt.) butter; **[es ist] alles in ~** (ugs.) everything's fine; **sie lässt sich** (*Dat.*) **nicht die ~ vom Brot nehmen** (ugs.) she doesn't let anyone put one over on her; **jmdm. die ~ aufs** *od.* **auf dem Brot nicht gönnen** (ugs.) begrudge sb. everything

Butter-: **~bemme** *die* (ostmd.) ▸ **~brot**; **~berg** *der* (ugs.) butter mountain; **~blume** *die* (Löwenzahn) dandelion; (Sumpfdotterblume) marsh marigold; (Hahnenfuß) buttercup; **~brot** *das* piece *or* slice of bread and butter; (zugeklappt) sandwich; **ein ~brot mit Schinken** a slice of bread and butter with ham on it/a ham sandwich; **für ein ~brot** (ugs.) for next to nothing; ‹*buy, sell*› for a song; **musst du mir ständig aufs ~brot streichen** *od.* **schmieren, dass ...?** (ugs.) do you have to keep rubbing it in that ...?; **~brot·papier** *das* greaseproof paper; **~creme** *die* buttercream; **~creme·torte** *die* buttercream cake; **~dose** *die* butter dish; **~fahrt** *die* (ugs.) sea trip to buy duty-free goods; **~fass**, ***~faß** *das* [butter] churn; **~fett** *das* butterfat; **~flöckchen** *das* flake of butter

Butterfly /ˈbatəflai/ *der;* **~s** 1 (Schwimmen) butterfly [stroke] 2 (Eiskunstlauf) split jump

butter·gelb *Adj.* butter yellow

butterig *Adj.* buttery

Butter-: ~käse *der* rich creamy cheese; **~keks** *der* butter biscuit; **~krem** *die* (ugs. auch:) *der* ▸**~creme**; **~messer** *das* butter knife; **~milch** *die* buttermilk

buttern

A *itr. V.* make butter

B *tr. V.* 1 butter; grease ‹*baking tray*› with butter 2 (ugs.: aufwenden) put (**in** + *Akk.* into)

butter-, Butter-: ~pilz *der* boletus lutens; **~säure** *die* (Chemie) butyric acid; **~schmalz** *das* clarified butter; **~stulle** *die* (nordd., bes. berlin.) ▸**~brot**; **~teig** *der* short pastry [made with butter]; **~weich**

A *Adj.* 1 beautifully soft; **eine ~weiche Landung** (fig.) a [really] soft landing; 2 (ohne Festigkeit) vague ‹*agreement, promise*›; **wenn man ihm schmeichelt, wird er ~weich** if you flatter him, he's like putty in your hands; 3 (Sportjargon) gentle ‹*shot, pass*›; B *adv.* 1 gently; **die Maschine landete ~weich** the machine landed gently; 2 (Sportjargon) gently

Buttje /ˈbʊtjə/ *der;* **~s, ~s, Buttjer** /ˈbʊtjɐ/ *der;* **~s, ~s** (nordd.) kid (coll.)

Büttner /ˈbʏtnɐ/ *der;* **~s, ~, Büttnerin** *die;* **~, ~nen** ▸**Böttcher**

Button /batn̩/ *der;* **~s, ~s** badge

Button-down-Kragen /batn̩ˈdaun-/ *der* button-down collar

buttrig ▸**butterig**

Butze·mann *der* (fam.) bogyman

bützen /ˈbʏtsn̩/ *tr., itr. V.* (rhein.) kiss

Butzen·scheibe *die* bullseye pane

Büx /bʏks/ *die;* **~, ~en, Buxe** /ˈbʊksə/ *die;* **~e, ~en** (nordd.) trousers *pl.*; pants *pl.* (Amer.); **zwei ~en** *od.* **Buxen** two pairs of trousers *or* (Amer.) pants

Buxtehude /bʊkstəˈhuːdə/ *in* **in/aus/nach ~** (fig. ugs.) at/from/to the back of beyond

Buy-out /ˈbaiaut/ *das;* **~s, ~s** (Wirtsch.) buyout

Buzzer /ˈbazɐ/ *der;* **~s, ~:** buzzer

BV *Abk.* (schweiz.) **= Bundesversammlung**

BVG *Abk.* 1 **= Bundesverwaltungsgericht** 2 **= Bundesverfassungsgericht** 3 **= Betriebsverfassungsgesetz**

b.w. *Abk.* **= bitte wenden** P.T.O.

BWL *Abk.* ▸**Betriebswirtschaftslehre**

Bypass /ˈbaipɑs/ *der;* **~es, Bypässe** (Med.) bypass

Byte /bait/ *das;* **~s, ~[s]** (DV) byte

Byzantiner /bʏtsanˈtiːnɐ/ *der;* **~s, ~, Byzantinerin** *die;* **~, ~nen** Byzantine

byzantinisch *Adj.* Byzantine; **das Byzantinische Reich** the Byzantine Empire

Byzantinismus *der;* **~** (geh. abwertend) obsequiousness; sycophancy

Byzantinistik *die;* **~:** Byzantine studies *pl.*, *no art.*

Byzanz /bʏˈtsants/ *(das);* **~':** Byzantium

bzgl. *Abk.* **= bezüglich**

bzw. *Abk.* **= beziehungsweise**

b

Cc

c, C /t͜seː/ *das;* ~, ~ 1 (Buchstabe) c/C 2 (Musik) [key of] C; *s. auch* **a, A**
C *Abk.* = **Celsius** C
ca. *Abk.* = **cirka** c.
Cabaret /kabaˈreː/ ▸ **Kabarett**
Cabrio ▸ **Kabrio**
Cabriolet /kabrioˈleː/ ▸ **Kabriolett**
Cache /kɛʃ/ *der;* ~, ~**s** (DV) cache
cachieren ▸ **kaschieren**
Café /kaˈfeː/ *das;* ~**s,** ~**s** café; **ins** ~ **gehen** go to a/the café
Cafeteria /kafetəˈriːa/ *die;* ~, ~**s** cafeteria
cal *Abk.* = **[Gramm]kalorie** cal.
Calcium ▸ **Kalzium**
Call /kɔːl/ *der;* ~**s,** ~**s** (Börsenw.) call [option]
Call·boy /ˈkɔːl.../ *der;* ~**s,** ~**s** call boy
Callgirl /ˈkɔːlgəːl/ *das;* ~**s,** ~**s** call girl
Callgirl·ring *der* call-girl ring
Calvados /kalvaˈdoːs/ *der;* ~, ~**:** calvados
calvinistisch ▸ **kalvinistisch**
Calypso /kaˈlɪpso/ *der;* ~**s,** ~**s** calypso
Camcorder /ˈkamkɔrdɐ/ *der;* ~**s,** ~ ▸ **Kamerarecorder**
Camembert /ˈkaməmbeːɐ̯/ *der;* ~**s,** ~**s** Camembert
Camion /ˈkamiõ̯/ *der;* ~**s,** ~**s** (schweiz.) lorry (Brit.); truck (Amer.)
Camouflage /kamuˈflaːʒə/ *die;* ~, ~**n** (bes. Milit.; veralt.) camouflage
camouflieren *tr. V.* (veralt.) camouflage
Camp /kɛmp/ *das;* ~**s,** ~**s** camp
campen /ˈkɛmpn̩/ *itr. V.* camp
Camper *der;* ~**s,** ~, **Camperin** *die;* ~, ~**nen** camper
Camping /ˈkɛmpɪŋ/ *das;* ~**s** camping; **zum** ~ **[nach X] fahren** go camping [in X]
Camping-: ~**ausrüstung** *die* camping equipment; ~**beutel** *der* duffle bag; ~**bus** *der* motor caravan; camper; ~**führer** *der* camping guide[book]; ~**kocher** *der* camping stove; ~**platz** *der* campsite; campground (Amer.); ~**stuhl** *der* [folding] camp chair; ~**tisch** *der* [folding] camp table
Campus /ˈkampʊs/ *der;* ~ (Hochschulw.) campus
Canaille ▸ **Kanaille**
Canasta /kaˈnasta/ *das;* ~**s** canasta
Cancan /kãˈkãː/ *der;* ~**s,** ~**s** cancan
Candela /kanˈdeːla/ *die;* ~, ~ (Physik) candela
Candle-Light-Dinner /ˈkɛndl̩lai̯t-/ *das* candlelit dinner
Cannabis /ˈkanabɪs/ *der;* ~**:** cannabis
Cannelloni /kanɛˈloːni/ *Pl.* cannelloni
Cañon /ˈkanjɔn/ *der;* ~**s,** ~**s** canyon
Canossa ▸ **Kanossa**
Cantilever·bremse /ˈkɛntɪliːvɐ/ *die* cantilever brake
Canto /ˈkanto/ *der;* ~**s,** ~**s** (Literaturw.) canto
Cantus /ˈkantʊs/ *der;* ~, ~ (Musik) cantus; principal *or* melody voice
Cape /keːp/ *das;* ~**s,** ~**s** cape
Cappuccino /kapʊˈtʃiːno/ *der;* ~**s,** ~**[s]** cappuccino
Capriccio /kaˈprɪt͜ʃo/ *das;* ~**s,** ~**s** (Musik) capriccio
Car /kaːɐ̯/ *der;* ~**s,** ~**s** (schweiz.) coach
Caravan /ˈka(ː)ravan/ *der;* ~**s,** ~**s** 1 (Kombi) estate car; station wagon (Amer.) 2 (Wohnwagen) caravan; trailer (Amer.)
Carbid ▸ **Karbid**
Cargo ▸ **Kargo**
Caritas /ˈkaːritas/ *die;* ~**:** Caritas (*Catholic welfare organization*); **ich bin doch nicht von der** ~**!** (ugs.) I'm not a charitable institution!
Carnet [de Passages] /karˈnɛ (də paˈsaːʒə)/ *das;* ~ **[**~**],** ~**s [**~**]** /karˈnɛ (də paˈsaːʒə)/ (Verkehrsw.) carnet
cartesianisch /karteˈzi̯aːnɪʃ/ *Adj.* Cartesian
Cartoon /karˈtuːn/ *der od. das;* ~**s,** ~**s** cartoon
carven /ˈkaːvn̩/ *itr. V.; mit sein* (Skifahren) carve
Carving /ˈkaːvɪŋ/ *das;* ~**[s]** (Skifahren) carving
Carving·ski *der* carving ski
Casanova /kazaˈnoːva/ *der;* ~**s,** ~**s** Casanova
Cäsar /ˈt͜sɛːzar/ *(der)* Caesar
Cäsaren- /t͜sɛˈzaːrən-/: ~**herrschaft** *die* dictatorship; ~**wahn·sinn** *der* [dictatorial] megalomania
Cäsarismus /t͜sɛzaˈrɪsmʊs/ *der;* ~**:** Caesarism; absolutism
Cäsaropapismus /t͜sɛzaropaˈpɪsmʊs/ *der;* ~**:** Caesaropapism *no art.*
Cashew·nuss, *Cashew·nuß /ˈkɛʃu-/ *die* cashew nut
Cashflow /kɛʃˈfloʊ/ *der;* ~**s** (Wirtsch.) [gross] cash flow
Casino ▸ **Kasino**
Cassata /kaˈsaːta/ *die od. das;* ~, ~**s** cassata
Cassette ▸ **Kassette**
casten /ˈkaːstn̩/ *tr. u. itr. V.* (Film, Ferns.) cast
Casting /ˈkaːstɪŋ/ *das;* ~**s,** ~**s** casting
Catch-as-catch-can /ˈkɛt͜ʃəzˈkɛt͜ʃˈkɛn/ *das;* ~**:** catch-as-catch-can; all-in wrestling
catchen /ˈkɛt͜ʃn̩/ *itr. V.* do all-in wrestling; **das Catchen** all-in wrestling
Catcher /ˈkɛt͜ʃɐ/ *der;* ~**s,** ~, **Catcherin** *die;* ~, ~**nen** all-in wrestler
Caterer /ˈkeɪtərɐ/ *der;* ~**s,** ~**:** caterer
Catsuit /ˈkɛtsjuːt/ *der;* ~**s,** ~**s** catsuit
Cayenne·pfeffer /kaˈjɛn-/ *der* cayenne [pepper]
CB-Funk /t͜seːˈbeː-/ *der;* ~**s** (Nachrichtent.) CB radio
cbm *Abk.* (veralt.) = **Kubikmeter** m³
ccm *Abk.* (veralt.) = **Kubikzentimeter** c.c.
CD /t͜seːˈdeː/ *die;* ~, ~**s** CD
CD-Brenner *der;* ~**s,** ~ (DV) CD burner; CD writer
CD-R *die;* ~, ~**s** (DV) CD-R
CD-ROM /t͜sedeˈrɔm/ *die;* ~, ~**[s]** (DV) CD-ROM
CD-ROM-Lauf·werk *das* (DV) CD-ROM drive
CD-RW *die;* ~, ~**s** (DV) CD-RW
CD-Spieler *der* CD player
CDU *Abk.* = **Christlich-Demokratische Union [Deutschlands]** [German] Christian Democratic Party

> **CDU — Christlich-Demokratische Union**
>
> One of the main German political parties. It was founded in 1945 and is committed to Christian and conservative values. The *CDU* is not active in Bavaria. See also **CSU**.

C-Dur /ˈt͜seː-/ *das* C major; *s. auch* **A-Dur**
C-Dur-Dreiklang *der* C major triad
Cedille /seˈdiːj(ə)/ *die;* ~, ~**n** (Sprachw.) cedilla
Cellist /t͜ʃɛˈlɪst/ *der;* ~**en,** ~**en, Cellistin** *die;* ~, ~**nen** ▸ **i S. 113** cellist; *s. auch* **-in**
Cello /ˈt͜ʃɛlo/ *das;* ~**s,** ~**s** *od.* **Celli** cello
Cello·konzert *das* cello concerto
Cellophan (Wz) *das;* ~**s, Cellophane** (Wz) /t͜seloˈfaːn(ə)/ *die;* ~**:** Cellophane ®
Celsius /ˈt͜sɛlzi̯ʊs/ ▸ **i S. 703** centigrade; Celsius (Phys.)
Celsius·skala *die* Celsius *or* centigrade scale
Cembalo /ˈt͜ʃɛmbalo/ *das;* ~**s,** ~**s** *od.* **Cembali** harpsichord
Cent /t͜sɛnt/ *der;* ~**s,** ~**[s]** ▸ **i S. 299** cent; **es kostet 50** ~**:** it costs 50 cents; **hast du ein paar einzelne** ~**s?** have you any single cent pieces?; **eine Briefmarke zu 60** ~**:** a 60 cent stamp; **es ist keinen** ~ **wert** (ugs.) it isn't worth a penny *or* (Amer.) a [red] cent; **bis auf den letzten** ~**:** down to the last penny *or* (Amer.) cent; **auf den** ~ **genau** correct to the last penny *or* (Amer.) cent; **auf den** ~ **sehen** look at *or* watch every penny *or* (Amer.) cent
Center /ˈsɛntɐ/ *das;* ~**s,** ~ 1 (Großmarkt) centre 2 (Einkaufszentrum) shopping centre *or* (Amer.) mall
Centime /sãˈtiːm/ *der;* ~**s,** ~**s** ▸ **i S. 299** centime
Ceran·kochfeld (Wz) /t͜seˈraːn-/ *das* Ceran ® hob (*type of ceramic hob*)
Cercle /ˈsɛrkl̩/ *der;* ~**s,** ~**s** 1 ~ **halten** (veralt.) hold court 2 (österr.: im Theater) front stalls *pl.*
Cervelat /ˈsɛrvəla/ *der;* ~**s,** ~**s** (schweiz.) cervelat [sausage]
ces, Ces /t͜sɛs/ *das;* ~ (Musik) C flat
Ces-Dur *das* C flat major; *s. auch* **A-Dur**
Ceylon /ˈt͜sai̯lɔn/ *(das);* ~**s** (hist.) Ceylon (Hist.)
Ceylonese *der;* ~**n,** ~**n, Ceylonesin** *die;* ~, ~**nen** (hist.) Ceylonese
cf. *Abk.* = **conferatur** cf.
C-Flöte /ˈt͜seː-/ *die* soprano recorder
Cha-Cha-Cha /ˈt͜ʃa ˈt͜ʃa ˈt͜ʃa/ *der;* ~**s,** ~**s** cha-cha-cha
Chaise /ˈʃɛːzə/ *die;* ~, ~**n** 1 (veralt.: Kutsche) [closed] chaise 2 (ugs. abwertend: Auto) jalopy; banger (Brit. sl.)
Chaiselongue /ʃɛzəˈlõːk/ *die;* ~, ~**n** *od.* ~**s** chaise longue
Chalet /ʃaˈleː/ *das;* ~**s,** ~**s** 1 Alpine [cowherd's] hut 2 (Landhaus) [Swiss] chalet
Chamäleon /kaˈmɛːleɔn/ *das;* ~**s,** ~**s** (auch fig.) chameleon
Chamois /ʃaˈmo̯a/ *das;* ~ 1 (Farbe) chamois; parchment [colour] 2 ▸ ~**leder**
Chamois·leder *das* chamois [leather]

Champagner /ʃamˈpanjɐ/ *der;* **~s, ~:** champagne (from Champagne)

champagner·farben *Adj.* champagne-coloured

Champagner·laune *die* festive mood

Champignon /ˈʃampɪnjɔn/ *der;* **~s, ~s** mushroom

Champion /ˈtʃɛmpi̯ən/ *der;* **~s, ~s** (Sport) champion; (Mannschaft) champions *pl.*

Chance /ˈʃãːsə/ *die;* **~, ~n** **1▸** (Gelegenheit) chance; **eine ~/keine ~/mehr ~n haben, etw. zu tun** have a chance/no chance/more chance of doing sth.; **die ~n [zu gewinnen] stehen eins zu hundert** the chances [of winning] are one in a hundred; (bes. beim Wetten) the odds [against winning] are 100:1 *or* a hundred to one; **ich gebe dir eine letzte ~:** I'll give you one last chance; **eine/keine ~ sehen, zu …** see a/no chance *or* hope of …; **sie rechnen sich** (*Dat.*) **eine ~ aus, 2 Punkte zu machen** they reckon they have a chance of scoring 2 points; **~n/eine ~ vergeben** (Sport) give away chances/a chance **2▸** *Pl.* (Aussichten) prospects; **seine ~n stehen gut/schlecht** his prospects are good/poor; **[bei jmdm] ~n haben** stand a chance [with sb.]

Chancen·gleichheit *die* (Päd., Soziol.) equality of opportunity *no art.*

chancen·los *Adj.* with no chance *postpos.*; **~ sein** have no chance

changieren /ʃãˈʒiːrən/ *itr. V.* shimmer (in different colours); iridesce; **~d** iridescent; **~de Seide** shot silk

Chanson /ʃãˈsõː/ *das;* **~s, ~s** chanson; cabaret-style song

Chansonette, Chansonnette /ʃãsɔˈnɛtə/ *die;* **~, ~n** chanteuse; (im Kabarett) cabaret singer

Chansonnier /ʃãsɔˈni̯eː/ *der;* **~s, ~s** singer/composer of chansons; chansonnier

Chansonniere /ʃãsɔˈni̯eːrə/ *die;* **~, ~n** singer/composer of chansons; chansonnière

Chanteuse /ʃãˈtøːzə/ *die;* **~, ~en** chanteuse

Chaos /ˈkaːɔs/ *das;* **~:** chaos *no art.*; **in der Wohnung herrschte ein einziges ~:** the flat (esp. Brit.) *or* (esp. Amer.) apartment was in total chaos

Chaos·theorie *die* (Physik) chaos theory

Chaot /kaˈoːt/ *der;* **~en, ~en, Chaotin** *die;* **~, ~nen** **1▸** (Politik) anarchist (trying to undermine society); (bei Demonstrationen) violent demonstrator **2▸** (salopp: unordentlicher Mensch) **ein [furchtbarer] Chaot sein** be [terribly] disorganized

chaotisch
A *Adj.* chaotic
B *adv.* chaotically; **es geht ~ zu** there is chaos

Chapeau claque /ʃapoˈklak/ *der;* **~ ~, ~x ~s** /ʃapoˈklak/ opera hat

Charade ▸ **Scharade**

Charakter /kaˈraktɐ/ *der;* **~s, ~e** /-ˈteːrə/ **1▸** character; personality; **etw. prägt** *od.* **formt den ~:** sth. moulds one's character *or* is character-forming; **die seinen ~ prägenden** *od.* **formenden Jahre** his formative years; **Geld verdirbt den ~:** money spoils people; **sie hat einen schwierigen/ist ein schwieriger ~:** she has/is a complex personality; **gegensätzliche ~e haben/sein** have entirely different personalities/be quite different in personality *or* character; **er ist ein mieser ~** (ugs.) he's a lousy so-and-so (coll.) **2▸** (**~stärke**) [strength of] character; **keinen ~ haben** lack [strength of] character; be spineless **3▸** (Eigenart) character; **die Mitteilung hat vertraulichen ~:** the communication is of a confidential nature

charakter-, Charakter-: ~an·lage *die* trait; **gute/schlechte ~anlagen haben** have good/bad qualities *or* a good/bad disposition; **~bild** *das* profile; **~bildend** *Adj.* character-forming; **~bildung** *die* formation of character; **jmds. ~bildung** the formation of sb.'s character; **~darsteller** *der* actor of complex parts; **~darstellerin** *die* actress of complex parts; **~eigenschaft** *die* characteristic; trait; **~fehler** *der* fault [of character]; **~fest** *Adj.* steadfast; **~festigkeit** *die* firmness *or* strength of character

charakterisieren *tr. V.* characterize

Charakterisierung *die;* **~, ~en** characterization; (Schilderung) portrayal

Charakteristik *die;* **~, ~en** characterization

Charakteristikum *das;* **~s, Charakteristika** (geh.) characteristic (+ *Gen. od.* **für** of)

charakteristisch
A *Adj.* characteristic, typical (**für** of)
B *adv.* characteristically; in a typical manner

charakteristischerweise *Adv.* characteristically [for him/her]

Charakter·kopf *der* striking head; **ein ~ sein** have a magnificent *or* striking head

charakterlich
A *Adj.* character *attrib.* ‹*defect, development, training*›; personal ‹*qualities*›; **~e Veränderungen** personality changes
B *adv.* in [respect of] character; **jmdn. ~ formen** mould sb.'s character; (schulen) give sb. character-training

charakter·los
A *Adj.* unprincipled; characterless, colourless ‹*style, playing, townscape*›; (niederträchtig) despicable; (labil) spineless
B *adv.* in an unprincipled fashion; (ohne Ausdruck) colourlessly; drearily; (niederträchtig) despicably; (labil) spinelessly

Charakterlosigkeit *die;* **~, ~en** **1▸** lack of principle; (Niederträchtigkeit) despicableness; (Labilität) weakness of character; spinelessness **2▸** (Handlung) unprincipled/despicable action; (Äußerung) unprincipled/despicable remark

Charakterologie /karakteroloˈgiː/ *die;* **~:** characterology *no art.*

charakter-, Charakter-: ~rolle *die* (Theater) complex part *or* character; **~schwach** *Adj.* of weak character *postpos.*; spineless; **~schwäche** *die* weakness of character; spinelessness *no pl.*; **~schwein** *das* (ugs. abwertend) unprincipled bastard (coll.); **~stärke** *die* strength of character; (Entschlossenheit) strength of mind; **~studie** *die* character study; **~voll** *Adj.* **1▸** (**~fest**) steadfast; showing strength of character *postpos., not pred.*; **2▸** (ausdrucksvoll) distinctive; ‹*house etc.*› of character; strongly characterized, individual ‹*features*›; **~zug** *der* characteristic

Charge /ˈʃarʒə/ *die;* **~, ~n** **1▸** (bes. Milit.: Dienstgrad, Person) rank; **die unteren ~n** the lower ranks (Mil.)/orders; **die oberen ~n** the upper ranks (Mil.)/echelons **2▸** (Theater: Nebenrolle) small character part

Charisma /ˈçaːrɪsma/ *das;* **~s, Charismen** charisma

charismatisch /çarɪsˈmaːtɪʃ/ *Adj.* charismatic

Charleston /ˈtʃarlstn̩/ *der;* **~, ~s** Charleston

charmant /ʃarˈmant/
A *Adj.* charming; **sich von seiner ~esten Seite zeigen** show one's most attractive side
B *adv.* charmingly; with much charm

Charme /ʃarm/ *der;* **~s** charm; **seinen ganzen ~ spielen lassen** *od.* **aufbieten** turn on all one's charm

Charmeur /ʃarˈmøːɐ̯/ *der;* **~s, ~s** *od.* **~e** charmer

Charmeuse /ʃarˈmøːz/ *die;* **~** (Textilw.) charmeuse

Charta /ˈkarta/ *die;* **~, ~s** (Politik) charter; **~ der Grundrechte** (EU) Charter of Fundamental Rights

Charter /ˈtʃartɐ/ *der;* **~s, ~s** charter agreement

Charter-: ~flug *der* charter flight; **~maschine** *die* chartered aircraft

chartern *tr. V.* charter ‹*aircraft, boat*›; hire [the services of] ‹*guide, firm*›

Charts /tʃarts/ *Pl.* charts

chassidisch /xaˈsiːdɪʃ/ *Adj.* (jüd. Rel.) Hasidic

Chassidismus *der;* **~** (jüd. Rel.) Hasidism *no art.*

Chassis /ʃaˈsiː/ *das;* **~** /ʃaˈsiː(s)/, **~** /ʃaˈsiːs/ (Kfz-W., Elektrot.) chassis

Chat /tʃɛt/ *der* (DV Jargon) chat

Chateaubriand /ʃatobriˈãː/ *das;* **~s, ~s** (Kochk.) Chateaubriand [steak]

Chatroom /ˈtʃɛtruːm/ *der;* **~s, ~s** (DV) chatroom

chatten /ˈtʃɛtn̩/ *itr. V.* (DV Jargon) chat

Chatter /ˈtʃɛtɐ/ *der;* **~s, ~, Chatterin** *die;* **~, ~nen** chat room user

Chauffeur /ʃɔˈføːɐ̯/ *der;* **~s, ~e** ▸ⓘ **S. 113** driver; (privat angestellt) chauffeur

Chauffeuse /ʃɔˈføːzə/ *die;* **~n, ~n,** ▸ⓘ **S. 113** (bes. schweiz.) driver; (privat angestellt) chauffeur; chauffeuse (dated)

chauffieren *tr., itr. V.* (veralt.) drive

Chaussee /ʃoˈseː/ *die;* **~, ~n** (veralt.) (surfaced) [high] road; highway (Amer.)

Chauvi /ˈʃoːvi/ *der;* **~s, ~s** (ugs. abwertend) male chauvinist (coll. derog.)

Chauvinismus /ʃoviˈnɪsmʊs/ *der;* **~:** chauvinism; **männlicher ~:** male chauvinism

Chauvinist *der;* **~en, ~en** (abwertend) chauvinist; (männlicher **~**) male chauvinist

Chauvinistin *die;* **~, ~nen** chauvinist

chauvinistisch (abwertend)
A *Adj.* chauvinistic; (männlich-**~**) male chauvinist
B *adv.* chauvinistically; (männlich-**~**) in a male chauvinist way

Check (schweiz.) ▸ **Scheck**

checken /ˈtʃɛkn̩/ *tr. V.* **1▸** (bes. Technik: kontrollieren) check; examine; **sich [vom Arzt] ~ lassen** (ugs.) have a check-up [from the doctor] **2▸** (salopp: begreifen) twig (coll.); (bemerken) spot; **ich habe das noch nicht gecheckt** I haven't got it yet **3▸** (Eishockey: stoppen) check ‹*player*›

Check·liste *die* checklist; (Passagierliste) passenger list

Check-up /tʃɛk|ˈap/ *der od. das;* **~[s], ~s** check-up

Cheerleader /ˈtʃiːɐ̯liːdɐ/ *der;* **~s, ~[s]** (Sport) cheerleader

Cheerleaderin *die;* **~, ~nen** (Sport) [female] cheerleader

Chef /ʃɛf/ *der;* **~s, ~s** **1▸** (Leiter) (einer Firma, Abteilung, Regierung) head; (der Polizei, des Generalstabs) chief; (einer Partei, Bande) leader; (Vorgesetzter) superior; boss (coll.); **wer ist denn hier der ~?** who's in charge here? **2▸** (salopp: Anrede) **hallo, ~:** hey, chief *or* squire (Brit. coll.); hey mister (Amer. coll.)

Chef- *in Zus.* chief

Chef-: ~arzt *der,* **~ärztin** *die: head of one or more specialist departments in a hospital;* (Direktor[in]) superintendent (*of small hospital*); **~dramaturg** *der,* **~dramaturgin** *die* (Theater) [chief] literary adviser; **~etage** *die* management floor; **Unruhe in den ~etagen auslösen** cause a flutter in the boardrooms; **~ideologe** *der,* **~ideologin** *die* leading ideologist

Chefin *die;* **~, ~nen** **1▸** (Leiterin) (einer Firma, Abteilung, Regierung) head; (einer Partei, Bande) leader; (Vorgesetzte) superior; boss (coll.) **2▸** (ugs.: Frau des Chefs) boss's wife (coll.) **3▸** (salopp: Anrede) missis (coll.); ma'am (Amer.)

Chef-: ~koch *der,* **~köchin** *die* ▸ⓘ **S. 113** chef; head cook; **~redakteur** *der,* **~redakteurin** *die* chief editor; (Verlagsw. auch) managing editor; **~sache** *die* matter for the boss; **er hat das Projekt zu seiner persönlichen ~sache erklärt** he took over the project himself; **~sekretärin** *die* director's secretary; **~visite** *die* senior consultant's round (in the wards)

Chemie /çeˈmiː/ *die;* **~** **1▸** (Wissenschaft) chemistry *no art.* **2▸** (ugs.: Chemikalien) chemicals *pl.*; **der Pudding ist reine ~:** the pudding is nothing but chemicals *or* is purely synthetic

Chemie-: ~arbeiter *der,* **~arbeiterin** *die* chemical worker; **~betrieb** *der* chemical firm; **~faser** *die* synthetic *or* man-made fibre; **~ingenieur** *der,* **~ingenieurin** *die* chemical engineer; **~laborant** *der,* **~laborantin** *die* chemical laboratory assistant; **~werker** *der,* **~werkerin** *die* (ugs.) chemical worker

Chemikalie /çemiˈkaːli̯ə/ *die;* **~, ~n** chemical

C

Chemiker /ˈçeːmikɐ/ *der;* ~**s,** ~, **Chemikerin** *die;* ~, ~**nen** ▸ **S. 113** (graduate) chemist; *s. auch* **-in**

Cheminée /ˈʃmɪne/ *das;* ~**s,** ~**s** (schweiz.) open fireplace

chemisch
A *Adj.* chemical; ~**er Versuch** chemistry experiment; **eine/die ~e Reinigung** a/the dry-cleaner's; (Vorgang) dry-cleaning; **die ~e Keule** Chemical Mace ®
B *adv.* chemically; ~ **bleichen** bleach with chemicals

chemisieren *tr. V.* (DDR) chemicalize; make increased use of chemicals in ‹*agriculture*›

chemo-, Chemo-: ~**techniker** *der,* ~**technikerin** *die* industrial chemist; (Chemieingenieur) chemical engineer; ~**therapeutisch** *Adj.* (Med.) chemotherapeutic; ~**therapie** *die* (Med.) chemotherapy; **mit einer ~therapie beginnen** start a course of chemotherapy

Chenille /ʃəˈnɪljə/ *die;* ~, ~**n** chenille

Cheque /ʃɛk/ ▸ **Scheck**

Cherrybrandy /ˈtʃɛri ˈbrɛndi/ *der;* ~**s,** ~**s** cherry brandy

Cherub /ˈçeːrʊp/ *der;* ~**s, Cherubim** /ˈçeːrubiːm/ *od.* **Cherubinen** /çeːruˈbiːnən/ (Rel.) cherub

cherubinisch *Adj.* cherubic

Chester·käse /ˈtʃɛstɐ-/ *der* (*usu. processed*) Cheddar cheese

chevaleresk /ʃəvaləˈrɛsk/ (geh.)
A *Adj.* chivalrous; gentlemanly
B *adv.* chivalrously

Chevreau·leder /ʃəˈvroː-/ *das* kid

Chianti /ˈki̯anti/ *der;* ~**s,** ~**s** Chianti

Chiasmus /ˈçi̯asmʊs/ *der;* ~ (Rhet.) chiasmus *no art.*

chic *usw.* ▸ **schick** *usw.*

Chicorée /ˈʃikore/ *der;* ~**s** *od. die;* ~**:** chicory

Chiffon /ˈʃɪfõ/ *der;* ~**s,** ~**s** chiffon

Chiffre /ˈʃɪfrə/ *die;* ~, ~**n** 1 (Zeichen) symbol 2 (Geheimzeichen) cipher; ~**n** cipher *sing.*; **in ~n** (*Dat.*) **schreiben** write in code 3 (in Annoncen) box number; **Zuschriften unter ~ …** reply quoting box no. … 4 (Rhet.) cipher

Chiffre·schrift *die* code

chiffrieren *tr. V.* [en]code; **chiffriert** coded; in [a secret] code *postpos.*

Chignon /ʃɪnˈjõː/ *der;* ~**s,** ~**s** chignon

Chihuahua /tʃiˈu̯au̯a/ *der;* ~**s,** ~**s** chihuahua

Chile /ˈtʃiːle, ˈçiːlə/ *(das);* ~**s** Chile

Chilene /tʃiˈleːnə, çiˈleːnə/ *der;* ~**n,** ~**n, Chilenin** *die;* ~, ~**nen** ▸ **S. 520** Chilean; *s. auch* **-in**

chilenisch *Adj.* ▸ **S. 520** Chilean

Chile·salpeter *der* Chile salpeter *or* nitre

Chili /ˈtʃiːli/ *der;* ~**s,** ~**es** 1 *Pl.* (Schoten) chillies 2 (Gewürz) chilli [powder] 3 ▸ **Chilisoße**

Chiliasmus /çiˈli̯asmʊs/ *der;* ~ (christl. Rel.) chiliasm *no art.*

Chili·soße *die* chilli sauce

chillen /ˈtʃɪlən/ *itr. V.* (Jugendspr.) chill out (coll.)

Chimäre /çiːˈmɛːrə/ *die;* ~, ~**n** 1 ▸ **Schimäre** 2 (Biol.) chimera

China /ˈçiːna/ *(das);* ~**s** China

China-: ~**kohl** *der* Chinese cabbage; (im Handel) Chinese leaves *pl.*; ~**kracher** *der* Chinese cracker; ~**papier** *das* rice paper

Chinchilla¹ /tʃɪnˈtʃɪla/ *das;* ~**s,** ~**s** 1 (Pelz) chinchilla 2 (Kaninchen) chinchilla [rabbit]

Chinchilla² *die;* ~, ~**s** (Zool.) chinchilla

Chinese /çiˈneːzə/ *der;* ~**n,** ~**n** ▸ **S. 520** Chinese; **zum ~n essen gehen** (ugs.) eat Chinese (coll.)

Chinesin *die;* ~, ~**nen** ▸ **S. 520** Chinese; *s. auch* **-in**

chinesisch ▸ **S. 520,** ▸ **S. 670**
A *Adj.* Chinese; ~**er Tee** China tea; **die Chinesische Mauer** the Great Wall of China
B *adv.* in the Chinese manner *or* style; ~ **essen** have a Chinese meal; eat Chinese (coll.)

-chinesisch *das;* -~**[s]** … jargon

Chinin /çiˈniːn/ *das;* ~**s** quinine

chinin·haltig *Adj.* containing quinine *postpos., not pred.*; ~ **sein** contain quinine

Chintz /tʃɪnts/ *der;* ~**:** chintz

Chip /tʃɪp/ *der;* ~**s,** ~**s** 1 (Spielmarke) chip 2 (Kartoffel~) [potato] crisp (Brit.) *or* (Amer.) chip 3 (Elektronik) [micro]chip

Chip·karte *die* smart card

Chippendale /ˈtʃɪpəndeɪl/ *das;* ~**[s]** Chippendale

Chiromant /çiroˈmant/ *der;* ~**en,** ~**en** palmist

Chiromantie *die;* ~**:** chiromancy *no art.*; palmistry *no art.*

Chiromantin *die;* ~, ~**nen** ▸ **Chiromant**

Chiropraktik *die;* ~ (Med.) chiropractic *no art.*

Chiropraktiker *der;* ~**s,** ~, **Chiropraktikerin** *die;* ~, ~**nen** ▸ **S. 113** (Med.) chiropractor

Chirurg /çiˈrʊrk/ *der;* ~**en,** ~**en** ▸ **S. 113** surgeon

Chirurgie /çirʊrˈgiː/ *die;* ~, ~**n** 1 (Disziplin) surgery *no art.* 2 (Abteilung) surgical department; (Station) surgical ward; **auf der ~ liegen** be in the surgical ward

Chirurgin *die;* ~, ~**nen** ▸ **S. 113** surgeon; *s. auch* **-in**

chirurgisch
A *Adj.* surgical
B *adv.* (operativ) surgically; by surgery

Chitin /çiˈtiːn/ *das;* ~**s** chitin

Chitin·panzer *der* (Zool.) chitinous exoskeleton

Chlor /kloːɐ̯/ *das;* ~**s** chlorine

Chloral /kloˈraːl/ *das;* ~**s** (Chemie) chloral

Chlorat /kloˈraːt/ *das;* ~**s,** ~**e** (Chemie) chlorate

chloren *tr. V.* chlorinate

chlor·haltig *Adj.* containing chlorine *postpos., not pred.*; ~**/stark ~ sein** contain chlorine/have a high chlorine content

Chlorid /kloˈriːt/ *das;* ~**s,** ~**e** (Chemie) chloride

chlorieren *tr. V.* (Chemie) chlorinate

chlorig *Adj.* ~**e Säure** (Chemie) chlorous acid

Chloroform /kloroˈfɔrm/ *das;* ~**s** chloroform

chloroformieren *tr. V.* chloroform

Chlorophyll /kloroˈfʏl/ *das;* ~**s** (Bot.) chlorophyll

Chlor-: ~**säure** *die* (Chemie) chloric acid; ~**wasser** *das* 1 (ugs.: gechlortes Wasser) chlorinated water; 2 (Chemie) chlorine water; ~**wasser·stoff** *der* (Chemie) hydrogen chloride

Choke /tʃoʊk/ *der;* ~**s,** ~**s, Choker** /tʃoʊkɐ/ *der;* ~**s,** ~ (Kfz-W.) [manual] choke

Cholera /ˈkoːlera/ *die;* ~ ▸ **S. 439** (Med.) cholera

Choleriker /koˈleːrikɐ/ *der;* ~**s,** ~, **Cholerikerin** *die;* ~, ~**nen** 1 choleric type *or* (Psych.) subject; **ein klassischer ~:** a textbook example of the choleric temperament 2 (ugs.: jähzorniger Mensch) irascible person; **ein ~ sein** have a short fuse

cholerisch
A *Adj.* irascible; choleric ‹*temperament*›
B *adv.* irascibly

Cholesterin /çolɛsteˈriːn/ *das;* ~**s** (Med.) cholesterol

Cholesterin·spiegel *der* (Physiol.) cholesterol level

Chor¹ /koːɐ̯/ *der;* ~**[e]s, Chöre** /ˈkøːrə/ 1 choir; (in Oper, Sinfonie) chorus; **im ~ rufen/brüllen** shout/roar in chorus 2 (Komposition; im Theater) chorus

Chor² *der od.* (selten:) *das;* ~**[e]s,** ~**e** *od.* **Chöre** 1 (Altarraum) choir 2 (Empore) choir loft; (mit der Orgel) organ loft

Choral /koˈraːl/ *der;* ~**s, Choräle** /koˈrɛːlə/ 1 (Kirchenlied) chorale 2 (gregorianischer ~) [Gregorian] chant

Choral-: ~**bearbeitung** *die* (Musik) arrangement of a chorale; ~**vor·spiel** *das* (Musik) chorale prelude

Choreograph /koreoˈgraːf/ *der;* ~**en,** ~**en** ▸ **S. 113** choreographer

Choreographie *die;* ~, ~**n** choreography

choreographieren *tr., itr. V.* choreograph

Choreographin *die;* ~, ~**nen** ▸ **S. 113** choreographer; *s. auch* **-in**

choreographisch *Adj.* choreographic

Chor-: ~**frau** *die* (kath. Rel.) canoness; ~**führer** *der,* ~**führerin** *die* (Theater) leader of the chorus; ~**gebet** *das* (kath. Rel.) canonical hour (*as part of divine office*); ~**gestühl** *das* choir stalls *pl.*; ~**herr** *der* (kath. Rel.) canon [regular]

Chorist *der;* ~**en,** ~**en** ▸ **Chorsänger**

Choristin *die;* ~, ~**nen** ▸ **Chorsängerin**

Chor-: ~**knabe** *der* choirboy; chorister; ~**konzert** *das* choral concert; ~**leiter** *der* chorus master; (des Kirchenchors) choirmaster; ~**leiterin** *die* chorus mistress; (eines Kirchenchors) choir mistress; ~**musik** *die* choral music; ~**rock** *der* surplice; ~**sänger** *der,* ~**sängerin** *die* member of the chorus

Chorus /ˈkoːrʊs/ *der;* ~, ~**se** (Jazz) theme

Chose /ˈʃoːzə/ *die;* ~, ~**n** (ugs.) 1 (Angelegenheit) business (derog.) 2 (Gegenstände) stuff; **die ganze ~:** the whole lot (coll.) *or* (coll.) shoot *or* (coll.) caboodle

Chow-Chow /tʃau̯ ˈtʃau̯/ *der;* ~**s,** ~**s** chow

Christ¹ /krɪst/ *der;* ~**en,** ~**en** Christian

Christ² *(der)* (Christus) Christ

christ-, Christ-: ~**baum** *der* 1 (bes. südd.) Christmas tree; **nicht alle auf dem ~baum haben** (ugs.) be dotty (Brit. coll.); be not quite all there (Brit. coll.); be missing some marbles (coll.); 2 (milit. Jargon: Leuchtsignale) target marker [flare]; ~**baum-** ▸ **Weihnachtsbaum-**; ~**demokrat** *der,* ~**demokratin** *die* (Politik) Christian Democrat; ~**demokratisch** (Politik) **A** *Adj.* Christian Democrat; **B** *adv.* in a Christian Democrat manner *or* spirit; ~**demokratisch regiert** governed by Christian Democrats

Christen-: ~**gemeinde** *die* Christian community; ~**glaube[n]** *der* Christian faith

Christenheit *die;* ~**:** Christendom *no art.*; **die ganze ~:** the whole Christian community; all Christians *pl.*

Christen·lehre *die* 1 (christl. Kirchen) [Church] teaching of Christian doctrine 2 (DDR Schulw.) Christian religious instruction

Christentum *das;* ~**s** Christianity *no art.*; (Glaube) Christian faith; **sich zum ~ bekennen** profess the Christian faith; declare oneself a Christian

Christen·verfolgung *die* persecution of Christians

Christ·fest *das* (veralt., noch südd., österr.) ▸ **Weihnachtsfest**

christianisieren /krɪsti̯aniˈziːrən/
A *tr. V.* Christianize; convert to Christianity
B *itr. V.* make conversions to Christianity

Christianisierung *die;* ~**:** Christianization

Christin *die;* ~, ~**nen** Christian; *s. auch* **-in**

christ-, Christ-: ~**katholisch** *Adj.* (schweiz.) ▸ **altkatholisch;** ~**kind** *das* 1 (Jesus) infant Jesus; Christ child; 2 (weihnachtliche Gestalt) Christ child (*as bringer of Christmas gifts*); **er glaubt noch ans ~kind** (fig. iron.) he still believes in Father Christmas; 3 (bes. südd., österr.: Geschenk) Christmas present; ~**kindchen** *das* ▸ ~**kind 1, 2**; ~**kindl** *das;* ~~**s** (südd., österr.) ▸ ~**kind 1, 2, 3**; ~**königs·fest** *das* (kath. Rel.) feast of Christ the King

> **Christkind**
>
> Traditionally, it is *das Christkind* (the Christ child) who brings Christmas presents to children on Christmas Eve. The concept of *der Weihnachtsmann* (Father Christmas or Santa Claus) is relatively new in Germany.

christlich
A *Adj.* Christian; **die ~e Seefahrt** (scherzh.) sea-

faring; **wir stehen um halb neun auf — eine halbwegs ~e Zeit** (ugs. scherzh.) we get up at half-past eight — a more or less civilized time
B *adv.* in a [truly] Christian spirit; **~ leben** live a Christian life; **Kinder ~ erziehen** give children a Christian upbringing; **~ geprägt** imbued with Christian principles

Christlichkeit *die;* ~: Christian spirit

Christ-: ~messe *die* (kath. Rel.) Christmas Mass; **~mette** *die* (kath. Rel.) Christmas Mass; (ev. Rel.) midnight service [on Christmas Eve]; **~nacht** *die* Christmas night

Christoph /ˈkrɪstɔf/ *(der)* Christopher

Christophorus /krɪsˈtoːforʊs/ *(der)*: **der heilige ~**: St Christopher

christ-, Christ-: ~rose *die* Christmas rose; **~sozial** (Politik) **A** *Adj.* Christian Socialist; **B** *adv.* on Christian Socialist lines; **~stollen** *der* [German] Christmas loaf *(with candied fruit, almonds, etc.)*

Christus /ˈkrɪstʊs/ *(der);* ~ *od.* **Christi** Christ; **1000 vor/nach Christi Geburt** 1000 BC/AD 1000

Christus-: ~dorn *der; Pl.* ~~e (Bot.) crown of thorns; **~kopf** *der* (Kunst) head of Christ; **~monogramm** *das* Christogram; chi-rho

Christ-vesper *die* (kath. u. ev. Rel.) Christmas Eve vespers *(with music)*

Chrom /kroːm/ *das;* ~s chromium

Chromatik /kroˈmaːtɪk/ *die;* ~ **1** (Musik) chromaticism **2** (Physik) chromatics *pl.*

chromatisch *Adj.* chromatic

chrom-, Chrom-: ~blitzend *Adj.* gleaming with chrome *postpos.*; **~dioxid-kassette** *die* chrome[-dioxide] cassette; **~gelb** *das* chrome yellow; **~leder** *das* chrome leather; **~nickel-stahl** *der* chrome-nickel steel

Chromosom /kromoˈzoːm/ *das;* ~s, ~en (Biol.) chromosome

Chromosomen-satz *der* (Biol.) chromosome set

Chromosphäre /kromoˈsfɛːrə/ *die* (Astron.) chromosphere

Chrom-stahl *der* chrome steel

Chronik /ˈkroːnɪk/ *die;* ~, ~en chronicle

chronisch
A *Adj.* (Med., auch ugs.) chronic; **an ~em Geldmangel leiden** (ugs.) suffer from a chronic shortage of money
B *adv.* (Med., auch ugs.) chronically

Chronist /kroˈnɪst/ *der;* ~en, ~en ▸ℹ S. 113 chronicler

Chronistik *die;* ~: historiography *no art.*

Chronistin *die;* ~, ~nen ▸ **Chronist**

Chronologie *die;* ~: chronology; **die ~ der Ereignisse** *od.* **des Geschehens** the sequence of events; **[nach] unserer/jüdischer ~**: according to our/the Jewish calendar

chronologisch
A *Adj.* chronological; **~er Fehler** mistake regarding the date
B *adv.* chronologically; in chronological order

Chronometer /kronoˈmeːtɐ/ *das;* ~s, ~: chronometer

chronometrisch
A *Adj.* chronometric
B *adv.* chronometrically

Chrysantheme /kryzanˈteːmə/ *die;* ~, ~n chrysanthemum

Chuzpe /ˈxʊtspə/ *die;* ~ (salopp abwertend) chutzpah; **die ~ haben, etw. zu tun** have the nerve to do sth. (coll.)

CIA /ˈsiːaɪˈeɪ/ *der od. die;* ~: CIA

Cicero *die od.* (schweiz.) *der;* ~, ~ (Druckw.) pica; 12-point type

Cidre /siːdɐ/ *der;* ~s [Normandy/Brittany] cider

Cimbal ▸ **Zimbal**

Cinch-: /ˈsɪntʃ-/ **~buchse** *die* (Elektrot.) cinch socket; **~stecker** *der* (Elektrot.) cinch plug

Cineast /sineˈast/ *der;* ~en, ~en, **Cineastin** *die;* ~, ~nen **1** (Filmschaffende[r]) filmmaker **2** (Kenner[in]) film expert; (Filmfan) film fan

circa ▸ **zirka**

Circe /ˈtsɪrtsə/ *die;* ~, ~n Circe; enchantress

Circulus vitiosus /ˈtsɪrkulʊs viˈtsioːzʊs/ *der;* ~ ~, **Circuli vitiosi** (geh.) vicious circle

Circus ▸ **Zirkus**

cis, Cis /tsɪs/ *das;* ~ (Musik) C sharp

Cis-Dur *das* (Musik) C sharp major; *s. auch* **A-Dur**

cis-Moll *das* (Musik) C sharp minor; *s. auch* **a-Moll**

Citoyen /sitoaˈjɛ̃ː/ *der;* ~s, ~s (politically aware) citizen

City /ˈsɪti/ *die;* ~, ~s city centre

City-ruf *der* area paging service

Clair-obscur /klɛrɔpsˈkyːɐ̯/ *das;* ~[s] (Kunst) chiaroscuro

Clan /klaːn/ *der;* ~s, ~e *od.* ~s **1** (salopp: Interessengemeinschaft) clique **2** (in Schottland; auch salopp: Familie) clan

Clan-chef *der,* **Clan-chefin** *die* tribal leader; (in Schottland, auch ugs.: Familienoberhaupt) head of the clan

Claque /ˈklakə/ *die;* ~: claque; hired applauders *pl.*

Claqueur /klaˈkøːɐ̯/ *der;* ~s, ~e claqueur; hired applauder

Clavicembalo /klaviˈtʃɛmbalo/ *das;* ~s, ~s (Musik) harpsichord

clean /kliːn/ *Adj.* (ugs.) clean (coll.); **~ werden** come off drugs

Clearing /ˈkliːrɪŋ/ *das;* ~s, ~s (Wirtsch.) clearing

clever /ˈklɛvɐ/
A *Adj.* (raffiniert) shrewd; (intelligent, geschickt) clever; smart
B *adv.; s. Adj.*: shrewdly; cleverly; smartly

Cleverness, *Cleverneß /ˈklɛvɐnɛs/ *die;* ~ ▸ **clever A**: shrewdness; cleverness; smartness (Amer.)

Cliché ▸ **Klischee**

Client /ˈklaiənt/ *der;* ~s, ~s (DV) client

Clinch /klɪntʃ/ *der;* ~[e]s **1** (Boxen) clinch; **in den ~ gehen** go into a clinch **2** (ugs.: Auseinandersetzung) conflict; **mit jmdm. im ~ liegen** be locked in dispute with sb.; **[mit jmdm.] in den ~ gehen** start quarrelling *or* wrangling [with sb.]

clinchen *itr. V.* (Boxen) go into a clinch

Clip /klɪp/ *der;* ~s, ~s **1** ▸ **Ohrklipp** **2** (Video~) video

Clipper Ⓦⓩ /ˈklɪpɐ/ *der;* ~s, ~ (veralt.) [long-haul] airliner *(on overseas routes)*

Clique /ˈklɪkə/ *die;* ~, ~n **1** (abwertend: Interessengemeinschaft) clique **2** (Freundeskreis) set; lot (coll.); (größere Gruppe) crowd (coll.); (Jugendliche) gang (coll.); **er gehört mit zur unserer ~**: he's one of our crowd (coll.) *or* lot (coll.)

Cliquen-: ~[un]wesen *das,* **~wirtschaft** *die* (ugs. abwertend) clique system

Clivia /ˈkliːvi̯a/ *die;* ~, **Clivien** (Bot.) clivia

Clochard /klɔˈʃaːr/ *der;* ~s, ~s down-and-out; tramp

Clog /klɔk/ *der;* ~s, ~s clog

Close-up /ˈkloʊs|ap/ *das;* ~[s], ~s close-up

Clou /kluː/ *der;* ~s, ~s (ugs.) main point; (Glanzpunkt) highlight; **der besondere ~**: the really special thing [about it]; **das ist doch gerade der ~**: but that's the great thing about it

Clown /klau̯n/ *der;* ~s, ~s clown; **sich zum ~ machen** make oneself look a fool *or* look ridiculous; **jmdn. zum ~ machen** make a clown of sb.; treat sb. as a clown

Clownerie /klau̯nəˈriː/ *die;* ~, ~n: ~[n] clowning *no pl.*

Clownin /ˈklau̯nɪn/ *die;* ~, ~nen clown; *s. auch* **Clown**

Club ▸ **Klub**

Cluster /ˈklastɐ/ *der;* ~s, ~[s] (Kernphysik, Musik, Sprachw.) cluster

cm *Abk.* ▸ℹ **S. 454 = Zentimeter** cm.

c-Moll /ˈtseː-/ *das* C minor; *s. auch* **a-Moll**

Co. *Abk.* **= Compagnie** Co.

Coach /koʊtʃ/ *der;* ~s, ~s ▸ℹ **S. 113** (Sport) coach; (bes. Fußball: Trainer) manager

coachen /ˈkoʊtʃn/ *tr., itr. V.* (Sport) coach; (Trainer sein) manage

Coaching /ˈkoʊtʃɪŋ/ *das;* ~s coaching

Coca /ˈkoːka/ *das;* ~s, ~s *od. die;* ~, ~s (ugs.) Coke ®

Cockerspaniel /ˈkɔkɐ-/ *der;* ~s, ~s cocker spaniel

Cockpit /ˈkɔkpɪt/ *das;* ~s, ~s cockpit; (bei großen Linienflugzeugen) flight deck

Cocktail /ˈkɔkteɪl/ *der;* ~s, ~s **1** (Getränk; auch Salat usw.) cocktail **2** (Party) cocktail party; (DDR: Empfang) reception

Cocktail-: ~empfang *der* [cocktail] reception; **~kleid** *das* cocktail dress; **~party** *die* cocktail party; **~schürze** *die* hostess apron

Code ▸ **Kode**

Codein ▸ **Kodein**

Codex ▸ **Kodex**

Cœur /køːɐ̯/ *das;* ~[s], ~[s] (Kartenspiel) hearts *pl.*; (einzelne Karte) heart; *s. auch* **Pik²**

Coffeeshop, Coffee-Shop /ˈkɔfiʃɔp/ *der* **1** coffee shop; **2** (Jargon) drug café

cognac /ˈkɔnjak/ *indekl. Adj.* cognac[-coloured]

Cognac Ⓦⓩ *der;* ~s, ~s Cognac

cognac-farben *Adj.* cognac[-coloured]

Coiffeur /koaˈføːɐ̯/ *der;* ~s, ~e, **Coiffeuse** /koaˈføːzə/ *die;* ~, ~n (schweiz., sonst geh.: Friseur/Friseuse) hairdresser; (Schöpfer/Schöpferin von Haarmoden) hairstylist

Coiffure /koaˈfyːɐ̯/ *die;* ~, ~n **1** (geh.: Frisierkunst) hairdressing; (Schöpfung von Haarmoden) hairstyling **2** (schweiz.: Frisiersalon) hairdresser's [salon]

Cola /ˈkoːla/ *das;* ~s, ~s *od. die;* ~, ~s (ugs.) Coke ®

Collage /kɔˈlaːʒə/ *die;* ~, ~n collage; (als Form/Technik) **die ~**: collage

Collie /ˈkɔli/ *der;* ~s, ~s collie

Colloquium ▸ **Kolloquium**

Colonia-kübel /koˈloːni̯a-/ *der* (österr.) dustbin; garbage *or* trash can (Amer.)

Color- /koˈloːɐ̯-/ (Fot.) **~film/~dia/~negativ** colour film/slide/negative

Colt Ⓦⓩ /kɔlt/ *der;* ~s, ~s Colt ® [revolver]

Combo /ˈkɔmbo/ *die;* ~, ~s small (jazz *or* dance) band; combo (sl.)

Come-back /kamˈbɛk/ *das;* ~s, ~s comeback; **ein ~ feiern** stage a comeback

COMECON, Comecon /ˈkɔmekɔn/ *der od. das;* ~: Comecon

Comic /ˈkɔmɪk/ *der;* ~s, ~s **1** comic strip; (Heft) comic **2** (Film) cartoon film

Comic-: ~figur *die* cartoon character; **~film** cartoon film; **~heft** *das* comic; **~held** *der* comic-strip hero; **~serie** *die* cartoon series

Comicstrip /ˈkɔmɪk ˈstrɪp/ *der;* ~[s], ~s comic strip

***Comic strip** /ˈkɔmɪk ˈstrɪp/ *der;* ~ ~[s], ~ ~s comic strip

Community /kɔˈmjuːniti/ *die;* ~, ~s community

Composer /kɔmˈpoːzɐ/ *der;* ~s, ~ (Druckw.) composer

Computer /kɔmˈpjuːtɐ/ *der;* ~s, ~: computer; **über ~** (Akk.) **gehen** *od.* **laufen** be computerized; be done by computer; **auf ~** (Akk.) **umstellen** computerize

computer-, Computer-: ~animation *die* (DV) computer animation; **~an-lage** *die* computer system; **~ausdruck** *der; Pl.* ~~s, ~~e computer printout; **~blitz** *der* (Fot.) computerized [electronic] flash; **~diagnostik** *die* (Med.) computer[-aided] diagnosis; **~gerecht** **A** *Adj.* computer-compatible; **B** *adv.* in computer-compatible form; **~gesteuert** *Adj.* computer-controlled; **~gestützt** *Adj.* computer-assisted

computerisieren *tr. V.* computerize ‹data, system›; (aufbereiten) make ‹data› computer-compatible

C

computer-, Computer-: ~kriminalität *die* computer crime; **~kunst** *die* computerized art; **~linguist** *der*, **~linguistin** *die* ▸ⓘ S. 113 computer linguist; **~linguistik** *die* computer linguistics; **~linguistisch** A *Adj.* computer-linguistic; B *adv.* in terms of computer linguistics; **~netzwerk** *das* (Elektrot.) computer network; **~satz** *der* (Druckw.) computer setting; **~simulation** *die*; (DV) computer simulation; **~spiel** *das* computer game; **~technik** *die* computer technology; **~tomographie** *die* (Med.) 1 (Methode) computer tomography; computed tomography; 2 (Bild) computed tomogram; computer tomogram; **~unterstützt** *Adj.* computer-aided; **~wissenschaftler** *der*, **~wissenschaftlerin** *die* ▸ⓘ S. 113 computer scientist

Comte /kõ:t/ *der*; ~, ~s (*French*) count

Comtesse /kõ'tɛs/ *die*; ~, ~n ▸**Komtess**

Conceptart /'kɔnsɛpt|a:ɐt/ *die*; ~ (Kunstwiss.) concept[ual] art

Concerto grosso /kɔn'tʃɛrto 'grɔso/ *das*; ~ ~, **Concerti grossi** (Musik) concerto grosso

conchieren /kõ'ʃi:rən/ *tr., itr. V.* conche

Concierge /kõ'si̯ɛrʃ/ *der/die*; ~, ~s concierge

Conditio sine qua non /kɔn'di:tsi̯o 'zi:nə 'kva: 'no:n/ *die*; ~ ~ ~ ~ (Philos.) sine qua non

Conférencier /kõferã'si̯e:/ *der*; ~s, ~s compère (Brit.); master of ceremonies

Confiserie ▸**Konfiserie**

Confiteor /kɔn'fi:teɔr/ *das*; ~ (kath. Rel.) Confiteor; general confession

Connaisseur /kɔnɛ'sø:ɐ/ *der*; ~s, ~s (geh.) connoisseur

Connection /kə'nɛkʃn/ *die*; ~, ~s connection

Consommé /kõsɔ'me:/ *die*; ~, ~s *od. das*; ~s, ~s (Kochk.) consommé

Container /kɔn'te:nɐ/ *der*; ~s, ~ 1 container; (für Müll) [refuse] skip; (für Altglas) bottle bank 2 (Wohn~, Büro~) Portakabin ®

Container-: ~bahn·hof *der* container station; **~hafen** *der* container port *or* terminal; **~schiff** *das* container ship; **~verkehr** *der* container traffic *no art.*

Contenance /kõtə'nã:s(ə)/ *die*; ~ (geh.) composure; **die ~ [be]wahren/verlieren** keep/lose one's composure *or* countenance

Content /'kɔntənt/ *der*; ~s, ~s (DV) content

Contergan Ⓦ /kɔntɛr'ga:n/ *das*; ~s thalidomide

Contergan·kind *das* thalidomide child

cool /ku:l/ (ugs.)
A *Adj.* 1 (gelassen) cool; **~ bleiben** keep one's cool (sl.) 2 (gut) cool (coll.); fabulous (coll.) 3 (reell) reliable; (anständig) decent; reasonable
B *adv.* 1 (gelassen) coolly 2 (gut) fabulously (coll.) 3 (anständig) decently; reasonably

Cool·jazz /'ku:l 'dʒɛz *od.* 'jats/ *der*; ~: cool jazz

Coolness /'ku:lnɛs/ *die*; ~ (ugs.) coolness

Copilot, Copilotin ▸**Kopilot**

Copyright /'kɔpirait/ *das*; ~s, ~s copyright

Copyshop /'kɔpiʃɔp/ *der* photocopy[ing] shop; copyshop

coram publico /'ko:ram/ (geh.) in public

Cord /kɔrt/ *der*; ~[e]s, ~e *od.* ~s cord; (~samt) corduroy

Cord-: ~an·zug *der* cord/corduroy suit; **~hose** *die* [pair *sing.* of] corduroy trousers *pl. or* cords *pl.*; **~jeans** *Pl.* corduroy jeans; cords

Cordon bleu /kɔrdõ'blø/ *das*; ~ ~, ~s ~s /kɔrdõ'blø/ (Kochk.) veal escalope cordon bleu

Cord-: ~rock *der* corduroy skirt; **~samt** *der* corduroy

Core /kɔ:/ *das*; ~[s], ~s (Kernphysik) core

Cornedbeef /'kɔ:nd 'bi:f/ *das*; ~s corned beef

Corner /'kɔ:nə/ *der*; ~s, ~ (österr. Fußball) corner [kick]

Cornflakes /'kɔ:nfleɪks/ *Pl.* cornflakes

Cornichon /kɔrni'ʃõ:/ *das*; ~s, ~s [fine-quality] gherkin

Corona ▸**Korona**

Corps ▸**Korps**

Corpus ▸**Korpus**

Corpus Delicti /'kɔrpʊs de'lɪkti/ *das*; ~ ~, **Corpora** /'kɔrpora/ **Delicti** 1 (Rechtsspr.) weapon [used] 2 (meist scherzh.: Beweisstück) piece of incriminating evidence

Corso ▸**Korso**

Cortison ▸**Kortison**

Costa Rica /'kɔsta 'ri:ka/ (*das*); ~s Costa Rica

Costa-Ricaner *der*; ~s, ~, **Costa-Ricanerin** *die*; ~, ~nen Costa Rican

costa-ricanisch *Adj.* Costa Rican

CO-Test /tse'|o:-/ *der* (Kfz-W.) exhaust emission test (*for carbon monoxide content*)

Couch /kautʃ/ *die*; ~, ~s; (schweiz. auch:) *der*; ~s, ~[e]s sofa; **auf die ~ müssen** (fig.) need to see a psychiatrist

Couch-: ~garnitur *die* three-piece suite; **~tisch** *der* coffee table

Couleur /ku'lø:ɐ/ *die*; ~, ~s 1 (Richtung) shade [of opinion]; persuasion; **Politiker jeglicher ~:** politicians of every shade of opinion *or* of every hue 2 (Studentenspr.: Band u. Mütze) fraternity colours *pl.*; **~ tragen** wear one's fraternity's colours

Coulomb /ku'lõ:/ *das*; ~s, ~ (Physik) coulomb

Count-down, Countdown /'kaunt'daun/ *der od. das*; ~s, ~s (Raumf., auch fig.) countdown

Countrymusic /'kantrɪmju:zɪk/ *die*; ~: country music

Coup /ku:/ *der*; ~s, ~s coup; **einen ~ landen** (ugs.) pull off a coup

Coupé /ku'pe:/ *das*; ~s, ~s 1 coupé 2 (österr., sonst veralt.: Abteil) compartment

Couplet /ku'ple:/ *das*; ~s, ~s satirical song (*with refrain*)

Coupon /ku'põ:/ *der*; ~s, ~s 1 (Gutschein) coupon; voucher; (im Café) ticket; (zum Abreißen) counterfoil; **auf** *od.* **für** *od.* **gegen diesen ~ bekommen Sie ...** for this voucher you will receive ... 2 (Finanzw.) [interest] coupon 3 (Stoff) piece; length

Cour /ku:ɐ/ *in* **einer Frau/Dame die ~ machen** *od.* **schneiden** (veralt.) pay court to a woman/lady

Courage /ku'ra:ʒə/ *die*; ~ (ugs.) courage; **im letzten Moment verließ sie die ~:** at the last moment she lost her nerve; *s. auch* **Angst**

couragiert /kura'ʒi:ɐt/
A *Adj.* (mutig) courageous; (beherzt) spirited
B *adv.* ▸A: courageously; spiritedly

Courtage /kʊr'ta:ʒə/ *die*; ~, ~n brokerage; broker's commission

Courtoisie /kʊrtoa'zi:/ *die*; ~, ~n (veralt.) courtesy

Cousin /ku'zɛ̃:/ *der*; ~s, ~s (male) cousin; *s. auch* **Grad 1**

Cousine /ku'zi:nə/ *die*; ~, ~n (female) cousin

Couturier /kutʏ'ri̯e:/ *der*; ~s, ~s couturier

Couvert /ku've:ɐ/ *das*; ~s, ~s 1 ▸**Kuvert** 2 (für Bettdecken) [quilt] cover

Cover /'kavɐ/ *das*; ~s, ~s 1 (von Illustrierten) cover 2 (von Schallplatten) sleeve

Cover·band, Cover-Band *die* cover band

Cover·girl *das* cover girl

covern /'kavɐn/ *tr. V.* cover ‹*song, record*›

Cover·version /'kavə.../ *die* cover [version]

Cowboy /'kaubɔy/ *der*; ~s, ~s cowboy

Cowboy-: ~hut *der* cowboy hat; stetson; **~stiefel** *der* cowboy boot

Cox Orange /'kɔks|orã:ʒə/ *der*; ~ ~, ~ ~: Cox's orange pippin

Crack /krɛk/ *der*; ~s, ~s ace; crack player; (Athlet) crack athlete; **ein ~ im Schwimmen/Radfahren** a crack swimmer/cyclist

Cracker /'krɛkɐ/ *der*; ~s, ~[s] cracker

Crash·kurs /'krɛʃ.../ *der* crash course

Credits /'krɛdɪts/ *Pl.* credits

Credo ▸**Kredo**

creme /kre:m/ *indekl. Adj.* cream

Creme /kre:m/ *die*; ~, ~s, (schweiz.:) ~n 1 (Kosmetik, Kochk.) cream 2 (oft iron.: Oberschicht) cream; top people; **die ~ der Gesellschaft** the cream of society

Crème de la Crème /'krɛ:mdəla'krɛ:m/ *die*; ~ (oft iron.) crème de la crème

creme·farben *Adj.* cream[-coloured]

cremen *tr. V.* ▸**eincremen**

Creme-: ~schnitte *die* cream slice; **~törtchen** *das* cream tart[let]; **~torte** *die* cream cake *or* gateau

cremig
A *Adj.* creamy; **etw. ~ schlagen** beat sth. into a cream
B *adv.* like cream

Crêpe[1] /krɛp/ *die*; ~, ~s (Kochk.) crêpe

Crêpe[2] *der*; ~, ~s ▸**Krepp**

Crescendo /krɛ'ʃɛndo/ *das*; ~s, ~s (Musik) crescendo

Creutzfeldt-Jakob-Krankheit /'krɔyts fɛlt'ja:kɔp.../ *die* ▸ⓘ S. 439 (Med.) Creutzfeldt-Jakob disease

Crew /kru:/ *die*; ~, ~s 1 (eines Schiffs/Flugzeugs) crew 2 (Gruppe) team 3 (Marine: Kadetten) group of cadets (in the same year); class

Croissant /kro̯a'sã:/ *das*; ~s, ~s croissant

Cromargan Ⓦ /kromar'ga:n/ *das*; ~s stainless [chrome-nickel] steel

Croquette ▸**Krokette**

Crosscountry /krɔs'kantri/ *das*; ~[s], ~s (Sport) cross-country [race]

Croupier /kru'pi̯e:/ *der*; ~s, ~s ▸ⓘ S. 113 croupier

cruisen /'kru:zn̩/ *itr. V.*; *mit sein* cruise

Crux /krʊks/ *die*; ~ 1 (Schwierigkeit) trouble (+ *Gen.*, **bei** with) 2 (Sorgen) **man hat seine ~ mit ihnen** they are a real trial; (sie sind eine Last) they are a real burden

C-Schlüssel /'tse:-/ *der* (Musik) C clef

ČSFR /tʃɛs|ɛf|'ɛr/ *Abk.* **Tschechoslowakei**

ČSSR /tʃe|ɛs|ɛs'|ɛr/ (hist.) ▸**ČSFR**

CSU *Abk.* **= Christlich-Soziale Union** CSU

> **CSU – Christlich-Soziale Union**
>
> The Bavarian sister party of the **CDU**. It was founded in 1946 and has enjoyed an absolute majority in Bavaria for over 30 years. Politically, it stands to the right of the **CDU**.

c.t. *Abk.* **= cum tempore; Beginn: 20 Uhr ~:** 8.15 p.m. start

CT (Med.) *Abk.* **= Computertomographie** CT

cum grano salis /kʊm 'gra:no 'za:lɪs/ (geh.) taken with a pinch of salt

cum laude /kʊm 'laudə/ (Hochschulw.) with distinction; *third of four grades of successful doctoral examination*

cum tempore /kʊm 'tɛmpore/ (Hochschulw.) 15 minutes after the time indicated

Cunnilingus /kuni'lɪŋgʊs/ *der*; ~, **Cunnilingi** (Sexualk.) cunnilingus

Cup /kap/ *der*; ~s, ~s cup

Cup·finale *das* (Fußball) Cup Final; (andere Sportarten) final of the Cup

Cupido /ku'pi:do/ (*der*); ~s (Myth.) Cupid

Curettage ▸**Kürettage**

Curie /kʏ'ri:/ *das*; ~[s], ~[s] (Physik) curie

Curling /'kə:lɪŋ/ *das*; ~s (Sport) curling

curricular /kuriku'la:ɐ/ *Adj.* (Päd.) curricular

Curriculum /ku'ri:kulʊm/ *das*; ~s, **Curricula** (Päd.) curriculum; (genauer festgelegt) syllabus

Curriculum·forschung *die* curricular research

Curry /'kœri/ *das*; ~s, ~s 1 (*auch: der*) curry powder 2 (Gericht) curry

Curry-: ~sauce, ~soße *die* curry sauce; **~wurst** *die*: *sliced fried sausage sprinkled with curry powder and served with ketchup*

Cursor /'kø:sɐ/ *der*; ~s, ~[s] cursor

Cut /kœt, kat/ *der*; ~s, ~s 1 (Sakko) morning coat 2 (Boxen) cut (esp. above the eye)

Cutaway /'kœtəve/ *der;* **~s, ~s ▸Cut 1**

cutten /'katn̩/ *tr., itr. V.* (Film, Rundf., Ferns.) cut; edit

Cutter /'katɐ/ *der;* **~s, ~, Cutterin** *die;* **~, ~nen ▸❶ S. 113** (Film, Ferns., Rundf.) editor

cuttern ▸cutten

Cuvée /ky've:/ *die;* **~, ~s**, *auch das;* **~s, ~s** cuvée

CVJM *Abk.* **1 = Christlicher Verein Junger Männer** YMCA **2 = Christlicher Verein Junger Menschen;** *combined form of YMCA and YWCA*

CVP *Abk.* (schweiz.) **= Christlich-demokratische Volkspartei** Christian Democratic People's Party

Cw-Wert /tse:'ve:-/ *der* (Technik) c_d [value]

Cyan /tsy̆a:n/ *das;* **~s** (Chem.) cyanogen

Cyanid /tsy̆a'ni:t/ *das;* **~s, ~e** (Chemie) cyanide

Cyber·sex /'sai̯bɐ/ *der* cybersex

Cyberspace /'sai̯bɐspe:s/ *der;* **~** (DV) cyberspace

Cyborg /'sai̯bɔ:k/ *der;* **~s, ~s** cyborg

Cymbal ▸Zimbal

Dd

d, D /de:/ *das;* ~, ~ **1** (Buchstabe) d/D **2** (Musik) [key of] D; *s. auch* **a, A**

D *Abk.* = **Damen**

da /da:/*Adv.* **1** (dort) there; **da draußen/drinnen/drüben/unten** out/in/over/down there; **da hinten/vorn[e]** [there] at the back/front; **da hinab/hinauf/hinüber** down/up/over that way; **geh da herum** go round that way; **he, Sie da!** hey, you there!; **der Kerl da** that fellow [over there]; **ich möchte von dem da** I'd like some of that one; **halt, wer da?** (Milit.) halt, who goes there?; **hallo, wer ist denn da?** (am Telefon) hello, who's that [speaking]?; **gleich sind wir da** we're almost there; we'll be there in a minute; **ach, da ist meine Brille!** so 'that's where my glasses are!; oh, 'there are my glasses!; **da bist du ja!** there you are [at last]!; **da, ein Reh!** look, [there's] a deer!; **da, wo die Straße nach X abzweigt** where the road to X turns off; at the turning for X; **da und da** at such-and-such a place; **da und dort** here and there; (manchmal) now and again *or* then
2 (hier) here; **da bin ich** here I am; **da hast du das Buch** here's the book; **da, nimm schon!** here [you are], take it!; *s. auch* **dahaben**
3 (zeitlich) then; (in dem Augenblick) at that moment; **ich hatte mich gerade ins Bett gelegt, da klingelte das Telefon** I had just got into bed when the telephone rang; **von da an** from then on; **in meiner Jugend, da war alles besser** back in my young days, everything was better [then]
4 (deshalb) **der Zug war schon weg, da habe ich den Bus genommen** the train had already gone, so I took the bus
5 (ugs.: in diesem Fall) **da kann man nichts machen** there's nothing one can do about it *or* that; **was gibts denn da zu lachen?** what's there to laugh about [there]?; what's funny about that?; **da kann ich [ja] nur lachen!** that's plain ridiculous!; that just makes me laugh!; **was tut man da?** what does one do in a case like this?
6 (altertümelnd: nach Relativpronomen; wird nicht übersetzt) **..., der da sagt** ..., who says
7 (hervorhebend; wird meist nicht übersetzt) **ich habe da einen Kollegen, der ...** I have a colleague who ...; **da fällt mir noch was ein** [oh yes] another thought strikes me
8 **da sein** be there; (hier sein) be here; (übrig sein) be left; **ist Herr X da?** is Mr X about *or* available?; **er ist schon da** he has already arrived; **der neue Katalog ist da** the new catalogue is in; **ist ein Brief für mich da?** is there a letter for me?; **es ist niemand da** there is nobody there/here; **es muss noch Brot da sein** there must be some bread left; **du musst essen, was da ist** you must eat what there is; **der Schlüssel ist wieder da** the key is back again; (ist gefunden worden) the key has turned up [again]; **ich bin gleich wieder da** I'll be right *or* straight back; **ich melde mich, wenn ich wieder da bin** I'll get in touch when I get back; **es ist/sie sind nur dazu da, zu ...** it only exists/they only exist to ...; its/their only purpose is to ...; **dafür** *od.* **dazu ist es ja da!** that's what it's [there] for!
9 **da sein** (sich ereignen) occur; ‹*moment*› have arrived; ‹*situation*› have arisen; **ein solcher Fall ist noch nie da gewesen** such a case has never occurred before *or* is unprecedented; **er überbot alles bisher Dagewesene** he surpassed all previous achievements
10 **da sein** (existieren, leben) be left; be still alive; **da warst du noch gar nicht da** (ugs.) you weren't around then; that was before your time; **sie war nur noch für ihn da** he had her to himself
11 **da sein** (ugs.: klar bei Bewusstsein sein) **ganz** *od.* **voll da sein** be completely with it (coll.); **ich bin noch nicht ganz da** I'm not quite with it yet (coll.); I haven't quite come round yet; **er ist [geistig] wieder voll da** he is in full possession of his faculties again
12 (*Note: in North German colloquial usage pronominal adverbs are often divided so that* **da** *appears on its own with the remainder of the adverb at the end of the clause; see footnotes under* **dabei**, **dafür**, **dagegen**, **daher**, **damit**, **danach**, **davon**, **davor**, **dazu**, **dazwischen**).

B *Konj.*
1 (weil) as; since; **da ich ein Feigling bin, wagte ich es nicht** being a coward *or* since I'm a coward I didn't dare to; **da es [gerade] regnet** as *or* seeing that it's raining
2 (geh.: als) when; **jetzt, da es feststand, dass ...** now that it was definite that ...

da-:

A *Bei den aus* **da-** *od.* **dar-** *und einer Präposition gebildeten Adverbien* (**dabei, dafür, damit, daran** *usw.*) *wird* **da[r]-** *im Allgemeinen durch* it *oder, wenn es sich auf einen Plural bezieht, durch* them *übersetzt; z. B.* **es gibt nur eine Tür, jeder muss dadurch** there is only one door and everyone has to pass through it; **die Tulpen sind schön; wie viel verlangen Sie dafür?** the tulips are nice; how much are you asking for them? *Wenn jedoch der Bestandteil* **da[r]-** *besonders betont ist, dann ist* that *bzw.* those *die angemessenere Übersetzung:* **also darauf willst du hinaus!** so that's what you're getting at! **Haben die Spritzen nicht geholfen? — Nein, dadurch ist ihm nur noch schlechter geworden** Didn't the injections help? — No, those only made him worse. *Wenn auf das Adverb ein* **dass** *mit Nebensatz folgt, bietet sich häufig die Formulierung* the fact that *an:* **dadurch gekennzeichnet, dass ...** characterized by the fact that ... *Wenn Haupt- u. Nebensatz dasselbe Subjekt haben oder wenn ein Infinitivsatz angeschlossen ist, kommt man durch die Verbindung von Präposition und Verbalsubstantiv zu einer eleganten Übersetzung:* **wir sind dafür, dass wir weitermachen** *od.* **weiterzumachen** we are in favour of continuing. *Das ist manchmal sogar bei verschiedenen Subjekten möglich, wenn man ein Possessivpronomen* (his, our *usw.*) *hinzusetzt:* **er ist dafür, dass wir weitermachen** he is in favour of our continuing

B *Die Einträge für diese Adverbien berücksichtigen nur einen Teil der möglichen Kontextbeispiele mit Verben oder Substantiven. Es empfiehlt sich deshalb, auch unter den jeweiligen Verben oder Substantiven nachzuschlagen; so kann man z. B. die Übersetzung für* **danach fragen** (ask about it/them) *über* **nach etw. fragen** *unter dem Stichwort* **fragen** *erschließen*

d. Ä. *Abk.* = **der Ältere**

> **DAAD — Deutscher Akademischer Austauschdienst**
>
> The German Academic Exchange Service is a joint organization of universities and other institutions of higher education for the promotion of academic exchange. The *DAAD* is the central source of information on study and research opportunities in Germany and abroad. It awards scholarships to students and academics and acts as a national agency for grants from the European Union.

da|behalten *unr. tr. V.* keep [there]; (hier behalten) keep here; **sie hat die Kinder gleich ~:** she simply kept the children at her place; **kann ich das Buch ~?** can I keep the book [here]?

da·bei *Adv.* **1** (bei etw.) with it/them; (bei jmdm.) with him/her/them; (beigeschlossen) enclosed; **eine Tankstelle mit einer Werkstatt ~:** a filling station with its own workshop [attached]; **nahe ~** (in der Nähe) near it; close by; **wir wollen es ~ lassen** (fig.) we'll leave it at that **2** (währenddessen) at the same time; (bei diesem Anlass) then; on that occasion; **er aß weiter und redete ~:** he went on eating and talked as he did so; **die ~ entstehenden Kosten** the expense involved; **er ist ~ gesehen worden, wie er das Geld nahm** he was seen [in the act of] taking the money; **eine unangenehme Reparatur — man muss ~ unterm Auto liegen** an unpleasant job — you have to lie under the car to do it; **ich hoffe, Sie haben alle ~ etwas gelernt** I hope you have all learned something from it *or* in the process; **eine Massenkarambolage — ~ gab es zwei Tote** a big pile-up — two people were killed [in it]; **~ kam es zu erbitterten Kämpfen** this gave rise to bitter fighting **3** (außerdem) **~ [auch] es war eiskalt und [auch] nass ~:** it was freezing cold and damp into the bargain; **er ist sehr beschäftigt, aber ~ immer freundlich** he is very busy but even so always friendly **4** (hinsichtlich des Erwähnten) about it/them; **was hast du dir denn ~ gedacht?** what were you thinking of?; what came over you?; **er hat sich nichts ~ gedacht** he saw no harm in it; **ich fühle mich ganz und gar nicht wohl ~:** I am not at all happy about it; **da ist doch nichts ~!** there's really no harm in it!; (es ist nicht schwierig) there's nothing to it!; *s. auch* **bleiben 5**; **da-** **5** (obwohl) but; **er suchte nach dem Brief, ~ hatte er ihn in der Hand** he was looking for the letter and all the time he had it in his hand **6** **~ sein** (anwesend sein) be there; be present (**bei** at); (teilnehmen) take part (**bei** in); **bei der Sitzung ~ sein** be at *or* attend the meeting; **~ sein ist alles!** it's taking part that counts; **Wer kommt mit? — Ich bin ~!** Who's coming? — Count me in!; **ein wenig Angst ist immer ~:** there is always an element of fear **7** **[gerade] ~ sein, etw. zu tun** be just doing sth.; **Spülst du das Geschirr? — Ich bin schon ~:** Will you wash up? — I'm already in the middle of it. *NB In senses* **1, 2,** *and* **4** *the word can occur in two parts in North German coll. usage, e.g.* **da ist eine Karte bei** there is a card with it

dabei-: ~|bleiben *unr. itr. V.; mit sein* (dort) stay there; be there; (bei einer Tätigkeit) stick to it; (bei einer Firma, der Armee) stay on; **~|haben** *unr. tr. V.* have with one; **ich habe kein Geld ~:** I haven't got any money with me *or* on me; **sie wollte die Kinder nicht ~haben** (ugs.) she didn't want to have the children there *or* around; ***~|sein** ▸**dabei 6, 7**; **~|sitzen** *unr. itr. V.* sit there; **~|stehen** *unr. itr. V.* stand by; stand there

da|bleiben *unr. itr. V.; mit sein* stay there; (hier bleiben) stay here; **[noch] ~:** stay on

da capo /da'ka:po/ 1 (Musik) da capo 2 (Beifallsruf) **~!** encore!

d'accord /da'ko:ɐ/ (bes. österr.) **mit jmdm. ~ gehen** *od.* **sein** agree with sb.

Dach /dax/ *das;* **~[e]s, Dächer** /'dɛçɐ/ 1 roof; **[ganz oben] unterm ~** *od.* (ugs. scherzh.) **unterm ~ juchhe** [right up] in the attic; **ein/kein ~ über dem Kopf haben** (ugs.) have a/no roof over one's head; **[mit jmdm.] unter einem ~ leben** live under the same roof [with *or* as sb.]; **etw. unter ~ und Fach bringen** get sth. [safely] under cover; bring in sth.; (fig.: erfolgreich beenden) get sth. all wrapped up; **unter ~ und Fach sein** be under cover; ‹*harvest*› be safely [gathered] in; (fig.: erfolgreich beendet) wrapped up; ‹*contract etc.*› be signed and sealed; **das ~ der Welt** (fig.) the roof of the world 2 (fig. ugs.) **jmdm. aufs ~ steigen** give sb. a piece of one's mind; ‹*superior officer etc.*› haul sb. over the coals; **jmdm. eins aufs ~ geben** bash sb. over the head; (tadeln) give sb. a dressing down; tear a strip off sb. (coll.); **eins aufs ~ bekommen** *od.* **kriegen** get a bash on the head; (eine Rüge erhalten) get it in the neck (coll.)

dach-, Dach-: ~antenne *die* roof aerial; roof antenna (Amer.); **~balken** *der* roof beam; **~boden** *der* loft; **auf dem ~boden** in the loft; **~decker** /-dɛkɐ/ *der;* **~~s, ~~, ~deckerin** *die;* **~~, ~~nen** ▸ⓘ **S. 113** roofer; (für Reetdächer) thatcher; **das kannst du halten wie ein ~decker** (ugs.) it's all the same to me; **~decker·arbeiten** *Pl.* roofing work *sing.;* (mit Reet) thatching work *sing.;* **~fenster** *das* skylight; (~gaube) dormer window; **~first** *der* [roof] ridge; **~fonds** *der* (Finanzw.) fund of funds; **~förmig** *Adj.* roof-shaped; **~förmiger Vorsprung** roof-like projection; **~garten** *der* 1 roof garden; 2 ▸**~terrasse**; **~gaube** *die* (bes. Bauw.) dormer window; **~gebälk** *das* roof timbers *pl.;* **~gepäckträger** *der* (Kfz-W.) roof rack; **~geschoss**, ***~geschoß** *das* attic [storey]; **~gesellschaft** *die* (Wirtsch.) holding company; **~gesims** *das* eaves *pl.;* **~gestühl** *das* ▸**~stuhl**; **~giebel** *der* gable; **~gleiche** /-glaiçə/ *die;* **~~, ~~n** (österr.) ▸**Richtfest**; **~hase** *der* (scherzh.) cat; moggie (coll.); **~kammer** *die* attic [room]; (ärmlich) garret; **~konstruktion** *die* 1 roof structure; (Entwurf) roof design; 2 (das Konstruieren) construction of the roof; **~lawine** *die: mass of snow sliding from a roof*

Dächlein /'dɛçlain/ *das;* **~s, ~:** little roof

Dach-: ~luke *die* skylight; **~organisation** *die* umbrella organization; **~pappe** *die* roofing felt; **~pfanne** *die* pantile; **~platte** *die* flat tile; (Schindel) shingle; (aus Schiefer) slate; **~reiter** *der* ridge turret; **~rinne** *die* gutter

Dachs /daks/ *der;* **~es, ~e** 1 (Tier) badger 2 (ugs.: unerfahrener Bursche) greenhorn; **er ist noch ein ganz junger ~:** he's still wet behind the ears 3 (ugs.: Kind) **vorlauter** *od.* **frecher kleiner ~:** little rascal; young whippersnapper

Dachs-: ~bär *der* (Jägerspr.) [male] badger; **~bau** *der; Pl.* **~~e** badger's earth *or* set

Dach-: ~schaden *der* 1 (ugs.) **einen ~schaden haben** be not quite right in the head; be slightly screwy (coll.); 2 (Schaden am ~) roof damage; **~schiefer** *der* roofing slate; **~schindel** *die* [roof] shingle; **~schräge** *die* roof angle; pitch of the roof

Dachs·hund *der* (fachspr.) ▸**Dackel 1**

Dächsin /'dɛksɪn/ *die;* **~, ~nen** [female] badger; badger sow

Dach-: ~sparren *der* rafter; **~stroh** *das* straw thatch; **~stübchen** *das* (veralt.) little attic room; (ärmlich) garret; **~stube** *die* (veralt.) ▸**~kammer**; **~stuhl** *der* roof truss

dachte /'daxtə/ *1. u. 3. Pers. Sg. Prät. v.* **denken**

Dach-: ~terrasse *die* roof terrace; **~traufe** *die* eaves *pl.;* **~verband** *der* ▸**~organisation**; **~wohnung** *die* attic flat (esp. Brit.) *or* (esp. Amer.) apartment; **~ziegel** *der* roof tile; **~ziegel·verband** *der* (Med.) [rib] strapping; **~zimmer** *das* attic room

Dackel /'dakl/ *der;* **~s, ~** 1 (Hund) dachshund 2 (Schimpfwort) clot (Brit. coll.)

Dackel-: ~beine *Pl.* (ugs. scherzh.) [stumpy] bow legs; **~blick** *der* (ugs.) innocent look; **mit ~blick** with a look of innocence

Dada /'dada/ *der;* **~[s]** 1 Dada 2 (Gruppe) Dada[ist group]

Dada-Bewegung *die* Dadaist movement; Dadaism

Dadaismus *der;* **~:** Dadaism *no art.*

Dadaist *der;* **~en, ~en, Dadaistin** *die;* **~, ~nen** Dadaist

dadaistisch *Adj.* Dadaist

daddeln /'dadl̩n/ *itr. V.* (ugs., bes. nordd.) **[am Computer] ~:** play computer games

da·dran (ugs.) ▸**daran**

da·drauf (ugs.) ▸**darauf**

da·draus (ugs.) ▸**daraus**

da·drin (ugs.) ▸**darin**

da·drinnen (ugs.) ▸**darinnen**

da·drüber (ugs.) ▸**darüber**

da·drum (ugs.) ▸**darum**

da·drunter (ugs.) ▸**darunter**

da·durch *Adv.* 1 (durch diese Öffnung hindurch) through it/them; (geh.: wodurch) through which; **soll ich dadurch gehen oder dadurch?** should I go through this one or that one *or* through here or through there? 2 (durch diesen Umstand) as a result; (durch dieses Mittel) in this way; by this [means]; **ich nehme den D-Zug, ~ bin ich zwanzig Minuten eher da** I'll take the express, that way I'll get there twenty minutes earlier; **er hat sich ~ selbst geschadet** by doing this he has damaged his own interests 3 **~, dass er es [nicht] tat, konnte er ...** as a result of [not] doing it *or* by [not] doing it he was able to ...; **~, dass er älter ist, hat er einige Vorteile** he has several advantages by virtue of being older *or* because he is older; *s. auch* **da-**

da·für *Adv.* 1 (für diese Sache, diesen Zweck) for it/them; **~ gebe ich gern etwas [Geld]** I'll gladly give some money for that; **~ haben wir Sie schließlich eingestellt!** after all, that's what we took you on for!; **Magenschmerzen? Pfefferminztee ist sehr gut ~** (ugs.) Stomach ache? Peppermint tea is very good for that; **~, dass ...** considering that ...; (damit) so that ...; **~ sorgen[, dass ...]** see to it [that ...]; **der Grund ~, dass ...** the reason why ... 2 (zugunsten dieser Sache) for it; **~ sein** be in favour [of it]; **ich bin ganz ~:** I'm all for it; **er ist nicht ~, dass sie allein fährt** he's against her going alone; **das ist ein/kein Beweis ~, dass ...** this is proof/no proof that ... *or* proves/does not prove that ...; **ein Beispiel ~ ist ...** an example of this is ...; **alles spricht ~, dass ...** all the evidence *or* everything suggests that ... 3 (als Gegenleistung) in return [for it]; (beim Tausch) in exchange; (stattdessen) instead; **heute hat er keine Zeit, ~ will er morgen kommen** he has no time today, so he wants to come tomorrow instead; **in Mathematik ist er zwar eine Niete, aber ~ kann er sehr gut zeichnen** he is useless at maths, but then *or* on the other hand he can draw very well 4 (als etw. [geltend]) **der Stein ist kein Rubin, aber man könnte ihn ~ halten** the stone is not a ruby, but one might think it was *or* take it for one; **er ist schon 60, aber ~ hält ihn niemand** he is 60 but nobody would think so; **sie ist ihre Mutter, nicht ihre Schwester, aber sie könnte ~ gelten** she is her mother, not her sister, though she could pass for it 5 **etwas/nichts ~ können** be/not be responsible; **~ kann er nichts[, dass ...]** it's not his fault [that ...]; he can't help it [that ...]; **die können sehr wohl etwas ~, dass es so ist** they are very much responsible for things being the way they are; *s. auch* **da-**. NB *In senses* **1, 2,** *and* **4** *the word can occur in two parts in North German coll. usage, e.g.* **da kriege ich nichts für** I'm getting nothing for it

dafür-: ~|halten *unr. itr. V.* (geh.) consider; be of the opinion; **nach meinem Dafürhalten** in my opinion; ***~|können** ▸**dafür 5**; **~|stehen** *unr. itr. V.* 1 (veralt.: bürgen) **~stehen, dass ...** guarantee that ...; **~stehen, wie sich die Kinder benehmen** be responsible for the way the children behave; 2 (österr.: sich lohnen) **das** *od.* **es steht [nicht] ~:** it is [not] worth it

DAG *Abk.* **= Deutsche Angestellten-Gewerkschaft** German Employees' Union

dagegen *Adv.* 1 (gegen das Genannte) against it/them; **der Wagen raste auf den Pfeiler zu und prallte ~:** the car careered towards the pillar and crashed into it; **er stieß aus Versehen ~:** he knocked into it by mistake; **ich protestiere energisch ~, dass Sie mich verleumden** I must protest strongly against this slander; **etwas ~ haben** have sth. against it; object [to it]; **ich habe nichts ~:** I've no objection; I don't mind; **haben Sie etwas** *od.* (ugs.) **was ~, wenn ...?** do you mind if ...?; **was hat er ~, dass wir Freunde sind?** why does he object to our being friends?; **~ sein** be opposed to it *or* against it; **die Mehrheit war ~, das Angebot anzunehmen** the majority was against *or* opposed to accepting the offer; **wir kennen kein Mittel ~:** we know of no cure for it; **~ kann man nichts machen** there is nothing one can do about it 2 *konjunktional* (im Vergleich dazu) by *or* in comparison; compared with that; (jedoch) on the other hand; **sein Sohn ist dunkelhaarig, seine Tochter ~ blond** his son has dark hair, but his daughter on the other hand is blonde 3 (als Gegenwert) in exchange; **er hat ein anderes Gerät ~ eingetauscht** he got another machine in exchange [for it]; *s. auch* **da-**. NB *In senses* **1, 3** *the word can occur in two parts in North German coll. usage, e.g.* **da kann niemand gegen sein** nobody can have any objection [to that]

dagegen-: ~|halten *unr. tr. V.* 1 (entgegnen) counter; (einwenden) object; **er hielt ~, dass ...** his rejoinder *or* answer was that ...; 2 (ugs.: vergleichen) hold it/them against; compare it/them with; **halte das Original ~:** compare it with the original; **~|setzen** *tr. V.* put forward [in opposition]; **„Das stimmt doch gar nicht", setzte er ~:** 'That's quite untrue,' he objected; **nichts ~zusetzen haben** offer no counter-argument; (nichts einwenden) make no objection; (es nicht leugnen) not deny it; **~|sprechen** *unr. itr. V.* be against it/them; **zahlreiche Gründe sprechen/nichts spricht ~, dass du ein paar Tage freinimmst** there are numerous reasons/there is no reason why you should not take a couple of days off; **was spricht ~?** what is the objection?; **~|stellen** *refl. V.* oppose it; **~|stemmen** *refl. V.* oppose it vigorously; fight it

da|haben *unr. tr. V.* (*Zusschr. nur im Inf. u. 2. Part.*) (ugs.) have [here]; (im Hause) have in the house; **mal sehen, ob ich noch eins dahabe** I'll see whether I've got one left

da·heim *Adv.* (bes. südd., österr., schweiz.) 1 (zu Hause) at home; (*nach Präp.*) home; **ich bin für niemanden ~:** I'm not at home to anybody; **~ anrufen** phone *or* ring home; **wie geht es ~?** how are things at home?; **sind Sie hier ~?** do you live here?; **bei mir ~:** at my place; **~ ist ~!** there's no place like home! (prov.); east, west, home's best (prov.) 2 (in der Heimat) [back] home; **bei uns ~:** back home where I/we come from; **nach ~ schreiben** write home; **wo bist du ~?** where do you come from?

Daheim *das;* **~s** (bes. südd., österr., schweiz.) home

Daheim·gebliebene *der/die; adj. Dekl.* one who stayed at home; **die ~n** those who stayed at home; those back home

da·her *Adv.* 1 (von dort) from there; **~ habe ich meine neuen Stiefel** that's where I got my new boots from; **von ~ droht keine Gefahr** there is no danger from 'that quarter;

~ **weht also der Wind!** (ugs.) so 'that's the way the wind blows! (fig.) 2 (durch diesen Umstand) hence; ~ **kommt seine gute Laune** that's why he's in a good mood; that's the reason for his good mood; **das/die Krankheit kommt ~, dass ...** the reason for this/the illness is that ...; ~ **der Name Bratkartoffel!** (scherzh.) that explains it; so that's why!; ~ **wusste er das** *od.* **hat er das** that's how he knew; that's where he got it from 3 *konjunktional* (deshalb) therefore; so 4 (bes. südd.: hierhin) here. NB *In senses* **1**, **2**, *and* **4** *the word can occur in two parts in coll. usage, e.g.* **da hast du die Klamotten her** that's where you got those clothes from

d

daher-, Daher-: ~**|bringen** *unr. tr. V.* (südd., österr.) 1 (mitbringen) bring [with one]; (nach Hause) bring home; 2 (abwertend: sagen) come out with (coll.); ~**|fliegen** *unr. itr. V.; mit sein* 1 (umherfliegen) fly around; 2 (heranfliegen) fly up; ~**geflogen kommen** come flying along; (auf jmdn. zu) come flying up; ~**gelaufen** *Adj.* (abwertend) that nobody's heard of *postpos.;* **jeder ~gelaufene Kerl** any guy who comes along; any Tom, Dick, or Harry; ~**gelaufene** *der/die; adj. Dekl.* (abwertend) nonentity; **jeder ~gelaufene** absolutely anybody [who comes along]; ~**|kommen** *unr. itr. V.* come along; (gemütlich) stroll along; (auf jmdn. zu) come/stroll up; (auftreten) turn up; **wie kann man nur in so einem Aufzug ~kommen?** how can one go around dressed like that?; ~**reden** (abwertend) A *itr. V.* 1 talk off the cuff; 2 (viel reden) blather on; **[so] dumm ~reden** talk [such] rubbish; B *tr. V.* 1 say off the cuff; 2 (wortreich sagen) prattle; **was er so ~redet** his blathering on; the things he comes out with

da·hier *Adv.* (österr., schweiz., sonst veralt.) here

da|hin 1 (nach dort) there; ~ **und dorthin** this way and that 2 (fig.) ~ **musste es kommen** it had to come to that; ~ **hat ihn seine Wettleidenschaft gebracht** that's where his betting mania has got him; **du wirst es ~ bringen, dass ...** you'll carry things *or* matters so far that ... 3 **bis ~:** to there; (zeitlich) until then; **bis ~ sind es 75 km** it's 75 km from here; **bis ~ sind es noch zehn Minuten** there are another ten minutes to go until then; **es steht mir bis ~** (ugs.) I am sick and tired of it *or* fed up to the back teeth with it (coll.) 4 /-'-/ (verloren, vorbei) ~ **sein** be *or* have gone; **mein neuer Mantel ist ~:** my new coat is ruined *or* (coll.) has had it 5 (in diesem Sinne) ~ **[gehend], dass ...** to the effect that ...; **man kann dieses Schreiben auch ~ [gehend] auslegen/verstehen, dass ...** one can also interpret/take this letter as meaning that ...

da·hinab *Adv.* down there; down that way

da·hinauf *Adv.* up there; up that way

da·hinaus *Adv.* out there; (in die Richtung) out that way

dahin-: ~**|bewegen** *refl. V.* move on one's way; ~**|dämmern** *itr. V.; mit sein* be semi-conscious; ~**|eilen** *itr. V.; mit sein* (geh.) hurry along *or* on one's way; ‹*time*› fly [past]

da·hinein *Adv.* in there; (hier hinein) in here

dahin-: ~**|fahren** *unr. itr. V.; mit sein* 1 (dichter.: wegfahren) depart; 2 (dichter.: vorbeifahren) go *or* pass on one's way; 3 (veralt.: sterben) pass away; depart this life (literary); ~**|fliegen** *unr. itr. V.; mit sein* (dichter.) 1 (wegfliegen) fly on its way; ‹*person*› fly away; 2 (vergehen) fly past; ~**|fließen** *unr. itr. V.; mit sein* (geh.) flow along *or* on its way

da·hingegen *Adv.* on the other hand

dahin-: ~**|gehen** *unr. itr. V.; mit sein* 1 (geh.: vergehen) pass; ‹*years*› go by; 2 (geh.: vorbeigehen) go *or* pass on one's way; 3 (verhüll.: sterben) pass away; ~**gestellt** *in* **es ist** *od.* **bleibt ~gestellt** it remains to be seen; **ob etwas Vernünftiges dabei herauskommt, sei ~gestellt** we must wait and see whether this produces any useful result; **etw. ~gestellt sein lassen** leave sth. open [for the moment]; ~**|jagen** *itr. V.; mit sein* (geh.) tear *or* race along; ~**|kümmern** *itr. V.; mit sein* (geh.) fade away; (im Gefängnis usw.) languish; ~**|leben** *itr. V.* live one's life; ~**|plätschern** *itr. V.; mit sein* **das Gespräch plätscherte an der Oberfläche ~:** the conversation was very superficial *or* remained at the level of small talk; ~**|raffen** *tr. V.* (geh. verhüll.) carry off; ~**|sagen** *tr. V.* say without thinking; **das war nur so ~gesagt** that was just a casual *or* off-the-cuff remark; ~**|scheiden** *unr. itr. V.; mit sein* (geh. verhüll.) pass away; depart this life (literary); ~**|schmelzen** *unr. itr.; mit sein* (auch fig.) melt away; **jmdn ~schmelzen lassen** (rühren) melt sb.'s heart; ~**|schwinden** *unr. itr. V.; mit sein* (geh.) 1 (abnehmen) dwindle; ‹*courage, interest, hope*› fade; 2 (vergehen) pass; ~**|siechen** *itr. V.; mit sein* (geh.) waste away; ~**|stehen** *unr. itr. V.* **[es] steht [noch] ~:** [it] remains to be seen

da·hinten *Adv.* over there

da·hinter *Adv.* behind it/them; (folgend) after it/them; **ein Haus mit einem Garten ~:** a house with a garden behind *or* at the back; **was sich wohl ~ verbirgt?** (fig.) what can be behind it?; **sich ~ klemmen** *od.* **setzen** *od.* **knien** (fig. ugs.) buckle down to it; pull one's finger out (coll.); ~ **kommen** (fig. ugs.) find out; **sich ~ machen** (fig. ugs.) get down to it; **mach dich ~!** get on with it!; ~ **stecken** (fig. ugs.: Grund, Ursache, Urheber sein) be behind it/them; **es steckt nichts/nicht viel ~** (fig. ugs.) there is nothing/not much to it/them; ~ **stehen** (fig.: dafür eintreten) be behind it/them; [fully] support it/them; (fig.: dazu stehen) stand by it/them; (fig.: dem zugrunde liegen) be behind it; be at the root of it; *s. auch* **da-**

***dahinter·her** *Adj.* (ugs.) ~ **sein** make a big effort; put oneself out; **nie macht ihr eure Aufgaben von euch aus, ich muss immer ~ sein** you never do your homework without being reminded, I've always got to keep on at you

dahinter|klemmen *usw.* ▸ **dahinter**

da|hinüber *Adv.* over/across there

da|hinunter *Adv.* down there; (in diese Richtung) down that way

dahin-: ~**|vegetieren** *itr. V.* **[elend] ~vegetieren** drag out a miserable existence; ~**|ziehen** A *unr. itr. V.; mit sein* go *or* move on one's way; ‹*clouds*› drift by; B *unr. refl. V.* ‹*path*› pass along

Dahlie /'da:li̯ə/ *die;* ~, ~**n** dahlia

Dakapo /da'ka:po/ *das;* ~**s**, ~**s** (Musik) encore

daktylisch /dak'tʏlɪʃ/ *Adj.* (Verslehre) dactylic

Daktylo- /'daktʏlo/: ~**graphin** /-'gra:fɪn/ *die;* ~, ~**nen** (schweiz.) typist; ~**skopie** /-sko'pi:/ *die;* ~, ~**n** dactyloscopy *no art.;* fingerprint identification *no art.*

Daktylus /'daktʏlʊs/ *der;* ~, **Daktylen** (Verslehre) dactyl

da-: ~**|lassen** *unr. tr. V.* (ugs.) leave [here]; (dort lassen) leave there; **[jmdm.] keine Nachricht ~lassen** leave [sb.] no message; ~**|liegen** *unr. itr. V.* lie there; ‹*building etc.*› stand there

Dalk /dalk/ *der;* ~**[e]s**, ~**e** (südd., österr. ugs.) [clumsy] clot (Brit. coll.); jerk (coll.)

Dalken *Pl.* (österr.) [yeast-dough] fritters

dalkert /'dalkɐt/ (südd., österr. ugs.)
A *Adj.* daft; ~**e Kuh** silly woman (derog.)
B *adv.* stupidly

Dalle /'dalə/ *die;* ~, ~**n** (bes. südd.) dent

Dalles /'daləs/ *der;* ~ (ugs.) **im ~ sein** be broke (coll.)

dalli /'dali/ *Adv.* (ugs.) **aber [ein bisschen] ~!** and make it snappy (coll.); **[~] ~!** get a move on!; (beim Laufen) come on, at the double!

Dalmatien /dal'ma:tsi̯ən/ *(das);* ~**s** Dalmatia

Dalmatiner /dalma'ti:nɐ/ *der;* ~**s**, ~, **Dalmatinerin** *die;* ~, ~**nen** Dalmatian

dalmatinisch *Adj.* Dalmatian

damalig /'da:ma:lɪç/ *Adj.* at that *or* the time *postpos.;* **der ~e Bundeskanzler** the then Federal Chancellor; the Federal Chancellor at that *or* the time; **das ~e Leben** life in those days; **die ~e Regierung** the government of the day; **unter den ~en Umständen** in the circumstances obtaining at the time; **im ~en Gallien** in what was then Gaul

damals /'da:ma:ls/ *Adv.* then; at that time; ~, **als ...** at the time *or* in the days when ...; **von ~:** of that time *or* those days; (aus dieser Zeit) from that time *or* those days; **seit ~:** since then; **wie es ~ war** what it was like in those days

Damast /da'mast/ *der;* ~**[e]s**, ~**e** damask

damasten *Adj.* (geh.) damask

Damaszener·klinge /damas'tse:nɐ-/ *die* Damascus blade

damaszieren /damas'tsi:rən/ *tr. V.* damascene ‹*blade, sword*›

Dämchen /'dɛ:mçən/ *das;* ~**s**, ~ 1 little lady 2 (Kind) [proper] little lady; little madam 3 (abwertend: Prostituierte) lady of the night

Dame /'da:mə/ *die;* ~, ~**n** 1 ▸❶ **S. 44**, ▸❶ **S. 143** (Frau) lady; **sehr verehrte** *od.* **meine ~n und Herren!** ladies and gentlemen; **was wünschen Sie, meine ~?** may I help you, madam?; **ein Abend mit ~n** a ladies' night; **die Abfahrt/die 200 Meter der ~n** (Sport) the women's downhill/200 metres; **bei den ~n siegte die deutsche Staffel** (Sport) the German team won in the women's event; **die ~ des Hauses** the lady of the house; **meine Alte ~** (veralt. scherzh.) my mater (dated sl.); **ganz ~ sein** be the complete lady; *s. auch* **Welt 6** 2 (Schach, Kartenspiele) queen 3 (Spiel) draughts (Brit.); checkers (Amer.) 4 (Doppelstein) king

Dame·brett *das* draughtboard (Brit.); checkerboard (Amer.)

Dämel /'dɛ:ml̩/ *der;* ~**s**, ~ (salopp) fool; **du ~!** you clot! (Brit. sl.); you jerk! (coll.)

Damen-: ~**bart** *der* [unwanted] facial hair; ~**begleitung** *die:* **in/ohne ~begleitung** in the company of a lady/unaccompanied; with/without a female companion; ~**bekanntschaft** *die* lady friend; **eine ~bekanntschaft machen** (ugs.) meet *or* get to know someone of the opposite sex; ~**besuch** *der* lady visitor/visitors; ~**besuch ist ab 20⁰⁰ untersagt** no female visitors after 8 p.m.; ~**binde** *die* sanitary towel (Brit.) *or* (Amer.) napkin; ~**doppel** *das* (Sport) women's doubles *pl.;* ~**einzel** *das* (Sport) women's singles *pl.;* ~**fahr·rad** *das* lady's bicycle; ~**friseur** *der* ladies' hairdresser; ~**fußball** *der* women's football; ~**garnitur** *die* set of women's underwear; ~**gesellschaft** *die* 1 ladies' party; 2 (Begleitung von ~) female company; **in ~gesellschaft** in the company of a lady/of ladies

damenhaft
A *Adj.* ladylike; ~**e Kleidung** clothes fit for a lady
B *adv.* like a lady; in a ladylike manner

Damen-: ~**kapelle** *die* women's band; ~**konfektion** *die* ladies' wear; ~**kränzchen** *das* (veralt.) ladies' circle; ~**mannschaft** *die* women's team; ~**rad** *das* lady's bicycle; ~**salon** *der* ladies' hairdressing salon (Brit.); beauty salon (Amer.); ~**sattel** *der* 1 side-saddle; **im ~sattel reiten** ride side-saddle; 2 (Fahrradsattel) ladies' saddle; ~**schneider** *der*, ~**schneiderin** *die* ▸❶ **S. 113** dressmaker; ~**schuh** *der* lady's shoe; ~**schuhe** ladies' shoes; ~**sitz** *der* (Reiten) **im ~sitz reiten** ride side-saddle; ~**stift** *das* (veralt.) home for elderly gentlewomen (*esp. members of the aristocracy*); ~**toilette** *die* 1 (WC) ladies' toilet; ladies' restroom (Amer.); 2 (Kleidung) ladies' [formal] wear; ~**unter·wäsche** *die* ladies' underwear; ~**wahl** *die* ladies' choice; **jetzt ist ~wahl** now it's the ladies' turn to choose their partners; ~**welt** *die* (scherzh.) **die ~welt** the ladies *pl.;* the fair sex

Dame-: ~**spiel** *das* 1 **das ~spiel** draughts (Brit.); checkers (Amer.); 2 (Partie) game of draught *or* (Amer.) checkers; ~**stein** *der* draughtsman (Brit.); checker (Amer.)

Dam·hirsch /'dam-/ *der* fallow deer; (männliches Tier) fallow buck

damisch /'da:mɪʃ/ (südd., österr. ugs.)
A *Adj.* 1 (dumm) stupid 2 (schwindlig) dizzy
B *adv.* (dumm) stupidly

da·mit
A *Adv.* 1 (mit dieser Sache) with it/them; **was will er ~ [machen]?** what's he going to do with

it/them?; **meint er mich ~?** does he mean me?; **ich bin gleich ~ fertig** I'll be finished in a moment; **du hast recht ~ gehabt** you were right there *or* about that; **er hatte nicht ~ gerechnet** he had not expected that *or* reckoned with that; **~ habe ich nichts zu tun** I have nothing to do with it/them; **er kommt immer wieder ~ an** he's for ever harping on it; **was ist denn ~?** what's the matter with it/them?; what about it/them?; **wie wäre es ~?** how about it?; **~ hat es noch Zeit** there's no hurry about that/those; **Schluss** *od.* **genug ~!** that's enough [of that]; **hör auf ~!** stop it!; **her ~!** let's have it/them!; hand it/them over! 2 (gleichzeitig) with that; thereupon 3 (daher) thus; as a result; **er hatte kein Alibi, und gehörte ~ zu den Verdächtigen** he had no alibi and was therefore one of the suspects; *s. auch* **da-**. *NB In sense* **1** *the word can occur in two parts in North German coll. usage, e.g.* **da habe ich nicht mit gerechnet** I didn't expect that
B *Konj.* so that; **er kam früher, ~ sie mehr Zeit hatten** *od.* (geh.) **hätten** he came earlier so that they would have more time

Dämlack /ˈdɛːmlak/ *der;* **~s, ~e** *od.* **~s** (salopp) clot (Brit. coll.); twerp (coll.); jerk (coll.)

dämlich /ˈdɛːmlɪç/ (ugs. abwertend)
A *Adj.* stupid
B *adv.* stupidly; **~ fragen** ask stupid questions

Dämlichkeit *die;* **~, ~en** (ugs. abwertend) 1 (Art) stupidity 2 (Handlung) piece of stupidity

Damm /dam/ *der;* **~[e]s, Dämme** /ˈdɛmə/ 1 (Schutzwall) embankment; levee (Amer.); (Deich) dyke; (Stau~) dam; (durch Wasser, Watt, Sumpf) causeway; (fig.) bulwark (**gegen** against); **einen ~ gegen etw. errichten** (fig.) form a barrier *or* defence against sth. 2 (Straßen~, Bahn~) embankment 3 (nord[ost]d.: Straße) road[way] 4 (fig.) **wieder/nicht auf dem ~ sein** (ugs.) be fit *or* in good shape again/not be fit *or* in good shape; **jmdn. wieder auf den ~ bringen** (ugs.) put sb. back on his/her feet 5 (Anat.) ▸ **S. 435** perineum

Dämm- insulating

Damm·bruch *der* ▸ **Damm:** breach in a dam/dyke; collapse of an embankment/a causeway

dämmen /ˈdɛmən/ *tr. V.* 1 (geh.: aufhalten) hold back; dam ‹*river, stream*›; stem ‹*flood*› 2 (Technik: nicht durchlassen) retain, keep in ‹*heat*›; (ausschließen) keep out ‹*noise, heat*›

Dämmer *der;* **~s** (dichter.) twilight; (Halbdunkel) half-light; **der ~ des Halbschlafs** (fig.) stupefied half-sleep

dämmerig ▸ **dämmrig**

Dämmer·licht *das* twilight; (trübes Licht) dim light

dämmern /ˈdɛmɐn/ *itr. V.* 1 **es dämmert** (morgens) it is getting light; (abends) it is getting dark; (mit Zeitangabe) it gets light/dark; **der Morgen dämmert** the day is dawning *or* breaking; **der Abend dämmert** dusk is falling 2 (ugs.: klar werden) **jmdn. ~:** dawn upon sb.; **mir dämmert da etwas** the penny is beginning to drop; (ich habe einen Verdacht) I am beginning to smell a rat; **jetzt dämmerts [bei] mir** now I'm beginning to understand 3 (im Halbschlaf) doze; **vor sich hin ~:** doze; (nicht klar bei Bewusstsein) be semi-conscious

Dämmer-: ~schlaf *der* 1 (Halbschlaf) half-sleep; doze; 2 (Med.) twilight sleep; **~schoppen** *der* [early] evening drink; **~stündchen** *das* early evening get-together; **~stunde** *die* (geh.) twilight hour; **in der ~stunde** at twilight *or* dusk

Dämmerung *die;* **~, ~en** 1 (Abend~) twilight; dusk; **in der [abendlichen] ~:** in the twilight *or* gloaming; **bei** *od.* **mit/vor Einbruch der ~:** at/before dusk *or* nightfall; **die Stunden der ~:** the twilight hours 2 (Morgen~) dawn; daybreak; **die ~ bricht an** dawn *or* day is breaking; **bei** *od.* **mit/vor Anbruch der ~:** at/before dawn *or* daybreak 3 (Halbdunkel) semi-darkness; half-light; **der Raum lag in tiefer ~:** the room was in deep shadow *or* gloom

Dämmer·zustand *der* 1 (Halbschlaf) half-sleep; doze 2 (Bewusstseinstrübung) semi-conscious state; coma

Dämm·platte *die* (Bauw.) insulating panel

dämmrig *Adj.* 1 **es ist** *od.* **wird schon ~** (morgens) it is beginning to get light; day is breaking; (abends) it is beginning to get dark; night is falling; **draußen ist es noch ~:** it is still quite dark outside 2 (halbdunkel) gloomy; dim ‹*light*›

Damm-: ~riss, *~riß *der* (Med.) perineal tear; **~schnitt** *der* (Med.) episiotomy

Dämmung *die;* **~, ~en** (Technik) insulation

Damm·weg *der* embankment/dyke path; (Verbindung durch Wasser, Watt, Sumpf) causeway

Damokles·schwert /ˈdaːmoklɛs-/ *das* (geh.) sword of Damocles

Dämon /ˈdɛːmɔn/ *der;* **~s, ~en** /dɛˈmoːnən/ 1 (böser Geist) demon; **gute und böse ~en** good and evil spirits 2 (geh.: im Menschen) daemon; daemonic inner force

dämonenhaft *Adj.* demoniac

Dämonie /dɛmoˈniː/ *die;* **~, ~n** (geh.) daemonic power; (eines Künstlers) daemonic genius; **eine** *od.* **die ~ des Schicksals** a cruel stroke of fate

dämonisch
A *Adj.* demonic; (teuflisch) diabolical
B *adv.* demonically

dämonisieren *tr. V.* demonize; portray as a demon/demons

Dämonisierung *die;* **~, ~en** demonization; portrayal as a demon/demons

Dämonismus *der;* **~:** demonism *no art.*

Dampf /dampf/ *der;* **~[e]s, Dämpfe** /ˈdɛmpfə/ 1 steam *no pl., no indef. art.;* (Rauch) smoke *no pl., no indef. art.;* (Physik) [water] vapour *as tech. term, no pl., no indef. art.;* **wallende Dämpfe** clouds of steam; **giftige Dämpfe einatmen** breathe in toxic vapour *or* fumes; **etw. mit ~ behandeln** steam sth.; **mit ~ betrieben [werden]** [be] steam-powered *or* steam-driven; **unter ~** (*Dat.*) **stehen** *od.* **sein** have steam up; **~ aufmachen** (veralt.: stärker feuern) get up [more] steam; (ugs.: energischer spielen) put on an effort; **da ist/aus etw. ist der ~ raus** (ugs.) it/sth. has lost its momentum; **~ ablassen** (auch ugs.: Ärger abreagieren) let off steam; **jmdm. ~ [unterm Hintern] machen** (ugs.) make sb. get on with it; put pressure on sb.; **~ drauf haben** (ugs.) be really shifting (coll.) *or* moving; (vital sein) be full of beans; **~ dahinter/hinter etw.** (*Akk.*) **machen** *od.* **setzen** (ugs.) (sich beeilen) get a move on/get a move on with sth.; (andere zur Eile treiben) get things *pl.*/sth. moving; **dieser Boxer hat ~ in den Fäusten** this boxer packs quite a punch 2 (ugs.: Angst) **vor jmdm./etw. [mächtigen** *od.* **unheimlichen] ~ haben** be [absolutely] terrified of sb./in a [blue] funk about sth. (coll.) 3 (bayr.: Alkoholrausch) **einen ~ haben** be drunk

Dampf-: ~antrieb *der* steam drive; (Eisenb.) steam traction; **mit ~antrieb** steam-driven; **~bad** *das* steam *or* Turkish bath; (Raum) steam *or* Turkish baths *pl.;* **~boot** *das* steamboat; **~bügel·eisen** *das* steam iron; **~druck** *der; Pl.* **~drücke** steam pressure

dampfen *itr. V.* 1 (Dampf abgeben) steam (**vor** + *Dat.* with, due to) 2 *mit sein* (fahren) steam 3 *mit sein* (ugs.: mit Zug, Schiff reisen) chug; (wegfahren) chug off

dämpfen /ˈdɛmpfn̩/ *tr. V.* 1 (mit Dampf garen) steam ‹*fish, vegetables, potatoes*› 2 (glätten) press with a damp cloth; (mit Dampfbügeleisen) steam iron 3 (mildern) muffle, deaden ‹*sound*›; attenuate ‹*high notes*›; dim, turn down ‹*lights*›; **die** *od.* **seine Stimme ~:** lower one's voice; **den Ton einer Trompete ~:** mute a trumpet; *s. auch* **gedämpft** 4 (abschwächen) cushion, absorb ‹*blow, impact, shock*›; damp ‹*vibrations*›; (fig.) temper, diminish ‹*joy*›; dampen ‹*enthusiasm*›; assuage ‹*sb.'s wrath*›; calm ‹*anger, excitement*›; (Wirtsch.) curb ‹*price rises*›; slow down ‹*inflation*›

Dampfer *der;* **~s, ~:** steamer; **mit dem ~ fahren** go by steamer; **auf dem falschen ~ sein** *od.* **sitzen** (fig. ugs.) be barking up the wrong tree; have got it wrong

Dämpfer *der;* **~s, ~** 1 (beim Klavier) damper; (bei Streich- u. Blasinstrumenten) mute 2 (fig.) **einen ~ bekommen** (ugs.) have one's enthusiasm dampened; (gerügt werden) be taken down a peg or two; **jmdm. einen ~ aufsetzen** dampen sb.'s enthusiasm 3 (Technik) damper; (Stoß~) shock absorber

Dampfer·linie *die* steamer service; (Gesellschaft) steamship line

dampf-, Dampf-: ~förmig *Adj.* vaporous; vapour *attrib.* ‹*state*›; **~hammer** *der* steam hammer; **~heizung** *die* steam heating

dampfig *Adj.* steamy; (dunstig) misty

Dampf-: ~kessel *der* boiler; **~kochtopf** *der* pressure cooker; **~kraft** *die* steam power; **~kraftwerk** *das* steam[-driven] power station; **~lok[omotive]** *die* steam locomotive *or* engine; **~maschine** *die* steam engine; **~nudel** *die* (südd., Kochk.) steamed yeast dumpling; **aufgehen wie eine ~nudel** (ugs.) fill out like a balloon; **~pfeife** *die* steam whistle; (mit Druckluft betrieben) compressed-air whistle; **~plauderer** *der,* **~plauderin** *die* (ugs. abwertend) chatterbox; babbler; **~reiniger** *der* steam cleaner; **~schiff** *das* steamer; (bes. hist.) steamship; ***~schiffahrt, ~schifffahrt** *die* steam navigation; **~turbine** *die* steam turbine

Dämpfung *die;* **~, ~en** 1 (der Stimme) lowering; (von hohen Tönen) attenuation; (von Licht) dimming; **~ des Schalls/der Töne** deadening of sound/sounds 2 (Stoß~) cushioning; absorption; (von Schwingungen) damping; (fig.) (von Freude, Leidenschaft) tempering; diminishing; (von Begeisterung) dampening; (von Wut, Aufregung) calming; (Wirtsch.: des Preisauftriebs) curbing; (der Konjunktur) slowing down

Dampf·walze *die* 1 steamroller 2 (ugs. scherzh.: Frau) mountain of flesh

Dam·wild *das* fallow deer *pl.*

da·nach *Adv.* 1 (zeitlich) after it/that; then; **noch tagelang ~:** for days after[wards]; **eine Stunde ~:** an hour later; **ich dusche gern kalt, ~ fühlt man sich gleich viel frischer** I like a cold shower, you feel really refreshed afterwards 2 (räumlich: dahinter) after it/them; **voran gingen die Eltern, ~ kamen die Kinder** the parents went in front, the children following after *or* behind; **Kommt Mainz vor oder nach Wiesbaden? — Danach** Is Mainz before or after Wiesbaden? — After 3 (ein Ziel angebend) towards it/them; **er sprang/griff ~:** he jumped/made a grab for it/them; **~ lasst uns alle streben** let us all strive for that 4 (entsprechend) in accordance with it/them; **ein Brief ist gekommen; ~ ist sie schon unterwegs** a letter has arrived, according to which she is already on her way; **~ zu urteilen** to judge by that; **ihr kennt die Regeln, nun richtet euch ~!** you know the rules, so stick to *or* abide by them; **~ steht mir nicht der Sinn,** (ugs.) **mir ist nicht ~:** I'm not in the mood; I don't feel like it; **es sieht ~ aus/~ aus, als ob ...** it looks like it/looks as though ...; **~ siehst du [gerade] aus!** (ugs. iron.) tell that to the Marines!; **es ist billig, aber es ist auch ~** (ugs.) it's cheap and looks it; **es ist nur ein kleiner Schnellimbiss, und das Essen ist auch ~:** it's only a small snack bar and the food's what you might expect; *s. auch* **da-**. NB *In sense* **4** *the word can occur in two parts in North German coll. usage, e.g.* **es ist billig, da ist es aber auch nach** it's cheap and looks it

Danaer·geschenk /ˈdaːnaɐ-/ *das* (geh.) Greek gift

Dancing /ˈdaːnsɪŋ/ *das;* **~s, ~s** (bes. österr.) 1 (Lokal) dance hall 2 (Veranstaltung) dance

Dandy /ˈdɛndi/ *der;* **~s, ~s** dandy

dandyhaft
A *Adj.* dandyish; foppish ‹*manner*›
B *adv.* like a dandy/dandies

Dandytum *das;* **~s** 1 (Art) dandyish nature 2 (Schicht) **das ~:** the dandies *pl.* (*as a group*)

Däne /ˈdɛːnə/ *der;* **~n, ~n** ▸ **S. 520** Dane; **er ist ~:** he is Danish *or* a Dane

da·neben *Adv.* 1 (an der/die Seite davon) next to *or* beside him/her/it/them *etc.* 2 (im Vergleich dazu) in comparison 3 (außerdem) in addition

d

[to that]; besides [that]; **man muss ~ auch berücksichtigen, wie schwer es ist** one must consider at the same time *or* as well how difficult it is; **4** **~ sein** (ugs.) ‹*reaction, remark*› be out of order (coll.); ‹*person*› (verwirrt sein) be in a complete daze; (sich unwohl fühlen) not be oneself; be under the weather (coll.); **die Entscheidung war total ~:** the decision was all wrong; **er sah völlig ~ aus** he looked a real freak (coll.)

daneben-: ~|benehmen *unr. refl. V.* (ugs.) blot one's copybook (coll.); spoil one's record; (sich aufführen) make an exhibition of oneself; **~|fallen** *unr. itr. V.; mit sein* miss; **~|gehen** *unr. itr. V.; mit sein* **1** (das Ziel verfehlen) miss [the target]; **2** (ugs.: fehlschlagen) misfire; be a flop (sl.); **das geht sowieso ~:** it won't be any good; **~|geraten** *unr. itr. V.; mit sein* (ugs.) **[jmdm.] ~geraten** go wrong [on sb.]; **~|greifen** *unr. itr. V.* **1** (vorbeigreifen) miss [one's aim] (*when reaching for sth.*); **beim Klavierspielen ~greifen** play a wrong note/some wrong notes on the piano; **2** (ugs.) **im Ausdruck ~greifen** (aus Unkenntnis) say the wrong thing; (aus Taktlosigkeit) put one's foot in it; **mit seiner Prognose ~greifen** be wide of the mark with one's prognosis; **~|halten** *unr. tr. V.* (ugs.: vergleichen) **wenn man X ~hält** when compared with X; **~|hauen** *unr. tr. V.;* **1** (nicht treffen) miss; **2** (ugs.: sich irren) be wide of the mark; **mit der Antwort hat er ziemlich ~gehauen** his answer was well wide of the mark *or* (coll.) way out; **~|liegen** *unr. itr. V.* (ugs.) be wide of the mark; **mit dieser Meinung liegst du aber sehr ~:** your estimation is quite wrong *or* (coll.) way out; **~|schießen** *unr. itr. V.* **1** (Ziel verfehlen) miss [the target]; **mit Absicht ~schießen** shoot to miss; **2** ▸ **~hauen 2**; ***~|sein** ▸ **daneben 4**; **~|tippen** *itr. V.* (ugs.) guess wrong; **~getippt!** wrong!; **~|treffen** *unr. itr. V.* miss [the target]; **~getroffen!** missed!

Dänemark /ˈdɛːnəmark/ (*das*); **~s** Denmark

dang /daŋ/ *1. u. 3. Pers. Sg. Prät. v.* **dingen**

da·nieden *Adv.* (dichter. veralt.) here below [on earth]

danieder|liegen *unr. itr. V.* (geh.) **1** (krank sein) be laid low; **schwer [krank]/sterbend ~:** lie seriously ill/dying **2** (Wirtsch.) ‹*trade, economy*› be depressed

Dänin *die; ~, ~nen* ▸ **i S. 520** Dane; Danish woman/girl; *s. auch* **-in**

dänisch /ˈdɛːnɪʃ/ *Adj.* ▸ **i S. 520**, ▸ **i S. 670** Danish; *s. auch* **deutsch**, **Deutsch**

dank /daŋk/ *Präp. mit Dat. u. Gen. im Sg. u. meist mit Gen. im Pl.* thanks to; **~ einem Zufall** *od.* **eines Zufalls** by chance; owing to a coincidence

Dank *der;* **~[e]s** **1** thanks *pl.*; **jmdm. seinen ~ abstatten** offer one's thanks to sb.; **jmdm. seinen [herzlichen/allerherzlichsten] ~ aussprechen** express one's/sincere/most sincere/thanks *or* gratitude to sb.; **jmdm. ~ sagen** thank sb.; offer one's thanks to sb.; **jmdm. [großen] ~ schulden** *od.* **schuldig sein** (geh.), **jmdm. zu [großem] ~ verpflichtet sein** owe sb. a [great] debt of gratitude; **kein Wort des ~es sagen** not say *or* offer a word of thanks; **als** *od.* **zum ~ dafür, dass ich seinen Hund in Pflege genommen hatte** as a way of saying 'thank you' to me for looking after his dog; **zum ~ dafür hat sie mir noch ins Gesicht gespuckt** (iron.) all the thanks I got was that she spat in my face; **und das ist nun der ~ dafür** (iron.) so that's all the thanks I get!; **zum ~ für seine Verdienste** in grateful recognition of his services; **mit vielem** *od.* **bestem ~ zurück** thanks for the loan; (bes. geschrieben) returned with thanks!; **etw. mit ~ annehmen** accept sth. with thanks; **von [tiefem] ~ erfüllt sein** (geh.) be filled with a [deep] sense of gratitude; **damit wird er [bei mir] wenig/keinen ~ ernten** he won't get much/any thanks [from me] for that **2** (in ~esformeln) **haben Sie ~!** please accept my thanks; **vielen/besten/herzlichen ~!** thank you very much; many thanks; **vielen ~, dass du mir beim Umzug geholfen hast** thank you very much for helping me with the move; **[nein,] vielen ~!** (iron.) no, thank you!; **tausend ~!** (ugs.) very many thanks [indeed]; *s. auch* **heiß**

Dank·adresse *die* [official] letter of thanks

dankbar

A *Adj.* **1** (voller Dank) grateful; (anerkennend) appreciative ‹*child, audience, etc.*›; **in ~er Anerkennung** (+ *Gen.*)/**Erinnerung an** (+ *Akk.*) in grateful recognition/memory of; **[jmdm.] für etw. ~ sein** be grateful [to sb.] for sth.; **sich ~ zeigen** show one's gratitude *or* appreciation; **sie sind für jede Abwechslung ~:** they are thankful for any diversion; **für eine baldige Antwort wären wir ~:** we should be grateful for an early reply; **ich wäre Ihnen sehr ~, wenn Sie … könnten** I should be very grateful if you could … **2** (lohnend) rewarding ‹*job, part, task, etc.*› **3** (ugs.: haltbar) hard-wearing ‹*material, clothes*›; (unempfindlich) easy-care ‹*garment, plant, etc.*›

B *adv.* gratefully; **etw. ~ annehmen** *od.* **entgegennehmen** accept sth. gratefully *or* with thanks; **jmdn. ~ anblicken** give sb. a look of gratitude

Dankbarkeit *die;* **~:** gratitude; **etw. aus ~ tun** do sth. out of gratitude; **in/mit [aufrichtiger/tiefer] ~:** in/with [sincere/deep] gratitude

Dank·brief *der* letter of thanks; thank-you letter

danke /ˈdaŋkə/ *Höflichkeitsformel* thank you; (ablehnend) no, thank you; **Darf ich Ihnen noch Tee nachgießen? — Ja ~[, gern]** May I pour you some more tea? — Yes, please[, I'd like some]; **Gefällt es Ihnen hier bei uns? — Ja ~, sehr sogar** Do you like it here? — Yes, thank you, very much; **nein ~, ~ nein** no, thank you; **Soll ich Ihnen helfen? — Danke, es geht schon** Shall I help you? — No thank you *or* No thanks, it's all right; **~ schön/sehr/vielmals** thank you very much; **~ schön sagen** say 'thank you'; **Wie gehts? — Mir gehts ~** (ugs.) How are you? — I'm OK [thanks] (coll.); **sonst gehts dir [wohl] ~!** (ugs.) what do you think you're doing?; have you taken leave of your senses?

danken

A *itr. V.* (Dank aussprechen) thank; **jmdm. für etw. [vielmals] ~:** thank sb. [very much] for sth.; **ich danke Ihnen vielmals** thank you very much; **er dankte kurz und verließ das Zimmer** he said a quick 'thank you' and left the room; **danke der [gütigen] Nachfrage!** (meist scherzh. od. iron.) thanks for asking; kind of you to ask; **Betrag ~d erhalten** [payment] received with thanks; **~d ablehnen** decline with thanks; **dafür danke ich bestens** (iron.) thanks a lot (coll.); **na, ich danke!** (ugs.) no, 'thank you!; **ich danke für Obst und Südfrüchte** (ugs.) no, thanks; *s. auch* **Knie**

B *tr. V.* **1** **[aber bitte,] nichts zu ~:** don't mention it; not at all; **es wird einem noch nicht einmal gedankt** you don't even get any thanks [for it]; **sie hat ihm seine Hilfe schlecht gedankt** she gave him a poor reward for his help; **er dankte ihnen ihre Güte mit Ungehorsam** (iron.) the only reward they got [from him] for their kindness was disobedience **2** (geh.: ver~) **jmdm. etw. ~:** owe sb. sth.; owe sth. to sb.; **nur diesem Umstand ist es zu ~, dass …** it was only thanks to this that …

dankens·wert *Adj.* commendable ‹*effort etc.*›; **es ist ~, dass er uns hilft** it is kind *or* very good of him to help [us]

dankenswerter·weise *Adv.* kindly; generously; **~ haben sich viele freiwillig gemeldet** commendably many have volunteered

Danke·schön *das;* **~s** thank you; **ein [herzliches] ~ sagen** express one's [sincere] thanks; **nicht einmal ein ~ bekommen** not get so much as a thank you

Dankes·wort *das; Pl.* **~e** word of thanks

Dank-: ~gebet *das* prayer of thanksgiving; **~gottes·dienst** *der* thanksgiving service; **~sagung** *die;* **~, ~en** (Text) expression of thanks; (Karte) note of thanks; (Brief) letter of thanks; **~schreiben** *das* letter of thanks

dann /dan/ *Adv.* **1** then; **was machen wir ~?** what shall we do then *or* after that?; **was ~?** what happens then?; **noch drei Tage, ~ ist Ostern** another three days and it will be Easter; **was soll ~ werden?** what will happen then?; **bis ~:** see you then; **~ und ~:** at such and such a time; (an dem und dem Tag) on such and such a date; **von ~ bis ~:** from such and such a date/time to such and such a date/time; **~ und wann** now and then **2** (räumlich: dahinter) **zuerst kam die Kapelle, ~ folgten die Pfadfinder** first came the band, then *or* followed by the Scouts; **an die Gärten schließt sich ~ Ödland an** then at the end of the gardens there is a piece of wasteland **3** (rangmäßig danach) **er ist der Klassenbeste, ~ kommt sein Bruder** he is top of the class, followed by his brother *or* then comes his brother **4** (unter diesen Umständen) **~ will ich nicht weiter stören** then *or* in that case I won't disturb you any further; **na ~!** well, that's different!; **[na,] ~ eben nicht!** in that case, forget it!; **~ bis morgen** see you tomorrow, then; **wenn er selbst nicht hinfahren kann, wer ~?** if he can't go there himself, who can?; **nur ~, wenn …** only if …; **lehnt er ab, ~ werden wir klagen** if he refuses, [then] we shall complain **5** (außerdem) **~ noch … then … as well; und ~ kommt noch die Mehrwertsteuer hinzu** and then there's VAT (Brit.) *or* (Amer.) tax to add on top of that; **zuletzt fiel ~ noch der Strom aus** finally to top it all there was a power failure **6** (demnach) **~ hast du also die ganze Zeit mit zugehört** so you've been listening the whole time **7** (schließlich) **es hat ~ doch noch geklappt** it was all right in the end

dannen /ˈdanən/ *Adv. in* **von ~** (veralt.) from thence (arch./literary); **von ~ eilen/gehen** hasten away/depart

dantesk /danˈtɛsk/ *Adj.* (geh.) Dantesque

dantisch /ˈdantɪʃ/ *Adj.* Dantean

Danzig /ˈdantsɪç/ (*das*); **~s** Gdansk; (vor 1945) Danzig

daran /daˈran/ *Adv.* **1** (an dieser/diese Stelle, an diesem/diesen Gegenstand) on it/them; **es klebt etwas ~:** something is sticking to it/them; **es hängt etwas ~:** something is hanging from it/them; **er klammert sich ~** (auch fig.) he clings to it; **~ riechen** take a sniff at it/them; **~ vorbei** past it/them; **kommen wir noch einmal ~ vorbei?** shall we be passing it/them again?; **dicht ~:** close to it/them; **nahe ~ sein, etw. zu tun** be on the point of doing sth. **2** (hinsichtlich dieser Sache) about it/them; **denken Sie ~:** think about it/them; **das Beste/Schlimmste ~:** the best/worst part of *or* about it/them; **~ ist nichts zu machen** there's nothing one can do about it; **~ wird sich nichts ändern** nothing will alter this fact; **kein Wort ~ ist wahr** not a word of it is true; **er arbeitet schon lange ~:** he has been working on it/them for a long time; **wir haben keinen Bedarf mehr ~:** we no longer have any need of it/them; **mir liegt viel ~:** it means a lot to me; **mir liegt ~, zu erfahren, wie er zu der Sache steht** I'd really like *or* I'd be interested to know his view of this matter; **Sie werden viel Freude ~ haben** you will get a lot of pleasure from it **3** (aufgrund dieser Sache) **ich wäre beinahe ~ erstickt** I almost choked on it; it almost made me choke; **er ist ~ gestorben** he died of it **4** (an diesen Vorgang) **~ anschließend** *od.* **im Anschluss ~ fand eine Diskussion statt** after that there was a discussion; *s. auch* **da-**; **dran**

daran- (*s. auch* **dran-**): **~|geben** *unr. tr. V.* (geh.) sacrifice; **~|gehen** *unr. itr. V.; mit sein* set about it; **~gehen, etw. zu tun** set about doing sth.; **~|machen** *refl. V.* (ugs.) set about it; (ernstlich) get down to it; **sich ~machen, etw. zu tun** get down to/set about doing sth.; **~|setzen** **A** *tr. V.* devote ‹*energy etc.*› to it; summon up ‹*ambition*› for it; (aufs Spiel setzen) risk ‹*one's life, one's honour*› for it; **er hat alles** *od.* **alle seine Kräfte ~gesetzt, um dieses Ziel zu erreichen** he spared no effort to achieve *or* devoted all his energy to achieving this aim; **B** *refl. V.* (ugs.: in Angriff nehmen) get down to it; **sich ~setzen, etw. zu tun** get down to doing sth.; **~|wenden** *unr. od. regelm. tr. V.* (geh.) devote ‹*time, effort*› to it

darauf /da'rauf/ *Adv.* 1) (auf dieser/diese Stelle) on it/them; (oben ~) on top of it/them; **er isst gern Frikadellen mit Senf ~:** he likes eating rissoles with mustard on top; **er goss Wasser ~:** he poured water on [to] it/them 2) (auf ein Ziel hin) **er hat ~ geschossen** he shot at it/them; **~ müsst ihr zugehen** that's what you must head towards *or* make for; **ich muss ~ dringen** I must insist on it; **er ist ganz versessen ~:** he is mad [keen] on it (coll.); **also darauf willst du hinaus** so 'that's what you're getting at; **~ wollen wir anstoßen!** let's drink to that! 3) (auf diese Angelegenheit) about it; **wir kamen nur kurz ~ zu sprechen** we only talked about it briefly *or* touched on it; **wie kommt du nur ~?** what makes you think that?; **wie kommst du ~, so etwas anzunehmen?** how do you come to assume such a thing? 4) (danach) after that; **erst ein Blitz, unmittelbar ~ ein Donnerschlag** first there was lightning, immediately followed by a clap of thunder; **ein Jahr ~/ kurz ~ starb er** he died a year later/shortly afterwards; **zuerst kamen die Kinder, ~ folgten die Festwagen** first came the children, then followed *or* followed by the floats; **dieser und der ~ folgende Wagen** this car and the one behind *or* following it; **am ~ folgenden Tag** the following day; next day 5) (infolgedessen, ~hin) because of that; as a result 6) **der Gutschein ist verfallen, ~ bekommen Sie nichts mehr** the voucher is out of date, you won't get anything on *or* for that; **~ fußen alle unsere Überlegungen** all our deliberations are based on it *or* this; *s. auch* **da-; drauf; tags**

darauf- (*s. auch* **drauf-**): **~folgend** ▸**darauf 4**; **~hin** /-'-/ *Adv.* 1) (infolgedessen) as a result [of this/that]; consequently; (zeitlich) thereupon; 2) (unter diesem Gesichtspunkt) with a view to this/that; **etw. ~hin prüfen, ob es geeignet ist** examine sth. to see whether it is suitable

daraus /da'raus/ *Adv.* 1) (aus diesem Raum, Behälter o. Ä. heraus) from it/them; out of it/them; **er holte eine Flasche und goss ~ ein** he fetched a bottle and poured out drinks from it; **sie öffnete den Koffer und holte ein Kleid ~ hervor** she opened the suitcase and took out a dress *or* took a dress out of it 2) (aus dieser Angelegenheit, Sache) from it/them; out of it/them; **wir alle wissen das und sollten ~ lernen** we all know that and should learn from it; **sie hat ihm nie einen Vorwurf ~ gemacht** she never reproached him for it *or* made an issue out of it; **mach dir nichts ~:** don't worry about it; **dieser Stoff ist hübsch, ~ nähe ich mir ein Kleid** this material is pretty, I'm going to make myself a dress out of it; **Kartoffeln sind nicht nur zum Essen da, viele machen Schnaps ~:** potatoes are not only for eating — a lot of people make schnapps from them; **~ ist eine große Firma geworden** it has become *or* turned into a large business; **was ist ~ geworden?** what has become of it?; **~ wird nichts** nothing will come of it 3) (aus dieser Quelle, Unterlage) from it/them; **~ geht eindeutig hervor, dass ...** from this it is clear that ...

darben /'darbn̩/ *itr. V.* (geh.) 1) (in Not leben) live in want; (sich sehr einschränken) go short; pinch and scrape; **die ~den Massen** the indigent *or* destitute masses; **wir haben sehr gedarbt** we suffered great want 2) (Hunger leiden) go hungry

dar|bieten (geh.)
A *unr. tr. V.* 1) (anbieten) offer; serve ‹*drinks, food*›; **die dargebotene Hand ausschlagen** (fig.) reject the proffered hand [of friendship] (fig.) 2) (aufführen, vortragen) perform; **es wurden Gedichte und Lieder dargeboten** a recital of poems and songs was presented
B *unr. refl. V.* **sich jmds. Blicken ~:** expose oneself to sb.'s gaze; **eine herrliche Aussicht bot sich uns dar** a marvellous view met our eyes

Darbietung *die;* **~, ~en** (geh.) 1) presentation 2) (Aufführung) performance; (beim Varietee usw.) act

dar|bringen *unr. tr. V.* offer; **jmdm. ein Ständchen ~:** serenade sb.

darein /da'rain/ *Adv.* (geh.) in it/them; *s. auch* **da-**

darein-: **~|finden** *unr. refl. V.* (geh.) come to terms with it; (sich daran gewöhnen) become accustomed to it; **~|fügen** *refl. V.* (geh.) resign oneself to it; **~|reden** *itr. V.* **jmdm. ~reden** meddle *or* interfere in sb.'s affairs/decisions *etc.;* (unterbrechen) interrupt sb.; **niemand hat ihm ~zureden** nobody has any right to [try to] tell him what to do; **~|setzen** *tr. V.* devote to it; **alles** *od.* **seine ganze Energie ~setzen, etw. zu tun** concentrate all one's efforts on doing sth.; **er setzt seinen ganzen Ehrgeiz ~, als erster fertig zu sein** he has made it his great ambition to finish first

darf /darf/ *1. u. 3. Pers. Sg. Präsens v.* **dürfen**

darfst /darfst/ *2. Pers. Sg. Präsens v.* **dürfen**

darin /da'rɪn/ *Adv.* 1) (in dieser Sache o. Ä.) in it/them; (drinnen) inside [it/them]; **die ~ enthaltenen Briefe** the letters contained in it/them *or* (formal) therein 2) (in dieser Hinsicht) in that respect; **~ stimme ich völlig mit Ihnen überein** I entirely agree with you there; *s. auch* **da-**

darinnen /da'rɪnən/ *Adv.* (geh.) in it/them; therein (formal)

dar|legen *tr. V.* explain; set forth ‹*reasons, facts*›; expound ‹*theory*›; **jmdm. etw. ~:** explain sth. to sb.; **etw. schriftlich ~:** set sth. out in writing

Darlegung *die;* **~, ~en** explanation

Darlehen /'da:ɐ̯le:ən/ *das;* **~s, ~:** loan; **ein ~ aufnehmen** get *or* raise a loan; **jmdm. ein ~ gewähren** give *or* grant sb. a loan

Darlehens-: **~kasse** *die* credit bank; **~nehmer** *der;* **~s, ~, ~nehmerin** *die;* **~~, ~~nen** (Bankw.) borrower; **~summe** *die* amount of the loan; **eine ~summe von ...** a loan amounting to ...; **~vertrag** *der* loan agreement

Darm /darm/ *der;* **~[e]s, Därme** /'dɛrmə/ 1) ▸ⓘ **S. 435** intestines *pl.;* bowels *pl.;* **[jmdm.] auf den ~ schlagen** give sb. diarrhoea; **den ~ entleeren** evacuate *or* empty one's bowels; **Erkrankungen des ~es** intestinal diseases 2) (als Saiten) gut 3) (als Wursthaut) skin

Darm-: **~ausgang** *der* ▸ⓘ **S. 435** (Anat.) anus; **~blutung** *die* ▸ⓘ **S. 439** (Med.) intestinal haemorrhage; **~bruch** *der* (Med.) enterocele; **~entleerung** *die* evacuation of the bowels; **~grippe** *die* ▸ⓘ **S. 439** gastric influenza; **~katarrh** *der* ▸ⓘ **S. 439** (Med.) enteritis; **~krebs** *der* cancer of the intestine *or* bowel; **~saite** *die* gut string; **~spiegelung** *die* (Med.) colonoscopy; **~spülung** *die* (Med.) enema; **~tätigkeit** *die* (Med.) functioning of the bowels; **~trägheit** *die* ▸ⓘ **S. 439** (Med.) constipation; **~trakt** *der* ▸ⓘ **S. 435** (Anat.) intestinal tract; **~verschlingung** *die* ▸ⓘ **S. 439** (Med.) volvulus; **~verschluss, *~verschluß** *der* ▸ⓘ **S. 439** (Med.) intestinal obstruction

darnach (veralt.) ▸**danach**

darneben (veralt.) ▸**daneben**

darnieder- ▸**danieder-**

darob /da'rɔp/ *Adv.* (veralt.) 1) (darüber) about it/them; **er wunderte sich ~, dass ...** he was surprised that ... 2) (deswegen) because of it; *s. auch* **da-**

Darre /'darə/ *die;* **~, ~n** 1) (Vorrichtung) [drying] kiln 2) (das ~n) drying

dar|reichen *tr. V.* (geh.) 1) (anbieten) proffer 2) (überreichen) **jmdm. ein Geschenk** *usw.* **~:** present sb. with a gift *etc.*

darren *tr. V.* dry

Darr-: **~gewicht** *das* [kiln-]dry weight (*of wood*); **~malz** *das* [kiln-]dried malt

darstellbar *Adj.* 1) (abbildbar) depictable; portrayable; **ist das grafisch ~?** can that be represented graphically?; **grafisch ~e Entwicklungen** developments which can be shown on a graph *or* diagram 2) (spielbar) playable ‹*part*› 3) (Chemie) **ein leicht ~er Stoff** a material which can easily be produced

dar|stellen
A *tr. V.* 1) (abbilden) depict; portray; **etw. grafisch ~:** present sth. graphically; (als Graph) show sth. on a graph; **wen/was stellt dieses Bild dar?** whom does this picture portray/what does this picture represent?; **die ~de Geometrie** descriptive geometry; **die ~de Kunst** the performing arts *pl.;* **ein ~der Künstler** a performer 2) (verkörpern) play; act; **den Othello ~:** play *or* act [the part of] Othello; **etwas/mehr/nichts ~:** make [a bit of] an impression/more of an impression/not make any sort of an impression; ‹*gift etc.*› look good/look better/not look anything special 3) (schildern) describe ‹*person, incident, etc.*›; present ‹*matter, argument*›; **falsch/verzerrt ~:** misrepresent/distort ‹*facts*›; **es wurde dann so dargestellt, als sei das unser Wunsch gewesen** it was then put in such a way as to suggest that we had wanted it; **so schlimm, wie du ihn darstellst, ist er auch nicht** he is not as bad as you make him out to be 4) (sein, bedeuten) represent; constitute; **das zweite Kind stellt eine große Belastung für sie dar** the second child means a heavy load for her 5) (Chemie) produce
B *refl. V.* 1) (sich erweisen, sich zeigen) prove [to be]; turn out to be; **sich jmdm. als ... ~:** appear to sb. as ...; **nach dem Bericht stellt sich die Sache ungefähr so dar** according to the report the situation appears to be roughly this 2) (sich selbst schildern) portray oneself (**als** + *Akk.* as); **sie lieben es, sich als Wohltäter darzustellen** they like to present themselves in the role of benefactors

Darsteller *der;* **~s, ~:** actor; **der ~ des Hamlet** the actor playing Hamlet; **berühmt als ~ des Hamlet** famous for his portrayal of Hamlet *or* as an interpreter of Hamlet

Darstellerin *die;* **~, ~nen** actress; *s. auch* **Darsteller**

darstellerisch
A *Adj.* acting *attrib.;* **das Darstellerische** the interpretative aspect; **eine einmalige ~e Leistung** a marvellous piece of acting; **ihre ~en Fähigkeiten** her abilities as an actress
B *adv.* from an acting point of view

Darstellung *die* 1) representation; (Schilderung) portrayal; (Bild) picture; **grafische/schematische ~:** diagram; (Graph) graph 2) (Beschreibung, Bericht) description; account; **bei seiner ~ der geschichtlichen Tatsachen** in his account *or* rendering of the historical facts 3) (einer Theaterrolle) interpretation; performance; (einer Szene usw.) performance; **seine ~ des Mephisto** his portrayal *or* interpretation of Mephisto; **etw. zur ~ bringen** portray sth.; (aufführen) perform sth. 4) (Chemie) production

Darstellungs-: **~form** *die* form of representation; **~mittel** *das* representational technique; (eines Schauspielers) acting technique

dar|tun *unr. tr. V.* (geh.) (darlegen) state ‹*fact, one's reasons*›; (erklären) explain; (demonstrieren) demonstrate; **er hat zur Genüge dargetan, wie ...** he gave a sufficient account of how ...

darüber *Adv.* 1) (über dem Genannten) over *or* above it/them; **~ liegen** be higher; **wir wohnen im zweiten Stock und er ~:** we live on the second floor and he lives above us; **sie liegen mit ihrem Angebot weit ~:** their offer is much higher; **~ stehen** (fig.) be above such things 2) (über es [hinweg]) over it/them; **~ führen zu wenige Brücken** too few bridges go across it/them; **~ hinaus** in addition [to that]; (noch obendrein) what is more; **~ hinaus sein** (zu alt dafür sein) be beyond that stage [now]; (es überwunden haben) have got over it; **~ fahren/steigen** run/climb over it/them; **sie fuhr rasch mit der Hand/mit einem Tuch ~:** she quickly ran her hand over it/wiped it with a cloth; **sich ~ machen** (fig. ugs.) get down to it/them; (zu essen beginnen) get stuck into it (coll.); (zu trinken beginnen) get to work on it 3) (über dieser/diese Angelegenheit) about it/them; **~ kann kein Zweifel bestehen** there can be no doubt about it; **ich habe fast den ganzen Tag ~ gesessen** I spent almost the whole day over *or* on it; **~ wollen wir hinwegsehen** we will

d

overlook it **4** (über diese Grenze, dieses Maß hinaus) above [that]; over [that]; **Kinder im Alter von 5 Jahren und ~:** children of 5 and over; **der Preis beträgt 50 Euro oder etwas ~:** the price is 50 euros or a bit more; **Ist es schon 12 Uhr? — Aber ja, es ist schon 10 Minuten ~:** Is it twelve o'clock yet? — Oh yes, it's already ten past; **man braucht 4 Wochen, manchmal auch etwas ~:** it takes four weeks, sometimes rather longer *or* more **5** (währenddessen) in the process; **es war ~ Abend geworden** meanwhile it had become evening **6** (währenddessen und deshalb) because of it/them; as a result; **der Film war so spannend, dass er ~ seine Sorgen vergaß** the film was so exciting that it made him forget his worries; *s. auch* **da-**

darüber|fahren *usw.* ▸**darüber 2**

darum /da'rʊm/ *Adv.* **1** (um diese Stelle herum) [a]round it/them; **ein Häuschen mit einem Garten ~ [herum]** a little house surrounded by a garden **2** (hinsichtlich dieser Angelegenheit) **ich werde mich ~ bemühen** I will try to deal with it; (versuchen, es zu bekommen) I'll try to get it; **sie wird nicht ~ herumkommen, es zu tun** she won't get out of *or* avoid doing it; **~ ist es mir nicht zu tun, ~ geht es mir nicht** that's not the point as far as I'm concerned; that's not what I'm after; **es geht mir ~, eine Einigung zu erzielen** my concern *or* aim is to reach an agreement **3** /'--/ (deswegen) because of that; for that reason; **ach, ~ ist er so schlecht gelaunt!** so that's why he's in such a bad mood!; **er ist zwar klein, aber ~ nicht schwach** he is small but that doesn't mean that he's weak; **Warum weinst du? — Darum!** Why are you crying? — Because!; *s. auch* **da-**

darum-: ~|binden *unr. tr. V.* tie [a]round it/them; **~|kommen** *unr. itr. V.*; *mit sein* lose it/them; **~kommen, etw. zu tun** miss the opportunity of doing sth.; miss out on [doing] sth. (coll.); **~|legen** *tr. V.* put around it/them

darunter /da'rʊntɐ/ *Adv.* **1** (unter dem Genannten/das Genannte) under *or* beneath it/them; **wir wohnen im 2. Stock und er ~:** we live on the second floor and he lives under us *or* on the floor below; **sie hatte nichts ~ an** she was wearing nothing underneath; **etw. ~ schreiben** write/type sth. underneath *or* at the bottom; (ab Unterschrift) sign sth. underneath *or* at the bottom; **seinen Namen/seine Unterschrift ~ setzen** put one's name/one's signature to it; **~ gehen** (ugs.: darunter passen) fit *or* go underneath **2** (unter dieser Grenze, diesem Maß) less; **10° oder etwas ~:** 10° or a bit less; **~ kann ich die Vase nicht verkaufen** I can't sell the vase for less; **Bewerber im Alter von 40 Jahren und ~:** applicants aged 40 and under; **~ tut er es nicht** (ugs.) he's not satisfied with anything less; **~ bleiben** remain lower; (niedriger sein) be lower; **viele forderten 20%, wir bleiben aber ~:** many demanded 20%, but we kept below this; **~ gehen** go below that; **~ liegen** be lower; (weniger bekommen) get less; **die Parallelklasse liegt mit ihren Leistungen ~:** the parallel class's performance is not as good **3** (unter dieser Sache) **was verstehen Sie ~?** what do you understand by that?; **was hat man ~ zu verstehen?** what is one to make of it/that?; what is it/that supposed to mean?; **sie hat sehr ~ gelitten** she suffered a great deal from *or* because of it/that **4** (unter dieser/diese Menge, dazwischen) amongst them; **in vielen Ländern, ~ der Schweiz** in many countries, including Switzerland; **~ fallen** be included; be amongst them; (in diese Kategorie fallen) come under it; **etw. ~ mischen** mix sth. in; mix sth. with it; **sich ~ mischen** mingle with it/them; *s. auch* **da-**

***darunter|bleiben** *usw.* ▸**darunter**

Darwinismus /darvi'nɪsmʊs/ *der;* **~:** Darwinism *no art.*

darwinistisch

A *Adj.* Darwinian; Darwinist

B *adv.* in Darwinian terms

das /das/

A *best. Art.* the; **~ Leben im Dschungel** life in the jungle; **~ Weihnachtsfest** Christmas; **~ Frankreich/London des 19. Jahrhunderts** nineteenth-century France/London; **~ Laufen/Sprechen fällt ihm schwer** walking/talking is difficult for him; **~ Gute/Schöne** what is good/beautiful

B *Demonstrativpron.* **1** *attr.* **das Kind/Buch/Auto war es** it was 'that child/book/car **2** *selbstständig* **das [da]** that one; **das [hier]** this one [here]; **~ mit dem blonden Haar/roten Umschlag** the one with the fair hair/red cover; **~ Schwein, ~!** the dirty pig!; **mein Auto, ~ ist kaputt** (ugs.) oh, my car — it's conked out (coll.)

C *Relativpron.* (Mensch) who; that; (Sache, Tier) which; that; **~ Mädchen, ~ da drüben entlanggeht** the girl walking along over there; **ich sah ein Mädchen/Hündchen, ~ aus dem Fenster schaute** I saw a girl/little dog looking out of the window

***da|sein** ▸**da A 8-11**

Da·sein *das* **1** (Vorhandensein) existence; **etw. ins ~ rufen** create sth.; (gründen) found sth. **2** (menschliche Existenz) life; **sich/jmdm. das ~ erleichtern** make life easier for oneself/sb.; **ein trauriges ~ führen** lead a miserable existence; *s. auch* **fristen**, **Kampf 3** (Zugegensein) presence

Daseins-: ~berechtigung *die* right to exist; **das findet darin** *od.* **dadurch seine ~berechtigung** this justifies its existence; **~form** *die* form *or* mode of existence; **~freude** *die* ▸**Lebensfreude**; **~kampf** *der* struggle for existence

da·selbst *Adv.* (geh. veralt.) there

da|sitzen *unr. itr. V.* **1** sit there **2** (ugs.: ohne etw. auskommen müssen) be left [there]; **ich saß ohne Geld da** I was stuck there without any money; **jetzt sitzen wir da!** now we're stuck!

dasjenige ▸**derjenige**

dass, *daß /das/ *Konj.* **1** that; **entschuldigen Sie bitte, ~ ich mich verspätet habe** please forgive me for being late; please forgive my being late; **ich weiß, ~ du Recht hast** I know [that] you are right; **ich verstehe nicht, ~ sie ihn geheiratet hat** I don't understand why she married him; **es ist schon 3 Jahre her, ~ wir zum letzten Mal im Theater waren** it is three years since *or* it was three years ago when we last went to the theatre **2** (nach Pronominaladverbien o. Ä.) [the fact] that; (bei gleichen Subjekten) **er leidet darunter, ~ er kleiner ist** he suffers from the fact that he is smaller *or* from being smaller; **Wissen erwirbt man dadurch, ~ man viel liest** one acquires knowledge by reading a great deal; (bei verschiedenen Subjekten) **das liegt daran, ~ du nicht aufgepasst hast** that is due to the fact that you did not pay attention; that comes from your not paying attention; **ich bin dagegen, ~ er geht** I am against his going **3** (mit Konsekutivsatz) that; **[so] ~:** so that; in such a way that; **ich bin so müde, ~ ich kaum gehen kann** I am so tired [that] I can hardly walk; **er lachte so [sehr], ~ ihm die Tränen in die Augen traten** he laughed so much that he almost cried **4** (mit Finalsatz) so that; **hilf ihm doch, ~ er endlich fertig wird** do help him so that he'll finally be ready/finished **5** (mit Wunschsatz) if only; **~ er doch käme!** if only he would come!; **~ ihn doch der Teufel hole!** to hell with him!; **~ mir das nicht noch einmal passiert!** see that it doesn't happen again!; **o ~ ich dich bald wieder sehe!** (poet.) oh that I may see you again soon! **6** (bedauernder Ausruf) **~ er so jung sterben musste!** how terrible *or* it's so sad that he had to die so young!; **~ mir das passieren musste!** why did it have to [go and] happen to me!; *s. auch* **als**, **[an]statt**, **auf**, **außer**, **nur**, **ohne**, **kaum**

dasselbe ▸**derselbe**

dasselbige ▸**derselbige**

Dassel·fliege *die* botfly

da|stehen *unr. itr. V.* **1** ([untätig] stehen) [just] stand there; **wie stehst du denn da!** what a way to stand!; **krumm ~:** slouch; **~ wie die Kuh** *od.* **der Ochs vorm neuen Tor** *od.* **Scheunentor** *od.* **vorm Berg** (salopp) be completely baffled **2** (in einer bestimmten Lage sein) find oneself; **gut/schlecht/[ganz] anders ~:** be in a good/bad/[quite] different position; **[ganz] allein ~:** be [all] alone in the world; **nun, wie stehe ich jetzt da?** (ugs.) just look at me now!; (bei einer bestimmten Leistung) how about that?; (verzweifelt) now I'm sunk! (coll.); **wie stehen wir denn jetzt vor den Nachbarn da?** what will the neighbours think of us now?; **mit leeren Händen/als Lügner** *usw.* **~:** be left empty-handed/looking like a liar *etc.*

Datei /da'tai̯/ *die;* **~, ~en** data file

Datei-: ~format *das* (DV) file format; **~manager** *der* (DV) file manager; **~name** *der* (DV) file name; **~verwaltung** *die* (DV) file management

Daten /'da:tn̩/ *Pl.* (Angaben) data; (persönliche ~) particulars; **die technischen ~ eines Typs** the technical specification *sing.* of a model; *s. auch* **Datum**

Daten-: ~abgleich *der* (DV) data synchronization; **~autobahn** *die* (DV) data highway; **~bank** *die; Pl.* **~~en** data bank; **~bestand** *der* database; **~erfassung** *die* data collection *or* capture; **~format** *das* (DV) ▸**Dateiformat**; **~handschuh** *der* dataglove; **~helm** *der* data helmet; virtual reality helmet; **~highway** /-hai̯weɪ/ *der;* **~~s, ~~s** ▸**~autobahn**; **~komprimierung** *die* data compression; **~schutz** *der* data protection; **~schutzbeauftragte** *der/die* data protection officer; **~technik** *die* data systems [engineering]; **~träger** *der* data carrier; **~typist** *der;* **~~en, ~~en**, **~typistin** *die;* **~~, ~~nen** data processing keyboarder; **~verarbeitung** *die* data processing *no def. art.*; **~verarbeitungs·anlage** *die* data processor; (größeres System) data processing system

datieren /da'ti:rən/

A *tr. V.* date; **vom 1. Mai datiert** dated 1 May; **archäologische Funde [ins 3. Jh.] ~:** date archaeological finds [to the third century AD]

B *itr. V.* (stammen) date (**aus** from); **der Brief datierte vom 4. Mai** the letter was dated 4 May

Dativ /'da:ti:f/ *der;* **~s, ~e** (Sprachw.) dative [case]; (Wort im ~) dative [form]; **im/mit dem ~ stehen** be in/take the dative [case]

Dativ·objekt *das* (Sprachw.) indirect object

dato /'da:to/ *in* **bis ~** (Kaufmannsspr., sonst ugs.) to date

Dato·wechsel *der* (Bankw.) time bill

Datscha /'datʃa/ *die;* **~, ~s** *od.* **Datschen, Datsche** /'datʃə/ *die;* **Datsche, Datschen** (DDR) dacha

Dattel /'datl̩/ *die;* **~, ~n** date

Dattel-: ~palme *die* date palm; **~traube** *die: popular name for various large, elongated black grapes*

Datterich /'datərɪç/ ▸**Tatterich**

Datum /'da:tʊm/ *das;* **~s, Daten** /'da:tn̩/ **1** ▸**ⓘ S. 143**, ▸**ⓘ S. 165** (Zeitangabe, Zeitpunkt) date; **das heutige ~:** the date today; today's date; **was für ein/welches ~ haben wir heute?** what is the date today?; **der Brief trägt das ~ vom 6. Mai** the letter is dated 6 May; **unter dem heutigen/gestrigen ~ übersandten wir Ihnen ...** in today's/yesterday's mail we sent you ...; **ein Schriftstück mit dem ~ versehen** date a document; **eine Entdeckung neueren ~s** a recent discovery **2** (Faktum) fact

Datums-: ~grenze *die* date line; **~stempel** *der* date stamp

Daube /'dau̯bə/ *die;* **~, ~n** **1** (am Fass) stave **2** (beim Eisschießen) tee

Dauer /'dau̯ɐ/ *die;* **~, ~n** **1** (Zeitraum) length; duration; **die ~ eines Vertrags** the term of a contract; **die ~ des Besuchs** the length of the visit; **von kurzer** *od.* **nicht von [langer] ~ sein** not last long; be short-lived; **für die ~ eines Jahres** *od.* **von einem Jahr** for a period of one year; **während der ~ unseres Aufenthalts** for the duration of our stay; (die ganze Zeit) throughout our whole stay **2** (Fortbestehen) **von ~ sein** last [long]; **ihr Glück hatte keine ~** *od.* **war nicht von ~:** her happiness was short-lived *or* did not last [long]; **auf die ~:** in the long run; **der Lärm ist auf die ~ nicht zu**

ℹ Datum

Im Englischen gibt es mehrere Möglichkeiten, das Datum zu schreiben oder zu sagen:

der 10. Mai
= (*geschrieben*) May 10, 10 May, May 10th, 10th May
= (*gesprochen*) May the tenth, the tenth of May *od.* (*amerik.*) May tenth

Die folgenden Beispiele beziehen sich auf die häufigsten Versionen, die überall in der englischsprachigen Welt verwendet werden: **May 10** bzw. **May 10th** für die schriftliche Form, die auch so im Briefkopf erscheint, und **May the tenth** für die gesprochene Form.

Selbstverständlich werden Daten auch nur mit Ziffern angegeben, vor allem in Geschäftsbriefen. Hier ist zu beachten, dass in den USA die Reihenfolge Monat, Tag, Jahr (mit Bindestrich) ist. Der Monat erscheint also an erster Stelle (**May 10th 2004** = 5-10-2004). Im britischen Gebrauch hingegen ist die Reihenfolge wie auch im deutschen Tag, Monat, Jahr (10.5.2004, oft auch mit Schrägstrich: 10/5/2004).

Der Wievielte?

Der Wievielte ist heute?
= What's the date [today]?
Heute ist der zehnte Mai
= Today is *od.* It's May the tenth
Am Wievielten ist die Hochzeit?
= What date is the wedding?
Die Hochzeit ist am 22.
= The wedding is on the 22nd (*gesprochen:* twenty-second)

	GESCHRIEBEN	GESPROCHEN
der 1. Mai	May 1st, May 1	May the first
der 21. Mai	May 21st, May 21	May the twenty-first
der 30. Mai 2005	May 30th *od.* May 30 2005 *od.* (*amerik.*) May 30, 2005	May the thirtieth two thousand and five
Montag, der 3. Mai	Monday May 3rd *od.* May 3	Monday May the third
21.5.66	21.5.66 *od.* (*amerik.*) 5-21-66	twenty-one five *od.* (*amerik.*) five twenty-one sixty-six

In welchem Jahr?

1900	1900	nineteen hundred
1905	1905	nineteen [oh] five, nineteen hundred and five
1920	1920	nineteen twenty[1]
das Jahr 2000	the year 2000	the year two thousand
im Jahr 2000	in the year 2000	in the year two thousand
2001	2001	two thousand and one
2020	2020	two thousand and twenty
230 n.Chr.	230 AD[2]	two hundred and thirty AD [ei'di:]
55 v.Chr.	55 BC[3]	fifty-five BC [bi'si:]
das 16. Jahrhundert	the 16th century	the sixteenth century

[1] Meist wird das **hundred and** bei der Jahresangabe weggelassen; es wird aber manchmal doch hinzugefügt, vor allem bei den Jahren 01 bis 09 des Jahrhunderts.

[2] = anno domini

[3] = before Christ

Wann?

am Freitag
= on Friday
am 6. März
= on March 6th (*gesprochen:* on March the sixth)
am Freitag, dem 6. März
= on Friday March 6th (*gesprochen:* on Friday March the sixth)

Beachten Sie, dass **the** nicht geschrieben und nur vor der Ordinalzahl für das Datum gesprochen wird.

Ausnahme: Wenn nur der Tag (ohne Angabe des Monats) genannt wird, wird **the** auch geschrieben:

Wir treffen uns am 6.
= We're meeting on the 6th
Der Termin ist am Ersten
= The deadline is on the first
Sie kommen am nächsten Ersten
= They are coming on the first of next month

Auch bei der Angabe des Monats wird **the** nicht verwendet:

im Juni
= in June
im Juni nächsten Jahres
= next June
letztes Jahr im Juni
= last June
Mitte Juni
= in the middle of June
Ende/Anfang Juni
= at the end/beginning of June

Vor Jahresangaben steht immer **in:**

1945 kam er aus dem Krieg zurück
= In 1945 he came back from the war

Für "im Jahr[e]" sagt man meist einfach **in; in the year ...** ist stilistisch etwas gehoben und bezieht sich meist auf geschichtliche Daten:

im Jahr[e] 55 v.Chr.
= in [the year] 55 BC
im Jahr[e] 27 n.Chr.
= in [the year] 27 AD

Sonstige Ausdrücke

vom 5. November an
= from November 5th [onwards]
ab kommendem Dienstag
= from next Tuesday
vom 21. bis zum 30.
= from the 21st to the 30th
Es wird bis Freitag/bis zum 14. fertig
= It will be ready by Friday/by the 14th
Es wird erst am Freitag fertig
= It won't be ready until Friday
um den 16. Mai [herum]
= around May 16th
in den Sechzigerjahren
= in the sixties *od.* 60s
in den Achtzigerjahren des 19. Jahrhunderts
= in the 1880s
der Roman des 19. Jahrhunderts
= the 19th century novel
ein Komponist des 17. Jahrhunderts
= a 17th century composer
ein Gebäude aus dem 14. Jahrhundert
= a 14th century building
Das Auto ist ein 1998er Modell/ist Baujahr 1998
= The car's a 1998 model
der Aufstand von 1912
= the 1912 uprising

ertragen the noise is not tolerable for any length of time; **auf die ~ möchte ich hier nicht wohnen** I wouldn't want to live here permanently *or* indefinitely; **auf ~:** permanently; for good; **er hat die Stelle jetzt auf ~:** his job is now permanent; he now has tenure (Amer. Sch./Univ.)

dauer-, Dauer-: ~arbeitslose *der/die* long-term unemployed person; **~auftrag** *der* (Finanzw.) standing order; **per** *od.* **durch ~auftrag** by standing order; **~ausweis** *der* long-term pass; **~belastung** *die* continual *or* constant strain; (Technik) permanent load; **~beschäftigung** *die* permanent job *or* (formal) position; **~brenner** *der* **1** (Ofen) slow-burning stove; **2** (ugs.: Theaterstück usw.) long-running success; (Schlager) evergreen; **~einrichtung** *die* permanent institution; **~erfolg** *der* long-running success; **~erscheinung** *die* permanent feature **(bei, in** of); **~frost** *der* long period of frost; **es herrschte ~frost** there was a long period of frost; **~gast** *der* **1** (im Hotel usw.) long-stay guest *or* resident; (scherzh.: Besucher) long-term visitor (*who outstays his/her welcome*); **2** (im Lokal) regular; **~geschwindigkeit** *die* cruising speed; **~haft A** *Adj.* **1** (von langer ~) [long-]lasting, enduring ‹*peace, friendship, etc.*›; **2** (haltbar) durable; hard-wearing; **B** *adv.* lastingly; with long-lasting effect; **~karte** *die* season ticket; **~lauf** *der* jogging *no art.*; **ein ~lauf** a jog; **einen ~lauf machen** go for a jog; go jogging; **im ~lauf** at a jog; **~leihgabe** *die* long-term loan; (auf unbegrenzte Zeit) permanent loan; **~lösung** *die* permanent solution; **~lutscher** *der* large lollipop; all-day sucker (Amer.); **~mieter** *der*, **~mieterin** *die* long-term tenant

dauern¹ *itr. V.* last; ‹*job etc.*› take; **der Film dauert zwei Stunden** the film lasts [for] *or* goes on for two hours; **bei ihm dauert alles furchtbar lange** everything takes him a terribly long time; **einen Moment, es dauert nicht lange** just a minute, it won't take long; **etw. dauert seine Zeit** sth. takes time; **ein Weilchen wird es schon noch ~:** it will be *or* take a little while longer; **es dauert mir zu lange** it takes too long for me; **das dauert** (ugs.) that will take [some] time; **diese Freundschaft wird ~** (geh.) this friendship will last *or* endure

dauern² *tr. V.* (geh.) **die Waisen dauerten ihn** he felt sorry for the orphans; **es dauert mich, dass ...** I regret *or* I am sorry that ...

dauernd
A *Adj.* constant, perpetual ‹*noise, interruptions, etc.*›; permanent ‹*institution*›; **~er Wohnsitz** permanent residence
B *adv.* constantly; (immer) always; the whole time; **er kommt ~ zu spät** he is for ever *or* keeps on arriving late

Dauer-: ~obst *das* fruit which keeps well; **~parker** *der*; **~~s, ~~, ~parkerin** *die*; **~~, ~~nen** long-term parker; (im Parkhaus) holder of a reserved parking space; **~redner** *der*, **~rednerin** *die* (abwertend) voluble speaker; **~regelung** *die* permanent arrangement; **~regen** *der* continuous rain; **~schach** *das* perpetual check; **~schaden** *der* (Med.) **ein ~schaden/~schäden** permanent damage *no indef. art.*; (Verletzung) permanent injury; **~stellung** *die* permanent position; **~stress** *der* permanent stress; **~strom** *der* (Elektrot.) constant current; **~test** *der* long-term test; **~ton** *der; Pl.* **~töne** continuous tone; **~welle** *die* perm; permanent wave; **sie will sich** (*Dat.*) **~wellen legen lassen** *od.* (ugs.) **machen lassen** she wants to have her hair permed; **~wurst** *die* smoked sausage (*with good keeping properties, esp. salami*); **~zustand** *der* permanent state

d

[of affairs]; **zum ~zustand werden** become permanent *or* a permanent state

Däumchen /ˈdɔymçən/ *das;* **~s, ~:** little thumb; **~ drehen** (ugs.) twiddle one's thumbs

Daumen /ˈdaumən/ *der;* **~s, ~ ▸❶ S. 435** thumb; **am ~ lutschen** suck one's thumb; (fig. ugs.) [sit there and] starve; **jmdm.** *od.* **für jmdn. den** *od.* **die ~ drücken** *od.* **halten** keep one's fingers crossed for sb.; **auf etw.** (*Dat.*) **den ~ haben, auf etw.** (*Akk.*) **den ~ halten** (ugs.) keep a careful eye *or* check on sth.; **jmdm. den ~ aufs Auge drücken** (ugs.) put the screws *pl.* on sb.; **[etw.] über den ~ peilen** (ugs.) make a guesstimate [of sth.] (coll.); **über den ~ gepeilt** at a rough estimate

daumen-, Daumen-: ~abdruck *der; Pl.* **~abdrücke** thumbprint; **~breit** *Adj.* as wide as your thumb *postpos.;* ≈ an inch across *postpos.;* **~lutscher** *der,* **~lutscherin** *die;* **~~, ~~nen** (oft abwertend) thumbsucker; **~nagel** *der* **▸❶ S. 435** thumbnail; **~register** *das* thumb index; **~schrauben** *Pl.* (hist.) thumbscrews; **jmdm. die ~schrauben anlegen** (fig.) put the screws on sb.

Däumling /ˈdɔymlɪŋ/ *der;* **~s, ~e** **1** (Märchengestalt) Tom Thumb **2** (Schutzkappe) thumbstall

Daune /ˈdaunə/ *die;* **~, ~n** down [feather]; **~n** down *sing.;* **man geht weich wie auf ~n** it's like walking on thistledown

daunen-, Daunen-: ~bett *das* down-filled quilt; **~kissen** *das* down[-filled] cushion; (für das Bett) down[-filled] pillow; **~weich** *Adj.* downy soft; as soft as down *postpos.*

Daus /daus/ (veralt.) *in* **ei der ~!, was der ~!** what the deuce *or* dickens! (coll.)

David /ˈdaːfɪt/ *(der)* David

David[s]·stern *der* Star of David

davon /daˈfɔn/ *Adv.* **1** (von dieser Stelle entfernt) from it/them; (von dort) from there; (mit Entfernungsangabe) away [from it/them]; **nur einige Meter ~ [entfernt] ist eine Mauer** there is a wall only a few metres away [from it]; **wir sind noch weit ~ entfernt** (fig.) we are still a long way from that; we still have a long way to go **2** (von dieser Stelle weg) from it/them; **sie konnte die Augen nicht ~ abwenden** she could not take her eyes off it *or* away from it; **dies ist die Hauptstraße und ~ zweigen einige Nebenstraßen ab** this is the main road and a few side roads branch off it **3** (hinsichtlich dieser Sache, darüber) about it/them; **er redet nur davon** he talks only of this; he talks of *or* about nothing else **4** (durch diese Angelegenheit verursacht, dadurch) by it/them; thereby; **~ betroffen sein** be affected by it/them; **~ wirst du krank** it will make you ill; **~ kriegt man Durchfall** you get diarrhoea from [eating] that/those; that gives/those give you diarrhoea; **das kommt ~!** (ugs.) [there you are,] that's what happens; (es geschieht dir usw. recht) it serves you/him/her/them right; **das kommt ~, dass du nicht genug schläfst** that's the result of [your] not getting enough sleep; **das hast du nun ~!** that's what comes of it!; **~ hast du doch nichts** you won't *or* don't get anything out of it; there's nothing in it for you **5** (als Teil eines Ganzen; dessen, deren) of it/them; **das Gegenteil ~ ist wahr** the opposite [of this] is true; **ich hätte gern ein halbes Pfund ~:** I would like half a pound of that/those; **geben Sie mir vier ~:** give me four of them; **hast du schon ~ gegessen/genommen?** have you had/taken some of that/those? **6** (aus diesem Material, auf dieser Grundlage) from *or* out of it/them; **hier ist Wolle, du kannst dir einen Schal ~ stricken** here is some wool, you can knit yourself a scarf with it; **~ kann man nicht leben** you can't live on that; *s. auch* **da-**. *NB The word can occur in two parts in North German coll. usage, e.g.* **da weiß ich nichts von** I don't know anything about it

davon-: ~|bleiben *unr. itr. V.; mit sein* keep away; **du sollst ~bleiben!** don't touch it/them!; leave it/them alone!; **~|fahren** *unr. itr. V.; mit sein* leave; (mit dem Auto) drive away *or* off; (mit dem Fahrrad, Motorrad) ride away *or* off; **dem ~fahrenden Zug nachschauen** look after the departing train; (aus dem Bahnhof) watch the train as it pulls out; **jmdm. ~fahren** leave sb. behind; **ich muss mich beeilen, sonst fährt mir der Bus ~:** I must hurry or the bus will leave without me *or* I'll miss the bus; **er fährt allen ~** (ist schneller als alle) he leaves the rest standing; **~|fliegen** *unr. itr. V.; mit sein* fly away *or* off; **~|gehen** *unr. itr. V.; mit sein* walk away *or* off; **~|kommen** *unr. itr. V.; mit sein* get away; escape; **mit dem Leben ~kommen** escape with one's life; **mit dem Schrecken/einer Geldstrafe ~kommen** get off with a fright/a fine; **~|lassen** *unr. tr. V. in* **die Finger ~lassen ▸Finger 1**; **~|laufen** *unr. itr. V.; mit sein* **1** (weglaufen) run away; **er ist mir ~gelaufen** he's made off; **es ist zum Davonlaufen** (ugs.) it really turns you off (coll.); it makes you want to run a mile; **2** (ugs.: überraschend verlassen) **jmdm. ~laufen** walk out on sb.; **dieser Partei laufen die Wähler ~:** the voters are deserting this party; **3** (unkontrollierbar steigen) spiral; **die Kosten des Projekts sind uns ~gelaufen** the costs of the project have got out of control; **die Preise laufen den Einkommen ~:** prices are outstripping incomes; **~|machen** *refl. V.* make off (**mit** with); **~|schleichen** *unr. itr. V. mit sein; auch refl. V.* slink off *or* away; **~|stehlen** *unr. refl. V.* (geh.) steal away; **~|tragen** *unr. tr. V.* **1** (wegtragen) carry away; take away ‹*rubbish*›; **2** (geh.: erringen) win, gain ‹*a victory, fame*›; **den Sieg ~tragen** win; be victorious; (Sport) be the winner/winners; **3** (geh.: sich zuziehen) receive, suffer ‹*injuries*›; **~|ziehen** *unr. itr. V.; mit sein* **1** (Sport) pull away; **2** (weggehen) go on one's way

davor /daˈfoːɐ̯/ *Adv.* **1** (vor dieser/diese Stelle) in front of it/them; **etw. ~ legen/stellen** put sth. in front of it/them; **sich ~ schieben** move in front of it/them; (es/sie bedecken) cover it/them; **sich ~ stellen** plant oneself in front of it/them; **ein Haus mit einem Garten ~:** a house with a garden at the front *or* in front; **Kommt Mainz vor oder nach Wiesbaden? — Davor** Is Mainz before or after Wiesbaden? — Before **2** (zeitlich) before [it/them]; **~ macht er einen Dauerlauf von 30 Minuten** he goes jogging for 30 minutes beforehand *or* first; **kurz ~ stehen** be close to it; (vor einer Tat) be about to do it **3** (in Verbindung mit bestimmten Verben und Substantiven) **wir haben ihn ~ gewarnt** we warned him of *or* about it/them; **er hat Angst ~, erwischt zu werden** he is afraid of being caught; **wir sind ~ geschützt** we are protected from it/them; *s. auch* **da-**. *NB In some uses under* **1** *and* **3** *the word occurs in North German colloquial usage in two parts, e.g.* **da habe ich keine Angst vor** I'm not afraid of it/them

***davor|legen** *usw.* **▸davor 1, 2**

dazu /daˈtsuː/ *Adv.* **1** (zusätzlich zu dieser Sache) with it/them; (gleichzeitig) at the same time; (außerdem) what is more; **~ reicht man am besten Salat** it's/they're best served with lettuce/salad; **er ist dumm und ~ auch noch frech** he is stupid and insolent into the bargain **2** (darüber) about *or* on it/them; **was meinen Sie ~?** what do you think about it?; what is your opinion on this? **3** (zu diesem Zweck) for it; (es zu tun) to do it **4** (zu diesem Ergebnis) to it; **ich kann nichts ~ tun** I can't do anything to help; **er ist zu alt ~:** he is too old for it; **~ reicht das Geld nicht** we haven't enough money for that; **~ sind sie ja da!** that's what they are there for!; **~ kann ich dir nur raten** I would strongly advise you to do it; **im Widerspruch** *od.* **Gegensatz ~:** contrary to this/that; **~ war sie nicht in der Lage** she was not in a position to do it *or* do so; **er hatte ~ keine Lust** he didn't want to *or* didn't feel like it; **ich komme nie ~/nie ~, es zu tun** I never get round to it/to doing it; **wie komme ich ~?** (ugs.) it would never occur to me; why on earth should I?; *s. auch* **da-**. *NB In senses* **2** *and* **4** *the word occurs in North German colloquial usage in two parts, e.g.* **da habe ich keine Lust zu** I don't feel like it

dazu-: ~|geben *unr. tr. V.* **1** (beisteuern) give towards it; **2** (zusätzlich geben) add; give as well; **3** (Kochk.) add; *s. auch* **Senf**; **~|gehören** *tr. V.* **1** (zu dieser Sache, Kategorie gehören) belong to it/them; (als Zusatz) go with it/them; **der Wein gehört ~** (ist nicht wegzudenken) the wine belongs with it; you have to have wine, it's all part of it; (ist im Preis inbegriffen) the wine is included [in the price]; **das gehört [mit] ~:** it's all part of it; (es ist Sitte) it's the done thing (coll.); **alles, was ~gehört** everything that goes with it/them; **2** (erforderlich sein) **sie hat alles, was ~gehört, um Karriere zu machen** she has what it takes to make a successful career; **es gehört Mut/schon einiges ~:** it takes courage/quite something; **~gehörig** *Adj.* **1** appropriate; which goes/go with it/them *postpos.;* (farblich usw. passend) matching; **ein Schloss und die ~gehörigen Schlüssel** a lock and the keys that fit it; **2** (erforderlich) necessary; **~|gesellen** *refl. V.* join in; (als Zuschauer) gather round; **~|kommen** *unr. itr. V.; mit sein* **1** (hinkommen) arrive [on the scene]; turn up; **2** (außerdem kommen) **es kommen noch einige Gäste ~:** there are still some guests to come; **kommt noch etwas ~?** (fig.) is there anything else [you would like]?; **~ kommt, dass ...** (fig.) what's more, ...; on top of that, ...; *s. auch* **kommen 13**; **~|lernen** *tr., itr. V.* **[etwas] ~lernen** learn [something new]; **man kann immer noch [etwas] ~lernen** there's always something [new] to learn

da·zu·mal *Adv.* (veralt., noch scherzh. altertümelnd) in those days; *s. auch* **Anno**

dazu-: ~|rechnen *tr. V.* add on; **wenn man noch ~rechnet ...** (fig.) when you also consider ...; **~|setzen** *refl. V.* sit down next to him/her/you/them; **darf ich mich ~setzen?** may I join you *or* sit here?; **~|tun** *unr. tr. V.* (ugs.) add; **das Seine ~tun** do one's bit; (mit Geld) chip in (coll.); **ohne jmds. Dazutun** without sb.'s help; (ohne jmds. Beteiligung) without involving sb.; **~|verdienen** *tr., itr. V.* earn ‹*sth.*› extra; (als Nebenbeschäftigung) earn ‹*sth.*› on the side; **seine Frau verdient noch [etwas] ~:** his wife earns something as well

dazwischen /daˈtsvɪʃn̩/ *Adv.* **1** in between; between them; (darunter) among them **2** (unterwegs) on the way; (währenddessen) during this

dazwischen-: ~|fahren *unr. itr. V.; mit sein* **1** (eingreifen) step in [and sort things out]; **2** (unterbrechen) break in; **~|funken** *itr. V.* (ugs.) put a spanner in the works; (sich einmischen) put one's oar in; **jmdm. ~funken** put a spoke in sb.'s wheel; mess it up for sb.; **~|kommen** *unr. itr. V.; mit sein* **1** (zwischen diese Dinge kommen) **mit dem Hemd/Finger ~kommen** get one's shirt/finger caught [in it]; **2** (als Störung auftreten) **[jmdm.] ~kommen** complicate matters [for sb.]; (es verhindern) prevent it; **mir ist etwas ~gekommen** I had problems; (immer noch) I've got problems; **wenn nur nichts ~kommt** as long as there are no hitches *or* complications; **3** (**~** an der Reihe sein) **[noch] ~kommen** come in between; **~|liegen** *unr. itr. V.* lie in between; **Jahre lagen ~:** years had passed; **da liegen doch schon Tage ~:** that was days ago; **die ~liegende Zeit/Strecke** the intervening period/distance; **die ~liegenden Ereignisse** the events which have/had occurred in the meanwhile; **~|reden** *itr. V.* **1** (unterbrechen) interrupt; **2** (umzustimmen versuchen) **jmdm. ~reden** try to make sb. change his/her mind; **~|rufen** **A** *unr. itr. V.* interrupt [by shouting]; **B** *unr. tr. V.* interrupt [loudly] with; interject; **~|schalten** *tr. V.* **1** (Elektrot.) insert; **2** (fig.) interpose; (vorteilhaft) use as an intermediary; **~|stehen** *unr. itr. V.* **1** (Einigung verhindern) be obstructive; stand in the way; **2** (zwischen diesen Gegensätzen stehen) be [somewhere] in the middle; **3** (zwischen den Erwähnten stehen) stand amongst them; **~|treten** *unr. itr. V.; mit sein* **1** (eingreifen) intervene; **sein Dazwischentreten** his intervention; **2** (Uneinigkeit verursachen) come between them

Dazzler /ˈdɛslɐ/ *der;* **~[s], ~** [gold] tooth jewel

DB *Abk.* **= Deutsche Bundesbahn** German Federal Railways

DBP *Abk.* (hist.) **= Deutsche Bundespost** German Federal Post Office

D-Day /'di:deɪ/ *der;* **~[s]** D-Day

DDR *Abk.* (hist.) **= Deutsche Demokratische Republik** GDR

DDR-Bürger *der,* **DDR-Bürgerin** *die* (hist.) GDR citizen

D-Dur /'de:-/ *das* D major; *s. auch* **C-Dur**

Deal /di:l/ *der od. das;* **~s, ~s** (salopp) deal

dealen /'di:lən/ *itr. V.* (ugs.) push drugs; **mit LSD ~:** push LSD

Dealer *der;* **~s, ~, Dealerin** *die;* **~, ~nen** (ugs.) pusher

Debakel /de'ba:kl̩/ *das;* **~s, ~:** debacle; fiasco; (schwere Niederlage) rout

Debatte /de'batə/ *die;* **~, ~n** debate (**über** + *Akk.* on); (Streit) argument (**über** + *Akk.* about); **etw. in die ~ werfen** introduce *or* bring sth. into the debate; **[nicht] zur ~ stehen** [not] be under discussion; (auf der Tagesordnung) [not] be on the agenda; **etw. zur ~ stellen** put sth. up for discussion

debattieren *tr., itr. V.* debate; (weniger formell) discuss; **[mit jmdm.] über etw. ~:** discuss sth. [with sb.]

Debattier·klub *der* debating society

Debet /'de:bɛt/ *das;* **~s, ~s** (Finanzw.) debit [side]

debil /de'bi:l/ *Adj.* **1** (Med.) mentally subnormal **2** (abwertend) feeble-minded

Debilität /debili'tɛ:t/ *die;* **~ 1** (Med.) mental subnormality **2** (abwertend) feeble-mindedness

Debit·karte /'de:bɪt-/ *die* (Finanzw.) debit card

Debitor /'de:bitɔr/ *der;* **~s, ~en** /debi'to:rən/, **Debitorin** *die;* **~, ~nen** (Finanzw.) debtor

Debüt /de'by:/ *das;* **~s, ~s** debut; **sein ~ [als Autor** *usw.***] geben** make one's debut [as an author *etc.*]

Debütant /deby'tant/ *der;* **~en, ~en** newcomer [making his debut]; (in einer Mannschaft, Truppe, usw.) new face

Debütantin *die;* **~, ~nen 1** ▸**Debütant 2** (in der Gesellschaft) debutante

Debütantinnen·ball *der* debutantes' ball

debütieren /deby'ti:rən/ *itr. V.* make one's debut

Dechant /dɛ'çant/ *der;* **~en, ~en** (kath. Kirche) dean

dechiffrieren *tr. V.* decipher ‹*code, message*›; decode ‹*message,* (*fig.*) *conventions*›

Deck /dɛk/ *das;* **~[e]s, ~s 1** (eines Schiffes) deck; **alle Mann an ~!** all hands on deck!; **auf ~ sein** be on deck; **unter ~ gehen** go below [decks]; **auf dem obersten/im mittleren/unteren ~:** on the top/middle/lower deck **2** (Park~) storey; level; **auf ~ 6 fahren** drive up to level 6 **3** (im Autobus) deck

Deck-: ~adresse *die* accommodation *or* (Amer.) cover address; **~an·strich** *der* top coat; **~auf·bauten** *Pl.* superstructure *sing.*; **~bett** *das* ▸**Oberbett**; **~blatt** *das* **1** (Bot.) bract; **2** (von Zigarre) wrapper; **3** (Titelblatt) title page

Deckchen *das;* **~s, ~ 1** small tablecloth **2** (Zier~, Häkel~) [small] crocheted mat *or* cover

Decke /'dɛkə/ *die;* **~, ~n 1** (Tisch~) tablecloth; **eine neue ~ auflegen** put a clean cloth on [the table] **2** (Woll~, Pferde~, auch fig.) blanket; (Reise~) rug; (Deckbett, Stepp~) quilt; (Tages~) bedspread; **sich** (*Dat.*) **die ~ über den Kopf ziehen** pull the covers *pl.* over one's head; **unter die ~ kriechen** slip under the covers; **sich nach der ~ strecken [müssen]** (ugs.) [have to] cut one's coat according to one's cloth; **mit jmdm. unter einer ~ stecken** (ugs.) be hand in glove with sb.; be in cahoots with sb. (coll.) **3** (Zimmer~) ceiling; **mir fällt die ~ auf den Kopf** (ugs.) (ich bekomme Platzangst) I feel claustrophobic *or* shut in; (ich langweile mich) I get sick of [the sight of] these four walls; **an die ~ gehen** (ugs.) hit the roof (coll.); **[vor Freude] [bis] an die ~ springen** jump for joy **4** (Radmantel) [outer] cover **5** (Fahrbahn~) surface **6** (Buchw.: Bucheinband) cover **7** (Jägerspr.: Haut, Fell) skin

Deckel /'dɛkl̩/ *der;* **~s, ~ 1** lid; (auf Flaschen, Gläsern usw.) top; (Schacht~, Uhr~, Buch~ usw.) cover **2** (Bier~) beer mat **3** (salopp: Kopfbedeckung) headgear *no pl.*; **jmdm. eins auf den ~ geben** (ugs.) haul sb. over the coals; take sb. to task

Deckel·krug *der* tankard (*with a lid*)

deckeln *tr. V.* **1** (ugs.) take to task; tell off **2** (Wirtsch.) cap ‹*expenditure*›

Deckelung *die;* **~, ~en** (Wirtsch.) capping

decken

A *tr. V.* **1** (breiten, legen) spread **2** (mit einem Dach o. Ä. versehen) roof ‹*house*›; cover ‹*roof*›; **ein Dach/Haus mit Ziegeln/Stroh ~:** tile/thatch a roof/house **3 den Tisch ~:** lay *or* set the table; **es ist [für fünf Personen] gedeckt** the table is set [for five] **4** (schützen) cover; (bes. Fußball: abschirmen) mark ‹*player*›; (vor Gericht usw.) cover up for ‹*accomplice, crime, etc.*› **5** (befriedigen) satisfy, meet ‹*need, demand*›; **mein Bedarf ist gedeckt** (ugs.) I've had enough **6** (Finanzw., Versicherungsw.) cover **7** (genau beschreiben) describe accurately; cover **8** (begatten) cover; ‹*stallion*› serve ‹*mare*›

B *itr. V.* **1** (Fußball) mark; (Boxen) keep up one's guard; **besser ~:** improve one's marking/guard **2** (den Tisch ~) lay *or* set the table **3** ‹*colour*› cover

C *refl. V.* **1** (Geom.) be congruent **2** (gleich sein) coincide; tally; **ihre Aussage deckt sich nicht mit seiner** her statement does not agree with his

Decken-: ~balken *der* ceiling beam; **~beleuchtung** *die* ceiling light; **~fluter** *der;* **~~s, ~~:** uplighter; **~gemälde** *das* ceiling painting; **~lampe** *die* ceiling light; **~malerei** *die* ceiling painting; **~träger** *der* [iron] ceiling joist; **~ventilator** *der* ceiling fan

Deck-: ~farbe *die* paint (*which covers well*); body colour; (für Gouachen) gouache colour; **~feder** *die* cover; tectrix (Ornith.); **~flügel** *der* elytron; **~haar** *das* **1** (bei Tieren) guard hair; **2** (bei Menschen) top hair; **~hengst** *der* stud horse; breeding stallion; **~mantel** *der,* **~mäntelchen** *das* (abwertend) cover; **unter dem ~mantel der Entwicklungshilfe** *usw.* using development aid *etc.* as a blind *or* cover; under the guise of development aid *etc.*; **~name** *der* alias; assumed name; (eines Spions, milit. Programms) code name; (einer Organisation) cover name; **~plane** *die* waterproof cover; (bes. geteert) tarpaulin; **~platte** *die* cover; **~station** *die* stud

Deckung *die;* **~, ~en 1** (das Schützen) covering (esp. Mil.); (Feuerschutz) covering fire; (Boxen, Fechten) guard; (bes. Fußball) marking; (Schach) protection **2** (Schutz; auch fig.) cover (esp. Mil.); (Schach) defence; (Boxen) guard; (bes. Fußball: die deckenden Spieler) defence; **~ nehmen, in ~ gehen** take cover; **~ suchen/in ~ bleiben** look for/stay under cover; **[volle] ~!** take cover! **3** (Finanzw.: das Begleichen) meeting; **zur ~ seiner Schulden** to meet his debts **4** (Finanzw.: Sicherheit) cover[ing]; **der Scheck ist ohne ~:** the cheque is not covered; **als ~ für seine Schulden** as security for his debts **5** (Befriedigung) satisfaction **6** (Übereinstimmung) **Pläne** *usw.* **zur ~ bringen** make plans *etc.* agree; bring plans *etc.* into line **7** (von Tieren: Begatten) covering; (einer Stute) service

deckungs-, Deckungs-: ~auf·lage *die* (Verlagsw.) break-even quantity; **~fehler** *der* (bes. Fußball) marking error; **~gleich** *Adj.* (Geom.) congruent; **unsere Meinungen sind ~gleich** (fig.) our opinions coincide *or* are the same

Deck-: ~weiß *das* opaque white; **~wort** *das; Pl.* **~wörter** code word

Decoder /de'ko:dɐ/ *der;* **~s, ~** (Elektronik) decoder

decodieren ▸**dekodieren**

Decrescendo /dekrɛ'ʃɛndo/ *das;* **~s, ~s** *od.* **Decrescendi** (Musik) decrescendo

Dedikation /dedika'tsi̯o:n/ *die;* **~, ~en** dedication

Dedikations·exemplar *das* presentation copy (*containing dedication*)

dedizieren /dedi'tsi:rən/ *tr. V.* dedicate; **jmdm. ein Exemplar ~:** inscribe a copy to sb.

Deduktion /deduk'tsi̯o:n/ *die;* **~, ~en** (Philos., Kybernetik) deduction

deduktiv /deduk'ti:f/ (Philos.)

A *Adj.* deductive

B *adv.* deductively; **~ folgern** conclude by deduction

deduzieren /dedu'tsi:rən/ *tr. V.* (bes. Philos.) deduce

Deern /de:ɐ̯n/ *die;* **~, ~s** (nordd.) lass

Deez ▸**Dez**

DEFA /'de:fa/*die;* **~** *Abk.* **= Deutsche Film-Aktiengesellschaft** (German film company)

de facto /de: 'fakto/ *Adv.* de facto (esp. Polit., Law); in reality

De-facto-Anerkennung *die* de facto recognition

Defaitismus *usw.* (schweiz.) ▸**Defätismus** *usw.*

Defäkation /defɛka'tsi̯o:n/ *die;* **~, ~en** (Med.) defecation

Defätismus /defɛ'tɪsmʊs/ *der;* **~** (oft abwertend) defeatism

Defätist *der;* **~en, ~en, Defätistin** *die;* **~, ~nen** (abwertend) defeatist

defätistisch (oft abwertend)

A *Adj.* defeatist

B *adv.* in a defeatist manner

defekt /de'fɛkt/ *Adj.* **1** defective; faulty; **~ sein** have a defect; be faulty; (nicht funktionieren) not be working **2** (fig.) deficient ‹*mind, understanding*›

Defekt *der;* **~[e]s, ~e 1** defect, fault (**an** + *Dat.* in) **2** ▸ⓘ **S. 439** (Psych., Med.) defect (**an** + *Dat.* in); **Heilung mit bleibendem ~:** cure leaving a permanent handicap

defektiv /defɛk'ti:f/ *Adj.* (Sprachw.) defective

Defektivum /defɛk'ti:vʊm/ *das;* **~s, Defektiva** (Sprachw.) defective

defensiv /defɛn'zi:f/

A *Adj.* **1** (verteidigend; auch Sport) defensive **2** (sicherheitsbewusst) safety-conscious

B *adv.* **1** (verteidigend; auch Sport) defensively **2** (sicherheitsbewusst) in a safety-conscious manner

Defensive *die;* **~, ~n 1** defensive; **in der ~:** on the defensive; **jmdn. in die ~ drängen** force sb. on [to] the defensive; **in die ~ geraten** go on [to] the defensive **2** (Sport) **die ~:** defensive play; **aus der ~ heraus** from defensive positions *pl.*

Defensiv-: ~krieg *der* defensive war; **~spiel** *das* (Sport) defensive play

Defilee /defi'le:/ *das;* **~s, ~s,** (auch:) **~n** parade; march past

defilieren /defi'li:rən/ *itr. V.; mit haben od. sein* **vor jmdm./etw. ~:** parade before *or* march past sb./sth.

definierbar *Adj.* definable; (identifizierbar) identifiable; **nicht [näher] ~:** indefinable; (nicht zu identifizieren) unidentifiable

definieren /defi'ni:rən/

A *tr. V.* define; (identifizieren) identify

B *refl. V.* (sich als etw. verstehen) describe oneself (**durch** in terms of)

Definition /definі'tsi̯o:n/ *die;* **~, ~en** definition

definitiv /defini'ti:f/

A *Adj.* definitive; final ‹*answer, decision*›; (sicher) definite

B *adv.* finally; (sicher) definitely

definitorisch /defini'to:rɪʃ/

A *Adj.* ‹*problem*› of definition; ‹*skill*› at defining

B *adv.* with regard to definition

defizient /defi'tsi̯ɛnt/ *Adj.* deficient

Defizit /'de:fitsɪt/ *das;* **~s, ~e 1** (Fehlbetrag) deficit **2** (Mangel) deficiency; **~ an etw.** (*Dat.*) lack of sth.

defizitär /defitsi'tɛ:ɐ̯/

A *Adj.* **1** (Defizit aufweisend) ‹*trade etc.*› which shows/showed a deficit *not pred.*; ‹*firm etc.*› which runs/ran at a loss *not pred.* **2** (Defizit verursachend) which leads/led to a deficit *postpos., not pred.*

d

B *adv.* **∼[er] arbeiten** *od.* **wirtschaften** show a [bigger] deficit; run at a [bigger] loss

Deflation /defla'tsi̯o:n/ *die;* **∼, ∼en** (Wirtsch.) deflation

deflationär /deflatsi̯o'nɛ:ɐ̯/, **deflationistisch** *Adj.* (Wirtsch.) deflationary

Deflations·politik *die* (Wirtsch.) deflationary policy

Deflektor /de'flɛktɔr/ *der;* **∼s, ∼en** /-'to:rən/ (Technik) deflector

Defloration /deflora'tsi̯o:n/ *die;* **∼, ∼en** (Med.) defloration

deflorieren /deflo'ri:rən/ *tr. V.* deflower

Deformation *die* **1** (Physik) deformation **2** ▸ⓘ **S. 439** (Med.) deformation; (Missbildung) deformity

deformieren *tr. V.* **1** (verformen) distort; put out of shape; **deformiert** out of shape *pred.*; distorted **2** (entstellen) deform (also fig.); (verunstalten) disfigure ‹*face etc.*›; (verstümmeln) mutilate

Deformierung *die* **1** (Verformung) deformation; distortion **2** (Entstellung) deformation; (Verunstaltung) disfigurement; (Verstümmelung) mutilation; (Missbildung) deformity

Deformität /defɔrmi'tɛ:t/ *die;* **∼, ∼en** ▸ⓘ **S. 439** (Med.) deformity

Defraudant /defrau̯'dant/ *der;* **∼en, ∼en** (veralt.) defrauder; swindler; (bei Unterschlagung) embezzler

Defroster /de'frɔstɐ/ *der;* **∼s, ∼** **1** (Gerät) defroster **2** (Spray) de-icer

deftig /'dɛftɪç/ (ugs.)

A *Adj.* **1** [good] solid *attrib.*, good and solid *pred.* ‹*meal etc.*›; [nice] big, [nice] fat ‹*sausage etc.*›; (tüchtig) [really] big ‹*surprise*›; sound ‹*hiding*›; (hoch) tremendous, (coll.) terrific ‹*price, bill, etc.*› **2** (derb) crude, coarse ‹*joke, speech, etc.*›

B *adv.* good and proper (coll.)

Degen[1] *der;* **∼s, ∼** (hist.) [doughty] warrior

Degen[2] /'de:gn̩/ *der;* **∼s, ∼** **1** (Waffe) [light] sword (*esp. for duelling*); (Rapier) rapier **2** (Sportgerät) épée

Degeneration /degenera'tsi̯o:n/ *die;* **∼, ∼en** degeneration (**zu** into)

Degenerations·erscheinung *die* sign of degeneration

degenerativ /degenera'ti:f/

A *Adj.* degenerative

B *adv.* **es ist ∼ verändert** it has degenerated

degenerieren /degene'ri:rən/ *itr. V.; mit sein* degenerate (**zu** into)

degeneriert *Adj.* degenerate; (überzüchtet) overbred

Degen-: **∼fechten** *das* épée [fencing] *no art.*; **∼klinge** *die* sword blade; **∼korb** *der* [sword] guard; **∼scheide** *die* scabbard

degoutant /degu'tant/ (geh.)

A *Adj.* disgusting

B *adv.* in a disgusting manner

degoutieren /degu'ti:rən/ *tr. V.* (geh.) disgust

degradieren /degra'di:rən/ *tr. V.* **1** (im Rang o. Ä.) demote; **vom Feldwebel zum einfachen Schützen degradiert werden** be demoted from [the rank of] sergeant to [a] mere private **2** (herabwürdigen) **jmdn./etw. zu etw. ∼:** reduce sb./sth. to [the level of] sth.

Degradierung *die;* **∼, ∼en** **1** (im Rang) demotion **2** (Herabwürdigung) degradation; reduction (**zu** to the level of)

Degression /degrɛ'si̯o:n/ *die;* **∼, ∼en** **1** (Wirtsch.) progressive reduction [of unit cost] **2** (Steuerw.) degression

degressiv /degrɛ'si:f/ *Adj.* (Wirtsch., Steuerw.) degressive

degustieren /degʊs'ti:rən/ *tr. V.* (bes. schweiz.) taste; sample

dehnbar *Adj.* **1** (elastisch) ‹*material etc.*› that stretches *not pred.*; elastic ‹*waistband etc.*›; stretch ‹*fabric*›; **etw. ist ∼:** sth. can be stretched **2** (fig.: vage) elastic; **das ist ein ∼er Begriff** it's a loose concept; that can mean what you want it to mean

Dehnbarkeit *die;* **∼** (auch fig.) elasticity

dehnen /'de:nən/

A *tr. V.* **1** stretch **2** (lang aussprechen) lengthen, draw out ‹*vowel, word*›; **etw. gedehnt sagen/aussprechen** say/pronounce sth. slowly; (lässig) drawl sth.

B *refl. V.* **1** stretch; **er dehnte sich wohlig** he stretched [himself] luxuriantly **2** (lange dauern) **sich endlos ∼:** go on for ever (coll.); go on and on; **die Minuten ∼ sich zu Stunden** the minutes seem like hours

Dehn·übung *die* stretching exercise

Dehnung *die;* **∼, ∼en** **1** (das Dehnen) stretching; (eines Vokals) lengthening **2** (Dehnbarkeit) elasticity

Dehnungs-: **∼fuge** *die* (Bauw.) expansion joint; **∼-h** *das* (Phon.) 'h' lengthening the preceding vowel; **∼zeichen** *das* (Phon.) length mark

dehydrieren *tr. V.* (Chemie) dehydrogenate

Deibel /'dai̯bl̩/ ▸**Deiwel**

Deich /dai̯ç/ *der;* **∼[e]s, ∼e** dyke; **mit etw. über den ∼ gehen** (nordd.) make off with sth.

Deich-: **∼bau** *der* building of a/the dyke; (allgemein) dyke-building; **∼bruch** *der* breach (Brit.) *or* (Amer.) break in the dyke; (Brechen des Deichs) breaching (Brit.) *or* (Amer.) breaking of the dyke; **∼genossenschaft** *die* ▸**∼verband**; **∼graf** *der* (veralt.) ▸**∼vorsteher**; **∼krone** *die* top of the dyke

Deichsel /'dai̯ksl̩/ *die;* **∼, ∼n** shaft; (in der Mitte) pole; (aus zwei Stangen) shafts *pl.*

Deichsel·kreuz *das* **1** (Griff) shaft handle **2** (Symbol) Y[-shaped] cross

deichseln *tr. V.* (ugs.) fix; (durch eine List) wangle (sl.)

Deich-: **∼verband** *der* association of owners of dyked land; **∼vorland** *das: land above mean high water mark on the seaward side of a dyke;* **∼vorsteher** *der,* **∼vorsteherin** *die* chairman of a 'Deichverband'

deifizieren /deifi'tsi:rən/ *tr. V.* (geh.) deify

dein[1] /dai̯n/ *Possessivpron.* your; (Rel., auch altertümelnd) thy; **viele Grüße von deinem Emil/deiner Karin/deinen Müllers** with best wishes, yours Emil/Karin/the Müllers; **∼ Wille geschehe** (Rel.: im Vaterunser) Thy will be done; **heute Abend kannst du ∼en Humphrey Bogart im Fernsehen sehen** you can watch your beloved Humphrey Bogart *or* that Humphrey Bogart of yours on television tonight; **das Buch dort, ist das ∼[e]s?** that book over there, is it yours?; **sind das ihre Schuhe oder ∼e?** are those her shoes or yours?; **das war nicht mein Wunsch, sondern ∼er** *od.* (geh.) **der ∼e** it was not my wish but yours; **ewig/stets der deine** (geh.) yours ever; **du und die ∼en** *od.* **Deinen** (geh.) you and yours *or* your family; **der/die deine** (geh.) your husband/wife; **das ∼e** *od.* **Deine** (geh.) your possessions *pl. or* property; **du musst das ∼e** *od.* **Deine tun** (was du kannst) you must do what you can; (**∼en** Teil) you must do your bit *or* share; *s. auch* **mein**[1]

dein[2] (geh. veralt.), **deiner** *Gen. des Personalpronomens* **du** (geh.) of you; **ich gedenke ∼(er)** *od.* (geh.) **∼ auf ewig** I will always remember you; **man lachte ∼er** they laughed at you

deiner·seits /'dai̯nɐ'zai̯ts/ *Adv.* (von deiner Seite) on your part; (auf deiner Seite) for your part

deines·gleichen *indekl. Pron.* people *pl.* like you; (abwertend) the likes *pl.* of you; your sort *or* kind; **unter ∼:** amongst your own sort *or* kind; **für dich und ∼** (abwertend) for your sort; for the likes of you

deines·teils *Adv.* for your part

deinet·halben (veralt.) ▸**deinetwegen 1**

deinet·wegen *Adv.* **1** because of you; on your account; (für dich) on your behalf; (dir zuliebe) for your sake; **ich habe mir ∼ große Sorgen gemacht** I have been very worried about you *or* on your account **2** (du hast nichts dagegen) **du hast gesagt, ∼ könnten wir gehen** you said we could go as far as you were concerned

deinet·willen *Adv. in* **um ∼:** for your sake

deinige /'dai̯nɪgə/ *Possessivpron.* (geh. veralt.) **der/die/das ∼:** yours; **die ∼n** *od.* **Deinigen** your family *sing.*; **das ∼** *od.* **Deinige:** what is yours; your property; **du musst das ∼** *od.* **Deinige tun** (was du kannst) you must do what you can; (deinen Teil) you must do your bit *or* share

Deismus /de'ɪsmʊs/ *der;* **∼:** deism *no art.*

deistisch *Adj.* deistic

Deiwel /'dai̯vl̩/ *der;* **∼s** (nordd.), **Deixel** /'dai̯ksl̩/ *der;* (südd.) **Deixels** devil; *s. auch* **Teufel**

de jure /de: 'ju:rə/ *Adv.* de jure; legally

De-jure-Anerkennung *die* de jure recognition

Deka /'dɛka/ *das;* **∼s, ∼s** (österr.) decagram; **12 ∼:** 12 decagrams

Dekade /de'ka:də/ *die;* **∼, ∼n** **1** (zehn Tage) ten days *pl.* **2** (zehn Jahre) decade

dekadent /deka'dɛnt/ *Adj.* decadent

Dekadenz /deka'dɛnts/ *die;* **∼:** decadence

dekadisch *Adj.* **∼es Zahlensystem** decimal system; **∼er Logarithmus** (Math.) common logarithm

Deka-: **∼eder** *das* (Geom.) decahedron; **∼gramm** *das* decagram; **∼liter** *der* decalitre

Dekalog /deka'lo:k/ *der;* **∼[e]s** (Rel.) decalogue

Dekan /de'ka:n/ *der;* **∼s, ∼e** **1** (Universität) dean **2** (kath. Kirche) dean **3** (ev. Kirche) superintendent

Dekanat /deka'na:t/ *das;* **∼s, ∼e** **1** (Universität) dean's office **2** (kath. Kirche) deanery **3** (Amt eines Dekans) office of dean

Dekanin *die;* **∼, ∼nen** ▸**Dekan**

dekartellisieren /dekartɛli'zi:rən/ *tr. V.* (Wirtsch.) decartelize

dekatieren /deka'ti:rən/ *tr. V.* (Textilw.) decatize

Deklamation /deklama'tsi̯o:n/ *die;* **∼, ∼en** **1** (Vortrag) recitation **2** (abwertend: hohles Gerede) [empty] rhetoric *no pl.*

deklamatorisch /deklama'to:rɪʃ/

A *Adj.* **1** (ausdrucksvoll) declamatory **2** (abwertend: hohl) rhetorical

B *adv.* **1** (ausdrucksvoll) expressively **2** (abwertend: hohl klingend) rhetorically; in expansive terms

deklamieren /dekla'mi:rən/ *tr., itr. V.* recite

Deklaration /deklara'tsi̯o:n/ *die;* **∼, ∼en** (Politik, Zoll-, Steuer-, Postwesen) declaration

deklarieren /dekla'ri:rən/ *tr. V.* declare; **etw. als etw. ∼:** declare sth. to be sth.; **zur atomwaffenfreien Zone deklariert werden** be declared a nuclear-free zone

deklassieren *tr. V.* **1** (Soziol.) disadvantage **2** (herabsetzen) reduce; downgrade **3** (Sport) outclass; (beim Rennen) leave standing

Deklassierung *die;* **∼, ∼en** **1** (Soziol.) disadvantaging; reduction in circumstances **2** (Herabsetzung) downgrading **3** (Sport) outclassing

deklinabel /dekli'na:bl̩/ *Adj.* (Sprachw.) declinable

Deklination /deklina'tsi̯o:n/ *die;* **∼, ∼en** **1** (Sprachw.) declension; **die starke/schwache ∼:** the strong/weak declension **2** (Astron., Physik) declination

deklinierbar *Adj.* (Sprachw.) declinable

deklinieren /dekli'ni:rən/ *tr. V.* (Sprachw.) decline; **ein Wort schwach/stark ∼:** decline a word as weak/strong

dekodieren *tr. V.* (fachspr.) decode

Dekolleté, Dekolletee /dekɔl'te:/ *das;* **∼s, ∼s** low[-cut] neckline; décolletage; **Kleid mit tiefem ∼:** very low-cut dress; dress with a plunging neckline

dekolletieren /dekɔl'ti:rən/ *tr. V.* make *or* cut with a low neckline

dekolletiert *Adj.* **1** (ausgeschnitten) décolleté; low-cut ‹*back, neckline*› **2** (Dekolleté tragend) **∼e Damen** ladies in low-cut dresses; **[tief] ∼ sein** *od.* **gehen** wear a [very] low-cut dress/[very] low-cut dresses

Dekolonisation *die* decolonization

dekolonisieren *tr. V.* decolonize

Dekompression *die* decompression

Dekompressions·kammer *die* decompression chamber

dekonstruieren *tr. V.* take apart; dismantle; (zerstören) demolish; (analysieren) deconstruct ‹*text*›

Dekonstruktion *die;* ~, ~**en** dismantling; (Zerstörung) demolition

Dekontamination *die* decontamination

Dekonzentration *die* (der Verwaltung) decentralization; (der Industrie usw.) deconcentration

Dekor /de'ko:ɐ̯/ *das;* ~**s**, ~**s** *od.* ~**e** [1] (Verzierung) decoration; (Muster) pattern; **ein Zimmer im ~ der Dreißigerjahre** a room in the 1930s style [2] (Theater, Film) décor; setting

Dekorateur /dekora'tø:ɐ̯/ *der;* ~**s**, ~**e**, **Dekorateurin** *die;* ~, ~**nen** ▸ⓘ **S. 113** (Schaufenster~) window dresser; (von Innenräumen) interior decorator *or* designer; (Dekorationsmaler) scene-painter

Dekoration /dekora'tsi̯o:n/ *die;* ~, ~**en** [1] (das Dekorieren) decoration; (von Schaufenstern) window dressing; **zur** ~: for decoration [2] (Schmuck, Ausstattung) decorations *pl.*; (Schaufenster~) window display; (Theater, Film) set; scenery *no pl.*; **bloße ~ sein** be purely for decoration purposes [3] (Orden[verleihung]) decoration

Dekorations-: ~**maler** *der,* ~**malerin** *die* interior decorator; (Theater) [stage] decorator; scene-painter; ~**stoff** *der* furnishing fabric; ~**stück** *das* part of the décor; (Theater) piece of scenery

dekorativ /dekora'ti:f/

[A] *Adj.* decorative

[B] *adv.* decoratively

dekorieren /deko'ri:rən/ *tr. V.* [1] (ausschmücken) decorate ‹*room etc.*›; dress ‹*shop window*› [2] (mit Orden auszeichnen) decorate (**mit** with); **hoch dekoriert** much decorated

Dekorierung *die;* ~, ~**en** ▸ **Dekoration 1, 3**

Dekorum /de'ko:rʊm/ *das;* ~**s** (veralt.) decorum *no art.*; **das ~ verletzen/wahren** offend against/observe the proprieties *pl.*

Dekostoff /'de:ko-/ *der* furnishing fabric

Dekrescendo ▸ **Decrescendo**

Dekret /de'kre:t/ *das;* ~**[e]s**, ~**e** decree

dekretieren *tr. V.* decree

dekuvrieren /deku'vri:rən/

[A] *tr. V.* (entlarven) expose

[B] *refl. V.* (schlechte Züge zeigen) reveal oneself; **sich als etw. ~:** reveal oneself to be sth.

Deleatur /dele'a:tʊr/ *das;* ~**s**, ~, **Deleatur-zeichen** *das* (Druckw.) deletion mark

Delegation /delega'tsi̯o:n/ *die;* ~, ~**en** delegation (**an** + *Akk.* to; **bei** at)

Delegations-chef *der,* **Delegations-chefin** *die* head of a/the delegation

delegieren /dele'gi:rən/ *tr. V.* [1] (abordnen) send as a delegate/as delegates (**zu** to); **jmdn. ins Komitee ~:** select sb. as one's representative on the committee [2] (übertragen) delegate ‹*task etc.*› (**an** + *Akk.* to)

Delegierte *der/die; adj. Dekl.* delegate; (Sport) representative (**bei** at)

Delegierten-: ~**konferenz** *die* delegates' *or* delegate conference; ~**versammlung** *die* delegates' *or* delegate assembly

delektieren /delɛk'ti:rən/

[A] *tr. V.* **jmdn. mit etw. ~:** entertain *or* regale sb. with sth.

[B] *refl. V.* **sich an etw.** (*Dat.*) **~:** regale oneself with sth.; (fig.) take delight in sth.

Delfin *usw.* ▸ **Delphin** *usw.*

delikat /deli'ka:t/

[A] *Adj.* [1] (wohlschmeckend) delicious; (fein) subtle, delicate ‹*bouquet, aroma*›; **~ riechen** have a delicate bouquet/aroma [2] (Diskretion erfordernd, heikel) delicate; (geh.: empfindlich) **in so persönlichen Dingen ist sie sehr ~:** she is very sensitive about such personal matters [3] (geh.: behutsam) discreet; (taktvoll) tactful; **~e Andeutung** subtle *or* discreet reference

[B] *adv.* [1] (lecker) deliciously [2] (geh.: behutsam) delicately; **etw. ~ behandeln** handle sth. tactfully *or* discreetly

Delikatesse /delika'tɛsə/ *die;* ~, ~**n** [1] (Leckerbissen) delicacy; (fig.) treat; **als besondere ~:** as a special delicacy/treat [2] (geh.: Feingefühl) delicacy; (Takt) tact; discretion; **eine Angelegenheit mit ~ behandeln** handle a matter discreetly

Delikatessen-geschäft, Delikatess-geschäft, ***Delikateßgeschäft** *das* delicatessen

Delikatess-gurke, ***Delikateß-gurke** *die* [fine-quality] gherkin

Delikt /de'lɪkt/ *das;* ~**[e]s**, ~**e** offence

delinquent /delɪŋ'kvɛnt/ *Adj.* (bes. Rechtsw.) delinquent; criminal ‹*conduct*›

Delinquent *der;* ~**en**, ~**en**, **Delinquentin** *die;* ~, ~**nen** offender

Delinquenz *die;* ~ (bes. Rechtsw.) delinquency

delirieren /deli'ri:rən/ *itr. V.* be delirious

Delirium /de'li:ri̯ʊm/ *das;* ~**s**, **Delirien** delirium; **im ~ liegen/sein** lie/be in a delirium; **im ~ reden** speak in one's delirium

Delirium tremens /-'tre:mɛns/ *das;* ~ ▸ⓘ **S. 439** (Med.) delirium tremens; **im ~ sterben** die in a state of delirium [tremens]

deliziös /deli'tsi̯ø:s/ (geh.)

[A] *Adj.* delicious; delectable; **~ schmecken** taste delicious

[B] *adv.* deliciously

Delle /'dɛlə/ *die;* ~, ~**n** [1] (ugs.) dent; **eine ~ in die Stoßstange fahren** drive into something and dent one's bumper [2] (Geogr.) hollow

delogieren *tr. V.* (bes. österr.) evict

Delphin[1] /dɛl'fi:n/ *der;* ~**s**, ~**e** dolphin

Delphin[2] *das;* ~**s** (Schwimmen) butterfly [stroke]

Delphinarium /dɛlfi'na:ri̯ʊm/ *das;* ~**s**, **Delphinarien** dolphinarium

Delphin-schwimmen *das* butterfly

delphisch /'dɛlfɪʃ/

[A] *Adj.* Delphic ‹*oracle*›; enigmatic ‹*remark etc.*›

[B] *adv.* enigmatically

Delta[1] /'dɛlta/ *das;* ~**[s]**, ~**[s]** (Buchstabe) delta

Delta[2] *das;* ~**s**, ~**s** *od.* **Delten** ▸ⓘ **S. 267** (Fluss~) delta

delta-, Delta-: ~**förmig** *Adj.* delta-shaped; triangular; deltaic ‹*estuary*›; ~**mündung** *die* delta [estuary]; ~**strahlen** *Pl.* (Kernphysik) delta rays

De-Luxe-Ausstattung /də'lyks-/ *die:* **eine ~ haben** be fitted with de luxe equipment; ‹*car etc.*› be a de luxe model; ‹*room*› have de luxe fittings

dem /de:m/

[A] *best. Art., Dat. Sg. v.* **der**[1] **A** *u.* **das A: ich gab ~ Mann/~ Kind das Buch** I gave the man/the child the book; I gave the book to the man/to the child; **hast du ~ Peter das Geld gegeben?** (ugs.) have you given Peter the money?; **ich half ~ Mann/~ Kind** I helped the man/the child; **er hat sich ~ Okkultismus zugewandt** he turned to occultism; **aus ~ Libanon/Baltikum kommen** come from Lebanon/the Baltic area; **~ Theater/Kino seinen Ruhm verdanken** owe one's fame to the stage/films

[B] *Demonstrativpron., Dat. Sg. v.* **der**[1] **B** *u.* **das B** [1] *attr.* **gib es dem Mann/Kind** give it to 'that man/child; **mit dem Messer kann man fast alles schneiden** you can cut almost anything with 'that knife [2] *selbstständig* **gib es nicht dem, sondern dem da!** don't give it to him, give it to that man/child *etc.*; **Zwiebeln schneide ich nicht mit dem [hier], sondern mit dem da** I chop onions with 'that knife, not with this one

[C] *Relativpron., Dat. Sg. v.* **der**[1] **C** *u.* **das C** (Mensch) **der Mann/das Kind, ~ ich das Geld gab** the man/the child to whom I gave the money *or* (coll.) [that] I gave the money to; **der Mann, ~ ich geholfen habe** the man whom *or* that I helped; (Sache) **das Messer, mit ~ ich Zwiebeln schneide** the knife with which I chop onions *or* (coll.) that I chop onions with

Demagoge /dema'go:gə/ *der;* ~**n**, ~**n** (abwertend) demagogue

Demagogie /demago'gi:/ *die;* ~, ~**n** (abwertend) demagogy

Demagogin *die;* ~, ~**nen** (abwertend) demagogue

demagogisch (abwertend)

[A] *Adj.* demagogic

[B] *adv.* by demagogic means; (zu ~en Zwecken) for demagogic purposes; **~ reden** talk like a demagogue

Demarche /de'marʃ(ə)/ *die;* ~, ~**n** (Dipl.) diplomatic move

Demarkation /demarka'tsi̯o:n/ *die;* ~, ~**en** demarcation; (Staatsgrenze) frontier

Demarkations-linie *die* demarcation line

demarkieren *tr. V.* demarcate

demaskieren

[A] *refl. V.* [1] (Maske ablegen) unmask; take one's mask off [2] (sich offenbaren) reveal oneself [as what one is]; appear in one's true colours; **sich als etw. ~:** reveal *or* show oneself to be sth.

[B] *tr. V.* (entlarven) unmask; expose; **jmdn. als etw. ~:** reveal sb. as sth.

Dementi /de'mɛnti/ *das;* ~**s**, ~**s** denial

dementieren

[A] *tr. V.* deny

[B] *itr. V.* deny it

Dementierung *die;* ~, ~**en** denial

dem-entsprechend

[A] *Adj.* appropriate; **das Wetter war schlecht und die Stimmung ~:** the weather was bad and the general mood was correspondingly bad *or* bad too; **Er hat eine Villa in Cannes und eine Luxusjacht. Sein Einkommen ist auch ~:** He has a villa in Cannes and a luxury yacht. And he has an income to match *or* to go with it

[B] *adv.* accordingly; (vor Adjektiven) correspondingly; **~ wird er bezahlt** he is paid accordingly

Demenz /de'mɛnts/ *die;* ~, ~**en** (Med.) dementia

dem-: ~**gegenüber** *Adv.* in contrast; (jedoch) on the other hand; ~**gemäß** [A] *adv.* [1] (infolgedessen) consequently; [2] (entsprechend) accordingly; [B] *Adj.* in accordance with it/them *postpos.*; (angemessen) appropriate; **ein Zimmer mit Vollpension kostet nur 18 Euro — das Essen ist ~gemäß** a room with full board only costs 18 euros — the food is what you'd expect [at that price]

Demimonde /dəmi'mõ:d/ *die;* ~ (abwertend) demi-monde

Demission *die;* ~, ~**en** (Politik) resignation; **jmdn. zur ~ zwingen** force sb. to resign; **um seine ~ bitten** ask to be relieved of one's duties

demissionieren *itr. V.* [1] (Politik: zurücktreten) resign [2] (schweiz.: kündigen) hand in one's notice (**auf** + *Akk.* for)

dem-: ~**jenigen** ▸ **derjenige**; ~**nach** *Adv.* therefore; (laut dessen) according to that; ~**nächst** *Adv.* in the near future; shortly; **~nächst in diesem Theater** coming soon [to this theatre]; (ugs. scherzh.) some time soon

Demo /'dɛmo/ *die;* ~, ~**s** (ugs.) demo; **auf der ~:** at the demo

Demo-band *das;* ~**[e]s**, **...bänder** (Jargon) demo tape

demobilisieren *tr. V.* [1] demobilize ‹*army, industry*› [2] (veralt.: entlassen) discharge ‹*soldier*›

Demobilisierung *die;* ~, ~**en** demobilization

Demodulation *die;* ~, ~**en** (Nachrichtent.) demodulation

Demo-graphie *die* demography *no art.*

demo-graphisch

[A] *Adj.* demographic

[B] *adv.* demographically

Demokrat /demo'kra:t/ *der;* ~**en**, ~**en** [1] democrat [2] (Parteimitglied) Democrat

Demokratie /demokra'ti:/ *die;* ~, ~**n** [1] (Prinzip) democracy *no art.*; **zur ~ zurückkehren** return to democracy *or* democratic government [2] (Staat) democracy

Demokratie-verständnis *das* understanding *or* conception of democracy

Demokratin *die;* ~, ~**nen** ▸**Demokrat**

demokratisch

A *Adj.* **1** democratic ‹*principle, process, etc.*› **2** (zur Demokratischen Partei gehörend) Democratic

B *adv.* democratically; **es wurde ~ gewählt** democratic elections were held; **bei uns geht es ~ zu** we run things on democratic lines; **~ eingestellt sein** have democratic attitudes

demokratisieren *tr. V.* **1** democratize; make democratic **2** (allgemein zugänglich machen) make generally available; make ‹*art*› generally accessible; bring ‹*art, fashion*› to the people

Demokratisierung *die;* ~ **1** (eines Staates, einer Institution) democratization **2** (das Zugänglichmachen); **die ~ der Mode/des Reisens** making fashion/travel generally available *or* accessible

demolieren /demo'li:rən/ *tr. V.* **1** (zerstören) wreck; smash up ‹*furniture*› **2** (österr.: abreißen) demolish

Demolierung *die;* ~, ~**en** **1** (Zerstörung) wrecking; (von Möbeln) smashing up **2** (österr.: Abriss) demolition

Demonstrant /demɔn'strant/ *der;* ~**en,** ~**en** demonstrator

Demonstrantin *die;* ~, ~**nen** demonstrator; *s. auch* **~-in**

Demonstration /demɔnstra'tsjo:n/ *die;* ~, ~**en** **1** (Protestkundgebung) demonstration (**für** in support of, **gegen** against) **2** (Bekundung, Veranschaulichung) demonstration; **zur ~ seines guten Willens** as a demonstration of *or* to demonstrate his good will

Demonstrations-: **~marsch** *der* demonstration; (gegen etw.) protest march; **~objekt** *das* exhibit (*used to demonstrate a point*); **~recht** *das* right to demonstrate; **~verbot** *das* ban on demonstrations; **~zug** *der* column *or* procession of demonstrators

demonstrativ /demɔnstra'ti:f/

A *Adj.* **1** (betont) demonstrative; pointed; **ein ~es Nein** an emphatic no **2** (Sprachw.) demonstrative **3** (anschaulich) graphic ‹*example etc.*›

B *adv.* pointedly; (aus Protest) in protest; **ich sah ~ weg** I intentionally looked the other way; **sie blieben ~ sitzen** they remained seated in protest *or* to make their point

Demonstrativ·pronomen *das* (Sprachwissenschaft) demonstrative pronoun

demonstrieren /demɔn'stri:rən/

A *itr. V.* demonstrate (**für** in support of, **gegen** against)

B *tr. V.* demonstrate; **jmdm. etw. ~:** demonstrate sth. to sb.

Demontage /demɔn'ta:ʒə/ *die;* ~, ~**n** (auch fig.) dismantling; (eines Schiffes) breaking-up; **soziale ~** (Politik) dismantling of the welfare state

demontieren *tr. V.* **1** (abbrechen) dismantle; (zerlegen) break up ‹*ship, aircraft*› **2** (abmontieren) take off **3** (fig.) eradicate ‹*prejudices*›; damage ‹*reputation*›

Demontierung *die;* ~, ~**en** ▸**Demontage**

Demoralisation /demoraliza'tsjo:n/ *die;* ~, ~**en** ▸**Demoralisierung**

demoralisieren *tr. V.* **1** (Moral untergraben) corrupt **2** (entmutigen) demoralize

Demoralisierung *die;* ~, ~**en** demoralization; (Sittenverfall) moral decline

Demoskop /demo'sko:p/ *der;* ~**en,** ~**en** opinion pollster

Demoskopie /demosko'pi:/ *die;* ~, ~**n** **1** (Meinungsforschung) [public] opinion research *no art.* **2** (Umfrage) opinion poll

Demoskopin *die;* ~, ~**nen** opinion pollster

demoskopisch

A *Adj.* opinion research ‹*institute, methods, data, etc.*›; ‹*data etc.*› from opinion polls *or* opinion research; **das ~e Ergebnis** the result of the opinion poll; **~e Umfrage** [public] opinion poll

B *adv.* through opinion polls *or* research; **etw. ~ untersuchen** conduct an opinion poll on sth.

Demo·tape /-teɪp/ *das od. der* ▸**Demoband**

dem·selben ▸**derselbe**

Demut /'de:mu:t/ *die;* ~**:** humility; **in** *od.* **mit ~:** with humility

demütig /'de:my:tɪç/

A *Adj.* humble; (respektvoll) respectful

B *adv.* humbly; (respektvoll) respectfully

demütigen

A *tr. V.* humiliate; humble ‹*sb.'s pride*›

B *refl. V.* humble oneself; **sich vor jmdm. ~:** humble oneself before sb.

Demütigung *die;* ~, ~**en** humiliation

Demuts·gebärde *die* (Verhaltensf.) attitude of submission

dem·zufolge *Adv.* consequently; therefore

den¹ /de:n/

A *best. Art., Akk. Sg. v.* **der¹ A: ich sah ~ Mann/~ Hund/~ Stein** I saw the man/the dog/the stone; **wir haben ~ „Faust" gelesen** we read 'Faust'; **hast du ~ Peter gesehen?** (ugs.) have you seen Peter?; **in ~ Libanon reisen** travel to Lebanon; **~ Sozialismus/Kapitalismus ablehnen** reject socialism/capitalism

B *Demonstrativpron., Akk. Sg. v.* **der¹ B: 1** *attr.* **ich meine den Mann/den Hund/den Stein, nicht ~ anderen** I mean 'that man/'that dog/'that stone, not the other **2** *selbstständig* **ich meine den [da]** I mean 'that one

C *Relativpron., Akk. Sg. v.* **der¹ C: der Mann/Hund/Stein, ~ ich gesehen habe** the man/dog/stone that I saw

den²

A *best. Art., Dat. Pl. v.* **der¹ A, die¹ A, das A: ich gab es ~ Männern/Frauen/Kindern** I gave it to the men/women/children; **ich habe mich mit ~ Berichten/Theorien/Büchern befasst** I dealt with the reports/theories/books; **er war bei ~ Müllers zu Besuch** (ugs.) he visited the Müllers

B *Demonstrativpron., Dat. Pl. v.* **der¹ B 1, die¹ B 1, das B 1: ich gab es den Männern/den Frauen/den Kindern** I gave it to 'those men/'those women/'those children

Denaturalisation *die;* ~, ~**en** denaturalization

denaturalisieren *tr. V.* denaturalize

denaturieren /denatu'ri:rən/

A *tr. V.* **1** (geh.: verändern) warp the personality of; (entmenschen) dehumanize **2** (bes. Chemie) denature ‹*alcohol, foodstuffs, protein, fissile material, etc.*›

B *itr. V.; mit sein* (geh.) **zu etw. ~:** degenerate into sth.

Dendrit /dɛn'dri:t/ *der;* ~**en,** ~**en** ▸**i S. 435** (Geol., Anat.) dendrite

denen /'de:nən/

A *Demonstrativpron., Dat. Pl. v.* **der¹ B 2, die¹ B 2, das B 2: gib es ~, nicht den anderen** give it to 'them, not to the others; **~ gehört das Buch** the book belongs to 'them; **~, die uns geholfen haben, helfen wir auch** we help those who have helped us

B *Relativpron., Dat. Pl. v.* **der¹ C, die¹ C das C: die Menschen, ~ wir Geld gegeben haben** the people to whom we gave money; **die Tiere, ~ er geholfen hat** the animals that he helped; **die Bücher, mit ~ sie aufgewachsen ist** the books she grew up with

dengeln /'dɛŋl̩n/ *tr. V.* (Landw.) sharpen (*by hammering out irregularities*)

Den Haag /de:n 'ha:k/ *(das);* ~**s** ▸**i S. 675** The Hague

denjenigen ▸**derjenige**

Denk-: **~an·satz** *der* intellectual approach; **~an·stoß** *der* something to think about; **jmdm. einen ~anstoß geben** give sb. food for thought; **~art** *die* way of thinking; **~auf·gabe** *die* brain-teaser

denkbar

A *Adj.* conceivable; **in einem Zustand, wie er schlimmer nicht ~ ist** in the worst state imaginable

B *adv.* (sehr, äußerst) extremely; **die Lösung ist ~ leicht** the solution could not be easier *or* is as easy as could be; **die ~ beste Methode** the best method imaginable

Denke *die;* ~, ~**n** (ugs.) way of thinking

denken /'dɛŋkn̩/

A *unr. itr. V.* think (**an** *od.* [*südd., österr.*] **auf** + *Akk.* of, **über** + *Akk.* about); **kleinlich/liberal/edel ~:** be petty-minded/liberal-minded/noble-minded; **spießig/reaktionär ~:** have a bourgeois/reactionary mind *or* bourgeois/reactionary views; **wie denkst du darüber?** what do you think about it?; what's your opinion of it?; **ich weiß nicht, wie ich darüber ~ soll** I don't know what to think *or* make of it; **erst ~, dann handeln** think before you act; **der Mensch denkt, [und] Gott lenkt** (Spr.) man proposes, God disposes; **Denken ist Glückssache** you/he/she *etc.* thought wrong; **~de Menschen** thinking people; **so darfst du nicht ~:** you mustn't think that; **schlecht von jmdm. ~:** think badly of sb.; **jmdm. zu ~ geben** make sb. think; (stutzig machen) make sb. suspicious; **denk mal, Eva hat sich verlobt!** just think, Eva has got engaged!; **denk mal an!** (spött.) just imagine!; imagine that!; **denk daran, dass .../zu ...** don't forget that .../to ...; **ich darf gar nicht an die Kosten ~:** I daren't think of the cost; the cost doesn't bear thinking about; **der wird noch an mich ~:** I'll give him something to remember; **das geschieht schon, solange ich ~ kann** this has been going on as long as I can remember; **ich muss an meine Familie ~:** I have to think of *or* consider my family; **an was für einen Schuh haben Sie denn gedacht?** what sort of shoe did you have in mind?; **ich komme nach Hause, denke an nichts Böses** I came home, quite unsuspecting; **ich denke nicht daran!** no way!; not on your life!; **ich denke nicht daran, das zu tun** I've no intention *or* I wouldn't dream of doing that

B *unr. tr. V.* think; **was sollen bloß die Nachbarn ~?** what will the neighbours think?; **einen Gedanken zu Ende ~:** think an idea through; **er dachte den gleichen Gedanken** the same thought occurred to him; **ich habe nichts Böses dabei gedacht** I didn't mean any harm [by it]; **das denke ich auch** I think so too; **ich denke schon** I think so; **was** *od.* **wie viel haben Sie denn gedacht?** how much did you have in mind?; **wer hätte das gedacht?** who would have thought it?; **[typischer Fall von] denkste!** (ugs.) how wrong can one be!; (da irrst du dich) that's what 'you think!; **da weiß man nicht, was man ~ soll** one doesn't know what to think; **das hätte ich nie von dir gedacht** I would never have thought it of you; **eine gedachte Linie** an imaginary line; **ein gedachter Punkt** an imaginary point

C *unr. refl. V.* **1** (sich vorstellen) think; imagine; **ich habe mir gedacht, dass wir ein paar Tage in Urlaub fahren** I was thinking *or* thought that we could go on holiday for a few days; **du kannst dir ~, dass ...** you can imagine that ...; as you can imagine, ...; **das kann ich mir ~/nicht ~:** I can well believe/cannot believe that; **das habe ich mir so gedacht** I imagined it like this; this is what I had in mind; **das hast du dir so gedacht!** that's what you thought; **das hättest du dir doch ~ können, dass ...** you should have realized that ...; **das habe ich mir [gleich] gedacht** that's [just] what I thought; (bei Verdacht) I thought *or* suspected as much; **das hätte ich mir ~ können!** I might have known it!; **ich denke mir mein[en] Teil** I can put two and two together *or* work things out for myself **2** **sich** (*Dat.*) **etw. bei etw. ~** (beabsichtigen) mean sth. by sth.; **ich habe mir nichts [Böses] dabei gedacht** I didn't mean any harm [by it]; **er denkt sich nichts dabei** he doesn't think anything of it; *s. auch* **gedacht**

Denken *das;* ~**s** thinking; (Denkweise) thought; **logisches/abstraktes ~:** logical/abstract thought

Denker *der;* ~**s,** ~, **Denkerin** *die;* ~, ~**nen** thinker

denkerisch

A *Adj.* intellectual

B *adv.* intellectually

Denker·stirn *die* (oft scherzh.) intellectual's high brow

denk-, Denk-: ~fabrik *die* think tank; **~fähig** *Adj.* capable of thinking *postpos.*; intellectually able; **~fähigkeit** *die* ability to think; intellectual capacity; **~faul** *Adj.* mentally lazy; **sei nicht so ~faul** use your brains; **~fehler** *der* flaw in one's reasoning; **das war ein ~fehler** that was poor thinking

Denk·mal *das;* **~s, Denkmäler** *od.* (geh.) **Denkmale** 1 (Monument) monument; memorial; **jmdm. ein ~ errichten** *od.* **setzen** erect *or* put up a memorial to sb.; **mit der Klinik hat er sich ein ~ gesetzt** (fig.) by building the clinic he has ensured that his name will live on 2 (Zeugnis) monument

Denkmal[s]-: ~pflege *die* preservation of historic monuments; **~schutz** *der* protection of historic monuments; **unter ~schutz stehen/stellen** be/put under a preservation order

Denk-: ~modell *das* hypothesis; **~pause** *die* pause for thought; **eine ~pause machen** *od.* **einlegen** pause for thought; (bei Verhandlungen usw.) have a break [to think things over]; **~schrift** *die* memorandum; **~sport·aufgabe** *die* brain-teaser; **~spruch** *der* maxim; motto; **~übung** *die* intellectual exercise

Denkungs·art *die* way of thinking

denk-, Denk-: ~vermögen *das:* **[kreatives] ~vermögen** ability to think [creatively]; **~weise** *die* way of thinking; [mental] attitude; **eine solch niedrige ~weise** such low-mindedness; **~würdig** *Adj.* memorable; **~würdigkeit** *die* 1 memorable nature; **der ~würdigkeit eines Ereignisses bewusst** aware how memorable an event is; 2 (Ereignis) memorable event; **~zettel** *der* warning; lesson; **jmdm. einen ~zettel verpassen** teach sb. a lesson; **~zettel·wahl** *die* (ugs.) election that sends a warning message

denn /dɛn/

A *Konj.* 1 (kausal) for; because 2 (geh.: als) than; **schöner/besser/größer ~ je [zuvor]** more beautiful/better/greater than ever 3 (konzessiv) **es sei ~, ...** unless ...; **ich spreche nicht mehr mit ihm, er müsste sich ~ geändert haben** (veralt.) I'm not speaking to him again unless he changes his ways; *s. auch* **geschweige**

B *Partikel* 1 (in Fragesätzen: oft nicht übersetzt) **Die Kirschen sind wahnsinnig teuer! — Wie viel kosten sie ~?** The cherries are frightfully expensive! — How much are they then?; **was ist ~ da los?** what 's going on there?; **ist er ~ krank gewesen?** has he been ill, then?; **wie geht es dir ~?** tell me, how are you?; **wer will ~ aufgeben?** who is talking of giving up?; **ist das ~ so wichtig?** is that really so important?; **was muss ich ~ machen?** what am I to do, then?; **wie hieß sie ~ noch?** now what was her name?; **wie heißt du ~?** tell me your name; **wieso ~?** why is that?; (stärker) what ever for?; **warum ~ nicht?** why ever not?; **was soll das ~?** what's all this about?; (wozu ist das gut?) what's this in aid of?; **was ~ [sonst]?** well, what [else] then?; **wohin [fahrt ihr] ~?** where [are you going] then? 2 (in Aussagesätzen verstärkend, oft folgernd) **so wollen wir ~ zur Abstimmung kommen** let's get on with the voting now; **das ist ~ doch die Höhe!** that really is the limit!; **er starb ~ auch bald** and so he soon died

C *Adv.* (nordd.: dann) then; **na, ~ man los!** right then, let's get going!

dennoch /ˈdɛnɔx/ *Adv.* nevertheless; even so; **ein höfliches und ~ eisiges Lächeln** a polite yet frosty smile

Denotat /denoˈtaːt/ *das;* **~s, ~e** (Sprachw.) denotation

Denotation /denotaˈtsi̯oːn/ *die;* **~, ~en** (Logik, Sprachw.) denotation

denselben ▸**derselbe**

dental /dɛnˈtaːl/

A *Adj.* (Anat., Med., Sprachw.) dental; **~e Laute** dentals

B *adv.* (Sprachw.) dentally

Dental *der;* **~s, ~e** (Sprachw.) dental

Dentist /dɛnˈtɪst/ *der;* **~en, ~en, Dentistin** *die;* **~, ~nen** (veralt.) dentist

Denunziant /denʊnˈtsi̯ant/ *der;* **~en, ~en, Denunziantin** *die;* **~, ~nen** (abwertend) informer; grass (sl.)

Denunziation /denʊntsi̯aˈtsi̯oːn/ *die;* **~, ~en** (abwertend) denunciation (*by an informer*)

denunziatorisch /denʊntsi̯aˈtoːrɪʃ/ *Adj.* (abwertend) 1 (denunzierend) **ein ~es Klima** a climate which favours informing; **~e Äußerungen seines eigenen Vaters** statements informing against him made by his own father 2 (öffentlich verurteilend) denunciatory; condemnatory

denunzieren /denʊnˈtsiːrən/ *tr. V.* (abwertend) 1 (anzeigen) denounce; (bei der Polizei) inform against; grass on (sl.) (**bei** to) 2 (als negativ hinstellen) denounce

Deo /ˈdeːo/ *das;* **~s, ~s, Deodorant** /de|odoˈrant/ *das;* **~s, ~s** (auch:) **~e** deodorant

deodorierend /de|odoˈriːrənt/ *Adj.* deodorant

Deo·spray *das* deodorant spray

Departement /departəˈmãː, *schweiz.:* departəˈmɛnt/ *das;* **~s, ~s** *od.* (schweiz.:) **~e** department

Dependance /depãˈdãːs/ *die;* **~, ~n** 1 (Hotelw.) annexe 2 (Zweigstelle) branch

Dependenz /depɛnˈdɛnts/ *die;* **~, ~en** 1 (Philos.) dependence (**von** on) 2 (Sprachw.) dependency

Dependenz·grammatik *die* (Sprachw.) dependency grammar

Depesche /deˈpɛʃə/ *die;* **~, ~n** (veralt.) telegram (**an** + *Akk.* to)

depeschieren (veralt.)

A *tr. V.* send a telegram giving ⟨*time of arrival etc.*⟩; **~, dass ...** wire that ... (coll.)

B *itr. V.* send a telegram (**an** + *Akk.* to)

deplaciert, deplatziert, *deplaziert /deplaˈtsiːɐ̯t/ *Adj.* out of place *pred.*; misplaced ⟨*remark etc.*⟩

Depolarisation *die* (Physik) depolarization

Deponie /depoˈniː/ *die;* **~, ~n** tip (Brit.); dump; **geordnete ~:** controlled tip (Brit.), sanitary landfill (Amer.) (*subsequently covered and planted with trees etc.*)

deponieren *tr. V.* 1 (im Safe o. Ä.) deposit (**bei** with) 2 (an einem bestimmten Platz) put

Deponierung *die;* **~:** depositing

Deportation /deportaˈtsi̯oːn/ *die;* **~, ~en** transportation (**in** + *Akk.*, **nach** to); (ins Ausland) deportation (**in** + *Akk.*, **nach** to)

deportieren /depɔrˈtiːrən/ *tr. V.* transport (**in** + *Akk.*, **nach** to); (ins Ausland) deport (**in** + *Akk.*, **nach** to)

Deportierte *der/die; adj. Dekl.* transportee; (ins Ausland) deportee

Depositar /depoziˈtaːɐ̯/ *der;* **~s, ~e, Depositär** /depoziˈtɛːɐ̯/ *der;* **~s, ~e** (Finanzw.) depositary

Depositen /depoˈziːtn̩/ *Pl.* (Finanzw.) deposits

Depot /deˈpoː/ *das;* **~s, ~s** 1 (Aufbewahrungsort) depot; (Lagerhaus) warehouse; (für Möbel usw.) depository; (im Freien, für Munition o. Ä.) dump; (für Straßenbahnen, Omnibusse) depot; garage; (in einer Bank) strongroom; safe deposit 2 (hinterlegte Wertgegenstände) deposits *pl.* 3 (Med.) deposit

Depot-: ~fett *das* (Biol., Med.) adipose; **~fund** *der* (Archäol.) cache [find]; **~geschäft** *das* (Finanzw.) safe-deposit business; **~präparat** *das* (Med.) depot preparation

Depp /dɛp/ *der;* **~en** (auch:) **~s, ~en** (auch:) **~e** (bes. südd., österr., schweiz. abwertend) 1 (Dummkopf) twit (coll.); nitwit (coll.); **und ich ~ bin darauf reingefallen** and like a fool I fell for it 2 (Schwachsinniger) cretin

deppert /ˈdɛpɐt/ (südd., österr. abwertend)

A *Adj.* stupid; (begriffsstutzig) thick

B *adv.* **stell dich doch nicht so ~ an** don't act so stupid

Depression /deprɛˈsi̯oːn/ *die;* **~, ~en** (Wirtsch., Psych., Met.) depression; **an ~en leiden** suffer from [fits *pl.* of] depression *sing.*

depressiv /deprɛˈsiːf/

A *Adj.* 1 depressive 2 (Wirtsch.) depressive ⟨*effect*⟩; depressed ⟨*phase*⟩

B *adv.* 1 **~ veranlagt sein** have a tendency towards depression 2 (Wirtsch.) **den Markt ~ beeinflussen** have a depressive influence on *or* depress the market

Depressivität /deprɛsiviˈtɛːt/ *die;* **~** (Psych.) depression

depri /ˈdeːpri/ *Adj.* (ugs.) glum; gloomy; **~ drauf sein** be down in the dumps

deprimieren /depriˈmiːrən/ *tr. V.* depress

deprimierend *Adj.* depressing

deprimiert

A *Adj.* depressed

B *adv.* dejectedly

Deputat /depuˈtaːt/ *das;* **~[e]s, ~e** 1 (Schulw.) teaching load; **mit einem halben ~ unterrichten** have half the normal teaching load 2 (Sachleistung) payment in kind; **ein ~ Kohlen/Milch** *usw.* **erhalten** receive free coal/milk *etc.*

Deputation /deputaˈtsi̯oːn/ *die;* **~, ~en** deputation; (bei Konferenzen) delegation

deputieren /depuˈtiːrən/ *tr. V.* depute; delegate; **jmdn. zu einer Konferenz ~:** depute *or* delegate sb. to attend a conference

Deputierte *der/die; adj. Dekl.* (Mitglied einer Deputation) delegate; (Abgeordnete[r]) deputy

der¹ /deːɐ̯/

A *best. Art. Nom.* the; **~ Kleine** the little boy; **~ Tod** death; **~ Montag/April/Winter** Monday/April/winter; **~ „Faust"** 'Faust'; **~ Dieter** (ugs.) Dieter; **~ Kapitalismus/Sozialismus/Buddhismus/Islam** capitalism/socialism/Buddhism/Islam; **~ 1. FC Köln** Cologne FC; **er ist der Fußballer/Komponist** he's 'the footballer/composer; **~ Washingtonplatz** Washington Square; **~ Bodensee/Mount Everest** Lake Constance/Mount Everest; **~ Iran/Sudan** Iran/the Sudan; **~ Mensch/Mann ist ...** man is .../men are ...

B *Demonstrativpron.* 1 *attr.* **der Mann war es** it was 'that man 2 *selbstständig* he; **der war es** it was 'him; **der und arbeiten!** (ugs.) [what,] him work! (coll.); **~ mit der Glatze** (ugs.) him with the bald head (coll.); **der [da]** (Mann/Junge) that man/boy; (Gegenstand, Tier) that one; **der [hier]** (Mann/Junge) this man/boy; (Gegenstand, Tier) this one; **der Idiot, ~!** (salopp) what an idiot!

C *Relativpron.* (Mensch) who; that; (Sache, Tier) which; that; **der Mann, ~ da drüben entlanggeht** the man walking along over there; **ich sah einen Mann/Hund, ~ aus dem Fenster schaute** I saw a man/dog looking out of the window

D *Relativ- u. Demonstrativpron.* the one who; **~ das getan hat** the man *etc.* who did it

der²

A *best. Art.* 1 *Gen. Sg. v.* **die¹ A: die Jacke ~ Frau** the woman's jacket; **die Form ~ Tasse** the shape of the cup; **das Wiehern ~ Stute** the neighing of the mare; the mare's neighing; **die Freuden ~ Liebe** the joys of love; **der Untergang ~ „Titanic"** the sinking of the Titanic; **am Ende ~ Hauptstraße** at the end of the High Street; **der Einfluss ~ NATO/UNO** the influence of NATO/the UN 2 *Dat. Sg. v.* **die¹ A: sein schwarzes Haar hat er von ~ Mutter** he got his black hair from his mother; **der Henkel an ~ Tasse** the handle of the cup; **sein Buch ist ~ Callas gewidmet** his book is dedicated to Callas; **in ~ Türkei** in Turkey; **seit ~ Aufklärung** since the Enlightenment 3 *Gen. Pl. v.* **der¹ A, die¹ A, das A: das Haus ~ Freunde** our/their *etc.* friends' house; **das Zimmer ~ Schwestern** our/their *etc.* sisters' room; **das Bellen ~ Hunde** the barking of the dogs

B *Demonstrativpron.* 1 *Gen. Sg. v.* **die¹ B: es ist das Kind der Frau, die gestern hier war** he's/she's the child of the woman who was here yesterday 2 *Dat. Sg. v.* **die¹ B** *attr.* **der Frau [da/hier] gehört es** it belongs to that woman there/this woman here; *selbstständig* **gib es der da!** (ugs.) give it to 'her; **alles nur wegen der** (ugs.) all because of her 3 *Gen. Pl. v.* **die¹ B: die Ansichten der Leute lehne ich ab** I reject the views of those people

C *Relativpron.; Dat. Sg. v.* **die¹ C** (Mensch) **die Frau,**

~ ich es gegeben habe the woman to whom I gave it; the woman I gave it to; (Tier, Sache) **die Katze, ~ er einen Tritt gab** the cat [that] he kicked; **die Lawine, unter ~ er begraben wurde** the avalanche under which he was buried

derangiert /derãˈʒiːɐ̯t/ *Adj.* dishevelled

der·art *Adv.* **jmdn. ~ schlecht/unfreundlich behandeln, dass ...;** treat sb. so badly/in such an unfriendly way that ...; **~ gute Vorbereitungen** such good preparations; **eine ~ schöne Frau** such a beautiful woman; **es hat lange nicht mehr ~ geregnet** it hasn't rained as hard as that for a long time; **sie hat ~ geschrien, dass ...** she screamed so much that ...

der·artig
A *Adj.* such; **ein ~er Wutausbruch** such a fit of fury; **Derartiges** things *pl.* like that; **etwas Derartiges** a thing like that; such a thing
B *adv.* ▸**derart**

derb /dɛrp/
A *Adj.* **1** strong, tough ‹*material*›; stout, strong, sturdy ‹*shoes*› **2** (kräftig) solid, substantial ‹*food*› **3** (kraftvoll, deftig) earthy ‹*scenes, humour*› **4** (unverblümt) crude, coarse ‹*expression, language*› **5** (unfreundlich) gruff
B *adv.* **1** strongly ‹*made, woven, etc.*› **2** (heftig) roughly **3** (kraftvoll, deftig) earthily; **um es einmal ~ zu sagen** to put it crudely **4** (unverblümt) crudely; coarsely **5** (unfreundlich) gruffly

Derbheit *die;* **~, ~en** **1** ▸**derb A 3, 4**: earthiness; crudity; coarseness **2** (Äußerung) crudity

derb·knochig *Adj.* big-boned

Derby /ˈdɛrbi/ *das;* **~s, ~s** **1** (Pferdesport) Derby **2** (Fußball) derby; **das ~ der beiden Lokalrivalen** the local derby

Deregulierung *die;* **~, ~en** deregulation

der·einst *Adv.* **1** (geh.) one *or* some day **2** (veralt.) once; at one time

der·einstig *Adj.* (geh.) future

deren /ˈdeːrən/
A *Relativpron.* **1** *Gen. Sg. v.* **die¹ C** *attr.* (Menschen) whose; (Sachen, Tiere) of which; **die Katastrophe, ~ Folgen furchtbar waren** the disaster, the consequences of which were frightful; *selbstständig* **die Großmutter, ~ wir uns gerne erinnern** our grandmother, of whom we have fond memories; **eine Anrede, ~ er sich gern bediente** a form of address which *or* that he liked to use **2** *Gen., Pl. v.* **der¹ C, die¹ C, das C** *attr.* (Menschen) whose; (Sachen, Tiere) **Maßnahmen, ~ Folgen wir noch nicht absehen können** measures, the consequences of which we cannot yet foresee
B *Demonstrativpron.* **1** *Gen. Sg. v.* **die¹ B** *attr.* **meine Tante, ihre Freundin und ~ Hund** my aunt, her friend and 'her dog; **die Universität und ~ Abteilungen** the university and its departments; *selbstständig* **Tante Frieda? Deren erinnere ich mich nicht mehr** Aunt Frieda? I don't remember 'her **2** *Gen. Pl. v.* **der¹ B, die¹ B, das B** *attr.* **meine Verwandten und ~ Kinder** my relatives and their children; **die Schulen und ~ Lehrpersonal** the schools and their teaching staff; *selbstständig* **Bücher/Kinder? Deren hat er genug** (geh.) Books/Children? He's got enough of those

derent-: ~halben *Adv.* (veralt.), **~wegen** *Adv.* **A** *relativ* on whose account; on account of whom; because of whom; (von Sachen) on account of which; because of which; **die Frau, ~wegen er seine Familie verlassen hat** the woman on whose account *or* for whom he left his family; **die Tasche, ~wegen du das ganze Haus abgesucht hast** the purse for which you searched the entire house; **B** *demonstrativ* because of them; **~willen** *Adv.* **A** *relativ* **um ~willen** for whose sake; for the sake of whom; (von Sachen) for the sake of which; **die Erbstücke, um ~willen sich die Kinder zerstritten** the heirlooms over which the children fell out; **die Parkplätze, um ~willen es so heiße Diskussionen gab** the car parks about which there were such impassioned debates; **B** *demonstrativ* **um ~willen** for her/their sake

derer /ˈdeːrɐ/ *Demonstrativpron.; Gen. Pl. v.* **der¹ B, die¹ B, das B;** *vorausweisend* **das Schicksal ~, die verschollen sind** the fate of those who are missing; **die Zahl ~, die das glauben, nimmt ab** the number of people who believe that is declining; **das Schloss ~ von Fleckenstein** (geh.) the castle of the family Fleckenstein

deret-: ▸**derent-**

der·gestalt *Adv.* (geh.) **~, dass ...** in such a way that ...; **Widrigkeiten, die uns ~ belasten[, dass ...]** adversities which weigh so heavily upon us [that ...]; **~ ausgerüstet/vorbereitet** thus equipped/prepared

der·gleichen *indekl. Demonstrativpron.* **1** *attr.* such; like that *postpos., not pred.* **2** *allein stehend* that sort of thing; such things *pl.;* things *pl.* like that; **nichts ~:** nothing of the sort; **es gibt ~ mehr** there's more of that sort of thing; **und ~ [mehr]** and suchlike; **nichts ~ tun** do nothing of the sort

Derivat /deriˈvaːt/ *das;* **~[e]s, ~e** (Chemie, Sprachw., Biol., Bankw.) derivative

Derivativ /derivaˈtiːf/ *das;* **~s, ~e** (Sprachw.) derivative

der·jenige /-jeːnɪɡə/, **die·jenige, das·jenige** *Pl.* **die·jenigen** *Demonstrativpron.* **1** *mit Relativsatz* **~, der ...** (Mensch) the one who ...; (Sache) the one which ...; **die Kinder ~n, die ...** the children of those who ...; **er ist immer ~, welcher** (ugs.) it's always him (coll.); **ach, du bist diejenige, welche** (ugs.) oh, so you're the one **2** *mit nachfolgendem Gen.* that; **diejenigen** those; **seine Frau ist charmanter als diejenige seines Bruders** (geh.) his wife is more charming than his brother's

derlei /ˈdeːɐ̯lai/ *indekl. Demonstrativpron.* **1** *attr.* such; like that *postpos., not pred.* **2** *selbstständig* that sort of thing; such things *pl.;* things *pl.* like that

der·maßen *Adv.* **~ schön** *usw.,* **dass ...** so beautiful *etc.* that ...; **ein ~ intelligenter Mensch** such an intelligent person; **er hat mich ~ belogen, dass ...** he has lied to me so much that ...

Dermatologe /dɛrmatoˈloːɡə/ *der;* **~n, ~n** dermatologist

Dermatologie /dɛrmatoloˈɡiː/ *die;* **~:** dermatology *no art.*

Dermatologin *die;* **~, ~nen** dermatologist

dermatologisch
A *Adj.* dermatological
B *adv.* dermatologically

Dermato·plastik *die* (Med.) dermatoplasty (Med.); plastic surgery

Dero /ˈdeːro/ *indekl. Pron.* (veralt.) Your

ders. *Abk.* **= derselbe**

derselbe /deːɐ̯ˈzɛlbə/, **dieselbe, dasselbe,** *Pl.* **dieselben** *Demonstrativpron.* **1** *attr.* the same; **~ Mann/dieselbe Frau/dasselbe Dorf** the same man/woman/village **2** *selbstständig* the same one; **er sagt immer dasselbe** he always says the same thing; **sie ist immer noch [ganz] dieselbe** she is still [exactly] the same; **es sind immer dieselben, die ...** it's always the same people *or* ones who ...; **noch einmal dasselbe, bitte** (ugs.) [the] same again please **3** *selbstständig* (Amtsspr. veralt.) the same; **~n/desselben** of same; **... des Angeklagten. Derselbe hatte ...:** ... of the defendant. He had ...

derselbige /deːɐ̯ˈzɛlbɪɡə/, **dieselbige, dasselbige,** *Pl.* **dieselbigen** (veralt.) ▸**derselbe**

der·weil[en]
A *Adv.* meanwhile; in the meantime
B *Konj.* while

Derwisch /ˈdɛrvɪʃ/ *der;* **~[e]s, ~e** dervish

der·zeit *Adv.* **1** (zurzeit) at present; at the moment **2** (veralt.: damals) at that time; then

der·zeitig *Adj.* **1** (jetzig) present; current **2** (veralt.: damalig) at that time *postpos.*

des¹ /dɛs/
A *best. Art.; Gen. Sg. v.* **der¹ A, das A: die Mütze ~ Jungen** the boy's cap; **das Wiehern ~ Pferdes** the neighing of the horse; the horse's neighing; **das Klingeln ~ Telefons** the ringing of the telephone; **er hat das schwarze Haar ~ Vaters** he has his father's black hair; **nördlich ~ Schillerplatzes** to the north of Schiller Square
B *Demonstrativpron.; Gen. Sg. v.* **der¹ B, das B: er ist der Sohn des Mannes, der gestern hier war** he's the son of the man who was here yesterday

des² (veralt.) **1** ▸**dessen** **2** ▸**wes**

des³, Des *das;* **~, ~** (Musik) D flat

Desaster /deˈzastɐ/ *das;* **~s, ~:** disaster

desavouieren /dɛs|avuˈiːrən/ *tr. V.* (geh.) **1** (bloßstellen) expose **2** (nicht anerkennen) repudiate

Desavouierung *die;* **~, ~en** ▸**desavouieren**: exposure; repudiation

Des-Dur *das* D flat major; *s. auch* **C-Dur**

desensibilisieren *tr. V.* (Fot., Med., fig.) desensitize

Deserteur /dezɛrˈtøːɐ̯/ *der;* **~s, ~e** (Milit.) deserter

desertieren *itr. V.; mit sein* (Milit., fig.) desert

Desertifikation *die;* **~, ~en** desertification

Desertion /dezɛrˈtsi̯oːn/ *die;* **~, ~en** (Milit.) desertion

des·gleichen *Adv.* likewise; **er ist Antialkoholiker, ~ seine Frau** he is a teetotaller, as is *or* and so is his wife; **es fehlt an Papier, ~ an Schreibmaschinen** there's a shortage of paper and also [of] typewriters

des·halb *Adv.* for that reason; because of that; **~ bin ich zu dir gekommen** that is why I came to you; **aber ~ ist sie nicht dumm** but that doesn't mean she is stupid; **~ also!** so that's why *or* the reason!; **er war krank, [und] ~ konnte er nicht kommen** he was ill, [and] so he couldn't come; **..., aber ~ könnt ihr gerne noch bleiben** ..., but you're still welcome so stay

Desiderat /dezideˈraːt/ *das;* **~[e]s, ~e, Desideratum** /dezideˈraːtʊm/ *das;* **~s, Desiderata** **1** (Buchw.) suggestion; **dieses Buch ist schon seit langem ein ~ in unserer Bibliothek** it was suggested a long time ago that our library should acquire this book **2** (geh.: Erwünschtes) desideratum

Design /diˈzai̯n/ *das;* **~s, ~s** design

Designat /dezɪˈɡnaːt/ *das;* **~[e]s, ~e** (Sprachw., Logik) designatum

Designation /dezɪɡnaˈtsi̯oːn/ *die;* **~, ~en** designation

Designer /diˈzai̯nɐ/ *der;* **~s, ~, Designerin** *die;* **~, ~nen** ▸**❶ S. 113** designer

Designer-: ~baby *das* (Jargon) designer baby; **~droge** *die;* **~~, ~~n** designer drug; **~möbel** *das* designer furniture

designieren /dezɪˈɡniːrən/ *tr. V.* (geh.) designate (**zu** as)

desillusionieren /dɛs|iluzi̯oˈniːrən/ *tr. V.* disillusion

Desillusionierung *die;* **~, ~en** disillusionment

Des·infektion /dɛs|-/ *die* disinfection; **zur ~:** to disinfect it/them

Desinfektions·mittel *das* disinfectant

des·infizieren *tr. V.* disinfect

Des·infizierung *die* disinfection

Des·information *die* disinformation *no indef. art.;* **~en** disinformation *sing.*

Des·integration *die* (Soziol., Psych.) disintegration

Des·interesse *das* lack of interest (**an** + *Dat.* in)

des·interessiert
A *Adj.* uninterested
B *adv.* uninterestedly

Deskription /deskrɪpˈtsi̯oːn/ *die;* **~, ~en** (geh.) description

deskriptiv /deskrɪpˈtiːf/
A *Adj.* descriptive
B *adv.* descriptively

Desktop /ˈdɛsktɔp/ *der;* **~s, ~s** (DV) desktop

Desktop·publishing /-pablɪʃɪŋ/ *das;* **~s** (DV) desktop publishing

Desodorant /dɛs|odo'rant/ ▸**Deodorant**

desolat /dezo'la:t/ *Adj.* (geh.) wretched

Des·organisation *die* (geh.) **1** disintegration **2** (fehlende Planung) disorganization *no indef. art.*; lack of organization

des·orientieren *tr. V.* disorientate

Des·orientiertheit, Des·orientierung *die*; **~:** confusion

Des·oxidation, Des·oxydation *die* (Chemie) deoxidation

Desoxiribonuklein·säure, Desoxyribonuklein·säure /dɛs|ɔksyribonukle'i:n-/ *die* (Biochemie) deoxyribonucleic acid

despektierlich /despɛk'ti:ɐ̯lɪç/ (geh.)
A *Adj.* (abfällig, geringschätzig) disparaging; (respektlos) disrespectful
B *adv.*; ▸**A:** disparagingly; disrespectfully

Desperado /dɛspe'ra:do/ *der*; **~s, ~s** desperado

desperat /dɛspe'ra:t/ *Adj.* (geh.) desperate; **eine ~e Stimmung** a mood of desperation

Despot /dɛs'po:t/ *der*; **~en, ~en** despot; (fig. abwertend) tyrant

Despotie /dɛspo'ti:/ *die*; **~, ~n** despotism

Despotin *die*; **~, ~nen** ▸**Despot**

despotisch
A *Adj.* despotic
B *adv.* despotically

Despotismus *der*; **~:** despotism

des·selben ▸**derselbe**

dessen /'dɛsn̩/
A *Relativpron.*; *Gen. Sg. v.* **der[1] C, das C** *attr.* (Mensch) whose; **der Onkel, ~ Besuch wir erwarten** the uncle from whom we are expecting a visit; (Sache, Tier) **der Garten, ~ Fläche 2000 m² beträgt** the garden, the area of which is 2,000 m²; *selbstständig* **der Großvater, ~ wir uns gern erinnern** our grandfather, of whom we have fond memories; **ein Sprichwort, ~ er sich gern bedient** a proverb which *or* that he likes to use
B *Demonstrativpron.*; *Gen. Sg. v.* **der[1] B, das B** *attr.* **mein Onkel, sein Sohn und ~ Hund** my uncle, his son, and 'his dog; **das Waldsterben und ~ Folgen** the death of the forests and its consequences; *selbstständig* **Onkel August? Dessen erinnere ich mich noch sehr gut** Uncle August? I remember 'him well

dessent-: ~halben (veralt.), **~wegen** *Adv.* **A** *relativ* on whose account; on account of whom; because of whom; (von Sachen) on account of which; because of which; **das Verbrechen, ~wegen er verurteilt wurde** the crime of which he was convicted; **B** *demonstrativ* because of him; (von Sachen) because of this; **~willen** *Adv.* **A** *relativ* **um ~willen** for whose sake; for the sake of whom; (von Sachen) for the sake of which; **das Treffen, um ~willen wir dorthin reisten** the meeting for which we travelled there; **B** *demonstrativ* **um ~willen** for his sake

***dessen·ungeachtet** ▸**ungeachtet**

Dessert /dɛ'se:ɐ̯/ *das*; **~s, ~s** dessert

Dessert-: ~teller *der* dessert plate; **~wein** *der* dessert wine

Dessin /dɛ'sɛ̃:/ *das*; **~s, ~s** **1** design; pattern **2** (Entwurf) design **3** (Billard) path [of the ball]

Dessous /dɛ'su:/ *das*; **~** /dɛ'su:(s)/, **~** /dɛ'su:s/ (geh.) (ladies') underwear *no indef. art.*

destabilisieren *tr. V.* (Politik) destabilize

Destabilisierung *die*; **~, ~en** (Politik) destabilization

Destillat /dɛstɪ'la:t/ *das*; **~[e]s, ~e** distillate

Destillateur /dɛstɪla'tø:ɐ̯/ *der*; **~s, ~e, Destillateurin** *die*; **~, ~nen** distiller

Destillation /dɛstɪla'tsi̯o:n/ *die*; **~, ~en** **1** (Chemie) distillation **2** (von Weinbrand) distilling; (Anlage) distillery

Destillator /dɛstɪ'la:tɔr/ *der*; **~s, ~en** /-la'to:rən/ still

Destille /dɛs'tɪlə/ *die*; **~, ~n** **1** bar **2** (Branntweinbrennerei) distillery

destillieren *tr. V.* **1** (Chemie) distil; **destilliertes Wasser** distilled water **2** (fig.) condense (**zu** into); **aus einer Dokumentation eine Reportage ~:** condense records into a report

Destillier·kolben *der* distillation flask

desto *Konj.*, *nur vor Komp.* **je eher, ~ besser** the sooner the better; **~ ängstlicher** the more anxious/anxiously; **ich schätzte ihn ~ mehr** I appreciated him all the more; **~ schlimmer für ihn** so much the worse for him; **~ besser für uns** all the better for us

Destruktion /destrʊk'tsi̯o:n/ *die*; **~, ~en** destruction

Destruktions·trieb *der* (Psych.) destructive urge

destruktiv /destrʊk'ti:f/
A *Adj.* destructive
B *adv.* destructively; **~ auf etw.** (*Akk.*) **wirken** have a destructive effect on sth.

Destruktivität /destrʊktivi'tɛ:t/ *die*; **~:** destructiveness

des·wegen *Adv.* ▸**deshalb**

Deszendent /destsɛn'dɛnt/ *der*; **~en, ~en** (Genealogie, Astrol.) descendant

Deszendenz·theorie *die* theory of evolution

Detail /de'tai̯/ *das*; **~s, ~s** detail; **ins ~ gehen** go into detail; **in allen ~s** in the fullest detail; **bis ins [kleinste] ~:** down to the smallest detail

detail-, Detail-: ~frage *die* question of detail; **~genau** **A** *Adj.* precisely detailed; **B** *adv.* in precise detail; **~getreu** **A** *Adj.* accurate in every detail *postpos.*; **B** *adv.* accurately in every detail; **~kenntnisse** *Pl.* detailed knowledge *sing.*

detaillieren /deta'ji:rən/ *tr. V.* explain ‹*plan, suggestion, etc.*› in detail; **etw. genauer ~:** explain sth. in more *or* greater detail

detailliert
A *Adj.* detailed
B *adv.* in detail; **sehr ~:** in great detail

detail-, Detail-: ~schilderung *die* detailed account; (Beschreibung) detailed description; **~versessen** **A** *Adj.* obsessively detailed; ‹*person*› obsessive about detail *pred.* **B** *adv.* in obsessive detail; **~versessen realistisch** with obsessively detailed realism

Detektei /detɛk'tai̯/ *die*; **~, ~en** [private] detective agency

Detektion /detɛk'tsi̯o:n/ *die*; **~, ~en** (fachspr.) detection

Detektiv /detɛk'ti:f/ *der*; **~s, ~e** ▸ⓘ **S. 113** [private] detective; **die ~e von Scotland Yard** the detectives from Scotland Yard

Detektiv-: ~büro *das* ▸**Detektei**; **~geschichte** *die* detective story

Detektivin *die*; **~, ~nen** ▸ⓘ **S. 113** [private] detective

detektivisch
A *Adj.* **mit ~em Scharfsinn** with the keen perception of a detective; **in ~er Kleinarbeit** by detailed detective work
B *adv.* like a detective

Detektiv·roman *der* detective novel

Detektor /de'tɛktɔr/ *der*; **~s, ~en** /-'to:rən/ (Technik, Funkw.) detector

Detergens /de'tɛrgɛns/ *das*; **~, Detergenzien** (Chemie) detergent

Determinante /detɛrmi'nantə/ *die*; **~, ~n** (Math., Biol.) determinant

Determination /detɛrmina'tsi̯o:n/ *die*; **~, ~en** (Philos., Biol., Psych.) determination

determinieren *tr. V.* determine

Determiniertheit *die*; **~** (Philos.) determined nature; **die gesellschaftliche ~ der Sprache** the socially determined nature of language

Determinismus *der*; **~** (Philos.) determinism *no art.*

deterministisch
A *Adj.* deterministic
B *adv.* deterministically

Detonation /detona'tsi̯o:n/ *die*; **~, ~en** detonation; explosion; **eine Bombe zur ~ bringen** detonate a bomb

detonieren /deto'ni:rən/ *itr. V.*; *mit sein* detonate; explode

Deubel /'dɔy̯bl̩/ *der*; **~s, ~** (nordd.) ▸**Teufel**

deucht /'dɔy̯çt/ *3. Pers. Sg. Präsens v.* **dünken**

deuchte *3. Pers. Sg. Prät. v.* **dünken**

Deut /dɔy̯t/ **keinen ~:** not one bit; **du bist keinen ~ besser als er** you're not one bit *or* whit better than he is

deutbar *Adj.* interpretable

Deutelei *die*; **~, ~en** (abwertend) speculation

deuteln /'dɔy̯tl̩n/ *itr. V.* quibble (**an** + *Dat.* about); **daran gibt es nichts zu ~:** there are no ifs and buts about it

deuten /'dɔy̯tn̩/
A *itr. V.* **1** point; **[mit dem Finger] auf jmdn./etw. ~:** point [one's finger] at sb./sth. **2** (hinweisen) **auf etw.** (*Akk.*) **~:** point to *or* indicate sth.; **sein Verhalten deutet darauf hin, dass …** his behaviour indicates that …
B *tr. V.* interpret; **die Zukunft ~:** read the future; **etw. falsch ~:** misinterpret sth.

Deuter *der*; **~s, ~** **1** interpreter **2** (österr.: Tipp) hint; clue

Deuterin *die*; **~, ~nen** interpreter

deutlich
A *Adj.* **1** clear; **daraus wird ~, dass/wie …** this makes it clear that/how … **2** (eindeutig) clear; plain; clear, distinct ‹*recollection, feeling*›; clear ‹*victory*›; **das ist ~:** that is [quite] plain *or* clear; **das war ~ [genug]** that was clear *or* plain enough; **~ werden** make oneself plain *or* clear; **muss ich noch ~er werden?** do I have to speak more plainly?
B *adv.* **1** clearly; **~ sichtbar/erkennbar/hörbar sein** be clearly *or* plainly visible/recognizable/audible **2** (eindeutig) clearly; plainly; **[klar und] ~ sagen, dass …** make it [perfectly *or* quite] clear that …; **jmdm. etw. ~ zu verstehen geben** make sth. clear *or* plain to sb.

Deutlichkeit *die*; **~, ~en** **1** clarity **2** (Eindeutigkeit) clearness; plainness; (von Erinnerungen) clearness; distinctness; **in** *od.* **mit aller ~ sagen, dass …** make it perfectly clear *or* plain that …; **seine Antwort ließ an ~ nichts zu wünschen übrig** his answer could not have been clearer **3** *Pl.* (Grobheiten) rude remarks

deutlichkeits·halber *Adv.* for the sake of clarity

deutsch /dɔy̯tʃ/ ▸ⓘ **S. 520**, ▸ⓘ **S. 670**
A *Adj.* **1** German; **die ~e Schrift** German script; **Deutscher Schäferhund** Alsatian; German shepherd [dog]; **mit typisch ~er Gründlichkeit** with typical Teutonic *or* German thoroughness; **Deutsche Mark** Deutschmark; German mark; **der Deutsche Orden** the Teutonic Order; **Deutsche Bundesbahn** German Federal Railway; **Deutsche Bundespost** German Federal Post Office; **Deutsche Demokratische Republik** German Democratic Republic; **Deutscher Fußball-Bund** German Football Association; **Deutscher Gewerkschaftsbund** German Trade Union Federation; **das Deutsche Reich** the German Reich *or* Empire; **Deutsche Presse-Agentur** German Press Agency; **Deutsches Rotes Kreuz** German Red Cross **2** (die Sprache betreffend) German; **die ~e Schweiz** German-speaking Switzerland; *s. auch* **Deutsch 1.**
B *adv.* **~ sprechen/schreiben** speak/write German; **~ geschrieben sein** be written in German; **~ fühlen** feel German; **etw. ~ aussprechen** pronounce sth. in a German way; **mit jmdm. ~ reden** *od.* **sprechen** (fig. ugs.) be blunt with *or* speak bluntly to sb.; **dieses Gebiet war damals ~ besetzt/verwaltet** this area was under German occupation/administration at that time

Deutsch *das*; **~[s]** ▸ⓘ **S. 670** **1** German; **gutes/fließend ~ sprechen** speak good/fluent German; **ein perfektes ~:** faultless *or* perfect German; **kein ~ [mehr] verstehen** (ugs.) not understand plain English; **auf/in ~:** in German; **was heißt das Wort auf ~?** what is the word in German?; what is the German for that word?; **auf [gut] ~** (fig. ugs.) in plain

d

English; ~ **sprechend** German-speaking **2▸** (Unterrichtsfach) German *no art.*; **er ist gut in ~:** he's good at German; **wen habt ihr in ~?** who do you have for German?

Deutsch·amerikaner *der*, **Deutsch·amerikanerin** *die* German-American

deutsch·amerikanisch *Adj.* German-American

Deutsch·arbeit *die* (Schulw.) German test

deutsch-deutsch *Adj.* intra-German

Deutsche[1] /ˈdɔytʃə/ *der/die; adj. Dekl.* ▸❶ **S. 520** German; **~[r] sein** be German; **er ist kein ~r** he's not German; **als ~r** as a German; **er hat eine ~ geheiratet** he married a German girl/woman

Deutsche[2] *das; adj. Dekl.* ▸❶ **S. 670** **1▸** German; **das ~ ist ...** German is ...; **aus dem ~n/ins ~ übersetzen** translate from/into German **2▸** (deutsche Eigenart) **alles ~:** all things *pl. or* everything German; **das typisch ~ daran** what is/was typically German about it

Deutsche Bibliothek

The German Library in Frankfurt am Main is the central archive of all German-language writing and the national bibliographical information centre of the Federal Republic. The first national library bringing together all German-language literature under one roof was set up in Leipzig in 1912. The division of Germany after the Second World War resulted in a new national library which was set up in 1947 in Frankfurt. After reunification in 1990 the German library in Leipzig was merged with the Frankfurt library.

Deutschen·feind *der*, **Deutschen·feindin** *die* anti-German; Germanophobe

deutsch·englisch *Adj.* Anglo-German ‹*relations, cooperation, etc.*›; German-English ‹*dictionary, anthology, etc.*›

Deutschen·hass, ***Deutschen·haß** *der* hatred of the Germans; Germanophobia *no indef. art.*

Deutsche Post

The previously state-run German postal system has undergone wide-ranging reforms in recent years which will effectively remove the *Deutsche Post* monopoly by 2007. The number of post offices has been reduced, but small post-office agencies can now be found in shops, newsagents, and petrol stations. German letter boxes are yellow. Postal charges are relatively high, but the service is very reliable.

Deutscher Kulturrat

The German Arts Council was founded in 1982 as a non-governmental commission representing cultural associations and institutions. The Arts Council comprises eight independent organizations, among them the Sociocultural Council (**Soziokultur**). The function of the *Kulturrat* is to co-ordinate, advise and inform on matters concerning cultural affairs, make recommendations on cultural policy, and further international cultural relations.

Deutscher Sportbund - DSB

Sports are a favourite leisure activity in Germany. Around 27 million people are members of a sports club, while another 12 million take part in sport. The German Sports Federation (*DSB*) has 16 regional sports federations and many individual sports associations. There are more than two and a half million volunteer coaches and officials working for the Sports Federation. Popular recreational sports are also promoted by the *DSB*, such as *Trimm dich* (Get fit), a programme aimed at physical fitness, and *Sport für alle* (Sport for all), a programme encouraging people to run, swim, cycle, ski and hike. About 750,000 people a year pass *DSB* tests and qualify for a gold, silver, or bronze sports medal.

Deutsche Telekom

The previously state-run German telecommunications service has undergone extensive reforms and gradual privatization and is now a public limited company. Since 1998 when the market was opened up to competition, *Deutsche Telekom* has ceased to have a monopoly.

Deutsche Welle

The German equivalent of the BBC World Service, this radio station is financed and controlled by the German government and broadcasts programmes on German politics, business, arts, and culture, aimed at listeners abroad.

deutsch-, Deutsch-: ~feindlich *Adj.* anti-German; Germanophobe; **~feindlichkeit** *die* Germanophobia *no indef. art.*; anti-German feeling; **~französisch** *Adj.* Franco-German ‹*relations, border, etc.*›; German-French ‹*dictionary, anthology, etc.*›; **der ~-Französische Krieg** the Franco-Prussian War; **~freundlich** *Adj.* pro-German; Germanophile; **~herren** *Pl.* (hist.) Teutonic Knights; **~herrenorden** *der* (hist.) Teutonic Order of Knights; **~kanadier** *der*, **~kanadierin** *die* German-Canadian

Deutschland *(das)*; **~s** Germany

Deutschland-: ~fahrt *die* trip through Germany; **~frage** *die* (Politik) German question; **~lied** *das* German national anthem; **~politik** *die* (innerdeutsche Politik) intra-German policy; (gegenüber Deutschlandpolitik) policy towards Germany; **~politisch** **A** *Adj.* ‹*speaker*› for intra-German affairs; ‹*committee*› on intra-German affairs; **B** *adv.* ‹*interested*› in intra-German affairs; **~politisch gesehen** from the point of view of intra-German affairs; **~reise** *die* trip to Germany; (Rundreise) tour of Germany

Deutschlandlied

This has been the German national anthem since 1922, when it was chosen by the first president of the Weimar Republic. The song entitled *Lied der Deutschen* (Song of the Germans) was written by Hoffmann von Fallersleben in 1841 and set to a melody composed by Joseph Haydn (1732-1809). The third stanza of the song (*Einigkeit und Recht und Freiheit ...*) is now used as the national anthem.

deutsch-, Deutsch-: ~lehrer *der*, **~lehrerin** *die* German teacher; **~schweiz** *die* (schweiz.) German-speaking Switzerland; **~schweizer** *der*, **~schweizerin** *die* German-Swiss; **~schweizerisch** *Adj.* German-Swiss; **~sowjetisch** *Adj.* German-Soviet; **~sprachig** *Adj.* **1▸** German-speaking; **~sprachige** *Pl.* German speakers; **2▸** (in ~er Sprache) German-language *attrib.* ‹*newspaper, edition, broadcast*›; ‹*teaching*› in German; ‹*literature*› written in German; **~sprachlich** *Adj.* German[-language *attrib.*]; ***~sprechend** ▸ **Deutsch 1**; **~stämmig** *Adj.* of German origin *postpos.*; **~stämmige** *Pl.* ethnic Germans; **~stunde** *die* German lesson

Deutschtum *das*; **~s** **1▸** (deutsche Wesensart) Germanness **2▸** (Volkszugehörigkeit) German nationality **3▸** (die Deutschen) Germans *pl.*

Deutschtümelei /-tyːməˈlai/ *die*; **~, ~en** (abwertend) jingoistic emphasis on things German

Deutsch·unterricht *der* German teaching; (Unterrichtsstunde) German lesson; **~ erteilen** *or* **geben** teach German; *s. auch* **Englischunterricht**; **Unterricht**

Deutung *die*; **~, ~en** interpretation

Deutungs·versuch *der* attempt at interpretation; **ein ~ dieser Parabel** an attempt to interpret this parable

Devalvation /devalvaˈtsi̯oːn/ *die*; **~, ~en** (Finanzw.) devaluation

Devise /deˈviːzə/ *die*; **~, ~n** motto; **sich** *(Dat.)* **etw. zur ~ machen** make sth. one's motto

Devisen *Pl.* foreign exchange *sing.*; (Sorten) foreign currency *sing. or* exchange *sing.*

Devisen-: ~abkommen *das* (Politik) foreign exchange agreement; **~bewirtschaftung** *die* foreign exchange control; **~börse** *die* foreign exchange market; **~bringer** *der* foreign exchange earner; **~geschäft** *das* foreign exchange business *or* dealings *pl.*; (einzelne Transaktion) foreign exchange transaction; **~kurs** *der* exchange rate; rate of exchange; **~markt** *der* foreign exchange market; **~schmuggel** *der* [foreign] currency smuggling; **~sperre** *die* exchange embargo; **~vergehen** *das* currency offence; breach of exchange control regulations

devot /deˈvoːt/ (geh.)
A *Adj.* **1▸** (abwertend) obsequious **2▸** (veralt.: demütig) humble
B *adv.* **1▸** (abwertend) obsequiously **2▸** (veralt.: demütig) humbly

Devotionalien /devotsi̯oˈnaːli̯ən/ *Pl.* (Rel.) devotional objects

Devotionalien-: ~handel *der* trade in devotional objects; **~händler** *der*, **~händlerin** *die* trader in devotional objects

Dextrose /dɛksˈtroːzə/ *die*; **~:** dextrose

Dez /deːts/ *der*; **~es, ~e** (salopp) nut (coll.); bonce (sl.)

Dez. *Abk.* = **Dezember** Dec.

Dezember /deˈtsɛmbɐ/ *der*; **~s, ~** ▸❶ **S. 165** December; *s. auch* **April**

Dezennium /deˈtsɛni̯ʊm/ *das*; **~s, Dezennien** (geh.) decennium; decade

dezent /deˈtsɛnt/
A *Adj.* quiet ‹*colour, pattern, suit*›; subdued ‹*lighting, music*›; discreet ‹*smile, behaviour*›; gentle ‹*irony*›
B *adv.* discreetly; ‹*dress*› unostentatiously

dezentral
A *Adj.* **1▸** non-central ‹*location*› **2▸** (von verschiedenen Stellen ausgehend) decentralized
B *adv.* **1▸** outside the centre **2▸** ▸**A 2**: decentrally

Dezentralisation *die*; **~, ~en** decentralization

dezentralisieren *tr. V.* decentralize

Dezentralisierung *die*; **~, ~en** decentralization

Dezenz /deˈtsɛnts/ *die*; **~** **1▸** discreetness **2▸** (Eleganz) unostentatious elegance

Dezernat /detsɛrˈnaːt/ *das*; **~[e]s, ~e** department

Dezernent /detsɛrˈnɛnt/ *der*; **~en, ~en**, **Dezernentin** *die*; **~, ~nen** head of department

dezi-, Dezi- /ˈdeːtsi-/ deci

Dezibel /detsiˈbɛl/ *das*; **~s, ~:** decibel

dezidiert /detsiˈdiːɐ̯t/ (geh.)
A *Adj.* firm ‹*demand, view*›; **mit einigen ~en Fragen** with some determined questioning
B *adv.* ‹*support, demand*› firmly; ‹*question*› determinedly

Dezi-: ~gramm *das* decigram; **~liter** *der od. das* decilitre

dezimal /detsiˈmaːl/ *Adj.* decimal

Dezimal-: ~bruch *der* ▸❶ **S. 826** decimal [fraction]; **~klassifikation** *die* decimal *or* Dewey classification; **~rechnung** *die* decimal arithmetic *no art.*; **~stelle** *die* decimal place; **~system** *das* decimal system; **~waage** *die* decimal balance; **~zahl** *die* ▸❶ **S. 826** decimal [number]

Dezime /deˈtsiːmə/ *die*; **~, ~n** (Musik) tenth

Dezi·meter *der od. das* decimetre

dezimieren /detsiˈmiːrən/
A *tr. V.* decimate
B *refl. V.* be drastically reduced

Dezimierung *die*; **~, ~en** **1▸** decimation **2▸** (starker Rückgang) drastic reduction *(Gen.* in)

DFB *Abk.* = **Deutscher Fußball-Bund**

DG *Abk.* = **Dachgeschoss**

DGB *Abk.* = **Deutscher Gewerkschaftsbund** German Trade Union Federation

DGB – Deutscher Gewerkschaftsbund

The biggest trade-union umbrella organization in Germany, with about 9 million members in 12 individual unions. In recent years, the *DGB* has pursued a policy of moderation in its pay demands.

dgl. *Abk.* **= dergleichen, desgleichen**

d. Gr. *Abk.* **= der/die Große**

d. h. *Abk.* **= das heißt** i.e.

Di. *Abk.* **= Dienstag** Tue[s].

Dia /'di:a/ *das;* **~s, ~s** slide; transparency

Diabetes /dia'be:tɛs/ *der;* **~ ▸❶ S. 439** diabetes

Diabetiker /dia'be:tikɐ/ *der;* **~s, ~, Diabetikerin,** *die;* **~, ~nen** diabetic

diabetisch *Adj.* diabetic

Dia·betrachter *der* [slide] viewer

Diabolik /dia'bo:lɪk/ *die;* **~** (geh.) diabolic malevolence

diabolisch (geh.)

A *Adj.* diabolic; diabolically malevolent

B *adv.* with diabolic malevolence

diachron /dia'kro:n/

A *Adj.* diachronic

B *adv.* diachronically

Diachronie /diakro'ni:/ *die;* **~** (Sprachw.) diachrony *no art.*

diachronisch *Adj.* **▸diachron**

Diadem /dia'de:m/ *das;* **~s, ~e** diadem

Diadochen /dia'dɔxn̩/ *Pl.* (geh.) rivals for the succession

Diadochen·kämpfe *Pl.* (geh.) power struggle *sing.*

Diagnose /dia'gno:zə/ *die;* **~, ~n** diagnosis; **eine ~ stellen** make a diagnosis

Diagnose·zentrum *das* diagnostic clinic

Diagnostik /dia'gnɔstɪk/ *die;* **~** (Med., Psych.) diagnostics *sing., no art.*

Diagnostiker *der;* **~s, ~, Diagnostikerin** *die;* **~, ~nen** (Med., Psych.) diagnostician

diagnostisch

A *Adj.* diagnostic

B *adv.* diagnostically

diagnostizieren /diagnɔsti'tsi:rən/

A *tr. V.* diagnose

B *itr. V.* **auf etw.** (*Akk.*) **~:** diagnose sth.

diagonal /diago'na:l/

A *Adj.* diagonal

B *adv.* diagonally; **etw. ~ lesen** (ugs.) skim through sth.

Diagonale *die;* **~, ~n** diagonal

Diagramm *das* graph; (von Gegenständen) diagram

Diakon /dia'ko:n/ *der;* **~s** *od.* **~en, ~e[n]** deacon

Diakonie /diako'ni:/ *die;* **~** (ev. Kirche) welfare and social work

Diakonin *die;* **~, ~nen** deaconess

diakonisch *Adj.* welfare and social ‹*work, facilities, etc.*›

Diakonisse /diako'nɪsə/ *die;* **~, ~n, Diakonissin** *die;* **~, ~nen** deaconess

dia·kritisch *Adj.* in **~es Zeichen** (Sprachw.) diacritical mark *or* sign; diacritic

Dialekt /dia'lɛkt/ *der;* **~[e]s, ~e** dialect; **~ sprechen** speak in dialect

dialektal /dialɛk'ta:l/ *Adj.* dialectal

dialekt-, Dialekt-: ~ausdruck *der; Pl.* **~ausdrücke** dialect expression; **~forschung** *die* dialect research; **~frei A** *Adj.* **~freies Deutsch sprechen** speak German without a trace of [any] dialect; **B** *adv.* **~frei sprechen** speak without a trace of [any] dialect

Dialektik /dia'lɛktɪk/ *die;* **~ 1▸** (Philos.) dialectics *pl.;* (Diamat) dialectic **2▸** (Gegensätzlichkeit) conflicting nature

Dialektiker *der;* **~s, ~, Dialektikerin** *die;* **~, ~nen** (Philos.) dialectician

dialektisch

A *Adj.* **1▸** (Philos.) dialectical **2▸ ▸dialektal**

B *adv.* dialectically

Dialer /'daɪəlɐ/ *der;* **~[s], ~** (DV) dialer

Dialog /dia'lo:k/ *der;* **~[e]s, ~e** dialogue

dialogisch *Adj.* dialogic; ‹*story*› in dialogue form

Dialyse /dia'ly:zə/ *die;* **~, ~n** (Physik, Chemie, Med.) dialysis

Dialyse-: ~patient *der,* **~patientin** *die* dialysis patient; **~zentrum** *das* dialysis centre

Diamant[1] /dia'mant/ *der;* **~en, ~en** diamond

Diamant[2] *die;* **~** (Druckw.) diamond ($4\frac{1}{2}$ *points Pica*); brilliant (*4 points Pica*)

diamanten *Adj.* diamond

Diamant[en]-: ~schleifer *der,* **~schleiferin** *die* diamond cutter; **~schmuck** *der* diamond jewellery; diamonds *pl.;* **~staub** *der* diamond dust

Diamat, DIAMAT /dia'ma(:)t/ *der;* **~** *Abk.* **= dialektischer Materialismus**

diametral /diame'tra:l/

A *Adj.* **1▸** (Geom.) diametral **2▸** (fig. geh.); diametrical ‹*opposition*›; diametrically opposed ‹*views*›; **im ~en Gegensatz zu etw. stehen** be diametrically opposed to sth.

B *adv.* (geh.) diametrically; **~ entgegengesetzt sein** be diametrically opposed

Dia-: ~positiv *das* slide; transparency; **~projektor** *der* slide projector; **~rahmen** *der* slide mount

Diärese /diɛ're:zə/ *die;* **~, ~n** (Sprachw., Metrik, Rhet., Philos.) diaeresis

Diarrhö, Diarrhöe /dia'rø:/ *die;* **~, Diarrhöen ▸❶ S. 439** (Med.) diarrhoea

Diaspora /di'aspora/ *die;* **~:** Diaspora

Diastole /di'astole/ *die;* **~, ~n** /dia'sto:lən/ (Med.) diastole

Diät /di'ɛ:t/ *die;* **~, ~en** diet; **eine ~ einhalten** keep to a diet; **nach einer ~ leben** live on a diet; **jmdn. auf ~ setzen** put sb. on a diet; **~ kochen** cook according to a/one's diet; **~ essen** be on a diet; **[strikt] ~ leben** keep to a [strict] diet

Diät-: ~assistent *der,* **~assistentin** *die* **▸❶ S. 113** dietitian; **~bier** *das* diabetic beer

Diäten *Pl.* [parliamentary] allowance *sing.*

Diätetik /diɛ'te:tɪk/ *die;* **~, ~en** dietetics *sing., no art.*

diätetisch *Adj.* dietetic; dietary; **eine ~e Lebensweise** living on a diet

Diät·fahrplan *der* (ugs.) diet

Diätist *der;* **~en, ~en, Diätistin** *die;* **~, ~nen** dietitian

Diät-: ~koch *der,* **~köchin** *die* dietary cook; **~kost** *die* dietary food; **~küche** *die* **1▸** dietary kitchen; **2▸** (Schonkost) dietary food; **~kur** *die* diet cure

Diatonik /dia'to:nɪk/ *die;* **~** (Musik) diatonicism; diatonic system

diatonisch *Adj.* (Musik) diatonic

Diät·plan *der* dietary plan; diet plan; diet

dich /dɪç/

A *Akk. des Personalpron.* **du** you

B *Akk. des Reflexivpron. der 2. Pers. Sg.* yourself; **wäschst du ~?** are you washing [yourself]?; **entschuldige ~!** apologize!

Dichotomie /dɪçoto'mi:/ *die;* **~, ~n** (Bot., Philos., Sprachw.) dichotomy

dicht /dɪçt/

A *Adj.* **1▸** thick ‹*hair, fur, plumage, moss*›; thick, dense ‹*foliage, fog, cloud*›; dense ‹*forest, thicket, hedge, crowd*›; heavy, dense ‹*traffic*›; densely ranked, close-ranked ‹*rows of houses*›; heavy ‹*snowstorm*›; (fig.) dense ‹*prose, dialogue, etc.*›; full, packed ‹*programme*›; **in ~er Folge** in rapid *or* quick succession **2▸** (undurchlässig) (für Luft) airtight; (für Wasser) watertight ‹*shoes*›; (für Licht) heavy ‹*curtains, shutters*›; **~ machen** seal ‹*crack*›; make airtight/watertight; seal the crack[s]/leak[s] in ‹*roof, window, etc.*›; waterproof ‹*material, umbrella, etc.*›; **nicht ganz ~ sein** (salopp) have a screw loose (coll.) **3▸** (ugs.: geschlossen) shut; closed

B *adv.* **1▸** densely ‹*populated, foliated*›; thickly, densely ‹*wooded*›; tightly, closely ‹*packed*›; **~ bebaut** heavily built up; **~ verschneit** thick with snow; **~ besetzt** full; packed; **~ behaart** [very] hairy; **~ an ~** *od.* **~ gedrängt stehen/sitzen** stand/sit close together; **das Dorf war ~ verschneit** the village was covered in a thick blanket of snow *or* was deep in snow; **~ bewachsene Hügel** hills covered with dense vegetation **2▸** (undurchlässig) tightly **3▸** *mit Präp.* (nahe) **~ neben** right next to; **sich ~ bei jmdm. halten** keep close to sb.; **~ daran** hard by; **~ nebeneinander** close together; **~ vor/hinter ihm** right *or* just in front of/behind him; **die Polizei ist ihm ~ auf den Fersen** the police are hard *or* close on his heels **4▸** (zeitlich: unmittelbar) **ich war ~ daran, es zu tun** I was just about to do it; **~ bevorstehen** be imminent; **das Fest steht ~ bevor** the party is almost upon us/them *etc.*

dicht·auf *Adv.* close behind

dichtbebaut *usw.* **▸dicht B 1**

Dichte /'dɪçtə/ *die;* **~ 1▸** (Physik, fig.) density **2▸** (Undurchdringlichkeit) **ein Nebel von solcher ~:** such [a] dense *or* thick fog

dichten[1] /'dɪçtn̩/

A *itr. V.* **[gut] ~:** make a good seal

B *tr. V.* make airtight/watertight; seal ‹*joint etc.*›; seal the crack[s]/leak[s] in ‹*window, roof, etc.*›

dichten[2]

A *itr. V.* **1▸** write poetry **2▸ sein ganzes Dichten und Trachten** all his thoughts and endeavours

B *tr. V.* (verfassen) write; compose

Dichter *der;* **~s, ~ ▸❶ S. 113** poet; (Schriftsteller) writer; author

Dichter·fürst *der* (veralt.) prince among poets; (Schriftsteller) prince among writers

Dichterin *die;* **~, ~nen ▸❶ S. 113** poet[ess]; (Schriftstellerin) writer; author[ess]

dichterisch

A *Adj.* poetic; (schriftstellerisch) literary

B *adv.;* **▸A:** poetically; literarily

Dichter-: ~komponist *der,* **~komponistin** *die* poet/writer and composer; **~kreis** *der* circle of poets; (von Schriftstellern) circle of writers; **~lesung** *die* reading (*by a poet or writer from his own works*)

Dichterling *der;* **~s, ~e** (abwertend) poetaster (derog.); rhymester (derog.)

Dichter-: ~schule *die* school of poets; (von Schriftstellern) school of writers; **~sprache** *die* poetic language

dicht-: ~gedrängt ▸dicht B 1; ~|halten *unr. itr. V.* (ugs.) keep one's mouth shut (coll.)

Dicht·kunst *die* **1▸** art of poetry **2▸** (Fähigkeit, Talent) poetic talent **3▸** (Poesie) poetry *no art.*

dicht|machen (ugs.)

A *tr. V.* shut; close; (endgültig) shut *or* close down; **die Polizei hat ihm die Bar dichtgemacht** the police shut *or* closed down his bar

B *itr. V.* **1▸** shut; close; (endgültig) shut *or* close down **2▸** (Sportjargon) **hinten ~:** close the game down at the back

Dichtung[1] *die;* **~, ~en 1▸** sealing; **zur ~ der Fugen** to seal the joints **2▸** (Vorrichtung) seal; (am Hahn usw.) washer; (am Vergaser, Zylinder usw.) gasket

Dichtung[2] *die;* **~, ~en 1▸** literary work; work of literature; (in Versform) poetic work; poem; (fig. ugs.) fiction; **~ und Wahrheit** fact and fiction; truth and fantasy; **Goethes „~ und Wahrheit"** Goethe's 'Poetry and Truth' **2▸** (Dichtkunst) literature; (in Versform) poetry

Dichtungs-: ~masse *die* sealing compound; sealant; **~mittel** *das* integral waterproofing agent *or* waterproofer; **~ring** *der,* **~scheibe** *die* sealing ring; (am Hahn) washer

dick /dɪk/

A *Adj.* **1▸** thick; thick, chunky ‹*pullover*›; stout ‹*tree*›; fat ‹*person, arms, legs, behind, etc.*›; big ‹*bust*›; **~ und rund** *od.* **fett sein** (ugs.) be round and fat; **~ werden** get fat; **das Kleid macht ~:** the dress makes you look fat; **Kuchen macht ~:** cakes are fattening *or* make you fat; **ein ~es Auto fahren** (fig. ugs.) drive a great big car (coll.); **ein Mädchen ~ machen** (salopp) put a girl in the club (sl.) **2▸** (mit Maßangaben) thick; **5 cm ~ sein** be 5 cm thick; **5 cm ~e Bretter** planks 5 cm thick; 5 cm thick planks **3▸** (stark)

thick ‹*carpet, wall, layer*›; **mit jmdm. durch ~ und dünn gehen** stay *or* stick with sb. through thick and thin; **es nicht so ~ haben** (ugs.) not be very well off **4** (ugs.: angeschwollen) swollen ‹*cheek, ankle, tonsils, etc.*› **5** (dicht, ~flüssig) thick ‹*hair, fog, soup, sauce, etc.*›; **im ~sten Verkehr** (fig. ugs.) in the heaviest traffic; **mitten in der ~sten Arbeit** (fig. ugs.) just when we're/they're *etc.* right up to our/their *etc.* necks in work (coll.) **6** (ugs.: außergewöhnlich groß) big ‹*mistake, order*›; hefty, (coll.) fat ‹*fee, premium, salary*›; **einen ~en Tadel verdienen** deserve heavy criticism; **jmdm. ein ~es Lob aussprechen** give sb. a great deal of prise *or* high praise; **das ~e Ende kommt noch** (ugs.) the worst is yet to come **7** (ugs.: eng) close ‹*friends, friendship, etc.*›
B *adv.* **1** **etw. ~ unterstreichen** underline sth. heavily; **sich ~ anziehen** wrap up warm[ly] **2** (mit Maßangabe) **etw. 5 cm ~ schneiden/auftragen** *usw.* cut/apply sth. 5 cm. thick **3** (stark) thickly; **~ geschminkt/bemalt** heavily made up; **~ auftragen** (ugs. abwertend) lay it on thick (sl.) **4** **~ geschwollen** (ugs.) badly swollen **5** **~ befreundet sein** (ugs.) be close friends

dick-, Dick-: ~bauch *der* (scherzh.) fatty; (mit Spitzbauch) pot belly; **~bauchig** *Adj.* large-bellied, big-bellied ‹*vase, pot, etc.*›; **~bäuchig** *Adj.* corpulent; portly; (mit Spitzbauch) pot-bellied ‹*person*›; **~darm** *der* ▸ⓘ **S. 435** (Anat.) large intestine

dicke *Adv.* (ugs.) easily; **wir haben noch ~ Zeit** we've got plenty of time; **von etw. ~ genug haben** have had quite enough of sth.; **jmdn./etw. ~ haben** (salopp) have had a bellyful of sb./sth.

Dicke¹ *die;* **~:** thickness; (von Menschen, Körperteilen) fatness

Dicke² *der/die; adj. Dekl.* **1** (ugs.) fatty (coll.); fat man/woman; **die ~n** (im Allgemeinen) fatties (coll.); fat people **2** (Kosename) podge (coll.)

dicken
A *tr. V.* thicken
B *itr. V.*; *auch mit sein* thicken

Dickerchen *das;* **~s, ~** (ugs. scherzh.) podge (coll.)

dicke|tun *unr. refl. V.* (ugs. abwertend) show off; (durch Reden) boast; brag; **sich mit etw. ~:** boast *or* brag about sth.; **sich mit seiner Kraft ~:** show off one's strength

dick-, Dick-: ~fellig (ugs. abwertend) **A** *Adj.* thick-skinned; **~fellig sein** have a thick skin; be thick-skinned; **B** *adv.* in a thick-skinned way; **~felligkeit** *die;* **~** (ugs. abwertend) insensitivity; **~flüssig** *Adj.* thick; viscous (as tech. term); **~flüssigkeit** *die* thickness; viscosity (as tech. term); **~häuter** *der;* **~s, ~:** pachyderm; (fig.) thick-skinned person

Dickicht /ˈdɪkɪçt/ *das;* **~[e]s, ~e** thicket; (im Wald) dense undergrowth *no indef. art.*; (fig.) jungle

dick-, Dick-: ~kopf *der* (ugs.) mule (coll.); **du bist ein ~kopf** you're as stubborn as a mule; **einen ~kopf haben** be stubborn *or* pigheaded; **~köpfig** (ugs.) **A** *Adj.* stubborn; pigheaded; **B** *adv.* stubbornly; pigheadedly; **~leibig** *Adj.* (geh.) corpulent; fat; (fig.) thick, fat ‹*document, book*›; **~leibigkeit** *die;* **~** (geh.) corpulence; fatness

dicklich *Adj.* **1** plumpish; chubby **2** (dickflüssig) thick

dick-, Dick-: ~macher *der* (ugs.) fattening food; **~milch** *die* sour milk; **~schädel** *der* ▸**~kopf**; **~schäd[e]lig** **A** *Adj.* stubborn; **B** *adv.* stubbornly; **~schalig** *Adj.* thick-skinned ‹*orange, tomato, etc.*›; **~|tun** *unr. refl. V.* ▸**dicketun**; **~wandig** *Adj.* thick-walled, thick-sided ‹*vessel, container*›; **~wanst** *der* (salopp abwertend) fatso (sl.)

Didaktik /diˈdaktɪk/ *die;* **~, ~en** **1** didactics *sing., no art.*; theory of teaching and methodology **2** (Unterrichtsmethode) teaching method

Didaktiker *der;* **~s, ~, Didaktikerin** *die;* **~, ~nen** **1** educationalist **2** (jmd. mit didaktischen Fähigkeiten) teacher

didaktisch
A *Adj.* didactic
B *adv.* didactically

die¹ /di:/
A *best. Art. Nom.* the; **~ Kleine** the little girl; **~ Liebe/Freundschaft** love/friendship; **~ „Iphigenie"** 'Iphigenia'; **die Helga** (ugs.) Helga; **~ Demokratie/Diktatur/Monarchie** democracy/dictatorship/monarchy; **~ Bardot** (ugs.) Bardot; **~ [Frankfurter] Eintracht** (ugs.) Eintracht Frankfurt; **sie ist die Sängerin/Schauspielerin** she's 'the singer/actress; **~ Marktstraße** Market Street; **~ Schweiz/Türkei** Switzerland/Turkey; **~ Frau/Menschheit** women *pl.*/mankind; **~ „Concorde"/„Klaus Störtebeker"** 'Concorde'/the 'Klaus Störtebeker'; **~ Kunst/Oper** art/opera
B *Demonstrativpron.* **1** *attr.* **die Frau war es** it was 'that woman **2** *selbstständig* she; **die war es** it was 'her; **die und arbeiten!** (ugs.) [what,] her work!; **~ mit dem Hund/den lila Haaren** (ugs.) her with the dog/purple hair; **die [da]** (Frau, Mädchen) that woman/girl; (Gegenstand, Tier) that one; **~ blöde Kuh, ~!** (fig. salopp) what a silly cow! (sl.)
C *Relativpron. Nom.* (Mensch) who; that; (Sache, Tier) which; that; **die Frau, ~ da drüben entlanggeht** the woman walking along over there; **ich sah eine Frau/Katze, ~ aus dem Fenster schaute** I saw a women/cat looking out of the window
D *Relativ- u. Demonstrativpron.* the one who; **~ das getan hat** the woman *etc.* who did it

die²
A *best. Art.* **1** *Akk. Sg. v.* **die¹ A: ich sah ~ Frau/Ratte** I saw the women/rat; **wir sahen ~ „Zauberflöte"** we saw the 'Magic Flute'; **hast du ~ Ute gesehen?** (ugs.) have you seen Ute?; **er hat ~ Callas geheiratet** (ugs.) he married Callas; **ich fuhr durch ~ Marktstraße** I drove through Market Street **2** *Nom. u. Akk. Pl. v.* **der¹ A, die¹ A, das A: [er fragte] ~ Männer/Frauen/Kinder** [he asked] the men/women/children
B *Demonstrativpron. Nom. u. Akk. Pl. v.* **der¹ B1, die¹ B1, das B1:** *attr.* **ich meine die Männer/Frauen/Kinder, die gestern hier waren** I mean those men/women/children who were here yesterday; *selbstständig* **ich meine die [da]** I mean 'them
C *Relativpron.* **1** *Akk. Sg. v.* **die¹ C:** (bei Menschen) **die Frau, ~ ich gesehen habe** the woman who *or* that I saw; (bei Sachen, Tieren) **die Straße, ~ ich entlangging** the street [that *or* which] I walked along; **die Maus, ~ die Katze fing** the mouse which *or* that the cat caught **2** *Nom. u. Akk. Pl. v.* **der¹ C, die¹ C, das C:** (bei Menschen) **die Männer/Frauen/Kinder, ~ ich gesehen habe/~ dort gehen** the men/women/children I saw/walking along over there; (bei Sachen, Tieren) **die Nägel/Birnen/Bücher, ~ da liegen/~ jemand da hingelegt hat** the nails/pears/books lying there/which somebody put there

Dieb /di:p/ *der;* **~[e]s, ~e** thief; **haltet den ~!** stop thief!

Dieberei *die;* **~, ~en** **1** (das Stehlen) thieving **2** (Diebstahl) theft

Diebes-: ~bande *die* (abwertend) gang of thieves; **~beute** *die* stolen goods *pl. or* property; **~gut** *das* stolen goods *pl. or* property; **~nest** *das* thieves' hideout; **~tour** *die* **auf ~tour gehen/sein** go/have gone [out] thieving *or* stealing; **auf ~touren sein** have been [out] thieving *or* stealing on a number of occasions

Diebin *die;* **~, ~nen** [woman] thief; *s. auch* **-in**

diebisch
A *Adj.* **1** thieving **2** (verstohlen) mischievous
B *adv.* mischievously; **sich ~ über etw.** (*Akk.*) **freuen** take a mischievous pleasure in sth.

Diebstahl /ˈdi:pʃta:l/ *der;* **~[e]s, Diebstähle** /ˈdi:p-ʃtɛ:lə/ theft; **einfacher ~:** theft; **schwerer ~:** burglary and theft; **räuberischer ~:** *robbery accompanied by use of violence to keep possession of the stolen property;* **[ein] geistiger ~:** plagiarism *no indef. art.*

Diebstahl·versicherung *die* insurance against theft

die·jenige, diejenigen ▸**derjenige**

Diele /ˈdi:lə/ *die;* **~, ~n** **1** hall[way] **2** (Fußbodenbrett) floorboard

dielektrisch /dieˈlɛktrɪʃ/ *Adj.* (Physik, Elektrot.) dielectric

dielen *tr. V.* lay floorboards in ‹*room*›; board ‹*floor*›

Dielen·brett *das* floorboard

dienen /ˈdi:nən/ *itr. V.* **1** be in service; **jmdm. ~:** serve sb.; **als Magd ~:** serve as a maid; **der Gerechtigkeit ~** (geh.) serve the cause of justice; **bei Hof ~:** wait *or* serve at court; *s. auch* **Herr** **2** (veralt.: Militärdienst tun) do military service; **beim Heer ~:** serve in the army; **acht Jahre ~:** do eight years' military service; *s. auch* **gedient B** **3** (nützlich sein) serve; **das dient einer guten Sache** it is in a good cause; **diese Maßnahmen ~ der Sicherheit am Arbeitsplatz** these measures help towards safety at work **4** (helfen) help (**in** + *Dat.* in); **womit kann ich ~?** what can I do for you?; can I help you?; **mit 20 Euro wäre mir schon gedient** 20 euros would do; **damit ist mir wenig gedient** it's not much help *or* use to me; **damit kann ich leider nicht ~:** I'm afraid I can't help you there **5** (verwendet werden) serve; **als Museum ~:** serve *or* be used as a museum; **als Ersatz/Vorwand ~:** serve as a substitute/pretext; **das soll dir als Warnung ~:** let that serve as *or* be a warning to you; **zur Unterstützung einer Theorie ~:** serve to support a theory

Diener *der;* **~s, ~:** servant; **einen ~ machen** (ugs.); bow; make a bow; *s. auch* **stumm**

Dienerin /ˈdi:nərɪn/ *die;* **~, ~nen** maid; servant

dienern *itr. V.* (abwertend) bow; (fig.) bow and scrape

Dienerschaft *die;* **~:** servants *pl.*; domestic staff

dienlich *Adj.* helpful; useful; **jmdm./einer Sache ~ sein** be helpful *or* of help to sb./sth.; **kann ich Ihnen mit etwas ~ sein?** (geh.) can I be of any assistance to you?

-dienst *der* service; **Schicht~:** shift work

Dienst /di:nst/ *der;* **~[e]s, ~e** **1** (Tätigkeit) work; (von Soldaten, Polizeibeamten, Krankenhauspersonal usw.) duty; **seinen ~ antreten** start work/go on duty; **zum ~ gehen** go to work/go on duty; **~ haben** be at work/on duty; ‹*doctor*› be on call; ‹*chemist*› be open; **~ habend** *od.* **tuend** duty ‹*officer*›; ‹*official, doctor*› on duty; **außerhalb des ~es** outside work/when off duty; **im ~ sein** be at work/on duty; **nicht im ~ sein** not be at work/be off duty; **der Unteroffizier vom ~** (Milit.) the duty NCO; **der Chef vom ~** (Zeitungsw.) the duty editor; **~ ist ~ und Schnaps ist Schnaps** (ugs.) you shouldn't mix business and pleasure **2** (Arbeitsverhältnis) post; **den** *od.* **seinen ~ quittieren** resign one's post; (Milit.) leave the service; ‹*officer*› resign one's commission; **jmdn. aus dem ~/seinen ~en entlassen** dismiss sb.; **jmdn. in ~ nehmen** (veralt.) employ *or* engage sb.; **in jmds. ~[en] sein** *od.* **stehen** (veralt.) be in sb.'s employ; **Major** *usw.* **außer ~ [sein]** [be a] retired major *etc.*; **im ~ einer guten Sache** (*Gen.*) **stehen** be in a good cause; **sich in den ~ einer guten Sache** (*Gen.*) **stellen** devote oneself to a good cause; **etw. in ~ stellen** put sth. into service *or* commission **3** (Tätigkeitsbereich) service; **der höhere ~ der Beamtenlaufbahn** the senior civil service; *s. auch* **öffentlich** **4** (Hilfe) **seine ~e [anbieten]** [offer] one's services; **jmdm. einen ~ tun** help sb.; **~ am Kunden** (ugs.) customer service; **seinen ~ tun** ‹*machine, appliance*› serve its purpose; **jmdm. gute ~e tun** serve sb. well; give sb. good service; **jmdm. mit etw. einen schlechten ~ erweisen** do sb. a disservice *or* a bad turn with sth.; **zu jmds. ~en** *od.* **jmdm. zu ~en sein** *od.* **stehen** (geh.) be at sb.'s disposal *or* service; **jmdm. den ~ versagen** fail sb. **5** (Hilfs~) service; (Nachrichten~, Spionage~) [intelligence] service **6** (Kunstwiss.) respond

dienst-, Dienst-: ~abteil *das* (Eisenb.) guard's compartment; **~adel** *der* (hist.) *nobility whose titles derive from being in the king's service;* **~ältest...** *Adj.* longest-serving

Diens·tag /diːns-/ *der* ▸ⓘ S. 165, ▸ⓘ S. 816 Tuesday; **am ~:** on Tuesday; (jeden ~) on Tuesday; **~, der 1. Juni** Tuesday the first of June; Tuesday, 1 June; **am ~, dem 1. Juni** *od.* **den 1. Juni** on Tuesday 1 June *or* June 1st; **er kommt ~:** he is coming on Tuesday; **die letzten ~e** the last few Tuesdays; **eines ~s** one Tuesday; **den ganzen ~ über** all day Tuesday; the whole of Tuesday; **ab nächsten** *od.* **nächstem ~:** from next Tuesday [onwards]; **die Nacht von ~ auf** *od.* **zum Mittwoch** Tuesday night; **~ in einer Woche** *od.* **in acht Tagen** Tuesday week; a week on Tuesday; **~ vor einer Woche** a week last Tuesday; **~ früh** Tuesday morning; *s. auch* **Dienstagabend, dienstagabends** *usw.*

Dienstag·abend *der* ▸ⓘ S. 816 Tuesday evening; Tuesday night (coll.); **[am] ~:** [on] Tuesday evening/night

dienstag·abends *Adv.* ▸ⓘ S. 816 [on] Tuesday evenings

dienstägig /ˈdiːnstɛːgɪç/ *Adj.* **die/unsere ~e Sendung** *usw.* Tuesday's programme *etc.*; the/our programme *etc.* on Tuesday

dienstäglich ▸ⓘ S. 816

A *Adj.* [regular] Tuesday

B *adv.* on Tuesday

dienstag-, Dienstag-: ~mittag *der* ▸ⓘ S. 816 Tuesday lunchtime; **~mittags** *Adv.* ▸ⓘ S. 816 Tuesday lunchtimes; **~morgen** *der* ▸ⓘ S. 816 Tuesday morning; **~morgens** *Adv.* ▸ⓘ S. 816 [on] Tuesday mornings; **~nachmittag** *der* ▸ⓘ S. 816 Tuesday afternoon; **~nachmittags** *Adv.* ▸ⓘ S. 816 [on] Tuesday afternoons; **~nacht** *die* ▸ⓘ S. 816 Tuesday night; **~nachts** *Adv.* ▸ⓘ S. 816 [on] Tuesday nights

diens·tags *Adv.* ▸ⓘ S. 816 on Tuesday[s]; **~ abends/morgens** on Tuesday evening[s]/morning[s]; on a Tuesday evening/morning

Dienstag·vormittag *der* ▸ⓘ S. 816 Tuesday morning

dienstag·vormittags *Adv.* ▸ⓘ S. 816 [on] Tuesday mornings

dienst-, Dienst-: ~alter *das* length of service; **er hat ein ~alter von 6 Jahren** he has 6 years of service; **~älteste** *der/die* longest-serving person; **~an·tritt** *der* commencement of one's duties; **~anweisung** *die* instruction; **laut ~anweisung** according to instructions *pl.*; **~auffassung** *die* conception of duty; **~aufsicht** *die* supervision; **die ~aufsicht liegt bei ...** ... has supervisory responsibility; **~aufsichts·beschwerde** *die* complaint to the supervising authority *(about a public servant or government department)*; **~ausweis** *der* [official] identity card; **~bar** *Adj.* **sich jmdm. ~bar erzeigen** (veralt.) show one's willingness to serve sb.; **ein ~barer Geist** (ugs. scherzh.) a ministering angel; **sich** *(Dat.)* **jmdn./etw. ~bar machen** get good service from sb./utilize sth.; **einer Sache** *(Dat.)* **jmdn./etw. ~bar machen** make sb./sth. serve sth.; **sich** *(Dat.)* **die Kräfte der Natur/die Atomenergie ~bar machen** harness the power of nature/atomic energy; **~barkeit** *die*; **~, ~en** 1) (geh.) **jmdn. in seine ~barkeit bringen** bring sb. under one's power; **in jmds. ~barkeit geraten** come under sb.'s power; 2) (hist.) bondage; servitude; 3) (jur.) easement; **~beflissen** A *Adj.* zealous; eager; B *adv.* zealously; eagerly; **~beflissenheit** *die* zeal; eagerness; **~beginn** *der* start of work; **vor/nach/bei ~beginn** before/after/at the start of work; **~bereich** *der* area of responsibility; **~bereit** *Adj.* ‹chemist› open *pred.*; ‹doctor› on call *or* duty; ‹dentist› on duty; **die nächste ~bereite Apotheke** the nearest chemist that is/was open; **~bereitschaft** *die*: **~bereitschaft haben** ‹chemist› be open; ‹doctor› be on call *or* duty; ‹dentist› be on duty; **~bezüge** *Pl.* salary *sing.*; **~bote** *der* servant; **~boten·eingang** *der* tradesmen's entrance; **~bezeichnung** *die* title; **~eid** *der* official oath; **~eifer** *der* zeal; eagerness; **~eifrig** A *Adj.* zealous; eager; B *adv.* zealously; eagerly; **~enthebung** *die* suspension from duty; **~fähig** *Adj.* fit for work *postpos.*; (Milit.) fit for service *postpos.*; **~fahrt** *die* ▸ **~reise**; **~frei** *Adj.* free ‹time›; **an ~freien Tagen** on days off; **~frei haben/bekommen** have/get time off; **am Montag ~frei haben** have Monday off; **Heiligabend ist ~frei** Christmas Eve is a holiday; **~gebrauch** *der*: **nur für den ~gebrauch bestimmt** for official use only; **~geheimnis** *das* 1) professional secret; (im Staats~) official secret; 2) professional secrecy; (im Staats~) official secrecy; **unter das ~geheimnis fallen** be a professional/official secret; **~geschäfte** *Pl.* business *sing.*; **in ~geschäften** on business; (von Beamten) on official business; **~gespräch** *das* 1) business meeting; (von Beamten) official meeting; 2) (Telefongespräch) business call; (von Beamten) official call; **~grad** *der* (Milit.) rank; **~grad·abzeichen** *das* (Milit.) insignia [of rank]; **~habend** ▸ **Dienst 1**; **~habende** *der/die*; *adj. Dekl.* (Offizier) duty officer; (Beamter/Arzt) official/doctor on duty; **~herr** *der*, **~herrin** *die* employer; **~hund** *der* dog used for police/security work; **ein Polizist mit seinem ~hund** a policeman with his dog; **~jahr** *das* year of service; **~jubiläum** *das* anniversary; **anlässlich seines 25-jährigen ~jubiläums** to mark his completion of 25 years' service; **~kleidung** *die* uniform; **~kleidung tragen** wear a uniform; **~leister** *der*; **~~s, ~~, ~leisterin** *die*; **~~, ~~nen** 1) (Firma, auch DV) service provider; 2) (Person) worker in the service sector; **~leistung** *die* (auch Wirtsch.) service

Dienstleistungs-: ~abend *der* late opening evening; **~bereich** *der* (Wirtsch.) ▸ **~sektor**; **~beruf** *der* (Wirtsch.) service[-sector] occupation; **~betrieb** *der* (Wirtsch.) business in the service sector; **~branche** *die* (Wirtsch.) 1) service industry; 2) ▸ **~sektor**; **~gesellschaft** *die* (Soziol.) service economy; **~gewerbe** *das* (Wirtsch.) service industries *pl.*; **~job** *der* (Wirtsch.) service[-sector] job; **~sektor** *der* (Wirtsch.) service sector **~unternehmen** *das* (Wirtsch.) service enterprise; service business; **~zentrum** *das* (Wirtsch.) service centre

dienstlich

A *Adj.* 1) business ‹call›; (im Staatsdienst) official ‹letter, call, etc.› 2) (offiziell) official; **~ werden** (ugs.) get businesslike and formal

B *adv.* on business; (im Staatsdienst) on official business

dienst-, Dienst-: ~mädchen *das* (veralt.) maid; **~magd** *die* (veralt.) maid; **~mann** *der*; *Pl.*: **~männer** *od.* **~leute** (veralt.) porter; **~marke** *die* [police] identification badge; ≈ warrant card (Brit.) *or* (Amer.) ID card; **~mütze** *die* regulation cap; **~nehmer** *der*; **~~s, ~~, ~nehmerin** *die*; **~~, ~~nen** (österr.) ▸ **Arbeitnehmer, Arbeitnehmerin**; **~ordnung** *die* official regulations *pl.*; **~personal** *das* servants *pl.*; (in einem Hotel) domestic staff; **~pflicht** *die* 1) compulsory service; 2) (bei Beamten) duty; **~pflichtig** *Adj.* liable for compulsory service *postpos.*; **~pistole** *die* service pistol; **~plan** *der* duty roster; **~rang** *der* (Milit.) rank; **~recht** *das* ≈ civil service law; **~rechtlich** A *Adj.* ≈ under civil service law *postpos.*; B *adv.* ≈ under civil service law; ≈ ‹regulated› by civil service law; **~reise** *die* business trip; **auf ~reise sein** be on a business trip *or* away on business; **~sache** *die* 1) official matter; 2) (Schreiben) official letter; 3) (Postw.) item of official mail; (Brief) official letter; **~schluss**, ***~schluß** *der* end of work; **um 17 Uhr ist ~schluss** work finishes at 5 o'clock; **nach ~schluss** after work; **~schluss haben** finish work/have finished work; **~schreiben** *das* official letter; **~stelle** *die* office; (Abteilung) department; **~stellen·leiter** *der*, **~stellen·leiterin** *die* office head; (einer Abteilung) department head; **~stempel** *der* official stamp; **~stunden** *Pl.* 1) working hours; **während der ~stunden** during working hours; 2) (Öffnungszeiten) **~stunden haben** be open; **~tauglich** *Adj.* (Milit.) fit for service *postpos.*; **~tuend** ▸ **Dienst 1**; **~tuende** *der/die*; *adj. Dekl.* ▸ **~habende**; **~unfähig** *Adj.* unfit for work *postpos.*; (Milit.) unfit for service *postpos.*; **~untauglich** *Adj.* (Milit.) unfit for service *postpos.*; **~vergehen** *das* offence against [official] regulations; **~verhältnis** *das*: *contractual relationship between employee and employer in the public service*; **ein ~verhältnis eingehen** become a public employee; **~verpflichten** *tr. V.* (*nur im Inf. u. 2. Part.*) conscript; **~vertrag** *der* contract of employment; **~vorschrift** *die* regulations *pl.*; (Milit.) service regulations; **~wagen** *der* official car; (Geschäftswagen) company car; **~weg** *der* proper *or* official channels *pl.*; **den ~weg gehen** *od.* **einhalten** go through the proper *or* official channels; **auf dem ~weg** through the proper *or* official channels; **~wohnung** *die* (von Firmen) company flat (esp. Brit.) *or* (esp. Amer.) apartment; (von staatlichen Stellen) government flat (esp. Brit.) *or* (esp. Amer.) apartment; (vom Militär) army/navy/air force flat (esp. Brit.) *or* (esp. Amer.) apartment; **~zeit** *die* 1) period of service; **eine ~zeit von 40 Jahren** 40 years' service; 2) (tägliche Arbeitszeit) working hours *pl.*; **außerhalb der ~zeit** outside working hours; **~zeugnis** *das* testimonial; **~zimmer** *das* office

dies /diːs/ ▸ **dieser**

dies·bezüglich

A *Adj.* relating to *or* regarding this *postpos., not pred.*

B *adv.* regarding this; on this matter

diese /ˈdiːzə/ ▸ **dieser**

Diesel /ˈdiːzl̩/ *der*; **~s, ~:** diesel

die·selbe ▸ **derselbe**

die·selbige ▸ **derselbige**

Diesel-: ~kraft·stoff *der* diesel fuel; **~lokomotive** *die* diesel locomotive; **~motor** *der* diesel engine; **~öl** *das* diesel oil

dieser /ˈdiːzɐ/, **diese, dieses, dies** *Demonstrativpron.* 1) *attr.* this; *Pl.* these; **dieses Buch/diese Bücher [da]** that book/those books [there]; **diesen Sommer/diese Weihnachten** this summer/this Christmas; **[zu] Anfang dieses Jahres/~ Woche** at the beginning of this year/this week; **in ~ Nacht wird es noch schneien/begann es zu schneien** it will snow tonight/it started to snow that night; **er hat ~ Tage Geburtstag** it's his birthday within the next few days; **ich habe ihn ~ Tage noch gesehen** I saw him the other day; **diese Inge ist doch ein Goldschatz/Idiot** that Inge is a treasure/an idiot, isn't she?; **wer ist denn diese Inge?** who is this Inge?; **diese Russen** these *or* those Russians 2) *selbstständig* **diese[r] [hier/da]** this one [here]/that one [there]; **diese** *Pl.* **[hier/da]** these [here]/those [there]; **dies alles** all this; **diese ..., jene ...** (geh.) the latter ..., the former ...; **dies und das,** (geh.) **dieses und jenes** this and that; **~ und jener** (geh.) (einige) some [people] *pl.*; (ein paar) a few [people] *pl.*; **~ oder jener** (geh.) (der eine oder andere) someone or other; (mancher) some people *pl.*

dieser·art (geh.)

A *indekl. Demonstrativpron.* of this/that kind *postpos.*

B *Adv.* in this/that way

dieses ▸ **dieser**

diesig *Adj.* hazy

dies-: ~jährig *Adj.* this year's; **unser ~jähriges Treffen** our meeting this year; **~mal** *Adv.* this time; **~seitig** *Adj.* 1) **das ~seitige Rheinufer** this side of the Rhine; **die ~seitigen Grenzdörfer** the villages on this side of the border; 2) (geh.) worldly; secular ‹world›; **~seits** A *Präp. mit Gen.* on this side of; B *Adv.* **~seits von** on this side of

Diesseits *das*; **~ im ~:** in this world; **das ~:** this world

Dietrich /ˈdiːtrɪç/ *der*; **~s, ~e** picklock; (Nachschlüssel) skeleton key

die·weil (veralt.)

A *Konj.* 1) (zeitl.) while 2) (kausal) because

B *adv.* in the meantime *or* the meanwhile

diffamatorisch /dɪfamaˈtoːrɪʃ/ *Adj.* (geh.) defamatory

diffamieren /dɪfaˈmiːrən/ *tr. V.* defame; **~de Äußerungen** defamatory utterances

Diffamierung *die;* ~, **~en** defamation; (Bemerkung) defamatory statement; **eine ~ des Gegners** defamation of one's opponent's character

Differential *usw.* ▸ **Differenzial** *usw.*

Differenz /dɪfəˈrɛnts/ *die;* ~, **~en** [1] (auch Math.) difference [2] (Meinungsverschiedenheit) difference [of opinion]

Differenz·betrag *der* difference

Differenzial /dɪfərɛnˈtsi̯aːl/ *das;* **~s, ~e** [1] (Math.) differential [2] (Technik) differential [gear]

Differenzial-: ~getriebe *das* (Technik) differential [gear]; **~gleichung** *die* (Math.) differential equation; **~rechnung** *die* (Math.) differential calculus

differenzier·bar *Adj.* [1] distinguishable [2] (Math.) differentiable

differenzieren
A *tr. V.* [1] be discriminating in ‹*judgement, opinion*›; (unterscheiden) differentiate [2] (Math.) differentiate [3] (DDR Landw.) grade
B *itr. V.* differentiate; make a distinction/distinctions (**zwischen** between); (bei einem Urteil, einer Behauptung) be discriminating; **genau ~:** make a precise distinction/precise distinctions
C *refl. V.* ‹*methods*› become more subtly differentiated; ‹*life, language*› become more complex; ‹*taste*› become more sophisticated

differenziert
A *Adj.* subtly differentiated ‹*methods, colours*›; complex ‹*life, language, person, emotional life*›; sophisticated ‹*taste*›; diverse ‹*range*›; **ein sehr ~er Bericht** a precise and subtle analysis
B *adv.* **~ urteilen** be discriminating in one's judgement; **etw. ~ darlegen** give a precise and subtle analysis of sth.

Differenziertheit *die;* ~ ▸ **differenziert** A: differentiation; complexity; sophistication; diversity

Differenzierung *die;* ~, **~en** (von Methoden) greater differentiation; (des Lebens, der Sprache) greater complexity; (des Geschmacks) greater sophistication

Differenz·menge *die* (Math.) **die ~ A\B** the complement of the set B relative to A

differieren /dɪfəˈriːrən/ *itr. V.* (geh.) differ (**um** by)

diffizil /dɪfiˈtsiːl/ *Adj.* (geh.) difficult; (kompliziert) complex; (peinlich genau) meticulous

diffus /dɪˈfuːs/
A *Adj.* [1] (Physik, Chemie) diffuse [2] (geh.) vague; vague and confused ‹*idea, statement, etc.*›
B *adv.* in a vague and confused way

Diffusion /dɪfuˈzi̯oːn/ *die;* ~, **~en** (Physik, Chemie) diffusion

Digestivum /digɛsˈtiːvʊm/ *das;* **~s, Digestiva** [1] digestive; digestant [2] (Chemie) digestive

digital /digiˈtaːl/ (DV)
A *Adj.* digital
B *adv.* digitally

Digital: ~anzeige *die* digital display; **~fernsehen** *das* digital television; **~foto** *das* digital photo

digitalisieren *tr. V.* (DV) digitalize

Digital-: ~kamera *die* digital camera; **~radio** *das* digital radio; **~rechner** *der* (DV) digital computer; (Taschenrechner) digital calculator; **~uhr** *die* digital clock; (Armbanduhr) digital watch

Dikta ▸ **Diktum**

Diktaphon /dɪktaˈfoːn/ *das;* **~s, ~e** Dictaphone ®

Diktat /dɪkˈtaːt/ *das;* **~[e]s, ~e** [1] dictation; **nach ~ schreiben** take dictation; **etw. nach ~ schreiben** write/type sth. from dictation [2] (das Diktierte) dictation; **ein ~ aufnehmen** take dictation [3] (Schulw.) dictation [4] (geh.: Befehl) dictate; (Politik) diktat; **das ~ der Mode** the dictates *pl.* of fashion

Diktator /dɪkˈtaːtɔr/ *der;* **~s, ~en** /-ˈtoːrən/, **Diktatorin** *die;* ~, **~nen** (auch fig.) dictator

diktatorisch
A *Adj.* (auch fig.) dictatorial
B *adv.* (auch fig.) dictatorially

Diktatur /dɪktaˈtuːɐ̯/ *die;* ~, **~en** (auch fig.) dictatorship

diktieren /dɪkˈtiːren/ *tr. V.* dictate

Diktier·gerät *das* dictating machine

Diktion /dɪkˈtsi̯oːn/ *die;* ~, **~en** (geh.) style and diction

Diktionär /dɪktsi̯oˈnɛːɐ̯/ *das od. der;* **~s, ~e** (veralt.) dictionary

Diktum /ˈdɪktʊm/ *das;* **~s, Dikta** (geh.) [1] dictum [2] (veralt.: Entscheid) dictum; pronouncement

dilatorisch /dilaˈtoːrɪʃ/ (geh.)
A *Adj.* dilatory
B *adv.* dilatorily; in a dilatory manner

Dildo /ˈdɪldo/ *der;* **~[s], ~s** dildo

Dilemma /diˈlɛma/ *das;* **~s, ~s** *od.* **Dilemmata** dilemma

Dilettant /dilɛˈtant/ *der;* **~en, ~en, Dilettantin** *die;* ~, **~nen** (auch abwertend) dilettante

dilettantisch (abwertend)
A *Adj.* dilettante; amateurish
B *adv.* amateurishly

Dilettantismus *der;* ~ (meist abwertend) dilettantism; amateurism

dilettieren /dilɛˈtiːrən/ *itr. V.* (geh.) dabble

Dill /dɪl/ *der;* **~[e]s, ~e,** *österr. auch:* **Dille** *die;* ~, **~n** (Gattung) Anethum; **Echter ~:** dill

Diluvium /diˈluːvi̯ʊm/ *das;* **~s** (Geol. veralt.) **das ~:** the Pleistocene

Dimension /dimɛnˈzi̯oːn/ *die;* ~, **~en** (Physik, fig.) dimension

-dimensional /dimɛnzi̯oˈnaːl/ *Adj.* -dimensional; **mehr~/drei~:** multi-/three-dimensional

dimensionieren *tr. V.* (Technik) dimension

Diminuendo /dimiˈnu̯ɛndo/ *das;* **~s, ~s** *od.* **Diminuendi** (Musik) diminuendo

diminutiv /diminuˈtiːf/ *Adj.* (Sprachw.) diminutive

Diminutiv *das;* **~s, ~e** (Sprachw.) diminutive

dimmen /ˈdɪmən/ *tr. V.* dim

Dimmer /ˈdɪmɐ/ *der;* **~s, ~** (Elektrot.) dimmer

DIN /diːn/ *Abk.* **= Deutsche Industrie-Norm[en]** *German Industrial Standard[s];* DIN; **= DIN-Format** DIN size; **DIN-A4-Format** A4

dinarisch /diˈnaːrɪʃ/ *Adj.* Dinaric

Diner /diˈneː/ *das;* **~s, ~s** [1] (geh.) [formal] dinner [2] (Abendessen) dinner

Ding[1] /dɪŋ/ *das;* **~[e]s, ~e** [1] (Gegenstand, Objekt) thing; **das ~ an sich** (Philos.) the thing-in-itself; **die Welt der ~e** (Philos.) the world of material objects; **jedes ~ hat zwei Seiten** there are two sides to everything; *s. auch* **Namen** [2] *Pl.* (Ereignisse) things; **nach Lage der ~e** the way things are; **wie die ~ stehen** as things stand; **über den ~en stehen** be above such things; *s. auch* **harren** [3] *Pl.* (Angelegenheiten) matters; **persönliche/private ~e** personal/private matters; **in ~en des Geschmacks** in matters of taste; **wie ich die ~e sehe** as I see things *or* matters; **reden wir von anderen ~en** let's talk about something else; **gut ~ will Weile haben** it takes time to do a thing well; **die letzten ~e** the last things; **ein ~ der Unmöglichkeit sein** be quite impossible; **das geht nicht mit rechten ~en zu** there's something funny about it; **vor allen ~en** above all [4] **guter ~e sein** (geh.) be in good spirits [5] (Hist.) ▸ **Thing**

Ding[2] *das;* **~[e]s, ~er** [1] (ugs.: Gegenstand, Sache) thing; **das ist ja ein ~!** that's really something; **ein ~ drehen** ‹*criminal*› pull a job (sl.); **jmdm. ein ~ verpassen** (salopp) clout sb. one (coll.); **mach keine ~er!** stop having me on (Brit. coll.); stop putting me on (Amer. coll.) [2] (ugs.: Mädchen) thing; creature [3] (salopp: Penis) thing (coll.); tool (sl.)

dingen *unr. tr. V.* [1] (geh.) hire; **ein gedungener Schreiberling** a mercenary hack; **ein gedungener Mörder** a hired killer [2] (veralt.: anstellen) hire; take on

ding·fest *in* **jmdn. ~ machen** arrest *or* apprehend sb.

Dinghi, Dingi /ˈdɪŋgi/ *das;* **~s, ~s** dinghy

dinglich *Adj.* [1] real; **die ~e Welt** the material world; the world of objects [2] (Rechtsspr.) real ‹*right, security, etc.*›

Dings[1] /dɪŋs/ *der/die;* ~ (ugs.: Mensch) thingamy (coll.); thingumajig (coll.); what's-his-name/-her-name

Dings[2] *das;* ~ (ugs.) [1] (Gegenstand) thingamy (coll.); thingumajig (coll.) what-d'you-call-it [2] (Ort) what's-its-name; what's-it-called

Dings·bums /-bʊms/ *der/die/das* ▸ **Dings**[1], **Dings**[2]

Ding·wort *das; Pl.* **Dingwörter** naming word

dinieren /diˈniːrən/ *itr. V.* (geh.) dine

Dinkel /ˈdɪŋkl̩/ *der;* **~s, ~** (Landw.) spelt

Dinner /ˈdɪnɐ/ *das;* **~s, ~[s]** dinner

Dino *der;* **~s, ~s** (ugs.) dinosaur

Dinosaurier /dinoˈzau̯ri̯ɐ/ *der;* **~s, ~** dinosaur

Diode /diˈoːdə/ *die;* ~, **~n** (Elektrot.) diode

Dioden·rücklicht *das* LED rear light

Diolen Ⓦⓩ /di̯oˈleːn/ *das;* **~s** (Textilind.) Terylene ®

dionysisch /di̯oˈnyːzɪʃ/
A *Adj.* Dionysiac; Dionysian
B *adv.* Dionysiacally

Diopter /diˈɔptɐ/ *das;* **~s, ~** (am Gewehr) [optical] sight; (an einer Kamera) [direct-vision] frame finder

Dioptrie /diɔpˈtriː/ *die;* ~, **~n** (Optik) dioptre

Dioskuren /di̯ɔsˈkuːrən/ *Pl.* (geh.) heavenly twins; inseparable friends

Dioxid /ˈdiː|ɔksiːt/ *das;* **~s, ~e, Dioxyd** /ˈdiː|ɔksyːt/ *das;* **~s, ~e** (Chemie) dioxide

Dioxin /ˈdiː|ɔksiːn/ *das;* **~s** (Chemie) dioxin

Diözesan *der;* **~en, ~en** member of the/a diocese

Diözese /di̯øˈtseːzə/ *die;* ~, **~n** diocese

Diphtherie /dɪfteˈriː/ *die;* ~, **~n** ▸ ❶ **S. 439** (Med.) diphtheria

diphtherisch *Adj.* (Med.) diphtherial

Diphthong /dɪfˈtɔŋ/ *der;* **~s, ~e** (Sprachw.) diphthong

diphthongieren /dɪftɔŋˈgiːrən/ *tr. V.* (Sprachw.) diphthongize

Diphthongierung *die;* ~, **~en** (Sprachw.) diphthongization

diphthongisch (Sprachw.)
A *Adj.* diphthongal
B *adv.* **etw. ~ aussprechen** pronounce sth. as a diphthong

Dipl.-Ing. *Abk.* **= Diplomingenieur** *academically qualified engineer*

Dipl.-Kfm. *Abk.* **= Diplomkaufmann** *holder of a diploma in commerce*

Dipl.-Landw. *Abk.* **= Diplomlandwirt** *holder of a diploma in agriculture*

diploid /diploˈiːt/ *Adj.* (Biol.) diploid

Diplom /diˈploːm/ *das;* **~s, ~e** [1] ≈ [first] degree (*in a scientific or technical subject*); (für einen Handwerksberuf) diploma; **sein ~ machen** do one's *or* a degree/diploma [2] (Urkunde) ≈ degree certificate (*in a scientific or technical subject*); (für einen Handwerksberuf) diploma

Diplom-: qualified

Diplom·arbeit *die* ≈ degree dissertation (*for a first degree in a scientific or technical subject*); (für einen Handwerksberuf) dissertation [submitted for a/the diploma]

Diplomat /diploˈmaːt/ *der;* **~en, ~en** ▸ ❶ **S. 113** (auch fig.) diplomat

Diplomaten-: ~gepäck *das* diplomatic bags *pl. or* baggage; **~koffer** *der* attaché case; executive case; **~pass, *~paß** *der* diplomatic passport; **~viertel** *das* embassy district

Diplomatie /diplomaˈtiː/ *die;* ~ [1] diplomacy [2] (die Diplomaten) diplomatic corps

Diplomatin *die;* ~, **~nen** ▸ ❶ **S. 113** (auch fig.) diplomat

diplomatisch (auch fig.)
A *Adj.* diplomatic
B *adv.* diplomatically

diplomieren *tr. V.* (Hochschulw.) **jmdn.** ~: award sb. a degree/diploma

diplomiert *Adj.* qualified

Diplom-: **~ingenieur** *der,* **~ingenieurin** *die* ▸ⓘ **S. 44,** ▸ⓘ **S. 113** *(academically)* qualified engineer; **~prüfung** *die* ≈ degree examination *(in a scientific or technical subject)*; (für einen Handwerksberuf) diploma examination

> **Diplomprüfung**
>
> Final (degree) examination at a university or equivalent higher education institution in a technical or scientific subject, especially in engineering, business administration, design, agriculture, and social work. On passing the exam, a degree or diploma is awarded.

Dipol /ˈdiːpoːl/ *der;* **~s, ~e** (Physik, Antenne) dipole

Dipol·antenne *die* dipole antenna

dippen /ˈdɪpn̩/ *tr. V.* (Seemannsspr.) dip ‹*flag*›

dir /diːɐ̯/
A *Dat. des Personalpron.* **du** to you; (nach Präpositionen) you; **ich gab es ~:** I gave it to you; **ich gab ~ das Buch** I gave you the book; **Freunde von ~:** friends of yours; **gehen wir zu ~:** let's go to your place; *s. auch* **mir A 1, 2**
B *Dat. des Reflexivpron. der 2. Pers. Sg.* yourself; **du willst ~ ein neues Kleid kaufen** you want to buy yourself a new dress; **nimm ~ noch von dem Braten** help yourself to some more roast; **hast du ~ seine Vorschläge genau überlegt?** have you given careful thought to his suggestions?; **hast du ~ gedacht, dass ...** did you think that ...

direkt /diˈrɛkt/
A *Adj.* direct
B *adv.* 1 (geradewegs) straight; directly 2 (sofort) directly; straight; **etw. ~ übertragen** broadcast sth. live 3 (nahe) directly; **~ am Marktplatz** right by the market square 4 (unmittelbar) direct; **sich ~ mit jmdm. verbinden lassen** get a direct line to sb. 5 (unverblümt) directly 6 (ugs.: geradezu) really; really, positively ‹*dangerous, witty*›

Direkt·bank *die;* **~, ~en** direct bank

direktemang /dirɛktəˈmaŋ/ *adv.* (landsch., bes. berlin.) straight; **~ neben** right next to

Direkt·flug *der* direct flight

Direktheit *die;* **~:** directness

Direktion /dirɛkˈtsi̯oːn/ *die;* **~, ~en** 1 management; (von gemeinnützigen, staatlichen Einrichtungen) administration 2 (die Geschäftsleiter) management 3 (Büroräume) managers' offices *pl.*

Direktions-: **~assistent** *der,* **~assistentin** *die* management trainee; **~sekretärin** *die* manager's secretary

Direktive /dirɛkˈtiːvə/ *die;* **~, ~n** (geh.) directive

Direkt·mandat *das* (Politik) **[über]** **~:** [by] direct mandate

Direktor /diˈrɛktɔr/ *der;* **~s, ~en** /...ˈtoːrən/ ▸ⓘ **S. 44,** ▸ⓘ **S. 113** 1 (einer Schule) headmaster; (eines Hochschulinstituts) director; (einer Fachschule o. dergl.) principal 2 (einer gemeinnützigen Einrichtung) director; (einer Strafanstalt) governor 3 (Wirtsch.) director; manager; (einer bestimmten Abteilung) manager

Direktorat /dirɛktoˈraːt/ *das;* **~[e]s, ~e** 1 (Amt, Amtszeit) (einer Schule) headship; (gemeinnütziger Einrichtungen) directorship 2 (Dienstzimmer) headmaster's/headmistress's office

Direktoren·sessel *der* (ugs.) directorship; managership

direktorial /dirɛktoˈri̯aːl/ *Adj.* directorial

Direktorin /dirɛkˈtoːrɪn/ *die;* **~, ~nen** ▸ⓘ **S. 44,** ▸ⓘ **S. 113** 1 (einer Schule) headmistress; (eines Hochschulinstituts) director; (einer Fachschule o. dergl.) principal 2 ▸**Direktor 2, 3;** *s. auch* **-in**

Direktorium /dirɛkˈtoːri̯ʊm/ *das;* **~s, Direktorien** board of directors

Direktrice /dirɛkˈtriːsə/ *die;* **~, ~n** head designer; (in einem Einzelhandelsgeschäft) manageress

Direkt-: **~saft** *der* juice direct from the fruit; **~sendung** *die* ▸**~übertragung; ~student** *der,* **~studentin** *die* (DDR) campus student; **~studium** *das* (DDR) campus course; **~übertragung** *die* live transmission *or* broadcast; **~verbindung** *die* 1 (Eisenb.) direct connection; through train; (Flugw.) direct flight; 2 (Fernspr.) direct [telephone] connection; **~versicherer** *der* direct insurer; **~versicherung** *die life insurance taken out by the employer on behalf of the employee;* **~wahl** *die* 1 direct election; **in** od. **durch ~wahl** by direct election; 2 (Fernspr.) direct dialling

Direx[1] /ˈdiːrɛks/ *der;* **~, ~e, Direx**[2] *die;* **~, ~en** (Schülerspr.) head

Dirigent /diriˈgɛnt/ *der;* **~en, ~en** ▸ⓘ **S. 113** conductor

Dirigenten-: **~pult** *das* conductor's rostrum; **~stab** *der,* **~stock** *der* [conductor's] baton

Dirigentin *die;* **~, ~nen** ▸ⓘ **S. 113** conductor

dirigieren /diriˈgiːrən/ *tr. V.* 1 *auch itr.* conduct 2 (führen) steer ‹*person*›; **jmdn. an einen Ort ~:** send sb. to a place 3 run ‹*business, company*› 4 (lenken) steer ‹*vehicle*›; (fahren) drive

Dirigismus /diriˈgɪsmʊs/ *der;* **~** (Wirtsch.) dirigisme

dirigistisch (Wirtsch.)
A *Adj.* dirigiste
B *adv.* in a dirigiste manner

Dirn /dɪrn/ *die;* **~, ~en** 1 (bayr., österr.) maid 2 (nordd.) girl; lass (esp. Scot.)

Dirndl /ˈdɪrndl̩/ *das;* **~s, ~:** dirndl

Dirndl·kleid *das* dirndl

Dirne /ˈdɪrnə/ *die;* **~, ~n** 1 prostitute 2 (veralt.: Mädchen) girl; lass (esp. Scot.)

Dirnen·viertel *das* red-light district

Dis /dɪs/ *das;* **~, ~** (Musik) D sharp

Disagio /dɪsˈ|aːdʒo/ *das;* **~s** (Finanzw.) disagio

Disc ▸**Disk**

Discjockey /ˈdɪskdʒɔke/ *der* ▸**Diskjockey**

Disco /ˈdɪskoː/ *die;* **~, ~s** disco

Discofox ▸**Diskofox**

Discount-: /dɪsˈkaʊnt/ discount; **~geschäft/~preis** discount shop/price

Discount·broker *der,* **Discount·brokerin** *die* ▸ⓘ **S. 113** discount broker

Dis-Dur *das* (Musik) D sharp major; *s. auch* **A-Dur**

Disengagement /dɪsɪnˈgeɪdʒmənt/ *das;* **~s** (Politik) disengagement

Disharmonie /*auch:* ˈ----/ *die* 1 (Musik) disharmony; discord; dissonance 2 (von Farben) clash 3 (geh.: Uneinigkeit) disagreement; disharmony *no indef. art.*; **solche ~n** such disharmony *sing. or* disagreements

disharmonieren *itr. V.* 1 (Musik) be discordant *or* dissonant 2 ‹*colours*› clash 3 (geh.: uneinig sein) disagree

disharmonisch *Adj.* 1 (Musik) disharmonious; discordant; dissonant 2 (nicht zusammenstimmend) clashing ‹*colours*› 3 (geh.: uneinig) disharmonious

Disjunktion /dɪsjʊŋkˈtsi̯oːn/ *die;* **~, ~en** (Logik) disjunction

disjunktiv /dɪsjʊŋkˈtiːf/ *Adj.* (Sprachw.) disjunctive

Disk /dɪsk/ *die;* **~, ~s** disc

Diskant /dɪsˈkant/ *der;* **~s, ~e** 1 **in einen schneidenden ~ umschlagen** ‹*voice*› become gratingly shrill 2 (einer Singstimme, beim Klavier) treble 3 (beim Cantus firmus) descant

Diskette /dɪsˈkɛtə/ *die;* **~, ~n** (DV) floppy disk

Disketten·lauf·werk *das* (DV) [floppy-]disk drive

Disk·jockey /ˈdɪskdʒɔke/ *der* disc jockey

Disko ▸**Disco**

Disko·fox, Disco·fox *der;* **~[es], ~e** disco fox

Diskont /dɪsˈkɔnt/ *der;* **~s, ~e** (Finanzw.) 1 discount 2 discount rate

Diskonten *Pl.* (Finanzw.) inland *or* domestic bills of exchange

Diskont·erhöhung *die* (Finanzw.) raising of the discount rate

diskontieren *tr. V.* (Finanzw.) discount

Diskontinuität *die;* **~, ~en** 1 discontinuity 2 (Politik) *principle that bills not passed before the end of a legislative period must be reintroduced in the next parliament*

Diskont·satz *der* (Finanzw.) discount rate

Diskothek /dɪskoˈteːk/ *die;* **~, ~en** 1 (Tanzlokal) discothèque 2 (Schallplatten) record collection 3 (Raum für Schallplatten) record library

diskreditieren /dɪskrediˈtiːrən/ *tr. V.* discredit

Diskrepanz /dɪskreˈpants/ *die;* **~, ~en** discrepancy (**zwischen** between)

diskret /dɪsˈkreːt/
A *Adj.* 1 (vertraulich) confidential ‹*discussion, report*›; (unauffällig) discreet ‹*action*› 2 (taktvoll) tactful ‹*behaviour, reserve*›; **sie ist sehr ~:** she is very discreet 3 (dezent) quiet ‹*colour, elegance*›; subtle ‹*perfume*› 4 (Technik, Physik, Math.) discrete
B *adv.* 1 (vertraulich) confidentially; **etw. ~ behandeln** treat sth. in confidence 2 (taktvoll) tactfully; **sich ~ zurückziehen** retire discreetly 3 (dezent) discreetly; **~ gemustert sein** have a subdued pattern

Diskretion /dɪskreˈtsi̯oːn/ *die;* **~** 1 (Verschwiegenheit, Takt) discretion; **in einer Angelegenheit äußerste/strengste ~ wahren** treat a matter in the strictest confidence; **~ [ist] Ehrensache** you can rely on my discretion 2 (Unaufdringlichkeit) discreetness

diskriminieren /dɪskrimiˈniːrən/ *tr. V.* 1 (herabwürdigen) disparage 2 (benachteiligen) discriminate against

Diskriminierung *die;* **~, ~en** 1 discrimination (**von** against) 2 (Handlung) act of discrimination; (Äußerung) discriminatory remark

Diskurs /dɪsˈkʊrs/ *der;* **~es, ~e** 1 (Abhandlung) discourse 2 (geh.: Unterhaltung) discourse *no indef. art.* (literary); conversation; **einen ~ [mit jmdm.] haben/führen** have *or* hold a conversation [with sb.] 3 (Wortwechsel) exchange [of words]; altercation 4 (Sprachw.) discourse

diskursiv /dɪskʊrˈziːf/ (Philos.)
A *Adj.* discursive
B *adv.* discursively

Diskus /ˈdɪskʊs/ *der;* **~** *od.* **~ses, Disken** *od.* **~se** (Leichtathletik) discus

Diskussion /dɪskʊˈsi̯oːn/ *die;* **~, ~en** discussion; (Gesprächsrunde, Tagesgespräch) discussion; debate; **etw. zur ~ stellen** put sth. up for discussion; **[nicht] zur ~ stehen** [not] be under discussion

Diskussions-: **~abend** *der* discussion [evening]; **~beitrag** *der* contribution to a/the discussion; **~grund·lage** *die* basis of a/the discussion; **als ~grundlage dienen** serve as a basis for [a/the] discussion; **~leiter** *der,* **~leiterin** *die* chair[man] [of the discussion]; **~teilnehmer** *der,* **~teilnehmerin** *die* participant [in a/the discussion]

Diskus-: **~werfen** *das;* **~~s** (Leichtathletik) [throwing the] discus; **das ~werfen ist ...** [throwing] the discus is ...; **die Meisterschaften im ~werfen** the discus championships; **~werfer** *der,* **~werferin** *die* discus-thrower; **~wurf** *der* (Leichtathletik) 1 (Disziplin) throwing the discus; **beim ~wurf** in the discus; 2 (einzelner Wurf) [discus] throw

diskutabel /dɪskuˈtaːbl̩/ *Adj.,* **diskutierbar** *Adj.* **[äußerst] ~:** [very well] worth considering *or* discussing *postpos.*

diskutieren /dɪskuˈtiːrən/
A *itr. V.* **über etw.** (*Akk.*) **~:** discuss sth.; **darüber wird viel zu viel diskutiert** there's much too much discussion about that; **darüber lässt**

sich ~: that's debatable; **wir haben stundenlang diskutiert** our discussion went on for hours
B *tr. V.* discuss
dis-Moll *das* (Musik) D sharp minor; *s. auch* **a-Moll**
disparat *Adj.* disparate
Dispatcher /dɪs'pɛtʃɐ/ *der;* **~s, ~. Dispatcherin** *die;* **~, ~nen** (DDR Technik) controller
Dispens /dɪs'pɛns/ *der;* **~es, ~e** (österr. u. kath. Kirche nur:) *die;* **~, ~en** (bes. kath. Kirche) dispensation (**von** from)
dispensieren *tr. V.* (auch fig.) dispense (form., Eccl.), excuse (**von** from)
Dispensierung *die;* **~, ~en** [1] (Befreiung) dispensation (form., Eccl.), exemption (**von** from) [2] (Pharm.) dispensing; **Wartezeit bei ~en** waiting period for dispensed *or* made-up prescriptions
Dispersion /dɪspɛr'zi̯o:n/ *die;* **~, ~en** (Physik, Chemie) dispersion
Dispersions·farbe *die* emulsion paint
Dispo /'dɪspo/ *der;* **~[s], ~s** (Jargon) overdraft facility
Disponent /dɪspo'nɛnt/ *der;* **~en, ~en** [1] (Wirtsch.) junior departmental manager [2] (am Theater) manager
Disponentin *die;* **~, ~nen** [1] (Wirtsch.) junior departmental manager [2] (am Theater) manageress
disponibel /dɪspo'ni:bl/ *Adj.* (verfügbar) available; (vielseitig einsetzbar) versatile
disponieren *itr. V.* [1] (verfügen) **über jmdn./etw. ~** (zur Verfügung haben) have sb./sth. at one's disposal; **nach Belieben über jmdn./etw. ~:** do just as one wishes *or* likes with sb./sth. [2] (vorausplanen) plan ahead
disponiert *Adj.* [1] **gut/schlecht ~ sein** be in good form *or* on form/be in bad form *or* off form [2] (Med.) **für** *od.* **zu etw. ~ sein** be disposed to sth.
Disposition /dɪspozi'tsi̯o:n/ *die;* **~, ~en** [1] (Verfügungsgewalt) right of disposal; **jmdm. zur** *od.* **zu jmds. ~ stehen** be at sb.'s disposal; **jmdm. etw. zur ~ stellen** place sth. at sb.'s disposal; **jmdn. zur ~ stellen** (Amtsspr.) suspend sb. [2] (Planung) arrangement; **~en treffen** make arrangements [3] (Gliederung) plan [4] (Med.: Anlage) disposition (**zu, für** to)
Dispositions·kredit *der* (Finanzw.) overdraft facility
Disput /dɪs'pu:t/ *der;* **~[e]s, ~e** (geh.) dispute, argument (**über** + *Akk.* about)
disputabel /dɪspu'ta:bl/ *Adj.* (geh.) disputable
Disputation /dɪsputa'tsi̯o:n/ *die;* **~, ~en** (Hochschulw., geh.: Streit) disputation
disputieren *itr. V.* (geh.) discuss; (streiten) dispute; **über etw.** (*Akk.*) **~:** discuss/dispute sth.
Disqualifikation *die* (auch Sport) disqualification
disqualifizieren *tr. V.* (auch Sport) disqualify
Disqualifizierung *die;* **~, ~en** (auch Sport) disqualification
Diss. *Abk.* **= Dissertation** diss.
Disse /'dɪsə/ *die;* **~, ~n** (ugs.) disco
Dissens /dɪ'sɛns/ *der;* **~es, ~e** (geh.) dissent *no indef. art.*; disagreement (**über** + *Akk.* over)
Dissertation /dɪsɛrta'tsi̯o:n/ *die;* **~, ~en** [doctoral] dissertation *or* thesis
Dissident /dɪsi'dɛnt/ *der;* **~en, ~en, Dissidentin,** *die;* **~, ~nen** dissident; (Rel.) nonbeliever
Dissimilation /dɪsimila'tsi̯o:n/ *die;* **~, ~en** (Sprachw., Biol.) dissimilation
dissimilieren *tr. V.* (Sprachw., Biol.) dissimilate
dissonant /dɪso'nant/ *Adj.* (Musik) dissonant
Dissonanz /dɪso'nants/ *die;* **~, ~en** (Musik) dissonance
Distanz /dɪs'tants/ *die;* **~, ~en** [1] (Abstand) distance; **in einiger ~:** some distance away; **~ zu etw. gewinnen** (fig.) distance oneself from sth. [2] (Rangunterschied, Zurückhaltung) **~ wahren** *od.* **halten** keep one's distance; **die soziale ~:** the social gap; **auf ~ bleiben** *od.* **gehen** keep one's distance [3] (Leichtathletik, Rennsport) distance; **gegen Ende der ~:** towards the end of the race [4] (Boxen: Abstand, Rundenzahl) distance; **jmdn. auf ~ halten** keep sb. at long range
distanzieren
A *refl. V.* **sich von jmdm./etw. ~:** dissociate oneself from sb./sth.
B *tr. V.* (Sport: überrunden) outdistance, outpace (**um** by); (schlagen) beat (**um** by)
distanziert
A *Adj.* distant; reserved; reserved ‹*politeness*›
B *adv.* in a distant *or* reserved manner; with reserve
Distel /'dɪstl/ *die;* **~, ~n** thistle
Distel·fink *der* goldfinch
Distichon /'dɪstɪçɔn/ *das;* **~s, Distichen** (Verslehre) distich
distinguiert /dɪstɪŋ'gi:ɐt/ (geh.)
A *Adj.* distinguished
B *adv.* in a distinguished manner
Distribution /dɪstribu'tsi̯o:n/ *die;* **~, ~en** (auch Wirtsch., Math., Sprachw.) distribution
distributiv /dɪstribu'ti:f/ *Adj.* (Sprachw., Math.) distributive
Distrikt /dɪs'trɪkt/ *der;* **~[e]s, ~e** district; area; (Bezirk) district
Disziplin /dɪstsi'pli:n/ *die;* **~, ~en** [1] (Ordnung) discipline; **~ halten** keep discipline; (sich diszipliniert verhalten) behave in a disciplined way [2] (Selbstbeherrschung) [self-]discipline [3] (Wissenschaftszweig, Sport) discipline
disziplinär /dɪstsipli'nɛ:ɐ/ (bes. österr.)
A *Adj.* disciplinary
B *adv.* **gegen jmdn. ~ vorgehen** take disciplinary action against sb.
disziplinarisch
A *Adj.* [1] disciplinary [2] (streng) severe
B *adv.* [1] **gegen jmdn. ~ vorgehen** take disciplinary action against sb.; **jmdm. ~ unterstellt sein** be answerable to sb. in matters of discipline [2] (streng) **jmdn. ~ bestrafen** punish sb. severely
Disziplinar-: ~maßnahme *die* disciplinary measure; **~strafe** *die* [1] (Sport) disciplinary penalty; **mit einer ~strafe rechnen müssen** have to expect disciplinary action; **eine hohe ~strafe** a heavy fine; **er erhielt eine ~strafe von 100 Euro** he was fined 100 euros; [2] (Eishockey) misconduct penalty; [3] (veralt.) disciplinary measure; **~verfahren** *das* disciplinary proceedings *pl.*
disziplinieren
A *tr. V.* discipline
B *refl. V.* discipline oneself
diszipliniert
A *Adj.* [1] (geordnet) well-disciplined [2] (beherrscht) disciplined
B *adv.* [1] (geordnet) in a well-disciplined way [2] (beherrscht) in a disciplined way
Disziplinierung *die;* **~, ~en** disciplining *no indef. art.*
disziplin-, Disziplin-: ~los A *Adj.* undisciplined; **B** *adv.* in an undisciplined way; **~losigkeit** *die;* **~:** lack of discipline; **~schwierigkeiten** *Pl.* discipline problems; problems in maintaining discipline
dithyrambisch *Adj.* (Literaturw.) dithyrambic
Dithyrambus /dity'rambʊs/ *der;* **~, Dithyramben** [1] (Literaturw.) dithyramb
dito /'di:to/ *Adv.* (Kaufmannsspr., auch ugs.) ditto
Diuretikum /diu're:tikʊm/ *das;* **~s, Diuretika** (Med.) diuretic
diuretisch *Adj.* (Med.) diuretic
Diva /'di:va/ *die;* **~, ~s** *u.* **Diven** [1] (Künstlerin) prima donna; diva; (Film~) great [film] star [2] (eingebildeter Mensch) prima donna
divenhaft
A *Adj.* diva-like
B *adv.* like a diva
divergent /divɛr'gɛnt/
A *Adj.* (auch fig., Math.) divergent
B *adv.* (auch fig., Math.) divergently; **~ verlaufen** diverge
Divergenz /divɛr'gɛnts/ *die;* **~, ~en** (auch Math.) divergence; (Meinungsverschiedenheit) divergence of opinion
divergieren *itr. V.* (auch Math.) diverge
divers... /di'vɛrs.../ *Adj.* various; (von derselben Sorte) several; **die ~esten ...** the most diverse ...
Diversifikation /divɛrzifika'tsi̯o:n/ *die;* **~, ~en** (Wirtsch.) diversification
diversifizieren /divɛrzifi'tsi:rən/ *tr., itr. V.* (Wirtsch.) diversify
Diversion /divɛr'zi̯o:n/ *die;* **~, ~en** (bes. DDR) subversion
Divertimento /divɛrti'mɛnto/ *das;* **~s, ~s** *u.* **Divertimenti** (Musik) divertimento
Divertissement /divɛrtɪsə'mã:/ *das;* **~s, ~s** (Musik) divertissement
Dividend /divi'dɛnt/ *der;* **~en, ~en** (Math.) dividend
Dividende /divi'dɛndə/ *die;* **~, ~n** (Börsenw., Wirtsch.) dividend
Dividenden·ausschüttung *die* (Börsenw., Wirtsch.) payment of the dividend/of dividends
dividieren /divi'di:rən/ *tr. V.* (Math.) divide
Divis /di'vi:s/ *das;* **~es, ~e** (Druckw.) hyphen
Division /divi'zi̯o:n/ *die;* **~, ~en** (Math., Milit.) division
Divisions·kommandeur *der* (Milit.) divisional commander
Divisor /di'vi:zɔr/ *der;* **~s, ~en** /-vi'zo:rən/ (Math.) divisor
Diwan /'di:va:n/ *der;* **~s, ~e** (veralt.: Sofa, Literaturw.: Gedichte) divan
Dixieland /'dɪksɪlɛnd/ *der;* **~[s]** Dixieland
d. J. *Abk.* [1] **= dieses Jahres** [2] **= der/die Jüngere**
DJH *Abk.* **= Deutscher Jugendherbergsverband** German Youth Hostel Association
DKP *Abk.* **= Deutsche Kommunistische Partei** Communist Party of Germany
DLF *Abk.* **= Deutschlandfunk**
DLRG *Abk.* **= Deutsche Lebens-Rettungs-Gesellschaft** German Life Saving Society
dm *Abk.* **= Dezimeter** dm
d. M. *Abk.* **= dieses Monats** inst.; **am 13. ~:** on the thirteenth inst.
DM *Abk.* **= D-Mark. = Deutsche Mark** DM
D-Mark /'de:-/ *die* Deutschmark
d-Moll /'de:-/ *das;* **~** (Musik) D minor; *s. auch* **a-Moll**
DNA *die;* **~, ~[s]** DNA
DNA: ~-Analyse *die* DNA analysis; **~-Probe** *die* DNA specimen
DNS *Abk.* (Chemie) **= Desoxyribonukleinsäure** DNA
do. *Abk.* **= dito** do.
Do. *Abk.* **= Donnerstag** Thur[s].
Dobermann /'do:bɐman/ *der;* **~s, Dobermänner** Dobermann [pinscher]
doch /dɔx/
A *Konj.* but
B *Adv.* [1] (je~) but [2] (dennoch) all the same; still; (trotzdem) nevertheless; all the same; (wider Erwarten) after all; **aber ich habe ihn ~ erkannt** but I recognized him all the same; but I still recognized him; **und ~:** and yet; **aber die Ausstellung war ~ ganz interessant** but the exhibition was actually quite interesting [3] (geh.: weil) **wusste er ~, dass ...** because he knew that ... [4] (als Antwort) **Das kannst du nicht! — Doch!** You can't do that! — [Oh] yes I can!; **Das stimmt nicht! — Doch!** That's not right! — [Oh] yes it is!; **Hast du keinen Hunger? — Doch!** Aren't you hungry? — Yes [I am]!; **~ schon, aber ...** yes, I do/he does *etc.*, but ... [5] (Angezweifeltes richtig stellend: tatsächlich) **er war also ~ der Mörder!** so he 'was the murderer!; **sie hat es also ~ gesagt** so she 'did say it [6] (etw. für unnütz erklärend) in any case; **du kannst mir ~ nicht helfen** there's nothing you can do to help me
C *Partikel* [1] (auffordernd, Ungeduld, Empörung ausdrückend) *oft nicht übersetzt* **das hättest du ~ wissen müssen** you [really] should have known that; **du hast ~ selbst gesagt, dass ...** (rechtfertigend) you did say yourself that ...; **gib mir ~ bitte mal die Zeitung** pass me the paper, please; **Kinder, seid ~ nicht so laut!**

don't make so much noise, children!; **reg dich ~ nicht so auf!** don't get so worked up!; **pass ~ auf!** [oh,] do be careful!; **das ist ~ nicht zu glauben** that's just incredible **2** (Zweifel ausdrückend) **du hast ~ meinen Brief erhalten?** you did get my letter, didn't you?; **es wird ihm ~ nichts passiert sein?** you don't think something has happened to him[, do you]? **3** (Bestätigung erwartend) **Sie kommen ~ morgen?** you will be coming tomorrow, won't you? **4** (Überraschung ausdrückend) *nicht übersetzt;* **das ist ~ Karl!** there's Karl! **5** (an Bekanntes erinnernd) **er ist ~ nicht mehr der Jüngste** he's not as young as he used to be[, you know]; **ich bin ~ deine Schwester** I 'am your sister[, you know] **6** (nach Vergessenem fragend) **wie war ~ sein Name?** now what was his name? **7** (verstärkt Bejahung/Verneinung ausdrückend) **gewiss/sicher ~:** [why] certainly; of course; **ja ~:** [yes,] all right *or* (coll.) OK; **nein ~:** [no,] of course not; **nicht ~!** (abwehrend) [no,] don't!; **sollen sie ~!** let them, then!; well, let them! **8** (Wunsch verstärkend) **wäre es ~ ...** if only it were ...

Docht /dɔxt/ *der;* **~[e]s, ~:** wick

Docht·schere *die* snuffers *pl.*

Dock /dɔk/ *das;* **~s, ~s** dock

Dock·arbeiter *der* dock worker; docker

Docke *die;* **~, ~n** **1** (Garnbündel) skein **2** (Getreidebündel) shock; stook **3** (südd.: Puppe) doll

docken¹ *tr. V.* shock, stook ‹*corn*›; wind ‹*thread*› into a skein/skeins

docken²

A *itr. V.* (Seew., Raumf.) dock

B *tr. V.* (Seew.) dock ‹*ship*›; put ‹*ship*› in dock

Docker *der;* **~s, ~:** docker

Dock·hafen *der* dock

> **documenta**
>
> This international contemporary art exhibition takes place in Kassel every four to five years. In 2002, *documenta* 11 showed works by 116 artists and artists' groups, and included drama, music, and film events. *documenta* 12 will take place in 2007. The events are heavily subsidized by the taxpayer and private sponsors.

Dodekaeder /dodeka'|eːdɐ/ *das;* **~s, ~** (Geom.) dodecahedron

Dodekaphonie /dodekafo'niː/ *die;* **~** (Musik) twelve-tone technique

Ködel /'døːdl̩/ *der;* **~s, ~** **1** (ugs.: Trottel) moron (coll.); thicko (coll.); **2** (ugs. nordd.: Penis) willy (coll.)

Doge /'doːʒə/ *der;* **~n, ~n** doge

Dogge /'dɔgə/ *die;* **~, ~n** **1** **Deutsche ~:** Great Dane **2** **Englische ~:** mastiff

Dogma /'dɔgma/ *das;* **~s, Dogmen** (bes. kath. Kirche, auch fig.) dogma

Dogmatik /dɔ'gmaːtik/ *die;* **~, ~en** **1** (Theol.) dogmatics *sing., no art.* **2** (fig. abwertend) dogmatism

Dogmatiker *der;* **~s, ~, Dogmatikerin** *die;* **~, ~nen** (Theol., auch fig.) dogmatist

dogmatisch (Theol., auch fig.)

A *Adj.* dogmatic

B *adv.* dogmatically

dogmatisieren *tr. V.* (Theol., auch fig.) dogmatize

Dogmatismus *der;* **~** (oft abwertend) dogmatism

Dogmen·geschichte *die* (Theol.) history of dogma

Dohle /'doːlə/ *die;* **~, ~n** jackdaw

Dohne /'doːnə/ *die;* **~, ~n** springe

Döhnkes /'døːnkəs/ *Pl.* (nordd.) stories; yarns

Doktor /'dɔktɔr/ *der;* **~s, ~en** /-'toːrən/ **1** (Titel) doctorate; doctor's degree; **den/seinen ~ machen** do a/one's doctorate; **den ~ haben** have a doctorate *or* doctor's degree; **zum ~ promoviert werden** be awarded one's doctorate *or* doctor's degree **2** ▸**i** **S. 44** (Träger) doctor; **er ist ~ der Philosophie** he is a Doctor of Philosophy; **guten Tag, Frau ~!** hello, Doctor; (Frau eines ~s) hello, Mrs X; **Herr ~ Krause** Doctor Krause **3** (ugs.: Arzt) doctor; **der Onkel ~** (Kinderspr.) the nice doctor; **~ spielen** play doctors and nurses

Doktorand /dɔkto'rant/ *der;* **~en, ~en** student taking his/her doctorate; **er ist ~ bei Professor Meier** he is studying for his doctorate under Professor Meier

Doktoranden·kolloquium *das* research students' colloquium

Doktorandin *die;* **~, ~nen** ▸**Doktorand**

Doktor·arbeit *die* doctoral thesis *or* dissertation (**über** + *Akk.* on)

Doktorat /dɔkto'raːt/ *das;* **~[e]s, ~e** **1** (veralt.: Doktorwürde) doctorate **2** (österr.) ▸**Doktorprüfung**

Doktor-: ~diplom *das* Ph. D. certificate; doctoral diploma (Amer.); **~examen** *das* ▸**~prüfung**; **~grad** *der* doctorate; doctor's degree; **den ~grad erwerben** gain *or* get one's doctorate *or* doctor's degree; **~hut** *der* **1** (Hut) doctor's cap; **2** (ugs.) ▸**~grad**

Doktorin *die;* **~, ~nen** doctor; *s. auch* **-in**

Doktor-: ~ingenieur *der* doctor of engineering science; **~mutter** *die* (ugs.) [thesis] supervisor; **~prüfung** *die* examination for a/one's doctorate; **~spiel** *das* game of doctors and nurses; **~spiele** *Pl.* playing at doctors and nurses; **~titel** *der* title of doctor; **den ~titel führen** (sich ~ nennen) call oneself doctor; (den ~grad haben) have a doctorate *or* doctor's degree; **~vater** *der* (ugs.) [thesis] supervisor; **~würde** *die* doctorate; doctor's degree

Doktrin /dɔk'triːn/ *die;* **~, ~en** doctrine

doktrinär /dɔktri'nɛːɐ̯/

A *Adj.* doctrinal; (abwertend: starr, einseitig) doctrinaire

B *adv.* doctrinally; (abwertend: starr, einseitig) in a doctrinaire way

Doktrinär *der;* **~s, ~e** **1** (Verfechter einer Doktrin) advocate of a/the doctrine **2** (abwertend) doctrinaire

Doku /'dɔku/ *die;* **~, ~s** (ugs.) **1** (Dokumentation) paperwork; bumf (coll.) **2** (Film, Bericht) documentary

Dokument /doku'mɛnt/ *das;* **~[e]s, ~e** **1** (Urkunde) document **2** (Zeugnis) document; record **3** (DDR: Parteibuch) party membership book

Dokumentalist /dɔkumɛnta'lɪst/ *der;* **~en, ~en, Dokumentalistin** *die;* **~, ~nen** (DDR), **Dokumentar** /dɔkumɛn'taːr/ *der;* **~s, ~e, Dokumentarin** *die;* **~, ~nen** documentalist

Dokumentar-: ~bericht *der* documentary report; **~film** *der* documentary [film]

dokumentarisch

A *Adj.* documentary

B *adv.* **etw. ~ belegen** provide documentary evidence of *or* for sth.; **etw. ~ festhalten** make a documentary record of sth.

Dokumentar-: ~literatur *die* documentary literature; **~theater** *das* documentary drama

Dokumentation /dɔkumɛnta'tsi̯oːn/ *die;* **~, ~en** **1** (das Dokumentieren) documentation **2** (Material) documentary account; (Bericht) documentary report **3** (das Beweisen) demonstration **4** (Beweis, Ausdruck) evidence

Dokumentations·zentrum *das* centre for documentation

dokumentieren

A *tr. V.* **1** (bekunden) demonstrate ‹*readiness, cast of mind, sympathy, interest*›; express, register ‹*protest*› **2** (belegen) document **3** (darstellen) record ‹*behaviour, event*›

B *refl. V.* (offenbar werden) **sich in** *od.* **an etw.** (*Dat.*) **~:** be demonstrated by sth.

Dolby Ⓦⓩ /'dɔlbi/ *das;* **~s** Dolby system ®

Dolce Vita /'dɔltʃə 'viːta/ *das od. die;* **~:** dolce vita; **~ machen** (ugs.) live a life of luxury and pleasure

Dolch /dɔlç/ *der;* **~[e]s, ~e** dagger

Dolch-: ~stich *der* stab [with a dagger]; **~stoß** *der* **1** (Stoß) dagger thrust; **2** (fig.: Hinterhalt) stab in the back; **~stoß·legende** *die* myth of the stab in the back

Dolde /'dɔldə/ *die;* **~, ~n** (Bot.) umbel

Dolden-: ~blütler *der* (Bot.) **1** (*aus der Ordnung ~blütler*) *plant of the order Umbelliflorae;* **2** ▸**~gewächs**; **~gewächs** *das* (Bot.) umbellifer

Dole /'doːlə/ *die;* **~, ~n** (südd.) drain

doll /dɔl/ (bes. nordd., salopp)

A *Adj.* **1** (ungewöhnlich) incredible; amazing **2** (verrückt) batty (coll.); *s. auch* **oll** **3** (großartig) fantastic (coll.); great (coll.); (iron.) great (coll.) **4** (schlimm) dreadful (coll.)

B *adv.* **1** (verrückt) like a madman **2** (großartig) fantastically [well] (coll.) **3** (sehr) ‹*hurt*› dreadfully (coll.), like mad; ‹*shake, rain*› good and hard (coll.); **es regnet immer ~er** it's chucking it down harder than ever (coll.); **sich ~ freuen** be terribly pleased (coll.)

Dollar /'dɔlaːɐ̯/ *der;* **~s, ~s** ▸**i** **S. 299** dollar; **zwei ~:** two dollars

Dollar-: ~kurs *der* dollar rate; **~zeichen** *das* dollar sign

Dolle *die;* **~, ~n** rowlock

Doll·punkt *der* (ugs.) bone of contention

Dolly /'dɔli/ *der;* **~s, ~s** (Film) dolly

Dolmetsch /'dɔlmɛtʃ/ *der;* **~[e]s, ~e** **1** (bes. österr.: ~er) interpreter **2** (geh.: Fürsprecher, Verkünder) spokesman (*Gen.* for)

dolmetschen

A *itr. V.* (übersetzen) act as interpreter (**bei** at); (als Dolmetscher arbeiten) work as *or* be an interpreter

B *tr. V.* act as interpreter at ‹*discussion etc.*›

Dolmetscher *der;* **~s, ~** ▸**i** **S. 113** interpreter; **sich über einen** *od.* **mithilfe eines ~ unterhalten** talk through an interpreter

Dolmetscherin *die;* **~, ~nen** ▸**i** **S. 113** ▸**Dolmetscher**; *s. auch* **-in**

Dolmetscher-: ~institut *das*, **~schule** *die* institute *or* school of interpreting

Dolomit /dolo'miːt/ *der;* **~s, ~e** (Geol.) dolomite

Dolomiten *Pl.* **die ~:** the Dolomites

Dom /doːm/ *der;* **~[e]s, ~e** **1** cathedral; (fig.) dome; **der Kölner ~, der ~ zu Köln** Cologne Cathedral **2** (Geol.) dome

Domäne /do'mɛːnə/ *die;* **~, ~n** **1** (Spezialgebiet) domain **2** (Staatsgut) demesne

Domestik /domɛs'tiːk/ *der;* **~en, ~en** (veralt. abwertend) domestic

Domestikation /domɛstika'tsi̯oːn/ *die;* **~, ~en** domestication

Domestike *der;* **~n, ~n** ▸**Domestik**

Domestikin *die;* **~, ~nen** (verhüll.) sub girl (coll.)

domestizieren /domɛsti'tsiːrən/ *tr. V.* domesticate; (fig.) tame; subdue

Dom-: ~freiheit *die* (hist.): *area of a city, usually around the cathedral, under the jurisdiction of the Church;* **~herr** *der* (kath. Rel.) canon

Domina¹ /'doːmina/ *die;* **~, Dominä** abbess; Mother Superior

Domina² *die;* **~, ~s** (verhüll.) mistress; dominatrix

dominant /domi'nant/

A *Adj.* (auch Biol.) dominant

B *adv.* dominantly

Dominant·akkord *der* (Musik) dominant chord

Dominante *die;* **~, ~n** **1** (Hauptmerkmal) dominant feature **2** (Musik) (Quint) dominant; (Dreiklang) ▸**Dominantakkord**

Dominant·sept·akkord *der* (Musik) dominant seventh chord

Dominanz /domi'nants/ *die;* **~, ~en** (auch Biol.) dominance

Dominanz·verhalten *das* dominance behaviour

dominieren /domi'niːrən/

A *itr. V.* dominate; ‹*aspect*› predominate, dominate; **~d** dominant

B *tr. V.* dominate

Dominikaner /domini'kaːnɐ/ *der;* **~s, ~, Dominikanerin** *die;* **~, ~nen** **1** (Mönch/Nonne) Dominican **2** (Einwohner/Einwohnerin der Dominikanischen Republik) Dominican

Dominikaner·orden *der* Dominican order

dominikanisch *Adj.* Dominican; **die Dominikanische Republik** the Dominican Republic

Domino[1] /'do:mino/ *der;* **~s, ~s** (Mantel, Person) domino

Domino[2] *das;* **~s, ~s** (Spiel) dominoes *sing.*

Domino[3] *der;* **~s, ~s** (österr.: ~stein) domino

Domino-: ~effekt *der* domino effect; **einen ~effekt auslösen** have *or* start a domino effect; **~spiel** *das* [1] dominoes *sing.;* [2] (~steine) [set *sing.* of] dominoes *pl.;* [3] (~partie) game of dominoes; **~stein** *der* [1] (Spielstein) domino; [2] (Gebäck) *small chocolate-covered cake with layers of marzipan, jam, and gingerbread*

Domizil /domi'tsi:l/ *das;* **~s, ~e** [1] (geh.) domicile; residence; **bei jmdm./in einer Stadt** *usw.* **~ nehmen** take up residence with sb./in a town *etc.* [2] (Finanzw.) place of payment

domizilieren *tr. V.* (Finanzw.) domicile

Dom-: ~kapitel *das* (kath. Kirche) cathedral chapter; **~kapitular** *der* (kath. Kirche) canon; **~pfaff** *der;* **~~en** *od.* **~~s, ~~e[n]** (Zool.) bullfinch; **~prediger** *der* (ev. Kirche) cathedral preacher; **~propst** *der* (kath. Kirche) dean; provost

Dompteur /dɔmp'tø:ɐ/ *der;* **~s, ~e, Dompteurin** *die;* **~, ~nen, Dompteuse** /dɔmp'tø:zə/ *die;* **~, ~n** tamer

Donau /'do:nau/ *die;* **~** ▸❶ **S. 267** Danube

Donau-: ~monarchie *die;* **~** (hist.) Austro-Hungarian Empire; **~schwaben** *Pl.: German settlers on the middle Danube*

Dönkes /'dœnkəs/ *Pl.* (nordd.) ▸**Döhnkes**

Donner /'dɔnɐ/ *der;* **~s, ~** (auch fig.) thunder; **der erste ~:** the first clap *or* peal of thunder; **wie vom ~ gerührt dastehen** *od.* **sein** be thunderstruck; **~ und Blitz** *od.* **Doria!** (veralt.) by Jove! (dated coll.)

Donner-: ~balken *der* (salopp) bog (Brit. sl.); latrine; (Sitzstange) latrine seat; **~getöse** *das* thunderous din; **~gott** *der* god of thunder; **~grollen** *das;* **~~s** rumbles of thunder; (fig.) rumbles of discontent; **~keil** *der* [1] (ugs.: Ausruf des Erstaunens) my word; [2] (Werkzeug, Belemnit) thunderstone; **~littchen** /-'lɪtçən/, **~lüttchen** /-'lʏtçən/ (nordd.: Ausruf des Erstaunens) my word; wow

donnern

[A] *itr. V.* [1] (unpers.) thunder; **es hat gedonnert und geblitzt** there was thunder and lightning [2] (fig.) ‹*gun*› thunder, boom [out]; ‹*engine*› roar; ‹*hooves*› thunder; **~der Applaus** thunderous applause [3] *mit sein* (sich laut fortbewegen) ‹*train, avalanche, etc.*› thunder [4] (ugs.: schlagen) thump, hammer (**an** + *Akk.,* **gegen** on) [5] *mit sein* (ugs.: prallen) **gegen etw. ~:** smash into sth.; **der Ball donnerte an die Latte** the ball slammed against the bar [6] (ugs.: schimpfen) **gegen etw. ~:** rage against sth.

[B] *tr. V.* [1] (ugs.: schleudern) sling (coll.); hurl [2] (ugs.: schlagen) slam; **jmdm. eine** *od.* **ein paar ~:** thump sb.; give sb. a good thumping [3] (ugs.: schimpfen) thunder

Donner·schlag *der* clap *or* peal of thunder; **die Nachricht traf uns wie ein ~:** the news completely stunned us

Donners·tag *der* ▸❶ **S. 165,** ▸❶ **S. 816** Thursday; *s. auch* **Dienstag**

donnerstags *Adv.* ▸❶ **S. 816** on Thursday[s]; *s. auch* **dienstags**

Donner-: ~stimme *die* thundering voice; **~wetter** *das* [1] (ugs.: Krach) row; **das wird ein [schönes] ~wetter geben** *od.* **setzen** that will cause a hell of a row (coll.); **ein ~wetter über sich ergehen lassen müssen** be given what for (coll.); [2] /'--'--/ (ugs.: Ausruf der Verärgerung) **zum ~wetter [noch einmal]!** damn it!; **warum, zum ~wetter, ...?** why, for Heaven's sake, ...?; [3] /'--'--/ (ugs.: Ausruf der Bewunderung) my word; wow

Don Quichotte /dɔnki'ʃɔt/ *(der)* Don Quixote

Donquichotterie /dɔnkiʃɔtə'ri:/ *die;* **~, ~n** quixotism; quixotry

Döntje/'dø:ntjə/ *der u. das;* **~s, ~s** (nordd.) [humorous] anecdote; funny story

doof /do:f/ (ugs. abwertend)

[A] *Adj.* [1] (einfältig) stupid; dumb (coll.); dopey (coll.); **~ bleibt ~[, da helfen keine Pillen]** once a fool, always a fool [2] (langweilig) boring [3] (ärgerlich) stupid

[B] *adv.* (beschränkt) stupidly; **da hat er vielleicht ~ geguckt** he didn't half make (Brit.) *or* really made a stupid face

Doofheit *die;* **~, ~en** (ugs. abwertend) [1] stupidity; dumbness (coll.) [2] (Äußerung) stupid *or* (coll.) dumb remark

Doofi /'do:fi/ *der;* **~s, ~s** (ugs.) dope (coll.); dummy; [stupid] twit (coll.); **steh nicht da wie Klein ~ mit Plüschohren!** stop looking so stupid!

Doofkopp /-kɔp/ *der;* **~s, Doofköppe** /-kœpə/, **Doofmann** *der;* **Doofmann[e]s, Doofmänner** (ugs. abwertend) dope (coll.); dummy; [stupid] twit (coll.)

dopen /'dɔpn̩/ *tr. V.* dope ‹*horse etc.*›; **jmdn. ~:** give sb. drugs; **gedopt sein** ‹*athlete*› have taken drugs; **sich ~:** take drugs

Doping /'dɔpɪŋ/ *das;* **~s, ~s** [1] (bei Sportlern) taking drugs; (das Verabreichen von Drogen) administering drugs [2] (von Pferden usw.) doping

Doping·kontrolle *die* (Sport) drug[s] test

Doppel /'dɔpl̩/ *das;* **~s, ~** [1] (Kopie) duplicate; copy [2] (Sport) doubles *sing. or pl.;* **im gemischten/das gemischte ~ gewinnen** win the mixed doubles; **ein ~:** a game of doubles; (im Turnier) a doubles match

doppel-, Doppel-: ~adler *der* double eagle; **~agent** *der,* **~agentin** *die* double agent; **~album** *das* double album *or* LP; **~-b** *das* (Musik) double flat; **~band** *der* double[-sized] volume; **~belastung** *die* double burden *or* load; **~belichtung** *die* (Fot.) double exposure; **~beschluss,** ***~beschluß** *der* (Politik) twin-track decision; **~besteuerung** *die* double taxation; **~bett** *das* double bed; **~blind·versuch** *der* (Med.) double-blind trial; **~bock** *das* extra-strong bock beer; **~bödig** /-bø:dɪç/ [A] *Adj.* ambiguous; [B] *adv.* ambiguously; **~bödigkeit** *die;* **~~, ~~en** ambiguity; **~bogen** *der* double sheet; **~bruch** *der* (Math.) compound *or* complex fraction; **~decker** *der;* **~~s, ~~** [1] (Flugzeug) biplane; [2] (Omnibus) double-decker [bus]; **~deutig** /-dɔytɪç/ [A] *Adj.* [1] ambiguous; [2] (anzüglich) suggestive; **eine ~deutige Bemerkung** a double entendre; [B] *adv.* [1] ambiguously; [2] (anzüglich) suggestively; **~deutigkeit** *die;* **~~, ~~en** [1] ambiguity; [2] (Anzüglichkeit) suggestiveness; (anzügliche Äußerung) double entendre; **~fenster** *das* double-glazed window; **~fenster haben** have double glazing; **~flinte** *die* double-barrelled shotgun; **~gänger** *der;* **~~s, ~~, ~gängerin** *die;* **~~, ~~nen** double; **~gleisig** [A] *Adj.* [1] (mit zwei Gleisen) double-tracked; [2] (zwielichtig) dubious; [B] *adv.* [1] (mit zwei Gleisen) **diese Strecke ist ~gleisig ausgebaut** this section is double-tracked *or* has two tracks; **~gleisig fahren** (fig.) adopt a two-pronged strategy; [2] (zwielichtig) dubiously; **~griff** *der* (Musik) double-stop; **~haus** *das* pair of semi-detached houses; **~haus·hälfte** *die* semi[-detached house]; **~heft** *das* double issue; **~hoch·zeit** *die* double wedding; **~kinn** *das* double chin; **~klick** *der;* **~~s, ~~s** (DV) double click; **~|klicken** *itr. V.* (DV) double-click; **~knoten** *der* double knot; **~konsonant** *der* (Sprachw.) double consonant; **~konzert** *das* double concerto; **~kopf** *der* (Kartenspiel) Doppelkopf; **~lauf** *der* double barrel; **~laut** *der* (Sprachw.) [1] (Diphthong) diphthong; [2] (~konsonant) double consonant; [3] (~vokal) double vowel; **~leben** *das* double life; **~moral** *die* double standards *pl.;* **~mord** *der* double murder

doppeln *tr. V.* [1] (südd., österr.) resole [2] (DV) reproduce

doppel-, Doppel-: ~naht *die* French seam; **~name** *der* double-barrelled name (Brit.); hyphenated name; **~pack** *der* double pack; twin pack; **im ~pack** in one [double] pack; (fig.) in double form; **Größenwahn im ~pack** (ugs. scherzh.) a double dose of megalomania; **~pass,** ***~paß** *der* (Fußball) one-two; **~punkt** *der* colon; **~reihig** *Adj.* ▸**zweireihig; ~rolle** *die* dual role; **~schicht** *die* double shift; **eine ~schicht fahren** work a double shift; **~schlag** *der* [1] (Musik) turn; [2] (Tennis, Tischtennis, Badminton) double hit; **~seite** *die* (Zeitungsw.) double page; **~seitig** [A] *Adj.* [1] (Zeitungsw.) two-page *attrib.;* double-page *attrib.;* [2] (Med.) double ‹*pleurisy, pneumonia*›; bilateral ‹*paralysis*›; [B] *adv.* [1] (Zeitungsw.) **~seitig gedruckt** printed across two pages *or* a double page; [2] (Med.) **~seitig gelähmt** paralysed on both sides; **~sieg** *der* first and second place; **einen ~sieg feiern** celebrate taking first and second place; **~sinnig** [A] *Adj.* ambiguous; [B] *adv.* ambiguously; **~spiel** *das* [1] (Sport) doubles *sing.* or *pl.;* [2] (abwertend: Unehrlichkeit) double game; **~steckdose** *die* (Elektrot.) double socket; **~stecker** *der* (Elektrot.) two-way plug *or* adapter; **~stöckig** *Adj.* two-storey ‹*house*›; double-decker *attrib.* ‹*bus*›; (fig.) double ‹*whisky etc.*›; **ein ~stöckiges Bett** a bunk bed; **~stunde** *die* double period

doppelt

[A] *Adj.* [1] (zweifach) double; dual ‹*nationality*›; **die ~e Länge/Breite/Menge** double *or* twice the length/breadth/quantity; **~e Buchführung** (Kaufmannsspr.) double-entry bookkeeping; **ein ~er Klarer** (ugs.) a double schnapps; **ein ~er Boden** a false bottom [2] (besonders groß, stark) redoubled ‹*enthusiasm, attention*›; **mit ~er Kraft arbeiten** work with twice as much energy;

[B] *adv.* [1] (zweimal) **~ konzentriert** double concentrated; **der Stoff liegt ~:** the material is double-width; **~ genäht hält besser** (Spr.) it's better to be on the safe side; better safe than sorry; **das ist ~ gemoppelt** (ugs.) that's just saying the same thing twice over; **~ so groß/alt wie ...** twice as large/old as ...; **~ so viel** twice as much; **das/diese Platte habe ich ~:** I have two of them/two copies of this record; **etw. ~ nehmen** double sth. up; **~ sehen** see double; **etw. ~ und dreifach bereuen/prüfen** regret sth. deeply/test and retest sth. [2] (ganz besonders, noch mehr) **~ einsam** twice as lonely; **sich ~ anstrengen** try twice as hard; **es ~ bereuen, dass ...** be even more sorry that ...

Doppelte[1] *das; adj. Dekl.* **das ~ bezahlen** pay twice as much; pay double; **um/auf das ~ steigen** triple/double; **etw. um das ~ erhöhen** triple sth.; **um das ~ größer** three times as large; **das ~ leisten** do double the work *or* twice as much work

Doppelte[2] *der; adj. Dekl.* (ugs.) double

doppelt·kohlen·sauer *Adj.* (Chemie) **...saures Natron** sodium bicarbonate; bicarbonate of soda; **...saurer Kalk** calcium bicarbonate

Doppelt·sehen *das;* **~s** (Med.) double vision; diplopia (Med.)

Doppel·tür *die* double door

Doppelung *die;* **~, ~en** doubling

doppel-, Doppel-: ~verdiener *der* [1] *Pl.* (Eheleute) married couple who are both earning; [2] (mit zwei Einkommen) person with an income from two jobs; **~verdiener sein** have an income from two jobs; **~verdienerin** *die* ▸**~verdiener 2; ~vokal** *der* (Sprachw.) double vowel; **~wandig** [A] *Adj.* double-walled; [B] *adv.* **~wandig isoliert** with double-wall insulation; **~zentner** *der* ▸❶ **S. 315** 100 kilograms; quintal; **~zimmer** *das* double room; **~züngig** /-tsʏŋɪç/ (abwertend) [A] *Adj.* two-faced; [B] *adv.* **~züngig reden** be two-faced; **~züngigkeit** *die;* **~~** (abwertend) ▸**~züngig**: double-facedness; two-facedness

Doppler·effekt *der;* **~[e]s** (Physik) Doppler effect

Dorado /do'ra:do/ ▸**Eldorado**

Dorf /dɔrf/ *das;* **~[e]s, Dörfer** /'dœrfɐ/ (auch ugs.: die Einwohner) village; **auf dem ~:** in the country; **vom ~ kommen** *od.* **stammen** come from the country; **aufs ~ ziehen** move to the country; **über die Dörfer** from village to village; **über die Dörfer fahren** drive on country roads; **das olympische ~:** the Olympic village; **das sind mir/für mich böhmische Dörfer** (ugs.) it's all Greek to me; **auf/über die Dörfer gehen** (Skat) lead the side suits; **aus** *od.* **in jedem ~ einen Hund haben** (Skat) have a more or less even distribution; *s. auch* **potemkinsch**

Dorf-: ~akademie *die* (DDR) village adult education centre; **~älteste** *der* village elder; **~anger** *der* village green; **~bewohner** *der*, **~bewohnerin** *die* villager

Dörfchen /ˈdœrfçən/ *das;* **~s, ~:** small village; hamlet

Dorf·depp *der* (bes. südd., österr.) village idiot

dörfisch
A *Adj.* rustic
B *adv.* rustically

Dorf-: ~jugend *die* young people *pl.* of the village; village youth; **~krug** *der* (nordd.) village inn *or* (Brit.) pub

Dörfler /ˈdœrflɐ/ *der;* **~s, ~, Dörflerin** *die;* **~, ~nen** villager

dörflich *Adj.* village *attrib.* ‹*life, traditions, etc.*›; (ländlich) rural ‹*character*›

Dorf-: ~polizist *der* village policeman; **~schenke** *die* village inn *or* (Brit.) pub; **~schönheit** *die* village beauty; **~schulze** *der* (veralt.) mayor of the/a village; **~trottel** *der* village idiot

dorisch /ˈdoːrɪʃ/ *Adj.* **1** (Archit.) Doric **2** (Musik) Dorian ‹*mode*›

Dorn[1] /dɔrn/ *der;* **~[e]s, ~en** (ugs. auch:) **Dörner** /ˈdœrnɐ/ **1** (an Rosen o. Ä.) thorn; **jmdm. ein ~ im Auge sein** annoy sb. intensely; **sein Weg war voller ~en** (fig. geh.) his life was no bed of roses **2** (Bot.) thorn; spine **3** (dichter.: ~busch) thorn bush

Dorn[2] *der;* **~[e]s, ~e** **1** (Metallstift) spike; (an der Gürtelschnalle) tongue **2** (Technik) (zum Weiten von Löchern o. Ä.) punch; (zum Biegen von Blechen o. Ä.) mandrel

Dorn·busch *der* thorn bush; **der brennende ~** (bibl.) the burning bush

dornen-, Dornen-: ~gestrüpp *das* tangle of thorn bushes; **~krone** *die* crown of thorns; **~reich** *Adj.* (fig. geh.) hard ‹*life, fate*›; thorny ‹*path*›; **~strauch** *der* thorn bush; **~voll** *Adj.* (fig. geh.) ▸ **~reich**

Dorn·fort·satz *der* ▸ⓘ **S. 435** (Anat.) spinous process

dornig *Adj.* **1** (mit Dornen) thorny **2** (geh.: schwierig) hard ‹*life, fate*›; thorny ‹*path, subject, question*›

Dorn-: ~röschen (*das*) the Sleeping Beauty; **~röschen·schlaf** *der* (iron.) long sleep

dorren /ˈdɔrən/ *itr. V.; mit sein* (geh.) dry up

dörren /ˈdœrən/
A *tr. V.* (trocken machen) dry
B *itr. V.; mit sein* dry

Dörr-: ~fleisch *das* (südd.) lean bacon; **~obst** *das* dried fruit; **~pflaume** *die* prune

dorsal /dɔrˈzaːl/ *Adj.* **1** (Med.) dorsal ‹*artery, nerve*›; spinal ‹*curvature*› **2** (Phon.) dorsal

Dorsch /dɔrʃ/ *der;* **~[e]s, ~e** cod; (junger Kabeljau) codling

dort /dɔrt/ *Adv.* there; **jmdn./etw. ~ behalten** keep sb./sth. there; **~ bleiben** stay there; *s. auch* **da A 1**

dort-: *~|**behalten** *usw.* ▸ **dort**; **~her** *Adv.* **[von] ~her** from there; **~hin** *Adv.* there; **bis ~hin** as far as there; **ich ging ~hin, wo der Wagen wartete** I went to where the car was waiting; **~hinab** *Adv.* down there; down that way; **~hinauf** *Adv.* up there; up that way; **bis ~hinauf** up to there; **~hinaus** *Adv.* out there; (in diese Richtung) out that way; **frech bis ~hinaus** (ugs.) [as] cheeky as anything; **das ärgert mich bis ~hinaus** (ugs.) that really gets me *or* my goat (coll.); **~hinein** *Adv.* in there; **~hinunter** *Adv.* down there

dortig *Adj.* there *postpos.*

dort·zu·lande *Adv.* (geh.) in that country; there

Döschen /ˈdøːsçən/ *das;* **~s, ~** ▸ **Dose 1**: small tin/box

Dose /ˈdoːzə/ *die;* **~, ~n** **1** (Blech~) tin; (Pillen~) box; (Zucker~) bowl **2** (Konserven~) can; tin (Brit.); (Bier~) can; **Bier aus der ~:** canned beer; beer in cans **3** (Steck~) socket

dösen /ˈdøːzn̩/ *itr. V.* (ugs.) doze; **vor sich hin ~:** doze

dosen-, Dosen-: ~bier *das* canned beer; **~fertig** *Adj.* ready in the can *or* (Brit.) tin *postpos.*; **~fleisch** *das* canned *or* (Brit.) tinned meat; **~milch** *die* canned *or* (Brit.) tinned milk; **~öffner** *der* can-opener; tin-opener (Brit.); **~pfand** *das* deposit on [drink] cans

dosierbar *Adj.* **etw. ist genau** *od.* **exakt ~:** sth. can be measured out in precise *or* exact doses

dosieren *tr. V.* **etw. ~:** measure out the required dose of sth.; (zuführen) administer the required dose of sth.; **ein Medikament genau/niedriger ~:** measure out/administer an exact/a smaller dose of a medicine; **sorgfältig dosierte Mengen** carefully measured doses; **seine Zuneigung sehr dosiert verteilen** (fig.) dispense one's affection in very small doses

Dosierung *die;* **~, ~en** **1** measuring out; (das Zuführen) administering; (fig.) dispensing **2** ▸ **Dosis**

dösig /ˈdøːzɪç/ (ugs.)
A *Adj.* **1** (schläfrig) drowsy; dozy **2** (benommen) dopey (coll.); **ich habe einen ganz ~en Kopf** my head is all muzzy **3** (unaufmerksam) dozy (coll.)
B *adv.* **1** (schläfrig) drowsily **2** (benommen) dopily (sl.) **3** (unaufmerksam) dozily (coll.)

Dosimeter /doziˈmeːtɐ/ *das;* **~s, ~** (Physik) dosimeter

Dosis /ˈdoːzɪs/ *die;* **~, Dosen** (auch fig.) dose; **die tägliche ~:** the daily dosage

Döskopp /ˈdøːskɔp/ *der;* **~s, Dösköppe** /ˈdøːskœpə/ (salopp) dozy twit (Brit. coll.); dimwit

Dossier /dɔˈsi̯eː/ *das*, (veraltet:) *der;* **~s, ~s** dossier

Dotation /dotaˈtsi̯oːn/ *die;* **~, ~en** endowment

Dotcom /ˈdɔtkɔm/ *das;* **~s, ~s** dot-com [company]

dotieren /doˈtiːrən/ *tr. V.* **1** **eine Position gut/mit 5 000 Euro ~:** offer a good salary/a salary of 5,000 euros with a position **2** (Physik) dope

dotiert
A *2. Part. v.* **dotieren**
B *Adj.* **hoch ~:** highly paid; **eine gut/mit 5 000 Euro im Monat ~e Stellung** a well-paid position/a position with a monthly salary of 5,000 euros; **das Rennen ist gut ~:** good prize money is being put up for the race

Dotierung *die;* **~, ~en** **1** (das Dotieren) **die ~ des Wettbewerbs/Rennens** putting up the prize money for the competition/race **2** (Entgelt) remuneration; salary; (Preis, Gewinn) prize

Dotter /ˈdɔtɐ/ *der od. das;* **~s, ~** **1** (Eigelb) yolk **2** (Zool.: Nährsubstanz) vitellus; yolk

dotter-, Dotter-: ~blume *die* marsh marigold; **~gelb** *Adj.* bright yellow; **~sack** *der* (Zool.) yolk sac

doubeln /ˈduːbl̩n/
A *tr. V.* stand in for ‹*actor*›; use a stand-in for ‹*scene*›; **sich ~ lassen** use *or* have a stand-in
B *itr. V.* **für jmdn. ~:** stand in for sb.

Double /ˈduːbl̩/ *das;* **~s, ~s** **1** (Ersatzdarsteller[in]) stand-in **2** (Doppelgänger, Sport: doppelter Gewinn) double **3** (Musik: Variation) double

Doublé /duˈbleː/ *das;* **~s, ~s** **1** (Schmuck) rolled gold **2** (Fechten) double hit

doublieren ▸ **dublieren**

Douglasie /duˈglaːzi̯ə/ *die;* **~, ~n, Douglas·fichte** /ˈduːglas-/, **Douglas·tanne** *die* Douglas fir *or* spruce

down /daʊn/ *Adj.* (salopp) down

Downhill /ˈdaʊnhɪl/ *das od. der;* **~s, ~s** (Sport) downhill; **Meisterschaft im ~:** downhill championship

Downhiller /ˈdaʊnhɪlɐ/ *der* **~s, ~, Downhillerin** *die;* **~, ~nen** (Sport) downhiller

Doyen /dɔa̯ˈjɛ̃ː/ *der;* **~s, ~s** doyen

Doyenne /dɔa̯ˈjɛn/ *die;* **~, ~n** doyenne

Dozent /doˈtsɛnt/ *der;* **~en, ~en, Dozentin** *die;* **~, ~nen** ▸ⓘ **S. 113** lecturer (**für** in); *s. auch* **-in**

Dozentur /dotsɛnˈtuːɐ̯/ *die;* **~, ~en** lectureship (**für** in)

dozieren /doˈtsiːrən/
A *itr. V.* **1** (lehren) lecture (**über** + *Akk.* on, **an** + *Dat.* at) **2** (belehrend reden) lecture
B *tr. V.* **„…", dozierte sie** '…,' she said in a lecturing tone

dpa /deːpeːˈ|aː/ *die;* **~** *Abk.* **= Deutsche Presse-Agentur** German Press Agency

Dr. *Abk.* ▸ⓘ **S. 44 = Doktor** Dr; *s. auch* **Dr. phil.**

Drache /ˈdraxə/ *der;* **~n, ~n** (Myth.) dragon

Drachen *der;* **~s, ~** **1** (Papier~) kite; **einen ~ steigen lassen** fly a kite **2** (salopp: zänkische Frau) dragon **3** (Fluggerät) hang-glider **4** (Segelboot) dragon

Drachen-: ~blut *das* (Myth.; Chemie) dragon's blood; **~fliegen** *das* (Sport) hang-gliding; **~saat** *die* (geh.) seeds *pl.* of discord

Dragée, Dragee /draˈʒeː/ *das;* **~s, ~s** dragée

Dragoner /draˈgoːnɐ/ *der;* **~s, ~** **1** (salopp: resolute Frau) battleaxe (coll.) **2** (hist.: Soldat) dragoon

Draht /draːt/ *der;* **~[e]s, Drähte** /ˈdrɛːtə/ **1** (dünnes Metall) wire **2** (Leitung) wire; cable; (Telefonleitung) line; wire **3** (Telefonverbindung) line; **per** *od.* **über ~:** by wire *or* cable; **hast du einen ~ zur Polizei?** (fig.) have you got a direct line to the police?; **heißer ~:** hot line; **auf ~ sein** (ugs.) be on the ball (coll.); **jmdn. auf ~ bringen** (ugs.) make sb. get a move on

Draht-: ~aus·löser *der* (Fot.) cable release; **~bürste** *die* wire brush

Drähtchen /ˈdrɛːtçən/ *das;* **~s, ~:** little wire

drahten *tr. V.* (veralt.) wire (coll.); (ins Ausland) cable; **an jmdn./nach Paris ~, dass …** wire/cable sb./Paris to say that …

Draht-: ~esel *der* (ugs. scherzh.) bike (coll.); **~funk** *der* wired radio; **~geflecht** *das* wire mesh; **~gitter** *das* wire netting *no indef. art.*; **~glas** *das* wire glass

drahtig *Adj.* wiry ‹*person, hair*›

draht-, Draht-: ~los (Nachrichtenw.) **A** *Adj.* wireless; **B** *adv.* **etw. ~los telegrafieren/übermitteln** radio sth.; **~schere** *die* wire cutters *pl.*; **~seil** *das* [steel] cable; **~seil·bahn** *die* cable railway; **~seil·künstler** *der*, **~seil·künstlerin** *die* tightrope walker; **~verhau** *der od. das* (Barriere) wire entanglement; (Käfig) wire enclosure; **~zange** *die* cutting pliers *pl.*; **~zaun** *der* wire fence; **~zieher** /-tsiːɐ/ *der* **1** (Beruf) wire-drawer; **2** (Hintermann) wire puller; **~zieherei** *die;* **~~, ~~en** wire works; **~zieherin** *die* ▸ **~zieher**

Drainage /drɛˈnaːʒə/ *die;* **~, ~n** (Med., Landw., Kfz-W.) drainage

drainieren /drɛˈniːrən/ *tr. V.* (Med., Landw.) drain

Draisine /drai̯ˈziːnə/ *die;* **~, ~n** **1** (Laufrad) dandy-horse **2** (Schienenfahrzeug) trolley

drakonisch /draˈkoːnɪʃ/
A *Adj.* Draconian
B *adv.* in a Draconian way

drall /dral/ *Adj.* strapping ‹*girl*›; full, rounded ‹*cheeks, face, bottom*›

Drall *der;* **~[e]s, ~e** **1** (bei Feuerwaffen) rifling **2** (eines Geschosses, Balls) spin; **er hat einen ~ nach rechts** (fig.) he leans to the right *or* has right-wing tendencies **3** (Physik) (Verdrehung) torsion; (Rotation) rotation; (Drehimpuls) angular momentum

Dralon Ⓦⓩ /ˈdraːlɔn/ *das;* **~s** Dralon ®

Drama /ˈdraːma/ *das;* **~s, Dramen** drama; **ein einziges/furchtbares ~** (fig.) an absolute/a terrible disaster; **das ~ um die Entführung** (fig.) the drama of *or* surrounding the hijack

Dramatik /draˈmaːtɪk/ *die;* **~:** drama

Dramatiker *der;* **~s, ~, Dramatikerin** *die;* **~, ~nen** dramatist

dramatisch
A *Adj.* dramatic

d

B *adv.* dramatically; **der Autor hat den Stoff ~ bearbeitet** the author adapted the material as a drama *or* for the stage

dramatisieren *tr. V.* dramatize

Dramaturg /drama'tʊrk/ *der;* **~en, ~en** (Theater) literary and artistic director (*who also plans the programme of performances and advises on choice of costumes, scenery, etc.*); (Rundf., Ferns.) script editor

Dramaturgie /dramatʊr'gi:/ *die;* **~, ~n** **1** (Dramenlehre) dramaturgy **2** (Gestaltung) dramatization **3** (Abteilung) (Theater) literary and artistic director's department; (Rundf., Ferns.) script department

Dramaturgin *die;* **~, ~nen** ▸**Dramaturg**

dramaturgisch

A *Adj.* dramaturgical; (gestalterisch) dramaturgical; dramatic; **die ~e Abteilung** (Theater) the literary and artistic director's department; (Rundfunk, Fernsehen) the script department

B *adv.* **~ wirkungsvoll in Szene gesetzt** staged effectively; **~ gerechtfertigt** justified on dramaturgical grounds

Dramolett /dramo'lɛt/ *das;* **~s, ~s** mini-drama

dran /dran/ *Adv.* (ugs.) **1** (an einer/eine Sache) **das Schild bleibt ~:** the sign stays up; **gib noch etwas Mehl ~:** add some more flour; **halt deine Hand mal hier ~:** put your hand on this; **häng das Schild ~!** put the sign up!; **ich komme/kann nicht ~:** I can't reach; **mach doch ein Schild ~:** put a sign up **2** **arm ~ sein** be in a bad way; **gut/schlecht ~ sein** be well off/badly off; (sich gut/schlecht fühlen) be well/not very well; **früh/spät ~ sein** be early/late; **an dem Gerücht ist was ~:** there is something in the rumour; **an ihm ist doch nichts ~:** he's got nothing going for him (coll.); (er ist sehr mager) there's nothing of him; **ich bin ~** *od.* (scherzh.) **am ~sten** (ich bin an der Reihe) it's my turn; I'm next; (ich werde zur Verantwortung gezogen) I'll be for the high jump *or* (sl.) for it (Brit.); I'll be under the gun (Amer.); **nicht wissen wie** *od.* **wo man ~ ist** not know where one stands; **nicht wissen wie** *od.* **wo man mit jmdm. ~ ist** not know where one is with sb.; ▸*auch:* **daran; ~bleiben; ~geben; ~hängen** *usw.;* **glauben**

Dränage /drɛ'na:ʒə/ *die;* **~, ~n** (auch Med.) drainage

dran|bleiben *unr. itr. V.; mit sein* (*ugs.*) (am Telefon) hold *or* (coll.) hang on; (das Programm weiter verfolgen) stay tuned; (an der Arbeit) stick at it (coll.); **am Gegner/an der Arbeit ~:** stick to one's opponent (coll.)/stick at one's work (coll.); *s. auch* **dran 1**

drang /draŋ/ *1. u. 3. Pers. Sg. Prät. v.* **dringen**

Drang *der;* **~[e]s, Dränge** /'drɛŋə/ **1** (Antrieb) urge; **ein ~ nach Bewegung/Freiheit** an urge to move/be free **2** (Bedrängnis) pressure

dränge /'drɛŋə/ *1. u. 3. Pers. Sg. Konjunktiv II v.* **dringen**

dran-: ~|geben *unr. tr. V.* give up ‹*time*›; give, sacrifice ‹*one's life*›; *s. auch* **dran 1**; **~|gehen** *unr. itr. V.; mit sein* (ugs.) **1** (berühren) touch; **2** (in Angriff nehmen) **~gehen, etw. zu tun** get down to doing sth.

Drängelei *die;* **~, ~en** (abwertend) **1** pushing [and shoving]; **hören Sie doch mit Ihrer ~ auf** stop pushing [and shoving] **2** (mit Wünschen, Bitten) pestering

drängeln /'drɛŋl̩n/ (ugs.)

A *itr. V.* **1** (schieben) push [and shove] **2** (auf jmdn. einreden) go on (coll.); **zum Aufbruch ~:** go on about it being time to leave (coll.)

B *tr. V.* **1** (schieben) push; shove **2** (einreden auf) pester; go on at (coll.)

C *refl. V.* **sich nach vorn/durch die Menge** *usw.* **~:** push one's way to the front/through the crowd *etc.*; **sich danach ~, etw. zu tun** (fig.) fall over oneself to do sth. (coll.)

drängen /'drɛŋən/

A *itr. V.* **1** (schieben) push; **die Menge drängte zum Ausgang** the crowd pressed towards the exit **2** (fordern) demand; **auf etw.** (*Akk.*) **~:** press for sth.; **zum Aufbruch ~:** insist that it is/was time to leave; **zur Eile ~:** hurry us/them *etc.* up; **darauf ~, dass ...** insist that ... **3** **die Zeit drängt** time is pressing; **~de Fragen/Probleme** pressing *or* urgent questions/problems **4** (Sport) press *or* push forward

B *tr. V.* **1** (schieben) push **2** (antreiben) press; urge; **jmdn. zur Bezahlung ~:** press sb. to pay; **es drängt mich, Ihnen zu sagen, dass ...** I feel I have to *or* must tell you that ...

C *refl. V.* ‹*visitors, spectators, etc.*› crowd, throng; ‹*crowd*› throng; **sich nach vorn/durch die Menge ~:** push one's way to the front/through the crowd; **sich in den Vordergrund ~** (fig.) make oneself the centre of attention

Dränger *der;* **~s, ~** ▸**Stürmer 2**

Drängerei *die;* **~, ~en** (abwertend) pushing [and shoving]

Drängler *der;* **~s, ~** (abwertend) aggressive driver; (zu dicht auffahrend) tailgater; **Raser und ~** *Pl.* recklessly fast and aggressive drivers

Dränglerin *die;* **~, ~nen** (abwertend) aggressive [woman] driver; (zu dicht auffahrend) tailgater

Drangsal /'draŋza:l/ *die;* **~, ~e** (geh.) (Not) hardship; (Qual) suffering

drangsalieren *tr. V.* (abwertend) (quälen) torment; (plagen) plague

dran-: ~|halten *unr. refl. V.* (ugs.) get a move on (coll.); *s. auch* **dran 1**; **~|hängen**[1] (ugs.)

A *tr. V.* **1** (aufwenden) **viel Zeit/Geld ~hängen** put a lot of time/money into it; **2** (anschließen) **ein paar Tage an seinen Urlaub ~hängen** add a few days on to one's holiday (Brit.) *or* (Amer.) vacation; **B** *refl. V.* (verfolgen) stay *or* (coll.) stick close behind; *s. auch* **dran 1**; **~|hängen**[2] *unr. itr. V.* **da hängt noch viel Arbeit ~:** it still needs a lot of work

dränieren /drɛ'ni:rən/ *tr. V.* (auch Med.) drain

dran-: ~|kommen *unr. itr. V.; mit sein* (ugs.) have one's turn; (beim Spielen) have one's turn *or* go; **ich kam als erste/erster ~:** it was my turn first; (beim Arzt, Zahnarzt usw.) I was the first one; **wer kommt jetzt ~?** who's next?; **jeder von uns kommt mal ~** (verhüll.) we've all got to go some time; **ich bin heute in Latein ~gekommen** (aufgerufen worden) I got picked on to answer in Latin today (coll.); *s. auch* **dran 1**; **~|kriegen** *tr. V.* (ugs.) **jmdn. ~kriegen** get sb.; (zum Arbeiten bringen) get sb. at it (coll.); **~|machen** *refl. V.* (ugs.) **sich ~machen, etw. zu tun** get down to doing sth.; **wenn sich die Kinder ~machen, ist der Kuchen gleich weg** once the children get started on it the cake won't last long; *s. auch* **dran 1**; **~|nehmen** *unr. tr. V.* (ugs.) (beim Friseur usw.) see to; (beim Arzt) see; **jmdn. ~nehmen** (in der Schule) pick on sb. [to answer]; **~|setzen** (ugs.) **A** *tr. V.* (einsetzen) **seine ganze Kraft ~setzen, etw. zu erreichen** put all one's energy into achieving sth.; **alles ~setzen** put everything into it; make every effort; **B** *refl. V.* (beginnen) get down to it

dransten /'dranstn̩/ ▸**dran 2**

dran|wollen *unr. itr. V.* (ugs.) want [to have] a turn; (beim Spielen) want [to have] a turn *or* go

Draperie /drapə'ri:/ *die;* **~, ~n** (veralt.) drapery

drapieren /dra'pi:rən/ *tr. V.* drape

Dräsine ▸**Draisine**

Drastik /'drastɪk/ *die;* **~** (eines Witzes, Schwanks) crude explicitness; (eines Berichts usw.) graphicness

drastisch

A *Adj.* **1** crudely explicit ‹*joke, story, etc.*›; graphic ‹*report, account*› **2** (empfindlich spürbar) drastic ‹*measure, means*›

B *adv.* **1** (grob) with crude explicitness; (deutlich) graphically **2** (einschneidend) drastically; ‹*punish*› severely

drauf /drauf/ *Adv.* (ugs.) on it; **da wäre ich nie ~ gekommen** I would never have thought of that; **da lege ich keinen Wert ~:** it's not important to me; **da zeigt sich, wer was ~ hat** that'll show who can and who can't; **da kannst du mal zeigen, was du ~ hast** here's your chance to show what you can do; **die Rolle/die dollsten Sprüche/90 Sachen ~ haben** have *or* know the part off pat (Brit.) *or* (Amer.) have the part down pat/have the most amazing patter/be doing 90; **~ und dran sein, etw. zu tun** be just about to do *or* be on the verge of doing sth.; **halt mal den Finger hier ~:** put your finger on here; **ich kriege den Deckel nicht ~:** I can't get the lid on; **der Deckel geht nicht ~:** the lid won't go on; **mach einen neuen Deckel ~:** put a new lid on [it]; **gut/schlecht** *usw.* **~ sein** (fig. ugs.) be in a good/bad *etc.* mood; *s. auch* **darauf 1-5**; **draufgehen**; **draufhalten** *usw.;* **scheißen**

drauf-, Drauf-: ~|bekommen *unr. tr. V.* (ugs.) *in* **eins ~bekommen** (gescholten werden) get it in the neck (coll.); (geschlagen werden) get a smack; **~gänger** *der;* **~~s, ~~:** daredevil; (veralt.: Frauenheld) ladykiller; **~gängerin** *die;* **~~, ~~nen** daredevil; **~gängerisch** *Adj.* daring; audacious; **~gängertum** *das;* **~s** daredevilry; **~|geben** *unr. tr. V.* (ugs.) **1** (dazugeben) **etw./was ~geben** add sth./add a bit on; **2** *in* **jmdm. eins ~geben** (schlagen) give sb. a smack; (zurechtweisen) put sb. in his/her place; **3** (österr.: als Zugabe) **etw. ~geben** play/sing/dance *etc.* sth. as an encore; **~|gehen** *unr. itr. V.; mit sein* (ugs.) **1** (umkommen) kick the bucket (sl.); **2** (verbraucht werden) go; **für etw. ~gehen** ‹*money*› go on sth.; **für diese Sitzungen geht immer viel Zeit ~:** these meetings always take up a lot of time; **3** (entzweigehen) get busted (coll.) *or* broken; **~|halten** *unr. itr. V.* (ugs.) shoot; **~halten und abdrücken** aim and fire; **~|hauen** *unr. itr. V.* (ugs.) **mein Arm tut noch weh, da darfst du nicht ~hauen** my arm still hurts, you're not to bash it; **einen ~hauen** have a booze-up (Brit. coll.); go on a binge (coll.); **~|kommen** *unr. itr. V.; mit sein* (ugs.) **jmdm. ~kommen** get on to sb.; **jmdm. ~kommen, dass er etw. tut** catch sb. doing sth.; *s. auch* **drauf**; **~kriegen** *tr. V.* (ugs.) **eins ~kriegen** (von einem Kind: geschlagen werden) get smacked; (besiegt werden) get a thrashing; **~|legen** (ugs.) **A** *tr. V.* **150 Euro/noch etwas ~legen** fork out (coll.) an extra 150 euros/a bit more; **B** *itr. V.* lay out (sl.); **ich lege dabei noch ~:** it's costing me money; *s. auch* **drauf**

drauf·los *Adv.* **nichts wie ~!** go on!

drauflos-: ~|arbeiten *itr. V.* work away; (anfangen zu arbeiten) get straight down to work; **~|gehen** *unr. itr. V.; mit sein* (ugs.) get going; **~|reden** *itr. V.* talk away; (anfangen zu reden) start talking away; **~|schimpfen** *itr. V.* (ugs.) curse away; (anfangen zu schimpfen) start cursing away; **~|wirtschaften** *itr. V.* (ugs. abwertend) splash out money right, left, and centre (Brit. coll.); throw one's money around

drauf-: ~|machen *tr. V.* **einen ~machen** (ugs.) paint the town red; **~|setzen** *tr. V.* **[noch] einen/eins ~setzen** (ugs.) go one better (+ *Dat.* than); **~|stehen** *unr. itr. V.* (ugs.) be on it; **~|zahlen** (ugs.) **A** *tr. V.* **noch etwas/1250 Euro ~zahlen** fork out (coll.) *or* pay a bit more/an extra 1,250 euros; **B** *itr. V.* (Unkosten haben) **ich zahle dabei noch ~:** it's costing me money; **diejenige sein, die immer nur ~zahlt** (fig.) be the one who makes all the sacrifices

draus /draus/ *Adv.* (ugs.) ▸**daraus**

draußen /'drausn̩/ *Adv.* **1** (außerhalb) outside; **hier/da ~:** out here/there; **~ vor der Tür** at the door; **nach/von ~:** outside/from outside; **„Hunde müssen ~ bleiben"** 'no dogs[, please]'; **bleib ~:** stay outside; **~ auf dem Land** (fig.) out in the country **2** (irgendwo) out there; **da/hier ~:** out there/here; **weit/weiter ~:** far/further out; **~ in der Welt** (fig.) in the world outside

Draußen·tag *der* (Schulw.) day for out-of-school activities and visits

DRB *Abk.* **= Deutschlandradio Berlin**

drechseln /'drɛksl̩n/ *tr. V.* turn; (fig. iron.) compose ‹*statement*›; turn ‹*phrase, verse*›

Drechsler *der;* **~s, ~:** turner

Drechsler-: ~arbeit *die* piece of turned work; **~arbeiten** [pieces *pl.* of] turned work *sing.*; **~bank** *die; Pl.* **~bänke** lathe

Drechslerei *die;* **~, ~en** turner's workshop; turnery

Drechslerin *die;* **~, ~nen** ▸**Drechsler**

Dreck /drɛk/ *der;* **~[e]s** 1 (ugs.) dirt; (sehr viel, Ekel erregend) filth; (Schlamm) mud; (Kot) mess; muck; **in den ~ fallen** fall in the dirt/mud/muck; **deine Hände sind schwarz vor ~:** your hands are filthy [dirty]; **vor ~ starren** be covered in dirt; be filthy [dirty]; **~ machen** make a mess; **~ am Stecken haben** have a skeleton in the cupboard (Brit.) *or* (Amer.) closet; **aus dem [gröbsten] ~ [heraus] sein** (ugs.) be over the worst; **jmdn. aus dem ~ ziehen** (ugs.) take sb. out of the gutter; **etw. in den ~ ziehen** *od.* **treten** drag sth. through the mud *or* mire; **im ~ stecken/sitzen** (ugs.) be in a [real] mess *or* in the mire; **mit ~ und Speck** (ugs.) unwashed; **jmdn./etw. mit ~ bewerfen** throw *or* (coll.) sling mud at sb./sth. 2 (salopp abwertend: Angelegenheit) **bei/wegen jedem ~ regt er sich auf** he gets worked up about every piddling little thing (coll.); **mach deinen ~ allein** do it yourself; **kümmere dich um deinen eigenen ~:** mind your own damn business; **ein ~** *od.* **der letzte ~ sein** (salopp abwertend) be the lowest of the low; **das geht dich einen ~ an** (salopp) none of your damned business (sl.); **er kümmert sich einen ~ darum** (salopp) he doesn't give a damn about it; **er hat uns einen ~ zu befehlen** (salopp) he's got no damn right to order us around; **jmdn. wie [den letzten] ~ behandeln** (ugs.) treat sb. like dirt 3 (salopp abwertend: Zeug) rubbish *no indef. art.;* junk *no indef. art.;* (Nahrungsmittel) junk *no indef. art.*

Dreck-: ~arbeit *die* (salopp) 1 (schmutzige Arbeit) dirty *or* messy work *no indef. art., no pl.;* dirty *or* messy job; 2 (minderwertige Arbeit) dirty *or* menial work *no indef. art., no pl.;* dirty *or* menial job; **~ding** *das; Pl.* **~~er** (salopp) 1 (schmutziges Ding) dirty *or* filthy thing; 2 (minderwertiges Ding) damn thing (coll.); **~eimer** *der* (südd. ugs.) rubbish bin; **~fink** *der* (salopp) filthy pig (coll.); (Kind, das etw. schmutzig macht) mucky pup (Brit. coll.); **~fleck** *der* (ugs.) stain; dirty mark

dreckig

A *Adj.* 1 (ugs.: schmutzig, ungepflegt, auch fig.) dirty; (sehr, Ekel erregend schmutzig, auch fig.) filthy; **mach dich nicht ~:** don't get yourself dirty 2 (salopp abwertend: unverschämt) cheeky 3 (salopp abwertend: gemein) dirty, filthy ‹*swine etc.*›; foul ‹*crime*›

B *adv.* 1 **es geht ihm ~** (ugs.) he's in a bad way 2 (salopp abwertend: unverschämt) cheekily; **~ grinsen** have a cheeky grin on one's face

Dreck-: ~loch (salopp abwertend) (Zimmer) dump (coll.); (Wohnung) dump (coll.); hole (coll.); **~nest** *das* (salopp abwertend) hole (coll.); dump (coll.); **~sack** *der* (derb) bastard (coll.); **der ~sack von Torhüter** that dirty bastard of a goalkeeper; **~sau** *die* (derb) dirty *or* filthy swine; **~schaufel** *die* (ugs.) dustpan; **~schleuder** *die* (derb abwertend) 1 (Mundwerk) foul mouth; **halt deine ~schleuder!** keep your filthy trap shut (sl.); 2 (Person) foul mouth; **~schwein** *das* (derb) dirty *or* filthy swine

Drecks-kerl *der* (derb) dirty *or* filthy swine

dreck-, Dreck-: ~spatz *der* 1 (fam.: Kind) grubby little so-and-so (coll.); (Kind, das etw. schmutzig macht) mucky pup (Brit. coll.); 2 (ugs.: Ärger erregender Mensch) filthy so-and-so (coll.); **~starrend** *Adj.* covered in filth *postpos.;* **~wetter** *das* (ugs. abwertend) lousy (coll.) *or* filthy weather; **~zeug** *das* (ugs. abwertend) rubbish *no indef. art.;* junk *no indef. art.;* (Nahrungsmittel) junk *no indef. art.*

Dreh /dre:/ *der;* **~s, ~s** (ugs.) 1 (Einfall, Kunstgriff) **den ~ heraushaben[, wie man es macht]** have [got] the knack [of doing it]; **auf/hinter den richtigen ~ kommen** get the knack *or* the hang of it (coll.) 2 *in* **um den ~:** about that

Dreh-: ~achse *die* axis [of rotation]; **~arbeiten** *Pl.* (Film) shooting *sing.* **(zu** of); **die ~arbeiten fanden in ... statt** the film was shot in ...; **~bank** *die; Pl.* **~bänke** lathe

drehbar

A *Adj.* revolving *attrib.* ‹*stand, stage*›; swivel *attrib.* ‹*chair*›; **~ sein** revolve/swivel

B *adv.* **~ gelagert** pivoted

Dreh-: ~bewegung *die* rotary motion; rotation; **sie machte eine rasche ~bewegung** she turned *or* spun round quickly; **~bleistift** *der* propelling pencil (Brit.); mechanical pencil (Amer.); **~brücke** *die* swing bridge; **~buch** *das* screenplay; [film] script; **~buch·autor** *der,* **~buch·autorin** *die* scriptwriter; (als Berufsbez.) screenwriter; scriptwriter; **~bühne** *die* revolving stage

drehen

A *tr. V.* 1 turn; **du kannst es ~ und wenden, wie du willst** (fig.) whichever way you look at it 2 (ugs.: einstellen) **das Radio laut/leise ~:** turn the radio up/down; **die Flamme klein/die Heizung auf klein ~:** turn the heat/heating down 3 (formen) twist ‹*rope, thread*›; roll ‹*cigarette*›; make ‹*pill*› by rolling; **sich** (*Dat.*) **eine [Zigarette] ~:** roll a cigarette 4 (Film) shoot ‹*scene*›; film ‹*report*›; make, shoot ‹*film*›; ‹*star*› make ‹*film*› 5 (ugs. abwertend: beeinflussen) **es so ~, dass ...** work it so that ... (coll.); **daran ist nichts zu ~ und zu deuteln** there are no two ways about it 6 (ugs. abwertend: anstellen) **etwas ~:** get up to sth.; *s. auch* **Ding**[2] **1, krumm, Mangel, Nase, Runde, Strick, Wolf**

B *itr. V.* 1 (Richtung ändern) ‹*car*› turn; ‹*wind*› change, shift 2 **an etw.** (*Dat.*) **~:** turn sth.; (spielend, aus Langeweile) twiddle sth.; **am Radio ~:** turn/twiddle a knob/knobs on the radio; **da muss einer dran gedreht haben** (salopp) somebody must have fiddled about *or* messed around with it 3 (Film) shoot [a/the film]; film

C *refl. V.* 1 turn; ‹*wind*› change, shift; (um eine Achse) turn; rotate; revolve; (um einen Mittelpunkt) revolve (**um** around); (sehr schnell) spin; **sie drehten sich im Tanz** they spun around; **mir dreht sich alles** (ugs.) everything's going round and round; **sich auf den Bauch ~:** turn over on to one's stomach 2 (ugs.: zum Gegenstand haben) **sich um etw. ~:** be about sth.; **es dreht sich darum, dass ...** it's about the fact that ...; **alles dreht sich um ihn** everything revolves around him; (er steht im Mittelpunkt des Interesses) he is the centre of attention 3 (österr. ugs.: aufbrechen) push off (coll.)

Dreher *der;* **~s, ~** 1 ▸ⓘ **S. 113** (Beruf) lathe operator 2 (Tanz) *Austrian folk dance, similar to the Ländler*

Dreherin *die;* **~, ~nen** ▸ⓘ **S. 113** ▸**Dreher 1**

Dreh-: ~feld *das* (Elektrot.) rotating field; **~impuls** *der* (Physik) angular momentum; **~kolben·motor** *der* rotary engine; **~kran** *der* revolving *or* slewing crane; **~kreuz** *das* turnstile; **~maschine** *die* lathe; **~moment** *das* (Physik) torque; **~orgel** *die* barrel organ; **~ort** *der* (Film) location; **~pause** *die* (Film) break in shooting; **~punkt** *der* pivot; (eines Sturms) centre; **der ~- und Angelpunkt einer Sache** (fig.) the key element in sth.; **~restaurant** *das* revolving restaurant; **~schalter** *der* rotary switch; **~scheibe** *die* (Eisenb.) turntable; (fig.) hub; **~strom** *der* (Elektrot.) three-phase current; **~stuhl** *der* swivel chair; **~tag** *der* (Film) day of shooting; **~tür** *die* revolving door

Drehung *die;* **~, ~en** 1 turn; (um eine Achse) turn; rotation; revolution; (um einen Mittelpunkt) revolution; (sehr schnell) spin; (beim Motor) revolution; **eine halbe/ganze ~:** a half/complete turn; **eine ~ um 180° [machen]** [do] a 180° turn; (fig.) [do] a complete about-face 2 (das Drehen) turning; (sehr schnell) spinning

Dreh-: ~wurm *der* 1 *in* **einen** *od.* **den ~wurm kriegen/haben** (salopp) get/feel giddy; 2 (Finne) coenurus; **~zahl** *die* revolutions *or* (coll.) revs (*esp. per minute*); **bei einer bestimmten ~zahl** at a particular number of revolutions *or* (coll.) revs per minute; **~zahl·bereich** *der:* **im unteren/oberen ~zahlbereich** at lower/higher revs (coll.); **~zahl·messer** *der;* **~~s, ~~:** revolution counter; rev counter (coll.); tachometer

drei *Kardinalz.* ▸ⓘ **S. 29,** ▸ⓘ **S. 729,** ▸ⓘ **S. 826** three; **er isst/arbeitet für ~:** he eats enough for three/does the work of three people; **aller guten Dinge sind ~!** all good things come in threes; (nach zwei missglückten Versuchen) third time lucky!; **nicht bis ~ zählen können** (ugs.) be as thick as two [short] planks (Brit. coll.); be dead from the neck up (coll.); *s. auch* **acht**[1]; **heilig 1**

Drei *die;* **~, ~en** three; **eine ~ schreiben/bekommen** (Schulw.) get a C; *s. auch* **Acht**[1] **1, 2, 4, 5; Zwei 2**

drei-, Drei-: ~achser *der;* **~~s, ~~** (ugs.) three-axled vehicle; **~achtel·takt** *der* (Musik) three-eight time; **~ad[e]rig** *Adj.* (Elektrot.) three-core; **~akter** *der;* **~~s, ~~:** three-act play; **~bändig** *Adj.* three-volume; **~bein** *das* (ugs.) three-legged stool; **~beinig** *Adj.* three-legged; **~bett·zimmer** *das* room with three beds; **~blättrig** *Adj.* (Bot.) three-leaved; trifoliate (Bot.)

3-D-Brille /draiˈde:-/ *die* 3-D glasses *pl.*

3-D-Effekt *der* 3-D effect

drei-, Drei-: ~dimensional **A** *Adj.* three-dimensional; **B** *adv.* three-dimensionally; in three dimensions; **einen Film ~dimensional sehen** watch a film in 3-D; **~eck** *das* 1 (Geom.) triangle; **das Goldene ~eck** the Golden Triangle; 2 (bes. Fußball) top corner; **~eckig** *Adj.* triangular; three-cornered; **~ecks·verhältnis** *das* eternal triangle; **~ein·halb** *Bruchz.* ▸ⓘ **S. 826** three and a half; **~einig** *Adj. in* **der ~einige Gott** (christl. Rel.) the triune God[head]; **~einigkeit** *die* (christl. Rel.) trinity; **die Heilige ~einigkeit** the [Holy] Trinity

Dreier *der;* **~s, ~** 1 (ugs.) ▸**Drei** 2 (ugs.: im Lotto) three winning numbers 3 (hist.: Münze) three-pfennig piece 4 (Golf) threesome 5 (ugs.: Sprungbrett) three-metre board; *s. auch* **Achter 3, 4**

Dreier-: ~kombination *die* (Ski) Alpine combined event; **~reihe** *die* row of three; **~takt** *der* (Musik) triple time

dreierlei *indekl. Gattungsz.* 1 *attr.* three kinds *or* sorts of; three different ‹*sorts, kinds, sizes, possibilities*› 2 *subst.* three [different] things

drei-, Drei-: ~fach *Vervielfältigungsz.* triple; **die ~fache Menge** three times *or* triple the amount; three times as much; **ein ~fach[es] Hoch!** three cheers!; **ein ~fach verschnürtes Paket** a parcel tied three times; **~fach verstärkt** triple reinforced; *s. auch* **achtfach**; **~fache** *das; adj. Dekl.* **das ~fache essen/kosten** eat/cost three times as much; **das ~fache von 3 ist 9** three times three is nine; **auf ein ~faches** *od.* **auf das ~fache steigen** treble; triple; *s. auch* **Achtfache**; **~faltigkeit** /-ˈ---/ *die;* **~~** (christl. Rel.) Trinity; **~farben·druck** /-ˈ---/ *der; Pl.* **~~e** 1 (Verfahren) three-colour process; **im ~farbendruck [gedruckt]** printed by the three-colour process; 2 (einzelner Druck) three-colour print; **~felder·wirtschaft** /-ˈ----/ *die* three-field *or* three-course system; **~fuß** *der* 1 (für Kessel usw.) trivet; tripod; 2 (Schemel) three-legged stool; 3 (zum Besohlen) three-way last; **~gang·schaltung** *die* three-speed gearbox *or* gears *pl.* *or* (Amer.) gear shift; **~gespann** *das* team of three horses; (fig.: von Direktoren o. Ä.) triumvirate; **eine Kutsche mit ~gespann** a three-horse carriage; **das unzertrennliche ~gespann** (fig.) the inseparable trio *or* threesome; **~gestrichen** *Adj.* (Musik) **das ~gestrichene C** the C two octaves above middle C; **~gestrichene Oktave** three-line octave; **~groschen·heft** /-ˈ---/ *das* (abwertend) cheap novelette; dime novel (Amer.)

Dreiheit *die;* **~:** trinity

drei-, Drei-: ~hundert *Kardinalz.* ▸ⓘ **S. 826** three hundred; **~jährig** *Adj.* (3 Jahre alt) three-year-old *attrib.;* (3 Jahre dauernd) three-year *attrib.;* *s. auch* **achtjährig**; **~jährlich** **A** *Adj.* three-yearly; triennial; **B** *adv.* every three years; triennially; *s. auch* **achtjährlich**; **~kampf** *der* (Sport) triathlon; **~kantig** *Adj.* three-sided; triangular; **~kantstahl** *der* (Technik) triangular section steel [rod]; **~käse·hoch** /-ˈ---/ *der;* **~~s, ~~s** (ugs. scherzh.) [little] nipper (Brit. sl.); little kid (sl.); **~klang** *der* triad; **~klassen-**

wahlrecht /ˈ-ˈ---/ *das* (hist.) three-class franchise; **~könige** /ˈ-ˈ--/ *(das)*; **~~:** Epiphany *sing.*; **an** *od.* **zu/nach ~könige** at/after Epiphany; **~köpfig** *Adj.* ‹*family, crew*› of three; three-headed ‹*monster*›; **~ländereck** /ˈ-ˈ--/ *das: region where three countries meet;* **~mal** *Adv.* three times; *s. auch* **achtmal**; **~malig** *Adj.* **eine ~malige Warnung/Wiederholung** three warnings/repeats; *s. auch* **achtmalig**; **~meilen·zone** /ˈ-ˈ---/ *die* three-mile zone; **~meter·brett** /ˈ-ˈ--/ *das* three-metre board

drein (ugs.) ▸ **darein**

drein-: ~|blicken *itr. V.* **mürrisch** *usw.* **~blicken** look morose *etc.*; **~|finden** *unr. refl. V.* (ugs.) get used to things; **~|reden** *itr. V.* (ugs.) **jmdm. ~reden** (sich einmischen) interfere in sb.'s affairs; (jmdm. Vorschriften machen) tell sb. what to do; **~|schauen** *itr. V.* ▸ **~blicken**; **~|schlagen** *unr. itr. V.* (ugs.) lay into him/her/them *etc.* (coll.)

drei-, Drei-: ~phasen·strom /ˈ-ˈ---/ *der* (Elektrot.) three-phase current; **~polig** *Adj.* (Elektrot.) three-core ‹*cable*›; three-pin ‹*adapter*›; **~punkt·gurt** *der* lap and diagonal belt; **~rad** *das* [1] (Kinderfahrrad) tricycle; [2] (Kleintransporter) three-wheeled van; **~räd[e]rig** *Adj.* three-wheeled; **~satz** *der,* **~satz·rechnung** *die* rule of three; **~schiffig** *Adj.* (Archit.) with a nave and two aisles *postpos.*; **~seitig** *Adj.* three-sided ‹*figure*›; three-page ‹*letter, leaflet, etc.*›; **~sekunden·regel** /-ˈ----/ *die* (Sport) three-second rule; **~silbig** *Adj.* trisyllabic; three-syllable *attrib.*; **~spaltig** (Druckw.) **A** *Adj.* three-column; *s. auch* **achtspaltig**; **B** *adv.* ‹*printed, set*› in three columns; **~spänner** *der;* **~~s, ~~:** three-horse carriage; **~spitz** *der* (hist.) tricorn; three-cornered hat; **~sprachig** **A** *Adj.* trilingual; **B** *adv.* [1] **~sprachig erzogen werden** be brought up speaking three languages; [2] ‹*written*› in three languages; *s. auch* **zweisprachig**; **~sprung** *der* triple jump

dreißig /ˈdraisɪç/ *Kardinalz.* ▸ⓘ **S. 29**, ▸ⓘ **S. 826** thirty; *s. auch* **achtzig**

Dreißig *die;* **~:** thirty

dreißiger *indekl. Adj.* **ein ~ Jahrgang** a '30 vintage; **die ~ Jahre** the thirties

Dreißiger[1] *der;* **~s, ~** (30-jähriger) thirty-year-old; *s. auch* **Achtziger**[1] **2, 3**

Dreißiger[2] *die;* **~, ~** (ugs. Briefmarke): thirty-cent/centime *etc.* stamp

Dreißiger[3] *Pl.* thirties; **eine Frau in den ~n** a woman in her thirties

Dreißigerin *die;* **~, ~nen** ▸ **Dreißiger**[1]

Dreißiger·jahre *Pl.* ▸ⓘ **S. 29**, ▸ⓘ **S. 165** thirties *pl.*

dreißig-, Dreißig-: ~jährig *Adj.* (30 Jahre alt) thirty-year-old *attrib.*; (30 Jahre dauernd) thirty-year *attrib.*; **der ~jährige Krieg** the Thirty Years' War; *s. auch* **achtjährig**; **~jährige** *der/die; adj. Dekl.* thirty-year-old

dreißigst... /ˈdraisɪçst.../ *Ordinalz.* ▸ⓘ **S. 165**, ▸ⓘ **S. 826** thirtieth; *s. auch* **acht...**; **achtzigst...**

Dreißigstel *das;* **~s, ~** ▸ⓘ **S. 826** thirtieth

dreist /draist/
A *Adj.* brazen; barefaced ‹*lie*›
B *adv.* brazenly

drei·stellig *Adj.* three-figure *attrib.* ‹*number, sum*›; *s. auch* **achtstellig**

Dreistigkeit *die;* **~, ~en** [1] (Art) brazenness; **er besaß die ~, zu ...** he had the audacity *or* cheek to ... [2] (Handlung) brazen act; (Bemerkung) brazen remark

drei-, Drei-: ~stimmig **A** *Adj.* ‹*song*› for three voices; three-voice ‹*choir*›; three-part ‹*singing*›; **B** *adv.* ‹*sing*› in three voices; ‹*play*› in three parts; **~stöckig** **A** *Adj.* three-storey *attrib.*; *s. auch* **achtstöckig**; **B** *adv.* ‹*build*› three storeys high; **~stufen·rakete** /ˈ-ˈ----/ *die* three-stage rocket; **~stündig** *Adj.* three-hour *attrib.*; *s. auch* **achtstündig**; **~stündlich** **A** *Adj.* three-hourly; **B** *adv.* every three hours; **~tage·bart** *der* three-day stubble; **~tägig** *Adj.* (3 Tage alt) three-day-old *attrib.*; (3 Tage dauernd) three-day *attrib.*; *s. auch* **achttägig**; **~täglich** **A** *Adj.* **in ~täglichem Wechsel** on a three-day rota; **B** *adv.* every three days; **~tausend** *Kardinalz.* ▸ⓘ **S. 826** three thousand; **~tausender** *der* mountain more than three thousand metres high; **~teiler** *der* (Mode) three-piece suit; **~teilig** *Adj.* three-part *attrib.* ‹*documentary, novel, etc.*›; three-piece *attrib.* ‹*suit*›; **~teilig sein** be in three parts/consist of three pieces; ***~viertel** ▸ **viertel**; **~viertel·lang** /ˈ-ˈ-/ *Adj.* three-quarter-length; **~viertel·liter·flasche** /---ˈ---/ *die* three-quarter-litre bottle; **~viertel·mehrheit** /ˈ-ˈ---/ *die* three-quarters majority; **~viertel·stunde** /---ˈ--/ *die* three-quarters of an hour; **~viertel·takt** /ˈ-ˈ--/ *der* three-four time; **im ~vierteltakt** in three-four time; **~wege·katalysator** *der* (Kfz-W.) three-way catalytic converter; **~wertig** *Adj.* [1] (Chemie) trivalent; [2] (Sprachw.) three-place *attrib.*; **~wöchentlich** **A** *Adj.* three-weekly; **B** *adv.* every three weeks; *s. auch* **achtwöchentlich**; **~wöchig** *Adj.* (3 Wochen alt) three-week-old *attrib.*; (3 Wochen dauernd) three-week *attrib.*; **~zack** *der;* **~~s, ~~e** trident; **~zackig** *Adj.* three-pointed; **~zehn** *Kardinalz.* ▸ⓘ **S. 29**, ▸ⓘ **S. 729**, ▸ⓘ **S. 826** thirteen; **jetzt schlägts aber ~zehn!** (ugs.) that's going too far; *s. auch* **achtzehn**; **~zehn·hundert** ▸ⓘ **S. 826** *Kardinalz.* one thousand three hundred; thirteen hundred; **~zehnt...** *Ordinalz.* thirteenth; *s. auch* **acht**; **~zehntel** *das* thirteenth; **~zeilig** *Adj.* three-line *attrib.*; **~zeilig sein** have three lines; **~zimmer·wohnung** *die* three-room flat (esp. Brit.) *or* (esp. Amer.) apartment

Dresche /ˈdrɛʃə/ *die;* **~** (salopp) walloping (coll.); thrashing; **~ kriegen** get a walloping (coll.) *or* thrashing

dreschen
A *unr. tr. V.* [1] thresh [2] (salopp: prügeln) wallop (coll.); thrash [3] (salopp: schießen) wallop (coll.) ‹*ball*›; **den Ball ins Netz ~:** slam the ball into the net (coll.); *s. auch* **Skat**
B *unr. itr. V.* [1] thresh [2] (salopp: schlagen) thump; bang; **mit der Faust auf den Tisch ~:** bang one's fist on the table; pound *or* bang the table with one's fist

Drescher *der;* **~s, ~, Drescherin** *die;* **~, ~nen** thresher

Dresch-: ~flegel *der* flail; **~maschine** *die* threshing machine

Dresden /ˈdreːsdn̩/ *(das);* **~s** ▸ⓘ **S. 675** Dresden

Dresd[e]ner /ˈdreːsd(ə)nɐ/ ▸ⓘ **S. 675**
A *indekl. Adj.* Dresden
B *der;* **~s, ~:** native of Dresden; (Einwohner) inhabitant of Dresden; *s. auch* **Kölner**

Dresd[e]nerin *die;* **~, ~nen** ▸ **Dresd[e]ner B**

Dress, *Dreß /drɛs/ *der;* **~** *od.* **Dresses, Dresse;** *(österr. auch die;* **~, Dressen)** [1] (Sportkleidung) kit (Brit.); (Fußball, Hockey usw.) kit (Brit.); strip (Brit. coll.) [2] (ugs.: Kleidung) outfit

Dresseur /drɛˈsøːɐ̯/ *der;* **~s, ~e, Dresseurin** *die;* **~, ~nen** [animal] trainer

dressierbar *Adj.* trainable; **nicht/gut ~:** untrainable/easy to train

dressieren *tr. V.* [1] train ‹*animal*›; **darauf dressiert sein, etw. zu tun** be trained to do sth.; **der Hund ist auf den Mann dressiert** the dog is trained to attack people [2] (Kochk.) dress ‹*poultry, fish, game*›; decorate ‹*cake etc.*›; pipe ‹*icing, marzipan, etc.*›

Dressing /ˈdrɛsɪŋ/ *das;* **~s, ~s** dressing

Dressman /ˈdrɛsmən/ *der;* **~s, Dressmen** male model

Dressur /drɛˈsuːɐ̯/ *die;* **~, ~en** [1] training; (fig. abwertend) conditioning [2] (Kunststück) trick [3] (~reiten) dressage

Dressur-: ~pferd *das* dressage horse; **~prüfung** *die* (Reiten) dressage [test]; **~reiten** *das* dressage

dribbeln /ˈdrɪbl̩n/ *itr. V.* (Ballspiele) dribble [the ball]

Dribbling /ˈdrɪblɪŋ/ *das;* **~s, ~s** (Ballspiele) piece of dribbling; **seine Stärken sind Kopfball und ~:** his strengths are heading and dribbling

Drift /drɪft/ ▸ **Trift 1**

driften *itr. V.; mit sein* (auch fig.) drift

Drill[1] /drɪl/ *der;* **~[e]s** drilling; (Milit.) drill

Drill[2] *der;* **~s, ~e** ▸ **Drillich**

Drill·bohrer *der* drill

drillen *tr. V.* [1] (auch Milit.) drill; **auf etw.** *(Akk.)* **gedrillt sein** be well-drilled in sth.; **jmdn. auf Angriff ~:** train sb. to attack [2] (Landw.) drill [3] (bohren) drill ‹*hole*›

Drillich /ˈdrɪlɪç/ *der;* **~s, ~e** drill

Drillich·zeug *das* [heavy cotton twill] overalls *pl.*

Drilling /ˈdrɪlɪŋ/ *der;* **~s, ~e** [1] (Geschwister) triplet [2] (Gewehr) triple-barrelled shotgun

Drill·maschine *die* (Landw.) drill

drin /drɪn/ *Adv.* [1] (ugs.: darin) in it; **da könnte für mich was ~ sein** something might come out of it [for me]; **das ist/mehr als 2 000 Euro sind nicht ~:** that/any more than 2,000 euros is not on (Brit. coll.) *or* (Amer. coll.) is no go; **es ist noch alles ~** (bei einem Fußballspiel usw.) there's still everything to play for; **nach drei Tagen ist man wieder ~** (wieder eingearbeitet) after three days you're back in the swing of things; *s. auch* **darin** [2] (ugs.: ~nen) inside; **hier/da ~:** in here/there; *s. auch* **~nen**

dringen /ˈdrɪŋən/ *unr. itr. V.* [1] *mit sein* (gelangen) ‹*water, smell, etc.*› penetrate, come through; ‹*news*› get through; **in etw.** *(Akk.)* **~:** get into *or* penetrate sth.; **durch etw. ~:** come through *or* penetrate sth.; ‹*person*› push one's way through sth.; **die Nachricht ist nicht bis zu mir gedrungen** the news did not get through to me; **in** *od.* **an die Öffentlichkeit ~:** get out; become public knowledge [2] *mit sein* (geh.: einwirken) **in jmdn. ~:** press *or* urge sb.; **mit Fragen/Ermahnungen in jmdn. ~:** ply sb. with questions/press warnings on sb.; **sich gedrungen fühlen, etw. zu tun** (veralt.) feel obliged *or* compelled to do sth. [3] (fordern) **auf etw.** *(Akk.)* **~:** insist upon sth.

dringend
A *Adj.* [1] (eilig) urgent [2] (eindringlich, stark) urgent ‹*appeal*›; strong ‹*suspicion, advice*›; compelling ‹*need*›
B *adv.* [1] (sofort) urgently [2] (zwingend) ‹*recommend, advise, suspect*› strongly; **jmdn. ~ bitten, etw. zu tun** insist that sb. does sth.; **~ erforderlich sein** be imperative *or* essential

dringlich /ˈdrɪŋlɪç/
A *Adj.* urgent
B *adv.* urgently; **jmdn. ~ bitten, etw. zu tun** plead hard with sb. to do sth.

Dringlichkeit *die;* **~:** urgency

Dringlichkeits·antrag *der* (Parl.) emergency motion

Drink /drɪŋk/ *der;* **~s, ~s** drink

drinnen /ˈdrɪnən/ *Adv.* inside; (im Haus) indoors; inside; **von ~:** from inside/indoors; **nach ~ gehen** go in[side]/indoors; **~ im Haus** indoors; **hier/da ~:** in here/there

drin-: ~|sitzen *unr. itr. V.* (ugs.) be right in it (coll.); **~|stecken** *itr. V.* (ugs.) [1] (beschäftigt sein) **[bis über beide Ohren] in etw.** *(Dat.)* **~stecken** be up to one's ears in sth. (coll.); [2] (vorhanden sein) **ich bin überzeugt, dass viel in ihm ~steckt** I am convinced he has a lot in him; **da steckt nichts für dich ~:** there's nothing in it for you; **da steckt viel Arbeit ~:** there's a lot of work in that; [3] (voraussehen können) **da steckt man nicht ~:** there's no [way of] telling; **~|stehen** *unr. itr. V.; südd. auch mit sein* **in etw.** *(Dat.)* **~stehen** be in sth.

dritt /drɪt/ *in* **wir waren zu ~:** there were three of us; **eine Ehe zu ~:** a ménage à trois; *s. auch* **acht**[2]

dritt... *Ordinalz.* ▸ⓘ **S. 165**, ▸ⓘ **S. 826** third; **wer ist der Dritte im Bunde?** who is the third person?; **in Gegenwart Dritter** in the presence of other people; **ein Drittes wäre noch zu erwägen** there is a third point that ought to be considered; **wenn zwei sich streiten, freut sich der Dritte** (Spr.) when two people argue, somebody else benefits; **der lachende Dritte** the one to benefit (*from a dispute between two others*); *s. auch* **acht...**

dritt·best... *Adj.* third-best

***Drittel** das; ~s, ~e (veralt.), **Drittel** das, (schweiz. meist der); ~s, ~ ▸ⓘ **S. 826** third

dritteln tr. V. split or divide ‹cost, profit› three ways; divide ‹number› by three

***dritte·mal, *dritten·mal** ▸**Mal¹**

drittens Adv. thirdly

> **Drittes Programm**
>
> One of the eight regional television channels run by the **ARD** and focusing on regional affairs and educational programmes.

dritt-, Dritt-: ~größt... Adj. third-largest; **~höchst...** Adj. third-highest; **~klassig** Adj. (meist abwertend) third-class ‹hotel, railway carriage›; third-rate ‹actor, novel, artist›; **~klässler, *~kläßler** der; ~~s, ~~, **~klässlerin, *~kläßlerin** die; ~~, ~~nen third-former; **~letzt...** Adj. antepenultimate; **~platzierte** der/die; adj. Dekl. (Sport) third-placed finisher; **~schuldner** der, **~schuldnerin** die (Rechtsw.) garnishee

Drive /draif/ der; ~s, ~s (auch Jazz, Golf, Tennis) drive

Dr. jur. Abk. = **doctor juris** LL D; s. auch **Dr. phil.**

DRK Abk. = **Deutsches Rotes Kreuz** German Red Cross

Dr. med. Abk. = **doctor medicinae** MD; s. auch **Dr. phil.**

Dr. med. dent. Abk. = **doctor medicinae dentoriae** DMD; s. auch **Dr. phil.**

drob /drɔp/ ▸**darob**

droben /'dro:bn̩/ Adv. (südd., österr., sonst geh.) up there; **da/hier ~**: up there/here

dröge /'drø:gə/ (nordd.)
[A] Adj. (auch fig.) dry
[B] adv. drily

Droge /'dro:gə/ die; ~, ~n drug; **unter ~n stehen** be on drugs

drogen-, Drogen-: ~abhängig Adj. addicted to drugs postpos.; **~abhängig sein/werden** be/become a drug addict; **~abhängige** der/die; adj. Dekl. drug addict; **~abhängigkeit** die drug addiction; **~handel** der drug trafficking; **~händler** der, **~händlerin** die drug dealer; **~missbrauch**, ***~mißbrauch** der drug abuse; **~süchtig** Adj. ▸**~abhängig**; **~süchtige** der/die drug addict; **~szene** die drug scene; **~tote** der/die drug-related death

Drogerie /drogə'ri:/ die; ~, ~n chemist's [shop] (Brit.); drugstore (Amer.)

Drogist der; ~en, ~en, **Drogistin** die; ~, ~nen ▸ⓘ **S. 113** chemist (Brit.); druggist (Amer.)

Droh·brief der threatening letter

drohen /'dro:ən/ itr. V. threaten; **er drohte ihm mit erhobenem Zeigefinger** he raised a warning finger to him; **jmdm. mit etw. ~**: threaten sb. with sth.; **die Regierung hat mit dem Abbruch der diplomatischen Beziehungen gedroht** the government threatened to break off diplomatic relations; **den Angeklagten droht die Todesstrafe** the accused are threatened with the death penalty; **ein Gewitter drohte** a storm was threatening

drohend
[A] Adj. impending ‹danger, strike, disaster›; threatening ‹gesture, clouds›
[B] adv. threateningly

Droh-: ~gebärde die threatening gesture; **~kulisse** die threatening scenario

Drohn /dro:n/ der; ~en, ~en, **Drohne** die; ~e, ~en drone

dröhnen /'drø:nən/ itr. V. [1] ‹voice, music› boom; ‹machine› roar; ‹room etc.› resound (**von** with); **~der Applaus** thunderous applause; **er brach in ~des Gelächter aus** he roared with laughter; **mir dröhnt der Schädel** (ugs.) my head's ringing [2] (Drogenjargon: Rausch verursachen) **das dröhnt** it gives you a high (coll.)

Dröhnung die; ~, ~en (Drogenjargon) [1] (Dosis) fix (sl.) [2] (Rausch) high (coll.)

Drohung die; ~, ~en threat; **eine ~ wahr machen** carry out a threat

drollig /'drɔlɪç/
[A] Adj. [1] (spaßig) funny; comical; (niedlich) sweet; cute (Amer.) [2] (seltsam) odd; peculiar; **werde nicht ~**: don't get funny
[B] adv. [1] (spaßig) comically; (niedlich) sweetly; cutely (Amer.) [2] (seltsam) oddly; peculiarly

Dromedar /'dro:meda:ɐ̯/ das; ~s, ~e dromedary

Drops /drɔps/ der od. das; ~, ~: fruit or (Brit.) acid drop; **saurer** od. **saures ~**: acid drop (Brit.); sour ball (Amer.)

drosch /drɔʃ/ 1. u. 3. Pers. Sg. Prät. v. **dreschen**

Droschke /'drɔʃkə/ die; ~, ~n [1] hackney carriage [2] (veralt.: Taxi) [taxi] cab

Droschken-: ~kutscher der hackney coachman; **~platz** der (Amtsspr.) taxi rank

Drossel¹ /'drɔsl̩/ die; ~, ~n thrush

Drossel² die; ~, ~n (Technik) ▸**~spule**, **~ventil**

Drossel·klappe die (Technik) throttle or butterfly valve

drosseln tr. V. [1] turn down ‹heating, air conditioning›; throttle back ‹engine›; reduce or restrict the flow of ‹steam, air›; check ‹flow› [2] (herabsetzen) reduce; cut back or down; reduce ‹speed›

Drossel·spule die (Elektrot.) choking coil

Drosselung die; ~, ~en ▸**drosseln**: turning down; throttling back; reduction or restriction of the flow; checking; reduction; cutback

Drossel·ventil das (Technik) throttle valve

Dr. phil. Abk. = **doctor philosophiae** Dr; **~ Hans Schulz** Dr Hans Schulz; Hans Schulz, Ph. D.; **sie ist ~, nicht Dr. med.** she is a Ph. D. or a Doctor of Philosophy, not a Doctor of Medicine

Dr. rer. nat. Abk. = **doctor rerum naturalium** Doctor of Natural Science

Dr. rer. pol. Abk. = **doctor rerum politicarum** Doctor of Political Science

Dr. theol. Abk. = **doctor theologiae** DD

drüben /'dry:bn̩/ Adv. [1] **dort** od. **da ~**: over there; **~ auf der anderen Seite** over on the other side [2] (in der DDR) in the East; (in der Bundesrepublik, in West-Berlin) in the West; **von ~ kommen** come from across the border/sea etc.

drüber /'dry:bɐ/ (ugs.) ▸**darüber**

drüber- (ugs.) ▸**darüber**

Druck¹ /drʊk/ der; ~[e]s, **Drücke** /'drʏkə/ [1] (Physik) pressure; **einen ~ im Kopf/Magen haben** (fig.) have a feeling of pressure in one's head/stomach [2] (das Drücken) **ein ~ auf den Knopf** a touch of or on the button [3] (Zwang) pressure; **auf jmdn. ~ ausüben** put pressure on sb.; **unter ~ stehen/handeln** be/act under pressure; **jmdn. unter ~ setzen** put pressure on sb.; **~ dahinter machen** (ugs.) put some pressure on; **in** od. **im ~ sein** (ugs.) be under pressure of time [4] Pl. **~s** (Drogenjargon: Injektion) fix (sl.); **sich** (Dat.) **einen ~ setzen** give oneself a fix (sl.)

Druck² der; ~[e]s, ~e [1] (das ~en) printing; (Art des Druckens) print; **in ~ gehen** go to press; **etw. in ~ geben** send sth. to press; **~ und Verlag Meier & Sohn** printed and published by Meier and Son; **im ~ erscheinen** appear in print; **im ~ sein** be being printed [2] (Bild, Grafik usw.) print [3] Pl. (fachspr.) **~s** (Textilw.) print [4] (~schrift) printed work; **frühe persische ~e** early printed works from Persia

Druck-: ~ab·fall der (Physik) drop or fall in pressure; **~an·zug** der pressure suit; **~anstieg** der (Physik) rise or increase in pressure; **~ausgleich** der (Physik, Med.) (Vorgang) equalization of pressure; (Zustand) balance of pressure; **~blei·stift** der propelling pencil; **~bogen** der printed sheet; **~buch·stabe** der block letter or capital

Drückeberger /'drʏkəbɛrgɐ/ der; ~s, ~ (ugs. abwertend) shirker

Drückebergerei die; ~ (ugs. abwertend) shirking

Drückebergerin die; ~, ~nen ▸**Drückeberger**

druck·empfindlich Adj. pressure-sensitive ‹material›; easily bruised ‹fruit›; ‹area of the body› sensitive to pressure

drucken tr., itr. V. print

drücken /'drʏkn̩/
[A] tr. V. [1] (pressen) press; press, push ‹button›; **jmdm. die Hand ~**: squeeze sb.'s hand; **jmdn. zur Seite/an die Wand ~**: push sb. aside/against the wall; **jmdn. ans Herz** od. **an sich** (Akk.) **~**: clasp sb. to one's breast; **jmdm. etw. in die Hand ~**: press sth. into sb.'s hand [2] (heraus~) squeeze ‹juice, pus› (**aus** out of) [3] (liebkosen) **jmdn. ~**: hug [and squeeze] sb. [4] (Druck verursachen, quetschen) ‹shoe, corset, bandage, etc.› pinch [5] (geh.: be~) ‹conscience› weigh heavily [up]on sb.; **jmds. Stimmung ~**: depress sb.'s spirits [6] (herabsetzen) push or force down ‹price, rate›; depress ‹sales›; bring down ‹standard›; **den Rekord ~**: beat or break the record; **den Rekord um zwei Sekunden ~**: take two seconds off the record [7] (Kartenspiel) discard [8] (Gewichtheben) press [9] (Drogenjargon: injizieren) **sich** (Dat.) **einen Schuss ~**: give oneself a fix (sl.)
[B] itr. V. [1] press; **auf den Knopf ~**: press or push the button; **„bitte ~"** 'push'; **die Hitze drückt** od. **ist ~d** (fig.) the heat is oppressive; **das drückte auf die Stimmung/unsere gute Laune** (fig.) it spoilt the atmosphere/dampened our spirits; s. auch **Tränendrüse** [2] (Druck verursachen) ‹shoe, corset, bandage› pinch; **der Rucksack drückt** the rucksack is pressing or digging into me [3] (herabsetzen) **auf etw.** (Akk.) **~**: push or force sth. down [4] (Drogenjargon) fix (sl.)
[C] refl. V. [1] **sich in die Ecke ~**: squeeze [oneself] into the corner; **die Kinder drückten sich ängstlich in die Ecke** the children huddled frightened in the corner; **sich aus dem Saal ~**: slip out of the hall [2] (ugs.) shirk; **sich vor etw.** (Dat.) **~**: get out of or dodge sth.; **sich vor einer Pflicht/Verantwortung/Aussprache ~**: shirk a duty/responsibility/avoid a frank discussion; **sich vor der Arbeit/ums Bezahlen ~**: get out of or avoid doing any work/paying

drückend Adj. [1] burdensome ‹responsibility›; grinding ‹poverty›; heavy ‹debt, taxes›; serious ‹worries› [2] (schwül) oppressive

Drucker der; ~s, ~ ▸ⓘ **S. 113** printer

Drücker der; ~s, ~ [1] (Tür~) handle; (eines Schnappschlosses) latch; (Abzug am Gewehr) trigger; **auf den letzten ~** (ugs.) at the very last minute [2] (Knopf) [push-]button; (Klingelknopf) [bell] push; **am ~ sitzen** od. **sein** (fig. ugs.) be in charge [3] (ugs.: Werber) hawker of magazine subscriptions [4] (ugs.: Unterton, Nuance) touch

Druckerei die; ~, ~en printing works; (Firma) printing house; printer's

Druckerei·arbeiter der, **Druckerei·arbeiterin** die print worker

Drucker·farbe die ▸**Druckfarbe**

Druckerin die; ~, ~nen ▸ⓘ **S. 113** printer

Drückerin die; ~, ~nen ▸**Drücker 3**

Druck·erlaubnis die permission to print; **die ~ verweigern** refuse to allow the book/article etc. to be printed

Drucker-: ~presse die ▸**Druckmaschine**; **~schwärze** die printer's or printing ink; **~sprache** die printers' terminology; **~zeichen** das printer's mark

druck-, Druck-: ~erzeugnis das piece of printed matter; **~erzeugnisse** printed matter sing.; **~fahne** die galley proof; **~farbe** die printer's or printing ink; **~fehler** der misprint; printer's error; **~fehler·teufel** der (scherzh.) misprint gremlin; **~fertig** Adj. ready for press pred.; **~fest** Adj. pressure-resistant; **~form** die [type] forme; **~frisch** Adj. hot off the press postpos.; **~grafik**, **~graphik** die (Kunstwiss.) graphic reproduction; **~kabine** die pressurized cabin; **~knopf** der [1] press stud (Brit.); snap fastener; [2] (an Geräten) push-button; **~kosten** Pl. printing costs

Drucklegung die; ~, ~en printing; **die ~** od. **mit der ~ beginnen** go to press

druck-, Druck-: ~luft *die* (Physik) compressed air; **~luft·bremse** *die* air brake; **~maschine** *die* printing press; **~messer** *der;* **~~s, ~~:** pressure gauge; **~mittel** *das* means of bringing pressure to bear (**gegenüber** on); **~papier** *das* printing paper; **~platte** *die* [printing] plate; **~posten** *der* (ugs.) cushy job (coll.); **~pumpe** *die* (Technik) pressure pump; **~punkt** *der* 1▸ (bei Waffen) first trigger pressure; 2▸ (bei Flugzeugen) centre of pressure; **~raum** *der* (Jargon) [safe] injection room; **~reif** A *Adj.* ready for publication; (~fertig) ready for press; (fig.) polished, perfectly formulated ‹*phrase, reply*›; B *adv.* ‹*speak*› in a polished manner; **~sache** *die* 1▸ (Postw.) printed matter; 2▸ (Druckw.) printed stationery; **~schrift** *die* 1▸ block letters *pl.*; 2▸ (Schriftart) type[face]; 3▸ (Schriftwerk) pamphlet

drucksen /ˈdrʊksn̩/ *itr. V.* (ugs.) hum and haw (coll.)

druck-, Druck-: ~stelle *die* mark (*where pressure has been applied*); (an Obst) bruise; **die ~stelle von der Zahnklammer** the tender spot where the brace has/had been pressing; **~stock** *der* block; **~taste** *die* push-button; **~technisch** A *Adj.* printing *attrib.* ‹*process*›; **ein ~technisches Problem** a problem from the point of view of printing; B *adv.* from the point of view of printing; **~type** *die* type; **~verband** *der* pressure bandage; **~verfahren** *das* printing process; **~vorlage** *die* printer's copy; **~wasserreaktor** *der* pressurized-water reactor; **~welle** *die* (Physik) shock wave; **~werk** *das* publication; printed work; **~wesen** *das* printing; **~zylinder** *der* (Fotoreproduktion) printing cylinder; (Offset~) impression cylinder

Drude /ˈdruːdə/ *die;* **~, ~n** (Myth.): *nocturnal female spirit that causes nightmares*

Druden·fuß *der* pentagram

druff /drʊf/ (ugs. landsch.) ▸ **drauf**

Druide /druˈiːdə/ *der;* **~n, ~n** (hist.) Druid

drum /drʊm/ *Adv.* (ugs.) 1▸ ▸ **darum** 2▸ [a]round; **um etw. ~ herum** [all] [a]round sth.; **ein Haus mit einem Garten ~:** a house with a garden [a]round it; **~ rumreden** beat about *or* (Amer.) around the bush; **eben ~:** that's precisely why; **seis ~:** never mind; [that's] too bad; **alles, was ~ und dran ist** *od.* **hängt** all the things that go with it; (bei einer Sachlage) all the circumstances; **alles** *od.* **das [ganze] Drum und Dran** (bei einer Mahlzeit) all the trimmings; (bei einer Feierlichkeit) all the palaver that goes with it (coll.)

drum- (ugs.) ▸ **darum-**

Drum·herum *das;* **~s** everything that goes/went with it

Drummer /ˈdramɐ/ *der;* **~s, ~, Drummerin** *die;* **~, ~nen** (Musik) drummer

Drums /drams/ *Pl.* (Musik) drums; **an den ~:** on [the] drums

drunten /ˈdrʊntn̩/ *Adv.* (südd., österr.) down there

drunter /ˈdrʊntɐ/ *Adv.* (ugs.) underneath; **es** *od.* **alles geht ~ und drüber** everything is topsy-turvy; things are completely chaotic; **das Drunter und Drüber** the confusion

drunter- (ugs.) ▸ **darunter-**

Drusch /drʊʃ/ *der;* **~[e]s, ~e** 1▸ threshing 2▸ (Ertrag) threshed corn; grain

Druse[1] /ˈdruːzə/ *der;* **~n, ~n** Druze

Druse[2] *die;* **~, ~n** 1▸ (Geol.) geode; druse 2▸ (Pferdekrankheit) strangles *sing.*

Drüse /ˈdryːzə/ *die;* **~, ~n** gland

Drüsen-: ~funktion *die* glandular function; **~schwellung** *die* glandular swelling

Drusin *die;* **~, ~nen** ▸ **Druse**[1]

drusisch *Adj.* Druze

DSB *Abk.* **= Deutscher Sportbund**

Dschihad /dʒiˈhat/ *der;* **~[s]** jihad

Dschingis Khan /ˈdʒɪŋɡɪsˈkaːn/ (*der*) Genghis Khan

Dschungel /ˈdʒʊŋl̩/ *der;* **~s, ~** (auch fig.) jungle; (von Konflikten, Leidenschaften) tangle

Dschungel-: ~fieber *das* jungle yellow fever; **~krieg** *der* jungle war; (Kriegsführung) jungle warfare

Dschunke /ˈdʒʊŋkə/ *die;* **~, ~n** junk

DSF *Abk.* (DDR) **= Gesellschaft für Deutsch-Sowjetische Freundschaft**

DSG *Abk.* **= Deutsche Schlafwagen- und Speisewagen-Gesellschaft**

dt. *Abk.* **= deutsch** G.

Dtzd. *Abk.* **= Dutzend** doz.

du /duː/ *Personalpron.; 2. Pers. Sg. Nom.* you; thou (arch.); **Du zueinander sagen** use the familiar form in addressing one another; say 'du' to each other; **[mit jmdm.] per Du sein** be on familiar terms *or* use the familiar form of address [with sb.]; **mit jmdm. auf Du und Du stehen** be on familiar terms with sb.; **~ Glücklicher/Idiot!** you lucky thing/you idiot!; **unser Vater, der ~ bist im Himmel** (bibl.) our Father which art in Heaven; **~, ich kann nicht länger warten** [listen,] I can't wait any longer; **du bist es** it's 'you; **mach du das doch** 'you do it; ▸ *auch* (*Gen.*) **deiner,** (*Dat.*) **dir,** (*Akk.*) **dich**

Du *das;* **~[s], ~[s]** 'du' *no art.;* the familiar form 'du'; **jmdm. das ~ anbieten** suggest to sb. that he/she use [the familiar form] 'du' *or* the familiar form of address

dual /duˈaːl/ *Adj.* dual

Dual *der;* **~s, ~e, Dualis** /duˈaːlɪs/ *der;* **~, Duale** (Sprachw.) dual

> **Duales System**
>
> This is a waste disposal and recycling system which was introduced in Germany in 1993 and is operated by the private company *DSD*. All packaging materials marked with the **Grüner Punkt** symbol are collected separately, and sorted into plastics, glass, paper, and metal for recycling. Non-recyclable and compostable waste is still collected by the local refuse collection service.

Dualismus *der;* **~** (Philos., geh.) dualism

dualistisch *Adj.* (Philos., geh.) dualistic

Dualität /dualiˈtɛːt/ *die;* **~:** duality

Dual·system *das* (Math.) binary system

Dub /dap/ *der;* **~[s]** (Mus.) dub

Dübel /ˈdyːbl̩/ *der;* **~s, ~:** plug; (Holz~) dowel

dübeln *tr. V.* **etw. ~:** fix sth. using a plug/plugs

dubios /duˈbi̯oːs/, **dubiös** /duˈbi̯øːs/ *Adj.* (geh.) dubious; **ich finde es ~, dass ...:** I find it suspicious that ...

Dublee /duˈbleː/ *das;* **~s, ~s** rolled gold [plate]

Dublette /duˈblɛtə/ *die;* **~, ~n** 1▸ duplicate 2▸ (bei Edelsteinen) doublet 3▸ (Boxen) one-two

dublieren /duˈbliːrən/ *tr. V.* 1▸ plate with gold 2▸ (Spinnerei) double; ply 3▸ (Kunstwiss.) reline

ducken /ˈdʊkn̩/
A *refl. V.* duck; (fig. abwertend) humble oneself (**vor** + *Dat.* before); (vor Angst) cower; **sich vor jmds. Fäusten ~:** duck to avoid sb.'s fists
B *tr. V.* 1▸ duck ‹*head [and shoulders]*› 2▸ (abwertend) (einschüchtern) intimidate; (demütigen) humiliate
C *itr. V.* humble oneself (**vor** + *Dat.* before)

Duckmäuser /ˈdʊkmɔyzɐ/ *der;* **~s, ~, Duckmäuserin** *die;* **~, ~nen** (abwertend) moral coward

duckmäuserisch (abwertend)
A *Adj.* ‹*behaviour etc.*› showing moral cowardice
B *adv.* ‹*behave*› in a way that shows moral cowardice

Duckmäusertum *das;* **~s** (abwertend) moral cowardice

Dudelei *die;* **~, ~en** (ugs. abwertend) (auf einem Blasinstrument) tootling; (aus dem Radio, Fernsehen usw.) drone; droning

Dudel·kasten *der* (salopp abwertend) (Radio) radio; (Plattenspieler) record player

dudeln /ˈduːdl̩n/
A *tr. V.* (auf Blasinstrument) tootle; (singen) sing tunelessly
B *itr. V.* ‹*radio, television, etc.*› drone on; ‹*barrel organ*› grind away

Dudel·sack *der* bagpipes *pl.*

Dudelsack·pfeifer *der;* **~s, ~, Dudelsack·pfeiferin** *die;* **~, ~nen** piper; bagpipe player

Duell /duˈɛl/ *das;* **~s, ~e** 1▸ duel; **jmdn. zum ~ [heraus]fordern** challenge sb. to a duel; **ein ~ auf Pistolen** a duel with pistols 2▸ (Sport) contest (*Gen.* between) 3▸ (Wortgefecht) duel of words

Duellant /duɛˈlant/ *der;* **~en, ~en** duellist

duellieren *refl. V.* fight a duel (**um** over)

Duett /duˈɛt/ *das;* **~[e]s, ~e** 1▸ (Musik) duet; **im ~ singen** sing a duet; **etw. im ~ singen** sing sth. as a duet; **im ~ schreien/heulen** (fig. ugs.) scream/weep in unison 2▸ (Duo, Paar) duo; pair

Dufflecoat /ˈdafəlkoʊt/ *der;* **~s, ~s** duffle coat

-duft *der:* **Flieder~/Veilchen~/Jasmin~** *usw.* scent of lilac/violets/jasmine *etc.*

Duft /dʊft/ *der;* **~[e]s, Düfte** /ˈdʏftə/ 1▸ pleasant smell; scent; (Zool.) scent; (von Parfüm, Blumen) scent; fragrance; (von Kaffee, frischem Brot, Tabak) aroma; (iron.) beautiful smell (iron.); **den ~ der großen, weiten Welt schnuppern** (fig.) get a taste of the big, wide world 2▸ (schweiz.: Raureif) hoar frost

Düftchen /ˈdʏftçən/ *das;* **~s, ~:** pleasant aroma *or* smell; (iron.) beautiful whiff *or* smell

Duft·drüse *die* (Zool.) scent gland

dufte /ˈdʊftə/ (ugs.)
A *Adj.* great (coll.)
B *adv.* ‹*dressed, behave*› smashingly (coll.); ‹*taste*› great (coll.)

duften /ˈdʊftn̩/ *itr. V.* smell (**nach** of); **nicht ~:** not smell; have no smell; **die Rosen ~ gut** the roses smell lovely *or* have a lovely scent; **es duftet nach Kaffee** it smells of coffee; there's a smell of coffee

duftend *Adj.* sweet-smelling; fragrant; **angenehm/stark ~:** pleasant-/strong-smelling

duftig *Adj.* 1▸ gossamer-fine ‹*dress, material*›; soft and fine ‹*hair*› 2▸ (dichter.) hazy

Duft-: ~kerze *die* scented candle; **~marke** *die* (Zool.) scent mark; **~note** *die* fragrance; **~öl** *das* aromatic oil; **~stoff** *der* 1▸ (Biol.) scent; 2▸ (bei Kosmetika) aromatic substance *or* essence; **~wasser** *das; Pl.* **~wässer** 1▸ (scherzh.: Parfüm) perfume; scent; 2▸ (Eau de Toilette) toilet water; **~wolke** *die* cloud of perfume

duhn /duːn/ ▸ **dun**

Dukaten /duˈkaːtn̩/ *der;* **~s, ~** (hist.) ducat

Dukaten-: ~esel *der* (ugs. scherzh.) **ein ~esel sein** be made of money; **~gold** *das* fine gold; **~scheißer** *der* (salopp) ▸ **~esel**

Duktus /ˈdʊktʊs/ *der;* **~** (geh.) characteristic style; (eines Gemäldes) characteristic lines *pl. or* style; (einer Handschrift) characteristic shape *or* appearance

dulden /ˈdʊldn̩/
A *tr. V.* 1▸ tolerate; put up with; **keinen Widerspruch ~:** tolerate *or* (literary) brook no contradiction; **die Arbeit duldet keinen Aufschub** the work will admit no delay 2▸ (Aufenthalt gestatten) **jmdn. ~:** tolerate *or* put up with sb.'s presence; **er war nur geduldet** his presence was only tolerated; he was here/there only on sufferance 3▸ (geh.: er~) endure
B *itr. V.* (geh.) suffer

Dulder *der;* **~s, ~, Dulderin** *die;* **~, ~nen** patient sufferer

Dulder·miene *die* (iron.) martyred expression; **mit ~:** with a martyred expression

duldsam /ˈdʊltzaːm/
A *Adj.* tolerant (**gegen** towards); (geduldig) patient
B *adv.* tolerantly; (geduldig) patiently

Duldsamkeit *die;* **~:** tolerance; (Geduld) patience

Duldung *die;* **~:** toleration; **stillschweigende ~:** tacit permission; connivance

Dumdum /ˈdʊmˈdʊm/ *das;* **~s, ~s, Dumdum·geschoss, *Dumdum·geschoß** *das* dumdum [bullet]

dumm /dʊm/, **dümmer** /ˈdʏmɐ/, **dümmst...** /ˈdʏmst.../

A *Adj.* **1** (nicht intelligent) stupid; stupid, thick, dense ‹*person*›; **jmdn. wie einen ~en Jungen behandeln** treat sb. like a stupid child; **[nicht] so ~ sein, wie man aussieht** [not] be as stupid as one looks; **sich ~ stellen** act stupid; **~ geboren, nichts dazugelernt** (salopp) stupid idiot! (coll.); **sich nicht für ~ verkaufen lassen** (ugs.) not be taken in; **du willst mich wohl für ~ verkaufen!** you're trying to have me on (Brit. coll.) *or* (Amer. coll.) put me on; **sich ~ und dämlich** *od.* **dusselig reden/verdienen/essen** (ugs.) talk till one is blue in the face/earn a fortune/ eat oneself silly **2** (unvernünftig) foolish; stupid; daft; **so etwas Dummes!** how stupid! **3** (ugs.: töricht, albern) idiotic; silly; stupid; **eine ~e Gans** a silly goose; **das ist mir [einfach] zu ~** (ugs.) I've had enough of it **4** (ugs.: unangenehm) nasty ‹*feeling, suspicion*›; annoying ‹*habit*›; awful (coll.) ‹*experience, business, coincidence*›; **so etwas Dummes!** how annoying!; **mir ist etwas Dummes passiert** something awful happened to me (coll.) **5** (ugs.: benommen) **mir ist ganz ~ im Kopf** my head is swimming

B *adv.* **1** (ugs.: töricht) foolishly; stupidly; **frag nicht so ~:** don't ask such silly *or* stupid questions **2** (ugs.: unangenehm) ‹*end*› badly *or* unpleasantly; **jmdm. ~ kommen** be cheeky *or* insolent to sb.

Dumm·beutel *der* (ugs. abwertend) nitwit (coll.); blockhead

Dummchen /ˈdʊmçən/ *das;* **~s, ~** ▸**Dummerchen**

dumm·dreist

A *Adj.* brashly impertinent

B *adv.* in a brashly impertinent manner

Dumme *der/die; adj. Dekl.* fool; **einen ~n finden, der etw. macht** find somebody stupid enough to do sth.; **die ~n werden nicht alle** there's one born every minute; **der ~ sein** (ugs.) be the loser

Dumme·jungen·streich *der* (ugs.) silly prank

Dummen·fang *der* (abwertend) duping of unsuspecting people; **auf ~ gehen/aus sein** go looking/be out looking for unsuspecting people to dupe

Dummerchen /ˈdʊmɐçən/ *das;* **~s, ~** (fam.) nitwit (coll.); ninny; silly little boy/girl

dummer·weise *Adv.* **1** (leider) unfortunately; (ärgerlicherweise) annoyingly; irritatingly **2** (törichterweise) foolishly; like a fool; stupidly

Dummheit *die;* **~, ~en** **1** stupidity; **wenn ~ weh täte, müsste er den ganzen Tag schreien** (salopp) he's as thick as two short planks (Brit. coll.) *or* (Amer.) as dumb as an ox **2** (unkluge Handlung) stupid *or* foolish thing; **es war eine große ~, deine Warnung nicht ernst zu nehmen** it was extremely stupid not to heed your warning; **[mach] keine ~en!** don't do anything stupid *or* foolish; **lauter** *od.* **nur ~en im Kopf haben** have a head full of silly ideas

Dumm·kopf *der* (ugs.) nitwit (coll.); [silly] fool *or* idiot; blockhead

dümmlich /ˈdʏmlɪç/

A *Adj.* simple-minded

B *adv.* ‹*grin, smile*› [rather] foolishly *or* stupidly

Dümmling /ˈdʏmlɪŋ/ *der;* **~s, ~e** (ugs.) dimwit (coll.)

Dumm·schwätzer *der,* **Dumm·schwätzerin** *die* (ugs. abwertend) driveller; **ein ~ sein** talk a load of rubbish

Dumms·dorf (*das*) (scherzh.) **ich bin doch nicht aus ~!** I wasn't born yesterday!; **du bist wohl aus ~!** you must be stupid!

dümpeln /ˈdʏmpl̩n/ *itr. V.* (Seemannsspr.) roll [gently]

dumpf /dʊmpf/

A *Adj.* **1** dull ‹*thud, rumble of thunder*›; muffled ‹*sound, thump*› **2** (muffig) musty **3** (stumpfsinnig) dull; dull and expressionless ‹*look*›; numb ‹*indifference*›; stifling ‹*small-town atmosphere*› **4** (undeutlich) dull ‹*pain, anger*›; dim ‹*memory, recollection*›; vague, hazy ‹*conception, idea*› **5** (veralt.: benommen) dazed; stupefied ‹*half-sleep*›

B *adv.* **1** ‹*echo*› hollowly; **~ auf etw.** (*Akk.*) **aufschlagen** land with a dull thud on sth. **2** (stumpfsinnig) apathetically; numbly; **~ vor sich hin blicken** gaze dully *or* apathetically into space **3** (undeutlich) vaguely ‹*remember*›

Dumpfheit *die;* **~** **1** (Stumpfsinn) torpor; apathy **2** (Benommenheit) numbness

dumpfig *Adj.* (muffig) musty; (moderig) fusty; mouldy; (stickig) stuffy ‹*atmosphere*›

Dumping /ˈdampɪŋ/ *das;* **~s** (Wirtsch.) dumping

Dumping·preis *der* dumping price

dun /duːn/ *Adj.* (nordd. salopp) plastered (sl.); well oiled (coll.)

Düne /ˈdyːnə/ *die;* **~, ~n** [sand] dune

Dung /dʊŋ/ *der;* **~[e]s** dung; manure

Dünge·mittel *das* fertilizer

düngen /ˈdʏŋən/

A *tr. V.* fertilize ‹*soil, lawn, etc.*›; spread fertilizer on ‹*field*›; scatter fertilizer around ‹*plants*›

B *itr. V.* ‹*person*› put on fertilizer; **gut ~** ‹*substance*› be a good fertilizer

Dünger *der;* **~s, ~:** fertilizer

Dung·haufen *der* dunghill; dung *or* manure heap

Düngung *die;* **~, ~en** **1** use of fertilizers; **die ~ mit Chemikalien** the use of chemical fertilizers **2** (Dünger) fertilizer

dunkel /ˈdʊŋkl̩/

A *Adj.* **1** dark; **es wird ~:** it's getting dark; **es wird um 22 h ~:** it gets dark about 10 o'clock; **im Dunkeln** in the dark; **im Dunkeln bleiben** (fig.) ‹*person*› remain unidentified; ‹*sb.'s identity etc.*› remain a mystery; ‹*future events*› remain uncertain; **im Dunkeln tappen** (fig.) grope around *or* about in the dark **2** (unerfreulich) dark ‹*chapter in one's life*›; black ‹*day*›; darker ‹*side of life*› **3** (fast schwarz) dark; **dunkles Brot** brown bread; **dunkles Bier** dark beer (darker than bitter); **eine dunkle Brille** dark glasses *pl.* **4** (tief) deep ‹*voice, note*› **5** (unbestimmt) vague; dim, faint, vague ‹*recollection*›; dark ‹*hint, foreboding, suspicion*›; **in dunkler Vorzeit** in the dim and distant past; **jmdn. [über etw.** (*Akk.*)**] im Dunkeln lassen** (fig.) leave sb. in the dark [about sth.] **6** (abwertend: zweifelhaft) dubious; shady; **dunkle Geschäfte machen** be involved in shady transactions *or* deals

B *adv.* **1** (tief) ‹*speak*› in a deep voice **2** (unbestimmt) vaguely; ‹*remember*› vaguely, dimly

Dunkel *das;* **~s** **1** (geh.) darkness; **im ~ der Nacht** (geh.) in the darkness of the night **2** (Rätselhaftigkeit) obscurity, mystery (**um** surrounding); **in ~ gehüllt sein** be shrouded in mystery

Dünkel /ˈdʏŋkl̩/ *der;* **~s** (geh. abwertend) (Überheblichkeit) arrogance; haughtiness; (Einbildung) conceit[edness]; **einen ungeheuren ~ haben** be immensely arrogant *or* conceited

dunkel-: **~äugig** *Adj.* dark-eyed; **~blau** *Adj.* dark blue; **~blond** *Adj.* light brown ‹*hair*›; ‹*person*› with light brown hair; **~blond sein** have light brown hair; **~braun** *Adj.* dark brown; **~grau** *Adj.* dark grey; **~grün** *Adj.* dark green; **~haarig** *Adj.* dark-haired

dünkelhaft

A *Adj.* (überheblich) arrogant; haughty; (eingebildet) conceited

B *adv.* (hochmütig) arrogantly; haughtily; (eingebildet) conceitedly

Dunkel·haft *die* confinement in a darkened cell

dunkel·häutig *Adj.* dark-skinned

Dunkelheit *die;* **~** **1** darkness; **bei ~:** during the hours of darkness; **bei Einbruch der ~:** at nightfall; *s. auch* **Einbruch** **2** (geh.: dunkle Tönung) darkness

Dunkel-: **~kammer** *die* darkroom; **~mann** *der* (abwertend) **1** shady character; **2** (veralt.: Obskurant) obscurantist

dunkeln

A *itr. V.* **1** (unpers.) **es dunkelt** (geh.) it is growing dark **2** *mit sein* grow *or* go darker; darken **3** (dichter.) ‹*evening, night*› fall

B *tr. V.* make darker; darken

dunkel-, Dunkel-: **~rot** *Adj.* dark red; (tiefrot) deep red; **~werden** *das;* **~~s** nightfall; **vor dem ~werden** before nightfall; **~ziffer** *die* number of unrecorded cases

dünken /ˈdʏŋkn̩/ (geh. veralt.)

A *unr. tr. V.* **mich dünkt, er hat Recht** methinks he is right (arch.)

B *refl. V.* **er dünkt sich etwas Besseres/ein Held [zu sein]** he regards himself as superior/ a hero; he thinks that he is superior/a hero

Dünkirchen /ˈdyːnkɪrçn̩/ (*das*); **~s** ▸❶ **S. 675** Dunkirk

dünn /dʏn/

A *Adj.* **1** thin ‹*slice, layer, etc.*›; slim ‹*book*› **2** (mager) thin ‹*person*›; **sich ~ machen** (scherzh.) squash *or* (Amer.) scrunch up [a bit] **3** (leicht) thin, light ‹*clothing, fabric*›; fine ‹*stocking*›; (fig.) thin, rarefied ‹*air*›; fine ‹*mist, rain*› **4** (spärlich) thin ‹*hair*›; sparse ‹*cover, vegetation*› **5** (wenig gehaltvoll) thin ‹*soup*›; weak, watery ‹*coffee, tea*›; watery ‹*beer*› **6** (~flüssig) thin ‹*paint, lubricating oil*›; runny ‹*batter*› **7** (schwach) thin ‹*voice*›; weak, faint ‹*smile*›; faint ‹*scent*›

B *adv.* **1** **~ geschnittene Wurst/~ geschnittener Käse** thinly sliced sausage/cheese; **etw. ~ auftragen** apply sth. thinly **2** (leicht) lightly ‹*dressed*› **3** (spärlich) **~ besiedelt/bevölkert** thinly *or* sparsely populated *or* inhabited; **~ gesät** (ugs.) rare; *s. auch* **säen** **4** (schwach) ‹*smile*› weakly, faintly

dünn-, Dünn-: **~besiedelt** *usw.* ▸**dünn B3**; **~bier** *das* (veralt.) small beer; **~brett·bohrer** *der,* **~brett·bohrerin** *die;* (salopp abwertend) **er ist ein ~brettbohrer** he likes to take the easy way out; **~darm** *der* ▸❶ **S. 435** (Anat.) small intestine; **~druck** *der Pl.* **~~e** thin-paper *or* India paper edition; **~druck·aus·gabe** *die* thin-paper *or* India paper edition; **~druck·papier** *das* India paper

Dünne[1] *die;* **~** (Technik) thinness

Dünne[2] *der/die; adj. Dekl.* (ugs.) thin man/ woman; **die ~n** thin people

dünne|machen ▸**dünnmachen**

dunnemals /ˈdʊnəmaːls/ ▸**anno**

dünn-, Dünn-: **~flüssig** *Adj.* thin; runny ‹*batter etc.*›; ***~gesät** ▸**dünn B3**; **~häutig** *Adj.* (auch fig.) thin-skinned; **~|machen** *refl. V.* (ugs.) make oneself scarce (coll.); **~pfiff** *der* (salopp), **~schiss**, ***~schiß** *der* (derb) the runs *pl.* (coll.); the shits *pl.* (coarse); **~wandig** *Adj.* thin-walled

Dunst /dʊnst/ *der;* **~[e]s, Dünste** /ˈdʏnstə/ **1** haze; (Nebel) mist **2** (Geruch) smell; (Ausdünstung) fumes *pl.*; (stickige, dumpfe Luft) fug (coll.); **jmdm. blauen ~ vormachen** (ugs.) pull the wool over sb.'s eyes; **keinen [blassen] ~ von etw. haben** (ugs.) have not the foggiest *or* faintest idea about sth.

Dunst·abzugs·haube *die* extractor hood

dunsten *itr. V.* (geh.) **1** smell, give off a smell (**nach** of) **2** (dampfen) steam

dünsten /ˈdʏnstn̩/ *tr. V.* steam ‹*fish, vegetables*›; braise ‹*meat*›; stew ‹*fruit*›

Dunst·glocke *die* pall of haze

dunstig *Adj.* **1** hazy; (neblig) misty **2** (verräuchert) smoky; (stickig) stuffy

Dunst·kreis *der* (fig.) orbit

Dunst·obst (österr.), **Dünst·obst** *das* stewed fruit

Dunst-: **~schicht** *die* layer of haze; (Nebelschicht) layer of mist; **~schleier** *der* veil of haze; (Nebelschleier) veil of mist; **~wolke** *die* cloud of smog; (stickige, dumpfe Luft) fug (coll.)

Dünung *die;* **~, ~en** swell

Duo /ˈduːo/ *das;* **~s, ~s** (Musik) **1** (Stück) duet **2** (Ausführende) ‹*piano etc.*› duet; (fig. scherzh.) duo; pair

Duodez- /duoˈdeːts/: **~band** *der* duodecimo *or* twelvemo edition; **~fürst** *der* (abwertend) princeling; petty *or* minor prince; **~fürstentum** *das* (abwertend) petty *or* minor princedom; **~staat** *der* (abwertend) minor state

Duo·dezimal·system *das* duodecimal system

düpieren /dyˈpiːrən/ *tr. V.* (geh.) dupe

Duplikat /dupliˈkaːt/ *das;* **~[e]s, ~e** duplicate

Duplikation /duplikaˈtsi̯oːn/ *die;* **~, ~en** (geh., Genetik) duplication

Duplizität /duplitsi'tɛ:t/ *die;* ~, ~**en** (geh.) duplication

Dur /du:ɐ/ *das;* ~ (Musik) major [key]; **in** ~ **enden** finish in a major key

Dur·akkord *der* (Musik) major chord

durativ /'du:rati:f/ *Adj.* (Sprachw.) durative

durch /dʊrç/

A *Präp. mit Akk.* **1** (räumlich) through; ~ **die Straßen/die Stadt bummeln** stroll through the streets/the town; ~ **ganz Europa reisen** travel all over *or* throughout Europe; ~ **einen Fluss waten** wade across a river; *s. auch* **Kopf** **2** (modal) by; **etw.** ~ **Boten/die Post schicken** send sth. by courier/post (Brit.) *or* mail; **etw.** ~ **Lautsprecher/das Fernsehen bekannt geben** announce sth. over the loudspeakers/on television; **sie ist** ~ **das Fernsehen bekannt geworden** she became famous through television; **etw.** ~ **jmdn. bekommen** get *or* obtain sth. through sb.; **zehn [geteilt]** ~ **zwei** ten divided by two **3** (österr.: zeitlich) ~ **Wochen/Jahre** for weeks/years; ~ **sein ganzes Leben** throughout *or* all his life

B *Adv.* **1** (hin~) **das ganze Jahr** ~: throughout the whole year; all year; **die ganze Zeit** ~: the whole time; all the time **2** (ugs.: vorbei) **es war 3 Uhr** ~: it was past *or* gone 3 o'clock **3** ~ **und** ~ **nass/überzeugt** wet through [and through]/completely *or* totally convinced; **jmdm.** ~ **und** ~ **gehen** go right through sb.; **er ist ein Lügner** ~ **und** ~: he's an out and out liar **4** **[durch etw.]** ~ **sein** be through *or* have got through [sth.]; **durch den Fluss** ~ **sein** be across *or* have got across the river; **ist die Post/der Briefträger schon** ~**?** has the mail arrived/has the postman (Brit.) *or* (Amer.) mailman been? **5** ~ **sein** (vorbeigefahren sein) ‹*train, cyclist*› have gone through; (abgefahren sein) ‹*train, bus, etc.*› have gone; (fertig sein) have finished; **durch etw.** ~ **sein** have got through sth.; **mit etw.** ~ **sein** have got through sth. **6** ~ **sein** (durchgescheuert sein) have worn through **7** ~ **sein** (reif sein) ‹*cheese*› be ripe **8** ~ **sein** (durchgebraten sein) ‹*meat*› be well done **9** ~ **sein** (angenommen sein) ‹*law, regulation*› have gone through; ‹*35-hour week etc.*› have been adopted **10** ~ **sein** (gerettet sein) ‹*sick or injured person*› be out of danger **11** **bei jmdm. unten** ~ **sein** be in sb.'s bad books **12** ~ **sein** (bestanden haben) have got through

durch|ackern (ugs.)

A *tr. V.* plough through

B *refl. V.* **sich durch etw.** ~: plough [one's way] through sth.

durch|arbeiten

A *tr. V.* **1** **die Nacht/Pause** *usw.* ~: work through the night/break *etc.* **2** (lesen und auswerten) work *or* go through ‹*book, article*› **3** (ausarbeiten) work out ‹*speech, essay*› **4** (durchkneten) work *or* knead thoroughly ‹*dough*›; massage *or* knead thoroughly ‹*muscles*›

B *itr. V.* work through

C *refl. V.* (auch fig.) work one's way through

durch|atmen *itr. V.* take a deep breath/deep breaths; breathe deeply

durch·aus *Adv.* **1** ~ **mitkommen wollen** [absolutely] insist on coming too; **das ist** ~ **nötig/zu empfehlen** it is absolutely necessary/definitely to be recommended; **Muss das sein? — Ja,** ~: Is that necessary? — Yes, absolutely; **wenn du** ~ **willst** if you really insist **2** (völlig) perfectly, quite ‹*correct, possible, understandable*›; **das ist** ~ **richtig** that is entirely right; **ich bin** ~ **Ihrer Meinung** I am entirely of your opinion; **man kann** ~ **vermuten, dass ...** one can quite reasonably suppose *or* assume that ...; **ein** ~ **annehmbarer Vorschlag/gelungener Abend** an eminently acceptable suggestion/a thoroughly successful evening **3** (verneint) **das hat** ~ **nichts damit zu tun** that's got nothing at all *or* whatsoever to do with it; ~ **nicht ins Wasser/darüber sprechen wollen** absolutely refuse to go into the water/talk about it; **es ist** ~ **nicht so einfach wie ...** it is by no means as easy as ...; **das ist** ~ **kein Scherz** it is certainly no joke; **für so etwas habe ich** ~ **kein Verständnis** I have absolutely no time for that sort of thing

durch|backen

A *itr. V.* bake through

B *tr. V.* **etw. richtig** ~: bake sth. right the way through

durch|beißen[1]

A *unr. tr. V.* bite through

B *unr. refl. V.* (ugs.) [manage to] struggle through

durch·beißen[2] *unr. tr. V.* bite through; **jmdm. die Kehle** ~: tear *or* rip sb.'s throat open

durch|bekommen *unr. tr. V.* **etw.** ~: get sth. through; (zerlegen) get *or* cut through sth.

durch|betteln *refl. V.* **sich überall** ~: beg one's way through life

durch|biegen

A *unr. tr. V.* **etw.** ~: bend sth. as far as possible; **seinen Rücken/sein Kreuz** ~: straighten one's back

B *unr. refl. V.* sag

durch|blasen

A *unr. tr. V.* **1** (durch Hindurchblasen reinigen) **etw.** ~: clear sth. by blowing through it **2** (treiben) **etw. durch etw.** ~: blow sth. through sth. **3** (durchdringen) ‹*wind*› blow right through ‹*person*›

B *unr. itr. V.* ~ **durch** ‹*wind*› blow through ‹*cracks, thin coat, etc.*›

durch|blättern[1], **durch·blättern**[2] *tr. V.* leaf through ‹*book, file, etc.*›

durch|bläuen, ***durch|bleuen** *tr. V.* (ugs.) **jmdn.** ~: give sb. a good hiding (coll.) *or* thrashing

Durch·blick *der* **1** (ugs.) **den [absoluten]** ~ **haben** know [exactly] what's going on; **den** ~ **verlieren** no longer know what's going on; lose track of what's going on **2** (Ausblick) view (**auf** + *Akk.* of)

durch|blicken *itr. V.* **1** look through; **durch etw.** ~: look through sth. **2** (ugs.) **ich blicke da nicht durch** I can't make head or tail of it; **blickst du bei dieser Aufgabe durch?** can you make head or tail of this exercise? **3** ~ **lassen, dass .../wie ...** hint that .../at how ...; **etw.** ~ **lassen** hint at sth.

durch|bluten[1] *itr. V.* **1** **die Wunde blutete durch** blood from the wound soaked through [the bandage/dressing *etc.*] **2** *mit sein* ‹*bandage etc.*› become soaked with blood

durch·bluten[2] *tr. V.* **1** supply ‹*body, limb, etc.*› with blood; **seine Beine sind schlecht durchblutet** the circulation in his legs is poor **2** (mit Blut tränken) **etw.** ~: soak sth. with blood

Durch·blutung *die* flow *or* supply of blood (+ *Gen.* to); [blood] circulation

durchblutungs·fördernd *Adj.* ‹*substance*› which stimulates the [blood] circulation; ~ **sein** stimulate the [blood] circulation

Durchblutungs·störung *die* disturbance of the blood supply

durch|bohren[1]

A *tr. V.* drill *or* bore through ‹*wall, plank*›; drill, bore ‹*hole*›

B *itr. V.* **durch etw.** ~: drill *or* bore through sth.

C *refl. V.* **sich durch etw.** ~ ‹*woodworm etc.*› bore its way through sth.; ‹*spear, iron paling*› go right through sth.

durch·bohren[2] *tr. V.* pierce; **jmdn. mit** ~**den Blicken ansehen** (fig.) look piercingly *or* penetratingly at sb.

durch|boxen (ugs.)

A *refl. V.* fight one's way through; (fig.) battle through

B *tr. V.* force *or* push through ‹*law, measure, bill, etc.*›; **einen Kandidaten** ~: bring pressure to bear to get a candidate appointed

durch|braten *unr. tr. V.* **etw.** ~: cook *or* roast sth. till it is well done; **ich möchte mein Steak durchgebraten** I'd like my steak well done

durch|brechen[1]

A *unr. tr. V.* **1** (zerbrechen) **etw.** ~: break sth. in two **2** (eine Öffnung brechen) **eine Tür/ein Fenster** ~: make a door/window

B *unr. itr. V.; mit sein* **1** break in two; **der Blinddarm/das Magengeschwür ist durchgebrochen** (Med.) the appendix has burst/the gastric ulcer has perforated **2** (hervorkommen) ‹*sun*› break through; ‹*new tooth*› come through; ‹*bud*› appear; (fig.) ‹*rage, hatred*› erupt **3** (einbrechen) fall through ‹*ice, floor, etc.*›; **durch etw.** ~: fall through sth. **4** (Milit.: sich einen Weg bahnen) break through

durch·brechen[2] *unr. tr. V.* break through ‹*sound barrier*›; break *or* burst through ‹*crowd barrier*›; ‹*car*› crash through ‹*railings etc.*›; (fig.) break ‹*law, convention*›

durch|brennen *unr. itr. V.; mit sein* **1** ‹*heating coil, light bulb*› burn out; ‹*fuse*› blow; **da ist ihm die Sicherung durchgebrannt** (fig. salopp) he blew a fuse (sl.) *or* his top (coll.) **2** (ugs.: weglaufen) (von zu Hause) run away; (mit der Kasse) run off; abscond; (mit dem Geliebten/der Geliebten) run off **3** (glühen) ‹*coals, logs*› glow

durch|bringen *unr. tr. V.* **1** ▸**durchbekommen** **2** (durch eine Kontrolle, über eine Grenze) **etw.** ~: get sth. through **3** (bei Wahlen) **jmdn.** ~: get sb. elected **4** (durchsetzen) get ‹*bill*› through; get ‹*motion*› passed; get ‹*proposal*› accepted **5** (versorgen) **seine Familie/sich** ~: support one's family/oneself **6** (verschwenden) get through

durch·brochen

A *2. Part. v.* **durchbrechen**[2]

B *Adj.* openwork *attrib.* ‹*stockings, shoes, etc.*›

Durch·bruch *der* **1** (Milit., Geol., fig.) breakthrough; **einer Idee** (*Dat.*) **zum** ~ **verhelfen** get an idea generally accepted **2** (Öffnung) opening; (durch Gewalteinwirkung) breach

durch|buchstabieren *tr. V.* **1** spell out **2** (Jargon) ▸**durchdeklinieren**

durch|bummeln[1] *itr. V.* (ugs.) **1** **bis zum Morgen** ~: live it up till morning (coll.) **2** *mit sein* ~ **durch** wander through ‹*park, exhibition, etc.*›

durch·bummeln[2] *tr. V.* **die Nacht** ~: be on the spree all night (coll.); **eine durchbummelte Nacht** a night on the spree (coll.)

durch|bürsten *tr. V.* brush ‹*hair*› thoroughly

durch|checken *tr. V.* check ‹*list, documents*› thoroughly; check ‹*car*› over thoroughly

durch·dacht

A *2. Part. v.* **durchdenken**

B *Adj.* **ein wenig/gut** ~**er Plan** a badly/well thought-out plan; **nicht [genügend]** ~ **sein** not be sufficiently well thought-out

durch|deklinieren *tr. V.* (Jargon) enumerate ‹*cases*›; rehearse ‹*ideas*›; ~, **wie man etw. macht** spell out how to do sth.

durch·denken *unr. tr. V.* think over *or* through

durch|diskutieren *tr. V.* discuss thoroughly

durch|drängen *refl. V.* **sich [durch etw.]** ~: push *or* force one's way through [sth.]

durch|drehen

A *tr. V.* put ‹*meat etc.*› through the mincer *or* (Amer.) grinder; chop ‹*nuts etc.*› in the blender

B *itr. V.* **1** *auch mit sein* (ugs.) crack up (coll.); go to pieces **2** ‹*wheels*› spin

durch|dringen[1] *unr. itr. V.; mit sein* **1** ‹*rain, sun*› come through; **durch etw.** ~: penetrate sth.; come through sth.; **bis zu jmdm.** ~ (fig.) ‹*rumour, story*› get through to sb. **2** (sich durchsetzen) **mit einem Vorschlag bei der Geschäftsleitung** ~: succeed in getting the management to accept one's suggestion; **der Redner drang mit seiner Stimme nicht durch** the speaker couldn't make himself heard

durch·dringen[2] *unr. tr. V.* **1** penetrate; **kaum zu** ~ **sein** be almost impenetrable **2** (erfüllen) **jmdn.** ~ ‹*idea*› take hold of sb. [completely]; **von der Wahrheit einer Behauptung durchdrungen sein** be totally convinced of the truth of a statement; **seine Schriften sind von diesen Ideen durchdrungen** his writings are imbued with these ideas

durch·dringend

A *Adj.* **1** (intensiv) piercing, penetrating ‹*voice, look, scream, sound*›; **mit** ~**em Blick** with a piercing *or* penetrating look **2** (penetrant) pungent, penetrating ‹*smell*›

B *adv.* **1** **jmdn.** ~ **ansehen** look at a person piercingly *or* penetratingly; give sb. a piercing or penetrating look 2 (penetrant) ~ **riechen/stinken** have a pungent *or* penetrating smell/stench

Durchdringung *die;* ~ 1 penetration; (Verschmelzung) fusion 2 (Erfassung) comprehension

durch|drücken *tr. V.* 1 **Püree** *usw.* **[durch ein Sieb/Tuch] ~:** press *or* pass purée *etc.* through a sieve/cloth 2 (strecken) straighten ‹*limb, back*›; **die Knie ~:** straighten one's legs 3 (ugs.: durchsetzen) manage to get ‹*extra holiday etc.*›; **seinen Antrag ~:** manage to force one's application through; **ein Gesetz im Parlament ~:** force a bill through Parliament

durch|dürfen *unr. itr. V.* (ugs.) be allowed through; **darf ich mal [hier] durch?** can I get through here?

durch·einander *Adv.* ~ **sein** ‹*papers, desk, etc.*› be in a mess *or* a muddle; (verwirrt sein) be confused *or* in a state of confusion; (aufgeregt sein) be flustered *or* (coll.) in a state; ~ **bringen** (in Unordnung bringen) get ‹*room, flat*› into a mess; get ‹*papers, file*› into a muddle; muddle up ‹*papers, file*›; (verwirren) confuse; (verwechseln) confuse ‹*names etc.*›; get ‹*names etc.*› mixed up; get ‹*names etc.*› muddled; **im Hause geht alles ~:** the whole house is in a muddle; **mir geht alles ~** (fig.) I'm getting everything muddled up; ~ **geraten** get in a muddle; ~ **kommen** ‹*pictures, papers, etc.*› get into a muddle; ‹*person*› get into a muddle, get confused; ~ **laufen** run [around] in all directions; ~ **reden** all talk at once *or* at the same time; **etw. ~ werfen** (durcheinander bringen) muddle *or* jumble sth. up; (verwechseln) mix *or* muddle sth. up; get sth. mixed *or* muddled up; **alles ~ essen/trinken** eat/drink everything indiscriminately

Durcheinander *das;* ~**s** 1 muddle; mess; **in wirrem ~** (fig.) in wild confusion 2 (Wirrwarr) confusion

***durcheinander|bringen** *usw.* ▸**durcheinander**

durch|essen *unr. refl. V.* 1 **sich bei jmdm. ~:** live on sb.'s hospitality 2 (scherzh.) **sich durch etw. ~:** eat one's way through sth.

durch|exerzieren *tr. V.* (ugs.) go through, practise ‹*rules, multiplication tables*›; rehearse ‹*situation*›

durch|fahren[1] *unr. itr. V.; mit sein* 1 **[durch etw.] ~:** drive through [sth.] 2 (nicht anhalten) go straight through; (mit dem Auto) drive straight through; (fahren, ohne umsteigen zu müssen) travel direct; go straight through; **durch eine Stadt ~:** go/drive straight through a town; go/drive through a town without stopping; **der Zug fährt [in H.] durch** the train doesn't stop [at H.]; **der Zug fährt bis München durch** the train is non-stop to Munich; **die [ganze] Nacht ~:** travel/drive [right] through the night

durch·fahren[2] *unr. tr. V.* 1 travel through; ‹*train*› pass through; (mit dem Auto) drive through 2 (zurücklegen) cover ‹*distance*›; complete ‹*course, lap*› 3 (durchzucken) **plötzlich durchfuhr ihn ein Schreck** he was seized with sudden fright; **auf einmal durchfuhr mich [der Gedanke], dass ...** suddenly the thought *or* it flashed through my mind that ...

Durch·fahrt *die* 1 (das Durchfahren) **„~ verboten"** 'no entry except for access'; **die ~ durch den Kanal** the passage through the canal; **bei der ~ durch den Tunnel** when passing through the tunnel 2 (Durchreise) **auf der ~ sein** be passing through; be on the way through 3 (Weiterfahrt) **die ~ freigeben** allow vehicles through; **freie ~ haben** have right of way 4 (Weg) thoroughfare; **„bitte [die] ~ freihalten"** 'please do not obstruct'

Durchfahrts·straße *die* main road through

Durch·fall *der* 1 ▸❶ **S. 439** diarrhoea *no art.* 2 (ugs.: Versagen) failure; **in der Prüfung einen ~ erleben** fail the exam (coll.)

durch|fallen *unr. itr. V.; mit sein* 1 fall through; **durch etw. ~:** fall through sth. 2 (ugs.: nicht bestehen) fail; flunk (Amer. coll.); **bei etw./in etw.** (*Dat.*)/**durch etw.** (*Akk.*) **~:** fail *or* flunk sth. 3 (ugs.: erfolglos sein) ‹*play, performance*› flop (sl.); be a flop (sl.) *or* failure; **bei der Kritik ~:** be a flop with (sl.) *or* fail to please the critics 4 (ugs.: verlieren) lose; not get in; be defeated; **bei der Wahl ~:** lose the election; be defeated in the election

durch|faulen *itr. V.; mit sein* rot through

durch|faxen *tr. V.* fax through; **jmdm. etw. ~:** fax sth. through to sb.

durch|fechten
A *unr. tr. V.* **seine Ansprüche/Forderungen ~:** fight successfully to establish one's claims/get one's demands accepted
B *refl. V.* **sich [im Leben] ~:** battle one's way through [life]

durch|fegen *tr. V.* sweep ‹*room*› [out] thoroughly

durch|feiern[1] *itr. V.* **[die ganze Nacht] ~:** celebrate all night

durch·feiern[2] *tr. V.* **die [ganze] Nacht ~:** spend all night celebrating; celebrate all night; **nach durchfeierter Nacht** after celebrating all night

durch|feilen *tr. V.* 1 file through 2 (bearbeiten) polish ‹*essay, speech, etc.*›

durch|finden *unr. refl. V.* find one's way through; **sich durch etw. ~:** find one's way through sth.; **sich durch das U-Bahn-System/in der Stadt ~:** find one's way around the underground (Brit.) *or* (Amer.) subway system/the town; **ich finde mich in diesem Kuddelmuddel nicht mehr durch** I can't make head or tail of this muddle

durch|fliegen[1] *unr. itr. V.; mit sein* 1 **[durch etw.] ~:** fly through [sth.]; **unter der Brücke ~:** fly under the bridge 2 (nicht zwischenlanden) fly non-stop 3 (ugs.: nicht bestehen) **[in einem Examen/bei einer Prüfung] ~:** fail [an exam (coll.)]

durch·fliegen[2] *unr. tr. V.* 1 fly through; fly over ‹*country*›; fly along ‹*air corridor*› 2 (zurücklegen) fly, cover ‹*distance*› 3 (lesen) glance through ‹*newspaper, post*›; skim through ‹*novel*›

durch|fließen[1] *unr. itr. V.; mit sein* **[durch etw.] ~:** flow through [sth.]

durch·fließen[2] *unr. tr. V.* flow through

Durch·flug *der* flight through; **der ~ durch den Luftkorridor/das Gebiet** the flight along the air corridor/over the area; **Passagiere auf dem ~:** transit passengers; **auf dem ~ [nach Kanada] sein** be in transit [to Canada]

Durch·fluss, *Durch·fluß *der* 1 (das Durchfließen) flow 2 (Öffnung in einem Damm) [discharge] opening; outlet; (zwischen Becken) connection channel

durch·fluten *tr. V.* (geh.) ‹*river*› flow through ‹*country*›; ‹*warmth, pleasant feeling*› flood through ‹*person*›; **Licht durchflutete den Raum** light flooded the room; the room was flooded with light

durch|formen *tr. V.* **etw. ~:** get sth. into its final shape; **etw. bis ins Einzelne ~:** work sth. out down to the last detail

durch|formulieren *tr. V.* finalize the [exact] wording of ‹*essay, thesis*›; **eine Rede ~:** prepare the wording of a speech in detail

durch·forschen *tr. V.* 1 search ‹*pocket, room, area, etc.*› thoroughly 2 (untersuchen) make a thorough investigation *or* examination of ‹*sources, literature on a subject*›; carry out research into ‹*subject*›

durch|forsten[1], **durch·forsten**[2] *tr. V.* 1 (Forstw.) thin 2 (durchsehen) sift through ‹*archives, regulations, etc.*›

durch|fragen *refl. V.* **sich [nach dem Bahnhof/zum Museum] ~:** find one's way [to the station/museum] by asking

durch|fressen[1]
A *unr. tr. V.* 1 **ein Loch durch etw. ~:** eat a hole through *or* in sth. 2 (zerstören, zersetzen) eat through; ‹*moths*› eat holes in ‹*pullover etc.*›
B *unr. refl. V.* 1 ‹*maggot, woodworm*› eat [its way] through; ‹*rust*› eat through 2 (ugs. abwertend) **sich bei jmdm. ~:** live on sb.'s hospitality 3 (durcharbeiten) plough through ‹*book, statistics, etc.*›

durch·fressen[2] *Adj.* **von Motten ~ sein** be moth-eaten *or* full of moth-holes; **ein von Säure ~er Kittel** a lab coat full of acid holes

durch|frieren *unr. itr. V.; mit sein* 1 get frozen stiff; get *or* become chilled to the marrow *or* bone; **durchgefroren sein** be frozen stiff *or* chilled to the bone 2 (gefrieren) ‹*water, lake*› freeze solid

durchfroren *Adj.* frozen ‹*face, hands*›; **~ sein** ‹*person*› be frozen stiff

durch|fühlen *tr. V.* **etw. durch etw. ~:** feel sth. through sth.; **jmds. Bitterkeit ~** (fig.) sense sb.'s bitterness

durchführbar *Adj.* practicable; feasible; workable; **ein leicht/schwer ~er Plan** a plan that is easy/difficult to carry out

Durchführbarkeit *die;* **~:** practicability; feasibility; workability

Durchführbarkeits·studie *die* feasibility study

durch|führen
A *tr. V.* 1 (verwirklichen) carry out ‹*intention*›; put into effect, implement ‹*decision, programme*›; carry out, put into effect, implement ‹*plan*›; put into practice ‹*idea*› 2 (ausführen) carry out ‹*work, installation, investigation*›; perform, carry out ‹*operation*›; take ‹*measurement*› 3 (veranstalten) make ‹*charity collection*›; hold ‹*meeting, election, examination*›; carry out ‹*census*› 4 (zu Ende führen) complete, finish ‹*task*›; carry through ‹*method, system*›; maintain, keep up ‹*role*›
B *itr. V.* **durch etw./unter etw.** (*Dat.*) ~ ‹*track, road*› go *or* run *or* pass through/under sth.

Durchfuhr-: ~handel *der* (Wirtsch.) transit trade; **~land** *das* (Wirtsch.) country of transit

Durch·führung *die* 1 (Verwirklichung) (einer Absicht) carrying out; (eines Plans, Programms) carrying out, implementation; **zur ~ kommen** *od.* **gelangen** (Papierdt.) ‹*decision, regulation*› be implemented; **zur ~ bringen** (Papierdt.) enforce ‹*regulation, law*› 2 (Ausführung) (einer Arbeit) carrying out; (einer Operation) performing; (einer Messung) taking 3 (Einhaltung) (einer Idee) carrying through; (von Richtlinien) putting into practice 4 (Veranstaltung) (eines Kongresses usw.) holding; (eines Wettbewerbs) staging

Durchführungs·verordnung *die* implementing order

durch|füttern *tr. V.* (ugs.) feed; support; **sich von jmdm. ~ lassen** live off sb.

Durch·gabe *die* (von Nachrichten, Meldungen) announcement; (von Gewinnzahlen) reading; **bei der ~ des Telegramms** when telephoning the telegram through

Durch·gang *der* 1 **„kein ~", „ ~ verboten"** 'no thoroughfare' 2 (Weg) passage[way] 3 (Phase) stage; (einer Versuchsreihe) run; (Sport, bei Wahlen, Wettbewerb) round 4 (Astron.) transit

durch·gängig
A *Adj.* general; (universell) universal; constant ‹*feature*›; general ‹*principle*›; continual, constant ‹*use*›
B *adv.* generally, universally ‹*accepted*›; **~ mit Maschine geschrieben sein** be typed throughout

Durchgangs-: ~bahn·hof *der* through station; **~lager** *das* transit camp; **~station** *die* (fig.) transitional stage; **~straße** *die* through road; thoroughfare; **~verkehr** *der* 1 through traffic; 2 (Transitverkehr) transit traffic

durch|geben *unr. tr. V.* announce ‹*news*›; give ‹*results, weather report, winning numbers*›; **eine Meldung im Radio/Fernsehen ~:** make an announcement on the radio/on television; **etw. in den Nachrichten ~:** announce sth. on the news; **telefonisch** *od.* **per Telefon ~:** telephone ‹*telegram*› through; give ‹*traffic information*› over the telephone; pass on ‹*report, results*› by telephone

durch|gehen
A *unr. itr. V.; mit sein* 1 **[durch etw.] ~:** go *or* walk through [sth.]; **„bitte weiter ~!"** 'pass *or* move right down, please' 2 (hindurchdringen) **[durch etw.] ~** ‹*rain, water*› come through [sth.]; ‹*wind*› go through [sth.] 3 (direkt zum Ziel führen) ‹*train, bus, flight*› go [right] through (**bis** to); go direct 4 (andauern) ‹*meeting, party, etc.*›

go on (**bis zu** until) 5 (verlaufen) ‹*path etc.*› go *or* run through (**bis zu** to); ‹*stripe*› go *or* run right through 6 (angenommen werden) ‹*application, claim*› be accepted; ‹*law*› be passed; ‹*motion*› be carried; ‹*bill*› be passed, get through 7 (hingenommen werden) ‹*discrepancy*› be tolerated; ‹*mistake, discourtesy*› be allowed to *or* let pass, be overlooked; **[jmdm.] etw. ~ lassen** let sb. get away with sth. 8 (davonstürmen) ‹*horse*› bolt 9 (ugs.: davonlaufen) **mit etw./jmdm. ~:** run off with sth./sb.; **sie ist ihrem Mann durchgegangen** she ran off and left her husband 10 (außer Kontrolle geraten) **die Nerven gehen mit ihm durch** he loses his temper; **ihr Temperament/ihre Begeisterung geht mit ihr durch** her temperament/enthusiasm gets the better of her 11 (ugs.: durchgebracht werden können) **[durch etw.] ~:** go through [sth.]; **hinter etw.** (*Dat.*) **~:** go through behind sth. 12 (ohne Unterbrechung zu Fuß gehen) walk without a break 13 (gehalten werden für) **für neu/30 Jahre** *usw.* **~:** be taken to be *or* pass for new/thirty *etc.*

B *unr. tr. V.; mit sein* go through ‹*newspaper, text*›; **etw. Punkt für Punkt/Wort für Wort ~:** go through sth. point by point/word by word

durch·gehend
A *Adj.* 1 continuous ‹*line, pattern, etc.*›; constantly recurring ‹*motif*› 2 (direkt) through *attrib.* ‹*train, carriage*›; direct ‹*flight, connection*›
B *adv.* 1 **~ geöffnet haben/bleiben** be/stay open all day; (Tag und Nacht) be/stay open 24 hours a day 2 (in einer Linie) **~ geknöpft werden/gefüttert sein** button all the way down/be lined throughout *or* fully lined

durch·geistigt *Adj.* spiritual ‹*person, appearance*›

durchgeknallt *Adj.* (ugs.) crazy

durch·geschwitzt
A *2. Part. v.* **durchschwitzen**
B *Adj.* ‹*person*› soaked *or* bathed in sweat; ‹*clothes*› soaked with sweat; sweat-soaked *attrib.* ‹*clothes*›

durch|gestalten *tr. V.* work ‹*theme, motif*› out in detail; portray ‹*experience*› in detail

durch|gießen *unr. tr. V.*; **etw. [durch etw.] ~:** pour sth. through [sth.]; **etw. durch ein Tuch ~:** strain sth. through a cloth

durch|gliedern *tr. V.* structure

durch|glühen¹
A *itr. V.; mit sein* 1 (entzweigehen) ‹*heating coil, light bulb*› burn out; ‹*fuse*› blow 2 (vollständig glühen) ‹*coals, log*› glow right through
B *tr. V.* **etw. ~:** heat sth. until it glows right through

durch·glühen² *tr. V.* (dichter.) **von etw. durchglüht sein** be aglow with sth.

durch|graben
A *unr. tr. V.* **einen Tunnel/Gang** *usw.* **[durch etw.] ~:** dig a tunnel/passage through [sth.]
B *unr. refl. V.* **sich [durch etw.] ~** ‹*miner*› dig his way through [sth.]; ‹*mole*› tunnel its way through [sth.]

durch|greifen *unr. itr. V.* 1 **[hart] ~:** take drastic measures *or* steps; **rücksichtslos/strenger ~:** take ruthless/more drastic measures *or* steps; **gegen die Demonstranten hart ~:** take drastic action against the demonstrators 2 **~ durch** reach through

durch|gucken *itr. V.* (ugs.) **[durch etw.] ~:** peep *or* look through [sth.]; **durch jmds. Fernglas ~:** have a look through sb.'s binoculars

durch|haben *unr. tr. V.* (ugs.) 1 have finished with ‹*book, newspaper*›; have got through ‹*song, discussion point*› 2 (zerteilt haben) have got through 3 (hindurchbewegt haben) **etw. [durch etw.] ~:** have got sth. through [sth.]

durch|hacken *tr. V.* hack *or* chop through; (mit einem Schlag) chop through

Durchhalte·appell *der* (bei einem Kampf) appeal to hold out; (bei einer schwierigen Aufgabe) appeal to see it through

durch|halten
A *unr. itr. V.* (bei einem Kampf) hold out; (bei einer schwierigen Aufgabe) see it through; (beim Rennen) stay the course
B *unr. tr. V.* stand ‹*strain, difficult working conditions*›; stand, keep up ‹*pace*›; **eine Diät ~:** keep to a diet

Durchhalte-: ~parole *die* (abwertend) exhortation to hold out; **~vermögen** *das* staying power; stamina; [power of] endurance

durch|hängen *unr. itr. V.* 1 sag 2 (ugs.) be washed out *or* drained

durch|hauen
A *regelm.* (*auch unr.*) *tr. V.* 1 **etw. ~:** chop *or* split sth. in half 2 (bahnen) **sich** (*Dat.*) **einen Weg durch etw. ~:** hack one's *or* a way through sth.
B *tr. V.* (ugs.) 1 (verprügeln) **jmdn. ~:** give sb. a good hiding (coll.) *or* (coll.) walloping 2 (zerstören) blow ‹*fuse*›; wreck ‹*power line*›
C *unr. refl. V.* **sich [durch etw.] ~:** hack one's way through [sth.]

durch|hecheln *tr. V.* (ugs. abwertend) gossip about ‹*person, behaviour*›

durch|heizen
A *tr. V.* 1 heat ‹*house, offices, etc.*› through 2 (ohne Pause heizen) heat ‹*house, offices, etc.*› continuously *or* day and night
B *itr. V.* have *or* keep the heating on

durch|helfen *unr. itr. V.* **jmdm. [durch etw.] ~:** help a person through [sth.]; **ich werde mir schon ~:** I'll manage *or* get by

durch|hören *tr. V.* 1 **etw. [durch etw.] ~:** hear sth. [through sth.] 2 (heraushören) sense, detect ‹*bitterness, envy, etc.*›

durch|hungern *refl. V.* get by *or* struggle along on very little to eat

durch·irren *tr. V.* wander *or* roam [aimlessly] through

durch|ixen *tr. V.* (ugs.) x out ‹*typing error*›

durch|kämmen¹ *tr. V.* 1 comb ‹*hair*› through 2 (durchsuchen) comb ‹*area etc.*›

durch·kämmen² *tr. V.* comb ‹*area etc.*›

durch|kämpfen
A *tr. V.* 1 fight ‹*case*› [right] to the end; fight one's way through ‹*adversity*› 2 (durchsetzen) force through
B *refl. V.* 1 **sich [durch etw.] ~:** fight *or* battle one's way through [sth.] 2 (durchstehen) battle *or* struggle through 3 (sich überwinden) **sich dazu ~, etw. zu tun** bring oneself to do sth.

durch|kauen *tr. V.* 1 **etw. [gut] ~:** chew sth. thoroughly *or* well 2 (ugs.: besprechen) go over and over

durch|klettern *itr. V.; mit sein* **[durch etw.] ~:** climb *or* clamber through [sth.]

durch|klicken (DV)
A *refl. V.* **sich zu etw. ~:** click through to sth.
B *tr. V* click through ‹*website, items, pages*› (**nach** in search of)

durch|klingeln *itr. V.* (nordd. ugs.) call *or* phone [up]; **bei jmdm. ~:** call *or* phone sb. [up]

durch|knallen *itr. V.; mit sein* (ugs.) 1 ‹*fuse*› blow; **[bei] ihm knallte die Sicherung durch** he blew his top (coll.); 2 (fig.: die Selbstbeherrschung verlieren) flip [out] (coll.)

durch|kneten *tr. V.* 1 knead ‹*dough etc.*› thoroughly 2 (ugs.: massieren) knead ‹*muscles etc.*› thoroughly; **jmdn. ~:** give sb. a good hard massage

durch|knöpfen *tr. V.* button ‹*dress, coat*› all the way down; **das Kleid wird hinten durchgeknöpft** the dress buttons all the way up the back; **ein durchgeknöpftes Kleid** a button-through dress

durch|kochen *tr. V.* boil ‹*stock, jam*› thoroughly

durch|kommen *unr. itr. V.; mit sein* 1 come through; (mit Mühe hindurchgelangen) get through; **durch etw. ~:** come/get through sth.; **es gab kein Durchkommen** there was no way through 2 (ugs.: beim Telefonieren) get through 3 (durchgehen, -fahren usw.) **durch etw. ~:** come *or* pass through sth.; **um fünf Uhr kommt der Zug [hier] durch** the train comes through [here] at five o'clock; **wenn du hier durchkommst, …** when you're passing through … 4 (sich zeigen) ‹*sun*› come out; ‹*character trait, upbringing*› come through, become apparent; **manchmal kommt sein Dialekt durch** (fig.) sometimes his dialect becomes noticeable; **bei ihm kommt der Lehrer durch** (fig.) the teacher in him comes through 5 (erfolgreich sein) **mit dieser Einstellung wird er [im Leben] nicht ~:** he won't get anywhere *or* far [in life] with an attitude like that; **mit Freundlichkeit und Verbindlichkeit kann man überall besser ~:** you'll get a lot further by being friendly and obliging; **damit kommst du bei mir nicht durch** you won't get anywhere with me like that; **mit so einer Entschuldigung kommt man bei ihm nicht durch** you won't get away with an excuse like that with him 6 (ugs.: überleben) pull through 7 (ugs.: durchdringen) **[durch etw.] ~** ‹*water, sand, etc.*› come through [sth.] 8 (durchgesagt werden) be announced; **die Nachricht kam im Fernsehen/Radio durch** the news was announced on television/the radio 9 (bestehen) get through; pass; **in einer Prüfung ~:** get through *or* pass an examination 10 (auskommen) manage; get by; **mit seiner Rente ~:** get by *or* manage on one's pension

durch|komponieren *tr. V.* 1 work ‹*story, play*› out in detail 2 (Musik) compose ‹*song*› with an individual setting for each verse; set ‹*poem*› to music with an individual setting for each stanza; **die Ballade ist durchkomponiert** the ballad is through-composed *or* durchkomponiert

durch|können *unr. itr. V.* (ugs.) 1 (durchgehen, -kommen dürfen) **[durch etw.] ~:** be able to go/come through [sth.]; **Sie können hier nicht durch** you can't go/come through here; **kann ich mal durch, bitte?** can I get by, please?; excuse me, please 2 (durchkommen) **[durch etw.] ~:** be able to get through [sth.]

durch|konstruieren *tr. V.* **etw. ~:** design and construct sth. with great attention to detail

durch|kreuzen¹ *tr. V.* cross through *or* out ‹*mistake, irrelevant information*›

durch·kreuzen² *tr. V.* 1 (vereiteln) thwart, frustrate ‹*plan, intention, ambition, policy*› 2 (geh.: durchfahren) cross ‹*continent, sea, etc.*›

durch|kriechen *unr. itr. V.; mit sein* **[durch etw.] ~:** crawl through [sth.]; **unter etw.** (*Dat.*) **~:** crawl [through] under sth.

durch|kriegen *tr. V.* (ugs.) ▸**durchbekommen**

durch|laden
A *unr. tr. V.* cock ‹*pistol etc.*› and rotate the cylinder
B *unr. itr. V.* cock the trigger and rotate the cylinder

Durchlass, *Durchlaß /ˈdʊrçlas/ *der;* **Durchlasses, Durchlässe** /ˈdʊrçlɛsə/ 1 (geh.) permission to pass; (Einlass) admittance; **sich** (*Dat.*) **~ verschaffen** obtain permission to pass/gain admittance 2 (Öffnung) gap; opening; (für Wasser) duct; conduit

durch|lassen *unr. tr. V.* 1 **jmdn. [durch etw.] ~:** let *or* allow sb. through [sth.]; **den Ball ~** (Sport) ‹*goalkeeper*› let a goal in 2 (durchlässig sein) let ‹*light, water, etc.*› through; (eindringen lassen) let ‹*light, water, etc.*› in 3 (ugs.: dulden) **jmdm. etw. ~:** let sb. get away with sth.

durchlässig /ˈdʊrçlɛsɪç/ *Adj.* 1 permeable; (porös) porous; (undicht) leaky; ‹*raincoat, shoe*› that lets in water 2 (offen) open ‹*system, border*›; **die Grenzen müssen ~er werden** the borders must be opened up further; **im Verteidigungsministerium gab es eine ~e Stelle** (fig.) there had been a leak/leaks at the defence ministry

-durchlässig *Adj.* **gas-/luft-/wasser~** *usw.* **sein** be permeable to gas/air/water *etc.*

Durchlässigkeit *die;* **~** 1 permeability; (Porosität) porosity; (Undichte) leakiness 2 (Offenheit) free interchange (+ *Gen.*, **zwischen** between)

Durchlaucht /ˈdʊrçlauxt/ *die;* **~, ~en: Ihre/Seine ~:** Her/His [Serene] Highness; **[Euer] ~:** Your [Serene] Highness

Durch·lauf *der* 1 (Sport, DV) run 2 (von Wasser) flow; **während des ~s des Wassers** while the water is flowing through 3 (Ferns.)

preview (*of programme to gain approval for broadcast*); (Rundf.) scrutiny

durch|laufen¹

A *unr. itr. V.; mit sein* 1▸ **[durch etw.] ~:** run through [sth.] 2▸ (durchrinnen) **[durch etw.] ~:** trickle through [sth.]; **der Kaffee ist durchgelaufen** the coffee is filtered 3▸ (passieren) ‹*runners*› run *or* pass through 4▸ (ohne Pause laufen) run without stopping 5▸ (fortlaufen) ‹*balcony, frieze*› run all the way along

B *unr. tr. V.* go through ‹*socks, soles of shoes*›

durch·laufen² *unr. tr. V.* 1▸ go *or* pass through ‹*phase, stage*› 2▸ (geh.: hindurchgehen durch) ‹*shudder, feeling, etc.*› run through 3▸ (zurücklegen) run, cover ‹*distance*›

durchlaufend

A *Adj.* continuous

B *adv.* ‹*numbered, marked*› in sequence

Durchlauf-: ~erhitzer *der; ~s, ~:* geyser; instantaneous water heater; **~zeit** *die* processing time; (DV) run duration

durch|lavieren *refl. V.* (ugs. abwertend) get along by dint of some smart manoeuvring

durch·leben *tr. V.* live through; experience; experience ‹*moments of bliss, terror, fright*›; **etw. wieder ~:** relive sth.

durch|legen *tr. V.* (ugs.) **die Straße/Leitung wird hier durchgelegt** the road/pipe will be laid through here

durch·leiden *unr. tr. V.* (geh.) endure; suffer

durch|leiten *tr. V.* **den Verkehr durch die Stadt ~:** direct the traffic through the town; **den Strom [durch das Gebiet] ~:** run electricity cables through [the area]

durch|lesen *unr. tr. V.* **etw. [ganz] ~:** read sth. [all the way] through; **wenn du das Buch durchgelesen hast** when you've finished reading the book; **sich** (*Dat.*) **etw. ~:** read sth. through; **etw. auf Fehler hin ~:** read sth. for errors

durch·leuchten *tr. V.* 1▸ x-ray ‹*patient, part of body*›; **sich ~ lassen** have an x-ray; **jmdm. den Magen ~:** x-ray sb.'s stomach 2▸ (fig.: analysieren) investigate ‹*case, matter, problem, etc.*› thoroughly *or* in depth; **jmds. Vergangenheit ~:** probe into *or* investigate sb.'s past; **jmdn. ~:** vet sb.

Durchleuchtung *die; ~, ~en* 1▸ (das Röntgen) x-ray examination; **jmdn. zur ~ ins Krankenhaus schicken** send sb. to hospital for an x-ray 2▸ (fig.: Analyse) [thorough] investigation; (von Bewerbern usw.) vetting

durch|liegen

A *unr. tr. V.* wear out ‹*mattress, bed*› [so that it sags in the middle]; **eine durchgelegene Matratze** a worn-out mattress

B *refl. V.* ‹*patient*› develop *or* get bedsores

durch·löchern *tr. V.* 1▸ make holes in; wear holes in ‹*socks, shoes*›; ‹*rust*› eat holes in; **jmdn./etw. mit Schüssen ~:** riddle sb./sth. with bullets; **völlig durchlöchert sein** be full of holes 2▸ (fig.: schwächen) undermine ‹*system*› completely; render ‹*principle*› meaningless

durch|lotsen *tr. V.* (ugs.) **ein Schiff [durch etw.] ~:** pilot a ship through [sth.]; **jmdn. [durch die Stadt] ~:** guide sb. through [the town]

durch|lüften¹

A *tr. V.* air ‹*room, flat, etc.*› thoroughly

B *itr. V.* air the place

durch·lüften² *tr. V.* (fachspr.) aerate ‹*soil*›; ventilate ‹*grain, woodpile*›

durch|machen (ugs.)

A *tr. V.* 1▸ undergo ‹*change*›; complete ‹*training course*›; go through ‹*stage, phase*›; serve ‹*apprenticeship*› 2▸ (erleiden) go through; **sie hat schlimme Zeiten/viel durchgemacht** she's been through some bad times/a lot; **eine schwere Krankheit ~:** suffer *or* have a serious illness 3▸ (durcharbeiten) work through ‹*lunch break, weekend, etc.*›

B *itr. V.* (durcharbeiten) work [right] through; (durchfeiern) celebrate all night/day *etc.*; keep going all night/day *etc.*

durch|manövrieren *tr. V.* **etw. [durch etw.] ~:** manoeuvre sth. through [sth.]; **jmdn. sicher durch alle Schwierigkeiten ~** (fig.) bring *or* lead sb. safely through all the difficulties

Durch·marsch *der* 1▸ **der ~ zur Grenze** the march through to the frontier; **auf dem ~ sein** be marching through 2▸ (salopp: Durchfall) **~ haben/bekommen** have/get the runs (coll.) 3▸ (Skat) **einen ~ machen** *take all the tricks when ramsch is called*

durch|marschieren *itr. V.; mit sein* **[durch etw.] ~:** march through [sth.]

durch|mengen *tr. V.* **[gut] ~:** mix ‹*ingredients etc.*› thoroughly

durch·messen *unr. tr. V.* (geh.) cross ‹*room*›; traverse ‹*time and space*›; **das Zimmer mit großen Schritten ~:** stride across the room; cross the room with long strides

Durchmesser *der; ~s, ~:* diameter; **das misst 3 m im ~:** it measures 3 m in diameter

durch|mischen¹ *tr. V.* **[gut/gründlich] ~:** mix ‹*ingredients etc.*› thoroughly

durch·mischen² *tr. V.* **etw. mit etw. ~:** mix sth. with sth.

durch|mogeln *refl. V.* (ugs. abwertend) cheat one's way through; (sich hineinmogeln) wangle one's way in (sl.); **sich bei einer Prüfung** *usw.* **~:** get through an examination *etc.* by cheating

durch|müssen *unr. itr. V.* (ugs.) **[durch etw.] ~:** have to go through [sth.]; **da werden wir ~** (fig.) we'll have to see it *or* the thing through

durch·mustern *tr. V.* (geh.) examine closely; scrutinize

durch|nagen *tr. V.* gnaw through

Durchnahme /'dʊrçna:mə/ *die; ~:* **bei ~ des Stoffes** while we/they *etc.* are/were going through the material

durch·nässen *tr. V.* soak; drench; **[völlig] durchnässt sein** be soaking wet *or* wet through; **mit durchnässten Kleidern** with soaking wet clothes

durch|nehmen *unr. tr. V.* deal with, do ‹*subject, topic*›; go through ‹*material*›

***durch|numerieren, durch|nummerieren** *tr. V.* number ‹*pages, seats, etc.*› consecutively from beginning to end

durch|organisieren *tr. V.* organize sth. well; **etw. perfekt ~:** organize sth. down to the last detail

durch|pauken *tr. V.* (ugs.) 1▸ force through ‹*law, regulation, etc.*› 2▸ (lernen) swot up (Brit.); bone up on (Amer.)

durch|pausen *tr. V.* trace

durch|peitschen *tr. V.* 1▸ **jmdn. ~:** give sb. a flogging; flog sb. 2▸ (ugs. abwertend) railroad ‹*law, application, etc.*› through

durch|pennen *itr. V.* (salopp) sleep through; **ich habe bis 11 Uhr durchgepennt** I kipped till 11 o'clock (coll.)

durch·pflügen *tr. V.* plough through

durch|planen *tr. V.* **etw. ~:** plan sth. well

durch|plumpsen *itr. V.; mit sein* (ugs.) 1▸ **[durch etw.] ~** ‹*person*› fall through [sth.]; ‹*small object*› drop *or* fall through [sth.] 2▸ (bei einer Prüfung) fail; flunk (Amer. coll.); **bei/in etw.** (*Dat.*) **~:** fail *or* flunk sth.

durch|pressen *tr. V.* mash ‹*potatoes*›; purée ‹*fruit*› (*by pressing through a sieve*); crush ‹*garlic*› (*in a press*); **Kartoffeln/Obst durch ein Sieb ~:** press *or* pass potatoes/fruit through a sieve

durch|proben *tr. V.* **etw. ~:** run through *or* rehearse sth. from beginning to end

durch|probieren *tr. V.* taste *or* try ‹*wines, cakes, etc.*› one after another; try on ‹*dresses, suits, etc.*› one after another

durch|prügeln *tr. V.* (ugs.) give sb. a real beating *or* (coll.) walloping; give ‹*naughty child*› a good hiding *or* (coll.) walloping

durch·pulsen *tr. V.* (geh.) ‹*blood*› pulse through; **buntes Leben durchpulste die Straßen** (fig.) the streets pulsated with life

durch|pusten *tr. V.* (ugs.) **etw. ~:** clear sth. by blowing through it

durch·queren *tr. V.* cross; travel across ‹*country*›; ‹*train*› pass *or* go through ‹*country*›

durch|quetschen *refl. V.* (ugs.) **sich [durch etw.] ~:** squeeze one's way through [sth.]

durch|rasen *itr. V.; mit sein* **[durch etw.] ~:** tear through [sth.]

durch|rasseln *itr. V.; mit sein* (salopp), **durch|rauschen** *itr. V.; mit sein* (ugs.) ▸**durchfallen 2**

durch|rechnen *tr. V.* calculate ‹*costs etc.*› [down to the last penny]; check ‹*bill*› thoroughly

durch|regnen *itr. V.* (unpers.) **in der Küche** *usw.* **regnet es durch** the rain is coming through in the kitchen *etc.*; **es regnet durchs Dach durch** the rain is coming [in] through the roof; **die ganze Nacht ~:** rain all [through the] night; *s. auch* **durchgeregnet**

Durchreiche *die; ~, ~n* [serving] hatch

durch|reichen *tr. V.* **etw. [durch etw.] ~:** pass *or* hand sth. through [sth.]

Durch·reise *die* journey through; **auf der ~ sein** be on the way through *or* passing through

durch|reisen¹ *itr. V.; mit sein* travel *or* pass through

durch·reisen² *tr. V.* travel through *or* across ‹*area, continent*›

Durch·reisende *der/die* person travelling through; **~ auf dem Weiterflug nach Rom** passengers travelling through *or* on to Rome

Durchreise·visum *das* transit visa

durch|reißen

A *unr. tr. V.* **etw. ~:** tear sth. in two *or* in half

B *unr. itr. V.; mit sein* ‹*fabric, garment*› rip, tear; ‹*thread, rope*› snap *or* break [in two]

durch|reiten *unr. itr. V.; mit sein* **[durch etw.] ~:** ride through [sth.]; **die ganze Nacht ~:** ride all night without stopping

durch|rennen *unr. itr. V.; mit sein* **[durch etw.] ~:** run through [sth.]

durch|rieseln¹ *itr. V.; mit sein* **[durch etw.] ~:** trickle through [sth.]

durch·rieseln² *tr. V.* ‹*feeling of horror or pleasure*› run through; **es durchrieselte sie kalt/heiß** a cold shiver ran through her/she felt a hot flush come over her

durch|ringen *unr. refl. V.* **sie hat sich endlich [zu einem Entschluss] durchgerungen** finally she managed to come to a decision; **wann wirst du dich dazu ~, es zu tun?** when are you going to bring yourself to do it?

durch|rinnen *unr. itr. V.; mit sein* **[durch etw.] ~:** run through [sth.]; **das Geld rinnt ihm zwischen den Fingern durch** (fig.) money burns a hole in his pocket

durch|rosten *itr. V.; mit sein* rust through

durch|rufen *unr. itr. V.* (ugs.) **[bei jmdm.] ~:** ring [sb.] up (Brit.)

durch|rühren *tr. V.* **etw. [gut] ~:** stir sth. [well]

durch|rutschen *itr. V.; mit sein* 1▸ **[durch etw.] ~** ‹*object*› slip through [sth.]; ‹*person*› slide through [sth.] 2▸ (ugs.: durchkommen) manage to get through without doing any work

durch|rütteln *tr. V.* **jmdn. ~:** shake sb. about badly

durchs /dʊrçs/ *Präp. + Art.* = **durch das**

durch|sacken *itr. V.; mit sein* ‹*aeroplane*› drop suddenly; (bei zu geringer Geschwindigkeit) stall

Durch·sage *die* announcement; (an eine bestimmte Person) message; **eine ~ machen** make an announcement

durch|sagen *tr. V.* ▸**durchgeben**

durch|sägen¹, durch·sägen² *tr. V.* saw through

Durch-: ~satz *der* 1▸ (DV) [processing] speed; 2▸ (fachspr.: Stoffmenge) throughput; **~satz·rate** *die* (DV) processing speed

durch|saufen *unr. itr. V.* (derb) **die ganze Nacht ~:** booze all night (sl.)

durch|sausen *itr. V.; mit sein* (ugs.) 1▸ **[durch etw.] ~:** shoot through [sth.] 2▸ (ugs.: durchfallen) **[durch eine Prüfung] ~:** fail *or* (Amer. coll.) flunk [an examination]

d

durch|schalten **A** *tr. V.* (Technik) connect ‹*telephone line*› through; put ‹*telephone call*› through; switch ‹*signal, current, etc.*› through **B** *itr. V.* (beim Autofahren) ‹*car driver*› change up [quickly]

durchschaubar *Adj.* transparent; **leicht/schwer ~ sein** be easy/difficult to see through; (verständlich) be easy/difficult to understand; **leicht ~** ‹*lie, plan, intention*› that is easy to see through *or* is easily seen through; **ein leicht/schwer ~er Mensch** a person who is easy/difficult to see through; **etw. ~ machen** make sth. easy to understand

durch|schauen¹ *itr. V.* ▸**durchsehen**

durch·schauen² *tr. V.* 1 see through ‹*lie, plan, intention, person, etc.*›; see ‹*situation*› clearly; **du bist durchschaut** I've/we've seen through you; I/we know what you're up to; **~, worum es wirklich geht** see what it's really all about 2 (verstehen) understand

durch|scheinen¹ *unr. itr. V.* **[durch etw.] ~** ‹*sun, light*› shine through [sth.]; ‹*colour, pattern*› show through [sth.]

durch·scheinen² *unr. tr. V.* (geh.) ‹*sun*› fill ‹*room*› with light; **von Sonnenlicht durchschienen** filled with sunlight

durchscheinend *Adj.* (lichtdurchlässig) translucent; (durchsichtig) transparent; diaphanous ‹*fabric*›; translucent ‹*skin etc.*›

durch|scheuern **A** *tr. V.* wear through; **ein durchgescheuertes Kabel** a worn cable **B** *refl. V.* wear through

durch|schieben *unr. tr. V.* **etw. [durch etw.] ~:** push sth. through [sth.]; **einen Brief unter der Tür ~:** push a letter under the door

durch|schießen¹ *unr. tr. V.* **durch etw. ~:** shoot through sth.; **den Ball zwischen den Bäumen ~:** shoot the ball [through] between the trees

durch·schießen² *unr. tr. V.* 1 **etw. ~:** shoot sth. through 2 (Buchbinderei) interleave 3 (Druckw.) space out 4 (Textilind.) interweave (**mit** with)

durch|schimmern *itr. V.* 1 **[durch etw.] ~** ‹*light*› shimmer through [sth.]; ‹*colour*› gleam through [sth.] 2 (fig.) ‹*qualities, emotions*› show through

durch|schlafen *unr. itr. V.* sleep [right] through; **die ganze Nacht ~:** sleep all night [without waking]

Durch·schlag *der* 1 (Kopie) carbon [copy] 2 (Küchengerät) colander; strainer 3 (Kfz-W.) puncture 4 (Werkzeug) punch 5 (Elektrot.) disruptive discharge

durch|schlagen¹ **A** *unr. tr. V.* 1 **etw. ~:** chop *or* split sth. in two 2 (schlagen) **ein Loch/einen Nagel [durch etw.] ~:** knock a hole through [sth.]/knock *or* drive a nail through [sth.] **B** *unr. itr. V.* 1 *mit sein* **[durch etw.] ~** ‹*dampness, water*› come through [sth.]; **das schlägt auf die Preise durch** (fig.) it has an effect on prices; **bei ihm schlägt die Mutter durch** (fig.) he takes after his mother; **der Aristokrat in ihm schlägt durch** the aristocrat in him comes out 2 *mit sein* ‹*fuse*› blow 3 (abführen) have a strong laxative effect; **bei jmdm. ~:** go straight through sb. **C** *refl. V.* 1 struggle along 2 (ein Ziel erreichen) (mit Gewalt) fight one's way through; (mit List) make one's way through

durch·schlagen² *unr. tr. V.* smash

durchschlagend *Adj.* resounding ‹*success*›; decisive ‹*effect, measures*›; conclusive ‹*evidence*›

Durchschlag·papier *das* copy paper

Durchschlags·kraft *die* 1 (Ballistik) penetrating power 2 (fig.: Wirkung) power; force

durch|schlängeln *refl. V.* **sich [durch etw.] ~** (auch fig.) thread one's way through [sth.]

durch|schleichen *unr. refl. V.* **sich [durch etw.] ~:** slip *or* creep through [sth.]

durch|schleppen *tr. V.* (ugs.) carry ‹*loss-making concern, non-productive worker*›; keep ‹*needy relation etc.*›

durch|schleusen *tr. V.* 1 (ugs.) **jmdn./etw. [durch etw.] ~:** guide sb./sth. through [sth.]; (durchschmuggeln) get sb./sth. through [sth.] 2 (Schifffahrt) **ein Schiff ~:** pass a ship through a lock

Durchschlupf /ˈdʊrçʃlʊpf/ *der;* **~[e]s, ~e** gap; (Loch) hole

durch|schlüpfen *itr. V.; mit sein* **[durch etw.] ~:** slip through [sth.]

durch|schmecken **A** *tr. V.* be able to taste (**bei** in) **B** *itr. V.* come through [too strongly]

durch|schmoren *itr. V.; mit sein* (ugs.) ‹*cable*› burn through; ‹*element*› burn out

durch|schmuggeln *tr. V.* **etw. [durch etw.] ~:** smuggle sth. through [sth.]

durch|schneiden¹ *unr. tr. V.* cut through ‹*thread, cable*›; cut ‹*ribbon, sheet of paper*› in two; cut ‹*throat, umbilical cord*›; **etw. in der Mitte ~:** cut sth. in half

durch·schneiden² *unr. tr. V.* 1 ▸**durchschneiden¹** 2 (geh.) ‹*road, river, valley*› cut through; ‹*bow of boat*› slice through ‹*waves*›; **das Land ist von Kanälen durchschnitten** the country is criss-crossed by canals

Durch·schnitt *der* 1 average; **im ~:** on average; **im ~ 110 km/h fahren** average 110 k.p.h.; do 110 k.p.h. on average 2 (Mittelmaß) **über/unter dem ~ liegen, guter/unterer ~ sein** be above/below average; **vom ~ abweichen** deviate from the norm 3 (ugs.: Mehrheit) majority; **der ~ ist ...** the majority [of people] *or* people in general are ... 4 (Math.) mean 5 (fachspr.) [cross] section

durchschnittlich **A** *Adj.* 1 average ‹*growth, performance, output*› 2 (ugs.: mehrheitlich) ordinary ‹*life, person, etc.*› 3 (mittelmäßig) modest ‹*intelligence, talent, performance, achievements*›; ordinary ‹*appearance*› **B** *adv.* ‹*produce, spend, earn, etc.*› on [an] average; **~ groß sein** be of average height; **~ begabt sein** be moderately talented

Durchschnitts-: **~alter** *das* average age; **~bürger** *der,* **~bürgerin** *die* average citizen; **~ehe** *die* ordinary marriage; (Statistik) average marriage; **~einkommen** *das* average income; **~geschwindigkeit** *die* average speed; **~gesicht** *das* ordinary face; **~leser** *der,* **~leserin** *die* average reader; **~lohn** *der* average wage; **~mensch** *der* average person; (Alltagsmensch) ordinary person; **für uns ~menschen** for ordinary people like ourselves; **~note** *die* (Schulw.) average grade; **~temperatur** *die* average temperature; **~wert** *der* average *or* mean value; **~zensur** *die* ▸**~note**

durch|schnüffeln¹, durch·schnüffeln² *tr. V.* (abwertend) poke *or* nose around in

Durchschreibe·block *der; Pl.* **~s** *od.* **Durchschreibeblöcke** duplicate pad

durch|schreiben *unr. tr. V.* make a carbon copy of

durch·schreiten *unr. tr. V.* (geh.) stride across ‹*room*›; stride through ‹*door, hall*›

Durch·schrift *die* carbon [copy]

Durch·schuss, ***Durch·schuß** *der* 1 bullet *or* gunshot wound (*where the bullet has passed right through*) 2 (Schuss): *shot in which the bullet passes through and emerges on the other side* 3 (Druckw.) (Zwischenraum) space; (Blindmaterial) lead 4 (Textilw.) weft; woof

durch|schütteln *tr. V.* **jmdn. ~:** give sb. a good shaking; **wir wurden im Bus tüchtig durchgeschüttelt** we were shaken about all over the place in the bus

durch·schweifen *tr. V.* (dichter.) roam *or* wander through; (fig.) ‹*gaze*› rove *or* wander

durch|schwimmen¹ *unr. itr. V.; mit sein* **[durch etw.] ~:** swim through [sth.]; **unter etw.** (*Dat.*) **~:** swim through under sth.

durch·schwimmen² *unr. tr. V.* swim ‹*the Channel, course, etc.*›

durch|schwindeln *refl. V.* get along by cheating and lying

durch|schwitzen, durch·schwitzen *tr. V.* **ich habe mein Hemd** *usw.* **durchgeschwitzt** *od.* **durchschwitzt** my shirt *etc.* is soaked in sweat; *s. auch* **durchgeschwitzt**

durch|segeln *itr. V.; mit sein* 1 **[durch etw.] ~:** sail through [sth.]; **zwischen den Felsen ~:** sail [through] between the rocks 2 (Schülerspr.: durchfallen) **[durch etw.] ~:** fail *or* (Amer. coll.) flunk sth.; **bei/in etw.** (*Dat.*) **~:** fail *or* flunk sth.

durch|sehen **A** *unr. itr. V.* 1 **[durch etw.] ~:** look through [sth.]; **durch dieses Glas kann man nicht ~:** you can't see through this type of glass 2 ▸**durchblicken 2** **B** *unr. tr. V.* 1 look *or* check through *or* over ‹*essay, homework, etc.*›; **etw. auf Fehler ~:** look *or* check through sth. for mistakes 2 (lesen) look through ‹*newspaper, magazine*›

durch|seihen *tr. V.* (Kochk.) strain; pass ‹*sauce, gravy*› through a sieve

***durch|sein** ▸**durch B 4-12**

durchsetzbar *Adj.* enforceable ‹*demand, claim*›; **diese Rentenerhöhung/Reform ist nicht ~:** it will be impossible to get this pension increase approved/to carry this reform through

durch|setzen¹ **A** *tr. V.* carry *or* put through ‹*programme, reform*›; carry through ‹*intention, plan*›; accomplish, achieve ‹*objective*›; enforce ‹*demand, claim*›; get ‹*resolution*› accepted; **~, dass etw. geschieht** succeed in getting sth. done; **seinen Willen ~:** have one's [own] way **B** *refl. V.* assert oneself; ‹*idea*› find *or* gain acceptance, become generally accepted *or* established; ‹*fashion*› catch on (coll.), find *or* gain acceptance; **sich gegen jmdn. ~:** assert oneself against sb.; **sich den Schülern gegenüber ~** ‹*teacher*› assert one's authority over the pupils

durch·setzen² *tr. V.* **eine Gruppe mit Spitzeln/ein Land mit Spionen ~:** infiltrate informers into a group/spies into a country; **mit Nadelbäumen durchsetzt sein** be interspersed with conifers

Durchsetzung *die;* **~** ▸**durchsetzen¹**: carrying through; putting through; accomplishment; achievement; enforcement; **zur ~ unserer Forderungen** to enforce our demands

durchsetzungs-, Durchsetzungs-: **~fähig** *Adj.* 1 [self-]assertive; 2 ▸**durchsetzbar**; **~fähigkeit** *die;* **~~** 1 [self-]assertiveness; 2 (von Reform, Projekt, Politik) realizable *od.* achievable nature; **~kraft** *die,* **~vermögen** *das* ability to assert oneself

Durch·sicht *die* look *or* check through; **nach [einer] ~ der Unterlagen** after looking *or* checking through the documents; **jmdm. etw. zur ~ geben** give sb. sth. to look *or* check through

durchsichtig *Adj.* 1 transparent; see-through, transparent ‹*nightdress, blouse*›; clear ‹*air, water*› 2 (durchschaubar) transparent; **etw. ~ machen** make sth. comprehensible

durch|sickern *itr. V.; mit sein* 1 seep through 2 (bekannt werden) ‹*news*› leak out; **es ist durchgesickert, dass ...** news has leaked out that ...

durch|sieben¹ *tr. V.* sift, sieve ‹*flour etc.*›; strain ‹*tea etc.*›; (fig.) sift [through] ‹*applicants etc.*›

durch·sieben² *tr. V.* ‹*bullets*› riddle; **von Kugeln durchsiebt** riddled with bullets

durch|sitzen **A** *unr. tr. V.* wear out ‹*chair, seat*›; **seine Hose ~:** wear through *or* out the seat of one's trousers **B** *unr. refl. V.* ‹*chair, seat*› wear out, become worn out

durchsoffen *Adj.* (derb) **eine ~e Nacht** a night on the booze (sl.)

durch|sollen *itr. V.* (ugs.) **[durch etw.] ~** ‹*cupboard, cable*› be supposed to go through [sth.]; **soll der Schrank hier durch?** is the cupboard to go through here?

durchsonnt /dʊrçˈzɔnt/ *Adj.* (dichter.) sun-drenched; sunny; sun-filled ‹*room, clearing*›

durch|spielen *tr. V.* 1 act ‹*scene*› through; play ‹*piece of music*› through 2 (fig.: durchgehen) go through ‹*alternatives, options*›; play ‹*part, role*› to the end; ‹*footballer*› play right through; **die ganze Nacht ~** ‹*card players etc.*› play all night [long]

durch|sprechen *unr. tr. V.* talk ‹*matter etc.*› over; discuss ‹*matter etc.*› thoroughly

durch|springen *unr. itr. V.; mit sein* **[durch etw.] ~:** jump *or* leap through [sth.]

durch|spülen *tr. V.* **etw. [gut/gründlich] ~:** rinse sth. thoroughly

durch|starten *itr. V.; mit sein* 1 (Flugw.) begin climbing again (instead of landing) 2 (Kfz-W.) accelerate away again

Durch·starter *der,* **Durch·starterin** *die* instant success; (Person auch) instant star; whizzkid (coll.)

durch|stechen[1] *unr. itr. V.* **mit einer Nadel** *usw.* **[durch etw.] ~:** stick a needle *etc.* through [sth.]

durch·stechen[2] *unr. tr. V.* pierce; cut through ‹*isthmus*›; **sich** (*Dat.*) **die Ohrläppchen ~ lassen** have one's ears pierced

durch|stecken *tr. V.* **etw. [durch etw.] ~:** put *or* (coll.) stick sth. through [sth.]

durch|stehen *unr. tr. V.* 1 stand ‹*pace, boring job, living with sb.*›; come through ‹*adventure, difficult situation*›; pass ‹*test*›; get over ‹*illness*› 2 (Ski) complete ‹*jump, run*› without falling

Durchsteh·vermögen *das* staying power; stamina; [power of] endurance

durch|steigen *unr. itr. V.; mit sein* 1 **[durch etw.] ~:** climb through [sth.] 2 (salopp: verstehen) get it (coll.); **da steige ich nicht durch** I don't get it (coll.)

durch|stellen *tr. V.* put ‹*call*› through (**in** + *Akk.*, **auf** + *Akk.* to)

durch|stemmen *tr. V.* chisel through, chisel a hole in ‹*wall*›

Durch·stich *der* 1 (Vorgang) cutting through; **der ~ der Landenge** *usw.* cutting through the isthmus *etc.* 2 (Verbindung) cut; cutting

Durchstieg /ˈdʊrçʃtiːk/ *der;* **~[e]s, ~e einen ~ in den Zaun schneiden** cut a hole in the fence [through which one can/could climb]

durch|stöbern[1] *tr. V.* (ugs.) search all through ‹*house*›; rummage through ‹*cupboard, case, etc.*›; scour ‹*wood, area*›

durch·stöbern[2] *tr. V.* (ugs.) 1 ▸**durchstöbern**[1] 2 (durchsuchen) rummage around ‹*shop*› (**nach** in search of); rummage through ‹*archives*› (**nach** in search of)

Durch·stoß *der* (Milit.) breakthrough

durch|stoßen[1] *unr. itr. V.* 1 **durch etw. ~:** knock a hole through sth.; break through sth. 2 *mit sein* (Milit.) break through (**bis zu** to)

durch·stoßen[2] *unr. tr. V.* break through; go through ‹*cloud layer*›; rupture ‹*hymen*›; smash ‹*pane of glass*›; **die feindlichen Linien ~** (Milit.) break through the enemy lines

durch|streichen[1] *unr. tr. V.* 1 cross through *or* out; delete; (in Formularen) delete 2 (passieren) **Gemüse/die Sauce [durch ein Sieb] ~:** pass vegetables through a sieve/strain the sauce [through a sieve]

durch·streichen[2] *unr. tr. V.* (geh.) roam ‹*area*›; rove, roam ‹*foreign parts*›

durch·streifen *tr. V.* 1 (geh.) roam, wander through ‹*fields, countryside*› 2 (kontrollieren) patrol

durch|strömen[1] *itr. V.; mit sein* **[durch etw.] ~:** flow through [sth.]; (fig.) ‹*people, crowd*› stream *or* pour through [sth.]

durch·strömen[2] *tr. V.* flow through

durch|strukturieren *tr. V.* **etw. ~:** structure sth. well; **ein gut durchstrukturierter Artikel** a well-structured article

durch|stylen *tr. V.* give a completely integrated design/style to ‹*premises, rooms etc.*›

durch|suchen[1] *tr. V.* search through

durch·suchen[2] *tr. V.* search ‹*house, car*› (**nach** for); frisk, search ‹*person*› (**nach** for); search, scour ‹*area*› (**nach** for)

Durchsuchung *die;* **~, ~en** search; **zur ~ einer Wohnung** in order to search a flat

Durchsuchungs·befehl *der* search warrant

durch|tanzen[1]
A *itr. V.* **die ganze Nacht ~:** dance all night; dance the night away; **bis zum Morgen ~:** dance until morning
B *tr. V.* wear out ‹*shoes*› [by] dancing

durch·tanzen[2] *tr. V.* **die Nacht ~:** spend the night dancing; dance all night; **nach einer durchtanzten Nacht** after a night of *or* spent dancing

durch|testen *tr. V.* 1 **jedes einzelne Gerät ~:** test each device individually 2 (gründlich testen) **etw. ~:** test sth. thoroughly

durch·toben *tr. V.* (geh.) rage through

durch|trainieren *tr. V.* get ‹*athlete, team, body*› into condition; **ein gut durchtrainierter Körper** a body in peak condition

durch·tränken *tr. V.* (geh.) soak *or* saturate [completely]; soak, steep ‹*fruit*›

durch|treiben *unr. tr. V.* 1 **Menschen/Tiere [durch etw.] ~:** drive people/animals through [sth.] 2 (durchschlagen) **einen Nagel** *usw.* **[durch etw.] ~:** drive a nail *etc.* through [sth.]

durch|trennen[1], **durch·trennen**[2] *tr. V.* cut [through] ‹*wire, rope*›; sever ‹*nerve, umbilical cord*›

durch|treten
A *unr. tr. V.* press ‹*clutch pedal, brake pedal*› right down; depress ‹*clutch pedal, brake pedal*› completely
B *unr. itr. V.* 1 *mit sein* **[durch etw.] ~** ‹*liquid, gas*› come through [sth.] 2 *mit sein* (ugs.: weitergehen) ‹*passenger*› move along down (*in bus, train*)

durchtrieben (abwertend)
A *Adj.* crafty; sly
B *adv.* craftily; slyly

Durchtriebenheit *die;* **~:** craftiness; slyness

durch|trinken *unr. itr. V.* **die ganze Nacht ~:** drink all night; **bis zum Morgen ~:** drink right through till morning

durch|tropfen *itr. V.; mit sein* **[durch etw.] ~** ‹*water*› drip through [sth.]

durch|wachen[1] *itr. V.* stay awake; **die ganze Nacht ~:** stay awake all night

durch·wachen[2] *tr. V.* **die Nacht/mehrere Nächte ~:** stay awake all night/[for] several nights running; **die Nacht am Bett des Kranken ~:** keep watch through the night at the patient's bedside

durch|wachsen[1] *unr. itr. V.; mit sein* **[durch etw.] ~** ‹*plant*› grow through sth.

durch·wachsen[2]
A *Adj.* 1 **mit Unkraut ~ sein** ‹*lawn*› have weeds growing in it; **~er Speck** streaky bacon 2 (ugs. scherzh.) so-so
B *adv.* **ihr geht es ~:** she has her ups and downs

durch|wagen *refl. V.* (ugs.) **sich [durch etw.] ~:** dare to go through sth.; venture through sth.

Durchwahl *die* 1 direct dialling 2 **mein Apparat ist mit/hat keine ~:** I have/don't have an outside line 3 ▸**Durchwahlnummer**

durch|wählen *itr. V.* 1 dial direct; **direkt nach Nairobi ~:** dial Nairobi direct; **in ein Land ~:** dial a country direct 2 (bei Nebenstellenanlagen) dial straight through

Durchwahl·nummer *die* number of the/one's direct line

durch|walken *tr. V.* 1 (durchkneten) **jmdn. ~** ‹*masseur*› give sb. a good, hard massage; **die Wäsche ~:** use a vigorous kneading action to get the washing clean 2 (ugs.: verprügeln) **jmdn. ~:** give sb. a good belting; (als Strafe) give sb. a good hiding

durch|wandern[1] *itr. V.; mit sein* walk *or* hike without a break; **den ganzen Tag ~:** walk *or* hike all day

durch·wandern[2] *tr. V.* walk *or* hike through

durch|wärmen[1], **durch·wärmen**[2] *tr. V.* **jmdn. ~:** warm sb. up

durch|waschen *unr. tr. V.* (ugs.) **etw. ~:** wash sth. through

durch|waten[1] *itr. V.; mit sein* **[durch etw.] ~:** wade through [sth.]

durch·waten[2] *tr. V.* wade across

durch·weben *regelm.* (*dichter. auch unr.*) *tr. V.* interweave (**mit** with)

durchweg /ˈdʊrçvɛk/, (österr. ugs.) **durchwegs** /ˈdʊrçveːks/ *Adv.* without exception; **er umgibt sich ~ mit Leuten, die …** he surrounds himself exclusively with people who …; **die Vegetation ist ~ öde** the vegetation is uniformly dreary

durch|wehen[1] *itr. V.* **durch etw. ~** ‹*wind*› blow through sth.

durch·wehen[2] *tr. V.* (geh.) ‹*breeze*› waft through; (fig.) pervade

durch|weichen[1] *itr. V.; mit sein* ‹*cardboard, paper*› become *or* go [soft and] soggy

durch·weichen[2] *tr. V.* make ‹*earth, path, etc.*› sodden; **völlig durchweicht sein** (fig.) be drenched; be sopping wet

durch|werfen *unr. tr. V.* **etw. [durch etw.] ~:** throw sth. through [sth.]

durch|wetzen wear out ‹*clothes*›; wear through ‹*sleeves*›; **eine durchgewetzte Hose** a worn-out pair of trousers

durch|winden *unr. refl. V.* **sich [durch etw.] ~** ‹*river*› wind its way through [sth.]; ‹*person*› thread one's way through [sth.]

durch·wirken *tr. V.* ▸**durchweben**

durch|witschen *itr. V.* (ugs.) **[durch etw.] ~:** slip through [sth.]; **jmdm. ~** ‹*word*› escape sb.

durch|wollen *unr. itr. V.* (ugs.) 1 **[durch etw.] ~** (durchgehen wollen) want to go through [sth.]; (durchkommen wollen) want to come through [sth.]; **unter etw.** (*Dat.*) **~:** want to go through under sth. 2 (ein Hindernis durchqueren) **[durch etw.] ~:** want to get through [sth.]

durch|wühlen[1]
A *tr. V.* rummage through, ransack ‹*drawers, cupboard, case*› (**nach** in search of, looking for); turn ‹*room, house*› upside down (**nach** in search of, looking for)
B *refl. V.* (ugs.) **sich durch das Blumenbeet/die Erde ~** ‹*mole*› dig up the flower bed/burrow through the earth; **sich durch einen Aktenstoß ~** (fig.) plough through a pile of documents

durch·wühlen[2] *tr. V.* 1 ▸**durchwühlen**[1] **A** 2 (aufwühlen) churn up

durch|wurschteln, durch|wursteln *refl. V.* (salopp) muddle through

durch|zählen *tr. V.* count; count up ‹*money, people*›

durch|zechen[1] *itr. V.* **bis zum Morgen ~:** drink until morning

durch·zechen[2] *tr. V.* **die Nacht ~:** spend all night drinking; **eine durchzechte Nacht** a night of drinking

durch|zeichnen *tr. V.* ▸**durchpausen**

durch|ziehen[1]
A *unr. tr. V.* 1 **jmdn./etw. [durch etw.] ~:** pull sb./sth. through [sth.]; **ein Gummiband [durch etw.] ~:** draw an elastic through [sth.] 2 (ugs.: durchführen) get through ‹*syllabus, programme*›; **wir müssen die Sache ~:** we must see the matter through 3 (bis zum Anschlag ziehen) pull ‹*oar, saw blade*› right through 4 (salopp: rauchen) smoke; **einen [Joint] ~:** smoke a joint (sl.) 5 (erstellen) dig ‹*ditch*› through; **eine Mauer [durch den Saal] ~:** build a wall across [the room]
B *unr. itr. V.; mit sein* 1 **[durch ein Gebiet** *usw.***] ~:** pass through [an area *etc.*]; ‹*soldiers*› march through [an area *etc.*] 2 (Kochk.) ‹*fruit, meat, etc.*› soak; **gut durchgezogen sein** be well soaked

durch·ziehen[2] *unr. tr. V.* 1 pass through ‹*land, area*› 2 (durchsetzen) ‹*river, road, ravine*› run through, traverse ‹*landscape*›; **von blauen Adern durchzogener Marmor** marble veined with blue 3 (enthalten sein in) ‹*theme, motif, etc.*› run through ‹*book etc.*› 4 (durchdringen) ‹*pain*› shoot through ‹*person*›; ‹*smell, scent*› suddenly

d

ℹ dürfen

1. Erlaubnis

ich darf = I may *od.* can

Wann darf ich nach Hause gehen?
= When may *od.* can I go home?

Er sagte mir, ich dürfte sofort nach Hause gehen
= He told me I could go home right away

Bei der Übersetzung von *dürfte* in dieser Konstruktion (indirekter Rede) ist **could** vorzuziehen, da **might** sich etwas gespreizt anhört.

In der Vergangenheit und in Fällen, wo *dürfen* qualifiziert wird, arbeitet man am besten mit **be allowed to:**

Sie durfte die Katze streicheln
= She was allowed to stroke the cat

Ich darf nur bis hierher kommen
= I am only allowed to come this far

Ich darf nie meine Meinung sagen
= I'm never allowed to say what I think, I can never speak my mind

Er darf nicht reiten, weil er es mit dem Rücken hat
= He isn't allowed to *od.* He can't ride because he has back trouble

(Weiteres zum negativen Gebrauch finden Sie unter 2.).

Wenn *dürfen* ohne zweites Verb allein steht, übersetzt man auch am besten mit **be allowed [to]:**

Wir haben nicht gedurft
= We weren't allowed to

Darf man das?
= Is that allowed?

Bei Höflichkeitsformeln mit *darf/dürfte ich ...* handelt es sich um höfliche Bitten um Erlaubnis, logischerweise ist die Übersetzung also **may/might I ...:**

Darf/Dürfte ich Sie begleiten?
= May/Might I accompany you?

Lediglich bei der Formel *darf ich Sie bitten ...* kommen andere Übersetzungen in Betracht:

Darf ich Sie bitten, hereinzukommen?
= Would you please come in?

Im erweiterten Sinne von "Grund haben zu" = **can:**

Wir dürfen annehmen, dass ...
= We can assume that ...

Ich darf mich nicht beklagen
= I can't *od.* mustn't complain

2. Verbot

Das darf man/darfst du/dürfen Sie nicht tun

Solche Beispiele lassen sich auf verschiedene Art übersetzen, je nachdem, welcher Aspekt betont wird. Will man betonen, dass die Handlung nicht erlaubt ist, sagt man "That's not allowed". Ist man entsetzt über einen Verstoß gegen die Sitten, sagt man "You can't do that!". Aber vor allem, wenn man ein Verbot ausspricht oder jemandem von etwas abrät, heißt es "You mustn't do that":

Das darfst du unter keinen Umständen erwähnen
= You mustn't mention that under any circumstances

Das gilt aber nicht nur für die Anrede in der zweiten Person:

Sie darf nicht alleine fahren
= She mustn't go on her own

Er darf es nicht wissen
= He must not know about it

Auch bei Vorschriften oder dergleichen sagt man **must not:**

Hier darf man nicht rauchen
= You must not smoke here, There's no smoking here

Dieser Stoff darf nicht nass werden
= This material must not get wet

Ähnliche Beispiele in der Vergangenheit, die Missbilligung ausdrücken, werden mit **should not have** übersetzt:

Das hätte sie nicht sagen dürfen
= She shouldn't have said that

3. dürfte

Außer in Höflichkeitsformeln wird dieser Konjunktiv II meist mit **should** oder **ought to** übersetzt:

Jetzt dürften sie dort angekommen sein
= They should be there by now

Das dürfte schon möglich sein
= That should *od.* ought to be possible

Bei einer Schätzung sagt man aber **must:**

Sie dürfte in den Achtzigern sein
= She must be in her eighties

Und bei einer Vorhersage kann man **will probably** sagen:

Es dürfte ein Gewitter geben
= There will probably be a storm

---

fill ‹*room*›; (fig.) ‹*feeling, awareness*› come over ‹*person*›

durch·zucken *tr. V.* ‹*lightning, beam of light*› flash across; **jmdn. ~** (fig.) ‹*thought*› flash through *or* cross sb.'s mind

Dụrch·zug *der* **1▸** draught; **~ machen** create a draught; **auf ~ schalten** (ugs.), **die Ohren auf ~ stellen** (ugs.) let it go in one ear and out the other **2▸** (das Durchziehen) passage through; (von Truppen) march through; **nach dem ~ des Schlechtwettergebietes** (Met.) once the area of bad weather has moved through

Dụrchzügler /-t̮sy:klɐ/ *der;* **~s, ~** (Zool.) bird of passage

Dụrchzugs·recht *das* (Völkerr.) right to march troops through

durch|zwängen
A *tr. V.* **etw. [durch etw.] ~:** force *or* squeeze [sth.] through [sth.]
B *refl. V.* **sich [durch etw.] ~:** force *or* squeeze one's way through [sth.]

Dur·drei·klang *der* (Musik) major triad

dürfen /ˈdʏrfn̩/
A *unr. Modalverb; 2. Part.* **dürfen: 1▸** (Erlaubnis haben zu) **etw. tun ~:** be allowed *or* permitted to do sth.; **darf ich [das tun]?** may I [do that]?; **das darf man nicht tun** that is not allowed; one mustn't do that; **nein, das darfst du nicht** no you may not; **hier darf man nicht rauchen** smoking is prohibited here; **ich darf morgen nicht verschlafen** I mustn't oversleep tomorrow; **du darfst nicht lügen/jetzt nicht aufgeben!** you mustn't tell lies/give up now!; **ihm darf nichts geschehen** nothing must happen to him; **das darf nicht wahr sein** (ugs.) that's incredible; **das hätte nicht kommen ~** (ugs.) he/you *etc.* shouldn't have said that **2▸** (in Höflichkeitsformeln) **darf ich rauchen?** may I smoke?; **darf ich Sie bitten, das zu tun?** could I ask you to do that?; **darf** *od.* **dürfte ich mal Ihre Papiere sehen?** may I see your papers?; **darf ich um diesen Tanz bitten?** may I have [the pleasure of] this dance?; **was darf es sein?** (im Laden) can I help you?; (was möchten Sie zum Trinken haben?) what can I get you to drink?; **darf ich bitten?** (um einen Tanz) may I have the pleasure?; (einzutreten) won't you come in?; **Ruhe, wenn ich bitten darf!** will you please be quiet! **3▸** (Grund haben zu) **ich darf Ihnen mitteilen, dass ...** I am able to inform you that ...; **darf ich annehmen, dass ...?** can I assume that ...?; **sie darf sich nicht beklagen** she can't complain; she has no reason to complain; **da darf sie sich nicht wundern** that shouldn't surprise her; **das darfst du mir glauben** you can take my word for it **4▸** *Konjunktiv II + Inf.* **das dürfte der Grund sein** that is probably the reason; (ich nehme an, dass das der Grund ist) that must be the reason; **es dürfte einfach sein, das zu tun** it should be *or* ought to be easy to do it; **das dürfte reichen** that should be enough
B *unr. tr., itr. V.* **er hat nicht gedurft** he was not allowed *or* permitted to; **darf ich ins Theater?** may I go to the theatre?; **darfst du das?** are you allowed to?; **Darf ich? — Ja, Sie ~:** May I? — Yes, you may

durfte /ˈdʊrftə/, *1. u. 3. Pers. Sg. Prät. v.* **dürfen**

dürfte /ˈdʏrftə/ *1. u. 3. Pers. Sg. Konjunktiv II v.* **dürfen**

dürftig /ˈdʏrftɪç/
A *Adj.* **1▸** (ärmlich) poor; scanty, meagre ‹*meal*›; scanty, poor ‹*clothing*› **2▸** (abwertend: unzulänglich) poor ‹*substitute, performance, light*›; feeble, poor ‹*explanation*›; lame, feeble ‹*excuse*›; scanty ‹*knowledge, evidence, results*›; sparse ‹*growth of hair*›; paltry, meagre ‹*income*› **3▸** (kümmerlich, unansehnlich) puny ‹*tree, person*›
B *adv.* **1▸** ‹*live*› poorly; scantily ‹*dressed*› **2▸** (abwertend: unzulänglich) skimpily, scantily ‹*furnished*›; poorly ‹*attended*›; ‹*report, formulate*› sketchily; thinly ‹*concealed*›

Dụ̈rftigkeit *die;* **~ ▸dürftig: 1▸** (Ärmlichkeit) poorness; scantiness; meagreness **2▸** (abwertend: Unzulänglichkeit) poorness; feebleness; lameness; scantiness; sparseness; paltriness; meagreness

dürr /dʏr/ *Adj.* **1▸** withered ‹*branch*›; dry, dried up, withered ‹*grass, leaves*›; arid, barren ‹*ground, earth*› **2▸** (mager) skinny, scraggy, scrawny ‹*legs, arms, body, person*› **3▸** (unergiebig) lean ‹*years*›; bare ‹*words, description*›

Dụ̈rre *die;* **~, ~n 1▸** (Trockenheit) drought **2▸** (Dürrheit) aridity; barrenness; (fig.: der Sprache) dryness

Dụ̈rre-: ~jahr *das* year of drought; **~kata·strophe** *die* catastrophic drought; **~peri·ode** *die* period of drought

Durst /dʊrst/ *der;* **~[e]s** thirst; **~ haben** be thirsty; **~ bekommen** get *or* become thirsty; **seinen ~ löschen** *od.* **stillen** quench *or* slake one's thirst; **ich habe ~ auf ein Bier** *od.* **nach einem Bier** I could just drink a beer; **~ nach Ruhm/Wissen** (fig. geh.) a thirst for fame/knowledge; **ein Glas** *od.* **einen/etliche über den ~ trinken** (ugs. scherzh.) have one/a few too many; **Fisch macht ~:** fish makes one thirsty

dụrsten *itr. V.* (geh.) **1▸** thirst; **~ müssen** have to go thirsty **2▸ ▸dürsten**

dụ̈rsten /ˈdʏrstn̩/ (dichter.)
A *tr. V.* (unpers.) **mich dürstet** *od.* **es dürstet mich** I am thirsty; **ihn dürstete nach Rache** (fig.) he thirsted *or* was thirsty for revenge
B *itr. V.* **nach Rache/Gerechtigkeit** *usw.* **~:** thirst for revenge/justice *etc.*

dụrstig *Adj.* thirsty; **das macht ~:** it makes you thirsty; it gives you a thirst

dụrst-, Dụrst-: ~löscher *der* thirst-quencher; **~löschend, ~stillend** *Adj.* thirst-quenching; **~strecke** *die* lean period *or* time; **~streik** *der* refusal of fluids (*as a means of protest*); **in einen ~streik treten** refuse fluids

Dur-: ~ton·art *die* (Musik) major key; **~ton·leiter** *die* (Musik) major scale

Dusch·bad *das* shower [bath]

Dusche /ˈdʊʃə/ *die;* ~, ~n shower; **unter die ~ gehen** take *or* have a shower; **unter der ~ sein** be in the shower; **eine heiße/kalte ~ nehmen** take *or* have a hot/cold shower; **eine kalte ~ [für jmdn.] sein, wie eine kalte ~ [auf jmdn.] wirken** (ugs.) be like a cold douche *or* a douche of cold water [on sb.]

duschen
A *itr., refl. V.* take *or* have a shower; **[sich] warm/kalt ~:** take *or* have a warm/cold shower
B *tr. V.* **jmdn. ~:** give sb. a shower

Düse /ˈdyːzə/ *die;* ~, ~n (Technik) nozzle; (eines Vergasers) jet

Dusel /ˈduːzl̩/ *der;* ~s [1] (ugs.) luck; **~ haben** be jammy (Brit. coll.) *or* lucky; **sie hat [einen] ~ gehabt** her luck was in (coll.); she was jammy (Brit. coll.) *or* lucky; **so ein ~:** that was lucky [2] (nordd.: Schwindelgefühl) daze; **einen ~ haben** feel dizzy [3] (nordd.: Rausch) fuddle; **im ~ sein** be in a fuddle

duselig *Adj.* (ugs.) (angetrunken) fuddled; tipsy; muzzy; (benommen) muzzy; (schlaftrunken) drowsy

duseln *itr. V.* (ugs.) doze

düsen *itr. V.; mit sein* (ugs.) dash

Düsen-: ~an·trieb *der* jet propulsion; **mit ~antrieb** jet-propelled; **~bomber** *der* jet bomber; **~clipper** *der* jet airliner; **~flug·zeug** *das* jet aeroplane *or* aircraft *or* plane; **~jäger** *der* jet fighter; **~maschine** *die* jet [aeroplane *or* aircraft *or* plane]; **~motor** *der* jet engine; **~trieb·werk** *das* jet power plant; jet engine

Dussel /ˈdʊsl̩/ *der;* ~s, ~ (ugs.) dope (coll.); idiot; clot (Brit. coll.)

Dusselei *die;* ~ (ugs.) stupidity

dusselig, dusslig, *dußlig (ugs.)
A *Adj.* [1] gormless (Brit. coll.); stupid; idiotic [2] (nordd.: benommen) dopey (coll.); muzzy
B *adv.* gormlessly (Brit. coll.); stupidly

duster /ˈduːstɐ/ *Adj.* (nordd.) dark

düster /ˈdyːstɐ/
A *Adj.* [1] dark; gloomy; dim ‹*light*›; dark ‹*background*› [2] (bedrückend) gloomy, dismal ‹*day, weather, surroundings*›; sombre ‹*colour, music*›; gloomy, sombre ‹*atmosphere, picture*› [3] (unheilvoll) gloomy ‹*forecast, conception, etc.*›; dark ‹*foreboding*› [4] (schwermütig) gloomy ‹*expression, look, person*›; gloomy, depressing ‹*atmosphere*›; gloomy, dark ‹*thoughts*› [5] (obskur) shady ‹*business, affair*› [6] (unklar) hazy ‹*idea*›; dim, hazy ‹*conception*›
B *adv.* (schwermütig) gloomily

Düsterheit, Düsterkeit *die;* ~, **Düster·nis** *die;* ~ (geh.) [1] ▸**düster 1**: darkness; gloom; dimness [2] ▸**düster 2**: gloominess; dismalness; sombreness [3] ▸**düster 4**: gloominess; depressingness; darkness

Dutt /dʊt/ *der;* ~[e]s, ~e *od.* ~s bun

Dutte *die;* ~, ~n (österr. ugs.) teat

Dutyfree-shop, Duty-free-Shop /ˈdjuːtɪˈfriːʃɔp/ *der* duty-free shop

Dutzend /ˈdʊtsn̩t/ *das;* ~s, ~e [1] *Pl.* ~: dozen; **ein [ganzes]/halbes ~:** a dozen/half a dozen; **zwei ~:** two dozen; **ein ~ Eier** a dozen eggs; **das ~ Schnecken kostet** *od.* **kosten 16 Euro** snails cost 16 euros a dozen; **davon gehen 12 auf ein ~** (ugs.) there is nothing special about it [2] **~e** (eine Menge) dozens; **sie kamen in** *od.* **zu ~en** they came in [their] dozens (coll.)

dutzend-, Dutzend-: ~fach A *Adj.* dozens of *attrib.;* **B** *adv.* a dozen times; dozens of times; **~gesicht** *das* (abwertend) nondescript face; **~mal** ▸**Mal**[1]; **~mensch** *der* (abwertend) nondescript *or* run-of-the-mill person; **~typ** *der* (abwertend) nondescript *or* run-of-the-mill type; **~ware** *die* (abwertend) cheap mass-produced item; **~ware sein** be a cheap mass-produced item; **~weise** *Adv.* ‹*arrive, leave*› in [their] dozens (coll.); **Artikel ~weise kaufen/verkaufen** buy/sell articles by the dozen

Duz·bruder *der* (veralt.) ▸**Duzfreund**

duzen /ˈduːtsn̩/ *tr. V.* call 'du' (*the familiar form of address*); **sich ~:** call each other 'du'; **sich mit jmdm. ~:** call sb. 'du'; *s. auch* **siezen**

Duz-: ~freund *der,* **~freundin** *die* good friend (*whom one addresses with 'du'*); **~fuß** *der:* **in mit jmdm. auf [dem] ~fuß stehen** (ugs. veralt.) use [the familiar form] 'du' *or* the familiar form of address with sb.

DV *Abk.* **= Datenverarbeitung** DP

DVD *die;* ~, ~s DVD

DVD-: ~-Brenner *der* (DV) DVD burner; DVD writer; **~-Laufwerk** *das* (DV) DVD drive; **~-R** *die;* ~, ~s (DV) DVD-R; **~-Recorder, DVD-Rekorder** *der* DVD recorder; **~-RW** *die;* ~, ~s (DV) DVD-RW; **~-Spieler** *der* DVD player; **~-Video** *das* DVD video

DVP *Abk.* (DDR) **= Deutsche Volkspolizei**

DW *Abk.* **= Deutsche Welle**

dwars /dvars/ *Adv.* (Seemannsspr.) abeam

Dynamik /dyˈnaːmɪk/ *die;* ~ [1] (Physik) dynamics *sing., no art.* [2] (Triebkraft) dynamism [3] (Musik) dynamics [4] (Versicherungsw.) **eine Lebensversicherung mit ~:** ≈ index-linked life insurance (linked to changes in the national product)

Dynamiker *der;* ~s, ~, **Dynamikerin** *die;* ~, ~nen dynamo (fig.)

dynamisch /dyˈnaːmɪʃ/
A *Adj.* [1] (auch fig.) dynamic; **~e Renten** ≈ index-linked pensions (linked to changes in the national product); **eine ~e Lebensversicherung** ≈ index-linked life insurance (linked to changes in the national product) [2] (Physik) dynamic; **~e Gesetze** laws of dynamics [3] (Musik) dynamic
B *adv.* dynamically

dynamisieren *tr. V.* [1] **etw. ~:** make sth. dynamic; give sth. dynamism [2] (anpassen) adjust ‹*pension*›

Dynamisierung *die;* ~, ~en [1] **eine ~ der Agrarpolitik** making the agricultural policy more dynamic; **die ~ einer Bewegung auslösen** give a movement dynamism [2] (Anpassung) adjustment (*of pension*)

Dynamismus *der;* ~: dynamism

Dynamit /dynaˈmiːt/ *das;* ~s dynamite; **~ in den Fäusten/Beinen haben** (fig.) pack a powerful punch/have a powerful shot

Dynamo /dyˈnaːmo/ *der;* ~s, ~s dynamo

Dynast /dyˈnast/ *der;* ~en, ~en (hist.) dynast

Dynastie *die;* ~, ~n dynasty

dynastisch *Adj.* dynastic

Dys·funktion /dʏs-/ *die* ▸**ⓘ S. 439** (Med., Psych., Soziol.) dysfunction

Dystonie /dʏstoˈniː/ *die;* ~, ~n ▸**ⓘ S. 439** (Med.) dystonia; **vegetative ~:** neurodystonia

D-Zug /ˈdeː-/ *der* fast *or* express train; **ein alter Mann/eine alte Frau ist doch kein ~!** (salopp) I'm too old to hurry

D-Zug-: ~-Tempo *das* (ugs.) **im ~-Tempo** in double-quick time; **~-Zuschlag** *der* fast train supplement

d

Ee

e, E /eː/ *das;* ~, ~ [1] (Buchstabe) e/E [2] (Musik) [key of] E; *s. auch* **a, A**

E *Abk.* = **Europastraße**

Eau de Cologne /'oː də ko'lɔnjə/ *das od. die;* ~, **Eaux de Cologne** /'oː-/ eau de Cologne

Ebbe /'ɛbə/ *die;* ~, ~**n** [1] (Bewegung) ebb tide; **nach Eintritt der** ~: once the tide starts/had started to go out; ~ **und Flut** ebb and flow [2] (Zustand) low tide; **es ist** ~: the tide is out; **bei** ~: at low tide; when the tide is/was out; **es herrschte** ~ **in seinem Geldbeutel** *od.* **in seiner Kasse** (fig. ugs.) he was short of cash (coll.)

Ebbe-und-Flut-Kraftwerk *das* tidal power station

ebd. *Abk.* = **ebenda, ebendort** ibid.

eben /'eːbn̩/

[A] *Adj.* [1] (flach) flat [2] (glatt) level ‹*ground, path, stretch*› [3] (veralt.: gleichmäßig) even, smooth ‹*gait*›

[B] *adv.* [1] (gerade jetzt) just; **hast du** ~ **etwas gesagt?** did you just say something? [2] (kurz) [for] a moment; **kann ich Sie** ~ **sprechen?** can I speak to you [for] a moment *or* minute? [3] (gerade noch) just [about]; **etw.** ~ **noch schaffen** only just manage sth. [4] (genau) precisely; **aus** ~ **diesem Grunde** for this very reason; for precisely this reason; **aus** ~ **diesem Grunde brauchen wir das Geld** that is exactly *or* precisely why we need the money; **ja,** ~: yes, exactly *or* precisely; **ja,** ~ **das meine ich auch** yes, that's just *or* exactly what I think

[C] *Partikel* [1] **nicht** ~: not exactly [2] (nun einmal) simply; **das ist** ~ **so** that's just the way it is; **so gut ich** ~ **kann** as well as I can in the circumstances

eben-, Eben-: ~**bild** *das* image; **ganz jmds.** ~**bild sein** be the spitting image of sb.; ~**bürtig** /-bʏrtɪç/ *Adj.* equal; **jmdm. ein** ~**bürtiger Gegner sein** be sb.'s equal; be a match for sb.; **jmdm.** ~**bürtig sein** be equal to sb.; be sb.'s equal; **die beiden waren sich** ~**bürtig** they were [both] equal; ~**da** *Adv.* ibid. *abbr.*; ibidem; ~**der**, ~**die**, ~**das** *Demonstrativpron.* ~**das meine ich** that's exactly what I mean; ~**die, von der wir sprachen** the very one we were talking about; ~**der war krank** he was the very one who was ill; ~**derselbe**, ~**dieselbe**, ~**dasselbe** *Demonstrativpron.* the very same ‹*person, thing*›; ~**dieselbe meine ich** she's just the one I mean; ~**dasselbe wollte ich auch kaufen** I wanted to buy the very same thing; ~**deshalb**, ~**deswegen** *Adv.* that is/was precisely [the reason] why; ~**dieser**, ~**diese**, ~**dieses** *Demonstrativpron.* ~**dieses Thema wurde behandelt** this very topic was discussed; ~**diese Regeln gelten in allen Abteilungen** these same rules apply in all departments; ~**dieser wurde genannt** he was the very one who was mentioned

Ebene *die;* ~, ~**n** [1] (flaches Land) plain; **in der** ~: on the plain [2] (Geom., Physik) plane; **zwei sich schneidende** ~**n** two intersecting planes [3] (Stufe) level; **auf einer rein wissenschaftlichen** ~: on a purely scientific plane *or* level; **auf höchster** ~: at the highest level; *s. auch* **schief**

eben-: ~**erdig** [A] *Adj.* ground level; (in Gebäuden) ground-floor; one-storey ‹*house*›; ~**erdig sein** be on ground level/on the ground floor *or* (Amer.) first floor; [B] *adv.* at ground level; (in Gebäuden) on the ground floor *or* (Amer.) first floor; ~**falls** *Adv.* likewise; as well; **der Botschafter war** ~**falls eingeladen** the ambassador was likewise invited; the ambassador was invited as well; **danke,** ~**falls** thank you, [and] [the] same to you

Eben-holz *das* ebony

ebenholz-farben *Adj.* ebony

eben-, Eben-: ~**maß** *das* (der Gesichtszüge) regularity; (des Körperbaus) symmetry; even proportions *pl.*; (von Versen) regularity; harmony; ~**mäßig** [A] *Adj.* regular ‹*features*›; well-proportioned ‹*figure*›; regular, harmonious ‹*verse*›; **von** ~**mäßigem Wuchs** of even proportions; [B] *adv.* ~**mäßig geformt** *od.* **gestaltet** regularly shaped; ~**mäßigkeit** *die;* ~ ▸**Ebenmaß**

eben-so *Adv.* [1] *mit Adjektiven, Adverbien, Indefinitpronomina* just as; ~ **groß/schön/gut wie ... sein** be just as big/beautiful/good as ...; **ein** ~ **frecher wie dummer Kerl** a fellow who is/was as impudent as he is/was stupid; **er ist/arbeitet** ~ **fleißig wie geschickt** he is as diligent as he is skilful/works as diligently as he does skilfully; ~ **gern mag ich Erdbeeren [wie ...]** I like strawberries just as much [as ...]; ~ **gern würde ich an den Strand gehen** I would just as soon go to the beach; ~ **gut hätte er zu Hause bleiben können** he might just as well have stayed at home; **ich kann** ~ **gut ein Taxi nehmen** I can just as easily take a taxi; ~ **lange** for the same length of time; ~ **sehr/viel** just as much; ~ **wenig** just as little; **man kann dieses** ~ **wenig wie jenes tun** one cannot do this, any more than that; **er aß kein Gemüse,** ~ **wenig mochte er Obst** he didn't eat vegetables and he didn't like fruit either; he didn't eat vegetables, nor did he like fruit [2] *mit Verben* in exactly the same way; (in demselben Maße) just as much; **ich glaube, er wird es** ~ **machen wie wir** I think he'll do exactly the same as we [do]; **bei Tag** ~ **wie bei Nacht** in the daytime as well as by night; **er ist dagegen, und ich denke** ~: he's against it, and so am I; **mir geht es** ~: it's just the same for me

***ebenso-gern** *usw.* ▸**ebenso 1**

eben-solch... *Demonstrativpron.* the same; **ich habe ebensolche Angst/Kopfschmerzen wie du** I am just as afraid as you are/I have a headache too

***ebenso-sehr** *usw.* ▸**ebenso 1**

Eber /'eːbɐ/ *der;* ~**s**, ~: boar; **wie ein angestochener** ~ (salopp) like a [raving] maniac

Eber-esche *die* rowan; mountain ash

ebnen *tr. V.* level ‹*ground*›; **jmdm. den Weg** *od.* **die Bahn** ~ (fig.) smooth the way for sb.; **das Geld seines Vaters ebnete ihm alle Wege** (fig.) his father's money opened [up] all doors for him

E-Book /'iːbʊk/ *das;* ~**[s]**, ~**s** e-book

E-Business /'iː-/ *das;* ~: e-business

echauffieren /eʃɔ'fiːrən/ *tr. V.* (geh.) [1] make hot; **sich** ~: get hot [2] (aufregen) excite; **sich** ~: get excited

echauffiert *Adj.* (geh.) [1] hot [2] (aufgeregt) excited

Echo /'ɛço/ *das;* ~**s**, ~**s** echo; **das** ~ **auf die Ankündigung/den Vorschlag** (fig.) the response to the announcement/the suggestion; **das** ~ **in der Presse** (fig.) the press reaction; the reaction in the press; **ein breites** ~ **finden** meet with a wide response

Echo-effekt *der* echo effect

echoen /'ɛçoən/

[A] *itr. V.* (unpers.) **es echot** there is an echo

[B] *tr. V.* (gedankenlos wiederholen) echo

Echo-: ~**lot** *das* [1] (Seew.) echo sounder; sonic depth finder; [2] (Flugw.) sonic altimeter; ~**lotung** *die* (Seew.) echo-sounding

Echse /'ɛksə/ *die;* ~, ~**n** (Zool.) [1] saurian [2] (Eidechse) lizard

echt /ɛçt/

[A] *Adj.* [1] (nicht nachgemacht) genuine ‹*gold, fur, coin, Scotch whisky, Persian carpet*›; authentic, genuine ‹*signature, document*›; **ist das** ~**?** is that real gold/fur *etc.?*; **ein** ~**er Picasso** a genuine Picasso [2] (wahr) true, real ‹*love, friendship*›; real, genuine ‹*concern, sorrow, emergency, need*›; **sind seine Gefühle** ~**?** is he sincere?; **sie hat noch** ~**e Gefühle** her emotions are still natural ones [3] (typisch) real, typical ‹*Bavarian, American, etc.*› [4] (Math.) proper ‹*fraction*› [5] (Textilw., Chemie) fast ‹*dye*› [6] (reinrassig) thoroughbred ‹*horse*›; pedigree ‹*dog, cattle*›

[B] *adv.* [1] (ugs. verstärkend) really; **ich habe mich** ~ **gefreut** I was really pleased; **das ist** ~ **wahr/blöd** that's absolutely true/stupid; **das war eine Frechheit, aber** ~: it was a piece of downright cheek [2] (typisch) typically; **das ist** ~ **amerikanisch/Frau/Klaus** that's typically American/just like a woman/Klaus all over [3] (unverfälscht) **das Armband ist** ~ **golden** the bracelet is real gold

echt-, Echt-: ~**gold** *das* real *or* genuine gold; ~**golden** *Adj.* real *or* genuine gold; ~**haar-perücke** *die* [real] hair wig

Echtheit *die;* ~ [1] genuineness; (einer Unterschrift, eines Dokuments) authenticity; genuineness [2] (Textilw., Chemie) fastness

echt-, Echt-: ~**silber** *das* real silver; genuine silver; ~**silbern** *Adj.* real silver; genuine silver; ~**zeit** *die* (DV) real time

Eck /ɛk/ *das;* ~**s**, ~**e** [1] (südd., österr.: ~e) corner; **über(s)** ~: diagonally [2] (Sport: Torecke~) **das lange/kurze** ~: the far/near corner [of the goal]

Eckart /'ɛkart/ *der:* in **der getreue** ~ (fig.) a faithful supporter

Eck-: ~**ball** *der* (Sport) corner [kick/hit/throw]; **einen** ~**ball treten** take a corner; **einen** ~**ball verwandeln** score from a corner; ~**bank** *die; Pl.* ~**bänke** corner seat; ~**daten** *Pl.* basic information *sing.*

Ecke /'ɛkə/ *die;* ~, ~**n** [1] corner; **am liebsten hätte ich mich in eine** ~ **verkrochen** I felt like creeping off into a corner; **an der** ~: on *or* at the corner; **Nietzschestr.,** ~ **Goethestr.** on the corner of Nietzschestrasse and Goethestrasse; Nietzschestrasse at Goethestrasse (Amer.); **um die** ~: round the corner; **um die** ~ **biegen** turn the corner; go/come round the corner; **jmdn. in die** ~ **drängen** (fig.) get sb. in a corner (fig.); **es brennt an allen** ~**n [und Enden** *od.* **Kanten]** (fig.) there's a terrible commotion everywhere (coll.); **das Auto klapperte an allen** ~**n [und Enden** *od.* **Kanten]** every nut and bolt in the car rattled; **jmdn. um die** ~ **bringen** (salopp) bump sb. off (coll.); **mit jmdm. um** *od.* **über**

sieben ∼n verwandt sein (ugs.) be distantly related to sb.; *s. auch* **fehlen 6** [2] (Ballspiele) corner; **eine ∼ treten** take a corner; **den Ball zur ∼ schlagen** put the ball over for a corner; **in die lange/kurze ∼:** in[to] the far/near corner; **eine lange/kurze ∼ treten** take a long/short corner [3] (Boxen) corner [4] (ugs.: Gegend) corner; **ihr wohnt in einer schönen ∼:** you live in a lovely spot [5] (ugs., bes. nordd.: Strecke) **ich komme noch eine ∼ mit** I'll come a little way/a bit further with you; **bis dahin ist es noch eine ganze ∼:** it's still quite some way there; **er ist eine ganze ∼ besser als du** (fig.) he is a whole lot better than you are [6] (keilförmiges Stück) wedge; **eine ∼ Käse** a wedge of cheese

Ecken·steher *der* (ugs.) street loafer

Ecker /ˈɛkɐ/ *die;* ∼, ∼n [1] (Buch∼) beech nut [2] (selten: Eichel) acorn

Eck-: **∼fahne** *die* (Sport) corner flag; **∼fenster** *das* corner window; **∼grundstück** *das* corner site; **∼haus** *das* corner house; house on the/a corner; (einer Häuserreihe) end house

eckig
[A] *Adj.* [1] square; angular ‹*features*› [2] (ruckartig) jerky ‹*movement, walk, gait*›
[B] *adv.* **sich ∼ bewegen** move jerkily

Eck-: **∼kneipe** *die: small friendly pub on a street corner;* **∼laden** *der; Pl.* **∼läden** corner shop; **∼lohn** *der* (Wirtsch.) basic *or* minimum wage; **∼pfeiler** *der* corner pillar; (fig.) cornerstone; **∼platz** *der* end seat; **∼punkt** *der* framework principle; **∼schrank** *der* corner cupboard; **∼sitz** *der* ▸▸**∼platz**; **∼sofa** *das* corner sofa; **∼stein** *der* [1] cornerstone; head stone; (fig.) cornerstone; [2] (Kartenspiel) ▸**Karo**; **∼stoß** *der* (Fußball) corner kick; **∼tisch** *der* corner table; **∼turm** *der* angle tower; **∼wert** *der* (Wirtsch.) standard [of value]; **∼zahn** *der* ▸❶ **S. 435** canine tooth; **∼zimmer** *das* corner room; **∼zins** *der; Pl.* **∼∼en** (Finanzw.) *official minimum interest rate on savings*

Eclair /eˈklɛːɐ̯/ *das;* ∼s, ∼s éclair

Ecofin /ˈeːkofin/ *der;* ∼[s] (EU) Ecofin

Ecofin-Rat *der* (EU) Ecofin Council

Economy /iˈkɔnəmi/ *die;* ∼ (Flugw.) economy [class]; **in der ∼:** in economy [class]; **∼ fliegen** fly economy

Economy·klasse /iˈkɔnəmi-/ *die* economy class; tourist class; **in der ∼ fliegen** fly economy [class]

Ecstasy /ˈɛkstəsi/ *das;* ∼s Ecstasy

Ecuador /ekua̯ˈdoːɐ̯/ *(das);* ∼s Ecuador

Ecuadorianer /ekua̯doˈri̯aːnɐ/ *der;* ∼s, ∼, **Ecuadorianerin** *die;* ∼, ∼nen Ecuadorean

Edamer Käse /ˈeːdamɐ-/ *der* Edam cheese

Edda /ˈɛda/ *die;* ∼: [Elder] Edda; **die jüngere ∼:** the Younger Edda

edel /ˈeːdl̩/
[A] *Adj.* [1] (reinrassig) thoroughbred ‹*horse*›; species ‹*rose*› [2] (großmütig) noble[-minded], high-minded ‹*person*›; noble ‹*thought, gesture, feelings, deed*›; honourable ‹*motive*›; **seine edle Gesinnung** his nobility of mind *or* noble-mindedness [3] (geh.: wohlgeformt) finely shaped; **von edlem Wuchs** of noble stature [4] (geh.: vortrefflich) fine ‹*wine*›; high-grade ‹*wood, timber*›; **die edlen Teile** (scherzh.) the vital parts [of the body] [5] (veralt.: adlig) noble; **aus edlem Geschlecht** of noble stock
[B] *adv.* **∼ handeln** act nobly; **∼ geformt** finely fashioned

Edel-: **∼fäule** *die* (Winzerspr.) noble rot; **∼feder** *die* (ugs.) distinguished writer; **∼frau** *die* (hist.) noblewoman; **∼fräulein** *das* (hist.) [unmarried] noblewoman; **∼gas** *das* (Chemie) noble *or* inert *or* rare gas; **∼hirsch** *der* ▸**Rothirsch**; **∼holz** *das* high-grade wood; high-grade timber

Edeling /ˈeːdəlɪŋ/ *der;* ∼s, ∼e (hist.) ▸**Edelmann**

edel-, Edel-: **∼kastanie** *die* sweet chestnut; Spanish chestnut; **∼kitsch** *der* grandly pretentious kitsch; **∼mann** *der; Pl.* **∼leute** *od.* **∼männer** (hist.) nobleman; noble; **∼metall** *das* [1] precious metal; [2] (Chem.) noble metal; **∼mut** *der* (geh.) nobility of mind; noble-mindedness; magnanimity; **∼mütig** *Adj.* (geh.) noble-minded; magnanimous; **∼nutte** *die* (salopp) high-class tart (sl.); **∼pilz·käse** *der* blue[-veined] cheese; **∼reis** *das* scion; **∼rost** *der* patina; **∼schnulze** *die* (abwertend) example of pretentious schmaltz; **der Film/Roman war eine ∼schnulze** the film/novel was pretentious schmaltz; **∼stahl** *der* (rostfreier Stahl) stainless steel; (Sonderstahl) special steel

Edel·stein *der* precious stone; gem[stone]; **mit ∼en besetzt** set with precious stones; **ein synthetischer ∼:** a synthetic stone; an artificial stone

edelsteinbesetzt *Adj.* set with precious stones *postpos.*

Edelstein·schleifer *der,* **Edelstein·schleiferin** *die* gem cutter

edel-, Edel-: **∼süß** *Adj.* (fachspr.) **∼süßer Wein** fine sweet wine (*esp. made from grapes affected by noble rot*); **∼tanne** *die* silver fir; **∼weiß** *das;* **∼∼[es], ∼∼e** edelweiss; **∼wild** *das* ▸**Rotwild**; **∼zwicker** *der* Edelzwicker (*fine Alsatian wine*)

Eden /ˈeːdn̩/ [1] *in* **der Garten ∼** (bibl.) the Garden of Eden [2] *das;* ∼[s] (Paradies) earthly paradise

edieren /eˈdiːrən/ *tr. V.* edit

Edikt /eˈdɪkt/ *das;* ∼[e]s, ∼e (hist.) edict

Edition /ediˈtsi̯oːn/ *die;* ∼, ∼en (das Herausgeben) editing; (Ausgabe) edition

E-Dur *das* (Musik) E major; *s. auch* **A-Dur**

EDV *Abk.* **= elektronische Datenverarbeitung** EDP

EEF *Abk.* (EU) **= Europäischer Entwicklungsfonds** EDF

EEG *Abk.* **= Elektroenzephalogramm** EEG; **ein EEG machen lassen** have an EEG

Efeu /ˈeːfɔy̯/ *der;* ∼s ivy

efeu·bewachsen *Adj.* ivy-covered; ivy-clad

Efeu·ranke *die* ivy twine; ivy bind

Effeff /ɛfˈlɛf/ *in* **etw. aus dem ∼ beherrschen** *od.* **verstehen** know sth. inside out; **etw. aus dem ∼ machen/können** do/be able to do sth. just like that (coll.)

Effekt /ɛˈfɛkt/ *der;* ∼[e]s, ∼e effect; **im ∼:** in the end; **im ∼ läuft beides auf das Gleiche hinaus** in effect the two *or* both come to the same thing

Effekten /ɛˈfɛktn̩/ *Pl.* (Finanzw.) securities

Effekten-: **∼bank** *die; Pl.* **∼∼en** investment bank (*also acting as an issuing house*); **∼börse** *die* stock exchange; **∼geschäft** *das* dealing in securities; **∼makler** *der,* **∼maklerin** *die* stockbroker

Effekt·hascherei /-haʃəˈrai̯/ *die;* ∼, ∼en (abwertend) straining for effect; showiness; **ohne jede ∼:** without any showiness; **billige ∼:** cheap straining for effect

effektiv /ɛfɛkˈtiːf/
[A] *Adj.* [1] (wirksam) effective; **ein ∼er Schutz** an effective form of protection [2] (tatsächlich) effective ‹*profit, price, benefit*›
[B] *adv.* [1] effectively [2] (ugs.: ganz bestimmt) really; **ich weiß ∼ nichts** I really haven't a clue (coll.); **da ist ∼ nichts zu machen** there's really nothing that can be done about it

Effektivität /ɛfɛktiviˈtɛːt/ *die;* ∼: effectiveness

Effektiv·lohn *der* real wage[s]

effekt·voll
[A] *Adj.* effective ‹*speech, poem, contrast, pattern*›; dramatic ‹*pause, gesture, entrance*›
[B] *adv.* effectively

Effet /ɛˈfeː/ *der;* ∼s, ∼s spin; (Billard) side; **den Ball mit ∼ schlagen** put spin/side on the ball

effizient /ɛfiˈtsi̯ɛnt/
[A] *Adj.* (geh.) efficient
[B] *adv.* efficiently

Effizienz /ɛfiˈtsi̯ɛnts/ *die;* ∼, ∼en (geh.) efficiency; (Wirksamkeit) effectiveness

Effizienz·steigerung *die* (Wirtsch.) improved efficiency

EFRE *Abk.* (EU) **= Europäischer Fonds für Regionalenentwicklung** ERDF

EFTA /ˈɛfta/ *die;* ∼ *Abk.* **= Europäische Freihandelsassoziation** EFTA; European Free Trade Association

EG *Abk.* [1] (EU) **= Europäische Gemeinschaft[en]** EC [2] **= Erdgeschoss**

egal /eˈgaːl/
[A] *Adj.* [1] (ugs.: einerlei) **es ist jmdm. ∼:** it makes no difference to sb.; it's all the same to sb.; (es kümmert ihn nicht) sb. couldn't care less; it's all the same to sb.; **das ist ∼:** that doesn't make any difference; **das kann dir doch ∼ sein** that's none of your business; that's no concern of yours; **[ganz] ∼, wie/wer/warum/wo/ob ...** no matter how/who/why/where/whether ... [2] (ugs.: gleich[artig]) identical; **∼ sein** be the same *or* identical; **sie hat nicht zwei ∼e Stühle** (ugs.) she hasn't got two chairs the same
[B] *adv.* [1] **Bretter ∼ schneiden** cut planks to the same size [2] (bes. ostm.: fortwährend) constantly

egalisieren *tr. V.* [1] (Sport) equal ‹*record*›; **den Vorsprung des Gegners ∼:** wipe out the opponent's lead; **den Punktvorsprung ∼:** level the scores [2] (Textilw.) level ‹*colour*› [3] (Technik, Handw.) smooth; dress ‹*leather*›

egalitär /egaliˈtɛːɐ̯/
[A] *Adj.* egalitarian
[B] *adv.* in an egalitarian way

Egalität *die;* ∼: equality

Egel /ˈeːgl̩/ *der;* ∼s, ∼: leech

Egge /ˈɛgə/ *die;* ∼, ∼n (Landw.) harrow

eggen *tr. V.* (Landw.) harrow

EGMR *Abk.* **= Europäischer Gerichtshof für Menschenrechte** ECHR

Ego /ˈeːgo/ *das;* ∼, ∼s (Psych.) ego

Egoismus /egoˈɪsmʊs/ *der;* ∼, **Egoismen** [1] (Selbstsucht) egoism; **gesunder ∼:** healthy self-esteem [2] *Pl.* (egoistische Eigenschaften) egoistic traits; **wo persönliche Egoismen aufeinander stoßen** where individual egos clash

Egoist /egoˈɪst/ *der;* ∼en, ∼en, **Egoistin** *die;* ∼, ∼nen egoist

egoistisch
[A] *Adj.* egoistic[al]
[B] *adv.* egoistically

egoman /egoˈmaːn/
[A] *Adj.* egomaniacal **er kam mir zu ∼ vor** he seemed too much of an egomaniac to me
[B] *adv.* like an egomaniac/egomaniacs

Egomane /egoˈmaːnə/ *der;* ∼n, ∼n, **Egomanin** *die;* ∼, ∼nen egomaniac

egomanisch
[A] *Adj.* egomaniacal
[B] *adv.* like an egomaniac/egomaniacs

Ego-Shooter /ˈeːgoʃuːtɐ/ *der;* ∼s, ∼ (DV) first-person shooter; FPS

Ego·trip /ˈeːgo-/ *der* (ugs.) ego trip

Egozentrik /egoˈtsɛntrɪk/ *die;* ∼: egocentric attitude

Egozentriker *der;* ∼s, ∼, **Egozentrikerin** *die;* ∼, ∼nen egocentric

egozentrisch
[A] *Adj.* egocentric
[B] *adv.* egocentrically; **∼ denken** be egocentric in the way one thinks

eh[1] /eː/ *Interj.* (ugs.) [1] hey [2] (was?) **das hast du nicht erwartet, ∼?** you didn't expect that, did you [,eh]?

eh[2] *Adv.* [1] (bes. südd., österr.: sowieso) anyway; in any case; **es ist ∼ alles zu spät** it's too late anyway *or* in any case [2] **seit ∼ und je** for as long as anyone can remember; for donkey's years (coll.); **wie ∼ und je** just as before; **es sieht aus wie ∼ und je** it looks the same as ever *or* the same as it always 'has done

ehe /ˈeːə/ *Konj.* before; **∼ ihr nicht still seid, kann ich euch das Märchen nicht vorlesen** I can't read you the fairy story until you're quiet; **∼ ich das tue, gehe ich lieber ins Gefängnis** I would rather go to prison than do it

Ehe /ˈeːə/ *die;* ∼, ∼n marriage; **eine glückliche ∼ führen** be happily married; lead a happy married life; die ~ brechen (geh. veralt.) commit adultery; jmdm. die ~ versprechen promise to marry sb.; mit jmdm. eine ~ eingehen marry sb.; ihre ~ wurde vor dem Standesamt/in der Kirche geschlossen they were married in a registry office/in church; Geld/Kinder in die ~ mitbringen bring money/children into the marriage; in erster ~ war sie mit einem Arzt verheiratet her first husband was a doctor; aus erster ~: from his/her first marriage; in wilder ~ leben (veralt.) live in sin (dated); eine ~ zur linken Hand (hist.) a morganatic *or* left-handed marriage; *s. auch* Hafen[1] 6; Stand; wild A 2

e

ehe-, Ehe-: ~ähnlich *Adj.* ein ~ähnliches Verhältnis a common law marriage; in einem ~ähnlichen Verhältnis leben live [together] as man and wife; cohabit; **~anbahnung** *die* ▸ ~vermittlung; **~berater** *der*, **~beraterin** *die* marriage guidance counsellor; **~beratung** *die* [1] marriage guidance (Brit.); marriage counselling; [2] ▸ ~beratungsstelle; **~beratungs·stelle** *die* marriage guidance centre (Brit.); marriage counseling center (Amer.); **~bett** *das* marriage bed; (Doppelbett) double bed; **~brechen** *unr. itr. V.; nur im Inf. u. 1. Part. gebr.* (geh. veralt.) commit adultery; du sollst nicht ~brechen (bibl.) thou shalt not commit adultery; **~brecher** *der* adulterer; **~brecherin** *die*; ~~, ~~nen adulteress; **~brecherisch** *Adj.* adulterous; **~bruch** *der* adultery

ehe·dem *Adv.* (geh.) formerly; in former times; wie ~: as in former times; von ~: of former times

ehe-, Ehe-: ~feindlich *Adj.* [1] (der Ehe abgeneigt) misogamic ‹*attitude, tendencies*›; [2] (die Ehe erschwerend) ein ~feindlicher Beruf an occupation which is difficult to combine with marriage; **~frau** *die* (im Verhältnis zum ~mann) wife; (im Verhältnis zu anderen) married woman; **~freuden** *Pl.* (scherzh.) joys of married life; **~gatte** *der* (geh.) husband; spouse; beide ~gatten both husband and wife; **~gattin** *die* (geh.) wife; spouse; **~gelübde** *das* (geh.) marriage vows *pl.*; **~gemeinschaft** *die* marriage partnership; **~glück** *das* wedded *or* married bliss; **~hälfte** *die* (scherzh.) better half (joc.); **~hindernis** *das* (Rechtsw.) impediment to marriage; **~jahr** *das* year of marriage; **~joch** *das* (scherzh.) yoke of marriage *or* matrimony; sich ins ~joch begeben get hitched (coll.); **~kandidat** *der*, **~kandidatin** *die* (scherzh.) marriage candidate; **~krach** *der* (ugs.) row; quarrel; er hat immer ~krach zu Hause he is always having rows at home with his wife; sie hatten ihren ersten ~krach they had the first row of their married life; **~krise** *die* marital crisis; **~leben** *das* married life; **~leute** *Pl.* married couple *sing.*; die beiden ~leute the husband and wife

ehelich

[A] *Adj.* [1] (die Ehe betreffend) marital; matrimonial; conjugal ‹*rights, duties*›; ~e Gemeinschaft marriage partnership; ~es Zusammenleben married life [2] (aus einer Ehe stammend) legitimate ‹*child*›; ein Kind für ~ erklären declare a child legitimate; legitimate a child

[B] *adv.* sich ~ verbinden (geh.) enter into [holy] wedlock

ehelichen *tr. V.* (veralt., scherzh.) wed

ehe·los *Adj.* celibate

Ehelosigkeit *die*; ~: celibacy

ehemalig /ˈeːəmalɪç/ *Adj.* former; ein ~er Offizier a former *or* one-time officer; meine ~e Wohnung my old flat (esp. Brit.) *or* (esp. Amer.) apartment; seine ~e Frau his ex-wife; seine Ehemalige/ihr Ehemaliger (ugs.) his/her ex (coll.)

ehemals /ˈeːəmals/ *Adv.* (geh., veralt.) formerly; in former times

ehe-, Ehe-: ~mann *der* husband; als ~mann as a married man; **~müde** *Adj.* tired of married life *postpos.*; **~mündig** *Adj.* (Rechtsspr.) of marriageable age *postpos.*; ~mündig sein be of marriageable age *or* of an age to marry; **~mündigkeit** *die* (Rechtsspr.) being of marriageable age; vor Eintritt der ~mündigkeit before attaining marriageable age; **~paar** *das* married couple; ein älteres ~paar an elderly [married] couple; **~partner** *der*, **~partnerin** *die* marriage partner

eher /ˈeːɐ/ *Adv.* [1] (früher) earlier; sooner; ich war ~ da als er I was there earlier *or* sooner than he was; je ~, desto lieber *od.* besser the sooner the better [2] (lieber) rather; sooner; ~ will ich sterben als mit ihr zusammenwohnen I'd rather *or* sooner die than live with her; alles ~ als das anything but that [3] (wahrscheinlicher) more likely; (leichter) more easily; das ist schon ~ möglich that's more likely; er ist schon ~ mein Typ he's more my type; umso ~, als ... [all] the more so as *or* because ... [4] (mehr) er ist ~ faul als dumm he is lazy rather than stupid; he's more lazy than stupid (coll.); ~ wie ein Beamter als wie ein Künstler aussehen look more like a civil servant than an artist; seine Wohnung ist ~ klein his flat (esp. Brit.) *or* (esp. Amer.) apartment is rather on the small side; es geht ihm ~ besser he's rather better; alles ~ sein als ... be anything but ...

Ehe-: ~recht *das* (Rechtsw.) marriage law; laws governing marriage; **~ring** *der* wedding ring

ehern /ˈeːɐn/ *Adj.* (dichter.) bronze; (eisern) iron; (fig.: unbeugsam) iron ‹*will, law*›; mit ~er Stirn brazenly

Ehe-: ~sakrament *das* (kath. Rel.) sacrament of marriage; **~scheidung** *die* divorce; **~schließung** *die* wedding *or* marriage ceremony; standesamtliche ~schließung registry office wedding

ehest... /ˈeːəst.../

[A] *Adj.* zum ~en Termin at the earliest possible date; bei ~er Gelegenheit at the earliest opportunity

[B] *adv.* [1] (noch am liebsten) best of all; am ~en wäre er nach Peru gefahren best of all he'd have liked to go to Peru [2] (noch am wahrscheinlichsten) most likely; am ~en möglich sein be most likely *or* the most likely possibility; mit diesem Werkzeug wirst du es noch am ~en schaffen you'll manage it easiest with this tool; am ~en könnte man ihn/es mit ... vergleichen he/it could be most nearly compared to ...

Ehe·stand *der* marriage *no art.*; matrimony *no art.*; in den ~ treten (geh.) enter into matrimony

Ehestands·darlehen *das*: *low-interest government-backed loan available to young married couples*

ehestens /ˈeːəstn̩s/ *Adv.* [1] (frühestens) at the earliest; ~ [am] Dienstag [on] Tuesday at the earliest; ~ in drei Wochen in three weeks at the earliest [2] (österr.: baldmöglichst) as soon as possible

ehe-, Ehe-: ~stifter *der*, **~stifterin** *die* matchmaker; **~streit** *der* marital *or* matrimonial dispute; **~vermittlung** *die* [1] arrangement of introductions between people wishing to marry; ~vermittlung durch Computer matching prospective marriage partners by computer; [2] (Institut) marriage bureau; **~vermittlungs·institut** *das* marriage bureau; **~versprechen** *das* promise of marriage; **~vertrag** *der* (Rechtsw.) marriage contract; **~weib** *das* (veralt., scherzh.) spouse (arch., joc.); **~widrig** (Rechtsspr.) [A] *Adj.* extramarital ‹*relations*›; ~widriges Verhalten behaviour constituting a matrimonial offence; [B] *adv.* sich ~widrig verhalten commit a matrimonial offence; **~zwist** *der* ▸ ~streit

Ehr-: ~ab·schneider *der*, **~ab·schneiderin** *die* calumniator; vilifier; **~auf·fassung** *die* conception of honour

ehrbar

[A] *Adj.* (geh.) respectable, worthy ‹*person, occupation*›; honourable ‹*intentions*›; ~e Leute respectable *or* worthy people

[B] *adv.* respectably

Ehrbarkeit *die*; ~: respectability; worthiness

Ehr·begriff *der* conception of honour

Ehre /ˈeːrə/ *die*; ~, ~n [1] (Ansehen) honour; seine ~ verlieren/bewahren lose/preserve one's self-respect; jmdm./einer Sache [alle] ~ machen do sb./sth. [great] credit; in ~n alt werden (geh.) grow old without dishonour; jmds. Andenken (*Akk.*) in ~n halten honour sb.'s memory; etw. um der ~ willen tun do sth. for the honour of it; zu ihrer ~ sei gesagt, ... in fairness to her *or* to do her justice it should be said ...; [ich] hab *od.* habe die ~ (österr., südd.) pleased to meet you; auf ~ und Gewissen in all truthfulness *or* honesty; er fragte mich auf ~ und Gewissen, ob ich ... he asked me whether in all truthfulness *or* honesty I ...; auf ~!, bei meiner ~! upon my [word of] honour!; dein Eifer in [allen] ~n, aber ... your enthusiasm is not in doubt *or* in question, but ...; deine Meinung in [allen] ~n, aber ich halte das nicht für richtig with [all] due respect to your opinion, I still think that it is wrong; ~ verloren, alles verloren (Spr.) take away my good name and take away my life (prov.) [2] (Zeichen der Wertschätzung) jmdm./einer Sache ~ antun pay tribute to sb./sth.; jmdm./einer Sache zu viel ~ antun overvalue sb./sth.; die ~ haben, etw. zu tun (geh.) have the honour of doing sth.; wir geben uns die ~, die Vermählung unserer Tochter bekannt zu geben (geh.) we have much pleasure in announcing *or* are very pleased to announce the marriage of our daughter; wir geben uns die ~, Sie zu einem Gartenfest einzuladen (geh.) we request the pleasure of your company at a garden party; we have the honour of inviting you to a garden party; sich (*Dat.*) etw. zur ~ anrechnen give oneself credit for sth.; regard sth. as being to one's credit; jmdm. zur ~ gereichen (geh.) bring honour to sb.; etw. zur ~ Gottes tun do sth. to the glory of God; ~, wem ~ gebührt [give] credit where credit is due; jmdm. die letzte ~ erweisen pay one's last respects to sb.; mit ihr kannst du ~/keine ~ einlegen she's a/no credit to you; damit kannst du [keine] ~ einlegen that does you [no] credit; mit diesen Manieren legst du keine ~ ein you won't get very far with manners like that; der Wahrheit (*Dat.*) die ~ geben tell the truth; um der Wahrheit die ~ zu geben to tell the truth; to be [perfectly] honest; mit ~n with honour; mit ~n überhäuft loaded with honours; er wurde in ~n entlassen he went into an honourable retirement; zu ~n des Staatsbesuchs/des Königs in honour of the state visit/of the king; wieder zu ~n kommen come back into favour [3] (Ehrgefühl) sense of honour; (Selbstachtung) self-esteem; pride; jmdm. gegen die ~ gehen offend sb.'s sense of honour; ein Mann von ~ (geh.) a man of honour; er hat keine ~ im Leib[e] he doesn't have an ounce of integrity in him; jmdn. bei seiner ~ packen *od.* fassen appeal to sb.'s sense of honour [4] (veralt.: Jungfräulichkeit) honour [5] (Golf) honour

ehren *tr. V.* [1] (Ehre erweisen) honour; ihre Einladung ehrt uns sehr we are greatly honoured by her invitation; für seine Verdienste wurde er mit einem Orden geehrt he was awarded a medal in recognition of his services; man ehrte den ausländischen Gast mit einem Empfang a reception was held in honour of the foreign guest; sehr geehrter Herr Müller!/sehr geehrte Frau Müller! Dear Herr Müller/Dear Frau Müller; hoch geehrt highly honoured [2] (Ehre machen) deine Hilfsbereitschaft ehrt dich your willingness to help does you credit; sein Vertrauen ehrt mich I'm honoured by his confidence in me [3] (veralt.: achten) respect; du sollst Vater und Mutter ~ (bibl.) honour thy father and thy mother

ehren-, Ehren-: ~ab·zeichen *das* medal; **~amt** *das* honorary position *or* post; **~amtlich** [A] *Adj.* honorary ‹*position, membership*›; voluntary ‹*help, worker*›; [B] *adv.* in an honorary capacity; (freiwillig) on a voluntary basis; **~bezeigung** *die* salute

Ehren·bürger *der*, **Ehren·bürgerin** *die* honorary citizen; ein ~/eine ~in der Stadt a freeman of the town/city; jmdn. zum ~ der Stadt ernennen give sb. the freedom of the town/city

Ehren·bürger-: ~recht *das,* **~würde** *die:* **jmdm. das ~recht** *od.* **die ~würde verleihen** admit sb. as a freeman

Ehren-: ~dame *die* lady-in-waiting; **~dienst** *der* (geh.) **seinen ~dienst leisten** have the privilege of serving; **~doktor** *der* 1 honorary doctor; 2 (Titel) honorary doctorate; **~doktor·würde** *die* honorary doctorate; **~erklärung** *die:* **eine ~erklärung [für jmdn.]** a statement that aspersions cast on sb. are without foundation; **~formation** *die* (Milit.) guard of honour; **~fried·hof** *der* war cemetery; **~garde** *die* guard of honour; **~gast** *der* guest of honour; **~geleit** *das* official escort; **~gericht** *das* disciplinary tribunal *or* court; (Standesgericht) professional tribunal

ehrenhaft
A *Adj.* honourable ‹*intentions, person*›; **ein ~er Mann** an honourable man; a man of honour
B *adv.* ‹*act*› honourably

Ehrenhaftigkeit *die;* **~:** sense of honour; **die ~ seiner Absichten** the honourableness of his intentions

ehren-, Ehren-: ~halber *Adv.* **jmdm. den Doktortitel ~halber verleihen** confer an honorary doctorate on sb.; **Doktor ~halber** honorary doctor; **~handel** *der; Pl.* **~händel** (veralt.) affair of honour; **~hof** *der* court of honour; **~karte** *die* complimentary ticket; **~kodex** *der* code of honour; **~kompanie** *die* guard of honour; **~kränkung** *die* (Rechtsspr.) affront; insult; **~legion** *die* Legion of Honour; **~loge** *die* VIP box; box reserved for VIPs; **~mal** *das; Pl.* **~~e** *od.* **~mäler** monument; **~mann** *der* man of honour; **~mitglied** *das* honorary member; **~nadel** *die* badge of honour (in the form of a lapel-pin); **~name** *der:* **den ~namen ... erhalten/tragen** be honoured by being given/by bearing the name ...; **~pflicht** *die* bounden duty; **es ist meine ~pflicht, diese Aufgabe zu erfüllen** I'm honour bound to perform this task; **~platz** *der* place of honour; **die ~plätze** the seats of honour; **~präsident** *der,* **~präsidentin** *die* honorary president; **~preis** *der* special prize; special award; **~rechte** *Pl.* **die bürgerlichen ~rechte** civil rights *or* liberties; *s. auch* **Aberkennung**; **~rettung** *die:* **zu jmds. ~rettung etw. sagen** say sth. to clear sb.'s name; **zu ihrer ~rettung muss ich sagen, dass ...** it must be said in her defence that ...; **~rührig** *Adj.* defamatory ‹*allegations*›; insulting ‹*behaviour*›; **etw. ist ~rührig** sth. is an insult to sb.'s honour; **~runde** *die* lap of honour; **eine ~runde laufen/fahren** *usw.* do a lap of honour; **eine ~runde drehen** (Schülerspr.) repeat *or* (Brit.) stay down a year [at school]; **~sache** *die* 1 (~pflicht) **das ist ~sache** that is a point of honour; **Verschwiegenheit ist ~sache** I/we feel honour bound to stay silent; **~sache!** you can count on me!; 2 (Angelegenheit der Ehre) **es handelt sich um eine ~sache** my/our *etc.* reputation *or* good name is at stake; **~salut** *der* salute; **man begrüßte ihn mit einem ~salut** a salute was fired to welcome him; **~schuld** *die* debt of honour; **~senator** *der* honorary member of the/a university senate; **~spalier** *das* guard of honour; **~tag** *der* (geh.) special day; **~titel** *der* 1 (für besondere Dienste) [honorary] title; 2 (ehrende Anrede, Bezeichnung) title; **~tor** *das,* **~treffer** *der* (Sport) consolation goal; **~tribüne** *die* VIP stand; **~urkunde** *die* certificate; **~voll** A *Adj.* honourable ‹*peace, death, compromise, occupation*›; creditable, gallant ‹*attempt, conduct*›; B *adv.* ‹*act*› honourably; **~vorsitzende** *der/die* honorary chairman; **~wache** *die* 1 (Wachtposten) guard of honour; 2 (Dienst) **Soldaten zur ~wache abkommandieren** detail soldiers to form a guard of honour; **~wache halten** keep vigil; **~wert** *Adj.* (geh.) worthy, honourable ‹*person, occupation*›; **die ~werte Gesellschaft** the Mafia; **~wort** *das Pl.* **~~e: ~wort[!/?]** word of honour[!/?]; **sein ~wort brechen** break one's word; **auf [mein] ~wort** [I] promise; **großes ~wort!** (scherzh.) scout's honour! (joc.); **Urlaub auf ~wort** (Milit.) parole; **~wörtlich** A *Adj.* solemn ‹*agreement, promise*›; ‹*agreement, promise*› on one's honour; B *adv.* **es war ~wörtlich ausgemacht, dass ...** he/they *etc.* had promised faithfully *or* made a solemn promise that ...; **~zeichen** *das* decoration

ehrerbietig /ˈeːɐ̯lɛɐ̯biːtɪç/
A *Adj.* (geh.) respectful; **sein ~es Gehabe** his deferential manner
B *adv.* ‹*greet*› respectfully

Ehrerbietung *die;* ~ (geh.) respect

Ehr·furcht *die* reverence (**vor** + *Dat.* for); **[große] ~ vor jmdm./etw. haben** have [a great] respect for sb./sth.; **~ vor dem Leben** reverence for life; **jmdm. ~ einflößen** fill sb. with awe; **er hat vor nichts ~:** he has no respect for anything; nothing is sacred to him

ehrfurchtgebietend
A *Adj.* awe-inspiring ‹*personality, cathedral*›; awesome ‹*silence*›; authoritative ‹*voice*›
B *adv.* **~ auftreten** have an imposing presence

ehrfürchtig
A *Adj.* reverent
B *adv.* reverently

ehrfurchts-: ~los A *Adj.* irreverent; B *adv.* irreverently; **~voll** (geh.) A *Adj.* reverent; **mit ~voller Miene** with a reverential expression; B *adv.* reverently

ehr-, Ehr-: ~gefühl *das* sense of honour; (Selbstachtung) self-esteem; pride; **falsches ~gefühl** a misplaced sense of honour; **~geiz** *der* ambition; **sie hatte den ~geiz, Pilotin zu werden** her ambition was *or* it was her ambition to become a pilot; **seinen ~geiz dareinsetzen, etw. zu tun** make it one's ambition to do sth.; **~geizig** A *Adj.* ambitious; **wenig ~geizig sein** be lacking in ambition; B *adv.* ambitiously; **~geizling** /-gaitslɪŋ/ *der;* **~~s, ~~e** (ugs. abwertend) pushy individual (coll.); pusher

ehrlich
A *Adj.* 1 honest ‹*person, face, answer, deal*›; genuine ‹*concern, desire, admiration*›; upright ‹*character*›; honourable ‹*intentions*›; (wahrheitsgetreu) truthful ‹*answer, statement*›; **wenn ich ~ bin** if you want my honest opinion; **der ~e Finder gab die Brieftasche beim Fundbüro ab** the person who found the wallet handed it in (Brit.) *or* (Amer.) turned it in at the lost-property office; **dem ~en Finder winkt eine Belohnung von 10% der Gesamtsumme** a reward of 10% is offered [for the return of the money]; **~ währt am längsten** (Spr.) honesty is the best policy (prov.) 2 (veralt.: anständig) **seinen Namen wieder ~ machen** restore one's good name; **ein ~es Handwerk** an honest trade
B *adv.* honestly; **etw. ~ teilen** share sth.; **~ spielen** play fairly; **es ~ mit jmdm. meinen** play straight with sb.; **~ gesagt** quite honestly; to be honest

ehrlicherweise *Adv.* 1 in all honesty; **etw. ~ zugeben** own up and admit sth. 2 (selten: ehrlich) honestly

Ehrlichkeit *die;* ~ ▸**ehrlich A 1**: honesty; genuineness; uprightness; honourableness; truthfulness

ehr-, Ehr-: ~los A *Adj.* dishonourable; B *adv.* dishonourably; **~los aus dem Leben scheiden** depart this life in dishonour; **~losigkeit** *die;* **~~:** dishonourableness; **~pusselig, ~pusslig,** ***~pußlig** *Adj.* (ugs.) ‹*person*› who is pompously concerned about his/her reputation

ehrsam *Adj.* (geh. veralt.) respectable, worthy ‹*people, occupation*›

Ehrsamkeit *die;* **~:** respectability

ehr-, Ehr-: ~sucht *die* (veralt.) inordinate ambition; **~süchtig** *Adj.* (veralt.) inordinately ambitious; overambitious

Ehrung *die;* **~, ~en** 1 (das Ehren) **die ~ der Preisträger** the prize-giving (Brit.) *or* (Amer.) awards ceremony; **bei der ~ der Sieger** when the winners were awarded their medals/trophies; **für jmdn. die höchste ~ sein** be the supreme accolade for sb. 2 (Ehrenerweisung) honour

ehr-, Ehr-: ~verlust *der* (Rechtsw.) loss of civil rights; (hist.) attainder; **~würden** (*der*); **~~s** (kath. Kirche, veralt.) **Euer ~würden** Reverend Father; **~würden Bruder Martin/Schwester Notburga** brother Martin/sister Notburga; **~würdig** *Adj.* 1 (ehrfurchtgebietend) venerable ‹*person*›; **ein ~würdiges Alter haben** ‹*person*› have reached a grand old age; ‹*building*› be of great age; 2 (kath. Kirche) **~würdiger Vater/~würdige Mutter** Reverend Father/Mother

ei /ai̯/ *Interj.* 1 hey; (abschätzig) oho; *s. auch* **Daus** 2 (Kinderspr.) **ei [ei] machen** stroke sb. [affectionately]; **mach mal ei!** stroke me!

Ei /ai̯/ *das;* **~[e]s, ~er** 1 egg; (Physiol., Zool.) ovum; **aus dem ~ schlüpfen** hatch [out]; **verlorene** *od.* **pochierte ~er** poached eggs; **russische ~er** egg mayonnaise; Russian eggs; **sie geht wie auf [rohen] ~ern** (fig.) she is walking very carefully; **das ist ein [dickes] ~!** (ugs.) that's terrible; **ach, du dickes ~!** (ugs.) dash it! (Brit. coll.); darn it! (Amer. coll.); **das ~ des Kolumbus** (fig.) an inspired discovery; **wie aus dem ~ gepellt sein** (fig.) be dressed to the nines; **sich gleichen wie ein ~ dem anderen** be as like as two peas in a pod; **das ~ will klüger sein als die Henne** (fig.) stop trying to teach your grandmother to suck eggs; **ein ~ legen** lay an egg; (ugs.: einen Plan ausbrüten) hatch [out] a plan; (derb: seine große Notdurft verrichten) have (Brit.) *or* (Amer.) take a shit (coarse); *s. auch* **Apfel**; **bewerfen**; **Pfanne**; **roh**; **ungelegt** 2 **~er** (derb: Hoden) balls (coarse); nuts (Amer. coarse) 3 (salopp) **zwölf ~er** twelve marks; (zwölf Pfund) twelve quid (coll.); (zwölf Dollar) twelve bucks (coll.) 4 (Sportjargon: Ball) ball

eia /ˈai̯a/ ▸**ei 2**

eiapopeia /ai̯apoˈpai̯a/ *Interj.* (Kinderspr.) hushaby[e]; **~ machen** lull the baby to sleep

EIB *Abk.* (EU) = **Europäische Investitionsbank** EIB

Eibe /ˈai̯bə/ *die;* **~, ~n** yew [tree]

Eibisch /ˈai̯bɪʃ/ *der;* **~[e]s, ~e** (Bot.) marsh mallow

Eich-: ~amt *das* local weights and measures office (Brit.); local bureau of standards (Amer.); **~baum** *der* oak tree; **~behörde** *die* ≈ Weights and Measures Inspectorate (Brit.); ≈ National Bureau of Standards (Amer.)

Eiche /ˈai̯çə/ *die;* **~, ~n** oak [tree]; (Holz) oak [wood]

Eichel /ˈai̯çl̩/ *die;* **~, ~n** 1 (Frucht) acorn 2 ▸➊ **S. 435** (Anat.) glans 3 *Pl.* (Spielkartenfarbe) acorns *pl.*; *s. auch* **Pik²**

Eichel·häher *der* jay

eichen¹ *tr. V.* calibrate ‹*measuring instrument, thermometer*›; standardize ‹*weights, measures, containers, products*›; adjust ‹*weighing scales*›; **darauf bin ich geeicht** (ugs.) that's in my line (coll.)

eichen² *Adj.* oak[en] ‹*furniture*›

Eichen-: ~baum *der* oak tree; **~blatt** *das* oak leaf; **~holz** *das* oak [wood]; **ein Schreibtisch aus ~holz** an oak writing desk; **~laub** *das* 1 oak leaves *pl.*; 2 (Auszeichnung) garland of oak [leaves]; **~sarg** *der* oak[en] coffin *or* (Amer.) casket; **~wald** *der* oak wood; (größer) oak forest

Eich·gewicht *das* standard weight

Eich·hörnchen *das,* **Eich·kätzchen** *das* (landsch.), **Eich·katze** *die* (landsch.) squirrel

Eich-: ~maß *das* standard measure; **~stempel** *der* verification stamp; **~strich** *der* [engraved] line showing the correct measure; **ein Glas bis zum ~strich füllen** fill a glass up to the line

Eid /ai̯t/ *der;* **~[e]s, ~e** oath; **einen ~ leisten** *od.* **ablegen** swear *or* take an oath; **einen ~ auf die Bibel schwören** swear an oath on the [Holy] Bible; **einen ~ auf die Verfassung schwören** solemnly swear to preserve, protect, and defend the constitution; **unter ~ [stehen]** [be] under *or* on oath; **etw. auf seinen ~ nehmen** swear to sth.; **ich nehme es auf meinen ~, dass ...** I swear that ...; **der ~ des Hippokrates** the Hippocratic oath; **an ~es statt erklären, dass ...** (Rechtsspr.) attest in an statutory declaration that ...

Eidam /ˈai̯dam/ *der;* **~s, ~e** (veralt.) son-in-law

e

e

Eid·bruch *der* breach of one's oath; (Rechtsw.) perjury *no indef. art.*; **einen ~ begehen** break one's oath

eid·brüchig *Adj.* treacherous ‹*allies*›; **~ werden** break one's oath; (Rechtsw.) perjure oneself

Eidechse /ˈaidɛksə/ *die*; **~, ~n** lizard

Eider- /ˈaidɐ-/: **~daune** *die* eider down; **~ente** *die* eider [duck]

eides-, Eides-: **~belehrung** *die* (Rechtsw.) *caution to those about to take the oath*; **~formel** *die* (jur.) wording of the oath; **die ~formel nachsprechen** repeat the [words of the] oath; **~stattlich** **A** *Adj.* (Rechtsw.) **eine ~stattliche Erklärung** a statutory declaration; **B** *adv.* **~stattlich erklären** *od.* **versichern, dass ...** attest in a statutory declaration that ...

Eidetik /aiˈdeːtɪk/ *die*; **~** (Psych.) eidetic ability

eidetisch *Adj.* (Psych.) eidetic

eid-, Eid-: **~genosse** *der* Swiss; (Verbündeter) confederate; **~genossenschaft** *die*: **die Schweizerische ~genossenschaft** the Swiss Confederation; **~genössisch** *Adj.* Swiss

eidlich
A *Adj.* made under oath *postpos.*
B *adv.* on oath

Ei·dotter *der od. das* egg yolk

eier-, Eier-: **~becher** *der* eggcup; **~brikett** *das* ovoid; **~farbe** *die*: *paint for decorating eggs as Easter gifts*; **~frucht** *die* eggplant; aubergine; **~hand·granate** *die* Mills bomb *or* grenade; **~kohle** *die* egg coal; **~kopf** *der* **1** (salopp) egg-shaped head; **2** (ugs.: Intellektueller) egghead (coll.); **~kuchen** *der* pancake; (Omelett) omelette; **~laufen** *das* egg-and-spoon race; **~legend** *Adj.* (Biol.) oviparous; egg-laying; **~likör** *der* egg flip; egg nog; **~löffel** *der* egg spoon

eiern *itr. V.* **1** (ugs.: ungleichmäßig rotieren) wobble **2** *mit sein* (salopp: sich wackelnd fortbewegen) roll

eier-, Eier-: **~nudel** *die* egg noodle; **~pfann·kuchen** *der* ▸ **~kuchen**; **~pflaume** *die* egg-plum; **~punsch** *der* egg flip; egg nog; **~salat** *der* egg salad; **~schale** *die* eggshell; **er hat noch die ~schalen hinter den Ohren** (fig.) he's still wet behind the ears (fig.); **~schalen·farben** *Adj.* off-white; **~schwamm** *der* (bes. österr.) chanterelle; **~speise** *die* **1** egg dish; **2** (österr.) scrambled egg; **~stich** *der* (Kochk.) cooked-egg garnish; royale; **~stock** *der* ▸ ❶ **S. 435** (Physiol., Zool.) ovary; **~stock·entzündung** *die* (Med.) ovaritis; **~tanz** *der* (ugs.) (um eine heikle Angelegenheit) intricate manoeuvring *no indef. art.*; (zwischen unangenehmen Alternativen) treading carefully *no art.*; **einen [richtigen] ~tanz aufführen** *od.* **vollführen** engage in [really] intricate manoeuvring/tread [very] carefully; **~uhr** *die* egg timer; **~wärmer** *der* egg cosy

Eifer /ˈaifɐ/ *der*; **~s** enthusiasm; (Eifrigkeit) eagerness; (Emsigkeit) zeal; **etw. voller ~ tun** do sth. with great enthusiasm; **in ~ geraten** become excited *or* heated; **etw. im ~ [des Gefechts] vergessen** forget sth. in the excitement; *s. auch* **blind A 3**

Eiferer *der*; **~s, ~, Eiferin** *die*; **~, ~nen** (geh.) zealot

eifern *itr. V.* **1** (abwertend) **für etw. ~:** agitate for sth.; **gegen etw. ~:** rail *or* agitate against sth. **2** (geh.: heftig streben) strive; **nach Macht ~:** strive for power

Eifer·sucht *die* jealousy (**auf** + *Akk.* of); **etw. aus ~ tun** do sth. out of jealousy

Eifersüchtelei /-zʏçtəˈlai/ *die*; **~, ~en** petty jealousy

eifer·süchtig
A *Adj.* jealous (**auf** + *Akk.* of)
B *adv.* jealously

Eifersuchts-: **~drama** *das* **1** (Bühnenwerk) drama of jealousy; **2** (fig.) [dramatic] tale of jealousy; **~szene** *die* display of jealousy; **sie machte ihm eine ~szene** in a fit of jealousy she made a scene; **~tragödie** *die* tragedy due to jealousy; **es handelte sich um eine ~tragödie** the tragedy was the result of jealousy

Eiffel·turm /ˈaifl̩-/ *der* Eiffel Tower

ei·förmig *Adj.* egg-shaped

eifrig
A *Adj.* eager; constant ‹*reader*›; enthusiastic ‹*supporter, collector*›; (fleißig) assiduous; **die ganz Eifrigen** the really keen ones; **~ bei einer Sache sein** show keen interest in doing sth.
B *adv.* eagerly; **~ dabei sein, etw. zu tun** be busy doing sth.; **sich ~ um etw. bemühen** set about sth. eagerly; **sich ~ bemühen, etw. zu tun** set about doing sth. eagerly; **~ bemüht sein, etw. zu tun** be eager to do sth.

Ei·gelb *das*; **~[e]s, ~e** egg yolk; **drei ~:** the yolks of three eggs; three [egg] yolks

eigen /ˈaign̩/ *Adj.* **1** (jmdm. selbst gehörend) own; (selbstständig) separate; **mein ~er Bruder** my own brother; **eine ~e Wohnung haben** have one's own flat (esp. Brit.) *or* (esp. Amer.) apartment; **ein Zimmer mit ~em Eingang** a room with a separate entrance; **etw. mit ~en Augen sehen** see sth. with one's [very] own eyes; **seine ~e Meinung** his own opinion; **auf ~en Füßen** *od.* **Beinen stehen** stand on one's own two feet; **sich** (*Dat.*) **etw. zu *~** *od.* **Eigen machen** adopt sth.; **etw. sein *~** *od.* **Eigen nennen** (geh., iron.) call sth. one's own; **meinem Lehrer zu *~** *od.* **Eigen** (geh.) [dedicated] to my teacher **2** (kennzeichnend) characteristic; **mit einer ihr ~en Gebärde** with a gesture characteristic of her; with a characteristic gesture; **mit allem ihr ~en Charme** with all her characteristic charm **3** (landsch.: gewissenhaft) particular; **mit etw. ~ sein** be particular about sth. **4** (veralt.: seltsam) peculiar; strange; odd; **mir ist so ~ zumute** I feel so strange; I have the strangest feeling

-eigen *Adj.* **1** (im Besitz von) belonging to the ‹*school, company, community*› **2** (zugehörig) intrinsic to the ‹*body, language*›; inherent in the ‹*system, period*›

Eigen ▸ **eigen 1**

eigen-, Eigen-: **~art** *die* (Wesensart) particular nature; (Zug) peculiarity; **eine ~art dieser Stadt** one of the characteristic features of this city; **ihre merkwürdigen ~arten** her strange peculiarities; **~artig** *Adj.* peculiar; strange; odd; **~artigerweise** *Adv.* strangely [enough]; oddly [enough]; **~artigkeit** *die* **1** peculiarity; strangeness; oddness; **2** (**~artige** Verhaltensweise) peculiarity; eccentricity; oddity; **~bau** *der*; *Pl.* **~~ten** **1** (das Selbstbauen) **Möbel/ein Haus im ~bau herstellen** make one's own furniture/build one's own house; **eine Anleitung zum ~bau einer Solaranlage** instructions for building one's own solar array; **das Haus ist im ~bau entstanden** I built the house myself/he built the house himself *etc.*; **2** (das Selbstanbauen) **der ~bau ist ...:** growing your own is ...; **Gemüse/Tabak im ~bau produzieren** grow one's own vegetables/tobacco; **3** (etw. Selbstgebautes) **das Haus ist ein ~bau** *od.* **ist Marke ~bau** I built the house myself/he built the house himself *etc.*; **4** (etw. Selbstangebautes) **probier doch mal unseren ~bau** try one/some we grew ourselves; **Marke ~bau sein** be home-grown; **~bedarf** *der* own requirements *pl.*; (eines Landes) domestic requirements *pl.*; **~bericht** *der*: **„~bericht"** 'report from our own correspondent'; **nur die Lokalberichte sind ~berichte** only the local news reports are by staff reporters; **~besitz** *der* (Rechtsspr.) personal property; **~brötelei** /-brøːtəˈlai/ *die*; **~~, ~~en** taking an [unduly] independent line; **~brötler** /-brøːtlɐ/ *der*; **~~s, ~~, ~brötlerin** *die*; **~~, ~~nen** loner; lone wolf; **~brötlerisch** **A** *Adj.* solitary; **B** *adv.* **sich ~brötlerisch verhalten** behave like a loner *or* a lone wolf; **~dynamik** *die* inherent dynamism; **eine ~dynamik entwickeln** develop a momentum of its own; **~finanzierung** *die* self-financing *no art.*; **etw. in ~finanzierung tun** finance sth. oneself; **~funktion** *die* (Math., Phys.) eigenfunction; **~geschmack** *der*: **ein ~geschmack** a taste of its/their own; its/their own particular taste; **der ~geschmack des Fleisches** the meat's own taste; **~gesetzlich** **A** *Adj.* **die ~gesetzliche Entwicklung der Wirtschaft** the development of the economy according to its own laws; **B** *adv.* according to its/their own laws; **~gesetzlichkeit** *die* inherent laws *pl.*; **~gewicht** *das* **1** own weight; **2** (Wirtsch.: Nettogewicht) net weight; **~goal** *das* (österr.) ▸ **~tor**; **~händig** **A** *Adj.* personal ‹*signature*›; personally inscribed ‹*dedication*›; holographic ‹*will, document*›; **B** *adv.* **etw. ~händig unterschreiben/übergeben** sign/present sth. personally; **„~händig abzugeben"** 'to be delivered to the addressee in person'; **~heim** *das* house of one's own; **der Trend zum ~heim** the trend towards owning a house of one's own

> **Eigenheim**
>
> The level of home ownership in Germany is rising but is still far lower than in Britain. Many people happily live in rented flats or houses, but most dream of buying or building their *Eigenheim* (own home) one day and save up towards it through the system of **Bausparen**. German houses tend to be large and solidly built, usually with cellars, and are therefore relatively expensive. First-time buyers are usually middle-aged and expect to stay in their home for the rest of their lives.

Eigenheit *die*; **~, ~en** peculiarity

eigen-, Eigen-: **~initiative** *die* initiative of one's own; **auf ~initiative** on one's own initiative; **~interesse** *das* personal interest; **~kapital** *das* (Wirtsch.) equity capital; **~leben** *das* life of one's own; **ein ~leben haben** *od.* **führen** live one's own life; **sein ~leben bewahren** continue to live a life of one's own; **~liebe** *die* amour propre; **~lob** *das* self-praise; **~lob stinkt!** (ugs.) self-praise is no recommendation; **~mächtig** **A** *Adj.* unauthorized ‹*decision*›; (selbstherrlich) high-handed; **B** *adv.* **~mächtig handeln** act on one's own authority; (selbstherrlich) act high-handedly; **er ist ~mächtig mit meinem Auto gefahren** he took my car without permission; **etw. ~mächtig tun** do sth. without asking; **~mächtiger·weise** *Adv.* ▸ **~mächtig B**; **~mächtigkeit** *die*; *Pl.* **~~en** **1** high-handedness; **2** (**~mächtige** Handlung) unauthorized action; **~mittel** *Pl.* own resources; **aus ~mitteln** out of *or* from one's own resources; **~name** *der* proper name; (Ling.) proper noun; **~nutz** *der*; **~~es** self-interest; **~nützig** /-nʏtsɪç/ **A** *Adj.* self-interested, self-seeking ‹*person*›; selfish ‹*motive*›; **B** *adv.* selfishly; **~produktion** *die*: **aus ~produktion** home-made; home-grown ‹*fruit, vegetables, etc.*›; **das ist eine ~produktion** I/they *etc.* made it myself/themselves *etc*; **~regie** *die*: **etw. in ~regie tun** undertake sth. oneself

eigens *Adv.* specially; **~ für diesen Zweck** specifically for this purpose; **~ aus diesen Gründen** just *or* solely for these reasons

Eigenschaft *die*; **~, ~en** (von Menschen, Tieren, Pflanzen) quality; characteristic; (von Sachen, Stoffen) property; **in seiner ~ als Mann/Vorsitzender** as a man/in his capacity as chairman

Eigenschafts·wort *das*; *Pl.* **Eigenschaftswörter** adjective

eigen-, Eigen-: **~sinn** *der* obstinacy; stubbornness; **~sinnig** **A** *Adj.* obstinate; stubborn; **B** *adv.* obstinately; stubbornly; **~sinnigkeit** *die*; **~~:** obstinacy; stubbornness; **~sinnigkeiten** obstinate *or* stubborn behaviour *sing.*; **~staatlich** *Adj.* **1** (souverän) sovereign; **2** (den **~en** Staat betreffend) national; **~staatlichkeit** *die*; **~~:** sovereignty; (von Bundesstaaten) statehood; **~ständig** **A** *Adj.* independent; **B** *adv.* independently; **~ständigkeit** *die*; **~~:** independence; **~sucht** *die* selfishness; **~süchtig** **A** *Adj.* selfish; **B** *adv.* selfishly

eigentlich /ˈaigntlɪç/
A *Adj.* (wirklich) actual; real; (wahr) true; (ursprünglich) original; **die ~e Bedeutung eines Wortes** the original meaning of a word; **das Eigentliche** the essential thing
B *Partikel* **1** (tatsächlich, genau genommen) actually; really; **~ nicht** not really **2** (Verstärkung) **wann erscheint ~ der letzte Band?/warum kommst du ~ nicht mehr zu uns?** tell me,

when will the last volume come out/why have you stopped coming to see us?; **~ müsste ich ja jetzt gehen, aber ...** really, I ought to go now, but ...; **es ist ~ schade, dass ...** actually, it's a pity that ...; **sind sie ~ verheiratet?** are they in fact married?; **wohnen Sie ~ in Köln oder in Bonn?** is it in Cologne or Bonn that you live?; **wussten Sie ~ schon, dass ...?** were you actually aware that ...?; **warst du ~ schon [ein]mal da?** have you in fact ever been there?; **ist daraus ~ was geworden?** (ugs.) did it ever come to anything?; **was soll das ~?** what's it all about?; **wer sind Sie ~?** who do you think you are?; **wissen Sie ~, wer ich bin?** do you know who 'I am?; **rauchen Sie ~ viel?** do you actually smoke a lot?; **was muss ~ noch alles passieren, bevor ...?** what else has got to happen before ...?; **was denkst du dir ~?** what do you think you're doing?; **was willst du ~?** what exactly do you want?

Eigentlichkeit *die;* ~ (geh.) authenticity

Eigen·tor *das* (Ballspiele, fig.) own goal; **ein ~ schießen** score an own goal; **zum ~ für jmdn. werden** (fig.) backfire on sb.

Eigentum *das;* **~s** [1] property; (einschließlich Geld usw.) assets *pl.*; **geistiges ~:** [one's own] intellectual creation; **sie haben sein geistiges ~ verwendet** they used his idea/ideas; **sich an fremdem ~ vergreifen** steal [2] (Recht des Eigentümers) ownership (**an** + *Dat.* of) [3] (veralt.: Grundbesitz) property

Eigentümer /ˈaignty:mɐ/ *der;* **~s, ~:** owner; (Hotel~, Geschäfts~) proprietor; owner

Eigentümerin *die* owner; (Hotel~, Geschäfts~) proprietress; proprietor; owner

eigentümlich /ˈaignty:mlɪç/

A *Adj.* [1] (typisch) peculiar; characteristic; **eine ihm ~e Geste** a gesture peculiar to him *or* characteristic of him [2] (eigenartig) peculiar; strange; odd

B *adv.* peculiarly; strangely; oddly

eigentümlicherweise *Adv.* strangely enough; oddly enough

Eigentümlichkeit *die;* **~, ~en** [1] (Eigenartigkeit) peculiarity; strangeness [2] (typischer Zug) peculiarity

Eigentums-: ~bildung *die* acquisition of assets; **~delikt** *das* offence against property; **~recht** *das* right of ownership; **~rechte geltend machen** claim one's proprietary rights; **~streuung** *die* distribution of assets; **~vorbehalt** *der* (Rechtsw.) reservation of proprietary rights; **~wohnung** *die* owner-occupied flat (esp. Brit.); condominium *or* co-op apartment (Amer.); **eine ~wohnung kaufen** buy a flat (Brit.) *or* (Amer.) an apartment

eigen-, Eigen-: ~verantwortlich

A *Adj.* responsible; **eine ~verantwortliche Tätigkeit** a job with responsibility; a responsible job; **B** *adv.* **~verantwortlich handeln** act on one's own authority; **etw. ~verantwortlich bestimmen/entscheiden** decide sth. on one's own responsibility; **~verantwortung** *die* own responsibility; (des Einzelnen) personal responsibility; (Selbstständigkeit) independence; **die Patienten wollen mehr ~verantwortung** the patients want to have more responsibility of their own; **~vorsorge** *die* personal pension provision; **~wärme** *die* (Biol.) body temperature; **~wert** *der* intrinsic value; (Math., Phys.) eigenvalue; **~willig** *Adj.* [1] self-willed ‹*person*›; individual ‹*style, idea*›; [2] (~sinnig) obstinate; stubborn; **~willigkeit** *die;* **~~, ~~en** [1] (von Menschen) individualism; independence of mind; (einer Behauptung, eines Kunstwerks, eines Stils usw.) originality; unconventionality; [2] (Handlung) display of self-will

eigne, eigner ▸ **eigen**

eignen

A *refl. V.* be suitable; **sich als** *od.* **zum Lehrer ~:** be suitable as a teacher; **er würde sich gut als** *od.* **zum Handwerker ~** he would make a good craftsman; **das Buch eignet sich gut als Geschenk** this book makes a good present; **für solche Arbeiten eignet er sich besonders** he is particularly well suited for that kind of work; *s. auch* **geeignet**

B *itr. V.* (geh., veralt.: eigen sein) **jmdm. eignet etw.** sb. possesses sth.

Eigner *der;* **~s, ~, Eignerin** *die;* **~, ~nen** owner

Eignung *die;* **~:** suitability; aptitude; **seine ~ für diesen Beruf/als Lehrer** his suitability for this profession/as a teacher; **seine ~ zum Fliegen** his aptitude for flying

Eignungs-: ~prüfung *die,* **~test** *der* aptitude test

Ei·klar, *das;* **~s, ~** (österr.) ▸ **Eiweiß 1**

Eiland /ˈailant/ *das;* **~[e]s, ~e** (veralt., dichter.) isle (poet.)

Eil- /ail-/: **~bote** *der* special messenger; **etw. durch einen ~boten zustellen lassen** send sth. by special delivery *or* express; **„durch** *od.* **per ~boten"** (veralt.) 'express'; **~brief** *der* express letter

Eile /ˈailə/ *die;* **~:** hurry; **ich habe [große] ~:** I'm in a [great] hurry; **ich habe keine ~:** I'm not in a *or* any hurry; **die Sache hat ~:** it's urgent *or* a matter of urgency; **die Sache hat keine ~:** there's no hurry; it's not urgent; **[immer] in ~ sein** [always] be in a hurry; **in der ~:** in her/our *etc.* hurry; **in aller ~:** in great haste; **jmdn. zur ~ antreiben** hurry sb. up

Ei·leiter *der* ▸❶ **S. 435** (Anat.) Fallopian tube

Eileiter-: ~entzündung *die* salpingitis; **~schwangerschaft** *die* tubal pregnancy

eilen

A *itr. V.* [1] *mit sein* hurry; hasten; (besonders schnell) rush; **nach Hause ~:** hurry/rush home; **jmdm. zu Hilfe ~:** rush to sb.'s aid; **eile mit Weile** (Spr.) more haste, less speed (prov.) [2] (dringend sein) ‹*matter*› be urgent; **„eilt!"** 'urgent'; **„eilt sehr!"** 'immediate'; **es eilt mir damit** it's urgent; I'm in a hurry; **es eilt ihm mit dem Umzug** he is in a hurry to move

B *refl. V.* hurry; make haste

eilends *Adv.* (unverzüglich) immediately; without delay; (geh.: geschwind) hastily

eil-, Eil-: ~fertig (geh.) **A** *Adj.* [1] (vorschnell) rash; [2] (dienstbeflissen) zealous; **B** *adv.*; *s. Adj.* rashly; zealously; **~fertigkeit** *die* ▸ **~fertig**: rashness; zeal; **~fracht** *die* express freight; express goods *pl.*; **etw. per** *od.* **als ~fracht senden** send sth. express freight; **~gut** *das* fast freight; express goods *pl.*; **etw. als ~gut schicken** send sth. by fast freight

eilig

A *Adj.* [1] (schnell) hurried; **mit ~en Schritten** hurriedly; **es ~ haben** be in a hurry; **es weniger ~ haben** be in less of a hurry [2] (dringend) urgent ‹*news*›; **~ sein** be urgent; **es [sehr] ~ mit etw. haben** be in a [great] hurry about sth.; **etw. Eiliges** sth. urgent; an urgent matter; **nichts Eiligeres zu tun haben, als ...** (iron) have nothing better to do than...; **er hatte nichts Eiligeres zu tun, als allen davon zu erzählen** he couldn't wait to tell everybody about it

B *adv.* hurriedly; **~ laufen** run hurriedly; hurry

Eil-: ~marsch *der* (Milit.) forced march; **~paket** *das* express parcel; **~schritt** *der:* **im ~schritt laufen** walk with short, quick steps; **~sendung** *die* express consignment; (Brief) express letter; (Paket) express parcel; **~tempo** *das* (ugs.) **im ~tempo** in a rush; **im ~tempo ging es zum Bahnhof** we/they *etc.* rushed to the station; **~verfahren** *das* (jur.) summary proceedings *pl.*; **etw. im ~verfahren erledigen** (fig. ugs.) do sth. in a rush; **~zug** *der* semi-fast train; stopping train (Brit.); **~zustellung** *die* (Postw.) express delivery

Eimer /ˈaimɐ/ *der;* **~s, ~** [1] bucket; (Milch~) pail; (Abfall~) bin; **ein ~ [voll] Wasser** a bucket of water; **es gießt wie aus ~n** (ugs.) it's raining cats and dogs (coll.); it's coming down in buckets (coll.); **im ~ sein** (salopp) be up the spout (coll.); **mein Wagen ist im ~** (salopp) my car is a total wreck; **unsere Stimmung war im ~** (salopp) the atmosphere was totally ruined; **seine Gesundheit ist im ~** (salopp) he's a physical wreck [2] (ugs. abwertend: altes Schiff) tub

Eimer·bagger *der* bucket dredger

eimer·weise *Adv.* by the bucketful; in bucketfuls

ein[1] /ain/

A *Kardinalz.* ▸❶ **S. 826** one; **~ Dollar/~e Meile/~ Jahr** one dollar/mile/year; **in ~em Tag** in one day; in a single day; **~ einziger Tag/Mensch** one single day/person; **ich will dir noch ~[e]s sagen** there's one more thing I'd like to tell you; **~[e]s gefällt mir daran/an ihr nicht** there's one thing I don't like about it/her; **das ~e Gute daran ist ...** the only good thing about it is ...; **das ~e, das ich brauche** the one thing I need; **~er von beiden** one of the two; one or the other; **~er für alle, alle für ~en** one for all and all for one; **~ für alle Mal, *~ für allemal** once and for all; **~ und derselbe** one and the same; **er war ihr Ein und Alles** he was everything to her; **das Buch bietet alles in ~em** the book has everything in one volume; **in ~em fort** (geh.) continuously; all the time

B *unbest. Art.* a/an; **~ Kleid/Apfel/Mensch/Hotel** a dress/an apple/a human being/a[n] hotel; **~ Held/~ ehrlicher Mensch** a hero/an honest man/woman; **~ bisschen** *od.* **wenig** a little [bit]; **~ anderer** somebody else; **~ jeder** (geh.) each and every one; **~e Kälte ist das hier!** it's freezing here!; **~e Frechheit ist das!** what absolute cheek!; **was für ~ Wein!** what superb wine!; **was für ~e Unordnung!** what a mess!; **was für ~ Kleid hast du gekauft?** what sort of dress did you buy?; **das konnte nur ~ Beethoven schaffen** only a Beethoven could do that; **er besaß ~en Klee und ~en Picasso** he owned a Klee and a Picasso

C *Indefinitpron.* [1] (irgendeiner) one [2] (man) one; (jemand) someone; somebody; **wie soll das ~er wissen?** how is one supposed to know that?; **das mach mal ~em verständlich** try explaining that to anybody; **~e/~er/~[e]s der besten** one of the best [people/things]; **~s war offen und ~s zu** one was open and one shut; **kaum ~er** hardly anybody; **~er von uns/euch** one of us/you; **~er namens Mayer** (meist abwertend) a certain Mayer; **ist ~er bereit, mir zu helfen?** is anyone willing to help me?; **~er nach dem anderen** one after the other; one by one; **der ~e kommt, der andere geht** one comes, the other goes; **die ~en ..., die anderen ...** some ..., the others ...; **er trinkt ganz gerne ~en** (ugs.) he likes [to have] a drink; **sieh [mal] ~er an!** (ugs.) [now just] look at that!; **du bist [mir] ~e/~er!** (iron.) you are a [right] one (coll.); **das ist ~e/~er!** (ugs.) she's/he's quite a one (coll.); **er ist belesen wie selten ~er** he's uncommonly well read [3] (der-/die-/dasselbe) **~er Meinung sein** be of the same opinion; **es kommt alles auf ~[e]s heraus** it all comes to the same thing [in the end]

ein[2] (elliptisch) **~ — aus** (an Schaltern) on — off; **~ und aus gehen** go in and out; **bei jmdm. ~ und aus gehen** be a regular visitor at sb.'s house; **ich wusste nicht ~ noch aus** I didn't know where to turn *or* what to do

ein·achsig *Adj.* single-axle

ein·adrig *Adj.* (Elektrot.) single-core

Einakter /ˈainlaktɐ/ *der;* **~s, ~:** one-act play

einander /aiˈnandɐ/ *reziprokes Pron.* (geh.) each other; one another; **sie grüßten ~:** they greeted each other *or* one another; **liebet ~** (bes. bibl.) love one another; **~ widersprechende Behauptungen** mutually contradictory statements

ein|arbeiten *tr. V.* [1] (ausbilden) train ‹*employee*›; **er arbeitet sich gerade ein** he is training at present; **sich in etw.** (*Akk.*) **~:** become familiar *or* familiarize oneself with sth. [2] (einfügen) incorporate ‹*quotation etc.*› (**in** + *Akk.* into); **sie arbeitete einige Verzierungen in die Decke ein** she worked some patterns into the cover

Einarbeitung *die;* **~, ~en** training; **die ~ in das neue Sachgebiet fiel ihm schwer** he found it difficult to familiarize himself with the new subject

Einarbeitungs·zeit *die* training period

ein·armig

A *Adj.* one-armed; **ein Einarmiger** a one-armed man

B *adv.* ~ **Gewichte stemmen** lift weights with one hand

ein|äschern /ˈainɛʃɐn/ *tr. V.* **1** (niederbrennen) **ein Gebäude ~:** burn a building to the ground *or* down; reduce a building to ashes; **eine Stadt ~:** reduce a town to ashes **2** cremate ‹*corpse*›; **ich werde mich ~ lassen** I am going to be cremated

Einäscherung *die;* ~, ~**en** **1** (das Niederbrennen) **die ~ des Gebäudes** the burning down of the building; **die ~ der Stadt** the destruction of the town by fire **2** (Leichenverbrennung) cremation

Einäscherungs·halle *die* crematorium

ein|atmen *tr., itr. V.* breathe in

einatomig /ˈain|atoːmɪç/ *Adj.* (Chemie, Physik) monatomic

ein·äugig *Adj.* one-eyed; single-lens ‹*camera*›; **unter Blinden ist der Einäugige König** (Spr.) in the kingdom of the blind the one-eyed man is king (prov.)

Ein·bahn·straße *die* one-way street; **eine ~, aus der es kein Zurück mehr gab** (fig.) a path from which there could be no turning back (fig.); **das Verhältnis darf keine ~ sein** there must be give and take on both sides

ein|balsamieren *tr. V.* embalm ‹*corpse*›; **du kannst dich ~ lassen** (fig. ugs.) you might as well give up

Ein·band *der* binding; [book] cover

Einband-: ~deckel *der* (Buchw.) board; **~entwurf** *der* cover design

ein·bändig *Adj.* one-volume

ein·basisch *Adj.* (Chemie) monobasic

Ein·bau *der; Pl.* ~**ten** **1** (das Einbauen) fitting; (eines Motors) installation **2** (Einfügung) incorporation; insertion **3** *Pl.* (Eingebautes) fitted shelves/cupboards

ein|bauen *tr. V.* **1** build in, fit ‹*cupboard, kitchen*› **2** (Technik) install ‹*engine, motor*› **3** (einfügen) insert, incorporate ‹*chapter*›

Einbau·küche *die* fitted kitchen

Ein·baum *der* dugout [canoe]

Einbau-: ~möbel *das* piece of built-in furniture; (Schrank) built-in cupboard; (Regal) fitted shelves *pl.*; **teure ~möbel** expensive built-in furniture *sing.*; (Schränke) expensive built-in cupboards; (Regale) expensive fitted shelves **~schrank** *der* built-in cupboard; (für Kleidung) built-in wardrobe

ein|begreifen *unr. tr. V.* (geh.) include; **MWSt einbegriffen** including VAT

ein|behalten *unr. tr. V.* **1** (zurückbehalten) withhold **2** (Amtsspr.: festsetzen) detain

ein·beinig *Adj.* one-legged

ein|bekennen *unr. tr. V.* (geh., bes. österr.) ▸**eingestehen**

Ein·bekenntnis *das* (geh., bes. österr.) ▸**Eingeständnis**

ein|berechnen *tr. V.* ▸**einkalkulieren**

ein|berufen *unr. tr. V.* **1** summon; call; **eine Versammlung/Sitzung ~:** call *or* convene a meeting; **den Bundestag ~:** summon the Bundestag; **eine Versammlung nach Berlin/eine Sitzung für den 30. Mai ~:** call a meeting in Berlin/for 30 May **2** (zur Wehrpflicht) call up; conscript; draft (Amer.); **~ werden** be called up *or* conscripted; be drafted (Amer.)

Ein·berufene *der/die; adj. Dekl.* conscript; draftee (Amer.)

Ein·berufung *die* **1** (das Einberufen) calling; **die ~ des Parlaments** the summoning of Parliament **2** (zur Wehrpflicht) call-up; conscription; draft (Amer.)

Einberufungs-: ~befehl *der,* **~bescheid** *der* call-up papers *pl.*; draft card (Amer.)

ein|beschreiben *unr. tr. V.* (Geom.) inscribe ‹*circle*›; **einem Dreieck einen Kreis ~:** inscribe a circle in a triangle

ein|bestellen *tr. V.* (Amtsspr.) summon

ein|betonieren *tr. V.* concrete in; **etw. in etw.** (*Akk.*) **~:** concrete sth. into sth.

ein|betten *tr. V.* **1** embed (**in** + *Akk.* in); **das Haus liegt eingebettet in ein Tal** the house nestles in a valley **2** (Sprachw.) **eingebettete Sätze** embedded sentences

Einbett-: ~kabine *die* single-berth cabin; **~zimmer** *das* single room

ein|beulen

A *tr. V.* **etw. ~:** dent sth.; make a dent in sth.; **ein eingebeulter Kotflügel** a dented mudguard

B *refl. V.* become dented

ein|beziehen *unr. tr. V.* include; **etw. in etw.** (*Akk.*) **~:** include sth. in sth.; **jmdn. in eine Diskussion ~:** involve sb. *or* get sb. involved in a discussion

Ein·beziehung *die,* (schweiz.) **Ein·bezug** *der* inclusion; **unter ~ aller Faktoren** taking all factors into account

ein|biegen

A *unr. itr. V.* ▸❶ **S. 800**; *mit sein* turn; **in eine Straße ~:** turn into a street; **[nach] links/rechts ~:** turn left/right

B *unr. tr. V.* bend

C *unr. refl. V.* bend inwards

ein|bilden *refl. V.* **1** **sich** (*Dat.*) **etw. ~:** imagine sth.; **sich** (*Dat.*) **~, dass ...** imagine that ...; **ich bilde mir ein, dass ich ihn in der Stadt gesehen habe** (ugs.) I think I saw him in town; **eine eingebildete Krankheit** an imaginary illness; **was bildest du dir eigentlich ein?** (ugs.) what do you think you are doing? **2** (ugs.: übermäßig stolz sein) **er bildet sich** (*Dat.*) **ganz schön viel ein** he thinks no end of himself (coll.); he fancies himself no end (coll.); **sich** (*Dat.*) **ziemlich viel auf etw. ~:** be terribly conceited about sth. (coll.); **darauf brauchst du dir nichts einzubilden** there's no need to be stuck-up about it

Ein·bildung *die;* ~, ~**en** **1** (Fantasie) imagination **2** (falsche Vorstellung) fantasy; **das ist alles nur ~:** it's all in the mind **3** (Hochmut) conceitedness; **~ ist auch eine Bildung** (ugs.) you're kidding yourself/he's kidding himself *etc.* (coll.)

Einbildungs-: ~kraft *die,* **~vermögen** *das* [powers *pl.* of] imagination; imaginative powers *pl.*

ein|bimsen *tr. V.* (ugs.) **jmdm. etw. ~:** drum sth. into sb.

ein|binden *unr. tr. V.* **1** bind ‹*book*›; **etw. neu ~:** rebind sth. **2** (einfügen) **er war in bestimmte Konventionen/Wertvorstellungen eingebunden** (fig.) he was bound by certain conventions/subject to certain values; **in die Verantwortung eingebunden** constrained by responsibility **3** (integrieren) **das Dorf muss in das Verkehrsnetz eingebunden werden** the village must be linked into the transport system; **den Einzelnen in ein Kollektiv ~:** make the individual part of a group; **in ein System eingebunden bleiben** remain part of a system **4** (einhüllen) wrap; bandage ‹*limb*›

Ein·bindung *die* **1** (Integration) integration; **die ~ der Bundesrepublik in die EG** the fact that the Federal Republic forms part of the European Community **2** (Bindung, Festgelegtsein) **gegen die zu starke ~ durch den Vertrag setzte er sich zur Wehr** he fought against being bound *or* tied too closely by the contract

ein·blätt[e]rig *Adj.* (Bot.) monophyllous

ein|bläuen *tr. V.* **jmdm. etw. ~:** drum *or* hammer sth. into sb.

ein|blenden (Rundf., Ferns., Film)

A *tr. V.* insert; **eine Nachricht in eine Sendung ~:** interrupt a programme with a news flash; **Geräusche/Musik/Szenen nachträglich ~:** dub in sounds/music/scenes

B *refl. V.* **sich in ein Fußballspiel ~:** go over to a football match; **sich in eine Direktübertragung ~:** link up with a live transmission

Ein·blendung *die* (Rundf., Ferns., Film) insertion; (Rückblende) flashback (**in** + *Akk.* to)

***ein|bleuen** ▸**einbläuen**

Ein·blick *der* **1** (Sicht) **den ~ in den Garten verhindern** obstruct the view of the garden; **~ in etw.** (*Akk.*) **haben** be able to see into sth. **2** (Durchsicht) **~ in etw. nehmen** take a look at *or* examine sth.; **jmdm. ~ in etw.** (*Akk.*) **gewähren** allow *or* permit sb. to look at *or* examine sth.; **keinen ~ in etw.** (*Akk.*) **haben** not be permitted to look at *or* examine sth. **3** (Kenntnis) insight; **[einen] ~ in etw. haben/gewinnen** have/gain an insight into sth.

ein|bohnern *tr. V.* wax ‹*floor, stairs*›

ein|bohren

A *tr. V.* drill; bore

B *refl. V.* **sich in etw.** (*Akk.*) **~:** bore into sth.

ein|brechen

A *unr. itr. V.* **1** *mit haben od. sein* break in; **in eine Bank/ein Geschäft ~:** break into a bank/shop; **bei jmdm. ~:** burgle sb.; **bei uns wurde eingebrochen** we were burgled; we had a break-in **2** *mit sein* (einstürzen) ‹*roof, ceiling*› fall in, cave in **3** *mit sein* (durchbrechen) fall through; **beim Eislaufen ~:** fall *or* go through the ice while skating **4** *mit sein* (eindringen) **in ein Land ~:** invade a country; **in die Verteidigungslinie ~:** break through the line of defences **5** *mit sein* (geh.: beginnen) ‹*night, darkness*› fall; ‹*winter*› set in **6** *mit sein* (salopp: scheitern) **[ganz schön] ~:** come [badly] unstuck (coll.); come a [fearful] cropper (coll.) **7** *mit sein* (hineinstürzen) burst in; **in etw.** (*Akk.*) **~:** burst into sth.

B *unr. tr. V.* break down ‹*door, wall*›; demolish ‹*chimney*›

Einbrecher *der;* ~**s**, ~: burglar

Einbrecher·bande *die* gang of burglars

Einbrecherin *die;* ~, ~**nen** burglar

ein|bremsen

A *tr. V.* **1** (Jargon) put the brakes on ‹*growth, development*›; rein in, curb ‹*person*›; check ‹*illness*›; reduce ‹*noise*›; **2** (langsamer machen) slow down (**auf** + *Akk.* to); **ein Auto elektronisch ~:** restrict the speed of a car electronically.

B *itr. V.* **in eine Kurve ~:** brake for a corner; **beim Einbremsen in den Orbit** while slowing to go into orbit

Einbrenne /ˈainbrɛnə/ *die;* ~, ~**n** (Kochk.: bes. südd., österr.) roux

ein|brennen

A *unr. tr. V.* **ein Zeichen in Holz/auf eine Platte ~:** burn a design into wood/bake a design on to a plate; **einem Tier das Brandzeichen ~:** brand an animal

B *unr. refl. V.* (geh.) **das Erlebnis hatte sich tief in sein** *od.* **seinem Gedächtnis eingebrannt** the experience had engraved itself on his memory

ein|bringen

A *unr. tr. V.* **1** (hineinschaffen) bring *or* gather in ‹*harvest*›; **ein Schiff in den Hafen ~:** bring a ship into port; **das Werkstück in die Maschine ~:** put the workpiece into the machine **2** (verschaffen) **jmdm. viel Geld ~:** bring sb. [in] a lot of money; **Gewinn/Zinsen ~:** yield a profit/bring in interest; **jmdm. Ruhm/Ehre ~:** bring sb. fame/honour; **das hat nichts als Ärger eingebracht** that's caused nothing but trouble; **das bringt nichts ein** it isn't worth it **3** (Parl.: vorlegen) introduce ‹*bill*›; **einen Antrag im Parlament ~:** introduce a bill into parliament; bring a bill before parliament **4** (in eine Gemeinschaft, Gesellschaft usw.) invest ‹*capital, money*›; **etw. in eine Ehe ~:** bring sth. into a marriage; **etw. [in eine Situation] ~:** contribute sth. [to a situation] **5** (festsetzen) catch, capture ‹*escaped prisoners*› **6** (Druckw.) take in ‹*lines*›

B *unr. refl. V.* **sich in eine Beziehung ~:** make one's own contribution to a relationship

Einbringung *die;* ~ **1** (Festsetzung) capture **2** (Parl.: von Gesetzen) introduction

ein|brocken *tr. V.* (ugs.) **sich/jmdm. etw. [Schönes] ~, sich/jmdm. eine schöne Suppe ~:** land oneself/sb. in the soup *or* in it (coll.); **das hast du dir selbst eingebrockt** you've only yourself to thank for that (coll.)

Ein·bruch *der* **1** burglary; break-in; **ein ~ in eine Bank** a break-in at a bank; **einen ~ verüben** commit a burglary **2** (das Einstürzen) collapse; **ein ~ der Börsenkurse** (fig.) a slump in stock market prices **3** (Vorstoß) breakthrough; **der ~ des Feindes in ein Land** the enemy invasion of a country; **der ~ einer Kälte-/Hitzewelle** (fig.) the onset of a cold wave *or* spell/a heat wave **4** (Beginn) **vor ~ der Dunkelheit** before it gets dark; **der ~ des Winters** the onset of winter; **bei ~ der Nacht** at nightfall; when night closes/closed in; **bei ~ des Winters** when winter sets/set in **5** (salopp: das Scheitern) **einen ~ erleiden** take a drubbing *or* hiding (coll.) **6** (Geol.) area of subsidence

einbruch[s]-, Einbruch[s]-: ~diebstahl *der* burglary; breaking and entering; **~gefahr** *die:* **„~gefahr"** 'danger — thin ice'; **~sicher** *Adj.* burglar-proof

ein|buchten *tr. V.* (salopp) **jmdn. ~:** lock sb. up (coll.); put sb. away (coll.); *s. auch* **eingebuchtet**

Einbuchtung *die;* **~, ~en** **1** **eine ~ der Straße** a bend in the road; **eine ~ der Küste** a bay; an inlet **2** (Delle) dent; **die ~ der Autotür** the dent in the car door

ein|buddeln *tr. V.* (ugs.) bury; **sich ~:** dig oneself in

einbürgern ▸**❶ S. 520**

A *tr. V.* naturalize ‹*person, plant, animal*›; introduce ‹*custom, practice*›

B *refl. V.* ‹*custom, practice*› become established; ‹*person, plant, animal*› become naturalized; **sich in einer Sprache ~:** become established as part of a language; **das hat sich hier so eingebürgert** it has become the practice here

Einbürgerung *die;* **~, ~en** naturalization

Ein·buße *die* loss; **schwere ~n erleiden** suffer heavy losses; **eine ~ an etw.** (*Dat.*) a loss of sth.; **das bedeutet eine [finanzielle] ~ für mich** I shall be worse off financially

ein|büßen

A *tr. V.* lose; (durch eigene Schuld) forfeit; **sein Geld/seine Freiheit/sein Leben ~:** lose/forfeit one's money/one's freedom/one's life

B *itr. V.* **sie büßte an Ansehen ein** her reputation suffered

Ein·cent·stück *das* one-cent piece

ein|checken *tr., itr. V.* (Flugw.) check in

ein|cremen *tr. V.* put cream on ‹*hands, back*›; **sich ~:** put cream on; **jmdm./sich die Hände/den Rücken ~:** put cream on sb.'s/one's hands/back

ein|dämmen *tr. V.* **1** dam ‹*river*›; embank, dyke ‹*land*› **2** (aufhalten) check; stem

ein|dämmern *itr. V.; mit sein* doze off

Eindämmung *die;* **~, ~en** ▸**eindämmen**: damming; dyking; checking, stemming; **eine ~ des Drogenhandels scheint unmöglich** it seems impossible to stem the flow of drugs

ein|dampfen *tr. V.* (Chemie) evaporate

ein|decken

A *refl. V.* stock up; **sich [für den Winter] mit etw. ~:** stock up with sth. [for the winter]

B *tr. V.* (ugs.: überhäufen) **jmdn. mit Arbeit/Fragen ~:** swamp sb. with work/questions; **mit etw. eingedeckt sein** be swamped with sth.

Eindecker *der;* **~s, ~** (Flugw.) monoplane

ein|deichen *tr. V.* dyke ‹*land*›; dyke, embank ‹*river*›

ein|dellen *tr. V.* (ugs.) dent [in]

eindeutig /ˈaindɔytɪç/

A *Adj.* **1** (klar) clear; clear, definite ‹*proof*› **2** (nur eine Deutung zulassend) unambiguous ‹*concept*›

B *adv. s. Adj.* clearly; unambiguously

Eindeutigkeit *die;* **~, ~en** **1** ▸**eindeutig**: clarity; unambiguity **2** (scherzh.: unanständiger Witz) crudity

ein|deutschen *tr. V.* Germanize

Eindeutschung *die;* **~, ~en** **1** Germanization **2** (eingedeutschtes Wort) Germanized word

ein|dicken *tr., itr. V.* thicken

ein·dimensional *Adj.* one-dimensional; unidimensional; (fig.) one-dimensional ‹*personality*›

ein|docken *tr. V.* (Schiffbau) dock

ein|dosen *tr. V.* can; tin (Brit.)

ein|dösen *itr. V.* (ugs.) *mit sein* doze off

ein|drängen

A *itr. V.; mit sein* **auf jmdn. ~:** crowd around sb.; **Eindrücke/Erinnerungen drängten auf ihn ein** (fig.) impressions/memories crowded in [up]on him

B *refl. V.* push one's way in; force one's way in

ein|drecken /ˈaindrɛkn̩/ *tr. V.* (ugs.) **etw./sich ~:** get sth./oneself filthy; (mit Schlamm usw.) get sth./oneself covered in *or* with muck (coll.)

ein|drehen *tr. V.* **1** (hin~) screw in ‹*light bulb*› (**in** + *Akk.* into) **2** **sich** (*Dat.*) **die Haare ~:** put one's hair in curlers *or* rollers; **sich** (*Dat.*) **die Haare ~ lassen** have one's hair curled

ein|dreschen *unr. itr. V.* (ugs.) **auf jmdn. ~:** lay into sb. (coll.)

ein|dringen *unr. itr. V.; mit sein* **1** **in etw.** (*Akk.*) **~:** penetrate into sth.; ‹*vermin*› get into sth.; ‹*bullet*› pierce sth.; (allmählich) ‹*water, sand, etc.*› seep into sth.; **er drang in sie ein** he penetrated her (sexually); **die ~de Kaltluft** the cold air that blows in **2** (einbrechen) **in ein Gebäude ~:** force an entry *or* one's way into a building; **Feinde sind in das Land eingedrungen** (geh.) enemies invaded the country; **in eine Gesellschaft ~** (fig.) be an uninvited guest **3** (bedrängen) set upon, attack ‹*person*›; **mit Fragen auf jmdn. ~:** besiege *or* ply sb. with questions; **auf jmdn. ~[, etw. zu tun]** (fig.) press *or* urge sb. [to do sth.]

ein·dringlich

A *Adj.* urgent ‹*warning, entreaty*›; impressive ‹*voice*›; forceful, powerful ‹*speech, words*›

B *adv.* ‹*urge*› strongly; ‹*talk*› insistently; **jmdn. auf das Eindringlichste warnen** warn sb. most urgently

Ein·dringlichkeit *die;* **~** ▸**eindringlich**: urgency; impressiveness; forcefulness

Eindringling /ˈaindrɪŋlɪŋ/ *der;* **~s, ~e** intruder

Ein·druck *der;* **~[e]s, Eindrücke** **1** (Vorstellung, Wirkung) impression; **einen ~ haben/gewinnen** have/get *or* gain an impression; **jmdn. nach dem ersten ~ beurteilen** judge sb. by first impressions; **einen guten ~ machen** make a good impression; **~ auf jmdn. machen** make an impression on sb.; **Eindrücke gewinnen** receive impressions; **er macht den ~ eines sehr gewissenhaften Menschen** he gives the impression of being a very conscientious person; **er konnte sich des ~s nicht erwehren, dass ...** (geh.) he had the strong impression that ...; he could not help thinking *or* feeling that ...; **sie stand noch unter dem ~ dieses schrecklichen Erlebnisses** she was still haunted by this terrible experience; **er stand noch ganz unter dem ~ seiner Indienreise** he was still under the spell of his journey to India; **er tat es nur, um [bei ihr] ~ zu schinden** (ugs.) he only did it to impress [her] **2** (Spur) impression

ein|drücken *tr. V.* **1** (verbiegen, zerbrechen) smash in ‹*mudguard, bumper*›; stave in ‹*side of ship*›; smash ‹*pier, column, support*›; break ‹*window*›; crush ‹*ribs*›; flatten ‹*nose*›; **der Wind drückte alle Fenster ein** the wind blew all the windows in **2** (hineindrücken) **etw. [in etw.** (*Akk.*)**] ~:** press *or* push sth. in[to sth.]

eindrucks-: ~los **A** *Adj.* unimpressive; **B** *adv.* unimpressively; **~voll** **A** *Adj.* impressive; **B** *adv.* impressively

ein|dübeln *tr. V.* **etw. in die Wand ~:** fix sth. into the wall with a plug/dowel

eine ▸**ein¹**

ein|ebnen *tr. V.* level; **der Unterschied ist eingeebnet worden** (fig.) the difference has been eliminated

Einebnung *die;* **~, ~en** levelling; (fig.) elimination; **bei der ~ des Grundstücks** during the levelling of the site

Ein·ehe *die* monogamy *no art.*

eineiig /ˈainlaiɪç/ *Adj.* identical ‹*twins*›

ein·eindeutig *Adj.* one-to-one ‹*correspondence, relationship*›; **eine ~e Abbildung** a representation having a one-to-one correspondence with its original

ein·ein·halb *Bruchz.* ▸**❶ S. 826** one and a half; **~ Stunden/Jahre** an hour/a year and a half; one and a half hours/years

ein·ein·halb·fach *Vervielfältigungsz.* one and a half times; **die ~e Anzahl/Menge** one and a half times the number/amount

Ein·eltern·familie *die* single-parent family

einen *tr. V.* (geh.) unite

ein|engen *tr. V.* **1** **jmdn. ~:** restrict sb.'s movement[s]; **sich eingeengt fühlen** feel hemmed in *or* shut in **2** (fig.: einschränken) restrict; restrict, narrow down ‹*concept*›; **jmdn. in seiner Freiheit ~:** restrict *or* curb sb.'s freedom

einer ▸**ein¹**

Einer *der;* **~s, ~** **1** (Math.) unit **2** (Sport) single sculler; **im ~:** in the single sculls

einerlei /ˈainɐlai/

A *Adj.* (unwichtig) **~, ob/wo/wer** *usw.* no matter whether/where/who *etc.*; **es ist ~:** it makes no difference; **es ist ihm ~:** it is all the same *or* all one to him; (es kümmert ihn nicht) he does not care at all

B *indekl. Gattungsz.* **von ~ Sorte** of one *or* of the same kind; **mit ~ Maß gemessen werden** be assessed according to one *or* the same standard

Einerlei *das;* **~s** monotony; **das tägliche ~:** the monotony of everyday life; the daily grind (coll.)

einerseits /ˈainɐˈzaits/ *Adv.* on the one hand; **~ ..., andererseits ...** on the one hand ..., on the other hand ...

Einer·stelle *die* (Math.) units place

eines ▸**ein¹**

eines·teils *Adv.* on the one hand; **~ ..., ander[e]nteils ...** on the one hand ..., on the other hand ...

Ein·euro·münze *die* one-euro coin

Ein·euro·stück *das* one-euro piece

ein|exerzieren *tr. V.* drill, train ‹*soldier, pupil, etc.*›; **jmdm. etw. ~:** drill *or* train sb. in sth.

ein·fach

A *Adj.* **1** (nicht mehrfach) single ‹*knot, ticket, journey*›; **zweimal ~ [nach] Köln** two singles to Cologne **2** (nicht schwierig) simple, easy ‹*task*›; **das ist ~:** that is simple *or* easy; **sich** (*Dat.*) **etw. [zu] ~ machen** make sth. [too] easy for oneself; **warum ~, wenn es auch kompliziert geht!** (scherzh.) the other way would be too simple, I suppose! **3** (einleuchtend) simple ‹*explanation, reason*›; **aus dem ~en Grund, weil ...** for the simple reason that ... **4** (bescheiden) simple ‹*person, manner, life, dress, etc.*›; plain, simple ‹*food*›; **er war nur ein ~er Mann** he was just an ordinary man; *s. auch* **Verhältnis**

B *adv.* **1** (bescheiden, einleuchtend) simply; **sich betont ~ kleiden** dress very simply **2** (nicht mehrfach) **etw. ~ falten** fold sth. once

C *Partikel* (verstärkend) simply; just; **das ist ~ unmöglich** that is simply *or* just impossible; **ich begreife es ~ nicht** I simply *or* just cannot understand it; **es ist ~ nicht zu begreifen, dass ...** it's simply incomprehensible that ...

Einfachheit *die;* **~** **1** (einfache Gestaltung) simplicity; **von verblüffender ~ sein** be of astonishing simplicity; **der ~ halber** for the sake of simplicity; for simplicity's sake **2** (Bescheidenheit) simplicity; (der Nahrung) plainness; simplicity

ein|fädeln

A *tr. V.* **1** thread ‹*needle, tape*› (**in** + *Akk.* into); thread up ‹*sewing machine*›; **einen [neuen] Faden ~:** [re]thread the needle **2** (ugs.: geschickt einleiten) engineer ‹*scheme, plot*›; **das hat sie fein/schlau eingefädelt** she worked that nicely/craftily (coll.)

B *refl. V.* (Verkehrsw.) filter in; **sich in den fließenden Verkehr ~:** filter into the flow of traffic

C *itr. V.* (Skisport) become entangled in the gate

ein|fahren

A *unr. itr. V.; mit sein* come in; ‹*train*› come *or* pull in; **in den Bahnhof ~:** come *or* pull into the station; **der Zug nach Hamburg ist soeben auf Gleis 5 eingefahren** the Hamburg train has just arrived at platform 5

B *unr. tr. V.* **1** bring in ‹*harvest*› **2** (beschädigen) knock down ‹*wall*›; smash in ‹*mudguard*› **3** (Kfz-W.) run in ‹*car*› **4** (Technik) retract ‹*undercarriage, antenna*› **5** (Wirtsch.) make ‹*profit, loss*›; set up ‹*record*›

C *unr. refl. V.* **1** **sich mit einem Fahrzeug ~:** get used to a vehicle **2** (sich einspielen) **der**

e

neue Produktionsprozess hat sich eingefahren the new production process is now running smoothly; *s. auch* **eingefahren**

Einfahr·signal *das* (Eisenb.) home signal

Ein·fahrt *die* **1** (das Hineinfahren) entry; **Vorsicht bei der ~ des Zuges!** stand clear [of the edge of the platform], the train is approaching **2** (Zufahrt) entrance; (Autobahn~) slip road; **„keine ~"** 'no entry'; **der Zug hat noch keine ~/hat ~ auf Gleis 5** the train is not yet able to pull in/is now approaching platform 5

Ein·fall *der* **1** (Idee) idea; **ein sonderbarer ~:** a strange notion *or* idea; **auf den ~ kommen, etw. zu tun** have *or* get the idea of doing sth.; **sie hat Einfälle wie ein altes Haus** (scherzh.) she gets some strange ideas **2** (Licht~) incidence (Optics) **3** (in ein Land usw.) invasion (**in** + *Akk.* of) **4** (geh.: plötzliches Einsetzen) (des Winters) onset; **bei ~ der Nacht** at nightfall

ein|fallen *unr. itr. V.; mit sein* **1** **jmdm. fällt etw. ein** sb. thinks of sth.; sth. occurs to sb.; **fällt dir etwas ein, was wir tun könnten?** can you think of anything we can do?; **ihm fallen immer wieder neue Ausreden ein** he can always think of *or* (coll.) come up with new excuses; **was fällt dir denn ein!** what do you think you're doing?; how dare you?; **lass dir das ja nicht ~!** don't you dare!; **sich** (*Dat.*) **etw. ~ lassen [müssen]** [have to] think of sth.; **das fällt mir nicht im Schlaf** *od.* **im Traum[e] ein** I wouldn't dream of it *or* such a thing **2** (in Erinnerung kommen) **ihr Name fällt mir nicht ein** I cannot think of her name; **plötzlich fiel ihm seine Frau ein** suddenly he thought of his wife; **es wird dir schon [wieder] ~:** it will come [back] to you; **plötzlich fiel ihr ein, dass …** (merkte sie) suddenly she realized that …; (erinnerte sie sich daran) suddenly she remembered that … **3** (von Licht) come in **4** (gewaltsam eindringen) **in ein Land ~:** invade a country **5** (einstimmen, mitreden usw.) join in; **in den Gesang ~:** join in the singing; **in ein Gespräch ~:** break into a conversation; **„Ja, natürlich", fiel er ein** 'Yes, of course,' he put in **6** (geh.: plötzlich beginnen) ‹*winter*› set in; ‹*night*› fall; ‹*storm*› break

einfalls-, Einfalls-: ~los **A** *Adj.* unimaginative; lacking in ideas; **B** *adv.* unimaginatively; without imagination; **~losigkeit** *die; ~~:* unimaginativeness; lack of ideas; **~reich** **A** *Adj.* imaginative; full of ideas; **B** *adv.* imaginatively; with imagination; **~reichtum** *der* imaginativeness; wealth of ideas; **~tor** *das* gateway

Einfall·straße *die* (Verkehrsw.) access road

Einfall[s]·winkel *der* (Physik) angle of incidence

Einfalt /ˈainfalt/ *die; ~* **1** (Beschränktheit) simpleness; simple-mindedness **2** (geh.: Reinheit) simplicity; innocence; **~ des Herzens** simplicity of heart

einfältig /ˈainfɛltɪç/ *Adj.* **1** (arglos) simple; naive; artless; naive ‹*remarks*›; **sei nicht so ~!** don't be so naive! **2** (beschränkt) simple; simple-minded

Einfältigkeit *die; ~* **1** (Arglosigkeit) simplicity; naivety; artlessness **2** (Beschränktheit) simpleness; simple-mindedness

Einfalts·pinsel *der* (ugs. abwertend) nincompoop

Ein·familien·haus *das* house (as opposed to block of flats etc.)

ein|fangen
A *unr. tr. V.* **1** catch, capture ‹*fugitive, animal*› **2** (geh.: wiedergeben) capture ‹*atmosphere, aura, etc.*›
B *unr. refl. V.* (ugs.: bekommen) **sich** (*Dat.*) **eine Erkältung** *usw.* **~:** catch *or* get a cold *etc.*; **sich** (*Dat.*) **eine Tracht Prügel ~:** get a beating

ein|färben *tr. V.* **1** dye ‹*material, hair*›; **eine kommunistisch eingefärbte Zeitung** (fig.) a newspaper with a communist slant **2** (Druckw.) ink

ein·farbig, (österr.) **ein·färbig**
A *Adj.* ‹*material, dress*› of one colour; plain ‹*material, dress*›
B *adv.* **das Sofa ~ beziehen** cover the sofa in material of one colour; **die Wände ~ streichen** paint the walls all one colour

ein|fassen *tr. V.* border, hem, edge ‹*material, dress, tablecloth*›; frame ‹*picture*›; set ‹*gem*›; edge ‹*lawn, flower bed, grave*›; curb ‹*source, spring*›

Ein·fassung *die* ▸ **einfassen:** border; hem; edging; frame; setting; (von Brunnen, Quellen) enclosure

ein|fetten *tr. V.* grease; dubbin ‹*leather*›; **sich** (*Dat.*) **die Haut/Hände ~:** rub cream into one's skin/hands

ein|finden *unr. refl. V.* (eintreffen) arrive; (sich treffen) meet; (zusammenkommen) gather; (sich melden) be present; (fig.) ‹*opportunity etc.*› occur; **sich bei jmdm. ~:** report to sb.

ein|flechten *unr. tr. V.* **sich** (*Dat.*) **Bänder ins Haar ~:** plait *or* braid ribbons into one's hair; **ein Muster in einen Korb ~:** weave a pattern into a basket; **in eine Rede ein paar Scherze ~:** work a couple of jokes into a speech; **Episoden in einen Roman ~:** weave episodes into a novel; **wenn ich das kurz ~ darf** if I could turn to this for a moment

ein|flicken *tr. V.* (ugs.) stitch on; (fig.) shove in (coll.)

ein|fliegen
A *unr. tr. V.* **1** fly in ‹*supplies, troops*› **2** flight-test, test-fly ‹*aircraft*› **3** (Wirtsch.) make ‹*profit, loss*›
B *unr. itr. V.; mit sein* **1** fly in; **eingeflogen kommen** come over by air; **in ein Gebiet ~:** fly into *or* enter a territory **2** (in einen geschlossenen Raum) ‹*bees, doves, etc.*› fly in; **in etw.** (*Akk.*) **~:** fly into sth.

ein|fließen *unr. itr. V.; mit sein* flow in; **von Norden fließt Kaltluft nach Westeuropa ein** (fig.) a cold northerly airstream is moving into Western Europe; **etw. in ein Gespräch ~ lassen** (fig.) slip sth. into a conversation; **~de Kalt-/Warmluft** (Met.) an inflow of cold/warm air

ein|flößen *tr. V.* **1** **jmdm. Tee/Medizin ~:** pour tea/medicine into sb.'s mouth; **jmdm. mit Gewalt Alkohol ~:** force alcohol *or* drink down sb.['s throat] **2** (fig.) **jmdm. Angst ~:** put fear into sb.; arouse fear in sb.; **jmdm. Vertrauen ~:** inspire sb. with confidence; **jmdm. Ehrfurcht/Mut ~:** fill sb. with awe/courage; inspire awe/courage in sb.

Ein·flug *der:* **~ einer feindlichen Maschine** an incursion by an enemy aircraft; **beim ~ in feindliches Hoheitsgebiet** while flying into enemy territory

Einflug-: ~loch *das* (Zool.) entrance [hole]; **~schneise** *die* (Flugw.) approach path

Ein·fluss, *Ein·fluß *der* **1** influence; **~ auf jmdn./etw. haben/ausüben** have/exert an influence on sb./sth.; **das entzieht sich meinem ~:** I have no influence over that; that is beyond my control; **unter jmds. ~** (*Dat.*) **stehen** be under sb.'s influence; **unter dem ~ von Alkohol** under the influence of alcohol; **~ auf etw.** (*Akk.*) **nehmen** influence sth.; **[einen] großen ~ besitzen** have a great deal of influence *or* sway **2** (Met.) inflow **3** (fig.: von Kapital usw.) influx

einfluss-, *einfluß-, Einfluss-, *Einfluß-: ~bereich *der,* **~gebiet** *das* sphere of influence; **~los** *Adj.* uninfluential; lacking in influence *postpos.*; **~nahme** *die; ~~:* exertion of influence (**auf** + *Akk.* on); (Versuch) **~nahme auf jmdn.** attempt to influence sb.; **~reich** *Adj.* influential; **~sphäre** *die* sphere of influence

ein|flüstern
A *tr. V.* (oft abwertend) **wer hat dir denn diesen Unsinn eingeflüstert?** who has put this nonsense into your head?; **lass dir nicht solche albernen Gerüchte ~:** don't be taken in by such silly gossip
B *itr. V.* (flüsternd sprechen) whisper

Einflüsterung *die; ~, ~en* (geh. abwertend) blandishment

ein|fordern *tr. V.* demand ‹*payment*›; demand payment of ‹*money, outstanding debts*›; **ein Gutachten ~:** ask for a report

ein·förmig
A *Adj.* monotonous
B *adv.* monotonously

Ein·förmigkeit *die; ~, ~en* monotony

ein|fressen *unr. refl. V.* **sich in etw.** (*Akk.*) **~:** eat into sth.

ein|frieden, ein|friedigen *tr. V.* (geh.) enclose ‹*plot of land*›

Einfriedung, Einfriedigung *die; ~, ~en* means of enclosure; (Zaun) fence; (Hecke) hedge; (Mauer) wall

ein|frieren
A *unr. itr. V.; mit sein* **1** ‹*water*› freeze, turn to ice; ‹*pond*› freeze over; ‹*pipes*› freeze up; ‹*ship*› be frozen in; **ihr Lächeln war eingefroren** (fig.) her smile had frozen (fig.) **2** (fig.) ‹*wages, credit*› be frozen; ‹*negotiations*› break down
B *unr. tr. V.* **1** deep-freeze ‹*food*› **2** (beenden) freeze ‹*credit, project, plan*›; break off, suspend ‹*negotiations*›; suspend ‹*inquiry*›

ein|frosten *tr. V.* ▸ **einfrieren B 1**

ein|fuchsen *tr. V.* (ugs.) **jmdn. auf etw.** (*Akk.*) **~:** drill sb. in sth.; **ein eingefuchster Spezialist/Trainer** an experienced specialist/trainer; **auf etw.** (*Akk.*) **eingefuchst sein** be well practised in sth.

ein|fügen
A *tr. V.* fit in; **etw. in etw.** (*Akk.*) **~:** fit sth. into sth.; **etw. in einen Text ~:** insert sth. into a text; **ich möchte noch ~, dass …** (fig.) I would like to add that …
B *refl. V.* adapt; **sich in etw.** (*Akk.*) **~:** adapt oneself to sth.; **sich überall gut ~:** fit in well anywhere

Ein·fügung *die* insertion

ein|fühlen *refl. V.* **sich in jmdn. ~:** empathize with sb.; **ich kann mich gut in deine Lage ~:** I know exactly how you feel; I can well understand how you feel; **er kann sich gut in eine Rolle/in einen anderen ~:** he is good at getting into a part/putting himself in another person's place; **sich in die Atmosphäre des alten Moskau ~:** get the feel of the atmosphere in old Moscow

einfühlsam *Adj.* understanding; sensitive ‹*interpretation, performance*›

Einfühlsamkeit *die; ~:* sensitivity

Ein·fühlung *die; ~:* empathy (**in** + *Akk.* with)

Einfühlungs·vermögen *das* ability to empathize; **mit ausgesprochenem ~ spielen/übersetzen** play/translate with great sensitivity for the work

Ein·fuhr *die; ~, ~en* **1** (das Einführen) import; importing **2** (das Eingeführte) import

ein|führen
A *tr. V.* **1** (importieren) import ‹*goods, technology*› **2** (als Neuerung) introduce ‹*fashion, method, technology*› **3** (ein-, unterweisen) introduce; initiate; **jmdn. in etw.** (*Akk.*) **~:** introduce sb. to sth.; initiate sb. into sth.; **jmdn. in sein Amt ~:** install sb. in office; **der neue Kollege wurde eingeführt** our *etc.* new colleague was introduced to *or* initiated into his new job **4** (hineinschieben) introduce, insert ‹*catheter etc.*› (**in** + *Akk.* into) **5** (vorstellen) introduce; **jmdn. bei seinen Eltern ~:** introduce sb. to one's parents; **eine junge Dame in die Gesellschaft ~:** bring a young lady out; **jmdn. bei Hofe ~:** present sb. at court
B *refl. V.* **1** (sich vorstellen) introduce oneself; **du hast dich nicht sehr gut eingeführt** you didn't make a very good first impression **2** (Kaufmannsspr.) ‹*shop, company*› become established

Einfuhr-: ~erlaubnis, ~genehmigung *die* import licence; **~hafen** *der* port of entry; **~kontingent** *das* import quota; **~land** *das* importing country; importer; **~lizenz** *die* import licence; **~sperre** *die,* **~stopp** *der* embargo *or* ban on imports

Ein·führung *die* **1** introduction; **eine ~ in die Naturwissenschaften** an introduction to the natural sciences; **ihre ~ in die Gesellschaft/bei Hof** her introduction to society/her presentation at court; **die ~ in sein Amt** his installation in office **2** (Einarbeitung) introduction; initiation; induction **3** (das Hineinschieben) introduction; insertion

Einführungs-: ~kurs[us] *der* (Schulw.) introductory course; **~preis** *der* (Kaufmannsspr.) introductory price

Einfuhr-: ~verbot *das* ▸▸**~sperre**; **~zoll** *der* import duty

ein|füllen *tr. V.* **etw. in etw.** (*Akk.*) **~:** pour *or* put sth. into sth.; **Wasser in eine Flasche ~:** fill a bottle with water

Einfüll·stutzen *der* (an Tanks) filler pipe; (an Haushaltsgeräten) filling spout

ein|füttern *tr. V.* (DV) feed in; **einem Computer Daten ~:** feed data into a computer

Ein·gabe *die* **1** (Gesuch) petition; (Beschwerde) complaint **2** (das Verabreichen) administration; **die ~ der Tabletten sollte alle zwei Stunden erfolgen** the tablets are to be taken every two hours **3** (DV) input

Eingabe-: ~gerät *das* (DV) input device; **~maske** *die* (DV) input mask; **~taste** *die* (DV) enter key

Ein·gang *der* **1** (Tür, Pforte, Portal usw.) entrance; **der ~ eines Hauses/eines Parks** the entrance of *or* to a house/a park; **„kein ~"** 'no entry'; **in etw.** (*Akk.*) **~ finden** (fig.) become established in sth. **2** (von Post, Geld) receipt **3** (eingetroffene Post) incoming mail **4** (Elektrot.) input

ein·gängig
A *Adj.* catchy ‹*song, melody*›; **ihr war das [nicht] ~** (geh.) it was [in]comprehensible to her
B *adv.* **etw. ~ erklären** explain sth. simply and clearly

eingangs
A *Adv.* at the beginning; at the start
B *Präp. + Gen.* **~ der Kurve/Fußgängerzone** where the bend/pedestrian precinct begins *or* starts; **~ des Jahres** at the beginning *or* start of the year

Eingangs-: ~buch *das* (Buchf.) 'goods inward' book; **~datum** *das* (Bürow.) date of receipt; **~formel** *die* preamble; **~halle** *die* entrance hall; (eines Hotels, Theaters) foyer; **~pforte** *die* gateway; **~stempel** *der* (Bürow.) date stamp; **~tür** *die* (von Kaufhaus, Hotel usw.) [entrance] door; (von Wohnung, Haus usw.) front door

ein|geben *unr. tr. V.* **1** (verabreichen) give; **jmdm. Medizin ~:** give *or* administer medicine to sb. **2** (DV) input; **etw. in den Computer ~:** input sth. into the computer **3** (geh.: zu denken veranlassen) **jmdm. eine Idee ~:** inspire sb. with an idea; **jmdm. den Wunsch ~, etw. zu tun** prompt sb. to do sth.

ein·gebildet
A *2. Part. v.* **einbilden**
B *Adj.* **1** (imaginär) imaginary ‹*illness*›; **ein ~er Kranker** a malade imaginaire; **~e Schwangerschaft** false pregnancy **2** (arrogant) conceited; **auf etw.** (*Akk.*) **~ sein** be conceited about sth.; *s. auch* **Affe**

ein·geboren *Adj.* **1** native ‹*population etc.*› **2** (geh.: angeboren) inborn; innate **3** (Rel.) **Gottes ~er Sohn** the only begotten Son of God

Eingeborene *der/die; adj. Dekl.* (veralt.) native

eingebuchtet
A *2. Part. v.* **einbuchten**
B *Adj.* indented ‹*coastline*›

Eingebung *die;* **~, ~en** inspiration; **es muss eine glückliche ~ gewesen sein** the idea was an inspiration; **einer ~ folgend** acting on a sudden impulse

eingedenk /ˈaingədɛŋk/ *Adj.* **einer Sache** (*Gen.*) **~ sein/bleiben** (geh.) be mindful of sth.; **~ dieser Sache ...** bearing this in mind ...; **~ der Tatsache, dass ...** bearing in mind that ...

ein·gefahren
A *2. Part. v.* **einfahren**
B *Adj.* long-established; deep-rooted ‹*prejudice*›; **sich auf** *od.* **in ~en Bahnen** *od.* **Gleisen bewegen** go on in the same old way

ein·gefallen
A *2. Part. v.* **einfallen**
B *Adj.* gaunt ‹*face*›; sunken, hollow ‹*cheeks*›

eingefleischt /ˈaingəflaiʃt/ *Adj.* confirmed ‹*bachelor*›; inveterate ‹*smoker*›; deep-rooted, ingrained ‹*habit, prejudice*›

ein|gehen
A *unr. itr. V.; mit sein* **1** (eintreffen) arrive; be received; **der Brief ist nicht bei uns eingegangen** we have not received the letter **2** (aufgenommen werden) **in die Geschichte ~:** go down in history; **in die Weltliteratur ~:** find one's/its place in world literature; **in die ewige Ruhe ~** (dichter.) pass away; **in das Reich Gottes ~:** enter the kingdom of Heaven **3** (schrumpfen) shrink **4** (Bezug nehmen) **auf eine Frage/ein Problem ~/nicht ~:** go into *or* deal with/ignore a question/problem **5** (entgegenkommen, sich widmen) **auf jmdn. ~:** be responsive to sb.; **auf jmdn. nicht ~:** ignore sb.'s wishes **6** **auf ein Angebot ~/nicht ~:** accept/reject an offer **7** (sterben) ‹*animal, plant*› die; **ihm war die Kuh eingegangen** the cow had died on him (coll.); **die Blumen gehen eine nach der anderen ein** the flowers are dying off **8** (Bankrott gehen) ‹*shop*› close down; ‹*newspaper, business*› close down, fold [up] **9** (einleuchten) **ihm geht alles leicht ein** he's quick on the uptake (coll.); he cottons on to things quickly (coll.); **es will ihr nicht ~, dass ...** she can't grasp the fact that ...
B *unr. tr. V.* enter into ‹*contract, matrimony*›; take ‹*risk*›; accept ‹*obligation*›; **darauf gehe ich jede Wette ein** (ugs.) I'll bet you anything on that (coll.)

eingehend
A *Adj.* detailed ‹*discussion, explanation, report*›; **~e Verhandlungen** negotiations on every detail
B *adv.* in detail; **~er** in more detail

ein·gekeilt
A *2. Part. v.* **einkeilen**
B *Adj.* (von beiden Seiten) wedged in (**in, zwischen** + *Dat.* between); (von allen Seiten) hemmed in (**in** among); **mein Auto war ~:** my car was boxed in

Ein·gekochte *das;* **~n** ▸**Eingemachte 1**

Ein·gemachte *das;* **~n** **1** preserved fruit/vegetables **2** (fig.: Substanz) **ans ~ gehen** (ugs.) draw on one's reserves; **jetzt gehts ans ~** (ugs.) now comes the crunch

ein|gemeinden *tr. V.* incorporate ‹*village*› (**in** + *Akk.*, **nach** into)

Eingemeindung *die;* **~, ~en** incorporation

ein·genommen
A *2. Part. v.* **einnehmen**
B *Adj.* **1** (eingebildet) **von sich ~ sein** be conceited; **von etw. ~ sein** be conceited about sth. **2** (begeistert) **von jmdm./etw. ~ sein** be taken with sb./sth.; (dauerhaft) like sb. very much/be very fond of sth.

ein·geschlechtig *Adj.* (Bot.) unisexual

ein·geschnappt
A *2. Part. v.* **einschnappen**
B *Adj.* (ugs.: beleidigt) huffy

ein·geschossig *Adj.* single-storey; one-storey; *s. auch* **achtstöckig**; **einstöckig**

ein·geschränkt
A *2. Part. v.* **einschränken**
B *Adj.* **~es Haltverbot** prohibition of stopping except for certain purposes; **in ~en Verhältnissen leben** live in reduced circumstances
C *adv.* **~ leben** live in reduced circumstances

ein·geschrieben
A *2. Part. v.* **einschreiben**
B *Adj.* registered ‹*letter, member*›; enrolled ‹*student*›

ein·geschworen
A *2. Part. v.* **einschwören**
B *Adj.* dedicated (**auf** + *Akk.* to); **ein ~er Freund/Gegner** a sworn friend/enemy; **die beiden waren darauf ~:** the two had agreed on it

ein·gesessen
A *2. Part. v.* **einsitzen**
B *Adj.* established

Ein·gesessene *der/die; adj. Dekl.* established resident

ein·gespannt
A *2. Part. v.* **einspannen**
B *Adj.* **stark ~:** very busy

ein·gespielt
A *2. Part. v.* **einspielen**
B *Adj.* in practice; **aufeinander ~:** playing well together

ein·gesprengt
A *2. Part. v.* **einsprengen**
B *Adj.* **mit ~en Kiefern/Heideflächen/Fremdwörtern** with a sprinkling of conifers/a few areas of heathland/occasional foreign words

eingestandenermaßen *Adv.* admittedly

Ein·geständnis *das* confession; admission

ein|gestehen *unr. tr. V.* admit, confess ‹*guilt*›; admit, confess to ‹*mistake, theft*›; **[sich] ~, dass ...** admit [to oneself] that ...

ein·gestellt
A *2. Part. v.* **einstellen**
B *Adj.* **fortschrittlich/modern ~:** progressively minded/not at all old-fashioned in one's views; **ich weiß nicht, wie er [politisch] ~ ist** I don't know what his [political] views are

ein·gestrichen[1] *2. Part. v.* **einstreichen**

ein·gestrichen[2] *Adj.* (Musik) **das ~e A** the A above middle C; **das ~e C** middle C

Eingeweide /ˈaingəvaidə/ *das;* **~s, ~:** entrails *pl.*; innards *pl.*; **der Hunger wühlte in seinen ~n** (geh.) raging hunger gnawed his insides

Eingeweide·bruch *der* (Med.) hernia

Ein·geweihte *der/die; adj. Dekl.* initiate

ein|gewöhnen
A *refl. V.* get used *or* accustomed to one's new surroundings; accustom oneself to one's new surroundings; **er hat sich hier gut eingewöhnt** he's settled down here very well; **sich an seinem neuen Arbeitsplatz/in eine neue Tätigkeit ~:** settle in at one's new place of work/get used to a new job
B *tr. V.* **jmdn. in etw.** (*Akk.*) **~:** get sb. used *or* accustomed to sth.

Ein·gewöhnung *die* (am Arbeitsplatz usw.) settling in *no art.*; **die ~ in seiner neuen Umgebung/an seinem neuen Arbeitsplatz fiel ihm schwer** he found it difficult to get used to his new surroundings/place of work

ein·gewurzelt
A *2. Part. v.* **einwurzeln**
B *Adj.* ingrained; **ein tief ~es Misstrauen** a deeply rooted *or* deep-seated mistrust

ein|gießen *unr. tr.* (*auch itr.*) *V.* pour in; **etw. in etw.** (*Akk.*) **~:** pour sth. into sth.; **den Kaffee/die Limonade ~:** pour [out] the coffee/lemonade

ein|gipsen *tr. V.* **1** (Handw.) **einen Nagel/Haken ~:** fix a nail/hook in with plaster **2** (Med.) **ein Bein/einen Arm ~:** put *or* set a leg/arm in plaster

Ein·glas *das* (veralt.) monocle

eingleisig /ˈainglaizɪç/
A *Adj.* single-track ‹*railway line*›
B *adv.* **eine ~ befahrene Strecke** a single-track line; **~ denken/ausgerichtet sein** (fig.) be narrow in one's outlook; be narrow-minded

Eingleisigkeit *die* **~** (fig.) narrowness

ein|gliedern
A *tr. V.* integrate (**in** + *Akk.* into); incorporate ‹*village, company*› (**in** + *Akk.* into); (einordnen) include (**in** + *Akk.* in)
B *refl. V.* **sich in etw.** (*Akk.*) **~:** fit into sth.

Ein·gliederung *die* ▸**eingliedern**: integration; incorporation; inclusion

ein|graben *unr. tr. V.* **1** bury ‹*box, treasure*› (**in** + *Akk.* in); sink ‹*pile, pipe*› (**in** + *Akk.* into); **sich in etw.** (*Akk.*) **~** ‹*claws*› dig into sth.; **der Krebs grub sich in den Sand ein** the crab buried itself in the sand **2** (einpflanzen) plant ‹*tree, bush*› (**in** + *Akk.* in) **3** (eindrücken) make, leave ‹*imprint, hole*› (**in** + *Akk.* in) **4** (geh.: einmeißeln) engrave ‹*inscription, epitaph, etc.*› (**in** + *Akk.* on); **der Fluss hatte sich tief ins Tal eingegraben** (fig.) the river had carved a deep channel in the valley

ein|gravieren *tr. V.* engrave (**in** + *Akk.* on)

ein|greifen *unr. itr. V.* **1** (Einfluss nehmen) intervene (**in** + *Akk.* in); **entschieden ~:** take decisive action; **das Eingreifen** intervention **2** (Technik) **in etw.** (*Akk.*) **~:** mesh with sth.

eingreifend *Adj.* drastic, radical ‹*change*›; far-reaching ‹*consequences*›

Eingreif·truppe *die* (Milit.) strike force

ein|grenzen *tr. V.* 1 enclose; **von** *od.* **mit etw. eingegrenzt werden** be enclosed by sth. 2 (fig.: beschränken) limit, restrict ‹*topic, discussion, etc.*› (**auf** + *Akk.* to); restrict, circumscribe ‹*freedom, rights, etc.*›

Ein·griff *der* 1 intervention (**in** + *Akk.* in); **ein staatlicher ~ in die Wirtschaft** state intervention in the economy; **ein ~ in jmds. Intimsphäre** (*Akk.*) an intrusion upon sb.'s privacy; **ein ~ in jmds. Rechte** an infringement of sb.'s rights 2 (Med.) operation 3 (Schlitz) fly

ein|gruppieren *tr. V.* **jmdn. in eine Gehaltsstufe ~:** place sb. on a step on the salary scale

Ein·gruppierung *die* grading

ein|hacken *itr. V.* **auf jmdn./aufeinander/etw. ~:** peck at sb./each other/sth.; **auf jmdn. ~** (fig. ugs.) pick on sb.

ein|haken

A *tr. V.* 1 (mit Haken befestigen) fasten 2 **jmdn. ~:** take sb.'s arm; link arms with sb.; **die Demonstranten hakten sich ein** the demonstrators linked arms; **sie gingen eingehakt** they walked arm in arm

B *refl. V.* **sich bei jmdm. ~:** link arms with sb.; take sb.'s arm

C *itr. V.* (ugs.) butt in; **bei einem Punkt ~:** [butt in and] take up a point

ein·halb·mal *Wiederholungsz., Adv.* half; **~ so viel/groß/teuer** half as much/big/expensive

Ein·halt *der:* **in jmdm./einer Sache ~ gebieten** *od.* **tun** (geh.) stop *or* halt sb./sth.

ein|halten

A *unr. tr. V.* keep ‹*appointment*›; meet ‹*deadline, commitments*›; keep to ‹*diet, speed limit, agreement*›; observe ‹*regulation*›; **die Gesetze ~:** obey the laws; **den Kurs ~:** stay on course

B *unr. itr. V.* (geh.) stop; (vorübergehend) pause; stop; **mit/in etw.** (*Dat.*) **~:** stop doing sth.

Ein·haltung *die* (einer Verabredung) keeping; (einer Vorschrift) observance; **die ~ der Diät/Vereinbarung/des Tempolimits** keeping to the diet/agreement/speed limit; **die ~ eines Termins** meeting a deadline; **die ~ des Kurses** staying on course

ein|hämmern

A *itr. V.* **auf etw.** (*Akk.*) **~:** hammer on sth.; **auf jmdn. ~** (fig.) pummel *or* pound sb.

B *tr. V.* **jmdm. etw. ~:** hammer *or* drum sth. into sb. *or* sb.'s head

ein|handeln

A *tr. V.* **etw. für/gegen etw. ~:** barter sth. for sth.

B *refl. V.* 1 (ugs.: hinnehmen müssen) **sich** (*Dat.*) **etw. ~:** let oneself in for sth. (coll.) 2 (ugs.: sich zuziehen) catch, get ‹*disease*›

einhändig /ˈainhɛndɪç/

A *Adj.* one-handed

B *adv.* with [only] one hand

ein|händigen *tr. V.* **jmdm. etw. ~:** hand sth. over to sb.

Einhand·segler *der* single-handed yachtsman; (Boot) single-hander; single-handed dinghy/yacht

Einhand·seglerin *die* single-handed yachtswoman

ein|hängen

A *tr. V.* hang ‹*door*›; fit ‹*window*›; put down ‹*receiver*›

B *itr. V.* (Fernspr.: auflegen) hang up

C *refl. V.* **sich bei jmdm. ~:** take sb.'s arm; link arms with sb.; **sie gingen eingehängt** they walked arm in arm

ein|hauchen *tr. V.* (dichter.) **jmdm./einer Sache etw. ~:** breathe sth. into sb./sth.

ein|hauen

A *unr. tr. V.* 1 (zertrümmern) smash [in] ‹*window*›; break down ‹*door*›; **jmdm. den Schädel ~** (ugs.) bash sb.'s head in (coll.) 2 (hineinschlagen) drive in, knock in ‹*nail*› 3 (einmeißeln) carve

B *unr. itr. V.* 1 (einschlagen) **auf jmdn. ~:** lay into sb. 2 (ugs.: essen) stuff oneself (coll.)

ein|heben *unr. tr. V.* 1 hang, fit ‹*door*›; fit ‹*window*›; put *or* lift ‹*wagon, train*› back on the rails 2 (südd., österr.) levy ‹*tax, fine*›; charge ‹*sum, fee*›

Einhebung *die;* **~, ~en** (südd., österr.) ▸ **einheben 2**: levying; charging

ein|heften *tr. V.* file

ein|heilen *itr. V.* (Med.) ‹*graft*› take

ein·heimisch *Adj.* native, indigenous ‹*population, plant*›; native ‹*culture, traditions*›; home *attrib.* ‹*team*›

Einheimische *der/die; adj. Dekl.* local

ein|heimsen /ˈainhaimzn̩/ *tr. V.* (ugs.) collect ‹*medals, good marks*›; rake in (coll.) ‹*money, profits*›

Ein·heirat *die* marriage (**in** + *Akk.* into); **durch ~ in die Familie** by marrying into the family

ein|heiraten *itr. V.* **in eine Familie ~:** marry into a family

Einheit *die;* **~, ~en** 1 unity 2 (Maß~, Milit.) unit

einheitlich

A *Adj.* 1 (in sich geschlossen) unified; integrated; **der Film hatte keine ~e Handlung** there was no unity of action in the film 2 (unterschiedslos) uniform ‹*dress*›; standardized ‹*education*›; standard ‹*procedure, practice*›

B *adv.* **~ gekleidet sein** be dressed the same; **die Prüfungsbestimmungen ~ regeln** standardize the examination regulations; **~ gestaltet sein** be designed along the same lines; **alle waren ~ ausgebildet** they had all had the same training

Einheitlichkeit *die;* **~** (der Kleidung) uniformity; (der Ausbildung, des Verfahrens) standard nature

Einheits-: ~brei *der* monotonous uniformity; **~essen** *das* institutional food; **~format** *das* standard size; **~front** *die* united front; **~gewerkschaft** *die* general trade union; **~kleidung** *die* uniform; **~kurzschrift** *die* unified shorthand [system]; **~liste** *die* (Politik) unified list [of candidates]; single list [of candidates]; **~partei** *die* united party; **Sozialistische ~partei Deutschlands** (DDR) Socialist Unity Party of Germany; **~preis** *der* standard *or* fixed price; **~staat** *der* centralized state; **~tarif** *der* standard tariff; **~währung** *die* single currency; **[europäische] ~währung** single [European] currency; **~wert** *der* (Steuerw.) rateable value

ein|heizen

A *tr. V.* put on ‹*stove, boiler*›; heat ‹*room*›

B *itr. V.* 1 (ugs.: zur Eile antreiben) **jmdm. ~:** chivvy sb. along (coll.) 2 (ugs.: bedrängen) **jmdm. ~:** go on at sb. (coll.)

einhellig /ˈainhɛlɪç/

A *Adj.* unanimous

B *adv.* unanimously

Einhelligkeit *die;* **~:** unanimity

ein·her|gehen *unr. itr. V.;* *mit sein* 1 (geh.: gemächlich gehen) walk about *or* around 2 (fig.: begleitet sein) **mit etw. ~:** be accompanied by sth.

einhöck[e]rig *Adj.* one-humped

ein|holen

A *tr. V.* 1 (erreichen) **jmdn./ein Fahrzeug ~:** catch up with sb./a vehicle 2 make up ‹*arrears, time*›; pull back ‹*lead*› 3 (einziehen) haul in, pull in ‹*nets*›; lower ‹*flag*› 4 (ugs.: einkaufen) buy, get ‹*groceries*› 5 (erbitten) ask for, seek ‹*reference, advice*›; make ‹*enquiries*›

B *itr. V.* (ugs.) **~ gehen** go shopping

Einhol-: ~netz *das* (ugs.) string bag; **~tasche** *die* (ugs.) shopping bag

Ein·horn *das* unicorn

Einhufer /ˈainhu:fɐ/ *der;* **~s, ~** (Zool.) soliped; solidungulate

ein|hüllen *tr. V.* **sich/jmdn. in etw.** (*Akk.*) **~:** wrap oneself/sb. up in sth.; **der Schnee/Nebel hatte die Gipfel eingehüllt** snow blanketed the peaks/the peaks were shrouded in mist

ein·hundert *Kardinalz.* ▸ **S. 826** a *or* one hundred; *s. auch* **hundert**; **Hundert**

einig /ˈainɪç/ *Adj.* 1 (einmütig) **sich** (*Dat.*) **~ sein** be agreed *or* in agreement; **sich** (*Dat.*) **~ werden** reach agreement; **mit jmdm. über etw.** (*Akk.*) **~ sein** be in agreement *or* agree with sb. about *or* on sth.; **mit jmdm. über etw.** (*Akk.*) **~ werden** reach agreement *or* agree with sb. about *or* on sth.; **in seiner Sache ~ gehen** agree *or* be agreed about *or* on a matter 2 (geeint) united ‹*nation*›

einig... /ˈainɪɡ.../ *Indefinitpron. u. unbest. Zahlwort* 1 *Sg.* (etwas) some ‹*effort, hope, courage*›; **bei ~em guten Willen** with a measure of good will; **in ~er Entfernung** some distance away 2 *Pl.* (mehrere) some; **~e wenige** a few; **~e Hundert** several hundred; **~e Dreißig** thirty or so 3 *Sg. u. Pl.* (beträchtlich) **~er Ärger** quite a bit *or* quite a lot of trouble; **ich könnte dir über ihn ~es erzählen** I could tell you a thing *or* two about him; **dazu gehört schon ~es** it takes something to do that

ein|igeln /ˈain|i:ɡl̩n/ *refl. V.* 1 (sich einrollen) curl up into a ball 2 (sich zurückziehen) hide oneself away 3 (Milit.) take up a position of all-round defence

***einige·mal** ▸ **Mal**¹

einigen

A *tr. V.* unite

B *refl. V.* come to an agreement; reach an agreement; **sich auf jmdn./etw. ~:** agree on sb./sth.; **sich mit jmdm. [über etw.]** (*Akk.*) **~:** come to *or* reach an agreement with sb. [about sth.]

einigermaßen *Adv.* rather; somewhat; **~ zufrieden** fairly *or* reasonably satisfied; **Wie gehts dir? — ~:** How are you? — Not too bad; **das Essen war ~** (ugs.) the meal was OK (coll.) *or* all right

***einig|gehen** ▸ **einig 1**

Einigkeit *die;* **~** 1 (Einheit, Eintracht) unity 2 (Übereinstimmung) agreement

Einigung *die;* **~, ~en** 1 (Übereinkunft) agreement; **[über etw.** (*Akk.*)**] eine ~ erzielen** come to *or* reach [an] agreement [on sth.] 2 (Vereinigung) unification

Einigungs-: ~vertrag *der* (Politik) unification treaty; **~versuch** *der* attempt to reach [an] agreement

ein|impfen *tr. V.* 1 (ugs.) **jmdm. etw. [immer wieder] ~:** drum sth. into sb. [over and over again] 2 (Med.: einspritzen) **jmdm./einem Tier etw. ~:** inject sb./an animal with sth.

ein|jagen *tr. V.* **jmdm. Angst/einen Schrecken ~:** give sb. a fright

ein·jährig *Adj.* 1 (ein Jahr alt) one-year-old *attrib.*; one year old *pred.*; (ein Jahr dauernd) **eine ~e Strafe** a one-year sentence; **eine ~e Abwesenheit** an absence of a *or* one year; a year's absence; **eine ~e Frist** a period of a *or* one year 2 (Bot.) annual

Einjährige¹ *das; adj. Dekl.* (Schulw. veralt.) *school-leaving examination taken after six years at secondary school*

Einjährige² *der/die; adj. Dekl.* one-year-old

ein|kalkulieren *tr. V.* 1 (einplanen) take into account 2 (mitberechnen) take into account; include

Ein·kammer·system *das* (Politik) unicameral system

ein|kapseln

A *tr. V.* encapsulate

B *refl. V.* encapsulate oneself; (fig.) withdraw into one's shell

Einkaräter /ˈainkarɛ:tɐ/ *der;* **~s, ~:** one-carat gem

einkarätig /ˈainkarɛ:tɪç/ *Adj.* one-carat

ein|kassieren *tr. V.* 1 (einnehmen) collect 2 (ugs.: entwenden) pinch (coll.); nick (Brit. coll.) 3 (salopp: festnehmen) pinch (coll.); nab (coll.)

Ein·kauf *der* 1 (Besorgung) buying; **[einige] Einkäufe machen** *od.* **erledigen** do some shopping 2 (eingekaufte Ware) purchase; **ein guter/schlechter ~:** a good/bad buy 3 (für ein Unternehmen) buying; purchasing; **einen ~ tätigen** make a purchase 4 (Kaufmannsspr.) buying *or* purchasing department; **die Abteilung ~:** the buying *or* purchasing department 5 (Sport) (von Spielern) purchase; (eingekaufter Spieler) new signing; **der Verein tätigte einige Einkäufe** the club bought some players 6 (einer Teilhaberschaft) **der ~ in eine Firma**

buying oneself into a firm

ein|kaufen

A *itr. V.* **1** (Einkäufe machen) shop; ~ **gehen** go shopping; do the *or* some shopping; **beim Bäcker/im Supermarkt** ~: shop at the baker's/the supermarket; **da hast du aber teuer eingekauft** you paid high prices there **2** (Kaufmannsspr.) do the buying *or* purchasing

B *tr. V.* **1** buy; purchase; buy in ‹*stores, provisions*›; **etw. billig/günstig** ~: buy sth. cheaply/at a favourable price **2** (Sport) buy ‹*player*›

C *refl. V.* **sich in ein Seniorenheim** ~: buy a place in an old people's home; **sich in eine Firma** ~: buy oneself into a firm

Ein·käufer *der,* **Ein·käuferin** *die* ▸ℹ S. 113 (Berufsbez.) buyer; purchaser

Einkaufs-: ~**abteilung** *die* ▸**Einkauf 4**; ~**bummel** *der* [leisurely] shopping expedition; **einen** ~**bummel machen** go on a shopping expedition; ~**genossenschaft** *die* purchasing cooperative; ~**korb** *der* shopping basket; (im Geschäft) [wire] basket; ~**meile** *die* [main] shopping street; ~**netz** *das* string bag; ~**passage** *die* shopping arcade *or* (Amer.) mall; ~**preis** *der* (Kaufmannsspr.) wholesale price; ~**quelle** *die:* **eine gute** ~**quelle für etw. sein** a good place to buy sth.; ~**tasche** *die* shopping bag; ~**tüte** *die* shopping bag; ~**wagen** *der* [shopping] trolley (Brit.) *or* (Amer.) cart; ~**zentrum** *das* shopping centre; (Großmarkt) hypermarket; ~**zettel** *der* shopping list

Einkehr /'ainke:ɐ̯/ *die;* ~ **1** (geh. veralt.) stop; ~ **halten** stop; make a stop **2** (geh.: Sammlung) ~ **halten** take stock of oneself and one's attitudes; **eine Stunde der** ~: time for reflection and taking stock

ein|kehren *itr. V.; mit sein* **1** stop; **in einem Wirtshaus** ~: stop at an inn **2** (geh.: sich einstellen) come

ein|keilen *tr. V.* **mein Auto ist eingekeilt** my car is boxed in; **die Fans keilten die Spieler ein** the fans mobbed the players; *s. auch* **eingekeilt**

ein·keim·blättrig *Adj.* (Bot.) monocotyledonous

ein|kellern *tr. V.* store in the/a cellar

ein|kerben *tr. V.* cut *or* carve a notch/notches in; notch; **Zeichen in etw.** (*Akk.*) ~: carve signs on sth.

Einkerbung *die;* ~, ~**en** (Kerbe) notch

ein|kerkern *tr. V.* (geh.) incarcerate

Einkerkerung *die;* ~, ~**en** incarceration

ein|kesseln *tr. V.* (bes. Milit.) surround; encircle

Einkesselung *die;* ~, ~**en** (bes. Milit.) encirclement

ein|kitten *tr. V.* fix in with putty

einklagbar *Adj.* legally recoverable ‹*debts*›; **nicht alle Rechte sind** ~: not all rights can be obtained through legal action

ein|klagen *tr. V.* sue for ‹*damages, compensation, etc.*›; **etw.** ~: take legal action in order to gain *or* obtain sth.; **Schulden** ~: sue for the recovery of debts

ein|klammern *tr. V.* **etw.** ~: put sth. in brackets; bracket sth.

Ein·klang *der* **1** (Übereinstimmung) harmony; **im** ~ **mit jmdm. sein** be in accord *or* agreement with sb.; **im** *od.* **in** ~ **mit etw. stehen** accord with sth.; **zwei Dinge in** ~ **[miteinander] bringen** harmonize two things; **die Hausarbeit mit einem Beruf in** ~ **bringen** combine housework and a career **2** (Musik) unison

ein|klappen *tr. V.* fold up; shut, close ‹*knife*›

ein|klarieren *tr. V.* (Zollw., Seew.) clear

Ein·klassen·schule *die* one-room school

ein·klassig *Adj.* (Schulw.) one-room ‹*school*›; **der** ~**e Unterricht** the teaching of children of different age groups in one class

ein|kleben *tr. V.* stick in; **Fotos ins Album** ~: stick photos into the album

ein|kleiden *tr. V.* **1** **sich/jmdn.** ~: clothe oneself/sb.; **sich/jmdn. neu** ~: fit oneself/sb. out with a new set of clothes; **sich/jmdn. völlig neu** ~: buy oneself/sb. a complete new wardrobe **2** (mit einer Uniform versehen) kit out ‹*soldier*›; clothe ‹*priest, nun*› **3** (fig.: umschreiben) couch; **Ermahnungen in Fabeln** ~: couch warnings in the form of fables

ein|klemmen *tr. V.* **1** (quetschen) catch; **jmdm./sich die Hand [in etw.** (*Dat.*)**]** ~: catch *or* trap sb.'s/one's hand [in sth.]; *s. auch* **Schwanz 1** **2** (fest einfügen) clamp

ein|klicken *refl. V.* (DV) **sich in eine Homepage/eine Webseite** ~: visit *or* access a home page/a Web site; **sich in das Netz** ~: go online

ein|klinken

A *tr. V.* latch ‹*door*›; engage ‹*latch*›

B *itr. V.; mit sein* ‹*door*› click to *or* shut

ein|klopfen *tr. V.* knock in ‹*nail*›; pat in ‹*cream*›

ein|kneifen *unr. tr. V.* ▸**Schwanz 1**

ein|knicken

A *tr. V.* bend; crease over ‹*paper*›; (brechen) snap; **mit eingeknickten Knien** with knees bent

B *itr. V.; mit sein* bend; (brechen) snap; **sie knickte beim Gehen ein** she went over on her ankle while walking along

ein|knöpfen *tr. V.* **etw. in etw.** (*Akk.*) ~: button sth. into sth.

ein|kochen

A *tr. V.* preserve ‹*fruit, vegetables*›

B *itr. V.* thicken; **eine eingekochte Soße** a thickened sauce

ein|kommen *unr. itr. V.; mit sein* **1** (geh.: nachsuchen) **[bei jmdm.] um etw.** ~ (geh.) apply [to sb.] for sth. **2** (veralt.: eingehen) ‹*money*› come in **3** (Sport, Seemannsspr.) come in; **als Erster/Letzter** ~: come in first/last

Einkommen *das;* ~**s**, ~: income; ~ **aus Grundbesitz/unselbstständiger Arbeit** income from property/from employment

einkommens-, Einkommens-: ~**grenze** *die* income limit; ~**los** *Adj.* without an income *postpos.;* ~**los sein** have no income; be without an income; ~**schwach** *Adj.* low-income *attrib.;* ~**stark** *Adj.* high-income *attrib.*

Einkommen·steuer *die* income tax

Einkommensteuer·erklärung *die* income tax return

einkommensteuerpflichtig /-pflɪçtɪç/ *Adj.* liable for income tax *postpos.*

ein|köpfen *tr., itr. V.* (Fußball) head in; **er köpfte zum 1:0 ein** he headed in to make it *or* the score 1-0

ein|kreisen *tr. V.* **1** (durch einen Kreis markieren) **etw.** ~: put a circle round sth. **2** (umzingeln) surround ‹*person*›; surround, encircle ‹*house, town, troops*› **3** (fig.: eingrenzen) circumscribe ‹*problem*›

Einkreisung *die;* ~, ~**en** encirclement

ein|kriegen (ugs.)

A *tr. V.* ▸**einholen A 1**

B *refl. V.* control oneself; **sie konnte sich vor Lachen nicht** ~: she couldn't stop laughing

Einkünfte /'ainkʏnftə/ *Pl.* income *sing.* **(aus** from); **feste** ~: a regular income

ein|kuppeln *itr. V.* (Kfz-W.) engage the clutch

ein|laden[1] *unr. tr. V.* load **(in** + *Akk.* into) ‹*goods*›

ein|laden[2] *unr. tr. V.* invite; **jmdn. zum Essen** ~: invite sb. for a meal; (im Restaurant) invite sb. out for a meal; **jmdn. in sein Landhaus/auf sein Boot** ~: invite sb. to one's country house/on to one's boat; **ich lade euch alle ein** this is on me; **sich** ~ (scherzh.) invite oneself; **jmdn. auf ein Bier/einen Kaffee** ~: invite sb. for a beer/a coffee; **jmdn. zu sich nach Hause** ~: invite sb. over

einladend

A *Adj.* inviting ‹*impression, atmosphere*›; tempting, appetizing ‹*meal*›; ~**e Worte** words of invitation

B *adv.* invitingly

Ein·ladung *die* invitation; **einer** ~ (*Dat.*) **folgen** accept an invitation

Einladungs-: ~**karte** *die* invitation [card]; ~**schreiben** *das* [written] invitation

Ein·lage *die* **1** (in einem Brief) enclosure **2** (Kochk.) *vegetables, meat balls, dumplings, etc. added to a clear soup;* **eine Brühe mit** ~: a clear soup with meat balls/dumpling *etc.* **3** (Schuh~) arch support **4** (Einschiebsel) **eine witzige** ~: a witty *or* humorous aside; **eine musikalische** ~: a musical interlude **5** (eingelegte Verzierung) inlay **6** (Zahnmed.) temporary filling **7** (Finanzw.) (Guthaben) deposit; (Beteiligung) investment; **die** ~**n bei den Banken** bank deposits **8** (Schneiderei) padding; (Versteifung) interfacing

ein|lagern

A *tr. V.* store; lay in ‹*stores*›

B *refl. V.* **sich [in etw.** (*Akk.*)**]** ~: be deposited [in sth.]

Ein·lagerung *die* **1** (Aufbewahren) storage **2** (das Abgelagerte) deposit

ein|langen *itr. V.; mit sein* (österr.) arrive

Einlass, *Einlaß /'ainlas/ *der;* **Einlasses, Einlässe** /'ainlɛsə/ **1** admission, admittance **(in** + *Akk.* to); **sich** (*Dat.*) ~ **verschaffen** gain admission *or* admittance; ~ **fordern** demand entry *or* admission; **jmdm.** ~ **gewähren** grant sb. admission *or* admittance **2** (veralt.: Eingang) entrance

ein|lassen

A *unr. tr. V.* **1** (hereinlassen) admit; let in **2** (einfüllen) run ‹*water*› **3** (einpassen) **etw. in etw.** (*Akk.*) ~: set sth. into sth.

B *unr. refl. V.* **1** (meist abwertend) **sich mit jmdm.** ~: get mixed up *or* involved with sb.; **sie lässt sich mit vielen Männern ein** she goes with lots of different men (coll.) **2** **sich auf etw.** (*Akk.*) ~: get involved in sth.; **sich auf einen Streit** ~: be drawn into *or* get involved in an argument; **auf dein Vorhaben lasse ich mich nicht ein** I don't want anything to do with your plan **3** (Rechtsw.) testify; **sich dahin gehend** ~, **dass ...** testify that ...; make a statement to the effect that ...

Einlass·karte, *Einlaß·karte *die* admission ticket

Einlassung *die;* ~, ~**en** (Rechtsw.) testimony; statement; **nach eigenen** ~**en** according to his/her *etc.* own testimony

Ein·lauf *der* **1** (Med.) enema; **jmdm. einen** ~ **machen** give sb. an enema **2** (Sport: Passieren der Ziellinie) finish; **beim** ~: at the finish **3** (Sport: Beginn einer Rennphase) **beim** ~ **in die Gerade/das Stadion** entering the straight/the stadium **4** (Sport: Reihenfolge) placings *pl.;* **es gab folgenden** ~: the placings were as follows

ein|laufen

A *unr. itr. V.; mit sein* **1** (Sport) **ins Stadion** ~: run into *or* enter the stadium; **in die letzte Runde** ~: start the last lap **2** (ankommen) **der Zug/das Schiff läuft ein** the train/ship is coming in; **das Schiff läuft in den Hafen ein** the ship is coming into *or* entering port **3** (kleiner werden) ‹*clothes*› shrink **4** (hineinfließen) run in **5** (eingehen) ‹*news, information*› come in

B *unr. tr. V.* **1** wear in ‹*shoes*› **2** **jmdm. das Haus** *od.* **die Tür** *od.* **die Bude** ~ (ugs.) pester sb. all the time

C *unr. refl. V.* (Sport) warm up

Einlauf·wette *die* (Pferdesport) place bet

ein|läuten *tr. V.* ring in ‹*Sunday, New Year*›; **die letzte Runde** ~ (Sport) ring the bell to signal *or* for the start of the last lap; (Boxen) ring the bell for the [start of the] last round

ein|leben *refl. V.* settle down; **sich an einem Ort** ~: settle down in a place; **sich in einem Haus** ~: settle in in a house; **sich gut** ~: settle down well

Einlege·arbeit *die* (Kunsthandwerk) inlaid work; (Gegenstand) piece of inlaid work

ein|legen *tr. V.* **1** **etw. in etw.** (*Akk.*) ~: put sth. in sth.; **einen Film in eine Kamera** ~: put *or* load a film into a camera; **den ersten Gang** ~: engage first gear; **einen schnelleren Gang** *od.* **ein schnelleres Tempo** ~ (fig.) get a move on (coll.) **2** (Kochk.) pickle; **eingelegte Zwiebeln/Heringe** pickled onions/herrings **3** (Kunsthandwerk) **in die Truhe waren Blumenmuster eingelegt** the chest had been inlaid with flower patterns 4 (Friseurhandwerk) set ‹hair›; **sich/jmdm. die Haare ~:** set one's/sb.'s hair 5 (einschieben) put in, insert ‹*film extracts etc.*›; put on ‹*trains, buses*›; **eine Pause ~:** take a break 6 (geltend machen) lodge ‹*protest*›; **sein Veto gegen etw. ~:** use one's veto against sth.; veto sth.; **ein gutes Wort für jmdn. ~:** put in a good word for sb.; *s. auch* **Ehre 2**

Einleger *der;* **~s,** ~, **Einlegerin** *die;* **~, ~nen** (Bankw.) depositor

Einlege·sohle *die* insole

ein|leiten *tr. V.* 1 (beginnen) institute, start ‹*search*›; introduce, take ‹*measures, steps*›; open ‹*negotiations, investigation, inquest*›; induce ‹*birth*›; launch, open ‹*campaign*› 2 (eröffnen) introduce ‹*chapter*›; **der Roman leitete eine neue Epoche ein** the novel ushered in a new epoch; **einige ~de Worte sprechen** say a few words of introduction; make a few introductory remarks 3 (hineinleiten) lead ‹*water*› (**in** + *Akk.* into); discharge ‹*effluent*›

Ein·leitung *die* 1 (einleitender Teil) introduction; **die ~ eines Aufsatzes/Buches** the introduction to an essay/book 2 (einer Suche) institution; (von Maßnahmen) introduction; (einer Untersuchung, von Verhandlungen) opening; (einer Geburt) induction; (einer Kampagne) launching; opening 3 (Eröffnung) **als** *od.* **zur ~ des Empfanges** to open *or* start the reception; **ein Feuerwerk bildete die ~:** the opening event was a firework display 4 **die ~ giftiger Abwässer in etw.** (*Akk.*) the discharge of poisonous effluents into sth.

ein|lenken

A *itr. V.* 1 (nachgeben) give way; make concessions; **sein Einlenken führte zu einem Kompromiss** by giving way *or* making concessions he enabled a compromise to be reached 2 *mit sein* (einbiegen) **in eine Straße ~:** turn into a street

B *tr. V.* steer ‹*boat, rocket, etc.*›

ein|lesen

A *unr. refl. V.* **sich in ein Buch ~:** get into a book

B *unr. tr. V.* (DV) feed in; input; **etw. in den Speicher ~:** read sth. into the memory

ein|leuchten *tr. V.* **jmdn. ~:** be clear to sb.; **es leuchtet ihr nicht ein, dass sie es allein machen soll** she doesn't see why she should do it by herself; **das will mir nicht ~:** I don't see that

ein·leuchtend

A *Adj.* plausible

B *adv.* plausibly

ein|liefern *tr. V.* **einen Brief bei der Post ~:** take a letter to the post office; **jmdn. ins Krankenhaus/Gefängnis ~:** take sb. to hospital/jail; **wir mussten unsere Großmutter ins Krankenhaus ~ [lassen]** we had to have our grandmother admitted to hospital

Ein·lieferung *die* admission (**in** + *Akk.* to); **die ~ eines Verurteilten [ins Gefängnis]** taking a convicted prisoner to jail; **er wehrte sich gegen seine ~ ins Krankenhaus** he fought against being admitted to hospital

Einlieferungs·schein *der* 1 receipt 2 (Postw.) certificate of posting

ein·liegend *Adj.* (Papierdt.) enclosed; **~ übersenden wir Ihnen ...** please find enclosed ...

Einlieger·wohnung *die* ≈ granny flat (esp. Brit.)

ein|lochen

A *tr. V.* (salopp) **jmdn. ~:** put sb. away (coll.); put sb. behind bars (coll.)

B *tr., itr. V.* (Golf) hole; (Billard) pot ‹*ball*›

ein|loggen *refl. V.* (DV) log in *or* on; **sich in etw.** (*Akk.*) *od.* **bei etw. ~:** log into *or* on to sth.

einlösbar *Adj.* redeemable; **das Versprechen ist nicht ~:** the promise can't be kept

ein|lösen *tr. V.* 1 cash ‹*cheque*›; cash [in] ‹*token, voucher, bill of exchange*›; redeem ‹*pledge, pawned article*›; **man wollte [mir] den Scheck nicht ~:** they wouldn't cash the cheque [for me] 2 (geh.: erfüllen) redeem ‹*pledge*›; **sein Wort ~:** keep one's word

Ein·lösung *die* (von Schecks) cashing; (von Pfändern, Versprechen) redemption

ein|lullen *tr. V.* (ugs.) **jmdn. ~:** lull sb. to sleep; (fig.) lull sb.'s suspicions

ein|machen *tr. V.* preserve ‹*fruit, vegetables*›; (in Gläser) bottle

Einmach·glas *das* preserving jar

einmal

A *Adv.* 1 (ein Mal) once; **noch ~ so groß [wie]** twice as big [as]; **etw. noch ~ tun** do sth. again; **~ mehr** once more *or* again; **~ sagt er dies, ein andermal das** first he says one thing, then another; **~ ist keinmal** (Spr.) just once won't matter; it won't matter just this once; **auf ~:** all at once; suddenly; (zugleich) at once 2 /ˈ-ˈ-/ (später) some day; one day; (früher) once; **es war ~ ein König, der ...** once upon a time there was a king who ...

B *Partikel* 1 **daran ist nun ~ nichts mehr zu ändern** there's nothing more that can be done about it; **nicht ~:** not even; **wieder ~:** yet again; **wir wollen die Sache erst ~ in Ruhe besprechen** let's discuss the matter quietly first 2 **alle ~ zuhören!** listen everybody!; **hör ~ auf zu reden!** stop talking, will you!

Einmal·eins *das;* **~:** [multiplication] tables *pl.*; **das kleine/große ~:** tables from 1 to 10/11 to 20; **das ~ der Kochkunst/Politik** (fig.) the fundamentals *pl.* of cookery/politics

Einmal·handtuch *das* disposable towel

einmalig

A *Adj.* 1 unique ‹*opportunity, chance*›; one-off, single ‹*payment, purchase*› 2 (hervorragend) superb ‹*film, book, play, etc.*›; (ugs.) fantastic (coll.) ‹*girl, woman*›

B *adv.* (ugs.) really fantastic *or* superb (coll.); **das Fest war ~ schön** the party was really superb *or* really fantastic (coll.)

Einmaligkeit *die;* **~:** uniqueness

Einmal·zahlung *die* one-off payment

Ein·mann-: ~betrieb *der* 1 (Firma) one-man business; 2 (Arbeitsweise) one-man operation; **~bus** *der* one-man bus; **~wagen** *der* one-man bus/tram (Brit.) *or* (Amer.) trolley

Ein·marsch *der* 1 entry; **der ~ ins Stadion** the march into the stadium 2 (Besetzung) invasion (**in** + *Akk.* of)

ein|marschieren *itr. V.; mit sein* 1 march in; **ins Stadion ~:** march into the stadium 2 (gewaltsam besetzen) **in ein Land ~:** march into *or* invade a country

ein|massieren *tr. V.* massage *or* rub in

Einmaster /ˈai̯nmastɐ/ *der;* **~s,** ~ (Seemannsspr.) single-master

ein|mauern *tr. V.* 1 immure ‹*prisoner, traitor*›; wall in ‹*relic, treasure*› 2 (ins Mauerwerk einfügen) **etw. in die Wand** *usw.* **~:** set sth. into the wall *etc.*

ein|meißeln *tr. V.* **etw. in etw.** (*Akk.*) **~:** carve sth. into *or* on sth. [with a chisel]

Ein·meter·brett *das* one-metre board

ein|mieten *refl. V.* **sich in einer Villa ~:** rent a villa; **sich in einer Pension ~:** rent a room in a boarding house

ein|mischen

A *refl. V.* interfere (**in** + *Akk.* in); **wenn ich mich kurz ~ darf** if I may butt in for a moment

B *tr. V.* mix in

Ein·mischung *die* interference (**in** + *Akk.* in); **verzeihen Sie meine ~:** excuse my butting in

einmonatig *Adj.* 1 (einen Monat alt) one-month-old *attrib.* 2 (einen Monat dauernd) one-month *attrib.*; *s. auch* **achtmonatig**

ein·monatlich

A *Adj.* monthly; *s. auch* **achtmonatlich A**

B *adv.* monthly; once a month

ein·motorig *Adj.* single-engined

ein|motten *tr. V.* **etw. ~:** put sth. into mothballs; (fig.) mothball sth.

ein|mumme[l]n *tr. V.* (ugs.) wrap up; **sich [warm] ~:** wrap up *or* wrap oneself up [warmly]

ein|münden *itr. V.; auch mit sein* 1 flow in; enter; **in einen Fluss ~:** flow into *or* enter a river 2 (enden) **in etw.** (*Akk.*) **~:** lead into sth.

Ein·mündung *die* 1 **die ~ der Mosel in den Rhein** the confluence of the Rhine and the Moselle; **die ~ des Kanals in den Fluss** the point where the canal flows into the river 2 (von Straßen) **die ~ der Straße in die Hauptstraße/den Platz** the junction of the street and the main road/the point where the road comes out into the square

einmütig /ˈai̯nmy:tɪç/

A *Adj.* unanimous

B *adv.* unanimously

Einmütigkeit *die;* **~:** unanimity (**über** + *Akk.* on)

ein|nachten *itr. V.* (unpers.) (schweiz.) get dark

ein|nähen *tr. V.* 1 (festnähen) sew in; **etw. in etw.** (*Akk.*) **~:** sew sth. into sth. 2 (enger nähen) take in

Einnahme *die;* **~, ~en** 1 income; (Staats~) revenue; (Kassen~) takings *pl.* 2 (von Arzneimitteln) taking; **wir empfehlen die ~ einer leichten Mahlzeit** it is advisable to take a light meal; **die ~ der Tabletten muss regelmäßig erfolgen** the tablets must be taken regularly 3 (einer Stadt, Burg) capture; taking; **die ~ Berlins** the capture *or* taking of Berlin

Einnahme·quelle *die* source of income; (des Staates) source of revenue

ein|nässen *tr., itr. V.* wet ‹*bed*›; **er nässt noch ein** he's still wetting the bed

ein|nebeln

A *tr. V.* shroud; blanket

B *refl. V.* 1 (Milit.) put up a smokescreen 2 (unpers.) **es hat sich eingenebelt** a mist has come down

ein|nehmen *unr. tr. V.* 1 (kassieren) take; (verdienen) earn; **er hat nicht viel an Trinkgeld eingenommen** he didn't make much by way of tips 2 (zu sich nehmen) take ‹*medicine, tablets*›; **eine Mahlzeit ~** (geh.) take a meal; partake of a meal (literary) 3 (besetzen) capture, take ‹*town, fortress*› 4 **seinen Platz ~:** take one's place; (sich setzen) take one's seat *or* place; **eine Haltung/einen Standpunkt ~** (fig.) take up *or* adopt an attitude/a position; **eine wichtige Stellung in der Kunst/Literatur ~** (fig.) occupy an important place in the artistic/literary world 5 (ausfüllen) take up ‹*amount of room*› 6 (beeinflussen) **jmdn. für sich ~:** win sb. over; **jmdn. gegen sich ~:** turn sb. against one; **gegen jmdn. eingenommen sein** be prejudiced against sb.; **von sich eingenommen sein** think a lot of oneself (coll.); be very taken with oneself

einnehmend *Adj.* winning ‹*manner*›; **ein ~es Wesen haben** (scherzh.) take everything one can get

ein|nicken *itr. V.; mit sein* (ugs.) nod off (coll.)

ein|nisten *refl. V.* 1 (meist abwertend: sich niederlassen) **sich bei jmdm. ~:** park oneself on sb. (coll.) 2 (ein Nest bauen) build a nest/their nests; nest 3 (Med.) **das befruchtete Ei nistet sich im Uterus ein** the fertilized ovum is implanted in the uterus

Ein·öde *die* barren *or* featureless waste; (Einsamkeit) isolation; **die weißen ~n Alaskas** the white wastes of Alaska

Einöd·hof *der* (südd., österr.) isolated farm

ein|ölen *tr. V.* 1 (mit Öl einreiben) **sich/jmdn. ~:** put *or* rub oil on oneself/sb. 2 (ölen) oil

ein|ordnen

A *tr. V.* 1 (einfügen) arrange; put in order; **etw. in Aktenordner ~:** sort sth. into files; file sth.; **Briefe in Fächer ~:** sort letters and place them in their correct pigeon-holes 2 (klassifizieren) classify; categorize, classify ‹*writer, thinker, artist*›

B *refl. V.* 1 (Verkehrsw.) get into the correct lane; **sich nach rechts/links ~:** get into the right-hand/left-hand lane; **„~"** 'get in lane' 2 (sich einfügen) **sich [in die Gemeinschaft] ~:** fit in[to the community]

Ein·ordnung *die* (in Karteien usw.) arranging; (Klassifizierung) classification

ein|packen

A *tr. V.* 1 pack (**in** + *Akk.* in); (einwickeln) wrap [up] 2 (ugs.: warm anziehen) wrap up; **jmdn./sich warm/gut ~:** wrap sb./oneself up warmly

B *itr. V.* (ugs.) **er kann ~:** he's had it (coll.); **pack**

ein! (hör auf!) pack it in! (coll.); give it a rest! (coll.); (verschwinde!) get lost! (coll.)

ein|parken *tr., itr. V.* park

Ein·parteien-: one-party

ein|passen
A *tr. V.* fit; install; **etw. in etw.** (*Akk.*) **~:** fit sth. into sth.
B *refl. V.* fit in

ein|pauken *tr. V.* **etw. ~:** mug up (Brit.) *or* (Amer.) bone up on sth. (coll.); **jmdm. etw. ~:** drum *or* hammer sth. into sb.

ein|pegeln *refl. V.* settle down (**bei** at)

Einpeitscher /ˈainpaitʃɐ/ *der;* **~s, ~, Ein·peitscherin** *die;* **~, ~nen 1** (Agitator) rabble-rouser **2** (Parl.) whip

ein|pendeln
A *refl. V.* settle down; cease to fluctuate
B *itr. V.; mit sein* commute; **die aus dem Umland ~den Beschäftigten** the workers commuting in from the surrounding area

Ein·pendler *der* commuter; *s. auch* **Auspendler**

ein|pennen *itr. V.; mit sein* (salopp) drop *or* doze off

Ein·personen-: ~haushalt *der* single-person household; **~stück** *das* (Theater) monodrama

ein|pferchen *tr. V.* **1** (zusammendrängen) **eingepfercht stehen/sein** stand/be crammed *or* crushed together **2** pen in ‹*animals*›

ein|pflanzen *tr. V.* **1** plant ‹*flowers, shrubs, etc.*›; **jmdm. einen Sinn für Gerechtigkeit ~** (fig.) implant in sb. a sense of justice **2** (Med.) implant; **jmdm. ein Organ ~:** implant an organ in[to] sb.

ein|pfropfen *tr. V.* graft (**in** + *Akk.* on)

Ein·phasen-Wechselstrom *der* (Physik, Elektrot.) single-phase current

einphasig *Adj.* (Physik, Elektrot.) single-phase

ein|pinseln *tr. V.* brush; paint ‹*wound*›

ein|planen *tr. V.* **etw. ~:** include sth. in one's plans; **diese Verzögerung war nicht eingeplant** we/they *etc.* didn't plan on this delay

ein|pökeln *tr. V.* (Kochk.) salt

ein·polig *Adj.* (Physik, Elektrot.) single-pole

ein|prägen
A *tr. V.* **1** stamp (**in** + *Akk.* into, on) **2** (fig.) **sich** (*Dat.*) **etw. ~:** memorize sth.; commit sth. to memory; **jmdm. ~, pünktlich zu sein** impress on sb. the importance of being punctual
B *refl. V.* **das prägte sich ihm [für immer] ein** it made an [indelible] impression on him; **Werbetexte prägen sich einem leicht ein** advertising slogans are catchy

einprägsam
A *Adj.* easily remembered; catchy, easily remembered ‹*tune, melody, slogan*›
B *adv.* **er hat das sehr ~ dargelegt** he expounded it in a way that made it easy to remember

ein|prasseln *itr. V.; mit sein* **auf jmdn./etw. ~:** rain down on sb./sth.; **die Fragen der Zuhörer prasselten auf ihn ein** the audience showered him with questions

ein|pressen *tr. V.* press in; **etw. in etw.** (*Akk.*) **~:** press sth. into sth.

ein|programmieren *tr. V.* (DV) input ‹*data, figures, etc.*›; programme in ‹*function, property*›

ein·prozentig *Adj.* one per cent *attrib.*; of one per cent *postpos.*

ein|prügeln
A *itr. V.* **auf jmdn./ein Tier ~:** beat sb./an animal
B *tr. V.* **jmdm. etw. ~** (fig.) drub *or* beat sth. into sb.

ein|pudern *tr. V.* powder; **sich** (*Dat.*) **das Gesicht ~:** powder one's face

ein|quartieren
A *tr. V.* quarter, billet ‹*troops*›; **die Opfer wurden vorläufig in Hotels einquartiert** the victims were given temporary accommodation in hotels; **sie quartierten ihre Freunde bei ihren Eltern ein** they put their friends up with their parents
B *refl. V.* **sich bei jmdm. ~** (Milit.) be quartered with *or* billeted on sb.; **sich auf einem Bauernhof/bei seinen Eltern ~:** stay on a farm/with one's parents

Einquartierung *die;* **~, ~en 1** (Milit.) quartering; billeting **2 [sechs Mann] ~ haben** have [six] soldiers billeted on one

ein|quetschen *tr. V.* ▸**einklemmen**

Ein·rad *das* unicycle

einräd[e]rig *Adj.* one-wheeled

ein|rahmen *tr. V.* frame; **sich** (*Dat.*) **etw. ~ lassen** have sth. framed; **er saß da, von zwei Damen eingerahmt** (fig.) he sat flanked by two ladies; **den Brief solltest du dir ~ lassen** (iron.) you ought to *or* should get that letter framed

ein|rammen *tr. V.* **1** ram in; **etw. in den Boden ~:** ram sth. into the ground **2** (zertrümmern) smash up ‹*car*›; break *or* batter down ‹*door*›

ein|rasten *itr. V.; mit sein* (Technik) engage

ein|räuchern *tr. V.* envelope in smoke; **ein Zimmer ~:** fill a room with smoke; **die Gardinen ~:** get *or* make the curtains smoky; **jmdn. mit Tränengas ~:** use tear gas against sb.

ein|räumen *tr. V.* **1** (einordnen) put away; **etw. in etw.** (*Akk.*) **~:** put sth. away in sth.; **Bücher wieder [ins Regal] ~:** put books back [on the shelf] **2** (füllen) **er musste seinen Schrank ~:** he had to put his things away in his cupboard; **das Zimmer wieder ~:** put everything *or* all the furniture back into the room **3** (zugestehen) admit; concede; **jmdm. etw. ~:** admit sth. to sb.; **jmdm. einen Platz ~:** reserve sb. a seat; **jmdm. ein Recht/einen Kredit ~:** give *or* grant sb. a right/loan; **jmdm. das Recht ~, etw. zu tun** give *or* grant sb. the right to do sth. **4** (Sprachw.) **~de Konjunktion** concessive conjunction

ein|rechnen *tr. V.* include, take account of ‹*costs etc.*›; **nicht eingerechnet die Trinkgelder** not including the tips

ein|reden
A *tr. V.* **jmdm. etw. ~:** talk sb. into believing sth.; **er redete ihr ein, es zu kaufen** he persuaded her to buy it; he talked her into buying it; **sich** (*Dat.*) **~, dass ...** persuade oneself that...; **das redest du dir bloß ein** you're just imagining it
B *itr. V.* **auf jmdn. ~:** talk insistently to sb.; **laut/beruhigend auf jmdn. ~:** keep talking to sb. loudly/soothingly

ein|regnen
A *refl. V.* (unpers.) **es hat sich eingeregnet** it's begun to rain steadily
B *itr. V.; mit sein* get soaked [to the skin]

ein|regulieren *tr. V.* (Technik) set ‹*temperature*› (**auf** + *Akk.* at); **ein falsch einreguliertes Hörgerät** a wrongly adjusted hearing aid

ein|reiben *unr. tr. V.* **Salbe [in die Haut] ~:** rub ointment in[to one's skin]; **jmdm. den Rücken ~:** rub lotion/ointment *etc.* into sb.'s back; **sich** (*Dat.*) **den Nacken/das Gesicht mit etw. ~:** rub sth. into one's neck/face

ein|reichen *tr. V.* **1** submit ‹*application*›; hand in, submit ‹*piece of work, dissertation, thesis*›; lodge, make ‹*complaint*›; tender ‹*resignation*› **2** (jur.) file ‹*suit, petition for divorce*›

ein|reihen
A *refl. V.* **sich in etw.** (*Akk.*) **~:** join sth.
B *tr. V.* **jmdn. in eine Kategorie/Gruppe ~:** place sb. in a category/group; **sich in eine Gruppe** *usw.* **~:** become part of a group *etc.*

Einreiher *der;* **~s, ~:** single-breasted suit/jacket

einreihig /ˈainraiɪç/
A *Adj.* single-breasted ‹*suit*›
B *adv.* in a single row *or* line; **ein ~ geknöpfter Mantel** a single-breasted overcoat

Ein·reise *die* entry; **bei der ~ nach Frankreich/in die Schweiz** on entry into France/Switzerland; **jmdm. die ~ verweigern** refuse sb. entry

Einreise·erlaubnis *die* entry permit

ein|reisen *itr. V.; mit sein* enter; **nach Schweden ~:** enter Sweden

Einreise-: ~verbot *das:* **jmdm. ~verbot erteilen** refuse sb. entry; **~visum** *das* entry visa

ein|reißen
A *unr. tr. V.* **1** (abreißen) pull *or* tear down ‹*building*› **2** (einen Riss machen in) tear; rip **3 sich** (*Dat.*) **einen Dorn ~:** prick oneself on a thorn; **sich** (*Dat.*) **einen Splitter ~:** get a splinter in one's hand/foot *etc.*
B *unr. itr. V.; mit sein* **1** (einen Riss bekommen) tear; rip **2** (ugs.: sich verbreiten) become a habit; **etw. ~ lassen** allow sth. to *or* let sth. become a habit; **eine Gewohnheit ~ lassen** allow a habit to catch on (coll.) *or* spread

Einreiß·haken *der* ceiling hook

ein|reiten
A *unr. itr. V.; mit sein* ride in; **in etw.** (*Akk.*) **~:** ride into sth.
B *unr. refl. V.* warm up; **sich mit einem Pferd ~:** get used to riding a horse

ein|renken *tr. V.* **1** (Med.) set; reduce (Med.); **jmdm. den Fuß/Arm [wieder] ~:** [re]set sb.'s foot/arm **2** (ugs.: bereinigen) **etw. ~:** sort *or* straighten sth. out; **das renkt sich ein** that will sort *or* straighten itself out

ein|rennen
A *unr. tr. V.* (aufbrechen) break down ‹*door*›; **jmdm. [wegen etw.] das Haus** *od.* **die Bude ~** (ugs.) pester sb. all the time [for sth.]; *s. auch* **offen**
B *unr. refl. V.* (ugs.: sich verletzen) **sich** (*Dat.*) **den Kopf an etw.** (*Dat.*) **~:** bash *or* bang one's head on *or* against sth.

ein|richten
A *refl. V.* **1 sich gemütlich/schön ~:** furnish one's home comfortably/beautifully; **sich an einem Ort häuslich ~:** make oneself at home in a place **2** (auskommen) **sich [mit seinem Gehalt] ~:** get by *or* make ends meet [on one's salary] **3** (sich vorbereiten) **sich auf jmdn./etw. ~:** prepare for sb./sth.; **darauf war sie nicht eingerichtet** she was not prepared for that
B *tr. V.* **1** furnish ‹*flat, house*›; fit out ‹*shop, restaurant, hobby room*›; equip ‹*laboratory*› **2** (ermöglichen) arrange; **das lässt sich ~:** that can be arranged; **es so ~, dass ...** arrange things so that ... **3** (eröffnen) open ‹*branch, shop*›; set up ‹*advisory centre*›; start, set up ‹*business*›; **sich** (*Dat.*) **ein Geschäft/eine Modeboutique ~:** start a business/open a fashion boutique **4** (Med.) set; reduce (Med.) **5** (umformen) arrange ‹*piece of music*›; adapt ‹*play, novel, etc.*› **6** (Math.) **eine gemischte Zahl ~:** reduce a mixed number

Ein·richter *der,* **Ein·richterin** *die* fitter

Ein·richtung *die* **1** (das Einrichten) (einer Wohnung) furnishing; (eines Musikstücks) arrangement; (eines Theaterstücks) adaptation; (Med.) setting; reducing (Med.) **2** (Mobiliar) furnishings *pl.* **3** (Geräte) **~en** (Geschäfts~) fittings; (Labor~) equipment *sing.*; **sanitäre ~en** sanitary facilities; sanitation *sing.* **4** (Institution, Gewohnheit) institution; **öffentliche/staatliche ~en** public/state institutions

Einrichtungs-: ~gegen·stand *der* piece of furniture; **~haus** *das* [large] furniture store

ein|ritzen *tr. V.* carve; **seinen Namen in einen Stamm ~:** carve one's name on a tree trunk

ein|rollen
A *tr. V.* roll up ‹*carpet etc.*›; **sich/jmdm. die Haare ~:** put one's/sb.'s hair in curlers *or* rollers; **sich ~** ‹*hedgehog, cat*› curl up
B *itr. V.; mit sein* **1** roll in; **der Zug rollt ein** the train is coming in

ein|rosten *itr. V.; mit sein* go rusty; rust up; **er ist/seine Knochen sind eingerostet** (fig.) his joints have stiffened up

ein|rücken
A *itr. V.; mit sein* **1** (Milit.: einmarschieren) move in; **in ein Land ~:** march into a country; **wieder in die Kaserne ~:** return to barracks **2** (Milit. veralt.: eingezogen werden) report for duty
B *tr. V.* **1** (Schriftw.) indent ‹*line, heading, etc.*› **2** (Zeitungsw.) insert ‹*advertisement, article*›

ein|rühren *tr. V.* stir in; **etw. in etw.** (*Akk.*) **~:** stir sth. into sth.

e

ein|rüsten *tr. V.* (Bauw.) put up *or* erect scaffolding around ‹*building*›

eins /ains/

A *Kardinalz.* ▸ⓘ **S. 29**, ▸ⓘ **S. 729**, ▸ⓘ **S. 826** one; **es ist ~:** it is one o'clock; **Punkt ~:** on the stroke of one; at one o'clock precisely; **halb ~:** half past twelve; **Viertel nach/vor ~:** [a] quarter past/to one; **gegen/vor ~:** around/before one; **~ zu null** one-nil; **~ zu ~:** one all; **~ zu null für dich!** (ugs.) that's one up to you!; **die Nummer ~ sein** (fig.) be number one; **„~, zwei, drei!"** 'ready, steady, go'; **... und ~, zwei, drei, weg war er** and in a jiffy (coll.) *or* in no time he was gone; **~ a,** (Kaufmannsspr. meist) **1 a** top-quality; **seine Arbeit ~ a erledigen** (ugs.) do a first-class job; *s. auch* **acht**[1]

B *Adj.* **mir ist alles ~:** it's all the same *or* all one to me; **den Schrei hören und zu Hilfe eilen war für sie ~:** the moment she heard the cry, she was hurrying to help; **mit jmdm. über etw.** (*Akk.*) **~ sein/werden** be in/reach agreement with sb. about *or* on sth.; **sich mit jmdm. ~ wissen/fühlen** be/feel at one with sb.

C *Indefinitpron.* ▸**ein**[1] **C 2, 3**

Eins *die;* **~, ~en** **1** one; **wie eine ~ stehen** (ugs.) stand as straight as a ramrod; **sie kocht/spielt Klavier wie eine ~** (ugs.) she's a fantastic cook/piano player (coll.); *s. auch* **Acht**[1] **1, 5, 7** **2** (Schulnote) one; A; *s. auch* **Zwei 2**

Ein·saat *die* sowing

ein|sacken[1] *tr. V.* **1** (in Säcke füllen) **etw. ~:** put sth. into sacks **2** (ugs.: einstecken) grab; pocket ‹*money*›

ein|sacken[2] *itr. V.; mit sein* sink in; ‹*building, pavement*› subside

ein|sagen *itr. V.* (südd., österr.) **er sagte ihr ein** he whispered the answer to her

ein|sägen *tr. V.* **etw. ~:** saw into sth.

ein|salben *tr. V.* **den Arm ~:** rub ointment on *or* into one's arm; **sich/jmdn. ~:** rub ointment on [oneself]/rub ointment on sb.

ein|salzen *tr. V.* salt ‹*fish, meat*›

einsam *Adj.* **1** (verlassen) lonely ‹*person, decision*›; **~ leben** live a lonely *or* solitary life; **sich ~ fühlen** feel lonely **2** (einzeln) solitary ‹*rock, tree, wanderer*›; **~e Spitzenklasse sein** (ugs.) be in a class of its/his/her own **3** (abgelegen) isolated; **~ liegen** be situated miles from anywhere **4** (menschenleer) empty; deserted; **~ und verlassen [da]liegen** lie [there] lonely and deserted

Einsamkeit *die;* **~, ~en** **1** (Verlassenheit) loneliness **2** (Alleinsein) solitude **3** (Abgeschiedenheit) isolation

ein|sammeln *tr. V.* **1** (auflesen) pick up; gather up; **die Kinder/Betrunkene ~** (ugs.) pick up *or* collect the children/pick up drunks **2** (sich aushändigen lassen) collect in; collect ‹*tickets*›

ein|sargen *tr. V.* **einen Toten ~:** put the body of a dead person into a coffin; **lass dich doch ~!** (salopp) [go and] get stuffed! (Brit. sl.); go to hell! (sl.)

Ein·satz *der* **1** (eingesetztes Teil) (in Tischdecke, Kopfkissen usw.) inset; (in Kochtopf, Nähkasten usw.) compartment **2** (eingesetzter Betrag) stake; **den ~ erhöhen** raise the stakes *pl.* **3** (das Einsetzen) (von Maschinen, Gewehren, Wasserwerfern, Schlagstöcken) use; (von Truppen) deployment; **unter ~ seines Lebens** at the risk of his life; **zum ~ kommen** *od.* **gelangen** (Papierdt.) ‹*machine*› come into operation; ‹*police, troops*› be brought into action, be used; ‹*reserve player*› be brought on *or* used; **jmdn./etw. zum ~ bringen** use sb./sth. **4** (Engagement) commitment; dedication; **~ zeigen** show commitment *or* dedication; **der ~ hat sich gelohnt** the effort was worthwhile **5** (Milit.) **im ~ sein/fallen** be in action *or* on active service/die in action; **einen ~ fliegen** (Luftwaffe) fly a mission **6** (Musik) **der ~ der Instrumente** the entry of the instruments; **der ~ der Violinen kam zu spät** the violins came in too late

einsatz-, Einsatz-: **~befehl** *der* **1** (Befehl zum ~) order to go into action; **2** (Verantwortung) **den ~befehl haben** have operational command; **~bereit** *Adj.* **1** (bereit, sich einzusetzen) ‹*worker*› ready to work; ‹*athlete*› fit to compete; **2** (bereit, eingesetzt zu werden) ready for use; **3** (Milit.) combat-ready *attrib.*; ready for action *postpos.*; **~bereitschaft** *die* ▸**~bereit**: readiness to work; fitness to compete; readiness for use; combat-readiness; readiness for action; **~fähig** *Adj.* **1** (fähig, sich einzusetzen) ‹*athlete*› fit to compete; **2** (verfügbar) fit ‹*player*›; ‹*washing machine etc.*› in working order; **~freudig** *Adj.* enthusiastic; **~gebiet** *das* area of use; sphere of application; (von Personal) area *or* field of work; (von Truppen) field of operations; area of deployment; **~gruppe** *die,* **~kommando** *das* task force; **~leiter** *der,* **~leiterin** *die* **1** (des ~kommandos) head of operations; **2** (des ~es) leader of the task force; **~plan** *der* plan of action; **~wagen** *der* (der Polizei) police car; (der Feuerwehr) fire engine; (Notarztwagen) ambulance; (der Straßenbahn) relief; **~zentrale** *die* operations centre

ein|sauen *tr. V.* (derb) **sich/etw. ~:** get oneself/sth. covered in muck (coll.)

ein|saugen *unr.* (*auch regelm.*) *tr. V.* suck in ‹*air, liquid*›; breathe [in] ‹*fresh air*›; **die Bienen saugen den Nektar ein** the bees suck the nectar

ein|säumen *tr. V.* **1** (Schneiderei) hem **2** (einfassen) edge ‹*flower bed, vegetable-patch*›; surround ‹*property*›

ein|schalten

A *tr. V.* **1** switch *or* turn on ‹*radio, TV, electricity, etc.*›; **einen anderen Sender ~:** switch *or* tune to another station **2** (fig.: beteiligen) call in ‹*press, police, expert, etc.*›; **jmdn. in die Verhandlungen ~:** bring sb. into the negotiations **3** (einfügen) take ‹*break*›

B *refl. V.* **1** switch [itself] on; come on **2** (eingreifen) intervene (**in** + *Akk.* in)

Einschalt·quote *die* (Rundf.) listening figures *pl.*; (Ferns.) viewing figures *pl.*

Ein·schaltung *die* **1** (Einschalten) switching *or* turning on **2** (Beteiligung) calling in **3** (Sprachw.) parenthesis

ein|schärfen *tr. V.* **jmdm. etw. ~:** impress sth. [up]on sb.; **jmdm. ~, etw. zu tun** impress upon sb. that he/she must do sth.

ein|scharren *tr. V.* (vergraben) bury; (lieblos begraben) **jmdn. ~:** bury sb. hurriedly

ein|schätzen *tr. V.* **1** judge ‹*person*›; assess ‹*situation, income, damages*›; (schätzen) estimate; **jmdn./eine Situation falsch ~:** misjudge sb./a situation; **jmdn./eine Leistung hoch/niedrig ~:** think highly/not think highly of sb./an achievement; **wie ich die Lage einschätze** as I see the situation **2** (Steuerw.) assess

Ein·schätzung *die* **1** ▸**einschätzen**: judging; assessment; estimation; **nach seiner/meiner ~:** in my estimation *or* judgement **2** (Steuerw.) assessment

ein|schäumen *tr. V.* **1** (mit Schaum bedecken) lather; **sich/jmdm. die Haare ~:** lather one's/sb.'s hair **2** (mit Schaumstoff umhüllen) **etw. ~:** wrap sth. in foam [material]

ein|schenken *tr., itr. V.* **1** (eingießen) pour [out]; **jmdm. etw. ~:** pour out sth. for sb. **2** (füllen) fill [up] ‹*glass, cup*›; **er schenkte immer wieder ein** he kept on filling up my glass/cup/our/their *etc.* glasses/cups

ein|scheren *itr. V.; mit sein* (Verkehrsw.) **in** *od.* **auf eine Fahrspur ~:** get *or* move into a lane; **nach links/rechts ~:** get *or* move into the left-hand/right-hand lane; **in eine Lücke ~:** move into a space; **er scherte vor mir ein** he cut in in front of me

ein|schicken *tr. V.* send in; **etw. zur Reparatur ~:** send sth. [in] to be repaired

ein|schieben *unr. tr. V.* **1** (hineinschieben) push in; **den Ball zum 1:0 ~** (Fußballjargon) put the ball away to make it *or* the score 1-0 **2** (einfügen) put in; insert; put on ‹*trains, buses*›; fit in ‹*client, patient*›; **etw. in etw.** (*Akk.*) **~:** put *or* insert sth. into sth.

Ein·schienen·bahn *die* monorail

ein|schießen

A *unr. tr. V.* **1** (zerstören) demolish ‹*wall, building*› by gunfire; **das Fenster [mit einem Ball] ~** (fig.) smash the window [with a ball] **2** (treffsicher machen) try out, test ‹*gun etc.*› **3** (hineinschießen) insert ‹*dowel, plug*› **4** (Sport) kick in ‹*ball*›; **den Ball zum 1 : 1 ~:** shoot a goal to make it *or* the score 1-1 **5** (einzahlen) inject ‹*capital, cash, etc.*› (**in** + *Akk.* into) **6** (Druckw.) interleave; insert **7** (Weberei) **den Faden ~:** shoot the weft; pick

B *unr. refl. V.* **1** (treffsicher werden) **sich [auf etw.** (*Akk.*)**] ~:** find *or* get the range [of sth.] **2** (Sport) find *or* get the range **3** (angreifen) **sich [immer mehr] auf jmdn./etw. ~:** make sb./sth. the target of [increasingly frequent] attacks

ein|schiffen

A *tr. V.* embark ‹*passengers*›; load ‹*cargo*›

B *refl. V.* embark (**nach** for)

Einschiffung *die;* **~, ~en** ▸**einschiffen**: embarkation; loading

Einschiffungs·hafen *der* port of embarkation

ein|schlafen *unr. itr. V.; mit sein* **1** fall asleep; go to sleep; **über der Zeitung ~:** fall asleep over the paper; **beim Fernsehen ~:** fall asleep while watching television *or* in front of the television; **ich kann nicht ~:** I can't get to sleep **2** (verhüll.: sterben) pass away (euphem.) **3** (gefühllos werden) go to sleep; **mein Bein ist eingeschlafen, mir ist das Bein eingeschlafen** my leg has gone to sleep **4** (aufhören) peter out

ein|schläfern *tr. V.* **1** (in Schlaf versetzen) **jmdn. ~:** send sb. to sleep **2** (betäuben) **jmdn. ~:** put sb. to sleep **3** (schmerzlos töten) **ein Tier ~:** put an animal to sleep **4** (beruhigen) soothe, salve ‹*conscience*›; dull ‹*critical faculties*›

einschläfernd

A *Adj.* soporific

B *adv.* **~ wirken** have a soporific effect

Einschläferung *die;* **~, ~en** **1** (Betäubung) anaesthesia *no art.* **2** (Tötung) **der Tierarzt empfahl die ~:** the vet recommended putting the animal to sleep **3** (Beruhigung) ▸**einschläfern 4**: soothing; salving; dulling

Ein·schlag *der* **1** (Einschlagen) **wir sahen den ~ des Blitzes/der Bomben** we saw the lightning strike/the bombs land **2** (Stelle) **wir sahen die Einschläge der Kugeln/der Bomben** we saw the bullet holes/where the bombs had fallen *or* landed **3** (Anteil) element; **eine Familie mit südländischem ~:** a family with southern blood in it; **mit nihilistischem ~:** with an element of nihilism **4** (Kfz-W.) (des Lenkrads) turning; (der Räder) lock **5** (Forstw.) felling

ein|schlagen

A *unr. tr. V.* **1** (hin~) knock in; hammer in; **etw. in etw.** (*Akk.*) **~:** knock *or* hammer sth. into sth. **2** (zertrümmern) smash [in] **3** (einwickeln) wrap up ‹*present*›; cover ‹*book*›; **ein Kind in eine warme Decke ~:** wrap a child up in a warm blanket **4** (wählen) take ‹*route, direction*›; take up ‹*career*›; adopt ‹*policy*›; **einen Kurs ~:** follow a course; (fig.) follow *or* pursue a course; **einen anderen Kurs ~** (auch fig.) change *or* alter course **5** (Kfz-W.) turn ‹[*steering*] *wheel*› **6** (Schneiderei: umlegen) take in; take up ‹*trousers*› **7** (Forstw.) fell ‹*trees*›

B *unr. itr. V.* **1** (auftreffen) ‹*bomb*› land; ‹*lightning*› strike; **bei uns hat es eingeschlagen** our house was struck by lightning **2** (einprügeln) **auf jmdn./etw. ~:** rain blows on *or* beat sb./sth. **3** (durch Händedruck) shake [hands] on it; (fig.) accept; **schlag ein!** shake on it! **4** (Kfz-W.) **nach links/rechts ~:** steer to the left/right **5** (sich erfolgreich entwickeln) come along *or* on well **6** (Erfolg haben) be a success

einschlägig /ˈainʃlɛːgɪç/

A *Adj.* specialist ‹*journal, shop*›; relevant ‹*literature, passage*›

B *adv.* **er ist ~ vorbestraft** he has previous convictions for a similar offence/similar offences; **der ~ vorbestrafte Angeklagte** the accused, who has/had previous convictions for a similar offence/similar offences

ein|schleichen *unr. refl. V.* steal *or* sneak *or* creep in; (fig.) creep in; **sich in etw.** (*Akk.*) **~:** steal *or* sneak *or* creep into sth.; **der Verdacht**

schleicht sich ein, dass ... one has a sneaking suspicion that ...

ein|schleifen
A *unr. tr. V.* **1** (eingraben) cut in; **etw. in etw.** (*Akk.*) **~:** cut sth. into sth. **2** (Technik: einpassen) grind in
B *unr. refl. V.* (bes. Psych.) become established

ein|schleimen *refl. V.* (ugs. abwertend) insinuate oneself (**in** + *Akk.* into); **sich bei jmdm. ~:** suck up to sb. (coll.)

ein|schleppen *tr. V.* tow in ‹*ship, yacht, etc.*›; bring in, introduce ‹*disease, pest*›; **Typhus in ein Land ~:** bring *or* introduce typhus into a country

ein|schleusen *tr. V.* smuggle in; **Agenten in ein Land/eine Terroristengruppe ~:** infiltrate agents into a country/a terrorist group

ein|schließen *unr. tr. V.* **1** **etw. in etw.** (*Dat.*) **~:** lock sth. up [in sth.]; **jmdn./sich ~:** lock sb./oneself in; **jmdn. in ein[em] Zimmer ~:** lock sb. [up] in a room; **sich in ein[em] Zimmer ~:** lock oneself in a room **2** (umgeben) ‹*wall*› surround, enclose; ‹*people*› surround, encircle **3** (einbegreifen) **etw. in etw.** (*Akk.*) **~:** include sth. in sth.

einschließlich
A *Präp. mit Gen.* (stark dekl. Substantiv im Sg. ohne Artikel od. Attribut bleibt ungebeugt) including; inclusive of; **~ der Unkosten** including expenses; **die Kosten ~ Porto** costs including *or* inclusive of postage; **sie verlor ihre Handtasche ~ aller Papiere** she lost her handbag and all the papers which were in it
B *adv.* **bis ~ 30. Juni** up to and including 30 June; **bis Montag ~:** up to and including Monday

ein|schlummern *itr. V.; mit sein* **1** (geh.: einschlafen) fall asleep **2** (verhüll.: sterben) pass away (euphem.)

Ein·schluss, *Ein·schluß *der* **1** (Einbeziehung) inclusion; **alle Staaten unter** *od.* **mit ~ dieses Landes** all states, including this country **2** (Geol.) inclusion

ein|schmeicheln *refl. V.* **sich bei jmdm. ~:** ingratiate oneself with sb.

einschmeichelnd *Adj.* beguiling ‹*music, voice*›; ingratiating ‹*manner*›

ein·schmeißen *unr. tr. V.* (salopp) smash [in] ‹*window*›

ein|schmelzen *unr. tr. V.* melt down

ein|schmieren *tr. V.* (ugs.) **1** (einfetten) (mit Creme) cream ‹*face, hands, etc.*›; (mit Fett) grease; (mit Öl) oil; **die Kinder schmierten meine Schuhe mit Zahncreme ein** the children smeared toothpaste on my shoes *or* smeared my shoes with toothpaste **2** (schmutzig machen) **sich/etw. ~:** make *or* get oneself/sth. mucky (coll.) *or* dirty; **sich mit Eis ~:** get oneself covered in ice cream

ein|schmuggeln *tr. V.* **1** (unerlaubt einführen) smuggle in; **etw. in ein Land** (*Akk.*) **~:** smuggle sth. into a country **2** (ugs.: unerlaubt Zutritt verschaffen) **sich in etw.** (*Akk.*) **~:** sneak into sth.; **jmdn. in etw.** (*Akk.*) **~:** smuggle *or* sneak sb. into sth.

ein|schnappen *itr. V.; mit sein* **1** ‹*door, lock*› click to **2** (ugs.: schmollen) go into a huff; *s. auch* **eingeschnappt B**

ein|schneiden
A *unr. tr. V.* **1** (hin~) make a cut in; cut; ‹*rope*› cut into ‹*wrists*›; **das Papier an den Ecken ~:** make a cut at each of the corners of the paper **2** (einritzen) carve; **ein tief eingeschnittenes Tal** a deeply carved valley
B *unr. itr. V.* **das Kleid schneidet an den Schultern ein** the dress cuts into my shoulders

einschneidend *Adj.* drastic, radical ‹*measure, change*›; drastic, far-reaching ‹*effect*›

ein|schneien *itr. V.; mit sein* ‹*person, car*› get snowed in; become snowbound; ‹*village, farm*› get snowed in, be cut off by snow; ‹*mountain pass*› be closed by snow; **eingeschneit sein** be snowed in

Ein·schnitt *der* **1** (Schnitt) cut; incision (Med.); **einen ~ machen** make a cut *or* (Med.) incision **2** (eingeschnittene Stelle) cut; (Med.) incision; (im Gebirge) cleft **3** (Zäsur) break **4** (einschneidendes Ereignis) [decisive] turning point; decisive event

ein|schnüren *tr. V.* **1** **sich/jmdm. die Taille ~:** lace one's/sb.'s waist; **sich ~:** lace oneself up [in one's corset] **2** (einengen) cut in; **es schnürt mich ein** it cuts into me

ein|schränken
A *tr. V.* **1** (verringern) reduce, curb ‹*expenditure, consumption, power*›; **das Trinken/Rauchen/Essen ~:** cut down on the amount one drinks/smokes/eats **2** (einengen) limit; restrict; **jmdn. in seinen Rechten/seiner Bewegungsfreiheit ~:** limit *or* restrict sb.'s rights/freedom of movement **3** (relativieren) qualify, modify ‹*remark*›
B *refl. V.* economize; cut back on spending; **sich finanziell ~ müssen** have to cut back on one's spending; **sich im Rauchen/Trinken sehr ~:** cut down drastically on the amount one smokes/drinks; *s. auch* **eingeschränkt**

Einschränkung *die;* **~, ~en** **1** restriction; limitation; **jmdm. ~en auferlegen** impose restrictions on sb.; **sich** (*Dat.*) **erhebliche finanzielle ~en auferlegen müssen** have to make considerable economies **2** (Vorbehalt) reservation; **nur mit ~[en]** only with reservations *pl.*; **ohne ~[en]** without reservation; **mit der ~, dass ...** with the [one] reservation that ...

ein|schrauben *tr. V.* screw in

Einschreibe-: ~brief *der* registered letter; **~gebühr** *die* **1** (Postw., Hochschulw.) registration fee; **2** (in Vereinen usw.) membership fee

ein|schreiben *unr. tr. V.* **1** (hineinschreiben) write up **2** (Postw.) register ‹*letter*›; **einen Brief ~ lassen** register a letter; send a letter by registered mail; *s. auch* **eingeschrieben B** **3** (eintragen) **sich/jmdn. [in eine Liste] ~:** write sb.'s/one's name down [on a list]; enter sb.'s/one's name [on a list]; **sich an einer Universität ~:** register at a university; **sich für einen Abendkurs ~:** enrol for an evening class; *s. auch* **eingeschrieben** **4** (DV) input

Ein·schreiben *das* (Postw.) registered letter; **per ~:** by registered mail

Ein·schreibung *die* (Hochschulw.) registration; (für einen Abendkurs) enrolment

ein|schreien *unr. itr. V.* **auf jmdn. ~:** shout at sb.

ein|schreiten *unr. itr. V.* intervene; **gegen jmdn./etw. ~:** take action against sb./sth.; **das Einschreiten der Polizei** intervention by the police

ein|schrumpfen *itr. V.; mit sein* shrivel up; (fig.) dwindle

Ein·schub *der* (Schrift- u. Druckw.) insertion

ein|schüchtern *tr. V.* intimidate; **sich ~ lassen** let oneself be intimidated; **wir lassen uns nicht ~:** we won't be intimidated

Einschüchterungs·versuch *der* attempt at intimidation

ein|schulen *tr. V.* **eingeschult werden** start school; **Sie müssen Ihr Kind mit 6 Jahren ~ lassen** you must ensure that your child starts school when he or she reaches the age of 6

Ein·schulung *die:* **die Anforderungen für die ~ erfüllen** meet the requirements for starting school; **wir müssen die ~ verlegen** we must postpone the date on which he/she starts school

Einschulungs·alter *das* age at which children start school

Ein·schuss, *Ein·schuß *der* **1** bullet wound; wound at point of entry **2** (Raumf.) **nach dem ~ in die Mondumlaufbahn** after the rocket has/had been put into orbit around the moon *or* into moon orbit **3** (Weberei) weft; woof **4** (Sport) **zum ~ kommen** shoot a goal

Einschuss-, *Einschuß-: ~loch *das* bullet hole; **~stelle** *die* wound at point of entry; bullet wound

ein|schütten *tr. V.* pour in; **etw. in etw.** (*Akk.*) **~:** pour sth. into sth.; **den Schweinen das Futter ~:** pour the pigs their feed

ein|schweben *itr. V.; mit sein* glide in

ein|schweißen *tr. V.* **1** weld in; **etw. in etw.** (*Akk.*) **~:** weld sth. into sth. **2** (in Klarsichtfolien) **etw. ~:** seal sth. in transparent film

ein|schwenken *itr. V.; mit sein* **1** turn in; **in die Toreinfahrt ~:** turn into the gateway; **nach links ~:** wheel left **2** (fig.) fall into line; **er schwenkte auf einen neuen politischen Kurs ein** he changed course politically

ein|schwören *unr. tr. V.* **1** (durch Treueschwur binden) **jmdn. ~:** swear sb. in **2** (verpflichten) **jmdn. auf etw.** (*Akk.*) **~:** swear sb. to sth.; **▸eingeschworen**

ein|segnen *tr. V.* **1** (ev. Religion landsch.: konfirmieren) confirm **2** (kath. Religion: weihen) consecrate

Ein·segnung *die* **▸einsegnen:** confirmation; consecration

ein|sehen *unr. tr. V.* **1** (überblicken) see into ‹*building, garden, etc.*› **2** (prüfend lesen) look at, see ‹*files*› **3** (erkennen) see; realize **4** (begreifen) understand, see

Einsehen *das;* **~s: ein ~ haben** have *or* show [some] understanding; **kein ~ haben** have *or* show no understanding

ein|seifen *tr. V.* **1** **jmdn./sich/etw. ~:** lather sb./oneself/sth.; **jmdn. mit Schnee ~** (ugs.) rub snow in sb's face **2** (ugs.: betrügen) **jmdn. ~:** con sb. (coll.); put one over on sb. (coll.)

ein·seitig
A *Adj.* **1** on one side *postpos.*; unrequited ‹*love*›; one-sided ‹*friendship*›; **er hat eine ~e Lähmung** he's paralysed down one side **2** (tendenziös) one-sided, biased ‹*view, statement, etc.*›; one-sided ‹*person*› **3** (nicht abwechslungsreich) unbalanced ‹*diet*›; one-sided ‹*education*›; **ein sehr ~er Mensch** a person with narrow interests
B *adv.* **1** **etw. ~ bedrucken** print sth. on one side **2** (tendenziös) one-sidedly **3** (nicht abwechslungsreich) **sich ~ ernähren** have an unbalanced diet; **sehr ~ ausgebildet sein** have had a very one-sided education

Einseitigkeit *die;* **~, ~en** (Voreingenommenheit) one-sidedness; bias

ein|senden *unr.* (*auch regelm.*) *tr. V.* send [in]; **etw. einem Verlag** *od.* **an einen Verlag ~:** send sth. to a publisher

Ein·sender *der,* **Ein·senderin** *die;* **~, ~nen** sender; (bei einem Preisausschreiben) entrant; **die Einsender von Fotos werden gebeten ...** we [would] ask all those who send in photographs ...

Einsende·schluss, *Einsende·schluß *der* closing date

Ein·sendung *die* letter/card/contribution/article *etc.*; (bei einem Preisausschreiben) entry

ein|senken *tr. V.* sink ‹*pile etc.*›; **etw. in etw.** (*Akk.*) **~:** sink sth. into sth.

Einser *der;* **~s, ~** (ugs.) **1** (Schulnote) one; A; *s. auch* **Zweier 1** **2** (Buslinie) number one [bus]

einsetzbar *Adj.* **1** ‹*part*› that can be inserted; **2** (anwendbar) (von Dingen) usable; (von Personen) employable; (Milit.) deployable ‹*troops, weapons*›; **vielseitig** *od.* **multifunktional ~:** versatile

ein|setzen
A *tr. V.* **1** (hineinsetzen) put in; put in, fit ‹*window*›; insert, put in ‹*tooth, piece of fabric, value, word*›; **etw. in etw.** (*Akk.*) **~:** put/fit/insert sth. into sth.; **Karpfen in einen Teich ~:** stock a pond with carp **2** (Verkehrsw.) put on ‹*special train etc.*› **3** (ernennen, in eine Position setzen) appoint; **jmdn. zum** *od.* **als Erben ~:** appoint *or* name sb. one's heir; **jmdn. in ein Amt ~:** appoint sb. to an office; **der Monarch glaubte sich von Gott eingesetzt** the monarch believed he held his office by divine right **4** (in Aktion treten lassen) use ‹*weapon, machine*›; bring into action, use ‹*troops, police*›; bring on, use ‹*reserve player*›; **seine ganze Kraft ~:** use all one's strength **5** (aufs Spiel setzen) stake ‹*money*› **6** (riskieren) risk; put at risk; **sein Leben/seinen Ruf ~:** risk one's life/reputation; put one's life/reputation at risk
B *itr. V.* start; begin; ‹*storm*› break; **mit etw. ~:** start *or* begin sth.; **dann setzte Regen ein** then it started *or* began to rain; **wenn [die]**

e

e

Ebbe/Flut einsetzt when the tide begins to ebb/flow
C *refl. V.* 1 (sich engagieren) **ich werde mich dafür ~, dass Sie mehr Geld bekommen** I shall do what I can to see that you get more money; **sich für die Annahme des Gesetzes/die Rettung der Flüchtlinge ~:** do what one can to see that the law is passed/the refugees are saved; **sich selbstlos für die Armen ~:** lend aid unselfishly to the poor; **der Schüler/Minister setzt sich nicht genug ein** the pupil is lacking application/the minister is lacking in commitment 2 (Fürsprache einlegen) **sich für jmdn. ~:** support sb.'s cause

Einsetzung *die; ~, ~en* appointment (**in** + *Akk.* to)

Ein·sicht *die* 1 (das Einsehen) view (**in** + *Akk.* into) 2 (Einblick) **~ in die Akten nehmen** take *or* have a look at the files; **jmdm. ~ in etw.** (*Akk.*) **gewähren** allow sb. to look at *or* see sth. 3 (Erkenntnis) insight; **zu der ~ kommen, dass ...** come to realize that ...; come to the realization that ... 4 (Vernunft) sense; reason; (Verständnis) understanding; **~ mit jmdm. haben** show [some] understanding for sb.; **zur ~ kommen** come to one's senses

einsichtig
A *Adj.* 1 (verständnisvoll) understanding; **jeder Einsichtige muss zugeben, dass ...** anyone with any understanding of the situation must concede that ... 2 (verständlich) comprehensible, understandable, clear; **ihm war nicht ~, warum ...** it was not clear to him why ...; he was not clear why ...
B *adv.* **sehr ~ vorgehen** show a great deal of understanding

Einsichtnahme *die; ~, ~n* (Papierdt.) **nach ~ in die Akten** after studying the files; **die Baupläne liegen zur ~ aus** the building plans are available for inspection

einsichts-: ~los *Adj.* 1 (verständnislos) lacking in understanding *postpos.*; 2 (reuelos) without remorse *postpos.*; **~voll** *Adj.* understanding

ein|sickern *itr. V.; mit sein* seep in; (fig.) trickle in

Einsiedelei /ainzi:dəˈlai/ *die; ~, ~en* hermitage; (fig.) [country] retreat

Ein·siedler *der*, **Ein·siedlerin** *die* hermit; (fig.) recluse

einsiedlerisch *Adj.* hermit-like; solitary

Einsiedler-: ~klause *die* hermitage; **~krebs** *der* hermit crab

ein·silbig
A *Adj.* 1 monosyllabic ‹*word*› 2 (fig.) taciturn ‹*person*›; monosyllabic ‹*answer*›
B *adv.* (fig.) ‹*answer*› in monosyllables

Einsilbigkeit *die; ~* (fig.) taciturnity

ein|singen *unr. refl. V.* get oneself into voice; ‹*choir*› get itself into voice

ein|sinken *unr. itr. V.* 1 sink in; **in etw.** (*Dat.*) **~:** sink into sth. 2 (zusammenfallen) ‹*roof*› sag; **eingesunkene Wangen** sunken cheeks

ein|sitzen *unr. itr. V.* (Rechtsw.) serve a prison sentence; **er sitzt für drei Jahre ein** he is serving three years *or* a three-year sentence

Einsitzer *der; ~s, ~:* single-seater

einsitzig *Adj.* single-seater *attrib.*

ein|sortieren *tr. V.* sort ‹*books, papers, etc.*› and put them away; **Briefmarken/Fotos in ein Album ~:** put stamps/photos into an album; **Karteikarten ~:** file cards; **Briefe in Fächer ~:** sort letters into pigeonholes

ein·spaltig (Druckw.)
A *Adj.* single-column *attrib.*
B *adv.* ‹*print, set*› in one column

ein|spannen *tr. V.* 1 harness ‹*horse*› 2 (in etw. spannen) **den Bogen [in die Schreibmaschine] ~:** put the sheet of paper in[to the typewriter]; **Stoff in einen Stickrahmen ~:** fix cloth into an embroidery frame; **das Werkstück [in den Schraubstock] ~:** clamp the work [in the vice] 3 (ugs.: heranziehen) rope in (coll.); **er wollte uns für seine Zwecke ~:** he wanted to use us for his own ends; *s. auch* **eingespannt B**

Einspänner /ˈainʃpɛnɐ/ *der; ~s, ~* 1 one-horse carriage 2 (österr. Gastr.) black coffee with whipped cream (*served in a glass*)

einspännig
A *Adj.* one-horse *attrib.* ‹*carriage*›
B *adv.* **~ fahren** drive a one-horse carriage

ein|sparen *tr. V.* save, cut down on ‹*costs, expenditure*›; save ‹*time*›; save, economize on ‹*energy, electricity, gas, materials*›; **Stellen/Arbeitsplätze ~:** cut down on the number of posts/cut down on staff

Einspar·potenzial *das* potential saving

Einsparung *die; ~, ~en* saving (**an** + *Dat.* in); **~en an Kosten/Energie/Material** savings *or* economies in costs/energy/materials; **durch ~ an** *od.* **von Material** by economizing on *or* saving materials

Einsparungs·maßnahme *die* economy measure

ein|speicheln *tr. V.* insalivate

ein|speichern *tr. V.* (DV) feed in; input; **einem Computer etw. ~:** feed sth. into a computer

ein|speisen *tr. V.* (Technik, DV) feed in; **etw. in etw.** (*Akk.*) **~:** feed sth. into sth.

ein|sperren *tr. V.* **jmdn. ~:** lock sb. up

ein|spielen
A *refl. V.* 1 ‹*musician, athlete, team, etc.*› warm up; (zum Saisonbeginn) ‹*athlete, team*› get into practice; **sich aufeinander ~** (fig.) get used to each other's ways *or* one another; *s. auch* **eingespielt A** 2 (funktionieren) get going [properly]
B *tr. V.* 1 (einbringen) make; bring in; **der Film hat seine Unkosten eingespielt** the film has covered its costs 2 play *or* break in ‹*musical instrument*› 3 (aufnehmen) record

Einspiel·ergebnis *das* (Film, Theater) box office takings *pl.*

ein|spinnen *unr. refl. V.* (Zool.) ‹*insect*› spin a cocoon around itself

einsprachig /ˈainʃpra:xɪç/
A *Adj.* monolingual
B *adv.* **~ aufwachsen** grow up speaking only one language; *s. auch* **zweisprachig**

ein|sprechen *unr. itr. V.* ▸ **einreden B**

ein|sprengen *tr. V.* **etw. ~:** sprinkle sth. with water; damp sth.; *s. auch* **eingesprengt**

Einsprengsel /ˈainʃprɛŋsl/ *das; ~s, ~:* embedded particles *pl.*; **mit einigen philosophischen** *usw.* **~n** (fig.) with a sprinkling of philosophy *etc.*

ein|springen
A *unr. itr. V.; mit sein* 1 (als Stellvertreter) stand in; (fig.: aushelfen) step in and help out; **für jmdn. ~:** stand in for sb./step in and help sb. out 2 (Turnen) **in den Handstand ~:** perform a dive to handstand
B *unr. refl. V.* (Ski) do practice jumps

Einspritz|düse *die* injection nozzle

ein|spritzen *tr. V.* (auch Kfz-W.) inject; **jmdm. etw. ~:** inject sb. with sth.

Einspritz-: ~motor *der* fuel-injection engine; **~pumpe** *die* injection pump

Ein·spruch *der* 1 (Einwand) objection (**gegen** to); **~ gegen etw. erheben** raise an objection to sth. 2 (Rechtsw.) objection; (gegen Urteil, Entscheidung) appeal; **[gegen etw.] ~ einlegen** raise an objection [to sth.]; (gegen Urteil, Entscheidung) lodge an appeal [against sth.]

ein|sprühen *tr. V.* **die Windschutzscheibe mit einem Entfroster ~:** spray de-icer on [to] the windscreen (Brit.) *or* (Amer.) windshield; **sich** (*Dat.*) **das Haar ~:** put hairspray on one's hair

einspurig /ˈainʃpu:rɪç/
A *Adj.* single-track ‹*road*›
B *adv.* **die Autobahn ist nur ~ befahrbar** only one lane of the motorway is open

Eins·sein *das* (geh.) oneness

einst /ainst/ *Adv.* (geh.) 1 (früher) once 2 (der~) some *or* one day; **~ wird kommen der Tag, da ...** (dichter., veralt.) the day will come when ...

ein|stampfen *tr. V.* pulp ‹*books*›

Ein·stand *der* 1 (zum Dienstantritt) **seinen ~ geben** celebrate starting a new job 2 (Sport: erstes Spiel) debut; **seinen ~ geben** make one's debut; play one's first match 3 (Tennis) deuce

ein|stanzen *tr. V.* (Technik) stamp in; **etw. auf etw.** (*Akk.*)/**in etw.** (*Akk.*) **~:** stamp sth. into *or* on sth.

ein|stauben *itr. V.; mit sein* get dusty; get covered in dust; **eingestaubt sein** be dusty; be covered in dust

ein|stäuben *tr. V.* (mit Mehl) dust

ein|stechen
A *unr. itr. V.* 1 (mit einer Stichwaffe) **auf jmdn. ~:** stab sb. 2 (Kartenspiel) trump; play a trump
B *unr. tr. V.* pierce, make ‹*hole*›; **eine Nadel in etw.** (*Akk.*) **~:** stick *or* push a needle into sth.; **den Teig mit einer Gabel ~:** prick the dough with a fork

ein|stecken *tr. V.* 1 (in etw. stecken) put in; **etw. in etw.** (*Akk.*) **~:** put sth. into sth.; **das Bügeleisen ~:** plug in the iron; **er steckte die Pistole/das Messer wieder ein** he put the pistol back in the holster/the knife back in the sheath 2 (mitnehmen) **[sich** (*Dat.*)**] etw. ~:** take sth. with one; put sth. in one's pocket/case *etc.* 3 mail ‹*letter*› 4 (abwertend: für sich behalten) pocket ‹*money, profits*› 5 (hinnehmen) take ‹*criticism, defeat, etc.*›; take, swallow ‹*insult*› 6 (ugs.: übertreffen) outclass ‹*competitors, opponents*›

Einsteck-: ~kamm *der* comb; **~tuch** *das; Pl.* **~tücher** dress handkerchief

ein|stehen *unr. itr. V.* 1 (garantieren) **für jmdn. ~:** vouch for sb.; **dafür ~, dass ...** vouch [for the fact] that ... 2 (verantwortlich gemacht werden) **für etw. ~:** take responsibility for *or* assume liability for sth.; **für jmdn. ~:** take responsibility for *or* assume liability for sb.'s debts/misdeeds *etc.*; (jmdm. treu bleiben) stand by sb.

Einsteige·diebstahl *der* (Rechtsw.) *burglary involving entering, but not breaking into, a property*

ein|steigen *unr. itr. V.; mit sein* 1 (in ein Fahrzeug) get in; **in ein Auto ~:** get into a car; **in den Bus ~:** get on the bus; **vorn/hinten ~** (ins Auto) get into the front/back; (in den Bus) get on at the front/back 2 (eindringen) **durch ein Fenster/über den Balkon ~:** climb in *or* get in through a window/over the balcony 3 (ugs.: sich engagieren) **in ein Geschäft/die Politik ~:** go into a business/into politics; **in die Frauenbewegung ~:** get involved in the women's movement; **[mit zwei Millionen] in ein Unternehmen ~:** take a [two million pound *etc.*] stake in a company 4 (Bergsteigen) **in eine Felswand ~:** tackle a rock face 5 (Sport) tackle; **hart ~:** go in hard

Einsteiger *der; ~s, ~*, **Einsteigerin** *die; ~, ~nen* (in einen Beruf) newcomer (**in** + *Akk.* to); **Kameras, die sich für ~ eignen** cameras suitable for the beginner

einstellbar *Adj.* adjustable; **das ist genau ~:** it can be adjusted *or* set exactly

ein|stellen
A *tr. V.* 1 (einordnen) put away ‹*books etc.*› 2 (unterstellen) put in ‹*car, bicycle*›; **das Auto [in die Garage] ~:** put the car in [the garage] 3 (auch itr.) (beschäftigen) take on, employ ‹*workers*›; **„VW stellt wieder ein"** 'VW is taking on new workers again'; **„wir stellen ein: Schweißer"** 'we have vacancies for welders' 4 (regulieren) adjust; set; focus ‹*camera, telescope, binoculars*›; adjust ‹*headlights*›; **die Kamera auf die richtige Entfernung ~:** set the camera to the correct distance; **das Radio laut/leiser ~:** put the radio on loud/turn the radio down; **ein Radio auf einen Sender ~:** tune a radio to a station; tune in to a station; **ein Programm [an der Waschmaschine] ~:** select a programme [on the washing machine] 5 (beenden) stop; call off ‹*search, strike*›; **das Feuer ~:** cease fire; **die Zeitung hat ihr Erscheinen eingestellt** the newspaper has ceased publication; **ein Gerichtsverfahren ~:** abandon court proceedings; **die Arbeit ~** ‹*factory*› close; ‹*workers*› stop work 6 (Sport) equal ‹*record*› 7 (Sport: vorbereiten) **eine Mannschaft defensiv/offensiv ~:** train a team to play defensive/attacking football
B *refl. V.* 1 (ankommen, auch fig.) arrive 2 (eintreten) ‹*pain, worry*› begin; ‹*success*› come; ‹*symptoms,*

consequences› appear; **starkes Erbrechen stellte sich ein** he/she began to vomit violently **3** (einrichten) **sich auf etw.** (*Akk.*) **~:** prepare oneself *or* get ready for sth.; **sich schnell auf neue Situationen ~:** adjust quickly to new situations; **sie war nicht auf Gäste eingestellt** she was not prepared for guests; **sich auf jmdn. ~:** adapt to sb.

Einstell·hebel *der* adjusting lever

ein·stellig *Adj.* single-figure *attrib.* ‹*number*›

Einstell·platz *der* parking space; (auf eigenem Grundstück) carport

Ein·stellung *die* **1** (von Arbeitskräften) employment; taking on **2** (Regulierung) adjustment; setting; (eines Fernglases, einer Kamera) focusing; (von Scheinwerfern) adjustment **3** (Beendigung) stopping; (einer Suchaktion, eines Streiks) calling off; **die ~ der Produktion veranlassen** order that production be stopped; **er drohte mit der ~ der Zahlungen** he threatened to stop the payments **4** (Sport) **die ~ eines Rekordes** the equalling of a record **5** (Ansicht) attitude; **ihre politische/religiöse ~:** her political/religious views *pl.* **6** (Film) take

Einstellungs-: ~bedingung *die* requirement [for appointment]; **~gespräch** *das* interview; **~sperre** *die*, **~stopp** *der* freeze on recruitment; **~termin** *der* starting date

einstens /ˈai̯nstn̩s/ (geh., veralt.) ▸**einst**

Ein·stich *der* **1** insertion **2** (~stelle) puncture; prick

ein|sticken *tr. V.* embroider (**in** + *Akk.* on)

Ein·stieg *der*; **~[e]s, ~e 1** (Eingang) entrance; (Tür) door/doors **2** (das Einsteigen) entry; **„kein ~"** 'exit only' **3** (Bergsteigen) **der ~ in die Nordwand** the start of the assault on the north face; **beim ~ in den Kamin** at the start of the climb up the chimney; **ein guter ~:** a good point to start the climb **4** (fig.) **der ~ in diese Problematik ist schwierig** these are difficult problems to approach

Einstieg·luke *die* hatch

Einstiegs·droge *die* come-on drug

einstig *Adj.* former

ein|stimmen

A *itr. V.* join in; (veralt.: zustimmen) agree; **in den Gesang ~:** join in the singing; **in das [allgemeine] Lachen ~** (fig.) join in the [general] laughter

B *tr. V.* **jmdn. auf etw.** (*Akk.*) **~:** get sb. in the [right] mood for sth.

einstimmig

A *Adj.* **1** (Musik) **ein ~es Lied** a song for one voice **2** (einmütig) unanimous ‹*decision, vote*›

B *adv.* **1** (Musik) **~ singen** sing in unison **2** (einmütig) unanimously

Einstimmigkeit *die*; **~:** unanimity; **~ erzielen** achieve unanimity; reach unanimous agreement

Ein·stimmung *die*: **zur** *od.* **als ~ auf etw.** to get in the [right] mood for sth.

ein|stippen *tr. V.* (bes. nordd.) dip; dunk

einst·mals *Adv.* (geh., veralt.) formerly; in former times

ein·stöckig

A *Adj.* single-storey *attrib.*; one-storey *attrib.*; **hier sind die meisten Häuser ~:** most of the houses here have one storey

B *adv.* **hier darf nur ~ gebaut werden** single-storey *or* one-storey buildings only may be built here

ein|stöpseln *tr. V.* **1** plug in ‹*telephone, electrical device*› **2** put in, push in ‹*cork etc.*›

ein|stoßen *unr. tr. V.* **1** (gewaltsam öffnen) break down ‹*door, wall*›; smash [in] ‹*window*›; smash ‹*mirror*› **2** (durch Anstoßen verletzen) break ‹*nose, ribs*›; **sich** (*Dat.*) **den Kopf ~:** bang one's head

ein|strahlen

A *itr. V.* **1** (hineinscheinen) shine in; **das ~de Licht** the light shining in **2** **auf etw.** (*Akk.*) **~** ‹*sun*› irradiate sth.

B *tr. V.* (Physik, Technik) direct ‹*beam etc.*›

Ein·strahlung *die* irradiation; (Sonnen~) insolation

ein|streichen *unr. tr. V.* **1** **Brot mit Butter usw. ~:** spread butter *etc.* on bread **2** (ugs.: für sich behalten) pocket ‹*money, winnings, etc.*›; (ugs. abwertend) rake in (coll.) ‹*money, profits, etc.*› **3** (Theater) cut ‹*script, play*›

ein·streifig (Verkehrsw.)

A *Adj.* single-lane

B *adv.* in a single lane

ein|streuen *tr. V.* **1** **etw. mit Sand ~:** strew *or* scatter sand on sth. **2** (einfügen) **er streute witzige Bemerkungen in seinen Vortrag ein** he sprinkled his lecture with witty remarks

ein|strömen *itr. V.*; *mit sein* ‹*water*› pour *or* flood *or* stream in; ‹*air, light*› stream in; (fig.) ‹*crowd, supporters*› stream *or* pour in

ein·strophig *Adj.* one-verse *attrib.* ‹*poem, song*›; ‹*poem, song*› consisting of one verse; **das Gedicht ist ~:** the poem consists of *or* has one verse *or* stanza

ein|studieren *tr. V.* rehearse

ein·studiert *Adj.* (abwertend) studied

Einstudierung *die*; **~, ~en 1** rehearsal **2** (Inszenierung) production

ein|stufen *tr. V.* classify; categorize; **jmdn. in eine Kategorie/eine höhere Steuerklasse ~:** put sb. in a category/a higher income-tax bracket

ein·stufig *Adj.* single-stage ‹*rocket*›

Einstufung /ˈai̯nʃtuːfʊŋ/ *die*; **~, ~en** classification; categorization

ein|stülpen *tr. V.* push in

ein·stündig *Adj.* one-hour *attrib.* ‹*wait, delay*›; **nach ~em Warten** after a wait of one hour; after an hour's wait; *s. auch* **achtstündig**

ein|stürmen *itr. V.* **mit Fragen/Bitten auf jmdn. ~:** besiege sb. with questions/requests

Ein·sturz *der* collapse

ein|stürzen *itr. V.*; *mit sein* **1** collapse; **eine Welt stürzte für sie ein** (fig.) her whole world collapsed *or* fell apart **2** (fig.) **auf jmdn. ~** ‹*worries, problems*› crowd in [up]on sb.

Einsturz·gefahr *die* danger of collapse; **„Achtung, ~!"** 'danger — building unsafe'

einst·weilen *Adv.* **1** (vorläufig) for the time being; temporarily **2** (inzwischen) in the meantime; meanwhile

einstweilig *Adj.* (Amtsspr.) temporary; **eine ~e Verfügung/Anordnung** (Rechtsw.) a temporary injunction/order; **in den ~en Ruhestand versetzt werden** be suspended from duty

ein|suggerieren *itr. V.* **jmdm. etw. ~:** instil sth. into sb. by suggestion

Eins·werden *das* (geh.) becoming one *no art.*; **das ~ der Liebenden** the union of the lovers

Eins-zu-eins-Umsetzung *die* (eines Plans, eines Konzepts) exact implementation

ein·tägig *Adj.* one-day *attrib.*; **ein ~er Ausflug** a day tour; *s. auch* **achttägig**

Eintags·fliege *die* (Zool.) mayfly; (fig. ugs.) seven-day wonder; (kein Dauerzustand) passing phase

ein|tanzen *refl. V.* warm up

Ein·tänzer *der* (veralt.) gigolo

ein|tasten *tr. V.* (Technik) key in

ein|tauchen

A *tr. V.* immerse; **den Pinsel in die Farbe ~:** dip the brush in the paint; **den Zwieback in den Tee ~:** dunk *or* dip the rusk in the tea

B *itr. V.*; *mit sein* dive in; ‹*submarine*› dive

Ein·tausch *der* exchange; **im ~ gegen etw.** in exchange for sth.

ein|tauschen *tr. V.* exchange (**gegen** for)

ein·tausend *Kardinalz.* ▸**i S. 826** a *or* one thousand; *s. auch* **acht**[1]

ein|teilen *tr. V.* **1** divide up; classify ‹*plants, species*›; **den Kuchen in zwölf Stücke ~:** divide *or* cut the cake [up] into twelve pieces **2** (disponieren, verplanen) organize; plan [out]; **sein Geld [besser] ~:** plan *or* organize one's finances [better]; **sich** (*Dat.*) **seine Arbeit ~:** organize *or* plan [out] one's work; **sich seine Vorräte ~:** plan out how to make one's provisions last **3** (delegieren, abkommandieren) **jmdn. für etw.** *od.* **zu etw. ~:** assign sb. to sth.

Einteiler *der*; **~s, ~** (Mode) one-piece bathing suit

einteilig /ˈai̯ntai̯lɪç/ *Adj.* one-piece ‹*dress, bathing suit*›

Ein·teilung *die* **1** (Gliederung) division; dividing up; (Biol.) classification **2** (planvolles Disponieren) organization; planning; **bei besserer ~ seines Gehalts würde er ...** if he planned out better how to spend his salary, he would... **3** (Delegierung, Abkommandierung) assignment

Eintel /ˈai̯ntl̩/ *das* (*schweiz. meist der*); **~s, ~:** whole

ein|tippen *tr. V.* (in die Kasse) register; (in einen Rechner) key in

eintönig /ˈai̯ntøːnɪç/

A *Adj.* monotonous ‹*landscape, work, life*›

B *adv.* monotonously; ‹*read*› in a monotone

Eintönigkeit *die*; **~:** monotony

Ein·topf *der*, **Eintopf·gericht** *das* (Kochk.) stew

Ein·tracht *die* harmony; concord; **in ~ leben** live in harmony

ein·trächtig

A *Adj.* harmonious

B *adv.* harmoniously; **~ zusammenleben** live together in harmony

Eintrag /ˈai̯ntraːk/ *der*; **~[e]s, Einträge** /ˈai̯ntrɛːɡə/ **1** (das ~en) entering **2** (Aktennotiz) entry; **ein ~ ins Register** an entry in the register

ein|tragen *unr. tr. V.* **1** (einschreiben) enter; copy out ‹*essay*›; **einen Aufsatz in sein Heft ~:** copy an essay into one's exercise book; (einzeichnen) mark in; enter; **seinen Namen** *od.* **sich [in eine Liste] ~:** enter one's name [on a list] **2** (Amtsspr.) register; **sich ~ lassen** register; **etw. auf seinen Namen ~ lassen** have sth. registered in one's name; **ein eingetragenes Warenzeichen** a registered trade mark **3** (einbringen) bring in ‹*money*›; bring ‹*criticism*›; win ‹*goodwill*›; **das Geschäft trägt [einen] Gewinn ein** the business makes a profit; **das hat ihm nur Undank eingetragen** that only brought him ingratitude

einträglich /ˈai̯ntrɛːklɪç/ *Adj.* profitable, lucrative ‹*business, sideline*›; lucrative ‹*work, job*›

Eintragung *die*; **~, ~en 1** (das Eintragen) entering; **die ~ der Zinsen vornehmen lassen** have the interest entered [in one's account book]; **eine ~ ins Grundbuch bezahlen** pay to have a property *etc.* entered in the land register **2** (Eingetragenes) entry

ein|träufeln *tr. V.* **sich/jmdm. Augentropfen ~:** put drops in one's/sb.'s eyes; **jmdm. ein Medikament ~:** administer *or* give a medicine to sb. in drops

ein|treffen *unr. itr. V.*; *mit sein* **1** (ankommen) arrive **2** (verwirklicht werden) ‹*prophecy*› come true

Ein·treffen *das* arrival; **ich glaube nicht an das ~ dieser Prophezeiung** I don't believe that this prophecy will come true

ein|treiben *unr. tr. V.* **1** (kassieren) collect ‹*taxes, debts*›; (durch Gerichtsverfahren) recover ‹*debts, money*›; **das Geld ~ lassen** take action to obtain the money **2** (hineintreiben) drive in ‹*nail, stake*›

Eintreibung *die*; **~, ~en** (von Steuern, Schulden) collection; (durch Gerichtsverfahren) recovery

ein|treten

A *unr. itr. V.* **1** *mit sein* (einen Raum betreten) enter; **in ein Zimmer ~:** enter a room; **bitte, treten Sie ein!** please come in; **die Eintretenden** those entering **2** *mit sein* (Mitglied werden) **in einen Verein/einen Orden ~:** join a club/enter a religious order **3** *mit sein* (Raumfahrt) **in die Erdumlaufbahn/Erdatmosphäre ~:** enter Earth orbit/the Earth's atmosphere **4** *mit sein* **in eine neue/schwierige Phase ~:** be entering a new/difficult phase; **in Verhandlungen ~:** enter into negotiations; **in die Beweisaufnahme ~** (Rechtsw.) proceed to hearing the evidence **5** *mit sein* (sich ereignen) occur; ‹*silence*› descend; ‹*thaw*› set in; ‹*darkness, night*› set in, fall; **bald trat eine Besserung ein** there was soon an improvement; **bei Eintreten der Dunkelheit** at nightfall; when darkness sets/set in; **das Unerwartete war eingetreten** the unexpected had occurred *or* happened **6** *mit sein*

(sich einsetzen) **für jmdn./etw. ~:** stand up for sb./sth.; (vor Gericht) speak in sb.'s defence 7 **auf jmdn./etw. ~:** kick sb./sth.
B *unr. tr. V.* kick in ‹*door, window, etc.*›
C *unr. refl. V.* **sich** (*Dat.*) **etw. ~:** get sth. in one's foot

ein|trichtern *tr. V.* (salopp) **jmdm. etw. ~:** drum sth. into sb.; **jmdm. ~, dass ...** drum into sb. that ...

Ein·tritt *der* 1 entry; entrance; **sich** (*Dat.*) **[in etw.** (*Akk.*)**] ~ verschaffen** gain entry [to sth.]; **beim ~ in die Adoleszenz** (fig.) when entering adolescence; **vor dem ~ in die Verhandlungen** (fig.) before entering into negotiations 2 (Beitritt) **der ~ in einen Verein/einen Orden** joining a club/entering a religious order 3 (von Raketen) entry; **beim ~ [in die Erdatmosphäre]** on entry [into the Earth's atmosphere] 4 (Zugang, ~sgeld) admission; **[der] ~ [ist] frei** admission [is] free; **jmdm. den ~ [in etw.** (*Akk.*)**] verwehren** refuse sb. admission [to sth.] 5 (Beginn) (des Winters) onset; **vor/nach ~ der Dunkelheit** before/after nightfall *or* dusk 6 (eines Ereignisses) occurrence; (der Menstruation, Wehen) onset; **bei ~ des Todes** when death occurs

Eintritts-: ~geld *das* admission charge *or* fee; entrance charge *or* fee; **~karte** *die* admission *or* entrance ticket; **~preis** *der* admission *or* entrance charge

ein|trocknen *itr. V.; mit sein* 1 ‹*paint, blood*› dry; ‹*water, toothpaste*› dry up 2 (verdorren) ‹*leather*› dry out; ‹*berry, fruit*› shrivel

ein|trüben *refl. V.* (Met.) cloud over; become overcast; **es trübt sich ein** it's clouding over

Ein·trübung *die* cloudy spell

ein|trudeln *itr. V.; mit sein* (ugs.) drift in (coll.)

ein|tunken *tr. V.* (landsch.) **etw. in etw.** (*Akk.*) **~:** dip *or* dunk sth. in sth.

ein|tüten *tr. V.* bag

ein|üben *tr. V.* 1 (sich aneignen) practise; **jede einzelne seiner Gesten wirkt sorgfältig eingeübt** all of his gestures seem carefully rehearsed 2 (proben, trainieren) **mit jmdm. etw. ~:** practise sth. with sb.

Ein·übung *die* 1 (Aneignung) acquisition 2 (Proben, Trainieren) practising

Ein·uhr-: one o'clock ‹*news, train*›

ein·und·ein·halb ▸ⓘ S. 826 ▸**anderthalb**

ein·und·zwanzig *Kardinalz.* twenty-one

Einung *die;* **~, ~en** (dichter.) ▸**Einigung 2**

ein|verleiben /-fɛɐ̯laibn̩/
A *tr. V.* annex ‹*land, country*›
B *refl. V.* (sich zu Eigen machen) assimilate, absorb ‹*knowledge, experience*›; (scherzh.: zu sich nehmen) put away (coll.)

Einvernahme *die;* **~, ~n** (Rechtsw., bes. österr. u. schweiz.) examination

ein|vernehmen *unr. tr. V.* (Rechtsw., bes. österr. u. schweiz.) examine

Ein·vernehmen *das;* **~s** harmony; (Übereinstimmung) agreement; **in freundschaftlichem/gutem ~ [mit jmdm.]** on friendly/good terms [with sb.]; *s. auch* **setzen A 3**

ein·vernehmlich (Amtsspr.)
A *Adv.* conjointly
B *adj.* conjoint

einverstanden *Adj.* **mit jmdm. ~ sein** (einer Meinung) be in agreement with sb.; agree with sb.; **mit jmdm./etw. ~ sein** (zufrieden) approve of sb./sth.; **sich [mit etw.] ~ erklären** agree [to sth.]; express one's agreement [to sth.]; **~!** (ugs.) okay! (coll.); agreed!

ein·verständlich (geh.)
A *Adj.* mutually agreed; ‹*divorce*› by mutual consent
B *adv.* by mutual consent

Ein·verständnis *das* 1 (Billigung) consent (**zu** to), approval (**zu** of); **im ~ mit jmdm. handeln** act with sb.'s consent; **Ihr ~ vorausgesetzt** with your approval; if you are agreed 2 (Übereinstimmung) agreement; **zwischen ihnen herrscht ~:** there is agreement between them

Ein·waage *die* (Kaufmannsspr.) contents *pl.*

ein|wachsen[1] *unr. itr. V.; mit sein* grow into the flesh; **eingewachsen** ingrown ‹*toenail*›

ein|wachsen[2] *tr. V.* wax

Einwand *der;* **~[e]s, Einwände** /ˈainvɛndə/ objection (**gegen** to)

Ein·wanderer *der,* **Ein·wanderin** *die* immigrant

ein|wandern *itr. V.; mit sein* immigrate (**in** + *Akk.* into)

Ein·wanderung *die* immigration; **eine Zunahme der ~en** an increase in the number of immigrants

Einwanderungs-: ~behörde *die* immigration authorities *pl.*; **~land** *das* country of immigration; **~quote** *die* immigration quota; **~welle** *die* wave of immigrants

einwand·frei
A *Adj.* 1 (ohne Fehler) flawless; perfect; impeccable ‹*behaviour*›; **das Fleisch ist noch ~:** the meat is still perfectly fresh 2 (eindeutig) indisputable, definite ‹*proof*›; watertight ‹*alibi*›
B *adv.* 1 perfectly; flawlessly; ‹*behave*› impeccably 2 beyond question *or* doubt; **es ist ~ erwiesen, dass ...** it has been proved beyond question *or* doubt that ...

einwärts /ˈainvɛrts/ *Adv.* inwards; **~ gebogen** concave

einwärts·gebogen ▸**einwärts**

ein|weben *tr. V.* weave in; **etw. in etw.** (*Akk.*) **~:** weave *or* work sth. into sth.

ein|wechseln *tr. V.* 1 (wechseln, umtauschen) change ‹*money*› 2 (Sport) substitute ‹*player*›

ein|wecken *tr. V.* preserve; preserve, bottle ‹*fruit, vegetables*›

Einweck-: ~glas *das* preserving jar; **~gummi** *der,* **~ring** *der* rubber seal (*for preserving jar*); **~topf** *der* preserving pan

Ein·weg-: ~flasche *die* non-returnable bottle; **~packung** *die* disposable pack; **~pfand** *das* deposit on a/the disposable container; **~spiegel** *der* one-way mirror; **~spritze** *die* disposable [hypodermic] syringe; **~verpackung** *die* disposable container

ein|weichen *tr. V.* soak

ein|weihen *tr. V.* 1 open [officially] ‹*bridge, road*›; dedicate ‹*monument*›; consecrate ‹*church*› 2 (ugs. scherzh.: zum ersten Mal benutzen) christen (coll.) 3 (vertraut machen) **jmdn. in etw.** (*Akk.*) **~:** let sb. in on sth.; **jmdn. in die Kunst des Strickens/in das Schachspiel ~:** initiate sb. into the art of knitting/the mysteries of chess

Einweihung *die;* **~, ~en** [official] opening

ein|weisen *unr. tr. V.* 1 **jmdn. in ein Krankenhaus ~:** have sb. admitted to hospital; **die Flüchtlinge wurden in eine Wohnung/ein Lager eingewiesen** the refugees were assigned a flat (esp. Brit.) *or* (esp. Amer.) apartment/sent to a camp 2 (in eine Tätigkeit) **jmdn. [in eine/die Arbeit] ~:** introduce sb. to a/the job; show sb. what a/the job involves 3 (in ein Amt) install; **jmdn. in sein Amt ~:** install sb. 4 (Verkehrsw.) direct

Ein·weisung *die* 1 (Unterbringung) **~ in ein Krankenhaus** admission to a hospital; **sich gegen die ~ in ein Lager wehren** fight against being sent to a camp 2 introduction; **er wurde mit der ~ der neuen Mitarbeiter betraut** he was given the task of introducing the new members of staff to their jobs 3 (Amtseinführung) installation

ein|wenden *unr.* (*auch regelm.*) *tr. V.* **dagegen lässt sich manches/vieles ~:** there are a number of things/is a lot to be said against that; **dagegen ist nichts einzuwenden** there can be no objection to that; **„...", wandte er ein** '...,' he objected; **gegen etw. nichts einzuwenden haben** have no objection to sth.; have nothing against sth.

Ein·wendung *die* objection [**gegen** to]

ein|werben *tr. V.* attract ‹*money, sponsorship*›

ein|werfen
A *unr. tr. V.* 1 mail ‹*letter, mail*›; put in, insert ‹*coin*› 2 (zertrümmern) smash, break ‹*window*› 3 (Ballspiele) throw in ‹*ball*› 4 (bemerken, sagen) throw in ‹*remark*›; **„...", warf sie ein** '...,' she interjected
B *unr. itr. V.* (Ballspiele) (vom Rand) take the throw-in; (ins Tor) score

ein·wertig *Adj.* 1 (Chemie) monovalent ‹*atom*› 2 (Sprachw.) one-place ‹*verb*›

ein|wickeln *tr. V.* 1 wrap [up] ‹*article, present*›; **jmdn./sich in etw.** (*Akk.*) **~:** wrap sb./oneself [up] in sth. 2 (ugs.) **jmdn. ~** (überreden) get round sb.; (überlisten) take sb. in

Einwickel·papier *das* wrapping paper

ein|wiegen[1] *tr. V.* **jmdn. ~:** lull sb. to sleep; (in der Wiege) **ein Kind ~:** rock a child to sleep

ein|wiegen[2] *unr. tr. V.* (Kaufmannsspr.) weigh out

ein|willigen *itr. V.* agree, consent (**in** + *Akk.* to); **in ein Angebot ~:** accept an offer

Einwilligung *die;* **~, ~en** agreement; consent; **seine ~ zu etw. geben** give one's consent to sth.; **ihre ~ in das Angebot** her acceptance of the offer

ein|winken *tr. V.* (Verkehrsw.) guide in ‹*aircraft*›; guide *or* direct in ‹*car*›; **ein Auto in eine Parklücke ~:** guide *or* direct a car into a parking space

ein|wirken
A *itr. V.* 1 (beeinflussen) **auf jmdn. ~:** influence sb.; exert *or* have an influence on sb.; **beruhigend auf jmdn. ~:** exert a soothing *or* calming influence on sb. 2 (eine Wirkung ausüben) have an effect (**auf** + *Akk.* on); **man lasse die Creme ~:** let the cream work in
B *tr. V.* (Handarb., Textilw.) work in; **etw. in etw.** (*Akk.*) **~:** work sth. into sth.

Ein·wirkung *die* (Einfluss) influence; (Wirkung) effect; **unter ~ von Drogen stehen** be under the influence of drugs

ein·wöchig *Adj.* one-week *attrib.*; week-old ‹*baby*›; week-long ‹*conference*›

Einwohner *der;* **~s, ~, Einwohnerin** *die;* **~, ~nen** inhabitant; **die Stadt hat 3 Millionen ~:** the town has 3 million inhabitants *or* a population of 3 million

Einwohner·meldeamt *das: local government office for registration of residents*

Einwohnermeldeamt

Anybody who moves to Germany or relocates within Germany is legally obliged to register their address with the *Einwohnermeldeamt* within a week.

Einwohnerschaft *die;* **~:** population; inhabitants *pl.*

Einwohner·zahl *die* population

Ein·wurf *der* 1 (Einwerfen) insertion; (von Briefen) mailing 2 (Ballspiele) throw-in; **ein falscher ~:** a foul throw 3 (Öffnung) (eines Briefkastens) slit; (einer Tür) letter box 4 (Zwischenbemerkung) interjection; (kritisch) objection; **einen kritischen ~ machen** raise an objection

ein|wurzeln *itr.* (*auch refl.*) *V.* root; (fig.) take root

Ein·zahl *die* (Sprachw.) singular

ein|zahlen *tr. V.* pay in; deposit; **Geld auf sein Konto ~:** pay *or* deposit money into one's account; **die Miete ~:** pay in the rent

Ein·zahlung *die* payment; deposit; (Überweisung) payment

Einzahlungs-: ~beleg *der* counterfoil; **~schalter** *der* paying-in counter (Brit.); deposit counter (Amer.); **~schein** *der* pay[ing]-in slip (Brit.); deposit slip

ein|zäunen *tr. V.* fence in; enclose; **ein Grundstück [mit etw.] ~:** fence a property in [with sth.]

Einzäunung *die;* **~, ~en** 1 (das Einzäunen) fencing-in; enclosure 2 (Zaun) fence; enclosure

ein|zeichnen *tr. V.* draw *or* mark in; **etw. in eine Karte ~:** draw *or* mark sth. in on a map

ein·zeilig *Adj.* 1 one-line *attrib.*; *s. auch* **achtzeilig** 2 **eine ~e Küche** a fitted kitchen arranged along one wall

Einzel /ˈaintsl̩/ *das;* **~s, ~** (Sport) singles *pl.*; **der Sieger im ~:** the winner in the singles; **~ spielen** to play a singles match

Einzel-: ~aktion *die* independent action; **~an·fertigung** *die* custom-made article; (Fahrzeug) custom-built model; **~ausgabe** *die* separate edition; **~band** *der* individual *or* single volume; **~bett** *das* single bed; **~buchstabe** *der* (Druckw.) single [piece of] type; single sort; **~darstellung** *die* (eines Themas) individual treatment; (Abhandlung) monograph; **~disziplin** *die* (bes. Leichtathletik) single event; **~erscheinung** *die* isolated occurrence; **~fahrer** *der,* **~fahrerin** *die* (Motorsport) solo rider; **~fahr·schein** *der* single; **~fall** *der* 1 particular case; **im ~fall** in particular cases; 2 (Ausnahme) isolated case; exception; **~feuer** *das* (Milit.) independent fire; **~frage** *die* individual question

Einzelgänger /-gɛŋɐ/ *der;* **~s, ~** 1 solitary person; loner 2 (Tier) lone animal

Einzelgängerin *die;* **~, ~nen** solitary person; loner

Einzelgängertum *das;* **~s** solitariness

Einzel-: ~gehöft *das* solitary farm; **~gewerkschaft** *die* member union; **~grab** *das* separate *or* individual grave; **~haft** *die* solitary confinement

Einzel·handel *der* retail trade; **das kostet im ~ 200 Euro** it retails at 200 euros; **etw. im ~ kaufen** buy sth. retail

Einzelhandels-: ~geschäft *das* retail shop; retail store (Amer.); **~kauffrau** *die* retail saleswoman; **~kaufmann** *der* retail salesman; **~preis** *der* retail price

Einzel-: ~händler *der,* **~händlerin** *die* retailer; retail trader; **~haus** *das* detached house

Einzelheit *die;* **~, ~en** 1 detail 2 (einzelner Umstand) particular; **bis in alle ~en** down to the last detail; **in ~en gehen** go into detail

Einzel-: ~interesse *das* individual interest; **~kind** *das* only child

Einzeller /ˈaintsɛlɐ/ *der;* **~s, ~** (Biol.) unicellular organism

einzellig /ˈaintsɛlɪç/ *Adj.* (Biol.) unicellular; single-cell *attrib.*

einzeln *Adj.* 1 (für sich allein) individual; **die ~en Bände eines Werkes** the individual *or* separate volumes of a work; **jede ~e Insel** each individual island; **ein ~er Schuh/Handschuh** an odd shoe/glove; **jede ~e ist ein Kunstwerk** each individual one is a work of art; **schon ein ~es von diesen Gläsern** just one of these glasses on its own; **„bitte ~ eintreten"** 'please enter one [person] at a time'; **alle Teile ~ verpacken** pack each piece individually; **~ reisen** travel alone *or* on one's own; **wir sind alle ~ gekommen** we all came separately; **sich um jeden ~en Gast kümmern** look after each guest individually; **~ stehend** solitary 2 (allein stehend) solitary ‹*building, tree*›; **eine ~e Dame/ein ~er Herr** a single lady/gentleman 3 *Pl.* (wenige) a few; (einige) some; **~e Regenschauer** scattered *or* isolated showers 4 *substantivisch* (~er Mensch) **der/jeder Einzelne** the/each individual; **als Einzelner** as an individual; **jeder Einzelne der Betroffenen wurde angehört** every [single] one of those concerned was given a hearing; **ein Einzelner** one individual; **für einen Einzelnen geeignet** suitable for one person 5 *substantivisch* **Einzelnes** (manches) some things *pl.*; **das Einzelne** the particular; **vom Einzelnen zum Allgemeinen** from the particular to the general; **etw. im Einzelnen besprechen** discuss sth. in detail; **ins Einzelne gehen** go into detail[s *pl.*]; **bis ins Einzelne** right down to the last detail

einzeln·stehend ▸ **einzeln 1**

Einzel-: ~person *die* one person; individual; **als ~person** as an individual; **~preis** *der* individual price; **~rad·aufhängung** *die* (Kfz-W.) independent suspension; **~richter** *der,* **~richterin** *die* judge sitting singly; **~schicksal** *das* individual fate *or* destiny; **~staat** *der* individual state; **~stück** *das* individual piece *or* item; **~stunde** *die* private lesson; **~teil** *das* individual *or* separate part; **etw. in [seine] ~teile zerlegen** take sth. to pieces; **~therapie** *die* (Med.) individual therapy; **~unterricht** *der* individual tuition; **~wertung** *die* (Sport) individual placings *pl.*; **~wesen** *das* individual [being]; **der Mensch als ~wesen** man as an individual; **~wettbewerb** *der* (Sport) individual event; **~zelle** *die* 1 (für ~haft) single cell; 2 (Biol.) single cell; **~zimmer** *das* single room

ein|zementieren *tr. V.* cement in

einziehbar *Adj.* 1 (Technik) retractable 2 (Finanzw.) recoverable

Einzieh·decke *die* duvet (Brit.); continental quilt (Brit.); stuffed quilt (Amer.)

ein|ziehen

A *unr. tr. V.* 1 put in ‹*duvet*›; thread in ‹*tape, elastic*› 2 (einbauen) put in ‹*wall, ceiling*› 3 (einholen) haul in, pull in ‹*net*›; retract, draw in ‹*feelers, claws*›; **den Kopf ~:** duck; **der Hund zog den Schwanz ein** the dog put its tail between its legs; *s. auch* **Schwanz 1** 4 (einatmen) breathe in ‹*scent, fresh air*›; inhale ‹*smoke*› 5 (einberufen) call up, conscript ‹*recruits*› 6 (beitreiben) collect; **er lässt die Miete vom Konto ~:** he pays his rent by direct debit 7 (beschlagnahmen) confiscate; seize 8 (aus dem Verkehr ziehen) withdraw, call in ‹*coins, banknotes*› 9 (Amtsspr.: einholen) **Informationen/Erkundigungen ~:** gather information/make enquiries 10 (Druckw.) indent ‹*paragraph*›

B *unr. itr. V.; mit sein* 1 (eindringen) ‹*liquid*› soak in 2 (einkehren) enter; **der Frühling zieht ein** (geh.) spring comes *or* arrives; **dann zog bei uns wieder Ruhe ein** then we had peace and quiet again; **ins Parlament ~:** enter parliament 3 (in eine Wohnung) move in

Ein·ziehung *die* 1 (Einberufung) call-up; conscription; drafting (Amer.) 2 (Beitreibung) collection 3 (von Eigentum) confiscation, seizure; (von Münzen, Banknoten usw.) withdrawal

einzig /ˈaintsɪç/

A *Adj.* 1 (alleinig) only; single; (intensivierend nach „ein" od. „kein") single; **der ~e Sohn** the only son; **unser Einziger/unsere Einzige** our only son/daughter; **nur ein Einziger** only one; **nicht ein ~es Stück** not one single piece; **es blieb nur ein ~er Ausweg** there was only one way out; **ihre ~e Freude war ihre Tochter** her daughter was her one and only joy; **das Einzige, was er sah, war ...** the only thing he saw was ... 2 (völlig) complete; absolute; one long ‹*torment*› 3 (geh.: unvergleichlich) unique; unparalleled; **~ in ihrer/seiner Art** unique in her/his/its [own] way

B *adv.* 1 (ganz besonders) singularly; extraordinarily; **ein ~ schöner Tag** an extraordinarily beautiful day 2 (ausschließlich) only; **das ~ Wahre** the only thing; **das ~ Vernünftige/Richtige** the only sensible/right thing [to do]; **~ und allein** nobody/nothing but; solely; **~ ihm wollte sie sich anvertrauen** he was the only one she would confide in

einzig·artig

A *Adj.* unique

B *adv.* uniquely; **~ schön** extraordinarily beautiful

Einzigartigkeit *die,* **Einzigkeit** *die* uniqueness

einzigst... *Adj.* (ugs.) ▸ **einzig A**

Ein·zimmer-: ~apartment *das,* **~appartement** *das,* **~wohnung** *die* one-room flat (esp. Brit.) *or* (esp. Amer.) apartment

ein|zuckern *tr. V.* sprinkle with sugar

Ein·zug *der* 1 entry (**in** + *Akk.* into); **der ~ des Winters** (geh.) the advent of winter; **[seinen] ~ halten** make one's entrance; **mit strahlendem Sonnenschein hielt der Frühling [seinen] ~:** glorious sunshine marked the beginning of spring; **der ~ ins Parlament** entry into parliament 2 (in eine Wohnung) move 3 (Druckw.) indentation

Einzugs-: ~bereich *der,* **~gebiet** *das* catchment area

ein|zwängen *tr. V.* squeeze *or* hem in; ‹*corset*› constrict

Ein·zylinder·motor *der* single-cylinder engine

Eis /ais/ *das;* **~es** 1 ice; **eine Flasche auf ~ legen** put a bottle on ice; **ein Whisky mit ~:** a whisky with ice *or* on the rocks; **etw. auf ~ legen** (fig. ugs.) put sth. on ice; shelve sth.; **jmdn. auf ~ legen** (fig. salopp) put sb. out of harm's way; **~ laufen** ice-skate 2 (Speise~) ice cream; **ein ~ am Stiel** an ice lolly (Brit.) *or* (Amer.) ice pop

Eis-: ~bahn *die* ice rink; **~bär** *der* polar bear; **~behälter** *der* ice bucket; **~becher** *der* 1 (~portion) ice cream sundae; 2 (Gefäß) [ice cream] sundae dish; **~bein** *das* 1 (Kochk.) knuckle of pork; 2 **ich habe ~beine** (ugs. scherzh.) my feet are like ice; **~berg** *der* iceberg; **die Spitze eines ~bergs** the tip of an iceberg; **~beutel** *der* ice bag; ice pack; **~blume** *die* frost flower; **~bombe** *die* (Gastr.) bombe glacée; **~brecher** *der* ice-breaker; **~café** *das* ice cream parlour

Ei·schnee *der* stiffly beaten egg white

Eis-: ~creme *die* ice cream; **~diele** *die* ice cream parlour

Eisen /ˈaizn̩/ *das;* **~s, ~** 1 iron; **aus ~ sein** be made of iron; **die ~ verarbeitende Industrie** the iron-processing industry; **die ~ schaffende Industrie** the iron-and-steel-producing industry 2 (Werkzeug, Werkstück usw., Golf~) iron; (Jägerspr.) trap; **jmdn. in ~ legen** (veralt.) put sb. in irons; (fig.) **ein heißes ~ anfassen** *od.* **anpacken** grasp the nettle; **das ist ein heißes ~:** that is a hot potato; **noch ein/mehrere ~ im Feuer haben** have another iron/several irons in the fire; **man muss das ~ schmieden, solange es heiß ist** (Spr.) strike while the iron is hot (prov.) 3 **jmdn./etw. zum alten ~ werfen** (ugs.) throw sb./sth. on [to] the scrap heap; **zum alten ~ gehören** belong on the scrap heap; **jmdn. zum alten ~ zählen** write sb. off [as too old]

Eisen·bahn *die* 1 railway; railroad (Amer.); **mit der ~ fahren** go *or* travel by train *or* rail; **es ist [die] [aller]höchste ~** (ugs.) it's high time; it's getting late 2 (Bahnstrecke) railway line; railroad track (Amer.) 3 (Verwaltung) railway[s]; railroad (Amer.) 4 (Spielbahn) train *or* railway set

Eisenbahn-: ~abteil *das* railway *or* (Amer.) railroad compartment; **~bau** *der* railway *or* (Amer.) railroad construction; **~brücke** *die* railway bridge; railroad bridge (Amer.)

Eisenbahner *der;* **~s, ~** ▸❶ **S. 113** railwayman; railway worker; railroader (Amer.)

Eisenbahner·gewerkschaft *die* railwaymen's union

Eisenbahnerin *die;* **~, ~nen** ▸❶ **S. 113** railway worker; railroader (Amer.)

Eisenbahner·streik *der* railway *or* (Amer.) railroad strike

Eisenbahn-: ~fähre *die* train ferry; **~gesellschaft** *die* railway *or* (Amer.) railroad company; **~knotenpunkt** *der* railway *or* (Amer.) railroad junction; **~netz** *das* railway *or* (Amer.) railroad network; **~schaffner** *der,* **~schaffnerin** *die* railway guard; railroad conductor (Amer.); **~tunnel** *der* railway *or* (Amer.) railroad tunnel; **~unglück** *das* train crash; **~wagen** *der* railway carriage; railroad car (Amer.); (Güterwagen) railway wagon; railroad car (Amer.); **~waggon** *der* (veralt.) ▸ **~wagen**

eisen-, Eisen-: ~bergwerk *das* iron mine; **~beschlag** *der* piece of ironwork; **~beschläge** ironwork *sing.*; **~beschlagen** *Adj.* ‹*chest, door, gate*› with iron fittings; iron-tipped ‹*boot*›; **~erz** *das* iron ore; **~farbe** *die* ferric oxide paint; **~feilspan** *der* iron filing; **~fresser** *der* (ugs. abwertend) big mouth (coll.); **~gerüst** *das* iron scaffolding *no indef. art.*; **~gießerei** *die* (Verfahren) iron smelting; (Betrieb) iron foundry; **~guss**, ***~guß** *der* (das Gießen) iron casting; (Guss~guss) cast iron; **~haltig** *Adj.* iron-bearing ‹*stone*›; ‹*food*› containing iron; **~hammer** *der* 1 steam hammer; 2 (bild. Kunst) trimming hammer; **~hart** *Adj.* as hard as iron *or* as a rock; (fig.) ‹*person*› as hard as nails; iron ‹*will*›; **~hut** *der* 1 (Bot.) monkshood; wolfsbane; 2 (Hist.) iron hat

Eisen·hütte *die* ironworks *sing. or pl.*; iron foundry

Eisenhütten-: ~industrie *die* iron industry; **~werk** *das* ▸ **Eisenhütte**

eisen-, Eisen-: ~industrie *die* iron industry; **~kern** *der* (Elektrot.) ferrite core; **~kette** *die* iron chain; **~kitt** *der* iron cement; **~kraut** *das* (Bot.) vervain; **~kur** *die* course of iron treatment; **~legierung** *die* iron alloy; **~mangel** *der* (Med.) iron deficiency; **~nagel** *der* iron nail; **~oxid, ~oxyd** *das* (Chemie) iron oxide; **~präparat** *das* iron preparation; **~ring** *der* iron ring; **~säge** *die* hacksaw; **~schaffend** ▸ **Eisen 1**; **~schwamm** *der* (Metall.) sponge iron; **~span** *der* iron filing; **~spat** *der* (Mineral.) siderite; **~stange** *die* iron bar; **~staub** *der* iron filings *pl.*; **~sulfat** *das* (Chemie) ferrous sulphate; **~teil** *das* iron part; **~träger** *der* iron girder; **~verarbeitend** ▸ **Eisen 1**; **~verhüttung** *die* iron smelting; **~vitriol** *das* (Chemie) green vitriol; copperas; ferrous sulphate; **~waren** *Pl.* ironmongery *sing.*; **~waren·händler** *der*, **~waren·händlerin** *die* ▸ⓘ **S. 113** ironmonger; **~zeit** *die* Iron Age

e

eisern /ˈaizɐn/

A *Adj.* **1** (aus Eisen) iron; **~e Lunge** (Med.) iron lung; **der ~e Vorhang** (Theater) the safety curtain; **der Eiserne Vorhang** (Pol.) the Iron Curtain; **das Eiserne Kreuz** the Iron Cross; **die Eiserne Jungfrau** the Iron Maiden **2** (unerschütterlich) iron ‹*discipline*›; unflagging ‹*energy*›; **mit ~em Willen** with a will of iron; **Eiserne Hochzeit** 65th wedding anniversary **3** (unerbittlich) iron; unyielding; iron ‹*discipline*›; **mit ~em Besen [aus]kehren** *od.* **[aus]fegen** make a ruthlessly clean sweep; **der Eiserne Kanzler** the Iron Chancellor **4** (bleibend) **~er Bestand** emergency stock; **eine ~e Reserve** emergency reserves *pl.*; **die ~e Ration** the iron rations *pl.*; (fig.) one's last reserves *pl. or* standby

B *adv.* **1** (unerschütterlich) resolutely; **~ bei etw. bleiben** stick tenaciously to sth.; **~ schweigen** remain resolutely silent; **sich ~ an etw.** (*Akk.*) **halten** keep resolutely to sth.; **~ sparen/trainieren** save/train with iron determination **2** (unerbittlich) **~ Widerstand leisten** put up steadfast resistance; **~ durchgreifen** take drastic measures *or* action; **~ auf Disziplin bedacht sein** insist on iron discipline

Eises·kälte *die* icy cold

eis-, Eis-: ~fach *das* freezing compartment; **~fischerei** *die* ice fishing; **~fläche** *die* sheet *or* surface of ice; **~frau** *die* (ugs.) ice cream woman; **~frei** *Adj.* ice-free; free of ice *postpos.*; **~gang** *der* drift ice; **~gekühlt** *Adj.* iced ‹*drink*›; **~glatt** *Adj.* **1** icy ‹*road*›; **2** /ˈ-ˈ-/ (ugs.) ‹*floor, steps*› as slippery as ice; **~glätte** *die* black ice; **~grau** *Adj.* steely grey; **eine ~graue Alte** a hoary old woman; **~heilige** *in* **die ~heiligen** [*feast days of*] *Three Saints (12, 13, 14 May)*; **~hockey** *das* ice hockey

eisig

A *Adj.* **1** (kalt wie Eis) icy ‹*wind, cold*›; icy [cold] ‹*water*›; **es ist ~:** it's icy cold; it's freezing **2** (kalt ablehnend) frosty, icy ‹*atmosphere*›; frosty ‹*smile*›

B *adv.* **1** **~ kalt** ice-cold ‹*drink*›; freezing cold ‹*weather*› **2** (ablehnend) ‹*smile*› frostily; **~ schweigen** maintain an icy silence; **jmdn. ~ empfangen** give sb. a frosty *or* icy reception

***eisig·kalt** ▸ **eisig B 1**

eis-, Eis-: ~kaffee *der* iced coffee; **~kalt** **A** *Adj.* **1** ice-cold ‹*drink*›; freezing cold ‹*weather*›; **sich ~kalt anfühlen** feel freezing cold; **2** (völlig gefühllos) icy; ice-cold ‹*technocrat, businessman*›; **ein ~kalter Blick** a cold look; **B** *adv.* **1** **es lief mir ~kalt über den Rücken** a cold shiver went down my spine; **2** **etw. ~kalt tun** (kaltblütig) do sth. in cold blood; (lässig) do sth. without turning a hair; **jmdn. ~kalt ansehen/abweisen** give sb. an icy *or* frosty look/ coldly reject sb.'s request; **er ging ~kalt hin und sagte ...** he went over there, cool as you like, and said ...; **~kanal** *der* (Sportjargon) toboggan run; **~karte** *die* (Gastron.) ice cream menu; **~keller** *der* ice cellar; **~kraut** *das* (Bot.) ice plant; **~kristall** *der* ice crystal; **~kübel** *der* ice bucket

Eis·kunst-: ~lauf *der* figure skating; **~laufen** *das* figure skating; **~läufer** *der*, **~läuferin** *die* figure skater

eis-, Eis-: ~lauf *der* ice skating; ***~|laufen** ▸ **Eis 1**; **~laufen** *das;* **~~s** ice skating; **~läufer** *der*, **~läuferin** *die* ice skater; **~mann** *der* (ugs.) ice cream man; **~maschine** *die* ice cream maker; freezer (Amer.); **~meer** *das:* **das Nördliche/Südliche ~meer** the Arctic/Antarctic Ocean; **~pickel** *der* (Bergsteigen) ice pick

Ei·sprung *der* (Physiol.) ovulation

eis-, Eis-: ~regen *der* sleet; **~revue** *die* ice show; **~schicht** *die* layer of ice; **~schießen** *das* (Sport) ▸ **~stock-schießen**; ***~schnellauf** *usw.* ▸ **~schnelllauf** *usw.*; **~schnell·lauf** *der*, **~schnell·laufen** *das;* **~~s** speed skating; **~schnell·läufer** *der*, **~schnell·läuferin** *die* speed skater; **~scholle** *die* ice floe; **~schrank** *der* refrigerator; **~spalte** *die* crevasse; **~sport** *der* ice sports *pl.*; **~stadion** *das* ice rink; **~stock** *der* (Sport) ice stick; **~stock·schießen** *das;* **~~s** (Sport) ice stick shooting; Bavarian curling; **~tanz** *der* (Sport) ice dancing; **~tee** *der* iced tea; **~vogel** *der* **1** kingfisher; **2** (Falter) white admiral; **~waffel** *die* [ice cream] wafer; **~wasser** *das* **1** (~kaltes Wasser) ice-cold water; **2** (Wasser mit ~stücken) iced water; **3** (Schmelzwasser) meltwater; **~wein** *der: wine made from grapes frozen on the vine;* **~würfel** *der* ice cube; **~zapfen** *der* icicle; **~zeit** *die* ice age; **~zeitlich** *Adj.* ice-age *attrib.*, of the ice age *postpos.*

> **Eisschießen, Eisstockschießen**
>
> Ice-stick shooting or Bavarian curling is a popular sport in Bavaria and Austria. Many thousands of enthusiasts meet up every Sunday in winter for matches. There are two kinds of *Eisschießen*: long-distance curling, in which the aim is to slide the ice stick, a heavy metal plate with a handle, as far as possible across the ice (distances of over 200 metres have been achieved); and a more skilful version played on a 42-metre long and 4-metre wide area of ice, in which players slide a metal-plated wooden ice stick as close as possible to the *Daube*, a wooden tee.

eitel /ˈaitl̩/ *Adj.* **1** (abwertend) vain; **~ wie ein Pfau [sein]** [be] as proud as a peacock **2** (veralt.: nichtig) vain ‹*hope*›; futile, vain ‹*endeavour*›; empty, idle ‹*talk*› **3** *indekl.* (veralt.: rein) pure; **~ Freude** pure joy

Eitelkeit *die;* **~, ~en** vanity

Eiter /ˈaitɐ/ *der;* **~s** pus

Eiter-: ~beule *die* boil; abscess; **~herd** *der* pus focus; suppurative focus; **~pickel** *der* spot; pimple

eitern *itr. V.* suppurate

eitrig *Adj.* suppurating; festering

Ei·weiß *das* **1** (des Hühnereis) egg white; albumen; **~ und Dotter trennen** separate the egg white and the yolk; **drei ~:** the whites of three eggs **2** (Chemie, Biol.) protein

eiweiß-, Eiweiß-: ~arm *Adj.* low-protein *attrib.*; low in protein *postpos.*; **~bedarf** *der* protein requirement; **~haltig** *Adj.* ‹*food*› containing protein; **~mangel** *der* protein deficiency; **~reich** *Adj.* high-protein *attrib.*; rich in protein *postpos.*

Ejakulation /ejakulaˈt͜si̯oːn/ *die;* **~, ~en** (Physiol.) ejaculation

EK *Abk.* **1** (EU) **= Europäische Kommission** **2** **= Eisernes Kreuz** Iron Cross

EKD *Abk.* **= Evangelische Kirche in Deutschland**

ekel /ˈeːkl̩/ *Adj.* (veralt.) **1** nauseating; disgusting; vile **2** (verwerflich) nasty; odious

Ekel[1] *der;* **~s** **1** (Abscheu) disgust; loathing; revulsion; **[einen] ~ vor etw.** (*Dat.*) **haben** have a loathing *or* revulsion for sth.; **[ein] ~ packte/erfüllte ihn** he was seized by/filled with disgust *etc.*; **ein ~ stieg in ihr hoch** she was overcome by a feeling of disgust *etc.*; **Ekel erregend** disgusting; nauseating; revolting; **Ekel erregende Krankheiten** diseases which could cause offence **2** (Überdruss) loathing; **einen ~ vor etw. entwickeln** come to loathe sth.

Ekel[2] *das;* **~s, ~** (ugs. abwertend) horror; **er ist ein [altes] ~:** he is a perfect horror *or* quite obnoxious

ekel·erregend *Adj.* ▸ **Ekel**[1] **1**

ekelhaft

A *Adj.* disgusting, revolting, nauseating ‹*sight*›; nasty (coll.), horrible ‹*weather, person*›; **~ riechen/schmecken** smell/taste disgusting *or* revolting

B *adv.* **1** in a disgusting *or* revolting *or* nauseating way **2** (ugs.: sehr) terribly (coll.), dreadfully (coll.) ‹*cold, hot*›

ekeln /ˈeːkl̩n/

A *refl. V.* be *or* feel disgusted *or* sickened; **sie ekelt sich vor Schlangen/Spinnen** *usw.* she finds snakes/spiders *etc.* repulsive; **sich vor jmdm./etw. ~:** find sb./sth. disgusting *or* revolting

B *tr., itr. V.* (unpers.) **es ekelt mich** *od.* **mir ekelt davor** I find it disgusting *or* revolting

C *tr. V.* **1** **Hunde ~ ihn** he finds dogs repulsive **2** (vertreiben) **jmdn. aus dem Haus ~:** hound sb. out of the house

EKG *Abk.* **= Elektrokardiogramm** ECG; **ein ~ machen lassen** have an ECG

Eklat /eˈkla(ː)/ *der;* **~s, ~s** (geh.) (Aufsehen, Skandal) sensation; stir; (Konfrontation) row; altercation; **es kam zum ~:** it came to a row *or* [major] confrontation

eklatant /eklaˈtant/ (geh.)

A *Adj.* **1** (offensichtlich) striking ‹*difference*›; flagrant, scandalous ‹*offence*› **2** (sensationell) sensational; spectacular

B *adv.* flagrantly; **~ gegen etw. verstoßen** be in flagrant breach of sth.

Eklektiker /eˈklɛktikɐ/ *der;* **~s, ~, Eklektikerin** *die;* **~, ~nen** eclectic

eklektisch

A *Adj.* eclectic

B *adv.* eclectically

Eklektizismus /eklɛktiˈt͜sɪsmʊs/ *der;* **~:** eclecticism

eklig /ˈeːklɪç/

A *Adj.* **1** disgusting, revolting, nauseating ‹*sight*›; nasty (coll.), horrible ‹*weather, person*›; **~ riechen/schmecken** smell/taste disgusting *or* revolting **2** (ugs.: gemein) mean; nasty; **sich ~ benehmen** be mean *or* nasty

B *adv.* **1** in a disgusting *or* revolting *or* nauseating way **2** (ugs.: sehr) terribly (coll.), dreadfully (coll.) ‹*hot, cold*›

Eklipse /eˈklɪpsə/ *die;* **~, ~n** (Astron.) eclipse

Ekliptik /eˈklɪptɪk/ *die;* **~, ~en** (Astron.) ecliptic

Ekstase /ɛkˈstaːzə/ *die;* **~, ~n** ecstasy; **in ~ geraten** go into ecstasies; become ecstatic; **jmdn. in ~ versetzen** send sb. into ecstasies; make sb. ecstatic

ekstatisch /ɛkˈstaːtɪʃ/

A *Adj.* ecstatic

B *adv.* ecstatically

Ektoderm /ˈɛktodɛrm/ *das;* **~s, ~e** (Zool.) ectoderm

Ekto·plasma /ɛkto-/ *das* (Biol.; Parapsychologie) ectoplasm

Ekzem *das;* **~s, ~e** (Med.) eczema

ekzematös /ɛkt͜semaˈtøːs/ *Adj.* (Med.) eczematous

EL *Abk.* **= Esslöffel** dessertspoonful

Elaborat /elaboˈraːt/ *das;* **~[e]s, ~e** (geh. abwertend) pathetic concoction

elaboriert *Adj.* (geh.) elaborate ‹*style*›; elaborated; **ein ~er Code** (Sprachw.) an elaborated code

Elan /eˈlaːn/ *der;* **~s** zest; vigour

elan·voll

A *Adj.* zestful; vigorous

B *adv.* zestfully; vigorously

Elaste /eˈlastə/ *Pl.* (Chemie) elastomers

Elastik /e'lastɪk/ *das;* **~s, ~s** *od. die;* **~, ~en** elasticated material; stretch fabric

elastisch
A *Adj.* 1 (dehnbar) elasticated ‹*material*›; springy, resilient ‹*surface*› 2 (geschmeidig) supple, lithe ‹*person, body*› 3 (flexibel) flexible ‹*tactics, rules*›
B *adv.* 1 (geschmeidig) supply; lithely; **sein ~ federnder Gang** his supple *or* lithe walk 2 (flexibel) flexibly

Elastizität /elastitsi'tɛ:t/ *die;* **~** 1 (Dehnbarkeit) elasticity; (Federkraft) springiness 2 (Geschmeidigkeit) suppleness 3 (Flexibilität) flexibility

Elativ /'e:lati:f/ *der;* **~s, ~e** (Sprachw.) absolute superlative; elative

Elb-Florenz /'ɛlp-/ *das* Dresden

Elb·kähne *Pl.* (nordd. scherzh.) clodhoppers (coll.)

Elch /ɛlç/ *der;* **~[e]s, ~e** elk; (in Nordamerika) moose

Elch-: ~bulle *der* bull elk; **~kuh** *die* cow elk; **~test** *der* elk test

Eldorado /ɛldo'ra:do/ *das;* **~s, ~s** eldorado; **ein ~ der** *od.* **für Taucher** (fig.) a divers' paradise

Elefant /ele'fant/ *der;* **~en, ~en** elephant; **wie ein ~ im Porzellanladen** (ugs.) like a bull in a china shop; *s. auch* **Mücke**

Elefanten-: ~baby *das* baby elephant; *s. auch* **~küken**; **~bulle** *der* bull elephant; **~haut** *die* elephant skin; **eine ~haut haben** (fig. ugs.) be thick-skinned; **~herde** *die* elephant herd; **~hochzeit** *die* (Wirtsch. scherzh.) giant merger; **~kuh** *die* cow elephant; **~küken** *das:* **er ist ein richtiges ~küken** (ugs. scherzh.) he looks just like a baby elephant; **~rennen** *das* (ugs. scherzh.) race between two juggernauts

Elefantiasis /elefan'ti:azɪs/ *die;* **~** (Med.) elephantiasis

elefantös /eləfan'tø:s/ *Adj.* 1 elephantine (also fig.); 2 (Jugendspr.) fantastic; wicked (coll.)

elegant /ele'gant/
A *Adj.* 1 (geschmackvoll) elegant, stylish ‹*dress, appearance*›; elegant ‹*society*›; **die ~e Welt** elegant society 2 (harmonisch) elegant, graceful ‹*movement*›; neat ‹*solution*› 3 (kultiviert) elegant, civilized ‹*taste*›; elegant ‹*style*›; civilized ‹*manner*›
B *adv.* elegantly, stylishly ‹*dressed*›; **sich ~ aus der Affäre ziehen** get oneself gracefully out of it

Eleganz /ele'gants/ *die;* **~:** elegance; stylishness; **zeitlose/sportliche/lässige ~:** timeless/sporty/casual elegance

Elegie /ele'gi:/ *die;* **~, ~n** elegy

elegisch /e'le:gɪʃ/
A *Adj.* 1 (Dichtk.) elegiac 2 (fig.: wehmütig) elegiac; mournful; plaintive
B *adv.* **~ gestimmt sein** feel in a mournful mood

elektrifizieren /elɛktrifi'tsi:rən/ *tr. V.* electrify

Elektrifizierung *die;* **~, ~en** electrification

Elektrik /e'lɛktrɪk/ *die;* **~, ~en** electrics *pl.*

Elektriker *der;* **~s, ~**, **Elektrikerin** *die;* **~, ~nen** electrician

elektrisch
A *Adj.* electric ‹*current, light, heating, shock*›; electrical ‹*resistance, wiring, system*›; **der ~e Stuhl** the electric chair
B *adv.* **~ kochen** cook with electricity; **~ geladen sein** be electrically charged; be charged with electricity; **sich ~ rasieren** use an electric shaver

Elektrische *die;* **~n, ~n** (veralt.) tram (Brit.); streetcar (Amer.)

elektrisieren
A *tr. V.* 1 (Med.) treat using electricity 2 (fig.: entflammen) electrify
B *refl. V.* give oneself *or* get an electric shock

Elektrizität /elɛktritsi'tɛ:t/ *die;* **~** (Physik) electricity; (elektrische Energie) electricity; [electric] power

Elektrizitäts-: ~erzeugung *die* generation of electricity; **~gesellschaft** *die* electricity company; **~versorgung** *die* [electric] power supply; **~werk** *das* power station; **~zähler** *der* electricity meter

elektro-, Elektro-: ~antrieb *der* electric drive; **~artikel** *der* electrical appliance; **~auto** *das* electric car; **~chemie** *die* electrochemistry *no art.*; **~chemisch** A *Adj.* electrochemical; B *adv.* electrochemically; **~chirurgie** *die* electrosurgery *no art.*

Elektrode /elɛk'tro:də/ *die;* **~, ~n** electrode

elektro-, Elektro-: ~dynamik *die* (Physik) electrodynamics *sing., no art.*; **~dynamisch** (Physik) A *Adj.* electrodynamic; B *adv.* electrodynamically; **~enzephalogramm** *das* (Med.) electroencephalogram; **~fahrzeug** *das* electric vehicle; **~gerät** *das* electrical appliance; **~geschäft** *das* electrical shop *or* (Amer.) store; **~handwerk** *das* electrical trade; **~herd** *der* electric cooker; **~industrie** *die* electrical goods industry; **~ingenieur** *der,* **~ingenieurin** *die* ▸ⓘ S. 113 electrical engineer; **~installateur** *der,* **~installateurin** *die* ▸ⓘ S. 113 electrical fitter; electrician; **~kardiogramm** *das* (Med.) electrocardiogram; **~karren** *der* electric trolley; **~konzern** *der* electrical company

Elektrolyse /elɛktro'ly:zə/ *die;* **~, ~n** (Chemie, Physik) electrolysis

elektrolysieren *tr. V.* (Chemie) electrolyse

Elektrolyt /elɛktro'ly:t/ *der;* **~en** *od.* **~s, ~en** *od.* **~e** electrolyte

elektrolytisch *Adj.* electrolytic

elektro-, Elektro-: ~magnet *der* electromagnet; **~magnetisch** A *Adj.* electromagnetic; B *adv.* electromagnetically; **~magnetismus** *der* electromagnetism *no art.*; **~mechanik** *die* electrical engineering *no art.*; **~mechanisch** A *Adj.* electromechanical; B *adv.* electromechanically; **~meter** *der* electrometer; **~mobil** *das;* **~s, ~e** electric car; **~monteur** *der,* **~monteurin** *die* ▸**~installateur**; **~motor** *der* electric motor

Elektron /e'lɛktrɔn/ *das;* **~s, ~en** /-'tro:nən/ (Kernphysik) electron

Elektronen-: ~blitz *der* electronic flash; **~blitz·gerät** *das* (Fot.) electronic flash; **~[ge]hirn** *das* (ugs.) electronic brain (coll.); **~hülle** *die* electron shell; **~mikroskop** *das* electron microscope; **~optik** *die* electron optics *sing., no art.*; **~rechner** *der* electronic computer; **~röhre** *die* electron tube *or* valve; **~strahl** *der* (Physik) electron beam; **~theorie** *die* electron theory; **~volt** *das* electron volt

Elektronik /elɛk'tro:nɪk/ *die;* **~** 1 electronics *sing., no art.* 2 (Bestandteile) electronic parts *pl.*; electronics *pl.*

Elektroniker *der;* **~s, ~**, **Elektronikerin** *die;* **~, ~nen** ▸ⓘ S. 113 electronics engineer

Elektronik·schrott *der* scrapped electronic equipment

elektronisch
A *Adj.* electronic
B *adv.* electronically

Elektro-: ~ofen *der* (Technik) electric furnace; **~rasierer** *der* electric shaver *or* razor; **~rasur** *die* shaving *no art.* with an electric shaver *or* razor; **~schock** *der* (Med.) electric shock; **~schweißer** *der,* **~schweißerin** *die* arc welder

Elektroskop /elɛktro'sko:p/ *das;* **~s, ~e** electroscope

elektro-, Elektro-: ~smog *der* (Jargon) electronic smog; **~statisch** A *Adj.* electrostatic; B *adv.* electrostatically; **~technik** *die* electrical engineering *no art.*; **~techniker** *der,* **~technikerin** *die* 1 electronics engineer; 2 (Elektriker[in]) electrician; **~technisch** A *Adj.* electrotechnical; **~technische Industrie** electrical *or* electrotechnical industry; B *adv.* electrotechnically; **~therapie** *die* (Med.) electrotherapy; **~wagen** *der* electric vehicle

Element /ele'mɛnt/ *das;* **~[e]s, ~e** 1 element; **die vier ~e** the four elements; **die entfesselten ~e** (geh.) the raging elements; **er war/fühlte sich in seinem ~:** he was/felt in his element; **zwielichtige/kriminelle ~e** shady/criminal elements; **die ~e der Mathematik/Grammatik** *usw.* the elements *or* rudiments of mathematics/grammar *etc.* 2 (Bauteil) element; (einer Schrankwand) unit 3 (Elektrot.) cell; battery

elementar /elemɛn'ta:ɐ̯/
A *Adj.* 1 (grundlegend) fundamental ‹*requirement, right, condition, insight, significance*› 2 (einfach) elementary, rudimentary ‹*knowledge*›; **ihm fehlen die ~sten Kenntnisse** he lacks the most elementary *or* rudimentary knowledge 3 (naturhaft) elemental ‹*force, forces*›
B *adv.* with elemental force

Elementar-: ~begriff *der* elementary *or* basic concept; **~gewalt** *die* elemental force; **~kenntnisse** *Pl.* elementary *or* rudimentary knowledge *sing.*; **~mathematik** *die* elementary mathematics *sing., no art.*; **~stufe** *die* (Schulw.) preschool level; **~teilchen** *das* (Physik) elementary particle; **~unterricht** 1 (Einführungsunterricht) elementary instruction; 2 (Unterricht in der ~stufe) preschool teaching

Elen /'e:lɛn/ *das od. der;* **~s, ~** ▸**Elch**

elend /'e:lɛnt/
A *Adj.* 1 wretched, miserable ‹*existence, life, conditions, environment*›; **eines ~en Todes sterben** die a miserable death 2 (krank) **sich ~ fühlen** feel wretched *or* (coll.) awful; **mir ist/wird ~:** I feel/I am beginning to feel awful *or* terrible (coll.) 3 (gemein) despicable ‹*person, coward, allegation*› 4 (ugs.: besonders groß) dreadful (coll.) ‹*hunger, pain*›
B *adv.* 1 (jämmerlich) wretchedly; miserably; **~ zugrunde gehen** come to a miserable *or* wretched end 2 (ugs.: intensivierend) dreadfully (coll.)

Elend *das;* **~s** 1 (Leid) misery; wretchedness; **das ganze Leben ist ein ~:** life is just a complete misery; **es ist ein ~ mit ihm** (ugs.) he's enough to drive you to despair; **das heulende ~ kriegen** (ugs.) start blubbering hysterically; **..., da kann man das heulende ~ kriegen** it's enough to make you weep; **wie das leibhaftige ~ aussehen** (ugs.) look like death warmed up (coll.); **ein langes ~** (ugs. scherzh.) a beanpole; *s. auch* **Häufchen** 2 (Armut) misery; destitution; **jmdn. ins ~ stürzen** plunge sb. into misery

elendig, elendiglich *Adv.* (geh.) miserably; wretchedly; **~ zugrunde gehen** perish miserably; come to a wretched *or* miserable end

Elends-: ~gestalt *die* [poor] wretch; wretched figure; **~quartier** *das* slum [dwelling]; **~viertel** *das* slum area

Eleve /e'le:və/ *der;* **~n, ~n**, **Elevin** *die;* **~, ~nen** 1 (Theater, Ballett) student 2 (Land- und Forstwirtsch.) trainee 3 (veralt. geh.: Schüler, Jünger) acolyte; disciple

elf /ɛlf/ *Kardinalz.* ▸ⓘ S. 29, ▸ⓘ S. 729, ▸ⓘ S. 826 eleven; *s. auch* **acht**[1]

Elf[1] *die;* **~, ~en** 1 eleven; *s. auch* **Acht**[1] **1, 5, 7** 2 (Sport) team; side

Elf[2] *der;* **~en, ~en** elf

Elfe /'ɛlfə/ *die;* **~, ~n** fairy

Elfen·bein *das* ivory; **schwarzes ~** (fig.) black ivory

Elfenbein·arbeit *die* ivory piece

elfen·beinern *Adj.* ivory

elfenbein-, Elfenbein-: ~farben *Adj.* ivory-coloured; **~küste** *die* Ivory Coast; **~schnitzerei** *die* 1 ivory carving; 2 (Gegenstand) ivory carving; **~turm** *der* (fig.) ivory tower

elfenhaft *Adj.* elfish; elfin

Elfen-: ~königin *die* elfin queen; fairy queen; **~reigen** *der* fairy dance

Elfer *der;* **~s, ~** 1 (Fußballjargon) penalty 2 (landsch.: Zahl Elf) eleven 3 (Buslinie) number eleven

elferlei *indekl. Gattungsz.* 1 *attr.* eleven kinds *or* sorts of; eleven different ‹*sorts, kinds, sizes,* possibilities› [2] *subst.* eleven [different] things

Ẹlfer-: ~rat *der: carnival committee consisting of eleven members;* **~wette** *die* (Sport) *football pools [entry] requiring eleven selections;* **er hat sieben Richtige in der ~wette** he's got seven out of eleven on the pools

ẹlf-: ~fach *Vervielfältigungsz.* elevenfold; **die ~fache Menge** eleven times the amount; *s. auch* **achtfach**; **~mal** *Wiederholungsz.* eleven times; *s. auch* **achtmal**

Elf·meter *der* (Fußball) penalty; **einen ~ schießen** take a penalty

Elfmeter-: ~punkt *der* (Fußball) penalty spot; **~schießen** *das;* **~~s** (Fußball) **durch ~schießen** by *or* on penalties; **es gab ein ~schießen** it was decided on penalties; **~schütze** *der,* **~schützin** *die* (Fußball) penalty taker; **~tor** *das* (Fußball) penalty

elft *in* **wir waren zu ~:** there were eleven of us; *s. auch* **acht²**

ẹlft... *Ordinalz.* **►ⓘ S. 165**, **►ⓘ S. 826** eleventh; *s. auch* **acht...**

elf·tausend *Kardinalz.* eleven thousand

Elftel /ˈɛlftl̩/ *das;* **~s, ~:** eleventh

***ẹlfte·mal, *elftenmal** **►Mal¹**

ẹlftens *Adv.* eleventh

elidieren /eliˈdiːrən/ *tr. V.* [1] (geh.: streichen) delete [2] (Sprachw.) elide

Elimination /eliminaˈt͡si̯oːn/ *die;* **~, ~en** elimination

eliminieren /elimiˈniːrən/ *tr. V.* eliminate

Eliminierung *die;* **~, ~en** elimination

Elisabeth /eˈliːzabɛt/ *(die)* Elizabeth

elisabethanisch *Adj.* Elizabethan

Elision /eliˈzi̯oːn/ *die;* **~, ~en** elision

elitär /eliˈtɛːɐ̯/

[A] *Adj.* [1] elitist; **ein ~es Bewusstsein** an elite-awareness [2] (zu einer Elite gehörend) elite *attrib.*

[B] *adv.* **er denkt/verhält sich ~:** he thinks/behaves in an elitist fashion

Elite /eˈliːtə/ *die;* **~, ~n** elite; **die ~ der Sportler** the sporting elite

Elite-: ~denken *das* elitist thinking; elitism; **~truppe** *die* (Milit.) elite *or* crack force

Elixier /elɪˈksiːɐ̯/ *das;* **~s, ~e** elixir

Ẹll·bogen *der;* **~s, ~ ►ⓘ S. 435** elbow; **er/sie hat keine ~** (fig. ugs.) he/she isn't pushy enough (coll.)

Ẹllbogen-: ~freiheit *die* elbow room; **~gesellschaft** *die* (abwertend) society where the weakest go to the wall; **~mensch** *der* (abwertend) pushy individual (ugs.)

Ẹlle /ˈɛlə/ *die;* **~, ~n** [1] **►ⓘ S. 435** (Anat.) ulna [2] (frühere Längeneinheit) cubit [3] (veralt.: Maßstock) ≈ yardstick; **alles mit einer ~ messen** (fig.) measure everything by the same yardstick

Ẹllen·bogen **►Ellbogen**

ẹllen·lang *Adj.* (ugs.) ‹*list*› as long as your arm; interminable ‹*lecture, sermon*›; terribly long (coll.) ‹*letter*›

Ellipse /ɛˈlɪpsə/ *die;* **~, ~n** ellipse; (Sprachw., Rhet.) ellipsis

Ellipsen·bahn *die* elliptical orbit

ellipsen·förmig

[A] *Adj.* elliptical

[B] *adv.* elliptically

elliptisch /ɛˈlɪptɪʃ/

[A] *Adj.* elliptical

[B] *adv.* elliptically

Elms·feuer /ˈɛlms-/ *das* (Met.) St. Elmo's fire

Eloge /eˈloːʒə/ *die;* **~, ~n** (geh.) eulogy

E-Lok *die* (veralt.) electric locomotive *or* engine

eloquent /eloˈkvɛnt/ (geh.)

[A] *Adj.* eloquent

[B] *adv.* eloquently

Eloquenz *die;* **~** (geh.) eloquence

Elritze /ˈɛlrɪt͡sə/ *die;* **~, ~n** (Zool.) minnow

Elsass, *Elsaß /ˈɛlzas/ *das;* **~** *od.* **Ẹlsasses** Alsace; **im/aus dem ~:** in/from Alsace

Elsässer /ˈɛlzɛsɐ/

[A] *indekl. Adj.* Alsatian

[B] *der;* **~s, ~:** Alsatian

Ẹlsässerin *die;* **~, ~nen** Alsatian; *s. auch* **-in**

ẹlsässisch *Adj.* Alsatian

Ẹlsass-Lothringen, *Elsaß-Lothringen *(das)* (hist.) Alsace-Lorraine

Elstar /ˈɛlstar/ *der;* **~, ~** Elstar [apple]

Elster /ˈɛlstɐ/ *die;* **~, ~n** (Zool.) magpie; **wie eine ~ stehlen** be light-fingered; **eine diebische ~** (fig.) a pilferer

Elter /ˈɛltɐ/ *das od. der;* **~s, ~n** (Biol.) parent

ẹlterlich *Adj.* parental

Ẹltern *Pl.* parents; **nicht von schlechten ~ sein** (fig. ugs.) be quite something

ẹltern-, Ẹltern-: ~abend *der* (Schulw.) parents' evening; **~aktiv** *das* (DDR: Schulw.) parents' committee; **~bei·rat** *der* (Schulw.) parents' association; **~haus** *das* parental home; **aus einem armen/katholischen ~haus kommen** come from a poor/Catholic home; **~liebe** *die* parental love; **~los** [A] *Adj.* parentless; orphaned; **ein ~loses Kind** a child without parents; an orphan; [B] *adv.* **~los aufwachsen** grow up an orphan *or* without parents

Ẹlternschaft *die;* **~** [1] (Schulw.) parents' association [2] (Elternsein) parenthood; **geplante ~:** planned parenthood

Ẹltern-: ~sprech·tag *der* parents' day; **~teil** *der* parent; **~versammlung** *die* parents' meeting; **~zeit** *die* [period of] parental leave

> **Elternzeit**
>
> A German mother or father who looks after a child at home is entitled to up to three years' extended maternity or paternity leave. At the end of this *Elternzeit* (formerly called *Erziehungsurlaub*) they are entitled to return to their old job. Around 95% of German mothers take time out of work for at least one year after the birth.

elysäisch /elyˈzɛːɪʃ/, **elysisch** /eˈlyːzɪʃ/ *Adj.* (dichter.) Elysian

Elysium /eˈlyːzi̯ʊm/ *das;* **~s, Elysien** /eˈlyːzi̯ən/ (dichter.) Elysium

EM *Abk.* **= Europameisterschaft[en]**

Email /eˈmai̯/ *das;* **~s, ~s, Emaille** /eˈmaljə/ *die;* **~, ~n** enamel

E-Mail /ˈiːmeːl/ *die;* **~, ~s** (DV) email

Email[le]-: ~arbeit *die* (Kunst) [1] enamel; [2] (**~malerei**) enamel painting; **~geschirr** *das* enamelware; **~waren** *Pl.* enamelware *sing.*

emaillieren *tr. V.* enamel

E-Mail-Wurm *der* e-mail worm

Emanation /emanaˈt͡si̯oːn/ *die;* **~, ~en** (Philos.) emanation

Emanze /eˈmant͡sə/ *die;* **~, ~n** (ugs., auch abwertend) women's libber (coll.)

Emanzipation /emant͡sipaˈt͡si̯oːn/ *die;* **~, ~en** emancipation; **die ~ der Frau** the emancipation *or* liberation of women

Emanzipations·bewegung *die* liberation movement

emanzipatorisch /emant͡sipaˈtoːrɪʃ/ *Adj.* (geh.) emancipatory ‹*education*›

emanzipieren /emant͡siˈpiːrən/

[A] *refl. V.* **sich [von jmdm./etw.] ~:** emancipate oneself [from sb./sth.]

[B] *tr. V.* emancipate

emanzipiert *Adj.* emancipated; emancipated, liberated ‹*woman*›

Embargo /ɛmˈbargo/ *das;* **~s, ~s** embargo

Emblem /ɛmˈbleːm/ *das;* **~s, ~e** emblem

Embolie /ɛmboˈliː/ *die;* **~, ~n** (Med.) embolism

Embonpoint /ãbõˈpo̯ɛ̃ː/ *der od. das;* **~s** (geh. scherzh.) embonpoint

Embryo /ˈɛmbryo/ *der;* **~s, ~nen** /-yˈoːnən/ *od.* **~s** embryo

Embryoblast *der;* **~en, ~en** (Biol.) cyst

embryonal *Adj.* (Med., Biol., fig.) embryonic

Embryonen-: ~forschung *die* (Gentechnik) embryo research; **~schutz** *der* embryo protection; **~schutz·gesetz** *das* Embryo Protection Act

Emendation /emɛndaˈt͡si̯oːn/ *die;* **~** (Literaturw.) emendation

emeritieren /emeriˈtiːrən/ *tr. V.* confer emeritus status on; **ein emeritierter Professor** an emeritus professor; a professor emeritus

Emeritierung *die;* **~, ~en seit seiner ~:** since he has been an emeritus professor

Emeritus /eˈmeːritʊs/ *der;* **~, Emeriti** (geh.) emeritus professor

Emigrant /emiˈgrant/ *der;* **~en, ~en** emigrant; (Flüchtling) emigré

Emigranten·presse *die* emigré press

Emigrantin *die;* **~, ~nen ►Emigrant**

Emigration /emigraˈt͡si̯oːn/ *die;* **~, ~en** [1] (das Emigrieren) emigration; **die innere ~:** inner emigration (*particularly during the Nazi period in Germany*) [2] (die Fremde) exile; **in der ~ leben** live in exile [3] (die Emigranten) emigrés *pl.*

emigrieren /emiˈgriːrən/ *itr. V.; mit sein* emigrate

eminent /emiˈnɛnt/

[A] *Adj.* (geh.) eminent; **von ~er Bedeutung sein** be of the utmost significance

[B] *adv.* eminently; **das ist ~ wichtig** that is of the utmost importance

Eminenz /emiˈnɛnt͡s/ *die;* **~, ~en ►ⓘ S. 44** (kath. Kirche) eminence; **Eure/Seine ~:** Your/His Eminence; **eine graue ~:** an éminence grise; a grey eminence

Emir /ˈeːmɪr/ *der;* **~s, ~e** emir

Emirat *das;* **~[e]s, ~e** emirate

Emissär /emɪˈsɛːɐ̯/ *der;* **~s, ~e** emissary

Emission /emɪˈsi̯oːn/ [1] (Physik, Ökologie) emission [2] (Ausgabe [von Briefmarken, Wertpapieren]) issue

emissions·arm *Adj.* low-emission; **~ sein** be low in emissions

Emissions·schutz·gesetz *das* anti-pollution law

Emitter /eˈmɪtɐ/ *der;* **~s, ~** (Technik) emitter

emittieren *tr. V.* [1] (Finanzw.) issue [2] (in die Luft abblasen) emit

EMK *Abk.* **= Europäische Menschenrechtskonvention** (EU) ECHR

Emmchen /ˈɛmçən/ *Pl.* (ugs. veralt.) marks

Emmentaler /ˈɛmɛntaːlɐ/ *der;* **~s, ~:** Emmenthal [cheese]

e-Moll *das* E minor; *s. auch* **a-Moll**

Emotion /emoˈt͡si̯oːn/ *die;* **~, ~en** emotion

emotional

[A] *Adj.* emotional ‹*person, reaction, etc.*›; emotive ‹*topic, question*›

[B] *adv.* emotionally

emotionalisieren *tr. V.* (geh.) arouse emotions in, emotionalize ‹*person*›; emotionalize ‹*issue*›

Emotionalität *die;* **~:** emotionalism; emotionality

emotionell *Adj.* **►emotional**

emotions·geladen *Adj.* emotionally charged

E-Motor *der* electric motor

Empathie /ɛmpaˈtiː/ *die;* **~** (Psych.) empathy

empfahl /ɛmˈpfaːl/ *1. u. 3. Pers. Sg. Prät. v.* **empfehlen**

empfand /ɛmˈpfant/ *1. u. 3. Pers. Sg. Prät. v.* **empfinden**

Empfang /ɛmˈpfaŋ/ *der;* **~[e]s, Empfänge** [1] (Entgegennahme) receipt; **bei ~:** on receipt; **etw. in ~ nehmen** accept sth.; **mit einer Strafpredigt in ~ genommen werden** (iron.) be welcomed *or* greeted with a dressing-down; **zahlbar bei ~:** payable on receipt [2] (Funkw., Rundf., Ferns.) reception; **auf ~ gehen/bleiben** (Funkw.) switch over to 'receive'/stay on 'receive' [3] (geh.: Begrüßung) reception [4] (festliche Veranstaltung) reception [5] (Rezeption) reception [desk]

empfangen
A *unr. tr. V.* **1** (geh.) receive; **einen Gast bei sich ~:** receive a guest at home; **die Sakramente ~** (Rel.) receive the sacraments **2** (Funkw., Rundf., Ferns.) receive **3** (begrüßen) receive, greet ‹*person*›; **jmdn. mit Blumen ~:** greet sb. with flowers **4** (geh.: angeregt werden zu) conceive ‹*idea*›; **eine Anregung [von jmdm.] ~:** receive a stimulus from sb. **5** (geh.) **ein Kind ~:** conceive a child
B *unr. itr. V.* (geh.: schwanger werden) conceive

-empfänger *der* (Renten~ usw.) recipient of …

Empfänger /ɛmˈpfɛŋɐ/ *der;* **~s, ~ 1** recipient; (eines Briefs) addressee; **~ unbekannt/verzogen/unbekannt verzogen** not known at this address/gone away/gone away, address unknown **2** (Empfangsgerät) receiver

Empfängerin *die;* **~, ~nen** ▸**Empfänger 1**

empfänglich *Adj.* **1** (leicht zugänglich) receptive (**für** to) **2** (beeinflussbar) susceptible; **für jmds. Charme/Schönheit ~ sein** be susceptible to sb.'s charm/beauty

Empfänglichkeit *die;* **~ 1** (Zugänglichkeit) receptivity, receptiveness (**für** to) **2** (Beeinflussbarkeit) susceptibility (**für** to)

Empfängnis *die;* **~:** conception

empfängnis·verhütend *Adj.* **ein ~es Mittel** a contraceptive; **~ wirken** act as a contraceptive

Empfängnis·verhütung *die* contraception

Empfängnisverhütungs·mittel *das* contraceptive

Empfängnis·zeit (Rechtsw.) time of conception

empfangs-, Empfangs-: ~antenne *die* (Rundf., Ferns.) [receiving] aerial (Brit.) *or* (Amer.) antenna; **~berechtigt** *Adj.* authorized to receive payment/goods *postpos.;* **eine ~berechtigte Person** an authorized recipient; **~bereich** *der* (Rundf., Ferns.) reception area; **~bereit** *Adj.* (Rundf., Ferns.) ready to receive programmes; (Fernspr.) ready to receive calls/faxes; **~bestätigung** *die* receipt; **~chef** *der* head receptionist; **~dame** *die* receptionist; **~gerät** *das* (Funkw., Rundf., Ferns.) receiver; **~halle** *die* reception lobby; **~saal** *der* reception hall; **~station** *die* (Funkw., Rundf., Ferns.) receiving station; (Raumfahrt) tracking station; **~zimmer** *das* reception room

empfehlen /ɛmˈpfe:lən/
A *unr. tr. V.* **1** **jmdm. etw./jmdn. ~:** recommend sth./sb. to sb.; **der empfohlene Richtpreis** (Wirtsch.) the recommended price; **~ Sie mich Ihrer Gattin** (geh.) convey my respects to your wife; **dieser Arzt/dies ist sehr zu ~:** this doctor/this is to be highly recommended **2** (veralt.: anvertrauen) commend (*Dat.* to)
B *unr. refl. V.* **1** (geh.: sich verabschieden und gehen) take one's leave; **darf ich mich ~?** may I take my leave? **2** (unpers.) **es empfiehlt sich, … zu …** it's advisable to … **3** (geh.: sich als geeignet erweisen) **sich [durch/wegen etw.] ~:** commend oneself/itself [because of sth.]

empfehlens·wert *Adj.* **1** to be recommended *postpos.;* recommendable **2** (ratsam) advisable

Empfehlung *die;* **~, ~en 1** recommendation; **sie kam auf ~:** she came on somebody's recommendation **2** (~sschreiben) letter of recommendation; testimonial **3** (höflicher Gruß) **„eine ~ an Ihre Frau Mutter"** '[kind] regards to your mother'; **„mit freundlicher ~"** 'with kindest regards'

Empfehlungs·schreiben *das* letter of recommendation; testimonial

empfiehl /ɛmˈpfi:l/ *Imperativ Sg. v.* **empfehlen**

empfiehlst *2. Pers. Sg. Präsens v.* **empfehlen**

empfiehlt *3. Pers. Sg. Präsens v.* **empfehlen**

empfinden /ɛmˈpfɪndn̩/ *unr. tr. V.* **1** (wahrnehmen) feel ‹*pain, pleasure, bitterness, etc.*›; **etwas/nichts für jmdn. ~:** feel something/nothing for sb. **2** (auffassen) **etw. als Beleidigung ~:** feel sth. to be an insult; **jmdn. als Eindringling ~:** feel sb. to be an impostor; **das empfinde ich nicht so** I feel differently about it

Empfinden *das;* **~s** feeling; **für mein** *od.* **nach meinem ~:** to my mind

empfindlich
A *Adj.* **1** (sensibel, feinfühlig, auch fig.) sensitive; **hoch ~:** highly sensitive; fast ‹*film*›; **eine ~e Stelle** a tender spot **2** (leicht beleidigt) sensitive, touchy ‹*person*› **3** (anfällig) **zart und ~:** delicate; **~ gegen Viruserkrankungen** prone to virus infections **4** (spürbar) severe ‹*punishment, shortage*›; harsh ‹*punishment, measure*›; sharp ‹*increase*›
B *adv.* **1** **~ auf etw.** (*Akk.*) **reagieren** (sensibel) be susceptible to sth.; (beleidigt) react oversensitively to sth. **2** (spürbar) ‹*punish*› severely, harshly; ‹*increase*› sharply **3** (intensivierend) ‹*hurt*› badly; bitterly ‹*cold*›; **der Streik machte sich für die Verbraucher sofort ~ bemerkbar** the strike had an immediate effect on the consumers

Empfindlichkeit *die;* **~, ~en** ▸**empfindlich:** sensitivity; touchiness; severity; harshness; (eines Films) speed; **ihre ~ gegen Infektionen** her proneness *or* susceptibility to infections

empfindsam
A *Adj.* sensitive ‹*nature*›; (gefühlvoll) sentimental
B *adv.* sensitively; (gefühlvoll) sentimentally

Empfindsamkeit *die;* **~:** sensitivity; (Literaturw.) sentimentality

Empfindung *die;* **~, ~en 1** (sinnliche Wahrnehmung) sensation; sensory perception **2** (Gefühl) feeling; emotion

empfindungs-, Empfindungs-: ~los *Adj.* **1** (körperlich) numb; without sensation *pred.;* **2** (seelisch) insensitive; unfeeling; **~losigkeit** *die;* **~~ 1** (körperlich) numbness; lack of sensation; **2** (Gefühlskälte) insensitivity; lack of feeling; **~nerv** *der* sensory nerve; **~vermögen** *das* **1** (physisch) sensory perception; **2** (seelisch) sensitivity

empfing /ɛmˈpfɪŋ/ *1. u. 3. Pers. Sg. Prät. v.* **empfangen**

empfohlen /ɛmˈpfo:lən/
A *2. Part. v.* **empfehlen**
B *Adj.* recommended

empfunden /ɛmˈpfʊndn̩/ *2. Part. v.* **empfinden**

Emphase /ɛmˈfa:zə/ *die;* **~, ~n** (geh.) emphasis

emphatisch /ɛmˈfa:tɪʃ/
A *Adj.* (geh.) emphatic
B *adv.* emphatically

Empire[1] /ãˈpi:ɐ̯/ *das;* **~[s]** Empire

Empire[2] /ˈɛmpaɪə/ *das;* **~[s]** (Hist.) Empire

Empire·stil /ãˈpi:ɐ̯-/ *der* Empire style

Empirie /ɛmpiˈri:/ *die;* **~ 1** (Methode) empirical method **2** (Erfahrungswissen) empirical knowledge

Empiriker *der;* **~s, ~, Empirikerin** *die;* **~, ~nen** empiricist

empirisch
A *Adj.* empirical
B *adv.* empirically

Empirismus *der;* **~:** empiricism

empor /ɛmˈpo:ɐ̯/ *Adv.* (geh.) upwards; up

empor-: ~|arbeiten *refl. V.* (geh.) work one's way up; **~|blicken** *itr. V.* (geh.) look upwards *or* (literary) heavenwards; **zum Himmel ~blicken** raise one's eyes heavenwards (literary)

Empore *die;* **~, ~n** gallery

empören /ɛmˈpø:rən/
A *tr. V.* fill with indignation; incense; outrage
B *refl. V.* **1** (zornig werden) **sich über jmdn./etw. ~:** become indignant *or* incensed *or* outraged about sb./sth. **2** (geh.: sich auflehnen) **sich gegen jmdn./etw. ~:** rebel *or* rise against sb./sth.

empörend
A *Adj.* outrageous
B *adv.* outrageously

Empörer *der;* **~s, ~, Empörerin** *die;* **~, ~nen** (geh.) rebel

empörerisch *Adj.* (geh.) rebellious

empor-: ~|heben *unr. tr. V.* (geh.) raise; **~|kommen** *unr. itr. V.; mit sein* (geh.) **1** (nach oben kommen) come up; **2** (fig.: aufsteigen) rise

Emporkömmling /-kœmlɪŋ/ *der;* **~s, ~e** (abwertend) upstart; parvenu

empor-: ~|ragen *itr. V.* (geh.) rise [up]; **über etw.** (*Akk.*) **~ragen** tower above sth.; **~|recken A** *tr. V.* (geh.) raise; **B** *refl. V.* rise; **~|schauen** *itr. V.* (geh.) raise one's eyes; **~|schwingen** *unr. refl. V.* (geh.) **sich ~schwingen** swing oneself aloft; **sich zu großen Taten ~schwingen** (fig.) rise to great deeds; **~|steigen** *unr. itr. V.; mit sein* (geh.) **1** climb up; **an etw.** (*Dat.*) **~steigen** climb [up] sth.; **einen Berg/die Treppe ~steigen** climb a mountain/the stairs; **2** ‹*balloon, kite*› rise aloft; **~|streben** *itr. V.; mit sein* (geh.) soar upwards; **ein ~strebender Künstler** an aspiring artist

empört
A *Adj.* outraged ‹*letter, look*›; **über jmdn./etw. ~ sein** be outraged about sb./at *or* about sth.
B *adv.* **jmdn./etw. ~ zurückweisen** reject sb./sth. indignantly *or* angrily

Empörung *die;* **~, ~en 1** outrage **2** (geh.: Aufstand) rebellion; uprising

empor|züngeln *itr. V.; mit sein* (geh.) ‹*flames*› leap up

emsig /ˈɛmzɪç/
A *Adj.* (fleißig) industrious, busy ‹*person*›; (geschäftig) bustling ‹*activity*›; (übereifrig) sedulous; **ein ~es Treiben** bustling activity; a hustle and bustle; **~ wie die Ameisen** *od.* **Bienen sein** be busy as bees
B *adv.* (fleißig) industriously; busily; (übereifrig) sedulously

Emsigkeit *die;* **~** (Fleiß) industriousness; business; (Übereifer) sedulousness

Emu /ˈe:mu/ *der;* **~s, ~s** (Zool.) emu

Emulgator /emʊlˈga:tɔr/ *der;* **~s, ~en** /-gaˈto:rən/ (Chemie) emulsifying agent; emulsifier

Emulsion /emʊlˈzi̯o:n/ *die;* **~, ~en** (Chemie, Fot., Kosmetik) emulsion

E-Musik *die;* **~:** serious music

en bloc /ãˈblɔk/ *Adv.* en bloc

end-, End-: ~abnehmer *der,* **~abnehmerin** *die* (Wirtsch.) ultimate buyer; **~abrechnung** *die* final account; **~achtziger**[1] *der;* **~~s, ~~:** man in his late eighties; **~achtziger**[2] *Pl.* **die ~achtziger:** the late eighties; **~achtzigerin** *die* **~~, ~~nen** woman in her late eighties; **~bahnhof** *der* terminus; **~betont** *Adj.* (Sprachw.) ‹*word*› with final stress; **das Wort „Berlin" ist ~betont** the word 'Berlin' is stressed on the final syllable; **~betonung** *die* (Sprachw.) final stress; **~betrag** *der* final amount

Endchen *das;* **~s, ~:** little bit; small piece

End·darm *der* ▸**i S. 435** (Anat.) (Dickdarm) large intestine; colon; (Afterdarm) rectum

End-: ~dreißiger[1] *der;* **~~s, ~~:** man in his late thirties; **~dreißiger**[2] *Pl.* **die ~dreißiger** the late thirties; **~dreißigerin** *die;* **~~, ~~nen** woman in her late thirties

Ende /ˈɛndə/ *das;* **~s, ~n** ▸**i S. 29,** ▸**i S. 165**
1 end; **am ~ der Straße/Stadt** at the end of the road/town; **am ~ der Welt** (scherzh.) at the back of beyond; **etw. am richtigen/falschen ~ anfassen** (fig.) go about sth. the right/wrong way; **am/bis/gegen ~ des Monats/der Woche/des Jahres/des Jahrhunderts** at/by/towards the end of the month/week/year/century; **~ April** at the end of April; **bis ~ der Woche** by the end of the week; **am ~ des Buchs/Films** at the end of the book/film; **das ~ des Films hat mir nicht gefallen** I didn't like the ending of the film; **~ zwanzig** *od.* **der Zwanziger/fünfzig** *od.* **der Fünfziger sein** be in one's late twenties/fifties; **wenn die beiden sich zanken, finden sie kein ~:** once those two start quarrelling they never stop; **zu ~ sein** ‹*patience, hostility, war*› be at an end; **die Schule/das Kino/das Spiel ist zu ~:** school is over/the film/game has finished; **zu ~ gehen** ‹*period of time*› come to an end; ‹*supplies, savings*› run out; ‹*contract*› expire; **etw. zu**

~ **führen** *od.* **bringen** finish sth.; **ein Buch zu ~ lesen** read a book to the end; **alles hat ein ~** *od.* **muss ein ~ haben** everything has to [come to an] end sometime; **~ gut, alles gut** all's well that ends well (prov.); **ein/kein ~ nehmen** come to an end/never come to an end; **einer Sache/seinem Leben ein ~ machen** *od.* **setzen** (geh.) put an end to sth./take one's life; **am ~ sein** (ugs.) be at the end of one's tether; **ich bin mit meiner Geduld am ~:** my patience is at an end; **mit etw. am ~ sein** be at *or* have reached the end of sth.; **mit ihm geht es zu ~** (verhüll.) he is nearing his end; **das ~ vom Lied** (ugs.) the end of the story; **am ~** (schließlich) when all is said and done; **am ~ wird er der Täter sein** (nordd.) he's probably the culprit; **das ~ der Wurst** the end [piece] of the sausage **2** (ugs.: kleines Stück) bit; piece; **ein ~ Schnur** a bit *or* piece of string **3** (ugs.: Strecke) **ein ganzes ~:** a pretty long way **4** (Jägerspr.) point **5** (Seemannsspr.) rope

End·effekt *der:* **im ~:** in the end; in the final analysis

endeln /ˈɛndl̩n/ *tr. V.* (bayr., österr.) turn in [and oversew] ‹*hem, seam*›

endemisch /ɛnˈdeːmɪʃ/
A *Adj.* (Biol., Med.) endemic
B *adv.* endemically

enden *itr. V.* **1** end; ‹*programme*› end, finish; **der Zug endet in Berlin/hier** this train terminates in Berlin/here; **gut ~:** end well; **das wird nicht gut ~:** it's bound to end in disaster; **nicht ~ wollender Beifall** unending applause **2** (sterben) *mit sein* **in der Gosse/im Gefängnis ~:** end up in the gutter/in prison; (dort sterben) die in the gutter/end one's days in prison

End·ergebnis *das* final result

en détail /ãdeˈtaj/ *Adv.* **1** (im Einzelnen) in detail **2** (Kaufmannsspr. veralt.) retail

end-, End-: ~fünfziger¹ *der;* **~~s, ~~:** man in his late fifties; **~fünfziger²** *Pl.* **die ~fünfziger** the late fifties; **~fünfzigerin** *die;* **~~, ~~nen** woman in her late fifties; **~geschwindigkeit** *die* ▸ **Höchstgeschwindigkeit**; **~gültig** **A** *Adj.* final ‹*consent, answer, decision*›; conclusive ‹*evidence*›; **etwas/nichts Endgültiges sagen/hören** say/hear something/nothing definite; **B** *adv.* **das ist ~gültig vorbei** that's all over and done with; **sich ~gültig trennen** separate for good; **das ist jetzt ~gültig entschieden** it's been decided once and for all; **~gültigkeit** *die* finality; (von Beweisen) conclusiveness; **~haltestelle** *die* terminus

endigen /ˈɛndɪgn̩/ *itr. V.* (veralt.) ▸ **enden**

Endivie /ɛnˈdiːvi̯ə/ *die;* **~, ~n** endive

end-, End-: ~kampf *der* (Sport) final; (Milit.) final battle; **~kunde** *der,* **~kundin** *die* consumer; **~lager** *das* [permanent] disposal site; [permanent] depository; **~|lagern** *tr. V.* dispose of [permanently]; **~lagerung** *die* permanent disposal (*of nuclear waste*); **~lauf** *der* (Sport) final; **~lauf·teilnehmer** *der,* **~lauf·teilnehmerin** *die* finalist

endlich
A *Adv.* **1** (nach langer Zeit) at last; **na ~ [kommst du]!** [so you've arrived] at [long] last; **bist du ~ so weit?** are you ready at last?; **siehst du ~ ein, dass du Unrecht hattest?** do you see now that you were wrong?; **halt ~ den Mund!** why don't you shut up?; **lass mich ~ in Ruhe mit deinem Geschwätz!** stop your babbling and leave me in peace **2** (schließlich) in the end; eventually; **wir kamen ~ doch zu einer Einigung** we did reach an agreement in the end *or* eventually
B *Adj.* finite ‹*size, number*›

Endlichkeit *die;* **~:** finiteness

end·los
A *Adj.* **1** (ohne Ende) infinite; (ringförmig) endless, continuous ‹*belt, chain*› **2** (nicht enden wollend) endless ‹*road, desert, expanse, etc.*›; endless, infinite ‹*patience*›; interminable ‹*speech*›
B *adv.* **~ lange dauern** be interminably long; go on and on; **~ lange reden** talk interminably; **~ warten** wait for ages

Endlos·formular *das:* **ein ~:** continuous stationery; form paper (Amer.)

Endlosigkeit *die;* **~:** infinity; endlessness

Endlos·schleife *die* endless loop

End-: ~lösung *die* **1** (selten: endgültige Lösung) final solution; **2** (ns. verhüll.) Final Solution (*to the Jewish question*); **~moräne** *die* terminal moraine

End-: ~neunziger¹ *der;* **~~s, ~~:** man in his late nineties; **~neunziger²** *Pl.* **die ~neunziger** the late nineties; **~neunzigerin** *die;* **~~, ~~nen** woman in her late nineties

Endogamie /ɛndogaˈmiː/ *die;* **~** (Völkerk.) endogamy *no art.*

endogen /ɛndoˈgeːn/ *Adj.* (Med., Psych., Bot.) endogenous

Endoskop /ɛndoˈskoːp/ *das;* **~s, ~e** (Med.) endoscope

endotherm /ɛndoˈtɛrm/ *Adj.* (Physik, Chemie) endothermic

End-: ~phase *die* final stages *pl.;* **~produkt** *das* final *or* end product; **~punkt** *der* end; (einer Reise) last stop; **~reim** *der* end rhyme; **~resultat** *das* final result; **~runde** *die* (Sport) final; **~runden·teilnehmer** *der,* **~runden·teilnehmerin** *die* (Sport) finalist; **~sechziger¹** *der;* **~~s, ~~** man in his late sixties; **~sechziger²** *Pl.* **die ~sechziger** the late sixties; **~sechzigerin** *die;* **~~, ~~nen** woman in her late sixties; **~siebziger¹** *der;* **~~s, ~~:** man in his late seventies; **~siebziger²** *Pl.* **die ~siebziger** the late seventies; **~siebzigerin** *die;* **~~, ~~nen** woman in her late seventies; **~sieg** *der* (bes. ns.) final *or* ultimate victory; **~silbe** *die* [word-]final syllable; **~spiel** *das* **1** (Sport) final; **2** (Schach) endgame; **~spurt** *der* (bes. Leichtathletik) final spurt; **einen guten ~spurt haben** have a good finish; be good in the final spurt; **~stadium** *das* final stage; (Med.) terminal stage; **Krebs im ~stadium** terminal cancer; **~stand** *der* (Sport) final result; **~station** *die* terminus; **~station Krankenhaus** (fig.) finishing up in hospital; **~stück** *das* end; (eines Brotes) crust; **~summe** *die* [sum] total

Endung *die;* **~, ~en** (Sprachw.) ending

endungs·los *Adj.* (Sprachw.) without an ending *postpos., not pred.;* uninflected

end-, End-: ~verbraucher *der,* **~verbraucherin** *die* (Wirtsch.) consumer; **~verbraucher·preis** *der* retail price; **~vierziger¹** *der;* **~~s, ~~:** man in his late forties; **~vierziger²** *Pl.* **die ~vierziger** the late forties; **~vierzigerin** *die;* **~~, ~~nen** woman in her late forties; **~zeit** *die* (Rel.) last days [of the world]; **~zeitlich** *Adj.* (Rel.) apocalyptic; **~ziel** *das* (einer Reise) final destination; (Zweck) ultimate aim *or* goal; **~ziffer** *die* final number; **das Los mit der ~ziffer 4** the coupon with a number ending in 4; **~zustand** *der* final state; **~zwanziger¹** *der;* **~~s, ~~:** man in his late twenties; **~zwanziger²** *Pl.* **die ~zwanziger** the late twenties; **~zwanzigerin** *die;* **~~, ~~nen** woman in her late twenties; **~zweck** *der* ultimate purpose *or* object

Energie /enɛrˈgiː/ *die;* **~, ~n** **1** (Physik) energy **2** (Tatkraft) energy; vigour

energie-, Energie-: ~arm *Adj.* ‹*country*› lacking in energy resources; **~bedarf** *der* energy requirement; **~bewusst,** *__~bewußt__ *Adj.* energy-conscious; **~bündel** *das* (ugs.) bundle of energy; **~effizient** **A** *Adj.* energy-efficient; **B** *adv.* in an energy-efficient manner; **~form** *die* form of energy; **~geladen** *Adj.* energetic, dynamic ‹*person*›; **~gewinnung** *die* energy production; **~haushalt** *der* (Physiol.) energy balance; (Wirtsch.) control of the use of energy; **~intensiv** *Adj.* energy-intensive; **~krise** *die* energy crisis; **~los** *Adj.* lacking [in] energy *postpos.;* sluggish; **~politik** *die* energy policy; **~politisch** **A** *Adj.* **~politische Maßnahmen/Programme** energy measures/programmes; **B** *adv.* in terms of energy policy; **~quelle** *die* energy source; source of energy; **neuzeitliche ~quellen** modern sources of energy; **~reich** *Adj.* energy-rich; **~reichtum** *der* energy wealth; **~satz** *der* (Physik) principle of the conservation of energy; **~sparer** *der,* **~sparerin** *die* energy-saver; **~spar·lampe** *die* energy-saving lamp; **~spender** *der* energy-giving substance; **~träger** *der* energy source; **~verbrauch** *der* energy consumption; **~verschwendung** *die* **1** wasting of energy; **2** (Verschwendung von Tatkraft) waste of energy; **~versorgung** *die* energy supply; **der ~versorgung** (*Dat.*) **dienen** serve to supply energy; **~wirtschaft** *die* energy sector; **~zufuhr** *die* supply of energy

energisch /eˈnɛrgɪʃ/
A *Adj.* **1** (tatkräftig) energetic, vigorous ‹*person*›; firm ‹*action*›; **~ werden** put one's foot down **2** (von starkem Willen zeugend) determined; forceful; **ein ~es Kinn** a strong chin **3** (entschlossen) forceful, firm ‹*voice, words*›
B *adv.* **1** (tatkräftig) **~ durchgreifen** take drastic action; **etw. ~ verteidigen** defend sth. vigorously **2** (entschlossen) ‹*reject, say*› forcefully, firmly; ‹*stress*› emphatically; ‹*deny*› strenuously

enervieren /enɛrˈviːrən/ *tr. V.* (geh.) enervate

Enfant terrible /ãfãtɛˈribl/ *das;* **~ ~, ~s ~s** (geh.) enfant terrible

eng /ɛŋ/
A *Adj.* **1** (schmal) narrow ‹*valley, road, bed*›; **einen ~en Horizont** *od.* **Gesichtskreis haben** (fig.) have a narrow *or* limited outlook **2** (dicht) close ‹*writing*› **3** (fest anliegend) close-fitting, tight; **ein ~es Kleid** a close-fitting dress; **der Anzug/Rock ist zu ~:** the suit/skirt is too tight **4** (beschränkt) narrow, restricted ‹*interpretation, concept*›; cramped, constricted ‹*room, space*› **5** *im Komp. u. Sup.* (begrenzt) **in die ~ere Wahl kommen** be short-listed (Brit.); **in der ~eren Wahl sein** be on the shortlist (Brit.); **im ~eren Sinne** in the stricter sense **6** (nahe) close ‹*friend*›; **im ~sten Freundeskreis** among close friends; **die Hochzeit fand im ~sten Kreis der Familie statt** the wedding was attended by close relatives [only]; **die ~ere Verwandtschaft/Heimat** one's immediate relatives/home [area]
B *adv.* **1** (dicht) **~ schreiben** write closely together; **~ [zusammen]sitzen/-stehen** sit/stand close together; **~ bedruckt/beschrieben** closely-printed/closely-written ‹*page*› **2** (fest anliegend) **~ anliegen/sitzen** fit closely; **~ anliegend** tight-fitting, close-fitting ‹*dress etc.*› **3** (beschränkt) **etw. zu ~ auslegen** interpret sth. too narrowly; **das siehst du zu ~** (ugs.) there's more to it than that; **~ begrenzt** limited; restricted **4** (nahe) closely ‹*related*›; **mit jmdm. ~ befreundet sein** be a close friend of sb.; **die beiden ~ befreundeten Herren/Ehepaare** the two gentlemen/[married] couples, who are/were close friends

Engadin /ˈɛŋgadiːn/ *das;* **~s** Engadine

Engagement /ãgaʒəˈmãː/ *das;* **~s, ~s** **1** (Einsatz) involvement; **sein ~ für etw.** his commitment to sth.; **sein ~ gegen etw.** his committed stand against sth. **2** (eines Künstlers) engagement

engagieren /ãgaˈʒiːrən/
A *refl. V.* commit oneself, become committed (**für** to); **sich politisch ~:** become politically involved; **sich in einer Organisation ~:** be active in an organization; **sich in einem Land/Geschäft ~** (verhüllend) become involved in a country/business
B *tr. V.* (unter Vertrag nehmen) engage ‹*artist, actor, etc.*›

engagiert *Adj.* **1** (entschieden für etw. eintretend) committed ‹*literature, film, director*›; **politisch/sozial ~ sein** be politically/socially committed *or* involved **2** (angestellt) engaged ‹*artist, actor, etc.*›

Engagiertheit *die;* **~:** commitment; involvement

eng·anliegend *usw.* ▸ **eng B**

Enge /ˈɛŋə/ *die;* **~, ~n** **1** confinement; restriction **2** (veralt.: Engpass) (Meeres~) strait; (Kanal~) narrows *pl.;* **jmdn. in die ~ treiben** (fig.) drive sb. into a corner

Engel /ˈɛŋl/ *der;* ~s, ~: angel; **ich habe die ~ [im Himmel] singen** *od.* **pfeifen hören** (ugs.) it hurt like hell; **sie ist mein guter/ein rettender/ein wahrer ~:** she is my good/a guardian/a real angel; **er ist [auch] nicht gerade ein ~:** he's not exactly an angel

Engelchen *das;* ~s, ~, **Engelein** *das;* ~s, ~: little angel

engel-, Engel-: **~haft** *Adj.* angelic; **~macher** *der,* **~macherin** *die* backstreet abortionist; **~schar** *die* heavenly host; host of angels

Engels-: **~geduld** *die* patience of a saint; **~gesicht** *das* angelic face

engel[s]-gleich *Adj.* angelic

Engels-haar *das* angel's hair

Engel[s]-kopf *der* cherub

Engels-: **~miene** *die* innocent look; **~musik** *die* heavenly music; **~zungen** *Pl. in* **mit ~zungen auf jmdn. einreden** use all one's powers of persuasion on sb.

Engerling /ˈɛŋɐlɪŋ/ *der;* ~s, ~e grub

eng-herzig
A *Adj.* petty
B *adv.* in a petty way

Eng-herzigkeit *die;* ~: pettiness

England *(das);* ~s **1** England **2** (ugs.: Großbritannien) Britain

Engländer /ˈɛŋlɛndɐ/ *der;* ~s, ~ ▸ℹ S. 520 **1** Englishman/English boy; **er ist ~:** he is English *or* an Englishman; **die ~:** the English **2** (ugs.: Brite) British person/man; Britisher (Amer.); **die ~:** the British **3** (Schraubenschlüssel) monkey wrench

Engländerin *die;* ~, ~nen ▸ℹ S. 520 **1** Englishwoman/English girl; **sie ist ~:** she is English *or* an Englishwoman **2** (ugs.: Britin) British person/woman; **die ~nen sind ...** British women are ...

england-freundlich *Adj.* anglophile

englisch[1] ▸ℹ S. 520, ▸ℹ S. 670
A *Adj.* English; **~-deutsch** Anglo-German; English-German ‹*dictionary*›; ‹*book*› in English and German; **die ~e Sprache/Literatur** the English language/English literature; **die ~e Krankheit** (veralt.) rickets; **Englisch Horn** (fachspr.) ▸**Englischhorn**; **~e Bulldogge** bulldog
B *adv.* **~ sprechen** speak English; **~ [gebraten]** rare; underdone; **ein ~ abgefasster Artikel** an article in English; *s. auch* **deutsch, Deutsche**[2]

englisch[2] *Adj.* **der Englische Gruß** the Angelic Salutation; the Ave Maria; the Hail Mary; **die Englischen Fräulein** *Institute of the Blessed Virgin Mary;* the 'English Ladies'; the 'English Virgins'

Englisch *das;* ~[s] ▸ℹ S. 670 English; **ein gutes/fehlerfreies ~ sprechen** speak good/perfect English; **das moderne ~/~ Chaucers** present day/Chaucerian English; *s. auch* **Deutsch**

englisch-, Englisch-: **~horn** *das* (Musik) cor anglais; **~lehrer** *der,* **~lehrerin** *die* 'English teacher; **~sprachig** *Adj.* **1** (in englischer Sprache) English-language ‹*book, magazine*›; **die ~sprachige Literatur** literature written in English; **2** (Englisch sprechend) English-speaking ‹*population, area*›; **~unterricht** *der* English teaching; (Unterrichtsstunde) English lesson; **er gibt ~unterricht** he teaches English; **sie arbeitet im ~unterricht gut mit** she always pays attention in English lessons; **das habe ich im ~unterricht gelernt** I learnt that in English

Englishwaltz /ˈɪŋglɪʃ ˈwɔ(:)l(t)s/ *der;* ~, ~: slow waltz

eng-maschig
A *Adj.* **1** close-meshed ‹*fabric*› **2** (Sport) tight
B *adv.* **1** ~ **stricken/gestrickt sein** knit/be knitted tightly **2** (Sport) **~ spielen** play tightly

Eng-pass, *Eng-paß *der* **1** [narrow] pass; defile **2** (fig.: in der Versorgung usw.) bottleneck

en gros /ãˈgro/ (Kaufmannsspr.) wholesale

eng-, Eng-: **~stirnig** **A** *Adj.* (abwertend) narrow-minded ‹*person*›; **B** *adv.* **~stirnig denken/handeln** be narrow-minded in the way one thinks/acts; **~stirnigkeit** *die;* ~~: narrow-mindedness; ***~verwandt** ▸**eng B4**; **~zeilig** *Adv.* with the lines closely spaced

Enjambement /ãʒãbəˈmã:/ *das;* ~s, ~s (Verslehre) enjambment

Enkel[1] /ˈɛŋkl/ *der;* ~s, ~ (nordd.) ankle

Enkel[2] *der;* ~s, ~ **1** grandson **2** (Nachfahr) grandchild; **selbst unsere ~ werden sich daran erinnern** even our grandchildren and great-grandchildren will remember it

Enkelin *die;* ~, ~nen granddaughter

Enkel-: **~kind** *das* grandchild; **~sohn** *der* grandson; **~tochter** *die* granddaughter

Enklave /ɛnˈkla:və/ *die;* ~, ~en enclave

enkodieren /ɛnkoˈdi:rən/ *tr. V.* encode

en masse /ãˈmas/ (ugs.) en masse

en miniature /ãminjaˈty:r/ in miniature; **der Eiffelturm ~:** the Eiffel Tower in miniature; a miniature Eiffel Tower

enorm /eˈnɔrm/
A *Adj.* enormous ‹*sum, costs*›; tremendous (coll.) ‹*effort*›; immense ‹*strain*›; vast ‹*knowledge, sum*›
B *adv.* tremendously (coll.) ‹*expensive, practical*›; **~ verdienen** earn an enormous amount *or* vast sums [of money]; **~ viel/viele** a tremendous (coll.) *or* an enormous amount/a tremendous (coll.) *or* an enormous number; **sich ~ freuen** (ugs.) be tremendously (coll.) pleased

en passant /ãpaˈsã/ **1** (beiläufig) en passant; in passing **2** (Schach) en passant

Enquete /ãˈke:t(ə)/ *die;* ~, ~n **1** survey **2** (österr.: Arbeitstagung) meeting for discussion

Ensemble /ãˈsã:bl/ *das* **1** (Gruppe) ensemble; **das ~ eines Theaters** the company of a theatre **2** (Auftritt) ensemble **3** (Kleidungsstück) outfit; ensemble **4** (geh.: Gesamtheit) ensemble

Ensemble-: **~mitglied** *das* member of the ensemble/company; **~musik** *die* light music

entarten *itr. V.; mit sein* degenerate; **entartet** degenerate; **zu** *od.* **in** (*Akk.*) **etw. ~:** degenerate into sth.

Entartung *die;* ~, ~en degeneration

Entartungs-erscheinung *die* sign of degeneration; **das führte zu ~en** this led to degeneracy

entasten, entästen *tr. V.* (Forstw.) disbranch

entäußern *refl. V.* (geh.) **1** **sich einer Sache** (*Gen.*) **~** (entsagen) renounce sth.; (weggeben) relinquish *or* give up sth. **2** (Philos.) be realized

Entäußerung *die* **1** (geh.: Verzicht) renunciation **2** (Weggabe) giving up **3** (Philos.) realization

entbehren /ɛntˈbe:rən/
A *tr. V.* **1** (geh.: vermissen) miss ‹*person*› **2** (verzichten) do without; spare; **etw./jmdn. nicht ~ können** not be able to spare sth./sb.; not be able to do without sth./sb.; **viel[es] ~ müssen** have to go without [a lot of things]
B *itr. V.* (geh.: ermangeln) **einer Sache** (*Gen.*) **~:** lack *or* be without sth.

entbehrlich *Adj.* dispensable; unnecessary ‹*action*›

Entbehrlichkeit *die;* ~: superfluousness; dispensability

Entbehrung *die;* ~, ~en privation; **große ~en auf sich** (*Akk.*) **nehmen** make great sacrifices

entbehrungs-: **~reich, ~voll** *Adj.* ‹*life, years*› of privation

entbeinen *tr. V.* bone

entbieten *unr. tr. V.* (geh.) **1** offer ‹*best wishes, greetings*›; **jmdm. seine Grüße ~:** present one's compliments to sb. **2** (veralt.: kommen lassen) summon

entbinden
A *unr. tr. V.* **1** (befreien) **jmdn. von einem Versprechen ~:** release sb. from a promise; **seines Amtes** *od.* **von seinem Amt entbunden werden** be relieved of [one's] office **2** (Geburtshilfe leisten) **jmdn. ~:** deliver sb.; deliver sb.'s baby; **von einem Jungen/Mädchen entbunden werden** give birth to a boy/girl
B *unr. itr. V.* (gebären) give birth; **zu Hause ~:** have one's baby at home

Entbindung *die* **1** (das Gebären) **eine schwere/schmerzfreie ~:** a difficult/painless delivery *or* birth; **zur ~ in die Klinik müssen** have to go to hospital for the delivery *or* to have the baby; **bei der ~ anwesend sein** be present at the birth **2** (Befreiung) release; **um die ~ von seinem Amt bitten** ask to be relieved of one's duties

Entbindungs-: **~saal** *der* delivery room; **~station** *die* maternity ward

entblättern
A *refl. V.* **1** ‹*trees, shrubs*› shed its/their leaves **2** (scherzh.: sich ausziehen) strip; take one's clothes off
B *tr. V.* strip ‹*trees*› [of leaves]

entblöden *refl. V.* **sich nicht ~, etw. zu tun** (geh. abwertend) have the effrontery to do sth.

entblößen
A *refl. V.* take one's clothes off; ‹*exhibitionist*› expose oneself; (sein wahres Gesicht zeigen) show oneself as one really is/was
B *tr. V.* **1** **den Arm ~:** uncover one's arm; **entblößt** bare; **mit entblößtem Kopf** without a hat; **sein Schwert ~** (dichter.) unsheathe one's sword **2** (fig.) reveal ‹*feelings, thoughts*›

entbrennen *unr. itr. V.; mit sein* (geh.) **1** (beginnen) ‹*battle*› break out; ‹*quarrel*› flare up **2** (ergriffen werden) **in Liebe entbrannt sein** be passionately in love; **in Zorn entbrannt sein** be inflamed with anger

Entchen /ˈɛntçən/ *das;* ~s, ~: duckling

entdecken
A *tr. V.* **1** (finden) discover; **eine Insel/ein chemisches Element ~:** discover an island/a chemical element **2** (ausfindig machen) **jmdn. ~:** find *or* spot sb.; **wir konnten ihn in dem Gewühl nicht ~:** we couldn't find him in the crowd; **etw. ~:** find *or* discover sth. **3** (überraschend bemerken) discover ‹*theft*›; come across ‹*acquaintance*› **4** (veralt.: offenbaren) **jmdm. etw. ~:** reveal *or* (arch.) discover sth. to sb.
B *refl. V.* (veralt.: anvertrauen) **sich jmdm. ~:** confide in sb.

Entdecker *der;* ~s, ~: discoverer; (Forschungsreisender) explorer

Entdecker-freude *die* joy of discovery

Entdeckerin *die;* ~, ~nen ▸**Entdecker**

Entdeckung *die;* ~, ~en discovery

Entdeckungs-reise *die* voyage of discovery; (zu Lande) expedition; **auf ~/~n gehen** (fig. scherzh.) go exploring

Ente /ˈɛntə/ *die;* ~, ~n **1** (Vogel, Fleisch) duck; **eine lahme ~** (ugs.) a slowcoach (coll.); **sein Wagen ist eine richtige lahme ~** (ugs.) his car totally lacks oomph (coll.) *or* has no pick-up (Amer. sl.) **2** (ugs.: Falschmeldung) canard; spoof (coll.) **3** **kalte ~:** [cold] punch **4** (ugs.: Auto) Citroën 2 CV car **5** (ugs.: Uringefäß) [bed] bottle

entehren *tr. V.* dishonour; **~d** degrading

Entehrung *die* dishonouring

enteignen *tr. V.* expropriate

Enteignung *die* expropriation

enteilen *itr. V.; mit sein* (geh.) hasten away; (fig.) ‹*hours, years, etc.*› fly by

enteisen *tr. V.* de-ice

enteisenen *tr. V.* remove the iron from; **stark/schwach enteisent** with a very low/slightly reduced iron content

Entelechie /ɛnteleˈçi:/ *die;* ~, ~n (Philos.) entelechy

Enten-: **~braten** *der* roast duck; **~brust** *die* (Gastr.) breast of duck; duck's breast; **~ei** *das* duck's egg; **~feder** *die* duck's feather; **~flott** *das;* ~~s (nordd.) ▸**~grütze**; **~gericht** *das* duck dish; **~grütze** *die* duckweed; **~jagd** *die* duck shooting; **eine ~jagd** a duck shoot; **~junge** *das* duckling; **~klein** *das;* ~s (Kochk.) duck's giblets *pl;* **~küken** *das* duckling; **~schnabel** *der* **1** duck's bill; **2** (Schuh) duckbill; **~tanz**

ℹ Entfernung

1 Meter = one metre = 3 feet 3.4 inches *od.* 1.094 yards
1 Kilometer = one kilometre = 1094 yards *od.* 0.6214 mile

Wie weit ist es von A nach B?
= How far is it *od.* What's the distance from A to B?
Es sind/Die Entfernung beträgt beinahe 600 Kilometer
= It's/The distance is nearly 600 kilometres
≈ It's/The distance is nearly 370 miles
Es ist ziemlich weit [entfernt]
= It's quite a long way [away]
Hannover liegt weiter vom Meer entfernt als Bremen
= Hanover is further from the sea than Bremen
Magdeburg liegt näher an Berlin als Braunschweig
= Magdeburg is closer to Berlin than Brunswick
A und B sind gleich weit entfernt
= A and B are the same distance away
Er traf das Ziel aus einer Entfernung von 50 Metern
= He hit the target from a distance of 50 metres
eine Autofahrt von achtzig Kilometern/zwanzig Minuten
= an eighty-kilometre *od.* ≈ a fifty-mile/twenty-minute drive
eine Stunde/zwei Stunden Fahrt [mit dem Auto]
= an hour's/two hours' drive, a one-hour/two-hour drive
Es sind nur zehn Minuten zu Fuß
= It's only a ten-minute walk *od.* ten minutes on foot

der: dance imitating the quacking and movements of ducks

Entente /ã'tã:t(ə)/ *die;* **~, ~n** (Politik) entente

Enten-: ~teich *der* duck pond; **~wal** *der* bottle-nosed whale

Enter·beil *das* boarding pike

enterben *tr. V.* disinherit

Enter·brücke *die* boarding bridge

Enterbung *die;* **~, ~en** disinheritance

Enter·haken *der* grapnel; grappling iron

Enterich /'ɛntərɪç/ *der;* **~s, ~e** drake

entern /'ɛntɐn/
A *tr., itr. V.* board ‹*ship*›
B *itr. V.; mit sein* **in die Masten ~** (Seemannsspr.) climb the rigging
C *tr. V.* (ugs.: erklettern) climb ‹*fence, wall, etc.*›; climb on to ‹*lorry, etc.*›

Enter·säbel *der* (hist.) cutlass

Entertainer /'ɛntɐteːnɐ/ *der;* **~s, ~, Entertainerin** *die;* **~, ~nen** ▸ℹ **S. 113** entertainer

Entertainment /ɛntɐ'teːnmɛnt/ *das;* **~s** entertainment

Enter·taste /'ɛntɐ-/ *die* (DV) enter key

entfachen *tr. V.* (geh.) **1** kindle, light ‹*fire*›; **einen Brand ~:** start a fire **2** (fig.: hervorrufen) provoke, start ‹*quarrel, argument*›; arouse ‹*passion, enthusiasm*›

entfahren *unr. itr. V.; mit sein* **ihm entfuhr ein Fluch/ein Seufzer** he swore inadvertently/he let out a sigh

entfallen *unr. itr. V.; mit sein* **1** (aus dem Gedächtnis) **der Name/das Wort ist mir ~:** the name/word escapes me *or* has slipped my mind; **das ist mir ~:** I have forgotten **2** (zugeteilt werden) **auf jmdn./etw. ~:** be allotted to sb./sth.; **auf jeden Erben entfielen 10 000 Euro** each heir received 10,000 euros; **auf jeden Miteigentümer ~ 50 000 Euro** (müssen bezahlt werden) each of the joint owners has to pay 50,000 euros **3** (wegfallen) lapse; **für Kinder ~ diese Gebühren** these charges do not apply *or* are not applicable to children; **aus Zeitmangel ~:** be omitted for lack of time **4** (geh.) **jmds. Händen ~:** slip *or* fall from sb.'s hands

entfalten
A *tr. V.* **1** (auseinander falten) open [up]; unfold, spread out ‹*map etc.*›; ‹*plant*› open ‹*leaves*› **2** (zeigen) show, display ‹*ability, talent*› **3** (darlegen) expound ‹*ideas, thoughts*›; present ‹*plan*› **4** (entwickeln) begin to show *or* display ‹*interest, enthusiasm, etc.*›
B *refl. V.* **1** (sich entwickeln) ‹*personality, talent*› develop; **sich frei ~:** develop one's own personality to the full **2** (sich öffnen) ‹*flower, parachute*› open [up]

Entfaltung *die;* **~, ~en** **1** (Entwicklung) development; **die ~ der Persönlichkeit** the development of one's personality; **zur ~ kommen** *od.* **gelangen** develop **2** (Darstellung) display; (eines Plans) exposition; presentation

entfärben
A *tr. V.* take the colour out of ‹*material, clothing*›
B *refl. V.* ‹*material, clothing, etc.*› fade

Entfärber *der* colour *or* dye remover

entfernen
A *tr. V.* **1** remove ‹*stain, wart, etc.*›; take out ‹*tonsils etc.*›; **jmdn. von** *od.* **aus der Schule ~:** expel sb. [from school]; **jmdn. aus seinem Amt ~:** dismiss sb. from his office **2** (geh.: fortbringen) remove
B *refl. V.* go away; **sich vom Weg ~:** go off *or* leave the path; **sich unerlaubt von der Truppe ~:** go absent without leave; **sich aus der Stadt/dem Büro ~:** leave [the] town/the office; **langsam entfernten sich die Schritte** the footsteps slowly receded

entfernt
A *Adj.* **1** ▸ℹ **S. 224** (fern) remote; **das ist** *od.* **liegt weit ~ von der Stadt** it is a long way from the town *or* out of town; **er ist weit davon ~, das zu tun** (fig.) he does not have the slightest intention of doing that; **10 km/zwei Stunden [von einem Punkt] ~:** 10 km/two hours away [from a place] **2** (weitläufig) slight ‹*acquaintance*›; distant ‹*relation*› **3** (schwach) slight, vague ‹*resemblance*›
B *adv.* **1** (fern) remotely; **das stört mich nicht im Entferntesten** that does not bother me in the slightest *or* in the least; **er dachte nicht ~** *od.* **im Entferntesten daran, das zu tun** he did not have the slightest intention of doing that **2** (weitläufig) slightly ‹*acquainted*›; distantly ‹*related*›; **mit jmdm. ~ verwandt sein** be distantly related to sb. **3** (schwach) slightly, vaguely; **sich ~ an etw.** (*Akk.*) **erinnern** remember sth. vaguely; have a vague recollection of sth.

Entfernung *die;* **~, ~en** **1** ▸ℹ **S. 224** (Abstand) distance; (beim Schießen) range; **in einer ~ von 100 m** at a distance/range of 100 m.; 100 m. away; **auf eine ~ von 100 m** from a distance of 100 m.; **aus der ~:** from a distance **2** (das Beseitigen) removal **3** (das Weggehen) **unerlaubte ~ von der Truppe** absence without leave

Entfernungs·messer *der;* **~s, ~** (Gerät) rangefinder

entfesseln *tr. V.* unleash ‹*war, riot, etc.*›; raise ‹*laughter etc.*›; **die entfesselten Elemente** *od.* **Naturgewalten** the raging elements; **entfesselte Leidenschaften** (geh.) unbridled passions

Entfesselungs·künstler *der,* **Entfesselungs·künstlerin** *die* escapologist

entfetten *tr. V.* skim ‹*milk*›; scour ‹*wool*›; dry ‹*skin*›

Entfettungs·kur *die* diet to remove one's excess fat

entflammbar *Adj.* **1** inflammable **2** (begeisterungsfähig) easily roused

entflammen
A *tr. V.* arouse ‹*enthusiasm etc*›; **jmdn. für etw. ~:** arouse sb.'s enthusiasm for sth.
B *itr. V.; mit sein* **1** ‹*hatred etc.*› flare up; ‹*battle, strike*› break out; **er ist [in Liebe] für sie entflammt** he became enraptured with her; (Zustand) he is passionately in love with her

entflechten *unr.* (*auch regelm.*) *tr. V.* **1** (entwirren) disentangle **2** (Wirtsch.) break up ‹*cartel etc.*›

Entflechtung *die;* **~, ~en** (Wirtsch.) breaking-up; break-up

entfleuchen *itr. V.; mit sein* (altertümelnd scherzh.) get *or* run away

entfliegen *unr. itr. V.; mit sein* fly away; **gestern ist uns** (*Dat.*) **unser Kanarienvogel entflogen** yesterday our canary got away; **„Wellensittich entflogen"** 'budgerigar lost'

entfliehen *unr. itr. V.; mit sein* **1** escape; **jmdm. ~:** escape from sb.; **dem Alltag ~** (geh.) escape from the daily routine **2** (geh.: entschwinden) ‹*time*› fly by

entfremden
A *tr. V.* **1** (fremd machen) **jmdn. einer Sache** (*Dat.*) **~:** alienate *or* estrange sb. from sth.; **etw. seinem Zweck ~:** use sth. for a different purpose **2** (Philos., Soziol.) **entfremdet** alienated ‹*person, work, etc.*›
B *refl. V.* **sich jmdm./einer Sache ~:** become estranged from sb./unfamiliar with sth.

Entfremdung *die;* **~, ~en** **1** alienation; estrangement; **die ~ von jmdm./etw.** alienation *or* estrangement from sb./sth.; **die ~ zwischen Regierung und Volk** the government's alienation from the people **2** (Philos., Soziol.) alienation

entfrosten *tr. V.* defrost ‹*refrigerator etc.*›; defrost, de-ice ‹*windscreen etc.*›

Entfroster *der;* **~s, ~:** defroster; de-icer

entführen *tr. V.* **1** kidnap, abduct ‹*child etc.*›; hijack ‹*plane, lorry, etc.*› **2** (scherzh.: mitnehmen) steal; make off with

Entführer *der,* **Entführerin** *die* ▸**entführen 1**: kidnapper; abductor; hijacker

Entführung *die* ▸**entführen 1**: kidnap; kidnapping; abduction; hijack; hijacking; **„Die ~ aus dem Serail"** 'Il Seraglio'

entgegen
A *Adv.* **1** (auf ... zu) towards; **der Sonne ~!** on towards the sun! **2** (zuwider) **alles, was ihnen ~ war** everything they did not like
B *Präp. mit Dat.* **~ meinem Wunsch** against my wishes; **~ dem Befehl** contrary to orders

entgegen-, Entgegen-: ~|arbeiten *itr. V.* **jmdm./einer Sache** (*Dat.*) **~arbeiten** work against sb./sth.; **~|blicken** *itr. V.* (geh.) **1** **jmdm. freudig/böse ~blicken** happily/angrily watch sb. coming; **2** (fig.) **der Zukunft froh/mit Bangen ~blicken** look towards the future with joy/fear; **~|branden** *itr. V.; mit sein* (geh.) **dem Künstler brandete Beifall ~:** the artist received *or* was greeted with a great wave of applause; **~|bringen** *unr. tr. V.* (fig.) **jmdm. Liebe/Verständnis ~bringen** show sb. love/understanding; **~|eilen** *itr. V.; mit sein* **1** **jmdm. ~eilen** hurry to meet sb.; **2** (fig.) **einer Sache** (*Dat.*) **~eilen** rush towards sth.; **~|fahren** *unr. itr. V.; mit sein* **jmdm. ~fahren** come/go to meet sb.; **~|fiebern** *itr. V.* **einem Ereignis ~fiebern** look forward to an event with nervous anticipation; **~|gehen** *unr. itr. V.; mit sein* **1** **jmdm. [ein Stück] ~gehen** go [a little way] to meet sb.; **2** (fig.) **einer Katastrophe/schweren Zeiten ~gehen** be heading for *or* towards a catastrophe/hard times; **der Vollendung/dem Ende ~gehen** be approaching completion/its end; **~gesetzt**
A *Adj.* **1** (umgekehrt) opposite ‹*end, direction*›; **sie gingen in ~gesetzter Richtung davon** they went off in opposite directions; **2** (gegensätzlich) opposing; **~gesetzter Meinung sein** hold opposing views; **das ~gesetzte tun** do

the opposite; **B** *adv.* **genau ~gesetzt handeln/denken** do/think exactly the opposite; **~|halten** *unr. tr. V.* **1** **jmdm. etw. ~halten** offer sth. to sb.; **2** (fig.: einwenden) **einem Argument ein anderes ~halten** counter an argument with another; **~halten, dass ...** counter that ...; **~|kommen** *unr. itr. V.; mit sein* **1** (zukommen auf) **jmdm. ~kommen** come to meet sb.; **der ~kommende Verkehr** oncoming traffic; **2** (Zugeständnisse machen) **jmdm. ~kommen** be accommodating towards sb.; **dem Verhandlungspartner ~kommen** make concessions to one's opposite number in the negotiations; **sie/das kam unseren Wünschen ~:** she complied with our wishes/it was what we wanted; **3** (entsprechen) **einer Sache** (*Dat.*) **~kommen** comply with *or* fit in with sth.; **~kommen** *das;* **~~s, ~~** **1** (Konzilianz) cooperation; **wenn er etwas mehr ~kommen gezeigt hätte** if he had shown a little more willingness to cooperate; **2** (Zugeständnis) concession; **zu keinem ~kommen bereit sein** be unwilling to make any concessions; **~kommend** *Adj.* obliging; **~kommenderweise** *Adv.* obligingly; **~|laufen** *unr. itr. V.; mit sein* **1** **jmdm. ~laufen** run to meet sb.; **2** (sich widersprechen) **einander ~laufen** conflict with each other; **~nahme** *die;* **~~** (Amtsdt.) receipt; **bei ~nahme** on receipt; **~|nehmen** *unr. itr. V.* receive; **ein Paket ~nehmen** accept a parcel; **~|schlagen** *unr. itr. V.* **1** *mit sein* **eine Rauchwolke/ein übler Geruch schlug mir ~:** I encountered a cloud of smoke/a foul smell; **ihm schlug eine Welle der Entrüstung ~:** he was met by a wave of indignation; **2** (geh.) **die Herzen schlugen ihm ~:** their/our *etc.* hearts went out to him; **~|schleudern** *tr. V.* fire ‹*answer, remark*›, hurl ‹*abuse, threats*› (**jmdm.** at sb.); **~|sehen** *unr. itr. V.* **1** **einer Sache** (*Dat.*) **~sehen** look forward to sth.; **einem Ereignis freudig ~sehen** look forward eagerly to an event; **2** (~blicken) **den eintreffenden Gästen ~sehen** watch the guests arriving; **~|setzen** *tr. V.* **1** **einer Sache** (*Dat.*) **etw. ~setzen** oppose sth. with sth.; **einer Sache** (*Dat.*) **Widerstand ~setzen** resist sth.; **2** (gegenüberstellen) **einer Behauptung/einem Argument etw. ~setzen** counter a claim/an argument with sth.; **~|stehen** *unr. itr. V.* **1** (hinderlich sein) **einer Sache** (*Dat.*) **~stehen** stand in the way of sth.; **dem steht nichts ~:** there's no reason why not; **2** (im Gegensatz stehen zu) **einer Sache** (*Dat.*) **~stehen** conflict with sth.; **~|stellen** *tr. V.:* **▸~setzen 2**; **~|strecken** *tr. V.* **jmdm. etw. ~strecken** hold sth. out towards sb.; **~|treten** *unr. itr. V.; mit sein* **1** (in den Weg treten) go/come up to; **einem Angreifer ~treten** go into action against an attacker; **Schwierigkeiten** (*Dat.*) **~treten** stand up to difficulties; **einem Angriff ~treten** answer an attack; **2** (sich wehren gegen) **Vorwürfen/Anschuldigungen ~treten** answer reproaches/accusations; **~|wirken** *itr. V.* **einer Sache** (*Dat.*) **~wirken** [actively] oppose sth.; **die Regierung sollte diesem Missbrauch ~wirken** the Government should do something to halt this abuse

entgegnen /ɛnt'ge:gnən/ *tr. V.* retort; reply; **einer Sache** (*Dat.*) **etw. ~:** say sth. in reply to sth.; **jmdm. ~, dass ...** reply that ...

Entgegnung *die;* **~, ~en** retort; reply; **als ~ darauf** in reply

entgehen *unr. itr. V.; mit sein* **1** (entkommen) escape; **einer Gefahr/Strafe** (*Dat.*) **~:** escape *or* avoid danger/punishment **2** (versäumt, ausgelassen werden) miss; **das darf man sich** (*Dat.*) **nicht ~ lassen** that is not to be missed **3** (nicht bemerkt werden) **jmdm. entgeht etw.** sb. misses sth.; sb. fails to see sth.; **ihm ist nicht entgangen, dass ...** it has not escaped his notice that ...

entgeistert /ɛnt'gaistɐt/ *Adj.* dumbfounded; **jmdn. ~ anstarren** stare at sb. in amazement *or* astonishment

Entgelt /ɛnt'gɛlt/ *das;* **~[e]s, ~e** payment; fee; **gegen** *od.* **für ein geringes ~:** for a small fee; **ohne ~:** free of charge

entgelten *unr. tr. V.* (geh.) pay for (also fig.); **jmdm. eine Arbeit ~:** pay sb. for a job; **jmdn. etw. ~ lassen** make sb. pay for sth.

entgeltlich (Papierdt.)
A *Adj.* payable
B *adv.* on payment of a fee

entgiften *tr. V.* decontaminate ‹*substance etc.*›; detoxicate ‹*body etc.*›

Entgiftung *die;* **~, ~en** decontamination; detoxication

entgleisen *itr. V.; mit sein* **1** be derailed; **der Zug ist entgleist** the train was derailed; **das Entgleisen** the derailment **2** (in Gesellschaft) make *or* commit a/some faux pas

Entgleisung *die;* **~, ~en** **▸entgleisen:** **1** derailment **2** faux pas

entgleiten *unr. itr. V.; mit sein* (geh.) **1** slip; **jmds. Händen ~:** slip from sb.'s hands **2** (fig.) **jmdm. entgleitet etw.** sb. loses his/her grip on sth.

entgräten *tr. V.* fillet; bone; **entgräteter Fisch** filleted fish

enthaaren *tr. V.* remove hair from; depilate (formal)

Enthaarungs·mittel *das* hair remover; depilatory

enthalten[1]
A *unr. tr. V.* contain
B *unr. refl. V.* **sich einer Sache** (*Gen.*) **~:** abstain from sth.; **sich der Stimme ~:** abstain; **sich jeder Meinung/Äußerung ~:** refrain from giving any opinion/making any comment

enthalten[2] *Adj.* **in etw.** (*Dat.*) **~ sein** be contained in sth.; **die im Wasser ~en Stoffe** the substances contained in water; **wie oft ist 4 in 12 ~?** how many times does 4 go into 12?; **das ist im Preis ~:** that is included in the price

enthaltsam
A *Adj.* abstemious; (sexuell) abstinent
B *adv.* **in Bezug auf etw.** (*Akk.*) **~ sein** be moderate regarding sth.; **~ leben** live in abstinence

Enthaltsamkeit *die;* **~:** abstinence

Enthaltung *die* abstention; **mit 20 Stimmen bei 3 ~en gewählt werden** be elected by 20 votes with 3 abstentions

enthärten *tr. V.* soften ‹*water*›

Enthärter *der;* **~s, ~:** [water] softener

Enthärtungs·mittel *das* [water] softener

enthaupten *tr. V.* (geh.) behead

Enthauptung *die;* **~, ~en** (geh.) beheading

enthäuten *tr. V.* skin

entheben *unr. tr. V.* (geh.) relieve; **jmdn. seines Amtes ~:** relieve sb. of his/her office; **aller Sorgen enthoben sein** be relieved of all one's cares; **einer Verpflichtung enthoben werden** be released from an obligation

entheiligen *tr. V.* desecrate, profane ‹*sabbath*›

enthemmen *tr., itr. V.* **jmdn. ~:** make sb. lose his/her inhibitions; free sb. from his/her inhibitions; **Alkohol enthemmt** alcohol takes away one's inhibitions

enthemmend
A *Adj.* disinhibitory ‹*effect, etc.*›
B *adv.* **~ wirken** take away sb.'s inhibitions

enthemmt
A **▸enthemmen**
B *Adj.* uninhibited

Enthemmtheit *die;* **~, Enthemmung** *die* loss of inhibition[s]; disinhibition (Psych.)

enthüllen
A *tr. V.* **1** unveil ‹*monument etc.*›; reveal ‹*face, etc.*› **2** (offenbaren) reveal ‹*truth, secret*›; disclose ‹*secret*›; (Zeitungsw.) expose ‹*scandal*›
B *refl. V.* (sich offenbaren) **sich [jmdm.] ~:** be revealed [to sb.]; **sich als etw. ~:** be revealed as *or* turn out to be sth.

Enthüllung *die;* **~, ~en** **▸enthüllen:** **1** (das Enthüllen) unveiling; revelation; disclosure; exposé **2** (das Enthüllte) revelation; disclosure

Enthüllungs-: ~geschichte *die* exposé; **~journalismus** *der* investigative journalism; **~journalist** *der,* **~journalistin** *die* investigative journalist; **~roman** *der* exposé novel; **~story** *die* exposé

enthülsen *tr. V.* shell; pod

Enthusiasmus /ɛntu'zi̯asmʊs/ *der;* **~:** enthusiasm

Enthusiast *der;* **~en, ~en, Enthusiastin** *die;* **~, ~nen** enthusiast

enthusiastisch
A *Adj.* enthusiastic
B *adv.* enthusiastically

Entität /ɛnti'tɛ:t/ *die;* **~, ~en** (Philos.) entity

entjungfern *tr. V.* deflower

Entjungferung *die;* **~, ~en** defloration

entkalken *tr. V.* decalcify

entkeimen *tr. V.* **1** (keimfrei machen) sterilize ‹*water etc.*› **2** (Triebe entfernen von) remove the shoots from ‹*potatoes etc.*›

entkernen *tr. V.* **1** core ‹*apple etc.*›; stone, remove stone from ‹*plum etc.*›; remove pips from ‹*grape etc.*› **2** (Städtebau) reduce the density of ‹*town*›

entkleiden *tr. V.* (geh.) **1** **jmdn./sich ~:** undress sb./undress; **die entkleidete Leiche einer Unbekannten** the unclothed body of an unknown woman **2** (berauben) strip; **jmdn. einer Sache** (*Gen.*) **~:** strip sb. of sth.

Entkleidung *die* undressing

entknoten
A *tr. V.* untie, undo ‹*string etc.*›; unravel ‹*wool etc.*›
B *refl. V.* (fig.) ‹*plot etc.*› unravel itself

entkoffeiniert /ɛntkɔfei'ni:ɐt/ *Adj.* decaffeinated

Entkolon[ial]isierung *die* decolonization

entkommen *unr. itr. V.; mit sein* escape; **jmdm./einer Sache ~:** escape *or* get away from sb./sth.; **es gibt kein Entkommen** there is no escape

entkorken *tr. V.* uncork ‹*bottle*›

entkräften /ɛnt'krɛftn̩/ *tr. V.* **1** weaken; **völlig ~:** exhaust; **von etw. [völlig] entkräftet sein** be [utterly] exhausted by sth. **2** (widerlegen) refute, invalidate ‹*argument etc.*›; remove ‹*suspicion etc.*›

Entkräftung *die;* **~, ~en** **1** debility; **völlige ~:** exhaustion; **an** *od.* **vor ~** (*Dat.*) **sterben** die of exhaustion **2** (Widerlegung) refutation; invalidation

entkrampfen
A *tr. V.* **1** relax ‹*body etc.*›; loosen, relax ‹*muscles etc.*› **2** (fig.) ease ‹*situation, tension*›
B *refl. V.* **1** relax **2** (fig.) ‹*atmosphere etc.*› become relaxed

Entkrampfung *die;* **~, ~en** **▸entkrampfen:** relaxation; loosening; easing

entkriminalisieren *tr. V.* decriminalize

entladen
A *unr. tr. V.* unload ‹*vehicle, ship, luggage, gun*›; discharge ‹*battery*›; *s. auch* **beladen**[1] **1**
B *unr. refl. V.* **1** ‹*storm*› break **2** (fig.: hervorbrechen) ‹*anger etc.*› erupt; ‹*aggression etc.*› be released; **sich in etw.** (*Dat.*) **~:** release itself in sth. **3** (Elektrot.) ‹*battery*› run down **4** ‹*gun*› go off

Entladung *die* **▸entladen A, B 2**: unloading; discharge; eruption; release; **etw. zur ~ bringen** (fig.) cause sth. to erupt

entlang
A *Präp. mit Akk. u. Dat.* along; **den Weg ~, ~ dem Weg** along the path
B *Adv.* along; **hier/dort ~, bitte!** this/that way please!

entlang-: ~|fahren *unr. itr. V.; mit sein* **1** drive along; **die Straße/den** *od.* **am Fluss ~fahren** drive *or* go down the street/along the river; **2** (streichen) go along; **er fuhr mit dem Finger die** *od.* **an der Tischkante ~:** he ran his finger along the edge of the table; **~|führen** **A** *tr. V.* lead along; **jmdn. die Straße ~führen** lead sb. along *or* down the street; **B** *itr. V.* (verlaufen) run *or* go along; **die Straße führt am** *od.* **den Fluss ~:** the road runs *or* goes along the river; **~|gehen** *unr. itr. V.; mit sein* ‹*person*› go *or* walk along; **bitte gehen Sie hier ~:** [go] this way please; **~|kommen** *unr. itr. V.; mit sein* come along;

~|**laufen** *unr. itr. V.; mit sein* **1** go *or* walk/ run along; **2** (verlaufen) go *or* run along

entlarven *tr. V.* expose; **jmdn. als Schwindler ~:** expose sb. as *or* show sb. to be a swindler

Entlarvung *die; ~, ~en* exposure

Entlass-, *Entlaß- (südd.) ▸**Entlassungs-**

entlassen *unr. tr. V.* **1** (aus dem Gefängnis) release; (aus dem Krankenhaus, der Armee) discharge; **jmd. wird aus der Schule ~:** sb. leaves school; **jmdn. aus der** *od.* **seiner Staatsbürgerschaft ~:** release sb. from citizenship **2** (aus einem Arbeitsverhältnis) dismiss; (wegen Arbeitsmangels) make redundant (Brit.); lay off; **bei einer Firma ~ werden** be dismissed from/be made redundant (Brit.) *or* laid off by a company **3** (geh.: gehen lassen) release

Entlassung *die; ~, ~en* **1** (aus dem Gefängnis) release; (aus dem Krankenhaus, der Armee) discharge; (aus der Schule) leaving; **~ aus der Staatsbürgerschaft** release from citizenship **2** (aus einem Arbeitsverhältnis) dismissal; (wegen Arbeitsmangels) redundancy (Brit.); laying off **3** (~sschreiben) notice of dismissal; (wegen Arbeitsmangels) redundancy notice (Brit.); pink slip (Amer.)

Entlassungs-: ~feier *die* (Schulw.) school-leaving *or* (Amer.) graduation ceremony; **~gesuch** *das* resignation; **~papiere** *Pl.* (eines Soldaten) discharge papers; (eines Häftlings) release papers; **~schreiben** *das* (Arbeitsw.) notice of dismissal; (wegen Arbeitsmangels) redundancy notice (Brit.); pink slip (Amer.); **~welle** *die* wave of job losses

entlasten *tr. V.* **1** (Rechtsspr.) exonerate ‹*defendant*› **2** (Beanspruchung mindern) **jmdn. ~:** relieve *or* take the load off sb.; **den Verkehr ~:** ease the traffic; **den Kreislauf ~:** relieve the strain on the circulation **3** (erleichtern) **sein Gewissen ~:** ease *or* relieve one's conscience **4** (Finanzw.) **sein Konto ~:** pay off the amount owed on one's account **5** (Kaufmannsspr.) approve the actions of ‹*chairman, board, etc.*›

Entlastung *die; ~, ~en* **1** (Rechtsw.) exoneration; defence; **zu jmds. ~:** in sb.'s defence **2** (Minderung der Belastung) relief; **die ~ eines Menschen/des Körpers/der Straßen** relief of the burden on a person/the body/the roads **3** (Person od. Sache) **eine große ~ für seinen Vater** a great help to his father; **eine ungeheure ~ für den Ortsverkehr** an enormous relief for local traffic **4** (Erleichterung) easing; relief; **wir senden Ihnen Ihre Unterlagen zu unserer ~ zurück** we are returning your documents for safe keeping **5** (Finanzw.) **die ~ eines Kontos** paying off the amount owed on an account **6** (Kaufmannsspr.) approval of the actions of ‹*chairman, board, etc.*›

Entlastungs-: ~material *das* (Rechtsw.) evidence for the defence; **~zeuge** *der* (Rechtsw.) witness for the defence; defence witness; **~zug** *der* (Eisenb.) relief train

entlauben
A *tr. V.* strip ‹*branch*›; defoliate ‹*forest, area*›
B *refl. V.* ‹*tree*› shed its leaves; **entlaubte Äste** bare branches

Entlaubung *die; ~, ~en* defoliation

Entlaubungs·mittel *das* defoliant

entlaufen *unr. itr. V.; mit sein* run away; **jmdm. ~:** run away from sb.; **ein ~er Sträfling/Sklave** an escaped convict/a runaway slave; **„Hund ~"** 'dog missing *or* lost'

entlausen *tr. V.* delouse

Entlausung *die; ~, ~en* delousing

entledigen *refl. V.* (geh.) **1** **sich jmds./einer Sache** *(Gen.)* **~:** dispose of *or* rid oneself of sb./sth. **2** **sich eines Kleidungsstücks ~:** remove an item of clothing **3** (erledigen) **sich einer Aufgabe/einer Schuld/seiner Pflichten ~:** carry out a task/discharge a debt/one's duty

entleeren
A *tr. V.* **1** empty ‹*ashtray etc.*› **2** evacuate ‹*bowels, bladder*›
B *refl. V.* **1** (leer werden) empty; become empty **2** (fig.: seinen Sinn verlieren) ‹*concept, tradition*› lose its meaning

Entleerung *die* **1** (das Leermachen) emptying **2** (fig.: von Werten, Begriffen) erosion **3** (Med.) evacuation

entlegen *Adj.* **1** (entfernt) out-of-the-way ‹*place*› **2** (abwegig) remote, little-known ‹*word, expression*›; out-of-the-way, odd ‹*theory etc.*›

entlehnen *tr. V.* borrow *(Dat.,* **aus** from)

Entlehnung *die; ~, ~en* borrowing; **das Wort ist eine ~ aus dem Lateinischen** the word is borrowed *or* a borrowing from the Latin

entleiben *refl. V.* (geh. veralt.) take one's own life

entleihen *unr. tr. V.* borrow; **entliehene Bücher** borrowed books

Entleiher *der; ~s, ~,* **Entleiherin** *die; ~, ~nen* borrower

Entlein /ˈɛntlain/ *das; ~s, ~:* duckling; **ein hässliches ~** (ugs. scherzh.) an ugly duckling

entlieben *refl. V.* fall out of love (**von** with); (Paar) fall out of love with one another

entloben *refl. V.* break off one's *or* the engagement

Entlobung *die; ~, ~en* breaking off [of] one's *or* the engagement

entlocken *tr. V.* (geh.) **jmdm. etw. ~:** elicit sth. from sb.; **jmdm. Begeisterung ~:** arouse enthusiasm in sb.; **jmdm. ein Geheimnis ~:** worm a secret out of sb.; **jmdm. ein Lächeln ~:** draw a smile from sb.

entlohnen, (bes. schweiz.) **entlöhnen** *tr. V.* pay; **jmdn. [für etw.] ~:** pay sb. [for sth.]

Entlohnung *die; ~, ~en* payment; (Lohn) pay

entlüften *tr. V.* **1** ventilate **2** (Technik) bleed ‹*brakes, radiator, etc.*›

Entlüfter *der; ~s, ~* **1** ventilator **2** (Technik) bleeder

Entlüftung *die* ventilation; (Anlage) ventilation [system]

Entlüftungs-: ~an·lage *die* ventilation system; **~ventil** *das* air-release valve

entmachten *tr. V.* deprive of power

Entmachtung *die; ~, ~en* deprivation of power

entmannen *tr. V.* castrate; (fig.) emasculate

Entmannung *die; ~, ~en* castration; (fig.) emasculation

entmaterialisieren *tr. V.* (bes. Philos.) dematerialize

entmenschen, entmenschlichen *tr. V.* **1** dehumanize **2** (verrohen) brutalize

entmenscht *Adj.* brutalized

entmieten *tr. V.* (Amtsspr.) drive out the tenants of

entmilitarisieren *tr. V.* demilitarize; **eine entmilitarisierte Zone** a demilitarized zone

Entmilitarisierung *die* demilitarization

entminen *tr. V.* clear of mines

entmisten *tr. V.* muck out

entmotten *tr. V.* (Technik) de-mothball

entmündigen *tr. V.* (Rechtsw.) incapacitate; (fig.) deprive of the right of decision

Entmündigung *die; ~, ~en* (jur.) incapacitation; (fig.) deprivation of the right of decision

entmutigen *tr. V.* discourage; dishearten; **lass dich nicht ~:** don't be discouraged

Entmutigung *die; ~, ~en* discouragement

Entmythologisierung *die* demythologization

Entnahme *die; ~, ~n* (von Wasser) drawing; (von Geld, Blutprobe) taking; (von Blut) extraction; (von Organen) removal

entnazifizieren /ɛntnatsifiˈtsiːrən/ *tr. V.* denazify

Entnazifizierung *die; ~, ~en* denazification

entnehmen *unr. tr. V.* **1** (herausnehmen aus) **etw. [einer Sache** *(Dat.)*] **~:** take sth. [from sth.]; **der Kasse Geld ~:** take money out of the till; **jmdm. Blut/eine Blutprobe ~:** take a blood sample from sb.; **Organe ~:** remove organs **2** (ersehen aus) gather; **einer Sache** *(Dat.)* **etw. ~ können** be able to gather sth. from sth.; **wie wir Ihrem Schreiben ~, ...** we gather from your letter that ...

entnerven *tr. V.* **jmdn. ~:** wear sb. down

entnervend *Adj.* wearing; **eine ~e Warterei** a nerve-racking wait; **der Lärm ist ~:** the noise is wearing on the nerves

entnervt *Adj.* **~ sein** be worn down; have reached *or* be at the end of one's tether; **von etw. ~ sein** have been worn down by sth.; **der ~e Beamte/Lehrer sagte ...:** the official/teacher, who had reached the end of his tether, said ...; **er gab ~ auf** he had reached the end of his tether and gave up

entölen *tr. V.* remove fat from ‹*cocoa*›; **stark/schwach entölt** with very low/slightly reduced fat content *postpos., not pred.*

Entomologe *der; ~, ~n* ▸**❶ S. 113** entomologist

Entomologie /ɛntomoloˈgiː/ *die; ~:* entomology *no art.*

Entomologin *die; ~, ~nen* ▸**❶ S. 113** entomologist

Entourage /ãtuˈraːʒə/ *die; ~, ~n* **1** entourage; **2** (Umgebung) surroundings

entpacken *tr.V.* (DV) unpack

entpflichten *tr. V.* release

entprivatisieren *tr. V.* nationalize; take out of the private sector

entpuppen *refl. V.* **sich als etw./jmd. ~:** turn out to be sth./sb.

entquellen *unr. itr. V.; mit sein* (geh.) **einer Sache** *(Dat.)* **~:** pour from sth.; **Tränen entquollen ihren Augen** tears streamed from her eyes

entrahmen *tr. V.* skim ‹*milk*›

entraten *unr. itr. V.* (geh.) **jmds./einer Sache ~:** dispense with sb./sth.; **einer Sache** *(Gen.)* **~ müssen** have to do without sth.

enträtseln
A *tr. V.* decipher ‹*code etc.*›; understand, fathom ‹*behaviour etc.*›
B *refl. V.* ‹*mystery, secret, etc.*› be solved

entrechten *tr. V.* **jmdn. ~:** deprive sb. of his/her rights

Entrechtete *der/die; adj. Dekl.* person deprived of his/her rights

Entrecote /ãtrəˈkoːt/ *das; ~s, ~s* (Kochk.) entrecôte

Entree /ãˈtreː/ *das; ~s, ~s* **1** (Kochk.) entrée **2** (Eingang) [entrance] hall **3** (Erscheinen) entrance **4** (bes. österr.: Eintrittsgeld) entrance *or* admission fee

entreißen *unr. tr. V.* **1** (wegnehmen) **jmdm. etw. ~:** snatch sth. from sb. **2** (retten vor) **jmdn. dem Tod ~:** save sb. from imminent death **3** (geh.: befreien von) **jmdn./etw. dem Vergessen ~:** rescue sb./sth. from oblivion

entrichten *tr. V.* (Amtsspr.) pay ‹*fee*›; **jede Familie musste dem Krieg ihren Tribut ~** (fig.) the war took its toll of every family

entriegeln *tr. V.* unbolt

entrinden *tr. V.* strip the bark off; decorticate

entringen (geh.)
A *unr. tr. V.* (wegnehmen) **jmdm. etw. ~:** wrest sth. from sb.
B *unr. refl. V.* **sich [einer Sache** *(Dat.)*] **~:** escape [from sth.]; **ein Seufzer entrang sich ihrer Brust** she heaved a sigh

entrinnen *unr. itr. V.; mit sein* (geh.) **1** (entgehen) **einer Sache** *(Dat.)* **~:** escape sth. **2** (dichter.) ‹*time*› fly by

entrollen
A *tr. V.* (geh.) unroll
B *refl. V.* (fig.) unfold

Entropie /ɛntroˈpiː/ *die; ~, ~n* (fachspr.) entropy

entrosten *tr. V.* derust

entrücken *tr. V.* (geh.) **jmdn. ~:** carry sb. [far] away (fig.) *(Dat.* from); **entrückt** carried away; transported; (gedankenverloren) lost in reverie; **jmdm./einer Sache entrückt sein** be far away from sb./sth.; **in eine bessere Welt entrückt** transported to a better world

Entrücktheit *die; ~, ~en* (geh.) reverie; **in völliger ~:** completely lost in reverie

ℹ Entschuldigungen

Ziemlich formell

Wir bedauern, Ihnen mitteilen zu müssen, dass ...
= We regret to have to inform you that ...
Ich muss Ihnen leider mitteilen, dass ...
= I am sorry to have to inform you that ...
Ich bedaure sehr, dass ich Sie enttäuschen musste
= I greatly *od.* very much regret that I have had to disappoint you
Es tut mir aufrichtig Leid, dass ich Sie im Stich gelassen habe
= I am really sorry to have let you down *od.* that I have let you down
Ich muss mich bei Ihnen [in aller Form] entschuldigen, dass ich Sie fälschlich beschuldigt habe
= I owe you an [unreserved] apology *od.* I must apologize [unreservedly] for accusing you wrongly
Ich muss Sie für meinen Fehler um Entschuldigung/ Verzeihung bitten
= I must ask you to excuse/forgive my mistake
Wir bitten Sie für unser Versehen um Entschuldigung
= We apologize for our oversight
Sie müssen entschuldigen, dass ich erst heute schreibe
= You must forgive me *od.* Please forgive me for not writing earlier
Bitte entschuldigen Sie unser Versehen
= Please excuse our oversight
Entschuldigen Sie bitte, können Sie mir sagen, wie spät es ist?
= Excuse me, can you tell me the time?
Entschuldigen Sie die Störung, aber haben Sie meine Uhr gesehen?
= I'm sorry to bother you, but have you seen my watch?

Weniger formell

Tut mir Leid, da kann ich nicht helfen
= Sorry, I can't help you there
Tut mir Leid, dass ich dir so viel Mühe mache
= [I'm] sorry to be such a nuisance
Verzeihung! od. Tut mir Leid! Es war alles nur ein dummes Missverständnis!
= Sorry! It was all a stupid misunderstanding
Leider muss ich jetzt gehen
= I'm afraid I'll have to go now
Sei mir nicht böse! Ich konnte nichts dafür
= Don't be cross [with me]! I couldn't help it

entrümpeln /ɛnt'rʏmpl̩n/ *tr. V.* clear out

Entrümpelung *die;* ~, ~en clear-out; clearing out

entrußen *tr. V.* clear of soot

entrüsten
A *refl. V.* **sich [über etw.** (*Akk.*)**] ~:** be indignant [at *or* about sth.]
B *tr. V.* (empören) **jmdn. ~:** make sb. indignant; **über etw.** (*Akk.*) **entrüstet/aufs Höchste entrüstet sein** be indignant/outraged at sth.; **etw. entrüstet tun** do sth. indignantly

Entrüstung *die* indignation (**über** + *Akk.* at, about)

entsaften *tr. V.* extract the juice from

Entsafter *der;* ~s, ~: juice extractor

entsagen *itr. V.* (geh.) **einem Genuss ~:** renounce *or* forgo a pleasure; **der Welt ~:** renounce the world; **sie musste lernen zu ~:** she had to learn self-denial

Entsagung *die;* ~, ~en (geh.) renunciation; **viele ~en auf sich** (*Akk.*) **nehmen** renounce many things

entsagungs·voll *Adj.* 1 full of self-denial *postpos.* 2 (Entsagungen verlangend) full of privation *postpos.*

entsalzen *tr. V.* desalinate

Entsalzung *die;* ~, ~en desalination

Entsalzungs·anlage *die* desalination plant; (bei Erdölgewinnung) brine separator

Entsatz *der* (Milit.) 1 relief 2 (~truppe) relief troops *pl.*

entsäuern *tr. V.* deacidify; disacidify

entschädigen *tr. V.* compensate (**für** for); **jmdn. für etw. ~** (fig.) make up for sth.

Entschädigung *die* compensation *no indef. art.*

entschädigungs-, Entschädigungs-: ~los *Adj., adv.* without compensation; **~summe** *die* compensation *no indef. art.*

entschärfen *tr. V.* 1 defuse, deactivate ‹*bomb etc.*›; control ‹*avalanche*›; blunt ‹*edge etc.*›; make ‹*hill, slope*› less steep; alleviate ‹*disaster, crisis*› 2 (fig.) defuse ‹*situation*›; tone down ‹*discussion, criticism*›

Entschärfung *die;* ~, ~en 1 (von Bomben usw.) defusing; deactivation 2 (fig.) defusing; toning down

Entscheid /ɛnt'ʃait/ *der;* ~[e]s, ~e decision

entscheiden
A *unr. refl. V.* 1 decide; **sich für/gegen jmdn./etw. ~:** decide on *or* in favour of/against sb./sth.; **sich nicht ~ können** be unable to make up one's mind 2 (unpers.) **morgen entscheidet es sich, ob ...** I/we/you will know tomorrow whether ...
B *unr. itr. V.* **über etw.** (*Akk.*) **~:** decide on *or* settle sth.
C *unr. tr. V.* 1 (bestimmen) decide on ‹*dispute*›; **der Richter entschied, dass ...** the judge decided *or* ruled that ... 2 (den Ausschlag geben für) decide ‹*outcome, result*›

entscheidend
A *Adj.* crucial ‹*problem, question, significance*›; decisive ‹*action*›; **die ~e Stimme** the deciding vote; **etwas/nichts Entscheidendes** something/nothing crucial *or* decisive
B *adv.* **jmdn./etw. ~ beeinflussen** have a crucial *or* decisive influence on sb./sth.; **sich/etw. ~ verändern** change/change sth. decisively

Entscheider *der;* ~s, ~, **Entscheiderin** *die;* ~, ~nen decision maker

Entscheidung *die* decision; (Gerichts~) ruling; (Schwurgerichts~) verdict; **etw. steht vor der ~:** sth. is just about to be decided; **einer ~** (*Dat.*) **ausweichen** avoid making a decision; **jmdn. vor die ~ stellen, etw. zu tun** leave the decision to sb. to do sth.

Entscheidungs-: ~befugnis *die* decision-making powers *pl.;* **~frage** *die* (Sprachw.) yes-no *or* polar question; **~gewalt** *die* power of decision; **~hilfe** *die* help *or* assistance in reaching a decision; **~kampf** *der* decisive struggle; (Milit.) decisive battle; **~schlacht** *die* decisive battle; **~spiel** *das* (Sport) deciding match; (bei gleichem Rang) play-off; **~träger** *der,* **~trägerin** *die* decision-maker

entschieden
A *2. Part. v.* **entscheiden**
B *Adj.* 1 (entschlossen) determined; resolute 2 (eindeutig) definite
C *adv.* resolutely; **etw. ~** *od.* **auf das Entschiedenste ablehnen** reject sth. emphatically *or* categorically; **jmdm. sehr ~ antworten** give sb. a very definite answer; **das geht ~ zu weit** that is going much too far

Entschiedenheit *die;* ~: decisiveness; **etw. mit ~ behaupten/verneinen** state/deny sth. categorically; **etw. mit ~ fordern** demand sth. emphatically

entschlacken *tr. V.* cleanse

Entschlackung *die;* ~, ~en cleansing

entschlafen *unr. itr. V.; mit sein* 1 (verhüll.: sterben) pass away; fall asleep (euphem.); **sanft ~:** pass away peacefully 2 (geh.: einschlafen) fall asleep

entschleiern *tr. V.* (geh.) 1 (fig.) reveal; uncover; **ein Geheimnis ~:** reveal a secret 2 unveil ‹*face*›

entschließen *unr. refl. V.* decide; make up one's mind; **sich ~, etw. zu tun** decide *or* resolve to do sth.; **sich dazu ~:** decide to do it; **sich zu einer Reise/zur Heirat ~:** decide to make a journey/to marry; **ich kann mich zu nichts ~:** I can't make up my mind; **sich anders ~:** change one's mind

Entschließung *die* resolution

entschlossen
A *2. Part. v.* **entschließen**
B *Adj.* determined, resolute ‹*person*›; determined ‹*look etc.*›; **fest ~ [sein], etw. zu tun** [be] absolutely determined to do sth.
C *adv.* **~ handeln/durchgreifen** act resolutely *or* with determination/take determined action; **kurz ~:** on the spur of the moment; (als Reaktion) immediately

Entschlossenheit *die;* ~: determination; resolution; **in wilder ~:** fiercely determined; with fierce determination

entschlummern *itr. V.; mit sein* 1 (dichter.: einschlafen) fall asleep 2 ▸**entschlafen 1**

entschlüpfen *itr. V.; mit sein* 1 escape; slip away 2 ‹*remarks, words*› slip out

Entschluss, *Entschluß *der* decision; **seinen ~ ändern** change one's mind; **aus eigenem ~:** on one's own initiative; of one's own volition

entschlüsseln *tr. V.* decipher; decode

Entschlüsselung *die;* ~, ~en deciphering; decoding

entschluss-, *entschluß-, Entschluss-, *Entschluß-: ~freudig *Adj.* decisive; **~kraft** *die* decisiveness; **~los** A *Adj.* indecisive; B *adv.* indecisively

entschuldbar *Adj.* excusable; pardonable

entschulden *tr. V.* free of debts; **einen Betrieb ~:** write off a business's debts

entschuldigen ▸ℹ **S. 227**
A *refl. V.* apologize; **sich bei jmdm. wegen** *od.* **für etw. ~:** apologize to sb. for sth.; **sich in aller Form ~:** apologize formally; make a formal apology
B *tr.* (*auch itr.*) *V.* excuse ‹*person*›; **die Mutter entschuldigte ihren Sohn in der Schule** the mother had her son excused from school; **sich ~ lassen** ask to be excused; **sein Verhalten ist durch nichts zu ~:** his behaviour is inexcusable; **~ Sie [bitte]!** (bei Fragen, Bitten) excuse me; (bedauernd) excuse me; I'm sorry; **Sie müssen ~, dass ...** I'm sorry, but ...

entschuldigend
A *Adj.* apologetic; **~e Worte** words of apology
B *adv.* apologetically

Entschuldigung *die;* ~, ~en 1 (Rechtfertigung) excuse; **etw. zu seiner ~ sagen/anführen** say sth. in one's defence 2 (schriftliche Mitteilung) [excuse] note; letter of excuse 3 ▸ℹ **S. 227** (Höflichkeitsformel) **~!** (bei Fragen, Bitten) excuse me; (bedauernd) excuse me; [I'm] sorry; **jmdn. für** *od.* **wegen etw. um ~ bitten** apologize to sb. for sth. 4 (entschuldigende Äußerung) apology

Entschuldigungs-: ~grund *der* excuse; **~schreiben** *das* letter of apology

entschweben *itr. V.; mit sein* (geh., häufig iron.) waft away

entschwefeln *tr. V.* (Chemie) desulphurize

entschwinden *unr. itr. V.; mit sein* (geh.) 1 disappear; vanish; **jmds. Blicken ~:** disappear *or* vanish from sb.'s view *or* sight 2 (vergehen) ‹*time*› fly by

entseelt /ɛnt'zeːlt/ *Adj.* (geh.) lifeless, dead (also fig.)

entsenden *unr.* (*auch regelm.*) *tr. V.* dispatch

Entsendung *die* (geh.) dispatch

entsetzen
A *refl. V.* be horrified; **sich vor** *od.* **bei dem Anblick von etw. ~:** be horrified at the sight of sth.
B *tr. V.* 1 (erschrecken) horrify; **über etw.** (*Akk.*) **entsetzt sein** be horrified by sth.; **entsetzt starren** stare in horror 2 (Milit.) relieve

Entsetzen *das;* **~s** horror; **vor ~ stumm** speechless with horror; **mit ~ bemerken** notice to one's horror; **ihn befiel lähmendes ~:** he was paralysed with horror

Entsetzens·schrei *der* cry of horror

entsetzlich
A *Adj.* 1 horrible, dreadful ‹*accident, crime, etc.*› 2 (ugs.: stark) terrible ‹*thirst, hunger*›; **einen ~en Durst haben** have a terrible thirst; be terribly thirsty
B *adv.* terribly (coll.); awfully; **es ist ~ kalt/warm/dunkel** it is terribly (coll.) *or* awfully cold/warm/dark

Entsetzlichkeit *die;* **~, ~en** horribleness; dreadfulness

entseuchen *tr. V.* decontaminate

entsichern *tr. V.* **eine Pistole ~:** release the safety catch of a pistol; **das Gewehr war entsichert/nicht entsichert** the rifle had the safety catch off/on

entsinnen *unr. refl. V.* **sich jmds./einer Sache ~:** remember sb./sth.; **sich an jmdn./etw. ~:** remember sb./sth.

Entsolidarisierung *die* loss of solidarity

entsorgen *tr. V.* (Amtsspr., Wirtsch.) dispose of ‹*waste etc.*›; **eine Stadt/ein Kernkraftwerk ~:** dispose of a town's/a nuclear power station's waste

Entsorgung *die;* **~, ~en** (Amtsspr., Wirtsch.) waste disposal

entspannen
A *tr. V.* 1 (lockern) relax ‹*body etc.*›; relax, loosen ‹*muscles*› 2 (von Spannung befreien) relax the tension of ‹*spring*›; reduce the surface tension of ‹*water*›
B *refl. V.* 1 ‹*person*› relax 2 (fig.) ‹*situation, tension*› ease

Entspannung *die* 1 relaxation 2 (politisch) easing of tension; détente

Entspannungs-: **~politik** *die* policy of détente; **~übung** *die* relaxation exercise

entspiegeln *tr. V.* bloom; **entspiegeltes Glas** coated glass

entspinnen *unr. refl. V.* develop; arise

entsprechen *unr. itr. V.* 1 (übereinstimmen mit) **einer Sache** (*Dat.*) **~:** correspond to sth.; **der Wahrheit/den Tatsachen ~:** be in accordance with the truth/the facts; **den Erwartungen ~:** live up to one's expectations; **sich** (*Dat.*) *od.* (geh.) **einander ~:** correspond 2 (nachkommen) **einem Wunsch/einer Bitte ~:** comply with a wish/request; **den Anforderungen ~:** meet the requirements; **dem Anlass ~:** be appropriate for the occasion; **dem Zweck ~:** suit the purpose

entsprechend
A *Adj.* 1 corresponding; (angemessen) appropriate ‹*payment, reply, etc.*› 2 (dem~) in accordance *postpos.*; **das Wetter war schlecht und die Stimmung ~:** the weather was bad and the mood was the same 3 (zuständig) relevant ‹*department etc.*›; ‹*person*› concerned
B *adv.* 1 (angemessen) appropriately 2 (dem~) accordingly
C *Präp. mit Dativ:* **~ einer Sache** in accordance with sth.; **der Anweisung ~ handeln** act in accordance with *or* according to instructions; **es geht ihm den Umständen ~:** he is as well as can be expected [in the circumstances]

Entsprechung *die;* **~, ~en** 1 (Übereinstimmung) correspondence 2 (Analogie) parallel; **in einer Sache seine ~ haben** *od.* **finden** have its counterpart in sth.; **für dieses Wort gibt es keine deutsche ~:** there is no German equivalent for this word

entsprießen *unr. itr. V.; mit sein* (geh.) **einer Sache** (*Dat.*) **~:** spring from sth.; (fig.: hervorgehen aus) come from sth.

entspringen *unr. itr. V.; mit sein* 1 ▸ ❶ **S. 267** ‹*river*› rise, have its source 2 (entstehen aus) **einer Sache** (*Dat.*) **~:** spring from sth. 3 (entweichen aus) escape; **ein entsprungener Häftling** an escaped prisoner; **dem Irrenhaus entsprungen sein** (scherzh.) be crazy

entstaatlichen *tr. V.* denationalize

Entstalinisierung /ɛntʃtaliniˈziːrʊŋ/ *die;* **~:** destalinization

entstammen *itr. V.; mit sein* come from; (herrühren von) derive from; **einer Sache** (*Dat.*) **~:** come/derive from sth.

entstauben *tr. V.* dust; remove the dust from; (fig.) bring up to date

entstehen *unr. itr. V.; mit sein* 1 originate; ‹*quarrel, friendship, etc.*› arise; ‹*work of art*› be created; ‹*building, town, etc.*› be built; ‹*industry*› emerge; ‹*novel etc.*› be written; **im Entstehen [begriffen] sein** be being created/built/written/be emerging 2 (gebildet werden) be formed (**aus** from, **durch** by) 3 (sich ergeben) occur; (als Folge) result; **jmdm. ~ Kosten** sb. incurs costs; **hoffentlich ist nicht der Eindruck entstanden, dass …** I/we hope I/we have not given the impression that …

Entstehung *die;* **~:** origin; **die ~ des Lebens/der Arten** the origin of life/species; **die ~ dieser Stadt/Industrie** the building of this town/the emergence of this industry

Entstehungs-: **~geschichte** *die* history of the origin[s]; **~ort** *der* place of origin; **~ursache** *die* [original] cause; **~zeit** *die* time of origin; (Datum) date of origin

entsteigen *unr. V.; mit sein* (geh.) **einer Kutsche** (*Dat.*) *usw.* **~:** alight from a coach *etc.*

entsteinen *tr. V.* stone

entstellen *tr. V.* 1 disfigure ‹*person*›; distort ‹*face*› 2 (verfälschen) distort ‹*text, facts*›

Entstellung *die* 1 (Entstelltsein) disfigurement 2 (Verfälschung) distortion

entstielen *tr. V.* remove the stalks from

entstören *tr. V.* (Elektrot.) suppress ‹*engine, distributor, electrical appliance*›

Entstörungs·stelle *die* fault repair service

entströmen *tr. V.; mit sein* (geh.) pour out; ‹*gas*› escape; (fig.) ‹*crowd*› pour *or* stream out

enttabuisieren *tr. V.* (geh.) free from taboos

enttarnen *tr. V.* uncover; (fig.) discover; **etw. als etw. ~:** reveal sth. as sth.

Enttarnung *die* uncovering

enttäuschen
A *tr. V.* disappoint; **unsere Hoffnungen wurden enttäuscht** our hopes were dashed; **jmdn. angenehm ~:** come as a pleasant surprise to sb.
B *itr. V.* **etw./jmd. enttäuscht** sth./sb. is disappointing *or* a disappointment

enttäuscht *Adj.* disappointed; dashed ‹*hopes*›; **von jmdm. ~ sein** be disappointed in sb.; **von** *od.* **über etw. ~ sein** be disappointed by *or* at sth.

Enttäuschung *die* disappointment (**für** to); **jmdm. eine ~ bereiten** be a disappointment to sb.

entthronen *tr. V.* 1 (geh.) dethrone ‹*monarch*› 2 (fig.: verdrängen) take the title away from ‹*champion etc.*›; remove ‹*magnate*› from power

Entthronung *die;* **~, ~en** (auch fig.) dethronement

entvölkern /ɛntˈfœlkɐn/
A *tr. V.* depopulate
B *refl. V.* become depopulated *or* deserted

Entvölkerung *die;* **~, ~en** depopulation

ent·wachsen *unr. itr. V.; mit sein* **einer Sache** (*Dat.*) **~:** grow out of *or* outgrow sth.; *s. auch* **Kinderschuh**

entwaffnen *tr. V.* (auch fig.) disarm

entwaffnend
A *Adj.* disarming
B *adv.* disarmingly

Entwaffnung *die;* **~:** disarming; (der Bevölkerung, eines Landes) disarmament

entwalden *tr. V.* deforest

entwarnen *itr. V.* sound *or* give the all-clear

Entwarnung *die* [sounding of the] all-clear

entwässern
A *tr. V.* 1 drain ‹*meadow, area*› 2 (Med.) dehydrate
B *itr. V.* (abfließen) flow

Entwässerung *die;* **~, ~en** 1 drainage 2 (Kanalisation) drainage [system]

Entwässerungs-: **~an·lage** *die* drainage system; **~graben** *der* drainage ditch; **~netz** *das* drainage network

entweder *Konj.* **~ … oder** either … or

Entweder-oder, *Entweder-Oder *das;* **~, ~:** **es gibt kein ~:** there is no alternative *or* are no alternatives; **es gibt nur ein ~:** a choice has to be made

entweichen *unr. itr. V.; mit sein* 1 (ausströmen) escape; **ihrem Gesicht entwich alles Blut** (geh.) the blood drained from her face 2 (geh.: entfliehen) escape

entweihen *tr. V.* desecrate; profane

Entweihung *die;* **~:** desecration; profanation

entwenden *tr. V.* (geh.) purloin (*Dat.* **from**)

entwerfen *unr. tr. V.* 1 design ‹*furniture, dress*›; (fig.) draw ‹*picture*› 2 (ausarbeiten) draft ‹*novel etc.*›; draw up ‹*plans etc.*›

entwerten *tr. V.* 1 cancel ‹*ticket, postage stamp*› 2 (Finanzw.) devalue ‹*currency*›

Entwerter *der;* **~s, ~:** ticket-cancelling machine

> **Entwerter**
>
> In many German cities, *Entwerter* (ticket-cancelling machines) are located on **U-Bahn** and **S-Bahn** platforms, or on trains, trams, or buses. When travelling on public transport in Germany it is important to remember to cancel (*entwerten*) the ticket in one of the machines. The ticket, even if just bought from the driver, is not valid without the stamp from the *Entwerter*.

Entwertung *die* ▸**entwerten**: cancellation; cancelling; devaluation

entwesen *tr. V.* (Amtsspr.) disinfest

Entwesung *die;* **~, ~en** (Amtsspr.) disinfestation

entwickeln
A *refl. V.* develop (**aus** from, **zu** into); **sie ist körperlich voll entwickelt** she is [physically] fully developed
B *tr. V.* give off, produce ‹*vapour, smell*›; show, display ‹*ability, characteristic*›; develop ‹*weapons, equipment, process, photograph, film*›; elaborate ‹*theory, ideas*›; **hoch entwickelt** highly developed

Entwickler *der;* **~s, ~** (Fot.) developer

Entwickler·bad *das* (Fot.) developing bath

Entwicklung *die;* **~, ~en** 1 development; (von Dämpfen usw.) production; **in der ~ sein** ‹*young person*› be adolescent *or* in one's adolescence; **in seiner [körperlichen] ~ zurückbleiben** be physically underdeveloped; **eine bestimmte ~ nehmen** show certain developments; **eine positive ~ zeichnet sich ab** positive developments *pl.* can be seen; **die ~ geht dahin, dass …** the trend is that …; **etw. befindet sich in der ~:** sth. is [still] in the development stage 2 (Darlegung) elaboration 3 (Fot.) development; developing

entwicklungs-, Entwicklungs-: **~abschnitt** *der* stage of development; **~alter** *das* adolescence; **~dienst** *der* development aid service; **~fähig** *Adj.* capable of development; **~gebiet** *das* development area; **~geschichte** *die* history of the development; **die ~geschichte der Menschheit/der Meerestiere** the evolution of man/of marine animals; **~geschichtlich** A *Adj.* historical; (stammesgeschichtlich) evolutionary; B *adv.* **~geschichtlich bedeutsam** important historically/as regards evolution; **sich ~geschichtlich verändert haben** have evolved; **~helfer** *der,* **~helferin** *die* development aid worker; **~hilfe** *die* [development] aid; **~jahre** *Pl.* adolescence *sing.;* **in die ~jahre kommen** reach adolescence; **~kosten** *Pl.* development costs; **~land** *das* developing country; **~ministerium** *das* ministry of development aid; **~phase** *die* stage of development; ~**politik** *die* development aid policy; ~**roman** *der* (Literaturw.) novel showing the development of an individual's character; ~**stand** *der* level of development; ~**störung** *die* developmental disturbance; ~**stufe** *die* stage of development; ~**zeit** *die* 1 ▸ ~**alter**; 2 (~zeitraum) period of development

entwinden (geh.)
A *unr. tr. V.* **jmdm. etw. ~:** wrest sth. from sb.
B *unr. refl. V.* **sich jmdm./einer Sache ~:** wrest *or* free oneself from sb./sth.

entwirrbar *Adj.* **das Garnknäuel war kaum ~:** the ball of thread could scarcely be unravelled; **die vielen Handlungsstränge waren kaum ~:** the strands of the plot could scarcely be untangled

entwirren
A *tr. V.* 1 unravel, disentangle ‹*wool etc.*› 2 (fig.) unravel, sort out ‹*situation etc.*›
B *refl. V.* sort itself out

entwischen *itr. V.; mit sein* (ugs.) get away; **aus dem Gefängnis ~:** get out of jail; **jmdm. ~:** give sb. the slip (coll.)

entwöhnen /ɛntˈvøːnən/ *tr. V.* 1 wean ‹*baby*› 2 (geh.) **jmdn. einer Sache** (*Dat.*) **~:** break sb. of the habit of [doing] sth.; **jmdn. [von einer Sucht] ~:** cure sb. [of an addiction]

entwürdigen *tr. V.* degrade

entwürdigend
A *Adj.* degrading
B *adv.* ‹*treat sb.*› in a degrading manner; degradingly ‹*low*›

Entwürdigung *die* degradation

Entwurf *der* 1 design 2 (Konzept) draft; **der ~ zu einem Roman** the outline *or* draft of a novel

entwurmen *tr. V.* worm

entwurzeln *tr. V.* uproot ‹*tree etc., person*›; **ein entwurzelter Mensch** a rootless person

Entwurzelung *die; ~, ~en* uprooting

entzaubern *tr. V.* (geh.) 1 free ‹*person*› from the spell; break the spell on ‹*person*› 2 **entzaubert werden** (die Poesie, den Zauber verlieren) lose its magic

entzerren *tr. V.* 1 (Technik) correct; rectify 2 (Fot.) rectify

Entzerrer *der; ~s, ~* 1 (Technik) equalizer 2 (Fot.) rectifier;

entziehen
A *unr. tr. V.* 1 take away; **etw. jmdm./einer Sache ~:** take sth. away from sb./sth.; **jmdm. den Führerschein ~:** take sb.'s driving licence away; **jmdm. das Wort ~:** ask sb. to stop [speaking] 2 (nicht zugestehen) withdraw; **jmdm. das Vertrauen ~:** withdraw one's confidence in sb. 3 (entfernen von, aus) **etw. einer Sache** (*Dat.*) **~:** remove sth. from sth. 4 (herausziehen aus) **etw. einer Sache** (*Dat.*) **~:** extract sth. from sth. 5 (ugs.: entwöhnen) get ‹*addict*› off drugs; dry ‹*alcoholic*› out (coll.)
B *unr. refl. V.* **sich jmds. Armen/Umklammerung ~:** free oneself from sb.'s arms/embrace; **ihrem Reiz konnte ich mich nicht ~:** I could not resist her/their charms; **sich der Gesellschaft** (*Dat.*) **~** (geh.) withdraw from society; **sich seinen Pflichten** (*Dat.*) **~:** shirk *or* evade one's duty; **sich einer Untersuchung** (*Dat.*) **~** (geh.) elude an investigation; **das entzieht sich meiner Kontrolle/Kenntnis** that is beyond my control/knowledge

Entziehung *die* 1 withdrawal; loss 2 (~skur) withdrawal treatment *no indef. art.*; **eine ~ machen** take withdrawal treatment

Entziehungs-: ~**anstalt** *die* treatment centre; clinic; ~**kur** *die* course of withdrawal treatment; withdrawal programme

entzifferbar *Adj.* decipherable

entziffern *tr. V.* 1 decipher ‹*writing*› 2 (entschlüsseln) decipher, decode ‹*message*›

Entzifferung *die; ~, ~en* ▸ **entziffern**: deciphering; decoding

entzippen *tr. V.* (DV) unzip

entzücken
A *tr. V.* delight; **etw. entzückt jmdn.** sth. delights sb. *or* fills sb. with delight
B *refl. V.* (geh.) **sich an etw.** (*Dat.*) **~:** be enraptured by sth.

Entzücken *das; ~s* (geh.) delight, joy (**an** + *Dat.* in)

entzückend
A *Adj.* delightful; **das ist ja ~!** (iron.) [that's] charming!
B *adv.* delightfully

entzückt *Adj.* delighted; **von/über etw.** (*Akk.*) **~ sein** be delighted by/at sth.

Entzückung *die; ~, ~en* (geh.) joy; rapture

Entzug *der; ~[e]s* 1 withdrawal; (das Herausziehen) extraction 2 ▸ **Entziehung 2**

Entzugs·erscheinung *die* withdrawal symptom

entzündbar *Adj.* 1 (brennbar) [in]flammable 2 (fig.: erregbar) easily roused

entzünden
A *tr. V.* 1 (geh.: anzünden) light ‹*fire*›; strike, light ‹*match*› 2 (geh.: erregen) kindle, arouse ‹*passion*›; arouse ‹*hatred*›
B *refl. V.* 1 catch fire; ignite 2 (anschwellen) become inflamed; **entzündete Augen haben** have inflamed eyes 3 (geh.: entstehen) **sich an etw.** (*Dat.*) **~** ‹*quarrel*› be sparked off by sth.; ‹*temper*› flare at sth.

entzündlich *Adj.* 1 [in]flammable ‹*substance*› 2 (Med.) inflammatory

Entzündlichkeit *die; ~:* [in]flammability

Entzündung *die; ~, ~en* inflammation

entzündungs·hemmend *Adj.* anti-inflammatory; antiphlogistic (Med.)

Entzündungs·herd *der* focus of inflammation

entzwei *Adj.* (geh.) in pieces

entzwei|brechen (geh.)
A *unr. tr. V.* break into pieces
B *unr. itr. V.; mit sein* break into pieces

entzweien
A *refl. V.* **sich [mit jmdm.] ~:** fall out [with sb.]
B *tr. V.* cause ‹*persons*› to fall out

entzwei- (geh.): ~**|gehen** *unr. itr. V.; mit sein* (zerbrechen) break; (nicht mehr funktionieren) cease to function; ~**|machen** *tr. V.* break; ~**|schlagen** *unr. tr. V.* smash to pieces

Entzweiung *die; ~, ~en:* **eine ~ herbeiführen** cause the two friends/countries *etc.* to fall out

en vogue /ãˈvoːk/ (geh.) **~ sein** be fashionable *or* in vogue

Enzephalogramm /ɛntsefaloˈgram/ *das; ~s, ~e* (Med.) encephalogram

Enzian /ˈɛntsi̯aːn/ *der; ~s, ~e* 1 (Bot.) gentian 2 (Schnaps) enzian liqueur

enzian·blau *Adj.* gentian-blue

Enzyklika /ɛnˈtsyːklika/ *die; ~, Enzykliken* encyclical

Enzyklopädie /ɛntsyklopɛˈdiː/ *die; ~, ~n* encyclopedia

enzyklopädisch
A *Adj.* encyclopedic
B *adv.* encyclopedically

Enzyklopädist *der; ~en, ~en* encyclopedist

Enzym /ɛnˈtsyːm/ *das; ~s, ~e* (Chemie) enzyme

eo ipso /ˈeːo ˈɪpso/ (geh.) ipso facto

Eolithikum /eoˈliːtikʊm/ *das; ~s* eolithic period

Epaulett /epoˈlɛt/ *das; ~s, ~s,* **Epaulette** *die; ~, ~n* epaulette

Epen ▸ **Epos**

ephemer /efeˈmeːɐ̯/ *Adj.* (geh.) ephemeral

Epidemie /epideˈmiː/ *die; ~, ~n* (auch fig.) epidemic

epidemisch
A *Adj.* epidemic
B *adv.* as/like an epidemic

Epidermis /epiˈdɛrmɪs/ *die; ~, Epidermen* (Biol.) epidermis

Epidiaskop /epidiaˈskoːp/ *das; ~s, ~e* epidiascope

epigonal /epigoˈnaːl/ *Adj.* (geh.) ▸ **epigonenhaft**

Epigone /epiˈgoːnə/ *der; ~n, ~n* (geh.) imitator

epigonenhaft *Adj.* (geh.) imitative; unoriginal

Epigonentum *das; ~s* (geh.) imitativeness; unoriginality

Epigonin *die; ~, ~nen* ▸ **Epigone**

Epigramm /epiˈgram/ *das; ~s, ~e* (Literaturw.) epigram

Epigrammatik *die; ~* (Literaturw.) epigrammatism

epigrammatisch *Adj.* epigrammatic

Epik /ˈeːpɪk/ *die; ~* (Literaturw.) epic poetry

Epiker *der; ~s, ~,* **Epikerin** *die; ~, ~nen* epic poet

Epikureer /epikuˈreːɐ/ *der; ~s, ~,* **Epikureerin** *die; ~, ~nen* 1 (Philos.) Epicurean 2 (geh.) epicurean

epikureisch *Adj.* 1 (Philos.) Epicurean 2 (geh.) epicurean

Epilepsie /epilɛˈpsiː/ *die; ~, ~n* ▸ **❶ S. 439** (Med.) epilepsy *no art.*

Epileptiker /epiˈlɛptikɐ/ *der; ~s, ~,* **Epileptikerin** *die; ~, ~nen* epileptic

epileptisch *Adj.* epileptic

Epilog /epiˈloːk/ *der; ~s, ~e* epilogue

Epiphanias /epiˈfaːni̯as/ *das; ~:* Epiphany *no art.*

Epiphanie /epifaˈniː/ *die; ~* (Rel.) epiphany

episch /ˈeːpɪʃ/
A *Adj.* epic
B *adv.* in epic terms

Episkop /epiˈskoːp/ *das; ~s, ~e* episcope

Episkopal·kirche *die* 1 Episcopal church 2 (ev. Kirche) Protestant church

Episkopat /epɪskoˈpaːt/ *das od. der; ~[e]s, ~e* (Theol.) 1 (Amt) episcopate 2 (Gesamtheit der Bischöfe) episcopate; episcopacy

Episode /epiˈzoːdə/ *die; ~, ~n* episode

episodenhaft, episodisch
A *Adj.* episodic
B *adv.* episodically

Epistel /eˈpɪstl̩/ *die; ~, ~n* 1 (bibl.) epistle 2 (kath. Kirche) epistle; lesson; **jmdm. die ~ lesen** (fig. veralt.) read sb. a lesson

Epitaph /epiˈtaːf/ *das; ~s, ~e* (geh.) 1 epitaph 2 (Gedenktafel) memorial plaque

Epithel /epiˈteːl/ *das; ~s, ~e* (Biol.) epithelium

Epitheton /eˈpiːtetɔn/ *das; ~s, Epitheta* (Sprachw.) epithet

Epizentrum *das* (Geol.) epicentre

epochal /epɔˈxaːl/ *Adj.* epochal; epoch-making; epoch-making ‹*invention*›; (fig. iron.) world-shattering; monumental

Epoche /eˈpɔxə/ *die; ~, ~n* epoch; **~ machen** be epoch-making

epoche·machend *Adj.* epoch-making

Epos /ˈeːpɔs/ *das; ~, Epen* epic [poem]; epos

Eprouvette /epruˈvɛt/ *die; ~, ~n* (österr.) test tube

Equipage /ekviˈpaːʒə/ *die; ~, ~n* (veralt.) equipage

Equipe /eˈkɪp/ *die; ~, ~n* team

er /eːɐ̯/ *Personalpron. 3. Pers. Sg. Nom. Mask.* he; (betont) him; (bei Dingen/Tieren) it; (bei männlichen Tieren) he/him; it; **„Er"** (auf Handtüchern, an Türen) 'His'; **~ war es, nicht sie** it was him, not her; **ich weiß mehr als ~:** I know more than he does; I know more than him (coll.); **„Er, 42, Witwer ..."** 'widower, 42 ...'; **bring Er den Wein!** (veralt.) fetch the wine!; *s. auch* **ihm**; **ihn**; **seiner**

Er *der; ~, ~s* (ugs.) he; **ist es ein ~ oder eine Sie?** is it a he or a she?

erachten *tr. V.* (geh.) consider; **etw. als** *od.* **für seine Pflicht ~:** consider sth. [to be] one's duty; **etw. als** *od.* **für notwendig ~:** consider *or* think sth. necessary

Erachten *das:* **in meinem ~ nach, meines ~s** in my opinion

erahnen *tr. V.* imagine; guess

e

e

erarbeiten *tr. V.* 1 (erwerben) work for; **[sich (*Dat.*)] ein Vermögen ~:** make [oneself] a fortune 2 (zu Eigen machen) work on; study; **[sich (*Dat.*)] einen Text ~:** understand a text by working on it 3 (erstellen) work out ‹*plan, programme, etc.*›

Erb- /'ɛrp-/ : **~adel** *der* hereditary nobility; (Titel) hereditary title; **~an·lage** *die* (Biol.) hereditary disposition; **~an·spruch** *der* claim to an/the inheritance; **~an·teil** *der* share of an/the inheritance

erbarmen /ɛɐ̯'barmən/
A *refl. V.* (geh.) **sich jmds./einer Sache ~:** take pity on sb./sth.; **Herr, erbarme dich unser!** Lord, have mercy upon us
B *tr. V.* **jmdn. ~:** arouse sb.'s pity; move sb. to pity

Erbarmen *das;* **~s** pity; **mit jmdm. ~ haben** take pity on *or* feel pity for sb.; **er kennt kein ~:** he knows no pity *or* mercy; **zum ~:** pitifully; pathetically; **zum ~ sein** be pitiful *or* pathetic

erbarmens·wert *Adj.* pitiful

erbärmlich /ɛɐ̯'bɛrmlɪç/
A *Adj.* 1 (elend) wretched 2 (unzulänglich) pathetic 3 (abwertend: gemein) mean; wretched 4 (sehr groß) terrible ‹*hunger, thirst, fear, etc.*›
B *adv.* (intensivierend) terribly ‹*cold, hot, thirsty, hungry, etc.*›

Erbärmlichkeit *die;* ~ 1 (Elend) wretchedness 2 (abwertend: Gemeinheit) meanness; wretchedness

erbarmungs-, Erbarmungs-: ~los A *Adj.* merciless; B *adv.* mercilessly; **~losigkeit** *die;* **~~:** mercilessness; **~würdig** *Adj.* pitiful

erbauen
A *tr. V.* 1 build 2 (geh.: erheben) uplift; edify; **wir waren von seinen Plänen wenig erbaut** we were not exactly delighted about his plans
B *refl. V.* (geh.: sich erfreuen) **sich an etw.** (*Dat.*) **~:** be uplifted *or* edified by sth.

Erbauer *der;* **~s, ~, Erbauerin** *die;* **~, ~nen** architect

erbaulich *Adj.* edifying

Erbauung *die;* ~ (Freude) edification

Erbauungs·literatur *die* devotional literature

erb-, Erb-: ~bauer *der;* **~~n, ~~n** 1 *farmer owning property by hereditary right;* 2 *(in ~pacht) farmer with hereditary right of tenure;* **~begräbnis** *das* 1 *right to be buried in the family grave;* 2 ▸**Familiengrab**; **~berechtigt** *Adj.* entitled to inherit; entitled to an/the inheritance; **die ~berechtigten** the heirs; **~biologisch** *Adj.* genetic; **ein ~biologisches Gutachten** the opinion of an expert in genetics

Erbe[1] /'ɛrbə/ *das;* **~s** 1 (Vermögen) inheritance; **das väterliche/mütterliche ~:** patrimony/maternal inheritance; **sein ~ antreten** come into one's inheritance 2 (Vermächtnis) heritage; legacy

Erbe[2] *der;* **~n, ~n** heir; **der rechtmäßige/mutmaßliche ~:** the rightful heir/heir presumptive; **jmdn. zum** *od.* **als ~n einsetzen** appoint sb. as one's heir; **am Ende war alles nur für die lachenden ~n** (ugs.) in the end it was all just for others to inherit; **die ~n** (fig.) future generations

Erbe·aneignung, Erbe·rezeption *die* (DDR) acquainting oneself with the nation's cultural heritage

erbeben *itr. V.; mit sein* (geh.) 1 shake; tremble 2 (fig.: erregt werden) shake; quiver

erb-, Erb-: ~eigen *Adj.* inherited; **~eigenschaft** *die* (Biol.) hereditary characteristic; **~einsetzung** *die* (Rechtsw.) appointment of an/one's heir

erben *tr. (auch itr.) V.* inherit; **bei mir ist nichts zu ~** (ugs.) you won't get anything out of me

Erben·gemeinschaft *die* [community of] joint heirs

erbetteln *tr. V.* get by begging; **um eine Mahlzeit zu ~:** to beg for a meal

erbeuten /ɛɐ̯'bɔytn̩/ *tr. V.* carry off, get away with ‹*valuables, prey, etc.*›; capture ‹*enemy plane, tank, etc.*›

erb-, Erb-: ~fähig *Adj.* (Rechtsspr.) heritable; **~faktor** *der* hereditary factor; **~fall** *der* (Rechtsw.) inheritance; **~fehler** *der* hereditary defect; **~feind** *der,* **~feindin** *die* 1 traditional enemy; 2 (verhüll.: Teufel) arch fiend

Erb·folge *die* 1 succession; **die gesetzliche ~:** intestate succession 2 (Thronfolge) succession

Erbfolge-: ~krieg *der* war of succession; **~recht** *das* law of succession

Erb-: ~forschung *die* genetics *sing., no art.;* **~gut** *das* (Biol.) genotype; genetic make-up; **~hof** *der* ancestral estate; (fig. Pol.) perquisite

erbieten *unr. refl. V.* (geh.) **sich ~, etw. zu tun** offer to do sth.

Erbin *die;* **~, ~nen** heiress

erbitten
A *unr. tr. V.* (geh.) request; **„baldige Antwort erbeten"** 'early reply appreciated'
B *unr. refl. V.* (veralt.) **sich ~ lassen, etw. zu tun** be prevailed upon to do sth.

erbittern *tr. V.* enrage; incense

erbittert
A *Adj.* bitter ‹*resistance, struggle*›
B *adv.* **~ kämpfen** wage a bitter struggle

Erbitterung *die;* **~:** bitterness

Erb·krankheit *die* hereditary disease

erblassen /ɛɐ̯'blasn̩/ *itr. V.; mit sein* (geh.) go *or* turn pale; blanch (literary); *s. auch* **Neid**

Erblasser /'ɛrplasɐ/ *der;* **~s, ~** (Rechtsw.) testator

Erblasserin *die;* **~, ~nen** (Rechtsw.) testatrix

Erb-: ~last *die* inherited burden; [negative] legacy; **~lehen** *das* (hist.) hereditary fief; **~lehre** *die* (Biol.) genetics *sing.*

erbleichen *itr. V.; mit sein* (geh.) go *or* turn pale; blanch (literary)

erblich
A *Adj.* hereditary ‹*title, disease*›
B *adv.* **er ist ~ belastet** he suffers from a hereditary condition; (scherzh.) it runs in his family

Erblichkeit *die;* ~ (auch Biol.) heritability

erblicken *tr. V.* (geh.) 1 catch sight of; see 2 (fig.) see; **sie erblickte in mir eine Konkurrentin** she saw me as a rival; she saw a rival in me

erblinden *itr. V.; mit sein* 1 go blind; lose one's sight 2 (matt werden) go *or* become dull

Erblindung *die;* **~:** loss of sight

erblonden *itr. V.; mit sein* (scherzh.) go blonde

erblühen *itr. V.; mit sein* (geh.) 1 bloom; blossom 2 (sich entfalten) blossom

Erb-: ~masse *die* 1 (Biol.) genotype; genetic make-up; 2 (Rechtsspr.) estate; **~monarchie** *die* hereditary monarchy; **~onkel** *der* (ugs. scherzh.) rich uncle

erbosen /ɛɐ̯'bo:zn̩/ (geh.)
A *tr. V.* infuriate
B *refl. V.* **sich über etw.** (*Akk.*) **~:** become furious about sth.

erbost *Adj.* angry, furious (**über** + *Akk.* at)

erbötig /ɛɐ̯'bø:tɪç/ *Adj.* (veralt.) **sich ~ machen, etw. zu tun** offer to do sth.

Erb-: ~pacht *die* 1 (Rechtsw.) hereditary lease; 2 (hist.) fee simple; **~prinz** *der,* **~prinzessin** *die* heir to the throne

erbrechen
A *unr. tr. V.* 1 bring up ‹*food*› 2 (geh.: aufbrechen) break open ‹*safe etc.*› 3 (veralt.: öffnen) open ‹*letter, seal*›
B *unr. itr., refl. V.* (geh.: sich übergeben) **[sich] ~:** vomit; be sick

Erbrechen *das;* **~s** vomiting; **bis zum ~** (ugs.) ad nauseam

Erb·recht *das* (Rechtsw.) 1 law of inheritance 2 (Anspruch) right of inheritance

erbringen *unr. tr. V.* 1 produce ‹*proof, evidence*› 2 (liefern) produce ‹*result etc.*›; yield ‹*amount*›; result in ‹*savings etc.*›; **die vorgesehene Leistung ~:** do the required work 3 (aufbringen) raise ‹*funds etc.*›; put up ‹*money etc.*›

Erbrochene /ɛɐ̯'brɔxənə/ *das; adj. Dekl.* vomit

Erb·schaden *der* (Genetik) hereditary defect

Erbschaft *die;* **~, ~en** inheritance; **eine ~ machen** come into an inheritance; **die ~ des Kolonialismus** (fig.) the legacy of colonialism

Erbschafts·anspruch *der* claim to an/the inheritance

Erbschaft[s]·steuer *die* estate *or* death duties *pl.*

Erb-: ~schein *der* certificate of inheritance; **~schleicher** *der* (abwertend) legacy hunter; **~schleicherei** *die;* **~~, ~~en** (abwertend) legacy hunting; **~schleicherin** *die* ▸**~schleicher**; **~schuld** *die* (Rechtsw.) inherited debt

Erbse /'ɛrpsə/ *die;* **~, ~n** pea; **grüne/getrocknete** *od.* **gelbe ~n** green/dried peas

erbsen·groß *Adj.* pea-size; the size of a pea *postpos.*

Erbs[en]·püree *das* pease pudding

Erbsen-: ~suppe *die* 1 pea soup; 2 (ugs.: Nebel) pea-souper; **~zähler** *der;* **~~s, ~~, ~zählerin** *die* **~~, ~~nen** (ugs. abwertend) nit-picker (coll.)

Erb-: ~stück *das* heirloom; **~sünde** *die* original sin; **~tante** *die* (ugs. scherzh.) rich aunt; **~teil** *das* 1 share of an/the inheritance; 2 (fig.: Anlage) inherited trait; **~träger** *der* (Biol.) gene; **~vertrag** *der* testamentary contract; **~verzicht** *der* renunciation of the/an inheritance

Erd-: ~achse *die* earth's axis; **~altertum** *das* (Geol.) Palaeozoic [era]; **~anziehung** *die* earth's gravitational pull; **~apfel** *der* (bes. österr.) ▸**Kartoffel**; **~arbeiten** *Pl.* (Bauw.) earth-moving *sing.;* **~atmosphäre** *die* earth's atmosphere; **~bahn** *die* earth's orbit; **~ball** *der* (geh.) globe; earth; **~beben** *das* earthquake

erdbeben-, Erdbeben-: ~gebiet *das* earthquake area; **~herd** *der* seismic focus; hypocentre; **~messer** *der;* **~~s, ~~:** seismograph; **~sicher** *Adj.* earthquake-proof ‹*building, construction*›; ‹*region etc.*› free from earthquakes; **~warte** *die* seismological station; **~welle** *die* seismic wave

Erdbeer·bowle *die* strawberry punch

Erd·beere *die* strawberry

erdbeer·farben *Adj.* strawberry-coloured

Erd-: ~beschleunigung *die* acceleration of gravity; **~bestattung** *die* burial; interment; **~bevölkerung** *die* earth's population; **~bewegung** *die* 1 (in der **~kruste**) tremor; 2 (Bauw.) excavation; earthwork; **~bewohner** *der,* **~bewohnerin** *die* inhabitant of the earth; (Science-Fiction) earthling; **~boden** *der* ground; earth; **etw. dem ~boden gleichmachen** raze sth. to the ground; **sie ist wie vom ~boden verschluckt** it's as if the earth *or* ground had swallowed her up; **er wäre am liebsten in den ~boden versunken** he wished the earth *or* ground could have swallowed him up; **vom ~boden verschwinden** disappear from *or* off the face of the earth; **~bohrer** *der* (Technik) drill

Erde /'e:ɐ̯də/ *die;* **~, ~n** 1 (Erdreich) soil; earth; **ein Klumpen ~:** a lump of earth; **etw. in die ~ rammen** ram sth. into the ground; **zu ~ werden** (geh. verhüll.) turn to dust 2 (fester Boden) ground; **etw. auf die ~ legen/stellen** put sth. down [on the ground]; **zu ebener ~:** on the ground floor *or* (Amer.) the first floor; **auf der ~ bleiben** (fig.) keep one's feet on the ground (fig.); **mit beiden Beinen** *od.* **Füßen fest auf der ~ stehen** (fig.) have one's feet firmly on the ground (fig.); **unter der ~ liegen** (geh. verhüll.) be in one's grave; **jmdn. unter die ~ bringen** (ugs.) bury sb.; (fig.: töten) be the death of sb. (coll.) 3 (Gebiet) **ein ruhiges/idyllisches Fleckchen ~:** a peaceful/idyllic spot; **in heimatlicher/fremder ~ begraben werden** be buried in one's native soil/in foreign soil; *s. auch* **Taktik** 4 (Welt) earth; world; **auf ~n** (bibl.), **auf der ~:** on earth; **die fernsten Winkel der ~:** the farthest corners of the globe; **auf der ganzen ~:** throughout the world 5 (Planet) Earth; **der Mars, der Jupiter**

und die ~: Mars, Jupiter, and [the] Earth [6] (Elektrot.) earth

erden *tr. V.* (Elektrot.) earth

Erden-: ~bürger *der,* **~bürgerin** *die* earth-dweller; **ein neuer/kleiner ~bürger** (scherzh.) a new arrival; **~da·sein** *das* (geh.) earthly existence; **~jammer** *der* (dichter.) earthly misery; misery of the world

erdenkbar *Adj.* ▸**erdenklich**

erdenken *unr. tr. V.* think *or* make up; **eine erdachte Geschichte** a made-up story

Erden·kind *das* (geh.) child of the earth (literary); mortal

erdenklich *Adj.* conceivable; imaginable; **alle** *od.* **jede ~e Mühe** every conceivable *or* the greatest possible trouble

Erden-: ~kloß *der* (veralt.: Mensch) lump of clay; **~leben** *das* (geh.) earthly existence; **~wurm** *der* (dichter. veralt.) earthly being; mortal

Erd·erwärmung *die* warming of the earth

erd-, Erd-: ~fern *Adj.* [1] (Astron.) remote, distant ‹*planet*›; distant ‹*orbit*›; [2] (dichter.) spiritual ‹*world etc.*›; **~ferne** *die* [1] (Astron.) apogee; [2] (dichter.) remoteness [from the world]; **~gas** *das* natural gas; **~gebunden** *Adj.* (geh.) close to nature *postpos.*; **~geist** *der* earth spirit; **~geruch** *der* earthy smell; **~geschichte** *die* history of the earth; **~geschichtlich** [A] *Adj.* relating to the earth's history *postpos., not pred.*; [B] *adv.* in relation to the earth's history; **~geschoss, *~geschoß** *das* ground floor; first floor (Amer.); **im ~geschoss** on the ground floor; **~gravitation** *die* [earth's] gravitation; **~haufen** *der* mound of earth; **~hörnchen** *das; ~s, ~* (Zool.) chipmunk; ground squirrel

erdichten *tr. V.* manufacture; **das ist alles erdichtet** it's all a pure fabrication

erdig *Adj.* [1] earthy ‹*mass, smell, taste*› [2] (geh.: mit Erde beschmutzt) muddy

erd-, Erd-: ~innere *das* interior of the earth; **~kabel** *das* underground cable; **~karte** *die* map of the earth; **~kern** *der* earth's core; **~klumpen** *der* lump of earth; clod [of earth]; **~kreis** *der* (dichter.) world; **~kröte** *die* toad; **~kruste** *die* earth's crust; **~kugel** *die* [1] (Planet) terrestrial globe; earth; [2] (Globus) globe; **~kunde** *die* geography; **~kundlich** [A] *Adj.* geographical; [B] *adv.* geographically; **~leitung** *die* (Elektrot.) earth [connection]

Erdling /ˈeːɐ̯tlɪŋ/ *der; ~s, ~e* (Science-Fiction) earthling

erd-, Erd-: ~loch *das* hole in the ground; (Milit.) foxhole; **~magnetismus** *der* terrestrial magnetism; **~massen** *Pl.* masses of earth; **~metall** *das* (Chemie) group III metal; **~mittel·alter** *das* (Geol.) Mesozoic [era]; **~mittel·punkt** *der* centre of the earth; **~nah** *Adj.* [1] (Astron.) close to the earth *postpos.*; [2] (geh.) down-to-earth; **~nuss, *~nuß** *die* peanut; groundnut; **~nuss·butter, *~nuß·butter** *die* peanut butter; **~nuss·öl, *~nuß·öl** *das* groundnut oil; **~ober·fläche** *die* earth's surface; **~öl** *das* oil; petroleum (as tech. term); **~öl exportierende/produzierende Länder** oil-exporting/oil-producing countries

erdolchen *tr. V.* (geh.) stab to death

erdöl-, Erdöl-: ~exportierend ▸**Erdöl**; **~feld** *das* oilfield; **~förderland** *das* oil-producing country; **~gewinnung** *die* oil production; **~leitung** *die* oil pipeline; **~produkt** *das* oil product; **~produzent** *der* oil-producing country; **~produzierend** ▸**Erdöl**; **~raffinerie** *die* oil refinery

Erd-: ~pol *der* terrestrial pole; **~reich** *das* soil

erdreisten *refl. V.* **sich ~, etw. zu tun** have the audacity to do sth.

erdröhnen *itr. V.; mit sein* [1] (ertönen) roar [2] (beben) shake

erdrosseln *tr. V.* strangle

Erdrosselung *die; ~, ~en* strangling

Erd·rotation *die* rotation of the earth

erdrücken *tr. V.* [1] crush [2] (fig.: belasten) overwhelm; **die ständigen Geldsorgen erdrückten ihn** he was oppressed by the continual worries about money [3] (fig.: nicht gelten lassen) overshadow; **die Schrankwand erdrückt den kleinen Raum** these wall units are too overpowering in the small room

erdrückend
[A] *Adj.* overwhelming ‹*evidence, superiority*›; oppressive ‹*heat, silence*›
[B] *adv.* overwhelmingly

Erd-: ~rutsch *der* landslide; landslip; **ein politischer ~rutsch** a political landslide; **~rutsch·sieg** *der* (Politik) landslide victory; **~satellit** *der* earth satellite; **~schatten** *der* shadow of the earth; **~schicht** *die* [1] layer of earth; [2] (Geol.) stratum; **~schluss, *~schluß** *der* (Elektrot.) accidental earth contact; **~scholle** *die* lump of earth; clod [of earth]; **~spalte** *die* fissure [in the ground]; **~stoß** *der* earth tremor; **~teil** *der* continent; **~trabant** *der* (geh.) earth satellite

erdulden *tr. V.* endure ‹*sorrow, misfortune*›; tolerate ‹*insults*›; (über sich ergehen lassen) undergo

Erd-: ~um·drehung *die* rotation of the earth; **eine ~umdrehung** one revolution of the earth; **~um·fang** *der* circumference of the earth; **~umkreisung** *die* orbit of the earth; **~um·lauf·bahn** *die* orbit [of the earth]; **in die ~umlaufbahn eintreten** enter into orbit; **~um·rundung** *die* (eines Schiffs) circumnavigation of the earth; (eines Raumschiffs) orbit of the earth; **~umseg[e]lung** *die* circumnavigation of the earth

Erdung *die; ~, ~en* (Elektrot.) [1] (das Erden) earthing [2] (Leitung) earth [connection]

erd-, Erd-: ~verbunden, ~verhaftet, ~verwachsen *Adj.* (geh.) close to nature *postpos.*; **~wall** *der* wall of earth; (Milit., Straßenbau) earthwork; **~wärts** *Adv.* (geh.) earthward[s]; **~zeit·alter** *das* geological era

ereifern *refl. V.* **sich über etw.** (*Akk.*) **~:** get excited about sth.; **sich schnell/unnötig ~:** quickly get worked up/get worked up about nothing

Ereiferung *die; ~:* excitement

ereignen *refl. V.* happen; ‹*accident, mishap*› occur

Ereignis /ɛɐ̯ˈlaignɪs/ *das; ~ses, ~se* event; occurrence; **ein aufregendes/historisches ~:** an exciting/historical event; **das fröhliche ~ eurer Hochzeit** the happy occasion of your marriage; **die ~se überstürzten sich** everything seemed to happen at once; **ein freudiges ~:** a happy event; **große ~se werfen ihren Schatten voraus** coming events cast their shadows before

ereignis-: ~los [A] *Adj.* uneventful; [B] *adv.* uneventfully; **~reich** [A] *Adj.* eventful; [B] *adv.* eventfully

ereilen *tr. V.* (geh.) **der Tod ereilte ihn** he died suddenly; **das gleiche Schicksal ereilte ihn** he met the same fate

Erektion /erɛkˈtsi̯oːn/ *die; ~, ~en* erection

Eremit /ereˈmiːt/ *der; ~en, ~en* hermit

Eremitage /eremiˈtaːʒə/ *die; ~, ~n* hermitage

Eremiten·leben *das* hermit's life

ererben *tr. V.* (veralt.) inherit ‹*money, characteristics*›

ererbt *Adj.* inherited ‹*fortune, ability*›; inherited, hereditary ‹*characteristic etc.*›

erfahrbar *Adj.* **~ sein** be able to be experienced; **einem Kind etw. ~ machen** bring sth. within a child's experience

erfahren¹ *unr. tr. V.* [1] find out; learn; (hören) hear; **etw. Wichtiges/Neues/Einzelheiten ~:** find out something important/new/some details; **etw. von jmdm. ~:** find sth. out from sb.; **etw. über jmdn./etw. ~:** find out *or* hear sth. about sb./sth.; **etw. von etw. ~:** find out *or* learn/hear sth. about sth.; **etw. durch jmdn./etw. ~:** learn of sth. from sb./sth. [2] (geh.: erleben) experience; **viel Leid/Kummer ~:** suffer much sorrow/anxiety; *s. auch* **Leib 1** [3] (mitmachen) undergo ‹*change, experience, development, etc.*›; suffer ‹*setback*›

erfahren² *Adj.* experienced

Erfahrung *die; ~, ~en* experience; **über reiche/langjährige ~en verfügen** have extensive/years of experience; **eine Frau mit ~:** a woman of experience; **~en sammeln** gain experience *sing.*; **~en austauschen** share one's experiences; **bittere ~en sammeln müssen** have bitter experiences; **die ~ machen, dass ...** learn by experience that ...; **durch ~ lernen** learn through experience; **aus ~ sprechen** speak from experience; **wir haben schlechte ~en mit ihm/damit gemacht** our experience of him/it has not been very good; **etw. in ~ bringen** discover sth.

erfahrungs-, Erfahrungs-: ~aus·tausch *der* exchange of experiences; **~bericht** *der* report; **~gemäß** *Adv.* in our/my experience; **~gemäß ist es so, dass ...** experience shows that ...; **~mäßig** [A] *Adj.* empirical; [B] *adv.* empirically; **~tat·sache** *die* empirical fact; **~wert** *der* figure drawn from past experience; **~wissenschaft** *die* empirical science

erfassbar, *erfaßbar *Adj.* ascertainable

erfassen *tr. V.* [1] (mitreißen) catch [2] (begreifen) grasp ‹*situation, implications, etc.*›; **etw. intuitiv ~:** have an intuitive grasp of sth.; **du hast es erfasst!** (meist iron.) you've got it! [3] (registrieren) register; record; **einen repräsentativen Bevölkerungsdurchschnitt ~:** record information on *or* from a representative cross section of the population [4] (einbeziehen) cover [5] (packen) seize; **Angst/Freude erfasste ihn** he was seized by fear/overcome with joy

Erfasser *der; ~s, ~,* **Erfasserin** *die; ~, ~nen* keyboarder

Erfassung *die* registration; **eine ~ der gesamten Bevölkerung/des Wohnraums** a survey of the whole population/of living space

erfinden *unr. tr. V.* [1] invent [2] (ausdenken) make up ‹*story, words*›; make up, invent ‹*excuse*›; **sie hat die Arbeit [auch] nicht erfunden** (iron.) she is a lazy so-and-so (coll.); **das ist alles erfunden** it is pure fabrication; *s. auch* **Pulver 2**

Erfinder *der; ~s, ~,* **Erfinderin** *die; ~, ~nen* [1] inventor [2] (Urheber) creator; **das ist nicht im Sinne des ~s** (ugs.) that's not what it was meant for

Erfinder·geist *der* inventive genius

erfinderisch *Adj.* inventive; (schlau) resourceful

Erfinder·schutz *der: protection of inventors;* ≈ patent law

erfindlich *Adj.* **nicht ~ sein** be unclear; **mir ist nicht ~, warum ...** I do not see why ...

Erfindung *die; ~, ~en* [1] invention; **die ~en der Raumfahrttechnik** inventions in the field of space technology; **eine ~ machen** invent something; **er hat viele ~en gemacht** he has many inventions to his credit [2] (Ausgedachtes) invention; fabrication

erfindungs-, Erfindungs-: ~gabe *die* inventiveness; **~reich** [A] *Adj.* imaginative; [B] *adv.* imaginatively; **~reichtum** *der* capacity for invention

erflehen *tr. V.* (geh.) beg; **jmds. Hilfe/Hilfe von jmdm. ~:** beg sb.'s help/beg help from sb.; **Vergebung ~:** beg for forgiveness

Erfolg /ɛɐ̯ˈfɔlk/ *der; ~[e]s, ~e* ▸**i S. 331** success; **viel/keinen ~ haben** be very successful/be unsuccessful; **etw. mit/ohne ~ tun** do something successfully/without success; **ohne ~ bleiben** remain unsuccessful; **der ~ blieb aus** success was not forthcoming; **einen ~ erzielen** *od.* **erringen** achieve success; **von ~ begleitet/gekrönt sein** be accompanied by/crowned with success; **der ~ war, dass ...** (ugs.) the upshot was that ...

erfolgen *itr. V.; mit sein* take place; occur; **nach erfolgtem Umbau** when reconstruction has/had been completed; **auf seine Beschwerden**

erfolgte keine Reaktion there was no reaction to his complaints; **es erfolgte keine weitere Stellungnahme** no further statement was forthcoming

erfolg-, Erfolg-: ~gekrönt *Adj.* (geh.) crowned with success; **~los** A *Adj.* unsuccessful; B *adv.* unsuccessfully; **~losigkeit** *die;* **~~:** lack of success; **~reich** A *Adj.* successful; B *adv.* successfully

erfolgs-, Erfolgs-: ~aussicht *die* prospect of success; **~autor** *der,* **~autorin** *die* successful author; **~beteiligung** *die* profit sharing; **~chance** *die* chance of success; **~denken** *das:* **das rücksichtslose ~denken** the thoughtless worship of success; **~erlebnis** *das* feeling of achievement; **dieses ~erlebnis tat ihm gut** this experience of success did him good; **~film** *der* successful film; **~honorar** *das* contingent fee; **~kurve** *die* path of success; (eines Produkts) sales graph; **~meldung** *die* report of success; **~mensch** *der* successful individual; **~modell** *das* (erfolgreiches Modell) successful model; (Vorbild) recipe for success; **~prämie** *die* (eines Vertreters) commission; (eines Arbeiters) bonus; **~quote** *die* success rate; (bei Prüfungen) pass rate; **~rezept** *das* recipe for success; **~roman** *der* successful novel; **~story** *die* success story; **~stück** *das* (Theater) successful play; **~verwöhnt** *Adj.* spoilt by success *postpos.*; too accustomed to success *postpos.*; **~zahl** *die,* **~ziffer** *die* high success figure; (Wirtsch.) profit figure; **~zwang** *der* pressure to succeed

erfolg·versprechend *Adj.* promising

erforderlich *Adj.* required; necessary

erforderlichenfalls *Adv.* (Amtsspr.) should it be necessary

erfordern *tr. V.* require; demand; **wenn es die Umstände ~:** if circumstances require

Erfordernis *das;* **~ses, ~se** requirement

erforschen *tr. V.* discover ‹*facts, causes, etc.*›; explore ‹*country*›; find out ‹*truth*›; **sein Gewissen ~:** search one's conscience

Erforscher *der,* **Erforscherin** *die* researcher; (Forschungsreisender) explorer

Erforschung *die* research (+ *Gen.* into); (der Erde, des Weltalls usw.) exploration

erfragen *tr. V.* ascertain; **Einzelheiten zu ~ bei ...** further details can be obtained from ...

erfrechen *refl. V.* (veralt., scherzh.) **sich ~, etw. zu tun** have the audacity to do sth.

erfreuen

A *tr. V.* please; **wir möchten Sie mit einem kleinen Geschenk ~:** we should like to give you a small present; **diese gute Nachricht hat uns sehr erfreut** we were very pleased to hear the good news; **sehr erfreut!** pleased to meet you

B *refl. V.* 1 **sich an etw.** (*Dat.*) **~:** take pleasure in sth. 2 (geh.: genießen) **sich einer Sache** (*Gen.*) **~:** enjoy sth.; **sich bester Gesundheit ~:** enjoy the best of health

erfreulich *Adj.* pleasant; **eine ~e Mitteilung** a piece of good news; **es ist sehr ~ zu hören, dass es Ihnen besser geht** it's very good to hear that you're better; **etwas/wenig/nichts Erfreuliches** something/hardly anything/nothing pleasant

erfreulicherweise *Adv.* happily

erfrieren

A *unr. itr. V.; mit sein* 1 ‹*person, animal*› freeze to death; ‹*plant, harvest, etc.*› be damaged by frost; suffer frost damage; **er ist ganz erfroren** (ugs.) he's absolutely frozen 2 (fig.: erstarren) freeze; ‹*feelings*› cool

B *unr. refl. V.* **sich** (*Dat.*) **die Finger/Ohren ~:** get frostbite in one's fingers/ears

Erfrierung *die;* **~, ~en** ▸ⓘ **S. 439** frostbite *no pl.*; **~en an den Händen/Füßen** frostbitten hands/feet

Erfrierungs·tod *der* death from exposure

erfrischen

A *tr.* (*auch itr.*) *V.* 1 (beleben) refresh; **ein Abendspaziergang erfrischt sehr** an evening walk is very refreshing 2 (anregen) stimulate

B *refl. V.* freshen oneself up

erfrischend (auch fig.)

A *Adj.* refreshing

B *adv.* refreshingly

Erfrischung *die;* **~, ~en** (auch fig.) refreshment

Erfrischungs-: ~getränk *das* soft drink; **eisgekühlter Tee ist ein herrliches ~getränk** iced tea is a wonderfully refreshing drink; **~raum** *der* refreshment room; **~stand** *der* refreshment stand; **~trunk** *der* (geh.) refreshing drink; **~tuch** *das; Pl.* **~tücher** tissue wipe; towelette

erfühlen *tr. V.* (geh.) sense

erfüllbar *Adj.* **~e Wünsche/Bedingungen** wishes which can be granted/conditions which can be met; **Ihre Wünsche/Bedingungen sind nicht ~:** your wishes cannot be granted/your conditions cannot be met

erfüllen

A *tr. V.* 1 grant ‹*wish, request*›; fulfil ‹*contract*›; carry out ‹*duty*›; meet ‹*condition*›; **seinen Zweck ~:** serve its purpose; **der Tatbestand des Totschlags ist erfüllt** this constitutes a case of manslaughter 2 (füllen) fill; **die Luft war von süßem Duft erfüllt** a sweet perfume filled the air; **ein erfülltes Leben** (geh.) a full life 3 (stark beschäftigen) overcome; **eine Sehnsucht erfüllte sein Herz** a longing came over him; **jmdn. mit etw. ~** (geh.) fill sb. with sth. 4 (Math.) satisfy

B *refl. V.* ‹*wish*› come true

Erfüllung *die:* **die ~ von Pflichten** the performance of duties; **sie glaubte nicht mehr an die ~ ihrer Wünsche** she no longer believed that her wishes would be granted; **in ~ gehen** come true; **in etw.** (*Dat.*) **~ finden** find fulfilment in sth.

Erfüllungs-: ~gehilfe *der* (bes. Rechtsspr.) vicarious agent; (fig. abwertend) henchman; **~gehilfin** *die* (Rechtsw.) vicarious agent; (fig. abwertend) henchwoman; **~ort** *der* (Rechtsw.) place of performance; **~politik** *die* (bes. ns.) *policy of unconditional fulfilment of the reparations and disarmament clauses of the Treaty of Versailles;* **~tag** *der* (Rechtsw.) day for settlement (*of debts*)

erfunden

A *2. Part. v.* **erfinden**

B *Adj.* **eine ~e Geschichte** a fictional story; **das Abenteuer ist doch nur ~:** the adventure is just made up; **frei ~:** completely fictitious

Erg /ɛrk/ *das;* **~s, ~** (Physik) erg

ergänzen /ɛɐ̯ˈgɛntsn̩/

A *tr. V.* 1 (vervollständigen) complete; (erweitern) add to; replenish ‹*supply*›; amplify ‹*remark, statement, etc.*›; amend ‹*statute*›; **etw. wieder ~:** make sth. up; **er ergänzte seine Sammlung durch** *od.* **um einige wertvolle Stücke** he added some valuable pieces to his collection 2 (hinzufügen) **~[d hinzufügen]** add ‹*remark*› 3 (hinzukommen zu) **eine Jacke ergänzte das Sommerkleid** a jacket complemented the summer dress; **der neue Mitarbeiter ergänzt das Team hervorragend** the new employee makes up the team admirably 4 **sie ~ einander** *od.* **sich** they complement each other

B *refl. V.* **sich durch etw. ~:** be augmented by sth.

Ergänzung *die;* **~, ~en** 1 (Vervollständigung) completion; (Erweiterung) enlargement; **die ~ der Arbeitsgruppen** making up the working groups; **zur ~ des Gesagten/einer Sammlung** to amplify what has been said/in order to enlarge a collection; **die ~ eines Gesetzes** the amendment of a statute; **die ~ der Vorräte** the replenishment of supplies 2 (Zusatz) addition; (zu einem Gesetz) amendment 3 (zusätzliche Bemerkung) further remark 4 (Sprachw.: Objekt) object

Ergänzungs-: ~ab·gabe *die* (Steuerw.) surtax; **~band** *der* supplementary volume; supplement; **~bindestrich** *der* (Sprachw.) hyphen; **~frage** *die* 1 (Sprachw.) wh-question; 2 (Zusatzfrage) supplementary question

ergattern *tr. V.* (ugs.) manage to grab

ergaunern *tr. V.* get by underhand means; **wo hast du [dir] das Fahrrad ergaunert?** (ugs.) where did you pinch *or* swipe that bike? (coll.)

ergeben[1]

A *unr. refl. V.* 1 (sich fügen) **sich in etw.** (*Akk.*) **~:** submit to sth.; **sich in sein Schicksal ~:** resign oneself *or* become resigned to one's fate 2 (kapitulieren) surrender (**jmdm.** to sb.); **sich [der Polizei** (*Dat.*)**] ~:** give oneself up [to the police] 3 (folgen, entstehen) ‹*opportunity, difficulty, problem*› arise (**aus** from); **bald ergab sich ein angeregtes Gespräch** soon a lively discussion was taking place; **es ergab sich so** it just turned out that way 4 (sich hingeben) **sich jmdm. ~:** give oneself to someone; **sich einer Sache** (*Dat.*) **~:** abandon oneself to sth.; **sich dem Alkohol/**(ugs.) **Suff ~:** take to alcohol/drink *or* the bottle

B *unr. tr. V.* result in; **die Ernte ergab rund 400 Zentner Kartoffeln** the harvest produced about 400 hundredweight of potatoes; **eins und eins ergibt zwei** one and one makes two

ergeben[2]

A *Adj.* 1 (zugeneigt) devoted 2 (resignierend) **mit ~er Miene** with an expression of resignation 3 (geh.: devot) obsequious; **~sten Dank** (veralt.) humblest thanks; **Ihr sehr ~er ...** (geh.) yours most obediently, ...; **Ihr ~ster** *od.* **sehr ~er Diener** (veralt.) your most obedient servant (arch.)

B *adv.* 1 devotedly 2 with resignation 3 (geh.) obsequiously; **jmdm. ~st danken** (veralt.) thank sb. most humbly

Ergebenheit *die;* **~** 1 (Treue) devotion 2 (Sichfügen) resignation

Ergebenheits·adresse *die* declaration of loyalty; (an Monarchen) loyal address

Ergebnis *das;* **~ses, ~se** result; **zu einem ~ kommen** reach a conclusion; **zu einem ~ führen** produce a result; **ohne ~ bleiben** lead to nothing

ergebnis·los

A *Adj.* fruitless ‹*discussion*›; **die Verhandlungen blieben/verliefen ~/wurden ~ abgebrochen** negotiations remained inconclusive/proceeded unprofitably/were broken off without a conclusion having been reached

B *adv.* fruitlessly

ergebnis·reich *Adj.* fruitful

Ergebung *die;* **~:** resignation

ergebungs·voll

A *Adj.* humble

B *adv.* humbly

ergehen

A *unr. refl. V.* 1 (äußern) **sich in etw.** (*Dat.*) **~:** indulge in sth.; **sich in endlosen Reden ~:** get carried away in endless speeches 2 (geh.: lustwandeln) take a turn

B *unr. itr. V.; mit sein* 1 (geh.: erlassen werden) ‹*law*› be enacted; **an ihn erging der Ruf einer bekannten Universität** he was offered a chair at a well-known university; **die Einladungen ergingen an alle Mitglieder** the invitations went to all members 2 *unpers.* (widerfahren) **jmdm. ergeht es gut/schlecht** things go well/badly for sb. 3 **etw. über sich** (*Akk.*) **~ lassen** let sth. wash over one

ergiebig /ɛɐ̯ˈgiːbɪç/ *Adj.* rich ‹*deposits, resources*›; productive ‹*mine*›; fertile ‹*fisheries, topic*›; **der neue Kaffee ist nicht so ~/ist ~er** the new coffee does not go as far/goes further

Ergiebigkeit *die;* **~** ▸**ergiebig**: richness; productivity; fertility; **wegen der ~ des Kaffees/Tees** because the coffee/tea goes a long way

ergießen *unr. refl. V.* pour; **die Abwässer ~ sich in den Fluss** the effluent pours out into the river; **eine Menschenmasse ergoss sich in das Stadion** a mass of people poured into the stadium

erglänzen *itr. V.; mit sein* (geh.) ‹*sun, light*› appear; ‹*sea, diamonds*› begin to sparkle

erglühen *itr. V.; mit sein* (geh.) 1 glow; **in Liebe [zu jmdm.] erglüht sein** be passionately in love [with sb.] 2 (rot werden) redden

ergo /ˈɛrgo/ *Adv.* ergo

Ergo·meter *das;* **~s, ~** (Med.) ergometer

Ergonomie /ɛrgono'mi:/ *die;* ~, **Ergonomik** /ɛrgo'no:mɪk/ *die;* ~ ergonomics *sing., no art.*

ergonomisch
A *Adj.* ergonomic
B *adv.* ergonomically

ergötzen (geh.)
A *tr. V.* enthral; captivate
B *refl. V.* **sich an etw.** (*Dat.*) **~:** be delighted by sth.

Ergötzen *das;* **~s** (geh.) delight

ergötzlich (geh.)
A *Adj.* delightful
B *adv.* delightfully

ergraben *unr. tr. V.* excavate

ergrauen *itr. V.; mit sein* go *or* turn grey; **in Ehren ergraut sein** (fig.) have grown old with honour; **ein im Dienst ergrauter Beamter** (fig.) an official of long standing

ergreifen *unr. tr. V.* [1] (greifen) grab; **jmds. Hand ~:** grasp sb.'s hand [2] (festnehmen) catch ‹*thief etc.*› [3] (fig.: erfassen) seize; **von blindem Zorn ergriffen** (geh.) in the grip of blind anger [4] (fig.: aufnehmen) **einen Beruf ~:** take up a career; **die Initiative/eine Gelegenheit ~:** take the initiative/an opportunity [5] (fig.: bewegen) move

ergreifend
A *Adj.* moving; **das ist ja ~** (iron.) how moving
B *adv.* movingly

Ergreifung *die;* ~ [1] (des Schuldigen) capture [2] (der Macht) seizure

ergriffen *Adj.* moved

Ergriffenheit *die;* **~: vor ~ schweigen** be too moved to speak; **vor ~ weinen** be moved to tears; **voller ~:** deeply moved

ergrimmen (geh.)
A *itr. V.; mit sein* be angry; **über etw.** (*Akk.*) **ergrimmt sein** be angry about something
B *tr. V.* infuriate

ergründbar *Adj.* ▸**ergründen**: ascertainable; discoverable; graspable; fathomable

ergründen *tr. V.* ascertain; discover ‹*cause*›; grasp ‹*concept*›; fathom ‹*mystery*›

Ergründung *die* ▸**ergründen**: ascertainment; discovery; grasping; fathoming

Erguss, *Erguß *der* [1] (Med.) (Blut~) bruise; contusion; (Samen~) ejaculation [2] (geh. abwertend) outburst; **ein poetischer ~:** a poetic outpouring [3] (Geol.) eruption

erhaben *Adj.* [1] (weihevoll) solemn ‹*moment*›; awe-inspiring ‹*sight*›; sublime ‹*beauty*› [2] (überlegen) **über etw.** (*Akk.*) **~ sein** be above sth.; **über jeden Zweifel ~:** beyond all criticism [3] (hervortretend) uneven ‹*surface*›; embossed ‹*pattern*›

Erhabenheit *die;* **~:** grandeur; **eine Landschaft von solcher ~:** a landscape of such awe-inspiring grandeur; **die ~ des Augenblicks** the solemn grandeur of the moment

Erhalt *der;* **~[e]s** (Amtsdt.) [1] receipt; **den ~ eines Briefes bestätigen** acknowledge receipt of a letter; **bei ~ zahlen** pay on receipt [2] ▸**Erhaltung**

erhalten
A *unr. tr. V.* [1] (empfangen, bekommen) receive ‹*letter, news, gift*›; be given ‹*order*›; get ‹*good mark, impression*›; **eine hohe Geldstrafe ~:** be fined heavily; **er erhielt 3 Jahre Gefängnis** he was sentenced to 3 years in prison [2] (bewahren) preserve ‹*town, building*›; conserve ‹*energy*›; **diese Kleider sind noch gut ~:** these clothes are still in good condition; **jmdn. am Leben ~:** keep sb. alive; **er ist noch gut ~** (scherzh.) he is well preserved [3] (unterhalten) support [4] (als Endprodukt gewinnen) obtain ‹*sugar, oil, etc.*›
B *unr. refl. V.* (überdauern) survive

Erhalter *der,* **Erhalterin** *die* (Bewahrer[in]) preserver; (der Familie) breadwinner

erhältlich /ɛɐ̯'hɛltlɪç/ *Adj.* obtainable

Erhaltung *die;* ~ (des Friedens) maintenance; (der Arten, von Kunstschätzen) preservation; (der Energie) conservation

Erhaltungs·satz *der* (Physik) principle of conservation

erhängen *tr. V.* **jmdn./sich ~:** hang sb./oneself; **Tod durch Erhängen** death by hanging

erhärten *tr. V.* [1] strengthen ‹*suspicion, assumption*›; substantiate ‹*claim*› [2] ▸**härten A**

Erhärtung *die;* **~, ~en** [1] (Bekräftigung) substantiation [2] ▸**Härtung**

erhaschen *tr. V.* (geh., auch fig.) catch

erheben
A *unr. tr. V.* [1] (emporheben) raise ‹*one's arm/hand*›; **das Glas ~:** raise one's glass; **[hoch] erhobenen Hauptes** with head held high; **mit hoch erhobenen Armen** with arms raised *or* held high; **die Stimme ~:** raise one's voice [2] (verlangen) levy ‹*tax*›; charge ‹*fee*› [3] (befördern) **jmdn. in den Adelsstand ~:** elevate sb. to the nobility [4] (sammeln) gather, collect ‹*data, material*› [5] (vorbringen) **Anklage ~:** bring *or* prefer charges; **Protest ~:** make a protest; *s. auch* **Einspruch 1** [6] *auch itr.* (geh.: erbauen) ‹*art*› edify; ‹*music*› uplift [7] (bes. südd., österr.: feststellen) ascertain ‹*cause etc.*›
B *unr. refl. V.* [1] (aufstehen) rise; **sich von seinem Platz ~:** rise from one's seat [2] (rebellieren) rise up (**gegen** against) [3] (aufsteigen) ‹*bird, balloon*› rise [4] (hinauswachsen) **sich über etw.** (*Akk.*) **~:** rise above sth. [5] (emporragen) ‹*tower, mountain*› rise [6] (geh.: sich besser dünken) **sich über jmdn. ~:** feel superior to sb. [7] (geh.: beginnen) ‹*cry*› ring out; ‹*storm*› rise

erhebend *Adj.* uplifting

erheblich /ɛɐ̯'he:plɪç/
A *Adj.* considerable
B *adv.* considerably

Erhebung *die;* **~, ~en** [1] (Anhöhe) elevation [2] (Aufstand) uprising [3] (Umfrage) survey [4] (Einziehen) (von Steuern) levying; (von Gebühren) charging [5] (Beförderung) elevation; **seine ~ in den Adelsstand** his elevation to the nobility [6] (seelische Erbauung) uplift

Erhebungs·zeitraum *der* (Statistik) period during which information is/was collected

erheischen *tr. V.* (geh.) demand; command ‹*admiration*›

erheitern
A *tr. V.* **jmdn. ~:** cheer sb. up
B *refl. V.* (geh.) be amused; **seine Züge erheiterten sich** his face brightened up

Erheiterung *die;* **~, ~en** amusement

erhellen
A *tr. V.* [1] (beleuchten) light up, illuminate ‹*room, sky*› [2] (erklären) shed light on, illuminate ‹*reason, relationship*›
B *refl. V.* (geh.: sich aufheitern) ‹*eyes, face*› brighten
C *itr. V.* (veralt.: hervorgehen) **daraus erhellt, dass ...** it follows *or* is evident from this that ...

Erhellung *die;* ~ (Erklärung) illumination

erhitzen
A *tr. V.* [1] (heiß machen) heat ‹*liquid*›; **jmdn. ~:** make sb. hot [2] (fig.: erregen) **die Gemüter ~:** make feelings run high
B *refl. V.* [1] heat up; ‹*person*› become hot [2] (fig.: sich erregen) ‹*feelings*› become heated

erhitzt *Adj.* heated

Erhitzung *die;* **~, ~en** heating; (Hitze) heat

erhoffen *tr. V.* **sich** (*Dat.*) **viel/wenig von etw. ~:** expect a lot/little from sth.; **die erhoffte Änderung/Lohnerhöhung** the change/pay rise we/they etc. had expected

erhöhen
A *tr. V.* [1] **eine Mauer [um einen Meter] ~:** make a wall [one metre] higher [2] (steigern) increase, raise ‹*prices, productivity, etc.*›; **erhöhte/leicht erhöhte Temperatur haben** have a [high]/slight temperature; **erhöhter Blutdruck** somewhat high blood pressure; **erhöhte Gefahr** increased danger; **erhöhte Vorsicht** extra care [3] (Musik) raise ‹*note*›
B *refl. V.* ‹*rent, prices*› rise

Erhöhung *die;* **~, ~en** [1] (Höhermachen) raising; **die ~ der Schornsteine/Deiche** increasing the height of the chimneys/dykes [2] **eine ~ der Preise/Steuern** an increase in prices/taxes; **eine ~ des Blutdrucks** a rise in blood pressure; **die ~ einer Dosis** the increasing of a dose [3] (Musik) raising [of a note] [4] (Anhöhe) hill

Erhöhungs-: ~winkel *der* (Waffent.) angle of elevation; **~zeichen** *das* (Musik) sharp [sign]

erholen *refl. V.* [1] (sich ausruhen) **sich [gut] ~:** have a [good] rest; (entspannen) relax [thoroughly]; **die Kurse haben/die Wirtschaft hat sich erholt** (fig.) the rates of exchange have/the economy has recovered [2] ▸ℹ **S. 439** (genesen) **sich von etw. ~:** recover from something

erholsam *Adj.* restful ‹*weekend, holiday*›; **wandern ist sehr ~:** walking is very refreshing

Erholung *die;* ~ [1] ▸ℹ **S. 439 ~ brauchen** *od.* **nötig haben** need a rest; **nach der langen Krankheit hat er ~ nötig** he needs to recuperate after his long illness; **zur ~ fahren** go on holiday to rest/relax; (nach einer Krankheit) go on holiday to convalesce; **eine ~ sein** be relaxing; **~ suchende Menschen** people seeking relaxation [2] (fig.) refreshing change

erholungs-, Erholungs-: ~aufenthalt *der* holiday; **~bedürftig** *Adj.* in need of a rest *postpos.*; **~bedürftig sein** need a rest; **~gebiet** *das* holiday area; **~heim** *das* holiday home; **~ort** *der* resort; **~pause** *die* break; **~reif** *Adj.* (ugs.) ▸**~bedürftig**; **~reise** *die* holiday trip; **~suchend** *Adj.* seeking relaxation *postpos.*; **~suchende** *der/die adj. Dekl.* holidaymaker; **~urlaub** *der* holiday for convalescence; **~wert** *der* recreational value; **~zentrum** *das* leisure centre

erhören *tr. V.* (geh.) hear ‹*plea, prayer*›; **einen Liebhaber ~** (veralt.) yield to a lover

erigieren /eri'gi:rən/ *itr. V.; mit sein* become erect; **erigiert** erect

Erika /'e:rika/ *die;* **~, ~s** *od.* **Eriken** /-kən/ (Bot.) erica

erinnerlich *Adj.* **wie ~:** as will be recalled; **soviel mir ~ ist** as I recall; **das ist mir nicht mehr ~:** I cannot remember that any more

erinnern /ɛɐ̯'|ɪnɐn/
A *refl. V.* **sich an jmdn./etw. [gut/genau] ~:** remember sb./sth. [well/clearly]; **sich [daran] ~, dass ...** remember *or* recall that ...; **wenn ich mich recht erinnere** if I remember rightly; **sich jmds./einer Sache ~** (geh.) remember *or* recall sb./sth.
B *tr. V.* [1] (ins Bewusstsein rufen) **jmdn. an etw./jmdn. ~:** remind sb. of sth./sb.; **jmdn. daran ~, etw. zu tun** remind sb. to do sth. [2] (ugs., bes. nordd.) **jmdn./etw. ~:** remember sb./sth.
C *itr. V.* [1] **jmd./etw. erinnert an jmdn./etw.** sb./sth. reminds one of sb./sth. [2] (zu bedenken geben) **an etw.** (*Akk.*) **~:** remind sb. of sth.; **ich möchte daran ~, dass ...** let us not forget *or* overlook that ...

Erinnerung *die;* **~, ~en** [1] memory (**an** + *Akk.* of); **etw. [noch gut] in ~ haben** [still] remember sth. [well]; **etw. aus der ~ aufschreiben/sagen** write/say sth. from memory; **wenn mich die ~ nicht täuscht** if my memory does not deceive me; **sich** (*Dat.*) **etw. in die ~ zurückrufen** call something to mind again; **nach meiner ~, meiner ~ nach** as far as I remember; **seinen ~en nachhängen** lose oneself in one's memories; **jmdn./etw. in guter ~ behalten** have pleasant memories of sb./sth.; **zur ~ an jmdn./etw.** in memory of sb./sth.; **zur ~ an die Gefallenen wurde ein Denkmal errichtet** a monument was erected to the memory of those who had fallen [2] (~sstück) remembrance; souvenir [3] *Pl.* (Autobiographie) memoirs [4] (Zahlungsaufforderung) reminder

Erinnerungs-: ~bild *das* memory; **~foto** *das* souvenir snapshot; **~lücke** *die* gap in one's memory; **da habe ich eine ~lücke** my mind is a blank about that; **~medaille** *die* commemorative coin; **~schreiben** *das* reminder; **~stück** *das* keepsake; (von einer Reise) souvenir; **~vermögen** *das* memory; **~wert** *der* sentimental value

Erinnye /e'rɪnʏə/ *die;* **~, ~n** (Myth.) Fury; Erinys

erjagen *tr. V.* [1] (erbeuten) catch [2] (gewinnen) win ‹*fame*›; make ‹*money, fortune*›

erkalten *tr. V.; mit sein* cool; ‹*limbs*› grow cold; (fig.) ‹*passion, feeling*› cool

erkälten *refl. V.* ▸❶ S. 439 catch cold; **sich** (*Dat.*) **den Magen ~:** get a chill on one's stomach; *s. auch* **Blase 3**

Erkältung *die;* ~, ~**en** ▸❶ S. 439 cold; **sich** (*Dat.*) **eine ~ zuziehen** *od.* (ugs.) **holen** catch a cold

Erkältungs·krankheit *die* cold

erkämpfen *tr. V.* win; **den Sieg ~:** gain a victory; **sich** (*Dat.*) **etw. ~ müssen** have to fight for sth.

erkaufen *tr. V.* 1▸ (durch Opfer) win; **etw. teuer ~:** win sth. at great cost 2▸ (durch Geld) buy; **sich** (*Dat.*) **etw. ~:** buy oneself sth.

erkennbar
A *Adj.* recognizable; (sichtbar) visible; (schwach sichtbar) discernible
B *adv.* recognizably; (sichtbar) visibly

erkennen
A *unr. tr. V.* 1▸ (deutlich sehen) make out; **die Fingerabdrücke waren deutlich zu ~:** the fingerprints were clearly visible 2▸ (identifizieren) recognize (**an** + *Dat.* by); **der Täter wurde nicht erkannt** the culprit was not identified; **sich zu ~ geben** reveal one's identity; **sich als etw. zu ~ geben** reveal oneself to be sth. 3▸ (einschätzen) recognize; perceive; acknowledge ‹*error, mistake*›; **„erkenne dich selbst!"** 'know thyself!' 4▸ (geh. veralt: begatten) know (arch.)
B *unr. itr. V.* 1▸ (Rechtsspr.) **auf Freispruch ~:** grant an acquittal; **das Gericht erkannte auf 6 Jahre Gefängnis** the court passed a sentence of six years' imprisonment 2▸ (Sport) **auf Elfmeter/Freistoß ~:** award a penalty/free kick

erkenntlich *Adj.* 1▸ **sich [für etw.] ~ zeigen** show one's appreciation for sth. 2▸ ▸**erkennbar**

Erkenntlichkeit *die;* ~, ~**en** 1▸ (Dankbarkeit) gratitude 2▸ (Geschenk) token of gratitude

Erkenntnis *die;* ~, ~**se** 1▸ (Einsicht) discovery; **wissenschaftliche/wichtige/gesicherte ~se** scientific findings/important discoveries/firm insights; **zu der ~ kommen, dass ...** come to the realization that ... 2▸ (das Erkennen) cognition; **der Baum der ~** (bibl.) the tree of knowledge

erkenntnis-, Erkenntnis-: ~**drang** *der* thirst for knowledge; ~**kritik** *die* (Philos.) critique of knowledge; ~**prozess**, *~**prozeß** *der* cognitive process; ~**theoretisch** (Philos.) A *Adj.* epistemological; B *adv.* epistemologically; ~**theorie** *die* (Philos.) theory of knowledge; epistemology *no art.*; ~**vermögen** *das* powers *pl.* of cognition

erkennungs-, Erkennungs-: ~**dienst** *der* police records department; ~**dienstlich** A *Adj.* ~**dienstliche Behandlung** fingerprinting and photographing; B *adv.* **Personen ~dienstlich erfassen** investigate persons through the police records department; **jmdn. ~dienstlich behandeln** take sb.'s fingerprints and photograph; ~**marke** *die* identification disc; ~**melodie** *die* (einer Sendung) theme music; (eines Senders) signature tune; ~**zeichen** *das* sign [to recognize sb. by]

Erker /ˈɛrkɐ/ *der;* ~**s**, ~: bay window

Erker-: ~**fenster** *das* bay window; ~**zimmer** *das* room with a bay window

erkiesen *unr. tr. V.* (veralt. geh.) choose

erklärbar *Adj.* explicable; **etw. ist ~:** sth. can be explained; **aus ~en Gründen** for reasons which can easily be explained

erklären
A *tr. V.* 1▸ explain; **jmdm. etw. ~:** explain sth. to sb.; **etw. an einem Beispiel ~:** explain sth. with an example 2▸ (begründen) explain (**durch** by) 3▸ (mitteilen) state; declare; announce ‹*one's resignation*›; **jmdm. den Krieg ~:** declare war on sb. 4▸ (bezeichnen) **jmdn. für tot ~:** pronounce sb. dead; **etw. für ungültig/verbindlich ~:** declare sth. to be invalid/binding; **die Ehe wurde für ungültig erklärt** the marriage was declared void; **jmdn. zu etw. ~:** name sb. as sth.
B *refl. V.* 1▸ **sich einverstanden/bereit ~:** declare oneself [to be] in agreement/willing; **sich zu einer Sache ~:** make a statement on sth.; **sich für jmdn./etw. ~** (geh.) declare one's support for sb./sth.; **sich gegen jmdn./etw. ~:** declare one's opposition to sb./sth.; **sich jmdm. ~** (geh. veralt.) declare one's love to sb. 2▸ (seine Begründung finden) be explained; **das erklärt sich einfach/von selbst** that is easily explained/self-evident

erklärend
A *Adj.* explanatory; **mit einigen ~en Worten** with a few words of explanation
B *adv.* by way of explanation

erklärlich *Adj.* understandable; **es ist mir einfach nicht ~, wie ...** I just can't understand how ...

erklärlicherweise *Adv.* understandably

erklärt *Adj.* declared ‹*opponent, intention*›; **er war der ~e Mittelpunkt** he was regarded by all as the centre of attraction

erklärtermaßen *Adv.* on one's own admission

Erklärung *die;* ~, ~**en** 1▸ (Darlegung) explanation 2▸ (Mitteilung) statement; **eine ~ abgeben** make a statement

Erklärungs-: ~**not** *die:* **in ~not geraten** *od.* **kommen** come under pressure for failing to offer an explanation; ~**versuch** *der* attempt at an explanation

erklecklich /ɛɐ̯ˈklɛklɪç/ *Adj.* considerable ‹*sum, profit*›

erklettern *tr. V.* climb to the top of ‹*rock, wall, mountain*›; climb to ‹*summit*›

erklimmen *unr. tr. V.* (geh.) climb ‹*wall, tree*›; **die oberste Stufe der Erfolgsleiter ~** (fig.) reach the top of the ladder to success

erklingen *unr. itr. V.; mit sein* ring out; **Musik ~ hören** hear the sound of music; **es erklang die Nationalhymne** the national anthem was played

erkoren /ɛɐ̯ˈkoːrən/ *2. Part. v.* **erkiesen**

erkranken *itr. V.* ▸❶ S. 439; *mit sein* become ill (**an** + *Dat.* with); **er ist an einer Lungenentzündung erkrankt** he's got an inflammation of the lungs; **schwer erkrankt sein** be seriously ill; **ein erkrankter Kollege** a sick colleague

Erkrankung *die;* ~, ~**en** ▸❶ S. 439 (eines Menschen, Tieres) illness; (eines Körperteils) disease

Erkrankungs·fall *der:* **im ~:** in event of illness; **die Versicherung schließt Erkrankungsfälle nicht ein** the insurance does not cover illness

erkühnen *refl. V.* (geh.) **sich ~, etw. zu tun** dare to do sth.

erkunden *tr. V.* reconnoitre ‹*terrain*›; **die Situation ~:** find out what the situation is

erkundigen *refl. V.* **sich nach jmdm./etw. ~:** ask after sb./enquire about sth.; **sich ~, ob/wann ...** enquire whether/when ...; *s. auch* **Befinden**

Erkundigung *die;* ~, ~**en** enquiry; ~**en einholen** *od.* **einziehen** make enquiries

Erkundung *die;* ~, ~**en** (meist Milit.) reconnaissance; **auf ~ gehen** go out on reconnaissance

Erkundungs-: ~**fahrt** *die* exploratory trip; **eine ~fahrt machen** go exploring; **eine ~fahrt durch die Umgebung machen** explore the area; ~**flug** *der* reconnaissance flight; ~**trupp** *der* reconnaissance party

erkünstelt /ɛɐ̯ˈkʏnst]ɪt/ *Adj.* (abwertend) ▸**gekünstelt A**

Erlag·schein /ɛɐ̯ˈlaːk-/ *der* (österr.) ▸**Zahlkarte**

erlahmen *itr. V.; mit sein* 1▸ tire; become tired; ‹*strength*› flag 2▸ (nachlassen) ‹*enthusiasm etc.*› wane

erlangen *tr. V.* gain; obtain ‹*credit, visa*›; reach ‹*age*›

Erlangung *die;* ~: attainment; (eines Kredits, Visums) obtaining; (von Stimmen) gaining; **zur ~ der Doktorwürde** for the degree of doctor

Erlass, ***Erlaß** /ɛɐ̯ˈlas/ *der;* **Erlasses, Erlasse** 1▸ (Anordnung) decree; **der ~ eines Ministers** a decree by a minister; a ministerial decree 2▸ (Straf~, Schulden~ usw.) remission 3▸ (Verfügung) (eines Gesetzes, einer Bestimmung) enactment; (eines Dekrets) issue; (eines Verbots) imposition

erlassen *unr. tr. V.* 1▸ (verkünden) enact ‹*law*›; declare ‹*amnesty*›; issue ‹*warrant*› 2▸ (verzichten auf) remit ‹*sentence*›; **~ Sie es mir, das zu schildern** (geh.) excuse me from having to describe it

erlauben
A *tr. V.* 1▸ allow; **jmdm. ~, etw. zu tun** allow sb. to do sth.; **~ Sie mir, das Fenster zu öffnen?** (geh.) would you mind if I opened the window?; **es ist nicht erlaubt, den Rasen zu betreten** it is forbidden to walk on the grass; **[na], ~ Sie mal!** (ugs.) do you mind! (coll.); **was ~ Sie sich!** how dare you!; **erlaubt ist, was gefällt** do what you feel like doing; **was nicht verboten ist, das ist erlaubt** if something's not forbidden then it's allowed 2▸ (ermöglichen) permit; **meine Gesundheit erlaubt es mir nicht** my health does not permit me to do it; **meine Zeit erlaubt es mir nicht** time does not allow
B *refl. V.* 1▸ (sich die Freiheit nehmen) **sich** (*Dat.*) **etw. ~:** permit oneself sth.; **du hast dir in letzter Zeit ziemlich viele Freiheiten erlaubt** you have been taking a lot of liberties recently; **sie erlaubt sich** (*Dat.*) **in letzter Zeit grobe Nachlässigkeiten** she's allowed herself to become extremely negligent recently; **über seine berufliche Leistung kann ich mir kein Urteil ~:** I do not feel free to comment on his professional competence; **sich** (*Dat.*) **alles ~:** do just as one pleases; **sich** (*Dat.*) **einen Scherz [mit jmdm.] ~:** play a trick [on sb.] 2▸ (sich leisten) **sich** (*Dat.*) **etw. ~:** treat oneself to sth.; **das/solche teuren Geschenke kannst du dir nicht ~:** you cannot afford it/such expensive presents

Erlaubnis *die;* ~, ~**se** permission; (Schriftstück) permit; **jmdn. um ~ bitten, etw. zu tun** ask sb.'s permission *or* sb. for permission to do sth.; **jmdm. die ~ erteilen/verweigern, etw. zu tun** give/refuse sb. permission to do sth.

Erlaubnis·schein *der* permit

erlaucht /ɛɐ̯ˈlauxt/ *Adj.* (geh.) illustrious

Erlaucht *die;* ~, ~**en** (veralt.) **Ihre/Seine ~:** Her Ladyship/His Lordship; **Euer ~:** Your Ladyship/Lordship

erläutern *tr. V.* explain; comment on ‹*picture etc.*›; annotate ‹*text*›; **näher ~:** clarify; ~**de Anmerkungen** explanatory notes

Erläuterung *die* explanation; (zu einem Bild usw.) commentary; (zu einem Text) [explanatory] note

Erle /ˈɛrlə/ *die;* ~, ~**n** alder

erlebbar *Adj.* ‹*situation etc.*› that can be experienced; **etw. ist ~:** sth. can be experienced

erleben *tr. V.* experience; **etwas Schönes/Schreckliches ~:** have a pleasant/terrible experience; **das habe ich noch nie erlebt!** I've never heard of such a thing!; **er hat viel erlebt** he has seen a lot of life; **große Abenteuer ~:** have great adventures; **er wollte erst etwas ~:** he wanted to live it up a bit first; **so ängstlich hatte er sie noch nie erlebt** he had never seen her so afraid before; **etw. bewusst/intensiv ~:** be fully aware of sth./experience sth. to the full; **sie wünschte sich nur, die Hochzeit ihrer Tochter noch zu ~:** her only remaining wish was to be at her daughter's wedding; **er wird das nächste Jahr nicht mehr ~:** he won't see next year; **dieser Film erlebte einen völligen Reinfall** this film was a complete flop (coll.); **du kannst was ~!** (ugs.) you won't know what's hit you!; **sich als etw. ~:** feel oneself to be sth.; *s. auch* **erlebt**

Erleben *das* experience; **etw. aus eigenem ~ kennen** know sth. from one's own experience

Erlebens·fall *der* (Versicherungsw.) **im ~:** in the event of survival; **eine Versicherung auf den ~:** endowment assurance

Erlebnis *das;* ~**ses**, ~**se** experience; **das war ein ~:** what an experience!

Erlebnis-: ~**aufsatz** *der* (Schulw.) essay based on personal experience; ~**fähigkeit** *die* (Psych.) capacity for experience;

~hunger *der* thirst for experience; **~welt** *die* (für den Besucher) world of experiences; (des inneren Erlebens) [inner] world of experiences

erlebt *Adj.* **~e Rede** inner monologue; **~e Geschichte** a first-hand account

erledigen
A *tr. V.* 1 (ausführen) **einen Auftrag ~:** deal with a task; **ich muss noch einige Dinge ~:** I must see to a few things; **so, damit wäre die Angelegenheit endlich erledigt** so now the matter is finally settled; **sie hat alles pünktlich erledigt** she got everything done on time; **schon erledigt!** that's already done 2 (erschöpfen) finish (coll.) ‹*person*›; **der Umzug hat ihn völlig erledigt** the move finished him off completely (coll.) 3 (ugs.: töten) knock off (coll.); (fig.: zerstören) destroy
B *refl. V.* ‹*matter, problem*› resolve itself; **damit hat sich die Sache erledigt** that's that; **vieles erledigt sich von selbst** a lot of things sort them'selves out

erledigt *Adj.* closed ‹*case*›; (ugs.) worn out ‹*person*›

Erledigung *die;* **~, ~en** 1 (Durchführung) carrying out; (Beendigung) completion; (einer Angelegenheit) settling; **um baldige ~ wird gebeten** please give this matter your prompt attention 2 (Besorgung) **er hat noch einige ~en zu machen** he's got one or two more things to see to

erlegen *tr. V.* 1 shoot ‹*animal*› 2 (österr.: entrichten) pay ‹*fee, charge*›

erleichtern
A *tr. V.* 1 (einfacher machen) make easier; **jmdm./sich die Arbeit ~:** make sb.'s/one's work easier 2 (befreien) relieve; **das hat ihn [sehr] erleichtert** that came as a [great] relief to him; **erleichtert aufatmen** breathe a sigh of relief 3 (Gewicht verringern, fig.) lighten; **sein Herz/sein Gewissen ~:** open one's heart/unburden one's conscience; **jmdn. um etw. ~** (ugs. scherzh.) relieve sb. of sth.
B *refl. V.* (verhüll.: seine Notdurft verrichten) relieve oneself

Erleichterung *die;* **~, ~en** 1 (Vereinfachung) **zur ~ der Arbeit** to make the work easier 2 (Befreiung) relief; **mit ~:** with relief; **voller ~:** with great relief; **~ empfinden** feel relieved 3 (Verbesserung, Milderung) alleviation; **es gab weitere ~en im Reiseverkehr** there was a further easing of travel restrictions

erleiden *unr. tr. V.* suffer

erlernbar *Adj.* learnable; **es ist leicht ~:** it can be easily learnt *or* is easy to learn; **eine ~e Fähigkeit** a faculty which can be acquired

erlernen *tr. V.* learn

erlesen[1] *unr. tr. V.* (geh. veralt.) choose

erlesen[2] *Adj.* superior ‹*wine*›; choice ‹*dish*›; **ein ~er Geschmack** a discriminating taste

Erlesenheit *die;* **~:** exquisiteness

erleuchten *tr. V.* 1 light; **Blitze erleuchteten den Himmel** the sky was lit up by flashes of lightning; **hell erleuchtete Fenster** brightly lit windows 2 (geh.: mit Klarheit erfüllen) inspire

Erleuchtung *die;* **~, ~en** inspiration; **ihm kam eine ~:** he had a flash of inspiration

erliegen *unr. itr. V.; mit sein* 1 succumb (*Dat.* to); **einem Irrtum ~:** be misled; **im Kampf ~** (veralt.) be vanquished in battle; **zum Erliegen kommen** come to a standstill; **etw. zum Erliegen bringen** bring sth. to a standstill 2 (zum Opfer fallen) **einer Krankheit** (*Dat.*) **~:** die from an illness

Erl·könig /'ɛrl-/ *der* 1 **„Der ~"** 'The erl-king' 2 (Kfz-Jargon) test model

erlogen *Adj.* made up; untruthful ‹*story*›

Erlös /ɛɐ̯'lø:s/ *der;* **~es, ~e** proceeds *pl.*; **vom ~ seiner Bilder leben** live on the income from the sale of one's paintings

erlöschen *unr. itr. V.; mit sein* 1 ‹*fire*› go out; **ein erloschener Vulkan** an extinct volcano; **die Lichter waren schon erloschen** the lights were already out 2 (nachlassen) ‹*hope, feelings*› wane 3 (aussterben) ‹*family, clan*› die out 4 (zu bestehen aufhören) ‹*claim, obligation*› cease; ‹*firm, membership*› cease to exist

erlösen *tr. V.* save, rescue (**von** from); **jmdn. von seinen Schmerzen ~:** release sb. from pain; **von einer Sorge erlöst sein** be relieved of a worry; **von einer Krankheit erlöst werden** (verhüll.) be released from an illness; **jmdn. ~** (ugs. scherzh.) take over from sb.; **und erlöse uns von dem Übel** *od.* **Bösen** (bibl.) and deliver us from evil

erlösend *Adj.* **das ~e Wort sprechen** say the magic word; **~ wirken** come as a relief

Erlöser *der;* **~s, ~** 1 saviour 2 (christl. Rel.) redeemer

Erlöserin *die;* **~, ~nen** ▸ **Erlöser 1**

Erlösung *die* release (**von** from); (christl. Rel.) redemption; **es war eine ~ zu wissen, dass ...** it was a relief to know that ...

ermächtigen *tr. V.* authorize; **[dazu] ermächtigt sein, etw. zu tun** be authorized to do sth.

Ermächtigung *die;* **~, ~en** authorization

Ermächtigungs·gesetz *das* (Politik, bes. ns.) Enabling Act

ermahnen *tr. V.* admonish; tell (coll.); (warnen) warn

Ermahnung *die* admonition; (Warnung) warning

ermangeln *itr. V.* (geh.) **einer Sache** (*Gen.*) **~:** lack sth.

Ermang[e]lung *die;* **~** *in* **in ~** (+ *Gen.*) (geh.) in the absence of; **in ~ eines Besseren** for lack of anything better

ermannen *refl. V.* (geh.) **sich ~, etw. zu tun** pluck up courage to do sth.

ermäßigen
A *tr. V.* reduce
B *refl. V.* be reduced

Ermäßigung *die* reduction

ermatten (geh.)
A *itr. V.; mit sein* ‹*person*› become exhausted; (fig.) ‹*enthusiasm*› wane
B *tr. V.* (matt machen) exhaust, tire ‹*person*›

ermattet *Adj.* exhausted

Ermattung *die;* **~:** weariness; fatigue

ermessen *unr. tr. V.* estimate, gauge ‹*consequences, implications*›; **daran können Sie ~, wie/ob ...** that will give you some idea of how/whether ...; **die Bedeutung von etw. ~:** appreciate the significance of sth.

Ermessen *das;* **~s** estimation; **nach eigenem ~:** in one's own estimation; **in jmds. ~** (*Dat.*) **liegen** be at sb.'s discretion; **nach menschlichem ~:** as far as anyone can judge; **etw. in jmds.** (*Akk.*) **~ stellen** leave sth. to sb.'s discretion

Ermessens-: ~entscheidung *die* discretionary decision; **~frage** *die* matter of discretion; **~missbrauch,** ***~mißbrauch** *der* abuse of one's powers of discretion; **~spiel·raum** *der* powers *pl.* of discretion; discretionary powers *pl.*

ermitteln
A *tr. V.* 1 (herausfinden) ascertain, determine ‹*facts*›; discover ‹*culprit, hideout, address*›; establish, determine ‹*identity, origin*›; decide ‹*winner*› 2 (errechnen) calculate ‹*quota, rates, data*›
B *itr. V.* (Rechtsw.) investigate; **gegen jmdn. ~:** investigate sb.; **in einer Sache ~:** investigate sth.

Ermittlung *die;* **~, ~en** 1 (das Ermitteln) ▸ **ermitteln 1**: ascertainment; determination; discovery; establishment; **die ~ eines Gewinners** deciding a winner 2 (Untersuchung) investigation

Ermittlungs-: ~arbeit *die* investigatory work; **~aus·schuss,** ***~aus·schuß** *der* committee of inquiry; **~beamte** *der,* **~beamtin** *die* investigating officer; **~richter** *der,* **~richterin** *die* examining magistrate; **~verfahren** *das* (Rechtsw.) preliminary inquiry

ermöglichen *tr. V.* enable; **jmdm. etw. ~:** make sth. possible for sb.; **um einen besseren Gedankenaustausch zu ~:** to facilitate a better exchange of ideas

ermorden *tr. V.* murder; (aus politischen Gründen) assassinate

Ermordung *die;* **~, ~en** murder; (aus politischen Gründen) assassination

ermüden
A *itr. V.; mit sein* 1 (müde werden) tire; become tired 2 (Technik) ‹*metal*› fatigue
B *tr. V.* (müde machen) tire; make tired

ermüdend *Adj.* tiring

Ermüdung *die;* **~, ~en** 1 tiredness; **vor ~:** from tiredness 2 (Technik) metal fatigue

Ermüdungs-: ~erscheinung *die* sign of fatigue; **~zustand** *der* state of fatigue

ermuntern *tr. V.* 1 **jmdn. [dazu] ~, etw. zu tun** encourage sb. to do sth.; **jmdn. zum Reden/zu einem Verbrechen ~:** encourage sb. to talk/to commit a crime 2 (veralt.: wach machen) liven up ‹*person*›

ermunternd
A *Adj.* encouraging
B *adv.* encouragingly

Ermunterung *die;* **~, ~en** 1 (Aufheiterung) enlivenment; **zur ~ der Anwesenden** to the amusement of those present 2 (Ermutigung) encouragement 3 (ermunternde Worte) words *pl.* of encouragement

ermutigen *tr. V.* 1 encourage 2 ▸ **ermuntern 1**

ermutigend
A *Adj.* encouraging
B *adv.* encouragingly

Ermutigung *die;* **~, ~en** 1 encouragement; **zur ~:** to encourage 2 (ermutigende Worte) words *pl.* of encouragement

ernähren
A *tr. V.* 1 feed ‹*young, child*›; **mit der Flasche ernährt werden** be bottle-fed 2 (unterhalten) keep ‹*family, wife*›; **das ernährt seinen Mann** it provides a good living
B *refl. V.* feed oneself; **sich von etw. ~:** live on sth.; ‹*animal*› feed on sth.; **sich vegetarisch ~:** live on a vegetarian diet

Ernährer *der;* **~s, ~, Ernährerin** *die;* **~, ~nen** breadwinner; provider

Ernährung *die;* **~** 1 (das Ernähren) feeding 2 (Nahrung) diet; **gesunde/ungesunde ~:** a healthy/an unhealthy diet 3 (Versorgung) feeding; **zur ~ der Familie beitragen** contribute to feeding the family

ernährungs-, Ernährungs-: ~bedingt *Adj.* caused by diet *postpos.*; diet-related; **~lage** *die* state of nutrition; **~lehre** *die* (Med.) dietetics *sing., no art.*; **~ministerium** *das* Ministry of Food; **~störung** *die* ▸ ❶ **S. 439** (Med.) nutritional disorder; **~weise** *die* diet; **~wissenschaft** *die* dietetics *sing., no art.*; **~wissenschaftler** *der,* **~wissenschaftlerin** *die* nutritionist

ernennen *unr. tr. V.* 1 **jmdn. zu etw. ~:** make sb. sth. 2 (bestimmen) appoint ‹*deputy, ambassador*›

Ernennung *die* appointment (**zu** as)

Ernennungs·urkunde *die* certificate of appointment

erneuerbar *Adj.* renewable; **~e Energien** renewable energy sources

Erneu[e]rer *der;* **~s, ~, Erneuerin** *die;* **~, ~nen** reviver

erneuern
A *tr. V.* 1 (auswechseln) replace 2 (wiederherstellen) renovate ‹*roof, building*›; (fig.) thoroughly reform ‹*system*› 3 (beleben) resume ‹*relations*› 4 (verlängern lassen) extend, renew ‹*permit, licence, contract*›
B *refl. V.* ‹*nature, growth*› renew itself

Erneuerung *die* 1 (Auswechslung) replacement 2 (Wiederherstellung) renovation; (fig.) thorough reform; **demokratische/religiöse ~:** democratic/religious revival 3 (von Beziehungen) resumption 4 (Verlängerung eines Vertrages usw.) renewal; extension

erneuerungs·bedürftig *Adj.* in need of replacement *postpos.*

Erneuerungs·schein *der* (Börsenw.) talon

erneut
A *Adj.* renewed
B *adv.* once again

erniedrigen *tr. V.* [1] (demütigen) humiliate; **sich [selbst] ~:** lower oneself; **wer sich selbst erniedrigt, wird erhöht werden** (bibl.) he that shall humble himself shall be exalted [2] (heruntersetzen) lower, reduce ‹*price, pressure*› [3] (Musik) lower ‹*note*›

erniedrigend *Adj.* humiliating

Erniedrigung *die;* ~, ~en [1] (Demütigung) humiliation [2] (Senkung) lowering; reduction (+ *Gen.* in) [3] (Musik) lowering

Erniedrigungs·zeichen *das* (Musik) flat sign

ernst /ɛrnst/

[A] *Adj.* [1] serious ‹*face, expression, music, doubts*›; **~ bleiben** remain serious; keep a straight face (coll.) [2] (aufrichtig) genuine ‹*intention, offer*› [3] (gefahrvoll) serious ‹*injury*›; grave ‹*situation*›; **etwas Ernstes** something serious

[B] *adv.* seriously; **jmdn./etw. ~ nehmen** take sb./sth. seriously; **es ~ mit etw. meinen** be serious about sth.; **~ gemeint** serious ‹*offer, reply*›; sincere ‹*wish*›

Ernst[1] *der;* ~[e]s [1] (ernster Wille) seriousness; **das ist mein [voller] ~:** I mean that [quite] seriously; **es ist mir [bitterer] ~ damit** I'm [deadly] serious about it; **etw. im ~ sagen** say sth. in all seriousness; **etw. im ~ meinen** mean sth. seriously; **allen ~es** in all seriousness; **etw. mit ~ betreiben** apply oneself seriously to sth.; **[mit etw.] ~ machen** be serious [about sth.]; **er will jetzt ~ machen und morgen nach Peru fliegen** now he wants to turn words into action and fly to Peru tomorrow [2] (Wirklichkeit) **daraus wurde [blutiger/bitterer] ~:** it became [deadly] serious; **der ~ des Lebens** the serious side of life; **dann beginnt der ~ des Lebens** then life begins in earnest [3] (Gefährlichkeit) **der ~ der Lage** the seriousness of the situation [4] (gemessene Haltung) gravity

Ernst[2] *(der);* ~s Ernest

Ernst·fall *der:* **eine Übung für den ~:** a practice for the real thing; **im ~:** when the real thing happens

ernst·gemeint ▸**ernst B**

ernsthaft

[A] *Adj.* serious; **etwas/nichts Ernsthaftes** something/nothing serious

[B] *adv.* seriously; **jmdn. ~ an etw.** (*Akk.*) **erinnern** give sb. a stern reminder about sth.

Ernsthaftigkeit *die;* ~: seriousness

ernstlich

[A] *Adj.* [1] (nachdrücklich) serious ‹*doubt, attempt, intention*› [2] (aufrichtig) genuine ‹*wish*› [3] (gefährlich) serious ‹*threat, danger, risk*›

[B] *adv.* [1] (nachdrücklich) seriously; **er hat ~ gefordert, dass ...** he has demanded in all seriousness that ... [2] (aufrichtig) genuinely ‹*sorry, repentant*›; **jmdm. ~ böse sein** be seriously annoyed with sb. [3] (gefährlich) seriously ‹*ill, threatened*›; **~ gefährdet sein** be in serious danger

-ernte *die;* -~, -~n ... harvest; (Ertrag) ... crop

Ernte /ˈɛrntə/ *die;* ~, ~n [1] (das ~n) harvest; **bei der ~ sein** be bringing in the harvest; **während der ~:** at harvest time; **reiche/furchtbare ~ halten** (fig. geh.) take a heavy/terrible toll [2] (Ertrag) crop; **die ~ einbringen** bring in the harvest; **die ~ an Getreide/Kartoffeln/Tabak** the grain/potato/tobacco crop; **ihm ist die ganze ~ verhagelt** (fig.) he's had a bad blow

Ernte-: **~arbeit** *die* harvest work; **~arbeiter** *der,* **~arbeiterin** *die* harvester; **~aus·fall** *der* crop failure; **~dank·fest** *das* harvest festival; **~ein·satz** *der* assistance with the harvest; **jmdn. zum ~einsatz aufrufen** call upon sb. to help with the harvest; **~ertrag** *der* yield; **~maschine** *die* harvester; **~monat** *der* month of the harvest

> **Erntedankfest**
>
> Harvest festival is not a legal holiday in Germany, but is celebrated with church services on the first Sunday in October in many rural areas. In Switzerland there is a thanksgiving holiday for a good harvest in mid-September.

ernten *tr. V.* harvest ‹*cereal, fruit*›; (fig.) get ‹*mockery, ingratitude*›; win ‹*fame, praise*›

Ernte-: **~wagen** *der* harvest wagon; **~wetter** *das:* **gutes/schlechtes ~wetter haben** have good/bad weather for the harvest; **~zeit** *die* harvest time; **in der ~zeit** at harvest time

ernüchtern *tr. V.* [1] (nüchtern machen) sober up [2] (fig.) **jmdn. [völlig] ~:** bring sb. down to earth [with a bang]; **~d** sobering

Ernüchterung *die;* ~, ~en (fig.) disillusionment

Eroberer /ɛɐ̯ˈ|oːbərɐ/ *der;* ~s, ~, **Eroberin** *die;* ~, ~nen conqueror

erobern *tr. V.* [1] conquer ‹*country*›; take ‹*town, fortress*› [2] (fig.) conquer ‹*woman, market*›; seize ‹*power*›; **[sich** (*Dat.*)**] die Herzen ~:** win hearts; **eine Stadt/ein Land ~** (scherzh.) take a town/country by storm; *s. auch* **Sturm 2**

Eroberung *die;* ~, ~en (auch fig. scherzh.) conquest; (einer Stadt, Festung) taking; **die ~ der Macht** the seizing of power; **~en machen** make conquests; *s. auch* **ausgehen 8**

Eroberungs-: **~drang** *der* thirst for conquest; **~feld·zug** *der* campaign of conquest; **~krieg** *der* war of conquest

eröffnen

[A] *tr. V.* [1] open ‹*shop, gallery, account*›; start ‹*business, practice*› [2] (beginnen) open ‹*meeting, conference*›; **das Feuer ~:** open fire; **eine Veranstaltung mit Musik ~:** begin an event with music [3] (mitteilen) **jmdm. etw. ~:** reveal sth. to sb. [4] **ein Testament ~:** read a will [5] (Rechtsw., Wirtsch.) **den Konkurs ~:** institute bankruptcy proceedings; **das Verfahren ~:** begin proceedings [6] **jmdm. neue Möglichkeiten ~:** open up new possibilities to sb.

[B] *itr. V.* (Börsenw.) ‹*stock exchange*› open

[C] *refl. V.* (sich bieten) **sich jmdm. ~** ‹*opportunity, possibility*› present itself

Eröffnung *die* [1] opening; (einer Sitzung) start; (einer Schachpartie) opening [move] [2] (Mitteilung) revelation; **ich muss dir eine ~ machen** I have something to tell you [3] (Testaments~) reading [4] (Wirtsch.) **die ~ des Konkurses** the institution of bankruptcy proceedings

Eröffnungs-: **~an·sprache** *die* opening speech; **~beschluss**, ***~beschluß** *der* (Rechtsw.) decision to begin court proceedings; **~bilanz** *die* (Wirtsch.) opening balance; **~feier** *die* opening ceremony; **~kurs** *der* (Börsenw.) opening price; **~spiel** *das* (Sport) opening game; **~tag** *der* (einer Ausstellung, eines Kongresses usw.) first day; (eines Geschäftes usw.) first day of opening; **~variante** *die* (Schach) opening variation; **~wehen** *Pl.* (Med.) dilation pains

erogen /eroˈgeːn/ *Adj.* erogenous ‹*zone*›

erörtern /ɛɐ̯ˈ|œrtɐn/ *tr. V.* discuss

Erörterung *die;* ~, ~en discussion

Eros /ˈeːrɔs/ *der;* ~ [1] (Gott) Eros [2] (sinnliche Liebe) erotic love

Eros·center, Eros-Center *das* [licensed] brothel; eros centre

Erosion /eroˈzi̯oːn/ *die;* ~, ~en erosion

Erosions·schutz *der* protection against erosion

Erotik /eˈroːtɪk/ *die;* ~: eroticism

Erotika /eˈroːtika/ ▸**Erotikon**

Erotiker *der;* ~s, ~, **Erotikerin** *die;* ~, ~nen [1] eroticist [2] (Autor[in]) erotic writer

Erotikon /eˈroːtikɔn/ *das;* ~s, **Erotika** [1] erotic work; **Erotika** erotica [2] *Pl.* (Mittel) aphrodisiacs

erotisch

[A] *Adj.* erotic

[B] *adv.* erotically

erotisieren *tr. V.* arouse sexual desire in; **~d wirken** have an erotic effect

Erotomane /erotoˈmaːnə/ *der;* ~n, ~n erotomaniac

Erotomanie *die;* ~: erotomania

Erotomanin *die;* ~, ~nen erotomaniac

Erpel /ˈɛrpl̩/ *der;* ~s, ~: drake

erpicht /ɛɐ̯ˈpɪçt/ *Adj.:* *in* **auf etw.** (*Akk.*) **~ sein** be keen on sth.

erpressbar, ***erpreßbar** *Adj.* blackmailable; susceptible to blackmail *postpos.*

Erpressbarkeit, *Erpreßbarkeit *die;* ~: susceptibility to blackmail; **dem Verdacht der ~ begegnen** counter the suspicion of being susceptible to blackmail

erpressen *tr. V.* [1] (nötigen) blackmail; **jmdn. mit etw. ~:** blackmail sb. with sth. [2] (erlangen) extort ‹*money, confession*› (**von** from)

Erpresser *der;* ~s, ~: blackmailer

Erpresser·brief *der* blackmail letter

Erpresserin *die;* ~, ~nen blackmailer

erpresserisch

[A] *Adj.* blackmailing *attrib.*; **diese Maßnahme ist ~:** this action amounts to blackmail; **in ~er Absicht** for the purpose of blackmail

[B] *adv.* **~ vorgehen** use blackmail

Erpresser·methoden *Pl.* blackmail *sing.*

Erpressung *die* blackmail *no indef. art.*; (von Geld, Geständnis) extortion; *s. auch* **räuberisch A 1**

Erpressungs·versuch *der* blackmail attempt

erproben *tr. V.* test ‹*medicine*› (**an** + *Akk.* on); **jmds. Zuverlässigkeit ~:** put sb.'s reliability to the test; **ein erprobter Soldat** an experienced soldier; **das ist seit langem erprobt** it is tried and tested

Erprobung *die;* ~, ~en testing

Erprobungs·flug *der* test *or* proving flight

erquicken /ɛɐ̯ˈkvɪkn̩/ *tr. V.* (geh.) refresh; **das Herz ~:** gladden one's heart; **ich will euch ~** (bibl.) and I will give you rest

erquickend *Adj.* (geh.) refreshing

erquicklich (geh.)

[A] *Adj.* pleasant

[B] *adv.* pleasantly

Erquickung *die;* ~, ~en (geh.) refreshment; **der Schlaf brachte ihm keine ~:** the sleep did not refresh him

Errata ▸**Erratum**

erraten *unr. tr. V.* guess; **du hast es ~!** (iron.) you've guessed it!

erratisch /eˈraːtɪʃ/ *Adj.* (Geol.) erratic

Erratum /eˈraːtʊm/ *das;* ~s, **Errata** (Druck- u. Schriftw.) erratum

errechenbar *Adj.* calculable; **leicht/genau ~ sein** be easily/accurately calculated

errechnen

[A] *tr.* (*auch itr.*) *V.* [1] (ausrechnen) calculate ‹*sum*›; **wie er errechnete** according to his calculations [2] (erwarten) count on ‹*chance, advantage*›

[B] *refl. V.* (Papierdt.) **sich aus etw. ~:** be calculated from sth.

erregbar *Adj.* excitable

Erregbarkeit *die;* ~: excitability

erregen

[A] *tr. V.* [1] annoy [2] (sexuell) arouse [3] (verursachen) arouse; **Aufsehen/Ärgernis ~:** cause a stir/annoyance; *s. auch* **öffentlich**

[B] *refl. V.* **sich über etw.** (*Akk.*) **~:** get excited about sth.

erregend *Adj.* exciting; (sexuell) arousing

Erreger *der;* ~s, ~ ▸❶ **S. 439** (Med.) pathogen

erregt

[A] *Adj.* excited; (sexuell) aroused; **die ~en Gemüter** the hot tempers

[B] *adv.* excitedly

Erregung *die* [1] excitement; (sexuell) arousal; **in starke ~ geraten** become extremely excited; **vor ~:** with excitement [2] (Verursachung) **~ öffentlichen Ärgernisses** (Rechtsspr.) causing a public nuisance; **~ von Missfallen** incurring displeasure

Erregungs·zustand *der* state of excitement; (sexuell) [state of] arousal

erreichbar *Adj.* [1] within reach *postpos.*; **in ~er Höhe** at a reachable height [2] **der Ort ist mit dem Auto/Zug ~:** the place can be reached by car/train; **leicht ~ sein** be easy to reach; be easily reachable [3] **er ist [telefonisch] ~:** he can be contacted [by telephone]

erreichen *tr. V.* 1 reach; **den Zug ~:** catch the train; **etw. ist zu Fuß/mit dem Bus/schnell zu ~:** sth. can be reached on foot/by bus/quickly 2 (in Verbindung treten mit, ansprechen) reach ‹*viewers*›; **er ist telefonisch/um 10 Uhr/zu Hause zu ~:** he can be contacted by telephone/at 10 o'clock/at home 3 (durchsetzen) achieve ‹*goal, aim*›; **bei jmdm. etwas/nichts ~:** get somewhere/not get anywhere with sb.

Erreichung *die;* **~:** reaching *no art.*; **bei** *od.* **mit ~ der Altersgrenze/Volljährigkeit** on reaching the age limit/one's majority

erretten *tr. V.* (geh.) save

Erretter *der*, **Erretterin** *die* (geh.) saviour

errichten *tr. V.* 1 build ‹*house, bridge, etc.*› 2 (aufstellen) erect, put up ‹*rostrum, barrier, etc.*› 3 (einrichten) found ‹*company*›; set up ‹*fund*›

erringen *unr. tr. V.* gain ‹*victory*›; reach ‹*first etc. place*›; win ‹*majority*›; gain, win ‹*sb.'s trust*›

erröten *itr. V.; mit sein* blush (**vor** with); **jmdn. zum Erröten bringen** make sb. blush

Errungenschaft /ɛɐ̯ˈrʊŋənʃaft/ *die;* **~, ~en** achievement; **meine neueste ~** (ugs. scherzh.) my latest acquisition

Ersatz *der;* **~es** 1 replacement; **als ~ für jmdn.** in place of sb. 2 (Entschädigung) compensation 3 (Milit.) reserve

ersatz-, Ersatz-: ~anspruch *der* claim for damages; **~ansprüche stellen** claim damages; **~ball** *der* (Sport) new ball; **~bank** *die; Pl.* **~bänke** (Sport) substitutes' bench; **~befriedigung** *die* (Psych.) vicarious satisfaction; **~dienst** *der: community service as an alternative to military service;* **~dienstleistende** *der; adj. Dekl.: person carrying out alternative service;* **~frau** *die* replacement; (Sport) substitute; **~gewebe** *das* (Med.) replacement tissue; **~heer** *das* reserve army; **~kasse** *die* private health insurance company; **~los** A *Adj.* without replacement *postpos.;* B *adv.* **etw. ~los streichen** cancel sth.; **ein Gesetz ~los streichen** strike a law from the statute books; **~mann** *der; Pl.* **~männer** *od.* **~leute** replacement; (Sport) substitute; **~mine** *die* refill; **~mittel** *das* substitute; **~pflichtig** *Adj.* liable to pay compensation *postpos.;* **~rad** *das* spare wheel; **~reifen** *der* spare tyre; **~religion** *die* substitute religion; **~spieler** *der,* **~spielerin** *die* (Sport) substitute [player]

Ersatz·teil *das* (bes. Technik) spare part; spare (Brit.)

Ersatzteil-: ~lager *das* [spares] store; **~medizin** *die* spare-part surgery

Ersatz-: ~truppe *die* (Milit.) reserve troops *pl.;* **~weise** *Adv.* as an alternative

ersaufen *unr. itr. V.; mit sein* 1 (salopp) drown 2 (überflutet werden) flood

ersäufen /ɛɐ̯ˈzɔyfn̩/ *tr. V.* drown; **seinen Kummer im Alkohol ~** (fig.) drown one's sorrows [in drink]

erschaffen *unr. tr. V.* create; **wie Gott ihn ~ hat** (scherzh. verhüll.) in his birthday suit

Erschaffer *der;* **~s, ~, Erschafferin** *die;* **~, ~nen** creator; (Gott) Creator

Erschaffung *die* creation

erschallen *unr. od. regelm. itr. V.; mit sein* ‹*song, call*› ring out; ‹*music*› sound

erschaudern *itr. V.; mit sein* (geh.) shudder (**bei** at)

erschauern *itr. V.; mit sein* (geh.) tremble (**vor** + *Dat.* with)

erscheinen *unr. itr. V.; mit sein* 1 (sichtbar werden, sich zeigen, auftreten) appear; **jmdm. ~:** appear to sb.; **in der Schule/am Arbeitsplatz ~:** put in an appearance at school/at work; **vor Gericht ~:** appear in court; **um frühzeitiges/rechtzeitiges/zahlreiches Erscheinen wird gebeten** an early/a punctual arrival/a full turnout is requested 2 (herausgegeben werden) ‹*newspaper, periodical*› appear; ‹*book*› be published 3 (sich darstellen) **jmdm. ratsam/unverständlich ~:** seem advisable/incomprehensible to sb.; *s. auch* **Licht 1**

Erscheinung *die;* **~, ~en** 1 (Vorgang) phenomenon; (Alters~, Krankheits~ usw.) symptom; **in ~ treten** become evident; **das Fest der ~ des Herrn** (christl. Rel.) [the Feast of the] Epiphany 2 (äußere Gestalt) appearance; **eine stattliche/elegante ~ sein** be an imposing/elegant figure 3 (Vision) apparition; **eine ~/~en haben** see a vision/visions

Erscheinungs-: ~bild *das* appearance; **vom ~bild her** judging by appearance; **~fest** *das* Epiphany *no art.;* **~form** *die* manifestation; **~jahr** *das* year of publication; **~ort** *der* place of publication; **~tag** *der* day of publication; publication day; **~weise** *die* 1 ▸ **~form;** 2 **die ~weise einer Zeitung** the frequency of publication of a newspaper; **wöchentliche/monatliche ~weise** weekly/monthly publication; **„~weise: vierteljährlich"** 'published quarterly'; **~welt** *die* world perceived through the senses

erschießen *unr. tr. V.* shoot dead; **Tod durch Erschießen** death by firing squad; **erschossen sein** (fig. ugs.) be completely whacked (Brit. coll.); **dann kann ich mich ~** (ugs.) I might as well end it all (coll.); *s. auch* **Flucht 1, standrechtlich B**

Erschießung *die;* **~, ~en** shooting; **eine sofortige/standrechtliche ~:** a summary execution [by firing squad]; **zur ~ abgeführt werden** be led away to be shot

Erschießungs·kommando *das* firing squad

erschlaffen *itr. V.; mit sein* 1 (kraftlos werden) ‹*muscle, limb*› become limp; (fig.) ‹*resistance, will*› weaken; **seine Spannkraft war erschlafft** he had lost his vigour 2 (welk werden) ‹*skin*› grow slack

Erschlaffung *die;* **~** 1 (das Müdewerden) weakening 2 (das Welkwerden) **bei ~ der Haut** when the skin grows slack

erschlagen[1] *unr. tr. V.* strike dead; kill; (ugs.: erschöpfen) wear out; **vom Blitz ~ werden** be struck dead by lightning; **jmdn. mit Argumenten ~** (fig.) defeat sb. with arguments

erschlagen[2] *Adj.* (ugs.) 1 (erschöpft) worn out 2 (verblüfft) **wie ~ sein** be flabbergasted (coll.) *or* thunderstruck

erschleichen *unr. refl. V.* (abwertend) **sich** (*Dat.*) **etw. ~:** get sth. by devious means; **sich** (*Dat.*) **jmds. Gunst/Vertrauen ~:** worm oneself into sb.'s favour/confidence

erschließbar *Adj.* ascertainable ‹*facts*›; **~e Rohstoffquellen** sources of raw materials which can be tapped; **~e Absatzmärkte** markets which can be opened up

erschließen
A *unr. tr. V.* 1 (zugänglich machen) develop ‹*area, building land*›; open up ‹*market*›; **jmdm. etw. ~** (fig.) make sth. accessible to sb.; **er hat mir ganz neue Welten erschlossen** he opened up a whole new world to me 2 (nutzbar machen) tap ‹*resources, energy sources*› 3 (ermitteln) deduce ‹*meaning, wording*›
B *unr. refl. V.* 1 (verständlich werden) **sich jmdm. ~:** become accessible to sb. 2 (geh.: sich offenbaren) **sich jmdm. ~:** confide in sb.

Erschließung *die* 1 (von Bauland) development; (von Märkten) opening up 2 (von Rohstoffen) tapping 3 **zur ~ des Textes** in order to grasp the meaning of the text

Erschließungs·kosten *Pl.* (Bauw.) development costs *pl.*

erschöpfen
A *tr. V.* (auch fig.) exhaust; **seine Kräfte ~:** drain one's strength
B *refl. V.* 1 (sich beschränken) **darin ~ sich ihre Kenntnisse** her knowledge does not go beyond that 2 (zu Ende gehen) ‹*supplies, stores*› run out; **seine Ideen haben sich erschöpft** he has run out of ideas

erschöpfend
A *Adj.* exhaustive
B *adv.* exhaustively

erschöpft *Adj.* exhausted

Erschöpfung *die* exhaustion; **bis zur ~:** to the point of exhaustion; **vor ~ einschlafen/umfallen** fall asleep from exhaustion/drop with exhaustion

Erschöpfungs-: ~tod *der* death from exhaustion; **den ~tod sterben** die from exhaustion; **~zu·stand** *der* state of exhaustion; **Müdigkeit und ~zustände** tiredness and exhaustion

erschrecken[1] *unr. itr. V.; mit sein* be startled; **vor etw.** (*Dat.*) *od.* **über etw.** (*Akk.*) **~:** be startled by sth.; **erschrick nicht!** don't be startled; **er war zutiefst/zu Tode erschrocken** he was frightened out of his wits/frightened to death

erschrecken[2] *tr. V.* frighten; scare; **du hast mich aber erschreckt!** you really gave me a scare

erschrecken[3] *unr. od. regelm. refl. V.* get a fright; **erschrick dich nicht!** don't be frightened

erschreckend
A *Adj.* alarming
B *adv.* alarmingly

erschrocken
A *2. Part. v.* **erschrecken**[1]
B *Adj.* frightened; **sie wandte sich ~ ab** she turned away in fright

erschüttern *tr. V.* (auch fig.) shake; **die Nachricht hat uns erschüttert** we were shaken by the news; **über etw.** (*Akk.*) **erschüttert sein** be shaken by sth.; **das kann mich nicht ~** (ugs.) that doesn't worry me

erschütternd *Adj.* deeply distressing ‹*account, picture, news*›; deeply shocking ‹*conditions*›

Erschütterung *die;* **~, ~en** 1 (Bewegung) (durch LKWs usw.) vibration; (der Erde) tremor; **wirtschaftliche ~en** (fig.) economic upheavals 2 (Ergriffenheit) shock; (Trauer) distress 3 **das trug zur ~ meines Glaubens/Vertrauens bei** that helped to shake my faith/confidence

erschütterungs-: ~fest *Adj.* shockproof; **~frei** A *Adj.* vibrationless; free from *or* without vibration *postpos.;* **ein ~freier Transport von etw.** transporting sth. without jolting; B *adv.* without vibration

erschweren
A *tr. V.* **etw. ~:** make sth. more difficult; **etw. durch etw. ~:** impede *or* hinder sth. by sth.
B *refl. V.* **sich [durch etw.] ~:** be hindered [by sth.]

erschwerend
A *Adj.* complicating ‹*factor*›; **~e Umstände** (Rechtsw.) aggravating circumstances
B *adv.* **es kommt ~ hinzu, dass er ...** to make matters worse he ...; **das kommt ~ hinzu** that is an added problem

Erschwernis *die;* **~, ~se** difficulty

Erschwernis·zulage *die: bonus for particularly hard work or shift work*

Erschwerung *die;* **~, ~en: eine ~ für etw.** an impediment to sth.; **das ist eine ~ seiner Tätigkeit** that makes his job more difficult

erschwindeln *refl. V.* get by swindling; **sich** (*Dat.*) **etw. von jmdm. ~:** swindle sb. out of sth.

erschwinglich *Adj.* reasonable ‹*price*›; **für jmdn. nicht ~ sein** not be within sb.'s reach; **dort sind die Mieten noch ~:** the rents there are still affordable

ersehen *unr. tr. V.* see; **aus etw. zu ~ sein** be evident from sth.

ersehnen *tr. V.* (geh.) long for

ersetzbar *Adj.* replaceable

ersetzen *tr. V.* 1 replace; **etw./jmdn. durch etw./jmdn. ~:** replace sth./sb. by sth./sb.; **Talent durch Fleiß ~:** substitute hard work for talent; **ihn wird niemand ~ können** nobody will be able to take his place 2 (erstatten) **jmdm. einen Schaden ~:** compensate sb. for damages; **die Fahrtkosten ~:** reimburse travel expenses

Ersetzung *die;* **~, ~en** (von Kosten usw.) reimbursement; **die ~ von Schäden** compensation for damage

ersichtlich *Adj.* apparent; **ohne ~en Grund** for no apparent reason; **etw. ist klar/nicht ~:** sth. is quite obvious/not clear; **hieraus ist ~, dass ...** it is apparent from this that ...; **die Lieferbedingungen sind aus dem Kaufvertrag ~:** the conditions of delivery are contained in the contract of sale

ersinnen *unr. tr. V.* (geh.) devise

e

ersitzen
A *unr. refl. V.* (abwertend) **als Beamter ersitzt man sich eine ansehnliche Pension** as a civil servant you get a considerable pension just by staying in your job long enough
B *unr. tr. V.* (Rechtsspr.) obtain by prescription

erspähen *tr. V.* (geh.) espy (literary); catch sight of; **einen Vorteil ~** (fig.) see an advantage

ersparen *tr. V.* **1** (erwerben) save ‹*money*›; **sein/ihr erspartes Geld** *od.* **Erspartes** his/her savings **2** (fern halten von) save, spare ‹*trouble, bother*›; save ‹*work*›; **er konnte ihr diese peinlichen Fragen nicht ~:** he could not spare her these awkward questions; **es bleibt einem nichts erspart** (ugs.) at least I/you *etc.* could have been spared that

Ersparnis *die;* **~, ~se** **1** (*österr. auch das;* **~ses, ~se**) (ersparte Summe) savings *pl.* **2** (Einsparung) saving

Ersparnis·kasse *die* (schweiz.) savings bank

Ersparte *das; adj. Dekl.* **das ~** (bestimmte Summe) the money saved; (allgemein) savings *pl.*

ersprießlich *Adj.* (geh.) profitable, fruitful ‹*contacts, collaboration*›; **das ist nicht sehr ~:** that is not very pleasant

erst /eːɐ̯st/
A *Adv.* **1** (zu~) first; **~ einmal** first [of all]; **wenn er ~ einmal in Wut gerät** once he becomes angry; **~ noch** first; **eine solche Frau muss ~ noch geboren werden** such a woman has not yet been born **2** (nicht eher als) **eben ~:** only just; **er will ~ in vierzehn Tagen/einer Stunde zurückkommen** he won't be back for a fortnight (Brit.) *or* for two weeks/for an hour; **~ nächste Woche/um 12 Uhr** not until next week/12 o'clock; **er war ~ zufrieden, als ...** he was not satisfied until ...; **~ im 19. Jh. ...** it was not until the nineteenth century that ... **3** (nicht mehr als) only; **~ eine Stunde/halb so viel** only an hour/half as much; **sie ist mit ihrer Arbeit ~ am Anfang** she is only just beginning her work
B *Partikel* **so was lese ich gar nicht ~:** I don't even start reading that sort of stuff; **jetzt tue ich es ~ recht!** that makes me even more determined to do it; **er ist schon ziemlich arrogant, aber ~ seine Frau** he is quite arrogant but his wife is even worse

erst... *Ordinalz.* **1** ▸**i** **S. 165,** ▸**i** **S. 826** first; **der ~e Stock** the first *or* (Amer.) second floor; **etw. das ~e Mal tun** do sth. for the first time; **am Ersten [des Monats]** on the first [of the month]; **am nächsten Ersten** on the first [day] of next month; **als Erstes** first of all; **der/die Erste** the first person; **als Erster/Erste etw. tun** be the first to do sth.; **Karl der Erste** Charles the First; **fürs Erste** for the moment; **der/die/das ~e beste ...** the first suitable ...; **sie kaufte das ~e beste Kleid, das sie sah** she bought the first dress she saw; *s. auch* **zum 8** **2** (best...) **das ~e Hotel** the best hotel; **der/die Erste [der Klasse]** the top boy/girl [of the class]; **sie kam als Erste ins Ziel** she was the first to reach the finish; **die Erste** (Sportjargon: erste Mannschaft) the first team

> **Das Erste**
>
> Also called *Erstes Programm*, this is the first German public TV channel, broadcast by the **ARD**. Programming includes news, information, films, and entertainment. There is a limited amount of advertising, which is concentrated in blocks at certain times of day and not after 8 p.m.

erstarken *itr. V.; mit sein* (geh.) regain one's strength; (fig.) grow stronger

Erstarkung *die;* **~** (geh.) strengthening

erstarren *itr. V.; mit sein* **1** (starr werden) ‹*jelly, plaster*› set; **ihm erstarrte das Blut in den Adern** (fig.) the blood ran cold in his veins **2** (steif werden) ‹*limbs, fingers*› grow stiff **3** **vor Schreck/Entsetzen ~:** be paralysed by fear/with horror **4** (geh.: leblos werden) ossify

Erstarrung *die;* **~** **1** (Starrheit) numbness **2** (von Lava) solidification; (von Eisen) hardening **3** (von Gliedern) stiffening **4** (fig.: Absterben) ossification

erstatten *tr. V.* **1** reimburse ‹*expenses*› **2** **Anzeige gegen jmdn. ~:** report sb. [to the police]; **jmdm. Bericht über etw.** (*Akk.*) **~:** report on sth. to sb.; **[über etw.** (*Akk.*)**] Meldung ~:** report [sth.]

Erstattung *die;* **~, ~en** **1** (von Kosten) reimbursement **2** **die ~ einer Anzeige** the reporting of something [to the police]; **er sah von der ~ einer Anzeige ab** he refrained from reporting it/us *etc.* to the police; **die ~ einer Meldung** the making of a report

erstattungs·fähig *Adj.* refundable ‹*amount, tax, costs*›; **~e Medikamente** medication whose cost can be refunded

Erst-: ~auf·führung *die* premiere; **~auf·lage** *die* first impression

erstaunen *tr. V.* astonish; amaze; **es erstaunte ihn nicht sonderlich** he wasn't particularly surprised

Erstaunen *das;* **~s** astonishment; amazement; **jmdn. in ~ versetzen** astonish *or* amaze sb.

erstaunlich
A *Adj.* astonishing, amazing ‹*achievement, number, amount*›; **das Erstaunliche ist, dass ...** the astonishing *or* amazing thing is that ...; **das Erstaunliche an diesem Vorfall** the astonishing *or* amazing thing about this incident
B *adv.* astonishingly; amazingly

erstaunlicher·weise *Adv.* astonishingly *or* amazingly [enough]

erstaunt *Adj.* astonished; amazed

erst-, Erst-: ~ausgabe *die* first edition; **~ausrüstung** *die* (Kfz-W.) original fittings *pl.*; **~ausstattung** *die* original furnishings *pl.*; **~begehung** *die* first journey (+ *Gen.* to); (eines Berges) first ascent (+ *Gen.* of); **~best...** *Adj.* **der ~beste Wagen, der ihr angeboten wurde** the first car she was offered; **die ~beste Frau, die ihm über den Weg lief** the first woman he met; **bei ~bester Gelegenheit** at the first opportunity; **~beste** *der/die/das; adj. Dekl.* ▸**Nächstbeste**; **~besteigung** *die* first ascent; **Hillary gelang die ~besteigung des Mount Everest** Hillary made the first successful ascent of Mount Everest; **~druck** *der; Pl.* **~~e** ▸**~ausgabe**

erstechen *unr. tr. V.* stab [to death]

erstehen
A *unr. tr. V.* (geh.: kaufen) purchase
B *unr. itr. V.; mit sein* (geh.) **1** (entstehen) ‹*difficulties, problems*› arise **2** (auf~) rise; **„Christ ist erstanden"** 'Christ is risen'

Erste-Hilfe-Ausrüstung *die* first-aid kit

Erste-Hilfe-Leistung *die* administering of first aid; **zur ~ verpflichtet sein** be obliged to give first aid

ersteigen *unr. tr. V.* climb

ersteigern *tr. V.* buy [at an auction]

Ersteigung *die* ascent

erstellen *tr. V.* (Papierdt.) **1** (bauen) build **2** (anfertigen) make ‹*assessment*›; draw up ‹*plan, report, list*›

Erstellung *die* **1** (Bau) construction; building **2** (Anfertigung) ▸**erstellen 2**: making; drawing up

***erste·mal, *ersten·mal** ▸**Mal**[1]

erstens /ˈeːɐ̯stn̩s/ *Adv.* firstly; in the first place

erster... /ˈeːɐ̯stɐ.../ *Adj.* former; **Ersteres** *od.* **das Erstere trifft hier zu** the former is the case here

ersterben *unr. itr. V.; mit sein* (geh.) ‹*flame*› die down; ‹*singing, murmuring*› die away; ‹*smile*› fade

Erste[r]-Klasse-Abteil *das* first-class compartment

erst-, Erst-: ~geboren *Adj.* first-born; **der/die ~geborene** the first-born child; **~gebot** *das* first *or* opening bid; **~geburt** *die* **1** first-born child; **2** **[das Recht der] ~geburt** (Rechtsw.) [right of] primogeniture; **~geburts·recht** *das* right of primogeniture; **~genannt** *Adj.* mentioned first *postpos.*; **der ~genannte** the one mentioned first

ersticken
A *itr. V.; mit sein* suffocate; (sich verschlucken) choke; **an einem Knochen ~:** choke on a bone; **vor Lachen ~** (ugs.) choke with laughter; **zum Ersticken sein** ‹*heat*› be stifling; **in Arbeit ~** (ugs.) be swamped with work; **in Geld ~** (ugs.) be rolling in money
B *tr. V.* **1** (töten) suffocate; **die Tränen erstickten ihre Stimme** (fig.) she was choked by tears; **der Widerstand wurde erstickt** (fig.) resistance was suppressed; **etw. sofort** *od.* **im Keim ~** (fig.) nip sth. in the bud **2** (löschen) smother ‹*flames*›

Erstickung *die;* **~** **1** (Sterben) suffocation; asphyxiation **2** (Löschen) smothering; **zur ~ der Flammen** to smother the flames

Erstickungs-: ~gefahr *die* danger of suffocation; **~tod** *der* death from suffocation; **den ~tod sterben** die from suffocation

erst-, Erst-: ~instanz *die* (Rechtsw.) court of first instance; **~klassig** **A** *Adj.* first-class; **~klassige Bedingungen** excellent conditions; **B** *adv.* superbly; **da kann man ~klassig essen** you can get a first-class meal there; **da wird man ~klassig bedient** the service there is first-class; **~klässler, *~kläßler** *der;* **~~s, ~~,** **~klässlerin, *~kläßlerin** *die;* **~~, ~~nen** (südd., schweiz.) *pupil in first class of primary school;* first-year pupil; **~kommunion** *die* (kath. Rel.) first communion; **~liga·klub** *der* (Sport) first division *or* premier-league club; **~liga·spiel** *das* (Sport) first division *or* premier-league match; **~liga·verein** *der* (Sport) first division *or* premier-league club; **~ligist** *der* (Sport) (Person) first division *or* premier-league player; (Mannschaft) first division *or* premier-league team; **~ligistin** *die* (Sport) first division *or* premier-league player

Erstling *der;* **~s, ~e** first work

Erstlings-: ~ausstattung *die* first layette; **~film** *der* first film; **~roman** *der* first novel; **~werk** *das* first work

erstmalig
A *Adj.* first
B *adv.* for the first time

erstmals *Adv.* for the first time

Erst·platzierte, *Erst·plazierte *der/die; adj. Dekl.* (Sport) *person gaining one of the first [three] places*

erstrahlen *itr. V.; mit sein* shine; **der ganze Park erstrahlte im Lichterglanz** the whole park was aglow with light

erstrangig *Adj.* **1** (vordringlich) of top priority *postpos.*; **von ~er Bedeutung** of the utmost importance **2** ▸**erstklassig A**

erstreben *tr. V.* strive for

erstrebens·wert *Adj.* ‹*ideals etc.*› worth striving for; desirable ‹*situation*›

erstrecken *refl. V.* **1** (sich ausdehnen) stretch; **sich bis an etw.** (*Akk.*) **~:** extend as far as sth.; **sich über ein Gebiet ~:** extend over *or* cover an area **2** (dauern) **sich über 10 Jahre ~:** carry on for 10 years **3** (betreffen) **sich auf jmdn./etw. ~:** affect sb./sth.; ‹*laws, regulations*› apply to sb./sth.

erstreiten *unr. tr. V.* (geh.) gain; **sich** (*Dat.*) **etw. ~ müssen** have to fight to get sth.; **sich ein Recht ~ müssen** have to fight for a right

Erst-: ~schlag *der* first strike; **~schlag·waffe** *die* first-strike weapon; **~sendung** *die* first broadcast; **~stimme** *die* first vote

Ersttags-: ~brief *der* (Philat.) first-day cover; **~stempel** *der* (Philat.) first-day stamp

Erst·täter *der,* **Erst·täterin** *die* (Rechtsw.) first offender

erstunken /ɛɐ̯ˈʃtʊŋkn̩/ *in* **~ und erlogen sein** (salopp) be a pack of lies

erstürmen *tr. V.* take ‹*fortress, town*› by storm; **den Gipfel ~** (geh.) conquer the summit

Erstürmung *die;* **~, ~en** storming

Erst-: ~wagen *der* main car; **~wähler** *der,* **~wählerin** *die* first-time voter

ersuchen *tr. V.* (geh.) ask; **jmdn. um etw. ~:** request sth. of sb.; **jmdn. ~, etw. zu tun** request sb. to do sth.

Ersuchen *das;* **~s, ~:** request (**an** + *Akk.* to); **auf ~ von .../des ...** at the request of ...

ertappen *tr. V.* catch ‹*thief, burglar*›; **jmdn. dabei ~, wie er etw. tut** catch sb. in the act of doing sth.; **jmdn. beim Mogeln ~:** catch sb. cheating; **sich bei etw. ~:** catch oneself doing sth.; *s. auch* **frisch A 1**

ertasten *tr. V.* **etw. ~:** make out sth. by touch; **sich** (*Dat.*) **seinen Weg ~:** feel one's way

erteilen *tr. V.* give ‹*advice, information*›; give, grant ‹*permission*›; **Unterricht ~:** teach; **Klavier-/Deutschunterricht ~:** give piano/German lessons; *s. auch* **Auftrag 1**; **Lektion**; **Wort 2**

Erteilung *die* giving; **die ~ der Arbeitsgenehmigung** granting of a work permit

ertönen *itr. V.; mit sein* [1] (laut werden) sound; **er ließ seine tiefe Stimme ~:** his deep voice rang out [2] (geh.) **von etw. ~:** resound with sth.

Ertrag /ɛɐ̯'tra:k/ *der;* **~[e]s, Erträge** /ɛɐ̯'trɛ:gə/ [1] (landwirtschaftliche Produkte) yield [2] (Gewinn) return

ertragen *unr. tr. V.* bear ‹*pain, shame, uncertainty*›; **etw. mit Geduld/Fassung ~:** bear sth. patiently/take sth. calmly; **es ist nicht mehr zu ~:** I can't stand it any longer; **Frauen können mehr Schmerz ~ als Männer** women can stand *or* tolerate more pain than men; **er musste große Schmerzen ~:** he had to endure great pain

ertrag·fähig *Adj.* [1] (Gewinn bringend) profitable ‹*investment etc.*› [2] (fruchtbar) fertile ‹*soil*›

Ertrag·fähigkeit *die* ▸**ertragfähig**: profitability; fertility

erträglich /ɛɐ̯'trɛ:klɪç/

A *Adj.* [1] bearable ‹*pain*›; tolerable ‹*conditions, climate*›; **die Grenze des Erträglichen erreichen** be as much as one can endure [2] (ugs.: annehmbar) tolerable

B *adv.* (ugs.: annehmbar) tolerably

ertrag-: ~los *Adj.* unprofitable ‹*business*›; unproductive ‹*land, soil*›; **~reich** *Adj.* lucrative ‹*business*›; productive ‹*land, soil*›

ertrags-, Ertrags-: ~arm *Adj.* unprofitable ‹*year*›; poor ‹*soil*›; **~ein·buße** *die* decrease in profits; **~lage** *die* profit situation; profits; **~minderung** *die* decrease in profits

Ertrag[s]-: ~steigerung *die* increase in profits; **~steuer** *die* (Wirtsch.) tax on profits

ertränken *tr. V.* drown; **seinen Kummer/seine Sorgen im Alkohol ~** (fig.) drown one's sorrows [in drink]

erträumen *refl. V.* dream of; **sie ist die Frau, die er sich** (*Dat.*) **erträumt hat** she's the woman of his dreams; **erträumte Welten** imaginary worlds

ertrinken *unr. itr. V.; mit sein* be drowned; drown; (fig.) be inundated; **in einer Flut von Anfragen ~** (fig.) be inundated with inquiries

Ertrinkende *der/die; adj. Dekl.* drowning person

ertrotzen *tr. V.* **sich** (*Dat.*) **etw. ~:** obtain sth. by sheer defiance

Ertrunkene *der/die; adj. Dekl.* drowned person

ertüchtigen

A *tr. V.* toughen up ‹*body*›

B *refl. V.* **sich körperlich ~:** get/keep oneself fit

Ertüchtigung *die;* **~, ~en** fitness; **jmdn. zur körperlichen ~ anhalten** encourage sb. to keep [himself/herself] physically fit

erübrigen

A *tr. V.* spare ‹*money, time*›; **etw. Geld/Zeit ~ können** have some money/time to spare

B *refl. V.* be unnecessary; **es erübrigt sich, noch länger darüber zu sprechen** there's no point in talking about it any longer

eruieren /eru'i:rən/ *tr. V.* find out; **jmdn. ~** (österr.) trace sb.

Eruierung *die;* **~, ~en** investigation; **die ~ des Täters** (österr.) the tracing of the culprit

Eruption /erʊp'tsi̯o:n/ *die;* **~, ~en** (Geol., Med.) eruption

Eruptiv·gestein /erʊp'ti:f-/ *das* (Geol.) eruptive rock

erwachen *itr. V.; mit sein* (geh.) awake; wake up; (fig.) awake; **aus tiefem Schlaf ~:** awake from a deep sleep; **aus der Narkose ~:** come round; **aus seinen Tagträumen ~:** snap out of one's daydreams; **ein neuer Tag erwacht** (geh.) a new day dawns

Erwachen *das;* **~s** (auch fig.) awakening; **es wird ein böses ~ [für ihn] geben** (fig.) it'll be a rude awakening [for him]

erwachsen[1] *unr. itr. V.; mit sein* [1] grow (**aus** out of); ‹*rumour*› spread [2] (sich ergeben) ‹*difficulties, tasks*› arise

erwachsen[2]

A *Adj.* grown-up *attrib.*; **~ sein** be grown up; **~ werden** reach adulthood

B *adv.* ‹*behave*› in an adult way

Erwachsene *der/die; adj. Dekl.* adult; grown-up

Erwachsenen-: ~alter *das* adulthood; **~bildung** *die* adult education *no art.*

Erwachsen·sein *das* being an adult/adults *no art.*

erwägen *unr. tr. V.* consider

erwägens·wert *Adj.* worth considering *postpos.*; worthy of consideration *postpos.*

Erwägung *die;* **~, ~en** consideration; **etw. in ~ ziehen** consider sth.; take sth. into consideration

erwählen *tr. V.* (geh.) choose

Erwählte *der/die; adj. Dekl.* (Freund[in]) sweetheart; (Bevorrechtigte) **er gehört zu den wenigen ~n** he belongs to the select few

erwähnen *tr. V.* mention; **etw. mit keinem Wort ~:** make no mention of sth.; **jmdn. lobend ~:** speak in praise of sb.; **es muss lobend erwähnt werden, dass ...** it must be said in his/her *etc.* praise that ...; **bereits erwähnt** aforementioned *attrib.*; **oben erwähnt** above mentioned *attrib.*

erwähnens·wert *Adj.* worth mentioning *postpos.*

Erwähnung *die;* **~, ~en** mention; **das verdient [keine] ~:** that is [not] worth mentioning

erwandern *tr., refl. V.* **er hat [sich** (*Dat.*)**] ganz Frankreich erwandert** he's walked all round France

erwärmen

A *tr. V.* [1] (warm machen) heat; **das erwärmte uns** (*Dat.*) **das Herz** (fig.) that warmed our hearts [2] (fig.: gewinnen) **jmdn. für etw. ~:** win sb. over to sth.

B *refl. V.* (warm werden) ‹*air, water*› warm up; **sich für jmdn./etw. ~** (fig.) warm to sb./sth.; **für diese Idee kann ich mich nicht ~:** I cannot work up any enthusiasm for this idea

Erwärmung *die;* **~: eine ~ der Luft/des Wassers** an increase in air/water temperature; **bei ~ der Flüssigkeit** when the liquid is heated

erwarten *tr. V.* [1] expect ‹*guests, phone call, post*›; **etw. ungeduldig/sehnlich ~:** wait impatiently/eagerly for sth; **jmdn. am Bahnhof ~:** wait for sb. at the station; **wir ~ ihn um 7 Uhr** we are expecting him at 7 o'clock; **ein Kind ~:** be expecting a baby; be expecting (coll.); **ich kann meinen Urlaub kaum ~:** I can hardly wait for my holiday [2] (rechnen mit) **etw. von jmdm. ~:** expect sth. of sb.; **von jmdm. ~, dass er etw. tut** expect sb. to do sth.; **es ist** *od.* (geh.) **steht zu ~, dass ...** it is to be expected that ...; **wider Erwarten** contrary to expectation; **[sich** (*Dat.*)**] von etw. viel/wenig/nichts ~:** expect a lot/little/nothing from sth.

Erwartung *die;* **~, ~en** expectation; **~en in etw.** (*Akk.*) **setzen** have expectations of sth.; **die in ihn gesetzten ~en erfüllten sich nicht** the hopes placed in him were not fulfilled; **in freudiger ~:** in joyful anticipation; **die ~en [nicht] erfüllen** [not] come up to one's expectations

erwartungs-, Erwartungs-: ~gemäß *Adv.* as expected; **~horizont** *der* level of expectations; **~voll** A *Adj.* expectant; B *adv.* expectantly

erwecken *tr. V.* [1] (auf~) wake; **jmdn. vom Tode ~:** bring sb. back to life [2] (erregen) arouse ‹*longing, mistrust, pity*›; **den Eindruck ~, als ...** give the impression that ...

Erweckung *die;* **~, ~en** [1] (Auf~) resurrection [2] (Erregung) arousal [3] (Mystik) religious awakening [4] (ev. Theol.) religious revival

Erweckungs·bewegung *die* revivalist movement

erwehren *refl. V.* (geh.) **sich jmds./einer Sache ~:** fend *or* ward sb./sth. off; **sie konnte sich des Gefühls/des Eindrucks nicht ~, dass ...** she could not help feeling/thinking that ...

erweichen

A *tr. V.* soften; **jmdn./jmds. Herz ~** (fig.) soften sb.'s heart; **sich ~ lassen** (fig.) yield

B *itr. V.; mit sein* (aufweichen) become soft

Erweichung *die;* **~, ~en** softening

erweisen

A *unr. tr. V.* [1] prove; **es ist erwiesen, dass ...** it has been proved that ... [2] (bezeigen) **jmdm. Achtung ~:** show respect to sb.; **jmdm. einen Gefallen ~:** do sb. a favour; **~ Sie mir die Ehre** (geh.) do me the honour

B *unr. refl. V.* **sich als etw. ~:** prove to be sth.; **seine Behauptungen haben sich als falsch erwiesen** his assertions have proved false

erweislich *Adv.* (geh.) demonstrably

erweitern

A *tr. V.* widen ‹*river, road*›; expand ‹*library, business*›; enlarge ‹*collection*›; dilate ‹*pupil, blood vessel*›; extend ‹*power*›; **seinen Horizont/seine Kenntnisse ~:** broaden one's horizons/knowledge; **einen Bruch ~** (Math.) reduce a fraction to higher terms; **eine erweiterte Neuauflage** a new, expanded edition; **erweiterte Oberschule** (DDR) (Stufe) ≈ sixth form; (Schule) ≈ sixth-form college

B *refl. V.* ‹*road, river*› widen; ‹*pupil, blood vessel*› dilate; **sich zu etw. ~:** widen into sth.

Erweiterung *die;* **~, ~en** ▸**erweitern**: widening; expansion; enlargement; dilation; extension; **die ~ eines Bruchs** the reduction of a fraction; **zur ~ seiner Fremdsprachenkenntnisse ...** to increase his knowledge of foreign languages ...

Erweiterungs·bau *der; Pl.* **Erweiterungs·bauten** extension

Erwerb /ɛɐ̯'vɛrp/ *der;* **~[e]s** [1] **der ~ des Lebensunterhaltes** earning a living [2] (Arbeit) occupation; **ohne ~ sein** be unemployed [3] (Aneignung) acquisition [4] (Kauf) purchase [5] (das Erworbene) earnings *pl.*

erwerben *unr. tr. V.* [1] (verdienen) earn; (fig.) win ‹*fame*›; **sich** (*Dat.*) **großen Ruhm ~:** win great fame; **jmds. Vertrauen ~:** win *or* earn sb.'s trust [2] (sich aneignen) gain ‹*experience, influence*›; acquire, gain ‹*knowledge*› [3] acquire ‹*property, works of art, etc.*›; **etw. käuflich ~** (Papierdt.) purchase sth. [4] (Biol., Psych.) acquire

erwerbs-, Erwerbs-: ~fähig *Adj.* capable of gainful employment *postpos.*; able to work *postpos.*; **~fähigkeit** *die* ability to work; **~leben** *das* working life; **im ~leben stehen** be working; **~los** *Adj.*: ▸**arbeitslos**; **~lose** *der/die; adj. Dekl.*: ▸**Arbeitslose**; **~minderung** *die*: **eine ~minderung** a reduction in one's/sb.'s capacity for work; **~mittel** *das* means of livelihood; **~quelle** *die* source of income; **~sinn** *der* business sense; **~tätig** *Adj.* gainfully employed; **~tätige** *der/die; adj. Dekl.* person in work; **die ~tätigen** those in work; **~unfähig** *Adj.* incapable of gainful employment *postpos.*; unable to work *postpos.*; **~unfähigkeit** *die* inability to work; **~zweig** *der* source of employment

Erwerbung *die* [1] (Aneignung) acquisition [2] (Erworbenes) acquisition; (Gekauftes) purchase

erwidern /ɛɐ̯'vi:dɐn/ *tr. V.* [1] reply; **etw. auf etw.** (*Akk.*) **~:** say sth. in reply to sth.; **auf diese Beleidigung wusste sie nichts zu ~:** she could not think of a reply to this insult [2] (reagieren auf) return ‹*greeting, visit*›; reciprocate ‹*sb.'s feelings*›

Erwiderung *die;* ~, ~**en** 1 (Antwort) reply (**auf** + *Akk.* to) 2 ▸ **erwidern 2**: return; reciprocation

erwiesen
A *2. Part. v.* **erweisen**
B *Adj.* proved; **eine ~e Tatsache** a proven fact; **das ist doch längst ~:** that has long since been proved

erwiesener·maßen *Adv.* as has been proved; **er hat ~ die Unwahrheit gesagt** it has been proved that he didn't tell the truth

erwirken *tr. V.* obtain ‹*permit, release*›

erwirtschaften *tr. V.* **etw. ~:** obtain sth. by careful management

erwischen *tr. V.* (ugs.) 1 (fassen, ertappen, erreichen) catch ‹*culprit, train, bus*›; **jmdn. beim Abschreiben ~:** catch sb. copying 2 (greifen) grab; **jmdn. am Ärmel ~:** grab sb. by the sleeve 3 (bekommen) manage to catch *or* get 4 (unpers.) **es hat ihn erwischt** (ugs.) (er ist tot) he has bought it (sl.); (er ist krank) he has got it; (er ist verletzt) he's been hurt; (scherzh.: er ist verliebt) he's got it bad (coll.)

erwünscht /ɛɐ̯ˈvʏnʃt/ *Adj.* wanted; **das ~e Resultat** the desired result; **deine Anwesenheit ist dringend ~:** your presence is urgently required

erwürgen *tr. V.* strangle

Erz /ɛrts *od.* eːɐ̯ts/ *das;* ~**es**, ~**e** ore

Erz-: ~**abbau** *der* mining of ore; ~**ader** *die* vein of ore

erzählen *tr.* (*auch itr.*) *V.* tell ‹*joke, story*›; **jmdm. etw. ~:** tell sb. sth.; **erzähl keine Märchen!** (ugs.) don't tell stories!; **dem werde ich was ~!** (ugs.) (zurechtweisend) I'll have something to say to him!; (ablehnend) I'll tell him where to get off! (coll.); **einen Traum/ein Erlebnis ~:** recount a dream/an experience; **jmdm. von etw. ~:** tell sb. about sth.; **von etw. ~:** talk about sth.; **etw. von jmdm.** *od.* **über jmdn. ~:** tell sth. about sb.; **das kannst du einem anderen** *od.* (ugs.) **deiner Großmutter ~!** tell that to the [horse] marines (Brit. coll.); pull the other leg *or* one (coll.); **du kannst mir viel ~** (ugs.) you can say what you like

erzählens·wert *Adj.* ‹*things, stories*› worth telling

Erzähler *der,* **Erzählerin** *die;* ~, ~**nen** 1 storyteller; **der Erzähler eines Romans** the narrator of a novel 2 (Autor) writer [of stories]; narrative writer; **„Deutsche Erzähler"** 'Stories by German Authors'; 'German Narrative Writers'

erzählerisch *Adj.* narrative *attrib.*

Erzähl-: ~**gut** *das* narrative [writing]; ~**kunst** *die* narrative art; ~**technik** *die* narrative technique

Erzählung *die;* ~, ~**en** 1 account; **ich kenne sie nur aus ~en** I only know her from what other people have said about her 2 (literarischer Text) story; (märchenhafte, fantastische Geschichte) tale; **die in die ~ eingebetteten Dialoge** the dialogue embedded in the narrative

Erzähl-: ~**weise** *die* 1 narrative style; 2 (Literaturw.) narrative form; ~**zeit** *die* (Literaturw.) narrative time

erz-, Erz-: ~**bergbau** *der* ore mining *no art.;* ~**bergwerk** *das* ore mine; ~**bischof** *der* archbishop; ~**bischöflich** *Adj.* archiepiscopal; ~**bistum** *das,* ~**diözese** *die* archbishopric; archdiocese

erzen *Adj.* (geh.) bronze

Erz·engel *der* archangel

erzeugen *tr. V.* 1 produce; generate ‹*electricity*› 2 (österr.: anfertigen) manufacture; produce

Erzeuger *der;* ~**s**, ~ 1 (Vater) father; **er ist zwar mein ~, aber ich betrachte ihn nicht als Vater** I may be his child, but I do not regard him as a father 2 (Produzent) producer; **vom ~ zum Verbraucher** from producer to consumer 3 (österr.: Hersteller) manufacturer

Erzeugerin *die;* ~, ~**nen** ▸ **Erzeuger 2, 3**

Erzeuger-: ~**land** *das* country of origin; ~**preis** *der* manufacturer's price

Erzeugnis *das* (auch fig.) product; **landwirtschaftliche ~se** agricultural products *or* produce

Erzeugung *die* 1 (das Bewirken) creation 2 (das Produzieren) (von Lebensmitteln usw.) production; (von Industriewaren) manufacture; (Strom~) generation 3 (österr.: Herstellung) manufacture

erz-, Erz-: ~**feind** *der,* ~**feindin** *die* arch enemy; ~**gang** *der* lode of ore; ~**gauner** *der,* ~**gaunerin** *die* (ugs.) arch villain; ~**gehalt** *der* ore content; ~**grube** *die* ore mine; ~**haltig** *Adj.* ore-bearing; ~**herzog** *der* archduke; ~**herzogin** *die* archduchess; ~**hütte** *die* ore-smelting works *sing.*

erziehbar *Adj.* educable; **der Junge ist sehr schwer ~:** the boy is a very difficult child

erziehen *unr. tr. V.* 1 (bilden u. fördern) bring up; (in der Schule) educate; **ein Kind streng/sehr frei ~:** give a child a strict/very liberal upbringing/education 2 (anleiten) **jmdn. zum Verbrecher ~:** bring sb. up to criminal ways; **ein Kind zu Sauberkeit und Ordnung ~:** bring a child up to be clean and tidy; **jmdn./sich dazu ~, etw. zu tun** train sb./oneself to do sth.; *s. auch* **erzogen B**

Erzieher *der;* ~**s**, ~, **Erzieherin** *die;* ~, ~**nen** ▸❶ **S. 113** educator; (Pädagoge) educationalist; (Lehrer) teacher

erzieherisch ▸ **pädagogisch A 1, B 1**

erziehlich *Adj.* (bes. österr.) educational

Erziehung *die* 1 (das Erziehen) upbringing; (Schul~) education; **eine gute ~ genießen** enjoy a good education 2 (Manieren) upbringing; breeding; **seine gute ~ vergessen** forget oneself

erziehungs-, Erziehungs-: ~**anstalt** *die* (veralt.) approved school; Borstal (Brit.); ~**berater** *der,* ~**beraterin** *die* (Berufsbez.) child guidance counsellor; ~**beratung** *die* 1 (Beraten) child guidance; 2 (Beratungsstelle) child guidance clinic; ~**berechtigt** *Adj.* having parental authority *postpos., not pred.;* **sein Großvater wurde ~berechtigt** his grandfather became his [legal] guardian; ~**berechtigte** *der/die; adj. Dekl.* parent or [legal] guardian; ~**frage** *die* question of upbringing; ~**heim** *das* community home; ~**maßnahme** *die* measure used in bringing up a child; ~**methode** *die* educational method; teaching method; ~**roman** *der* (Literaturw.) novel describing the development of an individual's character; ~**wesen** *das* educational system; education; ~**wissenschaft** *die* education; ~**wissenschaften studieren** study education *sing.;* ~**wissenschaftler** *der,* ~**wissenschaftlerin** *die* educationalist

> **Erziehungsgeld**
>
> A state benefit paid for up to two years to any mother or father who stays at home after the birth of a child to look after it. In 98% of cases, it is still the mother who claims *Erziehungsgeld*. Although this benefit is means-tested, almost all families receive some money for the first six months of the baby's life. In addition to this, parents receive *Kindergeld* (child benefit) for each child.

erzielen *tr. V.* reach ‹*agreement, compromise, speed*›; achieve ‹*result, effect*›; make ‹*profit*›; obtain ‹*price*›; score ‹*goal*›

erzittern *itr. V.; mit sein* 1 [begin to] shake *or* tremble; **etw. ~ lassen** shake sth. 2 (geh.) quiver; tremble

erz-, Erz-: ~**konservativ** *Adj.* ultra-conservative; ~**lager·stätte** *die* ore deposit; ~**lügner** *der,* ~**lügnerin** *die* inveterate liar; ~**lump** *der* (abwertend) [low-down] scoundrel

erzogen
A *2. Part. v.* **erziehen**
B *Adj.* **gut/schlecht ~ sein** have been brought up/not have been brought up properly

erz-, Erz-: ~**reaktionär** *Adj.* ultra-reactionary; ~**reaktionär** *der,* ~**reaktionärin** *die* ultra-reactionary; ~**schurke** *der,* ~**schurkin** *die* (abwertend) ▸ **Erzlump**

erzürnen (geh.)
A *tr. V.* anger; (stärker) incense; **erzürne ihn nicht** don't make him angry
B *refl. V.* **sich über jmdn./etw. ~:** become *or* grow angry with sb./about sth.

Erz-: ~**vater** *der* (Rel.) patriarch; ~**verhüttung** *die* ore smelting; ~**vorkommen** *das* ore deposit

erzwingen *unr. tr. V.* force; **sich** (*Dat.*) **den Zutritt ~:** force an entry; **etw. von jmdm. ~:** force sth. out of sb.

erzwungenermaßen *Adv.* under duress

es[1] /ɛs/ *Personalpron.; 3. Pers. Sg. Nom. u. Akk. Neutr.* 1 (*s. auch Gen.* **seiner;** *Dat.* **ihm**) (bei Dingen) it; (bei weiblichen Personen) she/her; (bei männlichen Personen) he/him 2 *bezieht sich auf ein Nomen mit beliebigem Genus* **Wer ist der Mann? — Es muss der Bruder des Gastgebers sein** Who is that man? — He/It must be the host's brother; **es waren Studenten** they were students; **keiner will es gewesen sein** no one will admit to it; **ich bin es** it's me; it is I (formal); **er/sie ist es** it's him/her; it is he/she (formal); **wir sind es** it's us; it is we (formal); **ich bin/wir sind es, der/die ...** I am the one/we are the ones who ...; (förmlicher) it is I/it is we who ... 3 *bezieht sich auf ein Adj.* **wir sind traurig, ihr seid es auch** we are sad, and you are too *or* so are you 4 *bezieht sich auf ein Prädikat* it; **er hat gelogen, will es aber nicht zugeben** he lied, but won't admit it; **er hatte es nicht anders erwartet** he hadn't expected anything else; **Wird man ihn dafür bestrafen? — Ich befürchte es** Will he be punished for it? — I fear so 5 *kündigt Subjekt od. Subjekt- und Objektsatz an* **es war einmal ein König** once upon a time there was a king; **es gibt keinen anderen Weg** there is no other way; **es war Karl, der ...** it was Karl who ...; **es ist schön, dass ...** it is nice that ...; **es wundert mich, dass ...** I'm surprised that ...; **es sei denn, [dass] ...** unless ... 6 *bezieht sich auf einen Sachverhalt* **es ist genug!** that's enough; **wir schaffen es** we'll manage it 7 *bei unpersönlicher Witterungsangabe* **es regnet/schneit/donnert** it rains/snows/thunders; (jetzt) it is raining/snowing/thundering; **es blitzt** there is lightning; **es stürmt** it is blowing a gale 8 *bei unpersönlicher Darstellung* **es hat geklopft** there was a knock; **es klingelte** there was a ring; **es klingelt** someone is ringing; **es knistert** there is something rustling; **in diesem Haus spukt es** this house is haunted; **es friert mich** I am cold 9 *bei Zustands- u. Artsätzen* **es ist 9 Uhr/spät/Nacht** it is 9 o'clock/late/night-time; **es wird schöner** the weather is improving; **es wird kälter** it's getting colder; **es wird Frühling** spring is on the way; **es geht ihm gut/schlecht** he is well/unwell 10 *bei passivischer Konstruktion* **es wird gelacht** there is laughter; **es wird um 6 Uhr angefangen** we/they *etc.* start at 6 o'clock; **es wurde uns befohlen, das Gebäude zu verlassen** we were ordered to leave the building 11 *bei reflexiver Konstruktion* **es lässt sich aushalten** it is bearable; **es lebt sich gut hier** it's a good life here 12 *als formales Objekt* **er hat es gut** he has it good; it's all right for him; **er meinte es gut** he meant well; **sie hat es mit dem Herzen** (ugs.) she has got heart trouble *or* something wrong with her heart; **er hat es mit seiner Sekretärin** (salopp) he's making it with his secretary (sl.); *s. auch* **haben A 14**

es[2], **Es**[1] *das;* ~, ~ (Musik) E flat

Es[2] *das;* ~, ~ (Psych.) id

Es[3] *der;* ~, ~ (österr., ugs.) schilling

ESA *Abk.* **= European Space Agency** ESA

E-Saite *die* E-string

Eschatologie /ɛsçatoloˈgiː/ *die;* ~, ~**n** /-ən/ (Theol.) eschatology *no art.*

eschatologisch *Adj.* eschatological

Esche /ˈɛʃə/ *die;* ~, ~**n** (Bot.) ash

Es-Dur *das* E flat major; *s. auch* **A-Dur**

Esel /ˈeːzl̩/ *der;* ~**s**, ~ 1 donkey; ass; **bepackt** *od.* **beladen wie ein ~ sein** be loaded down like a packhorse; **den hat der ~ im Galopp verloren** (salopp) he just appeared from nowhere (coll.); **wenn es dem ~ zu wohl wird, geht er aufs Eis** (Spr.) you'll/he'll *etc.* come unstuck one of these days **2▸** (ugs.: Dummkopf) ass (coll.); idiot (coll.); **so ein alter ~:** what a stupid ass *or* idiot (coll.); **du ~:** you ass!; *s. auch* **ich**

Eselei *die;* ~, ~**en** (ugs.) stupidity; **das war aber eine ~!** (Handlung) that was a stupid *or* silly thing to do; (Bemerkung) that was a stupid *or* silly thing to say

Eselein *das;* ~**s,** ~: little donkey

Esel-: ~füllen *das* ass-foal; **~hengst** *der* he-donkey; jackass

Eselin *die;* ~, ~**nen** she-donkey; jenny[-ass]

Esels-: ~brücke *die* (ugs.) mnemonic; **~milch** *die* ass's milk; **~ohr** *das* (ugs.) **1▸ ~ohren haben** (fig.) have donkey's ears; **2▸** (umgeknickte Stelle) dog-ear; **ein Buch voller ~ohren** a dog-eared book; **~stute** *die* she-donkey; jenny[-ass]

Esel·treiber *der,* **Esel·treiberin** *die* donkey driver

ESF *Abk.* (EU) = **Europäischer Sozialfonds** ESF

Eskalation /ɛskala'tsi̯o:n/ *die;* ~, ~**en** escalation

eskalieren *tr., itr. V.* escalate

eskamotieren /ɛskamo'ti:rən/ *tr. V.* conjure away; **Fakten ~:** explain facts away by sleight of hand

Eskapade /ɛska'pa:də/ *die;* ~, ~**n** escapade; (Seitensprung) amorous adventure

Eskapismus /ɛska'pɪsmʊs/ *der;* ~ (Psych.) escapism *no art.*

eskapistisch *Adj.* escapist

Eskimo /'ɛskimo/ *der;* ~**[s],** ~**[s]** ▸**i S. 520** Eskimo

Eskimo·frau *die* Eskimo woman

eskimoisch *Adj.* ▸**i S. 670** Eskimo

Eskimo·rolle *die* (Kanusport) Eskimo roll

Eskorte /ɛs'kɔrtə/ *die;* ~, ~**n** escort; (fig.) entourage; **eine ~ der Polizei** a police escort

eskortieren *tr. V.* escort

es-Moll *das* E flat minor; *s. auch* **a-Moll**

esoterisch /ezo'te:rɪʃ/

A *Adj.* esoteric

B *adv.* esoterically

Espe /'ɛspə/ *die;* ~, ~**n** aspen

Espen·laub *das:* in **wie ~ zittern** shake like a leaf

Esperanto /ɛspe'ranto/ *das;* ~**[s]** ▸**i S. 670** Esperanto

Esplanade /ɛspla'na:də/ *die;* ~, ~**n** esplanade

Espresso¹ /ɛs'prɛso/ *der;* ~**s,** ~**s 1▸** *dark blend of roasted coffee* **2▸** (Getränk) espresso [coffee]

Espresso² *das;* ~**[s],** ~**[s]** (Lokal) espresso [bar]

Espresso·maschine *die* espresso [machine]

Esprit /ɛs'pri:/ *der;* ~**s** esprit

Essai /'ɛse, ɛ'se:/ ▸**Essay**

Ess·apfel, *Eß·apfel *der* eating apple; eater (Brit.)

Essay /'ɛse/ *der od. das;* ~**s,** ~**s** essay

Essayist *der;* ~**en,** ~**en, Essayistin** *die;* ~, ~**nen** ▸**i S. 113** essayist

essayistisch *Adj.* essayistic; **seine ~e Begabung** his talent as an essayist

essbar, *eßbar *Adj.* edible; **ist etwas Essbares im Haus?** (ugs.) is there anything to eat in the house?; **nicht ~ sein** be inedible

Ess·besteck, *Eß·besteck *das* knife, fork, and spoon; **unser ~:** our cutlery; **zwei ~e** two sets of knife, fork, and spoon

Esse /'ɛsə/ *die;* ~, ~**n 1▸** (bes. ostmd.) chimney **2▸** (Herd) hearth; forge

Ess·ecke, *Eß·ecke *die* dining area

essen /'ɛsn̩/ *unr. tr., itr. V.* eat; eat, drink ‹*soup*›; **mittags isst er meist im Restaurant** he usually lunches *or* has lunch at a restaurant; **etw. gern ~:** like sth.; **möchten Sie ein Stück Kuchen ~?** would you like a piece of cake?; **was gibt es zu ~?** what's for lunch/dinner/supper?; **von etw. ~:** eat some of sth.; **jmdm. etwas zu ~ machen** get sb. something to eat; **sich satt ~:** eat one's fill; **den Teller leer ~:** clear one's plate; **er isst mich noch arm!** he'll eat me out of house and home!; **gut ~:** have a good meal; (immer) eat well; **warm/kalt ~:** have a hot/cold meal; **das Kind isst schlecht** the child doesn't eat very much *or* has a poor appetite; **Kranke müssen gut ~:** you must eat properly when you're ill; **~ gehen** got out for a meal; **er isst bei seiner Tante** he has his meals with his aunt; **es wird nichts so heiß gegessen, wie es gekocht wird** (Spr.) nothing is ever as bad as it seems; **selber ~ macht fett** (ugs.) I'm all right, Jack (coll.); *s. auch* **Abend 1; Mittag¹ 1; Mittag²**

Essen *das;* ~**s,** ~ **1▸ beim ~ sein** be having lunch/dinner/supper; **lasst euch nicht beim ~ stören** don't let me/us disturb your meal; **zum ~ gehen** go to lunch; **jmdn. zum ~ einladen** invite sb. for a meal **2▸** (Mahlzeit) meal; (Fest~) banquet; **zehn ~:** ten meals; **ein ~ [für jmdn.] geben** give a banquet [in sb.'s honour] **3▸** (Speise) food; **[das] ~ machen/kochen** get/cook the meal; **das ~ warm stellen** keep the lunch/dinner/supper hot; **das ~ wird kalt** lunch/dinner/supper is getting cold; the food is getting cold; **~ fassen!** (Soldatenspr.) come and get it!; **~ auf Rädern** meals on wheels **4▸** (Verpflegung) food; **~ und Trinken** food and drink

Essen·fassen *das* (Soldatenspr.) **zum ~!** come and get it!; **beim ~:** at mess time

Essen[s]-: ~ausgabe *die* **1▸** (das Ausgeben) serving of meals; **die ~ausgabe ist zwischen 12 und 14 Uhr** meals are *or* lunch is served between 12 [o'clock] and 2 o'clock; **2▸** (Stelle) serving hatch; **~marke** *die* meal ticket; **~rest** *der* leftover scrap; (zwischen Zähnen, an der Kleidung usw. haften geblieben) food particle; **~reste** *Pl.* leftovers/food particles; **~zeit** *die* mealtime; **während der ~zeit** during *or* at mealtimes

Essential /ɪ'sɛnʃl/ *das;* ~**s,** ~**s** essential

essentiell ▸**essenziell**

Essenz /ɛ'sɛnts/ *die;* ~, ~**en** essence

essenziell /ɛsɛn'tsi̯ɛl/

A *Adj.* (geh., auch Chemie, Biol.) essential

B *adv.* (geh.) essentially

Esser *der;* ~**s,** ~, **Esserin** *die;* ~, ~**nen: sie ist eine gute/schlechte Esserin** she has a healthy/poor appetite; **ein zusätzlicher Esser, den es zu ernähren gilt** an extra mouth to feed

Ess-, *Eß-: ~geschirr *das* **1▸** pots and pans; **2▸** (Milit.) mess kit; **~gewohnheiten** *Pl.* eating habits

Essig /'ɛsɪç/ *der;* ~**s,** ~**e** vinegar; **~ und Öl** oil and vinegar; **es ist mit etw. ~** (ugs.) sth. has fallen through completely (coll.)

essig-, Essig-: ~baum *der* staghorn sumac; **~essenz** *die* vinegar essence; **~flasche** *die* vinegar bottle; **~gurke** *die* pickled gherkin; **~sauce** *die* vinaigrette; French dressing; **~sauer** *Adj.* acetic; **~saure Tonerde** basic aluminium acetate; **~säure** *die* (Chemie) acetic acid; **~soße** *die:* ▸**~sauce**; **~-und-Öl-Ständer** *der* cruet stand; **~wasser** *das* water with a little vinegar added

ess-, *eß-, Ess-, *Eß-: ~kastanie *die* sweet chestnut; **~kohle** *die* dry steam coal; **~kultur** *die* gastronomy; **~löffel** *der* (Suppenlöffel) soup spoon; (für Nach-, Vorspeise) dessert spoon; **~löffel·weise** *Adv.* (abmessend) in dessertspoonfuls; (steigernd) by the spoonful; **~lokal** *das* restaurant; **~lust** *die* desire for something to eat; **~napf** *der* bowl; **~paket** *das* food parcel; **~platz** *der* dining area; **~stäbchen** *das* chopstick; **~teller** *der* dinner plate; **~tisch** *der* dining table; **~waren** *Pl.* food *sing.;* **~zimmer** *das* dining room; (Möbel) dining room suite

Establishment /ɪs'tɛblɪʃmənt/ *das;* ~**s,** ~**s** Establishment

Este /'e:stə/ *der;* ~**n,** ~**n** Estonian

Ester /'ɛstɐ/ *der;* ~**s,** ~ (Chemie) ester

Estin *die;* ~, ~**nen** Estonian

Estland *(das);* ~**s** Estonia

Estländer *der;* ~**s,** ~, **Estländerin** *die;* ~, ~**nen** ▸**Este, Estin**

estländisch, estnisch *Adj.* ▸**i S. 670** Estonian; *s. auch* **deutsch; Deutsch**

Estrade /ɛs'tra:də/ *die;* ~, ~**n 1▸** (veralt.) estrade; dais; platform **2▸** (DDR) open-air show

Estragon /'ɛstragɔn/ *der;* ~**s** tarragon

Estrich /'ɛstrɪç/ *der;* ~**s,** ~**e 1▸** composition *or* jointless floor **2▸** (schweiz.) attic; loft

Eszett /ɛs'tsɛt/ *das;* ~, ~: [the letter] ß

Eta /'e:ta/ *das;* ~**[s],** ~**s** eta

etablieren /eta'bli:rən/

A *tr. V.* (gründen) establish; set up

B *refl. V.* **1▸** (sich niederlassen) ‹*shop*› open up; ‹*chain store*› open up *or* set up branches; **sich als Juwelier ~:** set up as a jeweller; open up a jeweller's shop **2▸** (sich einrichten) settle in **3▸** (gesellschaftlich) become established

etabliert *Adj.* established; **er ist jetzt so entsetzlich ~** (abwertend) he is now so terribly conservative; **die Etablierten** the Establishment

Etablissement /etablɪs(ə)'mã:/ *das;* ~**s,** ~**s** establishment

Etage /e'ta:ʒə/ *die;* ~, ~**n** floor; storey; **in** *od.* **auf der dritten ~ wohnen** live on the third *or* (Amer.) fourth floor

Etagen-: ~bett *das* bunk bed; **~haus** *das* block of flats (esp. Brit.) *or* (esp. Amer.) apartments; **~heizung** *die: central heating serving one floor of a building;* **~wohnung** *die: flat (esp. Brit.) or (esp. Amer.) apartment occupying an entire floor*

Etagere /eta'ʒe:rə/ *die;* ~, ~**n** (veralt.) étagère; whatnot

Etappe /e'tapə/ *die;* ~, ~**n 1▸** (Teilstrecke) stage; leg; (Rennsport) stage **2▸** (Stadium) stage **3▸** (Milit.) back area; base; **jmdn. in die ~ versetzen** move sb. back behind the lines

etappen-, Etappen-: ~hase *der,* **~hengst** *der* (Soldatenspr. salopp) base wallah (Mil. coll.); **~sieg** *der* (Rennsport) stage win; **der heutige ~sieg ging an …** the winner of today's stage was …; **~weise** *Adv.* by *or* in stages; **~wertung** *die* (Rennsport) daily points classification; **~ziel** *das* (Sport) finish of the stage

Etat /e'ta:/ *der;* ~**s,** ~**s** budget

etat-, Etat-: ~ausgleich *der* balancing of the budget; **~defizit** *das* budgetary deficit; **~kürzung** *die* cut in the budget; **die ~kürzungen im Bildungswesen** the cuts in the education budget; the education cuts; **~mäßig A** *Adj.* **1▸** (im ~) budgetary ‹*expenditure*›; **2▸** (eingeplant) budgeted ‹*post, position*›; **der ~mäßige Mittelstürmer** (Fußballjargon) the regular centre forward; **B** *adv.* in the budget; **~stärke** *die* (Milit.) planned strength

etc. *Abk.* = **et cetera** etc.

et cetera /ɛt'tse:tera/ et cetera; **~ pp.** /-'---pe'pe:/ (ugs. scherzh.) and so on and so forth (coll.)

etepetete /e:təpe'te:tə/ *Adj.* (ugs.) fussy; finicky; pernickety (coll.)

Eternit Ⓦ /etɛr'ni:t/ *das od. der;* ~**s** asbestos cement

ETH *Abk.* = **Eidgenössische Technische Hochschule** Swiss Federal Institute of Technology

Ethernet /'i:θənɛt/ *das* (DV) Ethernet

Ethik /'e:tɪk/ *die;* ~, ~**en 1▸** (Sittenlehre) ethics *sing.* **2▸** (sittliche Normen) ethics *pl.* **3▸** (Werk über ~) ethical work

Ethiker *der;* ~**s,** ~, **Ethikerin** *die;* ~, ~**nen 1▸** (Philos.) moral philosopher **2▸** (Moralist) moralist

ethisch

A *Adj.* ethical

B *adv.* ethically

Ethnie /ɛt'ni:/ *die;* ~, ~**n** (Völkerk.) ethnos

ethnisch /'ɛtnɪʃ/

A *Adj.* ethnic; **~e Säuberung** ethnic cleansing

e

B *adv.* ethnically

Ethno *der;* **~s** ethnic music

Ethnograph /ɛtno'gra:f/ *der;* **~en, ~en** ethnographer

Ethnographie *die;* **~, ~n** ethnography *no art.*

Ethnographin *die;* **~, ~nen** ethnographer

Ethnologe /ɛtno'lo:gə/ *der;* **~n, ~n** ethnologist

Ethnologie *die;* **~, ~n** ethnology *no art.*

Ethnologin *die;* **~, ~nen** ethnologist

ethnologisch

A *Adj.* ethnological

B *adv.* ethnologically

Ethno·pop *der* ethnic pop [music]

Ethologie /etolo'gi:/ *die;* **~, ~n** ethology *no art.*

Ethos /'e:tɔs/ *das;* **~:** ethos; **das berufliche ~ der Ärzteschaft** doctors' professional ethics *pl.*

Etikett /eti'kɛt/ *das;* **~[e]s, ~en** *od.* **~e** *od.* **~s** label; **jmdn./etw. mit einem ~ versehen** (fig.) pin a label on sb./sth.

Etikette[1] *die;* **~, ~n** (schweiz., österr.) ▸ **Etikett**

Etikette[2] *die;* **~, ~n** etiquette; **die ~ wahren** observe the proprieties; **gegen die ~ verstoßen** commit a breach of etiquette

Etiketten·schwindel *der* (abwertend) playing with names

etikettieren /etikɛ'ti:rən/ *tr. V.* label

etlich... /'ɛtlɪç.../ *Indefinitpron. u. unbest. Zahlwort* **1** (ugs. verstärkend) *Sg.* quite a lot of; *Pl.* quite a few; a number of; **vor ~en Wochen** several *or* some weeks ago **2** *Sg.* (veralt.: wenig) a little; **Etliches bemerken** make a few remarks *or* comments; **Etliches sagen** say a few things **3** *Pl.* (veralt.: einige) a few; some; **~e der Gefangenen** a few *or* some of the prisoners

***etliche·mal** ▸ **Mal[1]**

Etrusker /e'trʊskɐ/ *der;* **~s, ~, Etruskerin** *die;* **~, ~nen** Etruscan

etruskisch *Adj.* ▸ⓘ **S. 670** Etruscan; *s. auch* **deutsch**

Etsch *die;* **~:** Adige

Etüde /e'ty:də/ *die;* **~, ~n** (Musik) étude

Etui /ɛt'vi:/ *das;* **~s, ~s** case

etwa /'ɛtva/

A *Adv.* **1** (ungefähr) about; approximately; **~ 50 m/2 Wochen** about 50 m/2 weeks; **~ so groß wie ...** about as large as ...; **wie lange wird die Fahrt ~ dauern?** roughly how long will the journey take?; **~ so** roughly like this; **das lässt sich ~ so erklären** you could perhaps explain it like this; **in ~:** to some *or* a certain extent *or* degree; **können Sie mir in ~ sagen, wann ...?** can you give me any idea when ...? **2** (beispielsweise) for example; for instance; **vergleicht man ~ ...** for example, if one compares ...; **wie ~ ...** as, for example ... **3** (schweiz.: bisweilen) from time to time; now and then

B *Part.* (womöglich) **hast du das ~ vergessen?** you haven't forgotten that, have you?; **störe ich ~?** am I disturbing you at all?; **falls sie ~ doch mitgeht, ...** if she does happen to go ...; **du glaubst doch nicht ~, dass ...?** surely you don't think that ...?; **sie darf nicht ~ glauben, dass ...** she mustn't think that ...

etwaig... /'ɛtva(:)ɪg.../ *Adj.* (Papierdt.) possible ‹*delays*›; **~e Mängel/Beschwerden** any faults/complaints [which might arise]; **bei ~en Beschwerden** in the event of any complaints

etwas /'ɛtvas/ *Indefinitpron.* **1** something; (fragend, verneinend) anything; **~ sagen/hören/sehen** say/hear/see something; **hast du ~ gesagt?** did you say something?; **irgend~:** something; **erzähl ihm einfach irgend~:** just tell him anything!; **es muss ~ geschehen** something has to *or* must be done; **wenn sie es wagt, dir ~ zu tun** if she dares to do anything to you; **~ gegen jmdn. haben** have something against sb.; **sie haben ~ miteinander** (ugs.) there is something going on between them; **~ für sich haben** (ugs.) have something in it; **dein Argument hat ~ für sich** (ugs.) there's something in your argument; **so ~:** a thing like that; **[so] ~ wie ...** something like ...; **so ~ habe ich noch nie gesehen** I've never seen anything like it; **nein, so ~:** would you believe it! **2** *attr.* something; (fragend, verneinend) anything; **~ Schönes/Neues/Unangenehmes** something beautiful/new/unpleasant; **so ~ Schönes habe ich noch nie gesehen** I've never seen anything so beautiful before; **~ anderes** something else; (fragend, verneinend) anything else; **das ist ~ anderes** (ugs.) that's different **3** (Bedeutsames) **aus ihm wird ~:** he'll make something of himself *or* his life; **es zu ~ bringen** get somewhere; **~ gelten** count for something; **das will ~ heißen** that really is something **4** (ein Teil) some; (fragend, verneinend) any; **~ von dem Geld** some of the money; **kann ich auch ~ davon haben?** can I have some of it too?; **er weiß ~ von dieser Sache** he knows something about this matter; **sie hat ~ von einer Künstlerin an sich** (*Dat.*) she has *or* there is something of the artist about her **5** (ein wenig) a little; **noch ~ Milch** a little more *or* some more milk; **kannst du mir ~ Geld leihen?** can you lend me some money?; **~ lauter/besser** a little louder/better; **[noch] ~ spielen/lesen** play/read for a little while [longer]; **~ Englisch** a little *or* some English

Etwas *das;* **~, ~:** something; **ein hilfloses ~:** a helpless little thing; **das gewisse ~:** that certain something

etwelch... /'ɛtvɛlç.../ *Indefinitpron.* (schweiz., österr.) some

Etymologe /etymo'lo:gə/ *der;* **~n, ~n** etymologist

Etymologie *die;* **~, ~n** etymology

Etymologin *die;* **~, ~nen** etymologist

etymologisch (Sprachw.)

A *Adj.* etymological

B *adv.* etymologically

etymologisieren *tr. V.* (Sprachw.) etymologize

Et-Zeichen /'ɛt-/ *das* ampersand

Etzel /'ɛtsl̩/ *(der)* Attila the Hun

EU *Abk.* **= Europäische Union** EU

euch /ɔyç/

A *Dat. u. Akk. Pl. des Personalpron.* **ihr** you; ye (Bibl./arch.); **ich gebe ~ das** I'll give you it; I'll give it to you

B *Dat. u. Akk. Pl. des Reflexivpron. der 2. Pers. Pl.* yourselves

Eucharistie /ɔyçarɪs'ti:/ *die;* **~, ~n** (kath. Rel.) Eucharist

eucharistisch *Adj.* (kath. Rel.) Eucharistic

euer[1] /'ɔyɐ/ *Possessivpron.* your; **Grüße von eu[e]rer Helga/eu[e]rem Hans** Best wishes, Yours, Helga/Hans; **Eu[e]re** *od.* **Euer Exzellenz** Your Excellency; **ist das/sind das eure?** is that/are they yours?; **es ist der Eu[e]re** (geh.) it is yours; **die Eu[e]ren** *od.* **Euern** (geh.) your family; **nehmt euch das Eu[e]re** (geh.) take what is yours; **ihr müsst das Eu[e]re dazu tun** you must do your share; **ich verbleibe auf immer die Eu[e]re ...** (veralt.) I remain, yours for ever, ...; *s. auch* **dein[1]**

euer[2] *Gen. des Personalpron.* **ihr** (geh.) **wir werden ~ gedenken** we will remember you

euerseits ▸ **eurerseits**

euersgleichen ▸ **euresgleichen**

euert-: **~halben** ▸ **eurethalben**; **~wegen** ▸ **euretwegen**; **~willen** ▸ **euretwillen**

Eugenik /ɔy'ge:nɪk/ *die;* **~** (Med.) eugenics *sing.*

eugenisch *Adj.* (Med.) eugenic

EuGH *Abk.* **= Europäischer Gerichtshof** ECJ

Eukalyptus /ɔyka'lʏptʊs/ *der;* **~, Eukalypten** *od.* **~:** eucalyptus

Eukalyptus·bonbon *das* eucalyptus cough sweet (Brit.); cough drop

Euklid /ɔy'kli:t/ *(der)* Euclid

euklidisch *Adj.* (Math.) Euclidean

Eule /'ɔylə/ *die;* **~, ~n** **1** owl; **~n nach Athen tragen** carry coals to Newcastle; send owls to Athens **2** (salopp abwertend: Frau) old boot (sl.)

eulen-, Eulen-: **~haft** *Adj.* owlish; owl-like; **~spiegel** *der* joker; *s. auch* **Till**; **~spiegelei** *die;* **~~, ~~en** caper; **~vogel** *der* (Zool.) owl

Eumel /'ɔyml̩/ *der;* **~s, ~** (Jugendspr.) twerp (coll. derog.)

Eunuch /ɔy'nu:x/ *der;* **~en, ~en, Eunuche** *der;* **~en, ~en** eunuch

Eunuchen·stimme *die* (ugs.) squeaky, high-pitched voice

Euphemismus /ɔyfe'mɪsmʊs/ *der;* **~, Euphemismen** (geh., Sprachw.) euphemism

euphemistisch (geh., Sprachw.)

A *Adj.* euphemistic

B *adv.* euphemistically

euphonisch /ɔy'fo:nɪʃ/ *Adj.* (Sprachw., Musik) euphonic

Euphorie /ɔyfo'ri:/ *die;* **~, ~n** (bes. Med., Psych.) euphoria; **in [eine] ~ verfallen** go into a state of euphoria

euphorisch (bes. Med., Psych.)

A *Adj.* euphoric

B *adv.* euphorically

Euphrat /'ɔyfrat/ *der;* **~[s]** ▸ⓘ **S. 267** Euphrates

Eurasien /ɔy'ra:zi̯ən/ *(das);* **~s** Eurasia

Eurasier *der;* **~s, ~, Eurasierin** *die;* **~, ~nen** Eurasian

eurasisch *Adj.* Eurasian

Euratom /ɔyra'to:m/ *die;* **~:** Euratom

eure /'ɔyrə/ ▸ **euer[1]**

eurer·seits *Adv.* (von eurer Seite) on your part; (auf eurer Seite) for your part

eures·gleichen *indekl. Pron.* people *pl.* like you; (abwertend) the likes *pl.* of you; your sort *or* kind; *s. auch* **deinesgleichen**

euret-: **~halben** /-halbn̩/ (veralt.), **~wegen** *Adv.* (wegen euch) because of you; on your account; (für euch) on your behalf; (euch zuliebe) for your sake; **ich mache mir ~wegen keine Sorgen** I don't worry about you; **~willen** *Adv.* **um ~willen** for your sake

Eurhythmie /ɔyrʏt'mi:/ *die;* **~** **1** (bes. Tanz, Gymnastik) eurhythmics *sing., no art.* **2** (Med.) eurhythmia

eurige /'ɔyrɪgə/ *Possessivpron.* (geh., veralt.) **der/die/das ~:** yours; **das ~** *od.* **Eurige** (Angelegenheit) your affairs; (Besitz) what is yours

Euro *der;* **~[s], ~[s]** ▸ⓘ **S. 299** euro; **zwei ~ fünfzig kosten** cost two euros fifty; *s. auch* **umdrehen[1]**

Euro-: **~cent** *der* euro cent; eurocent; **~cheque** /'ɔyroʃɛk/ *der;* **~s, ~s** Eurocheque

> **Eurocheque**
>
> The Eurocheque is the standard cheque issued by banks in Germany. It is backed up by the *Eurochequekarte*, which can also be used at cash machines and for payments in shops. Although plastic cards have become more popular in Germany, many people (and shops and restaurants) still prefer cash.

Eurocheque·karte *die* Eurocheque card

Euro-: **~dollar** *der* (Wirtsch.) Eurodollar; **~kommunismus** *der* Eurocommunism; **~krat** /-'kra:t/ *der;* **~~en, ~~en, ~kratin** *die;* **~~, ~~nen** Eurocrat; **~land** *(das);* **~s** Euroland

Europa /ɔy'ro:pa/ *(das);* **~s** Europe

Europa: **~abgeordnete** *der/die* Member of the European Parliament; **~cup** *der* (Sport) European cup

Europäer /ɔyro'pɛ:ɐ/ *der;* **~s, ~, Europäerin** *die;* **~, ~nen** European

Europa·flagge *die* flag of the Council of Europe

europäisch /ɔyro'pɛ:ɪʃ/ *Adj.* European; **die Europäische Gemeinschaft/Europäischen Gemeinschaften** the European Community/European Communities; **Europäischer Ausrichtungs- und Garantiefonds für die Landwirtschaft** (EU) European Agricultural

Guidance and Guarantee Fund; **Europäischer Entwicklungsfonds** (EU) European Development Fund; **Europäischer Gerichtshof** European Court of Justice; **Europäischer Gerichtshof für Menschenrechte** European Court of Human Rights; **Europäische Investitionsbank** European Investment Bank; **Europäische Kohle- und Stahlgemeinschaft** European Coal and Steel Community; **Europäisches Parlament** (EU) European Parliament; **Europäisches Polizeiamt** European Police Office; **Europäischer Rat** European Council; **Europäische Raumfahrtbehörde** European Space Agency; **Europäischer Rechnungshof** (EU) European Court of Auditors; **Europäischer Regionalentwicklungsfonds** European Regional Development Fund; **Europäischer Sozialfonds** European Social Fund; **Europäische Union** European Union; **Europäische Währungsunion** European Monetary Union; **Europäische Wirtschaftsgemeinschaft** European Economic Community; **Europäische Zentralbank** European Central Bank

europäisieren *tr. V.* Europeanize

Europäisierung *die;* ~, ~**en** Europeanization

europa-, Europa-: ~**meister** *der,* ~**meisterin** *die* (Sport) European champion; ~**meisterschaft** *die* (Sport) 1 (Wettbewerb) European Championship; 2 (Sieg) championship of Europe, European title; ~**minister** *der,* ~**ministerin** *die* minister for Europe; ~**müde** *Adj.* disillusioned with the Common Market *postpos.;* ~**parlament** *das* European Parliament *or* Assembly; ~**parlamentarier** *der,* ~**parlamentarierin** *die* Member of the European Parliament *or* Assembly; ~**pokal** *der* (Sport) ▸ **Europacup**; ~**politik** *die* policy towards the EEC; ~**rat** *der* Council of Europe; ~**rekord** *der* (Sport) European record; ~**straße** *die* European long-distance road; ~**wahlen** *Pl.* European elections; ~**weit** A *Adj.* Europe-wide; ‹*study, regulation*› covering the whole of Europe; B *adv.* in the whole of Europe; **etw.** ~**weit ausdehnen** extend sth. to the whole of Europe

Europol /ˈɔyːropoːl/ *(die);* ~**:** Europol

Euro·scheck *der* ▸ **Eurocheque**

euro·skeptisch *Adj.* Eurosceptic

Euro·skeptizismus *der;* ~**:** Euroscepticism

Euro·vision *die* Eurovision

euro·zentrisch *Adj.* Eurocentric

Euro·zone *die* eurozone

Eurythmie ▸ **Eurhythmie 1**

eustachische Röhre /ɔysˈtaxɪʃə/ *die;* ~**n** ~, ~**n** ~**n** ▸ ❶ **S. 435** (Med., Zool.) Eustachian tube

Euter /ˈɔytɐ/ *das od. der;* ~**s**, ~**:** udder

Euthanasie /ɔytanaˈziː/ *die;* ~**:** euthanasia *no art.*

ev. *Abk.* **= evangelisch** ev.

e. V., E. V. *Abk.* **= eingetragener Verein**

Eva¹ /ˈeːfa *od.* ˈeːva/ *(die)* Eve; *s. auch* **Adam¹**

Eva² *die;* ~, ~**s** (ugs. scherzh.: Frau) **sie ist eine richtige** ~**:** she's a real little Eve

evakuieren /evakuˈiːrən/ *tr. V.* evacuate

Evakuierte *der/die; adj. Dekl.* evacuee

Evakuierung *die;* ~, ~**en** evacuation

Evaluation /evaluaˈtsi̯oːn/ *die;* ~, ~**en** 1 (geh.) valuation 2 (Päd.) evaluation

Evangelien·buch *das* Gospel

evangelikal /evaŋgeliˈkaːl/ *Adj.* (christl. Kirche) evangelical

evangelisch /evaŋˈgeːlɪʃ/ *Adj.* 1 Protestant; **die** ~**e Kirche** the Protestant Church 2 (des Evangeliums) evangelical

evangelisch-lutherisch *Adj.* Lutheran

evangelisch-reformiert *Adj.* Reformed

evangelisieren *tr. V.* evangelize

Evangelist *der;* ~**en**, ~**en** evangelist

Evangelium /evaŋˈgeːli̯ʊm/ *das;* ~**s**, **Evangelien** 1 (auch fig.) gospel; **alles, was ihr Mann sagte, war [ein]** ~ **für sie** she took everything her husband said as gospel 2 (christl. Rel.) Gospel; **das** ~ **des Johannes** St. John's Gospel

Evas- /ˈeːfas- *od.* ˈeːvas-/: ~**kostüm** *das: in* **im** ~**kostüm** (ugs. scherzh.) in her birthday suit/their birthday suits (coll. joc.); in the altogether (coll. joc.); ~**tochter** *die* (scherzh.) **eine echte** ~**tochter** a real little Eve

Eventual- /evɛnˈtu̯aːl-/: ~**fall** *der* eventuality; contingency; **für den** ~**fall** should the eventuality arise; ~**haushalt** *der* (Politik) contingency reserve

Eventualität /evɛntu̯aliˈtɛːt/ *die;* ~, ~**n** eventuality; contingency

eventuell /evɛnˈtu̯ɛl/

A *Adj.* possible ‹*objections, difficulties, applicants*›; ‹*objections, difficulties*› which might occur; **bei** ~**en Schäden** in the event *or* case of damage

B *adv.* possibly; perhaps; **wir werden** ~ **morgen kommen** we may [possibly] come tomorrow; **können wir** ~ **bei euch übernachten?** can we stay the night at your house, if necessary?

Evergreen /ˈɛvəgriːn/ *der;* ~**s**, ~**s** old favourite

evident /eviˈdɛnt/ *Adj.* (geh.) 1 (einleuchtend) convincing ‹*argument, proof*›; evident, self-evident ‹*truth*› 2 (offenkundig) evident, obvious ‹*disadvantage*›

Evidenz /eviˈdɛnts/ *die;* ~, ~**en** (geh.) (einer Behauptung, eines Beweises) convincingness; (eines Satzes, einer Wahrheit) self-evidence

Evolution /evoluˈtsi̯oːn/ *die;* ~, ~**en** evolution

evolutionär /evolutsi̯oˈnɛːɐ̯/

A *Adj.* evolutionary

B *adv.* by evolution

Evolutions·theorie *die* theory of evolution

evozieren /evoˈtsiːrən/ *tr. V.* (geh.) evoke

evtl. *Abk.* **= eventuell**

EW *Abk.* **= Elektrizitätswerk**

Ewer /ˈeːvɐ/ *der;* ~**s**, ~ (nordd.) ketch-rigged sailing barge

E-Werk *das* ▸ **Elektrizitätswerk**

EWG *Abk.* **= Europäische Wirtschaftsgemeinschaft** EEC

ewig /ˈeːvɪç/

A *Adj.* eternal, everlasting ‹*life, peace*›; eternal, undying ‹*love*›; (abwertend) never-ending; **die Ewige Stadt** the Eternal City; **der Ewige Jude** the Wandering Jew; **ein** ~**er Student** (scherzh.) an eternal student; **das** ~**e Einerlei** the unending *or* never-ending monotony; **seit** ~**en Zeiten** for ages (coll.); for donkey's years (coll.); **das** ~**e Licht** (kath. Rel.) the Sanctuary Lamp

B *adv.* eternally; for ever; ~ **warten** wait for ever; ~ **dauern** take ages; ~ **halten** last for ever *or* indefinitely; **auf** ~**:** for ever; **sein Name wird** ~ **leben** his name will live for-ever; ~ **und drei Tage** (ugs.) for ever and a day; ~ **kommt er mit denselben Problemen an** (ugs.) he is for ever coming along with the same problems; *s. auch* **immer 1**

Ewig·gestrige *der/die; adj. Dekl.* (abwertend) **ein** ~**r sein** be an old reactionary

Ewigkeit *die;* ~, ~**en** 1 eternity; **in** ~**:** for ever and ever; **in die** ~ **eingehen** (geh. verhüll.) find eternal rest 2 (ugs.) **es dauert eine [ganze]** ~**:** it takes [absolutely] ages (coll.); **es ist eine [kleine]** ~ **her** it was ages ago (coll.); **es muss** ~**en her sein, dass ...** it must be ages since … (coll.); **seit** ~**en** for ages (coll.); **in alle** ~**:** for ever

Ewigkeits-: ~**sonntag,** *der* ▸ **Totensonntag**; ~**wert** *der* (geh.) **es besitzt** ~**wert** it will last for ever

ewiglich *Adv.* (dichter. veralt.) for ever; till the end of time

Ewig·weibliche *das; adj. Dekl.* (geh.) **das** ~**:** the essential Feminine

EWS *Abk.* **= Europäisches Währungssystem** EMS

EWU *Abk.* **= Europäische Währungsunion** EMU

ex /ɛks/ *Adv.* (ugs.) 1 **etw. ex trinken** drink sth. down in one (coll.); knock sth. back in one (sl.); **ex!** down in one! (sl.) 2 (salopp: tot) **der ist ex** he's snuffed it (sl.)

Ex¹ *der;* ~, ~ *od.* ~**e** ex

Ex² *die;* ~, ~ *od.* ~**e** ex

Ex- (vor Personenbez.: vormalig) ex-

exakt /ɛˈksakt/

A *Adj.* exact; precise; **eine** ~**e Beschreibung** a precise description

B *adv.* ‹*work etc.*› accurately; ~ **[um] 12 Uhr** at 12 o'clock precisely; ~**!** exactly!; precisely!

Exaktheit *die;* ~**:** precision; exactness

exaltieren /ɛksalˈtiːrən/ *refl. V.* get overexcited *or* worked up

exaltiert

A *Adj.* (hysterisch) overexcited; (überspannt) exaggerated ‹*behaviour, gestures*›; (überschwänglich) effusive

B *adv.* (hysterisch) overexcitedly; (überschwänglich) effusively

Exaltiertheit *die;* ~, ~**en** ▸ **exaltiert:** overexcitedness; exaggeratedness; effusiveness

Examen /ɛˈksaːmən/ *das;* ~**s**, ~ *od.* **Examina** /ɛˈksaːmina/ examination; exam (coll.); **ein** ~ **machen** *od.* **ablegen** sit *or* take an examination; ~ **haben** (ugs.) have examinations; **im** ~ **sein** *od.* **stehen** be in the middle of one's examinations; **im** ~ **durchfallen** fail the examination

Examens-: ~**angst** *die* examination nerves *pl.;* ~**arbeit** *die: written work presented for an examination;* ~**kandidat** *der,* ~**kandidatin** *die* examination candidate

examinieren *tr. V.* 1 examine; **eine examinierte Krankenschwester** a qualified nurse 2 (ausfragen) question 3 (veralt. geh.: prüfend untersuchen) scrutinize ‹*appearance*›; investigate ‹*affair, matter*›

ex cathedra /ɛksˈka(ː)tedra/ (kath. Rel.) ex cathedra

Exe /ˈɛksə/ *die;* ~, ~**n** (ugs.) ex

Exegese /ɛkseˈgeːzə/ *die;* ~, ~**n** (Theol.) exegesis

Exeget /ɛkseˈgeːt/ *der;* ~**en**, ~**en** (Theol.) exegete

exekutieren /ɛksekuˈtiːrən/ *tr. V.* 1 execute 2 (österr.) ▸ **pfänden**

Exekution /ɛksekuˈtsi̯oːn/ *die;* ~, ~**en** 1 execution 2 (österr.) ▸ **Pfändung**

Exekutions·kommando *das* firing squad

exekutiv /ɛksekuˈtiːf/ *Adj.* (bes. Politik, Rechtsw.) executive

Exekutiv·ausschuss, ***Exekutiv·ausschuß** *der* executive committee

Exekutive /ɛksekuˈtiːvə/ *die;* ~, ~**n** (Rechtsw., Politik) executive

Exekutiv-: ~**gewalt** *die* (Politik) executive power; ~**organ** *das* (Politik) executive body

Exekutor /ɛkseˈkuːtɔr/ *der;* ~**s**, ~**en**, **Exekutorin** *die;* ~, ~**nen** (österr.) bailiff

Exempel /ɛˈksɛmpl̩/ *das;* ~**s**, ~**:** example; **ein** ~ **[an jmdm.] statuieren** make an example [of sb.]; **zum** ~ (veralt.) for example; *s. auch* **Probe 1**

Exemplar /ɛksɛmˈplaːɐ̯/ *das;* ~**s**, ~**e** specimen; (Buch, Zeitung, Zeitschrift) copy

exemplarisch /ɛksɛmˈplaːrɪʃ/

A *Adj.* exemplary; **eine** ~**e Strafe** an exemplary punishment; a deterrent sentence; ~ **für etw. sein** be typical of sth.

B *adv.* by means of an example/examples; **jmdn.** ~ **bestrafen** punish sb. as an example to others

exemplifizieren /ɛksɛmplifiˈtsiːrən/ *tr. V.* (geh.) exemplify; **etw. an einem Beispiel** ~**:** illustrate sth. by an example

Exequien /ɛˈkseːkvi̯ən/ *Pl.* (kath. Kirche) exequies

exerzieren /ɛksɛrˈtsiːrən/

A *itr. V.* (Milit.: Übungen machen) drill

B *tr. V.* 1 (Milit.: ausbilden) drill ‹*soldiers*› 2 (ugs.: üben) practise 3 (ausführen) employ ‹*technique, method*›; follow ‹*procedure*›

Exerzier-: ~munition *die* (Milit.) dummy ammunition; **~platz** *der* (Milit.) parade ground; **~reglement** *das* (Milit.) drill regulations *pl.*

Exerzitien /ɛksɛrˈtsiːtsi̯ən/ *Pl.* (kath. Rel.) religious *or* spiritual exercises

Exhaustor /ɛksˈhaustɔr/ *der;* **~s, ~en** (Technik) extractor fan

exhibitionieren /ɛkshibitsi̯oˈniːrən/ *itr., refl. V.* (Psych.) expose oneself

Exhibitionismus *der;* ~ (Psych., fig.) exhibitionism

Exhibitionist *der;* **~en, ~en, Exhibitionistin** *die;* **~, ~nen** (Psych., fig.) exhibitionist

exhibitionistisch (Psych.)
A *Adj.* exhibitionist
B *adv.* **er ist ~ veranlagt** he has exhibitionist tendencies

exhumieren /ɛkshuˈmiːrən/ *tr. V.* exhume

Exhumierung *die;* **~, ~en** exhumation

Exil /ɛˈksiːl/ *das;* **~s, ~e** exile; **ins ~ gehen** go into exile

Exilant /ɛksiˈlant/ *der;* **~en, ~en, Exilantin** *die;* **~, ~nen** exile

Exil·heimat *die* home in exile

exiliert /ɛksiˈliːɐ̯t/ *Adj.* exiled

Exilierte *der/die; adj. Dekl.* exile

Exil-: ~literatur *die* literature written in exile; **~regierung** *die* government in exile

existent /ɛksɪsˈtɛnt/ *Adj.* existing; existent; **jmdn./etw. als nicht ~ betrachten** treat sb./sth. as if he/she/it did not exist

Existentialismus *usw.* ▸ **Existenzialismus** *usw.*

Existenz /ɛksɪsˈtɛnts/ *die;* **~, ~en** **1** (Dasein) existence; **die nackte ~ retten** to escape with one's life **2** (Lebensgrundlage) livelihood; **sich** (*Dat.*) **eine ~ aufbauen** build a life for oneself; **jmdm. eine gesicherte ~ bieten** offer sb. a secure livelihood *or* living **3** (Mensch) **zweifelhafte ~en** dubious characters; **eine verkrachte ~** (ugs.) a deadbeat

existenz-, Existenz-: ~angst *die* angst; existential fear; **~bedingungen** *Pl.* living conditions; conditions of life; **~berechtigung** *die* right to exist; **diese Institution hat keine ~berechtigung mehr** there is no longer any justification for the existence of this institution; **~fähig** *Adj.* able to exist *or* to survive *postpos.*; **~frage** *die* matter of life and death; **~grundlage** *die* basis of one's livelihood; **~gründung** *die* [business] start-up

Existenzialismus /ɛksɪstɛntsi̯aˈlɪsmʊs/ *der;* ~ (Philos.) existentialism *no art.*

Existenzialist *der;* **~en, ~en, Existenzialistin** *die;* **~, ~nen** existentialist

existenzialistisch
A *Adj.* existentialist
B *adv.* **~ beeinflusst** influenced by existentialism

existenziell /ɛksɪstɛnˈtsi̯ɛl/ *Adj.* (Philos.) existential; **in etw.** (*Dat.*) **eine ~e Bedrohung sehen** see in sth. a threat to one's existence

Existenz-: ~kampf *der* struggle for existence; **~minimum** *das* subsistence level; **am Rande des ~minimums leben** live at subsistence level; **die Löhne der Teepflücker liegen unter dem ~minimum** the tea pickers earn less than a living wage; **~philosophie** *die* existential philosophy *no art.*; **~recht** *das* right to exist

existieren /ɛksɪsˈtiːrən/ *itr. V.* exist

Exitus /ˈɛksitʊs/ *der;* ~ (Med.) death; **„~", konstatierte der Arzt** 'she's/he's dead,' confirmed the doctor

exkl. *Abk.* = **exklusiv[e]** excl.

Exklave /ɛksˈklaːvə/ *die;* **~, ~n** exclave

exklusiv /ɛkskluˈziːf/
A *Adj.* exclusive
B *adv.* exclusively; **[über etw.** (*Akk.*)**] ~ berichten** run an exclusive report [on sth.]

Exklusiv·bericht *der* exclusive [report]

exklusive /ɛkskluˈziːvə/ *Präp. + Gen.* (Kaufmannsspr.) exclusive of; excluding

Exklusiv·interview *das* exclusive interview

Exklusivität /ɛkskluziviˈtɛːt/ *die;* **~:** exclusiveness; exclusivity

Exklusiv·vertrag *der* exclusive contract

Ex·kommunikation *die* (kath. Kirche) excommunication

ex·kommunizieren *tr. V.* (kath. Kirche) excommunicate

Ex·könig *der* ex-king

Ex·königin *die* ex-queen

Exkrement /ɛkskreˈmɛnt/ *das;* **~[e]s, ~e** (bes. Med., Zool.) excrement; **menschliche ~e** human excrement *sing.*

Exkret /ɛksˈkreːt/ *das;* **~[e]s, ~e** (Med., Zool.) excretion; **~e** excreta; excretions

Exkulpation /ɛkskʊlpaˈtsi̯oːn/ *die;* **~, ~en** (Rechtsw.) exculpation

exkulpieren /ɛkskʊlˈpiːrən/ *tr. V.* (Rechtsw.) exculpate

Exkurs /ɛksˈkʊrs/ *der;* **~es, ~e** digression; (in einem Buch) excursus

Exkursion /ɛkskʊrˈzi̯oːn/ *die;* **~, ~en** study trip *or* tour

Exlibris /ɛksˈliːbriːs/ *das;* **~, ~** (Buchw., Grafik) ex libris; bookplate

Exmatrikulation /ɛksmatrikulaˈtsi̯oːn/ *die;* **~, ~en** (Hochschulw.) *removal of a student's name from the register on leaving a university*

exmatrikulieren /ɛksmatrikuˈliːrən/ *tr. V.* (Hochschulw.) **jmdn./sich ~:** remove sb.'s name/have one's name removed from the university register

Ex·meister *der,* **Ex·meisterin** *die* (Sport) ex-champion

exmittieren /ɛksmɪˈtiːrən/ *tr. V.* (Rechtsw.) evict

Exmittierung *die;* **~, ~en** (Rechtsw.) eviction

Exodus /ˈɛksodʊs/ *der;* **~, ~se** (geh.) exodus

exogen /ɛksoˈgeːn/ *Adj.* (Med., Psych., Bot.) exogenous

exorbitant /ɛksɔrbiˈtant/
A *Adj.* (geh.) exorbitant ‹*price*›
B *adv.* exorbitantly

Exorzismus /ɛksɔrˈtsɪsmʊs/ *der;* **~, Exorzismen** (Rel.) exorcism

Exorzist *der* (Rel.) exorcist

Exot /ɛˈksoːt/ *der;* **~en, ~en** **1** (Mensch) strange foreigner **2** (Tier, Pflanze) exotic

Exotin *die;* **~, ~nen** ▸ **Exot 1**

exotisch
A *Adj.* exotic
B *adv.* exotically

Expander /ɛksˈpandɐ/ *der;* **~s, ~** (Sport) chest expander

expandieren /ɛkspanˈdiːrən/ *tr., itr. V.* expand

Expansion /ɛkspanˈzi̯oːn/ *die;* **~, ~en** expansion

expansionistisch *Adj.* (Politik) expansionist

expansions-, Expansions-: ~drang *der* expansionism (esp. Pol.); (von Firma) drive to expand; **~freudig** *Adj.* **1** (Politik) expansionist; **2** (Wirtsch.) **~freudige Unternehmen** businesses which are eager to expand; **~kraft** *die* (Physik, Technik) expansive force; **~krieg** *der* expansionist war; **~politik** *die* **1** expansionism; expansionist policy; **2** (Wirtsch.) policy of expansion

expansiv /ɛkspanˈziːf/
A *Adj.* **1** (Politik) expansionist **2** (Wirtsch.) expansionary
B *adv.* in an expansionary manner

expatriieren /ɛkspatriˈiːrən/ *tr. V.* (Politik, Rechtsw.) expatriate

Expedient /ɛkspeˈdi̯ɛnt/ *der;* **~en, ~en, Expedientin** *die;* **~, ~nen** **1** dispatch clerk **2** (im Reisebüro) travel agency clerk

expedieren /ɛkspeˈdiːrən/ *tr. V.* dispatch; send; **jmdn. an einen anderen Ort ~** (ugs.) pack sb. off somewhere else (coll.)

Expedition /ɛkspediˈtsi̯oːn/ *die;* **~, ~en** **1** expedition **2** (Versandabteilung) dispatch department

Expeditions-: ~korps *das* (Milit.) expeditionary force; **~leiter** *der,* **~leiterin** *die* leader of the/an expedition

Experiment /ɛksperiˈmɛnt/ *das;* **~[e]s, ~e** experiment; **mach keine ~e!** (ugs.) (sei vorsichtig) don't take any unnecessary risks!; (bleib bei dem, was du kennst) why experiment unnecessarily?; **ein filmisches ~:** an experimental film

Experimental- /ɛksperimɛnˈtaːl-/: **~film** *der* experimental film; **der ~film** experimental cinema; **~physik** *die* experimental physics

experimentell /ɛksperimɛnˈtɛl/
A *Adj.* experimental
B *adv.* experimentally; **etw. ~ beweisen/bestätigen** prove/confirm sth. experimentally *or* by experiment

experimentieren *itr. V.* experiment; **mit etw. ~:** experiment on *or* with sth.

experimentier-, Experimentier-: ~freudig *Adj.* keen to experiment; **~stadium** *das* experimental stage; **~theater** *das* experimental theatre

Experte /ɛksˈpɛrtə/ *der;* **~n, ~n** expert (**für** in)

Experten·system *das* (DV) expert system

Expertin *die;* **~, ~nen** expert (**für** in)

Expertise /ɛkspɛrˈtiːzə/ *die;* **~, ~n** expert's report; **eine ~ [über etw.] einholen** obtain an expert opinion [on sth.]

explizieren /ɛkspliˈtsiːrən/ *tr. V.* (geh.) explicate

explizit /ɛkspliˈtsiːt/
A *Adj.* explicit
B *adv.* ‹*describe, define*› explicitly

explizite /ɛksˈpliːtsɪte/ *Adv.* (geh.) explicitly

explodieren /ɛksploˈdiːrən/ *itr. V.; mit sein* (auch fig.) explode; ‹*costs*› rocket

Explosion /ɛksploˈzi̯oːn/ *die;* **~, ~en** explosion; **etw. zur ~ bringen** detonate sth.; **eine ~ der Rohstoffpreise** (fig.) an explosion in the price of raw materials

explosions-, Explosions-: ~artig
A *Adj.* explosive, astronomical ‹*growth, increase*›; **B** *adv.* ‹*rise*› astronomically; **~gefahr** *die* danger of explosion; **„~gefahr!"** '[Danger,] Explosives!'; **~herd** *der* **1** centre of the explosion; **2** (Unruheherd) trouble spot; **~krater** *der* crater; (Bombenkrater) bomb crater; **~motor** *der* internal combustion engine; **~welle** *die* shock wave

explosiv /ɛksploˈziːf/
A *Adj.* **1** (auch fig.) explosive **2** (Sprachw.) explosive; plosive; **~e Laute** plosives
B *adv.* explosively; **~ reagieren** (fig.) react violently

Explosiv-: ~geschoss, *~geschoß *das* explosive device; **~laut** *der* (Sprachw.) explosive; plosive; **~stoff** *der* ▸ **Sprengstoff**

Explosivität /ɛksplozivi ˈtɛːt/ *die* explosiveness

> **Expo 2000**
> Germany's first world fair from June to October 2000 was located in Hanover. Its aims were to combine hi-tech industrial development with cultural exhibits and environmental solutions.

Exponat /ɛkspoˈnaːt/ *das;* **~[e]s, ~e** exhibit

Exponent /ɛkspoˈnɛnt/ *der;* **~en, ~en** (Math.) exponent; (fig.) leading exponent

Exponential- /ɛksponɛnˈtsi̯aːl-/ (Math.) exponential ‹*function, equation, curve*›

Exponentin *die;* **~, ~nen** leading exponent

exponieren /ɛkspoˈniːrən/ *tr. V.* (geh.) (der Aufmerksamkeit aussetzen) **jmdn./sich ~:** draw attention to sb./oneself; (der Gefahr aussetzen) lay sb./oneself open to attack

exponiert *Adj.* exposed

Export[1] /ɛksˈpɔrt/ *der;* **~[e]s, ~e** **1** (das ~ieren) export; exporting; **der ~ nach Afrika** exports to Africa **2** (das ~ierte) export

Export² *das;* **~s, ~s** export; **zwei ~:** two export

Export-: ~ab·teilung *die* export department; **~artikel** *der* export; **~bier** *das* export beer

Exporteur /ɛkspɔr'tøːɐ̯/ *der;* **~s, ~e** (Wirtsch.) exporter

Export-: ~firma *die* exporter; **~geschäft** *das* 1) export business; 2) (geschäftlicher Abschluss) export deal; **~handel** *der* export trade; **~händler** *der,* **~händlerin** *die* exporter

exportieren *tr., itr. V.* export

Export-: ~kauffrau *die* export saleswoman; **~kaufmann** *der* export salesman; **~markt** *der* export market; **~quote** *die: ratio of the value of exports to that of the national product*

Exposé /ɛkspo'zeː/ *das;* **~s, ~s** 1) exposé; report 2) (eines Drehbuchs, Romans usw.) outline

Exposition /ɛkspozi'tsi̯oːn/ *die;* **~, ~en** exposition

express, *expreß /ɛks'prɛs/ *Adv.* 1) (schnell) express 2) (veralt.: absichtlich) on purpose; deliberately

Express, *Expreß *der;* **~es, ~e** (bes. österr.) express [train]

Express-, *Expreß-: ~brief *der* (veralt.) express letter; **~gut** *das* express freight; express goods *pl.*; **etw. als ~gut schicken** send sth. by express goods

Expressionismus /ɛksprɛsi̯o'nɪsmʊs/ *der* expressionism *no art.*

Expressionist *der;* **~en, ~en, Expressionistin** *die;* **~, ~nen** expressionist

expressionistisch
A *Adj.* expressionist
B *adv.* expressionistically; ‹*influenced*› by expressionism

expressis verbis /ɛks'prɛsiːs-/ (geh.) explicitly

expressiv /ɛksprɛ'siːf/ *Adj.* expressive; creative ‹*dance*›

Express-, *Expreß-: ~reinigung *die* express [dry-]cleaning service; **~zug** *der* (bes. schweiz.) express [train]

Expropriation /ɛkspropria'tsi̯oːn/ *die;* **~, ~en** (geh., Soziol.) expropriation

exquisit /ɛkskvi'ziːt/
A *Adj.* exquisite
B *adv.* exquisitely

Exquisit·geschäft *das* (DDR) shop selling foreign and luxury goods (*for GDR currency*)

ex tempore /ɛks'tɛmpore/ *Adv.* (Theater) extempore

Extempore *das;* **~s, ~s** (Theater) improvisation; extemporization

extemporieren *itr. V.* (Theater) improvise; extemporize

extensiv /ɛkstɛn'ziːf/
A *Adj.* (auch Landw.) extensive
B *adv.* 1) (auch Landw.) extensively 2) (Rechtsw.) **ein Gesetz ~ auslegen** give an extensive interpretation to a law

Exterieur /ɛkste'ri̯øːɐ̯/ *das;* **~s, ~s** *u.* **~e** (geh.) (von Menschen) appearance; (von Gebäuden) exterior

extern /ɛks'tɛrn/ (Schulw.)
A *Adj.* external; **ein ~er Schüler** a day boy/girl
B *adv.* **eine Prüfung ~ ablegen** take an examination as an external candidate

Externe *der/die; adj. Dekl.* (Schulw.) day boy/girl; (Prüfling) external candidate

exterritorial /ɛkstɛrito'ri̯aːl/ *Adj.* (Völkerr.) extraterritorial

Exterritorialität /ɛkstɛritori̯ali'tɛːt/ *die* (Völkerr.) extraterritoriality

extra /'ɛkstra/
A *Adv.* 1) (gesondert) ‹*pay*› separately; **Getränke werden ~ berechnet** drinks are extra; (ugs. auch attr.) **ein ~ Bett** a spare bed 2) (zusätzlich, besonders) extra; **~ fein gemahlener Kaffee** extra-fine ground coffee; **dafür brauche ich aber noch 10 Euro ~:** but I need another 10 euros for that; **etwas ~ Schönes** something particularly nice 3) (eigens) especially; **etw. ~ für jmdn. tun** do sth. especially *or* just for sb.; **~ deinetwegen** just because of you 4) (ugs.: absichtlich) **etw. ~ tun** do sth. on purpose
B *Adj.* (bayr., österr.) **~ sein** be fussy *or* hard to please

Extra *das;* **~s, ~s** extra

extra-, Extra-: ~aus·gabe *die* 1) (Zeitung) special edition; extra; 2) (Geldausgabe) extra *or* additional expense; **~blatt** *das* special edition; extra; **~fahrt** *die* (bes. schweiz.) special excursion; **~fein** *Adj.* (ugs.) really good; superb; **~galaktisch** *Adj.* (Astron.) extragalactic

extrahieren /ɛkstra'hiːrən/ *tr. V.* (Med., Chem.) extract

Extrakt /ɛks'trakt/ *der;* **~[e]s, ~e** 1) *fachspr. auch das* extract 2) (Zusammenfassung) summary; synopsis

Extraktion /ɛkstrak'tsi̯oːn/ *die;* **~, ~en** (Med., Chem.) extraction

extra-, Extra-: ~ordinarius *der* (Hochschulw.) extraordinary professor; **~polation** /-polatsi̯oːn/ *die;* **~~, ~~en** (Math.) extrapolation; **~polieren** *tr., itr. V.* (Math.) extrapolate; **~post** *die* (hist.) post-chaise; **mit ~post** (veralt.) by express post; **~ration** *die* extra ration; **~terrestrisch** /-tɛrɛstrɪʃ/ *Adj.* (Astron.) extraterrestrial; **~tour** *die* (ugs. abwertend) **sich** (*Dat.*) **ständig irgendwelche ~touren leisten** keep doing things off one's own bat (Brit.) *or* on one's own initiative

extravagant /-va'gant/
A *Adj.* flamboyant; flamboyantly furnished ‹*flat*›
B *adv.* flamboyantly

Extravaganz /-va'gants/ *die;* **~, ~en** 1) flamboyance 2) *Pl.* **seine ~en** his flamboyance *sing.*

extravertiert /-vɛr'tiːɐ̯t/ *Adj.* (Psych.) extrovert[ed]

Extravertiertheit *die;* **~** (Psych.) extroversion

Extra·wurst *die* 1) (fig. ugs.) **eine ~ bekommen** get special treatment *or* special favours; **sie will immer eine ~ [gebraten] haben** she always expects to get special treatment 2) (österr.) ▸**Lyoner**

extrem /ɛks'treːm/
A *Adj.* extreme
B *adv.* extremely; **das Unternehmen hat sich ~ vergrößert** the business has expanded enormously; **~ reagieren** react in an extreme manner

Extrem *das;* **~s, ~e** extreme; **von einem ~ ins andere fallen** go from one extreme to another

Extrem·fall *der* extreme case

Extremismus *der;* **~, Extremismen** extremism; **alle Extremismen** all forms of extremism

Extremist *der;* **~en, ~en, Extremistin** *die;* **~, ~nen** extremist

extremistisch *Adj.* extremist

Extremität /ɛkstremi'tɛːt/ *die;* **~, ~en** 1) extremity 2) (das Extremsein) extremeness

Extrem-: ~punkt *der* (Math.) extremum; **~situation** *die* extreme situation; extremity; **~sportart** *die* extreme sport; **~sportler** *der* extreme sportsman; **~sportlerin** *die* extreme sportswoman; **~wert** *der* (Math.) extremum

extrovertiert /ɛkstrovɛr'tiːɐ̯t/ ▸**extravertiert**

exzellent /ɛkstsɛ'lɛnt/ (geh.)
A *Adj.* excellent
B *adv.* excellently

Exzellenz /ɛkstsɛ'lɛnts/ *die;* **~, ~en** ▸**❶ S. 44** Excellency; **Eure/Seine ~:** Your/His Excellency

Exzenter /ɛks'tsɛntɐ/ *der;* **~s, ~** (Technik) tappet

Exzenter·welle *die* (Technik) camshaft; tappet shaft

Exzentriker /ɛks'tsɛntrikɐ/ *der;* **~s, ~, Exzentrikerin** *die;* **~, ~nen** eccentric

exzentrisch
A *Adj.* eccentric
B *adv.* eccentrically

Exzentrizität /ɛkstsɛntritsi'tɛːt/ *die;* **~, ~en** eccentricity

exzeptionell /ɛkstsɛptsi̯o'nɛl/ *Adj.* (geh.) unusual; exceptional ‹*case, circumstances*›; (hervorragend) exceptional

exzerpieren /ɛkstsɛr'piːrən/ *tr. V.* (geh.) extract ‹*reference*›; excerpt ‹*book*›

Exzerpt /ɛks'tsɛrpt/ *das;* **~[e]s, ~e** excerpt

Exzess, *Exzeß /ɛks'tsɛs/ *der;* **~es, ~e** excess; **etw. bis zum ~ treiben** carry sth. to excess

exzessiv /ɛkstsɛ'siːf/
A *Adj.* excessive
B *adv.* excessively

Eyeliner /'ai̯lai̯nɐ/ *der;* **~s, ~:** eyeliner

EZB *Abk.* **= Europäische Zentralbank** ECB

E-Zug *der* semi-fast train; stopping train (Brit.)

e

f, F /ɛf/ *das;* ~, ~ 1 (Buchstabe) f/F; **nach Schema F** according to a set pattern *or* routine 2 (Musik) [key of] F; *s. auch* **a, A**

f. *Abk.* = **folgend** f.

F *Abk.* = **Fahrenheit** F

Fa. *Abk.* = **Firma**

Fabel /ˈfa:bl̩/ *die;* ~, ~n 1 (Literaturw.) (Gattung) fable; (Kern einer Handlung) plot 2 (Erfundenes) story; tale; fable; **[jmdm.] eine ~ auftischen** spin [sb.] a yarn; **ins Reich der ~ gehören** belong in the realm of fantasy

Fabel-: ~**buch** *das* book of fables; ~**dichter** *der,* ~**dichterin** *die* writer of fables

fabelhaft
A *Adj.* 1 (ugs.: großartig) fantastic (coll.); **das ist ja ~:** that's [just] fantastic 2 (unglaublich) fabulous ‹riches›
B *adv.* (ugs.) fantastically (coll.); fabulously (coll.)

Fabel-: ~**tier** *das* mythological *or* fabulous creature; ~**welt** *die* fairy tale world; fabulous world

Fabrik /faˈbri:k/ *die;* ~, ~en factory; (Papier~, Baumwollspinnerei) mill; **eine chemische ~:** a chemical works; **in die ~ gehen** (ugs.) work in a factory

Fabrik·anlage *die* factory; (Maschinen) factory plant

Fabrikant /fabriˈkant/ *der;* ~en, ~en, **Fabrikantin** *die;* ~, ~nen manufacturer

Fabrik·arbeiter *der,* **Fabrik·arbeiterin** *die* ▸ℹ **S. 113** factory worker

Fabrikat /fabriˈka:t/ *das;* ~[e]s, ~e product; (Marke) make

Fabrikation /fabrikaˈtsi̯o:n/ *die;* ~: production; **die ~ einstellen** stop production

Fabrikations-: ~**fehler** *der* manufacturing fault; factory fault; ~**prozess,** *~**prozeß** *der,* ~**verfahren** *das* manufacturing process

fabrik-, Fabrik-: ~**besitzer** *der,* ~**besitzerin** *die* factory owner; ~**direktor** *der,* ~**direktorin** *die* works *or* production manager; ~**gebäude** *das* factory building; ~**gelände** *das* factory site; ~**neu** *Adj.* brand-new

fabriks-, Fabriks- (bes. österr.) ▸ **fabrik-, Fabrik-**

Fabrik-: ~**schiff** *das* factory ship; ~**schorn·stein** *der* factory chimney; ~**tor** *das* factory gate

fabrizieren /fabriˈtsi:rən/ *tr. V.* 1 (ugs. abwertend) knock together (coll.); **Unsinn ~:** make a mess of things 2 (veralt.: herstellen) manufacture; produce

fabulieren /fabuˈli:rən/ *itr. V.* invent stories; spin yarns

Fabulier·lust *die* delight in making up stories

Facelift /ˈfeɪslɪft/ *das;* ~[s], ~s facelift

Facelifting /ˈfeɪslɪftɪŋ/ *das;* ~[s], ~s facelift

Facette /faˈsɛtə/ *die;* ~, ~n facet

facetten-, Facetten-: ~**auge** *das* compound eye; ~**reich** *Adj.* multifaceted; ~**schliff** *der* faceting; **ein Schmuckstein mit ~schliff** a faceted gem

Fach /fax/ *das;* ~[e]s, **Fächer** /ˈfɛçɐ/ 1 compartment; (für Post) pigeonhole; **ein ~ für Wäsche** a shelf for linen; *s. auch* **Dach 1** 2 (Studienrichtung, Unterrichtsfach) subject; (Wissensgebiet) field; (Berufszweig) trade; **ein Meister seines ~es** a master of his trade; **das schlägt [nicht] in mein ~:** that is [not] my province; **vom ~ sein** be an expert; **ein Mann vom ~:** an expert

fach-, Fach-: ~**arbeiter** *der,* ~**arbeiterin** *die* skilled worker; craftsman; ~**arzt** *der,* ~**ärztin** *die* ▸ℹ **S. 113** specialist (**für** in); ~**ausdruck** *der,* ~**begriff** *der* technical *or* specialist term; ~**bereich** *der* (Hochschulw.) faculty; school; (in der Schule) department; ~**bezogen** *Adj.* specialized ‹*training*›; ~**blatt** *das* specialist journal; ~**buch** *das* (Abhandlung) specialist book; (Nachschlagewerk) reference book; (Lehrbuch) textbook; ~**chinesisch** *das* (abwertend) technical mumbo-jumbo (coll.)

fächeln /ˈfɛçl̩n/
A *tr. V.* fan
B *itr. V.* ‹*breeze*› blow gently

Fächer /ˈfɛçɐ/ *der;* ~s, ~: fan; (fig.) range

fächer-, Fächer-: ~**artig** A *Adj.* fan-like; B *adv.* like a fan; ~**besen** *der* (Gartenbau) wire-tooth rake; ~**gewölbe** *das* fan vault

fächern
A *refl. V.* fan out
B *tr. V.* (fig.) diversify; **das Angebot ist breit gefächert** there is a wide range to choose from

Fächer·palme *die* fan palm

Fächerung *die;* ~, ~en (fig.) diversity

fach-, Fach-: ~**frau** *die* expert; ~**fremd** *Adj.* **~fremde Methoden** methods alien to the subject; **~fremde Ausdrücke/Vorstellungen** layman's terms/ideas; ~**gebiet** *das* field; ~**gelehrte** *der/die* specialist (**für** in); ~**gerecht** A *Adj.* correct; B *adv.* correctly; ~**geschäft** *das* specialist shop; **ein ~geschäft für Sportartikel/Eisenwaren** *usw.* a specialist sports shop/ironmonger's; ~**gespräch** *das* technical discussion; ~**gruppe** *die* section; ~**handel** *der* specialist shops *pl.*; ~**hoch·schule** *die* college (*offering courses in a special subject*); **~hochschule für Musik** academy of music; ~**idiot** *der* (abwertend) *person who has no interests outside his/her subject;* ~**jargon** *der* (abwertend) technical jargon; ~**kenntnis** *die* specialized *or* specialist knowledge; ~**kraft** *die* skilled worker; ~**kreise** *Pl.* **in ~n** in specialist circles; ~**kundig** A *Adj.* knowledgeable; B *adv.* **jmdn. ~kundig beraten** give sb. informed *or* expert advice; ~**lehrer** *der,* ~**lehrerin** *die* subject teacher

> **Fachhochschule**
>
> This type of college provides shorter, more vocational and practical courses than those available at a **Hochschule**. A third of new students now enrol at a *Fachhochschule* to take the **Diplomprüfung**.

> **Fachhochschulreife**
>
> ▸ **Fachoberschule**

fachlich
A *Adj.* specialist ‹*knowledge, work*›; technical ‹*problem, explanation, experience*›; **~e Ausbildung/Qualifikation** training/qualification in the subject
B *adv.* **etw. ~ beurteilen** give a professional opinion on sth.; **~ qualifiziert** qualified in the subject

fach-, Fach-: ~**literatur** *die* specialist literature; (bes. naturwissenschaftlich auch) technical literature; **in der medizinischen ~literatur** in the specialist medical literature; ~**mann** *der; Pl.* ~**männer** *od.* ~**leute** expert; ~**männisch** A *Adj.* expert; B *adv.* **jmdn. ~männisch beraten** give sb. expert advice; ~**oberschule** *die: college specializing in particular subjects;* ~**personal** *das* specialist staff; ~**presse** *die* specialist/technical publications *pl.*; *s. auch* ~**literatur**; ~**richtung** *die* ▸ **Fach 2**

> **Fachoberschule**
>
> This vocationally orientated college takes students with an intermediate school certificate and leads to the *Fachhochschulreife*, which qualifies students for the **Fachhochschule**. Courses last for two to three years and cover theoretical instruction as well as on-the-job training.

Fachschaft *die;* ~, ~en 1 (einer Berufsgruppe) professional association 2 (von Studenten) student body of the/a faculty

fach-, Fach-: ~**schule** *die* technical college; ~**simpelei** /-zɪmpəˈlai/ *die;* ~, ~~en (ugs. abwertend) shop talk; ~**simpeleien** shop talk *sing.*; ~**simpeln** /-zɪmpl̩n/ *itr. V.* (ugs. abwertend) talk shop; ~**sprache** *die* technical terminology *or* language; ~**sprachlich** *Adj.* technical; ~**tagung** *die* [specialist] conference; ~**terminus** *der* specialist/technical term; *s. auch* ~**literatur**; ~**text** *der* specialist text; ~**übergreifend** A *Adj.* inter-disciplinary ‹*teaching*›; B *adv.* ‹*think, argue*› along interdisciplinary lines; ‹*teach*› using interdisciplinary methods; ~**verband** *der* trade association; ~**welt** *die* experts *pl.*; **in der ~welt** among experts

Fach·werk *das* 1 (Bauweise) half-timbered construction 2 (Balkengerippe) half-timbering

Fachwerk·haus *das* half-timbered house

Fach-: ~**wissen** *das* specialist knowledge [of the subject]; ~**wissenschaftler** *der,* ~**wissenschaftlerin** *die* specialist; ~**wort** *das; Pl.* ~**wörter** technical *or* specialist term; ~**wörterbuch** *das* specialist/technical dictionary; *s. auch* ~**literatur**; ~**zeitschrift** *die* specialist/technical journal; *s. auch* ~**literatur**

Fackel /ˈfakl̩/ *die;* ~, ~n torch; **die ~ des Krieges** (fig.) the flames of war; **die ~ der Revolution/der Hoffnung** (fig.) the flame of revolution/hope; **von ~n erleuchtet sein** be torchlit *or* lit by torches; **wie lebende ~n** like human torches

fackeln *itr. V.* (ugs.) shilly-shally (coll.); dither; **nicht lange gefackelt!** no shilly-shallying! (coll.); don't dither about!

Fackel-: ~**schein** *der* torchlight; **im ~schein** by torchlight; ~**träger** *der,* ~**trägerin** *die* torch-bearer; ~**zug** *der* torchlight procession

fad /fa:t/ (bes. südd., österr.) ▸ **fade**

Fädchen /ˈfɛ:tçən/ *das;* ~s, ~: short, thin thread

fade /ˈfa:də/ *Adj.* 1 (schal) insipid; **ein ~r Beigeschmack** (fig.) a flat aftertaste 2 (bes. südd., österr.: langweilig) dull 3 (südd., österr.: zimperlich)

sei nicht ~! don't be such a sissy!

fädeln /ˈfɛːdl̩n/ *tr. V.* thread; **etw. auf eine Schnur ~:** thread sth. on to a string

Faden¹ /ˈfaːdn̩/ *der;* **~s, Fäden** /ˈfɛːdn̩/ [1] (Garn) thread; **ein ~:** a piece of thread; **sich wie ein roter ~ durch etw. ziehen** run like a thread through sth.; **der rote ~** (fig.) the central theme; **den ~ verlieren** (fig.) lose the thread; **er hat** *od.* **hält alle Fäden in der Hand** (fig.) he holds the reins; **er hält alle Fäden fest in der Hand** (fig.) he keeps a tight rein on everything; **an einem dünnen** *od.* **seidenen ~ hängen** (fig.) hang by a single thread; **seine Fäden spinnen** (fig.) spin a web of intrigue; **keinen trockenen ~ mehr am Leibe haben** (ugs.) be wet through *or* soaked to the skin; *s. auch* **Strich 8** [2] (fig.) **ein schmaler ~ Blut** a thin trickle of blood; **graue Fäden im Haar haben** have a grey hair here and there; **Fäden ziehen** ‹*cheese etc.*› be soft and stringy [3] (Med.) suture; **die Fäden ziehen** remove the stitches

Faden² *der;* **~s, ~** (Seemannsspr.) fathom

faden-, Faden-: ~kreuz *das* cross hairs *pl.*; **~lauf** *der* grain [of the cloth]; **~molekül** *das* linear molecule; **~nudeln** *Pl.* (Kochk.) vermicelli *sing.*; **~scheinig** /-ʃainɪç/ *Adj.* [1] (fig. abwertend: nicht glaubhaft) threadbare ‹*morality*›; flimsy ‹*argument, reason, excuse*›; [2] (abgewetzt) threadbare ‹*clothes*›; **~spiel** *das* cat's cradle; **~stärke** *die* thickness (*of wool*); **~wurm** *der* (Zool.) threadworm

Fadheit *die;* **~, ~en** ▸ **fade 1, 2**: insipidness; dullness

Fagott /faˈgɔt/ *das;* **~[e]s, ~e** bassoon

Fagottist *der;* **~en, ~en, Fagottistin** *die;* **~, ~nen** bassoonist

Fähe /ˈfɛːə/ *die;* **~, ~n** (Jägerspr.) (Fuchsfähe) vixen; bitch; (Dachsfähe) sow; bitch

fähig /ˈfɛːɪç/ *Adj.* [1] (begabt) able; capable; **ich halte ihn für einen ~en Kopf** I think he has an able mind [2] (bereit, in der Lage) **zu etw. ~ sein** be capable of sth.; **er ist zu allem ~:** he is capable of anything; **~ sein, etw. zu tun** be capable of doing sth.

Fähigkeit *die;* **~, ~en** [1] ability; capability; **menschliche ~en** human faculties; **geistige ~en** intellectual faculties *or* abilities; **praktische ~en** practical skills; **jmds. ~en wecken** awaken sb.'s talents; **seine ~en für etw. einsetzen** use one's abilities for sth. [2] (Imstandesein) ability (**zu** to)

Fähigkeits·nachweis *der* certificate of proficiency

fahl /faːl/ *Adj.* pale; pallid; wan ‹*light, smile*›; **~ schien der Mond ins Zimmer** the moon shone wanly into the room

fahl-: ~blau *Adj.* pale blue; **~blond** *Adj.* ash-blond; **~gelb** pale yellow

Fahlheit *die;* **~:** paleness; pallor

Fähnchen /ˈfɛːnçən/ *das;* **~s, ~** [1] little flag; **~ schwenken** wave flags [2] (ugs. abwertend: Kleid) **ein billiges ~:** a cheap frock (Brit.) *or* dress

fahnden /ˈfaːndn̩/ *itr. V.* search (**nach** for)

Fahndung *die;* **~, ~en** search

Fahndungs-: ~aktion *die* search operation; **~apparat** *der:* **der gesamte ~apparat der Polizei ist eingesetzt worden** the police have committed all their available resources to the search; **~blatt** *das,* **~liste** *die* wanted list

Fahne /ˈfaːnə/ *die;* **~, ~n** [1] flag [2] (fig.) **etw. auf seine ~n schreiben** espouse the cause of sth.; **seine ~ nach dem Wind[e] hängen** trim one's sails to the wind; **mit fliegenden ~n zu jmdm./etw. übergehen** *od.* (abwertend) **überlaufen** openly and suddenly turn one's coat; **zu den ~n eilen** (veralt.) join the colours; **jmdn. zu den ~n rufen** (veralt.) call sb. to the colours [3] (ugs.: Alkoholgeruch) smell of alcohol on sb.'s breath; **eine ~ haben** reek of alcohol [4] (Druckw.) galley

fahnen-, Fahnen-: ~eid *der* oath of allegiance; **~flucht** *die* desertion; **~flucht begehen** desert; **~flüchtig** *Adj.* **~flüchtig werden/sein** desert/be a deserter; **~geschmückt** *Adj.* decorated with flags *postpos.*; **~korrektur** (Druckw.) (Fahne) galley proof; (Korrekturlesen) **die ~korrektur muss bald erfolgen** the galley proofs will have to be read soon; **~mast** *der,* **~stange** *die* flagpole; **das Ende der ~stange ist erreicht** (fig.) that's as far as we/they *etc.* can go; **~träger** *der,* **~trägerin** *die* standard-bearer; **~weihe** *die* consecration of the flag

Fähnlein /ˈfɛːnlain/ *das;* **~s, ~** (hist.) small troop

Fähnrich /ˈfɛːnrɪç/ *der;* **~s, ~e** (Milit.) **~,** (Marine) **~ zur See** ensign

Fahr·ausweis *der* [1] (Amtsspr.: Fahrschein) ticket [2] (schweiz.: Führerschein) driving licence

Fahr·bahn *die* carriageway; **die linke/rechte ~:** the left-hand/right-hand side of the road; **beim Überqueren der ~:** when crossing the road *or* (formeller) carriageway

Fahrbahn-: ~belag *der* road surface; **~breite** *die* road width; **~markierung** *die* road marking

fahrbar *Adj.* ‹*table, bed*› on castors; mobile ‹*crane, kitchen, etc.*›; **ein ~er Untersatz** (ugs.) wheels *pl.* (joc.)

fahr·bereit *Adj.* ‹*car etc.*› in running order; **wir sind ~:** we're ready to go

Fahr·bereitschaft *die* motor pool

Fähr·betrieb *der* ferry service; (von mehreren Fähren) ferry services *pl.*

Fahr-: ~bücherei *die* mobile library; **~damm** *der* (bes. berlin.) ▸ **~bahn**; **~dienst·leiter** *der,* **~dienst·leiterin** *die* (Eisenb.) train controller; **~draht** *der* overhead contact wire

Fähre /ˈfɛːrə/ *die;* **~, ~n** ferry

Fahr·eigenschaft *die* (Kfz-W.) handling characteristic; **~en** handling

fahren /ˈfaːrən/

A *unr. itr. V.; mit sein* [1] ▸ **i S. 310** (als Fahrzeuglenker) drive; (mit dem Fahrrad, Motorrad usw.) ride; (mit dem Kinderroller) scooter; (auf Skiern) ski; (mit Rollschuhen) [roller-]skate; (mit Schlittschuhen) [ice-]skate; (mit dem Rodelschlitten) toboggan; **mit dem Auto ~:** drive; (her~ auch) come by car; (hin~ auch) go by car; **mit dem Fahrrad/Motorrad ~:** cycle/motorcycle; come/go by bicycle/motorcycle; **mit 80 km/h ~:** drive/ride at 80 k.p.h.; **links/rechts ~:** drive on the left/right; (abbiegen) bear *or* turn left/right; **langsam ~:** drive/ride slowly; **langsamer ~:** slow down; **gegen etw. ~:** go into sth.; **wie fährt man am schnellsten zum Bahnhof?** what is the quickest route to the station [by car/motorcycle *etc.*]?

[2] (mit dem Auto usw. als Mitfahrer; mit dem Bus, der Straßenbahn, U-Bahn, dem Taxi, Zug, Schiff, Luftschiff, Schlitten usw., ugs. mit dem Flugzeug) go; (mit dem Aufzug/der Rolltreppe/der Seilbahn/dem Skilift) take the lift (Brit.) *or* (Amer.) elevator/escalator/cable car/ski lift; (mit der Achterbahn, dem Karussell usw.) ride (**auf** + *Dat.* on); (per Anhalter) hitch-hike; **mit dem Auto/Bus/Zug** *usw.* **~:** go by car/bus/train *etc.*; **erster/zweiter Klasse/zum halben Preis ~:** travel *or* go first/second class/at half-price; **ich fahre nicht gern [im] Auto/Bus** I don't like travelling in cars/buses; **fährst du mit mir?** are you coming with me?; **sollen wir ~ oder zu Fuß gehen?** shall we go by car/bus *etc.* or walk?; **mit Chauffeur ~:** be driven round by a chauffeur; **ich will noch mal ~!** (auf der Achterbahn usw.) I want to have another ride!

[3] (reisen) go; **in Urlaub ~:** go on holiday; **ins Wochenende gefahren sein** (vom Arbeitsplatz aus gesehen) have left for the weekend; (von zu Hause) have gone away for the weekend; *s. auch* **Himmel 2**; **Hölle 1**

[4] (los~) go; leave

[5] ‹*motor vehicle, train, lift, cable car*› go; ‹*ship*› sail; **mein Auto fährt nicht** my car won't go; **der Wagen fährt sehr ruhig** the car is very quiet *or* runs very quietly; **der Aufzug fährt heute nicht** the lift (Brit.) *or* (Amer.) elevator is out of service today

[6] (verkehren) run; **der Bus fährt alle fünf Minuten/bis Goetheplatz** the bus runs *or* goes every five minutes/goes to Goetheplatz; **hier fährt dreimal täglich eine Fähre** there are three ferries a day from here; **von München nach Passau fährt ein D-Zug** there's a fast train from Munich to Passau

[7] (mit bestimmtem Treibstoff) **mit Diesel/Benzin ~:** run on diesel/petrol (Brit.) *or* (Amer.) gasoline; **mit Dampf/Atomkraft ~:** be steam-powered/atomic-powered

[8] (schnelle Bewegungen ausführen) **in die Kleider ~:** leap into one's clothes; **in die Höhe ~:** jump up [with a start]; **der Blitz ist in einen Baum gefahren** the lightning struck a tree; **jmdm. an die Kehle ~:** leap at sb.'s throat; **sich** (*Dat.*) **mit der Hand durch das Haar ~:** run one's fingers through one's hair; **was ist denn in dich gefahren?** (fig.) what's got into you?; **der Schreck fuhr ihm in die Glieder** (fig.) the shock went right through him; **ein Gedanke fuhr ihm durch den Kopf** (fig.) an idea flashed through his mind; **jmdm. über den Mund ~** (fig.) shut sb. up; **aus der Haut ~** (ugs.) blow one's top (coll.); **etw. ~ lassen** (loslassen) let sth. go; (fig.: aufgeben) abandon sth.

[9] (Erfahrungen machen) **gut/schlecht mit jmdm./einer Sache ~:** get on well/badly with sb./sth.; **er ist schlecht damit gefahren, den Arbeitsplatz zu wechseln** his change of job turned out badly for him

B *unr. tr. V.* [1] (fortbewegen) drive ‹*car, lorry, train, etc.*›; ride ‹*bicycle, motorcycle*›; **ein Boot ~:** sail a boat; **Auto/Motorrad/Roller ~:** drive [a car]/ride a motorcycle/scooter; **Kahn** *od.* **Boot/Kanu ~:** go boating/canoeing; **Ski ~:** ski; **Schlitten ~:** toboggan; **Rollschuh ~:** [roller-]skate; **Schlittschuh ~:** [ice-]skate; **Aufzug/Rolltreppe ~:** ride up and down in the lift (Brit.) *or* (Amer.) elevator/on the escalator; **Sessellift ~:** ride in a/the chairlift; **U-Bahn ~:** ride on the underground (Brit.) *or* (Amer.) subway

[2] *mit sein* ([als Strecke] zurücklegen) drive; (mit dem Motorrad, Fahrrad) ride; take ‹*curve*›; **einen Umweg/eine Umleitung ~:** make a detour/follow a diversion; **der Zug fährt jetzt eine andere Strecke** the train takes a different route now; **er fährt seine 26. Runde** he is on his twenty-sixth lap

[3] (befördern) drive, take ‹*person*›; take ‹*thing*›; ‹*vehicle*› take; ‹*ship, lorry, etc.*› carry ‹*goods*›; (zum Sprecher) drive, bring ‹*person*›; bring ‹*thing*›; ‹*vehicle*› bring; **jmdn. über den Fluss ~:** ferry sb. across the river

[4] *mit sein* (mit einer bestimmten Geschwindigkeit) **50/80 km/h ~:** do 50/80 k.p.h.; **hier muss man 50 km/h ~:** you've got to keep to 50 k.p.h. here

[5] *meist mit sein* (als Teilnehmer mit~ bei) **ein Rennen ~:** take part in a race

[6] *meist mit sein* (erzielen) **einen Rekord ~:** set a record; **1:23:45/eine gute Zeit ~:** do *or* clock 1.23.45/a good time

[7] *mit sein* (leisten) **der Wagen fährt 210 km/h** the car will do 210 k.p.h.

[8] (in einen schlechten Zustand bringen) **ein Auto schrottreif** *od.* **zu Schrott ~:** write off a car; (durch lange Beanspruchung) run *or* drive a car into the ground; **eine Beule in den Kotflügel ~:** dent the wing; **jmdm. eine Schramme in den Kotflügel ~:** scratch sb.'s wing

[9] (als Treibstoff benutzen) use ‹*diesel, regular, etc.*›

[10] (auf Roll-, Schlittschuhen ausführen) skate

[11] (Technik: bedienen) operate; **einen Hochofen ~:** control a blast furnace

[12] (Rundf.: senden) broadcast ‹*programme*›

[13] (arbeiten) **eine Sonderschicht ~:** do *or* work an extra shift

C *unr. refl. V.* [1] **sich gut ~** ‹*car*› handle well, be easy to drive; **wie fährt sich so ein Rennboot?** how does a power boat like that handle?

[2] *mit sein* (unpers.) **in dem Wagen fährt es sich bequem** the car gives a comfortable ride; **auf dieser Straße/mit dem Zug fährt es sich angenehm** this road is pleasant to drive on/it's pleasant travelling by train

fahrend *Adj.* itinerant; **~er Sänger** wandering minstrel; **~es Volk** travelling people *pl.*

Fahrenheit ▸ **Grad 3**

***fahren|lassen** ▸ **fahren A8**

Fahrens·mann *der; Pl.* **Fahrensmänner** *od.* **Fahrensleute** (Seemannsspr.) sailor

f

Fahrer *der;* **~s, ~** ▸ⓘ **S. 113** driver; **„Nicht mit dem ~ sprechen!“** 'Passengers must not talk to the driver'

Fahrerei *die;* **~, ~en** (Fahrweise) driving; (dauerndes Fahren) driving/riding around

Fahrer-: ~flucht *die:* **wegen ~flucht** for failing to stop after [being involved in] an accident; **~flucht begehen** fail to stop after [being involved in] an accident; **~haus** *das* [driver's] cab

Fahrerin *die;* **~, ~nen** ▸ⓘ **S. 113** driver; *s. auch* **-in**

fahrerisch

A *Adj.* **~es Können** driving skill; skill as a driver

B *adv.* **jmdm. ~ überlegen sein** be a better driver than sb.

Fahrer·kabine *die* [driver's] cab

Fahr-: ~erlaubnis *die* (Amtsspr.) driving licence; **jmdm. die ~erlaubnis entziehen** disqualify sb. from driving; **~fehler** *der* driving error; **~gast** *der* passenger; **~geld** *das* fare; **~geld·erstattung** *die* reimbursement of travelling expenses; **~gelegenheit** *die* means of transport; **~gemeinschaft** *die* car pool; **~geschwindigkeit** *die* speed; **~gestell** *das* [1] (Kfz-W.) chassis; [2] (bei Kränen, Eisenbahnwagen, Maschinen) bogie (Brit.); (Lafette) gun carriage; (beim Flugzeug) undercarriage; [3] (scherzh.: Beine) legs *pl.*

Fähr·hafen *der* ferry terminal

fahrig /ˈfaːrɪç/ *Adj.* nervous, agitated ‹*movements*›; nervous and fidgety ‹*student, pupil*›

Fahrigkeit *die;* **~:** nervousness and fidgetiness

Fahr·karte *die* ticket; **eine ~ schießen** (ugs.) miss completely

Fahrkarten-: ~ausgabe *die* ticket office; **~automat** *der* ticket machine; **~kontrolleur** *der,* **~kontrolleurin** *die* (im Bus) inspector; (im Zug) ticket inspector; **~schalter** *der* ticket window; **~verkäufer** *der,* **~verkäuferin** *die* ticket office clerk

fahr-, Fahr-: ~kilometer *der* (im Bus) kilometre [travelled]; (eines Autos) kilometre [covered]; **~komfort** *der* [passenger] comfort; **~kunst** *die* driving skills *pl.;* **~lässig** **A** *Adj.* negligent ‹*behaviour*›; **~lässige Tötung/Körperverletzung** (Rechtsw.) causing death/injury through *or* by [culpable] negligence; **B** *adv.* negligently; **er hat den Tod des Fußgängers ~lässig verschuldet** he was responsible for *or* guilty of causing the death of the pedestrian through *or* by culpable negligence; **~lässigkeit** *die* negligence; **~lehrer** *der,* **~lehrerin** *die* ▸ⓘ **S. 113** driving instructor; **~leistung** *die* performance

Fähr-: ~linie *die* (Strecke) ferry route; (Unternehmen) ferry line; **~mann** *der; Pl.* **~männer** *od.* **~leute** ▸ⓘ **S. 113** ferryman

Fahrnis *die;* **~, ~se** (Rechtsw.) chattels *pl.;* movables *pl.*

Fährnis *die;* **~, ~se** (veralt.) peril

Fahr·personal *das* crew

Fahr·plan *der* [1] timetable; schedule (Amer.); **den ~ einhalten** run to schedule *or* on time [2] (ugs.: Vorhaben) plans *pl.;* **den ~ durcheinander bringen** upset the entire schedule *or* all the arrangements

fahrplan·mäßig

A *Adj.* scheduled ‹*departure, arrival*›; **der verspätete Schnellzug nach Köln, ~e Abfahrt 16.30 ...** the delayed fast train to Cologne, due to depart at 16.30, ...

B *adv.* ‹*depart, arrive*› according to schedule, on time

Fahr·praxis *die* driving experience

Fahr·preis *der* fare

Fahrpreis-: ~anzeiger *der* taximeter; **~erhöhung** *die* fare increase; increase in fares; **~ermäßigung** *die* reduction in fares; **eine ~ermäßigung erhalten** be given concessionary fares

Fahr·prüfung *die* driving test

Fahr·rad *das* bicycle; cycle; **mit dem ~ fahren** cycle; ride a bicycle

Fahrrad-: ~computer *der* cycle computer; **~fahrer** *der,* **~fahrerin** *die* cyclist; **~händler** *der,* **~händlerin** *die* bicycle dealer; **etw. beim ~händler kaufen** buy sth. from a/the bicycle shop; **~handlung** *die* bicycle shop; **~kette** *die* bicycle chain; **~kurier** *der* bicycle *or* bike messenger; bicycle *or* bike courier; **~lampe** *die* bicycle lamp; **~pumpe** *die* bicycle pump; **~schlüssel** *der* [1] (für das Schloss) bicycle-lock key; [2] (Schraubenschlüssel) bicycle spanner; **~ständer** *der* bicycle rack *or* stand; **~weg** *der* cycle path

Fahr·rinne *die* shipping channel; fairway

Fahr·schein *der* ticket

Fahrschein-: ~automat *der* ticket machine; **~entwerter** *der* ticket cancelling machine; **~heft** *das* book of tickets

Fähr·schiff *das* ferry

Fahr-: ~schule *die* [1] (Unternehmen) driving school; [2] (ugs.: Unterricht) driving lessons *pl;* **~schüler** *der,* **~schülerin** *die* [1] learner driver; [2] *pupil who must use transport to get to school;* **~sicherheit** *die* safe driving *no art.;* **die ~sicherheit erhöhen** make driving safer; **~spur** *die* traffic lane; **die ~spur wechseln/beibehalten** change lanes/stay in one's lane

> **Fahrschule**
>
> Learner drivers in Germany have to take lessons from a qualified driving instructor at a *Fahrschule* (driving school) in a specially adapted car with dual controls. It is quite common to have 20 or 30 driving lessons before taking the driving test, as there is no other way of getting driving practice on the road.

fährst /fɛːɐ̯st/ *2. Pers. Sg. Präsens v.* **fahren**

Fahr-: ~stil *der* style of driving; (mit dem Rad) style of riding; (auf Skiern) style of skiing; **~streifen** *der* ▸ **~spur**

Fahr·stuhl *der* lift (Brit.); elevator (Amer.); (für Lasten) hoist; **mit dem ~ fahren** take the lift/elevator

Fahrstuhl-: ~führer *der,* **~führerin** *die* lift attendant (Brit.); elevator operator (Amer.); **~schacht** *der* lift shaft (Brit.); elevator shaft (Amer.)

Fahr·stunde *die* driving lesson

-fahrt *die;* **~, ~en: Frankreich~/Ostasien~:** trip to France/East Asia

fährt /fɛːɐ̯t/ *3. Pers. Sg. Präsens v.* **fahren**

Fahrt /faːɐ̯t/ *die;* **~, ~en** [1] ▸ⓘ **S. 224** (das Fahren) journey; **„während der ~ nicht hinauslehnen!“** 'do not lean out of the window while the train is in motion'; **freie ~ haben** have a clear run; (fig.) have been given the green light [2] (Reise) journey; (Schiffsreise) voyage; **auf der ~:** on the journey [3] (kurze Reise, Ausflug) trip; (Wanderung) hike; **eine ~ [nach/zu X] machen** go on *or* take a trip [to X]; **eine ~ ins Blaue machen** (mit dem Auto) go for a drive; (Veranstaltung) go on a mystery tour; **auf ~ gehen** (veralt.) go hiking [4] (Geschwindigkeit) **in voller ~:** at full speed; **die ~ verlangsamen** slow down; decelerate; **die ~ beschleunigen** speed up; accelerate; **die ~ aufnehmen** gather speed; pick up speed; **kleine ~ machen** (Seemannsspr.) sail slowly; **in ~ kommen** *od.* **geraten** (ugs.) get going; (böse werden) get worked up; **jmdn. in ~ bringen** (ugs.) get sb. going; (böse machen) get sb. worked up [5] (Seemannspr.) **Kapitän auf großer ~:** foreign trade master; **das Patent für kleine ~:** master's certificate for coastal trade *or* home trade

fahr·tauglich *Adj.* fit to drive *postpos.*

Fahr·tauglichkeit *die* fitness to drive

fahrt-, Fahrt-: ~ausweis *der* ▸ **Fahrausweis; ~bereit** ▸ **fahrbereit; ~dauer** *die* travelling time

Fährte /ˈfɛːɐ̯tə/ *die* tracks *pl.;* trail; **die ~ aufnehmen** pick up the trail *or* scent; **Hunde auf die ~ setzen** put hounds on the track; **jmds. ~ verfolgen** track sb.; **die richtige ~ finden** (fig.) get on the right track; **die falsche ~ verfolgen** (fig.) be on the wrong track; **jmdn. auf eine falsche ~ locken** (fig.) put sb. on the wrong track

Fahrten-: ~buch *das* [1] (Kontrollbuch) logbook; [2] (Tagebuch) [rambler's] diary; **~messer** *das* sheath knife; **~schreiber** *der* tachograph; **~schwimmer** *der,* **~schwimmerin** *die* advanced swimmer; **den ~schwimmer machen** (ugs.) take the advanced swimmer's test

Fahrt·kosten *Pl.* (für öffentliche Verkehrsmittel) fare/fares; (für Autoreisen) travel costs; **die ~ erstatten** pay travelling expenses

Fahr·treppe *die* escalator

Fahrt·richtung *die* direction; **in ~ Innenstadt** in the direction of the town centre; **die Autobahn ist in ~ Norden gesperrt** the northbound carriageway of the motorway is closed; **in ~ parken** park in the direction of the traffic; **die ~ ändern** change direction; **gegen die ~ sitzen** (im Zug) sit with one's back to the engine/(im Bus) facing backwards; **in ~ sitzen** (im Zug) sit facing the engine/(im Bus) facing forwards

Fahrtrichtungs·anzeiger *der* (Kfz-W.) [1] (Blinklicht) [direction] indicator [2] (Hinweistafel) destination board

Fahrt·schreiber *der* ▸ **Fahrtenschreiber**

fahr·tüchtig *Adj.* ‹*driver*› fit to drive; ‹*vehicle*› roadworthy

Fahr·tüchtigkeit *die* (des Fahrers) fitness to drive; (des Fahrzeugs) roadworthiness

Fahrt-: ~unterbrechung *die* break [in the journey]; stop; **eine ~unterbrechung ist [nicht] möglich** passengers may [not] break their journey; **~wind** *der* airflow; **~ziel** *das* destination

fahr·untüchtig *Adj.* ‹*driver*› unfit to drive; ‹*vehicle*› unroadworthy

Fähr·verbindung *die* ferry link

Fahr-: ~verbot *das* disqualification from driving; driving ban; **jmdm. [ein] ~verbot erteilen** ban *or* disqualify sb. from driving; **~verhalten** *das* [1] (des Fahrers) behaviour as a driver; [2] (des Fahrzeuges) performance

Fähr·verkehr *der* ferry traffic

Fahr-: ~wasser *das* shipping channel; fairway; **in ein gefährliches ~wasser geraten** (fig.) get on to dangerous ground; **in ein politisches ~wasser geraten** (fig.) stumble into a political minefield; **in jmds. ~wasser schwimmen** *od.* **segeln** (fig.) follow [along] in sb.'s wake; **~weise** *die* way of driving; **seine ~weise** the way he drives; **~werk** *das* [1] (Flugw.) undercarriage; [2] (Kfz-W.) ▸ **~gestell; ~wind** *der* [1] (Segelfliegen) wind; [2] ▸ **Fahrtwind; ~zeit** *die* travelling time; **eine ~zeit von wenigen Minuten/Stunden** a few minutes'/hours' travelling time; **nach einer ~zeit von zwei Stunden** after travelling for two hours

Fahr·zeug *das* vehicle; (Luft~) aircraft; (Wasser~) vessel

Fahrzeug-: ~bau *der* motor manufacturing industry; **~brief** *der* ▸ **Kraftfahrzeugbrief; ~führer** *der,* **~führerin** *die* driver of a/the motor vehicle; **~halter** *der,* **~halterin** *die* registered keeper [of a/the vehicle]; **~kolonne** *die* convoy of vehicles; **~papiere** *Pl.* vehicle documents *pl.;* **~verkehr** *der* traffic

Faible /ˈfɛːbl̩/ *das;* **~s, ~s** liking; (Schwäche) weakness; **ein ~ für etw. haben** have a weakness for sth.

fair /fɛːɐ̯/

A *Adj.* fair **(gegen** to)

B *adv.* fairly; **~ spielen** play fairly *or* (coll.) fair

fairer·weise /ˈfɛːrɐ-/ *Adv.* to be fair

Fairness, *Fairneß /ˈfɛːɐ̯nɛs/ *die;* **~:** fairness

Fairness·pokal, *Fairneß·pokal *der* (Sport) *cup for the most sporting competitor*

Fairplay /ˈfɛəˈpleɪ/ *das;* **~:** fair play

Fait accompli /fɛtakõˈpli/ *das;* **~, Faits accomplis** (geh.) fait accompli

Fäkalien /fɛˈkaːli̯ən/ *Pl.* faeces *pl.*

Fäkal·sprache *die* lavatorial language

faken /ˈfeɪkn̩/ *tr. V.* fake; forge ‹*document, letter, photograph, information, etc.*›; **gefakte Dreadlocks** fake dreadlocks

Fakir /ˈfaːkiːɐ̯, *österr.:* faˈkiːɐ̯/ *der;* **~s, ~e** fakir

Faksimile /fakˈziːmile/ *das;* **~s, ~s** facsimile

Faksimile-: ~aus·gabe *die* facsimile edition; **~druck** *der; Pl.* **~~e** printed facsimile

Fakt /fakt/ *das od. der;* **~[e]s, ~en** *od.* **~s** fact

Fakten ▸**Faktum**

Fakten-: ~material *das* facts *pl.;* **~wissen** *das* factual knowledge

Faktion /fakˈtsi̯oːn/ *die;* **~, ~en** (veralt., schweiz.) faction

faktisch

A *Adj.* real; actual; **der ~e Nachteil/Nutzen** the practical disadvantage/usefulness

B *adv.* **1** **das bedeutet ~ ...** it means in effect ...; **es ist ~ möglich/unmöglich** it is in actual fact possible/impossible **2** (bes. österr. ugs.: praktisch, eigentlich) more or less; virtually

Faktor /ˈfaktɔr/ *der;* **~s, ~en** /-ˈtoːrən/ **1** (auch Math.) factor; **der auslösende ~:** the immediate cause; **ein konstanter ~** (Math.) a constant **2** (Berufsbez.) (in einer Setzerei) composing-room foreman *or* supervisor; (in einer Druckerei) [printing-room] foreman *or* supervisor

Faktorei *die;* **~, ~en** (hist.) foreign trading post; factory (Hist.)

Faktotum /fakˈtoːtʊm/ *das;* **~s, ~s** *od.* **Faktoten** (scherzh.) factotum

Faktum /ˈfaktʊm/ *das;* **~s, Fakten** fact

Faktur /fakˈtuːɐ̯/ *die;* **~, ~en** (Kaufmannsspr. veralt.) invoice

fakturieren *itr. V.* do invoicing

Fakturier-maschine *die* invoicing machine

Fakturist *der;* **~en, ~en, Fakturistin** *die;* **~, ~nen** invoice clerk

Fakultas /faˈkʊltas/ *die;* **~, Fakultäten** /fakʊlˈtɛːtn̩/ (Schulw.) qualification to teach; **die ~ für etw. haben** be qualified to teach sth.

Fakultät /fakʊlˈtɛːt/ *die;* **~, ~en** (Hochschulw.) **1** (Abteilung) faculty; **die philosophische/medizinische/juristische ~:** the faculty of arts/medicine/law; **die ~ wechseln** change faculty **2** (Lehrer und Studenten) staff and students (*of a faculty*) **3** (Räumlichkeiten) faculty building **4** (Math.) factorial; **5 ~:** factorial 5

fakultativ /fakʊltaˈtiːf/

A *Adj.* optional ‹*subject, participation*›

B *adv.* optionally

Falange /faˈlaŋge/ *die;* **~:** Falange

Falangist *der;* **~en, ~en, Falangistin** *die;* **~, ~nen** Falangist

falb /falp/ *Adj.* (geh.) dun-coloured

Falbe /ˈfalbə/ *der;* **~n, ~n** dun [horse]

Falbel /ˈfalbl̩/ *die;* **~, ~n** (Textilw.) furbelow; flounce

Falke /ˈfalkə/ *der;* **~n, ~n** (auch Politik fig.) hawk

Falken-beize *die* falconry

Falkenier /falkəˈniːɐ̯/ *der;* **~s, ~e** ▸**Falkner**

Falkländer /ˈfalklɛndɐ/ *der;* **~s, ~, Falkländerin** *die;* **~, ~nen** Falklander

Falkland-inseln *Pl.* Falkland Islands; Falklands

Falkner *der;* **~s, ~, Falknerin** *die;* **~, ~nen** falconer

Falknerei *die;* **~, ~en** **1** (Falkenbeize) falconry **2** (Anlage) hawk house

Fall[1] /fal/ *der;* **~[e]s, Fälle** /ˈfɛlə/ **1** (Sturz) fall; **zu ~ kommen** have a fall; **durch** *od.* **über etw.** (*Akk.*) **zu ~ kommen** (fig.) come to grief because of sth.; **jmdn. zu ~ bringen** (fig.) bring about sb.'s downfall; **der ~ einer Stadt** (fig.) the fall of a town; *s. auch* **Hochmut** **2** (das ~en) descent; **der freie ~:** free fall **3** (Ereignis, Vorkommnis) case; (zu erwartender Umstand) eventuality; **für den äußersten** *od.* **schlimmsten ~, im schlimmsten ~:** if the worst comes to the worst; **im besten ~:** at best; **es ist [nicht] der ~:** it is [not] the case; **gesetzt den ~:** assuming; supposing; **für den ~, dass es morgen schön ist** in case it's fine tomorrow; **im ~e einer Veränderung** in the event of a change; **auf jeden ~:** in any case; **auf alle Fälle** in any case; **auf keinen ~:** on no account; **das ist doch ein ganz klarer ~:** it's perfectly clear; **jmds. ~ sein** (fig. ugs.) be sb.'s cup of tea; **klarer ~** (ugs.) it goes without saying; **in jedem ~:** in any case; **der ~ ist [für mich] erledigt** [as far as I'm concerned] that's the end of it **4** (Rechtsw., Med., Grammatik) case; **der 1./2./3./4. ~** (Grammatik) the nominative/genitive/dative/accusative case

Fall[2] *das;* **~[e]s, ~en** (Seemannsspr.) halyard

Fall-: ~beil *das* guillotine; **~beispiel** *das* case in point; (Paradefall) textbook case; **~beschleunigung** *die* (Physik) gravitational acceleration

Falle /ˈfalə/ *die;* **~, ~n** **1** (auch fig.) trap; **in die ~ gehen** walk into the trap; **jmdm. eine ~ stellen** (fig.) set a trap for sb.; **jmdn. in eine ~ locken** (fig.) lure sb. into a trap; **jmdm. in die ~ gehen** (fig.) fall into sb.'s trap; **in der ~ sitzen** (fig.) be in a spot **2** (salopp: Bett) **in die ~ gehen** turn in (coll.); **sich in die ~ hauen** hit the sack *or* hay (coll.) **3** (Riegel am Türschloss) catch; latch

fallen *unr. itr. V.; mit sein* **1** fall; **etw. ~ lassen** drop sth.; **immer [wieder] auf die Füße ~** (fig. ugs.) always land on one's feet; **sich ins Gras/Bett/Heu ~ lassen** fall on to the grass/into bed/into the hay; (fig.) **jmdn. ~ lassen** drop sb.; **einen Plan ~ lassen** abandon a plan; **eine Bemerkung ~ lassen** let fall a remark; **einen Hinweis ~ lassen** drop a hint; *s. auch* **Decke 3**; **Gewicht**; **Groschen 2**; **Rahmen 2**; **Schoß 1**; **Schuppe 1**; **stehen**; **Stein 2**; **Stuhl 1**; **Tür**; **Wasser 1**; **Wolke**; **Würfel 2** **2** (hin~, stürzen) fall [over]; **auf die Knie/in den Schmutz ~:** fall to one's knees/in the dirt; **über einen Stein ~:** trip over a stone; **im Fallen hat er den Schirmständer umgerissen** he pulled the umbrella stand over as he fell; *s. auch* **gefallen B**; **Kopf 1**; **Mund**; **Nase 1** **3** (sinken) ‹*prices*› fall; ‹*temperature, water level*› fall, drop; ‹*fever*› subside; **im Preis ~:** go down *or* fall in price; *s. auch* **Arm 1**; **Hals 1**; **Knie 1**; **Rücken 1**; **Schloss 1**; **Zügel 1** **4** (an einen bestimmten Ort gelangen, dringen) ‹*light, shadow, glance, choice, suspicion*› fall; **die Wahl fiel auf ihn** the choice fell on him **5** (abgegeben, erzielt werden) ‹*shot*› be fired; (Sport) ‹*goal*› be scored **6** (nach unten hängen) ‹*hair*› fall; **die Haare ~ ihr ins Gesicht/auf die Schulter** her hair falls over her face/to her shoulders **7** (im Kampf sterben) die; fall (literary); **im Krieg ~:** die in the war; **er ist bei Verdun gefallen** he died *or* fell at Verdun **8** (aufgehoben, beseitigt werden) ‹*ban*› be lifted; ‹*tax*› be abolished; ‹*obstacle*› be removed; ‹*limitation*› be overcome; *s. auch* **Opfer 2**; **Tisch** **9** (zu einer bestimmten Zeit stattfinden) **in eine Zeit ~:** occur at a time; **mein Geburtstag fällt auf einen Samstag** my birthday falls on a Saturday; **in diese Zeit fällt der Höhepunkt der romantischen Dichtung** that time saw the heyday of Romantic poetry **10** (zu einem Bereich gehören) **in/unter eine Kategorie ~:** fall into *or* within a category; **unter ein Gesetz/eine Bestimmung ~:** come under a law/a regulation **11** (zu~, zuteil werden) **eine Erbschaft/ein Gebiet fällt an jmdn.** an inheritance/a piece of territory falls to sb.; **er ist seinen Feinden in die Hände gefallen** he has fallen into the hands of his enemies **12** (geäußert werden) ‹*decision*› be taken *or* made; **scharfe Worte/Bemerkungen fielen** harsh words were spoken/harsh remarks were made **13** (verfallen) **in Trümmer ~:** collapse in ruins; **in Schwermut ~:** be overcome by melancholy; **in einen Dialekt ~:** lapse into a dialect; **in Trab ~:** break into a trot; *s. auch* **Last 3**; **Rolle 6**; **Ungnade** **14** (erobert werden) ‹*town, stronghold*› fall **15** (geh.: ab~) slope; fall

fällen /ˈfɛlən/ *tr. V.* **1** fell ‹*tree, timber*› **2** (verkünden) **ein Urteil ~** ‹*judge*› pass sentence; ‹*jury*› return a verdict; **einen Schiedsspruch ~:** make a ruling **3** (Milit.: zum Angriff senken) lower ‹*bayonet*› **4** (Chemie) precipitate

***fallen|lassen** ▸**fallen 1**

Fallen-steller *der;* **~s, ~, Fallen-stellerin** *die;* **~, ~nen** trapper

Fall-: ~geschwindigkeit *die* (Physik) velocity of fall; **~gesetz** *das* (Physik) law of gravity; **~gitter** *das* portcullis; **~grube** *die* pitfall; **~höhe** *die* **1** (Physik) height of fall; **2** (Literaturw.) extent of a/the dramatic hero's fall

fallieren *itr. V.* (Finanzw.) go bankrupt

fällig /ˈfɛlɪç/ *Adj.* **1** due; **eine ~e Reform** an overdue reform; **der Kerl ist ~** (ugs.) he's in for it (sl.) **2** (zu bezahlen) ‹*sum of money*› payable, due; **ein ~er Wechsel/~e Zinsen** a bill to mature/interest payable

Fälligkeit *die;* **~, ~en** (Wirtsch.), **Fälligkeits-termin** *der* settlement date; date of payment

Fall-obst *das* windfalls *pl.*

Fall-out /fɔːlˈlaʊt/ *der;* **~s, ~s** (Kernphysik) fall-out

Fall-: ~reep *das* (Seemannsspr.) jack ladder; **~rückzieher** *der* (Fußball) bicycle kick

falls /fals/ (Konj.) **1** (wenn) if; **~ es regnet/schneit** if it rains/snows **2** (für den Fall, dass) in case; **~ es regnen sollte** in case it should rain

Fall-schirm *der* parachute; **mit dem ~ abspringen** (im Notfall) parachute out; (als Sport) make a [parachute] jump; **mit dem ~ über Belgien abspringen** parachute out over Belgium; (als Soldat, Spion) parachute into Belgium

Fallschirm-: ~jäger *der* (Luftwaffe) paratrooper; **~springen** *das;* **~~s** parachuting *no art.;* **~springer** *der,* **~springerin** *die* parachutist

Fall-: ~strick *der* trap; snare; **jmdm. ~stricke legen** (fig.) set traps for sb.; **~studie** *die* case study; **~sucht** *die* (veralt.) falling sickness (arch.); **~tür** *die* trapdoor

Fällungs-mittel *das* (Chemie) precipitant

fall-, Fall-: ~weise *Adv.* (österr.) ▸**gelegentlich B 1**; **~wind** *der* katabatic wind; **~wurf** *der* (Handball) falling throw

falsch /falʃ/

A *Adj.* **1** (unecht, imitiert) false ‹*teeth, plait*›; imitation ‹*jewellery*›; **Falsche Akazie** (Bot.) false acacia; **~er Hase** (Kochk.) meat loaf **2** (gefälscht) counterfeit, forged ‹*banknote*›; false, forged ‹*passport*›; assumed ‹*name*› **3** (irrig, fehlerhaft) wrong ‹*impression, track, pronunciation*›; wrong, incorrect ‹*answer*›; **auf der ~en Fährte sein** be on the wrong track; **logisch ~ sein** be logically false; **an den Falschen geraten** come to the wrong man; **alle Aufgaben ~ [gelöst] haben** have got all one's exercises wrong; **etw. in die ~e Kehle** *od.* **den ~en Hals bekommen** (fig. ugs.) take sth. the wrong way; *s. auch* **Licht 1**, **Pferd 1** **4** (unangebracht) false ‹*shame, modesty*› **5** (irreführend) false ‹*statement, promise*›; **unter Vorspiegelung ~er Tatsachen** under false pretences **6** (abwertend: hinterhältig) false ‹*friend*›; **ein ~er Hund** (salopp) a two-faced so-and-so (sl.); **eine ~e Schlange** (fig.) a snake in the grass; **ein ~es Spiel [mit jmdm.] treiben** play false with sb.; *s. auch* **Fuffziger** **7** (bes. nordd.: erzürnt) angry

B *adv.* **1** (fehlerhaft) wrongly; incorrectly; **~ singen** sing wrongly; **~ gehen/fahren** go the wrong way; **etw. ~ verstehen** misunderstand sth.; **die Uhr geht ~:** the clock is wrong; **~ informiert** *od.* **unterrichtet sein** be misinformed; **~ liegen** (ugs.) be mistaken; **~ herum** (verkehrt) back to front; the wrong way round; (auf dem Kopf) upside down; (links) inside out; *s. auch* **herum 1**, **verbinden A 8** **2** (irreführend) **~ schwören** lie on oath; **~ spielen** cheat

Falsch *der;* **~s** (geh., veralt.) *in* **an jmdm. ist kein ~:** sb. is guileless; **ohne ~ sein** be completely guileless

Falsch-: ~aus·sage *die* (Rechtsspr.) **[eidliche] ~aussage** false testimony *or* evidence; **uneidliche ~aussage** false statement [not on oath]; **~eid** *der* (Rechtsspr.) unintentional false statement under oath

fälschen /ˈfɛlʃn̩/ *tr. V.* forge, fake ‹*signature, document, passport*›; forge ‹*painting*›; forge, counterfeit ‹*coin, banknote*›; falsify ‹*history*›

Fälscher *der;* ~s, ~, **Fälscherin** *die;* ~, ~nen forger; counterfeiter

Falsch-: ~**fahrer** *der,* ~**fahrerin** *die* ▸**Geisterfahrer**; ~**geld** *das* counterfeit money

Falschheit *die;* ~ **1** (Hinterhältigkeit) duplicity; deceitfulness **2** (Unechtheit) falseness; (Fehlerhaftigkeit) wrongness

fälschlich

A *Adj.* false ‹*claim, accusation*›; (irrtümlich) mistaken, false ‹*assumption, suspicion*›

B *adv.* falsely, wrongly ‹*claim, accuse*›; mistakenly, falsely ‹*assume, suspect*›

fälschlicher·weise *Adv.* by mistake; mistakenly

falsch-, Falsch-: *~|**liegen** ▸**falsch B1**; ~**meldung** *die* false report; ~**münzer** /'-mʏntsɐ/ *der;* ~~s, ~~: forger; counterfeiter; ~**münzerei** /-mʏntsə'rai/ *die;* ~~, ~~en forgery; counterfeiting; ~**münzerin** *die;* ~~, ~~nen ▸~**münzer**; *~|**spielen** ▸**falsch B2**; ~**spieler** *der,* ~**spielerin** *die* cheat; (erwerbsmäßig) card sharp[er]

Fälschung *die;* ~, ~en **1** fake; counterfeit **2** (das Fälschen) forging; counterfeiting

fälschungs·sicher *Adj.* secure against forgery

Falsett /fal'zɛt/ *das;* ~[e]s, ~e (Musik) falsetto [voice]

Falsifikat /falzifi'ka:t/ *das;* ~[e]s, ~e forgery; fake

Falsifikation /falzifika'tsi̯o:n/ *die;* ~, ~en falsification

falsifizieren /falzifi'tsi:rən/ *tr. V.* falsify

faltbar *Adj.* collapsible ‹*box, boat*›

Falt-: ~**blatt** *das* leaflet; (in Zeitungen, Zeitschriften, Büchern) insert; ~**boot** *das* collapsible boat

Fältchen /'fɛltçən/ *das;* ~s, ~: wrinkle

Falte /'faltə/ *die;* ~, ~n **1** crease; **~n schlagen** crease **2** (im Stoff) fold; (mit scharfer Kante) pleat **3** (Hautfalte) wrinkle; line; **die Stirn in ~n legen** *od.* **ziehen** (nachdenklich) knit one's brow; (verärgert) frown **4** (Geol.) fold

fälteln /'fɛltl̩n/ *tr. V.* pleat

falten

A *tr. V.* fold; **die Hände ~:** fold one's hands

B *refl. V.* (auch Geol.) fold; ‹*skin*› wrinkle, become wrinkled

falten-, Falten-: ~**bildung** *die* (auch Geol.) folding; (der Haut) wrinkling; ~**frei** *Adj.* creaseless ‹*fit*›; ~**gebirge** *das* [range of] fold mountains; ~**los** *Adj.* uncreased ‹*garment*›; unwrinkled ‹*skin*›; ~**reich** *Adj.* heavily pleated ‹*robe*›; heavily lined ‹*face*›; ~**rock** *der* pleated skirt; ~**wurf** *der* arrangement of the folds

Falter *der;* ~s, ~ (Nacht~) moth; (Tag~) butterfly

faltig **1** *Adj.* ‹*clothes*› gathered [in folds]; wrinkled ‹*skin, hands*› **2** (zerknittert) creased

-fältig /-fɛltɪç/ *Adj., adv.* -fold; **hundert~/tausend~:** hundredfold/thousandfold

Falt-: ~**karte** *die* folding map; ~**karton** *der* collapsible cardboard box; ~**rad** *das* folding bicycle; ~**tür** *die* folding door

Faltung *die;* ~, ~en (Geol.) fold

Falz /falts/ *der;* ~es, ~e **1** (Buchbinderei) (scharfe Faltlinie) fold; (Übergang zwischen Buchdeckel und -rücken) groove; (angehefteter Leinenstreifen) guard; stub **2** (bei Briefmarken) hinge **3** (Bauw., Holzverarb.) rebate; rabbet **4** (Technik) lock seam; double seam

falzen *tr. V.* (Buchbinderei) fold; (Technik) seam

Falz·maschine *die* **1** (Buchbinderei) folding machine **2** (Technik) seaming machine

Fama /'fa:ma/ *die;* ~ (geh.) rumour; **es geht die ~, dass ...** there is a rumour that ...

familial /fami'li̯a:l/ *Adj.* (Soziol.) familial

familiär /fami'li̯ɛ:ɐ̯/

A *Adj.* **1** family ‹*problems, worries*›; **aus ~en Gründen** for family reasons **2** (zwanglos) familiar; informal; informal ‹*tone, relationship*›

B *adv.* (zwanglos) **sich ~ ausdrücken** to talk in a familiar way

Familiarität /famili̯ari'tɛ:t/ *die;* ~, ~en familiarity

Familie /fa'mi:li̯ə/ *die;* ~, ~n **1** family; ~ **Meyer** the Meyer family; ~ **haben** have a family; **eine ~ gründen** (heiraten) marry; (Kinder bekommen) start a family; **das bleibt in der ~:** it will stay in the family; it will go no further; **das kommt in den besten ~n vor** it happens in the best families; **das liegt in der ~:** it runs in the family **2** (Biol.) family

familien-, Familien-: ~**album** *das* family album; ~**angehörige** *der/die* member of the family; ~**angelegenheit** *die* family affair *or* matter; **in dringenden ~angelegenheiten** on urgent family business; ~**anschluss**, *~**anschluß** *der* personal contact [with a/the family]; ~**anzeigen** *Pl.* births, deaths, and marriages; ~**besitz** *der* family property; **im ~besitz** in the family's possession; **dieses Stück ist aus altem ~besitz** this piece is a family heirloom; ~**betrieb** *der* family business *or* firm; ~**bibel** *die* family bible; ~**bild** *das* (Foto) family photograph; (Gemälde) family picture; ~**chronik** *die* family history; ~**ehre** *die* family honour; ~**feier** *die* family party; ~**feindlich** *Adj.* ‹*policy etc.*› hostile to the family; ~**flasche** *die* family-sized bottle; ~**forschung** *die* genealogy; ~**freundlich** **A** *Adj.* family-friendly; **B** *adv.* in a family-friendly way; ~**fürsorge** *die* family welfare service; ~**gerecht** *Adj.* ‹*accommodation etc.*› suiting the needs of families; ~**grab** *das* family grave; ~**gruft** *die* family vault; ~**krach** *der* (ugs.) family row; **bei uns gibt es oft ~krach** we often have family rows; ~**kreis** *der* family circle; **im engsten ~kreis** in the immediate family; ~**leben** *das* family life; ~**minister** *der,* ~**ministerin** *die: minister responsible for family matters;* ~**mitglied** *das* member of the family; ~**name** *der* surname; family name; ~**oberhaupt** *das* head of the family; ~**pass**, *~**paß** *der* family passport; ~**planung** *die* family planning *no art.;* ~**politik** *die* policy/policies relating to the family; ~**recht** *das* family law; ~**roman** *der* family saga; ~**schmuck** *der* family jewels *pl.;* family jewellery; ~**sinn** *der* sense of commitment to the family; ~**stand** *der* marital status; ~**stück** *das* family heirloom; ~**tragödie** *die* family tragedy; ~**treffen** *das* family meeting; ~**unternehmen** *das* family business; ~**vater** *der:* **~vater sein** be the father of a family; **ein guter ~vater** a good husband and father; ~**verhältnisse** *Pl.* family circumstances; family background; **aus geordneten ~verhältnissen kommen** have a stable family background; ~**vorstand** *der* (Amtsspr.) head of the family; ~**wappen** *das* family coat of arms; ~**zusammenführung** *die* reuniting of families; ~**zuwachs** *der* addition[s] to the family; **~zuwachs bekommen/erwarten** have/expect an addition to the family

famos /fa'mo:s/ (veralt.)

A *Adj.* splendid

B *adv.* splendidly

famulieren /famu'li:rən/ *itr. V.* (Med.) do one's clinical training

Famulus /'fa:mulʊs/ *der;* ~, ~se *od.* **Famuli** /'fa:muli/ **1** (Med.) *medical student doing his/her clinical training;* intern (Amer.) **2** (veralt., scherzh.: Assistent) famulus

Fan /fɛn/ *der;* ~s, ~s fan

Fanal /fa'na:l/ *das;* ~s, ~e (geh.) torch; **ein ~ für etw. setzen** light a torch for sth.

Fan·artikel *der* piece of fan merchandise; ~ *Pl.* fan merchandise *sing.*

-fanatiker *der,* **-fanatikerin** *die:* **Frischluft~/Fußball~:** fresh air/football fanatic

Fanatiker /fa'na:tikɐ/ *der;* ~s, ~, **Fanatikerin** *die;* ~, ~nen fanatic; (religiös) fanatic; zealot

fanatisch

A *Adj.* fanatical

B *adv.* fanatically

fanatisieren *tr. V.* rouse to fanaticism; **der fanatisierte Mob** the fanatically excited mob

Fanatismus *der;* ~: fanaticism

fand /fant/ *1. u. 3. Pers. Sg. Prät. v.* **finden**

Fandango /fan'daŋgo/ *der;* ~s, ~s fandango

Fanfare /fan'fa:rə/ *die;* ~, ~n **1** herald's trumpet; **die ~ blasen** play the ceremonial trumpet **2** (Signal) fanfare; flourish; **~n erklingen** fanfares are sounded **3** (Musikstück) fanfare **4** (am Auto) musical [air] horn

Fanfaren-: ~**klang** *der* sound of the fanfare; ~**zug** *der* parade of trumpeters

Fang /faŋ/ *der;* ~[e]s, **Fänge** /'fɛŋə/ **1** (Tierfang) trapping; (von Fischen) catching; **zum ~ auslaufen** put to sea [to fish] **2** (Beute) bag; (von Fischen) catch; haul; **einen guten ~ machen** *od.* **tun** (fig.) make a good catch **3** *Pl.* (Jägerspr.: Fuß eines Raubvogels) talons *pl.;* claws *pl.;* **was er einmal in den Fängen hat, rückt er nicht wieder heraus** (fig. ugs.) once something gets into his clutches, he doesn't let go **4** *Pl.* (Jägerspr.: ~zähne) fangs *pl.*

Fang-: ~**arm** *der* (Zool.) tentacle; ~**ball** *der* catch; ~**eisen** *das* (Jagdw.) trap

Fan·gemeinde *die* community of fans

fangen

A *unr. tr. V.* **1** (ergreifen, fassen) catch, trap ‹*bird, animal*›; catch ‹*fish*›; **die Katze fängt eine Maus** the cat catches a mouse; **eine ~** (südd., österr. ugs.) get a clip round the ear (coll.) **2** (gefangen nehmen) catch, capture ‹*fugitive etc.*›; **gefangene Soldaten** captured soldiers; **in Frankreich/Russland gefangen sein** be a prisoner of war in France/Russia; **von etw. [ganz] gefangen sein** (fig.) be [quite] enthralled by sth.; **sich gefangen geben** give oneself up; surrender; **jmdn./ein Tier gefangen halten** hold sb. prisoner *or* captive/keep an animal in captivity; **jmdn. gefangen nehmen** capture sb.; take sb. prisoner; (fig.: begeistern) captivate *or* enthral sb.; **jmds. Aufmerksamkeit gefangen halten** rivet sb.'s attention; **jmdn. gefangen halten** (fig.: faszinieren) hold sb. enthralled; **jmdn. gefangen setzen** (geh.) imprison sb. **3** *auch itr.* (auf~) catch ‹*ball*›; **er kann gut/nicht ~:** he's good/not good at catching

B *unr. refl. V.* **1** (in eine Falle geraten, nicht mehr frei kommen) get *or* be caught; **der Wind fängt sich in etw.** sth. catches the wind; *s. auch* **Schlinge 2** **2** (wieder in die normale Lage kommen) **sich [gerade] noch ~:** [just] manage to steady oneself; **sich wieder ~** (fig.) recover

Fangen *das;* ~s: **~ spielen** play tag *or* catch

Fänger /'fɛŋɐ/ *der;* ~s, ~, **Fängerin** *die;* ~, ~nen catcher; (von Großwild) hunter

fang-, Fang-: ~**flotte** *die* fishing fleet; ~**frage** *die* catch question; trick question; ~**frisch** *Adj.* fresh; freshly caught ‹*fish*›; ~**gebiet** *das* fishing ground; ~**leine** *die* **1** (Seemannsspr.) (eines Schiffs) hawser; (eines Bootes) mooring rope; **2** (Fallschirmspringen) shroud line; ~**netz** *das* **1** (Fischereiw.) [fishing] net; **2** (Flugw.) arrester gear; **3** (Artistik) safety net

Fango·packung /'faŋgo-/ *die* (Med.) fango pack

Fang-: ~**prämie** *die* bounty; ~**quote** *die* (Fischereiw.) catch quota; ~**riemen** *der* [binding] strap; ~**schaltung** *die* (Fernspr.) tracing device; interception circuit; ~**schuss**, *~**schuß** *der* (Jagdw.) coup de grâce; ~**zeit** *die* season

Fan- /fɛn-/: ~**klub** *der* fan club; ~**post** *die* fan mail

Fantasie /fanta'zi:/ *die;* ~, ~n **1** imagination; **mit [viel]/ohne [jede] ~:** [very] imaginatively *or* with [a lot of] imagination/[very] unimaginatively *or* without [any] imagination; **eine schmutzige ~ haben** have a dirty mind **2** (Produkt der Fantasie) fantasy **3** (Musik) fantasia

fantasie-los

A *Adj.* unimaginative

B *adv.* unimaginatively

Fantasielosigkeit *die;* ~: lack of imagination; (Eintönigkeit) dullness

fantasieren

A *itr. V.* **1** indulge in fantasies, fantasize (**von** about); **fantasierst du, oder sagst du die**

Wahrheit? are you making it up or telling the truth? 2 (Med.: irrereden) talk deliriously
B *tr. V.* **was fantasierst du da?** what's all that nonsense?

fantasie·voll
A *Adj.* imaginative
B *adv.* imaginatively

Fantasie·vor·stellung *die* figment of the imagination

Fantast /fan'tast/ *der;* ~en, ~en dreamer; starry-eyed idealist

Fantasterei *die;* ~, ~en fantasy; (Wunschtraum) pipe dream

Fantastin *die;* ~, ~nen ► **Fantast**

fantastisch
A *Adj.* 1 fantastic; ‹*idea*› divorced from reality; **eine ~e Erzählung** a tale of fantasy 2 (ugs.: großartig) fantastic (coll.); terrific (coll.)
B *adv.* (ugs.) fantastically (coll.); **~ tanzen/kochen** (ugs.) dance/cook fantastically (coll.) *or* incredibly well

Faraday·käfig /'fɛrədɪ-/ *der* (Physik) Faraday cage

Farb-: ~abstimmung *die* colour balance; colour harmony; **~band** *das; Pl.* **~bänder** [typewriter] ribbon; **~beutel** *der* paint bomb; **~bild** *das* 1 (Aufnahme) colour photo; 2 (Illustration) colour picture; **~dia** *das* colour slide; colour transparency; **~druck** *der; Pl.* **~~e** colour print *or* reproduction; **~drucker** *der* (DV) colour printer

Farbe /'farbə/ *die;* ~, ~n 1 colour; **~ bekommen/verlieren** get some colour/lose one's colour; **an ~ gewinnen/verlieren** (fig.) become more/less colourful; **die ~ wechseln** ‹*person*› blanch 2 (Farbstoff) (für Textilien) dye; (für Holz, Metall, Stein usw.) paint; **~n mischen/auftragen** mix/apply paint; **die ~n laufen ineinander/verblassen** the colours are running together/are fading; **etw. in den schwärzesten/glühendsten ~n malen** *od.* **schildern** (fig.) paint the gloomiest possible picture/a rosy picture of sth. 3 (Buntheit) colour; **der Film ist in ~:** the film is in colour 4 (Symbol eines Landes, einer Vereinigung) **~n** colours; **die ~n seines Landes vertreten** represent one's country; **die ~ wechseln** (fig.) change sides 5 (Spielkarten) suit; **eine ~ bedienen** follow suit; **~ bekennen** (fig. ugs.) come clean (coll.)

farb-, Farb-: ~echt *Adj.* colour-fast; **~effekt** *der* colour effect; **~empfindlich** *Adj.* 1 colour-sensitive ‹*film*›; 2 (nicht ~echt) non-colour-fast

Färbe·mittel *das* dye

-farben *Adj., adv.* **erd~/erdbeer~/ creme~/ haut~:** earth-/strawberry-/cream-/skin-coloured; **creme~ angestrichen** painted cream

färben /'fɛrbn̩/
A *tr. V.* 1 dye ‹*wool, material, hair*›; **etw. grün/schwarz/beige ~:** dye sth. green/black/beige; **sich** (*Dat.*) **das Haar blond ~ lassen** have one's hair dyed blond 2 *meist im 2. Part.* (verändert darstellen) **eine politisch gefärbte Rede** a speech with a political slant; **ein gefärbter Bericht** a biased report
B *refl. V.* change colour; **sich schwarz/rot** *usw.* **~:** turn black/red *etc.*
C *itr. V.* (ugs.: ab~) **der Stoff/die Bluse färbt** the material/the blouse runs

farben-, Farben-: ~blind *Adj.* colour-blind; **~freudig** *Adj.,* **~froh** *Adj.* colourful; **~industrie** *die* paint industry; **~lehre** *die* theory of colour; **~pracht** *die* colourful splendour; **~prächtig** *Adj.* vibrant with colour *postpos.;* **~sinn** *der* colour sense; sense of colour; **~spiel** *das* play of colours; **~test** *der* (Psych.) colour test; **~tragend** *Adj.* ‹*student fraternity*› using traditional colours

Färber *der;* ~s, ~ ►**i** S. 113 dyer

Färberei *die;* ~, ~en 1 (Betrieb) dyeworks *sing.* 2 (Verfahren) dyeing

Färberin *die;* ~, ~nen ►**i** S. 113 dyer

Farb-: ~fernsehen *das* colour television; **~fernseher** *der* (ugs.) colour telly (coll.) *or* television; **~fernseh·gerät** *das* colour television [set]; **~film** *der* colour film; **~filter** *der, fachspr. meist: das* colour filter; **~fleck** *der* paint spot; **~foto** *das* colour photo; **~fotografie** *die* 1 (Verfahren) colour photography; 2 (Foto) colour photograph; **~gebung** *die;* ~~, ~~en, **~gestaltung** *die* colouring; choice of colours

farbig
A *Adj.* 1 coloured 2 (bunt, fig.: anschaulich, lebhaft) colourful ‹*dress, picture, description, tale*›; **~e [Kirchen]fenster** stained-glass [church] windows
B *adv.* colourfully

-farbig *Adj., adv.* ► **-farben**

Farbige *der/die; adj. Dekl.* coloured man/woman; coloured; **die ~n in Amerika/Südafrika** the coloured people in America/the Coloureds in South Africa

Farbigkeit *die;* ~ (auch fig.) colourfulness

Farb-: ~karte *die* colour chart *or* guide; **~klecks** *der* paint spot *or* splash; (nicht aufgesogen) blob of paint; paint spot; **~kombination** *die* colour combination; **~komposition** *die* colour composition

farblich
A *Adj.* in colour *postpos.;* as regards colour *postpos.*
B *adv.* **etw. ~ aufeinander abstimmen** match sth. in colour

farb-, Farb-: ~los *Adj.* (auch fig.) colourless; clear ‹*varnish*›; neutral ‹*shoe polish*›; **~losigkeit** *die;* ~~ (auch fig.) colourlessness; **~negativ** *das* (Fot.) colour negative; **~schicht** *die* layer of paint; (beim Auftragen) coat of paint; **~skala** *die* colour range; **~stift** *der* 1 (Buntstift) coloured pencil; 2 (Filzstift) coloured felt-tip *or* pen; **~stoff** *der* 1 (Med., Biol.) pigment; 2 (für Textilien) dye; 3 (für Lebensmittel) colouring; **~ton** *der; Pl.* **~töne** shade; **~tupfen**, **~tupfer** *der* spot of colour

Färbung *die;* ~, ~en 1 (Farbgebung) colouring; colour 2 (das Färben) dyeing 3 (fig.: Tendenz) slant

Farb-: ~walze *die* (Druckw.) ink[ing] roller; **~wechsel** *der* 1 (wechselndes Auftreten von ~en) variation in colour; 2 (Zool.) ability to change skin colour

Farce /'farsə/ *die;* ~, ~n 1 (auch fig.) farce 2 (Kochk.) stuffing; (mit Fleisch) forcemeat

farcieren *tr. V.* (Kochk.) fill; stuff

Farm /farm/ *die;* ~, ~en farm

Farmer *der;* ~s, ~, **Farmerin** *die;* ~, ~nen farmer

Farn /farn/ *der;* ~[e]s, ~e fern

Farn-: ~kraut *das* fern; **~wedel** *der* fern frond

Färse /'fɛrzə/ *die;* ~, ~n heifer

Fasan /fa'za:n/ *der;* ~[e]s, ~e[n] pheasant

Fasanerie /fazanə'ri:/ *die;* ~, ~n pheasantry

faschieren *tr. V.* (österr.) mince

Faschierte *das; adj. Dekl.* (österr.) minced meat; mince

Faschine /fa'ʃi:nə/ *die;* ~, ~n (Straßenbau) fascine; faggot

Fasching /'faʃɪŋ/ *der;* ~s, ~e *od.* ~s [pre-Lent] carnival; **im ~:** at carnival time

> **Fasching, Fastnachtszeit**
>
> This is the carnival season, which begins in November and ends on *Aschermittwoch* for Lent. Depending on the region it is called *Karneval*, *Fastnacht*, *Fasnet*, or *Fasching* and is celebrated in Germany, Austria, and Switzerland. Every town and village has its own carnival customs. Whether it is the *Kölner Karneval* or the *Münchner Fasching*, celebrations reach a climax in the last week, especially on *Rosenmontag* and *Faschingsdienstag*, when revellers dress up for masked balls and there are parades of floats through the streets. On those two days people might even go to work in fancy dress. Originally the masks and wild dances served to drive away evil spirits, but now it's just a time for fooling about. On Ash Wednesday everything returns to normal.

Faschings-: ~ball *der* carnival ball; **~kostüm** *das* fancy-dress costume [for carnival]; **~zug** *der* carnival procession

Faschismus /fa'ʃɪsmʊs/ *der;* ~: fascism *no art.;* **Opfer des ~:** victim of fascism

Faschist *der;* ~en, ~en, **Faschistin** *die;* ~, ~nen fascist

faschistisch *Adj.* fascist

faschistoid /faʃɪsto'i:d/ *Adj.* fascistic

Fascho /'faʃo/ *der;* ~s, ~s (Jargon) fascist pig (coll. derog.)

Fase /'fa:zə/ *die;* ~, ~n (Technik) bevel [edge]; chamfer [edge]

Faselei *die;* ~, ~en (ugs. abwertend) drivel; twaddle

faseln /'fa:zl̩n/ *itr. V.* (ugs. abwertend) drivel; blather

fasen /'fa:zn̩/ *tr. V.* (Technik) bevel; chamfer

Faser /'fa:zɐ/ *die;* ~, ~n fibre; **mit jeder ~ seines Herzens an etw.** (*Dat.*) **hängen** (fig. geh.) love sth. with every fibre of one's being

Faser·glas *das* (Technik) fibreglass

faserig *Adj.* fibrous ‹*paper*›; stringy ‹*meat*›

fasern *itr. V.* fray

faser-, Faser-: ~pflanze *die* fibre plant; **~schonend** *Adj.* gentle [to fabrics]; **~stoff** *der* fibrous material

Fas·nacht /'fas-/ *die* (bes. südd.) ► **Fastnacht**

Fass, *Faß /fas/ *das;* **Fasses, Fässer** /'fɛsɐ/ barrel; (Öl~, Benzin~ usw.) drum; (kleines Bier~) keg; (kleines Sherry~, Portwein~ usw.) cask; (Butter~) churn; **Bier vom ~:** draught beer; **Wein vom ~:** wine from the wood; **er ist [so] dick wie ein ~** (ugs.) he's as fat as a barrel; **er säuft wie ein ~** (ugs.) he drinks like a fish; **das schlägt dem ~ den Boden aus** (ugs.) that takes the biscuit (Brit. coll.) *or* (coll.) cake; **das bringt das ~ zum Überlaufen** that's the last straw; **ein ~ ohne Boden sein** be an endless drain on sb.'s resources; **ein ~ aufmachen** (ugs.) paint the town red

Fassade /fa'sa:də/ *die;* ~, ~n 1 facade; frontage 2 (abwertend: äußere Erscheinung) facade; front; **das ist nur [noch] ~:** it is just a facade *or* front; **sie hat eine hübsche ~:** she is pretty on the outside

Fassaden-: ~kletterer *der;* ~s, ~, **~kletterin** *die* cat burglar; **~lift** *der* [workmen's/window cleaners'] cradle; **~reiniger** *der;* ~~s, ~~, **~reinigerin** *die;* ~~, ~~nen *worker who cleans the exteriors of buildings*

fassbar, *faßbar *Adj.* 1 (greifbar, konkret) tangible, concrete ‹*results*› 2 (verständlich) comprehensible

Fass-, *Faß-: ~bier *das* draught beer; beer on draught; **~binder** *der,* **~binderin** *die;* ~~, ~~nen (bes. südd., österr.) cooper

Fässchen, *Fäßchen /'fɛsçən/ *das;* ~s, ~: small barrel; [small] cask

fassen /'fasn̩/
A *tr. V.* 1 (greifen) grasp; take hold of; **jmdn. am Arm ~:** take hold of sb.'s arm; **jmdn. bei der Hand ~:** take hold of sb.'s hand; take sb. by the hand; **etw. zu ~ bekommen** get a hold on sth.; **fass!** get *or* grab it/him!; *s. auch* **Ehre 3**; **Fuß 2**; **Kopf 1**; **Nase 1**; **Schopf 1**; **Stier 1**; **Wurzel 1** 2 (festnehmen) catch ‹*thief, culprit*› 3 ►**i S. 582** (aufnehmen können) ‹*hall, tank*› hold 4 (begreifen) **ich kann es nicht ~:** I cannot take it in; **das ist [doch] nicht zu ~!** it's incredible 5 (in verblasster Bedeutung) make, take ‹*decision*›; **Vertrauen** *od.* **Zutrauen zu jmdm. ~:** begin to feel confidence in *or* to trust sb.; **Mut ~:** take courage; **er konnte keinen klaren Gedanken ~:** he could not think clearly; *s. auch* **Auge 1**; **Herz 2** 6 (in eine Fassung bringen) set, mount ‹*jewel*›; curb ‹*spring, well*› 7 (formulieren, gestalten) **etw. in Worte/Verse ~:** put sth. into words/verse; **einen Begriff eng/weit ~:** define a concept narrowly/widely 8 (geistig erfassen) grasp 9 (als Ladung aufnehmen) take on ‹*load, goods*› 10 (Soldatenspr.) draw ‹*rations, supplies, ammunition*›
B *itr. V.* 1 (greifen) **nach etw. ~:** reach for sth.; **in etw.** (*Akk.*) **~:** put one's hand in sth.; **an**

f

etw. (*Akk.*) ~: touch sth.; **ins Leere ~:** grasp thin air **2** (einrasten) ‹*screw*› bite; ‹*cog*› mesh
C *refl. V.* **1** pull oneself together; recover [oneself]; **sich [schnell/allmählich] wieder ~:** recover [quickly/gradually] **2** **sich kurz ~:** be brief; *s. auch* **Geduld**

fässer·weise *Adv.* by the barrel

fasslich, *faßlich *Adj.* comprehensible; intelligible; **etw. in [leicht] ~er Form schreiben** write sth. in an easily comprehensible way

Fasson /fa'sõ:/ *die;* ~, ~s style; shape; **keine ~ mehr haben** have become shapeless; **jeder muss nach seiner [eigenen]** *od.* **auf seine [eigene] ~ selig werden** everyone has to work out his own salvation

Fasson·schnitt *der* short back and sides

Fassung *die;* ~, ~en **1** (sprachliche, künstlerische Form) version **2** (Selbstbeherrschung, Haltung) composure; self-control; **die ~ bewahren** keep one's composure; **die ~ verlieren** lose one's self-control; **jmdn. aus der ~ bringen** upset *or* ruffle sb.; **etw. mit ~ tragen** bear sth. calmly; **nach ~ ringen** struggle to retain one's composure **3** (für Glühlampen) holder **4** (von Juwelen) setting; (Bilder~, Brillen~) frame

fassungs-, Fassungs-: ~kraft *die* ►**Auffassungsgabe**; **~los** *Adj.* stunned; **ich war einfach ~los** (ugs.) I was completely bewildered; **~los vor Schmerz sein** be beside oneself with grief; **jmdn. ~los anstarren** gaze at sb. in bewilderment; **~losigkeit** *die;* ~~: state of bewilderment; **~vermögen** *das* ►**❶ S. 582** capacity

fast /fast/ *Adv.* almost; nearly; **~ nie** almost never; hardly ever; **~ nirgends** hardly anywhere; **~ nichts** almost nothing; hardly anything

fasten *itr. V.* fast; **das lange/kurze Fasten** the long/short fast

Fasten *Pl.* **1** (~zeit vor Ostern) Lent *sing.* **2** (Bußübungen) Lenten works of penance

Fasten-: ~kur *die* drastic reducing diet; **eine ~kur machen** be/go on a drastic reducing diet; **~predigt** *die* (kath. Rel.) Lent[en] sermon; **~zeit** *die* **1** (Rel.) time of fasting; **2** (kath. Rel.) Lent

Fast·nacht *die* **1** (Faschingsdienstag) Shrove Tuesday **2** (Karneval) carnival; Shrovetide; **während der ~:** at Shrovetide; at carnival time; **~ feiern** celebrate Shrovetide *or* the carnival

fast·nächtlich *Adj.* Shrovetide; carnival

Fastnachts-: ~brauch *der* Shrovetide custom; **~dienstag** *der* Shrove Tuesday; **~kostüm** *das* [carnival] fancy dress; **~spiel** *das* (Literaturw.) Shrovetide play; **~treiben** *das* [carnival] hustle and bustle; **~zeit** *die* Shrovetide; **~zug** *der* carnival procession

Faszikel /fas'tsi:kl/ *der;* ~s, ~: fascicle

Faszination /fastsina'tsio:n/ *die;* ~: fascination; **eine ~ auf jmdn. ausüben** fascinate sb.

faszinieren /fastsi'ni:rən/ *tr. V.* fascinate

faszinierend
A *Adj.* fascinating;
B *adv.* fascinatingly

fatal /fa'ta:l/ *Adj.* **1** (peinlich, misslich) awkward; embarrassing; **~e Folgen haben** have unfortunate consequences; **sich als ~ erweisen** prove [to be] rather unfortunate **2** (verhängnisvoll) fatal

fataler·weise *Adv.* unfortunately

Fatalismus *der;* ~: fatalism

Fatalist *der;* ~en, ~en, **Fatalistin** *die;* ~, ~nen fatalist

fatalistisch
A *Adj.* fatalistic
B *adv.* fatalistically

Fata Morgana /'fa:ta mɔr'ga:na/ *die;* ~, **Fata Morganen** *od.* ~s Fata Morgana; mirage; (fig.) illusion

Fatum /'fa:tʊm/ *das;* ~s, **Fata** (geh.) fate; destiny

Fatzke /'fatskə/ *der;* ~n *od.* ~s, ~n *od.* ~s (ugs. abwertend) twit (Brit. coll.); jerk (coll.)

fauchen /'fauxn/ *itr. V.* **1** ‹*cat*› hiss; ‹*tiger*› snarl; (fig.) ‹*engine*› hiss **2** (sich gereizt äußern) snarl

faul /faul/
A *Adj.* **1** (verdorben) rotten, bad ‹*food*›; bad ‹*tooth*›; rotten ‹*wood*›; foul, stale ‹*air*›; foul ‹*water*› **2** (träge) lazy; idle; **zu ~ zu etw. sein/zu ~ sein, etw. zu tun** be too lazy *or* idle for sth./to do sth.; **er hat heute seinen ~en Tag** (ugs.) he's having a lazy day today; **er, nicht ~, übernahm die Leitung** he was not slow in taking over; **auf der ~en Haut liegen/sich auf die ~e Haut legen** take it easy **3** (ugs.: nicht einwandfrei) bad ‹*joke*›; dud ‹*cheque*›; false ‹*peace*›; lame ‹*excuse*›; shabby ‹*compromise*›; shady ‹*business, customer*›; **das ist doch [alles] ~er Zauber** it's [all] quite bogus; **etwas ist ~ im Staate Dänemark** something is rotten in the state of Denmark **4** (säumig) bad ‹*debtor*›
B *adv.* (träge) lazily; idly

Faul·baum *der* alder buckthorn; alder dogwood

Fäule /'fɔylə/ *die;* ~: foulness

faulen *itr. V.; meist mit sein* ‹*vegetables, fruit, straw, leaves, wood*› rot; ‹*water*› go foul, stagnate; ‹*meat*› go off, putrefy; ‹*fish*› go off, go bad

faulenzen /'faulɛntsn/ *itr. V.* laze about; loaf about (derog.)

Faulenzer *der;* ~s, ~: idler; lazybones *sing.* (coll.)

Faulenzerei *die;* ~, ~en (abwertend) idleness; laziness

Faulenzerin *die;* ~, ~nen ►**Faulenzer**

Faulenzer·leben *das* life of idleness

Faul·gas *das* sludge *or* sewage gas

Faulheit *die;* ~: laziness; idleness; **vor ~ stinken** (ugs.) be bone idle

faulig *Adj.* stagnating ‹*water*›; putrefying ‹*meat*›; ‹*meat*› which is going bad; rotting ‹*vegetables, fruit*›; foul, putrid ‹*smell*›; **~ schmecken/riechen** taste/smell bad *or* off

Fäulnis /'fɔylnɪs/ *die;* ~: rottenness; (fig.) decadence; degeneracy; **in ~ übergehen** begin to rot

Fäulnis-: ~bakterie *die* putrefactive bacterium; **~erreger** *der* putrefactive agent; organism causing putrefaction

Faul-: ~pelz *der* (fam.) lazybones *sing.* (coll.); **~schlamm** *der* sludge; **~tier** *das* **1** (Zool.) sloth; **2** (ugs.: ~enzer) ►**Faulpelz**

Faun /faun/ *der;* ~[e]s, ~e faun

Fauna /'fauna/ *die;* ~, **Faunen** (Zool.) fauna

faunisch
A *Adj.* (geh.) **1** (naturhaft) faun-like **2** (sinnesfroh) lascivious
B *adv.* lasciviously

Faust /faust/ *die;* ~, **Fäuste** /'fɔystə/ fist; **eine ~ machen, die Hand zur ~ ballen** clench one's fist; **die ~ ballen/öffnen** clench/unclench one's fist; **mit den Fäusten auf jmdn. losgehen** fly at sb. with one's fists; **jmdn. mit der ~ ins Gesicht schlagen** punch sb. in the face; **das passt wie die ~ aufs Auge** (ugs.) (passt nicht) that clashes horribly; (passt) that matches perfectly; **er passt zu ihr wie die ~ aufs Auge** (ugs.) they are like chalk and cheese *or* like night and day; **die ~ im Nacken spüren** (fig.) begin to feel the pressure; **die ~/Fäuste in der Tasche ballen** (fig.) be seething inwardly; **auf eigene ~:** on one's own initiative; off one's own bat (coll.); **mit der ~ auf den Tisch schlagen** *od.* **hauen** (fig.) put one's foot down

Faust-: ~abwehr *die* (Ballspiele) save with the fists; **~ball** *der* faustball

Fäustchen /'fɔystçən/ *das;* ~s, ~: fist; **sich** (*Dat.*) **ins ~ lachen** laugh up one's sleeve; (aus finanziellen Gründen) laugh all the way to the bank

faust·dick
A *Adj.* as thick as a man's fist *postpos.*; **eine ~e Lüge** (fig.) a barefaced lie
B *adv.* **er hat es ~ hinter den Ohren** (ugs.) he's a crafty *or* sly one

Fäustel /'fɔystl/ *der;* ~s, ~: club hammer; stonemason's hammer

fausten *tr. V.* fist, punch ‹*ball*›

faust-, Faust-: ~formel *die* handy formula; rule of thumb; **~groß** *Adj.* as big as a fist *postpos.*; **~handschuh** *der* mitten; **~hieb** *der* punch

faustisch *Adj.* (geh.) Faustian

Faust-: ~kampf *der* (geh.) pugilism; boxing; (Wettkampf) boxing contest; **~kämpfer** *der* (geh.) pugilist; boxer; **~keil** *der* (Archäol.) handaxe

Fäustling /'fɔystlɪŋ/ *der;* ~s, ~e mitten

Faust-: ~pfand *das* security; (fig.) bargaining-counter; **ein ~pfand verlangen** demand security; **~recht** *das* rule of force; **~regel** *die* rule of thumb; **~schlag** *der* punch; **jmdm. einen ~schlag versetzen** punch sb.

Fauteuil /fo'tø:j/ *der;* ~s, ~s (bes. österr., sonst veralt.) armchair

Fauvismus /fo'vɪsmʊs/ *der;* ~ (bild. Kunst) fauvism *no art.*

Fauxpas /fo'pa/ *der;* ~, ~: faux pas

favorisieren /favori'zi:rən/ *tr. V.* **1** (geh.: bevorzugen) favour **2** (Sport) **er ist klar favorisiert** he is the clear favourite

Favorit /favo'ri:t/ *der;* ~en, ~en favourite

Favoriten·rolle *die* position as favourite

Favoritin *die;* ~, ~nen favourite

Fax /faks/ *das;* ~, ~[e] fax

Fax·anschluss, *Fax·anschluß *der* fax line

faxen *tr. V.* fax

Faxen *Pl.* (ugs.) **1** (dumme Späße) fooling around; **nur ~ im Sinn** *od.* **Kopf haben** do nothing but fool around *or* play the fool; **lass die ~!** stop fooling around *or* playing the fool! **2** (Grimassen) **~ machen** *od.* **schneiden** make *or* pull faces

Fax·gerät *das* fax machine

Fax·nummer *die* fax number

Fayence /fa'jã:s/ *die;* ~, ~n faience

Fazialis /fa'tsia:lɪs/ *der;* ~ ►**❶ S. 435** (Anat.) facial nerve

Fazit /'fa:tsɪt/ *das;* ~s, ~s *od.* ~e result; **das ~ [aus etw.] ziehen** sum [sth.] up

FCKW *Abk.* = **Fluorchlorkohlenwasserstoff** CFC

FCKW-frei *Adj.* CFC-free

FDGB *Abk.* (DDR) = **Freier Deutscher Gewerkschaftsbund**

FDJ *Abk.* (DDR) = **Freie Deutsche Jugend** Free German Youth

FDJler /ɛfde:'jɔtlɐ/ *der;* ~s, ~, **FDJlerin** *die;* ~, ~nen (DDR) Free German Youth member

FDP, F.D.P. *Abk.* = **Freie Demokratische Partei**

> **FDP — Freie Demokratische Partei**
>
> The German Liberal party, which was founded in 1948. This relatively small party tends to gain only 5 to 10% of the vote at general elections, but it has held the balance of power in various coalition governments both with the **SPD** and the **CDU/CSU**. It supports a free-market economy and the freedom of the individual.

F-Dur /'ɛf-/ *das* (Musik) [key of] F major; *s. auch* **A-Dur**

Feature /'fi:tʃɐ/ *das;* ~s, ~s *od. die;* ~, ~s (Rundf., Ferns., Zeitungsw.) feature

Feber /'fe:bɐ/ *der;* ~[s], ~ (österr.) February

Febr. *Abk.* = **Februar** Feb.

Februar /'fe:brua:ɐ/ *der;* ~[s], ~e ►**❶ S. 165** February; *s. auch* **April**

Fecht-: ~bahn *die* [fencing] piste; **~boden** *der* (Studentenspr.) fencing room

fechten /'fɛçtn/ *unr. itr., tr. V.* **1** fence; **für etw. ~** (fig. geh.) fight for sth. **2** (geh.: im Krieg kämpfen) fight

Fechten *das;* ~s fencing *no art.*

Fechter *der;* ~s, ~: fencer

Fechter·flanke *die* (Turnen) flank vault

Fechterin *die;* ~, ~nen fencer; *s. auch* **-in**

Fecht-: ~hand·schuh *der* fencing glove; **~hieb** *der* cut; **~kampf** *der* rapier fight;

(Sport) fencing bout; **~maske** *die* fencing mask; **~meister** *der*, **~meisterin** *die* fencing master; **~sport** *der* fencing; **~stellung** *die* fencing stance; **~waffe** *die* fencing weapon

Fedajin /feda'ji:n/ *der;* **~[s], ~:** fedayin

Feder /'fe:dɐ/ *die;* **~, ~n** [1] (Vogel~) feather; (Gänse~) quill; (lange Hut~) plume; **leicht wie eine ~ sein** be as light as a feather; **in die ~n kriechen** (ugs.) turn in (coll.); **[noch] in den ~n liegen** (ugs.) [still] be in one's bed; **er ließ ~n** *od.* **musste ~n lassen** (ugs.) he did not come out [of it] unscathed; **sich mit fremden ~n schmücken** strut in borrowed plumes [2] (zum Schreiben) nib; (mit Halter) pen; (Gänse~) quill [pen]; **ein Mann der ~** (geh.) a man of letters; **eine spitze ~ führen** (geh.) wield a sharp pen; **aus berufener ~ stammen** (geh.) come from an authoritative source; **jmdm. etw. in die ~ diktieren** dictate sth. to sb.; **zur ~ greifen** (geh.) take up one's pen [3] (Technik) spring [4] (Tischlerei) tongue

Feder·antrieb *der* (Technik) clockwork

Feder·ball *der* [1] (Spiel) badminton [2] (Ball) shuttlecock

Federball-: ~schläger *der* badminton racket; **~spiel** *das* [1] badminton; [2] (Zubehör) badminton rackets and shuttlecock

feder-, Feder-: ~bein *das* (Technik) (am Auto) suspension strut; (am Motorrad) telescopic arm; **~bett** *das* duvet (Brit.); continental quilt (Brit.); stuffed quilt (Amer.); **~blume** *die* artificial flower [made of feathers]; **~boa** *die* feather boa; **~busch** *der* [1] (Hutzierde) plume; [2] (eines Vogels) crest; **~fuchser** /-fʊksɐ/ *der;* **~~s, ~~, ~fuchserin** *die;* **~~, ~~nen** (abwertend) pen-pusher; **~führend** *Adj.* in charge *postpos.*; **der ~führende Redakteur** the chief editor; **~führung** *die:* **unter der ~führung des Ministers** under the overall control of the minister; **die ~führung haben** have overall control; be in overall charge; **~gewicht** (Schwerathletik) [1] (Gewichtsklasse) featherweight; *s. auch* **Fliegengewicht 1**; [2] (Sportler) featherweight; **~gewichtler** *der;* **~~s, ~~:** featherweight; **~halter** *der* fountain pen; **~kiel** *der* quill; **~kissen** *das* feather cushion; (im Bett) feather pillow; **~kleid** *das* (geh.) plumage; **~kraft** *die* [1] tension [of a/the spring]; [2] (Elastizität) springiness; **~leicht** [A] *Adj.* ‹*person*› as light as a feather; featherweight ‹*object*›; [B] *adv.* as lightly as a feather; **~lesen** *das:* **nicht viel ~lesen[s] mit jmdm./etw. machen** give sb./sth. short shrift; make short work of sb./sth.; **ohne viel ~lesen[s], ohne langes ~lesen** without much ado; **viel zu viel ~lesen[s] machen** make far too much fuss; **~mappe** *die* pen and pencil case; **~messer** *das* penknife

federn

[A] *itr. V.* ‹*springboard, floor, etc.*› be springy; **in den Knien ~:** bend at the knees; **ein ~der Gang** a springy *or* bouncy walk; **mit ~den Schritten** with a spring in one's step

[B] *tr. V.* [1] (mit einer Federung versehen) spring; **das Auto ist gut/schlecht gefedert** the car has good/poor suspension; **das Bett ist gut gefedert** the bed is well-sprung [2] *s. auch* **teeren**

Feder-: ~ohr *das* ear tuft; plumicorn; **~schaft** *der* shaft of a/the feather; **~schmuck** *der* [1] (Kopfschmuck) feather headdress; [2] (geh.: Gefieder) plumage; **~spiel** *das* (Jägerspr.) lure; **~skizze** *die* pen-and-ink sketch; **~strich** *der* stroke of the pen; **du hast noch keinen ~strich getan** (fig. ugs.) you have not yet put pen to paper

Federung *die;* **~, ~en** (in Möbeln) springs *pl.*; (Kfz-W.) suspension

Feder-: ~vieh *das* (ugs.) poultry; **~waage** *die* spring balance; **~weiße** *der; adj. Dekl.* new wine; **~werk** *das* spring mechanism; **~wild** *das* game birds *pl.*; **~wisch** *der* feather duster; **~wolke** *die* wispy *or* fleecy cloud; **~zeichnung** *die* pen-and-ink drawing

Fee /fe:/ *die;* **~, ~n** fairy

Feed-back /'fi:dbɛk/ *das;* **~s, ~s** feedback

Feeling /'fi:lɪŋ/ *das;* **~s, ~s** feeling; (Geschicklichkeit) feel

feenhaft *Adj.* fairy-like

Feen-: ~königin *die* fairy queen; queen of the fairies; **~reich** *das* Fairyland; **ins ~reich** to Fairyland

Fege·feuer *das* purgatory

fegen /'fe:gn̩/

[A] *tr. V.* [1] (bes. nordd.: säubern) sweep [2] (schnell entfernen) brush; **etwas vom Tisch ~:** brush sth. off the table; (fig.) brush sth. aside; **den Gegner vom Platz ~** (Sportjargon) wipe the floor with one's opponent/opponents [3] (schnell treiben) sweep; drive [4] (bes. südd.: blank reiben) scour ‹*pots, pans*› [5] *auch itr.* (Jägerspr.) fray; **die Hirsche ~ [ihr Geweih]** the stags fray [their heads]

[B] *itr. V.* [1] sweep up [2] *mit sein* (rasen, stürmen) sweep; tear (coll.)

Feger *der;* **~s, ~** (ugs.) live wire

Fehde /'fe:də/ *die;* **~, ~n** feud; **mit jmdm. in ~ liegen** be at feud with sb.; **literarische/politische ~n [mit jmdm.] austragen/ausfechten** (fig. geh.) carry on/fight out literary/political controversies [with sb.]

Fehde·hand·schuh *der* (geh.) **jmdm. den ~ hinwerfen** *od.* **vor die Füße werfen** throw down the gauntlet to sb.; **den ~ aufnehmen** *od.* **aufheben** take up the gauntlet

fehl /fe:l/ *Adv.* **~ am Platz[e] sein** be out of place

Fehl *in* **ohne ~ [und Tadel] sein** (geh.) be faultless *or* beyond reproach

Fehl·anzeige *die* [1] (ugs.: Ausdruck der Verneinung) no chance (coll.) [2] (Milit.) nil return

fehlbar *Adj.* fallible

Fehlbarkeit *die;* **~:** fallibility

Fehl-: ~bedienung *die* incorrect operation; **~besetzung** *die:* **so viele ~besetzungen** so many examples of miscasting; **[als Ophelia] eine ~besetzung sein** be miscast [in the role of Ophelia]; **~bestand** *der* shortage; deficiency; **~betrag** *der* (bes. Kaufmannsspr.) deficit; **~bildung** *die* ▸ℹ **S. 439** (Med.) deformity; malformation; **~diagnose** *die* incorrect diagnosis; **~druck** *der; Pl.* **~~e** (Philat.) misprint; **~ein·schätzung** *die* false assessment; (einer Entwicklung) misjudgement

fehlen *itr. V.* [1] (nicht vorhanden sein) **ihm fehlt der Vater/das Geld** he has no father/no money; **ihr fehlt der Sinn dafür** she lacks a *or* has no feeling for it [2] (ausbleiben) be missing; be absent; **[un]entschuldigt ~:** be absent with[out] permission; **du darfst bei dieser Party nicht ~:** you mustn't miss this party; **diese Zutat darf bei dieser Soße nicht ~:** this ingredient is a must in this sauce [3] (verschwunden sein) be missing; be gone; **in der Kasse fehlt Geld** money is missing *or* has gone from the till [4] (vermisst werden) **er/das wird mir ~:** I shall miss him/that [5] (erforderlich sein) be needed; **zwei Punkte ~ nur noch** only two points are still needed; **ihm ~ noch zwei Punkte zum Sieg** he needs only two points to win; **es fehlte nicht viel, und ich wäre eingeschlafen** I all but fell asleep; **das fehlte mir gerade noch [zu meinem Glück], das hat mir gerade noch gefehlt** (ugs.) that's all I needed [6] *unpers.* (mangeln) **es fehlt an Lehrern** there is a lack of teachers; **es fehlt am Nötigsten** what is most needed is lacking; **bei ihnen fehlt es am Nötigsten** they lack what is most needed; **es an nichts ~ lassen** provide everything that is needed; **an mir soll es nicht ~:** I shall do my part; **es fehlt an allen Ecken und Enden** *od.* **Kanten [bei jmdm.]** sb. is short of everything [7] (krank sein) **was fehlt Ihnen?** what seems to be the matter?; **fehlt dir etwas?** is there something wrong?; are you all right?; **mir fehlt nichts** I'm all right; there is nothing wrong with me [8] **weit gefehlt!** (geh.) far from it! [9] (geh.: sündigen) do wrong; sin

Fehl-: ~entscheidung *die* wrong decision; **~entwicklung** *die* abortive development

Fehler *der;* **~s, ~** [1] (Unrichtigkeit, Irrtum) mistake; error; (Sport) fault; **der Schiedsrichter entschied** *od.* **erkannte auf ~:** the referee called a fault [2] (schlechte Eigenschaft) fault; shortcoming; (Gebrechen) [physical] defect; **sein ~ ist, dass er …** it is a fault of his that … [3] (schadhafte Stelle) flaw; blemish; **Textilien/Porzellan mit kleinen ~n** textiles/porcelain with small flaws *or* imperfections

fehler·frei

[A] *Adj.* faultless, perfect ‹*piece of work, dictation, etc.*›; correct ‹*measurement*›; **ein ~es Deutsch sprechen/schreiben** speak/write faultless *or* perfect German; (Reiten) **ein ~er Durchgang** a clear round

[B] *adv.* without any mistakes; (Reiten) without any faults; **ich spreche französisch, aber nicht ~:** I can speak French, but not perfectly

Fehler·grenze *die* margin of error; tolerance; **die ~ liegt bei 30%** there's a 30% margin of error

fehlerhaft *Adj.* faulty; defective; imperfect ‹*pronunciation*›; incorrect ‹*measurement*›; **eine ~e Stelle im Material** a defect in the material

fehler-, Fehler-: ~los [A] *Adj.* flawless; [B] *adv.* flawlessly; without a mistake; **etw. ~los schreiben/aufsagen** write/recite sth. without a mistake; **~quelle** *die* source of error; **~quote** *die* (Statistik, Schulw.) error rate; **~rechnung** *die* calculus of accidental error; **~suche** *die* [1] (bei der Reparatur) **ein Gerät zur ~suche** a device for detecting faults; [2] (zur Kontrolle) **bei der ~suche** when checking for faults; (DV: im Programm) when checking for errors; **~zahl** *die* number of mistakes *or* errors

fehl-, Fehl-: ~farbe *die* (Kartenspiel) (Farbe, die einem Spieler fehlt) void suit; (Farbe, die nicht Trumpf ist) plain suit; **mit einer ~farbe bedienen** follow with a non-trump card; **~geburt** *die* miscarriage; **~|gehen** *unr. itr. V.; mit sein* (geh.) [1] (sich irren) go *or* be wrong; **in einer Annahme ~gehen** be wrong in an assumption; [2] (sich verlaufen) lose one's way; **Sie können nicht ~gehen** you cannot go [far] wrong; [3] (nicht treffen) ‹*shot*› miss [the mark]; **~griff** *der* mistake; wrong choice; **einen ~griff tun** make a mistake *or* the wrong choice; **~information** *die* piece of wrong information; **einer ~information aufsitzen** (ugs.) have been given wrong information; **auf einer ~information beruhen** be based on [a piece of] incorrect information; **~interpretation** *die* misinterpretation; **~investition** *die* (bes. Wirtsch.) [1] bad investment; [2] (ugs.: Gegenstand) **eine [glatte] ~investition sein** be a [total] waste of money; **~kalkulation** *die* miscalculation; **~kauf** *der* (ugs.) bad buy; **~konstruktion** *die:* **eine ~konstruktion sein** be badly designed; **~leistung** *die* (Psych.) slip; mistake; **eine freudsche ~leistung** a Freudian slip; **~|leiten** *tr. V.* (geh.) misdirect; misdirect, misroute ‹*transport, convoy*›; **~pass,** ***~paß** *der* (Ballspiele) bad pass; **~planung** *die* [piece of] bad planning *no art.*; **~schlag** *der* failure; **~|schlagen** *unr. itr. V.; mit sein* fail; ‹*hopes*› come to nothing; **~schluss,** ***~schluß** *der* wrong conclusion; **~sichtig** /-zɪçtɪç/ *Adj.* ‹*person*› with defective vision; **~sichtigkeit** *die;* **~~:** defective vision; **~start** *der* [1] (Leichtathletik) false start; [2] (Flugw.) faulty start; [3] (Raumf.) abortive launch; **~tritt** *der* [1] (falscher Tritt) false step; [2] (geh.: Verfehlung) slip; indiscretion; (veralt.: gesellschaftlich verpönte Liebesbeziehung) indiscretion; **einen ~tritt begehen, sich eines ~tritts schuldig machen** commit an indiscretion; **~urteil** *das* [1] (Rechtsw.) **ein ~urteil fällen** ‹*jury*› return a wrong verdict; ‹*judge*› pass a wrong judgement; [2] (falsche Beurteilung) error of judgement; **ein ~urteil über etw.** (*Akk.*) **abgeben** make an incorrect assessment of sth.; **~verhalten** *das* [1] (fehlerhaftes Verhalten) incorrect conduct; **~verhalten beim Überholen** incorrect action when overtaking; [2] (anormales Verhalten) aberrant behaviour; **~versuch** *der* (Gewichtheben, Hochsprung) unsuccessful attempt; failure; (Weitsprung) foul jump; **~zündung** *die* (Technik) misfire

Fehn /fe:n/ *das;* **~[e]s, ~e** fen; marsh

Fehn·kultur *die* (Landw.) *method of cultivation which puts marshland to agricultural use*

feien /ˈfaiən/ *tr. V.; meist im 2. Part.* (geh.) protect (**gegen** against); **gegen Tropenkrankheiten gefeit sein** be immune to tropical diseases

Feier /ˈfaiɐ/ *die;* ~, ~**n** 1 (Veranstaltung) party; (aus festlichem Anlass) celebration; **zu** *od.* **anlässlich einer Begebenheit eine** ~ **veranstalten** celebrate an occasion with a party; **eine** ~ **in kleinem Rahmen/im Familienkreis** a small/family celebration/party; **keine** ~ **ohne Meier** (scherzh.) he/she *etc.* never misses a party 2 (Zeremonie) ceremony; **die** ~ **des heiligen Abendmahls** the celebration of Holy Communion; **zur** ~ **des Tages** (oft scherzh.) to mark the day; in honour of the occasion

Feier·abend *der* 1 (Zeit nach der Arbeit) evening; **den** ~ **genießen** enjoy one's evening; **schönen** ~**!** have a nice evening 2 (Arbeitsschluss) finishing time; **nach** ~**:** after work; ~ **machen** finish work; knock off; **für mich ist** ~**, dann ist** *od.* **mache ich** ~ (fig. ugs.) I'm finished; I've had enough (coll.)

Feierabend-: ~**beschäftigung** *die* leisure pursuit; spare-time interest; ~**heim** *das* (DDR) old people's home; ~**lektüre** *die* leisure-time reading

Feierei *die;* ~, ~**en** (ugs. abwertend) **diese ständige** ~**:** these endless parties

feierlich

A *Adj.* 1 ceremonial; solemn; **eine** ~**e Handlung** a ceremonial act; **eine** ~**e Stille** a solemn silence; **das ist ja [schon] nicht mehr** ~ (ugs.) it's got beyond a joke 2 (emphatisch) solemn ‹*declaration*›

B *adv.* 1 solemnly; ceremoniously; **jmdm. ist** ~ **zumute** sb. is in a solemn mood *or* frame of mind; ~ **verabschiedet werden** be given a ceremonious farewell 2 (emphatisch) solemnly ‹*declare, swear, etc.*›

Feierlichkeit *die;* ~, ~**en** 1 (Würde, Ernst) solemnity 2 (feierliche Veranstaltung) celebration; festivity

feiern

A *tr. V.* 1 (festlich begehen) celebrate ‹*birthday, wedding, etc.*›; **man muss die Feste** ~**, wie sie fallen** you have to enjoy yourself while you can 2 (ehren, umjubeln) acclaim ‹*artist, sportsman, etc.*›; **ein gefeierter Sportler/Dichter** a celebrated sportsman/poet; **Triumphe** ~**:** win the highest acclaim

B *itr. V.* (lustig beisammen sein) celebrate; have a party

feier-, Feier-: ~**schicht** *die* (Arbeitswelt) cancelled shift; **eine** ~**schicht einlegen müssen** have one's shift cancelled; ~**stunde** *die* ceremony; **jmdn. in/mit einer** ~**stunde ehren** hold a ceremony in sb.'s honour; ~**tag** *der* holiday; **ein gesetzlicher/kirchlicher** ~**tag** a public holiday/religious festival; **an Sonn- und** ~**tagen** on Sundays and public holidays; **jmdm. schöne** ~**tage wünschen** wish sb. a good holiday; **für mich ist heute ein** ~**tag** (fig.) today is a very special *or* a red letter day for me; ~**täglich** *Adj.* solemn ‹*silence, mood*›; ~**tags** *Adv.* **sonn- und** ~**tags** on Sundays and public holidays; ~**tags·arbeit** *die* working *no art.* on public holidays; ~**tags·stimmung** *die* Sunday mood

feig, feige /faik, ˈfaigə/

A *Adj.* cowardly

B *adv.* like a coward/like cowards; in a cowardly way

Feige *die;* ~, ~**n** fig

Feigen-: ~**baum** *der* fig tree; ~**blatt** *das* 1 (Blatt) fig leaf; 2 (fig.: Verhüllung) front; cover; ~**kaktus** *der* Indian fig; prickly pear

Feigheit *die;* ~**:** cowardice; cowardliness; ~ **vor dem Feind** (Milit.) cowardice in the face of the enemy

Feigling *der;* ~**s,** ~**e** coward

feil /fail/ *Adj.* (veralt.) for sale *postpos.;* (fig.) venal; **eine** ~**e Dirne** (veralt.) a harlot; **für Geld ist nicht alles** ~**:** money can't buy everything

feil|bieten *unr. tr. V.* (geh.) offer ‹*goods*› for sale

Feile *die;* ~, ~**n** file; **etw. mit einer** ~ **bearbeiten** file sth.

feilen *tr., itr. V.* file; **etw. passend/rund** ~**:** file sth. to fit/into a round shape; **sich** (*Dat.*) **die Fingernägel** ~**:** file one's [finger]nails

feil|halten *unr. tr. V.* (veralt.) offer ‹*goods*› for sale

feilschen /ˈfailʃn̩/ *itr. V.* haggle (**um** over); **nach langem/hartem Feilschen** after a long/hard bout of haggling

Feil-: ~**span** *der* filing; ~**staub** *der* filings *pl.*

fein /fain/

A *Adj.* 1 (zart) fine ‹*material, line, mesh, etc.*› 2 (aus kleinsten Teilchen bestehend) fine ‹*sand, powder*›; finely ground ‹*flour*›; finely granulated ‹*sugar*›; **etw.** ~ **mahlen** grind sth. fine; **etw.** ~ **schleifen** fine-grind sth.; ~ **gemahlen** finely ground; ~ **geschnitten** finely chopped; (fig.: schön geformt) delicate, finely shaped ‹*face, hands, etc.*› 3 (hochwertig) high-quality ‹*fruit, soap, etc.*›; fine ‹*silver, gold, etc.*›; fancy ‹*cakes, pastries, etc.*›; **nur das Feinste vom Feinen kaufen** buy only the best; **vom Feinsten** of the finest *or* highest quality 4 (ugs.: erfreulich) great (coll.); marvellous 5 (~ geschnitten) finely shaped, delicate ‹*hands, features, etc.*› 6 (scharf, exakt) keen, sensitive ‹*hearing*›; keen ‹*sense of smell*›; **eine** ~**e Nase für etw. haben** (fig.) have a good nose for sth. 7 (listig, gerissen) cunning ‹*move, scheme*› 8 (ugs.: anständig, nett) great (coll.), splendid ‹*person*›; **eine** ~**e Verwandtschaft/Gesellschaft** (iron.) a fine *or* nice family/crowd 9 (einfühlsam) delicate ‹*sense of humour*›; keen ‹*sense, understanding*›; **ein** ~**es Gespür für etw. haben** have a good feeling for sth. 10 (gediegen, vornehm) refined ‹*gentleman, lady*›; **du bist dir wohl zu** ~ **dafür!** (ugs.) I suppose you think it's beneath you; **sich** ~ **machen** (ugs.) dress up; *s. auch* **Herr 1**

B *adv.* 1 (gut, günstig) ~ **[he]raus sein** (ugs.) be sitting pretty (coll.); **Unterschiede** ~ **herausarbeiten** bring out subtle differences 2 (listig, gerissen) ~ **ausgeklügelt** cleverly thought out 3 (ugs.: bekräftigend) **etw.** ~ **säuberlich aufschreiben** write sth. down nice and neatly; ~ **brav sein** be a good boy/girl

Fein-: ~**ab·stimmung** *die* (Technik) fine tuning; ~**arbeit** *die* detailed work; (Technik) precision work; ~**bäckerei** *die* patisserie; ~**bearbeitung** *die* (Technik) finishing; ~**blech** *das* thin sheet metal

°feind, Feind /faint/ (geh.) *in* **jmdm./einer Sache** ~ **sein** be hostile towards sb./sth.

-feind *der* ...hater; **ein Hunde**~**/Fernseh**~ **sein** be anti dogs/television

Feind *der;* ~**[e]s,** ~**e** 1 enemy; **er ist ein** ~ **des Alkohols** he is opposed to alcohol; **sich** (*Dat.*) ~**e machen** make enemies; **sich** (*Dat.*) **jmdn. zum** ~ **machen** make an enemy of sb.; **liebet eure** ~**e** (bibl.) love thine enemy; **„**~ **hört mit"** 'careless talk costs lives' 2 (feindliche Truppen) enemy *constr. as pl.*; **[nichts wie] ran an den** ~ (fig. ugs.) get/let's get going *or* (coll.) stuck in

Feind-: ~**berührung** *die* (Milit.) contact with the enemy; ~**bild** *das* concept of the enemy

Feindes-: ~**hand** *die* (veralt.) **in** ~**hand geraten** *od.* **fallen** fall into the hands of the enemy; **von** ~**hand fallen** fall at the hands of the enemy; ~**land** *das* (veralt.) enemy territory

Feind·flug *der* (Luftwaffe) operational flight [over enemy territory]

Feindin *die;* ~, ~**nen** ▸ **Feind 1**

feindlich

A *Adj.* 1 hostile 2 (Milit.) enemy ‹*attack, broadcast, activity*›

B *adv.* in a hostile manner; with hostility

-feindlich *adj.* anti-‹*Soviet, American, EU, government, etc.*›; **familienfeindliche/kinderfeindliche Gesetze** laws which are hostile towards families/children

Feindlichkeit *die;* ~, ~**en** hostility (**gegenüber** towards); ~**en** hostilities

Feind·mächte *Pl.* enemy powers *pl.*

Feindschaft *die;* ~, ~**en** enmity; **zwischen ihnen herrscht bittere** ~**:** they are bitter enemies; **sich** (*Dat.*) **jmds.** ~ **zuziehen** make an enemy of sb.

feind·selig

A *Adj.* hostile; **sich** ~ **gegen jmdn. zeigen** show hostility towards sb.

B *adv.* **sich** ~ **ansehen** look at each other in a hostile manner *or* with hostility

Feind·seligkeit *die;* ~, ~**en** hostility; ~**en** (Milit.) hostilities

fein-, Fein-: ~**einstellung** *die* fine adjustment; ~**frost** *der* (DDR) deep-frozen foods *pl.;* ~**fühlig** **A** *Adj.* sensitive; **B** *adv.* sensitively; ~**fühligkeit** *die;* ~~**:** sensitivity; ~**gebäck** *das* [fancy] cakes and pastries *pl.;* ~**gefühl** *das* sensitivity; ~**gehalt** *der* fineness; ~**geist** *der* man/woman of culture; ~**gemahlen** ▸ **fein A2**; ~**geschnitten** ▸ **fein A2**; ~**gewicht** *das* fineness; ~**glied[e]rig** *Adj.* delicate; slender; ~**gold** *das* fine gold; ~**guss,** *~**guß** *der* (Metall) precision casting

Feinheit *die;* ~, ~**en** 1 (zarte Beschaffenheit) fineness; delicacy 2 (Nuance, Andeutung) subtlety; **die stilistischen** ~**en** the stylistic subtleties *or* nuances 3 (Vornehmheit) refinement

fein-, Fein-: ~**körnig** *Adj.* 1 fine-grained, fine ‹*sand, gravel, etc.*›; finely granulated ‹*sugar*›; 2 (Fot.) fine-grain ‹*film*›; ~**kost** *die* delicatessen *pl.;* ~**kost·geschäft** *das* delicatessen; *~**|machen** ▸ **fein A 10**; ~**maschig** *Adj.* finely meshed, fine-mesh *attrib.* ‹*net etc.*›; ~**mechanik** *die* precision engineering *no art.;* ~**mechaniker** *der*, ~**mechanikerin** *die* ▸ **❶ S. 113** precision engineer; ~**mechanisch** *Adj.* precision ‹*instrument*›; ~**mess·gerät,** *~**meß·gerät** *das* precision measuring instrument; ~**motorik** *die* fine motor functions *pl.;* ~**motorisch** *Adj.* fine motor ‹*skills, ability*›; ~**nervig** *Adj.* sensitive; ~**säuberlich** *Adj.* (österr.) ▸ **säuberlich**; ~**|schleifen** ▸ **fein A 2**; ~**schmecker** *der;* ~~**s,** ~~, ~**schmeckerin** *die;* ~~, ~~**nen** gourmet; ~**schmecker·lokal** *das* gourmet restaurant; ~**schnitt** *der* 1 (Tabak) fine cut; 2 (Film) final editing; ~**silber** *das* fine silver; ~**sinnig** **A** *Adj.* sensitive and subtle; **B** *adv.* in a sensitive and subtle manner; ~**sinnigkeit** *die;* ~~**:** sensitivity and subtlety

Feins·liebchen *das* (dichter. veralt.) sweetheart

Fein-: ~**struktur** *die* (Physik, Med.) fine structure; ~**strumpf·hose** *die* sheer tights *pl. or* pantyhose; ~**unze** *die:* **eine** ~**unze Gold/Silber** an ounce of fine gold/silver; ~**wäsche** *die* delicates *pl.;* ~**wasch·mittel** *das* mild detergent

feist *Adj.* (meist abwertend) fat ‹*face, fingers, etc.*›; **mit einem** ~**en Grinsen** (fig.) with a leer

feixen /ˈfaiksn̩/ *itr. V.* (ugs.) smirk

Felchen /ˈfɛlçn̩/ *der;* ~**s,** ~**:** whitefish

Feld /fɛlt/ *das;* ~**[e]s,** ~**er** 1 (geh.: unbebaute Bodenfläche) country[side]; **freies** ~**:** open country[side] 2 (bebaute Bodenfläche) field; **auf dem** ~ **arbeiten** work in the field; **das** ~ **bestellen** till the field 3 (Sport: Spiel~) pitch; field [of play] 4 (auf Formularen) box; space; (auf Brettspielen) space; (auf dem Schachbrett) square; (in Kassettendecken) panel 5 (Tätigkeitsbereich) field; sphere; **das** ~ **der Wissenschaften** the field of science; **ein weites** ~ **[sein]** (fig.) [be] a wide sphere 6 (veralt.: Schlacht~) field [of battle]; **ins** ~ **rücken** *od.* **ziehen** (veralt.) go into battle; **gegen/für jmdn./etw. ins** ~ **ziehen** (fig.) crusade against/for sb./sth.; **das** ~ **behaupten** stand one's ground; **in der Politik behaupten nach wie vor Männer das** ~**:** politics is still dominated by men; **das** ~ **räumen** leave; get out; **jmdm. das** ~ **überlassen** hand over to sb.; leave sb. a clear field; **jmdn. aus dem** ~**[e] schlagen** eliminate sb.; get rid of sb.; **jmdm. das** ~ **streitig machen** compete with sb.; **etw. gegen jmdn./etw. ins** ~ **führen** bring up sth. against sb./sth. 7 (Sport: geschlossene Gruppe) field 8 (Physik, Sprachw.) field

feld-, Feld-: ~**ahorn** *der* field maple; ~**arbeit** *die* 1 work in the field; 2 (Wissensch.) fieldwork; ~**bahn** *die* narrow-gauge railway; light railway; ~**bau** *der* agriculture; ~**bett** *das* camp bed; ~**blume** *die* field flower; wild flower; ~**ein[wärts]** /-ˈ-(-)/

Adv. across the field/fields; ~**flasche** *die* (Milit.) canteen; water bottle; ~**forschung** *die* (Wissensch.) fieldwork; ~**frucht** *die* arable crop; ~**geistliche** *der* (Milit. veralt.) army chaplain; ~**gottesdienst** *der* field service; ~**grau** *Adj.* field-grey; ~**hand·ball** *der* field handball; fieldball; ~**hase** *der* common hare; European hare

Feld·herr *der* (veralt.) commander

Feldherrn-: ~**kunst** *die* (veralt.) strategy; ~**stab** *der* (veralt.) field marshal's baton

feld-, Feld-: ~**hockey** *das* (Sport) [field] hockey; ~**huhn** *das* partridge; ~**hüter** *der,* ~**hüterin** *die: guard protecting crops from birds, thieves, etc.*; ~**jäger** *der* (Polizist) military policeman; **die** ~**jäger** the military police; ~**küche** *die* (bes. Milit.) field kitchen; ~**lager** *das* (veralt.) encampment; ~**lazarett** *das* field hospital; ~**linien** *Pl.* (Physik) field lines; ~**marschall** *der* ►ⓘ **S. 44** Field Marshal; ~**marsch·mäßig** **A** *Adj.* in full marching order *postpos.*; **B** *adv.* ~**marschmäßig angetreten/ausgerüstet sein** be lined up/be in full marching order; ~**maus** *die* [European] common vole

Feld·post *die* forces' (Brit.) *or* (Amer.) military postal service

Feldpost-: ~**brief** *der* forces' (Brit.) *or* (Amer.) military letter; ~**nummer** *die* forces' (Brit.) *or* (Amer.) military postal code

Feld-: ~**prediger** *der* (veralt.) army chaplain; ~**rain** *der* balk; baulk; ~**salat** *der* corn salad; lamb's lettuce

Feldscher /'fɛltʃeːɐ̯/ *der;* ~**s,** ~**e** (Milit.) **1** (hist.: Wundarzt) [unqualified] army doctor **2** (DDR) medical orderly

Feld-: ~**schlacht** *die* (veralt.) battle [in the field]; ~**schütz** *der;* ~~**en,** ~~**en** field guard; ~**spat** /-ʃpaːt/ *der* feldspar; ~**spieler** *der,* ~**spielerin** *die* player (excluding goalkeeper); ~**stärke** *die* (Physik) field strength; ~**stecher** *der;* ~~**s,** ~~**:** binoculars *pl.*; field glasses *pl.*; ~**stein** *der* stone; boulder; ~**studie** *die* (Wissensch.) field study; ~**theorie** *die* (Sprachw.) field theory; ~**überlegenheit** *die* (Sport) superiority; ~**versuch** *der* (Wissensch.) field experiment; ~**verweis** *der* (Sport) sending-off; **einen** ~**verweis gegen jmdn. aussprechen** send sb. off [the field]

Feld-Wald-und-Wiesen- (ugs.) run-of-the-mill; common-or-garden

Feld·webel /-veːbl̩/ *der;* ~**s,** ~ ►ⓘ **S. 44** (Milit.) sergeant

Feld·weg *der* path; track

Feld·weibel /-vaibl̩/ *der;* ~**s,** ~ (schweiz. Milit.) sergeant

Feld-: ~**zeichen** *das* (hist.) standard; flag; ~**zug** *der* (Milit., fig.) campaign

Felg·auf·schwung *der* (Turnen) upward circle forwards

Felge /'fɛlgə/ *die;* ~, ~**n** **1** (Radkranz) [wheel] rim; **die Reifen auf die** ~**n montieren** put the tyres on the wheels **2** (Turnen) circle

Felgen·bremse *die* (Technik) rim brake

Felg·um·schwung *der* (Turnen) circle

Fell /fɛl/ *das;* ~**[e]s,** ~**e** **1** (Haarkleid) fur; (Pferde~, Hunde~, Katzen~) coat; (Schaf~) fleece; skin; **ein weiches/glänzendes** ~**:** a soft/shiny coat; **einem Tier das** ~ **abziehen** skin an animal; **jmdm. das** ~ **über die Ohren ziehen** (fig. salopp) take sb. for a ride (coll.) **2** (Material) fur; furskin; **ein Mantel aus [braunem]** ~**:** a [brown] fur coat **3** (abgezogene behaarte Haut) skin; hide; **ihm sind die** *od.* **alle** ~**e weg-** *od.* **davongeschwommen** (fig.) he has had all his hopes dashed **4** (salopp: Haut des Menschen) skin; (fig.) **ihm** *od.* **ihn juckt das** ~ (ugs.) he is asking for a good hiding (coll.); **sich** (*Dat.*) **ein dickes** ~ **anschaffen** (ugs.) become thick-skinned; **ein dickes** ~ **haben** (ugs.) be thick-skinned *or* have a thick skin; **jmdm. das** ~ **versohlen** (ugs.) tan sb.'s hide; give sb. a good hiding (coll.); **das** ~ **versaufen** (ugs.) have a good drink to sb.'s memory

Fellache /fɛ'laxə/ *der;* ~**n,** ~**n, Fellachin** *die;* ~, ~**nen** fellah

Fellatio /fɛ'laːtsi̯o/ *die;* ~**:** fellatio *no art.*

Fell·eisen *das* (veralt.) knapsack

Fell-: ~**handel** *der* skin trade; ~**jacke** *die* fur jacket; ~**mütze** *die* fur cap

Fels /fɛls/ *der;* ~**en,** ~**en** **1** (Gestein) rock **2** (geh.: ~en) rock; **wie ein** ~ **in der Brandung stehen** stand as firm as a rock; *s. auch* **wachsen**[1] **1**

Fels-: ~**bild** *das* rock painting; ~**block** *der; Pl.* ~**blöcke** rock; boulder

Felsen /'fɛlzn̩/ *der;* ~**s,** ~**:** rock; (an der Steilküste) cliff

felsen-, Felsen-: ~**bucht** *die* bay lined by cliffs; cliff-lined bay; ~**fest** **A** *Adj.* firm; unshakeable ‹*opinion, belief*›; **B** *adv.* ‹*believe, be convinced*› firmly; ~**grab** *das* rock tomb; ~**grotte** *die* grotto; cave; ~**höhle** *die* rock cave; ~**klippe** *die* rocky cliff; **an einer** ~**klippe zerschellen** be dashed to pieces on a rock; ~**küste** *die* rocky coast *or* coastline; ~**riff** *das* rocky reef; ~**tor** *das* (Geogr.) rock arch

Fels-: ~**geröll** *das* rocks *pl.*; boulders *pl.*; ~**haken** *der* (Bergsteigen) piton

felsig *Adj.* rocky

Fels-: ~**massiv** *das* [rock] massif; ~**nase** *die* ledge; ~**schlucht** *die* gorge; ravine; ~**spalte** *die* crevice [in the rock]; ~**vorsprung** *der* ledge; ~**wand** *die* rock face; **in der** ~**wand** on the rock face

fem. *Abk.* = **feminin** fem.

Feme /'feːmə/ *die;* ~, ~**n** **1** (hist.) vehmgericht **2** (Geheimgericht) kangaroo court

Feme-: ~**gericht** *das* ►**Feme**; ~**mord** *der* lynching

feminin /femi'niːn/ *Adj.* **1** (geh.: weiblich) feminine ‹*characteristic, behaviour*› **2** (abwertend: unmännlich) effeminate ‹*man, type*› **3** (Sprachw.) feminine

Femininum /'feːminiːnʊm/ *das;* ~**s, Feminina** feminine noun

Feminismus *der;* ~, **Feminismen** **1** (Frauenbewegung) feminism *no art.* **2** ►ⓘ **S. 439** (Med., Zool.) feminism *no art.*

Feminist *der;* ~**en,** ~**en, Feministin** *die;* ~, ~**nen** feminist

feministisch *Adj.* feminist

Femme fatale /famfa'tal/ *die;* ~, **Femmes fatales** (geh.) femme fatale

Fenchel /'fɛnçl̩/ *der;* ~**s** fennel

Fenchel-: ~**knolle** *die* fennel; ~**öl** *das* fennel oil; ~**tee** *der* fennel tea

Fender /'fɛndɐ/ *der;* ~**s,** ~ (Seew.) fender

Fenn /fɛn/ *das;* ~**[e]s,** ~**e** (bes. nordd.) fen

Fennek /'fɛnɛk/ *der;* ~**s,** ~**s** *od.* ~**e** fennec

Fenster /'fɛnstɐ/ *das;* ~**s,** ~ (auch DV) window; **im** ~ **liegen** be leaning out of the window; **[sein] Geld zum** ~ **hinauswerfen** (fig.) throw [one's] money down the drain; **weg vom** ~ **sein** (ugs.) be right out of it

Fenster-: ~**bank** *die; Pl.* ~**bänke** window sill; window ledge; ~**bogen** *der* (Archit.) window arch; ~**brett** *das* ►►~**bank**; ~**brief[umschlag]** *der* window envelope; ~**brüstung** *die* window breast; ~**flügel** *der* [side of a/the] window; ~**front** *die* window frontage; ~**gips** *der* (Med.) fenestrated plaster; ~**gitter** *das* window grille *or* grating; ~**glas** *das; Pl.* ~**gläser** **1** window glass; **2** (ungeschliffenes Glas) plain glass; **eine Brille aus** ~**glas** glasses with plain glass lenses; ~**griff** *der* window catch; ~**heber** *der* (Kfz.-W.) window regulator; (elektrisch) window [regulator] mechanism; **das Auto hat elektrische** ~**heber** this car has electric windows; ~**kitt** *der* window putty; ~**klappe** *die* shutter opening; ~**kreuz** *das* mullion and transom; ~**kurbel** *die* window handle; ~**laden** *der; Pl.* ~**läden,** *auch* ~~**:** [window] shutter; ~**leder** *das* wash leather

fensterln /'fɛnstɐln/ *itr. V.* (bes. südd., österr.) climb through one's sweetheart's window

fenster-, Fenster-: ~**los** *Adj.* windowless; ~**nische** *die* window recess; ~**öffnung** *die* window opening; ~**platz** *der* window seat; seat by the window; ~**putzer** *der;* ~~**s,** ~~, ~**putzerin** *die;* ~~, ~~**nen** ►ⓘ **S. 113** window cleaner; ~**rahmen** *der* window frame; ~**ritze** *die* gap between window pane and frame; ~**rose** *die* (Archit.) rose window; ~**scheibe** *die* window pane; ~**sims** *der od. das* ►►~**bank**; ~**sturz** *der* **1** **der Prager** ~**sturz** (Hist.) the Defenestration of Prague; **2** (~abschluss) [window] lintel; ~**verband** *der* (Med.) fenestrated dressing

Ferial·tag /fe'ri̯aːl-/ *der* (österr.) ►**Ferientag**

Ferien /'feːri̯ən/ *Pl.* **1** (Arbeitspause) holiday (Brit.); vacation (Amer.); (Werks~) shutdown; holiday (Brit.); (Parlaments~) recess; (Hochschul~) vacation; **in den großen/während der großen** ~**:** in/during the summer holidays/vacation; ~ **haben** have a *or* be on holiday/vacation; **das Parlament geht in die** ~**:** parliament goes into recess **2** (Urlaub) holiday[s *pl.*] (Brit.); vacation (Amer.); **in die** ~ **fahren** go on holiday/vacation

Ferien- holiday… (Brit.); vacation… (Amer.); *s. auch* **Urlaubs-**

Ferien-: ~**arbeit** *die* vacation work; **eine** ~**arbeit** a vacation job; ~**aufenthalt** *der* holiday (Brit.); vacation (Amer.); ~**beginn** *der* start of the school holidays/vacation; ~**dorf** *das* holiday/vacation village; ~**erlebnis** *das* holiday/vacation experience; ~**gast** *der* holiday/vacation guest; ~**haus** *das* holiday/vacation house; ~**heim** *das* holiday/vacation home; ~**kind** *das: child on a state-subsidized holiday/vacation in the country or at the seaside;* ~**kolonie** *die* [children's] holiday/vacation camp; ~**kurs** *der* vacation course; ~**lager** *das* holiday/vacation camp; ~**ordnung** *die* holiday/vacation dates *pl.*; ~**ort** *der* holiday/vacation resort; **ein idyllischer** ~**ort** an idyllic holiday/vacation spot *or* spot for a holiday/vacation; ~**paradies** *das* holiday[-maker's]/vacation[er's] paradise; ~**reise** *die* holiday/vacation trip; ~**sonder·zug** *der* special holiday/vacation train; holiday/vacation special; ~**tag** *der* day [of one's holiday (Brit.) *or* (Amer.) vacation]; ~**zeit** *die* holiday (Brit.); vacation (Amer.); **zu Beginn der** ~**zeit** at the beginning of the holidays/vacation; ~**zentrum** *das* holiday/vacation centre *or* resort

Ferkel /'fɛrkl̩/ *das;* ~**s,** ~ **1** (junges Schwein) piglet **2** (ugs. abwertend) pig; **du [altes]** ~**!** you [dirty] pig!

Ferkelei *die;* ~, ~**en** (ugs. abwertend) (Benehmen) filthy behaviour; (Bemerkung) dirty remark; **seine** ~**en** his filth *sing. or* smut *sing.*

ferkeln *itr. V.* **1** (Ferkel werfen) farrow **2** (ugs. abwertend) be filthy

Fermate /fɛr'maːtə/ *die;* ~, ~**n** (Musik) pause

Ferment /fɛr'mɛnt/ *das;* ~**[e]s,** ~**e** (veralt.) ferment (arch.); enzyme

Fermentation /fɛrmɛnta'tsi̯oːn/ *die;* ~, ~**en** fermentation

fermentieren *tr. V.* ferment

fern /fɛrn/

A *Adj.* **1** (räumlich) distant, far-off, faraway ‹*country, region, etc.*›; **jmdn./etw. von jmdm./etw.** ~ **halten** keep sb./sth. away from sb./sth.; **sich von jmdm./etw.** ~ **halten** keep away from sb./sth. **2** (zeitlich) distant ‹*past, future*›; **eine Geschichte aus** ~**en Tagen** a story from far-off days; **in [nicht allzu]** ~**er Zukunft** in the [not too] distant future; **der Tag ist nicht mehr** ~**:** the day is not far off; **der Frieden ist** ~**er denn je** peace is farther away than ever

B *adv.* ~ **von der Heimat [sein/leben]** [be/live] far from home; **etw. von** ~ **betrachten** look at sth. from a distance; **von** ~ **betrachtet** (fig.) looked at from a distance; **so von** ~ **betrachtet würde ich …** looking at it from a distance, I should …; **das liegt mir** ~**:** that is the last thing I want to do; **es liegt mir** ~**, das zu tun** I shouldn't dream of doing that; **das sei** ~ **von mir, dass ich dich jemals verraten werde** (geh.) heaven forbid that I should ever betray you; **jmdm.** ~ **stehen** (geh.) not be on close terms with sb.; *s. auch* **Osten 3**; **nahe B 1**

C *Präp. mit Dat.* (geh.) far [away] from; a long way from; ~ **der Heimat [leben]** [live] far from home *or* a long way from home

fern-, Fern-: ~ab /-'-/ (geh.) **A** *Adv.* far away; **~ab von aller Zivilisation** far [away] from all civilization; **B** *Präp. mit Dat.* **~ab aller Zivilisation** far [away] from all civilization; **~amt** *das* (veralt.) telephone exchange; **~auslöser** *der* (Fot.) remote shutter release; **~bahn** *die* main-line railway; **~bahn·hof** *der* main-line station; **~beben** *das* (Geol.) distant earthquake; **~bedienung** *die* remote control; **~bereich** *der* (bes. Fot.) distance; **~|bleiben** *unr. itr. V.; mit sein* (geh.) stay away; **dem Unterricht ~bleiben** stay away from lessons; **~blick** *der* view

ferne *in* **von ~** (geh.) from far off *or* away

Ferne *die;* **~, ~n** **1** (räumlich) distance; **etw. in weiter ~ erblicken** see sth. in the far distance; **ein Gruß aus der ~:** greetings from afar *or* far away; **in die ~ ziehen** (geh.) travel to far-off parts [of the world] **2** (Zukunft) future; (Vergangenheit) past; **das liegt noch/schon in weiter ~:** that is still far off *or* a long time away/that was a long time ago

ferner *Adv.* **1** in addition; furthermore; **er rangiert unter „~ liefen"** (fig.) he is an also-ran **2** (geh.: künftig) in [the] future; **auch ~ etw. tun** continue to do sth.

ferner... *Adj.* (Papierdt.) further

ferner·hin *Adv.* **1** in [the] future; **wir werden ihn auch ~ unterstützen** we shall continue to support him. **2** ▸**ferner 1**

fern-, Fern-: ~fahrer *der,* **~fahrerin** *die* ▸❶ **S. 113** long-distance lorry driver (Brit.) *or* (Amer.) trucker; **~fahrer·lokal** *das* transport café; **~fahrt** *die* long run *or* trip; **~flug** *der* long-distance *or* long-haul flight; **~gelenkt** *Adj.* remote-controlled; (fig.: durch Geheimdienste usw.) controlled; **eine ~gelenkte Rakete** a guided missile; **~geschoss,** ***~geschoß** *das* (Milit.) long-range missile; **~gespräch** *das* long-distance call; trunk call; **ein ~gespräch mit jmdm./London führen** speak to *or* with sb./London long-distance; **~gesteuert** *Adj.* ▸**~gelenkt**; **~glas** *das; Pl.* **~gläser** binoculars *pl.*; **etw. mit dem ~glas erkennen** make sth. out with binoculars; **~|gucken** *itr. V.* (ugs.) watch telly (coll.) *or* the box (coll.); ***~|halten** ▸**fern A1**; **~heizung** *die* district heating system; **~her** *Adv.* (geh.) **[von] ~her** from afar; **~hin** *Adv.* (geh.) far off; **~kopierer** *der* fax machine; **~kurs[us]** *der* correspondence course; **~laster** *der* (ugs.) long-distance lorry (Brit.) *or* (Amer.) truck; **~last·fahrer** *der,* **~last·fahrerin** *die* long-distance lorry driver (Brit.) *or* (Amer.) trucker; **~last·zug** *der* [long-distance] articulated lorry; **~lehr·gang** *der* correspondence course; **~leihe** *die* **1** (Dienststelle) inter-library loans department; **2** (Leihverkehr) inter-library loan system; **ein Buch über [die] ~leihe bestellen** order a book through inter-library loans; **~leitung** *die* **1** (Postw.) long-distance line; **2** (Energiewirtsch.) long-distance cable; **~|lenken** *tr. V.* operate by remote control; **~lenkung** *die* remote control; **~lenk·waffen** *Pl.* guided missiles; **~licht** *das* (Kfz-W.) full beam; **das ~licht anhaben** drive on full beam; ***~|liegen** ▸**fern B**

Fern·melde-: ~amt *das* telephone exchange; **~gebühren** *Pl.* telephone charges; **~netz** *das* telecommunications network; **~satellit** *der* communications satellite; **~technik** *die* telecommunications *sing., no art.*; **~truppe** *die* (Milit.) signal corps; **~turm** *der* telecommunications tower; **~verkehr** *der* telecommunication; **~wesen** *das* telecommunications *pl.*

fern-, Fern-: ~mündlich **A** *Adj.* telephone ‹*communication*›; **B** *adv.* by telephone; **~ost** *in* **in/aus** *usw.* **~ost** in/from etc. the Far East; **in/nach ~ost** in/to the Far East; **~östlich** *Adj.* Far Eastern; **eine ~östliche Schönheit** an oriental beauty; **~rohr** *das* telescope; **~ruf** *der* telephone number; **~ruf: 45678** telephone *or* tel.: 45678; **~schach** *das* correspondence chess; **~schaltung** *die* remote control system; **durch ~schaltung** by remote control; **~schreiben** *das* telex [message]; **~schreiber** *der* telex [machine]; teleprinter; **~schriftlich** **A** *Adj.* telex ‹*message*›; **B** *adv.* by telex; **~schuss,** ***~schuß** *der* (Ballspiele) long-range shot

Fernseh-: ~abend *der* evening in front of the television; **~ansager** *der,* **~ansagerin** *die* television announcer; **~ansprache** *die* television address; **~anstalt** *die* television organization; **~antenne** *die* television aerial (Brit.) *or* (Amer.) antenna; **~apparat** *der* television [set]; **~auftritt** *der* television appearance; **~aufzeichnung** *die* telerecording; **~bericht** *der* television report; **~bild** *das* television picture; **~diskussion** *die* [television] discussion programme; **~duell** *das* televised [head-to-head] debate; **~empfang** *der* television reception

fern|sehen *unr. itr. V.* watch television

Fern·sehen *das;* **~s** television; **im ~:** on television; **vom** *od.* **im ~ übertragen werden** be televised; be shown on television; **das ~ brachte eine Sendung über ...** (*Akk.*) they showed a programme about ... on television

Fern·seher *der;* **~s, ~** (ugs.) **1** (Gerät) telly (Brit. coll.); TV; television **2** (Zuschauer) [television] viewer

Fernseh-: ~fassung *die* television version; **~film** *der* television film; **~frau** *die* woman in television; (im Fernsehen auftretend) woman on television; [female] television personality; **~gebühren** *Pl.* television licence fee; **~gerät** *das* television [set]; **~interview** *das* television interview; **~journalist** *der,* **~journalistin** *die* ▸❶ **S. 113** television reporter; **~kamera** *die* television camera; **~kanal** *der* television channel; **~leute** *Pl.* television people; **~lotterie** *die* television lottery; **~macher** *der,* **~macherin** *die* ▸❶ **S. 113** television programme maker; **~magazin** *das* [TV] magazine programme; **~mann** *der* man in television; (im Fernsehen auftretend) man on television; television personality; **~moderator** *der,* **~moderatorin** *die* ▸❶ **S. 113** television presenter; **~nachrichten** *Pl.* television news; **~produktion** *die* television production; **~programm** *das* **1** (Sendungen) television programmes *pl.*; **2** (Kanal) television channel; **3** (Blatt, Programmheft) television [programme] guide; **~publikum** *das* viewing public; **~rechte** *Pl.* television rights; **~reporter** *der,* **~reporterin** *die* moderator television reporter; **~satellit** *der* television satellite; **~schirm** *der* television screen; **~sender** *der* television station; (technische Anlage) television transmitter; **~sendung** *die* television programme; **~serie** *die* television series; (Fortsetzungsgeschichte) television serial; **~sessel** *der* television chair; **~show** *die* television show; **~spiel** *das* television play; **~spot** *der* television commercial; **~sprecher** *der,* **~sprecherin** *die* ▸**~ansager**; **~star** *der* television star; **~station** *die* television station; **~studio** *das* television studio; **~team** *das* television crew; **~techniker** *der,* **~technikerin** *die* ▸❶ **S. 113** television engineer; **~truhe** *die* television cabinet; **~turm** *der* television tower; **~übertragung** *die* television broadcast; **~werbung** *die* television advertising; **~zeitschrift** *die* TV magazine; **~zuschauer** *der,* **~zuschauerin** *die* television viewer

Fern·sicht *die* (Aussicht) view; (gute Sicht) visibility

fern·sichtig *Adj.* ▸**weitsichtig**

Fern·sprech- (bes. Amtsspr.) ▸**Telefon-**

Fernsprech-: ~amt *das* telephone [area] office; **~ansage·dienst** *der* telephone information service; **~an·schluss,** ***~an·schluß** *der* telephone line; **noch keinen ~anschluss haben** not yet be connected to the telephone network; **~apparat** *der* telephone; **~auftrags·dienst** *der* telephone services *pl.*; **ich möchte mich vom ~auftragsdienst wecken lassen** I'd like to book an alarm call; **~auskunft** *die* directory enquiries *sing., no art.*; **eine Telefonnummer über die** *od.* **von der ~auskunft bekommen** get a [telephone] number from *or* through directory enquiries; **~automat** *der* coin-box telephone; pay phone; **~buch** *das* telephone book *or* directory

Fern·sprecher *der* telephone

Fernsprech-: ~gebühren *Pl.* telephone charges; **~nummer** *die* telephone number; **~säule** *die* roadside telephone; **~teilnehmer** *der,* **~teilnehmerin** *die* telephone subscriber; telephone customer (Amer.); **~verbindung** *die* telephone connection *or* link; **~verkehr** *der* telephone communication; **~zelle** *die* telephone booth *or* (Brit.) box; call box (Brit.)

fern-, Fern-: ***~|stehen** ▸**fern B**; **~|steuern** *tr. V.* ▸**~lenken**; **~steuerung** *die* (Technik) remote control; (fig.: durch Geheimdienste usw.) control; **~straße** *die* [principal] trunk road; major road; **~studium** *das* **1** (Studium ohne personale Medien) correspondence course; ≈ Open University course (Brit.); **2** (DDR) extramural studies *pl.*; **~trauung** *die* marriage by proxy; **~universität** *die* ≈ Open University (Brit.); **~unterricht** *der* correspondence courses *pl.*; **~verkehr** *der* long-distance traffic; **~verkehrs·mittel** *das* form of long-distance transport; **~verkehrs·straße** *die* ▸**~straße**; **~wahl** *die* (Postw.) [automatic] trunk dialling; long-distance dialling; **~wärme** *die* district heating; **~weh** *das* (geh.) wanderlust; **~ziel** *das* **1** (zeitlich) long-term aim; **etw. als ~ziel anstreben** aim for sth. in the long term; **2** (räumlich) distant destination; **~zug** *der* long-distance train

Ferrit /fɛ'ri:t/ *der;* **~s, ~e** ferrite

Ferrit·antenne *die* ferrite-rod aerial *or* (Amer.) antenna

Ferro- /fɛro-/ ferro-

Ferro·magnetismus *der* ferromagnetism

Ferse /'fɛrzə/ *die;* **~, ~n** ▸❶ **S. 435** heel; **jmdm. in die ~n treten** kick sb. in the heel; (fig.) **sich an jmds. ~n** (*Akk.*)**/sich jmdm. an die ~n heften** stick [hard] on sb.'s heels; **jmdm. [dicht] auf den ~n sitzen** *od.* **sein** (ugs.) be [hard *or* close] on sb.'s heels; **jmdm. auf den ~n bleiben** stick on sb.'s heels; stay on sb.'s tail; **ich habe die Polizei auf den ~n** (ugs.) the police are on my tail; **er hatte Löcher in den ~n** he had holes in the heels of his socks

Fersen-: ~bein *das* ▸❶ **S. 435** (Anat.) heel bone; calcaneum; **~geld** *in* **~geld geben** (ugs. scherzh.) take to one's heels

fertig /'fɛrtɪç/ *Adj.* **1** (völlig hergestellt) finished ‹*manuscript, picture, etc.*›; **etw. ~ machen** finish sth.; **etw. ~ stellen** complete *or* finish sth.; **das Essen ist ~:** lunch/dinner *etc.* is ready; **und ~ ist der Lack** *od.* **die Laube** (ugs.) and there you are; and bob's your uncle (Brit. coll.) **2** (zu Ende) finished; **[mit etw.] ~ sein/werden** have finished/finish [sth.]; **bist du ~?** have you finished?; **mit jmdm. ~ sein** (ugs.) be finished *or* through with sb.; **mit etw. ~ werden** (fig.) cope with sth.; **sie wird mit dem Jungen einfach nicht mehr ~** (ugs.) she cannot cope with the boy any more **3** (bereit, verfügbar) ready (**zu, für** for); **zum Abmarsch/Start ~ sein** be ready to march/ready for take-off; **etw. ~ machen** get sth. ready; **sich für etw. ~ machen** get ready for sth.; **auf die Plätze — ~ — los!** on your marks, get set, go! (Sport); (bei Kindern auch:) ready, steady, go! **4** (ugs.: erschöpft) shattered (coll.); **mit den Nerven ~ sein** be at the end of one's tether; **jmdn. ~ machen** (erschöpfen) wear sb. out; (schikanieren) wear sb. down; (deprimieren) get sb. down; (salopp: zusammenschlagen, töten) do sb. in (sl.); (ugs.: zurechtweisen) tear sb. off a strip (coll.); **der Lärm macht mich [ganz] ~:** that noise is getting me down **5** (reif) mature ‹*person, artist, etc.*› **6** **etw. ~ bekommen** *od.* **bringen** *od.* (ugs.) **kriegen** manage sth; **so etwas bringst** *od.* **bekommst** *od.* (ugs.) **kriegst auch nur du ~!** (iron.) only you could manage to do a thing like that!; **ich brächte** *od.* **bekäme** *od.* (ugs.) **kriegte es nicht ~, jmdn. zu erschießen** I couldn't bring myself to shoot anybody; **der bringt** *od.* **bekommt** *od.* (ugs.) **kriegt das ~!** (iron.) I wouldn't put it past him; **sie bringt** *od.*

bekommt od. (ugs.) kriegt es ~ und sagt ihr das she is capable of saying that to her

fertig-, Fertig-: **~bau** der; Pl. ~~ten **1** (Gebäude) prefabricated building; **2** (Herstellung) prefabricated building; prefabrication; **~bau·weise** die prefabricated construction; prefabrication; etw. in ~bauweise errichten build sth. by the prefabricated method; ***~|bekommen**, ***~|bringen** ▸fertig 6

fertigen tr. V. make; von Hand/maschinell gefertigte Waren hand-made/machine-produced goods

Fertig-: **~erzeugnis** das, **~fabrikat** das finished product; **~gericht** das ready-to-serve meal; ein ~gericht aus der Dose a meal out of or from a tin (Brit.) or (Amer.) can; **~haus** das prefabricated house; prefab (coll.)

Fertigkeit die; ~, ~en skill; eine ~ in etw. (Dat.) haben be skilled in or at sth.; ~ im Zeichnen/Nähen skill in or at drawing/sewing

fertig-, Fertig-: ***~|kriegen** ▸fertig 6; ***~|machen** ▸fertig 1, 4; **~produkt** das finished product; ***~|stellen** ▸fertig 1; **~stellung** die completion; **~teil** das prefabricated part

Fertigung die; ~: production; manufacture

Fertigungs- production

Fertigungs-: **~kosten** Pl. production or manufacturing costs; **~verfahren** das production or manufacturing process

Fertig·ware die finished product

Fertilität /fɛrtili'tɛ:t/ die; ~ (Biol., Med.) fertility

fes, Fes¹ /fɛs/ das; ~, ~ (Musik) F flat

Fes² /fe:s/ der; ~[es], ~[e] fez

fesch /fɛʃ/ Adj. **1** (bes. österr.: hübsch) smart ‹woman, suit, etc.› **2** (österr.: nett) good; sei ~ und komm mit! be a sport and come too!

Fessel¹ /'fɛsl/ die; ~, ~n (auch fig.) fetter; shackle; (Kette) chain; jmdm. ~n anlegen, (geh.) jmdn. in ~n legen fetter sb./put sb. in chains

Fessel² die; ~, ~n ▸❶ S. 435 (Anat.) **1** (bei Huftieren) pastern **2** (bei Menschen) ankle

Fessel-: **~ballon** der captive balloon; **~gelenk** das (Zool.) pastern joint

fesseln tr. V. **1** tie up; (mit Ketten) chain up; jmdn. an etw. (Akk.) ~: tie/chain sb. to sth.; jmdn. an Händen und Füßen ~: tie sb. hand and foot; jmdm. die Hände auf den Rücken ~: tie sb.'s hands behind his/her back; ans Bett/Haus/an den Rollstuhl gefesselt sein (fig.) be confined to [one's] bed/tied to the house/confined to a wheelchair; jmdn. an sich (Akk.) ~ (fig.) bind sb. to oneself **2** (faszinieren) ‹book› grip; ‹work, person› fascinate; ‹personality› captivate; ‹idea› possess; das Buch hat mich so gefesselt I was so gripped by the book; jmdn. durch etw. ~: captivate sb. with sth.

fesselnd
A Adj. compelling
B adv. compellingly

Fesselung, Fesslung, ***Feßlung** die; ~, ~en (Schach) block

fest /fɛst/
A Adj. **1** (nicht flüssig od. gasförmig) solid; ~e Nahrung solid food; ~e Gestalt od. Form[en] annehmen take on a definite shape **2** (straff) firm, tight ‹bandage› **3** (kräftig) firm ‹handshake›; (tief) sound ‹sleep› **4** (haltbar, solide) sturdy ‹shoes›; tough, strong ‹fabric›; solid ‹house, shell› **5** (energisch) firm ‹tread›; steady ‹voice›; eine ~e Hand brauchen (fig.) need a firm hand **6** (unbeirrbar) der ~en Überzeugung od. Meinung sein, dass ... be firmly convinced or of the firm opinion that ... **7** (endgültig) firm ‹appointment, date›; eine ~e Zusage machen make a firm or definite commitment; s. auch Fuß 2 **8** (konstant) fixed, permanent ‹address›; fixed ‹income›; einen ~en Freund/eine ~e Freundin haben have a steady boyfriend/girlfriend; in ~en Händen sein (fig.) be spoken for; einen ~en Platz in etw. (Dat.) haben (fig.) be firmly established in sth. **9** (Milit. veralt.) fortified ‹position›
B adv. **1** (straff) ‹tie, grip› tight[ly] **2** (ugs. auch feste) (tüchtig) ‹work› with a will; ‹eat› heartily; ‹sleep› soundly; ~ zuschlagen plant a solid punch; er schläft [gerade] ~: he is fast asleep; ~ zulangen tuck in; ~ feiern have a real celebration; immer ~[e] drauf od. druff! (salopp) get stuck in! (coll.); let him/them have it! **3** (unbeirrbar) ‹believe, be convinced› firmly; sich auf jmdn./etw. ~ verlassen rely one hundred per cent on sb./sth. **4** (endgültig) firmly; definitely; etw. ~ vereinbaren come to a firm or definite arrangement about sth. **5** (auf Dauer) permanently; ~ angestellt permanent ‹employee›; ~ angestellt sein be permanently employed or a permanent member of staff; ~ befreundet sein be close friends; (als Paar) be going steady; jmdn. ~ einstellen give sb. a permanent job; employ sb. as a permanent member of staff; ~ besoldet full-time [and] salaried

Fest das; ~[e]s, ~e **1** (Veranstaltung) celebration; (Party) party; man muss die ~e feiern, wie sie fallen you don't get a chance for a celebration every day of the week; es ist mir ein ~ (scherzh.) [it's] my pleasure **2** (Feiertag) festival; (Kirchenfest) feast; festival; bewegliches/unbewegliches ~: movable/immovable feast; frohes ~! happy Christmas/Easter!

fest-, Fest-: **~akt** der ceremony; **~angestellt** ▸fest B5; **~angestellte** der/die permanent employee; **~ansprache** die address; **~|backen** itr. V. (landsch.) stick; **~|beißen** unr. refl. V. sich in etw. (Dat.) ~beißen ‹dog etc.› sink its teeth firmly into sth.; sich an einem Problem ~beißen (fig.) get bogged down in a problem; **~beleuchtung** die festive lighting; in ~beleuchtung erstrahlen be ablaze with festive illuminations; **~besoldet** ▸fest B5; **~besoldete** der/die; adj. Dekl. full-time member of staff; **~betrag** der fixed amount; **~|binden** unr. tr. V. tie [up]; etw. an einem Baum/Pfosten ~binden tie sth. to a tree/post; **~|bleiben** unr. itr. V.; mit sein stand firm; **~|drehen** tr. V. screw [up] tight

feste Adv. (ugs.) ▸fest B 2

Feste die; ~, ~n (veralt.) fortress; castle

fest-, Fest-: **~essen** das banquet; **~|fahren** unr. itr., refl. V. (itr. V. mit sein) get stuck; (fig.) get bogged down; der Wagen hat sich od. ist ~gefahren the car got stuck; **~|fressen** unr. refl. V. **1** (sich verklemmen) ‹engine› seize up; ‹saw› get stuck; **2** (fig.: sich einprägen) sich in jmdm. ~fressen become fixed in sb.'s mind; **~|frieren** unr. itr. V.; mit sein freeze up; freeze solid; **~gabe** die (geh.) gift; **~gefügt** ▸fügen A2; **~gelage** das ▸Gelage; **~geld** das (Bankw.) time deposit; **~gottesdienst** der festival service; **~|haken** **A** tr. V. (befestigen) hook up; etw. an etw. (Dat.) ~haken hook sth. to sth.; **B** refl. V. get caught (an + Dat. on); **~halle** die festival hall; **~|halten** **A** unr. tr. V. **1** (halten, packen) hold on to; jmdn. am Arm ~halten hold on to sb.'s arm; etw. mit den Händen ~halten hold sth. in one's hands; **2** (nicht weiterleiten) withhold ‹letter, parcel, etc.›; **3** (verhaftet haben) hold, detain ‹suspect›; **4** (aufzeichnen, fixieren) record; capture; etw. in Bild und Ton ~halten record or capture sth. in sound and vision; etw. mit der Kamera ~halten capture sth. with the camera; **5** (konstatieren) record; ~halten, dass ... record the fact that ...; **B** unr. refl. V. (sich anklammern) sich an jmdm./etw. ~halten hold on to sb./sth.; halt dich ~! hold tight!; (fig. ugs.) brace yourself!; **C** unr. itr. V. an jmdm./etw. ~halten stand by sb./sth.; **~|hängen** unr. itr. V. get caught; [mit etw.] an/in etw. (Dat.) ~hängen get [sth.] caught on/in sth.

festigen /'fɛstɪgn̩/
A tr. V. strengthen ‹friendship, alliance, marriage, etc.›; consolidate ‹position›; in sich (Dat.) gefestigt sein be strong
B refl. V. ‹friendship, ties› become stronger

Festigkeit die; ~ **1** (Entschlossenheit) firmness **2** (Standhaftigkeit) steadfastness; resolution; sein Ziel mit ~ verfolgen pursue one's aim with [great] resolution **3** (von Stoffen) strength

Festigkeits·lehre die [theory of] strength of materials

Festigung die; ~: strengthening; (einer Stellung) consolidation

Festival /'fɛstivəl/ das; ~s, ~s festival

Festival·besucher der, **Festival·besucherin** die visitor to a/the festival

Festivität /fɛstivi'tɛ:t/ die; ~, ~en (veralt., scherzh.) festivity; celebration

fest-, Fest-: **~|klammern** **A** tr. V. etw. [an etw. (Dat.)] ~klammern clip sth. on [to sth.]; Wäsche an der Leine ~klammern peg washing [up] on the line; **B** refl. V. sich an jmdm./etw. ~klammern cling [on] to sb./sth.; **~|kleben** **A** itr. V.; mit sein stick (an + Dat. to); **B** tr. V. stick; etw. an etw. (Dat.) ~kleben stick sth. to sth.; **~kleid** das evening dress; die Stadt legte ihr ~kleid an (fig. geh.) the town took on a festive look; **~kleidung** die formal dress; **~|klemmen** **A** itr. V.; mit sein ~geklemmt sein be stuck or jammed; **B** tr. V. wedge; jam; **~|klopfen** tr. V. bang ‹nail› in or home; bang ‹floorboard› down; (fig.) finalize ‹agreement›; **~|knoten** tr. V. etw. an etw. (Dat.) ~knoten tie sth. to sth.; **~komitee** das festival committee; **~komma** das (DV) fixed point; **~körper** der (Physik) solid; **~körper·physik** die solid-state physics sing., no art.; **~|krallen** refl. V. sich in etw. (Dat.) ~krallen dig its claws into sth.; sich an jmdm. ~krallen cling to sb. with its claws; ‹person› cling [on] to sb.; **~land** das **1** (Kontinent) continent; (im Gegensatz zu den Inseln) mainland; das europäische ~land the continent of Europe/the European mainland; **2** (fester Boden) land; auf dem ~land on dry land; **~ländisch** Adj. **1** (kontinental) continental ‹climate, shelf, etc.›; **2** (im Gegensatz zu den Inseln) mainland attrib.; **~land[s]·sockel** der (Geogr.) continental shelf; **~|laufen** **A** unr. itr., refl. V. (itr. V. mit sein) ‹ship› run aground, get stuck; ‹wheels› jam, get jammed; (fig.) ‹negotiations› reach a deadlock; ‹policy› get bogged down; das Schiff hat sich od. ist im Packeis ~gelaufen the ship has got stuck in the pack ice; **B** refl. V. (Sport) die Stürmer liefen sich immer wieder ~: the forwards could not find a way through [the defence]; **~legbar** Adj. das ist [nicht] eindeutig ~legbar it can[not] definitely be established; **~|legen** tr. V. **1** (verbindlich regeln) fix ‹time, deadline, price›; arrange ‹programme›; etw. gesetzlich ~legen prescribe sth. by law; **2** (verpflichten) sich [auf etw. (Akk.)] ~legen [lassen] commit oneself [to sth.]; jmdn. [auf etw. (Akk.)] ~legen tie sb. down [to sth.]; **3** (Bankw.) tie up ‹money›; **~legung** die; ~~, ~~en ▸festlegen: **1** fixing; arrangement; **2** commitment

festlich
A Adj. **1** festive ‹atmosphere› **2** (einem Fest gemäß) formal ‹dress›
B adv. **1** festively **2** (einem Fest gemäß) formally; etw. ~ begehen celebrate sth.

Festlichkeit die; ~, ~en **1** (Feier) celebration **2** (der Stimmung, Atmosphäre) festiveness; (Feierlichkeit, Würde) solemnity

fest-, Fest-: **~|liegen** unr. itr. V. **1** (nicht weiterkommen) be stuck; **2** (~stehen) have been fixed; ‹programme› have been arranged; **3** (Bankw.) ‹money› be tied up; **~|machen** **A** tr. V. **1** (befestigen) fix; (fig.) demonstrate ‹characteristic, fault›; **2** (~ vereinbaren) arrange ‹meeting etc.›; **3** (Seemannsspr.) moor ‹boat›; **B** itr. V. (Seemannsspr.) ▸anlegen B 1; **~mahl** das (geh.) banquet; **~meter** der od. das cubic metre (of solid timber); **~|nageln** tr. V. **1** (befestigen) nail (an + Dat. to); wie ~genagelt dastehen (ugs.) stand there as though rooted to the spot; **2** (ugs.: ~legen) jmdn. [auf etw. (Akk.)] ~nageln tie sb. down [to sth.]; sich auf etw. (Akk.) ~nageln lassen let oneself be tied [down] to sth.; **~nahme** die; ~~, ~~n arrest; bei seiner ~nahme when he was/is arrested; **~|nehmen** unr. tr. V. arrest; jmdn. vorläufig ~nehmen take sb. into custody

Feston /fɛs'tõ:/ das; ~s, ~s festoon

fest-, Fest-: **~platte** die (DV) hard disk; **~platz** der fairground; **~preis** der (Wirtsch.)

fixed price; **~programm** *das* festival programme; **~rede** *die* speech; **~redner** *der*, **~rednerin** *die* speaker; **~|rennen** *unr. refl. V.* **1** (ugs.) get tangled up; **2** (Sport) ▸ **~laufen B**; **~saal** *der* banqueting hall; (Ballsaal) ballroom; **~|saugen** *regelm. (auch unr.) refl. V.* attach itself (**an** + *Dat.* to); **~schmaus** *der* (veralt.) banquet; feast; **~schmuck** *der* festive decorations *pl.*; **im ~schmuck erstrahlen** be festively decorated; **~|schnallen** *tr. V.* tie (**an** + *Dat.* to); **der Pilot schnallte sich am Sitz ~:** the pilot strapped *or* fastened himself in; **~|schrauben** *tr. V.* screw [up] tight; **~|schreiben** *unr. tr. V.* establish; **~|schrift** *die* commemorative volume; (für Gelehrten) Festschrift; **~|setzen A** *tr. V.* **1** (~legen) fix ‹*time, deadline, price*›; lay down ‹*duties*›; **2** (in Haft nehmen) detain; **B** *refl. V.* **1** ‹*dust*› collect, settle; ‹*idea*› take root; **diese Idee hat sich bei ihm ~gesetzt** this idea has become fixed in his mind; **2** (ugs.: sich niederlassen) establish oneself; **~setzung** *die*; **~~, ~~en** ▸ **~setzen A: 1** fixing; laying down; **2** (selten) detention; **~|sitzen** *unr. itr. V.* **1** (haften) be stuck; **2** (nicht mehr weiterkommen) be stuck; **~spiel** *das* **1** *Pl.* festival; **die Bayreuther/Edinburger ~spiele** the Bayreuth/Edinburgh Festival *sing.*; **2** (Bühnenstück) festival production; **~spiel·haus** *das* festival theatre; **~|stecken A** *tr. V.* (befestigen) pin up; **B** *regelm. (auch unr.) itr. V.* (nicht weiterkommen) be stuck; **~|stehen** *unr. itr. V.* **1** (~gelegt sein) ‹*order, appointment, etc.*› have been fixed; **2** (unumstößlich sein) ‹*decision*› be definite; ‹*fact*› be certain; **~ steht** *od.* **es steht ~, dass ...** it is certain *or* definite that ...; **es steht ~, dass sie keine Chance haben** they certainly have no chance; **~stellbar** *Adj.* **1** (zu ermitteln) ascertainable; **die Ursache ist nicht mehr ~stellbar** the cause can no longer be ascertained *or* established; **2** (wahrnehmbar) detectable; diagnosable ‹*illness*›; **3** (arretierbar) lockable; securable ‹*lock*›; **~|stellen** *tr. V.* **1** (ermitteln) establish ‹*identity, age, facts*›; **das lässt sich [nicht] mit Sicherheit ~stellen** it can[not] be established with certainty *or* for certain; **2** (wahrnehmen) detect; diagnose ‹*illness*›; **er stellte ~, dass er sich geirrt hatte** he realized that he was wrong; **sie musste ~stellen, dass ...** she realized that ...; **die Ärzte konnten nur noch den Tod ~stellen** all the doctors could do was [to] confirm that the patient/victim *etc.* was dead; **3** (aussprechen) state ‹*fact*›; **ich muss ~stellen, dass ...** I must *or* am bound to say that ...; **4** (arretieren) secure, lock ‹*moving part*›; secure ‹*lock*›

Feststell-: ~hebel *der* locking lever; **~taste** *die* shift lock

Fest·stellung *die* **1** (Ermittlung) establishment **2** (Wahrnehmung) realization; **die ~ machen, dass ...** realize that ... **3** (Erklärung) statement; **die ~ treffen, dass ...** observe that ...

Fest-: ~stimmung *die* festive atmosphere *or* mood; **~stoff·rakete** *die* solid-fuel rocket; **~tafel** *die* (geh.) banquet table

Fest·tag *der* **1** holiday; (Kirchenfest) [religious] feast day; (Ehrentag) special day **2** (Festspieltag) [day of a/the] festival; **die Berliner ~e** the Berlin Festival *sing.*

Festtags·stimmung *die* festive atmosphere *or* mood

fest-: ~|treten *unr. tr. V.* tread down; **das tritt sich ~:** don't worry, it's good for the carpet (iron.); **~umrissen** ▸ **umreißen²**

Festung *die*; **~, ~en 1** (Verteidigungsanlage) fortress **2** (hist.: Haft) imprisonment [in a fortress]

Festungs-: ~anlage *die* fortification; **~graben** *der* moat; **~haft** *die* (hist.) imprisonment [in a fortress]; **~mauer** *die* wall of a/the fortress

fest-, Fest-: ~veranstaltung *die* official function; **~verwurzelt** ▸ **verwurzelt**; **~verzinslich** *Adj.* (Bankw.) fixed-interest *attrib.*; fixed-income *attrib.*; **~vortrag** *der* lecture; **~|wachsen** *unr. itr. V.; mit sein* **an** *od.* **auf etw.** (*Dat.*) **~wachsen** grow on [to] sth.; **~wiese** *die* festival site; **~zeit** *die* holiday (Brit.) *or* (Amer.) vacation [period]; **~zelt** *das* marquee; **~|ziehen** *unr. tr. V.* pull tight; **~zug** *der* procession; **~|zurren** *tr. V.* lash down [securely]

fetal /feˈtaːl/ *Adj.* (Med.) fetal

Fete /ˈfeːtə/ *die*; **~, ~n** (ugs.) party; **eine ~ geben** *od.* **feiern** have *or* throw a party

Fetisch /ˈfeːtɪʃ/ *der*; **~s, ~e** (Völkerk., fig.) fetish

Fetischismus *der*; **~:** fetishism *no art.*

Fetischist *der*; **~en, ~en**, **Fetischistin** *die*; **~, ~nen** fetishist

fett /fɛt/

A *Adj.* **1** (~reich) fatty ‹*food*›; **~er Speck** fat bacon; **das Fleisch war zu ~:** there was too much fat on the meat **2** (sehr dick) fat **3** (ugs.: üppig, reich) fat ‹*inheritance, wallet*›; **~e Jahre/Zeiten** rich years/good times; **~e Beute machen** make a rich haul **4** (ertragreich) rich ‹*soil*›; luxuriant ‹*vegetation*› **5** (Druckw.) bold; (breiter, größer) extra bold; **etw. ~ drucken** print sth. in bold/extra bold [type]; **~ gedruckt** bold

B *adv.* **~ essen** eat fatty foods; **~ kochen** use a lot of fat [in cooking]; **~ lachen** guffaw

Fett *das*; **~[e]s, ~e 1** fat; **pflanzliche/tierische ~e** vegetable/animal fats; (fig.) **das ~ abschöpfen** (ugs.) cream off the best; **sein ~ [ab]bekommen** *od.* **[ab]kriegen** (ugs.) get one's come-uppance (Amer.); **sein ~ [weg]haben** (ugs.) have been put in one's place *or* taught a lesson; **im ~ schwimmen** (ugs.) be rolling in it (coll.) **2** (~gewebe) fat; **~ ansetzen** ‹*animal*› fatten up; ‹*person*› put on weight; **die Gans hat viel ~:** the goose has a lot of fat on it; **~ schwimmt oben** (Spr.) fat people never drown!; (fig.) the rich never suffer

fett-, Fett-: ~absaugung *die* liposuction; **~ansatz** *der* fat; **er neigt zu ~ansatz** he tends to get fat *or* to put on weight easily; **~arm A** *Adj.* low-fat ‹*food*›; low in fat *pred.*; **B** *adv.* **~arm essen** eat low-fat foods; **~auge** *das* speck of fat; **~bauch** *der* (ugs.) paunch; fat stomach; **~bedarf** *der* fat requirement; **~creme** *die* enriched [skin] cream; **~depot** *das* (Physiol.) fat depot; **~druck** *der* bold type; **in ~druck** in bold [type]

fetten

A *tr. V.* (mit Fett einreiben) grease

B *itr. V.* (Fett absondern) be greasy

fett-, Fett-: ~film *der* greasy film; **~fleck[en]** *der* grease mark *or* spot; **~frei** *Adj.* non-fat; **~gebäck** *das*, **~gebackene** *das*; *adj. Dekl.* cakes *pl.* fried in fat; **~gedruckt** ▸ **fett A5**; **~gehalt** *der* fat content; **~geschwulst** *die* fatty tumour; **~gewebe** *das* ▸ **❶ S. 435** fatty tissue; **~haltig** *Adj.* fatty; **[sehr] ~haltig sein** contain [a lot of] fat; **~henne** *die* (Bot.) stonecrop; **Große ~henne** orpine; **~herz** *das* fatty heart; fat heart

fettig *Adj.* greasy; oily; greasy ‹*skin, saucepan, etc.*›

fett-, Fett-: ~kloß *der* (ugs. abwertend) fatty; fatso (sl.); **~leber** *die* ▸ **❶ S. 439** (Med.) fatty liver; **~leibig** *Adj.* obese; **~leibigkeit** *die*; **~~:** obesity; **~löslich** *Adj.* fat-soluble; **~näpfchen** *das*: **in [bei jmdm.] ins ~näpfchen treten** (scherzh.) put one's foot in it [with sb.]; **~polster** *das* subcutaneous fat *no indef. art.*; fat pad; **~reich A** *Adj.* high-fat ‹*food*›; **B** *adv.* **~reich essen** eat high-fat foods; **~sack** *der* (salopp abwertend) fatso (sl.); **~säure** *die* (Chemie) fatty acid; **~schicht** *die* layer of fat; **~stift** *der* **1** (Schreibgerät) grease pencil; lithographic pencil; **2** (Lippenstift) lip salve; **~stoffwechsel** *der* fat metabolism; **~sucht** *die* ▸ **❶ S. 439** (Med.) obesity; **~triefend** *Adj.* dripping with fat *postpos.*; **~wanst** *der* (salopp abwertend) fatso (sl.); **~wulst** *der od. die* roll of fat

Fetus /ˈfeːtʊs/ *der*; **~** *od.* **~ses, ~se** *od.* **Feten** (Med.) fetus

fetzen /ˈfɛtsn̩/ *tr. V.* (ugs.) tear; **die Musik/Platte fetzt unheimlich** (Jugendspr.) the music/record is really mind-blowing (coll.)

Fetzen *der*; **~s, ~ 1** scrap; **die Tapete hängt in ~ von der Wand** the wallpaper is hanging [off the wall] in shreds; **das Kleid ist in ~:** the dress is in tatters; **etw. in ~ [zer]reißen** tear sth. to pieces *or* shreds; **in ~ gehen** (ugs.) fall apart *or* to pieces; **dass die ~ fliegen** (ugs.) like mad (coll.) **2** (abwertend: billiges Kleid) **ein billiger ~:** cheap rags *pl.*

feucht /fɔyçt/ *Adj.* damp ‹*cloth, wall, hair*›; tacky ‹*paint*›; humid ‹*climate*›; sweaty, clammy ‹*hands*›; moist ‹*lips*›; lubricated ‹*condom*›; **die ~e Schnauze des Hundes** the dog's wet nose; **Oberhemden müssen ~ gebügelt werden** shirts must be ironed damp; **Gardinen ~ aufhängen** hang curtains while [they are] still damp; **etw. ~ abwischen** wipe sth. with a damp cloth; **eine ~e Aussprache haben** (scherzh.) spit when one speaks; **ein ~er Abend** (fig. ugs.) a boozy evening (coll.); **~e Augen bekommen** be close to tears; **das geht dich einen ~en Schmutz** *od.* **Kehricht an** (ugs.) that's none of your business

Feucht·biotop *das* (Ökol.) wetland

Feuchte *die*; **~:** humidity

feucht-, Feucht-: ~fröhlich *Adj.* (ugs. scherzh.) merry ‹*company*›; boozy (coll.) ‹*evening*›; **~gebiet** *das* wet area; **~heiß** *Adj.* hot and humid

Feuchtigkeit *die* **1** (leichte Nässe) moisture **2** (das Feuchtsein) dampness; **die ~ des Bodens/der Luft** the wetness of the soil/humidity of the air

Feuchtigkeits-: ~creme *die* (Kosmetik) moisturizing cream; moisturizer; **~gehalt** *der* moisture content; (der Luft) humidity; **~grad** *der* moisture level; (der Luft) humidity; **~messer** *der*; **~~s, ~~:** hygrometer; **~schutz** *der* (Bauw.) damp protection; protection against damp

feucht-: ~kalt *Adj.* cold and damp; **~warm** *Adj.* muggy; humid

feudal /fɔyˈdaːl/

A *Adj.* **1** feudal ‹*system*› **2** (aristokratisch) aristocratic ‹*regiment etc.*› **3** (ugs.: vornehm) plush ‹*hotel etc.*›

B *adv.* (ugs.: vornehm) **~ essen** have a slap-up meal (coll.); **~ Urlaub machen** have a plush holiday

Feudal-: ~gesellschaft *die* feudal society; **~herr** *der* feudal lord; **~herrschaft** *die* feudalism

Feudalismus *der*; **~:** feudalism *no art.*

feudalistisch *Adj.* feudalistic

Feudal-staat *der* feudal state

Feuer /ˈfɔyɐ/ *das*; **~s, ~ 1** fire; **[ein Gegensatz] wie ~ und Wasser sein** be as different as chalk and cheese; **das Essen aufs ~ stellen/vom ~ nehmen** put the food on to cook/take the food off the heat; **jmdn. um ~ bitten** ask sb. for a light; **jmdm. ~ geben** give sb. a light; **das olympische ~:** the Olympic flame *or* torch; **mit dem ~ spielen** play with fire; **er ist ganz ehrlich, für ihn** *od.* **dafür lege ich die Hand ins ~:** he is totally honest, I'd swear to it; **~ speiend** fire-breathing ‹*dragon*›; ‹*volcano*› spewing fire; *s. auch* **brennen B 1 2** (Brand) fire; blaze; **~!** fire!; **[für etw.] ~ und Flamme sein** be full of enthusiasm [for sth.]; **~ fangen** catch fire; (fig.: sich verlieben) be smitten; (fig.: sich schnell begeistern) be fired with enthusiasm; **für jmdn. durchs ~ gehen** go through hell and high water for sb.; **zwischen zwei ~ geraten** be caught between the devil and the deep blue sea; **jmdm. ~ unter dem Hintern machen** (salopp) put a squib under sb. **3** (Milit.) fire; **unter feindliches ~ geraten** come under enemy fire; **das ~ einstellen** cease fire; **jmdn./etw. unter ~ nehmen** fire on sb./sth.; **[gebt] ~!** fire!; **~ frei!** open fire! **4** (Leuchten, Funkeln) sparkle; blaze; **ihre Augen sprühten ~:** her eyes blazed [with fire] **5** (innerer Schwung) fire; passion; **das ~ der Jugend** the fire *or* passion of youth; **das Pferd/der Wein hat [viel] ~:** the horse has [a lot of] spirit/the wine is strong and full-bodied

feuer-, Feuer-: ~alarm *der* fire alarm; **~alarm geben** raise the [fire] alarm; **~anzünder** *der*; **~~s, ~~:** firelighter; **~befehl** *der* (Milit.) order to fire;

~bekämpfung *die* firefighting; **~bereit** *Adj.* (Milit.) ready to fire *postpos.*; **~beständig** *Adj.* fire-resistant; **~bestattung** *die* cremation; **~bock** *der* firedog; andiron; **~bohne** *die* (Bot.) scarlet runner [bean]; **~büchse** *die* 1 (Technik) firebox; 2 (veralt.: Gewehr) musket; **~eifer** *der* enthusiasm; zest; **~einstellung** *die* cessation of fire; (Waffenstillstand) ceasefire; **~fest** *Adj.* heat-resistant ‹*dish, plate*›; fireproof ‹*material*›; **~flüssig** *Adj.* molten ‹*rock, lava*›; **~gefahr** *die* fire hazard *or* risk; **bei ~gefahr** when there is a risk of fire; **~gefährlich** *Adj.* [in]flammable; **~gefecht** *das* gun battle; **~haken** *der* poker; **~holz** *das* firewood; **~kult** *der* fire cult

Feuerland *(das)*; **~s** Tierra del Fuego

Feuerländer *der*; **~s, ~**, **Feuerländerin** *die*; **~, ~nen** Fuegian

Feuer-: ~leiter *die* (bei Häusern) fire escape; (beim ~wehrauto) [fireman's] ladder; (fahrbar) turntable ladder; **~lösch·boot** *das* fireboat; **~löscher** *der* fire extinguisher; **~melder** *der* fire alarm

feuern

A *tr. V.* 1 (ugs.: entlassen) fire (coll.); sack (coll.) 2 (ugs.: schleudern, werfen) fling; **jmdm. eine ~** (salopp) belt sb. one 3 (heizen) fire ‹*stove*›; **mit Holz ~:** have wood fires

B *itr. V.* (Milit.) fire (**auf** + *Akk.* at)

feuer-, Feuer-: ~patsche *die* fire beater; **~pause** *die* (Milit.) lull in the fighting; **~polizei** *die: authorities responsible for fire precautions and firefighting;* **~probe** *die* 1 (Prüfung) test; **die ~probe bestehen** pass the [acid] test; 2 (Gottesurteil) ordeal by fire; **~qualle** *die* stinging jellyfish; **~rad** *das* 1 (~werkskörper) Catherine wheel; 2 (Wagenrad) fire wheel; **~rot** *Adj.* fiery red; flaming red; **~rot werden** (fig.) turn crimson *or* scarlet; **~salamander** *der* fire salamander; **~säule** *die* column of fire

Feuers·brunst *die* (geh.) great fire; conflagration

feuer-, Feuer-: ~schein *der* fiery glow; glow of the/a fire; **~schiff** *das* lightship; **~schlucker** *der*, **~schluckerin** *die* fire-eater; **~schutz** *der* 1 (Brandschutz) fire prevention *or* protection; 2 (Milit.) covering fire; **jmdm. ~schutz geben** cover sb.; **~sicher** A *Adj.* fireproof; B *adv.* **etw. ~sicher in einem Safe deponieren** deposit sth. in a fireproof safe; **~sirene** *die* fire siren; **~speiend** ▸ **Feuer 1**; **~spritze** *die* fire hose; **~stätte** *die* hearth; **~stein** *der* flint; **~stelle** *die* [camp]fire; **~stellung** *die* (Milit.) firing position; **~stuhl** *der* (ugs. scherzh.) [motor]bike (coll.); machine; **~taufe** *die* baptism of fire; **~teufel** *der* (Pressejargon) arsonist; **~tod** *der* (geh.) [death at] the stake; **den ~tod erleiden** be burnt at the stake; **~treppe** *die* fire escape; **~überfall** *der* armed attack

Feuerung *die*; **~, ~en** 1 (Verbrennungsvorrichtung) firing [system] 2 (das Heizen) heating 3 (Brennstoff) fuel

Feuer-: ~versicherung *die* fire insurance; **~wache** *die* fire station; **~waffe** *die* firearm; **~wasser** *das* (ugs.) firewater (coll.)

Feuer·wehr *die*; **~, ~en** fire service; **das ging ja wie die ~** (ugs.) that was quick; **der fährt ja wie die ~** (ugs.) he drives like a maniac

Feuerwehr-: ~auto *das* fire engine; **~beil** *das* fireman's axe; **~mann** *der*; *Pl.* **~männer** *od.* **~leute** ▸ S. 113 fireman; **~übung** *die* fire service drill; firefighting exercise

Feuer-: ~werk *das* firework display; (~werkskörper) fireworks *pl.*; (fig.) barrage; **~werks·körper** *der* firework; **~zangen·bowle** *die: burnt rum and red wine punch;* **~zeug** *das* lighter; **~zone** *die* (Milit.) firing zone

Feuilleton /fœjəˈtõ:/ *das*; **~s, ~s** 1 (Teil einer Zeitung) arts section 2 (literarischer Beitrag) [literary] article

Feuilletonismus *der*; **~** (oft abwertend) literary journalese

Feuilletonist *der*; **~en, ~en**, **Feuilletonistin** *die*; **~, ~nen** arts writer *or* correspondent

feuilletonistisch

A *Adj.* (unterhaltend) literary journalistic ‹*style*›; (abwertend) glib, facile ‹*essay etc.*›

B *adv.* in a literary journalistic style; (abwertend) glibly

Feuilleton·teil *der* arts section

feurig *Adj.* 1 fiery ‹*horse, spice, wine*›; passionate ‹*speech*› 2 (geh.: feuerrot) flaming ‹*sky, red, etc.*› 3 (geh.: funkelnd) blazing ‹*precious stone*›

Fez /fe:ts/ *der*; **~es** (ugs.) lark (coll.); **~ machen** lark about (coll.); **hört mit dem ~ auf!** stop larking about (coll.)

ff /ɛfˈɛf/ *Abk.* **= sehr fein** superior-quality ‹*sweets, cakes and pastries, etc.*›

ff. *Abk.* **= folgende [Seiten]** ff.

Ffm. *Abk.* **= Frankfurt am Main**

Fiaker /ˈfi̯akɐ/ *der*; **~s, ~** (österr.) hackney carriage; cab

Fiale /ˈfi̯a:lə/ *die*; **~, ~n** (Archit.) pinnacle

Fiasko /ˈfi̯asko/ *das*; **~s, ~s** fiasco; **unser Urlaub war ein einziges ~:** our holiday was a total disaster (coll.)

Fibel /ˈfi:bl̩/ *die*; **~, ~n** 1 (Lesebuch) reader; primer 2 (Lehrbuch) handbook; guide

Fiber /ˈfi:bɐ/ *die*; **~, ~n** fibre

Fibrille /fiˈbrɪlə/ *die*; **~, ~n** (Med.) fibril

Fibrin /fiˈbri:n/ *das*; **~s** (Med.) fibrin

Fibrom /fiˈbro:m/ *das*; **~s, ~e** ▸ **S. 439** (Med.) fibroma

Fiche /fi:ʃ/ *der od. das*; **~s, ~s** (Informationst.) [micro]fiche

ficht /fɪçt/ *Imperativ Sg. u. 3. Pers. Sg. Präsens v.* **fechten**

Fichte *die*; **~, ~n** 1 spruce 2 (Rottanne) Norway spruce

Fichten-: ~brett *das* spruce board; **~holz** *das* spruce [wood]; **~nadel** *die* spruce needle; **~nadel·öl** *das* spruce oil; pine needle oil; **~wald** *der* spruce forest

Fick /fɪk/ *der*; **~s, ~s** (vulg.) fuck (coarse)

ficken *tr., itr. V.* (vulg.) fuck (coarse); **mit jmdm. ~:** fuck sb. (coarse); **sie ließ sich von ihm ~:** she let him fuck her (coarse)

Fickerei *die*; **~, ~en** (vulg.) 1 (das Ficken) fucking (coarse) 2 (sexuelles Abenteuer) fuck (coarse)

fick[e]rig /ˈfɪk(ə)rɪç/ *Adj.* (landsch.: nervös) nervous

Fideikommiss, *Fideikommiß /fideikɔˈmɪs/ *das*; **Fideikommisses, Fideikommisse** (Rechtsspr.) entail; entailed estate

fidel /fiˈde:l/ *Adj.* (ugs.) jolly, merry ‹*company, person*›; **ein ~es Haus sein** be a *or* the cheerful type

Fidibus /ˈfi:dibʊs/ *der*; **~** *od.* **~ses, ~** *od.* **~se** (scherzh.) spill

Fidschianer /fɪˈdʒi̯a:nɐ/ *der*; **~s, ~**, **Fidschianerin** *die*; **~, ~nen** Fijian

Fidschi·inseln /ˈfɪdʒi-/ *Pl.* **die ~:** Fiji; the Fiji Islands

Fieber /ˈfi:bɐ/ *das*; **~s** 1 ▸ **S. 439**, ▸ **S. 703** [high] temperature; (über 38 °C) fever; **~ haben** have a [high] temperature/a fever; **hohes/ansteigendes ~ haben** have a high/rising temperature; **~ messen/bei jmdm. ~ messen** take one's/sb.'s temperature; **im ~:** in one's fever 2 (geh.: Besessenheit) fever; **vom ~ des Ehrgeizes gepackt sein** be consumed with ambition; **das ~ der Ungeduld hatte ihn ergriffen** he was in a fever of impatience; **im ~ der Erwartung** in a fever of anticipation; **im ~ des Wahlkampfs** in the heat of the election campaign

fieber-, Fieber-: ~anfall *der* attack *or* bout of fever; **~fantasie** *die* [feverish] delirium; **~flecke[n]** *Pl.* fever spots; fever rash *sing.*; **~frei** *Adj.* ‹*person*› free from fever; **er ist wieder ~frei** his temperature is back to normal; **~glänzend** *Adj.* (geh.) feverish ‹*eyes*›

fieber·haft

A *Adj.* 1 feverish, febrile ‹*infection, state, condition*› 2 (angestrengt, hektisch) feverish ‹*activity*›; **eine ~e Tätigkeit entfalten** become feverishly active

B *adv.* feverishly; **~ überlegen** think desperately hard

fieberig *Adj.* ▸ **fiebrig**

Fieber-: ~kurve *die* temperature chart; **~messer** *der*; **~~s, ~~** ▸ **~thermometer**; **~mücke** *die* (Zool.) malaria mosquito

fiebern *itr. V.* 1 (Fieber haben) have *or* run a temperature 2 (sehr aufgeregt sein) **vor Aufregung/Erwartung** *(Dat.)* **~:** be in a fever of excitement/anticipation 3 (heftig verlangen) **nach etw. ~:** long desperately for sth.

fieber-, Fieber-: ~phantasie ▸ **~fantasie**; **~senkend** *Adj.* antipyretic; **~senkende Mittel** antipyretics; **~thermometer** *das* [clinical] thermometer; **~wahn** *der* (geh.) [feverish] delirium; **im ~wahn** in his/her delirium

fiebrig *Adj.* (auch fig.) feverish

Fiedel /ˈfi:dl̩/ *die*; **~, ~n** (veralt., scherzh.) fiddle

fiedeln *tr., itr. V.* (scherzh., abwertend) fiddle; **eine Melodie ~:** play a tune on the fiddle

Fiedler /ˈfi:dlɐ/ *der*; **~s, ~**, **Fiedlerin** *die*; **~, ~nen** (scherzh., abwertend) fiddler

fiel /fi:l/ *1. u. 3. Pers. Sg. Prät. v.* **fallen**

fiepen /ˈfi:pn̩/ *itr. V.* 1 ‹*dog*› whimper; ‹*bird*› cheep 2 (Jägerspr.) ‹*deer*› call

fies /fi:s/

A *Adj.* (ugs.) 1 (charakterlich) nasty ‹*person, character*›; **das finde ich ~:** I think that's mean 2 (geschmacklich) horrid (coll.); awful (coll.)

B *adv.* in a nasty way

Fiesling /ˈfi:slɪŋ/ *der*; **~s, ~e** (salopp abwertend) creep (coll.)

Fifa, FIFA /ˈfi:fa/ *die*; **~:** FIFA; International Football Federation

fifty-fifty /ˈfɪftɪˈfɪftɪ/ *Adv.* (ugs.) *in* **~ machen** go fifty-fifty; **die Sache wird am Ende wohl ~ ausgehen** things will no doubt work out even in the end

Figaro /ˈfi:garo/ *der*; **~s, ~s** (scherzh.) hairdresser

Fight /fait/ *der*; **~s, ~s** (Sport) fight

fighten /ˈfaitn̩/ *itr. V.* (Sport) fight

Fighter /ˈfaitɐ/ *der*; **~s, ~**, **Fighterin** *die*; **~, ~nen** fighter

Figur /fiˈgu:ɐ̯/ *die*; **~, ~en** 1 (Wuchs, Gestalt) (einer Frau) figure; (eines Mannes) physique; **eine gute/schlechte ~ machen** cut a good/poor *or* sorry figure 2 (Bildwerk) figure 3 (geometrisches Gebilde) shape 4 (Spielstein) piece 5 (Persönlichkeit) figure 6 (literarische Gestalt) character; **die komische ~** (Theater) the comic character *or* figure; **eine komische ~:** a figure of fun 7 (Tanzen, Eissport usw.) figure; **~en laufen** skate figures 8 (salopp: Mensch) character (coll.) 9 (Musik, Sprachw.) figure

figural /figuˈra:l/ *Adj.* figured

Figural·musik *die* figurate *or* florid music

Figuration /figuraˈtsi̯o:n/ *die*; **~, ~en** (Musik, Kunstwiss.) figuration

figurativ /figuraˈti:f/ (Sprachw., Kunstw.)

A *Adj.* figurative

B *adv.* figuratively

figurieren *itr. V.* (geh.) figure

Figurine /figuˈri:nə/ *die*; **~, ~n** 1 (Kunstwiss.) figurine 2 (bes. Theater) costume design

figürlich /fiˈgy:ɐ̯lɪç/

A *Adj.* (Kunstwiss.) figured

B *adv.* (in Bezug auf die Figur) as far as her figure/his physique is concerned

Figur·problem *das* (ugs.) weight problem

Fiktion /fɪkˈtsi̯o:n/ *die*; **~, ~en** fiction

fiktional /fɪktsi̯oˈna:l/ *Adj.* (geh.) fictional ‹*significance*›; ‹*work*› of fiction

fiktiv /fɪkˈti:f/ *Adj.* (geh.) fictitious

Filament /filaˈmɛnt/ *das*; **~s, ~e** (Bot., Astron.) filament

Filet[1] /fiˈle:/ *das*; **~s, ~s** (Textilw.) filet; netting

Filet[2] *das*; **~s, ~s** fillet; (Rinder~, Schweine~) fillet; filet

Filet·arbeit *die* (Handarb.) filet; netting

filetieren /file'ti:rən/ *tr. V.* (Kochk.) fillet
Filet-: ~**nadel** *die* netting needle; ~**steak** *das* fillet steak; ~**stück** *das* (fig.) choice morsel
Filial·betrieb *der* branch
Filiale /fi'lia:lə/ *die;* ~, ~**n** branch
Filial·generation *die* (Genetik) filial generation
Filialist *der;* ~**en**, ~**en**, **Filialistin** *die;* ~, ~**nen** (Wirtsch.) chain-store owner
Filial-: ~**kirche** *die* daughter church; subsidiary church; ~**leiter** *der*, ~**leiterin** *die* ▸❶ **S. 113** branch manager; ~**netz** *das* branch network
Filibuster /fili'bastɐ/ *das;* ~**[s]**, ~ (Parl.) filibuster
filigran /fili'gra:n/ *Adj.* filigreed
Filigran *das;* ~**s**, ~**e** filigree
Filigran-: ~**arbeit** *die* [piece of] filigree work; ~**schmuck** *der* filigree [jewellery]
Filipina /fili'pi:na/ *die;* ~, ~**s** Filipina
Filipino *der;* ~**s**, ~**s** Filipino
Filius /'fi:liʊs/ *der;* ~, ~**se** (scherzh.) son
Film /fɪlm/ *der;* ~**[e]s**, ~**e** [1] (Fot.) film [2] (Kinofilm) film; movie (Amer. coll.); **da ist bei ihm der ~ gerissen** (fig. ugs.) he's had a mental blackout; **der deutsche/brasilianische ~:** the German/Brazilian cinema [3] (~branche) films *pl.*; **beim ~ sein** be in films [4] (dünne Schicht) film
Film-: ~**amateur** *der*, ~**amateurin** *die* amateur film-maker; ~**archiv** *das* film library *or* archive; ~**atelier** *das* film studio; ~**aufnahme** *die* shot; **mit den ~aufnahmen beginnen** start filming *or* shooting; ~**aus·rüstung** *die* filming equipment; ~**bar** *die* [porno] film club; ~**bericht** *der* film report; ~**branche** *die* films *pl., no art.;* ~**bühne** *die* [1] (Bildbühne) film window; [2] ▸**Filmtheater**; ~**cutter** *der*, ~**cutterin** *die* film editor; ~**diva** *die* (veralt.) screen goddess
Filme·macher *der*, **Filme·macherin** *die* ▸❶ **S. 113** film-maker
filmen
A *tr. V.* [1] film [2] (ugs.: hereinlegen) **jmdn. ~:** take sb. for a ride (coll.)
B *itr. V.* film; make a film/films
Film-: ~**festival** *das* film festival; ~**festspiele** *Pl.* film festival *sing.*; ~**fritze** *der* (salopp) film guy (coll.); ~**geschäft** *das* film business *or* industry; ~**groteske** *die* film grotesquerie; ~**held** *der* screen hero; ~**heldin** *die* screen heroine; ~**industrie** *die* film industry
filmisch
A *Adj.* cinematic ‹*art etc.*›
B *adv.* cinematically
Film-: ~**kamera** *die* film camera; (Schmalfilmkamera) cine camera; ~**kassette** *die* (Fot.) film cassette *or* cartridge; ~**klub** *der* film club *or* society; ~**komödie** *die* film comedy; comedy film; ~**kopie** *die* [film] print; copy of a/the film; ~**kritik** *die* [1] (Besprechung) film review; [2] (~kritiker) film critics *pl.*; ~**kritiker** *der*, ~**kritikerin** *die* film critic; ~**kulisse** *die* film set; **das wäre eine ideale ~kulisse** that would be an ideal setting for a film; ~**kunst** *die* cinematic art; ~**kunst·theater** *das* film theatre; ~**lein·wand** *die* cinema screen; ~**material** *das* [1] (Fot., Film: Aufnahmematerial) film; [2] (~e zu einem Thema) film material; ~**musik** *die* film music; (eines einzelnen ~s) theme music
Filmographie /fɪlmogra'fi:/ *die;* ~, ~**n** filmography *no art.*
film-, Film-: ~**palast** *der* picture palace (dated); cinema; ~**plakat** *das* film poster; ~**preis** *der* film award; ~**produzent** *der*, ~**produzentin** *die* film producer; ~**projektor** *der* film projector; ~**rechte** *die Pl.* film rights; ~**regisseur** *der*, ~**regisseurin** *die* ▸❶ **S. 113** film director; ~**reif** **A** *Adj.* fit for the silver screen *postpos.*; cinematic ‹*scenario*›; **B** *adv.* in true cinematic style; ~**riss**, *~**riß** *der:* in **einen ~riss haben** (ugs.) have a mental blackout; ~**rolle** *die* [1] (schauspielerische Rolle) film part *or* role; **jmdm. eine ~rolle anbieten** offer sb. a part in a film; [2] (Spule) reel of film; ~**schaffende** *der/die; adj. Dekl.* film-maker; ~**schauspieler** *der* ▸❶ **S. 113** film actor; ~**schauspielerin** *die* ▸❶ **S. 113** film actress; ~**spule** *die* film reel; ~**stadt** *die* [1] (Studiokomplex) film studios *pl.*; [2] (Zentrum) centre of the film industry; ~**star** *der* ▸❶ **S. 113** film star; ~**studio** *das* film studio; ~**technik** *die* film technology *no art.*; ~**theater** *das* cinema; ~**titel** *der* film title; ~**verleih** *der* film distributor[s]; ~**vorführer** *der;* ~~**s**, ~~, ~**vorführerin** *die;* ~~, ~~**nen** ▸❶ **S. 113** film projectionist; ~**vorstellung** *die* film show; ~**wirtschaft** *die* film business *or* industry; ~**zensur** *die* film censorship; (Gremium) film censors *pl.*; censor (coll.)
Filou /fi'lu:/ *der* (abwertend) [1] (Spitzbube) dog (derog.); rogue [2] (Verführer) devil (derog.)
Filter /'fɪltɐ/ *der,* (fachspr. meist) *das;* ~**s**, ~**:** filter; **Zigaretten ohne/mit ~:** plain/[filter-]tipped cigarettes
filter-, Filter-: ~**fein** *Adj.* finely ground *attrib.*, filter-fine *attrib.* ‹*coffee*›; **Kaffee ~fein mahlen** grind coffee fine[ly]; ~**kaffee** *der* filter coffee; ~**mund·stück** *das* filter tip
filtern *tr. V.* filter
Filter-: ~**papier** *das* filter paper; ~**presse** *die* (Technik) filter press; ~**staub** *der* filter dust; ~**tüte** *die* filter; ~**zigarette** *die* [filter-]tipped cigarette
Filtrat /fɪl'tra:t/ *das;* ~**[e]s**, ~**e** (Technik) filtrate
Filtration /fɪltra'tsio:n/ *die;* ~, ~**en** (Technik) filtration
filtrieren *tr. V.* filter
Filz /fɪlts/ *der;* ~**es**, ~**e** [1] (Material) felt [2] (filzartig Verschlungenes) mass; mat [3] (ugs. abwertend: geiziger Mensch) miser; skinflint [4] (Bierdeckel) beer mat [5] (~hut) felt hat [6] (ugs. abwertend: Korruption) corruption; graft (coll.)
filzen
A *itr. V.* felt
B *tr. V.* [1] (ugs.: durchsuchen) search ‹*room, car, etc.*›; frisk ‹*person*› [2] (salopp: berauben) do over (sl.) [3] (salopp: schlafen) kip (Brit. coll.)
Filz·hut *der* felt hat
filzig *Adj.* [1] (verfilzt) felted ‹*wool*›; matted ‹*hair*› [2] (ugs.: geizig) mean; tight-fisted
Filz-: ~**latschen** *der* (ugs.) slipper; ~**laus** *die* (Zool.) crab louse
Filzokratie /fɪltsokra'ti:/ *die;* ~, ~**n** (abwertend) corruption; graft (coll.)
Filz-: ~**pantoffel** *der* slipper; ~**schreiber** *der* felt-tip pen; ~**stiefel** *der* felt boot; ~**stift** *der* felt-tip pen
Fimmel /'fɪml/ *der;* ~**s**, ~ (ugs. abwertend) **einen ~ für etw. haben** have a thing about sth. (coll.); **du hast wohl einen ~!** there must be something the matter with you; you must be dotty (Brit.); **das ist ein ~ von ihm** it's a strange habit of his; (Idee) it's a funny idea he has (coll.)
final /fi'na:l/ *Adj.* (Philos., Sprachw.) final
Finale /fi'na:lə/ *das;* ~**s**, ~**[s]** [1] (Sport: Endkampf) final; **im ~ stehen** be in the final [2] (spektakulärer Abschluss; Musik: Schlusssatz, -szene) finale
Final·gegner *der*, **Final·gegnerin** *die* (Sport) opponent in the final
Finalist *der;* ~**en**, ~**en**, **Finalistin** *die;* ~, ~**nen** (Sport) finalist
Finalität /finali'tɛ:t/ *die;* ~, ~**en** (bes. Philos.) finality
Final·satz *der* (Sprachw.) final clause
Finanz /fi'nants/ *die;* ~ [1] (Geldwesen) finance *no art.* [2] (~leute) financial world
Finanz-: ~**amt** *das* [1] (Behörde) ≈ Inland Revenue; **Ärger mit dem ~amt** trouble with the taxman; [2] (Gebäude) tax office; ~**aristokratie** *die* financial aristocracy; ~**ausgleich** *der: equalization of revenue and costs between government and local authorities;* ~**ausschuss** *der* finance committee; ~**beamte** *der*, ~**beamtin** *die* ▸❶ **S. 113** tax officer; ~**buchhalter** *der*, ~**buchhalterin** *die* ▸❶ **S. 113** financial accountant; ~**buchhaltung** *die* financial accountancy; ~**dienstleister** *der*, ~**dienstleisterin** *die* financial service provider; ~**dinge** *Pl.* financial matters
Finanzen *Pl.* [1] (ugs.: finanzielle Verhältnisse) finances [2] (Finanz- und Geldwesen) finance *sing.*; **die Abteilung ~:** the finance department [3] (Einkünfte des Staates) [government] finances
Finanz-: ~**genie** *das* financial wizard; ~**gericht** *das: court dealing with tax disputes;* ~**gruppe** *die* [financial] syndicate; ~**hilfe** *die* financial aid; ~**hoheit** *die* fiscal prerogative
finanziell /finan'tsiɛl/
A *Adj.* financial
B *adv.* financially; **jmdn. ~ unterstützen** give sb. financial support; **~ gesichert sein** be financially secure
Finanzier /finan'tsie:/ *der;* ~**s**, ~**s** financier
finanzieren *tr. V.* [1] finance; (fig.: bezahlen) pay for; **frei/staatlich finanziert sein** be privately financed/financed by the state [2] (Kaufmannsspr.: auf Kredit kaufen) buy on credit; **etw. langfristig ~:** obtain long-term credit for sth.
Finanzierung *die;* ~, ~**en** [1] financing [2] (Gewährung eines Kredits) credit *no indef. art.*; **eine langfristige ~:** long-term credit
Finanzierungs·plan *der* financial plan
finanz-, Finanz-: ~**kapital** *das* financial capital; ~**kontrolle** *die* (Wirtsch.) financial control; ~**kraft** *die* financial strength; ~**kräftig** *Adj.* financially powerful; ~**lage** *die* financial situation; ~**markt** *der* financial market; ~**minister** *der*, ~**ministerin** *die* minister of finance; ≈ Chancellor of the Exchequer (Brit.); ≈ Secretary of the Treasury (Amer.); ~**ministerium** *das* Ministry of Finance; (in GB u. USA) ≈ Treasury; ~**not** *die* financial difficulties *pl.*; ~**planung** *die* financial planning; ~**politik** *die* (des Staates, eines Unternehmens) financial policy; (allgemeine) politics of finance; ~**politisch** **A** *Adj.* ‹*questions etc.*› relating to financial policy; **B** *adv.* from the point of view of financial policy; ~**reform** *die* financial reform; ~**schwach** *Adj.* financially weak; ~**spritze** *die* (ugs.) cash injection; ~**stark** *Adj.* financially strong; ~**verwaltung** *die: regional department with responsibility for settling fiscal matters;* ≈ Board of Inland Revenue (Brit.); ≈ Internal Revenue Service (Amer.); ~**wesen** *das* [1] system of public finances; **ein Ausdruck aus dem ~wesen** a financial expression; [2] ▸~**verwaltung**; ~**wirtschaft** *die* public finances *pl.*; ~**wissenschaft** *die* public finance
finassieren /fina'si:rən/ *itr. V.* (abwertend) use trickery
Findel·kind /'fɪndl-/ *das* foundling
finden /'fɪndn/
A *unr. tr. V.* [1] (entdecken) find; **eine Spur von jmdm. ~:** get a lead on sb.; **keine Spur von jmdm. ~:** find no trace of sb.; **er/das ist nicht zu ~:** he/it is not to be found; **ich weiß nicht, was er an ihr findet** I don't know what he sees in her [2] (erlangen, erwerben) find ‹*work, flat, wife, etc.*›; **Freunde ~:** make friends; **die Kraft/den Mut dazu ~, etw. zu tun** find the strength/the courage to do sth. [3] (heraus~) find ‹*solution, mistake, pretext, excuse, answer*›; **einen Ausweg ~:** see a way out [4] (einschätzen, beurteilen) **etw. gut/richtig ~:** think sth. is good/right; **wie ~ Sie dieses Bild?** what do you think of this painting?; **nichts bei etw. ~:** not mind sth.; **ich finde nichts dabei** I don't mind; **wie finde ich denn das?** (ugs.) well, really! [5] (erhalten) **Hilfe [bei jmdm.] ~:** get help [from sb.]; *s. auch* **Anklang 1**; **Beifall 2**; **Gefallen²**; **Gehör**; **Verwendung 1** [6] (vor~) find; **er fand das Haus verlassen** he found the house deserted
B *unr. refl. V.* **sich ~:** turn up; **es fand sich niemand/jemand, der das tun wollte** nobody wanted to do that/there was somebody who wanted to do that; **das/es wird sich alles ~** (das wird sich aufklären) it will all work out all

right; **sich in sein Schicksal/seine Lage/seine neue Rolle ∼** (geh.) come to terms with one's fate/situation/new role

C *unr. itr. V.* **zu jmdm. ∼:** find sb.; **nach einem Ort ∼:** find the way to a place; **nach Hause ∼:** find the way home; **zu sich selbst ∼** (fig.) come to terms with oneself; **er gehört zu diesen Nachtmenschen, die nicht ins Bett ∼ können** he is one of these night owls who just will not go to bed; **das Kind findet schon allein zur Schule** the child knows the way to school by himself/herself

Finder *der;* **∼s, ∼, Finderin** *die;* **∼, ∼nen** finder; *s. auch* **ehrlich A 1**

Finder·lohn *der* reward [for finding sth.]

Fin de Siècle /fɛ̃dˈsjɛkl/ *das;* **∼:** fin de siècle; **die Kunst/Literatur des ∼:** fin de siècle art/literature

findig *Adj.* resourceful; **ein ∼er Kopf** a resourceful person; **er ist ∼ im Aufspüren von Antiquitäten** he ist good at finding antiques

Findling /ˈfɪntlɪŋ/ *der;* **∼s, ∼e** 1 (Findelkind) foundling 2 (Geol.) erratic block

Findlings·block *der; Pl.* **Findlingsblöcke** (Geol.) erratic block

Finesse /fiˈnɛsə/ *die;* **∼, ∼n** 1 (Kunstgriff) trick; **alle ∼n von etw. beherrschen** know all the tricks of sth. 2 *meist Pl.* (in der Ausstattung) refinement; **mit allen ∼n ausgestattet** equipped with every refinement 3 (Schlauheit) flair

fing /fɪŋ/ *1. u. 3. Pers. Sg. Prät. v.* **fangen**

Finger /ˈfɪŋɐ/ *der;* **∼s, ∼** 1 ▸ⓘ **S. 435** finger; **mit dem ∼ auf jmdn./etw. zeigen** (auch fig.) point one's finger at sb./sth.; **den ∼ an die Lippen legen** put one's finger to one's lips; **einen Ring am ∼ tragen** have a ring on one's finger; **den ∼ am Abzug haben** have one's finger on the trigger; **mit den ∼n schnippen** snap one's fingers; **sich** (*Dat.*) **die ∼ wund schreiben** write one's fingers to the bone 2 (fig.) **das Geld zerrinnt ihm unter** *od.* **zwischen den ∼n** money just runs through his fingers; **wenn man ihm den kleinen ∼ reicht, nimmt er gleich die ganze Hand** if you give him an inch he takes a mile; **die ∼ davon lassen/von etw. lassen** (ugs.) steer clear of it/of sth.; **sie macht keinen ∼ krumm** (ugs.) she never lifts a finger; **lange ∼ machen** (ugs.) get itchy fingers; **er rührte keinen ∼:** he wouldn't lift a finger; **ich würde mir alle [zehn] ∼ danach lecken** (ugs.) I'd give my eye teeth for it; **die ∼ in etw.** (*Dat.*)**/im Spiel haben** (ugs.) have a hand in sth./have one's finger in the pie; **sich** (*Dat.*) **die ∼ schmutzig machen** get one's hands dirty; **sich** (*Dat.*) **die ∼ verbrennen** (ugs.) burn one's fingers (fig.); **etw. an den ∼n abzählen können** be able to count sth. on the fingers of one hand; **sich** (*Dat.*) **etw. an den [fünf** *od.* **zehn] ∼n abzählen können** be able to see sth. straight away; **eine[n] an jedem ∼ haben** (ugs. scherz.) have one for every day of the week; **jmdm. auf die ∼ sehen** *od.* **gucken** (ugs.) keep a sharp eye on sb.; **jmdm. auf die ∼ klopfen** (ugs.) rap sb. across the knuckles; **sich** (*Dat.*) **etw. aus den ∼n saugen** (ugs.) make sth. up; **ihm** *od.* **ihn juckt es in den ∼n [, etw. zu tun]** (ugs.) he is itching [to do sth.]; **dann juckts mir in den ∼n** (ugs.) then I get restless; **jmdm. in die ∼ fallen** *od.* **geraten** (ugs.) fall into sb.'s hands; **etw. in die ∼ bekommen** *od.* **kriegen** (ugs.) get hold of sth.; **wenn ich den in die ∼ kriege!** (ugs.) wait till I get my hands on him! (coll.); **sich** (*Dat.*) **in den ∼ geschnitten haben** (ugs.) have another think coming (coll.); **etw. mit spitzen ∼n anfassen** hold sth. at arm's length; **etw. mit dem kleinen ∼ machen** (ugs.) do sth. with one's eyes shut; **jmdn. um den [kleinen] ∼ wickeln** (ugs.) wrap sb. round one's little finger; **jmdm. unter die ∼ kommen** *od.* **geraten** (ugs.) fall into sb.'s hands; **der elfte ∼** (salopp scherzh.) one's third leg (coll. joc.) 3 (Teil des Handschuhs) finger

finger-, Finger-: ∼abdruck *der; Pl.* **∼abdrücke** fingerprint; **jmdm. ∼abdrücke abnehmen** take sb.'s fingerprints; **∼beere** *die* ▸ⓘ **S. 435** (Anat.) finger pad; **∼breit** *Adj.* as wide as a finger *postpos.;* half an inch wide *postpos.;* **∼breit** *der;* **∼∼, ∼∼** (Maßeinheit) finger's width; (fig.) inch; **sie war nicht bereit, einen ∼breit abzuweichen** (fig.) she was not prepared to budge an inch; **∼dick** *Adj.* as thick as a finger *postpos.;* **Brot ∼dick mit etw. bestreichen** spread bread thickly with sth.; **∼druck** *der; Pl.* **∼drücke** touch of a finger; **∼fertig** *Adj.* nimble-fingered; **∼fertigkeit** *die* dexterity; **∼food** /ˈfɪŋɐfuːt/ *das;* **∼[s]** finger food

Finger-: ∼gelenk *das* ▸ⓘ **S. 435** finger joint; **∼glied** *das* ▸ⓘ **S. 435** phalanx; **∼hakeln** /-haːkl̩n/ *das;* **∼∼s** finger-wrestling; **∼hand·schuh** *der* glove [with fingers]; **∼hut** *der* 1 thimble; **ein ∼hut [voll]** (fig.) a thimbleful; 2 (Bot.) foxglove; **∼knochen** *der,* **∼knöchel** *der* ▸ⓘ **S. 435** knuckle; **∼kuppe** *die* ▸ⓘ **S. 435** fingertip

fingern

A *itr. V.* fiddle; **an etw.** (*Dat.*) **∼:** fiddle with sth.; **nach etw. ∼:** fumble [around] for sth.

B *tr. V.* **etw. aus der Tasche ∼:** fish sth. out of one's pocket

Finger-: ∼nagel *der* ▸ⓘ **S. 435** fingernail; **an den ∼nägeln kauen** bite one's nails; **er gönnt ihr nicht das Schwarze unterm ∼nagel** (fig.) he grudges her everything; **∼rechnen** *das* counting on one's fingers *no art.;* **er beherrscht schon das ∼rechnen** he can already count on his fingers; **∼ring** *der* ring; **∼satz** *der* (Musik) fingering; **∼schale** *die* finger bowl; **∼schnippen** *das;* **∼∼s** snapping one's fingers; **sich mit ∼schnippen melden** attract attention by snapping one's fingers

Finger·spitze *die* ▸ⓘ **S. 435** fingertip; **Künstler/musikalisch bis in die ∼n sein** (fig.) be an artist/be musical to the tips of one's fingers; **das muss man in den ∼n haben** (fig.) you have to have a feel for it

Fingerspitzen·gefühl *das* feeling; **ein [besonderes] ∼ für etw. haben** have a [special] feeling for sth.

Finger-: ∼sprache *die* deaf-and-dumb language; (alphabetische Zeichen) deaf-and-dumb alphabet; **∼übung** *die* (Musik) finger exercise; **∼zeig** /-tsaik/ *der;* **∼∼s, ∼∼e** tip-off; **einen ∼zeig erhalten** be given a hint; ‹*police*› be tipped off, get a tip-off; **für sie war es ein ∼zeig des Schicksals** she took it as a sign

fingieren /fɪnˈgiːrən/ *tr. V.* fake ‹*accident, break-in*›; **ein fingierter Name** a false name; **ein fingierter Briefwechsel** (in der Literatur) an imaginary correspondence

Finish /ˈfɪnɪʃ/ *das;* **∼s, ∼s** finish

finit /fiˈniːt/ *Adj.* (Sprachw.) finite

Fink /fɪŋk/ *der;* **∼en, ∼en** finch

Finken-: ∼schlag *der* finch's song; **∼vogel** *der* finch

Finn-Ding[h]i /ˈfɪndɪŋgi/ *das;* **∼s, ∼s** Finn dinghy

Finne[1] /ˈfɪnə/ *der;* **∼n, ∼n** ▸ⓘ **S. 520** Finn

Finne[2] *die;* **∼, ∼n** 1 (Zool.) fin 2 (am Hammer) peen

Finnen·dolch *der* [short, wide-bladed] dagger

Finnin *die;* **∼, ∼nen** ▸ⓘ **S. 520** Finn

finnisch *Adj.* ▸ⓘ **S. 520,** ▸ⓘ **S. 670** Finnish; **der Finnische Meerbusen** the Gulf of Finland; *s. auch* **deutsch, Deutsch, Deutsche**[2]

Finnland /ˈfɪnlant/ *(das);* **∼s** Finland

Finnlandisierung /fɪnlandiˈziːrʊŋ/ *die;* **∼** (Pol.) Finlandization

Finn·wal *der* (Zool.) fin whale; common rorqual

finster /ˈfɪnstɐ/

A *Adj.* 1 dark; **im Finstern** in the dark 2 (düster) dark ‹*house, forest, alleyway*›; dimly-lit ‹*pub, district*› 3 (dubios) shady ‹*plan, affair*›; **eine ∼e Gestalt** a sinister figure 4 (verdüstert, feindselig) **eine ∼e Miene [aufsetzen]** [assume] a black expression; **∼e Gedanken gegen jmdn. hegen** have evil intentions against sb. 5 (fig.) **in diesen ∼en Zeiten** in these dark times; **aus dem ∼en Mittelalter** from the Dark Ages; **im Finstern tappen** be groping in the dark

B *adv.* **jmdn. ∼ ansehen** give sb. a black look; **∼ entschlossen sein, etw. zu tun** be grimly determined to do sth.

Finsternis *die;* **∼, ∼se** 1 darkness; (auch bibl., fig.) dark; **rabenschwarze ∼:** pitch darkness; **in tiefer ∼ liegen** be shrouded in darkness; **die Mächte/das Reich der ∼:** the powers of darkness/the Kingdom of Darkness; **eine ägyptische ∼:** stygian gloom 2 (Astron.) eclipse

Finte /ˈfɪntə/ *die;* **∼, ∼n** 1 trick; **jmdn. durch eine ∼ täuschen** deceive sb. by trickery; **alle ∼n nützen Ihnen nichts** no trickery will help you 2 (Fechten) feint

finten·reich *Adj.* (geh.) skilful, tricky ‹*opponent*›

finzelig, finzlig /ˈfɪnts(ə)lɪç/ *Adj.* (ugs.) **∼e Arbeit** fiddly work; **∼e Schrift** tiny writing

fipsig /ˈfɪpsɪç/ *Adj.* (ugs.) undersized

Firlefanz /ˈfɪrləfants/ *der;* **∼es** (ugs. abwertend) 1 (Tand, Flitter) frippery; trumpery 2 (Unsinn) nonsense; **∼ machen** fool around

firm /fɪrm/ *Adj.* **in etw.** (*Dat.*) **∼ sein** be well up in sth.; know sth. thoroughly

Firma /ˈfɪrma/ *die;* **∼, Firmen** 1 firm; company; **in einer ∼ arbeiten** work for a firm *or* company; **die ∼ ist erloschen** the company has been struck from the register; **„Fa. W. Bert & Söhne"** 'W. Bert & Sons' 2 (ugs. abwertend: Sippschaft) bunch (sl.)

Firmament /fɪrmaˈmɛnt/ *das;* **∼[e]s** (dichter.) firmament

firmen *tr. V.* (kath. Rel.) confirm

firmen-, Firmen-: ∼aufdruck *der* company letter heading; **∼chef** *der,* **∼chefin** *die* ▸ **∼inhaber**; **∼eigen** *Adj.* company *attrib.;* belonging to the company *postpos.;* **∼eigen sein** belong to the company; **ein ∼eigener LKW/eine ∼eigene Kantine** a company lorry (Brit.) *or* truck/canteen; **∼inhaber** *der,* **∼inhaberin** *die* owner of the/a company; **∼intern** A *Adj.* internal; internal company *attrib.;* B *adv.* internally; within the company; **∼logo** *der od. das* company logo; **∼name** *der* name of a/the company *or* firm; **∼schild** *das* company's name plate; **∼stempel** *der* company stamp; firm's stamp; **∼wagen** *der* company car; **∼zeichen** *das* trademark

firmieren *itr. V.* trade

Firmling /ˈfɪrmlɪŋ/ *der;* **∼s, ∼e** (kath. Rel.) confirmation candidate

Firm·pate *der,* **Firm·patin** *die* sponsor

Firmung *die;* **∼, ∼en** confirmation; **jmdm. die ∼ erteilen** confirm sb.

firn /fɪrn/ *Adj.* mature ‹*wine*›

Firn *der;* **∼[e]s** firn

Firn·feld *das* firn field

Firnis /ˈfɪrnɪs/ *der;* **∼ses, ∼se** varnish

Firn·schnee *der* firn snow

First /fɪrst/ *der;* **∼[e]s, ∼e** ridge

First-: ∼höhe *die* height [to the ridge of the roof]; **eine ∼höhe von 8,50 m aufweisen** be 8.50 m high; **∼ziegel** *der* ridge tile

Fis /fɪs/ *das;* **∼, ∼** (Musik) [key of] F sharp

Fisch /fɪʃ/ *der;* **∼[e]s, ∼e** 1 fish; **[fünf] ∼e fangen** catch [five] fish; **sie hatten viele ∼e im Netz** they had a good catch; **Fliegende ∼e** flying fish; **gesund und munter wie ein ∼ im Wasser** as fit as a fiddle; **stumm wie ein ∼ sein** keep a stony silence; (fig.) **kleine ∼e** (ugs.) small fry; **faule ∼e** (ugs.) lame excuses; **die ∼e füttern** (ugs. scherzh.) be seasick 2 (Nahrungsmittel) fish; **das ist weder ∼ noch Fleisch** (fig.) that's neither fish nor fowl 3 (Astrol.) **die ∼e** Pisces; the Fishes; **er ist [ein] ∼:** he is a Piscean; **im Zeichen der ∼e geboren sein** be born under [the sign of] Pisces 4 (Druckerspr.) *letter from the wrong fount*

fisch-, Fisch-: ∼abfälle *Pl.* fish scraps; **∼adler** *der* (Zool.) osprey; **∼arm** *Adj.* poor as regards fish; **∼auge** *das* 1 fish eye; **er hat große, hervorquellende ∼augen** (fig.) he's

ⓘ Fläche

1 Quadratzentimeter	= one square centimetre (sq. cm)	= 0.155 square inch (sq. in.)
1 Quadratmeter	= one square metre (sq. m)	= 10.764 square feet (sq. ft) *od.* 1.196 square yards (sq. yds)
1 Hektar	= one hectare (ha)	= 2.471 acres
1 Quadratkilometer	= one square kilometre (sq. km)	= 0.386 square mile

Wie viel Wohnfläche hat die Wohnung?
= What is the floor area of the flat *od.* (*amerik.*) apartment?

Das Zimmer hat 16 m² [Fläche]
= The room has an area of 16 sq. m,
≈ the room has an area of 170 sq. ft.

ein Gebäude mit 8 000 m² Bürofläche
= a building with 8,000 sq. m,
≈ a building with 86,000 sq. ft of office space

Er bewirtschaftet 400 Hektar [Land]
= He farms 400 hectares [of land],
≈ he farms 1,000 acres [of land]

ein Gut von 400 ha
= an estate of 400 ha,
≈ an estate of 1,000 acres

eine Fläche von etwa 100 km²
= an area of about 100 sq. km,
≈ an area of about 40 square miles

got big, protruding fish-like eyes; 2 (Fot.) fish-eye lens; **~becken** *das* fish pond; **~bein** *das* whalebone; **~bestand** *der* fish population; **~besteck** *das* fish knife and fork; **~blase** *die* 1 (Schwimmblase) fish sound; 2 (Archit.) vesica piscis; **~blut** *das* fish blood; **~blut in den Adern haben** (fig.) be a cold fish; **~brötchen** *das* fish roll; **~bude** *die: stall selling pickled and smoked fish;* **~bulette** *die* fishcake; **~dampfer** *der* steam trawler; **~ei** *das* fish egg

fischen
A *tr. V.* 1 fish for; **Forellen/Aale ~:** fish for trout/eels 2 (ugs.) **etw. aus etw. ~:** fish sth. out of sth.
B *itr. V.* fish; **~ gehen** go fishing; **nach etw. ~:** fish for sth.; **nach Komplimenten ~** (fig.) fish for compliments; *s. auch* **trüb A 1**

Fischer *der;* **~s, ~** ▸ⓘ **S. 113** 1 fisherman 2 (ugs.: Angler) angler

Fischer-: ~boot *das* fishing boat; **~dorf** *das* fishing village

Fischerei *die;* **~:** fishing; **von der ~ leben** make a/one's living from fishing

Fischerei-: ~fahrzeug *das* fishing vessel; **~flotte** *die* fishing fleet; **~grenze** *die* fishing limit; **~hafen** *der* fish dock; (Hafenort) fishing port; **~ industrie** *die* fishing industry; **~recht** *das* 1 fishing rights *pl.;* right of fishery (Law); 2 (Rechtsvorschriften) fishing laws *pl.;* **~schiff** *das* fishing vessel; **~schutzboot** *das* fishery protection vessel; **~wesen** *das* fisheries *pl.*

Fischer·hütte *die* fisherman's hut

Fischerin *die;* **~, ~nen** ▸ⓘ **S. 113** 1 fisherwoman 2 (ugs.: Angler) angler

Fischer-: ~kate *die* ▸ **~hütte**; **~netz** *das* fishing net; **~ring** *der* (kath. Rel.) Fisherman's Ring

Fisch-: ~fabrik *die* fish cannery; **~fabrikschiff** *das* factory ship

Fisch·fang *der* fishing; **vom ~ leben** make a/one's living by fishing; **auf ~ gehen** go fishing

Fischfang-: ~flotte *die* fishing fleet; **~gebiet** *das* fishing grounds *pl.;* fishery

fisch-, Fisch-: ~filet *das* fish fillet; **~frau** *die* fishwife; **~frikadelle** *die* fishcake; **~futter** *das* fish food; **~gabel** *die* fish fork; **~gang** *der* (Gastr.) fish course; **~gericht** *das* fish dish; **~geruch** *der* smell of fish; **~geschäft** *das* fishmonger's [shop] (Brit.); fish store (Amer.); **~gräte** *die* fish bone; **~grät[en]·muster** *das* (Textilw.) herringbone pattern; **ein Mantel/ein Anzug mit ~grätenmuster** a herringbone coat/suit; **~gräten·stich** *der* herringbone stitch; **~gründe** *Pl.* fishing grounds; **~guano** *der* fish guano; **~handel** *der* fish trade; **~händler** *der,* **~händlerin** *die* ▸ⓘ **S. 113** fishmonger (Brit.); fish dealer (Amer.); (Großhändler) fish wholesaler; **~konserve** *die* canned fish; **~kutter** *der* fishing trawler; **~laden** *der; Pl.* **~läden** ▸ **~geschäft**; **~laich** *der* (Zool.) fish spawn; **~lokal** *das* ▸ **~restaurant**; **~markt** *der* fish market; **~mehl** *das* fishmeal; **~messer** *das* fish knife; **~milch** *die* (Zool.) milt; **~otter** *der* otter; **~pass,** ***~paß** *der* fish ladder; **~reich** *Adj.* rich in fish *postpos.;* **~reiher** *der* (Zool.) common heron; **~restaurant** *das* fish restaurant; seafood restaurant; **~reuse** *die* fish trap; **~schuppe** *die* fish scale; **~schwanz** *der* fish's tail; **~schwarm** *der* shoal of fish; **~stäbchen** *das* (Kochk.) fish finger; **~sterben** *das* death of the fish; **~suppe** *die* fish soup; **~teich** *der* fish pond; **~vergiftung** *die* fish poisoning; **~wanderung** *die* (Zool.) fish migration; **~weib** *das* (meist abwertend) fishwife; **~wilderei** *die* illicit fishing; **~wirt** *der,* **~wirtin** *die* fish farmer; **~wirtschaft** *die* fishing industry; **~zaun** *der* fish weir; fishgarth; **~zucht** *die* fish farming; **~zug** *der* 1 (ugs.: Gewinn bringendes Unternehmen) killing; 2 (Fischereiw.) draught

Fis-Dur *das* (Musik) F sharp major; *s. auch* **A-Dur**

Fisimatenten /fizima'tɛntn̩/ *Pl.* (ugs.) messing about *sing.;* **mach keine ~!** stop messing about; **es ist besser, Sie machen keine ~:** it will be better if you don't try anything silly

fiskalisch /fɪs'ka:lɪʃ/ *Adj.* fiscal

Fiskus /'fɪskʊs/ *der;* **~, Fisken** *od.* **~se** Government (*as managing the State finances*); **das Erbe fällt dem ~ zu** the estate falls to the Crown (Brit.)/the Government (Amer.)

fis-Moll *das* (Musik) F sharp minor; *s. auch* **a-Moll**

fisselig /'fɪsəlɪç/ *Adj.* (bes. nordd.) 1 (dünn, fein) fine ‹*wool, material*› 2 (umständlich) fiddly ‹*work*›

fisseln /'fɪsl̩n/ *itr. V.* (unpers.) (bes. nordd.) drizzle; **es fisselt** it is drizzling

Fissur /fɪ'su:ɐ̯/ *die;* **~, ~en** ▸ⓘ **S. 439** (Med.) fissure

Fistel /'fɪstl̩/ *die;* **~, ~n** (Med.) fistula

fisteln /'fɪstl̩n/ *itr. V.* speak in a thin high-pitched voice

Fistel·stimme *die* 1 (hohe Stimme bei Männern) thin high-pitched voice 2 (Musik) falsetto [voice]

fit /fɪt/ *Adj.* fit; **jmdn. ~ machen** get sb. fit; **sich ~ halten** keep fit; **das hält ~:** it keeps you fit

Fitness, ***Fitneß** /'fɪtnɛs/ *die;* **~:** fitness

Fitness-, *Fitneß-: ~raum *der* fitness room; **~studio** *das* fitness centre; fitness studio; **~training** *das* fitness training; **~zentrum** *das* fitness centre

Fittich /'fɪtɪç/ *der;* **~[e]s, ~e** (dichter.) wing; pinion; **jmdn. unter seine ~e nehmen** (ugs. scherzh.) take sb. under one's wing

Fitting /'fɪtɪŋ/ *das;* **~s, ~s** (Technik) fitting

Fitzel /'fɪtsl̩/ *der od. das;* **~s, ~** (bes. nordd.) morsel

Fitzelchen *das;* **~s, ~** (ugs.) scrap; **nicht ein ~ war von seinem Reichtum übrig geblieben** he did not have a penny of his fortune left

fix /fɪks/
A *Adj.* 1 (ugs.: flink, wendig) quick; **ein ~er Bursche** a bright lad 2 (ugs.) **~ und fertig** (fertig vorbereitet) quite finished; (völlig erschöpft) completely shattered (coll.) 3 (festgelegt) fixed ‹*cost, salary*›; **eine ~e Idee** an idée fixe
B *adv.* (ugs.) quickly; **das geht ganz ~:** it won't take a jiffy (coll.); **mach ~!** hurry up!

Fixativ /fɪksa'ti:f/ *das;* **~s, ~e** fixative

Fixe /'fɪksə/ *die;* **~, ~n** (Drogenjargon) needle

fixen /'fɪksn̩/ *itr. V.* 1 (Drogenjargon: spritzen) fix (sl.) 2 (Börsenw.) bear

Fixer *der;* **~s, ~, Fixerin** *die;* **~, ~nen** 1 (Drogenjargon) fixer 2 (Börsenw.) bear

Fix·geschäft *das* (Wirtsch.) purchase for delivery at a fixed time

Fixier·bad *das* (Fot.) fixer

fixierbar *Adj.* definable

fixieren /fɪ'ksi:rən/ *tr. V.* 1 (scharf ansehen) fix one's gaze on; **jmdn./etw. scharf/kühl ~:** gaze sharply/coldly at sb./sth. 2 (geh.: schriftlich niederlegen) take down ‹*interview, report, statement*› 3 (geh.: verbindlich bestimmen) fix ‹*date*›; **der Zeitpunkt ist auf den 12. Mai fixiert worden** the date has been fixed as the twelfth of May 4 (Fot.) fix 5 (Med.: festmachen) set 6 (Psych.) **er ist stark auf seine Mutter fixiert** he has a strong mother fixation; **sich auf** (*Akk.*)/**an** (*Dat.*) **etw. ~:** devote oneself *or* give oneself up entirely to sth.

Fixier·salz *das* (Fot.) hypo

Fixierung *die;* **~, ~en** 1 (starres Festlegen, -halten) **die ~ auf eine Frage** concentration on a question; **die ~ auf seine Mutter** his mother fixation 2 (Festlegung) determination

Fixigkeit *die;* **~** (ugs.) speed

Fix-: ~punkt *der* fixed point; **~stern** *der* (Astron.) fixed star

Fixum /'fɪksʊm/ *das;* **~s, Fixa** basic salary

Fix·zeit *die* core time

Fjord /fjɔrt/ *der;* **~[e]s, ~e** fjord

FKK *Abk.* = **Freikörperkultur** nudism *no art.;* naturism *no art.*

FKK-: ~-Anhänger *der,* **~-Anhängerin** *die* nudist; naturist; **~-Strand** *der* nudist beach

Fla /fla:/ *die;* **~:** anti-aircraft defence; AA defence

flach /flax/ *Adj.* 1 (eben) flat ‹*countryside, region, roof*›; **das ~e Land** the flat country; **sich ~ hinlegen** lay oneself [down] flat; **mit der ~en Hand** with the flat of one's hand 2 ▸ⓘ **S. 374** (niedrig) low ‹*heels, building*›; flat ‹*shoe*› 3 ▸ⓘ **S. 267,** ▸ⓘ **S. 374** (nicht tief) shallow ‹*water, river, etc., dish*› 4 (abwertend: nichtssagend, unwesentlich) shallow

flach-, Flach-: ~bau *der; Pl.* **~~ten** low building; **~bett·scanner** *der* (DV) flatbed scanner; **~bildschirm** *der* (DV) flat screen; **~bogen** *der* (Archit.) segmental arch; **~brüstig** *Adj.* flat-chested; **~dach** *das* flat roof; **~druck·verfahren** *das* planographic printing method

Fläche /'flɛçə/ *die;* **~, ~n** 1 (ebenes Gebiet) area; **auf einer ~ von 20 m²** over an area of 20 square metres 2 (Ober~, Außenseite) surface 3 ▸ⓘ **S. 262** (Math.) area; (einer dreidimensionalen Figur) side; face 4 (weite Land~, Wasser~) expanse 5 (von Kristallen) facet

Flach·eisen *das* 1 (gewalztes Eisen) flat bar 2 (Werkzeug) scorper

flächen-, Flächen-: ~ausdehnung *die* area; **~blitz** *der* sheet lightning; **~brand** *der* extensive blaze; **sich zu einem ~brand ausweiten** (fig.) spread like wildfire; **~deckend** A *Adj.* ‹*supply, vaccinations, etc.*› with blanket coverage; comprehensive ‹*network*›; B *adv.* across the whole area/country *etc.;* **~gleich** *Adj.* of equal area *postpos.;* equal in area *postpos.;* **~haft** A *Adj.* extensive; B *adv.* extensively; **~inhalt** *der* (Math.)

area; **~maß** *das* (Math.) unit of square measure; **~nutzungs·plan** *der* land development plan; **~staat** *der* territorial state; **~stilllegung** *die* set-aside; **~tarifvertrag** *der* industry-wide pay agreement; **~wirkung** *die* surface effect

flach-, Flach-: ~|fallen *itr. V.; mit sein* (ugs.) ‹*trip*› fall through; ‹*event*› be cancelled; **das Kino fällt für dich heute ~:** you won't be going to the cinema today; **diese Subventionen sollen ~fallen** these subsidies will not be continued; **~feile** *die* flat file; **~glas** *das* sheet glass; **~hang** *der* slip-off slope

Flachheit *die;* ~, **~en** [1] (abwertend) shallowness [2] (Bemerkung) platitude

flächig

[A] *Adj.* [1] (abgeflacht) flat ‹*features, shape*› [2] (ausgedehnt) extensive ‹*area*› [3] (Kunstw.) two-dimensional ‹*style, representation*›

[B] *adv.* extensively

flach-, Flach-: ~kopf *der* (abwertend) numskull; **~küste** *die* (Geogr.) beach; **~land** *das* lowland; **~länder** *der;* **~~s, ~~, ~länderin** *die;* **~~, ~~nen** lowlander; **~|legen** [A] *refl. V.* (ugs.) lie down; [B] *tr. V.* (zu Boden strecken) floor ‹*opponent*›; **~|liegen** *unr. itr. V.* (ugs.) be flat on one's back; **~mann** *der* (ugs. scherzh.) hip flask; **~meißel** *der* flat chisel; **~moor** *das* (Geog.) low-moor bog; **~pass, *~paß** *der* (Fußball) low pass; **einen ~pass [auf jmdn.] spielen** make a low pass [to sb.]; **~relief** *das* low relief; **~rennen** *das* (Sport) flat race

Flachs /flaks/ *der;* **~es** [1] flax [2] (ugs.: Ulk) **das war doch nur ~:** I/he *etc.* was just having you on (Brit. coll.) *or* (Amer. coll.) putting you on; **ganz ohne ~:** no kidding (coll.)

flachs·blond *Adj.* flaxen ‹*hair*›

Flach·schuss, *Flach·schuß *der* (Fußball) low shot

flachsen /ˈflaksn̩/ *itr. V.* **mit jmdm. ~** (ugs.) joke with sb.; **gerne ~:** like a joke

Flachserei *die;* ~, **~en** (ugs.) joking; **das war doch nur ~:** it was just a joke

Flachs·kopf *der* flaxen-haired person; **beide Kinder waren ~köpfe** both of the children were flaxen-haired

Flach-: ~strecke *die* (Leichtathletik) flat race; **~zange** *die* flat tongs *pl.*; **~ziegel** *der* flat tile

flackern /ˈflakɐn/ *itr. V.* flicker; **~des Kaminfeuer/Licht/~de Augen** flickering fire/light/eyes; **Erregung flackerte in seinem Blick** his eyes glinted with excitement

Flacker·schein *der* flickering light

Fladen /ˈflaːdn̩/ *der;* **~s,** ~ [1] *flat, round unleavened cake made with oat or barley flour;* ≈ [large] oatcake (Scot.) [2] (Kuh~) cowpat

Fladen·brot *das* unleavened bread

Flagellant /flagɛˈlant/ *der;* **~en, ~en, Flagellantin** *die;* ~, **~nen** flagellant

Flagellantismus *der;* ~ (Med., Psych.) flagellantism *no art.*

Flagellation /flagɛlaˈtsi̯oːn/ *die;* ~ (Med., Psych.) flagellation

Flagellum /flaˈgɛlʊm/ *das;* **~s, Flagellen** (Biol.) flagellum; (Peitsche) scourge

Flagge /ˈflagə/ *die;* ~, **~n** flag; **unter neutraler ~ fahren** sail under a neutral flag; **die ~ streichen** (fig.) strike the flag (fig.); **~ zeigen** (fig.) show one's colours; **unter falscher ~ segeln** (fig.) sail under false colours

flaggen

[A] *itr. V.* put out the flags; **überall war geflaggt** the flags were flying everywhere

[B] *tr. V.* **die Straßen sind geflaggt** the flags have been put out in the streets

Flaggen-: ~alphabet *das* international code of signals; **~ehrung** *die* ►**~parade**; **~gala** *die* flag dressing; **~gruß** *der* flag salute; **~leine** *die* halyard; **~mast** *der* flagstaff; **~parade** *die* flag-raising/flag-lowering ceremony; **~signal** *das* code flag signal; **~tuch** *das; Pl.* **~~e** bunting

Flagg-: ~leine *die* halyard; **~offizier** *der* flag officer; **~schiff** *das* flagship

flagrant /flaˈgrant/ *Adj.* flagrant

Flair /flɛːɐ̯/ *das od. der;* **~s** [1] (Fluidum, Aura) air; **ein ~ von etw. haben** have an air of sth. [2] (Talent) flair; **ein ~ für etw. haben** have a flair for sth.

Flak /flak/ *die;* ~, ~ (Milit.) anti-aircraft gun; AA gun

Flak-: ~feuer *das* anti-aircraft fire; flak; **wir wurden unter ~feuer genommen** we came under anti-aircraft fire *or* flak; **~geschütz** *das* anti-aircraft gun; AA gun; **~helfer** *der* anti-aircraft auxiliary

Flakon /flaˈkõː/ *das od. der;* **~s, ~s** bottle

Flak-: ~scheinwerfer *der* anti-aircraft searchlight; **~soldat** *der* anti-aircraft soldier; **~stellung** *die* anti-aircraft position; AA position

flambieren /flamˈbiːrən/ *tr. V.* flambé; **flambiert** flambé; flambéed

Flamboyant /flãbo̯aˈjãː/ *der;* **~s, ~s** (Bot.) flamboyant tree; royal poinciana tree

Flamboyant·stil *der* (Archit.) Flamboyant style

Flame /ˈflaːmə/ *der;* **~n, ~n** ►ℹ **S. 520** Fleming

Flamenco /flaˈmɛŋko/ *der;* **~[s], ~s** flamenco

Flamin, Flämin /ˈflɛːmɪn/ *die;* ~, **~nen** ►ℹ **S. 520** Fleming; *s. auch* **-in**

Flamingo /flaˈmɪŋgo/ *der;* **~s, ~s** flamingo

flämisch /ˈflɛːmɪʃ/ *Adj.* ►ℹ **S. 520**, ►ℹ **S. 670** Flemish

Flämmchen /ˈflɛmçən/ *das;* **~s, ~:** [small] flame

Flamme /ˈflamə/ *die;* ~, **~n** [1] flame; **etw. auf kleiner/großer ~ kochen** cook sth. on a low/high flame *or* gas; **in [hellen] ~n stehen** be in flames; **in ~n aufgehen** go up in flames [2] (Brennstelle) burner; **ein Gasherd mit drei ~n** a gas stove with three burners [3] (ugs. veralt.: Freundin) flame

flammen /ˈflamən/ *itr. V.* (geh.) blaze

Flammen·blume *die* (Bot.) phlox

flammend *Adj.* [1] flaming; **~es Haar** flaming red hair [2] (fig.) fiery ‹*speech*›; **~e Anklagen und Protestaktionen** fervent accusations and protests

Flammen-: ~meer *das* (geh.) sea of flame[s]; **~tod** *der* (geh.) death by burning; **er konnte sie vor dem ~tod retten** he was able to save them from burning to death; **sie erlitt den ~tod** she was burnt to death; **~werfer** *der* (Milit.) flame-thrower

Flammeri /ˈflaməri/ *der;* **~[s], ~s** (Kochk.) flummery

Flandern /ˈflandɐn/ *(das);* **~s** Flanders

Flanell /flaˈnɛl/ *der;* **~s, ~e** flannel; **ein Anzug aus ~:** a flannel suit

Flanell-: ~anzug *der* flannel suit; **~hose** *die* flannel trousers *pl.*

Flaneur /flaˈnøːɐ̯/ *der;* **~s, ~e, Flaneurin** *die;* ~, **~nen** (geh.) flâneur; stroller

flanieren /flaˈniːrən/ *itr. V.; mit Richtungsangabe mit sein* stroll

Flanier·meile *die* (ugs.) promenade for strollers

Flanke /ˈflaŋkə/ *die;* ~, **~n** [1] (Weiche) flank [2] (Ballspiele) centre; **eine ~ geben** *od.* **schlagen** centre the ball; **eine ~ direkt aufnehmen** pick up a centre [3] (Teil des Spielfeldes) wing; **über die [rechte/linke] ~ spielen** play on the [right/left] wing [4] (Turnen) flank vault [5] (Milit.) flank [6] (Fechten) lower outside target

flanken *itr. V.* [1] (Ballspiele) **[in die Mitte] ~:** centre the ball [2] (Turnen) flank vault; **über etw.** (*Akk.*) **~:** flank vault over sth.

Flanken-: ~ball *der* (Ballspiele) centre; **~deckung** *die* (Milit.) flank defence; **~schutz** *der* (Milit.) flank protection

flankieren *tr. V.* flank; **von jmdm./etw. flankiert werden** be flanked by sb./sth.; **~de Maßnahmen** (fig.) additional measures

Flansch /flanʃ/ *der;* **~[e]s, ~e** (Technik) flange

Flappe /ˈflapə/ *die;* ~, **~n** (bes. nordd.; ugs.) **eine ~ ziehen** sulk; **halt die ~!** shut up! (coll.)

Flaps /flaps/ *der;* **~es, ~e** (ugs.) lout

flapsig /ˈflapsɪç/ (ugs.)

[A] *Adj.* rude

[B] *adv.* rudely

Flasche /ˈflaʃə/ *die;* ~, **~n** [1] bottle; **eine ~ Wein/Bier/Milch** a bottle of wine/beer/milk; **etw. auf ~n abfüllen** *od.* **ziehen** bottle sth.; **gibst du deinem Kind immer noch die ~?** are you still bottle-feeding your child?; **ich muss dem Kind noch die ~ geben** I must just feed the baby; **ein Tier mit der ~ großziehen** rear an animal by bottle; **zur ~ greifen** (fig.) take to the bottle [2] (ugs. abwertend) (Feigling) wet (coll.); (unfähiger Mensch) **eine [richtige] ~ sein** be [completely] useless; **du ~!** you useless item! (coll.)

flaschen-, Flaschen-: ~batterie *die* (ugs.) hoard of bottles; **~baum** *der* (Bot.) custard apple tree; sweetsop tree; **~bier** *das* bottled beer; **~bofist, ~bovist** *der* (Bot.) devil's tobacco pouch; **~bürste** *die* bottle brush; **~etikett** *das* label [on a/the bottle]; **~gärung** *die* fermentation in the bottle; **~gas** *das* bottled gas; **~gestell** *das* bottle rack; **~grün** *Adj.* bottle-green; **~hals** *der* (auch fig.) bottleneck; **~halter** *der* bottle cage; **~kind** *das* bottle-fed baby; **waren Sie ein Brustkind oder ein ~kind?** were you breast-fed or bottle-fed?; **~korken** *der* cork; **~kürbis** *der* (Bot.) bottle-gourd; **~milch** *die* [1] (abgefüllte Milch) bottled milk; [2] (Nahrung) [liquid] baby food; baby milk; **~öffner** *der* bottle opener; **~pfand** *das* deposit [on a/the bottle]; **~post** *die* message in a/the bottle; **~regal** *das* bottle rack; **~wein** *der* wine by the bottle; **offene und ~weine** wine by the bottle or by the glass; **~weise** *Adv.* by the bottleful; **~zug** *der* block and tackle

Flaschner /ˈflaʃnɐ/ *der;* **~s,** ~, **Flaschnerin** *die* (südd., schweiz.) plumber

Flatrate /ˈflɛtreɪt/ *die;* ~, **~s** flat rate

Flatschen /ˈfla(ː)tʃn̩/ *der;* **~s,** ~ (ugs.) (Lehm~) lump; (Tapeten~) strip

Flatter /ˈflatɐ/ *in* **die ~ machen** (salopp) beat it (coll.)

Flatter-: ~geist *der* fickle person; **~gras** *das* millet grass

flatterhaft *Adj.* fickle

Flatterhaftigkeit *die;* **~:** fickleness

Flatter·mann *der* (salopp) [1] (nervöse Unruhe) jitters *pl.* (coll.); **einen ~ haben** have the jitters; (zitternde Hände) be shaking all the time [2] (scherzh.: Brathuhn) roast chicken

flattern *itr. V.* [1] *mit Richtungsangabe mit sein* flutter; **der Vogel flatterte in seinem Käfig** the bird fluttered its wings in its cage [2] (zittern) ‹*hands*› shake; ‹*eyelids*› flutter; **seine Nerven flatterten** (fig.) he got in a flap (coll.) [3] *mit sein* (vom Wind weitergetragen werden) flutter; **zu Boden** *od.* **auf den Boden ~:** flutter to the ground; **plötzlich flattert mir eine Postkarte auf den Tisch** (fig.) suddenly a postcard appears on the table [4] (die Haftung verlieren) ‹*ski, wheel*› lose its grip

Flatter-: ~satz *der* (Druckw.) unjustified setting; **~tier** *das* (Zool.) flying mammal; **~zunge** *die* (Musik) tonguing

flau /flau̯/

[A] *Adj.* [1] (schwach, matt) slack ‹*breeze*›; flat ‹*atmosphere*› [2] (leicht übel) queasy ‹*feeling*›; **mir ist ~ [vor Hunger]** I feel queasy [with hunger]

[B] *adv.* (Kaufmannsspr.) **das Geschäft geht ~:** business is slack; **die Börse eröffnete ~:** the market got off to a slow start

Flaum /flau̯m/ *der;* **~[e]s** [1] fuzz [2] (**~feder**) down

Flaum·bart *der* downy beard

Flaumer *der;* **~s,** ~ (schweiz.) mop

Flaum-: ~feder *die* down feather; **~haar** *das* down

flaumig *Adj.* [1] downy [2] (österr.: schaumig, porös) fluffy

Flausch /flau̯ʃ/ *der;* **~[e]s, ~e** brushed wool

flauschig *Adj.* fluffy

Flausch·jacke *die* brushed-wool jacket

f

Flause /ˈflauzə/ *die;* ~, ~n (ugs.) 1 (Unsinn) **er hat nur ~n im Kopf** he can never think of anything sensible; **jmdm. die ~n austreiben** knock some sense into sb.; **lass doch die albernen ~n** stop messing about (coll.) 2 (Ausflucht) excuse; **~n machen** make excuses

Flaute /ˈflautə/ *die;* ~, ~n 1 (Seemannsspr.) calm 2 (Kaufmannsspr.) fall[-off] in trade; **in der ~:** in the doldrums; **es herrscht eine [allgemeine] ~:** trade is [generally] slack 3 (Sport: Tiefpunkt) **sie überwanden die ~:** they got over the bad patch [in the game]

Fläz /flɛːts/ *der;* ~es, ~e (ugs. abwertend) lout

fläzen *refl. V.* (ugs. abwertend) **sich in den/im Sessel ~:** flop into/lounge in the armchair

Flebbe /ˈflɛbə/ *die;* ~, ~n (salopp) identity card

Flechse /ˈflɛksə/ *die;* ~, ~n sinew

Flecht·arbeit *die* piece of wickerwork; **~en** wickerwork *sing.*

Flechte /ˈflɛçtə/ *die;* ~, ~n 1 (Bot.) lichen 2 ▸ⓘ S. 439 (Med.) eczema 3 (geh.: Zopf) plait

flechten *unr. tr. V.* plait ‹*hair*›; weave ‹*basket, mat*›; **etw. zu einem Korb ~:** weave sth. into a basket; weave a basket out of sth.; **jmdn. aufs Rad ~** (hist.) break sb. on the wheel

Flechter *der;* ~s, ~, **Flechterin** *die;* ~, ~nen basket weaver

Flecht-: **~werk** *das* 1 (Geflecht) wickerwork; 2 (Archit.) wattle and daub; **~zaun** *der* wicker fence

Fleck /flɛk/ *der;* ~[e]s, ~e 1 (verschmutzte Stelle) stain; **voller ~e sein** be covered in stains; **~e machen** leave stains; **das macht keine ~e** that does not leave stains *or* does not stain; **einen ~ auf der [weißen] Weste haben** (fig. ugs.) have blotted one's copybook 2 (andersfarbige Stelle) patch; **ein weißer ~ auf der Landkarte** a piece of uncharted territory; an uncharted region; *s. auch* **blau** 3 (Stelle, Punkt) spot; **er rührte sich nicht vom ~:** he didn't move an inch; **auf demselben ~ stehen** stand in the same place; **wir brachten den Stein nicht vom ~:** we couldn't budge the stone; **ich bin nicht vom ~ gekommen** (fig.) I didn't get anywhere; **am falschen ~ sparen** (fig.) save on the wrong things; **vom ~ weg** (fig.) on the spot; *s. auch* **Herz 1**

Fleckchen *das;* ~s, ~: spot; **ein schönes ~ Erde** a lovely little spot

flecken *itr. V.* stain

Flecken *der;* ~s, ~ 1 ▸ **Fleck 1, 2** 2 (Ortschaft) little place

flecken-, Flecken-: **~entfernungs·mittel** *das* stain *or* spot remover; **~los** A *Adj.* 1 spotless; 2 (einwandfrei, tadellos) without blemish *postpos.;* B *adv.* spotlessly

Fleck·entferner *der;* ~s, ~, **Fleck·entfernungs·mittel** *das,* **Flecken·wasser** *das* stain *or* spot remover

Fleckerl·teppich *der* (bayr., österr.) patchwork rug

Fleck·fieber *das* ▸ⓘ S. 439 (Med.) typhus

fleckig /ˈflɛkɪç/ *Adj.* 1 (verschmutzt) stained; **ganz ~:** full of stains 2 (gepunktet) speckled ‹*apple*›; blotchy ‹*face, skin*›

fleddern /ˈflɛdɐn/ *tr. V.* plunder, rob ‹*person*›; (salopp) ransack ‹*desk etc.*›

Fleder·maus /ˈfleːdɐ-/ *die* bat

Fledermaus·ärmel *der* (Textilw.) batwing sleeve

Fleder·wisch *der* feather duster

Fleet /fleːt/ *das;* ~s, ~e (nordd.) canal

Flegel /ˈfleːgl̩/ *der;* ~s, ~ (abwertend) lout

Flegel·alter *das* ▸ **Flegeljahre**

Flegelei *die;* ~, ~en (abwertend) loutish behaviour; **eine solche ~/solche ~en** such loutish behaviour

flegelhaft
A *Adj.* (abwertend) loutish; boorish ‹*tone of voice*›
B *adv.* loutishly

Flegel·jahre *Pl.* uncouth adolescence *sing.;* **in die ~ kommen/aus den ~n heraus sein** reach/be past the awkward age *sing.*

flegeln *refl. V.* (abwertend) **sich auf ein Sofa/in einen Sessel ~:** flop on to a sofa/into an armchair

flehen /ˈfleːən/ *itr. V.* plead; **[bei jmdm.] um etw. ~:** plead [with sb.] for sth.; **mit ~der Stimme** with a pleading voice; **zu Gott/zum Himmel [um etw.] ~:** beg God/Heaven [for sth.]

flehentlich *Adv.* (geh.) pleadingly

Fleisch /flaiʃ/ *das;* ~[e]s 1 (Muskelgewebe) flesh; **das nackte ~:** one's bare flesh; **das rohe ~:** one's raw flesh; **viel ~ zeigen** (ugs.) show a lot of flesh; (fig.) **sein eigen[es] ~ und Blut** (geh.) his own flesh and blood; **jmdm. in ~ und Blut übergehen** become second nature to sb.; **sich** (*Dat.*) **ins eigene ~ schneiden** cut off one's nose to spite one's face; **vom ~ fallen** (ugs.) waste away; **~ fressend** (Biol.) carnivorous 2 (Nahrungsmittel) meat 3 (Frucht~) flesh 4 **den Weg allen ~es gehen** (geh.) go the way of all flesh; **~ geworden** (dichter.) incarnate (Theol.); ‹*innocence, virtue, etc.*› personified

fleisch-, Fleisch-: **~abfälle** *Pl.* meat scraps; **~arm** A *Adj.* ‹*diet*› low in meat; B *adv.* **ich esse sehr ~arm** I eat very little meat; **~beschau** *die* meat inspection; (ugs. scherzh.) cattle market; **~beschauer** *der,* **~beschauerin** *die* meat inspector; **~brocken** *der* chunk of meat; **~brühe** *die* (mit Einlage) meat soup; (klar) bouillon; consommé; **~einlage** *die* added meat; **mit ~einlage** with meat added; **~einwaage** *die* meat content

Fleischer /ˈflaiʃɐ/ *der;* ~s, ~, **Fleischerin** *die;* ~, ~nen ▸ⓘ S. 113 butcher; *s. auch* **Bäcker**

Fleischerei *die;* ~, ~en butcher's shop; **in der ~:** at the butcher's; *s. auch* **Bäckerei**

Fleischer-: **~geselle** *der,* **~gesellin** *die* butcher; **~haken** *der* meat hook; **~handwerk** *das* butchery trade; **~hund** *der* large fierce dog; **ein Gemüt wie ein ~hund haben** (ugs.) be a cold-blooded sort (coll.); **~laden** *der; Pl.* **~läden** ▸ **Fleischerei**; **~meister** *der,* **~meisterin** *die* master butcher; **~messer** *das* butcher's knife

Fleisches·lust *die* (geh.) carnal lust

fleisch-, Fleisch-: **~esser** *der,* **~esserin** *die* meat eater; **~extrakt** *der* meat extract; **~farben, ~farbig** *Adj.* flesh-coloured; **~fliege** *die* meat fly; **~fondue** *das* (Kochk.) meat fondue; **~fressend** ▸ **Fleisch 1**; **~fresser** *der* (Biol.) carnivore; **~füllung** *die* (Kochk.) meat stuffing; (in Pasteten) meat filling; **~gang** *der* (Gastr.) meat course; **~gericht** *das* meat dish; **~geworden** ▸ **Fleisch 4**; **~haken** *der* meat hook; **~hauer** *der,* **~hauerin** *die;* ~~, ~~nen (österr.) butcher

fleischig *Adj.* plump ‹*hands, face*›; fleshy ‹*leaf, fruit*›

Fleisch-: **~käse** *der* meat loaf; **~kloß** *der* 1 (Kochk.) meat ball; 2 ▸ **~klumpen**; **~klößchen** *das* small meat ball; **~klumpen** *der* (ugs.) 1 (großes Stück ~klumpen) chunk of meat; 2 (abwertend: Mensch) mound of flesh; **~konserve** *die* tin of meat (Brit.); can of meat (Amer.); **~konserven** tinned meat (Brit.); canned meat (Amer.)

fleischlich *Adj.* 1 (veralt.) **~e Kost** *od.* **Nahrung** meat 2 (geh. veralt.) carnal; **allem Fleischlichen entsagen** renounce the flesh

fleisch-, Fleisch-: **~los** A *Adj.* 1 ‹*meal*› without meat; 2 (hager, mager) bony ‹*hands, face*›; B *adv.* ‹*cook*› without meat; **~maschine** *die* (südd., österr.) ▸ **~wolf**; **~messer** *das* carving knife; **~pastete** *die* (Kochk.) pâté; **~preis** *der* price of meat; **die ~preise** the meat prices; **~ration** *die* meat ration; **~salat** *der* (Kochk.) meat salad; **~seite** *die* (Gerberei) flesh side; **~stück** *das* piece of meat; **~topf** *der* meat pot; **sich nach den ~töpfen Ägyptens sehnen/zurücksehnen** long for/long to return to the good life; **~vergiftung** *die* food poisoning [from meat]; **~waren** *Pl.* meat products; **~- und Wurstwaren** meat and sausages; **~werdung** *die;* ~~ (dicht.) incarnation; **~wolf** *der* mincer; **etw. durch den ~wolf drehen** put sth. through the mincer; mince sth.; **~wunde** *die* flesh wound; **~wurst** *die* pork sausage

Fleiß /flais/ *der;* ~es 1 (eifriges Streben) hard work; (Eigenschaft) diligence; **mit großem ~:** diligently; **mit ihrem beharrlichen ~:** with her unceasing application; **viel ~ auf etw.** (*Akk.*) **verwenden** put a lot of effort into sth.; **durch ~ etw. erreichen** achieve sth. by hard work; **im ~ nachlassen** become slack; **ohne ~ kein Preis** (Spr.) success never comes easily 2 (veralt., südd.: Absicht) **mit ~:** on purpose

Fleiß·arbeit *die* task requiring great diligence; **eine reine ~** (abwertend) a [diligent but] routine piece of work

fleißig /ˈflaisɪç/
A *Adj.* 1 (arbeitsam) hard-working; **~e Hände** willing hands; **sie sind ~ wie die Bienen** *od.* **Ameisen** they work like beavers 2 (von Fleiß zeugend) **eine ~e Arbeit** a diligent piece of work 3 (regelmäßig, häufig) **ein ~er Besucher** a frequent visitor (*Gen.* to) 4 (unermüdlich) indefatigable ‹*collector*›; great ‹*walker*›
B *adv.* 1 ‹*work, study*› hard; **~ lernen** learn as much as one can 2 (unermüdlich) ‹*drink, spend*› steadily; ‹*collect*› regularly; **immer ~ hauen** keep on hitting 3 (regelmäßig) frequently; **geh nur ~ spazieren** do as much walking as you can

Fleiß·prüfung *die: examination to assess application*

flektierbar *Adj.* (Sprachw.) inflectional

flektieren /flɛkˈtiːrən/ (Sprachw.)
A *tr. V.* inflect
B *itr. V.* be inflected

flennen /ˈflɛnən/ *itr. V.* (ugs. abwertend) blubber

fletschen /ˈflɛtʃn̩/ *tr., itr. V.* **die Zähne** *od.* **mit den Zähnen ~:** bare one's teeth; **mit gefletschten Zähnen** with bared teeth

fleucht /flɔyçt/ ▸ **kreucht**

Fleurop Ⓦⓩ /ˈflɔyrɔp/ *die* Interflora ®

Flex *die;* ~, ~e (ugs.) angle grinder [with cutting disc]

flexen /ˈflɛksn̩/ *itr. V.* work with an/the angle grinder

flexibel /flɛˈksiːbl̩/
A *Adj.* flexible
B *adv.* flexibly

Flexibilität /flɛksibiliˈtɛːt/ *die;* ~: flexibility

Flexion /flɛˈksi̯oːn/ *die;* ~, ~en 1 (Sprachw.) inflexion; (von Adjektiven, Substantiven) declension; (von Verben) conjugation 2 ▸ⓘ S. 439 (Med.) flexion

flexions-, Flexions-: **~endung** *die* (Sprachw.) inflectional suffix *or* ending; **~los** *Adj.* (Sprachw.) uninflected

Flexo·druck /ˈflɛkso-/ *der* (Druckw.) flexographic printing

flicht *Imperativ Sg. u. 3. Pers. Sg. Präsens v.* **flechten**

Flick·arbeit *die* repair; **mit einer ~ beschäftigt sein** be repairing *or* mending something

flicken /ˈflɪkn̩/ *tr. V.* mend ‹*trousers, dress*›; repair ‹*engine, cable*›; mend, repair ‹*wall, roof*›; **etw. notdürftig ~:** patch sth. up

Flicken *der;* ~s, ~: patch

Flicken-: **~decke** *die* patchwork quilt; **~teppich** *der* patchwork rug

Flickflack /ˈflɪkflak/ *der;* ~s, ~s (Turnen) flikflak

Flick-: **~korb** *der* sewing basket; **~schneider** *der,* **~schneiderin** *die* (veralt.) mending tailor; **~schuster** *der* 1 (veralt. abwertend) cobbler; 2 (fig.: Nichtskönner) bungler; **~schusterei** *die* (fig. abwertend) bungling; **~schusterin** *die* ▸ **~schuster**; **~werk** *das* (abwertend) botched-up job; **~wort** *das; Pl.* **~wörter** filler; **~zeug** *das* repair kit

Flieder /ˈfliːdɐ/ *der;* ~s, ~: lilac

flieder-, Flieder-: **~duft** *der* scent of lilac; **~farben, ~farbig** *Adj.* lilac; **~strauch** *der* lilac bush; **~tee** *der* elderberry tea

Fliege /ˈfliːɡə/ *die;* ~, ~n 1 fly; **die Menschen starben wie die ~n** people were dying like flies; **er tut keiner ~ etwas zuleide/könnte keiner ~ etwas zuleide tun** he wouldn't/couldn't hurt a fly; (fig.) **ihn stört die ~ an der Wand** the least little thing annoys him; **zwei ~n mit einer Klappe schlagen** kill two birds with one stone; **die** *od.* **'ne ~ machen** (salopp) beat it (coll.) 2 (Schleife) bow tie 3 (Bärtchen) shadow

fliegen

A *unr. itr. V.* 1 *mit sein* fly; **das ~de Personal** the air crew; **im Wind ~:** be flying in the wind; **mit ~den Rockschößen** with flapping coat-tails; **die Funken flogen** sparks flew about; **in die Luft ~:** blow up; *s. auch* **Fahne 2** 2 *mit sein* (ugs.: geworfen werden) **aus der Kurve ~:** skid off a/the bend; **vom Pferd/Fahrrad ~:** fall off a/the horse/bicycle 3 *mit sein* (ugs.: entlassen werden) be sacked (coll.); get the sack (coll.); **auf die Straße/aus einer Stellung ~:** get the sack (coll.); be thrown out; **von der Schule ~:** be chucked out [of the school] (coll.) 4 *mit sein* (ugs.: hinfallen, stürzen) fall; **in einen Graben ~:** fall into a ditch; **über etw.** (*Akk.*) **~:** trip over sth.; **durch das Examen/eine Prüfung ~** (fig.) fail the exam/a test 5 *mit sein* **auf jmdn./etw. ~** (ugs.) go for sb./sth.; **er fliegt auf Blondinen** he makes a beeline for blondes 6 *meist mit sein* (flattern, zittern) ‹*pulse*› race; **sein Atem fliegt** he is gasping for breath; **er flog am ganzen Körper** he was trembling all over 7 *mit sein* (eilen, rasen) fly; race; **das Pferd flog wie ein Pfeil über die Bahn** the horse raced or flew over the track like a shot from a gun; **ihre Hand flog über das Papier** her hand flew over the paper; **in ~der Eile** *od.* **Hast** in a mad rush

B *unr. tr. V.* 1 (steuern, ~d befördern) fly ‹*aircraft, passengers, goods*› 2 *auch mit sein* (~d ausführen) **einen Einsatz ~:** fly a mission; **einen Umweg ~:** make a detour; **eine Kurve ~:** describe a curve; **einen Looping ~:** loop the loop; **einen Angriff ~** (Milit.) make an attack

C *refl. V.* **die Maschine fliegt sich gut/schlecht** the plane flies well/badly; **es fliegt sich gut/schlecht hier/heute** the flying is good/bad here/today

fliegend *Adj.* flying; **ein ~er Händler** a pedlar; **~e Bauten** mobile buildings; **der Fliegende Holländer** the Flying Dutchman

Fliegen-: ~draht *der* fly screen; **~dreck** *der* fly droppings *pl.*; **~fänger** *der* flypaper; **~fenster** *das* wire-mesh window; **~gewicht** *das* (Schwerathletik) 1 flyweight; **die Meisterschaften im ~gewicht** the flyweight championships; **im ~gewicht starten** compete at flyweight; 2 ▸ **~gewichtler**; **~gewichtler** /-ɡəvɪçtlɐ/ *der;* ~~s, ~~: flyweight; **~klatsche** *die* fly swat; **~kopf** *der* (Druckw.) *piece of type turned over to print as black oblong;* **~pilz** *der* fly agaric; **~schnäpper** *der;* ~~s, ~~ (Zool.) flycatcher; **~schrank** *der* meat safe

Flieger *der;* ~s, ~ 1 pilot; **er ist bei den ~n** (Milit.) he's in the air force 2 (Radsport) sprinter 3 (Artistik) trapeze artist 4 (Zool.) flyer

Flieger-: ~abwehr *die* ▸ **Flugabwehr**; **~abzeichen** *das* (Milit.) flying badge; **~alarm** *der* air-raid warning; **~angriff** *der* air raid

Fliegerei *die;* ~: flying *no art.*

Flieger·horst *der* (Milit.) military airfield

Fliegerin *die;* ~, ~nen [woman] pilot

fliegerisch *Adj.* aeronautical; **~e Eigenschaften** handling characteristics; handling *sing.*

Flieger-: ~jacke *die* flying jacket; **~krankheit** *die* altitude sickness; **~rennen** *das* (Radsport) sprint; **~schule** *die* flying school; **~sprache** *die* airmen's jargon; **~staffel** *die* (Milit.) [flying] squadron

Flieh·burg *die* refuge

fliehen /ˈfliːən/

A *unr. itr. V.*; *mit sein* (flüchten) flee (**vor** + *Dat.* from); (aus dem Gefängnis usw.) escape (**aus** from); **ins Ausland/über die Grenze ~:** flee the country/escape over the border

B *unr. tr. V.* (geh.: meiden) shun

fliehend *Adj.* sloping ‹*forehead*›; receding ‹*chin*›

Flieh·kraft *die* (Physik) centrifugal force

Fliese /ˈfliːzə/ *die;* ~, ~n tile; **etw. mit ~n auslegen** tile sth.

fliesen *tr. V.* tile

Fliesenleger /-leːɡɐ/ *der;* ~s, ~, **Fliesenlegerin** *die;* ~, ~nen ▸ℹ **S. 113** tiler

Fließ-: ~arbeit *die* assembly line production; **~band** *das; Pl.* **~bänder** conveyor belt; **am ~band arbeiten** *od.* (ugs.) **stehen** work on the assembly line; **am ~band gefertigt werden** be produced on the assembly line; **~band·arbeit** *die* assembly-line work; **~band·arbeiter** *der,* **~band·arbeiterin** *die* assembly-line worker; **~band·fertigung** *die* assembly-line production

fließen /ˈfliːsn̩/ *unr. itr. V.; mit sein* 1 ▸ℹ **S. 267** flow; **ein Bach ist ein ~des Gewässer** a stream is a body of running water; **ein Zimmer mit ~dem [warmem und kaltem] Wasser** a room with [hot and cold] running water; **„Alles fließt", sagte Heraklit** 'All is flux', said Heraclitus; (unpers.) **es floss Blut** blood was shed 2 ▸ℹ **S. 670** (fig.) **viele Devisen flossen ins Land** a great deal of foreign currency flowed into the country; **die Gaben flossen reichlich** donations were pouring in; **die Nachrichten aus diesem Gebiet flossen nur spärlich** news from this area came in very infrequently; **der Verkehr war ~d** the traffic kept moving; **die Grenzen [zwischen zwei Gebieten] sind ~d** the dividing line [between two areas] is blurred; **~de Übergänge** fluid transitions; **die Verse flossen ihm aus der Feder** the verses flowed from his pen; **eine Sprache ~d sprechen** speak a language fluently

Fließ-: ~grenze *die* (Technik) yield point; **~heck** *das* (Kfz-W.) fastback; **~komma** *das* (DV) floating point; **~satz** *der* (Druckw.) undisplay

Flimmer-: ~epithel *das* (Biol.) ciliated epithelium; **~kasten** *der,* **~kiste** *die* (ugs.) telly (coll.); box (coll.)

flimmern /ˈflɪmɐn/ *itr. V.; mit Richtungsangabe mit sein* ‹*water, air, surface*› shimmer; ‹*film*› flicker; **ihm flimmerte es vor den Augen** everything was swimming in front of his eyes; **über den Bildschirm ~** (ugs.) be served up on the box (coll.)

flink /flɪŋk/

A *Adj.* nimble ‹*fingers*›; sharp ‹*eyes*›; quick ‹*hands*›; **~ wie ein Wiesel** as quick as a flash; **er hat noch ~e Beine** *od.* **ist noch ~ auf den Beinen** (ugs.) he's still nippy on his pins (coll.)

B *adv.* quickly; **mit etw. ~ bei der Hand sein** be very ready to do sth.; **aber ein bisschen ~!** (ugs.) and be quick about it!

Flinkheit *die;* ~ ▸ **flink A**: nimbleness; sharpness; quickness

flink·züngig /-tsʏŋɪç/

A *Adj.* eloquent

B *adv.* eloquently

Flinte /ˈflɪntə/ *die;* ~, ~n shotgun; **alles, was ihm vor die ~ kommt** everything he gets in his sights; **der soll mir nur vor die ~ kommen!** (fig. salopp) if I can just get my hands on him; **die ~ ins Korn werfen** (fig.) throw in the towel

Flinten-: ~knall *der* gunfire; **ein ~knall** a gunshot; **~kugel** *die* shotgun pellet; **~lauf** *der* shotgun barrel; **~weib** *das* (abwertend) soldier in skirts

Flip /flɪp/ *der;* ~s, ~s flip

Flipchart *das;* ~s, ~s flip chart

Flipflop·schaltung /ˈflɪpflɔp-/ *die* (Elektrot.) flip-flop circuit

Flipper /ˈflɪpɐ/ *der;* ~s, ~, **Flipper·automat** *der* pinball machine; **~ spielen** play pinball

flippern /ˈflɪpɐn/ *itr. V.* (ugs.) play pinball

flirren /ˈflɪrən/ *itr. V.* (geh.) ‹*heat, light, dust, etc.*› shimmer

Flirt /flœrt/ *der;* ~s, ~s flirtation; **einen ~ mit jmdm. anfangen/haben** start flirting with sb./flirt with sb.

flirten *itr. V.* flirt

Flittchen /ˈflɪtçən/ *das;* ~s, ~ (ugs. abwertend) floozie

Flitter /ˈflɪtɐ/ *der;* ~s, ~ 1 (täuschender Glanz) frippery; trumpery 2 (Metallplättchen) sequin

Flitter-: ~gold *das* Dutch metal; **~kram** *der* (ugs. abwertend) frippery; trumpery

flittern *itr. V.* (ugs. scherzh.) honeymoon

Flitter-: ~wochen *Pl.* honeymoon *sing.*; **in die ~wochen fahren** go on one's honeymoon; **~wöchner** *der;* ~~s, ~~, **~wöchnerin** *die* (ugs. scherzh.) honeymooner

Flitz[e]·bogen /ˈflɪts(ə)-/ *der* bow; (fig.) **gespannt sein wie ein ~:** be on tenterhooks; **ich bin gespannt wie ein ~, ob er kommen wird** I'm dying to see if he will come; **auf etw.** (*Akk.*) **gespannt sein wie ein ~:** be on tenterhooks waiting for sth.

flitzen /ˈflɪtsn̩/ *itr. V.; mit sein* (ugs.) shoot; dart; **ich flitze mal gerade zum Fleischer** I'll just dash to the butcher's; **nach rechts und links ~:** dart to either side

Flitzer *der;* ~s, ~ (ugs.) sporty job (coll.)

floaten /ˈfloʊtn̩/ *tr., itr. V.* (Wirtsch.) float

Floating /ˈfloʊtɪŋ/ *das;* ~s, ~s (Wirtsch.) floating

F-Loch /ˈɛf-/ *das* (Musik) F-hole

flocht /flɔxt/ *1. u. 3. Pers. Sg. Prät. v.* **flechten**

Flöckchen /ˈflœkçən/ *das;* ~s, ~ (Schnee~) flake; (Staub~) bit of fluff

Flocke /ˈflɔkə/ *die;* ~, ~n 1 **eine ~ Watte/Wolle** a bit of cotton wool/tuft of wool 2 (Schnee~) flake; **es schneit in dicken ~n** it's snowing large flakes 3 (Schaum~) blob; (Staub~) piece of fluff 4 *Pl.* (salopp: Geld) dough (coll.); dosh (Brit. coll.)

Flocken-: ~blume *die* (Bot.) centaury; **~wirbel** *der* (geh.) whirl of snowflakes

flockig *Adj.* fluffy; **~er Schaum** blobs *pl.* of foam; **Butter ~ rühren** cream butter

flog /floːk/ *1. u. 3. Pers. Sg. Prät. v.* **fliegen**

floh /floː/ *1. u. 3. Pers. Sg. Prät. v.* **fliehen**

Floh /floː/ *der;* ~[e]s, **Flöhe** /ˈfløːə/ 1 flea; (fig.) **lieber einen Sack [voll] Flöhe hüten, als ...** even if you paid me a million pounds I wouldn't ...; **jmdm. einen ~ ins Ohr setzen** (ugs.) put an idea into sb.'s head; **die Flöhe husten** *od.* **niesen hören** (ugs.) know it all before it happens 2 *Pl.* (salopp: Geld) dough *sing.* (coll.); bread *sing.* (coll.)

Floh·biss, *Floh·biß *der* flea bite

flöhen /ˈfløːən/ *tr. V.* flea

Floh-: ~hüpfen *das;* ~~s (Kinderspiel) tiddlywinks; **~kino** *das* (ugs.) fleapit (coll.); **~kraut** *das* (Bot.) fleabane; **~markt** *der* flea market; **~zirkus** *der* flea circus

> **Flohmarkt**
>
> There is a *Flohmarkt* (flea market) on Sundays in most big cities. Stalls set up along a main street, in a park or central square to sell knick-knacks, second-hand clothes, cheap antiques, furniture, and other bargains.

Flom[en] /ˈfloːm(ən)/ *der;* ~s (nordd.) leaf fat

Flop /flɔp/ *der;* ~s, ~s (ugs.) flop (coll.)

Floppydisk *die;* ~, ~s floppy disk; floppy

Flor[1] /floːɐ̯/ *der;* ~s, ~e (geh.) 1 (Blütenpracht) **im ~ stehen** be in full bloom; **einen zweiten ~ entfalten** have a second flush 2 (Blumenfülle) display

Flor[2] *der;* ~s, ~e, *selten:* **Flöre** /ˈfløːrə/ 1 (zartes Gewebe) gauze 2 (Faserenden) pile 3 ▸ **Trauerflor**

Flora /ˈfloːra/ *die;* ~, **Floren** flora

floral /floˈraːl/ *Adj.* floral; **ein ~es Meer** a sea of flowers

Flor·band *das; Pl.* **Florbänder** black band; mourning band

Florentiner[1] /florɛnˈtiːnɐ/ *der;* ~s, ~ ▸ℹ **S. 675** Florentine

Florentiner[2] *der;* ~s, ~ 1 (Hut) picture hat 2 (Gebäck) florentine

Florentinerin *die;* ~, ~nen Florentine

f

florentinisch *Adj.* Florentine

Florenz /flo'rɛnts/ *(das);* **Florenz' ▸ℹ S. 675** Florence

Florett /flo'rɛt/ *das;* **~[e]s, ~e** [1] (Stoßwaffe) foil; **mit dem ~ fechten** fence with a foil [2] (~fechten) foils *sing.*; foil fencing *no art.*

Florett-: ~fechten *das* foil fencing *no art.*; **~fechter** *der,* **~fechterin** *die* foil fencer

Flor·fliege *die* (Zool.) green lacewing

florieren /flo'ri:rən/ *itr. V.* ‹*business*› flourish; **ein [gut] ~der Laden** a flourishing shop

Florist /flo'rɪst/ *der;* **~en, ~en, Floristin** *die;* **~, ~nen ▸ℹ S. 113** [1] (Blumenbinder) [qualified] flower arranger [2] (Kenner einer Flora) botanist [3] (Blumenhändler) florist

Flor·teppich *der* pile carpet

Floskel /'flɔskl̩/ *die;* **~, ~n** cliché; **der Brief enthält nichts außer abgedroschenen ~n** the letter is full of clichés *or* hackneyed phrases

floskelhaft

A *Adj.* cliché-ridden; clichéd

B *adv.* **sich ~ ausdrücken** talk in clichés

floss, *floß /flɔs/ *1. u. 3. Pers. Sg. Prät. v.* **fließen**

Floß /flo:s/ *das;* **~es, Flöße** /'flø:sə/ [1] raft [2] (an der Angel) float

flöß·bar *Adj.* navigable by raft *postpos.*

Flosse /'flɔsə/ *die;* **~, ~n** [1] (Zool., Flugw.) fin [2] (zum Tauchen) flipper [3] (ugs. scherzh. od. abwertend: Hand) paw

flößen /'flø:sn̩/ *tr., itr. V.* float; **Baumstämme [auf dem Fluss] ~:** raft tree trunks [on the river]

Flossen·füß[l]er *der* (Zool.) pinniped

Flößer /'flø:sɐ/ *der;* **~s, ~: ▸ℹ S. 113** raftsman

Flößerei /flø:sə'rai̯/ *die;* **~:** rafting

Flößerin *die;* **~, ~nen ▸ℹ S. 113** raftswoman

Floß-: ~fahrt *die* voyage by raft; **~gasse** *die* channel for rafts; **~holz** *das* rafted wood

Flotation /flota'tsi̯o:n/ *die;* **~, ~en** (bes. Hüttenw.) flotation

Flöte /'flø:tə/ *die;* **~, ~n** [1] (Musik) flute; (Block~) recorder; **~ spielen** play the flute/recorder; **die ~ des Pan** the pipes of Pan [2] (Skat) **die [ganze] ~ herunterspielen** play a [straight] flush [3] (hohes Glas) flute

flöten /'flø:tn̩/

A *itr. V.* [1] ‹*bird*› flute [2] (Flöte spielen) play the flute/recorder [3] (ugs.: affektiert sprechen) pipe; **in den sanftesten Tönen ~:** speak in wheedling tones [4] **~ gehen** (ugs.) go for a burton (Brit. coll.); ‹*money*› go down the drain; ‹*time*› be wasted

B *tr. V.* whistle ‹*song, tune*›

flöten-, Flöten-: *~|gehen ▸flöten A4; ~kessel *der* whistling kettle; **~konzert** *das* [1] (Musikstück) flute concerto; [2] (Veranstaltung) flute concert; **~musik** *die* flute music; **~register** *das* (Musik) flute stop; **~spiel** *das* flute-playing; **~spieler** *der,* **~spielerin** *die* flute player; **~ton** *der; Pl.* **~töne** sound of a flute; **jmdm. die ~töne beibringen** (fig. ugs.) teach sb. a thing or two (coll.)

Flötist /flø'tɪst/ *der;* **~en, ~en, Flötistin** *die;* **~, ~nen ▸ℹ S. 113** flautist

flott /flɔt/

A *Adj.* [1] (ugs.: schwungvoll) lively ‹*music, dance, pace, style*›; snappy ‹*dialogue*›; **den ~en Otto haben** (salopp) have the runs (coll.) [2] (ugs.: schick, modisch) smart ‹*hat, suit, car*› [3] (munter, hübsch) stylish; smart; **~ aussehen** look attractive [4] (leichtlebig) **ein ~es Leben führen** be fast-living [5] (fahrbereit, wiederhergestellt) seaworthy ‹*vessel*›; (ugs.) roadworthy ‹*vehicle*›; airworthy ‹*aircraft*›; **mein Auto ist wieder ~:** my car ist back on the road again

B *adv.* ‹*work*› quickly; ‹*dance, write*› in a lively manner; ‹*be dressed*› smartly

flott|bekommen *unr. tr. V.:* **▸flottkriegen**

Flotte /'flɔtə/ *die;* **~, ~n** fleet

Flotten-: ~abkommen *das* naval treaty; **~chef** *der* commander-in-chief of the/a fleet; **~kommando** *das* fleet command; **~parade** *die* naval parade; **~stütz·punkt** *der* naval base; **~verband** *der* naval unit

Flottille /flɔ'tɪl(j)ə/ *die;* **~, ~n** flotilla

Flottillen·admiral *der* rear admiral

flott-: ~|kommen *unr. itr. V.* get afloat; **~|kriegen** *tr. V.* get ‹*boat*› afloat; get ‹*car*› going; **~|machen** *tr. V.* refloat ‹*ship*›; get ‹*car*› back on the road; **~weg** *Adv.* (ugs.) **~weg arbeiten** keep at it

Flöz /flø:ts/ *das;* **~es, ~e** (Bergbau) seam

Fluch /flu:x/ *der;* **~[e]s, Flüche** /'fly:çə/ [1] (Kraftwort) curse; oath; **ein derber/lästerlicher ~:** a vulgar/blasphemous oath; **einen ~ ausstoßen/unterdrücken** utter/suppress an oath [2] (Verwünschung) curse; **einen ~ gegen jmdn. ausstoßen** utter a curse against sb. [3] (Unheil, Verderben) curse; **ein ~ liegt über/lastet auf jmdm.** there's a curse on sb.; **das ist der ~ der bösen Tat** that's the wages of sin

fluch·beladen *Adj.* (geh.) accursed

fluchen *itr. V.* [1] (Flüche ausstoßen) curse; swear; **auf/über jmdn./etw. ~:** swear at *or* curse sb./sth. [2] (verwünschen) (geh.) curse; **jmdm./einer Sache ~:** curse sb./sth.

Flucht[1] /flʊxt/ *die;* **~** [1] (Fliehen, Flüchten) flight; **auf/während der ~:** while fleeing; (von Gefangenen) on the run; **jmdn. auf der ~ erschießen** shoot sb. while he/she is trying to escape; **auf** *od.* **während der ~ erschossen werden** be shot while trying to escape; **in wilder ~ davonjagen** run away in mad panic; **die ~ aus dem Gefängnis/aus einem Land** the escape from prison/from a country; **den Bankräubern/Gefangenen gelang die ~:** the bank robbers/prisoners succeeded in escaping; **die ~ ergreifen** ‹*prisoner*› make a dash for freedom; (fig.) make a dash for it; **jmdn. in die ~ schlagen** put sb. to flight; *s. auch* **Ägypten** [2] (Ausweichen) refuge; **ihr blieb nur noch die ~ in den Alkohol/das Rauschgift** the only thing left to her was to take refuge in alcohol/drugs; **die ~ in die Krankheit/Anonymität** taking refuge in illness/anonymity; **die ~ in die Krankheit antreten** take refuge in illness; **die ~ aus der Wirklichkeit/Verantwortung** escape from reality/responsibility; **die ~ nach vorn antreten** take the bull by the horns; **die ~ in die Öffentlichkeit antreten** make a public statement

Flucht[2] *die;* **~, ~en** [1] (Bauw.: Häuser~, Arkaden~) row; **die ~ der Fenster** the line of the windows [2] (Zimmer~) suite

flucht-, Flucht-: ~artig A *Adj.* hurried; hasty; **B** *adv.* hurriedly; hastily; **~auto** *das* getaway car; **~burg** *die* refuge

flüchten /'flʏçtn̩/

A *itr. V.; mit sein* **vor jmdm./etw. ~:** flee from sb./sth.; **vor der Polizei ~:** run away from the police; (mit Erfolg) escape from the police; **zu jmdm. ~:** take refuge with sb.; **ins Ausland ~:** escape abroad; **unter ein schützendes Dach ~:** take shelter under a protective roof

B *refl. V.* **sich in ein Bauernhaus ~:** take refuge in a farmhouse; **sich aufs Dach ~:** escape on to the roof

Flucht-: ~fahrzeug *das* getaway vehicle; **~gefahr** *die* risk of an escape attempt; **es besteht ~gefahr/keine ~gefahr** there's a/no risk of an escape attempt; **~helfer** *der,* **~helferin** *die* person who aids/aided an/the escape; **~hilfe** *die* aiding an escape

flüchtig /'flʏçtɪç/

A *Adj.* [1] (flüchtend) fugitive; **er ist noch ~:** he ist still at large; **ein ~er Dieb/Verbrecher** a wanted thief/criminal [2] (oberflächlich) cursory; superficial ‹*insight*›; **eine ~e Arbeit** a hurried piece of work [3] (eilig, schnell) quick; short ‹*visit, greeting*›; fleeting ‹*glance*› [4] (vergänglich) fleeting ‹*moment*›; quickly changing ‹*moods*›; sudden ‹*temper, whim*› [5] (Chemie) volatile

B *adv.* [1] (oberflächlich) cursorily [2] (eilig) hurriedly

Flüchtigkeit *die;* **~, ~en** [1] (Oberflächlichkeit) cursoriness [2] **▸Flüchtigkeitsfehler** [3] (Vergänglichkeit) fleetingness [4] (Chemie) volatility

Flüchtigkeits·fehler *der* slip; (tadelnswert) careless mistake

Flucht·kapital *das* (Wirtsch.): *capital which has been sent out of the country to evade tax*

Flüchtling /'flʏçtlɪŋ/ *der;* **~s, ~e** refugee

Flüchtlings-: ~ausweis *der* refugee's identity card; **~elend** *das* hardship among refugees; **~lager** *das* refugee camp; **~treck** *der* long stream of refugees

Flucht-: ~linie *die* vanishing line; **~plan** *der* escape plan; **~punkt** *der* (Kunstwiss.) vanishing point; **~reaktion** *die* (Verhaltensf.) escape reaction; **~verdacht** *der:* **es besteht [kein] ~verdacht** he/she is [not] likely to try to escape; **~versuch** *der* escape attempt; **einen ~versuch unternehmen** *od.* **machen** attempt to escape; **~weg** *der* escape route; **sich** (*Dat.*) **den ~weg offenhalten** keep a way out open; **sich** (*Dat.*) **den ~weg freischießen** shoot one's way out

fluch·würdig *Adj.* (geh.) monstrous

Flug /flu:k/ *der;* **~[e]s, Flüge** /'fly:gə/ [1] flight; **im ~:** in flight; **die Urlaubstage/Stunden vergingen [wie] im ~e** the holiday/hours flew by [2] (~reise) flight [3] (Skispringen) jump; **einen ~ [sicher] stehen** land safely [4] (Jägerspr.) flock

flug-, Flug-: ~abwehr *die* (Milit.) anti-aircraft defence; **~abwehr·rakete** *die* (Milit.) anti-aircraft missile; **~angst** *die* fear of flying; **~asche** *die* fly ash; **~bahn** *die* trajectory; **~ball** *der* (Tennis) volley; **~begleiter** *der* **▸ℹ S. 113** steward; **~begleiterin** *die* **▸ℹ S. 113** stewardess; **~benzin** *das* aviation fuel; **~bereit** *Adj.* ready for take-off *postpos.*; **~betrieb** *der* air traffic; **~bild** *das* (Zool.) flight silhouette; **~blatt** *das* pamphlet; leaflet; **~boot** *das* flying boat; **~daten·schreiber** *der* flight recorder; **~dauer** *die* flight time; **~dienst** *der* [1] (~verkehr) air service; [2] (Überwachungsdienst) air traffic control; **~dienst·leiter** *der,* **~dienst·leiterin** *die* air traffic controller; **~drache** *der* (Zool.) flying dragon; **~drachen** *der* hang-glider; **~echse** *die* (Zool.) pterosaurian; **~eigenschaft** *die* flying characteristic

Flügel /'fly:gl̩/ *der;* **~s, ~** [1] wing; **mit den ~n schlagen** flap its/their wings; **die ~ hängen lassen** (fig. ugs.) become disheartened; **jmdm. die ~ stutzen** *od.* **beschneiden** (fig.) clip sb.'s wings; **das verlieh ihm ~** (fig. geh.) that gave *or* lent him wings (literary) [2] (Altar~) wing; (Fensterflügel) casement; (Nasen~) nostril; **der linke/rechte ~ der Lunge** the left/right lung [3] (Klavier) grand piano; **jmdn. auf dem ~ begleiten** accompany sb. on the piano [4] (Milit., Ballspiele) wing; **über die ~ spielen/angreifen** play/attack on the wings [5] (Tragfläche, Partei~, Gebäude~) wing [6] (Schrauben~) vane; (Windmühlen~) sail

flügel-, Flügel-: ~altar *der* winged altar; **~decke** *die* (Zool.) elytron; wing case; **~fenster** *das* casement window; **~horn** *das* (Musik) flugelhorn; **~lahm** *Adj.* [1] ‹*bird*› with an injured wing; **einen Vogel ~lahm schießen** wing a bird; [2] (fig.: mutlos, kraftlos) lacking energy *postpos.*; limping ‹*organization*›; **~mutter** *die; Pl.* **~n** wing nut; **~pumpe** *die* rotary pump; **~rad** *das* [1] impeller wheel; [2] (als Symbol) winged wheel; **~ross, *~roß** *das* (Myth.) winged horse; **~schlag** *der* beat of [its/their] wings; **~schlagend** *Adj.* beating its/their wings; **~spann·weite** *die* (Flugw., Zool.) wing span; **~stürmer** *der,* **~stürmerin** *die* (Ballspiele) wing forward; winger; **~tür** *die* double door

flug-, Flug-: ~entfernung *die* distance by air; **~erfahrung** *die* flying experience; **~fähig** *Adj.* airworthy; **~feld** *das* airfield; **~gast** *der* [air] passenger

flügge /'flʏgə/ *Adj.* fully-fledged; (fig.: selbstständig) independent

Flug-: ~geschwindigkeit *die* (eines Flugzeugs) flying speed; (eines Vogels) speed of flight; **~gesellschaft** *die* airline; **~hafen** *der* airport; **~hafen Frankfurt** Frankfurt airport;

ℹ Flüsse

Im Englischen gibt es nur das eine Wort **river,** das (oft großgeschrieben) vor dem Flussnamen eingesetzt werden kann:

die Seine
= the [river *od.* River] Seine

Eine Ausnahme im Englischen wie im Deutschen:

der Sankt-Lorenz-Strom
= the St Lawrence River

Bei Ortsnamen steht einfach **on** ohne Artikel:

Walton-on-Thames *Stockton-on-Tees*
Ross-on-Wye

Heute fehlt oft der Bindestrich.

am rechten Weserufer
= on the right bank of the Weser

ein Haus am Fluss
= a house by *od.* on the river

Der Fluss führt Hochwasser
= The river is in flood *od.* in full spate

Der Fluss führt sehr wenig Wasser
= The river is very low

Die Drau, ein rechter Nebenfluss der Donau, ist in ihrem Unterlauf schiffbar
= The Drava, a tributary of the Danube on its right bank, is navigable in its lower reaches

Der Rhein entspringt in der Schweiz und mündet in die Nordsee
= The Rhine rises in Switzerland and flows into the North Sea

Das Schiff ist in der Elbmündung gesunken
= The ship sank in the mouth of the Elbe *od.* the Elbe estuary

An der Mündung der Mosel in den Rhein befindet sich das Deutsche Eck
= At the point where the Moselle flows into the Rhine is the Deutsche Eck

Münden liegt am Zusammenfluss von Werra und Fulda [zur Weser]
= Münden lies at the confluence of the Werra and Fulda [which then become the Weser]

Flusssprache

flussaufwärts/flussabwärts fahren
= to go upstream/downstream *od.* up/down [the] river

rheinaufwärts/rheinabwärts fahren
= to go up/down the Rhine

die linksrheinischen Landesteile
= the parts of the country on the left bank of the Rhine

~hafen·gebühr *die* airport tax; **~hafen·restaurant** *das* airport restaurant; **~hafer** *der* (Bot.) wild oat; **~höhe** *die* altitude; **in einer ~höhe von ...** at an altitude of ...; **~hund** *der* (Zool.) flying fox; **~ingenieur** *der*, **~ingenieurin** *die* flight engineer; **~kapitän** *der*, **~kapitänin** *die* ▸ℹ **S. 113** captain; **~kilometer** *der* [air] kilometre; **~körper** *der* space vehicle; **~lärm** *der* aircraft noise; **~lehrer** *der*, **~lehrerin** *die* ▸ℹ **S. 113** flying instructor; **~leiter** *der*, **~leiterin** *die* flight controller; **~linie** *die* 1 (Strecke) air route; 2 (Gesellschaft) airline; **~loch** ▸ **Einflugloch**; **~lotse** *der*, **~lotsin** *die* ▸ℹ **S. 113** air traffic controller; **~meile** *die* air mile; **~motor** *der* aircraft engine; **~objekt** *das* flying object; **ein unbekanntes ~objekt** an unidentified flying object; **~personal** *das* flight personnel; **~plan** *der* flight schedule; **~platz** *der* airfield; aerodrome; **~preis** *der* air fare; **~reise** *die* air journey; **~route** *die* air route

flugs /flʊks/ *Adv.* (veralt.) swiftly

flug-, Flug-: **~sand** *der* wind-borne sand; **~saurier** *der* (Zool.) pterosaurian; **~schanze** *die* (Skifliegen) ski jump (*used for ski-flying*); **~schein** 1 pilot's licence; 2 (**~**ticket) air ticket; **~schneise** *die* air corridor; **~schreiber** *der* flight recorder; **~schrift** *die* pamphlet; **~schüler** *der*, **~schülerin** *die* trainee pilot; **~sicherung** *die* air traffic control; **~simulator** *der* flight simulator; **~sport** *der* aerial sports; **~steig** *der* pier; (Ausgang) **~steig 5** gate 5; **~stunde** *die* hour's flying time; **zwei ~stunden entfernt** two hours away by air; **~tauglich** *Adj.* ‹*pilot*› fit to fly; **~technik** *die* 1 (Technologie) aeronautical engineering; 2 (fliegerisches Können) flying technique; **~technisch** A *Adj.* aeronautical; B *adv.* aeronautically; **~ticket** *das* air ticket; **~touristik** *die* tourism by air; **~tüchtig** *Adj.* ▸ **~fähig**; **~unfähig** *Adj.* flightless ‹*bird*›; (vorübergehend) ‹*bird*› unable to fly; ‹*aircraft*› not airworthy; **~verbindung** *die* air connection; **~verbot** *das* flight ban; (*für bestimmte Person, Fluggesellschaft*) flying ban; **~verkehr** *der* air traffic; **der ~verkehr nimmt ständig zu** the volume of air traffic is continually increasing; **~wetter** *das* flying weather; **~wetter·dienst** *der* meteorological service [for aviation]; **~zeit** *die* flight time

Flug·zeug *das*; **~[e]s, ~e** aeroplane (Brit.); airplane (Amer.); aircraft; **mit dem ~ reisen** travel by plane *or* air

Flugzeug-: **~absturz** *der* plane crash; **~bau** *der* aircraft construction; **~besatzung** *die* crew; **~entführer** *der*, **~entführerin** *die* [aircraft] hijacker; **~entführung** *die* [aircraft] hijack[ing]; **~halle** *die* hangar; **~industrie** *die* aircraft industry; **~katastrophe** *die* air disaster; **~konstrukteur** *der*, **~konstrukteurin** *die* aircraft designer; **~modell** *das* model aeroplane; **~mutterschiff** *das* seaplane carrier; **~träger** *der* aircraft carrier; **~typ** *der* model of aircraft; **~unglück** *das* plane crash; **~wrack** *das* wreckage of the/a plane **zwei ~wracks** the wreckage of two planes

Fluidum /ˈfluːidʊm/ *das*; **~s, Fluida** aura; atmosphere; **von ihr/davon geht ein gewisses ~ aus** she/it exudes a certain aura; **das ~ des Künstlers** the aura *or* atmosphere surrounding the artist

Fluktuation /flʊktu̯aˈtsi̯oːn/ *die*; **~, ~en** (bes. Wirtsch., Soziol.) fluctuation (*Gen.* in)

fluktuieren /flʊktuˈiːrən/ *itr. V.* (bes. Wirtsch., Soziol.) fluctuate

Flunder /ˈflʊndɐ/ *die*; **~, ~n** flounder

Flunkerei /flʊŋkəˈrai̯/ *die*; **~, ~en** (ugs.) 1 (Flunkern) storytelling 2 (Lügengeschichte) tall story

flunkern /ˈflʊŋkɐn/ *itr. V.* tell stories

Flunsch /flʊnʃ/ *der*; **~[e]s, ~e** *od. die*; **~, ~en** (ugs.) pout; **eine[n] ~ ziehen** *od.* **machen** pout

Fluor[1] /ˈfluːɔr/ *das*; **~s** (Chemie) fluorine

Fluor[2] *der*; **~s** (Med.) vaginal discharge

Fluor·chlor·kohlen·wasserstoff *der* (Chemie) chlorofluorocarbon

Fluoreszenz /fluorɛsˈtsɛnts/ *die*; **~:** fluorescence

fluoreszieren *itr. V.* fluoresce; be fluorescent; **das Wasser fluoresziert** the water is fluorescent; **eine ~de Flüssigkeit** a fluorescent liquid

Fluor·gehalt *der* (Chemie) fluorine content

Fluorid /fluoˈriːt/ *das*; **~[e]s, ~e** (Chemie) fluoride

Fluor·test *der* (Paläont.) fluorine test

Fluppe /ˈflʊpə/ *die*; **~, ~n** (ugs.) fag (coll.)

Flur[1] /fluːɐ̯/ *der*; **~[e]s, ~e** (Korridor) corridor; (Diele) [entrance] hall; **im/auf dem ~:** in the corridor/hall

Flur[2] *die*; **~, ~en** 1 (landwirtschaftliche Nutzfläche) farmland *no indef. art.*; **die ~ bereinigen** reallocate land; **die ~en** the fields 2 (geh.: offenes Kulturland) fields *pl.*; **allein auf weiter ~ sein** *od.* **stehen** (fig.) be all alone in the world; **er stand mit seiner Ansicht allein auf weiter ~:** he was a lone voice in the wilderness

Flur-: **~begehung** *die* inspection of fields; **~bereinigung** *die* reallocation of land; **~fenster** *das* hall window/window in a/the corridor; **~form** *die* layout of fields; **~garderobe** *die* hall stand; **~hüter** *der*, **~hüterin** *die* field guard; **~name** *der*: *name of a feature of the local landscape*; **~schaden** *der* damage *no pl., no indef. art.* to farmland; **~tür** *die* front door

Fluse /ˈfluːzə/ *die*; **~, ~n** (bes. nordd.) bit of fluff

flusen *itr. V.* shed fluff

Fluss, *Fluß /flʊs/ *der*; **Flusses, Flüsse** /ˈflʏsə/ 1 ▸ℹ **S. 267** river; **die Stadt liegt am ~:** the town stands on the river; **am ~ sitzen** sit by the river 2 (fließende Bewegung) flow; **der ~ des Verkehrs** the flow of traffic; **die Dinge sind noch im ~:** things are in a state of flux; **in ~ kommen** *od.* **geraten** get going; get under way; **etw. in ~ bringen** get sth. going

fluss-, *fluß-, Fluss-, *Fluß-: **~aal** *der* (Zool.) freshwater eel; **~ab[wärts]** *Adv.* ▸ℹ **S. 267** downstream; **~arm** *der* river branch; river arm; **~auf[wärts]** *Adv.* ▸ℹ **S. 267** upstream; **~barsch** *der* (Zool.) perch; **~bett** *das* river bed

Flüsschen, *Flüßchen /ˈflʏsçən/ *das*; **~s, ~:** small river

Fluss-, *Fluß-: **~dampfer** *der* river steamer; **~diagramm** *das* (DV, Arbeitswiss.) flow chart; **~ebene** *die* flood plain; **~fisch** *der* freshwater fish; **~gott** *der* (Myth.) river god; **~göttin** *die* river goddess; **~hafen** *der* river port

flüssig /ˈflʏsɪç/
A *Adj.* 1 liquid ‹*nourishment, fuel*›; molten ‹*ore, glass*›; melted ‹*butter*›; runny ‹*honey*›; **sie konnte nur ~e Nahrung zu sich nehmen** she could only take liquids; **etw. ~ machen** melt sth.; **~es Brot** (scherzh.) beer 2 (fließend, geläufig) fluent; **~er Verkehr** free-flowing traffic 3 (verfügbar, solvent) **~es Kapital/Geld** ready capital/money; **~es Vermögen** liquid assets; **einen Betrag ~ machen** make a sum of money available; **wieder ~ sein** (ugs.) have got some cash to play with again (coll.); **nicht ~ sein** (ugs.) be skint (Brit. coll.) *or* (coll.) [flat] broke
B *adv.* ‹*write, speak*› fluently; **der Verkehr lief ~:** the traffic was flowing freely; **~ ernährt werden müssen** be only able to take liquids

Flüssig·gas *das* liquid gas

Flüssigkeit *die*; **~, ~en** 1 liquid; (auch Gas) fluid 2 (Geläufigkeit) fluency

Flüssigkeits-: **~aufnahme** *die* intake of fluids; **~maß** *das* liquid measure

Flüssig·kristall·anzeige *die* (Technik) liquid crystal display

***flüssig|machen** ▸ **flüssig A 3**

Flüssigseife *die* liquid soap

Fluss-, *Fluß-: **~krebs** *der* (Zool.) crayfish; **~landschaft** *die* 1 (Geogr.) fluvial topography; 2 (Gemälde) river landscape; **~lauf** *der* course of a/the river; **~mittel** *das* (Technik) flux; **~mündung** *die* river mouth; (mit Gezeiten) estuary; **~name** *der* river name; **~niederung** *die* flood plain; **~pferd** *das* hippopotamus; **~regulierung** *die* river control; **~schifffahrt, *~schiffahrt** *die* river traffic; (Navigation) river navigation; **~spat** *der* fluorite; fluorspar; **~tal** *das* river valley; **~ufer** *das* river bank; **das diesseitige/jenseitige ~ufer** the near/opposite bank [of the river]; **~wasser** *das* river water

Flüster-: ~gewölbe *das* whispering gallery; **~laut** *der* whisper; **~laute von sich geben** whisper

flüstern /ˈflʏstɐn/

A *itr. V.* whisper; **sich ~d unterhalten/verständigen** speak/communicate in whispers; **leises, beschwörendes Flüstern** quiet, pleading whispers

B *tr. V.* whisper; **jmdm. etw. ins Ohr ~:** whisper sth. in sb.'s ear; **jmdm. [et]was ~** (ugs.) give sb. something to think about; **das kann ich dir ~** (ugs.) I can promise you that

Flüster-: ~parole *die* rumour; **~propaganda** *die* underground propaganda; **~ton** *der; Pl.* **~töne** whisper; **im ~ton sprechen** speak in whispers; **~tüte** *die* (ugs.) megaphone; **~witz** *der* underground joke

Flut /fluːt/ *die;* **~, ~en 1** tide; **die ~ steigt/ebbt ab** the tide is coming in/going out; **die steigende ~:** the incoming *or* rising tide; **mit der ~ aus-/einlaufen** sail with the tide/come in on the tide **2** (geh.: Wassermasse) flood; **aufgewühlte/schmutzige ~en** turbulent/dirty waters; **in den ~en umkommen** die in the floods; **eine ~ von Protesten** (fig.) a flood of protests

fluten

A *itr. V.; mit sein* (geh.) flood; **in etw.** (*Akk.*) **~:** flood sth.; **Sonnenlicht flutete in den Raum** sunlight streamed into the room

B *tr. V.* (Seemannsspr.: unter Wasser setzen) flood

Flut-: ~höhe *die* height of the tide; **~katastrophe** *die* flood disaster; **~licht** *das* floodlight; **~licht·anlage** *die* floodlight installation; floodlights *pl.*

flutschen /ˈflʊtʃn̩/ *itr. V.* (ugs., bes. nordd.) **1** *mit sein* (gleiten) slip; **jmdm. aus den Fingern/Händen ~:** slip out of sb.'s fingers/hands **2** (glatt vonstatten gehen) go smoothly; **es flutscht nur so** it's going extremely well

Flut-: ~warnung *die* flood warning; **~welle** *die* tidal wave

fluvial /fluˈvi̯aːl/ *Adj.* (Geol.) fluvial

Flyer /ˈflaiɐ/ *der;* **~s, ~:** flyer

fm *Abk.* **= Festmeter** solid m³

f-Moll /ˈɛf-/ F minor; *s. auch* **a-Moll**

focht /fɔxt/ *1. u. 3. Pers. Sg. Prät. v.* **fechten**

Fock /fɔk/ *die;* **~, ~en** (Seew.) foresail; (auf einer Jacht) jib

Fock·mast *der* foremast

> **Focus**
>
> A relatively new weekly news and current affairs magazine published in Munich. It was set up in 1993 and is aimed at a centre-right readership, especially businesspeople and professionals. *Focus* has become a serious competitor of **Der Spiegel**, with shorter, easier-to-read articles and a more modern presentation.

föderal /fødeˈraːl/ *Adj.* ▸ **föderativ**

Föderalismus *der;* **~:** federalism *no art.*

föderalistisch *Adj.* federalist

Föderation /fødera'tsi̯oːn/ *die;* **~, ~en** federation

föderativ /fødera'tiːf/

A *Adj.* federal

B *adv.* federally

fohlen /ˈfoːlən/ *itr. V.* foal

Fohlen *das;* **~s, ~:** foal

Föhn /føːn/ *der;* **~[e]s, ~e 1** (Wind) föhn; **es war ~:** the föhn was blowing; **bei ~:** when the föhn is/was blowing **2** (Haartrockner) hairdryer; **sich** (*Dat.*) **die Haare mit dem ~ trocknen** blow-dry one's hair

föhnen /ˈføːnən/ *tr. V.* blow-dry

Föhn·krankheit *die* illness caused by föhn conditions

Föhre /ˈføːrə/ *die;* **~, ~n** (landsch.) ▸ **Kiefer²**

Fokus /ˈfoːkʊs/ *der;* **~, ~se** (Optik, Med.) focus

fokussieren *tr., itr. V.* (Optik) focus

Fokussierung *die;* **~, ~en** (Optik, fig.) focusing (**auf** + *Akk.* **on**)

Folge /ˈfɔlgə/ *die;* **~, ~n 1** (Auswirkung) consequence; (Ergebnis) consequence; result; **das kann böse ~n nach sich ziehen** that could have dire consequences; **die ~n tragen müssen** have to take the consequences; **an den ~n eines Unfalls/eines Herzleidens sterben** die as a result of an accident/a heart condition; **etw. zur ~ haben** result in sth.; lead to sth. **2** (Aufeinander~) succession; (zusammengehörend) sequence; (einer Sendung) episode; (eines Romans) instalment; (einer Zeitschrift) issue; **in rascher ~:** in quick succession; **in ~:** in a row; in succession; **das dritte Mal in ~:** the third time in a row *or* running; **eine ~ von Bildern/Tönen** a sequence of pictures/notes; **eine Fortsetzung in 10 ~n** a serialization in ten episodes **3 einem Aufruf/einem Befehl/einer Einladung ~ leisten** (Amtsspr.) respond to an appeal/obey *or* follow an order/accept an invitation

Folge-: ~erscheinung *die* consequence; **~jahr** *das* following year; **~kosten** *Pl.* resulting costs; **~kriminalität** *die: crime arising from the need to acquire drugs etc.;* **~lasten** ▸ **~kosten**

folgen /ˈfɔlgn̩/ *itr. V.* **1** *mit sein* follow; **jmdm./einer Sache ~:** follow sb./sth.; **jmdm. im Amt/in der Regierung ~:** succeed sb. in office/in government; **auf etw.** (*Akk.*) **~:** follow sth.; come after sth.; **einer Rede/einem Vortrag ~ [können]** [be able to] follow a speech/a lecture; **kannst du mir ~?** (oft scherzh.) do you follow me?; **jmds. Beispiel** (*Dat.*) **~:** follow sb.'s example; **aus etw. ~:** follow from sth.; **daraus folgt, dass ...** it follows from this that ... **2** (gehorchen) *auch mit sein* **jmds. Anordnungen/Befehlen ~:** follow *or* obey sb.'s orders; **seiner inneren Stimme/seinem Gefühl ~:** listen to one's inner voice/be ruled by one's feelings

folgend... *Adj.* following; **der/die/das Folgende** the next in order; **er sagte das Folgende ...** he said this ...; **Folgendes** *od.* **das Folgende** the following [words *pl.*/passage *etc.*]; **aus Folgendem** *od.* **dem Folgenden geht hervor, dass ...** it will be seen from what follows that ...; **alle Folgenden** all those who come/came after; **im Folgenden** *od.* **in Folgendem** in [the course of] the following discussion/passage *etc.*; **der/die Folgende** the one who follows/followed; **die Folgenden** those following

folgendermaßen *Adv.* as follows; (so) in the following way

folgen-: ~los *Adj.* without consequences *postpos.*; **das ist nicht ~los geblieben** that hasn't been without its consequences; **~reich** *Adj.* ‹*decision, event*› fraught with consequences; (bedeutsam) momentous; **~schwer** *Adj.* fateful ‹*error, omission*›; ‹*error, omission, accident*› with serious consequences

folge·richtig

A *Adj.* logical ‹*decision, conclusion*›; consistent ‹*behaviour, action*›

B *adv.* ‹*think, develop, conclude*› logically; ‹*act, behave*› consistently

Folge·richtigkeit *die* (einer Entscheidung, Schlussfolgerung) logicality; (eines Verhaltens, einer Handlung) consistency

folgern /ˈfɔlgɐn/

A *tr. V.* **~, dass ...** conclude that ...; **etw. aus etw. ~:** deduce *or* infer sth. from sth.

B *itr. V.* **richtig ~:** draw a/the correct conclusion; **voreilig ~:** jump to conclusions

Folgerung *die;* **~, ~en** conclusion

Folge-: ~satz *der* (Sprachw.) consecutive clause; **~schaden** *der* **1** damaging aftereffects; **2** (Versicherungsw.) consequential damage

folge·widrig

A *Adj.* illogical ‹*conclusion*›; inconsistent ‹*behaviour*›

B *adv.* ‹*conclude*› illogically; ‹*behave*› inconsistently

Folge·zeit *die* ensuing *or* following weeks/months/years *pl.*

folglich /ˈfɔlklɪç/ *Adv.* consequently; as a result; (ugs.: deshalb) consequently; therefore

folgsam

A *Adj.* obedient

B *adv.* obediently

Folgsamkeit *die;* **~:** obedience

Foliant /foˈli̯ant/ *der;* **~en, ~en** folio

Folie /ˈfoːli̯ə/ *die;* **~, ~n 1** (Metall~) foil; (Plastik~) film **2** (Druckw.: Farbschicht) [blocking] foil

Folio /ˈfoːli̯o/ *das;* **~s, Folien** *od.* **~s** folio

Folio·band *der; Pl.* **~bände** folio volume

Folklore /fɔlkˈloːrə/ *die;* **~ 1** (Überlieferung) folklore **2** (Musik) folk music

Folklore·bluse *die* peasant blouse

Folkloristik *die;* **~:** [study of] folklore

folkloristisch

A *Adj.* folkloric

B *adv.* in a folkloric way

Folk·song /ˈfoʊk-/ *der* folk song

Follikel /fɔˈliːkl̩/ *der;* **~s, ~** ▸ **❶ S. 435** (Med., Bot.) follicle

Follikel·sprung *der* (Med.) ovulation

Folter /ˈfɔltɐ/ *die;* **~, ~n 1** torture; **bei jmdm. die ~ anwenden** use torture on sb.; **die ~ abschaffen** abolish the use of torture **2** (**~bank**) rack; **jmdn. auf die ~ legen** put sb. on the rack; **jmdn. auf die ~ spannen** (fig.) keep sb. in an agony of suspense **3** (geh.: peinigende Qual) torment

Folter·bank *die; Pl.* **Folterbänke** rack

Folterer *der;* **~s, ~, Folterin** *die;* **~, ~nen** torturer

Folter-: ~kammer *die,* **~keller** *der* torture chamber; **~knecht** *der* torturer

foltern

A *tr. V.* **1** torture **2** (fig. geh.) torment

B *itr. V.* use torture

Folter·qual *die* **1** agony of torture **2** (fig. geh.) torment; **~en erdulden** suffer torment; **jmdm. wahre ~en bereiten** be sheer torment to sb.

Folterung *die;* **~, ~en** torture; **nach tagelangen ~en** after days of torture

Folter·werkzeug *das* instrument of torture

Fön Ⓦⓩ /føːn/ *der;* **~[e]s, ~e** hairdrier; **sich** (*Dat.*) **die Haare mit dem ~ trocknen** blow-dry one's hair

Fond¹ /fõː/ *der;* **~s, ~s** (geh.) rear compartment; back; **im ~ sitzen** sit in the back [seat]

Fond² *der;* **~s, ~s** (Kochk.) juices *pl.*

Fondant /fõˈdãː/ *der od. das;* **~s, ~s** fondant

Fonds /fõː/ *der;* **~** /fõː(s)/, **~** /fõːs/ **1** (Vermögensreserve) fund; **einen ~ bilden** set up a fund **2** *Pl.* (Finanzw.) government stocks; government bonds

Fondue /fõˈdyː/ *die;* **~, ~s** *od. das;* **~s, ~s** (Kochk.) fondue

Fondue-: ~gabel *die* fondue fork; **~gerät** *das* fondue set

***fönen** ▸ **föhnen**

Fono- ▸ **Phono-**

Font /fɔnt/ *der;* **~s, ~s** (DV) font

Fontäne /fɔnˈtɛːnə/ *die;* **~, ~n** jet; (Springbrunnen) fountain

Fontanelle /fɔntaˈnɛlə/ *die;* **~, ~n** ▸ **❶ S. 435** (Anat.) fontanelle

foppen /ˈfɔpn̩/ *tr. V.* (ugs.) **jmdn. ~:** pull sb.'s leg (coll.); put sb. on (Amer. coll.); **jmdn. mit etw. ~:** make fun of sb. with sth.; **jmdn. mit einem Spitznamen ~:** make fun of sb. by calling him/her by his/her nickname

forcieren /fɔrˈsiːrən/ *tr. V.* **1** step up ‹*production*›; redouble, intensify ‹*efforts*›; speed up, push forward ‹*developments*›; **das Tempo/Rennen ~** (Sport) force the pace; **er drängte auf eine forcierte Durchführung des Planes** he pressed for the plan to be forced through **2** (Milit.) force ‹*pass, stronghold, etc.*›

Forcierung *die;* **~, ~en** ▸ **forcieren**: stepping up; redoubling; intensification; speeding up; pushing forward; forcing

Förde /ˈføːɐ̯də/ *die;* **~, ~n** long narrow inlet

Förder-: ~anlage *die* (Technik) conveyor; **~band** *das; Pl.* **~bänder** (Technik) conveyor belt

Förderer /ˈfœrdərɐ/ *der;* **~s, ~ 1** (Gönner) patron **2** ▸ **Förderanlage**

Förderin *die;* **~, ~nen** ▸ **Förderer 1**

Förder-: ~korb *der* (Bergbau) cage; **~leistung** *die* (Bergbau, Technik) output; production

förderlich *Adj.* beneficial; **für jmdn./etw. ~ sein** be beneficial *or* of benefit to sb./sth.; **guten Beziehungen ~ sein** be conducive to *or* promote good relations

Förder·maschine *die* (Bergbau) winding engine

fordern /ˈfɔrdɐn/ *tr. V.* **1** (verlangen) demand; **sein Recht ~:** demand one's rights; **Rechenschaft von jmdm. ~:** call sb. to account; **das Unglück hat 200 Menschenleben gefordert** the disaster claimed 200 lives **2** (in Anspruch nehmen) make demands on; **gefordert werden** have demands made on one; **von etw. gefordert werden** be stretched by sth.; **jmdn. zu stark ~:** make excessive *or* too many demands on sb.; **von einem Gegner gefordert werden** be stretched by an opponent **3** (zum Zweikampf) **jmdn. [zum Duell] ~:** challenge sb. [to a duel]; **jmdn. auf Pistolen/Säbel ~** (veralt.) challenge sb. to a duel with pistols/sabres

fördern /ˈfœrdɐn/ *tr. V.* **1** promote ‹*trade, plan, project, good relations*›; patronize, support ‹*artist, art*›; further ‹*investigation*›; foster ‹*talent, tendency, new generation*›; improve ‹*appetite*›; aid ‹*digestion, sleep*›; **~d auf etw.** (*Akk.*) **wirken** have a beneficial effect on sth. **2** (Bergbau, Technik) mine ‹*coal, ore*›; extract ‹*oil*›

Förder-: ~schacht *der* (Bergbau) winding shaft; **~stufe** *die* (Schulw.): *phase of mixed-ability teaching intended to reveal the aptitudes and abilities of individual pupils*; **~turm** *der* (Bergbau) headframe; headgear

-förderung *die*: **Erdöl~/Erdgas~:** extraction of petroleum/natural gas; **Silber~/Kali~:** mining of silver/potash

Forderung *die*; **~, ~en** **1** (Anspruch) demand; (in bestimmter Höhe) claim; **eine ~ erfüllen** meet a demand/a claim **2** (Kaufmannsspr.) claim (**an** + *Akk.* against); **eine ~ einklagen** sue for payment of a debt **3** (zum Duell) challenge; **eine ~ auf Pistolen/Säbel** (veralt.) a challenge to a duel with pistols/sabres

Förderung *die*; **~, ~en** **1** ▸ **fördern 1**: promotion; patronage; support; furthering; fostering; improvement; aiding **2** (Bergbau, Technik) output; (das Fördern) mining; (von Erdöl) extraction; **die ~ steigt** output is increasing

Förderungs·maßnahme *die* supportive measure

förderungs·würdig *Adj.* worthy *or* deserving of support *postpos.*

Förder-: ~verein *der* support association; (von Freunden einer Sache) supporters' association; **~wagen** *der* (Bergbau) mine car

Forelle /foˈrɛlə/ *die*; **~, ~n** trout; **~ blau** (Kochk.) blue trout

Forellen-: ~teich *der* trout pond; **~zucht** *die* trout farming

Forensik /foˈrɛnzɪk/ *die*; **~** **1** forensic science; forensics *sing.* **2** (Krankenhaus[abteilung]) forensic [psychiatric *or* psychiatry] clinic

forensisch /foˈrɛnzɪʃ/ *Adj.* **1** forensic **2** (veralt.: rhetorisch) oratorical

Forke /ˈfɔrkə/ *die*; **~, ~n** (bes. nordd.) fork

Form /fɔrm/ *die*; **~, ~en** **1** (Gestalt) shape; **es hat die ~ einer Kugel/eines Rechtecks** it has the form of a sphere/rectangle; **[feste] ~[en] annehmen** take definite shape; **die Demonstration nahm hässliche ~en an** the demonstration began to look ugly; **in ~ von Tabletten/Briefmarken/Lebensmitteln/Subventionen** in the form of tablets/stamps/food/subsidies; **aus der ~ gehen** (ugs. scherzh.) lose one's figure **2** (bes. Sport: Verfassung) form; **in ~ sein** be on form; **in guter ~ sein** be in good form; **in schlechter ~ sein** be off form; **sich in ~ bringen** get on form; **zu großer ~ auflaufen** (Jargon) hit peak form **3** (vorgeformtes Modell) mould; (Back~) baking tin **4** (Gestaltungsweise, Erscheinungs~, Darstellungs~) form; **musikalische/künstlerische ~:** musical/artistic form; **~ und Inhalt** form and content; **etw. in angemessene ~ kleiden** present sth. in an appropriate form **5** (Umgangs~) form; **ein Mensch ohne ~en** an ill-mannered person; **die ~[en] wahren** observe the proprieties; **etw. der ~ halber tun** do sth. for the sake of form *or* as a matter of form; **in aller ~:** formally

formal /fɔrˈmaːl/

A *Adj.* formal; **ein ~er Fehler** a technical error; (Rechtsw.) procedural error

B *adv.* formally; **eine ~ gute Lösung** a good solution from the point of view of form; **~ im Recht sein** be technically in the right

Formaldehyd /ˈfɔrm|aldehyːt/ *der*; **~s** (Biol., Med.) formaldehyde

Formalie /fɔrˈmaːli̯ə/ *die*; **~, ~n** formality

Formalin Ⓦⓩ /fɔrmaˈliːn/ *das*; **~s** formalin

formalisieren *tr. V.* formalize

Formalisierung *die*; **~, ~en** formalization

Formalismus *der*; **~, Formalismen** formalism

Formalist *der*; **~en, ~en**, **Formalistin** *die*; **~, ~nen** formalist

formalistisch

A *Adj.* formalistic

B *adv.* formalistically

Formalität /fɔrmaliˈtɛːt/ *die*; **~, ~en** formality

formaliter /fɔrˈmaːlitɐ/ *Adv.* (geh.) formally

formal·juristisch, formal·rechtlich

A *Adj.* technical; **ein rein ~er Standpunkt** a narrowly legalistic view

B *adv.* technically

Form·anstieg *der* (Sport) improvement in form

Format /fɔrˈmaːt/ *das*; **~[e]s, ~e** **1** size; (Buch~, Papier~, Bild~) format **2** (Persönlichkeit) stature; **ihm fehlt das menschliche ~:** he lacks real personal stature; **eine Frau von ~:** a woman of stature **3** (besonderes Niveau) quality; **etw. hat/ist ohne ~:** sth. has/lacks class

formatieren *tr. V.* (DV) format

Formatierung *die*; **~, ~en** (DV) formatting

Formation /fɔrmaˈtsi̯oːn/ *die*; **~, ~en** **1** (Herausbildung, Anordnung) formation; (einer Generation, Gesellschaft) development **2** (Gruppe) group; **eine Hamburger ~** (Tanzsport) a team from Hamburg **3** (Milit.) (von Flugzeugen) formation; (von Soldaten) unit **4** (Geol., Bot.) formation

Formations-: ~flug *der* **1** (Flug in Formation) formation flying; **2** (Raumflug) alignment of orbits; **~tanz** *der* (Tanzsport) formation dancing

formbar *Adj.* malleable; soft ‹*bone*›; (fig.) malleable, pliable ‹*character, person*›

Formbarkeit *die*; **~:** malleability; (fig.) malleability; pliability

form-, Form-: ~beständig *Adj.* **~beständig sein** keep its/their shape; **~blatt** *das* form; **~brief** *der* form letter

Formel /ˈfɔrml̩/ *die*; **~, ~n** formula; **die ~ des Eides** the wording of the oath; **~ 1/2** (Motorsport) Formula One/Two; **~-1-Fahrer/-Wagen** Formula One driver/car

formelhaft

A *Adj.* stereotyped ‹*style, mode of expression*›; **eine ~e Wendung** a stereotyped phrase

B *adv.* **sich ~ ausdrücken** talk in stereotyped phrases

Formelhaftigkeit *die*; **~:** stereotyped character

Formel·kram *der* (ugs.) **die Chemie mit ihrem ~:** chemistry and its awful formulae *pl.*

formell /fɔrˈmɛl/

A *Adj.* formal

B *adv.* formally; **die Einladung wurde rein ~ ausgesprochen** the invitation was made only as a matter of form; **er ist nur ~ im Recht** he's only technically in the right

Formel-: ~sammlung *die* formulary; **~sprache** *die*: **die ~sprache der Physik** the language of formulae as used in physics; **die mathematische ~sprache** the language of mathematical formulae; **~zeichen** *das* symbol

formen

A *tr. V.* **1** (gestalten) form; shape; **etw. in Ton/Gips ~:** shape *or* form sth. in clay/plaster; **schön geformte Möbel/Hände** finely shaped furniture/hands; **Laute/Silben ~:** form sounds/syllables **2** (bilden, prägen) mould, form ‹*character, personality*›; mould ‹*person*›; **jmdn. zu etw. ~:** mould sb. into sth.

B *refl. V.* take on a shape; (fig.) form; take shape

formen-, Formen-: ~lehre *die* **1** (Sprachw., Biol.) morphology; **2** (Musik) theory of [musical] form; **~reich** *Adj.* with its/their great variety of forms; **~reich sein** display a great variety of forms; **~reichtum** *der* great variety of forms; wealth of forms; **~sprache** *die* form language

Former *der*; **~s, ~**, **Formerin** *die*; **~, ~nen** moulder

Formerei *die*; **~, ~en** moulding department

form-, Form-: ~fehler *der* **1** (in einem Verfahren, Dokument) irregularity; **2** (Taktlosigkeit) faux pas; breach of etiquette; **~frage** *die* formality; **~gebung** *die*; **~~, ~~en** design; **~gerecht** **A** *Adj.* correct; proper; **B** *adv.* correctly; properly; **~gestalter** *der*, **~gestalterin** *die* ▸ **Designer**; **~gestaltung** *die* ▸ **Design**

formidabel /fɔrmiˈdaːbl̩/ *Adj.* **1** (geh.: außergewöhnlich) superb **2** (veralt.: besorgniserregend) formidable

formieren

A *tr. V.* form ‹*team, party, organization*›; **der Feldherr formierte seine Truppen auf dem Hügel** the commander drew up his troops on the hill

B *refl. V.* **1** (sich aufstellen) form; **wir formierten uns zu einer Gruppe** we formed ourselves into a group; **sich neben der Tribüne ~:** assemble beside the rostrum **2** (sich zusammenschließen) be formed; **die formierte Gesellschaft** (hist.) the aligned society

Formierung *die*; **~, ~en** formation; (von Truppen) drawing up

-förmig /-fœrmɪç/ -shaped; *s. auch* **ei-**, **gabel-**, **kugelförmig** *usw.*

Form·krise *die* (Sport) bad patch; **in einer ~ sein** *od.* **stecken** be off form

förmlich /ˈfœrmlɪç/

A *Adj.* **1** formal; **warum denn so ~?** why [be] so formal? **2** (regelrecht) positive; **ein ~er Schreck durchfuhr ihn** he got a real fright; **einen ~en Abscheu verspüren** feel positive revulsion

B *adv.* **1** (steif, unpersönlich, offiziell) formally **2** (geradezu) **sich ~ fürchten** be really afraid; **~ außer sich sein** be quite beside oneself; **jmdn. ~ zwingen, etw. zu tun** positively force sb. to do sth.

Förmlichkeit *die*; **~, ~en** formality; **in aller ~ um etw. bitten** (veraltend) formally request sth.; **die juristischen ~en** the legal formalities; **bitte keine ~en!** please don't stand on ceremony!

form-, Form-: ~los **A** *Adj.* **1** informal; **einen ~losen Antrag stellen** make an application without the official form[s]; apply informally; **2** (gestaltlos) shapeless; **B** *adv.* informally; **~losigkeit** *die*; **~~** **1** informality; **2** (Gestaltlosigkeit) shapelessness; **~sache** *die* formality; **das ist [eine] reine ~sache** that is purely a formality; **~schön** *Adj.* elegant; **~tief** *das* (Sport) bad patch; **er steckt** *od.* **befindet sich in einem ~tief** he's badly off form

Formular /fɔrmuˈlaːɐ̯/ *das*; **~s, ~e** form

formulieren /fɔrmuˈliːrən/ *tr. V.* formulate; **eine Frage noch einmal ~:** reformulate *or* rephrase a question

Formulierung *die*; **~, ~en** **1** (das Formulieren) formulation; (eines Entwurfes, Gesetzes) drafting **2** (formulierter Text) formulation; **politische/wissenschaftliche ~en** political/scientific phraseology *sing.*

Formung *die*; **~, ~en** **1** (Gestaltung) design; **die strenge ~ des Sonetts** strict sonnet form **2** (Bildung, Erziehung) moulding; (des Charakters) moulding; forming

form-, Form-: ~veränderung *die* change in shape; **~verstoß** *der* ▸ **~widrigkeit**; **~vollendet** **A** *Adj.* perfectly executed ‹pirouette, bow, etc.›; ‹poem› perfect in form; B adv. **etw. ~vollendet tun** do sth. faultlessly; **~vorschrift** die statutory form; **~widrig** A Adj. improper ‹behaviour, expression›; B adv. improperly; **~widrigkeit** die impropriety

forsch /fɔrʃ/
A Adj. self-assertive; forceful; **einen ~en Eindruck machen** seem self-assertive or forceful; **mit ~en Schritten** with a brisk step; briskly
B adv. self-assertively; forcefully

forschen itr. V. [1] (suchen) **nach jmdm./etw. ~:** search or look for sb./sth.; **jmdn. ~d** od. **mit ~dem Blick betrachten** look at sb. searchingly; give sb. a searching look [2] (als Wissenschaftler) research; do research; **auf einem Gebiet ~:** research or do research in a field; **in [alten] Quellen ~:** research into [ancient] sources

Forscher der; ~s, ~ ▸❶ S. 113 [1] (Wissenschaftler) researcher; research scientist [2] (Forschungsreisender) explorer

Forscher-: **~drang** der [1] (Wissensdurst) thirst for new knowledge; [2] (Entdeckerfreude) urge to explore; **~geist** der inquiring mind

Forscherin die; ~, ~nen ▸❶ S. 113 ▸**Forscher**

forscherisch
A Adj. research attrib.; **~e Arbeit** research work
B adv. **~ arbeiten** do research [work]

Forscher·team das research team

Forschheit die; ~: self-assertiveness; forcefulness

Forschung die; ~, ~en research; **~en [auf einem Gebiet] betreiben** do research [in a field]; **~ und Lehre** teaching and research

Forschungs-: **~anstalt** die research establishment; **~arbeit** die [1] piece of research; [2] ▸**Forschung**; **~auftrag** der research assignment; **~bericht** der research report; **~ergebnis** das result of the research; **~gebiet** das field of research; **~gegen·stand** der research topic; **~institut** das research institute; **~labor[atorium]** das research laboratory; **~methode** die research method; **~programm** das research programme; **~rakete** die research rocket; **~reaktor** der research reactor; **~reise** die expedition; **~reisende** der/die explorer; **~satellit** der research satellite; **~schiff** das research vessel; **~stipendium** das research grant; **~tätigkeit** die research work; **~vorhaben** das research project; **~zentrum** das research centre; **~zweck** der purpose of the research; **für ~zwecke** for research purposes

Forst /fɔrst/ der; ~[e]s, ~e[n] forest

Forst-: **~amt** das forestry office; **~beamte** der, **~beamtin** die forestry official

Förster /ˈfœrstɐ/ der; ~s, ~ ▸❶ S. 113 forest warden; forester; ranger (Amer.)

Försterei die; ~, ~en ▸**Forsthaus**

Försterin die; ~, ~nen ▸❶ S. 113 ▸**Förster**

forst-, Forst-: **~frevel** der offence against the forest law; **~frevel begehen** break the forest law; **~haus** das forester's house; **~ingenieur** der, **~ingenieurin** die senior forestry official (with academic qualifications); **~nutzung** die [commercial] exploitation of forests; **~recht** das forest law; **~revier** das forest district; **~schaden** der damage no pl., no indef. art. to the forest; **~schädling** der forest pest; **~verwaltung** die Forestry Commission; **~wesen** das forestry; **~wirtschaft** die forestry; **~wirtschaftlich** A Adj. commercial; B adv. commercially

Forsythie /fɔrˈzyːtsi̯ə/ die; ~, ~n [1] forsythia [2] Pl. (Zweige) sprigs of forsythia

fort /fɔrt/ Adv. [1] (weg) **sie ist schon ~:** she has already gone or left; **ihre Brille war ~:** her glasses had gone or had vanished; **~ mit dir!** be off with you!; away with you!; **~ mit ihr/damit!** take her/it away!; away with her/it!; **[schnell] ~!** run for it! [2] (weiter) **nur immer so ~:** just carry on as you are or like that; **und so ~:** and so on; and so forth; **in einem ~:** continuously

Fort /foːɐ̯/ das; ~s, ~s fort

fort-, Fort-: **~an** /-ˈ-/ Adv. from now/then on; **~bestand** der continuation; (eines Staates) continued existence; **~|bestehen** unr. itr. V. remain; continue; ‹nation› remain in existence; (beim Alten bleiben) remain the same; remain as before; **~|bewegen** A tr. V. move; shift; B refl. V. move [along]; **~bewegung** die locomotion; **~bewegungs·mittel** das means of transport; **~|bilden** tr. V. **sich/jmdn. ~bilden** continue one's/sb.'s education; **die Lehrlinge wurden ~gebildet** the apprentices were given further training; **~bildung** die further education; (beruflich) further training; **~bildungs·kurs** der further education course; (beruflich) training course; **~|bleiben** unr. itr. V.; mit sein fail to come; **du bist so lange ~geblieben!** you've been away so long!; **sein Fortbleiben beunruhigte mich** I was worried when he didn't turn up; **~|bringen** unr. tr. V.: ▸**wegbringen**; **~dauer** die continuation; **~|dauern** itr. V. continue; **fortdauernder Widerstand** continuing/(in der Vergangenheit) continued resistance; **unter fortdauernden Beschuss geraten** come under continuous bombardment; **~|denken** unr. itr. V.: ▸**wegdenken**

forte /ˈfɔrtə/ Adv. (Musik, Pharm.) forte

Forte das; ~s, ~s od. **Forti** (Mus.) forte

fort-, Fort-: **~|eilen** itr. V.; mit sein (geh.) hurry off or away; hasten away; **~|entwickeln** A tr. V. **etw. ~entwickeln** develop sth. further; B refl. V. develop; **~|erben** refl. V. be passed on; be handed down; **sich auf jmdn. ~erben** pass to sb.; be handed down to sb.; **~|fahren** A unr. itr. V. [1] mit sein (abreisen) leave; (einen Ausflug machen) go out; [2] auch mit sein (weitermachen) **~fahren [,etw. zu tun]** continue or go on [doing sth.]; **in seiner Rede ~fahren** continue or go on with one's speech; **bitte, fahren Sie ~:** please continue; please go on; B unr. tr. V. drive away; **jmdn. [mit dem Auto] ~fahren** drive or take sb. away [in a car]; **etw. [mit einem Auto] ~fahren** take sth. away [in a car]; **~fall** der ending; discontinuation; **~|fallen** unr. itr. V.; mit sein ‹obstacle, misgiving› be removed; ‹words› be omitted; ‹conditions› no longer apply; ‹subsidy› be discontinued; ‹advantage› be lost; **ein Kapitel ~fallen lassen** delete a chapter; **~|fliegen** unr. itr. V.; mit sein: ▸**wegfliegen**; **~|führen** A tr. V. [1] lead away; [2] (~setzen) continue, keep up ‹tradition, business›; continue, carry on ‹another's work›; B itr. V. **von etw. ~führen** lead away from sth.; **~führung** die ▸**~führen A 2**; continuation; keeping up; carrying on; **sich zur ~führung von jmds. Geschäften bereit erklären** declare one's readiness to carry on sb.'s business; **~gang** der [1] departure (**aus** from); [2] (Weiterentwicklung) progress; **seinen ~gang nehmen** progress; **~|geben** unr. tr. V. ▸**weggeben**; **~|gehen** unr. itr. V.; mit sein [1] (weggehen) leave; **geh ~!** go away!; **geh nicht ~!** don't go away!; don't leave!; [2] (andauern, verlaufen) continue; go on; **~geschritten** Adj. advanced; **in ~geschrittenem Alter** at an advanced age; **zu ~geschrittener Tageszeit** at a late hour; **die Krankheit befindet sich in einem ~geschrittenen Stadium** the disease has reached an advanced stage; **~geschrittene** der/die; adj. Dekl. advanced student/player; **ein Kurs[us] für ~geschrittene** a course for advanced students; an advanced course; **~geschrittenen·kurs[us]** der advanced course; **~gesetzt** A Adj. continual; constant; **~gesetzter Betrug/~gesetzte Untreue** repeated fraud/embezzlement; B adv. continually; constantly; **~|haben** unr. tr. V.: ▸**weghaben 1**; **~hin** Adv. (veralt.) henceforth; henceforward

fortissimo /fɔrˈtɪsimo/ Adv. (Musik) fortissimo

Fortissimo das; ~s, ~s od. **Fortissimi** (Musik) fortissimo

fort-, Fort-: **~|jagen** tr. V.: ▸**wegjagen**; **~|kommen** unr. itr. V.; mit sein [1] ▸**wegkommen 1, 2, 4, 6**; [2] (Erfolg haben) get on; do well; **in der Schule/im Beruf ~kommen** get on at school/in one's job; **~kommen** das; ~~s [1] (das Vorwärtskommen, auch beruflich) progress; **das wird für mein ~kommen nützlich sein** that will help me get ahead or get on; [2] (Lebensunterhalt) living; **sein ~kommen finden** make a living; **das Gehalt reichte gerade für sein ~kommen** the money was just enough for him to get by on; **~|können** unr. itr. V.: ▸**wegkönnen**; **~|lassen** unr. tr. V.: ▸**weglassen**; **~|laufen** unr. itr. V.; mit sein [1] ▸**weglaufen**; [2] (sich ~setzen) continue; **~laufend** A Adj. continuous; **die ~laufende Handlung der Fernsehserie** the ongoing plot of the television series; **~laufende Hefte** consecutive issues; B adv. continuously; **~laufend nummeriert** numbered consecutively; **~|leben** itr. V.: ▸**weiterleben**; **~|legen** tr. V. put down or aside; **~|loben** tr. V.: ▸**wegloben**; **~|machen** (ugs.) A refl. V. get away; B itr. V.: ▸**weitermachen A**; **~|müssen** unr. itr. V.: ▸**wegmüssen**; **~|nehmen** unr. tr. V. take away; **~|pflanzen** refl. V. [1] (sich vermehren) reproduce [oneself/itself]; [2] (sich verbreiten) ‹idea, mood› spread; ‹sound, light› travel, propagate; **~pflanzung** die [1] (Vermehrung) reproduction; [2] (Verbreitung) transmission; (von Schall, Licht) propagation; (von Ideen) spread; **~pflanzungs·fähig** Adj. capable of reproduction postpos.; **~pflanzungs·medizin** reproductive medicine; **~pflanzungs·trieb** der reproductive instinct; **~|räumen** tr. V.: ▸**wegräumen**; **~|reisen** itr. V.; mit sein: ▸**abreisen**; **~|reißen** unr. tr. V. [1] (wegreißen) tear away; **die Fluten rissen alles mit sich ~:** the floods swept everything away; [2] (begeistern) **jmdn. ~reißen** carry or sweep sb. along; **jmdn. zu Beifallsstürmen ~reißen** rouse sb. to tumultuous applause; **~|rennen** unr. itr. V.; mit sein (ugs.) run off or away; **~satz** der (Biol.) process; **~|schaffen** tr. V. take or carry away; **~|scheren** refl. V. (ugs.) **scher dich ~!** clear off! (coll.); **~|scheuchen** tr. V. shoo or chase away; **~|schicken** tr. V.: ▸**wegschicken**; **~|schieben** unr. tr. V.: ▸**wegschieben**; **~|schleichen** unr. itr., refl. V.: ▸**wegschleichen**; **~|schleppen** refl., tr. V.: ▸**wegschleppen**; **~|schleudern** tr. V. fling away; **~|schreiben** unr. tr. V. update; (in die Zukunft) project forward; **~schreibung** die updating; (in die Zukunft) forward projection; **~|schreiten** unr. itr. V.; mit sein ‹process› progress, continue; ‹time› move on; **die Zeit ist [weit] ~geschritten** it is getting on or late; **der Sommer ist [weit] ~geschritten** we are well into summer; **das ~schreiten** progress; **~schreitend** Adj. progressive; **mit ~schreitender Jahreszeit** as the year goes/went on; **mit ~schreitendem Alter** with advancing age; with the passing of the years; **~schritt** der progress; **~schritte** progress sing.; **ein ~schritt** a step forward; **das ist schon ein ~schritt** that is some progress at least; **große ~schritte machen** make great progress; **~schrittlich** A Adj. progressive; B adv. progressively; **~schrittlichkeit** die; ~~: progressiveness; **~schritts·feindlich** Adj. anti-progressive; **~schritts·gläubig** Adj. **~schrittsgläubig/zu ~schrittsgläubig sein** put one's/too much faith in progress; **das ~schrittsgläubige 19. Jahrhundert** the nineteenth century with its implicit faith in progress; **~schritts·gläubigkeit** die belief or faith in progress; **~|schwemmen** tr. V. sweep away; **~|sehnen** refl. V. long to go; **~|setzen** A tr. V. continue; carry on; **den Weg zu Fuß/mit dem Auto ~setzen** continue by foot/car; B refl. V. continue; **~setzung** die; ~setzung, ~setzungen [1] (das ~setzen) continuation; **[s]eine ~setzung finden** resume; [2] (anschließender Teil) instalment; **in ~setzungen erscheinen** be published in instalments; **~setzung von S. 7** continued from p. 7; **~setzung folgt** to be continued; **~setzungs·roman** der serial; serialized novel; **~|spülen** tr. V.: ▸**wegspülen**; **~|stehlen** unr. refl. V. steal or sneak away; **~|stoßen** unr. tr. V.: ▸**wegstoßen**; **~|stürzen** itr. V.; mit sein rush off or away;

~|tragen *unr. tr. V.:* ▸**wegtragen**; **~|treiben** **A** *unr. tr. V.* **1** (ver-, wegtreiben) drive off *or* away; **er hat seinen Sohn ~getrieben** he made it impossible for his son to stay; **es trieb mich bald ~:** I soon felt I had to leave; **2** (vorwärts treiben) sweep away; **B** *itr. V.; mit sein* float away

Fortuna /fɔr'tuːna/ *(die)* Fortune; **~ lachte** *od.* **lächelte ihm** (geh.) Fortune smiled upon him

Fortune /fɔr'tyːn/ *die;* **~,** *eingedeutscht:* **Fortüne** /fɔr'tyːnə/ *die;* **~:** luck; **keine/wenig ~ haben** have no/not much luck

fort-: **~|währen** *itr. V.* (geh.) ▸**~dauern**; **~|während** **A** *Adj.* continual; incessant; **B** *adv.* continually; incessantly; **~|werfen** *unr. tr. V.:* ▸**wegwerfen**; **~|wirken** *itr. V.* continue to have an effect; **das wirkt in uns ~:** the effect of it persists in us; **sein Vorbild wirkt in ihnen ~:** his example continues to exert an influence on them; **das Fortwirken antiker Motive** the continuing influence of ancient motifs; **~|wollen** *unr. itr. V.* **1** ▸**wegwollen**; **2** (vorwärts wollen) want to move; **seine Füße wollten nicht recht ~:** his feet did not seem to be able to carry him; **~|zaubern** *tr. V.* **etw. ~zaubern** make sth. disappear; **~|zerren** *tr. V.:* ▸**wegzerren**; **~|ziehen** *unr. tr., itr. V.:* ▸**wegziehen**

Forum /'foːrʊm/ *das;* **~s, Foren** *od.* **Fora** **1** (Personenkreis, Plattform, röm. Marktplatz) forum **2** *Pl. nur* **Foren** (Aussprache) (über Literatur) symposium; (über Politik) forum discussion

fossil /fɔ'siːl/ *Adj.* fossilized; fossil *attrib.*

Fossil *das;* **~s, ~ien** fossil

Foto[1] /'foːto/ *das;* **~s, ~s,** (schweiz.:) *die;* **~, ~s** photo; **~s machen** *od.* (ugs.:) **schießen** take photos; **auf einem ~:** in a photo

Foto[2] *der;* **~s, ~s** (bes. südd. ugs.) camera

Foto-: **~album** *das* photo album; **~apparat** *der* camera; **~atelier** *das* photographic studio; **~ecke** *die* [mounting] corner

fotogen /foto'geːn/ *Adj.* photogenic

Foto·geschäft *das* photographic shop

Foto·graf *der;* **~en, ~en** ▸❶ **S. 113** photographer

Fotografie *die;* **~, ~n** **1** photography *no art.* **2** (Lichtbild) photograph

fotografieren
A *tr. V.* photograph; take a photograph/photographs of; **sie lässt sich gern/ungern ~:** she likes/does not like being photographed *or* having her photograph taken; **Katzen lassen sich gut ~:** cats photograph well
B *itr. V.* take photographs; **er fotografiert gut** *od.* **kann gut ~:** he is a good photographer; **[das] Fotografieren [ist] verboten!** photography prohibited

Fotografin *die;* **~, ~nen** ▸❶ **S. 113** photographer

fotografisch
A *Adj.* photographic
B *adv.* photographically

foto-, Foto-: **~kopie** *die* photocopy; **~kopieren** *tr., itr. V.* photocopy; **~kopierer** *der,* **~kopier·gerät** *das* photocopier; photocopying machine

Foto-: **~labor** *das* photographic laboratory; **~modell** *das* ▸❶ **S. 113** **1** photographic model; **2** (verhüll.: Prostituierte) model; **~montage** *die* photomontage; **~papier** *das* photographic paper; **~realismus** *der* (bild. Kunst) photorealism *no art.;* **~reporter** *der,* **~reporterin** *die* ▸❶ **S. 113** press photographer; newspaper photographer; **~safari** *die* photographic safari; **~satz** *der* (Druckw.) ▸**Lichtsatz**; **~shooting** /-ʃuːtɪŋ/ *das;* **~[s], ~s** photo shoot; **~tapete** *die* panoramic wallpaper; **~tasche** *die* camera bag; **~termin** *der* photocall; **~wettbewerb** *der* photographic competition; **~zeitschrift** *die* photographic magazine

Fötus ▸**Fetus**

Fotze /'fɔtsə/ *die;* **~, ~n** **1** (vulg.: Vulva) cunt (coarse) **2** (vulg.: Frau) cunt (coarse) **3** (bayr. u. österr. ugs.: Mund) gob (sl.)

foul /faul/ *Adv.* (Sport) **~ spielen** play dirty; be a dirty player; **er hat gerade ~ gespielt** he has just committed a foul

Foul *das;* **~s, ~s** (Sport) foul **(an** + *Dat.* on)

Foul·elf·meter *der* (Fußball) penalty [for a foul]; **einen ~ verhängen** *od.* **geben** award *or* give a penalty

foulen /'faulən/ (Sport)
A *tr. V.* foul
B *itr. V.* commit a foul

Fox /fɔks/ *der;* **~[es], ~e** **1** ▸**Foxterrier** **2** ▸**Foxtrott**

Fox·terrier *der* fox terrier

Fox·trott /-trɔt/ *der;* **~s, ~e** *od.* **~s** foxtrot; **~ tanzen** foxtrot

Foyer /foa'jeː/ *das;* **~s, ~s** foyer

FPÖ *Abk.* **= Freiheitliche Partei Österreichs**

> **FPÖ — Freiheitliche Partei Österreichs**
>
> The Austrian Freedom Party, also known as *Die Freiheitlichen*, was founded in 1955. It is right-wing and is the third largest party. It advocates a 1000-Euro minimum monthly wage and stricter asylum policies.

Fr.[1] *Abk.* **= Franken** SFr.

Fr.[2] *Abk.* **= Frau**

Fr.[3] *Abk.* **= Freitag** Fri.

Fracht /fraxt/ *die;* **~, ~en** **1** (Schiffs~, Luft~) cargo; freight; (Bahn~, LKW-~) goods *pl.;* freight; **volle/halbe ~ führen** carry full/half freight **2** (~kosten) (Schiffs~, Luft~) freight; freightage; (Bahn~, LKW-~) carriage

Fracht-: **~brief** *der* consignment note; waybill; **~dampfer** *der* (veralt.) steam freighter

Frachten·bahnhof *der,* **Frachtenstation** *die* (österr.) ▸**Güterbahnhof**

Frachter *der;* **~s, ~:** freighter

fracht-, Fracht-: **~flugzeug** *das* cargo *or* freight plane; **~frei** **A** *Adj.* carriage-free ‹*delivery*›; **B** *adv.* ‹*deliver*› carriage free; **~führer** *der,* **~führerin** *die* carrier; **~geld** *das* ▸**Fracht 2**; **~gut** *das* slow freight; slow goods *pl.;* **etw. als ~gut schicken** send sth. by slow goods; **~kosten** *Pl.:* ▸**Fracht 2**; **~raum** *der* [cargo] hold; (Platz) [cargo] space; **~schiff** *das* cargo ship

Frack /frak/ *der;* **~[e]s, Fräcke** /'frɛkə/ tails *pl.;* evening dress; **einen ~ tragen** wear tails *or* evening dress; **im ~ erscheinen** turn up in tails *or* evening dress; **jmdm. saust der ~** (fig. ugs. scherzh.) sb. gets the wind up (coll.)

Frack-: **~hemd** *das* dress shirt; **~sausen** *das: in* **~sausen haben** (ugs.) get the wind up (coll.); **~schoß** *der* coat-tail; **~weste** *die* waistcoat (*worn with evening dress*)

Frage /'fraːgə/ *die;* **~, ~n** **1** question; **jmdm.** *od.* **an jmdn. eine ~ stellen** put a question to sb.; **jmdm. eine ~ beantworten/auf jmds. ~** (*Akk.*) **antworten** reply to *or* answer sb.'s question; **eine ~ [zu etw.] haben** have a question [on sth.]; **sind noch ~n?** are there any questions?; **an jmdn. eine ~ richten** direct a question to sb.; **darf ich Ihnen eine ~ stellen?** may I put a question?; **eine ~ verneinen/bejahen** give a negative/positive answer to a question; **auf eine dumme ~ bekommt man eine dumme Antwort** ask a silly question [and you get a silly answer] **2** (Problem) question; (Angelegenheit) issue; **es erhebt sich/bleibt die ~, ob ...** the question arises/remains whether ...; **eine soziale/politische ~:** a social/political issue; **die deutsche ~:** the German problem; **das ist [nur] eine ~ der Zeit** that is [only] a question *or* matter of time **3** *in* **das ist noch sehr die ~:** that is still very much the question; **das ist die große ~:** that is the big question; **das ist gar keine ~:** there's no doubt *or* question about it; **es ist** *od.* **steht außer ~, dass ...** there is no doubt that ...; there is no question but that ...; **in ~:** ▸**infrage**; **ohne ~:** without question

Frage-: **~bogen** *der* questionnaire; (Formular) form; **~bogen·aktion** *die* poll; **~fürwort** *das* ▸**Interrogativpronomen**

fragen
A *tr., itr. V.* **1** ask; **er fragt immer so klug** he always asks *or* puts such astute questions; **neugierig/erstaunt ~:** ask inquisitively/in amazement; **gezielt ~:** ask *or* put well-aimed questions; **frag nicht so dumm!** (ugs.) don't ask such silly questions; **das fragst du noch?** (ugs.) need you ask?; **~ Sie lieber nicht** (ugs.) don't ask!; **da fragst du mich zu viel** that I don't know; I really can't say; **jmdn. ~d ansehen** look at sb. inquiringly; give sb. a questioning look; **~ kostet nichts** there is no harm in asking **2** (sich erkundigen) **nach etw. ~:** ask *or* inquire about sth.; **jmdn. nach/wegen etw. ~:** ask sb. about sth.; **nach dem Weg ~:** ask the way; **nach Einzelheiten ~:** ask for details; **nach jmds. Meinung ~:** ask [for] sb.'s opinion; **nach jmdm. ~** (jmdn. suchen) ask for sb.; (über jmdn. Fragen stellen) ask about sb.; (nach jmds. Befinden ~) ask after *or* about sb.; **wenn ich ~ darf** if you don't mind my asking; (ungeduldig) may I ask? **3** (nach~) ask for; **jmdn. um Rat/Erlaubnis ~:** ask sb. for advice/permission **4** (verneint: sich nicht kümmern) **nach jmdm./etw. nicht ~:** not care about sb./sth.; **ich frage den Teufel** *od.* **einen Dreck danach** (salopp) I couldn't care less [about it] (coll.); I don't give a damn about it (sl.)
B *refl. V.* **sich ~, ob ...** wonder whether ...; **das frage ich mich auch** I was wondering that, too; (unpers.) **es fragt sich [nur], ob/wann ...** the [only] question is whether/when ...

Fragen·komplex *der* set of problems

Fragerei *die;* **~, ~en** (abwertend) questions *pl.*

Frage-: **~satz** *der* interrogative sentence/clause; **ein direkter/indirekter ~satz** a direct/an indirect question; **~stellung** *die* **1** (Formulierung) formulation of a/the question; **durch eine geschickte ~stellung** by skilled questioning; **2** (Problem) problem; **~stunde** *die* (Parl.) question time; **~-und-Antwort-Spiel** *das* question-and-answer game; **~zeichen** *das* question mark; **ein ~zeichen setzen** put a question mark; **etw. mit einem [dicken/großen] ~zeichen versehen** (fig.) put a [big] question mark over sth. (fig.); **dastehen/dasitzen wie ein ~zeichen** (ugs.) stand/sit like a hunchback

fragil /fra'giːl/ *Adj.* (geh.) fragile

fraglich /'fraːklɪç/ *Adj.* **1** (unsicher) doubtful **2** (betreffend) in question *postpos.;* relevant; **zur ~en Zeit** at the time in question; at the relevant time

fraglos *Adv.* without question; unquestionably

Fragment /fra'gmɛnt/ *das;* **~[e]s, ~e** fragment

fragmentarisch /fragmɛn'taːrɪʃ/
A *Adj.* fragmentary
B *adv.* **ein ~ überlieferter Text** a text preserved only as fragments/a fragment; **es ist nur ~ erhalten** it is preserved only in fragmentary form

frag·würdig *Adj.* **1** questionable **2** (zwielichtig) dubious

Fragwürdigkeit *die;* **~, ~en** **1** questionableness **2** (Zwielichtigkeit) dubiousness

fraktal *Adj.* (Math.) fractal

Fraktion /frak'tsi̯oːn/ *die;* **~, ~en** **1** (Parl.) parliamentary party; (mit zwei Parteien) parliamentary coalition **2** (Sondergruppe) faction **3** (Chemie) fraction

fraktionell /fraktsi̯o'nɛl/ *Adj.* within a/the party/group *postpos.;* internal ‹*conflict, agreement*›

fraktions-, Fraktions-: **~beschluss,** ***~beschluß** *der* party/coalition decision; **~chef** *der,* **~chefin** *die* ▸**~führer**; **~führer** *der,* **~führerin** *die* leader of the parliamentary party/coalition; **~kollege** *der,* **~kollegin** *die* fellow parliamentary party/coalition member; **~los** *Adj.* independent; **~mitglied** *das* member of a/the parliamentary party/coalition; **~sitzung** *die* meeting of the parliamentary party/coalition; **~stärke** *die* **1** *minimum number of elected members necessary for a party to be allowed to form a parliamentary group;* **2** (Größe der Fraktion) size of the parliamentary party; **~vorsitzende** *der/die* ▸**~führer**; **~zwang** *der* obligation to vote in accordance with party policy; **den**

~zwang aufheben allow a free vote

Fraktur /frak'tu:ɐ/ *die;* ~, **~en** [1] ▸ⓘ **S. 439** (Med.) fracture [2] (Schriftart) Fraktur; **mit jmdm. ~ reden** (ugs.) talk straight with sb.

Franc /frã:/ *der;* ~, **~s** ▸ⓘ **S. 299** franc

Franchise /'frɛntʃaɪz/ *das;* ~ (Wirtsch.) franchise

frank /fraŋk/ *Adv.* **~ und frei** frankly and openly; openly and honestly

Franke *der;* **~n, ~n** [1] Franconian [2] (hist.) Frank

Franken[1] *(das);* **~s** Franconia

Franken[2] *der;* **~s,** ~ ▸ⓘ **S. 299** [Swiss] franc

Frankfurter[1] /'fraŋkfʊrtɐ/ *die;* ~, ~ (Wurst) frankfurter

Frankfurter[2] ▸ⓘ **S. 675**

A *indekl. Adj.* Frankfurt

B *der;* **~s, ~:** Frankfurter; *s. auch* **Kölner**

> **Frankfurter Allgemeine Zeitung (FAZ)**
>
> One of Germany's most serious and widely respected daily newspapers. It was founded in 1945 and is published in Frankfurt am Main. It tends to have a centre-left to liberal outlook. The *Frankfurter Rundschau* is another Frankfurt daily, with a circulation of almost 200,000.

Frankfurterin *die;* ~, **~nen** ▸**Frankfurter**[2] **B**

frankieren /fraŋ'ki:rən/ *tr. V.* frank

Frankiermaschine *die* franking machine

Fränkin *die;* ~, **~nen** ▸**Franke**

fränkisch /'frɛŋkɪʃ/ *Adj.* [1] Franconian [2] (hist.) Frankish; *s. auch* **deutsch, Deutsch, badisch**

franko /'fraŋko/ *Adv.* (Kaufmannsspr. veralt.) carriage paid; (mit der Post) post-free

Franko·kanadier *der,* **Franko·kanadierin** *die* French Canadian

frankophil /-'fi:l/ *Adj.* Francophile

frankophon /-'fo:n/ *Adj.* Francophone

Frank·reich *(das);* **~s** France

Franktireur /frãti'rø:ɐ/ *der;* **~s, ~e** *od.* **~s** (hist.) franc tireur

Franse /'franzə/ *die;* ~, **~n** strand [of a/the fringe]; **die ~n der Decke/des Teppichs** the fringe of the rug/the carpet

fransen *itr. V.:* ▸**ausfransen A**

fransig

A *Adj.* frayed ‹*shirt, trousers*›; straggly ‹*hair*›

B *adv.* **das Haar hing ihr ~ ins Gesicht** her hair hung down over her face in untidy strands

Franz[1] /frants/ *(der)* Francis

Franz[2] *das;* ~ (Schülerspr.) French

Franz·branntwein *der* (veralt.) alcoholic liniment

Franziskaner /frantsɪs'ka:nɐ/ *der;* **~s,** ~, **Franziskanerin** *die;* ~, **~nen** Franciscan

Franziskaner-: ~kloster *das* Franciscan monastery; **~orden** *der* (kath.) Franciscan Order

Franzose /fran'tso:zə/ *der;* **~n, ~n** [1] ▸ⓘ **S. 520** Frenchman; **er ist ~:** he is French *or* a Frenchman; **die ~n** the French [2] (ugs.: Schraubenschlüssel) screw wrench

Franzosen·krankheit *die* (veralt.) French disease (dated); syphilis

Französin /fran'tsø:zɪn/ *die;* ~, **~nen** ▸ⓘ **S. 520** Frenchwoman

französisch ▸ⓘ **S. 520,** ▸ⓘ **S. 670**

A *Adj.* French; **ein ~es Bett** a double bed; **die Französische Schweiz** French-speaking Switzerland; **die Französische Revolution** the French Revolution; **die ~e Krankheit** (veralt.) ▸**Franzosenkrankheit**

B *adv.* **es ~ machen** (salopp) have oral sex; **sich [auf] ~ empfehlen** *od.* **verabschieden** (ugs.) take French leave; *s. auch* **deutsch, Deutsche**[2]

Französisch *das;* **~[s]** ▸ⓘ **S. 670** French; *s. auch* **Deutsch**

französischsprachig *Adj.* [1] French-speaking ‹*person, area*›; **Französischsprachige** French speakers [2] (in französischer Sprache) French-language *attrib.* ‹*newspaper, edition, broadcast*›; ‹*teaching, song*› in French; ‹*literature*› written in French

frappant /fra'pant/ *Adj.* striking ‹*similarity*›; remarkable ‹*success, discovery*›

frappieren /fra'pi:rən/ *tr. V.* (geh.) astonish; astound

frappierend *Adj.* astonishing; remarkable

Fräse /'frɛ:zə/ *die;* ~, **~n** [1] (für Holz) moulding machine; (für Metall) milling machine [2] ▸**Fräser 1** [3] (Boden~) rotary cultivator

fräsen *tr. V.* [1] shape ‹*wood*›; mill ‹*metal*›; form ‹*groove, thread*› [2] (Landw.) hoe [with a rotary cultivator]

Fräser *der;* **~s,** ~ [1] (Werkzeug) cutter [2] ▸ⓘ **S. 113** (Metallbearb.) milling-machine operator; (Holzverarb.) moulding-machine operator

Fräserin *die;* ~, **~nen** ▸**Fräser 2**

Fräs·maschine *die* ▸**Fräse 1**

fraß /fra:s/ *1. u. 3. Pers. Sg. Prät. v.* **fressen**

Fraß *der;* **~es** [1] (Tiernahrung) food; **einem Tier etw. als** *od.* **zum ~ vorwerfen** feed an animal with sth.; **jmdm. etw. zum ~ hin-** *od.* **vorwerfen** (fig. abwertend) let sb. have sth. [2] (derb: schlechtes Essen) muck; swill; **ein abscheulicher/widerlicher ~:** disgusting/repulsive muck [3] **vom ~ befallen sein** have been eaten away

Frater /'fra:tɐ/ *der;* **~s, Fratres** /'fra:tre:s/ (kath. Kirche) lay brother

fraternisieren /fraterni'zi:rən/ *itr. V.* (geh.) fraternize

Fraternisierung *die;* **~:** fraternization

Fratz /frats/ *der;* **~es, ~e,** (österr.:) **~en, ~en** [1] (ugs.: niedliches Kind) [little] rascal; **ein süßer ~:** a sweet little rascal [2] (bes. südd., österr.: ungezogenes Kind) brat

Fratze /'fratsə/ *die;* ~, **~n** [1] (hässliches Gesicht) hideous face; hideous features *pl.;* **sein Gesicht war zu einer ~ deformiert** his face was hideously deformed [2] (ugs.: Grimasse) grimace; **jmdm. ~n schneiden** pull faces at sb. [3] (abwertend: Gesicht) mug (coll.)

fratzenhaft *Adj.* grotesque; hideous

Frau *die;* ~, **~en** [1] woman; **zur ~ werden** (verhüll.) lose one's virginity; **typisch** *od.* **echt ~** (ugs.) typical of a woman; **die Gleichberechtigung der ~:** equal rights for women; **von ~ zu ~:** woman to woman [2] (Ehefrau) wife; **wie Mann und ~ zusammenleben** live together as man *or* husband and wife; **jmdn. zur ~ nehmen** (veralt.) take sb. to wife (arch.); **er hat eine Französin zur ~:** his wife is French; **willst du meine ~ werden?** will you be my wife? [3] ▸ⓘ **S. 44,** ▸ⓘ **S. 143** (Titel, Anrede) **~ Schulze** Mrs Schulze; **~ Professor/Dr. Schulze** Professor/Dr. Schulze; **~ Ministerin/Direktorin/Studienrätin Schulze** Mrs/Miss/Ms Schulze; **~ Ministerin/Professor/Doktor** Minister/Professor/doctor; **~ Vorsitzende/Präsidentin** Madam Chairman/President; (in Briefen) **Sehr geehrte ~ Schulze** Dear Madam; (bei persönlicher Bekanntschaft) Dear Mrs/Miss/Ms Schulze; **[Sehr verehrte] gnädige ~:** [Dear] Madam; **gute ~** (veralt.) good lady; **Ihre ~ Gemahlin/Mutter** (geh.) your lady wife/lady mother (dated); your wife/mother [4] (Herrin) lady; mistress; **die ~ des Hauses** the lady of the house; **Unsere Liebe ~** (kath. Rel.) Our Lady

Frauchen /'frauçən/ *das;* **~s,** ~ [1] (ugs.: Ehefrau) wifie [2] (Herrin eines Hundes) mistress

frauen-, Frauen-: ~arbeit *die* [1] (Erwerbstätigkeit) women's employment; [2] (für Frauen geeignete Arbeit) women's work; [3] (gesellschaftspolitisch) work for the women's movement; **in der ~arbeit tätig sein** work in the women's movement; **~arzt** *der,* **~ärztin** *die* gynaecologist; **~beruf** *der* women's occupation; **~bewegung** *die* women's movement; **~domäne** *die* women's domain; **eine reine ~domäne sein** be purely the domain of women; **~emanzipation** *die* female emancipation; women's emancipation; **~fachschule** *die* women's technical college; **~farn** *der* (Bot.) lady fern; **~feind** *der* misogynist; **~feindlich** *Adj.* anti-women; **~frage** *die* issue of women's rights; **~funk** *der* women's [radio] programmes *pl.;* **~fußball** *der* women's football; **~gefängnis** *das* women's prison; **~geschichten** *Pl.* (ugs.) affairs with women; **~gestalt** *die* female character; **~haar** *das* [1] woman's hair; [2] (Bot.) haircap moss; **~haar·farn** *der* (Bot.) maidenhair fern; **~hand** *die:* *in* **von zarter ~hand** from the fair hand of a lady; **von zarter ~hand gepflegt** nursed by a woman's tender care; **~haus** *das* [1] women's refuge; [2] (veralt.) brothel; [3] (Völkerk.) unmarried girls' dormitory; **~heilkunde** *die* gynaecology; **~held** *der* ladykiller; **~herz** *das* female heart; **sich auf ~herzen verstehen** know the way to a woman's heart; **~kleider** *Pl.* women's clothes; **~klinik** *die* gynaecological hospital *or* clinic; **~kloster** *das* convent; nunnery; **~krankheit** *die,* **~leiden** *das* gynaecological disorder; **Facharzt für ~krankheiten** gynaecologist; **~liebling** *der* favourite with the ladies; **~lohn** *der* women's pay *no indef. art.;* **~los** *Adj.* all-male; **~mörder** *der* killer of women; **~orden** *der* (kath. Rel.) women's order; **~recht** *das* women's right; **~rechtlerin** /-rɛçtlərɪn/ *die;* **~~, ~~nen** feminist; Women's Libber (coll.); **~sache** *die:* **das ist ~sache** that's a woman's job; **~schänder** *der;* **~~s, ~~:** rapist; **~schuh** *der* (Bot.) lady's slipper; **~schwarm** *der* heart-throb; **~seite** *die* women's page

> **Frauenhaus**
>
> A refuge run by a group of women for battered wives and their children. Women's refuges are supported by charitable groups and offer advice and provisional accommodation.

Frauens·person *die* (veralt.) female

Frauen-: ~sport *der* women's sport; **~station** *die* women's ward; **~stimme** *die* [1] woman's voice; [2] (Parl.) **die ~stimmen** the women's vote *sing.;* **~stimmrecht** *das* ▸**~wahlrecht**; **~tausch** *der* (Völkerk.) exchange of wives

Frauentum *das;* **~s** (geh.) womanhood

Frauen-: ~turnen *das* ladies' *or* women's gymnastics *sing.;* **~über·schuss,** ***~über·schuß** *der* surplus of women; **~verband** *der* women's association; **~wahl·recht** *das* women's franchise; women's right to vote; **~zeitschrift** *die* women's magazine; **~zimmer** *das* [1] (abwertend) female; [2] (veralt., landsch.) woman

Fräulein /'frɔylain/ *das;* **~s,** ~ (ugs. **~s**) [1] (junges ~) young lady; (ältliches ~) spinster [2] ▸ⓘ **S. 44,** ▸ⓘ **S. 143** (Titel, Anrede) **~ Mayer/Schulte** Miss Mayer/Schulte; **[sehr verehrtes] gnädiges ~ [X]** Dear Miss X [3] (veralt.: Angestellte) **~, wollen Sie ...** Miss, would you ...; **das ~ hat uns schlecht bedient** the girl gave us bad service [4] (Kellnerin) **~, wir möchten zahlen** [Miss,] could we have the bill (Brit.) *or* (Amer.) check, please?; **das ~ kommt gleich** the waitress is just coming [5] **das ~ vom Amt** (veralt.) the operator

fraulich

A *Adj.* feminine; (reif) womanly

B *adv.* in a feminine/womanly way; **sich ~ kleiden** dress femininely/in a womanly way

Fraulichkeit *die;* **~:** femininity; (reifes Wesen) womanliness

Frauschaft *die;* ~, **~en** (bes. Sport) women's team

Freak /fri:k/ *der;* **~s, ~s** freak (coll.)

frech /frɛç/

A *Adj.* [1] (respektlos, unverschämt) impertinent; impudent; cheeky; barefaced ‹*lie*›; **ein ~er Kerl** an impertinent chap; **~ werden/sein** become/be impertinent; **etw. mit ~er Stirn behaupten** (fig.) have the barefaced cheek to say sth.; **~ wie Dreck** *od.* **Oskar sein** (bes. berlin.) be a cheeky devil (coll.) [2] (keck, kess) saucy

B *adv.* (respektlos, unverschämt) impertinently; impudently; cheekily; **jmdn. ~ anlügen** tell sb. barefaced lies; **jmdm. etw. ~ ins Gesicht**

sagen say sth. quite unashamedly to sb.'s face; **jmdm. ~ ins Gesicht lachen** laugh in sb.'s face

Frech·dachs *der* (ugs., meist scherzh.) cheeky little thing

Frechheit *die;* ~, **~en** 1 impertinence; impudence; cheek; **die ~ haben, etw. zu tun** have the impertinence *etc.* to do sth.; **das ist der Gipfel der ~!** that is the height of impertinence! 2 (Äußerung) impertinent *or* impudent *or* cheeky remark; **sich** (*Dat.*) **~en erlauben** be impertinent; **was erlauben Sie sich für ~en?** how dare you be so impertinent?

Frechling *der;* **~s, ~e** (geh.) impudent rascal

Freecall·nummer /ˈfriːkɔːl-/ *die* freefone number

Freesie /ˈfreːziə/ *die;* ~, **~n** freesia

Fregatte /freˈgatə/ *die;* ~, **~n** 1 (Marine) frigate 2 (abwertend: Frau) **eine alte/aufgetakelte ~:** an old bag/overdressed old bag

Fregatten·kapitän *der* commander

frei /frai/

A *Adj.* 1 (unabhängig) free ‹*man, will, life, people, decision, etc.*›; **eine ~e Reichsstadt/Hansestadt** (hist.) a free imperial/Hanseatic city

2 (nicht angestellt) freelance ‹*writer, worker, etc.*›; **die ~en Berufe** the independent professions

3 (ungezwungen) free and easy; lax (derog.); **ein ~es Benehmen haben** behave in a free and easy/lax way; **es herrschte ein ~er Ton** there was an informal atmosphere; **~e Liebe** free love

4 (in Freiheit) free; at liberty *pred.*; **~ lebende Tiere** animals living in the wild; **~ herumlaufen** ‹*person*› run around scot-free

5 (offen) open; **ein ~es Gelände/~er Platz** open ground/an open square; **unter ~em Himmel** in the open [air]; outdoors; **auf ~er Strecke** (Straße) on the open road; (Eisenbahn) between stations; **ins Freie gehen** walk out into the open; **im Freien sitzen/übernachten** sit out of doors/spend the night in the open; **ständig im Freien übernachten** sleep rough

6 (unbesetzt) vacant; unoccupied; free; **ein ~er Stuhl/Platz** a vacant *or* free chair/seat; **Entschuldigung, ist hier noch ~?** excuse me, is this anyone's seat *etc.?*; **eine ~e Stelle** a vacancy; **ein Bett ist [noch] ~:** one bed is [still] free *or* not taken; **ist der Tisch ~?** is this table free?; **sind Sie ~?** are you free?; **den Weg/die Kreuzung ~ machen** clear the path/junction; **[jmdm.] Platz ~ lassen** leave [sb.] some space; **einige Seiten ~ lassen** leave some pages blank; **Ring ~!** (Boxen) seconds out!

7 (kostenlos) free ‹*food, admission*›; **~e Verpflegung** free board; **der Eintritt ist ~:** admission is free [of charge]; **20 kg Gepäck ~ haben** have *or* be allowed a 20 kilogram baggage allowance; **Lieferung ~ Haus** carriage free; **~e Kost und Logis** (veralt.) free board and lodging

8 (ungenau) **eine ~e Übersetzung** a free *or* loose translation; **~ nach einer Vorlage** based [loosely] on a source

9 (ohne Vorlage) improvised; **in ~er Improvisation** in spontaneous improvisation

10 (uneingeschränkt) free; **~e Meinungsäußerung/Religionsausübung** free expression of opinion/practice of religion; **die ~e Arzt-/Berufswahl** the free choice of doctor/profession; **der Zug hat ~e Fahrt** the train can proceed; **der ~e Fall** (Physik) free fall

11 **von etw. ~/~ von etw. sein** be free of sth.; **~ von Schuld/Schmerzen sein** be free of guilt/pain; **~ von Fehlern** without faults; **nicht ~ von Überheblichkeit** not without arrogance

12 (verfügbar) spare; free; **jede ~e Minute/Stunde** every spare *or* free minute/hour; **ich habe heute ~:** I've got today off; **er hat seinen ~en Sonnabend/Abend** this is his Saturday/evening off; **sich** (*Dat.*) **~ nehmen** (ugs.) take some time off; **er ist noch/nicht mehr ~:** he is still/no longer unattached

13 (ohne Hilfsmittel) **eine ~e Rede** an extempore speech; **aus ~er Hand zeichnen** draw freehand

14 (unbekleidet) bare; **das Kleid lässt die Schultern ~:** the dress leaves the shoulders bare; *s. auch* **freimachen B1**

15 (bes. Fußball) unmarked; **der ~e Mann** the sweeper; **~ stehen** be [standing] unmarked

16 (Chemie, Physik) free; **~ werden** (bei einer Reaktion) be given off; **Elektronen werden ~:** electrons are released

17 (in festen Wendungen) **~e Hand haben** have a free hand; **jmdm. ~e Hand lassen** give sb. a free hand; **aus ~en Stücken** (ugs.) of one's own accord; voluntarily; **jmdn. auf ~en Fuß setzen** set sb. free; **auf ~em Fuß** (von Verbrechern etc.) at large; **~ ausgehen** get away scot-free; get away with it; **ich bin so ~!** if I may …

B *adv.* ‹*act, speak, choose*› freely; ‹*translate*› freely, loosely; **etw. ~ heraus sagen** say sth. freely; **eine Rede ~ halten** make a speech without notes; **ein ~ praktizierender Arzt** a doctor in private practice; **die Personen sind/die Geschichte ist ~ erfunden** the characters are/the story is entirely fictional; **~ in der Luft schweben** hang in mid-air

frei-, Frei-: **~aktie** *die* (Börsenw.) bonus share; **~bad** *das* open-air *or* outdoor swimming pool; **~ballon** *der* free balloon; **~bank** *die; Pl.* **~bänke** *place in slaughterhouse where lower-grade meat is sold;* **~|bekommen** **A** *unr. itr. V.* (ugs.) get time off; **ich habe nachmittags ~bekommen** I've got the afternoon off; **B** *unr. tr. V.* **jmdn./etw. ~bekommen** get sb./sth. released; **~beruf·ler** *der;* **~~s, ~~, ~beruflerin** *die;* **~~, ~~nen** freelancer; freelance; **~beruflich** ▸ⓘ **S. 113** **A** *Adj.* self-employed; freelance ‹*journalist, editor, architect, etc.*›; ‹*doctor, lawyer*› in private practice; **B** *adv.* **~beruflich tätig sein/arbeiten** work freelance/practise privately; **~betrag** *der* (Steuerw.) [tax] allowance; **~beuter** /-bɔytɐ/ *der;* **~~s, ~~** 1 (hist.: Pirat) freebooter; 2 (abwertend) exploiter; **~beuterei** *die;* **~~** 1 (hist.: Piraterie) freebootery; 2 (abwertend) exploitation; **~beuterin** *die;* **~~, ~~nen** ▸**~beuter**; **~bier** *das* free beer; **~bleibend** (Kaufmannsspr.) **A** *Adj.* **~bleibendes Angebot** provisional offer; **B** *adv.* **die Preise verstehen sich ~bleibend** prices are subject to alteration; **~bord** *der* (Schifffahrt) freeboard; **~brief** *der* 1 *in* **kein ~brief für etw. sein** be no excuse for sth.; **jmdm. einen ~brief für etw. geben** *od.* **ausstellen** give sb. a licence for sth.; **einen ~brief für etw. haben/einen ~brief haben, etw. zu tun** have authority for sth./to do sth.; (fig.) have a licence for sth./to do sth.; **etw. als ~brief für etw. ansehen/betrachten** regard sth. as a charter for sth.; 2 (hist.: Urkunde) charter; **~demokrat** *der,* **~demokratin** *die* Free Democrat; **~denker** *der,* **~denkerin** *die* free thinker; **~denkertum** *das;* **~~s** free thought; free-thinking

Freie *der/die; adj. Dekl.* (hist.) freeman/freewoman

freien

A *tr. V.* (veralt.) marry; wed; **jung gefreit hat nie gereut** (Spr.) marry young and you won't regret it

B *itr. V.* **um ein Mädchen ~:** court *or* woo a girl

Freier *der;* **~s, ~** 1 (veralt.) suitor 2 (salopp: Kunde einer Dirne) punter (coll.)

Freiers·füße *Pl. in* **auf ~n gehen** (scherzh.) be courting

frei-, Frei-: **~exemplar** *das* (Buch) free copy; (Zeitung) free issue; **~fahr·schein** *der* free ticket; **~fahrt** *die* free trip; (auf Karussell) free turn *or* ride; **~fläche** *die* open space; **~flug** *der* free flight; **~frau** *die,* **~fräulein** *das* baroness; **~gabe** *die* 1 release; **die ~gabe der Wechselkurse** the lifting of controls on exchange rates; 2 (Übergabe) opening [to the public]; **~|geben** **A** *unr. tr. V.* 1 release ‹*prisoner, footballer*›; decontrol ‹*exchange rates*›; **jmdm. den Weg ~geben** let sb. through; 2 open ‹*motorway*›; pass ‹*film*›; **etw. für den Verkehr/die Öffentlichkeit ~geben** open sth. to traffic/to the public; **der Film ist ab 18 ~gegeben** the film has been passed 18; **B** *unr. tr., itr. V.* **jmdm. ~geben** give sb. time off; **sich** (*Dat.*) **zwei Tage ~geben lassen** take two days off; **~gebig** /-geːbɪç/ *Adj.* generous; open-handed; **~gebig gegen jmdn. sein** (veralt.) be generous to sb.; **[nicht] sehr ~gebig mit etw. sein** be [not] very generous *or* open-handed with sth.; **~gebigkeit** *die;* **~~:** generosity; open-handedness; **~gehege** *das* outdoor *or* open-air enclosure; **~geist** *der* free thinker; **~geistig** *Adj.* free-thinking; **~gelände** *das* piece of open ground; (Film) studio lot; **~gelassene** *der/die; adj. Dekl.* (hist.) freedman/freedwoman; **~gepäck** *das* baggage allowance; **~grenze** *die* (Steuerw.) tax exemption limit; **~gut** *das* (Zollw.) duty-free goods *pl.*; **~|haben** *unr. tr., itr. V.* (ugs.) **ich habe [am** *od.* **den] Montag ~:** I've got Monday off; **~hafen** *der* free port; **~|halten** *unr. tr. V.* 1 treat; **er hielt das ganze Lokal ~:** he stood drinks for everyone in the pub (Brit.) *or* (Amer.) bar; 2 (offenhalten) keep ‹*entrance, roadway*› clear; **Einfahrt ~halten!** no parking in front of entrance; keep clear; 3 (reservieren) **jmdm.** *od.* **für jmdn. einen Platz ~halten** keep a place for sb.; **sich ~halten** keep oneself free of engagements; **~hand·bücherei** *die* open-access library; **~handel** *der* free trade; **~handels·zone** *die* free-trade zone; **~händig** /-hɛndɪç/ **A** *Adj.* 1 freehand ‹*drawing*›; offhand ‹*shooting*›; 2 (Amtsspr.) private ‹*sale*›; **B** *adv.* 1 ‹*cycle*› without holding on; ‹*draw*› freehand; ‹*shoot*› offhand; 2 (Amtsspr.) ‹*sell*› privately; **~hand·zeichnen** *das* freehand drawing

-freiheit *die;* **-~:** **Gebühren~/Porto~:** freedom from dues/postal charges; **Bewegungs~:** freedom of movement; **Entscheidungs~:** freedom of decision *or* choice

Freiheit *die;* ~, **~en** 1 freedom; **~, Gleichheit, Brüderlichkeit** Liberty, Equality, Fraternity; **die persönliche ~:** personal freedom *or* liberty; **die ~ der Presse** Press freedom; the freedom of the Press; **die akademische ~:** academic freedom; **jmdm. völlige ~ lassen** give sb. a completely free hand; **die ~ der Meere** (Rechtsw.) the freedom of the seas; **einem Gefangenen/Tier die ~ schenken** give a prisoner his/an animal its freedom; **jmdn. in ~ setzen** set sb. free 2 (Vorrecht) freedom; privilege; **[besondere] ~en genießen** enjoy [special] privileges; **sich** (*Dat.*) **gegen jmdn. ~en herausnehmen** take liberties with sb.; **die dichterische ~:** poetic licence; **sich** (*Dat.*) **die ~ nehmen, etw. zu tun** take the liberty of doing sth.

freiheitlich

A *Adj.* liberal ‹*philosophy, conscience*›; **~ und demokratisch** free and democratic

B *adv.* liberally; **~ gesinnt sein** have liberal ideas

Freiheitliche *der/die; adj. Dekl.* (Politik) member of the Freedom Party; **die ~n** the Freedom Party

> **Die Freiheitlichen**
>
> ▸ FPÖ

freiheits-, Freiheits-: **~beraubung** *die* (jur.) wrongful detention; **~bewegung** *die* liberation movement; **~drang** *der* desire for freedom; **~entzug** *der* imprisonment; **jmdn. zu zwei Jahren ~entzug verurteilen** sentence sb. to two years' imprisonment; **~kampf** *der* struggle for freedom; **~kämpfer** *der,* **~kämpferin** *die* freedom fighter; **~krieg** *der* war of liberation; **die ~kriege** (hist.) the War of Liberation; **~liebe** *die* love of freedom *or* liberty; **~liebend** *Adj.* freedom-loving; **~rechte** *Pl.* civil rights; **~statue** *die* Statue of Liberty; **~strafe** *die* (Rechtsw.) term of imprisonment; prison sentence; **er wurde zu einer ~strafe von fünf Jahren/zu einer lebenslänglichen ~strafe verurteilt** he was sentenced to five years' imprisonment/given a life sentence

frei-, Frei-: **~heraus** *Adv.* frankly; openly; **~heraus gesagt …** to put it frankly …; **~herr** *der* ▸ⓘ **S. 44** baron; **~herrlich** *Adj.* baronial

Freiin /ˈfraiɪn/ *die;* ~, **~nen** baroness

f

frei-, Frei-: **~|kämpfen** *tr. V.* liberate; **sich ~kämpfen** fight one's way out; **~karte** *die* complimentary *or* free ticket; **~|kaufen** *tr. V.* ransom ‹*hostage*›; buy the freedom of ‹*slave*›; **sich von der Verantwortung/Schuld ~kaufen** (fig.) buy off one's responsibility/guilt; **~kirche** *die* Free Church; **~|kommen** *unr. itr. V.*; *mit sein* **aus dem Gefängnis ~kommen** be released from prison; leave prison; **aus jmds. Fängen ~kommen** escape from sb.'s clutches; **~körper·kultur** *die* nudism *no art.*; naturism *no art.*; **~korps** *das* (hist.) volunteer corps

Freiland *das* open ground; **etw. im ~ anbauen** grow sth. outdoors *or* in the open

Freiland-: **~anbau** *der* (Landw.) **der ~anbau von Gemüse** growing vegetables outdoors *or* in the open; **Gemüse aus ~anbau** crops grown outdoors *or* in the open; **~ei** *das* free-range egg; **~gemüse** *das* outdoor vegetables *pl.*; **~hähnchen** *das* free-range chicken; **~haltung** *die* (Landw.) keeping of animals on free range; **Fleisch aus ~haltung** free-range meat; **~henne** *die* free-range hen; **~huhn** *das* free-range chicken; **~tomate** *die* outdoor tomato; **~versuch** *der* (Landw., Biol.) outdoor trial

frei-, Frei-: **~|lassen** *unr. tr. V.* set free; release; **~lassung** *die*; **~~, ~~en** release; **~lauf** *der* (Technik) neutral gear; (beim Fahrrad) free wheel; **im ~lauf fahren** ‹*driver*› coast in neutral; ‹*cyclist*› freewheel; **~|laufen** *unr. refl. V.* (bes. Fuß- und Handball) run into *or* find space; **~lebend** ▸**frei A4**; **~|legen** *tr. V.* uncover; **~leitung** *die* (Technik) overhead cable

freilich *Adv.* **1** (einschränkend) **er arbeitet schnell, ~ nicht sehr gründlich** he works quickly, though admittedly he's not very thorough; **deine Theorie klingt zwar überzeugend, ~ ist eine wichtige Einschränkung zu machen** your theory sounds convincing, it's true, but there is one important reservation to be made; **ich werde morgen einmal bei dir vorbeischauen, lange bleiben kann ich ~ nicht** I'll call in on you tomorrow, though I shan't be able to stay long; **sie hat sehr viel Talent, ~ fehlt es ihr an Ausdauer** she has a great deal of talent, but she does lack staying power **2** (einräumend) **man muss ~ bedenken, dass ...** one must of course bear in mind that ...; **~ scheinen die Tatsachen gegen meine Überlegungen zu sprechen ...** admittedly the facts seem to contradict my ideas, but ...; **sie war sehr wütend auf ihren Mann, wozu sie ~ auch allen Grund hatte** she was furious with her husband, and of course she had every reason to be **3** (bes. südd.: selbstverständlich) of course; **ja ~:** [why] yes; of course

Frei·licht-: **~bühne** *die* ▸**~theater**; **~museum** *das* open-air *or* outdoor museum; **~theater** *das* open-air *or* outdoor theatre

frei-, Frei-: **~los** *das* **1** free [lottery] ticket; **2** (Sport) bye; **durch ~los die nächste Runde erreichen** get a bye into the next round; **~|machen** **A** *refl. V.* (ugs.: ~nehmen) **sich [für etw.] ~machen** take time off [for sth.]; **B** *tr. V.* **1** (entkleiden) **den Oberkörper ~machen** strip to the waist; **sich ~machen** strip; **2** (Postw.) put a stamp on; (freistempeln) frank; **etw. mit 80 Cent ~machen** put an 80-cent stamp on sth.; **~machung** *die*; **~~** (Postw.) franking; **~marke** *die* postage stamp; **~maurer** *der* Freemason; **~maurerei** *die*; **~~:** Freemasonry; **~maurer·loge** *die* Freemasons' lodge; **~mut** *der* candidness; frankness; **mit ~mut sprechen** speak candidly *or* frankly; **~mütig** **A** *Adj.* candid; frank; **B** *adv.* candidly; frankly; **~mütigkeit** *die*; **~~:** candidness; frankness; **~platz** *der* **1** ([Hoch]schulw.) scholarship; **2** (Sitzplatz) free seat; **~|pressen** *tr. V.* **jmdn. ~pressen** obtain sb.'s release by threats; **~raum** *der* (Psych., Soziol.) space *no indef. art.* to be oneself; **unpolitische ~räume** areas where politics is not involved; **~religiös** *Adj.* non-denominational; **~sass**, ***~saß**, **~sasse** *der*; **~sassen**, **~sassen** (hist.) yeoman; tenant farmer; **~schaffend** *Adj.* freelance; **Steuervergünstigungen für Freischaffende** tax concessions to self-employed persons; **~|schalten** *tr. V.* (Elektrot.) launch ‹*website*›; provide ‹*Internet connection*›; **den Internetzugang ~schalten** activate Internet access; **~schaltung** *die* (Elektrot.) launch; activation; **~schar** *die* (hist.) corps of irregulars; **~schärler** /-ʃɛːɐ̯lɐ/ *der*; **~~s, ~~**, **~schärlerin** *die*; **~~, ~~nen** irregular [soldier]; **~|schaufeln** *tr. V.* clear ‹*road*› by shovelling; dig ‹*person*› free; **~|schießen** *unr. tr., refl. V.* **sich** (*Dat.*) **den Weg ~schießen** shoot one's way out; **jmdn. ~schießen** free sb. [in a gun battle]; **~|schwimmen** *unr. refl. V.* **sich ~schwimmen** pass the 15-minute swimming test; **inzwischen hat er sich ~geschwommen** (fig.) he has now got over his initial difficulties; **~|setzen** *tr. V.* **1** (Physik, Chemie, Med.) release ‹*energy*›; emit ‹*rays, electrons, neutrons*›; release, give off ‹*gas*›; **2** (Arbeitsw.) release ‹*staff*›; (verhüll.) make ‹*staff*› redundant; **~setzung** *die*; **~~, ~~en** **1** (Physik, Chemie, Med.) (von Energie, Gas) release; (von Strahlung usw.) emission; **2** (Arbeitsw.) release (*of staff*); (verhüll.) redundancy; **~sinn** *der* (veralt.) liberalism; **~sinnig** *Adj.* (veralt.) liberal; broad-minded; **~spiel** *das* free turn; **~|spielen** **A** *tr. V.* (Ballspiele) **jmdn./sich ~spielen** create space for sb./oneself; **B** *refl. V.* (auf der Bühne) settle into the performance; **~sprech·anlage**, **~sprech·einrichtung** *die* hands-free kit; **~|sprechen** *unr. tr. V.* **1** (Rechtsw.) acquit; **jmdn. von einer Anklage ~sprechen** acquit sb. of a charge; **2** (für unschuldig erklären) exonerate (**von** from); **3** (Handw.) release ‹*apprentice*›; **~sprechung** *die*; **~~, ~~en** **1** (Rechtsw.) acquitting; **2** (Handw.) release; **~spruch** *der* (Rechtsw.) acquittal; **~staat** *der* (veralt.) free state; **der ~staat Bayern** the Free State of Bavaria; **~statt**, **~stätte** *die* (geh.) sanctuary; **~|stehen** *unr. itr. V.* **1** **es steht jmdm. ~, etw. zu tun** sb. is free to do sth.; **2** ‹*flat, house*› be empty *or* vacant; ‹*storeroom etc.*› be empty; **~stelle** *die* ▸**~platz 1**; **~|stellen** *tr. V.* **1** **jmdm. etw. ~stellen** leave sth. up to sb.; let sb. decide sth.; **2** (befreien) release ‹*person*›; **jmdn. vom Wehrdienst ~stellen** exempt sb. from military service; **~stellung** *die* release; (befristet) leave; **~stempel** *der* (Postw.) postmark

Frei·stil *der* (Sport) **1** ▸**~ringen** **2** ▸**~schwimmen**

Freistil-: **~ringen** *das* freestyle wrestling; **~schwimmen** *das* freestyle swimming

Frei-: **~stoß** *der* (Fußball) free kick; **einen ~stoß schießen** *od.* **treten** take a free kick; **~stunde** *die* free hour; (Schulstunde) free period

Frei·tag *der* ▸**❶ S. 165**, ▸**❶ S. 816** Friday; **ein schwarzer ~:** a black day; *s. auch* **Dienstag**, **Dienstag-**

freitags *Adv.* ▸**❶ S. 816** on Friday[s]; *s. auch* **dienstags**

frei-, Frei-: **~tod** *der* (verhüll.) suicide *no art.*; **den ~tod wählen** choose to take one's own life; **~tragend** *Adj.* (Bauw.) suspended ‹*floor*›; cantilever ‹*bridge*›; **~treppe** *die* [flight of] steps; **~übung** *die* (Sport) keep-fit exercise; **~übungen machen** do keep-fit exercises; **~umschlag** *der* stamped addressed envelope; s.a.e.; **~verkehr** *der* (Bankw.) unofficial market; kerb dealings *pl.*; **~wache** *die* (Seemannsspr.) watch below; **~weg** *Adv.* (ugs.) **wir können ~weg reden** we can talk freely *or* openly; **sag es ~weg** say it straight out; **~wild** *das* fair game; **zum ~wild werden** become fair game; **~willig** **A** *Adj.* voluntary ‹*decision*›; optional ‹*subject*›; **~willige Feuerwehr** volunteer fire brigade; **B** *adv.* voluntarily; of one's own accord; **sich ~willig melden** volunteer; **~willig aus dem Leben scheiden** choose to end one's life; **~willige** *der/die*; *adj. Dekl.* volunteer; **~willige vor!** volunteers take one step forward!; **sich als ~williger zu etw. melden** volunteer for sth.; **~wurf** *der* free throw; **~zeichen** *das* **1** (volkst.) dialling tone; **2** (Nachrichtenw.) ringing tone; **~zeichnungs·klausel** *die* (Rechtsw.) exemption clause

Frei·zeit *die* **1** spare time; leisure time; (Arbeitsw.) time off in lieu; **in** *od.* **während der ~:** in/during one's spare time **2** (Zusammenkunft) [holiday/weekend] course; (der Kirche) retreat

Freizeit-: **~angebot** *das* range of leisure activities; **~anzug** *der* leisure suit; **~beschäftigung** *die* hobby; leisure pursuit; **~gesellschaft** *die* (Soziol.) leisure society; **~gestaltung** *die* (Soziol., Päd.) leisure activity; **~hemd** *das* sports shirt; **~industrie** *die* leisure industry; **~kleidung** *die* casual clothes *pl.*; leisure wear (Commerc.); **~park** *der* amusement park; **~wert** *der*: **eine Stadt mit hohem ~wert** a town with many leisure amenities

frei-, Frei-: **~zügig** **A** *Adj.* **1** (großzügig) generous, liberal ‹*dosage, spending*›; liberal, flexible ‹*interpretation of rule etc.*›; **~zügig im Geldausgeben** generous with one's money; **2** (gewagt, unmoralisch) risqué, daring ‹*remark, film, dress*›; permissive ‹*attitude*›; **3** (~ in der Wahl des Wohnsitzes) **~zügig sein** enjoy freedom of domicile; **ein ~zügiges Leben führen** live a nomadic life; be always on the move; **B** *adv.* **Geld ~zügig ausgeben** be generous with one's money; **ein Gesetz ~zügig auslegen** interpret a law flexibly; **~zügigkeit** *die*; **~~** **1** (Großzügigkeit) liberalness; (in Geldsachen) generosity; (von Interpretation) flexibility; **2** permissiveness; **3** (freie Wahl des Wohnsitzes) freedom of domicile **4** (EU) **~zügigkeit der Arbeit** freedom of movement of labour

fremd /frɛmt/ *Adj.* **1** foreign ‹*country, government, customs, language*› **2** (nicht eigen) other people's; of others *postpos.*; **~es Eigentum** other people's property; the property of others; **sich in ~e Angelegenheiten mischen** interfere in other people's business; **etw. ohne ~e Hilfe schaffen** do sth. without anyone else's help; **unter ~em Namen** under an assumed name; **unter ~em Namen schreiben** write under a nom de plume *or* pseudonym; **~e Welten** other worlds; *s. auch* **Feder 1** **3** (unbekannt) strange; **eine ~e Umgebung** strange *or* unknown surroundings *pl.*; **Rockmusik war ihr ~:** she knew nothing about rock music; **Hinterhältigkeit ist ihm ~:** underhandedness is foreign to his nature; **er fühlte sich sehr ~:** he felt very much a stranger; **sich** (*Dat.*) *od.* **einander ~ werden** become estranged; grow apart; **die Anziehungskraft des Fremden** the attraction of the unfamiliar **4** (anders geartet) strange

fremd-, Fremd-: **~arbeiter** *der*, **~arbeiterin** *die* (veralt., schweiz.) foreign worker; **~artig** *Adj.* strange; (exotisch) exotic; **~artigkeit** *die* strangeness; (Exotik) exoticness; **~bestimmt** *Adj.* (Politik, Wirtsch., Soziol.) heteronomous; **~bestimmung** *die* (Politik, Wirtsch., Soziol.) heteronomy; **~bezug** *der* (Wirtsch.) outsourcing

Fremde¹ /ˈfrɛmdə/ *der/die*; *adj. Dekl.* **1** (Unbekannte[r]) stranger **2** (Ausländer) foreigner; alien (Admin. lang.) **3** (Besucher, Tourist) visitor

Fremde² *die*; **~** (geh.) foreign parts *pl.*; abroad; **in die ~ ziehen** go off to foreign parts; go abroad

Fremd·einwirkung *die* (Rechtsspr.) **ohne ~:** without any other person *or* vehicle being involved; **der Unfall passierte ohne ~:** no other vehicle was involved in the accident; **liegt ~ vor?** was any other person involved?

fremdeln, (schweiz.) **fremden** *itr. V.* be afraid of strangers

fremden-, Fremden-: **~bett** *das* hotel bed; **~buch** *das* hotel register; **~feindlich** *Adj.* hostile to strangers/foreigners *postpos.*; xenophobic; **~feindlichkeit** *die* hostility to strangers/foreigners; xenophobia; **~führer** *der*, **~führerin** *die* tourist guide; **~heim** *das* guest house; boarding house; **~industrie** *die* tourist industry; tourist trade; **~legion** *die* foreign legion; **~legionär** *der* legionnaire; **~pass**, ***~paß** *der* alien's passport; **~polizei** *die: police department dealing with aliens;* **~verkehr** *der* tourism *no art.;* **~zimmer** *das* [1] (Hotelzimmer) room; **~zimmer frei!** vacancies (Brit.); vacancy (Amer.); [2] (Gastzimmer) guest room

fremd-, Fremd-: ~erregung *die* (Technik) separate excitation; **~finanzierung** *die* (Finanzw.) financing from outside sources; **~|gehen** *unr. itr. V.; mit sein* (ugs.) be unfaithful

Fremdheit *die; ~:* strangeness; (Zurückhaltung) reserve

fremd-, Fremd-: ~herrschaft *die* foreign domination *no art. or* rule *no art.;* **~kapital** *das* (Wirtsch.) outside capital; **~körper** *der* [1] (Med., Biol.) foreign body; [2] (fig.) **ein ~körper sein/ sich** *(Dat.)* **wie ein ~körper vorkommen** be/feel out of place; **~ländisch** /-lɛndɪʃ/ *Adj.* foreign; (exotisch) exotic

Fremdling *der; ~s, ~e* (veralt.) stranger

Fremd·sprache *die* foreign language

Fremdsprachen-: ~korrespondentin *die* ▸ⓘ **S. 113** bilingual/multilingual secretary; **~unterricht** *der* teaching of foreign languages

fremd-, Fremd-: ~sprachig *Adj.* bilingual/multilingual ‹*staff, secretary*›; foreign ‹*literature*›; foreign-language ‹*edition, teaching*›; **~sprachlich** *Adj.* foreign-language ‹*teaching*›; foreign ‹*word*›; **~stoff** *der* (Med.) foreign substance; **~verschulden** *das* involvement of another person; **ein ~verschulden an diesem Unfall ist unwahrscheinlich** it is unlikely that anyone else was involved in the accident; **~wort** *das; Pl.* **~wörter** foreign word; **Liebe ist für ihn ein ~wort** (fig.) he doesn't know the meaning of the word love; **~wörter·buch** *das* dictionary of foreign words

frenetisch /fre'ne:tɪʃ/

A *Adj.* frenetic ‹*applause*›

B *adv.* ‹*applaud*› frenetically

frequentieren *tr. V.* frequent ‹*pub, café*›; use ‹*library*›; **eine stark frequentierte Straße** a heavily used road

Frequenz /fre'kvɛnts/ *die; ~, ~en* [1] (Physik) frequency; (Med.: Puls~) rate [2] (Besucherzahl) **die Schule hat eine geringe ~:** the school has low numbers; **die ~ der Touristen** (bes. österr., schweiz.) the number of tourists; **die ~ des Elternabends war gut** attendance at the parents' evening was good [3] (Verkehrsdichte) traffic density

Frequenz-: ~bereich *der* frequency range; **~modulation** *die* frequency modulation

Fresko /'frɛsko/ *das; ~s,* **Fresken** (Kunstwiss.) fresco

Fresko·malerei *die* (Kunstwiss.) fresco; fresco painting

Fressalien /frɛ'sa:li̯ən/ *Pl.* (ugs. scherzh.) grub (coll.)

Fress·beutel, *Freß·beutel *der* [1] (ugs.: Brotbeutel) lunch bag [2] (für Pferde) nosebag

Fresse /'frɛsə/ *die; ~, ~n* (derb) [1] (Mund) gob (sl.); trap (sl.); **eine große ~ haben** (fig.) have a big mouth (coll.); **die ~ weit aufreißen** (fig.) shoot one's mouth off (sl.); **[ach] du meine ~!** bloody hell! (sl.); **die ~ halten** keep one's trap *or* gob shut (sl.) [2] (Gesicht) mug (coll.); **jmdm. die ~ polieren** smash sb.'s face in (sl.); **jmdm. eins vor** *od.* **auf die ~ geben** smash sb. in the face (sl.)

fressen

A *unr. tr. V.* [1] ‹*animal*› eat; (sich ernähren von) feed on; **einem Tier zu ~ geben** feed an animal; **sich satt ~:** eat its/her/his fill; **sich dick [und rund] ~:** get fat by overeating [2] (ugs.: verschlingen) swallow up ‹*money, time, distance*›; drink ‹*petrol*› [3] (zerstören) eat away [4] (derb: von Menschen) guzzle; (fig.) **er wird dich schon nicht ~** (salopp) he won't eat you (coll.); **etw. ge~ haben** (ugs.) have understood sth.; **jmdn. ge~ haben** (ugs.) hate sb.'s guts (coll.); **jmdn. zum Fressen gern haben** like sb. so much one could eat him/her

B *unr. itr. V.* [1] (von Tieren) feed; **friss, Vogel, oder stirb!** (fig.) you've got no option [2] (zerstören) **an etw.** *(Dat.)* **~** ‹*rust*› eat away at sth.; ‹*fire*› begin to consume sth.; **Ärger und Sorgen fraßen an ihm** irritation and worry gnawed at him [3] (derb: von Menschen) stuff oneself *or* one's face (sl.); **er frisst für drei** he eats enough for three

C *unr. refl. V.* **sich durch/in etw.** *(Akk.)* **~:** eat one's way through/into sth.

Fressen *das; ~s* [1] (Futter) (für Hunde, Katzen usw.) food; (für Vieh) feed [2] (derb, oft abwertend: Essen) grub (coll.); **das ist ein gefundenes ~ für sie** (fig.) that's just what she needed; that's a real gift for her; **erst kommt das ~, dann kommt die Moral** you can't moralize on an empty stomach

-fresser *der; ~s, ~* (ugs. abwertend) **Kommunisten~:** Communist-hater

Fresser *der; ~s, ~* [1] (Tier) **ein guter/langsamer ~:** a good/slow eater [2] (derb: Mensch) hungry mouth to feed

Fresserei *die; ~, ~en* (derb abwertend) guzzling; stuffing; **eine große ~:** a big blowout (sl.)

Fresserin *die; ~, ~nen* ▸ **Fresser 2**

fress-, *freß-, Fress-, *Freß-: ~gier *die* (abwertend) (bei Tieren) voracity; (bei Menschen) greed; gluttony; **~gierig** *Adj.* voracious ‹*animal*›; greedy, gluttonous ‹*person*›; **~korb** *der* (ugs.) [1] (Verpflegungskorb) picnic basket; [2] (Geschenkkorb) hamper; **~lust** *die* (ugs.) desire for food; **~napf** *der* feeding bowl; **~paket** *das* (ugs.) food parcel; **~sack** *der* (derb) greedy pig (sl.); **~sucht** *die* [morbid] craving for food; **~trog** *der* [feeding] trough; **~welle** *die* (scherzh.) wave of gluttony *or* overeating; **~werkzeuge** *Pl.* (Zool.) trophi; **~zelle** *die* (Biol.) scavenger cell

Frettchen /'frɛtçən/ *das; ~s, ~* (Zool.) ferret

Freude /'frɔydə/ *die; ~, ~n* [1] joy; (Vergnügen) pleasure; (Wonne) delight; **~ an etw.** *(Dat.)* **haben** take pleasure in sth.; **~ am Leben haben** enjoy life; **die ~ an der Natur** enjoyment of nature; **das war eine große ~ für uns** that was a great pleasure for us; **eine wahre/reine ~:** a real pleasure *or* joy; **das war nicht gerade eine reine ~ für mich** it was not exactly fun for me; **jmdm. eine ~ machen** *od.* **bereiten** make sb. happy; **etw. aus lauter** *od.* **reiner ~ tun** do sth. out of sheer joy; (aus Spaß) do sth. just for the pleasure oft it; **vor ~ hüpfen/in die Hände klatschen** jump for joy/clap one's hands with joy; **zu unserer ~:** to our delight; **zu meiner ~ kann ich Ihnen mitteilen, dass ...** I am pleased to be able to inform you that ...; **jmdm. die ~ verderben** spoil sb.'s enjoyment; **seine helle ~ an etw.** *(Dat.)* **haben** be delighted about sth.; **herrlich und in ~n leben** live happily; **geteilte ~ ist doppelte ~** (Spr.) a pleasure shared is a pleasure doubled; **Freud und Leid** (geh.) joy and sorrow; **mit ~n** with pleasure [2] *Pl.* (Annehmlichkeit) **die ~n des Alltags/der Liebe** the pleasures of everyday life/ the joys of love

Freuden-: ~botschaft *die* glad news; **~fest** *das* celebration; **ein ~fest feiern** hold a celebration; **~feuer** *das* bonfire; **~gebrüll** *das,* **~geheul** *das,* **~geschrei** *das* cries *or* shouts of joy *pl.;* **~haus** *das* house of pleasure; **~mädchen** *das* (verhüll.) woman of easy virtue; **~rausch** *der* transport of joy; **~schrei** *der* cry *or* shout of joy; **einen ~schrei ausstoßen** shout for joy; **~spender** *der* (geh.) source of pleasure; **~sprung** *der* joyful leap; **einen ~sprung machen** jump for joy; **~tag** *der* joyous *or* happy day; **~tanz** *der: in* **einen [wilden** *od.* **wahren] ~tanz aufführen** *od.* **vollführen** dance for joy; **~taumel** *der* transport of delight *or* joy; **~träne** *die:* **~tränen weinen** *od.* **vergießen** cry *or* weep tears of happiness *or* joy

freude-: ~strahlend *Adj.* beaming with joy; radiant with joy; **mit ~strahlendem Gesicht** beaming with delight *or* joy; **~trunken** *Adj.* (dichter.) delirious with joy

Freudianer /frɔy'di̯a:nɐ/ *der; ~s, ~,* **Freudianerin** *die; ~, ~nen* Freudian

freudianisch *Adj.* Freudian

freudig

A *Adj.* [1] joyful, happy ‹*face, feeling, greeting*›; joyous ‹*heart*›; **in ~er Erwartung** in joyful anticipation [2] (erfreulich) delightful ‹*surprise*›; **ein ~es Ereignis** (verhüll.) a happy event; **eine ~e Nachricht** good news; glad tidings (literary)

B *adv.* **~ erregt** happy and excited; **von etw. ~ überrascht sein** be surprised and delighted about sth.; **etw. ~ tun** do sth. gladly *or* with pleasure; **etw. ~ erwarten** look forward to sth. with pleasure; **jmdn./etw. ~ begrüßen** give sb./sth. a warm welcome; **~ arbeiten/ seine Pflicht tun** work cheerfully/do one's duty willingly

-freudig *Adj.* [1] (Freude an etw. zeigend) **lese~:** fond of reading [2] (schnell bereit, etw. zu tun) **experimentier~/kauf~:** keen *or* eager to experiment/buy; **beifalls~/entscheidungs~:** very ready to applaud/take decisions

Freudigkeit *die; ~:* joyfulness; (Begeisterung) enthusiasm

freud·los

A *Adj.* joyless ‹*days, existence*›; cheerless ‹*surroundings*›

B *adv.* joylessly; **~ arbeiten** work unenthusiastically

freudsch, *Freudsch /frɔytʃ/ *Adj.* Freudian

freud·voll

A *Adj.* joyful; joyous; happy

B *adv.* joyfully; joyously; happily

freuen /'frɔyən/

A *refl. V.* be pleased *or* glad (**über** + *Akk.* about); (froh sein) be happy; **ich freue mich über das Geschenk** I am pleased with the present; **sich zu früh ~:** get carried away *or* rejoice too soon; **sich an jmdm./etw. ~** (geh.) take pleasure in sb./sth.; **sich auf etw.** *(Akk.)* **~:** look forward to sth.; **sich auf jmdn. ~:** look forward to seeing sb.; **sich mit jmdm. ~:** rejoice with sb.; **sich für jmdn. ~:** be pleased *or* glad for sb.; **ich freue mich, Ihnen mitteilen zu können, dass ...** I am pleased to be able to inform you that ...

B *tr. V.* please; **es freut mich, dass ...** I am pleased *or* glad that ...; **freut mich!** pleased to meet you; **es hat mich aufrichtig gefreut, Ihre Bekanntschaft zu machen** I'm delighted *or* very pleased to have met you; **das hat ihn sehr gefreut** he was very pleased about it

***freund, Freund** /frɔynt/ (geh. veralt.) *in* **jmdm. ~ sein/bleiben** be/remain friends with sb.; **jedem Menschen ~ sein** be a friend to all men

Freund *der; ~es, ~e* [1] friend; **unter ~en sein** be among friends; **jmdn. zu seinen ~en rechnen** regard *or* count sb. as a friend; **~e in der Not gehen hundert** *od.* **tausend auf ein Lot** (Spr.) friends are hard to find when you really need them; **~ und Feind** friend and foe; **dicke ~e sein** (ugs.) be bosom pals *or* buddies (coll.); **du bist mir ja ein feiner ~!** (iron.) you're a fine friend! [2] (Verehrer, Geliebter) boyfriend; (älter) gentleman friend [3] (Anhänger, Liebhaber) lover; **ein ~ der Musik/Kunst/des Weines** a lover of music/art/wine; **ich bin kein ~ von großen Worten** (fig.) I am not one for fine words [4] (Anrede) **~[e]!** my friend[s]!; **hallo, alter ~!** hello, old friend!

Freundchen *das; ~s, ~* (Anrede; [scherzh.] drohend) my friend

Freundes-: ~hand *die* (geh.) hand of friendship; **~kreis** *der* circle of friends; **im engen ~kreis** among close friends; **~treue** *die* (geh.) loyalty as a friend

Freund-Feind-Denken *das* us-and-them attitude

Freundin *die; ~, ~nen* [1] friend [2] (Geliebte) girlfriend; (älter) lady friend

freundlich

A *Adj.* [1] (liebenswürdig) kind ‹*face*›, friendly ‹*reception*›; friendly ‹*smile*›; fond ‹*farewell*›; **zu jmdm. ~ sein** be kind to sb.; **er war so ~, mir zu helfen** he was kind *or* good enough to help me; **würden Sie so ~ sein, mir den Weg zum Bahnhof zu zeigen?** would you be so kind *or* good as to show me the way to the station?; **bitte recht ~!** smile, please! [2] (angenehm) pleasant ‹*weather, surroundings*›; pleasant, congenial ‹*atmosphere*›; pleasant, mild ‹*climate*›; **eine ~e Stimmung/Tendenz an der Börse** (Kaufmannsspr.) a favourable mood/trend on the Stock Exchange [3] (freundschaftlich) friendly, amiable ‹*person, manner*›; friendly ‹*disposition, attitude, warning*›

B *adv.* [1] (freundschaftlich) **jmdn. ~ anhören/begrüßen** listen to/greet sb. amiably; **jmdm. ~ danken** thank sb. kindly; **jmdm. ~ gesinnt sein** be well-disposed towards sb. [2] (angenehm) **die Morgensonne schien ~ in das Zimmer** the morning sun cast its friendly light into the room

-freundlich *adj.* [1] (wohlgesinnt) pro-; **regierungs~:** pro-government; **presse~:** friendly to the press *postpos.* [2] (-gerecht) **familien~/fußgänger~:** catering for the interests of families/pedestrians *postpos., not pred.*; **haut~:** kind to the skin *postpos.*; **benutzer~:** user-friendly

freundlicher·weise *Adv.* kindly; **sie hat mich ~ mit dem Auto mitgenommen** she was kind enough to take me in the car

Freundlichkeit *die*; ~, ~en [1] (Liebenswürdigkeit, Gefälligkeit) kindness; **würden Sie die ~ haben, mit uns mitzukommen?** would you be so kind as to come with us?; **jmdm. ein paar ~en sagen** to make a few kind remarks to sb.; **jmdm. ~en erweisen** show kindness to sb.; be kind to sb. [2] (angenehme Art) pleasantness; friendliness; (eines Zimmers, Hauses) cheerfulness

freund·nachbarlich *Adj.* good-neighbourly

Freundschaft *die*; ~, ~en [1] friendship; **die ~ zwischen uns/ihnen** the friendship between us/them; **mit jmdm. ~ schließen** make *or* become friends with sb.; **jmdm. etw. in aller ~ sagen** tell sb. sth. as a friend [2] (DDR: Gruß der FDJ) **~!** *greeting of the Free German Youth organization* [3] (DDR: Pioniergruppe) *school branch of the Pioneer organization*

freundschaftlich

A *Adj.* friendly; amicable; **ein ~er Hinweis** a friendly piece of advice; **mit jmdm. auf ~em Fuße stehen** be on friendly *or* amicable terms with sb.

B *adv.* in a friendly way; amicably; **jmdm. ~ auf die Schulter klopfen** give sb. a friendly pat on the shoulder

Freundschafts-: ~bande *Pl.* (geh.) bonds of friendship; **~besuch** *der* (bes. Politik) goodwill visit; **~bezeigung** *die*; ~~, ~~en (geh.) gesture of friendship; **~dienst** *der* service rendered out of friendship; **jmdm. einen ~dienst erweisen** render sb. a service out of friendship; **~pakt** *der* (Politik) pact of friendship; **~preis** *der*: **etw. zu einem ~preis verkaufen** sell sth. at a specially reduced price; **~ring** *der* ring given as a token of friendship; **jmdm. einen ~ring schenken** give sb. a ring as a token of friendship; **~spiel** *das* (Sport) friendly match *or* game; friendly (coll.); **~treffen** *das* (bes. DDR) friendly meeting; **~vertrag** *der* (Politik) treaty of friendship

Frevel /ˈfreːfl̩/ *der*; ~s, ~ (geh., veralt.) crime; outrage; **einen ~ an jmdm./etw. begehen** commit a crime against sb./sth.; **~ gegen Gott** sacrilege

frevelhaft (geh.)

A *Adj.* wicked ‹*deed, rebellion, person*›; criminal ‹*stupidity*›

B *adv.* wickedly

freveln *itr. V.* (geh.) **an jmdm./gegen etw. ~:** commit a crime against sb./sth.; **gegen das Gesetz ~:** violate the law

Frevel·tat *die* (geh.) wicked deed; heinous crime

freventlich /ˈfreːfn̩tlɪç/ *Adj.* (veralt.) ▸ **frevelhaft**

Frevler *der*; ~s, ~, **Frevlerin** *die*; ~in, ~innen evildoer; wicked person; (gegen Gott) sacrilegious person; (Lästerer) blasphemer

frevlerisch *Adj.* ▸ **frevelhaft**

friderizianisch /frideriˈt̮si̯aːnɪʃ/ of Frederick the Great *postpos., not pred.*

Friede /ˈfriːdə/ *der*; ~ns, ~n [1] (älter, geh.) ▸ **Frieden** [2] (geh.) **~ sei mit euch** peace be with you; **~ seiner Asche** (*Dat.*) God rest his soul; **~ auf Erden** peace on earth; **ruhe in ~n** Rest in Peace

Frieden *der*; ~s, ~ [1] peace; **[mit dem Feind] ~ schließen** make peace [with the enemy]; **mit jmdm. ~ schließen** make one's peace with sb.; **mitten im ~:** in the middle of peacetime; **der eheliche/häusliche ~:** marital/domestic peace; **zwischen Gegnern ~ stiften** make peace between opponents; **um des lieben ~s willen** for the sake of peace and quiet; **er kann keinen ~ finden** he can find no peace; **der ~ der Natur** the peace *or* tranquillity of nature; **lass mich in ~!** (ugs.) leave me in peace!; leave me alone!; **seinen ~ mit jmdm. machen** make one's peace with sb.; **ich traue dem ~ nicht** (ugs.) it's too good to be true [2] (~sschluss) peace settlement; **den ~ diktieren** dictate the terms for peace *or* the terms of the peace settlement

friedens-, Friedens-: ~angebot *das* peace offer; **~apostel** *der* (spött.) peacemaker; **~appell** *der*, **~auf·ruf** *der* appeal for peace; **einen ~appell** *od.* **~aufruf an die Völker richten** call upon the nations to make peace; **~bedingungen** *Pl.* peace terms; terms for peace; **~bemühungen** *Pl.* efforts to bring about peace; **~bewegung** *die* peace movement; **~bruch** *der* violation of the peace; **~demonstration** *die* peace demonstration; **~diktat** *das* dictated peace terms *pl.*; **das ~diktat der Siegermächte** the peace terms dictated by the victorious nations; **~engel** *der* angel of peace (poet.); messenger of peace; **~fahrt** *die* (DDR) Peace Race; **~forschung** *die* peace studies *pl., no art.*; **~freund** *der*, **~freundin** *die* lover of peace; **~fürst** *der* (bibl.) Prince of Peace; **~garantie** *die* guarantee of peace; **~gefährdend** *Adj.* representing a threat to peace *postpos., not pred.*; **~gespräche** *Pl.* peace talks; **~glocken** *Pl.* **die ~glocken läuten** the bells are ringing to proclaim the peace; **~göttin** *die* goddess of peace; **~grenze** *die* (DDR) *frontier serving as guarantee of peace, esp. Oder-Neisse-Line*; **~kämpfer** *der*, **~kämpferin** *die* pacifist; **~konferenz** *die* peace conference; **~kundgebung** *die* peace rally; **~kuss**, ***~kuß** *der* (kath. Rel.) kiss of peace; pax; **~lager** *das* (DDR) *bloc of peace-loving nations*; **~liebe** *die* love of peace; **~nobel·preis** *der* Nobel Peace Prize; **~pfeife** *die* pipe of peace; **mit jmdm. die ~pfeife rauchen** (fig.) make one's peace with sb.; **lasst uns die ~pfeife rauchen!** (fig.) let us make peace; **~pflicht** *die* (Arbeitswelt) *obligation on employers and unions to avoid conflicts resulting in industrial action while a/the wages agreement is in force*; **~politik** *die* policy of peace; **~richter** *der*, **~richterin** *die*: *lay magistrate dealing with minor offences*; ≈ Justice of the Peace; **~schluss**, ***~schluß** *der* peace settlement; **nach dem ~schluss** after the peace settlement had been reached; **~sehnsucht** *die* longing for peace; **~sicherung** *die* peacekeeping; **~stärke** *die* (Milit.) peacetime strength; **~stifter** *der*, **~stifterin** *die* peacemaker; **~symbol** *das* symbol of peace; **~taube** *die* dove of peace; **~truppe** *die* peacekeeping force; **~verhandlungen** *Pl.* peace negotiations; peace talks; **~vertrag** *der* peace treaty; **~wille** *der* desire for peace; **~wirtschaft** *die* peacetime economy; **~zeiten** *Pl.* peacetime *sing.*

fried·fertig *Adj.* peaceable ‹*person, character*›; peaceful ‹*intentions*›; **selig sind die Friedfertigen** (bibl.) blessed are the peacemakers

Fried·fertigkeit *die*; ~: peaceableness

Fried·hof *der* cemetery; (Kirchhof) graveyard; churchyard

Friedhofs-: ~gärtner *der*, **~gärtnerin** *die* cemetery gardener; **~kapelle** *die* cemetery chapel; **~ruhe** *die*, **~stille** *die* stillness *or* quiet of the graveyard; (fig.) deathly stillness; deathly quiet; **~wärter** *der*, **~wärterin** *die* cemetery attendant

friedlich /ˈfriːtlɪç/

A *Adj.* [1] (nicht kriegerisch) peaceful; **auf ~em Wege** by peaceful means [2] (ruhig, verträglich) peaceable, peaceful ‹*character, person*›; peaceful, tranquil ‹*life, atmosphere, valley*›; **sei ~!** (ugs.) be quiet!

B *adv.* ‹*live, sleep*› peacefully; **einen Streit ~ schlichten/beilegen** settle an argument peaceably *or* peacefully

Friedlichkeit *die*; ~: peaceableness; peacefulness; (der Atmosphäre, eines Tals) peacefulness; tranquillity

fried·liebend *Adj.* peace-loving

fried·los

A *Adj.* [1] (geh.: ruhelos) **er entsagte der ~en Welt** he renounced the unquiet world [2] (hist.: geächtet) outlawed ‹*person*›

B *adv.* [1] (geh.: ruhelos) **~ durchwanderte er die Welt** he wandered through the world, never finding peace [2] (hist.: geächtet) ‹*live*› as an outlaw

Friedrich /ˈfriːdrɪç/ (*der*) Frederick; **~ der Große** Frederick the Great

Friedrich Wilhelm *der*; ~ ~s, ~ ~s (ugs. scherzh.: Unterschrift) monicker (coll. joc.)

fried·voll *Adj.* (geh.) peaceful; tranquil

Fried·wald *der* woodland cemetery

frieren /ˈfriːrən/ *unr. itr. V.* [1] (Kälte empfinden) be *or* feel cold; **erbärmlich/sehr ~:** be freezing/terribly cold; **er fror an den Händen/Beinen** he had [freezing] cold hands/legs [2] *mit sein* (gefrieren) freeze; **das Wasser/der Boden ist gefroren** the water/the ground is *or* has frozen; **steif gefroren sein** be frozen stiff; **blau gefroren sein** be blue with cold [3] (unpers.: Kälte empfinden) **mich/ihn/sie friert [es]** I am/he/she is cold [4] (unpers.: ge~) **es friert/hat gefroren** it is/was freezing; *s. auch* **Stein**

Fries /friːs/ *der*; ~es, ~e (Archit., Textilw.) frieze

Friese /ˈfriːzə/ *der*; ~n, ~n, **Friesin** *die*; ~, ~nen Frisian

friesisch *Adj.* ▸ ❶ **S. 670** [East] Frisian

frigid[e] /friˈgiːd(ə)/ *Adj.* frigid

Frigidität /frigidiˈtɛːt/ *die*; ~: frigidity

Frikadelle /frikaˈdɛlə/ *die*; ~, ~n rissole

Frikandeau /frikanˈdoː/ *das*; ~s, ~s (Kochk.) fricandeau

Frikassee /frikaˈseː/ *das*; ~s, ~s (Kochk.) fricassee; **aus jmdm. ~ machen** (salopp, scherzh.) make mincemeat of sb. (coll.)

frikassieren *tr. V.* fricassee

Frikativ /frikaˈtiːf/ *der*; ~s, ~e (Sprachw.) fricative

Friktion /frɪkˈt̮si̯oːn/ *die*; ~, ~en friction

frisch /frɪʃ/

A *Adj.* [1] fresh; new-laid ‹*egg*›; fresh, clean ‹*linen*›; clean ‹*underwear*›; wet ‹*paint*›; **~e Luft schöpfen** *od.* (ugs.) **schnappen** get some fresh air; **mit ~en Kräften** with renewed strength; **~en Mut fassen** take heart again; **sich ~ machen** freshen oneself up; **jmdn. auf ~er Tat ertappen** catch sb. red-handed; **die Erinnerung daran ist noch ganz ~:** the memory of it is still quite fresh [in sb.'s mind] [2] (munter) fresh; **~ und munter sein** (ugs.) be bright and cheerful; **~, fromm, fröhlich, frei** fresh, pious, cheerful, free (motto of 19th century physical education enthusiasts) [3] (kühl) fresh ‹*wind, breeze*›; chilly ‹*night, air*› [4] (leuchtend) lively ‹*colours*›

B *adv.* freshly; **~ gelegte Eier** new-laid eggs; **~ gebackenes Brot/gefallener Schnee** freshly baked bread/fallen snow; **Bier, ~ vom Fass** beer straight from the barrel; **~ gewaschen sein** ‹*person*› have just had a wash; ‹*garment*› have just been washed; **~ rasiert sein** have just had a shave; **er kommt ~ von der Universität** he has come straight from the university; **er kommt ~ vom Friseur** he has just been to the hairdresser's; **~ geputzte Schuhe/ausgehobene Gräber/gestrichene Bänke** newly cleaned shoes/dug graves/painted seats; **„Vorsicht, ~ gestrichen!"** 'wet paint'; **etw. ~ verputzen lassen** have sth. replastered; **die Betten ~ beziehen** put fresh or clean sheets on the beds; **ein ~ gebackenes Ehepaar** (ugs.) a newly-wed couple; newlyweds *pl.*; **ein ~ gebackener Doktor** (ugs.) a newly qualified doctor; **~ gewagt ist halb gewonnen** (Spr.) nothing ventured, nothing gained (prov.)

frisch·auf *Adv.* (veralt.) let us be off

Frische *die;* ~ 1 freshness 2 (Lebhaftigkeit, frisches Aussehen) **jugendliche ~:** youthful freshness; **geistige ~:** mental alertness; **körperliche ~:** physical fitness; vigour; **in voller körperlicher und geistiger ~:** hale and hearty in mind and body; **in erstaunlicher ~:** with amazing sprightliness; **in rosiger ~:** with a rosy freshness; **bis morgen in alter ~!** (ugs.) see you tomorrow! 3 (Kühle, Reinheit) freshness; **~ für den ganzen Tag** all-day freshness 4 (von Farben) liveliness

Frisch·ei *das* new-laid egg

frischen *tr. V.* (Hüttenw.) refine

frisch-, Frisch-: ~fisch *der* fresh fish; **~fleisch** *das* fresh meat; **~gebacken** ▸ **frisch B**; **~gemüse** *das* fresh vegetables *pl.*; **~gewaschen** *Adj.* ▸ **frisch B**; **~gewicht** *das* weight when packed; **~halte·beutel** *der* airtight bag; **~halte·folie** *die* cling film; **~halte·packung** *die* airtight pack; **~käse** *der* curd cheese

Frischling *der;* ~s, ~e 1 (Jägerspr.) young boar 2 (scherzh.) new boy *or* girl

frisch-, Frisch-: ~luft *die* fresh air; **~luft·zufuhr** *die* fresh air supply; **~milch** *die* fresh milk; **~obst** *das* fresh fruit; **~wasser** *das* fresh water; **~weg** *Adv.* uninhibitedly; **~weg antworten** answer right away; **~zelle** *die* (Med.) living cell; **~zellen·therapie** *die* (Med.) Niehans's therapy

Friseur /fri'zøːɐ̯/ *der;* ~s, ~e ▸ ❶ S. 113 1 hairdresser; (Herren~) hairdresser; barber 2 (~salon) (für Frauen) hairdresser's (Brit.); beauty salon (Amer.); (für Herren) hairdresser's; barber's; *s. auch* **Bäcker**

Friseurin *die;* ~, ~nen ▸ ❶ S. 113 ▸ **Friseur 1**

Friseur·salon *der* hairdressing *or* hairdresser's salon (Brit.); (für Frauen) beauty salon (Amer.); (für Herren) barber shop (Amer.)

Friseuse /fri'zøːzə/ *die;* ~, ~n ▸ ❶ S. 113 hairdresser

Frisier·creme *die* hair cream

frisieren /fri'ziːrən/ *tr. V.* 1 **jmdn./sich ~:** do sb.'s/one's hair; **sich ~ lassen** have one's hair done; **[sich (*Dat.*)] die Haare ~:** do one's hair; **eine elegant frisierte Dame** an elegantly coiffured lady; **er war immer sorgfältig frisiert** he was always well-groomed 2 (ugs.: verfälschen) doctor ‹*reports, statistics*›; fiddle (coll.) ‹*accounts*› 3 (Kfz-W.) soup up (coll.) ‹*engine, vehicle*›

Frisier-: ~haube *die* (hood-type) hairdrier; **~kommode** *die* dressing table; **~salon** *der* ▸ **Friseursalon**; **~spiegel** *der* dressing table mirror; **~stab** *der* curling tongs *pl.*; **~um·hang** *der* cape

Frisör ▸ **Friseur**

Frisöse ▸ **Friseuse**

friss, *friß /frɪs/ *Imperativ Sg. v.* **fressen**

frisst, *frißt *2. u. 3. Pers. Sg. Präsens v.* **fressen**

Frist /frɪst/ *die;* ~, ~en 1 (Zeitspanne) time; period; **die ~ für die Anmeldung läuft ab** the time allowed for registration is running out; **[sich (*Dat.*)] eine ~ von 3 Wochen setzen** set [oneself] a time limit of 3 weeks; **die ~ verlängern** extend the deadline; **in kürzester ~:** within a very short time 2 (begrenzter Aufschub) extension; **jmdm. drei Tage [als] ~ geben** give sb. three days' time; **eine letzte ~ von einem Monat** a final extension of one month 3 (Zeitpunkt) date; deadline; **[bis] zu dieser ~:** by that date

fristen *tr. V.* **ein kümmerliches Dasein** *od.* **Leben ~:** eke out a wretched existence; barely manage to survive

Fristen-: ~lösung *die,* **~regelung** *die* abortion limit

frist-, Frist-: ~gemäß, ~gerecht *Adj., adv.* within the specified time *postpos.*; (bei Anmeldung usw.) before the closing date *postpos.*; **wir bitten Sie um eine ~gerechte Wahrnehmung der Liefertermine** it is requested that delivery dates should be met; **~los** A *Adj.* instant ‹*dismissal*›; B *adv.* without notice; **jmdn.** *od.* **jmdm. ~los kündigen, jmdn. ~los entlassen** dismiss sb. without notice; **jmdm. ~los die Wohnung kündigen** ask sb. to quit without notice; **~verlängerung** *die* extension [of the/a time limit]

Frisur /fri'zuːɐ̯/ *die;* ~, ~en hairstyle; hairdo (coll.)

***Friteuse** ▸ **Fritteuse**

***fritieren** ▸ **frittieren**

Frittate /frɪ'taːtə/ *die;* ~, ~n (bes. österr.) pancake

Fritte /'frɪtə/ *die;* ~, ~n (ugs.) chip

Fritten·bude *die* (ugs.) chip stand; chippy (Brit. coll.); fries stand (Amer.)

Fritteuse /frɪ'tøːzə/ *die;* ~, ~n deep fryer

frittieren /frɪ'tiːrən/ *tr. V.* deep-fry

-fritze /'frɪtsə/ *der;* ~n, ~n (ugs., abwertend) man

frivol /fri'voːl/ *Adj.* 1 (schamlos) suggestive ‹*remark, picture, etc.*›; risqué ‹*joke*›; earthy ‹*man*›; flighty ‹*woman*› 2 (leichtfertig) frivolous; irresponsible

Frivolität /frivoli'tɛːt/ *die;* ~, ~en 1 ▸ **frivol 1**: suggestiveness; risqué nature; earthiness; flightiness 2 (frivole Bemerkung) risqué remark

Frivolitäten·arbeit *die* (Handarb.) tatting

Frl. *Abk.* = **Fräulein**

froh /froː/

A *Adj.* 1 ▸ ❶ S. 331 (glücklich) happy; cheerful ‹*person, mood*›; **jmdn. ~ machen** make sb. happy; cheer sb. up; **~e Ostern** happy Easter; **~e Weihnachten** happy *or* merry Christmas; **~es Fest** happy Christmas/Easter *etc.*; **~en Herzens** with a glad heart 2 (ugs.: erleichtert) pleased, glad (**über** + *Akk.* about); **du kannst ~ sein, dass ...** you can be thankful *or* glad that ...; **da bin ich aber ~ [, dass ...]** I am glad [that ...]; **seines Lebens nicht mehr ~ werden** not enjoy life any more; **der soll seines Lebens nicht mehr ~ werden** we'll make his life a misery 3 (erfreulich) good ‹*news*›; happy ‹*event*›

B *adv.* **~ gelaunt** cheerful

froh-, Froh-: ~botschaft *die* (geh.) glad tidings *pl.*; **~gelaunt** ▸ **froh B**; **~gemut** A *Adj.* happy; B *adv.* happily; in good spirits

fröhlich /'frøːlɪç/

A *Adj.* ▸ ❶ S. 331 cheerful; happy; **~e Ostern** happy Easter; **~e Weihnachten** happy *or* merry Christmas; **eine ~e Gesellschaft** a happy crowd of people; **~es Treiben** merrymaking; **~e Spiele** fun and games; **~e Tänze** dancing and merrymaking

B *adv.* (unbekümmert) blithely; cheerfully

Fröhlichkeit *die;* ~: cheerfulness; (eines Festes, einer Feier) gaiety

froh·locken *itr. V.* (geh.) 1 (Schadenfreude empfinden) rejoice; gloat; **heimlich ~:** secretly rejoice 2 (jubeln) rejoice; exult; **frohlocket dem Herrn** sing joyfully unto the Lord

Froh-: ~natur *die* 1 happy *or* cheerful nature; 2 (Mensch) cheerful person; **~sinn** *der* cheerfulness; gaiety

fromm /frɔm/, **frommer** *od.* **frömmer** /'frœmɐ/, **frommst...** *od.* **frömmst...**

A *Adj.* 1 pious, devout ‹*person*›; devout ‹*Christian*›; **ein ~es Leben führen** lead a devout life; **~e Reden führen** talk piously 2 (scheinheilig) **ein ~er Augenaufschlag** a look of wide-eyed innocence; **~es Getue** pious affectation 3 (wohl gemeint) **eine ~e Lüge** a white lie; **einer ~en Täuschung unterliegen** deceive oneself; **ein ~er Wunsch** a pious hope 4 (brav) docile; **~ wie ein Lamm** meek as a lamb 5 (veralt.: rechtschaffen) worthy ‹*person*›

B *adv.* (gläubig) piously; (brav) docilely; **~ und rechtschaffen leben** (veralt.) live a worthy life

Frömmelei *die;* ~, ~en (abwertend) 1 affected piety 2 (Handlung) sanctimonious act; ~en sanctimonious behaviour *sing.*

frömmeln /'frœmḷn/ *itr. V.* (abwertend) affect piety; **eine ~de Betschwester** an over-pious woman; **~des Geschwätz** sermonizing

frommen *itr. V.* (unpers.) (veralt.) **das frommt uns [nicht]** it will avail us [nothing]; *s. auch* **Nutz**

frömmer ▸ **fromm**

Frömmigkeit /'frœmɪçkait/ *die;* ~: piety; devoutness

Frömmler /'frœmlɐ/ *der;* ~s, ~, **Frömmlerin** *die;* ~, ~nen (abwertend) [pious] hypocrite

frömmst ... ▸ **fromm**

Fron /froːn/ *die;* ~, ~en 1 (hist.) corvée; **schwere ~ leisten** do hard forced labour 2 (geh.: aufgezwungene Mühsal) drudgery

Fron·arbeit *die* ▸ **Fron 1**

Fronde /'frõːdə/ *die;* ~, ~n (geh.) [political] faction

Fron·dienst *der* 1 ▸ **Fron 1** 2 (schweiz.) voluntary work

fronen *itr. V.* 1 (hist.) do forced labour 2 (geh.: unter Zwang arbeiten) slave; toil

frönen /'frøːnən/ *itr. V.* (geh.) **einer Neigung/einem Laster ~:** indulge an inclination/in a vice; **dem Alkohol ~:** indulge one's craving for alcohol; **einem Hobby ~:** devote oneself to a hobby

Fron·leichnam (*das*); ~s [the feast of] Corpus Christi

Fronleichnams·prozession *die* Corpus Christi procession

Front /frɔnt/ *die;* ~, ~en 1 (Gebäude~) front; facade 2 (Kampfgebiet) front [line]; **an die ~ gehen** go to the front; **er war an der ~:** he fought at the front 3 (Milit.: vorderste Linie) front line; **auf breiter ~:** on a broad front; **in vorderster ~ kämpfen** fight at the very front; **die ~en haben sich verhärtet** (fig.) attitudes have hardened; **zwischen die ~en geraten** (fig.) be caught in the crossfire; **an zwei ~en kämpfen** (fig.) fight on two fronts; **klare ~en schaffen** clarify one's position 4 (Milit.: einer Truppe) **die ~ abnehmen/abschreiten** inspect the troops/guard of honour *etc.*; **gegen jmdn./etw. ~ machen** (fig.) make a stand against sb./sth. 5 (Sport) **in ~ [liegen]** [be] in front *or* in the lead; **in ~ gehen** go in front; **die Mannschaft lag mit 5:0 in ~:** the team was leading 5-0 6 (Gruppe) front; **die Nationale ~** (DDR) the National Front 7 (Met.) front

Front·abschnitt *der* (Milit.) sector of the front

frontal /frɔn'taːl/

A *Adj.* 1 (von vorn) head-on ‹*collision*› 2 (nach vorn) frontal ‹*attack*›

B *adv.* ‹*collide*› head-on; ‹*attack*› from the front

Frontal-: ~an·griff *der* frontal attack; **zum ~angriff übergehen** go over to a frontal attack; **~unterricht** *der* (Päd.) teacher-centred teaching; **~zusammenstoß** *der* head-on collision

Front-: ~an·trieb *der* (Kfz-W.) front-wheel drive; **~begradigung** *die* (Milit.) straightening of the front; **~bericht** *der* (Milit.) report *or* dispatch from the front; **~dienst** *der* (Milit.) front-line service; service at the front; **~ein·satz** *der* (Milit.) front-line action; **~erfahrung** *die* (Milit.) experience of the front; **~frau** *die* frontwoman

Frontispiz /frɔnti'spiːts/ *das;* ~es, ~e 1 (Archit.) pediment; frontispiece 2 (Buchw.) frontispiece

Front-: ~kämpfer *der* (Milit.) front-line soldier; **~linie** *die* (Milit.) front line; **~mann** *der* frontman; **~scheibe** *die* windscreen (Brit.); windshield (Amer.); **~schwein** *das* (Soldatenspr.) front-line soldier; **~seite** *die* front page; **~soldat** *der* (Milit.) front-line soldier; **~stellung** *die* 1 (entschiedene Gegnerschaft) hostile stance; 2 (Fechten) guard position; **~urlaub** *der* (Milit.) leave from the front; **~wechsel** *der* (fig.) U-turn; volte-face

fror /froːɐ̯/ *1. u. 3. Pers. Sg. Prät. v.* **frieren**

Frosch /frɔʃ/ *der;* ~[e]s, **Frösche** /'frœʃə/ 1 frog; **einen ~ in der Kehle** *od.* **im Hals haben** have a frog in one's throat; **sei kein ~**

(ugs.) don't be a spoilsport ② (Musik) nut ③ ▸**Knallfrosch**

Frosch-: ~auge *das* [frog's] eye; **[richtige] ~augen haben** (fig.) have [real] goggle-eyes; **~hüpfen** *das;* **~~s** leapfrog; **~klemme** *die* (Technik) stone tongs; nippers *pl.;* **~könig** *der* Frog Prince; **~laich** *der* frogspawn; **~löffel** *der* (Bot.) water plantain; **~lurch** *der* (Zool.) anuran; salientian; **~mann** *der* frogman; **~perspektive** *die* worm's-eye view; **etw. aus der ~perspektive fotografieren** make a low-angle shot of sth.; **etw. aus der ~perspektive betrachten** (fig.) take a very narrow view of sth.; **~schenkel** *der* frog's leg; **~teich** *der* frog pond; **~test** *der* (Med.) male frog test

Frost /frɔst/ *der;* **~[e]s, Fröste** /'frœstə/ ① frost; **es herrscht** *od.* **ist [strenger] ~:** there is a [severe] frost; it is [very] frosty ② (Kälteempfindung) fit of shivering

frost-, Frost-: ~anfällig *Adj.* sensitive *or* susceptible to frost *postpos.;* **~auf·bruch** *der* frost damage *no indef. art.;* **wegen der ~aufbrüche** because of the frost damage; **~beständig** *Adj.* frost-resistant; **~beule** *die* chilblain; **~boden** *der* frozen soil; (ständig) permafrost; **~ein·bruch** *der* sudden frost

frösteln /'frœstl̩n/ *itr. V.* ① feel chilly; **vor Kälte/Müdigkeit ~:** shiver with cold/tiredness; **mich überkommt** *od.* **durchläuft ein Frösteln** I feel a sudden chill ② (unpers.) **es fröstelt ihn, ihn fröstelt** he feels chilly

frosten *tr. V.* (fachspr.) deep-freeze

Froster *der;* **~s, ~:** freezing compartment

frost-, Frost-: ~frei *Adj.* **ein ~freier Winter** a winter without frost; **die Nacht war ~frei** there was no frost during the night; **~gefahr** *die* danger of frost; **~grenze** *die* (Met.) 0 °C isotherm; (Geol.) frost line

frostig /'frɔstɪç/

A *Adj.* (auch fig.) frosty

B *adv.* frostily; **sie lächelte ~:** she smiled frostily *or* icily; **jmdn. ~ empfangen** give sb. a frosty reception

Frostigkeit *die;* **~:** frostiness

frost-, Frost-: ~klirrend *Adj.* crisp and frosty; **~salbe** *die* chilblain ointment; **~schaden** *der* frost damage; **durch die vielen ~schäden** due to extensive frost damage; **~schutz** *der* frost protection; protection from frost; **~schutz·mittel** *das* ① frost protection agent; ② (Kfz-W.) antifreeze; **~sicher** *Adj.* frostproof; **~warnung** *die* (Met.) frost warning; **~wetter** *das* freezing weather; frost

Frottee /frɔ'te:/ *das u. der;* **~s, ~s** terry towelling

Frottee-: ~handtuch *das* terry towel; **~kleid** *das* towelling dress

Frottier- /frɔ'ti:ɐ-/ ▸**Frottee-**

frottieren /frɔ'ti:rən/ *tr. V.* rub; towel; **sich ~:** rub oneself down

Frotzelei *die;* **~, ~en** (ugs.) ① teasing ② (Bemerkung) teasing remark

frotzeln /'frɔtsl̩n/

A *tr. V.* tease; **jmdn. wegen einer Sache ~:** tease sb. about sth.

B *itr. V.* **über jmdn./etw. ~:** make fun of sb./sth.

Frucht /frʊxt/ *die;* **~, Früchte** /'frʏçtə/ ① fruit; **Früchte tragen** (auch fig.) bear fruit; **Früchte ansetzen** start to fruit; **jmdm. wie eine reife ~ in den Schoß fallen** drop into sb.'s lap; **verbotene Früchte** (fig.) forbidden fruits; **die ~ ihres Leibes** (fig. geh.) the fruit of her womb ② (geh.: Ertrag) fruit; **reiche Früchte tragen** bear rich fruit ③ (landsch.: Getreide) corn; crops *pl.;* **die ~ steht gut/schlecht [auf dem Halm]** the corn is coming on well/looks bad

frucht·bar *Adj.* fertile ‹*soil, field, man, woman*›; prolific ‹*breed*›; fruitful ‹*work, idea*›; fruitful, rewarding ‹*conversation*›; **eine Idee** *usw.* **für etw. ~ machen** allow sth. to benefit from an idea *etc.*

Fruchtbarkeit *die;* **~** ▸**fruchtbar**: fertility; prolificness; fruitfulness

Fruchtbarkeits·kult *der* fertility cult

frucht-, Frucht-: ~becher *der* ① (Eisbecher) fruit sundae; ② (Bot.) cupule; **~blase** *die* ▸ **S. 435** (Anat.) amniotic sac; **~bonbon** *das od. der* fruit drop; **~bringend** *Adj.* fruitful; rewarding

Früchtchen /'frʏçtçən/ *das;* **~s, ~** (ugs. abwertend: Tunichtgut) good-for-nothing; **ein nettes/sauberes ~:** a right good-for-nothing

Frucht-: ~ein·waage *die* net weight [of fruit]; **~eis** *das* fruit ice cream

fruchten *tr. V.* **nichts ~:** be no use; be of no avail; **[bei jmdm.] nicht[s] ~:** have no effect [on sb.]

Frucht-: ~fleisch *das* flesh; pulp; **~fliege** *die* fruit fly; **~folge** *die* (Landw.) rotation of crops

fruchtig *Adj.* fruity

frucht-, Frucht-: ~joghurt *der od. das* fruit yoghurt; **~kapsel** *die* (Biol.) capsule; **~knoten** *der* (Bot.) ovary; **~los** *Adj.* fruitless, vain ‹*efforts*›; **alle Anstrengungen blieben ~los** all efforts proved in vain; **~losigkeit** *die;* **~~:** fruitlessness; **~presse** *die* fruit squeezer; **~saft** *der* fruit juice; **~salat** *der* fruit salad; **~säure** *die* fruit acid; **~stand** *der* (Bot.) multiple fruit; **~wasser** *das; Pl.* **~wässer** ▸ **S. 435** (Anat.) amniotic fluid; waters *pl.* (coll.); **~wasser·untersuchung** *die* (Med.) amniocentesis; **~zucker** *der* fruit sugar; fructose

Fructose /frʊk'to:zə/ *die;* **~** (Chemie) fructose

frugal /fru'ga:l/

A *Adj.* frugal

B *adv.* frugally

früh /fry:/

A *Adj.* ① early; **am ~en Morgen/Abend** early in the morning/evening; **von ~er Kindheit an** from early childhood ② (vorzeitig) premature; **ein ~es Ende finden** come to an untimely end; **einen ~en Tod sterben** die an untimely *or* premature death

B *adv.* ① early; **~ am Tage/morgens** early in the day/morning; **~ genug kommen** arrive in [good] time; **~er oder später** sooner or later; **seine ~ verstorbene Mutter** his mother, who died young; **der ~ vollendete Dichter Keats** the poet Keats, whose life ended so soon; **ein ~ Vollendeter** one whose genius was cut off by his untimely death ② (morgens) **heute/morgen/gestern ~:** this/tomorrow/yesterday morning; **um fünf Uhr ~:** at five o'clock in the morning; **von ~ bis spät** from morning till night; from dawn to dusk; *s. auch* **aufstehen**; **früher**

früh-, Früh-: ~auf *in* **von ~auf** from early childhood on[wards]; **~aufsteher** *der;* **~~s, ~~, ~aufsteherin** *die;* **~~, ~~nen** early riser; early bird (coll.); **~beet** *das* cold frame; (geheizt) [heated] frame

Früh·bucher *der;* **~s, ~, Früh·bucherin** *die;* **~, ~nen** early booker; person who books early; **~** *Pl.* early bookers; those who book early

Frühbucher·rabatt *der* discount for early booking

früh-, Früh-: ~christlich *Adj.* early Christian; **~diagnose** *die* (Med.) early diagnosis; **~dienst** *der* early duty; (im Betrieb) early shift; **~dienst haben** be on early duty/shift

Frühe *die;* **~: in der ~** (geh.) in the early morning; **in aller ~:** at the crack of dawn

Früh·ehe *die* early marriage

früher /'fry:ɐ/

A *Adj.* ① (vergangen) earlier; former; **in ~en Zeiten** in the past; in former times; **aus ~en Zeiten/Jahrhunderten** from the past/from past centuries; **eine ~e Auflage** an earlier edition ② (ehemalig) former ‹*owner, occupant, friend*›

B *adv.* formerly; **~ war er ganz anders** he used to be quite different at one time; **meine Bekannten von ~:** my former acquaintances; **ich kenne ihn [noch] von ~ [her]** I know him from some time ago; **diese Dinge waren ihm von ~ [her] vertraut** he had already been familiar with such things; **an ~ denken** think back

Früh·erkennung *die* (Med.) early recognition *or* diagnosis

frühestens /'fry:əstn̩s/ *Adv.* at the earliest; **~ in einer Woche/morgen** in a week/tomorrow at the earliest

frühest·möglich /'fry:əst'mø:klɪç/ *Adj.* earliest possible

früh-, Früh-: ~geburt *die* ① premature birth; ② (Kind) premature baby; **~gemüse** *das* early vegetables *pl.;* **~geschichte** *die* ancient history; **die ~geschichte Europas** the early history of Europe; early European history; **~geschichtlich** *Adj.* **~geschichtliche Funde** finds dating back to early history; **aus ~geschichtlicher Zeit** dating back to early history; **~gottes·dienst** *der* early service; **~herbst** *der* early autumn; **~invalide** *der/die* premature invalid

Früh·jahr *das* ▸ **S. 395** spring; **im ~:** in spring

Frühjahrs-: ~kollektion *die* spring collection; **~messe** *die* (Wirtsch.) spring trade fair; **~müdigkeit** *die* springtime tiredness; **~putz** *der* spring-cleaning

früh-, Früh-: ~kapitalismus *der* early capitalism *no art.;* **~kapitalistisch** *Adj.* early capitalist; **~kartoffel** *die* early potato; **~kindlich** *Adj.* (Psych.) in early childhood *postpos.;* **~konzert** *das* [early] morning concert; **~kultur** *die* ① (Geschichte) early culture; ② (Gartenbau) forcing; **bei der ~kultur wachsen die Pflanzen schneller** when forced, plants grow more quickly

Frühling /'fry:lɪŋ/ *der;* **~s, ~e** ▸ **S. 395** spring; **im ~:** in [the] spring; **[im] ~ vergangenen/nächsten Jahres** last/next spring; in spring last/next year; **der ~ kommt** spring is coming; **vor dem nächsten ~:** before next spring; **im ~ 1979** in the spring of 1979; **im ~ des Lebens** (geh.) in the springtime of one's life; **seinen zweiten ~ erleben** (fig. iron.) relive one's youth

frühlings-, Frühlings-: ~anfang *der* first day of spring; **~gefühl** *das:* **~gefühle haben/bekommen** (ugs. scherzh.) feel/get frisky (coll.); **~haft** *Adj.* ▸ **S. 395** springlike; **~lied** *das* song about spring; **~punkt** *der* (Astron.) vernal equinox; **~rolle** *die* (Kochk.) spring roll; **~tag** *der* spring day; **~wetter** *das* spring weather; **~zeit** *die* (geh.) spring [time]; springtide (literary)

früh-, Früh-: ~messe, ~mette *die* (kath. Kirche) early [morning] mass; **~morgendlich** **A** *Adj.* early morning *attrib.;* **B** *adv.* in the early morning; **~morgens** /-'--/ *Adv.* early in the morning; **~nebel** *der* early morning fog/mist; **~neuhochdeutsch** *das* Early New High German; **~reif** *Adj.* precocious ‹*child*›; early ‹*fruit, vegetables*›; **~rente** *die* early retirement pension; **~rentner** *der,* **~rentnerin** *die: person who has retired early;* **~rentner werden/sein** retire/have retired early; **~schicht** *die* early shift; **~schicht haben** be on the early shift; **~schoppen** *der* morning drink; (um Mittag) lunchtime drink; **~sommer** *der* early summer; **~sport** *der* early-morning exercise; **~stadium** *das* early stage; **im ~stadium** at an early stage; **~start** *der* (Sport) false start

Früh·stück *das;* **~s, ~e** ① breakfast; **das erste ~:** breakfast; **das zweite ~:** mid-morning snack ② (ugs.: Pause) morning break; coffee break

> **Frühstück**
>
> Breakfast in Germany typically consists of strong coffee, slices of bread or fresh rolls with butter, jam, honey, sliced cheese and meat, and maybe a boiled egg. For working people and schoolchildren, who have little time for breakfast first thing in the morning, a *zweites Frühstück* is common at around 10 a.m.

frühstücken

A *itr. V.* breakfast; have breakfast; **gut/ausgiebig ~:** have a good/hearty breakfast

B *tr. V.* **Brot/Eier ~:** breakfast on bread/eggs; have bread/eggs for breakfast

Frühstücks-: ~brot *das* sandwiches *pl.* [for morning snack]; **~fernsehen** *das* breakfast television; **~fleisch** *das* luncheon meat; **~kartell** *das* (Wirtsch. Jargon) informal, illegal cartel; **~pause** *die* morning break; coffee break; **~speck** *der* bacon; bacon rashers *pl.*; **~teller** *der* tea plate

früh-, Früh-: ~verstorben ▸**früh B1**; **~vollendet** ▸**früh B1**; **~warn·system** *das* early warning system; **~werk** *das* early work; (gesamtes) early works *pl.*; **~zeit** *die* (einer Kulturstufe) early period; (eines Künstlers) early life; **~zeitig A** *Adj.* **1** (früh) early; **2** (vorzeitig) premature; untimely ‹*death*›; **der ~zeitige Winter** the early onset of winter; **B** *adv.* **1** (früh) early; (im Leben, in der Entwicklung) at an early stage; **das Verbrechen wurde ~zeitig aufgedeckt** the crime was uncovered at an early stage; **jmdn. ~zeitig benachrichtigen** let someone know in good time; **2** (vorzeitig) prematurely; **~zug** *der* early [morning] train; **~zündung** *die* (Technik) pre-ignition

Fruktose ▸**Fructose**

Frust /frʊst/ *der;* **~[e]s** (ugs.) frustration; **ihre Arbeit war der absolute ~:** her work was a real drag (coll.); **der große ~ überkam ihn** he began to feel really browned off (coll.)

frusten /ˈfrʊstn̩/ *tr. V.* (ugs.) frustrate

Frustration /frʊstraˈtsi̯oːn/ *die;* **~, ~en** (Psych.) frustration

frustrieren /frʊsˈtriːrən/ *tr. V.* frustrate

frustrierend *Adj.* frustrating

FS *Abk.* **= Fernschreiben**

F-Schlüssel *der* (Musik) bass clef; F-clef

FU[B] *Abk.* **= Freie Universität [Berlin]**

Fuchs /fʊks/ *der;* **~es, Füchse** /ˈfʏksə/ **1** fox; **dort sagen sich ~ und Hase** *od.* **die Füchse gute Nacht** (scherzh.) it's in the middle of nowhere *or* at the back of beyond **2** (ugs.: schlauer Mensch) **ein schlauer ~:** a sly *or* cunning devil **3** (Fell, Pelz) fox [fur] **4** (Pferd) chestnut; (heller) sorrel **5** (ugs.: rothaariger Mensch) carrot-top **6** (Tagfalter) tortoiseshell **7** (Studentenspr.) *first-year member of a student fraternity*

Fuchs-: ~bandwurm *der* fox tapeworm; **~bau** *der; Pl.* **~e** fox den

Füchschen /ˈfʏksçən/ *das;* **~s, ~:** little fox

fuchsen

A *tr. V.* annoy; vex

B *refl. V.* **sich [über etw.** (*Akk.*)**] ~:** be annoyed [about sth.]

Fuchs-: ~falle *die* fox trap; **~fell** *das* fox fur

Fuchsie /ˈfʊksi̯ə/ *die;* **~, ~n** (Bot.) fuchsia

fuchsig *Adj.* **1** (ugs.: wütend) mad (coll.); furious **2** ginger ‹*hair*›

Füchsin /ˈfʏksɪn/ *die;* **~, ~nen** vixen

fuchs-, Fuchs-: ~jagd *die* fox hunt; (Schleppjagd) drag-hunt; **~loch** *das* ▸**Fuchsbau**; **~pelz** *der* fox fur; **~rot** *Adj.* ginger; **~schwanz** *der* **1** [fox's] brush; [fox] tail; **2** (Bot.) amaranth; love-lies-bleeding; **3** (Werkzeug) hand saw; **~teufels·wild** *Adj.* (ugs.) livid (coll.); hopping mad (coll.)

Fuchtel /ˈfʊxtl̩/ *die;* **~, ~n 1** (ugs.: strenge Zucht) **jmdn. unter der/seiner ~ haben/halten** have/keep sb. under one's thumb **2** (österr.: zänkische Frau) shrew

fuchteln *itr. V.* (ugs.) **mit etw. ~:** wave sth. about; **mit etw. vor jmds. Gesicht/Nase ~:** wave sth. in sb.'s face

fuchtig /ˈfʊxtɪç/ *Adj.* (ugs.) mad (coll.); furious

Fuder /ˈfuːdɐ/ *das;* **~s, ~ 1** (Wagenladung) cartload **2** (ugs.: große Menge) load (coll.) **3** (fachspr.: Weinfass) tun

fuder·weise *Adv.* (ugs.) by the ton; **er isst das ~:** he eats tons of it

fuffzehn /ˈfʊf-/ (ugs.) ▸**fünfzehn**

fuffzig /ˈfʊftsɪç/ (ugs.) ▸**fünfzig**

Fuffziger *der;* **~s, ~** (ugs.) fifty-cent piece; **ein falscher ~** (salopp) a real crook

Fug /fuːk/ *der:* in **mit ~ [und Recht]** rightly; justifiably

Fuge[1] /ˈfuːgə/ *die;* **~, ~n 1** joint; (Zwischenraum) gap; **der Stuhl/Tisch kracht in allen ~n** (ugs.) every joint in the chair/table creaks; **aus den ~n gehen** *od.* **geraten/sein** (fig.) be turned completely upside down (fig.) **2** (Sprachw.) juncture

Fuge[2] *die;* **~, ~n** (Musik) fugue

fugen /ˈfuːgn̩/ *tr. V.* **1** (verbinden) join, joint ‹*timber*› **2** (ausfüllen) point ‹*brickwork*›; grout ‹*tiles*›

fügen /ˈfyːgn̩/

A *tr. V.* **1** (hinzu~) place; set; **etw. zu etw. ~** (fig.) add sth. to sth.; **Wort an Wort ~:** string words together; **sie fügte Masche an Masche** she joined up the stitches one by one **2** (geh.: zusammen~) put together; **aus roten Ziegeln gefügt** built with red bricks; **lose gefügte Bretter** loosely jointed boards; **Bestandteile zu einem Ganzen ~** (fig.) join parts together to form a whole; **fest gefügt** (fig.) firmly established **3** (geh.: bewirken) ‹*fate*› ordain, decree; ‹*person*› arrange; **der Zufall hat es gefügt, dass …** fate decreed that …

B *refl. V.* **1** (sich ein~) **sich in etw.** (*Akk.*) **~:** fit into sth.; **im Garten fügte sich ein Beet an das andere** in the garden one flower bed followed the next **2** (gehorchen) **sich ~:** fall into line; **sich jmdm./einer Sache** (*Dat.*) **~:** fall into line with sb./sth.; **er muss lernen, sich zu ~:** he must learn to toe the line; **sich in sein Schicksal ~:** submit to *or* accept one's fate **3** (geh.: geschehen) **es fügt sich gut, dass … ** it is fortunate that …; **die Umstände scheinen sich günstig zu ~:** circumstances seem to be favourable

fugenlos

A *Adj.* smooth ‹*concrete wall*›; **eine ~e Trockenmauer** a dry stone wall with no gaps

B *adv.* **die Tür schließt ~:** the door fits exactly

Fugen·zeichen *das* (Sprachw.) juncture marker

füglich *Adv.* (veralt.) with reason; justifiably

fügsam

A *Adj.* obedient

B *adv.* obediently

Fügsamkeit *die;* **~:** obedience

Fügung *die;* **~, ~en 1 eine ~ Gottes** divine providence; **eine ~ des Schicksals** a stroke of fate; **in etw.** (*Dat.*) **eine glückliche ~ sehen** see providence at work in sth. **2** (Sprachw.) construction

fühlbar

A *Adj.* **1** noticeable ‹*lack, improvement, change, difference*› **2** (wahrnehmbar) perceptible ‹*touch, sound*›

B *adv.* **1** noticeably **2** (wahrnehmbar) perceptibly

fühlen /ˈfyːlən/

A *tr., itr. V.* feel ‹*pain, warmth, etc.*›; **jmdm. den Puls ~:** feel sb.'s pulse; **einen Drang/eine Kraft in sich** (*Dat.*) **~:** feel in oneself an urge/a strength; **jmdn. seine Verachtung ~ lassen** show sb. one's contempt; **[Mitleid] mit jmdm. ~:** feel [sympathy] for sb.

B *refl. V.* **sich krank/matt ~:** feel sick/weary; **sich bedroht/verfolgt ~:** feel threatened/persecuted; **sich zu jmdm. hingezogen/von jmdm. abgestoßen ~:** feel drawn to/repelled by sb.; **sich schuldig/betrogen ~:** feel guilty/betrayed; **sich zu etw. berufen ~:** feel called to be sth.; **sich zu etw. verpflichtet ~:** feel obliged *or* an obligation to do sth.; **sich als Künstler ~:** feel oneself to be an artist; feel one is an artist; **der fühlt sich aber** (ugs.) he's really pleased with himself

C *itr. V.* (tastend prüfen) **nach etw. ~:** feel for sth.

Fühler *der;* **~s, ~ 1** (Tentakel) feeler; antenna; **seine/die ~ ausstrecken** put out feelers **2** ▸**Mess~**

Fühl[er]·lehre *die* feeler gauge

fühl·los *Adj.* (geh. veralt.) unfeeling

Fühlung *die;* **~:** contact; **mit jmdm. ~ bekommen/[auf]nehmen** get into contact with sb.; **mit einer Organisation/Regierung ~ haben** be in contact with an organization/a government

Fühlungnahme *die;* **~:** initial contact; **die diplomatische ~ ist erfolgt** diplomatic contact has been established

fuhr /fuːɐ̯/ *1. u. 3. Pers. Sg. Prät. v.* **fahren**

Fuhrbetrieb *der* ▸**Fuhrunternehmen**

Fuhre /ˈfuːrə/ *die;* **~, ~n 1** (Wagenladung) load; **eine ~ Sand/Kies** a load of sand/gravel **2** (Transport) (Taxi) fare; (Laster) trip; journey

führen /ˈfyːrən/

A *tr. V.* **1** (geleiten, bringen) lead; **jmdn. an der Hand ~/zum Tisch ~:** lead sb. by the hand/to the table; **ein Tier an der Leine ~:** walk an animal on a lead; **jmdn. durch ein Haus/eine Stadt ~:** show sb. around a house/town; **jmdn. ins Theater/zu einem Ball ~:** take sb. to the theatre/to a ball; **durch das Programm führt [Sie] Klaus Frank** Klaus Frank will present the programme; **jmdn. auf die richtige Spur ~:** put sb. on the right track; **eine Klasse zum Abitur ~:** take a class through to Abitur level; **ein Land ins Chaos ~:** plunge a country into chaos

2 (verkaufen) stock, sell ‹*goods*›

3 (durch~) **Gespräche/Verhandlungen ~:** hold conversations/negotiations; **ein Orts-/Ferngespräch ~:** make a local/long-distance call; **ein unruhiges Leben ~:** lead a turbulent life; **eine glückliche Ehe ~:** be happily married; **einen Prozess [gegen jmdn.] ~:** take legal action [against sb.]

4 (verantwortlich leiten) manage, run ‹*company, business, pub, etc.*›; lead ‹*party, country*›; command ‹*regiment*›; chair ‹*committee*›; **eine Reisegruppe ~:** be courier to a group of tourists

5 (gelangen lassen) take; **die Straße/Reise führte uns durch einen Wald** the road/journey took us through a forest; **was führt Sie zu mir?** what brings you to me?

6 (Amtsspr.) drive ‹*train, motor, vehicle*›; navigate ‹*ship*›; fly ‹*aircraft*›

7 (bewegen) **die Hand an die Mütze/Stirn ~:** raise one's hand to one's cap/forehead

8 (verlaufen lassen) take; **die neue Autobahn um die Stadt ~:** take the new motorway round the city

9 (als Kennzeichnung, Bezeichnung haben) bear; **etw. in seinem Wappen ~:** have *or* bear sth. on one's coat of arms; **das Auto führt das Kennzeichen …** the car bears the registration number …; **das Schiff führt die schwedische Flagge** the ship is flying the Swedish flag; **einen Titel/Künstlernamen ~:** have a title/use a stage name; **den Titel „Professor" ~:** use the title of professor

10 (angelegt haben) keep ‹*diary, list, file*›

11 (befördern) carry; **die Leitung führt Gas** the pipe carries gas; **der Lkw führt Kohle** the truck *or* (Brit.) lorry is carrying coal; **der Zug führt einen Speisewagen** the train has a dining car; **der Fluss führt Hochwasser** the river is in flood

12 (registrieren) **jmdn. in einer Liste/Kartei ~:** have sb. on a list/on file; **in einer Liste geführt werden** appear on a list; **wir ~ hier keinen Müller** there is no Müller here

13 (tragen) **etw. bei** *od.* **mit sich ~:** have sth. on one; **eine Waffe/einen Ausweis bei sich ~:** carry a weapon/a pass

14 (handhaben) wield ‹*weapon*›

B *itr. V.* **1** lead; **die Straße führt nach …/durch …** the road leads *or* goes to …/goes through …; **die Brücke führt über den Bach** the bridge goes over the stream; **das Rennen führt über zehn Runden** the race is over ten laps; **das führt zu weit** (fig.) that would be taking things too far

2 (an der Spitze liegen) lead; be ahead; **nach Punkten ~:** be ahead on points; **in der Tabelle ~:** be the league leaders; be at the top of the league; **mit 3:1 ~:** be leading 3-1

3 (ein Ergebnis haben) **zu etw. ~:** lead to sth.; **zum Ziel ~:** bring the desired result; **das führt zu nichts** (ugs.) that won't get you/us *etc.* anywhere (coll.)

C *refl. V.* **sich gut/schlecht ~:** conduct oneself *or* behave well/badly; **er wurde frühzeitig aus dem Gefängnis entlassen, weil er sich gut geführt hatte** he got remission for good behaviour

führend *Adj.* leading ‹*politician, figure, role*›; high-ranking ‹*official*›; prominent ‹*position*›; **auf einem Gebiet/in einer Sache ~ sein** be a leader in a field/in sth.

Führer *der;* **~s, ~** [1] (Leiter) leader; **der ~** (ns.) the Führer [2] (Fremden~) guide [3] (Handbuch) guide[book] (**durch** to) [4] (Amtsspr., schweiz.: Fahrer) driver

Führer-: ~befehl *der* (ns.) Führer's order; **~eigenschaft** *die* quality of leadership; **~hauptquartier** *das* (ns.) Führer's headquarters *pl.*; Hitler's headquarters *pl.*; **~haus** *das* driver's cab

Führerin *die;* **~, ~nen** ▸ **Führer 1, 2, 4**

führer-, Führer-: ~kult *der* leader cult; **~los** [A] *Adj.* [1] (ohne An~) leaderless; [2] (ohne Lenker) driverless ‹*car*›; pilotless ‹*aircraft*›; unmanned ‹*boat*›; [B] *adv.* [1] (ohne An~) without a leader; [2] (ohne Lenker) ▸ **A 2**: without a driver; without a pilot; unmanned; **~natur** *die* [1] leader figure; [2] (Wesensart) **er hat eine starke ~natur** he is clearly a born leader; **~persönlichkeit** *die* ▸ **~natur 1**; **~prinzip** *das* (bes. ns.) leadership principle

Führerschaft *die;* **~:** leadership

Führer-: ~schein *der* driving licence (Brit.); driver's license (Amer.); **den ~schein machen** (ugs.) learn to drive; **jmdm. den ~schein entziehen** take away sb.'s licence; ban *or* disqualify sb. from driving; **~schein·entzug** *der* disqualification from driving; driving ban; **~sitz** *der* driving seat; driver's seat; **~stand** *der* driver's cab

Führ·hand *die* (Boxen) leading hand

Fuhr-: ~lohn *der* (an die Spedition) carriage charge; (an den Fahrer) carriage money; **~mann** *der; Pl.* **~leute** [1] carter; (einer Kutsche) driver; [2] (Astron.) **der ~mann** the Charioteer; **~park** *der* transport fleet

Führ·ring *der* (Pferdesport) paddock

Führung *die;* **~, ~en** [1] ▸ **führen A 4**: management; running; leadership; command; chairmanship; **die politische ~ übernehmen** take over political control *or* the political leadership [2] (Fremden~) guided tour; **an einer ~ teilnehmen** go on a guided tour [3] (führende Position) lead; **auf einem Gebiet/in etw.** (*Dat.*) **die ~ haben** be leading *or* the leader/leaders in a field/in sth.; **in ~ liegen/gehen** (Sport) be in/go into the lead [4] (Erziehung) guidance; **eine feste ~:** a firm hand; firm guidance [5] (leitende Gruppe) leaders *pl.*; (einer Partei) leadership; (einer Firma) directors *pl.*; (eines Regiments) commanders *pl.* [6] (Betragen) conduct; **wegen guter ~ vorzeitig entlassen werden** get remission for good behaviour [7] (eines Registers, Protokolls usw.) keeping [8] (das Handhaben von Waffen) wielding [9] (Amtsspr.) (eines Kfz) driving; (eines Flugzeugs) flying [10] (eines Titels usw.) use [11] (Technik) guide

Führungs-: ~anspruch *der* claim to leadership; **einen ~anspruch erheben** lay claim to the leadership; **~aufgabe** *die* (im Betrieb) management function; (Politik) leadership function; **~gremium** *das* executive committee; **~kraft** *die* manager; **~krise** *die* (Politik) leadership crisis; (Wirtsch.) boardroom crisis; **~riege** *die* management team; (Politik) leadership team; **~rolle** *die* role as leader; **~schiene** *die* (Technik) guide rail; **~spitze** *die* (Politik) top leadership; (im Betrieb) top management; **~stab** *der* (Milit.) high command; (im Betrieb) top management; **~tor** *das,* **~treffer** *der* (Sport) *goal which puts the/a team in the lead;* **das ~tor erzielen** score the goal which puts one's team in the lead; **~wechsel** *der* (Politik) change of leadership; (Wirtsch.) change of director/directors; **~zeugnis** *das document issued by police certifying that holder has no criminal record*

fuhr-, Fuhr-: ~unternehmen *das* haulage business; **~unternehmer** *der,* **~unternehmerin** *die* haulage contractor; **~werk** *das* cart (*drawn by horse[s], ox[en], etc.*); (veralt.: Wagen) (horse-drawn) carriage; **~werken** *itr. V.* (ugs.) **mit etw. ~werken** wave sth. about; **sie ~werkte nervös mit ihrer Handtasche** she fumbled nervously with her handbag

Fülle /ˈfʏlə/ *die;* **~** [1] (große Menge) wealth; abundance; **eine ~ von Arbeit** an enormous amount of work; **in ~:** in plenty; in abundance [2] (Intensität) **die ganze ~ des Lebens** the fullness *or* richness of life; **die ~ seines Glücks** the extent of his happiness [3] (Körper~) corpulence; (von Wein) full-bodiedness; (von Haar) fullness; **zur ~ neigen** tend to corpulence; **sie ließ sich mit ihrer ganzen ~ auf das Sofa fallen** she let her whole weight drop on to the sofa

füllen

[A] *tr. V.* [1] (voll machen, an~) fill; **eine Flasche/ein Glas [mit etw.] ~:** fill a bottle/a glass with sth.; **bis zum Rand gefüllt sein** be full to the brim; **der Saal ist bis auf den letzten Platz/halb gefüllt** the hall is completely/half full; *s. auch* **gefüllt B** [2] (fig.) fill in ‹*gap, time*› [3] (mit einer Füllung versehen) stuff ‹*fowl, tomato, apple, mattress, toy*›; fill ‹*tooth*›; *s. auch* **gefüllt B** [4] (schütten) pour; **etw. in Flaschen ~:** bottle sth.; **etw. in Säcke ~:** put sth. into sacks [5] (einnehmen) fill ‹*space etc.*›

[B] *refl. V.* (voll werden) fill [up]; **sich mit etw. ~:** fill up with sth.

Füllen *das;* **~s, ~** (geh.) foal

Füller *der;* **~s, ~** [1] (ugs.) [fountain] pen [2] (Zeitungsw.) filler

Füll-: ~feder·halter *der* fountain pen; **~gewicht** *das* net weight; **~horn** *das* horn of plenty; (fig.) cornucopia

füllig *Adj.* corpulent, portly ‹*person*›; ample, portly ‹*figure*›; full ‹*face*›; ample ‹*bosom*›

Füll-: ~masse *die* filler; **~material** *das* (Druckw.) furniture; spacing material

Füllsel /ˈfʏlzl̩/ *das;* **~s, ~** [1] (Lückenfüller) padding [2] (in Lebensmitteln) filling; (in Geflügel) stuffing

Füllung *die;* **~, ~en** [1] (in Geflügel, Paprika) stuffing; (in Pasteten, Kuchen) filling; (in Schokolade, Pralinen) centre; (in Kissen, Matratzen) stuffing [2] (Zahnmed.) filling [3] (Teil der Tür) panel [4] (das Vollmachen) filling

Füll·wort *das; Pl.* **Füllwörter** filler; (Sprachw., Literaturw.) expletive

fulminant /fʊlmiˈnant/ *Adj.* brilliant

Fummel /ˈfʊml̩/ *der;* **~s, ~** (salopp) [1] rags *pl.* [2] (von Transvestiten) drag [outfit]; **im ~:** in drag

Fummelei *die;* **~, ~en** (ugs.) [1] twiddling; **das ist eine furchtbare ~:** it's terribly fiddly [2] (Petting) petting; groping (coll.) [3] (Fußballjargon) dribbling

fummelig (ugs. abwertend)

[A] *Adj.* fiddly

[B] *adv.* with much fumbling; **~ zu bedienen sein** be fiddly to operate

fummeln

[A] *itr. V.* [1] (ugs.: fingern) fiddle; **an etw.** (*Dat.*) **~:** fiddle [around] with sth.; **nach etw. ~:** grope for *or* feel for sth. [2] (ugs.: erotisch) pet [3] (Fußballjargon) dribble

[B] *tr. V.* **etw. in etw.** (*Akk.*)**/aus etw. ~** (ugs.) get sth. in sth./out of sth.

Fund /fʊnt/ *der;* **~[e]s, ~e** (auch Archäol.) find; (wissenschaftliche Entdeckung) discovery

Fundament /fʊndaˈmɛnt/ *das;* **~[e]s, ~e** [1] (Bauw.) foundations *pl.*; **das ~ legen** *od.* **mauern** lay the foundations; **etw. bis auf die ~e abreißen** raze sth. to the ground; **etw. in seinen ~en erschüttern** (fig.) strike at the very foundations of sth.; **das ~ zu etw. legen** (fig.) lay the foundations for sth.; **an den ~en rütteln** (fig.) rock the very foundations [2] (Basis) base; basis; **ein solides ~ haben** have a solid base

fundamental /fʊndamɛnˈtaːl/ *Adj.* fundamental

Fundamentalismus *der;* **~:** fundamentalism

Fundamentalist *der;* **~en, ~en, Fundamentalistin** *die;* **~, ~nen** fundamentalist; *s. auch* **-in**

Fundamental·satz *der* fundamental theorem

fundamentieren *tr. V.* (Bauw.) **ein Gebäude ~:** lay the foundations of a building; **schlecht fundamentiert sein** (auch fig.) have weak foundations

Fund-: ~amt *das* (bes. österr.), **~büro** *das* lost property office (Brit.); lost and found office (Amer.); **~gegenstand** *der* [1] ▸ **~sache**; [2] (Archäol.) find; **~grube** *die* treasure house

Fundi /ˈfʊndi/ *der;* **~s, ~s,** *die;* **~, ~s** (ugs.) fundamentalist

fundieren /fʊnˈdiːrən/ *tr. V.* [1] (geistig begründen, untermauern) underpin; **ein wissenschaftlich fundierter Vortrag** a scientifically sound lecture [2] (geh.: festigen) sustain [3] (finanziell sichern) strengthen [financially]; **ein gut fundiertes Unternehmen** a [financially] sound business

fündig /ˈfʏndɪç/ *Adj.* **~ sein** yield something; **~ werden** make a find; (bei Bohrungen) make a strike

Fund-: ~ort *der* place *or* site where sth. is/was found; **~sache** *die* article found; **~sachen** lost property *sing.*; **~stätte** *die,* **~stelle** *die* ▸ **Fundort**; **~unterschlagung** *die* (Rechtsw.) larceny by finding

Fundus /ˈfʊndʊs/ *der;* **~, ~** [1] (Requisition) equipment store [2] (Grundstock, -lage) **einen [reichen] ~ von/an etw.** (*Dat.*) **haben** have a [rich] fund of sth.; **kein eigentlicher geistiger ~:** no real intellectual resources *pl.*

fünf /fʏnf/ *Kardinalz.* ▸ⓘ **S. 29,** ▸ⓘ **S. 729,** ▸ⓘ **S. 826** five; **~[e] gerade sein lassen** (fig. ugs.) let sth. pass; **man muss manchmal ~[e] gerade sein lassen** (ugs.) one has to turn a blind eye sometimes; **es ist ~ Minuten vor zwölf** it is five minutes to twelve; **~ Minuten vor zwölf** (fig.) at the eleventh hour; at the last minute; *s. auch* **acht¹**; **Finger 2**; **Sinn 1**

Fünf *die;* **~, ~en** five; **eine ~ schreiben/bekommen** (Schulw.) get an E; *s. auch* **Acht¹ 1, 4, 5, 7**; **Zwei 2**

fünf-, Fünf-: ~akter /-aktɐ/ *der;* **~s, ~~:** five-act play; **~eck** *das* pentagon; **~eckig** *Adj.* pentagonal; five-cornered

Fünfer *der;* **~s, ~** (ugs.) [1] (Geldschein, Münze) five [2] (ugs.: Ziffer) five [3] (Lottogewinn) five out of six [4] (ugs.: Sprungturm) five-metre board; *s. auch* **Achter 3, 4**

fünferlei *indekl. Gattungsz.* [1] *attr.* five kinds *or* sorts of; five different *attrib.* ‹*sorts, kinds, sizes, possibilities*› [2] *subst.* five [different] things

fünf-, Fünf-: ~euro·schein *der* five-euro note; **~fach** *Vervielfältigungsz.* fivefold; quintuple; *s. auch* **achtfach**; **~fache** *das; adj. Dekl.* five times as much; quintuple; *s. auch* **Achtfache**; **~fältig** *Adj.* (veralt.) ▸ **~fach**; **~flach** *das;* **~~s, ~~e, ~flächner** *der;* **~~s, ~~:** pentahedron; **~franken·stück** *das* five-franc piece; **~füßig** *Adj.* (Verslehre) five-foot; **~füßiger Jambus/Trochäus** iambic/trochaic pentameter; **~gang·getriebe** *das* five-speed gearbox; **~hebig** *Adj.* (Verslehre) ▸ **~füßig**; **~hundert** *Kardinalz.* ▸ⓘ **S. 826** five hundred; *s. auch* **hundert**; **~hunderter** *der* (ugs.) 500-euro/-dollar *etc.* note; **~hundert·jahr·feier** *die* quincentenary; **~jahr[es]·plan** *der* five-year plan; **~jährig** *Adj.* (5 Jahre alt) five-year-old; (5 Jahre dauernd) five-year; *s. auch* **achtjährig**; **~jährlich** [A] *Adj.* five-yearly; quinquennial; [B] *adv.* every five years; *s. auch* **achtjährlich**; **~kampf** *der* (Sport) pentathlon; **der moderne ~kampf** the Modern Pentathlon; **~kämpfer** *der,* **~kämpferin** *die* (Sport) pentathlete; **~köpfig** *Adj.* ‹*family, crew*› of five; five-headed ‹*monster*›

Fünfling /ˈfʏnflɪŋ/ *der;* **~s, ~e** quintuplet; quin (coll.)

fünf-, Fünf-: ~mal *Adv.* five times; *s. auch* **achtmal**; **~malig** *Adj.* **eine ~malige Wiederholung** five repeats; *s. auch* **achtmalig**; **~meter·plattform** *die* (Wasserspringen) five-metre platform; **~meter·raum** *der* (Fußball) goal area; **~prozentig** *Adj.* five per cent; **~prozent·klausel** *die* (Politik) five per cent clause; **~seitig** *Adj.* five-page ‹*letter, leaflet*›; *s. auch* **achtseitig**; **~silber** *der;* **~~s, ~~** ▸ **Fünfsilbler**; **~silbig** *Adj.* five-syllable; pentasyllabic; **~silbler** *der;* **~~s,**

~~ (Verslehre) five-syllable line; **~stellig** *Adj.* five-figure ‹*number, sum*›; *s. auch* **achtstellig**; **~stöckig** *Adj.* five-storey *attrib.*; *s. auch* **achtstöckig**; **~strophig** /-ʃtro:fɪç/ *Adj.* of five stanzas *or* verses *postpos., not pred.*

Fünfprozentklausel

The five per cent clause introduced in 1953 stipulates that only parties gaining at least five per cent of the valid second votes or at least three constituency seats can be represented in parliament. The clause can be waived in the case of national minorities.

fünft /fʏnft/ *in* **wir/sie waren zu ~:** there were five of us/them; *s. auch* **acht²**

fünft... *Ordinalz.* ▸ⓘ **S. 165**, ▸ⓘ **S. 826** fifth; *s. auch* **acht...**

fünf-, Fünf-: **~tage·woche** *die* five-day [working] week; **~tägig** *Adj.* five-day; *s. auch* **achttägig**; **~tausend** *Kardinalz.* ▸ⓘ **S. 826** five thousand; *s. auch* **tausend**

Fünfte *der/die; adj. Dekl.* fifth; **Kaiser Karl V.** *od.* **der ~:** the Emperor Charles V; *s. auch* **Achte**

fünfteilig *Adj.* five-part; *s. auch* **achtteilig**

fünftel /ˈfʏnftl̩/ *Bruchz.* ▸ⓘ **S. 826** fifth; *s. auch* **achtel**

Fünftel *das* (*schweiz. meist der*); **~s, ~:** ▸ⓘ **S. 826** fifth

***fünfte·mal, *fünften·mal** ▸**Mal¹**

fünftens /ˈfʏnftn̩s/ *Adv.* fifthly; in the fifth place

fünf-, Fünf-: **~tonner** *der;* **~~s, ~~:** five-tonner; **~uhr·tee** *der* [afternoon] tea; **~viertel·takt** /-ˈ---/ *der* five-four time; **~zehn** *Kardinalz.* ▸ⓘ **S. 29**, ▸ⓘ **S. 729**, ▸ⓘ **S. 826** fifteen; *s. auch* **achtzehn**; **~zehn·jährig** *Adj.* (15 Jahre alt) fifteen-year-old *attrib.*; (15 Jahre dauernd) fifteen-year *attrib.*; *s. auch* **achtjährig**; **~zehnt...** *Ordinalz.* ▸ⓘ **S. 165** fifteenth; *s. auch* **acht...**

fünfzig /ˈfʏnftsɪç/ *Kardinalz.* ▸ⓘ **S. 29**, ▸ⓘ **S. 826** fifty; *s. auch* **achtzig**

Fünfzig *die;* **~:** fifty

Fünfzig·cent·stück *das* fifty-cent piece

fünfziger *indekl. Adj.* **die ~ Jahre** the fifties; *s. auch* **achtziger**

Fünfziger¹ *der;* **~s, ~** 1 (ugs.) fifty-cent piece 2 (50-jähriger) fifty-year-old; *s. auch* **Achtziger¹ 2, 3**

Fünfziger² *die;* **~, ~** (ugs. Briefmarke) fifty-cent/centime *etc.* stamp

Fünfziger³ *Pl.* fifties; *s. auch* **Achtziger³**

Fünfzigerin *die;* **~, ~nen** ▸**Fünfziger¹ 2**

Fünfziger·jahre *Pl.* ▸ⓘ **S. 29**, ▸ⓘ **S. 165** fifties *pl.*

fünfzig-, Fünfzig-: **~euro·schein** *der* fifty-euro note; **~jährig** *Adj.* (50 Jahre alt) fifty-year-old *attrib.*; (50 Jahre dauernd) fifty-year *attrib.*; *s. auch* **achtjährig**

fünfzigst... /ˈfʏnftsɪçst.../ *Ordinalz.* ▸ⓘ **S. 826** fiftieth; *s. auch* **acht...**; **achtzigst...**

fungieren /fʊŋˈgi:rən/ *itr. V.* **als etw. ~** ‹*person*› act as sth.; ‹*word etc.*› function as sth.

Funk /fʊŋk/ *der;* **~s** 1 (drahtlose Übermittlung) radio; **jmdn./etw. über ~** (*Akk.*) **anfordern** ask for sb./sth. by radio 2 (Rund~) radio; **beim ~ sein** (ugs.) *od.* **arbeiten** be (coll.) *or* work in radio

Funk-: **~amateur** *der,* **~amateurin** *die* ▸ⓘ **S. 113** radio ham; **~anlage** *die* radio set; **~ausstellung** *die* radio and television exhibition; **~bake** *die* radio beacon; **~bearbeitung** *die* radio adaptation; adaptation for radio; **~bericht** *der* radio report; **~bild** *das* radio photograph

Fünkchen /ˈfʏŋkçən/ *das;* **~s, ~** ▸**Funke 2**

Funk·dienst *der* radio communication service

Funke /ˈfʊŋkə/ *der;* **~ns, ~n** 1 (glühendes Teilchen) spark; **~n sprühen** send out a shower of sparks; (fig.) ‹*eyes*› flash; **ein ~n sprühendes Feuer** a fire sending out showers of sparks; **~n sprühend raste die Lok vorbei** the engine thundered past, giving off showers of sparks 2 (fig.) **der ~ der Begeisterung/Revolution** the spark of enthusiasm/revolution; **der auslösende ~ für meinen Entschluss war ...** what finally triggered my decision was ...; **ein/kein ~** *od.* **Fünkchen [von] Verstand/Ehrgefühl/Mitleid** a/not a glimmer of understanding/shred of honour/scrap of sympathy; **arbeiten, dass die ~n stieben** *od.* **fliegen** (fig.) work like mad (coll.)

funkeln /ˈfʊŋkl̩n/ *itr. V.* ‹*light, star*› twinkle, sparkle; ‹*gold, diamonds*› glitter, sparkle; ‹*eyes*› blaze

funkel·nagel·neu *Adj.* (ugs.) brand new; spanking new (coll.)

funken /ˈfʊŋkn̩/

A *tr. V.* radio; ‹*transmitter*› broadcast; **SOS ~:** send out an SOS

B *itr. V.; unpers.* (fig. ugs.) **es hat gefunkt** (es hat Streit gegeben) the sparks flew; (die Sache geht in Ordnung) it's worked out OK (coll.); (man hat sich verliebt) something clicked between them/us (coll.); **es hat bei ihm gefunkt** the penny's dropped [with him] (coll.)

funken-, Funken-: **~bildung** *die* sparking *no art.*; **~entladung** *die* spark discharge; **~fänger** *der* (Eisenb.) spark arrester; **~flug** *der* flying sparks *pl.*; **~mariechen** *das;* **~~s, ~~:** red-coat girl (in Rhenish carnival); **~regen** *der* shower of sparks; **~sprühend** ▸**Funke 1**

funk·entstören *tr. V.* fit with a suppressor/suppressors; suppress

Funk·entstörung *die* suppression of interference

Funker *der;* **~s, ~,** **Funkerin** *die;* **~, ~nen** ▸ⓘ **S. 113** radio operator

Funk-: **~fernsteuerung** *die* radio control; **~feuer** *das* ▸**~bake**; **~gerät** *das* radio set; (tragbar) walkie-talkie; **~haus** *das* broadcasting centre; **~kolleg** *das* radio-based [adult education] course; **~loch** *das* (Fernsprechw.) area with no signal; reception blackspot; **~meldung** *die* radio message *or* report; **~mess·technik,** ***~meß·technik** *die* radar; **~navigation** *die* radio navigation; **~ortung** *die* radio position-finding; **~peiler** *der;* **~~s, ~~,** **~peilerin** *die;* **~~, ~~nen** [radio] direction-finder; **~peilung** *die* [radio] direction-finding; **~signal** *das* radio signal; **~sprech·gerät** *das* radiophone; (tragbar) walkie-talkie; **~sprech·verkehr** *der* radio telephony; **~spruch** *der* radio signal; (Nachricht) radio message; **~station** *die,* **~stelle** *die* radio station; **~stille** *die* radio silence; **bei ihm herrscht ~stille** (fig.) he's keeping quiet; **~störung** *die* [radio] interference; (mit Absicht) jamming; **~streife** *die* [police] radio patrol; **~streifen·wagen** *der* radio patrol car; **~taxi** *das* radio taxi; **~technik** *die* radio technology; **~telegramm** *das* radio telegram

Funktion /fʊnkˈtsi̯o:n/ *die;* **~, ~en** 1 function 2 (Tätigkeit, Arbeiten) functioning; working; **außer/in ~ sein** be out of/in operation; **in ~** (*Akk.*) **treten** come into operation; **jmdn./etw. außer ~ setzen** put sb./sth. out of operation 3 (Amt, Stellung) function; **in seiner ~ als ...** in his function as ... 4 (Math., Sprachw.) function

funktional /fʊŋktsi̯oˈna:l/

A *Adj.* functional

B *adv.* functionally

Funktionalismus *der;* **~:** functionalism

Funktionär /fʊŋktsi̯oˈnɛ:ɐ̯/ *der;* **~s, ~e,** **Funktionärin** *die;* **~, ~nen** official; functionary

funktionell /fʊŋktsi̯oˈnɛl/

A *Adj.* functional

B *adv.* functionally

Funktionen·theorie *die* (Math.) theory of functions

funktionieren *itr. V.* work; function; **die gut ~de Organisation** the smooth organization

funktions-, Funktions-: **~fähig** *Adj.* able to function *or* work *pred.*; **~fähigkeit** *die* ability to function; **~gerecht** **A** *Adj.* functional; **B** *adv.* functionally; **~jacke** *die* multi-function jacket; multi-activity jacket; **~kleidung** *die* activity clothing; **~los** *Adj.* ‹*person*› without a job to do; functionless ‹*equipment, object*›; **~los werden** become unnecessary; **~sicher** **A** *Adj.* operatively sound; **B** *adv.* properly; **~störung** *die* ▸ⓘ **S. 439** (Med.) functional disorder; dysfunction; **~taste** *die* (DV) function key; **~tüchtig** *Adj.* working ‹*equipment, part*›; sound ‹*organ*›; **~unterwäsche** *die* activity underwear; **~verb** *das* (Sprachw.) empty verb; **~wäsche** *die* outdoor underwear; **~wechsel** *der* change in function

Funk-: **~turm** *der* radio tower; **~verbindung** *die* radio contact; **~verkehr** *der* radio communication; **~wagen** *der* radio patrol car; **~weg** *der:* **auf dem ~weg** by radio; **~zelle** *die* (Elektrot.) radio cell

Funzel /ˈfʊntsl̩/ *die;* **~, ~n** (ugs. abwertend) useless lamp *or* light; **bei dieser ~:** in this gloomy light

funz[e]lig (ugs. abwertend)

A *Adj.* dim ‹*light*›; dimly lit ‹*screen*›

B *adv.* dimly

für /fy:ɐ̯/

A *Präp. mit Akk.* 1 for; **~ etw. trainieren/kämpfen** train/fight for sth.; **~ jmdn. bestimmt sein** be meant for sb.; **das ist nichts ~ mich** that's not for me; **Lehrer/Professor/Minister ~ etw. sein** be a teacher/professor/minister of sth.; **zu jung/alt ~ etw. sein** be too young/old for sth.; **~ sich** by oneself; on one's own; **er ist am liebsten ganz ~ sich** what he most prefers is being completely on his own; **jetzt habe ich eine Küche ganz ~ mich** now I've a kitchen all to myself; **das ist gut ~ Husten** that's good for coughs; **sich ~ jmdn. freuen/schämen** be pleased/ashamed for sb.; **~ etw. verurteilt werden** be condemned for sth.; **etw. ~ 50 Euro kaufen** buy sth. for 50 euros; **~ diese Jahreszeit ist es viel zu kalt** it's much too cold for this time of year; **~ 20 Minuten/drei Tage** for 20 minutes/three days; **~ morgen** for tomorrow; **~ immer** for ever; for good; **~ gewöhnlich** usually; **~ nichts und wieder nichts** for absolutely nothing 2 (zugunsten) for; **~ jmdn./etw. stimmen/sein** vote/be for *or* in favour of sb./sth.; **das hat etwas ~ sich** it has something to be said for it; **das Für und Wider** the pros and cons *pl.* 3 (als) **etw. ~ ungültig/zulässig erklären** declare sth. invalid/admissible; **jmdn. ~ tot erklären** declare sb. dead 4 (anstelle) for; **~ jmdn. einspringen** take sb.'s place; **~ zwei arbeiten** do the work of two people 5 (als Stellvertreter) for; on behalf of; **~ jmdn. eine Erklärung abgeben** make an announcement on sb.'s behalf 6 (um) **Jahr ~ Jahr/Tag ~ Tag** year after year/day after day; **Punkt ~ Punkt/Schritt ~ Schritt** point by point/step by step; **Wort ~ Wort** word for word; *s. auch* **was A**

B *adv.* (veralt.) **~ und ~:** for ever [and ever]; unto all generations (bibl.)

Furage /fuˈra:ʒə/ *die;* **~** (Milit. veralt.) 1 (Verpflegung) rations *pl.* 2 (Futter) forage

furagieren *itr. V.* (Milit. veralt.) forage

für·bass, *für·baß *Adv.* (veralt., noch scherzh.) onwards; **~ gehen/schreiten** proceed on one's way

Für·bitte *die* intercession; **[bei jmdm.] für jmdn. ~ einlegen** intercede [with sb.] for sb.

Furche /ˈfʊrçə/ *die;* **~, ~n** 1 furrow; **[mit dem Pflug] ~n ziehen** plough furrows; **~n im Gesicht/auf der Stirn haben** have a furrowed face/brow 2 (Wagenspur) rut 3 (Rille) groove

furchen *tr. V.* (geh.) 1 (Linien bilden) furrow; **die Stirn/die Brauen ~:** furrow one's brow 2 (Rillen ziehen) make ‹*ruts*›; make ruts in ‹*ground, track*›

Furcht /fʊrçt/ *die;* **~:** fear; **~ vor jmdm./etw. haben** fear sb./sth.; **~ vor Gespenstern haben** be afraid of ghosts; **von ~ erfasst sein** (geh.) be seized by fear *or* dread; **jmdm. ~ einflößen** frighten sb.; **aus ~ vor jmdm./etw.** for fear of sb./sth.; **jmdn. in ~ und Schrecken versetzen** fill sb. with terror; terrify sb.

furchtbar

A *Adj.* 1 awful; frightful; dreadful; **~ aussehen** look awful *or* frightful; **es war mir ~, das tun zu müssen** it was awful [for me] to have to do it 2 (ugs.: unangenehm) awful (coll.); terrible

(coll.); **ein ~er Angeber/Pedant** an awful *or* frightful show-off/pedant (coll.)
B *adv.* (ugs.) awfully (coll.); terribly (coll.); **~ lachen [müssen]** laugh oneself silly (coll.); **das ist ~ einfach/teuer** it's awfully simple/expensive; **es dauerte ~ lange** it took an awfully long time; **jmdn. ~ beschimpfen/verprügeln** give sb. an awful talking-to/beating

furcht·einflößend *Adj.* frightening; fearsome; **es wirkte ~ auf uns** it frightened us

fürchten
A *refl. V.* **sich [vor jmdm./etw.] ~:** be afraid *or* frightened [of sb./sth.]; **es ist/war zum Fürchten** it is/was quite frightening; **du siehst in diesem Anzug ja zum Fürchten aus** (scherzh.) you look quite frightful in that suit
B *tr. V.* fear; be afraid of; **jmdn./etw. ~:** fear *or* be afraid of sb./sth.; **jmdn./etw. wegen etw. ~:** fear sb./sth. because of sth.; **er war als strenger Prüfer gefürchtet** he was feared as a strict examiner; **ein gefürchteter Kritiker** a feared critic; **der gefürchtete Augenblick** the moment they/we *etc.* had been fearing; **Gott ~:** fear God; **ich fürchte, [dass] ...** I'm afraid [that] ...
C *itr. V.* **für** *od.* **um jmdn./etw. ~:** fear for sb./sth.

fürchterlich *Adj.* ▸**furchtbar**

furcht·erregend *Adj.* frightening

furcht·los
A *Adj.* fearless
B *adv.* fearlessly

Furcht·losigkeit *die;* **~:** fearlessness

furchtsam /ˈfʊrçtzaːm/
A *Adj.* timid; fearful
B *adv.* timidly; fearfully

Furchtsamkeit *die;* **~, ~en** timidity; fearfulness

Furchung *die;* **~, ~en** (Biol.) cleavage; segmentation

fürder[hin] /ˈfʏrdɐ(hɪn)/ *Adv.* (veralt.) in future

für·einander *Adv.* for one another; for each other

Furie /ˈfuːri̯ə/ *die;* **~, ~n** Fury; **er rannte wie von ~n gehetzt davon** he ran off as if the devil were on his tail; **sie wurde zur ~** (fig.) she started acting like a woman possessed; **wie ~n gingen sie aufeinander los** they went for each other like wildcats

furios /fuˈri̯oːs/ *Adj.* (geh. veralt.) rousing; stirring

für·lieb|nehmen** *unr. itr. V.* (veralt.) ▸vorliebnehmen**

fürnehm /ˈfyːɐ̯neːm/ *Adj.* (veralt., scherzh.) ▸**vornehm**

Furnier /fʊrˈniːɐ̯/ *das;* **~s, ~e** veneer

furnieren *tr. V.* veneer; **[mit] Eiche furniert sein** have an oak veneer

Furore /fuˈroːrə/ *in* **~ machen** cause a sensation *or* stir

fürs /fyːɐ̯s/ *Präp. + Art.* **1** = **für das** **2** **~ Erste** for the time being

Für·sorge *die;* **~** **1** (umsorgende Hilfe) care **2** (veralt.: Sozialhilfe) welfare **3** (veralt.: Sozialamt) social services *pl.* **4** (ugs.: Unterstützungsgeld) social security (Brit.); welfare (Amer.)

Fürsorge-: **~amt** *das* (veralt.) welfare office; **~empfänger** *der,* **~empfängerin** *die* (ugs.) recipient of social security; **~empfänger sein** receive social security; **~erziehung** *die* upbringing in [local authority] care

für·sorgend
A *Adj.* caring; thoughtful
B *adv.* caringly; thoughtfully

Fürsorge·pflicht *die* (jur.) *employer's obligation to ensure the welfare of his/her employees*

Fürsorger *der;* **~s, ~,** **Fürsorgerin** *die;* **~, ~nen** (veralt.) welfare worker

Fürsorge·unterstützung *die* (veralt.) social security (Brit.); welfare (Amer.)

für·sorglich
A *Adj.* considerate; thoughtful
B *adv.* considerately; thoughtfully

Fürsorglichkeit *die;* **~:** considerateness; thoughtfulness

Für·sprache *die* support; **bei jmdm. für jmdn. ~ einlegen** put in a good word for sb. with sb.

Fürsprech /ˈfyːɐ̯ʃprɛç/ *der;* **~s, ~e** (veralt., geh.) ▸**Fürsprecher**

Für·sprecher *der,* **Für·sprecherin** *die* **1** advocate; **in jmdm. einen ~ haben** have an advocate in sb. **2** (schweiz.) ▸**Rechtsanwalt**

Fürst /fʏrst/ *der;* **~en, ~en** prince; **der ~ der Hölle/Finsternis** (fig.) the Prince of Hell/Darkness; **gehe nie zu deinem ~, wenn du nicht gerufen wirst** (scherzh.) do not meet trouble half way

Fürst-: **~abt** *der* (hist.) prince-abbot; **~bischof** *der* (hist.) prince-bishop

Fürsten-: **~geschlecht** *das,* **~haus** *das* royal house; **~hof** *der* prince's palace; **~krone** *die* prince's coronet; **~spiegel** *der: novel giving guidance for the conduct of princes;* **~stand** *der* rank of prince

Fürstentum *das;* **~s, Fürstentümer** /-tyːmɐ/ principality; **das ~ Liechtenstein/Monaco** the Principality of Liechtenstein/Monaco

Fürstin *die;* **~, ~nen** princess

fürstlich
A *Adj.* **1** royal **2** (fig.: üppig) handsome; lavish
B *adv.* handsomely; lavishly; **~ speisen** enjoy a sumptuous meal

Fürstlichkeit *die;* **~, ~en** royal personage

Furt /fʊrt/ *die;* **~, ~en** ford

Furunkel /fuˈrʊŋkl̩/ *der od. das;* **~s, ~** ▸**i S. 439** boil; furuncle

Furunkulose /furʊŋkuˈloːzə/ *die;* **~, ~n** ▸**i S. 439** (Med.) furunculosis

für·wahr *Adv.* (geh. veralt.) of a truth (arch.); in truth (literary)

Für·witz *der;* **~es** (veralt.) ▸**Vorwitz**

Für·wort *das; Pl.* **Fürwörter** pronoun

Furz /fʊrts/ *der;* **~es, Fürze** /ˈfʏrtsə/ (derb) fart (coarse); **einen ~ lassen** let off a fart; **jeder ~** (fig.) the slightest thing

furzen *itr. V.* (derb) fart (coarse)

Fusel /ˈfuːzl̩/ *der;* **~s, ~** (ugs. abwertend) rotgut (coll. derog.)

Fusel-: **~geruch** *der* (ugs. abwertend) smell of cheap alcohol; **~öl** *das* fusel oil

Füsilier /fyziˈliːɐ̯/ *der;* **~s, ~e** (schweiz., sonst veralt.) fusilier

füsilieren *tr. V.* (veralt.) execute by firing squad

Fusion /fuˈzi̯oːn/ *die;* **~, ~en** **1** amalgamation; (von Konzernen) merger **2** (Naturw.) fusion

fusionieren *itr. V.* merge

Fusionmusic /ˈfjuːʒənmjuːzɪk/ *die;* **~:** fusion

Fusions·reaktor *der* (Physik) fusion reactor

Fuß /fuːs/ *der;* **~es, Füße** /ˈfyːsə/ **1** ▸**i S. 435** foot; (südd., österr., schweiz.) leg; **sich** (*Dat.*) **den ~ verstauchen/brechen** sprain one's ankle/break a bone in one's foot; **mit bloßen Füßen** barefoot; with bare feet; **jmdm. auf den ~ treten** tread on sb.'s foot; **zu ~ gehen** go on foot; walk; **über seine eigenen Füße stolpern** trip over one's own feet; **gut/schlecht zu ~ sein** be a good/bad walker; **ich habe keinen ~ vor die Tür gesetzt** I did not set foot outside the door; **sich** (*Dat.*) **gegenseitig auf die Füße treten** tread on each other's toes; **jmdm. auf dem ~e folgen** follow at sb.'s heels; **bei ~!** heel!; **nimm die Füße weg!** (ugs.) move your feet!; **Gewehr bei ~ stehen** stand with ordered arms **2** (fig.) **stehenden ~es** (veralt., geh.) without delay; instanter (arch.); **[festen] ~ fassen** find one's feet; **kalte Füße kriegen** (ugs.) get cold feet (coll.); **sich** (*Dat.*) **die Füße nach etw. ablaufen** *od.* **wund laufen** chase round everywhere for sth.; **sich auf eigene Füße stellen** stand on one's own feet; **auf freiem ~ sein** be at large; **jmdn. auf freien ~ setzen** set sb. free; **auf großem ~ leben** live in great style; **mit jmdm. auf freundschaftlichem/gespanntem ~ stehen** *od.* **leben** be on friendly/less than friendly terms with sb.; **jmdm. auf die Füße treten** (ugs.) give sb. a good talking-to; **auf dem ~e folgen** follow swiftly; **jmdn. auf dem falschen ~ erwischen** (Sportjargon) wrong-foot sb.; **jmdn./etw. mit Füßen treten** trample on sb./sth.; **jmdm. etw. vor die Füße werfen** throw sth. in sb.'s face; **jmdm. zu Füßen liegen** (geh.) (bewundern) adore *or* worship sb.; (anflehen) go on one's bended knee to sb.; **jmdm. etw. zu Füßen legen** (geh.) lay sth. at sb.'s feet; *s. auch* **eigen 1**; **Erde 2**; **fallen 1**; **Gefängnis 1**; **Grab** *usw.* **3** (tragender Teil) (einer Lampe) base; (eines Weinglases) foot; (eines Schranks, Sessels, Klaviers) leg; **auf tönernen** *od.* **schwachen** *od.* **schwankenden Füßen stehen** (fig.) be unsoundly based **4** (eines Berges) foot; (einer Säule) base **5** *Pl.:* **~** ▸**i S. 224**, ▸**i S. 374**, ▸**i S. 454** (Längenmaß) foot; **zwei/drei ~:** two/three feet *or* foot **6** (Teil des Strumpfes) foot

fuß-, Fuß-: **~abdruck** *der; Pl.* **~abdrücke** footprint; **~abstreifer**, **~abtreter** *der;* **~~s, ~~:** shoe scraper; **~abwehr** *die* (Ballspiele) kick save; **~angel** *die* mantrap; (fig.) trap; **er hat sich in den ~angeln dieser Paragraphen verstrickt** he has got entangled in these legal clauses; **~bad** *das* **1** footbath; **2** (ugs. scherzh.) pool in the saucer

Fuß·ball *der* **1** (Ballspiel) football; soccer **2** (Ball) football; soccer ball

Fuß·ballen *der* ▸**i S. 435** the ball of the/one's foot

Fußballer *der;* **~s, ~,** **Fußballerin** *die;* **~, ~nen** footballer; soccer player

fußballerisch *Adj.* footballing

fußball-, Fußball-: **~groß** *Adj.* the size of a football *postpos.;* **~klub** *der* ▸**~verein**; **~mannschaft** *die* football team; **~meisterschaft** *die* football championship; **~platz** *der* football ground; (Spielfeld) football pitch; **~schuh** *der* football boot; **~spiel** *das* **1** football match; **2** (Sportart) football *no art.;* **~spieler** *der,* **~spielerin** *die* football player; **~tor** *das* [football] goal; **~toto** *das od. der* football pools *pl.;* **~verband** *der* football association; **~verein** *der* football club

Fuß-: **~bank** *die; Pl.* **~bänke** footstool; **~bekleidung** *die* footwear; **~bett** *das* footbed; **~boden** *der* floor

Fußboden-: **~belag** *der* floor covering; **~heizung** *die* underfloor heating

fuß-, Fuß-: **~breit** *Adj.* foot-wide; **~breit sein** be a foot wide; **~breit** *der;* **~~, ~~:** foot; **er wollte keinen ~breit nachgeben** (fig.) he would not budge an inch; **~bremse** *die* foot brake; **~brett** *das* foot rest

Füßchen /ˈfyːsçən/ *das;* **~s, ~:** [little] foot

Fussel /ˈfʊsl̩/ *die;* **~, ~n** *od. der;* **~s, ~[n]** fluff; **ein[e] ~:** a piece of fluff; some fluff

fusselig *Adj.* covered in fluff *postpos.;* (ausgefranst) frayed; **sich** (*Dat.*) **den Mund ~ reden** (salopp) talk till one is blue in the face (coll.)

fusseln *itr. V.* make fluff

fußen *itr. V.* **auf etw.** (*Dat.*) **~:** be based on sth.

Fuß·ende *das* foot

fuß-, Fuß-: **~fall** *der* kowtow; **einen ~fall vor jmdm. machen** (fig.) kowtow to sb.; **~fällig** **A** *Adj.* humble; **B** *adv.* **1** **sie flehte den Fürsten ~fällig um Gnade an** she fell on her knees before the prince, begging him for mercy; **2** (fig.) humbly; **~fehler** *der* **1** (bes. Hockey) kick; **2** (Tennis) foot fault; **~fesseln** *Pl.* shackles (*on the feet*); **~frei** *Adj.* ankle-length ‹*dress, skirt, etc.*›

Fußgänger /-gɛŋɐ/ *der;* **~s, ~:** pedestrian

Fußgänger·brücke *die* footbridge

Fußgängerin *die;* **~, ~nen** ▸**Fußgänger**

Fußgänger-: **~tunnel** *der* pedestrian subway; **~übergang** *der,* **~über·weg** *der* pedestrian crossing; **~unter·führung** *die* pedestrian subway; **~verkehr** *der* pedestrian traffic; **~zone** *die* pedestrian precinct

fuß-, Fuß-: **~geher** *der,* **~geherin** *die* (österr.) pedestrian; **~gelenk** *das* ▸**i S. 435** ankle; **~gymnastik** *die* foot exercises *pl.;* **~hebel** *der* foot pedal; **~hoch** **A** *Adj.*

ankle-high ‹*grass etc.*›; ankle-deep ‹*water etc.*›; **B** *adv.* ‹*rise, lie*› ankle-deep

-füßig /-fy:sɪç/ *adj.* -footed ‹*animal*›; -legged ‹*chair, stool, insect*›; -foot ‹*line*›

fuß-, Fuß-: ~kalt *Adj.* **das Zimmer ist ~kalt** the room has a cold floor; **~kettchen** *das* anklet; **~knöchel** *der* ▸ℹ **S. 435** ankle bone; **~krank** *Adj.* **~krank sein/werden** have/get bad feet; **~lage** *die* (Med.) footling presentation; **~lahm** *Adj.* footsore [and weary]; (fig.: energielos) lethargic; **~lappen** *der* foot cloth; **~leiden** *das* foot complaint; **~leiste** *die* skirting board (Brit.); baseboard (Amer.)

fusslig, *fußlig ▸**fusselig**

Füßling /'fy:slɪŋ/ *der;* **~s, ~e** foot (*of sock, stocking*)

Fuß-: ~marsch *der* march; **ein ~marsch von zwei Stunden** (fig.) two hours' steady walk; **~matte** *die* doormat; **~nagel** *der* ▸ℹ **S. 435** toenail; **~note** *die* footnote; **~pfad** *der* footpath; **~pflege** *die* foot treatment; (beruflich) chiropody; **zur ~pflege gehen** go to the chiropodist's; **~pfleger** *der,* **~pflegerin** *die* ▸ℹ **S. 113** chiropodist; **~pilz** *der,* **~pilz·erkrankung** *die* ▸ℹ **S. 439** athlete's foot; **~puder** *der* foot powder; **~punkt** *der* **1** (Math.) foot [of the perpendicular]; **2** (Astron.) nadir; **~raste** *die* foot rest; **~ring** *der* leg ring; **~rücken** *der* instep; **~sack** *der* footmuff; **~schalter** *der* foot switch; **~schaltung** *die* foot gear change control; **~schemel** *der* footstool; **~schweiß** *der* foot perspiration; **~sohle** *die* ▸ℹ **S. 435** sole [of the/one's foot]; **meine ~sohlen** the soles of my feet; **~soldat** *der* (veralt.) foot soldier; **~spitze** *die:* ▸ℹ **S. 435 auf den ~spitzen gehen/stehen** walk/stand on tiptoe; **~sprung** *der* (ins Wasser) feet-first jump; **einen ~sprung machen** jump feet first; **~spur** *die* footprint; (Fährte) line of footprints; tracks *pl.;* **~stapfen** *der* footprint; **in jmds. ~stapfen** (*Akk.*) **treten** (fig.) follow in sb.'s footsteps; **~steig** *der* **1** (veralt.) footpath; **2** (Gehsteig) pavement (Brit.); sidewalk (Amer.); **~stütze** *die* foot rest; **~tritt** *der* **1** kick; **jmdm./einer Sache einen ~tritt geben** *od.* **versetzen** (fig.) give sb./sth. a kick; **einen ~tritt bekommen** (fig.) get a kick in the teeth (coll.); **2** (Auftreten) **jmdn. an seinem ~tritt erkennen** recognize sb. by his/her step; **~truppe** *die* (Milit.) infantry; **~volk** *das* **1** (hist.) footmen *pl.;* **2** (abwertend: Untergeordnete) lower ranks *pl.;* dogsbodies *pl.* (coll.); **~wanderung** *die* ramble; **~waschung** *die* (kath. Rel.) pedilavium; foot washing; **~weg** *der* **1** (Gehweg, Bürgersteig) footpath; **2** (Gehen zu ~weg) walk; **eine Stunde/zwei Stunden ~weg** one hour's/two hours' walk; **~zehe** *die* (ugs.) toe

Fut /fʊt/ *die;* **~, ~en** (vulg.) ▸**Fotze 1**

Futon /'fu:tɔn/ *der;* **~s, ~s** futon

futsch /fʊtʃ/ *Adj.* (salopp) **~ sein** have gone for a burton (Brit. coll.)

Futter¹ /'fʊtɐ/ *das;* **~s** (Tiernahrung) feed; (für Pferde, Kühe) fodder; **dem Vieh ~ geben** feed the cattle; **gut im ~ sein** *od.* **stehen** (ugs.) be well-fed

Futter² *das;* **~s 1** (von Kleidungsstücken) lining **2** (Bauw.) casing **3** (Tech.) chuck

Futterage /fʊtə'ra:ʒə/ *die;* **~** (ugs.) grub (coll.)

Futteral /fʊtə'ra:l/ *das;* **~s, ~e** case

Futter-: ~beutel *der* nosebag; **~getreide** *das* fodder cereal; forage cereal; **~klee** *der* red clover; **~krippe** *die* manger; (fig.) **an der ~krippe sitzen** (ugs.) be in clover; **an die ~krippe kommen** (ugs.) get on the gravy train (coll.); **~mittel** *das* animal food

futtern (ugs.)
A *tr. V.* eat
B *itr. V.* feed; **futtert nur ordentlich!** tuck in; have a good feed

füttern¹ /'fʏtɐn/ *tr. V.* feed; **Vieh mit etw. ~:** feed cattle on sth.; **„bitte nicht ~!"** 'please do not feed the animals'; **etw. ~:** use sth. for feed; (für Haustiere) use sth. for food; **einen Computer mit etw. ~** (fig.) feed a computer with sth.; **jmdn. mit Bonbons/Schokolade ~:** stuff sb. with sweets/chocolate

füttern² *tr. V.* **1** (mit Futter² ausstatten) line; **mit Taft/Seide gefüttert** lined with taffeta/silk **2** (ausmauern, auskleiden) case

Futter-: ~napf *der* bowl; **~neid** *der* **1** (Verhaltensf.) jealousy [as regards food]; **2** (fig. ugs.: Neid) jealousy; envy; **~pflanze** *die* fodder plant; forage plant; **~rübe** *die* mangold; mangel-wurzel; **~silo** *der od. das* fodder silo; **~suche** *die* search for food; **auf ~suche/bei der ~suche** searching for food; **~trog** *der* feeding trough

Fütterung¹ *die;* **~, ~en** feeding

Fütterung² *die;* **~, ~en** (von Kleidungsstücken) lining

Futter·verwerter *der:* **ein guter/schlechter ~ sein** fatten up well/badly; (fig. salopp) ‹*person*› get fat easily/never get fat

Futter·verwerterin *die:* **eine gute/schlechte ~ sein** (fig. salopp) ‹*person*› get fat easily/never get fat

Futur /fu'tu:ɐ̯/ *das;* **~s, ~e** (Sprachw.) future [tense]; **das erste/zweite ~:** future/future perfect [tense]

Futurismus *der;* **~:** Futurism *no art.*

futuristisch 1 Futurist **2** (die Futurologie betreffend) futuristic

Futurologe /futuro'lo:gə/ *der;* **~n, ~n, Futurologin** *die;* **~, ~nen** futurologist

Futurologie *die;* **~:** futurology

Futurum /fu'tu:rʊm/ *das;* **~s, Futura** (veralt.) ▸**Futur**

F-Zug /'ɛf-/ *der* [long-distance] express train

f

Gg

g, G /geː/ *das;* ~, ~ ① (Buchstabe) g/G ② (Musik) [key of] G; *s. auch* **a, A**

g *Abk.* ① **= Gramm** g ② **= Groschen**

gab /gaːp/ *1. u. 3. Pers. Sg. Prät. v.* **geben**

Gabardine /ˈgabardiːn/ *der;* **~s** *od. die;* **~:** gabardine

gäbe /ˈgɛːbə/ *1. u. 3. Pers. Sg. Konjunktiv II v.* **geben;** *s. auch* **gang**

Gabe /ˈgaːbə/ *die;* **~, ~n** ① (geh.: Geschenk) gift; present; **eine ~ Gottes** a gift of God ② (Almosen, Spende) alms *pl.;* (an eine Sammlung) donation; **eine milde/fromme ~:** alms *pl.;* **um eine ~ bitten** beg for alms ③ (geh.: Begabung, Talent) gift; **die ~ haben, etw. zu tun** have the gift *or* (iron.) knack of doing sth. ④ (Med.: Verabreichung) administration ⑤ (Med.: Dosis) dose

Gabel /ˈgaːbl̩/ *die;* **~, ~n** ① (Essgerät) fork ② (Heu~, Mist~) pitchfork ③ (Telefon~) rest; cradle ④ (Fahrrad~) fork ⑤ (Ast~) fork ⑥ (Jägerspr.) fork ⑦ (Deichsel) shafts *pl.*

gabel-, Gabel-: ~bissen *der* ① piece of pickled herring; ② ▸**Appetithappen; ~bock** *der* (Zool.) pronghorn [antelope]; **~deichsel** *die* shafts *pl.;* **~förmig** **A** *Adj.* forked; **B** *adv.* **sich ~förmig teilen** fork; **~frühstück** *das* cold buffet; fork lunch

gabeln
A *refl. V.* fork; (fig.: sich teilen) divide; **ein gegabelter Ast/Stock** a forked branch/stick
B *tr. V.* fork ‹*hay, straw*›

Gabel-: ~schlüssel *der* flat spanner; **~stapler** *der* forklift truck

Gabelung *die;* **~, ~en** fork

Gabel-: ~weihe *die* (Zool.) red kite; **~zinke** *die* prong

Gaben·tisch *der* gift table (*at Christmas and on birthdays*); **ein reich gedeckter ~:** a table overflowing with gifts

Gabun /gaˈbuːn/ *das;* **~s,** (österr.) **Gabon** /gaˈboːn/ *(das);* **~s** Gabon

gack, gack /ˈgak ˈgak/ *Interj.* cluck, cluck

gackern /ˈgakɐn/ *itr. V.* ① cluck ② (ugs.: kichern, lachen) cackle

Gaffel /ˈgafl̩/ *die;* **~, ~n** (Seemannsspr.) gaff

Gaffel-: ~schoner *der* (Seemannsspr.) fore-and-aft schooner; **~segel** *das* (Seemannsspr.) gaff sail

gaffen /ˈgafn̩/ *itr. V.* (abwertend) gape; gawp (coll.)

Gaffer *der;* **~s, ~, Gafferin** *die;* **~, ~nen** gaper; starer

Gag /gɛk/ *der;* **~s, ~s** ① (Theater, Film) gag ② (Besonderheit) gimmick

Gagat /gaˈgaːt/ *der;* **~[e]s, ~e** jet

Gage /ˈgaːʒə/ *die;* **~, ~n** salary; (für einzelnen Auftritt) fee

gähnen /ˈgɛːnən/ *itr. V.* ① yawn; **im Saal herrschte ~de Leere** the hall was totally empty ② (geh.: sich auftun) ‹*chasm, abyss*› yawn; ‹*hole*› gape; **ein ~der Abgrund** a yawning abyss

Gala /ˈgaːla, *auch* ˈgala/ *die;* **~** ① (Festkleidung) formal dress; gala dress; **sich in ~ werfen** (ugs. scherzh.) put on one's best bib and tucker (coll.) ② (~vorstellung) gala

Gala-: ~abend *der* ▸**~vorstellung; ~diner** *das* formal dinner; banquet; **~empfang** *der* gala reception; formal reception

galaktisch /gaˈlaktɪʃ/ *Adj.* galactic; **~er Nebel** [galactic] nebula

Galaktose /galakˈtoːzə/ *die;* **~, ~n** (Biol.) galactose

Galan /gaˈlaːn/ *der;* **~s, ~e** (ugs. abwertend) lover boy (coll. derog.)

galant /gaˈlant/
A *Adj.* ① (veralt.) gallant ② (amourös) amorous ‹*adventure*›; **~e Dichtung** galant poetry (*of the late 17th century*)
B *adv.* gallantly

Galanterie /galantəˈriː/ *die;* **~, ~n** (veralt.) gallantry

Galanterie·waren *Pl.* (veralt.) fashion accessories *pl.*

Gala-: ~uniform *die* full-dress uniform; **~vorstellung** *die* gala performance

Galaxie /galaˈksiː/ *die;* **~, ~n** (Astron.) galaxy

Galaxis /gaˈlaksɪs/ *die;* **~** (Astron.) Galaxy

Gäle /ˈgɛːlə/ *der;* **~n, ~n** Gael

Galeere /gaˈleːrə/ *die;* **~, ~n** galley

Galeeren-: ~sklave *der* galley slave; **~sträfling** *der* galley slave

Galeone /galeˈoːnə/ *die;* **~, ~n** (hist.) galleon

Galerie /galəˈriː/ *die;* **~, ~n** ① gallery ② (scherzh.: beträchtliche Anzahl) **eine [ganze] ~ von etw.** a [whole] array of sth. ③ (bes. österr., schweiz.: Tunnel) tunnel ④ (Teppich) runner

Galerist /galəˈrɪst/ *der;* **~en, ~en, Galeristin** *die;* **~, ~nen** gallery owner

Galgen /ˈgalgn̩/ *der* ① gallows *sing.;* gibbet; **jmdn. zum [Tode am] ~ verurteilen** condemn sb. to [death on] the gallows; **jmdn. an den ~ bringen** (ugs.) bring sb. to the gallows; **am ~ enden** end up on the gallows ② (Mikrofon~) boom

Galgen-: ~frist *die* reprieve; **~humor** *der* gallows humour; **~strick** *der,* **~vogel** *der* (ugs. abwertend) rogue

Galicien /gaˈliːtsi̯ən/ *(das);* **~s** Galicia (in Spain)

Galiläa /galiˈlɛːa/ *(das);* **~s** Galilee

Galiläer /galiˈlɛːɐ/ *(der);* **~s, ~, Galiläerin** *die;* **~, ~nen** Galilean

Galilei /galiˈleːi/ *(der)* Galileo

Gälin *die;* **~, ~nen** ▸**Gäle**

Galions·figur /gaˈli̯oːns-/ *die* figurehead

gälisch /ˈgɛːlɪʃ/ *Adj.* ▸❶ **S. 670** Gaelic

Galizien /gaˈliːtsi̯ən/ *(das);* **~s** Galicia (in E. Europe)

Gall·apfel *der* oak apple; gall

Galle[1] /ˈgalə/ *die;* **~, ~n** ① ▸❶ **S. 435** (~nblase) gall [bladder] ② (Sekret) (bei Tieren) gall; (bei Menschen) bile; **bitter wie ~:** extremely bitter; **mir lief die ~ über** *od.* **kam die ~ hoch** (fig.) my blood boiled; **seine ~ verspritzen** (fig.) give bitter vent to one's feelings

Galle[2] *die;* **~, ~n** (Bot.) gall

galle·bitter *Adj.* extremely bitter

Gallen-: ~blase *die* ▸❶ **S. 435** gall bladder; **~gang** *der* bile duct; **~kolik** *die* ▸❶ **S. 439** biliary colic; **~leiden** *das* ▸❶ **S. 439** gall-bladder complaint; **~stein** *der* ▸❶ **S. 439** gallstone; **~wege** *Pl.* biliary tract *sing.;* bile ducts

Gallert /ˈgalɐt/ *das;* **~[e]s** jelly

gallert·artig *Adj.* jelly-like

Gallerte /gaˈlɛrtə/ *die;* **~, ~n** ▸**Gallert**

Gallien /ˈgali̯ən/ *(das);* **~s** Gaul

Gallier /ˈgali̯ɐ/ *der;* **~s, ~, Gallierin** *die;* **~, ~nen** Gaul

gallig *Adj.* ① (bitter) **einen ~en Geschmack haben, ~ schmecken** taste of bile ② (verbittert) caustic ‹*remark, humour, person*›

Gallions·figur *die* ▸**Galionsfigur**

gallisch *Adj.* Gallic

Gallium /ˈgali̯ʊm/ *das;* **~s** (Chemie) gallium

Gallizismus /galiˈtsɪsmʊs/ *der;* **~, Gallizismen** Gallicism

Gallone /gaˈloːnə/ *die;* **~, ~n** gallon

Gall-: ~seife *die* gall soap; **~wespe** *die* (Zool.) gall wasp

Galopp /gaˈlɔp/ *der;* **~s, ~s** *od.* **~e** ① (Gangart) gallop; **im ~:** at a gallop; **in ~ fallen** break into a gallop; **in vollem** *od.* **gestrecktem ~:** at full gallop; **etw. im ~ machen** (fig. ugs.) race through sth. ② (Tanz) galop

Galopp·bahn *die* (Pferdesport) racetrack; racecourse

Galopper *der;* **~s, ~** (Pferd) racehorse; (Reiter) jockey

Galopperin *die;* **~, ~nen** jockey

galoppieren *itr. V.; meist mit sein* gallop; **die ~de Schwindsucht/Inflation** galloping consumption/inflation

Galopp-: ~rennbahn *die* ▸**Galoppbahn; ~rennen** *das* (Pferdesport) race

Galosche /gaˈlɔʃə/ *die;* **~, ~n** galosh

galt /galt/ *1. u. 3. Pers. Sg. Prät. v.* **gelten**

galvanisch /galˈvaːnɪʃ/ *Adj.* galvanic

Galvaniseur /galvaniˈzøːɐ̯/ *der;* **~s, ~e, Galvaniseurin** *die;* **~, ~nen** electroplater

galvanisieren *tr. V.* electroplate

Galvano /galˈvaːno/ *das;* **~s, ~s** (graf. Technik) electro[type]

Galvano-: ~meter *das* (Technik) galvanometer; **~plastik** *die* ① electroforming; ② (Druckw.) electrotyping; **~skop** *das;* **~~s, ~~e** (Technik) galvanoscope

Gamasche /gaˈmaʃə/ *die;* **~, ~n** gaiter; (bis zum Knöchel reichend) spat

Gamaschen·hose *die* [pair of] leggings *pl.*

Gambe /ˈgambə/ *die;* **~, ~n** (Musik) viola da gamba

Gambia /ˈgambi̯a/ *(das);* **~s** the Gambia

Gambit /gamˈbɪt/ *das;* **~s, ~s** (Schach) gambit

Gamelan /ˈgaːməlan/ *das;* **~s, ~s, Gamelang** /ˈgaːməlaŋ/ *das;* **~s, ~s** (Musik) gamelan

Gamet /gaˈmeːt/ *der;* **~en, ~en** (Biol.) gamete

Gamma /ˈgama/ *das;* **~[s], ~s** gamma

Gamma-: ~funktion *die* (Math.) gamma function; **~strahlen** *Pl.* (Physik, Med.) gamma rays

Gammel /ˈgaml̩/ *der;* **~s** (ugs.) junk (coll.)

Gammelei *die;* **~** (ugs.) drifting around; bumming around (Amer. coll.)

gammelig /ˈgam(ə)lɪç/ *Adj.* (ugs.) ① (ungenießbar) bad; rotten; **der Fisch/das Fleisch/der Käse ist ~:** the fish/meat/cheese has gone off ② (unordentlich) scruffy; **~ aussehen/herumlaufen** look scruffy/go round looking scruffy

Gammel-Look *der* scruffy *or* untidy look; **sie erschien im ~:** she appeared dressed as a dropout (coll.)

gammeln /ˈgamḷn/ *itr. V.* 1 (ugs.) (verderben) go bad; go off 2 (nichts tun) loaf around; bum around (Amer. coll.)

Gammler /ˈgamlɐ/ *der;* **~s, ~, Gammlerin** *die;* **~, ~nen** (ugs.) dropout (coll.)

gammlig ▸**gammelig**

Gams /gams/ *die;* **~, ~en** (Jägerspr., südd.) ▸**Gämse**

Gams·bart, Gäms·bart /ˈgɛms-/ *der: tuft of chamois hair used as a hat decoration*

Gäms·bock *der* chamois buck

Gämse /ˈgɛmzə/ *die:* **~, ~n** chamois

gang /gaŋ/ *in* **~ und gäbe sein** be quite usual; be the usual *or* accepted thing

Gang[1] /gaŋ/ *der;* **~[e]s, Gänge** /ˈgɛŋə/ 1 (Gehweise) walk; gait; **jmdn. am ~ erkennen** recognise sb. by the way he/she walks; **gemessenen ~es einherschreiten** (geh.) walk with a measured step 2 (zu einem Ort) **einen ~ in die Stadt machen** go to town; **sein erster ~ führte ihn in die Kneipe** the first place he went to was the pub; **jmdn. auf seinem letzten ~ begleiten** (fig. geh.) accompany sb. to his/her last *or* final resting place; **einen schweren ~ tun** *od.* **gehen [müssen]** (fig.) [have to] do a difficult thing 3 (Besorgung) **ich habe noch einige Gänge zu machen** I still have some errands to do; **jmdm. einen ~ abnehmen** do an errand for sb. 4 (Bewegung) running; **die Maschine hatte einen ruhigen ~:** the machine ran quietly; **etw. in ~ bringen** *od.* **setzen** get sth. going; **etw. in ~ halten** keep sth. going; **in ~ sein** be going; **die Maschine ist in ~:** the machine is running; **in ~ kommen** get going; get off the ground 5 (Verlauf) course; **der ~ der Ereignisse/Verhandlungen** the course of events/negotiations; **seinen [gewohnten] ~ gehen** go on as usual; **im ~[e] sein** be in progress; **gegen ihn ist etwas im ~[e]** (ugs.) moves are being made against him 6 (Technik) gear; **den ersten ~ einlegen** engage first gear; **in den ersten ~ [zurück]schalten** change [down] into first gear; **einen ~ zulegen** (fig. ugs.) get a move on (coll.); **einen ~ zurückschalten** (fig. ugs.) take things a bit easier 7 (Flur) (in Zügen, Gebäuden usw.) corridor; (Verbindungs~) passage[way]; (im Theater, Kino, Flugzeug) aisle; **auf dem ~:** in the corridor/hall[way] 8 (unterirdisch) tunnel; passage[way]; (im Bergwerk) gallery; (eines Tierbaus) tunnel; (von Insekten) gallery; tunnel 9 (Kochk.) course 10 (Fechten) bout; **einen ~ ausfechten** *od.* **austragen** fight a bout 11 (Geol.) vein; seam 12 (Technik) ▸**Gewinde~**

Gang[2] /gɛŋ/ *die;* **~, ~s** (Bande) gang

Gang·art *die* walk; way of walking; gait; (eines Pferdes) gait; **eine schnellere ~ anschlagen** step up the pace; (Pferdesport) increase to a faster pace *or* gait; **eine langsamere ~ einlegen** (fig.) take things more easily

gangbar *Adj.* passable; **nicht ~:** impassable; **jmdm. einen ~en Weg zeigen** (fig.) show sb. a feasible *or* practicable way

Gängel·band /ˈgɛŋəl-/ *das: in* **jmdn. am ~ führen** keep sb. in leading reins; **am ~ gehen** be in leading reins

Gängelei *die;* **~, ~en** (ugs.) spoon-feeding; **sie war seine ~ leid** she was tired of being treated like a child by him

gängeln /ˈgɛŋḷn/ *tr. V.* (ugs.) **jmdn. ~:** boss sb. around; tell sb. what to do

gang·genau *Adj.* accurate

Gang·genauigkeit *die* accuracy

gängig /ˈgɛŋɪç/ *Adj.* 1 (üblich) common; (aktuell) current 2 (leicht verkäuflich) popular; in demand *postpos.* 3 (im Umlauf) current 4 (beweglich) **[wieder] ~ machen** get ‹*mechanism*› working [again]; loosen [again] ‹*lock, screw, etc.*›

Ganglien·zelle /ˈgaŋ(g)liən-/ *die* (Med.) ganglion cell

Ganglion /ˈgaŋ(g)liɔn/ *das;* **~s, Ganglien** /ˈgaŋ(g)liən/ (Med.) ganglion

Gangrän /gaŋˈgrɛːn/ *die;* **~, ~en** *od. das;* **~s, ~e** ▸ⓘ **S. 439** (Med.) gangrene

Gang·schaltung *die* (Technik) gear system; (Art) gear change; **hat dein Auto Automatik oder ~?** has your car got an automatic or manual gearbox?; **ein Fahrrad mit ~:** a bicycle with gears

Gangsta·rap /ˈgɛŋsta-/ *der* gangsta rap

Gangster /ˈgɛŋstɐ/ *der;* **~s, ~** (abwertend) gangster

Gangster-: ~bande *die* gang [of criminals]; **~boss,** ***~boß** *der* (ugs.) gang boss; **~braut** *die* gangster's moll (coll.); **~methoden** *Pl.* (abwertend) gangster tactics; **~stück** *das* piece of villainy

Gangstertum *das;* **~s** gangsterism

Gangway /ˈgɛŋweɪ/ *die;* **~, ~s** gangway

Ganove /gaˈnoːvə/ *der;* **~n, ~n** (ugs. abwertend) crook (coll.)

Gans /gans/ *die;* **~, Gänse** /ˈgɛnzə/ 1 goose 2 (Braten) [roast] goose 3 (abwertend: weibliche Person) **eine [dumme/alberne/blöde] ~:** a silly goose

Gänschen /ˈgɛnsçən/ *das;* **~s, ~** 1 (junge Gans) gosling 2 (kleine Gans, naives Mädchen) little goose

Gänse-: ~blümchen *das* daisy; **~braten** *der* roast goose; **~brust** *die* (Kochk.) breast of goose; **~ei** *das* goose egg; **~feder** *die* goose feather; goose quill; **~fett** *das* goose fat; **~füßchen** *das* (ugs.) ▸**Anführungszeichen**; **~geier** *der* griffon vulture; **~haut** *die* (fig.) gooseflesh; goose pimples *pl.*; **eine ~haut bekommen** *od.* **kriegen** get gooseflesh *or* goose pimples; **ihm läuft eine ~haut über den Rücken** a cold shiver runs down his spine; **~junge** *das* gosling; **~kiel** *der* goose quill; **~klein** *das;* **~s** (Kochk.) braised trimmings of goose; gänseklein; **~leber** *die* goose liver; **~leber·pastete** *die* pâté de foie gras; **~marsch** *der: in* **im ~marsch** in single *or* Indian file

Ganser /ˈganzɐ/ *der;* **~s, ~** (südd., österr.), **Gänserich** /ˈgɛnzərɪç/ *der;* **~s, ~e** gander

Gänse-: ~schmalz *das* goose dripping; **~wein** *der* (ugs. scherzh.) water; Adam's ale *or* wine (coll. joc.)

Ganter /ˈgantɐ/ *der;* **~s, ~** (nordd.) ▸**Gänserich**

ganz /gants/

A *Adj.* 1 (gesamt) whole; entire; **den ~en Tag/das ~e Jahr** all day/year; **die ~e Welt/Stadt** the whole world/town; **~ Europa/Afrika** the whole of Europe/Africa; **wir fuhren durch ~ Frankreich** we travelled all over France; **diese Arbeit fordert den ~en Mann** this work requires all one's efforts; **~e Arbeit leisten** do a complete *or* proper job; **die ~e Geschichte** *od.* **Sache** (ugs.) the whole story *or* business 2 (ugs.: alle) **die ~en Kinder/Leute/Gläser** *usw.* all the children/people/glasses *etc.*; **die ~e Stadt/Straße** everybody in the town/street 3 ▸ⓘ **S. 826** (vollständig) whole; **~e Zahlen** whole numbers; **eine ~e Note** (Musik) a semibreve (Brit.); a whole note (Amer.); **im Ganzen sechs Tage/drei Jahre** six days/three years in all *or* altogether; **im Ganzen ist seine Leistung gut** on the whole *or* all in all his performance is good; **der ~e Shakespeare** (ugs.) the whole of Shakespeare (coll.) 4 (ugs.: ziemlich [viel]) **eine ~e Menge/ein ~er Haufen** quite a lot/quite a pile; **~e Nächte/Tage** whole nights/days 5 (ugs.: unversehrt) intact; **etw. wieder ~ machen** mend sth. 6 (ugs.: nur) all of; **~e 14 Jahre alt/10 Euro** all of fourteen [years old]/ten euros; **mit ~en drei Mann kann ich die Arbeit unmöglich schaffen** with only three men I can't possibly get the work done 7 (richtig) **ein ~er Mann** a real man; *s. auch* **groß A 11; Herz 2**

B *adv.* 1 (vollkommen) quite; **etw. ~ Blödes sagen** say sth. really stupid; **das ist mir ~ egal** it's all the same to me; I don't care; **etw. ~ vergessen** completely *or* quite forget sth.; **du bist ja ~ nass!** you're all wet!; **etwas ~ anderes** something quite different; **etw. ~ allein tun** *od.* **machen** do sth. entirely on one's own; **nicht ~:** not quite; **~ deiner Meinung!** I quite agree [with you]; **~ besonders** especially; **er hat sich ~ besonders viel Mühe gegeben** he took particular trouble; **~ wie Sie wollen** just as you like; **sie ist ~ die Mutter/der Vater** she's the image of *or* just like her mother/father; **sie ist ~ Dame** she is quite the lady; **~ und gar** totally; utterly; **es ist ~ und gar nicht wahr** it is utterly *or* totally untrue; **etw. ~ oder gar nicht machen** do sth. properly or not at all; **ein Buch ~ lesen** read a book from cover to cover *or* all the way through 2 (sehr, ziemlich) quite; **es ist mir ~ recht** it's quite all right with me; **~ gut/nett** quite good/nice; *s. auch* **Ohr**

Ganze *das; adj. Dekl.* 1 (Einheit) whole; **das ~ im Auge behalten** keep looking at the whole; **etw. als ~s betrachten** see sth. as a whole 2 (alles) **das ~:** the whole thing; **das ~ gefällt mir gar nicht** I don't like anything about it; **aufs ~ gehen** (ugs.) go the whole hog (coll.); **es geht ums ~:** everything's at stake

Gänze /ˈgɛntsə/ *in* **in seiner/ihrer ~** (geh.) in its/their entirety; **zur ~** (bes. österr.) entirely; completely

Ganzheit *die;* **~, ~en** entirety; (Einheit) unity; **etw. in seiner ~ erfassen** grasp sth. in its entirety

ganzheitlich *Adj.* (Päd.) integrated

Ganzheits-: ~medizin *die* holistic medicine; **~methode** *die* (Päd.) 'look and say' method; **~psychologie** *die* 'Ganzheit' psychology; holism; **~unterricht** *der* (Päd.) integrated teaching

ganz·jährig

A *Adj.* **die ~e Trockenperiode** the dry period lasting all year

B *adv.* **~ geöffnet** open throughout the year *or* all the year round

Ganz·leder *das* (Buchw.) **in ~ [gebunden]** bound in [full] leather

Ganzleder·band *der* (Buchw.) [full-]leather-bound volume

ganz·leinen *Adj.* 1 (Textilw.) pure linen 2 (Buchw.) **ein ~er Einband** a cloth binding

Ganzleinen·band *der* (Buchw.) cloth-bound book

gänzlich /ˈgɛntslɪç/

A *Adv.* completely; entirely; **~ unangebracht** quite inappropriate *or* out of place

B *Adj.* complete; total

Ganz·massage *die* whole-body massage

ganz-, Ganz-: ~sache *die* (Postw., Philat.) entire; **~seitig A** *Adj.* whole-page; **B** *adv.* **~seitig inserieren** (einmal) take a whole-page advertisement; (auf Dauer) use whole-page advertising; **~tägig A** *Adj.* all-day; **eine ~tägige Arbeit** a full-time job; **B** *adv.* all day

ganz·tags *Adv.* **~ arbeiten** work full-time

Ganztags-: ~beschäftigung *die* full-time job; **~schule** *die* all-day school; (System) all-day schooling *no art.*

Ganz·wort·methode *die* (Päd.) 'look and say' method

GAP *Abk.* (EU) **= gemeinsame Agrarpolitik** CAP

gar[1] /gaːɐ̯/ *Adj.* 1 cooked; done *pred.*; **etw. ist ~ [gekocht]/erst halb ~:** sth. is cooked *or* done/only half-cooked *or* half-done; **etw. ~ kochen** cook sth. [until it is done] 2 (Landw.) ready for cultivation *postpos.*; **der Kompost ist ~:** the compost is ready for use

gar[2] *Partikel* 1 (überhaupt) **~ nicht [wahr]** not [true] at all; **sie konnte ~ nicht anders handeln** there was nothing else at all that she could do; **~ nicht so übel** not bad at all; **das habe ich ~ nicht gewusst** I had no idea that that was so; **~ nichts** nothing at all *or* whatsoever; **ich habe ~ keinen Hunger** I'm not at all *or* not in the least hungry; **~ niemand** *od.* **keiner** nobody at all *or* whatsoever; **~ keines** not a single one; **~ kein Geld** no money at all 2 (südd., österr., schweiz.: verstärkend) **~ zu** only too; **es waren ~ zu viele Leute da** there were just too many people there; **er wäre ~ zu gern gekommen** he would so much have liked to come; **~ so** so very; **sei doch nicht ~ so stur!** don't be so [damned] stubborn 3 (geh.: so~) even; **die Zeitungen setzten sich ~ für den Attentäter ein** the papers even came out in support of the assassin; **ich glaube ~, sie weint** I do believe she's crying 4 (geh. veralt.: erst) **er ist unangenehm genug,**

g

und ~ sein Bruder! he's unpleasant enough, and as for his brother! [5] (veralt.: sehr) very; **du bist ~ früh gekommen** you have indeed come early; **~ mancher** many a one *or* person; *s. auch* **ganz B 1**

Garage /ga'ra:ʒə/ *die;* **~, ~n** garage

Garagen-: ~einfahrt *die* garage entrance; **~firma** *die* garage start-up; **~wagen** *der* garaged car

garagieren *tr. V.* (österr., schweiz.) park

Garant /ga'rant/ *der;* **~en, ~en** guarantor

Garantie /garan'ti:/ *die;* **~, ~n** [1] (Gewähr) guarantee; **eine ~ für etw.** a guarantee of sth.; **für etw. keine ~ übernehmen** not guarantee sth.; **wir haben unter ~ nicht genug Geld** (ugs.) we're dead certain not to have enough money (coll.) [2] (Kaufmannsspr.) guarantee; warranty; **die ~ auf** *od.* **für das Auto ist abgelaufen** the guarantee on the car has run out; **eine ~ auf etw.** (*Akk.*) **geben** guarantee sth.; **für** *od.* **auf etw.** (*Akk.*) **ein Jahr ~ erhalten** get a one year guarantee on sth. [3] (Sicherheit) guarantee; surety

Garantie-: ~anspruch *der* right to claim under [the] guarantee; **~frist** *die* guarantee period; **~lohn** *der* guaranteed minimum wage

garantieren
[A] *tr. V.* guarantee; **jmdm. etw. ~:** guarantee sb. sth.
[B] *itr. V.* **für etw. ~:** guarantee sth.; **ich kann für den Hund nicht ~:** I can't say for sure what the dog will do

garantiert *Adv.* (ugs.) **wir kommen ~ zu spät** we're dead certain to arrive late (coll.)

Garantie·schein *der* guarantee [certificate]

Garantin *die;* **~, ~nen** ▸ **Garant**

Garaus /'ga:ɐ̯laus/ *in* **jmdm. den ~ machen** do sb. in (coll.); **dem Ungeziefer/Unkraut den ~ machen** get rid of the vermin/weeds; **einem Gerücht den ~ machen** scotch a rumour

Garbe[1] /'garbə/ *die;* **~, ~n** [1] (Getreide~) sheaf [2] (Geschoss~) burst of fire; **eine ~ abfeuern** fire a burst

Garbe[2] *die;* **~, ~n** ▸ **Schafgarbe**

Gär·bottich *der* fermenter

Garçonnière /garsõ'ni̯ɛ:r/ *die;* **~, ~n** (österr.) bedsitter

Garde /'gardə/ *die;* **~, ~n** [1] (Leib~) guard [2] (Gruppe) team; **von der alten ~ sein** (ugs.) be one of the old guard [3] (Milit.: Elitetruppe) the Guards *pl.*; **bei der ~:** in the Guards

Garde·maß *das* [1] (hist.) *minimum height for belonging to the Prussian Guards* [2] (scherzh.) **~ haben** be as tall as a tree; **mit deinem ~ solltest du Basketballspieler werden** with your height you ought to be a basketball player

Gardenie /gar'de:ni̯ə/ *die;* **~, ~n** (Bot.) gardenia

Garde·regiment *das* Guards regiment

Garderobe /gardə'ro:bə/ *die;* **~, ~n** [1] (Oberbekleidung) wardrobe; clothes *pl.*; **für diesen Anlass fehlt ihm die passende ~:** he hasn't got suitable clothes for this occasion; **für ~ wird nicht gehaftet!** clothes are left at the owner's risk [2] (Flur~) coat rack; **etw. an die ~ hängen** hang sth. up on the coat rack [3] (Raum) clothes cupboard *or* (Amer.) closet [4] (im Theater o. Ä.) cloakroom; checkroom (Amer.); **etw. an der ~ abgeben** hand sth. in at the cloakroom [5] (Ankleideraum) dressing room

Garderoben-: ~frau *die* ▸❶ **S. 113** cloakroom *or* (Amer.) checkroom attendant; **~marke** *die* cloakroom *or* (Amer.) checkroom ticket; **~spiegel** *der* hall mirror; **~ständer** *der* coat stand

Garderobier /gardəro'bi̯e:/ *der;* **~s, ~s** ▸❶ **S. 113** dresser

Garderobiere /gardəro'bi̯e:rə/ *die;* **~, ~n** ▸❶ **S. 113** [1] dresser [2] (veralt.) ▸ **Garderobenfrau**

Gardine /gar'di:nə/ *die;* **~, ~n** [1] net curtain [2] (landsch., veralt.) curtain; *s. auch* **schwedisch**

Gardinen-: ~leiste *die* curtain rail; **~predigt** *die* (ugs.) telling-off (coll.); (einer Ehefrau zu ihrem Mann) curtain lecture; **jmdm. eine ~predigt halten** give sb. a [good] telling-off (coll.)/a curtain lecture; **~ring** *der* curtain ring; **~röllchen** *das* curtain runner; **~stange** *die* curtain rail; **~stoff** *der* curtain material

Gardist *der;* **~en, ~en** guardsman

garen /'ga:rən/ *tr., itr. V.* cook; **Fleisch/Gemüse ~ [lassen]** cook meat/vegetables

gären /'gɛ:rən/
[A] *regelm.* (*auch unr.*) *itr. V.* ferment; (fig.) seethe; **es gärt in ihm/der Masse** he/the crowd is seething [with anger]/afire [with hatred/passion]
[B] *regelm.* (*auch unr.*) *tr. V.* ferment ‹*beer, tobacco*›

Gär·futter *das* (Landw.) silage *no pl.*

gar-, Gar-: ~gekocht ▸ **gar**[1] **1**; **~küche** *die* snackbar

Gär·mittel *das* ferment; fermenting agent

Garn /garn/ *das;* **~[e]s, ~e** [1] (Faden) thread; (zum Weben, Stricken) yarn; (Näh~) cotton [2] (Seew.) yarn [3] (Seemannsspr.: Geschichte) *in* **[s]ein ~ spinnen** spin a yarn [4] (Jagdw., Fischereiw.: Netz) net; **jmdm. ins ~ gehen** (fig.) fall *or* walk into sb.'s trap

Garnele /gar'ne:lə/ *die;* **~, ~n** shrimp

Gar·nichts *der od. das;* **~, ~e** (abwertend) [absolute] nonentity

garnieren /gar'ni:rən/ *tr. V.* [1] (schmücken) decorate (*mit* with) [2] (Gastr.) garnish

Garnierung *die;* **~, ~en** [1] garnish [2] (Vorgang) garnishing

Garnison /garni'zo:n/ *die;* **~, ~en** garrison

Garnison·stadt *die* garrison town

Garnitur /garni'tu:ɐ̯/ *die;* **~, ~en** [1] (zusammengehörige Stücke) set; (Wäsche) set of [matching] underwear; (Schreibtisch~) desk set; (Möbel) suite; **eine zwei-/dreiteilige ~:** a two-piece/three-piece suite [2] (ugs.) **die erste/zweite ~:** the first/second-rate people *pl.*; **zur ersten/zweiten ~ gehören, erste/zweite ~ sein** be first-/second-rate [3] (Gastr.) garnishing; garniture

Garn-: ~knäuel *das od. der* ball of thread; (zum Weben) ball of yarn; **~rolle** *die* reel; bobbin; (von Nähgarn) cotton reel; **~spule** *die* spool

Gär·prozess, ***Gär·prozeß** *der* ▸ **Gärungsprozess**

Garrotte /ga'rɔtə/ *die;* **~, ~n** garrotte

garstig /'garstɪç/ *Adj.* [1] (boshaft) nasty (**zu** to); bad ‹*behaviour*›; nasty, naughty, (coll.) horrid ‹*child*› [2] (abscheulich) horrible; nasty

Garstigkeit *die;* **~, ~en** [1] nastiness; (eines Kindes) naughtiness, (coll.) horridness [2] (Handlung) piece of nastiness; **~en** nastiness *sing.*; horridness *sing.* (coll.) [3] (Äußerung) nasty *or* (coll.) horrid remark

Gärtchen /'gɛrtçən/ *das;* **~s, ~:** little garden

Garten /'gartn̩/ *der;* **~s, Gärten** /'gɛrtn̩/ garden; **ein [kleines] Stück ~:** a [small] bit of garden; **der ~ Eden** the Garden of Eden; **quer durch den ~** (ugs.: verschiedene Sorten Gemüse) all sorts of different vegetables; (oft spöttisch: in bunter Vielfalt) all sorts; a real mixture; *s. auch* **botanisch**; **zoologisch**

Garten-: ~abfall *der* garden waste; **~anlage** *die* garden; (öffentlich) park; gardens *pl.*; **~arbeit** *die* gardening; **~architekt** *der,* **~architektin** *die* landscape gardener; **~bank** *die; Pl.* **~bänke** garden seat

Garten·bau *der* horticulture

Gartenbau-: ~betrieb *der* market garden; **~ingenieur** *der,* **~ingenieurin** *die* horticulturist

Garten-: ~blume *die* garden flower; **~erde** *die* garden mould; **~fest** *das* garden party; **~freund** *der,* **~freundin** *die* amateur gardener; **~gerät** *das* garden tool; **~gestaltung** *die* landscaping; **~haus** *das* [1] (Haus im Garten) summerhouse; garden house; [2] (Hinterhaus) *dwelling situated at or forming the rear of a house and having its own garden;* **wir wohnen in der Goethestr. 10, im ~haus** we live at 10, Goethestrasse, at the back; **~hecke** *die* garden hedge; **~land** *das* gardening land; **~laube** *die* summerhouse; garden house; **~lokal** *das* beer garden; (Restaurant) open-air café; **~mauer** *die* garden wall; **~möbel** *das* piece of garden furniture; **teure ~möbel** expensive garden furniture *sing.*; **~party** *die* ▸ **~fest**; **~schau** *die* horticultural show; **~schirm** *der* sunshade; **~schlauch** *der* garden hose; **~stadt** *die* garden city; **~stuhl** *der* garden chair; **~wirtschaft** *die* ▸ **~lokal**; **~zaun** *der* garden fence; **~zwerg** *der* [1] garden gnome; [2] (salopp abwertend) little runt

Gärtner /'gɛrtnɐ/ *der;* **~s, ~** ▸❶ **S. 113** gardener

Gärtnerei *die;* **~, ~en** [1] nursery [2] (Gartenarbeit) gardening

Gärtnerin *die;* **~, ~nen** ▸❶ **S. 113** gardener

Gärtnerin·art *die: in* **Schweinefleisch** *usw.* **nach ~** (Gastr.) pork *etc.* jardinière

gärtnerisch
[A] *Adj.* **der ~e Pflanzenbau** the growing of garden plants; **~er Betrieb** nursery
[B] *adv.* **sich gern ~ betätigen** enjoy gardening

Gärung *die;* **~, ~en** [1] fermentation; **etw. zur ~ ansetzen** start sth. fermenting [2] (Erregung) ferment; **in ~ sein** be in [a state of] ferment

Gärungs-: ~mittel *das* ▸ **Gärmittel**; **~prozess,** ***~prozeß** *der* fermentation process

Gar·zeit *die* (Kochk.) cooking time

Gas /ga:s/ *das;* **~es, ~e** [1] gas; **jmdn. mit ~ vergiften** gas sb.; **mit ~ heizen** have gas heating; **mit ~ kochen** cook with gas; use gas for cooking; **jmdm. das ~ abdrehen** (fig. salopp) force sb. out of business; **etw. aufs ~ stellen** put sth. on the cooker *or* the gas [2] (Treibstoff) petrol (Brit.); gasoline (Amer.); gas (Amer. coll.); **ohne ~ den Berg hinunterfahren** drive down the mountain without using any petrol *etc.*; **~ wegnehmen** decelerate; take one's foot off the accelerator; **~ geben** accelerate; put one's foot down (coll.); (ugs. fig.: schneller gehen) step on it (coll.) [3] (ugs.: ~pedal) accelerator; gas pedal (Amer.); **aufs ~ treten** put one's foot down (coll.); **vom ~ gehen** take one's foot off the accelerator

gas-, Gas-: ~anschluss, ***~anschluß** *der* gas connection; (~hahn) gas tap; **~anstalt** *die* ▸ **~werk**; **~anzünder** *der* gas lighter; **~austausch** *der* (Biol., Med.) gaseous exchange; **~automat** *der* coin-in-the-slot gas meter; **~bade·ofen** *der* gas water heater; **~behälter** *der* gasholder; gasometer; **~beheizt** *Adj.* gas-heated; **ein ~beheizter Backofen** a gas oven; **~beleuchtung** *die* gas lighting; **~beton** *der* (Bauw.) cellular *or* aerated concrete; **~bombe** *die* gas bomb; **~brand** *der* (Med.) gas gangrene; **~brenner** *der* gas burner; **~dicht** *Adj.* gas-tight; **~druck** *der; Pl.* **~drücke** gas pressure; **~entladung** *die* (Physik) gas discharge; **~entwicklung** *die* formation of gas; **~explosion** *die* gas explosion; **~fabrik** *die* gasworks *sing.*; **~feuerung** *die* gas firing; **~feuerzeug** *das* gas lighter; **~flamme** *die* gas flame; **~flasche** *die* gas cylinder; (für einen Herd, Ofen) gas bottle; gas container; **~förmig** *Adj.* gaseous; **~fuß** *der* (ugs.) **einen nervösen ~fuß haben** rev up impatiently at the lights (coll.); **~gemisch** *das* mixture of gases; **~gerät** *das* gas appliance; **~geruch** *der* smell of gas; **~hahn** *der; Pl.* **~hähne,** (fachspr.) **~~en** gas tap; **den ~hahn aufdrehen** (ugs. verhüll.) end it all (coll. euphem.); **jmdm. den ~hahn abdrehen** (salopp) force sb. out of business; **~hebel** *der* accelerator pedal; gas pedal (Amer.); **~heizung** *die* gas heating; **~herd** *der* gas cooker; **~hülle** *die* atmosphere; **~kammer** *die* gas chamber; **~kessel** *der* gasholder; gasometer; **~kocher** *der* camping stove; **~koks** *der* gas coke; **~krieg** *der* gas war; (Kriegführung) gas warfare; **~lampe**, **~laterne** *die* gas lamp; **~leitung** *die* gas pipe; (Hauptrohr) gas main; **~-Luft-Gemisch** *das* (Kfz-W.) fuel-and-air mixture; **~mann** *der* (ugs.) gas man;

~maske *die* gas mask; **~ofen** *der* gas heater

Gasolin /gazo'li:n/ *das;* **~s** gasoline

Gasometer /gazo'me:tɐ/ *der* (veralt.) gasometer; gasholder

GASP *Abk.* (EU) **= gemeinsame Außen- und Sicherheitspolitik** CFSP

Gas-: ~pedal *das* accelerator [pedal]; gas pedal (Amer.); **~pistole** *die* pistol that fires gas cartridges; **~rechnung** *die* gas bill; **~rohr** *das* gas pipe; (Hauptrohr) gas main; **~schlauch** *der* gas hose

Gasse /'gasə/ *die;* **~, ~n** 1 lane; narrow street; (österr.) street; **auf der ~:** in the lane *or* narrow street; **die Salzburger Altstadt ist von kleinen, engen ~n durchzogen** the old part of Salzburg is a maze of little, narrow streets and alleyways *or* passages; **[für jmdn.] eine ~ bilden** (fig.) make way *or* clear a path [for sb.]; **wir machten eine ~ für das Brautpaar** (fig.) we lined up to make a passage for the bride and groom; **jmdm./sich eine ~ durch die Menge bahnen** (fig.) clear a path for sb./force one's way through the crowd 2 (Fußball) opening; **eine ~ öffnen** make an opening 3 (Rugby) line-out 4 (Kegeln) **in die rechte/linke ~ zielen/werfen** *aim/throw at the right-hand/left-hand gap between the lines of skittles*

gassen-, Gassen-: ~hauer *der* (ugs.) popular song; **~junge** *der* (abwertend) street urchin; **~seitig** *Adj.* (österr.) ‹*room etc.*› facing the street; **~seitig sein** face the street; **~wohnung** *die* (österr.) flat facing the street; **~wort** *das; Pl.* **~wörter** coarse word; **er benutzt die ordinärsten ~wörter** he uses the most vulgar gutter language

Gassi /'gasi/ *in* **~ gehen** (ugs.) go walkies (Brit. coll.)

Gast[1] /gast/ *der;* **~[e]s, Gäste** /'gɛstə/ 1 (auch zahlender ~) guest; **ungebetene Gäste** (auch fig.) uninvited guests; (bei einer Party usw. auch) gatecrashers; **das Glück war ein seltener ~ bei ihr** (fig.) she hadn't known much happiness; **bei jmdm. zu ~ sein** be sb.'s guest/guests; **jmdn. zu ~ haben** have sb. as one's guest/guests; **jmdn. zu ~ laden** *od.* **bitten** (geh.) request the pleasure of sb.'s company 2 (Besucher eines Lokals) patron 3 (Besucher) visitor; **ein ~ in einem Land** a visitor to a country; **als ~ im Studio war X** the studio guest was X 4 (Künstler[in]) guest star

Gast[2] *der;* **~[e]s, ~en** *od.* **Gäste** (Seemannsspr.) man; (Boots~) crewman; (Signal~) signalman

Gas-tanker *der* gas tanker

Gast-: ~arbeiter *der,* **~arbeiterin** *die* immigrant *or* foreign *or* guest worker; **~bett** *das* (im Hotel) bed; (im Haus) spare bed; **~dozent** *der,* **~dozentin** *die* (Hochschulw.) visiting lecturer

> **Gastarbeiter**
>
> The term used for workers from foreign countries, mainly Turkey, former Yugoslavia, and Italy, many of whom came to Germany in the 60s and 70s. Despite the time that they have lived in Germany and the fact that their children have grown up there, integration is still a widely discussed issue.

Gäste-: ~buch *das* guest book; **~handtuch** *das* guest towel; **~haus** *das* guest house; **~WC** *das* guest toilet; **~zimmer** *das* (privat) guest room; spare room; (im Hotel) room

gast-, Gast-: ~familie *die* host family; **~frei** *Adj.* hospitable; **~freiheit** *die* hospitality; **~freund** *der* (veralt.) 1 (~geber) host; 2 (Besucher) guest; **~freundin** *die* (veralt.) 1 (~geberin) hostess; 2 (Besucher) guest; **~freundlich** *Adj.* hospitable; **~freundschaft** *die* hospitality; **~gebend** *Adj.* host ‹*city, nation, etc.*›; **die ~gebende Mannschaft** the home team *or* side; **~geber** *der* 1 host; 2 (Sport) **der/die ~geber** the home team *or* side; **~geberin** *die* hostess; **~geschenk** *das* gift [for one's host/hostess]; **~haus** *das,* **~hof** *der* inn; **~hörer** *der,* **~hörerin** *die: student who with permission attends lectures and seminars at a university without working for a degree;* auditor (Amer.)

gastieren *itr. V.* appear as a guest; give a guest performance; **das Orchester gastiert in N.** the orchestra is giving a guest performance in N; **der ~de Tenor** the guest tenor

Gast-: ~konzert *das* guest concert; **~land** *das* host country

gastlich
A *Adj.* hospitable; **~e Aufnahme finden** have a hospitable reception; be received hospitably
B *adv.* hospitably

Gastlichkeit *die;* **~:** hospitality

Gast-: ~mahl *das* (geh.) banquet; **Platons „~mahl"** Plato's 'Symposium'; **~mannschaft** *die* (Sport) visiting team

Gas-tod *der* death by gassing; **den ~ erleiden** be gassed

Gast-: ~professor *der,* **~professorin** *die* visiting professor; **~recht** *das* right to hospitality; **jmdm. ~recht gewähren/das ~recht verweigern** grant/refuse sb. hospitality; **~recht genießen** enjoy the privileges of a guest; **das ~recht missbrauchen** abuse one's position as a guest; **~redner** *der,* **~rednerin** *die* guest speaker

Gastritis /gas'tri:tɪs/ *die;* **~, Gastritiden** ▸**❶ S. 439** (Med.) gastritis

Gast-rolle *die* guest role *or* part; **in einer ~ auftreten** make a guest appearance; appear as a guest

gastro-, Gastro- /gastro:-/: **~nom** /-'no:m/ *der;* **~~en, ~~en** restaurateur; **~nomie** /-no'mi:/ *die;* **~~** 1 (Gaststättengewerbe) restaurant trade; (Versorgung, Service) catering *no art.;* 2 (Kochk.) gastronomy; **~nomin** *die;* **~~, ~~nen** restaurateur; **~nomisch** /-'no:mɪʃ/ *Adj.* gastronomic; **~skopie** /-sko'pi:/ *die;* **~~** (Med.) gastroscopy

Gast-spiel *das* guest performance; **ein [kurzes] ~ geben** (fig. scherzh.) stay for a short time

Gastspiel-reise *die* tour; **eine ~ durch Japan** a tour of Japan; **auf ~:** on tour

Gast-stätte *die* public house (Brit.); (Speiselokal) restaurant

Gaststätten-gewerbe *das* pub/restaurant trade

Gast-stube *die* bar; (in einem Speiselokal) restaurant

Gas-turbine *die* gas turbine

Gast-: ~vorlesung *die* guest lecture; **~vorstellung** *die* guest performance; **~wirt** *der* ▸**❶ S. 113** publican; landlord; (eines Restaurants) [restaurant] proprietor *or* owner; (Pächter) restaurant manager; **~wirtin** *die* ▸**❶ S. 113** ▸**~wirt:** publican; landlady; [restaurant] proprietress *or* owner; restaurant manageress; **~wirtschaft** *die* ▸**~stätte; ~zimmer** *das* ▸**Gästezimmer**

Gas-: ~uhr *die* gas meter; **~verbrauch** *der* gas consumption; **~verflüssigung** *die* (Technik, Physik) liquefaction of gases; **~vergiftung** *die* gas-poisoning *no indef. art.;* **~versorgung** *die* gas supply; **~wasch-flasche** *die* (Technik) gas washer; (Chemie) gas-washing bottle; **~werk** *das* gasworks *sing.;* **~wolke** *die* cloud of gas; **~zähler** *der* gas meter

Gate /geɪt/ *das;* **~s, ~s** (Flugw.) gate

Gatt /gat/ *das;* **~[e]s, ~en** *od.* **~s** (Seemannsspr.) eyelet hole

GATT /gat/ *das;* **~:** GATT

Gatte /'gatə/ *der;* **~n, ~n** 1 (geh.: Ehemann) husband 2 *Pl.* (veralt.: Eheleute) couple; husband and wife

Gatten-: ~liebe *die* (geh.) conjugal love; love of one's husband/wife; **~mord** *der* (Rechtsw., sonst geh.) murder of one's husband/wife

Gatter /'gatɐ/ *das;* **~s, ~** 1 (Zaun) fence; (Lattenzaun) fence; paling 2 (Tor) gate 3 (Jägerspr.: Gehege) [game] preserve 4 (Pferdesport) rails *pl.* 5 (Textilw.) creel 6 (Elektronik) gate

Gatter-: ~säge *die* (Technik) gang saw; **~tor** *das* gate

Gattin /'gatɪn/ *die;* **~, ~nen** (geh.) wife; **die besten Grüße an Ihre ~:** my regards to your lady wife

Gattung /'gatʊŋ/ *die;* **~, ~en** 1 kind; sort; (Kunst~) genre; form; **Menschen/Dinge verschiedener ~:** all sorts of people/things of different kinds *or* sorts 2 (Biol.) genus 3 (Milit.) service

Gattungs-: ~begriff *der* generic concept; **~name** *der* generic name; **~zahlwort** *das* (Sprachw.) *numeral showing how many different kinds* ('achterlei' etc.); variative numeral

Gau /gau/ *der;* **~[e]s, ~e** 1 *tribal district in Germanic times* 2 (ns.: Organisationseinheit) *administrative district during the Nazi period* 3 (Gebiet) region

Gäu /gɔy/ *das;* **~[e]s, ~e** (österr., schweiz.) ▸**Gau 1**

GAU *der;* **~s, ~s: = größter anzunehmender Unfall** MCA; maximum credible accident

Gaube /'gaubə/ *die;* **~, ~n** dormer [window]

Gauchheil /'gauxhail/ *der;* **~[e]s, ~e** (Bot.) anagallis; pimpernel

Gaucho /'gautʃo/ *der;* **~[s], ~s** gaucho

Gaudi /'gaudi/ *das;* **~s** (*bayr., österr.: die;* **~**) (ugs.) bit of fun; **eine große ~ haben** have a lot of *or* great fun; **eine ~ sein** be a lot of *or* great fun

Gaudium /'gaudiʊm/ *das;* **~s** amusement; entertainment; **zum allgemeinen ~:** to everyone's amusement; to the amusement of everyone *or* all

Gaukel-bild *das* (veralt.) phantasm; **ein ~ deiner Fantasie** a figment of your imagination

Gaukelei *die;* **~, ~en** (geh.) 1 (Vorspiegelung) trickery *no indef. art., no pl.;* **~en** trickery *sing.; tricks* 2 (Possenspiel) trick

gaukeln /'gaukl̩n/ *itr. V.; mit sein* (dichter.) ‹*glow-worm*› flicker; ‹*butterfly*› flutter; **der ~de Flug der Fledermäuse** the dancing flight of the bats

Gaukel-spiel *das* (geh.) deception

Gaukler *der;* **~s, ~** 1 (veralt.: Taschenspieler) itinerant entertainer 2 (geh.: Betrüger) charlatan; mountebank; trickster 3 (Zool.) bateleur [eagle]

Gauklerin *die;* **~, ~nen** ▸**Gaukler 1, 2**

Gaul /gaul/ *der;* **~[e]s, Gäule** /'gɔylə/ 1 (abwertend) nag (derog.); hack (derog.) 2 (veralt.) horse; **einem geschenkten ~ schaut man nicht ins Maul** (Spr.) never look a gift-horse in the mouth

Gau-leiter *der* (ns.) gauleiter

Gaullismus /go'lɪsmʊs/ *der;* **~:** Gaullism

Gaumen /'gaumən/ *der;* **~s, ~** 1 ▸**❶ S. 435** palate; roof of the mouth; **der weiche/harte ~:** the soft/hard palate 2 (geh.: Geschmacksorgan) palate; **das ist etwas für einen verwöhnten ~:** this is something for the real gourmet

Gaumen-: ~freude *die* (geh.), **~kitzel** *der* (geh.) delicacy; **~laut** *der* guttural; **~mandel** *die* ▸**❶ S. 435** (Anat.) [palatine] tonsil; **~platte** *die* upper [dental] plate; **~segel** *das* ▸**❶ S. 435** (Anat.) soft palate; velum (Anat.); **~spalte** *die* ▸**❶ S. 439** (Med.) cleft palate; **~zäpfchen** *das* uvula

Gauner /'gaunɐ/ *der;* **~s, ~** 1 (abwertend) crook (coll.); rogue; **ein ausgemachter/kleiner ~:** an out-and-out crook (coll.) *or* rogue/a small-time crook (coll.) 2 (ugs.: schlauer Mensch) cunning devil (coll.); sly customer (coll.)

Gauner-bande *die* gang *or* band of crooks (coll.)

Gaunerei *die;* **~, ~en** swindle; (das Gaunern) swindling

Gaunerin *die;* **~, ~nen** ▸**Gauner**

Gauner-komödie *die* comedy thriller

gaunern
A *itr. V.* swindle; cheat
B *refl. V.* **sich durchs Leben ~:** cheat one's way through life

Gauner-: ~sprache *die* thieves' cant *or* Latin; **~streich** *der,* **~stück** *das* swindle; piece of roguery

g

gautschen /ˈgautʃn̩/ *tr. V.* [1] (Papierherstellung) couch [2] (Druckw.) **jmdn. ~:** give sb. a ducking (initiation ceremony for those finishing an apprenticeship in the printing trade)

Gautscher *der;* **~s, ~, Gautscherin** *die;* **~, ~nen** (Papierherstellung) coucher

Gaza·streifen /ˈgaːza-/ *der* Gaza Strip

Gaze /ˈgaːzə/ *die;* **~, ~n** gauze; (Draht~) gauze; [wire] mesh

Gaze-: **~bausch** *der* gauze swab; **~binde** *die* gauze bandage

Gazelle /gaˈtsɛlə/ *die;* **~, ~n** gazelle

Gaze·schleier *der* gauze veil

Gazette /gaˈtsɛtə/ *die;* **~, ~n** newspaper; rag (coll. derog.)

Gaze·tupfer *der* ▸ **Gazebausch**

G-Dur /ˈgeː-/ *das* (Musik) G major; *s. auch* **A-Dur**

geachtet
A *2. Part. v.* **achten**
B *Adj.* respected; **hoch ~:** highly respected *or* regarded; **~ und respektiert** esteemed and respected; **bei jmdm. ~ sein** be respected *or* held in esteem by sb.

Geächtete *der/die; adj. Dekl.* outlaw

Geächze *das;* **~s** groaning; groans *pl.*

Geäder /gəˈ|ɛːdɐ/ *das;* **~s** venation; veins *pl.;* (beim Menschen) veins *pl.*

geadert, geädert *Adj.* veined

Geäfter /gəˈ|ɛftɐ/ *das;* **~s, ~** (Jägerspr.) dew-claws *pl.*

Gealbere *das;* **~s** (ugs. abwertend) messing about *or* around (coll.)

geartet *Adj.* **es ist [ganz] anders ~, als ich mir vorgestellt hatte** it is [quite] different [in kind] from what I'd imagined; **wie [auch] immer die Situation ~ ist** whatever the situation may be; **kein wie auch immer ~er Reiz** no stimulus of any kind; **dieses besonders ~e Material** this special material; **sie ist so ~, dass ...** her nature is such that ...; **gutmütig ~:** good-natured; **sie ist ganz anders ~:** she is quite different; she has quite a different nature

Geäst /gəˈ|ɛst/ *das;* **~[e]s** branches *pl.;* boughs *pl.*

geb. *Abk.* [1] **= geboren** [2] **= geborene**

Gebäck /gəˈbɛk/ *das;* **~[e]s, ~e** cakes and pastries *pl.;* (Kekse) biscuits *pl.;* (Törtchen) tarts *pl.*

gebacken *2. Part. v.* **backen**

Gebäck-: **~schale** *die* cake dish; **~zange** *die* cake tongs *pl.*

Gebälk /gəˈbɛlk/ *das;* **~[e]s, ~e** [1] (Balkenwerk) beams *pl.;* (Dach~) rafters *pl.;* **es knistert** *od.* **kracht im ~** (fig.) there are signs that things are beginning to fall apart (fig.) [2] (antike Archit.) entablature

Geballere *das;* **~s** (ugs. abwertend) banging

geballt /gəˈbalt/
A *2. Part. v.* **ballen**
B *Adj.* concentrated; **mit ~er Kraft einen neuen Angriff starten** concentrate one's forces in a new attack; **eine ~e Ladung** (Milit.) a concentrated charge; **jmdm. eine ~e Ladung Sand ins Gesicht werfen** (fig. ugs.) chuck a load of sand in sb.'s face (coll.)

gebar *1. u. 3. Pers. Sg. Prät. v.* **gebären**

Gebärde /gəˈbɛːɐ̯də/ *die;* **~, ~n** gesture; **mit vielen ~n** with much gesticulation

gebärden *refl. V.* **sich seltsam/wie ein Rasender/wie toll ~:** behave *or* act oddly/like a madman/as if one were mad

Gebärden-: **~spiel** *das* gestures *pl.;* gesticulation[s *pl.*]; **~sprache** *die* (Zeichensprache) sign language; (Taubstummensprache) deaf-and-dumb language

gebären /gəˈbɛːrən/ *unr. tr. V.* bear; give birth to; **jmdn. ein Kind ~** (geh.) bear sb. a child; **wo bist du geboren?** where were you born?; **einen Gedanken/eine Idee ~** (fig.) generate a thought/give birth to an idea; *s. auch* **geboren**

Gebaren *das;* **~s** (oft abwertend) conduct; behaviour

gebär·freudig *Adj.* prolific

Gebär·mutter *die; Pl.* **Gebärmütter** ▸ ❶ **S. 435** womb

Gebärmutter·krebs *der* ▸ ❶ **S. 439** (Med.) cancer of the womb

gebauchpinselt /gəˈbauxpɪnzl̩t/ *in* **sich ~ fühlen** (ugs. scherzh.) feel flattered

Gebäude /gəˈbɔydə/ *das;* **~s, ~** [1] (Bauwerk) building [2] (Gefüge) structure; **kunstvolles ~:** edifice; **das ~ einer Theorie/Wissenschaft** the structure of a theory/of a science; **ein ~ von Lügen** a tissue of lies

Gebäude-: **~komplex** *der* complex of buildings; **~teil** *der* part of the building

gebaut
A *2. Part. v.* **bauen**
B *Adj.* **gut ~ sein** have a good figure; **gut ~e Mannequins** models with good figures; **so wie du ~ bist ...** (ugs.) with a figure like yours ...; (fig.) you being what you are ... (coll.)

gebe·freudig *Adj.* generous; open-handed

Gebein *das;* **~[e]s, ~e** [1] *Pl.* (geh.: Skelett) bones *pl.;* (sterbliche Reste) [mortal] remains [2] **ihr fuhr der Schreck durchs ~** (veralt.) her whole body shook with fear

Gebell *das;* **~[e]s** barking; (der Jagdhunde) baying; (fig.: von Geschützen) booming

geben /ˈgeːbn̩/
A *unr. tr. V.* [1] give; (reichen) give; hand; pass; **jmdm. zu essen/trinken ~:** give sb. something to eat/drink; **jmdm. [zur Begrüßung] die Hand ~:** shake sb.'s hand [in greeting]; **~ Sie mir bitte Herrn N.** please put me through to Mr N.; **ich gäbe viel darum, wenn ich das machen könnte** I'd give a lot to be able to do that; **jmdm. etw. in die Hand ~:** give sb. sth.; **etw. [nicht] aus der Hand ~:** [not] let go of sth.; **ich gebe Ihnen die Vase für 130 Euro** I'll let you have the vase for 130 euros; **~ Sie mir bitte eine Schachtel Zigaretten/ein Bier** I'll have a packet of cigarettes/a beer, please; **können Sie mir zwei Plätze ~?** can you give me *or* let me have two seats?; **jmdm. seine ganze Liebe ~** (fig.) give sb. all one's love; **Geben ist seliger denn Nehmen** (Spr.) it is more blessed to give than to receive (prov.)
[2] (über~) **jmdn. zu jmdm. in die Lehre ~:** apprentice sb. to sb.; **etw. in Druck** (*Akk.*) *od.* **zum Druck ~:** send sth. to press *or* to be printed; **jmdm. etw. als** *od.* **zum Pfand ~:** give sb. sth. as [a] security; **etw. [bei jmdm.] in Verwahrung ~:** hand sth. in [to sb.] for safe keeping; **etw. zur Reparatur ~:** take sth. [in] to be repaired; **etw. zur Post ~:** post sth.; *s. auch* **Pflege**
[3] (gewähren) give; **jmdm. eine Genehmigung/ein Interview ~:** give sb. permission/an interview; **einen Elfmeter/eine Ecke ~** (Sport) award a penalty/corner
[4] (bieten) give; **es hat mir nichts ge~:** I didn't gain anything from *or* get anything out of it; **jmdm. ein gutes/schlechtes Beispiel ~:** set sb. a good/bad example
[5] (versetzen) give; **jmdm. einen Klaps/Tritt ~:** give sb. a slap/kick; **es jmdm. ~** (ugs.: jmdm. die Meinung sagen) give sb. what for (coll.); (jmdn. verprügeln) let sb. have it; **gib [es] ihm!** (ugs.) let him have it!
[6] (erteilen) give; **Unterricht ~:** teach; **eine Lektion ~:** give a lesson; **Französisch ~:** teach French; **jmdm. Antwort ~:** give sb. an answer; **jmdm. Auskunft/Aufschluss ~:** give sb. information
[7] (hervorbringen) give ‹*milk, shade, light*›; **etw. gibt Flecken** (ugs.) sth. stains
[8] (veranstalten) give, throw ‹*party*›; give, lay on ‹*banquet*›; give ‹*dinner party, ball*›; **ein Fest ~:** give *or* hold a party *or* celebration
[9] (aufführen) give ‹*concert, performance*›; **das Theater gibt nächste Woche den „Faust"** the theatre is putting on 'Faust' next week; **was wird heute ge~?** what's on today?; **die Schauspielerin gibt ihr Debüt** the actress is making her debut
[10] (er~) **drei mal drei gibt neun** three threes are nine; three times three is *or* makes nine; **eins plus eins gibt zwei** one and one is *or* makes two; **das gibt [k]einen Sinn** that makes [no] sense; **ein Wort gab das andere** one word led to another
[11] (vermitteln) give; **jmdm./einer Sache neue Impulse/Anregungen ~:** give sb./sth. a fresh impulse/stimulus; **etw. ist jmdm. nicht ge~:** sb. just hasn't got sth.; **es ist ihm nicht ge~, eine gute Rede zu halten** he just hasn't got what it takes to be a good speaker
[12] (äußern) **etw. von sich ~:** utter sth.; **Unsinn/dummes Zeug von sich ~** (abwertend) talk nonsense/rubbish; **keinen Laut/Ton von sich ~:** not make a sound
[13] **viel/wenig auf etw.** (*Akk.*) **~:** set great/little store by sth.
[14] (hinzu~) add; put in; **etw. an das Essen ~:** add sth. to *or* put sth. into the food
[15] (ugs.: erbrechen) **alles wieder von sich ~:** bring *or* (coll.) sick everything up again
[16] (Ballspiele: ab~) pass; **den Ball nach links ~:** pass the ball [to the] left
[17] (darstellen) play ‹*role*›
B *unr. tr. V.* (unpers.) [1] (vorhanden sein) **es gibt** there is/are; **es gibt einen/keinen Gott** God exists/does not exist; **das gibt es wohl häufiger** it happens all the time; **dass es so etwas heutzutage überhaupt noch gibt!** I'm surprised that such things still go on nowadays; **zu meiner Zeit gab es das nicht** it wasn't like that in my day; **gibt es noch etwas?** (ugs.) is there anything else?; **das gibt es ja gar nicht** I don't believe it; you're joking (coll.); **Ein Hund mit fünf Beinen? Das gibt es ja gar nicht** A dog with five legs? There's no such thing!; **was gibt es Neues?** what's new? (coll.); **bei mir gibts nichts Neues** I haven't got any news; **Kommen Sie herein. Was gibt es?** Come in. What's the matter *or* (coll.) what's up?; **was gibts denn da?** what's going on over there?; **was es nicht alles gibt!** (ugs.) what will they think of next?; **gibt es dich auch noch?** (ugs.) are you still around? (coll.); **da gibts nichts** (ugs.) there's no denying it *or* no doubt about it; **da gibts nichts, da würde ich sofort protestieren** there's nothing else for it, I'd protest immediately in that case
[2] (angeboten werden) **was gibt es zu essen/trinken?** what is there to eat/drink?; **was gibt es denn zum Mittagessen?** what's for lunch?; **heute gibts Schweinefleisch** we're having pork today; **im Theater/Fernsehen gibt es heute Abend ...** ... is on at the theatre/on television this evening
[3] (einsetzen) **morgen gibt es Schnee/Sturm** it'll snow tomorrow/there'll be a storm tomorrow; **es gibt Scherereien/Streit** there'll be trouble/a row; **gleich/sonst gibts was** (ugs.) there'll be trouble in a minute/otherwise
C *unr. itr. V.* [1] (Karten austeilen) deal; **wer gibt?** whose deal is it?
[2] (Sport: aufschlagen) serve
D *unr. refl. V.* [1] **sich [natürlich/steif] ~:** act *or* behave [naturally/stiffly]; **er gab sich nach außen hin gelassen** he gave the appearance of being relaxed; **deine Art, dich zu ~:** the way you behave
[2] (nachlassen) **das Fieber wird sich ~:** his/her *etc.* temperature will drop; **sein Eifer wird sich bald ~:** his enthusiasm will soon wear off *or* cool; **das gibt sich/wird sich noch ~:** it will get better

gebenedeit /gəbeneˈdait/ *Adj.* (christl. Rel.) blessed; **die ~e Jungfrau** the Blessed Virgin Mary

Geber *der;* **~s, ~** [1] (veralt.: Gebender) giver; donor [2] (Technik) transducer

Geberin *die;* **~, ~nen** ▸ **Geber 1**

Geber-: **~land** *das* donor country; **~laune** *die* generous mood; **in ~laune** in a generous mood

Gebet /gəˈbeːt/ *das;* **~[e]s, ~e** prayer; **ein ~ sprechen** say a prayer; **sein ~ verrichten** say one's prayers *pl.;* **das ~ des Herrn** (geh.) the Lord's Prayer; **jmdn. ins ~ nehmen** (ugs.) give sb. a dressing down; take sb. to task

Gebet·buch *das* prayer book

gebeten *2. Part. v.* **bitten**

gebets-, Gebets-: **~mühle** *die* prayer wheel; **~mühlenhaft** **A** *Adj.* mantra-like ‹*announcement, statement, repetition*›; **B** *adv.*

‹repeat, assert› mantra-like; **~teppich** *der* (islam. Rel.) prayer mat

gebeut /gəˈbɔyt/ (veralt.) *3. Pers. Sg. Präsens v.* **gebieten**

gebiert /gəˈbiːɐ̯t/ *3. Pers. Sg. Präsens v.* **gebären**

Gebiet /gəˈbiːt/ *das;* **~[e]s, ~e** 1 (Landstrich) region; area 2 (Staats~) territory 3 (Bereich) field; sphere; **auf dem ~ der Wirtschaft/Politik** in the field *or* sphere of economics/politics 4 (Fach) field; **auf einem ~ führend sein** be the leader in a field

gebieten (geh.)
A *unr. tr. V.* 1 (befehlen, fordern) command; order; **jmdm. ~, etw. zu tun** command *or* order sb. to do sth.; **eine Respekt ~de Persönlichkeit** a figure who commands/commanded respect 2 (erfordern) demand; bid; *s. auch* **Einhalt**
B *unr. itr. V.* 1 **über etw.** (*Akk.*) **~:** command sth.; have command over sth.; **über ein Land/Volk ~:** hold sway over a country/people 2 (verfügen) **über Geld ~:** have money at one's disposal; **er gebietet über beträchtliche Körperkräfte** he is a man of considerable strength

Gebieter *der;* **~s, ~** (veralt.) master; **~ über 400 Sklaven** master of 400 slaves

Gebieterin *die;* **~, ~nen** (veralt.) mistress

gebieterisch (geh.)
A *Adj.* imperious; (herrisch) domineering; overbearing; peremptory ‹*tone*›
B *adv.* imperiously; **die Lage erfordert ~, dass ...** the situation makes it [absolutely] imperative that ...

gebiets-, Gebiets-: ~abtretung *die* cession *or* ceding of territory; **~anspruch** *der* territorial claim; **~fremd** *Adj.* (nicht wohnhaft) non-resident; (nicht heimisch) non-native ‹*animal, species*›; **~körperschaft** *die* (Rechtsw.) regional authority; **~reform** *die* local government reorganization; **~weise** *Adv.* locally; in some areas

Gebilde /gəˈbɪldə/ *das;* **~s, ~** (Gegenstand) object; (Bauwerk) construction; structure; (Form) shape; **ein kompliziertes geistiges ~** (fig.) a complicated intellectual construct; **diese Dinge sind ~ seiner Fantasie** (fig.) these things are products of his imagination

gebildet
A *2. Part. v.* **bilden**
B *Adj.* educated; (kultiviert) cultured; **er ist sehr ~:** he is very well educated; **vielseitig ~:** broadly educated; **er ist vielseitig ~:** he has a broad education; **akademisch ~ sein** have had an academic training
C *adv.* **sich ~ unterhalten** have a cultured conversation

Gebimmel *das;* **~s** (ugs.) ringing; (von kleinen Glocken) tinkling

Gebinde *das;* **~s, ~** (Blumenarrangement) arrangement; (Bund, Strauß) bunch; (von kleinen Blumen) posy

Gebirge /gəˈbɪrgə/ *das;* **~s, ~** 1 mountain range; range of mountains; **ein ~ von Schutt** (fig.) a mountain of rubble (fig.) 2 (Gebirgsgegend) mountains *pl.* 3 (Bergbau) rock

gebirgig *Adj.* mountainous

Gebirgs-: ~ausläufer *der* foothill; **~bach** *der* mountain stream; **~bahn** *die* mountain railway; **~bewohner** *der,* **~bewohnerin** *die* mountain dweller; **~jäger** *der* (Milit.) 1 (Soldat) mountain soldier; 2 *Pl.* (Waffengattung) mountain troops *pl.*; **~kamm** *der* mountain ridge *or* crest; **~kette** *die* mountain chain *or* range; **~klima** *das* mountain climate; **~landschaft** *die* mountainous region; (Ausblick) mountain scenery; (Gemälde) mountain landscape; **~massiv** *das* massif; **~pass,** ***~paß** *der* mountain pass; **~stock** *der* massif; **~truppe** *die* (Milit.) ▸**~jäger** 2; **~volk** *das* mountain people; (Stamm) mountain tribe; **~zug** *der* mountain range

Gebiss, *Gebiß *das;* **Gebisses, Gebisse** 1 ▸ⓘ **S. 435** (Zähne) set of teeth; teeth *pl.*; **sein ~ zeigen/entblößen** bare one's teeth 2 (Zahnersatz) denture; plate (coll.); (für die Zähne beider Kiefer) dentures *pl.*; set of false teeth; false teeth *pl.*; **ein [künstliches] ~ anpassen** fit a denture/dentures *or* [a set of] false teeth 3 (am Pferdezaum) bit

gebissen /gəˈbɪsn̩/ *2. Part. v.* **beißen**

Gebläse /gəˈblɛːzə/ *das;* **~s, ~** (Technik) fan; (Kfz-W.: am Vergaser) supercharger

Gebläse·motor *der* (Kfz-W.) supercharged engine

geblasen *2. Part. v.* **blasen**

geblichen /gəˈblɪçn̩/ *2. Part. v.* **bleichen**

Geblödel *das;* **~s** (ugs.) silly chatter; twaddle (coll.)

geblümt /gəˈblyːmt/ *Adj.* 1 flowered 2 (geziert) flowery ‹*style etc.*›

Geblüt /gəˈblyːt/ *das;* **~[e]s** (geh.) blood; **von königlichem ~ sein** be of royal blood; **eine Prinzessin von ~:** a princess of the blood

gebogen
A *2. Part. v.* **biegen**
B *Adj.* bent; **eine aufwärts ~e Nase** an upturned nose

geboren /gəˈboːrən/
A *2. Part. v.* **gebären**
B *Adj.* **blind/taub ~ sein** be born blind/deaf; **Frau Anna Schmitz ~e Meyer** Mrs Anna Schmitz née Meyer; **sie ist eine ~e von Schiller** she is a von Schiller by birth; **der ~e Schauspieler** *usw.* **sein** be a born actor *etc.*; **zum Musiker** *usw.* **~ sein** be born to be a musician *etc.*; be a born musician *etc.*

geborgen
A *2. Part. v.* **bergen**
B *Adj.* safe; secure; **sich bei jmdm. ~ fühlen** feel safe and secure with sb.; **sicher und ~ sein** be safe and secure

Geborgenheit *die;* **~:** security

geborsten /gəˈbɔrstn̩/ *2. Part. v.* **bersten**

gebot *1. u. 3. Pers. Sg. Prät. v.* **gebieten**

Gebot *das;* **~[e]s, ~e** 1 (Grundsatz) precept; **das ~ der Fairness/Höflichkeit verlangt es, dass ...** fairness/politeness demands that ...; **das oberste/erste ~:** the highest precept; **die Zehn ~e** (Rel.) the Ten Commandments 2 (Vorschrift) regulation 3 (geh.: Befehl) command; (Verordnung) decree; **auf jmds. ~** (*Akk.*) **[hin]** at sb.'s command 4 *in* **jmdm. zu ~[e] stehen** (geh.) be at sb.'s command/disposal 5 (Erfordernis) **ein ~ der Vernunft/Klugheit** a dictate of reason/good sense; **es ist ein ~ der Vernunft/Klugheit, etw. zu tun** reason/good sense dictates that one does sth.; **es ist das ~ der Stunde, nicht länger zu zögern** (geh.) our present predicament demands that we hesitate no longer; **etw. ist das ~ der Stunde** (geh.) sth. is the order of the day 6 (Kaufmannsspr.) bid; **verkaufe X gegen ~:** offers [are] invited for X

geboten
A *2. Part. v.* **bieten, gebieten**
B *Adj.* (ratsam) advisable; (notwendig) necessary; (unbedingt ~) imperative; **mit der ~en Sorgfalt** with [all] due care; **mit dem ~en Respekt** with all due respect

Gebots·schild *das* (Verkehrsw.) regulatory sign

Gebr. *Abk.* **= Gebrüder** Bros.

gebracht /gəˈbraxt/ *2. Part. v.* **bringen**

gebrandmarkt *2. Part. v.* **brandmarken**

gebrannt /gəˈbrant/ *2. Part. v.* **brennen**

gebraten *2. Part. v.* **braten**

Gebräu /gəˈbrɔy/ *das;* **~[e]s, ~e** (meist abwertend) brew; concoction (derog.)

Gebrauch *der* 1 (Benutzung) use; **für den persönlichen/täglichen ~:** for personal/daily use; **vor ~ gut schütteln!** shake well before use; **von etw. ~ machen** make use of sth.; **von seinem Recht ~ machen** avail oneself of *or* exercise one's rights *pl.*; **außer ~ kommen** fall into disuse; **etw. in ~ nehmen** start using sth.; **etw. in** *od.* **im ~ haben** be using sth.; **in** *od.* **im ~ sein** be in use 2 (Brauch) custom

gebrauchen *tr. V.* use; **das kann ich gut ~:** I can make good use of that; I can just do with that (coll.); **er ist zu nichts zu ~** (ugs.) he is useless; **sie ist zu allem zu ~:** she is always a useful person to have around; **den Verstand/eine List ~:** use one's common sense/a subterfuge; **er könnte einen neuen Mantel ~** (ugs.) he could do with *or* (coll.) use a new coat; **ich kann jetzt keine Störung ~** (ugs.) I don't want to be disturbed just now

gebräuchlich /gəˈbrɔyçlɪç/ *Adj.* 1 (üblich) normal; usual; customary 2 (häufig) common

gebrauchs-, Gebrauchs-: ~anleitung *die,* **~anweisung** *die* instructions *pl. or* directions *pl.* [for use]; **~artikel** *der* basic consumer item; **~artikel** *Pl.* basic consumer goods; **~fähig** *Adj.* usable; in working order *pred.*; **etw. ~fähig machen** make sth. usable; put sth. in working order; **~fertig** *Adj.* ready for use *pred.*; **~gegenstand** *der* item of practical use; **~grafik, ~graphik** *die* commercial art; **~grafiker, ~graphiker** *der,* **~grafikerin, ~graphikerin** *die* commercial artist; **~gut** *das* consumer item; **~güter** consumer goods; **langlebige ~güter** consumer durables; **~muster** *das* (Rechtsw.) registered design; **~musterschutz** *der* (Rechtsw.) protection of designs; **~spuren** *Pl.* signs of usage; (Verschleiß) signs of wear; **~wert** *der* utility value

gebraucht
A *2. Part. v.* **brauchen, gebrauchen**
B *Adj.* second-hand ‹*bicycle, clothes, etc.*›; used, second-hand ‹*car*›; used ‹*handkerchief*›; **etw. ~ kaufen** buy sth. second-hand

Gebraucht-: ~wagen *der* used *or* second-hand car; **~wagen·händler** *der,* **~wagen·händlerin** *die* used-car dealer; second-hand car dealer; **~ware** *die* second-hand item; **~waren** second-hand goods

Gebrause *das;* **~s** (des Meeres, der Wellen) thundering; roar[ing]; booming; (des Sturms, Windes) roar[ing]; (des Verkehrs) roar

gebrechen *unr. itr. V.* (unpers.) (geh.) **jmdm. gebricht etw., jmdm. gebricht es an etw.** (*Dat.*) sb. is lacking in *or* lacks sth.

Gebrechen *das;* **~s, ~** (geh.) affliction

gebrechlich *Adj.* infirm; frail; **die Alten und Gebrechlichen** the aged and infirm

Gebrechlichkeit *die;* **~:** infirmity; frailty

gebrochen /gəˈbrɔxn̩/
A *2. Part. v.* **brechen**
B *Adj.* 1 (fehlerhaft) **~es Englisch/Deutsch** broken English/German 2 (niedergedrückt) broken; **er ist ein ~er Mensch** he is a broken man 3 (gestört) **ein ~es Verhältnis zu jmdm./etw. haben** have a disturbed relationship to sb./sth.
C *adv.* **~ Deutsch sprechen** speak broken German

Gebrodel *das;* **~s** boiling; bubbling; (fig.) turmoil

Gebrüder *Pl.* 1 (Kaufmannsspr.) **die ~ Meyer** Meyer Brothers 2 (veralt.) **die ~ Schulze** the brothers Schulze

Gebrüll *das;* **~[e]s** 1 roaring; (von Rindern) bellowing 2 (ugs.) (lautes Schreien) bellowing; yelling; (einer Menschenmenge) roaring; **auf sie mit ~!** (scherzh.) go for *or* get them! 3 (ugs.: lautes Weinen) bawling

Gebrumm *das;* **~[e]s** (von Bären) growling; (von Flugzeugen, Bienen) droning; (von Insekten) buzz[ing]; **ein zustimmendes ~** (fig.) a growl of assent

Gebrumme *das;* **~s** (ugs. abwertend) (von Flugzeugen, Motorrädern, Bienen) droning; (von Insekten) buzz[ing]

gebückt
A *2. Part. v.* **bücken**
B *Adj.* **in ~er Haltung** bending forward; **~ gehen** walk with a stoop

gebügelt *2. Part. v.* **bügeln;** *s. auch* **geschniegelt**

Gebühr /gəˈbyːɐ̯/ *die;* **~, ~en** 1 charge; (Maut) toll; (Anwalts~) fee; (Fernseh~) licence fee; (Vermittlungs~) commission *no pl.*; fee; (Post~) postage *no pl.*; **~ bezahlt Empfänger** postage will be paid by addressee 2 **jmds. Leistungen nach ~ anerkennen** give due recognition to sb.'s achievements; **ich werde dich nach ~ belohnen** I shall reward you appropriately; **über ~** (*Akk.*) unduly; excessively

g

gebühren (geh.)
A *itr. V.* **jmdm. gebührt Achtung** *usw.* **[für etw.]** sb. deserves respect *etc.* [for sth.]; respect *etc.* is due to sb. [for sth.]
B *refl. V.* **wie es sich gebührt** as is fitting *or* proper; **er bewahrte die Haltung, wie es sich für einen König gebührt** he kept his composure, as befitted a king

Gebühren·anzeiger *der* (Fernspr.) telephone meter

gebührend
A *Adj.* fitting; proper; (angemessen) fitting; suitable; **in ~em Abstand** at a proper distance; **mit ~er Sorgfalt** with due care; **jmdm. die ~e Achtung erweisen** show sb. due *or* proper respect; show sb. the respect due to him/her
B *adv.* fittingly; in a fitting manner

gebührender·maßen, gebührender·weise *Adv.* fittingly; in a fitting manner

gebühren-, Gebühren-: ~einheit *die* (Fernspr.) [tariff] unit; **~erhöhung** *die* ▸**Gebühr 1**: increase in charges/fees; (Erhöhung der Fernsehgebühren) licence fee increase; **~erlass, *~erlaß** *der* ▸**Gebühr 1**: remission of charges/fees; (der Fernsehgebühren) remission of the licence fee; **~ermäßigung** *die* ▸**Gebühr 1**: reduction of charges/fees; **~frei** **A** *Adj.* free of charge *pred.*; post-free ‹*letter, packet, etc.*›; **B** *adv.* free of charge; **einen Brief ~frei schicken** send a letter post-free; **~marke** *die* revenue stamp; fiscal stamp; **~ordnung** *die* ▸**Gebühr 1**: scale of charges/fees; **~pflichtig** **A** *Adj.* **eine ~pflichtige Verwarnung** a fine and a caution; **B** *adv.* **jmdn. ~pflichtig verwarnen** fine and caution sb.; **~vignette** *die* [Swiss] motorway fee sticker

gebührlich *Adj.* (veralt.) ▸**gebührend**

gebunden
A *2. Part. v.* **binden**
B *Adj.* [1] (verpflichtet) bound; **an ein Versprechen/das Haus ~ sein** be bound by a promise/tied to one's home; **sich [an etw.** (*Akk.*)**] ~ fühlen** feel bound by sth. [2] (verlobt) engaged; (verheiratet) married [3] (festgesetzt) fixed ‹*book prices*›

Gebundenheit *die;* **~: ein Gefühl der ~:** a feeling of being tied [down]

Geburt /gə'buːɐ̯t/ *die;* **~, ~en** ▸ⓘ **S. 520** birth; **von ~ an** from birth; **vor/nach Christi ~:** before/after the birth of Christ; **von hoher ~ sein** (geh.) be of noble birth; **ein Deutscher/Engländer von ~:** a German/Englishman by birth; **das war eine schwere ~** (fig. ugs.) it wasn't easy; it took some doing (coll.)

geburten-, Geburten-: ~beschränkung *die* population control; **~kontrolle** *die* birth control; **~rate** *die* birth rate; **~regelung** *die* birth control; **~rückgang** *der* decrease in the birth rate; **~schwach** *Adj.* **ein ~schwacher Jahrgang** a year with a low birth rate; **~stark** *Adj.* **ein ~starker Jahrgang** a year with a high birth rate; **~überschuss, *~überschuß** *der* excess of births over deaths; **~ziffer** *die* birth rate

gebürtig /gə'bʏrtɪç/ *Adj.* **ein ~er Schwabe** a Swabian by birth; **aus Ungarn/Paris ~ sein** be Hungarian/Parisian by birth

Geburts-: ~anzeige *die* birth announcement; **~datum** *das* date of birth; **~fehler** *der* congenital defect; **~haus** *das:* **das ~haus Beethovens** the house where Beethoven was born; Beethoven's birthplace; **~helfer** *der* ▸ⓘ **S. 113** (Arzt) obstetrician; (Laie) assistant [at a/the birth]; **~helferin** *die* ▸ⓘ **S. 113** obstetrician; (Hebamme) midwife; **~hilfe** *die* (Med.) obstetrics *sing.*; (von einer Hebamme) midwifery; **~jahr** *das* year of birth; **1848 ist das ~jahr der Demokratie in Deutschland** (fig.) the year 1848 marks the birth of democracy in Germany; **~ort** *der* place of birth; birthplace; **~schein** *der* ▸**~urkunde**; **~stadt** *die* native town/city; **~stunde** *die* hour of birth; **die ~stunde des Reiches schlug, als er den Thron bestieg** (fig.) with his accession to the throne the empire was born

Geburts·tag *der* [1] ▸ⓘ **S. 331** birthday; **jmdm. zum ~ gratulieren** wish sb. [a] happy birthday *or* many happy returns of the day; **sich** (*Dat.*) **etw. zum ~ wünschen** want sth. for one's birthday; **er hat morgen ~:** it's his birthday tomorrow [2] (Geburtsdatum) date of birth

Geburtstags-: ~feier *die* birthday party; **~geschenk** *das* birthday present; **~kind** *das* (scherzh.) birthday boy/girl; **~torte** *die* birthday cake; **~überraschung** *die* birthday surprise

Geburts-: ~trauma *das* (Med., Psych.) birth trauma; **~ur·kunde** *die* birth certificate; **~wehen** *Pl.* labour pains; (fig.) birth pangs; **~zange** *die* obstetric forceps *pl.*

Gebüsch /gə'bʏʃ/ *das;* **~[e]s, ~e** bushes *pl.*; clump of bushes; **ein niedriges ~:** a clump of low bushes; some low bushes *pl.*; **sich im ~ verstecken** hide in the bushes

Geck /gɛk/ *der;* **~en, ~en** (abwertend) dandy; fop

geckenhaft
A *Adj.* dandyish; foppish
B *adv.* **er kleidet sich ~:** he dresses like a dandy

Gecko /'gɛko/ *der;* **~s, ~s** *od.* **~nen** /-'--/ (Zool.) gecko

gedacht /gə'daxt/
A *2. Part. v.* **denken, gedenken**
B *Adj.* **für jmdn./etw. ~ sein** be meant *or* intended for sb./sth.; **so war das nicht ~:** that wasn't what I intended

Gedächtnis /gə'dɛçtnɪs/ *das;* **~ses, ~se** [1] memory; **den Alten lässt sein ~ im Stich** the old man's memory fails him; **sich** (*Dat.*) **etw. ins ~ [zurück]rufen** recall sth.; **etw. aus dem ~ aufsagen** recite sth. from memory; **jmdm. etw. aus dem ~ sagen** tell sb. sth. from memory; **das ist meinem ~ entfallen** it has slipped my mind; **das ist mir noch frisch im ~:** it is still fresh in my memory; **du hast ein kurzes ~** (ugs.) you have a short memory; **jmds. ~** (*Dat.*) **nachhelfen** jog sb.'s memory; **ein ~ wie ein Sieb haben** (ugs.) have a memory like a sieve (coll.) [2] (Andenken) memory; remembrance; **zum ~ an jmdn.** in memory *or* remembrance of sb.

Gedächtnis-: ~feier *die* ▸**Gedenkfeier**; **~gottes·dienst** *der* service of remembrance; memorial service; **~hilfe** *die* ▸**~stütze**; **~lücke** *die* gap in one's memory; **~rede** *die* ▸**Gedenkrede**; **~schwäche** *die* weak *or* poor memory; (Med., Psych.) defective *or* weakened memory; **~schwund** *der* loss of memory; amnesia; **~störung** *die* (bes. Med., Psych.) defect of memory; memory defect; **~stütze** *die* memory aid; mnemonic

gedämpft
A *2. Part. v.* **dämpfen**
B *Adj.* subdued ‹*mood*›; subdued, soft ‹*light*›; subdued, muted ‹*colour*›; muffled ‹*sound*›; **mit ~er Stimme** in a low *or* hushed voice; **~e Schwingungen** (Physik) damped vibrations

Gedanke *der;* **~ns, ~n** [1] thought; **ein guter/vernünftiger ~:** a good/sensible idea; **einen ~n aufgreifen** take up an idea; **einen ~n zu Ende denken** follow a thought through; **seinen ~n nachhängen** abandon oneself to one's thoughts; **jmdn. auf andere ~n bringen** take sb.'s mind off things; **in ~n verloren** *od.* **versunken [sein]** [be] lost *or* deep in thought; **er war ganz in ~n** he was lost in thought; **in ~n ganz woanders sein** have one's mind on something completely different; be miles away (coll.); **mit seinen ~n nicht bei der Sache sein** have one's mind on something else; **ich bin in ~n immer bei dir** I'm always with you in my thoughts; **sich mit einem ~n vertraut machen** get used to an idea; **~n sind frei** thoughts are free; **jmds. ~n lesen** read sb.'s thoughts *or* mind; **~n lesen können** be able to read people's thoughts *or* to mind-read; **sich** (*Dat.*) **[um jmdn./etw.** *od.* **wegen jmds./etw.] ~n machen** be worried [about sb./sth.]; **mach dir keine ~n** (ugs.) don't worry; **sich über etw.** (*Akk.*) **~n machen** (länger nachdenken) think about *or* ponder sth. [2] **der ~ an etw.** (*Akk.*) the thought of sth.; **bei dem ~n, hingehen zu müssen** at the thought of having to go; **kein ~ [daran]!** (ugs.) out of the question!; no way! (coll.); **kein ~ daran, dass ich rechtzeitig fertig werde** (ugs.) there's no chance that I'll be finished on time [3] *Pl.* (Meinung) ideas; **seine eigenen ~n über etw. haben** have one's own ideas about sth.; **seine ~n [über etw.** (*Akk.*)**] austauschen** exchange views [about sth.] [4] (Einfall) idea; **das bringt mich auf einen ~n** that gives me an idea; **mir kommt ein ~:** I've had an idea; **mir kam der ~, wir könnten ...** it occurred to me that we could ...; **auf dumme ~n kommen** (ugs.) get silly ideas (coll.); **sich mit dem ~n tragen, etw. zu tun** entertain the idea of *or* consider doing sth.; **mit dem ~n spielen[, etw. zu tun]** be toying with the idea [of doing sth.] [5] (Idee) idea; **der ~ des Friedens** the idea of peace

gedanken-, Gedanken-: ~armut *die* paucity of ideas; unoriginality; **~aus·tausch** *der* exchange of ideas; **~blitz** *der* (ugs. scherzh.) brainwave (coll.); **~flug** *der* flight of intellect; **~freiheit** *die* freedom of thought; **~gang** *der* train of thought; **~gebäude** *das* edifice of ideas; **~gut** *das* thought; **christliches ~gut** Christian thought; **staatszersetzendes ~gut** subversive ideas *pl.*; **~lesen** *das* mind-reading; **~los** **A** *Adj.* (unüberlegt) unconsidered; thoughtless; (oberflächlich) thoughtless; (zerstreut) absent-minded; **B** *adv.* (zerstreut) absent-mindedly; (unüberlegt) without thinking; thoughtlessly; **~losigkeit** *die;* **~~:** (Zerstreutheit) absent-mindedness; (Unüberlegtheit) lack of thought; thoughtlessness; **~lyrik** *die* (Literaturw.) philosophical poetry; **~reichtum** *der* (eines Menschen) fertility of ideas; (eines Werkes) wealth of ideas; **~schritt** *der* logical step; **~spiel** *das* intellectual pastime *or* game; **~splitter** *der* ▸**Aphorismus**; **~sprung** *der* mental leap; jump from one idea to another; **~strich** *der* dash; **~übertragung** *die* telepathy *no indef. art.*; thought transference *no indef. art.*; **~verloren** *Adv.* lost in thought; **~voll** **A** *Adj.* pensive; thoughtful; **B** *adv.* pensively; thoughtfully; **~vorbehalt** *der* (Rechtsw.) mental reservation; **~welt** *die* intellectual world

gedanklich /gə'daŋklɪç/
A *Adj.* intellectual; **ein ~er Fehler** an error in reasoning; **die ~e Klarheit in diesem Werk** the clarity of thought in this work
B *adv.* intellectually

Gedärm /gə'dɛrm/ *das;* **~[e]s, ~e** ▸ⓘ **S. 435** intestines *pl.*; bowels *pl.*, (eines Tieres) entrails *pl.*

Gedeck *das;* **~[e]s, ~e** [1] place setting; cover; **ein ~ auflegen** lay *or* set a place [2] (Menü) set meal [3] (Getränk) drink [with a cover charge]

gedeckt
A *2. Part. v.* **decken**
B *Adj.* subdued; muted; *s. auch* **Apfelkuchen**

Gedeih *in* **auf ~ und Verderb** for good or ill; for better or [for] worse; **jmdm. auf ~ und Verderb ausgeliefert sein** be entirely at sb.'s mercy

gedeihen /gə'daiən/ *unr. itr. V.; mit sein* [1] thrive; (wirtschaftlich) flourish; prosper; **gut/schlecht gediehen sein** have/not have thrived [2] (fortschreiten) progress; **noch nicht sehr weit gediehen sein** have not yet progressed very far

gedeihlich
A *Adj.* (geh.) thriving, flourishing, successful ‹*business*›; successful ‹*development, cooperation*›; beneficial ‹*effect etc.*›
B *adv.* successfully

ge·denken *unr. itr. V.* [1] (geh.: zurückdenken, sich erinnern) **jmds./einer Sache** *od.* (schweiz.) **jmdm./einer Sache** (*Dat.*) **~:** remember sb./sth.; (erwähnen) recall sb./sth.; (in einer Feier) commemorate sb./sth. [2] (beabsichtigen) intend

Gedenken *das;* **~s** (geh.) remembrance; memory; **Worte des ~s** words of remembrance; **zum ~ an jmdn./etw.** in memory *or* remembrance of sb./sth.

Gedenk-: ~feier *die* commemoration; commemorative ceremony; **~gottesdienst** *der* ▸ **Gedächtnisgottesdienst**; **~marke** *die* (Philat.) commemorative stamp; **~minute** *die* minute's silence; **eine ~minute einlegen** observe a minute's silence; **~münze** *die* commemorative coin; **~rede** *die* commemorative speech; **~stätte** *die* memorial; **~stein** *der* memorial *or* commemorative stone; **~stunde** *die* hour of commemoration; **~tafel** *die* commemorative plaque; **~tag** *der* day of remembrance; commemoration day

Gedicht *das;* **~[e]s, ~e** poem; **Goethes ~e** Goethe's poetry *sing. or* poems; **das Steak/Kleid ist ein ~** (fig. ugs.) the steak is just superb/the dress is just heavenly

Gedicht-: ~interpretation *die* interpretation of a poem; **~sammlung** *die* collection of poems; (von mehreren Dichtern) anthology of poetry *or* verse; poetry anthology

gediegen /gə'di:gn̩/

A *Adj.* **1** (solide) solid, solidly made ‹*furniture*›; sound, solid ‹*piece of work*›; well-made ‹*clothing*›; **~e Kenntnisse/ein ~es Wissen** sound knowledge; **ein ~er Charakter** a sterling character **2** (rein) pure ‹*gold, silver, etc.*›; (in der Natur rein vorkommend) native ‹*metal*› **3** (ugs.: komisch) hilarious; **eine ~e Marke/Type sein** be good fun (coll.) **4** (wunderlich) odd; peculiar

B *adv.* **~ gebaut/verarbeitet** solidly built/made

Gediegenheit *die;* **~:** solidity; (von Kleidung) sound manufacture; (von Metall) purity

gedieh /gə'di:/ *1. u. 3. Pers. Sg. Prät. v.* **gedeihen**

gediehen *2. Part. v.* **gedeihen**

gedient /gə'di:nt/

A *2. Part. v.* **dienen**

B *Adj.* **ein ~er Soldat** a former soldier

Gedinge *das;* **~s, ~** (Bergmannsspr.: Akkordlohn) piece rate pay; (Vereinbarung) piecework agreement; **im ~ arbeiten** work on a piecework basis

Gedöns /gə'dø:ns/ *das;* **~es** (landsch.) fuss; **ein ~ machen** make a fuss

Gedränge *das;* **~s 1** (das Drängeln) pushing and shoving; (Menschenmenge) crush; crowd; **vor der Theaterkasse herrschte ein großes ~:** there was a big crush in front of the box office **2** *in* **ins ~ kommen** *od.* **geraten** get into difficulties **3** **mit dem Termin/der Zeit ins ~ kommen** *od.* **geraten** have problems meeting the deadline/get into difficulties through lack of time **4** (Rugby) scrum; scrummage

gedrängt

A *2. Part. v.* **drängen**

B *Adj.* compressed, condensed ‹*account*›; terse, succinct ‹*style, description*›; crowded ‹*timetable, agenda*›

C *adv.* **~ schreiben** write succinctly *or* tersely; **etw. ~ behandeln** treat sth. in a condensed form

gedroschen /gə'drɔʃn̩/ *2. Part. v.* **dreschen**

gedrückt

A *2. Part. v.* **drücken**

B *Adj.* dejected, depressed ‹*mood*›

gedrungen /gə'drʊŋən/

A *2. Part. v.* **dringen**

B *Adj.* stocky; thickset

Gedrungenheit *die;* **~:** stockiness

Gedudel *das;* **~s** (ugs. abwertend) tootling; (im Radio) noise

Geduld /gə'dʊlt/ *die;* **~:** patience; **meine ~ ist erschöpft/am Ende** my patience is exhausted/at an end; **die ~ verlieren** lose one's patience; **keine ~ [zu etw.] haben** have no patience [with sth.]; **mit jmdm. ~ haben** be patient with sb.; **haben Sie bitte noch ein wenig ~:** please bear with me/us *etc.* a little while longer; **ihm riss die ~:** his patience snapped *or* gave way; **mir reißt die ~:** my patience is wearing thin; I'm losing all patience; **sich in ~ fassen** exercise *or* have patience; **mit ~ und Spucke** (fig. salopp) with a little patience [and ingenuity]

gedulden *refl. V.* be patient; **~ Sie sich bitte ein paar Minuten** please be so good as to wait a few minutes

geduldig

A *Adj.* patient; **ein ~er Patient** a good patient; **~ wie ein Lamm** meek as a lamb

B *adv.* patiently

Gedulds-: ~faden *der:* *in* **mir/ihm** *etc.* **reißt der ~faden** (ugs.) my/his *etc.* patience is wearing thin; **~probe** *die* trial of one's patience; **das ist eine harte ~probe für mich** that sorely tries my patience; **auf eine harte ~probe gestellt werden** have one's patience sorely tried; **~spiel** *das* puzzle; (fig.) Chinese puzzle

gedungen /gə'dʊŋən/ *2. Part. v.* **dingen**

gedunsen /gə'dʊnzn̩/ *Adj.* ▸ **aufgedunsen**

gedurft /gə'dʊrft/ *2. Part. v.* **dürfen**

geeignet

A *2. Part. v.* **eignen**

B *Adj.* suitable; (richtig) right; **er ist der ~e Mann für diese Aufgabe** he's the right man for this job; **im ~en Augenblick** at the right moment; **ich war für diese Arbeit nicht ~:** I wasn't suited to the work; **er ist zum Lehrer ~:** he makes a good teacher; **das Fernsehprogramm ist ~, die Leute zu vergraulen** the television schedule is designed to put people off

-geeignet *adj.* suitable for ...; ...-friendly; **rollstuhl~:** suitable for wheelchairs; wheelchair-friendly; **medien~:** media-friendly; **familien~:** family-friendly

Geest /ge:st/ *die;* **~:** *sandy heathland on N. German coast*

Gefahr *die;* **~, ~en 1** (gefährliche Lage) danger; (Bedrohung) danger; threat; **die ~en meines Berufs** the hazards of my job; **die ~en des Dschungels** the perils of the jungle; **eine ~ für jmdn./etw.** a danger to sb./sth.; **in ~ kommen/geraten** get into danger; **jmdn./etw. in ~ bringen** put sb./sth. in danger; **sich in ~ begeben** put oneself in danger; expose oneself to danger; **in ~ sein** be in danger; ‹*rights, plans*› be in jeopardy *or* peril; **außer ~ sein** be out of danger; **bei ~:** in case of emergency; **sie liebt die ~:** she likes living dangerously **2** (Risiko) risk; **jmdn./sich einer ~ aussetzen** run *or* take a risk; **es besteht die ~, dass ...** there is a danger *or* risk that ...; **auf die ~ hin, dass das passiert** at the risk of that happening; **~ laufen, etw. zu tun** risk *or* run the risk of doing sth.; **auf eigene ~:** at one's own risk; **wer sich in ~ begibt, kommt darin um** if you keep on taking risks, you'll come to grief eventually

gefahr·bringend *Adj.* dangerous

gefährden /gə'fɛ:ɐ̯dn̩/ *tr. V.* endanger; jeopardize ‹*enterprise, success, position, etc.*›; (aufs Spiel setzen) put at risk; **sich ~:** put oneself in danger

gefährdet *Adj.* ‹*people, adolescents, etc.*› at risk *postpos.*

Gefährdung *die;* **~, ~en 1** endangering; (eines Unternehmens, einer Position usw.) jeopardizing **2** (Gefahr) threat (+ *Gen.* to)

gefahren *2. Part. v.* **fahren**

Gefahren-: ~bereich *der* danger area *or* zone; **~herd** *der* source of danger; **~quelle** *die* source of danger; **~zone** *die* danger zone *or* area; **~zulage** *die* danger money *no indef. art.*

gefährlich /gə'fɛ:ɐ̯lɪç/

A *Adj.* dangerous; (gewagt) risky; **ein Mann im ~en Alter** (fig.) a man at a dangerous age; **[für jmdn./etw.] ~ sein** be dangerous [for sb./sth.]; **er könnte mir ~ werden** he could be a threat *or* a danger to me; (fig.) I could fall for him [in a big way]; **das ist [alles] nicht so ~:** it's not disastrous; **ein ~er Plan/~es Unternehmen** a risky plan/enterprise; **ein ~es Spiel treiben** play a dangerous game

B *adv.* dangerously

Gefährlichkeit *die;* **~:** dangerousness; (Gewagtheit) riskiness

gefahr·los

A *Adj.* safe

B *adv.* safely

Gefahr·losigkeit *die;* **~:** safety; safeness

Gefährt *das;* **~[e]s, ~e** (geh.) vehicle

Gefährte *der;* **~n, ~n, Gefährtin** *die;* **~, ~nen** (geh.) companion; (Ehemann/Ehefrau) partner in life

gefahr·voll *Adj.* dangerous; perilous

Gefälle /gə'fɛlə/ *das;* **~s, ~ 1** (Neigungsgrad) slope; incline; (eines Flusses) drop; (einer Straße) gradient; **ein ~ von fünf Prozent** a gradient of one in twenty *or* of five per cent; **das Gelände hat ein leichtes ~:** the land slopes gently **2** (Unterschied) difference; **das geistige/soziale ~:** the difference in intellect/social class

gefallen[1] *unr. itr. V.* **1** **das gefällt mir** I like it; **das gefällt ihm gut/gar nicht** he likes it very much *or* (coll.) a lot/doesn't like it at all; **es gefiel ihr, wie er sich bewegte** she liked the way he moved; **zu ~ wissen** know how to make oneself liked [by everyone]; **weißt du, was mir an dir/dem Bild so gut gefällt?** do you know what I like so much about you/the picture?; **mir gefällt es hier** I like it here; **er gefällt mir [ganz und gar] nicht** (ugs.: sieht krank aus) he looks in a bad way to me (coll.); **die Sache gefällt mir nicht** (ugs.) I don't like [the look of] it (coll.); **wenn es dem Herrn gefällt** (geh.) if it please God; if it is God's will **2** (ugs.) *in* **sich** (*Dat.*) **etw. ~ lassen** put up with sth.; **das lasse ich mir nicht länger ~:** I won't put up with it *or* stand for it any longer; **das lasse ich mir ~!** there's nothing I like better; that's just the job (coll.) **3** (abwertend) **sich** (*Dat.*) **in einer Rolle ~:** enjoy *or* like playing a role; fancy oneself in a role (coll.); **er gefällt sich in der Rolle des Intellektuellen** he likes playing the intellectual; **er gefällt sich in Übertreibungen** he likes to exaggerate

gefallen[2]

A *2. Part. v.* **fallen, gefallen**

B *Adj.* fallen ‹*angel etc.*›; **ein ~es Mädchen** (veralt.) a fallen woman

Gefallen[1] *der;* **~s, ~:** favour; **jmdm. einen ~ tun** *od.* **erweisen** do sb. a favour; **tu mir den** *od.* **einen ~, und ...!** (ugs.) do me a favour and ...; **jmdn. um einen ~ bitten** ask a favour of sb.

Gefallen[2] *das;* **~s** pleasure; **etw. mit ~ betrachten** get pleasure from *or* enjoy looking at sth.; **~ an jmdm./aneinander finden** like sb./each other; **an etw.** (*Dat.*) **~ finden** get *or* derive pleasure from sth.; enjoy sth.; **jmdm. etw. zu ~ tun** do sth. to please sb.

Gefallene *der; adj. Dekl.* soldier killed in action; **die ~n** the fallen; those killed *or* those who fell in action

Gefallenen·denkmal *das* war memorial

Gefälle·strecke *die* incline

ge·fällig

A *Adj.* **1** (hilfsbereit) obliging; helpful; **jmdm. ~ sein** oblige *or* help sb.; **sich ~ zeigen/[als] ~ erweisen** show oneself willing to oblige *or* help **2** (anziehend) pleasing; agreeable; pleasant, agreeable ‹*programme, behaviour*› **3** (gewünscht) **folgen Sie mir, wenns ~ ist!** follow me, if you please; **noch ein Kaffee ~?** would you like *or* care for another coffee?

B *adv.* pleasingly; agreeably

Gefälligkeit *die;* **~, ~en 1** (Hilfeleistung) favour; **jmdm. eine [kleine] ~ erweisen** do sb. a [small] favour **2** (Hilfsbereitschaft) obligingness; helpfulness; **etw. aus reiner ~ tun** do sth. just to be obliging **3** (ansprechende Art) agreeableness; pleasantness

Gefälligkeits-akzept *das,* **Gefälligkeits·wechsel** *der* (Bankw.) accommodation bill

gefälligst /gə'fɛlɪçst/ *Adv.* (ugs.) kindly; **lass das ~!** kindly stop that

Gefäll·strecke *die* ▸ **Gefällestrecke**

Gefall·sucht *die* (veralt.) vanity

gefall·süchtig *Adj.* (veralt.) vain

gefangen *2. Part. v.* **fangen**

Gefangene *der/die; adj. Dekl.* **1** prisoner; captive; **~ machen** take prisoners **2** (Häftling, Kriegs~) prisoner

Gefangenen-: ~austausch *der* exchange of prisoners; **~befreiung** *die* (Rechtsw.) aiding and abetting the escape of a prisoner; **~haus** *das* (österr.) ▸ **Gefängnis**; **~lager** *das* prisoner of war camp; prison camp

gefangen-, Gefangen-: ***~|halten** ▸**fangen A2**; **~nahme** *die;* **~~, ~~nen** capture; **bei seiner ~nahme** when he was captured; ***~|nehmen** ▸**fangen A2**

Gefangenschaft *die;* **~, ~en** captivity; **in ~ sein/geraten** be a prisoner/be taken prisoner; **in russischer ~ sein** be a prisoner of the Russians

***gefangen|setzen** ▸**fangen A2**

Gefängnis /gəˈfɛŋnɪs/ *das;* **~ses, ~se** [1] (Strafanstalt) prison; gaol; **jmdn. ins ~ bringen/werfen** put/throw sb. in[to] prison; **im ~ sein** *od.* **sitzen** be in prison; **ins ~ kommen** be sent to prison; **mit einem Bein** *od.* **Fuß im ~ stehen** be only just on the right side of the law [2] (Strafe) imprisonment; **darauf steht ~:** that is punishable by imprisonment *or* a prison sentence; **ein Vergehen mit ~ bestrafen** punish an offence with imprisonment; **jmdn. zu zwei Jahren ~ verurteilen** sentence sb. to two years' imprisonment *or* two years in prison

Gefängnis-: ~arzt *der,* **~ärztin** *die* prison doctor; **~direktor** *der,* **~direktorin** *die* prison governor; **~geistliche** *der/die* prison chaplain; **~haft** *die* imprisonment; **~hof** *der* prison yard; **~kleidung** *die* prison uniform; **~mauer** *die* prison wall; **~strafe** *die* prison sentence; **eine ~strafe verbüßen** *od.* (ugs.) **absitzen** serve a prison sentence; **eine ~strafe von sechs Monaten** six months' imprisonment; six months in prison; **jmdn. zu einer ~strafe [von acht Monaten] verurteilen** send sb. to prison [for eight months]; **~wärter** *der,* **~wärterin** *die* ▸ⓘ **S. 113** prison officer; [prison] warder; **~zelle** *die* prison cell

Gefasel *das;* **~s** (ugs. abwertend) twaddle (coll.); drivel (derog.)

Gefäß /gəˈfɛːs/ *das;* **~es, ~e** [1] (Behälter) vessel; container [2] ▸ⓘ **S. 435** (Med.) vessel [3] (Fechten) coquille

gefäß-, Gefäß-: ~erweiternd (Med.) **A** *Adj.* vasodilating; **B** *adv.* **~erweiternd wirken** have a vasodilating effect; **~erweiterung** *die* ▸ⓘ **S. 439** (Med.) vasodilation; vascular dilation; **~leiden** *das* ▸ⓘ **S. 439** (Med.) vascular complaint

gefasst, *gefaßt /gəˈfast/
A *2. Part. v.* **fassen**
B *Adj.* [1] (beherrscht) calm; composed; **mit ~er Haltung** with composure; **mit ~er Stimme** in a calm voice [2] *in* **auf etw.** *(Akk.)* **[nicht] ~ sein** [not] be prepared for sth.; **sich auf etw.** *(Akk.)* **~ machen** prepare oneself for sth.; **der kann sich auf was ~ machen** (ugs.) he'll catch it *or* be for it (coll.)
C *adv.* calmly; with composure

Gefasstheit, *Gefaßtheit *die* calmness; composure

gefäß-, Gefäß-: ~verengend (Med.) **A** *Adj.* vasoconstrictive; **B** *adv.* **~verengend wirken** have a vasoconstrictive effect; **~verengung** *die* ▸ⓘ **S. 439** (Med.) vaso-constriction; vascular constriction; **~wand** *die* ▸ⓘ **S. 435** (Med.) vascular wall

Gefecht *das;* **~[e]s, ~e** [1] battle; engagement (Milit.); **ein schweres/kurzes ~:** fierce fighting/a skirmish; **sich** *(Dat.)***/dem Feind ein ~ liefern** engage each other/the enemy in battle; **die Truppen ins ~ führen** lead the troops into battle; **ein hitziges ~** (fig.) a heated exchange; **jmdn./etw. außer ~ setzen** put sb./sth. out of action; **klar zum ~!** (Marine) clear for action! [2] (Fechten) bout; *s. auch* **Eifer**

gefechts-, Gefechts-: ~ausbildung *die* (Milit.) combat training; battle training; **~bereich** *der* (Milit.) battle zone; battle area; combat zone (Amer.); **~bereit** *Adj.* (Milit.) ready for action *or* battle *postpos.;* combat-ready; **~bereitschaft** *die* (Milit.) readiness for action; readiness for battle; **sich in ~bereitschaft befinden** be ready for action *or* battle; **~einheit** *die* (Milit.) fighting unit; **~klar** *Adj.* ▸**~bereit**; **~kopf** *der* (Milit.) warhead; **~mäßig** (Milit.) **A** *Adj.* ‹*equipment*› for active service; combat ‹*firing practice, formation, etc.*›; **B** *adv.* **~mäßig ausgerüstet** equipped for active service *or* for battle; **~pause** *die* lull in the fighting; **~stand** *der* (Milit.) battle headquarters *pl.;* command post; (Luftw.) operations room; **~stärke** *die* (Milit.) fighting strength; **~turm** *der* (Milit.) turret; **~übung** *die* (Milit.) combat exercise; field exercise

gefedert *2. Part. v.* **federn**

gefehlt
A *2. Part. v.* **fehlen**
B *Adj.* **weit ~!** wide of the mark!

Gefeilsche *das;* **~s** haggling

gefeit *2. Part. v.* **feien**

gefestigt
A *2. Part. v.* **festigen**
B *Adj.* assured ‹*beliefs*›; secure ‹*person*›; established ‹*tradition*›

Gefiedel *das;* **~s** (abwertend) fiddling

Gefieder /gəˈfiːdɐ/ *das;* **~s, ~:** plumage; feathers *pl.*

gefiedert *Adj.* [1] (mit Federn) feathered; **unsere ~en Freunde** our feathered friends [2] (Bot.) pinnate; **paarig/unpaarig ~:** abruptly pinnate/odd-pinnate

Gefilde /gəˈfɪldə/ *das;* **~s, ~** (geh.) **anmutige/sonnige ~:** pleasant/sunny climes (literary); **die ~ der Seligen** (griech. Myth.) the Elysian Fields; **wieder in heimatlichen ~n sein** (scherzh.) be back under one's native skies

gefingert
A *2. Part. v.* **fingern**
B *Adj.* (Bot.) digitate[d]; palmate

gefinkelt /gəˈfɪŋkl̩t/ *Adj.* (österr.) cunning; crafty; shrewd

geflammt
A *2. Part. v.* **flammen**
B *Adj.* mottled, wavy-grained ‹*wood*›; mottled ‹*tile*›; watered, moiré ‹*silk, fabric*›

Geflatter *das;* **~s** fluttering

Geflecht *das;* **~[e]s, ~e** [1] (Flechtwerk) wickerwork *no art.;* **ein ~ aus Binsen** interlaced rushes *pl.* [2] (fig.: dichtes Netz) tangle; **ein wirres/dichtes ~ von Zweigen und Wurzeln** a tangled/dense network of twigs and roots

gefleckt
A *2. Part. v.* **flecken**
B *Adj.* spotty, blotchy ‹*skin, face*›; spotted ‹*leopard skin*›

Geflenne *das;* **~s** (ugs. abwertend) bawling; blubbering

Geflimmer *das;* **~s** (auf dem Bildschirm, auf der Filmleinwand) flickering; (von Sternen) twinkling

geflissentlich /gəˈflɪsn̩tlɪç/
A *Adj.* [1] (absichtlich) deliberate [2] (Amtsspr. veralt.: freundlich) **zu Ihrer ~en Kenntnisnahme/Beachtung** for your information/for your esteemed consideration
B *adv.* deliberately; **jmdm. ~ aus dem Wege gehen** studiously avoid sb.

geflochten /gəˈflɔxtn̩/ *2. Part. v.* **flechten**

geflogen /gəˈfloːgn̩/ *2. Part. v.* **fliegen**

geflohen /gəˈfloːən/ *2. Part. v.* **fliehen**

geflossen /gəˈflɔsn̩/ *2. Part. v.* **fließen**

Gefluche *das;* **~s** (ugs. abwertend) swearing; cursing

Geflügel *das;* **~s** (Federvieh, Fleisch) poultry

Geflügel-: ~farm *die* poultry farm; **~haltung** *die* poultry farming; **~händler** *der,* **~händlerin** *die* poulterer; **~handlung** *die* poulterer's [shop]; **~pest** *die* avian flu; **~salat** *der* chicken salad/turkey salad *etc.;* **~schere** *die* poultry shears *pl.*

geflügelt *Adj.* winged ‹*insect, seed*›; **ein ~es Wort** (fig.) a standard *or* familiar quotation

Geflügel-: ~zucht *die* poultry breeding; **~züchter** *der,* **~züchterin** *die* poultry breeder

Geflunker *das;* **~s** (ugs.) fibbing (coll.)

Geflüster *das;* **~s** whispering

gefochten /gəˈfɔxtn̩/ *2. Part. v.* **fechten**

Gefolge *das;* **~s, ~** [1] (Begleitung) entourage; retinue; **etw. im ~ haben** lead to sth.; bring sth. in its wake [2] (Trauergeleit) cortège

Gefolgschaft *die;* **~, ~en** [1] (Gehorsam) **jmdm. ~ leisten** obey *or* follow sb.; give one's allegiance to sb.; **jmdm. die ~ aufsagen** *od.* **kündigen** refuse to obey sb. any longer; renounce one's allegiance to sb.; **jmdm. die ~ verweigern** refuse to obey *or* follow sb.; refuse to give sb. one's allegiance [2] (hist.) *band of young nobles bound to a peer leader by an oath of fealty;* ≈ followers *pl.*

Gefolgs-: ~frau *die* (bes. Politik) [female] follower; **~mann** *der; Pl.* **~männer** *od.* **~leute** *member of a Gefolgschaft;* ≈ follower; (fig.) follower

Gefrage *das;* **~s** (abwertend) questions *pl.*

gefragt
A *2. Part. v.* **fragen**
B *Adj.* ‹*artist, craftsman, product*› in great demand; sought-after ‹*artist, craftsman, product*›; **~ sein** *od.* **werden** be in great demand

gefräßig /gəˈfrɛːsɪç/ *Adj.* (abwertend) greedy; gluttonous; voracious ‹*animal, insect*›

Gefräßigkeit *die;* **~** (abwertend) greediness; gluttony; (von Tieren) voracity

Gefreite /gəˈfraitə/ *der; adj. Dekl.* ▸ⓘ **S. 44** (Milit.) lance corporal (Brit.); private first class (Amer.); (Marine) able seaman; (Luftw.) aircraftman first class (Brit.); airman third class (Amer.)

gefressen *2. Part. v.* **fressen**

Gefrier-: ~anlage *die* freezing plant; **~apparat** *der* freezing unit; freezer

gefrieren
A *unr. itr. V.; mit sein* (auch fig.) freeze; *s. auch* **Blut**
B *unr. tr. V.* (einfrieren) freeze

gefrier-, Gefrier-: ~fach *das* freezing compartment; **~fleisch** *das* frozen meat; **~gemüse** *das* frozen vegetables *pl.;* **~getrocknet** *2. Part. v.* **~trocknen**; **~gut** *das* frozen food; **~punkt** *der* ▸ⓘ **S. 703** freezing point; **Temperaturen über/unter dem ~punkt** temperatures above/below freezing; **~raum** *der* freezer; deep-freeze room; **~schrank** *der* [upright] freezer; **~schutz·mittel** *das* ▸**Frostschutzmittel**; **~|trocknen** *tr. V.; meist im Inf. u. 2. Part.* freeze-dry; **~truhe** *die* [chest] freezer

gefroren /gəˈfroːrən/ *2. Part. v.* **frieren, gefrieren**

Gefror[e]ne *das; adj. Dekl.* (südd., österr.) ice cream

Gefrotzel *das;* **~s** (ugs.) ribbing (coll.)

gefrustet *Adj.* (ugs.) frustrated

Gefuchtel *das;* **~s** gesticulating

Gefüge *das;* **~s, ~** [1] (Zusammengefügtes) structure; construction; **ein ~ aus Balken/Steinen** a construction of beams/stones [2] (Aufbau, Struktur) structure; **das syntaktische ~:** the syntactical structure; **das wirtschaftliche/soziale ~:** the economic/social fabric

gefügig *Adj.* submissive; compliant; docile ‹*animal*›; **ein ~es Werkzeug** (fig.) a willing tool; **sich** *(Dat.)* **jmdn. ~ machen/jmdn. seinen Wünschen ~ machen** make sb. submit to one's will/one's wishes

Gefügigkeit *die;* **~:** submissiveness; compliance; (von Tieren) docility

Gefühl *das;* **~s, ~e** [1] (Wahrnehmung) sensation; feeling; **ein ~ für Wärme und Kälte haben** be able to feel *or* tell the difference between hot and cold; **kein ~ im Arm haben** have no feeling in one's arm; **ein ~ des Schmerzes/der Kälte** a sensation of pain/cold [2] (Gemütsverfassung) feeling; **ein ~ der Einsamkeit/der Scham** a sense *or* feeling of loneliness/shame; **ein beglückendes/beängstigendes ~ überkam/ergriff sie** she was filled with a feeling of happiness/gripped by a feeling of anxiety; **kein ~ haben** have no feelings; **mit gemischten ~en** with mixed feelings; **drei Euro sind das höchste der ~e** (ugs.) three euros is the most I'm prepared to pay; (was man dafür verlangen kann) it won't fetch more than three euros [3] (Ahnung) feeling; **ein/das ~ haben, als ob …** have a/the feeling that …; **etw. im ~ haben** have a feeling *or* a premonition of sth. [4] (Verständnis, Gespür) sense; instinct; **ein ~ für Rhythmus/Gut und Böse** a sense of rhythm/right and wrong; **sich auf sein ~ verlassen** trust one's feelings *or* instinct; **etw. nach ~ tun** do sth. by instinct

gefühlig *Adj.* (abwertend) mushy, mawkish ‹*play, film, etc.*›; mawkish ‹*person*›

gefühl·los *Adj.* [1] (ohne Wahrnehmung) numb; ~ **gegen Schmerzen** insensitive to pain [2] (herzlos, kalt) unfeeling; callous

Gefühllosigkeit *die;* ~ [1] numbness; lack of sensation [2] (Mangel an Mitleid) unfeelingness; callousness

gefühls-, Gefühls-: ~aktiv *Adj.* supersensitive, extra sensitive ‹*condom*›; **~arm** *Adj.* lacking in feeling; **~armut** *die* lack of feeling; **~ausbruch** *der* outburst [of emotion]; **~betont** **A** *Adj.* emotional ‹*speech, argument*›; **B** *adv.* **~betont handeln** be guided by one's emotions; **~chaos** *das* emotional turmoil; **~dinge** *Pl.* emotional matters *pl.*; **~duselei** /-du:zəˈlai̯/ *die;* ~~ (ugs. abwertend) mawkishness; mawkish sentimentality; **~kalt** *Adj.* [1] cold; unfeeling; [2] (frigide) frigid; **~kälte** *die* [1] coldness; unfeelingness; [2] (Frigidität) frigidity; **~leben** *das* emotional life; **~mäßig** **A** *Adj.* emotional ‹*reaction*›; ‹*action*› based on emotion; **B** *adv.* **es hat sich ~mäßig auf ihn stark ausgewirkt** it has affected him deeply; **rein ~mäßig würde ich sagen, dass ...** my own, purely instinctive, feeling would be to say that ...; **~mensch** *der* emotionalist; person guided by his/her emotions; **~nerv** *der* sensory nerve; **~regung** *die* emotion; ***~roheit**, **~rohheit** *die* callousness; **~sache** *die* matter of feel *or* instinct; **~tiefe** *die* (geh.) depth of feeling; **~überschwang** *der* flood of emotion; **in seinem ~überschwang** carried away by emotion; **~welt** *die* emotions *pl.*

gefühl·voll
A *Adj.* [1] (empfindsam) sensitive [2] (ausdrucksvoll) expressive
B *adv.* sensitively; expressively; with feeling

gefüllt
A *2. Part. v.* **füllen**
B *Adj.* **~e Bonbons** sweets (Brit.) *or* (Amer.) candies with centres; **~e Tomaten/Paprikaschoten** stuffed tomatoes/peppers; **~er Flieder/~e Geranien** double lilac/geraniums; **eine [gut] ~e Brieftasche** a well-stuffed *or* bulging wallet

Gefummel *das;* ~s (ugs. abwertend) [1] fiddling (coll.); **lass doch das ~ an der Tischdecke!** stop fiddling with the tablecloth! [2] (erotisch) pawing (coll.)

gefunden /gəˈfʊndn̩/ *2. Part. v.* **finden;** *s. auch* **Fressen 2**

gefurcht
A *2. Part. v.* **furchen**
B *Adj.* lined; wrinkled

gefürchtet
A *2. Part. v.* **fürchten**
B *Adj.* dreaded; feared ‹*despot, opponent*›

gefüttert *2. Part. v.* **füttern**

gegabelt
A *2. Part. v.* **gabeln**
B *Adj.* forked ‹*branch, stick, tail*›

Gegacker *das;* ~s [1] (dauerndes Gackern) cackling [2] (ugs.: Kichern) giggling

gegangen *2. Part. v.* **gehen**

gegeben
A *2. Part. v.* **geben**
B *Adj.* [1] (vorhanden) given; **etw. als ~ voraussetzen/hinnehmen** take sth. for granted; **aus ~em Anlass** for certain reasons (specified or not); **aus ~em Anlass kann ich nicht umhin, auch einige Worte der Kritik zu äußern** [there are reasons why] I cannot refrain from offering some criticisms; **unter den ~en Umständen** in these circumstances; **eine ~e Größe/Zahl** (Math.) a given magnitude/number [2] (passend) right; proper; **das ist das Gegebene** that's the best thing; **zu ~er Zeit** in due course; at the appropriate time

gegebenen·falls *Adv.* should the occasion arise; (wenn nötig) if necessary; (auf einem Formular) if applicable

Gegebenheit *die;* ~, ~en condition; (Tatsache) fact; **die wirtschaftlichen und sozialen ~en** the economic and social conditions

gegen /ˈgeːgn̩/
A *Präp. mit Akk.* [1] towards; (an) against; **das Dia ~ das Licht halten** hold the slide up to *or* against the light; **~ die Tür schlagen** bang on the door; **~ etw. stoßen** knock into *or* against sth.; **das ist [nicht] ~ Sie gerichtet** that is [not] aimed against you; **ein Mittel ~ Husten/Krebs** a cough medicine/a cure for cancer; **~ jmdn. spielen/gewinnen** play [against] sb./win against sb.; **etwas/nichts ~ jmdn. haben** have something/nothing against sb.; **~ die Abmachung** contrary to *or* against the agreement; **~ alle Vernunft/bessere Einsicht** against all reason/one's better judgement; **~ jmds. Willen/Befehl** against *or* contrary to sb.'s wishes/orders [2] ▸❶ **S. 729** (ungefähr um) **~ Abend/Morgen** towards evening/dawn; **~ 4⁰⁰ nachts** around 4 a. m. *or* 4 o'clock in the morning [3] (im Vergleich zu) compared with; in comparison with; **~ gestern** compared with yesterday; **ich wette hundert ~ eins, dass er ...** I'll bet you a hundred to one he ... [4] (im Ausgleich für) for; **etw. ~ bar verkaufen/tauschen** sell/exchange sth. for cash; **etw. ~ Quittung erhalten** receive sth. against a receipt [5] (veralt.: gegenüber) **~ jmdn. freundlich/höflich sein** be pleasant/polite to *or* towards sb.; **~ jmdn./sich streng sein** be strict with sb./oneself
B *Adv.* ▸❶ **S. 729** (ungefähr) about; around

Gegen-: ~angebot *das* counter-offer; **~angriff** *der* counter-attack; **zum ~angriff ansetzen** mount *or* launch a counter-attack; **~antrag** *der* (im Parlament) countermotion; **~anzeige** *die* (Med.) contraindication; **~argument** *das* counter-argument; **~beispiel** *das* example to the contrary; counter-example; **~beschuldigung** *die* countercharge; counter accusation; **~besuch** *der* return visit; **~bewegung** *die* [1] countermovement; [2] (Musik) (bei der Melodie) inversion; (bei Tonleitern usw.) contrary motion; **~beweis** *der* evidence to the contrary, counter-evidence *no indef. art., no pl.*; **den ~beweis antreten** *od.* **führen** produce evidence to the contrary *or* counter-evidence; **~buchung** *die* (Buchf.) cross-entry

Gegend /ˈgeːgn̩t/ *die;* ~, ~en [1] (Landschaft) landscape; (geographisches Gebiet) region; **die ~ ist flach/gebirgig** the region is flat/mountainous; **durch die ~ latschen/kurven** (salopp) traipse around (coll.)/drive around; **in der ~ herumbrüllen** (salopp) bawl one's head off (coll.) [2] (Umgebung) area; neighbourhood; (Stadtviertel) district; neighbourhood; (Einwohnerschaft) neighbourhood; **in der ~ von/um Hamburg** in the Hamburg area; **in der ~ des Parks** in the neighbourhood of the park; **ein Einbrecher/eine Jugendbande macht die ~ unsicher** (ugs.) there is a burglar about in the neighbourhood/a gang of youths are making a nuisance of themselves in this area [3] **in der ~ des Magens/der Leber** in the region of the stomach/the liver [4] (Richtung) direction

Gegen-: ~darstellung *die:* **eine ~darstellung [der Sache]** an account [of the matter] from an opposing point of view; **~demonstration** *die* counter-demonstration; **~dienst** *der* service in return; (Gefälligkeit) favour in return; **~druck** *der; Pl.* **~drücke** counterpressure; (fig.) resistance

gegen·einander *Adv.* [1] against each other *or* one another; (im Austausch) **man tauschte die Geiseln ~ aus** the hostages were exchanged; **es ist schwierig, diese beiden Begriffe/Epochen ~ abzugrenzen** it is difficult to distinguish these two concepts/to divide these two periods from each other; **die beiden haben etwas ~:** those two have got something against each other; **zwei Dinge ~ halten** hold two things up together *or* side by side; (vergleichen) compare two things; put two things side by side; **~ prallen** collide; **Bretter/Fahrräder ~ stellen** stand planks/bicycles [up] against one another [2] (zueinander) to[wards] each other *or* one another

Gegen·einander *das;* ~s conflict

***gegeneinander|halten** *usw.:* ▸**gegeneinander**

gegen-, Gegen-: ~entwurf *der* alternative draft; **~erklärung** *die* counter-statement; rebuttal; **~fahrbahn** *die* opposite carriageway; **~forderung** *die* [1] countercondition; [2] (Forderung eines Schuldners) counterclaim; **~frage** *die* question in return; counterquestion; **auf eine Frage mit einer ~frage antworten** answer a question with another question; **~gabe** *die* (geh.) present *or* gift in return; **~gerade** *die* (Leichtathletik) back straight; **~gewalt** *die* counter-violence; **~gewicht** *das* counterweight; **ein ~gewicht zu** *od.* **gegen etw. bilden** (fig.) counterbalance sth.; **~gift** *das* antidote; **~grund** *der* ▸**Grund 3**; **~|halten** **A** *unr. tr., itr. V.* (nordd. ugs.) **[die Hand/den Finger] ~halten** hold one's hand/finger against it. **B** *unr. itr. V.* resist; (kämpfen) fight back; **politisch ~halten** offer political resistance; **~kandidat** *der,* **~kandidatin** *die* opposing candidate; rival candidate; **~klage** *die* (Rechtsw.) counterclaim; countercharge; **~klage [gegen jmdn.] erheben** bring a counterclaim *or* countercharge/countercharges *pl.* [against sb.]; **~kläger** *der,* **~klägerin** *die* (Rechtsw.) counterclaimant; **~könig** *der,* **~königin** *die* (hist.) rival claimant to the throne; **~kraft** *die* opposing force; counterforce; **~kultur** *die* counterculture; alternative culture; **~kurs** *der* (Flugw.) reciprocal course; **auf ~kurs gehen** set a reciprocal course; (fig.) steer an opposite course; **~läufig** **A** *Adj.* opposed ‹*pistons*›; contra-rotating ‹*propellers*›; **eine ~läufige Entwicklung/Tendenz** (fig.) a reverse development/trend; **B** *adv.* **sich ~läufig bewegen** ‹*pistons*› be opposed; ‹*propellers*› contra-rotate; **~leistung** *die* service in return; consideration; **als ~leistung für etw.** in return for sth.; **zu einer ~leistung bereit sein** be prepared to do sth. in return; **~|lenken** *itr. V.* turn the wheel to correct the line; **~|lesen** *unr. tr. V.* read as a check

Gegen·licht *das* (bes. Fot.) back-lighting

Gegenlicht·aufnahme *die* (Fot.) photograph taken/taking a picture against the light; contre-jour photograph

gegen-, Gegen-: ~liebe *die:* **in [bei jmdm.] ~liebe finden** *od.* **auf ~liebe stoßen** find favour [with sb.]; **~maßnahme** *die* countermeasure; **~meinung** *die* opposing *or* dissenting view; **~mittel** *das* (gegen Gift) antidote; (gegen Krankheit) remedy; **ein ~mittel für ein Gift/~ eine Krankheit** an antidote for *or* to a poison/a remedy for a disease; **~mutter** *die; Pl.* **~~n** (Technik) locking nut; locknut; **~offensive** *die* (Milit.) counter-offensive; **~papst** *der* (hist.) antipope; **~part** *der* (geh.) counterpart; (Gegner) opponent; **~partei** *die* opposing side; other side; (Sport) opposing side *or* team; **~plan** *der* (DDR Wirtsch.) counterplan (*to supplement the national economic plan*); **~pol** *der* (auch fig.) opposite pole; (Math.) antipole; **~probe** *die* [1] (einer Behauptung, These) cross-check; **durch die ~probe** by cross-checking; **die ~probe machen** carry out a cross-check; (bei einer Rechnung) work the sum the other way round; [2] (bei Abstimmungen durch Handzeichen od. Aufstehen) recount in which the opposite motion is put; **~propaganda** *die* counter-propaganda; **~rechnung** *die* contra account; check account; **[jmdm.] die ~rechnung aufmachen** make out a contra account for sb.; (fig.) reply with one's own set of figures; **~rede** *die* [1] (geh.: Erwiderung) reply; rejoinder; **Rede und ~rede** dialogue; **ein amüsantes Spiel von Rede und ~rede** an amusing series of exchanges; [2] (Widerrede) contradiction; (Einspruch) objection; **~reformation** *die* (hist.) Counter-Reformation; **~revolution** *die* counter-revolution; **~richtung** *die* opposite direction; **~ruder** *das* (Flugw.) [1] (zur Erleichterung des Steuerns) servo tab; [2] (zur Einhaltung der Fluglage) trim tab; **~satz** *der* [1] (**~teil**) opposite; **einen schroffen/diametralen ~satz zu etw./jmdm. bilden** contrast sharply with/be diametrically opposed to sth./sb.; **im ~satz zu** in contrast to *or* with; unlike; **~sätze ziehen**

sich an opposites attract; **2** (Widerspruch) conflict; **im krassen/scharfen ~satz zu etw. stehen** be in stark/sharp conflict with sth.; **3** *Pl.* (Meinungsverschiedenheiten) **~sätze abbauen/überbrücken** reduce/reconcile differences; **~sätzlich** **A** *Adj.* conflicting ‹*views, opinions, etc.*›; **~sätzliche Fronten** opposing alignments; **B** *adv.* **etw. ~sätzlich beurteilen** judge sth. completely differently; **~schlag** *der* counterstroke; **zum ~schlag ausholen** prepare to counter-attack *or* strike back; **~seite** *die* **1** (einer Straße, eines Flusses usw.) other side; far side; **2** ▸ **~partei**; **~seitig** **A** *Adj.* **1** (wechselseitig) mutual ‹*aid, consideration, love, consent, services*›; reciprocal ‹*aid, obligation, services*›; **in ~seitiger Abhängigkeit stehen** be mutually dependent; be dependent on each other *or* one another; **2** (beide Seiten betreffend) **eine ~seitige Abmachung** a bilateral arrangement; **in ~seitigem Einvernehmen** by mutual agreement; **B** *adv.* **sich ~seitig helfen/überbieten** help/outdo each other *or* one another; **~seitigkeit** *die;* **~~:** reciprocity; **auf ~seitigkeit** (*Dat.*) **beruhen** be mutual; **~sinn** *der:* **in im ~sinn** in the opposite direction; **~spieler** *der,* **~spielerin** *die* **1** (Widersacher) opponent; **2** (Sport) opposite number; **3** (Theater) antagonist; **~spionage** *die* counter-espionage; **~sprechanlage** *die* intercom [system]; (Fernspr.) duplex system; **~sprechverkehr** *der* two-way communication

Gegen·stand *der* **1** (Ding, Körper) object; **Gegenstände des täglichen Gebrauchs/Bedarfs** objects *or* articles of everyday use **2** (Thema) subject; topic; **etw. zum ~ haben** deal with sth.; be concerned with sth. **3** (Objekt, Ziel) **der ~ seiner Zuneigung/seines Hasses** the object of his affections/of his hatred; **zum ~ der Kritik werden** become the target *or* butt of criticism **4** (österr.: Schulfach) subject

gegenständlich /ˈgeːgn̩ʃtɛntlɪç/ *Adj.* (Kunst) representational; (Philos.) objective

gegenstands·los *Adj.* **1** (hinfällig) invalid; **das hat unsere Pläne ~ gemacht** that's made nonsense of our plans **2** (grundlos, unbegründet) unsubstantiated, unfounded ‹*accusation, complaint*›; baseless ‹*fear*›; unfounded ‹*jealousy*› **3** (abstrakt) non-representational; abstract

Gegenstands·wort *das; Pl.* **Gegenstands·wörter** (Sprachw.) concrete noun

gegen-, Gegen-: **~|steuern** *itr. V.* **1** ▸ **~lenken**; **2** (fig.) take countermeasures; **~stimme** *die* **1** vote against; **ohne ~stimme** unanimously; **das Gesetz passierte mit 380 Jastimmen und 80 ~stimmen das Parlament** the law was passed by Parliament by 380 votes to 80; **2** (~teilige Meinung) dissenting voice; **3** (Musik) counterpart; **~stoß** *der* **1** ▸ **~schlag**; **2** ▸ **~angriff**; **~strömung** *die* countercurrent; **~stück** *das* **1** (Pendant) companion piece; (fig.) counterpart; **2** ▸ **~teil**; **~teil** *das* opposite; **im ~teil** on the contrary; **ganz im ~teil** far from it; quite the reverse; **die Stimmung schlug ins ~teil um** the mood changed completely; **~teilig** *Adj.* opposite; contrary; **~teiliger Meinung/Ansicht sein** hold the opposite opinion *or* view; be of the opposite opinion; **~teilige Aussagen** contradictory statements; **~tor** *das,* **~treffer** *der* (Sport) goal for the other side; **ein ~tor** *od.* **einen ~treffer hinnehmen müssen** concede a goal

gegen·über

A *Präp. mit Dat.* **1** ▸ ❶ **S. 800** (auf der entgegengesetzten Seite) opposite; **~ dem Bahnhof/Rathaus, dem Bahnhof/Rathaus ~:** opposite the station/town hall **2** (in Bezug auf) **~ jmdm.** *od.* **jmdm. ~ freundlich/streng sein** be kind to/strict with sb.; **~ einer Sache** *od.* **einer Sache ~ skeptisch sein** be sceptical about sth.; **~ uns** *od.* **uns ~ brauchst du wirklich keine Hemmungen zu haben** you really needn't have any inhibitions with us **3** (im Vergleich zu) compared with; in comparison with; **~ jmdm. im Vorteil sein** have an advantage over sb.

B *Adv.* ▸ ❶ **S. 800** opposite; **er wohnt schräg ~:** he lives diagonally opposite

Gegen·über *das;* **~s, ~** **1** (gegenübersitzende/-stehende Person) person [sitting/standing] opposite; (Gesprächspartner) person one is talking to **2** (Bewohner eines gegenüberliegenden Gebäudes) person living opposite; **kein ~ haben** have no one living opposite

gegenüber-, Gegenüber-: **~|liegen** *unr. itr. V.* **sich** (*Dat.*) *od.* **einander ~liegen** face each other *or* one another; **auf der ~liegenden Seite/am ~liegenden Ufer** on the opposite side/bank; **~|sehen** *unr. refl. V.* **sich jmdm./etw. ~sehen** find oneself facing sb./sth.; **sich einer Sache** (*Dat.*) **~sehen** (fig.) be faced with sth.; **~|sitzen** *unr. itr. V.* **jmdm./sich ~sitzen** sit opposite *or* facing sb./each other; **~|stehen** *unr. itr. V.* **1** (zugewandt stehen) **jmdm./einer Sache ~stehen** stand facing sb./sth.; **jmdm. Auge in Auge ~stehen** confront sb. face to face; **Schwierigkeiten/Problemen ~stehen** (fig.) be faced *or* confronted with difficulties/problems; **2** (eingestellt sein) **jmdm./einer Sache feindlich/wohlwollend ~stehen** be ill/well disposed towards sb./sth.; **jmdm./einer Sache misstrauisch ~stehen** be mistrustful of sb./sth.; *s. auch* **ablehnend**; **3** (Sport) **sich ~stehen** face each other *or* one another; meet; **4** (im Widerstreit stehen) **sich ~stehen** stand directly opposed to each other *or* one another; **~|stellen** *tr. V.* **1** (konfrontieren) confront; **jmdn. einem Zeugen ~stellen** to confront sb. with a witness; **2** (in Beziehung bringen) compare; **~stellung** *die* **1** (Konfrontation) confrontation; **2** (Vergleich) comparison; **~|treten** *unr. itr. V.; mit sein* face; **Schwierigkeiten** (*Dat.*) **~treten** face [up to] difficulties

Gegen-: **~verkehr** *der* oncoming traffic; **~vorschlag** *der* counter-proposal

Gegenwart /-vart/ *die;* **~** **1** present; (heutige Zeit) present [time *or* day]; **bis in die ~ fortwirken** continue [down] to the present day; **die Literatur/Musik der ~:** contemporary literature/music **2** (Anwesenheit) presence; **in ~ von anderen** in the presence of others **3** (Grammatik) present [tense]

gegenwärtig /-vɛrtɪç/

A *Adj.* **1** present; (heutig) present[-day]; current **2** (geh.: erinnerlich) **ich habe die Begebenheit nicht ~:** I cannot recall the event; **sich** (*Dat.*) **etw. ~ halten** keep sth. in mind **3** (veralt.: anwesend, zugegen) present; **bei etw. ~ sein** be present at sth.; **in dieser mittelalterlichen Stadt ist die Geschichte überall ~** (fig.) history is all around one in this medieval town

B *adv.* at present; at the moment; (heute) at present; currently

gegenwarts-, Gegenwarts-: **~bezogen** *Adj.* relevant to the present day *or* to today *postpos.*; **~fern** *Adj.* remote from the present *postpos.*; **~fremd** *Adj.* out of touch with the present *or* with today; **~kunde** *die* (Schulw.) political and social studies *sing., no art.*; **~kunst** *die* contemporary art *no art.*; **~literatur** *die* contemporary literature *no art.*; **~nah[e]** **A** *Adj.* relevant to the present day *or* to today *postpos.*; (aktuell) topical; **B** *adv.* **~nah denken** be up to date in one's thinking; **~nah unterrichten** teach in accordance with contemporary ideas; **~sprache** *die* present-day language; **die deutsche ~sprache** modern German; **~stück** *das* contemporary play

gegen-, Gegen-: **~wehr** *die* resistance; **[keine] ~wehr leisten** put up [no] resistance; **~welt** *die* alternative world; **~wert** *der* equivalent; **der volle ~wert für das gestohlene Auto** the full replacement value of the stolen car; **~wind** *der* head wind; **~winkel** *der* (Math.) opposite angle; **~wirkung** *die* reaction; **~|zeichnen** *tr. V.* countersign; **~zug** *der* **1** (Brettspiele, fig.) countermove; (Polit.) reciprocal gesture; **im ~zug** (fig.) in return for; **2** (entgegenkommender Zug) train in the opposite direction; **3** ▸ **~angriff**

gegessen /gəˈgɛsn̩/ *2. Part. v.* **essen**

geglichen /gəˈglɪçn̩/ *2. Part. v.* **gleichen**

geglitten /gəˈglɪtn̩/ *2. Part. v.* **gleiten**

Geglitzer *das;* **~s** (von Edelsteinen) glitter; sparkle; (von Sternen) twinkling

geglommen /gəˈglɔmən/ *2. Part. v.* **glimmen**

Geglucks[e] *das;* **~[e]s** chuckling; (lauter) chortling; **lass doch mal dein ~:** stop [that] chuckling/chortling

Gegner /ˈgeːgnɐ/ *der;* **~s, ~** **1** adversary; opponent; (Rivale) rival; **ein ~ der Todesstrafe sein** oppose *or* be an opponent of **2** (Sport) opponent; (Mannschaft) opposing team; **der ~ war für uns viel zu stark** the opposition was far too strong for us **3** (feindliches Heer) enemy

Gegnerin *die;* **~, ~nen** **1** ▸ **Gegner 1** **2** (Sport) opponent

gegnerisch *Adj.* **1** opposing **2** (Sport) opposing ‹*team, player, etc.*›; opponents' ‹*goal*› **3** (Milit.) enemy

Gegnerschaft *die;* **~** **1** (Einstellung) hostility; antagonism **2** (Gesamtheit der Gegner) opposition

gegolten /gəˈgɔltn̩/ *2. Part. v.* **gelten**

gegoren /gəˈgoːrən/ *2. Part. v.* **gären**

gegossen /gəˈgɔsn̩/ *2. Part. v.* **gießen**

gegriffen /gəˈgrɪfn̩/ *2. Part. v.* **greifen**

Gegrinse *das;* **~s** (abwertend) grinning

Gegröle *das;* **~s** (ugs. abwertend) [raucous] bawling and shouting; (Gesang) raucous singing

Gegrunze *das;* **~s** (abwertend) grunting

Gehabe *das;* **~s** (abwertend) affected behaviour; **ihr wichtigtuerisches ~:** her pompous behaviour

gehaben *refl. V.* (veralt., noch scherzh.) *in* **gehab dich wohl!/gehabt euch wohl!/~ Sie sich wohl!** farewell!

Gehaben *das;* **~s** (geh. veralt.) behaviour; demeanour

gehabt

A *2. Part. v.* **haben**

B *Adj.* (ugs.: schon da gewesen) same old (coll.); usual; **wie ~:** as before; **[es ist] alles wie ~:** everything's just the same *or* just as before

Gehackte /gəˈhaktə/ *das; adj. Dekl.* mince[meat]; **~s vom Rind/Schwein** minced beef/pork

Gehalt[1] *der;* **~[e]s, ~e** **1** (gedanklicher Inhalt) meaning; **intellektueller/religiöser ~:** intellectual/religious content **2** (Anteil) content; **ein hoher ~ an Gold/Blei** a high gold/lead content

Gehalt[2] *das, österr. auch: der;* **~[e]s, Gehälter** /gəˈhɛltɐ/ salary; **ein hohes/niedriges ~ beziehen** draw a large/small salary; **1 000 Euro ~, ein ~ von 1 000 Euro** a salary of 1,000 euros

gehalten

A *2. Part. v.* **halten**

B *Adj.* **1** (geh.) **~ sein, etw. zu tun** be obliged *or* required to do sth. **2** (Mus.) held; tenuto

gehalt·los *Adj.* unnutritious ‹*food*›; ‹*wine*› lacking in body; (fig.) vacuous; empty; lacking in substance *postpos., not pred.*

Gehaltlosigkeit *die;* **~** (von Nahrungsmitteln) lack of nutritional value; (fig.) vacuousness; emptiness; lack of substance

Gehalts-: **~abrechnung** *die* salary statement; payslip; **~abzug** *der* deduction from salary; **~anspruch** *der* salary claim; pay claim; **~aufbesserung** *die* increase in salary; **zur ~aufbesserung** in order to increase one's salary; **~auszahlung** *die* payment of salary/salaries; **~empfänger** *der,* **~empfängerin** *die* salary earner; **~erhöhung** *die* salary increase; rise [in salary]; (regelmäßig) increment; **~forderung** *die* salary claim; pay claim; **~gruppe** *die* salary group *or* bracket; (innerhalb einer Firma) grade; **~konto** *das: account into which the/one's salary is paid;* **~kürzung** *die* salary cut; cut in salary; **~liste** *die* payroll; **auf jmds. ~liste** (*Dat.*) **stehen** (fig.) be on sb.'s payroll; be in sb.'s pocket; **~pfändung** *die* attachment of earnings; **~streifen** *der* payslip; **~stufe** *die* salary bracket; **~vorrückung**

die; ~~, ~~**en** (österr.) increment; ~**vorschuss**, *~**vorschuß** *der* advance [on one's salary]; ~**zahlung** *die* payment of salary/salaries; ~**zulage** *die* salary increase; (regelmäßig) increment; (zusätzlich) bonus

gehalt·voll *Adj.* nutritious, nourishing ‹*food*›; full-bodied ‹*wine*›; ‹*novel, speech*› rich in substance *postpos.*

Gehänge *das;* ~**s**, ~ 1 (Girlande) festoon; (Kranz) garland; (Ohrring) ear pendant 2 (österr.: Bergabhang) slope 3 (Jagdw., sonst veralt.) belt (*with scabbard for hunting knife, sword, etc.*) 4 (vulg.: Hoden) balls (coarse)

gehangen *2. Part. v.* **hängen¹**

Gehängte /gəˈhɛŋtə/ *der/die; adj. Dekl.* hanged man/woman; **die** ~**n** the hanged

geharnischt /gəˈharnɪʃt/

A *Adj.* 1 (scharf, energisch) sharp, sharply-worded, strongly-worded ‹*letter, protest, reply*›; strongly-worded ‹*speech, article*› 2 (hist.: gepanzert) **ein** ~**er Ritter** a knight in armour

B *adv.* sharply

gehässig /gəˈhɛsɪç/ *Adj.* (abwertend) spiteful; ~ **von jmdm. reden/sprechen** be spiteful about sb.

Gehässigkeit *die;* ~, ~**en** 1 (Wesen) spitefulness 2 (Äußerung) spiteful remark

gehauen *2. Part. v.* **hauen**

gehäuft

A *2. Part. v.* **häufen**

B *Adj.* **ein** ~**er Teelöffel/Esslöffel** a heaped teaspoon/tablespoon

C *adv.* in large numbers

Gehäuse /gəˈhɔyzə/ *das;* ~**s**, ~ 1 (einer Maschine, Welle) casing; housing; (einer Kamera, Uhr) case; casing; (einer Lampe) housing; (Pistolen~, Gewehr~) casing 2 (Schnecken~ usw.) shell 3 (Kern~) core 4 (Sportjargon: Tor) goal

geh·behindert *Adj.* able to walk only with difficulty *postpos.*; disabled; **sie ist stark** ~: she can walk only with great difficulty

Geh·behinderung *die* disability [which makes walking difficult]

Gehege *das;* ~**s**, ~ 1 (Jägerspr.: Revier) preserve; **jmdm. ins** ~ **kommen** (fig.) poach on sb.'s preserve; **sich** (*Dat.*) **[gegenseitig] ins** ~ **kommen** (fig.) encroach on each other's territory 2 (im Zoo) enclosure

geheim

A *Adj.* 1 secret; **streng** ~: top *or* highly secret; **etw.** ~ **halten** keep sth. secret; ~ **tun** (ugs. abwertend) be secretive (**mit** about); **im Geheimen** in secret; secretly; **Geheimer Rat** (hist.) (Gremium) Privy Council; (Mitglied) privy councillor 2 (mysteriös) mysterious

B *adv.* ~ **abstimmen** vote by secret ballot

geheim-, Geheim-: ~**abkommen** *das* secret agreement; ~**agent** *der,* ~**agentin** *die* secret agent; ~**befehl** *der* secret order; ~**bund** *der* secret society; ~**bündelei** *die;* ~~ (veralt.) membership of an illegal secret society; ~**code** *der* ▸~**kode**; ~**dienst** *der* secret service; ~**diplomatie** *die* secret diplomacy; (neben der offiziellen Diplomatie) behind-the-scenes diplomacy; ~**fach** *das* secret compartment; (Schublade) secret drawer; ~**gang** *der* secret passage; *~|**halten** ▸**geheim A 1**

Geheim·haltung *die* observance of secrecy; **zur** ~ **verpflichtet sein** be pledged to secrecy

Geheimhaltungs·pflicht *die* obligation to maintain secrecy

Geheim-: ~**kode** *der* secret code; ~**lehre** *die* esoteric doctrine; ~**material** *das* secret papers *pl. or* documents *pl.*; **militärisches** ~**material** secret military papers *or* documents

Geheimnis *das;* ~**ses**, ~**se** 1 secret; **ein** ~ **lüften/enträtseln** unravel a secret; **vor jmdm. [keine]** ~**se haben** have [no] secrets from sb.; **jmdn. in die** ~**se einer Sache einweihen** initiate *or* let sb. into the secrets of sth.; **ein/kein** ~ **aus etw. machen** make a big/no secret of sth.; **das ist das ganze** ~: that's all there is to it; **ein offenes** *od.* **öffentliches** ~: an open secret 2 (Unerforschtes) mystery; secret; **die** ~**se der Natur/des Lebens** the mysteries *or* secrets of nature/life

geheimnis-, Geheimnis-: ~**krämer** *der* (ugs.) mystery-monger; ~**krämerei** *die;* ~~ ▸~**tuerei**; ~**krämerin** *die* ▸~**krämer**; ~**träger** *der,* ~**trägerin** *die* person cleared for access to secret information; ~**tuerei** *die;* ~~ (ugs. abwertend) secretiveness; mystery-mongering; ~**tuerisch** (ugs. abwertend) A *Adj.* secretive; B *adv.* secretively; ~**umwittert**, ~**umwoben** *Adj.* (geh.) shrouded in mystery *postpos.*; mysterious; ~**verrat** *der* (Rechtsspr.) betrayal of secrets; ~**voll** A *Adj.* mysterious; **auf** ~**volle Weise** in a mysterious way; mysteriously; B *adv.* mysteriously; ~**voll tun** be mysterious; act mysteriously

Geheim·nummer *die* 1 (Bankw.) personal identification number; PIN 2 (Telefonnummer) ex-directory number; unlisted number (Amer.)

Geheim-: ~**polizei** *die* secret police; ~**polizist** *der,* ~**polizistin** *die* member of the secret police

Geheim·rat *der* Privy Councillor (*purely honorary title*)

Geheimrats·ecken *Pl.* (ugs. scherzh.) receding hairline *sing.*; **er hat schon** ~: he's receding *or* going bald [at the temples] already

geheim-, Geheim-: ~**rezept** *das* secret recipe; ~**sache** *die* classified information *no indef. art., no pl.*; ~**schrift** *die* secret writing *no indef. art., no pl.*; cipher; ~**sender** *der* secret transmitter; ~**sitzung** *die* secret session; closed meeting; ~**sprache** *die* secret language; ~**tinte** *die* invisible ink; *~**tip**, ~**tipp** *der* inside tip; *~|**tun** ▸**geheim A1**; ~**tür** *die* secret door; ~**vertrag** *der* secret treaty *or* agreement; ~**waffe** *die* (Milit.) secret weapon; ~**wissenschaft** *die* occult science; ~**zeichen** *das* secret sign

Geheiß *das;* ~**es** (geh.) behest (literary); command; **auf jmds.** ~: at sb.'s behest *or* command

gehemmt

A *2. Part. v.* **hemmen**

B *Adj.* inhibited

gehen /ˈgeːən/

A *unr. itr. V.; mit sein* 1 (sich zu Fuß fortbewegen) walk; go; **auf und ab** ~: walk up and down; **über die Straße** ~: cross the street; **wo er geht und steht** wherever he goes *or* is; no matter where he goes *or* is; **etw. geht durch die Presse** (fig.) sth. is in the papers

2 (sich irgendwohin begeben) go; **schwimmen/tanzen** ~: go swimming/dancing; **schlafen** ~: go to bed; **zu jmdm.** ~: go to see sb.; go and see sb. (coll.); **zum Arzt** ~: go to the doctor; **nach London/Mannheim** ~: move to London/Mannheim; **aufs Amt/auf den Markt** ~: go to the office/the market; **an die Arbeit** ~ (fig.) get down to work; **er geht auf die 60** (fig.) he is approaching *or* (coll.) pushing 60; **in sich** (*Akk.*) ~: take stock of oneself

3 (regelmäßig besuchen) attend; **in die** *od.* **zur Schule** ~: be at *or* attend school; **wie viele Jahre musst du noch in die Schule** ~? how many more years have you got at school?

4 (weg~) go; leave; **ich muss jetzt/bald** ~: I must leave now/soon; **Sie können** ~: you may go; **gegangen werden** (ugs. scherzh.) be sacked (coll.); **der Minister/Offizier musste** ~: the Minister/officer had to resign; **er ist von uns gegangen** (verhüll.) he has passed away *or* passed over (euphem.); **jmdn. lieber** ~ **als kommen sehen** be always glad to see the back of sb.; **geh mir mit deinen politischen Schlagworten** spare me the political slogans; **jmdn. gehen lassen** (ugs.: in Ruhe lassen) leave sb. alone

5 (ugs.: [ab]fahren) leave; **der Zug geht um zehn Uhr** the train leaves at ten o'clock

6 (in Funktion sein) work; **etw. geht wieder/nicht mehr** sth. is working again/has stopped working; **meine Uhr geht falsch/richtig** my watch is wrong/right; **das Telefon/die Klingel geht ununterbrochen** the telephone/the bell never stops ringing

7 (möglich sein) **ja, das geht** yes, I/we can manage that; **das geht nicht** that can't be done; that's impossible; (ist nicht zulässig) that's not on (Brit. coll.); no way (coll.); **Donnerstag geht auch** Thursday's a possibility *or* all right too; **es geht einfach nicht, dass du so spät nach Hause kommst** it simply won't do for you to come home so late; **es geht leider nicht anders** unfortunately there's nothing else for it; **das wird schwer/schlecht** ~: that will be difficult; **auf diese Weise geht es nicht/sicher** it won't/is bound to work this way

8 (ugs.: gerade noch an~) **es geht so** it could be worse; **das Essen ging ja noch, aber der Wein war ungenießbar** the food was passable, but the wine was undrinkable; **Wie war die Feier? — Es ging so** How was the party? — [It was] all right *or* [It] could have been worse; **Hast du gut geschlafen? — Es geht** Did you sleep well? — Not too bad *or* So-so; **der Anfang ging, aber der Schluss des Films war idiotisch** the film began fairly well, but the end was absolutely stupid

9 (sich entwickeln) **der Laden/das Geschäft geht gut/gar nicht** the shop/business is doing well/not doing well at all; **schief** ~ (ugs.: schlecht ausgehen) go wrong; **es wird schon schief** ~ (iron.) it'll all turn out OK (coll.); **gut** ~ (gut ausgehen) turn out well; **es ist noch einmal gut gegangen** it worked out all right again this time; **es geht alles nach Wunsch/Plan** everything is going according to plan; **alles geht drunter und drüber** (ugs.) everything's at sixes and sevens; **die Anfangszeile geht ...** (fig.) the first line goes *or* runs ...; **wie geht die Melodie?** (fig.) how does the tune go?; what's the tune?; **vor sich** ~: go on; happen

10 (sich ausdehnen bis) **das Wasser geht mir bis an die Knie** the water comes up to *or* reaches my knees; **ich gehe ihm bis zu den Schultern** I come up to his shoulders; **in die Hunderte/Tausende** ~: run into [the] hundreds/thousands; **das geht über mein Vermögen/meinen Horizont** (fig.) that is beyond me; **diese Nachricht würde über ihre Kräfte** ~ (fig.) this news would be too much for her; **es geht [doch] nichts über ...** (+ *Akk.*) (fig.) there is nothing like *or* nothing to beat ...; nothing beats ...; **das geht zu weit** (fig.) that's going too far

11 (unpers.) **jmdm. geht es gut/schlecht** (gesundheitlich) sb. is well *or* (coll.) fine/not well; (geschäftlich) sb. is doing well/badly; **wie geht es dir/Ihnen?** how are you?; **mir geht es ähnlich** it's the same with me; same here (coll.); **wie gehts, wie stehts?** (ugs.) how are things?; **wenn sie das rausfindet, gehts dir schlecht!** (ugs.) if she finds out, you'll be [in] for it

12 (unpers.) (sich um etw. handeln) **es geht um mehr als ...** there is more at stake than ...; **jmdm. geht es um etw.** sth. matters to sb.; **ihr geht es nur um Geld** she only thinks about money; **worum geht es hier?** what is this all about?; **bei dieser Sache geht es um viel Geld** this involves a great deal of money; **wenn es ums Geld geht, versteht er keinen Spaß** he takes money matters very seriously; **Ich hätte eine Frage. — Worum geht es denn?** I have a question. — What [is it] about?; *s. auch* **darum 2**

13 (tätig werden) **in den Staatsdienst/in die Industrie/die Politik** ~: join the Civil Service/go into industry/politics; **zum Film/Theater** ~: go into films/on the stage; **ins Kloster** ~: enter a monastery/convent; **als Kellner/Prostituierte** ~: work as *or* be a waiter/prostitute

14 (ugs.: sich kleiden) **gut/schlecht gekleidet** ~: be well/badly dressed; **in Kurz/Lang** ~: wear a short/long dress/skirt; **als Zigeuner/Matrose** ~: go as a gypsy/a sailor

15 (ugs.: sich zu schaffen machen an) **du sollst nicht an meine Sachen** ~: you must not mess around with my things; (benutzen) you must not take my things; **die Kinder sind an den Kuchen/das Geld gegangen** the children have been at the cake/money (coll.)

16 (ein Liebespaar sein) **mit jmdm.** ~: go out with sb.

17 (absetzbar sein) **[gut/schlecht]** ~: sell [well/slowly]

18 (passen) go; **in den Kofferraum geht nur**

g

ein Koffer only one case will go into the boot **19** (aufgeteilt werden) **etw. geht in zwei/drei Teile** sth. is shared out *or* divided two/three ways **20** (verlaufen) go; **die Straße geht geradeaus/nach links** the road goes *or* runs straight ahead/turns to the left; **wohin geht diese Straße?** where does this road go *or* lead to? **21** (gerichtet sein auf) **nach der Hauptstraße ~:** face the main road; **die Fenster ~ alle nach Süden** all the windows face south; **gegen jmdn./etw. ~** (fig.) be aimed *or* directed at sb./sth.; **das geht gegen meine Überzeugung** that goes against my convictions **22** (als Maßstab nehmen) **nach jmdm./etw. ~:** go by sb./sth.; **wenn es nach mir geht, fangen wir jetzt an** I'd be quite happy if we began now **23** ▸**aufgehen 4** **24** **sich ~ lassen** lose control of oneself; (sich vernachlässigen) let oneself go
B *unr. tr. V.* (zurücklegen) **eine Strecke ~:** cover *or* do a distance; **er ist eine Strecke mit uns gegangen** he walked with us for some of the way; **einen Umweg ~:** make a detour; **10 km ~:** walk 10 km.; **einen Weg in 30 Minuten ~:** do a walk in 30 minutes; **seine eigenen Wege ~** (fig.) go one's own way; **lerne doch, deine eigenen Wege zu ~** (fig.) learn to stand on your own two feet
C *unr. refl. V.* (unpers.) **in diesen Schuhen geht es sich sehr bequem** these shoes are very comfortable [to walk in]; **auf dem Weg ging es sich schlecht** the going on the track was difficult

Gehen *das;* **~s** **1** walking; **er hat Schmerzen beim ~:** it hurts him to walk **2** (Leichtathletik) walking; **der Sieger im 50-km-~:** the winner of the 50 km walk

Gehenkte /gəˈhɛŋktə/ *der/die; adj. Dekl.* hanged man/woman; **die ~n** the hanged

***gehen|lassen** ▸**gehen A 4, 24**

Geher /ˈgeːɐ/ *der;* **~s, ~, Geherin** *die;* **~, ~nen** **1** (Leichtathletik) walker **2** (Bergsteigen) hill/mountain walker

geheuer /gəˈhɔyɐ/ *Adj.* **1** **in diesem Gebäude ist es nicht ~:** this building is eerie; this building feels as if it's haunted (coll.); **in der Ruine soll es nicht ganz ~ sein** there is said to be something eerie about the ruins **2** **ihr war doch nicht [ganz] ~:** she felt [a little] uneasy **3** **diese Angelegenheit ist nicht ganz ~:** there's something odd *or* suspicious about this business

Geheul *das;* **~[e]s** **1** (auch fig.) howling **2** (ugs. abwertend: Weinen) bawling; wailing

Geheule *das;* **~s** ▸**Geheul 2**

geh·fähig *Adj.* ‹*patient*› who is able to walk *postpos., not pred.*; walking ‹*wounded*›; **~ sein** be able to walk

Geh·gips *der: plaster which allows the patient to walk*

Gehilfe /gəˈhɪlfə/ *der;* **~n, ~n, Gehilfin** *die;* **~, ~nen** **1** qualified assistant **2** (veralt.: Helfer/Helferin) helper; assistant

Gehirn *das;* **~[e]s, ~e** **1** ▸❶ **S. 435** brain **2** (ugs.: Verstand) mind; **sein ~ anstrengen** *od.* **sich** (*Dat.*) **das ~ zermartern** rack one's brain[s]

gehirn-, Gehirn-: **~amputiert** *Adj.* (salopp abwertend) brain-dead (coll.); **~blutung** *die* ▸❶ **S. 439** (Med.) cerebral haemorrhage; encephalorrhagia (Med.); **~chirurgie** *die* brain surgery; **~erschütterung** *die* ▸❶ **S. 439** (Med.) concussion; **~erweichung** *die* ▸❶ **S. 439** (Med.) softening of the brain; encephalomalacia (Med.); **~haut** *die* ▸**Hirnhaut**; **~haut·entzündung** *die* ▸**Hirnhautentzündung**; **~kasten** *der* (salopp scherzh.) [thick] skull; **~schlag** *der* ▸❶ **S. 439** (Med.) stroke; [cerebral] apoplexy *no art.* (Med.); **~substanz** *die* brain matter; **graue/weiße ~substanz** grey/white matter; **~tätigkeit** *die* brain activity; **~tumor** *der* ▸**Hirntumor**; **~wäsche** *die* brainwashing *no indef. art.*; **jmdn. einer ~wäsche unterziehen** brainwash sb.; **~zelle** *die* brain cell

gehoben /gəˈhoːbn̩/
A *2. Part. v.* **heben**
B *Adj.* **1** higher ‹*income*›; senior ‹*position*›; **der ~e Dienst** the higher [levels of the] Civil Service; **die ~e Beamtenlaufbahn einschlagen** ≈ enter the Civil Service as an Administrative Trainee (Brit.); **der ~e Mittelstand** the upper middle class **2** (anspruchsvoll) **Kleidung für den ~en Geschmack** clothes for those with discerning taste; **Artikel für den ~en Bedarf** luxury goods; **die ~e Unterhaltungsliteratur** upmarket popular literature **3** (gewählt) elevated, refined ‹*language, expression*› **4** (feierlich) festive ‹*mood*›; **in ~er Stimmung sein** be in high spirits
C *adv.* **sich ~ ausdrücken** use elevated *or* refined language

Gehöft /gəˈhœft, -ˈhøːft/ *das;* **~[e]s, ~e** farm[stead]

geholfen /gəˈhɔlfn̩/ *2. Part. v.* **helfen**

Gehölz /gəˈhœlt̮s/ *das;* **~es, ~e** **1** (Wäldchen) copse; spinney (Brit.) **2** *Pl.* (Holzgewächse) woody plants

Gehör /gəˈhøːɐ̯/ *das;* **~[e]s** [sense of] hearing; **ein scharfes/gutes ~ haben** have acute/good hearing; **[etw.] nach dem ~ singen/spielen** sing/play [sth.] by ear; **das absolute ~ [haben]** (Musik) [have] absolute pitch; **~/kein ~ finden** meet with *or* get a/no response; **jmdm./einer Sache [kein] ~ schenken** [not] listen to sb./sth.; **sich** (*Dat.*) **~ verschaffen** make oneself heard; **um ~ bitten** ask for a hearing; **ein Lied/Gedicht/Musikstück zu ~ bringen** (geh.) sing a song/recite a poem/perform a piece of music

gehorchen /gəˈhɔrçn̩/ *itr. V.* **1** (Gehorsam leisten) **jmdm. ~:** obey sb. **2** (sich leiten, lenken lassen) **einer Sache** (*Dat.*) **~:** respond to sth.; **das Auto gehorchte dem Fahrer nicht mehr** the car wouldn't respond when the driver turned the wheel; **einer Laune/Stimmung** (*Dat.*) **~:** yield to a caprice/mood

gehören
A *itr. V.* **1** (Eigentum sein) **jmdm. ~:** belong to sb.; **das Haus gehört uns nicht** the house doesn't belong to us; we don't own the house; **der Jugend gehört die Zukunft** the future belongs to the young; **dir will ich ~** (dichter.) I want to be yours; **ihr Herz gehört einem anderen** (geh.) her heart belongs to another **2** (Teil eines Ganzen sein) **zu jmds. Freunden ~:** be one of sb.'s friends; **zu jmds. Aufgaben ~:** be part of sb.'s duties **3** (passend sein) **dein Roller gehört doch nicht in die Küche!** your scooter does not belong in the kitchen!; **das gehört nicht/durchaus hierher** that is not to the point/is very much to the point; **dieses Problem/Thema gehört nicht/durchaus hierher** this problem/topic is not relevant/certainly relevant here; **du gehörst ins Bett** you should be in bed **4** (nötig sein) **es hat viel Fleiß dazu gehört, dieses Projekt durchzuführen** it took *or* called for a lot of hard work to carry through this project; **dazu gehört sehr viel/einiges** that takes a lot/something; **dazu gehört nicht viel** that doesn't take much; **auf diese Weise sein Geld zu verdienen, dazu gehört nicht viel** earning one's living like this is nothing to be proud of **5** (bes. südd.) **er gehört geohrfeigt** he deserves *or* (coll.) needs a box round the ears; **du gehörst eingesperrt** (ugs.) you ought to be locked up
B *refl. V.* (sich schicken) be fitting; **es gehört sich [nicht], ... zu ...** it is [not] good manners to ...; **wie es sich gehört** comme il faut; **benimm dich, wie es sich gehört** behave properly

Gehör·gang *der* ▸❶ **S. 435** (Anat.) auditory canal

gehörig
A *Adj.* **1** (gebührend) proper; **jmdm. den ~en Respekt/die ~e Achtung erweisen** show sb. proper *or* due respect **2** (ugs.: beträchtlich) **ein ~er Schrecken/eine ~e Portion Mut/Ausdauer** a good fright/a good deal of courage/perseverance **3** (zu~) **zu etw. ~ sein** be part of sth.; belong to sth.; **jmdm. ~ sein** (geh.) belong to sb.; be owned by sb.; **[nicht] zur momentanen Fragestellung ~:** [not] relevant to the question [under discussion]
B *adv.* **1** (gebührend) properly **2** (ugs.: beträchtlich) **~ essen/trinken** eat/drink properly *or* heartily; **er hat ~ geschimpft** he didn't half grumble (coll.); *s. auch* **Marsch¹ 2; Meinung**

Gehör·knöchelchen *Pl.* ▸❶ **S. 435** (Anat.) auditory ossicles

gehör·los *Adj.* deaf

Gehörn /gəˈhœrn/ *das;* **~[e]s, ~e** **1** horns *pl.* **2** (Jägerspr.) antlers *pl.*

Gehör·nerv *der* ▸❶ **S. 435** auditory nerve

gehörnt *Adj.* **1** (mit einem Gehörn) horned; (mit einem Geweih) antlered **2** (scherzh. verhüll.: betrogen) cuckolded; **ein ~er Ehemann** a cuckold

Gehör·organ *das* organ of hearing

gehorsam /gəˈhoːɐ̯zaːm/
A *Adj.* **1** (artig, brav) obedient; **jmdm. ~ sein** (geh.) be obedient to sb. **2** (veralt. als Höflichkeitsformel) humble; (als Briefschluss) **Ihr ~ster Diener** your most obedient servant
B *adv.* (veralt. als Höflichkeitsformel) humbly

Gehorsam *der;* **~s** obedience; **~ gegenüber jmdm.** obedience to sb.; **jmdm. ~ leisten/den ~ verweigern** obey/refuse to obey sb.

Gehorsamkeit *die* obedience

Gehorsams-: **~pflicht** *die* (Milit.) duty to obey orders; **~verweigerung** *die* (Milit.) insubordination; refusal to obey orders

Gehör·sinn *der* [sense of] hearing

Geh·rock *der* frock coat

Gehrung /ˈgeːrʊŋ/ *die;* **~, ~en** (Handw., Technik) mitre [joint]

Geh·steig *der* pavement (Brit.); sidewalk (Amer.)

Geht·nicht·mehr *das: in* **bis zum ~** (salopp) ad nauseam; **das habe ich bis zum ~ erklärt/gehört** I've explained it ad nauseam *or* till I'm blue in the face (coll.)/I've heard it so often I'm sick of it (coll.)

Gehupe *das;* **~s** honking; hooting

Geh-: **~versuch** *der* (eines Kindes) attempt at walking; (nach einem Unfall) attempt at walking again; **~weg** *der* ▸**~steig**; **~werkzeuge** *Pl.* (ugs. scherzh.) legs

GEI *Abk.* (EU) **= Gericht erster Instanz** CFI

Geier /ˈgai̯ɐ/ *der;* **~s, ~:** vulture; **hol dich/hols der ~** (ugs.) to hell with you/it (coll.); **weiß der ~** (salopp) God only knows (coll.); Christ knows (sl.)

Geifer /ˈgaifɐ/ *der;* **~s** **1** (Speichel) slaver; spittle; slobber; (von Tieren) slaver; slobber; (schäumend) foam; froth **2** (geh. abwertend: Gehässigkeit) venom; vituperation

Geiferer *der;* **~s, ~, Geiferin** *die;* **~, ~nen** (geh. abwertend) vituperator; venomous speaker/writer *etc.*

geifern *itr. V.* **1** slaver; slobber **2** (abwertend: gehässig reden) **gegen jmdn./über etw.** (*Akk.*) **~:** discharge one's venom at sb./sth.

Geige /ˈgaigə/ *die;* **~, ~n** violin; fiddle (coll./derog.); **~ spielen** play the violin; **die erste ~ spielen** (ugs.) play first fiddle; call the tune; **die zweite ~ spielen** (ugs.) play second fiddle

geigen
A *itr. V.* **1** (ugs.: Geige spielen) play the fiddle (coll.) *or* the violin **2** (ugs.: von Insekten) chirp; chirr
B *tr. V.* **1** (ugs.: auf der Geige spielen) **einen Walzer/ein Solo ~:** play a waltz/a solo on the fiddle (coll.) *or* violin; **jmdm. die Meinung ~:** give sb. a piece of one's mind **2** (salopp: koitieren mit) lay (sl.); shag (sl.); have it off with (sl.)

Geigen-: **~bau** *der* violin making; **~bauer** *der;* **~~s, ~~, ~bauerin** *die;* **~~, ~~nen** ▸❶ **S. 113** violin-maker; **~bogen** *der* violin bow; **~hals** *der* neck of the/a violin; **~kasten** *der* violin case; **~musik** *die* violin music; **~saite** *die* violin string; **~spiel** *das* violin-playing; **~spieler** *der,* **~spielerin** *die* violin player

Geiger *der;* **~s, ~, Geigerin** *die;* **~, ~nen** ▸❶ **S. 113** violin player; violinist

Geiger·zähler *der* (Physik) Geiger counter

geil /gail/
A *Adj.* **1** (oft abwertend: sexuell erregt) randy; horny (sl.); (lüstern) lecherous; **auf jmdn. ~ sein** lust for *or* after sb.; **~e alte Männer** old lechers;

dirty old men 2 (Landw.) rank ‹*vegetation, growth, plant*›; over-rich, over-manured ‹*soil*› 3 (ugs.) great (coll.); fabulous (coll.)
B *adv.* 1 (oft abwertend) lecherously 2 (Landw.) **~ wuchern/emporschießen** grow rank 3 (Jugendspr.) fabulously (coll.)

Geilheit *die; ~* ▸**geil A**: 1 randiness; horniness (sl.); lecherousness 2 (Landw.) rankness; overrichness

Geisel /ˈgaizl̩/ *die; ~, ~n* hostage; **jmdn. als ~ behalten** *od.* **festhalten** hold sb. hostage; **jmdn. als** *od.* **zur ~ nehmen** take sb. hostage

Geisel-: ~drama *das* (Pressejargon) hostage drama; **~gangster** *der* (Pressejargon) ▸**~nehmer**; **~nahme** *die; ~~, ~~n* taking of hostages; **„Bankraub mit ~nahme zweier Kunden"** 'Bank raid. Two customers taken hostage'; **~nehmer** *der; ~~s, ~~,* **~nehmerin** *die; ~~, ~~nen* terrorist/guerrilla *etc.* holding the hostages

Geisha /ˈgeːʃa/ *die; ~, ~s* geisha

Geiß /gais/ *die; ~, ~en* 1 (südd., österr., schweiz.: Ziege) [nanny] goat 2 (Jägerspr.) doe

Geiß-: ~bart *der* 1 (Bot.) goat's beard; 2 (österr.: Spitzbart) goatee; **~blatt** *das* (Bot.) honeysuckle; woodbine

Geißel /ˈgaisl̩/ *die; ~, ~n* 1 (hist., auch fig.) scourge 2 (Biol.) flagellum 3 (bes. südd.: Peitsche) whip

geißeln *tr. V.* 1 (anprangern, tadeln) castigate 2 (plagen) plague 3 (hist.: züchtigen) scourge

Geißel·tierchen *das* (Biol.) flagellate

Geißelung *die; ~, ~en* 1 (Anprangern) castigation 2 (hist.: Züchtigung) scourging

Geiß·fuß *der* 1 (Bot.) Aegopodium; **gewöhnlicher ~:** ground elder; goutweed 2 (Handw., Technik) V-shaped gouge

Geißlein *das; ~s, ~:* little goat

Geißler /ˈgaislɐ/ *der; ~s, ~,* **Geißlerin** *die; ~, ~nen* ▸**Flagellant**

Geist /gaist/ *der; ~[e]s, ~er* 1 (Verstand) mind; **jmds. ~ ist verwirrt/gestört** sb. is mentally deranged/disturbed; **jmdm. mit etw. auf den ~ gehen** (salopp) get on sb.'s nerves with sth.; **den** *od.* **seinen ~ aufgeben** (geh./ugs. scherzh., auch fig.) give up the ghost; **im ~[e]** in my/his *etc.* mind's eye; **im ~ werde ich dabei sein** I shall be there in spirit; **den** *od.* **seinen ~ aushauchen** (geh. verhüll.) breathe one's last; pass away; **der ~ ist willig, aber das Fleisch ist schwach** (bibl.) the spirit is willing, but the flesh is weak 2 (Scharfsinn) wit; **einen sprühenden ~ haben** have a sparkling wit; **Mangel an ~:** lack of intellect *or* intelligence 3 (innere Einstellung) spirit; **im ~ der Zeit** in the spirit of the age; **ein schlechter ~ in der Mannschaft** poor morale in the team; **wes ~es Kind er/sie** *usw.* **ist** the kind of person he/she *etc.* is 4 (denkender Mensch) mind; intellect; **ein großer/kleiner ~:** a great mind/a person of limited intellect; **hier** *od.* **da scheiden sich die ~er** this is where opinions differ; **große ~er stört das nicht** (ugs. scherzh.) it doesn't worry me/her *etc.*; not to worry (coll.) 5 (Mensch mit bestimmten Eigenschaften) spirit; **ein dienstbarer ~** (ugs. scherzh.) a servant 6 (überirdisches Wesen) spirit; **der Heilige ~** (christl. Rel.) the Holy Ghost *or* Spirit; **der böse ~:** the evil spirit 7 (Gespenst) ghost; **~er gehen im Schloss um/spuken im Schloss** the castle is haunted; **von allen guten ~ern verlassen sein** have taken leave of one's senses; be out of one's mind

Geister-: ~bahn *die* ghost train; **~beschwörer** *der; ~~s, ~~,* **~beschwörerin** *die; ~~, ~~nen* exorcist; (der die ~ heraufbeschwört) necromancer; **~beschwörung** *die* exorcism; (das Heraufbeschwören) necromancy; **~erscheinung** *die* apparition; phantom; **~fahrer** *der,* **~fahrerin** *die: person driving on the wrong side of the road or the wrong carriageway;* **~geschichte** *die* ghost story

geisterhaft
A *Adj.* ghostly; spectral; eerie ‹*atmosphere*›
B *adv.* eerily

Geister·hand *die:* in **wie von** *od.* **durch ~:** as if by an invisible hand

geistern /ˈgaistɐn/ *itr. V.; mit sein* ‹*ghost*› wander; (fig.) wander like a ghost; **Irrlichter geisterten über das Moor** will o' the wisps drifted eerily across the moor; **diese Idee geisterte immer noch durch seinen Kopf** he still had this idea in his head

Geister-: ~seher *der,* **~seherin** *die* ghost-seer; (Hellseher) visionary; **~stadt** *die* ghost town; **~stunde** *die* witching hour

geistes-, Geistes-: ~abwesend A *Adj.* absent-minded; B *adv.* absent-mindedly; **~abwesenheit** *die* absent-mindedness; **~anlage** *die* intellectual ability *or* gift; **~arbeiter** *der,* **~arbeiterin** *die* brainworker; **~armut** *die* poverty of mind; **~art** *die* cast of mind; **~blitz** *der* (ugs.) brainwave; flash of inspiration; **~gaben** *Pl.* intellectual gifts; **~gegenwart** *die* presence of mind; **~gegenwärtig** A *Adj.* quick-witted; B *adv.* with great presence of mind; **~geschichte** *die* history of ideas; intellectual history; **~geschichtlich** A *Adj.* ‹*work, method, etc.*› relating to the history of ideas, relating to intellectual history; **eine ~geschichtliche Tradition** an intellectual tradition; a tradition of ideas; B *adv.* **etw. ~geschichtlich einordnen** place sth. in the history of ideas; **~gestört** *Adj.* mentally disturbed; **~größe** *die* 1 (Kraft des Geistes) greatness of mind; 2 (Mensch) genius; intellectual giant; **~haltung** *die* attitude [of mind]; **~kraft** *die* mental ability; **~kräfte** *Pl.* mental powers; **~krank** *Adj.* mentally ill; [mentally] deranged; **~kranke** *der/die* mentally ill person; (im Krankenhaus) mental patient; **~krankheit** *die* mental illness; **~leben** *das* intellectual life; **~richtung** *die* school of thought; **~riese** *der,* **~riesin** *die* (ugs.) great genius; **~schaffende** *der/die; adj. Dekl.* (bes. DDR) intellectual; **~schärfe** *die* keenness of intellect; **~schwäche** *die* feeble-mindedness; mental deficiency; **~störung** *die* mental disturbance *or* disorder; **~strömung** *die* current of thought; **~tätigkeit** *die* mental activity; **~verfassung** *die* state of mind; mental state; **~verwandt** *Adj.* spiritually akin; **wir sind ~verwandt** we are kindred spirits; **~verwirrung** *die* mental confusion; (~gestörtheit) [mental] derangement; **~welt** *die* (geh.) 1 (Welt des Geistes) world of the mind; 2 (Gesamtheit der geistig Interessierten) intelligentsia; **~wissenschaften** *Pl.* arts; humanities; **~wissenschaftler** *der,* **~wissenschaftlerin** *die* arts scholar; scholar in the humanities; **~wissenschaftlich** A *Adj.* **~wissenschaftliche Fächer** arts subjects; B *adv.* ‹*interested, be distinguished*› in arts subjects; **~zustand** *der* mental condition; mental state; **jmdn. auf seinen ~zustand untersuchen lassen** have sb.'s mental condition examined; **du solltest dich mal auf deinen ~zustand untersuchen lassen** (ugs.) you need your head examined (coll.)

Geist·heiler *der,* **Geist·heilerin** *die* faith healer

geistig
A *Adj.* 1 intellectual; (Psych.) mental; **~e und körperliche Arbeit** physical work and brainwork; **er verlebte seine Rentnerjahre in ~er Frische** he remained mentally alert throughout the years of his retirement; **der ~e Vater/Urheber** the spiritual father/author; **in ~er Umnachtung** (geh.) in a state of mental derangement; **das ~e Erbe** the spiritual legacy; **~es Eigentum** intellectual property; **~er Diebstahl** plagiarism; **ein ~es Band** (fig. geh.) a spiritual bond; **~-kulturell** intellectual and cultural; **das ~-kulturelle Leben** (bes. DDR) the intellectual and cultural scene; **ein ~-kulturelles Zentrum** (bes. DDR) a centre of learning and the arts; **~-schöpferische Arbeit** (bes. DDR) intellectual and creative work 2 (alkoholisch) **~e Getränke** alcoholic drinks *or* beverages
B *adv.* **~ träge/rege sein** be mentally lazy/active; **~ überlegen** intellectually superior; **~ zurückgeblieben** mentally retarded; **~ weggetreten sein** (ugs.) be miles away (coll.)

Geistigkeit *die; ~:* intellectuality

geistlich *Adj.* sacred ‹*song, music*›; religious ‹*order*›; religious, devotional ‹*book, writings*›; spiritual ‹*matter, support*›; spiritual, religious ‹*leader*›; ecclesiastical ‹*office, dignitary*›; **der ~e Stand** the clergy; **in den ~en Stand eintreten** take holy orders

Geistliche[1] *der; adj. Dekl.* ▸❶ **S. 113** clergyman; priest; (einer Freikirche) minister; (Militär~, Gefängnis~) chaplain

Geistliche[2] *die* ▸❶ **S. 113** [woman] priest

Geistlichkeit *die; ~:* clergy

geist-, Geist-: ~los *Adj.* (dumm) dim-witted; witless; (ohne ernsten Gehalt) trivial; shallow ‹*conversation*›; **~losigkeit** *die; ~~* (Dummheit) dim-wittedness; witlessness; (Trivialität) triviality; **~reich** A *Adj.* (amüsant) witty; (elegant) elegant; (klug) clever; (unterhaltsam) entertaining; **nicht gerade ~reich aussehen** (ugs.) look pretty stupid (coll.); B *adv.; s. Adj.:* wittily; elegantly; cleverly; entertainingly; **~sprühend** *Adj.* brilliantly witty; **~tötend** *Adj.* soul-destroying ‹*work, job*›; stupefyingly boring ‹*chatter, drivel*›; **~voll** *Adj.* brilliantly witty ‹*joke, satire*›; brilliant ‹*idea*›; intellectually stimulating ‹*conversation, book*›

Geiz /gaits/ *der; ~es* (abwertend) meanness; (Knauserigkeit) miserliness

geizen *itr. V.* 1 (übertrieben sparsam sein) be mean; **mit etw. ~:** be mean *or* stingy with sth.; **mit Lob ~** (fig.) be sparing with one's praise; **sie geizt nicht mit ihren Reizen** (fig. iron.) she doesn't mind displaying her charms 2 (veralt.: heftig verlangen) **nach etw. ~:** crave [for] sth.; (gierig) be greedy for sth.

Geiz·hals *der* (abwertend) skinflint

geizig *Adj.* mean; (knauserig) miserly

Geiz·kragen *der* (ugs. abwertend) skinflint

Gejammer[e] *das; ~s* (abwertend) yammering (coll.); bellyaching (sl.)

Gejauchze *das; ~s* rejoicing; jubilation; **ihr ~ hallte durch das ganze Haus** their joyful cheers echoed through the house

Gejaul[e] *das; ~s* (abwertend) howling

Gejohl[e] /gəˈjoːl(ə)/ *das; ~s* (abwertend) howling; **mit lautstarkem ~:** with loud howls *pl.*

gekannt /gəˈkant/ *2. Part. v.* **kennen**

Gekeif[e] /geˈkaif(ə)/ *das; ~s* scolding; nagging

Gekicher *das; ~s* giggling

Gekicke *das; ~s* (ugs. abwertend) kicking the ball around

Gekläff[e] *das; ~[e]s* (abwertend; auch fig.) yapping

Geklapper *das; ~s* clatter[ing]

Geklatsch[e] *das; ~s* (abwertend) 1 (Beifallklatschen) clapping 2 (Tratsch) gossiping

gekleidet
A *2. Part. v.* **kleiden**
B *Adj.* dressed; **gut/schlecht ~ sein** be well/badly dressed

Geklimper *das; ~s* (abwertend) plunking

Geklingel *das; ~s* (abwertend) ringing

geklungen /gəˈklʊŋən/ *2. Part. v.* **klingen**

Geknall[e] *das; ~s* (ugs. abwertend) banging; (von Schüssen, einer Peitsche) cracking; (von Korken) popping

Geknatter *das; ~s* (eines Autos, Motors, Motorrades) clattering; (eines Maschinengewehrs) rattling; (eines Segels) flapping; (eines Radios) crackle

geknickt
A *2. Part. v.* **knicken**
B *Adj.* (ugs.) dejected; downcast

gekniffen *2. Part. v.* **kneifen**

Geknister *das; ~s* rustling; rustle; (von Holz, Feuer) crackling; crackle

gekommen *2. Part. v.* **kommen**

gekonnt /gəˈkɔnt/
A *2. Part. v.* **können**
B *Adj.* accomplished; (hervorragend ausgeführt) masterly
C *adv.* in an accomplished manner; (hervorragend) in masterly fashion

gekoren /gəˈkoːrən/ *2. Part. v.* **küren, kiesen**

Gekrächz[e] *das;* **~s** cawing; (einer heiseren Stimme) croaking; (von Papageien) squawking

Gekrakel *das;* **~s** (ugs. abwertend) scrawl; scribble

Gekreisch[e] *das;* **~s** (von Vögeln) screeching; (von Menschen) shrieking; squealing; (von Rädern, Bremsen) squealing

gekrischen /gə'krɪʃn/ *2. Part. v.* **kreischen**

Gekritzel[e] *das;* **~s** (abwertend) scribble; scrawl

gekrochen *2. Part. v.* **kriechen**

Gekröse /gə'krø:zə/ *das;* **~s, ~** 1 (Kochk.) (vom Kalb) tripe; (vom Schwein) chitterlings *pl.*; (von Geflügel) giblets *pl.* 2 ▸ **S. 435** (Anat.) mesentery

gekünstelt /gə'kʏnstl̩t/

A *Adj.* artificial; **ein ~es Lächeln** a forced smile; **ein ~es Benehmen** affected behaviour

B *adv.* **er lächelte ~:** he gave a forced smile; **sie spricht immer so ~:** she always talks so affectedly

Gel /ge:l/ *das;* **~s, ~e** (Chemie) gel

Gelaber[e] *das;* **~s** (ugs. abwertend) rabbiting (coll.) *or* babbling on

Gelächter /gə'lɛçtɐ/ *das;* **~s, ~:** laughter; **ein lautes/schallendes ~:** loud/ringing laughter; **in ~ ausbrechen** burst out laughing; *s. auch* **homerisch**

gelackmeiert /gə'lakmaiɐt/ *Adj.* (salopp scherzh.) had (sl.); conned (coll.); **ich bin/du bist** *usw.* **der/die Gelackmeierte** I'm/you're *etc.* the one who's been had (sl.)

geladen

A *2. Part. v.* **laden**

B *in* **~ sein** be furious *or* (coll.) livid; **[auf jmdn./etw.] ~ sein** be furious *or* (Brit. coll.) livid [with sb./about sth.]

Gelage *das;* **~s, ~:** feast; banquet; (abwertend) orgy of eating and drinking

Gelähmte *der/die; adj. Dekl.* paralytic

Gelände /gə'lɛndə/ *das;* **~s, ~** 1 (Landschaft) ground; terrain; **das ~ steigt an/fällt ab** the ground rises/falls; **das ~ durchkämmen/erkunden** comb/reconnoitre the ground 2 (Grundstück) site; (von Schule, Krankenhaus usw.) grounds *pl.*; **das ~ absperren** cordon off the area 3 (Milit.) **~ gewinnen/verlieren** gain/lose ground

gelände-, Gelände-: **~darstellung** *die* (Geogr.) relief mapping; **~fahrt** *die* cross-country drive; (das Fahren) cross-country driving; **~fahrzeug** *das* cross-country vehicle; **~gängig** *Adj.* cross-country *attrib.* ‹*vehicle*›; ‹*vehicle*› suitable for cross-country driving; **~lauf** *der* (Leichtathletik) cross-country run; (Wettbewerb) cross-country race; (das Laufen) cross-country running

Geländer /gə'lɛndɐ/ *das;* **~s, ~:** banisters *pl.*; handrail; (am Balkon, an einer Brücke) railing[s *pl.*]; (aus Stein) balustrades; parapet

Gelände-: **~reifen** *der* cross-country tyre; **~ritt** *der* 1 cross-country ride; 2 (Reitsport) endurance competition; **~spiel** *das* scouting game; **~sport** *der* scrambling; **~übung** *die* (Milit.) field exercise; **~wagen** *der* ▸ **~fahrzeug**

gelang *3. Pers. Sg. Prät. v.* **gelingen**

gelänge *3. Pers. Sg. Konjunktiv II v.* **gelingen**

gelangen *itr. V.; mit sein* 1 **an etw.** (Akk.)**/zu etw. ~:** arrive at *or* reach sth.; **ans Ziel ~:** arrive at *or* reach one's destination; **an die Öffentlichkeit ~:** reach the public; leak out; **in jmds. Besitz ~:** come into sb.'s possession; **in den Besitz von etw. ~:** gain possession of sth. 2 (fig.) **zu Geld ~** (durch Arbeit) make money; (durch Erbe) come into money; **zu Ansehen ~:** gain esteem *or* standing; **zu Ehre ~:** attain honour; **zu Ruhm ~:** achieve fame; **an die Macht ~:** come to power; **zu der Erkenntnis ~, dass ...** come to the realization that ...; realize that ... 3 *als Funktionsverb* **zur Aufführung ~:** be presented *or* performed; **zur Auszahlung/Verteilung ~:** be paid [out]/distributed

Gelass, *Gelaß /gə'las/ *das;* **Gelasses, Gelasse** (geh.) [small, dark] room *or* chamber; (Verlies) dungeon

gelassen

A *2. Part. v.* **lassen**

B *Adj.* calm; (gefasst) composed; **~ bleiben** keep calm *or* cool

C *adv.* calmly

Gelassenheit *die;* **~:** calmness; (Gefasstheit) composure

Geläster *das;* **~s** (abwertend) making malicious remarks

Gelatine /ʒela'ti:nə/ *die;* **~:** gelatine

Geläuf *das;* **~[e]s, ~e** 1 (Jägerspr.) tracks *pl.*; track; spoor 2 (Sport) track, course

gelaufen *2. Part. v.* **laufen**

geläufig

A *Adj.* 1 (vertraut) familiar, common ‹*expression, concept*›; **etw. ist jmdm. ~:** sb. is familiar with sth. 2 (fließend, perfekt) fluent

B *adv.* fluently; **~ Englisch sprechen** speak fluent English; speak English fluently; be fluent in English

Geläufigkeit *die;* **~** 1 (Bekanntheit) familiarity 2 (Perfektion) fluency

gelaunt /gə'launt/ **gut ~:** good-humoured; cheerful; **froh ~:** cheerful; **schlecht ~:** ill-tempered; bad-tempered; **übel ~:** ill-tempered; ill-humoured; **gut/schlecht ~ sein** be in a good/bad mood; **wie ist sie ~?** what sort of mood is she in?; **zu etw. ~ sein** (veralt.) be in the mood for sth.

Geläut *das;* **~[e]s, ~e** 1 (Glocken) chime 2 ▸ **Geläute**

Geläute *das;* **~s** ringing; (harmonisch) chiming

gelb /gɛlp/ *Adj.* yellow; **die ~e Gefahr** (abwertend) the yellow peril; **die ~e Karte** (Fußball) the yellow card; **vor Neid ~ werden** turn green with envy; **der Gelbe Fluss/das Gelbe Meer** the Yellow River/Sea; **das Gelbe vom Ei** the egg yolk; **das ist nicht das Gelbe vom Ei** (fig. ugs.) that's no great shakes (sl.); **Gelbe Seiten** (Wz) *Pl.* Yellow Pages ®

Gelb *das;* **~s, ~** *od.* (ugs.) **~s** yellow; **bei ~ über die Ampel fahren** go through *or* crash the lights on amber; *s. auch* **Blau**

gelb·braun *Adj.* yellowish-brown

Gelbe /'gɛlbə/ *der/die; adj. Dekl.* (abwertend) Oriental

gelb-, Gelb-: **~fieber** *das* ▸ **S. 439** (Med.) yellow fever; **~filter** *der od.* (fachspr. meist) *das* (Fot.) yellow filter; **~grün** *Adj.* yellowish-green; **~körper** *der* ▸ **S. 435** (Anat.) corpus luteum; **~kreuz** *das* mustard gas

gelblich

A *Adj.* yellowish; yellowed ‹*paper*›; sallow ‹*skin*›

B *adv.* **~ grün** yellowish-green

gelb-, Gelb-: **~sucht** *die* ▸ **S. 439** (Med.) jaundice; icterus (Med.); **~süchtig** *Adj.* jaundiced; **~wurz[el]** *die* (Bot.) turmeric

Geld /gɛlt/ *das;* **~es, ~er** ▸ **S. 299** 1 money; **großes ~:** large denominations *pl.*; **kleines/bares ~:** change/cash; **etw. bedeutet bares ~:** sth. is worth hard cash; **~ scheffeln** rake in the money; **etw. für teures ~ erwerben** pay a lot of money for sth.; **es ist für ~ nicht zu haben** money cannot buy it; **mit ~ nicht umgehen können** be hopeless about money; **das ist hinausgeworfenes ~:** that is a waste of money *or* (coll.) money down the drain; **ohne ~ dastehen** be left penniless; **ins ~ gehen** (ugs.) run away with the money (coll.); **~ stinkt nicht** (Spr.) money has no smell; **~ regiert die Welt** (Spr.) money makes the world go round; **~ allein macht nicht glücklich [**(scherzh.)**, aber es hilft]** (Spr.) money isn't everything[, but it helps]; **~ und Gut** (geh.) all one's wealth and possessions; **hier liegt das ~ auf der Straße** (fig.) the streets here are paved with gold; **das große ~ machen** make a lot of money; **sein ~ unter die Leute bringen** spend one's money; **jmdm. das ~ aus der Tasche ziehen** get *or* wheedle money out of sb.; **~ wie Heu haben, im ~ schwimmen** be rolling in money *or* in it (coll.); **nicht für ~ und gute Worte** (ugs.) not for love or money; **zu ~ kommen** get hold of [some] money; **etw. zu ~ machen** turn sth. into money *or* cash 2 (größere Summe) money; **öffentliche/staatliche ~er** public/state money *sing. or* funds 3 (Börsenw.) ▸ **Geldkurs**

geld-, Geld-: **~adel** *der* financial aristocracy; **~angelegenheit** *die* money *or* financial matter; **seine ~angelegenheiten regeln** settle one's affairs; **~anlage** *die* investment; **~automat** *der* cash dispenser; **~betrag** *der* sum *or* amount [of money]; **~beutel** *der* (bes. südd.) purse; **auf dem** *od.* **seinem ~beutel sitzen** (ugs. abwertend) be tight-fisted; **~bombe** *die* night-safe box; **~börse** *die* purse; **~briefträger** *der*, **~briefträgerin** *die: postman/postwoman who delivers items containing money or on which money is payable;* **~buße** *die* fine; **~entwertung** *die* depreciation of the/a currency; **~erwerb** *der* 1 **zum ~erwerb arbeiten** work [in order] to earn money; **seine Malerei dient nicht dem ~erwerb** he does not paint for the money; 2 (Tätigkeit) **seinem ~erwerb nachgehen** earn one's living; **~forderung** *die* claim [for money]; **eine ~forderung an jmdn. haben** have a claim against sb.; **~frage** *die* question of money; **~geber** *der*, **~geberin** *die* financial backer; (für Forschungen usw.) sponsor; **~geschäft** *das* financial transaction; money transaction; **~geschenk** *das* gift of money; **~gier** *die* (abwertend) greed; avarice; **~gierig** *Adj.* (abwertend) greedy; avaricious; **~hahn** *der: in* **[jmdm.] den ~hahn ab-** *od.* **zudrehen** (ugs.) cut off sb.'s supply of money; **~haus** *das* financial institution; **~heirat** *die:* **das ist eine reine ~heirat** he just married her for her money/she just married him for his money; **~herrschaft** *die* plutocracy

geldig *Adj.* (österr.) rich; wealthy

Geld-: **~institut** *das* financial institution; **~karte** *die* cash card; **~katze** *die* (hist.) *large leather purse worn on or as a belt;* **~klemme** *die* (ugs.) financial straits *pl. or* difficulties *pl.*; **~knappheit** *die* shortage of money; **~kurs** *der* (Börsenw.) bid price; **~leute** ▸ **~mann**

geldlich *Adj.* financial

Geld-: **~mangel** *der* lack of money; **~mann** *der; Pl.* **~leute** financier; **~markt** *der* (Wirtsch.) money market; **~mittel** *Pl.* financial resources; funds; **~not** *die* financial straits *pl. or* difficulties *pl.*; **~politik** *die* monetary policy; **~prämie** *die* cash bonus; (~preis) cash prize; **~preis** *der* cash prize; (bei einem Turnier) prize money; **~quelle** *die* source of income; (für den Staat) source of revenue; **~sache** *die* ▸ **~angelegenheit**; **~sack** *der* 1 money bag; 2 (veralt.) ▸ **~beutel**; 3 (ugs. abwertend: geiziger Mensch) money bags *sing.*; **~schein** *der* ▸ **S. 299** banknote; bill (Amer.); **~schöpfung** *die* (Finanzw.) creation of money; **~schrank** *der* safe; **~schrank·knacker** *der*, **~schrank·knackerin** *die* (ugs.) safe-breaker; safe-cracker; **~schuld** *die* [money *or* financial] debt; **~schwemme** *die* (ugs.) glut of money; **~schwierigkeiten** *Pl.* financial difficulties *or* straits; **~sorgen** *Pl.* money troubles; financial worries; **~sorte** *die* (Bankw.) currency; **~spende** *die* donation; contribution; **~spritze** *die* ▸ **Finanzspritze**; **~strafe** *die* fine; **jmdn. zu einer ~strafe verurteilen** fine sb.; **~stück** *das* ▸ **S. 299** coin; **~summe** *die* sum [of money]; **~tasche** *die* purse; **~umlauf** *der* circulation of money; **~umtausch** *der* ▸ **~wechsel**; **~verlegenheit** *die* (verhüll.) financial embarrassment; **in ~verlegenheit sein** be financially embarrassed; **~verleiher** *der*, **~verleiherin** *die* moneylender; **~verlust** *der* financial loss; **~verschwendung** *die* waste of money; **das wäre reinste ~verschwendung** that would be a sheer waste of money; **~wasch·anlage** *die* (ugs.) money-laundering scheme; **~wechsel** *der* exchanging of money; **„~wechsel"** 'bureau de change'; 'change'; **~wert** *der* 1 (Wert eines Gegenstandes) cash value; 2 (innerer ~wert) value of money; (äußerer ~wert) value of the/a currency; **~wesen** *das* finance *no art.*; **~zuwendung** *die* allowance [of money]; (~geschenk) gift of money

ℹ Geld

Britisches Geld

GESCHRIEBEN	GESPROCHEN
1p	one p
2p	two p *od.* pence
50p	fifty p *od.* pence
£1	one pound, a pound
£1.03	one pound three p *od.* three pence*
£1.20	one pound twenty [p *od.* pence]*
£1.99	one pound ninety-nine
£20	twenty pounds
£100	one hundred *od.* a hundred pounds
£1,000	one thousand *od.* a thousand pounds
£1,000,000	one million *od.* a million pounds
£5,000,000	five million pounds

100 Pence sind ein Pfund
= 100 pence make one pound, There are 100 pence in a pound

* Normalerweise sagt man immer 'p' bzw 'pence' nach einer Zahl zwischen 1 und 19, die auf eine Pfundzahl folgt; bei 20 Pence oder mehr wird das 'p' bzw 'pence' hier meist weggelassen.

Amerikanisches Geld

GESCHRIEBEN	GESPROCHEN
1c	one cent, a cent
10c	ten cents, a dime*
25c	twenty-five cents, a quarter*
$1	one dollar, a dollar
$1.50	one dollar fifty [cents]
$5.99	five dollars ninety-nine
$200	two hundred dollars
$1,000	one thousand *od.* a thousand dollars
$1,000,000	one million *od.* a million dollars
$100,000,000	one hundred *od.* a hundred million dollars

100 Cent sind ein Dollar
= 100 cents make one dollar, There are 100 cents in a dollar

* Diese Bezeichnungen beziehen sich meist auf die Münzen mit diesen Werten.

Geld in Euroland

GESCHRIEBEN	GESPROCHEN
1c or 1ct	one cent, a cent
25cts	twenty-five cents
€1	one euro
€1.50	one euro fifty [cents]
€2	two euros
€2.75	two euros seventy-five [cents]
€100	one hundred *od.* a hundred euros
€200	two hundred euros
€1,000	one thousand *od.* a thousand euros
€1,000,000	one million *od.* a million euros
€50,000,000	fifty million euros

100 Cent sind ein Euro
= 100 cents make one euro

der Wert des Pfundes gegenüber dem Euro
= the value of the pound against the euro

Schweizerisches Geld

GESCHRIEBEN	GESPROCHEN
90c	ninety centimes
1 SF	one [Swiss] franc, a [Swiss] franc
2,000 SF	two thousand [Swiss] francs

Münzen und Scheine

GB:

ein Zwanzigpencestück = a 20p *od.* 20 pence piece	***ein Pfundstück*** = a pound coin
ein Fünfzigpencestück = a 50p *od.* 50 pence piece	***ein Fünfpfundschein*** = a five-pound note

USA:

ein Fünfcentstück = a nickel	***ein Dollarstück*** = a dollar coin
ein Zehncentstück = a dime	***ein Dollarschein*** = a dollar bill
ein Vierteldollarstück = a quarter	***ein Zehndollarschein*** = a ten-dollar bill

Man sieht, dass für die kleineren Werte (unter 1 Pfund bzw. 1 Dollar) *Stück* durch 'piece' übersetzt wird, sonst durch 'coin'. Auch dass die Währungseinheit (pound, dollar, euro usw.) vor 'piece', 'coin', 'note' oder 'bill' im Singular bleibt. Das gilt ebenfalls für Euro und Cent.

ein Fünfzigcentstück
= a 50 cent piece

ein Eineurostück
= a one-euro coin

ein Zweieurostück
= a two-euro coin

ein Zwanzigeuroschein
= a twenty-euro note *od.* (*amerik.*) bill

Sonstige Ausdrücke

Was od. Wie viel kostet das?
= What *od.* How much does it cost?

Es kostet knapp 200 €/etwas über 200 €
= It costs just under/just over 200 €

Die Kartoffeln kosten 30p das Pfund
= The potatoes are 30p a pound

100 Euro in bar
= 100 euros in cash

etwas bar/in Pfund bezahlen
= to pay for something in cash/in pounds

bargeldlose Zahlung
= cashless payment

Kann ich mit Scheck/mit Kreditkarte zahlen?
= Can I pay by cheque/by credit card?

ein Scheck über 50 Pfund
= a cheque for £50

ein Reisescheck in Dollar/Pfund [Sterling]
= a dollar/sterling traveller's cheque *od.* (*amerik.*) traveler's check

Können Sie auf einen Zwanzigeuroschein herausgeben?
= Can you change *od.* give me change for a twenty-euro note *od.* (*amerik.*) bill?

Ich will Euros in Dollar wechseln
= I want to change euros into dollars

Allgemeine Bemerkungen: 1. Im Englischen steht bei Zahlen über tausend ein Komma dort, wo im Deutschen ein Spatium steht. 2. Das Wort 'million' ist kein Substantiv (wie *Million* im Deutschen), sondern ein Adjektiv. Deshalb kein **s** bei mehreren Millionen (zwei Millionen Pfund = two million pounds).

Siehe auch □ **Zahlen.**

geleckt
A *2. Part. v.* **lecken²**
B *Adj. in* **wie ~ aussehen** (ugs.) look all spruced up

Gelee /ʒe'le:/ *der od. das;* **~s, ~s** jelly; **Aale in ~:** jellied eels

Gelege *das;* **~s, ~** (von Vögeln) clutch of eggs; (von Reptilien, Insekten) batch of eggs

gelegen
A *2. Part. v.* **liegen**
B *Adj.* **1** (passend) convenient; **das kommt mir ~:** that comes just at the right time for me **2** (liegend) situated; **hoch ~:** high-lying

Gelegenheit *die;* **~, ~en** **1** (günstiger Augenblick) opportunity; **jmdm. [die] ~ geben, etw. zu tun** give sb. the opportunity of doing *or* to do sth.; **die ~ nutzen** make the most of the opportunity; **bei nächster ~:** at the next opportunity; **bei ~:** some time; **~ macht Diebe** opportunity makes the thief (prov.); **die ~ beim Schopf[e] fassen** *od.* **ergreifen** grab *or* seize the opportunity with both hands **2** (Anlass) occasion; **ein Anzug für alle ~en** a suit that can be worn on any occasion

Gelegenheits-: ~arbeit *die* casual work; **~arbeiter** *der,* **~arbeiterin** *die* casual worker; **~dieb** *der,* **~diebin** *die* opportunist thief; **~dichtung** *die* occasional poetry; **~kauf** *der* bargain

gelegentlich
A *Adj.* occasional
B *adv.* **1** (manchmal) occasionally **2** (bei Gelegenheit) some time
C *Präp. + Gen.* (Amtsspr.) on the occasion of

gelehrig /gə'le:rɪç/
A *Adj.* ‹*child*› who is quick to learn *or* quick at picking things up; ‹*animal*› that is quick to learn
B *adv.* **sich ~ anstellen** be quick to learn

Gelehrigkeit *die;* **~:** quickness to learn

gelehrsam *Adj.* **1** ▸ **gelehrig** **2** (veralt.: gelehrt) learned; erudite

Gelehrsamkeit *die;* **~:** learning; erudition

gelehrt
A *2. Part. v.* **lehren**
B *Adj.* **1** (kenntnisreich) learned; erudite **2** (auf gründlichen Kenntnissen beruhend) scholarly **3** (abwertend: schwer verständlich) highbrow
C *adv.* **1** learnedly; eruditely **2** (abwertend: schwer verständlich) in a highbrow way

Gelehrte *der/die; adj. Dekl.* scholar; **darüber streiten sich die ~n** *od.* **sind sich die ~n noch nicht einig** the experts disagree on that; (fig.) that's a moot point

Gelehrten-: ~dasein *das* scholarly life *or* existence; **~streit** *der* dispute among scholars

Geleise *das;* **~s, ~** (österr., sonst geh.) ▸ **Gleis**

Geleit *das;* **~[e]s, ~e** **1** (geh.: das Begleiten) **sie bot uns ihr ~ an** she offered to accompany *or* escort us; **freies** *od.* **sicheres ~** (Rechtsw.) safe conduct; **jmdm. das ~ geben** (geh.) accompany *or* escort sb.; **jmdm. das letzte ~ geben** (geh. verhüll.) attend sb.'s funeral; **zum ~:** as a preface; **„zum ~"** 'preface' **2** (Eskorte) escort; (Gefolge) entourage; retinue

geleiten *tr. V.* (geh.) escort; (begleiten) accompany; escort; **jmdn. zur Tür ~:** see sb. to the door; show sb. out

Geleit-: ~schiff *das* (Milit.) escort vessel; **~schutz** *der* (Milit.) escort; **jmdm. ~schutz geben** provide an escort for sb.; **~wort** *das; Pl.* **~~e** (geh.) preface; **~zug** *der* (Milit.) convoy

gelen /'ge:lən/ *tr. V.* gel ‹*hair*›

Gelenk /gə'lɛŋk/ *das;* **~[e]s, ~e** **1** ▸ ℹ **S. 435** joint; **es kracht** *od.* **knackt in den ~en** my/your *etc.* joints creak **2** (Technik) joint; (Scharnier~) hinge

Gelenk-: ~entzündung *die* ▸ ℹ **S. 439** (Med.) arthritis; **~fahrzeug** *das* articulated vehicle

gelenkig
A *Adj.* agile ‹*person*›; (geschmeidig) supple ‹*limb*›
B *adv.* **1** agilely **2** (Technik) **~ gelagert** (mittels Scharnier) hinge-mounted; (mittels Drehzapfen) swivel-mounted

Gelenkigkeit *die;* ~: agility; (von Gliedmaßen) suppleness

Gelenk-: **~kapsel** *die* ▸ⓘ **S. 435** (Anat.) joint capsule; articular capsule; **~kopf** *der* (Anat.) head of a/the bone; **~pfanne** *die* ▸ⓘ **S. 435** (Anat.) socket of a/the joint; **~rheumatismus** *der* ▸ⓘ **S. 439** (Med.) articular rheumatism; **~schmiere** *die* (Anat.) synovial fluid; **~welle** *die* (Kfz-W.) cardan shaft

gelernt
A *2. Part. v.* **lernen**
B *Adj.* qualified

gelesen *2. Part. v.* **lesen**

Gelichter *das;* ~s (veralt. abwertend) rabble; riff-raff

Geliebte /gəˈliːptə/ *der/die; adj. Dekl.* **1** lover/mistress **2** (geh. veralt.) beloved

geliefert
A *2. Part. v.* **liefern**
B *Adj. in* ~ **sein** (salopp) be sunk (coll.); have had it (coll.)

geliehen /gəˈliːən/ *2. Part. v.* **leihen**

gelieren /ʒeˈliːrən/ *itr. V.* set

Gelier·zucker *der* preserving sugar

gelind[e]
A *Adj.* **1** (schonend) mild **2** (geh. veralt.: mild, sanft) mild ‹*climate*›; light ‹*punishment*›; slight ‹*pain*›
B *adv.* mildly; ~ **gesagt** to put it mildly

gelingen /gəˈlɪŋən/ *unr. itr. V.; mit sein* succeed; **es gelang ihr, es zu tun** she succeeded in doing it; **es gelang ihr nicht, es zu tun** she did not succeed in doing it; she failed to do it; **möge dir dein Vorhaben ~:** I hope you succeed with *or* accomplish your plan; **das wollte ihr nicht ~:** she couldn't seem to manage it; **eine gelungene Arbeit** a successful piece of work; *s. auch* **gelungen B**

Gelingen *das;* ~s success; **auf ein gutes ~ hoffen** hope for success; **jmdm. gutes ~ wünschen** wish sb. every success; **gutes ~!** the best of luck!

gelitten /gəˈlɪtn̩/ *2. Part. v.* **leiden**

gell[1] /gɛl/
A *Adj.* (geh.) piercing; shrill
B *adv.* ~ **aufschreien** let out *or* give a piercing scream *or* shriek

gell[e][2] /ˈgɛl(ə)/ *Interj.* (südd.) ▸ **gelt**

gellen /ˈgɛlən/ *itr. V.* **1** (hell schallen) ring out; **ein Schrei gellte durch die Nacht** a scream *or* shriek pierced the night; **jmdm. in den Ohren ~:** make sb.'s ears ring; **~des Gelächter** shrill peals of laughter; **~d aufschreien** let out *or* give a piercing scream *or* shriek **2** (nachhallen) ring; **uns gellten die Ohren** our ears rang; **von etw. ~:** ring with sth.

geloben *tr. V.* (geh.) vow; **Besserung/Armut ~:** promise solemnly to improve/take a vow of poverty; **jmdm. Treue ~:** vow to be faithful to sb.; **sich** (*Dat.*) **~, etw. zu tun** vow to oneself *or* make a solemn resolve to do sth.; **das Gelobte Land** the Promised Land

Gelöbnis /gəˈløːpnɪs/ *das;* **~ses, ~se** (geh.) vow; **ein ~ ablegen** *od.* **leisten** make *or* take a vow

gelogen *2. Part. v.* **lügen**

gelöst /gəˈløːst/
A *2. Part. v.* **lösen**
B *Adj.* relaxed

Gelöstheit *die;* ~: relaxed mood

Gelse /ˈgɛlzə/ *die;* **~, ~n** (österr.) mosquito, gnat

gelt /gɛlt/ *Interj.* (südd., österr. ugs.) **~, du bist mir doch nicht böse?** you're not angry with me, are you?; **er kommt doch morgen zurück, ~?** he'll be coming back tomorrow, won't he *or* (coll.) right?

gelten /ˈgɛltn̩/
A *unr. itr. V.* **1** (gültig sein) be valid; ‹*banknote, coin*› be legal tender; ‹*law, regulation, agreement*› be in force; ‹*price*› be effective; **etw. gilt für jmdn.** sth. applies to sb.; **das gilt auch für dich/Sie!** (ugs.) that includes you!; that goes for you too!; **das gilt nicht!** that doesn't count!; **~de Preise** current prices; **nach ~dem Recht** in accordance with the law as it [now] stands; **die ~de Meinung** the generally accepted opinion; **etw. [nicht] ~ lassen** [not] accept sth. **2** (angesehen werden) **als etw. ~:** be regarded as sth.; be considered [to be] sth.; **er galt als klug/Favorit** he was regarded as clever/the favourite; he was considered [to be] clever/the favourite **3** (+ *Dat.*) (bestimmt sein für) be directed at; **die Bemerkung gilt dir** the remark is aimed at you; **der Beifall galt auch dem Regisseur** the applause was also for the director
B *unr. tr. V.* **1** (wert sein) **sein Wort gilt viel/wenig** his word carries a lot of/little weight; **was gilt die Wette?** what do you bet?; **etw. gilt jmdm. mehr als …** sth. is worth *or* means more to sb. than … **2** *unpers.* (darauf ankommen, dass) **es gilt, Zeit zu gewinnen/rasch zu handeln** it is essential to gain time/act swiftly; **es gilt einen Versuch** the only thing to do is to make an attempt **3** *unpers.* (geh.: auf dem Spiel stehen) **es gilt dein Leben** *od.* **deinen Kopf** your life is at stake

geltend *in* **etw. ~ machen** assert sth.; **einige Bedenken/einen Einwand ~ machen** express some doubts/raise an objection; **sich ~ machen** begin to show; begin to make itself/themselves felt; *s. auch* **gelten A 1**

Geltendmachung *die;* ~ (Amtsspr.) assertion

Geltung *die;* ~ **1** (Gültigkeit) validity; **~ haben** ‹*banknote, coin*› be legal tender; ‹*law, regulation, agreement*› be in force; ‹*price*› be effective; **für jmdn. ~ haben** apply to sb. **2** (Wirkung) recognition; **jmdm./sich/einer Sache ~ verschaffen** gain *or* win recognition for sb./oneself/sth.; **an ~ verlieren** ‹*value, principle, etc.*› lose its importance, become less important; **etw. zur ~ bringen** show something to its best advantage; **zur ~ kommen** show to [its best] advantage

Geltungs-: **~bedürfnis** *das* need for recognition; **~bereich** *der* scope; **unter den ~bereich eines Gesetzes fallen** come within the scope of a law; **~bereich dieser Verordnung ist Hessen** the area in which the regulation is in force is Hesse; **~dauer** *die* period of validity; **die ~dauer des Vertrags/Gesetzes** the period during which the agreement/law is in force; **~drang** *der* ▸ **~sbedürfnis**; **~sucht** *die* [pathological] craving for recognition; **~trieb** *der* (~bedürfnis) need for recognition; (~sucht) craving for recognition

Gelump[e] /gəˈlʊmp(ə)/ *das;* ~s (ugs. abwertend) **1** (Plunder) junk; rubbish **2** (Gesindel) riff-raff; rabble

gelungen /gəˈlʊŋən/
A *2. Part. v.* **gelingen**
B *Adj.* **1** (ugs.: spaßig) priceless; **das finde ich ~:** what a laugh! **2** (ansprechend) inspired

Gelüst *das;* **~[e]s, ~e, Gelüste** *das;* **~es, ~e** (geh.) longing; strong desire; (zwingend, krankhaft) craving; **ein ~ nach** *od.* **auf etw.** (*Akk.*) **haben** have a longing *or* a strong desire/a craving for sth.

gelüsten *tr. V.* (unpers.) **es gelüstet ihn nach …** he has a longing for …; (zwingend, krankhaft) he has a craving for …

gemach /gəˈmaː(ː)x/ *Adv.* (veralt.) **[nur/immer] ~!** not so fast!; take it easy!

Gemach /gəˈma(ː)x/ *das;* **~[e]s, Gemächer** /gəˈmɛ(ː)çɐ/ (veralt. geh.) apartment

gemächlich /gəˈmɛ(ː)çlɪç/
A *Adj.* leisurely; **ein ~es Leben führen** take life easily
B *adv.* in a leisurely manner; **~ wandern** stroll

Gemächlichkeit *die;* ~: leisureliness; **etw. mit ~ machen** do sth. at a leisurely pace

gemacht
A *2. Part. v.* **machen**
B *in* **ein ~er Mann sein** (ugs.) be a made man; **zu** *od.* **für etw. [nicht] ~ sein** (ugs.) [not] be made for sth.; **ich bin nicht dazu ~, einen solchen Posten auszufüllen** I'm not cut out for a job like this

Gemächt *das;* **~[e]s, Gemächte** *das;* **~es** (scherzh., veralt.) privy parts *pl.* (arch.)

Gemahl *der;* **~s, ~e** (geh.) consort; husband; **bitte grüßen Sie Ihren Herrn ~:** please give my regards to your husband

Gemahlin *die;* **~, ~nen** (geh.) consort; wife; **eine Empfehlung an die Frau ~:** my compliments to your wife

gemahnen *tr., itr. V.* (geh.) **jmdn. an etw.** (*Akk.*) **~:** remind sb. of sth.; **diese Gedenktafel soll an die Opfer beider Weltkriege ~:** this memorial plaque is to commemorate the dead of two World Wars

Gemälde /gəˈmɛːldə/ *das;* **~s, ~:** painting

Gemälde-: **~ausstellung** *die* exhibition of paintings; **~galerie** *die* picture gallery; **~sammlung** *die* collection of paintings

gemäß /gəˈmɛːs/
A *Präp. + Dat.* in accordance with; **~ Paragraph 15/Artikel 12** under section 15/article 12
B *Adj.* **jmdm./einer Sache ~ sein** be appropriate for sb./to sth.; **eine deinen Leistungen ~e Arbeit** a job suited to your abilities

-gemäß *Adj.* in accordance with ‹*tradition etc.*›; **berufs~:** in accordance with the standards of the profession; **art~:** appropriate [for the species *postpos.*]

gemäßigt
A *2. Part. v.* **mäßigen**
B *Adj.* moderate; modest ‹*lifestyle*›; more restrained ‹*version*›; qualified ‹*optimism*›; temperate ‹*climate*›

Gemäuer /gəˈmɔyɐ/ *das;* **~s, ~:** walls *pl.*; (Ruine) ruin

Gemauschel *das;* **~s** (ugs. abwertend) under-hand dealing

Gemecker[e] *das;* **~s** **1** (von Schafen, Ziegen) bleating **2** (abwertend: Lachen) cackling **3** (ugs. abwertend: Nörgelei) griping (coll.); grousing (sl.); moaning

gemein
A *Adj.* **1** (abstoßend) coarse, vulgar ‹*joke, expression*›; nasty ‹*person*› **2** (niederträchtig) mean; base, dirty ‹*lie*›; mean, dirty ‹*trick*›; **du bist ~!/das ist ~ [von dir]!** you're mean *or* nasty!/that's mean *or* nasty [of you]! **3** (ärgerlich) infuriating; damned annoying (coll.) **4** (Bot., Zool., sonst veralt.: allgemein vorkommend) common; **der ~e Mann** the ordinary man; the man in the street; **ein ~er Soldat** a common soldier **5** (veralt.: all~) general; **das ~e Wohl** the common good; **etw. mit jmdm./etw. ~ haben** have sth. in common with sb./sth.; **sich mit jmdm. ~ machen** associate with sb.; **das ist ihnen ~:** they have that in common; they share that
B *adv.* **1** (niederträchtig) **jmdn. ~ behandeln** treat sb. in a mean *or* nasty way **2** (ugs.: sehr) **sich ~ verletzen** injure oneself badly; **es hat ganz ~ weh getan** it hurt like hell (coll.); **~ kalt** terribly *or* hellish cold (coll.)

Gemein·besitz *der* common property

Gemeinde /gəˈmaində/ *die;* **~, ~n** **1** (staatliche Verwaltungseinheit) municipality; (ugs.: ~amt) local authority; **die ~ X** the municipality of X; **einen Zug durch die ~ machen** (fig. ugs.) go on a pub crawl (Brit. coll.); go barhopping (Amer. coll.) **2** (Seelsorgebezirk) (christlich) parish; (nicht-christlich) community; (Mitglieder) parish; parishioners *pl.* **3** (Bewohner) community; local population **4** (Gottesdienstteilnehmer) congregation **5** (Anhängerschaft) body of followers; **die ~ seiner Anhänger** his following

> **Gemeinde**
>
> The lowest level of local government, run by a local council chaired by the *Bürgermeister* (mayor). *Gemeinden* have their own budget, with income from local taxes. They pass local legislation and administer local affairs.

gemeinde-, Gemeinde-: **~abgaben** *Pl.* local taxes; **~amt** *das* local authority; (Gebäude) municipal offices *pl.*; **~beamte** *der,* **~beamtin** *die* local government official; **~behörde** *die* local authority; **~bezirk** *der* **1** municipality; district; **2** (österr.) ward; **~eigen** *Adj.* municipal ‹*swimming pool, sports centre, etc.*›; **~eigen sein** be municipally owned; **~haus** *das* parish hall; **~mitglied** *das* parishioner; **~ordnung** *die* [state] law governing local authorities; **~pflege** *die* parish welfare work; **~rat** *der* 1 (Gremium) local council; 2 (Mitglied) local councillor; **~rätin** *die* ▸**~rat 2**; **~schwester** *die* district nurse; **~steuer** *die* local tax

gemein·deutsch *Adj.* standard German

Gemeinde-: ~verwaltung *die* local administration; **~vor·stand** *der* local council; **~wahl** *die* ▸**Kommunalwahl**; **~zentrum** *das* community centre

gemein-, Gemein-: ~eigentum *das* (Politik, Wirtsch.) public property; **~gefährlich** *Adj.* dangerous to the public; **~gefährlich sein** be a danger to the public; **ein ~gefährlicher Verbrecher** a dangerous criminal; **~gültig** *Adj.* ▸**allgemein gültig**; **~gültigkeit** *die* ▸**Allgemeingültigkeit**; **~gut** *das* (geh.) common property

Gemein·heit *die; ~, ~en* 1 (niederträchtige Gesinnung) meanness; nastiness; **etw. aus ~ tun/sagen** do/say sth. out of meanness *or* nastiness 2 (gemeine Handlung) mean *or* nasty *or* dirty trick; **das war eine ~:** that was a mean *or* nasty thing to do/say 3 (unerfreulicher Umstand) **so eine ~!** (ugs.) what a damned nuisance!

gemein-, Gemein-: ~hin *Adv.* commonly; generally; **wie man ~hin vermutet/annimmt** as is commonly *or* generally supposed/assumed; **~kosten** *Pl.* (Wirtsch.) overheads; overhead expenses; **~nutz** *der;* **~~es** public good; **~nutz geht vor Eigennutz** the public interest comes first; **~nützig** /-nʏtsɪç/ *Adj.* serving the public good *postpos., not pred.;* (wohltätig) charitable; **eine ~nützige Institution** a charitable *or* non-profit-making institution; **~platz** *der* platitude; commonplace

gemeinsam

A *Adj.* 1 common ‹*interests, characteristics*›; mutual ‹*acquaintance, friend*›; joint ‹*property, account*›; shared ‹*experience*›; **der Gemeinsame Markt** the Common Market; **~e Agrarpolitik** (EU) Common Agricultural Policy; **~e Außen- und Sicherheitspolitik** (EU) Common Foreign and Security Policy; **~e europäische Sicherheits- und Verteidigungspolitik** (EU) Common European Security and Defence Policy; **~e Interessen/Merkmale haben** have interests/characteristics in common; **~e Kasse machen** pool funds *or* resources; **größter ~er Teiler** (Math.) highest common denominator; **kleinstes ~es Vielfaches** (Math.) lowest common multiple 2 (miteinander unternommen) joint ‹*undertaking, consultations*›; joint, concerted ‹*efforts, action, measures*›; **[mit jmdm.] ~e Sache machen** join forces *or* up [with sb.] 3 (übereinstimmend) **ihnen ist nur das ~:** that's the only thing they have in common; **das blonde Haar ist ihnen ~:** they both have blond hair; **viel Gemeinsames haben** have a lot in common

B *adv.* together; **es gehört ihnen ~:** it is owned by them jointly

Gemeinsamkeit *die; ~, ~en* 1 (gemeinsames Merkmal) common feature; point in common; **zwischen den beiden Parteien gab es keine ~en** there was no common ground between the two parties 2 (Einheit) community of interest; **ein Gefühl der ~:** a sense of community

Gemeinschaft *die; ~, ~en* 1 community; **die ~ der Heiligen** (Rel.) the communion of saints; **die Europäische ~:** the European Community 2 (Verbundenheit) coexistence; **in unserer Klasse herrscht keine echte ~:** there is no real sense of community in our class; **in ~ mit jmdm.** together *or* jointly with sb.

gemeinschaftlich

A *Adj.* common ‹*interests, characteristics*›; joint ‹*property, undertaking*›; mutual ‹*acquaintance, friend*›; joint, concerted ‹*efforts, action*›

B *adv.* together; **wir führen die Firma ~:** we run the firm jointly *or* together

Gemeinschafts-: ~anschluss, ***~anschluß** *der* (Fernspr.) party line; **~antenne** *die* community aerial (Brit.) *or* (Amer.) antenna; **~arbeit** *die* 1 (gemeinschaftliches Arbeiten) joint work; **etw. in ~arbeit tun** do sth. jointly; **sozialistische ~arbeit** (DDR) collective socialist work *or* efforts *pl.;* 2 (Ergebnis der Zusammenarbeit) joint product *or* effort; **~aufgabe** *die* 1 common *or* shared task; 2 (Bundesrepublik Deutschland) *major project for which Land and Federation are jointly responsible;* **~beichte** *die* (christl. Rel.) public confession; **~gefühl** *das* community spirit; **~küche** *die* (in einem Wohnheim usw.) shared kitchen; **~kunde** *die* social studies *sing.;* **~leben** *das* communal life; **~produktion** *die* (von einem Film, Buch usw.) co-production; **~raum** *der* common room (Brit.); **~schule** *die* non-denominational school; **~sendung** *die* (Rundf., Ferns.) joint transmission; **~sinn** *der* community spirit; **~werbung** *die* joint advertising; **~werbung machen** run a joint advertisement; **~wesen** *das* social being *or* animal; **~zelle** *die* shared cell

gemein-, Gemein-: ~schuldner *der,* **~schuldnerin** *die* (Rechtsw.) [declared] bankrupt; **~sinn** *der* public spirit; **~sprache** *die* (Sprachw.) standard language; ordinary language; **~verständlich** **A** *Adj.* generally comprehensible *or* intelligible; **B** *adv.* **sich ~verständlich ausdrücken** make oneself generally comprehensible *or* intelligible; **~wesen** *das* community; (staatlich) political unit; polity; **~wohl** *das* public *or* common good; **etw./jmd. dient dem ~wohl** sth. is/sb. acts in the public interest

Gemenge *das; ~s, ~* 1 (Gemisch) mixture (**aus, von** of) 2 (Durcheinander) jumble; (von Menschen) crowd 3 (Landw.) mixed crop

Gemengsel /gəˈmɛŋzl̩/ *das; ~s, ~:* mixture; (von Gerüchen, Düften) medley

gemessen

A *2. Part. v.* **messen**

B *Adj.* 1 (würdevoll) measured ‹*steps, tones, language*›; deliberate ‹*words, manner of speaking*›; **~en Schrittes** with measured tread *or* steps *pl.* 2 (an~) **in ~em Abstand** *od.* **~er Entfernung** at a respectful distance; **in ~er Bescheidenheit** with due modesty 3 (veralt.: zurückhaltend) reserved

C *adv.* **~ schreiten** walk with measured tread *or* steps *pl.;* **~ sprechen** speak in measured tones

Gemessenheit *die; ~* 1 (Würde) ▸**gemessen B 1**: measuredness; deliberateness; **in aller ~:** slowly and with all due solemnity 2 (An~) respectfulness 3 (veralt.: Zurückhaltung) reserve

Gemetzel *das; ~s, ~* (abwertend) bloodbath; massacre

gemieden /gəˈmiːdn̩/ *2. Part. v.* **meiden**

Gemisch *das; ~[e]s, ~e* (auch fig.) mixture (**aus, von** of); mix (coll.); (Kfz-W.) mixture

gemischt

A *2. Part. v.* **mischen**

B *Adj.* 1 mixed; **~e Kost** a varied diet; **eine ~e Klasse** a mixed *or* coeducational *or* (coll.) coed class 2 (abwertend: anrüchig) **eine ~e Gesellschaft** a disreputable crowd

C *adv.* (abwertend: anrüchig) **es geht sehr ~ zu** there are all sorts of goings-on

gemischt-, Gemischt-: ~rassig, ~rassisch *Adj.* multiracial; **~rassige Badestrände** desegregated bathing beaches; **~waren·handlung** *die* (veralt.) general store

Gemme /ˈgɛmə/ *die; ~, ~n* 1 (Edelstein) engraved gem; (Intaglio) intaglio; (Kamee) cameo 2 (Biol.: Zelle) gemma

gemocht /gəˈmɔxt/ *2. Part. v.* **mögen**

gemolken *2. Part. v.* **melken**

gemoppelt /gəˈmɔpl̩t/ ▸**doppelt B 1**

Gemotze *das; ~s* (salopp) grumbling; fault-finding; crabbing (coll.)

***Gems·bart, *Gems·bock, *Gemse** ▸**Gäms·bart** *usw.*

Gemunkel *das; ~s* rumours *pl.;* whispers *pl.*

Gemurmel *das; ~s* murmuring

Gemüse /gəˈmyːzə/ *das; ~s, ~:* vegetables *pl.;* **ein ~:** a vegetable; **frisches/gekochtes ~:** fresh/cooked vegetables; **junges ~** (fig. ugs.) youngsters *pl.;* **dieses junge ~ kann man doch nicht ernst nehmen** (fig. ugs.) these young whippersnappers *pl.* can't be taken seriously

Gemüse-: ~anbau *der* growing of vegetables; (Handelsgärtnerei) market gardening; **~beet** *das* vegetable patch *or* plot; **~beilage** *die* vegetables *pl.;* **~eintopf** *der* vegetable stew; **~frau** *die* vegetable seller; **~garten** *der* vegetable *or* kitchen garden; (Teil eines Gartens) vegetable patch *or* plot; **~händler** *der,* **~händlerin** *die* ▸❶ **S. 113** greengrocer; **~konserve** *die* canned *or* (Brit.) tinned vegetables *pl.;* (in einem Glas) preserved vegetables *pl.;* **~laden** *der; Pl.* **~läden** greengrocer's [shop]; **~mann** *der* vegetable seller; **~pflanze** *die* vegetable; **~platte** *die* vegetable dish; (als Beilage) dish of assorted vegetables; **~saft** *der* vegetable juice; **~suppe** *die* vegetable soup

gemusst, *gemußt /gəˈmʊst/ *2. Part. v.* **müssen**

Gemüt /gəˈmyːt/ *das; ~[e]s, ~er* 1 (Gefühlsleben) nature; disposition; **ein sonniges/kindliches ~ haben** (iron.) be [really] naive 2 (Empfindungsvermögen) heart; soul; **viel/wenig ~ haben** be soft-hearted/hard-hearted; **das rührt ans** *od.* **ist etw. fürs ~:** that touches the heart *or* tears at one's heartstrings; **jmdm. aufs ~ schlagen** *od.* **gehen** make sb. depressed; **sich** (*Dat.*) **etw. zu ~e führen** (beherzigen) take sth. to heart; (essen od. trinken) treat oneself to sth. 3 (Mensch) soul; **einfache/romantische ~er** simple/romantic souls; **etw. erhitzt/erregt die ~er** sth. makes feelings run high; **die ~er haben sich beruhigt** feelings have cooled down

gemütlich

A *Adj.* 1 (behaglich) snug; cosy; gemütlich (literary); (bequem) comfortable; **mach es dir ~!** make yourself comfortable *or* at home! 2 (ungezwungen) informal; **ein ~es Beisammensein** an informal get-together 3 (umgänglich) sociable; friendly; (gelassen) easygoing 4 (gemächlich) leisurely; **ein ~es Tempo** a leisurely *or* comfortable pace

B *adv.* 1 (behaglich) cosily; (bequem) comfortably 2 (ungezwungen) **~ beisammensitzen** sit pleasantly together; **sich ~ unterhalten** have a pleasant chat 3 (gemächlich) at a leisurely *or* comfortable pace; unhurriedly

Gemütlichkeit *die; ~* 1 (Behaglichkeit) snugness 2 (Zwanglosigkeit) informality; **die ~ stören** disturb the atmosphere *or* mood of informality 3 (Gemächlichkeit) **in aller ~:** quite unhurriedly; **da hört [sich] doch die ~ auf** (fig. ugs.) that's going too far

gemüts-, Gemüts-: ~arm *Adj.* insensitive; cold; **~art** *die* nature; disposition; **~bewegung** *die* emotion; **~krank** *Adj.* (Med., Psych.) emotionally disturbed; **~krankheit** *die* emotional disorder; **~lage** *die* emotional state; **~mensch** *der* (ugs.) (gutmütiger Mensch) good-natured *or* even-tempered person; (etwas langsamer Mensch) phlegmatic person; **du bist [vielleicht] ein ~mensch!** (iron. abwertend) you're the soul of tact, I must say!; (du bist naiv) you'll be lucky!; **~regung** *die* emotion; **~ruhe** *die* peace of mind; **in aller ~ruhe** (ugs.) (ohne Sorge) completely unconcerned; (ohne Hast) as if there were all the time in the world; **~verfassung** *die,* **~zustand** *der* emotional state

gemüt·voll *Adj.* warm-hearted; (empfindsam) sentimental

gen /gɛn/ *Präp. + Akk.* (veralt., bibl., noch dichter.) towards; toward; **~ Süden/Osten** *usw.* southwards/eastwards, *etc.;* **einen Blick ~ Himmel werfen** throw a glance heavenwards

Gen /geːn/ *das; ~s, ~e* (Biol.) gene

Gen- GM ‹*maize, rape etc.*›

genagelt /gəˈnaːgl̩t/

A *2. Part. v.* **nageln**

B *Adj.* **~e Schuhe** hobnailed boots

genannt /gəˈnant/ *2. Part. v.* **nennen**

genant /ʒeˈnant/ *Adj.* 1 (veralt.: peinlich) embarrassing 2 (bes. südd.: schüchtern) shy; bashful

g

g

genas /gəˈnaːs/ *1. u. 3. Pers. Sg. Prät. v.* **genesen**

genäschig /gəˈnɛʃɪç/ *Adj.* ▸**naschhaft**

genau /gəˈnau/

A *Adj.* **1** (exakt) exact; precise; **eine ~e Waage** accurate scales *pl.*; **die ~e Uhrzeit** the exact *or* right time; **~e Untersuchungen** accurate *or* precise investigations; **Genaues/Genaueres wissen** know the/more exact *or* precise details; **ich weiß nichts Genaues/Genaueres** I don't know anything definite/more definite **2** (sorgfältig, gründlich) meticulous, painstaking ‹*person*›; careful ‹*study*›; precise ‹*use of language*›; detailed, thorough ‹*knowledge*›

B *adv.* **1** exactly; precisely; **~ um 8⁰⁰** at 8 o'clock precisely; at exactly 8 o'clock; **die Uhr geht [auf die Minute] ~:** the watch/clock keeps perfect time; **die Schuhe passten ihm ~:** the shoes fitted him perfectly **2** (gerade, eben) just; **~ reichen** be just enough **3** (als Verstärkung) just; exactly; precisely; **~ das habe ich gesagt** that's just *or* exactly what I said **4** (als Zustimmung) exactly; precisely; quite [so] **5** (sorgfältig) **~ arbeiten/etw. ~ durchdenken** work/think sth. out carefully *or* meticulously; **jmdn. ~ kennen** know exactly what sb. is like; **etw. ~ beachten** observe sth. meticulously *or* painstakingly; **es mit etw. [nicht so] ~ nehmen** be [not too] particular about sth.; **~ genommen** strictly speaking

***genau·genommen** ▸**genau B 5**

Genauigkeit *die;* **~** **1** (Exaktheit) exactness; exactitude; precision; (einer Waage) accuracy **2** (Sorgfalt) meticulousness

genau·so ▸**ebenso**

genaustens *Adv.* **etw. ~ durchdenken/beachten** think sth. out/observe sth. most meticulously

Gen·check /-tʃɛk/ *der;* **~s, ~s** gene check

Gendarm /ʒanˈdarm/ *der;* **~en, ~en** (österr., sonst veralt.) village *or* local policeman *or* constable

Gendarmerie /ʒandarməˈriː/ *die;* **~, ~n** (österr., sonst veralt.) village *or* local constabulary

Gen-: ~defekt *der* genetic defect; **~diagnostik** *die* genetic diagnosis

Genealoge /genealoːgə/ *der;* **~n, ~n** ▸ⓘ **S. 113** genealogist

Genealogie /genealoˈgiː/ *die;* **~, ~n** genealogy

Genealogin *die;* **~, ~nen** ▸ⓘ **S. 113** ▸**Genealoge**

genealogisch *Adj.* genealogical

genehm /gəˈneːm/ *Adj.: in* **jmdm. ~ sein** (geh.) (jmdm. passen) be convenient to *or* suit sb.; (jmdm. angenehm sein) be acceptable to sb.

genehmigen *tr. V.* approve ‹*plan, alterations*›; grant, approve ‹*application*›; authorize ‹*stay*›; grant, agree to ‹*request*›; give permission for ‹*demonstration*›; **sich** (*Dat.*) **etw. ~** (ugs.) treat oneself to sth.; **sich** (*Dat.*) **einen ~** (ugs.) have a drink

Genehmigung *die;* **~, ~en** **1** (eines Plans, Antrags, einer Veränderung) approval; (eines Aufenthalts) authorization; (einer Bitte) granting; (einer Demonstration) permission (*Gen.* for); **jmdm. die ~ zur Eröffnung einer Gaststätte verweigern** refuse [to grant] sb. a licence to open a restaurant/pub **2** (Schriftstück) permit; (Lizenz) licence

genehmigungs-, Genehmigungs-: ~pflicht *die* (Rechtsspr.) obligation to obtain official approval; **der ~pflicht unterliegen** require official approval; **~pflichtig** *Adj.* requiring official approval *postpos.*; **~pflichtig sein** require official approval; **Demonstrationen sind ~pflichtig** demonstrations require official permission

geneigt /gəˈnaikt/

A *2. Part. v.* **neigen**

B *Adj. in* **~ sein** *od.* **sich ~ zeigen, etw. zu tun** be inclined to do sth.; (bereit sein) be ready *or* willing to do sth.; **jmdm./einer Sache ~ sein** (geh.) be well-disposed towards sb./sth.; **~er Leser** (veralt.) gentle reader

Geneigtheit *die;* **~** **1** inclination; disposition; (Bereitschaft) readiness; willingness **2** (Wohlwollen) goodwill (**gegenüber, für** towards)

Genera ▸**Genus**

General /genəˈraːl/ *der;* **~s, ~e** *od.* **Generäle** /genəˈrɛːlə/ ▸ⓘ **S. 44** (auch kath. Rel.) general; **Herr ~:** General

General-: ~amnestie *die* general amnesty; **~angriff** *der* general offensive; **~anwalt** *der* (EU) Advocate General; **~bass,** ***~baß** *der* (Musik) [basso] continuo; thorough bass; **~beichte** *die* (kath. Rel.) general confession; **~bevollmächtigte** *der/die* (Rechtsw.) general agent; universal agent [with full powers of attorney]; (Politik) plenipotentiary; (in einer Firma) general manager; **~bundes·anwalt** *der,* **~bundes·anwältin** *die* Chief Federal Prosecutor; **~direktion** *die* top management; **~direktor** *der* chairman; president (Amer.); **~direktorat** *das* (EU) Directorate-General; **~direktorin** *die* chairwoman; president (Amer.); **~feldmarschall** /---'---/ *der* (Milit.) ▸**Feldmarschall**; **~gouverneur** *der* Governor-General; **~inspekteur** *der* (Milit.) inspector general; **~intendant** *der,* **~intendantin** *die* artistic director

generalisieren *tr., itr. V.* generalize

Generalisierung *die;* **~, ~en** generalization

Generalissimus /genəraˈlɪsimʊs/ *der;* **~, ~se** *od.* **Generalissimi** /-ˈlɪsimi/ (Milit.) generalissimo

Generalist *der;* **~en, ~en, Generalistin** *die;* **~, ~nen** generalist

Generalität /genəraliˈtɛːt/ *die;* **~, ~en** (Milit.) **die ~:** the generals *pl.*

general-, General-: ~klausel *die* (Rechtsw.) blanket *or* general clause; **~konsul** *der,* **~konsulin** *die* consul general; **~konsulat** *das* consulate general; **~leutnant** *der* (Milit.) lieutenant general; (Luftw.) air marshal (Brit.); **~major** *der* (Milit.) major-general; (Luftw.) air vice-marshal (Brit.); **~musik·direktor** /----'----/ *der,* **~musik·direktorin** *die* musical director; **~nenner** *der* ▸**Hauptnenner**; **~präventiv** *Adj.* (Rechtsspr.) ‹*judgement*› acting as a general deterrent; **~probe** *die* **1** (auch fig.) dress *or* final rehearsal; **2** (Sport: letztes Testspiel) final trial; **~sekretär** *der,* **~sekretärin** *die* Secretary General; (einer Partei) general secretary; **~staatsanwalt** /---'---/ *der,* **~staatsanwältin** *die* chief public prosecutor (*in a Higher Regional Court*)

Generals·rang *der* rank of general

General·stab *der* (Milit.) general staff

Generalstabs-: ~chef *der* chief of the general staff; **~karte** *die* (hist.) ordnance survey map (*scale 1 : 100,000*); **~offizier** *der* general staff officer

general-, General-: ~streik *der* general strike; **~überholen** *tr. V.; nur im Inf. und 2. Part. gebr.* (bes. Technik) **etw. ~überholen** give sth. a general overhaul; **etw. ~überholen lassen** have sth. generally overhauled; **~überholung** *die* general overhaul; **~versammlung** *die* general meeting; **die ~versammlung der Vereinten Nationen** the General Assembly of the United Nations; **~vertreter** *der,* **~vertreterin** *die* general representative; **~vertretung** *die* ▸**Alleinvertretung**; **~vollmacht** *die* (Rechtsw.) full *or* unlimited power of attorney

Generation /genəraˈtsi̯oːn/ *die;* **~, ~en** generation

Generations-: ~konflikt *der* generation gap; **~problem** *das* generation problem; **~unterschied** *der* generation gap; **~wechsel** *der* **1** new generation; **ein ~wechsel ist notwendig** new blood is needed; **2** (Biol.) alternation of generations

generativ /genəraˈtiːf/ *Adj.* **1** (Biol.) generative ‹*cell, nucleus, etc.*›; sexual ‹*reproduction*› **2** (Sprachw.) generative

Generator /genəˈraːtɔr/ *der;* **~s, ~en** /---'--/ **1** generator **2** (Gas~) producer

Generator·gas *das* producer gas

generell /genəˈrɛl/

A *Adj.* general

B *adv.* generally; **man kann ganz ~ sagen, dass ...** generally speaking *or* in general, it can be said that ...; **es sollte sonnabends ~ schulfrei sein** all schools should close on Saturdays

generieren *tr. V.* (geh.; Sprachw.) generate

Generikum /geˈneːrikʊm/ *das;* **~s, Generika** generic product; (Pharm.) generic drug

generisch

A *Adj.* generic

B *adv.* generically

generös /genəˈrøːs/ (geh.)

A *Adj.* generous

B *adv.* generously

Generosität /genərozi'tɛːt/ *die;* **~** (geh.) generosity

genervt *Adj.* annoyed

Genese /geˈneːzə/ *die;* **~, ~n** genesis

genesen /gəˈneːzn̩/ *unr. itr. V.; mit sein* **1** (geh.) recover; recuperate; (fig.) recover; **von einer Krankheit ~:** recover from an illness **2** (veralt. dichter.) **eines Knaben ~:** be delivered of a son

Genesende *der/die; adj. Dekl.* convalescent

Genesis /ˈgɛnezɪs/ *die;* **~:** genesis; **die ~** (bibl.) [the Book of] Genesis

Genesung *die;* **~, ~en** (geh.) recovery

Genesungs-: ~heim *das* convalescent home; **~prozess,** ***~prozeß** *der* [process of] recovery; **~urlaub** *der* (Milit.) convalescent leave

Genetik /geˈneːtɪk/ *die;* **~** (Biol.) genetics *sing., no art.*

Genetiker *der;* **~s, ~, Genetikerin** *die;* **~, ~nen** ▸ⓘ **S. 113** geneticist

genetisch (Biol.)

A *Adj.* genetic

B *adv.* genetically

Genezareth /geˈneːtsarɛt/ (*das*); **~s** Gennesaret; **der See ~:** the Sea of Galilee

Genf /gɛnf/ (*das*); **~s** ▸ⓘ **S. 675** Geneva

Genfer ▸ⓘ **S. 675**

A *der;* **~s, ~:** Genevese

B *Adj.* Genevese; **der ~ See** Lake Geneva; **die ~ Konvention** the Geneva Convention; *s. auch* **Kölner**

Genferin *die;* **~, ~nen** ▸**Genfer A**

Genfer·see *der;* **~s** (schweiz.) Lake Geneva

Gen·forschung *die* (Biol.) genetic research

genial /geˈni̯aːl/

A *Adj.* brilliant ‹*idea, invention, solution, etc.*›; **ein ~er Mensch** a [man/woman of] genius; **ein ~er Künstler/Musiker** an inspired artist/musician; an artist/musician of genius

B *adv.* brilliantly

genialisch

A *Adj.* **1** brilliant; **ein ~er Musiker** a brilliant musician; a musical genius **2** (exaltiert) **ein ~er Hauch** a touch of the eccentric genius

B *adv.* **1** like a genius **2** (exaltiert) like an eccentric genius

Genialität /geniali'tɛːt/ *die;* **~:** genius

Genick /gəˈnɪk/ *das;* **~[e]s, ~e** ▸ⓘ **S. 435** back *or* nape of the neck; **sich das ~ brechen** (auch fig.) break one's neck; **jmdn. beim ~ packen** grab sb. by the scruff of the neck; **ein Schlag ins ~:** a blow to the back of the neck; **jmdm./einer Sache das ~ brechen** (ugs.) ruin sb./sth.; **jmdm. im ~ sitzen** (ugs.) haunt sb.

Genick-: ~schlag *der* blow to the back of the neck; rabbit punch; **~schuss,** ***~schuß** *der* shot through the base of the skull; **~starre** *die* stiffness of the neck

Genie[1] /ʒeˈniː/ *das;* **~s, ~s** genius; **sie ist ein ~ im Kochen** she is a brilliant cook

Genie[2] *die;* **~, ~s** (schweiz. Milit.) ▸**Genietruppe**

genieren /ʒeˈniːrən/

A *refl. V.* be *or* feel embarrassed (**wegen** about); **sich vor jmdm. ~:** be *or* feel embarrassed *or* shy in sb.'s presence; **greifen Sie zu, ~ Sie sich nicht!** help yourself — don't be shy!

B *tr. V.* (veralt.) disturb

genierlich /ʒeˈniːrlɪç/ *Adj.* (ugs.) [1] (peinlich) embarrassing [2] (schüchtern) shy

genießbar *Adj.* (essbar) edible; (trinkbar) drinkable; **er ist heute nicht ∼** (fig. ugs.) he is unbearable today

genießen /gəˈniːsn̩/ *unr. tr. V.* [1] enjoy; **er hat eine gute Ausbildung genossen** he had [the benefit of] a good education; **er genießt Vertrauen in der Partei** he has the confidence of the Party [2] (geh.: essen/trinken) eat/drink; **das Fleisch ist nicht/nicht mehr zu ∼:** the meat is inedible/no longer edible; **er ist heute nicht zu ∼** (fig. ugs.) he is unbearable today

Genießer *der;* **∼s, ∼, Genießerin** *die;* **∼, ∼nen er ist ein richtiger Genießer** he is a regular 'bon viveur'; he really knows how to enjoy life [to the full]; **sie ist eine stille Genießerin** she enjoys life [to the full] in her own quiet way

genießerisch
A *Adj.* appreciative; sensuous ‹*lips*›
B *adv.* appreciatively; ‹*drink, eat*› with relish

Genie-: **∼streich** *der* (auch iron.) stroke of genius; **∼truppe** *die* (schweiz. Milit.) engineer corps; **∼zeit** *die* (Literaturw.) Storm and Stress Period

genital /geniˈtaːl/ *Adj.* genital

Genital·apparat *der* ▸**Geschlechtsapparat**

Genitale *das;* **∼s, Genitalien** /geniˈtaːli̯ən/, **Genital·organ** *das* ▸**ⓘ S. 435** genital organ; **die männlichen/weiblichen Genitalien** the male/female genitals *or* genital organs *or* genitalia

Genitiv /ˈgeːnitiːf/ *der;* **∼s, ∼e** (Sprachw.) genitive [case]; (Wort im ∼) genitive; **im/mit dem ∼ stehen** be in/take the genitive [case]

Genitiv-: **∼attribut** *das* genitive attribute; **∼objekt** *das* genitive object

Genius /ˈgeːni̯ʊs/ *der;* **∼, Genien** /ˈgeːni̯ən/ [1] (Geist) guardian spirit; genius; **∼ loci** /- ˈloːtsi/ (geh.) genius loci [2] (geh.: Schöpferkraft) [creative] genius [3] (Mensch, Gottheit) genius

Gen-: **∼manipulation** *die* genetic manipulation; **∼manipuliert** *Adj.* genetically engineered; genetically manipulated; **∼mutation** *die* gene mutation

Genom /geˈnoːm/ *das;* **∼s, ∼e** (Biol.) genome

genomisch *Adj.* (Biol.) genomic

genommen /gəˈnɔmən/ *2. Part. v.* **nehmen**

genoppt /gəˈnɔpt/
A *2. Part. v.* **noppen**
B *Adj.* knop ‹*yarn, wool*›; pimpled ‹*rubber*›; ‹*suit*› made of knop yarn

Genörgel /gəˈnœrgl̩/ *das;* **∼s** (abwertend) grumbling; moaning; (Krittelei) carping

genoss, *genoß /gəˈnɔs/ *1. u. 3. Pers. Sg. Prät. v.* **genießen**

Genosse /gəˈnɔsə/ *der;* **∼n, ∼n** [1] ▸**ⓘ S. 44** comrade; **„∼ General/Professor"** *usw.* 'Comrade General/Professor' *etc;* **er ist kein ∼ der Partei** he is not a party member [2] (veralt.: Kamerad) comrade; companion; **... und ∼n** (abwertend) ... and his/her/their ilk [3] (Wirtsch. veralt.) member of a/the cooperative

genossen /gəˈnɔsn̩/ *2. Part. v.* **genießen**

Genossenschaft *die;* **∼, ∼en** cooperative

Genossenschaftler *der;* **∼s, ∼, Genossenschaftlerin** *die;* **∼, ∼nen** member of a/the cooperative

genossenschaftlich
A *Adj.* cooperative; collective ‹*ownership*›; jointly owned ‹*property*›
B *adv.* on a cooperative basis

Genossenschafts-: **∼bank** *die; Pl.* **∼∼en** credit cooperative *or* union; **∼bauer** *der;* **∼∼n, ∼∼n** (bes. DDR) member of a/the farming cooperative; **∼betrieb** *der* cooperative

Genossin *die;* **∼, ∼nen** [1] ▸**Genosse 1:** comrade [2] (veralt.: Kameradin) companion

Geno·typ /geno-/, **Geno·typus** *der* (Biol.) genotype

Genozid /-ˈtsiːt/ *der od. das;* **∼[e]s, ∼e** *od.* **∼ien** /-ˈtsiːdi̯ən/ genocide; **der** *od.* **das ∼ der Nazis an den Juden** the genocide perpetrated by the Nazis against the Jews

Gen·pool /-puːl/ *der* gene pool

Genre /ˈʒãːrə/ *das;* **∼s, ∼s** genre

Genre-: **∼bild** *das* genre picture; genre painting; **∼malerei** *die* genre painting

Gent[1] /dʒɛnt/ *der;* **∼s, ∼s** (iron.) dandy

Gent[2] /gɛnt/ *(das);* **∼s** ▸**ⓘ S. 675** Ghent

Gen-: **∼technik** *die,* **∼technologie** *die* genetic engineering *no art.;* **∼technisch**
A *Adj.* genetic engineering ‹*techniques, research etc.*›; ‹*research, developments etc.*› in genetic engineering; **B** *adv.* by genetic engineering; **∼technisch verändert** genetically modified

Genua /ˈgeːnu̯a/ *(das);* **∼s** ▸**ⓘ S. 675** Genoa

Genuese /geˈnueːzə/ *der;* **∼n, ∼n** Genoese

Genueser ▸**ⓘ S. 675**
A *der;* **∼s, ∼:** Genoese
B *Adj.* Genoese; *s. auch* **Kölner**

Genueserin *die;* **∼, ∼nen, Genuesin** *die;* **∼, ∼nen** Genoese

genuesisch *Adj.* Genoese

genug /gəˈnuːk/ *Adv.* enough; **er hat ∼ Geld/Geld ∼:** he has enough *or* sufficient money; **das ist ∼:** that's enough *or* sufficient; **er hat ∼ gearbeitet** he has done enough work; **ich habe jetzt ∼ [davon]** now I've had enough [of it]; **∼ davon!** enough of that!; **nicht ∼ damit, dass er faul ist, er ist auch frech** not only is he lazy, he is cheeky as well; **∼ der Worte** (geh.) I/we/you have talked long enough; **er ist Manns ∼, um zu ...** he is man enough to ...; **das ist ihm nicht gut ∼:** that is not good enough for him; **sich** *(Dat.)* **selbst ∼ sein** be quite happy in one's own company; **er kann nicht ∼ kriegen** (ugs.) he is very greedy; **davon kann er nicht ∼ kriegen** (ugs.) he can't get enough of it (fig. coll.); **von Bach kann ich nicht ∼ kriegen** (ugs.) I can always listen to Bach's music

Genüge /gəˈnyːgə/ (geh.) *in* **jmdm. ∼ tun** *od.* **leisten** satisfy sb.; **einer Anordnung/einer Pflicht ∼ tun** *od.* **leisten** comply with an order; fulfil a duty *or* an obligation; **der Gerechtigkeit wurde ∼ getan** justice was done; **zur ∼** (ausreichend) enough; sufficiently; (im Übermaß) quite enough; **etw. zur ∼ kennen** know sth. only too well; be only too familiar with sth.

genügen *itr. V.* [1] be enough *or* sufficient; **diese Wohnung genügt für uns** this flat is adequate for us; **das genügt mir** that is enough *or* sufficient [for me]; that will do [for me]; (das befriedigt mich) that satisfies me [2] (erfüllen) satisfy; **den Anforderungen ∼:** satisfy *or* meet *or* fulfil the requirements; **den Bestimmungen ∼:** comply with the regulations; **einer Pflicht ∼:** fulfil a duty *or* an obligation

genügend
A *Adj.* [1] enough; sufficient [2] (befriedigend) satisfactory
B *adv.* enough; sufficiently; **∼ lange** long enough; **∼ Geld/Zeit haben** have enough *or* sufficient money/time

genugsam *Adv.* (geh.) sufficiently; **das Thema dürfte ∼ diskutiert sein** the subject has probably been adequately discussed

genügsam /gəˈnyːkzaːm/
A *Adj.* modest ‹*life*›; **ein ∼er Mensch** a person who lives modestly; **Schafe sind sehr ∼e Tiere** sheep can live *or* subsist on very little; **in Bezug auf Kleidung ist sie sehr ∼:** she does not spend a great deal on clothes
B *adv.* **∼ leben** live modestly

Genügsamkeit *die;* **∼: sie weiß, was ∼ heißt** she knows what it means to live modestly; **wegen ihrer ∼ sind Schafe ...** as they can live *or* subsist on very little, sheep are ...

genug|tun *unr. itr. V.* (veralt.) *in* **er konnte sich** *(Dat.)* **nicht ∼, sie/es zu loben** he couldn't praise her/it enough

Genugtuung /-tuːʊŋ/ *die;* **∼, ∼en** satisfaction; **es ist mir eine ∼, das zu hören** it gives me satisfaction to hear that; **∼ über etw.** *(Akk.)* **empfinden** feel satisfied *or* a sense of satisfaction about sth.; **[für etw.] ∼ verlangen** demand satisfaction [for sth.]

genuin /genuˈiːn/ *Adj.* (geh.) genuine

Genus /ˈgɛnʊs/ *das;* **∼, Genera** /ˈgɛnera/ (Sprachw.) gender

Genuschel /gəˈnʊʃl̩/ *das;* **∼s** (meist abwertend) mumbling

Genuss, *Genuß /gəˈnʊs/ *der;* **Genusses, Genüsse** /gəˈnʏsə/ [1] consumption; **der ∼ von schmerzstillenden Mitteln/Heroin** the use *or* taking of painkillers/heroin [2] (Wohlbehagen) **etw. mit/ohne ∼ essen/trinken** eat/drink sth. with/without relish; **etw. mit ∼ lesen** enjoy reading sth.; **das Konzert/der Kuchen ist ein ∼:** the concert is thoroughly enjoyable/the cake is delicious; **die Genüsse des Lebens** the pleasures *or* good things of life; **in den ∼ von etw. kommen** enjoy sth.; **in den ∼ einer Rente kommen** receive a pension

genuss·freudig, *genuß·freudig *Adj.* pleasure-loving

Genuss·gift, *Genuß·gift *das* (Amtsspr.) *stimulant etc.* (▸**Genussmittel**) *dangerous to health*

genüsslich, *genüßlich /gəˈnʏslɪç/
A *Adj.* appreciative; comfortable ‹*feeling*›; (schadenfroh) gleeful
B *adv.* appreciatively; ‹*eat, drink*› with relish; (schadenfroh) ‹*smile*› gleefully; **sich ∼ im Sessel zurücklehnen** lie back luxuriously in the armchair

genuss-, *genuß-, Genuss- *Genuß-: **∼mensch** *der* hedonist; **∼mittel** *das: tea, coffee, alcoholic drinks, tobacco, etc.;* **∼reich** *Adj.* very *or* highly enjoyable; **∼schein** *der* (Börsenw.) [profit] participation certificate; **∼sucht** *die* (oft abwertend) craving for pleasure; **∼süchtig** *Adj.* (oft abwertend) pleasure-seeking; **∼voll A** *Adj.* (erfreulich) very *or* highly enjoyable; (genüsslich) appreciative; **B** *adv.* appreciatively; ‹*eat, drink*› with relish

gen·verändert *Adj.* genetically modified

Geodäsie /-dɛˈziː/ *die;* **∼:** geodesy *no art.*

Geodät *der;* **∼en, ∼en, Geodätin** *die;* **∼, ∼nen** ▸**ⓘ S. 113** geodesist

geodätisch *Adj.* geodetic

Geo·dreieck Ⓦⓩ *das* geometry set square

Geograph /-ˈgraːf/ *der;* **∼en, ∼en** ▸**ⓘ S. 113** geographer

Geographie *die;* **∼:** geography *no art.*

Geographin *die;* **∼, ∼nen** ▸**ⓘ S. 113** geographer

geographisch
A *Adj.* geographic[al]
B *adv.* geographically

Geologe /-ˈloːgə/ *der;* **∼n, ∼n** ▸**ⓘ S. 113** geologist

Geologen·hammer *der* geologist's hammer

Geologie *die;* **∼:** geology *no art.*

Geologin *die;* **∼, ∼nen** ▸**ⓘ S. 113** geologist

geologisch
A *Adj.* geological;
B *adv.* geologically

Geo·meter *der;* **∼s, ∼** [1] ▸**Geodät** [2] (veralt.) geometer; geometrician

Geometrie *die;* **∼:** geometry *no art.*

geometrisch
A *Adj.* geometric[al]
B *adv.* geometrically

Geo·morphologie *die* geomorphology *no art.*

Geo·physik *die* geophysics *sing., no art.*

Geo·politik *die* geopolitics *sing., no art.*

geo·politisch *Adj.* geopolitical

geordnet
A *2. Part. v.* **ordnen**
B *Adj.* **in ∼en Verhältnissen leben** live a settled life; **∼e Verhältnisse schaffen** put things on a proper footing; **ein ∼er Rückzug** (Milit.) an orderly retreat

Georg /geˈɔrk, ˈgeːɔrk/ *(der)* George

Georgien /geˈɔrgi̯ən/ *(das);* **∼s** Georgia

g

Georgier /ɡeˈɔrɡi̯ɐ/ *der;* ∼**s,** ∼, **Georgierin** *die;* ∼, ∼**nen** Georgian

Geo·wissenschaft *die* geoscience *no art.*

Geozentrik /ɡeoˈtsɛntrɪk/ *die;* ∼ (Astron.) geocentric system

geozentrisch *Adj.* (Astron.) geocentric

Gepäck /ɡəˈpɛk/ *das;* ∼**[e]s** [1] luggage (Brit.); baggage (Amer.); (am Flughafen) baggage; **mit leichtem** ∼ **reisen** travel light; **das** ∼ **aufgeben/einchecken** hand in *or* check in the luggage; check the baggage (Amer.) [2] (Milit.) kit

Gepäck-: ∼**abfertigung** *die* [1] ▸**Gepäck 1**: checking in the luggage/baggage; [2] (Schalter) (am Bahnhof) luggage office (Brit.); baggage office (Amer.); (am Flughafen) baggage check-in; ∼**ablage** *die* luggage rack (Brit.); baggage rack (Amer.); ∼**annahme** *die* [1] ▸**Gepäck 1**: checking in the luggage/baggage; **bei der** ∼**annahme** when checking in the luggage/baggage; [2] (Schalter) [in-counter of the] luggage office (Brit.) *or* baggage office (Amer.); (zur Aufbewahrung) [in-counter of the] left-luggage office (Brit.) *or* checkroom (Amer.); (am Flughafen) baggage check-in; ∼**aufbewahrung** *die* [1] **Schäden, die während der** ∼**aufbewahrung entstanden sind** damage to items in left luggage (Brit.) *or* the checkroom (Amer.); [2] (Schalter) left-luggage office (Brit.); checkroom (Amer.); (Schließfächer) luggage lockers (Brit.); baggage lockers (Amer.); ∼**aufbewahrungs·schein** *der* left-luggage ticket (Brit.); baggage check (Amer.); ∼**aufgabe** *die* ▸∼**abfertigung 1, 2**; ∼**ausgabe** *die* [1] (am Bahnhof) returning the luggage (Brit.) *or* (Amer.) baggage; (am Flughafen) reclaiming of baggage; [2] (Schalter) [out-counter of the] luggage office (Brit.) *or* (Amer.) baggage office; (zur Aufbewahrung) [out-counter of the] left-luggage office (Brit.) *or* (Amer.) checkroom; (am Flughafen) baggage reclaim; ∼**beförderung** *die* (mit der Bahn) conveyance of luggage (Brit.) *or* (Amer.) baggage; (mit einem Flugzeug) conveyance of baggage; ∼**fach** *das* (Jargon) luggage compartment; ∼**karren** *der* ▸∼ **1**: luggage/baggage trolley; ∼**kontrolle** *die* baggage check; ∼**marsch** *der* (Milit.) route march with full kit; ∼**netz** *das* ▸∼**ablage**; ∼**raum** *der* ▸**Gepäck 1**: luggage/baggage compartment; ∼**schalter** *der* ▸∼**annahme 2**; ∼**schein** *der* luggage ticket (Brit.); baggage check (Amer.); ∼**schließfach** *das* luggage locker (Brit.); baggage locker (Amer.); ∼**stück** *das* ▸∼ **1**: piece *or* item of luggage/baggage; ∼**träger** *der* [1] porter; [2] (am Fahrrad) carrier; rack; ∼**verladung** *die* baggage handling; ∼**versicherung** *die* ▸**Gepäck 1**: luggage/baggage insurance; ∼**wagen** *der* luggage van (Brit.); baggage car (Amer.)

Gepard /ˈɡeːpart/ *der;* ∼**s,** ∼**e** cheetah; hunting leopard

gepfeffert
[A] *2. Part. v.* **pfeffern**
[B] *Adj.* (ugs.) [1] (unverschämt) steep (coll.) ‹*price, rent, etc.*› [2] (hart) tough ‹*question, problem, speech*›; tough, harsh ‹*words, criticism*› [3] (derb) crude ‹*joke, oath, language, talk*›; spicy ‹*story*›

Gepfeife *das;* ∼**s** (ugs. abwertend) [continuous, tuneless] whistling

gepfiffen /ɡəˈpfɪfn̩/ *2. Part. v.* **pfeifen**

gepflegt
[A] *2. Part. v.* **pflegen**
[B] *Adj.* [1] well-groomed, spruce ‹*appearance*›; neat ‹*clothing*›; cultured ‹*conversation*›; cultured, sophisticated ‹*atmosphere, environment*›; stylish ‹*living*›; well-kept, well-tended ‹*garden, park*›; well-kept ‹*street*›; well cared-for ‹*hands, house*› [2] (hochwertig) choice ‹*food, drink*›
[C] *adv.* ∼ **essen** dine in style; ∼ **essen gehen** dine at a good restaurant; **sich** ∼ **ausdrücken** express oneself in a cultured manner

Gepflegtheit *die;* ∼ [1] **die [äußere]** ∼: a well-groomed appearance; smartness of appearance [2] (Kultiviertheit) **die** ∼ **seines Stils** his cultured style

gepflogen /ɡəˈpfloːɡn̩/ *2. Part. v.* **pflegen D**

Gepflogenheit *die;* ∼, ∼**en** (geh.) (Sitte, Brauch) custom; tradition; (Gewohnheit) habit; (Verfahrensweise) practice

Geplänkel /ɡəˈplɛŋkl̩/ *das;* ∼**s,** ∼ [1] (Wort∼) banter *no indef. art.* [2] (Milit. veralt.) skirmish

Geplapper *das;* ∼**s** (ugs., oft abwertend) prattling; **das** ∼ **des Babys** the baby's babbling

Geplärr[e] *das;* ∼**s** (ugs. abwertend) bawling

Geplätscher *das;* ∼**s** splashing; **das seichte** ∼ **der Unterhaltung** (fig.) the superficial *or* polite exchange of pleasantries

geplättet
[A] *2. Part. v.* **plätten**
[B] *Adj.* (salopp) flabbergasted

Geplauder *das;* ∼**s** (geh.) chatting

Gepolter *das;* ∼**s** [1] clatter; **sie rannten mit** ∼ **die Treppe hinunter** they clattered down the stairs [2] (Schimpfen) grumbling; moaning

Gepräge *das;* ∼**s,** ∼ [1] (Münzk.) strike [2] (geh.: Merkmal) [special] character; (Aura, Ambiente) aura; **einer Sache** (*Dat.*) **ihr** ∼ **geben** give sth. its character

Geprahle *das;* ∼**s** (abwertend) bragging; boasting

Gepränge /ɡəˈprɛŋə/ *das;* ∼**s** (geh.) pomp; splendour; **mit festlichem/feierlichem** ∼: with pomp and pageantry/in solemn splendour

Geprassel *das;* ∼**s** (von Kies usw.) rattle; (von Feuer) crackle; crackling

gepriesen *2. Part. v.* **preisen**

gepunktet
[A] *2. Part. v.* **punkten**
[B] *Adj.* spotted ‹*tie, blouse, etc.*›; (regelmäßig) polka-dot; dotted ‹*line*›

Gequake *das;* ∼**s** (ugs.) croaking; (von Enten) quacking

Gequäke *das;* ∼**s** (ugs.) bawling

gequält
[A] *2. Part. v.* **quälen**
[B] *Adj.* forced ‹*smile, gaiety*›; pained ‹*expression*›

Gequassel, Gequatsche *das;* ∼**s** (ugs. abwertend) jabbering

Gequengel[e] *das;* ∼**s** (ugs. abwertend) whimpering; (Drängelei) nagging; (Nörgelei) carping

Gequieke *das;* ∼**s** (ugs.) squealing

Gequietsche *das;* ∼**s** (ugs.) squeaking; (von Bremsen, Reifen, Kränen) squealing; screeching; (von Menschen) squealing, shrieking

gequollen *2. Part. v.* **quellen**

Ger /ɡeːɐ̯/ *der;* ∼**[e]s,** ∼**e** (hist.) spear, javelin (*of ancient Germanic peoples*)

gerade /ɡəˈraːdə/, (ugs.) **grade** /ˈɡraːdə/
[A] *Adj.* [1] straight; ∼ **geschnitten** cut straight; **in** ∼**r Linie von jmdm. abstammen** (fig.) be descended in a direct line from sb.; **den** ∼**n Weg verfolgen** (fig.) keep to the straight and narrow [2] (nicht schief) upright; ∼ **gewachsen sein** ‹*plant*› have grown straight; ‹*person*› have grown up straight; ∼ **sitzen/stehen** sit up/stand up straight; **etw.** ∼ **halten** hold sth. straight; **den Kopf** ∼ **halten** hold one's head up; **sich bei Tisch** ∼ **halten** sit up straight at the table; **etw.** ∼ **legen** put *or* set sth. straight; **etw.** ∼ **klopfen** hammer sth. straight; **etw.** ∼ **machen** straighten sth. [out]; **etw.** ∼ **richten** straighten sth. [out]; put *or* set sth. straight [3] (aufrichtig) forthright; direct [4] (genau) **das** ∼ **Gegenteil** the direct *or* exact opposite [5] (Math.) even ‹*number*›
[B] *Adv.* [1] (soeben, ugs.: für kurze Zeit) just; **halt** ∼ **[mal] fest!** just hold this [for a moment]; **haben Sie** ∼ **Zeit?** do you have time just now?; ∼ **erst** only just; **wir wollten diese Sache** ∼ **noch besprechen** we were just going to discuss the matter [2] (direkt) right; ∼ **gegenüber/um die Ecke** right opposite/just round the corner; **jmdm.** ∼ **in die Augen schauen** look sb. straight in the eyes [3] (knapp) just; ∼ **noch** only just; **er hat das Examen** ∼ **so bestanden** he just scraped through the examination; ∼ **so viel, dass ...** just enough to ...; ∼ **noch rechtzeitig** only just in time [4] (eben) just; ∼ **diese Angelegenheit** precisely *or* just this matter [5] (ausgerechnet) ∼ **du/dieser Idiot** you/this idiot, of all people; **warum** ∼ **ich/heute?** why me of all people/today of all days?; ∼ **seine Toleranz wurde ihm als Schwäche angerechnet** it was precisely his tolerance which was regarded as a weakness
[C] *Partikel* [1] (besonders) particularly; **nicht** ∼: not exactly [2] (ugs.: erst recht) **nun** *od.* **jetzt [tue ich es]** ∼: [you] just watch me; [you] just try and stop me now; **nun** *od.* **jetzt [tue ich es]** ∼ **nicht** now I certainly shan't [do it]

Gerade *die;* ∼**n,** ∼**n** [1] (Geom.) straight line [2] (Leichtathletik) straight [3] (Boxen) straight-arm punch; **linke/rechte** ∼: straight left/right

gerade·aus ▸❶ **S. 800**
[A] *Adv.* straight ahead; ‹*walk, drive*› straight on, straight ahead; **immer** ∼ **gehen/fahren** carry straight on
[B] *adj.* **er ist sehr** ∼ (fig.) he is very straightforward *or* direct

gerade-: ∼**|biegen** *unr. tr. V.* (ugs.: bereinigen) straighten out; put right; *∼**|halten** ▸**gerade A2**; ∼**heraus** /----ˈ-/ (ugs.) [A] *Adv.* **etw.** ∼**heraus sagen** say sth. straight out; **jmdm.** ∼**heraus sagen/jmdn.** ∼**heraus fragen** tell/ask sb. straight; ∼**heraus gesagt** quite frankly; to be quite frank; [B] *adj.* straightforward; direct; *∼**|klopfen** *usw.* **gerade A2**

geraden·wegs ▸**geradewegs**

***gerade|richten** ▸**gerade A2**

gerädert
[A] *2. Part. v.* **rädern**
[B] *Adj.* (ugs.) whacked (coll.); tired out; **wie** ∼ **sein/sich wie** ∼ **fühlen** be/feel whacked (coll.) *or* tired out

gerade-: *∼**|sitzen** ▸**gerade A2**; ∼**so** ▸**ebenso**; ∼**|stehen** *unr. itr. V.* (fig.: einstehen) **für etw.** ∼**stehen** accept responsibility for sth.; **für jmdn.** ∼**stehen** answer for sb.; ∼**wegs** *Adv.* [1] straight; [2] (ohne Umschweife) straight away; directly; **er kam** ∼**wegs zum Thema** he came straight to the point; ∼**zu** [A] *Adv.* [1] really; perfectly; (beinahe) almost; **das ist** ∼**zu lächerlich** that is downright ridiculous; **ein** ∼**zu ideales Beispiel** an absolutely perfect example; [2] (landsch.: unverblümt) bluntly; directly; [B] *adj.* (landsch.: unverblümt) blunt; direct

Gerad·heit *die;* ∼: straightforwardness

gerad-, Gerad-: ∼**linig** /-liːnɪç/ [A] *Adj.* [1] straight; direct, lineal ‹*descent, descendant*›; [2] (aufrichtig) straightforward; [B] *adv.* [1] ∼**linig verlaufen** run in a straight line; [2] (aufrichtig) ∼**linig handeln/denken** be straightforward; ∼**linigkeit** *die;* ∼∼ [1] straightness; [2] (Aufrichtigkeit) straightforwardness; ∼**sinnig** *Adj.* straightforward; honest

gerammelt
[A] *2. Part. v.* **rammeln**
[B] *Adv.: in* ∼ **voll** (ugs.) [jam-]packed (coll.); packed out (coll.)

gerändert *Adj.* **rot** ∼**e Augen** red-rimmed eyes; **schwarz** ∼**es Papier** black-edged paper

Gerangel /ɡəˈraŋl̩/ *das;* ∼**s** (ugs.) [1] scrapping (coll.) [2] (abwertend: Kampf) free-for-all; scramble; **ein** ∼ **um etw.** a scramble for sth.; a free-for-all for sth.

Geranie /ɡeˈraːni̯ə/ *die;* ∼, ∼**n** geranium

gerann /ɡəˈran/ *3. Pers. Sg. Prät. v.* **gerinnen**

gerannt /ɡəˈrant/ *2. Part. v.* **rennen**

Geraschel *das;* ∼**s** (ugs.) rustling

Gerassel /ɡəˈrasl̩/ *das;* ∼**s** rattling; rattle

gerät /ɡəˈrɛːt/ *3. Pers. Sg. Präsens v.* **geraten**

Gerät /ɡəˈrɛːt/ *das;* ∼**[e]s,** ∼**e** [1] piece of equipment; (Fernseher, Radio) set; (Garten∼) tool; (Küchen∼) utensil; (Mess∼) instrument; **landwirtschaftliche** ∼**e** agricultural implements; **elektrische** ∼**e** electrical appliances [2] (Turnen) piece of apparatus; **an den** ∼**en turnen** do gymnastics on the apparatus [3] (Ausrüstung) equipment *no pl.*; (des Anglers) tackle; (des Handwerkers) tools *pl.*

Geräte·haus *das* (Feuerwehr) appliance room

geraten[1] *unr. itr. V.; mit sein* [1] get; **in ein Unwetter** ∼: be caught in a storm; **unter ein Auto** ∼: be run over by a car; **an jmdn.** ∼: meet sb.; **an den Richtigen/Falschen** ∼:

g

come to the right/wrong person; **in Panik/Wut/Ekstase ~:** panic *or* get into a panic/fly into a rage/go into a state of ecstasy; *s. auch* **Gesellschaft 1**; **Verdacht**; **Verruf** *usw.* [2] (gelingen) turn out well; **das Essen ist [ihr] gut ~:** the meal [she cooked] turned out well; **sie ist zu kurz/lang ~** (scherzh.) she has turned out on the short/tall side; **die Tapeten sind zu bunt ~:** the wallpaper turned out to be too colourful [3] (ähneln) **nach jmdm. ~:** take after sb. [4] (werden) **zu etw. ~:** turn into *or* become sth.

geraten²
A *2. Part. v.* **raten, geraten¹**
B *Adj.* advisable; **es scheint mir ~, ...** I think it advisable ...

Geräte-: ~raum *der* [1] [sports] equipment store; [2] (für Gartengeräte usw.) tool shed; **~schuppen** *der* tool shed; **~turnen** *das* apparatus gymnastics *sing.*

Geratewohl *in* **wir fuhren aufs ~ los** (ugs.) we went for a drive just to see where we ended up; **er hat sich aufs ~ einige Firmen ausgewählt** (ugs.) he selected a few firms at random; **sie ist aufs ~ in die Prüfung gegangen** (ugs.) she took the examination on the off chance [of passing]

Gerätschaften /gəˈrɛːtʃaftn̩/ *Pl.* (Werkzeug) tools; (Küchengeräte) utensils

gerätst *2. Pers. Sg. Präsens v.* **geraten**

Geratter *das;* **~s** (ugs.) clatter; (von Schüssen) rattle

Geräucherte /gəˈrɔyçɐtə/ *das;* **~n;** *adj. Dekl.* smoked *or* cured meat (*usually ham or bacon*)

geraum *Adj.* (geh.) considerable; **nach ~er Zeit** after some [considerable] time

geräumig /gəˈrɔymɪç/ *Adj.* spacious ‹*room*›; roomy ‹*cupboard, compartment*›

Geräumigkeit *die;* **~** (eines Zimmers) spaciousness; (eines Schrankes, Kofferraums) roominess

Geraune *das;* **~s** (geh.) whispering; (Gemurmel) murmuring

Geraunze *das;* **~s** (österr., südd. abwertend) grumbling; moaning; grousing (coll.)

Geräusch /gəˈrɔyʃ/ *das;* **~[e]s, ~e** sound; (unerwünscht) noise

geräusch-, Geräusch-: ~arm A *Adj.* quiet; B *adv.* quietly; **~empfindlich** *Adj.* sensitive to noise *pred.*; **~empfindliche Menschen** people who are sensitive to noise; **~kulisse** *die* [1] background noise; [2] (akustische Untermalung) [background] sound effects; **~los** A *Adj.* silent; noiseless; B *adv.* [1] silently; without a sound; noiselessly; [2] (fig. ugs.: ohne Aufsehen) without [any] fuss; quietly; **~losigkeit** *die;* **~~:** quietness; noiselessness; **~pegel** *der* noise level; **~voll** A *Adj.* noisy; B *adv.* noisily

Geräusper /gəˈrɔyspɐ/ *das;* **~s** noise of throat-clearing

gerben /ˈgɛrbn̩/ *tr. V.* tan ‹*hides, skins*›; **von Wind und Wetter gegerbte Haut** (fig.) skin tanned by wind and sun

Gerber *der;* **~s, ~:** tanner

Gerbera /ˈgɛrbəra/ *die;* **~, ~[s]** gerbera

Gerberei *die;* **~, ~en** [1] tannery [2] (das Gerben) tanning

Gerberin *die;* **~, ~nen** ▸ **Gerber**

Gerber·lohe *die* tanning bark

Gerbung *die;* **~, ~en** tanning

gerecht
A *Adj.* [1] just ‹*verdict, punishment*›; (unparteiisch) just; fair; **ein ~er Richter/Lehrer** an impartial judge/a just teacher; **~ gegen jmdn. sein** be fair *or* just to sb.; **eine ~e Sache** a just cause; **~er Zorn** righteous anger; **jmdm./einer Sache ~ werden** do justice to sb./sth.; **einer Aufgabe/der Belastung ~ werden** cope with a task/the strain [2] (bibl.) **der ~e Gott** our righteous Lord; **die Gerechten** the righteous
B *adv.* justly; ‹*judge, treat*› fairly

-gerecht *Adj.* [1] (passend) **kind~/behinderten~:** suitable for children/the disabled *postpos.*; **umwelt~:** harmless to the environment *postpos.* [2] (entsprechend) **protokoll~:** in accordance with protocol *postpos.*; **leistungs~:** productivity- *or* output-related

gerechterweise *Adv.* in [all] fairness; to be fair

gerechtfertigt
A *2. Part. v.* **rechtfertigen**
B *Adj.* justified

Gerechtigkeit *die;* **~** [1] justice; **~ üben** (geh.) act justly; be just; **jmdm. ~ widerfahren lassen** (geh.) treat sb. justly; **um der ~ willen** in order that justice be done [2] (Recht) **die ~ nimmt ihren Lauf** the law takes its course [3] (christl. Rel.) **die ~ Gottes** the righteousness of God [4] (geh.: Justiz) **jmdn. den Händen der ~ übergeben** hand sb. over to be dealt with by the courts

gerechtigkeits-, Gerechtigkeits-: ~fanatiker *der,* **~fanatikerin** *die* stickler for the law; **~fimmel** *der* (ugs. abwertend) exaggerated concern for justice; **~gefühl** *das* sense of justice; **~liebend** *Adj.* **~liebend sein** have a love of justice; **ein ~liebender Mensch** a person with a love of justice; **~sinn** *der* sense of justice

Gerede *das;* **~s** (abwertend) [1] (ugs.) talk; **das ewige ~ darüber ändert doch nichts** talking about it all the time won't change anything [2] (Klatsch) gossip; **jmdn. ins ~ bringen** bring sb. into disrepute; **ins ~ kommen** get into disrepute

geregelt
A *2. Part. v.* **regeln**
B *Adj.* regular, steady ‹*job*›; orderly, well-ordered ‹*life*›; **~er Katalysator** computer-controlled catalytic converter

gereichen *itr. V.* (geh.) **jmdm. zur Ehre/zum Vorteil ~:** redound to sb.'s honour *or* credit/advantage

gereift
A *2. Part. v.* **reifen**
B *Adj.* mature; **sie ist jetzt geistig ~:** she has now matured as a person

gereizt
A *2. Part. v.* **reizen**
B *Adj.* irritable; touchy
C *adv.* irritably; **~ reagieren** react angrily; **~ lächeln** smile wearily

Gereiztheit *die;* **~:** irritability; touchiness

Gerenne /gəˈrɛnə/ *das;* **~s** (ugs.) running *or* racing about

gereuen *tr. V.* (geh. veralt.) **sein Zornesausbruch gereute ihn** he regretted his angry outburst; (unpers.) **es gereute ihn, dass ...** he regretted that ...; **es gereute ihn** he was sorry

Geriater /geˈri̯aːtɐ/ *der;* **~s, ~, Geriaterin** *die;* **~, ~nen** ▸ℹ **S. 113** (Med.) geriatrician; geriatrist

Geriatrie *die;* **~:** geriatrics *sing., no art.*

geriatrisch *Adj.* geriatric

Gericht¹ /gəˈrɪçt/ *das;* **~[e]s, ~e** [1] (Institution) court; **jmdn. dem ~** *od.* **den ~en übergeben** *od.* **ausliefern** hand sb. over to be dealt with by the courts; **~ erster Instanz** (EU) Court of First Instance; **jmdn. vor ~ laden** *od.* **zitieren** summon sb. to appear in court; **vor ~ erscheinen/aussagen** appear/testify in court; **vor ~ stehen** be on *or* stand trial; **mit einem Fall vor ~ gehen** take a case to court [2] (Richter) bench; **Hohes ~!** Your Honour!; **das ~ zieht sich zur Beratung zurück** the bench retires for discussion [3] (Gebäude) court [house] [4] *in* **das Jüngste** *od.* **Letzte ~** (Rel.) the Last Judgement; **mit jmdm. [hart** *od.* **scharf] ins ~ gehen** (zurechtweisen) take sb. [severely] to task; (bestrafen) punish sb. [severely]; **über jmdn. ~ halten** *od.* **zu ~ sitzen** sit in judgement on sb.

Gericht² *das;* **~[e]s, ~e** dish; **~e aus der Dose** canned *or* (Brit.) tinned food *sing.*

gerichtlich
A *Adj.* judicial; forensic ‹*psychology, medicine*›; legal ‹*proceedings*›; court ‹*order*›; **~e Zuständigkeit** [legal] jurisdiction; **eine ~e Vorladung** a summons from the court; **ein ~es Nachspiel haben** have legal consequences; **die Sache wird ein ~es Nachspiel haben** the matter will end up in court
B *adv.* **jmdn. ~ verfolgen** prosecute sb.; take sb. to court; **gegen jmdn. ~ vorgehen** take legal action against sb.; take sb. to court; **etw. ~ bezeugen/beeiden** testify/swear to sth. in court; **jmdn. ~ für tot erklären** pronounce sb. legally dead

gerichts-, Gerichts-: ~akte *die* court record; **~arzt** *der,* **~ärztin** *die* specialist in forensic medicine; **~ärztlich** *Adj.* forensic [medical] ‹*report, test, investigation*›; **~assessor** *der,* **~assessorin** *die: law student appointed as judge or court official for trial period after his/her second state examination*

Gerichtsbarkeit *die;* **~, ~en** jurisdiction; **der staatlichen ~ nicht unterliegen** be immune from legal proceedings by the State

gerichts-, Gerichts-: ~beschluss, ***~beschluß** *der* decision of the/a court; the/a court's decision; **~bezirk** *der* jurisdictional district; **~diener** *der,* **~dienerin** *die* ▸ℹ **S. 113** [court] usher; **~dolmetscher** *der,* **~dolmetscherin** *die* court interpreter; **~entscheid** *der,* **~entscheidung** *die* decision of the/a court; the/a court's decision; **~ferien** *Pl.* recess *sing.*; vacation *sing.*; **~gebäude** *das* court house; **~herr** *der* (hist.) [highest] judicial authority; **der oberste ~herr** the supreme judicial authority; **~hof** *der* [1] Court of Justice; **der Oberste/Internationale/Europäische ~hof** the Supreme/International/European Court of Justice; [2] (früher: Kollegialgericht) tribunal, Court of Justice (*with more than one judge*); **Hoher ~hof!** if it please the court; **~hoheit** *die* supreme legal authority; **~kosten** *Pl.* legal costs; costs of the case; **~kundig** *Adj.* ▸ **~notorisch**; **~medizin** *die* forensic medicine *no art.*; **~mediziner** *der,* **~medizinerin** *die* specialist in forensic medicine; **~medizinisch** A *Adj.* forensic [medical] ‹*examination, report*›; B *adv.* **etw. ~medizinisch feststellen** establish sth. by forensic [medical] tests; **~notorisch** *Adj.* (Rechtsspr.) ‹*person, event, fact*› known to the court; **~präsident** *der* senior judge; **~referendar** *der,* **~referendarin** *die: law student who has passed his/her first state examination*; **~reporter** *der,* **~reporterin** *die* legal correspondent; **~saal** *der* courtroom; **Ruhe im ~saal!** silence in court!; **~schreiber** *der,* **~schreiberin** *die* clerk of the court; **~stand** *der* (Rechtsspr.) place of jurisdiction; **~tag** *der* court day; **Mittwoch ist ~tag** the court sits on Wednesdays; **~termin** *der* (strafrechtlich) date of the/a trial; (zivil) date of the/a hearing; **~urteil** *das* judgement [of the court]; **~verfahren** *das* legal proceedings *pl.*; **ein ~verfahren einleiten** institute legal *or* court proceedings; **ohne ~verfahren** without trial; **~verfassung** *die* constitution of the courts; **~verhandlung** *die* (strafrechtlich) trial; (zivil) hearing; **~verwaltung** *die* administration of the courts; **~vollzieher** *der;* **~~s, ~~, ~vollzieherin** *die;* **~~, ~~nen** bailiff; **~weg** *der:* **auf dem ~weg** through the courts; by taking legal proceedings; **~weibel** *der;* **~~s, ~~** (schweiz.) court usher; **~wesen** *das* judicial system

gerieben
A *2. Part. v.* **reiben**
B *Adj.* (ugs.) artful

Geriebenheit *die;* **~** (ugs.) artfulness

gerieren /geˈriːrən/ *refl. V.* (geh.) **sich als etw. ~:** talk and act as if one were sth.

Geriesel *das;* **~s** trickling; trickle; (von Schnee) gentle fall

geriffelt
A *2. Part. v.* **riffeln**
B *Adj.* corrugated ‹*surface, sheet metal*›; fluted ‹*column*›; ribbed ‹*glass*›

gering /gəˈrɪŋ/
A *Adj.* [1] (nicht groß, niedrig) low ‹*temperature, pressure, price*›; low, small ‹*income, fee*›; little ‹*value*›; small ‹*quantity, amount*›; short ‹*distance, time*›; **in ~er Entfernung** a short distance away; **von/in ~er Höhe** low/low down; **der Abstand wird ~er** the gap is closing *or* getting smaller; **um ein Geringes** (veralt.) a little [bit]; (um wenig Geld) for a trifle *or* a mere bagatelle; (fast) nearly; almost [2] (unbedeutend)

g

slight; minor ‹*role*›; **meine ~ste Sorge** the least of my worries; **das Geringste** the least; **nicht das Geringste** nothing at all; **nicht im Geringsten** not in the slightest *or* least [3] (veralt.: niedrig stehend) humble ‹*origin, person*›; **kein Geringerer als …** no less a person than … [4] (geh.: schlecht) poor, low, inferior ‹*quality, opinion*›; poor ‹*knowledge*›
[B] *adv.* **~ von jmdm. sprechen/denken** speak badly/have a low opinion of sb.; **~ achten** *od.* **schätzen** *+Akk.* (verachten) have a low opinion of, think very little of ‹*person, achievement*›; set little store by ‹*success, riches*›; (missachten) disregard ‹*warning*›; make light of ‹*danger*›; **sein eigenes Leben ~ achten** *od.* **schätzen** have scant regard for one's own life

***gering|achten** ▸ **gering B**

Gering·achtung *die* ▸ **Geringschätzung**

geringelt
[A] *2. Part. v.* **ringeln**
[B] *Adj.* curly; ‹*hair*› in ringlets; ‹*pattern, socks, jumper*› with horizontal stripes

gering·fügig /-fy:gɪç/
[A] *Adj.* slight ‹*difference, deviation, improvement*›; slight, minor ‹*alteration, injury*›; small, trivial ‹*amount*›; minor, trivial ‹*detail*›
[B] *adv.* slightly

Geringfügigkeit *die;* ~, **~en** [1] triviality; insignificance; **eine Beschwerde wegen ~ ablehnen** dismiss a complaint because of its trivial nature [2] (Kleinigkeit) triviality; trifle; (Angelegenheit auch) trivial matter

***gering|schätzen** ▸ **gering B**

gering·schätzig /-ʃɛtsɪç/
[A] *Adj.* disdainful; contemptuous; disparaging ‹*remark*›
[B] *adv.* disdainfully; contemptuously; **von jmdm. ~ sprechen** speak disparagingly of sb.

Geringschätzigkeit *die;* **~:** disdain[fulness]; contempt[uousness]

Gering·schätzung *die* [1] (Verachtung) disdain; contempt [2] (Missachtung) disregard; **die ~ des Lebens** a scant regard for life

geringsten·falls *Adv.* (geh.) at the very least

Gering·verdiener *der,* **Gering·verdienerin** *die* low earner

gerinnen *unr. itr. V.; mit sein* [1] coagulate; ‹*blood*› coagulate, clot; ‹*milk*› curdle; *s. auch* **Blut** [2] (fig. geh.) **zu etw. ~:** develop into *or* become sth.

Gerinnsel /gəˈrɪnzl̩/ *das;* **~s,** ~ [1] (Blut) clot [2] (veralt.: Rinnsal) streamlet; rivulet

Gerinnung *die;* ~, **~en** coagulating; (von Blut auch) clotting; (von Milch) curdling

gerinnungs-: ~fähig *Adj.* coagulable; **sein Blut ist nicht ~fähig** his blood does not clot properly; **~hemmend** *Adj.* anticoagulant

Gerippe *das;* **~s,** ~ [1] skeleton; **sie ist bis zum ~ abgemagert** (fig.) she has lost so much weight that she is only skin and bones [2] (fig.) framework; (von Schiffen, Gebäuden) skeleton; (Grundriss, Entwurf) outline

gerippt /gəˈrɪpt/ *Adj.* ribbed ‹*fabric, garment*›; fluted ‹*glass, column*›; laid ‹*paper*›

gerissen /gəˈrɪsn̩/
[A] *2. Part. v.* **reißen**
[B] *Adj.* (ugs.) crafty

Gerissenheit *die;* **~:** craftiness

geritten *2. Part. v.* **reiten**

geritzt
[A] *2. Part. v.* **ritzen**
[B] *Adj.* (salopp) *in* **etw. ist ~:** sth. is [all] settled; **ist ~!** will do! (coll.)

Germ /gɛrm/ *der;* **~[e]s,** *österr. auch: die;* ~ (südd., österr.) yeast

Germane /gɛrˈma:nə/ *der;* **~n, ~n** (hist.) ancient German; Teuton; (scherzh.) Teutonic type; **die alten ~n** the ancient Germanic peoples *or* Teutons; **die Skandinavier sind ~n** the Scandinavians are of Germanic *or* Teutonic origin

Germanentum *das;* **~s** (Kultur) Germanic *or* Teutonic culture; (germanische Völker) Germanic *or* Teutonic world

Germania /gɛrˈma:ni̯a/ *(die)* Germania

Germanien /gɛrˈma:ni̯ən/ *(das);* **~s** (hist.) Germania

Germanin *die;* ~, **~nen** ancient German; Teuton

germanisch *Adj.* (auch fig.) Germanic; Teutonic; **Germanisches Seminar** Institute of Germanic Studies

germanisieren *tr. V.* Germanize

Germanisierung *die;* **~:** Germanization

Germanismus *der;* ~, **Germanismen** (Sprachw.) Germanism

Germanist *der;* **~en, ~en** Germanist; German scholar

Germanistik *die;* **~:** German studies *pl., no art.*

Germanistin *die;* ~, **~nen** Germanist; German scholar

germanistisch *Adj.* **~e Studien** German studies; **eine ~e Zeitschrift** a periodical on *or* devoted to German studies; **Germanistisches Seminar** Institute of German Studies

Germanium /gɛrˈma:ni̯ʊm/ *das;* **~s** (Chemie) germanium

germanophil /gɛrmanoˈfi:l/ *Adj.* Germanophile

germanophob /gɛrmanoˈfo:p/ *Adj.* Germanophobe

gern[e] /ˈgɛrn(ə)/; **lieber** /ˈli:bɐ/, **am liebsten** /-ˈli:pstn̩/ *Adv.* [1] (mit Vergnügen) **etw. ~ tun** like *or* enjoy *or* be fond of doing sth.; **er spielt lieber Tennis als Golf** he prefers playing tennis to golf; **etw. ~ essen/trinken** like sth.; **am liebsten trinkt er Wein** he likes wine best; **ja, ~/aber ~:** yes, of course; certainly!; **Kommst du mit? — Ja, ~!** Are you coming too? — Yes I'd like to!; **[das ist] ~ geschehen** it is *or* was a pleasure; **jmdn. ~ haben** like *or* be fond of sb.; **er hat sie lieber als dich** he likes her more than he does you; **sie hat ihn am liebsten** she likes him best; **sie hat** *od.* **sieht es lieber/am liebsten, wenn …** she likes it better/likes it best if …; **~ gesehen sein/werden** be welcome; **der kann mich ~ haben!** (ugs.) he can go to hell! (coll.); he can get stuffed! (sl.) [2] (drückt Billigung aus: durchaus) **das glaube ich ~:** I can quite *or* well believe that; **das kannst du ~ tun/haben** you are welcome to do/have that [3] (drückt Wunsch aus) **ich hätte ~ einen Apfel** I would like an apple; **er wäre ~ mitgekommen** he would have liked to come along; **ich wäre lieber [zu Fuß] gegangen** I would rather have walked; **das hättest du lieber nicht tun sollen** it would have been better if you had not done that; **lass das lieber** better not do that; **noch ein Stück Kuchen? — Lieber nicht** Another piece of cake? — I'd rather not; (aus Vernunftsgründen) I'd better not; **ich bleibe heute lieber im Bett** I'd better stay in bed today [4] (gewöhnlich) **etw. ~ tun** usually do sth. [5] (ugs.: leicht, oft) soon

Gerne·groß *der;* ~, **~e** (ugs. scherzh.) **er ist ein [kleiner] ~:** he likes to act big (coll.)

Geröchel *das;* **~s** rattle in the throat; (eines Sterbenden) [death] rattle

gerochen *2. Part. v.* **riechen**

Geröll /gəˈrœl/ *das;* **~s, ~e** detritus; debris; (größer) boulders *pl.;* (im Gebirge auch) scree

Geröll-: ~halde *die* scree [slope]; **~schutt** *der* detritus; debris; **~wüste** *die* boulder-strewn wilderness; (Geogr.) rock desert

geronnen /gəˈrɔnən/ *2. Part. v.* **rinnen, gerinnen**

Gerontokratie /gerɔntokraˈti:/ *die;* ~, **~n** (hist., Völkerk.) gerontocracy

Gerontologie *die;* ~ (Med.) gerontology *no art.*

Geröstete /gəˈrø:stətə, gəˈrœstətə/ *Pl.; adj. Dekl.* (südd., österr.) sauté potatoes

Gerste /ˈgɛrstə/ *die;* **~:** barley

Gersten-: ~grütze *die* [1] barley groats; [2] (Brei) porridge *or* gruel made from barley; **~kaffee** *der: coffee substitute produced from malted barley;* **~kaltschale** *die* (scherzh.) fruit of the barley; **~korn** *das* [1] (Frucht) barleycorn; [2] (Augenentzündung) sty; **~saft** *der* (scherzh.) beer; **~schrot** *der od. das* bruised *or* ground barley; **~zucker** *der* barley sugar

Gerte /ˈgɛrtə/ *die;* ~, **~n** switch

gerten·schlank *Adj.* slim *or* slender and willowy

Geruch /gəˈrʊx/ *der;* **~[e]s, Gerüche** /gəˈrʏçə/ [1] smell; odour; (von Blumen) scent; fragrance; (von Brot, Kuchen) smell; aroma; **ein ~ nach/der ~ von frischem Brot** a/the smell of freshly-baked bread; **einen unangenehmen ~ verbreiten** give off an unpleasant smell *or* odour *or* a stench [2] (Geruchssinn) sense of smell [3] (geh.: Ruf) reputation; **im ~ stehen, etw. zu sein/getan zu haben** be reputed to be sth./to have done sth.

geruch·los *Adj.* odourless; (ohne Duft) unscented, scentless ‹*flower etc.*›

geruchs-, Geruchs-: ~belästigung *die* nuisance caused by the smell *or* stench; **~bindend** *Adj.* deodorant; **~empfindlich** *Adj.* sensitive to smells *postpos.;* **~empfindung** *die* [1] olfactory sensation; [2] ▸ **~sinn; ~nerv** *der* ▸ ❶ **S. 435** olfactory nerve; **~organ** *das* olfactory organ; **~sinn** *der* sense of smell; olfactory sense; **~stoff** *der* aromatic essence; (von Tieren) scent; **~verschluss, *~verschluß** *der* [anti-siphon] trap

Gerücht /gəˈrʏçt/ *das;* **~[e]s, ~e** rumour; **ein ~ in die Welt** *od.* **in Umlauf setzen** start a rumour; **es geht das ~, dass …** there's a rumour going round that …; **das halte ich für ein ~!** (ugs.) I can't believe that!

Gerüchte-: ~küche *die* (ugs. abwertend) hotbed of rumours; **~macher** *der,* **~macherin** *die* (abwertend) rumour-monger

geruch·tilgend *Adj.* deodorant

gerücht·weise *Adv.* **ich habe ~ vernommen** *od.* **gehört, dass …** I've heard a rumour that …; I've heard it rumoured that …; **~ verlautet, er sei …** rumour has it *or* it is rumoured that he is …

gerufen *2. Part. v.* **rufen**

geruhen *tr. V.* (geh. veralt.; sonst iron.) **~, etw. zu tun** condescend *or* deign to do sth.

gerührt
[A] *2. Part. v.* **rühren**
[B] *Adj.* touched (also iron.); moved

geruhsam
[A] *Adj.* peaceful; quiet; leisurely ‹*stroll*›; **jmdm. eine ~e Nacht wünschen** wish sb. a restful night
[B] *adv.* leisurely; (ungestört) quietly

Geruhsamkeit *die;* **~:** peacefulness; quietness; (eines Spaziergangs) leisureliness

Gerumpel *das;* **~s** bumping and banging; (von Lastwagen usw.) rumbling

Gerümpel /gəˈrʏmpl̩/ *das;* **~s** (abwertend) junk; [useless] rubbish

Gerundium /geˈrʊndi̯ʊm/ *das;* **~s, Gerundien** (Sprachw.) gerund

Gerundiv /gerʊnˈdi:f/ *das;* **~s, ~e** /-ˈdi:və/ (Sprachw.) gerundive

gerundivisch *Adj.* (Sprachw.) gerundival

gerungen /gəˈrʊŋən/ *2. Part. v.* **ringen**

Gerüst /gəˈrʏst/ *das;* **~[e]s, ~e** scaffolding *no pl., no indef. art.;* (fig.: eines Romans usw.) framework

Gerüst-: ~bau *der* erection of the scaffolding; **„~bau: H. Müller, Mannheim"** 'scaffolding by H. Müller, Mannheim'; **~bauer** *der;* **~~s, ~~, ~bauerin** *die;* **~~, ~~nen** scaffolder

gerüttelt
[A] *2. Part. v.* **rütteln**
[B] *Adj.: in* **~ voll** (veralt.) [jam-]packed; **ein ~ Maß** (veralt.) a good measure

ges, Ges /gɛs/ *das;* ~, ~ (Musik) [key of] G flat; *s. auch* **a, 1**

Gesabber /gəˈzabɐ/ *das;* **~s** [1] slavering; slobbering; (eines Babys) dribbling [2] (salopp: Gerede) rabbiting (Brit. coll.); babbling

Gesalbte /gəˈzalptə/ *der/die; adj. Dekl.* (Rel., hist.) **er/sie kehrte als ~r/~ von Rom zurück**

he/she returned anointed from Rome; **Christus, der ~:** Christ, the Lord's Anointed

gesalzen
A *2. Part. v.* **salzen**
B *Adj.* (salopp) **1** (sehr hoch) *steep* (coll.) ‹*price, bill*› **2** (derb ausgedrückt) crude ‹*joke, language*›; spicy ‹*story*›

Gesalzene *das; adj. Dekl.* salt[ed] meat

gesammelt
A *2. Part. v.* **sammeln**
B *Adj.* concentrated ‹*attention, energy*›; intense ‹*fear*›; **~e Werke** collected works

gesamt *Adj.* whole; entire; **das ~e Vermögen** the entire *or* total wealth; **die ~en Werke** the complete works

Gesamt *das; ~s* ▸ **Gesamtheit**

gesamt-, Gesamt-: ~ansicht *die* general *or* overall view; **~auflage** *die* (Druckw.) total edition; (einer Zeitung) total circulation; **~ausgabe** *die* (Druckw.) complete edition; **~betrag** *der* total amount; **~bild** *das* general *or* overall view; (fig.) general *or* overall picture; **~darstellung** *die* general account *or* description; **~deutsch** *Adj.* all-German; **~deutschland** (*das*) all Germany; **~eindruck** *der* general *or* overall impression; **~einkommen** *das* total income; **~ergebnis** *das* overall result; **~erscheinung** *die* general appearance; **~fläche** *die* total area; **~gesellschaftlich** *Adj.* (Soziol.) of society *or* the community as a whole *postpos.*; **~gewicht** *das* total weight; **das zulässige ~gewicht** the permissible maximum weight

gesamthaft (schweiz.)
A *Adj.* ▸ **gesamt**
B *adv.* ▸ **insgesamt**

Gesamtheit *die;* ~ **1** **die ~ der Beamten** all civil servants; **die ~ der Bevölkerung** the whole of the *or* the entire population; **die Verleger in ihrer ~:** publishers as a whole **2** ▸ **Allgemeinheit**

Gesamt·hochschule *die*

> **Gesamthochschule**
>
> A type of university established in some *Länder* following reforms in the 60s and combining **Hochschule** and **Fachhochschule** under one roof, thereby offering greater flexibility and a wider choice of subjects to the student.

gesamt-, Gesamt-: ~kapital *das* total capital; **~katalog** *der* complete catalogue; (Katalog der Bestände mehrerer Bibliotheken) union catalogue; **~lage** *die* general *or* overall situation; **~note** *die* overall mark; **~produktion** *die* total production *or* output; **~schaden** *der* total damage; **ein ~schaden von 1 000 Euro** total damage amounting to 1,000 euros; **~schau** *die* overview; **in der ~schau** [when] viewed overall; taking the overall view; **~schuldner** *Pl.* (Rechtsw.) joint debtors; **~schule** *die* comprehensive [school]; **eine integrierte ~schule** an all-ages comprehensive [school]; **eine kooperative ~schule** *a comprehensive [school] which retains ability bands corresponding to the traditional types of school: Hauptschule, Realschule, and Gymnasium;* **~sieg** *der* (Sport) overall victory; **~sieger** *der,* **~siegerin** *die* (Sport) overall winner; **~stärke** *die* total strength; **~strafe** *die* (Rechtsw.) concurrent sentence; **~summe** *die* ▸ **~betrag**; **~um·satz** *der* total turnover; **~unterricht** *der* (Schulw.) interdisciplinary teaching *no art.*; **~verband** *der* (Wirtsch.) general *or* national association; **~volumen** *das* (Wirtsch.) total volume; **das ~volumen des Verteidigungsetats** the total size of the defence budget; **~werk** *das* oeuvre; (Bücher) complete works *pl.*; **~wert** *der* total value; **~wirtschaft** *die* economy as a whole; national economy; **~wirtschaftlich** **A** *Adj.* overall economic ‹*development etc.*›; ‹*development etc.*› of the economy as a whole; **B** *adv.* **~wirtschaftlich vertretbar** justifiable from the point of view of the economy as a whole; **~zahl** *die* total number; **~zusammenhang** *der* general *or* overall context

> **Gesamtschule**
>
> A comprehensive secondary school introduced in the 70s and designed to replace the traditional division into **Gymnasium**, **Realschule**, and **Hauptschule**. Pupils are taught different subjects at their own level and may take any of the school-leaving exams, including the **Abitur**.

gesandt /gəˈzant/ *2. Part. v.* **senden**

Gesandte *der/die; adj. Dekl.* envoy; **der päpstliche ~:** the papal legate *or* nuncio

Gesandtin *die;* **~, ~nen** envoy

Gesandtschaft *die;* **~, ~en** legation

Gesandtschafts·rat *der,* **Gesandtschafts·rätin** *die* counsellor at a/the legation

Gesang /gəˈzaŋ/ *der;* **~[e]s, Gesänge** /gəˈzɛŋə/ **1** singing **2** (Lied) song; *s. auch* **gregorianisch** **3** (Literaturw.) canto

Gesang·buch *das* hymn book; **das richtige/falsche ~buch haben** (ugs. scherzh.) belong to the right/wrong [religious] denomination; (in der Politik) belong to the right/wrong [political] party

gesanglich
A *Adj.* vocal; **großes ~es Talent haben** have great talent as a singer
B *adv.* vocally

Gesang[s]-: ~lehrer *der,* **~lehrerin** *die* singing teacher; **~stunde** *die* singing lesson; **~unterricht** *der* singing instruction; **~unterricht nehmen/geben** take/give singing lessons *pl.*

Gesang·verein *der* choral society; **mein lieber Herr ~!** (salopp) my godfathers!; ye gods [and little fishes]!

Gesäß /gəˈzɛ:s/ *das;* **~es, ~e** ▸ **ⓘ S. 435** backside; buttocks *pl.*

Gesäß-: ~falte *die* ▸ **ⓘ S. 435** (Anat.) gluteal fold; gluteal furrow; **~muskel** *der* ▸ **ⓘ S. 435** (Anat.) gluteal muscle; **~tasche** *die* back pocket

gesättigt
A *2. Part. v.* **sättigen**
B *Adj.* (Chemie) **~e Fettsäuren** saturated fatty acids

Gesäusel /gəˈzɔyzl̩/ *das;* **~s** (von Wind) whispering; murmuring; (von Blättern) rustling; whispering; (ugs. abwertend: Schmeichelei) flannel (coll.)

gesch. *Abk.* = **geschieden**

Geschädigte /gəˈʃɛ:dɪçtə/ *der/die; adj. Dekl.* injured party

geschaffen *2. Part. v.* **schaffen A**

geschafft
A *2. Part. v.* **schaffen B, C**
B *Adj.* (ugs.) all in (coll.)

-geschäft *das* **1** (Laden) **Schuh~/Lebensmittel~/Feinkost~:** shoe shop/food shop/delicatessen [shop]; shoe store/food store/delicatessen [store] (Amer.) **2** (Transaktion) **Bank~/Kompensations~:** bank/barter transaction; (Absatz) **Weihnachts~:** Christmas trade **3** (Aufgabe) **Amts~e/Staats~e** official/state duties

Geschäft /gəˈʃɛft/ *das;* **~[e]s, ~e** **1** business; (Abmachung) [business] deal *or* transaction; **die ~e gehen gut** business is good; **mit jmdm. ~e/ein ~ machen** do business with sb./strike a bargain *or* do a deal with sb.; **in ein ~ einsteigen** go into a business; **in ~en reisen/unterwegs sein** travel/be travelling on business; **mit jmdm. ins ~ kommen** go into business with sb.; **~ ist ~:** business is business; **das ~ mit der Angst** trading on people's fears **2** (Absatz) business *no art.*; **das ~ blüht** business *or* trade is booming **3** (Profit) profit; **mit etw. ein gutes/schlechtes ~ machen** make a good/poor profit on sth.; **diese Unternehmung war für uns [k]ein ~:** this venture was [not] a financial success for us **4** (Firma) business; **ein ~ führen** run *or* manage a business; **ins ~ gehen** (südd.) go to work **5** (Laden) shop; store (Amer.); (Kaufhaus) store **6** (Aufgabe) task; duty; **seinen ~en nachgehen** go about one's business **7** **sein großes/kleines ~ erledigen** *od.* **machen** (ugs. verhüll.) do big jobs *or* number two/small jobs *or* number one (child language)

geschäfte-, Geschäfte-: ~halber *Adv.* (in Geschäften) on business; (wegen Geschäften) because of business; **~macher** *der* (abwertend) profit-seeker; **~macherei** *die;* **~~** (abwertend) profit-seeking *no pl.*; **~macherin** *die* ▸ **~macher**

geschäftig
A *Adj.* bustling; **ein ~es Treiben** bustling activity; hustle and bustle
B *adv.* **~ hin und her laufen** bustle about

Geschäftigkeit *die;* **~:** bustle

Geschaftlhuber /gəˈʃaftl̩hu:bɐ/ *der;* **~s, ~** (bes. südd., österr. abwertend) officious meddler

geschäftlich
A *Adj.* **1** business *attrib.* ‹*conference, appointment*›; **das Geschäftliche besprechen** discuss business [matters] **2** (sachlich, kühl) businesslike
B *adv.* **1** on business; **er hat dort ~ zu tun** he has [some] business to do there; **ich habe nächste Woche ~ in Hamburg zu tun** I have to be in Hamburg next week on business; **Wie geht es Ihnen? — Meinen Sie ~ oder privat?** How are you doing? — Do you mean how's business or how am I personally? **2** (sachlich, kühl) in a businesslike way *or* manner

geschäfts-, Geschäfts-: ~ablauf *der* business *no art.*; **~abschluss,** ***~abschluß** *der* conclusion of the/a business transaction *or* deal; **einen ~abschluss tätigen** conclude a business transaction *or* deal; **~anteil** *der* share in the/a business; **~aufgabe** *die* closure of the/a business; **zur ~aufgabe gezwungen werden** be forced to close down; **„Ausverkauf wegen ~aufgabe!"** 'closing-down sale'; 'going-out-of-business sale' (Amer.); **~auto** *das* ▸ **~wagen**; **~bedingungen** *Pl.* terms [and conditions] of trade; **~beginn** *der* opening time; **eine Schlange hatte sich vor ~beginn gebildet** a queue (Brit.) *or* (Amer.) line had formed before the shop opened; **~bereich** *der* portfolio; **Minister ohne ~bereich** Minister without portfolio; **~bericht** *der* company report; (jährlich) annual report; **~beziehungen** *Pl.* business dealings; **in ~beziehungen mit einer Firma stehen** have business dealings with a firm; **~beziehungen zu China** business contacts with China; **~brief** *der* business letter; **~bücher** *Pl.* books; accounts; **~eröffnung** *die* opening of a/the shop *or* (Amer.) store; **~fähig** *Adj.* (Rechtsspr.) legally competent; **~fähigkeit** *die* (Rechtsspr.) legal competence; **~feld** *das* business segment; **~frau** *die* ▸ **ⓘ S. 113** businesswoman; **~freund** *der,* **~freundin** *die* business associate; **~führend** *Adj.* managing ‹*director*›; executive ‹*chairman*›; **die ~führende Regierung** the caretaker government; **~führer** *der* **1** (leitender Angestellter) manager; **2** (Vereinswesen) secretary; **~führerin** *die* **1** (leitende Angestellte) manageress; manager; **2** (Vereinswesen) secretary; **~führung** *die* management; **~gang** *der* **1** business *no art.*; **2** (Dienstweg) **den normalen ~gang gehen** go through the normal channels; **3** (Besorgung) errand; **~gebaren** *das* business *no art.*; business practices *pl.*; **~geheimnis** *das* business secret; **~geist** *der* business acumen *or* sense; **~haus** *das* **1** business [house]; firm; **2** (Gebäude) office block (*with or without shops*); **~idee** *die* business concept; **~inhaber** *der,* **~inhaberin** *die* owner *or* proprietor of the/a business; **~interesse** *das:* **das ~interesse/die ~interessen** the interests *pl.* of the business; **~jahr** *das* financial year; **~jubiläum** *das* anniversary of the firm; **die Firma feiert ihr fünfzigjähriges ~jubiläum** the firm is celebrating its fiftieth anniversary; **~kapital** *das* working capital; **~kosten** *Pl.*: **in auf ~kosten [gehen]** [be] on expenses; **~kundig** *Adj.* ‹*person*› with business experience; **~lage** *die* **1** (wirtschaftliche Lage) **die ~lage der Firma** the [business] position of the firm; **die allgemeine ~lage** the general business situation; **2** (Ort) **in guter ~lage** well

g

situated [for business]; **~leben** *das* business [life]; **er steht seit vierzig Jahren im ~leben** he's been active in business [life] for forty years; **~leitung** *die* ▸**~führung**; **~leute** ▸**~mann**; **~mann** *der; Pl.* **~leute** ▸**ⓘ S. 113** businessman; **~mäßig** *Adj.* businesslike; **~methoden** *Pl.* business methods; **~ordnung** *die* standing orders *pl.*; (im Parlament) [rules *pl.* of] procedure; **Antrag zur ~ordnung** procedural motion; **Fragen zur ~ordnung** questions on points of order; **zur ~ordnung!** point of order!; **~papiere** *Pl.* business documents *or* papers; **~partner** *der*, **~partnerin** *die* business partner; **~politik** *die* business *or* trading policy; **~räume** *Pl.* business premises; (Büroräume) offices; **~reise** *die* business trip; **auf ~reise sein** be on a business trip; **~rückgang** *der* decline *or* fall-off in business; **~schädigend** *Adj.* bad for business; ‹*conduct*› damaging to the interests of the company; **~schluss**, ***~schluß** *der* closing time; **nach ~schluss** after business hours; (im Büro) after office hours; **~sinn** *der* business sense *or* acumen; **~sitz** *der* place of business; **eingetragener ~sitz** registered office[s]; **~stelle** *die* **1▸** (einer Bank, Firma) branch; (einer Partei, eines Vereins) office; **2▸** (Rechtsspr.) court office; **~straße** *die* shopping street; **~stunden** *Pl.* business hours; (im Büro) office hours; **~tätigkeit** *die* business activity *no indef. art.*; **~träger** *der*, **~trägerin** *die* (Dipl.) chargé d'affaires; **~tüchtig** *Adj.* able, capable, efficient ‹*businessman, landlord, etc.*›; **eine ~tüchtige Frau** an able *or* capable businesswoman; **~tüchtigkeit** *die* business ability *or* efficiency; **~übergabe** *die* transfer of the business; **~übernahme** *die* takeover of the business; **~unfähig** *Adj.* (Rechtsspr.) legally incompetent; **~unfähigkeit** *die* (Rechtsspr.) legal incompetence; **~verbindung** *die* business connection; **~verkehr** *der* business; business dealings *pl.*; **~viertel** *das* business quarter; (Einkaufszentrum) shopping district; **~wagen** *der* company car; **~welt** *die* **1▸** business world *or* community; **2▸** ▸**~leben**; **~zeit** *die* business hours *pl.*; (im Büro) office hours *pl.*; **~zentrum** *das* ▸**~viertel**; **~zimmer** *das* office; **~zweck** *der* business aim; business purpose; **~zweig** *der* branch of the/a business

geschah /gəˈʃaː/ *3. Pers. Sg. Prät. v.* **geschehen**

Geschäker /gəˈʃɛːkɐ/ *das;* **~s** flirting

Gescharre *das;* **~s** (abwertend) scraping; (mit den Füßen) scraping of feet; (von Hühnern) scratching

Geschaukel *das;* **~s** rocking; (auf See) rolling

gescheckt /gəˈʃɛkt/ *Adj.* spotted ‹*cow, bull, rabbit, etc.*›; skewbald ‹*horse*›; (mit weißen Flecken auf schwarzem Fell) piebald ‹*horse*›

geschehen /gəˈʃeːən/ *unr. itr. V.; mit sein* **1▸** (passieren) happen; occur; **so tun, als wäre nichts ~**: act as if nothing had happened; **~ ist ~**: what's done is done; **so ~ ...** (veralt.) this came to pass ... **2▸** (ausgeführt werden) be done; **die Tat/der Mord geschah aus Eifersucht** the deed was done/the murder was committed out of jealousy; **es muss etwas ~**: something must be done; **was geschieht damit?** what's to be done with it?; **er ließ es ~**: he let it happen **3▸** (widerfahren) **jmdm. geschieht etw.** sth. happens to sb.; **es geschieht dir nichts** nothing will happen to you; **das geschieht ihm recht** it serves him right **4▸ ihm ist ein Unrecht ~**: he's been wronged **5▸ es ist um ihn ~**: it's all up with him; **es ist um seine Gesundheit/Stellung ~**: his health is ruined/he has lost his job; **als er sie sah, war es um ihn ~**: he was lost the moment he saw her

Geschehen *das;* **~s, ~** (geh.) **1▸** (Ablauf der Ereignisse) events *pl.*; happenings *pl.*; **das politische ~**: political events *pl.* **2▸** (Vorgang) action

Geschehnis *das;* **~ses, ~se** (geh.) event

gescheit /gəˈʃait/

A *Adj.* **1▸** (intelligent) clever; **daraus werde ich nicht ~**: I can't make head or tail of it **2▸** (ugs.: vernünftig) sensible; **sei doch ~**: be sensible; **nichts/etwas Gescheites** nothing/something sensible; **gibt es etwas Gescheites zu essen?** is there anything decent to eat?; **du bist wohl nicht ganz** *od.* **nicht recht ~**: you can't be quite right in the head; you must be off your head (coll.)

B *adv.* cleverly

Gescheitheit *die;* **~**: cleverness

Geschenk /gəˈʃɛŋk/ *das;* **~[e]s, ~e** present; gift; **jmdm. ein ~ machen** give sb. a present; **jmdm. etw. zum ~ machen** make sb. a present of sth.; give sth. to sb. as a present; **kleine ~e erhalten die Freundschaft** (Spr.) small gifts preserve friendships; **ein ~ des Himmels** a godsend

Geschenk-: ~artikel *der* gift; **~packung** *die* gift pack; **~papier** *das* gift wrapping paper; **~sendung** *die* (Postw.) parcel containing a gift/gifts; **„~sendung"** 'gift [only]'

Gescherr /gəˈʃɛr/ ▸**Herr 3**

geschert /gəˈʃeːɐt/ *Adj.* (südd., österr. salopp) stupid; idiotic

Gescherte *der; adj. Dekl.* (südd., österr. salopp) stupid git (sl.)

Geschichte /gəˈʃɪçtə/ *die;* **~, ~n** **1▸** (auch Wissenschaft, Darstellung) history; **die ~ Frankreichs** the history of France; **die englische ~**: English history; **Alte/Mittlere/Neue ~**: ancient/medieval/modern history; **~ machen** make history; **in die ~ eingehen** (geh.) go down in history; **etw. gehört der ~** (*Dat.*) **an** sth. belongs to *or* is part of history **2▸** (Erzählung) story; (Fabel, Märchen) story; tale **3▸** (ugs.: Sache) **das sind alte ~n** that's old hat (coll.); **das ist [wieder] die alte ~**: it's the [same] old story [all over again]; **das sind ja schöne ~n!** (iron.) that's a fine thing *or* state of affairs! (iron.); **die ganze ~**: the whole business *or* thing; **mach keine ~n!** don't do anything silly; **Du wirst doch nicht krank werden. Mach keine ~n!** You won't fall ill. Don't be [so] silly!; **mach keine langen ~n** don't make a [great] fuss

Geschichten-: ~buch *das* story book; **~erzähler** *der*, **~erzählerin** *die* storyteller

geschichtlich

A *Adj.* **1▸** historical **2▸** (bedeutungsvoll) historic

B *adv.* historically; **etw. ~ betrachten** consider sth. from a historical point of view *or* perspective

Geschichtlichkeit *die;* **~** (Philos.) historicity

geschichts-, Geschichts-: ~atlas *der* historical atlas; **~auffassung** *die* conception *or* view of history; **~bewusst** *Adj.* historically aware; aware of history *pred.*; **~bewusstsein**, ***~bewußtsein** *das* awareness of history; historical awareness; **~bild** *das* ▸**~auffassung**; **~buch** *das* history book; **~drama** *das* (Literaturw.) historical drama; **~epoche** *die* historical epoch; **~fälschung** *die* falsification of history; **~forscher** *der*, **~forscherin** *die* historian; **~forschung** *die* historical research; **~klitterung** *die;* **~~, ~~en** deliberately biased account of history; **~lehrer** *der*, **~lehrerin** *die* history teacher; **~los** *Adj.* ‹*country, society, people, etc.*› without a history *or* past; (ohne ~bewusstsein) with no sense of its own history; **~philosophie** *die* philosophy of history; **~philosophisch A** *Adj.* ‹*writings*› on/‹*studies*› in/‹*interpretation*› according to/‹*view of the world*› based on the philosophy of history; **B** *adv.* **etw. ~philosophisch interpretieren** interpret sth. from the point of view of the philosophy of history; **~schreiber** *der*, **~schreiberin** *die* historian; (Chronist) chronicler; **~schreibung** *die* historiography; **~unterricht** *der* history teaching; (Unterrichtsstunde) history lesson; **im ~unterricht nehmen sie den Dreißigjährigen Krieg durch** in history they are doing the Thirty Years War; *s. auch* **Englischunterricht**; **~werk** *das* historical work; **~wissenschaft** *die* [science of] history; **~wissenschaftler** *der*, **~wissenschaftlerin** *die* [academic] historian; **~zahl** *die* [historical] date

Geschick[1] /gəˈʃɪk/ *das;* **~[e]s, ~e** **1▸** (geh.: Schicksal) fate; **ihn ereilte sein ~**: he met his fate; **ein glückliches/gutes ~**: a kindly Providence **2▸** *Pl.* (Lebensumstände) destiny *sing.*

Geschick[2] *das;* **~[e]s** skill; **ein ~ für etw. haben** be skilled at sth.

Geschicklichkeit *die;* **~**: skilfulness; skill; **es zu großer ~ in etw.** (*Dat.*) **bringen** become very skilful at sth.

Geschicklichkeits-: ~fahren *das;* **~~s** (Motorsport) manoeuvring tests *pl.*; **~spiel** *das* game of skill

geschickt

A *2. Part. v.* **schicken**

B *Adj.* **1▸** (gewandt) skilful; (fingerfertig) skilful; dexterous; **~ im Klettern sein** be an agile climber **2▸** (klug) clever; adroit **3▸** (südd.: geeignet) suitable (**für** for)

C *adv.* **1▸** (gewandt) skilfully; (fingerfertig) skilfully; dexterously **2▸** (klug) cleverly; adroitly

Geschicktheit *die;* **~** ▸**Geschicklichkeit**

Geschiebe *das;* **~s, ~** **1▸** (ugs.) pushing and shoving **2▸** (Geol.) debris

geschieden *2. Part. v.* **scheiden**

Geschiedene *der/die; adj. Dekl.* divorcee; **seine ~**: his ex-wife; **ihr ~r** her ex-husband

geschienen *2. Part. v.* **scheinen**

Geschimpfe *das;* **~s** (ugs.) cursing; (das Tadeln) scolding

Geschirr /gəˈʃɪr/ *das;* **~[e]s, ~e** **1▸** (Riemenzeug) harness; **dem Pferd das ~ anlegen** harness the horse; put the harness on the horse; **sich ins ~ legen** (kräftig ziehen) pull hard; (angestrengt arbeiten) work like a slave **2▸** (Teller, Tassen usw.) crockery; (benutzt) dishes *pl.*; (zusammenpassend) [dinner/tea] service; (Küchen~) pots and pans *pl.*; kitchenware; **das gute/beste ~**: the good/best china; **feuerfestes ~**: ovenware set; **das ~ abwaschen** wash up *or* do the dishes **3▸** (veralt.: Gefäß) pot

Geschirr-: ~aufzug *der* dumb waiter; **~reiniger** *der* dishwasher detergent; **~schrank** *der* china cupboard; **~spülen** *das;* **~~s** washing-up; **~spüler** *der;* **~~s, ~~** **1▸** washer-up; **2▸** ▸**~spülmaschine**; **~spülerin** *die;* **~~, ~~nen** ▸**~spüler 1**; **~spül·maschine** *die* dishwashing machine; dishwasher; **~spülmittel** *das* washing-up liquid; **~tuch** *das; Pl.* **~tücher** tea towel; drying-up cloth (Brit.); dish towel (Amer.)

Geschiss, ***Geschiß** /gəˈʃɪs/ *das;* **Geschisses** (derb) fuss and bother (coll.)

geschissen /gəˈʃɪsn̩/ *2. Part. v.* **scheißen**

Geschlabber *das;* **~s** (ugs.) **1▸** (das Schlabbern) slurping **2▸** (bei Kleidern) **das ~ ihres langen Rocks** the flapping of her long skirt **3▸** (Brei, Pudding usw.) mush

geschlafen *2. Part. v.* **schlafen**

geschlagen *2. Part. v.* **schlagen**

Geschlecht *das;* **~[e]s, ~er** **1▸** sex; **männlichen/weiblichen ~s sein** be male/female; **Jugendliche beiderlei ~s** young people of both sexes; **das starke ~** (ugs. scherzh.) the stronger sex; **das schwache/schöne/zarte ~** (ugs. scherzh.) the weaker/fair/gentle sex **2▸** (Generation) generation; **die nachfolgenden ~er** future generations **3▸** (Sippe) family; **von altem ~**: of ancient lineage; **das ~ der Habsburger** the house of Habsburg; **ein edles ~**: a noble house **4▸** (Sprachw.) gender **5▸** (Geschlechtsteil) sex **6▸** (dichter.: Gattung) **das menschliche ~** *od.* **das ~ der Menschen** the human race; **das ~ der Götter** the gods

Geschlechter-: ~folge *die* succession of generations; **die ~folgen** the generations; **~trennung** *die* segregation of the sexes

geschlechtlich

A *Adj.* sexual

B *adv.* **mit jmdm. ~ verkehren** have sexual intercourse with sb.

Geschlechtlichkeit *die;* **~:** sexuality

geschlechts-, Geschlechts-: **~akt** *der* sex[ual] act; **~apparat** *der* (Fachspr.) genital organs *pl.*; genitals *pl.*; **~bestimmung** *die* **1** (Festlegung) sex determination; **2** (Feststellung) determination of sex; (von Tieren auch) sexing; **eine ~bestimmung vornehmen** determine the sex of a baby/an animal; **~chromosom** *das* (Biol.) sex chromosome; **~drüse** *die* ▸**i S. 435** (Anat., Zool.) gonad; **~erziehung** *die* sex education; **~gebunden** **A** *Adj.* sex-linked; **B** *adv.* **~gebunden weitervererbt werden** be passed on in a way which shows sex-linkage; **~genosse** *der*, **~genossin** *die* (fachspr.) person/animal of the same sex; **~genossen** *Pl.* those of the same sex; **ein ~genosse** another of the same sex; **~hormon** *das* sex hormone; **~krank** *Adj.* ‹*person*› suffering from VD *or* a venereal disease; **~krank sein** have VD; be suffering from a venereal disease; **~krankheit** *die* ▸**i S. 439** venereal disease; **~leben** *das* sex life; **~los** *Adj.* (Biol.) asexual; (fig.) sexless; **~lust** *die* sexual desire *or* lust; **~merkmal** *das* sex[ual] characteristic; **~organ** *das* ▸**i S. 435** sex[ual] organ; genital organ; **~partner** *der*, **~partnerin** *die* sex partner; **~reif** *Adj.* sexually mature; **~reife** *die* sexual maturity; **~rolle** *die* (Soziol.) sex role; **~spezifisch** *Adj.* (Soziol.) sex-specific; **~teil** *das:* ▸**i S. 435 die ~teile/das ~teil** the genitals *pl.*; **~trieb** *der* sex[ual] drive *or* urge; **~umwandlung** *die* sex change; change of sex; **~unterschied** *der* difference between the sexes; **~verkehr** *der* sexual intercourse; **~wort** *das; Pl.* **~wörter** ▸**Artikel**; **~zelle** *die* gamete

geschlichen *2. Part. v.* **schleichen**

geschliffen
A *2. Part. v.* **schleifen**
B *Adj.* polished, refined ‹*style, manners, etc.*›; polished ‹*sentence*›
C *adv.* in a polished manner

Geschliffenheit *die;* **~, ~en** refinement; (des Stils) polish

geschlissen /gəˈʃlɪsn̩/ *2. Part. v.* **schleißen**

geschlossen
A *2. Part. v.* **schließen**
B *Adj.* **1** (gemeinsam) united ‹*action, front*›; unified ‹*procedure*›; *s. auch* **Gesellschaft** **2** (zusammenhängend) **eine ~e Ortschaft** a built-up area; **eine ~e Linie von Demonstranten** a solid line of demonstrators **3** (abgerundet) **eine [in sich] ~e Persönlichkeit** a well-rounded personality; **ein ~es Bild/~er Eindruck** a full *or* complete picture/impression
C *adv.* **~ für etw. stimmen/sein** vote/be unanimously in favour of sth.; **wir verließen ~ unser Büro** we walked out in a body *or* en masse; **~ gegen etw. vorgehen** take concerted action against sth.; **~ hinter jmdm. stehen** be solidly behind sb.; **die ganze Gruppe stand ~ auf** the whole group rose with one accord

Geschlossenheit *die;* **~** **1** (Gemeinschaft) unity **2** (Einheitlichkeit) unity; uniformity **3** **die ~ der Handlung** the tight construction of the plot

Geschluchze *das;* **~s** (ugs.) sobbing; **hör mit dem ~ auf!** stop your blubbering *or* (sl.) blubbing

geschlungen /gəˈʃlʊŋən/ *2. Part. v.* **schlingen**

Geschlürfe *das;* **~s** (ugs. abwertend) slurping

Geschmack /gəˈʃmak/ *der;* **~[e]s, Geschmäcke** /gəˈʃmɛkə/ *od. ugs. scherzh.:* **Geschmäcker** /gəˈʃmɛkɐ/ **1** taste; **einen schlechten ~ im Munde haben** have a bad *or* nasty taste in one's mouth; **einen guten/schlechten ~ haben** have good/bad taste; **das ist [nicht] mein** *od.* **nach meinem ~:** that is [not] to my taste; **jmds. ~** (*Akk.*) **treffen** guess sb.'s taste exactly; **das verstößt gegen den guten ~:** that offends against good taste; **im ~ jener Zeit eingerichtet** furnished in the style of that period; **von erlesenem ~:** exquisitely tasteful; showing exquisite taste; **die Geschmäcker sind verschieden** (ugs. scherzh.) tastes differ; **über ~ lässt sich nicht streiten** there's no accounting for taste[s]; **an etw.** (*Akk.*) **~ finden** *od.* **gewinnen** acquire a taste for sth.; take a liking to sth.; **einer Sache** (*Dat.*) **~ abgewinnen** come *or* grow to like sth.; **sie kann solchen Bildern keinen ~ abgewinnen** she cannot appreciate such pictures; **auf den ~ kommen** acquire the taste for it; get to like it **2** (Geschmackssinn) sense of taste

Geschmäckle /gəˈʃmɛklə/ *das;* **~s** nasty taste; **(ein) ~ haben** leave a bad taste in the mouth

geschmacklich
A *Adj.* as regards taste *postpos.*; **zur ~en Verfeinerung** to improve the taste *or* flavour
B *adv.* as regards taste

geschmacklos
A *Adj.* **1** (ohne Geschmack) tasteless; insipid **2** (unschön, taktlos) tasteless; **~ sein** be in bad taste; ‹*person*› be lacking in taste
B *adv.* tastelessly

Geschmacklosigkeit *die;* **~, ~en** **1** lack of [good] taste; bad taste; **diese Gebäude sind ~en** these buildings are examples of bad taste **2** (Unverschämtheit) tastelessness; bad taste; **das ist eine ~ ersten Ranges!** that is the height of bad taste! **3** (Äußerung) tasteless remark; (Handlung) tasteless behaviour *sing., no indef. art.*

geschmacks-, Geschmacks-: **~empfindung** *die* sense of taste; **~frage** *die* question *or* matter of taste; **~knospe** *die* ▸**i S. 435** (Zool., Anat.) taste bud; **~neutral** *Adj.* tasteless; flavourless; **~richtung** *die* **1** flavour; **2** (Geschmack, Vorliebe) taste

Geschmack[s]·sache *die: in* **das ist ~:** that is a question *or* matter of taste

geschmacks-, Geschmacks-: **~sicher** **A** *Adj.* showing a sure sense of taste *or* sound taste *postpos.*; **~sicher sein** show a sure sense of taste *or* sound taste; **B** *adv.* with a sure sense of taste; **~sinn** *der* sense of taste; **~stoff** *der* flavouring; **~verirrung** *die* (abwertend) lapse of taste; **an** *od.* **unter ~verirrung** (*Dat.*) **leiden** (ugs.) suffer from a lapse in taste; **~verstärker** *der* flavour enhancer

geschmack·voll
A *Adj.* tasteful; **die Bemerkung war nicht sehr ~:** the remark was not in very good taste
B *adv.* tastefully

Geschmatze *das;* **~s** (ugs. abwertend) smacking one's lips *no art.*; (beim Essen) noisy eating *no art.*; **hör mit dem ~ auf!** stop making so much noise when you're eating!

Geschmeide /gəˈʃmaidə/ *das;* **~s, ~** (geh.) jewellery *no pl.*; (einzelnes Schmuckstück) piece of jewellery

geschmeidig
A *Adj.* **1** (schmiegsam) sleek ‹*hair, fur*›; supple, soft ‹*leather, boots, skin*›; smooth ‹*dough*› **2** (gelenkig) supple ‹*fingers*›; supple, lithe ‹*body, movement, person*› **3** (fig.: anpassungsfähig) adaptable
B *adv.* **1** (gelenkig) agilely **2** (fig.) adaptably

Geschmeidigkeit *die;* **~** ▸**geschmeidig A:** sleekness; suppleness; softness; smoothness; litheness; adaptability

Geschmeiß *das;* **~es** **1** (veralt., auch fig.) vermin **2** (Jägerspr.) droppings *pl.*

Geschmiere *das;* **~s** (ugs. abwertend) **1** [filthy] mess **2** (Geschriebenes) scribble; scrawl **3** (Machwerk) rubbish; bilge (sl.)

geschmissen /gəˈʃmɪsn̩/ *2. Part. v.* **schmeißen**

geschmolzen *2. Part. v.* **schmelzen**

Geschmorte /gəˈʃmoːɐ̯tə/ *das; adj. Dekl.* (ugs.) braised meat

Geschmunzel *das;* **~s** (ugs.) smiling; **allgemeines ~ auslösen** make everyone smile

Geschmuse *das;* **~s** (ugs.) cuddling; (eines Pärchens) kissing and cuddling

Geschnäbel *das;* **~s** (ugs.) **1** (von Vögeln) billing **2** (ugs. scherzh.: Geküsse) billing and cooing

Geschnatter *das;* **~s** (ugs.) **1** (das Schnattern) cackling; cackle **2** (abwertend: das Sprechen) chatter[ing]; nattering (coll.)

Geschnetzelte *das; adj. Dekl. small, thin slices of meat [cooked in sauce]*

geschniegelt
A *2. Part. v.* **schniegeln**
B *Adj.* (ugs. abwertend) nattily dressed; **~ und gebügelt** *od.* **gestriegelt** all spruced up

geschnitten /gəˈʃnɪtn̩/ *2. Part. v.* **schneiden**

geschnoben *2. Part. v.* **schnauben**

geschoben /gəˈʃoːbn̩/ *2. Part. v.* **schieben**

geschollen *2. Part. v.* **schallen**

gescholten /gəˈʃɔltn̩/ *2. Part. v.* **schelten**

Geschöpf /gəˈʃœpf/ *das;* **~[e]s, ~e** **1** creature; **ein ~ Gottes** one of God's creatures **2** (erfundene Gestalt) creation

geschoren *2. Part. v.* **scheren**

Geschoss[1], ***Geschoß** *das;* **Geschosses, Geschosse** projectile; (Kugel) bullet; (Rakete) rocket; missile; (Granate) shell; grenade

Geschoss[2], ***Geschoß** *das;* **Geschosses, Geschosse** (Etage) floor; (Stockwerk) storey; **im ersten ~:** on the first (Brit.) *or* (Amer.) second floor

Geschoss·bahn, *Geschoß·bahn *die* trajectory

geschossen /gəˈʃɔsn̩/ *2. Part. v.* **schießen**

Geschoss·hagel, *Geschoß·hagel *der* hail of bullets

-geschossig
A *Adj.* -storey; **ein~/zwei~/mehr~:** single-storey/two-storey/multi-storey; **unser Wohnhaus ist zwei~:** our house has two storeys
B *adv.* **drei~ bauen** build three storeys high

geschraubt
A *2. Part. v.* **schrauben**
B *Adj.* (ugs. abwertend) stilted ‹*language, construction*›; (schwülstig) affected, pretentious ‹*way of speaking, style*›
C *adv.* **sich ~ ausdrücken** express oneself in an affected *or* a pretentious manner *or* way

Geschraubtheit *die;* **~:** stiltedness; (Schwulst) affectedness; pretentiousness

Geschrei *das;* **~s** **1** shouting; shouts *pl.*; (durchdringend) yelling; yells *pl.*; (schrill) shrieking; shrieks *pl.*; (von Verletzten, Tieren) screaming; screams *pl.*; **hört mit dem ~ auf** stop that shouting *or* yelling **2** (ugs.: das Lamentieren) fuss; to-do; **ein großes ~ wegen etw. machen** make *or* kick up a great fuss about sth.; make a great to-do about sth.

Geschreibsel /gəˈʃraipsl̩/ *das;* **~s** (ugs. abwertend) rubbish; bilge (sl.)

geschrieben *2. Part. v.* **schreiben**

***geschrieen, geschrien** /gəˈʃriː(ə)n/ *2. Part. v.* **schreien**

geschritten *2. Part. v.* **schreiten**

geschunden *2. Part. v.* **schinden**

Geschütz *das;* **~es, ~e** [big] gun; piece of artillery; **die ~e** the artillery *sing.*; the [big] guns; **grobes** *od.* **schweres ~ auffahren** (fig. ugs.) bring up the big guns *or* heavy artillery (fig.)

Geschütz-: **~bedienung** *die* (Milit.) gun crew; **~donner** *der* roar *or* booming of the [big] guns *or* the artillery; **~feuer** *das* artillery fire; shellfire; **~stand** *der*, **~stellung** *die* (Milit.) gun emplacement

geschützt
A *2. Part. v.* **schützen**
B *Adj.* **1** sheltered **2** (unter Naturschutz) protected

Geschwader /gəˈʃvaːdɐ/ *das;* **~s, ~** (Marine) squadron; (Luftwaffe) wing (Brit.); group (Amer.)

Geschwafel *das;* **~s** (ugs. abwertend) waffle

Geschwätz *das;* **~es** (ugs. abwertend) **1** (Gerede) prattle; prattling **2** (Klatsch) gossip; tittle-tattle

Geschwatze, Geschwätze *das;* **~s** (ugs. abwertend) chatter[ing]; nattering (coll.)

geschwätzig *Adj.* (abwertend) talkative

Geschwätzigkeit *die;* **~** (abwertend) talkativeness; **sie neigt ein bisschen zur ~:** she tends to be rather talkative

g

❶ Geschwindigkeiten

In Großbritannien und den USA werden Geschwindigkeiten im Straßenverkehr sowie im Schienenverkehr und im Luftverkehr noch meist in Meilen in der Stunde (**miles per hour** *oder* **miles an hour, mph**) gemessen.

100 km/h = 62,14 Meilen in der Stunde

Aber immer öfter werden diese Geschwindigkeiten auch als Kilometer in der Stunde (**kilometres** *od.* (*amerik.*) **kilometers per hour, kph**) angegeben.

Das britische Tempolimit in geschlossenen Ortschaften liegt bei 30 Meilen in der Stunde (ungefähr 50 km/h). Andere Grenzen liegen bei 40 (≈ 65 km/h), 50 (= 80 km/h), 60 (≈ 100 km/h), und auf der Autobahn 70 Meilen in der Stunde (≈ 110 km/h).

Wie schnell od. Mit welcher Geschwindigkeit fuhr der Wagen?
= How fast was the car going?, What speed was the car doing?

Der Wagen fuhr mit 120 Stundenkilometern
≈ The car was going at *od.* doing 75 [miles an hour]

Sie fuhr mit Vollgas/mit Höchstgeschwindigkeit
= She was driving flat out/at full speed

Das Auto fährt 200 Kilometer Spitze
≈ The car will do 125 [miles an hour] flat out, The car's top speed is 125 [miles an hour]

Du hast das Tempolimit überschritten
= You were exceeding the speed limit

Sie rasten dahin/fuhren in rasendem Tempo
= They were tearing along/going at a crazy speed

Wir mussten im Kriechtempo fahren
= We had to go at a crawl *od.* were reduced to a crawl

Lichtgeschwindigkeit, Schallgeschwindigkeit

Die Schallgeschwindigkeit beträgt 330 Meter pro Sekunde
= The speed of sound is 330 metres per second (m/s)

die Schallmauer durchbrechen
= break the sound barrier

Die Lichtgeschwindigkeit beträgt 300 000 Kilometer pro Sekunde
= The speed of light is 186,300 miles per second

mit Lichtgeschwindigkeit
= at the speed of light

geschweift
[A] *2. Part. v.* **schweifen**
[B] *Adj.* (gebogen) curved; **~e Klammern** (Druckw.) braces

geschweige *Konj.* **~ [denn]** let alone; never mind

geschwiegen *2. Part. v.* **schweigen**

geschwind /gəˈʃvɪnt/ (bes. südd.)
[A] *Adj.* swift; quick
[B] *adv.* swiftly; quickly; **~!** be quick!; **ich laufe ~ zum Kaufmann** I'm just dashing to the grocer's

Geschwindigkeit *die;* **~, ~en** ▸❶ **S. 310** speed; **mit großer/hoher ~:** at great/high speed; **mit einer ~ von 50 km/h** at a speed of 50 kmh; **überhöhte ~:** excessive speed; **die ~ erhöhen/drosseln** *od.* **verringern** increase/reduce speed; speed up/slow down; **Europa der verschiedenen/der zwei ~en** (Politik) multi-speed/two-speed Europe

Geschwindigkeits-: **~abfall** *der* loss of speed; drop in speed; **~begrenzung** *die,* **~beschränkung** *die* speed limit; **die ~beschränkung nicht beachten** exceed the speed limit; **~kontrolle** *die* speed check; **~messer** *der;* **~~s, ~~:** speedometer; **~überschreitung** *die* exceeding the speed limit *no art.;* speeding; **~zunahme** *die* increase in speed; increase in velocity (Phys.)

Geschwirr *das;* **~s** (von Pfeilen) whizzing; (von Insekten) buzzing

Geschwister /gəˈʃvɪstɐ/ *das;* **~s, ~** [1] *Pl.* brothers and sisters; **Hans und Maria sind ~:** Hans and Maria are brother and sister [2] (bes. Biol., Psych.) sibling

Geschwisterkind *das* (veralt.) [1] (Neffe/Nichte) nephew/niece [2] (Cousin/Cousine) cousin

geschwisterlich
[A] *Adj.* brotherly/sisterly ‹*affection, love*›
[B] *adv.* **das Geld ~ teilen** divide the money fairly among everybody

Geschwister-: **~liebe** *die* [1] brotherly/sisterly love *or* affection; [2] (Inzest) love affair between a brother and [a] sister; **~paar** *das* brother and sister; **zwei ~paare** two sets of brother and sister

geschwollen
[A] *2. Part. v.* **schwellen**
[B] *Adj.* [1] swollen [2] (fig. abwertend) pompous; bombastic
[C] *adv.* pompously; bombastically

geschwommen /gəˈʃvɔmən/ *2. Part. v.* **schwimmen**

geschworen
[A] *2. Part. v.* **schwören**
[B] *Adj. in* **ein ~er Feind** *od.* **Gegner von etw. sein** be a sworn enemy of sth.

Geschworene, (österr.:) **Geschworne** *der/die; adj. Dekl.* juror; **die ~n** the jury

Geschworenen-: **~bank** jury box; (fig.) jury; **~gericht** *das* ▸**Schwurgericht**

Geschwulst /gəˈʃvʊlst/ *die;* **~, Geschwülste** /gəˈʃvʏlstə/ tumour

geschwunden *2. Part. v.* **schwinden**

geschwungen
[A] *2. Part. v.* **schwingen**
[B] *Adj.* curved

Geschwür /gəˈʃvyːɐ̯/ *das;* **~s, ~e** ▸❶ **S. 439** ulcer; (Furunkel) boil; (fig.) running sore

Ges-Dur *das* (Musik) G major; *s. auch* **C-Dur**

gesehen /gəˈzeːən/ *2. Part. v.* **sehen**

Geselchte /gəˈzɛlçtə/ *das; adj. Dekl.* (südd., österr.) smoked meat

Gesell /gəˈzɛl/ *der;* **~en, ~en** (veralt.), **Geselle** /gəˈzɛlə/ *der;* **~n, ~n** [1] journeyman [2] (Kerl) fellow

-geselle *der:* **Tischler~/Fleischer~:** journeyman-carpenter/-butcher

gesellen *refl. V.* **sich zu jmdm. ~:** join sb.; (fig.: hinzukommen) **dazu gesellten sich noch Krankheit und finanzielle Unsicherheit** together with this came illness and financial insecurity

Gesellen-: **~brief** *der* journeyman's diploma *or* certificate; **~prüfung** *die* examination to become a journeyman; apprentice's final examination; **~stück** *das: piece of work produced by an apprentice in order to qualify as a journeyman*

gesellig
[A] *Adj.* [1] sociable; gregarious; **ein ~er Abend/~es Beisammensein** a convivial *or* sociable evening/a friendly get-together [2] (Biol.) gregarious
[B] *adv.* **~ leben** live gregariously; be gregarious; **~ zusammensitzen** sit [together] and chat [sociably]

Geselligkeit *die;* **~, ~en** [1] (Umgang) **die ~ lieben** enjoy [good] company [2] (geselliger Abend) social gathering

Gesellin *die;* **~, ~nen** journeyman; journeywoman (rare)

Gesellschaft *die;* **~, ~en** [1] society; **eine geschlossene ~:** a closed community *or* society; **die ~ verändern** change society; **~ bekommen** get company; **in schlechte ~ geraten** get into bad company; **jmdm. ~ leisten** keep sb. company; **die Damen der ~:** society ladies; **zur ~ gehören** belong to society; **jmdn. in die ~ einführen** introduce sb. into society; **die ~ Jesu** (kath. Rel.) the Society of Jesus; **zur ~:** to be sociable; **sich in guter ~ befinden** (fig. scherzh.) be in good company [2] (Veranstaltung) party; **eine ~ geben** give a party; **eine geschlossene ~:** a private function *or* party [3] (Kreis von Menschen) group of people; crowd; (abwertend) crew; lot (coll.) [4] (Wirtschaft) company; **~ mit beschränkter Haftung** limited liability company

Gesellschafter *der;* **~s, ~** [1] (Unterhalter) **ein glänzender ~:** a brilliant conversationalist; **ein guter ~ sein** be good company [2] (verhüll.: Callboy) [male] escort (euphem.) [3] (Wirtsch.) partner; (Teilhaber) shareholder; **stiller ~:** sleeping partner; silent partner (Amer.)

Gesellschafterin *die;* **~, ~nen** [1] [lady] companion [2] (verhüll.: Callgirl) escort (euphem.) [3] (Wirtsch.) partner; (Teilhaber) shareholder

gesellschaftlich
[A] *Adj.* [1] social; **die ~en Verhältnisse** social conditions [2] (Soziol.) society; **die ~e Produktion** production by society; **~es Eigentum an etw.** (*Dat.*) social ownership of sth. [3] (DDR) ‹*work etc.*› in the service of the community
[B] *adv.* [1] socially; **sich ~ unmöglich machen** put oneself beyond the pale of society [2] (DDR) **~ nützliche Tätigkeit** socially useful activity; **~ aktiv sein** *od.* **sich ~ betätigen** be actively involved in service to the community

gesellschafts-, Gesellschafts-: **~abend** *der* social evening; **~anzug** *der* dress suit; **~dame** *die* (veralt.) ▸**Gesellschafterin 1**; **~fähig** *Adj.* (auch fig.) socially acceptable; **~feindlich** *Adj.* anti-social; **~form** *die* form of society; social system; **~formation** *die* (Soziol.) social system; **~kapital** *das* (Wirtsch.) capital of a/the company; **~klasse** *die* social class; **~kritik** *die* social criticism; **~kritiker** *der,* **~kritikerin** *die* critic of society; **~kritisch** [A] *Adj.* critical of society *postpos.;* **die ~kritischen Elemente bei Fontane** the elements of social criticism in Fontane; [B] *adv.* **etw. ~kritisch interpretieren** interpret sth. from the point of view of social criticism; **~lehre** *die* (veralt.) sociology; (Schulfach) social studies *pl., no art.;* **~ordnung** *die* social order; **~politik** *die* social policy; **~politisch** [A] *Adj.* socio-political; [B] *adv.* socio-politically; **~raum** *der* function room; (auf Schiffen) saloon; **~reise** *die* group tour; **~roman** *der* social novel; **~schicht** *die* stratum of society; **~spiel** *das* parlour *or* party game; **~struktur** *die* structure of society; **die japanische ~struktur** the structure of Japanese society; **~stück** *das* [1] (Theater) comedy of manners; [2] (Malerei) genre painting; **~system** *das* social system; **~tanz** *der* ballroom dance; (das Tanzen) ballroom dancing; **~vertrag** *der* [1] (Philos.) social contract; [2] (Rechtsw.) memorandum *or* articles of association; **~wissenschaften** *Pl.* social sciences; **~wissenschaftlich** *Adj.* sociological ‹*studies, analyses*›; **~wissenschaftliche Fächer** social-science subjects

gesessen /gəˈzɛsn̩/ *2. Part. v.* **sitzen**

Gesetz /gəˈzɛts/ *das;* **~es, ~e** [1] law; (geschrieben) statute; **ein ~ verabschieden/einbringen** pass/introduce a bill; **[zum] ~ werden** become law; **vor dem ~:** in [the eyes of the] law; **das ~ der Serie** *the expectation that future events will continue the pattern of past ones;* **das ~ des Handelns** the need *or* necessity to act; **das ~ des Handelns an sich reißen** seize the initiative; **etw. hat seine eigenen ~e** (fig.) sth. is a law unto itself [2] (Regel) rule; law; **jmdm. höchstes ~ sein** be sb.'s golden rule; *s. auch* **aufheben 3**; **einhalten A**

Gesetz-: **~blatt** *das* law gazette; **~buch** *das* statute book; **das Bürgerliche ~buch** the Civil Code; **~entwurf** *der* bill

gesetzes-, Gesetzes-: **~brecher** *der*, **~brecherin** *die;* **~~, ~~nen** lawbreaker; **~hüter** *der*, **~hüterin** *die* (iron.) guardian of the law; **~initiative** *die* legislative initiative; **~kraft** *die* force of law; legal force; **~kraft haben** have the force of law *or* legal force; **~kraft erlangen** become law; be placed on the statute book; **~kundig** *Adj.* well versed in the law *postpos.*; **~lücke** *die* loophole in the law; **~novelle** *die* amendment; **~sammlung** *die* legal digest; **~tafel** *die* (hist.) tablet on which laws are written; **die ~tafeln** (bibl.) the Tables of the Law; the Two Tables; **~text** *der* wording of the/a law; **~treu** **A** *Adj.* law-abiding; **B** *adv.* in accordance with the law; **~treue** *die* law-abidingness; **~übertretung** *die* violation of the law; **~vorlage** *die* bill; **~werk** *das* corpus *or* body of laws

gesetz-, Gesetz-: **~gebend** *Adj.* legislative; **die ~gebende Versammlung/Gewalt** the legislative assembly *or* the legislature/the legislative power; **~geber** *der* legislator; lawmaker; (Organ) legislature; **~gebung** *die;* **~:** legislation; law-making; **~gebungshoheit** *die* supreme authority to make *or* enact laws; supreme legislative power *or* authority; **~kundig** *Adj.:* ▸**gesetzeskundig**

gesetzlich
A *Adj.* legal ‹*requirement, definition, representative, interest*›; legal, statutory ‹*obligation*›; statutory ‹*holiday*›; lawful, legitimate ‹*heir, claim*›; **~es Zahlungsmittel** legal tender; **~e Kündigungsfrist** statutory period of notice
B *adv.* legally; **~ verankert sein** be established in law; **~ geschützt** registered ‹*patent, design*›; ‹*symbol*› registered as a trade mark; **~ geschützt/verboten sein** be protected/forbidden by law

Gesetzlichkeit *die;* **~** **1** (Gesetzmäßigkeit) conformity to a [natural] law/[natural] laws; **einer ~ folgen** obey a law/laws **2** (geregelter Zustand) **~ wieder herstellen** restore law and order; **außerhalb der ~ liegen** be illegal

gesetz-, Gesetz-: **~los** *Adj.* lawless; **~losigkeit** *die;* **~~:** lawlessness; **~mäßig** **A** *Adj.* **1** law-governed ‹*development, process*›; **~mäßig sein** be governed by *or* obey a [natural] law/ [natural] laws; **2** (~lich) legal; (rechtmäßig) lawful; legitimate; **B** *adv.* in accordance with a [natural] law/[natural] laws; **~mäßigkeit** *die* **1** conformity to a [natural] law/[natural] laws; **~mäßigkeiten im Verhalten von Tieren entdecken** discover laws governing animal behaviour; **2** (~lichkeit) legality; (Rechtmäßigkeit) lawfulness; legitimacy

gesetzt
A *2. Part. v.* **setzen**
B *Adj.* staid; **eine Dame ~en Alters** a woman of mature years

Gesetztheit *die;* **~:** staidness

gesetz·widrig
A *Adj.* illegal; unlawful
B *adv.* illegally; unlawfully

Gesetz·widrigkeit *die* **1** illegality; unlawfulness **2** *Pl.* (Handlungen) unlawful acts

Geseufze *das;* **~s** sighing

Gesicht[1] /gəˈzɪçt/ *das;* **~[e]s, ~er** **1** ▸**❶ S. 435** face; **das ~ abwenden** turn one's face away; **ein fröhliches ~ machen** look pleasant *or* cheerful; **über das ganze ~ strahlen** (ugs.) beam all over one's face; **sich** (*Dat.*) **eine Zigarette ins ~ stecken** (ugs.) stick a cigarette in one's mouth (coll.); (fig.) **sein wahres ~ zeigen** show oneself in one's true colours; show one's true character; **jmdm. wie aus dem ~ geschnitten sein** be the [very *or* dead] spit [and image] of sb.; **ihm fiel das Essen aus dem ~** (ugs. scherzh.) he threw up (coll.); **das ist ein Schlag ins ~:** that is a slap in the face; **jmdm. ins ~ lachen** laugh in sb.'s face; **jmdm. ins ~ lügen** lie to sb.'s face; **jmdm. etw. ins ~ sagen** say sth. to sb.'s face; **jmdm. nicht ins ~ sehen können** be unable to look sb. in the face; **den Tatsachen ins ~ sehen** face the facts; **jmdm. [nicht] zu ~[e] stehen** [not] become sb.: **solche Unhöflichkeit steht dir nicht zu ~[e]** such impoliteness ill becomes you; **jmdm. ins ~ springen** (ugs.) go for sb.; **ein bekanntes/fremdes ~:** a familiar *or* well-known/unknown *or* strange face; **ein anderes ~ aufsetzen** *od.* **machen** put on a different expression; **das ~ wahren** *od.* **retten** save one's face; **das ~ verlieren** lose face; **ein ~ machen wie drei** *od.* **acht** *od.* **vierzehn Tage Regenwetter** look as miserable as sin; **ein langes ~/lange ~er machen** pull a long face; **ein schiefes ~ machen** make a wry face; **ein ~ ziehen** *od.* **machen** make *or* pull a face; **~er schneiden** pull *or* make faces; **das stand ihm im ~ geschrieben** it was written all over his face **2** (fig.: Aussehen) **das ~ einer Stadt** the appearance of a town; **die vielen ~er Chinas** the many faces of China; **diese Pläne haben noch kein ~:** these plans still have no definite shape *or* form; **ein anderes ~ bekommen** take on a different complexion *or* character **3** (geh., veralt.: Sehvermögen) sight; **das zweite ~ [haben]** [have] second sight; **jmdn./etw. aus dem ~ verlieren** lose sight of sb./sth.; **jmdn./etw. zu ~ bekommen** set eyes on *or* see sb./sth.; **jmdm. zu ~ kommen** (Amtsspr.) be seen by sb.

Gesicht[2] *das;* **~[e]s, ~e** (geh.) vision; **ein ~/~e haben** have a vision/visions

gesichts-, Gesichts-: **~ausdruck** *der; Pl.* **~ausdrücke** expression; look; **~creme** *die* face cream; **~erker** *der* (ugs. scherzh.) conk (coll.); hooter (Brit. coll.); schnozzle (Amer. sl.); **~farbe** *die* complexion; **~feld** *das* field of vision *or* view; **~hälfte** *die* side of the face; **seine rechte ~hälfte** the right side of his face; **~haut** *die* ▸**❶ S. 435** facial skin; **~kontrolle** *die* identity check (*before granting admittance to nightclub etc.*); **~kreis** *der* (veralt.) **1** field of view; field *or* range of vision; **jmdn. aus dem ~kreis verlieren** (fig.) lose touch with sb.; **2** (Horizont) horizon; outlook; **seinen ~kreis erweitern** broaden one's horizons *pl.*; **~lähmung** *die* facial paralysis; **~los** *Adj.* faceless; **~lotion** *die* face lotion; **~maske** *die* **1** (Larve) mask; **2** (Med.) face mask; **3** (Kosmetik) face mask; face pack; **4** (Sport) face guard; **~muskel** *der* ▸**❶ S. 435** facial muscle; **~nerv** *der* ▸**❶ S. 435** facial nerve; **~partie** *die* part of the face; **ihre untere ~partie** the lower part of her face; **~pflege** *die* care of one's face; **ihre tägliche ~pflege** her daily facial; **zur ~pflege benutzt sie nur Wasser und Seife** all she uses on her face is soap and water; **~plastik** *die* (Med.) plastic surgery *no art.* on the face; **~puder** *der* face powder; **~punkt** *der* point of view; **etw. unter einem anderen/neuen ~punkt betrachten** consider sth. from a different/new point of view; **~rose** *die* ▸**❶ S. 439** (Med.) facial erysipelas; **~schnitt** *der* [cast *sing.* of] features *pl.*; **~sinn** *der* visual faculty; **~verlust** *der* loss of face; **~wasser** *das; Pl.* **~wässer** face lotion; **~winkel** *der* **1** angle of vision; visual angle; **2** ▸**~punkt**; **~züge** *Pl.* features

Gesims *das;* **~es, ~e** cornice

Gesinde /gəˈzɪndə/ *das;* **~s, ~** (veralt.) [domestic] servants *pl.*; (auf einem Bauernhof) [farm] hands *pl.*

Gesindel /gəˈzɪndl/ *das;* **~s** (abwertend) rabble; riff-raff *pl.*; **lichtscheues ~:** shady characters *pl.*

Gesinde·stube *die* (veralt.) servants' quarters *pl.*; (auf einem Bauernhof) quarters *pl.* for the farmhands

Gesinge *das;* **~s** (ugs. abwertend) singing

gesinnt /gəˈzɪnt/ *Adj.* **christlich/sozial ~ [sein]** [be] Christian-minded/public-spirited; **jmdm. freundlich/übel ~ sein** be well-disposed/ill-disposed towards sb.

Gesinnung *die;* **~, ~en** [basic] convictions *pl.*; [fundamental] beliefs *pl.*; **eine niedrige ~:** a low cast of mind

gesinnungs-, Gesinnungs-: **~freund** *der*, **~freundin** *die*, **~genosse** *der*, **~genossin** *die* like-minded person; **seine ~freunde** *od.* **~genossen** people of the same mind as himself; **~los** (abwertend) **A** *Adj.* unprincipled; **B** *adv.* in an unprincipled manner; **~losigkeit** *die;* **~~:** lack of principle; **~lump** *der* (ugs. abwertend) time-server; **~schnüffelei** *die* (abwertend) snooping around to find out people's political convictions; political snooping; **~täter** *der*, **~täterin** *die* lawbreaker motivated by moral *or* political convictions; **~treu** *Adj.* loyal; **~treue** *die* loyalty; **~wandel** *der*, **~wechsel** *der* change *or* shift of attitude *or* views

gesittet /gəˈzɪtət/
A *Adj.* **1** well-behaved; well-mannered ‹*behaviour*› **2** (zivilisiert) civilized
B *adv.* **1** **sich ~ benehmen** *od.* **aufführen** be well-behaved **2** (zivilisiert) in a civilized manner

Gesittung *die;* **~** (geh.) cultured behaviour

Gesocks /gəˈzɔks/ *das;* **~** (salopp abwertend) riff-raff; rabble

Gesöff /gəˈzœf/ *das;* **~[e]s, ~e** (salopp abwertend) muck (coll.); awful stuff (coll.)

gesogen /gəˈzoːgn̩/ *2. Part. v.* **saugen**

gesondert /gəˈzɔndɐt/
A *Adj.* separate
B *adv.* separately

gesonnen /gəˈzɔnən/
A *2. Part. v.* **sinnen**
B *Adj.* **~ sein, etw. zu tun** feel disposed to do sth.

gesotten /gəˈzɔtn̩/ *2. Part. v.* **sieden**

Gesottene *das; adj. Dekl.* (landsch.) boiled meat

Gespann /gəˈʃpan/ *das;* **~[e]s, ~e** **1** (Zugtiere) team; **ein ~ Ochsen** a yoke *or* team of oxen **2** (Wagen) horse and carriage; (zur Güterbeförderung) horse and cart **3** (Menschen) couple; pair

gespannt
A *2. Part. v.* **spannen**
B *Adj.* **1** (erwartungsvoll) eager; expectant; rapt ‹*attention*›; **ich bin ~, ob ...** I'm keen *or* eager to know/see whether ...; *s. auch* **Flitz[e]bogen** **2** (konfliktbeladen) tense ‹*situation, atmosphere*›; strained ‹*relations, relationships*›
C *adv.* eagerly; expectantly; **die Kinder hörten seinen Erzählungen ~ zu** the children listened with rapt attention to his stories

Gespanntheit *die* **1** eager expectancy; **voller ~ die Entwicklung verfolgen** follow the developments with tense interest **2** (Gereiztheit) tenseness

gespaßig (bayr., österr.) ▸**spaßig**

Gespenst /gəˈʃpɛnst/ *das;* **~[e]s, ~er** **1** ghost; **~er sehen** (fig.) be imagining things **2** (geh.: Gefahr) spectre

Gespenster-: **~geschichte** *die* ghost story; **~glaube** *der* belief in ghosts

gespensterhaft *Adj.* ghostly

gespenstern *itr. V.* **in etw.** (*Dat.*) **~:** haunt sth.

Gespenster·stunde *die* witching hour

gespenstig, gespenstisch *Adj.* ghostly; ghostly, eerie ‹*appearance*›; eerie ‹*building, atmosphere*›

***gespieen, gespien** /gəˈʃpiː(ə)n/ *2. Part. v.* **speien**

Gespiele *der;* **~n, ~n, Gespielin** *die;* **~, ~nen** (geh. veralt.) **1** playmate **2** (abwertend: Geliebte[r]) lover

Gespinst /gəˈʃpɪnst/ *das;* **~[e]s, ~e** gossamer-like material; **das ~ der Seidenraupe** the cocoon of the silkworm; **ein ~ von Lügen** (fig.) a tissue of lies

gesplissen /gəˈʃplɪsn̩/ *2. Part. v.* **spleißen**

gesponnen /gəˈʃpɔnən/ *2. Part. v.* **spinnen**

Gespons[1] /gəˈʃpɔns/ *der;* **~es, ~e** (veralt., noch scherzh.) spouse; (Bräutigam) bridegroom

Gespons[2] *das;* **~es, ~e** (veralt., noch scherzh.) spouse; (Braut) bride

gespornt
A *2. Part. v.* **spornen**
B *Adj.* ▸**gestiefelt**

g

Gespött /gəˈʃpœt/ *das;* **~[e]s** mockery; ridicule; **jmdn./sich zum ~ machen** make sb./oneself a laughing stock

Gespräch /gəˈʃprɛːç/ *das;* **~[e]s, ~e** 1 conversation; (Diskussion) discussion; **das ~ auf etw.** (*Akk.*) **bringen** bring *or* steer the conversation round to sth.; **ein ~ über etw.** (*Akk.*) a conversation *or* talk about sth.; **~e** (Politik) talks; discussions; **der Gegenstand des ~[e]s** the subject *or* topic under discussion; **ein ~ mit jmdm. führen** have a conversation *or* talk with sb.; **jmdn. in ein ~ verwickeln** engage sb. in conversation; **mit jmdm. ins ~ kommen** (sich unterhalten) get into *or* engage in conversation with sb.; (fig.: sich annähern) enter into a dialogue with sb.; **im ~ sein** be under discussion; **als neuer Vorsitzender ist Herr X im ~:** Mr X's name is being discussed in connection with the chairmanship 2 (Telefongespräch) call (**mit** to); **ein ~ anmelden** make *or* place a call; **ein ~ für Sie!** there's a call for you! 3 (ugs.: ~sgegenstand) **das ~ der Stadt/der Familie** the talk of the town/the whole family; **das ~ der letzten Wochen** the talking point for the last few weeks

gesprächig *Adj.* talkative; **der Alkohol machte ihn ~:** the alcohol loosened his tongue

Gesprächigkeit *die;* **~:** talkativeness

gesprächs-, Gesprächs-: ~bereit *Adj.* ready to talk *postpos.;* (zu Verhandlungen bereit auch) ready for discussions *postpos.;* (Telefon) **sind Sie jetzt ~bereit?** are you ready to speak now?; **~bereitschaft** *die* readiness for discussions; **~dauer** *die* (Fernspr.) call time; **~einheit** *die* ▸ **Gebühreneinheit**; **~fetzen** *der* fragment *or* snatch of conversation; **~form** *die* **in ~form** in the form of a dialogue; in dialogue form; **~gebühr** *die* call charge; **~gegenstand** *der* topic of conversation; (Diskussionsgegenstand) subject of the discussion; **~gegenstand war ...** the subject *or* topic of conversation/the subject of the discussion was ...; **~kreis** *der* discussion group; **~leiter** *der,* **~leiterin** *die* discussion leader; chairman; **~partner** *der,* **~partnerin** *die:* **wer war ihr ~partner?** who was she talking to?; **meine heutige ~partnerin wird die Innenministerin sein** today I shall be talking to the Minister of the Interior; **der Kanzler und seine ~partner** the Chancellor and his partners in the talks; **~pause** *die* break in the discussions *or* talks; **~stoff** *der* subjects *pl. or* topics *pl.* of conversation; **ihr geht nie der ~stoff aus** she never runs out of things to talk about; **~teilnehmer** *der,* **~teilnehmerin** *die* participant in the discussion; **~thema** *das* topic of conversation; **~therapie** *die* (Psych.) therapy by means of conversation; **~weise** *Adv.* in [the course of] conversation; **~zeit** *die* (Fernspr.) call time; **Ihre ~zeit ist abgelaufen** the time allowed for your call has run out

gespreizt
A *2. Part. v.* **spreizen**
B *Adj.* (abwertend) stilted; affected
C *adv.* (abwertend) in a stilted *or* an affected manner

Gespreiztheit *die;* **~** (abwertend) stiltedness; affectedness

gesprenkelt
A *2. Part. v.* **sprenkeln**
B *Adj.* mottled; speckled ‹*egg*›

Gespritzte *der; adj. Dekl.* (südd.) wine with soda water

gesprochen /gəˈʃprɔxn̩/ *2. Part. v.* **sprechen**

gesprossen /gəˈʃprɔsn̩/ *2. Part. v.* **sprießen**

Gesprudel *das;* **~s** bubbling

gesprungen *2. Part. v.* **springen**

Gespür /gəˈʃpyːɐ̯/ *das;* **~s** feel; **sie hat ein feines ~ für Unaufrichtigkeiten** she quickly senses when somebody is being insincere

gest. *Abk.* = **gestorben** d.

Gestade /gəˈʃtaːdə/ *das;* **~s, ~** (dichter.) shore(s)

Gestagen /gɛstaˈgeːn/ *das;* **~s, ~e** (Med.) gestagen

Gestalt /gəˈʃtalt/ *die;* **~, ~en** 1 build; **von kräftiger ~, kräftig von ~:** of powerful *or* strong build; **zierlich von ~:** petite; **klein von ~:** small in stature; of small build 2 (Mensch, Persönlichkeit) figure; **eine zwielichtige ~:** a shady character 3 (in der Dichtung) character 4 (Form) form; **die ~ des neuen Hochhauses** the shape of the new tower block; **~ annehmen** *od.* **gewinnen** take shape; **einer Sache** (*Dat.*) **~ geben** *od.* **verleihen** give shape [and form] to sth.; (etw. ausdrücken) express sth.; **in ~ von einer Sache** *od.* **einer Sache** (*Gen.*) in the form of sth.; **sich in seiner wahren ~ zeigen** show one's true character; show [oneself in] one's true colours

gestalten
A *tr. V.* fashion, shape, form ‹*vase, figure, etc.*›; design ‹*furnishings, stage set, etc.*›; lay out ‹*public gardens*›; dress ‹*shop window*›; mould, shape ‹*character, personality*›; arrange ‹*party, conference, etc.*›; frame ‹*sentence, reply, etc.*›; **etw. moderner ~:** modernize sth.; **etw. künstlerisch/literarisch ~:** give artistic/literary form to sth.
B *refl. V.* turn out; **sich schwieriger ~ als erwartet** turn out *or* prove to be more difficult than had been expected; **er fragte sich, wie sich seine Zukunft ~ würde** he wondered what the future would hold for him

Gestalter *der;* **~s, ~, Gestalterin** *die;* **~, ~nen** creator

gestalterisch *Adj.* creative; artistic; **vom ~en Standpunkt** creatively; artistically

gestalt·los *Adj.* shapeless; formless; **eine ~e Masse** an amorphous mass

Gestalt·psychologie *die* Gestalt psychology

Gestaltung *die;* **~, ~en** 1 ▸ **gestalten**: fashioning; shaping; forming; designing; laying out; dressing; moulding; shaping; arranging; framing; **die literarische ~ dieses historischen Ereignisses** the literary representation of this historic event; **Hochschule für ~:** academy of art and design; **die künstlerische ~ des Films** the artistic direction of the film 2 (Gestaltetes) form

Gestaltungs-: ~form *die* form; **~kraft** *die* creative power; **~prinzip** *das* formal principle

Gestammel *das;* **~s** stammering; stuttering; **seine Antwort war nur ein ~:** he was only able to stammer *or* stutter out a reply

Gestampfe *das;* **~s** stamping; **das ~ der Baumaschinen** the pounding *or* thumping of the construction plant

gestand *1. u. 3. Pers. Sg. Prät. v.* **gestehen**

gestanden
A *2. Part. v.* **stehen, gestehen**
B *Adj.* **ein ~er Mann** a grown man; **ein ~er Parlamentarier** an experienced *or* seasoned parliamentarian

geständig *Adj.* **~ sein** have confessed; **wenn Sie ~ wären** if you confessed; **der ~e Entführer** the self-confessed kidnapper

Geständnis /gəˈʃtɛntnɪs/ *das;* **~ses, ~se** confession; **ein ~ ablegen** make a confession; **ich muss dir ein ~ machen** I must make a confession to you

Gestänge /gəˈʃtɛŋə/ *das;* **~s, ~** 1 (Stangen) struts *pl.* 2 (Technik) linkage; (des Kolbens) connecting rod

Gestank /gəˈʃtaŋk/ *der;* **~[e]s** (abwertend) stench; stink

Gestänker /gəˈʃtɛnkɐ/ *das;* **~s** (ugs.) trouble-making

Gestapo /geˈstaːpo/ *die;* **~** (ns.) Gestapo

Gestapo·methoden *Pl.* (abwertend) Gestapo methods

gestatten /gəˈʃtatn̩/
A *tr., itr. V.* permit; allow; **jmdm. ~, etw. zu tun** permit *or* allow sb. to do sth.; **„Rauchen nicht gestattet!"** 'no smoking'; **~ Sie eine Bemerkung** allow *or* permit me to make a remark; **~ Sie, dass ich ...** may I ...?; **wenn Sie ~:** if I may; **wenn es die Umstände ~:** if circumstances permit *or* allow; circumstances permitting
B *refl. V.* (geh.) **sich** (*Dat.*) **etw. ~:** allow oneself sth.; **wenn ich mir eine Bemerkung ~ darf** if I may be so bold as to make a remark; **sich** (*Dat.*) **~, etw. zu tun** take the liberty of doing sth.; **ich gestatte mir, Sie zu diesem Fest einzuladen** I have pleasure in inviting you to this celebration

Geste /ˈgɛstə, ˈgeːstə/ *die;* **~, ~n** (auch fig.) gesture

Gesteck /gəˈʃtɛk/ *das;* **~[e]s, ~e** flower arrangement

gestehen *tr., itr. V.* confess; **die Tat** *usw.* **~:** confess to the deed *etc.*; **jmdm. seine Gefühle ~:** confess one's feelings to sb.; **ich muss ~, dass ...** I must confess that ...; **offen gestanden ...** frankly *or* to be honest ...

Gestehungs·kosten *Pl.* (Wirtsch.) production costs

Gestein *das;* **~[e]s, ~e** rock

Gesteins-: ~ader *die* rock seam; **~art** *die* type of rock; **~brocken** *der* rock; **~formation** *die* rock formation; **~kunde** *die* petrology; **~masse** *die* rock mass; mass of rock; **~probe** *die* rock sample; **~schicht** *die* stratum *or* layer of rock

Gestell /gəˈʃtɛl/ *das;* **~[e]s, ~e** 1 (für Weinflaschen) rack; (zum Wäschetrocknen) horse; (für Pflanzen) planter 2 (Unterbau) frame; (eines Wagens) chassis; (fig. salopp) legs *pl.* 3 (salopp: dünne Person) scarecrow; **sie ist ein dünnes ~:** she's as skinny as a rake

Gestellung *die;* **~, ~en** 1 (Milit., hist.) reporting *no art.* for military service 2 (Amtsspr.) provision; **er bat um die ~ weiterer LKWs** he requested that more trucks *or* (Brit.) lorries be made available

Gestellungs·befehl *der* (Milit., hist.) call-up papers *pl.*

gestelzt
A *2. Part. v.* **stelzen**
B *Adj.* stilted; affected
C *adv.* in a stilted *or* an affected manner

gesten·reich /ˈgɛstn̩-, ˈgeːstn̩-/
A *Adj.* accompanied by many gestures *postpos.*
B *adv.* with much gesturing

gestern /ˈgɛstɐn/ *Adv.* ▸ **i S. 816** 1 yesterday; **~ Morgen/Abend/Mittag** yesterday morning/evening/[at] midday yesterday; **seit ~:** since yesterday; **~ vor einer Woche** a week ago yesterday; **die Zeitung von ~:** yesterday's [news]paper; **die Welt/die Mode von ~:** the world of yesterday *or* yesteryear/yesterday's fashions *pl.*; **das Gestern** yesterday; the past; **im Gestern leben** live in the past; **von ~ sein** be outdated *or* outmoded; **sie ist nicht von ~** (ugs.) she wasn't born yesterday (coll.)

Gestichel /gəˈʃtɪçl̩/ *das;* **~s** (ugs. abwertend) snide remarks *pl. or* comments *pl.* (coll.)

gestiefelt *Adj.* booted; **der ~e Kater** Puss in Boots; **~ und gespornt** (ugs. scherzh.) ready and waiting

gestiegen *2. Part. v.* **steigen**

gestielt *Adj.* (Bot.) stemmed, petiolate ‹*leaf*›; stemmed, pedunculate ‹*flower*›; stalked ‹*fruit*›

Gestik /ˈgɛstɪk/ *die;* **~:** gestures *pl.*

Gestikulation /gɛstikulaˈtsi̯oːn/ *die;* **~, ~en** gesticulation

gestikulieren /gɛstikuˈliːrən/ *itr. V.* gesticulate

gestimmt
A *2. Part. v.* **stimmen**
B *Adj.* **freudig/heiter ~:** in a joyful/cheerful mood *pred.*

Gestimmtheit *die;* **~, ~en** mood

Gestirn *das;* **~[e]s, ~e** heavenly body; (Stern) star

gestirnt *Adj.* (geh.) starry

gestoben /gəˈʃtoːbn̩/ *2. Part. v.* **stieben**

Gestöber /gəˈʃtøːbɐ/ *das;* **~s, ~:** snowstorm

gestochen /gəˈʃtɔxn̩/
A *2. Part. v.* **stechen**
B *Adj.* **eine ~e Handschrift** extremely neat *or* careful handwriting
C *adv.* **~ scharfe Bilder** crystal clear photographs

gestohlen /gəˈʃtoːlən/
A *2. Part. v.* **stehlen**
B *Adj.* **der/das kann mir ~ bleiben** (ugs.) he can

get lost (coll.)/you can keep it (coll.)

Gestöhne *das;* ~s groaning

gestorben /gəˈʃtɔrbn̩/ *2. Part. v.* **sterben**

gestört /gəˈʃtøːɐ̯t/
A *2. Part. v.* **stören**
B *Adj.* disturbed; **ein ~es Verhältnis zu jmdm./etw. haben** have a disturbed relationship with sb./sth.; **geistig ~ sein** be mentally disturbed *or* unbalanced

gestoßen *2. Part. v.* **stoßen**

Gestotter /gəˈʃtɔtɐ/ *das;* ~s (ugs., meist abwertend) stuttering; stammering; **das ~ des Motors** (fig.) the spluttering of the engine

Gestrampel *das;* ~s (ugs.) kicking about; (beim Radfahren) pedalling

Gesträuch /gəˈʃtrɔyç/ *das;* **~[e]s, ~e** shrubbery; bushes *pl.*

gestreckt
A *2. Part. v.* **strecken**
B *Adj.* full ‹*gallop*›; 180° ‹*angle*›; flat ‹*trajectory*›

gestreift
A *2. Part. v.* **streifen**
B *Adj.* striped; **längs ~:** with vertical stripes *postpos.*; vertically striped; ‹*material*› with lengthwise stripes; **quer ~:** diagonally striped; (horizontal) horizontally striped

Gestreite *das;* ~s (ugs.) quarrelling; squabbling; bickering

gestreng *Adj.* (veralt.) strict; severe; stern

gestresst
A *2. Part. v.* **stressen**
B *Adj.* stressed; stressful ‹*life*›

gestrichen
A *2. Part. v.* **streichen**
B *Adj.* level ‹*measure*›; **ein ~er Teelöffel [Zucker** *usw.***]** a level teaspoon[ful] [of sugar *etc.*]
C *adv.* **~ voll** full to the brim; *s. auch* **Hose 2; Nase 2**

gestrig /ˈgɛstrɪç/ *Adj.* yesterday's; **der ~e Abend** yesterday evening; (spät) last night; **der ~e Tag** yesterday; **unser ~es Gespräch** our conversation yesterday; **die ewig Gestrigen** (fig.) those who live in the past

gestritten /gəˈʃtrɪtn̩/ *2. Part. v.* **streiten**

Gestrüpp /gəˈʃtrʏp/ *das;* **~[e]s, ~e** undergrowth

gestuft
A *2. Part. v.* **stufen**
B *Adj.* stepped ‹*gable, façade*›; terraced ‹*landscape, slope*›; graduated ‹*colours, shades*›; (fig.: ab~) staggered ‹*working hours*›

Gestühl /gəˈʃtyːl/ *das;* **~[e]s, ~e** seats *pl.*; (Kirchen~) pews *pl.*

Gestümper /gəˈʃtʏmpɐ/ *das;* ~s (ugs. abwertend) ham-fisted performance; **das ist kein literarisches Kunstwerk, das ist abgeschmacktes ~:** that's no work of literature, it's banal rubbish; **ihr ~ auf der Violine** her amateurish efforts *pl.* on the violin

gestunken /gəˈʃtʊŋkn̩/ *2. Part. v.* **stinken**

Gestus /ˈgɛstʊs/ *der;* ~ (geh.) **1** (Attitüde) air **2** ▸ **Gestik**

Gestüt /gəˈʃtyːt/ *das;* **~[e]s, ~e** stud [farm]

Gesuch /gəˈzuːx/ *das;* **~[e]s, ~e** request (**um** for); (Antrag) application (**um** for); **ein ~ einreichen/zurückziehen** submit/withdraw a request/an application

Gesuchsteller /-ʃtɛlɐ/ *der;* **~s, ~, Gesuchstellerin** *die;* **~, ~nen** (Amtsspr. veralt.) petitioner

gesucht
A *2. Part. v.* **suchen**
B *Adj.* **1** (begehrt) [much] sought-after; **einer der ~esten Dirigenten** one of the most sought-after conductors **2** (gekünstelt) affected ‹*style*›; laboured ‹*expression*›; far-fetched ‹*comparison*›
C *adv.* ‹*express oneself*› affectedly

Gesudel /gəˈzuːdl̩/ *das;* ~s (abwertend) scrawl; (fig.: schlechte Literatur) rubbish

Gesülze /gəˈzʏltsə/ *das;* ~s (salopp) drivel (**von** about ‹*topic*›, from ‹*speaker*›)

Gesumm /gəˈzʊm/ *das;* **~[e]s** buzzing; humming

Gesums /gəˈzʊms/ *das;* **~es** (ugs.) fuss (**um** about); **dein ~:** the fuss you make

gesund /gəˈzʊnt/; **gesünder** /gəˈzʏndɐ/, *seltener:* **gesunder, gesündest...** /gəˈzʏndəst.../, *seltener:* **gesundest...** *Adj.* **1** ▸ ℹ **S. 439** healthy; healthy, strong ‹*constitution*›; (fig.) viable, financially sound ‹*company, business*›; **wieder ~ werden** get better; recover; **~ sein** ‹*person*› be healthy; (im Augenblick) be in good health; **jmdn. ~ pflegen** nurse sb. back to health; **~ und munter** hale and hearty; **frisch und ~:** fit and well; **aber sonst bist du ~?** (ugs. iron.) [are] you sure you're feeling all right? (coll.); **bleib ~!** look after yourself!; **das ist ~ für ihn** (fig.) that will do him good **2** (natürlich, normal) healthy ‹*mistrust, ambition, etc.*›; sound ‹*construction*›; healthy, sound ‹*attitude, approach*›; **der ~e Menschenverstand** common sense

gesund-, Gesund-: **~|beten** *tr. V.* **jmdn. ~beten** heal sb. *or* restore sb. to health by prayer; **~beten** *das;* **~~s** faith healing *no art.*; healing by prayer; **~beter** *der;* **~~s, ~~, ~beterin** *die;* **~~, ~~nen** faith healer; **~beterei** *die;* **~beterei** ▸ **~beten**; **~brunnen** *der* (geh.) **die Beschäftigung mit der Jugend/dieser Urlaub ist für mich der reinste ~brunnen** working with young people keeps me young and healthy/this holiday is doing wonders to restore me to health

Gesunde /gəˈzʊndə/ *der/die; adj. Dekl.* healthy person

gesunden *itr. V.; mit sein* ‹*person*› recover, get well, regain one's health; ‹*tissue*› heal; (fig.) ‹*economy etc.*› recover

Gesundheit *die;* ~ ▸ ℹ **S. 439** health; **von zarter ~ sein** have a delicate constitution; **bei bester ~ sein** be in the best of health; **auf jmds. ~** (*Akk.*) **trinken/anstoßen** drink sb.'s health; **~ und ein langes Leben!** your very good health!; (als Geburtstagswunsch) many happy returns!; **~!** (ugs.: Zuruf beim Niesen) bless you!

gesundheitlich
A *Adj.* **~e Betreuung** health care; **sein ~er Zustand** [the state of] his health; **aus ~en Gründen** for reasons of health
B *adv.* **wie geht es Ihnen ~?** how are you?; **~ geht es ihm nicht sehr gut** he is not in very good health

gesundheits-, Gesundheits-: **~amt** *das* [local] public health department; **~apostel** *der* (spött.) health fanatic; **~attest** *das* certificate of health; health certificate; **~behörde** *die* public health authority; **~fabrik** *die* (abwertend) *large, impersonal hospital dispensing assembly-line treatment;* **~fördernd** *Adj.* conducive to health *postpos.*; good for one's health *postpos.*; healthy ‹*food, diet, climate, etc.*›; **~fürsorge** *die* medical welfare services *pl.*; **~gefährdung** *die* risk to health; **~halber** *Adv.* for reasons of health; for health reasons; **~lehre** *die* ▸ **Hygiene 3**; **~lenker** *der* (ugs. scherzh.) 'sit up and beg' handlebars; **~minister** *der,* **~ministerin** *die* minister of health; Health Secretary (Brit.); **~ministerium** *das* ministry of health; **~pflege** *die* health care; **~reform** *die* (ugs.) health service reform; **~schaden** *der* ▸ ℹ **S. 439** damage *no pl., no indef. art.* to [one's] health; **das kann ~schäden bewirken** that can damage one's health; **einen bleibenden ~schaden davontragen** suffer permanent damage to one's health as a result; **trotz eines leichten ~schadens ...** despite a slight disability ...; **~schädlich** *Adj.* detrimental to [one's] health *postpos.*; unhealthy; **Rauchen ist ~schädlich** smoking can damage your health; **~schutz** *der* (DDR) [system of] preventive health care; **~system** *das* health-care system; **~vorsorge** *die* health care; **~wesen** *das* [public] health service; **~zeugnis** *das* certificate of health; health certificate; **~zustand** *der* state of health

gesund-: **~|machen** *refl. V.* (ugs.) make a pile (coll.); **~|schreiben** *unr. tr. V.* pass ‹*person*› fit; **~|schrumpfen** *itr.* (*auch refl.*) *V.* (ugs.) ‹*industry, firm*› be slimmed down; **eine Firma ~schrumpfen lassen** slim a firm down; **~|stoßen** *unr. refl. V.* (salopp) grow fat (coll.)

Gesundung *die;* ~ (geh., auch fig.) recovery

gesungen /gəˈzʊŋən/ *2. Part. v.* **singen**

gesunken /gəˈzʊŋkn̩/ *2. Part. v.* **sinken**

Gesurre /gəˈzʊrə/ *das;* ~s (von Insekten) buzzing; (einer Filmkamera) whirring

GESVP *Abk.* (EU) = **gemeinsame europäische Sicherheits- und Verteidigungspolitik** CESDP

Getäfel /gəˈtɛːfl̩/ *das;* ~s panelling

getäfelt *2. Part. v.* **täfeln**

getan /gəˈtaːn/ *2. Part. v.* **tun**

Getändel *das;* ~s (veralt.) dalliance

geteilt
A *2. Part. v.* **teilen**
B *Adj.* (Bot.) **~e Blätter** compound leaves

Getier *das;* **~[e]s** (geh.) **1** (Tiere) animals *pl.*; wildlife **2** (einzelnes Tier) animal/insect

getigert /gəˈtiːgɐt/ *Adj.* **1** (mit ungleichen Flecken) patterned like a tiger *postpos.* **2** (mit Querstreifen) striped

Getobe *das;* ~s romping *or* charging about

Getose *das;* ~s roar

Getöse *das;* ~s [thunderous] roar; (von vielen Menschen) din; **mit ~:** with a roar

getragen
A *2. Part. v.* **tragen**
B *Adj.* solemn ‹*music, voice, etc.*›
C *adv.* solemnly

Geträller *das;* ~s (von Vögeln) trilling; (von Menschen) warbling

Getrampel *das;* ~s (ugs.) tramping; (als Zeichen des Beifalls, der Ablehnung) stamping

Getränk /gəˈtrɛŋk/ *das;* **~[e]s, ~e** drink; beverage (formal)

Getränke-: **~automat** *der* drinks machine *or* dispenser; **~bude** *die* drinks stand *or* kiosk; **~karte** *die* list of beverages; (in einem Restaurant) wine list; **~stand** *der* drinks stand *or* kiosk; **~steuer** *die: tax on alcoholic drinks*

Getrappel *das;* ~s (von Hufen, Pferden) clatter; (von Füßen) patter; **das ~ der Tänzer** the patter of the dancers' feet

Getratsch[e] *das;* ~s (ugs. abwertend) gossip; gossiping

getrauen *refl. V.* dare; **sich [nicht]** od. (seltener:) **sich** (*Dat.*) **es [nicht] ~, etw. zu tun** [not] dare to do sth.; **ich getraue mich nicht über die Straße** I dare not cross the road; **ich getraue mir den doppelten Salto noch nicht** I dare not attempt the double somersault yet

Getreide /gəˈtraidə/ *das;* ~s grain; corn; **~ anbauen** grow cereals *pl. or* grain

Getreide-: **~anbau** *der* growing of cereals *or* grain; **~art** *die* kind of grain *or* cereal; **~börse** *die* corn exchange; **~ernte** *die* grain harvest; **~feld** *das* cornfield; **~flocken** *Pl.* cereal flakes; **~halm** *der* corn stalk; **~handel** *der* corn trade; **~korn** *das* [cereal] grain; **~land** *das* **1** corn-growing country; **2** (Ackerland) corn land; **~produkt** *das* cereal *or* grain product; **~schädling** *der* grain pest; **~speicher** *der* grain silo

getrennt
A *2. Part. v.* **trennen**
B *Adj.* separate; **~e Kasse führen** pay separately
C *adv.* ‹*pay*› separately; ‹*sleep*› in separate rooms; **[von jmdm.] ~ leben** live apart [from sb.]

Getrennt·schreibung *die: writing a lexical item as two or more separate words;* **beachten Sie bitte die ~ von „so viel"** please remember that 'so viel' is written as two words

getreten *2. Part. v.* **treten**

getreu
A *Adj.* (geh.) **1** (genau entsprechend) exact ‹*wording*›; true, faithful ‹*image*› **2** (treu) faithful, loyal ‹*friend, servant*›; **~ bis in den Tod** faithful unto death
B *adv.* (geh.) **1** (genau entsprechend) ‹*report, describe*› faithfully, accurately **2** (treu) faithfully, loyally
C *präpositional* (geh.) **~ einem Versprechen/einer Abmachung handeln** act in accordance with a promise/an agreement

Getreue *der/die; adj. Dekl.* faithful *or* loyal follower

g

getreulich *Adv.* ▸**getreu B**

Getriebe *das;* **~s, ~** 1 gears *pl.*; (in einer Maschine) gear system; (~kasten) gearbox 2 (Betriebsamkeit) hustle and bustle

Getriebe-: ~bremse *die* transmission brake; **~gehäuse** *das* gearbox casing; **~kasten** *der* gearbox

getrieben *2. Part. v.* **treiben**

Getriebe·schaden *der* gearbox damage

Getriller /gəˈtrɪlɐ/ *das;* **~s** trilling

getroffen *2. Part. v.* **treffen, triefen**

getrogen /gəˈtroːgn̩/ *2. Part. v.* **trügen**

Getrommel *das;* **~s** (ugs.) drumming

getrost

A *Adj.* confident; **sei ~!** take heart!

B *adv.* 1 (zuversichtlich) confidently 2 (ruhig) **du kannst das Kind ~ allein lassen** you need have no qualms about leaving the child on its own; **du kannst mir ~ glauben, dass ...** you can take my word for it that ...; **man kann ~ behaupten, dass ...** one can safely say that ...

getrüffelt *Adj.* ‹*pheasant etc.*› [served *or* garnished] with truffles

getrunken *2. Part. v.* **trinken**

Getto /ˈgɛto/ *das;* **~s, ~s** ghetto

Getto·bildung *die* creation of a ghetto/of ghettos

Getue /gəˈtuːə/ *das;* **~s** (ugs. abwertend) fuss (**um** about); **ein ~ machen** kick up *or* make a fuss; (sich wichtig machen) put on airs

Getümmel /gəˈtʏml̩/ *das;* **~s** tumult; **das fröhliche/dichte ~:** the merry/crowded bustle; **mitten im dichtesten** *od.* **dicksten ~:** in the thick of it

getupft

A *2. Part. v.* **tupfen**

B *Adj.* speckled ‹*garment, fabric, etc.*›

Getuschel *das;* **~s** (ugs.) whispering

geübt /gəˈlyːpt/

A *2. Part. v.* **üben**

B *Adj.* experienced, accomplished, proficient ‹*horseman, speaker, etc.*›; trained, practised ‹*eye, ear*›; **in etw.** (*Dat.*) **~ sein** be proficient at sth.

Gevatter /gəˈfatɐ/ *der;* **~s** *od.* (älter:) **~n, ~n** (veralt.) 1 (Pate) godfather; **[bei jmdm.] zu ~ stehen** act as *or* be [sb.'s] godfather; **jmdn. zu ~ bitten** ask sb. to act as *or* be godfather; **~ Tod** (dicht. veralt.) (im Märchen) Godfather Death; (fig.) the Grim Reaper; **bei etw. ~ stehen** (scherzh.) be the inspiration behind sth. 2 (veralt., noch scherzh.) **Grüß Gott, ~!** greetings, friend!

Gevatterin *die;* **~, ~nen** 1 (Patin) godmother 2 (veralt., noch scherzh.) ▸**Gevatter 2**

Geviert *das;* **~[e]s, ~e** 1 (veralt.) ▸**Quadrat** 2 (Druckw.) quadrat; quad

GEW *Abk.* = **Gewerkschaft Erziehung und Wissenschaft** Educators' Union

Gewächs /gəˈvɛks/ *das;* **~es, ~e** 1 (Pflanze) plant 2 (Weinsorte) wine; (Weinjahrgang) vintage 3 ▸ i **S. 439** (Med.: Geschwulst) growth

gewachsen

A *2. Part. v.* **wachsen**

B *in* **jmdm./einer Sache ~ sein** be a match for sb./be equal to sth.

Gewächs·haus *das* greenhouse; glasshouse; (Treibhaus) hothouse

gewagt

A *2. Part. v.* **wagen**

B *Adj.* 1 (kühn) daring; (gefährlich) risky 2 (fast anstößig) risqué ‹*joke, song, etc.*›; daring ‹*neckline etc.*›

gewählt

A *2. Part. v.* **wählen**

B *Adj.* refined, elegant ‹*style, manner of expression, etc.*›; refined ‹*taste*›

C *adv.* in a refined manner; elegantly

Gewähltheit *die;* **~** (des Ausdrucks) refinement; (der Kleidung) elegance

gewahr /gəˈvaːɐ̯/ *in* **jmdn./etw.** *od.* (geh.) **jmds./einer Sache ~ werden** catch sight of sb./sth.; **etw.** (*Akk.*) *od.* (geh.) **einer Sache** (*Gen.*) **~ werden** (etw. erkennen, feststellen) become aware of sth.

Gewähr /gəˈvɛːɐ̯/ *die;* **~:** guarantee; **für etw. ~ leisten/die ~ geben** guarantee sth.; **die ~ für etw. übernehmen/bieten** guarantee sth.; **keine ~ übernehmen** be unable to guarantee sth.; **die Angaben erfolgen ohne ~:** no responsibility is accepted for the accuracy of this information; **ohne ~** (auf Fahrplänen usw.) subject to change

gewahren *tr. V.* (geh.) become aware of

gewähren

A *tr. V.* 1 (zugestehen) give; grant, give ‹*asylum, credit, loan*›; **jmdm. einen Aufschub ~:** grant *or* allow sb. a period of grace 2 (erfüllen) grant; **jmdm. seinen Wunsch/seine Bitte** *usw.* **~:** grant sb.'s wish/request *etc.* 3 (bieten) offer ‹*advantage*›; give ‹*pleasure, joy*›

B *itr. V.: in* **jmdn. ~ lassen** let sb. do as he/she likes; **lass ihn nur ~:** leave him alone

gewähr·leisten *tr. V.* guarantee; ensure ‹*safety*›

Gewähr·leistung *die* 1 guarantee; (von Sicherheit) ensuring 2 ▸**Mängelhaftung**

Gewahrsam /gəˈvaːɐ̯zaːm/ *der;* **~s** 1 (Obhut) safe keeping; **etw. in ~ nehmen/behalten** take sth. into safe keeping/keep sth. safe; **jmdm. etw. in ~ geben** give sth. to sb. for safe keeping 2 (Haft) custody; **jmdn. in ~ bringen** take sb. into custody; **jmdn. in polizeilichen ~ bringen** hand sb. over to the police; **sich in [polizeilichem] ~ befinden** be in [police] custody

Gewährs-: ~mann *der; Pl.* **~männer** *od.* **~leute, ~person** *die* informant; source

Gewährung *die;* **~** ▸**gewähren A:** granting; giving; offering

Gewalt /gəˈvalt/ *die;* **~, ~en** 1 (Macht, Befugnis) power; **die elterliche/richterliche ~:** parental/judicial power *or* authority; **jmdn. in seiner ~ haben** have sb. in one's power; **jmdn./ein Land in seine ~ bekommen/bringen** catch sb./bring a country under one's control; **in** *od.* **unter jmds. ~** (*Dat.*) **stehen** be in sb.'s power; **die ~ über sein Fahrzeug verlieren** (fig.) lose control of one's vehicle; **sich/seine Beine in der ~ haben** have oneself under control/have control over one's legs 2 (Willkür) force; **der ~ weichen** yield to force; **etw. mit ~ zu erreichen suchen** try to achieve sth. by force; **sich** (*Dat.*) **~ antun [müssen]** [have to] force oneself; **er versuchte mit aller ~, seinen Ehrgeiz zu befriedigen** he did everything he could to achieve his ambition; **etw. mit [aller] ~ wollen** want sth. desperately 3 (körperliche Kraft) force; violence; **~ anwenden** use force *or* violence; **etw. mit ~ öffnen** force sth. open; **mit roher/brutaler ~:** with brute force; **einer Frau ~ antun** (geh. verhüll.) violate a woman 4 (geh.: elementare Kraft) force; **die ~ der Leidenschaft/Rede** (fig.) the power of passion/oratory; **höhere ~ [sein]** [be] an act of God; **im Falle höherer ~:** in the case of an act of God/acts of God

gewalt-, Gewalt-: ~akt *der* act of violence; **~androhung** *die* threat of violence; **~anwendung** *die* use of force *or* violence; **~bereit** *Adj.* ready to use violence *postpos.*; **~einwirkung** *die:* **keinerlei Spuren von ~einwirkung aufweisen** show no signs of violence; **durch ~einwirkung sterben** die as a result of violence

Gewalten-: ~teilung *die,* **~trennung** *die* separation of powers

Gewalt-: ~herrschaft *die* tyranny; despotism; **~herrscher** *der,* **~herrscherin** *die* tyrant; despot

gewaltig

A *Adj.* 1 (immens) enormous, huge ‹*sum, amount, difference, loss*›; tremendous ‹*progress*› 2 (imponierend) mighty, huge, massive ‹*wall, pillar, building, rock*›; monumental ‹*literary work etc.*›; mighty ‹*spectacle of nature*› 3 (mächtig; auch fig.) powerful

B *adv.* (ugs.: sehr, überaus) **sich ~ irren/täuschen** be very much mistaken; **es wundert mich/imponiert mir ~:** I'm amazed/tremendously impressed; **etw. ist ~ gestiegen/gesunken** sth. has risen/dropped sharply

-gewaltige *der/die; adj. Dekl.* boss; **die Zeitungs~n** the press barons

Gewaltigkeit *die;* **~** (von Mauern, Felsen, Gebäuden usw.) mightiness; massiveness

gewalt-, Gewalt-: ~kur *die* (ugs.) drastic measures *pl. or* methods *pl.*; drastic treatment *no indef. art.*; **~los** A *Adj.* non-violent; B *adv.* without violence; **~losigkeit** *die;* **~~:** non-violence; **~marsch** *der* forced march; **~maßnahme** *die* violent measure; **er schreckte vor ~maßnahmen nicht zurück** he was not afraid to use force; **~mensch** *der* the brutal person; brute

gewaltsam

A *Adj.* forcible ‹*expulsion*›; enforced ‹*separation*›; violent ‹*death*›; **ein ~es Ende nehmen** meet a violent death

B *adv.* forcibly; **~ die Tür öffnen** open the door by force; **sich ~ zurückhalten/wach halten** exercise the utmost restraint/force oneself to keep awake; **~ ums Leben kommen** meet a violent death

Gewaltsamkeit *die;* **~:** violence

gewalt-, Gewalt-: ~streich *der* bold surprise action; **~tat** *die* ▸**~verbrechen**; **~tätig** *Adj.* violent; **~tätigkeit** *die* 1 (gewalttätige Art) violence; 2 ▸**~akt**; **~verbrechen** *das* crime of violence; **~verbrecher** *der,* **~verbrecherin** *die* violent criminal; **~verzicht** *der* renunciation of the use of force; **~verzichts·abkommen** *das* non-aggression treaty

Gewand *das;* **~[e]s, Gewänder** /gəˈvɛndɐ/ (geh.) robe; gown; (Abendkleid) gown; **geistliche Gewänder** vestments; **im neuen ~** (fig.) dressed up as new; **ab nächster Woche erscheint die Zeitung in einem neuen ~** (fig.) from next week the newspaper will have a new look

gewandet *Adj.* (veralt./scherzh.) clad; apparelled (arch.)

Gewand-: ~haus *das* (hist.) cloth hall; **~meister** *der* wardrobe master; **~meisterin** *die* wardrobe mistress

gewandt /gəˈvant/

A *2. Part. v.* **wenden**

B *Adj.* skilful; (körperlich) agile; expert ‹*skier*›; **ein ~es Auftreten/~e Umgangsformen** an easy, confident manner/easy social manners

C *adv.* skilfully; (körperlich) agilely

Gewandtheit *die;* **~** ▸**gewandt B:** skill; skilfulness; agility; expertness; easiness

gewann /gəˈvan/ *1. u. 3. Pers. Sg. Prät. v.* **gewinnen**

gewärtig /gəˈvɛrtɪç/ *in* **einer Sache** (*Gen.*) **~ sein** (geh.) be prepared for sth.; **~ sein, dass ...** expect that ...

gewärtigen *tr. V.* (geh.) (erwarten) expect; (gefasst sein auf) be prepared for

Gewäsch /gəˈvɛʃ/ *das;* **~[e]s** (ugs. abwertend) twaddle; garbage (Amer. coll.)

gewaschen *2. Part. v.* **waschen**

Gewässer /gəˈvɛsɐ/ *das;* **~s, ~** stretch of water; **ein fließendes/stehendes ~:** a stretch of running/standing water; **sich in arktische ~ wagen** venture into Arctic waters

Gewässer-: ~kunde *die* hydrography *no art.*; **~schutz** *der* prevention of water pollution

Gewebe *das;* **~s, ~** 1 (Stoff) fabric 2 ▸ i **S. 435** (Med., Biol.) tissue

Gewebe·probe *die* (Med., Biol.) tissue sample

Gewebs-: ~transplantation *die,* **~verpflanzung** *die* (Med.) tissue graft

Gewehr /gəˈveːɐ̯/ *das;* **~[e]s, ~e** rifle; (Schrot~) shotgun; **mit dem ~ auf jmdn./etw. zielen** aim [one's rifle/shotgun] at sb./sth.; **~ ab!** (Milit.) order arms!; **das ~ über!** (Milit.) shoulder arms!; **präsentiert das ~!** (Milit.) present arms!; **~ bei Fuß stehen** be at the ready

Gewehr-: ~feuer *das* rifle fire; **~kolben** *der* rifle/shotgun butt; **~kugel** *die* rifle bullet; **~lauf** *der* rifle/shotgun barrel; **~riemen** *der* rifle/shotgun sling; **~schloss, *~schloß** *das* lock of a rifle/shotgun; **~schuss, *~schuß** *der* rifle shot

ℹ Gewichte

1 Gramm = one gram = 0.035 ounce (oz)
1 Kilogramm = one kilogram = 2.205 pounds (lb)
1 Tonne = one tonne = 2, 205 lb *od.* 19.684 hundredweight (cwt)

Es ist zu beachten, dass das britische Pfund (**pound**) nur 454 Gramm wiegt. Dagegen ist die britische Tonne (**ton**) etwas schwerer als die metrische (1 016 kg).

Personen

Wie viel wiegen Sie?
= How much do you weigh?, What's your weight?
Ich wiege 76 Kilo
≈ I weigh 12 stone (*brit.*) *od.* 168 pounds (*amerik.*)
Er hat zugenommen
= He has put on weight
Sie hat stark abgenommen
= She has lost a lot of weight
Mit mehr als 114 Kilo hat er Übergewicht
= At over 18 stone (*brit.*) *od.* 250 pounds (*amerik.*) he is overweight

Dinge

Wie viel wiegt das Paket?
= How much does the parcel weigh?, What's the weight of the parcel?
Es wiegt ungefähr zwei Kilo
= It weighs about two kilograms,
≈ it weighs about four pounds
Mein Gepäck hat fünf Kilo Übergewicht
= My baggage is five kilograms over weight,
≈ My baggage is ten pounds over weight
A hat das gleiche Gewicht wie B
= A is the same weight as B
A und B sind gleich schwer
= A and B are the same weight
125 Gramm Leberwurst
= 125 grams of liver sausage,
≈ 4 oz of liver sausage
6 Pfund Kartoffeln
≈ 6 pounds of potatoes
They are sold by the kilo
= Sie werden kiloweise verkauft
eine 500-Gramm-Schachtel Pralinen
≈ a pound box of chocolates

Geweih /gəˈvai/ *das;* **~[e]s, ~e** antlers *pl.;* **~e/ein ~:** sets of antlers/a set of antlers

Geweih·stange *die* (Jägerspr.) beam; main trunk

gewellt
A *2. Part. v.* **wellen**
B *Adj.* wavy ‹*hair, leaves*›; undulating ‹*fields, country, putting green*›; warped ‹*floor*›

Gewerbe *das;* **~s, ~** **1** business; (Handel, Handwerk) trade; **ein dunkles/schmutziges ~:** a shady/dirty business; **in einem ~ tätig sein** be in a trade/business; **das horizontale ~** (ugs. scherzh.), **das älteste ~ der Welt** (verhüll. scherzh.) the oldest profession [in the world] (joc.) **2** (kleine Betriebe) [small and medium-sized] businesses and industries

Gewerbe·aufsicht *die: enforcement of laws governing health and safety and conditions of work*

Gewerbe·aufsichts·amt *das* ≈ factory inspectorate (*authority with responsibility for* **Gewerbeaufsicht**)

Gewerbe-: ~betrieb *der* (des Handels) commercial enterprise; business; (der Industrie) industrial enterprise; business; **~freiheit** *die* right to carry on a business *or* trade; **~gebiet** *das* trading estate; **~lehrer** *der,* **~lehrerin** *die* teacher in a trade school; **~ordnung** *die* laws *pl.* governing trade and industry; **~park** *der* business park; **~schein** *der* licence to carry on a business *or* trade; **~schule** *die* trade school; **~steuer** *die* trade tax; **~tätigkeit** *die* business activities *pl.;* **~treibende** *der/die; adj. Dekl.* tradesman/tradeswoman; **~zweig** *der* branch of trade

gewerblich
A *Adj.* commercial; business *attrib.;* (industriell) industrial; trade *attrib.* ‹*union, apprentice*›; **~e Nutzung** use for commercial *or* business/industrial purposes
B *adv.* **~ tätig sein** work; **etw. ~ nutzen** use sth. for commercial *or* business/industrial purposes

gewerbs·mäßig
A *Adj.* professional; **~e Unzucht** prostitution; **ein ~er Hehler** a receiver of stolen goods
B *adv.* **etw. ~ betreiben** do sth. professionally *or* for gain

Gewerkschaft /gəˈvɛrkʃaft/ *die;* **~, ~en** **1** trade union **2** (veralt.: Bergbauunternehmen) *mining company whose capital is divided into shares of no par value*

Gewerkschaft[l]er *der;* **~s, ~, Gewerkschaft[l]erin** *die;* **~, ~nen** trade unionist

gewerkschaftlich
A *Adj.* [trade] union *attrib.;* ‹*rights, duties*› as a [trade] union member; **~er Vertrauensmann/~e Vertrauensfrau** shop steward; **der ~e Kampf** the struggle of the trade union movement
B *adv.* **~ organisiert sein** belong to a [trade] union; **sich ~ engagieren** devote oneself to trade union work

gewerkschafts-, Gewerkschafts-: ~arbeit *die* work for *or* on behalf of the/a [trade] union; **~bewegung** *die* [trade] union movement; **~boss,** ***~boß** *der* (ugs. abwertend) [trade] union boss; **~bund** *der* federation of trade unions; ≈ Trades Union Congress (Brit.); ≈ AFL-CIO (Amer.); **~eigen** *Adj.* owned by a [trade] union *postpos.;* **~führer** *der,* **~führerin** *die* [trade] union leader; **~funktionär** *der,* **~funktionärin** *die* [trade] union official; **~kongress,** ***~kongreß** *der* ▸ **~tag**; **~mitglied** *das* member of a [trade] union; **~tag** *der* [trade] union conference

Gewese *das;* **~s** (ugs.) fuss; **ein großes ~ um etw. machen** kick up *or* make a lot of fuss about sth.

gewesen
A *2. Part. v.* **sein¹**
B *Adj.* (bes. österr.) former

gewichen *2. Part. v.* **weichen**

gewichst /gəˈvɪkst/
A *2. Part. v.* **wichsen**
B *Adj.* (ugs.) smart

Gewicht /gəˈvɪçt/ *das;* **~[e]s, ~e** ▸ℹ **S. 315** (auch Physik, auch fig.) weight; **ein ~ von 75 kg/ein großes ~ haben** weigh 75 kg/be very heavy; **das zulässige ~:** the maximum permitted weight; the weight limit; **das spezifische ~** (Physik) the specific gravity; **sein ~ halten** stay the same weight; **etw. nach ~ verkaufen** sell sth. by weight; **seine Meinung/eine adlige Abstammung hat noch großes ~:** his opinion still carries a great deal of weight/it still counts for a great deal to be of noble descent; **einer Sache** (*Dat.*) **[kein] ~ beimessen** *od.* **beilegen** attach [no] importance to sth.; **sein ganzes ~ in die Waagschale werfen** throw one's whole weight behind it; **auf etw.** (*Akk.*) **~ legen** attach importance to sth.; **[nicht] ins ~ fallen** be of [no] consequence

gewichten *tr. V.* **1** (Statistik) weight **2** (Schwerpunkte festsetzen) evaluate

Gewicht-: ~heben *das;* **~~s** weightlifting; **~heber** *der;* **~~s, ~~, ~heberin** *die;* **~~, ~~nen** weightlifter

gewichtig *Adj.* **1** (veralt.: schwer) heavy; weighty; **jmd. ist ~** (scherzh.) sb. is impressively large **2** (bedeutungsvoll) weighty, important ‹*reason, question, decision, etc.*›; **eine ~e Persönlichkeit** an important person *or* figure; **~ tun** act pompously; **ein ~es Gesicht machen** (iron.) put on *or* assume an air of importance

Gewichtigkeit *die;* **~** ▸ **gewichtig 2**: importance; weightiness

gewichts-, Gewichts-: ~abnahme *die* decrease *or* reduction in weight; (**~verlust**) loss of weight; **~angabe** *die* indication of weight; **~klasse** *die* **1** (Sport) weight [division *or* class]; **2** (Kaufmannsspr.) weight class; **Eier nach ~klassen sortieren** grade eggs according to weight; **~los** *Adj.* **1** ▸ **schwerelos A**; **2** (bedeutungslos) lacking in substance *postpos.;* **~problem** *das* weight problem; **~verlagerung** *die* shift *or* transfer of weight; (fig.) shift in *or* of emphasis; **~verlust** *der* loss of weight; **~zunahme** *die* increase in weight

Gewichtung *die;* **~, ~en** evaluation

gewieft /gəˈviːft/ *Adj.* (ugs.) cunning; wily

gewiegt
A *2. Part. v.* **wiegen²**
B *Adj.* ▸ **gewieft**

Gewieher /gəˈviːɐ/ *das;* **~s** **1** (Wiehern) neighing **2** (salopp: Gelächter) guffawing; braying laughter

gewiesen *2. Part. v.* **weisen**

gewillt /gəˈvɪlt/ *Adj.:* in **~/nicht ~ sein, etw. zu tun** be willing/unwilling to do sth.

Gewimmel *das;* **~s** throng; milling crowd; (von Insekten) teeming mass

Gewimmer *das;* **~s** whimpering

Gewinde *das;* **~s, ~** **1** (Technik) thread **2** (veralt.: Girlande) garland

Gewinde-: ~bohrer *der* [screw] tap; **~gang** *der* turn [of a thread]; **~schneiden** *das;* **~~s** thread-cutting; (innen) tapping; **~stift** *der* grub screw

Gewinn /gəˈvɪn/ *der;* **~[e]s, ~e** **1** (Reinertrag) profit; **aus etw. ~ schlagen** *od.* **ziehen** make a profit out of sth.; **mit ~ wirtschaften** operate at a profit *or* profitably; **etw. mit ~ verkaufen** sell sth. at a profit **2** (Preis einer Lotterie) prize; (beim Wetten, Kartenspiel usw.) winnings *pl.;* **die ~e auslosen** draw the winners *or* winning numbers; **jedes zweite Los ist ein ~:** every other ticket is a winner **3** (Nutzen) gain; profit; **das war ein großer ~ für uns** we gained a great deal *or* profited greatly from it; **der neue Spieler ist ein [großer] ~ für unsere Mannschaft** the new player is a valuable addition to our team **4** (Sieg) win; **auf ~ stehen** (Schach) be in a winning position

gewinn-, Gewinn-: ~anteil *der* (Wirtsch.) share of the profits; **~beteiligung** *die* (Wirtsch.) profit sharing; (Betrag) profit-sharing bonus; **gegen ~beteiligung** in return for a share of the profits; **~bringend** *Adj.* **1** profitable; lucrative; **2** (nutzbringend) profitable; valuable ‹*knowledge, information*›; **~chance** *die* chance of winning; **~einbruch** *der* (Wirtsch.) slump in profits

gewinnen /gəˈvɪnən/
A *unr. tr. V.* **1** (siegen in) win ‹*contest, race, etc.*›; **es [nicht] über sich ~, etw. zu tun** (geh. veralt.) [not] bring oneself to do sth.; *s. auch* **Spiel 2** **2** (erringen, erreichen, erhalten) gain, win ‹*respect, sympathy, etc.*›; gain ‹*time, lead, influence, validity, confidence*›; win ‹*prize*›; **Klarheit über etw.** (*Akk.*) **~:** become clear in one's mind about sth.; **wie gewonnen, so zerronnen** (Spr.) easy come, easy go; *s. auch* **Abstand 3**; **Oberhand** **3** (Unterstützung erlangen) **jmdn. für etw. ~:** win sb. over [to sth.]; **jmdn. als Kunden/Freund ~:** win sb. as a customer/friend **4** (abbauen, fördern) mine, extract ‹*coal, ore, metal*›; recover ‹*oil*› **5** (erzeugen) produce (**aus** from); (durch

Recycling) reclaim; recover

B *unr. itr. V.* [1] win (bei at); in der Lotterie ~: win [a prize] in the lottery; jedes zweite Los gewinnt! every other ticket [is] a winner! [2] (sich vorteilhaft verändern) improve [3] (zunehmen) an Höhe/Fahrt ~: gain height/gain *or* pick up speed; an Bedeutung ~: gain in importance

gewinnend
A *Adj.* winning, engaging, winsome ‹*manner, smile, way*›; charming ‹*manners*›
B *adv.* ‹*smile*› winningly, engagingly, winsomely

Gewinner *der;* ~s, ~ , **Gewinnerin** *die;* ~, ~nen winner

Gewinner·straße *die* (Sport, Jargon) auf der ~ sein be set *or* heading for victory

gewinn-, Gewinn-: ~los *das* winning ticket; ~mitnahme *die* (Börsenw.) profit-taking *no indef. art.*; ~nummer *die* winning number; ~quote *die* share of prize money; ~satz *der* (Sport) über fünf ~sätze spielen (Tennis) play the best of five sets; (Tischtennis) play the best of five games; der fünfte Satz war ihr ~satz (Tennis) she won in the fifth set; (Tischtennis) she won in the fifth game; ~spanne *die* profit margin; ~spiel *das* prize game; ~streben *das* pursuit of profit; ~sucht *die* greed for profit; ~süchtig *Adj.* greedy for profits *pred.*; in ~süchtiger Absicht (Rechtsspr.) with the intention of making unreasonably high profits; ~trächtig *Adj.* profitable; lucrative

***Gewinnummer** *die* ▸ Gewinnnummer

Gewinn-und-Verlust-Rechnung *die* (Wirtsch.) profit and loss account

Gewinnung *die;* ~ [1] (von Kohle, Erz usw.) mining; extraction; (von Öl) recovery; (von Metall aus Erz) extraction [2] (Erzeugung) production

Gewinn-: ~warnung *die* (Wirtsch.) profit[s] warning; ~zahl *die* winning number

Gewinsel *das;* ~s (abwertend) [1] whimpering; whining [2] (das Klagen, Bitten) whining

Gewirr *das;* ~[e]s [1] (wirres Knäuel) tangle [2] (Durcheinander) ein ~ von Ästen a maze of branches; ein ~ von Paragraphen a maze *or* jungle of regulations; ein ~ von Stimmen a [confused] babble of voices

Gewisper *das;* ~s whispering

gewiss, *gewiß /gəˈvɪs/
A *Adj.* [1] (nicht sehr viel/groß) certain; in gewisser Beziehung in some respects; eine gewisse Ähnlichkeit/Distanz a certain resemblance/distance; *s. auch* Etwas; Maß[1] 4 [2] (sicher) certain (+ *Gen.* of); etw. ist jmdm. ~: sb. is certain *or* sure of sth.; wir können seiner Hilfe ~ sein we can be certain *or* sure of his help; we can count on his help; man weiß nichts Gewisses nothing certain *or* definite is known
B *adv.* certainly; ja *od.* aber ~ [doch]! but of course!; du hast ~ nichts dagegen, wenn ... I'm sure you won't mind if ...; ich weiß es ganz ~: I'm sure *or* certain of it

Gewissen *das;* ~s, ~ conscience; ein gutes/schlechtes ~: a clear/guilty *or* bad conscience; ruhigen ~s etw. tun do sth. with a clear conscience; mit gutem ~: with a clear conscience; ein gutes ~ ist ein sanftes Ruhekissen (Spr.) one can sleep more easily with a clear conscience; sich (*Dat.*) kein ~ daraus machen, etw. zu tun have no scruples *or* qualms about doing sth.; etw./jmdn. auf dem ~ haben have sth./sb. on one's conscience; jmdm. ins ~ reden [, etw. zu tun] have a serious talk with sb. [and persuade him/her to do sth.]; *s. auch* Wissen

gewissenhaft
A *Adj.* conscientious
B *adv.* conscientiously

Gewissenhaftigkeit *die;* ~ conscientiousness

gewissen·los
A *Adj.* conscienceless; unscrupulous; er ist vollkommen ~: he is completely without conscience
B *adv.* ~ handeln act with a complete lack of conscience

Gewissenlosigkeit *die;* ~ [1] (gewissenloses Wesen) lack of conscience [2] (gewissenloses Handeln) unscrupulous act; wie konntest du eine solche ~ begehen? how could you show such a lack of conscience?

Gewissens-: ~bisse *Pl.* pangs of conscience; sich (*Dat.*) ~bisse über etw. (*Akk.*) machen have a guilty conscience about sth.; ~entscheidung *die* decision on a matter of conscience; ~frage *die* question *or* matter of conscience; matter for one's conscience; ~freiheit *die* freedom of conscience; ~gründe *Pl.* reasons of conscience; aus ~gründen for reasons of conscience; ~konflikt *der* moral conflict; ~not *die* moral dilemma; ~qual *die:* ~qual[en] agonies *pl.* of conscience

gewissermaßen *Adv.* (sozusagen) as it were; (in gewissem Sinne) to a certain extent

Gewissheit, *Gewißheit *die;* ~, ~en certainty; wir haben noch keine ~, ob ... we still do not know for certain whether ...; sich (*Dat.*) ~ verschaffen find out for certain; zur ~ werden turn into certainty

gewisslich, *gewißlich *Adv.* (veralt.) ▸ gewiss B

Gewitter /gəˈvɪtɐ/ *das;* ~s, ~ thunderstorm; (fig.) storm

Gewitter·front *die* storm front

gewitterig *Adj.* ▸ gewittrig

gewittern *itr. V.* (unpers.) es gewitterte/wird bald ~: there was/will soon be thunder and lightning

Gewitter-: ~neigung *die* likelihood of thunderstorms; ~regen *der,* ~schauer *der* thundery shower; ~sturm *der* thunderstorm; ~wolke *die* thundercloud

gewittrig /gəˈvɪtrɪç/ *Adj.* thundery; ~e Schwüle sultry heat

gewitzigt /gəˈvɪtsɪçt/ *Adj.* [1] (klüger geworden) wiser; durch Erfahrung/Schaden ~ sein have learnt from experience/one's mistakes [2] ▸ gewitzt

gewitzt /gəˈvɪtst/ *Adj.* shrewd; ein ~er Junge a smart lad

gewoben /gəˈvoːbn̩/ *2. Part. v.* weben

Gewoge *das;* ~s (von einem Kornfeld usw.) waving; (von Gedanken) surge; das ~ der Menschenmenge the surging back and forth of the crowd

gewogen
A *2. Part. v.* wiegen
B *Adj.* (geh.) well disposed, favourably inclined (+ *Dat.* towards)

Gewogenheit *die;* ~ (geh.) favourable attitude; bei aller ~, die ich Ihnen entgegenbringe, kann ich nicht ... although I'm favourably disposed towards you, I can't ...

gewöhnen /gəˈvøːnən/
A *tr. V.* jmdn. an jmdn./etw. ~: get sb. used *or* accustomed to sb./sth.; accustom sb. to sb./sth.; Kinder an Sauberkeit ~: get children used to being clean and tidy; an jmdn./etw. gewöhnt sein be used *or* accustomed to sb./sth.
B *refl. V.* sich an jmdn./etw. ~: get used *or* get *or* become accustomed to sb./sth.; accustom oneself to sb./sth.; sich daran ~ müssen, dass ... have to get used to the fact that ...

Gewohnheit /gəˈvoːnhai̯t/ *die;* ~, ~en habit; die ~ haben, etw. zu tun be in the habit of doing sth.; das ist ihm zur ~ geworden this has become a habit with him; sich (*Dat.*) etw. zur ~ machen make a habit of sth.; nach alter ~: from long-established habit; etw. aus ~ tun do sth. out of habit *or* from force of habit; die Macht der ~: the force of habit

gewohnheits-, Gewohnheits-: ~gemäß *Adv.* as is/was his/her *etc.* custom; ~mäßig A *Adj.* habitual ‹*drinker etc.*›; automatic ‹*reaction etc.*›; B *adv.* [1] (regelmäßig) habitually; [2] (einer Gewohnheit folgend) as is/was my/his *etc.* habit; ~mensch *der* creature of habit; ~recht *das* (Rechtsw.) [1] (System) common law; [2] (einzelnes Recht) established right; ~sache *die* matter *or* question of habit; ~tier *das* (scherzh.) creature of habit; der Mensch ist ein ~tier man is a creature of habit; ~trinker *der,* ~trinkerin *die* habitual drinker; ~verbrecher *der,* ~verbrecherin *die* (Rechtsw.) habitual criminal

gewöhnlich /gəˈvøːnlɪç/
A *Adj.* [1] (alltäglich) normal; ordinary; im ~en Leben in ordinary *or* everyday life; ein ~er Sterblicher an ordinary mortal [2] (gewohnt, üblich) usual; normal; customary [3] (abwertend: ordinär) common
B *adv.* [1] [für] ~: usually; normally; wie ~: as usual [2] (abwertend: ordinär) in a common way

Gewöhnlichkeit *die;* ~ (abwertend) commonness

gewohnt
A *2. Part. v.* wohnen
B *Adj.* [1] (vertraut) usual; zur ~en Zeit/Stunde at the usual *or* normal *or* customary time; in ~er *od.* auf ~e Weise in the/one's usual manner *or* way [2] etw. (*Akk.*) ~ sein be used *or* accustomed to sth.; es ~ sein, etw. zu tun be used *or* accustomed to doing sth.

gewohntermaßen *Adv.* as usual

Gewöhnung *die;* ~ [1] habituation (an + *Akk.* to) [2] (Sucht) habit; addiction

gewöhnungs·bedürftig *Adj.* which takes some getting used to *postpos.*; ~ sein take some getting used to

Gewölbe /gəˈvœlbə/ *das;* ~s, ~ vault; das blaue ~ des Himmels (fig.) the blue vault of the sky; das ~ der Burg the vaults *pl.* of the castle

Gewölk /gəˈvœlk/ *das;* ~[e]s clouds *pl.*

gewollt
A *2. Part. v.* wollen
B *Adj.* [1] (willentlich) deliberate [2] (erwünscht) desired [3] (gekünstelt) forced
C *adv.* ~ lachen/lächeln give a forced laugh/smile

gewonnen /gəˈvɔnən/ *2. Part. v.* gewinnen

geworben /gəˈvɔrbn̩/ *2. Part. v.* werben

geworfen /gəˈvɔrfn̩/ *2. Part. v.* werfen

gewrungen /gəˈvrʊŋən/ *2. Part. v.* wringen

Gewühl *das;* ~[e]s [1] milling crowd; das ~ der Menschenmassen the milling crowd [of people] [2] (das Wühlen) rooting about

gewunden *2. Part. v.* winden

gewunken /gəˈvʊŋkn̩/ (landsch.) *2. Part. v.* winken

gewünscht
A *2. Part. v.* wünschen
B *Adj.* desired; (erhofft) hoped-for

gewürfelt
A *2. Part. v.* würfeln
B *Adj.* (kariert) check; checked

Gewürge *das;* ~s [1] retching [2] (abwertend: umständliches Vorgehen) rigmarole

Gewürm /gəˈvʏrm/ *das;* ~[e]s, ~e (oft abwertend) worms *pl.*; (fig. geh.) swarm of diminutive creatures

Gewürz *das;* ~es, ~e spice; (würzende Zutat) seasoning; condiment; (Kraut) herb; verschiedene ~e various herbs *or* spices

Gewürz-: ~essig *der* ▸ Kräuteressig; ~gurke *die* pickled gherkin; ~mischung *die* mixed spices *pl.*/herbs *pl.*; ~nelke *die* clove; ~traminer *der* Gewürztraminer

Gewusel /gəˈvuːzl̩/ *das;* ~s (landsch.) ▸ Gewimmel

gewusst, *gewußt *2. Part. v.* wissen

Geysir /ˈgai̯zɪr/ *der;* ~s, ~e geyser

gez. *Abk.* = gezeichnet sgd.

gezähnt /gəˈtsɛːnt/ *Adj.* (Bot.) dentate

Gezänk /gəˈtsɛŋk/ *das;* ~[e]s, **Gezanke** /gəˈtsaŋkə/ *das;* Gezankes (abwertend) quarrelling

Gezappel *das;* ~s (ugs., oft abwertend) wriggling

Gezeiten *Pl.* tides

Gezeiten-: ~kraft·werk *das* tidal power station; ~strom *der* tidal current; ~tafel *die* tide table

Gezerre *das;* ~s wrangling

Gezeter *das;* ~s (abwertend) scolding; nagging

g

Geziefer /gəˈtsiːfɐ/ *das;* ~s (veralt.) ▸ **Ungeziefer**

geziehen /gəˈtsiːən/ *2. Part. v.* **zeihen**

gezielt

A *2. Part. v.* **zielen**

B *Adj.* well-aimed ‹*shot, throw*›; specific ‹*questions, measures, etc.*›; deliberate ‹*insult, indiscretion*›; well-directed ‹*advertising campaign*›; well-directed ‹*help*›; targeted ‹*publicity, measure*›; pointed ‹*question*›; dedicated ‹*research*›; selective ‹*purchases*›

C *adv.* ‹*proceed, act*› purposefully, in a purposeful manner; ~ **schießen** shoot with precision; (um zu töten) shoot to kill; ~ **getötet werden** be targeted and killed; ~ **nach etw. forschen** search specifically for sth.; ‹*ask*› specifically; **jmdm.** ~ **helfen** give sb. specific help

geziemen (geh. veralt.)

A *itr. V.* **jmdm. [nicht]** ~: [ill] befit sb.

B *refl. V.* be proper *or* right; **sich für jmdn.** ~: befit sb.; **es geziemt sich nicht, so mit deiner Mutter zu reden** it isn't proper *or* right for you to talk to your mother like that

geziemend (geh.)

A *Adj.* fitting; proper, due ‹*respect*›; **in ~er Weise** in a proper manner; **mit ~en Worten** with a few fitting remarks; **mit der ihr ~en Bescheidenheit** with fitting modesty

B *adv.* in a fitting manner

geziert

A *2. Part. v.* **zieren**

B *Adj.* (abwertend) affected

C *adv.* (abwertend) affectedly

Geziertheit *die;* ~ (abwertend) affectedness

Gezirp[e] *das;* ~s (oft abwertend) chirping; chirruping

gezogen /gəˈtsoːgn̩/ *2. Part. v.* **ziehen**

Gezücht *das;* ~[e]s, ~e (geh. abwertend) riffraff *pl.*; rabble

Gezüngel /gəˈtsʏŋl̩/ *das;* ~s **das** ~ **der Schlange/Schlangen** the flicking *or* darting of the snake's tongue/snakes' tongues; **das** ~ **der Flammen** (fig.) the flickering of the flames

Gezweig *das;* ~[e]s (geh.) branches *pl.*

Gezwitscher *das;* ~s twittering; chirping; chirruping

gezwungen /gəˈtsvʊŋən/

A *2. Part. v.* **zwingen**

B *Adj.* forced ‹*laugh, smile, etc.*›; stiff ‹*behaviour*›

C *adv.* ‹*laugh*› in a forced way *or* manner; ‹*behave*› stiffly

gezwungenermaßen *Adv.* of necessity; **etw.** ~ **machen** be forced to do sth.

GG *Abk.* = **Grundgesetz**

ggf. *Abk.* = **gegebenenfalls**

Ghana /ˈgaːna/ *(das);* ~s Ghana

Ghanaer *der;* ~s, ~, **Ghanaerin** *die;* ~, ~nen Ghanaian

Ghetto ▸ **Getto**

Ghostwriter /ˈgəʊstraɪtə/ *der;* ~s, ~ ghost writer; **von ~n geschrieben werden** be ghosted

gib /giːp/ *Imperativ Sg. Präsens v.* **geben**

Gibbon /ˈgɪbɔn/ *der;* ~s, ~s (Zool.) gibbon

gibst /giːpst/ *2. Pers. Sg. Präsens v.* **geben**

gibt /giːpt/ *3. Pers. Sg. Präsens v.* **geben**

Gicht[1] /gɪçt/ *die;* ~, ~en (Metall.) 1 (Öffnung) throat [of the/a furnace] 2 (Oberteil des Hochofens) top [of the/a furnace] 3 (Menge) charge

Gicht[2] *die;* ~ ▸ⓘ **S. 439** gout

gicht·brüchig *Adj.* (veralt.) gouty; **die Gichtbrüchigen** (bibl.) those that had the palsy

gichtig, gichtisch *Adj.* gouty

Gicht·knoten *der* gouty concretion

gicht·krank *Adj.* gouty

gicksen /ˈgɪksn̩/ (bes. md.)

A *itr. V.* (einen Schrei ausstoßen) squeak

B *tr. V.* (stechen, stoßen) **jmdn.** ~: jab sb.; **jmdn.** *od.* **jmdm. in die Seite** ~: jab sb. in the side

Giebel /ˈgiːbl̩/ *der;* ~s, ~ 1 gable 2 (von Portalen) pediment

Giebel-: ~**dach** *das* gable roof; ~**feld** *das* (Archit.) tympanum; ~**fenster** *das* gable window; ~**seite** *die* gable end; ~**wand** *die* gable wall

Gier /giːɐ̯/ *die;* ~ 1 greed (**nach** for); **mit solcher** ~: so greedily; ~ **nach Macht/Ruhm** lust *or* craving for power/craving for fame; ~ **nach Zigaretten** greedy desire for cigarettes; ~ **nach Leben** passionate desire for life 2 (Lüsternheit) lust

gieren[1] *itr. V.* (geh.) **nach etw.** ~: crave for sth.; **nach Macht/Rache** ~: lust for power/revenge

gieren[2] *itr. V.* (Seemannsspr.) yaw

gierig

A *Adj.* greedy; avid ‹*reader, desire*›; **nach etw.** ~ **sein** be greedy for sth.

B *adv.* greedily

Gieß·bach *der* [mountain] torrent; (nach starkem Regen) swollen [mountain] stream

gießen /ˈgiːsn̩/

A *unr. tr. V.* 1 (rinnen lassen/schütten) pour (**in** + *Akk.* into, **über** + *Akk.* over) 2 (verschütten) spill (**über** + *Akk.* over) 3 (be~) water ‹*plants, flowers, garden*› 4 cast ‹*machine part, statue, candles, etc.*›; cast, found ‹*metal*›; found ‹*glass*›; **Blei zu Kugeln** ~: cast lead into bullets

B *unr. itr. V.* 1 **ich muss im Garten noch** ~: I still have to water the garden 2 *unpers.* (ugs.) pour [with rain]; **es gießt in Strömen** it is coming down in buckets; it's raining cats and dogs

Gießer *der;* ~s, ~, **Gießerin** *die;* ~, ~nen caster; founder

Gießerei *die;* ~, ~en 1 (Betrieb) foundry 2 (Zweig der Metallindustrie) casting; founding

Gieß-: ~**form** *die* (Gießerei) [casting] mould; ~**grube** *die* (Gießerei) casting pit; ~**harz** *das* (Technik) cast resin; ~**kanne** *die* watering can

Gießkannen·prinzip *das* (scherzh.) principle of 'equal shares for all'

Gieß-: ~**kelle** *die* (Gießerei) casting ladle; ~**pfanne** *die* (Gießerei) pouring *or* teeming ladle

Gift /gɪft/ *das;* ~[e]s, ~e 1 poison; (Schlangen~) venom; **jmdm.** ~ **[ein]geben** poison sb.; ~ **[aus]legen** put poison down 2 (fig.) ~ **für jmdn./etw. sein** be extremely bad for sb./sth.; **sein** ~ **verspritzen** (ugs.) spit venom (fig.); ~ **und Galle speien** *od.* **spucken** (sehr wütend sein) be in a terrible rage; (gehässig reagieren) give vent to one's spleen; **du kannst** ~ **darauf nehmen** (ugs.) you can bet your life on it; *s. auch* **blond**

Gift-: ~**becher** *der* (hist.) cup of poison; ~**drüse** *die* (Zool.) poison gland

giften (ugs.)

A *tr. V.* (böse machen) rile (coll.); infuriate

B *refl. V.* (sich ärgern) be furious

C *itr. V.* (gehässig reden) **gegen jmdn./etw.** ~: be nasty about sb./sth.

gift-, Gift-: ~**frei** *Adj.* non-toxic; non-poisonous; ~**gas** *das* poison gas; ~**grün** *Adj.* garish green

giftig

A *Adj.* 1 poisonous; venomous, poisonous ‹*snake*›; toxic, poisonous ‹*substance, gas, chemical*› 2 (ugs.: bösartig) venomous, spiteful ‹*remark, person, words, etc.*›; venomous ‹*look*›; ~ **werden** turn nasty 3 (grell, schreiend) garish, loud ‹*colour*›

B *adv.* venomously

Gift-: ~**küche** *die* (scherzh.) chemical laboratory (*with its unpleasant products*); ~**mischer** *der,* ~**mischerin** *die;* ~~, ~~nen 1 (ugs. abwertend) maker of poisons; 2 (ugs. scherzh.: Apotheker) chemist; ~**mord** *der* [murder by] poisoning; ~**mörder** *der,* ~**mörderin** *die* poisoner; ~**müll** *der* toxic waste; ~**müll·deponie** *die* toxic [waste] tip *or* dump; ~**pfeil** *der* poisoned arrow; ~**pflanze** *die* poisonous plant; ~**pilz** *der* poisonous mushroom; [poisonous] toadstool; ~**schlange** *die* poisonous *or* venomous snake; ~**schrank** *der* poison cabinet *or* cupboard; ~**spinne** *die* poisonous spider; ~**stachel** *der* poisonous sting; ~**stoff** *der* poisonous *or* toxic substance; ~**trank** *der* (geh.) poisoned drink; ~**wolke** *die* toxic cloud; ~**zahn** *der* poison fang; ~**zwerg** *der* (ugs. abwertend) [nasty] spiteful little man

Giga- /giga-/ giga‹*hertz etc.*›

Gigant /giˈgant/ *der;* ~en, ~en 1 (geh.: Riese) giant 2 (sehr beeindruckende Sache, Person) giant; titan; ~**en der Landstraße/des Meeres** (fig.) juggernauts of the road/leviathans of the ocean

gigantisch *Adj.* gigantic; huge ‹*success*›

Gigantomanie /gigantomaˈniː/ *die;* ~ (geh.) craze for the huge and spectacular

gigantomanisch *Adj.* obsessed with spectacular size *postpos.*; ‹*building*› which reveals an obsession with spectacular size; **sich ins G~e steigern** take on absurdly huge proportions

Gigerl /ˈgiːgɐl/ *der od. das;* ~s, ~n (südd., österr. ugs.) dandy; fop

giggeln /ˈgɪgl̩n/ *itr. V.* giggle

Gigolo /ˈʒiːgolo/ *der;* ~s, ~s gigolo

Gilb /gɪlp/ *der;* ~s yellowing

Gilde /ˈgɪldə/ *die;* ~, ~n 1 (hist.) guild 2 (Interessengruppe) fraternity

gilt /gɪlt/ *3. Pers. Sg. Präsens v.* **gelten**

Gimpel /ˈgɪmpl̩/ *der;* ~s, ~ 1 (Vogel) bullfinch 2 (ugs. abwertend: einfältiger Mensch) ninny; simpleton

Gin /dʒɪn/ *der;* ~s, (Sorten:) ~s gin

Ginfizz /ˈdʒɪnfɪs/ *der;* ~, ~ gin fizz

ging /gɪŋ/ *1. u. 3. Pers. Sg. Prät. v.* **gehen**

Ginseng /ˈgɪnzɛŋ/ *der;* ~s, ~s ginseng

Ginster /ˈgɪnstɐ/ *der;* ~s, ~ broom; (Stechginster) gorse; furze

Gipfel /ˈgɪpfl̩/ *der;* ~s, ~ 1 peak; (höchster Punkt des Berges) summit; **den** ~ **besteigen/bezwingen** climb the peak/conquer the peak *or* summit 2 (Höhepunkt) height; (von Begeisterung, Glück, Ruhm, Macht auch) peak; **auf dem** ~ **der Macht/des Ruhmes** at the height of one's power/fame; **der** ~ **der Geschmacklosigkeit/Dummheit** (ugs.) the height of bad taste/stupidity; **das ist [doch] der** ~! (ugs.) that's the limit! 3 (veralt.: Wipfel) top 4 (~konferenz) summit

Gipfel-: ~**buch** *das* (Alpinistik) summit book; *book kept on a mountain summit, into which successful climbers can enter their names;* ~**gespräch** *das* summit talks *pl.*; ~**konferenz** *die* summit conference; ~**kreuz** *das* cross on the summit of a/the mountain

gipfeln *itr. V.* **in etw.** *(Dat.)* ~: culminate in sth.

Gipfel-: ~**punkt** *der* highest point; top; (fig.) high point; **der** ~ **seines künstlerischen Schaffens** the peak of his artistic powers; ~**stürmer** *der,* ~**stürmerin** *die* climber attempting the/an ascent; (erfolgreich) conqueror of the/a mountain; (fig.: Aktie) high flier; (fig.: Person die ein hohes Ziel erreicht) scaler of the heights

Gips /gɪps/ *der;* ~es, (Sorten:) ~e plaster; gypsum (Chem.); (zum Modellieren) plaster of Paris; **einen Arm in** ~ **legen** put an arm in plaster; **drei Monate im** ~ **liegen** be laid up in plaster for three months

Gips-: ~**abdruck** *der; Pl.* ~**abdrücke**, ~**abguss**, *~**abguß** *der* plaster cast; ~**bein** *das* (ugs.) **ich komme mit meinem** ~**bein nicht mit** I can't keep up, with this plaster on my leg; **durch ein** ~**bein behindert werden** be hindered by having one's leg in plaster

gipsen *tr. V.* 1 plaster ‹*wall, ceiling*›; put ‹*leg, arm, etc.*› in plaster 2 (ausbessern) repair with plaster

Gipser *der;* ~s, ~, **Gipserin** *die;* ~, ~nen ▸ⓘ **S. 113** plasterer

Gips-: ~**figur** *die* plaster [of Paris] figure; ~**korsett** *das* (Med.) plaster jacket; ~**modell** *das* plaster model; ~**verband** *der* plaster cast

Giraffe /giˈrafə/ *die;* ~, ~n giraffe

Girant /ʒiˈrant/ *der;* ~en, ~en, **Girantin** *die;* ~, ~nen (Finanzw.) endorser

girieren /ʒiˈriːrən/ *tr. V.* (Finanzw.) endorse

Girl /gøːɐ̯l/ *das;* ~s, ~s 1 (ugs., oft scherzh.: Mädchen) girl 2 (Tänzerin) chorus girl

Girlande /gɪrˈlandə/ *die;* ~, ~n festoon

g

Girlie /ˈgœrli/ *das;* **~s, ~s** girlie
Giro /ˈʒiːro/ *das;* **~s, ~s,** *österr. auch* **Giri** (Finanzw.) **1** (Überweisung) giro **2** (Vermerk) endorsement
Giro-: ~bank *die; Pl.* **~~en** (Finanzw.) clearing bank; **~konto** *das* (Finanzw.) current account
girren /ˈgɪrən/ *itr. V.* (auch fig.) coo
Gis, gis /gɪs/ *das;* **~, ~** (Musik) G sharp
Gischt /gɪʃt/ *der;* **~[e]s, ~e** *od. die;* **~, ~en** **1** (Schaumkronen) foam; surf **2** (Sprühwasser) spray
gischten *itr. V.* (geh.) spray up
Gis-Dur *das* (Musik) G sharp major; *s. auch* **A-Dur**
gis-Moll *das* (Musik) G sharp minor; *s. auch* **a-Moll**
Gitarre /giˈtarə/ *die;* **~, ~n** guitar
Gitarren-: ~griff *der* guitar fingering; fingering on the guitar; **~spieler** *der,* **~spielerin** *die* guitar player; guitarist
Gitarrist *der;* **~en, ~en, Gitarristin** *die;* **~, ~nen** ▸❶ **S. 113** guitarist
Gitter /ˈgɪtɐ/ *das;* **~s, ~** **1** (parallele Stäbe) bars *pl.*; (Drahtgeflecht vor Fenster-, Türöffnungen) grille; (in der Straßendecke, im Fußboden) grating; (Geländer) railing[s *pl.*]; (Spalier) trellis; (feines Draht~) mesh; (Kamin~) [fire]guard; **hinter ~n** (ugs.) behind bars **2** (Physik, Chemie) lattice **3** (Math., Elektronik, auf Landkarten) grid
Gitter-: ~bett *das* cot; **~fenster** *das* barred window; **~mast** *der* (Technik) pylon; lattice tower; **~netz** *das* (Kartographie) grid; **~rost** *der* grating; **~stab** *der* bar; **~struktur** *die* (Physik) lattice structure; **~tor** *das* iron-barred gate; **~werk** *das* ironwork; (kunstvoller) wrought-iron work; **~zaun** *der* railing[s *pl.*]; (mit gekreuzten Stäben) lattice-[work] fence
Glace /ˈglasə/ *die;* **~, ~n** (schweiz.) ice cream
Glacé-/glaˈseː/: **~hand·schuh** *der* kid glove; **jmdn./etw. mit ~handschuhen anfassen** (ugs.) handle sb./sth. with kid gloves; **~leder** *das* glacé leather
glacieren /glaˈsiːrən/ *tr. V.* (Kochk.) glaze
Glacis /glaˈsiː/ *das;* **~, ~** (Milit.) glacis
Gladiator /glaˈdi̯aːtɔr/ *der;* **~s, ~en** /-ˈtoːrən/ gladiator
Gladiole /glaˈdi̯oːlə/ *die;* **~, ~n** gladiolus
Glamour /ˈglɛmə/ *der od. das;* **~s** glamour
Glamour·girl *das* glamour girl
glamourös /glamuˈrøːs/
A *Adj.* glamorous
B *adv.* glamorously
Glanz /glants/ *der;* **~es** **1** (von Licht, Sternen) brightness; brilliance; (von Haar, Metall, Perlen, Leder usw.) shine; lustre; sheen; (von Augen) shine; brightness; lustre; **den ~ verlieren** ‹*diamonds, eyes*› lose their sparkle; ‹*metal, leather*› lose its shine; **etw. auf ~ polieren** polish sth. till it shines; **welch ~ in meiner Hütte!** (scherzh. iron.) to what do I owe the honour of this visit? (iron.) **2** (der Jugend, Schönheit) radiance; (des Adels usw.) splendour; **zu neuem ~ kommen** acquire new splendour; **mit ~** (ugs.) with flying colours; **mit ~ und Gloria** (ugs. iron.) in grand style
Glanz·abzug *der* (Fot.) glossy print
glänzen /ˈglɛntsn̩/ *itr. V.* **1** (Glanz ausstrahlen) shine; ‹*car, hair, metal, paintwork, etc.*› gleam; ‹*elbows, trousers, etc.*› be shiny; **vor Sauberkeit ~:** be so clean [that] it shines; **sein Gesicht glänzte vor Freude** his face shone with joy *or* pleasure **2** (Bewunderung erregen) shine (**bei** at); **durch Wissen/Können ~:** be outstanding for one's knowledge/ability; **in einer Rolle ~:** shine in a role; **durch Abwesenheit ~** (iron.) be conspicuous by one's absence
glänzend (ugs.)
A *Adj.* **1** shining; gleaming ‹*car, hair, metal, paintwork, etc.*›; shiny ‹*elbows, trousers, etc.*› **2** (bewundernswert) brilliant ‹*idea, career, victory, pupil, prospects, etc.*›; splendid, excellent, outstanding ‹*references, marks, results, etc.*›; **in ~er Laune/Form sein** be in a splendid mood/in splendid form
B *adv.* **~ mit jmdm. auskommen** get on very well with sb.; **es geht mir/uns ~:** I am/we are very well; (finanziell) I am/we are doing very well *or* very nicely; **eine Aufgabe ~ lösen** solve a problem brilliantly
glanz-, Glanz-: ~kohle *die* glance coal; **~leistung** *die* (auch iron.) brilliant performance; **~licht** *das; Pl.* **~~er** (bild. Kunst) highlight; **einer Sache** (*Dat.*) **[noch einige] ~lichter aufsetzen** give sth. [more] sparkle; **~los** *Adj.* dull; lacklustre; **~nummer** *die* star turn; **diese Rezitation ist seine ~nummer** this recitation is his pièce de résistance; **~papier** *das* glossy paper; **~parade** *die* (Sport) superb *or* outstanding save; **~politur** *die* high-gloss polish; **~punkt** *der* high spot; highlight; **~rolle** *die* star role; **~stück** *das* **1** (Meisterwerk) pièce de résistance; **2** (der kostbarste Gegenstand) showpiece; **~voll** **A** *Adj.* **1** (ausgezeichnet) brilliant; sparkling ‹*variety number*›; **2** (prachtvoll) magnificent; **B** *adv.* **1** (ausgezeichnet) brilliantly; **eine Prüfung ~voll bestehen** pass an examination with flying colours; do brilliantly in an examination; **2** (prachtvoll) **Louis XIV pflegte ~voll Hof zu halten** Louis XIV used to hold court in glittering style; **~zeit** *die* heyday; **ihre ~zeit ist vorüber** she's had her day
Glas /ˈglaːs/ *das;* **~es, Gläser** /ˈglɛːzɐ/ **1** glass; **unter ~:** behind glass; ‹*plants*› under glass; **„Vorsicht, ~!"** 'glass — handle with care'; **du bist nicht aus ~** (ugs.) you make a better door than you do window (coll.) **2** (Trinkgefäß) glass; **zwei ~** *od.* **Gläser Wein/Bier** two glasses of wine/beer; **ein ~ über den Durst trinken** (ugs. scherzh.), **zu tief ins ~ gucken** (ugs. scherzh.) have one too many *or* (coll.) one over the eight **3** (Behälter aus ~) jar; **ein ~ Marmelade/Honig** a jar of jam/honey **4** (geh.: Brillen~) lens; **Gläser** (veralt.: Brille) spectacles; glasses **5** (Fern~) binoculars *pl.*; [field] glasses *pl.*; (Opern~) opera glasses *pl.*
glas-, Glas-: ~artig *Adj.* vitreous; glassy; **~auge** *das* glass eye; **~ballon** *der* carboy; **~baustein** *der* glass brick *or* block; **~bläser** *der* ▸❶ **S. 113** glass-blower; **~bläserei** /-blɛːzəˈrai̯/ *die;* **~~, ~~en** **1** glass-blowing; **2** (Betrieb) glass-blowing works *sing. or pl.*; **~bläserin** *die* ▸**~bläser**
Gläschen /ˈglɛːsçən/ *das;* **~s, ~** **1** (kleines Trinkglas) [little] glass **2** (kleines Gefäß aus Glas) [little] [glass] jar

Glascontainer
▸ **Recycling**

Glas·dach *das* glass roof
Glaser *der;* **~s, ~** ▸❶ **S. 113** glazier
Glaserei *die;* **~, ~en** **1** (Betrieb) glazing business; (Werkstatt) glazier's workshop **2** glazier's trade
Glaserin *die;* **~, ~nen** ▸❶ **S. 113** ▸**Glaser**
gläsern /ˈglɛːzɐn/ *Adj.* **1** (aus Glas) glass; **ein ~er Abgeordneter** (fig.) a member of parliament who has no secrets **2** (dichter.: wie Glas) glassy
glas-, Glas-: ~fabrik *die* glassworks *sing. or pl.*; **~faser** *die* glass fibre; **~fenster** *das* [glass] window; **bemalte ~fenster** stained-glass windows; **~fiber** *die* ▸**~faser**; **~fiber·stab** *der* (Leichtathletik) glass-fibre pole; **~flasche** *die* glass bottle; **~flügler** *der;* **~~s, ~~** (Zool.) clearwing; **~fluss,** ***~fluß** *der* paste; **~geschirr** *das* glassware; **~hart** **A** *Adj.* **1** /ˈ--/ (hart) solid ‹*ice*›; rigid ‹*plastic*›; (spröde) brittle; **2** /ˈ-ˈ-/ (Sport) cracking ‹*shot*›; solid ‹*punch*›; **B** *adv.* **1** **~hart gefroren** frozen hard; **2** (Sport) **seine Rechte ~hart schlagen** have a solid right; **~haus** *das* greenhouse; glasshouse; **wer [selbst] im ~haus sitzt, soll nicht mit Steinen werfen** (Spr.) those who live in glass houses shouldn't throw stones (prov.); **~hütte** *die* glassworks *sing. or pl.*
glasieren *tr. V.* **1** (glätten und haltbar machen) glaze **2** (Kochk.) ice ‹*cake etc.*›; glaze ‹*meat*›
glasig *Adj.* **1** (starr) glassy ‹*stare, eyes, etc.*› **2** (Kochk.: durchsichtig) transparent
glas-, Glas-: ~kasten *der* **1** glass case; (kleiner) glass box; **2** (ugs.: Raum) glass box; **~keramik** *die* devitrified glass; **~kinn** *das* (Sportjargon) vulnerable chin; **~klar** *Adj.* (auch fig.) crystal clear; **~knochen·krankheit** *die* ▸❶ **S. 439** brittle bone disease; **~kolben** *der* glass flask; (einer Glühbirne) glass bulb; **~körper** *der* ▸❶ **S. 435** (Anat.) vitreous body; **~kugel** *die* glass ball; (einer Wahrsagerin) crystal ball; (Murmel) marble; **~malerei** *die* stained glass; (Verfahren) glass staining; **~papier** *das* glass *or* sand paper; **~perle** *die* glass bead; **~platte** *die* glass plate; (eines Tisches) glass top; (im Fenster) pane of glass; **~röhrchen** *das* small glass tube; **~scheibe** *die* sheet of glass; (im Fenster) pane of glass; **~scherbe** *die* piece of broken glass; **~scherben** [pieces of] broken glass; **~schleifer** *der,* **~schleiferin** *die* **1** glass cutter; **2** (Optik) glass grinder; **~schneider** *der* glass-cutter; **~schrank** *der* glass-fronted cabinet; (mit Wänden aus Glas) glass cabinet; **~splitter** *der* splinter of glass; **~stein** *der* ▸**~baustein**; **~tür** *die* glass door
Glasur /glaˈzuːɐ̯/ *die;* **~, ~en** **1** (Schmelz) glaze **2** (Kochk.) (auf Kuchen) icing; (auf Fleisch) glaze
glas-, Glas-: ~veranda *die* glassed-in veranda; **~vitrine** *die* glass showcase; **~waren** *Pl.* glassware *sing.*; **~watte** *die* ▸**~wolle**; **~weise** *Adv.* by the glass; **~wolle** *die* glass wool; **~ziegel** *der* glass tile
glatt /glat/
A *Adj.* **1** smooth; straight ‹*hair*›; **etw. ~ bügeln/hobeln** iron/plane sth. smooth; **etw. ~ machen** smooth sth. out; **den Boden ~ machen** level the ground; **sich** (*Dat.*) **die Haare ~ kämmen** comb one's hair straight; **etw. ~ ziehen** pull sth. straight; **~ rasiert** clean shaven; **eine ~e Eins/Fünf** a clear A/E **2** (rutschig) slippery **3** (komplikationslos) smooth ‹*landing, journey*›; clean, straightforward ‹*fracture*› **4** (ugs.: offensichtlich) downright, outright ‹*lie*›; outright ‹*deception, fraud*›; sheer, utter ‹*nonsense, madness, etc.*›; pure, sheer ‹*invention*›, flat ‹*refusal*›; complete ‹*failure*›; **~er Mord sein** be tantamount to murder **5** (allzu gewandt) smooth
B *adv.* **1** **die Rechnung geht ~ auf** the calculation works out exactly; **stricken Sie die ersten zehn Reihen ~ rechts** start with ten rows of plain knitting **2** (komplikationslos) smoothly; **jmdn. ~ schlagen/besiegen** beat/defeat sb. decisively; **~ gehen** (ugs.) go smoothly **3** (ugs.: rückhaltlos) **jmdm. etw. ~ ins Gesicht sagen** tell sb. sth. straight to his/her face; **etw. ~ ablehnen/leugnen** reject/deny sth. flatly; **etw. ~ vergessen** completely *or* clean forget sth. **4** (abwertend: allzu gewandt) smoothly
***glatt|bügeln** ▸**glatt A1**
Glätte /ˈglɛtə/ *die;* **~** **1** (ebene Beschaffenheit) smoothness **2** (Rutschigkeit) slipperiness **3** (abwertend: allzu große Gewandtheit) smoothness
Glatt·eis *das* glaze; ice; (auf der Straße) black ice; **jmdn. aufs ~ führen** (fig.) catch sb. out; **aufs ~ geraten** (fig.) get on to tricky ground
Glatteis·bildung *die* formation of black ice
Glätt·eisen *das* (schweiz.) ▸**Bügeleisen**
Glatteis·gefahr *die* danger of black ice
glätten
A *tr. V.* smooth out ‹*piece of paper, banknote, etc.*›; smooth [down] ‹*feathers, fur, etc.*›; plane ‹*wood etc.*›; **jmds. Zorn/aufgebrachte Stimmung ~** (fig.) calm sb.'s anger/smooth sb.'s ruffled feathers
B *refl. V.* ‹*waves*› subside; ‹*sea*› become calm *or* smooth; (fig.) subside; die down; **ihre Stirn glättete sich** her frown vanished
C *tr., itr. V.* (schweiz.) ▸**bügeln**
Glätterin *die;* **~, ~nen** (schweiz.) ▸**Büglerin**
glatt-: *~|gehen *usw.:* ▸**glatt B2, A1;** **~|machen** *tr. V.* (ugs.: begleichen) settle ‹*account etc.*›; ***~rasiert** ▸**glatt A1**; **~weg** *Adv.* (ugs.) **etw. ~weg ablehnen/ignorieren** turn sth. down flat/just *or* simply ignore sth.; **das ist ~weg erlogen/erfunden** that's a downright lie/that's pure invention;

***~|ziehen** ▸ glatt A1; **~züngig** /-t͜syŋɪç/ *Adj.* (geh. abwertend) smooth-tongued; glib

Glatze /ˈglat͜sə/ *die;* ~, **~n** bald head; (kahle Stelle) bald patch; **eine ~ haben/bekommen** be/go bald; **sich eine ~ schneiden lassen** (ugs.) have one's hair cropped very short all over; **ein Mann mit ~:** a man with a bald head; a bald-headed man

Glatz·kopf *der* [1] (Kopf) bald head [2] (ugs.: Person) baldhead

glatz·köpfig *Adj.* bald[-headed]

Glaube /ˈglaubə/ *der;* **~ns** [1] (gefühlsmäßige Bindung) faith (**an** + *Akk.* in); (Überzeugung, Meinung) belief (**an** + *Akk.* in); **den ~n an jmdn./etw. verlieren** lose faith in sb./sth.; **jmdm./jmds. Worten ~n schenken** believe sb./what sb. says; **[bei jmdm.] ~n finden** be believed [by sb.]; **guten ~ns sein, dass ...** be quite convinced that ...; **in dem ~n leben, dass ...** live in the belief that ...; **lass ihn in seinem ~n** don't disillusion him; **jmdn. bei** *od.* **in dem ~n lassen, dass ...** let sb. believe that ...; **[der] ~ versetzt Berge** *od.* **kann Berge versetzen** faith can move mountains; **sich in dem ~n wiegen, dass ...** labour under the illusion that ...; **in gutem** *od.* **im guten ~n** in good faith [2] (religiöse Überzeugung, Religion, Bekenntnis) faith; **den ~n verlieren** lose one's [religious] faith; **den ~n an Gott verlieren** lose one's faith *or* belief in God

glauben

A *tr. V.* [1] (annehmen, meinen) think; believe; **ich glaube, ja** I think *or* believe so; **ich glaube, nein** *od.* **nicht** I don't think so; I think *or* believe not; **jmdn. etw. ~ machen wollen** try to make sb. believe sth. [2] (für wahr halten) believe; **jmdm. [etw.] ~:** believe sb.; **ich glaube ihm seine Geschichte** I believe his story; **das glaubst du doch selbst nicht!** [surely] you can't be serious; **sie glaubt ihm jedes Wort** she believes every word he says; **ob du es glaubst oder nicht ...** believe it or not ...; **wer hätte das [je] geglaubt?** who would [ever] have thought it?; **wer hätte [je] geglaubt, dass ...** who would [ever] have believed *or* thought that ...; **du glaubst [gar] nicht, wie ...** you have no idea how ...; **wers glaubt, wird selig** (ugs. scherzh.) if you believe that, you'll believe anything; **das ist doch kaum zu ~** (ugs.) it's incredible [3] (fälschlich annehmen) **wir glaubten ihn tot/in Sicherheit** we thought *or* believed him [to be] dead/safe; **sich allein/unbeobachtet ~:** think *or* believe oneself [to be] alone/unobserved

B *itr. V.* [1] (vertrauen) **an jmdn./etw./sich [selbst] ~:** believe in *or* have faith in sb./sth./oneself [2] (gläubig sein) hold religious beliefs; believe; **fest/unbeirrbar ~:** have a strong/unshakeable religious belief [3] (von der Existenz von etw. überzeugt sein) believe (**an** + *Akk.* in); **an Gott ~:** believe in God [4] **dran ~ müssen** (salopp: getötet werden) buy it (coll.); (salopp: sterben) peg out (coll.); kick the bucket (sl.); **heute muss sie dran ~ und Küchendienst machen** (ugs.: ist an der Reihe) today it is her turn to be lumbered with working in the kitchen (coll.)

Glauben *der;* **~s** ▸ Glaube

glaubens-, Glaubens-: ~artikel *der* article of faith; **~bekenntnis** *das* [1] (auch fig.: Überzeugung) creed; *s. auch* **apostolisch 1**; [2] (Konfessionsangehörigkeit) religion; **~bruder** *der* co-religionist; fellow-believer; **~dinge** *Pl.* matters of faith; **~eifer** *der* religious zeal; **~frage** *die* question of faith *or* belief; **~freiheit** *die* religious freedom; freedom of worship; **~gemeinschaft** *die* religious sect; denomination; **~kampf** *der* religious war; war of religion; **~lehre** *die* doctrine; (Dogma) dogma; (Dogmatik) dogmatics *sing.*; **~sache** *die* (ugs.) matter of faith *or* belief; **~satz** *der* doctrine; dogma; **~schwester** *die* ▸ ~bruder; **~spaltung** *die* schism; **~stark** *Adj.* deeply religious; **~streit** *der* religious dispute; **~wahrheit** *die* religious truth; **~wechsel** *der* change of religion

Glauber·salz /ˈglaubɐ-/ *das* (Chemie) Glauber's salt

glaubhaft

A *Adj.* credible; believable

B *adv.* convincingly

Glaubhaftigkeit *die;* ~ credibility

Glaubhaft·machung *die;* ~ (Rechtsspr.) substantiation

gläubig /ˈglɔybɪç/

A *Adj.* [1] (religiös) devout; **sehr/zutiefst ~ sein** be very/deeply religious [2] (vertrauensvoll) trusting; **~e Anhänger** faithful followers

B *adv.* [1] (religiös) devoutly [2] (vertrauensvoll) trustingly

-gläubig *Adj.* having a blind trust in ‹*authority, drugs, Hitler, the Party, etc.*›

Gläubige *der/die; adj. Dekl.* believer; **die ~n** the faithful

Gläubiger *der;* **~s,** ~, **Gläubigerin** *die;* ~, **~nen** creditor

Gläubiger·schutz *der* (Rechtsw.) creditor protection

Gläubigkeit *die;* ~ [1] (religiöse Überzeugung) religious faith [2] (Vertrauen) trustfulness

glaublich *Adj.* **es ist kaum ~:** it is scarcely *or* hardly credible

glaub·würdig

A *Adj.* credible; believable; **von ~er Seite/aus ~er Quelle** from reliable quarters/a reliable source

B *adv.* convincingly

Glaubwürdigkeit *die* credibility

Glaukom /glauˈkoːm/ *das;* **~s, ~e** ▸ ❶ S. 439 (Med.) glaucoma

glazial /glaˈt͜si̯aːl/ *Adj.* (Geol.) glacial

Glazial *das;* **~s, ~e** (Geol.) glacial epoch

gleich /glai̯ç/

A *Adj.* [1] (identisch, von derselben Art) same; (~berechtigt, ~wertig, Math.) equal; **~ bleiben** remain *or* stay the same; ‹*speed, temperature, etc.*› remain *or* stay constant *or* steady; ‹*prices*› remain unchanged, stay the same; **sich** (*Dat.*) **~ bleiben** stay the same; **das bleibt sich [doch] ~** (ugs.) it makes no difference; **~ bleibend** constant, steady ‹*temperature, speed, etc.*›; **in ~ bleibendem Abstand** at a steady distance; **zur ~en Zeit/im ~en Augenblick** at the same time/at the same moment; **~er Lohn für ~e Arbeit** equal pay for equal work; **~es Recht für alle** equal rights for all; **dreimal zwei [ist] ~ sechs** three times two equals *or* is six; **das Gleiche wollen/beabsichtigen** have the same objective[s *pl.*]/intentions *pl.*; **das Gleiche gilt auch für dich** the same applies to *or* goes for you too; **das kommt auf das Gleiche** *od.* **aufs Gleiche heraus** it amounts *or* comes to the same thing; **der/die Gleiche bleiben** remain *or* stay the same; **Gleiches mit Gleichem vergelten** pay sb. back in his/her own coin *or* in kind; **Gleich und Gleich gesellt sich gern** (Spr.) birds of a feather flock together (prov.) [2] (ugs.: ~gültig) **es ist mir völlig** *od.* **ganz ~:** it's all the same to me; I couldn't care less (coll.); **ganz ~, wer anruft, ...** no matter who calls, ...

B *adv.* [1] (übereinstimmend) **groß/alt** *usw.* **sein** be the same height/age *etc.*; **~ gut/schlecht** *usw.* equally good/bad *etc.* [2] (in derselben Weise) **~ aufgebaut/gekleidet** having the same structure/wearing identical clothes; **alle Menschen ~ behandeln** treat everyone alike; **~ denkend** *od.* **gesinnt** like-minded; **~ lautend** identical, identically worded ‹*texts etc.*›; homonymous ‹*words*› (Ling.) [3] (sofort) at once; right *or* straight away; (bald) in a moment *or* minute; **ich komme ~:** I'm just coming; **es muss nicht ~ sein** there's no immediate hurry; **ich bin ~ wieder da** I'll be back in a moment *or* minute; I'll be right back; **es ist ~ zehn Uhr** it is almost *or* nearly ten o'clock; **das habe ich [euch] ~ gesagt** I told you so; what did I tell you?; **warum nicht ~ so?** why didn't you do that/say so in the first place?; **bis ~!** see you later! [4] (räumlich) right; immediately; just; **~ rechts/links** just *or* immediately on the right/left; **~ um die Ecke** just round the corner [5] (geh.: schon, auch) **wenn er ~ reich war, ...** rich though he was, ...; **ob er ~ unschuldig war, ...** although he was innocent, ...

C *Präp.* + *Dat.* (geh.) like; **einem silbernen Band ~:** like a silver ribbon

D *Partikel* [1] **nun wein nicht ~/sei nicht ~ böse** don't start crying/don't get cross; **da könnte man doch ~ in die Luft gehen/aus der Haut fahren** it's enough to drive you up the wall (coll.) [2] (in Fragesätzen) **wie hieß er ~?** what was his name [again]?; **was wollte ich ~ sagen?** what was I going to say?

gleich-, Gleich-: ~alt[e]rig /-alt[ə]rɪç/ *Adj.* of the same age (**mit** as); **die beiden sind ~alt[e]rig** they are both the same age; **Gleichalt[e]rige** *Pl.* people/children of the same age; **~artig** A *Adj.* of the same kind *postpos.* (+ *Dat.* as); (sehr ähnlich) very similar (+ *Dat.* to); B *adv.* in the same way; **~artigkeit** *die* great similarity; **~bedeutend** *Adj.* **~bedeutend mit** synonymous with; ‹*action*› tantamount to; **~berechtigt** *Adj.* having *or* enjoying *or* with equal rights *postpos.*; **~berechtigte Partner/Mitglieder** equal partners/members; **~berechtigt sein** have *or* enjoy equal rights; **~berechtigt mit jmdm. sein** have the same rights as sb.; **Gleichberechtigte** *Pl.* people who have *or* enjoy equal rights; **~berechtigung** *die* equal rights *pl.*; equality; **für die ~berechtigung der Frauen kämpfen** fight for equal rights *or* equality for women; ***~|bleiben** ▸ gleich A 1; **~bleibend** *Adj.* **~bleibend sein** remain *or* stay the same; ‹*temperature, speed, etc.*› remain *or* stay constant *or* steady; *s. auch* **gleich A 1**; **~denkend** ▸ gleich B 2

gleichen *unr. itr. V.* **jmdm./einer Sache ~:** be like *or* resemble sb./sth.; (sehr ähnlich aussehen) closely resemble sb./sth.; **sich** (*Dat.*) **~:** be alike; (sehr ähnlich aussehen) closely resemble each other; **nichts gleicht dem Zauber dieser Musik** nothing can equal *or* there is nothing to equal the enchanting quality of this music

gleichen·orts *Adv.* (schweiz.) in the same place

gleichermaßen *Adv.* equally

gleich-, Gleich-: ~falls *Adv.* (auch) also; (ebenfalls) likewise; **danke ~falls!** thank you, [and] the same to you; **~farbig** *Adj.* of the same colour *postpos.*; **~förmig** A *Adj.* [1] (einheitlich) uniform; uniform, even ‹*light*›; steady ‹*development*›; [2] (langweilig, monoton) monotonous; B *adv.* [1] (einheitlich) uniformly; [2] (langweilig, monoton) monotonously; **~förmig sprechen** speak in a monotone; **~förmigkeit** *die;* ~~ [1] (Einheitlichkeit) uniformity; [2] (Monotonie) monotony; **~geschlechtlich** *Adj.* homosexual; **~gesinnt** ▸ gleich B2; **~gesinnte** *der/die; adj. Dekl.* like-minded person; **mit ~gesinnten** with like-minded people

Gleich·gewicht *das* [1] balance; **das ~ halten/verlieren** keep/lose one's balance; **aus dem ~ kommen** lose one's balance; **im ~ sein** be in equilibrium; **ihr ~ ist leicht gestört** her sense of balance is slightly impaired [2] (Ausgewogenheit) balance; **das europäische ~:** the balance of power in Europe; **das ~ der Kräfte** the balance of power [3] (innere Ausgeglichenheit) equilibrium; **aus dem ~ geraten** lose one's equilibrium; **sein ~ bewahren/verlieren** keep *or* retain/lose one's equilibrium; **jmdn. aus dem ~ bringen** throw sb. off balance

Gleichgewichts-: ~lage *die* equilibrium; **~organ** *das* ▸ ❶ S. 435 (Anat.) organ of equilibrium; **~sinn** *der* sense of balance; **~störung** *die* disturbance of one's sense of balance; **~störungen** impaired balance *sing.*

gleich·gültig

A *Adj.* [1] (teilnahmslos) indifferent (**gegenüber** towards); **sie war ihm [nicht] ~** (verhüll.) he was [by no means] indifferent to her [2] (belanglos) trivial, unimportant ‹*matter, question, etc.*›; trivial ‹*conversation*›; **es ist ~, ob ...** it does not matter whether ...; **das ist mir [vollkommen] ~:** it's a matter of [complete] indifference to me

B *adv.* indifferently; ‹*look on*› with indifference

Gleich·gültigkeit *die* indifference (**gegenüber** towards)

Gleichheit *die;* ~, **~en** [1] (Identität) identity; (Ähnlichkeit) similarity; **bei ~ der Punktzahl** if the teams/players *etc.* are level on points [2] (gleiche Rechte) equality

g

Gleichheits-: **∼[grund]satz** *der* principle of equality before the law; **∼zeichen** *das* equals sign

gleich-, Gleich-: **∼klang** *der* harmony; **∼|kommen** *unr. itr. V.; mit sein* 1 (entsprechen) amount to; be tantamount to; 2 (die gleiche Leistung erreichen) **jmdm./einer Sache [an etw.** (*Dat.*)**] ∼kommen** equal sb./sth. [in sth.]; **jmdm. an Erfolg/Schnelligkeit ∼kommen** equal *or* match sb.'s success/match sb. for speed; **∼lauf** *der* (Technik) synchronism; **∼laufend** *Adj.* parallel (**mit** with); **∼lautend** *Adj.* ▸**gleich B 2**; **∼|machen** *tr. V.* make equal; **der Tod macht alle Menschen ∼:** Death is the great leveller; *s. auch* **Erdboden**; **∼macherei** *die;* **∼∼, ∼∼en** (abwertend) levelling down (derog.); egalitarianism; **∼macherisch** *Adj.* (abwertend) egalitarian; **∼maß** *das* 1 (Ebenmaß) (von Bewegung, Strophen) regularity; (von Zügen, Proportionen) symmetry; 2 (Ausgeglichenheit) equilibrium; **∼mäßig** A *Adj.* regular ‹*interval, rhythm*›; uniform ‹*acceleration, distribution*›; even ‹*heat*›; **∼mäßige Atemzüge** regular breathing *sing.*; B *adv.* ‹*breathe*› regularly; **etw. ∼mäßig verteilen/auftragen** distribute sth. equally/apply sth. evenly; **∼mäßig hohe Temperaturen** constantly high temperatures; **∼mäßigkeit** *die* ▸**∼mäßig**: regularity; uniformity; evenness; **∼mut** *der* (*veralt., landsch. auch: die;* **∼∼**) equanimity; calmness; composure; **etw. mit ∼mut hinnehmen/ertragen** accept/bear sth. with equanimity; **∼mütig** A *Adj.* calm; composed; unruffled ‹*calm*›; B *adv.* with equanimity; calmly; **∼mütigkeit** *die;* **∼∼** ▸**∼mut**; **∼namig** /-na:mɪç/ *Adj.* 1 of the same name *postpos.*; 2 (Math.) **∼namige Brüche** fractions with a common denominator; **Brüche ∼namig machen** reduce fractions to a common denominator; 3 (Physik) like ‹*charges, poles*›

Gleichnis *das;* **∼ses, ∼se** (Allegorie) allegory; (Parabel) parable

gleichnishaft

A *Adj.* (allegorisch) allegorical; (parabolisch) parabolic

B *adv.* allegorically/parabolically

gleich-, Gleich-: **∼rangig** /-raŋɪç/ A *Adj.* ‹*principle, problem, etc.*› of equal importance *or* status; equally important ‹*principle, problem, etc.*›; ‹*official, job*› of equal rank; B *adv.* **alle Punkte ∼rangig behandeln** give all points equal treatment; **∼|richten** *tr. V.* (Elektrot.) rectify; **∼richter** *der* (Elektrot.) rectifier

gleichsam *Adv.* (geh.) as it were; so to speak; **∼ als [ob] ...** just as if ...

gleich-, Gleich-: **∼|schalten** *tr. V.* (abwertend) force *or* bring into line; **∼schaltung** *die* (abwertend) Gleichschaltung; **∼schenk[e]lig** *Adj.* (Math.) isosceles; **∼schritt** *der* marching in step; **im ∼schritt** in step; **im ∼schritt marsch!** forward march!; **∼schritt halten** keep in step; **∼|sehen** *unr. itr. V.* **jmdm./einer Sache ∼sehen** look like sb./sth.; **∼seitig** *Adj.* (Math.) equilateral; **∼|setzen** *tr. V.* **zwei Dinge ∼setzen** equate two things; **etw. einer Sache** (*Dat.*) *od.* **mit etw. ∼setzen** equate sth. with sth.; **sich mit jmdm. ∼setzen** put oneself on the same level as *or* on a level with sb.; **Ludwig XIV. setzte sich mit seinem Staat ∼:** Ludwig XIV identified himself with his state; **∼setzung** *die;* **∼∼, ∼∼en: die ∼setzung von sozialistischen und fortschrittlichen Ideen** equating socialist and progressive ideas; **die ∼setzung der Arbeiter mit den Vertretern der Intelligenz** placing the workers on the same level as the members of the intelligentsia; **∼silbig** *Adj.* having the same number of syllables *postpos., not pred.*; **∼silbig sein** have the same number of syllables; **∼sinnig** A *Adj.* ‹*fluctuations etc.*› in the same direction; B *adv.* in the same direction; **∼stand** *der* 1 (Sport: gleicher Spielstand) **den ∼stand herstellen/erzielen** level the score; **beim ∼stand von 1:1** with the scores level at 1 all; **das Spiel wurde beim ∼stand von 1:1 beendet** the match ended in a 1 all draw; 2 (Politik) balance of forces; **∼|stehen** *unr. itr. V.* be equal (*Dat.* to, with); (Sport) be level; **∼|stellen** *tr. V.* **zwei Dinge ∼stellen** equate two things; **etw. einer Sache** (*Dat.*) *od.* **mit etw. ∼stellen** equate sth. with sth.; **jmd. [mit] jmdm. ∼stellen** put sb. on the same level as *or* on a level with sb.; (gleiche Rechte zugestehen) put sb. on an equal footing with sb.; **∼stellung** *die:* **die rechtliche ∼stellung unehelicher Kinder** giving equal rights to illegitimate children; **soziale ∼stellung** social equality; **∼strom** *der* (Elektrot.) direct current; **∼|tun** *unr. tr. V.* **es jmdm. ∼tun** match *or* equal sb.; (nachahmen) copy sb.; **es jmdm. an** *od.* **in etw.** (*Dat.*) **∼tun** match *or* equal sb. in sth.; **es jmdm. an Schnelligkeit ∼tun** match *or* equal sb. for speed

Gleichung *die;* **∼, ∼en** equation; **die ∼ ging nicht auf** (fig.) things did not work out as planned

gleich-, Gleich-: **∼viel** /-'- *od.* '--/ *Adv.* no matter; **∼viel wohin** no matter where; **∼viel ob es leicht oder schwer geht/du darüber böse bist** regardless of whether it's easy or difficult/even if you are angry about it; **∼wertig** *Adj.* 1 (Sport: gleich stark) evenly matched ‹*opponents, teams*›; 2 (von gleichem Wert) of equal *or* the same value *postpos.*; ‹*performances*› of the same standard; 3 (Chemie) equivalent; **∼wertigkeit** *die:* **wie ist ∼wertigkeit der Arbeit zu definieren?** how can you define what constitutes equal work?; **die ∼wertigkeit beider Inszenierungen steht außer Frage** that the two productions are of an equal standard is beyond question; **∼wink[e]lig** *Adj.* (Geom.) equiangular; **∼wohl** /-'- *od.* '--/ A *Adv.* nevertheless; nonetheless; B *Konj.* (selten, noch landsch.) although; **∼zeitig** A *Adj.* simultaneous; B *adv.* 1 (zur gleichen Zeit) simultaneously; at the same time; 2 (auch noch) at the same time; **∼zeitigkeit** *die;* **∼∼** simultaneity; simultaneousness; (von historischen Ereignissen) contemporaneity; contemporaneousness; **∼|ziehen** *unr. itr. V.* catch up; draw level

Gleis /glais/ *das;* **∼es, ∼e** 1 (Fahrspur) track; line; rails *pl.*; permanent way *as Brit. tech. term;* (Bahnsteig) platform; (einzelne Schiene) rail; **auf ∼ 5 einlaufen** ‹*train*› arrive at platform 5; **„das Überschreiten der ∼e ist verboten!"** 'passengers must not cross the line'; **aus dem ∼ springen/kommen** jump/leave the rails; **ein totes ∼:** an unused siding 2 (fig.) **auf** *od.* **in ein falsches ∼ geraten** get on [to] the wrong track; **jmdn. aufs tote ∼ schieben** put sb. out of harm's way (fig.); **etw. auf ein totes ∼ schieben** shelve sth. indefinitely; **jmdn. aus dem ∼ bringen** *od.* **werfen** put sb. off [his/her stroke]; (von jmdm. psychisch nicht bewältigt werden) upset *or* affect sb. deeply; **sie/alles wird wieder ins rechte ∼ kommen** she'll be all right/everything will sort itself out; **alles wieder ins [rechte] ∼ bringen** put things *or* matters right again; **aus dem ∼ kommen** go off the rails (fig.); **er/alles ist wieder im ∼:** he's/everything's all right again; **sich in ausgefahrenen ∼en bewegen** be in a rut

Gleis-: **∼anlage** *die* [railway] lines *pl. or* tracks *pl.*; **∼anschluss**, ***∼anschluß** *der* siding; **∼bau** *der* track laying; construction of permanent way (Brit.); **∼bremse** *die* (Eisenb.) rail brake; **∼kette** *die* (Technik) caterpillar track

Gleisner /'glaisnɐ/ *der;* **∼s, ∼, Gleisnerin** *die;* **∼, ∼nen** (veralt.) hypocrite

gleisnerisch *Adj.* (veralt.) hypocritical

gleißen /'glaisn̩/ *itr. V.* (dichter.) blaze

Gleis-: **∼sperre** *die* (Eisenb.) scotch block; **∼waage** *die* weighbridge

Gleit-: **∼bahn** *die* (Flugw.) glide path; **∼boot** *das* hydroplane

gleiten /'glaitn̩/ *unr. itr. V.; mit sein* 1 glide; ‹*hand*› slide; **ein Lächeln glitt über ihr Gesicht** a smile passed over her face; **aus dem Sattel/ins Wasser ∼:** slide out of the saddle/slide *or* slip into the water; **jmdm. aus den Händen ∼:** slip from sb.'s hands; **er ließ das Geld in seine Tasche ∼:** he slipped the money into his pocket 2 (ugs.: in Bezug auf Arbeitszeit) work flexitime

gleitend *Adj.* **∼e Arbeitszeit** flexitime; flexible working hours *pl.*; **∼e Lohnskala** index-linked wage scale

Gleiter *der;* **∼s, ∼** glider

gleit-, Gleit-: **∼fläche** *die* slide; (für Schiffe) slipway; (am Ski) sole [of the ski]; **∼flug** *der* glide; **im ∼flug landen** glide-land; **zum ∼flug ansetzen** go into a glide; **∼flugzeug** *das* glider; **∼klausel** *die* (Rechtsw.) escalator clause; **∼kufe** *die* (Fliegerspr.) skid; **∼laut** *der* (Sprachw.) glide; **∼schiene** *die* guide *or* slide rail; **∼schirm** *der* paraglider; **∼schutz** *der* (Kfz-W.) anti-skid protection; (Bauteil) anti-skid device; **∼sicher** *Adj.* non-slip ‹*shoe, surface, etc.*›; non-skid ‹*tyre*›; **∼zeit** *die* 1 (Zeitspanne) flexible working hours *pl. or* starting and finishing times *pl.*; 2 **drei Stunden ∼zeit** three hours flexitime; 3 (ugs.: gleitende Arbeitszeit) flexitime; flexible working hours *pl.*

Glencheck /'glɛntʃɛk/ *der;* **∼[s], ∼s** 1 (Material) glen-check cloth 2 (Anzug) glen-check suit

Gletscher /'glɛtʃɐ/ *der;* **∼s, ∼** glacier

Gletscher-: **∼bach** *der* glacial stream; **∼brand** *der* glacier burn; **∼eis** *das* glacial ice; **∼mühle** *die* glacier mill; moulin; **∼spalte** *die* crevasse; **∼tisch** *der* (Geol.) glacier table; **∼tor** *das* (Geol.) glacier snout

glibberig /'glɪbərɪç/ *Adj.* (bes. nordd.) slippery; (schleimig) slimy

glich /glɪç/ *1. u. 3. Pers. Sg. Prät. v.* **gleichen**

Glied /gli:t/ *das;* **∼[e]s, ∼er** 1 ▸❶ **S. 435** (Körperteil) limb; (Finger∼, Zehen∼) joint; phalanx (Anat.); **kein ∼ rühren können** be unable to move a muscle; **der Schreck sitzt** *od.* **steckt ihm noch in den ∼ern** he is [still] shaking with the shock; **der Schreck fuhr ihr in die** *od.* **durch alle ∼er** the shock made her shake all over 2 (Ketten∼, auch fig.) link 3 (Teil eines Ganzen) section; part; (Mit∼) member; (eines Satzes) part; (einer Gleichung) term; **ein nützliches ∼ der Gesellschaft** a useful member of society 4 ▸❶ **S. 435** (Penis) penis 5 (Mannschaftsreihe) rank 6 (geh. veralt.: Generation) generation

glieder-, Glieder-: **∼bau** *der* limb structure; **∼füßer** *der;* **∼∼s, ∼∼** (Zool.) arthropod; **∼lahm** *Adj.* stiff-limbed

gliedern /'gli:dɐn/

A *tr. V.* structure; organize ‹*thoughts*›; **nach Eigenschaften ∼:** classify according to properties; **in Teile ∼:** arrange in parts; **einen Aufsatz in drei Teile ∼:** divide an essay into three sections; **hierarchisch gegliedert** hierarchically structured

B *refl. V.* **sich in Gruppen/Abschnitte** *usw.* **∼:** divide *or* be divided into groups/sections *etc.*

Glieder-: **∼puppe** *die* jointed doll; (als Modell für Maler o. Ä.) lay figure; **∼reißen** *das;* **∼∼s** (ugs.), **∼schmerz** *der* rheumatic pains *pl.*; **∼tier** *das* (Zool.) member of the Articulata; **die ∼tiere** the Articulata

Gliederung *die;* **∼, ∼en** 1 (Aufbau, Einteilung) structure; **in militärischer ∼:** in military formation; **die ∼ eines Buches in Kapitel** the division of a book into chapters 2 (das Gliedern) structuring; (von Gedanken) organization; (nach Eigenschaften) classification; (in Teile) arrangement 3 (ns.: Gruppe) section

Glieder·zucken *das;* **∼∼s** twitching of the limbs

glied-, Glied-: **∼maße** /-ma:sə/ *die;* **∼, ∼n** limb; **∼satz** *der* (Sprachw.) subordinate clause; **∼staat** *der* member *or* constituent state; **∼weise** *Adv.* in ranks

glimmen /'glɪmən/ *unr. od. regelm. itr. V.* glow; **in seinen Augen glomm ein gefährlicher Funke** (fig.) there was a dangerous glint in his eyes

Glimmer *der;* **∼s, ∼** mica

glimmern *itr. V.* glimmer; ‹*lake etc.*› glisten

Glimm-: **∼lampe** *die* (Elektrot.) glow lamp; **∼stängel**, ***∼stengel** *der* (ugs. scherzh.) fag (coll.); ciggy (coll.)

glimpflich /'glɪmpflɪç/

A *Adj.* 1 **der Unfall nahm ein ∼es Ende** the accident turned out not to be too serious; **sie**

g

war über den ~en Ausgang der Angelegenheit erfreut she was glad to have got off so lightly [2] (mild) lenient ‹*sentence, punishment*›
[B] *adv.* [1] (ohne Schaden) **~ davonkommen** get off lightly; **es ist ~ abgegangen** it turned out not to be too bad [2] (mild) mildly; leniently

glitschen /ˈglɪtʃn̩/ *itr. V.; mit sein* (ugs.) slip; **jmdm. aus der Hand ~:** slip out of sb.'s hand

glitschig /ˈglɪtʃɪç/ *Adj.* (ugs.) slippery

glitt /glɪt/ *1. u. 3. Pers. Sg. Prät. v.* **gleiten**

Glitzer *der;* **~s** glitter

glitz[e]rig /ˈglɪts(ə)rɪç/ *Adj.* (ugs.) glistening ‹*snow*›; sparkling, glittering ‹*diamond, decorations*›

glitzern /ˈglɪtsɐn/ *itr. V.* ‹*star*› twinkle; ‹*diamond, decorations*› sparkle, glitter; ‹*snow, eyes, tears*› glisten

Glitzer·stein *der* imitation gem[stone]

glitzrig ▸ **glitz[e]rig**

global /gloˈbaːl/
[A] *Adj.* [1] (weltweit) global; worldwide [2] (umfassend) general, all-round ‹*education*›; overall ‹*control, planning, etc.*› [3] (allgemein) general
[B] *adv.* [1] (weltweit) worldwide; globally [2] (umfassend) in overall terms; **~ gesteuert werden** be subject to overall control [3] (allgemein) in general terms; **~ gerechnet** in round figures

globalisieren *tr. V.* globalize

Globalisierung *die;* **~, ~en** globalization

Globalisierungs·gegner *der,* **Globalisierungs·gegnerin** *die* opponent of globalization

Globalismus /globaˈlɪsmʊs/ *der;* **~** globalism

Globalität /globaliˈtɛːt/ *die;* **~:** global nature; (Bedeutung) global importance

Global-: **~steuerung** *die* (Wirtsch.) overall control; **~strategie** *die* global *or* worldwide strategy

Globen ▸ **Globus**

Globetrotter /ˈgloːbətrɔtɐ/ *der;* **~s, ~, Globetrotterin** *die;* **~, ~nen** globetrotter

Globus /ˈgloːbʊs/ *der;* **~** *od.* **~ses, Globen** /ˈgloːbn̩/ [1] globe [2] (salopp: Kopf) nut (coll.); bonce (Brit. sl.)

Glöckchen /ˈglœkçən/ *das;* **~s, ~** [little] bell

Glocke /ˈglɔkə/ *die;* **~, ~n** [1] (auch: Tür~, Taucher~, Blüte) bell; **etw. an die große ~ hängen** (ugs.) tell the whole world about sth.; **wissen, was die ~ geschlagen hat** (ugs.) know what one is in for (coll.) [2] (Hut) cloche [3] (Käse~, Butter~, Kuchen~) cover; bell [4] (Fechten) coquille

glocken-, Glocken-: **~balken** *der* [bell] yoke; **~blume** *die* (Bot.) bell flower; campanula; **~förmig** [A] *Adj.* bell-shaped; widely flared ‹*skirt etc.*›; [B] *adv.* **~förmig geschnitten** widely flared; **~geläute** *das* pealing *or* ringing of bells; **~gießer** *der* bell-founder; **~gießerei** /----'-/ *die* bell foundry; **~gießerin** *die* ▸ **~gießer**; **~guss,** ***~guß** *der* bell-founding *no art.*; **~heide** *die* (Bot.) bell heather; **~hell** [A] *Adj.* bell-like; **eine ~helle Stimme** a high, clear voice; [B] *adv.* **~hell lachen** give a high, clear laugh; **~klang** *der* pealing *or* ringing of bells; **~klöppel** *der* [bell-]clapper; **~läuten** *das;* **~~s** pealing *or* ringing of bells; **~mantel** *der* (Gussform) cope; **~rein** [A] *Adj.* as clear as a bell *postpos.*; [B] *adv.* as clear as a bell; **~rock** *der* widely flared skirt; **~schlag** *der* stroke; **beim ~schlag um acht Uhr** on the stroke of eight o'clock; **mit dem** *od.* **auf den ~schlag** (ugs.) on the dot (coll.); **~seil** *das* bell rope; **~spiel** *das* [1] carillon; (mit einer Uhr gekoppelt auch) chimes *pl.*; [2] (Instrument) glockenspiel; **~strang** *der* ▸ **~seil**; **~stube** *die* belfry; **~stuhl** *der* bell cage; **~ton** *der; Pl.* **~töne** stroke of a/the bell; **~töne** the sound of a/the bell/of bells; **~turm** *der* bell tower; belfry; **~weihe** *die* (kath. Rel.) baptism *or* blessing of a/the bell; **~zeichen** *das* ring of a/the bell; **auf das ~zeichen** when the bell rings/rang; **~zug** *der* (Klingelschnur) bell pull; (**~seil**) bell rope

glockig /ˈglɔkɪç/ ▸ **glockenförmig**

Glöckner /ˈglœknɐ/ *der;* **~s, ~** (veralt.) bell-ringer; **der ~ von Notre Dame** the Hunchback of Notre Dame

glomm /glɔm/ *1. u. 3. Pers. Sg. Prät. v.* **glimmen**

Gloria[1] /ˈgloːria/ *das;* **~s** *od. die;* **~** (iron.) glory

Gloria[2] *das;* **~s, ~s** (Rel.) gloria; **das große/kleine ~:** the greater/lesser doxology

Glorie /ˈgloːri̯ə/ *die;* **~, ~n** [1] (geh.: Ruhm) glory [2] (geh.: Lichtschein) glory; (um den Kopf, um einen Stern) halo

Glorien·schein *der* glory; (um den Kopf, fig.) halo

Glorifikation /glorifikaˈtsi̯oːn/ *die;* **~, ~en** glorification

glorifizieren /glorifiˈtsiːrən/ *tr. V.* glorify

Glorifizierung *die;* **~, ~en** glorification

Gloriole /gloˈri̯oːlə/ *die;* **~, ~n** [1] (auch fig.) glory [2] (um den Kopf) halo; aura

glorios /gloˈri̯oːs/ (iron.)
[A] *Adj.* brilliant
[B] *adv.* brilliantly

glor·reich /ˈgloːɐ̯-/
[A] *Adj.* glorious
[B] *adv.* gloriously

glosen /ˈgloːzn̩/ *itr. V.* (landsch./dichter.) ▸ **glimmen**

Glossar /glɔˈsaːɐ̯/ *das;* **~s, ~e** glossary

Glosse /ˈglɔsə/ *die;* **~, ~n** [1] (in den Medien) commentary [2] (spöttische Bemerkung) sneering *or* (coll.) snide comment [3] (Sprachw., Literaturw.) gloss

Glossen·schreiber *der,* **Glossen·schreiberin** *die* commentator

glossieren *tr. V.* [1] commentate on [2] (bespötteln) sneer at [3] (Sprachw., Literaturw.) gloss

Glottal /glɔˈtaːl/ *der;* **~s, ~e** (Phon.) glottal stop

Glottis /ˈglɔtɪs/ *die;* **~, Glottides** /ˈglɔtideːs/ (Anat.) glottis

Glotz·auge *das* [1] *Pl.* (salopp abwertend) goggle eyes; **~n machen/bekommen** go goggle-eyed; goggle [2] ▸ ❶ **S. 439** (Med.) exophthalmus

glotz·äugig *Adj.* goggle-eyed

Glotze /ˈglɔtsə/ *die;* **~, ~n** (salopp) box (coll.); goggle-box (Brit. coll.)

glotzen *itr. V.* (abwertend) goggle; gawk, gawp (coll.)

Glotz·kiste *die* (salopp) box (coll.); goggle-box (Brit. coll.)

Glotzophon /glɔtsoˈfoːn/ *das;* **~s, ~e** (salopp scherzh.) ▸ **Glotze**

Gloxinie /glɔˈksiːni̯ə/ *die;* **~, ~n** (Bot.) gloxinia

Glubsch·augen /ˈglʊpʃ-/ *Pl.* (nordd.) ▸ **Glupschaugen**

gluck /glʊk/ *Interj.* [1] (für das Glucken) cluck [2] (für das Gluckern) glug; **~, ~, weg war er** (scherzh.) glug, glug, and he went under; **~, ~ machen** (ugs. scherzh.) have a few (sl.)

Glück /glʏk/ *das;* **~[e]s** [1] luck; **ein großes/unverdientes ~:** a great/an undeserved stroke of luck; **[es ist/war] ein ~, dass ...** it's/it was lucky that ...; **er hat [kein] ~ gehabt** he was [un]lucky; **sie hatte das ~, zu ...** she was lucky enough to ...; **bei jmdm. ~ mit etw. haben** succeed in getting sb. to agree to sth.; **bei jmdm. kein ~ haben** get no joy out of sb.; **~ bei Frauen haben** be successful with women; **bei der Auslosung kein ~ haben** have no luck in the draw; **~ im Unglück haben** be quite lucky in the circumstances; **jmdm. ~ wünschen** wish sb. [good] luck; **jmdm. viel ~ zum Geburtstag wünschen** wish sb. a very happy birthday; **viel ~!** [the] best of luck!; good luck!; **~ bringen** bring [good] luck; **~ muss der Mensch haben** my/his *etc.* luck must have been in; **mehr ~ als Verstand haben** have more luck than judgement; **er weiß noch nichts von seinem ~** (iron.) he doesn't know what's in store for him yet; **sein ~ versuchen** *od.* **probieren** try one's luck; **sein ~ machen** make one's fortune; **auf gut ~:** trusting to luck; **er hatte sich auf gut ~ beworben** he had applied on the off chance; **sie wählte ein Buch auf gut ~:** she chose a book at random; **von ~ sagen** *od.* **reden können** consider *or* count oneself lucky; **zum ~** *od.* **zu meinem/seinem** *usw.* **~:** luckily *or* fortunately [for me/him *etc.*]; **~ auf!** (Bergmannsgruß) good luck!; **~ ab!** (Fliegergruß) happy landings!; good luck! [2] (Hochstimmung) happiness; **das häusliche ~:** domestic bliss; **sie ist sein ganzes ~:** she means everything to him; **jmdn. zu seinem ~ zwingen** make sb. do what is good for him/her; **man kann niemanden zu seinem ~ zwingen** you can lead a horse to water but you can't make him drink; **du hast/das hat mir gerade noch zu meinem ~ gefehlt** (iron.) you're/that's all I needed; **jeder ist seines ~es Schmied** (Spr.) life is what you make it; **~ und Glas, wie leicht bricht das** (Spr.) happiness is such a fragile thing [3] (Fortuna) fortune; luck; **das ~ ist launisch** fortunes change; **er ist ein Liebling des ~s** fortune has always smiled upon him; **das ~ war ihm hold** (geh.) fortune smiled [up]on him

glück·bringend *Adj.* lucky

Glucke /ˈglʊkə/ *die;* **~, ~n** brood-hen; mother hen

glucken *itr. V.* [1] (brüten) brood [2] (ugs.: herumsitzen) sit around [3] (Laut hervorbringen) cluck

glücken *tr. V.; mit sein* succeed; be successful; **etw. glückt jmdm.** sb. is successful with sth.; **ein geglückter Versuch** a successful attempt; **die Flucht ist nicht geglückt** the escape [attempt] failed; **es glückt jmdm., etw. zu tun** sb. manages to do sth.

gluckern /ˈglʊkɐn/ *itr. V.* gurgle; glug

glück·haft *Adj.* (geh.) happy

Gluck·henne *die* ▸ **Glucke**

glücklich
[A] *Adj.* [1] ▸ ❶ **S. 331** (von Glück erfüllt) happy (**über** + *Akk.* about); **wunschlos/unsagbar ~ sein** be perfectly happy; **Geld allein macht nicht ~:** money by itself won't bring happiness; **du Glücklicher!** you lucky thing!; lucky you!; **wer ist denn der/die Glückliche?** who is the lucky man/woman/girl *etc.*? [2] (erfolgreich) lucky ‹*winner*›; successful ‹*outcome*›; safe ‹*journey*›; happy ‹*ending*› [3] (vorteilhaft) fortunate; **ein ~er Zufall** a happy coincidence; a lucky chance; *s. auch* **Hand 6**
[B] *adv.* [1] (erfolgreich) successfully [2] (vorteilhaft, zufrieden) happily ‹*chosen, married*› [3] (endlich) eventually; at last

glücklicher·weise *Adv.* fortunately; luckily

glück·los *Adj.* luckless ‹*enterprise*›; unhappy ‹*existence etc.*›

Glück·sache ▸ **Glückssache**

Glücks-: **~bote** *der,* **~botin** *die* bearer of good news *or* glad tidings; **~botschaft** *die* good news *sing.*; glad tidings *pl.*; **~bringer** *der;* **~~s, ~~:** lucky *or* good-luck charm; [lucky] mascot; (Person) [lucky] mascot; **~bringerin** *die;* **~~, ~~nen** [lucky] mascot

glück·selig
[A] *Adj.* blissfully happy ‹*person*›; blissfully happy, blissful ‹*time, experience, etc.*›
[B] *adv.* blissfully

Glück·seligkeit *die;* **~:** bliss; blissful happiness

glucksen /ˈglʊksn̩/ *itr. V.* [1] ▸ **gluckern** [2] (lachen) chuckle; ‹*baby*› gurgle

Glücks-: **~fall** *der* piece *or* stroke of luck; **~fee** *die:* **sie war seine ~fee** she [always] brought him good luck; **~gefühl** *das* feeling of happiness; **~göttin** *die* goddess of fortune; Fortune *no art.*; **~güter** *Pl.* (geh.) riches; **~käfer** *der* ▸ **Marienkäfer**; **~kind** *das* lucky person; **er/sie ist ein ~kind** he/she was born lucky; **~klee** *der* four-leaf *or* four-leaved clover; **~linie** *die* line of fortune; **~pfennig** *der* lucky penny; **~pilz** *der* (ugs.) lucky devil (coll.) *or* beggar (coll.); **~rad** *das* wheel of fortune; **~ritter** *der* (abwertend) adventurer; fortune hunter; **~ritterin** *die;* **~~, ~~nen** (abwertend) adventuress; fortune hunter

g

Glück[s]·sache *die:* **das ist ~:** it's a matter of luck

Glücks-: ~schwein *das: model of a pig as a symbol of good luck or as a good-luck charm;* **~spiel** *das* [1] game of chance; **dem ~spiel verfallen sein** be addicted to gambling; [2] (fig.) matter of luck; lottery; **~spieler** *der,* **~spielerin** *die* gambler; **~stern** *der* lucky star; **~strähne** *die* lucky streak; **eine ~strähne haben** have hit a lucky streak; have a run of good luck; **~tag** *der* lucky day

glück·strahlend
[A] *Adj.* radiant; radiantly happy
[B] *adv.* **sie verkündete uns ~, dass sie heiraten werde** she was radiant with happiness *or* radiantly happy as she told us she was going to get married

Glücks-: ~treffer *der* [1] (Gewinn) bit *or* piece of luck; [2] (beim Schießen) lucky hit; fluke; **~umstand** *der* fortunate circumstance; **~zahl** *die* lucky number

glück·verheißend *Adj.* (geh.) auspicious, propitious ‹*sign, omen*›; ‹*smile*› which holds/held out the promise of happiness

Glück·wunsch *der* ▸ⓘ **S. 331** congratulations *pl.;* **herzlichen ~ zur Beförderung!** [many] congratulations on your promotion!; **herzlichen ~ zum Geburtstag!** happy birthday!; many happy returns of the day!; **jmdm. die herzlichsten Glückwünsche übermitteln/senden** convey/send one's congratulations to sb.

Glückwunsch-: ~adresse *die* message of congratulation; congratulatory message; **~karte** *die* congratulations card; (zum Geburtstag, zu Weihnachten usw.) greetings card; **~schreiben** *das* letter of congratulation; congratulatory letter; **~telegramm** *das* telegram of congratulations; congratulatory telegram; (zum Geburtstag, zu Weihnachten usw.) greetings telegram

Glucose /glu'ko:ze/ *die;* ~ (Chemie) glucose

Glüh-: ~birne *die* light bulb; **~draht** *der* filament

glühen /'gly:ən/
[A] *itr. V.* [1] (leuchten) glow; (fig.) ‹*eyes, cheeks, etc.*› be aglow, glow; **heiß glühte die Sonne über der Wüste** (fig.) the sun was burning down on the desert; **ihr Körper glühte im Fieber** (fig.) her body was burning with fever [2] (geh.: erregt sein) burn; **in Liebe/Leidenschaft ~:** burn with love/passion; **vor Begeisterung ~:** be fired with enthusiasm
[B] *tr. V.* (zum Leuchten bringen) heat until red-hot

glühend
[A] *Adj.* [1] (heiß) red-hot ‹*metal etc.*›; (fig.) blazing ‹*heat*›; burning ‹*hatred*›; flushed, burning ‹*cheeks*› [2] (begeistert) ardent ‹*admirer etc.*›; passionate ‹*words, letter, etc.*›
[B] *adv.* [1] (heiß) **~ heiß** scorching *or* blazing hot; **~ rot** red-hot [2] (begeistert) ‹*love*› passionately; ‹*admire*› ardently; **jmdn. ~ beneiden** be intensely envious of sb.

***glühend·heiß** *usw.* ▸ **glühend B1**

Glüh-: ~faden *der* filament; **~kerze** *die* (Kfz-W.) glow plug; **~lampe** *die* light bulb; **~ofen** *der* (Technik) annealing furnace; **~strumpf** *der* gas mantle; **~wein** *der* mulled wine; glühwein; **~würmchen** *das* (ugs.) (weiblich) glow-worm; (männlich) firefly

Glukose ▸ **Glucose**

Glupsch·augen /'glʊpʃ-/ *Pl.* (nordd.) goggle-eyes; **~ machen** *od.* **bekommen** go goggle-eyed; goggle

Glut /glu:t/ *die;* ~, **~en** [1] embers *pl.;* (von einer Zigarette) [burning] ash; (fig.) [blazing] heat; (des Fiebers) [burning] heat; **die ~ ihrer Wangen** the flush on her cheeks; **die ~ des Abendhimmels** the glow of the evening sky [2] (geh.: Leidenschaft) passion; **die ~ seiner Leidenschaft** the ardour of his passion; **die ~ seines Hasses** the fire of his hatred

Glutamat /gluta'ma:t/ *das;* **~[e]s, ~e** (Chemie) glutamate

Glutamin /gluta'mi:n/ *das;* **~s, ~e** (Chemie) glutamine

Glutamin·säure *die* (Chemie) glutamic acid

glut-, Glut-: ~äugig *Adj.* fiery-eyed; **~hauch** *der* (dichter.) scorching *or* sweltering heat; **~heiß** *Adj.* blazing *or* swelteringly hot; **~hitze** *die* blazing *or* sweltering heat; **~rot** *Adj.* fiery red; **~voll** [A] *Adj.* passionate; [B] *adv.* passionately

Glycerin (fachspr.) ▸ **Glyzerin**

Glykogen /glyko'ge:n/ *das;* **~s** (Med., Biol.) glycogen

Glykol /gly'ko:l/ *das;* **~s, ~e** (Chemie) [ethylene] glycol

Glyzerin /glytse'ri:n/ *das;* **~s** glycerine; glycerol (Chem.)

Glyzerin-creme *die* glycerine cream

Glyzine, Glyzinie /gly'tsi:n(i)ə/ *die;* **~, ~n** wisteria

GmbH *Abk.* **= Gesellschaft mit beschränkter Haftung** ≈ plc, PLC

g-Moll /'ge:-/ *das* (Musik) G minor; *s. auch* **a-Moll**

Gnade /'gna:də/ *die;* ~, **~n** [1] (Gewogenheit) favour; **die ~ [des Königs] erlangen/verlieren** gain/lose [the king's] favour; **die ~ haben, etw. zu tun** (iron.) graciously consent to do sth. (iron.); **vor jmdm.** *od.* **vor jmds. Augen ~ finden** find favour with sb. *or* in sb.'s eyes; **jmdm. auf ~ und** *od.* **oder Ungnade ausgeliefert sein** be [completely] at sb.'s mercy; **etw. aus ~ [und Barmherzigkeit] tun** do sth. out of the kindness of one's heart; **in ~n wieder aufgenommen werden** be restored to favour; **bei jmdm. in [hohen] ~n stehen** (geh.) stand high in sb.'s favour; **von jmds. ~n** by the grace of sb. [2] (Rel.: Güte) grace [3] (Milde) mercy; **~ walten lassen** show mercy; be lenient; **~ vor** *od.* **für Recht ergehen lassen** temper justice with mercy [4] (veraltete Anrede) **Euer** *od.* **Ihro** *od.* **Ihre ~n** Your Grace

gnaden *itr. V. in* **gnade mir/dir Gott!** God *or* Heaven help me/you!

gnaden-, Gnaden-: ~akt *der* act of mercy; **~beweis** *der,* **~bezeigung** *die;* **~~, ~~en** token of [his/her *etc.*] favour; **~bild** *das* (kath. Rel.) *picture of Christ, the Virgin Mary, or a saint, possessing miraculous powers;* **~brot** *das:* **jmdm./einem Tier das ~brot geben** keep sb./an animal in his/her/its old age; **einem Pferd das ~brot geben** put a horse out to grass; **~erweis** *der;* **~~es, ~~e** (Rechtsw.) pardon; **~frist** *die* reprieve; **jmdm. eine ~frist von 4 Wochen gewähren** give sb. four weeks' grace; **ihm bleibt eine ~frist von einer Woche** he has a week left; **~gesuch** *das* plea for clemency; **~halber** *Adv.* as a favour; (Rechtsw.) as an act of mercy; **~instanz** *die: person in whom or authority in which the right of pardon is vested;* **~los** (auch fig.) [A] *Adj.* merciless; [B] *adv.* mercilessly; **~losigkeit** *die;* **~~:** mercilessness; **~reich** *Adj.* (geh.) gracious; **~schuss, *~schuß** *der* coup de grâce (by shooting); **einem Pferd den ~schuss geben** put a horse out of its misery [by shooting it]; **~stoß** *der* coup de grâce (*with sword etc.*); **~tod** *der* euthanasia; mercy killing; **jmdm. den ~tod gewähren** allow sb. to die; **~voll** *Adj.* (geh.) gracious; **~weg** *der:* **auf dem ~weg** by a pardon; **ihm steht der ~weg offen** he can ask *or* has the right to ask for a pardon

gnädig /'gnɛ:dɪç/
[A] *Adj.* [1] (oft iron.) gracious; **er war so ~, mich nach Hause zu begleiten** (iron.) he condescended to take me home; (Anrede) **~es Fräulein/~e Frau** madam; **~er Herr** (veralt.) sir; **die ~e Frau/das ~e Fräulein/der ~e Herr** (veralt.) madam/the young lady/the master; **die Gnädige** (spött.) her ladyship [2] (glimpflich) lenient, light ‹*sentence etc.*› [3] (Rel.) gracious ‹*God*›; **Gott ist allen Sündern ~:** God is merciful to *or* has mercy on all sinners; **Gott sei uns ~:** [may] the good Lord preserve us
[B] *adv.* [1] (oft iron.) graciously [2] (glimpflich) **das ist ~ abgegangen** it turned out not to be too bad; **machen Sie es ~ mit mir** (scherzh.) have mercy on me (joc.)

Gneis /gnais/ *der;* **~es, ~e** (Geol.) gneiss

Gnom /gno:m/ *der;* **~en, ~en** gnome; (fig.: ugs.) little twerp (coll.)

gnomen·haft *Adj.* gnome-like

Gnosis /'gno:zɪs/ *die;* ~ (Rel.) gnosis

Gnostiker /'gnɔstikɐ/ *der;* **~s, ~. Gnostikerin** *die;* **~, ~nen** (Rel.) gnostic

gnostisch *Adj.* (Rel.) gnostic

Gnostizismus /gnɔsti'tsɪsmʊs/ *der;* ~ (Rel.) gnosticism *no art.*

Gnu /gnu:/ *das;* **~s, ~s** gnu

Go /go:/ *das;* **~:** go

Goal /go:l/ *das;* **~s, ~s** (österr., schweiz. Sport) goal

Goal-: ~getter /-gɛtɐ/ *der;* **~~s, ~~** (Sport) goal scorer; **~keeper** /-ki:pɐ/ *der;* **~~s, ~~** (Sport, bes. österr. u. schweiz.) goalkeeper

Gobelin /gobə'lɛ̃:/ *der;* **~s, ~s** Gobelin [tapestry]

Gobelin·stickerei *die* Gobelin embroidery

Go-cart ▸ **Gokart**

Gockel /'gɔkl̩/ *der;* **~s, ~** (bes. südd., sonst ugs. scherzh.) cock; **stolz wie ein ~:** [as] proud as a peacock; **ein verliebter alter ~** (fig.) an amorous old goat (coll.)

Gockel·hahn *der; Pl.* **Gockel·hähne** ▸ **Gockel**

Godemiché /go:dmi'ʃe:/ *der;* **~, ~s** dildo

Goetheana /gøte'a:na/ *Pl.* works by and on Goethe

> **Goethe-Institut**
>
> An organization promoting German language and culture abroad. It is based in Munich and runs about 140 institutes in over 70 countries, offering German language classes, cultural events such as exhibitions, films and seminars, and a library of German books and magazines and other documentation, which is open to the public.

goethesch, *Goethesch /'gø:təʃ/, **goethisch, *Goethisch** /'gø:tɪʃ/ *Adj.* Goethean; **die ~en Gedichte** Goethe's poems; the poems of Goethe

Go-go-Girl /'go:gogø:gl/ *das* go-go girl *or* dancer

Goi /'go:i/ *der;* **~[s], Gojim** /'go:jɪm/ goy

Go-in /go:'ɪn/ *das;* **~s, ~s: ein ~ veranstalten** disrupt the/a meeting

Gokart /'go:kart/ *der;* **~s, ~s** go-kart (Brit.); kart

Golan·höhen /go'la:n-/ *Pl.* Golan Heights

gold /gɔlt/ *Adj.: in* **uns geht's ja noch ~** (ugs.) we're still doing just marvellously

Gold *das;* **~[e]s** gold; **etw. ist aus ~:** sth. is [made of] gold; **ein Barren ~:** a gold bar *or* ingot; **das schwarze ~** (fig.) black gold (fig.); **das flüssige ~** (fig.) liquid gold (fig.); **es ist nicht alles ~, was glänzt** (Spr.) all that glitters *or* glistens is not gold (prov.); **treu wie ~ sein** be absolutely loyal *or* faithful; **etw. in ~ bezahlen** pay for sth. in gold; **~ in der Kehle haben** (fig.) have a golden voice; **jmd. ist nicht mit ~ zu bezahlen** sb. is worth his/her weight in gold (fig.); **etw. ist nicht mit ~ zu bezahlen** *od.* **aufzuwiegen** sth. is invaluable; **olympisches ~:** Olympic gold; **er hat bereits dreimal olympisches ~ geholt** he has already won three Olympic gold medals *or* golds

gold-, Gold-: ~ader *die* vein of gold; **~ammer** *die* yellowhammer; **~arbeit** *die* goldwork; (Gegenstand) piece of goldwork; **~auflage** *die* gold plating *no indef. art.;* **~barren** *der* gold bar *or* ingot; **~barsch** *der* ▸ **Rotbarsch; ~bestand** *der* gold reserves *pl.;* **~bestickt** *Adj.* embroidered with gold [thread] *postpos.;* **~betresst, *~betreßt** *Adj.* trimmed with gold braid *postpos.;* **~blech** *das* rolled gold; **~blond** *Adj.* golden ‹*hair etc.*›; **~borte** *die* gold braid; **~braun** *Adj.* golden brown; **~broiler** *der* (DDR) spit-roasted chicken; **~brokat** *der* gold brocade; **~deckung** *die* gold cover; **~doublé** *das* ▸ **~dublee; ~druck** *der* gold tooling; **~dublee** *das* rolled gold; **~echt** *Adj.* (ugs.) completely genuine ‹*person*›

golden
[A] *Adj.* [1] gold ‹*bracelet, watch, etc.*›; **das Goldene**

Kalb (bibl.) the golden calf; **der Tanz ums Goldene Kalb** the worship of the golden calf *or* Mammon; **eine ~e Schallplatte** a gold disc; **die Goldene Bulle** (hist.) the Golden Bull; **das Goldene Vlies** (Myth.) the Golden Fleece; (Orden) the [order of the] Golden Fleece; **das Goldene Buch [der Stadt]** the [town's] visitors' book; **die Goldene Stadt** the Golden City (Prague) **2** (dichter.: goldfarben) golden **3** (herrlich) golden ‹*days, memories, etc.*›; blissful ‹*freedom etc.*›; **der ~e Westen** the promised land in the West; **~e Worte/Lehren** words of wisdom/wise teachings; **einen ~en Humor haben** have a wonderful sense of humour; **ein ~es Herz haben** have a heart of gold; **die ~e Mitte** *od.* **den ~en Mittelweg finden/wählen** find/strike a happy medium; **das goldene Zeitalter** the Golden Age; **die ~en zwanziger [Jahre]** the roaring twenties; **der goldene Schnitt** (Math.) the golden section

B *adv.* like gold

gold-, Gold-: ~esel *der* (ugs.) **ich bin auch kein ~esel** I'm not made of money (coll.); **~faden** *der* gold thread; **~farben, ~farbig** *Adj.* gold-coloured; golden; **~fasan** *der* golden pheasant; **~feder** *die* gold nib; **~fieber** *das* gold fever; **~folie** *die* gold foil; **~fuchs** *der* **1** (Pferd) golden chestnut [horse]; **2** (veralt.: **~stück**) gold coin *or* piece; **~füllung** *die* gold filling; **~fund** *der* gold find *or* strike; **~gefasst, *~gefaßt** *Adj.* gold-rimmed ‹*glasses*›; ‹*jewel*› mounted in gold; **~gehalt** *der* gold content; **~gelb** *Adj.* golden yellow; **~gerändert** *Adj.* ‹*plate etc.*› edged with gold; gold-rimmed ‹*glasses*›; **~glänzend** *Adj.* shining gold; **~gräber** *der;* **~~s, ~~, ~gräberin** *die;* **~~, ~~nen** gold-digger; **~grube** *die* (auch fig.) gold mine; **~haltig** *Adj.* gold-bearing; auriferous; **~hamster** *der* golden hamster

goldig

A *Adj.* (niedlich, landsch.: nett) sweet

B *adv.* sweetly

Gold-: ~junge *der* **1** (Kosewort) good [little] boy; **2** (Sportjargon) gold medallist; gold-medal winner; **~käfer** *der* **1** rose chafer; rose beetle; **2** (ugs.: reiches Mädchen) rich girl; **~kette** *die* gold chain; **~kind** *das* (ugs. Kosew.) little treasure (coll.); **mein ~kind** my precious (coll.); my pet; **~klumpen** *der* gold nugget; **~krone** *die* (Zahnmed.) gold crown; **~kurs** *der* (Börsenw.) price of gold; gold price; **~küste** *die;* **~~** (Geogr.) Gold Coast; **~lack** *der* **1** gold lacquer; **2** (Bot.) wallflower; **~lager·stätte** *die* gold deposit; **~legierung** *die* gold alloy; **~leiste** *die* gilt strip *or* fillet; **~macher** *der* alchemist; **~mädchen** *das* (Sportjargon) gold medallist; gold-medal winner

Gold·medaille *die* gold medal

Goldmedaillen-: ~gewinner *der,* **~gewinnerin** *die* gold medallist; gold-medal winner

gold-, Gold-: ~mine *die* gold mine; **~münze** *die* gold coin; **~papier** *das* gold[-coloured] paper; **~parität** *die* (Wirtsch.) gold parity; **~pool** *der* (Wirtsch.) gold pool; **~preis** *der* price of gold; gold price; **~probe** *die* gold assay; **~rahmen** *der* gold *or* gilt frame; **~rausch** *der* gold fever; **~regen** *der* **1** (Bot.) laburnum; golden rain; **2** (Feuerwerk) golden rain; **3** (Reichtum) riches *pl.*; wealth; **~reif** *der* (geh.) gold ring; (Armband) gold bracelet; **~reserve** *die* gold reserve; **~richtig** (ugs.) **A** *Adj.* absolutely *or* dead right; **du bist ~richtig, so wie du bist** you're perfectly all right as you are; **B** *adv.* absolutely right; **~schatz** *der* **1** (Schatz) gold treasure; (verborgen auch) hoard of gold; **2** (Kosew.) treasure

Gold·schmied *der* ▸ **i S. 113** goldsmith

Goldschmiede-: ~arbeit *die* piece of goldwork; **~handwerk** *das* goldsmith's craft; goldwork *no art.*; **~kunst** *die* goldsmith's art; goldwork *no art.*

Gold-: ~schmiedin *die* ▸ **Goldschmied**; **~schmuck** *der* gold jewelry *or* (Brit.) jewellery; **~schnitt** *der* gilt edging; **~schrift** *die* gold lettering; **~staub** *der* gold dust; **~stück** *das* (hist.) gold piece; **sie ist ein ~stück** (fig.) she is a [real] treasure; **~sucher** *der,* **~sucherin** *die* gold prospector; **~ton** *der; Pl.* **~töne** golden colour; **~topas** *der* yellow topaz; **~tresse** *die* gold braid; **~überzug** *der* layer of gold plate; **~uhr** *die* gold watch; **~vorkommen** *das* gold deposit; **~waage** *die* gold balance; **alles** *od.* **jedes Wort auf die ~waage legen** (wörtlich nehmen) take everything *or* every word [too] literally; (vorsichtig äußern) weigh one's words very carefully; **~währung** *die* (Wirtsch.) currency tied to the gold standard; **~waren** *Pl.* gold articles; **~wäscher** *der;* **~~s, ~~:** gold washer; **~wert** *der* **1** (Wert des **~es**) value of gold; **2** (Wert in **~**) value in gold; **~zahn** *der* (ugs.) gold tooth

Golem /ˈgoːlɛm/ *der;* **~s** golem

Golf¹ /gɔlf/ *der;* **~[e]s, ~e** gulf; **der ~ von Neapel** the Bay of Naples

Golf² *das;* **~s** (Sport) golf

Golf·ball *der* golf ball

Golfer *der;* **~s, ~, Golferin** *die;* **~, ~nen** golfer

Golf-: ~hose *die* golf[ing] trousers *pl.*; **~mütze** *die* golf[ing] cap; **~platz** *der* golfcourse; **~schläger** *der* golf club; **~schuh** *der* golf[ing] shoe; **~spieler** *der,* **~spielerin** *die* golfer; **~staat** *der* Gulf State; **~strom** *der* Gulf Stream; **~turnier** *das* golf tournament

Golgatha /ˈgɔlgata/ *das;* **~[s]** (bibl.) Golgotha; **für ihn war diese Niederlage/dieser Verlust ein ~** (fig. geh.) this defeat/loss caused him much pain and suffering

Goliath /ˈgoːli̯at/ *der;* **~s, ~s** Goliath

Gomorrha /goˈmɔra/ ▸ **Sodom**

Gondel /ˈgɔndl̩/ *die;* **~, ~n** gondola

Gondel-: ~bahn *die* **1** (Seilbahn) cable railway; **2** (schweiz.) ▸ **Sessellift**; **~fahrt** *die* trip in a gondola; gondola trip

gondeln *itr. V.; mit sein* (ugs.) **1** (mit einem Boot) cruise **2** (reisen) travel around **3** (herumfahren) drive *or* cruise around; **durch die Stadt ~:** drive *or* cruise around town

Gondoliera /gɔndoˈli̯eːra/ *die;* **~, Gondolieren** [female] gondolier

Gondoliere /gɔndoˈli̯eːrə/ *der;* **~s, Gondolieri** gondolier

Gong /gɔŋ/ *der;* **~s, ~s** gong

gongen *itr. V.* **es hat gegongt** the gong has sounded; **der Butler gongte zum Abendessen** the butler sounded the gong for dinner

Gong·schlag *der* stroke of the/a gong; **beim ~:** when the gong sounds/sounded

gönnen /ˈgœnən/ *tr. V.* **1** (zugestehen) **jmdm. etw. ~:** not begrudge sb. sth.; **ich gönne ihm diesen Erfolg von ganzem Herzen** I'm delighted *or* very pleased for him that he has had this success; **jmdm. den Misserfolg ~** (iron.) delight in sb.'s misfortune **2** (zukommen lassen) **sich/jmdm. etw. ~:** give *or* allow oneself/sb. sth.; **sie gönnte sich** (*Dat.*) **einen großen Cognac** she treated herself to a large cognac; **sie gönnte ihm keinen Blick/kein Wort** she didn't spare him a single glance/she didn't say a single word to him

Gönner *der;* **~s, ~** patron

gönnerhaft (abwertend)

A *Adj.* patronizing; **mit ~er Miene** with a patronizing expression [on his/her face]

B *adv.* patronizingly; in a patronizing manner

Gönnerin *die;* **~, ~nen** patroness

Gönner·miene *die* (abwertend) patronizing expression; **mit ~:** with a patronizing expression [on his/her face]

Gonokokkus /gonoˈkɔkʊs/ *der;* **~, Gonokokken** (Med.) gonococcus

Gonorrhö[e] /gɔnoˈrøː/ *die;* **~, Gonorrhöen** /gɔnoˈrøːən/ ▸ **i S. 439** (Med.) gonorrhoea

Goodwill /ˈgʊdˈwɪl/ *der;* **~s** **1** (Ansehen) good name **2** (Wohlwollen) goodwill

Goodwill-: ~reise *die* goodwill trip (**nach** to); **~tour** *die* goodwill tour (**durch** of)

Göpel /ˈgøːpl̩/ *der;* **~s, ~:** whim

Gopher /ˈgoʊfɐ/ *der;* **~s, ~** (DV) gopher

gor /goːɐ̯/ *3. Pers. Sg. Prät. v.* **gären**

Gör /gøːɐ̯/ *das;* **~[e]s, ~en** (nordd., oft abwertend) ▸ **Göre**

gordisch /ˈgɔrdɪʃ/ *Adj.* **der Gordische Knoten** the Gordian knot; **ein ~er Knoten** (fig.) a Gordian knot (fig.)

Göre /ˈgøːrə/ *die;* **~, ~n** (nordd., oft abwertend) **1** (Kind) child; kid (coll.); brat (coll. derog.) **2** (freches Mädchen) [cheeky *or* saucy] little madam (coll.)

Gorilla /goˈrɪla/ *der;* **~s, ~s** **1** gorilla **2** (ugs.: Leibwächter) heavy (coll.)

Gosch[e] /ˈgɔʃ(ə)/ *die;* **~, Goschen, Goschen** /ˈgɔʃn̩/ *die;* **~, ~** (südd., österr. meist abwertend) mouth; **eine große/freche Gosche** *od.* **Goschen haben** (derb) have a big mouth (coll.)/be a cheeky so-and-so (coll.); **die Gosche** *od.* **Goschen halten** (derb) shut one's gob *or* trap (sl.)

Gospel /ˈgɔspl̩/ *das od. der;* **~s, ~s, Gospel·song** *der;* **~s, ~s** gospel song

goss, *goß /gɔs/ *1. u. 3. Pers. Sg. Prät. v.* **gießen**

Gosse /ˈgɔsə/ *die;* **~, ~n** gutter; (fig. abwertend) **aus der ~ kommen** come from the gutter; **in der ~ enden** end up in the gutter; **jmdn.** *od.* **jmds. Namen durch die ~ ziehen** drag sb.'s name through the mud

Gossen-: ~jargon *der,* **~sprache** *die* (abwertend) gutter language; language of the gutter

Gote¹ /ˈgoːtə/ *der;* **~n, ~n** Goth

Gote² *der;* **~n, ~n** (bes. südd.: Pate) godfather

Gote³ *die;* **~, ~n** (bes. südd.: Patin) godmother

Gotha /ˈgoːta/ *der;* **~:** *almanac containing information on the nobility of Europe*

Gotik /ˈgoːtɪk/ *die;* **~** (Stil) Gothic [style]; (Epoche) Gothic period

Gotin *die;* **~, ~nen** ▸ **Gote¹**

gotisch *Adj.* Gothic; **die ~e Schrift** Gothic [script]

Gott /gɔt/ *der;* **~es, Götter** /ˈgœtɐ/ **1** God; **~ Vater** God the Father; **hier ruht in ~ ...** here lies ...; **~ segne dich!** God bless you!; **~es Mühlen mahlen langsam** (Spr.) the mills of God grind slowly; **bei ~ ist kein Ding unmöglich** (Spr.) with God all things are possible; **grüß [dich] ~!** (landsch.) hello!; **behüt dich ~!** (südd., österr.) goodbye! God bless!; **vergelts ~!** (landsch.) thank you! God bless you!; **großer** *od.* **mein ~!** good God!; **o** *od.* **ach [du lieber] ~!** goodness me!; **weiß ~:** God *or* heaven knows; **~ behüte** God *or* Heaven forbid; **~ steh mir bei** God help me; **gebe ~, dass alles gut ausgeht** please God, may everything turn out all right; **wie ~ ihn/sie geschaffen hat** (scherzh.) in his/her birthday suit (joc.); in the altogether (joc.); **~ und die Welt** all the world and his wife; **über ~ und die Welt quatschen** (ugs.) talk about everything under the sun (coll.); **~ sei Dank!** (ugs.) thank God!; **~ seis geklagt!** alas; **um ~es Willen** (bei Erschrecken) for God's sake; (bei einer Bitte) for heaven's *or* goodness' sake; **tue es in ~es Namen** (ugs.) do it and have done with it; **da sei ~ vor!** God forbid!; **~ soll mich strafen, wenn ...** may God strike me down if ...; **so ~ will** (ugs.) God willing; **~ hab ihn selig** God rest his soul; **wie ~ in Frankreich leben** (ugs.) live in the lap of luxury; **den lieben ~ einen guten Mann sein lassen** (ugs.) take things as they come; **ein Wetter, dass [es] ~ erbarm** (ugs.) abominable weather; **er spielt/kocht, dass [es] ~ erbarm** his playing/cooking is abominable; **dem lieben ~ den Tag stehlen** laze the day away; **er/sie ist ganz und gar von ~ verlassen** (ugs.) he/she has quite taken leave of his/her senses **2** (übermenschliches Wesen) god; **wie ein junger ~ spielen/tanzen** play/dance divinely; **das wissen die Götter** (ugs.) God *or* heaven only knows; **es war ein Bild für die Götter** (ugs.) it was priceless (coll.)

gott·ähnlich *Adj.* godlike

Gottchen *in* **[ach] ~!** oh dear!

Gott·erbarmen *das: in* **zum ~ sein** (mitleiderregend) be pitiful; (schlecht) be pathetic; **zum ~ schreien** cry out pitifully; **zum ~ spielen/**

g

singen play/sing pathetically

Götter-: ~bild *das* idol; **~bote** *der* messenger of the gods; **~dämmerung** *die* (nord. Myth.) twilight of the gods; (fig.) end of civilization; götterdämmerung; **~gatte** *der* (ugs. scherzh.) lord and master (coll. joc.)

gott·ergeben
A *Adj.* meek
B *adv.* meekly

Gott·ergebenheit *die* meekness

götter-, Götter-: ~gestalt *die* god; **~gleich** *Adj.* godlike; **~sage** *die* 1) (Myth.) mythology of the gods; 2) (Sage von einem Gott) myth about a god/the gods; **~speise** *die* 1) (Myth.) food of the gods; 2) (Kochk.) jelly; **~trank** *der* (Myth.) drink of the gods; **~vater** *der* (Myth.) father of the gods

gottes-, Gottes-: ~acker *der* (geh.) God's Acre *no art.* (literary); graveyard; **~begriff** *der* conception of God; **~beweis** *der* proof of the existence of God; **~dienst** *der* service; **den ~dienst besuchen** go to church; **~erkenntnis** *die* knowledge of God; **~friede** *der* (hist.) Truce of God; **~furcht** *die* fear of God; **~fürchtig** *Adj.* god-fearing; **~gabe** *die* gift from God; **~gelehrte** *der* (veralt.) theologian; **~gnadentum** *das;* **~~s** (hist.) divine right [of kings]; **~haus** *das* (geh.) house of God; **~krieger** *der* warrior of God; jihad fighter; **~lästerer** *der*, **~lästerin** *die* blasphemer; **~lästerlich** A *Adj.* blasphemous; B *adv.* blasphemously; **~lästerung** *die* blasphemy; **~lohn** *der* God's reward; **um ~lohn** for love; **~mann** *der* (geh.) man of God; **~sohn** *der* Son of God; **~staat** *der* theocracy; **~urteil** *das* (hist.) trial by ordeal

gott-: ~froh *Adj.* (ugs.) very *or* (Brit. coll.) jolly glad; **~gefällig** *Adj.* (geh.) pleasing to God *postpos.;* **~gegeben** *Adj.* God-given; **~gesandt** *Adj.* sent by God *postpos.;* **~geweiht** *Adj.* dedicated to God *postpos.;* **~gewollt** *Adj.* ordained by God *postpos.;* **~gläubig** *Adj.* 1) (veralt.) religious; 2) (ns.) **~gläubig sein** be a theist but of no particular denomination

Gottheit *die;* ~, **~en** 1) (Gott, Göttin) deity 2) (geh.: Gottsein) divinity 3) (geh.: Gott) **die ~:** the Godhead

Göttin /ˈgœtɪn/ *die;* ~, **~nen** goddess

göttlich /ˈgœtlɪç/
A *Adj.* 1) (Gott eigen od. ähnlich; herrlich) divine ‹*grace, beauty, etc.*›; **die ~e Gerechtigkeit** divine justice 2) (einem Gott zukommend) god-like ‹*status etc.*›; **jmdm. ~e Verehrung entgegenbringen** worship sb. as if he/she were a God
B *adv.* (herrlich) divinely

Göttlichkeit *die;* ~: divinity

gott-, Gott-: ~lob *adv.* thank goodness; **es hat ~lob nicht geschneit** it didn't snow, thank goodness; **~los** A *Adj.* 1) (verwerflich) ungodly, wicked ‹*life etc.*›; impious ‹*words, speech, etc.*›; (pietätlos) irreverent; 2) (~ leugnend) godless ‹*theory etc.*›; B *adv.* (verwerflich) irreverently; **~losigkeit** *die;* ~~ 1) (Verwerflichkeit) ungodliness; wickedness; (von der Rede) impiety; 2) (Unglauben) godlessness; **~mensch** *der* God-man; **~sei·bei·uns** *der;* ~~ (verhüll.) **der ~seibeiuns** the Evil One

gotts·erbärmlich, gotts·jämmerlich
A *Adj.* (salopp) 1) (erbärmlich) dreadful (coll.) 2) (stark) dreadful (coll.); terrible (coll.); God-awful (sl.)
B *adv.* terribly (coll.); dreadfully (coll.)

gott-, Gott-: ~vater *der* God the Father; **~verdammich** /-fɛɐ̯ˈdamɪç/ *Interj.* (derb) God damn it (sl.); God Almighty (coll.); **~verdammt** *Adj.* (salopp), **~verflucht** *Adj.* (salopp) goddamn[ed] (sl.); **~vergessen** *Adj.* 1) (~los) godless; 2) ▸**gottverlassen**; **~verlassen** *Adj.* 1) (ugs.: abseits) godforsaken; 2) (von ~ verlassen) forsaken by God *postpos.;* **sich ~verlassen fühlen** feel that God has forsaken one; **~vertrauen** *das* trust in God; **~voll** A *Adj.* 1) (ugs.: komisch) priceless (coll.); 2) (herrlich) divine; B *adv.* divinely

Götze /ˈgœtsə/ *der;* **~n, ~n** (auch fig.) idol

Götzen-: ~anbeter *der* ▸**~diener**; **~anbeterin** *die* ▸**~dienerin**; **~bild** *das* idol; graven image (bibl.); (fig.) idol; **~diener** *der* idolater; (fig.) worshipper; **~dienerin** *die* idolatress; (fig.) worshipper; **~dienst** *der* idolatry *no art.;* (fig.) worship; **~dienst leisten** practise idolatry; **~verehrung** *die* idolatry *no art.*

Götz·zitat /ˈgœts-/ *das: the insulting remark 'du kannst mich am Arsch lecken' or the like, frequently used in altercations; a verbal equivalent of the V-sign*

Gouache /gu̯a[:]ʃ/ *die;* ~, **~n** gouache

Gouda /ˈgauda/ *der;* **~s, ~s, Gouda·käse** *der* Gouda [cheese]

Goulasch ▸**Gulasch**

Gourmand /gʊrˈmã:/ *der;* **~s, ~s** gourmand

Gourmet /gʊrˈmɛ/ *der;* **~s, ~s** gourmet

Gourmet·tempel *der* gourmet retreat; gourmet temple

goutieren /guˈti:rən/ *tr. V.* (geh.) appreciate

Gouvernante /guvɛrˈnantə/ *die;* ~, **~n** ▸ⓘ **S. 113** governess

gouvernanten·haft
A *Adj.* schoolmarmish (coll.)
B *adv.* like a schoolmarm (coll.)

Gouvernement /guvɛrnəˈmã:/ *das;* **~s, ~s** 1) (Regierung) government; (Verwaltung) administration 2) (Verwaltungsbezirk) province

Gouverneur /guvɛrˈnø:ɐ̯/ *der;* **~s, ~e** governor

Grab /gra:p/ *das;* **~[e]s, Gräber** /ˈgrɛ:bɐ/ grave; **das ~ meiner Träume/Hoffnungen** (fig.) the end of my dreams/hopes; **er würde sich im ~[e] herumdrehen** (fig. ugs.) he would turn in his grave; **das Heilige ~:** the Holy Sepulchre; **das ~ des Unbekannten Soldaten** the tomb of the Unknown Soldier *or* Warrior; **verschwiegen wie ein** *od.* **das ~ sein** (ugs.) keep absolutely mum (coll.); **ein feuchtes** *od.* **nasses ~ finden,** (geh.) **sein ~ in den Wellen finden** go to a watery grave; meet a watery end; **sich** (*Dat.*) **selbst sein ~ schaufeln** (fig.) dig one's own grave (fig.); **mit einem Fuß** *od.* **Bein im ~[e] stehen** (fig.) have one foot in the grave (fig.); **jmdn. an den Rand des ~es bringen** (fig. geh.) drive sb. to distraction; **jmdn. ins ~ bringen** be the death of sb.; **jmdm. ins ~ folgen** (geh.) follow sb. to the grave; **etw. mit ins ~ nehmen** (geh.) take sth. with one to the grave; **bis ins** *od.* **ans ~** (fig. geh.) [right up] to the end; **jmdn. zu ~e tragen** (geh.) bury sb.; **seine Pläne/Hoffnungen zu ~e tragen** (fig. geh.) abandon one's plans/hopes

Grab·beigabe *die* burial object

grabbeln /ˈgrabl̩n/ *itr. V.* (ugs., bes. nordd.) grope [about]; rummage [about]

Grab·denkmal *das* ▸**Grabmal**

graben
A *unr. tr. V.* 1) dig ‹*hole, grave, etc.*›; dig, carve ‹*groove*›; **Furchen/Falten in jmds. Gesicht ~** (fig.) carve *or* etch lines/wrinkles in sb.'s face 2) (gewinnen) cut ‹*turf*›; mine ‹*coal etc.*› 3) (geh.: ein~) carve; engrave
B *unr. itr. V.* dig (**nach** for); **seine Zähne/Hände in etw.** (*Akk.*) **~** (geh.) sink *or* bury one's teeth/hands in sth.
C *unr. refl. V.* (geh.) **sich in etw. ~:** dig into sth.; **es grub sich ihm ins Gedächtnis** (fig.) it became imprinted *or* engraved in his memory

Graben *der;* **~s, Gräben** /ˈgrɛ:bn̩/ 1) ditch 2) (Schützengraben) trench; **im ~ liegen** lie in the trenches 3) (Festungsgraben) moat 4) (Geol.) rift valley; graben

Graben-: ~bruch *der* (Geol.) graben; **~kampf** *der*, **~krieg** *der* trench warfare *no pl., no indef. art.*

Gräber-: ~feld *das* [large] cemetery; **~fund** *der* grave find

Grabes-: ~kälte *die* (geh.) deathly cold; **~luft** *die* (geh.) grave-like *or* tomb-like air *no pl., no indef. art.;* **~ruhe** *die*, **~stille** *die* deathly silence *or* hush; **~stimme** *die* (ugs.) sepulchral voice

Grab-: ~fund *der* ▸**Gräberfund**; **~geläut[e]** *das* [death] knell; **~gesang** *der* dirge; funeral hymn; (fig.) death knell; **~gewölbe** *das* vault; (in Kirche, Dom) crypt; **~hügel** *der* grave mound; **~inschrift** *die* inscription [on a/the gravestone]; epitaph; **~kammer** *die* burial chamber; **~kreuz** *das* cross [on the/a grave]; **~lege** *die;* **~~, ~~n** burial place; **~legung** *die;* **~~, ~~en** 1) (christl. Rel.) entombment of Christ; 2) (Kunst) **die ~legung Christi** the Entombment of Christ; **~licht** *das; Pl.* **~er** grave light; **~mal** *das; Pl.* **~mäler,** *geh.* **~~e** monument; (~stein) gravestone; **das ~mal des Unbekannten Soldaten** the tomb of the Unknown Soldier *or* Warrior; **~platte** *die* memorial slab; (aus Metall) memorial plate; **~rede** *die* funeral oration *or* speech; **~schänder** *der;* **~~s, ~~, ~schänderin** *die;* **~~, ~~nen** desecrator of a/the grave/of [the] graves; **~schändung** *die* desecration of a/the grave/of [the] graves

grabschen /ˈgrapʃn̩/
A *tr. V.* grab; snatch
B *itr. V.* **nach etw. ~:** grab at sth.

Grab-: ~spruch *der* epitaph; **~stätte** *die* tomb; grave; **~stein** *der* gravestone; tombstone; **~stelle** *die* burial plot

gräbst /grɛ:pst/ *2. Pers. Sg. Präsens v.* **graben**

gräbt *3. Pers. Sg. Präsens v.* **graben**

Grabung *die;* ~, **~en** (bes. Archäol.) excavation

Grabungs·fund *der* archaeological find

Grab·urne *die* funeral urn

Gracht /graxt/ *die;* ~, **~en** canal

grad. *Abk.* = **graduiert**

grad-, Grad- ▸**gerad[e]-, Gerad[e]-**

Grad /gra:t/ *der, als Maßeinheit: das;* **~[e]s, ~e** 1) degree; **Verbrennungen ersten/zweiten ~es** first-/second-degree burns; **ein Verwandter ersten/zweiten ~es** an immediate relation/a relation once removed; **Vettern ersten ~es** first cousins; **bis zu einem gewissen ~[e]** to a [certain] degree; **in hohem ~e** to a great *or* large extent; **er ist mir in höchstem ~e unsympathisch** I dislike him intensely; **in geringem ~e** to a slight extent; slightly 2) (akademischer ~) degree; (Milit.) rank 3) ▸ⓘ **S. 703** (Maßeinheit, Math., Geogr.) degree; **20 ~ Celsius/Fahrenheit** *usw.* 20 degrees Centigrade *or* Celsius/Fahrenheit *etc.;* **10 ~ Wärme/Kälte** 10 degrees above zero/below [zero]; **39 ~ Fieber haben** have a temperature of 39 degrees; **minus 5 ~/5 ~ minus** minus 5 degrees; **null ~:** zero; **etw. auf 90 ~ erhitzen** heat sth. to [a temperature of] 90 degrees; **Gleichungen zweiten ~es** equations of the second degree; quadratic equations; **sich um hundertachtzig ~ drehen** (fig.) completely change [one's views]; **der 50. ~ nördlicher Breite** [latitude] 50 degrees North; **die Insel liegt auf dem 42. ~ östlicher Länge** the longitude of the island is 42 degrees East

Grad-: ~bogen *der* graduated arc; **~einteilung** *die* graduation

Gradient /graˈdi̯ɛnt/ *der;* **~en, ~en** (bes. Math., Physik) gradient

gradieren *tr. V.* graduate; calibrate

Gradier·werk *das* thorn-house; graduation-house

grad-, Grad-: ~linig ▸**geradlinig**; **~mäßig** ▸**graduell**; **~messer** *der;* **~~s, ~~:** gauge, yardstick (**für** of); **~netz** *das* network of parallels and meridians

graduell /graˈdu̯ɛl/
A *Adj.* gradual ‹*development etc.*›; slight ‹*difference etc.*›
B *adv.* gradually; by degrees; ‹*different*› in degree

graduieren
A *tr. V.* 1) (an Hochschulen) award a degree to; graduate (Amer.) 2) ‹*in Grade einteilen*› graduate; calibrate
B *itr. V.* (an Hochschulen) graduate

graduiert *Adj.* graduate; **ein ~er Ingenieur/eine ~e Ingenieurin** an engineering graduate

Graduierte *der/die; adj. Dekl.* graduate

Graduierung *die;* ~, **~en** graduation

Grad·unterschied *der* difference of *or* in degree

grad·weise *Adv.* gradually; by degrees
Graecum /ˈgrɛ:kʊm/ *das;* **~s** (Prüfung) examination in Greek; (Qualifikation) qualification in Greek
Graf /gra:f/ *der;* **~en, ~en** **1** count; (britischer ~) earl **2** (Titel) Count; (britischer ~) Earl; **~ Koks [von der Gasanstalt]** (salopp scherzh.), **~ Rotz [von der Backe]** (salopp abwertend) Lord Muck (Brit. joc.)
Grafen·stand *der* **1** (Rang eines Grafen) rank of count; (in Großbritannien) rank of earl; earldom; **jmdn. in den ~ erheben** confer the rank of count/earl upon sb. **2** (Gesamtheit der Grafen) counts *pl.;* (in Großbritannien) earls *pl.*
Graffito /graˈfi:to/ *der od. das;* **~[s], Graffiti** **1** (Kunst) graffito **2** *Pl.* (Kritzelei) graffiti
Grafik /ˈgra:fɪk/ *die;* **~, ~en** **1** (Gestaltung, grafisches Schaffen) graphic art[s *pl.*] **2** (Kunstwerk) graphic; (Druck) print **3** (Illustration) diagram
Grafiker ▸**Graphiker**
Gräfin /ˈgrɛ:fɪn/ *die;* **~, ~nen** countess; (Titel) Countess
grafisch ▸**graphisch**
Grafit ▸**Graphit**
gräflich /ˈgrɛ:flɪç/ *Adj.* count's *attrib.;* of the count *postpos., not pred.;* (in Großbritannien) earl's; of the earl
Grafschaft *die;* **~, ~en** **1** (Amtsbezirk des Grafen) count's land; (in Großbritannien) earldom **2** (Verwaltungsbezirk) county
Graham·brot /ˈgra:ham-/ *das* wholemeal (Brit.) *or* (Amer.) wheatmeal bread
gräko- /ˈgrɛ:ko-/ Graeco-; **~lateinisch** Graeco-Latin
Gral /gra:l/ *der;* **~[e]s: der [Heilige] ~:** the [Holy] Grail
Grals-: ~hüter *der* keeper of the [Holy] Grail; (fig.) guardian; **~hüterin** *die* (fig.) guardian; **~ritter** *der* knight of the [Holy] Grail
gram /gra:m/ *in* **jmdm. ~ sein** be aggrieved at sb.
Gram *der;* **~[e]s** (geh.) grief; sorrow; **aus ~ um** *od.* **über etw.** (*Akk.*) out of grief *or* sorrow at sth.; **vom** *od.* **von ~ gebeugt sein** be bowed down with grief *or* sorrow
grämen /ˈgrɛ:mən/
A *tr. V.* grieve
B *refl. V.* grieve (**über** + *Akk.*, **um** over); **sich wegen etw. ~:** worry about sth.
gram·erfüllt
A *Adj.* grief-stricken; sorrowful
B *adv.* sorrowfully
Gram·färbung *die* (Bakteriol.) Gram's method
gram·gebeugt *Adj.* bowed down with grief *or* sorrow *postpos.*
grämlich /ˈgrɛ:mlɪç/
A *Adj.* morose; sullen; morose ‹*thought*›
B *adv.* morosely; sullenly
Gramm /gram/ *das;* **~s, ~e** ▸**❶ S. 315** gram; **250 ~ Käse** 250 grams of cheese
Grammatik /graˈmatɪk/ *die;* **~, ~en** **1** grammar **2** (Lehrbuch) grammar [book]
grammatikalisch /gramatiˈka:lɪʃ/ *Adj.* ▸**grammatisch**
Grammatik·regel *die* grammatical rule; rule of grammar
grammatisch
A *Adj.* grammatical
B *adv.* grammatically
Gramm·atom *das* (Chemie, Physik) gram-atom
Grammel /ˈgraml̩/ *die;* **~, ~n** (bayr., österr.) ▸**Griebe**
Grammophon Ⓦⓩ /gramoˈfo:n/ *das;* **~s, ~e** gramophone; phonograph (Amer.); **auf dem ~ spielen** (ugs.) play records
Grammophon·trichter *der* gramophone *or* (Amer.) phonograph horn
Grammy /ˈgrɛmi/ *der;* **~[s], ~s** Grammy
gram-: ~negativ *Adj.* (Bakteriol.) Gram-negative; **~positiv** *Adj.* (Bakteriol.) Gram-positive
Granat /graˈna:t/ *der;* **~[e]s, ~e** **1** (Schmuckstein) garnet **2** (Garnele) [common] shrimp
Granat·apfel *der* pomegranate
Granat·[apfel]baum *der* pomegranate [tree]
Granate /graˈna:tə/ *die;* **~, ~n** shell; (Hand~) grenade
granaten·voll *Adj.* (ugs.) absolutely plastered (sl.); totally canned (Brit. sl.)
Granat-: ~feuer *das* shellfire *no pl., no indef. art.;* **~splitter** *der* shell splinter; **~trichter** *der* shell crater; **~werfer** *der* (Milit.) mortar
Grand /grã: *od.* graŋ/ *der;* **~s, ~s** (Skat) grand; **~ Hand** grand solo; **~ ouvert** open grand
Grande /ˈgrandə/ *der;* **~n, ~n** (hist.) grandee
Grandeur /grãˈdø:ɐ̯/ *die;* **~:** grandeur
Grandezza /granˈdɛt̮sa/ *die;* **~:** grandeur; **mit ~:** with a grand air
Grand·hotel /ˈgrã:-/ *das* luxury *or* five-star hotel
grandios /granˈdi̯o:s/
A *Adj.* magnificent
B *adv.* magnificently
Grand Prix /grãˈpri:/ *der;* **~** /-pri:(s)/, **~** /-pri:s/ Grand Prix
Grandseigneur /grãsɛnˈjø:ɐ̯/ *der;* **~s, ~s** *od.* **~e** (geh.) grand seigneur
Granit /graˈni:t/ *der;* **~s, ~e** granite; **auf ~ beißen** (fig.) bang one's head against a brick wall (fig.); **bei jmdm. auf ~ beißen** (fig.) get nowhere with sb. (fig.)
Granit·block *der; Pl.* **Granitblöcke** block of granite; granite block
graniten *Adj.* **1** granite; granitic (Geol.) **2** (geh.: hart) granitic; granite; (fig.) rigid; inflexible; granitic
Granit·gestein *das* granitic rock
Granne /ˈgranə/ *die;* **~, ~n** awn; beard
Grant /grant/ *der;* **~s** (südd., österr. ugs.) **[wegen etw.] einen ~ haben/bekommen** be in/get into a bad mood [because of sth.]
granteln /ˈgrantl̩n/ *itr. V.* (südd., österr. ugs.) grumble (**über** + *Akk.*, **gegen** about)
grantig /ˈgrantɪç/ (südd., österr. ugs.)
A *Adj.* bad-tempered; grumpy
B *adv.* bad-temperedly; grumpily
Grantler /ˈgrantlɐ/ *der;* **~s, ~, Grantlerin** *die;* **~, ~nen** (südd., österr. ugs.) grumbler
Granulat /granuˈla:t/ *das;* **~[e]s, ~e** (bes. Chemie) granules *pl.*
granulieren *itr., tr. V.* (bes. Chemie) granulate
Grapefruit /ˈgre:pfru:t/ *die;* **~, ~s** grapefruit
Grapefruit·saft *der* grapefruit juice
Graph¹ /gra:f/ *der;* **~en, ~en** (Math., Naturw.) graph
Graph² *das;* **~s, ~e** (Sprachw.) graph
Graphem /graˈfe:m/ *das;* **~s, ~e** (Sprachw.) grapheme
Graphie /graˈfi:/ *die;* **~, ~n** (Sprachw.) written form
Graphik /ˈgra:fɪk/ *die;* **~, ~en** **1** (Gestaltung, graphisches Schaffen) graphic art[s *pl.*] **2** (Kunstwerk) graphic; (Druck) print **3** (Illustration) diagram
Graphiker *der;* **~s, ~, Graphikerin** *die;* **~, ~nen** ▸**❶ S. 113** [graphic] designer; (Künstler[in]) graphic artist
graphisch
A *Adj.* **1** graphic; **das ~e Gewerbe** (veralt.) the printing trade **2** (schematisch) graphic; diagrammatic; **eine ~e Darstellung** a diagram; (Math.: ein Graph) a graph **3** (Sprachw.) graphic
B *adv.* graphically
Graphit /graˈfi:t/ *der;* **~s, ~e** graphite
graphit·grau *Adj.* dark grey
Graphit·stift *der* lead pencil
Graphologe /grafoˈlo:gə/ *der;* **~n, ~n** ▸**❶ S. 113** graphologist
Graphologie *die;* **~:** graphology *no art.*
Graphologin *die;* **~, ~nen** ▸**❶ S. 113** graphologist
graphologisch
A *Adj.* graphological
B *adv.* graphologically; ‹*analysed, interpreted*› by a graphologist
grapschen /ˈgrapʃn̩/ ▸**grabschen**
Gras /gra:s/ *das;* **~es, Gräser** /ˈgrɛ:zɐ/ grass; **wo er hinhaut, da wächst kein ~ mehr** (fig. ugs.) one blow from him and you'd be out cold (coll.); **das ~ wachsen hören** (ugs. spött.) read too much into things; **über etw.** (*Akk.*) **~ wachsen lassen** (ugs.) let the dust settle on sth.; **ins ~ beißen [müssen]** (salopp) bite the dust (coll.)
gras-, Gras-: ~bahn *die* (Sport) grass track; **~bedeckt, ~bewachsen** *Adj.* grass-covered; grassy; **~büschel** *das* tuft of grass; **~decke** *die* covering of grass
grasen *itr. V.* **1** graze **2** (ugs.: suchen) **nach etw. ~:** search for sth.
gras-, Gras-: ~fläche *die* area of grass; (Rasen) lawn; **~fleck** *der* **1** patch of grass; **2** (auf der Kleidung) grass stain; **~fresser** *der* (Zool.) herbivore; **~frosch** *der* grass frog; **~grün** *Adj.* grass-green; **~halm** *der* blade of grass; **~hüpfer** *der* (ugs.) grasshopper; **~land** *das* grassland; **~mäher** *der*, **~mäh·maschine** *die* grass mower; [grass-]mowing machine; **~mücke** *die* warbler; **~narbe** *die* turf; **~nelke** *die* thrift; **~pflanze** *die* gramineous plant (Bot.); grass
Grass /gra:s/ *das;* **~** (Drogenjargon) grass (sl.)
grassieren /graˈsi:rən/ *itr. V.* ‹*disease etc.*› rage, be rampant; ‹*craze etc.*› be [all] the rage; ‹*rumour*› be rife
Gras·ski *der* grass ski
grässlich, *gräßlich /ˈgrɛslɪç/
A *Adj.* **1** (abscheulich) horrible; terrible ‹*accident*› **2** (ugs.: unangenehm) dreadful (coll.); awful **3** (ugs.: sehr stark) terrible (coll.); awful
B *adv.* **1** (abscheulich) horribly; terribly **2** (ugs.: unangenehm) terribly (coll.) **3** (ugs.: sehr) terribly (coll.); dreadfully (coll.); **~ frieren** be terribly *or* dreadfully cold (coll.)
Grässlichkeit, *Gräßlichkeit *die;* **~, ~en** **1** (Abscheulichkeit) horribleness; (eines Unfalls) terribleness **2** (unangenehme Art) dreadfulness (coll.); awfulness **3** (grässliche Handlung) atrocity
Gras-: ~steppe *die* (Geogr.) [grassy] steppe; **~streifen** *der* strip of grass; (längs einer Straße) grass verge; **~teppich** *der* (geh.) sward (literary)
Grat /gra:t/ *der;* **~[e]s, ~e** **1** (Bergrücken) ridge **2** (Archit.) hip **3** (Technik) burr
Gräte /ˈgrɛ:tə/ *die;* **~, ~n** **1** [fish] bone **2** (salopp: Knochen) bone; **sich** (*Dat.*) **die ~n brechen** get badly smashed up (sl.); **jmdm. alle** *od.* **sämtliche ~n brechen** break every bone in sb.'s body (coll.)
gräten-, Gräten-: ~los *Adj.* boneless; **~muster** *das* herringbone [pattern]; **ein Jackett mit ~muster** a herringbone jacket; **~schritt** *der* (Skifahren) herringbone [step]
Gratifikation /gratifikaˈt̮si̯o:n/ *die;* **~, ~en** bonus
gratinieren /gratiˈni:rən/ *tr. V.* (Gastr.) brown [the top of]; **gratinierter Blumenkohl** cauliflower au gratin
gratis /ˈgra:tɪs/ *Adv.* free [of charge]; gratis; **~ und franko** (ugs.) for free (coll.)
Gratis-: ~aktie *die* (Börsenw.) bonus share; **~anzeiger** *der* (schweiz.) [free] advertisement paper; **~exemplar** *das* free copy; **~muster** *das*, **~probe** *die* free sample; **~vorstellung** *die* free performance
Grätsche /ˈgrɛ:t͡ʃə/ *die;* **~, ~n** (Turnen) straddle; (Sprung) straddle vault; **in die ~ gehen** go into the straddle position
grätschen
A *tr. V.* **die Beine ~:** straddle one's legs
B *itr. V.; mit sein* straddle; do *or* perform a straddle; **über ein Gerät ~:** do a straddle vault over a piece of apparatus
Grätsch-: ~sitz *der* (Turnen) straddle position; **~sprung** *der* (Turnen) astride jump; (über ein Gerät) straddle vault; **~stellung** *die* (Turnen) straddle position
Gratulant /gratuˈlant/ *der;* **~en, ~en, Gratulantin** *die;* **~, ~nen** well-wisher; **sie war die erste ~in** she was the first to offer her congratulations

g

Gratulation /gratula'tsi̯o:n/ *die;* ~, ~en **1** (Glückwunsch) congratulations *pl.;* **~en entgegennehmen** receive congratulations; **meine [herzliche] ~!** [many] congratulations! **2** (das Gratulieren) **sie kamen zur ~:** they came to congratulate him/her/them

Gratulations-: ~besuch *der* congratulatory visit; **~cour** *die;* ~~, ~~en reception; **~schreiben** *das* letter of congratulation[s]; congratulatory letter

gratulieren *itr. V.* **jmdm. ~:** congratulate sb.; **jmdm. zum Geburtstag ~:** wish sb. many happy returns [of the day]; **jmdm. zum Examen ~:** congratulate sb. on passing his/her exam; **[ich] gratuliere!** congratulations!; **zu dieser Tochter kann ich Ihnen/er sich nur ~:** you are/he is lucky to have a daughter like her

Grat·wanderung *die* ridge walk; (fig.) balancing act

grau /grau̯/
A *Adj.* **1** grey; **~ werden** go grey; **~ im Gesicht** grey- *or* ashen-faced; **eine ~e Stadt** (fig.) a grey *or* drab town; **deine ~en Zellen** (ugs.) your grey matter (coll.); **~ in ~:** grey and drab **2** (trostlos) dreary; drab; depressing; **der ~e Alltag** the dull routine *or* monotony of daily life; **alles ~ in ~ sehen** always see the gloomy side of things; **alles ~ in ~ malen** paint a gloomy *or* bleak picture of things **3** (zwischen legal und illegal) grey; **der ~e Markt** the grey market **4** (unbestimmt) vague; **in ~er Vorzeit/Ferne** in the dim and distant past/future
B *adv.* **~ meliert** greying ‹*hair*›

Grau *das;* ~s, ~ **1** grey **2** (Trostlosigkeit) dreariness; drabness

grau-, Grau-: ~äugig *Adj.* grey-eyed; **~bart** *der* (ugs.) greybeard; **~bärtig** *Adj.* grey-bearded; **~blau** *Adj.* grey-blue; **~brot** *das: bread made with rye- and wheat-flour*

Grau·bünden /-'bʏndn̩/ *(das);* ~s the Grisons

Gräuel /'grɔy̆əl/ *der;* ~s, ~ (geh.) **1** (Abscheu) horror; **~ vor etw.** *(Dat.)* **empfinden** have a horror of sth.; **er/sie/es ist mir ein ~:** I loathe *or* detest him/her/it; **es ist ihm ein ~, das zu tun** he loathes *or* detests doing it **2** (~tat) atrocity

Gräuel-: ~geschichte *die,* **~märchen** *das* horror story; **~meldung** *die* report of an/the atrocity/of atrocities; **~propaganda** *die* atrocity propaganda; stories *pl.* of atrocities; **~tat** *die* atrocity

grauen[1] *itr. V.* (geh.) **der Morgen/der Tag graut** morning is breaking; day is dawning *or* breaking

grauen[2] *itr. V.* (unpers.) **ihm graut [es] davor/vor ihr** he dreads [the thought of] it/he's terrified of her; **mir graut es, wenn ich nur daran denke** I dread the [mere] thought of it

Grauen *das;* ~s, ~ **1** horror (**vor** + *Dat.* of); **ein Bild des ~s** a scene of horror **2** (Schreckbild) horror

grauen·erregend *Adj.* horrifying

grauen·haft, grauen·voll
A *Adj.* **1** horrifying **2** (ugs.: sehr unangenehm) terrible (coll.); dreadful (coll.)
B *adv.* **1** horrifyingly **2** (ugs.: sehr unangenehm) terribly (coll.); dreadfully (coll.)

grau-, Grau-: ~gans *die* grey goose; greylag [goose]; **~grün** *Adj.* grey-green; **~guss,** ***~guß** *der* (Technik) grey iron; **~haarig** *Adj.* grey-haired; **~kopf** *der* (ugs.) **1** (~es Haar) grey hair; **einen ~kopf haben** have grey hair; **2** (Mensch) grey-headed man/woman

graulen /'graulən/
A *tr. V.* drive out; **jmdn. aus dem Haus ~:** drive sb. out of the house
B *refl. V.* **sich [vor jmdm./etw.] ~:** be scared *or* frightened [of sb./sth.]
C *tr., itr. V.* (unpers.) **davor graulte [es] ihm/ihn** he dreaded it; **mir/mich grault bei dem Gedanken, dass ...** I shudder at the thought that ...

graulich *Adj.* scary

gräulich[1] /'grɔy̆lɪç/ *Adj.* greyish

gräulich[2]
A *Adj.* **1** (entsetzlich) horrifying **2** (unangenehm) awful
B *adv.* **1** (entsetzlich) horrifyingly **2** (unangenehm) terribly

grau·meliert ▸ **grau B**

Graupe /'graupə/ *die;* ~, ~n **1** (Gerstenkorn) grain of pearl barley; (Weizenkorn) grain of hulled wheat; **~n** pearl barley *sing.*/hulled wheat *sing.* **2** *Pl.* (Gericht) pearl barley *sing.*

Graupel /'graupl̩/ *die;* ~, ~n soft hail pellet; **~n** soft hail; graupel

graupeln *itr. V.* (unpers.) **es graupelt** there's soft hail falling

Graupel-: ~regen *der* shower of soft hail; **der ~regen behinderte den Verkehr** the soft hail impeded the flow of traffic; **~schauer** *der* shower of soft hail; **der Regen ging in ~schauer über** the rain turned to soft hail

Graupen·suppe *die* barley soup *or* broth

Graus /graus/ *der;* ~es **1** **es ist ein ~:** it's terrible; **es ist ein ~ mit dem Jungen** the boy's impossible (coll.); **o ~!** (ugs. scherzh.) oh horror! (joc.) **2** (veralt.: ~en) horror

grausam
A *Adj.* **1** cruel; **~ gegen jmdn. sein** be cruel to sb. **2** (furchtbar) terrible; dreadful **3** (ugs.: sehr schlimm) terrible (coll.); dreadful (coll.)
B *adv.* **1** cruelly; **sich ~ für etw. rächen** take cruel revenge for sth. **2** (furchtbar) terribly, dreadfully; **~ ums Leben kommen** die a horrible death **3** (ugs.: sehr stark) terribly (coll.); dreadfully (coll.)

Grausamkeit *die;* ~, ~en **1** cruelty **2** (Handlung) act of cruelty; (Gräueltat) atrocity

grau-, Grau-: ~schimmel *der* **1** (Pferd) grey [horse]; **2** (Pilz) grey mould; **~schwarz** *Adj.* grey-black

grausen
A *tr., itr. V.* (unpers.) **es grauste ihm** *od.* **ihn davor/vor ihr** he dreaded [the thought of] it/he was terrified of her; **es graust ihr** *od.* **sie, wenn sie nur an die Prüfung denkt** she dreads the [mere] thought of the exam; **uns grauste vor der langen Fahrt** we were dreading the long journey
B *refl. V.* **sich vor etw./jmdm. ~:** be terrified by *or* dread sth./be terrified of sb.

Grausen *das;* ~s horror; **das kalte ~ kriegen** (ugs.) be scared stiff *or* to death (coll.)

grausig ▸ **grauenhaft**

grauslich (bes. bayr., österr.) ▸ **grässlich**

grau-, Grau-: ~specht *der* grey-headed woodpecker; **~tier** *das* (ugs. scherzh.) (Esel) ass; donkey; (Maultier) mule; **~ton** *der; Pl.* **~töne** [shade of] grey; **~wal** *der* grey whale; **~weiß** *Adj.* greyish white; **~zone** *die* grey area (fig.)

Graveur /gra'vø:ɐ̯/ *der;* ~s, ~e, **Graveurin** *die;* ~, ~nen ▸ ❶ **S. 113** engraver

Gravier-: ~anstalt *die* engraving establishment; engraver's; **~arbeit** *die* engraving

gravieren /gra'vi:rən/ *tr. V.* engrave; **etw. auf etw.** *(Akk.)* **~:** engrave sth. on sth.

gravierend *Adj.* serious, grave ‹*matter, accusation, error, etc.*›; important ‹*difference, decision, etc.*›; **~e Beweise** very strong evidence

Gravier·nadel *die* engraving needle

Gravierung *die;* ~, ~en engraving

Gravimetrie /gravime'tri:/ *die;* ~ (Chemie, Physik) gravimetry *no art.*

Gravis /'gra:vɪs/ *der;* ~, ~ (Sprachw.) grave [accent]

Gravitation /gravita'tsi̯o:n/ *die;* ~ (Physik, Astron.) gravitation

Gravitations-: ~feld *das* (Physik, Astron.) gravitational field; **~gesetz** *das* (Physik, Astron.) law of gravitation

gravitätisch
A *Adj.* grave; solemn
B *adv.* gravely; solemnly

gravitieren /gravi'ti:rən/ *itr. V.* (Physik, Astron.) gravitate

Gravur /gra'vu:ɐ̯/ *die;* ~, ~en, **Gravüre** /gra'vy:rə/ *die;* ~, ~n engraving

Grazie /'gra:tsi̯ə/ *die;* ~, ~n **1** (Anmut) grace; gracefulness **2** (Myth.) Grace **3** (scherzh.: junges Mädchen) beauty

grazil /gra'tsi:l/ *Adj.* (auch fig.) delicate

graziös /gra'tsi̯ø:s/
A *Adj.* graceful; (anmutig) charming
B *adv.* gracefully; (anmutig) charmingly

Gräzismus /grɛ'tsɪsmʊs/ *der;* ~, **Gräzismen** Graecism

Gräzist *der;* ~en, ~en, **Gräzistin** *die;* ~, ~nen expert on/student of ancient Greece

Greenhorn /'gri:nhɔ:n/ *das;* ~s, ~s greenhorn

Gregor /'gre:gɔr/ *(der)* Gregory

gregorianisch, *Gregorianisch /grego'ri̯a:nɪʃ/ *Adj.* Gregorian; **~er Gesang** Gregorian chant; **der ~e Kalender** the Gregorian calendar

Greif /grai̯f/ *der;* ~[e]s *od.* ~en, ~en **1** (Wappentier) griffin; gryphon **2** ▸ **~vogel**

Greif-: ~arm *der* (Technik) grasping arm; **~bagger** *der* grab-dredger

greif·bar
A *Adj.* **1** **etw. ~ haben** have sth. to hand; **~ sein** be within reach; **in ~er Nähe** (fig.) within reach; **der Urlaub ist in ~e Nähe gerückt** (fig.) the holiday is just coming up [now] **2** (deutlich) tangible; concrete **3** (ugs.: verfügbar) available
B *adv.* **~ nahe** (fig.) within reach

Greif·bewegung *die* grasping movement

greifen
A *unr. tr. V.* **1** (er~) take hold of; grasp; (rasch ~) grab; seize; **sich** *(Dat.)* **etw. ~:** help oneself to sth.; **jmdn. an den Händen ~:** take sb. by the hand; **aus dem Leben gegriffen sein** be taken from real life; **von hier scheint der See zum Greifen nah[e]** from here the lake seems close enough to reach out and touch; **zum Greifen nahe sein** ‹*end, liberation*› be imminent; ‹*goal, success*› be within sb.'s grasp **2** (fangen) catch; **den werde ich mir mal ~** (ugs.) I'll sort (Brit.) *or* (Amer.) straighten him out (coll.); **Greifen spielen** play tag **3** **einen Akkord ~** (auf dem Klavier usw.) play a chord; (auf der Gitarre usw.) finger a chord; **er kann noch keine Oktave ~:** he can't reach an octave yet **4** (schätzen) **tausend ist zu hoch/niedrig gegriffen** one thousand is an overestimate/underestimate; **sein Ziel ist zu hoch gegriffen** (fig.) he has set his sights too high (fig.)
B *unr. itr. V.* **1** **in/unter/hinter etw./sich** *(Akk.)* **~:** reach into/under/behind sth./one; **nach etw. ~:** reach for sth.; (hastig) make a grab for sth.; **zu Drogen/zur Zigarette ~:** turn to drugs/reach for a cigarette; **zu strengen Maßnahmen ~** (fig.) resort to *or* use tough measures; **nach der Macht ~** (fig.) try to seize power; **[jmdm.] ans Herz ~** (fig. geh.) tug at sb.'s heartstrings; **seine Argumentation greift zu kurz** (fig.) his arguments do not go far enough; **etw. greift um sich** sth. is spreading **2** (Technik) grip **3** (ugs.: spielen) **in die Tasten/Saiten ~:** sweep one's hand over the keys/across the strings **4** (wirken) take effect; **nicht mehr ~:** be no longer effective

Greifer *der;* ~s, ~ **1** (Technik) grab[-bucket] **2** (salopp abwertend: Polizist) cop (coll.)

Greiferin *die;* ~, ~nen ▸ **Greifer 2**

Greif-: ~fuß *der* (Zool.) prehensile foot; **~vogel** *der* (Zool.) diurnal bird of prey; **~zange** *die* tongs *pl.;* **~zirkel** *der* [outside] callipers *pl.*

greinen /'grai̯nən/ *itr. V.* (ugs. abwertend) grizzle (coll. derog.); (weinerlich klagen) whine

greis /grai̯s/ *Adj.* (geh.) aged; white ‹*hair, head*›; **~ werden** grow old

Greis *der;* ~es, ~e old man

Greisen·alter *das* old age; **im [hohen] ~:** in old age

greisen·haft
A *Adj.* old man's/woman's *attrib.;* aged; (von jüngeren Menschen) ‹*face etc.*› like that of an old man/woman
B *adv.* like an old man/woman

Greisen·haupt *das* (geh.) old head

Greisin *die;* ~, ~nen old woman *or* lady

grell /grɛl/
A *Adj.* 1 (hell) glaring, dazzling ‹*light, sun, etc.*› 2 (auffallend) garish, gaudy ‹*colour etc.*›; flashy, loud ‹*dress, pattern, etc.*› 3 (schrill) shrill, piercing ‹*cry, voice, etc.*›
B *adv.* 1 (hell) with glaring *or* dazzling brightness; ~ **beleuchtet** dazzlingly lit 2 (auffallend) **gegen** *od.* **von etw.** ~ **abstechen** contrast sharply with sth. 3 (schrill) shrilly; piercingly

grell-: ~**beleuchtet** ▸**grell B 1**; ~**bunt** *Adj.* gaudily coloured

Grelle /ˈgrɛlə/ *die;* ~, **Grellheit** *die;* ~ 1 (Helligkeit) dazzling brightness 2 (Auffälligkeit) garishness; gaudiness 3 (Schrillheit) shrillness; piercing quality

grell·rot *Adj.* garish *or* bright red

Gremium /ˈgreːmi̯ʊm/ *das;* ~**s, Gremien** committee

Grenadier /grenaˈdiːɐ̯/ *der;* ~**s,** ~**e** (Milit.) 1 (Infanterist) infantryman; **er kam zu den** ~**en** he went into *or* joined the infantry 2 (hist.) grenadier

grenz-, Grenz-: ~**abfertigung** *die* (Zollw.) passport control and customs clearance [at the/a border]; ~**baum** *der* ▸**Schlagbaum**; ~**beamte** *der,* ~**beamtin** *die* border official; ~**befestigung** *die* (Milit.) border fortification; ~**bereich** *der* 1 border *or* frontier zone *or* area; 2 (äußerster Bereich) limit[s *pl.*]; ~**berichtigung** *die* adjustment to a/the border; ~**bewohner** *der,* ~**bewohnerin** *die* inhabitant of a/the border *or* frontier zone; **die** ~**bewohner** [the] people living near the border *or* frontier; ~**bezirk** *der* border *or* frontier district; ~**debil** (ugs.) **A** *Adj.* thick (coll.); **B** *adv.* like a mental defective; stupidly

Grenze /ˈgrɛntsə/ *die;* ~, ~**n** 1 (zwischen Staaten) border; frontier; **die** ~ **zu Italien** the border with Italy; **die** ~ **passieren/überschreiten** cross the border *or* frontier; **über die** ~**n hinaus** beyond the borders of this country; **an der** ~ **wohnen** live on the border *or* frontier; **über die grüne** ~ **gehen** (ugs.) cross the border *or* frontier illegally 2 (zwischen Gebieten) boundary; **die** ~ **des Grundstücks** the boundary of the property 3 (gedachte Trennungslinie) borderline; dividing line 4 (Schranke) limit; **jmdm. [keine]** ~**n setzen** impose [no] limits on sb.; **einer Sache** (*Dat.*) **[keine]** ~**n setzen** set [no] limits to sth.; **alles hat seine** ~**n** there is a limit *or* are limits to everything; one must draw the line somewhere; **an seine** ~**n stoßen** reach its limit[s]; **an** ~**n stoßen** come up against limiting factors; **keine** ~**n kennen** know no bounds; **seine** ~**n kennen** know one's limitations; **jmdn. in seine** ~**n verweisen** put sb. in his/her place; **sich in** ~**n halten** (begrenzt sein) keep *or* stay within limits; **seine Leistungen hielten sich in** ~**n** his achievements were not [all that (coll.)] outstanding; **die** ~**n des Möglichen** the bounds of possibility

grenzen *itr. V.* **an etw.** (*Akk.*) ~: border [on] sth.; (fig.) verge on sth.

grenzen·los
A *Adj.* boundless; endless; (fig.) boundless, unbounded ‹*joy, wonder, jealousy, grief, etc.*›; unlimited ‹*wealth, power*›; limitless ‹*patience, ambition*›; extreme ‹*tiredness, anger, foolishness*›
B *adv.* endlessly; (fig.) beyond all measure

Grenzen·losigkeit *die;* ~: boundlessness; immensity; **bis zur** ~ **steigern** (fig.) increase beyond all measure

Grenzer *der;* ~**s,** ~, **Grenzerin** *die;* ~, ~**nen** (ugs.) 1 ▸**Grenzbewohner** 2 ▸**Grenzsoldat**

grenz-, Grenz-: ~**fall** *der* (nicht eindeutiger Fall) borderline case; (Sonderfall) limiting case; ~**fluss,** *~**fluß** *der* river forming a/the border *or* frontier; ~**formalitäten** *Pl.* passport and customs formalities [at the/a border]; ~**gänger** *der;* ~~**s,** ~~, ~**gängerin** *die;* ~~, ~~**nen** [regular] commuter across the border or frontier; ~**gebiet** *das* 1 border *or* frontier area *or* zone; 2 (Sachgebiet zwischen Disziplinen) adjacent field; **die Biochemie ist ein** ~**gebiet der Medizin** biochemistry is a field bordering on medicine; **im** ~**gebiet zwischen zwei Wissenschaften** in the area where two sciences meet; ~**konflikt** *der* border *or* frontier conflict; ~**kontrolle** *die* 1 border *or* frontier check; 2 (Personen) border officials *pl.*; ~**land** *das* border *or* frontier area; ~**linie** *die* 1 (Grenze) border; 2 (Sport) line (marking edge of playing area); ~**mark** *die; Pl.* ~~**en** (hist.) marches *pl.*; ~**nah** *Adj.* close to the border *or* frontier *postpos.*; ~**nutzen** *der* (Wirtsch.) marginal utility; ~**polizei** *die* border *or* frontier police; ~**posten** *der* border *or* frontier guard; ~**schutz** *der* 1 border *or* frontier protection; 2 (ugs.: Bundesgrenzschutz) border *or* frontier police; ~**situation** *die* borderline situation; ~**soldat** *der,* ~**soldatin** *die* border *or* frontier guard; ~**stadt** *die* border *or* frontier town; ~**stein** *der* boundary stone; ~**streitigkeit** *die* boundary dispute; (wegen einer Staatsgrenze) border *or* frontier dispute; ~**übergang** *der* 1 border crossing point; frontier crossing-point; [border] checkpoint; 2 (das Passieren der ~e) crossing of the border *or* frontier; ~**überschreitend** *Adj.* across the/a border *or* frontier/across the borders *or* frontiers *postpos., not pred.*; ~**überschreitung** *die* 1 crossing of the frontier/frontiers; 2 (fig.) crossing of the/a boundary (**zu** to); ~**verkehr** *der* [cross-]border traffic; frontier traffic; **der kleine** ~**verkehr** local [cross-]border *or* frontier traffic; ~**verlauf** *der* frontier line; ~**verletzung** *die* border *or* frontier violation; ~**wacht** *die* (schweiz.) border *or* frontier guard[s *pl.*]; ~**wall** *der* border *or* frontier rampart; ~**wert** *der* (Math.) limit; ~**wertig** **A** *Adj.* on the limit *postpos.*; **B** *adv.* ~**wertig eng** critically narrow; ~**wertig gutartiges Karzinom** borderline carcinoma; ~**zaun** *der* border fence; ~**zwischenfall** *der* border incident

Gretchen-: ~**frage** *die;* ~: crucial question; sixty-four-thousand-dollar question (coll.); ~**frisur** *die* chaplet hairstyle

***Greuel** *usw.* ▸**Gräuel** *usw.*

***greulich** ▸**gräulich**²

Greyerzer /ˈgrai̯ɐtsɐ/ *der;* ~**s,** ~ Gruyère

Griebe /ˈgriːbə/ *die;* ~, ~**n** crackling *no indef. art.*; greaves *pl.*

Grieben-: ~**fett** *das* bacon dripping; ~**schmalz** *das* dripping with crackling *or* greaves

Grieche /ˈgriːçə/ *der;* ~**n,** ~**n** ▸❶ **S. 520** Greek

Griechenland *(das);* ~**s** Greece

Griechentum *das;* ~**s** (Zivilisation) Hellenism *no art.*; Greek civilization; (Kultur) Greek culture

Griechin *die;* ~, ~**nen** ▸❶ **S. 520** Greek

griechisch ▸❶ **S. 520,** ▸❶ **S. 670**
A *Adj.* Greek ‹*language, mythology, island, etc.*›; Grecian, Greek ‹*vase, style, etc.*›; **die** ~**e Tragödie** Greek tragedy
B *adv.* ~ **sprechen/schreiben** speak/write in Greek; *s. auch* **deutsch**

Griechisch *das;* ~**[s]** ▸❶ **S. 670** Greek *no art.*; *s. auch* **Deutsch**

Griechische *das;* ~**n** 1 (Sprache) Greek *no art.* 2 (Eigenart) things Greek *pl.*; **alles** ~: all things *pl. or* everything Greek

griechisch-: ~**-orthodox** *Adj.* Greek Orthodox; ~**-römisch** *Adj.* (Ringen) Graeco-Roman

grienen /ˈgriːnən/ *itr. V.* (bes. nordd.) grin

Griesgram /ˈgriːsgraːm/ *der;* ~**[e]s,** ~**e** (abwertend) grouch (coll.)

griesgrämig /ˈgriːsgrɛːmɪç/
A *Adj.* grouchy (coll.); grumpy
B *adv.* in a grouchy (coll.) *or* grumpy manner

Grieß /griːs/ *der;* ~**es,** ~**e** semolina

Grieß-: ~**brei** *der* semolina; ~**kloß** *der,* ~**klößchen** *das* semolina dumpling

griff /grɪf/ *1. u. 3. Pers. Sg. Prät. v.* **greifen**

Griff *der;* ~**[e]s,** ~**e** 1 grip; grasp; **mit eisernem/festem** ~: with a grip of iron/a firm grip; **der** ~ **nach etw./in etw.** (*Akk.*)**/an etw.** (*Akk.*) reaching for sth./dipping into sth./taking hold of *or* grasping sth.; **der** ~ **zum Alkohol/zu Drogen** turning to alcohol/drugs; **[mit jmdm./etw.] einen guten/glücklichen** ~ **tun** make a good choice [with sb./sth.]; **einen** ~ **in die Ladenkasse tun** (verhüll.) put one's hand in the till; **der** ~ **nach der Macht** (fig.) the bid for *or* attempt to seize power 2 (beim Ringen, Bergsteigen) hold; (beim Turnen) grip; (bei der Arbeit) **jeder** ~ **muss sitzen** every movement must be exactly right; **mit wenigen** ~**en** with very little effort; ~**e kloppen** (Soldatenspr.) do rifle drill; **etw. im** ~ **haben** (etw. routinemäßig beherrschen) have the hang of sth. (coll.); (etw. unter Kontrolle haben) have sth. under control; **etw. in den** ~ **bekommen** *od.* (ugs.) **kriegen** get the hang *or* knack of sth. (coll.); acquire a grasp of *or* hold on sth. 3 (Knauf, Henkel) handle; (eines Gewehrs, einer Pistole) butt; (eines Schwerts) hilt 4 (Musik) finger placing; **schwierige** ~**e beherrschen** master difficult fingering 5 (Weberei) hand; handle

griff·bereit *Adj.* ready to hand *postpos.*

Griff·brett *das* (Musik) fingerboard

Griffel /ˈgrɪfl̩/ *der;* ~**s,** ~ 1 (Schreibgerät) slate pencil 2 (Bot.) style 3 (salopp: Finger) finger

Griffel·kasten *der* (veralt.) pencil box

griffig *Adj.* 1 (handlich) handy; ‹*tool etc.*› that is easy to handle; (fig.) handy, useful ‹*word, expression, etc.*› 2 (gut greifend) that grips well *postpos., not pred.*; non-slip ‹*surface, floor*›; **ein** ~**er Reifen** a tyre with good roadholding characteristics 3 (fest gewebt) ‹*cloth*› with a firm handle 4 (österr.: grobkörnig) coarse ‹*flour*›

Griffigkeit *die;* ~ 1 (Handlichkeit) handiness 2 (von Reifen, Straßen) grip 3 (Festigkeit des Gewebes) firm handle 4 (österr.: von Mehl) coarseness

Griff·loch *das* (Musik) fingerhole

Grill /grɪl/ *der;* ~**s,** ~**s** 1 (Feuerstelle) grill; (Rost) barbecue 2 (Kfz-W.) radiator grille

Grill·anzünder *der* grill lighter

Grille /ˈgrɪlə/ *die;* ~, ~**n** 1 (Insekt) cricket 2 (sonderbarer Einfall) whim; fancy; **er hat** ~**n im Kopf** (hat seltsame Ideen) his head is [stuffed] full of silly ideas; (hat trübselige Gedanken) he's in low spirits *or* (coll.) [down] in the dumps; (fig.) ~**n fangen** (veralt.) be in low spirits *or* (coll.) down in the dumps; **jmdm. die** ~**n vertreiben** *od.* **austreiben** (fig. veralt.) knock some sense into sb.

grillen
A *tr. V.* grill
B *itr. V.* **im Garten** ~: have a barbecue in the garden
C *refl. V.* (ugs.: bräunen) **sich in der Sonne** ~: soak up the sun

Grill-: ~**platz** *der* barbecue area; ~**spieß** *der* ≈ kebab

Grimasse /griˈmasə/ *die;* ~, ~**n** grimace; **eine** ~ **schneiden** *od.* **machen** grimace; pull a face

Grimm /grɪm/ *der;* ~**[e]s** (geh.) fury

Grimm·darm *der* ▸❶ **S. 435** (Anat.) colon

grimmen *tr., itr. V.* (unpers.) (veralt.) **es grimmt mir** *od.* **mich im Bauch/Magen** I have griping pains in my stomach

Grimmen *das;* ~**s** colic; griping pains *pl.*

grimmig
A *Adj.* 1 (zornig) furious ‹*person*›; grim ‹*face, expression*›; fierce, ferocious ‹*enemy, lion, etc.*› 2 (heftig) fierce, severe ‹*cold, hunger, pain, etc.*›
B *adv.* 1 (wütend) furiously; ~ **lachen** laugh grimly 2 (heftig) fiercely; ~ **kalt** bitterly *or* fiercely cold

Grind /grɪnt/ *der;* ~**[e]s,** ~**e** 1 (Flechte) impetigo 2 (Wundschorf) scab

grindig *Adj.* scabby

grinsen /ˈgrɪnzn̩/ *itr. V.* grin; (höhnisch) smirk

Grinsen *das;* ~**s ein fröhliches/unverschämtes** ~: a happy grin/an insolent smirk

Grip /grɪp/ *der;* ~**s** (fachspr.) grip

grippal /grɪˈpaːl/ *Adj.* influenzal; grippal

Grippe /ˈgrɪpə/ *die;* ~, ~**n** 1 ▸❶ **S. 439** influenza; flu (coll.) 2 (volkst.: Erkältung) cold

Grippe-: ~**epidemie** *die* influenza epidemic; ~**impfung** *die* influenza *or* (coll.) flu immunization; ~**welle** *die* wave of influenza *or* (coll.) flu

g

Grips /grɪps/ *der;* **~es** (bes. nordd. u. md. ugs.) brains *pl.*; nous (coll.); **streng deinen ~ an** use your brains *or* nous

Grisli·bär, *Grisly·bär, Grizzly·bär /ˈgrɪsli-/ *der* grizzly bear

grob /gro:p/

A *Adj.* **1** coarse ‹*sand, gravel, paper, sieve, etc.*›; thick ‹*wire*›; rough, dirty ‹*work*›; **~e Gesichtszüge** coarse features **2** (ungefähr) rough; **in ~en Umrissen** in rough outline **3** (schwerwiegend) gross; flagrant ‹*lie*›; **ein ~er Fehler/Irrtum** a bad mistake *or* gross error; **~er Unfug** disorderly conduct; **das Gröbste** the worst; **aus dem Gröbsten heraus sein** (ugs.) be over the worst **4** (barsch) coarse; rude; **~ werden** become abusive *or* rude **5** (nicht sanft) rough; **~ [zu jmdm.] sein** be rough [with sb.] **6** (heftig) fierce ‹*gust of wind*›; **~e See** (Seemannsspr.) rough sea

B *adv.* **1** coarsely; **~ gemahlen** coarsely ground; coarse-ground; **~ gesponnen** coarsely spun; coarse-spun; **ein ~ geschnittenes Gesicht haben** have coarse features *pl.* **2** (ungefähr) roughly; **~ gerechnet** *od.* **geschätzt** at a rough estimate; **etw. ~ umreißen/darlegen** present a rough outline/exposition of sth. **3** (schwerwiegend) grossly; **~ fahrlässig handeln** (Rechtsspr.) be guilty of gross negligence **4** (barsch) coarsely; rudely; **jmdm. ~ kommen** (ugs.) get rude with sb. **5** (nicht sanft) roughly

grob-, Grob-: ~blech *das* thick *or* heavy [steel] plate; **~einstellung** *die* rough adjustment; **~faserig** *Adj.* coarse-fibred; **~gemahlen** *usw.* ▸ **grob B 1**

Grobheit *die;* **~, ~en** **1** (Wesensart) rudeness; coarseness **2** (Äußerung) rude remark; (Handlung) [piece of] rudeness; **jmdm. ~en sagen/** (ugs.) **an den Kopf werfen** be extremely rude to sb. **3** (derbe Beschaffenheit) coarseness

Grobian /ˈgro:bi̯a:n/ *der;* **~[e]s, ~e** boor; lout

grob-: ~knochig *Adj.* big-boned; **~körnig** *Adj.* coarse ‹*sand, flour, etc.*›; (Fot.) coarse-grained ‹*film*›

gröblich /ˈgrø:plɪç/ (geh.)

A *Adj.* gross

B *adv.* grossly

grob-, Grob-: ~maschig *Adj.* wide-meshed ‹*sieve, net, etc.*›; loose-knit ‹*pullover etc.*›; **~motorik** *die* (Physiol.) basic motor functions *pl.*; **~motorisch** *Adj.* basic motor function *attrib.*; **~schlächtig** /-ʃlɛçtɪç/ *Adj.* heavily built; **eine ~schlächtige Darstellung** (fig.) a simplistic account; **~schmied** *der* (veralt.) blacksmith

Grog /grɔk/ *der;* **~s, ~s** grog

groggy /ˈgrɔgi/ *Adj.* **1** (Boxen) groggy **2** (ugs.: erschöpft) whacked [out] (coll.); all in (coll.)

grölen /ˈgrø:lən/

A *tr. V.* (ugs. abwertend) bawl [out]; roar, howl ‹*approval*›

B *itr. V.* bawl; **eine ~de Menge** a roaring crowd

Groll /grɔl/ *der;* **~[e]s** (geh.) rancour; resentment; **einen ~ auf jmdn./etw. haben** *od.* **gegen jmdn./etw. hegen** harbour resentment *or* a grudge against sb./sth.; **aus ~ über jmdn./etw.** from a grudge against sb./out of resentment at sth.; **ohne ~:** without rancour; with no ill feelings

grollen *itr. V.* (geh.) **1** (verstimmt sein) be sullen; **[mit] jmdm. ~:** bear a grudge against sb.; bear sb. a grudge **2** (dröhnen) rumble; ‹*thunder*› roll, rumble; **das Grollen des Donners** the roll *or* rumble of thunder

Grönland /ˈgrø:n.../ *(das);* **~s** Greenland

Grönländer *der;* **~s, ~, Grönländerin** *die;* **~, ~nen** Greenlander

Gros[1] /gro:/ *das;* **~** /gro:(s)/, **~** /gro:s/ bulk; main body; **das ~ der Betriebe** the greater *or* major part of industry

Gros[2] /grɔs/ *das;* **~ses, ~se** gross; **zwei ~:** two gross

Groschen /ˈgrɔʃn̩/ *der;* **~s, ~** **1** (Hist.: österreichische Münze) groschen **2** (ugs veralt.: Zehnpfennigstück) ten-pfennig piece; (fig.) penny; cent (Amer.); **Bonbons für einen** *od.* **zu einem ~:** ten pfennigs' worth of sweets; **[sich** *(Dat.)***] ein paar ~ verdienen** (ugs.) earn [oneself] a few pennies *or* pence; **die ~ zusammenhalten müssen** (ugs.) have to count every penny [one spends]; **der ~ ist [bei ihm] gefallen** (fig.) the penny has dropped; **bei ihr fällt der ~ pfennigweise** (fig.) she's a bit slow on the uptake

Groschen-: ~blatt *das* (abwertend) tabloid; cheap rag (derog.); **~roman** *der* (abwertend) cheap novel; dime novel (Amer.)

groß /gro:s/, **größer** /ˈgrø:sɐ/, **größt...** /ˈgrø:st.../

A *Adj.* **1** ▸ⓘ **S. 374** big; large ‹*house, window, area, room, etc.*›; large ‹*pack, size, can, etc.*›; great ‹*length, width, height*›; tall ‹*person*›; **~e Eier/Kartoffeln** large eggs/potatoes; **der ~e Zeiger** the big *or* minute hand; **ein ~er Buchstabe** a big *or* capital letter; **eine ~e Terz/Sekunde** (Musik) a major third/second; **ein ~es Bier, bitte** a pint, please; **im Großen einkaufen** buy in bulk; **die Großen Seen/der Große Salzsee** the Great Lakes/Great Salt Lake; **ein/zwei Nummern zu ~:** one size/two sizes too big

2 ▸ⓘ **S. 374** (eine bestimmte Größe aufweisend) **1 m^2/2 ha ~:** 1 m^2/2 ha in area; **sie ist 1,75 m ~:** she is 1.75 m tall; **doppelt/dreimal so ~ wie ...** twice/three times the size of ...

3 (älter) big ‹*brother, sister*›; **seine größere Schwester** his elder sister; **unsere Große/unser Großer** our eldest *or* oldest daughter/son; (von zwei Kindern) our elder *or* older daughter/son

4 (erwachsen) grown-up ‹*children, son, daughter*›; **[mit etw.] ~ werden** grow up [with sth.]; **die Großen** (Erwachsene) the grown-ups; (ältere Kinder) the older children; **Groß und Klein** old and young [alike]

5 (lange dauernd) long, lengthy ‹*delay, talk, explanation, pause*›; **ein ~er Zeitraum** a long period of time; **die ~en Ferien** (Schulw.) the summer holidays *or* (Amer.) long vacation *sing.*; **die ~e Pause** (Schulw.) [mid-morning] break

6 (beträchtlich) **eine ~e Zuhörerschaft/Kundschaft** a large audience/clientele; **~e Summen/Kosten** large sums/heavy costs; **eine ~e Familie** a big *or* large family; **eine ~e Auswahl** a wide selection *or* range; **~es Geld** notes *pl.*; **das ~e Geld machen** (ugs.) *od.* **verdienen** make big money

7 (außerordentlich) great ‹*pleasure, pain, hunger, anxiety, hurry, progress, difficulty, mistake, importance*›; intense ‹*heat, cold*›; high ‹*speed*›; **mit dem größten Vergnügen** with the greatest of pleasure; **eine ~e Freude empfinden** feel great pleasure; **ein ~er Lärm** a lot of noise; **~en Hunger haben** be very hungry; **ein ~er Esser/Bastler** a great *or* heavy eater/great handyman; **ihre/seine ~e Liebe** her/his great love; **~ im Geschäft sein** be in great demand

8 (gewichtig) great; major ‹*producer, exporter*›; great, major ‹*event*›; **ein ~er Augenblick/Tag** a great moment/day; **~e Worte/Gesten** grand *or* fine words/grand gestures; **[k]eine ~e Rolle spielen** [not] play a great *or* an important part; **sie hat Großes geleistet** she has achieved great things; **die Großen [der Welt]** the great figures [of our world]

9 (glanzvoll) grand ‹*celebration, ball, etc.*›; **in ~er Aufmachung/Garderobe** in all one's finery; **die ~e Dame/den ~en Herrn spielen** (iron.) play the fine lady/gentleman

10 (bedeutend) great, major ‹*artist, painter, work*›; **Otto der Große/Katharina die Große** Otto/Catherine the Great; *s. auch* **Karl**

11 (wesentlich) **die ~e Linie/der ~e Zusammenhang** the basic line/the overall context; **in ~en Zügen** *od.* **Umrissen** in broad outline; **im Großen [und] Ganzen** by and large; on the whole

12 (geh.: selbstlos) noble ‹*deed etc.*›; **ein ~es Herz haben** be great-hearted

13 (ugs.: ~artig) great (coll.); **das finde ich** *od.* **das ist ganz ~** (iron.) that's just great (coll. iron.); **~ in etw.** *(Dat.)* **sein** be a great one for sth.

14 (ugs.: ~spurig) **~e Reden schwingen** *od.* (salopp) **Töne spucken** talk big (coll.)

B *adv.* **1** **die Heizung** *usw.* **~/größer einstellen** turn the heating *etc.* up high/higher; **~ geschrieben werden** (fig.) be stressed *or* emphasized; **bei ihm wird Geldverdienen ~ geschrieben** earning money comes high on his list of priorities; **jmdn. ~ ansehen** stare hard at sb.; **~ machen** (Kinderspr.) do number two (child lang.); **~ und breit** at great length

2 (ugs.: aufwändig) **~ ausgehen** go out for a big celebration; **etw. ~ feiern** celebrate sth. in a big way; **jmdn./etw. ~ herausbringen** publicize sb./sth. with a big splash; **ein ~ angelegtes Projekt** a large-scale project; **ein ~ angelegter Angriff** a full-scale attack

3 (ugs.: besonders) greatly; particularly; **es lohnt [sich] nicht ~, das zu tun** there is not much point in doing that; **sich nicht ~ um jmdn./etw. kümmern** not bother *or* concern oneself greatly about sb./sth.; **wir haben nicht ~ darauf geachtet** we didn't pay much attention to it; **was gibt es da noch ~ zu diskutieren?** why do we need all this long discussion?; **niemand freute sich ~:** nobody was very pleased *or* (coll.) exactly overjoyed

4 (geh.: selbstlos) **~ handeln** act nobly; **fähig sein, ~ zu fühlen** be capable of noble sentiments

5 (ugs.: ~artig) **sie steht ganz ~ da** she has made it big (coll.) *or* made the big time (coll.)

6 (ugs.: ~spurig) **~ daherreden/auftreten** talk/act big (coll.)

groß-, Groß-: ~abnehmer *der,* **~abnehmerin** *die* bulk buyer *or* purchaser; **~admiral** *der* (Milit. hist.) Grand Admiral; **~aktion** *die* major campaign; big drive; **~aktionär** *der,* **~aktionärin** *die* (Wirtsch.) principal *or* major shareholder; **~alarm** *der* full-scale alarm; **~angelegt** ▸ **groß B2**; **~angriff** *der* (Milit.) full-scale attack; **~artig** **A** *Adj.* magnificent; splendid; wonderful ‹*person*›; **B** *adv.* magnificently; splendidly; **wir haben uns ~artig amüsiert** we had a marvellous time; **~artigkeit** *die* magnificence; splendour; **~aufgebot** *das* large contingent; (der Polizei, Feuerwehr) large force; (von Helfern) large number; **~aufnahme** *die* **1** (Film) close-up; **in ~aufnahme** in close-up; **2** (Fot.) ▸ **Nahaufnahme**; **~auftrag** *der* (Wirtsch.) large order; **~bank** *die; Pl.* **~~en** (Finanzw.) big bank; **die fünf ~banken** the Big Five; **~bauer** *der;* **~~n, ~~n** big farmer; **~betrieb** *der* large *or* big concern; large-scale enterprise; **~bourgeoisie** *die* (marx.) haute bourgeoisie; **~brand** *der* large fire *or* blaze

Groß·britannien *(das);* **~s** the United Kingdom; [Great] Britain

groß-, Groß-: ~buchstabe *der* capital [letter]; upper-case letter (Printing); **~bürgerlich** *Adj.* upper middle-class; **~bürgertum** *das* upper middle class; **~deutsch** *Adj.* (bes. ns.) Pan-German; **~deutschland** *(das)* (bes. ns.) *Germany after the anschluss of Austria*

Größe /ˈgrø:sə/ *die;* **~, ~n** **1** size; (Kleider~) **in ~ 38** in size 38; **sie trägt ~ 44** she is *or* takes size 44 **2** ▸ⓘ **S. 374** (Höhe, Körper~) height; **der ~ nach** by height **3** (Bedeutsamkeit, sittlicher Wert) greatness **4** (Ausmaß) **die ~ der Katastrophe** the [full] scale *or* extent of the catastrophe **5** (Genie) outstanding *or* important figure **6** (Math., Physik) quantity; **eine gegebene/**(auch fig.) **unbekannte ~:** a given/an unknown quantity

Groß-: ~ein·kauf *der* bulk purchase; **~einkauf machen** do all one's shopping at one time; **~ein·satz** *der* large-scale operation; **~eltern** *Pl.* grandparents; **~enkel** *der* great-grandchild; (Junge) great-grandson; **~enkelin** *die* great-granddaughter

Größen-: ~klasse *die* **1** size [group]; **Eier der ~klasse 2** class 2 eggs; **2** (Astron.) magnitude; **~ordnung** *die* **1** (Dimension) order [of magnitude]; **in einer ~ordnung von einer Milliarde Euro** in the order of a thousand million *or* a billion euros; **2** (Physik, Math.) order of magnitude

großen·teils *Adv.* largely; for the most part

größen-, Größen-: ~verhältnis *das* **1** (Maßstab) scale; **im ~verhältnis 1:10** on a scale of 1:10; **2** (Proportion) proportions *pl.*;

~wahn *der* (abwertend) megalomania; delusions *pl.* of grandeur; **~wahnsinnig** *Adj.* megalomaniacal; **er ist ~wahnsinnig** he's a megalomaniac

größer ▸ **groß**

groß-, Groß-: ~fahndung *die* large-scale search *or* manhunt; **~familie** *die* (Soziol.) extended family; (mehrere Kleinfamilien) composite family; **~feuer** *das* large fire *or* blaze; **~flughafen** *der* large *or* major airport; **~folio** *das* (Buchw.) large folio; **~format** *das* large size; (bei Büchern) large format *or* size; **~formatig** *Adj.* large-size; large-format ‹*book, photograph*›; large-scale ‹*sculpture, pattern*›; **~fürst** *der* (hist.) Grand Duke; **~fürstin** *die* (hist.) Grand Duchess; **~grundbesitz** *der* ownership of large estates; **~grundbesitzer** *der*, **~grundbesitzerin** *die* big landowner; **~handel** *der* wholesale trade; **~händler** *der*, **~händlerin** *die* wholesaler; **~handlung** *die* wholesale business; **~herzig** (geh.) **A** *Adj.* magnanimous; **B** *adv.* magnanimously; **~herzigkeit** *die*; **~~** (geh.) magnanimity; **~herzog** *der* Grand Duke; **~herzogin** *die* Grand Duchess; **~herzoglich** *Adj.* grandducal; **~herzogtum** *das* grand duchy; **~herzogtum Luxemburg** Grand Duchy of Luxembourg; **~hirn** *das* ▸❶ **S. 435** (Anat.) cerebrum; **~hirn·rinde** *die* ▸❶ **S. 435** (Anat.) cerebral cortex; **~industrie** *die* big industry; **~industrielle** *der/die* big industrialist; **~inquisitor** *der* (hist.) Grand Inquisitor

Grossist *der*; **~en, ~en, Grossistin** *die*; **~, ~nen** (Kaufmannsspr.) wholesaler

groß-, Groß-: ~jährig *Adj.* (veralt.) ‹*person*› who is of age; **~jährig werden/sein** come/be of age; **~jährigkeit** *die*; **~~** (veralt.) majority; **die ~jährigkeit erlangen** reach the age of majority; **~kampf·schiff** *das* (Milit. veralt.) capital ship; **~kapital** *das* (Wirtsch.) big business *or* capital; **~kapitalist** *der*, **~kapitalistin** *die* big capitalist; **~katze** *die* (Zool.) big cat; **~kauffrau** *die*, **~kaufmann** *der* merchant; **~kind** *das* (schweiz.) grandchild; **~klima** *das* (Met.) macroclimate; **~konzern** *der* big *or* large combine; **~kopfe[r]te** /-kɔpfətə/ *der; adj. Dekl.* (ugs. abwertend) high-up (coll.); (Intellektueller) egghead (coll.); **~kotzig** /-kɔtsɪç/ **A** *Adj.* (salopp abwertend) pretentious ‹*style*›; swanky (coll.) ‹*present etc.*›; boastful ‹*tone etc.*›; **B** *adv.* boastfully; **~kreuz** *das* Grand Cross; **~küche** *die* large kitchen (*of hotel, hospital, etc.*); **~kundgebung** *die* mass rally *or* meeting; **~macht** *die* great power; **die ~macht USA** the USA, one of the great powers; **~macht·stellung** *die* great power status; **~mama** *die* (ugs.) grandma (coll./child lang.); granny (coll./child lang.); **~manns·sucht** *die* (abwertend) craving for status; **~markt** *der* central market; **~maschig** *Adj.* wide-meshed; **~mast** *der* (Seemannsspr.) mainmast; **~maul** *das* (ugs. abwertend) bigmouth (coll.); braggart; **~mäulig** /-mɔylɪç/ *Adj.* (ugs. abwertend) big-mouthed (coll.); **~meister** *der* Grand Master; (Schach) grand master; **~mut** *die*; **~~**: magnanimity; generosity; **~mütig** /-myːtɪç/ **A** *Adj.* magnanimous; generous; **B** *adv.* magnanimously; generously; **~mutter** *die*; *Pl.* **~mütter 1** grandmother; **~mutter werden** become a grandmother; **das kannst du deiner ~mutter erzählen** (ugs.) tell that to the marines; **2** (ugs.: alte Frau) old lady; **~mütterlich** *Adj.* **1** grandmother's; **das ~mütterliche Haus** one's grandmother's house; **jmds. ~mütterliches Erbe** sb.'s inheritance from his/her/their grandmother; **2** (wie eine ~mutter) grandmotherly; **~neffe** *der* great-nephew; grandnephew; **~nichte** *die* great-niece; grandniece; **~offensive** *die* (Milit.) major *or* full-scale offensive; **~oktav** *das* (Buchw.) royal octavo; **~onkel** *der* great-uncle; granduncle; **~papa** *der* (ugs.) grandpa (coll./child lang.); grandad (coll./child lang.); **~rat** *der*, **~rätin** *die* (schweiz.) *member of a cantonal great council*; **~raum** *der* area; **im ~raum Hamburg** in the [Greater] Hamburg area; **~raum·abteil** *das* (Eisenb.) open carriage; **~raum·büro** *das* open-plan office; **~raum·flugzeug** *das* wide-bodied aircraft

großräumig /-rɔymɪç/
A *Adj.* extensive; over a wide *or* large area *post-pos., not pred.*; (viel Platz bietend) spacious, roomy ‹*office, house, etc.*›; wide-bodied ‹*aircraft*›
B *adv.* over a wide *or* large area; **eine ~ gebaute Stadt** a town [built] with plenty of open space; **ein ~ konzipiertes Flugzeug** an aircraft designed for high-capacity air transport

groß-, Groß-: ~raum·limousine *die* people carrier; MPV; **~raum·wagen** *der* (Verkehrsw.) open car; **~rechner** *der* (DV) mainframe [computer]; **~reinemachen** *das* (ugs.) thorough cleaning; spring-clean; **ein ~reinemachen veranstalten** spring-clean the house; **~schanze** *die* (Skisport) ninety-metre hill; **~schnauze** *die* (salopp) bigmouth (coll.); **~schnauzig** *Adj.* (salopp) big-mouthed (coll.); **~|schreiben** *unr. tr. V.* write ‹*word*› with a capital [initial] letter; write ‹*word*› with a capital; *s. auch* **groß B 1**; **~schreibung** *die* capitalization; **~segel** *das* (Seemannsspr.) mainsail; **~sprecher** *der*, **~sprecherin** *die* (abwertend) braggart; boaster; **~sprecherisch** *Adj.* (abwertend) boastful ‹*person*›; bragging *attrib.*, boastful ‹*words, manner, etc.*›; **~spurig** (abwertend) **A** *Adj.* boastful; (hochtrabend) pretentious ‹*word, language*›; grandiose ‹*plan*›; **B** *adv.* boastfully; (hochtrabend) pretentiously; **~stadt** *die* city; large town; **~städter** *der*, **~städterin** *die* city-dweller; urbanite; **~städtisch** *Adj.* [big-]city *attrib.* ‹*life*›; **der ~städtische Autoverkehr** traffic in the [big] cities; **Genf ist in vielem ~städtischer als Bern** in many ways Geneva is more of a big city than Berne; **~stadt·luft** *die* city air; (fig. ugs.: Atmosphäre) atmosphere of the big city (fig.); **~stadt·verkehr** *der* [big-]city traffic

größt... ▸ **groß**

Groß-: ~tante *die* great-aunt; grandaunt; **~tat** *die* (geh.) great feat; **~teil** *der* **1** (Hauptteil) major part; **zum ~teil** mostly; for the most part; **2** (nicht unerheblicher Teil) large part; **zu einem ~teil** largely; **~teils** *Adv.* largely

größten·teils *Adv.* for the most part

Größt·maß *das* **1** (zulässiges Maß) maximum size *or* dimensions *pl.* **2** (größtmöglicher Anteil) maximum amount

größt·möglich *Adj.* greatest possible

groß-, Groß-: ~tuer /-tuːɐ/ *der*; **~~s, ~~** (abwertend) braggart; boaster; **~tuerei** *die*; **~~** (abwertend) bragging; boasting; **~tuerin** *die*; **~~, ~~nen** ▸ **~tuer**, **~tuerisch** *Adj.* (abwertend) boastful; bragging; **~|tun A** *unr. itr. V.* boast; brag; **mit jmdm./etw. ~tun** boast *or* brag about sb./sth.; **mit seinen Kenntnissen ~tun** show off one's knowledge; **B** *unr. refl. V.* **sich mit jmdm./etw. ~tun** boast *or* brag about sb./sth.; **~unternehmen** *das* (Wirtsch.) large-scale enterprise; big concern; **~unternehmer** *der* (Wirtsch.) big businessman; **~unternehmerin** *die* (Wirtsch.) big businesswoman; **~vater** *der* grandfather; **~väterlich 1** *Adj.* grandfather's; **das ~väterliche Haus** one's grandfather's house; **jmds. ~väterliches Erbe** sb.'s inheritance from his/her/their grandfather; **2** (wie ein ~vater) grandfatherly; **~vater·stuhl** *der* (ugs.) easy chair; wing chair; **~veranstaltung** *die* mass rally *or* meeting; **~verbraucher** *der*, **~verbraucherin** *die* bulk *or* large consumer; **~verdiener** *der*, **~verdienerin** *die* big earner; **~versand·haus** *das* [large] mail order firm *or* house; **~vieh** *das* cattle and horses *pl.*; **~wesir** *der* (hist.) grand vizier; **~wetter·lage** *die* (Met.) macro weather situation; (fig.) general political situation; **~wild** *das* big game; **~wild·jagd** *die* big-game hunting *no art.*; **~wild·jäger** *der*, **~wild·jägerin** *die* big-game hunter; **~wörterbuch** *das* comprehensive dictionary; **~|ziehen** *unr. tr. V.* bring up; raise; rear ‹*animal*›; **~zügig A** *Adj.* **1** generous; generous, handsome ‹*tip*›; **2** (in ~em Stil) grand and spacious ‹*building, gardens, etc.*›; generous, liberal ‹*working conditions*›; large-scale ‹*measures*›; **B** *adv.* **1** generously; **sich ~zügig über etw.** (*Akk.*) **hinwegsetzen** be broad-minded enough to disregard sth.; **2** (in ~em Stil) **ein ~zügig eingerichtetes Büro** a handsomely equipped office; **die ~zügig angelegten Schlossgärten** the palace gardens, laid out on a grand scale; **~zügigkeit** *die* **1** generosity; **2** (~es Ausmaß) grand scale

grotesk /groˈtɛsk/
A *Adj.* grotesque
B *adv.* grotesquely

Grotesk *die*; **~** (Druckw.) Grotesque; sanserif

Groteske *die*; **~, ~n 1** (Ornamentik) grotesque **2** (Literaturwiss.) grotesque tale

grotesker·weise *Adv.* absurdly [enough]

Grotte /ˈgrɔtə/ *die*; **~, ~n** grotto

grotten·doof *Adj.* bloody stupid (sl.)

Grotten·olm *der* olm

grotten·schlecht (salopp)
A *Adj.* lousy (coll.); awful; abysmal
B *adv.* abysmally

grub /gruːp/ *1. u. 3. Pers. Sg. Prät. v.* **graben**

Grubber /ˈgrʊbɐ/ *der*; **~s, ~** (Landw.) cultivator

Grübchen /ˈgryːpçən/ *das*; **~s, ~**: dimple

Grube *die*; **~, ~n 1** pit; hole; **wer andern eine ~ gräbt, fällt selbst hinein** (Spr.) take care that you are not hoist with your own petard **2** (Bergbau) mine; pit; **in der ~ arbeiten/in die ~ einfahren** work/go down the mine **3** (veralt.: offenes Grab) grave; **in die** *od.* **zur ~ fahren** (veralt.) yield up the ghost (arch.)

Grübelei *die*; **~, ~en** pondering; (Melancholie) brooding

grübeln /ˈgryːbl̩n/ *itr. V.* ponder (**über** + *Dat.* on, over); (brüten) brood (**über** + *Dat.* over, about)

Gruben-: ~arbeiter *der*, **~arbeiterin** *die* miner; mineworker; **~bahn** *die* mine *or* pit tram *or* train; **~brand** *der* pit fire; **~gas** *das* firedamp; **~lampe** *die* miner's lamp; **~unglück** *das* pit *or* mine disaster; **~wasser** *das* pit *or* mine water

Grübler *der*; **~s, ~, Grüblerin** *die*; **~, ~nen** meditative person; (Melancholiker) brooder; brooding person

grüblerisch *Adj.* meditative; (melancholisch) brooding

grüezi /ˈgryːɛtsi/ *Adv.* (schweiz.) hello

Gruft /grʊft/ *die*; **~, Grüfte** /ˈgryftə/ **1** (Gewölbe) vault; (in einer Kirche) crypt **2** (offenes Grab) grave

grummeln /ˈgrʊml̩n/ *itr. V.* **1** (dröhnen) rumble; **man hörte den Donner/die Geschütze ~**: one could hear the rumble of thunder/the guns **2** (murmeln) mumble

Grummet /ˈgrʊmət/ *das*; **~s, Grumt** /grʊmt/ *das*; **Grumt[e]s** aftermath

grün /gryːn/ *Adj.* **1** green; **~er Salat** lettuce; **die Ampel ist ~** (ugs.) the lights are green; **wir haben ~e Weihnachten gehabt** we didn't have a white Christmas; **die Grüne Insel** the Emerald Isle; **~e Bohnen/Erbsen** French beans/green peas; **~es Holz** green timber; **~e Heringe** fresh herrings; **ein ~er Junge** (abwertend) a greenhorn; **~es Licht geben** give the go-ahead; **jmdn. ~ und blau** *od.* **gelb schlagen** (ugs.) beat sb. black and blue; **sich ~ und blau** *od.* **gelb ärgern** (ugs.) be livid (coll.) *or* furious; **du bist noch [zu] ~ hinter den Ohren** (abwertend) you're still [too] wet behind the ears (coll.); *s. auch* **Welle 1 2** (ugs.: wohlgesinnt) **ich bin ihr nicht ~**: she's not someone I care for; **die beiden sind sich** (*Dat.*) **nicht ~**: there's no love lost between them **3** (Politik) ecological; **ein ~er Abgeordneter** a Member belonging to the Green party

Grün *das*; **~s, ~** *od.* (ugs.) **~s 1** green; **die Ampel steht auf** *od.* **zeigt ~**: the lights *pl.* are at green; **das ist dasselbe in ~** (ugs.) it makes *or* there is no real difference **2** (Pflanzen)

g

greenery 3 (Golf) green 4 (Spielkartenfarbe) spades *pl.*; *s. auch* **Pik²**
Grün·anlage *die* green space; (Park) park
grün·blau *Adj.* greenish blue
Grund /grʊnt/ *der;* **~[e]s, Gründe** /'grʏndə/ 1 (Erdoberfläche) ground; **etw. bis auf den ~ abreißen** raze sth. to the ground; **etw. von ~ auf neu bauen** rebuild sth. from scratch; **den ~ zu etw. legen** (fig.) lay the foundations *pl.* of *or* for sth. (fig.); **sich in ~ und Boden schämen** be utterly ashamed; **etw. in ~ und Boden verdammen** condemn sth. outright; **jmdn. in ~ und Boden reden** shoot every one of sb.'s arguments to pieces; **etw. in ~ und Boden wirtschaften** bring *or* reduce sth. to rack and ruin 2 (eines Gewässers, geh.: eines Gefäßes) bottom; **auf ~ laufen** run aground; **ein Glas bis auf den ~ leeren** (geh.) drain a glass [to the dregs]; **im ~e seines Herzens/seiner Seele** (fig. geh.) at heart *or* deep down/in his innermost soul; **der Sache** (*Dat.*) **auf den ~ gehen/kommen** get to the bottom *or* root of the matter; **im ~e [genommen]** basically 3 (Ursache, Veranlassung) reason; (Beweg~) grounds *pl.*; reason; **es gibt keinen/nicht den geringsten ~ zu etw.** there is no/not the slightest reason for sth.; **allen ~ haben, etw. zu tun** have every *or* good reason to do *or* for doing sth.; **[k]einen ~ zum Feiern/Klagen haben** have [no] cause for [a] celebration/to complain *or* for complaint; **aus Gründen der Geheimhaltung/Sicherheit** for reasons of secrecy/security; **aus dem einfachen ~, weil ...** (ugs.) for the simple reason that ...; **ohne ersichtlichen ~:** for no obvious *or* apparent reason; **auf ~ ihrer Aussagen/dieser Lage** on the basis *or* strength of their statements/in view of this situation; **Gründe und Gegengründe** pros and cons; arguments for and against 4 (veralt., noch landsch.: Erdreich) soil; ground 5 (bes. österr.: ~besitz) land *no indef. art., no pl.*; (Bau~) plot [of land]; **~ und Boden** land 6 (veralt.: kleines Tal) valley 7 (Unter~) ground 8 **zu ~e** ▸**zugrunde**
grund-, Grund-: ~anschauung *die* fundamental ideas *pl. or* attitudes *pl.*; **seine politische ~anschauung** his basic political outlook; **~anständig** *Adj.* thoroughly decent; **~anstrich** *der* priming coat; **~ausbildung** *die* (Milit.) basic training; **~ausstattung** *die* basic equipment; **~bedeutung** *die* 1 fundamental *or* basic *or* essential meaning; 2 (Sprachw.) original meaning; **~bedingung** *die* basic condition; **~bedürfnis** *das* basic need; **~begriff** *der* basic *or* fundamental concept; **die ~begriffe der lateinischen Sprache** the rudiments of Latin; **~besitz** *der* 1 (Eigentum an Land) ownership of land; 2 (Land) land; landed property; **~besitzer** *der*, **~besitzerin** *die* landowner; **~bestandteil** *der* [basic] element; **~buch** *das* land register; **~buch·amt** *das* land registry; **~ehrlich** *Adj.* thoroughly honest; **~eigentum** *das* ▸**~besitz 1**; **~eigentümer** *der*, **~eigentümerin** *die* ▸**~besitzer**; **~einheit** *die* 1 (Physik) fundamental unit; 2 (DDR: organisatorische Einheit) local group; **~einstellung** *die* fundamental *or* basic attitude; **~eis** *das* anchor ice; ground ice; *s. auch* **Arsch 1**
gründen /'grʏndn̩/
A *tr. V.* 1 (neu schaffen) found, set up, establish ‹*organization, party, etc.*›; set up, establish ‹*business*›; start [up] ‹*club*›; **eine Familie/ein Heim ~:** start a family/set up home 2 (aufbauen) base ‹*plan, theory, etc.*› (**auf** + *Akk.* on)
B *itr. V.* **auf** *od.* **in etw.** (*Dat.*) **~:** be based on sth.
C *refl. V.* **sich auf etw.** (*Akk.*) **~:** be based on sth.
Gründer *der;* **~s, ~, Gründerin** *die;* **~, ~nen** founder
Gründer·jahre *Pl.: period* (1871-1873) *when many industrial firms were founded in Germany*
Grund-: ~erwerb *der* (Rechtsw.) acquisition of land; (Kauf) purchase of land; **~erwerb[s]·steuer** *die* (Steuerw.) land transfer tax
Gründer·zeit *die* ▸**Gründerjahre**
grund-, Grund-: ~falsch *Adj.* utterly wrong; **~farbe** *die* 1 (Malerei, Druckw.) primary colour; 2 (Untergrundfarbe) ground colour; **~fehler** *der* basic *or* fundamental mistake *or* error; **~fertigkeit** *die* basic skill; **~festen** *Pl.*: *in* **an den ~festen von etw. rütteln** shake the [very] foundations of sth.; **etw. in seinen** *od.* **bis in seine ~festen erschüttern** shake sth. to its [very] foundations; **~fläche** *die* 1 (eines Zimmers) [floor] area; 2 (Math.) base; **~form** *die* 1 (Hauptform) basic form; 2 (Urform) original form; 3 (Sprachw.) infinitive; (Satzbauplan) basic [grammatical] structure of a/the sentence; **~frage** *die* basic *or* fundamental issue *or* question; **die politischen ~fragen** the basic *or* fundamental political issues *or* questions; **~gebühr** *die* basic *or* standing charge; **~gedanke** *der* basic idea; **~gehalt¹** *der* (einer Theorie) basic idea; (eines Dramas) basic theme; **~gehalt²** *das* basic salary; **~gescheit** *Adj.* extremely clever *or* bright; **~gesetz** *das* 1 (Verfassung) Basic Law; 2 (wichtiges Gesetz) fundamental or basic law; **~gütig** A *Adj.* extraordinarily kind[ly]; B *adv.* with extraordinary kind[li]ness; **~haltung** *die* 1 (Sport: Körperhaltung) basic position; 2 (Einstellung) basic *or* fundamental attitude; **~herr** *der* (hist.) lord of the manor

> **Grundgesetz**
>
> The written German constitution which came into force in May 1949. It lays down the basic rights of German citizens, the relationship between **Bund** and *Länder* (▸ **Land**), and the legal framework of the German state.

Grundier·anstrich *der* priming coat
grundieren /grʊn'di:rən/ *tr. V.* prime; (Ölmalerei) ground; apply the ground to
Grundier·farbe *die* primer
Grundierung *die;* **~, ~en** 1 (das Grundieren) priming; (Ölmalerei) grounding; applying the ground (*Gen.* to) 2 (erster Anstrich) priming coat; (Ölmalerei) ground coat
Grund-: ~kapital *das* (Wirtsch.) equity *or* share capital; **~kenntnis** *die* basic knowledge *no pl.* (**in** + *Dat.* of); **~konzeption** *die* basic *or* fundamental conception; **~kurs** *der* basic course
Grund·lage *die* basis; foundation; **auf der ~:** on the basis; **jeder ~ entbehren** be completely unfounded *or* without any foundation; **die geistigen/theoretischen ~n** the intellectual/theoretical foundations; **die ~n einer Wissenschaft** the basic principles of a science; **auf breiter ~ arbeiten** work *or* operate on a broad basis; **iss mal tüchtig, damit du eine gute ~ hast** (ugs.) get a good meal inside you to line your stomach with (coll.)
Grundlagen·forschung *die* basic research
grund·legend
A *Adj.* fundamental, basic (**für** to); seminal ‹*idea, work*›
B *adv.* fundamentally; **sich ~ zu etw. äußern** make a statement of fundamental importance on sth.
Grund·legung *die;* ~ (fig.) laying of the foundations (*Gen.* for)
gründlich /'grʏntlɪç/
A *Adj.* thorough
B *adv.* 1 (gewissenhaft) thoroughly 2 (ugs.: gehörig) **sich ~ täuschen** be sadly *or* greatly mistaken; **sich ~ langweilen** be bored to tears (coll.); **~ mit etw. aufräumen** do away completely with sth.; **~ mit jmdm. abrechnen** really get even with sb.
Gründlichkeit *die;* **~:** thoroughness
Gründling /'grʏntlɪŋ/ *der;* **~s, ~e** (Zool.) gudgeon
grund-, Grund-: ~linie *die* 1 (Math.) base; 2 (Sport) baseline; 3 (Hauptzug) main *or* principal feature *or* characteristic; **~linien·spiel** *das* (Tennis) baseline play; **~lohn** *der* basic salary; **~los** A *Adj.* 1 (unbegründet) groundless; unfounded; 2 (ohne festen Boden) bottomless ‹*sea, depths, etc.*›; B *adv.* **sich ~los aufregen/ängstigen** be needlessly agitated/alarmed; **~los lachen** laugh for no reason [at all]; **jmdn. ~los verdächtigen** be suspicious of sb. without reason; **~mauer** *die* foundation wall; **das Haus war bis auf die ~mauern abgebrannt** the house had burnt to the ground; **~nahrungs·mittel** *das* basic food[stuff]; **~norm** *die* basic standard
Grün·donnerstag *der* Maundy Thursday
Grund-: ~ordnung *die* basic fundamental [constitutional] order; **~pfeiler** *der* foundation *or* main pillar; (einer Brücke) main pier; (fig.) main pillar; **~prinzip** *das* fundamental *or* basic principle; **~rechen·art**, **~rechnungs·art** *die* fundamental *or* basic arithmetical operation; **~recht** *das* basic *or* fundamental *or* constitutional right; **~regel** *die* fundamental *or* basic rule; **~rente** *die* 1 (Wirtsch.: Bodenrente) ground rent; 2 (Sozialw.) basic pension; **~riss**, ***~riß** *der* 1 (Bauw.) [ground] plan; 2 (Leitfaden) outline; **~satz** *der* principle; **aus ~satz** on principle; **sich** (*Dat.*) **etw. zum ~satz machen** make sth. a matter of principle; **ein Mann von ~sätzen** a man of principle; **~satz·entscheidung** *die* decision on fundamental principles; (Rechtsw.) ruling; **~satz·erklärung** *die* declaration of principle; **~satz·frage** *die* fundamental question
grund·sätzlich
A *Adj.* 1 fundamental ‹*difference, question, etc.*› 2 (aus Prinzip) ‹*rejection, opponent, etc.*› on principle 3 (allgemein) ‹*agreement, readiness, etc.*› in principle
B *adv.* 1 fundamentally; **zu etw. ~ Stellung nehmen** make a statement of principle on sth. 2 (aus Prinzip) as a matter of principle; on principle; **es ist ~ verboten** it is absolutely forbidden 3 (allgemein) in principle; **~ habe ich nichts dagegen einzuwenden, aber ...** basically *or* in principle I've nothing against it, but ...
Grund-: ~satz·programm *das* political programme; **~schnelligkeit** *die* (Sport) 1 maximum speed; 2 (angeboren) basic speed capability; **~schuld** *die* (Rechtsw., Finanzw.) land charge; encumbrance; **~schule** *die* primary school; **~schüler** *der* primary school pupil; **~schul·lehrer** *der*, **~schul·lehrerin** *die* ▸❶ **S. 113** primary-school teacher; **~sicherung** *die* (Politik) basic income payment; **~stein** *der* foundation stone; (fig.) foundation [stone]; **den ~stein zu etw. legen** lay the foundation stone of sth.; (fig.) lay the foundation[s *pl.*] for *or* of sth.; **~stein·legung** *die;* **~~, ~~en** laying of the foundation stone; **~stellung** *die* (Sport) basic position; **~steuer** *die* (Steuerw.) property tax [under German law]; **~stimmung** *die* prevailing mood; **eine pessimistische ~stimmung** a prevailing mood of pessimism; **~stock** *der* basis; foundation; (einer Sammlung) basis; nucleus; **~stoff** *der* 1 (Chemie: Element) element; 2 (Rohstoff) [basic] raw material; **~stoff·industrie** *die* basic industry

> **Grundschule**
>
> The primary school which all German children attend for four years from the age of 6 (some children do not start until they are 7). Lessons are intense but pupils only attend school for about 4 hours a day. At the end of the *Grundschule*, teachers and parents decide together which type of secondary school the child should attend.

Grund·stück *das* plot [of land]; (Baugrundstück) plot of land; building plot; **ein bebautes ~:** a developed site
Grundstücks-: ~makler *der*, **~maklerin** *die* ▸❶ **S. 113** estate agent; **~spekulant** *der*, **~spekulantin** *die* property speculator
grund-, Grund-: ~studium *das* basic course; **~stürzend** A *Adj.* fundamental; radical; B *adv.* fundamentally; radically; **~tendenz** *die* basic trend; **~text** *der* original text; **~ton** *der; Pl.* **~töne** 1 (Farbton) basic colour; 2 (~stimmung) basic or prevailing tone *or* mood; **ein optimistischer ~ton** a basic *or* prevailing mood of optimism; 3 (Musik) fundamental [tone]; root; **~übel**

i Grüße

Auf einer Postkarte

Schöne od. Herzliche Grüße aus Freiburg
= Greetings *od.* Best wishes from Freiburg
Es gefällt uns hier ausgezeichnet
= We're having a wonderful time
Bis bald
= See you soon
Es grüßen recht herzlich Stephan und Inge
= All best wishes, Stephan and Inge

Zum Geburtstag

Herzlichen Glückwunsch zum Geburtstag
= Many happy returns [of the day], Happy birthday
Alles Gute zum 60. Geburtstag
= All best wishes on your 60th birthday

Zu Weihnachten und zum neuen Jahr

Frohe Weihnachten!
= Happy Christmas!
Ein gesegnetes Weihnachtsfest und viel Glück im neuen Jahr
= Best wishes for a Happy *od.* Merry Christmas and a Prosperous New Year
Glückliches neues Jahr!, Prost Neujahr!
= Happy New Year!

Zu Ostern

Frohe Ostern!
= [Best wishes for a] Happy Easter

Zu einer Hochzeit

Dem glücklichen Paar alles Gute am Hochzeitstag und viel Glück in der Zukunft
= Every good wish to the happy couple *od.* to the bride and groom on their wedding day and in the years to come

Zu einer Prüfung

Viel Erfolg bei der bevorstehenden Prüfung
= Every success in your exams, The best of luck with your exams
Alles Gute zum/Viel Glück beim Abitur
≈ All good wishes/The best of luck with your A levels

Zum Umzug

Viel Glück im neuen Heim
= Every happiness in your new home

Bei einem Krankheitsfall

Gute Besserung!
= Get well soon!
Die besten Wünsche zur baldigen Genesung
= Best wishes for a speedy recovery

Gesprochene Grüße

Hier gibt es manchmal keine genauen bzw. gar keine richtigen Entsprechungen.

Bei Begegnungen

Guten Tag!
= Good morning/afternoon/evening (*je nach Tageszeit*); Hello! (*wirkt ungezwungener*)
Hallo!
= Hello [there]!, Hi [there]!
Guten Morgen!
= Good morning!
Guten Abend!
= Good evening!
Wie geht es Ihnen?/Wie gehts?
= How are you?
***Freut mich!* (bei Vorstellungen)**
= How do you do?

Beim Abschied

Auf Wiedersehen!
= Goodbye!
Tschüs!
= Bye now!
Bis bald!
= See you soon!
Machs gut!
= Look after yourself!, Take care!

Siehe auch □ **Briefeschreiben**

das basic evil; **~umsatz** *der* (Physiol.) basal metabolic rate

Gründung *die;* ~, ~en (Partei~, Vereins~) foundation; establishment; setting up; (Geschäfts~) setting up; establishing; (Klub~) starting [up]; **die ~ einer Familie** starting a family

Gründungs-: **~feier** *die* foundation ceremony; **~jahr** *das* year of foundation *or* establishment; **das ~jahr unseres Vereins** the year of the foundation of our organization; **~kapital** *das* (Wirtsch.) original *or* initial capital

grund-, Grund-: **~verkehrt** *Adj.* completely *or* entirely wrong; **~vermögen** *das* (Finanzw.) [landed] property; real estate; **~verschieden** *Adj.* totally *or* completely different; **~wahrheit** *die* fundamental *or* basic truth; **~wasser** *das* (Geol.) groundwater; **~wasser·spiegel** *der* water table; groundwater level; **~wehr·dienst** *der* basic military service; national service; **~wissen** *das* basic *or* elementary knowledge; **~wissenschaft** *die* basic discipline; **~wort** *das; Pl.* **~wörter** (Sprachw.) basic component; **~wort·schatz** *der* (Sprachw.) basic vocabulary; **~zahl** *die* cardinal [number]; **~zug** *der* essential feature; **etw. in seinen ~zügen darstellen** outline the essential features *or* essentials of sth.

Grüne[1] *das; adj. Dekl.* 1) green 2) **im ~n/ins ~:** [out] in/into the country 3) (ugs.: grüne Pflanzen) greenery; (Salat) green salad; (Gemüse) greens *pl.*; green vegetables *pl.*

Grüne[2] *der/die; adj. Dekl.* (Politik) member of the Green Party; **die ~n** the Greens

Grüne[3] *der; adj. Dekl.* (ugs.: Polizist) cop (coll.)

grünen *itr. V.* (geh.) be green; (grün werden) turn green; (fig. dichter.) spring up anew

Grüner Punkt

A symbol used to mark packaging materials which can be recycled. Any packaging carrying this logo is collected separately under the **Duales System** recycling scheme. Manufacturers have to buy a licence from the recycling company DSD (*Duales System Deutschland*) to entitle them to use this symbol.

grün-, Grün-: **~fink** *der* greenfinch; **~fläche** *die* green space; (im Park) lawn; **~futter** *das* (Landw.) green fodder; **~gelb** *Adj.* greenish yellow; **~gürtel** *der* green belt; **~kern** *der: dried unripe spelt grains (used to thicken soup)*; **~kohl** *der* curly kale; **~land** *das* (Landw.) (Wiese) meadow land; (Weide) pastureland; (mit ~futter bebaut) land used for growing green fodder

grünlich
A *Adj.* greenish
B *adv.* **~ gelb** greenish yellow

grün-, Grün-: **~pflanze** *die* foliage plant; **~schnabel** *der* (abwertend) [young] whippersnapper; (Neuling) greenhorn; **~span** *der* verdigris; **~specht** *der* green woodpecker; **~stichig** *Adj.* (Fot.) with a green cast *postpos., not pred.*; **~stichig sein** have a green cast; **~streifen** *der* central reservation; centre strip (grassed and often with trees and bushes); (am Straßenrand) grass verge

grunzen /ˈgrʊntsn̩/ *tr., itr. V.* grunt

Grün·zeug *das* (ugs.) ▸**Grüne**[1] **3**

Grunz·laut *der* grunt

Grüppchen /ˈgrʏpçən/ *das;* **~s, ~:** small group

Gruppe /ˈgrʊpə/ *die;* ~, ~n 1) (auch Sport, Math., Musik) group; **eine ~ Jugendlicher/Erwachsener** *od.* **von Jugendlichen/Erwachsenen** a group of juveniles/adults 2) (Klassifizierung) class; category; **die ~ der starken/schwachen Verben** the class of strong/weak verbs 3) (Milit.: kleine Einheit) ≈ section; (Luftwaffe) ≈ squadron

gruppen-, Gruppen-: **~arbeit** *die* group work; **~aufnahme** *die* ▸**~bild 1**; **~bild** *das* 1) (Fot.) group photograph; 2) (Gemälde) group portrait; **~dynamik** *die* (Sozialpsych.) group dynamics *sing., no art.*; **~führer** *der* 1) (Milit.) ≈ section commander *or* leader; 2) (Wirtsch.) team *or* group leader; 3) (ns.) SS lieutenant general; **~führerin** *die* ▸**~führer 2**; **~mitglied** *das* member of the/a group; **~reise** *die* (Touristik) group travel *no pl., no art.*; **eine ~reise nach London machen** travel to London with a group; **~sex** *der* group sex; **~sieg** *der* (Sport) top place in the group; **den ~sieg erreichen** win the group; **~sieger** *der,* **~siegerin** *die* (Sport) winner of the/a group; **~therapie** *die* (Psych.) group therapy; **~unterricht** *der* 1) (Päd.) teaching of groups; **etw. im ~unterricht lernen** learn sth. as part of a group; 2) (erteilter Unterricht) group instruction; **~versicherung** *die* (Versicherungsw.) group insurance; **~weise** *Adv.* in groups

gruppieren
A *tr. V.* arrange; **die Stühle um den Tisch ~:** arrange *or* set the chairs round the table; **Pflanzen nach verschiedenen Gesichtspunkten ~:** group plants according to different criteria
B *refl. V.* form a group/groups; **sie gruppierten sich um den Tisch** they arranged themselves in a group around the table

Gruppierung *die;* ~, ~en 1) (Personengruppe) grouping; group; (Politik) faction 2) (Anordnung) arrangement; grouping

Grus /gruːs/ *der;* **~es, ~e** 1) (Kohlenstaub) breeze; slack 2) (Geol.) detritus

Grusel /ˈgruːzl̩/ *der;* **~s** horror

Grusel-: **~effekt** *der* horror effect; **~film** *der* horror film; **~geschichte** *die* horror story

gruselig /ˈgruːzəlɪç/, **gruslig** /ˈgruːslɪç/ *Adj.* eerie; creepy; blood-curdling ⟨*apparition, scream*⟩; spine-chilling ⟨*story, film*⟩

gruseln
A *tr., itr. V.* (unpers.) **es gruselt jmdn.** *od.* **jmdm.** sb.'s flesh creeps; **es hat mich** *od.* **mir vor diesem Anblick gegruselt** this sight made my flesh creep *or* (coll.) gave me the creeps
B *refl. V.* be frightened; get the creeps (coll.); **mit leichtem Gruseln** with a small shiver of fear

gruslig ▸**gruselig**

Gruß /gruːs/ *der;* **~es, Grüße** /ˈgryːsə/ ▸**i S. 331** 1) greeting; (Milit.) salute; **jmdm. die Hand zum ~ reichen** (geh.) shake hands with sb.; **jmdm. herzliche Grüße senden** send sb. one's best regards *or* wishes; **viele Grüße** best wishes (**an** + *Akk.* to); **bestell Barbara bitte viele Grüße von mir** please give Barbara my regards; please remember me to Barbara; **einen [schönen] ~ an jmdn./von jmdm.** [best] regards *pl.* to/from sb.; **der Deutsche ~** (ns.) the Nazi salute 2) (im Brief) **mit herzlichen**

g

Grüßen [with] best wishes; **viele liebe Grüße euer Hans** love, Hans; **mit bestem ~/freundlichen Grüßen** Yours sincerely

Gruß·adresse *die* message of greetings

Grüß·august *der* (salopp scherzh. od. abwertend) public figurehead

grüßen /ˈgry:sn̩/ ▸ⓘ S. 331
A *tr. V.* 1) greet; (Milit.) salute; **grüß [dich] Gott!** (südd.) hello; **er hat mich nie gegrüßt** he never said hello to me; **grüß dich!** (ugs.) hello *or* (coll.) hi [there]! 2) (Grüße senden) **grüße deine Eltern [ganz herzlich] von mir** please give your parents my [kindest] regards; **jmdn. ~ lassen** send one's regards to sb.; **grüß mir die Familie** remember me to your family
B *itr. V.* say hello; (Milit.) salute; **Franz lässt ~:** Franz sends his regards

gruß-, Gruß-: ~formel *die* salutation; (am Briefende) [complimentary] close; **~los** *Adv.* without a word of greeting/farewell; **~wort** *das; Pl.* **~worte** 1) ▸ **~adresse**; 2) (Ansprache) [short] welcoming speech *or* address; **einige ~worte** a few words of welcome

Grütz·beutel *der* sebaceous cyst

Grütze /ˈgrʏtsə/ *die;* **~, ~n** 1) groats *pl.*; **rote ~:** red fruit pudding (*made with fruit juice, fruit and cornflour, etc.*) 2) (ugs.: Verstand) brains *pl.*; nous (coll.); **die hat [keine] ~ im Kopf** she's got [no] nous (coll.)

G-Saite /ˈge:-/ *die* (Musik) G-string

Gschaftlhuber ▸ **Geschaftlhuber**

gschert, Gscherte ▸ **geschert, Gescherte**

G-Schlüssel /ˈge:-/ *der* (Musik) ▸ **Violinschlüssel**

Gspusi /ˈkʃpu:zi/ *das;* **~s, ~s** (südd., österr. ugs.) 1) (Liebschaft) [love] affair 2) (Geliebte[r]) sweetheart

Guatemala /guateˈma:la/ *(das);* **~s** Guatemala

Guatemalteke /guatemalˈte:kə/ *der;* **~n, ~n, Guatemaltekin** *die;* **~, ~nen** Guatemalan

Guave /guˈa:və/ *die;* **~, ~n** guava

Guayana /guaˈja:na/ ▸ **Guyana**

gucken /ˈgʊkn̩/
A *itr. V.* (ugs.) 1) look; (heimlich) peep; **jmdm. über die Schulter ~:** look *or* peer over sb.'s shoulder; **lass [mich] mal ~!** let's have a look! (coll.); *s. auch* **Karte 7** 2) (hervorsehen) stick out 3) (dreinschauen) look; **finster/freundlich ~:** look grim/affable
B *tr. V.* (ugs.) **Fernsehen ~:** watch TV *or* (coll.) telly *or* (coll.) the box

Guck·fenster *das* judas [window]

Gucki /ˈgʊki/ *der;* **~s, ~s** (Fot.) [slide] viewer

Guck-: ~in-die-luft ▸ **Hans; ~kasten** *der* peep show; **~loch** *das* spyhole; peephole

Guerilla¹ /geˈrɪlja/ *die;* **~, ~s** 1) (Krieg) guerrilla war 2) (Einheit) guerrilla unit

Guerilla² *der;* **~s, ~s** (Kämpfer) guerrilla

Guerilla-: ~kämpfer *der,* **~kämpferin** *die* guerrilla; **~krieg** *der* guerrilla war; **eine Spezialausbildung für den ~krieg** special training in guerrilla warfare

Guerillero /-ˈje:ro/ *der;* **~s, ~s** guerrilla

Gugel·hupf /-hʊpf/ *der;* **~[e]s, ~e** (südd., österr.) gugelhupf

Güggeli /ˈgʏgəli/ *das;* **~s, ~** (schweiz.) roast chicken

Guillotine /gijoˈti:nə/ *die;* **~, ~n** guillotine

guillotinieren *tr. V.* guillotine

Guinea /giˈne:a/ *(das);* **~s** Guinea

Guineer /giˈne:ɐ/ *der;* **~s, ~, Guineerin** *die;* **~, ~nen** Guinean

Gulasch /ˈgʊlaʃ, ˈgu:laʃ/ *das od. der;* **~[e]s, ~e** *od.* **~s** goulash

Gulasch-: ~kanone *die* (Soldatenspr. scherzh.) field kitchen; **~suppe** *die* goulash soup

gülden /ˈgʏldn̩/ *Adj.* (dichter.) golden

Gulden /ˈgʊldn̩/ *der;* **~s, ~:** guilder; florin

Gülle /ˈgʏlə/ *die;* **~** (Landw.) ▸ **Jauche**

Gulli, Gully /ˈgʊli/ *der;* **~s, ~s** drain

gültig /ˈgʏltɪç/ *Adj.* valid; current ⟨*note, coin*⟩; **ein ~er Beweis** a valid proof; **das bisher ~e Gesetz** the law previously/hitherto in force; **diese Münze/dieser Geldschein ist nicht mehr ~:** this coin/note is no longer legal tender; **der Fahrplan ist ab 1. Oktober ~:** the timetable comes into operation on 1 October; **einen Vertrag als ~ anerkennen** recognize a contract as valid *or* legally binding; **eine Ehe für ~ erklären** declare a marriage [to be] legal *or* valid; **~ für zwanzig Fahrten sein** be valid *or* good for twenty journeys

Gültigkeit *die;* **~:** validity; (eines Gesetzes) [legal] force; **~ haben/erlangen** be/become valid; ⟨*law*⟩ be in/come into force; **die ~ verlieren** become invalid; **wann verliert diese Münze ihre ~?** when does this coin cease to be legal tender?; **einem Dokument ~ verleihen** validate a document

Gültigkeits-: ~dauer *die* period of validity; **~erklärung** *die* validation

Gummi¹ /ˈgʊmi/ *der od. das;* **~s, ~[s]** 1) [india] rubber 2) (~ring) rubber *or* elastic band

Gummi² *der;* **~s, ~s** 1) (Radier~) rubber; eraser 2) (salopp: Präservativ) rubber (sl.)

Gummi³ *das;* **~s, ~s** (~band) elastic *no indef. art.*

gummi-, Gummi-: ~arabikum /-aˈra:bikʊm/ *das;* **~~s** gum arabic; **~artig** *Adj.* rubbery; rubber-like ⟨*material*⟩; **~ball** *der* rubber ball; **~band** *das; Pl.* **~bänder** 1) rubber *or* elastic band; 2) (in Kleidung) elastic *no indef. art.*; **ein ~band einziehen** insert a piece of elastic; **~bär** *der,* **~bärchen** *das* jelly baby; **~baum** *der* (Zimmerpflanze) rubber plant; **~bereifung** *die* rubber tyres *pl.*; **~bonbon** *das* gumdrop; **~druck** *der* (Druckw.) flexography

gummieren *tr. V.* 1) gum 2) (Textilw.) rubberize

Gummierung *die;* **~, ~en** 1) (gummierte Fläche) gummed surface; (Textilw.) rubberized surface 2) (das Gummieren) gumming; (Textilw.) rubberizing

Gummi-: ~gutt *das;* **~~s** gamboge; **~handschuh** *der* rubber glove; **~harz** *das* gum resin; **~knüppel** *der* [rubber] truncheon; **~lack** *der* shellac; **~linse** *die* (Fot.) zoom lens; **~lösung** *die* rubber solution; **~mantel** *der* mackintosh (Brit.); raincoat; **~paragraph** *der* (ugs.) paragraph *or* section with an elastic interpretation; **~reifen** *der* rubber tyre; **~ring** *der* 1) rubber band; 2) (Spielzeug) rubber ring; quoit; 3) (Weckglasring) rubber seal; **~sauger** *der* rubber teat; **~schlauch** *der* rubber hose; **~schuh** *der* 1) rubber shoe; 2) ▸ **~überschuh**; **~schutz** *der* (veralt.) sheath; condom; **~sohle** *die* rubber sole; **~stiefel** *der* rubber boot; (für Regenwetter) wellington [boot] (Brit.); (bis zum Oberschenkel) wader; **~strumpf** *der* elastic stocking; **~tier** *das* rubber animal; (aufblasbar) inflatable animal; **~twist** *der od. das;* **~~s, ~~s** Chinese jump rope; **~überschuh** *der* galosh; rubber overshoe; **~waren** *Pl.* rubber goods; **~zelle** *die* padded cell; **~zug** *der* ▸ **~band 2**

Gunder·mann /ˈgʊndɐ-/ *der;* **~[e]s** (Bot.) ground ivy

Gunst /gʊnst/ *die;* **~** 1) favour; goodwill; **jmds. ~ erlangen** win *or* gain sb.'s favour; **in jmds. ~** *(Dat.) od.* **bei jmdm. in ~** *(Dat.)* **stehen** (geh.) enjoy sb.'s favour; be in favour with sb.; **jmdm. seine ~ bezeugen** show one's favour to sb.; **die ~ der Stunde/Lage nutzen** (fig.) take advantage of the favourable *or* propitious moment/situation; **zu jmds. ~en** in sb.'s favour 2) **zu ~en** ▸ **zugunsten**

Gunst·bezeigung *die* mark of favour *or* goodwill

günstig /ˈgʏnstɪç/
A *Adj.* 1) (vorteilhaft) favourable; propitious ⟨*sign*⟩; auspicious ⟨*moment*⟩; beneficial ⟨*influence*⟩; good, reasonable ⟨*price*⟩; **bei ~em Wetter** if the weather is favourable; weather permitting; **der Zug um 10 Uhr ist ~er** the 10 o'clock train is better *or* more convenient 2) (wohlwollend) well-disposed; favourably disposed; **das Glück war uns ~:** luck was on our side
B *adv.* 1) (vorteilhaft) favourably; **etw. ~ beeinflussen** have *or* exert a beneficial influence on sth.; **etw. ~ kaufen/verkaufen** buy/sell sth. at a good price; **das trifft sich ~:** that's a piece of luck 2) (wohlwollend) **jmdn./etw. ~ aufnehmen** receive sb./sth. well *or* favourably; **jmdn. ~ stimmen** put sb. in a favourable mood; **jmdn. für etw. ~ stimmen** make sb. well-disposed towards sth.; **jmdm./einer Sache ~ gesinnt sein** be well *or* favourably disposed towards sb./sth.

günstig[st]en·falls *Adv.* at best

Günstling /ˈgʏnstlɪŋ/ *der;* **~s, ~e** favourite

Günstlings·wirtschaft *die* (abwertend) favouritism

Guppy /ˈgʊpi/ *der;* **~s, ~s** (Zool.) guppy

Gurgel /ˈgʊrgl̩/ *die;* **~, ~n** throat; **jmdm. die ~ zudrücken** strangle *or* throttle sb.; **jmdm. die ~ durchschneiden** cut sb.'s throat; **jmdm. an die ~ springen/fahren** jump *or* leap at/go for sb.'s throat; **jmdm. an die ~ wollen** fly at sb.; **jmdm. die ~ abdrehen** *od.* **zudrücken** (fig. salopp) force *or* send sb. to the wall; **sein ganzes Geld durch die ~ jagen** (ugs.) drink all one's money away (coll.); **sich** *(Dat.)* **die ~ ölen** *od.* **schmieren** (ugs.) wet one's whistle (coll.)

gurgeln *itr. V.* 1) (spülen) gargle 2) (blubbern) gurgle

Gürkchen /ˈgʏrkçən/ *das;* **~s, ~** [cocktail] gherkin

Gurke /ˈgʊrkə/ *die;* **~, ~n** 1) cucumber; (eingelegt) gherkin; **saure ~n** pickled gherkins 2) (salopp scherzh.: Nase) hooter (coll.); snout (coll.) 3) (salopp abwertend: Auto) [old] banger (sl.)

Gurken-: ~hobel *der* cucumber slicer; **~salat** *der* cucumber salad; **~truppe** *die* (salopp) useless *or* feeble bunch (coll.)

gurren /ˈgʊrən/ *itr. V.* (auch fig.) coo

Gurt /gʊrt/ *der;* **~[e]s, ~e** strap; (Gürtel) belt; (im Auto, Flugzeug) [seat] belt

Gürtel /ˈgʏrtl̩/ *der;* **~s, ~** belt; **den ~ enger schnallen** (fig. ugs.) tighten one's belt (fig.)

Gürtel-: ~linie *die* waist[line]; **ein Schlag unter die ~linie** (Boxen) a punch *or* blow below the belt; **das war ein Schlag unter die ~linie** (fig. ugs.) that was hitting below the belt (fig. coll.); **~reifen** *der* radial[-ply] tyre; **~rose** *die* ▸ⓘ **S. 439** (Med.) shingles *sing. or pl.*; **~schnalle** *die* belt buckle; **~tier** *das* armadillo

gürten /ˈgʏrtn̩/ (geh. veralt.)
A *tr. V.* gird (arch./literary); **jmdn. mit dem Schwert ~:** gird sb. with his sword
B *refl. V.* **sich [zum Kampf] ~:** gird oneself; **sich mit dem Schwert ~:** gird on one's sword

Gurt·muffel *der* (ugs.) person not wearing a safety belt

Gurtstraffer *der;* **~s, ~** (Kfz.-W.) [seat-]belt tensioner

Guru /ˈgʊru/ *der;* **~s, ~s** guru

Guss, *Guß /gʊs/ *der;* **Gusses, Güsse** /ˈgʏsə/ 1) (das Gießen) casting; founding; **[wie] aus einem ~:** forming a unified *or* an integrated whole; fully coordinated ⟨*plan*⟩ 2) (ugs.: Regenschauer) downpour; **ein heftiger/wolkenbruchartiger ~:** a violent downpour/a cloudburst 3) (gegossenes Erzeugnis) casting; cast 4) (das Begießen) stream; (Med.) affusion 5) (auf Backwaren) icing; **eine Torte mit ~ überziehen** ice a gateau

guss-, *guß-, Guss-, *Guß-: ~asphalt *der* [poured] asphalt; **~beton** *der* cast concrete; **~eisen** *das* cast iron; **~eisern** *Adj.* cast-iron; **~form** *die* casting mould; **~naht** *die* (Gießerei) [casting] fin *or* flash; **~stahl** *der* cast steel

Gusto /ˈgʊsto/ *der;* **~s, ~s** 1) (Neigung) taste; liking; **nach jmds. ~ sein** be to sb.'s taste *or* liking 2) (Appetit) **~ auf etw.** *(Akk.)* **haben** feel like *or* fancy sth.

Gusto·stückerl *das* (österr.) star turn

gut /gu:t/; **besser** /ˈbɛsɐ/, **best...** /ˈbɛst.../
A *Adj.* 1) good; fine ⟨*wine*⟩; **in Französisch ~ sein** be good at French; **ist der Kuchen ~ geworden?** did the cake turn out all right?; **es wäre ~, wenn ...** it would be as well if ...; **also ~:** very well; all right; **schon ~:** [it's] all right *or* (coll.) OK; **nun ~:** very well *or* all right

[then]; **wie ~, dass ...** it's good that ...; **jetzt ist es aber ~!** (ugs.) that's enough!; **das ist ja alles ~ und schön** that's all very well *or* all well and good; **etwas Gutes zu essen/trinken** something good to eat/drink; **es ~ sein lassen** (ugs.) leave it at that; **lass es ~ sein** (ugs.) let's say no more about it; **das ist ~ gegen** *od.* **für Kopfschmerzen** it's good for headaches; **wer weiß, wozu das ~ ist** perhaps it's for the best; **das ist so ~ wie gewonnen** it's as good as won; **dieser Stürmer ist immer ~ für ein Tor** (ugs.) this forward is always likely to score goals; **~en Tag!** good morning/afternoon!; **~en Morgen!** good morning!; **~en Abend!** good evening!; **~e Nacht!** good night!; **etw. zu einem ~en Ende führen** bring sth. to a happy conclusion; **ein ~es neues Jahr** a happy new year; **Sie haben es noch nie so ~ gehabt** you've never had it so good; **er hat es doch ~ bei uns** he's well enough off with us; **ihr habt es ~:** it's all right for 'you; **mir ist nicht ~:** I'm not feeling well; I don't feel well; **alles Gute!** all the best!; **das bedeutet nichts Gutes** that's an ominous sign; **das ist zu viel des Guten** (iron.) that's overdoing it; **das Gute daran** the good thing about it; **~en Appetit!** enjoy your lunch/dinner *etc.!*; **es dürfte eine ~e Stunde [von hier] sein** it must be a good hour [from here]; **ein ~ Teil von etw.** a good deal *or* part of sth.; **~e Frau/~er Mann** (iron. Anrede) dear lady/my good man; **sich** (*Dat.*) **zu ~ für etw. sein** consider sth. beneath one *or* beneath one's dignity; **du bist ~!** (iron.) you're joking!; you must be joking!; **im Guten wie im Bösen haben wir uns bemüht ...** we've done everything we can to try ...; **jmdm. ~ sein** (ugs.) feel a lot of affection for sb.; **wieder ~ [mit jmdm.] sein** be friends [with sb.] again; **sei [bitte] so ~ und reich mir das Buch** would you be good *or* kind enough to pass me the book?; **im Guten auseinander gehen** part amicably *or* on amicable terms; **[jmdm.] ~ tun** do [sb.] good; **ein Schnaps tut ~ bei der Kälte** schnapps is good for you when it's cold
[2] (besonderen Anlässen vorbehalten) best; **sein ~er Anzug** his best suit; **die ~e Stube** the best room; **für ~** (ugs.) for best; for special occasions

B *adv.* [1] well; **~ reiten/schwimmen** be a good rider/swimmer; **etw. ~ können** be good at sth.; **seine Sache ~ machen** do well; **~ hören/sehen** [be able to] hear/see well *or* clearly; **[das hast du] ~ gemacht!** well done!; **du tätest ~ daran, darüber zu schweigen** you would do well *or* be wise to say nothing about it; **der Laden/das Geschäft geht ~:** the shop/business is doing well; **~ bezahlt** well-paid; **~ gehend** flourishing, thriving ‹*business*›; **~ gekleidet** well-dressed; **~ gemeint** well-meant; **~ unterrichtet** well-informed; **~ eine Stunde [von hier] entfernt** a good hour [from here]; **~ zwei Pfund wiegen** weigh a good two pounds; **~ und gern** (ugs.) easily; at least (ugs.); **so ~ wie nichts** next to nothing; **so ~ ich kann** as best I can; **~ und richtig handeln** do the right thing; **jmdm. ~ zureden** coax sb. [gently]; **mit jmdm. ~ stehen** *od.* **auskommen** be on good *or* friendly terms with sb.; get on well with sb.; **es ~ meinen** mean well; **es ~ mit jmdm. meinen** have sb.'s interests at heart; *s. auch* **anschreiben A 2**
[2] (mühelos) easily; **~ zu Fuß sein** (ugs.) be a strong walker; **hinterher hat** *od.* **kann man ~ reden** it's easy to be wise after the event; **du hast ~ lachen** it's all right for you to laugh; **es kann ~ sein, dass ...** it may well be that ...; **ich kann das nicht ~ tun** I can't very well do that; *s. auch* **besser, best...**

Gut *das;* **~[e]s, Güter** /ˈɡuːtɐ/ [1] (Eigentum) property; (Besitztum, auch fig.) possession; **ererbtes/gestohlenes ~:** inherited/stolen property; **irdische Güter** earthly goods *or* possessions; **die geistigen Güter des Volkes** the intellectual wealth *sing.* of the people; **bewegliche/unbewegliche Güter** movables/immovables; **das höchste ~** (fig.) the greatest good; **unrecht ~ gedeihet nicht** *od.* **tut selten gut** (Spr.) ill-gotten goods *or* gains never *or* seldom prosper [2] (landwirtschaftlicher Grundbesitz) estate [3] (Frachtgut, Ware) item; **Güter** goods; (Fracht~) freight *sing.*; goods (Brit.) [4] (das ~e) **~ und Böse** good and evil; **jenseits von ~ und Böse sein** (iron.) be past it (coll.) [5] (veralt.: Material) material [to be processed]

gut-, Gut-: ~achten *itr. V.* give an expert opinion; (in einem Prozess) act as an expert witness; **der ~de Arzt** the medical expert; **~achten** *das;* **~~s, ~~:** [expert's] report; **~achter** *der;* **~~s, ~~, ~achterin** *die;* **~~, ~~nen** expert; (in einem Prozess) expert witness; **~achtlich** **A** *Adj.* expert; **B** *adv.* **etw. ~achtlich prüfen/untersuchen lassen** commission an expert report on sth.; **~artig** *Adj.* [1] good-natured; [2] (nicht gefährlich) benign; **~artigkeit** *die* [1] good nature; goodnaturedness; [2] (Ungefährlichkeit) benignity; **~aussehend** ▸**aussehen**; **~bezahlt** ▸**gut B 1**; **~|bringen** *unr. tr. V.* (Kaufmannsspr.) ▸**~schreiben**; **~bürgerlich** **A** *Adj.* good middle class; **~bürgerliche Küche** good plain cooking; **~bürgerliches Zuhause** comfortable middle-class home; **B** *adv.* in a good middle-class way; ‹*grow up*› in good middle-class circumstances; **~bürgerlich essen** eat good plain food; **~dünken** *das;* **~~s** discretion; judgement; **nach [eigenem] ~dünken** at one's own discretion; **nach [eigenem/seinem] ~dünken mit jmdm./etw. verfahren** use one's own discretion in dealing with sb./sth.

Güte /ˈɡyːtə/ *die;* **~** [1] goodness; kindness; (~ Gottes) loving kindness; goodness; **er ist die ~ selbst** he is goodness *or* kindness itself; **sich mit jmdm. in ~ einigen** come to an amicable agreement with sb.; **ein Vorschlag zur ~:** a suggestion for an amicable agreement; **hätten Sie die ~, mir zu helfen?** (geh.) would you be kind *or* good enough to help me?; **[ach] du meine** *od.* **liebe ~!** (ugs.) my goodness!; goodness me [2] (Qualität) quality

Güte·klasse *die* grade; class

Gute·nacht·kuss, *Gute·nacht·kuß *der* goodnight kiss

Güter-: ~abfertigung *die* [1] (Abfertigung von Waren) dispatch of freight *or* (Brit.) goods; [2] (Annahmestelle) freight *or* (Brit.) goods office; **~austausch** *der* exchange of goods *or* commodities; **~bahnhof** *der* freight depot; goods station (Brit.); **~fern·verkehr** /-ˈ--/ *der* long-distance haulage *no art.*; **~gemeinschaft** *die* (Rechtsw.) community of property; **~nah·verkehr** /-ˈ--/ *der* short-distance haulage *no art.*; **~recht** *das* (Rechtsw.) law of property; **~transport** *der* transport *or* carriage of goods (Brit.) *or* freight; **~trennung** *die* (Rechtsw.) separation of property; **~verkehr** *der* freight *or* (Brit.) goods traffic; **~wagen** *der* goods wagon (Brit.); freight car (Amer.); **~zug** *der* goods train (Brit.); freight train (Amer.)

Güte-: ~siegel *das* ▸**~zeichen**; **~verfahren** *das* (Rechtsw.) conciliation procedure; (Verhandlung) conciliation meeting; **~zeichen** *das* quality mark

gut-, Gut-: *~|gehen ▸**gehen A 9, A 11**; **~gehend** ▸**gut B 1**; **~gekleidet** ▸**gut B 1**; **~gelaunt** ▸**gelaunt**; **~gemeint** ▸**gut B 1**; **~gläubig** *Adj.* innocently trusting; **~gläubigkeit** *die* innocent trust; **~|haben** *unr. tr. V.* **etw. bei jmdm. ~haben** be owed sth. by sb.; **~haben** *das* credit balance; **Sie haben ein ~haben von 450 Euro auf Ihrem Konto** your account is 450 euros in credit; **~|heißen** *unr. tr. V.* approve of; **~herzig** *Adj.* kind-hearted; good-hearted; **~herzigkeit** *die;* **~~:** kind-heartedness; good-heartedness

gütig /ˈɡyːtɪç/
A *Adj.* kindly; kind ‹*heart*›; **mit Ihrer ~en Erlaubnis** (geh./iron.) with your kind permission
B *adv.* **~ lächeln/nicken** give a kindly smile/nod

gütlich /ˈɡyːtlɪç/
A *Adj.* amicable
B *adv.* amicably; **sich ~ an etw.** (*Dat.*) **tun** regale oneself with sth.

gut-, Gut-: ~|machen *tr. V.* [1] (in Ordnung bringen) make good ‹*damage*›; put right, correct ‹*omission, mistake, etc.*›; **an jmdm. viel gutzumachen haben** have a lot to make up *or* make amends to sb. for; **wie soll/kann ich das ~machen?** how can I ever repay you?; **das ist nicht wieder gutzumachen** that cannot be put right; **ein nicht wieder gutzumachendes Unrecht** an irreparable injustice; [2] (Überschuss erzielen) make [a profit of] (**bei** on); (aufholen) **gegenüber der führenden Mannschaft fünf Sekunden ~machen** make up five seconds on the leading team; **~mütig** **A** *Adj.* good-natured; **B** *adv.* good-naturedly; **~mütig veranlagt sein** be good-natured; **~mütigkeit** *die;* **~~:** good nature; goodnaturedness; **~nachbarlich** **A** *Adj.* good-neighbourly ‹*relations etc.*›; **B** *adv.* as good neighbours; **~|sagen** *itr. V.* **für jmdn./etw. ~sagen** vouch for sb./sth.

Guts·besitzer *der,* **Guts·besitzerin** *die* owner of a/the estate; landowner

gut-, Gut-: ~schein *der* voucher, coupon (**für, auf** + *Akk.* for); **~|schreiben** *unr. tr. V.* credit; **etw. jmdm./jmds. Konto ~schreiben** credit sb./sb.'s account with sth.; **~schrift** *die* [1] (Betrag) credit; [2] (Bescheinigung) credit slip *or* note; [3] (Vorgang) crediting

Guts-: ~haus *das* manor house; **~herr** *der* lord of the manor; **~herren·art** *die:* **nach ~herrenart** (Kochk.) in a rich traditional style; (fig.) in an autocratic *or* a dictatorial style; **~herrin** *die* lady of the manor; **~hof** *der* estate; manor

Guts·verwalter *der,* **Guts·verwalterin** *die* steward; bailiff

Guttapercha /ɡʊtaˈpɛrça/ *die;* **~** *od. das;* **~[s]** gutta-percha

***gut·tun** ▸**gut A 1**

Guttural[laut] /ɡʊtuˈraːl(-)/ *der;* **~s, ~e** (Sprachw. veralt.) guttural

gut-, Gut-: ~unterrichtet ▸**gut B 1**; **~verdiener** *der,* **~verdienerin,** *die* above-average earner; **~willig** **A** *Adj.* willing; (entgegenkommend) obliging; **sich ~willig zeigen** be obliging; show willing (coll.); **B** *adv.* **etw. ~willig herausgeben/versprechen** hand sth. over voluntarily/promise sth. willingly *or* freely; **~willigkeit** *die;* **~~:** willingness; (Entgegenkommen) obligingness

Guyana /ɡuˈjaːna/ *(das);* **~s** Guyana

gymnasial /ɡʏmnaˈzi̯aːl/ *Adj.* ≈ grammar school ‹*education, syllabus*›

Gymnasial- ≈ grammar school ‹*education, teacher*›

Gymnasiast /ɡʏmnaˈzi̯ast/ *der;* **~en, ~en, Gymnasiastin** *die;* **~, ~nen** ≈ grammar-school pupil

Gymnasium /ɡʏmˈnaːzi̯ʊm/ *das;* **~s, Gymnasien** [1] (höhere Schule) ≈ grammar school; **neusprachliches ~:** ≈ grammar school stressing modern languages; **aufs ~ gehen** ≈ be at *or* attend grammar school [2] (in der Antike) gymnasium

> **Gymnasium**
>
> The secondary school which prepares pupils for the **Abitur**. The *Gymnasium* is attended after the **Grundschule** by the most academically-inclined pupils. They spend nine years at this school, and during the last three years they have some choice as to which subjects they study. See also **Schule**.

Gymnastik /ɡʏmˈnastɪk/ *die;* **~:** physical exercises *pl.*; (Turnen) gymnastics *sing.*

Gymnastik-: ~lehrer *der,* **~lehrerin** *die* teacher of physical exercises; **~saal** *der* gymnasium; gym (coll.)

gymnastisch *Adj.* gymnastic

Gynäkologe /ɡynɛkoˈloːɡə/ *der;* **~n, ~n** ▸ⓘ **S. 113** gynaecologist

Gynäkologie *die;* **~:** gynaecology *no art.*

Gynäkologin *die;* **~, ~nen** ▸ⓘ **S. 113** gynaecologist

gynäkologisch *Adj.* gynaecological

Gyroskop /ɡyroˈskoːp/ *das;* **~s, ~e** gyroscope

g

Hh

h

h, H /ha:/ *das;* ~, ~ 1) (Buchstabe) h/H 2) (Musik) [key of] B; *s. auch* **a, A**

h *Abk.* 1) = **Uhr** hrs 2) = **Stunde** hr[s]

H *Abk.* 1) = **Herren** 2) = **Haltestelle**

H. *Abk.* = **Heft** No.

ha¹ /ha(:)/ *Interj.* 1) (Überraschung) ha!; oh!; ah! 2) (Triumph) aha!

ha² *Abk.* = **Hektar** ha

hä /hɛ/ *Interj.* (salopp) eh

Haag /ha:k/ *(das) od. der;* **~s** ▸ S. 675 The Hague; *s. auch* **Den Haag**

Haar /ha:ɐ̯/ *das;* **~[e]s, ~e** 1) ▸ S. 435 (auch Zool., Bot.) hair; **blonde ~e** *od.* **blondes ~ haben** have fair hair; **echtes ~:** real hair; **sein echtes ~:** his own hair; **[sich** *(Dat.)***] das ~** *od.* **die ~e waschen** wash one's hair; **sich** *(Dat.)* **das ~** *od.* **die ~e schneiden lassen** have *or* get one's hair cut; **ihm geht das ~ aus** he's losing his hair; **sich** *(Dat.)* **die ~e [aus]raufen** (ugs.) tear one's hair [out] 2) (fig.) **ihr stehen die ~e zu Berge** *od.* **sträuben sich die ~e** (ugs.) her hair stands on end; **ein ~ in der Suppe finden** (ugs.) find something to quibble about *or* find fault with; **kein gutes ~ an jmdm./etw. lassen** (ugs.) pull sb./sth. to pieces (fig. coll.); **jmdm. die ~e vom Kopf fressen** (ugs. scherzh.) eat sb. out of house and home; **~e auf den Zähnen haben** (ugs. scherzh.) be a tough customer; **sich** *(Dat.)* **über** *od.* **wegen** *od.* **um etw. keine grauen ~e wachsen lassen** not lose any sleep over sth.; not worry one's head about sth.; **er wird dir kein ~ krümmen** (ugs.) he won't harm a hair of your head; **an einem ~ hängen** (ugs.) be touch-and-go; **das ist an den ~en herbeigezogen** (ugs.) that's far-fetched; **jmdm. aufs ~ gleichen** be the spitting image of sb.; **sie gleichen sich aufs ~:** they're as alike as two peas in a pod; **sich in die ~e geraten** *od.* **kriegen** (ugs.) quarrel, squabble (**wegen** over); **sich** *(Dat.)* **in den ~en liegen** (ugs.) be at loggerheads; **um ein ~** (ugs.) very nearly; **sie wäre um ein ~ abgestürzt** (ugs.) she came within an inch *or* an ace *or* a whisker of falling; **ich hätte sie um ein ~ verfehlt** (ugs.) I just missed her by a hair's breadth; **nicht [um] ein ~** *od.* **[um] kein ~ besser** (ugs.) not a whit *or* bit better

Haar-: **~analyse** *die* hair analysis; **~ansatz** *der* 1) hairline; 2) (unmittelbar an der Kopfhaut) roots *pl.*; **~ausfall** *der* loss of hair; hair loss; **~balg** *der; Pl.* **~bälge** hair follicle; **~band** *das; Pl.* **~bänder** hairband; **~besen** *der* broom; **~breit** *das: in* **nicht [um] ein** *od.* **[um] kein ~breit** not an inch; **~bürste** *die* hairbrush; **~büschel** *das* tuft of hair

haaren *itr. V.* moult; lose *or* shed its hair

Haar-: **~entferner** *der;* **~s, ~:** hair remover; depilatory; **~ersatz** *der* hairpiece

Haares·breite *die: in* **um ~:** by a hair's breadth; **nicht um ~ von etw. abweichen** not budge an inch from sth.

haar-, Haar-: **~farbe** *die* hair colour; **mit seiner ~farbe nicht zufrieden sein** be unhappy with the colour of one's hair; **welche ~farbe hatte der Dieb?** what colour hair did the thief have?; **~färbe·mittel** *das* hair dye; **~fein** *Adj.* fine as a hair *postpos.*; **ein ~feiner Sprung** a hairline crack; **~festiger** *der;* **~~s, ~~:** setting lotion; **~garn** *das* (Textilw.) hair yarn; **~gefäß** *das* ▸ S. 435 (Med.) capillary [vessel]; **~genau** (ugs.) A *Adj.* exact; B *adv.* exactly; **die Beschreibung trifft ~genau auf sie zu** the description fits her to a T (coll.); **etw. ~genau erzählen** relate sth. in great detail; **das stimmt ~genau** that is absolutely right

haarig *Adj.* 1) (behaart) hairy 2) (ugs.: heikel) tricky

haar-, Haar-: **~klammer** *die* hairgrip; **~kleid** *das* (geh.) coat; **~klein** A *Adj.* minute; B *adv.* in minute detail; **~klemme** *die* hairgrip; **~kranz** *der* 1) fringe *or* circle of hair; 2) (Frisur) chaplet [of plaited hair]; **~künstler** *der,* **~künstlerin** *die* (oft scherzh.) hair stylist; tonsorial artist (joc.); **~lack** *der* hair lacquer; **~los** *Adj.* hairless; (glatzköpfig) bald; **~mode** *die* hairstyle; **~nadel** *die* hairpin; **~nadel·kurve** *die* hairpin bend; **~netz** *das* hairnet; **~öl** *das* hair oil; **~pflege** *die* hair care; **~pflege·mittel** *das* hair-care product; **~pinsel** *der* fine animal-hair brush; **~pracht** *die* (scherzh.) magnificent head of hair; **~riss,** ***~riß** *der* hairline crack; **~röhrchen** *das* (Physik) capillary tube; **~scharf** A *Adj.* (sehr genau) razor-sharp ‹*remark*›; very fine ‹*distinction*›; very good ‹*memory*›; B *adv.* 1) (sehr nah) **das Auto blieb ~scharf vor dem Kind stehen** the car stopped only a hair's breadth from the child; **die Kugel flog ~scharf an ihm vorbei** the bullet missed him by a hair's breadth; **~scharf an jmdm. vorbeizielen** aim to just miss sb.; 2) (sehr genau) with great precision; **~schleife** *die* bow; hair ribbon; **~schmuck** *der* hair ornaments *pl.*; **~schneide·maschine** *die* electric clippers *pl.*; **~schnitt** *der* haircut; (modisch) hairstyle; **jmdm. einen ~schnitt machen** cut sb.'s hair; give sb. a haircut; **~schopf** *der* mop *or* shock of hair; **~schwund** *der* loss of hair; hair loss; **~seite** *die* 1) (Textilw.) right side; front; 2) (Gerberei) hair side; (eines Pelzes) fur side; **~sieb** *das* hair sieve; **~spalter** *der;* **~~s, ~~** (abwertend) hair-splitter; **~spalterei** *die;* **~~, ~~en** (abwertend) hair-splitting; **das ist doch ~spalterei** that's splitting hairs; **~spalterin** *die;* **~~, ~~nen** ▸ **~spalter**; **~spalterisch** *Adj.* (abwertend) hair-splitting; **~spange** *die* hairslide; **~spitze** *die* end of a hair; **die ~spitzen** the ends of the hairs; **~spray** *der od. das* hair spray; **~strähne** *die* strand of hair; **~sträubend** *Adj.* 1) (grauenhaft) hair-raising; horrifying; 2) (empörend) outrageous; shocking; **~teil** *das* hairpiece; **~tracht** *die* (veralt.) hairstyle; **~trockner** *der* hairdryer; **~wäsche** *die* shampoo; [hair] wash; **~wasch·mittel** *das* shampoo; **~wasser** *das; Pl.* **~wässer** hair lotion; **~wild** *das* (Jägerspr.) ground game; **~wuchs** *der* hair growth; growth of hair; **einen spärlichen/starken ~wuchs haben** have little/a lot of hair; **~wuchs·mittel** *das* hair restorer; **~wurzel** *die* root [of the/a hair]

Hab /ha:p/ *in* **~ und Gut** (geh.) possessions *pl.*; belongings *pl.*

Habacht·stellung *die* ▸ **Habtachtstellung**

Habe /'ha:bə/ *die;* **~** (geh.) possessions *pl.*; belongings *pl.*; **bewegliche ~:** movables *pl.*

Habeaskorpus·akte /ha:beas'kɔrpʊs-/ *die* (hist.) Habeas Corpus Act

haben

A *unr. tr. V.* 1) have; have got; **er hat nichts** (ugs.) he has nothing; **von ihm kannst du dir kein Geld borgen: er hat selber nichts** you can't borrow money from him: he hasn't got any himself; **wer hat, der hat** (scherzh./iron.) I/you *etc.* can afford it; **was man hat, das hat man** (scherzh./iron.) I'd rather have something than nothing; **da hast du das Geld** there's the money; **die ~s ja** (ugs.) they can afford it; **gute Kenntnisse ~:** be knowledgeable; **ich habe Zeit/keine Zeit** I have [got] [the] time/I have [got] no time *or* I haven't [got] any time; **die Sache hat Zeit** it's not urgent; it can wait (coll.); **wir ~ Mai/1998/den 15./Donnerstag/Sommer** it's May/1998/the 15th/Thursday/summer; **den Wievielten ~ wir heute?** what's the date today?; what's today's date?; **in Kalifornien ~ sie jetzt Nacht/fünf Uhr morgens** it's night-time/five o'clock in the morning now in California; **heute ~ wir schönes Wetter/30°** the weather is fine/it's 30° today; **wann hast du Urlaub?** when is your holiday?; *s. auch* **Datum 1**; **Schuld 2**

2) (empfinden) **Hunger/Durst ~:** be hungry/thirsty; **Sehnsucht nach etw. ~:** long for sth.; **Heimweh/Furcht ~:** be homesick/afraid; **Husten/Fieber/Schmerzen ~:** have [got] a cough/a temperature/have pain; **es an der Leber/auf der Brust ~** (ugs.) have [got] liver trouble *or* something wrong with one's liver/have [got] a bad chest; **was hast du denn?** (ugs.) what's the matter?; what's wrong?; **hast du was?** (ugs.) is [there] something the matter?; is [there] something wrong?; **ich kann das nicht ~** (ugs.) I can't stand it; **dich hats wohl** (ugs.) you must be mad *or* crazy

3) *mit Adj. u. „es"* **es gut/schlecht/schwer/eilig ~:** have it good (coll.)/have a bad time [of it]/have a difficult *or* tough time/be in a hurry; **wir ~ es sehr gemütlich hier** we are very comfortable here; **möchten Sie es etwas wärmer ~?** are you warm enough?

4) *mit „zu" u. Inf.* **nichts zu essen/trinken ~:** have nothing to eat/drink; **habt ihr nichts zu trinken?** haven't you got anything to drink?; **er hat nichts mehr zu erwarten** he can expect nothing more; (müssen) **du hast zu gehorchen** you must obey; **etw. zu tun/erledigen ~:** have [got] sth. to do *or* that one must do; **er hat zu tun** he's busy; (dürfen) **er hat mir nichts zu befehlen** he has [got] no right to order me about; **du hast dich hier nicht einzumischen** you should mind your own business

5) (sich zusammensetzen aus) **das Jahr hat 12 Monate** there are 12 months in a year; **ein Kilometer hat 1 000 Meter** there are 1,000 metres in a kilometre; **diese Stadt hat 10 000 Einwohner** this town has 10,000 inhabitants; **die USA ~ 50 Bundesstaaten** the USA is made up of 50 states

6) (bekommen) have; **kann ich heute dein Auto ~?** can I have your car today?; **sind diese Puppen noch zu ~?** can you still get these dolls?; **zu ~ sein** (ugs.) be unattached; (zum Beischlaf bereit sein) be available; **dafür ist er immer zu ~:** he's always game for that; **er ist immer für ein gutes Essen zu ~:** he always likes *or* enjoys a good meal; **für so etwas bin ich nicht zu ~:** I'm not one for *or* keen on things

like that; **da hast dus** (ugs.) there you are
7) (ugs.: in der Schule) **morgen ~ wir Geschichte** we've got history tomorrow; **wir ~ schon seit Monaten keine Chemie** we haven't done [any] chemistry for months
8) (ugs.: gebrauchen) **man hat das nicht mehr** it is no longer in use/in fashion; **hat man bei euch noch die alten Karbidlampen?** are you still using the old carbide lamps?
9) (ugs.: gefasst ~) have ‹*thief etc.*›; **jetzt hab' ich dich** now I've got you
10) (bekommen ~) **Nachricht von jmdm. ~:** have heard from sb.; **was** (ugs.)/**welche Note hast du diesmal in Physik?** what did you get in *or* for physics this time?
11) (gefunden ~) **~ Sie den Fehler?** have you found the mistake?; **ich habs!** (ugs.) I've got it!; **das werden wir gleich ~** (ugs.) we'll soon find out
12) (ugs.: repariert, beendet ~) **noch zwei Minuten, dann hab ichs** I'll be finished in a couple of minutes; **das werden wir gleich ~:** we'll soon fix that
13) *mit Präp.* **sie hat einen guten Freund an ihm** he is a good friend to her; **er weiß ja gar nicht, was er an dir hat** he doesn't realize how lucky he is to have you; **wir ~ viele Bilder an der Wand [hängen]** we have quite a lot of pictures up; **er hat immer Blumen auf dem Tisch [stehen]** he has always [got] flowers on the table; **ich habe meinen Wagen auf dem Parkplatz [stehen]** I've got my car in the car park; **etwas/nichts gegen jmdn.** *od.* **etw. ~:** have something/nothing against sb. *or* sth.; **sie hat alle Kollegen gegen sich** all her colleagues are against her; **etwas mit jmdm. ~** (ugs.) have a thing *or* something going with sb. (coll.); **hast du es schon einmal mit einer Frau gehabt?** (salopp) have you ever had it off with a woman? (sl.); **viel/wenig von jmdm. ~:** see a lot/little of sb.; **er hat etwas von einem Tyrannen/Faulpelz** he is a bit of a tyrant/lazybones; **etw. von etw. ~:** get sth. out of sth.; **ihn würde ich gerne zum Freund ~:** I would like [to have] him as a friend; **er hat eine Adlige zur Frau** he has [got] an aristocratic wife; *s. auch* **an**, **auf**, **bei** *usw.*
14) *unpers.* (bes. österr., südd.: vorhanden sein) **es hat ...** there is/are ...
B *refl. V.* 1) (ugs. abwertend: sich aufregen) make a fuss; **hab dich nicht so!** don't make *or* stop making such a fuss!
2) (ugs.: sich erledigt ~) **und damit hat es sich** *od.* **hat sich die Sache** then that's that; **hat sich was!** far from it!
C *Hilfsverb* have; **ich habe/hatte ihn eben gesehen** I have *or* I've/I had *or* I'd just seen him; **sie ~ gelacht** they laughed; **er hat das gewusst** he knew it; **wir suchten, bis wir ihn gefunden hatten** we kept looking until we [had] found him; **das hättest du früher machen können** you could have done that earlier

Haben *das;* **~s, ~** (Kaufmannsspr.) credit; (**~seite**) **etw. im ~ verbuchen** credit sth.; *s. auch* **Soll 1**

Habe·nichts *der;* **~, ~e** pauper

Haben-: ~seite *die* (Kaufmannsspr.) credit side; **~zinsen** *Pl.* interest *sing.* on deposits

Haber *der;* **~s** (südd., österr., schweiz.) ▸ **Hafer**

Hab·gier *die* (abwertend) greed

hab·gierig
A *Adj.* (abwertend) greedy
B *adv.* greedily

habhaft *in* **jmds./einer Sache ~ werden** catch *or* apprehend sb./get hold of sth.

Habicht /ˈhaːbɪçt/ *der;* **~s, ~e** 1) hawk 2) (Hühner~) goshawk

Habichts-: ~kraut *das* (Bot.) hawkweed; **~nase** *die* hooked *or* aquiline nose

Habilitand /habiliˈtant/ *der;* **~en, ~en, Habilitandin** *die;* **~, ~nen** person working on his/her habilitation thesis

Habilitation /habilitaˈtsi̯oːn/ *die;* **~, ~en** habilitation (qualification as a university lecturer)

Habilitations·schrift *die: postdoctoral thesis required in order to qualify as a university lecturer*

habilitieren /habiliˈtiːrən/
A *itr., refl. V.* habilitate (*qualify as a university lecturer*); **[sich] in Berlin/bei Prof. Schumacher ~:** habilitate at Berlin/under Professor Schumacher
B *tr. V.* **jmdn. ~:** habilitate sb.; confer on sb. his/her qualification as a university lecturer

Habit[1] /haˈbiːt/ *das od. der;* **~s, ~e** 1) (abwertend, iron.) outfit 2) (Amtskleidung) habit

Habit[2] /ˈhɛbɪt/ *das od. der;* **~s, ~s** (Psych.: Gewohnheit) habit

Habitat /habiˈtaːt/ *das;* **~s, ~e** (Biol.) habitat

habituell /habiˈtu̯ɛl/ *Adj.* habitual

Habitus /ˈha(ː)bitʊs/ *der;* **~** (geh.) 1) (Gesamterscheinungsbild) appearance and manner *or* bearing 2) (Haltung) attitude 3) (Benehmen) behaviour 4) (Med.) habitus

Habsburger /ˈhaːpsbʊrgɐ/ *der;* **~s, ~, Habsburgerin** *die;* **~, ~nen** (hist.) Habsburg

hab-, Hab-: ~seligkeiten *Pl.* [meagre] possessions *or* belongings; **~sucht** *die* (abwertend) greed; avarice; **~süchtig** (abwertend) **A** *Adj.* greedy; avaricious; **B** *adv.* greedily; avariciously

Habt·acht·stellung *die* attention; **in ~ stehen** stand to attention

hach /hax/ *Interj.* oh!

Haché /[h]aˈʃeː/ ▸ **Haschee**

Hachse /ˈhaksə/ *die;* **~, ~n** (südd.) 1) knuckle; **~ vom Kalb** knuckle of veal 2) (ugs. scherzh.) leg

Hack /hak/ *das;* **~s** (ugs., bes. nordd.) mince; minced meat

Hack-: ~beil *das* chopper; cleaver; **~braten** *der* (Kochk.) meat loaf; **~brett** *das* (Musik) dulcimer

Hacke[1] *die;* **~, ~n** hoe; (Pickel) pick[axe]

Hacke[2] *die;* **~, ~n** ▸ **S. 435** (bes. nordd. u. md.) heel; **sich** (*Dat.*) **die ~n nach etw. ablaufen** *od.* **abrennen** wear oneself out running around looking for sth.; *s. auch* **Ferse**

hacken
A *itr. V.* 1) (mit der Hacke arbeiten) hoe; **sich** (*Dat. od. Akk.*) **ins Bein ~:** cut one's leg [with a hoe/an axe *etc.*] 2) (picken) peck; **nach jmdm./etw. ~:** peck at sb./sth.; **der Papagei hat mir in den Finger gehackt** the parrot pecked my finger
B *tr. V.* 1) (mit der Hacke bearbeiten) hoe ‹*garden, flower bed, etc.*› 2) (mit der Axt zerkleinern) chop ‹*wood etc.*›; **etw. in Stücke ~:** chop sth. up 3) (ein Loch machen) chop, hack ‹*hole*› 4) (zerkleinern) chop [up] ‹*meat, vegetables, etc.*›

Hacker *der;* **~s, ~, Hackerin** *die;* **~, ~nen** (DV-Jargon) hacker

Hack-: ~fleisch *das* minced meat; mince; **aus jmdm. ~fleisch machen** (fig. ugs.) make mincemeat of sb.; **~frucht** *die* (Landw.) root crop; **~klotz** *der* chopping block; **~messer** *das* chopper; cleaver; **~ordnung** *die* (Verhaltensf.) pecking order

Häcksel /ˈhɛksl̩/ *der od. das;* **~s** (Landw.) chaff

Häcks[e]ler *der;* **~s, ~, Häcksel·maschine** *die* (Landw.) chaff-cutter

häckseln *tr. V.* chop [up] ‹*straw, hay, etc.*›

Hader /ˈhaːdɐ/ *der;* **~s** (geh.) discord

hadern *itr. V.* (geh.) 1) (streiten) quarrel 2) (unzufrieden sein) **mit etw. ~:** be at odds with sth.; **er haderte mit seinem Schicksal** he railed against his fate

Hadern·papier *das* (fachspr.) rag paper

Hades /ˈhaːdɛs/ *der;* **~** (griech. Myth.) Hades *no art.*

Hadschi /ˈhaːdʒi/ *der;* **~s, ~s** hadji

Hafen[1] /ˈhaːfn̩/ *der;* **~s, Häfen** harbour; port; (**~anlagen**) docks *pl.*; **der Hamburger ~:** the port of Hamburg; **ein Schiff läuft den ~ an/aus dem ~ aus/in den ~ ein** a ship is putting into/leaving/entering port *or* harbour; **in den ~ der Ehe einlaufen** (fig. scherzh.) taste the joys of married *or* wedded bliss

Hafen[2] *der;* **~s, ~** (südd., schweiz., österr.) pot; (Schüssel) bowl

Hafen-: ~amt *das* port *or* harbour authority; **~anlagen** *Pl.* docks; **~arbeiter** *der,* **~arbeiterin** *die* ▸ **S. 113** dock worker; docker; **~aus·fahrt** *die* harbour mouth; **~bahn** *die* harbour railway; **~becken** *das* harbour basin; dock; **~behörde** *die* port *or* harbour authority; **~blockade** *die* blockade of a/the harbour *or* port; **~ein·fahrt** *die* harbour entrance *or* mouth; **~gebühren** *Pl.,* **~geld** *das* harbour charges *pl.*; port dues *pl.*; **~kneipe** *die* dockland pub (Brit.) *or* (Amer.) bar; **~meister** *der,* **~meisterin** *die* harbour master; **~polizei** *die* port *or* dock police; **~rund·fahrt** *die* trip round the harbour; **~stadt** *die* port; **~viertel** *das* dock area; dockland *no art.*

Hafer /ˈhaːfɐ/ *der;* **~s** oats *pl.*; **jmdn. sticht der ~** (ugs.) sb. is feeling his oats

Hafer-: ~brei *der* porridge; **~flocken** *Pl.* rolled oats; porridge oats; **~grütze** *die* 1) oat groats; 2) (Brei) porridge; **~mehl** *das* oatmeal; **~sack** *der* nosebag; **~schleim** *der* gruel

Haff /haf/ *das;* **~[e]s, ~s** *od.* **~e** lagoon

Haflinger /ˈhaːflɪŋɐ/ *der;* **~s, ~:** Haflinger [horse]

Hafner *der;* **~s, ~, Hafnerin** *die;* **~, ~nen** (südd., österr., schweiz.) 1) (Töpfer) potter 2) (Ofensetzer) stove-fitter

-haft *Adj., adv.* -like

Haft /haft/ *die;* **~** 1) (Gewahrsam) custody; (aus politischen Gründen) detention; **jmdn. aus der ~ entlassen** release sb. from custody/detention; **sich in ~ befinden** be [held] in custody/detention; **jmdn. in ~ nehmen** take sb. into custody; (aus politischen Gründen) detain sb. 2) (Freiheitsstrafe) imprisonment; **jmdn. zu zwei Jahren ~ verurteilen** sentence sb. to two years in prison *or* two years' imprisonment

Haft-: ~anstalt *die* prison; **~aussetzung** *die* (Rechtsspr.) **der Verteidiger beantragte ~aussetzung** the defence counsel requested that the defendant be released from custody

haftbar *Adj.* (bes. Rechtsspr.) *in* **für etw. ~ sein** be [legally] responsible *or* liable for sth.; **jmdn. für etw. ~ machen** make *or* hold sb. [legally] liable for sth.

Haft-: ~befehl *der* (Rechtsw.) warrant [of arrest]; **einen ~befehl gegen jmdn. ausstellen** issue a warrant for sb.'s arrest; **~beschwerde** *die* (Rechtsw.) appeal against a remand in custody; **~creme** *die* (Pharm.) fixative cream; **~dauer** *die* term of imprisonment

haften[1] *itr. V.* 1) (festkleben) stick (**an/auf** + *Dat.* to); **~ bleiben** stick (**an/auf** + *Dat.* to) 2) (sich festsetzen) ‹*smell, dirt, etc.*› cling (**an** + *Dat.* to); **~ bleiben** ‹*mud, clay, dirt, etc.*› stick, cling (**an/auf** + *Dat.* to); ‹*smell, smoke*› cling (**an/auf** + *Dat.* to); (fig.: im Gedächtnis bleiben) stick; **[einem] in der Erinnerung ~** (fig.) stick in one's memory *or* mind; **~de Eindrücke** lasting impressions; **an ihm haftet ein Makel** (fig.) he carries a stigma; **seine Augen hafteten/sein Blick haftete an ...** (*Dat.*) (fig.) his eyes were/gaze was fixed on ... 3) ‹*tyre*› grip

haften[2] *itr. V.* 1) (einstehen) **für jmdn./etw. ~:** be responsible for sb./liable for sth.; (verantwortlich sein) **jmdm. für etw. ~:** be responsible *or* answerable to sb. for sth.; **für etw. nicht ~** ‹*company*› not accept liability for sth.; *s. auch* **Garderobe 1** 2) (Rechtsw., Wirtsch.) be liable

***haften|bleiben** ▸ **haften**[1] **1, 2**

haft-, Haft-: ~erleichterung *die* special privilege; **~fähig**[1] *Adj.* (Rechtsw.) fit to be kept in prison *postpos.*; **~fähig**[2] *Adj.* (klebend) adhesive; **~fähigkeit**[1] *die* (Rechtsw.) fitness to be kept in prison; **~fähigkeit**[2] *die* (von Materialien) adhesion

Häftling /ˈhɛftlɪŋ/ *der;* **~s, ~e** prisoner

Häftlings·kleidung *die* prison clothing

Haft·pflicht *die* 1) liability (**für** for) 2) ▸ **Haftpflichtversicherung**

haftpflichtig *Adj.* liable (**für** for)

Haftpflicht·versicherung *die* personal liability insurance; (für Autofahrer) third party insurance

h

haft-, Haft-: ~prüfung *die* (Rechtsw.) review of a/the remand in custody; **~psychose** *die* prison psychosis; **~reibung** *die* (Physik) static friction; **~richter** *der*, **~richterin** *die* (Rechtsw.) magistrate; **~schale** *die* contact lens; **~strafe** *die* (Rechtsspr. veralt.) prison sentence; **~unfähig** *Adj.* unfit to be kept in prison *postpos.*; **~unfähigkeit** *die* unfitness to be kept in prison

Haftung¹ *die;* **~:** adhesion; (von Reifen) grip

Haftung² *die;* **~, ~en** 1) (Verantwortlichkeit) liability; responsibility; *s. auch* **Garderobe** 2) (Rechtsw., Wirtsch.) liability; **Gesellschaft mit [un]beschränkter ~:** [un]limited [liability] company

Haft·verschonung *die* (Rechtsw.) suspended sentence

Hag /ha:k/ *der;* **~[e]s, ~e** (veralt., noch schweiz.) 1) (Hecke) hedge 2) (Wald) grove

Hagebutte /'ha:gəbʊtə/ *die;* **~, ~n** 1) (Frucht) rose hip 2) (ugs.: Heckenrose) dog rose

Hagebutten·tee *der* rose hip tea

Hage·dorn *der; Pl.* **~e** hawthorn

Hagel /'ha:gl̩/ *der;* **~s, ~** (auch fig.) hail; **ein ~ von Drohungen** a stream of threats

Hagel·korn *das* hailstone

hageln

A *itr., tr. V.* (unpers.) hail; **es hagelt** it is hailing; **es hagelte Steine und leere Bierdosen** (fig.) there was a hail of stones and empty beer cans; **es hagelte Drohungen/Fragen** (fig.) there was a stream of threats/flood of questions

B *itr. V.; mit sein* (fig.) **auf jmdn./etw. ~** ‹*stones, bombs, etc.*› rain down on sb./sth.

Hagel-: ~schaden *der* damage *no pl.* caused by hail; **~schauer** *der* [short] hailstorm; **~schlag** *der* hail; **~sturm** *der* hailstorm; **~zucker** *der* sugar crystals *pl.*

hager /'ha:gɐ/ *Adj.* gaunt ‹*person, figure, face*›; thin ‹*neck, arm, fingers*›

Hagerkeit *die;* **~** ▸**hager**: gauntness; thinness

Hage·stolz *der;* **~es, ~e** (veralt.) confirmed bachelor

haha /ha'ha(:)/ *Interj.* ha ha

Häher /'hɛ:ɐ/ *der;* **~s, ~:** jay

Hahn¹ /ha:n/ *der;* **~[e]s, Hähne** /'hɛ:nə/ 1) cock; (junger ~) cockerel; **~ im Korb sein** (ugs.) be cock of the walk; **nach ihr/danach kräht kein ~** (ugs.) no one could care less about her/it; **jmdm. den roten ~ aufs Dach setzen** (veralt.) set sb.'s house on fire 2) (Wetter~) weathercock

Hahn² *der;* **~[e]s, Hähne,** *fachspr.:* **~en** 1) tap; faucet (Amer.); (eines Fasses) tap; spigot; *s. auch* **abdrehen A 1** 2) (bei Waffen) hammer; **den ~ spannen** cock a/the gun

Hähnchen /'hɛ:nçən/ *das;* **~s, ~:** chicken; (junger Hahn) cockerel

Hahnen-: ~fuß *der* buttercup; **~fuß·gewächs** *das* ranunculus; **~kamm** *der* cockscomb; **~kampf** *der* 1) cockfighting; (einzelner Wettkampf) cockfight; 2) (Gymnastik) *hopping-game in which players barge each other and attempt to push each other off balance;* **~schrei** *der* cockcrow; **beim ersten ~schrei** at cockcrow; **~tritt·muster** *das* dog-tooth *or* dog's tooth check

Hahnrei /'ha:nrai/ *der;* **~s, ~e** (geh., veralt.) cuckold

Hai /hai/ *der;* **~s, ~e** (auch fig.) shark

Hai·fisch *der* shark

Haifisch·flossen·suppe *die* (Kochk.) sharkfin soup

Hain /hain/ *der;* **~[e]s, ~e** (dichter. veralt.) grove

Hain·buche *die* hornbeam

Haiti /ha'i:ti/ *(das);* **~s** Haiti

Haitianer /hai'tia:nɐ/ *der;* **~s, ~, Haitianerin** *die;* **~, ~nen** Haitian

haitianisch *Adj.* Haitian

Häkchen /'hɛ:kçən/ *das;* **~s, ~** 1) [small] hook; **was ein ~ werden will, krümmt sich beizeiten** (Spr.) there's nothing like starting young 2) (Zeichen) mark; (beim Abhaken) tick

Häkel-: ~arbeit *die* crocheting; crochet work; (etw. Gehäkeltes) a piece of crochet work *or* crocheting; **~decke** *die* crocheted tablecloth; (für ein Sofa, einen Stuhl usw.) crocheted cover

Häkelei *die;* **~, ~en** ▸**Häkelarbeit**

Häkel-: ~garn *das* crochet thread *or* yarn; **~muster** *das* crochet pattern

hakeln /'ha:kl̩n/

A *itr. V.* 1) (landsch.) finger-wrestle 2) (Fußball) trip the/an opposing player

B *tr. V.* 1) (Fußball) trip 2) (Ringen) **jmds. Bein/Fuß ~:** get sb. in a leg lock/foot lock

häkeln /'hɛ:kl̩n/ *tr., itr. V.* crochet

Häkel·nadel *die* crochet hook

haken /'ha:kn̩/

A *tr. V.* 1) hook (**an** + *Akk.* on to) 2) ([Eis]hockey) hook 3) (Fußball) ▸**hakeln B**

B *itr. V.* (klemmen) be stuck

Haken *der;* **~s, ~** 1) hook; **~ und Öse** hook and eye; **einen ~ schlagen** dart sideways; **mit ~ und Ösen** (fig. ugs.) by fair means or foul 2) (Zeichen) tick 3) (ugs.: Schwierigkeit) catch; snag; **wo ist der ~?** where's the catch?; **der ~ an etw.** *(Dat.)* the catch in sth. 4) (Boxen) hook

haken-, Haken-: ~förmig A *Adj.* hooked; hook-shaped; B *adv.* **~förmig gebogen** hooked; hook-shaped; **~kreuz** *das* swastika; **~leiter** *die* hook ladder; **~nase** *die* hooked nose; hook nose

Halali /hala'li:/ *das;* **~s, ~[s]** (Jägerspr.) 1) (Signal) mort 2) (Ende der Jagd) mort; kill

halb /halp/

A *Adj. u. Bruchz.* 1) ▸❶ **S. 729,** ▸❶ **S. 826** (die Hälfte von) half; **eine ~e Stunde/ein ~er Meter/ein ~es Glas** half an hour/a metre/a glass; **zum ~en Preis** [at] half price; **~ Europa/die ~e Welt** half of Europe/half the world; **es ist ~ eins** it's half past twelve; **5 Minuten vor/nach ~:** 25 [minutes] past/to; *s. auch* **Arm 3; Höhe 2; Note 1; Weg 4** 2) (unvollständig, vermindert) **die ~e Wahrheit** half [of] *or* part of the truth; **er macht keine ~en Sachen** he doesn't do things by halves; **er hat [nur] ~e Arbeit getan** he hasn't done the job properly; **nichts Halbes und nichts Ganzes [sein]** [be] neither one thing nor the other 3) (fast) **[noch] ein ~es Kind sein** be hardly *or* scarcely more than a child; **eine ~e Ewigkeit warten** wait [for] ages; **die ~e Stadt** half the town

B *adv.* 1) (zur Hälfte) **~ voll/leer** half-full/-empty; **~ lachend, ~ weinend** half laughing, half crying; **~ link.../recht...** (bes. Fußball) inside left/right; **~ links/rechts** (Fußball) [at] inside left/right; **~ links/rechts abbiegen** fork left/right 2) (unvollständig) **~ gar/angezogen** *od.* **bekleidet/wach/fertig** half-done *or* -cooked/half dressed/half awake/half-finished; **~ offen** half-open ‹*door etc.*›; open ‹*prison*›; **~ verdaut** (auch fig.) half-digested; **~ reif** half-ripe; **die Pflaumen sind erst ~ reif** the plums aren't fully ripe; **er hat seine Arbeit ~ getan** he has done some of his work; **die Verletzung war nur ~ so schlimm, wie er erst dachte** the injury was not as serious as he at first thought; **etw. nur ~ verstehen** only half understand sth.; **nur ~ zuhören** be only half listening; **nur ~ bei der Sache sein** be only half with it (coll.); *s. auch* **schlimm A 2** 3) (fast) **~ blind/verhungert/tot/erfroren/nackt** half blind/starved/dead/frozen/naked; **~ roh** half-cooked; half-done; **~ verwest** partially decomposed; **~ wild** half-wild ‹*animal, country*›; half-savage ‹*person*›; **ich bin schon ~ fertig** I'm nearly *or* almost finished; **~ so klug** half as clever; **~ und ~** (ugs.) more or less; **Gefällt es dir? — Halb und ~** (ugs.) Do you like it? — Sort of (coll.)

halb-, Halb-: ~affe *der* (Zool.) half-ape; prosimian; **~amtlich** *Adj.* semi-official; **~automatisch** A *Adj.* semi-automatic; B *adv.* semi-automatically; **~bekleidet** ▸**halb B 2; ~bildung** *die* (abwertend) superficial education; **~bitter** *Adj.* plain ‹*chocolate*›; **~blind** ▸**halb B 3; ~blut** *das* 1) (bei Pferden) cross-breed; 2) (Mischling) half-caste; half-breed; **~brille** *die* (pair of) half-moon glasses; **~bruder** *der* half-brother; **~dunkel** *Adj.* half-dark; **~dunkel** *das* semi-darkness

Halbe¹ *der od. die od. das; adj. Dekl.* (ugs.) half litre (*of beer etc.*); **ein ~s** a half litre

Halbe² *die; adj. Dekl.* (Musik) minim (Brit.); half note (Amer.)

Halb·edelstein *der* (veralt.) semi-precious stone

halbe-halbe *in* **[mit jmdm.] ~ machen** (ugs.) go halves [with sb.]

halber /'halbɐ/ *Präp. mit Gen.* (wegen) on account of; (um ... willen) for the sake of; **der Ordnung ~:** as a matter of form; **der Wahrheit ~:** to tell the truth

halb-, Halb-: ~erfroren ▸**halb B 3; ~fabrikat** *das* (Wirtsch.) semi-finished product; **~fertig** ▸**halb B 2; ~fett** A *Adj.* 1) (Druckw.) bold ‹*type*›; (schmaler, kleiner) semibold; 2) medium-fat ‹*cheese*›; B *adv.* **etw. ~fett drucken** print sth. in bold/semibold [type]; **~finale** *das* (Sport) semi-final; **~gar** ▸**halb B 2; ~gebildet** A *Adj.* (abwertend) half-educated; B *adv.* in a half-educated way; **~gebildete** *der/die; adj. Dekl.* (abwertend) half-educated person; **~gefror[e]ne** *das; adj. Dekl.* soft ice cream; ***~geschoß**, **~geschoss** *das* (Archit.) mezzanine [floor]; **~geschwister** *Pl.* half-brothers/half-sisters/half-brother[s] and -sister[s]; **~gott** *der* (Myth., fig. iron.) demigod; **~götter in Weiß** (ugs. iron.) [hospital] doctors

Halbheit *die;* **~, ~en** (abwertend) half measure

halb-, Halb-: ~herzig A *Adj.* half-hearted; B *adv.* half-heartedly; **~herzigkeit** *die;* **~~:** half-heartedness; **~hoch** A *Adj.* (bes. Sport) shoulder-high ‹*shot, pass, etc.*›; low ‹*shelf etc.*›; calf-length ‹*boot*›; B *adv.* **der Ball kam ~hoch** the ball came at shoulder height

halbieren *tr. V.* cut/tear ‹*object*› in half; halve ‹*amount, number*›; (Math.) bisect

halb-, Halb-: ~insel *die* peninsula; **~jahr** *das* six months *pl.*; half year; **im ersten/zweiten ~jahr** in the first/last six months [of the year]; **~jahres·bilanz** *die* half-yearly figures *pl. or* results *pl.*; **~jahres·zeugnis** *das* half-yearly report; **~jährig** *Adj.* 1) (ein ~es Jahr alt) six-month-old ‹*baby, pony, etc.*›; 2) (ein ~es Jahr dauernd) six-month ‹*contract, course, etc.*›; **~jährlich** A *Adj.* half-yearly; six-monthly; B *adv.* every six months; twice a year; **~jude** *der*, **~jüdin** *die* (bes. ns.) half-Jew; **~jude sein** be half Jewish; **~kanton** *der* demi-canton; **~kreis** *der* semicircle; **sich im ~kreis aufstellen** form a semicircle; **im ~kreis sitzen** sit in a semicircle; **~kreis·förmig** A *Adj.* semicircular; B *adv.* in a semicircle; **~kugel** *die* hemisphere; **~kugel·förmig** *Adj.* hemispherical; **~lang** *Adj.* mid-length ‹*hair*›; mid-calf length ‹*coat, dress, etc.*›; **[nun] mach [aber mal] ~lang!** (ugs.) hang on a minute! (coll.); **~laut** A *Adj.* low; quiet; B *adv.* in a low voice; in an undertone; **~leder** *das* (Buchw.) half-leather; ***~leer** ▸**halb B 1; ~leinen** *das* 1) (Gewebe) fifty-per-cent linen material; 2) (Buchw.) half-cloth; **~leiter** *der* (Elektronik) semiconductor; **~link...** ▸**halb B 1; ~linke** /'-'--/ *der* (bes. Fußball) inside left; **~links** ▸**halb B 1; ~mast** *Adv.* at half mast; **~mast flaggen** fly a flag/the flags at half mast; **~matt** *Adj.* (Fot.) semi-matt; **~messer** *der;* **~~s, ~~** (Math.) radius; **~metall** *das* (Chemie) semi-metal; **~militärisch** *Adj.* paramilitary; **~monatlich** A *Adj.* fortnightly; twice-monthly; B *adv.* fortnightly; twice monthly; **~monats·schrift** *die* fortnightly periodical; **~mond** *der* 1) (Mond) half-moon; **heute ist ~mond** there's a half-moon tonight; 2) (Figur) crescent; 3) (an Fingernägeln) half-moon; **~mond·förmig** *Adj.* crescent-shaped; ***~nackt** ▸**halb B 3;** ***~offen** ▸**halb B 2; ~offiziell** *Adj.* semi-official; **~part** *Adv.: in* **[mit jmdm.] ~part machen** (ugs.) go halves [with sb.]; **~pension** *die* half board; ***~recht...** ▸**halb B 1; ~rechte** /'-'--/ *der* (bes. Fußball) inside right; **~rechts**

▸**halb B 1**; ~**reif** ▸**halb B 2**; ~**rock** *der* waist petticoat; ~**roh** ▸**halb B 3**; ~**rund** *Adj.* semicircular; ~**rund** *das* semicircle; ~**satz** *der* [1] half-sentence; **der zweite ~satz** the second half of the sentence; **kein ~satz, nicht ein ~satz** not a single word; [2] (Rechtsw.) clause; ~**schatten** *der* [1] half shadow; [2] (Optik, Astron.) penumbra; ~**schlaf** *der* light sleep; **im ~schlaf liegen** be half asleep; doze; ~**schuh** *der* shoe; ~**schwergewicht** *das* (Schwerathletik) [1] light-heavyweight; *s. auch* **Fliegengewicht 1**; [2] ▸~**schwergewichtler**; ~**schwergewichtler** *der* (Schwerathletik) light-heavyweight; ~**schwester** *die* half-sister; ~**seide** *die* fifty-per-cent silk [mixture]; ~**seiden** *Adj.* [1] fifty-per-cent silk; [2] (ugs. abwertend: unmännlich) poofy (coll.); pansyish (coll.); [3] (ugs. abwertend: anrüchig) dubious ‹*business practice etc.*›; fast ‹*woman*›; ~**seitig** **A** *Adv.* [1] (Med.) **~seitig gelähmt sein** be hemiplegic; be paralysed down one side; [2] **ein Blatt ~seitig beschreiben** write on the left-hand/right-hand side of a sheet only; **B** *adj.* half-page ‹*article etc.*›; ~**staatlich** *Adj.* (DDR) partially state-controlled *or* state-run; ~**stark** *Adj.* (ugs. abwertend) rowdy; ~**starke** *der; adj. Dekl.* (ugs. abwertend) young rowdy; [young] hooligan; ~**stiefel** *der* half-boot; ankle boot; ~**stündig** *Adj.* half-hour; lasting half an hour *postpos., not pred.*; **eine ~stündige Fahrt** a half-hour journey; half an hour's journey; ~**stündlich** **A** *Adj.* half-hourly; **B** *adv.* half-hourly; every half an hour; ~**stürmer** *der,* ~**stürmerin** *die* (bes. Fußball) midfield player; ~**tägig** **A** *Adj.* half-day ‹*excursion etc.*›; part-time ‹*work, worker, etc.*›; (morgens/nachmittags) morning/afternoon ‹*work etc.*›; **B** *adv.* ‹*work*› part-time; (morgens/nachmittags) ‹*work*› [in the] mornings/afternoons; ~**täglich** **A** *Adj.* twice daily; **B** *adv.* twice a day; twice daily

halb·tags *Adv.* ▸❶ **S. 113** ‹*work*› part-time; (morgens/nachmittags) ‹*work*› [in the] mornings/afternoons

Halbtags-: ~**arbeit** *die,* ~**beschäftigung** *die* part-time job; (morgens/nachmittags) morning/afternoon job; ~**kraft** *die* part-time worker; part-timer; ~**schule** *die* half-day school

halb-, Halb-: ~**ton** *der; Pl.* ~**töne** [1] (Musik) semitone; half step (Amer.); [2] (Malerei) half-tone; *~**tot** ▸**halb B 3**; ~**totale** *die* (Film) medium shot; ~**trauer** *die* half mourning; **~trauer tragen** be in half mourning; ~**verdaut** ▸**halb B 2**; ~**verhungert** ▸**halb B 3**; ~**verwest** ▸**halb B 3**; ~**vokal** *der* (Phon.) semivowel; *~**voll** ▸**halb B 1**; *~**wach** ▸**halb B 2**; ~**wahrheit** *die* half-truth; ~**waise** *die* fatherless/motherless child; **er/sie ist ~waise** he/she has lost one of his/her parents; ~**wegs** /-ve:ks/ *Adv.* [1] to some extent; reasonably ‹*good, clear, comprehensible, etc.*›; **es geht mir ~wegs besser** I'm feeling a bit better; **kannst du dich nicht wenigstens ~wegs ordentlich benehmen?** can't you behave at all properly?; **ich kann ~wegs von meinem Einkommen leben** I can live fairly well on my income; [2] (veralt.: auf halbem Weg) halfway; ~**welt** *die* demi-monde; ~**welt·dame** *die* demi-mondaine; ~**weltergewicht** *das* [1] (Klasse) light welterweight; [2] (Sportler) light welterweight; ~**werts·zeit** *die* (Physik) half-life; ~**wild** ▸**halb B 3**; ~**wilde** *der/die: in* **wie die ~wilden** (ugs.) like [a bunch of] savages; ~**wissen** *das* (abwertend) superficial knowledge; smattering of knowledge; **sein medizinisches ~wissen** his smattering of medical knowledge; ~**wüchsig** /-vy:ksɪç/ *Adj.* adolescent; teenage; ~**wüchsige** *der/die; adj. Dekl.* adolescent; teenager; ~**zeit** *die* (bes. Fußball) [1] half; **die erste/zweite ~zeit** the first/second half; **während der ersten ~zeit seiner Amtsperiode** (fig.) during the first half of his period of office; [2] (Pause) half-time; **zur ~zeit seiner Regierungszeit** (fig.) halfway through his period of office; ~**zeit·pause** *die* (Sport) half-time; ~**zeit·pfiff** *der* (Sport) half-time whistle; ~**zeug** *das* (Wirtsch.) semi-finished product

Halde /'haldə/ *die;* ~, ~**n** [1] (Bergbau) slag heap; (von Vorräten) pile; (fig.) mountain; pile; **neue Wagen liegen massenhaft auf ~:** there are piles of unsold new cars; **Kartoffeln werden jetzt für die ~ produziert** the potatoes now being produced will simply go to swell existing stocks [2] (geh.: Hang) slope

half /half/ *1. u. 3. Pers. Sg. Prät. v.* **helfen**

Hälfte /'hɛlftə/ *die;* ~, ~**n** [1] half; **die ~ einer Sache** (*Gen.*) *od.* **von etw.** half [of] sth.; **Studenten bezahlen die ~ des Preises** students pay *or* (coll.) are half-price; **etw. in zwei gleiche ~n teilen** divide sth. in half *or* into two equal parts; **er füllte sein Glas nur bis zur ~:** he only half-filled his glass; **über die ~:** more than *or* over half; **um die ~ größer/kleiner** half as big/small again; **um die ~ zu viel/mehr** too much by half/half as much again; **etw. um die ~ steigern** increase sth. by half; **etw. zur ~ zahlen** pay half of sth.; **die gegnerische ~** (Sport) the opponents' half; **ich habe die ~ vergessen** I've forgotten half of it; **meine bessere ~** (ugs. scherzh.) my better half (coll. joc.) [2] (ugs.: Teil) part; **die größere ~ ihres Gehalts/des Publikums** the greater part of her salary/the majority of the audience

Halfter[1] /'halftɐ/ *der od. das;* ~**s,** ~, *veralt. auch die;* ~, ~**n** halter

Halfter[2] *die;* ~, ~**n,** *auch das;* ~**s,** ~**:** holster

halftern *tr. V.* halter

Halfter·riemen *der* halter strap

Hall /hal/ *der;* ~**[e]s,** ~**e** [1] (geh.) reverberation [2] (Echo) echo

Halle /'halə/ *die;* ~, ~**n** (Saal, Gebäude) hall; (Fabrik~) shed; (Hotel~, Theater~) lobby; foyer; (Sport~) [sports] hall; (Schwimm~) pool; **Tennis in der ~ spielen** play tennis indoors *or* on an indoor court; **in diesen heiligen ~n** (iron.) within these sacred halls (iron.)

halleluja /hale'lu:ja/ *Interj.* hallelujah!; (scherzh.: hurra) hurrah!

Halleluja *das;* ~**s,** ~**s** hallelujah; **das ~ aus Händels „Messias"** the Hallelujah Chorus from Handel's 'Messiah'

hallen *itr. V.* [1] reverberate; ring; ‹*shot, bell, cry*› ring out [2] (wider~) echo; **von etw. ~:** reverberate *or* echo with sth.

Hallen- indoor ‹*swimming pool, handball, football, hockey, tennis, championship, record, sport, etc.*›

Hallig /'halɪç/ *die;* ~, ~**en** small low island (*particularly one of those off Schleswig-Holstein*)

hallihallo /ha'lihalo/ *Interj.* (fam.) hello; hullo

Hallimasch /'halimaʃ/ *der;* ~**[e]s,** ~**e** (Bot.) honey agaric; honey mushroom

hallo *Interj.* [1] *meist* /'halo/ (am Telefon) hello; ~, **warte doch mal auf mich!** hey! wait for me!; ~, **gehört Ihnen diese Tasche?** excuse me! is this your bag? [2] *meist* /ha'lo:/ (überrascht) hello [3] *meist* /'halo/ (ugs., bes. Jugendspr. als Gruß) hi (coll.); hello

Hallo /ha'lo:/ *das;* ~**s,** ~**s** [1] cheering; cheers *pl.*; **mit großem ~:** with loud cheering *or* cheers [2] (Aufsehen) hullabaloo

hallöchen /ha'lø:çən/ *Interj.* (fam.) hello there

Hallodri /ha'lo:dri/ *der;* ~**s,** ~**[s]** (bayr., österr. ugs. abwertend) rogue

Hallstatt·zeit /'halʃtat-/ *die;* ~ (Archäol.) Hallstatt period

Halluzination /halutsina'tsio:n/ *die;* ~, ~**en** hallucination; **du hast wohl ~en** you must be seeing things

halluzinatorisch /halutsina'to:rɪʃ/ *Adj.* (Med., Psych.) hallucinatory

halluzinieren *itr. V.* (Med., Psych.) hallucinate; have hallucinations

halluzinogen /halutsino'ge:n/ *Adj.* (Med., Psych.) hallucinogenic

Halluzinogen *das;* ~**s,** ~**e** (Med., Psych.) hallucinogen

Halm /halm/ *der;* ~**[e]s,** ~**e** stalk; stem; **das Getreide/die Ernte auf dem ~:** the standing corn

Halma /'halma/ *das;* ~**s** halma

Hälmchen /'hɛlmçən/ *das;* ~**s,** ~**:** [small] stalk *or* stem

Halm·frucht *die* cereal

Halo /'ha:lo/ *der;* ~**[s],** ~**s** *od.* ~**nen** /-'--/ (Physik) halo

Halogen /halo'ge:n/ *das;* ~**s,** ~**e** (Chemie) halogen

Halogen- halogen ‹*lamp, headlamp*›

Hals /hals/ *der;* ~**es, Hälse** /'hɛlzə/ [1] ▸❶ **S. 435** neck; **sich** (*Dat.*) **den ~ brechen** break one's neck; **jmdm. um den ~ fallen** throw *or* fling one's arms around sb.['s neck]; **~ über Kopf** (ugs.) in a rush *or* hurry: **sich ~ über Kopf verlieben** fall head over heels in love; **sich** (*Dat.*) **nach jmdm./etw. den ~ verrenken** crane one's neck to see sb./sth.; **einen langen ~/lange Hälse machen** (ugs.) crane one's neck/their necks; **jmdm. den ~ abschneiden** *od.* **umdrehen** *od.* **brechen** (ugs.) drive sb. to the wall; **das kostete ihn** *od.* **ihm den ~** (ugs.) that did for him (coll.); **jmdn./etw. auf dem** *od.* **am ~ haben** (ugs.) be saddled with sb./sth. (coll.); **zu viel am ~ haben** (ugs.) have too much on one's plate (coll.); **sich jmdm. an den ~ werfen** (ugs.) throw oneself at sb.; **jmdm. jmdn. auf den ~ schicken** *od.* **hetzen** (ugs.) get *or* put sb. on [to] sb.; **sich** (*Dat.*) **jmdn./etw. auf den ~ laden** (ugs.) lumber *or* saddle oneself with sb./sth. (coll.); **bis über den ~ in etw.** (*Dat.*) **stecken** (ugs.) be up to one's ears *or* eyes in sth.; **jmdm. steht** *od.* **geht das Wasser bis zum** *od.* **an den ~** (ugs.: jmd. hat Schulden) sb. is up to his/her eyes in debt; (ugs.: jmd. hat Schwierigkeiten) sb. is up to his/her neck in it; **jmdm. mit etw. vom ~[e] bleiben** (ugs.) not bother sb. with sth.; **sich** (*Dat.*) **jmdn. vom ~[e] halten** (ugs.) keep sb. away: **dem Chef alle Besucher vom ~e halten** (ugs.) keep all visitors away from the boss [2] ▸❶ **S. 435** (Kehle) throat; **aus vollem ~[e]** at the top of one's voice; **er hat es in den falschen** *od.* **verkehrten ~ bekommen** (ugs.: falsch verstanden) he took it the wrong way; (ugs.: sich verschluckt) it went down [his throat] the wrong way; **er kann den ~ nicht voll [genug] kriegen** (ugs.) he can't get enough; he's insatiable; **das hängt/wächst mir zum ~[e] heraus** (ugs.) I'm sick and tired of it (coll.) [3] (einer Flasche) neck; **einer Flasche** (*Dat.*) **den ~ brechen** (ugs.) crack [open] a bottle [4] (Musik) (einer Note) stem; (eines Saiteninstruments) neck [5] (Anat.) neck; collum (Anat.); (Gebärmutter~) neck; cervix (Anat.)

hals-, Hals-: ~**ab·schneider** *der,* ~**ab·schneiderin** *die* (ugs. abwertend) shark; ~**abschneiderisch** *Adj.* cutthroat ‹*practice etc.*›; extortionate ‹*interest etc.*›; ~**aus·schnitt** *der* neckline; ~**band** *das; Pl.* ~**bänder** [1] (für Tiere) collar; [2] (Samtband) choker; neckband; [3] (veralt.: ~kette) necklace; ~**brecherisch** /-brɛçərɪʃ/ *Adj.* dangerous, risky ‹*climb, action, etc.*›; hazardous ‹*road*›; breakneck *attrib.* ‹*speed*›; ~**bruch** *der* ▸~**- und Beinbruch**

Hälschen /'hɛlsçən/ *das;* ~**s,** ~**:** [little] neck

halsen[1] *tr. V.* (veralt.) embrace

halsen[2] *itr. V.* (Seemannsspr.) wear

hals-, Hals-: ~**entzündung** *die* ▸❶ **S. 439** inflammation of the throat; ~**kette** *die* necklace; (für Hunde) chain; ~**kragen** *der* collar; ~**krause** *die* ruff; ~**länge** *die* (Pferdesport) neck; **um eine ~länge** by a neck; ~**-Nasen-Ohren-Arzt** *der,* ~**-Nasen-Ohren-Ärztin** *die* ear, nose, and throat specialist; ~**-Nasen-Ohren-Krankheiten** *Pl.* (Med.) diseases of the ear, nose, and throat; **Facharzt für ~-Nasen-Ohren-Krankheiten** ear, nose, and throat specialist; ~**schlagader** *die* ▸❶ **S. 435** carotid [artery]; ~**schmerzen** *Pl.* ▸❶ **S. 439** sore throat *sing.*; **[starke] ~schmerzen haben** have a[n extremely] sore throat; ~**starrig** /-ʃtarɪç/ **A** *Adj.* (abwertend) stubborn; obstinate; **B** *adv.* stubbornly; obstinately; ~**starrigkeit** *die;* ~**:** (abwertend) stubbornness; obstinacy; ~**stück** *das* (Kochk.) neck; ~**tuch** *das* cravat; (des Cowboys) neckerchief; ~**- und Beinbruch** *Interj.* (scherzh.) good luck!; best of luck!; ~**weh** *das* (ugs.)

h

▸~schmerzen; ~wickel *der* (Med.) compress (applied to the throat); ~wirbel *der* ▸❶ S. 435 (Anat.) cervical vertebra

halt[1] /halt/ *Partikel* (südd., österr., schweiz.) ▸**eben C 2**

halt[2] *Interj.* stop; (Milit.) halt; ~, **ich habe etwas vergessen** wait a minute *or* (coll.) hold on, I've forgotten something

Halt *der;* ~[e]s, ~e 1 (Stütze) hold; **seine Füße/Hände fanden keinen ~:** he couldn't find *or* get a foothold/handhold; **in diesen Schuhen haben meine Füße keinen ~:** these shoes don't give my feet any support; **den ~ verlieren** lose one's hold; **inneren ~ haben** be secure; **ohne jeden ~:** totally insecure; **er hat einen festen ~ an seinem Glauben** his faith gives him *or* provides him with a great sense of security 2 (Anhalten) stop; **einen ~ machen** make a stop; **zum ~ kommen** come to a stop *or* halt; **ohne ~:** non-stop; without stopping; **~ machen** stop; **vor jmdm./etw. nicht ~ machen** (fig.) not spare sb./sth.; **vor nichts und niemandem ~ machen** stop at nothing

haltbar *Adj.* 1 (nicht verderblich) **~ sein** ‹*food*› keep [well]; **etw. ~ machen** preserve sth.; **~ bis 5. 3.** use by 5 March 2 (nicht verschleißend) hard-wearing, durable ‹*material, clothes*› 3 (aufrechtzuerhalten) tenable ‹*hypothesis etc.*› 4 (Ballspiele) stoppable, savable ‹*shot*›; **der Ball war nicht ~:** the shot was unstoppable 5 (beizubehalten) maintainable ‹*position etc.*›; **die Position war nicht ~:** the position could not be maintained

Haltbarkeit *die;* ~ 1 **Lebensmittel von beschränkter ~:** perishable foods; **eine längere ~ haben** keep longer 2 (Strapazierfähigkeit) durability; **ein Teppich von größter ~:** an extremely hard-wearing carpet 3 (Glaubhaftigkeit) tenability

Haltbarkeits·dauer *die:* **Sahne, die eine ~ von 3 Monaten hat** cream which keeps for three months; **die ~ von verpackten Lebensmitteln muss auf der Packung angegeben werden** the date by which packed foodstuffs should be eaten must be shown on the pack

Halte-: ~bogen *der* (Musik) tie; ~bucht *die* (Verkehrsw.) lay-by (Brit.); turnout (Amer.); ~griff *der* 1 [grab] handle; (Riemen) [grab] strap; 2 (Budo, Ringen) pinning hold; ~gurt *der* seat belt; ~linie *die* (Verkehrsw.) stop line

halten

A *unr. tr. V.* 1 (auch Milit.) hold; **etw. an einem Ende/am Griff ~:** hold one end of sth./hold sth. by the handle; **jmdm. den Mantel ~:** hold sb.'s coat [for him/her]; **sich** (*Dat.*) **den Kopf/den Bauch ~:** hold one's head/stomach; **jmdn. an** *od.* **bei der Hand ~:** hold sb.'s hand; hold sb. by the hand; **jmdn./etw. im Arm ~:** hold sb./sth. in one's arms; **die Hand vor den Mund ~:** put one's hand in front of one's mouth; **etw. ins Licht/gegen das Licht ~:** hold sth. to/up to the light

2 (Ballspiele) save ‹*shot, penalty, etc.*›

3 (bewahren) keep; (beibehalten, aufrechterhalten) keep up ‹*speed etc.*›; maintain ‹*temperature, equilibrium*›; **einen Ton ~:** stay in tune; (lange an~) sustain a note; **den Takt ~:** keep time; **Diät ~:** keep to a diet; **den Kurs ~:** stay on course; **diese Forderungen lassen sich nicht ~** *od.* **sind nicht zu ~:** these demands cannot be kept up *or* maintained; **diese Behauptung lässt sich nicht ~:** this statement does not hold up; **mit jmdm. Kontakt** *od.* **Verbindung ~:** keep in touch *or* contact with sb.; **Ordnung/Frieden ~:** keep order/the peace; **Ruhe in der Klasse ~** ‹*teacher*› keep the class quiet; ‹*pupils*› keep quiet in class

4 (erfüllen) keep; **sein Wort/ein Versprechen ~:** keep one's word/a promise; **das Buch hielt nicht, was das Titelbild versprach** (fig.) the book didn't live up to the promise of the picture on its cover

5 (besitzen, beschäftigen, beziehen) keep ‹*chickens etc.*›; take ‹*newspaper, magazine, etc.*›; **ein Auto ~:** run a car; **sich** (*Dat.*) **eine Putzfrau ~:** have a woman to come in and clean

6 (einschätzen) **jmdn. für reich/ehrlich ~:** think sb. is *or* consider sb. to be rich/honest; **jmdn. für tot ~:** think sb. is dead; **ich halte es für das beste/möglich/meine Pflicht** I think it best/possible/my duty; **viel/nichts/wenig von jmdm./etw. ~:** think a lot/nothing/not think much of sb./sth.

7 (ab~, veranstalten) give, make ‹*speech*›; give, hold ‹*lecture*›; **Unterricht ~:** give lessons; teach; **seinen Winterschlaf ~:** hibernate; **seinen Mittagsschlaf ~:** have one's *or* an afternoon nap; **eine Mahlzeit ~** (veralt.) have a meal

8 (Halt geben) hold up, support ‹*bridge etc.*›; hold back ‹*curtain, hair*›; fasten ‹*dress*›

9 (zurück~) keep; **ihn hält hier nichts** there's nothing to keep him here; **es hält dich niemand** nobody's stopping you

10 (bei sich be~) **das Wasser ~:** hold one's water

11 (nicht aufgeben) **ein Geschäft** *usw.* **~:** keep a business *etc.* going

12 (behandeln) treat; **jmdn. streng ~:** be strict with sb.

13 (vorziehen) **es mit jmdm./etw. ~:** like sb./sth.; **es mehr** *od.* **lieber mit jmdm./etw. ~:** prefer sb./sth.

14 (verfahren) **es mit einer Sache so/anders ~:** deal with *or* handle sth. like this/differently; **wie haltet ihr es in diesem Jahr mit eurem Urlaub?** what are you doing about holidays this year?

15 (lassen, be~) keep; **für jmdn. das Essen warm ~:** keep sb.'s meal hot; **jmdn. jung/fit ~:** keep sb. young/fit; **jmdn. bei Laune/in Bewegung/in Atem ~:** keep sb. happy/on the go/in suspense

16 (gestalten) **das Badezimmer ist in Grün ge~:** the bathroom is decorated in green; **sie wollten das Esszimmer ganz in Eiche ~:** they wanted all oak furniture in the dining room; **die Rede war sehr allgemein ge~:** the speech was very general

B *unr. itr. V.* 1 (stehen bleiben) stop; **etw. zum Halten bringen** stop sth.; bring sth. to a stop; **halt [mal]** (fig. ugs.) hang *or* hold on [a minute] (coll.)

2 (unverändert, an seinem Platz bleiben) last; **der Nagel/das Seil hält nicht mehr länger** the nail/rope won't hold much longer; **die Tapete hält nicht** the wallpaper won't stay on; **diese Freundschaft hält nicht [lange]** (fig.) this friendship won't last [long]

3 (Sport) save; **er hat gut ge~:** he made some good saves

4 (beistehen) **zu jmdm. ~:** stand *or* stick by sb.

5 (zielen) aim (**auf** + *Akk.* at)

6 (Seemannsspr.) head; **auf etw.** (*Akk.*) **~:** head for *or* towards sth.

7 (sich beherrschen) **an sich** (*Akk.*) **~:** control oneself

8 (achten) **auf Ordnung ~:** attach importance to tidiness; **auf sich** (*Akk.*) **~:** take a pride in oneself

C *unr. refl. V.* 1 (sich durchsetzen, behaupten) **wir werden uns/die Stadt wird sich nicht länger ~ können** we/the town won't be able to hold out much longer; **das Geschäft wird sich nicht ~ können** the shop won't keep going [for long]; **der neue Regisseur konnte sich nicht ~:** the new director didn't last

2 (sich bewähren) **sich gut ~:** do well; make a good showing; **halte dich tapfer** be brave

3 (unverändert bleiben) ‹*weather, flowers, etc.*› last; ‹*milk, meat, etc.*› keep

4 (Körperhaltung haben) **sich schlecht/gerade/aufrecht ~:** hold *or* carry oneself badly/straight/erect

5 (bleiben) **sich auf den Beinen/im Sattel ~:** stay on one's feet/in the saddle

6 (gehen, bleiben) **sich links/rechts ~:** keep [to the] left/right; **sich südwärts/in Richtung Bahnhof ~:** keep going south/towards the station; **sich an jmds. Seite** (*Dat.*)**/hinter jmdm. ~:** stay *or* keep next to/behind sb.

7 (befolgen) **sich an etw. ~** (*Akk.*) **~:** keep to *or* follow sth.; **der Film hat sich nicht eng an den Roman ge~:** the film didn't keep *or* stick closely to the book

8 (sich wenden) **sich an jmdn. ~:** ask sb.; **halte dich an Peter, der ist immer hilfsbereit** stay *or* stick with Peter — he's always helpful

9 (ugs.: jung, gesund bleiben) **sie hat sich gut ge~:** she is well preserved for her age (coll.)

Halte-: ~platz *der* [taxi] rank (Brit.); [cab] stand (Amer.); ~punkt *der* stop

Halter *der;* ~s, ~ 1 (Fahrzeug~) keeper 2 (Tier~) owner 3 (Vorrichtung) holder; (Handtuch~) towel rail 4 (ugs.: Feder~) pen 5 (österr.) ▸**Viehhirt**

Halterin *die;* ~, ~nen ▸**Halter 1, 2**

Halterung *die;* ~, ~en support

Halte-: ~seil *das* supporting cable; (eines Ballons) mooring cable; ~signal *das* stop signal; ~stelle *die* stop; ~verbot *das* 1 „~verbot" 'no stopping'; **auf dieser Straße besteht ~verbot** stopping is prohibited in this street; **„absolutes/eingeschränktes ~verbot"** 'no stopping/no waiting'; 2 (Stelle) no-stopping zone; **hier ist ~verbot** this is a no-stopping zone; ~verbotsschild *das* no-stopping sign; ~vorrichtung *die* ▸**Halterung**

-haltig /-haltɪç/, (österr.) **-hältig** /-hɛltɪç/ **vitamin~/silber~** *usw.* containing vitamins/silver *etc. postpos., not pred.*; **vitamin~ sein** contain vitamins

halt-, Halt-: ~los *Adj.* 1 (labil) **~los sein** be a weak character; **ein ~loser Mensch** a weak character; 2 (unbegründet) unfounded; ~losigkeit *die;* ~~ 1 (Labilität) weakness of character; 2 (mangelnde Begründung) unfoundedness; *~|machen ▸**Halt 2**

Haltung *die;* ~, ~en 1 (Körper~) posture; (Sport) stance; (in der Bewegung) style; **~ annehmen** (Milit.) stand to attention 2 (Pose) manner 3 (Einstellung) attitude 4 (Fassung) composure; **~ zeigen/bewahren** keep one's composure 5 (Tier~) keeping

Haltungs-: ~fehler *der* 1 (Med.) bad posture; 2 (Sport) style fault; ~schaden *der* (Med.) bad posture; ~schäden bad posture

Halt·verbot *das* ▸**Halteverbot**

Halunke /haˈlʊŋkə/ *der;* ~n, ~n 1 (Schurke) scoundrel; villain 2 (scherzh.: Lausbub) rascal; scamp

Hämatit /hɛmaˈtiːt/ *der;* ~s, ~e (Geol.) haematite

Hämatologe /hɛmatoˈloːgə/ *der;* ~n, ~n (Med.) haematologist

Hämatologie *die;* ~ (Med.) haematology *no art.*

Hämatologin *die;* ~, ~nen ▸**Hämatologe**

Hämatom /hɛmaˈtoːm/ *das;* ~s, ~e (Med.) haematoma

Hamburg /ˈhambʊrk/ *(das);* ~s ▸❶ S. 675 Hamburg

Hamburger[1] ▸❶ S. 675

A *der;* ~s, ~: native of Hamburg; (Einwohner) inhabitant of Hamburg; **Schmidt ist ~:** Schmidt comes from Hamburg

B *indekl. Adj.* Hamburg; **der ~ Hafen** the harbour at Hamburg; Hamburg harbour; *s. auch* **Kölner**

Hamburger[2] *der;* ~s, ~ *od.* ~s (Frikadelle) hamburger

hamburgern *itr. V.* speak Hamburg dialect

hamburgisch *Adj.* Hamburg *attrib.*; of Hamburg *postpos.*

Häme /ˈhɛːmə/ *die;* ~: malice

Hameln /ˈhaːmḷn/ *(das);* ~s Hamelin; **der Rattenfänger von ~:** the Pied Piper of Hamelin

hämen /ˈhɛːmən/ *itr. V.* say maliciously

hämisch /ˈhɛːmɪʃ/

A *Adj.* malicious

B *adv.* maliciously

Hammel /ˈhaml̩/ *der;* ~s, ~ 1 wether 2 (Fleisch) mutton 3 (salopp abwertend) oaf; dolt

Hammel-: ~bein *das:* in **jmdm. die ~beine lang ziehen** (ugs.) give sb. a good telling-off; ~fleisch *das* mutton; ~herde *die* (salopp abwertend) flock of sheep; ~keule *die* leg of mutton; ~sprung *der* (Parl.) division

Hammer /ˈhamɐ/ *der;* ~s, **Hämmer** /ˈhɛmɐ/ 1 hammer; (Holz~) mallet; (Eis~) hammer axe; (eines Auktionators) hammer; gavel; ~ **und Sichel** hammer and sickle; ~ **und Zirkel** hammer and compasses (*on the GDR national flag*); **unter den ~ kommen** come under the hammer; **etw. unter den ~ bringen** auction sth. **2** (Technik) tup; ram **3** (Musik) hammer **4** (Leichtathletik) hammer **5** (ugs.: Fehler) bad mistake; (in einer Aufgabe) howler (coll.); **ein dicker ~:** an awful blunder; **er hat einen ~:** he must be round the bend (coll.) *or* (sl.) twist **6** (ugs.: Überraschung, Clou) real surprise; **das ist ein ~!** (großartig) that's fantastic! (coll.); (unerhört) that's quite outrageous! **7** ▸ℹ **S. 435** (Anat.) hammer; malleus

Hämmerchen /ˈhɛmɐçən/ *das;* **~s, ~:** [small] hammer

hammer-, Hammer-: ~förmig *Adj.* hammer-shaped; **~hai** *der* hammerhead [shark]; **~klavier** *das* (veralt.) pianoforte; **~kopf** *der* (auch Leichtathletik, Musik) hammerhead; **~mäßig** (Jugendspr.) **A** *Adj.* fantastic (coll.); awesome (coll.) ‹*music, film*›; **B** *adv.* ‹*play etc.*› fantastically well (coll.)

hämmern /ˈhɛmɐn/

A *itr. V.* **1** hammer; **es hämmert** sb. is hammering **2** (schlagen) hammer; (mit der Faust) hammer; pound; **gegen die Wand/die Tür ~:** hammer/pound on the wall/door **3** (klopfen) pound; ‹*pulse*› race

B *tr. V.* **1** hammer; beat, hammer ‹*tin, silver, etc.*›; beat ‹*jewellery*› **2** (ugs.) hammer *or* pound out ‹*melody etc.*› **3** (ugs.: einprägen) **jmdm. etw. in den Schädel ~:** hammer *or* knock sth. into sb.'s head (coll.) **4** (Fußballjargon) hammer, slam ‹*ball*›

Hammer-: ~schlag *der* **1** hammer blow; blow from a/the hammer; **2** (Boxen) rabbit punch; **3** (Faustball) smash; **4** (Technik) hammer scale; **~stiel** *der* handle *or* shaft of a/the hammer; **~werfen** *das;* **~~s** (Leichtathletik) throwing the hammer; **er ist Weltmeister im ~werfen** he's world champion in the hammer; **~werfer** *der,* **~werferin** *die* (Leichtathletik) hammer-thrower; **~werk** *das* **1** (veralt.) hammer mill; **2** (Musik) striking mechanism; **~wurf** *der* (Leichtathletik) **1** ▸ **~werfen; 2** (einzelner Wurf) hammer throw; **~zehe** *die* hammer toe

Hammond·orgel /ˈhɛmənd-/ *die* Hammond organ

Hämoglobin /hɛmogloˈbiːn/ *das;* **~s** (Physiol.) haemoglobin

Hämorrhoiden /hɛmoroˈiːdn̩/ *Pl.* (Med.) haemorrhoids; piles

Hämozyt /hɛmoˈt͜syːt/ *der;* **~en, ~en** (Physiol.) haemocyte

Hampelei *die;* ~ (ugs. abwertend) fidgeting

hampelig (ugs. abwertend)

A *Adj.* jerky; fidgety ‹*Person*›

B *adv.* jerkily

Hampel·mann /ˈhampl̩-/ *der* **1** jumping jack **2** (ugs. abwertend) puppet; **jmdn. zu einem/seinem ~ machen** make sb. one's puppet **3** (Gymnastik) side-straddle hop; jumping jack

hampeln *itr. V.* (ugs.) jump about

Hamster /ˈhamstɐ/ *der;* **~s, ~:** hamster

Hamster·backen *Pl.* chubby cheeks

Hamsterer *der;* **~s, ~** (ugs.) hoarder

Hamster·fahrt *die* foraging trip; **auf ~ gehen** go foraging

Hamsterin *die;* **~, ~nen** ▸ **Hamsterer**

Hamster·kauf *der* panic-buying *no pl.*; **Hamsterkäufe machen** panic-buy

hamstern *tr., itr. V.* **1** (horten) hoard; (Hamsterkäufe machen) panic-buy **2** (Lebensmittel tauschen) barter goods for food

Hand /hant/ *die;* **~, Hände** /ˈhɛndə/ **1** ▸ℹ **S. 435** hand; **mit der rechten/linken ~:** with one's right/left hand; **jmdm. die ~ geben** *od.* (geh.) **reichen** shake sb.'s hand; shake sb. by the hand; **jmdm. die ~ drücken/schütteln** press/shake sb.'s hand; **eine ~ frei haben** have a free hand; **ich habe keine ~ frei** my hands are full; **Hände hoch!** hands up!; **jmdm. die ~ küssen** kiss sb.'s hand; **jmdn. an die** *od.* (geh.) **bei der ~ nehmen** take sb. by the hand; **jmdm. etw. aus der ~ nehmen** take sth. out of sb.'s hand/hands; **etw. aus der ~ legen** put sth. down; **jmdm. aus der ~ lesen** read sb.'s hand *or* palm; **etw. in die/zur ~ nehmen** pick sth. up; **etw. in der ~/den Händen haben** *od.* (geh.) **halten** have got *or* hold sth. in one's hand/hands; **in die Hände klatschen** clap one's hands; **mit Händen und Füßen reden** use gestures to make oneself understood; **etw. mit der ~ schreiben/nähen** write/sew sth. by hand; **von ~:** by hand; **~ in ~ gehen** go *or* walk hand-in-hand; **eine Sonate für vier Hände** *od.* **zu vier Händen** a four-handed sonata; **jmdm. etw. in die ~ versprechen** promise sb. sth. faithfully; **eine ~/ein paar Hände voll Sand** a handful/a couple of handfuls of sand **2** (Fußball) handball **3** (Boxen) punch **4** (veralt., geh.: ~schrift) hand **5** (österr. ugs.: Arm) arm **6** (in Wendungen) **was hältst du davon — ~ aufs Herz!** what do you think? — be honest; **~ aufs Herz, ich habe ihn nicht gesehen** I haven't seen him, word of honour *or* (coll.) cross my heart; **eine ~ wäscht die andere** you scratch my back and I'll scratch yours; **Zuschüsse von öffentlicher ~:** subsidies from government funds *or* from the government; **die öffentlichen Hände** the local/regional authorities; **jmds. rechte ~:** sb's right-hand man; **ihm rutschte die ~ aus** (ugs.) he couldn't stop himself [hitting her/him *etc.*]; **jmdm. sind die Hände gebunden** sb.'s hands are tied; **~ und Fuß/weder ~ noch Fuß haben** (ugs.) make sense/no sense; **[bei etw. selbst mit] ~ anlegen** lend a hand [with sth.]; **die** *od.* **seine ~ aufhalten** *od.* **hinhalten** (ugs.) hold out one's hand; **jmds. ~ ausschlagen** (veralt. geh.) reject sb.; **keine ~ rühren** (ugs.) not lift a finger; **~ an sich legen** (geh.) take one's own life; **letzte ~ an etw.** (*Akk.*) **legen** put the finishing touches *pl.* to sth.; **jmdm. die ~ [zum Bund] fürs Leben reichen** (geh.) marry sb.; **sich** (*Dat.*) *od.* (geh.) **einander die ~ reichen können** be tarred with the same brush; **dann können wir uns die ~ reichen** snap!; shake!; **alle** *od.* **beide Hände damit voll haben, etw. zu tun** (ugs.) have one's hands full doing sth.; **er hat alle Hände voll zu tun** he's got his hands full; **sich** (*Dat.*) **die ~ für jmdn./etw. abhacken** *od.* **abschlagen lassen** (ugs.) do anything for sb./stake one's life on sth.; **jmdm. auf etw.** (*Akk.*) **die ~ geben** promise sb. sth.; **die Hände in den Schoß legen** sit back and do nothing; **bei etw. die** *od.* **seine Hände [mit] im Spiel haben** have a hand in sth.; **überall seine ~** *od.* **Hände im Spiel haben** have a finger in every pie; **die Hände über dem Kopf zusammenschlagen** (ugs.) throw up one's hands in horror; **die** *od.* **seine ~ über jmdn. halten** (geh.) protect sb.; **zwei linke Hände haben** (ugs.) have two left hands (coll.); **eine lockere** *od.* **lose ~ haben** (ugs.) hit out at the slightest provocation; **eine offene ~ haben** be open-handed; **eine glückliche ~ bei etw. haben** have a feel for the right choice in sth.; **dabei hat er eine glückliche ~ gehabt** he intuitively made the right choice; **eine glückliche ~ in etw.** (*Dat.*) **haben** have the right knack for sth.; **im Umgang mit Kindern hat er eine glückliche ~:** he's very good *or* has a way with children; **sie hat in solchen Dingen eine glückliche ~:** she has a [natural] flair for such things; **eine grüne ~ haben** (ugs.) have green fingers; **linker/rechter ~:** on *or* to the left/right; **an ~** (+ *Gen.*) with the help of; **an ~ dieses Berichts** from this report; **jmdm. etw. an die ~ geben** make sth. available to sb.; **jmdn. an der ~ haben** (ugs.) know [of] sb.; **[klar] auf der ~ liegen** (ugs.) be obvious; **jmdn. auf Händen tragen** lavish every kind of care and attention on sb.; **Möbel/ein Auto aus erster ~:** furniture/a car which has/had had one [previous] owner; **etw. aus erster ~ wissen** know sth. at first hand; have first-hand knowledge of sth.; **Kleidung aus zweiter ~:** second-hand clothes *pl.*; **das Auto ist aus zweiter ~:** the car has had two [previous] owners; **Leihgaben aus** *od.* **von privater ~:** loans from private collections; **jmdm. aus der ~ fressen** eat out of sb.'s hand (fig.); **etw. aus der ~ geben** (weggeben) let sth. out of one's hands; (aufgeben) give sth. up; **[aus der] ~ spielen** (Skat) play without using the widow *or* skat; **jmdm. etw. aus der ~ nehmen** relieve sb. of sth.; **etw. bei der ~ haben** (greifbar haben) have sth. handy; (parat haben) have sth. ready; **mit etw. schnell** *od.* **rasch bei der ~ sein** (ugs.) be ready with sth.; **[schon** *od.* **bereits] durch viele Hände gegangen sein** have been *or* have [been] passed through many hands; **die Vera ist schon durch viele Hände gegangen** (ugs.) she's been around a bit, has Vera (coll.); **~ in ~ arbeiten** work hand in hand; **Regierung und Rauschgifthändler arbeiteten ~ in ~:** the government and the drug dealers were working hand in glove; **mit etw. ~ in ~ gehen** go hand in hand with sth.; **hinter vorgehaltener ~:** off the record; **in die Hände spucken** spit on one's hands; (fig. ugs.) roll up one's sleeves (fig.); **jmdm./einer Sache in die Hände arbeiten** play into sb.'s hands/help bring sth. about; **jmdn./etw. in die ~** *od.* **Hände bekommen** *od.* **kriegen** lay *or* get one's hands on sb./get one's hands on sth.; **jmdm. in die Hände fallen** fall into sb.'s hands; **etw. in der ~ haben** have sth.; **jmdn. in der ~ haben** have *or* hold sb. in the palm of one's hand; **etw. in Händen halten** hold sth.; **etw. in jmds. ~** *od.* **Hände legen** (geh.) put sth. in sb.'s hands; **etw. in die ~ nehmen** take sth. in hand; **in jmds. ~** (*Dat.*) **sein** *od.* (geh.) **liegen** be in sb.'s hands; **in festen Händen sein** (ugs.) be spoken for *or* attached; **in sicheren** *od.* **guten Händen sein, sich in guten Händen befinden** be in safe *or* good hands; **jmdm. Informationen** *usw.* **in die ~** *od.* **Hände spielen** pass information *etc.* to sb.; **in jmds. ~** *od.* **Hände übergehen** pass into sb.'s hands; **mit Händen zu greifen sein** be as plain as a pikestaff; be perfectly obvious; **mit beiden Händen zugreifen** grab *or* seize the opportunity with both hands; **sich mit Händen und Füßen gegen etw. sträuben** *od.* **wehren** (ugs.) fight tooth and nail against sth.; **mit leeren Händen** empty-handed; **das mache ich mit der linken ~** (ugs.) I could do that with my eyes closed; **mit starker** *od.* **fester ~:** with a firm hand; **das Geld mit vollen Händen ausgeben** spend money like water; **um jmds. ~ anhalten** *od.* **bitten** (geh. veralt.) ask for sb.'s hand [in marriage]; **etw. unter den Händen haben** be working on sth.; **unter der ~:** on the quiet; **etw. unter der ~ erfahren** hear sth. through the grapevine; **jmdm. etw. unter der ~ mitteilen** tell sb. sth. secretly; **von jmds. ~ sterben** (geh.) die at sb.'s hand; **das geht ihm gut/leicht von der ~:** he finds that no trouble; **etw. von langer ~ vorbereiten** plan sth. well in advance; **die Nachteile/seine Argumente lassen sich nicht von der ~ weisen** *od.* **sind nicht von der ~ zu weisen** the disadvantages cannot be denied/his arguments cannot [simply] be dismissed; **von der ~ in den Mund leben** live from hand to mouth; **von ~ zu ~ gehen** be passed from hand to hand; **etw. zu treuen Händen nehmen** take sth. into one's care; **jmdm. etw. zu treuen Händen geben** give sth. to sb. for safe keeping; **zur linken/rechten ~:** on *or* to the left/right[-hand side]; **etw. zur ~ haben** have sth. handy; **ich habe kein Kleingeld zur ~:** I haven't got any change on me; **jmdm. zur ~ gehen** lend sb. a hand; **zu Händen [von] Herrn Müller** for the attention of Herr Müller; attention Herr Müller; *s. auch* **öffentlich A**

hand-, Hand-: ~ab·zug *der* **1** (Druckw.) proof pulled by hand; **2** (Fot.) print made by hand; **~akte** *die* file; **~apparat** *der* **1** (Fernspr.) handset; **2** (Bücher) set of reference books; reference collection; **~arbeit** *die* **1** handicraft; craft work; **etw. in ~arbeit herstellen** make sth. by hand; **2** (Gegenstand) handmade article; **das ist eine ~arbeit** that is handmade *or* made by hand; **3** (Arbeit aus Stoff, Wolle usw.) [piece of] needlework; (gestrickt) [piece of] knitting; (gehäkelt) [piece of] crocheting; **sie macht gerne ~arbeiten** she likes doing needlework/knitting/crocheting; **4** (ugs.:

~arbeitsunterricht) needlework; ~**arbeiten** *itr. V.* do needlework; ich kann nicht gut ~arbeiten I am not very good at needlework; ~**arbeiter** *der*, ~**arbeiterin** *die* manual worker

Handarbeits-: ~**geschäft** *das* wool and needlework shop; ~**korb** *der* workbasket; ~**lehrerin** *die* needlework teacher

Hand-: ~**aufheben** *das* (bei einer Wahl) show of hands; sich durch ~aufheben melden put one's hand up to speak/answer; ~**auflegen** *das;* ~~s (bes. Rel.) laying on *or* imposition of hands

Hand·ball *der* 1 (Spiel) handball 2 (Ball) handball

Hand·ballen *der* ▸ⓘ S. 435 ball of the thumb

Hand·baller *der;* ~s, ~, **Hand·ballerin** *die;* ~, ~nen (ugs.) handball player

Handball-: ~**mannschaft** *die* handball team; ~**spiel** *das* 1 handball match; 2 (Sportart) das ~spiel the game of handball; ~**spieler** *der*, ~**spielerin** *die* handball player

hand-, Hand-: ~**bedienung** *die* manual operation; eine Maschine mit ~bedienung a manually operated *or* hand-operated machine; ~**besen** *der* brush; ~**betrieb** *der* manual operation; mit ~betrieb manually operated; hand-operated; ~**betrieben** *Adj.* manually operated; hand-operated; ~**bewegung** *die* 1 movement of the hand; 2 (Geste) gesture; ~**bibliothek** *die* 1 reference library; 2 (~apparat) set of reference books; reference collection; ~**bohrer** *der* (mit Kurbel) hand-drill; (zum Vorbohren) gimlet; ~**bohrmaschine** *die* hand-drill; (elektrisch) drill; ~**brause** *die* shower handset; ~**breit** A *Adj.* ‹seam etc.› a few inches wide; ein ~breiter Abstand a gap of a few inches; B *adv.* a few inches; ~**breit** *die;* ~~, ~~: eine/zwei ~breit a few/several inches; keine ~breit barely an inch; ~**breite** *die:* ein Abstand/Streifen von einer ~breite a gap of a few inches/a strip a few inches wide; ~**bremse** *die* handbrake; ~**buch** *das* handbook; (technisches ~buch) manual

Händchen /'hɛntçən/ *das;* ~s, ~: [little] hand; ~ halten (ugs. scherzh.) hold hands; ein ~ haltendes junges Paar a young couple holding hands; für etw. ein ~ haben (fig. ugs.) have a knack for sth.; be good at sth.

Händchen·halten *das;* ~s (ugs. scherzh.) holding hands *no art.*

händchen·haltend ▸ Händchen

Hand·creme *die* hand cream

Hände ▸ Hand

Hände-: ~**druck** *der; Pl.* ~drücke handshake; ~**klatschen** *das;* ~~s clapping; applause

Handel[1] /'handl̩/ *der;* ~s 1 (Wirtschaft) trade; commerce; ~ und Industrie/~ und Gewerbe trade and industry 2 (~n) trade; der ~ mit Waffen/Drogen the traffic in arms/drugs 3 (Geschäftsverkehr) trade; der internationale/überseeische ~: international/overseas trade; ~ treiben trade; ~ treibend trading ‹nation›; ‹tribe› engaged primarily in trade; ein Produkt aus dem ~ ziehen take a product off the market; in den ~ kommen come on [to] the market; das ist [nicht mehr] im ~: it is [no longer] on the market; ~ und Wandel (veralt.) commercial and social life 4 (veralt.: Geschäft) business 5 (Vereinbarung) deal

Handel[2] *der;* ~s, Händel /'hɛndl̩/ (geh.) quarrel; einen ~ [mit jmdm.] austragen settle a quarrel [with sb.]; Händel anfangen/suchen start/ [try to] pick a quarrel

handelbar *Adj.* (Finanzw., Börsenw.) tradable; ~e Option traded option

Hand·elfmeter *der* (Fußball) penalty for handball

handeln

A *itr. V.* 1 trade; deal; mit *od.* in Gemüse/Gebrauchtwagen ~: deal in vegetables/second-hand cars; mit Waffen/Drogen ~: traffic in arms/drugs; mit jmdm. ~: trade *or* deal with sb.; en gros/en détail ~: be in the wholesale/retail trade; wir ~ en gros mit Spielwaren we are toy wholesalers 2 (feilschen) haggle; bargain; um den Preis ~: haggle over the price; mit ihm lässt sich [nicht] ~: he is [not] open to negotiation; er lässt nicht mit sich ~: it's impossible to bargain with him 3 (eingreifen) act; auf Befehl/aus Überzeugung ~: act on orders/out of conviction; im Affekt/in Notwehr ~: act in the heat of the moment/in self-defence 4 (verfahren) act; eigenmächtig/richtig/fahrlässig ~: act on one's own authority/correctly/carelessly 5 (sich verhalten) behave; gut/schlecht an jmdm. *od.* gegen jmdn. ~: behave well/badly towards sb. 6 von etw. *od.* über etw. (Akk.) ~ ‹book, film, etc.› be about *or* deal with sth.

B *refl. V.* (unpers.) bei dem Besucher handelte es sich um einen entfernten Verwandten the visitor was a distant relative; es handelt sich um ... it is a matter of ...; (es dreht sich um) it's about *or* it concerns ...; es handelt sich darum, dass die Presse nichts davon erfährt the important thing is that the press should not get wind of it

C *tr. V.* sell (für at, for); diese Papiere werden nicht an der Börse gehandelt these securities are not traded on the stock exchange; der US-Dollar wird jetzt zu 2 Euro gehandelt the US dollar is now valued at 2 euros

Handeln *das;* ~s 1 (das Feilschen) haggling; bargaining 2 (das Eingreifen) action 3 (Verhalten) action[s *pl.*]

handels-, Handels-: ~**abkommen** *das* trade agreement; ~**agent** *der*, ~**agentin** *die* (österr.) ▸ ~vertreter; ~**akademie** *die* (österr.) commercial college; ~**artikel** *der* commodity; ~**attaché** *der* commercial attaché; ~**bank** *die; Pl.* ~~en merchant bank; ~**beschränkung** *die* trade restriction; ~**beziehungen** *Pl.* trade relations; ~**bilanz** *die* 1 (eines Betriebes) balance sheet; 2 (eines Staates) balance of trade; eine aktive/passive ~bilanz a balance of trade surplus/deficit; ~**block** *der; Pl.* ~blöcke trading block; ~**boykott** *der* trade boycott; ~**delegation** *die* trade delegation; ~**einig**, ~**eins** in mit jmdm. ~einig *od.* ~eins werden/sein agree/have agreed terms *or* come/have come to an agreement with sb.; ~**firma** *die* [business *or* commercial] firm; business concern; ~**flagge** *die* merchant flag; ~**flotte** *die* merchant fleet; ~**geist** *der* business acumen *or* sense; ~**gericht** *das* commercial court; ~**gesellschaft** *die* company; offene ~gesellschaft general partnership; ~**gesetz** *das* commercial law; ~**gesetzbuch** *das* commercial code; ~**größe** *die* (Kaufmannsspr.) commercial size; ~**hafen** *der* commercial *or* trading port; ~**haus** *das* (veralt.) business house; firm; ~**kammer** *die* ▸ Industrie- und Handelskammer; ~**kette** *die* (Kaufmannsspr.) 1 (Weg der Ware) channel of distribution; 2 (Zusammenschluss von Händlern) voluntary chain; ~**klasse** *die* grade; ~**kontor** *das* (hist.) branch; ~**korrespondenz** *die* business correspondence; ~**lehrer** *der*, ~**lehrerin** *die* teacher of commercial subjects; ~**macht** *die* trading power; ~**marine** *die* merchant navy; ~**marke** *die* trade mark; ~**messe** *die* trade fair; ~**metropole** *die* commercial metropolis *or* centre; ~**minister** *der*, ~**ministerin** *die* minister of trade; (in UK) Secretary of State for Trade; Trade Secretary (coll.); ~**ministerium** *das* ministry of trade; (in UK) Department of Trade; ~**mission** *die* trade mission; ~**monopol** *das* trading monopoly; ~**name** *der* trade *or* business name; ~**nation** *die* trading nation; ~**niederlassung** *die* branch; ~**organ** *das* (DDR) branch; ~**organisation** *die* 1 trading organization; 2 (DDR) [*state-owned*] *commercial concern running shops, hotels, etc.;* ~**partner** *der*, ~**partnerin** *die* trading partner; ~**politik** *die* trade *or* commercial policy; ~**politisch** A *Adj.* relating to trade *or* commercial policy *postpos.;* vom ~politischen Standpunkt from the point of view of trade *or* commercial policy; B *adv.* as far as trade *or* commercial policy is concerned; ~**recht** *das* commercial law; ~**rechtlich** A *Adj.* relating to commercial law *postpos.;* ‹*offence*› against commercial law; B *adv.* from the point of view of commercial law; es ist ~rechtlich nicht erlaubt it is not allowed under commercial law; ~**register** *das* register of companies; ~**reisende** *der/die* ▸ ~vertreter; ~**schiff** *das* merchant ship; trading vessel; *~**schiffahrt**, ~**schifffahrt** *die* merchant shipping; (Schiffsverkehr) movement of merchant shipping; ~**schranke** *die* trade barrier; ~**schule** *die* commercial college; ~**schüler** *der*, ~**schülerin** *die* student at a commercial college; ~**schul·lehrer** *der*, ~**schul·lehrerin** *die* teacher at a commercial college; ~**spanne** *die* (Kaufmannsspr.) margin; ~**sperre** *die* trade embargo; ~**sprache** *die* trade language; language of commerce; ~**stadt** *die* trading town; (Großstadt) trading city; ~**straße** *die* (hist.) trade route; ~**üblich** *Adj.* ~übliche Praktiken/Größen normal *or* standard business practices/standard [commercial] sizes; ~üblich sein be normal *or* standard business practice

Händel·sucht *die* (geh. veralt.) quarrelsomeness

händel·süchtig *Adj.* (geh. veralt.) quarrelsome

Handels-: ~**unternehmen** *das* trading concern; ~**verbindung** *die* trade link; ~**vertrag** *der* trade agreement; ~**vertreter** *der*, ~**vertreterin** *die* ▸ⓘ S. 113 [sales] representative; travelling salesman/saleswoman; commercial traveller; ~**vertretung** *die* ▸ ~mission; ~**volumen** *das* (Wirtsch.) volume of trade; ~**ware** *die* commodity; „keine ~ware" (Postw.) 'no commercial value'; ~**weg** *der* 1 commercial artery; 2 (Weg der Ware) channel of distribution; ~**wert** *der* (Kaufmannsspr.) commercial value; ~**zentrum** *das* trading *or* commercial centre

handel·treibend ▸ Handel 3

hände-, Hände-: ~**ringend** *Adv.* 1 wringing one's hands; 2 (ugs.: dringend) ~ringend Leute suchen need staff urgently; ~ringend nach jmdm./etw. suchen search desperately for sb./sth.; ~**schütteln** *das;* ~~s hand-shaking *no pl.;* die ersten zehn Minuten vergingen mit ~schütteln the first ten minutes were spent shaking hands; ~**trockner** *der* hand-drier; ~**waschen** *das;* ~~s washing *no art.* one's hands; sie ging zum ~waschen ins Bad she went to the bathroom to wash her hands

hand-, Hand-: ~**feger** *der* brush; herumlaufen wie ein wild gewordener ~feger (salopp) (zerzaust) go round looking like a scarecrow; (aufgeregt) run around madly; ~**fertigkeit** *die* [manual] dexterity; ~**fest** A *Adj.* 1 (kräftig) robust; sturdy; 2 (deftig) substantial ‹*meal etc.*›; etwas Handfestes something substantial; 3 (gewichtig) solid, tangible ‹*proof*›; concrete ‹*suggestion*›; full-blooded, violent ‹*row*›; complete ‹*lie*›; well-founded ‹*argument*›; real, thorough ‹*beating*›; B *adv.* (deutlich) ‹*criticize*› severely; er hat mich ~fest belogen/betrogen he told me a complete lie/it was an out-and-out deception; ~**feuerlöscher** *der* hand fire extinguisher; ~**feuerwaffe** *die* handgun; ~feuerwaffen small arms; ~**fläche** *die* ▸ⓘ S. 435 palm [of one's/the hand]; flat of one's/the hand; ~**galopp** *der* (Reiten) canter; hand gallop; ~**gas** *das* (Kfz-W.) hand throttle; mit ~gas fahren drive using the hand throttle; ~**gearbeitet** *Adj.* handmade ‹*furniture, jewellery, etc.*›; ~**gefertigt** *Adj.* hand-made; ~**geknüpft** *Adj.* handwoven; ~**geld** *das* lump sum [payment]; ~**gelenk** *das* ▸ⓘ S. 435 wrist; ein loses *od.* lockeres ~gelenk haben (ugs.) lash out at the slightest provocation; aus dem ~gelenk [heraus] (ugs.) (unvermittelt) offhand; (ohne Mühe) effortlessly; as easily as anything (coll.); etw. aus dem ~gelenk schütteln (ugs.) do sth. just like that (coll.); ~**gemacht** *Adj.* handmade; ~**gemalt** *Adj.* hand-painted; ~**gemenge** *das* 1 fight; 2 (Milit.) hand-to-hand fighting *no indef. art.*; **~genäht** *Adj.* hand-sewn; **~gepäck** *das* hand baggage; **~geschliffen** *Adj.* hand-cut; **~geschmiedet** *Adj.* hand-wrought; **~geschöpft** *Adj.* hand-made; **~geschrieben** *Adj.* handwritten; **~gesponnen** *Adj.* hand-spun; **~gesteuert** *Adj.* manually operated; manually controlled ‹*vehicle*›; **~gestrickt** *Adj.* hand-knitted; (fig. abwertend) half-baked ‹*idea, theory, etc.*›; **~gewebt** *Adj.* handwoven; **~granate** *die* hand grenade; **~greiflich** **A** *Adj.* [1] (tätlich) **eine ~greifliche Auseinandersetzung** a scuffle; **~greiflich werden** start using one's fists; [2] tangible ‹*success, advantage, proof, etc.*›; palpable ‹*contradiction, error*›; obvious ‹*fact*›; **B** *adv.* [1] (tätlich) **sich ~greiflich auseinander setzen** come to blows; [2] (konkret fassbar) clearly; **~greiflichkeit** *die;* **~~, ~~en** [1] (eines Beweises) tangibility; (eines Widerspruchs, Fehlers) palpability; [2] (Tätlichkeit) scuffle; fight; **es kam zu/nicht zu ~greiflichkeiten** a fight broke out/there was no violence; **~griff** *der* [1] **ein falscher ~griff** a false move; **ein geschickter ~griff, und ...** one deft action and ...; **mit einem ~griff/wenigen ~griffen** in one movement/without much trouble; (schnell) in no time at all/next to no time; **jeder ~griff muss sitzen** every movement must be exactly right; **keinen ~griff [für jmdn.] tun** (fig.) not do anything to help sb.; [2] (am Koffer, an einem Werkzeug) handle; [3] (Haltegriff) grab handle; **~groß** *Adj.* ‹*hole, wound, etc.*› the size of a hand; **~habbar** /-ha:pba:ɐ̯/ *Adj.* handy; **kaum ~habbar** very difficult *or* awkward to manage; very unwieldy; **~habe** *die;* **~~, ~~n: eine [rechtliche] ~habe [gegen jmdn.]** a legal handle [against sb.]; **~haben** *tr. V.* [1] handle; operate ‹*device, machine*›; [2] (praktizieren) implement ‹*law etc.*›; **~habung** *die;* **~~, ~~en** [1] handling; (eines Gerätes, einer Maschine) operation; [2] (Durchführung) implementation; **~harmonika** *die* accordion

Handheld /ˈhɛnthɛlt/ *das;* **~s, ~s** (DV) hand-held [device]

Handikap /ˈhɛndikɛp/ *das;* **~s, ~s** (auch Sport) handicap

handikapen /ˈhɛndikɛpn̩/ *tr. V.* handicap

händisch /ˈhɛndɪʃ/ (österr. ugs.)
A *Adj.* manual
B *adv.* manually; by hand

Hand-: ~kamera *die* hand camera; **~kante** *die* edge of the/one's hand

Handkanten·schlag *der* chop

hand-, Hand-: ~karre *die,* **~karren** *der* handcart; **~käse** *der* (landsch.) *small, hand-formed curd cheese;* **~käse mit Musik** (landsch.) marinaded hand-formed curd cheese; **~koffer** *der* [small] suitcase; **~koloriert** *Adj.* hand-coloured; **~kurbel** *die* [hand-]crank; **~kuss, *~kuß** *der* kiss on sb.'s hand; **etw. mit ~kuss [an]nehmen/tun** accept/do sth. with [the greatest of] pleasure; **~lampe** *die* hand-lamp; inspection lamp

Hand·langer *der;* **~s, ~, Hand·langerin** *die;* **~, ~nen** [1] (Hilfsarbeiter[in]) labourer [2] (abwertend) lackey; general dogsbody [3] (abwertend: Büttel) henchman/henchwoman

Handlanger·dienst *der* (abwertend) **für jmdn. ~e leisten** do sb.'s dirty work for him/her

Hand·lauf *der* handrail

-händler *der* ‹*cattle-, furniture-, scrap-, stamp-*› dealer; ‹*coal-, corn-, scrap-, timber, wine*›merchant

Händler /ˈhɛndlɐ/ *der;* **~s, ~:** ▸ⓘ **S. 113** trader; tradesman/tradeswoman; **ein fliegender ~:** a hawker *or* street trader

Händlerin *die;* **~, ~nen** tradeswoman; *s. auch* **Händler**

Hand-: ~lese·kunst *die* palmistry *no art.*; **~lexikon** *das* concise encyclopedia

handlich /ˈhantlɪç/
A *Adj.* handy; easily carried ‹*parcel, suitcase*›; easily portable ‹*television, camera*›; manoeuvrable ‹*car*›
B *adv.* **~ verpackt** wrapped as a manageable parcel

Handlichkeit *die;* **~:** handiness; (eines Buches) handy size; (eines Autos) manoeuvrability

Hand-: ~linie *die* line of the hand; **~linien·deutung** *die* palmistry

Handlung *die;* **~, ~en** [1] (Vorgehen) action; (Tat) act; **eine symbolische/feierliche ~:** a symbolic/ceremonial act [2] (Fabel) plot; **Einheit der ~:** unity of action [3] (veralt.: Geschäft) business

handlungs-, Handlungs-: ~ablauf *der* action; **~arm** *Adj.* short on action *pred.;* **~bedarf** *der* need for action; **wir haben ~bedarf** we need action; **ein juristischer/politischer ~bedarf besteht** legal/political action is needed; **~bevollmächtigte** *der/die* authorized representative; **~fähig** *Adj.* [1] able to act *pred.;* working *attrib.* ‹*majority*›; [2] (Rechtsw.) able to act on one's own account *pred.;* **~fähigkeit** *die* [1] ability to act; [2] (Rechtsw.) ability to act on one's own account; **~freiheit** *die* freedom of action *or* to act; **~gehilfe** *der,* **~gehilfin** *die* (Kaufmannsspr.) employee (*on the business side of a firm*); **~reich** *Adj.* action-packed; **~reisende** *der/die* ▸**Handelsvertreter**; **~schema** *das* plot structure; **~spielraum** *der* scope for action; **~strang** *der* strand of the plot; **~unfähig** *Adj.* [1] unable to act *pred.;* [2] (Rechtsw.) unable to act on one's own account *pred.;* **~unfähigkeit** *die* [1] inability to act; [2] (Rechtsw.) inability to act on one's own account; **~vollmacht** *die* authority to act; **~weise** *die* behaviour; conduct

Hand-: ~mixer *der* hand mixer; **~mühle** *die* hand mill

Hand-out /ˈhɛndaut/ *das;* **~s, ~s** handout

Hand-: ~presse *die* hand press; **~pumpe** *die* hand pump; **~puppe** *die* glove *or* hand puppet; **~puppen·spiel** *das* glove puppet *or* hand puppet show; (Technik) glove *or* hand puppetry; **~rad** *das* handwheel; **~reichung** *die;* **~~, ~~en: eine ~reichung/~reichungen machen** lend a hand; **sie konnte nur einige ~reichungen machen** she couldn't help very much; **~rücken** *der* ▸ⓘ **S. 435** the back of the/one's hand; **auf beiden ~rücken tätowiert** with tattoos on the back of both hands; **~säge** *die* handsaw; **~satz** *der* (Druckw.) hand-setting; **etw. im ~satz herstellen** hand-set sth.; **~schelle** *die* handcuff; **jmdm. ~schellen anlegen** handcuff sb.; put handcuffs on sb.; **~schlag** *der* [1] handshake; **jmdn. mit ~schlag begrüßen** greet sb. by shaking hands; **etw. durch einen ~schlag besiegeln** shake hands on sth.; [2] *in* **er tat keinen ~schlag** (ugs.) he did not lift a finger

Hand·schrift *die* [1] handwriting; **eine deutliche/unleserliche ~:** clear/illegible handwriting [2] (Ausdrucksweise) personal style [3] (Text) manuscript

Handschriften-: ~deutung *die* graphology *no art.*; analysis of handwriting; **~kunde** *die* palaeography; **~probe** *die* sample of handwriting

Handschrift·leser *der* (DV) *optical character reader with handwriting recognition capability*

hand·schriftlich
A *Adj.* handwritten; **~e Quellen/Urkunden** manuscript sources/texts
B *adv.* by hand

Hand·schuh *der* glove

Handschuh-: ~fach *das* glove compartment *or* box; **~größe** *die* glove size; **welche ~größe haben Sie?** what size glove do you take?; **~macher** *der,* **~macherin** *die* glove maker

hand-, Hand-: ~schutz *der* hand guard; **~setzer** *der,* **~setzerin** *die* (Druckw.) hand compositor; **~signiert** *Adj.* signed; **~skizze** *die* freehand sketch; **~spiegel** *der* hand-mirror; **~spiel** *das* (Fußball) handball

Hand·stand *der* (Turnen) handstand; **einen ~ machen** do a handstand

Handstand·überschlag *der* (Turnen) handspring

Hand-: ~steuerung *die* [1] manual operation *or* control; [2] (Apparatur) manual control; **~streich** *der* (bes. Milit.) lightning *or* surprise attack; **in einem** *od.* **im ~streich** in a surprise *or* lightning attack; **~tasche** *die* handbag; **~teller** *der* ▸ⓘ **S. 435** palm [of the/one's hand]; **~trommel** *die* hand drum

Hand·tuch *das; Pl.* **Handtücher** towel; (Geschirrtuch) tea towel; tea cloth; **dieser Raum ist nicht mehr als ein ~** (ugs.) this room is nowhere near wide enough; **das ~ werfen** *od.* (ugs.) **schmeißen** (Boxen, fig.) throw in the towel

Handtuch·halter *der* towel rail

hand-, Hand-: ~umdrehen *in* **im ~umdrehen** in no time at all; **~verlesen** *Adj.* hand-picked; **~vermittlung** *die* (Fernspr.) connection by the operator; **über ~vermittlung laufen** be connected by the operator; ***~voll** *die;* **~~** (auch fig.) handful; **ein paar ~voll** a couple of handfuls; **~waffe** *die* hand weapon; **~wagen** *der* handcart; **~warm** **A** *Adj.* hand-hot; **B** *adv.* **etw. ~warm waschen** wash sth. in hand-hot water; **~wäsche** *die* washing by hand; **diese Pullover kommen in die ~wäsche** these pullovers will have to be washed by hand

-handwerk *das:* **Töpfer~/Bäcker~/Schuhmacher~:** potter's / baker's / shoemaker's trade

Handwerk *das* [1] craft; (als Beruf) trade; **ein ~ ausüben/betreiben** carry on/ply a trade [2] (Beruf) **sein ~ kennen** *od.* **verstehen/beherrschen** know one's job; ‹*tradesman*› know/be master of one's trade; **jmdm. das ~ legen** put a stop to sb.'s activities; **jmdm. ins ~ pfuschen** try to do sb.'s job for him/her [3] **das ~:** the craft professions *pl.*

Handwerker *der;* **~s, ~:** tradesman; craftsman; **die ~ im Haus haben** have the workmen in; **er ist ein guter ~:** he's a good craftsman

Handwerkerin *die;* **~, ~nen** tradeswoman; craftswoman

Handwerkerschaft *die;* **~:** skilled tradesmen *pl. or* craftsmen *pl.*

Handwerker·stand *der* artisan class

handwerklich *Adj.* [1] ‹*training, skill, ability*› as a craftsman; **ein ~er Beruf** a [skilled] trade [2] (fig.) technical

Handwerks-: ~beruf *der* [skilled] trade; **~betrieb** *der* workshop; **~bursche** *der* (veralt.) travelling journeyman (arch.); **~kammer** *die* Chamber of Crafts; **~meister** *der* master craftsman; **~meisterin** *die* master craftswoman; **~rolle** *die* register of qualified craftsmen; **~zeug** *das* tools *pl.*; (fig.) tools *pl.* of the trade

Hand·wörter·buch *das* concise dictionary

Hand·wurzel *die* ▸ⓘ **S. 435** wrist; carpus (Anat.)

Handwurzel·knochen *der* ▸ⓘ **S. 435** (Anat.) wristbone; carpal bone (Anat.)

Handy /ˈhɛndi/ *das;* **~s, ~s** mobile [phone]; cell phone (esp. Amer.)

Handy·nummer *die* mobile number

hand-, Hand-: ~zahm *Adj.* [1] so tame it/they can be handled; [2] (fig.) tamely obedient; biddable; **~zeichen** *das* [1] sign [with one's hand]; (eines Autofahrers) hand signal; **darf ich die Betroffenen um ihr ~zeichen bitten?** will those concerned please raise their hands; [2] (Abstimmung) show of hands; **durch ~zeichen** by a show of hands; **~zeichnung** *die* drawing; (Skizze) sketch; **~zettel** *der* handbill; leaflet

hanebüchen /ˈha:naby:çn̩/
A *Adj.* outrageous
B *adv.* outrageously; **~ lügen** tell the most outrageous lies

Hanf /hanf/ *der;* **~[e]s** [1] (Pflanze, Faser) hemp [2] (Samen) hempseed

Hanf·anbau *der* growing *or* cultivation of hemp

hanfen, hänfen /ˈhɛnfn̩/ *Adj.* hempen; hemp

Hänfling /ˈhɛnflɪŋ/ *der;* **~s, ~e** **1** (Vogel) linnet **2** (abwertend) weakling

Hanf-: ~seil *das,* **~strick** *der* hempen *or* hemp rope

Hang /haŋ/ *der;* **~[e]s, Hänge** /ˈhɛŋə/ **1** (Berg~) slope; hillside/mountainside; (Ski~) slope; **das Haus am ~:** the house on the hillside; **das Haus ist an einen ~ gebaut** the house is built on a slope **2** (Neigung) tendency; **einen ~ zum Träumen/Lügen** *usw.* **haben** have a tendency to dream/lie *etc.;* **einen ~ haben, etw. zu tun** tend to do sth. **3** (Turnen) hang

Hangar /ˈhaŋgaːɐ̯/ *der;* **~s, ~s** hangar

Hänge-: ~arsch *der* (derb) sagging backside (coll.); **~backe** *die* flabby cheek; **~bauch** *der* paunch; **~bauch·schwein** *das* pot-bellied pig; **~boden** *der* false *or* drop ceiling; **~brücke** *die* suspension bridge; **~brust** *die,* **~busen** *der* sagging breasts *pl.;* **~dach** *das* suspended roof; **~gleiter** *der* hang-glider; **~kleid** *das* tent dress; **~lampe** *die* pendant light; drop-light

hangeln /ˈhaŋl̩n/

A *itr. V.; meist mit sein* make one's way hand over hand; **an einem Seil über die Schlucht ~:** make one's way hand over hand along a rope over the ravine

B *refl. V.* **sich aufwärts/abwärts ~:** climb up/down hand over hand

Hänge·matte *die* hammock

hangen /ˈhaŋən/ (schweiz., landsch.) ▸ **hängen¹**

hängen¹ /ˈhɛŋən/ *unr. itr. V.; südd., österr., schweiz. mit sein* **1** hang; **die Bilder ~ [schon]** the pictures are [already] up; **der Schrank hängt voller Kleider** the wardrobe is full of clothes; **der Weihnachtsbaum hängt voller Süßigkeiten** the Christmas tree is laden with sweets; **sein Zimmer hängt voller Plakate** the walls of his room are covered with posters; **an einem Faden ~:** be hanging by a thread; **etw. ~ lassen** (vergessen) leave sth. behind; **die Nachbarn hingen aus den Fenstern** (fig.) the neighbours were hanging out of the windows **2** (sich festhalten) hang, dangle (**an** + *Dat.* from); **jmdm. am Hals ~:** hang round sb.'s neck; **der Junge hing an ihrem Arm** the boy hung on to her arm; *s. auch* **Rockzipfel**
3 (erhängt werden) hang; be hanged
4 (an einem Fahrzeug) be hitched *or* attached (**an** + *Dat.* to)
5 (herab~) hang down; **bis auf den Boden ~:** hang down to the ground; **die Pflanzen ließen ihre Blätter ~:** the leaves of the plants drooped; **die Beine ins Wasser ~ lassen** let one's legs dangle in the water; **der Anzug hängt ihm am Leib** the suit hangs loosely on him; **sich ~ lassen** (fig.) let oneself go; **lass dich nicht so ~!** (fig.) [you must] pull yourself together!
6 (unordentlich sitzen) **im Sessel ~** (erschöpft, betrunken) be *or* sit slumped in one's/the chair; (flegelhaft) lounge in one's/the chair
7 (geh.: schweben, auch fig.) hang (**über** + *Dat.* over)
8 (haften) cling, stick (**an/auf** + *Dat.* to); **~ bleiben** stick (**an/auf** + *Dat.* to); **ihre Augen hingen an seinen Lippen** (fig.) her eyes were fixed on his lips; **das bleibt an mir ~** (fig.) I've been stuck *or* landed with it (coll.); **von dem Vortrag blieb [bei ihm] nicht viel ~** (fig.) not much of the lecture stuck (coll.); **ein Verdacht bleibt an ihr ~** (fig.) suspicion rests on her
9 (fest~) **sie hing mit dem Rock am Zaun/in der Fahrradkette** her skirt was caught on the fence/in the bicycle chain; **mit dem Ärmel** *usw.* **an/in etw.** (*Dat.*) **~ bleiben** get one's sleeve *etc.* caught on/in sth.; **der Angriff blieb im Mittelfeld ~** (fig.) the attack broke down in mid-field; **sein Blick blieb an der Uhr ~** (fig.) his gaze rested on the clock; **ich bin bei Freunden ~ geblieben** (fig. ugs.) I got stuck talking to friends (coll.); **~ bleiben** (ugs.: in der Schule nicht versetzt werden) stay down; have to repeat a year
10 (ugs.: sich aufhalten, sein) hang around (coll.); **[schon wieder] am Radio/Telefon/vorm Fernseher ~:** have got the radio on [again]/be on the telephone [again]/be in front of the television [again]
11 (sich nicht trennen wollen) **an jmdm./etw. ~:** be very attached to sb./sth.; **am Geld/Leben ~:** love money/life
12 (sich neigen) lean; ‹*road*› slope to one side
13 (ugs.: angeschlossen sein) **an etw.** (*Dat.*) **~:** be on sth.
14 (ugs.: nicht weiterkommen) be stuck; **die Verhandlungen ~:** the talks are deadlocked
15 (ugs.: zurück sein) be behind
16 (verschuldet sein) **bei ihr hänge ich mit 2 000 Euro** I owe her 2,000 euros
17 (entschieden werden) **an/bei jmdm./etw. ~:** depend on sb./sth.
18 (Schach) ‹*man*› be en prise; (nicht beendet sein) ‹*game*› be adjourned
19 (ugs.: verbunden sein) **etw. hängt an etw.** (*Dat.*) sth. involves sth.
20 **jmdn. ~ lassen** (ugs.: jmdm. nicht helfen) let sb. down

hängen²

A *tr. V.* **1** **etw. in/über etw.** (*Akk.*) **~:** hang sth. in/over sth.; **etw. an/auf etw.** (*Akk.*) **~:** hang sth. on sth.; **den Hörer in die Gabel ~:** replace the receiver **2** (befestigen) hitch up (**an** + *Akk.* to); couple on ‹*railway carriage, trailer, etc.*› (**an** + *Akk.* to) **3** (~ lassen) hang; **seinen Arm aus dem Fenster ~:** put one's arm out of the window; **die Beine ins Wasser ~:** let one's legs dangle in the water **4** (er~) hang; **Tod durch Hängen** death by hanging; **mit Hängen und Würgen** by the skin of one's teeth **5** (ugs.: aufwenden) **an/in etw.** (*Akk.*) **~:** put ‹*work, time, money*› into sth.; spend ‹*time, money*› on sth. **6** (ugs.: anschließen) **jmdn./etw. an etw.** (*Akk.*) **~:** put sb./sth. on sth.; *s. auch* **Glocke 1; Nagel 2**

B *refl. V.* **1** (ergreifen) **sich an etw.** (*Akk.*) **~:** hang on to sth.; **sich jmdm. an den Hals ~:** cling to sb.'s neck; **sich ans Telefon ~** (fig. ugs.) get on the telephone; **sich an den Wasserhahn ~** (ugs. fig.) turn the tap on and drink thirstily from it **2** (sich festsetzen) ‹*smell*› cling (**an** + *Akk.* to); ‹*burr, hairs, etc.*› cling, stick (**an** + *Akk.* to) **3** (anschließen) **sich an jmdn. ~:** attach oneself to sb.; latch on to sb. (coll.); **sie hängt sich zu sehr an mich** she clings to me too much **4** (verfolgen) **sich an jmdn./ein Auto ~:** follow *or* (coll.) tail sb./a car **5** (binden) **sich an jmdn./etw. ~:** get *or* become attached to sb./sth.; **sie hängt sich zu sehr an materielle Werte** she's too attached to material values

Hangen *das;* **~s** *in* **mit ~ und Bangen** (geh.) in fear and trepidation

***hängen|bleiben** ▸ **hängen¹ 8, 9**

hängend *Adj.* hanging; **die Hängenden Gärten der Semiramis** the Hanging Gardens of Babylon; **mit ~em Kopf** with head hanging; **mit ~er Zunge** (fig.) gasping for breath

***hängen|lassen** ▸ **hängen¹ 1, 5, 20**

Hänge-: ~ohr *das* lop ear; **~partie** *die* (Schach) adjourned game; **~pflanze** *die* trailing plant

Hänger *der;* **~s, ~** **1** ▸ **Anhänger 2** **2** ▸ **Hängekleid** **3** (weiter Mantel) loose[-fitting] coat; tent coat

Hänge-: ~schrank *der* wall cupboard; **~schultern** *Pl.* round shoulders

hängig *Adj.* **1** (schweiz. Rechtsspr.) **~ sein** be in progress; continue; **ein ~er Prozess** a trial that is in progress **2** (fachspr.) sloping; **in ~er Lage** on a slope *or* an incline

Hang·lage *die* hillside location; **in ~:** in a hillside location

Hängolin /hɛŋoˈliːn/ *das;* **~s** (salopp scherzh.) *substance allegedly used in order to diminish sb.'s sex drive*

Hang-: ~täter *der,* **~täterin** *die* (Rechtsspr.) compulsive criminal; **~wind** *der* slope wind

Hängung *die;* **~, ~en** hanging

Hannover /haˈnoːfɐ/ *(das);* **~s** ▸ **ℹ S. 675** Hanover

Hannoveraner ▸ **ℹ S. 675**

A *der;* **~s, ~** (Einwohner, Pferd) Hanoverian

B *indekl. Adj.* Hanover; *s. auch* **Kölner**

Hannoveranerin *die;* **~, ~nen** Hanoverian

hannoversch /haˈnoːfɐʃ/ *Adj.* Hanoverian; **im Hannoverschen** in the Hanover area

Hans /hans/ *der;* **~, Hänse** /ˈhɛnzə/ **~ im Glück** lucky devil; (Märchenfigur) Hans in Luck; **~ Guckindieluft** dreamer; (Märchenfigur) Johnny-Head-in-[the-]Air; **jeder ~ findet seine Grete** every Jack shall have his Jill

Hansaplast (Wz) /hanzaˈplast/ *das;* **~[e]s** sticking plaster; Elastoplast ®

Hänschen /ˈhɛnsçən/ *das;* **~s, ~: was ~ nicht lernt, lernt Hans nimmermehr** what you don't learn as a child, you'll never learn as an adult; ≈ you can't teach an old dog new tricks

Hans·dampf *der;* **~[e]s, ~e: ~ [in allen Gassen]** Jack of all trades

Hanse /ˈhanzə/ *die;* **~** (hist.) Hanse; Hanseatic league

Hanseat /hanzeˈaːt/ *der;* **~en, ~en** **1** citizen of a Hanseatic city; **ein typischer ~** *someone with the dignified bearing regarded as typical of upper-class citizens of the Hanseatic cities* **2** (hist.) member of the Hanseatic League

Hanseatin *die;* **~, ~nen** ▸ **Hanseat 1**

hanseatisch *Adj.* Hanseatic

Hanse-: ~bund *der* ▸ **Hanse; ~kogge** *die* (hist.) Hansa cog

Hänselei *die;* **~, ~en** **1** teasing **2** (Bemerkung) teasing remark

hänseln /ˈhɛnzl̩n/ *tr. V.* tease

Hanse·stadt *die* Hanseatic city

> **Hansestadt**
>
> *Hansestädte* (Hanseatic cities), such as Bremen and Hamburg, were once part of an association of trading cities along the North Sea and Baltic coasts. The *Hanse* (Hanseatic League or Hansa) was formed in the 13th century to protect the economic interests of its members. Meetings were held at Lübeck, where members developed a system of commercial laws. The *Hanse* lasted as a powerful force until 1669.

Hans·wurst *der;* **~[e]s, ~e** **1** (dummer Mensch) clown **2** (Theater) fool; hanswurst

Hans·wurstiade /hansvʊrsˈti̯aːdə/ *die;* **~, ~n** **1** (Scherz) clowning; buffoonery **2** (Theater) harlequinade

Hantel /ˈhantl̩/ *die;* **~, ~n** (Sport) (kurz) dumbbell; (lang) barbell

hanteln *itr. V.* exercise with dumb-bells/barbells

hantieren /hanˈtiːrən/ *itr. V.* be busy; **sie hantierte mit einem Schraubenschlüssel an ihrem Auto** she was busy doing something to her car with a spanner

hapern /ˈhaːpɐn/ *itr. V.* (unpers.) **1** (fehlen) **es hapert an etw.** (*Dat.*) there's a shortage of sth.; **es hapert bei jmdm. an etw.** sb. is short of sth.; **ich wäre gerne mitgefahren, aber es hapert an der Zeit** I'd like to have gone, but I haven't got the time **2** (nicht klappen) **es hapert mit etw.** there's a problem with sth.; **bei ihr hapert es in Latein** she's poor at *or* weak in Latin

haploid /haploˈiːt/ *Adj.* (Biol.) haploid

Häppchen /ˈhɛpçən/ *das;* **~s, ~** **1** [small] morsel **2** (Appetithappen) canapé

Happen /ˈhapn̩/ *der;* **~s, ~:** morsel; **einen ~ essen** have a bite to eat; **ein fetter ~** (fig.) a real plum

Happening /ˈhɛpənɪŋ/ *das;* **~s, ~s** happening

happig /ˈhapɪç/ *Adj.* (ugs.) steep (coll.); **~e Preise** fancy prices (coll.); **das ist aber [ein bisschen] ~:** that's a bit much (coll.)

Happs /haps/ *der* (ugs.) mouthful; **in** *od.* **mit einem ~:** in one gulp; (fig.) in one go; **ein Buch mit einem ~ verschlingen** devour a book in one sitting

happy /ˈhɛpi/ (ugs.)

A *Adj.* happy

B *adv.* happily

Happyend /ˈhɛpiˈlɛnt/ *das;* **~s, ~s** happy ending

Harakiri /hara'ki:ri/ *das;* **~[s], ~s** hara-kiri *no art.;* **politisches ~ begehen** (fig.) commit political suicide; **gesellschaftliches ~ begehen** (fig.) ruin one's reputation

Härchen /'hɛ:ɐ̯çən/ *das;* **~s, ~:** little *or* tiny hair; **die feinen ~ in ihrem Nacken** the fine down on her neck

Hardcover /'ha:d'kavə/ *das;* **~s, ~s** (Buchw.) hardback

Hardtop /'ha:dtɔp/ *das od. der;* **~s, ~s** hardtop

Hardware /'ha:dwɛə/ *die;* **~, ~s** (DV) hardware

Harem /'ha:rɛm/ *der;* **~s, ~s** (auch ugs. scherzh.) harem

Harems-: ~dame *die* lady of the harem; **~wächter** *der* guardian of the harem

hären /'hɛ:rən/ *Adj.* (geh.) [made] of hair *postpos.;* hair

Häresie /hɛre'zi:/ *die;* **~, ~n** /-i:ən/ heresy

Häretiker /hɛ're:tikɐ/ *der;* **~s, ~, Häretikerin** *die;* **~, ~nen** heretic

häretisch *Adj.* heretical

Harfe /'harfə/ *die;* **~, ~n** harp

harfen

A *itr. V.* play the harp; harp

B *tr. V.* **ein Lied** *usw.* **~:** play a song *etc.* on the harp

Harfenist *der;* **~en, ~en, Harfenistin** *die;* **~, ~nen** harpist; harp player

Harfen·spiel *das* harp playing; (Musik) harp music

Harke /'harkə/ *die;* **~, ~n** rake; **jmdm. zeigen, was eine ~ ist** (fig. salopp) give sb. what for (coll.)

harken *tr. V.* rake

Harlekin /'harleki:n/ *der;* **~s, ~e** harlequin

Harlekinade /harleki'na:də/ *die;* **~, ~n** ▸ **Hanswurstiade**

Harm /harm/ *der;* **~[e]s** (geh. veralt.) distress; (über Verlorenes) grief

härmen /'hɛrmən/ *refl. V.* (geh.) grieve (**um** over)

harm·los

A *Adj.* **1** (ungefährlich) harmless; slight ‹*injury, cold, etc.*›; mild ‹*illness*›; safe ‹*medicine, bend, road, etc.*›; **eine ~e Grippe** a mild bout of flu **2** (arglos) innocent; harmless ‹*fun, pastime, etc.*›

B *adv.* **1** (ungefährlich) harmlessly **2** (arglos) innocently; **ich bin ganz ~ hingegangen** I went there quite innocently; **er hatte nur ~ gefragt** he only asked an innocent *or* inoffensive question; **ganz ~ tun** act innocent

Harmlosigkeit *die;* **~ 1** (Ungefährlichkeit) harmlessness; (einer Krankheit) mildness; (eines Medikamentes) safety **2** (Arglosigkeit, harmloses Verhalten) innocence; **in aller ~:** in all innocence

Harmonie /harmo'ni:/ *die;* **~, ~n** (auch fig.) harmony

Harmonie-: ~lehre *die* theory of harmony; **~musik** *die* music for wind instruments

harmonieren *itr. V.* **1** (zusammenpassen) harmonize; go together; match; **mit etw. ~:** harmonize *or* go together with sth. **2** (miteinander auskommen) get on well

Harmonik /har'mo:nɪk/ *die;* **~:** harmony

Harmonika /har'mo:nika/ *die;* **~, ~s** *od.* **Harmoniken** harmonica

Harmonika-: ~spieler *der,* **~spielerin** *die* harmonica player; **~tür** *die* folding door; accordion door

harmonisch

A *Adj.* **1** (Musik) harmonic ‹*tone, minor*› **2** (wohlklingend, zusammenpassend, übereinstimmend) harmonious **3** (Math.) **~e Teilung** harmonic division

B *adv.* **1** (Musik) harmonically **2** (wohlklingend, zusammenpassend, übereinstimmend) harmoniously; **~ zusammenleben** live together in harmony

harmonisieren *tr. V.* **1** (Musik) harmonize **2** (in Einklang bringen) coordinate; **etw. mit etw. ~** (Wirtsch.) bring sth. into line with sth.

Harmonisierung *die;* **~, ~en** harmonization

Harmonium /har'mo:ni̯ʊm/ *das;* **~s, Harmonien** harmonium

Harn /harn/ *der;* **~[e]s, ~e** (Med.) urine; **~ lassen** pass water; urinate

Harn-: ~blase *die* ▸ℹ **S. 435** bladder; **~drang** *der* desire to urinate *or* to pass water

Harnisch /'harnɪʃ/ *der;* **~s, ~e 1** armour **2** **in ~ sein** be in a furious temper; **jmdn. in ~ bringen** get sb.'s hackles up; make sb. see red; **in ~ geraten** get up in arms (**über** + *Akk.* over, about)

harn-, Harn-: ~lassen *das;* **~~s** urination *no pl., no art.;* **Schmerzen beim ~lassen haben** find it painful to urinate *or* pass water; **~leiter** *der* (Med.) ureter; **~röhre** *die* ▸ℹ **S. 435** (Anat.) urethra; **~säure** *die* (Med., Chemie) uric acid; **~stein** *der* (Med.) urinary calculus; **~stoff** *der* (Med., Chemie) urea; **~treibend A** *Adj.* diuretic; **B** *adv.* **~treibend wirken** have a diuretic effect; **~vergiftung** *die* (Med.) uraemia; **~wege** *Pl.* ▸ℹ **S. 435** (Med.) urinary tract *sing.;* **~wegsinfektion** *die* (Med.) infection of the urinary tract

Harpune /har'pu:nə/ *die;* **~, ~n** harpoon

Harpunier /harpu'ni:ɐ̯/ *der;* **~s, ~e** harpooner

harpunieren

A *tr. V.* harpoon

B *itr. V.* throw/fire the harpoon

Harpyie /har'py:jə/ *die;* **~, ~n** (Myth.) harpy

harren /'harən/ *itr. V.* (geh.) **jmds./einer Sache** *od.* **auf jmdn./etw. ~:** wait for *or* await sb./sth.; (fig.) await sb./sth.; **der Dinge ~, die da kommen sollen** wait and see what happens

harsch /harʃ/

A *Adj.* **1** (vereist) crusted ‹*snow*› **2** (barsch) harsh

B *adv.* harshly

Harsch *der;* **~[e]s** crusted *or* hard snow

harschen *itr. V.* ‹*snow*› freeze [over]

harschig *Adj.* ‹*snow*› frozen hard [on top]

Harsch·schnee *der* ▸ **Harsch**

hart /hart/; **härter** /'hɛrtɐ/, **härtest...** /'hɛrtəst.../

A *Adj.* **1** hard ‹*wood, bread, cheese, etc.*›; **~e** *od.* **~ gekochte Eier** hard-boiled eggs; **Eier ~ kochen** hard-boil eggs; **~ gefroren** frozen hard *or* solid; **~ werden** go hard; harden; ‹*cheese etc.*› go hard; *s. auch* **Brocken 2; Nuss 1; Schädel 1 2** (abgehärtet) tough; **~ im Nehmen sein** (Schläge ertragen können) be able to take a punch; (Enttäuschungen ertragen können) be able to take the rough with the smooth **3** (schwer erträglich) hard ‹*work, life, fate, lot, times*›; tough ‹*childhood, situation, job*›; harsh ‹*reality, truth*›; bitter ‹*disappointment*›; heavy, severe ‹*loss*›; severe ‹*hardship*›; **jmds. Geduld** *usw.* **auf eine ~e Probe stellen** sorely try sb.'s patience *etc.;* **ein ~er Schlag für jmdn. sein** be a heavy *or* severe blow for sb.; **es war ~ für ihn, darauf zu verzichten** it was hard for him to go without; **es ist sehr ~ für ihn, dass er nicht mitkommen darf** it's very hard on him that he can't come too **4** (streng) severe, harsh ‹*penalty, punishment, judgement*›; tough ‹*measure, law, course*›; hard, harsh ‹*words*›; harsh ‹*treatment*›; severe, hard ‹*features*›; **durch eine ~e Schule gegangen sein** have been through a hard school; **~ gegen jmdn. sein** be hard on sb. **5** (heftig) hard, violent ‹*impact, jolt*›; heavy ‹*fall*›; violent ‹*argument*› **6** (rau) rough ‹*game, opponent*› **7** (stabil) hard ‹*currency*› **8** (kalkig) hard ‹*water*› **9** hard, severe ‹*winter, frost*›; harsh ‹*accent, light, colour, contrast*›; hard ‹*consonant, drink, drug, pornography*› **10** (Physik) hard ‹*rays etc.*›

B *adv.* **1** **~ schlafen/sitzen** sleep on a hard bed/sit on a hard chair **2** (mühevoll) ‹*work*› hard; **es kommt mich ~ an** it is hard for me **3** (streng) severely; harshly; **~ durchgreifen** take tough measures; **jmdn. ~ anfassen** be tough with sb. **4** (heftig) **~ aneinander geraten** have a violent argument; have a real set-to (coll.); **jmdm. ~ zusetzen, jmdn. ~ bedrängen** press sb. hard; **~ bedrängt** hard-pressed; **~ umkämpft** bitterly contested; **jmdn. ~ treffen** hit sb. hard; **es geht ~ auf ~:** the chips are down **5** (nahe) close (**an** + *Dat.* to); **die Kugel ging ~ an seinem Kopf vorbei** the bullet just missed his head; **das ist ~ an der Grenze der Legalität/des Machbaren** that is very close to being illegal/that's nearing the limits of what's possible; **~ am Wind segeln** (Seemannsspr.) sail near *or* close to the wind; **~ auf ein Ziel zuhalten** (Seemannsspr.) hold steady on course for sth.

***hart·bedrängt** ▸ **hart B 4**

Hart·beton *der* granolithic concrete

Härte /'hɛrtə/ *die;* **~, ~n 1** (auch Physik) hardness **2** (Widerstandsfähigkeit) toughness **3** (schwere Belastung) hardship; **eine soziale ~:** a case of social hardship **4** (Strenge) severity **5** (Heftigkeit) (eines Aufpralls usw.) force; (eines Streits) violence **6** (Rauheit) roughness **7** (Stabilität) hardness **8** (von Wasser) hardness **9** (von Licht, Farbe) harshness; (von Frost) hardness

Härte-: ~ausgleich *der* (Sozialw.) hardship payment; **~fall** *der* **1** case of hardship; **2** (ugs.: Person) hardship case; **~fonds** *der* hardship fund; **~grad** *der* degree of hardness; **~mittel** *das* hardener

härten

A *tr. V.* harden; harden, temper ‹*steel*›; cure ‹*plastic*›

B *itr. V.* harden

härter ▸ **hart**

Härter *der;* **~s, ~** (Chemie) hardener

Härte·skala *die* (Mineral.) scale of hardness; hardness scale

härtest... ▸ **hart**

Härte·test endurance test; (fig.) acid test

Hart·faser·platte *die* hardboard

hart-, Hart-: ~gefroren, ~gekocht ▸ **hart A 1; ~geld** *das* coins *pl.;* small change; **~gesotten** *Adj.* **1** (gefühllos) hard-bitten; hard-boiled; **2** (unbelehrbar) hardened; **~gummi** *das* hard rubber; **~herzig A** *Adj.* hard-hearted; **B** *adv.* hard-heartedly; **~herzigkeit** *die;* **~~:** hard-heartedness; **~holz** *das* hardwood; **~käse** *der* hard cheese; **~laub·gewächs** *das* (Bot.) sclerophyll [plant]; sclerophyllous plant; **~löten** *tr., itr. V.* hard-solder; **~metall** *das* hard metal; **~näckig** /-nɛkɪç/ **A** *Adj.* **1** (eigensinnig) obstinate; stubborn; **2** (ausdauernd) persistent; dogged; inveterate ‹*liar*›; stubborn, dogged ‹*resistance*›; persistent ‹*questioning, questioner*›; **3** (langwierig) stubborn ‹*illness, stain*›; **B** *adv.* **1** (eigensinnig) obstinately; stubbornly; **2** (ausdauernd) persistently; doggedly; **~näckigkeit** *die;* **~~ 1** (Eigensinn) obstinacy; stubbornness; **2** (Ausdauer) persistence; doggedness; **3** (Langwierigkeit) stubbornness; **~packung** *die* cardboard packet; **~papier** *das* (Technik) laminated paper; **~pappe** *die* fibreboard; **~platz** *der* (Sport) (Tennis) hard court; (Fußball) asphalt pitch; **~schalig** /-ʃa:lɪç/ *Adj.* hardshell; hard-shelled; thick-skinned ‹*apple, pear, etc.*›; ***~umkämpft** ▸ **hart B 4**

Härtung *die;* **~, ~en** hardening; (von Stahl auch) tempering; (von Kunststoffen) curing

Hart-: ~weizen·grieß *der* semolina; **~wurst** *die* dry sausage

Harz /ha:ɐ̯ts/ *das;* **~es, ~e** resin

harzen

A *itr. V.* exude resin

B *tr. V.* resin; resinate ‹*wine*›

Harzer *der;* **~s, ~, Harzer Käse** *der;* **~ Käses, ~ Käse** Harz [Mountain] cheese

Harzer Roller *der;* **~ ~s, ~ ~ 1** ▸ **Harzer Käse 2** (Kanarienvogel) Harz Mountain roller

Harz·geruch *der* smell of resin

harzig *Adj.* **1** resinous **2** (schweiz.: zähflüssig) slow-moving ‹*traffic, queue*›

Harz·säure *die* resin acid

Hasard /ha'zart/ *das;* **~s: ~ spielen** (auch fig.) gamble

Hasardeur /hazar'dø:ɐ̯/ *der;* **~s, ~e** (abwertend) gambler

Hasard·spiel *das* **1** (Glücksspiel) game of chance **2** (Wagnis) gamble

h

Hasch /haʃ/ *das;* ~s (ugs.) hash (coll.)

Haschee /haˈʃeː/ (Kochk.) *das;* ~s, ~s hash

haschen¹ (veralt.)
A *tr. V.* catch
B *itr. V.* **nach etw. ~:** make a grab for sth.; **nach Komplimenten/Beifall ~** (fig.) fish *or* angle for compliments/applause

haschen² *itr. V.* (ugs.) smoke [hash] (coll.)

Haschen *das;* ~s tag

Häschen /ˈhɛːsçən/ *das;* ~s, ~: bunny

Hascher *der;* ~s, ~ (ugs.) hash smoker (coll.)

Häscher /ˈhɛʃɐ/ *der;* ~s, ~ (geh. veralt.) pursuer

Hascherin *die;* ~, ~nen ▸**Hascher**

Hascherl /ˈhaʃɐl/ *das;* ~s, ~n (südd., österr. ugs.) **armes ~!** poor thing *or* soul!; (Kind) poor little thing *or* soul!

Haschisch /ˈhaʃɪʃ/ *das od. der;* ~[s] hashish

Haschmich /ˈhaʃmɪç/ *in* **einen ~ haben** (salopp) have a screw loose (coll.)

Hase /ˈhaːzə/ *der;* ~n, ~n [1] hare; (männlicher ~) hare; buck; **ängstlich wie ein ~:** timid as a mouse; **ein alter ~ sein** (ugs.) be an old hand; **falscher ~** (Kochk.) meat loaf; **da liegt der ~ im Pfeffer** (ugs.) that's the real trouble; **sehen/wissen, wie der ~ läuft** (ugs.) see/know which way the wind blows; **mein Name ist ~** (ugs. scherzh.) I'm not saying anything [2] (landsch.) ▸**Kaninchen**

Hasel-: **~busch** *der* hazel [tree]; **~huhn** *das* hazel grouse *or* hen; **~kätzchen** *das* hazel catkin; **~nuss**, ***~nuß** *die* [1] hazelnut; [2] hazel [tree]; **~[nuss]·strauch**, ***~[nuß]·strauch** *der* hazel [tree]

hasen-, Hasen-: **~braten** *der* roast hare; **~fuß** *der* (spöttisch abwertend) coward; chicken (sl.); **~füßig** *Adj.* (spöttisch abwertend) cowardly; **~herz** *das* ▸**~fuß**; **~jagd** *die* hare shoot; **auf ~jagd gehen** go on a hare shoot; go hare shooting; **~klein** *das;* ~~s trimmings *pl.* of hare; **~panier** *in* **das ~panier ergreifen** take to one's heels; **~pfeffer** *der* (Kochk.) marinaded and stewed trimmings *pl.* of hare; **~rein** *Adj.* (Jagdw.) steady from hare; **er/das ist nicht ganz ~rein** (fig.) there's something fishy (coll.) about him/it; **~scharte** *die* ▸❶ **S. 439** (Med.) cleft lip

Häsin /ˈhɛːzɪn/ *die;* ~, ~nen doe [hare]

Haspel /ˈhaspl̩/ *die;* ~, ~n (Technik) [1] (für Garn) reel; bobbin; (für ein Seil, Kabel) drum [2] (Seilwinde) windlass

haspeln
A *tr. V.* wind
B *itr. V.* (ugs.: hastig reden) gabble

Hass, ***Haß** /has/ *der;* **Hasses** hate, hatred (**auf** + *Akk.*, **gegen** of, for); **~ auf** *od.* **gegen jmdn. empfinden** feel hatred of *or* for sb.; **sich** (*Dat.*) **jmds. ~ zuziehen** incur sb.'s hatred

hassen *tr., itr. V.* hate; *s. auch* **Pest**

hassens·wert *Adj.* hateful; odious

hass·erfüllt, ***haß·erfüllt**
A *Adj.* filled with hatred *or* hate *postpos.*
B *adv.* **jmdn. ~ ansehen** look at sb. with [one's] eyes full of hatred *or* hate

Hass·gefühl, ***Haß·gefühl** *das* feeling of hatred

hässlich, ***häßlich** /ˈhɛslɪç/
A *Adj.* [1] ugly; **~ wie die Nacht** as ugly as sin (coll.) [2] (gemein) nasty; hateful; **~ zu jmdm. sein** be mean *or* hateful to sb.; **das war ~ von dir** that was mean *or* nasty of you [3] (unangenehm) terrible (coll.), awful ‹*weather, cold, situation, etc.*›
B *adv.* [1] ‹*dress*› unattractively [2] (gemein) nastily; hatefully; **~ von jmdm. sprechen** be mean *or* nasty about sb. [3] (unangenehm) terribly (coll.); awfully

Hässlichkeit, ***Häßlichkeit** *die;* ~, ~en [1] (Aussehen) ugliness [2] (Gesinnung) meanness; nastiness; hatefulness [3] (Äußerung) mean remark

hass-, ***haß-**, **Hass-**, ***Haß-:** **~liebe** *die* love-hate relationship; **~tirade** *die* (abwertend) tirade of hatred *or* hate; **~verzerrt** *Adj.* twisted with hatred *or* hate *postpos.*

hast /hast/ *2. Pers. Sg. Präsens v.* **haben**

Hast *die;* ~: haste; **etw. in** *od.* **mit größter ~ tun** do sth. in great haste; **ohne ~:** unhurriedly; without hurrying *or* haste

haste /ˈhastə/ (ugs.) = **hast du; [was] ~, was kannste** as fast as he/you/they *etc.* can/could; **~ was, biste was** money talks

hasten *itr. V.; mit sein* hurry; hasten

hastig
A *Adj.* hasty; hurried
B *adv.* hastily; hurriedly; **sein Essen ~ herunterschlingen** gobble [down] one's food; **nur nicht so ~!** not so fast!

hat /hat/ *3. Pers. Sg. Präsens v.* **haben**

Hätschelei *die;* ~, ~en (abwertend) [1] ~[en] fondling; caressing [2] (das Verwöhnen) pampering

Hätschel·kind *das* pampered child; (fig.) darling

hätscheln /ˈhɛːtʃl̩n/ *tr. V.* [1] (liebkosen) fondle; caress [2] (verwöhnen) pamper; (fig.) lionize [3] (sich widmen) cherish ‹*idea, hope, etc.*›; nurse ‹*pain etc.*›

hatschen /ˈhaːtʃn̩/ *itr. V.; mit sein* (bayr., österr. ugs.) [1] (schlendern) stroll; saunter [2] (hinken) hobble; limp [3] (mühselig gehen) trudge

hatschi /haˈtʃiː/ *Interj.* atishoo; atchoo; **~ machen** (Kinderspr.) sneeze

hatte /ˈhatə/ *1. u. 3. Pers. Sg. Prät. v.* **haben**

hätte /ˈhɛtə/ *1. u. 3. Pers. Sg. Konjunktiv II v.* **haben**

***Hat-Trick, Hattrick** /ˈhɛttrɪk/ *der;* ~s, ~s [1] (Fußball, Handball) *three successive goals by the same player in the same half* [2] (Sport) hat trick

Hatz /hats/ *die;* ~, ~en [1] (Hetzjagd, auch fig. ugs.) hunt [2] (ugs., bes. bayr.: Eile, Stress) mad rush

hatzi /haˈtsiː/ ▸**hatschi**

Hau /hau/ *in* **einen ~ haben** (salopp) have a screw loose (coll.)

Häubchen /ˈhɔypçən/ *das;* ~s, ~ ▸**Haube 1, 5**

Haube /ˈhaubə/ *die;* ~, ~n [1] bonnet; (einer Krankenschwester) cap; **unter die ~ kommen** (ugs. scherzh.) get hitched (coll.); **unter der ~ sein** (ugs. scherzh.) be married; **jmdn. unter die ~ bringen** (ugs. scherzh.) marry sb. off [2] (Kfz-W.) bonnet (Brit.); hood (Amer.) [3] ▸**Trocken~** [4] (südd., österr.: Mütze) [woollen] cap [5] (Zool.) crest [6] (Bedeckung) cover; (über Teekanne, Kaffeekanne, Ei) cosy

Hauben-: **~lerche** *die* crested lark; **~taucher** *der* great crested grebe

Haubitze /hauˈbɪtsə/ *die;* ~, ~n (Milit.) howitzer; **voll wie eine ~ sein** (derb) be as pissed as a newt (sl.)

Hauch /haux/ *der;* ~[e]s, ~e (geh.) [1] (Atem, auch fig.) breath [2] (Luftzug) breath of wind; breeze [3] (leichter Duft) delicate smell; waft [4] (dünne Schicht) [gossamer-]thin layer; **ein ~ von Reif** a [thin] film of hoar frost [5] (Atmosphäre) air; feeling [6] (Anflug) hint; trace; **der ~ eines Lächelns** a ghost *or* hint of a smile

hauch·dünn
A *Adj.* gossamer-thin ‹*material, dress*›; wafer-thin, paper-thin ‹*layer, slice, majority*›; **ein ~er Sieg** (fig.) the narrowest of victories
B *adv.* **etw. ~ auftragen** apply sth. very sparingly; **etw. ~ schneiden** cut sth. wafer-thin *or* into wafer-thin slices

hauchen
A *itr. V.* breathe (**gegen, auf** + *Akk.* on)
B *tr. V.* (auch fig.: flüstern) breathe; **jmdm. etw. ins Ohr ~:** breathe sth. in sb.'s ear

hauch-, Hauch-: **~fein** *Adj.* extremely fine; **~laut** *der* (Phon.) aspirate; **~zart** *Adj.* extremely delicate; gossamer-thin

Hau·degen *der:* **[alter] ~:** old soldier *or* warhorse

Hau·drauf /hauˈdrauf/ *der;* ~s, ~s (ugs. abwertend) bruiser; (Tennisspieler) big hitter

Haue /ˈhauə/ *die;* ~, ~n [1] (südd., österr.: Hacke) hoe [2] (ugs.: Prügel) a hiding (coll.); **..., sonst gibts ~:** ... or you'll get a hiding

hauen
A *unr. tr. V.* [1] (ugs.: schlagen) belt; clobber (coll.); beat; **jmdn. windelweich/grün und blau ~:** beat sb. black and blue; **jmdn. zu Brei ~** (salopp) beat sb.'s brains in (sl.) [2] (ugs.: auf einen Körperteil) belt (coll.); hit; (mit der Faust auch) smash (sl.); punch; (mit offener Hand auch) slap; smack; **jmdn. ins Gesicht ~:** hit/belt/slap sb. in the face; **jmdm. das Heft um die Ohren ~:** clout (coll.) *or* hit sb. round the ears with the exercise book [3] (ugs.: hineinschlagen) knock; **einen Nagel in die Wand ~:** knock a nail into the wall [4] (herstellen) carve ‹*figure, statue, etc.*› (**in** + *Akk.* in); cut, chop ‹*hole*›; (mit einem Hammer) knock ‹*hole*›; **Stufen in den Fels ~:** cut steps in the rock [5] (mit einer Waffe schlagen) **jmdn. aus dem Sattel/vom Pferd ~:** knock sb. out of the saddle/off his/her horse; **das haut mich vom Stuhl** *od.* **aus dem Anzug** (salopp) I'm [absolutely] staggered (coll.) [6] (salopp: schleudern) sling (coll.); fling; (nachlässig schreiben) stick (coll.), scrawl ‹*comments, signature*› (**in** + *Akk.* in, **unter** + *Akk.* underneath); **jmdm. eine 6 ins Zeugnis ~** (fig.) stick a 6 on sb.'s report (coll.) [7] (landsch.: fällen) fell; cut down [8] (Bergbau) cut ‹*coal, ore*›
B *unr. itr. V.* [1] (ugs.: prügeln) **hau doch nicht schon wieder!** don't belt me again!; **er haut immer gleich** he's quick to hit out [2] *auch unr.* (auf einen Körperteil) belt; hit; (mit der Faust auch) punch; (mit offener Hand auch) slap; smack; **jmdm. auf die Schulter ~:** slap *or* clap sb. on the shoulder; **jmdm. ins Gesicht ~:** belt/slap sb. in the face [3] (ugs.: auf/gegen etw. schlagen) thump; **mit der Faust auf den Tisch ~:** thump the table [with one's fist]; **auf die Tasten ~:** thump on the keys; **auf den Putz** *od.* **Pudding ~** (fig. salopp) run riot [4] *mit sein* (ugs.: stoßen) bump; **mit dem Kopf/Bein gegen etw. ~:** bang *or* hit *or* bump one's head/leg against sth. [5] *mit sein* (ugs.: auftreffen) **auf etw.** (*Akk.*) **~:** hit sth.
C *unr. refl. V.* [1] (ugs.: sich prügeln) have a punch-up (coll.) *or* a fight; fight [2] (salopp: sich setzen, legen) fling *or* throw oneself; **sich ins Bett ~:** hit the sack (coll.)

Hauer *der;* ~s, ~ [1] ▸❶ **S. 113** (Bergmannsspr.) faceworker [2] (Jägerspr.) tusk; (fig.) fang [3] (südd., österr.: Winzer) winegrower

Häufchen /ˈhɔyfçən/ *das;* ~s, ~: [small *or* little] pile *or* heap; **wie ein ~ Unglück** *od.* **Elend aussehen/dasitzen** (ugs.) look a/sit there looking a picture of misery; **nur noch ein ~ Unglück** *od.* **Elend sein** (ugs.) be nothing but a small bundle of misery

Haufe /ˈhaufə/ *der;* ~ns, ~n (veralt.) ▸**Haufen**

häufeln /ˈhɔyfl̩n/ *tr. V.* [1] (Gartenbau) earth *or* hill up [2] (zu Häufchen schichten) pile *or* heap up

häufen /ˈhɔyfn̩/
A *tr. V.* heap, pile (**auf** + *Akk.* on to); (aufheben) hoard ‹*money, supplies*›
B *refl. V.* (sich mehren) pile up; *s. auch* **gehäuft**

Haufen /ˈhaufn̩/ *der;* ~s, ~ [1] heap; pile; **ein ~ Erde/trockenes Stroh** *od.* **trockenen Strohs** a heap *or* pile of earth/dry straw; **etw. zu ~ aufschichten** stack sth. up in piles; **alles auf einen ~ werfen** throw everything in a heap; **der Hund hat da einen ~ gemacht** (ugs.) the dog has done his business there (coll.); **etw. über den ~ werfen** (ugs.) (aufgeben) chuck sth. in (coll.); (zunichte machen) mess sth. up; **jmdn. über den ~ fahren/rennen** (ugs.) knock sb. down; run sb. over; **jmdn. über den ~ schießen** *od.* **knallen** (ugs.) gun *or* shoot sb. down (coll.) [2] (ugs.: große Menge) heap (coll.); pile (coll.); load (coll.); **ein ~ Arbeit/Bücher** a load *or* heap *or* pile of work/books (coll.); loads *or* heaps *or* piles of work/books (coll.); **ein ~ Unsinn** a load of rubbish *or* nonsense (coll.); **ein ~ Geld** loads of money (coll.); **einen ~ Geld machen** make a packet (coll.) [3] (Ansammlung von Menschen) crowd; **so viele Idioten auf einem ~** (ugs.) so many idiots in one place [4] (Gruppe) crowd (coll.); bunch (coll.) [5] (Soldatenspr.) troop

haufen-, Haufen-: **~dorf** *das* Haufendorf (irregular conglomerate village); **~weise** *Adv.* (ugs.) **~weise Geld ausgeben/Eis essen** spend loads of money/eat heaps *or* loads of ice cream (coll.); **~wolke** *die* (Met.) cumulus [cloud]

häufig /ˈhɔyfɪç/
A *Adj.* frequent
B *adv.* frequently; often

Häufigkeit *die;* ~, ~**en** frequency

Häufigkeits·zahl *die,* **Häufigkeits·ziffer** *die* frequency

Häuflein /ˈhɔyflain/ *das;* ~**s,** ~ **1▸** (kleine Menge) ▸**Häufchen** **2▸** (kleine Gruppe) handful

Häufung *die;* ~, ~**en** increasing frequency; **in dieser ~:** in these large numbers; (so oft) with this high frequency

Haupt /haupt/ *das;* ~**[e]s, Häupter** /ˈhɔyptɐ/ **1▸** (geh.: Kopf) head; **bloßen** *od.* **entblößten ~es** with one's head bared; **erhobenen ~es** with one's head [held] high; **gesenkten ~es** with head bowed; **gekrönte Häupter** crowned heads; **an ~ und Gliedern** completely; **zu jmds. Häupten** (in Kopfhöhe) at head height; (bei einem Liegenden) at sb.'s head; **jmdn. aufs ~ schlagen** vanquish sb. **2▸** (geh.: wichtigste Person) head

haupt-, Haupt-: **~abnehmer** *der,* **~abnehmerin** *die* main *or* principal *or* chief customer; **der ~abnehmer eines Produktes** the main buyer of a product; **~achse** *die* **1▸** (beim Fahrzeug) main axle; **2▸** (Geom.) principal axis; **~aktion** *die* ▸~ **und Staatsaktion**; **~aktionär** *der* principal shareholder; **~akzent** *der* (Phon.) main *or* primary stress; (fig.) main emphasis; **~altar** *der* high altar; **~amtlich** **A** *Adj.* full-time; **B** *adv.* **~amtlich tätig sein** work full-time *or* on a full-time basis; **~angeklagte** *der/die* (Rechtsw.) main *or* principal defendant; **~anschluss**, ***~anschluß** *der* (Fernspr.) main exchange line; **~arbeit** *die* main part of the work; **~argument** *das* main *or* principal argument; **~attraktion** *die* main attraction; **~augenmerk** *das* closest attention; **sein ~augenmerk galt ...** (+ *Dat.*) he paid closest attention to ...; **~bahnhof** *der* main station; **Amsterdam ~bahnhof** Amsterdam Central; **~belastungszeuge** *der* (Rechtsw.) principal *or* main *or* chief prosecution witness; **~beruf** *der* main occupation *or* job; **er ist im ~beruf Schreiner** his main occupation *or* job is that of carpenter; **~beruflich** **A** *Adj.* **seine ~berufliche Tätigkeit** his main occupation; **B** *adv.* **er ist ~beruflich als Elektriker tätig** his main occupation is that of electrician; **~beschäftigung** *die* main occupation; **~buch** *das* (Kaufmannsspr.) ledger; **~darsteller** *der* (Theater, Film) leading man; male lead; **~darstellerin** *die* (Theater, Film) leading lady; female lead; **~deck** *das* main deck; **~eingang** *der* main entrance; **~einnahmequelle** *die* main *or* principal source of income; (eines Staates) main *or* principal source of revenue

Häuptel /ˈhɔyptl̩/ *das;* ~**s,** ~**[n]** (südd., österr.) head (*of cabbage/lettuce*); **ein ~ Salat/Kohl** a [head of] lettuce/cabbage

Haupt·erbe *der* principal heir

Hauptes·länge *die:* *in* **jmdn. um ~ überragen** (geh.) be a head taller than sb.

Haupt-: **~fach** *das* **1▸** (Universität) main subject; major; **etw. im ~fach studieren** study sth. as one's main subject; **2▸** (Schule) main subject; **~farbe** *die* main *or* principal colour; **~fehler** *der* main *or* principal *or* chief mistake/(im Charakter) fault/(in einer Theorie, einem Argument) flaw; **~feind** *der,* **~feindin** *die* main *or* principal *or* chief enemy; **~feld** *das* (Sport) [main] bunch; **~feldwebel** *der* ▸ i **S. 44** (Milit.) **1▸** ≈ staff sergeant (Brit.); ≈ sergeant first class (Amer.); **2▸** (hist.) company sergeant major; **~figur** *die* main *or* principal character; **~film** *der* main feature *or* film; **~forderung** *die* main *or* principal *or* chief demand; **~frage** *die* main question; (Angelegenheit) main question *or* issue; **~gang** *der* **1▸** main corridor; **2▸** ▸~**gericht**; **~gasleitung** *die* gas main; **~gebäude** *das* main building; **~gegenstand** *der* main *or* principal *or* chief subject; **~gericht** *das* main course; **~geschäft** *das* **1▸** (Laden) main branch; **2▸** (größter Umsatz) peak sales *pl.*; (wichtigster Geschäftszweig) main line; **~geschäfts·stelle** *die* head office; **~geschäfts·straße** *die* main shopping street; **~geschäfts·zeit** *die* peak shopping hours *pl.*; **~gewicht** *das* main emphasis; **~gewinn** *der* first *or* top prize; **~grund** *der* main *or* principal *or* chief reason; **~hahn** *der; Pl.* **~hähne,** (fachspr.) **~~en** mains stopcock; **~interesse** *das* main interest; **~kampf·linie** *die* (Milit.) front [line]; **~kasse** *die* main cash desk; **~katalog** *der* main catalogue; **~last** *die* main burden; **~leitung** *die* (Gas-, Wasserleitung) main; (Stromleitung) main[s *pl.*]; **~leute** ▸~**mann**

Häuptling /ˈhɔyptlɪŋ/ *der;* ~**s,** ~**e** chief[tain]; (iron. abwertend) bigwig (coll.)

haupt-, Haupt-: **~macht** *die* (veralt.) main body [of the army]; **~mahlzeit** *die* main meal; **~mangel** *der* main *or* principal defect; **~mann** *der; Pl.* **~leute** **1▸** ▸ i **S. 44** (Milit.) captain; **2▸** (hist.) leader; **~masse** *die* bulk; **~merkmal** *das* main *or* principal *or* chief characteristic; **~mieter** *der,* **~mieterin** *die* [main] tenant; **~motiv** *das* **1▸** (Gegenstand) main *or* principal motif; **2▸** (Beweggrund) main *or* principal *or* chief motive; **~nahrung** *die* staple *or* main food; **~nenner** *der* (Math.) common denominator; **~person** *die* central figure; **sie will immer und überall die ~person sein** (fig.) she always wants to be the centre of everything *or* of attention; **~portal** *das* main portal; **~post** *die,* **~post·amt** *das* main post office; **~probe** *die* ▸**Generalprobe 1**; **~problem** *das* main *or* chief problem; **~produkt** *das* main *or* chief product; **~programm** *das* main programme; **ein Sexfilm im ~programm** a sex film as the main feature; **~punkt** *der* main point; **~quartier** *das* (Milit., auch fig.) headquarters *sing. or pl.*; **~quelle** *die* main *or* principal *or* primary source; **~redner** *der,* **~rednerin** *die* main *or* principal speaker; **~reise·zeit** *die* high season; peak [holiday] season; **~rolle** *die* leading *or* main role; lead; **die ~rolle spielen** play the leading role *or* the lead (**in** + *Dat.* in); **die ~rolle [in** *od.* **bei etw.] spielen** (fig.) play the leading role [in sth.]; **~runde** *die* (Fußball) main round; **~sache** *die* main *or* most important thing; **~sache, du bist gesund** (ugs.) the main thing is, you're in good health; **in der ~sache** mainly; in the main; **~sächlich** **A** *Adv.* mainly; principally; chiefly; **B** *adj.* main; principal; chief; **~saison** *die* high season; **~satz** *der* **1▸** (Sprachw.) main clause; (allein stehend) sentence; **2▸** (Musik) first subject; **3▸** (grundlegender Satz) first *or* basic principle; **~schalter** *der* **1▸** (Elektrot.) mains switch; **2▸** (in der Bank, Post) main counter; **~schiff** *das* (Archit.) nave; **~schlagader** *die* aorta; **~schlüssel** *der* master key; pass key; **~schulabschluss**, ***~schul·abschluß** *der* ≈ secondary school leaving certificate; **~schuld** *die* main share of the blame; **die ~schuld an etw.** (*Dat.*) **haben** bear the main part of the blame for sth.; **~schuldige** *der/die* person mainly to blame; (an einem Verbrechen) main *or* chief offender

Haupt·schule, *die* ≈ secondary school

> **Hauptschule**
>
> The secondary school which prepares pupils for the *Hauptschulabschluss* (school-leaving certificate). The *Hauptschule* aims to give the least academically-inclined children a sound educational grounding. Pupils stay at the *Hauptschule* for 5 or 6 years after the **Grundschule**. See also **Schule, Lehre.**

haupt-, Haupt-: **~schüler** *der,* **~schülerin** *die* pupil at a *Hauptschule*; **~schullehrer** *der,* **~schul·lehrerin** *die* teacher at a *Hauptschule*; **~schwierigkeit** *die* main *or* chief difficulty; **~segel** *das* (Seemannsspr.) mainsail; **~seminar** *das* (Hochschulw.) advanced seminar; **~sicherung** *die* (Elektrot.) mains fuse; **~sitz** *der* head office; headquarters *pl.*; **~sorge** *die* main worry; **~stadt** *die* capital [city]; **~städter** *der,* **~städterin** *die* citizen *or* inhabitant of the capital; **~städtisch** *Adj.* metropolitan; **~straße** *die* ▸ i **S. 800** **1▸** (wichtigste Geschäftsstraße) high *or* main street; **2▸** (Durchgangsstraße) main road; **~strecke** *die* (Eisenb.) main line; **~stütze** *die* main support; (fig.) mainstay; **~sünde** *die* (kath. Rel.) cardinal sin; **~tätigkeit** *die* main *or* principal activity; **~teil** *der* major part; **~thema** *das* main topic *or* theme; (Musik) main theme; **~ton** *der; Pl.* **~töne** **1▸** (Musik) principal note; **2▸** ▸~**akzent**; **~treffer** *der* ▸~**gewinn**; **~tribüne** *die* (Sport) main stand; **~übel** *das* main *or* chief evil; **~- und Staatsaktion** *die:* *in* **eine ~- und Staatsaktion aus etw. machen** make a big thing *or* a meal of sth. (coll.); **~unterschied** *der* main *or* principal *or* chief difference; **~ursache** *die* main *or* principal *or* chief cause; **~verantwortlich** *Adj.* mainly responsible (**für** for); **~verantwortliche** *der/die* person mainly responsible; **~verdiener** *der,* **~verdienerin** *die* principal *or* main wage earner; breadwinner; **~verhandlung** *die* (Rechtsw.) main hearing

Haupt·verkehr *der* bulk of the traffic

Hauptverkehrs-: **~straße** *die* main road; **~zeit** *die* rush hour

Haupt-: **~versammlung** *die* (Wirtsch.) shareholders' meeting; **~verwaltung** *die* head office; **~wache** *die* main police station; **~wachtmeister** *der,* **~wachtmeisterin** *die* ▸**Polizeihauptwachtmeister**; **~werk** *das* **1▸** (eines Künstlers) major *or* most important work; **2▸** (zentrales Werk mit mehreren Teilbetrieben) main works *sing. or pl.*; **3▸** (an der Orgel) great organ; **~wohnsitz** *der* main place of residence; **~wort** *das; Pl.* **~wörter** (Sprachw.) noun; **~zeuge** *der,* **~zeugin** *die* principal *or* main *or* chief witness; **~zug** *der* **1▸** (Eisenbahnw.) scheduled train; **2▸** (wichtigste Eigenschaft) main *or* principal feature; **~zweck** *der* main *or* chief purpose *or* aim

hau ruck /ˈhauˈrʊk/ *Interj.* heave[-ho]

Haus /haus/ *das;* ~**es, Häuser** /ˈhɔyzɐ/ **1▸** house; (Firmengebäude) building; **~ an ~ wohnen** be next-door neighbours; **~ an ~ mit jmdm. wohnen** live next door to sb.; **er ist gerade aus dem ~ gegangen** he has just gone out; **im ~ spielen** play indoors; **kommt ins ~, es regnet** come inside, it's raining; **Herrn X, im ~e** (auf Briefen) to Mr X (*living in the same block of flats, working in the same firm, etc.*); **das ~ Gottes** (geh.) the house of God; **das Weiße ~:** the White House; **~ und Hof** house and home; **jmdm. ins ~ stehen** (ugs.) be in store for sb.; *s. auch* **öffentlich A**
2▸ (Heim) home; **jmdm. das ~ verbieten** not allow sb. in one's *or* the house; **etw. ins ~/frei ~ liefern** deliver sth. to sb.'s door/free of charge; **das ~ auf den Kopf stellen** (ugs.) turn the place upside down; **außer ~[e] sein/essen** be/eat out; **ist Ihre Frau im ~[e]?** is your wife at home?; **nach ~e** home; **zu ~e** at home; **ich bin für niemanden zu ~e** I'm not at home to anybody; **wie geht es zu ~e?** how are things at home?; **zu ~e anrufen** phone home; **fühlt euch wie zu ~e** make yourselves at home; **sich zu ~e fühlen** (fig.) feel at home; **schon dreißig, und er wohnt noch zu ~e** he's already thirty and he's still living with his parents; **bei ihnen zu ~e** in their house/flat; (in ihrer Heimat) where they come from; **dieser Brauch ist in Holstein zu ~e** this custom comes from Holstein; **zu ~e spielen** (Sport) play at home; **das ~ hüten** stay at home *or* indoors; **jmdm. das ~ einrennen** (ugs.) be constantly on sb.'s doorstep; **jmdm. ins ~ schneien** (ugs.) descend on sb.; **auf einem Gebiet/in etw.** (*Dat.*) **zu ~e sein** (ugs.) be at home in a field/in sth.
3▸ (Theater) theatre; (Publikum) house; **das große/kleine ~:** the large/small theatre; **vor vollen/ausverkauften Häusern spielen** play to full *or* packed houses
4▸ (Gasthof, Geschäft) **das erste ~ am Platze** the best shop of its kind/hotel in the town/village *etc.*; **eine Spezialität des ~es** a speciality of the house

[5] (Firma) firm; business house; **das ~ Meyer** the firm of Meyer
[6] (geh.: Parlament) **das Hohe ~:** the House; **beide Häuser [im Parlament]** both Houses [of Parliament]; **Hohes ~!** ≈ Mr Speaker, Sir
[7] (geh.: Familie) household; **der Herr/die Dame des ~es** the master/lady of the house; **aus gutem ~e kommen** come from a *or* be of good family; **der Herr im eigenen ~ sein** be master in one's own house; **Grüße von ~ zu ~:** regards from all of us to all of you; **von ~[e] aus** (von der Familie her) by birth; (eigentlich) really; actually
[8] (~halt) household; **jmdm. das ~ führen** keep house for sb.; **~ halten** (veralt.) keep house; **jmdn. ins ~ nehmen** take sb. in and look after him/her
[9] (Dynastie) house; **das ~ Tudor/[der] Hohenzollern** the House of Tudor/Hohenzollern
[10] (ugs.: die ~bewohner) occupants *pl.* [of the house]; **das ganze ~:** the whole house
[11] (ugs. scherzh.: Mensch) **ein gelehrtes/lustiges** *usw.* **~:** a scholarly/amusing *etc.* sort (coll.)
[12] (Schnecken~) shell
[13] (Astrol.) house
[14] **~ halten** (sparsam sein) be economical (**mit** with); **mit seinen Kräften ~ halten** conserve one's strength

haus-, Haus-: ~altar *der* domestic altar; **~angestellte** *der/die* domestic servant; **~antenne** *die* external aerial (Brit.) *or* (Amer.) antenna; **~anzug** *der* (für Männer) leisure suit; (für Frauen) pyjama suit; **~apotheke** *die* medicine cabinet; **~arbeit** *die* [1] housework; [2] (Schulw.) item of homework; **~arbeiten aufhaben** (ugs.) have homework *sing.*; **~arrest** *der* [1] house arrest; [2] (in der Familie) **er bestraft seinen Sohn mit ~arrest** he punishes his son by keeping him in; **mein Bruder hat ~arrest** my brother is being kept in; **~arzt** *der,* **~ärztin** *die* [1] family doctor; [2] (eines Hotels, Heims) resident doctor; **~aufgabe** *die* piece of homework; **~aufgaben aufhaben** (ugs.) have homework *sing.*; **~aufgaben·hilfe** *die* assistance with homework; **~aufgaben·überwachung** *die* homework supervision; **~aufsatz** *der* homework essay; **~backen** [A] *Adj.* plain; unadventurous, boring ‹*clothes*›; [B] *adv.* ‹*dress*› unadventurously; **~ball** *der* [private] dance (*held at sb.'s house*); **~bar** *die* [1] (Möbelstück) cocktail cabinet; [2] (kleine Bar) [home] bar; **~bau** *der* housebuilding; **beim ~bau** when building a/one's house; **mit dem ~bau beginnen** start building a/one's house; **~besetzer** *der,* **~besetzerin** *die* squatter; **~besetzung** *die* (Vorgang) squatting; (Ergebnis) squat; **~besitzer** *der* houseowner; (Vermieter) landlord; **~besitzerin** *die* houseowner; (Vermieterin) landlady; **~besorger** *der;* **~~s, ~~, ~besorgerin** *die;* **~~, ~~nen** (österr.) ▸**Hausmeister[in]**; **~besuch** *der* house call; **~bewohner** *der,* **~bewohnerin** *die* occupant [of the house]; **~boot** *das* houseboat; **~brand** *der* [1] (Material) domestic fuel; [2] (Prozess) domestic heating; **~bursche** *der* pageboy

Häuschen /ˈhɔysçən/ *das;* **~s, ~** [1] little *or* small house [2] **[ganz** *od.* **rein] aus dem ~ sein** (ugs.) be [completely] over the moon (coll.); **[ganz** *od.* **rein] aus dem ~ geraten** *od.* **fahren** (ugs.) go wild with excitement; **jmdn. aus dem ~ bringen** (ugs.) get sb. wildly excited [3] (ugs.: Toilette) privy

haus-, Haus-: ~dame *die* housekeeper; **~detektiv** *der,* **~detektivin** *die* house detective; **~diener** *der,* **~dienerin** *die* domestic servant; **~drachen** *der* (ugs. abwertend) dragon (coll.); **~durchsuchung** *die* (österr.) ▸**~suchung**; **~ecke** *die* corner of the house; **~eigen** *Adj.* **der ~eigene Kindergarten** the company's/hotel's *etc.* own kindergarten; **das Hotel hat einen ~eigenen Swimmingpool/Strand** the hotel has its own swimming pool/[private] beach; **~eigentümer** *der,* **~eigentümerin** *die* ▸**~besitzer**; **~einfahrt** *die* [1] drive[way] [of the house]; [2] (österr.) ▸**~eingang**; **~eingang** *der* entrance [to the house]

hausen *itr. V.* [1] (ugs. abwertend: wohnen) live [2] (ugs. abwertend: Verwüstungen anrichten) **[furchtbar] ~:** cause *or* wreak havoc; **wie die Wandalen ~:** behave like vandals [3] (schweiz.: sparen) be economical

Häuser-: ~block *der; Pl.* **~~s** *od.* **~blöcke** block [of houses]; **~kampf** *der* (Milit.) house-to-house fighting *no indef. art.*; **~makler** *der,* **~maklerin** *die* ▸ⓘ **S. 113** estate agent; **~meer** *das* mass of houses; **~reihe** *die* row of houses; (aneinander gebaut) terrace [of houses]

Haus-: ~fassade *die* house front; **~flagge** *die* (Seew.) house flag; **~flur** *der* hall[way]; entrance hall; (im Obergeschoss) landing

Haus·frau *die* ▸ⓘ **S. 113** [1] housewife [2] (südd., österr.) ▸**~besitzerin**

Hausfrauen-: ~art *die:* **in nach** *od.* **auf ~art** home-made-style *attrib.*; **~pflicht** *die* housewifely duty

hausfraulich *Adj.* housewifely; **ihre ~en Fähigkeiten** her abilities as a housewife

Haus·freund *der* [1] friend of the family; family friend [2] (verhüll.: Liebhaber) man friend (euphem.)

Haus·freundin *die* ▸**Hausfreund 1**

Haus·friede[n] *der* (in der Familie) domestic peace; (zwischen Hausbewohnern) good relationships *pl.* between the tenants

Hausfriedens·bruch *der* (Rechtsw.) trespass

haus-, Haus-: ~gans *die* domestic goose; **~gast** *der* resident; guest; **~gebrauch** *der* domestic use; **das reicht für den ~gebrauch** (ugs.) it's good enough to get by (coll.); **Spielst du Klavier? — Ja, aber nur für den ~gebrauch** Do you play the piano? — Yes, but only well enough to get by (coll.); **~geburt** *die* home birth; **~gehilfin** *die* [home] help; **~geist** *der* [1] (Gespenst) [resident] ghost; [2] (scherzh.: ~angestellte) **unser guter ~geist** our faithful housekeeper; **~gemacht** *Adj.* home-made; **~gemeinschaft** *die* [1] (gemeinsamer Haushalt) household; **in einer ~gemeinschaft mit jmdm. leben** live together with sb.; [2] (Bewohner eines Hauses) occupants *pl.* of the block; **~gerät** *das* [1] (veralt.) household articles *pl.*; [2] ▸**~haltsgerät**

-haushalt *der* (bes. Biol., Med.) balance

Haus·halt *der* [1] household; **einen ~ gründen/auflösen** set up home/break up a household [2] (Arbeit im ~) housekeeping; **jmdm. den ~ führen** keep house for sb.; **im ~ helfen** help with the housework [3] (Politik) budget

haus|halten ▸**Haus 8, 14**

Haushälterin *die;* **~, ~nen** housekeeper

haushälterisch
[A] *Adj.* economical
[B] *adv.* **~ mit etw. umgehen** be economical with sth.; use sth. economically

haushalts-, Haushalts-: ~artikel *der* household article; **billige ~artikel** cheap household articles *or* goods; **~auflösung** *die* house clearance; **bei einer ~auflösung** when a house/flat is cleared; **~ausgleich** *der* (Politik) **den ~ausgleich garantieren** guarantee a balanced budget; **einen ~ausgleich herbeiführen** balance the budget; **~buch** *das* housekeeping book; **~debatte** *die* (Politik) budget debate; **~defizit** *das* budgetary deficit; **~frage** *die* budgetary question *or* issue; **~führung** *die* housekeeping; **~geld** *das* housekeeping money; **~gerät** *das* household appliance; **~gesetz** *das* (Amtsspr.) budget legislation; **~hilfe** *die* home help; **~jahr** *das* [1] (Rechnungsjahr) financial year; [2] (Lehrzeit in einem Haushalt) **sie machte ein ~jahr** she spent a year with a family, learning how to keep house; **~kasse** *die* housekeeping money; **die ~kasse war leer** there was no housekeeping money left; **diese alte Schachtel dient uns als ~kasse** we use this old box to keep the housekeeping money in; **~loch** *das* (Wirtsch.) budget deficit; **~mittel** *Pl.* budgetary funds; **~packung** *die* family pack; **~plan** *der* budget; **~politik** *die* budgetary policy; **~politisch** [A] *Adj.* related to budgetary policy *postpos.*; **~politische Erwägungen** considerations of budgetary policy; [B] *adv.* **~politisch gesehen** from the point of view of the budget; **~volumen** *das* total budget; **~waage** *die* kitchen scales *pl.*; **~waren** *Pl.* household goods

Haushaltung *die* [1] ▸**Haushalt 1** [2] (Haushaltsführung) housekeeping

Haushaltungs-: ~kosten *Pl.* housekeeping costs; **~vorstand** *der* head of the household

haus-, Haus-: ~herr *der* [1] (Familienoberhaupt) head of the household; [2] (als Gastgeber) host; [3] (Rechtsspr.) (Eigentümer) owner; (Mieter) occupier; [4] (südd., österr.) ▸**~besitzer**; [5] (Sportjargon) **die ~herren** the hosts; the home team *sing.*; **~herrin** *die* [1] (Familienoberhaupt) lady of the house; [2] (als Gastgeberin) hostess; [3] (südd., österr.) ▸**~besitzerin**; **~hoch** [A] *Adj.* ‹*flames/waves etc.*› as high as a house; (fig.) overwhelming ‹*superiority etc.*›; **die ~hohe Favoritin** the hot favourite; [B] *adv.* **~hoch türmten sich die Wellen** the waves were mountainous; (fig.) **~hoch gewinnen/jmdn. ~hoch schlagen** win hands down/beat sb. hands down; **jmdm. ~hoch überlegen sein** be vastly superior to sb.; **~huhn** *das* domestic chicken; **~hund** *der* domestic dog

hausieren *itr. V.* **[mit etw.] ~:** hawk [sth.]; peddle [sth.]; **mit einer Idee ~ [gehen]** (ugs. abwertend) hawk an idea around; **„Hausieren verboten"** 'no hawkers'

Hausierer *der;* **~s, ~, Hausiererin** *die;* **~, ~nen** ▸ⓘ **S. 113** pedlar; hawker

haus-, Haus-: ~intern [A] *Adj.* internal ‹*regulations, purposes, information*›; ‹*agreement, custom*› within the company; [B] *adv.* internally; within the company; **~jacke** *die* casual [wrapover] jacket (*worn at home*); **~jurist** *der,* **~juristin** *die* firm's lawyer; company lawyer; **~kapelle**[1] *die* private chapel; **~kapelle**[2] *die* resident band; **~katze** *die* domestic cat; **~kleid** *das* house dress; **~konzert** *das* concert given at home; **~lehrer** *der,* **~lehrerin** *die* private tutor

häuslich /ˈhɔyslɪç/
[A] *Adj.* [1] domestic ‹*bliss, peace, affairs, duties, etc.*›; **am ~en Kaminfeuer** at one's own fireside; *s. auch* **Herd 1** [2] (das Zuhause liebend) home-loving
[B] *adv.* **sich [bei jmdm./irgendwo] ~ niederlassen** *od.* **einrichten** (ugs.) make oneself at home [in sb.'s house/somewhere]

Häuslichkeit *die;* **~:** domesticity

Hausmacher-: ~art *die:* **in nach ~art** home-made-style *attrib.*; **~wurst** *die* home-made sausage

Haus-: ~macht *die* (hist.) allodium; (fig.) power base; **~mädchen** *das* ▸ⓘ **S. 113** [home] help

Haus·mann *der* ▸ⓘ **S. 113** *man who stays at home and does the housework;* (Ehemann) house-husband

Hausmanns·kost *die* plain cooking

Haus-: ~mantel *der* housecoat; **~märchen** *das* folk tale; **die ~märchen der Brüder Grimm** Grimms' Fairy Tales; **~marke** *die* [1] (Wein, Sekt) house wine; [2] (ugs.: bevorzugtes Getränk) usual *or* favourite tipple (coll.); [3] (Markenfabrikat einer Firma) own brand; **~maus** *die* house mouse; **~meier** *der* (hist.) mayor of the palace; **~meister** *der,* **~meisterin** *die* ▸ⓘ **S. 113** [1] caretaker; [2] (schweiz.) ▸**Hausbesitzer[in]**; **~mitteilung** *die* [1] (im Büro) [internal] memo; [2] (für Kunden) company newsletter; **~mittel** *das* household remedy; **~musik** *die* music at home; **~musik machen** play music at home; **~mutter** *die; Pl.* **~mütter** housemother; **~mütterchen** *das* (ugs. scherzh.) little housewife; **~nummer** *die* ▸ⓘ **S. 143** house number; **ihre ~nummer** the number of her house; **~ordnung** *die* house rules *pl.*; **~partei** *die* (österr.) tenant; **~postille** *die* (hist.): *collection of religious and devotional sayings and stories for the family;* (fig. ugs.) organ; **~putz** *der* spring-clean; (regelmäßig) clean-out; **beim ~putz helfen** help with the regular cleaning-out; ~**putz halten** *od.* **machen** spring-clean the house

Hausordnung

These are the house rules a tenant has to adhere to in order to maintain a harmonious relationship with neighbours. They might include the maintenance of common areas and other specific requirements relating to cleanliness, uniformity and appearance within the house or apartment block; for example, a tenant should never hang washing from a front window. But usually the *Hausordnung*, whether written or unwritten, refers to restrictions on noise, possibly even including running a late-night bath.

Haus·rat *der* household goods *pl.*

Hausrat·versicherung *die* [household *or* home] contents insurance

Haus-: ~**recht** *das* (Rechtsw.): *right of a householder or owner of a property to forbid sb. entrance or order sb. to leave;* **von seinem ~recht Gebrauch machen** forbid sb. entrance/order sb. to leave; ~**rind** *das* domestic ox; ~**sammlung** *die* house-to-house *or* door-to-door collection; ~**schaf** *das* domestic sheep; ~**schlachtung** *die* home slaughtering; **aus eigener ~schlachtung stammen** be home-slaughtered; ~**schlüssel** *der* front-door key; house key; ~**schneiderin** *die* visiting seamstress; ~**schuh** *der* slipper; ~**schwamm** *der* (Pilz) dry rot; ~**schwein** *das* domestic pig

Hausse /ˈhoːs(ə)/ *die;* ~, ~**n** (Börsenw.) rise [in prices]; (fig.) boom; ~ **haben** rise [on the Stock Exchange]; **auf ~ spekulieren** bull; speculate for a rise

Haus·segen *der* house blessing (devotional inscription placed in a house); **bei ihnen hängt der ~ schief** (ugs. scherzh.) they've been having a row

Haussier /(h)oˈsi̯eː/ *der;* ~**s,** ~**s** (Börsenw.) bull

Haus·stand *der* household; **einen [eigenen] ~ gründen** set up home [on their own]; **sie führt einen eigenen ~** she lives independently

Haussuchung *die;* ~, ~**en** house search

Haussuchungs·befehl *der* search warrant

Haus-: ~**technik** *die* domestic electrical and plumbing systems; ~**telefon** *das* internal telephone; ~**tier** *das* 1 pet; 2 (Nutztier) domestic animal; ~**tochter** *die: young girl living with a family in order to learn how to keep house;* ~**tor** *das* front entrance; ~**tür** *die* front door; **etw. direkt vor der ~tür haben** (ugs. fig.) have sth. on one's doorstep; ~**tyrann** *der,* ~**tyrannin** *die* (ugs.) tyrant [in one's own home]; ~**vater** *der* 1 (in einem Heim) housefather; (in einer Jugendherberge) warden; 2 (veralt.: Familienvater) paterfamilias; ~**verbot** *das* ban on entering the house/pub/restaurant *etc.;* ~**verbot haben/bekommen** be banned [from the house/pub/restaurant *etc.*]; **jmdm. ~verbot erteilen** ban sb. [from the house/pub/restaurant *etc.*]; ~**versammlung** *die* (DDR) tenants' meeting; ~**verwalter** *der,* ~**verwalterin** *die* manager [of the block]; ~**verwaltung** *die* management [of the block]; ~**wand** *die* [house] wall; ~**wart** *der;* ~~**[e]s,** ~~**e,** ~**wartin** *die;* ~~, ~~**nen** (landsch.) caretaker; ~**wesen** *das* (veralt.) household; ~**wirt** *der* landlord; ~**wirtin** *die* landlady

Haus·wirtschaft *die* 1 domestic science and home economics 2 (DDR Landw.) **individuelle** *od.* **persönliche ~:** *cooperative farmer's personal holding of land, buildings livestock, and equipment*

hauswirtschaftlich

A *Adj.* domestic; ~**e Kenntnisse** knowledge of domestic matters

B *adv.* ~ **interessiert/begabt** interested/talented in domestic matters

Hauswirtschafts-: ~**lehrerin** *die* ▸ⓘ **S. 113** domestic science and home economics teacher; ~**leiterin** *die* housekeeper; ~**schule** *die* college of domestic science and home economics

Haus-: ~**zelt** *das* ridge tent; ~**zins** *der; Pl.* ~~**e** (südd., schweiz.) ▸ **Miete**[1] **1**

Haut /haut/ *die;* ~, **Häute** /ˈhɔytə/ 1 ▸ⓘ **S. 435** skin; **sich** (*Dat.*) **die ~ abschürfen** graze oneself; **viel ~ zeigen** (ugs. scherzh.) show a lot of bare flesh (coll.); **nass bis auf die ~:** soaked to the skin; wet through; **nur noch ~ und Knochen sein** (ugs.), **nur noch aus ~ und Knochen bestehen** (ugs.) be nothing but skin and bone; **seine eigene ~ retten** save one's own skin; **seine ~ zu Markte tragen** (ugs.) risk one's neck (coll.); **seine ~ so teuer wie möglich verkaufen** (ugs.) sell oneself as dearly as possible; **sich seiner ~** (*Gen.*) **wehren** (ugs.) stand up for oneself; **aus der ~ fahren** (ugs.) go up the wall (coll.); **es ist zum Aus-der-~-Fahren** it's enough to drive *or* send you up the wall (coll.); **er/sie kann nicht aus seiner/ihrer ~ heraus** (ugs.) a leopard cannot change its spots (prov.); **sich in seiner ~ nicht wohl fühlen** (ugs.) feel uneasy; (unzufrieden sein) feel discontented [with one's lot]; **sich in seiner ~ wohl fühlen** (ugs.) feel contented [with one's lot]; **ich möchte nicht in deiner ~ stecken** (ugs.) I shouldn't like to be in your shoes (coll.); **mit heiler ~ davonkommen** (ugs.) get away with it; **jmdm. mit ~ und Haar[en] verfallen sein** (ugs.) be head over heels in love with sb.; **sich einer Aufgabe** (*Dat.*) **mit ~ und Haar[en] verschreiben** (ugs.) devote oneself completely *or* wholeheartedly to a task; **jmdm. unter die ~ gehen** (ugs.) get under sb.'s skin (coll.) 2 (Fell) skin; (von größerem Tier auch) hide; **auf der faulen ~ liegen** (ugs.) sit around and do nothing; **sich auf die faule ~ legen** (ugs.) sit back and do nothing 3 (Schale) skin 4 (dünne Schicht, Bespannung) skin 5 (Mensch) **eine gute/ehrliche ~:** a good/honest sort (coll.)

Haut-: ~**abschürfung** *die* graze; ~**arzt** *der,* ~**ärztin** *die* ▸ⓘ **S. 113** skin specialist; dermatologist; ~**atmung** *die* (Med., Zool.) cutaneous respiration; ~**ausschlag** *der* [skin] rash

Häutchen /ˈhɔytçən/ *das;* ~**s,** ~ 1 ▸ **Haut 3**: piece of skin 2 ▸ **Haut 4**: thin skin

Haut·creme *die* skin cream

Haute Couture /(h)oːtkuˈtyːɐ̯/ *die;* ~**:** haute couture

häuten /ˈhɔytn̩/

A *tr. V.* skin, flay ‹*animal*›; skin ‹*tomato, almond, etc.*›

B *refl. V.* shed its skin/their skins; ‹*snake*› shed *or* slough its skin

haut·eng *Adj.* skintight

Hautevolee /(h)oːtvoˈleː/ *die;* ~ (abwertend) upper crust (coll.)

haut-, Haut-: ~**falte** *die* fold [of skin]; ~**farbe** *die* [skin] colour; **wegen seiner ~farbe** because of the colour of his skin; ~**farben** *Adj.* skin-coloured; flesh-coloured; ~**freundlich** *Adj.* kind to the/one's skin *pred.*

-häutig /-ˈhɔytɪç/ *Adj.* -skinned

haut-, Haut-: ~**jucken** *das* itching *no indef. art.;* ~**krankheit** *die* skin disease; ~**krebs** *der* skin cancer; ~**nah** **A** *Adj.* 1 (unmittelbar) immediate ‹*contact*›; eyeball-to-eyeball ‹*confrontation*›; 2 (ugs.: packend, anschaulich) realistic and gripping ‹*description*›; 3 (Anat.) close to *or* immediately below the skin *postpos.;* **B** *adv.* 1 (unmittelbar) **mit etw. ~nah in Berührung/Kontakt kommen** come into very close contact with sth.; **jmdn. ~nah decken** *od.* **bewachen** (Sport Jargon) mark sb. very tightly *or* closely; (sehr eng) ~**nah tanzen** dance very close together; 2 (ugs.: packend, anschaulich) **etw. ~nah beschreiben** describe sth. in a realistic and gripping way; ~**öl** *das* body oil; ~**pflege** *die* skin care; ~**pilz** *der* fungus parasitic on the skin; cutaneous fungus (Med.); ~**reizung** *die* skin irritation; ~**schere** *die* cuticle scissors *pl.;* ~**schicht** *die* layer of skin; ~**schonend** *Adj.* kind to the/one's skin *pred.;* ~**transplantation** *die* (Med.) skin graft; ~**typ** *der* skin type

Häutung *die;* ~, ~**en** 1 ▸ **häuten A**: skinning; flaying 2 (das Sichhäuten) **Schlangen machen viele ~en durch** snakes shed *or* slough their skin many times; **eine Eidechse bei der ~:** a lizard shedding its skin

haut·verträglich *Adj.* kind to the/one's skin *pred.*

Havanna[1] /haˈvana/ *(das);* ~**s** ▸ⓘ **S. 675** Havana

Havanna[2] *die;* ~, ~**[s], Havanna·zigarre** *die* Havana [cigar]

Havarie /havaˈriː/ *die;* ~, ~**n** (Seew., Flugw., österr. auch: ~ eines Autos) accident; (Schaden) damage *no indef. art.;* average (Ins.); (fig.) breakdown

havarieren *itr. V.* (Seew., Flugw.) ‹*aircraft*› crash; ‹*ship*› have an accident; **zwei Militärmaschinen**/(österr.) **Autos havarierten** two military planes/cars collided; **ein havariertes Schiff** a damaged ship

Havarist *der;* ~**en,** ~**en** (Seew.) 1 (Schiff) damaged ship 2 (Eigentümer) owner of a/the damaged ship

Havaristin *die;* ~, ~**nen** ▸ **Havarist 2**

Hawaii /haˈvai̯/ *(das);* ~**s** Hawaii

Hawaii-: ~**gitarre** *die* Hawaiian guitar; ~**insein**, ~**-Inseln** *Pl.* Hawaiian Islands

hawaiisch *Adj.* Hawaiian

Haxe *die;* ~, ~**n** ▸ **Hachse**

H-Bombe /ˈhaː-/ *die* H-bomb

H-Dur /ˈhaː-/ *das* (Musik) B major; *s. auch* **A-Dur**

he /heː/ *Interj.* (ugs.) 1 (Zuruf, Ausruf) hey; ~ **[du], komm mal her!** hey [you], come here! 2 (zur Verstärkung einer Frage) eh

Headset /ˈhɛtsɛt/ *das;* ~**s,** ~**s** headset

Hearing /ˈhɪərɪŋ/ *das;* ~**[s],** ~**s** (bes. Politik) hearing

Heb·amme *die* ▸ⓘ **S. 113** midwife

Hebe-: ~**balken** *der,* ~**baum** *der* lever; ~**bühne** *die* hydraulic lift; ~**figur** *die* (Eis-, Rollkunstlauf) lift

Hebel /ˈheːbl̩/ *der;* ~**s,** ~ (auch Griff, Physik) lever; **den ~ ansetzen** position the lever; **da müssen wir den ~ ansetzen** (fig.) that's where we've got to start (coll.); **alle ~ in Bewegung setzen** (ugs.) move heaven and earth; **am längeren ~ sitzen** (ugs.) have the whip hand

Hebel-: ~**arm** *der* (Physik) lever arm; ~**gesetz** *das* (Physik) principle of the lever; ~**griff** *der* (Ringen) lever [hold]; ~**kraft** *die* leverage; ~**wirkung** *die* leverage

heben /ˈheːbn̩/

A *unr. tr. V.* 1 (nach oben bewegen) lift; raise ‹*baton, camera, glass*›; **eine Last ~:** lift a load; **die Hand/den Arm ~:** raise one's hand/arm; **schlurft nicht, hebt die Füße!** pick your feet up!; **100 kg/einen Rekord ~** (Sport) lift 100 kg./a record weight; **die Stimme ~** (geh.) raise one's voice; **einen ~** (ugs.) have a drink 2 (an eine andere Stelle bringen) lift; **jmdn. auf die Schulter/von der Mauer ~:** lift sb. [up] on to one's shoulders/[down] from the wall 3 (heraufholen) dig up ‹*treasure etc.*›; raise ‹*wreck*› 4 (verbessern) raise, improve ‹*standard, level*›; increase ‹*turnover, self-confidence*›; improve ‹*mood*›; enhance ‹*standing*›; boost ‹*morale*› 5 (unpers.) **es hebt jmdm. den Magen** sb.'s stomach heaves; **es hebt mich, wenn ich das sehe** it turns me over to see it (coll.)

B *unr. refl. V.* 1 (geh.: sich recken, sich erheben) rise; **sich auf die Zehenspitzen ~:** stand on tiptoe 2 (hochgehen, hochsteigen) rise; ‹*curtain*› rise, go up; ‹*mist, fog*› lift; **sich ~ und senken** rise and fall 3 ‹*sea, chest*› rise and fall, heave 4 (sich verbessern) ‹*mood*› improve; ‹*trade*› pick up; ‹*standard, level*› rise, improve, go up 5 (geh.: emporragen) rise [up]

Heber *der;* ~**s,** ~ 1 (Technik) jack 2 (Chemie) pipette 3 (Sport: Gewicht~) weightlifter

-hebig /-heːbɪç/ (Verslehre) -footed

Hebräer /heˈbrɛːɐ/ *der;* ~**s,** ~, **Hebräerin** *die;* ~, ~**nen** Hebrew

h

h

Hebraicum /he'bra:ikʊm/ *das;* **~s** qualifying examination in Hebrew (taken by theology students); **das ~ haben** have passed the Hebrew examination

hebräisch *Adj.* ▸❶ **S. 670** Hebrew

Hebung *die;* **~, ~en** [1] (Bergung) **die ~ eines Schiffes** the raising of a ship; **bei der ~ des Schatzes ...** when the treasure is/was dug up ... [2] (Verbesserung) raising; improvement; **zur ~ des Selbstvertrauens/der Moral** to improve sb.'s self-confidence/morale [3] (Geol.) uplift [4] (Verslehre) stressed syllable

Hechel /'hɛçl̩/ *die;* **~, ~n** (Landw.) card; hackle; heckle

Hechelei *die;* **~, ~en** (ugs. abwertend) backbiting *no pl.;* (Klatsch) gossip *no pl.*

hecheln¹
A *itr. V.* (ugs. abwertend) gossip
B *tr. V.* (Landw.) card; hackle; heckle

hecheln² *itr. V.* pant [for breath]

Hecht /hɛçt/ *der;* **~[e]s, ~e** [1] pike; **der ~ im Karpfenteich sein** (ugs.) be a new broom; be a live wire full of new ideas; (die erste Rolle spielen) be the kingpin [2] (ugs.: Bursche) **ein toller ~:** an incredible fellow [3] (Tabaksqualm) fug (coll.).

hechten *itr. V.; mit sein* dive headlong; make a headlong dive; (schräg nach oben) throw oneself sideways; (Schwimmen) perform *or* do a racing dive; (vom Sprungturm) perform *or* do a pike-dive; (Turnen) do a long fly

Hecht-: **~rolle** *die* (Turnen) piked roll; **~sprung** *der* [1] (Turnen) Hecht vault; [2] (Schwimmen) racing dive; (vom Sprungturm) pike-dive; **~suppe** *die:* in **es zieht wie ~suppe** (ugs.) there's a terrible draught (coll.)

Heck¹ /hɛk/ *das;* **~[e]s, ~e** *od.* **~s** [1] (Schiffs~) stern [2] (Flugzeug~) tail; **im ~ der Maschine** at the rear of the plane [3] (Auto~) rear; back

Heck² *das;* **~[e]s, ~e** (nordd.) gate

Heck·antrieb *der* (Kfz-W.) rear-wheel drive

Hecke *die;* **~, ~n** [1] hedge [2] (wild wachsend) thicket

Hecken-: **~landschaft** *die* landscape of fields and hedgerows; **~rose** *die* dogrose; **~schere** *die* hedge shears *pl.;* (elektrisch) hedge trimmer; **~schütze** *der,* **~schützin** *die* sniper

heck-, Heck-: **~fenster** *das* rear *or* back window; **~flosse** *die* tail fin; **~lastig** /-lastɪç/ **A** *Adj.* tail-heavy; **B** *adv.* **das Auto reagiert ~lastig** the car tends to be tail-heavy

Heckmeck /'hɛkmɛk/ *der;* **~s** (ugs. abwertend) [1] (Getue) fuss [2] (Unsinn) rubbish

Heck-: **~motor** *der* rear engine; **~scheibe** *die* rear *or* back window; **~tür** *die* back

heda /'he:da/ *Interj.* (veralt.) I say

Hederich /'he:dərɪç/ *der;* **~s, ~e** (Bot.) jointed charlock

Hedonismus /hedo'nɪsmʊs/ *der;* **~** (Philos.) hedonism *no art.*

Hedonist *der;* **~en, ~en, Hedonistin** *die;* **~, ~nen** (Philos.) hedonist

hedonistisch *Adj.* hedonistic

Hedschra /'hɛdʒra/ *die;* **~:** Hegira

Heer /he:ɐ̯/ *das;* **~[e]s, ~e** [1] (Gesamtheit der Streitkräfte) armed forces *pl.;* **das stehende ~:** the standing army; **in das ~ eintreten** join the services [2] (für den Landkrieg) army [3] (fig.: große Anzahl) army

Heeres-: **~bericht** *der* (Milit.) military communiqué; **~bestände** *Pl.* army supplies *or* stores; **~dienst** *der* military service; **~leitung** *die* (Milit.) army command staff; **die oberste ~leitung** the high command; **~reform** *die* army reform

Heer-: **~führer** *der* army commander; **~lager** *das* army camp; **~schar** *die* (veralt., noch fig.) host (arch.); *s. auch* **himmlisch A 1;** **~straße** *die* (veralt.) military road; **~wesen** *das* armed forces *pl.*

Hefe /'he:fə/ *die;* **~, ~n** [1] yeast; (fig.) driving force [2] (geh. abwertend: Abschaum) scum

Hefe-: **~gebäck** *das* pastry (*made with yeast dough*); **~kloß** *der* dumpling made with yeast dough; **aufgehen** *od.* **auseinander gehen wie ein ~kloß** (ugs. scherzh.) blow up like a balloon; **~kuchen** *der* yeast cake; **~pilz** *der* yeast fungus; **~teig** *der* yeast dough; **~zopf** *der* plaited bun

Heft¹ /hɛft/ *das;* **~[e]s, ~e** (geh.) (am Dolch, Messer) haft; handle; (am Schwert) hilt; **das ~ ergreifen** *od.* **in die Hand nehmen** (geh.) take control; **das ~ in der Hand haben/behalten** (geh.) be in/keep control; **jmdm. das ~ aus der Hand nehmen** (geh.) take control from sb.

Heft² *das;* **~[e]s, ~e** [1] (bes. Schule) exercise book [2] (Nummer einer Zeitschrift) issue; **Jahrgang 10, ~ 12** Volume 10, No. 12 [3] (kleines Buch) (small stapled) book

Heftchen *das;* **~s, ~** [1] (Comic) comic; (Groschenroman) novelette [2] (Block) book [of tickets/stamps *etc.*]

heften
A *tr. V.* [1] (mit einer Nadel) pin; fix; (mit einer Klammer) clip; fix; (mit Klebstoff) stick; **etw. an/in etw.** (*Akk.*) **~:** pin/stick/clip sth. to/into sth.; **etw. in einen Ordner ~:** put *or* insert sth. in[to] a file [2] (richten) **die Augen/den Blick auf jmdn./etw. ~:** fasten one's eyes/gaze on sb./sth. [3] (Schneiderei) tack; baste [4] (Buchbinderei) stitch; (mit Klammern) staple
B *refl. V.* [1] (verfolgen) **sich an jmds. Fersen** (*Akk.*) **~:** stick hard on sb.'s heels; **sich an jmds. Spur** (*Akk.*) **~:** get on the track of sb. [2] (geh.: knüpfen) **sich an etw.** (*Akk.*) **~:** be linked with sth. [3] (richten) ‹*eyes, look*› be fixed (**auf** + *Akk.* on)

Hefter *der;* **~s, ~:** [loose-leaf] file

Heft·garn *das* tacking thread; basting thread

heftig
A *Adj.* [1] violent ‹*storm, explosion, struggle, collision, argument, movement, passion*›; heavy ‹*rain, shower, blow*›; intense, burning ‹*hatred, desire*›; fierce ‹*controversy, criticism, competition*›; severe ‹*pain, cold*›; loud ‹*bang*›; rapid ‹*breathing*›; bitter ‹*weeping*› [2] (unbeherrscht) violent ‹*reaction, manner*›; ‹*person*› with a violent temper; heated, vehement ‹*tone, words*›; **~ werden/gleich ~ sein** fly into a temper/flare up
B *adv.* [1] ‹*rain, snow, breathe*› heavily; ‹*hit*› hard; ‹*hurt*› a great deal; ‹*quarrel, shiver*› violently; **~ weinen** bawl; cry loudly; **sich ~ verlieben** fall passionately *or* (coll.) madly in love [2] (unbeherrscht) ‹*answer*› angrily, heatedly; ‹*react*› angrily, violently

Heftigkeit *die;* **~** [1] ▸**heftig 1:** violence; heaviness; intensity; fierceness; severity; loudness; rapidity; bitterness [2] (Unbeherrschtheit) vehemence

Heft-: **~klammer** [1] staple; [2] ▸**Büroklammer;** **~maschine** *die* stapler; (Buchbinderei) stitcher; **~pflaster** *das* sticking plaster; **~zwecke** *die;* **~~, ~~n** ▸**Reißzwecke**

Hege /'he:gə/ *die;* **~** (Forstw., Jagdw.) care and protection; (fig.) care

Hegelianer /he:gə'li̯a:nɐ/ *der;* **~s, ~,** **Hegelianerin** *die;* **~, ~nen** Hegelian

hegelianisch *Adj.* Hegelian

Hegelianismus *der;* **~:** Hegelianism *no art.*

hegelsch, *Hegelsch /'he:gl̩ʃ/ *Adj.* Hegelian; **die ~e Staatsphilosophie** Hegel's political philosophy

hegemonial /hegemo'ni̯a:l/ *Adj.* hegemonic

Hegemonie /hegemo'ni:/ *die;* **~, ~n** /-ən/ hegemony

hegen *tr. V.* [1] (bes. Forstw., Jagdw.) look after, tend ‹*plants, animals*› [2] (geh.: umsorgen) look after; take care of; preserve ‹*old customs*›; **jmdn./etw. ~ und pflegen** lavish care and attention on sb./sth. [3] (in sich tragen) feel ‹*contempt, hatred, mistrust*›; cherish ‹*hope, wish, desire*›; harbour, nurse ‹*grudge, suspicion*›; **eine Abneigung gegen/eine gewisse Achtung für jmdn. ~:** have a dislike/a certain respect for sb.; **ich hege den Verdacht, dass ...** I have a suspicion that ...; **große Zweifel [an etw.** (Dat)**] ~:** have *or* entertain grave doubts [about sth.]

Hehl /he:l/ *in* **kein[en] ~ aus etw. machen** make no secret of sth.; **er macht kein[en] ~ daraus, dass ...** he makes no secret of the fact that ...

Hehler *der;* **~s, ~:** receiver [of stolen goods]; fence (coll.)

Hehlerei *die;* **~, ~en** (Rechtsw.) receiving [stolen goods] *no art.*

hehr /he:ɐ̯/ *Adj.* (geh.) majestic ‹*sight*›; glorious ‹*moment*›; noble ‹*ideal*›

hei /hai̯/ *Interj.* **~, war das eine Fahrt!** wow, what a trip!; **~, ist das ein Spaß!** oh *or* hey, what fun!

heia /'hai̯a/ (Kinderspr.) *in* **~ machen** go bye-byes *or* beddy-byes (child lang.)

Heia *die;* **~, ~[s], Heia·bett** *das* (Kinderspr.) bye-byes, beddy-byes (child lang.); **ab in die ~:** off to bye-byes *or* beddy-byes

heiapopeia *Interj.* ▸**eiapopeia**

Heide¹ /'hai̯də/ *der;* **~n, ~n** heathen; pagan; **das Kind ist ein kleiner ~:** the child is a little heathen

Heide² *die;* **~, ~n** [1] moor; heath; (~landschaft) moorland; heathland; **die Lüneburger ~:** the Luneburg Heath [2] ▸**~kraut**

Heide-: **~kraut** *das* heather; ling; **~land** *das* moorland; heathland

Heidel·beere /'hai̯dl̩-/ *die* bilberry; blueberry; whortleberry; **in die ~n gehen** (ugs.) go picking bilberries *etc.*

Heiden-: **~angst** *die* (ugs.) **eine ~angst vor etw.** (*Dat.*) **haben** be scared stiff of sth. (coll.); **er hatte eine ~angst vor der Fahrprüfung** he was in a blue funk about the driving test (coll.); **~arbeit** *die* (ugs.) a heck of a lot of work (coll.); **~geld** *das* (ugs.) a packet (coll.); a heck of a lot of money (coll.); **~krach** *der* (ugs.) [1] ▸**~lärm;** [2] (Streit) flaming row (coll.); **~lärm** *der* (ugs.) unholy *or* dreadful din *or* row (coll.); dreadful racket (coll.); **~mission** *die* missionary work; **~respekt** *der* (ugs.) healthy respect (**vor** + *Dat.* for); **~röschen** *das* ▸**Heideröschen 2;** **~schreck** *der* (ugs.) terrible fright (coll.); **ihr habt mir einen ~schreck eingejagt** you frightened the life out of me (coll.); **~spaß** *der* (ugs.) terrific fun (coll.); **es macht einen ~spaß** it's terrific fun (coll.); **~spektakel** *der* (ugs.) (Lärm) unholy *or* dreadful din *or* row (coll.); (Aufregung) great *or* (coll.) dreadful commotion; **~tempel** *der* heathen *or* pagan temple

Heidentum *das;* **~s** [1] (Zustand) heathenism; paganism [2] (die Heiden) the heathen *pl. or* pagans *pl.;* **das westliche ~:** the infidels *pl.* in the West

Heide·röschen *das* [1] rock rose (of genus Fumana) [2] (veralt.: Hundsrose) dogrose

heidi /hai̯'di:/ *Interj.* **[und] ~ begann die wilde Fahrt** away he/they *etc.* went; **~ gings den Berg hinunter** away he/they *etc.* went down the hill

Heidin *die;* **~, ~nen** heathen; pagan

heidnisch
A *Adj.* heathen; pagan
B *adv.* **~ leben** live a heathen *or* pagan life

Heid·schnucke *die;* **~, ~n** German Heath [sheep]

heikel /'hai̯kl̩/ *Adj.* [1] (schwierig) delicate, ticklish ‹*matter, subject*›; ticklish, awkward, tricky ‹*problem, question, situation*› [2] (wählerisch, empfindlich) finicky, fussy, fastidious (**in Bezug auf** + *Akk.* about); **in allen Dingen der Hygiene ist sie sehr ~:** she is very particular in all matters of hygiene

heil /hai̯l/ *Adj.* [1] (unverletzt) unhurt, unharmed ‹*person*›; **ein Wunder, dass seine Knochen ~ geblieben sind** it's a wonder he didn't break any bones; **~ ankommen** arrive safely *or* safe and sound; **etw. ~ überstehen** survive sth. unscathed; **sollte ich diese Angelegenheit ~ überstehen** (fig.) if I come out of this affair without getting my fingers burned; **aus etw. ~ herauskommen** come through sth. safely *or* unscathed; (fig.) survive sth.; *s. auch* **Haut 1** [2] (wieder gesund) **~ werden/wieder ~ sein** ‹*injured part*› heal [up]/have healed [up] [3] (nicht entzwei) intact; in one piece; **er hat nicht ein einziges ~es Hemd** he hasn't got a single shirt that doesn't need mending; **es**

gab nur noch wenige ~e Häuser only a few houses were undamaged; **eine ~e Welt** (fig.) an ideal *or* a perfect world

Heil *das;* ~**s** [1] (Wohlergehen) benefit; **sein ~ in etw.** *(Dat.)* **suchen** seek one's salvation in sth.; **bei jmdm./irgendwo sein ~ versuchen** try one's luck with sb./somewhere; **~ Hitler!** (ns.) heil Hitler!; **sein ~ in der Flucht suchen** seek refuge in flight; *s. auch* **Berg 1**; **Petri Heil**; **Ski** [2] (Rel.) salvation

Heiland /'hailant/ *der;* ~**[e]s,** ~**e** [1] (Christus) Saviour; Redeemer [2] (geh.: Retter) saviour

Heil-: ~**anstalt** *die* [1] (Anstalt für Kranke od. Süchtige) sanatorium; [2] (psychiatrische Klinik) mental hospital *or* home; ~**bad** *das* [1] (Kurort) spa; watering place; [2] (medizinisches Bad) medicinal bath

heilbar *Adj.* curable

Heilbarkeit *die;* ~: curability

heil·bringend *Adj.* saving; redeeming; **die ~e Botschaft** the message of salvation *or* redemption

Heil·butt *der* halibut

heilen

[A] *tr. V.* [1] ▸❶ **S. 439** cure ‹*disease*›; heal ‹*wound*›; **jmdn. ~:** cure sb.; restore sb. to health [2] (befreien) **jmdn. von etw. ~:** cure sb. of sth.; **davon/von ihm bin ich geheilt** (ugs.) I've been cured of it/my attachment to him

[B] ▸❶ **S. 439** *itr. V.; mit sein* ‹*wound*› heal [up]; ‹*infection*› clear up; ‹*fracture*› mend

Heiler *der;* ~**s,** ~ healer

heil-, Heil-: ~**erde** *die: pulverized earth with therapeutic properties, used in treating skin diseases and intestinal complaints;* ~**erfolg** *der* success (*of cure etc.*); **zum ~erfolg führen** lead to a successful cure

Heilerin *die;* ~, ~**nen** [female] healer

Heil-: ~**fasten** *das;* ~**fastens** fasting cure; ~**froh** *Adj.* very *or* (Brit. coll.) jolly glad; ~**gymnastik** *die* ▸**Krankengymnastik**

heilig *Adj.* [1] holy; **der Heilige Vater** the Holy Father; **der Heilige Stuhl** the Holy See; **die Heilige Jungfrau** the Blessed Virgin; **die ~e Barbara/der ~e Augustinus** Saint Barbara/Saint Augustine; **die Heilige Familie/Dreifaltigkeit** the Holy Family/Trinity; **der Heilige Geist** the Holy Spirit; **die Heiligen Drei Könige** the Three Kings *or* Wise Men; the Magi; **die ~e Taufe/Messe** Holy Baptism/Mass; **der ~e Sonntag** the Sabbath; **die Heilige Schrift** the Holy Scriptures *pl.*; **die Heilige Allianz** (hist.) the Holy Alliance; **das Heilige Römische Reich** (hist.) the Holy Roman Empire; **jmdn. ~ sprechen** canonize sb. [2] (besonders geweiht) holy; sacred; **~e Stätten** holy *or* sacred places; **der Heilige Abend/die Heilige Nacht** Christmas Eve/Night; **das Heilige Land** the Holy Land [3] (geh.: unantastbar) sacred ‹*right, tradition, cause, etc.*›; sacred, solemn ‹*duty*›; gospel ‹*truth*›; solemn ‹*conviction, oath*›; righteous ‹*anger, zeal*›; awed ‹*silence*›; **etw. ist jmdm. ~:** sth. is sacred to sb.; **bei allem, was mir ~ ist** by all that I hold sacred; **etw. ~ halten** keep *or* observe sth.; *s. auch* **hoch B 4** [4] (ugs.: groß) incredible (coll.); healthy ‹*respect*›; **seine ~e Not mit jmdm. haben** have a lot of trouble *or* a hard time with sb. [5] (veralt.: fromm) [extremely] devout *or* pious

Heilig·abend *der* Christmas Eve; *s. auch* **Weihnachten**

Heilige *der/die; adj. Dekl.* saint; **ein sonderbarer** *od.* **komischer ~r** (ugs. iron) a queer fish (coll.)

> **Heilige Drei Könige**
>
> Epiphany or Twelfth Night (6 January) is a public holiday in Austria and parts of southern Germany. In some places children dress up as the Three Kings and go from house to house to bless the homes for the coming year and collect money for charity. This is also traditionally the day when the Christmas tree is taken down.

heiligen *tr. V.* [1] keep, observe ‹*tradition, Sabbath, etc.*›; **die geheiligten Räume** (auch iron.) the inner sanctum; the holy of holies; **der Zweck heiligt die Mittel** the end justifies the means [2] (geh.: weihen) consecrate ‹*church*›; bless ‹*house, field, etc.*›

Heiligen-: ~**bild** *das* picture of a saint; ~**figur** *die* figure of a saint; ~**legende** *die* life of a saint; ~**schein** *der* gloriole; aureole; (um den Kopf) halo; **jmdn. mit einem ~schein umgeben** (fig.) be unable to see sb.'s faults; ~**verehrung** *die* veneration of the saints

***heilig|halten** ▸**heilig 3**

Heiligkeit *die;* ~ [1] holiness; **Seine/Euere ~** (Anrede) His/Your Holiness [2] (der Ehe, Taufe usw.) sanctity; sacredness; (geh.: des Zornes) righteousness; **die ~ des Eigentums** (geh.) the sanctity *or* inviolability of property

heilig-, Heilig-: ~**mäßig** [A] *Adj.* saintly; [B] *adv.* **~mäßig leben** lead a saintly life; *~**|sprechen** ▸**heilig 1**; ~**sprechung** *die;* ~~, ~~**en** (kath. Kirche) canonization

Heiligtum *das;* ~**s, Heiligtümer** shrine; **ein ~ für jmdn. sein** (fig.) be a sacred object to sb.; **sein Arbeitszimmer ist sein ~** (fig.) his study is his sanctuary *or* sanctum

Heiligung *die;* ~, ~**en** (geh.) [1] (das Heilighalten) observance [2] (Rechtfertigung) justification

heil-, Heil-: ~**klima** *das* healthy climate; **ein gutes ~klima** a healthy climate; ~**kraft** *die* healing *or* curative power; ~**kräftig** *Adj.* medicinal ‹*herb, plant, etc.*›; curative ‹*effect*›; ~**kraut** *das* medicinal *or* officinal herb; ~**kunde** *die* medicine; ~**kundig** *Adj.* skilled in medicine *or* the art of healing *postpos.*; ~**los** [A] *Adj.* hopeless, awful ‹*mess, muddle*›; utter, (coll.) terrible ‹*confusion*›; **eine ~lose Angst haben** be terrified *or* (coll.) terribly frightened; [B] *adv.* hopelessly; ~**massage** *die* curative massage; ~**massagen** massage treatment *sing., no indef. art.*; ~**methode** *die* curative treatment; method of treatment; ~**mittel** *das* (auch fig.) remedy (**gegen** for); (Medikament) medicament; ~**pädagoge** *der,* ~**pädagogin** *die* teacher of children with special needs; ~**pädagogik** *die* special education *no art.*; ~**pflanze** *die* medicinal *or* officinal plant *or* herb; ~**praktiker** *der,* ~**praktikerin** *die* ▸❶ **S. 113** non-medical practitioner; ~**quelle** *die* mineral spring

heilsam *Adj.* salutary ‹*lesson, effect, experience, etc.*›

Heils-: ~**armee** *die* Salvation Army; ~**botschaft** *die* message of salvation; ~**bringer** *der;* ~~**s,** ~~, ~**bringerin** *die;* ~~, ~~**nen** (Rel., auch fig.) bringer of salvation

Heil-: ~**schlaf** *der* (Med.) healing sleep; ~**serum** *das* (Med.) [antitoxic] serum

Heils-: ~**geschichte** *die* (Theol.) Heilsgeschichte; salvation-history; ~**lehre** *die* (auch fig.) doctrine of salvation

Heil·stätte *die* sanatorium; clinic

Heilung *die;* ~, ~**en** ▸❶ **S. 439** [1] (einer Wunde) healing; (von Krankheit, Kranken) curing; **wenig Hoffnung auf ~ haben** have little hope of being cured; **~ suchen** seek a cure [2] (das Gesundwerden) **die ~ dieser Fraktur dauert mehrere Wochen** this fracture will take several weeks to mend; **diese Salbe wird die ~ der Wunde beschleunigen** this ointment will help the wound to heal faster

Heilungs-: ~**prozess,** *~**prozeß** *der,* ~**verlauf** *der* healing process; (Rekonvaleszenz) process of recovery

Heil-: ~**verfahren** *das* [course of] treatment; ~**wirkung** *die* therapeutic *or* curative effect; ~**zweck** *der: in* **zu ~zwecken** for therapeutic *or* medicinal purposes

heim /haim/ *Adv.* home

Heim *das;* ~**[e]s,** ~**e** [1] (Zuhause) home; **ein eigenes ~:** a home of his/their *etc.* own [2] (Anstalt, Alters~) home; (für Obdachlose) hostel; (für Studenten) hall of residence; hostel [3] ▸**Erholungsheim**

Heim-: ~**abend** *der* social evening; ~**arbeit** *die* outwork; **eine ~arbeit suchen/bekommen** look for/get outwork; **etw. in ~arbeit herstellen lassen** have sth. produced by homeworkers; ~**arbeiter** *der,* ~**arbeiterin** *die* homeworker; outworker

Heimat /'haima:t/ *die;* ~, ~**en** [1] (~ort) home; home town/village; (~land) home; homeland; **ihr ist Frankreich zur zweiten ~ geworden** France has become her second home [2] (Ursprungsland) natural habitat; **Frankreich ist die ~ des Champagners** France is the home of champagne

Heimat-: ~**an·schrift** *die* home address; ~**dichter** *der,* ~**dichterin** *die* regional writer; ~**dichtung** *die* regional literature; ~**erde** *die* native soil; ~**film** *der* [sentimental] film in a[n idealized] regional setting; ~**forschung** *die* research into local history; ~**front** *die* (bes. ns.) home front; ~**hafen** *der* home port; ~**kunde** *die* local history, geography, and natural history; ~**land** *das* homeland; native land; (fig.) home

heimatlich *Adj.* [1] (zur Heimat gehörend) native ‹*dialect*›; **die ~en Berge** the mountains of [one's] home; **die ~e Landschaft/die ~en Bräuche** the landscape/customs of one's native land/district; *s. auch* **Gefilde** [2] (an die Heimat erinnernd) nostalgic ‹*emotions*›; **~e Klänge** sounds which evoke memories of home

heimat-, Heimat-: ~**lied** *das* song of one's homeland; ~**los** *Adj.* homeless; **durch den Krieg ~los werden** be displaced by the war; ~**lose** *der/die; adj. Dekl.* homeless person; **die ~losen** the homeless; ~**museum** *das* museum of local history; ~**ort** *der* [1] home town/village; [2] ▸~**hafen**; ~**recht** *das* right of domicile; ~**sprache** *die* native language; (Mundart) native dialect; ~**stadt** *die* home town; ~**verbunden** *Adj.* ‹*person*› with strong roots [in his/her native soil]; **~verbunden sein** have strong roots [in one's native soil]; ~**verein** *der* local history society; ~**vertrieben** *Adj.* expelled from his/her homeland *postpos.*; ~**vertriebene** *der/die* expellee [from his/her homeland]

heim-, Heim-: ~**|begeben** *unr. refl. V.* (geh.) make one's way home; go home; ~**|begleiten** *tr. V.* **jmdn. ~begleiten** take *or* see sb. home; ~**bewohner** *der,* ~**bewohnerin** *die* resident of a/the home; ~**|bringen** *unr. tr. V.* [1] ▸~**begleiten**; [2] bring home

Heimchen *das;* ~**s,** ~ [1] (ugs. abwertend: Frau) **~ [am Herd]** little hausfrau *or* housewife [2] (Grille) house cricket

Heim·computer *der* home computer

heim|dürfen *unr. itr. V.* be allowed [to go] home; **darf ich heim?** may I go home?

heimelig /'haiməlıç/ *Adj.* cosy

heim-, Heim-: ~**erzieher** *der,* ~**erzieherin** *die* ▸❶ **S. 113** *care worker in a home for children or young people;* ~**|fahren** [A] *unr. itr. V.; mit sein* drive home; [B] *unr. tr. V.* drive home; *s. auch* **fahren A 1, B 3**; ~**fahrt** *die* journey home; (mit dem Auto) drive home; ~**|finden** *unr. itr. V.* find one's way home; ~**|führen** *tr. V.* [1] (geleiten) take home; [2] (geh. veralt.: heiraten) **eine Frau ~führen** take a wife; **er führte sie ~:** he took her to wife (arch.); **er führte sie als seine Braut ~:** he took her for his bride; ~**gang** *der* (geh. verhüll.) passing away; **nach dem ~gang ihres Mannes** after her husband passed away; ~**gegangene** *der/die; adj. Dekl.* (geh. verhüll.) departed; **unser lieber ~gegangener** our dear departed friend/brother *etc.*; ~**|gehen** *unr. itr. V.; mit sein* [1] go home; [2] (geh. verhüll.: sterben) pass away; [3] (unpers.) **es geht ~:** I/we *etc.* are going home; ~**geschädigt** *Adj.* institutionalized; ~**|holen** *tr. V.* [1] fetch home; [2] (geh. verhüll.) **Gott hat ihn [zu sich] ~geholt** he has been called to his Maker; ~**industrie** *die* cottage industry

heimisch *Adj.* [1] (ein~) indigenous, native ‹*plants, animals, etc.*› (**in** + *Dat.* to); domestic, home ‹*industry*›; **die ~en Flüsse und Seen** the rivers and lakes of his/her *etc.* native land; **vor ~em Publikum** (Sport) in front of a home crowd [2] (zum Heim gehörend) **an den ~en Herd zurückkehren** go back home; **vom ~en Herd flüchten** get away from the house [3] **~ sein/sich ~ fühlen** be/feel at home; **~ werden**

h

settle in; ~ **werden in** (+ *Dat.*) settle into

heim-, Heim-: ~kehr *die;* ~~: return home; homecoming; **~|kehren** *itr. V.; mit sein* return home (**aus** from); **~kehrer** *der;* ~~**s**, ~~, **~kehrerin** *die;* ~~, ~~**nen** homecomer; **die ~kehrer aus dem Krieg/Urlaub** the soldiers returning from the war/the holidaymakers returning home; **~kind** *das* child brought up in a home; **ein ~kind adoptieren** adopt a child from a home; **~kino** *das* 1 home movies *pl.*; **eine Vorführung im ~kino** a home-movie show; 2 (ugs. scherzh.: Fernsehen) box (coll.); goggle-box (Brit. coll.); **~|kommen** *unr. itr. V.; mit sein* come *or* return home; **~|laufen** *unr. itr. V.; mit sein* run [back] home; **schnell ~laufen** dash home; **~leiter** *der* warden; (eines Kinder-/Jugendheims) superintendent; (eines Pflegeheims) director; **~leiterin** *die* warden; (eines Kinder-/Jugendheims) superintendent; (eines Pflegeheims) matron; **~leitung** *die* 1 warden's office; (eines Kinder-/Jugendheims) superintendent's office; (eines Pflegeheims) director's/matron's office; 2 (Person) ▸ **~leiter**, **~leiterin**; **~|leuchten** *itr. V.* (salopp) **jmdm. ~leuchten** give sb. a piece of one's mind (coll.)

heimlich

A *Adj.* 1 secret; secret, clandestine ‹*agreement, meeting*› 2 (österr.) ▸ **heimelig**

B *adv.* secretly; ‹*meet*› secretly, in secret; **sie schaute ~ auf die Uhr** she looked furtively at her watch; **er ist ~ weggelaufen** he slipped *or* stole away; **~, still und leise** (ugs.) on the quiet; quietly

Heimlichkeit *die;* ~, **~en** secret; **in aller ~:** in secret; secretly

Heimlichtuer /-tu:ɐ/ *der;* **~s**, ~, **Heimlichtuerin** *die;* ~, **~nen** (abwertend) secretive person

heim-, Heim-: ~mannschaft *die* (Sport) home team *or* side; **~|müssen** *unr. itr. V.* have to go home; **~niederlage** *die* (Sport) home defeat; **~ordnung** *die* rules of the/a home/hostel *etc.*; **~orgel** *die* home organ; **~platz** *der* place in a home/hostel *etc.*; **~recht** *das* (Sport) **~recht haben** be playing at home; **die Mannschaft mit ~recht** the home team *or* side; **~reise** *die* journey home; **~|schicken** *tr. V.* send home; **~schwach** *Adj.* (Sport) **~schwach sein** have a poor home record; **~sieg** *der* (Sport) home win; **~spiel** *das* (Sport) home match *or* game; **~stark** *Adj.* (Sport) **~stark sein** have a very good home record; **~statt** *die* (geh.) home; **~stätte** *die* 1 ▸ **Heimstatt**; 2 (Grundbesitz für Vertriebene) homestead (*for refugees etc.*); **~|suchen** *tr. V.* 1 (überfallen) ‹*storm, earthquake, epidemic*› strike; ‹*disease*› afflict; ‹*nightmares, doubts*› plague; ‹*catastrophe, fate*› overtake; **von Streiks/Dürre ~gesucht** strike-torn/drought-ridden; 2 (aufsuchen) ‹*visitor, salesman, etc.*› descend [up]on; **~suchung** *die;* ~~, ~~**en** affliction; visitation; **~|trauen** *refl. V.* dare to go home

Heim·tücke *die;* ~ (Bösartigkeit) [concealed] malice; (Hinterlistigkeit, fig.: einer Krankheit) insidiousness

heim·tückisch

A *Adj.* (bösartig) malicious; (fig.) insidious ‹*disease*›; (hinterlistig) insidious

B *adv.* maliciously

heim-, Heim-: ~vorteil *der* (Sport) advantage of playing at home; home advantage; **~wärts** /-vɛrts/ (nach Hause zu) home; (in Richtung Heimat) homeward[s]; **~weg** *der* way home; **sich auf den ~weg machen** set off [for] home; **haben Sie einen weiten ~weg?** have you got a long way to get home?

Heim·weh *das* homesickness; **nach jmdm./einem Ort ~ haben** pine for sb./be homesick for a place; **~ bekommen** get homesick

heimweh·krank *Adj.* homesick

heim-, Heim-: ~werker *der;* ~~**s**, ~~: handyman; do-it-yourselfer; **~werkerin** *die;* ~~, ~~**nen** handywoman; do-it-yourselfer; **~|wollen** *unr. itr. V.* want to go home; **~|zahlen** *tr. V.* **jmdm. etw. ~zahlen** pay sb. back *or* get even with sb. for sth.; **jmdm. in gleicher Münze ~zahlen** pay sb. back in the same coin; **~|ziehen** **A** *unr. itr. V.; mit sein* return home; **B** *unr. tr. V.* (unpers.) **es zog ihn ~:** he wanted to go home; **~zögling** *der* ▸ **~kind**

Hein /hain/ *in* **Freund ~** (verhüll.) [Angel of] Death

Heini /'haini/ *der;* **~s**, **~s** (ugs. Schimpfwort) idiot; halfwit; clot (Brit. coll.)

Heinzel·männchen /'haints̮l-/ *das;* **~s**, **~:** brownie

Heirat /'haira:t/ *die;* ~, **~en** marriage

heiraten

A *itr. V.* marry; get married; **~ müssen** (verhüll.) have to get married; **das Heiraten** marriage *no art.*; getting married *no art.*; **sie hat nach Amerika geheiratet** she got married and settled in America

B *tr. V.* marry

heirats-, Heirats-: ~absichten *Pl.* marriage plans; **ernsthafte ~absichten haben** seriously intend to marry *or* get married; **~alter** *das* marrying age; **im ~alter sein** be of an age to marry; **~annonce** *die* advertisement for a marriage partner; **~antrag** *der* proposal *or* offer of marriage; **jmdm. einen ~antrag machen** propose to sb.; **~anzeige** *die* 1 (Anzeige, dass jemand heiratet) announcement of a/the forthcoming marriage; 2 ▸ **~annonce**; **~fähig** *Adj.* ‹*person*› of marriageable age; **im ~fähigen Alter** of marriageable age; **~institut** *das* marriage bureau; **~kandidat** *der* (scherzh.) 1 (jmd., der heiraten will) husband-to-be; 2 (unverheirateter Mann) eligible bachelor; **~kandidatin** *die* (scherzh.) 1 bride-to-be; 2 (unverheiratete Frau) eligible single woman; **~lustig** *Adj.* (scherzh.) eager *or* keen to get married *postpos.*; **~markt** *der* (scherzh.) 1 (Zeitungsrubrik) matrimonial advertisements *pl.*; 2 (Veranstaltung) marriage market; **~schwindel** *der* fraud involving a spurious offer of marriage; **~schwindler** *der*, **~schwindlerin** *die: person who makes a spurious offer of marriage for purposes of fraud;* **~urkunde** *die* marriage certificate; **~vermittler** *der*, **~vermittlerin** *die* ▸ⓘ **S. 113** marriage broker; **~versprechen** *das* promise of marriage; **Bruch eines ~versprechens** (Rechtsw.) breach of promise

heisa /'haiza *od.* 'haisa/ *Interj.* (veralt.) hooray

heischen /'haiʃn/ *tr. V.* (geh.) 1 (fordern) demand 2 (veralt.: bitten um) ask for; (inständig) beg

heiser /'haizɐ/

A *Adj.* hoarse; (rauchig) husky; **sich ~ schreien/reden** shout/talk oneself hoarse

B *adv.* hoarsely; in a hoarse voice

Heiserkeit *die;* ~ ▸ **heiser**: hoarseness; huskiness

heiß /hais/

A *Adj.* 1 hot; hot, torrid ‹*zone*›; **brennend/glühend ~:** burning/scorching hot; **jmdm. ist ~:** sb. feels hot; **etw. ~ machen** heat sth. up; **ein Paar Heiße** (ugs.) a couple of hot sausages; **es überläuft mich ~ und kalt, es läuft mir ~ und kalt den Rücken hinunter** I feel hot and cold all over; **sie haben sich die Köpfe ~ geredet** the conversation/debate became heated; **dich haben sie wohl zu ~ gebadet?** (salopp) you must be off your rocker (coll.) 2 (heftig) heated ‹*debate, argument*›; impassioned ‹*anger*›; burning, fervent ‹*desire*›; fierce ‹*fight, battle*› 3 (innig) ardent, passionate ‹*wish, love*›; **~e Tränen weinen** weep bitterly; cry one's heart out; **~en Dank** (ugs.) thanks a lot! (coll.) 4 (aufreizend) hot ‹*rhythm etc.*›; sexy ‹*blouse, dress, etc.*›; **eine ~e Nummer** (ugs.) a [red-]hot number (coll.); **was für'n ~er Typ!** (salopp) what a guy! (coll.); *s. auch* **Sohle 1** 5 (ugs.: gefährlich) hot (coll.) ‹*goods, money*›; **das wird ein ~es Jahr** things are going to get pretty hot this year (coll.); **ein ~es Thema** a controversial subject; **ein ~es Geschäft** a risky business; **eine ~e Gegend** a rough district; *s. auch* **Eisen 2** 6 (ugs.: Aussichten habend) hot ‹*favourite, tip, contender, etc.*›; **auf einer ~en Spur sein** be hot on the scent 7 (ugs.: schnell) hot; *s. auch* **Ofen 5** 8 (ugs.: brünstig) on heat 9 (salopp: aufgereizt) **jmdn. ~ machen** turn sb. on (coll.) 10 (Physik) hot (coll.)

B *adv.* 1 (heftig) ‹*fight*› fiercely; **die Stadt wurde ~ umkämpft** the town was the object of fierce fighting; **es ging ~ her** things got heated; sparks flew (coll.); (auf einer Party usw.) things got wild; **~ umkämpft** fiercely contested or disputed; **~ umstritten** hotly debated ‹*matter, subject, etc.*›; highly controversial ‹*figure, director, etc.*› 2 (innig) **jmdn. ~ und innig lieben** love sb. dearly *or* with all one's heart; **etw. ~ ersehnen** long fervently for sth.; **~ geliebt** dearly beloved ‹*husband, son, etc.*›; beloved ‹*doll, car, etc.*›; **das ~ ersehnte Fahrrad** the bicycle he/she has longed for so fervently

heißa /'haisa/ ▸ **heisa**

heiß·blütig *Adj.* (leidenschaftlich) hot-blooded; ardent, passionate ‹*lover*›; (leicht erregbar) hot-tempered

heißen[1]

A *unr. itr. V.* 1 (den Namen tragen) be called; **ich heiße Hans** I am called Hans; my name is Hans; **er heißt mit Nachnamen Müller** his surname is Müller; **früher hat sie anders ge~:** she used to have a different name; **nach jmdm. ~:** be named *or* called after sb.; **und wie sie alle ~:** and the rest [of them]; **wie kann man nur Traugott ~?** how can anyone have a name like Traugott?; **so wahr ich … heiße** (ugs.) as sure as I'm standing here; **dann will ich Emil ~** (ugs.) then I'm a Dutchman (coll.) 2 (bedeuten) mean; **was heißt "danke" auf Französisch?** what's the French for 'thanks'?; **das will viel/nicht viel ~:** that means a lot/doesn't mean much; **was soll das denn ~?** what's that supposed to mean?; **was heißt hier: morgen?** what do you mean, tomorrow?; **das heißt** that is [to say] 3 (lauten) ‹*saying*› go; **wie heißt das Buch?** what's [the title *or* name of] the book?; **der Titel/sein Motto heißt …** the title/his motto is … 4 (unpers.) (man sagt) **es heißt, dass …** they say *or* it is said that …; **es heißt, dass sie unheilbar krank ist** she is said to be incurably ill; **wie es hieß, war sie unheilbar krank** they said *or* it was said [that] she was incurably ill; **es hieß allgemein, dass …** everybody said that …; **es soll nicht ~, dass …** never let it be said that … 5 (unpers.) (ist zu lesen) **in dem Gedicht/Roman/Artikel heißt es …** in the poem/novel/article it says that …; **wie heißt es doch gleich bei Goethe?** what was it Goethe said? 6 (unpers.) (geh.: es gilt) **jetzt heißt es aufgepasst!** you'd better watch out now!; **jetzt heißt es handeln!** now it's time to act *or* for action!

B *unr. tr. V.* 1 (geh.: auffordern) tell; bid; **jmdn. etw. tun ~:** tell sb. to do sth.; bid sb. do sth. 2 (geh.: bezeichnen) call; **jmdn. einen Lügner ~:** call sb. a liar; **jmdn. willkommen ~:** bid sb. welcome 3 (veralt.: einen Namen geben) name; call

heißen[2] *tr. V.* ▸ **hissen**

heiß-, Heiß-: ~ersehnt, ~geliebt ▸ **heiß B2**; **~getränk** *das* hot drink; **~getränke** (auf Speisekarten) hot beverages; **~hunger** *der:* **einen ~hunger auf etw.** (*Akk.*) *od.* **nach etw. [haben]** [have] a craving for sth.; **etw. mit [wahrem] ~hunger verschlingen** devour sth. ravenously; [absolutely (coll.)] wolf sth. down; **sich mit [wahrem] ~hunger auf etw.** (*Akk.*) **stürzen** (fig.) [absolutely (coll.)] devour sth.; **~hungrig** **A** *Adj.* ravenous; **B** *adv.* ravenously; voraciously; **~|laufen** **A** *unr. itr. V.; mit sein* run hot; ‹*engine*› run hot, overheat; **sie telefonierte so viel, dass die Drähte ~liefen** she made so many telephone calls that the wires were buzzing; **B** *unr. refl. V.* run hot; ‹*engine*› run hot, overheat

Heiß·luft *die* hot air

Heißluft-: ~backofen *der* fan oven; **~bad** *das* hot-air bath; **~ballon** *der* hot-air balloon; **~gerät** *das* (Trockner) hot-air dryer; (Herd) hot-air oven

heiß-, Heiß-: ~mangel *die* rotary ironer; **~sporn** *der* hothead; **~umkämpft, ~umstritten** ▸ **heiß B1**

Heiß·wasser-: ~bereiter *der;* ~~**s**, ~~: water heater; **~speicher** *der* hot-water tank with an immersion heater

heiter /ˈhaitɐ/ *Adj.* 1 (fröhlich) cheerful, happy ‹*person, nature*›; happy, merry ‹*laughter*›; **~ und zufrieden** happy and contented 2 (froh stimmend) cheerful ‹*music etc.*›; cheerful, bright ‹*colour, wallpaper, room, etc.*›; (amüsant) funny, amusing ‹*story etc.*›; **einer Sache** (*Dat.*) **die ~e Seite abgewinnen** look on the bright side of sth.; **das ist ja ~!** (ugs. iron.) that's just great *or* wonderful (iron.); **das kann ja ~ werden!** (ugs. iron.) that'll be fun (iron.) 3 (sonnig) fine ‹*weather*›; bright, fine ‹*day*›; **~ bis wolkig** generally fine, though cloudy in places

Heiterkeit *die*; ~ 1 (Frohsinn) cheerfulness 2 (Belustigung) merriment; **allgemeine ~ erregen** provoke *or* cause general merriment 3 (sonniges Wetter) brightness

Heiterkeits·ausbruch *der* burst of merriment

heizbar *Adj.* heated ‹*windscreen, room, etc.*›; **das Zimmer ist nicht/schwer ~:** the room has no heating/is difficult to heat

Heiz·decke *die* electric blanket

heizen /ˈhaitsn̩/

A *itr. V.* have the heating on; **der Ofen heizt gut** the stove gives off *or* throws out a good heat; **mit Kohle** *usw.* **~:** use coal *etc.* for heating

B *tr. V.* 1 (warm machen) heat ‹*room etc.*› 2 (an~) stoke ‹*furnace, boiler, etc.*›; **den Badeofen ~:** heat the bathwater; **sie ~ ihre Öfen mit Öl** their boilers are oil-fired 3 (als Brennstoff verwenden) burn

C *refl. V.* **sich gut/schlecht ~:** be easy/difficult to heat

Heizer *der*; **~s, ~, Heizerin** *die*; **~, ~nen** ▸ⓘ **S. 113** (einer Lokomotive) fireman; stoker; (eines Schiffes) stoker

Heiz-: ~fläche *die* heating surface; **~gerät** *das* heater; **~kessel** *der* boiler; **~kissen** *das* heating pad; **~körper** *der* radiator; **~kosten** *Pl.* heating costs; **~lüfter** *der* fan heater; **~material** *das* fuel [for heating]; **~ofen** *der* stove; heater; **ein elektrischer ~ofen** an electric heater; **~öl** *das* heating oil; fuel oil; **~periode** *die* heating period; **~platte** *die* hotplate; **~rohr** *das* heating pipe; **~sonne** *die* bowl fire; parabolic heater; **~strahler** *der* radiant heater

Heizung *die*; **~, ~en** 1 [central] heating *no pl., no indef. art.* 2 (ugs.: Heizkörper) radiator

Heizungs-: ~anlage *die* heating system; **~keller** *der* boiler room (in the basement); **~monteur** *der*, **~monteurin** *die* ▸ⓘ **S. 113** heating engineer; **~technik** *die* heating engineering

Heiz·wert *der* calorific value

Hektar /ˈhɛktaːɐ̯/ *das od. der*; **~s, ~e** ▸ⓘ **S. 262** hectare

Hektar·ertrag *der* (Landw.) yield per hectare

Hektik /ˈhɛktɪk/ *die*; **~:** hectic rush; (des Lebens) hectic pace; **wozu die ~?** (ugs.) what's the rush?; **nur keine ~!** (ugs.) take it easy!

Hektiker *der*; **~s, ~, Hektikerin** *die*, **~, ~nen** (ugs.) person in a rush

hektisch

A *Adj.* 1 (fieberhaft) hectic; **sie ist immer furchtbar ~:** she is always in a hectic rush; **nun mal nicht so ~!** take it easy! 2 (Med. veralt.) hectic; **~e Flecken** (fig.) red blotches

B *adv.* ‹*work, run to and fro*› frantically; **~ zugehen** be hectic; **~ leben** lead a hectic life

Hektographie /hɛktograˈfiː/ *die*; **~, ~n** 1 (veralt.: Verfahren) hectography *no art.* 2 (Kopie) hectographed *or* hectographic copy

hektographieren *tr. V.* 1 (veralt.) hectograph 2 (vervielfältigen) duplicate; copy

Hekto-: ~liter *der od. das* hectolitre; **~pascal** *das* hectopascal; **~watt** *das* hundred watts

Helanca Ⓦⓩ /heˈlaŋka/ *das*; **~:** nylon stretch fabric

helau /heˈlau̯/ *Interj.: cheer or greeting used at Carnival time*

Held /hɛlt/ *der*; **~en, ~en** hero; **du bist mir ein schöner** *od.* **netter ~** (scherzh.) a fine one you are!; **den ~en spielen** (abwertend) play the hero; **kein ~ in etw.** (*Dat.*) **sein** (ugs. scherzh. od. spött.) be no great shakes at sth. (coll.); **du bist nicht gerade ein ~ in der Schule** (ugs.) you're not exactly doing brilliantly at school; **der ~ des Tages/des Abends** the hero of the hour; **~ der Arbeit** (DDR) Hero of Labour

Helden-: ~brust *die* (scherzh./iron.) manly chest; **~darsteller** *der* (Theater) actor of heroic roles; **~dichtung** *die* (Literaturw.) epic *or* heroic poetry; **~epos** *das* (Literaturw.) heroic epic; **~friedhof** *der* military *or* war cemetery; **~gedenktag** *der* (veralt.) ≈ Remembrance Day (Brit.); Memorial Day (Amer.); **~gestalt** *die* hero

heldenhaft

A *Adj.* heroic

B *adv.* heroically

helden-, Helden-: ~lied *das* (Literaturw.) heroic song *or* lay; **~mut** *der* heroism; **~mütig** A *Adj.* heroic; B *adv.* heroically; **~pose** *die* (abwertend) heroic pose; **~rolle** *die* (Theater) part *or* role of the hero; **~sage** *die* (Literaturw.) heroic legend; (aus Norwegen, Island) heroic saga; **~stück** *das* (iron.) **das war kein ~stück** that was nothing to be proud of; **~tat** *die* heroic feat *or* deed; **das war keine ~tat** (spött.) that was nothing to be proud of; **~tenor** *der* 1 (Sänger) heroic *or* dramatic tenor; Heldentenor; 2 (Stimmlage) Heldentenor; **~tod** *der* (geh. verhüll.) death in action; **den ~tod sterben/finden** be killed in action

Heldentum *das*; **~s** heroism

Heldin *die*; **~, ~nen** heroine

helfen /ˈhɛlfn̩/ *unr. itr. V.* 1 (behilflich sein) **jmdm. ~ [etw. zu tun]** help *or* assist sb. [to do sth.]; lend *or* give sb. a hand [in doing sth.]; **jmdm. bei etw. ~:** help *or* assist sb. with sth.; **jmdm. in den/aus dem Mantel ~:** help sb. into *or* on with/out of *or* off with his/her coat; **jmdm. über die Straße/in den Bus ~:** help sb. across the road/on to the bus; **dem Kranken war nicht mehr zu ~:** the patient was beyond [all] help; **dir ist nicht zu ~** (ugs.) you're a hopeless case; **sich** (*Dat.*) **nicht mehr zu ~ wissen** be at one's wits' end; **sich immer zu ~ wissen** be able to take care of oneself; **dem werde ich ~, einfach die Schule zu schwänzen!** (ugs.) I'll teach him to play truant; **ich kann mir nicht ~, aber ...** I'm sorry, but [I have to say that] ... 2 (nützlich sein) help; **ein paar Tage Ruhe werden Ihnen sicher ~:** a couple of days' rest will certainly do you good; **das hilft gegen** *od.* **bei Kopfschmerzen** it is good for *or* helps to relieve headaches; **das hilft mir auch nichts** that's no help *or* good to me either; **hilf dir selbst, so hilft dir Gott** (Spr.) God helps those who help themselves; **da hilft alles nichts** there's nothing *or* no help for it; **da hilft kein Jammern und kein Klagen** it's no good *or* use moaning and groaning 3 (unpers.) **es hilft nichts** it's no use *or* good; **was hilfts?** what's the use *or* good?; **damit ist uns nicht geholfen** that is no help to us; that doesn't help us; **es hilft dir wenig zu jammern** it's not much good *or* use moaning

Helfer *der*; **~s, ~:** helper; (Mitarbeiter) assistant; (eines Verbrechens) accomplice; **ein ~ in der Not** a friend in need

Helferin *die*; **~, ~nen** ▸**Helfer**

Helfers·helfer *der*, **Helfers·helferin** *die* (abwertend) accomplice

Helikopter /heliˈkɔptɐ/ *der*; **~s, ~:** helicopter

helio-, Helio- /heli̯o-/ helio-

Heliograph /-ˈgraːf/ *der*; **~en, ~en** (Astron., Nachrichtenw.) heliograph

Heliographie /-graˈfiː/ *die*; **~** (Druckw., Nachrichtenw.) heliography *no art.*

Helioskop /-ˈskoːp/ *das*; **~s, ~e** (Astron.) helioscope

Heliostat /-ˈstaːt/ *der*; **~[e]s** *od.* **~en, ~en** (Astron.) heliostat

Heliotrop[1] *das*; **~s, ~e** (Pflanze, Farbe, Farbstoff) heliotrope

Heliotrop[2] *der*; **~s, ~e** (Schmuckstein) bloodstone; heliotrope

Helium /ˈheːli̯ʊm/ *das*; **~s** helium

Helix /ˈheːlɪks/ *die*; **~, Helices** /ˈheːlitseːs/ (Chemie) helix

hell /hɛl/

A *Adj.* 1 (von Licht erfüllt) light ‹*room etc.*›; well-lit ‹*stairs*›; **es wird ~:** it's getting light; **es war schon ~er Morgen/Tag** it was already broad daylight; **am ~en Tag** (ugs.) in broad daylight; **in ~en Flammen stehen** be in flames *or* ablaze 2 (klar) bright ‹*day, sky, etc.*›; **eine ~ere Zukunft** (fig. ugs.) a brighter *or* more promising future 3 (viel Licht spendend) bright ‹*light, lamp, star, etc.*› 4 (blass) light ‹*colour*›; fair ‹*skin, hair*›; light-coloured ‹*clothes*›; **~es Bier** ≈ lager 5 (akustisch) **ein ~er Ton/Klang** a high, clear sound; **eine ~e Stimme** a high, clear voice; **ein ~es Lachen** a ringing laugh 6 (klug) bright; intelligent; **ein ~er Kopf sein** be bright; **dort fehlt ein ~er Kopf** what is needed there is somebody with brains 7 (voll bewusst) lucid ‹*moment, interval*› 8 (ugs.: absolut) sheer, utter ‹*madness, foolishness, despair, nonsense*›; unbounded, boundless ‹*enthusiasm*›; unrestrained ‹*jubilation*›; **in ~e Wut geraten** fly into a blind rage; **er hat seine ~e Freude an ihr/daran** she/it is his great joy; **daran wirst du deine ~e Freude haben** (iron.) you'll soon find out what you've let yourself in for; *s. auch* **Schar**

B *adv.* 1 brightly; **~ erleuchtet** brightly-lit; **~ leuchtend** bright; **~ lodernd** blazing; **~ lodernde Flammen** raging flames 2 (in hoher Tonlage) **~ läuteten die Glocken** the bells rang out high and clear; **~ lachen** give a ringing laugh 3 (sehr) highly ‹*enthusiastic, delighted, indignant, etc.*›; (laut) **über diesen Unsinn musste er ~ lachen** he had to laugh heartily at this nonsense

hell-, Hell-: ~auf *Adv.* highly ‹*enthusiastic, indignant, etc.*›; **~auf lachen** laugh out loud; **~äugig** *Adj.* ‹*person*› with light-coloured eyes; **~blau** *Adj.* light blue; **~blond** *Adj.* very fair; light blonde; **~braun** *Adj.* light brown; **~-Dunkel-Adap[ta]tion** *die* adaptation to light and dark; **~dunkel·malerei** *die* chiaroscuro

helle *Adj.* (landsch.) bright; intelligent; **sei ~!** use your head!

Helle[1] *die*; **~** (geh.) ▸**Helligkeit**

Helle[2] *das*; *adj. Dekl.* ≈ lager

Hellebarde /hɛləˈbardə/ *die*; **~, ~n** (hist.) halberd

hellenisieren /hɛleniˈziːrən/ *tr. V.* Hellenize

Hellenismus *der*; **~:** Hellenism *no art.*

Hellenist *der*; **~en, ~en** Hellenist

Hellenistik *die*; **~:** classical Greek studies *pl.*, *no art.*

Hellenistin *die*; **~, ~nen** ▸**Hellenist**

hellenistisch *Adj.* Hellenistic; **die ~en Staaten** the states of Ancient Greece

Heller *der*; **~s, ~:** heller; **bis auf den letzten ~/bis auf ~ und Pfennig** (ugs.) down to the last penny *or* (Amer.) cent; **das ist keinen [roten** *od.* **lumpigen] ~ wert** (ugs.) it's not worth a penny *or* (Amer.) one red cent; **sie hat keinen [roten** *od.* **lumpigen] ~** (ugs.) she doesn't have a penny to her name *or* (Amer.) have one [red] cent; **keinen [roten] ~ für jmdn./etw. geben** (ugs.) not care tuppence about sb./sth.

***hell·erleuchtet** ▸**hell B 1**

hell-: ~farben, ~farbig *Adj.* light-coloured; **~gelb** *Adj.* light yellow; **~grau** *Adj.* light grey; **~grün** *Adj.* light green; **~haarig** *Adj.* fair[-haired]; **~häutig** *Adj.* fair[-skinned]; fair-skinned, pale-skinned ‹*race*›; **~hörig** *Adj.* 1 (aufmerksam) **~hörig werden** sit up and take notice (coll.); **jmdn. ~hörig machen** make sb. sit up and take notice (coll.); 2 (schalldurchlässig) badly *or* poorly soundproofed; 3 (veralt.: gut hörend) **~hörig sein** have keen hearing *or* sharp ears

***hellicht** ▸**helllicht**

Helligkeit *die*; **~, ~en** (auch Physik) brightness; **eine Lampe von größerer ~:** a brighter lamp

Helligkeits·regler *der* (Elektrot.) dimming control; dimmer; (beim Fernsehgerät) brightness

h

control; **Lichtschalter mit ~:** dimmer switch

hellleuchtend ▸**hell B 1**

hell·licht /'hɛlɪçt/ *Adj.*: *in* **es ist ~er Tag** it's broad daylight; **am ~en Tag** in broad daylight

helllodernd /'hɛlo:dn̩t/ ▸**hell B 1**

hell-, Hell-: ~rot *Adj.* light red; **~sehen** *unr. itr. V.; nur im Inf.* **~sehen können** have second sight; be clairvoyant; **~seher** *der,* **~seherin** *die* clairvoyant; **~seherisch** *Adj.* clairvoyant; **~seherische Begabung haben** have the gift of second sight; **~sichtig** *Adj.* 1 (durchschauend) perceptive; 2 (weitblickend) far-sighted; **~sichtigkeit** *die; ~~:* perceptiveness; **~wach** *Adj.* 1 (ganz wach) wide awake; 2 (ugs.: klug) bright; **~werden** *das; ~~s* daybreak *no art.*

Helm¹ /hɛlm/ *der;* **~[e]s, ~e** 1 (Kopfschutz) helmet; **~ ab zum Gebet!** (Milit.) helmets off for prayers! 2 (Archit.) (pyramidenförmig) helm *or* pyramidal roof; (kegelförmig) conical roof

Helm² *der;* **~[e]s, ~e** (einer Axt, eines Hammers usw.) helve; (eines Messers) haft; handle

Helm-: ~busch *der* plume; crest; **~dach** *das* ▸**Helm¹ 2**; **~zier** *die* crest

Helot /he'lo:t/ *der;* **~en, ~en** (hist.) Helot

Helotentum *das;* **~s** (hist.) helotism; helotry

hem /həm/ *Interj.* hem

Hemd /hɛmt/ *das;* **~[e]s, ~en** 1 (Oberhemd) shirt 2 (Unterhemd) [under]vest; undershirt 3 *in* **etw. wechseln wie das** *od.* **sein ~** (ugs. abwertend) change sth. as often as one changes one's clothes; **nass bis aufs ~ sein** be soaked to the skin; be wet through; **das ~ ist mir näher als der Rock** for me charity begins at home; **mach dir nicht ins ~** (salopp) don't get [all] uptight (coll.); **das zieht einem [ja] das ~ aus** (ugs.) that's terrible!; **für sie gibt er sein letztes** *od.* **das letzte ~ her** (ugs.) he'd sell the shirt off his back to help her; **jmdn. bis aufs ~ ausziehen** (ugs.) have the shirt off sb.'s back (coll.); **alles bis aufs ~ verlieren** (ugs.) lose almost everything

Hemd-: ~ärmel *der* (österr.) ▸**Hemdsärmel**; **~bluse** *die* shirt; **~blusen·kleid** *das* shirt-waist dress; **~brust** *die* shirt front; dicky (coll.)

Hemden·matz *der* (ugs. scherzh.) *small child wearing only a shirt or vest;* little bare-bum (coll.)

Hemd-: ~knopf *der* shirt button; **~kragen** *der* shirt collar

Hemds·ärmel *der* shirtsleeve; **in ~n** in [one's] shirtsleeves

hemdsärmelig /-ɛrməlɪç/ *Adj.* 1 (im Hemd) shirtsleeved *attrib.*; in [one's] shirtsleeves *postpos.* 2 (ugs.: leger) casual ‹*manner*›; informal ‹*style*›; **sich ~ geben** behave in a casual manner; **er ist mir zu ~:** he's too pally for my liking (coll.)

Hemd·zipfel *der* shirt tail

Hemisphäre /hemi'sfɛ:rə/ *die;* **~, ~n** hemisphere

hemmen /'hɛmən/ *tr. V.* 1 (verlangsamen) slow [down]; retard; **seinen Schritt ~:** slow one's pace; slow down 2 (aufhalten) check; stem ‹*flow*› 3 (beeinträchtigen) hinder; hamper; **jmdn. in seiner Entwicklung ~:** inhibit sb.'s development 4 (behindern) impede, hamper ‹*person*›; **die Verletzung hemmte sie beim Laufen** her injury made walking difficult

Hemmnis *das;* **~ses, ~se** obstacle, hindrance (**für** to)

Hemm·schuh *der* 1 (Hemmnis) obstacle, hindrance (**für** to) 2 (Eisenb.) slipper [brake] 3 (Bremsklotz) chock 4 (Bremse) skid; drag

Hemmung *die;* **~, ~en** 1 (Gehemmtheit) inhibition; **~en haben** have inhibitions; be inhibited; **ich hatte ~en, sie darum zu bitten** I felt awkward about asking her for it 2 (Bedenken) scruple; **keine ~en haben, etw. zu tun** have no scruples about doing sth. 3 (Hemmen) (des Wachstums, einer Entwicklung) inhibition

hemmungs·los A *Adj.* unrestrained; unrestrained, unbridled ‹*passion*›; (skrupellos) unscrupulous; **ein ~er Mensch** a person lacking in all restraint/an unscrupulous person B *adv.* unrestrainedly; without restraint; ‹*cry, laugh, scream*› uncontrollably; (skrupellos) unscrupulously

Hemmungslosigkeit *die;* **~:** lack of restraint; (Skrupellosigkeit) unscrupulousness

Hendl /'hɛndl̩/ *das;* **~s, ~[n]** (bayr., österr.) chicken; (Brathähnchen) [roast] chicken

Hengst /hɛŋst/ *der;* **~[e]s, ~e** (Pferd) stallion; (Kamel) male; (Esel) male; jackass

Hengst-: ~fohlen *das,* **~füllen** *das* colt; [male] foal

Henkel /'hɛnkl̩/ *der;* **~s, ~:** handle; (einer Kanne) handle; ear

Henkel-: ~kanne *die* jug; (größer) pitcher; **~kreuz** *das* ansate cross; ankh; **~mann** *der* (ugs.): *portable set of stacked containers for taking a hot meal to one's work*

henken /'hɛŋkn̩/ *tr. V.* (veralt.) hang

Henker *der;* **~s, ~** 1 hangman; (Scharfrichter, auch fig.) executioner 2 (salopp) **sich den ~ um etw. scheren** not give a damn about sth. (coll.); **scher dich** *od.* **geh zum ~!** go to blazes *or* to the devil! (coll.); **hols der ~!** damn [it]! (coll.); the devil take it! (coll.); **weiß der ~!** the devil only knows (coll.); **beim** *od.* **zum ~!** damn it! (coll.); hang it all! (coll.)

Henker[s]-: ~beil *das* executioner's axe; **~hand** *die:* **durch** *od.* **von ~hand** (geh.) at the hand of the executioner

Henkers-: ~knecht *der* hangman's assistant; (eines Scharfrichters) executioner's assistant; (fig.) henchman; **~mahlzeit** *die* last meal (*before execution*); (scherzh.) last slap-up meal (*before examination, operation, departure, etc.*)

Henna /'hɛna/ *die;* **~** *od.* *das;* **~[s]** henna

Henne /'hɛnə/ *die;* **~, ~n** hen

Hepatitis /hepa'ti:tɪs/ *die;* **~, Hepatitiden** ▸**❶ S. 439** (Med.) hepatitis

hepp /hɛp/ *Interj.* **und ~!** and there you are!

her /he:ɐ̯/ *Adv.* 1 **~ damit** give it to me; give it here (coll.); **~ mit dem Geld** hand over *or* give me the money; **Bier ~!** bring me/us some beer!; **vom Fenster ~:** from the window; **von weit ~:** from far away *or* a long way off; **sie ist von Köln ~:** she is or comes from Cologne 2 (zeitlich) **von ihrer Kindheit ~:** since childhood; **jmdn. von früher/von der Schulzeit ~ kennen** know sb. from earlier times/from one's schooldays; *s. auch* **früher B 3** **von der Konzeption ~:** as far as the basic design is concerned; **das ist von der Sache ~ nicht vertretbar** it is unjustifiable in the nature of the matter 4 **eine Woche/einige Zeit/lange ~ sein** be a week/some time/a long time ago; **es ist lange ~, dass ...** it is a long time since ...; **es ist schon einen Monat ~:** it was a month ago 5 **mit jmdm./etw. ist es nicht weit ~** (ugs.) sb./sth. isn't all that hot (coll.) 6 **hinter jmdm./etw. ~ sein** (ugs.) be after sb./sth.

herab /hɛ'rap/ *Adv.* **vom Gipfel ~ bis ins Tal** from the summit down to the valley; **bis ~ auf etw.** (*Akk.*) down to sth.; **die Treppe/den Berg ~:** down the stairs/the mountain; **von oben ~** (fig.) condescendingly; **er ist immer so von oben ~:** he's always so superior

herab-, Herab- (*s. auch* **herunter-**): **~|blicken** *itr. V.* (geh.) ▸**~sehen**; **~|flehen** *tr. V.* (geh.) **Gottes Hilfe ~flehen** beseech God's help; **Gottes Segen auf jmdn. ~flehen** call down God's blessing on sb.; **~|fließen** *unr. itr. V.; mit sein* (geh.) flow down; **~|hängen** *unr. itr. V.* 1 (nach unten hängen) hang [down] (**von** from); (fig.) ‹*clouds*› hang low [in the sky]; 2 (schlaff hängen) ‹*hair, arms, etc.*› hang down; **~hängende Schultern** drooping shoulders; **~|klettern** *itr. V.; mit sein* (geh.) climb down; descend; **~|kommen** *unr. itr. V.; mit sein* (geh.) come down; descend; **~|lassen** A *unr. tr. V.* let down; lower; B *unr. refl. V.* 1 (iron.: bereit sein) **sich ~lassen, etw. zu tun** condescend *or* deign to do sth.; 2 (iron. veralt.: leutselig sein) **sich zu jmdm. ~lassen** come down to sb.'s level; **~lassend** A *Adj.* condescending; patronizing (**zu** towards); B *adv.* condescendingly; patronizingly; in a condescending *or* patronizing manner; **~lassung** *die;* **~~:** condescension; **~|mindern** *tr. V.* 1 reduce; 2 (schlecht machen) belittle, disparage ‹*achievement, qualities, etc.*›; **~minderung** *die* belittlement; disparagement; **~|regnen** *itr. V.; mit sein* ‹*drops of rain*› fall; (fig.) rain down; **~|rieseln** *itr. V.; mit sein* (geh.) trickle down; ‹*snow*› fall gently; ‹*snowflakes*› float down; **~|sehen** *unr. itr. V.* 1 (nach unten sehen) look down (**auf** + *Akk.* on); 2 (geringschätzig betrachten) **auf jmdn. ~sehen** look down on sb.; **~|senken** *refl. V.* (geh.) ‹*night, evening*› fall; ‹*mist, fog*› settle, descend (**auf** + *Akk.* on, over); **~|setzen** *tr. V.* 1 (reduzieren) reduce, cut ‹*cost, price, working hours, etc.*›; reduce ‹*speed*›; **zu ~gesetzten Preisen** at reduced prices; **~gesetzte Waren** (ugs.) cut-price goods; 2 (abwerten) belittle; disparage; **~setzung** *die;* **~~:** ▸▸**~setzen**: 1 reduction, cut (*Gen.* in); 2 belittling; disparagement; **~|sinken** *unr. itr. V.; mit sein* 1 (nach unten sinken) sink [down]; (fig.) ‹*night*› fall; descend; ‹*mist, fog*› settle, descend (**auf** + *Akk.* on, over); 2 (moralisch absinken) sink; **~|steigen** *unr. itr. V.; mit sein* (geh.) descend; climb down; (vom Pferd) dismount; **~|stoßen** (geh.) A *unr. tr. V.* push down; **er hat ihn von der Klippe ~gestoßen** he pushed him off the cliff; B *unr. itr. V.; mit sein* swoop down; **~|stufen** *tr. V.* downgrade (**zu, auf** + *Akk.* to); **~|stürzen** A *itr. V.; mit sein* plummet down; **er stürzte vom Gerüst ~:** he fell from *or* off the scaffolding; **~stürzende Felsbrocken** falling rocks; B *refl. V.* throw oneself (**von** from *or* off); **~|würdigen** *tr. V.* belittle; disparage; **~würdigung** *die* belittling; disparagement; **~|ziehen** *unr. tr. V.* (geh.) 1 pull down; 2 (moralisch) **jmdn. zu sich/auf sein eigenes Niveau ~ziehen** drag sb. down to one's own level

Heraklit /hera'kli:t/ (*der*) Heraclitus

Heraldik /he'raldɪk/ *die;* **~:** heraldry *no art.*

Heraldiker *der;* **~s, ~, Heraldikerin** *die;* **~, ~nen** heraldist; expert in heraldry

heraldisch *Adj.* heraldic

heran /hɛ'ran/ *Adv.* **an etw.** (*Akk.*) **~:** close to *or* right up to sth.; **nur ~ zu mir!, immer ~!** come closer!

heran-, Heran-: ~|arbeiten *refl. V.* **sich an etw.** (*Akk.*) **~arbeiten** work one's way towards sth.; **~|bilden** A *tr. V.* train [up]; (auf der Schule, Universität) educate; B *refl. V.* (sich entwickeln) develop; **~|bringen** *unr. tr. V.* 1 (zu jmdm. bringen) bring [up] (**an** + *Akk.*, **zu** to); 2 (vertraut machen) **jmdn. an etw.** (*Akk.*) **~bringen** introduce sb. to sth.; **~|fahren** *unr. itr. V.; mit sein* drive up (**an** + *Akk.* to); **~|führen** A *tr. V.* 1 (in die Nähe führen) lead up; bring up ‹*troops*›; **aus dem Osten wird Kaltluft ~geführt** there is/will be a cold easterly airstream; 2 (nahe bringen) bring up (**an** + *Akk.* to); 3 (vertraut machen) **jmdn. an etw.** (*Akk.*) **~führen** introduce sb. to sth.; B *itr. V.* **an etw.** (*Akk.*) **~führen** lead to sth.; **~|gehen** *unr. itr. V.; mit sein* 1 go up (**an** + *Akk.* to); **näher ~gehen** go [up] closer; 2 (anpacken) **an ein Problem/eine Aufgabe/die Arbeit** *usw.* **~gehen** tackle a problem/a task/the work *etc.*; **an die Lösung eines Problems ~gehen** set about solving a problem; **~gehensweise** *die* approach (**an** + *Akk.* to); **~|holen** *tr. V.* fetch; **~|kommen** *unr. itr. V.; mit sein* 1 **an etw.** (*Akk.*) **~kommen** come *or* draw near to sth.; approach sth.; **lass es erst an dich ~kommen** (ugs.) cross that bridge when you get to it; **wir waren fast an den Fluss ~gekommen** we had almost reached the river; **ganz nahe an etw.** (*Akk.*) **~kommen** come right up to sth.; 2 (zeitlich) **der große Tag kam näher ~/war ~gekommen** the big day drew nearer/had arrived; 3 **an etw.** (*Akk.*) **~kommen** (erreichen) reach sth.; (erwerben) obtain sth.; get hold of sth.; **an den Motor** *usw.* **~kommen** get at the engine *etc.*; **an jmdn. ~kommen** (fig.) get hold of sb.; **er ist so verschlossen, man kommt nur schwer an ihn ~:** he's so reserved, it's very hard to get to know him; **an diesen Wissenschaftler kommt keiner ~** (fig.) there is no one who can compare with this scientist; **an jmds. Erfolg/**

Rekord ~kommen (fig.) equal sb.'s success/record; **~|machen** *refl. V.* (ugs.) **1** (beginnen) **sich an etw.** (*Akk.*) **~machen** get down to *or* (coll.) get going on sth.; **2** (nähern) **sich an jmdn. ~machen** chat sb. up (coll.); **~|nahen** *itr. V.; mit sein* (geh.) approach; draw near; **~|nehmen** *unr. tr. V.* **die Lehrlinge werden ganz schön ~genommen** the apprentices are really made to work [hard]; **der Lehrer nahm den Schüler tüchtig ~:** the teacher took the boy firmly in hand; **~|reichen** *itr. V.* **1** (erreichen) reach; **an die oberen Schrankfächer ~reichen** reach [up to] the top shelves; **2** (von gleicher Qualität sein) **an jmdn./etw. ~reichen** come *or* measure up to the standard of sb./sth.; **~|reifen** *itr. V.; mit sein* ‹*fruit, crops*› ripen; (fig.) ‹*plan*› mature; **zur Frau/zum Mann/zu einer großen Malerin ~reifen** mature into a woman/man/great painter; **in ihm reifte der Entschluss ~, ins Ausland zu gehen** (fig.) he became increasingly resolved to go abroad; **~|rücken** **A** *tr. V.* pull up ‹*table*›; draw *or* pull *or* bring up ‹*chair*›; **B** *itr. V.; mit sein* move *or* come closer *or* nearer; ‹*troops*› advance (**an** + *Akk.* towards); **dicht** *od.* **nah ~rücken** move up close (**an** + *Akk.* to); **mit seinem Stuhl ~rücken** draw *or* pull *or* bring one's chair up closer; **~|schaffen** *tr. V.* bring; (liefern) supply; **~|schleichen** *unr. itr. V. mit sein; refl. V.* **[sich an etw./jmdn.] ~schleichen** creep *or* sneak up [to sth./on sb.]; **~|tasten** *refl. V.* **sich [an etw.] ~tasten** grope *or* feel one's way [over to sth.]; (fig.) feel one's way [towards sth.]; **~|tragen** *unr. tr. V.* **1** bring [over]; **2** (vorbringen) **eine Bitte/Beschwerde an jmdn. ~tragen** go/come to sb. with a request/complaint; **~|trauen** *refl. V.* dare to approach; **sich an etw. ~trauen** (etw. in Angriff nehmen) dare to tackle sth.; **~|treten** *unr. itr. V.; mit sein* **1** (an eine Stelle treten) come/go up (**an** + *Akk.* to); **treten Sie nur näher ~!** come along!; [just] step this way!; **2** (sich ergeben) **Probleme/Fragen/Anfechtungen treten an jmdn. ~:** sb. is faced with problems/questions/accusations; **Zweifel treten an ihn ~:** he is assailed by doubts; **3** (sich wenden) **an jmdn. ~treten** approach sb.; **~|wachsen** *unr. itr. V.; mit sein* grow up; (fig.) develop; **zum Mann/zur Frau ~wachsen** grow up into *or* to be a man/woman; **die ~wachsende Generation** the rising *or* up-and-coming generation; **~wachsende** *der/die; adj. Dekl.* **1** young person; **viele ~wachsende** many young people; **2** (Rechtsw.) adolescent; **~|wagen** *refl. V.* venture near; dare to go near; **sich an etw.** (*Akk.*) **~wagen** venture near sth.; dare to go near sth.; (fig.) venture *or* dare to tackle *or* attempt sth.; **er wagte sich nicht an das Mädchen ~:** he did not dare to approach the girl; **~|ziehen** **A** *unr. tr. V.* **1** (an eine Stelle ziehen) pull *or* draw over; pull *or* draw up ‹*chair*›; **etw. zu sich ~ziehen** pull *or* draw sth. towards one; **etw. näher ~ziehen** pull *or* draw sth. closer *or* near (**an** + *Akk.* to); **2** (beauftragen) call *or* bring in; **weitere Arbeitskräfte ~ziehen** bring in more labour; **3** (in Betracht ziehen) refer to; (geltend machen) invoke; quote; **4** (großziehen) rear, raise ‹*animal*›; grow ‹*plant*›; (ugs.) rear, raise ‹*child*›; **5** (ausbilden) **jmdn. zu etw. ~ziehen** make *or* turn sb. into sth.; **B** *unr. itr. V.; mit sein* (auch fig.) approach; (Milit.) advance; **~|züchten** *tr. V.* **1** rear, raise ‹*animal*›; grow, cultivate ‹*plant, vegetable*›; **2** train up ‹*specialists, players, terrorists, etc.*›

herauf /hɛˈrauf/ *Adv.* up; **~ ist es beschwerlich** it's hard work coming up; **vom Tal ~:** up from the valley

herauf-: ~|arbeiten *refl. V.* **1** work one's/its way up; **2** (hocharbeiten) work one's way up; **~|bemühen** **A** *tr. V.* **jmdn. ~bemühen** trouble sb. to come up; **B** *refl. V.* take the trouble to come up; **würden Sie sich bitte ~bemühen?** (geh.) would you mind coming up?; **~|beschwören** *tr. V.* **1** (verursachen) cause, bring about ‹*disaster, war, crisis*›; cause, provoke ‹*dispute, argument*›; give rise to ‹*criticism*›; **2** (erinnern) evoke ‹*memories etc.*›; **~|bitten** *unr. tr. V.* **jmdn. ~bitten** ask sb. [to come] up; **~|bringen** *unr. tr. V.* bring up; **~|dämmern** *itr. V.; mit sein* ‹*day, morning*› dawn, break; (fig.) dawn; **~|dringen** *unr. itr. V.; mit sein* rise up [from below]; ‹*smell*› drift up [from below]; **von/aus etw. ~dringen** rise/drift up from sth.; **Lachen drang zu uns ~:** [the sound of] laughter reached our ears from below; **~|fahren** **A** *unr. itr. V.; mit sein* drive up; (mit einem Motorrad, Rad) ride up; **B** *unr. tr. V.* **jmdn. ~fahren** drive sb. up; **~|führen** **A** *itr. V.* **es führen zwei Wege ~:** there are two paths up; **B** *tr. V.* show ‹*person*› up; **~|kommen** *unr. itr. V.; mit sein* **1** (nach oben kommen) come up; **auf den Baum/die Mauer ~kommen** climb *or* get up the tree/up on the wall; **in das obere Stockwerk ~kommen** come up to the top floor; **2** (aufsteigen) rise; come up; **3** (bevorstehen) ‹*storm*› be approaching *or* gathering *or* brewing; **~|lassen** *unr. tr. V.* (ugs.) **jmdn. ~lassen** allow sb. [to come] up; let sb. [come] up; **~|reichen** **A** *tr. V.* hand *or* pass up; **B** *itr. V.* (ugs.: erreichen) **bis zu etw. ~reichen** reach up to sth.; **~|sehen** *unr. itr. V.* look up; **~|setzen** *tr. V.* increase, raise, put up ‹*prices, rents, interest rates, etc.*›; **~|steigen** *unr. itr. V.; mit sein* **1** (nach [hier] oben kommen) climb [up]; **2** (aufsteigen) rise; come up; ‹*mist, smoke*› rise; **3** (geh.: beginnen) ‹*day, morning*› dawn, break; ‹*night*› come on, fall; ‹*dawn*› break; ‹*new age*› dawn; **~|ziehen** **A** *unr. tr. V.* pull up; **B** *unr. itr. V.; mit sein* **1** (näher kommen) ‹*storm*› be approaching *or* gathering *or* brewing; (fig.) ‹*disaster*› be approaching; **2** ▸ **~steigen 3**

heraus /hɛˈraus/ *Adv.* out; **aus etw. ~ sein** be out of sth.; **aus der Schule ~ sein** have left school; **aus den Schulden/einem Dilemma** *usw.* **~ sein** have got *or* be out of debt/a dilemma *etc.*; **aus dem Gröbsten ~ sein** (ugs.) be over the worst; **fein ~ sein** (ugs.) be sitting pretty (coll.); **~ aus den Federn!/dem Bett!** rise and shine!/out of bed!; **~ mit dir!** get out of here!; **~ damit!** (gib her!) hand it over!; (weg damit!) get rid of it!; **~ mit der Sprache!** out with it!; **nach vorn ~ wohnen** live at the front; **aus einem Gefühl der Einsamkeit ~:** out of a feeling of loneliness

heraus-, Heraus-: ~|arbeiten **A** *tr. V.* **1** (aus Stein, Holz) fashion, carve (**aus** out of); **2** (hervorheben) bring out ‹*difference, aspect, point of view, etc.*›; develop ‹*observation, remark*›; **B** *refl. V.* work one's way out (**aus** of); **~|bekommen** **A** *unr. tr. V.* **1** (entfernen) get out (**aus** of); **2** (ugs.: lösen) work out ‹*problem, answer, etc.*›; solve ‹*puzzle*›; **3** (ermitteln) find out; **etw. aus jmdm. ~bekommen** get sth. out of sb.; **4** (als Wechselgeld bekommen) **5 Euro ~bekommen** get back 5 euros change; **ich bekomme noch 5 Euro ~:** I still have 5 euros [change] to come; **5** (von sich geben) ▸ **~bringen 8**; **B** *unr. itr. V.* (Wechselgeld bekommen) **richtig/falsch ~bekommen** (ugs.) get the right/wrong change; **~|bilden** *refl. V.* develop; **~|bitten** *unr. tr. V.* **jmdn. ~bitten** ask sb. to come out[side]; **darf ich Sie einen Moment ~bitten?** would you mind coming outside for a moment?; **~|boxen** *tr. V.* **1** (Fußball, Handball) punch out; **2** (befreien) bail out; **~|brechen** **A** *unr. tr. V.* knock out; (mit brutaler Gewalt) wrench out; pull up ‹*paving stone*›; **eine Tür/ein paar Fliesen aus der Wand ~brechen** knock out a hole [in the wall] for a doorway/knock a few tiles off the wall; **B** *unr. itr. V.; mit sein* ‹*anger, hatred*› burst forth, erupt; **aus dem Glas ist ein großer Splitter ~gebrochen** there's a large chip out of the glass; **~|bringen** *unr. tr. V.* **1** (nach außen bringen) bring out (**aus** of); **2** (nach draußen begleiten) show out; **3** (veröffentlichen) bring out; publish; (aufführen) put on, stage ‹*play*›; screen ‹*film*›; **4** (auf den Markt bringen) bring out; launch; **5** (populär machen) make widely known; **jmdn./etw. ganz groß ~bringen** launch sb./sth. in a big way; **6** (ugs.: ermitteln) ▸ **~bekommen A 3**; **7** (ugs.: lösen) ▸ **~bekommen A 2**; **8** (von sich geben) utter; say; **~|drehen** *tr. V.* unscrew; **~|drücken** *tr. V.* **1** **etw. ~drücken** squeeze sth. out (**aus** of); squeeze *or* press ‹*juice, oil*› out (**aus** of); **2** (vorwölben) stick out ‹*chest etc.*›; **~|dürfen** *unr. itr. V.* be allowed [to come/go] out; **~|fahren** **A** *unr. itr. V.; mit sein* **1** (nach außen fahren) **aus etw. ~fahren** drive out of sth.; (mit dem Rad, Motorrad) ride out of sth.; **der Zug fuhr aus dem Bahnhof ~:** the train pulled out of the station; **2** (fahrend ~kommen) come out; **3** (ugs.: schnell ~kommen) **aus dem Bett ~fahren** shoot *or* leap out of bed; **eilig fuhr sie aus dem Mantel ~:** she whipped off her coat; **4** (ugs.: entschlüpfen) ‹*word, remark, etc.*› slip out; **B** *unr. tr. V.* **1** **den Wagen/das Fahrrad [aus dem Hof] ~fahren** drive the car/ride the bicycle out [of the yard]; **jmdn. ~fahren** drive sb. out (**zu** to); **2** (Sport) **eine gute Zeit/einen Sieg ~fahren** record a good *or* fast time/a victory; **den zweiten Platz ~fahren** take second place; **~|fallen** *unr. itr. V.; mit sein* **aus etw. ~fallen** fall out of sth.; (anders sein als) stand out from sth.; (nicht mehr berücksichtigt werden) drop out of sth.; **aus der Förderung ~fallen** no longer receive sponsorship; **~|filtern** *tr. V.* filter out (**aus** of); (aussondern) select (**aus** from); **~|finden** **A** *unr. tr. V.* **1** (entdecken) find out; trace ‹*fault*›; **man fand ~, dass …** it was found *or* discovered that …; **2** (aus einer Menge) pick out (**aus** from [among]); find (**aus** among); **B** *unr. itr. V.* find one's way out (**aus** of); **C** *unr. refl. V.* find one's way out (**aus** of); **~|fischen** *tr. V.* (ugs.) fish out (coll.) (**aus** of); **sie hat sich** (*Dat.*) **einige hübsche Sachen ~gefischt** she picked out some nice things [for herself]; **~|fliegen** **A** *unr. itr. V.; mit sein* **1** fly out (**aus** of); **2** (aus etw. fallen) be thrown out (**aus** of); **3** (ugs.: entlassen werden) be fired *or* (coll.) sacked (**bei** from); **B** *unr. tr. V.* fly out (**aus** of); **~forderer** *der;* **~~s, ~~, ~forderin** *die;* **~~, ~~nen** (auch Sport) challenger; **~|fordern** **A** *tr. V.* **1** (auch Sport) challenge; **2** (heraufbeschwören) provoke ‹*person, resistance, etc.*›; invite ‹*criticism*›; court ‹*danger*›; **sein Schicksal ~fordern** tempt fate *or* providence; **B** *itr. V.* (provozieren) **zu etw. ~fordern** provoke sth.; **~fordernd** **A** *Adj.* provocative; (verlockend) provocative, inviting ‹*glance, smile, etc.*›; (Streit suchend) challenging, defiant ‹*words, speech, look*›; **B** *adv.: s. Adj.:* provocatively; invitingly; challengingly; defiantly

Heraus·forderung *die* (auch Sport) challenge; (Provokation) provocation

heraus-, Heraus-: ~|fühlen *tr. V.* sense; feel; **~|führen** **A** *tr. V.* **1** (nach außen führen) lead out; **2** (nach draußen führen) bring out; **was führt dich denn zu uns ~?** what brings you out to see us, then?; **B** *itr. V.* lead out (**aus** of); **~gabe** *die* **1** (von Eigentum, Personen, Geiseln usw.) handing over; (Rückgabe) return; **2** (das Veröffentlichen) publication; (Redaktion) editing; **~|geben** **A** *unr. tr. V.* **1** (nach außen geben) hand *or* pass out; **2** (aushändigen) hand over ‹*property, person, hostage, etc.*›; (zurückgeben) return; give back; **3** (als Wechselgeld zurückgeben) **5 Euro/zu viel ~geben** give 5 euros/too much change; **4** (veröffentlichen) publish; (für die Veröffentlichung bearbeiten) edit [for publication]; **5** issue ‹*stamp, coin, etc.*›; **6** (erlassen) issue; **B** *itr. V.* give change; **können Sie [auf 100 Euro] ~geben?** do you have *or* can you give me change [for 100 euros]?; **jmdm. falsch/richtig ~geben** give sb. the wrong/right change; **~geber** *der,* **~geberin** *die* publisher; (Redakteur) editor; **~|gehen** *unr. itr. V.; mit sein* **1** (nach außen gehen) go out; leave; **aus dem Saal ~gehen** go out of the hall; **aus sich ~gehen** come out of one's shell; **2** (sich entfernen lassen) ‹*stain, cork, nail, etc.*› come out; **~|greifen** *unr. tr. V.* pick out; select; **sich** (*Dat.*) **jmdn. ~greifen** pick *or* single sb. out (**aus** from); (fig.) take ‹*example, aspect, etc.*› (**aus** from); **~|haben** *unr. tr. V.* (ugs.) **1** (entfernt haben) have got ‹*stain, nail, cork, etc.*› out; **ich will ihn aus dem Verein ~haben** I want him out of the club; **2** (verstanden haben) have found out; **den Bogen** *od.* **Dreh ~haben[, wie man es macht]** have got the knack [of doing it]; **3** (gelöst haben) have worked out *or* solved ‹*problem*›; have solved ‹*puzzle*›; **er hat etwas anderes ~ als ich** we arrived at *or* got different answers; **ich habs ~!** I've done it!; **4** (ermittelt haben) know; have found out; **~|halten** **A** *unr. tr. V.* **1** (nach außen halten)

h

put *or* stick out (**aus** of); 2 (ugs.: fernhalten, nicht verwickeln) keep out (**aus** of); B *unr. refl. V.* keep *or* stay out; **halte du dich da ~!** you keep *or* stay out of this *or* it!; **~|hängen¹** *unr. itr. V.* hang out (**aus** of); **~|hängen²** *tr. V.* hang out (**aus** of); **~|hauen** *unr. tr. V.* 1 chop *or* cut down and clear ‹*tree*›; 2 (durch Hauen fertigen) carve ‹*figure, letters, relief, etc.*› (**aus** from, out of); 3 (ugs.: befreien) get out; (aus Schwierigkeiten) bail out; **~|heben** A *unr. tr. V.* 1 (nach außen heben) lift out (**aus** of); 2 (hervorheben) bring out; **es ist diese Eigenschaft, die ihn aus der Masse ~hebt** it is this quality that raises him above *or* sets him apart from the rest; **etw. durch Fettdruck aus dem übrigen Text ~heben** make sth. stand out from the rest of the text with bold type; B *unr. refl. V.* stand out (**aus** from); **~|helfen** *unr. itr. V.* **jmdm. ~helfen** (auch fig.) help sb. out (**aus** of); **er half ihr aus dem Zug ~:** he helped her off the train; **~|holen** *tr. V.* 1 (nach außen holen) bring out; **etw. aus einem brennenden Haus ~holen** get sth. out of a burning house; 2 (ugs.: abgewinnen) get out; gain, win ‹*victory, points*›; gain, take ‹*place*›; **er holte das Letzte aus sich ~:** he made an all-out *or* supreme effort; 3 (ugs.: erwirken) gain, win ‹*wage increase, advantage, etc.*›; get, achieve ‹*result*›; 4 (ugs.: durch Fragen) get out; **etw. aus jmdm. ~holen** get sth. out of sb.; 5 (ugs.: ~arbeiten) bring out ‹*difference, aspect, point of view*›; 6 (ausgleichen) make up ‹*time, points deficit, etc.*›; 7 (ugs.) **Geld aus jmdm. ~holen** get money out of *or* extract money from sb.; **~|hören** *tr. V.* 1 hear; 2 (erkennen) detect, sense (**aus** in); **~|kehren** *tr. V.* parade; **den Vorgesetzten ~kehren** parade the fact that one is in charge; **die Dame der Gesellschaft ~kehren** act the society lady; **~kehren, dass ...** parade the fact that ...; **~|kommen** *unr. itr. V.; mit sein* 1 (nach außen kommen) come out (**aus** of); **nach/in zwei Jahren wieder ~kommen** (ugs.) be let out after/in two years; 2 (ein Gebiet verlassen) **er ist nie aus seiner Heimatstadt ~gekommen** he's never been out of *or* never left his home town; **du kommst viel zu wenig ~:** you don't get out nearly enough; **wir kamen aus dem Staunen/Lachen nicht ~** (fig.) we couldn't get over our surprise/stop laughing; 3 (ugs.: einen Ausweg finden) get out (**aus** of); **aus einer Situation/den Sorgen ~kommen** get out of a situation/get over one's worries; **aus den Schulden ~kommen** get out of debt; 4 (ugs.: auf den Markt kommen) come out; **mit einem Produkt ~kommen** bring out *or* launch a product; 5 (erscheinen) ‹*book, timetable, etc.*› come out, be published, appear; ‹*coin, postage stamp*› be issued; ‹*play*› be staged; 6 (ugs.: bekannt werden) come out; 7 (ugs.: zur Sprache kommen) **mit etw. ~kommen** come out with sth.; 8 (ugs.: sich erfolgreich produzieren) **ganz groß ~kommen** make a big splash; 9 (deutlich werden) come out; ‹*colour*› show up; 10 (ugs.: ausgedrückt werden) sound; 11 (ugs.: sich als Resultat ergeben) **bei etw. ~kommen** come out of *or* emerge from sth.; **auf dasselbe ~kommen** amount to the same thing; **was kommt bei der Aufgabe ~?** what is the answer to the question?; **dabei kommt nichts ~:** nothing will come of it; **was soll dabei ~kommen?** what's that supposed to achieve?; 12 (ugs.: aus der Übung kommen) get out of practice; 13 (ugs.: ausspielen) lead; **wer kommt ~?** whose lead is it?; **mit etw. ~kommen** lead sth.; 14 (ugs.: gewinnen) ‹*number, person*› come up; 15 (schweiz.: ausgehen, enden) turn out; **~|kriegen** *tr. V.* (ugs.) ▸ **~bekommen**; **~|kristallisieren** A *tr. V.* 1 (Chemie) crystallize [out]; 2 (zusammenfassen) extract; B *refl. V.* 1 (Chemie) crystallize [out]; ‹*crystal*› form; 2 (entwickeln) crystallize (**aus** out of); **~|lassen** *unr. tr. V.* (ugs.) 1 (nach außen kommen lassen) let out (**aus** of); release (**aus** from); **abends lassen sie den Wachhund ~:** they let the guard dog loose in the evenings; 2 (weglassen) leave out (**aus** of); **~|laufen** A *unr. itr. V.; mit sein* 1 run out (**aus** of); (Fußball) ‹*goalkeeper*› come out; 2 (nach außen fließen) run out (**aus** of); B *unr. tr. V.* (Sport) win ‹*victory*›; build up ‹*lead*›; take ‹*first place etc.*›; **eine gute Zeit ~laufen** run *or* record a good time; **~|lesen** *unr. tr. V.* 1 (entnehmen) tell (**aus** from); 2 (interpretieren) **etw. aus etw. ~lesen** read sth. into sth.; 3 (auswählen) pick out (**aus** from); **~|locken** *tr. V.* 1 entice out (**aus** of); lure ‹*enemy, victim, etc.*› out (**aus** of); 2 (durch List) **Geld/ein Geheimnis aus jmdm. ~locken** wheedle money/worm a secret out of sb.; **jmdn. aus seiner Reserve ~locken** draw sb. out of his/her shell; **~|lösen** *tr. V.* (entfernen) remove (**aus** from); (herausnehmen) take out (**aus** of); **~|lügen** *unr. refl. V.* **sich aus etw. ~lügen** lie one's way out of sth.; **~|machen** (ugs.) A *tr. V.* take out; get out ‹*stain*›; B *refl. V.* come on well; (nach einer Krankheit) pick up; (finanziell) do well; **~|müssen** *unr. itr. V.* (ugs.) 1 **aus etw. ~müssen** have to leave sth.; **dieser Zahn muss ~:** this tooth has to come out; 2 (aufstehen müssen) have to get up; 3 (gesagt werden müssen) have to come out; **das musste einfach ~!** I simply had to get that off my chest (coll.); **~nehmbar** *Adj.* removable; detachable ‹*lining*›; **~|nehmen** *unr. tr. V.* 1 take out (**aus** of); 2 (ugs.: entfernen) take out, remove ‹*appendix, tonsils, tooth, etc.*›; **jmdm. den Blinddarm ~nehmen** take out *or* remove sb.'s appendix; **sich** (*Dat.*) **die Mandeln ~nehmen lassen** have one's tonsils out; **den Gang ~nehmen** (fig.) put the car into neutral; **ein Kind aus einer Schule ~nehmen** take a child away *or* remove a child from a school; 3 (Ballspiele) take off ‹*player*›; 4 (ugs.: erlauben) **sich** (*Dat.*) **Freiheiten ~nehmen** take liberties; **was nimmst du dir ~, mich so zu kritisieren!** how dare you criticize me like that!; **sich** (*Dat.*) **zu viel ~nehmen** go too far; **~|picken** *tr. V.* (fig.) pick out (**aus** of); **~|platzen** *itr. V.; mit sein* (ugs.) 1 (~lachen) burst out laughing; 2 (spontan äußern) **mit etw. ~platzen** blurt sth. out; **~|pressen** *tr. V.* 1 (aus etw. pressen) ▸ **~drücken 1**; 2 (erpressen) squeeze out ‹*money*› (**aus** from); wring out ‹*confession, concession*› (**aus** from); **~|putzen** *tr. V.* 1 (festlich kleiden) dress up; **sich ~putzen** get dressed up; 2 (festlich schmücken) deck out; **sich ~putzen** be decked out; **~|ragen** *itr. V.* 1 jut out, project (**aus** from); (sich erheben über) **aus etw. ~ragen** rise above sth.; 2 (hervortreten) stand out (**aus** from); **~ragend** *Adj.* outstanding; **~|reden** *refl. V.* (ugs.) talk one's way out (**aus** of); **~|reißen** *unr. tr. V.* 1 tear *or* rip out (**aus** of); pull up *or* out ‹*plant*›; pull out ‹*hair*›; pull up ‹*floor*›; rip out ‹*tiles*›; 2 (aus der Umgebung, der Arbeit) tear away (**aus** from); **die Krankheit hat ihn aus der Arbeit ~gerissen** the illness has interrupted his work; **jmdn. aus einem Gespräch/seiner Lethargie ~reißen** drag sb. away from a conversation/jolt *or* shake sb. out of his/her lethargy; **jmdn. aus seiner Traurigkeit ~reißen** take sb. out of himself/herself; 3 (ugs.: befreien) save; **~|rücken** A *tr. V.* 1 (nach außen rücken) move out (**aus** of); 2 (ugs.: hergeben) hand over; cough up (coll.) ‹*money*›; B *itr. V.; mit sein* **mit etw./der Sprache ~rücken** come out with sth./it; **~|rufen** A *unr. itr. V.* call *or* shout out (**aus** of); B *unr. tr. V.* call out; **jmdn. aus einer Sitzung ~rufen** call sb. out of a meeting; **das Publikum rief den Sänger mehrmals ~:** the audience called the singer back several times; **~|rutschen** *itr. V.; mit sein* 1 slip out (**aus** of); **ihm rutscht immer das Hemd aus der Hose ~:** his shirt is always coming out of his trousers; 2 (ugs.: entschlüpfen) ‹*remark etc.*› slip out; **die Bemerkung war ihr nur so ~gerutscht** the remark just slipped out somehow; **~|saugen** *unr.* (*auch regelm.*) *tr. V.* suck out (**aus** of); **~|schälen** *refl. V.* 1 (erkennbar werden) emerge (**aus** from); 2 (sich erweisen) **sich als etw. ~schälen** turn out *or* prove to be sth.; **~|schauen** *itr. V.* (landsch.) 1 look out (**aus/zu** of); 2 (hervorschauen) ‹*petticoat etc.*› be showing; ‹*shirt*› be hanging out; 3 (ugs.: zu erwarten sein) **dabei schaut etwas/nicht viel für ihn ~:** there's something/not much in it for him; **es schaut nichts dabei ~:** there's nothing to be gained by it; **~|schießen** *unr. itr. V.* 1 **aus einem Fenster/Auto ~schießen** shoot *or* fire from a window/car; 2 *mit sein* (sich schnell bewegen) shoot out (**aus** of); **ein Blutstrahl schoss aus der Wunde ~:** blood spurted from the wound; **~geschossen kommen** (ugs.) shoot out (**aus** of); **~|schlagen** A *unr. tr. V.* 1 knock out; 2 (ugs.: gewinnen) get ‹*discount, advantage, etc.*›; make ‹*money, profit*›; B *unr. itr. V.; mit sein* ‹*flames*› leap out (**aus** of); **~|schleichen** A *unr. itr. V.; mit sein* sneak *or* steal out (**aus** of); B *unr. refl. V.* sneak *or* steal out (**aus** of); **~|schleudern** *tr. V.* hurl *or* fling out (**aus** of); hurl ‹*accusations etc.*›; **die Straßenbahn wurde aus den Schienen ~geschleudert** the tram (Brit.) *or* (Amer.) streetcar was flung *or* thrown off the rails; **~|schlüpfen** *itr. V.; mit sein* slip out (**aus** of); **eine Bemerkung schlüpfte ihm ~:** a remark slipped out; **~|schmecken** A *tr. V.* **etw. ~schmecken [können]** be able to taste sth.; B *itr. V.* taste; **~|schmeißen** ▸ **rausschmeißen**; **~|schmuggeln** *tr. V.* smuggle out (**aus** of); **~|schneiden** *unr. tr. V.* cut out (**aus** of); **~|schrauben** *tr. V.* unscrew ‹*light bulb, screw*›; unscrew, screw off ‹*door handle, table leg, etc.*›; **~|schreiben** *unr. tr. V.* copy out (**aus** from); **~|schreien** *unr. tr. V.* **seine Wut/seinen Zorn/seinen Hass ~schreien** vent *or* give vent to one's anger/rage/hatred in a loud outburst; ***~|sein** ▸ **heraus**

heraußen /hɛ'rausn̩/ *Adv.* (südd., österr.) out here

heraus-: **~|springen** *unr. itr. V.; mit sein* 1 jump *or* leap out (**aus** of); 2 (sich lösen) come out; 3 ▸ **~schauen 3**; **~|sprudeln** A *itr. V.; mit sein* bubble out (**aus** of); B *tr. V.* **sie sprudelte die Worte ~:** the words tumbled from her lips; **~|stehen** *unr. itr. V.* protrude; stick out; **~|stellen** A *tr. V.* 1 put out[side]; **sie stellte das Geschirr zum Abendessen ~:** she got the china out ready for dinner; **einen Spieler ~stellen** (Sport) send a player off; 2 (hervorheben) emphasize; bring out; present, set out ‹*principles etc.*›; **eine Nebenfigur ~stellen** give prominence to a minor character; B *refl. V.* **es stellte sich ~, dass ...** it turned out *or* emerged that ...; **wie sich später ~stellte, hatte er ...** it turned out later that he had ...; **wer Recht hat, wird sich erst noch ~stellen müssen** it remains to be seen who is right; **es wird sich bald ~stellen, ob ...** we shall soon know *or* find out whether ...; **sich als falsch/wahr** *usw.* **~stellen** turn out *or* prove to be wrong/true *etc.*; **~|strecken** *tr. V.* stick out (**aus** of); **jmdm. die Zunge ~strecken** stick *or* put one's tongue out at sb.; **seinen Arm/Kopf zum Fenster ~strecken** stick *or* put one's arm/head out of the window; **~|streichen** *unr. tr. V.* 1 (ausstreichen) cross out; delete (**aus** from); 2 (hervorheben) point out; **er streicht gerne ~, dass ...** he likes everyone to know that ...; **~|strömen** *itr. V.; mit sein* 1 (ausströmen) ‹*water etc.*› pour out (**aus** of); ‹*gas*› escape (**aus** from); 2 (~kommen) ‹*Menschenmenge*› pour out (**aus** of); **~|stürzen** *itr. V.; mit sein* 1 (~fallen) fall out (**aus** of); 2 (eilen) rush *or* dash out (**aus** of); **~|suchen** *tr. V.* pick out; look out ‹*file*›; **~|tragen** *unr. tr. V.* carry outside; **die Kisten aus dem Haus ~tragen** carry the boxes out of the house; **~|treten** *unr. itr. V.; mit sein* 1 come out (**aus** of); **auf den Balkon ~treten** come *or* step out onto the balcony; 2 (sich abzeichnen) ‹*veins etc.*› stand out; **~|trommeln** *tr. V.* (ugs.) get out; **~|wachsen** *unr. itr. V.; mit sein* grow out (**aus** of); **~|werfen** *unr. tr. V.* 1 throw out (**aus** of); 2 ▸ **hinauswerfen**; **~|winden** *unr. refl. V.* wriggle out (**aus** of); **~|wirtschaften** *tr. V.* make ‹*profit etc.*› (**aus** out of); **~|wollen** *unr. itr. V.* want to come/go out (**aus** of); **er wollte nicht mit der Sprache ~:** he did not want to come out with it; **~|ziehen** A *unr. tr. V.* 1 pull out (**aus** of); 2 (wegbringen) pull out, withdraw ‹*troops etc.*›; 3 (exzerpieren, extrahieren) extract (**aus** from); B *unr. itr. V.; mit sein* move out (**aus** of)

herb /hɛrp/

A *Adj.* 1 [slightly] sharp *or* astringent ‹*taste*›; dry ‹*wine*›; [slightly] sharp *or* tangy ‹*smell, perfume*› 2 bitter ‹*disappointment, loss*›; severe ‹face, features›; austere ‹beauty› [3] (unfreundlich) harsh ‹words, criticism›; curt ‹greeting› [B] adv. bitterly ‹disappointed›

Herbarium /hɛrˈbaːri̯ʊm/ das; ~s, **Herbarien** /-ˈ-ri̯ən/ herbarium

herbei /hɛɐ̯ˈbai̯/ Adv. ~ **[zu mir]!** come [over] here!; **alle Mann** od. (ugs.) **alles ~!** come [over] here, everybody!

herbei-: ~**|bringen** unr. tr. V. bring [over]; ~**|eilen** itr. V.; mit sein hurry over; come hurrying up; ~**|führen** tr. V. produce, bring about ‹decision›; bring about, cause ‹downfall›; cause ‹accident›; **wenn nicht bald eine Entscheidung ~geführt wird** if no decision is reached soon; **den Tod ~führen** cause death; ~**|holen** tr. V. fetch; **sich** (Dat.) **etw. ~holen lassen** have sth. brought to one; **einen Arzt ~holen/~holen lassen** fetch/send for a doctor; ~**|kommen** unr. itr. V.; mit sein come up or along; **die Menschen kamen aus allen Richtungen ~:** people came from all directions; ~**|lassen** unr. refl. V. (iron.) **sich ~lassen, etw. zu tun** condescend or deign to do sth.; ~**|laufen** unr. itr. V.; mit sein come running up; ~**|rufen** unr. tr. V. call over; **Hilfe/einen Arzt ~rufen** summon help/call a doctor; ~**|schaffen** tr. V. bring; (besorgen) get; ~**|sehnen** tr. V. long for; **sie hatte den Urlaub sehr ~gesehnt** she had been longing for the holidays to arrive; ~**|strömen** itr. V.; mit sein come in crowds; come flocking; ~**|winken** tr. V. **jmdn. ~winken** beckon sb. over; ~**|wünschen** tr. V. long for; **jmdn. ~wünschen** long for sb. to come; ~**|ziehen** unr. tr. V. **etw. ~ziehen** pull or draw sth. up; draw ‹crowd etc.›; **jmdn. ~ziehen** draw sb. to one; **sich** (Dat.) **etw. ~ziehen** pull or draw sth. to one; s. auch **Haar 2**; ~**|zitieren** tr. V. **jmdn. ~zitieren** send for or summon sb.

her-: ~**|bekommen** unr. tr. V. get; ~**|bemühen** (geh.) [A] tr. V. **jmdn. ~bemühen** trouble sb. to come; [B] refl. V. take the trouble to come; ~**|beordern** tr. V. summon; send for

Herberge /ˈhɛrbɛrɡə/ die; ~, ~n [1] (veralt.: Gasthaus) inn [2] (Jugend~) [youth] hostel [3] (veralt.: Unterkunft) accommodation no indef. art.

Herbergs-: ~**mutter** die; Pl. ~**mütter**, ~**vater** der warden [of the/a youth hostel]

her-: ~**|bestellen** tr. V. **jmdn. ~bestellen** ask sb. to come; (~beordern) summon sb.; ~**|beten** ▸herunterbeten

Herbheit die; ~: ▸herb A 1, 2: [slight] sharpness or astringency; dryness; [slight] sharpness or tanginess; bitterness; severity; austerity

her|bitten unr. tr. V. **jmdn. ~:** ask sb. to come

Herbizid /hɛrbiˈtsiːt/ das; ~s, ~e herbicide

her|bringen unr. tr. V. **etw. ~:** bring sth. [here]

Herbst /hɛrpst/ der; ~[e]s, ~e ▸ⓘ S. 395 autumn; fall (Amer.); s. auch **Frühling**

Herbst-: ~**anfang** der beginning of autumn; ~**blume** die autumn flower

herbsten itr. V. (unpers.) (geh.) **es herbstet** autumn is coming or approaching

Herbst·ferien Pl. autumn half-term holiday sing.

herbstlich ▸ⓘ S. 395
[A] Adj. autumn attrib.; autumnal; (wie im Herbst) autumnal; **es wird ~:** autumn is coming
[B] adv. **sich ~ färben** take on the colours of autumn; **~ kühle Tage** cool autumn days; **es ist schon ~ kühl** there's already an autumn chill in the air

Herbst-: ~**monat** der [1] autumn month; [2] (veralt.) **der ~monat** September; ~**tag** der autumn day; ~**wetter** das autumnal weather; ~**zeitlose** die; ~~, ~~n od. adj. Dekl. (Bot.) meadow saffron

Herd /heːɐ̯t/ der; ~[e]s, ~e [1] (Kochstelle) cooker; stove; **das Essen auf dem ~ haben** (ugs.) be cooking something; **den ganzen Tag am ~ stehen** (ugs.) slave over a hot stove all day; **am heimischen** od. **häuslichen ~:** by one's own fireside; **eigener ~ ist Goldes wert** there's no place like home (prov.) [2] (Ausgangspunkt) centre (of disturbance/rebellion); (Geol.) focus [3] (Med.) focus; seat [4] (Technik) hearth

Herd·buch das (Landw.) herd book

Herde /ˈheːɐ̯də/ die; ~, ~n [1] (von Tieren) herd; **eine ~ Rinder** a herd of cattle; **eine ~ Schafe** a flock of sheep [2] (abwertend: Menschenmenge) crowd; **mit der ~ laufen, der ~ folgen** follow the herd or crowd [3] (fig.: kirchliche Gemeinde) flock

Herden-: ~**mensch** der (abwertend) ▸~tier 2; ~**tier** das [1] gregarious animal; [2] (abwertend: Mensch) sheep; ~**trieb** der (auch fig. abwertend) herd instinct

Herd·platte die (eines Elektroherdes) hotplate; (eines Kohlenherds) top

herein /hɛˈrai̯n/ Adv. **~!** come in!; **[immer] nur ~ mit dir!** come on in!

herein-: ~**|bekommen** unr. tr. V. (ugs.) get in ‹fresh stocks›; pick up ‹radio station›; recover ‹investment›; ~**|bemühen** (geh.) [A] tr. V. **jmdn. ~bemühen** trouble sb. to come in; [B] refl. V. take the trouble to come in; ~**|bitten** unr. tr. V. **jmdn. ~bitten** ask or invite sb. in; ~**|brechen** unr. itr. V.; mit sein [1] (geh.: hart treffen) **über jmdn./etw. ~brechen** ‹fate, disaster, misfortune, etc.› befall or overtake sb./sth.; [2] (geh.: beginnen) ‹night, evening, dusk› fall; ‹winter› set in; ‹storm› strike, break; [3] (überfluten) **über etw.** (Akk.) **~brechen** break over sth.; **eine Flut von Beschimpfungen brach über ihn ~** (fig.) he was engulfed in a flood of abuse; ~**|bringen** unr. tr. V. [1] bring in; **etw. in etw.** (Akk.) **~bringen** bring sth. into sth.; [2] (wettmachen) make up ‹loss›; make up for ‹delay›; recoup ‹costs›; ~**|drängen** itr. V.; mit sein push one's way in; **in etw.** (Akk.) **~drängen** push one's way into sth.; ~**|dürfen** unr. itr. V. (ugs.) be allowed in; **in etw.** (Akk.) **~dürfen** be allowed into sth.; **darf er ~?** may or can he come in?; ~**|fallen** unr. itr. V.; mit sein [1] ‹light› shine in; [2] (ugs.: betrogen werden) be taken for a ride (coll.); be done (coll.); **bei/mit etw. ~fallen** be taken for a ride with sth.; **auf jmdn./etw. ~fallen** be taken in by sb./sth.; ~**|führen** tr. V. **jmdn. ~führen** show sb. in; ~**|holen** tr. V. [1] bring in; [2] (ugs.: verdienen) make (coll.); ~**|kommen** unr. itr. V.; mit sein come in; **in das Haus/zur Tür ~kommen** come into the house/in through the door; **wie sind sie ~gekommen?** how did they get in?; ~**|kriegen** tr. V. (ugs.) ▸~bekommen; ~**|lassen** unr. tr. V. let or allow in; **jmdn. ins Zimmer ~lassen** let or allow sb. into the room; ~**|legen** tr. V. (ugs.) **jmdn. ~legen** take sb. for a ride (coll.) **(mit, bei** with); ~**|nehmen** unr. tr. V. [1] bring in; **etw. ins Haus ~nehmen** bring sth. into the house; [2] (in eine Liste) include; **etw. in sein Sortiment ~nehmen** start selling sth. as well; ~**|platzen** itr. V.; mit sein (ugs.) burst in; come bursting in; **in den Saal ~platzen** burst or come bursting into the hall; ~**|rasseln** itr. V.; mit sein (salopp) [1] (betrogen werden) **mit/bei etw. ~rasseln** be taken for a ride with sth. (coll.); [2] (in Schwierigkeiten geraten) get into deep water (coll.); ~**|regnen** itr. V. (unpers.) **es regnet ~:** the rain's coming in; ~**|reichen** [A] tr. V. hand or pass in; [B] itr. V. **etw. reicht in das Zimmer ~:** sth. comes [right] in to the room; ~**|reißen** unr. tr. V. (ugs.) ▸reinreißen; ~**|reiten** [A] unr. itr. V.; mit sein ride in; **in den Hof ~reiten** ride into the yard; [B] ▸reinreiten; ~**|rufen** unr. tr. V. **jmdn. ~rufen** call sb. in; ~**|schauen** itr. V. (landsch.) ▸~sehen; ~**|schleichen** unr. itr. V. mit sein; refl. V. creep or steal in; **[sich] ins Haus ~schleichen** creep or steal into the house; ~**|schneien** unr. itr. V. [1] mit sein (ugs.) turn up out of the blue (coll.); [2] (unpers.) **es schneit ~:** the snow's coming in; ~**|sehen** unr. itr. V. [1] see in; (~blicken) look in; **in etw.** (Akk.) **~sehen** see/look into sth.; [2] (kurz besuchen) look or drop in (**bei** on); ~**|spazieren** itr. V.; mit sein (ugs.) walk in; stroll in; **er ist einfach in das Zimmer ~spaziert** he simply walked straight into the room; **nur ~spaziert!** come right in!; ~**|stecken** tr. V. **den Kopf zur Tür ~stecken** ▸Tür; ~**|strömen** itr. V.; mit sein ‹water etc.› pour in; ‹people› pour or stream in; **in etw.** (Akk.) **~strömen** pour or stream into sth.; ~**|stürmen** itr. V.; mit sein rush or dash in; come rushing or dashing in; (wütend) storm in; come storming in; **ins Zimmer ~stürmen** rush/storm into the room; ~**|stürzen** itr. V.; mit sein rush in; burst in; **ins Zimmer ~stürzen** rush or burst into the room; ~**|tragen** unr. tr. V. carry in; **etw. ins Haus ~tragen** carry sth. into the house; ~**|wagen** refl. V. venture to come in; ~**|wollen** unr. itr. V. (ugs.) want to come in; **ins Haus ~wollen** want to come into the house

her-, Her-: ~**|fahren** [A] unr. itr. V.; mit sein come here; (mit einem Auto) drive or come here; (mit einem [Motor]rad) ride or come here; **hinter/vor jmdm./etw. ~fahren** drive/ride along behind/in front of sb./sth.; [B] unr. tr. V. **jmdn. ~fahren** drive sb. here; ~**fahrt** die journey here; ~**|fallen** unr. itr. V.; mit sein [1] **über jmdn. ~fallen** set upon or attack sb.; ‹animal› attack sb.; **mit Fragen/Vorwürfen über jmdn. ~fallen** (fig.) besiege sb. with questions/hurl reproaches at sb.; [2] (gierig zu essen beginnen) **über etw.** (Akk.) **~fallen** fall upon sth.; ~**|finden** unr. itr. V. find one's way here; ~**|führen** tr. V. [1] (geleiten) **jmdn. ~führen** bring sb. here; **ein Tier hinter/vor jmdm. ~führen** lead an animal along in front of/behind sb.; [2] (an einen Ort gelangen lassen) **was führt dich ~?** what brings you here?; ~**gang** der: **der ~gang der Ereignisse** the sequence of events; **jmdn. über den ~gang befragen** question sb. about what happened; **schildern Sie den ~gang des Überfalls** describe what happened during the attack; ~**|geben** unr. tr. V. [1] hand over; (weggeben) give away; **sein Geld für etw. ~geben** put one's money into sth.; **seinen Namen für etw. ~geben** lend one's name to sth.; allow one's name to be associated with sth.; **er hat sein Letztes ~gegeben** he gave everything he had; **sich für etw. ~geben** get involved in sth.; **dazu gebe ich mich nicht ~:** I won't have anything to do with it; [2] (reichen) give; **gib es ~!** hand it over!; [3] (erbringen) **der Boden gibt wenig ~:** the soil is poor; **das Thema wird viel ~geben** there's a lot to this topic; **was seine Beine ~gaben** as fast as his legs could carry him; ~**gebracht** [A] 2. Part. v. ~**bringen;** [B] Adj. time-honoured; ~**|gehen** unr. itr. V.; mit sein [1] (begleiten) **neben/vor/hinter jmdm. ~gehen** walk along beside/in front of/behind sb.; [2] (ugs.) **~gehen und etw. tun** just [go and] do sth.; [3] (südd., österr.: ~kommen) come [here]; [4] unpers. (ugs.) **auf der Party ging es hoch/lustig ~:** everyone had a whale of a time (coll.)/great fun at the party; **bei der Debatte ging es heiß ~:** the sparks really flew in the debate; ~**|gehören** ▸hierher gehören; ~**gelaufen** [A] 2. Part. v. ~**laufen;** [B] Adj. **dieser ~gelaufene Strolch** this good-for-nothing rascal from Heaven knows where; ~**|haben** unr. tr. V. (ugs.) **wo hat er/sie das ~?** where did he/she get that from?; ~**|halten** [A] unr. itr. V. **~halten müssen [für jmdn./etw.]** be the one to suffer [for sb./sth.]; **als Beweis für die Theorie ~halten** serve as proof of the theory; **der Mantel wird diesen Winter noch einmal ~halten müssen** the coat will have to do for one more winter; [B] unr. tr. V. hold out; ~**|holen** tr. V. fetch; **etw. von weit ~holen** get sth. from a long way away; **weit ~geholt** far-fetched; ~**|hören** itr. V. listen; **alle mal ~hören!** listen everybody

Hering /ˈheːrɪŋ/ der; ~s, ~e [1] herring; **wie die ~e** (fig.) packed together like sardines [2] (Zeltpflock) peg [3] (ugs.: sehr dünne Person) **ein [richtiger] ~ sein** be as thin as a rake

Herings-: ~**fänger** der (Schiff) herring boat; ~**filet** das herring fillet; ~**fischerei** die herring fishing; ~**salat** der herring salad

herinnen /hɛˈrɪnən/ Adv. (südd., österr.) in here

her-, Her-: ~**|jagen** [A] tr. V. **ein Tier ~jagen** drive or chase an animal here; **jmdn./ein Tier vor sich** (Dat.) **~jagen** drive or chase sb./an animal along ahead of one; [B] itr. V.; mit sein **hinter jmdm. ~jagen** chase or pursue sb.;

h

hinter etw. ~jagen (fig.) pursue sth.; ~|kommen unr. itr. V.; mit sein [1] come here; komm [mal] ~! come here!; sie wird mit Sicherheit ~kommen she'll definitely come; [2] (abstammen) come; wer weiß, wo das ~kommt (ugs.: warum das so ist) who can tell the reason?; [3] (~genommen werden) wo soll das Geld ~kommen? where is the money coming from?; ~kommen das; ~~s [1] (Brauch, Sitte) tradition; [2] ▸Herkunft 1; ~kömmlich /-kœmlıç/ Adj. conventional; traditional ‹custom›

Herkules /ˈhɛrkulɛs/ der; ~, ~se Hercules

Herkules·arbeit die Herculean task

herkulisch /hɛrˈku:lıʃ/ Adj. (geh.) Herculean

Herkunft /ˈhe:ɐ̯kʊnft/ die; ~, Herkünfte /ˈhe:ɐ̯kʏnftə/ [1] (soziale Abstammung) origin[s pl.]; einfacher (Gen.) od. von einfacher ~ sein be of humble origin or stock; sie ist ihrer ~ nach Amerikanerin she is of American descent or extraction [2] (Ursprung) origin

Herkunfts-: ~bezeichnung die indication of country of origin; ~land das country of origin

her-: ~|laufen unr. itr. V.; mit sein [1] vor/hinter/neben jmdm. ~laufen run [along] in front of/behind/alongside sb.; [2] (nachlaufen) hinter jmdm. ~laufen run after sb.; (fig.) chase sb. up; [3] (zum Sprechenden laufen) come on foot; (schneller) come running up; ich bin ~gelaufen I walked here; (schneller) I ran here; ~|leiten A tr. V. derive (aus, von from); etw. von jmdm. ~leiten derive sth. from sb.; B refl. V. sich von/aus etw. ~leiten derive or be derived from sth.; ~|locken tr. V. jmdn./ein Tier ~locken lure or entice sb./an animal here; ein Tier hinter sich (Dat.) ~locken entice an animal to follow one along; ~|machen (ugs.) A refl. V. [1] sich über etw. (Akk.) ~machen get stuck into sth. (coll.); sich über das Essen/die Geschenke ~machen fall upon the food/presents; [2] (~fallen) sich über jmdn. ~machen set on or attack sb.; B tr. V. wenig ~machen not look much (coll.); viel ~machen look great (coll.); nichts ~machen not look much at all (coll.); viel von jmdm./etw. ~machen make a lot of fuss about sb./sth.; wenig/nichts von jmdm./etw. ~machen not make a lot of/any fuss about sth.

Hermaphrodit /hɛrm|afroˈdi:t/ der; ~en, ~en (Biol., Med.) hermaphrodite

Hermelin[1] /hɛrməˈli:n/ das; ~s, ~e (Tier) ermine; (im Sommerfell) stoat

Hermelin[2] der; ~s, ~e (Pelz) ermine

Hermeneutik /hɛrmeˈnɔytık/ die; ~: hermeneutics sing., no art.

hermeneutisch Adj. hermeneutic

hermetisch /hɛrˈme:tıʃ/

A Adj. hermetic

B adv. hermetically; ein Dorf usw. ~ abriegeln seal a village etc. off completely

her|müssen unr. itr. V. (ugs.) das muss her I/we have to or must have it

her·nach Adv. (veralt.) after that

her|nehmen unr. tr. V. [1] (beschaffen) wo soll ich das Geld ~? where am I supposed to get the money from or find the money? [2] (bes. österr.: stark beanspruchen) die Arbeit/Krankheit/der Schicksalsschlag hat sie hergenommen the work/illness/blow of fate took it out of her [3] (ugs.: scharf tadeln) jmdn. ~: give sb. a good talking-to

her·nieder- in Zus. (geh.) down

heroben /heˈro:bn̩/ Adv. (südd., österr.) up here

Heroe /heˈro:ə/ der; ~n, ~n (geh.) hero

Heroen·kult der (geh.) hero worship

Heroin[1] /heroˈi:n/ das; ~s heroin

Heroin[2] /heˈro:ın/ die; ~, ~nen heroine

Heroine /heroˈi:nə/ die; ~, ~n (Theater) actress who plays heroine roles

heroin·süchtig Adj. addicted to heroin postpos.

heroisch Adj. heroic

heroisieren tr. V. make a hero of, heroize ‹person›; glorify ‹deed›

Heroismus der; ~: heroism

Herold /ˈhe:rɔlt/ der; ~[e]s, ~e herald

Herr /hɛr/ der; ~n (selten: ~en), ~en [1] (Mann) gentleman; ein feiner ~: a refined gentleman; ein feiner/sauberer ~ (iron.) a fine one; das Kugelstoßen/Finale der ~en (Sport) the men's shot-put/final; mein Alter ~ (ugs. scherzh.: Vater) my old man (coll.); Alter ~ (Studentenspr.) former member; (Sport) veteran [2] ▸❶ S. 44, ▸❶ S. 143 (Titel, Anrede) ~ Schulze Mr Schulze; ~ Professor/Dr. Schulze Professor/Dr Schulze; ~ Minister/Direktor/Studienrat Schulze Mr Schulze; ~ Minister/Professor/Doktor Minister/Professor/doctor; ~ Vorsitzender/Präsident Mr Chairman/President; Sehr geehrter ~ Schulze! Dear Sir; (bei persönlicher Bekanntschaft) Dear Mr Schulze; Sehr geehrte ~en! Dear Sirs; ~ Ober! waiter!; mein ~: sir; meine ~en gentlemen; meine ~en! (salopp) my God!; bitte sehr, der ~! there you are, sir; womit kann ich dem ~n dienen? (veralt.) can I help you, sir?; Ihr ~ Vater/Sohn/Gemahl (geh.) your father/son/husband [3] (Gebieter) master; ~! Gebt uns die Freiheit Sire, give us our freedom; er ist ~ über alle Menschen auf der Insel he rules over the whole population of the island; mein ~ und Gebieter (scherzh.) my lord and master (joc.); die ~en der Schöpfung (ugs. scherzh.) their lordships (coll. joc.); in diesem Land ist der König ~ über Leben und Tod in this country the king has the power of life and death; wie der ~, so's Gescherr like master, like man; sein eigener ~ sein be one's own master; ~ der Lage sein/bleiben be/remain master of the situation; einer Sache (Gen.) ~ werden get sth. under control; nicht mehr ~ seiner Sinne sein be no longer in control of oneself; aus aller ~en Länder[n] (geh.) from the four corners of the earth; from all over the world [4] (Besitzer) master (über + Akk. of) [5] (christl. Rel.: Gott) Lord; Gott der ~: Lord God; Brüder und Schwestern im ~n brothers and sisters in the Lord; der ~ der Heerscharen the Lord of Hosts; er ist ein großer Jäger/Angler vor dem ~n (scherzh.) he loves his hunting/angling

Herrchen das; ~s, ~: master

her|reichen

A tr. V. pass; hand

B itr. V. (bes. südd.) reach; be long enough

Her·reise die journey here

herren-, Herren-: ~abend der stag evening; ~artikel der [1] Pl. (Kleidung) menswear sing.; [2] (kleinere Bedarfsartikel) accessories for men; ~ausstatter der; ~~s, ~~: [gentle]men's outfitter; ~begleitung die: in/ohne ~begleitung in the company of a gentleman/unaccompanied; with/without a male companion; ~bekanntschaft die gentleman acquaintance; eine ~bekanntschaft machen make the acquaintance of a gentleman; ~besuch der gentleman visitor/visitors; ~besuch haben have a gentleman visitor/gentlemen visitors; ~besuch ist ab 20⁰⁰ untersagt no male visitors after 8 p.m.; ~doppel das (Sport) men's doubles pl.; ~einzel das (Sport) men's singles pl.; ~fahrrad das gent's or man's bicycle; ~friseur der men's hairdresser; ~haus das [1] (großes Wohnhaus) manor house; [2] (hist.) upper chamber; ~hemd das ▸Oberhemd; ~konfektion die menswear no pl., no indef. art.; ~leben das life of luxury and ease; ~los Adj. abandoned ‹car, luggage›; stray ‹dog, cat›; ~magazin das men's magazine; magazine for men; ~mensch der masterful person; (ns.) member of the master race; ~mode die men's fashion; ~partie die stag outing; ~rasse die (ns.) master race; ~reiter der (Reiten) amateur rider; ~salon der men's hairdressing salon; ~sattel der men's saddle; ~schnitt der Eton crop; ~schuh der man's shoe; ~schuhe men's shoes; ~toilette die [gentle]men's toilet; ~unterwäsche die men's underwear; ~volk das (bes. ns.) master race; ~zimmer das smoking room

Herr·gott der; ~s [1] (ugs.: Gott) der [liebe]/unser ~: the Lord [God]; God; ~ noch mal! for Heaven's sake!; for God's sake! [2] (südd., österr.: Kruzifix) crucifix

Herrgotts-: ~frühe die: in in aller ~frühe at the crack of dawn; ~schnitzer der, ~schnitzerin die (südd., österr.) carver of crucifixes (and figures of Christ and saints)

her·richten

A tr. V. [1] (bereitmachen) get ‹room, refreshments, etc.› ready; dress ‹shop window›; arrange ‹table› [2] (in Ordnung bringen) renovate; do up (coll.)

B refl. V. get ready

Herrin die; ~, ~nen mistress; (als Anrede) my lady

herrisch

A Adj. overbearing; peremptory; imperious

B adv. peremptorily; imperiously; ~ auftreten have a peremptory or imperious manner

herr·je, herrjemine /hɛrˈje:mine/ Interj. (ugs.) goodness gracious [me]; heavens [above]

herrlich

A Adj. marvellous; marvellous, glorious ‹weather›; magnificent, splendid ‹view›; magnificent, glorious ‹countryside›; magnificent, gorgeous ‹clothes›; marvellous, wonderful, splendid ‹meal›; ‹sth. tastes, looks, sounds› wonderful, marvellous

B adv. marvellously; ~ und in Freuden leben live in clover

Herrlichkeit die; ~, ~en [1] (Schönheit) magnificence; splendour; die ~ Gottes the glory of God; ist das die ganze ~? (iron.) is that all [there is]? [2] (herrliche Sache) marvellous or wonderful thing; (einer Sammlung) treasure

Herrschaft die; ~, ~en [1] rule; (Macht) power; unter jmds. ~ (Dat.) stehen be under sb.'s rule; die ~ an sich reißen/erringen seize/gain power; die ~ über jmdn./etw. ausüben/innehaben rule over or hold sway over sb./sth.; die ~ über sich/das Auto verlieren (fig.) lose control of oneself/the car [2] Pl. (Damen u. Herren) ladies and gentlemen; die älteren/jüngeren ~en the older/younger people; meine ~en! ladies and gentlemen!; darf ich die ~en bitten, Platz zu nehmen ladies and gentlemen/ladies/gentlemen, would you please take your seats; (Mann und Frau) would sir and madam care to take their seats, please; Ruhe bitte, ~! (ugs.) quiet please, all of you!; meine Alten ~en (ugs. scherzh.) my old man and old woman (coll.) [3] (veralt.: Dienstherr[in]) master/mistress [4] ~ [noch mal]! (ugs.) for Heaven's sake!

herrschaftlich Adj. [1] (zu einer Herrschaft gehörend) master's/mistress's ‹coach etc.› [2] (einer Herrschaft gemäß) grand

Herrschafts-: ~an·spruch der claim to power; ~form die system of government; ~system das system of rule

herrschen /ˈhɛrʃn̩/ itr. V. [1] (regieren) rule; ‹monarch› reign, rule; allein über jmdn./etw. ~: have absolute power over sb./sth. [2] (vorhanden sein) draußen ~ 30° Kälte it's 30° below outside; überall herrschte große Freude/Trauer there was great joy/sorrow everywhere; in der Stadt herrschte reges Leben the town was bustling with life; jetzt herrscht hier wieder Ordnung order has been restored here [3] (unpers.) prevail; es herrscht jetzt Einigkeit there is now agreement; es herrscht die Meinung, dass ... the prevailing opinion is that ...

herrschend Adj. [1] ruling ‹power, party, etc.›; reigning ‹monarch›; die Herrschenden the rulers; those in power [2] (vorhanden) prevailing ‹opinion, view, conditions, etc.›

Herrscher der; ~s, ~: ruler; ~ über ein Volk sein be [the] ruler of a people

Herrscher-: ~geschlecht das ruling dynasty; ~haus das ruling house

Herrscherin die; ~, ~nen ▸Herrscher

Herrscher·paar das ruler and his/her consort

Herrsch·sucht die thirst for power; (herrisches Wesen) domineering nature

herrsch·süchtig Adj. domineering

her-: ~|**rufen** *unr. tr. V.* call ‹dog›; **jmdn. ~rufen** call sb. [over]; **etw. hinter jmdm. ~rufen** call sth. after sb.; ~|**rühren** *itr. V.* **von jmdm./etw. ~rühren** come from sb./stem from sth.; ~|**sagen** *tr. V.* **etw. ~sagen** recite sth. mechanically; ~|**schaffen** *tr. V.* **jmdn./etw. ~schaffen** bring sb./sth. here; **das Geld ~schaffen** get the money; ~|**schenken** *tr. V.* (landsch.) give away; ~|**schicken** *tr. V.* **jmdn./etw. ~schicken** send sb./sth. here; **jmdn./etw. hinter jmdm. ~schicken** send sb./sth. after sb.; ~|**schieben** *unr. tr. V.* **etw. ~schieben** push sth. here; **etw. vor sich** *(Dat.)* **~schieben** push sth. along in front of one; (fig.) put sth. off; ~|**schleichen** **A** *unr. itr. V.; mit sein* creep [over] here; **B** *unr. refl. V.* **sich hinter jmdm. ~schleichen** creep along behind sb.; ~|**sehen** *unr. itr. V.* look [over] here *or* this way; **seht mal alle ~!** look here *or* this way, everyone!; **hinter jmdm. ~sehen** follow sb. with one's eyes; *~|**sein** ▸**her 1, 4, 5, 6**; ~|**stellen** *tr. V.* **1** (anfertigen) produce; manufacture; make; **ein Auto von Hand ~stellen** build a car by hand; **in Deutschland ~gestellt** made in Germany; **etw. serienmäßig ~stellen** mass-produce sth.; **2** (zustande bringen) establish ‹*contact, relationship, etc.*›; bring about ‹*peace, order, etc.*›; **eine Verbindung zwischen der Insel und dem Festland ~stellen** connect the island to the mainland; **3** (gesund machen) **sie** *od.* **ihre Gesundheit ist [ganz] ~gestellt** she has [quite] recovered; **4** (zum Sprechenden stellen) **etw. ~stellen** put sth. [over] here; **stell dich ~ [zu mir]** [come and] stand over here [next to *or* by me]

Her·steller *der;* **~s, ~** ▸❶ **S. 113** **1** (Produzent) producer; manufacturer **2** (Buchw.: Berufsbez.) production department worker

Hersteller·firma *die* manufacturer

Herstellerin *die;* **~, ~nen** ▸❶ **S. 113** ▸**Hersteller**

Her·stellung *die* **1** (Anfertigung) production; manufacture **2** ▸**herstellen 2**: establishment; bringing about

Herstellungs-: ~**fehler** *der* manufacturing fault; ~**kosten** *Pl.* production *or* manufacturing costs; ~**land** *das* country of manufacture; ~**verfahren** *das* production *or* manufacturing process

her-: ~|**stürzen** *itr. V.; mit sein* **1** (nachlaufen) **hinter jmdm. ~stürzen** rush after sb.; **2** (zum Sprecher) rush *or* come rushing here; ~|**tragen** *unr. tr. V.* **1** (zum Sprecher) **etw. ~tragen** carry sth. here; **2** (begleiten und tragen) **etw. hinter/vor jmdm. ~tragen** carry sth. along behind/in front of sb.; ~|**treiben** *unr. tr. V.* **1** (zum Sprecher) drive ‹*animal*› here; **jmdn. ~treiben** ‹*yearning, hunger, worry, etc.*› drive sb. here; **2** (antreiben) **etw. vor sich** *(Dat.)* **~treiben** drive sth. along in front of one; **der Spieler trieb den Ball vor sich** *(Dat.)* **~:** the player dribbled the ball; **der Wind trieb die Wolken vor sich** *(Dat.)* **~:** the wind drove *or* blew the clouds along

Hertz /hɛrts/ *das;* **~, ~** (Physik) hertz

herüben /hɛ'ry:bn̩/ *Adv.* (südd., österr.) over here

herüber /hɛ'ry:bɐ/ *Adv.* over; **die Fahrt von Amerika ~:** the journey over from America; **~ und hinüber** back and forth

herüber-: ~|**bitten** *unr. tr. V.* **jmdn. ~bitten** ask sb. [to come] over; ~|**bringen** *unr. tr. V.* **jmdn./etw. ~bringen** bring sb./sth. over; ~|**fahren** **A** *unr. itr. V.; mit sein* drive *or* come over; (mit dem Motorrad, Rad) come *or* ride over; **B** *unr. tr. V.* **jmdn./etw. ~fahren** drive sb./sth. over; ~|**fliegen** **A** *unr. itr. V.; mit sein* fly over; **B** *unr. tr. V.* **jmdn./etw. ~fliegen** fly sb./sth. over; ~|**geben** *unr. tr. V.* pass *or* hand over; ~|**grüßen** *itr. V.* **[zu jmdm.] ~grüßen** call across to sb. in greeting; ~|**holen** *tr. V.* **jmdn./etw. ~holen** bring sb./sth. over; ~|**kommen** *unr. itr. V.; mit sein* come over; **über den Zaun/Fluss ~kommen** get over the fence/across the river; **kommt doch ~:** come over!; ~|**lassen** *unr. tr. V.* **jmdn. ~lassen** let sb. come over; allow sb. to come over; ~|**laufen** *unr. itr. V.; mit sein* run *or* come running over; ~|**reichen** **A** *tr. V.* ▸**~geben**; **B** *itr. V.* **[über etw.** *(Akk.)***] ~reichen** reach across [sth.]; ~|**retten** **A** *tr. V.* retain; **etw. in die Gegenwart ~retten** preserve sth. [until the present day]; **B** *refl. V.* ‹*customs, hopes, etc.*› survive; ~|**schicken** *tr. V.* **jmdn./etw. ~schicken** send sb./sth. over; ~|**schwimmen** *unr. itr. V.; mit sein* swim over *or* across; ‹*boat*› float over *or* across; ~|**sehen** *unr. itr. V.* **[zu jmdm.] ~sehen** look across [at sb.]; ~|**wechseln** *itr. V.; mit sein od. haben* cross over; **er ist in unsere Partei ~gewechselt** he has swapped parties and joined ours; ~|**wehen** **A** *itr. V.* **1** (zum Sprecher) **von Osten/Westen ~wehen** blow across from the East/West; **zu uns ~wehen** blow in our direction *or* towards us; **2** *mit sein* ‹*scent*› waft across; ‹*sound*› be blown across; **B** *tr. V.* **Blätter/den Duft ~wehen** blow leaves/waft the scent across here; ~|**wollen** *unr. itr. V.* want to come over; **über den Zaun ~wollen** want to get over the fence; ~|**ziehen** **A** *unr. tr. V.* **etw. ~ziehen** pull sth. over; **jmdn. ~ziehen** (fig.) win sb. over; **B** *unr. itr. V.; mit sein* ‹*clouds, troops*› move across; (umziehen) move here

herum /hɛ'rʊm/ *Adv.* **1** (Richtung) round; **im Kreis ~:** round in a circle; **verkehrt/richtig ~:** the wrong/right way round; (mit Ober- und Unterseite) upside down/the right way up; **etw. falsch** *od.* **verkehrt ~ anziehen** put sth. on back-to-front/(Innenseite nach außen) inside out **2** (Anordnung) **um jmdn./etw. ~:** around sb./sth.; **um die Stadt ~ zog sich ein Grüngürtel** the town was surrounded by a green belt **3** (in enger Umgebung) **um jmdn. ~ sein** be around sb.; **um München/Berlin ~:** around Munich/Berlin **4** (ugs.: ungefähr) **um Weihnachten/Ostern ~:** around Christmas/Easter; **um 100 Euro/das Jahr 1050 ~:** around *or* about 100 euros/the year 1050 **5** (vorüber, vorbei) over; **~ sein** be over **6** **~ sein** (ugs.: überall bekannt geworden sein) have got around

herum-, Herum-: ~|**albern** *itr. V.* (ugs.) fool around *or* about; ~|**ärgern** *refl. V.* (ugs.) **sich mit jmdm./etw. ~ärgern** keep getting annoyed with sb./sth.; **sich mit einem Problem ~ärgern müssen** be plagued by a problem; ~|**balgen** *refl. V.* **sich [mit jmdm.] ~balgen** keep scrapping (coll.) [with sb.]; ~|**basteln** *itr. V.* (ugs.) **an etw.** *(Dat.)* **~basteln** mess about with sth.; ~|**bekommen** *unr. tr. V.* (ugs.) **1** (überreden) **jmdn. ~bekommen** talk sb. into it; **jmdn. ~bekommen, etw. zu tun** talk sb. into doing sth.; **2** (hinter sich bringen) [manage to] pass *or* spend ‹*time*›; ~|**blättern** *itr. V.* **in etw.** *(Dat.)* **~blättern** keep leafing through sth.; ~|**bohren** *itr. V.* (ugs.) **[in etw.** *(Dat.)***] ~bohren** keep poking [in sth.]; ~|**brüllen** *itr. V.* (ugs.) go on shouting one's head off (coll.); ~|**bummeln** *itr. V.* (ugs.) **1** *mit sein* (spazieren) stroll *or* wander around; **in der Stadt ~bummeln** stroll *or* wander around the town; **2** (trödeln) **[mit etw.] ~bummeln** dawdle [over sth.]; ~|**doktern** *itr. V.* (ugs.) **an jmdm./etw. ~doktern** have a go at treating sb./sth.; **an etw.** *(Dat.)* **~doktern** (fig.) fiddle *or* tinker around *or* about with sth.; ~|**drehen** **A** *tr. V.* (ugs.) turn ‹*key*›; turn over ‹*coin, mattress, hand, etc.*›; **den Kopf ~drehen** turn one's head; **B** *refl. V.* turn [a]round; **sich im Kreis ~drehen** turn right round; **sich [auf die andere Seite] ~drehen** turn over [on to one's other side]; **C** *itr. V.* (ugs.) **an etw.** *(Dat.)* **~drehen** fiddle [around *or* about] with sth.; ~|**drücken** *refl. V.* **1** (ugs.: vermeiden) **sich um etw. ~drücken** get out of *or* (coll.) dodge sth.; **2** (ugs.: sich aufhalten) hang around; **wo hast du dich ~gedrückt?** where have you been?; ~|**drucksen** *itr. V.* (ugs.) hum and haw (coll.); ~|**erzählen** *tr. V.* (ugs.) **etw. ~erzählen** spread sth. around; **er erzählte überall ~, dass ...** he went around telling everyone that ...; ~|**experimentieren** *itr. V.* **[an jmdm./etw.] ~experimentieren** carry out experiments [on sb./sth.]; ~|**fahren** (ugs.) **A** *unr. itr. V.; mit sein* **1** **um etw. ~fahren** drive *or* go round sth.; (mit einem Motorrad, Rad) ride *or* go round sth.; (mit einem Schiff) sail round sth.; **2** (irgendwohin fahren) drive/ride/sail around; **3** (sich plötzlich ~drehen) spin round; **4** (hin und her bewegen) **mit den Armen/dem Schirm** *usw.* **~fahren** wave one's arms/umbrella *etc.* about; **B** *unr. tr. V.* **jmdn. [in der Stadt] ~fahren** drive sb. around the town; ~|**flattern** *itr. V.; mit sein* (ugs.) **[um jmdn./etw.] ~flattern** flutter around [sb./sth.]; ~|**fliegen** (ugs.) **A** *unr. itr. V.; mit sein* **1** **[um etw.] ~fliegen** fly around [sth.]; **2** (salopp: ~liegen) ▸**rumfliegen A 2**; **B** *unr. tr. V.* **jmdn. ~fliegen** fly sb. around; ~|**fragen** *itr. V.* (ugs.) ask around (**bei** among); ~|**fuchteln** *itr. V.* (ugs.) **mit den Armen/einem Messer** *usw.* **~fuchteln** wave one's arms/a knife *etc.* around *or* about; ~|**führen** **A** *tr. V.* **1** **jmdn. [in der Stadt] ~führen** show sb. around the town; *s. auch* **Nase**; **2** (rund um etw. führen) **jmdn. um etw. ~führen** lead *or* take sb. round sth.; **3** (um etw. bauen) **die Straße um die Stadt ~führen** take the road round the town; **B** *itr. V.* **um etw. ~führen** ‹*road etc.*› go round sth.; ~|**fuhrwerken** *itr. V.* (ugs.) mess about; **mit einem Schraubenzieher an der Uhr ~fuhrwerken** fiddle around with the clock with the aid of a screwdriver; ~|**fummeln** *itr. V.* (ugs.) **1** **an etw.** *(Dat.)* **~fummeln** fiddle around with sth.; **2** (sich handwerklich beschäftigen) fiddle *or* mess around with sth.; **3** (betasten) **an jmdm. ~fummeln** touch sb. up (sl.); ~|**geben** *unr. tr. V.:* ▸**~reichen A**; ~|**gehen** *unr. itr. V.; mit sein* **1** **um etw. ~gehen** go *or* walk round sth.; **2** (ziellos gehen) walk around; **im Garten ~gehen** walk around the garden; **3** (die Runde machen) go around; (~gereicht werden) be passed *or* handed around; **etw. ~gehen lassen** circulate sth.; **4** (vergehen) pass; go by; ~|**geistern** *itr. V.; mit sein* (ugs.) wander around *or* about; (fig.) ‹*idea, rumour, etc.*› go round; **im Haus ~geistern** wander around the house [like a ghost]; **jmdm. im Kopf ~geistern** go round in sb.'s mind; ~|**gondeln** *itr. V.; mit sein* (salopp) travel around; **in der Weltgeschichte ~gondeln** travel around all over the place; ~|**hacken** *itr. V.* (ugs.) **1** (kritisieren) **auf jmdm. ~hacken** keep getting at sb. (coll.); **2** (mit einer Hacke bearbeiten) **auf etw.** *(Dat.)* **~hacken** hack away at sth.; ~|**hängen** *unr. itr. V.* (ugs.) **1** (aufgehängt sein) **überall ~hängen** be hung up all over the place; **2** ▸**rumhängen 1**; ~|**hantieren** *itr. V.* (ugs.) mess about; **an etw.** *(Dat.)* **~hantieren** mess about with sth.; ~|**hetzen** (ugs.) **A** *tr. V.* **jmdn. ~hetzen** rush sb. off his/her feet; **B** *itr. V.; mit sein* rush *or* chase around *or* about; ~|**horchen** *itr. V.* (ugs.) keep one's ears open; **horch mal ~, ob ...** keep your ears open and try and find out whether ...; ~|**irren** *itr. V.; mit sein* wander around *or* about; **im Wald ~irren** wander about the wood; ~**kauen** *itr. V.* **auf** *od.* **an etw.** *(Dat.)* **~|kauen** chew away at sth.; (fig.) wrestle with sth.; ~|**kommandieren** (ugs.) **A** *tr. V.* **jmdn. ~kommandieren** boss (coll.) *or* order sb. around *or* about; **B** *itr. V.* boss (coll.) *or* order people around *or* about; ~|**kommen** *unr. itr. V.; mit sein* (ugs.) **1** (vorbeikommen können) get round; **[mit etw.] um die Ecke** *usw.* **~kommen** get [sth.] round the corner *etc.*; **2** (sich ~bewegen) come round; **um die Ecke ~kommen** come round the corner; **3** (vermeiden können) **um etw. [nicht] ~kommen** [not] be able to avoid sth.; **darum ~kommen etw. zu tun** avoid doing sth.; get round doing sth. **um eine Operation/Entscheidung ~kommen** avoid having an operation/coming to a decision; **wir kommen nicht um die Tatsache ~, dass ...** we cannot get away *or* there is no getting away from the fact that ...; **4** (viel reisen) get around *or* about; **in der Welt ~kommen** see a lot of the world; **viel ~kommen** get around *or* about a lot *or* a great deal; **5** (umschließen können) **mit den Armen/der Hand/dem Seil um etw. ~kommen** get one's arms/hand/the rope [a]round sth.; ~|**kramen** *itr. V.* (ugs.) keep rummaging around *or* about; ~|**krebsen** *itr. V.* (ugs.) struggle; ~|**kriechen** *unr. itr. V.; mit sein* crawl around *or* about; **um etw. ~kriechen** crawl round sth.; ~|**kriegen** *tr. V.*

h

[1] (salopp) **jmdn. ~kriegen** talk sb. into it; (verführen) get sb. into bed (coll.); [2] (ugs.) ▸**~bekommen 2**; **~|kritisieren** *itr. V.* (ugs.) **an jmdm./etw. ~kritisieren** pick holes in sb./sth.; run sb./sth. down; **~|kutschieren** (ugs.) **A** *itr. V.; mit sein* drive around [aimlessly]; **B** *tr. V.* drive ‹*person*› about [with no particular destination]; **~|laborieren** *itr. V.* (ugs.) **an etw.** (*Dat.*) **~laborieren** try to get over sth.; **~|laufen** *unr. itr. V.; mit sein* [1] walk/(schneller) run around *or* about; **in der Stadt ~laufen** walk/(schneller) run around the town; [2] (umrunden) **um etw. ~laufen** walk *or* go round sth.; [3] (gekleidet sein) **wie ein Hippie ~laufen** go about looking *or* dressed like a hippie; **wie läufst du wieder ~!** what do you look like!; **~|liegen** *unr. itr. V.* (ugs.) lie around *or* about; **~|lümmeln** *refl. V.* (ugs.) lounge around; **~|lungern** *itr. V.* (salopp) loaf around; **~|machen** *itr. V.* (ugs.) be busy; (abwertend) mess about *or* around; **er fing an, an mir/meiner Bluse ~zumachen** he started trying to fondle me/undo my blouse; **~|mäkeln** *itr. V.* (ugs.) **[an jmdm./etw.] ~mäkeln** pick holes [in sb./sth.]; **am Essen ~mäkeln** moan (coll.) *or* grumble about the food; **~|nörgeln** *itr. V.* (ugs. abwertend) moan; grumble; **an jmdm./etw. ~nörgeln** moan *or* grumble about sb./sth.; **~|pfuschen** *itr. V.* (ugs. abwertend) **[an jmdm./etw.] ~pfuschen** mess about [with sb./sth.]; **~|posaunen** *tr. V.* (ugs.) broadcast; **sie posaunte im ganzen Dorf ~, dass ...** she broadcast to the whole village the fact that ...; **~|quälen** *refl. V.* (ugs.) **sich [mit einem Problem] ~quälen** struggle [with a problem]; **sich mit Rheuma/finanziellen Sorgen ~quälen** be plagued by rheumatism/financial worries; **~|rätseln** *itr. V.* (ugs.) **an etw.** (*Dat.*) **~rätseln** try to figure *or* puzzle sth. out; **~|reden** *itr. V.* (ugs.) **um etw. ~reden** talk round sth.; **red nicht lange um die Sache ~!** don't beat about the bush!; **~|reichen** (ugs.) **A** *tr. V.* **etw. ~reichen** pass sth. round; **jmdn. [überall] ~reichen** (fig.) introduce sb. everywhere; **B** *itr. V.* **[um etw.] ~reichen** reach round [sth.]; **~|reisen** *itr. V.; mit sein* (ugs.) travel around *or* about; **~|reißen** *unr. tr. V.* **den Wagen/das Pferd ~reißen** swing the car/horse round; *s. auch* **Steuer**[1]; **~|reiten** *unr. itr. V.; mit sein* [1] (ziellos reiten) ride around *or* about; **in der Gegend ~reiten** ride around the area; [2] (salopp; auf dasselbe zurückkommen) **auf etw.** (*Dat.*) **~reiten** go on about sth. (coll.); harp on sth.; [3] (salopp: kritisieren) **auf jmdm. ~reiten** keep getting at sb. (coll.); **~|rennen** *unr. itr. V.; mit sein* (ugs.) [1] (ziellos rennen) run around *or* about; [2] (im Bogen rennen) **um etw. ~rennen** run round sth.; **im Kreis ~rennen** run round in a circle; **~|rutschen** *itr. V.; mit sein* (ugs.) slide around *or* about; **~|scharwenzeln** *itr. V.; mit sein* (ugs. abwertend) **um jmdn. ~scharwenzeln** dance attendance on sb.; **~|schlagen** **A** *unr. tr. V.* **Papier/eine Decke** *usw.* **um etw. ~schlagen** wrap paper/a blanket *etc.* round sth.; **B** *unr. refl. V.* (ugs.) [1] (sich schlagen) **sich mit jmdm. ~schlagen** keep fighting *or* getting into fights with sb.; [2] (sich auseinander setzen) **sich mit Problemen/Einwänden ~schlagen** grapple with problems/battle against objections; **sich mit jmdm. [wegen etw.] ~schlagen** conduct a running battle with sb. [about sth.]; **~|schleichen** *unr. itr. V.; mit sein* (ugs.) creep around *or* about; **um etw. ~schleichen** creep round sth.; **~|schlendern** *itr. V.; mit sein* (ugs.) stroll around *or* about; **in der Stadt ~schlendern** stroll around *or* about the town; **~|schleppen** *tr. V.* (ugs.) **etw. um etw. ~schleppen** lug sth. round sth.; **eine Erkältung/ein Problem mit sich** (*Dat.*) **~schleppen** (fig.) go around with a cold/be worried by a problem; **die Probleme anderer mit sich** (*Dat.*) **~schleppen** (fig.) worry about other people's problems; **~|schnüffeln** *itr. V.* (ugs. abwertend) nose *or* snoop around *or* about (coll.); **in jmds. Schreibtisch ~schnüffeln** poke around *or* about in sb.'s desk (coll.); **in anderer Leute Angelegenheiten ~schnüffeln** poke one's nose into other people's affairs; **~|schubsen** *tr. V.* (ugs.) **jmdn. ~schubsen** push sb. around; ***~|sein** ▸**herum 3, 5, 6**; **~|sitzen** *unr. itr. V.* (ugs.) sit around *or* about; **um etw. ~sitzen** sit round sth.; **tatenlos ~sitzen** sit around *or* about doing nothing; **~|spielen** *itr. V.* (ugs.) **an/mit etw. ~spielen** keep playing [around *or* about] with sth.; **an seinen Knöpfen ~spielen** fiddle with one's buttons; **~|spionieren** *itr. V.* (ugs.) snoop *or* nose around *or* about (coll.); **~|sprechen** *unr. refl. V.* get around *or* about; **schnell hatte sich ~gesprochen, dass ...** it had quickly got around that ...; **~|spuken** *itr. V.* (ugs.) **in/auf etw.** (*Dat.*) **~spuken** haunt sth.; **ich möchte wissen, was in seinem Kopf ~spukt** (fig.) I'd like to know what's going on in his mind; **~|stänkern** *itr. V.* (ugs.) keep complaining; **~|stehen** *unr. itr. V.* (ugs.) stand around *or* about; **um etw. ~stehen** stand round sth.; **~|stöbern** *itr. V.* (ugs.) (in einem Schreibtisch usw.) keep rummaging around *or* about (**in** + *Dat.* in); **die Jagdhunde stöberten im Dickicht ~:** the hounds were hunting around in the thicket; **ich habe in der ganzen Wohnung ~gestöbert** I've hunted all over the house; **~|stochern** *itr. V.* poke around *or* about; **im Essen ~stochern** pick at one's food; **~|stoßen** *unr. tr. V.* (ugs.) **jmdn. ~stoßen** push sb. around; **~|streichen** *unr. itr. V.; mit sein* (abwertend) [1] (umherstreifen) roam around *or* about; [2] (lauernd umkreisen) **um jmdn./etw. ~streichen** prowl round sb./sth.; **~|streifen** *itr. V.; mit sein* (ugs.) roam around *or* about; **auf den Straßen ~streifen** roam the streets; **~|streiten** *unr. refl. V.* (ugs.) **sich [mit jmdm./etw.] ~streiten** keep quarrelling *or* wrangling [with sb.]; **~|streunen** *itr. V.; mit sein* (abwertend) roam around *or* about; **auf den Feldern ~streunen** roam the fields; **~|stromern** *itr. V.; mit sein* (salopp abwertend) roam around *or* about; **~|tanzen** *itr. V.; mit sein* (ugs.) [1] dance around *or* about; **im Zimmer ~tanzen** dance around *or* about the room; [2] (im Bogen um etw. tanzen) **um jmdn./etw. ~tanzen** dance round sb./sth.; **um jmdn. ~tanzen** (fig.) dance attendance on sb.; *s. auch* **Kopf 1**; **Nase 2**; **~|tollen** *itr. V.; mit sein* romp around *or* about; **auf dem Hof ~tollen** romp around the yard; **~|tragen** *unr. tr. V.* (ugs.) [1] (überallhin tragen) **jmdn./etw. ~tragen** carry sb./sth. around *or* about; **jmdn./etw. mit sich ~tragen** carry sb./sth. around with one; [2] **eine Idee/einen Plan mit sich ~tragen** nurse an idea/a plan; [3] (abwertend: weitererzählen) **etw. ~tragen** spread sth. around; **~|trampeln** *itr. V.; mit haben od. sein* **auf etw.** (*Dat.*) **~trampeln** trample [around] on sth.; trample all over sth.; **auf jmdm. ~trampeln** (fig.) walk all over sb.; **auf jmds. Nerven/Gefühlen ~trampeln** (fig.) really get on sb.'s nerves/trample on sb.'s feelings; **~|treiben** *unr. refl. V.* (ugs. abwertend) [1] (kein geordnetes Leben führen) **sich auf den Straßen/in Spelunken ~treiben** hang around the streets/(coll.) in dives; **sich mit Männern ~treiben** hang around with men; [2] (sich irgendwo aufhalten) **sich in der Welt ~treiben** roam *or* move about the world; **wo hast du dich nur ~getrieben?** where have you been?; **ich möchte wissen, wo er sich ~treibt** I'd like to know where he's got to; **~treiber** *der*, **~treiberin** *die*; **~~, ~~nen** (ugs.) layabout; (Streuner) vagabond; **~|trödeln** *itr. V.* (ugs.) dawdle around *or* about (**mit** over); **~|wälzen** (ugs.) **A** *tr. V.* **etw. ~wälzen** roll sth. over; **B** *refl. V.* roll around *or* about; **sich im Bett ~wälzen** toss and turn in bed; **sich im Schlamm ~wälzen** wallow in the mud; **~|wandern** *itr. V.; mit sein* [1] (ugs.: umhergehen) wander around *or* about; **im Garten ~wandern** wander around *or* about the garden; [2] (im Bogen um etw. wandern) **um den Berg/See** *usw.* **~wandern** hike around the mountain/the lake *etc.*; **~|werfen** **A** *unr. tr. V.* [1] (ugs.: umherwerfen) **etw. ~werfen** chuck (coll.) *or* throw sth. around *or* about; **etw. im Zimmer ~werfen** chuck (coll.) *or* throw sth. around *or* about the room; [2] (in eine andere Richtung drehen) throw ‹*helm, steering wheel, etc.*› [hard] over; **den Kopf ~werfen** turn one's head quickly; **B** *unr. refl. V.* **sich im Bett ~werfen** toss and turn in bed; **~|wickeln** *tr. V.* **etw. um etw. ~wickeln** wrap sth. round sth.; **~|wirbeln** **A** *tr. V.* **jmdn./etw. ~wirbeln** whirl *or* spin sb./sth. [a]round; **der Wind wirbelte die Blätter ~:** the wind whirled the leaves around *or* about; **B** *itr. V.; mit sein* spin *or* whirl [a]round; **~|wühlen** *itr. V.* **in etw.** (*Dat.*) **~wühlen** rummage *or* root around *or* about in sth.; **in jmds. Vergangenheit ~wühlen** (fig.) dig into sb.'s past; **~|wurschteln**, **~|wursteln** *itr. V.* (salopp) **mit etw. ~wurschteln** *od.* **~wursteln** mess *or* fiddle around *or* about with sth.; **~|zanken** *refl. V.* (ugs.) ▸**~streiten**; **~|zeigen** *tr. V.* (ugs.) **etw. ~zeigen** show sth. round; **~|ziehen** **A** *unr. itr. V.* move around *or* about; **im Land ~ziehen** move around *or* about the country; **um etw. ~ziehen** go round sth.; **B** *unr. tr. V.* (ugs.: mit sich ziehen) **jmdn./etw. ~ziehen** drag sb./sth. round (coll.); **C** *unr. refl. V.* **sich um etw. ~ziehen** ‹*fence, wall, river, etc.*› go *or* run round sth.; ‹*wood etc.*› surround sth.

herunten /hɛˈrʊntn̩/ *Adv.* (südd., österr.) down here

herunter /hɛˈrʊntɐ/ *Adv.* [1] (nach unten) down; **~ sein** (unten sein) be down; **von Kiel nach München ~** (fig.) from Kiel down to Munich [2] (fort) off; **~ vom Sofa!** [get] off the sofa!; **~ vom Baum/von der Mauer!** get *or* come down from that tree/wall! [3] **[körperlich] ~ sein** be in poor health; **er ist mit seiner Gesundheit/seinen Nerven ~:** he's in poor health/his nerves are in a bad state

herunter-: ~|bekommen *unr. tr. V.* (ugs.) [1] (essen können) be able to eat; (~schlucken) swallow; [2] (entfernen können) **etw. [von etw.] ~bekommen** be able to get sth. off [sth.]; **~|bemühen** **A** *tr. V.* **jmdn. ~bemühen** trouble sb. to come down; **B** *refl. V.* take the trouble to come down; **würden Sie sich bitte ~bemühen?** would you mind coming down?; **~|beten** *tr. V.* (abwertend) **etw. ~beten** recite sth. mechanically; **~|bitten** *unr. tr. V.* **jmdn. ~bitten** ask sb. [to come] down; **~|brechen** *unr. tr. V.* **etw. auf etw.** (*Akk.*) **~brechen** (auf bestimmte Verhältnisse übertragen) make sth. relevant to sth.; **~|brennen** *unr. itr. V.* [1] *mit sein* (vollkommen abbrennen) ‹*house, fire, etc.*› burn down; [2] ‹*sun*› burn *or* beat down; **~|bringen** *unr. tr. V.* [1] (nach unten bringen) bring down; [2] (zugrunde richten) ruin; [3] (ugs.: ~schlucken) ▸**~bekommen 1**; **~|drücken** *tr. V.* [1] (nach unten drücken) **etw. ~drücken** press sth. down; [2] (auf ein niedriges Niveau bringen, verringern) force down ‹*prices, wages, etc.*›; bring down ‹*temperature*›; reduce ‹*marks*›; **~|fahren** **A** *unr. itr. V.; mit sein* drive *or* come down; ‹*skier*› ski down; (mit einem Motorrad, Rad) ride down; **B** *unr. tr. V.* [1] **jmdn./etw. ~fahren** drive *or* bring sb. down/bring sth. down; [2] (DV) shut down; **~|fallen** *unr. itr. V.; mit sein* fall down; **vom Tisch/Stuhl ~fallen** fall off the table/chair; **die Treppe ~fallen** fall down the stairs; **jmdm. fällt etw. ~:** sb. drops sth.; **~|fliegen** *unr. itr. V.; mit sein* [1] (nach unten fliegen) fly down; [2] (ugs.) ▸**~fallen**; **~|geben** *unr. tr. V.* (ugs.) pass *or* hand down; **~|gehen** *unr. itr. V.; mit sein* [1] (nach unten gehen) come down; [2] (niedriger werden) ‹*temperature*› go down, drop, fall; ‹*prices*› come down, fall; **im Preis ~gehen** come down in price; [3] (die Höhe senken) **auf eine Flughöhe von 2 000 m ~gehen** descend to 6,000 ft.; **auf eine geringere Geschwindigkeit ~gehen** slow down; reduce speed; **mit den Preisen ~gehen** reduce one's/its prices; [4] **von etw. ~gehen** (ugs.: räumen) get off sth.; [5] (ugs.: sich lösen) come off; **~gekommen** **A** *2. Part. v.* **~kommen**; **B** *Adj.* poor ‹*health*›; dilapidated, run-down ‹*building*›; run-down ‹*area*›; down and out ‹*person*›; **ein [völlig] ~gekommenes Subjekt** a down-and-out; **~|handeln** *tr. V.* (ugs.) **einen Preis ~handeln** beat down a price; **100 Euro vom Kaufpreis ~handeln** get 100 euros knocked off the price (coll.); **~|hängen** *unr. itr. V.* hang down; **~|hauen** *unr. tr. V.* (ugs.) [1] (ohrfeigen) **jmdm. eine ~hauen** give sb. a clout round the ear (coll.); [2] (schlecht ausführen) dash off;

~|heben *unr. tr. V.* **etw. [von etw.] ~heben** lift sth. down [from sth.]; **~|helfen** *unr. itr. V.* (ugs.) **jmdm. ~helfen** help sb. down; **~|holen** *tr. V.* **1** (nach unten holen) **jmdn./etw. ~holen** fetch sb./sth. down; **2** (ugs.: abschießen) bring down; **~|klappen** *tr. V.* pull *or* put down ‹*seat*›; close ‹*lid*›; **seinen Kragen ~klappen** turn down one's collar; **~|klettern** *itr. V.; mit sein* climb down; **~|kommen** *unr. itr. V.; mit sein* **1** (kommen) come down; (nach unten kommen können) manage to come down; **2** (ugs.: verfallen) go to the dogs (coll.); **er ist so weit ~gekommen, dass ...** he has sunk so low that ...; **er ist gesundheitlich ~gekommen** his health has deteriorated; **3** (ugs.: wegkommen) **von Drogen/vom Alkohol ~kommen** come off drugs/alcohol; kick the habit (coll.); **von einer [schlechten] Note ~kommen** improve on a [bad] mark; **~|können** *unr. itr. V.* (ugs.) be able to get down; **~|kriegen** *tr. V.* (ugs.) ▸**runterkriegen**; **~laden** *unr. tr. V.* (DV) download; **~|lassen** *unr. tr. V.* (schließen) let down, lower ‹*blind, shutter*›; lower ‹*barrier*›; shut ‹*window*›; (nach unten gleiten lassen) wind down ‹*car window*›; **jmdn./etw. an etw.** (*Dat.*) **~lassen** lower sb./sth. by sth.; **die Hose ~lassen** take one's trousers down; **~|leiern** *tr. V.* (salopp) **1** (abwertend) drone out (coll.); **2** wind down ‹*car window*›; **~|machen** *tr. V.* (salopp) **1** (zurechtweisen) **jmdn. ~machen** give sb. a rocket (coll.); tear sb. off a strip (coll.); **2** (herabsetzen) slate (coll.); run down (coll.); **~|nehmen** *unr. tr. V.* take down; **die Arme ~nehmen** put one's arms down; **etw. von etw. ~nehmen** take sth. off sth.; **~|purzeln** *itr. V.; mit sein* (ugs.) **die Treppe ~purzeln** tumble down the stairs; **vom Stuhl ~purzeln** topple off the chair; **~|putzen** *tr. V.* (salopp) ▸**~machen 1**; **~|rasseln** (ugs.) **A** *tr. V.* rattle off; **B** *itr. V.; mit sein* rattle down; come rattling down; **~|reißen** *unr. tr. V.* (ugs.) **1** (nach unten reißen) pull down; **2** (abreißen) pull off ‹*plaster, wallpaper*›; tear down ‹*poster*›; **3** (salopp: ableisten) get through; **~|rutschen** *itr. V.; mit sein* (ugs.) slide down; ‹*trousers, socks*› slip down; **~|schalten** *itr. V.* (Kfz-Jargon) change down; **~|schießen** **A** *unr. tr. V.* shoot down ‹*bird, aircraft, etc.*›; **B** *unr. itr. V.* **1** **von einem Fenster aus ~schießen** shoot *or* fire down from a window; **2** *mit sein* (~stürzen) hurtle down; come hurtling down; **~|schlagen** *unr. tr. V.* **1** knock off; **den Stuck von der Wand ~schlagen** knock the stucco off the wall; **2** (nach unten wenden) turn ‹*collar etc.*› down; **~|schlucken** *tr. V.* swallow; **~|schrauben** *tr. V.* turn down ‹*wick etc.*›; **seine Ansprüche/Erwartungen ~schrauben** (fig.) reduce one's requirements/lower one's expectations; **~|sehen** *unr. itr. V.* **1** (nach unten sehen) look down; **2** (geringschätzig betrachten) **auf jmdn. ~sehen** look down [up]on sb.; ***~|sein** ▸**herunter 1, 3**; **~|setzen** *tr. V.* (ugs.) ▸**herabsetzen**; **~|spielen** *tr. V.* (ugs.) **1** (als unbedeutend darstellen) play down (coll.); **2** (ausdruckslos spielen) **etw. ~spielen** play sth. through mechanically; **~|steigen** *unr. itr. V.; mit sein* climb down; **~|stufen** *tr.V.* ▸**herabstufen**; **~|stürzen** **A** *itr. V.; mit sein* fall down; (steil herabfallen) ‹*aircraft, person, etc.*› plunge down; (~eilen) rush down; **vom Dach ~stürzen** fall off the roof; **B** *tr. V.* **1** (schnell trinken) gulp down; **2** **jmdn. ~stürzen** throw sb. down; **~|tragen** *unr. tr. V.* **etw. ~tragen** carry sth. down; **~|werfen** *unr. tr. V.* **1** (nach unten werfen) **etw. ~werfen** throw sth. down; **2** (ugs.: ~fallen lassen) drop; **~|wirtschaften** *tr. V.* (ugs.) **etw. ~wirtschaften** ruin sth./bring sth. to the brink *or* edge of ruin [by mismanagement]; **~|ziehen** **A** *unr. tr. V.* pull down; **jmdn. [auf seine Ebene] ~ziehen** (fig.) drag sb. down [to one's own level]; **B** *unr. itr. V.; mit sein* go *or* move down; (umziehen) move down

her·vor *Adv.* **aus etw. ~:** out of sth.; **aus der Ecke ~ kam ...** from out of the corner came ...

hervor-, Hervor-: ~|brechen *unr. itr. V.; mit sein* (geh.) **1** (zum Vorschein kommen) ‹*animal etc.*› burst out; ‹*sun*› break through; ‹*plant*› come up *or* through; **2** (sich äußern) ‹*feelings*› burst forth *or* out; **~|bringen** *unr. tr. V.* **1** (zum Vorschein bringen) bring out (**aus** of); produce (**aus** from); **2** (wachsen, entstehen lassen; auch fig.) produce; **3** (von sich geben) say; produce ‹*sound*›; **er brachte kein Wort/keinen Ton ~:** he could not utter a word/sound; **~|dringen** *unr. itr. V.; mit sein* (geh.) ‹*plant*› come up *or* through; **~|gehen** *unr. itr. V.; mit sein* (geh.) **1** (seinen Ursprung haben) **viele große Musiker gingen aus dieser Stadt ~:** this city produced many great musicians; **drei Kinder gingen aus der Ehe ~:** the marriage produced three children; there were three children from the marriage; **eines geht aus dem andern ~:** one thing evolves from another; **2** (herauskommen, sich ergeben) emerge (**aus** from); **aus etw. siegreich/als Sieger ~gehen** emerge victorious from sth.; **aus seinem Brief geht klar ~, dass ...** it is clear from his letter that ...; **3** (zu folgern sein) follow; **daraus geht ~, dass ...** from this it follows that ...; **~|gucken** *itr. V.* (ugs.) look out; **unter etw.** (*Dat.*) **~gucken** peep out from under sth.; **~|heben** *unr. tr. V.* emphasize; stress; **etw. durch Kursivdruck ~heben** make sth. stand out by using italics; **~hebung** *die* emphasis; **der ~hebung dienen** be [used] for emphasis; **~|holen** *tr. V.* take out (**aus** of); **ich muss meine alten Schulbücher ~holen** I must get out my old school books; **~|kehren** *tr. V.* ▸**herauskehren**; **~|kommen** *unr. itr. V.; mit sein* come out (**aus** of, **unter** + *Dat.* from under); **~|kramen** *tr. V.* (ugs.) dig out (also fig.); **die Vergangenheit ~kramen** dig up the past; **~|locken** *tr. V.* lure *or* entice ‹*person, animal*› out (**aus** of); **~|quellen** *unr. itr. V.; mit sein* well up; ‹*smoke*› pour out; **aus etw. ~quellen** stream from sth.; **unter dem Hut quoll ihr Haar ~:** her hair spilled out from under her hat; **~quellende Augen** bulging eyes; **~|ragen** *itr. V.* **1** (aus etw. ragen) project; jut out; ‹*cheekbones*› stand out; **aus dem Häusermeer ragte der Kirchturm ~:** the church spire stood out above the sea of houses; **2** (sich auszeichnen) stand out; **~ragend** **A** *Adj.* outstanding[ly good]; **B** *adv.* **~ragend geschult** outstandingly well trained; **~ragend spielen/arbeiten** play/work outstandingly well *or* excellently; **~ruf** *der* curtain call; **~|rufen** *unr. tr. V.* **1** (nach vorn rufen) **jmdn. ~rufen** call for sb. to come out; (Theater usw.) call sb. back; **sie wurde sechsmal ~gerufen** she had to take six curtain calls; **2** (verursachen) elicit, provoke ‹*response*›; arouse ‹*admiration*›; cause ‹*unease, disquiet, confusion, merriment, disease*›; provoke ‹*protest, displeasure*›; **~|sehen** *unr. itr. V.* be visible; (unerwünscht) show; **~|springen** *unr. itr. V.; mit sein* **1** (springend ~kommen) leap *or* jump out (**hinter** + *Dat.* from behind); **2** (vorspringen) project; jut out; ‹*nose*› stick out; **~|stechen** *unr. itr. V.* **1** (herausstehen) stick out (**aus** of); **2** (sich abheben) stand out; **~stechend** *Adj.* outstanding; striking; **~|stehen** *unr. itr. V.* protrude; stick out; ‹*cheekbones*› stand out; **~|stoßen** *unr. tr. V.* exclaim; **~|stürzen** *itr. V.; mit sein* rush *or* burst out (**hinter** + *Dat.* from behind); **~|suchen** *tr. V.* look out; **~|treten** *unr. itr. V.; mit sein* **1** emerge, step out (**hinter** + *Dat.* from behind); ‹*veins, ribs, etc.*› stand out; ‹*similarity etc.*› become apparent *or* evident; ‹*eyes*› bulge, protrude; **die Sonne trat aus den Wolken ~** (fig. geh.) the sun emerged *or* came out from behind the clouds; **2** (bekannt werden) make one's mark; make a name for oneself; **~|tun** *unr. refl. V.* **1** (Besonderes leisten) distinguish oneself; **sie hat sich nicht sonderlich ~getan** she did not exactly distinguish herself; **sich mit/als etw. ~tun** make one's mark with/as sth.; **2** (wichtig tun) show off; **~|wagen** *refl. V.* dare to come out (**aus** of); **du kannst dich wieder ~wagen** you can come out again; **~|zaubern** *tr. V.* conjure up; **er zauberte ein Päckchen Zigaretten ~:** as if by magic he produced a packet of cigarettes; **~|ziehen** *unr. tr. V.* pull out (**hinter** + *Dat.* from behind, **unter** + *Dat.* from under)

her|wagen *refl. V.* (ugs.) dare to come here

Her·weg *der:* **auf dem ~weg** on the way here

Herz /hɛrts/ *das;* **~ens, ~en** **1** ▸❶ **S. 435** (auch: herzförmiger Gegenstand, zentraler Teil) heart; **sie hat es am ~en** (ugs.) she has a bad heart; (fig.) **komm an mein ~, Geliebter** come into my arms, my darling; **jmdm. das ~ zerreißen** break sb.'s heart; **dabei dreht sich mir das ~ im Leib[e] um** it makes my heart bleed; **mir blutet das ~** (auch iron.) my heart bleeds; **mir lacht das ~ im Leibe** my heart sings; **ihm rutschte** *od.* **fiel das ~ in die Hose[n]** (ugs., oft scherzh.) his heart sank into his boots; **jmds. ~ höher schlagen lassen** make sb.'s heart beat faster; **jmdm. das ~ brechen** (geh.) break sb.'s heart; **das ~ auf dem rechten Fleck haben** have one's heart in the right place; **das ~ in die Hand** *od.* **in beide Hände nehmen** take one's courage in both hands; **jmdn./etw. auf ~ und Nieren prüfen** (ugs.) grill sb./go over sth. with a fine toothcomb; **ein Kind unter dem ~en tragen** (dichter.) be with child; be great with child (arch.); *s. auch* **drücken 1; klopfen A 2**

2 (meist geh.: Gemüt) heart; **ein treues ~ haben** be true-hearted; **ein warmes/gutes ~ haben** have a warm/good *or* kind heart; **die ~en bewegen/rühren** touch people's hearts; **von ~en kommen** come from the heart; **im Grunde seines ~ens** in his heart of hearts; **man kann einem Menschen nicht ins ~ sehen** one cannot see *or* look into another man's heart; **wes das ~ voll ist, des geht der Mund über** (prov.) when you're excited about something, it's difficult to stop talking about it; **ein ~ und eine Seele sein** be bosom friends; **jmds. ~ hängt an etw.** (*Dat.*) (jmd. möchte etw. sehr gerne behalten) sb. is attached to sth.; (jmd. möchte etw. sehr gerne haben) sb.'s heart is set on sth.; **sein ~ gehört der Musik/Literatur** *usw.* (geh.) music/literature *etc.* is his first love; **ihm war/wurde das ~ schwer** his heart was/grew heavy; **alles, was das ~ begehrt** everything one's heart desires; **nicht das ~ haben, etw. zu tun** not have the heart to do sth.; **sich** (*Dat.*) **ein ~ fassen** pluck up one's courage; take one's courage in both hands; **sein ~ an jmdn./etw. hängen** (geh.) give one's heart to sb./devote oneself to sth.; **sein ~ für etw. entdecken** (geh.) discover a passion for sth.; **ein ~ für die Armen und Kranken haben** feel for the sick and the poor; **ein ~ für Kinder/die Kunst haben** have a love of children/art; **jmdm. sein ~ ausschütten** pour out one's heart to sb.; **jmdm. das ~ schwer machen** sadden sb.'s heart; **das ~ auf der Zunge haben** wear one's heart on one's sleeve; **die** *od.* **alle ~en im Sturm erobern** (geh.) capture everybody's heart; **seinem ~en einen Stoß geben** [suddenly] pluck up courage; **seinem ~en Luft machen** (ugs.) give vent to one's feelings; **leichten ~ens** easily; happily; **schweren ~ens** with a heavy heart; **jmd./etw. liegt jmdm. am ~en** sb. has the interests of sb./sth. at heart; **jmdm. etw. ans ~ legen** entrust sb. with sth.; **jmd./etw. ist jmdm. ans ~ gewachsen** sb. has grown very fond of sb./sth.; **etw. auf dem ~en haben** have sth. on one's mind; **aus seinem ~en keine Mördergrube machen** speak freely *or* frankly; **aus tiefstem ~en** (geh.) from the bottom of one's heart; **jmdn. ins** *od.* **in sein ~ schließen** take to sb.; **jmdn. ins ~ treffen** cut sb. to the quick; **mit halbem ~en** (geh.) half-heartedly; **es nicht übers ~ bringen, etw. zu tun** not have the heart to do sth.; **von ~en gern** [most] gladly; **von ganzem ~en** (aufrichtig) with all one's heart; (aus voller Überzeugung) wholeheartedly; **sich** (*Dat.*) **etw. zu ~en nehmen** take sth. to heart; **habt ein ~ [mit dem armen Kerl]!** have pity [on the poor fellow]!; **mit ganzem ~en** (geh.) wholeheartedly; **ein Mann** *usw.* **nach jmds. ~en** a man *etc.* after sb.'s own heart; **jmdm. aus dem ~en sprechen** express just what sb. is/was thinking; **jmdm. sein ~ schenken** (geh.) give sb. one's heart; **die Dame seines ~ens** (geh., oft scherzh.) the woman of his heart; **von ~en**

h

kommen ‹*present*› be given with cordial feeling; ‹*congratulations, thanks, etc.*› come from the heart; **jmdm. zu ~en gehen** upset sb. deeply; *s. auch* **golden A 3**; **Luft 3**; **Stein 2**; **Stich 5**; **Zentnerlast**
3 (Kartenspiel) hearts *pl.*; *s. auch* **Pik²**
4 (Speise) heart; **ein Pfund ~ vom Schwein** a pound of pig's heart[s]
5 (Kosewort) **mein ~:** my dear

herz-, Herz-: ~allerliebste *der/die; adj. Dekl.* (veralt.) beloved; **~allerliebster mein** my beloved; my darling; **~anfall** *der* heart attack; ***~as, ~ass** *das* ace of hearts; **~asthma** *das* ▸❶ **S. 439** (Med.) cardiac asthma; cardiasthma; **~beklemmend** *Adj.* oppressive; **~beklemmung** *die* angina; **~beschwerden** *Pl.* heart trouble *sing.*; **~beutel** *der* ▸❶ **S. 435** (Anat.) pericardium; **~binkerl** /-bɪŋkɐl/ *das;* **~~s, ~~** (bayr., österr. ugs.) pet (coll.); darling; **~blatt** *das* 1 (Gartenbau) new, inner leaf; 2 (Kosewort) darling; **~blut** *das: in* **sein ~blut für jmdn./etw. hingeben** (geh. veralt.) sacrifice everything for sb./sth.; **~bube** *der* jack of hearts

Herzchen *das;* **~s, ~** 1 (abwertend: naive/unzuverlässige Person) simpleton/unreliable person 2 (Kosewort) darling; sweetheart 3 (kleines Herz) little heart

Herz-: ~chirurgie *die* heart *or* cardiac surgery; **~dame** *die* queen of hearts

Herzegowina /hɛrtse'go:vina/ *die;* **~:** Herzegovina

her|zeigen *tr. V.* (ugs.) show; **zeig [es] mal her!** let me see [it]!

Herze·leid *das* (veralt.) heartbreak

herzen *tr. V.* (veralt.) hug

herzens-, Herzens-: ~angelegenheit *die* (Liebesangelegenheit) affair of the heart; (Leidenschaft) passion; **~angst** *die* (geh.) deep anxiety; (bei unmittelbarer Bedrohung) [mortal] fear; **~bedürfnis** *das: in* **jmdm. ein ~bedürfnis sein** (geh.) be very important to sb.; **~bildung** *die* (geh.) sensitivity; **~brecher** *der* ladykiller (coll.); heartbreaker; **~brecherin** *die;* **~~, ~~nen** heartbreaker; **~grund** *der: in* **aus ~grund** from the bottom of one's heart; **~gut** /'--'-/ *Adj.* kind-hearted; good-hearted; **~güte** *die* (geh.) kindness of heart; kind-heartedness; goodness of heart; **~lust** *die: in* **nach ~lust** to one's heart's content; **~wunsch** *der* dearest *or* fondest wish

herz-, Herz-: ~entzündung *die* ▸❶ **S. 439** (Med.) ▸ **Karditis**; **~erfreuend** *Adj.* heart-warming; **~erfrischend** A *Adj.* refreshing; B *adv.* refreshingly; **~ergreifend** A *Adj.* heart-rending; B *adv.* heart-rendingly; **~erquickend** *Adj.* ▸ **~erfrischend**; **~erwärmend** A *Adj.* heart-warming. B *adv.* in a heart-warming manner; **~fehler** *der* heart defect; **~flimmern** *das* ▸❶ **S. 439** (Med.) (Kammerflimmern) ventricular fibrillation; (Vorhofflimmern) auricular fibrillation; **~förmig** *Adj.* heart-shaped; heart-shaped, cordate ‹*leaf*›; **~gegend** *die* area *or* region of the heart; **~geräusch** *das* ▸❶ **S. 439** (Med.) heart murmur

herzhaft
A *Adj.* 1 (kräftig) hearty 2 (nahrhaft) hearty, substantial ‹*meal*›; (von kräftigem Geschmack) tasty; **ein ~er Eintopf** a substantial/tasty stew 3 (veralt.: mutig) bold
B *adv.* 1 (kräftig) heartily; **~ gähnen** give a wide yawn 2 (nahrhaft) **er isst gern ~:** he likes to have a hearty meal 3 (veralt.: mutig) boldly

her|ziehen
A *unr. itr. V.* 1 *mit sein od. haben* (ugs.: abfällig reden) **über jmdn./etw. ~:** run sb./sth. down; pull sb./sth. to pieces 2 *mit sein* (mitgehen) **vor/hinter/neben jmdm./etw. ~:** walk along in front of/behind/beside sb./sth.; (marschieren) march along in front of/behind/beside sb./sth. 3 (umziehen) *mit sein* move here
B *unr. tr. V.* 1 (ugs.: zum Sprechenden bewegen) **etw. ~:** pull sth. over [here] 2 (mit sich führen) **jmdn./etw. hinter sich** (*Dat.*) **~:** pull sb./sth. along behind one

herzig
A *Adj.* sweet; dear; delightful
B *adv.* sweetly; delightfully

herz-, Herz-: ~infarkt *der* ▸❶ **S. 439** heart attack; cardiac infarction (Med.); **~innig** (veralt.), **~inniglich** (veralt.) A *Adj.* heartfelt; B *adv.* with heartfelt emotion; **jmdn. ~innig lieben** love sb. with all one's heart; **~insuffizienz** *die* ▸❶ **S. 439** (Med.) cardiac insufficiency; **~kammer** *die* ▸❶ **S. 435** (Anat.) ventricle; **~kasper** *der* (ugs.) racing heart; **ich krieg noch den ~kasper** my heart's racing; **~kirsche** *die* heart cherry; sweet cherry; **~klappe** *die* ▸❶ **S. 435** (Anat.) heart valve; **~klappen·fehler** *der* ▸❶ **S. 439** (Med.) valvular defect *or* insufficiency; **~klopfen** *das;* **~~s: jmd. hat ~klopfen** sb.'s heart is pounding; **jmd. bekommt ~klopfen** sb.'s heart starts to pound; **mit ~klopfen** with a pounding heart; **~kollaps** *der* ▸ **~versagen**; **~könig** *der* king of hearts; **~krampf** *der* heart spasm; **~krank** *Adj.* ‹*person*› with *or* suffering from a heart condition; **[sehr] ~krank sein/werden** have/get a [serious] heart condition; **~kranke Patienten** cardiac patients; **~kranke** *der/die* person with *or* suffering from a heart condition; (Patient) cardiac patient; **~kranz·gefäß** *das* ▸❶ **S. 435** coronary vessel; **~leiden** *das* heart condition

herzlich
A *Adj.* 1 (warmherzig) warm ‹*smile, reception*›; kind ‹*words*›; **~ zu jmdm. sein** be cordial towards sb. 2 ▸❶ **S. 331** (ehrlich gemeint) sincere; **~e Grüße/~en Dank** kind regards/many thanks; **sein ~es Beileid zum Ausdruck bringen** express one's sincere condolences *pl.*; **~[st] dein/euer Julius** (als Briefschluss) kind[est] regards, Julius; *s. auch* **Glückwunsch**
B *adv.* 1 (warmherzig) warmly; **der Empfang fiel sehr ~ aus** the reception was very cordial 2 ▸❶ **S. 331** (ehrlich gemeint) sincerely; ‹*congratulate*› heartily; **es grüßt euch ~ eure Viktoria** (als Briefschluss) kind regards, Victoria 3 (sehr) **~ wenig** very *or* (coll.) precious little; **~ schlecht** dreadful; **~ gern!** gladly; **etw. ~ satt haben** be heartily sick of sth.

Herzlichkeit *die* 1 ▸ **herzlich 1**: warmth; kindness 2 (Aufrichtigkeit) sincerity

herz-, Herz-: ~liebste *der/die* ▸ **~allerliebste**; **~los** A *Adj.* heartless; callous; B *adv.* heartlessly; callously; **~losigkeit** *die;* **~~, ~~en** 1 heartlessness; callousness; 2 (~lose Tat/Bemerkung) heartless act/remark; **~-Lungen-Maschine** *die* heart-lung machine; **~massage** *die* cardiac massage; heart massage; **~mittel** *das* (ugs.) heart pills *pl.*; **~muskel** *der* ▸❶ **S. 435** (Anat.) heart muscle; cardiac muscle

Herzog /'hɛrtso:k/ *der;* **~s, Herzöge** /'hɛrtsø:gə/ duke; **[Herr] Friedrich ~ von Meiningen** Frederick, Duke of Meiningen

Herzogin *die;* **~, ~nen** duchess

herzoglich *Adj.* ducal; of the duke *postpos., not pred.*; **die ~e Familie** the family of the duke

Herzogtum *das;* **~s, Herzogtümer** duchy

Herz·rhythmus *der* (Med.) heart rhythm; cardiac rhythm

Herzrhythmus·störung *die* ▸❶ **S. 439** (Med.) disturbance of the heart *or* cardiac rhythm

herz-, Herz-: ~schlag *der* 1 heartbeat; **einen ~schlag lang** (geh.) for a *or* one fleeting moment; 2 (Abfolge der ~schläge, auch fig. geh.) pulse; 3 ▸❶ **S. 439** (~versagen) heart failure; **an einem ~schlag sterben** die of heart failure; **~schmerz** *der* pain in the region of the heart; **~schrittmacher** *der* (Anat., Med.) [cardiac] pacemaker; **~schwäche** *die* cardiac insufficiency; **~spezialist** *der,* **~spezialistin** *die* heart specialist; **~stärkend** *Adj.* **ein ~stärkendes Mittel** a cardiac tonic; **~stärkend sein/wirken** act as a cardiac tonic; **~stillstand** *der* ▸❶ **S. 439** (Med.) cardiac arrest; **~stück** *das* (geh.) heart; **~tätigkeit** *die* action of the heart; **~tod** *der* [death from] heart failure *no art.*; **~ton** *der; Pl.* **~töne** (Med.) heart sound; cardiac sound; **~transplantation** *die* (Med.) heart transplantation

herzu /hɛɐ̯'tsu:/ *Adv.* (geh.) ▸ **herbei**

herz-, Herz-: ~verfettung *die* fatty degeneration of the heart; **~verpflanzung** *die* ▸ **~transplantation**; **~versagen** *das;* **~~s** ▸❶ **S. 439** heart failure; **~zentrum** *das* cardiac centre **~zerreißend** A *Adj.* heart-rending; B *adv.* heart-rendingly

Hesse /'hɛsə/ *der;* **~n, ~n** Hessian

Hessen *(das)* Hesse

Hessin *die;* **~, ~nen** ▸ **Hesse**

hessisch *Adj.* Hessian

Hetäre /he'tɛ:rə/ *die;* **~, ~n** hetaera

Hetera /'hɛtəra/ *die;* **~, ~s** hetero woman

hetero-, Hetero- /hetero-/ *in Zus.* hetero-

Hetero *der;* **~s, ~s** (ugs.) hetero (coll.)

heterodox /-'dɔks/ *Adj.* (Rel.) heterodox

Heterodoxie /-dɔ'ksi:/ *die;* **~, ~n** (Rel.) heterodoxy

heterogen /-'ge:n/ *Adj.* heterogeneous

Heterogenität /-geni'tɛ:t/ *die;* **~:** heterogeneity

heteronom /-'no:m/ *Adj.* (geh.; Zool.) heteronomous

Hetero·sexualität *die;* **~:** heterosexuality *no art.*

hetero·sexuell *Adj.* heterosexual

Hethiter /he'ti:tɐ/ *der;* **~s, ~, Hethiterin** *die;* **~, ~nen** Hittite

Hetz /hɛts/ *die;* **~, ~en** (österr. ugs.) **das war eine ~!** that was a [good] laugh; **seine ~ haben** have some fun; **aus ~:** for fun

Hetz·blatt *das* (abwertend) political smear-sheet

Hetze /'hɛtsə/ *die;* **~** 1 (große Hast) [mad] rush; **in großer ~:** in a mad rush *or* hurry; **heute war eine fürchterliche ~:** today was one mad rush 2 (abwertend: Aufhetzung) smear campaign; (gegen eine Minderheit) hate campaign; **eine ~ betreiben** mount *or* run a smear/hate campaign 3 (Jägerspr.) ▸ **Hetzjagd 1**

hetzen
A *tr. V.* 1 hunt; **ein Tier zu Tode ~:** hunt an animal to death; **die Hunde/die Polizei auf jmdn. ~:** set the dogs on [to] sb./get the police on to sb. 2 (antreiben) rush; hurry
B *itr. V.* 1 (in großer Eile sein) rush; **den ganzen Tag ~:** be in a rush all day long 2 *mit sein* (hasten) rush; hurry; (rennen) dash; race 3 (abwertend: Hass entfachen) stir up hatred; (schmähen) say malicious things; **gegen jmdn./etw. ~:** smear sb./agitate against sth.; **gegen eine Minderheit ~:** stir up hatred against a minority; **zum Krieg ~:** engage in warmongering; **bei jmdm. gegen jmdn. ~:** try to turn sb. against sb.

Hetzer *der;* **~s, ~:** malicious agitator

Hetzerei *die;* **~, ~en** 1 (Hast) [mad] rush 2 (ugs. abwertend: Aufwiegelei) malicious agitation 3 (ugs. abwertend: hetzerische Handlung/hetzerisches Wort) inflammatory act/word

Hetzerin *die;* **~, ~nen** ▸ **Hetzer**

hetzerisch *Adj.* inflammatory

Hetz-: ~hund *der* hound; hunting dog; **~jagd** *die* 1 (Jagdw.) hunting (*with hounds*); (einzelne Jagd) hunt (*with hounds*); 2 (Hast) [mad] rush; **~kampagne** *die* (abwertend) smear campaign; (gegen eine Minderheit) hate campaign; **~rede** *die* (abwertend) inflammatory speech; **~tirade** *die* (abwertend) inflammatory diatribe

Heu /hɔy/ *das;* **~[e]s** 1 hay; **~ machen** make hay 2 (ugs.: Geld) dough (coll.); **der hat vielleicht ~:** he's rolling in money *or* it (coll.); *s. auch* **Geld 1**

Heu-: ~blumen *Pl.: mixture of seeds, flowers, and grasses sieved from hay and used for medical purposes*; **~boden** *der* hayloft

Heuchelei *die;* **~, ~en** (abwertend) 1 (Verstellung) hypocrisy 2 (Äußerung) piece of hypocrisy; hypocritical remark

heucheln /'hɔyçl̩n/
A *itr. V.* be a hypocrite
B *tr. V.* feign ‹*joy, sympathy, etc.*›

Heuchler *der;* **~s, ~, Heuchlerin** *die;* **~, ~nen** hypocrite

heuchlerisch
A *Adj.* **1** (unaufrichtig) hypocritical **2** (geheuchelt) feigned ‹*interest, sympathy, etc.*›
B *adv.* hypocritically

heuen *itr. V.* (landsch.) make hay

heuer /ˈhɔyɐ/ *Adv.* (südd., österr., schweiz.) this year

Heuer *die;* ~, ~**n** (Seemannsspr.) **1** (Lohn) pay; wages *pl.* **2** (Anstellung) **auf einem Schiff [als Funker] ~ nehmen** join a ship [as wireless operator]; **auf einem Frachter ~ nehmen** ship on board a freighter; **eine ~ bekommen** get hired

Heu·ernte *die* **1** hay harvest; haymaking **2** (Ertrag) hay crop

Heuer·vertrag *der* (Seemannsspr.) contract of employment

Heu-: ~**fieber** *das* ▸ ~**schnupfen**; ~**forke** *die* (nordd.), ~**gabel** *die* hay fork; ~**haufen** *der* haystack; hayrick; *s. auch* **Stecknadel**

Heul·boje *die* **1** (Seew.) whistling buoy **2** (ugs. abwertend: Sänger) caterwauler

heulen /ˈhɔylən/ *itr. V.* **1** ‹*wolf, dog, jackal, etc.*› howl; (fig.) ‹*wind, gale*› howl; ‹*storm*› roar **2** ‹*siren, buoy, etc.*› wail **3** (ugs.: weinen) howl; bawl; **vor Wut/Schmerz/Freude ~:** howl and weep with rage/pain/howl with delight; **das ist zum Heulen** (ugs.) it's enough to make you weep; **Heulen und Zähneklappern** *od.* **Zähneknirschen** wailing and gnashing of teeth

Heuler *der;* ~**s,** ~ **1** (ugs.: Heulton) whine **2** (Feuerwerkskörper) wailing banshee **3** (salopp: tolle Sache) **das ist wirklich ein ~:** it's really great *or* fantastic (coll.); **das ist [ja] der letzte ~!** (iron.) it's bloody awful! (Brit. sl.) **4** (ugs.: Seehund) seal

Heulerei *die;* ~, ~**en** (abwertend) **1** (einer Sirene, Boje) wailing **2** (ugs.: heftiges Weinen) howling; bawling

Heulsuse /ˈhɔylzuːzə/ *die;* ~, ~**n** (ugs. abwertend) cry-baby

Heu-: ~**monat** *der,* ~**mond** *der* (veralt.) July; ~**pferd** *das* grasshopper; ~**reiter** *der* (österr.) ▸ ~**reuter**

heureka /ˈhɔyreka/ *Interj.* (geh.) eureka

Heu·reuter *der;* ~**s,** ~ (südd.) drying rack for hay

heurig /ˈhɔyrɪç/ *Adj.* (südd., österr., schweiz.) this year's ‹*harvest, crop, etc.*›; new ‹*potatoes, wine*›; **der ~e Sommer** this summer

Heurige *der; adj. Dekl.* (bes. österr.) **1** (Wein) new wine; **sie saßen beim ~n** they sat drinking the new wine **2** (Weinlokal) inn with new wine on tap

> **Heurige**
>
> This is an Austrian term for both a new wine and an inn with new wine on tap, especially an inn with its own vineyard in the environs of Vienna. On warm, late summer evenings Viennese wine devotees sit on wooden benches and sample the new wine of the year. A garland of pine twigs outside the gates of the *Heurige* shows that the barrel has been breached. See also **Besenwirtschaft**

Heuristik /hɔyˈrɪstɪk/ *die;* ~**:** heuristics *sing.*

heuristisch *Adj.* heuristic

Heu-: ~**schnupfen** *der* ▸❶ **S. 439** hay fever; ~**schober** *der* (südd., österr.) haystack; hayrick; ~**schrecke** *die* grasshopper; (in Afrika, Asien) locust; grasshopper; ~**stadel** *der* (südd., österr., schweiz.) [hay] barn

heut /hɔyt/ (ugs.) ▸ **heute**

heute /ˈhɔytə/ *Adv.* ▸❶ **S. 816** today; **~ früh** early this morning; **~ Morgen/Abend** this morning/evening; **~ Mittag** [at] midday today; **~ Nacht** tonight; (letzte Nacht) last night; **~ in einer Woche** a week [from] today; today week; **~ vor einer Woche** a week ago today; **seit ~:** from today; **ab ~, von ~ an** from today [on]; **bis ~:** until today; **bis ~ nicht** (erst ~) not until today; (überhaupt noch nicht) not to this day; (bis jetzt noch nicht) not as yet; **für ~:** for today; **die Zeitung von ~:** today's paper; **das Brot ist von ~:** it is today's bread; **das kann sich ~ oder morgen schon ändern** (ugs.) that can change at any time; **lieber ~ als morgen** (ugs.) the sooner, the better; **von ~ auf morgen** from one day to the next; **von ~ auf morgen sterben** die suddenly; **das geht nicht von ~ auf morgen** it can't be done at such short notice; **das Heute** the present; today; **der Bauernhof/die Frau von ~:** the farm/woman of today

heutig *Adj.* **1** (von diesem Tag) today's; **die ~e Post/Zeitung/Vorstellung** today's post/newspaper/performance; **der ~e Tag/am ~en Tage** today; **am ~en Abend** this evening; **bis zum ~en Tag** until the present day *or* today **2** (gegenwärtig) today's; of today *postpos.;* **die ~e Jugend/Generation** today's youth/generation; the youth/generation of today; **der ~e Stand der Forschung** the present state of research; **in der ~en Zeit** today; nowadays

heut·zu·tage *Adv.* nowadays

Heu-: ~**wagen** *der* hay cart; ~**wender** *der;* ~~**s,** ~~ (Landw.) tedder; tedding machine

Hexagon /hɛksaˈgoːn/ *das;* ~**s,** ~**e** (Math.) hexagon

Hexa·gramm /hɛksa-/ *das* hexagram

Hexameter /hɛˈksaːmetɐ/ *der;* ~**s,** ~ (Verslehre) hexameter

Hexe /ˈhɛksə/ *die;* ~, ~**n** **1** witch **2** (abwertend) **diese kleine ~:** this little minx

hexen
A *itr. V.* work magic; **ich kann doch nicht ~** (ugs.) I'm not a magician (coll.)
B *tr. V.* conjure up

Hexen-: ~**einmaleins** *das* magic formula; ~**haus** *das* witch's cottage; ~**jagd** *die* (auch fig.) witch-hunt; ~**kessel** *der:* **ein [wahrer] ~kessel sein** be [absolute] bedlam; **das Fußballstadion glich einem ~kessel** there was pandemonium *or* bedlam in the football ground; ~**meister** *der* sorcerer; ~**prozess,** *~**prozeß** *der* (hist.) witch trial; ~**ring** *der* **1** (von Pilzen) fairy ring; **2** (Jägerspr.) *circular run trodden by roedeer in the mating season;* ~**sabbat** *der* **1** (Zusammenkunft der ~) witches' sabbath; **2** (wüstes Treiben) orgy; ~**schuss,** *~**schuß** *der* lumbago *no indef. art.;* ~**verbrennung** *die* (hist.) burning of a witch/of witches; ~**verfolgung** *die* (hist.) witch-hunt

Hexer *der;* ~**s,** ~**:** sorcerer

Hexerei *die;* ~, ~**en** sorcery; witchcraft; (von Kunststücken usw.) magic; **das ist doch keine ~:** there's no magic about it

Hexode /hɛˈksoːdə/ *die;* ~, ~**n** (Elektrot.) hexode

hey /heɪ/ *Interj.* hey

HGB *Abk.* **= Handelsgesetzbuch**

hibbelig /ˈhɪbəlɪç/ (nordd. ugs.)
A *Adj.* jumpy; nervy
B *adv.* jumpily; nervously

hick /hɪk/ *Interj.* (ugs.) hic

Hickhack /ˈhɪkhak/ *das od. der;* ~**s,** ~**s** (ugs.) squabbling; bickering

hie /hiː/ *Adv.: in* **~ und da** (stellenweise) here and there; (von Zeit zu Zeit) now and then; from time to time; **~ ..., da ...** on the one hand ..., on the other [hand] ...

hieb /hiːp/ *1. u. 3. Pers. Sg. Prät. v.* **hauen**

Hieb *der;* ~**[e]s,** ~**e** **1** (Schlag) blow; (mit der Peitsche) lash; (im Fechten) cut; (fig.) dig (**gegen** at); **jmdm. einen ~ mit der Faust/einem Beil versetzen** punch sb./strike sb. with an axe **2** *Pl.* (ugs.: Prügel) hiding *sing.;* beating *sing.;* walloping *sing.* (coll.); **~e bekommen/kriegen** get a hiding *or* (coll.) walloping; **es gibt/setzt ~e!** you'll get a hiding *or* beating *or* (coll.) walloping

hieb·fest *Adj.: in* **hieb- und stichfest** watertight; cast-iron

Hieb·waffe *die* cutting weapon

hielt /hiːlt/ *1. u. 3. Pers. Sg. Prät. v.* **halten**

hienieden /hiːˈniːdn̩/ *Adv.* (bes. österr., sonst veralt.) here below; here in this world [below]

hier /hiːɐ̯/ *Adv.* **1** (an diesem Ort) here; **~ sein/bleiben** be/stay here; **jmdn./etw. ~ behalten/lassen** keep/leave sb./sth. here; **[von] ~ oben/unten** [from] up/down here; **~ vorn** here in front; **~ draußen/drinnen** out/in here; **~ entlang** along here; **von ~ [aus]** from here; **wo ist ~ die nächste Tankstelle?** where is the nearest petrol station (Brit.) *or* (Amer.) gas station around here?; **er ist nicht von ~:** he's not from this area *or* around here; **das Buch ~:** this book [here]; **~ spricht Hans Schulze** this is Hans Schulze [speaking]; **~ und da** *od.* **dort** (an manchen Stellen) here and there; (manchmal) [every] now and then; **~ und jetzt** *od.* **heute** (geh.) here and now; **das Hier und Jetzt** *od.* **Heute** (geh.) the here and now **2** (zu diesem Zeitpunkt) now; **von ~ an** from now on **3** (in diesem Zusammenhang, Punkt) here; **was gibt es ~ zu lachen?** what's funny [about this]?

hier-: *Bei den aus* **hier** *und einer Präposition gebildeten Adverbien* (**hieran, hierauf, hierbei** *usw.*) *werden im Folgenden* this, these *oder* here *zur Übersetzung verwendet* (hold on to this; on here; among these; about this). *Dies ist im Allgemeinen die angemessene Form der Übersetzung. Wenn der Bestandteil* **hier-** *weniger stark betont ist, kann man* this *oder* here *durch* it *ersetzen* (hold on to it; on it; about it). *Beispiele:* **er suchte einen starken Ast und lehnte die Leiter hieran** he looked for a strong branch and leaned the ladder against it; **sie ging zum Schuppen, um ihr Fahrrad hierhinter zu stellen** she went to the shed to put her bicycle behind it. *Ähnlich:* **hierunter befanden sich auch einige Deutsche** there were some Germans among them

hieran /ˈhiːˈran/ *Adv.* **1** (an dieser/diese Stelle) here; **sich ~ festhalten** hold on to this **2** (fig.) **im Anschluss ~:** immediately after this; **~ wird deutlich, dass ...** this shows clearly that ...; *s. auch* **hier-**

Hierarch /hieˈrarç/ *der;* ~**en,** ~**en** hierarch; high priest; (fig.: Chef) top man; chief; boss

Hierarchie /hierarˈçiː/ *die;* ~, ~**n** hierarchy

Hierarchin *die;* ~, ~**nen** chief; boss

hierarchisch
A *Adj.* hierarchical
B *adv.* hierarchically

hierauf /ˈhiːˈrauf/ *Adv.* **1** (auf dieser/diese Stelle) on here **2** (darauf) on this; **wir werden ~ zurückkommen** we'll come back to this **3** (danach) after that; then **4** (infolgedessen) whereupon; *s. auch* **hier-**

hierauf·hin *Adv.* hereupon

hieraus /ˈhiːˈraus/ *Adv.* **1** (aus dem eben Erwähnten) out of *or* from here **2** (aus dieser Tatsache, Quelle) from this **3** (aus diesem Material) out of this; *s. auch* **hier-**

*__hier|behalten__ ▸ **hier 1**

hier·bei *Adv.* **1** (bei dieser Gelegenheit) **Diese Übung ist sehr schwierig. Man kann sich ~ leicht verletzen.** This exercise is very difficult. You can easily injure yourself doing it; **Ich habe ihn gestern getroffen. Hierbei habe ich gleich ...** I met him yesterday, and straightaway I ... **2** (bei der erwähnten Sache) here; *s. auch* **hier-**

*__hier|bleiben__ ▸ **hier 1**

hier·durch *Adv.* **1** (hier hindurch) through here **2** (aufgrund dieser Sache) because of this; as a result of this **3** ▸ **hiermit**; *s. auch* **hier-**

hierein /ˈhiːˈrain/ *Adv.* in here; *s. auch* **hier-**

hier·für *Adv.* for this; **ich habe kein Interesse ~:** I have no interest in this; *s. auch* **hier-**

hier·gegen *Adv.* **1** (gegen die erwähnte Sache) against this **2** (gegen diese Stelle) against here **3** (im Gegensatz hierzu) in *or* by comparison with this; compared with this; *s. auch* **hier-**

hier·her *Adv.* here; **jmdn. ~ bemühen** trouble sb. to come here; **sich ~ bemühen** take the trouble to come here; **darf ich Sie ~ bitten?** would you come here please?; **wie bist du ~ gekommen?** how did you get here?; **komm mal ~!** come here!; **ich gehe bis ~ und nicht weiter** I'm going this far and no further; **bis ~**

h

und nicht weiter (als Warnung) so far and no further; **das gehört nicht ~** (fig.) that is not relevant [here]

hierher|bemühen *usw.* ▸ **hierher**

hier·herum *Adv.* 1 (an dieser Stelle herum) round here; (in diese Richtung) round this way 2 (ugs.: hier irgendwo) around here

hierher-: **~|wagen** *refl. V.* dare to come here; **~|ziehen** A *unr. tr. V.* **etw. ~ziehen** pull sth. here; B *unr. itr. V.; mit sein* (umziehen) move here

hier·hin *Adv.* here; **sie blickte bald ~, bald dorthin** she looked this way and that; **bis ~:** up to here *or* this point

hier·hinab *Adv.* down here

hier·hinauf *Adv.* up here

hier·hinaus *Adv.* 1 (an dieser Stelle) out here 2 (aus diesem Raum) out of here

hier·hinein *Adv.* in here

hier·hinter *Adv.* behind here; *s. auch* **hier-**

hier·hinunter *Adv.* 1 (unter diesen Gegenstand) under here 2 (an dieser Stelle) down here

hierin /ˈhiːˈrɪn/ *Adv.* 1 (in diesem Gegenstand) in here 2 (in dieser Angelegenheit) in this; *s. auch* **hier-**

***hier|lassen** ▸ **hier 1**

hier·mit *Adv.* with this/these; **~ ist der Fall erledigt** that puts an end to the matter; **~ erkläre ich, dass ...** (Amtsspr.) I hereby declare that ...; **~ wird bestätigt/bescheinigt, dass ...** (Amtsspr.) this is to confirm/certify that ...; *s. auch* **hier-**

hier·nach *Adv.* 1 (einer Sache entsprechend) in accordance with this/these 2 (demnach) according to this/these 3 (anschließend) after that; *s. auch* **hier-**

hier·neben *Adv.* beside this; next to this; *s. auch* **hier-**

Hieroglyphe /hieroˈglyːfə/ *die;* **~, ~n** hieroglyph; **~n** hieroglyphics

hier·orts *Adv.* here

***hier|sein** ▸ **hier 1**

hierüber /ˈhiːˈryːbɐ/ *Adv.* 1 (über dem Erwähnten) above here 2 (über das Erwähnte) over here 3 (das Erwähnte betreffend) about this/these 4 (geh.: währenddessen) **er war ~ eingeschlafen** he had fallen asleep while doing so; *s. auch* **hier-**

hierum /ˈhiːˈrʊm/ *Adv.* about this; (um ... herum) round here; **~ geht es gar nicht** that's not the point; it's not a question of that; *s. auch* **hier-**

hierunter /ˈhiːˈrʊntɐ/ *Adv.* 1 (unter diese[r] Stelle) under here 2 (unter der erwähnten Sache) **~ leiden** suffer from this; **etw. ~ verstehen** *od.* **sich** (*Dat.*) **etw. ~ vorstellen** understand sth. by this 3 (unter die genannte/der genannten Gruppe) among these; *s. auch* **hier-**

hier·von *Adv.* 1 (von dieser Stelle) from here 2 (von dieser Sache) of this; **~ zeugen** bear witness to this 3 (dadurch) because of this 4 (aus dieser Menge) of this/these 5 (aus diesem Material) out of this; *s. auch* **hier-**

hier·vor *Adv.* 1 (vor dieser/diese Stelle) in front of this *or* here 2 (vor der erwähnten Sache) **Respekt ~ haben** have respect for this; **Angst ~ haben** be afraid of this; *s. auch* **hier-**

hier·zu *Adv.* 1 (zu dieser Sache) with this; **vgl. ~:** cf. 2 (zu dieser Gruppe) **~ gehört/gehören ...** this includes/these include 3 (zu diesem Zweck) **ich kann dir ~ nur raten** I can only recommend you to do this/buy this/go *etc.*; **ich wünsche dir ~ viel Erfolg** I wish you every success with this; **~ reicht mein Geld nicht** I haven't got enough money for that 4 (hinsichtlich dieser Sache) about this; *s. auch* **hier-**

hierzu·lande *Adv.* (in diesem Land) [here] in this country; [here] in these parts; (in dieser Gegend) [here] in these parts

hiesig /ˈhiːzɪç/ *Adj.* local; **die ~e Gegend** this locality; **meine ~en Verwandten** my relatives here

hieß /hiːs/ *1. u. 3. Pers. Sg. Prät. v.* **heißen**

hieven /ˈhiːvn̩/ *tr. V.* heave

Hi-Fi-Anlage /ˈhaifi-/ *die* (Rundf.) hi-fi system

high /haɪ/ *Adj.* (ugs.) high (coll.)

Highlife /ˈhailaif/ *das;* **~[s]** (ugs.) high life; **bei uns ist heute ~:** we're living it up today; **~ machen** live it up

High Society /hai səˈsaɪətɪ/ *die;* **~ ~:** high society; **zur ~ ~ gehören** be a member of high society

Hightech-, High-Tech- /ˈhaiˈtɛk-/ *in Zus.* high-tech

hihi /hiˈhiː/, **hihihi** /hihiˈhiː/ *Interj.* he-he[-he]

Hilfe /ˈhɪlfə/ *die;* **~, ~n** 1 help; (für Notleidende) aid; relief; **wirtschaftliche/finanzielle ~:** economic aid/financial assistance; **jmdm. ~ leisten** help sb.; **mit ~** (+ *Gen.*) with the help *or* aid of; **ohne fremde ~:** unaided; without help *or* assistance; **jmdn. um ~ bitten**/(geh.) **ersuchen** ask sb. for help *or* assistance/request sb.'s help *or* assistance; **sein ~ suchender Blick ging zum Fenster** he looked towards the window, seeking help; **sich ~ suchend umschauen** look round for help; **sich ~ suchend an jmdn. wenden** turn to sb. for help; **um ~ rufen** shout for help; **jmdn. zu ~ rufen** call on sb. for help; **jmdm. zu ~ kommen/eilen** come/hurry to sb.'s aid *or* assistance; **zu ~!** help!; **jmds. Gedächtnis zu ~ kommen** (fig.) refresh sb.'s memory [for him/her]; **etw. zu ~ nehmen** use sth.; make use of sth.; **jmdm. eine große ~ sein** be a great help to sb.; **jmdm. ~n geben** give sb. some help; **einem Pferd ~n geben** give a horse aids; **erste ~:** first aid 2 (Hilfskraft) help; (im Geschäft) assistant

hilfe-, Hilfe-: **~leistung** *die* help; assistance; **finanzielle ~leistung** financial aid *or* assistance; **unterlassene ~leistung** (Rechtsspr.) failure to render assistance in an emergency; **~ruf** *der* cry for help; (Notsignal) distress signal; **~stellung** *die* (Turnen) 1 **jmdm. ~stellung geben** act as spotter for sb.; 2 (Person) spotter; **~suchend** ▸ **Hilfe 1**

hilf-, Hilf-: **~los** A *Adj.* 1 helpless; 2 (unbeholfen) awkward; B *adv.* 1 helplessly; 2 (unbeholfen) awkwardly; **~losigkeit** *die;* **~~** 1 helplessness; 2 (Unbeholfenheit) awkwardness; **~reich** (geh.) A *Adj.* helpful; B *adv.* **jmdm. ~reich zur Seite stehen** lend support to sb.; stand by sb.

hilfs-, Hilfs-: **~aktion** *die* relief programme; **~arbeiter** *der,* **~arbeiterin** *die* labourer; (in einer Fabrik) unskilled worker; **~bedürftig** *Adj.* 1 (schwach) in need of help *postpos.;* 2 (Not leidend) in need *postpos.;* needy; **~bedürftigkeit** *die* need; neediness; **~bereit** *Adj.* helpful; **~bereitschaft** *die* helpfulness; readiness *or* willingness to help; **~dienst** *der* 1 (Dienst zu Hilfszwecken) community work; 2 (Organisation) emergency service; (bei Katastrophen) [emergency] relief service; (für Autofahrer) [emergency] breakdown service; **~fonds** *der* aid *or* relief fund; **~geistliche** *der/die* (ev. u. kath. Kirche) curate; **~gelder** *Pl.* aid money *sing.;* **~konstruktion** *die* (Geom.) auxiliary construction; **~kraft** *die* assistant; **~lehrer** *der,* **~lehrerin** *die* assistant teacher; **~maßnahme** *die* aid *or* relief measure; **~mittel** *das* 1 (Mittel zur Erleichterung) aid; 2 *Pl.* (finanzielle Mittel) [financial] aid *sing.;* (materielle Mittel) aid *sing.;* supplies; **~motor** *der* auxiliary engine; **ein Fahrrad mit ~motor** a motor-assisted bicycle; **~organisation** *die* aid *or* relief organization; **~personal** *das* auxiliary staff; **~polizist** *der* reserve policeman; **~polizistin** *die* reserve policewoman; **~programm** *das* aid *or* relief programme; **~quelle** *die* 1 (Material) source; 2 (finanziell) source of [financial] aid; **~schule** *die* (veralt., noch ugs.) special school; **~schüler** *der* (veralt., noch ugs.) pupil at a special school; **~schul·lehrer** *der,* **~schul·lehrerin** *die* (veralt., noch ugs.) teacher at a special school; **~schwester** *die* nursing auxiliary; auxiliary nurse; **~sheriff** *der* deputy sheriff; **~truppe** *die* (Milit.) reserve unit; **~verb** *das* (Sprachw.) auxiliary [verb]; **~werk** *das* aid agency; **~willig** *Adj.* helpful; willing to help *postpos.;* **~willige** *der/die; adj. Dekl.* 1 person willing to help; **die ~willigen** the people willing to help; 2 (hist.) *volunteer from German occupied territory serving in German army in Second World War;* **~wissenschaft** *die* ancillary science; **~zeitwort** *das* ▸ **~verb**

Himalaja /hiˈmaːlaja/ *der;* **~[s] der/im ~:** the/in the Himalayas *pl.*

Him·beere /ˈhɪm-/ *die* raspberry

Himbeer-: **~eis** *das* raspberry ice [cream]; **~marmelade** *die* raspberry jam; **~saft** *der* raspberry juice; **~strauch** *der* raspberry bush

Himmel /ˈhɪml̩/ *der;* **~s, ~** 1 sky; **hoch am ~ stehen** be high in the sky; **eher stürzt der ~ ein, als dass er dir Geld leiht** (ugs.) never in a million years will he lend you any money (coll.); **unter freiem ~:** in the open [air]; outdoors; **~ und Erde** (Kochk.) *dish of puréed potato and apple with fried blood sausage and liver sausage;* **aus heiterem ~** (ugs.) out of the blue; **jmdn./etw. in den ~ heben** (ugs.) praise sb./sth. to the skies; **Fortschritte fallen nicht vom ~:** advances don't come overnight 2 (Aufenthalt Gottes) heaven; **in den ~ kommen** go to heaven; **im ~ sein** (verhüll.) be in heaven; **zum ~** *od.* **in den ~ auffahren,** (geh.) **gen ~ fahren** ascend into heaven; **Sohn des ~s** (hist.: Titel des chinesischen Kaisers) Son of Heaven; **~ und Hölle** (Kinderspiel) ≈ hopscotch; **jmdm. hängt der ~ voller Geigen** (geh.) sb. is walking on air; **~ und Hölle** *od.* **Erde in Bewegung setzen** move heaven and earth; **sie hat den ~ auf Erden** (geh.) life is heaven on earth for her; **jmdm. den ~ auf Erden versprechen** promise sb. the earth; **im sieb[en]ten ~ sein/sich [wie] im sieb[en]ten ~ fühlen** (ugs.) be in the seventh heaven; **etw. schreit zum ~:** sth. is scandalous *or* a scandal; **etw. stinkt zum ~** (salopp) sth. stinks to high heaven 3 (verhüll.: Schicksal) Heaven; **gerechter/gütiger/[ach] du lieber ~!** good Heavens!; Heavens above!; **dem ~ sei Dank** thank Heaven[s]; **das weiß der [liebe] ~** *od.* **das mag der liebe ~ wissen** Heaven [only] knows; **weiß der ~!** (ugs.) Heaven knows; **weiß der ~, wer .../wie .../wo .../wann ...** (ugs.) Heaven [only] knows who .../how .../where .../when ...; **um [des] ~s willen!** (Ausruf des Schreckens) good Heavens!; good God!; (inständige Bitte) for Heaven's sake; **~ noch [ein]mal!** for Heaven's *or* goodness' sake!; **~, Herrgott, Sakrament!** for Heaven's sake!; **~, Kreuz, Donnerwetter!** (salopp) damn and blast! (sl.); **~, Arsch und Zwirn!** (derb) bloody hell! (Brit. sl.) 4 (Baldachin) canopy

himmel-, Himmel-: **~an** *Adv.* (dichter.) heavenwards (poet.); up towards the sky; **~angst** *Adj.: in* **mir ist/wird ~angst** I am scared to death; **~bett** *das* four-poster bed; **~blau** *Adj.* sky-blue; azure; clear blue ⟨*eyes*⟩; **~donner·wetter** *Interj.: in* **~donnerwetter noch [ein]mal!** (salopp) hell's bells! (coll.)

Himmel·fahrt *die* (Rel.) 1 (Auffahrt in den Himmel) ascent to heaven; **Christi/Mariä ~:** the Ascension of Christ/the Assumption of the Virgin Mary 2 (Festtag) **[Christi] ~:** Ascension Day *no art.*

Himmelfahrts-: **~kommando** *das* 1 (Unternehmen) suicide mission *or* operation; 2 (Personen) suicide squad; **~nase** *die* (ugs. scherzh.) turned-up nose; **~tag** *der* Ascension Day *no art.*

himmel-, Himmel-: **~herr·gott** *Interj.: in* **~herrgott noch [ein]mal!** (salopp) hell's bells! (coll.); **~herr·gott·sakra** *Interj.* (österr., südd. salopp) bloody hell! (Brit. sl.); **~hoch** A *Adj.* soaring; towering; B *adv.* ⟨*rise up etc.*⟩ high into the sky; **~hoch jauchzend, zu Tode betrübt** up one minute, down the next; on top of the world one minute, down in the dumps the next; **~hund** *der* (derb)

ℹ Himmelsrichtungen

Die vier Himmelsrichtungen haben im Englischen nur die eine Form, die auch adjektivisch verwendet wird. (Es gibt andere Übersetzungen für die deutschen Adjektive *nördlich, südlich* usw.; s. unten):

Nord, Norden, Nord-	north
Ost, Osten, Ost-	east
Süd, Süden, Süd-	south
West, Westen, West-	west

Die weiteren, zusammengesetzten Bezeichnungen werden ähnlich wie im Deutschen gebildet:

Nordost, Nordosten	north-east
Nordwest, Nordwesten	north-west
Südost, Südosten	south-east
Südwest, Südwesten	south-west
Nordnordost, Nordnordosten	north-north-east
Nordnordwest, Nordnordwesten	north-north-west
Südsüdost, Südsüdosten	south-south-east
Südsüdwest, Südsüdwesten	south-south-west
Ostnordost, Ostnordosten	east-north-east
Westnordwest, Westnordwesten	west-north-west
Ostsüdost, Ostsüdosten	east-south-east
Westsüdwest, Westsüdwesten	west-south-west

Richtung

Der Wind kommt von Norden/Nordosten
= The wind is from the north/north-east
Wir fahren morgen nach Norden
= We are going north tomorrow
Die Nadel weist nach Norden
= The needle points to the north
der Zug nach Norden
= the northbound train
Das Schiff fährt nach Süden
= The ship is southward bound
Die Straße führt nach Südwesten
= The road runs south-west/south-westwards
Sie fuhren in Richtung Osten od. in östliche Richtung
= They were travelling eastwards *od.* in an easterly direction
Das Wohnzimmer geht nach Norden
= The sitting room faces north

Lage

Sie wohnen im Südwesten
= They live in the South-West
im Süden Englands, in Südengland
= in the South of England, in southern England
Im Norden ballten sich Gewitterwolken zusammen
= To the north storm clouds were gathering
Sie stammt aus dem Nordosten
= She comes from the North-East
Es liegt ein paar Kilometer westlich
= It's a few kilometres to the west
Es liegt weiter östlich
= It's further east
30 Kilometer südlich von Passau
= 30 kilometres [to the] south of Passau
etwas westlich der Insel
= a little to the west of the island

Adjektive

Nord-, Süd-, Ost-, West- bei geographischen Namen werden durch **North, South, East, West** übersetzt, solange es sich um ein ziemlich genau umgrenztes Gebiet handelt, also:

Nordamerika/Südamerika
= North America/South America
Westafrika/Ostafrika
= West Africa/East Africa
Nordkorea/Südkorea
= North Korea/South Korea
Westberlin/Ostberlin
= West Berlin/East Berlin

Aber:

Norditalien/Süditalien
= Northern/Southern Italy,

da es sich hier nicht um ein genau umgrenztes Gebiet handelt. Man kann auch sagen 'the North/South of Italy'; vor allem *Südfrankreich* = the South of France. Allerdings:

die Südstaaten
= the southern States
die Westmächte
= the Western Powers
Ostdeutschland/Westdeutschland
= East *od.* Eastern Germany/West *od.* Western Germany (*hierbei bezieht sich die jeweils erste Bezeichnung hauptsächlich auf die ehemalige DDR bzw. die alte BRD*)

Man beachte ferner:

die Westküste
= the West Coast
die Südseite
= the south side; (*eines Hauses*) the south front
die Eigernordwand
= the north face of the Eiger

Aber:

die Westfront/Ostfront
= the Western/Eastern Front

Da sie im Deutschen schon weniger spezifisch sind, liegt es nahe, die Adjektive *nördlich, südlich, westlich, östlich* mit **northern, southern, western, eastern** zu übersetzen, etwa in:

das südliche Afrika
= southern Africa (im Gegensatz zu *Südafrika* = South Africa)

Sofern die Adjektive eine politische Bedeutung haben, werden sie groß geschrieben:

westliche Journalisten
= Western journalists
die westlichen Länder
= the Western countries

Bei Winden (und Richtungen) hingegen verwendet man die Formen **northerly, southerly, westerly, easterly:**

nördliche Winde
= northerly winds, northerlies (im Gegensatz zu *der Nordwind* = the north wind)
Winde aus östlicher Richtung
= winds from an easterly direction, easterly winds

Für den Superlativ kann im Englischen auch eine mit den Adjektiven **northern, southern** usw. und dem Suffix **-most** gebildete Form stehen:

der östlichste Punkt
= the easternmost point, the most easterly point

---

unscrupulous bastard (coll.); (Draufgänger) daredevil; **~reich** *das* (christl. Rel.) kingdom of heaven; **ein ~reich für ...** I'd give anything for ...; *s. auch* **Mensch**[1] **2**

Himmels-: ~achse *die* (Astron.) celestial axis; **~äquator** *der* (Astron.) celestial equator; **~bahn** *die* (dichter.) path across the heavens

himmel·schreiend *Adj.* scandalous; outrageous; scandalous, appalling ‹*conditions, disgrace*›; arrant *attrib.* ‹*nonsense*›; **ihre Dummheit ist ~:** she is appallingly stupid; **eine ~e Ungerechtigkeit** an injustice that cries out to heaven

Himmels-: ~erscheinung *die* celestial phenomenon; **~fürst** *der* (christl. Rel.) King of heaven; **~gabe** *die* (geh.) gift from heaven; **~gegend** *die* ▸ **~richtung**; **~gewölbe** *das* **1** (dichter.) firmament; vault of heaven *or* the heavens; **2** (Astron.) sky; **~globus** *der* celestial globe; **~karte** *die* (Astron.) star map; **~königin** *die* (kath. Rel.) Queen of heaven; **~körper** *der* celestial body; **~kugel** *die* celestial sphere; **~kunde** *die* astronomy; **~kuppel** *die* ▸ **~gewölbe 1**; **~labor** *das* (Raumf., bes. DDR) space lab[oratory]; **~macht** *die* (geh.) heavenly power; **~pforte** *die* (dichter.) gates *pl.* of heaven; Pearly Gates (also joc.); **~pol** *der* (Astron.) celestial pole; **~richtung** *die* ▸ ℹ **S. 363** point of the compass; cardinal point; **die vier ~richtungen** the four points of the compass; **aus allen ~richtungen** from all directions; **in alle ~richtungen verstreut sein** be scattered to all four corners of the earth; **von hier aus führen Wege in alle ~richtungen** from this point paths radiate in all directions; **~schlüssel** *der* cowslip; (Waldschlüsselblume) oxlip; **~sphäre** *die* celestial sphere; **~spion** *der* (ugs.) spy-in-the-sky satellite (coll.); **~stürmer** *der*, **~stürmerin** *die* (geh.) unshakeable idealist; **~tor** *das*, **~tür** *die* (dichter.) gates *pl.* of heaven

himmel·stürmend *Adj.* (geh.) boundless ‹*enthusiasm*›; unbridled ‹*feelings*›; wildly ambitious ‹*plan*›

Himmels·zelt *das* (dichter.) firmament

himmel-: ~wärts *Adv.* (geh.) heavenwards; **~weit A** *Adj.* enormous, vast ‹*difference*›; **zwischen uns besteht ein ~weiter Unterschied** there's a world of difference between us; **B** *adv.* **~weit voneinander entfernt sein** be poles apart; **~weit von etw. entfernt sein** be nowhere near sth.

himmlisch
A *Adj.* **1** (den Himmel betreffend) heavenly; **der ~e Vater** our Heavenly Father; **die ~en Heerscharen** the heavenly host[s] **2** (göttlich) divine; **eine ~e Fügung** divine providence **3** (herrlich) heavenly; divine; wonderful ‹*weather, day, view*›
B *adv.* divinely; wonderfully, gloriously ‹*comfortable, warm*›

hin /hɪn/ *Adv.* **1** (räumlich) **zur Straße ~ liegen** face the road; **nach rechts ~ verlaufen** ‹*road*› go off to the right; **nach Frankfurt ~:** in the direction of Frankfurt; **bis zu dieser Stelle ~:** [up] to this point; as far as here; **sich zu etw. ~ erstrecken** stretch as far as sth.; **zur Straße ~ sind es 500 m** (landsch.) it's 500 m to the road; **über die ganze Welt ~** (veralt.) all over the world; throughout the world **2** (zeitlich) **gegen Mittag ~:** towards midday; **zum Herbst ~:** towards the autumn; as autumn approaches/approached; **über einen Monat ~:** for a whole month; **durch viele Jahre ~:**

for many years 3 (in Verbindungen) **nach außen ~:** outwardly; **auf meine Anweisung/meinen Rat ~:** on *or* in response to my instructions/ advice; **auf seine Bitte/seinen Anruf/eine Annonce ~:** at his request/in response to his [telephone] call/an advertisement; **selbst/ auch auf die Gefahr ~, einen Fehler zu begehen** even at the risk of making a mistake; **etw. auf eine spätere Erweiterung ~ planen** plan sth. with a view to future expansion; *s. auch* **vor** B 4 (in Wortpaaren) **~ und zurück** there and back; **einmal Köln ~ und zurück** a return [ticket] to Cologne; **Hin und zurück? — Nein, nur ~:** Return? — No, just a single; **~ und her** to and fro; back and forth; **~ und her beraten/reden** go backwards and forwards over the same old ground; **das Hin und Her** the toing and froing; **nach langem Hin und Her** after a great deal of argument; **das reicht/langt nicht ~ und nicht her** (ugs.) it's nowhere near enough; **Regen ~, Regen her** rain or no rain; **~ und wieder** [every] now and then 5 (elliptisch) **nichts wie ~!** what are we waiting for?; **~ zu ihm!** [hurry up,] to him!; **~ sein** (ugs.: hingegangen, -gefahren sein) have gone 6 **das ist noch lange ~:** that's not for a long time yet; **bis zu dem Termin ist es noch einige Zeit ~:** there's some time to go before the deadline 7 **von jmdm./etw. ganz ~ sein** (ugs.: hingerissen sein) be mad about sb./bowled over by sth. 8 **~ sein** (ugs.: nicht mehr brauchbar sein) have had it (coll.); **das Auto ist ~** (ugs.) the car is a write-off; **er ist ~** (salopp: tot) he has snuffed it *or* has pegged out (sl.); **wenn er richtig zuschlägt, bist du ~** (salopp: tot) if he really hits you you've had it (coll.) 9 **~ sein** (ugs.: verloren sein) be *or* have gone; **was ~ ist, ist ~:** what's done is done

hinab /hɪˈnap/ *Adv.* down; **den Hang ~:** down the slope; **ins Tal ~:** down into the valley; **den Fluss ~:** downstream; down the river; **bis ~ zu** down to

hinab- (*s. auch* **hinunter-**): **~|blicken** *itr. V.* look down; **~|senken** A *tr. V.* lower; sink ‹*foundations*›; B *refl. V.* slope down; **~|steigen** *unr. itr. V.; mit sein* climb down; (hinuntergehen) go down; **~|ziehen** A *unr. tr. V.* (auch fig.) **jmdn. ~ziehen** drag sb. down; B *unr. itr. V.; mit sein* (geh.) move down

hinan /hɪˈnan/ *Adv.* (geh.) ▸**hinauf**

hin|arbeiten *itr. V.* **auf etw.** (*Akk.*) **~:** work towards sth.; **auf eine Prüfung ~:** work for an examination; **auf einen Krieg ~:** work to bring about war

hinauf /hɪˈnauf/ *Adv.* up; **den Hügel ~:** up the hill; **die Treppe ~:** up the stairs; upstairs; **bis ~ zu** up to

hinauf-: ~|arbeiten *refl. V.* ▸**hocharbeiten**; **~|begeben** *unr. refl. V.* (geh.) go up[stairs]; **~|begleiten** *tr. V.* **jmdn. ~begleiten** accompany sb. up[stairs]; **~|bemühen** A *tr. V.* **jmdn. ~bemühen** trouble sb. to go up; B *refl. V.* take the trouble to go up; **~|bitten** *unr. tr. V.* **jmdn. ~bitten** ask sb. to go up; **~|blicken** *itr. V.* look up; **~|bringen** *unr. tr. V.* **jmdn./etw. ~bringen** take sb./sth. up[stairs]; **~|fahren** A *unr. itr. V.; mit sein* go up; (im Auto) drive up; (mit einem Motorrad) ride up; B *unr. tr. V.* **jmdn. ~fahren** drive *or* take sb. up; **~|fallen** *unr. itr. V.; mit sein* ▸**Treppe 1**; **~|führen** A *itr. V.* lead up; B *tr. V.* **jmdn. ~führen** show sb. up; **~|gehen** *unr. itr. V.; mit sein* 1 (nach oben gehen) go up; **die Treppe ~gehen** go up the stairs *or* upstairs; **auf 1000 Meter ~gehen** ‹*aircraft, pilot*› climb to 1,000 metres; 2 (nach oben führen) lead up; **es geht steil ~:** the road/ path climbs steeply; 3 (ugs.: steigen) ‹*prices, taxes, etc.*› go up; rise; 4 **mit dem Preis/der Miete ~gehen** (ugs.) put the price/rent up; **~|gelangen** *itr. V.; mit sein* [manage to] get up; **auf etw.** (*Akk.*) **~gelangen** [manage to] get up sth.; **~|helfen** *unr. itr. V.* **jmdm. [die Treppe] ~helfen** help sb. up [the stairs]; **~|klettern** *itr. V.; mit sein* climb up; **[auf] den Baum ~klettern** climb up the tree; **~|kommen** *unr. itr. V.; mit sein* 1 (nach oben kommen) come up; 2 (nach oben kommen können) [manage to] get up; **~|lassen** *unr. tr. V.* **jmdn. ~lassen** allow sb. to go up; let sb. go up; **~|laufen** *unr. itr. V.; mit sein* run up; **die Treppe ~laufen** run up the stairs; **~|reichen** A *tr. V.* hand *or* pass up; **jmdm. etw. ~reichen** hand *or* pass sth. up to sb.; B *itr. V.* **bis zu etw. ~reichen** reach up to sth.; **~|schauen** *itr. V.* (südd.) look up; **~|schicken** *tr. V.* send up; **~|schnellen** *itr. V.; mit sein* shoot up; **~|sehen** *unr. itr. V.* look up; **~|setzen** *tr. V.* 1 (erhöhen) raise; increase; put up; **die Preise ~setzen** increase *or* raise prices; 2 (nach oben setzen) **etw. auf etw.** (*Dat.*) **~setzen** put sth. up on sth.; **~|steigen** *unr. itr. V.; mit sein* climb up; (~gehen) go up; **~|tragen** *unr. tr. V.* carry *or* take up; **~|werfen** *unr. tr. V.* **etw. ~werfen** throw sth. up (**auf** + *Akk.* on to); **~|winden** *unr. refl. V.* 1 **sich [an etw.** (*Dat.*)**] ~winden** ‹*plant*› creep *or* climb up [sth.]; 2 (nach oben verlaufen) wind up; **~|ziehen** A *unr. tr. V.* pull up; B *unr. itr. V.; mit sein* move up; C *unr. refl. V.* (sich erstrecken) stretch up; ‹*pain*› spread up

hinaus /hɪˈnaus/ *Adv.* 1 (räumlich) out; **~ [mit dir]!** out you go!; out with you!; **zum Fenster ~:** out of the window; **hier/dort ~:** this/that way out; **nach hinten/vorne ~ wohnen/ liegen** live/be situated at the back/front; **durch die Tür ~:** out through the door; **über die Grenze ~:** beyond the frontier 2 (zeitlich) **auf Jahre ~:** for years to come; **bis über die Achtzig ~:** well past *or* over eighty; well into one's eighties 3 (etw. überschreitend) **über etw.** (*Akk.*) **~:** over and above *or* in addition to sth.; **über das Grab ~:** beyond the grave 4 **über etw.** (*Akk.*) **~ sein** (fig.) be past *or* beyond sth.; *s. auch* **darüber**

hinaus-, Hinaus-: ~|befördern *tr. V.* **jmdn. ~befördern** throw *or* (coll.) chuck sb. out; **~|begeben** *unr. refl. V.* go out; **~|begleiten** *tr. V.* **jmdn. ~begleiten** see sb. out; **~|beugen** *refl. V.* lean out; **sich zum Fenster ~beugen** lean out of the window; **~|bitten** *unr. tr. V.* **jmdn. ~bitten** ask sb. to go *or* step outside; **~|blicken** *itr. V.* look out (**aus** of); **~|bringen** *unr. tr. V.* 1 **jmdn./etw. ~bringen** take *or* see sb. out/ take sth. out (**aus** of); 2 (weiterbringen) **es nie über den untersten Dienstgrad ~bringen** never make it *or* get beyond the lowest grade; **~|bugsieren** *tr. V.* (ugs.) **jmdn. ~bugsieren** (mit Geschick) steer sb. out (**aus** of); (~befördern) hustle sb. out (**aus** of); **~|drängen** A *itr. V.; mit sein* push one's way out (**aus** of); ‹*crowd*› push its way out (**aus** of); B *tr. V.* **jmdn. ~drängen** push sb. out (**aus** of); (fig.) push sb. out (**aus** of); oust sb. (**aus** from); **~|dürfen** *unr. itr. V.* be allowed out (**aus** of); **darf ich bitte ~?** may I go out?; **~|eilen** *itr. V.; mit sein* hurry out (**aus** of); **~|ekeln** *tr. V.* (ugs.) **jmdn. ~ekeln** drive sb. out; **~|fahren** A *unr. itr. V.; mit sein* 1 **aus etw. ~fahren** (mit dem Auto) drive out of sth.; (mit dem Zweirad) ride out of sth.; ‹*car, bus*› go out of sth.; ‹*train*› pull out of sth.; **zum Flugplatz ~fahren** drive out to the airport; **aufs Meer ~fahren** head for the sea; 2 (herauskommen) shoot out (**aus** of); 3 (weiterfahren) **über etw.** (*Akk.*) **~fahren** go past sth.; B *unr. tr. V.* **jmdn./etw. ~fahren** drive *or* take sb./take sth. out; **~|fallen** *unr. itr. V.; mit sein* fall out (**aus** of); ‹*light*› come out (**aus** of); **~|finden** *unr. itr. V.* find one's way out (**aus** of); **er wird alleine ~finden** he'll find his own way out; **~|fliegen** A *unr. itr. V.; mit sein* 1 fly out (**aus** of); 2 (geworfen werden) be thrown out (**aus** of); fly out; 3 (ugs.: ~fallen) fall out (**aus** of); 4 (ugs.: ~geworfen werden) be chucked out (coll.); (als Arbeitnehmer) get the sack (coll.); be fired (coll.); (als Mieter) be thrown out (coll.); B *unr. tr. V.* fly out (**aus** of); **~|führen** A *tr. V.* 1 **jmdn. ~führen** show sb. out; 2 (retten) **die Partei aus der Krise ~führen** lead the party out of the crisis; **den Betrieb aus den roten Zahlen ~führen** get the business out of the red; 3 (weiterführen) **jmdn. über etw.** (*Akk.*) **~führen** take sb. beyond sth.; B *itr. V.* 1 (verlaufen) lead out (**aus** of); 2 (nach draußen gerichtet sein) lead out; 3 (weiter verlaufen, überschreiten) **über etw.** (*Akk.*) **~führen** go beyond sth.; **~|gehen** *unr. itr. V.; mit sein* 1 go out; **aus dem Zimmer ~gehen** go *or* walk out of *or* leave the room; 2 (gerichtet sein) **das Zimmer geht zum Garten/nach Westen ~:** the room looks out on to *or* faces the garden/faces west; **die Tür geht auf den Hof ~:** the door leads *or* opens into the yard; **die Schlafzimmer gehen nach hinten ~:** the bedrooms are at the back; 3 (verlaufen) lead; 4 (überschreiten) **über etw.** (*Akk.*) **~gehen** go beyond sth.; 5 (gesendet werden) go out; be sent out; 6 (unpers.) **wo geht es ~?** which is the way out?; **hier/da geht es ~:** this/that is the way out; **~|gelangen** *itr. V.; mit sein* 1 (nach draußen gelangen, auch fig.) [manage to] get out (**aus** of); 2 (weiter gelangen) **über etw.** (*Akk.*) **~gelangen** progress *or* get beyond sth.; **~|greifen** *unr. itr. V.* **über etw.** (*Akk.*) **~greifen** go beyond sth.; **~|gucken** *itr. V.* (ugs.) ▸**~blicken**; **~|halten** *unr. tr. V.* hold ‹*lamp, flag, etc.*› out; **den Kopf/die Hand [zum Fenster] ~halten** put *or* stick one's head/hand out [of the window]; **~|hängen**[1] *unr. itr. V.* hang out (**aus** of); **~|hängen**[2] *tr. V.* hang out (**aus** of); **~|heben** *unr. tr. V.* 1 **jmdn./etw. ~heben** lift sb./sth. out (**aus** of); **etw. aus dem Bus ~heben** lift sth. down from the bus; 2 (geh.: erheben) **jmdn. über die anderen ~heben** raise sb. above the others; **~|jagen** A *tr. V.* drive *or* chase out; **jmdn. ~jagen** (fig.: aus dem Haus) drive *or* turn sb. out; B *itr. V.; mit sein* rush *or* race out (**aus** of); **~|katapultieren** *tr. V.* 1 (mit dem Schleudersitz) eject; 2 (salopp: verdrängen) **jmdn. ~katapultieren** push sb. out (**aus** of); **~|kommen** *unr. itr. V.; mit sein* 1 come out (**aus** of); **ich bin schon seit zwei Tagen nicht mehr ~gekommen** I've not got *or* been out of the house for two days; 2 (ein Gebiet verlassen) **er ist nie aus dem Dorf/aus Europa ~gekommen** he has never been out of *or* outside his village/Europe; 3 (ugs.: einen Ausweg finden) get out (**aus** of); 4 **über etw.** (*Akk.*) **~kommen** (auch fig.) get beyond sth.; 5 ▸**~laufen 2**; **~|komplimentieren** *tr. V.* **jmdn. ~komplimentieren** show sb. the door; (verabschieden) usher sb. out [with a great show of courtesy]; **~|lassen** *unr. tr. V.* **jmdn. ~lassen** let sb. out; **~|laufen** *unr. itr. V.; mit sein* 1 run out (**aus** of); **zur Tür ~laufen** run out of the door; 2 (als Ergebnis haben) **auf etw.** (*Akk.*) **~laufen** lead to sth.; **das läuft auf dasselbe ~:** it comes to the same thing; **~|lehnen** *refl. V.* lean out; **sich zum Fenster ~lehnen** lean out of the window; **~|manövrieren** *tr. V.* **sich/jmdn./etw. aus etw. ~manövrieren** manoeuvre oneself/sb./sth. out of sth.; **~|müssen** *unr. itr. V.* (ugs.) have to get out (**aus** of); **~|nehmen** *unr. tr. V.* **jmdn./etw. ~nehmen** take sb./sth. out (**aus** of); **nimm den Mülleimer mit ~:** put *or* take the dustbin out when you go; **~|posaunen** *tr. V.* (ugs.) broadcast; **~posaunen, dass ...** broadcast the fact that ...; **~|ragen** *itr. V.* 1 (vertikal) rise up (**über** + *Akk.* above); (horizontal) jut out; project; 2 (übertreffen) **über seine Kollegen/die anderen Werke ~ragen** stand out from one's colleagues/the other works; **~|reden** *refl. V.* (südd., österr., schweiz.) talk one's way out (**aus** of); **~|reichen** A *tr. V.* **etw. ~reichen** hand *or* pass sth. out (**aus** of); **etw. zum** *od.* **aus dem Fenster ~reichen** hand *or* pass sth. out through the window; B *itr. V.* 1 (bis nach draußen reichen) reach *or* stretch (**bis zu** as far as); 2 (weiter reichen) **über etw.** (*Akk.*) **~reichen** go beyond sth.; **~|rennen** *unr. itr. V.; mit sein* run out; **aus etw. ~rennen** run out of sth.; **~|rücken** *tr. V.* 1 move out; 2 (verschieben) put off; postpone; **~|schaffen** *tr. V.* **jmdn./etw. ~schaffen** get sb./sth. out (**aus** of); **~|schauen** *itr. V.* (südd.) ▸**~blicken**; **~|scheren** *refl. V.* **scher dich ~!** get out of here!; **~|scheuchen** *tr. V.* chase out; **~|schicken** *tr. V.* 1 **jmdn. ~schicken** send sb. out; 2 (senden) send out; **~|schieben** A *unr. tr. V.* 1 (nach draußen schieben) **jmdn./etw. ~schieben** push sb./sth. out (**aus** of); 2 (aufschieben) put off; postpone; **eine Entscheidung [um einen Tag] ~schieben** put off *or* postpone *or* defer a decision [by one day]; B *unr. refl. V.* 1 (sich nach draußen schieben) push one's/its way out (aus of); 2 (sich verschieben) be put off *or* postponed; **~|schießen** *unr. itr. V.* 1 **aus dem Auto/zum Fenster ~schießen** fire from the car/the window; 2 *mit sein* (sich schnell ~bewegen) shoot out (aus of); ‹*water*› rush out (aus of); 3 (weiter bewegen) **über etw.** (*Akk.*) **~schießen** shoot past sth.; **über das Ziel ~schießen** (fig.) go too far; **~|schleichen** *unr. itr. V. mit sein; unr. refl. V.* creep *or* steal out (aus of); **~|schmeißen** *unr. tr. V.* (ugs.) ▸ **rausschmeißen**; **~|schmuggeln** *tr. V.* smuggle out (aus of); **~|schreien** A *unr. itr. V.* shout out; B *unr. tr. V.* (geh.) **seinen Hass/Zorn ~schreien** vent *or* give vent to one's hate/rage in a loud outburst; **~|schwimmen** *unr. itr. V.; mit sein* ‹*person*› swim out; ‹*object*› float out; **~|sehen** *unr. itr. V.* look out; **zum Fenster ~sehen** look out of the window; ***~|sein** ▸ **hinaus**; **~|setzen** A *tr. V.* **etw. ~setzen** put sth. out[side]; B *refl. V.* go and sit outside; **~|stehlen** *unr. refl. V.* sneak *or* steal out (aus of); **~|steigen** *unr itr. V.; mit sein* climb out (aus of); **zum Fenster ~steigen** climb out of the window; **~|stellen** A *tr. V.* 1 put out[side]; 2 (Sport) **einen Spieler ~stellen** send a player off; B *refl. V.* go and stand outside; **~stellung** *die* (Sport) sending-off; **~|strecken** *tr. V.* stick *or* put out (aus of); **den Arm/Kopf zum Fenster ~strecken** put *or* stick one's arm/head out of the window; **~|strömen** *itr. V.; mit sein* pour out (aus of); **~|stürzen** A *itr. V.; mit sein* 1 (~fallen) fall (aus out of); **zum Fenster ~stürzen** fall out of the window; 2 (~eilen) rush *or* dash out (aus of); **zur Tür ~stürzen** rush *or* dash out of the door; B *refl. V.* throw oneself out (aus of); **~|tragen** *unr. tr. V.* 1 (nach draußen tragen) **jmdn./etw. ~tragen** carry sb./sth. out; 2 (verbreiten) **etw. in alle Welt ~tragen** spread sth. throughout the world; 3 (weiter tragen) **über etw.** (*Akk.*) **~getragen werden** be carried across sth.; **aufs Meer ~getragen werden** be carried out to sea; **~|trauen** *refl. V.* venture out; dare to go out; **~|treiben** A *unr. tr. V.* drive out (aus of); **es treibt jmdn. in fremde Länder/die Welt ~:** sb. has an urge to travel to *or* see other countries/see the world; B *unr. itr. V.; mit sein* drift out; **~|treten** *unr. itr. V.; mit sein* step out (aus of); **ins Leben ~treten** go out into the world; **~|trompeten** *tr. V.* ▸ **~posaunen**; **~|wachsen** *unr. itr. V.; mit sein* 1 (größer werden) **über etw.** (*Akk.*) **~wachsen** grow taller than *or* up above sth.; 2 (~kommen) **über etw.** (*Akk.*) **~wachsen** outgrow sth.; **über jmdn./sich ~wachsen** surpass sb./rise above oneself; **~|wagen** *refl. V.* 1 venture out (aus of); **sich in die Dunkelheit ~wagen** dare [to] go out into the dark; 2 (sich weiter wagen) **sich über etw.** (*Akk.*) **~wagen** venture beyond *or* dare [to] go beyond sth.; **~|weisen** A *unr. tr. V.* **jmdn. ~weisen** order sb. out (aus of); B *unr. itr. V.* **ein Symbol weist über sich ~** (fig.) a symbol implies something more than itself; **~|werfen** *unr. tr. V.* 1 (nach draußen werfen) throw out (aus of); **etw. zur Tür ~werfen** throw sth. out of the door; 2 (nach draußen richten) **einen Blick ~werfen** take *or* have a look *or* glance outside; 3 (ugs.: entfernen) throw out; 4 (ugs.: ausschließen, die Wohnung kündigen) **jmdn. ~werfen** throw sb. out (aus of); (ugs.: entlassen) sack sb. (coll.); **~|wollen** *unr. itr. V.* (ugs.) want to get *or* go out (aus of); **[zu] hoch ~wollen** (fig.) aim [too] high; set one's sights [too] high; **worauf willst du ~?** (fig.) what are you getting *or* driving at?; **auf etwas Bestimmtes ~wollen** (fig.) have something particular in mind; **~wurf** *der* (ugs.) throwing out; (eines Angestellten) sacking (coll.); **~|ziehen** A *unr. tr. V.* 1 (nach draußen ziehen) **jmdn./etw. ~ziehen** pull *or* drag sb./sth. out (aus of); tow ‹*ship*› out; 2 (in die Ferne ziehen) **das Fernweh zog ihn in die Welt ~:** his wanderlust drove him out into the world; 3 (hinziehen) draw *or* drag out; prolong; protract; 4 (verzögern) put off; delay; 5 (unpers.) **es zog sie in die Natur ~:** she felt the urge to get out into the countryside; B *unr. itr. V.; mit sein* 1 (umziehen) move out; 2 (in die Ferne ziehen) go out (aus of); ‹*group, troops*› move out (aus of); 3 (nach draußen dringen) get out; C *unr. refl. V.* 1 (sich erstrecken) extend; 2 (sich hinziehen) drag on; 3 (sich verzögern) be delayed; **~|zögern** A *tr. V.* delay; put off; B *refl. V.* be delayed; be put off

hin-, Hin-: ~|bauen *tr. V.* build; put up; **~|begeben** *unr. refl. V.* **sich irgendwo ~begeben** go *or* proceed somewhere; **sich zu jmdm. ~begeben** go to see sb.; **~|begleiten** *tr. V.* **jmdn. ~begleiten** accompany sb. [there]; **~|bekommen** *unr. tr. V.* (ugs.) 1 (fertig bringen) **das hast du gut ~bekommen** you made a good job of that; 2 (in Ordnung bringen) **etw. ~bekommen** straighten sth. out; get sth. straightened out; put sth. right; **~|bemühen** A *tr. V.* **jmdn. ~bemühen** trouble sb. to go; B *refl. V.* take the trouble to go; **~|beordern** *tr. V.* **jmdn. ~beordern** order sb. [to go] there; **~|bestellen** *tr. V.* **jmdn. ~bestellen** tell sb. to be there; **~|biegen** *unr. tr. V.* (ugs.) **etw. ~biegen** sort sth. out; **wie hat er das bloß ~gebogen?** how did he manage *or* (sl.) wangle that?; **den werden wir schon ~biegen** we'll lick *or* knock him into shape (coll.); **~|blättern** *tr. V.* (ugs.) fork *or* shell out (coll.), pay out ‹*sum of money*›; **~blick** *der:* **in im** *od.* **in ~blick auf etw.** (*Akk.*) (wegen) in view of; (~sichtlich) with regard to; **~|blicken** *itr. V.* look; **zu jmdm. ~blicken** look [across] at sb.; **~|bringen** *unr. tr. V.* 1 **jmdn./etw. ~bringen** take sb./sth. [there]; 2 (verbringen) while away; (müßig) spend; 3 (ugs.: fertig bringen) manage

Hinde /ˈhɪndə/ *die;* ~, ~n (veralt.) hind

hin|denken *unr. itr. V.* **wo denkst du hin?** (ugs.) whatever are you thinking of?; what an idea!

hinderlich *Adj.* **~ sein** get in the *or* sb.'s way; **ein ~er Verband/Mantel** a bandage/a coat that gets in the way *or* is restricting; **jmds. Karriere** (*Dat.*)**/für jmds. Karriere ~ sein** be an obstacle to sb.'s career; **jmdm.** *od.* **für jmdn. ~ sein** be a nuisance to sb.; **sich als ~ erweisen** prove to be a hindrance

hindern /ˈhɪndɐn/ *tr. V.* 1 (abhalten) **jmdn. ~:** stop *or* prevent sb.; **jmdn. [daran] ~, etw. zu tun** prevent *or* stop sb. [from] doing sth.; **jmdn. am Sprechen ~:** prevent *or* stop sb. [from] speaking; **ich werde dich nicht ~** (iron.) I'm not stopping you 2 (be~) hinder, hamper ‹*person*›; impede, hamper, hinder ‹*growth, progress, etc.*›

Hindernis *das;* **~ses, ~se** 1 obstacle; **jmdm. ~se in den Weg legen** (fig.) put obstacles in sb.'s way 2 (Leichtathletik, Geländeritt) obstacle; (Springreiten) jump; obstacle; (Pferderennen) fence 3 (Golf) hazard

Hindernis-: ~lauf *der* (Leichtathletik) steeplechase; **~rennen** *das* (Pferdesport) steeplechase

Hinderung *die;* ~, **~en** hindrance

Hinderungs·grund *der:* **das ist kein ~ für mich** it does not prevent *or* stop me; **darin sehe ich keinen ~ für den Weiterbau** I do not see it as any reason why we should not continue with the construction

hin|deuten *itr. V.* 1 **auf jmdn./etw.** *od.* **zu jmdm./etw. ~:** point to sb./sth. 2 (aufmerksam machen) **auf etw.** (*Akk.*) **~:** draw *or* call attention to sth.; point sth. out; **darauf ~, dass …** draw *or* call attention to the fact that …; point out that … 3 (anzeigen) suggest; point to; **alles deutet darauf hin, dass …** everything suggests that …

Hindi /ˈhɪndi/ *das;* ~ ▸ ➊ **S. 670** Hindi

Hindin *die;* **~, ~nen** (veralt.) hind

hin|drängen
A *tr. V.* **jmdn. zu etw. ~:** force sb. towards sth.
B *itr. V.; mit sein* **zu jmdm. ~:** push one's way towards sb.
C *refl. V.* **sich zu jmdm./etw. ~:** push [one's way] towards sb./sth.

Hindu /ˈhɪndu/ *der;* **~[s], ~[s]** ▸ ➊ **S. 520** Hindu

Hinduismus *der;* **~:** Hinduism *no art.*

hinduistisch *Adj.* Hindu

hin·durch *Adv.* 1 (räumlich) **durch den Wald ~:** through the wood; **mitten/quer durch etw. ~:** straight through sth. 2 (zeitlich) **das ganze Jahr ~:** throughout the year; **den ganzen Tag/die ganze Nacht ~:** all day/night [long]; throughout the day/night; all through the day/night; **die ganze Zeit ~:** all the time; **durch all die Schwierigkeiten ~** (fig.) through all the difficulties

hindurch-: ~|finden *unr. itr., refl. V.* **[sich] durch etw. ~finden** find one's way through sth.; **~|gehen** *unr. itr. V.; mit sein* 1 walk *or* go through; **durch etw. ~gehen** walk *or* go through sth.; (fig.) go through sth.; **unter der Brücke ~gehen** walk *or* go under the bridge; 2 **durch etw. ~gehen** (dringen) go through sth.; (verlaufen, auch fig.) run through sth.; (passen) ‹*person, vehicle*› go *or* get through sth.; ‹*object*› go through sth.; **~|müssen** *unr. itr. V.* **durch etw. ~müssen** have to go through sth.; **~|sehen** *unr. itr. V.* 1 **[durch etw.] ~sehen** see through [sth.]; 2 (sichtbar sein) peep through; **~|ziehen** A *unr. tr. V.* **etw. [durch etw.] ~ziehen** pull *or* draw sth. through [sth.]; B *unr. itr. V.; mit sein* move through; C *unr. refl. V.* **sich durch etw. ~ziehen** run through sth.

hin-: ~|dürfen *unr. itr. V.* (ugs.) be allowed to go (zu to); **dort dürft ihr nicht mehr ~:** you're not to go there any more; **~|eilen** *itr. V.; mit sein* 1 hurry (zu to); **alle eilten ~:** everyone hurried there; 2 (sich schnell bewegen) ‹*train etc.*› speed (**über** + *Akk.* across); ‹*person*› rush (**über** + *Akk.* across)

hinein /hɪˈnain/ *Adv.* 1 (räumlich) in; **~ mit euch!** in you go!; in with you!; **in etw.** (*Akk.*) **~:** into sth.; **nur ~!** go *or* walk right in! 2 (zeitlich) **bis in den Morgen/tief in die Nacht ~:** till morning/far into the night

hinein-: ~|begeben *unr. refl. V.* go in[side]; **sich in etw.** (*Akk.*) **~begeben** enter sth.; **~|bekommen** *unr. tr. V.* (ugs.) **etw. [in etw.** (*Akk.*)**] ~bekommen** get sth. in[to sth.]; **~|bemühen** A *tr. V.* **jmdn. ~bemühen** trouble sb. to go in; B *refl. V.* take the trouble to go in; **~|bitten** *unr. tr. V.* **jmdn. ~bitten** ask *or* invite sb. in; **~|blicken** *itr. V.* look in; **in etw.** (*Akk.*) **~blicken** look into sth.; **~|bohren** A *tr. V.* **Löcher in die Wand ~bohren** drill holes in the wall; **den Finger in den Kuchen ~bohren** stick *or* poke one's finger into the cake; B *refl. V.* **sich in etw.** (*Akk.*) **~bohren** bore one's/its way into sth.; **~|bringen** *unr. tr. V.* 1 take in; **bringen Sie mir die Unterlagen ~:** bring me in the documents; **Ordnung in etw. ~bringen** (fig.) bring [some] order into sth.; **etw. in die Diskussion ~bringen** (fig.) introduce sth. into the discussion; **Schwung in etw.** (*Akk.*) **~bringen** put [some] life into sth.; liven sth. up; 2 (ugs.) ▸ **~bekommen**; **~|denken** *unr. refl. V.* **sich in jmdn./in jmds. Lage ~denken** put oneself in sb.'s position; **sich in ein Problem ~denken** think one's way into a problem; **~|drängen** A *itr. V. mit sein; refl. V.* **[sich] in etw.** (*Akk.*) **~drängen** push one's way into sth.; **[sich] in den Bus ~drängen** push one's way on to the bus; B *tr. V.* **jmdn. in etw.** (*Akk.*) **~drängen** push sb. into sth.; **jmdn. in eine Rolle ~drängen** (fig.) force sb. into a role; **~|dürfen** *unr. itr. V.* be allowed in; **in etw.** (*Akk.*) **~dürfen** be allowed into sth.; **~|fahren** A *unr. itr. V.; mit sein* 1 (mit dem Auto) drive in; (mit dem Zweirad) ride in; **in etw.** (*Akk.*) **~fahren** drive/ride into sth.; **der Zug fuhr [in den Bahnhof] ~:** the train pulled in[to the station]; 2 (ugs.) **in ein anderes Auto ~fahren** run into another car; 3 **in seine Kleider ~fahren** slip into one's clothes; B *unr. tr. V.* 1 **den Wagen in etw.** (*Akk.*) **~fahren** drive one's car into sth.; 2 **jmdn. in die Stadt ~fahren** drive sb. into town; **~|fallen** *unr. itr. V.; mit sein* fall in; **in etw.** (*Akk.*) **~fallen** fall into sth.; **sich in einen Sessel ~fallen lassen** drop into a chair; **~|finden** *unr. refl. V.* **sich in etw.** (*Akk.*) **~finden** (sich vertraut machen) get used to sth.; (sich abfinden) come to terms with sth.; **~|fliegen** A *unr. itr. V.; mit sein* 1 fly in; **in etw.** (*Akk.*) **~fliegen** fly into sth.; **zum Fenster ~fliegen** fly in through the window;

2 (geworfen werden) in etw. (Akk.) ~fliegen be thrown into sth.; B unr. tr. V. fly in; etw. in etw. (Akk.) ~fliegen fly sth. into sth.; ~|fressen A unr. tr. V. etw. in sich ~fressen ‹animal, (derb) person› gobble sth. down or up, wolf sth. down; seine Sorgen/seinen Ärger in sich ~fressen (fig.) bottle up one's worries/anger; B unr. refl. V. sich in etw. (Akk.) ~fressen eat into sth.; ~geboren Adj. in eine Zeit/Umwelt ~geboren born into an age/environment; ~|geheimnissen tr. V. etw. in etw. (Akk.) ~geheimnissen read sth. into sth.; ~|gehen unr. itr. V.; mit sein go in; in etw. (Akk.) ~gehen go into sth.; in den Eimer gehen 3 Liter ~: the bucket holds three litres; ~|geraten unr. itr. V.; mit sein in eine Schlägerei ~geraten get into a fight; ~|gießen unr. tr. V. pour in; etw. in etw. (Akk.) ~gießen pour sth. into sth.; ~|grätschen itr. V.; mit sein (bes. Fußball) [in jmdn.] ~grätschen make a sliding tackle [on sb.]; ~|gucken itr. V. (ugs.) look in; in etw. (Akk.) ~gucken look in[to] sth.; take a look in sth.; ~|halten A unr. tr. V. etw. in etw. (Akk.) ~halten put sth. into sth.; B unr. itr. V. (schießen) in die Menge ~halten fire into the crowd; ~|helfen unr. itr. V. jmdm. in den Mantel ~helfen help sb. on with his/her coat; jmdm. in den Bus ~helfen help sb. on to the bus; ~|horchen itr. V. (geh.) in etw. (Akk.) ~horchen tune in to sth.; in die Partei ~horchen gauge the mood of the party; in sich selbst ~horchen tune in to one's inner self; ~|hören A itr. V 1 [in ein Programm] ~hören listen in [to a programme]; in einen Titel ~hören listen to a track; (kurz) sample a track; 2 ▸hineinhorchen; B refl. V. sich in etw. ~hören listen to and get to know sth.; ~|interpretieren tr. V. etw. in etw. (Akk.) ~interpretieren read sth. into sth.; ~|jagen tr. V. drive or chase in; jmdn./ein Tier in etw. ~jagen drive or chase sb./an animal into sth.; ~|knien refl. V. (ugs.) sich in etw. (Akk.) ~knien get one's teeth into sth.; ~|kommen unr. itr. V.; mit sein 1 come in; in etw. (Akk.) ~kommen come into sth.; 2 (gelangen, auch fig.) get in; in etw. (Akk.) ~kommen get into sth.; 3 (sich ~finden) [wieder] in eine Sprache/ein Fach ~kommen get [back] into a language/subject; 4 (ugs.: hinzugefügt werden) in etw. (Akk.) ~kommen go into sth.; ~|kriechen unr. itr. V.; mit sein crawl in; in etw. (Akk.) ~kriechen crawl into sth.; s. auch reinkriechen; ~|kriegen tr. V. (ugs.) ▸~bekommen; ~|lachen itr. V. in sich ~lachen laugh to oneself; ~|lassen unr. tr. V. let or allow in; jmdn. ins Zimmer ~lassen let or allow sb. into the room; ~|laufen unr. itr. V.; mit sein 1 run in; (zu Fuß gehen) walk in; in etw. (Akk.) ~laufen run/walk into sth.; in sein Verderben ~laufen (fig.) be heading [straight] for disaster; in ein Fahrzeug ~laufen run under a vehicle; 2 (fließen) in etw. (Akk.) ~laufen run into sth.; ~|legen tr. V. 1 etw. [in etw. (Akk.)] ~legen put sth. in[to sth.]; seine ganze Liebe/sein ganzes Gefühl in etw. (Akk.) ~legen put all one's love/feeling into sth.; 2 ▸~interpretieren; 3 (ugs.) ▸hereinlegen; ~|lesen A unr. refl. V. ▸einlesen A; B unr. tr. V. ▸~interpretieren; ~|leuchten itr. V. 1 shine in; in etw. (Akk.) ~leuchten shine into sth.; 2 (Licht ~werfen) mit einer Lampe in den Keller ~leuchten shine a light into the cellar; 3 (fig.) in etw. (Akk.) ~leuchten throw light on sth.; ~|manövrieren tr. V. 1 etw. in etw. (Akk.) ~manövrieren manoeuvre sth. into sth.; 2 (in etw. bringen) jmdn./sich in eine verzwickte Lage ~manövrieren get or put sb./oneself into a tricky situation; ~|passen itr. V. fit in; in etw. (Akk.) ~passen fit into sth.; (fig.) fit in with sth.; ~|pfuschen itr. V. jmdm. in seine Arbeit ~pfuschen meddle or interfere in sb.'s work; ~|platzen itr. V.; mit sein (ugs.) burst in; in etw. (Akk.) ~platzen burst into sth.; ~|pressen tr. V. 1 (durch Pressen erzeugen) etw. in etw. (Akk.) ~pressen stamp sth. into sth.; 2 (in etw. pressen) etw. in etw. (Akk.) ~pressen press sth. into sth.; etw. in ein Schema ~pressen (fig.) force sth. into a pattern; ~|projizieren tr. V. etw. in etw. (Akk.) ~projizieren project sth. into sth.; ~|pumpen tr. V. 1 pump in; etw. in etw. (Akk.) ~pumpen pump sth. into sth.; 2 (fig. ugs.) Geld in etw./Drogen in jmdn. ~pumpen pump money into sth./drugs into sb.; ~|ragen itr. V. in den Himmel ~ragen rise up into the sky; ~|reden itr. V. 1 ins Leere ~reden talk to an empty hall/lecture theatre etc.; in die Stille ~reden break the silence with a remark/exclamation etc.; 2 (abwertend: sich einmischen) jmdm. in seine Angelegenheiten/Entscheidungen usw. ~reden meddle or interfere in sb.'s affairs/decisions etc.; ~|regnen itr. V. (unpers.) es regnet [ins Zimmer] ~: the rain is coming in[to the room]; es regnet bei uns ~: the rain is coming in through our roof; ~|reichen A tr. V. etw. [zum Fenster] ~reichen hand or pass sth. in [through the window]; B itr. V. 1 (lang genug sein) in etw. (Akk.) ~reichen reach into sth.; 2 (sich erstrecken) in etw. (Akk.) ~reichen extend into sth.; ~|reißen unr. tr. V. jmdn. in etw. (Akk.) ~reißen (auch fig.) drag sb. into sth.; ~|reiten A unr. itr. V.; mit sein ride in; in etw. (Akk.) ~reiten ride into sth.; B unr. tr. V. (ugs.) ▸reinreiten; ~|rennen unr. itr. V.; mit sein (ugs.) run in; race in; in etw. (Akk.) ~rennen run or race into sth.; in sein Verderben ~rennen (fig.) be heading [straight] for disaster; ~|riechen unr. itr. V. (ugs.) in eine Arbeit/eine Firma ~riechen get a taste of a job/a firm; ~|rufen A unr. tr. V. jmdn./etw. ~rufen call sb./sth. in; B unr. itr. V. in etw. (Akk.) ~rufen call into sth.; ~|schaffen tr. V. jmdn./etw. [in etw. (Akk.)] ~schaffen get sb./sth. in[to sth.]; ~|schauen itr. V. 1 (bes. südd., österr.) ▸~sehen; 2 (bes. südd., österr.: kurz besuchen) bei jmdm. ~schauen look in on sb.; ~|schaufeln tr. V. 1 shovel in; (fig.) pour in ‹money›; 2 (ugs.: essen) etw. in sich (Akk.) ~schaufeln shovel sth. down (coll.); ~|schieben A unr. tr. V. etw. in etw. (Akk.) ~schieben push sth. into sth.; (mit Wucht) shove sth. into sth.; B unr. refl. V. sich in etw. (Akk.) ~schieben penetrate into sth.; (störend) intrude into sth.; ein Meeresarm schiebt sich tief ins Land hinein an arm of the sea extends far inland; ~|schießen unr. itr. V. 1 in etw. (Akk.) ~schießen fire into sth.; in die Menge ~schießen fire into the crowd; 2 mit sein (sich schnell ~bewegen) ‹person, car› shoot in; ‹water› rush in; in etw. (Akk.) ~schießen shoot/rush into sth.; ~|schlagen unr. tr. V. einen Nagel/Pfahl [in etw. (Akk.)] ~schlagen knock or drive a nail/stake in[to sth.]; ein Loch in etw. (Akk.) ~schlagen knock or cut a hole in sth.; ~|schleichen A unr. itr. V.; mit sein [in etw. (Akk.)] ~schleichen creep or steal in[to sth.]; B unr. refl. V. sich [in etw. (Akk.)] ~schleichen creep or steal in[to sth.]; (fig.) ‹error› creep in[to sth.]; ~|schlingen unr. tr. V. etw. in sich ~schlingen devour sth.; ~|schlittern itr. V.; mit sein (ugs.) in eine Situation usw. ~schlittern stumble into a situation etc.; ~|schlüpfen itr. V.; mit sein slip in; ins Zimmer/in seinen Mantel ~schlüpfen slip into the room/one's coat; ~|schmuggeln tr. V. smuggle in; jmdn./etw. [in etw. (Akk.)] ~schmuggeln smuggle sb./sth. in[to sth.]; ~|schneien itr. V. 1 (unpers.) es schneit [in die Hütte] ~: the snow is coming in[to the hut]; 2 mit sein ▸hereinschneien 1; ~|schreiben unr. tr. V. write in; etw. in etw. (Akk.) ~schreiben write sth. in sth.; ~|schütten tr. V. pour in; etw. in etw. (Akk.) ~schütten pour sth. into sth.; etw. in sich ~schütten (fig.) knock sth. back (sl.); pour sth. down one's throat; ~|sehen unr. itr. V. look in; in etw. (Akk.) ~sehen look into sth.; in jmds. Zeitung ~sehen have a look at sb.'s paper; ~|setzen A tr. V. (auch ugs.: zuweisen) jmdn./etw. [in etw. (Akk.)] ~setzen put sb./sth. in[to sth.]; B refl. V. 1 sich in etw. (Akk.) ~setzen sit down in sth.; 2 (festsetzen) sich in die Ecken/die Teppiche ~setzen ‹dust, dirt› get right into the corners/the carpet; ~|spazieren itr. V.; mit sein walk or stroll in; nur ~spaziert! walk right [on] in!; ~|spielen A itr. V. da spielen viele Dinge/Faktoren ~: there are a lot of contributory factors; B tr. V. (Sport) den Ball [in den Strafraum usw.] ~spielen play the ball in[to the penalty area etc.]; ~|sprechen unr. itr. V. in etw. (Akk.) ~sprechen speak into sth.; ~|stecken tr. V. 1 etw. [in etw. (Akk.)] ~stecken put sth. in[to sth.]; 2 (ugs.: in etw. bringen) etw. [in etw. (Akk.)] ~stecken stick (coll.) or put sth. in sth.; 3 viel Geld in etw. (Akk.) ~stecken (ugs.) put or sink a lot of money into sth.; viel Arbeit in etw. (Akk.) ~stecken (ugs.) put a lot of work into sth.; ~|steigern refl. V. sich in große Erregung/seine Ängste/seine Wut ~steigern work oneself up into a state of great excitement/anxiety/into a rage; ~|stoßen A unr. tr. V. 1 thrust in; etw. in etw. (Akk.) ~stoßen thrust sth. into sth.; 2 (~bringen) jmdn. in etw. (Akk.) ~stoßen push sb. into sth.; (fig.) plunge sb. into sth.; B unr. itr. V.; mit sein in etw. (Akk.) ~stoßen (vordringen) push or thrust into sth.; (~steuern) drive or turn into sth.; ~|stürzen A itr. V.; mit sein 1 (~fallen) in etw. (Akk.) ~stürzen fall or plunge into sth.; 2 (nach innen eilen) rush or burst in; ins Zimmer ~stürzen rush or burst into the room; B tr. V. jmdn. in etw. (Akk.) ~stürzen hurl sb. into sth.; C refl. V. sich in etw. (Akk.) ~stürzen throw oneself or plunge into sth.; sich in die Arbeit ~stürzen (fig.) throw oneself into one's work; ~|tappen itr. V.; mit sein (ugs.) in etw. (Akk.) ~tappen grope one's way into sth.; (~geraten) walk [right] into sth.; ~|tragen unr. tr. V. 1 carry in; etw. in etw. (Akk.) ~tragen carry sth. into sth.; Schmutz ins Haus ~tragen bring dirt into the house; 2 (verbreiten) etw. in etw. (Akk.) ~tragen bring sth. into sth.; Unruhe in einen Betrieb ~tragen spread unrest in a firm; ~|treiben unr. tr. V. 1 jmdn./etw. in etw. (Akk.) ~treiben drive sb./sth. into sth.; ‹tide› carry sb./sth. into sth.; 2 (verwickeln) jmdn. in etw. (Akk.) ~treiben force sb. into sth.; 3 (in etw. schlagen) etw. [in etw. (Akk.)] ~treiben drive sth. in[to sth.]; ~|tun unr. tr. V. 1 (ugs.: in etw. tun) etw. [in etw. (Akk.)] ~tun put sth. in[to sth.]; 2 (vollführen) einen Blick [in etw. (Akk.)] ~tun take a look in[to sth.]; ~|versetzen refl. V. sich in jmdn. od. jmds. Lage ~versetzen put oneself in sb.'s position; ~|wachsen unr. itr. V.; mit sein 1 in das Haus/das Fleisch ~wachsen grow into the house/the or one's flesh; 2 (ugs.: ~passen) in ein Kleid usw. ~wachsen grow into a dress etc.; in die Uniform ~wachsen (fig.) come to identify with the or one's uniform; 3 (vertraut werden) in eine Aufgabe/Rolle ~wachsen get to know a job/get into or inside a part; ~|wagen refl. V. venture in; dare to go in; sich in etw. (Akk.) ~wagen venture into sth.; dare to go into sth.; ~|werfen unr. tr. V. 1 etw. [in etw. (Akk.)] ~werfen throw sth. in[to sth.]; 2 (fallen lassen) einen Blick [in etw. (Akk.)] ~werfen glance [at sth.]; ~|wollen unr. itr. V. (ugs.: ~gelangen wollen) want to get or go in; in etw. (Akk.) ~wollen want to go/get into sth.; das will mir nicht in den Kopf ~: I just or simply can't understand it; ~|ziehen A unr. tr. V. 1 (nach drinnen ziehen) pull or draw in; etw./jmdn. in etw. (Akk.) ~ziehen pull or draw sth./sb. into sth.; 2 (verwickeln) jmdn. in eine Angelegenheit/einen Streit/Skandal ~ziehen drag sb. into an affair/a dispute/scandal; B unr. itr. V.; mit sein 1 march in; in etw. (Akk.) ~ziehen march into sth.; 2 (nach innen ziehen) ‹smoke, fumes, etc.› drift in; in etw. (Akk.) ~ziehen drift into sth.; ~|zwängen A tr. V. etw. [in etw. (Akk.)] ~zwängen squeeze or force sth. in[to sth.]; B refl. V. squeeze in; sich in die Hose ~zwängen squeeze [oneself] into one's trousers; ~|zwingen unr. tr. V. jmdn. [in etw. (Akk.)] ~zwingen force sb. to go in[to sth.]; jmdn. in ein Schema/eine Rolle ~zwingen force sb. into a rigid pattern/a role

hin-, Hin-: ~|fahren A unr. itr. V.; mit sein 1 (an einen Ort fahren) go there; (mit einem Auto) drive or go there; (mit einem Fahrrad, Motorrad) ride or go there; wo ist er ~gefahren? where has he gone?; 2 (streichen) mit der Hand/den Fingern über etw. (Akk.) ~fahren run one's hand/fingers over sth.; **B** *unr. tr. V.* **jmdn. ~fahren** drive *or* take sb. there; **jmdn. zum Bahnhof ~fahren** drive *or* take sb. to the station; **~fahrt** *die* journey there; (Seereise) voyage out; **auf der ~fahrt** on the way *or* journey there/the voyage out; **~|fallen** *unr. itr. V.; mit sein* **1** (stürzen) fall down *or* over; **lang ~fallen** fall flat [on one's face/back]; **2** (herunterfallen) **jmdm. fällt etw. ~:** sb. drops sth.; **etw. ~fallen lassen** drop sth.; **~fällig** *Adj.* **1** (schwächlich) infirm; frail; **2** (ungültig) invalid; **~fälligkeit** *die* **1** (Schwäche) infirmity; frailty; **2** (Ungültigkeit) invalidity; **~|finden** *unr. itr. V.* find one's way there; **zu jmdm./zu einem Ort ~finden** find one's way to sb./a place; **~|fläzen**, **~|flegeln** *refl. V.* (ugs. abwertend) loll around *or* about; **~|fliegen** **A** *unr. itr. V.; mit sein* **1** fly there; **er fliegt heute ~:** he's flying [out] there today; **wo fliegt sie ~?** where is she flying to?; **2** (ugs.: fallen) come a cropper (coll.); fall over; **mit dem Fahrrad ~fliegen** come a cropper on one's bicycle (coll.); fall off one's bicycle; **B** *unr. tr. V.* **jmdn./etw. ~fliegen** fly sb./sth. [out] there; **~flug** *der* outward flight

hin·fort *Adv.* (geh.) henceforth; henceforward

hin|führen
A *tr. V.* **1** **jmdn. ~:** lead *or* take sb. there **2** (zu etw. bringen) **jmdn. zu etw. ~:** lead sb. to sth.
B *itr. V.* **zu etw. ~:** lead to sth.; **wo soll das ~?** what will it lead to?

hing /hɪŋ/ *1. u. 3. Pers. Sg. Prät. v.* **hängen**

Hin·gabe *die;* **~** **1** devotion; (Eifer) dedication; **etw. mit ~ tun** do sth. with dedication; **mit ~ tanzen** put one's whole soul into one's dancing **2** (geh.: das Opfern) **unter ~ des Lebens** at the cost of one's life

hin-, Hin-: **~gang** *der* (geh.) decease; demise; **~|geben** **A** *unr. tr. V.* (geh.) give; sacrifice; **sein Leben ~geben** lay down *or* sacrifice one's life; **B** *unr. refl. V.* **1** **sich einer Illusion/einem Genuss ~geben** entertain an illusion/abandon oneself to a pleasure; **2** (verhüll.) **sich einem Mann ~geben** give oneself to a man; **~gebend** *Adj.* devoted

Hingebung *die;* **~:** devotion

hingebungs·voll
A *Adj.* devoted
B *adv.* devotedly; with devotion; ‹*listen*› raptly, with rapt attention; ‹*dance, play*› with abandon

hin·gegen *Konj., Adv.* (jedoch) however; (andererseits) on the other hand

hin-: **~gegossen** *Adj.* (ugs. scherzh.) **wie ~gegossen auf der Couch liegen/sitzen** have draped oneself over the couch; **~|gehen** *unr. itr. V.; mit sein* **1** go [there]; **zu jmdm./etw. ~gehen** go to sb./sth.; **wo gehst du ~?** where are you going?; **2** (verstreichen) ‹*years, time*› pass, go by; **darüber gingen Jahre ~:** it took years; **3** (~gleiten) **sein Blick ging über die Landschaft ~:** he *or* his eyes scanned the landscape; **4** (tragbar sein) pass; **diesmal mag das noch ~gehen** I'll/we'll *etc.* let it pass this time; **~|gehören** *itr. V.* (ugs.) go; belong; ‹*person*› belong; **wo gehört das ~?** where does this go *or* belong *or* (coll.) live?; **~|gelangen** *itr. V.; mit sein* get there; **zu jmdm./etw. ~gelangen** get to sb./sth.; **~|geraten** *unr. itr. V.; mit sein* get there; **wie sind wir dort ~geraten?** how did we get there?; **wo ist er/der Brief ~geraten?** where has he/the letter got to?; **~gerissen** **A** *2. Part. v.* **~reißen;** **B** *Adj.* carried away; spellbound; **~gerissen der Musik lauschen** listen spellbound to the music; **~|gleiten** *unr. itr. V.; mit sein* **1** glide along; **die Hand über etw.** (*Akk.*) **~gleiten lassen** run one's hand over sth.; **den Blick über etw. ~gleiten lassen** (fig.) let one's gaze sweep over sth.; **2** (geh.: vergehen) slip away; **~|halten** *unr. tr. V.* **1** hold out; **jmdm. etw. ~halten** hold sth. out to sb.; **2** (warten lassen) **jmdn. ~halten** put sb. off; keep sb. waiting; **3** (Milit.: aufhalten) hold off

Hin·halte-: **~politik** *die* policy of procrastination; **~taktik** *die* delaying tactics *pl.*

hin-: **~|hängen** *tr. V.* (ugs.) hang up; **~|hauen** **A** *unr. tr. V.* **1** (salopp: aufgeben) chuck in (sl.); **den ganzen Kram ~hauen** chuck the whole thing in (sl.); **2** (salopp abwertend: flüchtig anfertigen) knock off (coll.); dash off; **3** (unpers. salopp) **es hat mich ~gehauen** I came a cropper (coll.); **4** (salopp: ~werfen) chuck down (coll.); **B** *unr. itr. V.* **1** (ugs.: schlagen) **[mit etw.] ~hauen** take a swipe [with sth.] (coll.); **2** *mit sein* (~fallen) fall [down] heavily; **3** (salopp: gut gehen) ‹*plan*› work [all right]; **es wird schon ~hauen** it'll work out *or* be all right *or* (coll.) OK; **4** (salopp: richtig sein) ‹*calculation*› be right; **so haut das nicht ~:** it's wrong as it stands; **C** *unr. refl. V.* (salopp) lie down and have a kip (coll.); **~|hören** *itr. V.* listen

Hinke·bein /ˈhɪŋkə-/ *das* (ugs.) **1** stiff *or* (coll.) gammy leg **2** (jmd., der hinkt) person with a limp *or* (coll.) a gammy leg

Hinkel·stein *der* menhir; standing stone

hinken /ˈhɪŋkn̩/ *itr. V.* **1** limp; walk with a limp; **auf** *od.* **mit dem rechten Bein ~:** have a limp in one's right leg **2** *mit sein* (~d gehen) limp; hobble **3** (fig.) ‹*line*› be clumsy *or* halting; ‹*rhyme*› be clumsy; ‹*comparison*› be poor *or* feeble

hin-, Hin-: **~|knallen** (ugs.) **A** *tr. V.* slam down; **B** *itr. V.; mit sein* fall [down] heavily; come a cropper (coll.); **~|knien** *refl. V.* kneel [down]; **~|kommen** *unr. itr. V.; mit sein* **1** get there; **nach Madrid ~kommen** get to Madrid; **wie kommt man zu ihm ~?** how do you get to his place?; **2** (an einen Ort gehören) go; belong; **wo kommen die Gläser ~?** where do the glasses go *or* belong?; **wo ist meine Uhr ~gekommen?** where has my watch got to *or* gone?; **wo kommen** *od.* **kämen wir ~, wenn ...** (fig.) where would we be if ...; **3** (ugs.: auskommen) **mit etw. ~kommen** manage with sth.; **4** (ugs.: in Ordnung kommen) work out *or* turn out all right *or* (coll.) OK; **5** (ugs.: stimmen) be right; **~|kriegen** *tr. V.* (ugs.) **1** (fertig bringen) **das hat sie toll ~gekriegt** she made a great job of that (coll.); **so genau wie auf der Vorlage kriege ich das nicht ~:** I won't be able to get it as accurate as it is on the pattern; **das wird er schon ~kriegen** he'll manage it all right *or* (coll.) OK; **2** (in Ordnung bringen) fix ‹*radio etc.*›; **jmdn. wieder ~kriegen** put sb. right; **~kunft** *die:* **in** *od.* **in ~kunft** (österr.) in future; **~|langen** *itr. V.* **1** (ugs.: fassen) **er langte ~ und steckte einige Uhren in seine Tasche** he reached over and stuck some watches in his pocket (coll.); **2** (salopp: zuschlagen) **[kräftig] ~langen** take a [hefty] swipe (coll.); **3** (salopp: sich bedienen) help oneself; **schön/ordentlich ~langen** help oneself in a big way (coll.); **4** (ugs.: ausreichen) be enough; **5** (ugs.: auskommen) manage; **~länglich** **A** *Adj.* sufficient; (angemessen) adequate; **B** *adv.* sufficiently; (angemessen) adequately; **etw. ist ~länglich bekannt** sth. is sufficiently well known; **~|lassen** *unr. tr. V.* (ugs.) **jmdn. ~lassen** allow sb. to go there; let sb. go there; **jmdn. zu etw. ~lassen** allow sb. to go to sth.; let sb. go to sth.; **~|laufen** *unr. itr. V.; mit sein* **1** (an einen Ort laufen) run there; **zu jmdm./zu einer Stelle ~laufen** run to sb./a place; **2** (zu Fuß gehen) walk [there]; **3** (zu jmdm./etw. gehen) **zum Anwalt/Arzt/Chef ~laufen** run to *or* rush off to the lawyer/doctor/boss; **~|legen** **A** *tr. V.* **1** (an eine Stelle legen) put; **sie legte den Kindern frische Wäsche ~:** she put out clean underwear for the children; **2** (weglegen) put down; **3** (zu Bett bringen) **jmdn. ~legen** lay sb. down; **4** (ugs.: bezahlen) pay *or* (coll.) shell out; **5** (salopp: ausführen) **eine hervorragende Rede ~legen** do a brilliant speech; **eine gekonnte Übung auf dem Trampolin ~legen** turn in a splendid performance on the trampoline; **B** *refl. V.* **1** lie down; **da legst du dich [lang] ~** (ugs.) you won't believe your ears; **2** (sich schlafen legen) lie down; **sich zeitig ~legen** have an early night; **sich zum Sterben ~legen** (geh.) lie down to die; **3** (ugs.: ~fallen) come a cropper (coll.); fall [down *or* over]; **~|leiten** *tr. V.* lead there; **etw. zu etw. ~leiten** lead sth. to sth.; **~|lenken** *tr. V.* **1** **etw. [zu etw.] ~lenken** steer sth. [to sth.]; **seine Schritte zum Bahnhof ~lenken** direct one's steps towards the station; **2** (fig.) steer ‹*conversation*› (**auf** + *Akk.* round to); direct ‹*attention*› (**auf** + *Akk.* towards); turn ‹*gaze*› (**auf** + *Akk.* towards); **~|machen** (salopp) **A** *tr. V.* **1** put up ‹*curtain, picture, fence, etc.*›; put on ‹*paint, oil, cream*›; put in ‹*comma etc.*›; put ‹*cross, ring, etc.*›; make ‹*dirty mark etc.*›; **2** (töten) do in (sl.); rub out (sl.); bump off (coll.); **B** *itr. V.* **1** (seine Notdurft verrichten) do one's/its business (coll.); **2** (landsch.: sich beeilen) hurry up; get a move on (coll.); **~|marschieren** *itr. V.; mit sein* march there; **~|metzeln**, **~|morden** *tr. V.* (geh.) massacre; slaughter; butcher; **~nahme** *die;* **~~:** acceptance; **~nehmbar** *Adj.* acceptable; **nicht ~nehmbar sein** be unacceptable; **~|nehmen** *unr. tr. V.* **1** (annehmen) accept; take; put up with, swallow, accept ‹*insult*›; **etw. als gegeben ~nehmen** take sth. for granted; accept sth. as a fact; **2** (ugs.: mitnehmen) **kannst du das Buch mit ~nehmen** can you take the book with you?; **~|neigen** **A** *tr. V.* incline; **den Kopf zu jmdm. ~neigen** incline *or* bend one's head towards sb.; **B** *refl. V.* lean [over]; **C** *itr. V.* **zu einer Auffassung** *usw.* **~neigen** incline to a point of view *etc.*

hinnen /ˈhɪnən/ *in* **von ~** (veralt. geh.) [from] hence; **von ~ scheiden** (verhüll.) depart this life; pass away *or* on

hin-, Hin-: **~|passen** *itr. V.* (ugs.) **1** (an eine Stelle passen) fit *or* go in; **2** (in die Umgebung passen) fit in; go; **~|pfeffern** *tr. V.* (ugs.) **1** (~werfen) fling *or* slam down; **2** (äußern) rap out; **~|pflanzen** **A** *tr. V.* plant; **B** *refl. V.* (ugs.) **sich vor jmdn. ~pflanzen** plant oneself in front of sb.; **~|reichen** **A** *tr. V.* hand; pass; **jmdm. etw. ~reichen** hand *or* pass sth. to sb.; **B** *itr. V.* **1** (erstrecken) reach; **bis zu etw. ~reichen** reach to *or* as far as sth.; **2** (ausreichen) be enough *or* sufficient; **3** (ugs.: auskommen) manage; **mit etw. ~reichen** manage on sth.; **~reichend** **A** *Adj.* sufficient; (angemessen) adequate; **B** *adv.* sufficiently; (angemessen) adequately; **~reise** *die* journey there; outward journey; (mit dem Schiff) voyage out; outward voyage; **die ~reise nach Rom** the journey to Rome; **[die] Hin- und Rückreise** the journey there and back; **~|reisen** *itr. V.; mit sein* travel there; **~|reißen** *unr. tr. V.* **1** **jmdn. zu sich ~reißen** pull sb. to one; **2** (begeistern) enrapture; **das Publikum zu Beifallsstürmen ~reißen** elicit thunderous *or* rapturous applause from the audience; **3** (verleiten) **jmdn. zu etw. ~reißen** drive sb. to sth.; **sich ~reißen lassen** let oneself get *or* be carried away; **~reißend** **A** *Adj.* enchanting ‹*person, picture, view*›; captivating ‹*speaker, play*›; **B** *adv.* enchantingly; **~|richten** *tr. V.* execute; **~richtung** *die* execution

Hinrichtungs-: **~kommando** *das* firing squad; **~stätte** *die* place of execution

hin-, Hin-: **~|rücken** **A** *tr. V.* **etw. ~rücken** move *or* push sth. over; **B** *itr. V.; mit sein* move over; **~|sagen** *tr. V.* say without thinking; (nur beiläufig sagen) say casually; **das hat er nur so ~gesagt** he just said it without thinking; **~|schaffen** *unr. tr. V.* **etw. ~schaffen** get sth. there; **etw. zum Bahnhof ~schaffen** get sth. to the station; **~|schauen** *itr. V.* (bes. südd., österr.) ▸**~sehen**; **~|scheiden** *unr. itr. V.; mit sein* (geh. verhüll.) pass away *or* over; **der ~geschiedene** the deceased *or* departed; **~|scheiden** *das;* **~~s** (geh. verhüll.) decease; demise; **~|scheißen** *unr. itr. V.* (derb) crap (coarse); **~|schicken** *tr. V.* send; **~|schieben** *unr. tr. V.* **jmdm. etw. ~schieben** push sth. over to sb.; **~schied** *der;* **~~[e]s, ~~e** (schweiz.) ▸**~~scheiden**; **~|schielen** *itr. V.* steal a glance/glances (**zu** at); **~|schlachten** *tr. V.* (geh.) massacre; slaughter; butcher; **~|schlagen** *unr. itr. V.* **1** (auf eine Stelle schlagen) strike; hit; **2** *mit sein* (ugs.: fallen) **[der Länge nach** *od.* **lang] ~schlagen** fall flat on one's face/back; **da schlag einer lang ~!** (ugs.) well I never (coll.); would you believe it! (coll.); **~|schleichen** *unr. itr. V. mit sein; unr. refl. V.* creep *or* steal over; **~|schleppen** **A** *refl. V.* **1** (mühsam gehen) drag oneself along; **sich zu etw. ~schleppen** drag oneself to sth.; **2** (sich ~ziehen) drag on; **B** *tr. V.* **1** (an einen Ort schleppen) **etw. ~schleppen** drag sth. there; **etw. zu etw. ~schleppen** drag sth. to sth.; **2** (verzögern) drag out;

h

~|**schmeißen** *unr. tr. V.* (salopp) [1] (werfen) chuck down (coll.); [2] (aufgeben) chuck in (coll.); ~|**schmelzen** *unr. itr. V.; mit sein* [1] ▸**zerschmelzen**; [2] (ugs. scherzh.: vergehen) swoon; **vor Rührung ~schmelzen** be overcome with emotion; ~|**schmieren** *tr. V.* (ugs.) (~schreiben) scrawl; scribble; (~malen) daub; ~|**schreiben** A *unr. tr. V.* write down; B *unr. itr. V.* (an eine Firma o. Ä. schreiben) write; ~|**schwinden** *unr. V.* ▸**dahinschwinden**; ~|**sehen** *unr. itr. V.* look; **ich kann nicht ~sehen** I can't [bear to] look; **bei genauerem ~sehen** on closer inspection; *~|**sein** ▸**hin**; ~|**setzen** A *tr. V.* [1] (an eine Stelle setzen) put; seat, put ‹*person*›; **das Kind ~setzen** sit the child/baby down; [2] (absetzen) put *or* set down; B *refl. V.* [1] sit down; **setzen Sie sich doch ~!** do sit down!; **wo soll ich mich ~setzen?** where should I sit?; **sich gerade ~setzen** sit up straight; **sich ~setzen und etw. tun** (fig.) sit down and do sth.; get down to doing sth.; [2] (ugs.: fallen) land on one's backside; [3] (salopp: überrascht sein) **er wird sich ~setzen** he won't believe his ears; ~**sicht** *die:* **in gewisser ~sicht** in a way/in some respect *or* ways; **in mancher ~sicht** in some respects *or* ways; **in jeder ~sicht** in every respect; **in finanzieller ~sicht** financially; **in ~sicht auf** (+ *Akk.*) with regard to; ~**sichtlich** *Präp. mit Gen.* (Amtsspr.) with regard to; (in Anbetracht) in view of; ~|**sinken** *unr. itr. V.; mit sein* (geh.) sink down; sink to the ground; ~|**sollen** *unr. itr. V.* (ugs.) **wo sollen die Sachen ~?** where do these things go?; where do you want these things [to go]?; **wo soll ich mit den Büchern ~?** where should I put the books?; what should I do with the books?; **sie weiß nicht, wo sie ~soll** she doesn't know where to go; ~**spiel** *das* (Sport) first leg; ~|**starren** *itr. V.* stare (**zu, nach** at); ~|**stellen** A *tr. V.* [1] (an eine Stelle stellen) put; put up ‹*building*›; put, park ‹*car*›; [2] (absetzen) put down; [3] (bezeichnen) **etw. als falsch ~stellen** make sth. out to be *or* represent sth. as false; **jmdn. als Lügner ~stellen** make sb. out to be *or* represent sb. as a liar; **jmdn. als Vorbild ~stellen** hold sb. up as an example; **er hat die Sache so ~gestellt, als seien wir die Schuldigen** he made it look as though it was our fault; B *refl. V.* [1] (sich an eine Stelle stellen) stand; ‹*driver*› park; **sich gerade ~stellen** stand up straight; **sich vor jmdn. ~stellen** stand in front of sb.; [2] (sich bezeichnen) **sich als unschuldig ~stellen** make out that one is innocent; ~|**steuern** A *tr. V.* steer; **das Boot zum Ufer ~steuern** steer the boat towards the bank; B *itr. V.; mit sein* [1] **zu etw. ~steuern** make *or* head for sth.; [2] (eine Absicht verfolgen) **auf etw.** (*Akk.*) **~steuern** aim at sth.; ~|**strecken** A *tr. V.* [1] stretch out; hold out; **jmdm. die Hand ~strecken** hold out one's hand to sb.; [2] (geh. veralt.: töten) fell; slay (liter.); B *refl. V.* [1] (sich ausgestreckt ~legen) stretch [oneself] out; lie down full length; [2] (sich erstrecken) extend, stretch (**bis an** + *Akk.* as far as); ~|**strömen** *itr. V.; mit sein* [1] ‹*river*› flow; [2] ‹*people*› flock there; **zu etw. ~strömen** flock to sth.; ~|**stürzen** *itr. V.; mit sein* [1] (~fallen) fall down [heavily]; [2] (~eilen) rush *or* dash there; **zum Ausgang ~stürzen** rush *or* dash towards the exit

hintan-, Hintan- /hɪnt'|an-/: ~|**setzen** *tr. V.* **etw. ~setzen** put sth. last; **Differenzen ~setzen** put *or* set aside differences; ~**setzung** *die;* ~~: **nur unter ~setzung persönlicher Interessen** only by putting personal interests last; ~|**stellen** *tr. V.* ▸~**setzen**

hinten /'hɪntn̩/ *Adv.* [1] (am rückwärtigen Ende) at the back; in *or* at the rear; **~ im Bus sitzen** sit in the back of the bus; **~ in die Straßenbahn einsteigen** get on at the back of the tram (Brit.) *or* (Amer.) streetcar; **ganz ~ im Garten/in der Garage/im Schrank** right at the back of the garden/the garage/the cupboard; **sich ~ anstellen** join the back of the queue (Brit.) *or* (Amer.) line; **nach ~ abgehen** move [off] towards the back; exit upstage (Theatre); **~ im Buch** at the back *or* end of the book; **weiter ~:** further back; (in einem Buch) further on; **von ~ anfangen** start from the end; **von ~ nach vorne** backwards; (in einem Buch) from back to front; (Bewegung) towards the front; **nach ~ gehen** go *or* walk to the back/into the room behind [2] (an/auf/von der Rückseite) **die Adresse steht ~ auf dem Brief** the address is on the back of the envelope; **~ auf der Münze** on the back *or* reverse of the coin; **~ am Haus** at the back *or* rear of the house; **nach ~ hinaus liegen/gehen** be at the back *or* rear; **von ~ kommen/jmdn. von ~ erstechen** come from behind/stab sb. from behind; **von ~ sah sie jünger aus** she looked younger from the back; **jmdn. von ~ erkennen** recognize sb. from the back; **jmdm. ~ drauffahren** (ugs.) run into the back of sb.; **~ und vorn[e] nichts haben** (salopp) be as flat as an ironing board (coll.) [3] (entfernt) **die anderen sind ganz weit ~:** the others are a long way back *or* behind; **~ in Sibirien** far away in Siberia; **~ im Wald** in the depths of the forest; deep in the forest; **ganz weit ~ konnte man die Bergspitzen erkennen** far away in the distance you could make out the mountain peaks [4] (in Wendungen) **jetzt heißt es Herr Meier ~, Herr Meier vorn** now it's Herr Meier this, and Herr Meier that; **~ und vorn[e] bedient werden** be waited on hand and foot; **das kann ~ und vorn[e] nicht stimmen** that cannot possibly be true; there is no way that can be true; **~ und vorn[e] betrogen werden** be cheated right, left and centre; **nicht [mehr] wissen, wo ~ und vorn[e] ist** (ugs.) not know whether one is coming or going; **~ nicht mehr hochkönnen** (ugs.) be in desperate straits; **jmdn. am liebsten von ~ sehen** (ugs.) be glad to see the back of sb.; **von ~ durch die Brust ins Auge** (salopp scherzh.) in a roundabout fashion *or* way

hinten-: ~**dran** *Adv.* (ugs.) at the back; **~dran einen Anhänger hängen** hitch a trailer on behind; ~**drauf** *Adv.* (ugs.) on the back; **jmdm. eins** *od.* **ein paar ~drauf geben** (ugs.) smack sb.'s bottom; ~**drein** *Adv.* ▸**hinterher**; ~**heraus** /'----/ *Adv.* **~heraus liegen/wohnen** be/live at the back; ~**herum** /'----/ *Adv.* (ugs.) [1] (um die hintere Seite herum) round the back; [2] (am Rücken) **mir ist ~herum kalt** my back's cold; [3] (ugs.: heimlich) **etw. ~herum erfahren** hear sth. indirectly; **Waren ~herum besorgen** get goods under the counter; ~**nach** *Adv.* (südd., österr.) ▸**hinterher**

hinten·über *Adv.* backwards

hintenüber-: ~|**fallen** *unr. itr. V.; mit sein* fall [over] backwards; ~|**kippen** *itr. V.; mit sein* tip [over] backwards; ~|**stürzen** *itr. V.; mit sein* ▸~**fallen**

hinter /'hɪntɐ/

A *Präp. mit Dat.* [1] behind; **~ dem Haus sein** be behind *or* at the back of the house; **~ jmdm. zurückbleiben** lag behind sb.; **eine große Strecke ~ sich haben** have put a good distance behind one; **~ der Mauer hervortreten** step out from behind the wall; **~ jmdm. stehen** (fig.) be behind sb.; back *or* support sb.; **~ etw.** (*Dat.*) **stehen** (fig.) support sth.; **jmdn. ~ sich haben** (fig.) have sb.'s backing; **sich ~ etw. verbergen** (fig.) ‹*person*› hide behind sth.; ‹*danger*› lie concealed behind sth.; ‹*purpose*› lie behind sth. [2] (nach) after; **3 km ~ der Grenze** 3 km beyond the frontier; **die nächste Station ~ Mannheim** the next stop after Mannheim [3] (in der Rangfolge) **~ jmdm. zurückstehen** lag behind sb.; **~ der Entwicklung/der Zeit zurückbleiben** lag behind in development/be behind in times; **er ist ~ unseren Erwartungen zurückgeblieben** he has fallen short of our expectations [4] (bewältigt) **eine Prüfung/Aufgabe ~ sich haben** (fig.) have got an examination/a job over [and done] with; **viele Enttäuschungen/eine Krankheit ~ sich haben** have experienced many disappointments/have got over an illness; **wenn er das Studium ~ sich hat** when he's finished his studies

B *Präp. mit Akk.* [1] behind; **~ das Haus gehen** go behind the house; **sich ~ jmdn./etw. stellen** (fig.) stand *or* get behind sb./support sth. [2] **~ jmdn. zurückfallen** fall behind sb. [3] **etw. ~ sich bringen** get sth. over [and done] with [4] (zeitlich) **~ etw. gehen/reichen** go back to before sth. [5] (fig.) **~ ein Geheimnis/die Wahrheit/seine Geschichte kommen** find out a secret/get to the truth/get to the bottom of his story

hinter... *Adj.* back; **das ~e Ende des Ganges/des Zimmers** the far end of the corridor/the far end *or* the back of the room; **das ~e Ende des Zuges** the back *or* rear [end] of the train; **die ~ste Reihe** the back row; **die Hinter[st]en** those [right] at the back

Hinter-: ~**achse** *die* rear *or* back axle; ~**ansicht** *die* rear *or* back view; ~**ausgang** *der* rear *or* back exit; ~**backe** *die* ▸ⓘ S. 435 (ugs.) buttock; **auf seine ~backen fallen** fall over on one's backside; ~**bänkler** /-bɛŋklɐ/ *der;* ~~s, ~~, ~**bänklerin** *die;* ~~, ~~**nen** (ugs.) inconspicuous backbencher; ~**bein** *das* hind leg; **sich auf die ~beine stellen** (ugs.) put up a fight; **sich auf die ~beine setzen** (ugs.) get *or* knuckle down and do some work

Hinterbliebene /-'bli:bənə/ *der/die; adj. Dekl.* [1] (Familienangehörige) **die ~n** the bereaved [family] [2] (jur.) surviving dependant

Hinterbliebenen·rente *die* [surviving] dependant's pension

hinter-, Hinter-: ~**bringen**[1] /--'--/ *unr. tr. V.* **jmdm. etw. ~bringen** inform sb. [confidentially] of sth.; ~|**bringen**[2] *unr. tr. V.* (landsch.) bring to the back; ~**deck** *das* (Seew.) afterdeck

hinter·einander *Adv.* [1] (räumlich) one behind the other; **sie liefen dicht ~:** they were running close behind one another; **~ fahren** drive/ride one behind the other; **~ gehen** walk in a single file *or* one behind the other; **~ schalten** +*Akk.* (Electrot.) connect ‹*lamps, etc.*› in series [2] (zeitlich) one after another *or* the other; **an drei Tagen ~:** for three days running *or* in succession

***hintereinander|fahren** *usw.* ▸**hintereinander**

hintereinander·weg *Adv.* (ugs.) one after the other

hinter-, Hinter-: ~**ein·gang** *der* rear *or* back entrance; ~**fotzig** /-fɔtsɪç/ *Adj.* (bayr.; sonst derb) underhand[ed]; ~**fragen** /--'--/ *tr. V.* examine; analyse; ~**fuß** *der* hind foot; ~**gebäude** *das* ▸~**haus**; ~**gedanke** *der* ulterior motive; **einen ~gedanken bei etw. haben** have an ulterior motive for sth.; ~**gehen**[1] /--'--/ *unr. tr. V.* deceive; **sie hat ihren Mann mit seinem besten Freund ~gangen** she deceived her husband by having an affair with his best friend; ~|**gehen**[2] *unr. itr. V.; mit sein* (landsch.) go to the back; **ins Lager ~gehen** go to the back of the store room

Hinterglas·malerei *die* (Kunst) [1] (Herstellung) verre églomisé [2] (Bild) verre églomisé picture

Hinter·grund *der* background; (der Bühne) back; (Theater: Kulisse) backcloth; backdrop; **der akustische/musikalische ~:** the background sounds/music; **im ~ der Bühne** at the back of the stage; **die Hintergründe dieser Verhaltensweise** (fig.) the background *sing.* to this behaviour; **jmdn./etw. in den ~ drängen** push sb./sth. into the background; **in den ~ treten/geraten** recede *or* fade into the background; **sich im ~ halten** keep in the background; **etw. im ~ haben** have sth. up one's sleeve

hinter·gründig

A *Adj.* enigmatic; cryptic

B *adv.* enigmatically; cryptically

Hintergründigkeit *die;* ~, ~**en** [1] (Eigenschaft) enigmaticness; crypticness [2] (Äußerung) enigmatic *or* cryptic remark

Hintergrund-: ~**information** *die* item *or* piece of background information; ~**informationen** [items *or* pieces of] background information *sing.;* ~**musik** *die* background music

hinter-, Hinter-: ~**halt** *der* ambush; **in einen ~halt geraten** be ambushed; **jmdn. aus dem ~halt überfallen** ambush sb.; **im ~halt lauern** lie in ambush; **jmdn. aus dem**

~halt angreifen (fig.) attack sb. without warning; make a surprise attack on sb.; **etw. im ~halt haben** have sth. up one's sleeve *or* in reserve; **~hältig** A *Adj.* underhand; B *adv.* in an underhand fashion *or* manner; **~hältigkeit** *die;* ~~, ~~**en** [1] (Eigenschaft) underhandedness; [2] (Handlung) underhand act; **~hand** *die* [1] (bei Tieren) hindquarters *pl.*; [2] **etw. in der ~hand haben** have sth. up one's sleeve *or* in reserve; **in der ~hand sein** *od.* **sitzen** (Kartenspiel) play last; **~haus** *das: dwelling situated at or forming the rear of a house [and accessible only from a courtyard]*

hinter·her *Adv.* [1] (räumlich) behind; **nichts wie ihm ~!** quick, after him!; **jmdm. ~ sein** (ugs.) be after sb.; *s. auch* **nichts** [2] (nachher) afterwards; **es ~ besser wissen** be wise after the event [3] **~ sein** (fig. ugs.: zurückgeblieben sein) be behind

hinterher-: **~|blicken** *itr. V.* **jmdm. ~blicken** follow sb. with one's eyes; gaze after sb.; **~|fahren** *unr. itr. V.; mit sein* (mit dem Auto/Fahrrad) drive/ride [along] behind (**jmdm.** sb.); (folgen) follow (**jmdm.** sb.); **~|gehen** *unr. itr. V.; mit sein* walk [along] behind (**jmdm.** sb.); (folgen) follow (**jmdm.** sb.); **~|hinken** *itr. V.; mit sein* [1] limp *or* hobble [along] behind (**jmdm.** sb.); [2] (fig.) **einer Sache** (*Dat.*) **~hinken** lag behind sth.; **mit etw. ~hinken** be behind with sth.; **~|kommen** *unr. itr. V.; mit sein* [1] (dahinter ankommen) follow behind; [2] (danach kommen) follow; come after; **~|laufen** *unr. itr. V.; mit sein* [1] run [along] behind (**jmdm.** sb.); [2] ▸**~gehen**; [3] (ugs.: für sich zu gewinnen suchen) **jmdm./etw. ~laufen** run after sb./sth.; **~|rennen** *unr. itr. V.; mit sein* [1] ▸**~laufen 1**; [2] (ugs.) ▸**~laufen 3**; **~|schicken** *tr. V.* **jmdm. jmdn./etw. ~schicken** send sb. after sb./send sth. on to sb.; ***~sein** ▸**hinterher**; **~|spionieren** *itr. V.* **jmdm. ~spionieren** spy on sb.; **~|telefonieren** *itr. V.* **jmdm./etw. ~telefonieren** chase sb./sth. up on the phone

hinter-, Hinter-: **~hof** *der* courtyard; **~kopf** *der* ▸❶ **S. 435** back of the/one's head; **etw. im ~kopf haben/behalten** (ugs.) have/keep sth. at the back of one's mind; **~lader** *der;* ~~**s**, ~~ (Waffenkunde) breech-loader; **~land** *das* hinterland; (Milit.) back area; **~lassen** /--'--/ *unr. tr. V.* [1] leave; (testamentarisch) leave; bequeath; **die ~lassenen Schriften** the posthumous works; [2] (zurücklassen) leave ‹*message, telephone number, etc.*›; **ein Zimmer in Unordnung ~lassen** leave a room in a muddle; [3] (verursachen) leave ‹*fingerprints, impression, etc.*›; **keine Spuren ~lassen** leave no trace[s] [behind]; **~lassene** /--'---/ *der/die; adj. Dekl.* (schweiz.) ▸**~bliebene**; **~lassenschaft** /--'---/ *die;* ~~, ~~**en** estate; **jmds. ~lassenschaft antreten** inherit sb.'s estate; (ugs. scherzh.) take over from sb.; **jmds. literarische ~lassenschaft** the writings that sb. has left to posterity; **~lastig** *Adj.* tail-heavy ‹*aircraft*›; stern-heavy ‹*ship*›; **~lauf** *der* (Jägerspr.) hind leg; **~legen** /--'--/ *tr. V.* deposit (**bei** with); (als Pfand) deposit, leave (**bei** with)

Hinterlegung *die;* ~, ~**en** ▸**hinterlegen**: depositing; leaving; **jmdn. gegen ~ einer Kaution freilassen** release sb. on bail

Hinterlegungs·schein *der* deposit receipt

hinter-, Hinter-: **~letzt...** *Adj.* (ugs.) ▸**allerletzt...**; **~list** *die* guile; deceit; (Verrat) treachery; **eine ~list** an underhand trick; a piece of deceit; **~listig** *Adj.* deceitful; (verräterisch) treacherous

hinterm /ˈhɪntɐm/ *Präp. + Art.* (ugs.) = **hinter dem**

Hinter-: **~mann** *der* [1] person behind; **sein ~mann** the person behind [him]; [2] (Gewährsmann) [secret] informant; [3] (jmd., der aus dem ~grund lenkt) **der ~mann/die ~männer** the brains behind the operation; **~mannschaft** *die* (Sport) defence

hintern *Präp. + Art.* (ugs.) = **hinter den**

Hintern /ˈhɪntɐn/ *der;* ~**s**, ~ ▸❶ **S. 435** (ugs.) behind; backside; bottom; **jmdm. den ~ verhauen** *od.* **versohlen** tan sb.'s hide; **jmdn.** *od.* **jmdm. in den ~ treten** kick sb. in the pants (coll.) *or* up the backside; (fig.) kick sb. in the teeth (fig.); **sich [vor Wut** *od.* **Ärger] in den ~ beißen** (salopp) kick oneself; **jmdm. in den ~ kriechen** (derb) lick sb.'s arse (coarse); suck up to sb. (coll.); **sich auf den ~ setzen** (salopp) (sich anstrengen) get *or* knuckle down to it; (aufs Gesäß fallen) fall on one's behind; (überrascht sein) be flabbergasted; **Hummeln** *od.* **Pfeffer im ~ haben** (salopp) have ants in one's pants (coll.); *s. auch* **abwischen 2**

Hinter-: **~pfote** *die* hind paw; **~rad** *das* back *or* rear wheel; **~rad·antrieb** *der* rear-wheel drive; **~reifen** *der* back *or* rear tyre

hinter·rücks /ˈhɪntɐrʏks/ *Adv.* [1] (von hinten) from behind [2] (veralt.: hinter jmds. Rücken) behind sb.'s back

hinters /ˈhɪntɐs/ *Präp. + Art.* (ugs.) = **hinter das**

hinter-, Hinter-: **~schiff** *das* stern; **~seite** *die* ▸**Rückseite**; **~sinn** *der* deeper meaning; **~sinnig** *Adj.* ‹*remark, story, etc.*› with a deeper meaning; subtle ‹*sense of humour*›

hinterst... /ˈhɪntɐst.../ ▸**hinter...**

hinter-, Hinter-: **~steven** *der* [1] (Seemannsspr.) sternpost; [2] (ugs. scherzh.: Gesäß) backside; behind; **~teil** *das* ▸❶ **S. 435** (ugs.: Gesäß) backside; behind; (eines Tieres) rump; **~treffen** *das* (ugs.) *in* **ins ~treffen geraten** *od.* **kommen** fall behind; **jmdn./etw. ins ~treffen bringen** put sb./sth. behind; **~treiben** /--'--/ *unr. tr. V.* foil, thwart, frustrate ‹*plan*›; prevent ‹*marriage, promotion*›; block ‹*law, investigation, reform*›; **~treibung** *die;* ~~, ~~**en** ▸**~treiben**: foiling; thwarting; frustration; prevention; blocking; **~treppe** *die* back stairs *pl.*; **~treppen·roman** *der* (abwertend) trashy novel; **~tupfingen** /-ˈtʊpfɪŋən/ *(das);* ~~**s** (ugs. spött.) the back of beyond; **~tür** *die* back door; **durch die** *od.* **durch eine ~tür** (auch fig.) by the back door; **sich** (*Dat.*) **eine ~tür offen halten** (fig.) leave oneself a way out (fig.); **~wäldler** /-vɛltlɐ/ *der;* ~~**s**, ~~ (spött.) backwoodsman; **~wäldlerin** *die;* ~~, ~~**nen** backwoods woman; **~wäldlerisch** *Adj.* (spött.) backwoods *attrib.* ‹*views, attitudes, manners, etc.*›; **~ziehen** /--'--/ *unr. tr. V.* misappropriate ‹*materials, goods*›; **Steuern ~ziehen** evade [payment of] tax; **~ziehung** *die* ▸**~ziehen**: misappropriation; evasion; **~zimmer** *das* back room

hintnach /hɪntˈnaːx/ *Adv.* (österr. ugs.) ▸**hinterher**

hin-: **~|tragen** *unr. tr. V.* **jmdn./etw. ~tragen** carry sb./take *or* carry sth. there; **etw. zu jmdm.** *od.* **jmdm. etw. ~tragen** take sth. to sb.; **~|treiben** A *unr. tr. V.* [1] (an eine Stelle treiben) **die Schafe ~treiben/zur Weide ~treiben** drive the sheep there/to the pasture; **die Strömung/der Wind trieb das Boot zum Ufer ~:** the current carried/the wind blew the boat to the shore; [2] (unpers.) **es trieb ihn immer wieder zu ihr ~:** something always drove him back to her; B *unr. itr. V.; mit sein* drift *or* float there; **~|treten** *unr. itr. V.* [1] *mit sein* **zu jmdm./etw. ~treten** step over to sb./sth.; **vor jmdn. ~treten** go up to sb.; [2] (gegen jmdn./etw. treten) kick him/her/it *etc.*

hintüber /hɪntˈ|yːbɐ/ *Adv.* ▸**hintenüber**

hin|tun *unr. tr. V.* (ugs.) put; **wo soll ich ihn bloß ~?** (fig.) I can't place him

hinüber /hɪˈnyːbɐ/ *Adv.* [1] over; across; **bis zur anderen Seite ~:** over *or* across to the other side; **~ und herüber** back and forth [2] (ugs.) **~ sein** (tot/unbrauchbar sein) have had it (coll.); (verdorben sein) be *or* have gone off; (eingeschlafen sein) have dropped off; (bewusstlos sein) be out for the count (coll.); (betrunken sein) be well away (coll.) *or* plastered (sl.)

hinüber-: **~|blicken** *itr. V.* look across; **zu** *od.* **nach jmdm. ~blicken** look across at sb.; **~|bringen** *unr. tr. V.* **jmdn./etw. ~bringen** take sb./sth. across *or* over (**auf + Akk., zu** to); **~|dämmern** *itr. V.; mit sein* [1] (einschlafen) drift off; [2] (geh. verhüll.: sterben) pass away in one's sleep; **~|fahren** A *unr. itr. V.; mit sein* (mit dem Auto/Fahrrad) drive/ride *or* go over *or* across; **über den Fluss ~fahren** cross the river; B *unr. tr. V.* **jmdn./ein Auto ~fahren** drive *or* take sb./drive a car over *or* across; **~|führen** A *tr. V.* **jmdn. über die Straße/die Grenze/in den Saal ~führen** take sb. across the road/guide sb. over *or* across the frontier/take *or* show sb. across to the hall; B *itr. V.* ‹*street, path, etc.*› lead *or* go over *or* across (**an** + *Akk.*, **nach** to); **über etw.** (*Akk.*) **~führen** lead *or* go over sth.; **~|gehen** *unr. itr. V.; mit sein* [1] walk *or* go over *or* across; **zu jmdm. ~gehen** go across *or* over to sb.; **ins Nebenzimmer ~gehen** go across into the next room; [2] (geh. verhüll.: sterben) pass away; **~|helfen** *unr. itr. V.* **jmdm. [über etw.** (*Akk.*)**] ~helfen** help sb. over *or* across [sth.]; **jmdm. auf die andere Seite ~helfen** help sb. over *or* across to the other side; **~|kommen** *unr. itr. V.; mit sein* [1] (nach drüben kommen) come over *or* across; (~überkommen können) get across; **über etw.** (*Akk.*) **~kommen** get across sth.; [2] (ugs.: Besuch machen) come over; pop over (coll.); **~|lassen** *unr. tr. V.* **jmdn. ~lassen** allow *or* let sb. over *or* across; **~|reichen** A *tr. V.* **[jmdm.] etw. ~reichen** pass *or* hand sth. across [to sb.]; B *itr. V.* [1] (sich erstrecken) extend [over *or* across]; [2] (lang genug sein) reach over *or* across; **über die Mauer ~reichen** reach over the wall; **~|retten** A *tr. V.* [1] (in Sicherheit bringen) **sein Vermögen in die Schweiz ~retten** save one's fortune by getting it over *or* across the border into Switzerland; [2] (bewahren) keep alive, preserve ‹*tradition etc.*›; B *refl. V.* [1] (sich in Sicherheit bringen) **sich ins Ausland ~retten** reach safety abroad; [2] (sich erhalten) ‹*customs, hopes, etc.*› survive; **~|rufen** A *unr. tr. V.* **jmdn. ~rufen** call sb. over; B *unr. itr. V.* call over; **~|schauen** *itr. V.* [1] (landsch.) ▸**~blicken**; [2] (ugs.: besuchen) **zu jmdm. ~schauen** look in on sb.; **~|schicken** *tr. V.* **jmdn./etw. ~schicken** send sb./sth. over; **~|schwimmen** *unr. itr. V.; mit sein* swim over *or* across; **~|sehen** *unr. itr. V.:* ▸**~blicken**; ***~|sein** ▸**hinüber**; **~|spielen** A *tr. V.* (Sport) cross ‹*ball*›; B *itr. V.* **das Weiß spielt ins Gelbliche ~:** the white is tinged with yellow *or* has a yellow tinge; **~|springen** *unr. itr. V.; mit sein* **über etw.** (*Akk.*)**/ein Hindernis ~springen** jump over sth./clear an obstacle; **~|steigen** *unr. itr. V.; mit sein* **[über etw.** (*Akk.*)**] ~steigen** climb over [sth.]; **~|wechseln** *itr. V.; mit haben od. sein* cross over; **zu einer anderen Partei ~wechseln** go over *or* switch to another party; **~|werfen** *unr. tr. V.* **etw. ~werfen** throw sth. over *or* across; **einen Blick ~werfen** (fig.) glance over *or* across; **~|ziehen** A *unr. tr. V.* **jmdn./etw. ~ziehen** draw sb. over/pull *or* draw sth. over *or* across; B *unr. itr. V.; mit sein* [1] (wandern) **über etw. ~ziehen** go over *or* across sth.; cross sth.; [2] (umziehen) move across

hin- und her-: **~|bewegen** *tr. V.* **etw. ~bewegen** move sth. to and fro *or* back and forth; **~|fahren** A *unr. itr. V.; mit sein* travel *or* go to and fro *or* back and forth; (mit dem Auto) drive to and fro *or* back and forth; (mit dem Fahrrad) ride to and fro *or* back and forth; B *unr. tr. V.* **jmdn. ~fahren** drive sb. to and fro *or* back and forth; **~|gehen** *unr. itr. V.; mit sein* walk up and down *or* to and fro; (aufgeregt) pace up and down *or* to and fro; **im Zimmer ~gehen** walk/pace up and down the room

Hinundher·gerede *das:* **bei diesem ~ kommt doch nichts heraus** we're going backwards and forwards over the same old ground and getting nowhere

hin- und her|pendeln *itr. V.; mit sein* ‹*person*› commute; ‹*bus*› shuttle to and fro

Hin- und Rück-: **~fahrt** *die* journey there and back; round trip (Amer.); **~flug** *der* outward and return flight; **~reise** *die,* **~weg** *der* journey there and back

hinunter /hɪˈnʊntɐ/ *Adv.* down; **den Berg ~:** down the mountain; **~ mit der Medizin!** (ugs.) get the medicine down!

hinunter-: **~|begeben** *unr. refl. V.* **sich ~begeben** go down; **sich die Treppe ~begeben** go downstairs; **~|blicken** *itr. V.* look down; **auf jmdn. ~blicken** (fig.) look down on sb.; **~|bringen** *unr. tr. V.* **jmdn./etw. ~bringen** take sb./sth. down; **~|fahren** A *unr. itr.*

V.; *mit sein* go down; (mit dem Auto) drive down; (mit dem Fahrrad) ride down; **B** *unr. tr. V.* **jmdn./ein Auto/eine Ladung ~fahren** drive *or* take sb. down/drive a car down/take a load down; **~|fallen** *unr. itr. V.; mit sein* fall down; **die Treppe ~fallen** fall down the stairs; **mir ist die Vase ~gefallen** I dropped the vase; **~|führen** **A** *tr. V.* **jmdn. ~führen** lead *or* guide sb. down; **B** *itr. V.* ‹*path, road, etc.*› lead *or* run down; **den Berg ~führen** lead *or* run down the mountain; **~|gehen** *unr. itr. V.; mit sein* [1] go down; (zu Fuß) go *or* walk down; ‹*aircraft*› descend; [2] ‹*path, road, etc.*› go *or* run down; **~|jagen** **A** *tr. V.* **jmdn. ~jagen** chase sb. down; **B** *itr. V.; mit sein* **die Treppe/Straße ~jagen** race down the stairs/street; **~|kippen** *tr. V.* [1] **etw. ~kippen** tip sth. down; [2] (ugs.: trinken) knock back (sl.); down; **~|klettern** *itr. V.; mit sein* climb down; **~|kommen** *unr. itr. V.; mit sein* come down; **die Treppe ~kommen** come downstairs; **~|lassen** *unr. tr. V.* [1] (mit einem Seil usw.) **jmdn./etw. ~lassen** lower sb./sth.; let sb./sth. down; [2] (erlauben) **jmdn. ~lassen** let sb. [go] down; **~|laufen** *unr. itr. V.; mit sein* [1] run down; (zu Fuß ~gehen) walk down; **die Treppe ~laufen** run/walk down the stairs *or* downstairs; [2] (nach unten fließen) run down; **an der Wand ~laufen** run down the wall; [3] (fig.) **ein Schauer lief ihm den Rücken ~:** a shiver ran down his spine; **~|reichen** **A** *tr. V.* pass *or* hand down; **B** *itr. V.* [1] (sich bis ~ erstrecken) reach down (**bis auf** + *Akk.* to); [2] (bis zu einer Stufe reichen) **bis zu jmdm. ~reichen** reach *or* extend down to sb.; **~|rutschen** *itr. V.; mit sein* slide down; **~|schauen** *itr. V.* (landsch.) ▸**~blicken**; **~|schlingen** *unr. tr. V.* gulp *or* gobble down; **~|schlucken** *tr. V.* [1] swallow; [2] (hinnehmen) swallow ‹*insult etc.*›; [3] (unterdrücken) bite back ‹*remark, oath, etc.*›; choke back ‹*tears, anger*›; **~|sehen** *unr. itr. V.* ▸**~blicken**; **~|springen** *unr. itr. V.; mit sein* [1] jump down; [2] (ugs.: schnell ~laufen) run down; **die Treppe ~springen** run down the stairs *or* downstairs; **~|spülen** *tr. V.* [1] **etw. [den Ausguss] ~spülen** swill sth. down [the sink]; **etw. [die Toilette] ~spülen** flush sth. down [the toilet]; [2] (ugs.: ~schlucken) wash down ‹*tablets etc.*›; **seinen Kummer [mit Alkohol] ~spülen** (fig.) drown one's sorrows [in drink]; **~|stürzen** **A** *itr. V.; mit sein* [1] fall *or* plunge down; **die Treppe ~stürzen** fall down the stairs *or* downstairs; [2] (ugs.: eilen) rush *or* race down; **B** *refl. V.* throw *or* fling oneself down; **sich von etw. ~stürzen** throw *or* fling oneself off sth.; **C** *tr. V.* [1] **jmdn. ~stürzen** throw *or* hurl sb. down; **jmdn. von den Klippen/in den Abgrund ~stürzen** push sb. off the cliff/over the precipice; [2] (ugs.: schnell trinken) gulp down; knock back (sl.); **~|tragen** *unr. tr. V.* **etw. ~tragen** carry sth. down; **~|werfen** *unr. tr. V.* throw down; **einen Blick ~werfen** (fig.) glance down; **~|ziehen** **A** *unr. itr. V.; mit sein* [1] (umziehen) move down; [2] (sich nach unten bewegen) move *or* go down; **B** *unr. tr. V.* **jmdn./etw. ~ziehen** pull sb./sth. down; **C** *unr. refl. V.* stretch *or* extend down

hin-, Hin-: **~|wagen** *refl. V.* dare [to] go there; venture there; **~wärts** *Adv.* on the way there; **~weg** *der* way there; **auf dem ~weg** on the way there; **für den ~weg** for the journey there

hin·weg *Adv.* [1] (geh.) **~ mit diesem Unrat!** away with this rubbish!; **~ mit dir!** away with you! [2] **über etw. ~:** over sth.; **über den Brillenrand ~:** over [the top of] his/her spectacles; **über alle Schwierigkeiten** *usw.* **~** (fig.) in spite of *or* despite all the difficulties *etc.*; **über jmdn. ~** (fig.) over sb.'s head; **über Jahre/lange Zeit ~:** for many years/a long time

hinweg-: **~|brausen** *itr. V.; mit sein* **über etw.** (*Akk.*) **~brausen** roar over sth.; **~|gehen** *unr. itr. V.; mit sein* (nicht beachten) **über etw.** (*Akk.*) **~gehen** pass over sth.; (sich über etw. fortbewegen, auch fig.) pass *or* sweep over sth.; **~|helfen** *unr. itr. V.* **jmdm. über etw.** (*Akk.*) **~helfen** help sb. [to] get over sth.; **~|kommen** *unr. itr. V.; mit sein* **über etw.** (*Akk.*) **~kommen** get over sth.; **~|lesen** *unr. itr. V.* **über etw.** (*Akk.*) **~lesen** read past sth. without noticing it; **~|raffen** *tr. V.* (geh.) carry off; **~|sehen** *unr. itr. V.* [1] **über jmdn./etw. ~sehen** see over sb. *or* sb.'s head/sth.; [2] (übersehen) **über jmdn. ~sehen** look past sb.; [3] (unbeachtet lassen) **über etw.** (*Akk.*) **~sehen** overlook sth.; **~|setzen** **A** *itr. V.; auch mit sein* **über etw.** (*Akk.*) **~setzen** leap *or* jump over sth.; **B** *refl. V.* **sich über etw.** (*Akk.*) **~setzen** ignore *or* disregard sth.; **~|täuschen** *tr. V.* **jmdn. über etw.** (*Akk.*) **~täuschen** blind sb. to sth.; deceive *or* mislead sb. about sth.; **darüber ~täuschen, dass ...** hide *or* obscure the fact that ...; **~|trösten** *tr. V.* **jmdn. über etw.** (*Akk.*) **~trösten** console sb. for sth.

Hinweis /ˈhɪnvais/ *der;* **~es, ~e** [1] (Wink) hint; tip; **jmdm. einen ~ geben** give sb. a hint; **wenn ich mir den ~ erlauben darf** if I may [just] point something out *or* draw your attention to something; **~e für den Benutzer** notes for the user; **~e aus der Bevölkerung** leads provided by the public [2] **unter ~ auf** (+ *Akk.*) with reference to [3] (Anzeichen) hint; indication

hin-: **~|weisen** **A** *unr. itr. V.* [1] (zeigen) **auf jmdn./etw. ~weisen** point to *or* indicate sb./sth.; [2] **auf etw.** (*Akk.*) **~weisen** (anzeigen) point to *or* indicate sth.; (verweisen) point sth. out; refer to sth.; **darauf ~weisen, dass ...** point to the fact that *or* indicate that/point out that ...; **B** *unr. tr. V.* **jmdn. auf etw.** (*Akk.*) **~weisen** point sth. out to sb.; draw sb.'s attention to sth.; **~weisend** *Adj.* (Grammatik) demonstrative ‹*pronoun, adjective, etc.*›

Hinweis-: **~schild** *das* sign; (Straßenschild) [road] sign; **~tafel** *die* information board

hin-, Hin-: **~|wenden** **A** *unr. tr. V.* turn (**zu** towards); **B** *unr. refl. V.* turn (**zu** to, towards); **wo soll ich mich jetzt noch ~wenden?** (ugs. fig.) where shall I turn now?; **~wendung** *die* change of direction (**zu** towards); **~|werfen** **A** *unr. tr. V.* [1] (an eine Stelle werfen) throw down; [2] (von sich werfen) throw *or* fling down; [3] (ugs.: aufgeben) chuck in (coll.); [4] (flüchtig schreiben) jot down; (flüchtig zeichnen) dash off; [5] (beiläufig äußern) drop [casually] ‹*remark*›; ask casually ‹*question*›; make casually ‹*accusation*›; say casually ‹*words*›; **eine [beiläufig] ~geworfene Bemerkung** a casual remark; [6] (ugs.: fallen lassen) drop; **B** *unr. refl. V.* **sich [vor jmdm.] ~werfen** throw oneself down [before sb.]

hin·wieder, hin·wiederum *Adv.* (veralt.) on the other hand

hin|wirken *itr. V.* **auf etw.** (*Akk.*) **~:** work towards sth.; **bei jmdm. darauf ~, dass er seine Meinung ändert** try to persuade sb. to change his opinion

Hinz /hɪnts/ *in* **~ und Kunz** (ugs. abwertend) every Tom, Dick and Harry

hin-: **~|zählen** *tr. V.* count out; **~|zaubern** *tr. V.* (ugs.) **etw. ~zaubern** produce sth. as if by magic; **~|zeigen** *itr. V.* point (**zu** to, towards); **~|ziehen** **A** *unr. tr. V.* [1] pull, draw (**zu** to, towards); [2] (zu etw., jmdm. treiben) draw, attract (**zu** to); **sich zu jmdm./etw. ~gezogen fühlen** be *or* feel attracted to sb./sth.; [3] (in die Länge ziehen) draw out; protract; [4] (verzögern) delay; put off; **B** *unr. itr. V.; mit sein* [1] (umziehen) move there; **wo ist sie ~gezogen?** where did she move to?; [2] (an einen Ort ziehen) move (**zu** towards); **am Himmel ~ziehen** (dichter.) sail across the sky; **C** *unr. refl. V.* [1] (sich erstrecken) drag on (**über** + *Akk.* for); [2] (sich verzögern) be delayed; **~|zielen** *itr. V.* **auf etw.** (*Akk.*) **~zielen** aim at sth.; ‹*policies, efforts, etc.*› be aimed at sth.

hin·zu *Adv.* in addition; besides; **dieses Gehalt und noch das Doppelte ~, dann wäre ich zufrieden** I'd be content with this salary and twice as much again *or* on top

hinzu-, Hinzu-: **~|bekommen** *unr. tr. V.* get in addition; **~|denken** *unr. refl. V.* **sich** (*Dat.*) **etw. ~denken** add sth. in one's imagination; **~|dichten** *tr. V.* **etw. ~dichten** make sth. up and add it; add sth. out of one's head; **~|fügen** *tr. V.* add; **~fügung** *die* addition; **unter ~fügung** (*Dat.*) **einer Sache** (*Gen.*) *od.* **von etw.** with the addition of sth.; **~|geben** *unr. tr. V.* [1] (dazugeben) **jmdm. etw. ~geben** give sth. to sb. in addition; [2] (hineingeben) add; **~|gesellen** *refl. V.* **sich [zu] jmdm./etw. ~gesellen** join sb./sth.; **~|gewinnen** *unr. tr. V.* gain in addition; **~|kommen** *unr. itr. V.; mit sein* [1] (zufällig kommen) arrive *or* appear [on the scene]; come along; **er kam gerade** *od.* **genau in dem Moment ~, als ...** he arrived *or* happened to arrive at the very moment when *or* just as ...; [2] (hinkommen) come along *or* up; [3] (sich anschließen) join; **zu etw. ~kommen** join sth.; [4] (~gefügt werden) **zu etw. ~kommen** be added to sth.; **zu der Grippe kam noch eine Lungenentzündung ~:** in addition to the flu he/she also contracted a lung infection; **es kommt noch ~, dass ...** there is also the fact that ...; **~|nehmen** *unr. tr. V.* add; **~|setzen** **A** *refl. V.* **sich zu jmdm./einer Gruppe** *usw.* **~setzen** join sb./a group *etc.*; **B** *tr. V.* add; **~|treten** *unr. itr. V.; mit sein* [1] come up; **zu jmdm./den anderen ~treten** come up to sb./join the others; [2] ▸**~kommen 4**; **~|tun** *unr. tr. V.* (ugs.) add; *s. auch* **dazutun**; **~|verdienen** *tr. V.* **etwas ~verdienen** earn a bit extra; **~|zählen** *tr. V.* add [on]; **~|ziehen** *unr. tr. V.* consult; call in; **~ziehung** *die* consultation; **unter ~ziehung einschlägiger Literatur** by consulting the relevant literature

Hiob /ˈhiːɔp/ (*der*) Job

Hiobs·botschaft *die* bad news

hipp, hipp, hurra /ˈhɪpˈhɪphʊˈraː/ *Interj.* hip, hip, hooray *or* hurrah

Hippe[1] /ˈhɪpə/ *die;* **~, ~n** pruning knife; (des Todes) scythe

Hippe[2] *die;* **~, ~n** (ugs. abwertend) bitch (derog.)

Hipphipphurra /hɪphɪphʊˈraː/ *das;* **~s, ~s** cheer; **dem Sieger ein dreifaches ~:** three cheers for the winner

Hippie /ˈhɪpi/ *der;* **~s, ~s** hippie (coll.)

Hippodrom /hɪpoˈdroːm/ *der od. das;* **~s, ~e** hippodrome

hippokratisch /hɪpoˈkraːtɪʃ/ *Adj.* **der ~e Eid** the Hippocratic oath

Hirn /hɪrn/ *das;* **~[e]s, ~e** [1] ▸**❶ S. 435** brain [2] (Speise; ugs.: Verstand) brains *pl.*; **sein ~ anstrengen** exercise one's mental faculties; **sich** (*Dat.*) **das ~ zermartern** rack one's brains; **welchem ~ ist das entsprungen?** whose brainchild is that?

hirn-, Hirn-: **~anhangs·drüse** *die* ▸**❶ S. 435** (Anat.) pituitary gland *or* body; **~gespinst** *das* (abwertend) fantasy; **~haut** ▸**❶ S. 435** *die* (Anat.) meninges *Pl.*; **~haut·entzündung** *die* ▸**❶ S. 439** (Med.) meningitis; **~infarkt** *der* (Med.) brain infarction; **~kasten** *der* (salopp scherzh.) ▸**Gehirnkasten**; **~los** (abwertend) **A** *Adj.* brainless; **B** *adv.* brainlessly; **~rinde** *die* ▸**❶ S. 435** (Anat.) cerebral cortex; **~rissig** *Adj.* (abwertend) crazy; crack-brained (coll.); **~stamm** *der* ▸**❶ S. 435** (Anat.) brainstem; **~tod** *der* (Med.) brain death; **~tot** *Adj.* brain-dead; **~tumor** *der* ▸**❶ S. 439** (Med.) brain tumour; **~verbrannt** *Adj.* (abwertend) crazy; crack-brained (coll.); **~windung** *die* ▸**❶ S. 435** (Med.) convolution *or* (Med.) gyrus of the brain

Hirsch /hɪrʃ/ *der;* **~[e]s, ~e** [1] deer [2] (Rothirsch) red deer [3] (männlicher Rothirsch) stag; hart [4] (Speise) venison [5] (Schimpfwort) bastard (coll.)

Hirsch-: **~brunft, ~brunst** *die* rut [of the stags]; **während der ~brunft** *od.* **~brunst** while the stags are in rut; **~fänger** *der* (Jägerspr.) [double-edged] hunting knife; **~geweih** *das* [stag's] antlers *pl.*; **ein ~geweih** a set of antlers; **~horn** *das* staghorn; **~horn·salz** *das* salt of hartshorn; ammonium carbonate; **~käfer** *der* stag beetle; **~kalb** *das* [male] deer calf; [male] fawn; **~kuh** *die* hind; **~leder** *das* buckskin; **~ragout** *das* (Kochk.) ragout of venison; **~steak** *das* (Kochk.) venison steak

Hirse /ˈhɪrzə/ *die;* **~, ~n** millet

Hirse·brei *der* millet gruel

Hirt /hɪrt/ *der;* **~en, ~en** herdsman; (Schaf~) shepherd

Hirte *der;* ~**n**, ~**n** ▸❶ **S. 113** (geh.) ▸**Hirt**; **der Gute** ~: the Good Shepherd

Hirten-: ~**amt** *das* (kath. Rel.) pastorate; pastoral office; ~**brief** *der* (kath. Rel.) pastoral letter; ~**dichtung** *die* (Literaturw.) pastoral *or* bucolic poetry; ~**hund** *der* sheepdog; ~**junge** *der,* ~**knabe** *der* (dicht.) shepherd boy; ~**mädchen** *das* shepherd girl; ~**spiel** *das* pastoral [play]; ~**stab** *der* 1 (geh.) shepherd's crook; 2 (kath. Rel.) pastoral staff; crosier; ~**täschel[kraut]** *das;* ~**s** (Bot.) shepherd's purse; ~**volk** *das* pastoral people

Hirtin *die;* ~, ~**nen** ▸❶ **S. 113** (veralt. selten) shepherdess

his, His /hɪs/ *das;* ~, ~ (Musik) B sharp; *s. auch* **a, 1**

hispanisieren /hɪspani'zi:rən/ *tr. V.* Hispanicize

Hispanist *der;* ~**en**, ~**en**, **Hispanistin** *die;* ~, ~**nen** Hispanist; Hispanicist

Hispanistik *die;* ~: study of Hispanic languages and literature; ≈ Hispanic studies

hissen /'hɪsn̩/ *tr. V.* hoist ‹*sail*›; hoist, run up ‹*flag*›

Histamin /hɪsta'mi:n/ *das;* ~**s** (Chemie) histamine

Histologie /hɪstolo'gi:/ *die;* ~ (Med.) histology *no art.*

histologisch *Adj.* (Med.) histological

Histörchen /hɪs'tø:ɐ̯çən/ *das;* ~**s**, ~ (scherzh.) anecdote

Historie /hɪs'to:ri̯ə/ *die;* ~, ~**n** (veralt.) 1 history 2 (Erzählung) story; tale

Historien-: ~**maler** *der* painter of historical scenes; historical painter; ~**malerei** *die* painting of historical scenes; historical painting; ~**malerin** *die* ▸~**maler**

Historiker /hɪs'to:rikɐ/ *der;* ~**s**, ~, **Historikerin** *die;* ~, ~**nen** historian

historisch
A *Adj.* 1 historical 2 (geschichtlich bedeutungsvoll) historic
B *adv.* 1 **das ist** ~ **belegt** this is historically attested; there is historical evidence for this; **etw.** ~ **erklären** explain sth. in historical terms; ~ **erwiesen sein** be historically proven; **etw.** ~ **betrachten** see sth. in the light of history *or* in historical terms 2 ~ **höchst bedeutsam** of historic importance

historisieren *itr. V.* (geh.) historicize

Historismus *der;* ~: historicism

Hit /hɪt/ *der;* ~**[s]**, ~**s** (ugs.) hit

Hitler- /'hɪtlɐ-/: ~**bärtchen** *das* (ugs.) Hitler moustache; ~**faschismus** *der* Hitlerite fascism; ~**gruß** *der* Nazi salute; ~**jugend** *die* Hitler Youth; ~**junge** *der* member of the Hitler Youth; ~**zeit** *die* Hitler era

Hit-: ~**liste** *die* top ten/twenty/thirty *etc.;* ~**parade** *die* hit parade

Hitze /'hɪtsə/ *die;* ~, (fachspr.:) ~**n** heat; **bei dieser** ~: in this heat; **etw. bei mittlerer/mäßiger** ~ **backen** bake sth. in a medium/moderate oven; **die fliegende** ~ **haben** (fig.) have [the] hot flushes; **sich in** ~ (*Akk.*) **reden** (fig.) get more and more excited as one talks; **in der** ~ **des Gefechts** in the heat of the moment

hitze-, Hitze-: ~**abweisend** *Adj.* heat-reflecting; ~**beständig** *Adj.* heat-resistant, heat-resisting ‹*metal etc.*›; heatproof, heat-resistant ‹*glass etc.*›; ~**bläschen** *das* heat spot; ~**empfindlich** *Adj.* sensitive to heat *postpos.;* heat-sensitive ‹*material*›; ~**frei** *Adj.* ~**frei haben/bekommen** have/be given the rest of the day off [school/work] because of excessively hot weather; ~**periode** *die* hot spell; spell *or* period of hot weather; (~welle) heat wave; ~**schild** *der* (Raumf.) heat shield; ~**wallung** *die* hot flush; ~**welle** *die* heat wave

hitzig *Adj.* 1 (heftig) hot-tempered; quick-tempered; ~ **werden** flare up; fly into a temper 2 (leidenschaftlich) hot-blooded ‹*person, race, etc.*›; hot ‹*blood*›; passionate ‹*supporter, advocate, etc.*› 3 (erregt) heated ‹*discussion, argument, words, etc.*› 4 (veralt.: fiebrig) fevered ‹*brow, cheeks, etc.*›; feverish ‹*red*› 5 (läufig) on *or* in heat *pred.*

Hitzigkeit *die;* ~ 1 (Heftigkeit) hot *or* quick temper 2 (Leidenschaftlichkeit) hot-bloodedness

hitz-, Hitz-: ~**kopf** *der* hothead; ~**köpfig** *Adj.* hot-headed; ~**pocke** *die* ▸**Hitzebläschen**; ~**schlag** *der* heatstroke

HIV *Abk.* = **humanes Immundefizienzvirus** HIV

HIV-: ~**-infiziert** *Adj.* HIV-infected; ~**-positiv** *Adj.* HIV-positive; ~**-Test** *der* HIV test

Hiwi /'hi:vi/ *der;* ~**s**, ~**s** laboratory *or* (coll.) lab/departmental/library assistant

HJ *Abk.* (ns.) = **Hitlerjugend**

hl *Abk.* = **Hektoliter** hl

hl. *Abk.* = **heilig** St.

hm /hm̩/ *Interj.* h'm; hem

H-Milch /'ha:-/ *die;* ~: long-life *or* UHT milk

h-Moll /'ha:-/ *das* (Musik) B minor; *s. auch* **a-Moll**

HNO-Arzt /ha:|ɛn'|o:-/ *der,* **HNO-Ärztin** *die* ENT specialist

HO /ha:|'o:/ *die;* ~ (DDR) 1 ▸**Handelsorganisation 2** 2 ▸~**-Geschäft**

hob /ho:p/ *1. u. 3. Pers. Sg. Prät. v.* **heben**

Hobby /'hɔbi/ *das;* ~**s**, ~**s** hobby

Hobby- amateur ‹*gardener, archaeologist, astronomer, etc.*›

Hobby·raum *der* hobby room

Hobel /'ho:bl̩/ *der;* ~**s**, ~ 1 plane 2 (Küchengerät) [vegetable] slicer

Hobel-: ~**bank** *die; Pl.* ~**bänke** carpenter's *or* woodworker's bench; ~**eisen** *das,* ~**messer** *das* plane iron

hobeln *tr., itr. V.* 1 plane; **an etw.** (*Dat.*) ~: plane sth. 2 (schneiden) slice

Hobel·span *der* shaving

hoch /ho:x/, **höher** /'hø:ɐ/, **höchst...** /'hø:çst.../
A *Adj.* 1 ▸❶ **S. 374** (von beträchtlicher Höhe) high; high, tall ‹*building*›; tall ‹*tree, mast*›; long ‹*grass*›; deep ‹*snow, water*›; long, tall ‹*ladder*›; high-ceilinged ‹*room*›; **10 m** ~: 10 m high; **eine hohe Stirn** a high forehead; **er bekommt eine hohe Stirn** he's receding; **von hoher Gestalt** (geh.) tall in stature; of tall stature; **hohe Absätze** high heels; **hohe Schuhe** (mit hohem Schaft) high boots; (mit hohen Absätzen) high-heeled shoes
2 (mengenmäßig groß) high ‹*price, wage, rent, speed, pressure, temperature, sensitivity*›; heavy ‹*fine*›; great ‹*weight*›; large ‹*sum, amount*›; high, large, big ‹*profit*›; severe, extensive ‹*damage*›; **einen hohen Blutdruck haben** have high blood pressure
3 (zeitlich fortgeschritten) great ‹*age*›; **ein hohes Alter erreichen** live to *or* reach a ripe old age; **es ist höchste Zeit, dass ...** it is high time that ...
4 (oben in einer Rangordnung) high ‹*birth, office*›; high-ranking ‹*officer, civil servant*›; senior ‹*official, officer, post*›; high-level ‹*diplomacy, politics*›; important ‹*guest, festival*›; **Verhandlungen auf höchster Ebene** top-level negotiations; **der hohe Adel** the higher ranks of the nobility; **eine hohe Ehre** a great honour; **mit höchster Diskretion/Eile** with the greatest discretion/urgency; **das Höchste Wesen** the Supreme Being; **sich zu Höherem berufen fühlen** feel called to higher things; **höchste Gefahr** extreme danger; **im höchsten Fall[e]** at the most; *s. auch* **Blödsinn**; **Gefühl 2**; **Gewalt 4**; **Haus 6**; **Jagd 1**; **Tier**; **Tochter 1**
5 (qualitativ ~ stehend) high ‹*standard, opinion*›; great ‹*responsibility, concentration, talent, happiness, good, importance*›; **die hohe Schule** (Reiten) haute école
6 (Musik) high ‹*voice, note*›; **das hohe C** top C
7 ▸❶ **S. 826** (Math.) **vier** ~ **zwei** four to the power [of] two; four squared
8 (in großer Höhe) high ‹*cloud, branch, etc.*›; **der hohe Norden** (fig.) the far North
9 (auf dem Höhepunkt) **das hohe Mittelalter** the High Middle Ages
10 *in* **das ist mir zu** ~ (ugs.) that's beyond me; that went over my head
B *adv.* 1 (in großer Höhe) high; ~ **oben am Himmel** high up in the sky; ~ **über uns** high above us; **die Sonne steht** ~: the sun is high in the sky; **wenn die Sonne am höchsten steht** when the sun is [at its] highest; ~ **zu Ross** (geh.) on horseback; **er wohnt drei Treppen** ~: he lives on the third (Brit.) *or* (Amer.) fourth floor; ~ **auf etw.** (*Dat.*) **sitzen** sit high up on sth.
2 (nach oben) up; **Kopf** ~! chin up! **die Flammen loderten** ~: the flames leapt up high; **zu** ~ **zielen** aim too high; **ein** ~ **aufgeschossener Junge** a very tall lad; **einen Ball** ~ **in die Luft werfen** throw a ball high in the air; **die Nase** ~ **tragen** walk around with one's nose in the air; **die Preise höher schrauben** (fig.) push up the prices; ~ **gesteckt** (fig.) ambitious ‹*goal, plan*›
3 (zahlenmäßig viel) highly ‹*taxed, paid*›; heavily ‹*taxed*›; ~ **verschuldet/versichert** heavily in debt/insured for a large sum [of money]; ~ **gewinnen/verlieren** (Sport) win/lose by a large margin; **wenn es** ~ **kommt** at [the] most
4 (dem Rang nach oben) **etw.** ~ **und heilig versprechen** promise sth. faithfully; ~ **hinauswollen** (ugs.) aim high; have great ambitions; **zu** ~ **hinauswollen** (ugs.) aim too high; be too ambitious; ~ **gestellt** ‹*person*› in a high position; important ‹*person*›; ~ **stehend** ‹*person*› of high standing; **geistig** ~ **stehend** intellectually distinguished; ‹*person*› of high intellect; **sittlich** ~ **stehend** high-minded
5 (sehr) highly ‹*gifted, delighted, satisfied, respected, regarded*›; most ‹*welcome*›; highly, greatly ‹*esteemed*›; **jmdm. etw.** ~ **anrechnen** consider sth. [to be] greatly to sb.'s credit; **jmdn.** ~ **verehren** esteem sb. highly *or* greatly
6 (zeitlich fortgeschritten) ~ **in den Siebzigern** well into his/her seventies
7 (Musik) high
8 (in Wendungen) **das Herz höher schlagen lassen** make sb.'s heart beat faster; **es ging** ~ **her** things were pretty lively; **sie kamen drei Mann** ~: three of them came; there were three of them; *s. auch* **höchst**

Hoch *das;* ~**s**, ~**s** 1 (~ruf) **ein [dreifaches]** ~ **auf jmdn. ausbringen** give three cheers for sb.; **ein** ~ **dem Gastgeber!** three cheers for the host! 2 (Met.) high

hoch-: ~**achtbar** *Adj.* highly respectable; *~|**achten** ▸**achten A**

Hoch·achtung *die* great respect; high esteem; ~ **vor jmdm. haben** have a great respect for sb.; hold sb. in high esteem; **meine** ~! may I congratulate you; **mit vorzüglicher** ~ (veralt.: Briefschluss) most respectfully yours (dated); yours faithfully

hochachtungs·voll *Adv.* (Briefschluss) yours faithfully

hoch-, Hoch-: ~**adel** *der* higher ranks *pl.* of the nobility; ~**adelig**, ~**adlig** *Adj.* from the higher ranks of the nobility *postpos.;* ~**adelig geboren** born into the higher ranks of the nobility; ~**aktuell** *Adj.* highly topical; ~**alpin** *Adj.* high alpine *attrib.* ‹*landscape, flora, fauna, etc.*›; ~**altar** *der* high altar; ~**amt** *das* (kath. Rel.) high mass; ~**angesehen** *Adj.* ▸**hoch B5**; ~**anständig** A *Adj.* very decent; B *adv.* very *or* most decently; ~**antenne** *die* roof aerial (Brit.) *or* (Amer.) antenna; ~|**arbeiten** *refl. V.* work one's way up; ~**bahn** *die* overhead railway; elevated railroad (Amer.); ~**barren** *der* (Sport) parallel bars *pl.* (*set at international height of 180 cm.*); ~**bau** *der* [building] construction *no art.;* ~**- und Tiefbau** [building] construction and civil engineering *no art.;* ~**befriedigt** *Adj.* highly satisfied; ~**begabt** ▸**begabt**; ~**beglückt** *Adj.* blissfully happy; ~**beinig** *Adj.* long-legged ‹*person, animal*›; ‹*table, sofa, etc.*› with long legs; ~**bejahrt** *Adj.* (geh.) ▸~**betagt**; ~|**bekommen** *unr. tr. V.* [manage to] lift; [manage to] do up ‹*zip*›; *~**beladen** ▸**beladen²**; ~**berühmt** *Adj.* very famous; ~**betagt** *Adj.* aged; ‹*person*› advanced in years *postpos.;* ~**betrieb** *der* (ugs.) **es herrschte** ~**betrieb im Geschäft** the shop was at its busiest; **heute herrschte** ~**betrieb im Büro** the office was very busy today; ~**bezahlt** ▸**bezahlen A**; ~|**biegen** A *unr. tr. V.* **etw.** ~**biegen** bend

h

sth. up[wards]; [B] *unr. refl. V.* bend up; **~|binden** *unr. tr. V.* tie up ‹*plant*›; put up ‹*hair*›; **~|blicken** *itr. V.* look up; **~blüte** *die* golden age; **~|bringen** *unr. tr. V.* [1] (nach oben bringen) bring up; [2] (ugs.: in die Wohnung bringen) bring in[to the flat (esp. Brit.) *or* (esp. Amer.) apartment]; [3] (gesund machen) **jmdn. ~bringen** put sb. on his/her feet; [4] (ugs.: ärgern) **jmdn. ~bringen** put sb.'s back up; **~burg** *die* stronghold; **~busig** *Adj.* high-bosomed; **~dekoriert** ▸**dekorieren 2**; **~deutsch** *Adj.* standard *or* High German; **die ~deutsche Lautverschiebung** the High German *or* second sound shift; **mit jmdm. ~deutsch sprechen** *od.* **reden** (ugs.) give sb. a piece of one's mind; **~deutsch** *das*, **~deutsche** *das* standard *or* High German; **~|dienen** *refl. V.* work one's way up; **~dotiert** ▸**dotiert**; **~|drehen** *tr. V.* [1] (in die Höhe drehen) wind up ‹*window, barrier, etc.*›; [2] (Technik) rev [up] (coll.) ‹*engine*›

> **Hochdeutsch**
>
> There are many regional variations and dialects in Germany, Austria, and Switzerland (64 per cent of Swiss people speak *Schwyzerdütsch*). *Hochdeutsch* is the standard German that can be understood by all German speakers. It is probably the only way for a Bavarian, Austrian or Swiss to communicate with a North German. Newspapers and other publications are generally printed in *Hochdeutsch*, which is regarded as 'proper' German.

Hoch·druck[1] *der; Pl.* **Hoch·drücke** [1] (Physik, Met.) high pressure [2] (Geschäftigkeit) **mit** *od.* **unter ~ arbeiten** (ugs.) work flat out *or* at full stretch; **in allen Abteilungen herrschte ~:** all departments were at full stretch [3] ▸❶ **S. 439** (Med.) high blood pressure; hypertension (Med.)

Hoch·druck[2] *der; Pl.* **~e** (Druckw.) [1] (Verfahren) relief *or* letterpress printing; **etw. im ~ herstellen/drucken** produce/print sth. by letterpress [2] (Erzeugnis) piece of letterpress work; **~e** letterpress work

Hochdruck·gebiet *das* high-pressure area

hoch-, Hoch-: ~ebene *die* plateau; tableland; **~empfindlich** ▸**empfindlich A1**; **~entwickelt** ▸**entwickeln B**; **~erhoben** ▸**erheben A1**; **~explosiv** *Adj.* (auch fig.) highly explosive; **~|fahren** [A] *unr. itr. V.; mit sein* [1] (ugs.: nach oben fahren) go up; (mit dem Auto) drive up; (mit dem Fahrrad, Motorrad) ride up; [2] (ugs.: nach Norden fahren) drive up; [3] (auffahren) start up; **aus dem Sessel ~fahren** start [up] from one's chair; **aus dem Schlaf ~fahren** wake up with a start; [4] (aufbrausen) flare up; [5] (DV) start [up]; boot [up]; [B] *unr. tr. V.* [1] (ugs.) **jmdn./etw. ~fahren** take sb./sth. up; **das Auto ~fahren** drive the car up; [2] (DV) start [up]; boot [up]; **~fahrend** *Adj.* arrogant; supercilious; **~fein** *Adj.* of the finest quality *postpos.*; **aus ~feiner Schokolade/~feinem Batist** of the finest chocolate/batiste; **~finanz** *die* high finance; **~fläche** *die* plateau; tableland; **~|fliegen** *unr. itr. V.; mit sein* fly up [into the air]; **~fliegend** *Adj.* ambitious ‹*plan, idea, etc.*›; **~flut** *die* high water *or* tide; (fig.) flood; **~form** *die* peak *or* top form; **~format** *das* upright format; **ein Bild/Blatt in ~format** a picture/sheet with an upright format; **~frequenz** *die* (Physik) high frequency; **~frequenz·technik** *die* radio-frequency engineering *no art.*; **~frisur** *die* upswept hairstyle; **~garage** *die* multistorey car park; **~geachtet** ▸**geachtet B**; **~gebildet** *Adj.* highly cultured; **~gebirge** *das* [high] mountains *pl.*; **~gebirgs·landschaft** *die* high-mountain region; **~geboren** *Adj.* (veralt.) highborn; **~geehrt** ▸**ehren 1**; **~gefühl** *das* [feeling of] elation; **im ~gefühl des Erfolges/Sieges** in his/her *etc.* elation at success/victory; **~|gehen** *unr. itr. V.; mit sein* [1] (steigen) go up; rise; [2] (ugs.: hinaufgehen) go up; **die Treppe ~gehen** go up the stairs *or* upstairs; [3] (ugs.: zornig werden) blow one's top (coll.); explode; [4] (ugs.: explodieren) ‹*bomb, mine*› go off; ‹*bridge, building, etc.*› go up; **etw. ~gehen lassen** (salopp) blow sth. up; [5] (ugs.: aufgedeckt werden) get caught *or* (coll.) nabbed; **jmdn. ~gehen lassen** ‹*informer*› grass *or* squeal on sb. (sl.); **die Polizei ließ den Rauschgiftring ~gehen** the police smashed the drug ring; **~geistig** *Adj.* highly intellectual; ***~gelegen** ▸**gelegen B 2**; **~gelehrt** *Adj.* extremely *or* very learned *or* erudite; **~gelobt** *Adj.* highly praised; **~gemut** /-gəmu:t/ (geh.) [A] *Adj.* cheerful; [B] *adv.* cheerfully; in good spirits; **~genuss**, ***~genuß** *der:* **in ein ~genuss sein** be a real delight; ‹*meal, concert, etc.*› be a real treat; **ihm zuzuhören ist ein ~genuss** he is a real delight to listen to; **~geschätzt** ▸**schätzen A2**; **~gescheit** *Adj.* ▸**~intelligent**; **~geschlossen** *Adj.* high-necked ‹*dress*›; **~geschwindigkeits·zug** *der* high-speed train; **~gesinnt** *Adj.* (geh.) high-minded; noble-minded; **~gespannt** *Adj.* great, high ‹*expectations*›; **~gesteckt** ▸**hoch B 2**; **~gestellt** ▸**hoch B 4**; **~gestimmt** *Adj.* (geh.) elated; **~gestochen** (ugs. abwertend) [A] *Adj.* [1] (anspruchsvoll) highbrow; (geschraubt) stilted ‹*style*›; [2] (eingebildet) conceited; stuck-up; [B] *adv.* in a highbrow way (coll.); **~gewachsen** ▸**wachsen**[1] **1**; **~gezüchtet** *Adj.* highly-bred ‹*animal*›; **ein ~gezüchteter Motor** a very finely tuned engine

Hoch·glanz *der:* **ein Foto in ~** (*Dat.*) a high-gloss print; **etw. auf ~** (*Akk.*) **polieren** polish sth. until it shines *or* gleams; **etw. auf ~** (*Akk.*) **bringen** give sth. a high polish; (fig.) make sth. spick and span

Hochglanz·folie *die* glazing sheet

hoch-, Hoch-: ~gradig [A] *Adj.* extreme; [B] *adv.* extremely; **~hackig** *Adj.* high-heeled ‹*shoe*›; **~|halten** *unr. tr. V.* [1] hold up ‹*arms*›; [2] (geh.: schützen) uphold ‹*truth, tradition, etc.*›; **jmds. Andenken ~halten** honour sb.'s memory; **~haus** *das* high-rise building; **~|heben** *unr. tr. V.* lift up; raise ‹*arm, leg, etc.*›; raise, hold up ‹*hand*›; **~herrschaftlich** *Adj.* palatial ‹*house, apartment*›; **~herzig** *Adj.* (geh.) magnanimous; generous; **~herzigkeit** *die;* **~~:** magnanimity; generosity; **~intelligent** *Adj.* highly intelligent; **~interessant** *Adj.* extremely *or* most interesting; fascinating; **~|jagen** *tr. V.* [1] scare up ‹*birds*›; forcibly rouse ‹*sleeper*›; [2] (Jargon) race, (coll.) rev up ‹*engine*›; [3] (ugs.: sprengen) blow up; **~|jubeln** *tr. V.* (ugs.) **jmdn./etw. ~jubeln** build sb. up as a star/sth. up as a hit; **~kant** *Adv.* [1] on end; [2] (ugs.) *in* **jmdn. ~kant hinauswerfen** *od.* (salopp) **rausschmeißen** chuck sb. out (sl.); throw sb. out on his/her ear (coll.); **~kant hinausfliegen** *od.* (salopp) **rausfliegen** be chucked out (sl.); be thrown out on one's ear (coll.); **~kantig** *Adv.* ▸**~kant**; **~karätig** /-ka'rɛ:tɪç/ *Adj.* [1] high-carat ‹*gold, diamond*›; [2] (fig.) top-flight (coll.); **~kirche** *die* High Church; **~|klappen** [A] *tr. V.* fold up ‹*chair, table*›; raise, lift up ‹*lid, car bonnet*›; turn up ‹*collar*›; [B] *itr. V.; mit sein* fold up; **~|klettern** *itr. V.; mit sein* (ugs.) climb up; **den Baum ~klettern** climb [up] the tree; **~kochen** *itr. V; mit sein* ‹*emotions*› run high; **die Stimmung ist hochgekocht** feelings are running high; **~|kommen** *unr. itr. V.; mit sein* (ugs.) [1] come up; [2] (vorwärts kommen) get on; [3] (aus dem Magen) **ihr kam das Essen ~:** she threw up (coll.) *or* brought up her meal; **es kommt einem ~, wenn ...** (fig.) it makes you sick when ...; [4] (sich erheben) get up; (sich erheben können) be able to get up; [5] (fig.) **in jmdm. ~kommen** rise up in sb.; **~konjunktur** *die* (Wirtsch.) boom; **auf dem Automarkt herrscht ~konjunktur** the car market is booming; there's a boom in car sales; **~|können** *unr. V.* (ugs.) be able to get up; **~konzentriert** *Adj.* highly concentrated; **~|krempeln** *tr. V.* roll up ‹*sleeve, trouser leg*›; **~|kriegen** *tr. V.* (ugs.) ▸**~bekommen**; **einen ~kriegen** (salopp) get it up (sl.); **~kultur** *die* advanced civilization *or* culture; **~|kurbeln** *tr. V.* wind up; **~|laden** *unr. tr. V.* (DV) upload; **~lage** *die* higher region; **~land** *das* highlands *pl.*; **~|leben** *itr. V.:* *in* **jmdn./etw. ~leben lassen** cheer sb./sth.; **er/unser Verein lebe ~!** three cheers for him/our club!; **der König lebe ~!** long live the king!; **~|legen** *tr. V.* **ein gebrochenes Bein ~legen** support a broken leg in a raised position; **die Beine ~legen** put one's feet up

Hoch·leistung *die* outstanding performance

Hochleistungs·sport *der* top-level sport

höchlich[st] /'hø:çlɪç(st)/ *Adv.* (veralt.) highly; greatly; most

hoch-, Hoch-: ~mittelalter *das* High Middle Ages; **~modern** [A] *Adj.* ultramodern; [B] *adv.* **~modern gekleidet/eingerichtet sein** be extremely fashionably dressed *or* dressed in the very latest fashions/be furnished in the very latest style; **~moor** *das* (Geogr.) high-moor bog; **~motiviert** ▸**motivieren 2**; **~mut** *der* arrogance; **~mut kommt vor dem Fall** (Spr.) pride goes before a fall (prov.); **~mütig** *Adj.* arrogant; **~näsig** /-nɛ:zɪç/ *Adj.* (abwertend) stuck-up; conceited; **~näsigkeit** *die;* **~~** (abwertend) conceitedness; **~nebel** *der* low stratus [cloud]; **~|nehmen** *unr. tr. V.* [1] lift *or* pick up; [2] (ugs.: verspotten) **jmdn. ~nehmen** pull sb.'s leg; [3] (ugs.: nach oben nehmen) **jmdn./etw. mit ~nehmen** take sb./sth. up with one; [4] (salopp: verhaften) run in; **~not·peinlich** *Adj.* (veralt.) ‹*interrogation*› under torture; **ein ~notpeinliches Verhör** (fig.: scherzh.) an inquisition; **~ofen** *der* blast furnace; **~offiziell** *Adj.* extremely formal; **~|päppeln** *tr. V.* (salopp) feed up; **~parterre** *das* upper ground floor; **~plateau** *das* high plateau; **~politisch** *Adj.* highly political; **~prozentig** *Adj.* high-proof ‹*spirits*›; **~punkt** *der* (Math.) maximum; **~qualifiziert** ▸**qualifiziert B 2**; **~rädrig** *Adj.* large-wheeled; **~|ragen** *itr. V.* rise *or* tower up; **~|rappeln** *refl. V.* ▸**aufrappeln**; **~|rechnen** project; **~rechnung** *die* (Statistik) projection; **~reck** *das* (Turnen) high *or* horizontal bar; **~rein** *Adj.* (fachspr.) 100% pure; hundred-per-cent pure; **~|reißen** *unr. tr. V.* whip up; pull up ‹*aircraft*›; **die Arme ~reißen** throw one's arms up; **~relief** *das* high relief; **~rot** *Adj.* bright red; **~rot im Gesicht werden** (aus Verlegenheit) go as red as a beetroot; **~ruf** *der* cheer; **~|rutschen** *itr. V.; mit sein* (ugs.) ‹*dress, shirt, etc.*› ride up; **~saison** *die* high season; **~|schaukeln** *tr. V.* (ugs.) blow up ‹*problem, incident, etc.*›; **sich [gegenseitig] ~schaukeln** goad each other; **~|scheuchen** *tr. V.* ▸**aufscheuchen**; **~|schieben** *unr. tr. V.* (ugs.) push up; **~|schießen** [A] *unr. tr. V.* send up, launch ‹*rocket, space probe, etc.*›; [B] *unr. itr. V.; mit sein* (auch fig.) shoot up; **~|schlagen** [A] *unr. tr. V.* turn up ‹*collar, brim*›; [B] *unr. itr. V.; mit sein* ‹*water, waves*› surge up; ‹*flames*› leap up; **Wellen der Begeisterung schlugen ~** (fig.) there was a great surge of enthusiasm; **~|schnellen** *itr. V.; mit sein* leap up; **~schrank** *der* wardrobe; **~|schrauben** [A] *tr. V.* [1] raise ‹*seat*› (*by screwing*); [2] (fig.) force up ‹*prices*›; step up, increase ‹*demands*›; raise ‹*expectations*›; [B] *refl. V.* circle up[wards]; **~|schrecken** ▸**aufschrecken**; **~|scrollen** (DV) *itr. u. tr. V.* scroll up

Hochschul·bildung *die* college/university education

Hoch-: ~schule *die* college; (Universität) university; **~schüler** *der*, **~schülerin** *die* college/university student

> **Hochschule**
>
> German *Hochschulen* (universities and colleges) have up to now generally not charged fees, but at least some *Länder* will in the near future introduce them. Anybody who has passed the **Abitur** is entitled to go to university (except for some subjects which have a **Numerus Clausus**). They tend to be very large and impersonal institutions. Students may receive a **BAföG** grant and often take more than the minimum 8 semesters (4 years) to complete their course.

Hochschul-: ~lehrer *der*, **~lehrerin** *die* ▸❶ **S. 113** college/university lecturer *or* teacher; **~studium** *das* college/university studies *pl., no art.;* **~wesen** *das* university and college system; (Bereich) higher education

hoch·schwanger *Adj.* in an advanced stage of pregnancy *postpos.;* very pregnant (coll.)

Hoch·see *die* open sea

hochsee-, Hochsee-: ~fischerei *die* deep-sea fishing *no art.;* **~flotte** *die* deep sea fleet; **~jacht** *die* ocean-going yacht; **~tüchtig** *Adj.* seaworthy

Hoch·seil *das* high wire

Hochseil-: ~akrobat *der,* **~akrobatin** *die,* **~artist** *der,* **~artistin** *die* ▸ℹ **S. 113** performer on the high wire

hoch-, Hoch-: ~sensibel **A** *Adj.* highly sensitive; **B** *adv.* ‹*treat, reflect, depict*› with great sensitivity; ‹*react*› very sensitively; **~sicherheits·trakt** *der* high-security wing; **~sitz** *der* (Jagdw.) raised hide; **~sommer** *der* high summer; midsummer; **~sommerlich** *Adj.* very summery ‹*weather etc.*›

Hoch·spannung *die* ① (Elektrot.) high voltage *or* tension; **Vorsicht, ~spannung!** danger — high voltage ② (gespannte Stimmung) high tension; **es herrscht ~spannung** there's a great deal of tension

Hochspannungs-: ~leitung *die* high voltage *or* high tension [transmission] line; power line; **~mast** *der* electricity pylon

hoch-, Hoch-: ~|spielen *tr. V.* blow up ‹*incident, affair, etc.*›; **~sprache** *die* standard language; **~sprachlich** **A** *Adj.* standard; **B** *adv.* **sich ~sprachlich ausdrücken** speak the standard language; **~|springen** *unr. itr. V.; mit sein* ① jump *or* leap up; **an jmdm. ~springen** ‹*dog etc.*› jump up at sb.; ② *nur im Inf. u. Part. gebr.* (Sport) do the high jump; **~springer** *der,* **~springerin** *die* (Sport) high jumper; **~sprung** *der* (Sport) high jump; (einzelner Sprung) jump; **~sprung·anlage** *die* (Sport) high jump apparatus

höchst /hø:çst/ *Adv.* extremely; most

höchst... ▸**hoch**

Höchstädt /'hø:çʃtɛt/ *(das);* **~s: die Schlacht bei ~:** the Battle of Blenheim

hoch-, Hoch-: ~stämmig *Adj.* standard ‹*rose*›; **~stand** *der* (Jagdw.) raised stand; **~stapelei** /-ʃta:pə'lai/ *die;* **~~, ~~en** ① fraud; **eine ~stapelei** a confidence trick; ② (Aufschneiderei) empty boasting; **~|stapeln** *itr. V.* ① perpetrate a fraud/frauds; ② (aufschneiden) make empty boasts; **~stapler** *der* ① confidence trickster; conman (coll.); ② (Aufschneider) fraud; **~staplerin** *die;* **~~, ~~nen** ① confidence trickster; ② (Aufschneiderin) fraud

Höchst-: ~belastung *die* extreme strain *or* stress *no indef. art.;* (Technik) maximum [safe] load; **~betrag** *der* maximum amount; **~bietende** *der/die; adj. Dekl.* highest bidder

hoch-: ~stehend ▸**hoch B 4**; **~|steigen** *unr. itr. V.; mit sein* ① climb; **die Treppe/Stufen ~steigen** climb the stairs/steps; ② ‹*bubbles, smoke, etc.*› rise; ‹*rocket*› go up; ③ (langsam entstehen) rise up; ‹*tears*› well up; **Freude/Wut stieg in ihr ~:** joy rose in her heart/rage rose [up] inside her

höchst·eigen *Adj.* (veralt.; noch scherzh.) **in ~er Person** in person

hoch-: ~|stellen *tr. V.* ① put up; ② (~klappen) turn up ‹*collar*›; ③ (Math.) **eine ~gestellte Zahl** a superior number; *s. auch* **hochgestellt**; **~|stemmen** *tr. V.* ① lift; ② (aufrichten) **sich/seinen Oberkörper ~stemmen** raise oneself [up]

höchsten·falls /'hø:çstn̩-/ *Adv.* at [the] most *or* the outside; at the very most

höchstens *Adv.* ① (nicht mehr als) at most; (bestenfalls) at best; **in ~** *od.* **~ in drei Fällen** in three cases at most ② (außer) **sie verreist nicht, ~ dass sie einmal zu ihren Verwandten fährt** she never goes away anywhere, apart from *or* except for visiting her relations once in a while

Höchst-: ~fall *der: in* **im ~fall** at [the] most *or* the outside; at the very most; **~form** *die* (bes. Sport) peak *or* top form; **~gebot** *das* highest bid *or* offer; **etw. gegen ~gebot verkaufen** sell sth. to the highest bidder; **„große Briefmarkensammlung gegen ~gebot zu verkaufen"** 'offers invited for large stamp collection'; **~geschwindigkeit** *die* ▸ℹ **S. 310** top *or* maximum speed; (Geschwindigkeitsbegrenzung) speed limit; **~grenze** *die* maximum

hoch|stilisieren *tr. V.* (abwertend) build up (**zu** into)

Hoch·stimmung *die* festive mood; high spirits *pl.;* **in ~ sein** be in a festive mood

höchst-, Höchst-: ~leistung *die* supreme performance; (Ergebnis) supreme achievement; (Technik) maximum performance; **~maß** *das:* **ein ~maß an etw.** *(Dat.)* a very high degree of sth.; **ein ~maß von etw.** *(Dat.)* a maximum [amount] of sth.; **~möglich** *Adj.* highest possible; **~persönlich** **A** *Adj.* personal; **B** *adv.* in person; **~preis** *der* (~möglicher Preis) highest price; (~zulässiger Preis) maximum price

Hoch·straße *die* overpass; flyover (Brit.)

hoch|streifen *tr. V.* pull up

höchst-, Höchst-: ~richterlich *Adj.* **eine ~richterliche Entscheidung** a ruling of the supreme court; **~satz** *der* maximum *or* top rate; **~selbst** *indekl. Pron.* (veralt., noch scherzh.) in person; **~stand** *der* highest level; **~strafe** *die* maximum penalty; **~wahrscheinlich** *Adv.* very probably; **~wert** *der* maximum value; **~zulässig** /*auch:* '-'--/ *Adj.* maximum [permissible] ‹*weight, speed, etc.*›

hoch-, Hoch-: ~tal *das* high[-lying] valley; **~tour** *die: in* **auf ~touren laufen** run at top *or* full speed; (intensiv betrieben werden) be in full swing; **einen Motor auf ~touren bringen** rev an engine up to full speed (coll.); **~tourig** /-tu:rɪç/ (Technik) **A** *Adj.* fast-revving (coll.) ‹*engine*›; **B** *adv.* **~tourig fahren** drive at high revs (coll.); **~trabend** (abwertend) **A** *Adj.* pretentious; high-flown; **B** *adv.* pretentiously; in a high-flown manner; **~|tragen** *unr. tr. V.* carry up; **~|treiben** *unr. tr. V.* ① (ugs.: hinauftreiben) drive up; **die Schafe den Berg ~treiben** drive the sheep up the mountain; ② (fig.) force *or* push up ‹*prices etc.*›; **~verdient** *Adj.* ‹*scientist etc.*› of outstanding merit; richly deserved ‹*victory, success, etc.*›; **~verehrt** *Adj.* highly respected *or* esteemed; (als Anrede) **meine ~verehrten Damen und Herren!** ladies and gentlemen!; **~verehrte Frau Schmidt** my dear Mrs Schmidt; **~verrat** *der* high treason; **~verräter** *der,* **~verräterin** *die* traitor; person guilty of high treason; **~verräterisch** *Adj.* traitorous; treasonable; ***~verschuldet** ▸**verschuldet**; **~verzinslich** *Adj.* (Finanzw.) ‹*security etc.*› yielding a high rate of interest; **~wald** *der* (Forstw.) high forest

Hoch·wasser *das* ▸ℹ **S. 267** (Flut) high tide *or* water; (Überschwemmung) flood; **der Fluss hat** *od.* **führt ~:** the river is in flood; **er hat ~** (ugs. scherzh.) his trousers are at half mast (coll.)

Hochwasser-: ~gefahr *die* flood danger; danger of flooding; **~hose[n]** *die* (scherzh.) trousers *pl.* at half mast (coll.); **~schaden** *der* flood damage

hoch-, Hoch-: ~|werfen *unr. tr. V.* **etw. ~werfen** throw sth. up; **eine Münze ~werfen** toss a coin; **~wertig** *Adj.* high-quality ‹*goods*›; highly nutritious ‹*food*›; **~wild** *das* (Jägerspr.) *larger game animals, e.g. deer, boar, chamois;* **~willkommen** *Adj.* very *or* most welcome; **~|winden** **A** *unr. tr. V.* wind up; weigh ‹*anchor*›; **B** *unr. refl. V.* wind one's/its way up; **~wirksam** *Adj.* highly *or* extremely effective; **~wohlgeboren** *Adj.* ▸ℹ **S. 44** (veralt.) high-born; **Euer Hochwohlgeboren** Your Honour; **~|wollen** *unr. itr. V.* (ugs.) want to get up; **~|wuchten** *tr. V.* (ugs.) heave up; **~würden** *(der);* **~~s** ▸ℹ **S. 44** (veralt.) Reverend Father; **~zahl** *die* (Math.) exponent

Hoch·zeit¹ *die* (geh.) Golden Age

Hochzeit² /'hɔxtsait/ *die;* **~, ~en** ▸ℹ **S. 331** wedding; **~ halten** *od.* **machen** (veralt.) get married; **grüne ~:** wedding day; **silberne/goldene ~:** silver/golden wedding [anniversary]; **man kann nicht auf zwei ~en tanzen** (fig. ugs.) you can't be in two places at once

Hochzeiter *der;* **~s, ~** (landsch.) [bride]-groom; **die ~:** the bride and groom

Hochzeiterin *die;* **~, ~nen** (landsch.) bride

Hochzeits-: ~anzeige *die* wedding announcement; **~feier** *die* wedding; **~flug** *der* (Zool.) nuptial flight; **~foto** *das* wedding photo; **~geschenk** *das* wedding gift *or* present; **~kleid** *das* ① (Brautkleid) wedding dress; ② (Zool.) (von Vögeln) nuptial plumage; (von Tieren) nuptial coloration; **~kuchen** *der* wedding cake; **~nacht** *die* wedding night; **~reise** *die* honeymoon [trip]; **wir haben unsere ~reise nach Berlin gemacht** we went to Berlin for our honeymoon; **~tag** *der* ▸ℹ **S. 331** ① wedding day; ② (Jahrestag) wedding anniversary; **~zug** *der* wedding procession

hoch-, Hoch-: ~|ziehen **A** *unr. tr. V.* ① (nach oben ziehen) pull up; pull up, raise ‹*shutters, blind*›; hoist, raise, run up ‹*flag*›; hoist ‹*sail*›; **die Schultern/Brauen ~ziehen** hunch one's shoulders/raise one's eyebrows; **die Nase ~ziehen** sniff [loudly]; ② **ein Flugzeug ~ziehen** put an aircraft into a steep climb; ③ (mauern) put up, build ‹*wall, building*›; **B** *unr. refl. V.* **sich [an etw.** *(Dat.)***] ~ziehen** pull oneself up [by hanging on to sth.]; **sich an etw.** *(Dat.)* **~ziehen** (fig.) latch on to sth.; **~zins·politik** *die* policy of keeping interest rates high; **~zufrieden** **A** *Adj.* highly satisfied; **B** *adv.* with great satisfaction

Hocke /'hɔkə/ *die;* **~, ~n** ① (Körperhaltung) squat; crouch; **in der ~ sitzen** squat; crouch; **in die ~ gehen** squat [down]; crouch down ② (Turnen) squat vault

hocken
A *itr. V.* ① *mit haben od. (südd.) sein* squat; crouch ② *mit haben od. (südd.) sein* (ugs.: sich aufhalten) sit around; **hinter einem Schreibtisch ~:** sit behind a desk ③ *mit sein* (südd.: sitzen) sit ④ *mit sein* (Turnen) perform *or* do a squat vault (**über** + *Akk.* over)
B *refl. V.* ① crouch down; squat [down] ② (südd.: sich setzen) sit down

Hocker *der;* **~s, ~:** stool

Höcker /'hœkɐ/ *der;* **~s, ~** ① hump; (auf der Nase) bump; (auf dem Schnabel) knob; **er hat einen ~:** he's humpbacked ② (Hügel) hillock; hump

Hocker·grab *das* (Archäol.) crouched burial

höckerig *Adj.* bumpy

Höcker·schwan *der* mute swan

Hockey /'hɔki/ *das;* **~s** hockey

Hockey-: ~schläger *der* hockey stick; **~spieler** *der,* **~spielerin** *die* hockey player

Hock-: ~sitz *der* (Turnen) squat; **~stand** *der* (Turnen) crouch

Hoden /'ho:dn̩/ *der;* **~s, ~** ▸ℹ **S. 435** testicle

Hoden-: ~bruch *der* ▸ℹ **S. 439** (Med.) scrotal hernia; **~sack** *der* ▸ℹ **S. 435** scrotum

Hoek van Holland /'hʊk 'fan 'hɔlant/ *(das);* **Hoeks van Holland** Hook of Holland

Hof /ho:f/ *der;* **~[e]s, Höfe** /'hø:fə/ ① courtyard; (Schul~) playground; (Gefängnis~) [prison] yard ② (Bauern~) farm; **in einen ~ einheiraten** marry into a farming family ③ (Herrscher, ~staat) court; **am ~ leben/verkehren** live at court/move in court circles; **die europäischen Höfe** the European royal courts; **jmdn. bei ~e einführen/vorstellen** present sb. at court; **~ halten** hold court ④ **jmdm. den ~ machen** (veralt.) pay court to sb. ⑤ (Aureole) corona; aureole ⑥ (in Namen von Hotels, z. B. „Bayerischer ~") (implying *or* suggesting a particular, e.g. Bavarian, style and a superior standard of accommodation)

hof-, Hof-: ~amt *das* (hist.) [hereditary] office at court; **~ball** *der* court ball; **~dame** *die* lady of the court; (Begleiterin der Königin) lady-in-waiting; **~dichter** *der* (hist.) court poet; **~etikette** *die* court etiquette; **~fähig** *Adj.*

h

ⓘ Höhe und Tiefe

Höhe

Wie hoch ist es?
= How high *od.* What height is it?

Es ist ungefähr neun Meter hoch
= It's about nine metres *od.*
≈ thirty feet high *od.* in height

A ist niedriger/höher als B
= A is lower/higher than B

A ist [genau] so hoch wie B
= A is [just] the same height *od.* as high as B

Die Türme sind gleich hoch
= The towers are the same height

Die Maschine flog in einer Höhe von 3 000 Metern
≈ The aircraft was flying at a height *od.* an altitude of 10,000 feet

Die Baumgrenze liegt bei etwa 2 000 Metern
≈ The treeline is at [a height of] about 6,500 feet

drei Meter hohe Wellen
≈ waves ten feet high

ein Berg von über 6 000 Metern od. von über 6 000 Meter Höhe
≈ a mountain of over 20,000 feet *od.* over 20,000 feet in height

Körpergröße

Wie groß ist sie?
= How tall *od.* What height is she?

Sie ist ein od. einen Meter achtundsechzig groß
≈ She's five foot six

ein 1,80 Meter großer Athlet
≈ an athlete six foot *od.* feet tall

Er ist kleiner als sein Bruder
= He's shorter *od.* smaller than his brother

A ist [genau] so groß wie B
= A is [just] the same height *od.* as tall as B

Sie sind gleich groß
= They are the same height

Tiefe

Wie tief ist od. Welche Tiefe hat der Fluss?
= How deep *od.* What depth is the river?

Er ist drei Meter tief od. hat eine Tiefe von drei Metern
= It's three metres deep,
≈ It's ten feet deep

Der Schatz liegt in einer Tiefe von fünfzehn Metern od. fünfzehn Meter tief
= The treasure is at a depth of fifteen metres *od.* is fifteen metres down,
≈ The treasure is at a depth of fifty feet *od.* is fifty feet down

A hat die gleiche Tiefe wie B
= A is the same depth as *od.* as deep as B

A und B sind gleich tief
= A and B are the same depth

A ist flacher od. seichter als B
= A is shallower than B

ein drei Meter tiefes Loch
≈ a hole three metres deep,
≈ a hole ten feet deep

h

presentable at court *pred.*; (fig.) [socially] acceptable

Hoffart /ˈhɔfart/ *die;* ~ (veralt. abwertend) overweening pride; haughtiness

hoffärtig /ˈhɔfɛrtɪç/ (veralt. abwertend)
A *Adj.* haughty
B *adv.* haughtily

hoffen /ˈhɔfn̩/
A *tr. V.* hope; **ich hoffe es/will es ~:** I hope so/can only hope so; **ich will es [doch wohl] ~:** I should hope so; **ich will nicht ~, dass sie das macht** I hope she doesn't do that; **ich will es nicht ~:** I hope not; **es bleibt zu ~, dass ...** let us hope that ...; **das wollen wir ~:** let's hope so; **~ wir das Beste** let's hope for the best
B *itr. V.* 1 (vertrauen) **auf etw.** (*Akk.*) **~:** hope for sth.; (Vertrauen setzen auf) **auf jmdn./etw. ~:** put one's trust *or* faith in sb./sth. 2 (Hoffnung haben) hope

hoffentlich /ˈhɔfn̩tlɪç/ *Adv.* hopefully; **~!** let's hope so; **~ ist ihr nichts passiert** I do hope nothing's happened to her; **es ist dir doch ~ recht** I hope it's all right with you

-höffig /-hœfɪç/ *adj.* promising to be rich in ‹*oil, gas, uranium, etc.*›

Hoffnung /ˈhɔfnʊŋ/ *die;* ~, **~en** hope; **seine ~ auf jmdn./etw. setzen** pin one's hopes *pl.* on sb./sth.; **keine ~ mehr haben, die ~ aufgegeben haben** have given up [all] hope; **sich** (*Dat.*) **[falsche] ~en machen** have [false] hopes; **jmdm. ~en machen** raise sb.'s hopes; **jmdm. auf etw.** (*Akk.*) **~en machen** lead sb. to expect sth.; **guter ~ sein** (veralt.) be expecting [a baby]; be with child (dated); **in der ~ auf etw.** (*Akk.*) in the hope of sth.

hoffnungs-, Hoffnungs-: ~froh (geh.) A *Adj.* hopeful; B *adv.* hopefully; ‹*smile etc.*› in happy anticipation; **~funke[n]** *der* (geh.) spark *or* glimmer of hope; **~lauf** *der* (Sport) repêchage; **~los** A *Adj.* hopeless; despairing ‹*person*›; B *adv.* hopelessly; **~losigkeit** *die;* **~~:** despair; (der Lage) hopelessness; **~schimmer** *der* (geh.) glimmer of hope; **~strahl** *der* (geh.) ray of hope; **~voll** A *Adj.* 1 hopeful; full of hope *pred.*; **jmdn. ~voll stimmen** give sb. cause to hope *or* make sb. hopeful; 2 (Erfolg versprechend) promising; B *adv.* 1 full of hope; 2 (Erfolg versprechend) promisingly

Hof-gang *der* exercise; **während des ~es** during the exercise period

hof-, Hof-: ~gesellschaft *die* court; *~**|halten** ▸**Hof** 3; **~haltung** *die* running of the court; (Haushalt) court; **~hund** *der* watchdog

hofieren /hoˈfiːrən/ *tr. V.* (geh.) pay court to

höfisch /ˈhøːfɪʃ/ *Adj.* courtly

Hof-: ~knicks *der* curtsy; **~kreise** *Pl.:* **in/aus ~kreisen** in/from court circles; **~leben** *das* life at court; court life

höflich /ˈhøːflɪç/
A *Adj.* polite; courteous; **etw. in ~em Ton fragen/sagen** ask/say sth. politely
B *adv.* politely; courteously

Höflichkeit *die;* ~, **~en** 1 politeness; courteousness; **etw. [nur] aus ~ tun/sagen** do/say sth. [only] to be polite *or* out of politeness 2 (höfliche Redensart) civility; courtesy

höflichkeits-, Höflichkeits-: ~besuch *der* courtesy visit; **~floskel, ~formel** *die* polite phrase; **~halber** *Adv.* to be polite; out of politeness

Hof·lieferant *der*, **Hof·lieferantin** *die* (veralt.) supplier to the court; **königlicher ~:** supplier to the royal court; (von Lebensmitteln) purveyor to the royal court

Höfling /ˈhøːflɪŋ/ *der;* **~s, ~e** courtier

Hof-: ~marschall *der* ▸ⓘ **S. 44** major-domo; **~meister** *der* (veralt.) court tutor and master of ceremonies; **~narr** *der* (hist.) court jester; **~prediger** *der* court chaplain; **~rat** *der* ▸ⓘ **S. 44** (veralt., noch österr.) *honorary title conferred on senior civil servant;* **~sänger** *der* (hist.) court minstrel; **~schranze** *die od. der* (veralt. abwertend) fawning courtier; **~staat** *der* court; **~theater** *das* court theatre; **~tor** *das* courtyard gate; **~tür** *die* courtyard door

HO-Geschäft /haːˈloː-/ *das* (DDR): *shop owned by the Handelsorganisation*

hohe... /ˈhoːə.../ ▸**hoch**

Höhe /ˈhøːə/ *die;* ~, **~n** 1 ▸ⓘ **S. 374** (Ausdehnung nach oben) height; **das ist ja die ~!** (ugs.) that's the limit! 2 (Entfernung nach oben) height; altitude; **in einer ~ von 4 000 m fliegen/eine ~ von 4 000 m erreichen** fly at/reach a height *or* altitude of 4,000 m.; **an ~ gewinnen/verlieren** gain/lose height *or* altitude; **in großen ~n** at great heights *or* high altitudes; **auf halber ~:** at mid-altitude 3 (Richtung) **etw. in die ~ heben** lift sth. up; **in die ~ [auf]steigen** rise up[wards] 4 (Gipfelpunkt) height; **auf der ~ seines Ruhmes/Könnens/Erfolges sein** be at the height of one's fame/ability/success; **auf der ~ sein** (fig. ugs.) (gesund sein) be fit; (sich wohl fühlen) feel fine; **nicht [ganz] auf der ~ sein** (fig. ugs.) be/feel a bit under the weather (coll.); not be/feel quite oneself 5 (messbare Größe) level; (von Einkommen) size; level; **die ~ der Geschwindigkeit/Temperatur** the speed/temperature level; **Unkosten/ein Stipendium in ~ von 5 000 Euro** expenses/a grant of 5,000 euros 6 (Linie) **auf gleicher ~ sein/fahren** be in line abreast *or* be level/travel in line abreast; **die Pferde waren auf gleicher ~:** the horses were neck and neck; **auf ~ des Leuchtturms/von Hull sein** (Seemannsspr.) be level with *or* abreast of the lighthouse/be off Hull 7 (hoher Grad) high level 8 (Anhöhe) hill; **die ~n und Tiefen des Lebens** (fig.) the ups and downs of life 9 (Math., Astron.) altitude 10 *Pl.* (Akustik) treble *sing.*

Hoheit /ˈhoːhait/ *die;* ~, **~en** 1 (Souveränität) sovereignty (**über** + *Akk.* over); **unter der ~ eines Staates stehen** be under the sovereignty of a state 2 ▸ⓘ **S. 44 Seine/Ihre ~:** His/Your Highness 3 (geh.: Würde) majestic dignity; majesty

hoheitlich *Adj.* 1 sovereign 2 (selten) ▸**hoheitsvoll**

hoheits-, Hoheits-: ~ab·zeichen *das* national emblem; **~gebiet** *das* [sovereign] territory; **~gewässer** *Pl.* territorial waters; **~recht** *das* right of the state; **~voll** *Adj.* majestic; stately ‹*gesture*›; **~zeichen** *das* national emblem

Hohe·lied *das* 1 (bibl.) Song of Songs 2 (fig. geh.) song of praise; **ein ~ der Liebe** a song in praise of love; *s. auch* **Lied**

höhen-, Höhen-: ~an·gabe *die* altitude reading; (auf Karten) altitude marking; **~angst** *die* fear of heights; **~flug** *der* (Flugw.) high-altitude flight; (fig.) flight; **im ~flug** at high altitude; **~gleich** (Verkehrsw.) A *Adj.* level ‹*crossing*›; B *adv.* at the same level; **~klima** *das* mountain climate; **~krankheit** *die* altitude sickness; **~lage** *die* altitude; **in ~lage** at high altitude; **in ~lagen über 1 500 m** at altitudes over 1,500 m.; **~leitwerk** *das* (Flugw.) tailplane; **~linie** *die* (Geogr.) contour [line]; **~luft** *die* mountain air; air at high altitude; **~marke** *die* (Vermessungsw.) benchmark; **~messer** *der;* **~~s, ~~:** altimeter; **~messung** *die* measurement of height; **~rekord** *der* altitude record; **~ruder** *das* (Flugw.) elevator; **~sonne** *die* 1 (Med.: Quarzlampe) ultraviolet lamp; sun lamp; 2 (Med.: Bestrahlung) ultraviolet radiation treatment; sun lamp treatment; 3 (Met.) high-altitude solar radiation; **~steuer** *das* (Flugw.) elevator control; **~strahlung** *die* (Physik) cosmic radiation; **~training** *das* (Sport) [high-]altitude training; **~unterschied** *der* altitude difference; difference in altitude; **~weg** *der* ridge path; **~winkel** *der* (Geom.) angle of elevation; **~zug** *der* (Geogr.) range of hills; (Bergkette) range of mountains; mountain range

Hohe·priester *der* (bibl.) high priest; *s. auch* **Priester**

Höhepunkt *der* high point; (einer Veranstaltung) high spot; highlight; (einer Laufbahn, des Ruhms) peak; pinnacle; (einer Krankheit) crisis; critical point; (einer Krise) turning point; (der Macht) summit; pinnacle; (des Glücks) height; (Orgasmus;

eines Stückes) climax; **auf dem ~ seiner Laufbahn stehen** be at the peak of one's career

höher /ˈhøːɐ/ 1 ▸**hoch** 2 **ein ~ gestellter Beamter** a senior official/civil servant; **die ~ gestellten Persönlichkeiten** the more prominent public figures

höher-, Höher-: ~gestellt ▸**höher** 2; *~|**schrauben** ▸**hoch** B 2; **~stufung** *die* upgrading

hohl /hoːl/

A *Adj.* 1 (leer) hollow; **sich innerlich ~ fühlen** (fig.) feel empty inside 2 (nach innen gebogen) cupped ‹*hand*›; sunken, hollow ‹*cheeks, eyes*›; concave ‹*lens, mirror*›; **ein ~es Kreuz** a hollow back 3 (dumpf) hollow ‹*sound, voice, etc.*› 4 (abwertend: geistlos) hollow, empty ‹*phrases, slogans*›; empty ‹*talk, chatter*›; shallow ‹*person*›

B *adv.* 1 (dumpf) hollowly 2 (abwertend: geistlos) inanely

hohl·äugig *Adj.* hollow-eyed; sunken-eyed

Hohl·block·stein *der* (Bauw.) hollow block

Höhle /ˈhøːlə/ *die;* ~, ~n 1 cave; (größer) cavern 2 (Tierbau) den; lair; (von Höhlenbrütern) nest; **sich in die ~ des Löwen begeben** (scherzh.) enter the lion's den 3 (abwertend: Wohnung) hole 4 (Augenhöhle) socket

Hohl·eisen *das* (Handw.) gouge; hollow chisel

höhlen /ˈhøːlən/ *tr. V.* hollow out; **steter Tropfen höhlt den Stein** (Spr.) these things take their toll eventually

Höhlen-: ~bär *der* cave bear; **~brüter** *der* (Zool.) bird that nests in holes; hole-nester; **~forscher** *der*, **~forscherin** *die* speleologist; (Sportler[in]) caver; **~forschung** *die* speleology; (als Sport) caving; **~malerei** *die* cave painting; **~mensch** *der* cave dweller; caveman; **~zeichnung** *die* cave painting

Hohlheit *die;* ~ 1 hollowness 2 (innere Leere, auch fig. abwertend) emptiness

hohl-, Hohl-: ~kopf *der* (abwertend) idiot (coll.); dimwit; **~köpfig** *Adj.* (abwertend) idiotic (coll.); blockheaded; **~körper** *der* hollow body; **~kreuz** *das* ▸❶ **S. 439** hollow back; lordosis (Med.); **~kugel** *die* hollow sphere; **~maß** *das* 1 (Maßeinheit) measure of capacity; 2 (Gefäß) dry/liquid measure; **~nadel** *die* (Med.) cannula; (für Einspritzungen) hypodermic needle; **~raum** *der* cavity; [hollow] space; **~raum·versiegelung** *die* (Kfz-W.) body-cavity sealing; **~saum** *der* (Handarb.) hemstitch; **~schliff** *der* hollow grinding; **eine Klinge mit ~schliff** a hollow-ground blade; **~spiegel** *der* concave mirror; **~tier** *das* coelenterate

Höhlung *die;* ~, ~en 1 (das Aushöhlen) excavation 2 (Vertiefung) hollow

hohl-, Hohl-: ~wangig *Adj.* hollow-cheeked; sunken-cheeked; **~weg** *der* defile; (Durchstich) cutting; **~ziegel** *der* perforated tile; (Dachziegel) concave tile

Hohn /hoːn/ *der;* ~[e]s scorn; derision; **jmdn. mit ~ und Spott überschütten** pour *or* heap scorn on sb.; **das ist der reine** *od.* **der blanke ~** (fig.) it is just grotesque; **~ lächeln/lachen** smile/laugh scornfully *or* derisively; **einer Sache ~ sprechen** fly in the face of sth.

höhnen /ˈhøːnən/ *itr. V.* (geh.) jeer; sneer

Hohn·gelächter *das* derisive *or* scornful laughter

höhnisch /ˈhøːnɪʃ/

A *Adj.* scornful; derisive

B *adv.* scornfully; derisively

hohn-: ~lächeln *itr. V.* **er ~lächelte** he smiled scornfully *or* derisively; **ein Hohnlächeln** a scornful or derisive smile; *s. auch* **Hohn**; **~lachen** *itr. V.* 1 laugh scornfully *or* derisively; **ein Hohnlachen** a scornful *or* derisive laugh; 2 (geh.: zuwiderlaufen) **einer Sache** (*Dat.*) **~lachen** fly in the face of sth.; *s. auch* **Hohn**; **~|sprechen** ▸**Hohn**

Höker /ˈhøːkɐ/ *der;* ~s, ~, **Hökerin** *die;* ~, ~nen (veralt.) (auf dem Markt) stallholder; (auf der Straße) street trader; street pedlar (Amer.)

hökern *itr. V.* (auf dem Markt) run a market stall; (auf der Straße) run a street stall

Hokuspokus /hoːkʊsˈpoːkʊs/ *der;* ~: hocus-pocus; (abwertend: Drum und Dran) fuss

hold /hɔlt/

A *Adj.* 1 (dichter. veralt.: anmutig) fair; lovely; lovely ‹*sight*›; sweet, lovely ‹*smile*›; **die ~e Weiblichkeit** (scherzh.) the fair sex; **mein ~er Gatte/meine ~e Gattin** (scherzh.) my beloved spouse (joc.) 2 *in* **jmdm./einer Sache ~ sein** (geh.) be well-disposed towards sb./sth.; (jmdn./etw. gern haben) be fond of sb./sth.; **das Glück war uns** (*Dat.*) **~**: fortune smiled upon us

B *adv.* sweetly

Holder *der;* ~s, ~ (bes. südd.) ▸**Holunder**

Holding /ˈhoʊldɪŋ/ *die;* ~, ~s holding company

Holding·gesellschaft *die* (Wirtsch.) holding company

Holdrio /ˈhɔldrio/ *das;* ~s, ~s halloo

hold·selig (dichter. veralt.)

A *Adj.* sweet; lovely; lovely ‹*sight, appearance*›

B *adv.* sweetly

holen /ˈhoːlən/

A *tr. V.* 1 fetch; get; **jmdn. aus dem Bett ~**: get *or* (coll.) drag sb. out of bed; **da/bei ihr ist nichts/nichts mehr zu ~** (fig.) you won't get anything/any more there/out of her 2 (ab~) fetch; pick up; collect; take away ‹*suspect, prisoner, etc.*› 3 (ugs.: erlangen) get, win ‹*prize*›; get, carry off, win ‹*medal, trophy, etc.*›; get, score ‹*points*›; **den Sieg ~**: win 4 (landsch.: kaufen) buy; get 5 (Seemannsspr.: herabziehen) take in ‹*sail*›; haul ‹*boat*› alongside

B *refl. V.* 1 (sich verschaffen) get; **sich** (*Dat.*) **Hilfe/Rat** *usw.* **~**: get [some] help/advice *etc.* 2 (erlangen) win, take ‹*championship, prize, etc.*›; **sich** (*Dat.*) **eine Niederlage ~**: be beaten; lose 3 (ugs.: sich zuziehen) catch; **sich** (*Dat.*) **[beim Baden** *usw.***] einen Schnupfen/die Grippe ~**: catch a cold/the flu [swimming *etc.*]; **sich** (*Dat.*) **den Tod ~** (fig.) catch one's death [of cold]

holla /ˈhɔla/ *Interj.* hallo; hello; hey

Holland /ˈhɔlant/ (*das*); ~s Holland

Holländer /ˈhɔlɛndɐ/ ▸❶ **S. 520**

A *der;* ~s, ~ 1 Dutchman; **er ist ~**: he is Dutch *or* a Dutchman; **die ~**: the Dutch 2 (Käse) Dutch cheese 3 (Papierherstellung) Hollander

B *indekl. Adj.* **~ Käse** Dutch cheese

Holländerin *die;* ~, ~nen ▸❶ **S. 520** Dutchwoman/Dutch girl

holländisch *Adj.* ▸❶ **S. 520** Dutch; *s. auch* **deutsch**; **Deutsch**

Holle *in* **Frau ~ schüttelt die Betten [aus]** (veralt.) it is snowing; the old woman is plucking her geese (dated)

Hölle /ˈhœlə/ *die;* ~, ~n 1 hell *no art.*; **in die ~ kommen** go to hell; **zur ~ fahren** (geh.) descend into hell; **jmdn. zur ~ wünschen** (geh.) wish sb. to hell; **zur ~ mit ihm/damit!** to hell with him/it (coll.) 2 (fig.) **die ~ ist los** (ugs.) all hell has broken loose (coll.); **es war die reinste ~**: it was pure hell (coll.); **die ~ auf Erden haben** suffer hell on earth; **jmdm. das Leben zur ~ machen** make sb.'s life hell (coll.); **jmdm. die ~ heiß machen** give sb. hell (coll.); **die grüne ~**: the jungle; *s. auch* **Vorsatz**

Höllen-: ~angst *die* (salopp) terror; **eine ~angst vor etw.** (*Dat.*) **haben** be scared to death of sth. (coll.); be terrified of sth.; **~fahrt** *die* (Myth., Rel.) descent into hell; **~feuer** *das* hellfire; **das ~feuer** the fires *pl.* of hell; **~fürst** *der* Prince of Darkness; **~hund** *der* (Myth.) hellhound; hound of hell; **~lärm** *der* (ugs.) diabolical noise *or* row (coll.); **~maschine** *die* infernal machine (arch.); time bomb; **~pein**, **~qual** *die* agony; **~qualen erleiden** suffer the torments of hell (fig.); suffer terrible agony *sing.*; **~spektakel** *das* (ugs.) ▸**~lärm**; **~stein** *der* lunar caustic; **~tempo** *das* (ugs.) breakneck speed; **in einem ~tempo** at breakneck speed

Holler /ˈhɔlɐ/ *der;* ~s, ~ (bes. südd., österr.) ▸**Holunder**

höllisch /ˈhœlɪʃ/

A *Adj.* 1 infernal; ‹*spirits, torments*› of hell 2 (schrecklich) terrible ‹*war, situation*›; fiendish, diabolical ‹*invention, laughter*›; **~e Schmerzen** terrible agony *sing.* 3 (ugs.: sehr groß) tremendous (coll.) ‹*noise, shock, respect*› (coll.); enormous (coll.) ‹*pleasure*›; **~e Angst vor etw.** (*Dat.*) **haben** be scared stiff of sth. (coll.)

B *adv.* (ugs.: sehr) terribly, hellishly (coll.) ‹*cold, difficult*›; **sich ~ zusammennehmen** make a tremendous effort to control oneself (coll.); **~ [genau] aufpassen** be tremendously careful (coll.); **es tut ~ weh** it hurts like hell (coll.)

Hollywood·schaukel /ˈhɔlɪwʊd-/ *die* swinging garden hammock

Holm /hɔlm/ *der;* ~[e]s, ~e 1 (Turnen) bar 2 (Leiter~) upright; side piece 3 (Geländer~) [banister] rail 4 (Flugw.) spar

Holocaust /holoˈkaust/ *der;* ~[s], ~s Holocaust

Hologramm /holoˈgram/ *das* (Physik) hologram

Holographie /hologra'fiː/ *die;* ~ (Physik) holography *no art.*

Holozän /holoˈtsɛːn/ *das;* ~s (Geol.) Holocene

holperig ▸**holprig**

holpern /ˈhɔlpɐn/ *itr. V.* 1 *mit sein* (fahren) jolt; bump 2 (schütteln) jolt 3 (stockend lesen) stumble [over one's words]

holprig /ˈhɔlprɪç/

A *Adj.* 1 (uneben) bumpy; uneven; rough 2 (stockend) stumbling, halting ‹*speech*›; clumsy ‹*verses*›; broken, halting ‹*English etc.*›

B *adv.* haltingly; **~ lesen** stumble over one's words when reading

Hol·schuld /ˈhoːl-/ *die* (Rechtsw.): *debt to be collected at the debtor's residence*

Holster /ˈhɔlstɐ/ *das;* ~s, ~: holster

holterdiepolter /hɔltɐdiˈpɔltɐ/ *Adv.* (ugs.) helter-skelter; **alles ging ~**: there was a mad rush

holüber /hoːlˈ|yːbɐ/ *Interj.* **[Fährmann] ~!** ferry[man]!

Holunder /hoˈlʊndɐ/ *der;* ~s, ~ 1 (Strauch) elder 2 (Früchte) elderberries *pl.*

Holunder-: ~beere *die* elderberry; **~strauch** *der* elder[berry] bush; **~tee** *der* elder tea

Holz /hɔlts/ *das;* ~es, **Hölzer** /ˈhœltsɐ/ 1 wood; (Bau~, Tischler~) timber; wood; **bearbeitetes ~**: timber (Brit.); lumber (Amer.); **ein Stück/Festmeter ~**: a piece of wood *or* timber/cubic metre of timber; **viel ~** (fig. ugs.) a hell of a lot (coll.); **[viel] ~ vor der Hütte** *od.* **Tür haben** (fig. ugs. scherzh.) be well stacked (coll.) *or* well endowed; **ich bin nicht aus ~**: I've got feelings, you know; **die ~ verarbeitende Industrie** the timber processing industry 2 (~art) wood; **aus dem ~ sein, aus dem man Minister/Helden macht** be cut out to be a minister/be of the stuff heroes are made of; **aus dem gleichen ~ [geschnitzt] sein** (fig.) be cast in the same mould; **aus anderem ~ [geschnitzt] sein** (fig.) be cast in a different mould 3 (Forstw.) felled trunk 4 (Golf) wood 5 **den Ball mit dem ~ schlagen/treffen** (Tennis, Badminton) hit the ball with the wood 6 *Pl.* ~ (Kegeln) skittle; ninepin; **gut ~!** have a good game! (skittle-players' greeting) 7 (Musik) woodwind 8 (Streich~) match 9 (veralt., Jägerspr.: Wald) wood

holz-, Holz-: ~apfel *der* 1 crab apple; 2 (Baum) crab apple tree; **~arbeiter** *der* ▸**~fäller**; **~arm** *Adj.* ‹*country*› with little timber of its own; **~arm sein** have little timber of its own; **~art** *die* kind of wood *or* timber; **~auge** *das: in* **~auge sei wachsam!** (scherzh.) better be careful; **~bearbeitung** *die* processing of timber; timber processing; (in der Tischlerei) woodworking; **~bein** *das* wooden leg; **~bläser** *der*, **~bläserin** *die* woodwind player; **~blas·instrument** *das* woodwind instrument; **~block** *der; Pl.* **~blöcke** block of wood; **~bock** *der* 1 (Gestell) wooden stand *or* trestle; 2 (Zecke) castor-bean tick; 3 (Käfer) poplar longhorn; **~bohrer** *der* 1 wood drill; 2 (Schmetterling) goat moth; carpenter moth; **~bündel** *das* bundle of wood

Hölzchen /ˈhœltsçən/ *das;* ~s, ~ 1 small piece of wood; (Stöckchen) stick 2 (Streichholz) match

Holz-: ~diele *die* plank; (für Fußböden) [floor]board; **~dübel** *der* wooden dowel; (in der Wand) wooden plug

holzen *itr. V.* (Fußballjargon) play dirty (coll.)

Holzerei *die;* ~, ~**en** [1] (Fußballjargon) dirty play; **eine** ~: a dirty game *or* match [2] (Prügelei) brawl; free-for-all

hölzern /ˈhœltsn̩/ *Adj.* (auch fig.) wooden

holz-, Holz-: ~**essig** *der* wood vinegar; ~**fäller** *der;* ~~**s,** ~~, ~**fällerin** *die;* ~~, ~~**nen** ►ⓘ **S. 113** woodcutter; lumberjack (Amer.); ~**feuer** *das* wood fire; ~**frei** *Adj.* wood-free ‹*paper*›; ~**gas** *das* wood gas; ~**geist** *der* wood spirit; ~**geschnitzt** *Adj.* carved wooden *attrib.;* carved in wood *pred.;* ~**hacker** *der,* ~**hackerin** *die* [1] (bes. österr.) ►~**fäller**; [2] (Fußballjargon) dirty player; ~**haltig** *Adj.* woody ‹*paper*›; ‹*paper*› containing mechanical wood pulp

Holz·hammer *der* [wooden] mallet

Holzhammer·methode *die* (ugs.) sledgehammer method

Holz-: ~**handel** *der* timber trade; ~**haus** *das* timber *or* wooden house

holzig *Adj.* woody

holz-, Holz-: ~**industrie** *die* timber industry; ~**kitt** *der* plastic wood; ~**klasse** *die* bottom class; (Eisenb.) third class; (Flugw.) economy [class]; peasant class (joc.); ~**klotz** *der* block of wood; (als Spielzeug) wooden block; **dasitzen wie ein** ~**klotz** (fig.) sit there like a stuffed dummy; ~**kohle** *die* charcoal; ~**kohlen·grill** *der* charcoal grill; ~**kopf** *der* [1] wooden head; [2] (salopp abwertend) blockhead; numbskull; ~**kreuz** *das* wooden cross; ~**lager** *das* timber yard; ~**leim** *der* wood glue; ~**leiste** *die* batten; ~**malerei** *die* painting on wood; wood painting; ~**nagel** *der* wooden nail; ~**pantine** *die* (landsch.), ~**pantoffel** *der* clog; ~**pflock** *der* wooden stake; ~**sandale** *die* wooden sandal; ~**schädling** *der* wood pest; ~**schale** *die* wooden bowl; ~**scheit** *das* piece of wood; (Brenn~) piece of firewood; ~**schläger** *der* (Golf) wood; ~**schneider** *der,* ~**schneiderin** *die* wood engraver; ~**schnitt** *der* [1] woodcutting *no art.;* [2] (Blatt) woodcut; ~**schnitt·artig** *Adj.* (fig.) simplistic; ~**schnitzer** *der* wood carver; ~**schnitzerei** *die* wood carving; ~**schnitzerin** *die* ►~**schnitzer**; ~**schraube** *die* wood screw; ~**schuh** *der* clog; ~**schuh·tanz** *der* clog dance; ~**schuppen** *der* [1] (aus ~) wooden shed; [2] (für ~) woodshed; ~**span** *der* [1] (zum Feueranzünden) stick of firewood; (zum Rühren usw.) small stick [of wood]; [2] (Hobelspan) [wood] shaving; ~**spielzeug** *das* wooden toy; ~**spiritus** *der* wood alcohol; ~**splitter** *der* splinter of wood; ~**stab** *der* wooden rod; ~**stich** *der* wood engraving; ~**stift** *der* ►~**nagel**; ~**stock** *der* [1] [wooden] stick; [2] (Grafik) wood block; ~**stoß** *der* pile of wood; ~**täfelung** *die* wood[en] panelling; ~**teer** *der* wood tar; ~**treppe** *die* wooden steps *pl.;* ~**verarbeitend** ►**Holz 1**; ~**verschlag** *der* [1] area divided off by a wooden partition; [2] (Schuppen) wooden shed; ~**waren** *Pl.* wooden articles; ~**weg** *der* (fig.): *in* **auf dem** ~**weg sein** *od.* **sich auf dem** ~**weg befinden** be on the wrong track (fig.); be barking up the wrong tree (fig.); **wenn du glaubst, du kannst das verhindern, so bist du auf dem** ~**weg** if you think you can prevent it, you're very much mistaken *or* (coll.) you've got another think coming; ~**wirtschaft** *die* timber industry; ~**wolle** *die* wood wool; ~**wurm** *der* woodworm

Homburg /ˈhɔmbʊrk/ *der;* ~**s,** ~**s** Homburg

Home-: ~**banking** /ˈhoʊmbɛŋkɪŋ/ *das;* ~~**s** home banking; ~**page** /ˈhoʊmpeɪdʒ/ *die;* ~, ~~**s** (DV) home page

homerisch /hoˈmeːrɪʃ/ *Adj.* Homeric; **ein** ~**es Gelächter** Homeric laughter

Home·trainer /ˈhoʊm-/ *der* exerciser

Hommage /ɔˈmaːʒ/ *die;* ~, ~**n** (geh.) tribute (**für** to)

homo *Adj.* (ugs.) queer (coll.)

Homo /ˈhoːmo/ *der;* ~**s,** ~**s** (ugs.) queer (coll.), homo (coll.)

Homo·ehe *die* (ugs.) single-sex marriage

homo-, Homo-: ~**erotisch** *Adj.* (geh.) homoerotic (Psych.); homosexual; ~**gen** /-ˈɡeːn/ *Adj.* homogeneous; ~**genisieren** *tr. V.* [1] (Chemie, Metallbearb.) homogenize; [2] (geh.) homogenize; integrate ‹*groups*›; ~**genität** /-ɡeniˈtɛːt/ *die;* ~~ (geh.) homogeneity; ~**log** /-ˈloːk/ *Adj.* (Biol., Math., Chemie) homologous; ~**logieren** *tr. V.* (Motorsport) homologate; ~**nym** /-ˈnyːm/ *Adj.* (Sprachw.) homonymous; ~**nym** *das;* ~~**s,** ~~**e** (Sprachw.) homonym; ~**nymie** /homonyˈmiː/ *die;* ~~ (Sprachw.) homonymy

homöo-, Homöo-/homøo-/ : ~**path** /-ˈpaːt/ *der;* ~~**en,** ~~**en** homeopath; ~**pathie** *die;* ~~: homeopathy *no art.;* ~**pathin** *die;* ~~, ~~**nen** ►~**path**; ~**pathisch** *Adj.* homeopathic

homo-, Homo-: ~**phil** /-ˈfiːl/ *Adj.* (geh.) homophile; ~**phon** *das;* ~~**s,** ~~**e** (Sprachw.) homophone; ~**sexualität** *die;* ~~: homosexuality; ~**sexuell** [A] *Adj.* homosexual; [B] *adv.* ~**sexuell veranlagt sein** have homosexual tendencies; ~**sexuelle** *der/die; adj. Dekl.* homosexual

Homunkulus /hoˈmʊŋkulʊs/ *der;* ~, ~**se** *od.* **Homunkuli** homunculus

Honduras /hɔnˈduːras/ *(das);* ~**'** Honduras

honen /ˈhoːnən/ *tr. V.* (Technik) hone

honett /hoˈnɛt/ *Adj.* (geh.) (rechtschaffen) honest; upright; (anständig) decent; (ehrenhaft) honourable

Hongkong /ˈhɔŋkɔŋ/ *(das);* ~**s** ►ⓘ **S. 675** Hong Kong

Honig /ˈhoːnɪç/ *der;* ~**s,** ~**e** honey; **jmdm.** ~ **um den Bart** (ugs.) *od.* (salopp) **ums Maul schmieren** (fig.) butter sb. up

honig-, Honig-: ~**biene** *die* honey bee; ~**brot** *das* bread and honey; **ein** ~**brot** a slice of bread and honey; ~**farben** *Adj.* honey-coloured; ~**gelb** *Adj.* honey-yellow; ~**kuchen** *der* honey cake; ~**kuchen·pferd** *das: in* **lachen** *od.* **grinsen** *od.* **strahlen wie ein** ~**kuchenpferd** (ugs. scherzh.) grin like a Cheshire cat; ~**lecken** *das: in* **das ist kein** ~**lecken** (ugs.) it is not a bed of roses; ~**melone** *die* honeydew melon; ~**schlecken** *das* ►~**lecken**; ~**süß** [A] *Adj.* ‹*grapes, taste, etc.*› as sweet as honey; (fig.) honey-sweet ‹*voice*›; **ein** ~**süßes Lächeln** (fig.) the sweetest of smiles; **mit** ~**süßer Stimme** (fig.) in honeyed tones; [B] *adv.* (fig.) ~**süß lächeln/antworten** smile a honey-sweet smile/answer in honeyed tones; ~**tau** *der* honeydew; ~**wabe** *die* honeycomb; ~**wein** *der* mead; ~**zelle** *die* honey[comb] cell

Honneur /(h)ɔˈnøːɐ̯/ *in* **die** ~**s machen** (veralt.) do the honours

Honorar /honoˈraːɐ̯/ *das;* ~**s,** ~**e** fee; (Autoren~) royalty

Honorar-: ~**konsul** *der,* ~**konsulin** *die* honorary consul; ~**professor** *der,* ~**professorin** *die: professor who is not primarily an academic and has no voice in faculty matters*

Honoratioren /honoraˈtsi̯oːrən/ *Pl.* notabilities

honorieren *tr. V.* [1] **jmdn.** ~: pay sb. [a/his/her fee]; **jmds. Leistung/Buch** ~: pay sb. [a/his/her fee] for his/her work/book [2] (würdigen) appreciate; (belohnen) reward [3] (Finanzw.) honour ‹*cheque*›

Honorierung *die;* ~, ~**en** [1] payment [2] (Würdigung) appreciation; (Belohnung) rewarding [3] (Finanzw.) honouring

honorig *Adj.* honourable; respectable

honoris causa /hoˈnoːrɪs ˈkau̯za/ *Adv.* honoris causa; **Doktor** ~: honorary doctor

hopfen /ˈhɔpfn̩/ *tr. V.* hop ‹*beer*›

Hopfen *der;* ~**s,** ~: hop; **bei ihm ist** ~ **und Malz verloren** (ugs.) he's a hopeless case

Hopfen-: ~**garten** *der* hop garden; ~**stange** *die* hop pole

hopp /hɔp/

[A] *Interj.* quick; look sharp

[B] *Adv.* in double-quick time; **bei ihm muss alles** ~ **gehen** he likes everything done in double-quick time

hoppe /ˈhɔpə/ *Interj.: in* ~, ~, **Reiter machen** (Kinderspr.) play gee-gees (*on sb.'s knee*)

hoppeln /ˈhɔpl̩n/ *itr. V.; mit sein* hop (**über** + *Akk.* across, over); (fig.) bump, jolt (**über** + *Akk.* across, over)

Hoppelpoppel /ˈhɔpl̩ˈpɔpl̩/ *das;* ~**s,** ~ [1] (bes. berlin.) ►**Bauernfrühstück** [2] (Getränk) ≈ egg flip

hoppla /ˈhɔpla/ *Interj.* oops; whoops

hopp|nehmen *unr. tr. V.* (salopp) nab (coll.); nick (coll.)

hops /hɔps/

[A] *Interj.* up; jump

[B] *Adj.* (salopp) ~ **sein** be gone; ‹*money*› have gone down the drain (coll.); (entzweigegangen sein) be broken

Hops *der;* ~**es,** ~**e** [little] jump

hopsala /ˈhɔpsala/, **hopsasa** /ˈhɔpsasa/ *Interj.* (Kinderspr.) oops-a-daisy (coll.); whoops-a-daisy (coll.)

hopsen *itr. V.; mit sein* (ugs.) (springen) jump; (hüpfen) ‹*animal*› hop; ‹*child*› skip; ‹*ball*› bounce

Hopser *der;* ~**s,** ~ (ugs.) [1] (kleiner Sprung) [little] jump [2] (Tanz) écossaise

Hopserei *die;* ~, ~**en** (ugs. abwertend) jumping about *or* around; (Tanzen) leaping about *or* around

hops-: ~**|gehen** *unr. itr. V.; mit sein* (salopp) [1] (umkommen) buy it (sl.); [2] (entzweigehen) get broken; (abhanden kommen) go missing; (unbrauchbar werden) ‹*car, machine, etc.*› pack up (coll.); ~**|nehmen** *unr. tr. V.* ►**hoppnehmen**

Hör·apparat *der* hearing aid

hörbar

[A] *Adj.* audible

[B] *adv.* audibly; (geräuschvoll) noisily

Hör-: ~**bereich** *der* audible range; range of hearing; ~**bild** *das* radio feature (*combining documentary and dramatic techniques*); ~**brille** hearing aid spectacles *pl.*

horchen /ˈhɔrçn̩/ *itr. V.* listen (**auf** + *Akk.* to); (heimlich zuhören) eavesdrop; listen; **an der Tür/Wand** ~: listen at the door/through the wall

Horcher *der;* ~**s,** ~, **Horcherin** *die;* ~, ~**nen** ►**Lauscher 1**

Horch-: ~**gerät** *das* sound locator; (Marine) hydrophone; ~**posten** *der* (Milit., auch fig. scherzh.) listening post

Horde[1] /ˈhɔrdə/ *die;* ~, ~**n** (auch Völkerk.) horde; (von Halbstarken) mob; crowd; **eine** ~ **Kinder** *od.* **von Kindern** a horde of children

Horde[2] *die;* ~, ~**n** (Gestell) rack

hören /ˈhøːrən/

[A] *tr. V.* [1] hear; **jmdn. kommen/sprechen** ~: hear sb. coming/speaking; **ich habe sagen** ~, **dass ...** I have heard it said that ...; **ich höre nichts** I can't hear anything; *s. auch* **Gras** [2] (an~) listen to, hear ‹*programme, broadcast, performance, etc.*›; hear ‹*singer, musician*›; **Rundfunk** *od.* **Radio** ~: listen to the radio; **den Angeklagten/Zeugen** ~: hear the accused/witness; **eine Vorlesung bei jmdm.** ~: go to *or* attend a lecture by sb.; **das lässt sich** ~: that's good news [3] (erfahren) hear; **etw. von jmdm.** ~: hear sth. from sb.; **er lässt nichts von sich** ~: I/we *etc.* haven't heard from him; **lass mal etwas von dir** ~! keep in touch; **etw. von jmdm. zu** ~ **bekommen** *od.* (ugs.) **kriegen** get a good talking-to from sb. (coll.) [4] (erkennen) **an etw.** (*Dat.*) ~, **dass ...** hear *or* tell by sth. that ...

[B] *itr. V.* [1] hear; **gut** ~: have good hearing; **schlecht** ~: have bad hearing; be hard of hearing; **nur auf einem Ohr** ~: be deaf in one ear; **höre ich recht?** am I hearing things?; **ich geb' dir gleich eine, dass dir Hören und Sehen vergeht** (ugs.) I'll give you such a clout in a minute that you'll be seeing stars for a week (coll.); **er raste über die Autobahn, dass uns Hören und Sehen verging** (ugs.) he tore along the motorway so fast that we were scared out of our wits (coll.) [2] (aufmerksam verfolgen) **auf etw.** (*Akk.*) ~: listen to sth. [3] (zu~) listen; **ich höre** I'm listening; **hörst du!** listen [here]!; **hörst du?** are you listening?; **man höre und staune** would you believe it!; wonders will never cease (iron.); **hör mal!/**~ **Sie**

mal! listen [here]!; **hört, hört!** aha, listen to this! 4 (befolgen) **auf jmdn./jmds. Rat ~:** listen to *or* heed sb./sb.'s advice; **alles hört auf mein Kommando!** (Milit.) I'm taking command; (scherzh.) everyone do as I say; **auf den Namen Monika ~:** answer to the name [of] Monika 5 (Kenntnis erhalten) **von jmdm./etw. ~:** hear of sb./sth.; **davon ~, dass ...** hear that ...; **von jmdm. ~** (Nachricht bekommen) hear from sb.; **Sie ~ noch von mir** you'll be hearing from me again; you haven't heard the last of this; **ich lasse wieder von mir ~:** I'll be in touch 6 (ugs.: gehorchen) do as one is told; **nicht ~ wollen** not do as one's told; **wer nicht ~ will, muss fühlen** (Spr.) if you don't do as you're told, you'll suffer for it

Hören·sagen *das;* **~s** hearsay; **vom ~:** by *or* from hearsay

Hörer *der;* **~s, ~** 1 listener 2 (Telefon~) receiver

Hörer·brief *der* listener's letter; **~e** listeners' letters

Hörerin *die;* **~, ~nen** listener

Hörer·kreis *der* audience

Hörerschaft *die;* **~, ~en** audience

Hör-: ~fehler *der* 1 **das war ein ~fehler** he/she *etc.* misheard; **~fehler ausschließen** exclude the possibility of mishearing [sth.]; 2 (Schwerhörigkeit) hearing defect; **~folge** *die* radio series; (in Fortsetzungen) radio serial; **~funk** *der* radio; **im ~funk** on the radio; **~gerät** *das* hearing aid; **~gewohnheit** *die* listening habits *pl.*

hörig *Adj.* 1 *in* **jmdm. ~ sein** be submissively dependent on sb.; (sexuell) be sexually dependent on *or* enslaved to sb.; be sb.'s sexual slave 2 (hist.) **die ~en Bauern** the serfs; **~ sein** be in bondage

Hörige *der/die; adj. Dekl.* (hist.) serf; bondsman/bondswoman

Hörigkeit *die;* **~** 1 enslavement; (sexuell) sexual dependence 2 (hist.) bondage; serfdom

Horizont /hori'tsɔnt/ *der;* **~[e]s, ~e** (auch Geol., fig.) horizon; **am ~:** on the horizon; **einen engen** *od.* **kleinen ~ haben** (fig.) have narrow horizons *pl.;* **seinen ~ erweitern** (fig.) widen *or* expand one's horizons *pl.;* **hinter dem ~:** below the horizon; **über jmds. ~** (*Akk.*) **gehen** (fig.) be beyond sb.; go over sb.'s head

horizontal /horitsɔn'ta:l/
A *Adj.* horizontal; *s. auch* **Gewerbe 1**
B *adv.* horizontally

Horizontale *die;* **~, ~n** 1 (Linie) horizontal line 2 (Lage) **die ~:** the horizontal; **etw. in die ~ bringen** lay sth. flat; **sich in die ~ begeben** (scherzh.) lie down

Hormon /hɔr'mo:n/ *das;* **~s, ~e** hormone

hormonal /hɔrmo'na:l/
A *Adj.* hormonal
B *adv.* hormonally

Hormon·behandlung *die* hormone treatment; **eine ~:** a course of hormone treatment

hormonell /hɔrmo'nɛl/ *Adj., adv.* ▸ **hormonal**

Hormon-: ~haushalt *der* hormone balance; **~präparat** *das* hormone preparation; **~spiegel** *der* hormone level

Hör·muschel *die* earpiece

Horn /hɔrn/ *das;* **~[e]s, Hörner** /'hœrnɐ/ 1 horn; **jmdm. Hörner aufsetzen** (fig. ugs.) cuckold sb.; **sich** (*Dat.*) **die Hörner ablaufen** *od.* **abstoßen** (fig.) sow one's wild oats 2 (Blasinstrument) horn; (Milit.) bugle; **ins gleiche ~ stoßen** (fig.) take the same line 3 *Pl.* **~e** (Substanz) horn 4 (Signal~) (eines Autos usw.) horn; hooter (Brit.); (eines Zuges) horn

horn·artig *Adj.* hornlike

Hornberger /'hɔrnbɛrgɐ/ *in* **wie das ~ Schießen ausgehen** all come to nothing

Horn-: ~blende *die* (Mineral.) hornblende; **~brille** *die* horn-rimmed spectacles *pl. or* glasses *pl.*

Hörnchen /'hœrnçən/ *das;* **~s, ~** 1 small *or* little horn 2 (Gebäck) croissant 3 (Nagetier) squirrel 4 ▸ **Lenkerhörnchen**

Hörner·klang *der* sound of horns

hörnern *Adj.* horn ‹*handle etc.*›; ‹*handle etc.*› [made] of horn

Horn·haut *die* 1 callus; hard *or* callused skin *no indef. art.* 2 ▸ⓘ **S. 435** (am Auge) cornea

Hornhaut-: ~entzündung *die* ▸ⓘ **S. 439** inflammation of the cornea; corneitis *no indef. art.* (Med.); keratitis *no indef. art.* (Med.); **~trübung** *die* corneal opacity; opacity of the cornea; **~übertragung** *die* corneal grafting

hornig *Adj.* horny

Hornisse /hɔr'nɪsə/ *die;* **~, ~n** hornet

Hornist *der;* **~en, ~en, Hornistin** *die;* **~, ~nen** 1 horn player 2 (Milit.) bugler

Horn-: ~kamm *der* horn comb; **~ochse** *der* (ugs.) stupid ass; **~signal** *das* blast on a/the horn; **~tier** *das* horned animal; **die ~tiere** the Bovidae

Hornung *der;* **~s, ~e** (veralt.) February

Hör·organ *das* ▸ **Gehörorgan**

Horoskop /horo'sko:p/ *das;* **~s, ~e** horoscope; **jmdm. das ~ stellen** cast sb.'s horoscope

horrend /hɔ'rɛnt/ *Adj.* shocking (coll.), horrendous (coll.) ‹*price*›; colossal (coll.) ‹*sum, amount, rent*›; shocking (coll.) ‹*blunder, mistake, lack of discipline*›

horrido /hɔri'do:/ *Interj.* (Jägerspr.) hurrah

Hör·rohr *das* 1 (Stethoskop) stethoscope 2 (Hörgerät) ear trumpet

Horror /'hɔrɔr/ *der;* **~s** horror; **einen ~ vor jmdm./etw. haben** loathe and fear sb./have a horror of sth.

Horror-: ~film *der* horror film; **~szenario** *das* horror scenario; **~trip** *der* (ugs.) bad trip; **der reinste ~trip sein** (fig.) be a nightmare

Hör-: ~saal *der* 1 lecture theatre *or* hall *or* room; 2 (Zuhörerschaft) audience; **~schwelle** *die* (Akustik) threshold of audibility *or* hearing

Horsd'oeuvre /ɔr'dœ:vr/ *das;* **~s, ~s** (Gastr.) hors d'oeuvre

Hör·spiel *das* 1 radio play 2 (Gattung) radio drama *no art.*

Horst /hɔrst/ *der;* **~[e]s, ~e** 1 (Nest) eyrie 2 (Forstw.) (Bäume) group of trees; (Gebüsch) group of bushes 3 (Geol.) horst 4 ▸ **Fliegerhorst**

horsten *itr. V.* nest

Hör·sturz *der* ▸ⓘ **S. 439** (Med.) acute hearing loss

Hort /hɔrt/ *der;* **~[e]s, ~e** 1 (dichter.: Goldschatz) hoard [of gold] 2 (geh.: Schutz) refuge; sanctuary; **ein ~ der Freiheit** a stronghold *or* bulwark of liberty 3 (geh.: Stätte) **ein ~ des Lasters/des Geistes** a hotbed of vice/a centre of intellectual activity 4 ▸ **Kinderhort**

horten *tr. V.* hoard; stockpile ‹*raw materials*›

Hortensie /hɔr'tɛnziə/ *die;* **~, ~n** hydrangea

Hör·test *der* hearing test

Hortnerin /'hɔrtnərɪn/ *die;* **~, ~nen** *supervisor in a day home for schoolchildren*

Hortung *die;* **~:** hoarding; (von Rohstoffen) stockpiling

ho ruck /'ho:'rʊk/ ▸ **hau ruck**

Hör-: ~vermögen *das* hearing; **~weite** *die* hearing range; **in/außer ~weite** in/out of hearing range *or* of earshot; **~zentrum** *das* (Anat.) auditory centre

hosanna /ho'zana/ ▸ **hosianna**

Höschen /'hø:sçən/ *das;* **~s, ~** 1 trousers *pl.;* pair of trousers; (kurzes ~) short trousers *pl.;* shorts *pl.;* pair of shorts; **heiße ~** (ugs. scherzh.) hot pants 2 (Slip) panties *pl.;* pair of panties

Hose /'ho:zə/ *die;* **~, ~n** 1 trousers *pl.;* pants *pl.* (*Amer.*); (Unter~) pants *pl.;* (Freizeit~) slacks *pl.;* (Bund~) breeches *pl.;* (Reit~) jodhpurs *pl.;* riding breeches *pl.;* **eine ~:** a pair of trousers/pants/slacks *etc.;* **eine kurze/lange ~:** [a pair of] short trousers *or* shorts/long trousers; **ein/zwei Paar ~n** one/two pairs of trousers; **in die ~n schlüpfen/steigen** slip/get one's trousers on; slip/get into one's trousers; **das Kind hat in die ~[n] gemacht/die ~ vollgemacht** the child has made a mess in its pants 2 (fig.) **[zu Hause** *od.* **daheim] die ~n anhaben** (ugs.) wear the trousers [at home]; **die ~n runterlassen** (salopp) come clean (coll.); **die ~[n] [gestrichen] voll haben** (salopp) be shitting oneself (coarse); be in a blue funk (coll.); **die ~n voll kriegen** (ugs.) get a good hiding (coll.); **jmdm. die ~n strammziehen** (ugs.) give sb. a good hiding (coll.); **in die ~[n] gehen** (salopp) be a [complete] flop (coll.); **sich [vor Angst] in die ~[n] machen** (salopp) shit oneself (coarse); get into a blue funk (sl.); **es ist tote ~** (Jugendspr.) there's nothing doing (coll.)

Hosen-: ~an·zug *der* trouser suit (Brit.); pant suit; **~aufschlag** *der* [trouser *or* (Amer.) pants] turn-up; **~band·orden** *der* Order of the Garter; **~bein** *das* trouser leg; pants leg (Amer.); **~boden** *der* seat of the/one's/sb.'s trousers *or* (Amer.) pants; **ein paar auf den ~boden bekommen** get a smacked bottom; **sich auf den ~boden setzen** (fig.) knuckle down to it; **jmdm. den ~boden stramm ziehen** (fig. ugs.) give sb. a good hiding (coll.); **~boje** *die* (Seew.) breeches buoy; **~bügel** *der* trouser hanger; **~bund** *der* waistband; **~klammer** *die* bicycle clip; **~knopf** *der* trouser button; pants button (Amer.); **~latz** *der* 1 (an Leder~) flap; (an Trachten~, Matrosen~) bib; 2 (landsch.) ▸ **~schlitz**; **~matz** *der* (ugs. scherzh.) toddler; [tiny] tot; **~naht** *die* trouser seam; pants seam (Amer.); **Hände an die ~naht!** (Milit.) thumbs on your trouser seams!; **~rock** *der* culottes *pl.;* divided skirt; **~rolle** *die* (Theater) breeches part; **~scheißer** *der* 1 (derb: Feigling) chicken (coll.); 2 (ugs. scherzh.) ▸ **~matz**; **~schlitz** *der* fly; flies *pl.;* **~spanner** *der* ▸ **~bügel**; **~stall** *der* (ugs. scherzh.) ▸ **~schlitz**; **~tasche** *die* trouser pocket; pants pocket (Amer.); **etw. wie seine ~tasche kennen** (fig. ugs.) know sth. like the back of one's hand; **~träger** *Pl.* braces; suspenders (Amer.); pair of braces/suspenders

hosianna /ho'zi̯ana/ *Interj.* (christl. Rel.) hosanna

Hospital /hɔspi'ta:l/ *das;* **~s, ~e** *od.* **Hospitäler** /hɔspi'tɛ:lɐ/ 1 hospital 2 (veralt.: Pflegeheim) nursing home (Brit.)

Hospitalismus *der;* **~** (Psych., Päd., Med.) hospitalism *no art.*

Hospitant /hɔspi'tant/ *der;* **~en, ~en, Hospitantin** *die;* **~, ~nen** 1 *person sitting in on a class/lecture* 2 ▸ **Gasthörer**

hospitieren *itr. V.* **bei jmdm. ~:** sit in on sb.'s lectures/seminars; **in einem Seminar/einer Vorlesung ~:** sit in on a seminar/lecture

Hospiz /hɔs'pi:ts/ *das;* **~es, ~e** 1 hospice 2 (Hotel) **[christliches] ~** *private hotel run in accordance with Protestant principles*

Host /hoʊst/ *der;* **~s, ~s** (DV) host

Hostess, *Hosteß /hɔs'tɛs/ *die;* **~, ~en** ▸ⓘ **S. 113** hostess

Hostie /'hɔsti̯ə/ *die;* **~, ~n** (christl. Rel.) host

Hostien- (christl. Religion): **~schrein** *der* tabernacle; **~teller** *der* paten

Hotel /ho'tɛl/ *das;* **~s, ~s** hotel

Hotel-: ~bar *die* hotel bar; **~boy** *der* ▸ⓘ **S. 113** page[boy]; bellboy (Amer.); **~direktor** *der* hotel manager; **~direktorin** *die* hotel manager[ess]; **~fach** *das* hotel trade; **~fachfrau** *die*, **~fachmann** *der* [qualified] hotel manager; **~fachfrau/-mann lernen** complete a hotel management course; **~fachschule** *die* school of hotel management; **~führer** *der* hotel guide

Hotel garni /-gar'ni:/ *das;* **~, Hotels garnis** bed-and-breakfast hotel

Hotel-: ~gast *der* hotel guest; **~halle** *die* hotel lobby

Hotelier /hotɛ'li̯e:/ *der;* **~s, ~s** ▸ⓘ **S. 113** hotelier

Hotel-: ~page *der* ▸ⓘ **S. 113** ▸ **~boy**; **~portier** *der* ▸ⓘ **S. 113** [hotel] commissionaire; **~zimmer** *das* hotel room

Hot: ~line /'hɔtlaɪn/ *die;* **~, ~s** hotline; **~spot** /'hɔtspɔt/ *der;* **~s, ~s** (DV) hotspot

hott /hɔt/ *Interj.* gee[-up]; *s. auch* **hü**

hotten /ˈhɔtn̩/ *itr. V.* (salopp) rave it up (coll.)

HQ *Abk.* = **Hauptquartier** HQ.

HR *Abk.* = **Hessischer Rundfunk** Hesse Radio

hrsg. *Abk.* = **herausgegeben** ed.

Hrsg. *Abk.* = **Herausgeber** ed.

Hs. *Abk.* = **Handschrift** MS.

HTML *die;* ~ (DV) HTML

hu /hu:/ *Interj.* **1** ugh **2** (bei Kälte) brrr **3** (zum Erschrecken) boo

hü /hy:/ *Interj.* **1** (vorwärts) giddap; gee[-up] **2** (halt) whoa; **einmal sagt sie ~ und einmal hott** (fig. ugs.) first she says one thing, then another

Hub /hu:p/ *der;* **~[e]s, Hübe** /ˈhy:bə/ (Technik) **1** (das Heben) lifting; **in einem ~:** in one lift; (bei einem Bagger) in one load **2** (Weg des Kolbens) stroke

Hubbel /ˈhʊbl̩/ *der;* **~s, ~** (bes. südd.) bump

hubbelig *Adj.* (bes. südd.) bumpy

Hub·brücke *die* (Technik) lift bridge

hüben /ˈhy:bn̩/ *Adv.* on this side; over here; **~ und** *od.* **wie drüben** on both sides

Hubertus·jagd /huˈbɛrtʊs-/ *die;* **~, ~en** (Jagdw.) St. Hubert's Day hunt

Hub-: **~höhe** *die* (Technik) (eines Krans) lifting height; (einer Schleuse) lift; (eines Kolbens) length of stroke; **~raum** *der* ▸ **S. 582** (Technik) piston displacement; swept volume; (Messgröße für die Leistungsfähigkeit eines Motors) cubic capacity

hübsch /hʏpʃ/

A *Adj.* **1** pretty; nice-looking ‹*boy, person*›; (reizvoll) nice, pleasant ‹*area, flat, voice, tune, etc.*›; nice ‹*phrase, idea, present*›; **ihr Hübschen** (ugs.) my pretty ones; **sich ~ machen** make oneself look nice **2** (ugs.: ziemlich groß) **eine ~e Stange Geld kosten** cost a pretty penny; **ein ~es Sümmchen** a tidy sum (coll.); a nice little sum; **ein ~es Stück Arbeit** a fair amount *or* quite a lot of work **3** (ugs. iron.: unangenehm) **das ist eine ~e Geschichte/hier herrschen ~e Zustände** this is a fine *or* pretty kettle of fish (coll.) *or* a fine state of affairs

B *adv.* **1** prettily; **sich ~ anziehen** dress nicely; wear nice clothes; **~ eingerichtet/gekleidet** nicely *or* attractively furnished/dressed; **~ singen/spielen** sing/play nicely **2** (ugs.: sehr) **~ kalt** perishing cold **3** (ugs.: ordentlich) **immer ~ der Reihe nach** everybody must take his turn; **sei ~ brav** be a good boy/girl; **immer ~ langsam** take it nice and slowly

Hub·schrauber *der;* **~s, ~:** helicopter

Hubschrauber-lande·platz *der* heliport; (kleiner) helicopter pad; landing pad

Hub-: **~stapler** *der* **1** stacker truck; **2** ▸ **Gabelstapler**; **~volumen** *das* ▸ **~raum**

huch /hʊx/ *Interj.* ugh; (bei Kälte) brrr

Hucke /ˈhʊkə/ *die;* **~, ~n** pannier; **jmdm. die ~ voll hauen** (fig. ugs.) give sb. a good hiding (coll.); (bei einer Prügelei) beat hell out of sb. (coll.); **jmdm. die ~ voll lügen** (fig. ugs.) tell sb. a pack of lies; **die ~ voll kriegen** (fig. ugs.) get a good hiding (coll.); (bei einer Prügelei) get a proper beating (coll.); *s. auch* **saufen C**

huckepack /ˈhʊkəpak/ *Adv.* (ugs.): *in* **jmdn. ~ tragen** carry sb. piggyback; give sb. a piggyback; **etw. ~ tragen** carry sth. piggyback; **jmdn./etw. ~ nehmen** take sb./sth. up on one's back

Hudelei *die;* **~, ~en** (bes. südd., österr.) **1** (Arbeitsweise) sloppiness **2** (Pfuscharbeit) sloppy *or* slipshod *or* slapdash work *no indef. art.*

hudelig (bes. südd., österr.)

A *Adj.* sloppy; slapdash; slipshod ‹*work*›

B *adv.* sloppily; in a sloppy *or* slipshod *or* slapdash manner

hudeln /ˈhu:dl̩n/ *itr. V.* (bes. südd., österr.) work sloppily; be sloppy *or* slapdash (**bei** in); **nur nicht ~!** don't be in such a hurry!; take it easy!

hudlig ▸ **hudelig**

Huf /hu:f/ *der;* **~[e]s, ~e** hoof; **einem Pferd die ~e beschlagen** shoe a horse

huf-, Huf-: **~eisen** *das* horseshoe; **~eisen·form** *die:* **in ~eisenform** in [the shape of] a horseshoe; **~eisenförmig** **A** *Adj.* horseshoe-shaped; **B** *adv.* in [the shape of] a horseshoe

Hufen·dorf *das: linear village in which each house has its own fields behind it*

Huf-: **~lattich** *der* coltsfoot; **~nagel** *der* horseshoe nail; **~schlag** *der* **1** (Klang) hoofbeats *pl.;* **2** (Stoß) kick [from a/the horse]; **~schmied** *der* farrier; blacksmith; **~schmiede** *die* farrier's *or* blacksmith's workshop

Hüft·bein *das* ▸ **S. 435** (Anat.) hip bone; innominate bone (Anat.)

Hüfte /ˈhʏftə/ *die;* **~, ~n** ▸ **S. 435** hip; **sie stand da, die Arme in die ~n gestemmt ...** she stood there, hands on hips *or* with arms akimbo; **sich in den ~n wiegen** swing one's hips; **aus der ~ schießen/feuern** shoot/fire from the hip

hüft-, Hüft-: **~gelenk** *das* ▸ **S. 435** (Anat.) hip joint; **~gelenk·entzündung** *die* coxitis; **~gürtel** *der,* **~halter** *der* girdle; **~hoch** **A** *Adj.* **~hoch sein** ‹*grass, wall*› be almost waist-high; ‹*water, snow, mud*› be almost waist-deep; **B** *adv.* **~hoch im Schlamm stehen** stand waist-deep in mud; **~hose** [pair *sing.*] of hipsters *pl.*

Huf·tier *das* hoofed animal; ungulate (Zool.)

Hüft-: **~knochen** *der* ▸ **Hüftbein**; **~nerv** *der* ▸ **S. 435** sciatic nerve; **~schwung** *der* (Ringen) cross-buttock; **~speck** *der* flab on *or* around the hips (coll.); hip flab (coll.); **~umfang** *der,* **~weite** *die* (Schneiderei) hip size

Hügel /ˈhy:gl̩/ *der;* **~s, ~** **1** hill; (fig.) heap; pile **2** (dichter.) grave mound

hügel-, Hügel-: **~ab** *Adv.* (geh.) downhill; **~an, ~auf** *Adv.* (geh.) uphill; **~grab** *das* (Archäol.) barrow; tumulus

hügelig *Adj.* hilly

Hügel-: **~kette** *die* chain *or* range of hills; **~land** *das* hill country

Hugenotte /hugəˈnɔtə/ *der;* **~n, ~n** Huguenot

hüglig ▸ **hügelig**

huh ▸ **hu**

hüh ▸ **hü**

Huhn /hu:n/ *das;* **~[e]s, Hühner** /ˈhy:nɐ/ **1** chicken; [domestic] fowl; (Henne) chicken; hen; **gebratenes ~:** roast chicken; **herumlaufen wie ein aufgescheuchtes ~** (ugs.) run about in a great panic (coll.); **da lachen [ja] die Hühner** (ugs.) you/he/she *etc.* must be joking (coll.); **ein blindes ~ findet auch mal ein Korn** (Spr.) anyone can have a stroke of luck once in a while; **mit den Hühnern aufstehen/zu Bett gehen** (scherzh.) get up with the lark/go to bed early **2** (ugs.: Mensch) **ein verrücktes/dummes/fideles ~:** a nutcase (coll.) *or* idiot/stupid twit (Brit. coll.) *or* idiot/cheerful sort (coll.) **3** (Jägerspr.) ▸ **Rebhuhn**

Hühnchen /ˈhy:nçən/ *das;* **~s, ~:** little *or* small chicken; **mit jmdm. [noch] ein ~ zu rupfen haben** (ugs.) [still] have a bone to pick with sb.

Hühner-: **~auge** *das* (am Fuß) corn; **jmdm. auf die ~augen treten** (fig. ugs.) tread on sb.'s corns *or* toes; **~augen·pflaster** *das* corn plaster; **~brühe** *die* chicken broth; **~brust** *die* ▸ **S. 439** **1** (Med.) chicken breast; pigeon breast; **2** (ugs.: flacher Brustkorb) scrawny chest; **~dieb** *der* chicken thief; **~dreck** *der* (ugs.) chicken dirt; **~ei** *das* hen's egg; **~farm** *die* chicken farm; **~frikassee** *das* chicken fricassee; fricassee of chicken; **~futter** *das* chicken feed; **~habicht** *der* [northern] goshawk; **~hof** *der* chicken run; **~hund** *der* ▸ **Vorstehhund**; **~klein** *das;* **~~s** trimmings *pl.* of chicken (in stew etc.); **~leiter** *die* chicken ladder; **~mist** *der* chicken droppings *pl.;* **~pest** *die* (Tiermed.) fowl pest; **~stall** *der* chicken coop; hen-coop; **~suppe** *die* chicken soup; **~vogel** *der* (Zool.) gallinaceous bird; **~zucht** *die* **1** chicken rearing *no art.;* chicken farming *no art.;* **2** (Betrieb) chicken farm

hui /hui/ *Interj.* whoosh; **außen ~ und innen pfui** (von Geräten usw.) the outside's fine but inside it's a different story; (von Personen) he/she seems very nice on the surface, but underneath it's a different story

Huld /hʊlt/ *die;* **~** (geh., veralt., noch iron.) (Gunst) favour; (Güte) graciousness; **jmdm. seine ~ schenken** bestow one's favour on sb.

huldigen /ˈhʊldɪgn̩/ *itr. V.* **1** **jmdm. ~:** pay tribute to *or* honour sb. **2** (geh.: anhängen) **einem Grundsatz/einer Ansicht/Mode ~:** hold [devotedly] to a principle/a point of view/follow a fashion; **dem Kartenspiel/Alkohol ~:** be addicted to cards/enjoy a few drinks **3** (hist.: Treue geloben) **jmdm. ~:** pay *or* render homage to sb.

Huldigung *die;* **~, ~en** **1** (Ehrung) tribute; homage; **einer Dame seine ~ darbringen** pay one's addresses *pl.* to a lady **2** (hist.: Treuegelöbnis) homage

Huldigungs·gedicht *das* panegyric

huld·reich, huld·voll (geh. veralt.)

A *Adj.* gracious

B *adv.* graciously

Hülle /ˈhʏlə/ *die;* **~, ~n** **1** (Umhüllung) cover; (für Ausweis, Zeitkarte) cover; holder; (für Füllhalter) case; (Schallplatten~) cover; sleeve; (fig.: eines Menschen) **die leibliche ~** (dicht.) this mortal frame (literary); **die sterbliche ~** (geh. verhüll.) the mortal remains *pl.* **2** (ugs. scherzh.: Kleidung) **seine** *od.* **die ~ fallen lassen** strip off [one's clothes] **3** **in ~ und Fülle,** (geh.) **die ~ und Fülle** in abundance; in plenty **4** (Bot.) involucre

hüllen *tr. V.* (geh.) wrap; **jmdn./sich in etw.** (*Akk.*) **~:** wrap sb./oneself in sth.; **in Dunkel** (*Akk.*) **gehüllt** (fig.) shrouded *or* veiled in obscurity; **in Wolken** (*Akk.*) **gehüllt** (fig.) enveloped in clouds

hüllenlos *Adj.* **1** (unverhüllt) plain; clear **2** (scherzh.: nackt) naked; in one's birthday suit *pred.* (joc.)

Hülse /ˈhʏlzə/ *die;* **~, ~n** **1** (Hülle) (für Füllhalter, Thermometer, Patrone) case; (für Film) [cassette] container; (für Impfstoff) capsule **2** (Bot.) pod; hull

Hülsen·frucht *die* **1** (Frucht) fruit of a leguminous plant; **Hülsenfrüchte** pulses **2** (Pflanze) legume; leguminous plant

human /huˈma:n/

A *Adj.* **1** (menschenwürdig) humane; **die modernen Großstädte müssen ~er werden** modern cities must provide a more humane environment for people to live in **2** (nachsichtig) considerate **3** (Med.) human

B *adv.* **1** (menschenwürdig) humanly **2** (nachsichtig) considerately

Human-: **~biologie** *die* human biology *no art.;* **~genetik** *die* human genetics *sing., no art.*

humanisieren *tr. V.* humanize

Humanisierung *die;* **~:** humanization

Humanismus *der;* **~:** humanism; (Epoche) Humanism *no art.*

Humanist *der;* **~en, ~en, Humanistin** *die;* **~, ~nen** **1** humanist; (hist.) Humanist **2** (Altsprachler) classical scholar; (Student) classics student

humanistisch *Adj.* **1** humanist[ic]; (hist.) Humanist **2** (altsprachlich) classical; **ein ~es Gymnasium** *secondary school emphasizing classical languages*

humanitär /humaniˈtɛ:ɐ̯/ *Adj.* humanitarian

Humanität /humaniˈtɛ:t/ *die;* **~:** respect for humanity

Humanitäts·duselei /-du:zəlai/ *die;* **~, ~en** (abwertend) **[eine] ~/~en** *Pl.* sentimental humanitarianism *sing.*

Human-: **~medizin** *die* human medicine *no art.;* **~mediziner** *der,* **~medizinerin** *die* practitioner of human medicine

Humanoide /humanoˈi:də/ *der;* **~n, ~n** **Humanoidin** *die;* **~, ~nen** humanoid

Human·versuch *der* (Med.) test on a human being/on human beings

Humbug /ˈhʊmbʊk/ *der;* **~s** (ugs. abwertend) humbug

Hummel /'hʊml̩/ *die;* ~, ~n bumble-bee; humble-bee; **eine wilde ~** (scherzh.) a proper tomboy; *s. auch* **Hintern**

Hummer /'hʊmɐ/ *der;* ~s, ~: lobster

Hummer-: **~cocktail** *der* (Kochk.) lobster cocktail; **~krabbe** *die* king prawn; **~majonäse**, **~mayonnaise** *die* (Kochk.) lobster mayonnaise

Humor /hu'mo:ɐ̯/ *der;* ~s, ~e [1] humour; (Sinn für ~) sense of humour; **etw. mit ~ tragen/nehmen** bear/take sth. with a sense of humour *or* cheerfully; **keinen [Sinn für] ~ haben** have no sense of humour; **er hat ~ — lässt mich mit der ganzen Arbeit allein hier sitzen** he's got a strange sense of humour, leaving me sitting here on my own with all the work; **~ ist, wenn man trotzdem lacht** it's not the end of the world; **der rheinische/englische ~:** Rhenish/English humour; the Rhinelander's/Englishman's sense of humour; **schwarzer ~:** black humour [2] (gute Laune) **den ~ nicht verlieren** remain good-humoured

Humoreske /humo'rɛskə/ *die;* ~, ~n [1] (Literaturwiss.) humorous sketch [2] (Musik) humoresque

humorig *Adj.* humorous

Humorist *der;* ~en, ~en, **Humoristin** *die;* ~, ~nen [1] (Autor[in]) humorist [2] (Vortragskünstler[in]) comedian

humoristisch
[A] *Adj.* humorous; **er ist ein großes ~es Talent** he has great talent to amuse
[B] *adv.* with humour

humor-, Humor-: **~los** [A] *Adj.* humourless; [B] *adv.* without humour; **~losigkeit** *die;* ~~: humourlessness; lack of humour; **~voll** [A] *Adj.* humorous; [B] *adv.* humorously; in a humorous way

Humpelei *die;* ~ (ugs.) hobbling; **er übertreibt ein bisschen mit seiner ~:** he's overdoing the limp a bit

humpeln /'hʊmpl̩n/ *itr. V.* [1] *auch mit sein* walk with *or* have a limp [2] *mit sein* (sich ~d fortbewegen) hobble; limp

Humpen /'hʊmpn̩/ *der;* ~s, ~: tankard; [beer] mug; (aus Ton auch) stein

Humus /'hu:mʊs/ *der;* ~: humus

humus-, Humus-: **~boden** *der,* **~erde** *die* humus soil; **~reich** *Adj.* ‹soil› rich in humus; rich ‹soil›

Hund /hʊnt/ *der;* ~es, ~e [1] dog; (Jagdhund) hound; dog; **ein junger ~:** a puppy *or* pup; **bei diesem Wetter würde man keinen ~ vor die Tür schicken** I wouldn't turn a dog out in weather like this; **da liegt der ~ begraben** (fig. ugs.) (Ursache) that's what's causing it; (Grund) that's the real reason; **da wird der ~ in der Pfanne verrückt** (salopp) it's quite incredible; **das ist zum Junge-~e-Kriegen** (ugs.) it's enough to drive you to despair; it's enough to drive you spare (Brit. coll.); **viele ~e sind des Hasen Tod** (Spr.) it's one against many; **~e, die bellen, beißen nicht** (Spr.) barking dogs seldom bite; **den letzten beißen die ~e** (fig.) late-comers must expect to be unlucky; **ein dicker ~** (ugs.: grober Fehler) a real bloomer (Brit. sl.) *or* (coll.) goof; **das ist ein dicker ~** (ugs.: Frechheit) that's a bit thick (coll.); **kalter ~** (ugs.): *gateau consisting of layers of biscuit and chocolate-flavoured filling;* **der Große ~/der Kleine ~** (Astron.) the Great[er] Dog/the Little *or* Lesser Dog; **bekannt sein wie ein bunter** *od.* **scheckiger ~:** be a well-known figure; **wie ~ und Katze leben** (ugs.) lead a cat-and-dog life; **damit kannst du keinen ~ hinter dem Ofen hervorlocken** that won't tempt anybody; **auf den ~ kommen** (ugs.) go to the dogs (coll.); **mit allen ~en gehetzt sein** (ugs.) be up to (coll.) *or* know all the tricks; **vor die ~e gehen** (ugs.) go to the dogs (coll.); (sterben) die; kick the bucket (coll.) [2] (salopp: Mann) bloke (Brit. coll.); (abwertend) bastard (coll.); **so ein blöder ~!** [what a] stupid bastard! [3] (Bergmannsspr.) [mine] car; tub

Hundchen, Hündchen /'hʏntçən/ *das;* ~s, ~ (kleiner Hund) little dog; (Koseform) doggie (coll.); (junger Hund) puppy; pup

hunde-, Hunde-: **~artige** *Pl.; adj. Dekl.* (Zool.) canines; **die ~artigen** the Canidae; **~ausstellung** *die* dog show; **~blick** *der* (fig. ugs.) doglike look; (ergeben) look of doglike devotion; **~blume** *die* dandelion; **~deckchen** *das* [1] dog coat; [2] (scherzh.: Gamasche) gaiter; **~dreck** *der* dog's mess *or* muck; **~elend** *Adj.* [really] wretched *or* awful; **~fänger** *der,* **~fängerin** *die* dog catcher; **~futter** *das* dog food; **~gespann** *das* dog team; **~halsband** *das* dog collar; **~halter** *der,* **~halterin** *die* (Amtsspr.) dog owner; **~haufen** *der* pile of dog mess; **~hütte** *die* (auch fig. abwertend) [dog] kennel; **~kalt** *Adj.* (ugs.) freezing cold; **~kälte** *die* (ugs.) freezing cold; **~klo[sett]** *das* dogs' toilet *or* lavatory; **~kot** *der* (geh.) dog dirt; **~kuchen** *der* dog biscuit; **~leben** *das* (ugs.) dog's life; **~marke** *die* [1] dog licence disc; dog tag; [2] (salopp scherzh.: Erkennungsmarke) (bei Soldaten) identity disc; dog tag (Amer. sl.); (bei der Polizei) ▸ **Kennmarke**; **~müde** *Adj.* (ugs.) dog-tired; **~narr** *der* fanatical dog lover; **~rasse** *die* breed of dog; **~rennen** *das* dog racing; greyhound racing; **ein Vermögen beim ~rennen verlieren** lose a fortune at the dog track *or* (coll.) on the dogs *pl.*

hundert /'hʊndɐt/ *Kardinalz.* [1] ▸ⓘ **S. 29**, ▸ⓘ **S. 826** a *or* one hundred; **mehrere/einige ~** *od.* **Hundert Menschen** several/a few hundred people; **auf ~ kommen/sein** (ugs.) blow one's top (coll.)/be in a raging *or* (coll.) flaming temper; *s. auch* **acht** [2] (ugs.: viele) hundreds of; **~ Neuigkeiten** lots of news

Hundert[1] *das;* ~s, ~e *od.* (nach unbest. Zahlwörtern) ~ [1] hundred; **ein halbes ~:** fifty; **fünf vom ~:** five per cent [2] *Pl.* (große Anzahl) **~e/hunderte von Menschen** hundreds of people; **von solchen Menschen gibt es unter ~en/hunderten nur einen** people like that are few and far between; **in die ~e/hunderte gehen** (ugs.) run into hundreds

Hundert[2] *die;* ~, ~en hundred

hundert·ein[s] *Kardinalz.* ▸ⓘ **S. 29**, ▸ⓘ **S. 826** a *or* one hundred and one

Hunderter *der;* ~s, ~ [1] (ugs.) hundred-euro/-dollar *etc.* note; **das wird mich einige ~ kosten** that will cost me a few hundred [euros/dollars *etc.*] [2] (Math.) hundred

hunderterlei *Gattungsz.; indekl.* (ugs.) [1] (von verschiedener Art) a hundred and one different ‹*answers, kinds, etc.*› [2] (viele) a hundred and one; **ich muss noch ~ besorgen** I still have a hundred and one things to see to

Hundert·euro·schein *der* hundred-euro note

hundert·fach *Vervielfältigungsz.* hundredfold; **die ~e Menge/der ~e Preis** a hundred times the amount/price; *s. auch* **achtfach**

Hundert·fünf·und·siebziger *der;* ~s, ~ (ugs. veralt.) homo (coll.); queer (sl.)

hundert·fünfzig·prozentig *Adj.* (ugs. iron.) overzealous ‹*official*›; fanatical ‹*nationalist, communist, etc.*›

Hundert·jahr·feier *die* centenary; centennial; **die ~ unserer Organisation** the centenary *or* centennial of our organization

hundert·jährig *Adj.* [1] (100 Jahre alt) [one-]hundred-year-old; **ein ~er Greis** a centenarian [2] (100 Jahre dauernd) **nach ~em Kampf** after a hundred years of war; **ihr/sein ~es Bestehen feiern** celebrate its centenary; **der Hundertjährige Krieg** (hist.) the Hundred Years' War; **der hundertjährige Kalender** the Century Almanac

hundert·mal *Adv.* a hundred times; **auch wenn du dich ~ beschwerst** (ugs.) however much *or* no matter how much you complain; *s. auch* **achtmal**

Hundert-: **~meter·hürdenlauf** *der* (Leichtathletik) hundred-metres hurdles *sing.;* **~meter·lauf** *der* (Leichtathletik) hundred metres *sing.;* **sie gehört zu den Weltbesten im ~meterlauf** she is among the world's best at a *or* the hundred metres

hundert·prozentig
[A] *Adj.* [1] [one-]hundred per cent *attrib.;* **~er Alkohol** pure alcohol [2] (ugs.: völlig) a hundred per cent, complete, absolute ‹*certainty, agreement, etc.*› [3] (ugs.: ganz sicher) completely *or* absolutely reliable [4] (ugs.: typisch) **ein ~er Konservativer/eine ~e Amerikanerin** a conservative/an American through and through
[B] *adv.* (ugs.) **ich bin nicht ~ sicher** I'm not a hundred per cent sure; **du kannst dich ~ auf ihn/darauf verlassen** you can rely on him/it absolutely *or* one hundred per cent; **~ Recht haben** be absolutely right; **etw. ~ wissen** know sth. for sure; **er wird das tun, ~:** he will do it, you can be a hundred per cent sure of that

Hundertschaft *die;* ~, ~en group of a hundred; **einige ~en der Polizei** several hundred police

hundertst... /'hʊndɐtst.../ *Ordinalz.* ▸ⓘ **S. 826** hundredth; **zum ~en Mal fragen** (ugs.) ask for the hundredth time; **vom Hundertsten ins Tausendste kommen** get carried away so that one subject just leads to another

hundertstel /'hʊndɐtstl̩/ *Bruchz.* ▸ⓘ **S. 826** hundredth; *s. auch* **achtel**

Hundertstel *das* (schweiz. *meist* **der**); ~s, ~: ▸ⓘ **S. 826** hundredth

Hundertstel·sekunde *die* hundredth of a second

hundert·tausend *Kardinalz.* ▸ⓘ **S. 826** a *or* one hundred thousand; **mehrere/viele ~** *od.* **Hunderttausend Menschen** several hundred thousand people/many hundreds of thousands of people

hundert·und·ein[s] *Kardinalz.* a *or* one hundred and one

hundert·zehn *Kardinalz.* ▸ⓘ **S. 826** a *or* one hundred and ten

Hundert·zehn·meter·hürden·lauf *der* (Leichtathletik) 110 metres hurdles *sing.*

Hunde-: **~salon** *der* poodle *or* dog parlour; **~scheiße** *die* (derb) dog shit (coarse); **~schlitten** *der* dog sledge; dog sled (Amer.); **~schnauze** *die* dog's muzzle *or* snout; **kalt wie eine ~schnauze sein** (fig. ugs.) be as cold as ice (fig.); **~sohn** *der* (abwertend) cur; **~steuer** *die* dog licence fee; **~streife** *die* dog patrol; **~wetter** *das* (ugs.) filthy *or* (coll.) lousy weather; **~zucht** *die* [1] dog breeding *no art.;* [2] (Betrieb) [breeding] kennels *pl.;* **~zwinger** *der* dog run

Hündin /'hʏndɪn/ *die;* ~, ~nen bitch

hündisch /'hʏndɪʃ/
[A] *Adj.* [1] (würdelos) doglike, servile ‹*obedience*›; doglike ‹*devotion*›; fawning, abject ‹*submissiveness*› [2] (gemein) mean; nasty
[B] *adv.* **jmdm. ~ ergeben sein** have a doglike devotion to sb.; **sich einer Sache** (*Dat.*) **~ unterwerfen** submit abjectly to sth.

hunds-, Hunds-: **~erbärmlich** (ugs.) [A] *Adj.* [1] [really] dreadful (coll.); [2] (verabscheuenswürdig) dirty *attrib.* ‹*lie, coward*›; **eine ~erbärmliche Gemeinheit** a dirty low-down thing to do/say; [B] *adv.* [1] (sehr) terribly (coll.), dreadfully (coll.) ‹*cold*›; [2] (sehr schlecht) [really] abysmally (coll.) *or* dreadfully (coll.); **~fott** /-fɔt/ *der;* ~~[e]s, ~~e *od.* **~fötter** /fœtɐ/ (derb abwertend) low-down bastard (coll.); **~föttisch** /-fœtɪʃ/ *Adj.* (derb abwertend) low-down *attrib.;* dirty *attrib.* ‹*coward*›; **~gemein** (ugs.) [A] *Adj.* [1] (abwertend: überaus gemein) really mean *or* shabby; dirty ‹*liar*›; **es war ~gemein, uns so hereinzulegen** it was a really mean *or* shabby trick to take us for a ride (coll.) like that; [2] (sehr stark) terrible (coll.), dreadful (coll.) ‹*cold, weather, pain, etc.*›; [B] *adv.* [1] (gemein) ‹*deceive, behave*› really meanly *or* shabbily; [2] (sehr stark) **das tut ~gemein weh** it hurts like hell (coll.) *or* terribly (coll.); **~gemeinheit** *die* (abwertend) really mean *or* shabby trick; **~miserabel** (salopp abwertend) [A] *Adj.* [really] lousy (coll.) *or* dreadful (coll.); [B] *adv.* ‹*behave*› [really] appallingly (coll.) *or* dreadfully (coll.); **~rose** *die* (Bot.) dog rose; wild briar; **~stern** *der* (Astron.) dog star; **~tage** *Pl.* dog days; **~veilchen** *das* dog violet; **~wut** *die* (veralt.) ▸ **Tollwut**

Hüne /'hy:nə/ *der;* ~n, ~n giant

Hünen·grab *das* megalithic tomb; (Hügelgrab) barrow; tumulus

hünenhaft *Adj.* gigantic ‹*build, stature*›

Hunger /ˈhʊŋɐ/ *der;* **~s** [1] **~ bekommen/haben** get/be hungry; **ich habe ~ wie ein Bär** *od.* **Wolf** I'm so hungry I could eat a horse; **sein ~ war groß** he was very hungry; **~ auf etw.** (*Akk.*) **haben** fancy sth.; feel like sth. (coll.); **~ leiden** go hungry; starve; **wissen, was ~ ist** know what it is to go hungry; **vor ~ sterben** die of starvation *or* hunger; starve to death; **seinen ~ stillen** satisfy one's hunger; **~ ist der beste Koch** (Spr.) hunger is the best sauce (prov.); **der ~ treibts rein** (ugs. scherzh.) if you're hungry enough, you'll eat anything [2] (Hungersnot) famine [3] (geh.: Verlangen) hunger; (nach Ruhm, Macht) craving; thirst; **~ nach Gerechtigkeit** powerful desire to see justice done

Hunger-: ~blockade *die* food blockade; **~dasein** *das* existence at starvation level *or* below subsistence level; **~gefühl** *das* feeling of hunger; **~haken** *der* (salopp abwertend) beanpole; **ein ~haken sein** be skin and bone; **~jahr** *das* hungry year; **~kur** *die* starvation diet; **eine ~kur machen** go on a starvation diet; **~leider** *der;* **~~s, ~~, ~leiderin** *die;* **~~, ~~nen** (ugs. abwertend) starving pauper; **~lohn** *der* (abwertend) starvation wage[s *pl.*]

hungern /ˈhʊŋɐn/

A *itr. V.* [1] go hungry; starve; **~, um schlank zu werden** be on a starvation diet in order to get slim; **jmdn. ~ lassen** let sb. starve; (als Strafe) starve sb. [2] (verlangen) **nach etw. ~:** hunger *or* be hungry for sth.; (nach Macht, Ruhm) crave sth.; thirst for sth.

B *refl. V.* **sich schlank ~:** go on a [slimming] diet; (mit totalem Verzicht auf Nahrung) slim by going on a starvation diet; **sich zu Tode ~:** starve oneself to death

C *tr. V.* (unpers.) (dichter.: verlangen) **jmdn. hungert nach etw.** sb. craves [for] sth. *or* hungers for sth.

Hunger-: ~ödem *das* ▸❶ **S. 439** (Med.) famine oedema; nutritional oedema; **~ration** *die* (ugs.) starvation rations *pl.*

hungers *in* **~ sterben** die of starvation *or* hunger; starve to death

Hungers·not *die* famine

Hunger-: ~streik *der* hunger strike; **in den ~streik treten** go on hunger strike; **~tod** *der* death from starvation; **den ~tod sterben** die of starvation; **~tuch** *das: in* **am ~tuch nagen** (ugs. scherzh.) be on the breadline; **~turm** *der* (hist.): *dungeon in which prisoners were starved to death*

hungrig *Adj.* [1] hungry; **das macht [einen] ~:** it makes you hungry *or* gives you an appetite; **~ nach etw. sein** fancy sth.; feel like sth. (coll.) [2] (geh.: begierig) hungry (**nach** for); **~ nach Anerkennung sein** crave recognition

Hunne /ˈhʊnə/ *der;* **~n, ~n** (hist.) Hun

Hupe /ˈhuːpə/ *die;* **~, ~n** horn; **auf die ~ drücken** sound the/one's horn

hupen *itr. V.* sound the *or* one's horn; **dreimal ~:** hoot three times; give three toots on the horn

Huperei *die;* **~:** honking; hooting

Hupf·dohle *die* (salopp) chorus girl

hupfen /ˈhʊpfn̩/ *itr. V.; mit sein* (südd., österr.) hop; **das ist gehupft wie gesprungen** (ugs.) it doesn't make any difference; it doesn't matter either way

hüpfen /ˈhʏpfn̩/ *itr. V.; mit sein* hop; ‹*ball*› bounce; ‹*lamb*› gambol; **über die Straße ~:** skip across the road; **Hüpfen spielen** play [at] hopscotch; **mein Herz hüpfte vor Freude** my heart leapt for joy; **das ist gehüpft wie gesprungen** (ugs.) ▸**hupfen**

Hupfer *der;* **~s, ~** (bes. südd., österr.), **Hüpfer** *der;* **~s, ~** skip; (auf einem Bein) hop

Hup-: ~konzert *das* (ugs. scherzh.) chorus of hooting; **~signal** *das* hoot; toot; **~verbot** *das* ban on sounding one's horn

Hürde /ˈhʏrdə/ *die;* **~, ~n** [1] (Leichtathletik, Reitsport, fig.) hurdle; **eine ~ nehmen/reißen** clear/knock over a hurdle; **eine ~ nehmen** (fig.) get over a hurdle

Hürden-: ~lauf *der* (Leichtathletik) hurdling; (Wettbewerb) hurdles *pl.*; hurdle race; **~läufer** *der*, **~läuferin** *die* (Leichtathletik) hurdler; **~rennen** *das* (Reitsport) hurdle race; **~rennen reiten** ride in a hurdle race

Hure /ˈhuːrə/ *die;* **~, ~n** (abwertend) whore

huren *itr. V.* (abwertend) whore; fornicate; **mit jmdm. ~:** fornicate with sb.

Huren-: ~bock *der* (abwertend) whoremonger; fornicator; **~kind** *das* (Druckw.) widow; **~sohn** *der* (abwertend) bastard (coll.); son of a bitch (derog.)

Hurerei *die;* **~, ~en** (abwertend) **~/~en** *Pl.* whoring *sing.*; fornication *sing.*

Huri /ˈhuːri/ *die;* **~, ~s** (islam. Rel.) houri

hurra /hʊˈraː/ *Interj.* hurray; hurrah; **~/Hurra schreien** cheer; *s. auch* **hipp, hipp, hurra**

Hurra *das;* **~s, ~s** cheer; **ein dreifaches ~:** three cheers *pl.*; **jmdn. mit ~ begrüßen** greet sb. with cheering *or* cheers *pl.*

hurra-, Hurra-: ~gebrüll *das*, **~geschrei** *das* [loud] cheering *or* cheers *pl.*; **~patriot** *der* (ugs. abwertend) flag-waving patriot; **~patriotisch** *Adj.* (ugs. abwertend) flag-waving ‹*speech etc.*›; **~patriotismus** *der* (ugs. abwertend) flag-waving patriotism; **~ruf** *der* cheering; cheers *pl.*

Hurrikan /ˈharɪkən/ *der;* **~s, ~s** hurricane

hurtig /ˈhʊrtɪç/

A *Adj.* rapid

B *adv.* quickly; ‹*work*› fast, quickly

Husar /huˈzaːɐ̯/ *der;* **~en, ~en** (hist.) hussar

Husaren-: ~streich *der*, **~stück** *das* daring coup

husch /hʊʃ/

A *Interj.* quick; quickly; **~, ~!** away with you!; be off with you!; (zu einem Tier) shoo!

B *Adv.* **das geht nicht so ~, ~:** it can't be rushed; **bei ihr muss alles ~, ~ gehen** she wants everything done in a hurry

Husch *der;* **~[e]s, ~e** *in* **in einem ~** (ugs.) in a flash; in no time at all

Husche /ˈhʊʃə/ *die;* **~, ~n** (ostmd.) [sudden] shower

huschen *itr. V.; mit sein* (lautlos u. leichtfüßig) ‹*person*› slip, steal; (lautlos u. schnell) flit, dart; ‹*mouse, lizard, etc.*› dart; ‹*smile*› flit; ‹*light*› flash; ‹*shadow*› slide *or* glide quickly

hussa /ˈhʊsa/, **hussasa** /ˈhʊsasa/ *Interj.* (bei der Jagd) tally-ho; halloo; (zum Pferd) gee-up

hüsteln /ˈhyːstl̩n/ *itr. V.* cough slightly; give a slight cough; **verlegen/vornehm ~:** cough with embarrassment/politely

husten /ˈhuːstn̩/

A *itr. V.* [1] cough; **auf etw.** (*Akk.*) **~** (salopp) not give a damn for sth. [2] (Husten haben) have a cough; be coughing

B *tr. V.* cough up ‹*blood, phlegm*›; **jmdm. etwas ~** (salopp spött.) tell sb. where he/she can get off (coll.)

Husten *der;* **~s, ~** ▸❶ **S. 439** cough; **~ haben** have a cough

Husten-: ~an·fall *der* ▸❶ **S. 439** coughing fit; fit of coughing; **~bonbon** *das* cough sweet (Brit.); cough drop; **~mittel** *das* cough medicine *or* mixture; **~reiz** *der* tickling in the throat; **den ~reiz nicht unterdrücken können** be unable to suppress the urge *or* need to cough; **~saft** *der* cough syrup; cough mixture; **~tee** *der: herb tea which soothes coughs;* **~tropfen** *Pl.* cough drops

Hut[1] /huːt/ *der;* **~es, Hüte** /ˈhyːtə/ [1] hat; **den ~ abnehmen/aufsetzen** take off/put on one's hat; **vor jmdm. den ~ ziehen** (abnehmen) take off one's hat to sb.; (zum Gruß) raise one's hat to sb.; **in ~ und Mantel** wearing one's hat and coat; with one's hat and coat on [2] (fig.) **da geht einem/mir der ~ hoch** (ugs.) it makes you/me mad *or* wild (coll.); **~ ab!** (ugs.) hats off to him/her *etc.*; I take my hat off to him/her *etc.*; **ein alter ~ sein** (ugs.) be old hat; **seinen ~ nehmen [müssen]** (ugs.) [have to] pack one's bags and go; **vor jmdm./etw. den ~ ziehen** (ugs.) take off one's hat to sb./sth.; **das kann er sich** (*Dat.*) **an den ~ stecken** (ugs. abwertend) he can keep it (coll.) *or* (sl.) stick it; **mit etw. nichts am ~ haben** (ugs.) have nothing to do with sth.; **jmdm. eins auf den ~ geben** (ugs.) give sb. a dressing down *or* (Brit. coll.) rocket; **eins auf den ~ kriegen** (ugs.) get a dressing down *or* (coll.) rocket; **verschiedene Interessen/Personen unter einen ~ bringen** (ugs.) reconcile different interests/the interests of different people [3] (Bot.) cap

Hut[2] *die;* **~** (geh.) keeping; care; **bei jmdm. in guter ~ sein** be in good hands with sb.; **auf der ~ sein** be on one's guard

Hut-: ~ab·lage *die* hat rack; **~band** *das; Pl.* **~bänder** hatband; (eines Damenhutes) hat ribbon

Hüte·junge *der* shepherd boy

hüten /ˈhyːtn̩/

A *tr. V.* look after; take care of; tend, keep watch over ‹*sheep, cattle, etc.*›; **etw. eifersüchtig ~:** guard sth. jealously; **ein Geheimnis ~** (fig.) keep *or* guard a secret; *s. auch* **Bett 1**

B *refl. V.* (vorsehen) be on one's guard; **sich vor jmdm./etw. ~:** be on one's guard against sb./sth.; **sich ~, etw. zu tun** take [good] care not to do sth.; **ich werde mich ~!** (ugs.) no fear!; not likely! (coll.)

Hüter *der;* **~s, ~:** guardian; custodian; **soll ich meines Bruders ~ sein?** (bibl.) am I my brother's keeper?; **ein ~ des Gesetzes** (scherzh.) a custodian of the law (coll.)

Hüterin *die;* **~, ~nen** guardian; custodian

Hut-: ~feder *die* hat feather; (größer) plume; **~geschäft** *das* hat shop; hatter's [shop]; (für Damen) hat shop; milliner's (shop); **~größe** *die* hat size; size of hat; **~krempe** *die* [hat] brim; **~macher** *der* ▸❶ **S. 113** hatter; hat maker; (für Damen) milliner; **~macherin** *die;* **~, ~nen** ▸❶ **S. 113** ▸**~macher**; **~mode** *die* (der Herren) fashion in gents' *or* gentlemen's hats; (der Damen) fashion in ladies' hats; **~nadel** *die* hatpin; **~schachtel** *die* hat box

Hutsche /ˈhʊtʃə/ *die;* **~, ~n** (südd., österr. ugs.) ▸**Schaukel**

Hut·schnur *die: in* **das geht mir über die ~** (ugs.) that's going too far

Hutsch·pferd *das* (südd., österr.) ▸**Schaukelpferd**

Hütte /ˈhʏtə/ *die;* **~, ~n** [1] hut; (Holz~) cabin; hut; (ärmliches Haus) shack; hut [2] (Eisen~) iron [and steel] works *sing. or pl.*; (Glas~) glassworks *sing. or pl.*; (Blei~) lead works *sing. or pl.* [3] (Jagd~) [hunting] lodge [4] (Seemannsspr.) poop

Hütten-: ~abend *der: evening social gathering or party in a mountain hut;* **~arbeiter** *der*, **~arbeiterin** *die* (in der Eisenhütte) worker in a/the iron/steel works; ironworker/steelworker; (in der Glashütte) glass worker; **~industrie** *die* iron and steel industry; **~käse** *der* cottage cheese; **~kombinat** *das* (DDR) metallurgical combine; **~schuh** *der* slipper sock; **~werk** *das* ▸**Hütte 2**; **~wesen** *das* (Technik) metallurgical engineering *no art.*; (~industrie) iron and steel industry

Hutze /ˈhʊtsə/ *die;* **~, ~n** (Kfz-T.) bulge

Hutzel /ˈhʊtsl̩/ *die;* **~, ~n** (bes. südd.) dried fruit; (Birne) dried pear

Hutzel·brot *das* (bes. südd.) fruit bread; **ein ~:** a fruit loaf

hutzelig *Adj.* (ugs.) wizened ‹*person, face*›; shrivelled, dried-up ‹*fruit*›

Hutzel-: ~männchen *das* brownie; **~weib** *das* wizened old woman

Hut·zucker *der* loaf sugar (in the shape of a cone)

Hyäne /ˈhyɛːnə/ *die;* **~, ~n** (auch fig. ugs.) hyena

Hyazinthe /hy̆aˈtsɪntə/ *die;* **~, ~n** hyacinth

hybrid /hyˈbriːt/ *Adj.* (bes. Biol.) hybrid

Hybride *der;* **~n, ~n** (Biol.) hybrid

Hybrid-: ~rechner *der* (DV) hybrid computer; **~züchtung** *die* (Biol.) cross-breeding; crossing

Hybris /ˈhyːbrɪs/ *die;* **~** (geh.) hubris

Hydra /ˈhyːdra/ *die;* **~, Hydren** hydra

Hydrant /hyˈdrant/ *der;* **~en, ~en** hydrant

Hydrat /hyˈdraːt/ *das;* **~[e]s, ~e** (Chemie) hydrate

Hydra[ta]tion /hydra[ta]'tsi̯o:n/ *die;* ~ (Chemie) hydration

Hydraulik /hy'drau̯lɪk/ *die;* ~ (Technik) **1** (Theorie) hydraulics *sing., no art.* **2** (Vorrichtungen) hydraulics *pl.*; hydraulic system

hydraulisch (Technik)
A *Adj.* hydraulic
B *adv.* hydraulically

Hydrid /hy'dri:t/ *das;* **~[e]s, ~e** (Chemie) hydride

hydrieren /hy'dri:rən/ *tr. V.* (Chemie) hydrogenate

Hydrierung *die;* ~ (Chemie) hydrogenation

hydro-, Hydro- /hydro-/ : **~biologie** *die* hydrobiology *no art.*; **~dynamik** *die* (Physik) hydrodynamics *sing., no art.*; **~dynamisch** *Adj.* (Physik) hydrodynamic; **~kultur** *die* (Gartenbau) hydroponics *sing.*; **~logie** *die;* **~~**: hydrology; **~logisch** **A** *Adj.* hydrological; **B** *adv.* hydrologically; **~lyse** /-'ly:zə/ *die;* **~~, ~~n** (Chemie) hydrolysis; **~meter** *das* current meter; (Senkwaage) hydrometer; **~phil** /-'fi:l/ *Adj.* **1** (Biol.) hydrophilous ‹*plant, insect*›; water-loving ‹*animal*›; **2** (Chemie) hydrophilic; **~phob** /-'fo:p/ *Adj.* **1** (Biol.) ‹*plant, animal*› that avoids water; **2** (Chemie) hydrophobic; **~pneumatisch** *Adj.* (Technik) hydropneumatic; **~technik** *die* hydraulic engineering *no art.*; **~therapie** *die* (Med.) hydrotherapy

Hydroxid, Hydroxyd *das;* **~[e]s, ~e** (Chemie) hydroxide

Hygiene /hy'gi̯e:nə/ *die;* ~ **1** (Gesundheitspflege) health care **2** (Sauberkeit) hygiene **3** (Med.) hygiene *no art.*; hygienics *sing., no art.*

hygienisch
A *Adj.* hygienic
B *adv.* hygienically

hygro-, Hygro- /hygro-/: **~meter** *das* (Met.) hygrometer; **~skop** /-'sko:p/ *das;* **~~s, ~~e** (Met.) hygroscope; **~skopisch** *Adj.* (Chemie) hygroscopic

Hymen /'hy:mən/ *das od. der;* **~s,** ~ ▸**❶ S. 435** (Anat.) hymen

Hymne /'hʏmnə/ *die;* **~, ~n** **1** hymn **2** (Nationalhymne) national anthem

hymnisch *Adj.* hymnic; **ein ~er Gesang** a paean [of praise]

Hymnus /'hʏmnʊs/ *der;* **~, Hymnen** (geh.) ▸**Hymne 1**

hyper·aktiv /'hy:pɐ-/
A *Adj.* hyperactive
B *adv.* hyperactively

Hyperbel /hy'pɛrbḷ/ *die;* **~, ~n** **1** (Geom.) hyperbola **2** (Rhet.) hyperbole

Hyperbel·funktion *die* (Math.) hyperbolic function

hyperbolisch /hypɐ'bo:lɪʃ/ (Math., Rhet.) hyperbolic

hyper-, Hyper- /hypɐ-/: **~korrekt** (ugs. abwertend, Sprachw.) **A** *Adj.* hypercorrect; **B** *adv.* in a hypercorrect way; **~kritisch** *Adj.* (abwertend) hypercritical; **~link** /'haipa.../ *der* (DV) hyperlink; **~modern** **A** *Adj.* ultra- modern; ultra-fashionable ‹*clothes*›; **B** *adv.* ultra-modernly; ‹*dress*› ultra-fashionably; **~nervös** **A** *Adj.* extremely jumpy *or* nervous; **B** *adv.* in an extremely jumpy *or* nervous way; **~sensibel** *Adj.* hypersensitive; **~text** /'haipa.../ *der* (DV) hypertext; **~tonie** /-to'ni:/ *die;* **~~, ~~n** ▸**❶ S. 439** (Med.) **1** hypertension; **2** (im Auge, Muskel) hypertonia; **~toniker** /-'to:nikɐ/ *der;* **~~s, ~~, ~tonikerin** *die;* **~~, ~~nen** (Med.) hypertensive; **~troph** /-'tro:f/ *Adj.* (Med.) hypertrophic; **~trophie** /-tro'fi:/ *die;* **~~** ▸**❶ S. 439** (Med.) hypertrophy

Hypnose /hʏp'no:zə/ *die;* **~, ~n** hypnosis; **jmdn. in ~ versetzen** put sb. under hypnosis; **unter ~ stehen** be under hypnosis

Hypno·therapie *die* hypnotherapy

Hypnotikum /hʏp'no:tikʊm/ *das;* **~s, Hypnotika** (Med.) hypnotic; soporific

hypnotisch *Adj.* hypnotic; hypnotic, soporific ‹*drug*›

Hypnotiseur /hʏpnoti'zø:ɐ̯/ *der;* **~s, ~e, Hypnotiseurin** *die;* **~, ~nen** hypnotist

hypnotisieren *tr. V.* hypnotize

Hypnotismus *der;* **~**: hypnotism *no art.*

Hypochonder /hypo'xɔndɐ/ *der;* **~s, ~, Hypochonderin** *die;* **~, ~nen** hypochondriac

Hypochondrie *die;* **~, ~n** ▸**❶ S. 439** (Med.) hypochondria *no art.*

hypochondrisch *Adj.* hypochondriac

hypo-, Hypo- /hypo-/: **~nym** /-'ny:m/ *das;* **~~s, ~~e** (Sprachw.) hyponym; **~physe** /-'fy:zə/ *die;* **~~, ~~n** ▸**❶ S. 435** (Anat.) hypophysis; **~stase** /-'sta:zə/ *die;* **~~, ~~n** **1** (Philos.) hypostasis; **2** (Sprachw.) establishment as an independent word; **~taktisch** /-'taktɪʃ/ *Adj.* (Sprachw.) hypotactic; **~taxe** /-'taksə/ *die* (Sprachw.) hypotaxis; **~tenuse** /-te'nu:zə/ *die;* **~~, ~~n** (Math.) hypotenuse; **~thalamus** *der* ▸**❶ S. 435** (Anat.) hypothalamus

Hypothek /-'te:k/ *die;* **~, ~en** **1** (Bankw.) mortgage; **eine ~ aufnehmen** take out a mortgage; **etw. mit einer ~ belasten** encumber sth. with a mortgage; mortgage sth. **2** (Bürde) burden

hypothekarisch /-te'ka:rɪʃ/
A *Adj.* **~e Sicherheiten bieten** offer a mortgage [on property] as security; **~e Belastungen** mortgage *sing*
B *adv.* **etw. ~ belasten** mortgage sth.

Hypotheken-: ~brief *der* (Bankw.) mortgage deed; **~gläubiger** *der,* **~gläubigerin** *die* (Bankw.) mortgagee; **~pfand·brief** *der* (Bankw.) mortgage bond; **~schuldner** *der,* **~schuldnerin** *die* (Bankw.) mortgagor; **~zins** *der; Pl.* **~~en** mortgage interest

hypo-, Hypo-: ~these /-'te:zə/ *die* hypothesis; **das ist eine reine ~these** that's pure hypothesis; **~thetisch** **A** *Adj.* hypothetical; **B** *adv.* hypothetically; **~tonie** /-to'ni:/ *die;* **~~, ~~n** ▸**❶ S. 439** (Med.) **1** (niedriger Blutdruck) hypotension; **2** (im Auge, Muskel) hypotonia; **~toniker** /-'to:nikɐ/ *der;* **~~s, ~~, ~tonikerin** *die;* **~~, ~~nen** hypotensive; **~zykloide** *die* (Math.) hypocycloid

Hysterie /hʏste'ri:/ *die;* **~, ~n** /-i:ən/ hysteria

Hysteriker /hʏs'te:rikɐ/ *der;* **~s, ~, Hysterikerin** *die;* **~, ~nen** hysterical person; hysteric

hysterisch
A *Adj.* hysterical; **einen ~en Anfall bekommen** have [a fit of] hysterics
B *adv.* hysterically

Hz *Abk.* **= Hertz** Hz

h

Ii

i, I /iː/ *das;* ~, ~: i/I; **das Tüpfelchen** *od.* **der Punkt auf dem** ~ (fig.) the final touch; *s. auch* **a, A**

i *Interj.* ugh; **i bewahre, i wo** (ugs) [good] heavens, no!

i. A. *Abk.* = **im Auftrag[e]** p.p.

iah /iː'aː/ *Interj.* hee-haw

iahen /iː'aːən/ *itr. V.* hee-haw; bray

IAO *Abk.* = **Internationale Arbeitsorganisation** ILO

ibd. *Abk.* = **ibidem** ibid.

iberisch /i'beːrɪʃ/ *Adj.* Iberian; **Iberische Halbinsel** Iberian Peninsula

Ibero·amerika /i'beːro-/ *(das)* Latin America

IBFG *Abk.* = **Internationaler Bund Freier Gewerkschaften** ICFTU (International Confederation of Free Trade Unions)

ibidem /i'biːdɛm/ *Adv.* ibidem

Ibis /'iːbɪs/ *der;* ~**ses,** ~**se** (Zool.) ibis

IC *Abk.* = **Intercity[zug]** IC

ICE *Abk.* = **Intercityexpress[zug]** ICE

> **ICE - Intercityexpresszug**
>
> This high-speed train runs at one- or two-hour intervals on a number of main routes in Germany, offering shorter journey times and better facilities than ordinary trains.

ich /ɪç/ *Personalpron.; 1. Pers. Sg. Nom.* I; **Wer ist da? — Ich bins!** Who's there? — It's me!; **Wer hat nun das gemacht? — Ich wars** Who did that? — I did *or* It was me; **Hat sie mich gerufen? — Nein,** ~: Was it she who called me? — No, I did; **und** ~ **Esel/Idiot habe es gemacht** and I, silly ass/idiot that I am, did it; and, like a fool, I did it; ~ **Idiot/Esel!** what an idiot I am!; I 'am an idiot!; **immer** ~ (ugs.) [it's] always me; ~ **selbst** I myself; ~ **nicht** not me; **Menschen wie du und** ~: people like you and I *or* me; *s. auch (Gen.)* **meiner,** *(Dat.)* **mir,** *(Akk.)* **mich**

Ich *das;* ~**[s],** ~**[s]** 1 self; **das eigene** ~: one's own self 2 (Psych.) ego

Ich-AG *die* self-employment business *(started by unemployed person with the help of a government subsidy and having either self-employed or company status)*

ich-, Ich-: ~**bewusstsein,** *~**bewußtsein** *das* self-awareness; ~**bezogen** A *Adj.* egocentric; (in der Kommunikation) egotistic; B *adv.* ~**bezogen denken** think in an egocentric way; ~**bezogenheit** *die;* ~~: egocentricity; (in der Kommunikation) egotism; ~**erzähler,** ~**-Erzähler** *der,* ~**erzählerin,** ~**-Erzählerin** *die* first-person narrator; ~**form** *die* first person; ~**laut,** ~**-Laut** *der* (Sprachw.) palatal fricative; ich-laut; ~**sucht** *die* (geh.) egoism; ~**süchtig** *Adj.* (geh.) egoistic[al]

Ichthyo·saurier /ɪçtÿo-/ *der* ichthyosaurus

Icon /'aikən/ *das;* ~**s,** ~**s** (DV) icon

ideal /ide'aːl/
A *Adj.* ideal
B *adv.* ideally; **das Haus liegt** ~: the house is ideally situated

Ideal *das;* ~**s,** ~**e** ideal; **er ist das** ~ **eines Vorgesetzten** he is the ideal *or* perfect boss (coll.)

Ideal-: ~**besetzung** *die* 1 (Film, Theater) ideal cast; 2 (Sport) ideal line-up; ~**bild** *das* ideal; ~**fall** *der* ideal case; **im** ~**fall** in ideal circumstances *pl.;* ~**figur** *die* ideal figure; ~**gestalt** *die* ideal; ~**gewicht** *das* ideal weight

idealisieren *tr. V.* idealize; **ein** ~**des Bild von etw.** an idealized picture of sth.

Idealisierung *die;* ~, ~**en** idealization

Idealismus *der;* ~ (auch Philos.) idealism

Idealist *der;* ~**en,** ~**en, Idealistin** *die;* ~, ~**nen** (auch Philos.) idealist

idealistisch (auch Philos.)
A *Adj.* idealistic
B *adv.* idealistically

ideal-, Ideal-: ~**konkurrenz** *die* (Rechtsw.) ▸**Tateinheit;** ~**linie** *die* (Sport) ideal line; ~**typisch** *Adj.* (Soziol.) ideal-typical; idealized; ~**typus** *der* (Soziol.) ideal type; ~**vorstellung** *die* ideal

Idee /i'deː/ *die;* ~, ~**n** 1 idea; **du hast [vielleicht]** ~**n** (iron.) you do get some ideas, don't you!; **auf eine** ~ **kommen** hit [up]on an idea; **wie bist du nur auf die** ~ **gekommen?** whatever gave you 'that idea?; **jmdn. auf eine** ~ **bringen** give sb. an idea; **eine fixe** ~: an obsession; an idée fixe; **er ist von der fixen** ~ **besessen, Rennfahrer zu werden** he is obsessed with the idea of becoming a racing driver 2 (ein bisschen) **eine** ~: a shade *or* trifle; **eine** ~ **[Salz/Pfeffer]** a touch [of salt/pepper]

ideell /ide'ɛl/
A *Adj.* non-material; (geistig-seelisch) spiritual
B *adv.* **etw.** ~ **unterstützen** support sth. in non-material ways

ideen-, Ideen-: ~**arm** *Adj.* lacking in ideas *postpos.;* ~**armut** *die* lack of ideas; ~**austausch** *der* exchange of ideas; ~**drama** *das* (Literaturw.) drama of ideas; ~**geber** *der,* ~**geberin** *die* source of ideas; **ihr** ~**geber** the source of their ideas; ~**gut** *das* ideas *pl.;* ~**los** *Adj.* devoid of *or* [completely] lacking in ideas *postpos.;* ~**losigkeit** *die;* ~~: [complete] lack of ideas; ~**reich** *Adj.* full of ideas *postpos.;* inventive; ~**reichtum** *der* inventiveness

Iden /'iːdn̩/ *Pl.* (hist.) **die** ~ **des März** the ides of March

Identifikation /idɛntifika'tsi̯oːn/ *die;* ~, ~**en** (auch Psych.) identification

Identifikations-: ~**figur** *die* person with whom sb./people can identify; **eine** ~**figur für Frauen** someone with whom women can identify; ~**nummer** *die* identification number; (PIN) personal identification number; PIN [number]

identifizierbar *Adj.* identifiable; recognizable ‹handwriting›

identifizieren /idɛntifi'tsiːrən/
A *tr. V.* identify
B *refl. V.* (auch Psych.) **sich mit jmdm./etw.** ~: identify with sb./sth.

Identifizierung *die;* ~, ~**en** (auch Psych.) identification

identisch /i'dɛntɪʃ/ *Adj.* identical; **möglicherweise sind der Einbrecher und der entsprungene Häftling** ~: it's possible that the intruder and the escaped prisoner are one and the same person

Identität /idɛnti'tɛːt/ *die;* ~: identity; **jmds.** ~ **feststellen** establish sb.'s identity; **die** ~ **dieser beiden Begriffe** the identity between these two concepts

identitäts-, Identitäts-: ~**diebstahl,** *der* identity theft; ~**krise** *die* identity crisis; ~**nachweis** *der* proof of identity; ~**stiftend** *Adj.* identifying ‹factor, clothing›; ~**stiftend sein** provide an identity; ~**verlust** *der* loss of identity

Ideogramm /ideo'gram/ *das;* ~**s,** ~**e** ideogram

Ideologe /ideo'loːgə/ *der;* ~**n,** ~**n** ideologue

Ideologie *die;* ~, ~**n** /-iːən/ ideology

Ideologie-: ~**begriff** *der* conception of ideology; ~**kritik** *die* ideological criticism

Ideologin *die;* ~, ~**nen** ideologue

ideologisch
A *Adj.* ideological
B *adv.* ideologically; **jmdn.** ~ **schulen** give sb. ideological instruction

ideologisieren *tr. V.* ideologize

Ideologisierung *die;* ~, ~**en** ideologization

Idiom /i'di̯oːm/ *das;* ~**s,** ~**e** (Sprachw.) idiom

Idiomatik /idi̯o'maːtɪk/ *die;* ~ (Sprachw.) idioms *pl.;* (Gebiet der Lexikologie) idiomology *no art.*

idiomatisch
A *Adj.* idiomatic
B *adv.* idiomatically

Idiosynkrasie /idi̯ozʏnkra'ziː/ *die;* ~, ~**n** ▸ⓘ **S. 439** 1 (Med.) idiosyncrasy 2 (Psych.) pathological aversion

Idiot /i'di̯oːt/ *der;* ~**en,** ~**en** 1 idiot 2 (ugs. abwertend) fool; (stärker) idiot (coll.)

Idioten-: ~**hang** *der,* ~**hügel** *der* (ugs. scherzh.) nursery slope

idioten·sicher *Adj.* (ugs. scherzh.) foolproof

Idioten·test *der* (ugs.) *range of medical and psychological tests designed to test suitability to hold a driving licence*

Idiotie /idi̯o'tiː/ *die;* ~, ~**n** /-iːən/ 1 idiocy 2 (ugs. abwertend: Dummheit) lunacy; madness; **seine** ~**n** his idiocies

Idiotikon /i'di̯oːtikɔn/ *das;* ~**s, Idiotiken** *od.* **Idiotika** dialect dictionary

Idiotin *die;* ~, ~**nen** 1 idiot 2 (ugs. abwertend) fool; (stärker) idiot

idiotisch
A *Adj.* 1 (Psych.) severely subnormal; idiotic (as tech. term) 2 (ugs. abwertend: unsinnig) stupid; (stärker) idiotic
B *adv.* 1 (schwachsinnig) idiotically 2 (ugs. abwertend: unsinnig) stupidly; (stärker) idiotically

Idiotismus *der;* ~, **Idiotismen** 1 (Krankheit) idiocy 2 (Äußerung der Idiotie) symptom of idiocy

Idol /i'doːl/ *das;* ~**s,** ~**e** (auch bild. Kunst) idol; **jmdn. als** ~ **vergöttern** idolize sb.

Idolatrie *die;* ~, ~**n** /-iːən/ (geh.) idolatry

Idyll /i'dʏl/ *das;* ~**s,** ~**e** idyll; **ein** ~ **für Erholungssuchende** an idyllic place *or* spot for those seeking relaxation and recreation

Idylle *die;* ~, ~**n** (auch Literaturw.) idyll

idyllisch
A *Adj.* (auch Literaturw.) idyllic
B *adv.* ~ **gelegen** in an idyllic spot

i. e. *Abk.* = **id est** i.e.

IG *Abk.* = **Industriegewerkschaft**

Igel /'iːgl̩/ *der;* ~**s,** ~: hedgehog

Igel-: **∼frisur** *die* (ugs. scherzh.), **∼schnitt** *der* (ugs. scherzh.) crew cut; **∼stellung** *die* (Milit.) hedgehog position

igitt[igitt] /iˈgɪt(iˈgɪt)/ *Interj.* ugh

Iglu /ˈiːglu/ *der od. das;* **∼s, ∼s** igloo

ignorant /ɪgnoˈrant/ *Adj.* (abwertend) ignorant

Ignorant *der;* **∼en, ∼en**, **Ignorantin** *die;* **∼, ∼nen** (abwertend) ignoramus

Ignoranz /ɪgnoˈrants/ *die;* **∼** (abwertend) ignorance

ignorieren *tr. V.* ignore

ihm /iːm/ *Dat. der Personalpron.* **er, es** 1 (nach Präpositionen) (bei Personen) him; (bei Dingen, Tieren) it; (bei männlichen Tieren) him; it 2 **gib es ∼:** give it to him; give him it; (dem Tier) give it to it/him; **ich sagte ∼, dass ...** I told him that ...; I said to him that ...; **∼ geht es gut** he's well; **∼ war, als habe man ∼ ins Gesicht geschlagen** he felt as if somebody had punched him in the face; **sie sah ∼ ins Gesicht** she looked him in the face; **sie hat ∼ etwas zu essen gekocht** she cooked him a meal; she cooked a meal for him; **sie kämmte ∼ das Haar** she combed his hair [for him]; **ich bin zu ∼ gegangen** I went to see him; **Freunde von ∼:** friends of his

ihn /iːn/ *Akk. des Personalpron.* **er** (bei Personen) him; (bei Dingen, Tieren) it; (bei männlichen Tieren) him; it

ihnen /ˈiːnən/ *Dat. des Personalpron.* **sie,** *Pl.* 1 (nach Präpositionen) them 2 **gib es ∼:** give it to them; give them it; **∼ geht es gut** they're well; **Freunde von ∼:** friends of theirs; *s. auch* **ihm**

Ihnen *Dat. von* **Sie** (Anrede) 1 (nach Präpositionen) you 2 **ich habe es ∼ gegeben** I gave it to you; I gave you it; **geht es ∼ gut?** are you well?; **Freunde von ∼:** friends of yours; *s. auch* **ihm**

ihr[1] /iːɐ̯/ *Dat. des Personalpron.* **sie,** *Sg.* (*nach Präpositionen*) (bei Personen) her; (bei Dingen, Tieren) it; (bei weiblichen Tieren) her; it; *s. auch* **ihm**

ihr[2] *Personalpron.; 2. Pers. Pl. Nom.* (Anrede an vertraute Personen) you; **ihr Lieben** (im Brief) dear all; *s. auch* (*Gen.*) **euer,** (*Dat., Akk.*) **euch**

ihr[3] *Possessivpron.* 1 (einer Person) her; **Ihre Majestät** Her Majesty; **das Buch dort, ist das ∼[e]s?** that book there, is it hers?; is that book hers?; **das ist nicht mein Mann, sondern ∼er** that is not my husband, but hers; **der/die/das ∼e** hers; **die ∼en** hers; **die ∼en** *od.* **Ihren** her family 2 (eines Tiers, einer Sache) its; (eines weiblichen Tiers) her; its; **die Lok fährt glatt ∼e 200 Sachen** (ugs.) the locomotive does a good 200 kilometres an hour 3 (mehrerer Personen, Tiere, Sachen) their; **das Haus am Ende der Straße ist ∼es** the house at the end of the street is theirs; **der/die/das ∼e** theirs; **die ∼en** theirs; **die ∼en** *od.* **Ihren** their family; **sie haben das ∼e** *od.* **Ihre getan** they did their bit; **sie haben das ∼e** *od.* **Ihre bekommen** they got their due *or* what was due to them

Ihr *Possessivpron.* (Anrede) your; **∼ Hans Meier** (Briefschluss) yours, Hans Meier; **welcher Mantel ist ∼er?** which coat is yours?; **der/die/das ∼e** yours; **die ∼en** yours; **Sie haben das ∼e getan** you have done your bit; *s. auch* **ihr[3]**

ihrer /ˈiːrɐ/ 1 *Gen. des Personalpron.* **sie,** *Sg.* (geh.) **wir gedachten ∼:** we remembered her 2 *Gen. des Personalpron.* **sie,** *Pl.* (geh.) **wir werden ∼ gedenken** we will remember them; **es waren ∼ zwölf** there were twelve of them

Ihrer *Gen. von* **Sie** (Anrede) (geh.) **wir werden ∼ gedenken** we will remember you

ihrerseits /-zaits/ *Adv.* 1 *Sg.* (von ihrer Seite) on her part; (auf ihrer Seite) for her part 2 *Pl.* (von ihrer Seite) on their part; (auf ihrer Seite) for their part

Ihrerseits *Adv.* (von Ihrer Seite) on your part; (auf Ihrer Seite) for your part

ihres·gleichen *indekl. Pron.* 1 *Sg.* people *pl.* like her; (abwertend) the likes of her; her sort *or* kind; **sie fühlt sich nur unter ∼ wohl** she only feels at home among people like herself *or* her own kind 2 *Pl.* people like them; (abwertend) the likes of them; their sort *or* kind; **sie sollten unter ∼ bleiben** they should stay among their own kind

Ihresgleichen *indekl. Pron.* people *pl.* like you; (abwertend) the likes of you; your sort *or* kind; **Sie sollten besser unter ∼ bleiben** you should stay among your own kind

ihret·halben (veralt.), **ihret·wegen** *Adv.* 1 *Sg.* (wegen ihr) because of her; on her account; (für sie) on her behalf; (ihr zuliebe) for her sake; **mach dir ∼ keine Sorgen** don't worry about her 2 *Pl.* (wegen ihnen) because of them; on their account; (für sie) on their behalf; (ihnen zuliebe) for their sake[s]; (um sie) about them

Ihrethalben (veralt.), **Ihretwegen** *Adv.* (wegen Ihnen) because of you; on your account; (für Sie) on your behalf; (Ihnen zuliebe) for your sake; *Pl.* for your sake[s]; (um Sie) about you

ihret·willen *Adv.: in* **um ∼** (Sg.) for her sake; (Pl.) for their sake[s]

Ihret·willen *Adv.: in* **um ∼** (Sg.) for your sake; (Pl.) for your sake[s]

ihrige /ˈiːrɪgə/ *Possessivpron.* (geh. veralt.) 1 *Sg.* **der/die/das ∼:** hers 2 *Pl.* **der/die/das ∼:** theirs; *s. auch* **deinige**

Ihrige *Possessivpron.* (Anrede) (geh. veralt.) **der/die/das ∼:** yours

Ihro /ˈiːro/ *indekl. Pron.* (veralt.) your; **∼ Gnaden** Your Grace

Ikebana /ikeˈbaːna/ *das;* **∼[s]** ikebana

Ikone /iˈkoːnə/ *die;* **∼, ∼n** icon

Ikonoklasmus /ikonoˈklasmʊs/ *der;* **∼, Ikonoklasmen** (geh.) iconoclasm

Ikosaeder /ikozaˈ|eːdɐ/ *das;* **∼s, ∼** (Math.) icosahedron

Ilex /ˈiːlɛks/ *die od. der;* **∼, ∼** (Bot.) holly

Ilias /ˈiːli̯as/ *die;* **∼:** Iliad

illegal /ˈɪlegaːl/

A *Adj.* illegal

B *adv.* illegally

Illegale *der/die; adj. Dekl.* illegal immigrant

Illegalität /ɪlegaliˈtɛːt/ *die;* **∼, ∼en** illegality

illegitim /ˈɪlegitiːm/ *Adj.* (geh.) illegitimate

Illegitimität *die;* **∼** (geh.) illegitimacy

illiquid /ˈɪlikviːt/ *Adj.* (Wirtsch.) insolvent

Illiquidität *die;* **∼** (Wirtsch.) insolvency

illoyal /ˈɪlo̯ajaːl/ *Adj.* (geh.) disloyal

Illoyalität *die;* **∼** (geh.) disloyalty

Illumination /ɪluminaˈtsi̯oːn/ *die;* **∼, ∼en** 1 (Beleuchtung) illumination; **die Stadt zeigte sich in festlicher ∼:** the town was festively lit 2 (von Handschriften) illumination

Illuminator /ɪlumiˈnaːtɔr/ *der;* **∼s, ∼en** /-ˈtoːrən/, **Illuminatorin** *die;* **∼, ∼nen** illuminator

illuminieren *tr. V.* illuminate

Illuminierung *die;* **∼, ∼en** illumination

Illusion /ɪluˈzi̯oːn/ *die;* **∼, ∼en** illusion; **sich** (*Dat.*) **∼en machen** delude oneself; **jmdm. die ∼en rauben** rob sb. of his/her illusions; **gib dich doch nicht der ∼ hin, du könntest damit irgendetwas erreichen** do not delude yourself that you could achieve anything by that

illusionär /ɪluzi̯oˈnɛːɐ̯/ *Adj.* (geh.) illusory ‹*conception, expectation, thing*›; fanciful ‹*demand, procedure, attempt*›

Illusionist *der;* **∼en, ∼en**, **Illusionistin** *die;* **∼, ∼nen** 1 (geh.) dreamer 2 (Zauberkünstler) illusionist

illusionistisch *Adj.* (Kunstw.) illusionistic

illusions·los

A *Adj.* [sober and] realistic; **∼ sein** have no illusions

B *adv.* without any illusions

illusorisch /ɪluˈzoːrɪʃ/ *Adj.* 1 (trügerisch) illusory 2 (zwecklos) pointless

illuster /ɪˈlʊstɐ/ *Adj.* (geh.) illustrious

Illustration /ɪlʊstraˈtsi̯oːn/ *die;* **∼, ∼en** illustration; **zur ∼ von etw. [dienen]** (fig.) [serve] to illustrate sth.

illustrativ /ɪlʊstraˈtiːf/

A *Adj.* (auch fig.) illustrative; **ein sehr ∼er Vortrag** (fig.) a very illuminating lecture

B *adv.* **etw. ∼ schildern** describe sth. graphically

Illustrator /ɪlʊsˈtraːtɔr/ *der;* **∼s, ∼en** /-ˈtoːrən/, **Illustratorin** *die;* **∼, ∼nen** illustrator

illustrieren *tr. V.* (auch fig.) illustrate; **eine illustrierte Zeitschrift** a magazine; **jmdm. etw. ∼:** illustrate sth. for sb.

Illustrierte *die; adj. Dekl.* magazine

Illustrierung *die;* **∼, ∼en** (auch fig.) illustration

Iltis /ˈɪltɪs/ *der;* **∼ses, ∼se** polecat; (Pelz) fitch

im /ɪm/ *Präp. + Art.* 1 **= in dem** 2 (räumlich) in the; **er wohnt im vierten Stock** he lives on the fourth floor; **im Theater** at the theatre; **er tritt im Zirkus auf** he is appearing in *or* performing with the circus; **im Fernsehen** on television; **im Bett** in bed; **im Spessart/Schwarzwald** in the Spessart/the Black Forest 3 (zeitlich) **im Mai/Januar** in May/January; **im Jahre 1648** in [the year] 1648; **im letzten Jahr** last year; **im Alter von 50 Jahren** at the age of 50 4 (Verlauf) **etw. im Sitzen tun** do sth. [while] sitting down; **noch im Laufen** while still running; **im Gehen/Kommen sein** be going/coming

i. m. *Abk.* (Med.) **= intramuskulär** IM

> **IM – inoffizieller Mitarbeiter**
>
> This term refers to 'unofficial collaborators' of the **Stasi**. These informers were often ordinary people in the former GDR who had been recruited or pressurized by the *Stasi* to spy on neighbours, family, and friends. However, some were prominent figures in the West.

Image /ˈɪmɪtʃ/ *das;* **∼[s], ∼s** /ˈɪmɪtʃs/ image

Image-: **∼kampagne** *die* (bes. Werbespr.) image campaign; **∼pflege** *die* cultivation of one's image; **∼schaden** *der* loss of image; **jmdm. ∼schaden zufügen** damage sb.'s image; **einen ∼schaden davontragen** suffer a loss of image, suffer damage to one's image

imaginär /imagiˈnɛːɐ̯/ *Adj.* (geh., Math.) imaginary

Imagination /imaginaˈtsi̯oːn/ *die;* **∼, ∼en** (geh.) imagination

imaginativ /imaginaˈtiːf/ *Adj.* (geh.) imaginative

Imagismus /imaˈgɪsmʊs/ *der;* **∼** (Literaturw.) imagism *no art.*

Imago /iˈmaːgo/ *die;* **∼, Imagines** /-gineːs/ 1 (Psych., Biol.) imago 2 (Kunstwiss.) *wax death mask of an ancestor*

Imam /iˈmaːm/ *der;* **∼s, ∼s** *od.* **∼e** imam

imbezil /ɪmbeˈtsiːl/, **imbezill** /ɪmbeˈtsɪl/ *Adj.* (Med.) imbecile

Imbiss, *Imbiß /ˈɪmbɪs/ *der;* **Imbisses, Imbisse** 1 (kleine Mahlzeit) snack 2 ▸ **Imbisslokal**

Imbiss-, *Imbiß-: **∼bude** *die* (ugs.) ≈ hot-dog stall *or* stand; **∼lokal** *das* café; **∼stand** *der* ▸ **∼bude**; **∼stube** *die* ▸ **∼lokal**

-imitat *das;* **-∼s, -∼e** imitation ‹*leather, wood, etc.*›

Imitation /imitaˈtsi̯oːn/ *die;* **∼, ∼en** imitation

Imitator /imiˈtaːtɔr/ *der;* **∼s, ∼en**, **Imitatorin** *die;* **∼, ∼nen** /-taˈtoːrən/ imitator; mimic; (im Kabarett usw.) impressionist

imitieren *tr. V.* imitate

Imker /ˈɪmkɐ/ *der;* **∼s, ∼** ▸ **S. 113** beekeeper; apiarist (formal)

Imkerei *die;* **∼, ∼en** 1 (Bienenzucht) bee-keeping *no art.;* (as tech. term) apiculture *no art.* 2 (Betrieb) apiary

Imkerin *die;* **∼, ∼nen** ▸ **S. 113** ▸ **Imker**

imkern *itr. V.* keep bees

immanent /ɪmaˈnɛnt/ *Adj.* 1 (geh.) inherent; **einer Sache** (*Dat.*) **∼ sein** be inherent in sth. 2 (Philos.) immanent

Immanenz /ɪmaˈnɛnts/ *die;* **∼** (Philos.) immanence

immateriell /ɪmateˈri̯ɛl/ *Adj.* (geh.) non-material

Immatrikulation /ɪmatrikula'tsjo:n/ *die;* ~, ~**en** **1** (Hochschulw.) registration **2** (schweiz.: eines Fahrzeugs) registration

immatrikulieren
A *tr. V.* **1** (Hochschulw.) register **2** (schweiz.) register ‹*vehicle*›
B *refl. V.* (Hochschulw.) register

Imme /'ɪmə/ *die;* ~, ~**n** (dichter.) bee

immens /ɪ'mɛns/
A *Adj.* immense
B *adv.* immensely; enormously ‹*expensive*›

immer /'ɪmɐ/ *Adv.* **1** always; **wie ~:** as always; as usual; **mach es wie ~!** do it the way you've/we've always done it; **~ dieser Nebel/dieser Streit** this fog never seems to lift/you're/they're *etc.* always arguing; **~ diese Kinder!** these wretched children!; **schon ~:** always; **~ und ewig** for ever; (jedesmal) always; **auf** *od.* **für ~ [und ewig]** for ever [and ever]; **sie haben sich für ~ getrennt** they've split up for good; **~ wieder** again and again; time and time again; **~ wieder von vorne anfangen** keep on starting from the beginning again; **~, wenn** every time that; whenever; **er ist ~ der Dumme** (ugs.) he's always the loser; **~ ich!** (ugs.) [it's] always me **2** **~** + *Komp.* (nach u. nach) **~ dunkler/häufiger** darker and darker/more and more often; **~ mehr** more and more; **~ mehr zunehmen** keep on increasing **3** (ugs.: jeweils) **es durften ~ zwei auf einmal eintreten** we/they were allowed in two at a time; **~ drei Stufen auf einmal** three steps at a time **4** (auch) **wo/wer/wann/wie [auch] ~:** wherever/whoever/whenever/however **5** (verstärkend) **~ noch, noch ~:** still **6** (ugs.: bei Aufforderung) **~ langsam!/mit der Ruhe!** take it easy!; **nur ~ zu!** keep it up!; **~ geradeaus!** keep [going] straight on; **~ der Nase nach!** keep following your nose!; **was treibst du denn ~?** what are you doing these days? **7** (irgend) **so schnell er ~ konnte** as fast as he possibly could

immer-, Immer-: **~dar** /-'da:ɐ/ *Adv.* (geh.) forever; [for] evermore; **~fort** *Adv.* all the time; constantly; **~grün** *Adj.* evergreen; **~grün** *das* periwinkle; **~hin** *Adv.* **1** (wenigstens) at any rate; anyhow; at least; **er hat es ~hin versucht** he tried, anyhow *or* at any rate; at least he tried; **er ist zwar nicht reich, aber ~hin!** he's not rich, it's true, but still; **2** (trotz allem) nevertheless; all the same; **3** (schließlich) after all

Immersion /ɪmɛr'zjo:n/ *die;* ~, ~**en** (Physik, Astron.) immersion

immer-: **~während** ▸**währen**; **~zu** *Adv.* (ugs.) the whole time; all the time; constantly

Immigrant /ɪmi'grant/ *der;* ~**en**, ~**en**, **Immigrantin** *die;* ~, ~**nen** immigrant

Immigration /ɪmigra'tsjo:n/ *die;* ~, ~**en** immigration

immigrieren *itr. V.; mit sein* immigrate

imminent /ɪmi'nɛnt/ *Adj.* (veralt.) imminent

Immission /ɪmi'sjo:n/ *die;* ~, ~**en** (fachspr.) *air pollution, noise, noxious substances, radiation, etc. constituting a private nuisance*

Immissions·schutz *der: protection against the effects of air pollution, noise, noxious substances, radiation, etc.*

immobil /'ɪmobi:l/ *Adj.* **1** (geh.) immobile; **~es Vermögen** immovable property; real estate *or* property **2** (Milit.) not on a war footing *postpos.*

Immobilien /ɪmo'bi:ljən/ *Pl.* [real] property *sing.*; real estate *sing.*; (Rubrik in Zeitungen) property *sing.*

Immobilien-: **~fonds** *der* (Finanzw.) real estate investment fund; **offener ~fonds** open-ended real estate investment fund; **geschlossener ~fonds** closed-end real estate investment fund; **~handel** *der* dealing *no art.* in real estate *or* in property; **~händler** *der*, **~händlerin** *die* ▸❶ **S. 113** estate agent; realtor (Amer.); **~makler** *der*, **~maklerin** *die* ▸❶ **S. 113** estate agent; realtor (Amer.)

immobilisieren *tr. V.* (Med.) immobilize

Immoralismus /ɪmora'lɪsmʊs/ *der;* ~ (geh.) immoralism

Immortelle /ɪmɔr'tɛlə/ *die;* ~, ~**n** everlasting [flower]; immortelle

immun /ɪ'mu:n/ **1** (Med., fig.) immune (**gegen** to) **2** (Rechtsspr.) **~ sein** have *or* enjoy immunity

immunisieren *tr. V.* immunize (**gegen** against)

Immunisierung *die;* ~, ~**en** immunization (**gegen** against)

Immunität /ɪmuni'tɛ:t/ *die;* ~, ~**en** **1** (Med.) immunity (**gegen** to) **2** (Rechtsspr.) immunity (**gegen** from)

Immunologie /ɪmunolo'gi:/ *die;* ~: immunology

Immun-: **~schwäche** *die* (Med.) immunodeficiency; immune deficiency; **eine ~schwäche haben** be immunodeficient; **~system** *das* (Med.) immune system; **~therapie** *die* (Med.) immunotherapy; immune therapy

Imp. *Abk.* **1** = **Imperfekt** imperf. **2** = **Imperativ** imper.

Impedanz /ɪmpe'dants/ *die;* ~, ~**en** (Elektrot.) impedance

Imperativ /'ɪmperati:f/ *der;* ~**s**, ~**e** **1** (Sprachw.) imperative **2** (Philos.) **[kategorischer] ~:** [categorical] imperative

imperativisch (Sprachw.)
A *Adj.* imperative
B *adv.* in the imperative

Imperativ·satz *der* imperative sentence

Imperator /ɪmpe'ra:tɔr/ *der;* ~**s**, ~**en** /-'to:rən/ (hist.) **1** (römischer Oberfeldherr) imperator **2** (Kaiser) emperor; **~ Rex** King Emperor

Imperfekt /'ɪmpɛrfɛkt/ *das;* ~**s**, ~**e**, **Imperfektum** /ɪmpɛr'fɛktʊm/ *das;* ~**s**, ~ (Sprachw.) imperfect [tense]

Imperialismus /ɪmperja'lɪsmʊs/ *der;* ~: imperialism *no art.*

Imperialist *der;* ~**en**, ~**en**, **Imperialistin** *die;* ~, ~**nen** imperialist

imperialistisch *Adj.* imperialistic

Imperium /ɪm'pe:rjʊm/ *das;* ~**s**, **Imperien** (hist., fig.) empire

impertinent /ɪmpɛrti'nɛnt/
A *Adj.* impertinent; impudent
B *adv.* impertinently; impudently

Impertinenz /ɪmpɛrti'nɛnts/ *die;* ~, ~**en** impertinence; impudence; **diese ~en** this impertinence *or* impudence *sing.*

Impetus /'ɪmpetʊs/ *der;* ~ **1** (Antrieb) impetus **2** (Schwung) verve; zest

Impf-: **~aktion** *die* vaccination *or* inoculation programme; **~arzt** *der*, **~ärztin** *die* vaccinator; inoculator; **~ausweis** *der* vaccination certificate

impfen /'ɪmpfn̩/ *tr. V.* ▸❶ **S. 439** **1** vaccinate; inoculate; **sich ~ lassen** be vaccinated *or* inoculated **2** (Biol., Landw.) inoculate

Impfling /'ɪmpflɪŋ/ *der;* ~**s**, ~**e** person who has been vaccinated; (zu impfende Person) person waiting to be vaccinated

Impf-: **~pass**, ***~paß** *der* vaccination certificate; **~pflicht** *die:* **die ~pflicht für die Pockenimpfung wurde aufgehoben** compulsory vaccination for smallpox was abolished; **~pistole** *die* inoculation injector; **~schaden** *der* vaccine damage *no pl., no indef. art.*; **~schutz** *der* protection given by vaccination; **~stoff** *der* vaccine

Impfung *die;* ~, ~**en** ▸❶ **S. 439** vaccination; inoculation

Impf-: **~zeugnis** *das* ▸**~ausweis**; **~zwang** *der* ▸**~pflicht**

Implantat /ɪmplan'ta:t/ *das;* ~**[e]s**, ~**e** (Med.) implant

Implantation /ɪmplanta'tsjo:n/ *die;* ~, ~**en** (Med.) implantation

implantieren *tr. V.* (Med.) implant; **jmdm. etw. ~:** implant sth. in sb.

implementieren *tr. V.* (DV) implement

Implikation /ɪmplika'tsjo:n/ *die;* ~, ~**en** (geh., Logik) implication

implizieren /ɪmpli'tsi:rən/ *tr. V.* (geh.) imply

implizit /ɪmpli'tsi:t/ (geh.)
A *Adj.* implicit
B *adv.* implicitly

implizite /ɪm'pli:tsite/ *Adv.* (geh.) implicitly

implodieren /ɪmplo'di:rən/ *itr. V.; mit sein* (fachspr.) implode

Implosion /ɪmplo'zjo:n/ *die;* ~, ~**en** (fachspr.) implosion

Imponderabilien /ɪmpɔndera'bi:ljən/ *Pl.* (geh.) imponderables

imponieren /ɪmpo'ni:rən/ *itr. V.* impress; **jmdm. durch etw./mit etw. ~:** impress sb. by sth.; **am meisten imponiert uns an ihm seine Ruhe** what impresses us most about him is his calmness

imponierend
A *Adj.* impressive
B *adv.* impressively

Imponier·gehabe[n] *das* (Verhaltensf.) display

Import /ɪm'pɔrt/ *der;* ~**[e]s**, ~**e** import; **den ~ erhöhen** increase imports; **eine Firma für ~ und Export** an import/export firm

Importeur /ɪmpɔr'tø:ɐ/ *der;* ~**s**, ~**e**, **Importeurin** *die;* ~, ~**nen** importer

Import·geschäft *das* **1** import business **2** (geschäftlicher Abschluss) import deal

importieren *tr., itr. V.* import

Import-: **~kauffrau** *die*, **~kaufmann** *der* importer; **~überschuss**, ***~überschuß** *der* import surplus

imposant /ɪmpo'zant/
A *Adj.* imposing; impressive ‹*achievement*›
B *adv.* imposingly

impotent /'ɪmpotɛnt/ *Adj.* impotent

Impotenz /'ɪmpotɛnts/ *die;* ~: impotence

imprägnieren /ɪmprɛ'gni:rən/ *tr. V.* **1** impregnate; (wasserdicht machen) waterproof **2** (fachspr.) carbonate ‹*wine*›

Imprägnierung *die;* ~, ~**en** ▸**imprägnieren 1, 2**: impregnation; waterproofing; carbonation

im·praktikabel *Adj.* impracticable

Impresario /ɪmpre'za:rjo/ *der;* ~**s**, ~**s** *od.* **Impresari** (veralt.) impresario

Impressen ▸**Impressum**

Impression /ɪmprɛ'sjo:n/ *die;* ~, ~**en** impression

Impressionismus *der;* ~: impressionism *no art.*

Impressionist *der;* ~**en**, ~**en**, **Impressionistin** *die;* ~, ~**nen** impressionist

impressionistisch *Adj.* impressionistic

Impressum /ɪm'prɛsʊm/ *das;* ~**s**, **Impressen** imprint

Imprimatur /ɪmpri'ma:tʊr/ *das;* ~**s**, (österr.:) /---'-/ *die;* ~ **1** (Buchw.) **das** *od.* (österr.) **die ~ [für etw.] erteilen** pass sth. for press **2** (kath. Kirche) imprimatur

Improvisation /ɪmproviza'tsjo:n/ *die;* ~, ~**en** improvisation

Improvisations·talent *das* gift *or* talent for improvisation

improvisieren *tr., itr. V.* improvise; **über ein Thema ~** (Musik) improvise on a theme

Impuls /ɪm'pʊls/ *der;* ~**es**, ~**e** **1** (Anstoß) stimulus; **von etw. gehen wichtige ~e aus** sth. is an important stimulus *sing.*; **einer Sache** (*Dat.*) **neue ~e geben** give sth. fresh stimulus *sing. or* impetus *sing.* **2** (innere Regung) impulse; **einem ~ folgen** act on [an] impulse; **etw. aus einem ~ heraus tun** do sth. on impulse **3** (Elektrot.) pulse **4** (Physik) impulse; (Produkt aus Masse u. Geschwindigkeit) momentum

Impuls-: **~geber** *der*, **~generator** *der* (Elektrot.) pulse generator

impulsiv /ɪmpʊl'zi:f/
A *Adj.* impulsive
B *adv.* impulsively

Impulsivität /ɪmpʊlzivi'tɛ:t/ *die;* ~: impulsiveness

Impuls·satz *der* (Physik) principle of the conservation of momentum

imstande /ɪm'ʃtandə/ *Adv.* **~ sein, etw. zu tun** (fähig sein) be able to do sth.; be capable of doing sth.; (die Möglichkeit haben) be in a position to do sth.; **zu etw. ~ sein** be capable of sth.; **er ist ~ und schiebt mir die Schuld in die Schuhe** he's [quite] capable of putting the blame on to me

in¹ /ɪn/
A *Präp. mit Dat.* 1▸ (auf die Frage: wo?) in; **er hat in Tübingen studiert** he studied at Tübingen; **in Deutschland/der Schweiz** in Germany/Switzerland; **sind Sie schon mal in China gewesen?** have you ever been to China?; **in der Schule/Kirche** at school/church; **in der Schule/Kirche steht noch eine alte Orgel** there's still an old organ in the school/church; **in einer Partei** in a party 2▸ (auf die Frage: wann?) in; **in zwei Tagen/einer Woche** in two days/a week; **in diesem Sommer** this summer; **[gerade] in dem Moment, als er kam** the [very] moment he came; **in diesem Jahr/Monat** this/that year/month 3▸ (auf die Frage: wie?) in; **in Farbe/Schwarzweiß** in colour/black and white; **in Deutsch/Englisch** in German/English 4▸ (fig.) **in Mathematik/Englisch** in mathematics/English; **sich in jmdm. täuschen** be wrong about sb. 5▸ **er hat es in sich** (ugs.) he's got what it takes (coll.); **der Schnaps/diese Übersetzung hat es in sich** (ugs.) this schnapps packs a punch (coll.)/this translation is a tough one 6▸ (Kaufmannsspr.) **in etw.** (Dat.) **handeln** deal in sth.; **er macht in Spirituosen** (ugs.) he deals in spirits
B *Präp. mit Akk.* 1▸ (auf die Frage: wohin?) into; **in die Stadt/das Dorf** into town/the village; **in die Schweiz** to Switzerland; **in die Kirche/Schule gehen** go to church/school; **in eine Partei eintreten** join a party 2▸ (auf die Frage: [bis] wann?) into; **bis in den Herbst** into the autumn 3▸ (fig.) **in die Millionen gehen** run into millions; **sich in jmdn. verlieben** fall in love with sb.; **in etw. einwilligen** agree *or* consent to sth.; *s. auch* **ins**

in² *Adj.* **in ~ sein** (ugs.) be in

-in *Bei der Übersetzung ins Englische wird das deutsche Suffix* **-in**, *mit dem feminine Substantive wie* **Lehrerin** *oder* **Kanadierin** *als Ableitungen von Maskulina gebildet werden, im Allgemeinen nicht übersetzt* (**Lehrerin** = teacher). *Soll jedoch betont werden, dass es sich um weibliche Personen im Gegensatz zu männlichen handelt, bieten sich folgende Übersetzungsmöglichkeiten an:* **Lehrerinnen gehen mit 60 in den Ruhestand** women teachers retire at sixty; **sie ist die bekannteste Kanadierin** she is the best-known Canadian woman; *gelegentlich sind Formulierungen wie* lady teachers *oder* Canadian lady *angebracht, wenn eine besonders höfliche Ausdrucksweise angestrebt wird. Sofern es sich um eine Nationalitätenbezeichnung handelt und die betreffende Person noch recht jung ist, findet man auch häufig die Form* Canadian girl. *In diesem Wörterbuch wurde aus Platzgründen auf die Darstellung solcher Möglichkeiten beim jeweiligen Einzelstichwort meist verzichtet*

in·adäquat
A *Adj.* (geh.) inadequate
B *adv.* inadequately

in·aktiv
A *Adj.* (geh., auch Chemie, Med.) inactive
B *adv.* **sich ~ verhalten** be inactive

In·aktivität *die;* ~ (geh., auch Chemie, Med.) inactivity

in·akzeptabel *Adj.* (geh.) unacceptable

In·angriffnahme /-na:mə/ *die;* ~, ~n (Amtsspr.) commencement; (eines Problems) tackling

In·anspruchnahme *die;* ~, ~n 1▸ (Amtsspr.) use; **bei häufiger ~ der Versicherung** if frequent [insurance] claims are made; **auf ~ seiner Rechte verzichten** waive one's rights 2▸ (starke Belastung) demands *pl.*; **die große berufliche ~:** the heavy demands made on him/her by his/her job 3▸ (von Maschinen, Material) use; (von Einrichtungen) utilization

in·artikuliert (geh.)
A *Adj.* inarticulate
B *adv.* inarticulately

In·augenscheinnahme *die;* ~, ~n (Amtsspr.) inspection; **nach ~ mehrerer Wohnungen** after inspecting several flats

Inaugural·dissertation /ɪnǀaugu'ra:l-/ *die* (doctoral) thesis

Inauguration /ɪnǀaugura'tsi̯o:n/ *die;* ~, ~en (geh.) inauguration

In·begriff *der* quintessence; **der ~ des Gelehrten/Spießers** the epitome of the scholar/petit bourgeois; the quintessential scholar/petit bourgeois; **der ~ der Schönheit/des Schreckens** the quintessence of beauty/terror; **sie ist der ~ der Tugend/des Bösen** she is virtue personified *or* itself/the embodiment of evil

inbegriffen *Adj.* included

In·besitznahme *die;* ~, ~n (Amtsspr.) appropriation

In·betriebnahme *die;* ~, ~n, **In·betriebsetzung** /-zɛtsʊŋ/ *die;* ~, ~en (Amtsspr.) 1▸ (von [öffentlichen] Einrichtungen) opening 2▸ (von Maschinen) bringing into service; **vor ~ der Maschine** before bringing the machine into service 3▸ (eines Kraftwerks) commissioning

Inbox *die;* ~, ~en (DV) in-box

In·brunst *die;* ~ (geh.) fervour; (der Liebe) ardour; **mit ~:** with fervour; **jmdn. mit ~ lieben** love sb. ardently

in·brünstig (geh.)
A *Adj.* fervent; ardent ‹*love*›
B *adv.* fervently; ‹*love*› ardently

Inbus·schlüssel Ⓦⓩ /'ɪnbʊs-/ *der* (Technik) Allen key

Indanthren Ⓦⓩ /ɪndan'tre:n/ *das;* ~s, ~e (Textilind.) indanthrene

Indefinit·pronomen /ɪndefi'ni:t-/ *das* (Sprachw.) indefinite pronoun

in·deklinabel *Adj.* (Sprachw.) indeclinable

in·dem *Konj.* 1▸ (während) while; (gerade als) as 2▸ (dadurch, dass) **~ man etw. tut** by doing sth. 3▸ (bes. südd.) **~ dass** because

Indemnität /ɪndɛmni'tɛ:t/ *die;* ~: ≈ parliamentary privilege

Inder /'ɪndɐ/ *der;* ~s, ~, **Inderin** *die;* ~, ~nen ▸ⓘ **S. 520** Indian

in·des (selten), **in·dessen**
A *Konj.* (geh.) 1▸ (während) while 2▸ (wohingegen) whereas
B *Adv.* 1▸ (inzwischen) meanwhile; in the meantime 2▸ (jedoch) however

Index /'ɪndɛks/ *der;* ~ *od.* ~es, ~e *od.* **Indizes** /'ɪnditse:s/ 1▸ (Register) index 2▸ (kath. Kirche) Index 3▸ (Math., Physik, Wirtsch.) index

Index·schaltung *die* index gears *pl.*

Index·zahl *die* (Wirtsch.) index [number]

in·dezent *Adj.* (geh.) indelicate

Indianer /ɪn'di̯a:nɐ/ *der;* ~s, ~ ▸ⓘ **S. 520** [American] Indian

Indianer-: **~geheul** *das* (scherzh.) **mit ~geheul** whooping and yelling like a Red Indian/[Red] Indians; **~häuptling** *der* Indian chief

Indianerin *die;* ~, ~nen ▸ⓘ **S. 520** [American] Indian

Indianer-: **~krapfen** *der* (österr.) ▸**Mohrenkopf 1**; **~reservat** *das* Indian reservation

indianisch *Adj.* ▸ⓘ **S. 520** Indian

Indien /'ɪndi̯ən/ *(das);* ~s India

In·dienst·stellung *die;* ~, ~en (Amtsspr.) commissioning

in·different
A *Adj.* (geh., fachspr.) indifferent
B *adv.* (geh.) indifferently

In·differenz *die;* ~, ~en (geh., auch Chemie, Med.) indifference

Indignation /ɪndɪgna'tsi̯o:n/ *die;* ~ (geh.) indignation

indigniert /ɪndɪ'gni:ɐ̯t/ *Adj.* indignant

Indigo /'ɪndigo/ *der od. das;* ~s, ~s indigo

indigo·blau *Adj.* indigo [blue]

Indikation /ɪndika'tsi̯o:n/ *die;* ~, ~en 1▸ (Med.: Heilanzeige) indication 2▸ (Rechtsw.) **[medizinische/soziale/ethische] ~:** [medical/social/ethical] grounds *pl.* for abortion

Indikativ /'ɪndikati:f/ *der;* ~s, ~e /-i:və/ (Sprachw.) indicative [mood]

indikativisch *Adj.* (Sprachw.) indicative

Indikator /ɪndi'ka:tɔr/ *der;* ~s, ~en /-ka'to:rən/ (auch Chemie, Technik) indicator

Indio /'ɪndi̯o/ *der;* ~s, ~s (*Central/South American*) Indian

in·direkt
A *Adj.* indirect; **~e Rede/eine ~e Frage** (Sprachw.) indirect *or* reported speech/an indirect question; **ein ~er Freistoß** (Sport) an indirect free kick
B *adv.* indirectly; **einen Freistoß ~ ausführen** (Sport) take an indirect free kick

indisch /'ɪndɪʃ/ ▸ⓘ **S. 520**
A *Adj.* Indian
B *adv.* **sie hat gestern ~ gekocht** she cooked an Indian meal yesterday

in·diskret *Adj.* indiscreet

In·diskretion *die;* ~, ~en indiscretion

in·diskutabel *Adj.* (abwertend) unworthy of discussion *pred.*

in·disponiert *Adj.* (geh.) indisposed

In·disposition *die* (geh.) indisposition

individualisieren *tr. V.* (geh.) individualize

Individualismus /ɪndividu̯a'lɪsmʊs/ *der;* ~ (Philos., geh.) individualism

Individualist *der;* ~en, ~en, **Individualistin** *die;* ~, ~nen (geh.) individualist

individualistisch *Adj.* (geh.) individualistic

Individualität /ɪndividu̯ali'tɛ:t/ *die;* ~, ~en (geh.) 1▸ individuality 2▸ (Persönlichkeit) personality

Individual·verkehr *der* private transport

Individuation /ɪndividu̯a'tsi̯o:n/ *die;* ~, ~en (Psych.) individuation

individuell /ɪndivi'du̯ɛl/
A *Adj.* 1▸ individual 2▸ (einem Einzelnen gehörend) private ‹*property, vehicle, etc.*›
B *adv.* individually; **etw. ~ gestalten** give sth. one's own personal touch; **das ist ~ verschieden** it varies from case to case

Individuum /ɪndi'vi:duʊm/ *das;* ~s, **Individuen** (auch Chemie, Biol.) individual; **ein fragwürdiges/verdächtiges ~** a dubious/suspicious individual *or* character

Indiz /ɪn'di:ts/ *das;* ~es, ~ien 1▸ (Rechtsw.) piece of circumstantial evidence; **~ien** circumstantial evidence *sing.* 2▸ (Anzeichen) sign (**für** of)

Indizes ▸**Index**

Indizien·beweis *der* (Rechtsw.) piece of circumstantial evidence; **~e** circumstantial evidence *sing.*

indizieren /ɪndi'tsi:rən/ *tr. V.* 1▸ (Med.) indicate 2▸ (kath. Kirche) **ein Buch ~:** place a book on the Index

indo-, Indo-/ɪndo-/: **~china** *(das)* Indo-China; **~europäer** *Pl.* ▸**~germanen**; **~europäisch** *Adj.* ▸**~germanisch**; **~germanen** *Pl.* Indo-Europeans; **~germanisch** *Adj.* ▸ⓘ **S. 670** Indo-European; Indo-Germanic

Indoktrination /ɪndɔktrina'tsi̯o:n/ *die;* ~, ~en indoctrination

indoktrinieren *tr. V.* indoctrinate

indolent /'ɪndolɛnt/ *Adj.* (geh., Med.) indolent

Indonesien /ɪndo'ne:zi̯ən/ *(das);* ~s Indonesia

Indonesier *der;* ~s, ~, **Indonesierin** *die;* ~, ~nen ▸ⓘ **S. 520** Indonesian

indonesisch *Adj.* ▸ⓘ **S. 520**, ▸ⓘ **S. 670** Indonesian

Indossament /ɪndɔsa'mɛnt/ *das;* ~[e]s, ~e (Finanzw.) endorsement

Indossant /ɪndɔ'sant/ *der;* ~en, ~en, **Indossantin** *die;* ~, ~nen (Finanzw.) endorser

Indossat /ɪndɔ'sa:t/ *der;* ~en, ~en, **Indossatin** *die;* ~, ~nen (Finanzw.) endorsee

indossieren *tr. V.* (Finanzw.) endorse

Induktanz /ɪndʊk'tants/ *die;* ~ (Elektrot.) inductance

Induktion /ɪndʊk'tsi̯o:n/ *die;* ~, ~en (Philos., Elektrot., Biol.) induction

Induktions-: **~maschine** *die* (Elektrot.) induction machine; **~ofen** *der* (Technik) induction furnace; **~schleife** *die* (Elektrot.) induction control loop; **~spule** *die* (Elektrot.) induction coil; **~strom** *der* (Elektrot.) induced current

induktiv /ɪndʊk'tiːf/ *Adj.* (Philos., Elektrot.) inductive

Induktivität /ɪndʊktivi'tɛːt/ *die;* **~, ~en** (Elektrot.) self-inductance; coefficient of self-induction

industrialisieren /ɪndʊstriali'ziːrən/ *tr. V.* industrialize

Industrialisierung *die;* **~:** industrialization

Industrie /ɪndʊs'triː/ *die;* **~, ~n** industry; **in die ~ gehen** (ugs.) go into industry; **in der ~ arbeiten** work in industry

Industrie-: **~abfall** *der* industrial waste; **~aktie** *die* industrial share; **~anlage** *die* industrial plant; **~ansiedlung** *die* setting-up of industry; **~arbeiter** *der,* **~arbeiterin** *die* industrial worker; **~archäologie** *die* industrial archaeology *no art.;* **~ausstellung** *die* industrial exhibition; **~betrieb** *der* industrial company *or* firm; **~erzeugnis** *das* industrial product; **~gebiet** *das* industrial area; **~gesellschaft** *die* (Soziol.) industrial society; **~gewerkschaft** *die* industrial union; **~kapitän** *der* captain of industry; **~kauffrau** *die,* **~kaufmann** *der: person with three years' business training employed on the business side of an industrial company;* **~landschaft** *die* industrial landscape

industriell /ɪndʊstri'ɛl/

A *Adj.* industrial; **die ~e Revolution** (hist.) the Industrial Revolution

B *adv.* industrially; **~ überlegen/rückständig** industrially more/less advanced

Industrielle *der/die; adj. Dekl.* industrialist

Industrie-: **~magnat** *der* industrial magnate; **~müll** *der* industrial waste; **~produkt** *das* industrial product; **~spionage** *die* industrial espionage; **~staat** *der* industrial nation; **~stadt** *die* industrial town; (größer) industrial city

Industrie- und Handels·kammer *die* Chamber of Industry and Commerce

Industrie-: **~unternehmen** *das* industrial concern *or* company; **~zweig** *der* branch of industry

induzieren /ɪndu'tsiːrən/ *tr. V.* (Philos., Elektrot.) induce

in·effektiv *Adj.* ineffective

in·effizient *Adj.* (geh.) inefficient

In·effizienz *die* (geh.) inefficiency

in·einander *Adv.* into each other; into one another; (zusammen) together; **die Farben fließen ~:** the colours run into each other *or* one another; **~ greifen** mesh or engage [with each other *or* one another]; mesh together; **sich ~ schieben** ‹vehicles› telescope; **~ verliebt sein** be in love with each other *or* one another; **~ verschlungene Ornamente** intertwined decorations; **ganz ~ aufgehen** be totally wrapped up in each other *or* one another; **~ übergehen** merge

***ineinander|fließen** *usw.:* ▸**ineinander**

in·existent *Adj.* (geh.) non-existent

infam /ɪn'faːm/

A *Adj.* disgraceful; **~e Schmerzen** (ugs.) dreadful pain *sing.* (coll.)

B *adv.* disgracefully; **~ weh tun** (ugs.) hurt like mad *or* hell (coll.)

Infamie /ɪnfa'miː/ *die;* **~, ~n** [1] disgracefulness [2] (Äußerung) disgraceful remark; (Handlung) disgraceful action

Infant /ɪn'fant/ *der;* **~en, ~en** (hist.) infante; (Thronfolger) principe

Infanterie /'ɪnfant(ə)riː/ *die;* **~, ~n** (Milit.) infantry

Infanterie-: **~regiment** *das* (Milit.) infantry regiment; **~stellung** *die* (Milit.) infantry position

Infanterist *der;* **~en, ~en** (Milit.) infantryman

infantil /ɪnfan'tiːl/ (Psych., Med., sonst abwertend)

A *Adj.* infantile

B *adv.* in an infantile way

Infantilismus *der;* **~, Infantilismen** (Psych., Med.) infantilism

Infantilität /ɪnfantili'tɛːt/ *die;* **~** [1] (abwertend) infantility [2] (Psych., Med.) infantilism

Infantin *die;* **~, ~nen** (hist.) infanta

Infarkt /ɪn'farkt/ *der;* **~[e]s, ~e** ▸ℹ **S. 439** (Med.) infarction

infarkt·gefährdet *Adj.* (Med.) ‹person› with a high risk of suffering a cardiac infarction

Infarkt·risiko *das* (Med.) infarction risk

Infekt /ɪn'fɛkt/ *der;* **~[e]s, ~e** ▸ℹ **S. 439** (Med.) infection; **ein grippaler ~:** an influenzal infection

Infektion /ɪnfɛk'tsi̯oːn/ *die;* **~, ~en** ▸ℹ **S. 439** (Med.) [1] (Ansteckung) infection [2] (ugs.: Entzündung) inflammation

Infektions-: **~gefahr** *die* (Med.) danger *or* risk of infection; **~herd** *der* (Med.) seat of the/an infection; **~krankheit** *die* ▸ℹ **S. 439** (Med.) infectious disease

infektiös /ɪnfɛk'tsi̯øːs/ *Adj.* (Med.) infectious

Inferiorität /ɪnferi̯ori'tɛːt/ *die;* **~** (geh.) inferiority

Inferioritäts·komplex *der* (Psych.) ▸**Minderwertigkeitskomplex**

infernalisch /ɪnfɛr'naːlɪʃ/ (geh.)

A *Adj.* infernal; **~ schmecken** taste dreadful

B *adv.* infernally; **~ stinken** stink dreadfully

Inferno /ɪn'fɛrno/ *das;* **~s** (geh.) inferno

Infiltrat /ɪnfɪl'traːt/ *das;* **~[e]s, ~e** (Med.) infiltrate

Infiltration /ɪnfɪltra'tsi̯oːn/ *die;* **~, ~en** (auch Med.) infiltration

infiltrieren *tr. V.* (auch Med.) infiltrate; **jmdm. etw. ~** (Med.) infiltrate sth. into sb.

in·finit *Adj.* (Sprachw.) infinite

Infinitesimal·rechnung /ɪnfinitezi'maːl-/ *die* (Math.) infinitesimal calculus

Infinitiv /'ɪnfinitiːf/ *der;* **~s, ~e** /-tiːvə/ (Sprachw.) infinitive

Infinitiv·satz *der* (Sprachw.) infinitive clause

infizieren /ɪnfi'tsiːrən/

A *tr. V.* (auch fig.) infect

B *refl. V.* become *or* get infected; **sich bei jmdm. ~:** be infected by sb.; catch an infection from sb.

in flagranti /ɪn fla'granti/ *Adv.* (geh.) in flagrante [delicto]

Inflation /ɪnfla'tsi̯oːn/ *die;* **~, ~en** (Wirtsch.) inflation; (Zeit der ~) period of inflation; **eine schleichende ~:** creeping inflation

inflationär /ɪnflatsi̯o'nɛːɐ̯/, **inflationistisch** *Adj.* inflationary

Inflations-: **~ausgleich** *der* increase to allow for inflation; **~politik** *die* policy of inflation; **~rate** *die* rate of inflation

in·flexibel *Adj.* [1] (auch fig.) inflexible [2] (Sprachw.) uninflected

In·flexibilität *die;* **~** (auch fig.) inflexibility

Influenz /ɪnflu'ɛnts/ *die;* **~, ~en** (Elektrot.) [electrostatic] induction

Influenza /ɪnflu'ɛntsa/ *die;* **~** (veralt.) influenza

Info /'ɪnfo/ *das;* **~s, ~s** (ugs.) handout

in·folge

A *Präp. + Gen.* as a result of; owing to

B *Adv.* **~ von etw.** (*Dat.*) as a result of *or* owing to sth.

infolge·dessen *Adv.* consequently; as a result of this

Informant /ɪnfɔr'mant/ *der;* **~en, ~en, Informantin** *die;* **~, ~nen** (auch Sprachw.) informant

Informanten·schutz *der* (Rechtsw.) protection of sources

Informatik /ɪnfɔr'maːtɪk/ *die;* **~:** computer science *no art.*

Informatiker *der;* **~s, ~, Informatikerin** *die;* **~, ~nen** computer scientist

Information /ɪnfɔrma'tsi̯oːn/ *die;* **~, ~en** [1] (auch Kybernetik) information *no pl., no indef. art.* (**über** + *Akk.* about, on); **eine ~:** [a piece of] information; **eine umfassende ~ der Öffentlichkeit zu diesen Vorfällen ist unbedingt notwendig** it is vital to inform the public fully about these incidents; **zu Ihrer ~:** for your information; **nach neuesten ~en** according to the latest information; **nähere ~en erhalten Sie ...** you can obtain more information ... [2] (Büro) information bureau; (Stand) information desk

Informations-: **~austausch** *der* exchange of information; **~büro** *das* information bureau *or* office; **~fluss,** ***~fluß** *der* flow of information; **~gesellschaft** *die* (Soziol.) information society; **~gespräch** *das* mutual briefing session; **~material** *das* informational literature; **~quelle** *die* source of information; **~stand** *der* [1] information stand; [2] (Zustand) **bei meinem jetzigen ~stand** with the information I have at present; **~theorie** *die* information theory *no art.;* **~vorsprung** *der* superior knowledge; **~zeitalter** *das* (Soziol.) information age

informativ /ɪnfɔrma'tiːf/

A *Adj.* informative

B *adv.* informatively

informatorisch /ɪnfɔrma'toːrɪʃ/ *Adj.* informatory

in·formell *Adj.* informal

informieren

A *tr. V.* inform (**über** + *Akk.* about); **falsch/einseitig informiert sein** be misinformed/have biased information; **aus gut informierten Kreisen** from well-informed circles

B *refl. V.* inform oneself, find out (**über** + *Akk.* about); **sich aus der Presse/in der Zeitung über etw.** (*Akk.*) **~:** inform oneself or find out about sth. from the press/the newspaper

in·frage *in* **etw. ~ stellen** call sth. into question; question sth.; **jmdn. ~ stellen** cast doubt on sb.; **das stellt unsere Glaubwürdigkeit ~:** it casts doubt on our credibility; **~ kommen** be possible; **für ein Stipendium kommen nur gute Schüler ~:** only good pupils can be considered for a grant; **dieses Kleid kommt für mich nicht ~:** I couldn't possibly wear this dress; **die für die Tat ~ kommenden Personen** those suspected of the crime; **das kommt nicht ~** (ugs.) that is out of the question

infra·rot /'ɪnfra-/ *Adj.* (Physik) infra-red

Infra·rot *das;* **~s** (Physik) infra-red radiation; **im ~:** in the infra-red

Infrarot-: **~film** *der* infra-red film; **~strahler** *der* [1] (Heizgerät) infra-red heater; [2] (Med.) infra-red lamp

Infra-: **~schall** *der* (Physik) infrasound; **~struktur** *die* infrastructure

Infusion /ɪnfu'zi̯oːn/ *die;* **~, ~en** (Med.) infusion; (durch den After) enema

Infusions·tierchen *das,* **Infusorium** /ɪnfu'zoːri̯ʊm/ *das;* **~s, Infusorien** (Biol.) infusorium

Ing. *Abk.* = **Ingenieur**

Ingebrauchnahme *die;* **~, ~n: vor ~ des Geräts** before operating the appliance

Ingenieur /ɪnʒe'ni̯øːɐ̯/ *der;* **~s, ~e** ▸ℹ **S. 113** [qualified] engineer

Ingenieur-: **~bau** *der; Pl.* **~~ten** civil engineering structure; **~büro** *das* firm of consulting engineers

Ingenieurin *die;* **~, ~nen** ▸ℹ **S. 113** [qualified] engineer

Ingenieur·schule *die* college of engineering

ingeniös /ɪnge'ni̯øːs/ (geh.)

A *Adj.* ingenious

B *adv.* ingeniously

Ingeniosität /ɪngeni̯ozi'tɛːt/ *die;* **~** (geh.) ingenuity

Ingredienz /ɪngre'di̯ɛnts/ *die;* **~, ~en** (bes. Pharm., Kochk.) ingredient

In·grimm *der* (geh.) inward rage *or* wrath

in·grimmig (geh.)

A *Adj.* wrathful ‹look, expression›

B *adv.* wrathfully

Ingwer /'ɪŋvɐ/ *der;* **~s, ~** [1] ginger [2] (Likör) ginger liqueur

Ingwer·bier *das* ginger beer

Inhaber /ˈɪnha:bɐ/ *der;* **~s, ~** [1] (einer Aktie, einer Lizenz, eines Rekords, eines Patents, eines Passes) holder; (eines Schecks) bearer; (eines Amtes) holder; incumbent [2] (Besitzer) owner; (eines Hotels, Restaurants, Ladens) owner; proprietor

Inhaberin *die;* **~, ~nen** [1] ▸**Inhaber 1** [2] ▸**Inhaber 2**: owner; proprietress

Inhaber·papier *das* (Wirtsch.) bearer security

inhaftieren /ɪnhafˈti:rən/ *tr. V.* take into custody; detain; **jmdn. zwei Tage lang ~:** keep sb. in custody *or* detain sb. for two days

Inhaftierte *der/die; adj. Dekl.* prisoner

Inhaftierung *die;* **~, ~en** detention

Inhalation /ɪnhalaˈtsi̯o:n/ *die;* **~, ~en** (Med.) inhalation

inhalieren

A *tr. V.* (Med./ugs.) inhale

B *itr. V.* (Med.) use an inhalant

In·halt *der;* **~[e]s, ~e** [1] contents *pl.* [2] (das Dargestellte/geistiger Gehalt) content; **etw. zum ~ haben** deal with *or* concern sth.; **ein Buch politischen ~s** a political book; **der ~ eines Wortes** the meaning of a word; **wir erhielten eine Nachricht des ~s, dass ...** (geh.) we received a message to the effect that ... [3] (bes. Math.) (Flächen~) area; (Raum~) volume

inhaltlich

A *Adj.* **die ~e Struktur des Dramas** the plot structure of the drama; **an ~en Gesichtspunkten gemessen** from the point of view of content

B *adv.* **~ ist der Aufsatz gut** the essay is good as regards content; **~ übereinstimmen** be the same in content

inhalts-, Inhalts-: ~an·gabe *die* summary [of contents]; synopsis; (eines Films, Dramas) [plot] summary; synopsis; **~bezogen** *Adj.* (Sprachw.) **~bezogene Grammatik** content[-oriented] grammar; **~erklärung** *die* declaration of contents; **~leer, ~los** *Adj.* lacking in content *postpos.*; meaningless ‹*word, phrase*›; empty ‹*life*›; **~reich** *Adj.* full ‹*life, discussion*›; **~schwer** *Adj.* weighty; **~übersicht** *die* summary [of contents]; **~verzeichnis** *das* table of contents; (auf einem Paket) list of contents; (als Überschrift) [table of] contents; **~voll** *Adj.* ▸**~reich**

inhärent /ɪnhɛˈrɛnt/ *Adj.* (geh., Philos.) inherent (+ *Dat.* in)

Inhärenz /ɪnhɛˈrɛnts/ *die;* **~** (Philos.) inherence

in·homogen *Adj.* (geh., fachspr.) inhomogeneous

In·homogenität *die;* **~** (geh., fachspr.) inhomogeneity

in·human *Adj.* [1] (unmenschlich) inhuman [2] (rücksichtslos) inhumane

In·humanität *die;* **~:** inhumanity

Initial /iniˈtsi̯a:l/ *das;* **~s, ~e** (selten), **Initiale** *die;* **~, ~n** initial [letter]

Initial-: ~zünder *der* detonator; **~zündung** *die* detonation

Initiation /initsi̯aˈtsi̯o:n/ *die;* **~, ~en** (Soziol., Völkerk.) initiation

Initiations·ritus *der* (Soziol., Völkerk.) initiation rite

initiativ /initsi̯aˈti:f/ *Adj.* **~ werden** take the initiative

Initiative *die;* **~, ~n** [1] (erster Anstoß) initiative; **die ~ ergreifen** take the initiative; **auf jmds. ~** (*Akk.*) **[hin]** on sb.'s initiative [2] (Entschlusskraft) initiative; **~ entwickeln/entfalten** develop initiative; **nur der ~** (*Dat.*) **der Opposition ist es zu verdanken, dass ...** it is only thanks to the Opposition that ... [3] ▸**Bürgerinitiative** [4] (Parl.) right to table *or* introduce a bill; (das Einbringen) tabling *or* introduction of a bill [5] (schweiz.) ▸**Volksbegehren**

Initiator /iniˈtsi̯a:tɔr/ *der;* **~s, ~en, Initiatorin** *die;* **~, ~nen** initiator; (einer Organisation) founder

initiieren /initsiˈi:rən/ *tr. V.* (geh.) initiate

Injektion /ɪnjɛkˈtsi̯o:n/ *die;* **~, ~en** (Med.) injection

Injektions-: ~nadel *die* hypodermic needle; **~spritze** *die* hypodermic syringe

injizieren /ɪnjiˈtsi:rən/ *tr. V.* (Med.) inject; **jmdm. etw. ~:** inject sb. with sth.

Injurie /ɪnˈju:ri̯ə/ *die;* **~, ~n** (geh., Rechtsw.) injury

Inka /ˈɪŋka/ *der;* **~[s], ~[s]** Inca

Inkarnation /ɪnkarnaˈtsi̯o:n/ *die;* **~, ~en** incarnation

Inkasso /ɪnˈkaso/ *das;* **~s, ~s** *od.* **Inkassi** (Finanzw.) collection

In·kaufnahme *die;* **~** (Amtsspr.) acceptance; **er konnte den Vertrag nur unter ~ von Verlusten abschließen** he could complete the contract only by accepting the losses involved

inkl. *Abk.* **= inklusive** incl.

inklusive /ɪnkluˈzi:və/

A *Präp.* + *Gen.* (bes. Kaufmannsspr.) inclusive of; including; **der Preis versteht sich ~ der Verpackung** the price includes *or* is inclusive of packing; **wir bezahlten ~ Frühstück 40 Euro** we paid 40 euros, breakfast included *or* including breakfast

B *Adv.* inclusive

Inklusiv·preis *der* inclusive price

inkognito /ɪnˈkɔgnito/ *Adv.* (geh.) incognito

Inkognito *das;* **~s, ~s** incognito

in·kommensurabel *Adj.* (geh., Math.) incommensurable

in·kommodieren /ɪnkɔmoˈdi:rən/ (geh.)

A *tr. V.* inconvenience; trouble; **jmdn. mit etw. ~:** trouble sb. with sth.

B *refl. V.* trouble oneself

in·kompatibel *Adj.* (fachspr.) incompatible

In·kompatibilität *die* (fachspr.) incompatibility

in·kompetent *Adj.* [1] (unfähig) incompetent [2] (bes. Rechtsspr.: nicht befugt) not competent *postpos.*; incompetent

In·kompetenz *die* incompetence

In·kongruenz *die* (Math.) incongruence

in·konsequent

A *Adj.* inconsistent

B *adv.* inconsistently

In·konsequenz *die* inconsistency

in·konsistent *Adj.* (geh.) inconsistent

in·konstant *Adj.* [1] (Physik) inconstant [2] (geh.) inconsistent; [constantly] shifting ‹*balance of power*›

in·konvertibel *Adj.* (Wirtsch.) inconvertible ‹*currency*›

in·korrekt

A *Adj.* incorrect; incorrect, improper ‹*dress, behaviour*›

B *adv.* incorrectly; **sich ~ kleiden/benehmen** dress/behave incorrectly *or* inproperly

Inkorrektheit *die;* **~, ~en** [1] (Fehlerhaftigkeit) incorrectness; (des Benehmens) incorrectness; impropriety [2] (Fehler) mistake; (inkorrektes Benehmen) breach of propriety; impropriety

In·kraftsetzung /-zɛtsʊŋ/ *die;* **~, ~en** (Amtsspr.) **mit ~ dieses Gesetzes** when this law is/was brought *or* put into force

In-Kraft-Treten, Inkrafttreten *das;* **~s: das ~ des Gesetzes erfolgt dann, wenn ...** the law comes into effect *or* force when ...

In·kreis *der* (Geom.) inscribed circle

inkriminieren /ɪnkrimiˈni:rən/ *tr. V.* (bes. Rechtsspr.) incriminate

Inkubation /ɪnkubaˈtsi̯o:n/ *die;* **~, ~en** ▸ⓘ **S. 439** (Med., Biol.) incubation

Inkubations·zeit *die;* **~, ~en** ▸ⓘ **S. 439** (Med.) incubation period

Inkubator /ɪnkuˈba:tɔr/ *der;* **~s, ~en** (Med.) incubator

Inkubus /ˈɪnkubʊs/ *der;* **~, Inkuben** incubus

in·kulant *Adj.* (Kaufmannsspr.) unaccommodating; disobliging

Inkulanz /ˈɪnkulants/ *die;* **~** (Kaufmannsspr.) disobligingness

Inkunabel /ɪnkuˈna:bl/ *die;* **~, ~n** (Buchw., Literaturw.) incunabulum

In·land *das* [1] (das eigene Land) **im ~:** at home; **im ~ hergestellte Waren, Produktionen des ~es** home-produced goods; **für das ~ bestimmte Waren** goods for the home market; **wir werden unseren Urlaub diesmal im ~ verbringen** we're not going abroad for our holidays this year; **im In- und Ausland** at home and abroad [2] (Binnenland) interior; inland; **im/ins ~:** inland

Inland·eis *das;* **~es** inland ice

Inländer /ˈɪnlɛndɐ/ *der;* **~s, ~, Inländerin** *die;* **~, ~nen** native citizen

Inland·flug *der* ▸**Inlandsflug**

inländisch *Adj.* domestic; internal, domestic ‹*trade, traffic*›; home, domestic ‹*market*›; home-produced, domestic ‹*goods*›

Inlands-: ~ab·satz *der* (Wirtsch.) domestic sales *pl.*; **~flug** *der* domestic flight; **~markt** *der* home *or* domestic market; **~porto** *das* inland postage; **~presse** *die* domestic press; **~verkehr** *der* internal *or* domestic traffic

In·laut *der;* **~[e]s, ~e** (Sprachw.) **im ~ stehen/vorkommen** occur in [word-]medial position *or* [word-]medially

Inlett /ˈɪnlɛt/ *das;* **~[e]s, ~e** *od.* **~s** (Stoff) tick; ticking; (Hülle) tick

in·liegend *Adj.* (Amtsspr., bes. österr.) ▸**einliegend**

Inliner /ˈɪnlaɪnɐ/ *der;* **~s, ~:** Rollerblade ®; in-liner

Inlineskate /ˈɪnlaɪnske:t/ *der;* **~s, ~s** Rollerblade ®; in-line skate

Inlineskater /ˈɪnlaɪnske:tɐ/ *der;* **~s, ~:** rollerblader; in-line skater

in·mitten

A *Präp.* + *Gen.* (geh.) in the midst of; surrounded by

B *Adv.* **~ von** in the midst of; surrounded by

inne /ˈɪnə/ **in einer Sache** (*Gen.*) **~ sein** (geh.) be [fully] aware of sth.

inne-/ˈɪnə-/: **~|haben** *unr. tr. V.* [1] (einnehmen) hold, occupy ‹*position*›; hold ‹*office*›; **die Führung/Leitung ~haben** be in charge; **einen Lehrstuhl ~haben** hold a [professorial] chair; [2] (geh.: besitzen) own; possess; **~|halten** *unr. itr. V.* pause; **in** *od.* **mit etw. ~halten** stop sth. for a moment; **er hielt in seiner Arbeit/im Laufen ~:** he stopped work/running for a moment; **er hielt mitten im Satz ~:** he stopped *or* paused in the middle of his sentence *or* in mid-sentence

innen /ˈɪnən/ *Adv.* [1] inside; (auf/an der Innenseite) on the inside; **etw. von ~ nach außen kehren** turn sth. inside out; **die Leitung verlief von ~ nach außen** the cable ran from the inside to the outside; **~ und außen** inside and out[side]; **nach ~ aufgehen** open inwards; **etw. von ~ besichtigen/ansehen** look round the/at the inside of sth.; **die Füße nach ~ setzen** turn one's feet in[wards]; **~ laufen** (Sport) run on the inside; **von ~ heraus** from within [2] (österr.: drinnen) inside; (im Haus) indoors

innen-, Innen-: ~ansicht *die* interior view; **~antenne** *die* indoor aerial; **~arbeiten** *Pl.* interior work *sing.*; **~architekt** *der*, **~architektin** *die* interior designer; **~aufnahme** *die* (Fot.) indoor photo[graph]; (Film) indoor *or* interior shot; **~ausstattung** *die:* **[eine] ~ausstattung** decoration and furnishings; (eines Autos) [an] interior trim; **~bahn** *die* (Sport) inside lane; **~beleuchtung** *die* [1] (eines Fahrzeugs) interior light; (beim Türöffnen aufleuchtend) courtesy light; [2] (im Zug, Flugzeug) interior lighting; **~dienst** *der:* **~dienst haben** be working in the office; ‹*policeman*› be on station duty; **im ~dienst tätig sein** work in the office; ‹*policeman*› do station duty; **~durchmesser** *der* internal diameter; **~einrichtung** *die* furnishings *pl.*; **~fläche** *die* inner surface; (der Hand) palm; **~geleitet** *Adj.* (Soziol.) self-directed; **~hof** *der* inner courtyard; (eines Klosters, Colleges) quadrangle; **~kurve** *die* inside bend; **die ~kurve nehmen** ‹*driver*› cut the corner; **~lager** *das* (Jargon) ▸**Tretlager**; **~leben** *das* [1] [inner] thoughts and feelings *pl.*; [2] (oft scherzh.: Ausstattung) inside; (eines Hauses) interior; (eines Autos, Fernsehers usw.) inner workings *pl.*; **~minister** *der*, **~ministerin** *die*

▸❶ S. 113 Minister of the Interior; ≈ Home Secretary (Brit.); ≈ Secretary of the Interior (Amer.); **~ministerium** *das* Ministry of the Interior; ≈ Home Office (Brit.); ≈ Department of the Interior (Amer.); **~pfosten** *der* (Ballspiele) inside of the post; **der rechte ~pfosten** the inside of the right-hand post; **~politik** *die* (eines Staates) home affairs *pl.*; (einer Regierung) domestic policy/policies *pl.*; **~politiker** *der*, **~politikerin** *die* politician concerned with home affairs; **~politisch** ▸~politik: **A** *Adj.* **~politische Fragen** matters of domestic policy; **der ~politische Kurs der Regierung** the government's domestic policy; **eine ~politische Debatte** a debate on home affairs/domestic policy; **B** *adv.* as regards home affairs/domestic policy; **~politisch betrachtet** from the point of view of home affairs/domestic policy; **~raum** *der* **1** inner room; **die ~räume des Hauses** the interior of the house; **2** (Platz im Innern) room inside; **ein Auto/Haus mit großem ~raum** a car/house with a spacious interior; **~rist** *der* (bes. Fußball) inside of the *or* one's foot; **~rolle** *die* hair curled under *no pl., no indef. art.*; **~seite** *die* inside; (eines Stoffes) wrong side; **~senator** *der*, **~senatorin** *die: minister for internal affairs* (in Bremen, Hamburg, Berlin); **~spiegel** *der* rear-view mirror; **~stadt** *die* town centre; downtown (Amer.); (einer Großstadt) city centre; **~stürmer** *der*, **~stürmerin** *die* (Ballspiele) inside forward; **~tasche** *die* inside pocket; **~temperatur** *die* inside temperature; **bei 22 °C ~temperatur** when the temperature inside is 22°C; when it's 22°C inside; **wir haben eine ~temperatur von 22 °C** the temperature inside is 22°C; **~wand** *die* interior wall; **~welt** *die* inner world; **sie hat sich ganz in ihre ~welt zurückgezogen** she withdrew completely into her own private world; **~winkel** *der* interior angle

inner... /ˈɪnɐ.../ *Adj.* **1** inner; inside ‹*pocket, lane*›; **die ~e Seite** the inside **2** (Med.) internal; **die ~en Organe** the internal organs; **eine ~e Blutung/~e Blutungen** *Pl.* internal bleeding; **die ~e Medizin** internal medicine; **die I~e** (Med. Jargon) the medical ward **3** (im Innern gefühlt) inner ‹*calm, impatience, etc.*› **4** (einer Sache innewohnend) internal ‹*structure, stability, etc.*› **5** (inländisch) internal

inner-: ~betrieblich A *Adj.* internal ‹*problem, question, regulation, agreement*›; **B** *adv.* internally; **~deutsch** *Adj.* **1** (Deutschland betreffend) **~deutsche Angelegenheiten** the internal *or* domestic affairs of Germany; Germany's internal *or* domestic affairs; **2** (hist.: die beiden deutschen Staaten betreffend) ‹*trade, relations, border*› between the two German states; **der Bundesminister für ~deutsche Beziehungen** the Federal Minister for Intra-German Relations

Innere /ˈɪnərə/ *das; adj. Dekl.* **1** inside; (eines Gebäudes, Wagens, Schiffes) interior; inside; (eines Landes) interior; **im ~n des Waldes** deep within the forest; **der Minister des Innern** the Minister of the Interior; *s. auch* **Innenminister 2** (Empfindung) inner being; **in seinem tiefsten ~n** in his heart of hearts; deep [down] inside; **wenn wir nur wüssten, was in ihrem ~n vorgeht** if only we knew what's going on inside her **3** (Kern) heart

Innereien /ɪnəˈraiən/ *Pl.* entrails; (Kochk.) offal *sing.*

inner: ~europäisch A *Adj.* internal European *attrib.*; **B** *adv.* within Europe; **~familiär A** *Adj.* within the family *postpos.*; **B** *adv.* within the family **~halb A** *Präp.* + *Gen.* **1** (im Innern) within, inside; **~ der Familie/Partei** (fig.) within the family/party; **2** (binnen) within; **~ einer Woche** within a week; **~ der Arbeitszeit** during *or* in working hours; **B** *Adv.* **1** (im Innern) **~ von** within; inside; **2** (im Verlauf) **~ von zwei Jahren** within two years

innerlich
A *Adj.* **1** (geistig-seelisch) inner; (nicht nach außen gezeigt) inward **2** (geh.) (nach innen gewandt) introvert[ed]; (nicht oberflächlich) inwardly directed **3** (im Körper) internal ‹*use, effect*›
B *adv.* **1** (geistig-seelisch) inwardly; **~ lachen** laugh inwardly *or* to oneself **2** (im Körper) **die Arznei muss ~ wirken/wird ~ angewendet** the medicine must work/is used internally

Innerlichkeit *die;* **~:** inwardness

inner-: ~parteilich *Adj.* **~parteiliche Auseinandersetzungen** internal [party] disputes; disputes within the party; **~parteiliche Diskussionen** discussions within the party; **~staatlich** *Adj.* internal; domestic; **~städtisch** *Adj.* urban

innerst... *Adj.* inmost; innermost; **ihre ~e Überzeugung** her deepest *or* most profound conviction

Innerste *das; adj. Dekl.* innermost being; **in meinem ~n** in my heart of hearts; deep [down] inside

innert /ˈɪnɐt/ *Präp.* + *Gen. od. Dat.* (schweiz., österr.) within

inne-: *~|sein ▸inne; **~|werden** *unr. itr. V.; mit sein (Zusammenschreibung nur im Inf. u. Part.)* (geh.) **einer Sache** (*Gen.*) **~werden** become [fully] aware of sth.; **~|wohnen** *itr. V.* (geh.) **etw. wohnt jmdm./einer Sache ~:** sb./sth. possesses sth.

innig /ˈɪnɪç/
A *Adj.* **1** heartfelt, deep ‹*affection, sympathy*›; heartfelt, fervent ‹*wish*›; intimate ‹*relation, relationship, friendship*›; **mein ~ster Dank** my sincerest thanks; **unsere ~sten Wünsche begleiten euch** our warmest wishes go with you **2** (Chemie) intimate
B *adv.* ‹*hope*› fervently; ‹*love*› deeply, with all one's heart; **~ verbunden sein** ‹*friends, families*› be very close

Innigkeit *die;* **~:** depth; (einer Beziehung, Freundschaft) intimacy; **die ~ seiner Worte** the depth of feeling in his words

inniglich /ˈɪnɪklɪç/ *Adj., adv.* (geh.) ▸innig

Innovation /ɪnovaˈtsi̯oːn/ *die;* **~, ~en** (Soziol., Wirtsch.) innovation

Innovations-schub *der* impetus for innovation

-innung *die:* **Fleischer~/Bäcker~:** butchers'/bakers' guild

Innung /ˈɪnʊŋ/ *die;* **~, ~en** [trade] guild; **die ganze ~ blamieren** (ugs. scherzh.) let the side down

in-offiziell
A *Adj.* unofficial
B *adv.* unofficially

in-operabel *Adj.* (Med.) inoperable

in-opportun *Adj.* (geh.) inopportune

in petto /ɪn ˈpɛto/ *in* **etw. ~ haben** (ugs.) have sth. up one's sleeve

in puncto /ɪn ˈpʊŋkto/ **~ Pünktlichkeit** *usw.* as regards punctuality *etc.*; where punctuality *etc.* is concerned

Input /ˈɪnpʊt/ *der od. das;* **~s, ~s** (fachspr.) input

Inquisition /ɪnkviziˈtsi̯oːn/ *die;* **~, ~en** (hist.) **1** Inquisition **2** (Untersuchung vor der ~) inquisition

Inquisitions-gericht *das* (hist.) court of the Inquisition

Inquisitor /ɪnkviˈziːtɔr/ *der;* **~s, ~en** /-ziˈtoːrən/ (hist.) inquisitor

ins /ɪns/ *Präp.* + *Art.* **1** = **in das 2 ~ Bett/Theater gehen** go to bed/the theatre; **er geriet ~ Stottern** he began to stutter; **etw. ~ Englische übersetzen** translate sth. into English

Insasse /ˈɪnzasə/ *der;* **~n, ~n 1** (Fahrgast) passenger; **die ~n eines Autos/Flugzeuges** the passengers in a car/an aircraft **2** (Bewohner) inmate

Insassen-versicherung *die* passenger insurance

Insassin *die;* **~, ~nen** ▸Insasse

ins-besond[e]re *Adv.* especially; particularly; in particular

In-schrift *die* inscription

Insekt /ɪnˈzɛkt/ *das;* **~s, ~en** insect; **~en fressend** (Biol.) insectivorous, insect-eating ‹*animals*›

insekten-, Insekten-: ~bekämpfung *die* insect control; **~fressend** ▸Insekt; **~fresser** *der* insectivore; insect eater; **~kunde** *die* entomology *no art.*; **~plage** *die* plague of insects; **~pulver** *das* insect powder; **~stich** *der* (einer Wespe, Biene) insect sting; (einer Mücke) insect bite; **~vertilgungs-mittel** *das* insecticide

Insektizid /ɪnzɛktiˈtsiːt/ *das;* **~s, ~e** (fachspr.) insecticide

Insel /ˈɪnzl̩/ *die;* **~, ~n** (auch fig.) island; **die ~ Helgoland** the island of Heligoland; **die ~ Man** the Isle of Man

Insel-bewohner *der*, **Insel-bewohnerin** *die* islander

Inselchen *das;* **~s, ~:** islet; little island

Insel-: ~gruppe *die* group of islands; **~lage** *die* island position; position as an island; **~reich** *das* island kingdom; **~republik** *die* island republic; **~staat** *der* island state; **~volk** *das* island race *or* people; **~welt** *die* islands *pl.*

Inserat /ɪnzeˈraːt/ *das;* **~[e]s, ~e** advertisement (*in a newspaper*); **sich auf ein ~ melden** reply to an advertisement; **ein ~ aufgeben** put in an advertisement; **am besten gibst du ein ~ auf** the best thing you can do is to put an advertisement in the paper

Inseraten-teil *der* advertisement section

Inserent /ɪnzeˈrɛnt/ *der;* **~en, ~en**, **Inserentin** *die;* **~, ~nen** advertiser

inserieren *itr., tr. V.* advertise; **[wegen etw.] in einer Zeitung ~:** advertise [sth.] in a newspaper

ins-geheim *Adv.* secretly

ins-gemein *Adv.* (veralt.) **die Naturwissenschaften ~ waren seine Leidenschaft** he had a passion for the natural sciences as a whole

ins-gesamt *Adv.* **1** in all; altogether; **es waren ~ 500** there were 500 in all *or* altogether **2** (alles in allem) all in all; **~ gesehen** all in all

Insider /ˈɪnsaɪdə/ *der;* **~s, ~:** insider; **~ der Rock-Szene** those in on the rock scene

Insider: ~handel *der* (Börsenw.) insider trading; **~tipp** *der* inside tip

Insigne /ɪnˈzɪɡnə/ *das;* **~s, Insignien** insignia

in-signifikant *Adj.* (geh.) insignificant

insinuieren /ɪnzinuˈiːrən/ *tr. V.* (vorgeben) pretend [to be]; (unterstellen) **~[, dass] ...** insinuate *or* make out that …

insistieren /ɪnzɪsˈtiːrən/ *itr. V.* (geh.) **auf etw.** (*Dat.*) **~:** insist on sth.

inskribieren /ɪnskriˈbiːrən/ (österr.)
A *itr. V.* register; **in Wien ~:** register at [the university of] Vienna
B *tr. V.* **Germanistik ~:** register to study German; **bei jmdm. Vorlesungen ~:** register to attend sb.'s lectures

Inskription /ɪnskrɪpˈtsi̯oːn/ (österr.) *die;* **~, ~en** registration

insofern
A *Adv.* /ɪnˈzoːfɛrn/ (in dieser Hinsicht) in this respect; to this extent; **~, als** in so far as; **die Vorstellung ist ~ irrig, als ...** this notion is wrong in so far as …
B *Konj.* /ɪnzoˈfɛrn/ (falls) provided [that]; so *or* as long as

in-solvent *Adj.* insolvent

In-solvenz *die;* **~, ~en** (bes. Wirtsch.) insolvency

Insolvenz-verfahren *das* (Wirtsch.) insolvency proceedings *pl.*

***insonderheit** ▸Sonderheit

insoweit /ɪnˈzoːvait/ *od.* /ɪnzoˈvait/ *Adv./Konj.* ▸insofern

in spe /ɪn ˈspeː/ future *attrib.*; **mein Schwiegersohn ~:** my future son-in-law

Inspekteur /ɪnspɛkˈtøːɐ̯/ *der;* **~s, ~e** (Milit.) Chief of Staff

Inspektion /ɪnspɛkˈtsi̯oːn/ *die;* **~, ~en 1** (Kontrolle) inspection **2** (Kfz-W.) service; **das Auto zur ~ bringen** take the car in for a service **3** (Behörde) inspectorate

Inspektions-reise *die* tour of inspection

Inspektor /ɪn'spɛktɔr/ *der;* **~s, ~en** /-'to:rən/, **Inspektorin** *die;* **~, ~nen** inspector; **das Gutachten des ~s Müller, ~ Müllers Gutachten** Inspector Müller's report; *s. auch* **-in**

Inspiration /ɪnspira'tsio:n/ *die;* **~, ~en** inspiration

inspirieren *tr. V.* inspire; **das inspirierte ihn zu einem Roman** it inspired him to write a novel; **sich von jmdm./etw. ~ lassen** be inspired by sb./sth.

Inspizient /ɪnspi'tsiɛnt/ *der;* **~en, ~en, Inspizientin** *die;* **~, ~nen** (Theater) stage manager; (Ferns., Rundf.) studio manager

inspizieren *tr. V.* inspect

Inspizierung *die;* **~, ~en** inspection

in·stabil *Adj.* (auch Physik, Technik) unstable

In·stabilität *die;* **~, ~en** (auch Physik, Technik) instability

Installateur /ɪnstala'tø:ɐ̯/ *der;* **~s, ~e, Installateurin** *die;* **~, ~nen ▸❶ S. 113** 1 (Klempner[in]) plumber 2 (Gas~) [gas] fitter 3 (Heizungs~) heating engineer 4 (Elektro~) electrician

Installation /ɪnstala'tsio:n/ *die;* **~, ~en** 1 installation 2 (Anlage) installation; (Rohre) plumbing *no pl.* 3 (schweiz., sonst veralt.: Amtseinführung) installation

installieren
A *tr. V.* 1 (einbauen) install 2 (geh.: in ein Amt einführen) install 3 (einrichten) set up
B *refl. V.* settle in

in·stand *Adv.* **etw. ist gut/schlecht ~:** sth. is in good/poor condition; **etw. ~ halten** keep sth. in good condition *or* repair *or* (funktionsfähig) in working order; **etw. ~ setzen/bringen** repair sth.; (funktionsfähig machen) get sth. into working order; **jmdn. ~ setzen, etw. zu tun** enable sb. to do sth.

instand-, Instand-: ~besetzen *tr. V.* **ein Haus ~besetzen** occupy and renovate a house *(illegally, to prove that its demolition is not desirable)*; **~besetzung** *die: illegal occupation and renovation;* **~haltung** *die* maintenance; upkeep; **~haltungs·kosten** *Pl.* maintenance costs

in·ständig
A *Adj.* urgent; insistent ‹*invitation*›
B *adv.* urgently; **~ um etw. bitten** beg for sth.; **jmdn. ~ bitten, etw. zu tun** beg *or* implore *or* beseech sb. to do sth.; **~ auf etw.** (Akk.) **hoffen** hope fervently for sth.

Instandsetzung *die;* **~, ~en** (Amtsspr.) repair; (Renovierung) renovation; **eine ~ der Brücke hätte sich nicht gelohnt** it would not have been worth repairing the bridge

Instanz /ɪn'stants/ *die;* **~, ~en** 1 authority; **durch alle ~en gehen** *od.* **alle ~en durchlaufen** go *or* pass through all the official channels; **in letzter ~ ist ... entscheidend** (fig.) in the final analysis, ... is decisive 2 (Rechtsw.) **[die] erste/zweite/dritte ~:** the court of first instance *or* court of original jurisdiction/the appeal court/the court of final appeal; **durch alle ~en gehen** go through all the courts

Instanzen·weg *der* official channels *pl.;* (Rechtsspr.) stages *pl.* of appeal; **den ~ nehmen** go through the official channels/the various stages of appeal

Instinkt /ɪn'stɪŋkt/ *der;* **~[e]s, ~e** instinct; **etw. aus ~ tun** do sth. instinctively; **den richtigen ~ für etw. haben** have a flair for sth.; **seinem ~ folgen** follow one's instincts *pl.*

Instinkt·handlung *die* instinctive action

instinktiv /ɪnstɪŋk'ti:f/
A *Adj.* instinctive
B *adv.* instinctively

instinkt·los
A *Adj.* insensitive
B *adv.* insensitively; **politisch ~ handeln** act with political insensitivity

Instinktlosigkeit *die;* **~, ~en** insensitivity; **eine ~ sein** be insensitive

Institut /ɪnsti'tu:t/ *das;* **~[e]s, ~e** 1 institute; **das ~ für Kernphysik** the Institute of Nuclear Physics 2 (Rechtsspr.) institution

Institution /ɪnstitu'tsio:n/ *die;* **~, ~en** (auch fig.) institution

institutionalisieren /ɪnstitutsionali'zi:rən/ *tr. V.* (geh.) institutionalize

institutionell /ɪnstitutsio'nɛl/ *Adj.* institutional

Instituts-: ~bibliothek *die* institute library; **~leiter** *der,* **~leiterin** *die* director of the/an institute

instruieren /ɪnstru'i:rən/ *tr. V.* 1 (in Kenntnis setzen) inform; **jmdn. über etw.** (Akk.) **~:** inform sb. about sth. 2 (anleiten) instruct; **jmdn. genau ~:** give sb. precise instructions

Instrukteur /ɪnstrʊk'tø:ɐ̯/ *der;* **~s, ~e, Instrukteurin** *die;* **~, ~nen** instructor

Instruktion /ɪnstrʊk'tsio:n/ *die;* **~, ~en** instruction

instruktiv /ɪnstrʊk'ti:f/
A *Adj.* instructive; informative
B *adv.* instructively; informatively

Instrument /ɪnstru'mɛnt/ *das;* **~[e]s, ~e** instrument

instrumental /ɪnstrumɛn'ta:l/ (Musik)
A *Adj.* instrumental
B *adv.* instrumentally; **~ musizieren** play instrumental music

Instrumental·begleitung *die* instrumental accompaniment

instrumentalisieren /ɪnstrumɛntali'zi:rən/ *tr. V.* 1 (Musik) set ‹*piece*› for instruments 2 (ausnutzen) exploit

Instrumentalismus *der;* **~** (Philos.) instrumentalism

Instrumental·musik *die* instrumental music

Instrumentarium /ɪnstrumɛn'ta:riʊm/ *das;* **~s, Instrumentarien** 1 (Technik) equipment; instruments *pl.* 2 (Musik) instruments *pl.;* **diese Oper verlangt ein großes ~:** this opera calls for a large number and range of instruments 3 (geh.: Gesamtheit der Mittel) apparatus

instrumentell /ɪnstrumɛn'tɛl/
A *Adj.* (mit Instrumenten) using instruments *postpos.;* **~e Hilfsmittel/Ausrüstung** equipment; instruments *pl.*
B *adv.* **etw. ~ untersuchen** investigate sth. using instruments; **~ gut/schlecht ausgerüstet** well/poorly equipped

Instrumenten-: ~bau *der* making of musical instruments; **~brett** *das* instrument panel; **~flug** *der* (Flugw.) flying on instruments; instrument-flying; **~kasten** *der* instrument housing; (tragbar) instrument case

instrumentieren
A *tr. V.* 1 (Musik: für das Orchester ausarbeiten) instrument; (für das Orchester umarbeiten) orchestrate 2 (Technik) instrument; equip with instruments
B *itr. V.* (Med.) **bei jmdm. ~:** assist sb. by handing him/her the instruments

In·subordination *die;* **~, ~en** (geh.) insubordination; **eine ~:** an act of insubordination

Insuffizienz /'ɪnzʊfitsiɛnts/ *die;* **~, ~en ▸❶ S. 439** (Med.) insufficiency

Insulaner /ɪnzu'la:nɐ/ *der;* **~s, ~, Insulanerin** *die;* **~, ~nen** (veralt., noch scherzh.) islander

insular /ɪnzu'la:ɐ̯/ *Adj.* insular

Insulin /ɪnzu'li:n/ *das;* **~s** insulin

Insulin·schock *der* **▸❶ S. 439** (Med.) insulin shock

inszenatorisch /ɪnstsena'to:rɪʃ/ *Adj.* directorial; **eine ~e Meisterleistung** a masterpiece of directing

inszenieren /ɪnstse'ni:rən/ *tr. V.* 1 stage, put on ‹*play, opera*›; (Regie führen bei) direct; (Ferns.) direct; produce 2 (oft abwertend) (einfädeln) engineer; (organisieren) stage

Inszenierung *die;* **~, ~en** 1 staging; (Regie) direction 2 (Aufführung) production; **Rigoletto in neuer ~:** a new production of 'Rigoletto' 3 (oft abwertend) (das Einfädeln) engineering; (das Organisieren) staging

intakt /ɪn'takt/ *Adj.* 1 (unbeschädigt) intact; undamaged; unspoiled ‹*region*› 2 (funktionsfähig) in [proper] working order *postpos.;* healthy ‹*economy*›; **einen ~en Organismus haben** be physically healthy

Intarsie /ɪn'tarziə/ *die;* **~, ~n** intarsia

integer /ɪn'te:gɐ/ *Adj.* **eine integre Persönlichkeit** a person of integrity; **~ sein** be a person of integrity

integral /ɪnte'gra:l/ *Adj.* integral

Integral *das;* **~s, ~e** (Math.) integral; (Zeichen) integral sign

Integral-: ~helm *der* integral helmet; **~rechnung** *die* 1 integral calculus; 2 (einzelne Rechnung) problem in integral calculus

Integration /ɪntegra'tsio:n/ *die;* **~, ~en** (auch Math.) integration

Integrations·figur *die* unifying figure

integrieren *tr. V.* (auch Math.) integrate; *s. auch* **Gesamthochschule; Gesamtschule**

integrierend *Adj.* integral ‹*part, component, element*›

Integrierung *die;* **~, ~en** (auch Math.) integration

Integrität /ɪntegri'tɛ:t/ *die;* **~:** integrity

Intellekt /ɪntɛ'lɛkt/ *der;* **~[e]s** intellect

intellektuell /ɪntɛlɛk'tuɛl/ *Adj.* intellectual

Intellektuelle *der/die; adj. Dekl.* intellectual

intelligent /ɪntɛli'gɛnt/
A *Adj.* intelligent
B *adv.* intelligently

Intelligenz /ɪntɛli'gɛnts/ *die;* **~, ~en** 1 intelligence 2 (Gesamtheit der Intellektuellen) intelligentsia 3 (veralt.: intelligentes Wesen) intelligence

Intelligenz·bestie *die* (ugs.) 1 egghead (coll.); brain (coll.) 2 (abwertend) clever-clever type

Intelligenzija /ɪntɛli'gɛntsija/ *die;* **~:** intelligentsia

Intelligenz·leistung *die* instance of intelligent behaviour; **das war mal eine ~ von dir!** (iron.) that was bright of you, I must say

Intelligenzler *der;* **~s, ~, Intelligenzlerin** *die;* **~, ~nen** (abwertend) intellectual

Intelligenz-: ~quotient *der* intelligence quotient; **~test** *der* intelligence test

intelligibel /ɪntɛli'gi:bl̩/ *Adj.* (Philos.) intelligible

Intendant /ɪntɛn'dant/ *der;* **~en, ~en, Intendantin** *die;* **~, ~nen** 1 (Theater) manager and artistic director; (Fernseh~, Rundfunk~) director general

Intendantur /ɪntɛndan'tu:ɐ̯/ *die;* **~, ~en ▸Intendanz 1**

Intendanz /ɪntɛn'dants/ *die;* **~, ~en** 1 (Amt) management and artistic directorship; (Ferns., Rundf.) director-generalship 2 (Büro) office of the manager and artistic director; (Ferns., Rundf.) director-general's office

intendieren /ɪntɛn'di:rən/ *tr. V.* (geh.) intend

Intensität /ɪntɛnzi'tɛ:t/ *die;* **~** (auch Physik) intensity

intensiv /ɪntɛn'zi:f/
A *Adj.* 1 (gründlich) intensive ‹*research, efforts, etc.*› 2 (kräftig) intense; strong ‹*smell, taste*› 3 (Landw.) intensive ‹*cultivation etc.*›
B *adv.* 1 (gründlich) intensively; ‹*think*› hard; **sich ~ mit etw. beschäftigen** be deeply involved with sth. 2 (kräftig) intensely; ‹*smell, taste*› strongly; **~ leuchten** shine with intense brightness 3 (Landw.) ‹*farm etc.*› intensively

-intensiv -intensive; **geruchs~:** strong-smelling

Intensiv-: ~anbau *der* (Landw.) intensive cultivation; **~haltung** *die* (Landw.) intensive rearing

intensivieren *tr. V.* intensify; increase ‹*exports*›; strengthen ‹*connections*›

Intensivierung *die;* **~, ~en** intensification; **bei einer ~ des Exports** by increasing exports *pl.*

Intensiv-: ~kurs *der* intensive course; **~station** *die* intensive-care unit

Intention /ɪntɛnˈtsi̯oːn/ *die;* ~, ~**en** intention; **das liegt nicht in seinen ~en** that is not his intention

intentional /ɪntɛntsi̯oˈnaːl/ (Philos.)
A *Adj.* intentional
B *adv.* intentionally

Inter-/ɪntɐ-/: ~**aktion** *die* (Psych., Soziol.) interaction; ~**aktiv** *Adj.* interactive; ~**aktivität** *die;* ~~: interactivity; ~**brigaden** *Pl.* (hist.) International Brigades

Inter·city /ɪntɐˈsɪti/ *der;* ~**s**, ~**s** (ugs.) intercity [train]

Intercity-: ~**express**, *~**-Expreß** *der* intercity express train; ~**expresszug**, *~**-Expreßzug** *der* intercity express train; ~**verkehr** *der* intercity [railway] traffic; ~**zug** *der* intercity train

inter-, Inter-: ~**dependent** *Adj.* (geh.) interdependent; ~**dependenz** *die* (geh.) interdependence *no pl.;* ~**disziplinär** A *Adj.* interdisciplinary; B *adv.* ~**disziplinär forschen** do interdisciplinary research

interessant /ɪntərɛˈsant/
A *Adj.* interesting; **sich ~ machen** attract attention to oneself; **das ist ja ~:** that's [very] interesting; **das Angebot ist für uns nicht ~:** the offer is of no interest to us *or* doesn't interest us
B *adv.* ~ **schreiben** write in an interesting way

interessanterweise *Adv.* interestingly enough

Interesse /ɪntəˈrɛsə/ *das;* ~**s**, ~**n** 1 interest; **[großes] ~ an jmdm./etw. haben** be [very] interested in sb./sth.; **~ für jmdn./etw. haben/zeigen** have/show an interest in sb./sth. 2 (Neigung) interest; **gemeinsame ~n haben** have interests in common; **im eigenen ~ handeln** act in one's own interest; **jmds. ~n wahrnehmen** look after *or* represent sb.'s interests; **in jmds. ~** (*Dat.*) **liegen** be in sb.'s interest; **es liegt in unser aller ~:** it's in all our interests *pl.*

interesse-, Interesse-: ~**halber** /-halbɐ/ *Adv.* out of interest; ~**los** A *Adj.* uninterested; B *adv.* without interest; uninterestedly; ~**losigkeit** *die;* ~~: lack of interest

Interessen-: ~**ausgleich** *der* reconciliation of [conflicting] interests; ~**bereich** *der*, ~**gebiet** *das* field of interest; ~**gegensatz** *der* ▸ ~**konflikt**; ~**gemeinschaft** *die* 1 **sich in einer ~gemeinschaft zusammenfinden** join together with others to pursue common interests; 2 (Wirtsch.) syndicate; ~**gruppe** *die* interest group; ~**kollision** *die* clash of interests; ~**konflikt** *der* conflict of interests; ~**lage** *die* interests *pl.;* ~**sphäre** *die* sphere of influence

Interessent /ɪntərɛˈsɛnt/ *der;* ~**en**, ~**en** 1 interested person; **wenn es genug ~en gibt** if enough people are interested; **auf die Anzeige haben sich zahlreiche ~en gemeldet** the advertisement attracted a large response; **~en werden gebeten ...** those interested are asked ... 2 (möglicher Käufer) potential buyer

Interessenten·kreis *der* market

Interessentin *die;* ~, ~**nen** ▸ **Interessent**

Interessen-: ~**verband** *der* [organized] interest group; ~**vertreter** *der*, ~**vertreterin** *die* representative [of sb.'s interests]; **~vertreter der Kubaner** those representing the interests of the Cubans; ~**vertretung** *die* 1 representation; 2 (Vertreter von ~) representative body

interessieren
A *refl. V.* **sich für jmdn./etw. ~:** be interested in sb./sth.
B *tr. V.* interest; **interessiert dich denn nicht, was passiert ist?** aren't you interested to know what happened?; **das interessiert mich nicht** I'm not interested [in it]; it doesn't interest me; **das hat dich zu ~:** you can't just ignore it; **das hat dich nicht zu ~:** it's none of your business; it's no concern of yours

interessiert *Adj.* interested; **an jmdm./etw. ~ sein** be interested in sb./sth.; **er ist daran ~, dass sie nichts davon erfahren** he doesn't want them to find out anything about it; **vielseitig ~ sein** have a wide range of interests; **~ zuhören** listen with interest

Interessiertheit *die;* ~: **das Prinzip der materiellen ~** (DDR): *principle that the individual can directly improve his own standard of living by working harder and more efficiently to achieve the goals of socialism*

inter-, Inter-: ~**ferenz** /-feˈrɛnts/ *die;* ~~, ~~**en** (Physik, Med., Sprachw.) interference *no pl.;* ~**feron** /-feˈroːn/ *das;* ~~**s**, ~~**e** (Med.) interferon; ~**fraktionell** /-fraktsi̯oˈnɛl/ A *Adj.* inter-party *attrib.;* B *adv.* **etw. ~fraktionell besprechen** discuss sth. on an inter-party basis; hold inter-party discussions about sth.; ~**hotel** /ˈ----/ *das* (DDR) Interhotel (*hotel intended mainly for visitors to the GDR*)

Interieur /ɛ̃teˈri̯øːɐ̯/ *das;* ~**s**, ~**s** *od.* ~**e** (auch bild. Kunst) interior

Interim /ˈɪnterɪm/ *das;* ~**s**, ~**s** (geh.) interim measure

interimistisch
A *Adj.* (geh.) interim *attrib.;* temporary; provisional
B *adv.* on an interim basis

Interims-: ~**lösung** *die* interim solution; ~**regierung** *die* caretaker government; ~**schein** *der* (Wirtsch.) scrip

Interjektion /ɪntɐjɛkˈtsi̯oːn/ *die;* ~, ~**en** (Sprachw.) interjection

inter-, Inter-: ~**kantonal** A *Adj.* intercantonal; B *adv.* on an inter-cantonal basis; ~**konfessionell** *Adj.* (geh.) interdenominational; interconfessional; ~**kontinental** *Adj.* (geh.) intercontinental; ~**kontinentalrakete** *die* (Milit.) intercontinental ballistic missile; ~**kulturell** A *Adj.* intercultural; B *adv.* interculturally; ‹*function*› on an intercultural basis; ‹*think*› in intercultural terms; **sich ~kulturell öffnen** open up to other cultures; ~**linear** *Adj.* (Literaturw.) interlinear; ~**linear·version** *die* interlinear version *or* translation; ~**ludium** /-ˈluːdi̯ʊm/ *das;* ~~**s**, ~**ludien** (Musik) interlude; ~**mezzo** /-ˈmɛtso/ *das;* ~~**s**, ~~**s** *od.* ~**mezzi** (Theat., Musik) intermezzo; (fig.) interlude; intermezzo; ~**ministeriell** A *Adj.* inter-ministerial; B *adv.* on an inter-ministerial basis; ~**mittierend** /-mɪˈtiːrənt/ *Adj.* (geh.) intermittent; lightning ‹*strike*›

intern /ɪnˈtɛrn/
A *Adj.* 1 internal; **diese Dinge müssen ~ bleiben** these matters must not become public knowledge 2 (im Internat wohnend) **ein ~er Schüler** a boarder
B *adv.* internally; **wir haben das Jubiläum nur ~ gefeiert** we only celebrated the anniversary among ourselves

-intern
A *Adj.* **firmen~e/klub~e/abteilungs~e Dinge** internal [company/club/departmental] matters; **eine firmen~e/klub~e Regelung** an arrangement within the company/club
B *adv.* **firmen~/klub~/abteilungs~:** within the company/club/department; internally

Interna ▸ **Internum**

internalisieren /ɪntɛrnaliˈziːrən/ *tr. V.* (Soziol., Psych.) internalize

Internalisierung *die;* ~, ~**en** (Soziol., Psych.) internalization

Internat /ɪntəˈnaːt/ *das;* ~**[e]s**, ~**e** 1 boarding school 2 (einer Schule angeschlossenes Heim) dormitory block

inter-, Inter-: ~**national** A *Adj.* international; B *adv.* internationally; ~**nationale** *die;* ~~, ~~**n** 1 (internationale Arbeiterassoziation) International; Internationale; 2 (Lied) Internationale; ~**nationalisieren** *tr. V.* internationalize; ~**nationalismus** *der* 1 (Politik) internationalism; **sozialistischer ~nationalismus** (DDR) socialist internationalism; 2 (Sprachw.) internationalism; ~**nationalistisch** *Adj.* (Politik) internationalistic

Internationalität *die;* ~: international character

Internats-: ~**schule** *die* boarding school; ~**schüler** *der*, ~**schülerin** *die* boarding school pupil; boarder

Interne *der/die; adj. Dekl.* boarder

Internet /ˈɪntɐnɛt/ *das;* ~**s**, ~**s** Internet; **im ~:** on the Internet

internet-, Internet-: ~**anbieter** *der*, ~**anbieterin** *die* (DV) Internet provider; ~**anschluss** *der*, *~**anschluß** *der* (DV) Internet connection; connection to the Internet; **einen ~anschluss haben** be connected to the Internet; ~**auftritt** *der* (DV) Internet presentation; ~**café** *das* Internet café; cybercafé; ~**fähig** *Adj.* (DV) Internet-capable; Internet-enabled; ~**handel** *der* Internet commerce; e-commerce; e-business; ~**jargon** *der* netspeak; ~**portal** *das* (DV) Internet portal; ~**provider** *der* (DV) Internet provider; ~**recherche** *die* Internet search; ~**seite** *die* (DV) Internet page; Web page

internieren *tr. V.* 1 (Milit.) intern 2 (Med.) **jmdn. [in einem Krankenhaus] ~:** confine sb. to [a] hospital

Internierte *der/die; adj. Dekl.* 1 (Milit.) internee 2 (Med.) patient confined to hospital

Internierung *die;* ~, ~**en** internment

Internierungs·lager *das* internment camp

Internist *der;* ~**en**, ~**en**, **Internistin** *die;* ~, ~**nen** (Med.) internist

Internum /ɪnˈtɛrnʊm/ *das;* ~**s**, **Interna;** (geh.) internal matter

inter-, Inter-: ~**parlamentarisch** *Adj.* (Politik) inter-parliamentary; ~**planetar[isch]** *Adj.* (Astron.) interplanetary; ~**pol** /ˈ---/ (*die*); ~: Interpol *no art.;* ~**polation** /-polaˈtsi̯oːn/ *die;* ~~, ~~**en** (Math., Sprachw.) interpolation; ~**polieren** *itr.* (*auch tr.*) *V.* (Math., Sprachw.) interpolate

Interpret /ɪntɐˈpreːt/ *der;* ~**en**, ~**en** interpreter (*of music, text, events, etc.*)

Interpretation /ɪntɐpretaˈtsi̯oːn/ *die;* ~, ~**en** interpretation (*of music, text, events, etc.*)

interpretatorisch /ɪntɐpretaˈtoːrɪʃ/
A *Adj.* interpretative
B *adv.* interpretatively

interpretieren *tr. V.* interpret ‹*music, texts, events, etc.*›; **etw. falsch ~:** misinterpret sth.; interpret sth. wrongly

Interpretin *die;* ~, ~**nen** ▸ **Interpret**

interpunktieren *tr., itr. V.* (Sprachw.) punctuate

Interpunktion /ɪntɐpʊŋkˈtsi̯oːn/ *die;* ~ (Sprachw.) punctuation

Interpunktions-: ~**regel** *die* punctuation rule; ~**zeichen** *das* punctuation mark

Interrail·karte /ˈɪntɐreɪl-/ *die* (Eisenbahnw.) Interrail card

Interregnum /ɪntɐˈrɛgnʊm/ *das;* ~**s**, **Interregnen** *od.* **Interregna** (Politik) interregnum

interrogativ /ɪntɐrogaˈtiːf/ *Adj.* (Sprachw.) interrogative

Interrogativ-: ~**pronomen** *das* interrogative pronoun; ~**satz** *der* interrogative sentence

Interruptus /ɪntɐˈrʊptʊs/ *der;* ~ (ugs.) withdrawal

Intershop /ˈɪntɐʃɔp/ *der;* ~**s**, ~**s** (DDR) Intershop (*shop where foreign goods and top-quality GDR goods were sold for freely convertible currency*)

inter-: ~**stellar** /-stɛˈlaːɐ̯/ *Adj.* (Astron.) interstellar; ~**subjektiv** *Adj.* (Psych.) intersubjective

Intervall /ɪntɐˈval/ *das;* ~**s**, ~**e** (Musik, Math.) interval

Intervall·training *das* (Sport) interval training

intervenieren /ɪntɐveˈniːrən/ *itr. V.* (geh., Politik) intervene; **bei jmdm. gegen etw. ~:** make representations to sb. about sth.; **für jmdn. ~:** intervene on sb.'s behalf

Intervention /ɪntɐvɛnˈtsi̯oːn/ *die;* ~, ~**en** (geh., Politik) intervention; (Protest) representations *pl.*

Interventions·krieg *der* war of intervention

Interview /ɪntɐˈvjuː/ *das;* ~**s,** ~**s** interview

interviewen /ɪntɐˈvjuːən/ *tr. V.* interview

Interviewer /ɪntɐˈvjuːɐ/ *der;* ~**s,** ~, **Interviewerin** *die;* ~, ~**nen** interviewer

Intervision *die;* ~**:** Intervision (alliance of Eastern European television corporations for pooling of programmes)

Inter·zonen-: ~**auto·bahn** *die* interzonal autobahn; ~**handel** *der* interzonal trade; ~**verkehr** *der* interzonal traffic; ~**zug** *der* interzonal train

Inthronisation /ɪntroniza'tsi̯oːn/ *die;* ~, ~**en** enthronement

inthronisieren *tr. V.* enthrone

intim /ɪn'tiːm/

A *Adj.* **1** intimate; **im** ~**en Kreis** among close friends; ~**e Beziehungen mit jmdm. haben** (verhüll.) have intimate relations with sb. (euphem.); **mit jmdm.** ~ **sein/werden** (verhüll.) be/become intimate with sb. (euphem.); ~**e Hygiene/Körperpflege** intimate personal hygiene **2** (tiefinnerlich) intimate; innermost

B *adv.* ~ **befreundet sein** be intimate friends; **mit jmdm.** ~ **verkehren** (verhüll.) have intimate relations with sb. (euphem.)

Intim-: ~**bereich** *der* **1** ▸ ~**sphäre; 2** (Genitalbereich) genital area; ~**feind** *der,* ~**feindin** *die: person whom one knows well and dislikes intensely;* ~**hygiene** *die* intimate personal hygiene

Intimität /ɪntimi'tɛːt/ *die;* ~, ~**en** intimacy; **es ist zu** ~**en gekommen** (verhüll.) intimacy took place (euphem.); ~**en austauschen** (verhüll.) be engaged in intimacy (euphem.)

Intim-: ~**kenner** *der,* ~**kennerin** *die:* **ein** ~**kenner von etw. sein** have an intimate knowledge of sth.; **von einem** ~**kenner der politischen Szene stammen** come from someone with an intimate knowledge of the political scene; ~**leben** *das* (verhüll.) intimate life; ~**pflege** *die* ▸ ~**hygiene;** ~**sphäre** *die* private life; **jmds.** ~**sphäre verletzen** invade sb.'s privacy; **jmdn. wegen Verletzung seiner** ~**sphäre verklagen** sue sb. for invasion of privacy; ~**spray** *der od. das* intimate deodorant

Intimus /'ɪntimʊs/ *der;* ~, **Intimi** intimate friend; (Vertrauter) confidant

Intim·verkehr *der* (verhüll.) intimate relations *pl.* (euphem.)

in·tolerant

A *Adj.* intolerant (**gegenüber** of); **sich** ~ **zeigen** display *or* show intolerance

B *adv.* intolerantly

In·toleranz *die;* ~, ~**en** intolerance (**gegenüber** of)

Intonation /ɪntona'tsi̯oːn/ *die;* ~, ~**en** (Sprachw., Musik) intonation

intonieren

A *tr. V.* **1** (Musik) (anstimmen) **etw.** ~**:** sing/play the first few bars of sth.; start to sing/play sth.; (Ton angeben) play/sing; **bitte intoniere ein a** please give me/us an A **2** (Musik: hervorbringen) **die Melodie sauber/weich** ~**:** play/sing the melody with clean/soft intonation **3** (Sprachw.) **etw. richtig/falsch/anders** ~**:** say sth. with the right/wrong/a different intonation

B *itr. V.* **1** (Musik) **er hat sauber/weich intoniert** he played/sang with clean/soft intonation **2** (Sprachw.) **richtig/falsch** ~**:** use the right/wrong intonation

Intoxikation /ɪntɔksika'tsi̯oːn/ *die;* ~, ~**en** ▸ **❶ S. 439** (Med.) intoxication (Med.)

intramuskulär /ɪntramʊsku'lɛːɐ̯/ (Med.)

A *Adj.* intramuscular

B *adv.* intramuscularly

Intranet *das;* ~**s,** ~**s** (DV) Intranet

intransitiv

A *Adj.* (Sprachw.) intransitive

B *adv.* intransitively

Intrauterin·pessar /ɪntra|ute'riːn-/ *das* (Med.) intra-uterine device

intravenös /ɪntrave'nøːs/ (Med.)

A *Adj.* intravenous

B *adv.* intravenously

intrigant /ɪntri'gant/ *Adj.* scheming

Intrigant *der;* ~**en,** ~**en, Intrigantin** *die;* ~, ~**nen** schemer; intriguer

Intrige /ɪn'triːgə/ *die;* ~, ~**n** intrigue

Intrigen-: ~**spiel** *das* intrigue; ~**wirtschaft** *die* (abwertend) constant scheming and intriguing

intrigieren *itr. V.* intrigue; scheme; **gegen jmdn.** ~**:** intrigue *or* scheme against sb.; **er intrigierte beim Chef gegen sie** he attempted to turn the boss against her with hints and insinuations

Intro /'ɪntro/ *das;* ~**s,** ~**s** intro (coll.); introduction

intro-, Intro-/ɪntro-/: ~**duktion** /-dʊk'tsi̯oːn/ *die;* ~~, ~~**en** (geh., Musik) introduction; ~**spektion** /-spɛk'tsi̯oːn/ *die;* ~~ (Psych.) introspection; ~**vertiert** /-vɛr'tiːɐ̯t/ *Adj.* (Psych.) introverted; **ein** ~**vertierter Mensch** an introvert; ~**vertiertheit** *die;* ~~ (Psych.) introversion

Intuition /ɪntui̯'tsi̯oːn/ *die;* ~, ~**en** intuition

intuitiv /ɪntui̯'tiːf/

A *Adj.* intuitive

B *adv.* intuitively

intus /'ɪntʊs/ *in* **etw.** ~ **haben** (ugs.) (begriffen haben) have got sth. into one's head; (gegessen od. getrunken haben) have put sth. away (coll.); **einen** ~ **haben** (ugs.) have had a few (coll.)

invalid /ɪnva'liːt/, **invalide** /ɪnva'liːdə/ *Adj.* invalid *attrib.*; ~ **sein** be an invalid

Invalide *der;* ~**n,** ~**n** invalid

Invaliden-: ~**heim** *das* home for the disabled and infirm; ~**rente** *die* (veralt./schweiz.) invalidity *or* disability pension; ~**versicherung** *die* (veralt., schweiz.) invalidity *or* disability insurance

Invalidin *die;* ~, ~**nen** ▸ **Invalide**

Invalidität /ɪnvalidi'tɛːt/ *die;* ~**:** invalidity

in·variabel *Adj.* invariable

Invasion /ɪnva'zi̯oːn/ *die;* ~, ~**en** (auch fig. scherzh.) invasion

Invasions·krieg *der* war of invasion

Invasor /ɪn'vaːzɔr/ *der;* ~**s,** ~**en, Invasorin** *die;* ~, ~**nen** invader

Invektive /ɪnvɛk'tiːvə/ *die;* ~, ~**n** (geh.) invective

Inventar /ɪnvɛn'taːɐ̯/ *das;* ~**s,** ~**e** **1** **[totes]** ~ (einer Firma) fittings and equipment *pl.*; (eines Hauses, Büros) furnishings and fittings *pl.*; (eines Hofes) machinery and equipment; **lebendes** ~**:** livestock; **zum** ~ **gehören** (fig.) ‹*person*› be part of the scenery **2** (Verzeichnis) inventory

inventarisieren *tr. V.* inventory; draw up *or* make an inventory of

Inventar·stück *das* [inventoried] item

Inventur /ɪnvɛn'tuːɐ̯/ *die;* ~, ~**en** stocktaking; ~ **machen** carry out a stocktaking; stocktake; (fig.) take stock

Inventur·liste *die* stock list; inventory list

Inversion /ɪnvɛr'zi̯oːn/ *die;* ~, ~**en** (fachspr.) inversion

Invest- /ɪn'vɛst-/ (DDR) ▸ **Investitions-**

investieren *tr., itr. V.* (auch fig.) invest (**in** + *Akk.* in); **Gefühle in jmdn.** ~ (fig.) become emotionally involved with sb.

investigativ /ɪnvɛstiga'tiːf/

A *Adj.* investigative ‹*journalist, journalism, weekly, etc.*›

B *adv.* investigatively

Investition /ɪnvɛsti'tsi̯oːn/ *die;* ~, ~**en** investment; **die privaten** ~**en sind zurückgegangen** private investment has fallen

Investitions-: ~**güter** *Pl.* (Wirtsch.) capital goods; ~**güter·industrie** *die* capital-goods industry; ~**lenkung** *die* investment control; ~**tätigkeit** *die* investment activity

Investitur /ɪnvɛsti'tuːɐ̯/ *die;* ~, ~**en** investiture

Investiv·lohn /ɪnvɛs'tiːf-/ *der* (Wirtsch.) *portion of worker's wages set aside for investment in the company's investment savings scheme*

Investment /ɪn'vɛstmɛnt/ *das;* ~**s,** ~**s** (Finanzw.) ▸ **Investition**

Investment-: ~**fonds** *der* investment fund; ~**gesellschaft** *die* investment trust; ~**papier** *das,* ~**zertifikat** *das* investment fund certificate

Investor /ɪn'vɛstɔr/ *der;* ~**s,** ~**en** /-'toːrən/ **Investorin** *die;* ~, ~**nen** (Wirtsch.) investor

involvieren /ɪnvɔl'viːrən/ *tr. V.* (geh.) involve

in·wendig

A *Adj.* inside ‹*pocket*›; inner ‹*part*›; (fig.) inner, inward ‹*happiness, strength*›

B *adv.* [on the] inside; (fig.) inwardly; deep down [inside]; **etw./jmdn. in- und auswendig kennen** (ugs.) know sth./sb. inside out

in·wie·fern *Adv.* (in welcher Hinsicht) in what way; (bis zu welchem Grade) to what extent; how far

in·wie·weit *Adv.* to what extent; how far

In·zahlungnahme *die;* ~, ~**n** part exchange; trade in (Amer.); **durch** ~ **Ihres Altgerätes ...** by taking your old appliance in part exchange ...; if you trade in your old appliance ...

Inzest /ɪn'tsɛst/ *der;* ~**[e]s,** ~**e** incest

Inzest·tabu *das* (Völkerk.) incest taboo

inzestuös /ɪntsɛs'tu̯øːs/ *Adj.* incestuous

In·zucht *die;* ~**:** inbreeding

in·zwischen *Adv.* **1** (seither) in the meantime; since [then]; **es hatte sich** ~ **nichts geändert** nothing had changed in the meantime *or* since **2** (bis zu einem Zeitpunkt) (in der Gegenwart) by now; (in der Vergangenheit) by then; (in der Zukunft) by then; by that time; **er hat/hatte sich** ~ **daran gewöhnt** he has/had got used to it by now/then; **bestell ihm** ~ **einen schönen Gruß!** (ugs.) till then, give him my regards **3** (währenddessen) meanwhile; in the meantime

IOK *Abk.* = **Internationales Olympisches Komitee** IOC

Ion /i̯oːn/ *das;* ~**s,** ~**en** (Physik, Chemie) ion

Ionen-: ~**austauscher** *der;* ~~**s,** ~~ (Physik, Chemie) ion exchanger; ~**beschleuniger** *der* (Elektronik) ion accelerator; ~**bindung** *die* (Physik, Chemie) ionic bond; ~**gitter** *das* (Chemie) ionic lattice; ~**strahl** *der* (Physik, Chemie) ion beam

Ionien /'i̯oːni̯ən/ *(das);* ~**s** Ionia

Ionisation /i̯oniza'tsi̯oːn/ *die;* ~, ~**en** (Physik, Chemie) ionization

ionisch *Adj.* **1** Ionic ‹*dialect, order, column*›; **das Ionische Meer** the Ionian Sea **2** (Musik) Ionian ‹*mode*›

ionisieren *tr. V.* (Physik, Chemie) ionize

Ionisierung *die;* ~, ~**en** ▸ **Ionisation**

Iono·sphäre /i̯ono-/ *die* ionosphere

Ionosphären- ionospheric

ionosphärisch *Adj.* ionospheric

i-Punkt, *I-Punkt /'iː-/ *der* dot over *or* on the i; **ein i ohne** ~**:** a dotless i; **bis auf den** ~ (fig.) down to the last detail

IQ *Abk.* = **Intelligenzquotient** IQ

i. R. *Abk.* = **im Ruhestand** retd.

Irak /i'raːk/ *(das);* ~**s** *od. der;* ~**[s]** Iraq; **in/nach/aus** *od.* **im/in den/aus dem** ~**:** in/to/from Iraq

Iraker *der;* ~**s,** ~, **Irakerin** *die;* ~, ~**nen** ▸ **❶ S. 520** Iraqi; *s. auch* **-in**

irakisch *Adj.* ▸ **❶ S. 520** Iraqi

Irak·krieg *der* Iraq War

Iran /i'raːn/ *(das);* ~**s** *od. der;* ~**[s]** Iran; *s. auch* **Irak**

Iraner *der;* ~**s,** ~, **Iranerin** *die;* ~, ~**nen** ▸ **❶ S. 520** Iranian; *s. auch* **-in**

iranisch *Adj.* ▸ **❶ S. 520** Iranian; **I**~**/das I**~**e** Iranian; *s. auch* **Deutsch**

Iranistik *die;* ~**:** Iranian studies *pl., no art.*

irden /'ɪrdn̩/ *Adj.* earthen[ware] ‹*bowl, pot, jug*›; ~**es Geschirr** earthenware

Irden·ware *die* earthenware

irdisch *Adj.* 1 earthly ‹*joys, paradise, love*›; mortal, earthly ‹*creature, being*›; temporal ‹*power, justice*›; worldly ‹*goods, pleasures, possessions*›; **dieses ~e Jammertal** this vale of tears; **die Irdischen** (dichter.) the mortals; **den Weg alles Irdischen gehen** go the way of all flesh; ‹*object*› go the way of all things; **alles Irdische ist vergänglich** all earthly things must fade 2 (zur Erde gehörig) terrestrial; **das ~e Leben** life on earth

Ire /ˈiːrə/ *der;* **~n, ~n** ▸ⓘ **S. 520** Irishman; **die ~n** the Irish; **er ist ~:** he is Irish *or* an Irishman

irgend /ˈɪrgn̩t/ *Adv.* 1 **~ so ein Politiker** (ugs.) some politician [or other]; **~ so etwas** something like that; something of the sort *or* kind; **führen Sie ~ so etwas?** do you stock anything like that? 2 (~wie) **wenn ~ möglich** if at all possible; **wenn ich Ihnen ~ helfen kann** if I can help you in any way; *s. auch* **irgendetwas, irgendjemand**

irgend-: ~ein *Indefinitpron.* 1 (attr.) some; (fragend, verneinend) any; **~ein Idiot** some idiot [or other]; **in ~einer Zeitung habe ich neulich gelesen, dass ...** I read in one of the papers recently that ...; **Welche Zeitung soll es sein? — Irgendeine** What newspaper do you want? — Just any; **~ein anderer Redakteur/~eine andere Zeitung/~ein anderes Buch** some other editor/newspaper/book; (fragend, verneinend) any other editor/newspaper/book; **~ein anderer/~eine andere** someone *or* somebody else; (fragend, verneinend) anyone *or* anybody else; **mehr als ~ein anderer** more than anyone *or* anybody else; 2 (subst.) **~einer/~eine** someone; somebody; (fragend, verneinend) anyone; anybody; **~eines** *od.* (ugs.) **~eins** any one; **~einer muss es machen** someone *or* somebody [or other (coll.)] must do it; **nicht ~einer** not just anyone; **~einmal** *Adv.* sometime; [at] some time [or other (coll.)]; **hast du schon ~einmal solchen Unsinn gehört?** have you ever heard such nonsense before?; **~etwas** *Indefinitpron.* something; (fragend, verneinend) anything; **~jemand** *Indefinitpron.* someone; somebody; somebody or other (coll.); (fragend, verneinend) anyone; anybody; **warum hast du nicht ~jemand[en] gefragt?** why didn't you ask someone *or* somebody?; **Haben Sie an jemand Bestimmtes gedacht? — Ach wo, ~jemand** Did you have anyone particular in mind? — Oh, anyone *or* anybody [will do]; **~wann** *Adv.* [at] some time [or other]; somewhen (coll.); (zu jeder beliebigen Zeit) [at] any time; **~wann einmal** [at] some time [or other]; **~was** *Indefinitpron.* (ugs.) something [or other]; (fragend, verneinend) anything; **[nimm] ~was** [take] anything [you like]; **ist ~was?** is [there] something wrong *or* the matter?; **~welch** *Indefinitpron.* some; (fragend, verneinend) any; **er raucht nicht ~welche Zigarren** he doesn't smoke just any *or* (coll.) any old cigars; **~wer** *Indefinitpron.* (ugs.) somebody or other (coll.); someone; somebody; (fragend, verneinend) anyone; anybody; **~wie** *Adv.* 1 somehow; somehow or other (coll.); **ich glaube nicht, dass ihr das noch ~wie schaffen könnt** I don't think there's any way you could do it; **wer ~wie kann, sollte helfen** anyone who can help in any way should do so; **kann man das ~wie anders/besser machen?** is there some other/better way of doing this?; **er tut mir ~wie Leid, aber ...** I feel sorry for him in a way, but ...; **ihr Lächeln war ~wie kalt** her smile was somehow *or* (coll.) sort of cold; 2 (ugs.: als Füllwort) **sie will ~wie auch kommen** I somehow think she wants to come too; **~wo** *Adv.* 1 somewhere; some place [or other] (coll.); (fragend, verneinend) anywhere; **ist hier ~wo ein Lokal?** is there a pub anywhere around here?; **~wo anders** somewhere/anywhere else; 2 (ugs.: ~wie) **er tut mir ~wo Leid, aber ...** I feel sorry for him in a way, but ...; **~woher** *Adv.* from somewhere; from some place; from somewhere or other (coll.); (fragend, verneinend) from anywhere; from any place; **Woher soll ich das nehmen? — [Von] ~woher** Where shall I get it from? — From anywhere *or* wherever you like; **~wohin** *Adv.* somewhere; somewhere or other (coll.); (fragend, verneinend) anywhere; **wollen wir ~wohin gehen?** shall we go out somewhere?; **Wohin soll ich die Socken werfen? — Irgendwohin** Where should I throw these socks? — Anywhere [will do *or* you like]; **~wo·mit** *Adv.* with something; with something or other (coll.); **~woran** *Adv.* **~woran erinnert mich dieses Gebäude** this building reminds me of something; **~woran werden wir es schon erkennen** we'll recognize it by something

Iridium /iˈriːdi̯ʊm/ *das;* **~s** (Chemie) iridium

Irin *die;* **~, ~nen** ▸ⓘ **S. 520** Irishwoman; **sie ist ~:** she is Irish *or* an Irishwoman

Iris /ˈiːrɪs/ *die;* **~, ~** ▸ⓘ **S. 435** (Bot., Anat.) iris

Iris·blende *die* (Fot.) iris [diaphragm]

irisch *Adj.* ▸ⓘ **S. 520**, ▸ⓘ **S. 670** Irish; **die Irische See** the Irish Sea; **Irisch-Republikanische Armee** Irish Republican Army; **~-römisches Bad** Turkish bath; *s. auch* **Deutsch**

Iris·diagnostik *die* (Med.) iridodiagnosis

irisieren *itr. V.* iridesce; be iridescent; **~d** iridescent

Irland /ˈɪrlant/ *(das);* **~s** Ireland; (die Republik) Ireland; Eire

Ironie /iroˈniː/ *die;* **~, ~n** irony; **etw. mit ~ sagen** say sth. ironically; **das war ~:** that was meant ironically *or* meant to be ironic; **die ~ des Lebens hat es mit sich gebracht, dass ...** it was one of life's ironies that ...; **die ~ des Schicksals wollte es, dass ...** it was one of the ironies of fate *or* an irony of fate that ...

ironisch
A *Adj.* ironic; ironical; **das Ironische in der Literatur** irony *or* the ironic in literature; **sie zieht alles ins Ironische** she tends to be ironic about everything
B *adv.* ironically

ironischer·weise *Adv.* ironically

ironisieren *tr. V.* ironize

Ironisierung *die;* **~, ~en** ironizing

irr /ɪr/ *Adj.* ▸ **irre A**

irrational /ˈɪratsi̯onaːl/
A *Adj.* irrational
B *adv.* irrationally

Irrationalismus *der;* **~, Irrationalismen** irrationalism

Irrationalität *die;* **~:** irrationality

irre /ˈɪrə/
A *Adj.* 1 (geistesgestört) mad, insane ‹*person*›; insane ‹*laughter*›; demented ‹*grin, look*›; insane, crazy ‹*idea, thought, suggestion*›; **davon kann man ja ~ werden** it's enough to drive you mad *or* crazy; **sich wie ~ gebärden** act *or* behave like a madman/madwoman 2 (salopp: stark) terrific (coll.); terrible (coll.); **eine ~ Arbeit** a hell of a job (coll.) 3 (salopp: faszinierend) amazing (coll.); *s. auch* **irrewerden**
B *adv.* (salopp) terrifically (coll.); terribly (coll.); **sich ~ freuen** be thrilled to bits (coll.)

Irre[1] /ˈɪrə/ *der/die; adj. Dekl.* madman/madwoman; lunatic; (fig.) fool; idiot; lunatic; **das sind alles ~:** they're all crazy *or* mad; **er fährt wie ein ~r** he drives like a maniac *or* lunatic; **er schreit/arbeitet wie ein ~r** he shouts/works like mad (coll.)

Irre[2] *die* (geh.) **in die ~ gehen** (sich verirren) go astray; (fig.: sich irren) make a mistake; **in die ~ führen** (fig.) be misleading; (täuschen) be deceptive; **jmdn. in die ~ führen** mislead sb.; (täuschen) deceive sb.

irreal /ˈɪreaːl/ *Adj.* 1 (unwirklich) unreal 2 (unrealistisch) unrealistic

Irrealis /ˈɪreaːlɪs/ *der;* **~, Irreales** [-leːs] (Sprachw.) hypothetical subjunctive

Irrealität *die;* **~** 1 unreality 2 (Sprachw.) **als Ausdruck der ~:** as an expression of the unreal *or* hypothetical

irre-, Irre-: ~|führen *tr. V.* mislead; (täuschen) deceive; **lassen Sie sich durch ... nicht ~führen** don't be misled *or* deceived by ...; **~führend** *Adj.* misleading; (täuschend) deceptive; **~führung** *die:* **das war eine bewusste ~führung** that was a deliberate attempt to mislead; **~führung der Öffentlichkeit** misleading the public; **~|gehen** *unr. V.; mit sein* (geh.) 1 (sich irren) be mistaken; 2 (sich verirren) go astray

irregulär /ˈɪreguleːɐ̯/ *Adj.* 1 (regelwidrig, Milit.) irregular 2 (abnorm) abnormal

irre|leiten *tr. V.* (geh.) 1 (verführen, täuschen) lead astray; **irregeleitete Emotionen/Jugend** misguided emotions/youth 2 (falsch leiten) **ein irregeleiteter Brief** a misdirected letter

irrelevant /ˈɪrelevant/ *Adj.* irrelevant (**für** to)

Ir·relevanz *die* irrelevance (**für** to)

irreligiös *Adj.* non-religious; unreligious ‹*person, science, country*›

irre|machen *tr. V.* 1 (verwirren) disconcert; put off; **lass dich durch ihn nicht ~:** don't be disconcerted *or* (coll.) put off by him 2 (zweifeln lassen) **jmdn. in seinem Glauben ~:** shake sb.'s faith; **sie ließ sich in ihrer Hoffnung/ihrem Plan nicht ~:** she would not let anything confound her hopes/her plan

irren /ˈɪrən/
A *refl. V.* be mistaken; **man kann sich auch mal ~:** everybody makes *or* we all make mistakes [sometimes]; **Sie ~ sich, wenn ...** you are making a mistake if ...; **ich irre mich oft bei Namen** I often get names mixed up; **er hat sich in einigen Punkten geirrt** he got a few things wrong; **Sie haben sich in der Person/Hausnummer geirrt** you've got the wrong person/number; **sich um 1 Euro ~:** be out by 1 euro; be 1 euro out; **ich habe mich in dir geirrt** I was wrong about you
B *itr. V.* 1 (sich ~) **da ~ Sie** you are mistaken *or* wrong there; **die Zeitungsberichte ~ in diesem Punkt alle** the newspaper reports are all wrong on this point; **Irren ist menschlich** to err is human (prov.) 2 *mit sein* (ziellos umherstreifen) wander; **durch die Straßen/den Park ~:** wander the streets/about in the park

irren-, Irren-: ~anstalt *die* (veralt. abwertend) mental home; madhouse (derog.); **~arzt** *der,* **~ärztin** *die* (veralt. abwertend) mad-doctor (arch.); **~haus** *das* (abwertend) [lunatic] asylum; madhouse (derog.); **das war das reinste ~haus** (ugs.) it was bedlam *or* an absolute madhouse; **er ist reif fürs ~haus** (ugs.) he'll crack up soon (coll.); **~häusler** *der;* **~~s, ~~,** **~häuslerin** *die;* **~~, ~~nen** (veralt. abwertend) lunatic (derog.); **~haus·reif** *Adj.* (ugs.) **sie ist bald ~hausreif** she'll crack up before long (coll.); **~witz** *der* (ugs.) loony joke (coll.); joke about lunatics

irreparabel /ɪrepaˈraːbl̩/ *Adj.* (nicht reparabel) irreparable; beyond repair *pred.*; (nicht zu beheben, Med.) irreparable ‹*loss, damage*›

Irre·sein *das* ▸ **manisch-depressiv**

irreversibel *Adj.* (fachspr.) irreversible

irre|werden *unr. itr. V* (geh.) **an jmdm. ~:** lose faith in sb.; **an sich** (*Dat.*) **selbst ~:** doubt oneself; **am Glauben ~:** begin to have agonizing doubts about one's faith

Irr-: ~fahrt *die* wandering; **meine Reise wurde zu einer endlosen ~fahrt** my journey turned into an endless series of wanderings; **~flug** *der* aimless flight; **~garten** *der* maze; labyrinth; **~glaube[n]** *der* 1 misconception; 2 (Rel.) heresy; heterodoxy; **~gläubige** *der/die* heretic

irrig /ˈɪrɪç/ *Adj.* erroneous ‹*impression, belief, assumption, etc.*›; false ‹*premise*›

Irrigation /ɪrigaˈtsi̯oːn/ *die;* **~, ~en** irrigation; (Med.: Spülung) douche

Irrigator /ɪriˈgaːtɔr/ *der;* **~s, ~en** /-gaˈtoːrən/ (Med.) irrigator

irrigerweise *Adv.* mistakenly; erroneously

Irritation /ɪritaˈtsi̯oːn/ *die;* **~, ~en** (Med., geh.) irritation

irritieren *tr., itr. V.* 1 (verwirren) bother; put off; **das irritiert** it's off-putting; **lass dich nicht dadurch ~:** don't be put off by it 2 (stören) disturb 3 (befremden) annoy; irritate

irr-, Irr-: ~läufer *der* (Postw.) misdirected letter/parcel; **~lehre** *die* (Rel.) heresy; heterodoxy; (fig.) false doctrine; **~licht** *das; Pl.*

~~**er** will o' the wisp; jack o' lantern; ~**lichter entstehen durch ...** will o' the wisp *or* jack o' lantern is caused by ...; ~**sinn** *der* 1 (Wahnsinn) insanity; madness; **er war dem ~sinn nahe** he was on the brink of madness; 2 (ugs. abwertend) madness; lunacy; **so ein ~sinn!** what lunacy!; ~**sinnig** A *Adj.* 1 (geistig gestört) insane; mad; (absurd) idiotic; **bist du ~sinnig?** are you mad?; **wie ~sinnig schreien/rasen** scream/rush like mad (coll.); 2 (ugs.: extrem) terrible (coll.), horrific (coll.) ‹*pain, screams, prices, etc.*›; terrific (coll.) ‹*speed, heat, cold*›; B *adv.* (ugs.) terribly (coll.); frightfully (coll.); ~**sinnig schuften** slog away like mad *or* crazy (coll.); ~**sinnige** *der/die; adj. Dekl.* madman/madwoman; lunatic; **sie schrie wie eine ~sinnige** she screamed like mad (coll.)

Irrtum *der;* ~**s, Irrtümer** /ˈɪrty:mɐ/ 1 (falsche Vorstellung, Fehlhandlung) fallacy; misconception; **im ~ sein** *od.* **sich im ~ befinden** be wrong *or* mistaken 2 (Fehler) mistake; error; ~**!** wrong!

irrtümlich /ˈɪrty:mlɪç/
A *Adj.* incorrect; wrong
B *adv.* by mistake; ~ **gemachte Angaben** inaccuracies; incorrect information *sing.*

irrtümlicherweise *Adv.* by mistake; **wie man oft ~ meint** as is often erroneously *or* mistakenly thought

Irrung *die;* ~, ~**en** (geh.) **die ~en und Wirrungen seiner verfehlten Jugend** the vagaries of his misspent youth

irr-, Irr-: ~**weg** *der* error; **diese Methode hat sich als ~weg erwiesen** this method has proved to be wrong; **auf ~wege geraten** (gedanklich) go off on the wrong track; (moralisch) depart from the straight and narrow; ~|**werden** *unr. itr. V.:* ▸**irrewerden**; ~**wisch** *der* flibbertigibbet; ~**witz** *der* (geh.) madness; lunacy; ~**witzig** *Adj.* (geh.) mad

Ischias /ˈɪʃi̯as/ *der od. das od. Med. die;* ~ ▸ⓘ **S. 439** sciatica

Ischias·nerv *der* ▸ⓘ **S. 435** sciatic nerve

ISDN *das;* ~**s** ISDN

Isegrim /ˈi:zəgrɪm/ *der;* ~**s,** ~**e** 1 (Myth.) **[Meister]** ~**:** Isegrim; Isgrin 2 (mürrischer Mann) crusty old man

Islam /ɪsˈla:m *od.* ˈɪslam/ *der;* ~**[s]: der ~:** Islam; **die Welt des ~[s]** the Islamic world; the world of Islam

islamisch *Adj.* Islamic; Islamitic

islamisieren *tr. V.* Islamize

Islamismus *der;* ~**:** Islamic fundamentalism; Islamism

Islamist *der;* ~**en,** ~**en, Islamistin** *die;* ~, ~**nen** Islamic fundamentalist; Islamist

islamistisch *Adj.* Islamic fundamentalist; Islamist

Island /ˈi:s-/ *(das);* ~**s** Iceland

Isländer /ˈi:slɛndɐ/ *der;* ~**s,** ~**, Isländerin** *die;* ~, ~**nen** ▸ⓘ **S. 520** Icelander

isländisch /ˈi:slɛndɪʃ/ *Adj.* ▸ⓘ **S. 520,** ▸ⓘ **S. 670** Icelandic; **I~/das I~e** Icelandic; *s. auch* **Deutsch**

Ismailit /ɪsmaiˈli:t/ *der;* ~**en,** ~**en** Ismaili

Ismus /ˈɪsmʊs/ *der;* ~, **Ismen** (abwertend) ism

iso-, Iso-, (vor Vokalen auch:) **is-, Is-** /i:z(o)-/ iso-

Iso·bar *das;* ~**s,** ~**e** (Physik) isobar

Iso·bare *die;* ~, ~**n** (Met.) isobar

Iso·drink /ˈi:zo-/ *der* isotonic drink

Isogamie /izogaˈmi:/ *die;* ~, ~**n** /-i:ən/ (Biol.) isogamy *no art.*

Isolation /izolaˈtsi̯o:n/ *die;* ~, ~**en** ▸**Isolierung**

Isolations-: ~**folter** *die* torture by solitary confinement; ~**haft** *die* solitary confinement

Isolator /izoˈla:tɔr/ *der;* ~**s,** ~**en** /-ˈto:rən/ insulator

Isolier·band *das; Pl.* **Isolierbänder** insulating tape

Isolier·baracke *die* isolation ward

isolieren *tr. V.* 1 isolate ‹*prisoner, patient, bacterium, element*›; **von der Umwelt isoliert** cut off from the outside world; **etw. isoliert betrachten** look at sth. out of context 2 (Technik) insulate ‹*wiring, wall, etc.*›; lag ‹*boilers, pipes, etc.*›; (gegen Schall) soundproof; insulate ‹*room, door, window, etc.*›

Isolierer *der;* ~**s,** ~**, Isoliererin** *die;* ~, ~**nen** insulation engineer

Isolier-: ~**kanne** *die* Thermos jug ®; vacuum jug; ~**schicht** *die* insulating layer; ~**station** *die* (Med.) isolation ward

Isolierung *die;* ~, ~**en** 1 (Absonderung, auch fig.) isolation; **in der ~:** in isolation; **in die ~ geraten** (fig.) become isolated *or* detached 2 (Technik) (das Isolieren) insulation; insulating; (von Kesseln, Röhren) lagging; (gegen Schall) soundproofing 3 (Isoliermaterial) insulation; (für Kessel, Röhren) lagging

Iso·matte /ˈi:zo-/ *die* thermal mat

Isomer /izoˈme:ɐ̯/ *das;* ~**s,** ~**e, Isomere** *das; adj. Dekl.* (Chemie) isomer

Isometrie /izomeˈtri:/ *die;* ~ (Biol., Geodäsie) isometry

isometrisch
A *Adj.* isometric
B *adv.* isometrically

Isotherme /izoˈtɛrmə/ *die;* ~, ~**n** (Met.) isotherm

Isotop /izoˈto:p/ *das;* ~**s,** ~**e** isotope

Isotopen·therapie *die* (Med.) radiotherapy

Israel /ˈɪsrae:l/ *(das);* ~**s** Israel; **das Volk ~** (bibl.) the Israelites; the people of Israel; **die Kinder ~[s]** (bibl.) the Children of Israel

Israeli *der;* ~**[s],** ~**[s]/** *die;* ~, ~**[s]** ▸ⓘ **S. 520** Israeli

israelisch *Adj.* ▸ⓘ **S. 520** Israeli

Israelit *der;* ~**en,** ~**en, Israelitin** *die;* ~, ~**nen** Israelite; *s. auch* **-in**

israelitisch *Adj.* Israelite

iss, *iß /ɪs/ *Imperativ Sg. v.* **essen**

isst, *ißt /ɪst/ *2. u. 3. Pers. Sg. Präsens v.* **essen**

ist /ɪst/ *3. Pers. Sg. Präsens v.* **sein**

Ist-: ~**aufkommen,** ~**-Aufkommen** *das* (Steuerw.) actual *or* real yield; ~**bestand,** ~**-Bestand** *der* (Kaufmannsspr.) actual stocks *pl.;* ~**stärke,** ~**-Stärke** *die* (Milit.) actual strength

Isthmus /ˈɪstmʊs/ *der;* ~, **Isthmen** isthmus

Ist-zustand, Ist-Zustand *der* current state

Itaker /ˈi:takɐ/ *der;* ~**s,** ~**, Itakerin** *die;* ~, ~**nen** (salopp abwertend) Eyetie (sl. derog.); dago (sl. derog.)

Italien /iˈta:li̯ən/ *(das);* ~**s** Italy

Italiener /itaˈli̯e:nɐ/ *der;* ~**s,** ~**, Italienerin** *die;* ~, ~**nen** ▸ⓘ **S. 520** Italian; *s. auch* **-in**

italienisch *Adj.* Italian; **I~/das I~e** ▸ⓘ **S. 520,** ▸ⓘ **S. 670** Italian; *s. auch* **Deutsch**

Italo·western /ˈi:talo-/ *der* Italian-made Western; spaghetti western (derog.)

IT-Branche /iˈte:-/ *die* IT sector

Item /ˈaɪtəm/ *das od. der;* ~**s,** ~**s** item

iterativ /iteraˈti:f/ *Adj.* iterative

i-Tüpfel[chen], *I-Tüpfel[chen] *das;* ~**s,** ~, (österr.) **i-Tüpferl, *I-Tüpferl** /ˈi:typfəl/ *das;* ~**s,** ~**n** final *or* finishing touch; **bis aufs [letzte] ~:** down to the last detail

i-Tüpfel-Reiter, *I-Tüpfel-Reiter *der,* **i-Tüpfel-Reiterin, *I-Tüpfel-Reiterin** (österr. ugs.) nit-picker (coll.)

i. v. *Abk.* (Med.) = **intravenös** IV

i. V. /i:ˈfau̯/ *Abk.* = **in Vertretung**

Iwan /ˈi:va(:)n/ *der;* ~**s,** ~**s** (salopp abwertend) Russki (derog.); Ivan (derog.); **der ~:** the Russkis *pl.;* Ivan

i. w. S. *Abk.* = **im weiteren Sinne**

i

Jj

j, J /jɔt, *österr.:* je:/ *das;* ~, ~: j/J; *s. auch* **a, A**

ja /ja:/ *Partikel* [1] (zustimmend) yes; **Wohnen Sie hier? — Ja** Do you live here? — Yes [, I do]; **Hast du ihm Bescheid gesagt? — Ja** Have you told him? — Yes [, I have]; **ja** *od.* **Ja zu etw. sagen** say yes to sth. [2] (bekräftigend) yes; **ja natürlich** *od.* **sicher!** [yes,] of course; [yes,] certainly; **o ja!** oh, yes!; **aber ja doch!** yes, of course [I/you *etc.* can/do *etc.*] [3] (nachgestellt) won't you/doesn't it *etc.*?; **du bleibst doch noch ein bisschen, ja?** but you'll stay on a bit, won't you *or* surely?; **das Kleid sieht doch gut aus, ja?** the dress looks nice, doesn't it? [4] **ich komme ja schon** I'm [just] coming; **Sie wissen ja, dass ...** you know, of course, that ...; **du kennst ihn ja** you know what he's like; you know him; **es schneit ja!** it's [actually] snowing!; **da seid ihr ja!** there you are! [5] (einschränkend) **er mag ja Recht haben** he may [well] be right [6] (unbedingt) **lass ja die Finger davon!** [just you] leave it alone!; **sag das ja nicht weiter!** don't [you dare] pass it on, whatever you do!; **damit er ja alles mitbekommt** to make sure he knows all *or* everything that's going on; **damit wir ja nicht zu spät kommen** so that there's no risk of us being late [7] (sogar) indeed; even; **ich schätze, ja bewundere ihn** I like him, indeed admire him *or* admire him even [8] (allerdings) oh; **ja, das waren noch Zeiten!** [yes], those were the days! [9] (fragend) (am Telefon usw.) **ja [bitte]?** yes?; **Sie kommen. — Ja?** They're coming. — Are they?; (ungläubig) **Der König ist tot. — Ja?** The King is dead. — [Is he] really?

Ja *das;* ~[s], ~[s] yes; **mit ~ stimmen** vote yes

Jacht /jaxt/ *die;* ~, ~en yacht

Jacht-: ~**hafen** *der* yacht harbour; marina; ~**klub** *der* yacht club

Jäckchen /'jɛkçən/ *das;* ~s, ~: jacket; (gestrickt) cardigan

Jacke /'jakə/ *die;* ~, ~n jacket; (gestrickt) cardigan; **das ist ~ wie Hose** (ugs.) it makes no odds (coll.); *s. auch* **saufen C**

Jacken-: ~**kleid** *das* dress and jacket combination; ~**tasche** *die* jacket pocket

Jacket·krone /'dʒɛkɪt-/ *die* (Zahnmed.) jacket crown

Jackett /ʒa'kɛt/ *das;* ~s, ~s jacket

Jade /'ja:də/ *der;* ~[s] *od. die;* ~: jade

jade·grün *Adj.* jade-green

Jagd /ja:kt/ *die;* ~, ~en [1] (Weidwerk) **die ~:** shooting; hunting; (Hetzjagd) hunting; **die ~ auf Hasen** hare hunting; (mit Hunden) hare coursing; **die ~ auf Federwild** shooting game birds; **~ auf Fasanen/Wildschweine machen** shoot pheasant/hunt wild boar; **auf der ~ sein** be hunting/shooting; **auf die ~ gehen** go hunting/shooting; **die hohe/niedere ~** (Jägerspr.) hunting for Hochwild/Niederwild [2] (Veranstaltung) shoot; (Hetzjagd) hunt [3] (Revier) preserve; shoot; **eine ~ pachten** rent a hunting preserve *or* shoot [4] (Verfolgung) hunt; (Verfolgungsjagd) chase; **auf jmdn./etw. ~ machen** hunt for sb./sth.; **die ~ nach Geld/Besitz** (fig.) the constant pursuit of money/possessions [5] (~gesellschaft) shooting party; (bei einer Hetzjagd) hunt; field; **die Wilde ~:** the Wild Hunt

Jagd-: ~**aufklärer** *der* (Luftwaffe) fighter-reconnaissance aircraft; ~**aufseher** *der,* ~**aufseherin** *die* game warden

jagdbar *Adj.* **~e Tiere** animals that can be hunted/shot

Jagd-: ~**beute** *die* bag; kill; **eine reiche/magere ~beute** a good/poor bag; ~**bomber** *der* (Luftwaffe) fighter-bomber; ~**falke** *der* falcon; ~**fieber** *das* hunting fever; **vom ~fieber gepackt** in the fever of the hunt; ~**flieger** *der* (Luftwaffe) fighter pilot; ~**flugzeug** *das* (Luftwaffe) fighter aircraft; ~**frevel** *der* poaching; ~**gebiet** *das* hunting ground[s *pl.*]; ~**geschwader** *das* (Luftwaffe) fighter wing; ~**gesellschaft** *die* shooting party; hunting party; (bei Hetzjagden) hunting party; ~**gewehr** *das* sporting gun; ~**glück** *das:* **~glück/kein ~glück haben** be lucky/unlucky [in the hunt]; ~**grund** *der* hunting ground; **in die ewigen ~gründe eingehen** go to the happy hunting grounds; ~**haus** *das* hunting *or* shooting lodge; hunting *or* shooting box; ~**herr** *der,* ~**herrin** *die* owner of a/the preserve *or* shoot; ~**horn** *das* hunting horn; ~**hund** *der* gun dog; (bei Hetzjagden) hunting dog; hound; ~**hütte** *die* hunting *or* shooting box; ~**messer** *das* hunting knife; ~**pächter** *der,* ~**pächterin** *die* game-tenant; ~**panzer** *der* (Milit.) anti-tank vehicle; tank destroyer; ~**rennen** *das* (Pferdesport) steeplechase; ~**revier** *das* preserve; shoot; (fig.) hunting ground; ~**schein** *der* game licence; **er hat den** *od.* **einen ~schein** (fig. ugs.) he's certified — the courts can't do anything about him; ~**schloss, *~schloß** *das* hunting seat *or* lodge; ~**springen** *das;* ~~s (Pferdesport) showjumping; ~**staffel** *die* (Luftwaffe) fighter squadron; ~**stock** *der* shooting stick; ~**stück** *das* (Malerei) hunting piece; ~**stuhl** *der* ▸ ~**stock**; ~**szene** *die* (bild. Kunst) hunting scene; ~**waffe** *die* hunting weapon; ~**wesen** *das* hunting; ~**wurst** *die* chasseur sausage; ~**zeit** *die* open *or* hunting *or* shooting season

jagen /'ja:gn̩/

A *tr. V.* [1] (verfolgen) hunt ‹*game, fugitive, criminal, etc.*›; shoot ‹*game, game birds*›; (hetzen) chase, pursue ‹*fugitive, criminal, etc.*›; (wegscheuchen) chase; run after; **von Todesfurcht/Gewissensbissen gejagt** stricken by the fear of death/by pangs of conscience; **ein Gedanke jagte den anderen** thoughts raced through his/her *etc.* mind [2] (in eine bestimmte Richtung treiben) drive ‹*animals*›; **den Ball ins Netz ~** (Fußballjargon) drive the ball into the net [3] (vertreiben) **den Feind aus dem Land ~:** drive the enemy out of *or* from the country; **jmdn. aus dem Haus ~:** throw sb. out of the house; **jmdn. aus dem Bett ~:** turn sb. out of bed; **jmdn. in die Flucht ~:** put sb. to flight; **damit kannst du mich ~** (ugs.) I can't stand it/that/them; *s. auch* **Gurgel** [4] (ugs.) **sich/jmdm. eine Spritze in den Arm ~:** jab *or* stick a needle in one's/sb.'s arm; **sich/jmdm. eine Kugel durch den Kopf ~:** blow one's/sb.'s brains out

B *itr. V.* [1] (Jägerspr.) **auf Rebhühner ~:** shoot partridge; **auf Hasen ~:** hunt *or* shoot hare [2] (die Jagd ausüben) go shooting *or* hunting; (auf Hetzjagd gehen) go hunting [3] **nach Geld/Glück ~:** chase after money/happiness [4] *mit sein* (eilen) race; rush; **Wolken ~ am Himmel** (fig.) clouds race *or* scud across the sky; **mit ~dem Puls** (fig.) with his/her *etc.* pulse racing

Jagen *das;* ~s, ~ (Forstw.) compartment

Jäger /'jɛ:gɐ/ *der;* ~s, ~ [1] hunter; (bei Hetzjagden) huntsman; **~ und Sammler** (Prähist.) hunters and gatherers [2] (Milit.) rifleman; jaeger [3] (Soldatenspr.: Jagdflugzeug) fighter

Jäger·art *die* (Kochk.) **Schnitzel nach ~:** escalope chasseur

Jägerei *die;* ~ [1] (das Jagen) shooting; hunting; (Hetzjagd) hunting [2] (Jagdwesen) hunting

Jäger·hut *der* huntsman's hat

Jägerin *die;* ~, ~**nen** huntress; huntswoman

Jäger-: ~**latein** *das* (scherzh.) [hunter's *or* huntsman's] tall story/stories; **das ist das reinste ~latein** that's all wild exaggeration; ~**rock** *der* hunting jacket; ~**schnitzel** *das* (Kochk.) escalope chasseur

Jägers·mann *der; Pl.* **Jägers·leute** (ugs. veralt.) ▸ **Jäger 1**

Jäger·sprache *die* hunting language

Jag·hund /'ja:k-/ *der* (schweiz.) ▸ **Jagdhund**

Jaguar /'ja:gua:ɐ̯/ *der;* ~s, ~e jaguar

jäh /jɛ:/

A *Adj.* (geh.) [1] (plötzlich, heftig) sudden; sudden, abrupt ‹*change, movement, stop*›; sudden, sharp ‹*pain*›; **er fand einen ~en Tod** he met his death suddenly; **ein ~es Erwachen** a sudden awakening; (fig.) a rude awakening [2] (steil) steep; precipitous ‹*slope, ravine, ridge*›

B *adv.* [1] (plötzlich) **die Stimmung schlug ~ um** the mood changed suddenly *or* abruptly [2] (steil) **dort ging es ~ in die Tiefe** the ground fell *or* dropped away steeply *or* abruptly at that point

jählings /'jɛ:lɪŋs/ *Adv.* (geh.) [1] (plötzlich) ‹*change, end, stop*› suddenly, abruptly; ‹*die, understand, wake up*› suddenly [2] (steil) steeply; precipitously

Jahr /ja:ɐ̯/ *das;* ~[e]s, ~e [1] ▸❶ **S. 165** (12 Monate) year; **ein halbes ~:** six months; **anderthalb ~e** eighteen months; a year and a half; **im ~[e] 1908** in [the year] 1908; **jedes ~:** every year; **jedes zweite ~:** [once] every two years; **alle halbe[n] ~ [mal]** (ugs.) [once] every six months; **alle ~e** every year; **1 000 Tonnen pro ~:** 1,000 tonnes per *or* a year; **100 000 € pro ~:** € 100,000 per annum; **lange ~e [hindurch]** for many years; **nach langen ~en** after many years; **vor langen ~en** many years ago; **~ für** *od.* **um ~:** year after year; **von ~ zu ~:** from one year to the next; from year to year; **ich war seit ~ und Tag nicht mehr dort** I haven't been there for many years; **zwischen den ~en** between Christmas and the New Year; **das Buch/der Sportler des ~es** the book/sportsman *or* sports personality of the year; **zu zehn ~en [Gefängnis] verurteilt werden** be sentenced to ten years [imprisonment]; **er ist Lehrling im zweiten ~:** he is an apprentice in his second year; **auf ~ und Tag** to the exact day; **nach ~ und Tag** after many years; **vor ~ und Tag** (mit Präteritum) many years ago; (mit Plusquamperfekt) many years before [2] ▸❶ **S. 29** (Lebens~) year; **er ist zwanzig ~e [alt]** he is twenty years old *or* of age; **Kinder bis zu zwölf ~en** children up to the age of twelve *or* up to twelve years of age; **Kinder über 14 ~e** children over the age of 14 *or* over 14 years of age; **Kinder ab zwei ~en** children of two years and over; **alle Männer zwischen 18 und 45 ~en** all men

j

ℹ Die Jahreszeiten

der Frühling, das Frühjahr = **spring**
der Sommer = **summer**
der Herbst = **autumn** (*brit.*), **fall** (*amerik.*)
der Winter = **winter**

Spricht man von einer Jahreszeit im Allgemeinen oder als Phänomen, verwendet man im Englischen oft keinen Artikel:

Der Frühling ist früh eingetroffen
= Spring came early
Der Sommer ist meine Lieblingsjahreszeit
= Summer *od.* The summer is my favourite time of year
Im Winter bleibe ich die meiste Zeit zu Hause
= In [the] winter I stay at home most of the time
Sie blühen zu Anfang/zu Ende des Frühjahrs
= They flower in [the] early/late spring

Eine Ausnahme bildet der amerikanische Ausdruck **fall**, der stets mit dem Artikel verwendet wird.

Im Herbst verfärbt sich das Laub
= The leaves change colour in [the] autumn *od.* (*amerik.*) in the fall

Spricht man aber von einem bestimmten Sommer usw., ist der Gebrauch ähnlich wie im Deutschen:

Der Sommer war verregnet
= The summer was wet
nächsten/letzten Winter
= next/last winter
Er blieb den ganzen Sommer
= He stayed all summer *od.* [for] the whole summer
Sie kommen diesen Herbst
= They are coming this autumn *od.* (*amerik.*) this fall
Er macht jeden Winter Skiurlaub
= He goes skiing every winter
Die letzten beiden Sommer waren wir in Griechenland
= The last two summers we were in Greece

Adjektive

frühlingshaft = springlike
herbstlich = autumnal
sommerlich = summery
winterlich = wintry

In ganz wenigen Fällen lässt sich das Adjektiv durch ein attributives **summer, winter** usw. übersetzen. Bei Kleidung etwa unterscheidet man nicht zwischen *winterlich/sommerlich* und *Winter-/Sommer-:*

Winterkleidung/winterliche Kleidung
= winter clothing
Sommerkleidung/sommerliche Kleidung
= summer clothing

Allerdings:

ein sommerliches Kleid
= a summery dress

Beachten Sie auch:

winterliche/sommerliche Temperaturen
= winter/summer temperatures

between the ages of 18 and 45; **mit 65 ~en** od. **im Alter von 65 ~en** at the age of 65; **seine ~e spüren** feel one's age; **das hat er schon in jungen ~en gelernt** he learned that at an early age *or* while he was still young; **für seine achtzig ~e ist er noch erstaunlich rüstig** he's amazingly sprightly for [a man of] eighty; **mit den ~en** as he/she *etc.* grows/grew older; **er ist um ~e gealtert** he's put on years; **in die ~e kommen** reach middle age

jahr·aus *Adv.* **~, jahrein** year in, year out

Jahr·buch *das* yearbook

Jährchen /ˈjɛːɐ̯çən/ *das;* **~s, ~** (scherzh.) year; **die paar ~, die ich noch zu leben habe!** the few short years I have left to live; **einige ~ auf dem Buckel haben** be knocking on a bit (coll.)

jahr·ein *Adv.;* ▸**jahraus**

jahre·lang
A *Adj.* [many] years of ‹*practice, imprisonment, experience, etc.*›; long-standing ‹*feud, friendship*›; **mit ~er Verspätung** years late
B *adv.* for [many] years; **sie ist schon ~ tot** she has been dead for [many] years; **man sprach noch ~ darüber** people were talking about it for years afterwards

jähren /ˈjɛːrən/ *refl. V.* **heute jährt sich [zum fünften Male] sein Todestag** today is the [fifth] anniversary of his death; **heute jährt sich zum zehntenmal, dass ...** it is ten years ago today that ...; it is ten years since ...

jahres-, Jahres-: ~abonnement *das* annual *or* yearly subscription; **~abrechnung** *die* annual accounts *pl.;* (Abrechnungsblatt) annual [statement of] account; **~abschluss**, ***~abschluß** *der* **1** (Wirtsch., Kaufmannsspr.) annual accounts *pl.;* **2** ▸**~ende**; **~anfang** *der* beginning *or* start of the year; **~ausgleich** *der* (Steuerw.) end-of-year adjustment; **den ~ausgleich beantragen** send in one's tax return; **~ausklang** *der* close of the year; **Musik zum ~ausklang** music at the close of the year; **~ausstoß** *der* (Wirtsch.) annual production; **~beginn** *der* beginning *or* start of the new year; **den ~beginn feiern** celebrate New Year; **~beitrag** *der* annual *or* yearly subscription; **~bestleistung** *die* (Sport) best performance of the season; **~bestzeit** *die* (Sport) fastest *or* best time of the season; **~bezüge** *Pl.* annual income *sing.;* **~bilanz** *die* (Wirtsch., Kaufmannsspr.) annual balance [of accounts]; (Dokument) annual balance sheet; **~durchschnitt** *der* yearly *or* annual average; **~einkommen** *das* annual income; **~ende** *das* end of the year; **~etat** *der* annual budget; **~frist** *die:* **in** od. **innerhalb** od. **binnen ~frist** within [a period of] a *or* one year; **vor ~frist** in less than a year; within [a period of] a *or* one year; (vor einem Jahr) a year ago; **nach ~frist** after [a period of] a *or* one year; **~gehalt** *das* annual salary; **zwei ~gehälter** two years' salary; **~hälfte** *die* half of *or* six months of the year; **die erste/zweite ~hälfte** the first/second half *or* six months of the year; **~hauptversammlung** *die* (Wirtsch.) annual general meeting; **~kapazität** *die* (Wirtsch.) annual *or* yearly capacity; **~karte** *die* yearly season ticket; **~miete** *die* annual *or* yearly rent; **eine Kaution in Höhe einer ~miete** a deposit equivalent to a year's rent; **~mittel** *das* annual mean; **im ~mittel fallen 3,2 cm Niederschlag** the mean annual precipitation is 3.2 cm; **~plan** *der* [economic, financial] plan for the year; **~produktion** *die* annual *or* yearly production; **~ring** *der* (Bot.) annual ring; **~rückblick** *der* end-of-the-year review; **~schluss**, ***~schluß** *der* ▸**~ende**; **~schlussbilanz**, ***~schlußbilanz** *die* ▸**~abschluss 1**; **~schrift** *die* annual; **~tag** *der* anniversary; **~tagung** *die* annual congress *or* conference *or* convention; **~temperatur** *die:* **die höchste/tiefste ~temperatur** the highest/lowest temperature of the year; **die mittlere ~temperatur** the mean temperature during the year; **eine mittlere ~temperatur von 9°C** a mean annual temperature of 9°C; **~umsatz** *der* annual turnover; **~urlaub** *der* annual holiday *or* (formal) leave *or* (Amer.) vacation; **~versammlung** *die* annual [general] meeting; **~vertrag** *der* one-year contract; **~wechsel** *der* turn of the year; **zum ~wechsel die besten Wünsche** best wishes for the New Year; **~wende** *die* **1** (geh.) ▸**~wechsel**; **2** turn of the year; **um die ~wende 1976/1977** around the end of 1976; around the beginning of 1977; **~zahl** *die* date; **ohne Angabe der ~zahl** with no indication of the date *or* year; **~zeit** *die* season; **für die ~zeit ist es kalt** it's cold for the time of the year; **trotz der vorgerückten ~zeit** although it is/was late in the year; **~zeitlich A** *Adj.* seasonal; **B** *adv.* **~zeitlich schwanken** vary with the seasons *or* according to the time of year; **~zeitlich bedingt sein** be governed by seasonal factors

Jahr·gang *der* **1** (Altersklasse) year; **der ~ 1900** those *pl.* born in 1900; **der ~ 1900 hat viele Gelehrte hervorgebracht** the year 1900 produced many scholars; **sie ist ~ 1943** she was born in 1943; **er ist mein ~:** he was born in the same year as I was; **welcher ~ sind Sie?** which year were you born in? **2** (eines Weines) vintage; **der 81er soll ein guter ~ werden** 81 should be a vintage year; **ein Edelzwicker ~ 1978** a 1978 Edelzwicker **3** (einer Zeitschrift) set [of issues] for a/the year; **die beiden letzten Jahrgänge** the sets of back numbers for the past two years **4** (eines Autos usw.) year; **ein Modell ~ 1950** a 1950 model

Jahr·gänger *der;* **~s, ~, Jahr·gängerin** *die;* **~, ~nen** (südd., schweiz.) **er ist mein Jahrgänger** he was born in the same year as I was

Jahr·hundert *das* ▸ℹ **S. 165** century; **das 18. ~:** the 18th century; **im 19. und 20. ~:** in the 19th and 20th centuries; **durch die ~e** over *or* through the centuries; **im ersten ~ vor/nach Christi Geburt** in the first century BC/AD; **die Literatur des 19. ~s** 19th-century literature; the literature of the 19th century

jahrhunderte-: ~alt *Adj.* centuries-old; **~lang A** *Adj.* age-long; **B** *adv.* for centuries; **das dauert noch ~lang** that will take centuries

Jahrhundert-: ~ereignis *das* hundred-year event; **~flut** *die* flood of the century; **~hälfte** *die:* **die erste/zweite ~hälfte** the first/second half of the century; **~hochwasser** *das* flood of the century; **~mitte** *die* middle of the century; **~projekt** *das* project of the century; **~sommer** *der* summer of the century; **~wein** *der* exceptional vintage wine; **~wende** *die* turn of the century; **aus der Zeit um die ~wende** from the turn of the century; **~werk** *das* achievement of the century

-jährig /ˈjɛːrɪç/ **1** ▸ℹ **S. 29** (... Jahre alt) **ein elfjähriges/halbjähriges Kind** an eleven-year-old/a six-month-old child; **kaum acht~:** hardly eight years old **2** (... Jahre dauernd) ... year's/years'; -year; **nach vierjähriger/halbjähriger Vorbereitung** after four years'/six months' preparation; **mit dreijähriger/halbjähriger Verspätung** three years/six months late

jährlich /ˈjɛːɐ̯lɪç/
A *Adj.* annual; yearly
B *adv.* annually; yearly; **einmal/zweimal ~:** once/twice a *or* per year; **ein Umsatz von 5 Millionen ~:** a turnover of five million per annum

Jahr·markt *der* fair; funfair; **ein ~ der Eitelkeit[en]** (fig.) a Vanity Fair

Jahrmarkts·bude *die* fairground booth

Jahr·millionen *Pl.* millions of years

Jahr·schießet *der;* **~s** (schweiz.) ▸**Schützenfest**

Jahr·tausend *das* thousand years; millennium; **vor ~en** thousands of years ago; **das dritte ~ nach Christi Geburt** the third millennium AD

jahrtausende-: ~alt *Adj.* age-old; **ein ~altes Gebäude** a building dating back thousands of years; **~lang A** *Adj.* age-long; **B** *adv.* for thousands of years; **das dauert ~lang** that will take thousands of years

Jahrtausend·wende *die* turn of the millennium

Jahr·zahl *die* (schweiz.) ▸**Jahreszahl**

Jahr·zehnt *das* decade

jahrzehnte·lang

A *Adj.* **das macht die ~e Übung** that's the result of decades of practice; **mit ~er Verspätung** decades late; **nach ~er Abwesenheit** after being away for decades

B *adv.* for decades

Jahve, (ökum.:) **Jahwe** /ˈjaːvə/ *(der);* **~s** Jehova; Yahweh

Jäh·zorn *der* violent anger; **er neigt zum ~:** he tends towards violent fits *or* outbursts of temper *or* anger; **in wildem ~ zuschlagen** lash out in blind anger *or* a blind rage

jäh·zornig

A *Adj.* violent-tempered; **ein ~er Charakter, ein ~es Temperament** a violent temper

B *adv.* in blind anger; in a blind rage

ja·ja *Part.* (ugs.) **1** (seufzend) **~[, so ist das Leben]** oh well[, that's life] **2** (ungeduldig) **~[, ich komme schon]!** OK, OK *or* all right, all right[, I'm coming]!

Jak /jak/ *der;* **~s, ~s** yak

Jakob /ˈjaːkɔp/ *(der)* James; (in der Bibel) Jacob; **ich weiß ja nicht, ob das der wahre ~ ist** I don't know if that is really quite the thing; **der billige ~:** the/a cheap jack

Jakobi /jaˈkoːbi/ *(das); indekl.* ▸**Jakobstag**

Jakobiner /jakoˈbiːnɐ/ *der;* **~s, ~** (hist.) Jacobin

Jakobiner·mütze *die* (hist.) cap of liberty; Phrygian cap

Jakobinertum *das;* **~s** Jacobinism *no art.*

jakobinisch *Adj.* Jacobin; Jacobinic

Jakobit /jakoˈbiːt/ *der;* **~en, ~en, Jakobitin** *die;* **~, ~nen** (hist.) Jacobite

Jakobi·tag *der* ▸**Jakobstag**

Jakobs·leiter *die* (Seemannsspr., Bot.) Jacob's ladder

Jakobs·tag *der* St. James's Day; Feast of St. James

Jalousette /ʒaluˈzɛtə/ *die;* **~, ~n, Jalousie** /ʒaluˈziː/ *die;* **~, ~n** venetian blind

Jalta /ˈjalta/ *(das);* **~s** Yalta

Jamaika /jaˈmaika/ *(das);* **~s** Jamaica

Jamaikaner *der;* **~s, ~, Jamaikanerin** *die;* **~, ~nen** Jamaican; *s. auch* **-in**

jamaikanisch *Adj.* Jamaican

Jamaika·rum *der* Jamaica rum

Jambe /ˈjambə/ *die;* **~, ~n** ▸**Jambus**

jambisch *Adj.* (Verslehre) iambic

Jamboree /dʒɛmbəˈriː/ *das;* **~[s], ~s** jamboree

Jambus /ˈjambʊs/ *der;* **~, Jamben** (Verslehre) iambus; iamb; **ein Drama in Jamben** a drama in iambic verse *or* in iambics

jammen /ˈdʒɛmən/ *itr. V.* (Jargon) jam (coll.)

Jammer /ˈjamɐ/ *der;* **~s** **1** (Wehklagen) [mournful] wailing **2** (Elend) misery; **ein Bild des ~s** a picture of misery; **es ist ein ~, dass ...** (ugs.) it's a crying shame that ...

Jammer-: ~bild *das* miserable sight; **~geschrei** *das* (von Menschen) wailing; moaning; (von Vögeln) squawking; squawks; **~gestalt** *die* **1** (elender Mensch) pitiful creature; **2** (ugs. abwertend) miserable wretch; **~lappen** *der* (ugs. abwertend) (Feigling) coward; (Schwächling) sniveller

jämmerlich /ˈjɛmɐlɪç/

A *Adj.* **1** (Jammer ausdrückend) pathetic; pitiful **2** (beklagenswert) miserable ‹*existence, conditions, etc.*›; wretched ‹*appearance, existence, etc.*› **3** (ärmlich) pathetic; pitiful ‹*conditions, clothing, housing*›; paltry, meagre ‹*quantity*›; pitiful, sorry ‹*state*› **4** (abwertend: minderwertig) contemptible ‹*person*›; pathetic, paltry ‹*wages, sum*›; pathetic, useless ‹*piece of work etc.*› **5** (sehr groß, stark) awful; terrible (coll.)

B *adv.* **1** (Jammer ausdrückend) pathetically; pitifully **2** (beklagenswert) miserably; hopelessly; pitifully; **~ versagen** fail miserably *or* hopelessly **3** (ärmlich) pitifully; miserably **4** (abwertend: schlecht) pathetically; hopelessly **5** (sehr, stark) terribly (coll.); **~ frieren** be frozen stiff

Jämmerlich·keit *die;* **~** **1** (Jammer) mournfulness **2** (Elend) wretchedness **3** (Ärmlichkeit) pitifulness; wretchedness **4** (abwertend) (eines Menschen) contemptibility; (einer Arbeit usw.) uselessness

Jämmerling /ˈjɛmɐlɪŋ/ *der;* **~s, ~e** (ugs. abwertend) (Feigling) chicken (coll.); (Schwächling) weakling

jammern

A *itr. V.* **1** wail; **ohne zu ~:** without so much as a groan; **Jammern und Klagen** groans and cries *pl.* **2** (sich beklagen) moan; grumble; **über sein Schicksal ~:** bemoan one's fate **3** (verlangen) cry [out]; **die Kinder jammerten nach einem Stück Brot** the children were crying out for *or* crying after a piece of bread

B *tr. V.* (geh.: Mitleid erregen) grieve; distress; **er/sein Elend jammert mich** his distress grieves me; my heart goes out to him in his distress

jammer-, Jammer-: ~schade *Adj.* (ugs.) **es ist ~schade, dass ...** it's a crying shame that ...; **es ist ~schade um ihn** it's a great pity about him; **~tal** *das* (geh.) vale of tears; **dieses irdische ~tal** this earthly vale of tears; **~voll** **A** *Adj.* **1** (Jammer ausdrückend) pathetic; pitiful ‹*cry etc.*›; **2** (beklagenswert) miserable; **B** *adv.* **1** (Jammer ausdrückend) pathetically; pitifully; **2** (beklagenswert) miserably; wretchedly

Jan. *Abk.* **= Januar**

Janker /ˈjaŋkɐ/ *der;* **~s, ~** (südd., österr.) Alpine jacket

Jänner /ˈjɛnɐ/ *der;* **~s, ~** (österr.), **Januar** /ˈjanuaːɐ̯/ *der;* **~[s], ~e** ▸ⓘ **S. 165** January; *s. auch* **April**

janus-, Janus-/ˈjaːnʊs-/: **~gesicht** *das,* **~kopf** *der* Janus face; **~köpfig** *Adj.* Janus-faced

Japan /ˈjaːpan/ *(das);* **~s** Japan

Japaner *der;* **~s, ~, Japanerin** *die;* **~, ~nen** ▸ⓘ **S. 520** Japanese; *s. auch* **-in**

japanisch *Adj.* ▸ⓘ **S. 520**, ▸ⓘ **S. 670** Japanese; **das Japanische Meer** the Sea of Japan; **Japanisch/das Japanische** Japanese; *s. auch* **Deutsch**

Japan·lack *der* Chinese *or* Japanese lacquer

Japan·papier *das* rice paper

Japs /japs/ *der;* **~es, ~e** (ugs. abwertend) Jap (derog.)

japsen /ˈjapsn̩/ *itr. V.* (ugs.) pant; **ich kann kaum noch ~:** I'm gasping for breath

Japser *der;* **~s, ~** (ugs.) gasp of breath

Jargon /jarˈgõː/ *der;* **~s, ~s** **1** (Gruppensprache) jargon; **der ~ der Juristen/Mediziner** legal/medical jargon; **der ~ der Journalisten** journalese; **der Berliner ~:** Berlin slang; **im „Spiegel"-~:** in the jargon of the 'Spiegel' **2** (abwertend: ungepflegte Ausdrucksweise) language; **er redet in einem ganz ordinären ~:** he uses very vulgar language

Ja·sager /-zaːgɐ/ *der;* **~s, ~** (abwertend) yes-man

Ja·sagerin *die;* **~, ~nen** (abwertend) yes-woman

Jasmin /jasˈmiːn/ *der;* **~s, ~e** **1** (Echter ~) jasmine **2** (Falscher ~) mock orange; syringa

Jasmin·tee *der* jasmine tea

Jaspis /ˈjaspɪs/ *der;* **~** *od.* **~ses, ~se** jasper

Jass, *Jaß /jas/ *der;* **Jasses** (schweiz.) jass *(card game)*

jassen *itr. V.* (schweiz.) play jass

Ja·stimme *die* yes-vote; **die ~n** the votes in favour; the ayes (Brit. Parl.)

jäten /ˈjɛːtn̩/ *tr., itr. V.* weed; **Unkraut ~:** weed; **Brennnesseln ~:** pull out *or* weed out stinging nettles

Jauche /ˈjauxə/ *die;* **~, ~n** **1** liquid manure **2** (ugs. abwertend) muck

Jauche·grube *die* liquid-manure reservoir

jauchen *tr., itr. V.* (Landw.) manure

jauchzen /ˈjauxtsn̩/ *itr. V.* **1** (laut jubeln) cheer; **vor Freude ~:** shout for joy; **der Säugling jauchzte laut** the baby gurgled with pleasure; **das Publikum jauchzte** the audience was in raptures **2** (veralt.) rejoice; **jauchzet dem Herrn** rejoice in the Lord

Jauchzer *der;* **~s, ~:** cry of delight

jaulen /ˈjaulən/ *itr. V.* ‹*dog, cat, etc.*› howl, yowl; ‹*wind*› howl; ‹*engine*› scream

Jause /ˈjauzə/ *die;* **~, ~n** (österr.) **1** snack; **eine ~ machen** have a snack **2** (Nachmittagskaffee) [afternoon] tea

Jausen·station *die* (österr.) café

jausnen *itr. V.* (österr.) have a snack

Java /ˈjaːva/ *(das);* **~s** Java

ja·wohl *Part.* **1** certainly; **~, Herr Oberst!** yes, sir! **2** (verstärkend) **Kant, ~ Kant** Kant, no less

jawoll /jaˈvɔl/ (ugs.) ▸**jawohl**

Ja·wort *das* consent; **jmdm. das ~ geben** consent to marry sb.; **sich** *(Dat.)* **das ~ geben** accept each other in marriage

Jazz /dʒɛs *od.* jats/ *der;* **~:** jazz

Jazz·band *die* jazz band

jazzen /ˈdʒɛsn̩ *od.* ˈjatsn̩/ *itr. V.* play jazz

Jazzer /ˈdʒɛsɐ *od.* ˈjatsɐ/ *der;* **~s, ~, Jazzerin** *die;* **~, ~nen** jazz musician

Jazz·fan *der* jazz fan

jazzig /ˈjatsɪç/ *Adj.* (ugs.) jazzy

Jazz-: ~kapelle *die* jazz band; **~keller** *der* jazz cellar; **~musik** *die* jazz music **~rock** *der* jazz-rock

je[1] /jeː/

A *Adv.* **1** (jemals) ever; **mehr/besser denn je** more/better than ever; **seit** *od.* **von je** always; for as long as anyone can remember; *s. auch* **eh**[2] **2** **2** (jeweils) **je zehn Personen** ten people at a time; **die Gruppen bestehen aus je acht Mitgliedern** the groups consist of eight members each; **die Kinder stellen sich je zwei und zwei auf** the children arrange themselves in twos *or* in pairs; **die Schränke sind je zwei Meter breit** the wardrobes are each two metres wide; **sie kosten je 30 Euro** they cost 30 euros each; **er gab den Mädchen je eine Birne** he gave each of the girls a pear; **in Schachteln mit** *od.* **zu je 10 Stück verpackt** packed in boxes of ten **3** (entsprechend) **je nach Gewicht/Geschmack** according to weight/taste

B *Präp. mit Akk.* per; for each; **je angebrochene Stunde** for each *or* per hour or part of an hour

C *Konj.* **1** **je länger, je lieber** the longer the better; **je früher du kommst, desto** *od.* **um so mehr Zeit haben wir** the earlier you come, the more time we'll have **2** **je nachdem** it all depends; **wir gehen hin, je nachdem [ob] wir Zeit haben oder nicht** we'll go, depending on whether we have the time or not; **Willst du mitgehen? — Je nachdem** (ugs.) Do you want to come too? — I'll see

je[2]

A *Interj.* **ach je, wie schade!** oh dear *or* dear me, what a shame!; *s. auch* **oje**

B *Adv.* (veralt.) **je nun** well now

Jeans /dʒiːnz/ *Pl. od. die;* **~, ~** **1** (Hose) jeans *pl.*; denims *pl.* **2** (Stoff) denim; jean[s] material

Jeans-: ~hose *die* [pair of] jeans; **~jacke** *die* denim jacket; **~stoff** *der* denim; jean[s] material

jeck /jɛk/ *Adj.* (rhein., meist abwertend) (leicht verrückt) stupid; daft; (wahnsinnig) crazy

Jeck *der;* **~en, ~en** (rhein.) **1** (abwertend: Verrückter) idiot **2** (Fastnachter) carnival clown

jede ▸**jeder**

jeden·falls *Adv.* **1** (gewiss) certainly; definitely **2** (zumindest) at any rate; **ich ~ habe keine Lust mehr** I at any rate *or* for one have had enough **3** (so viel steht fest) in any case; at any rate; anyway; **das steht ~ fest** that much is certain, in any case *or* at any rate *or* anyway

jeder /ˈjeːdɐ/, **jede, jedes** *Indefinitpron. u. unbest. Zahlwort*

A *attr.* **1** ▸ⓘ **S. 816** (alle) every; **jeder einzelne Schüler** every single pupil; **jeder zweite Bürger** one out of *or* in every two citizens; **der Zug fährt jeden Tag/viermal jeden Tag** the train runs every day/four times a day **2** (verstärkend) **das kann Ihnen jedes Kind sagen**

any child could tell you that; **ohne jeden Zweifel** without any doubt; **ohne jeden Grund** without any reason whatever; for no reason whatever 3 (alle einzeln) each; **jeder Mitspieler bekommt sechs Karten** each player receives six cards 4 (jeglicher) all; **jede Hilfe kam zu spät** all help came too late; **hier wurde jedes Maß überschritten** that went beyond all bounds; **Menschen jeden** *od.* **jedes Alters** people of all ages; **„nehme jede Arbeit an"** 'all offers of work accepted'

B *allein stehend* 1 (alle) everyone; everybody; **jeder** *od.* (geh.) **ein jeder darf mitkommen** everyone *or* everybody can come; **hier kennt jeder jeden** everybody knows everybody else here; (verstärkend) **jeder, der Lust hat, ist willkommen** anyone who wants to come is welcome; **das kann ja jeder** anyone can do that 2 (alle einzeln) **jedes der Kinder** every one *or* each of the children; **jeder für sich hat Recht** each of us/you/them *etc.* is right in his own way; **jeder von uns kann helfen** each *or* every one of us can help; **jedem nach seinem Verdienst** to each according to his merits

jeder-: **~art** *indekl. unbest. Gattungsz.; indekl.* any kind *or* sort *or* type of; **er ist bereit, ~art Arbeit anzunehmen** he is prepared to take any kind of work; **~lei** *indekl. unbest. Gattungsz.;* (geh.) all kinds *or* sorts of; **~mann** *Indefinitpron.* everyone; everybody; **hier kann ~mann mitmachen** everyone *or* everybody *or* anyone *or* anybody can come along and join in; **das ist ~manns Pflicht** that is everyone's *or* everybody's duty; **Schnecken sind nicht ~manns Sache/Geschmack** snails are not to everyone's *or* everybody's taste; **~zeit** *Adv.* [at] any time; **natürlich, ~zeit!** of course, any time!

jedes ▸ **jeder**

***jedes·mal** ▸ **Mal¹**

je·doch *Konj., Adv.* however; **es war ~ zu spät** it was too late, however; it was, however, too late

jedweder /ˈjeːtˈveːdɐ/, **jedwede, jedwedes** *Indefinitpron. u. unbest. Zahlwort* (nachdrücklich, veralt.) 1 *attr.* every; **ohne jedwede Rücksicht** without any consideration whatsoever 2 *allein stehend* everyone; everybody

Jeep (Wz) /dʒiːp/ *der;* **~s, ~s** jeep ®

jeglicher /ˈjeːklɪçɐ/, **jegliche, jegliches** *Indefinitpron. u. unbest. Zahlw.* ▸ **jeder A 3, B 2**

je·her /od. ˈ-ˈ-/ *Adv.* **seit** *od.* **von ~:** always; since *or* from time immemorial; **es wurde seit** *od.* **von ~ so gehandhabt, dass ...** the procedure has always been that ...

Jehova /jeˈhoːva/ ▸ **Zeuge**

jein /jain/ *Adv.* (scherzh.) yes and no

Je·länger·je·lieber *das;* **~s, ~** (Bot.) honeysuckle; woodbine

jemals /ˈjeːmaːls/ *Adv.* ever

jemand /ˈjeːmant/ *Indefinitpron.* someone; somebody; (fragend, verneinend) anyone; anybody; **ich kenne ~[en], der ...** I know someone *or* somebody who ...; **sich mit ~[em] treffen** to meet someone *or* somebody; **ist da ~?** is anybody there?; **ich glaube nicht, dass da ~ ist** I don't think there's anybody there; **~ anders/Fremdes** someone *or* somebody else/strange; **ein gewisser Jemand** (scherzh.) a certain somebody; **kaum ~:** hardly *or* scarcely anyone *or* anybody

Jemen /ˈjeːmən/ *(das);* **~s** *od. der;* **~[s]** Yemen; *s. auch* **Irak**

Jemenit /jeməˈniːt/ *der;* **~en, ~en, Jemenitin** *die;* **~, ~nen** Yemenite; Yemeni

jemenitisch *Adj.* Yemenite; Yemeni

jemine /ˈjeːmine/ *Interj.* (veralt.) **ach ~!** oh dear; dear me!

jener /ˈjeːnɐ/, **jene, jenes** *Demonstrativpron.* (geh.)

A *attr.* that; (im Pl.) those; **in jenem Haus dort** in that house [over] there; **vergleichen Sie dieses mit jenem Bild** compare this picture and that one; **zu jenem Zeitpunkt** at that time; **in jenen Tagen** in those days

B *allein stehend* that one; (im Pl.) those; **jene, die ...** those who ...; **ein Roman Bölls, in dem jener schildert, wie ...** a novel by Böll in which he describes how ...

jenseitig /ˈjeːn- *od.* ˈjɛn-/ *Adj.* 1 (gegenüberliegend) opposite; far, opposite ‹*bank, shore*› 2 (geh.) **die ~e Welt** *od.* **das Jenseitige** the next world; the hereafter

jenseits /ˈjeːn-/

A *Präp. mit Gen.* on the other side of; (in größerer Entfernung) beyond; **~ des Urals** beyond the Urals; **~ des Flusses** on the other *or* far *or* opposite side of the river; **sie ist schon ~ der Vierzig** she's already over *or* (coll.) the wrong side of forty

B *Adv.* beyond; on the other side; **~ vom Rhein** on the other side of *or* beyond the Rhine; **eine Welt ~ von Hass und Gewalt** a world free from hatred and violence; *s. auch* **gut D 2**

Jenseits *das;* **~:** hereafter; beyond; **ins ~ abgerufen** *od.* **abberufen werden** (geh. verhüll.) pass away; **jmdn. ins ~ befördern** (salopp) bump sb. off (coll.)

Jeremia /jereˈmiːa/ *(der);* **~s** Jeremiah

Jeremiade /jereˈmi̯aːdə/ *die;* **~** (geh., veralt.) jeremiad

Jersey¹ /ˈdʒøːɐ̯zi/ *der;* **~[s], ~s** (Textilind.) jersey

Jersey² *das;* **~s, ~s** (Sport: Trikot) jersey

Jersey·kleid *das* jersey dress

jerum /ˈjeːrʊm/ *Interj.* ▸ **ojerum**

Jesaja /jeˈzaːja/ *(der);* **~s** Isaiah

Jessas [na] /ˈjɛsas (naː)/ *Interj.* (österr.) my goodness

Jesuit /jeˈzu̯iːt/ *der;* **~en, ~en** (Rel., auch abwertend) Jesuit

Jesuiten-: **~general** *der* General of the Jesuits; **~orden** *der* order of Jesuits; Society of Jesus; **~schule** *die* Jesuit school

Jesuitentum *das;* **~s** Jesuitism

Jesus /ˈjeːzʊs/ *(der);* **Jesu** /ˈjeːzu/ Jesus; **~ Christus** Jesus Christ

Jesus-: **~kind** *das:* **das ~kind** the Infant Jesus; baby Jesus (child lang.); **~knabe** *der* ▸ **~kind**; **~latschen** *der* (scherzh.) Jesus sandal (joc.)

Jesus[, Maria und Josef] *Interj.* (veralt.) oh [my] Lord

Jet /dʒɛt/ *der;* **~[s], ~s** jet; **mit einem ~ fliegen/reisen** fly/travel by jet

Jet·flug *der* flight by jet

Jeton /ʒəˈtõː/ *der;* **~s, ~s** 1 (Spielmarke) gaming chip *or* token 2 (für das Telefon usw.) token

Jetset, *Jet-set /ˈdʒɛtsɛt/ *der;* **~s, ~s** jet set

jetten /ˈdʒɛtn̩/ *itr. V.; mit sein* (ugs.) jet

jetzig /ˈjɛtsɪç/ *Adj.* present; current; **in der ~en Zeit** at present; in present times

jetzo /ˈjɛtso/ (veralt.) ▸ **jetzt**

jetzt /jɛtst/ *Adv.* 1 (im Augenblick) at the moment; just now; **bis ~:** up to now; **bis ~ noch nicht** not yet; not so far; **von ~ an** *od.* **ab** from now on[wards]; **~ noch** still; **was, ~ [so spät] noch?** what, now?; **das geht nicht von ~ auf nachher** (ugs.) it can't be done at a moment's notice; **~ oder nie!** it's now or never; **~ ist aber Schluss!** that's [quite] enough! 2 (nun, nunmehr) now; **~ ist es aus mit uns** we've had it now; **sie ist gerade ~ weggegangen** she has just left; **~ endlich** [now,] at last; **~ erst [einmal]** just; **erst ~** *od.* **~ erst** only just; **schon ~:** already; **er ist ~ schon drei Wochen krank** he has been ill for three weeks now 3 (heutzutage) now; these days; nowadays 4 (landsch.: wohl) **von wem wird ~ der Brief sein?** now, who will that letter be from, I wonder?

Jetzt *das;* **~** (geh.) **das ~:** the present

Jetzt·zeit *die* present times *pl.;* **in der ~:** in present times; in our times

je·weilen *Adv.* (schweiz.) occasionally; once in a while

jeweilig /ˈjeːvailɪç/ *Adj.* 1 (in einem bestimmten Fall) particular; **nach den ~en Umständen** according to the particular circumstances 2 (zu einer bestimmten Zeit) current; of the time *postpos., not pred.;* **nach der ~en Mode** in the current fashion; in the fashion of the time 3 (zugehörig, zugewiesen) respective

jeweils /ˈjeːvails/ *Adv.* 1 (jedesmal) **~ am ersten/letzten Mittwoch des Monats** on the first/last Wednesday of each month 2 (zur jeweiligen Zeit) currently; at the time; **die ~ amtierende Regierung** the government of the day

Jg. *Abk.* = **Jahrgang**

Jh. *Abk.* = **Jahrhundert** c.

jiddeln /ˈjɪdl̩n/ ▸ **jüdeln**

jiddisch /ˈjɪdɪʃ/ *Adj.* ▸ⓘ **S. 670** Yiddish; **Jiddisch/das Jiddische** Yiddish; *s. auch* **Deutsch**

Jitterbug /ˈdʒɪtəbag/ *der;* **~:** jitterbug

Jiu-Jitsu /dʒiːuˈdʒɪtsu/ *das;* **~[s]** ju-jitsu

Jive /dʒaɪv/ *der;* **~:** jive; **~ tanzen** jive

Job¹ /joːp/ ▸ **Hiob**

Job² /dʒɔp/ *der;* **~s, ~s** ▸ⓘ **S. 113** (ugs.; auch DV) job

jobben /ˈdʒɔbn̩/ *itr. V.* (ugs.) do a job/jobs; **als Taxifahrer ~:** do [some] taxi-driving

Jobber /ˈdʒɔbɐ/ *der;* **~s, ~, Jobberin** *die;* **~, ~nen** (Börsenw.) [stock] jobber; (ugs. abwertend) jobber (derog.)

Job·maschine *die* (ugs.) job creator

Joch /jɔx/ *das;* **~[e]s, ~e** 1 (bei Zugtieren) yoke; **Ochsen/Kühe ins/unters ~ spannen** yoke oxen/cows; **das ~ der Tyrannei abschütteln** (fig. geh.) throw *or* cast off the yoke of tyranny 2 (Gespann, Feldmaß) **zwei ~ Ochsen/Land** two yoke of oxen/land 3 (Geogr.) col; saddle 4 (Archit.) bay

Joch·bein *das* ▸ⓘ **S. 435** (Anat.) zygomatic bone; malar bone

Jockei, Jockey /ˈdʒɔke *od.* ˈdʒɔki/ *der;* **~s, ~s** ▸ⓘ **S. 113** jockey

Jockey·mütze *die* jockey cap

Jod /joːt/ *das;* **~[e]s** iodine

Jodel·lied *das* yodelling song

jodeln /ˈjoːdl̩n/ *itr., tr. V.* yodel

jod·haltig *Adj.* iodiferous

Jodler *der;* **~s, ~** 1 (Person) yodeller 2 (kurzes Jodeln) yodel 3 ▸ **Jodellied**

Jodlerin *die;* **~, ~nen** yodeller

Jod-: **~tinktur** *die* tincture of iodine; iodine tincture; **~zahl** *die* (Chemie) iodine number; iodine value

Joga /ˈjoːga/ *der od. das;* **~[s]** yoga; **~ betreiben** *od.* (ugs.) **machen** practise *or* (coll.) do yoga

Joga·übung *die* yoga exercise

joggen /ˈdʒɔgn̩/ *itr. V.; mit Richtungsangabe mit sein* jog; **[zwei Kilometer] ~:** go jogging [for two km]

Jogging /ˈdʒɔgɪŋ/ *das;* **~s** jogging *no art.*

Joghurt /ˈjoːgʊrt/ *der od. das;* **~[s], ~[s]** yoghurt

Joghurt·becher *der* yoghurt pot (Brit.) *or* (Amer.) container

Jogi /ˈjoːgi/ *der;* **~s, ~s, Jogin** /ˈjoːgɪn/ *der;* **~s, ~s** yogi

Johann /ˈjoːhan/ *(der)* John

Johanna /joˈhana/ *(die):* **~ von Orléans** Joan of Arc

Johannes /joˈhanəs/

A *(der)* John; **~ der Täufer** John the Baptist

B *der;* **~, ~se** (salopp) ▸ **Jonny**

Johannes·evangelium *das* St John's Gospel; Gospel according to St John

Johanni /joˈhani/ *(das); indekl.* ▸ **Johannistag**

Johannis·beere *die* 1 (Frucht) currant; **rote/weiße/schwarze ~n** redcurrants/white currants/blackcurrants 2 (Strauch) currant [bush]; **rote/weiße/schwarze ~n** redcurrant/white currant/blackcurrant bushes

Johannisbeer-: **~saft** *der* currant juice; **~strauch** *der* currant bush

Johannis-: **~brot** *das* (Bot.) Saint-John's-bread; carob [bean]; **~brot·baum** *der* (Bot.) Saint-John's-bread; carob [tree]; **~feuer** *das* Saint John's fire; **~käfer** *der* (südd.)

▸**Leuchtkäfer**; **~kraut** *das* Saint John's wort; **~tag** *der* Saint John's the Baptist's day; **~trieb** *der* (Bot.) 1) (das Austreiben) Lammas growth; 2) (Trieb) Lammas shoot

Johanniter /jo:ha'ni:tɐ/ *der;* **~s, ~:** Knight of St. John of Jerusalem

Johanniter·orden *der* Order of [the Hospital of] St. John of Jerusalem

johlen /'jo:lən/
A *itr. V.* yell; (vor Wut) howl
B *tr. V.* **die Menge johlte Beifall/Pfuirufe** the crowd yelled *or* roared its approval/howled *or* roared its disapproval

Joint /dʒɔɪnt/ *der;* **~s, ~s** (ugs.) joint (coll.); **einen ~ kreisen lassen** pass a joint round

Jointventure, Joint Venture /'dʒɔɪnt 'ventʃə/ *das;* **~s, ~s** (Wirtsch.) joint venture

Jo-Jo /jo(:)'jo:/ *das;* **~s, ~s** yo-yo

Joker /'jo:kɐ *od.* dʒo:kɐ/ *der;* **~s, ~** (Kartensp.) joker

Jokus /'jo:kʊs/ *der;* **~, ~se** (veralt.) **seinen ~ mit etw./jmdm. haben** tease sth./sb.; make fun of sth./sb.

Jolle /'jɔlə/ *die;* **~, ~n** 1) (Sportboot) [sailing] yacht 2) (mit Schwert) keel-centreboard yawl 3) (Beiboot) yawl; jolly [boat]

Jollen·kreuzer *der* dinghy cruiser

Jongleur /ʒɔŋ'lø:ɐ/ *der;* **~s, ~e, Jongleurin** *die;* **~, ~nen** juggler

jonglieren *tr., itr. V.* juggle; **Bälle** *od.* **mit Bällen ~:** juggle with balls; **mit Zahlen ~:** juggle [about] with figures; **ich werde das schon irgendwie ~** (ugs.) I'll wangle (coll.) *or* work it somehow

Jonny /'dʒɔni/ *der;* **~s, ~s** (salopp: Penis) John Thomas (sl.)

Joppe /'jɔpə/ *die;* **~, ~n** heavy jacket

Jordan /'jɔrdan/ *der;* **~[s]** ▸**ⓘ S. 267** Jordan; **über den ~ gehen** (verhüll.) go the way of all flesh

Jordanien /jɔr'da:ni̯ən/ *(das);* **~s** Jordan

Jordanier *der;* **~s, ~, Jordanierin** *die;* **~, ~nen** Jordanian; *s. auch* **-in**

jordanisch *Adj.* Jordanian

Josef, Joseph /'jo:zɛf/ *(der)* Joseph

Joseph[s]·ehe *die* unconsummated marriage

Jot /jɔt/ *das;* **~, ~:** j, J; *s. auch* **a, 1**

Jota /'jo:ta/ *das;* **~[s], ~s** iota; **kein/nicht ein/um kein ~** (geh.) not an iota; not one jot

Joule /dʒu:l *od.* dʒaul/ *das;* **~[s], ~** (Physik) joule

Jour /ʒu:ɐ/ *der;* **~s, ~s** (veralt.) open house; **~ fixe** at-home

Journaille /ʒʊr'naljə *od.* ʒʊr'nai̯l/ *die;* **~** (veralt. abwertend) 1) (verantwortungslose Presse) yellow *or* gutter press 2) (Sensationsjournalisten) hacks *pl.* (derog.)

Journal /ʒʊr'na:l/ *das;* **~s, ~e** 1) (veralt.: Tageszeitung) journal (dated); newspaper 2) (geh.: Zeitschrift) journal; periodical; **ein ~ für Mode/Kunst** a fashion/an art journal *or* periodical 3) (veralt.: Tagebuch) journal (dated); diary 4) (Schiffstagebuch) log[book] 5) (Kaufmannsspr.) daybook

Journal·beamte *der,* **Journal·beamtin** *die* (österr.) official *or* officer [on duty]

Journalismus *der;* **~:** journalism *no art.*

Journalist *der;* **~en, ~en** ▸**ⓘ S. 113** journalist

Journalisten·deutsch *das* (oft abwertend) journalese

Journalistik *die;* **~:** journalism *no art.*

Journalistin *die;* **~, ~nen** ▸**ⓘ S. 113** journalist

journalistisch
A *Adj.* journalistic; **eine ~e Ausbildung** a training in journalism
B *adv.* journalistically; **~ tätig sein** work as *or* be a journalist

jovial /jo'vi̯a:l/ *Adj.* jovial

Jovialität /jovi̯ali'tɛ:t/ *die;* **~:** joviality

Joystick /'dʒɔɪstɪk/ *der;* **~s, ~s** (DV) joystick

jr. *Abk.* **= junior** Jr.

Jubel /'ju:bl̩/ *der;* **~s** (das Jauchzen) rejoicing; jubilation; (laut) cheering; **ein großer ~ brach aus** a loud cheer went up; **unter dem ~ der Zuschauer** amid the cheering *or* cheers of the spectators; **~, Trubel, Heiterkeit** an atmosphere of eat, drink, and be merry

Jubel-: ~feier *die* jubilee; anniversary; (Feierlichkeiten) jubilee *or* anniversary celebrations *pl.*; **~greis** *der* (scherzh.) old swinger (coll. joc.); **~jahr** *das* jubilee; **alle ~jahre [einmal]** once in a blue moon

jubeln
A *itr. V.* cheer; **über etw.** *(Akk.)* **~:** rejoice over sth.; celebrate sth.; **~de Instrumente/Klänge** (dichter.) joyful instruments/sounds
B *tr. V.* **Beifall ~:** applaud; give applause; **„Hurra!", jubelte er** 'hurrah!' he cried delightedly

Jubel-: ~paar *das* couple celebrating their wedding anniversary; **~perser** *der* (ugs. abwertend) person hired to cheer in the/a crowd; **~ruf** *der* cheer; joyful shout; (religiös) exultation; shout of praise

Jubilar /jubi'la:ɐ/ *der;* **~s, ~e** man celebrating his anniversary/birthday

Jubilarin *die;* **~, ~nen** woman celebrating her anniversary/birthday

Jubiläum /jubi'lɛ:ʊm/ *das;* **~s, Jubiläen** anniversary; (eines Monarchen) jubilee; **fünfundzwanzigjähriges/fünfzigjähriges ~:** twenty-fifth/fiftieth anniversary/jubilee; **hundertjähriges ~:** hundredth anniversary; centenary; **500-jähriges/1 000-jähriges ~:** quincentenary/millenary; **sein 25-jähriges ~ bei der Firma begehen** celebrate 25 years with the firm

Jubiläums-: ~ausgabe *die* jubilee edition; **~ausstellung** *die* jubilee exhibition; **~heft** *das* jubilee issue

jubilieren *itr. V.* (geh. veralt.) jubilate (literary); rejoice; **die Lerche trällerte ~d** the lark sang joyfully

juchhe /jʊx'he:/, **juchhei** /jʊx'hai̯/, **juchheirassa[ssa]** /jʊx'hai̯rasa(sa)/ (veralt.), **juchheißa** /jʊx'hai̯sa/ *Interj.* (veralt.) hurrah

Juchten /'jʊxtn̩/ *der od. das;* **~s** 1) (Leder) Russia [leather] 2) (Duftstoff) Russian leather

juchzen /'jʊxtsn̩/ *itr. V.* (ugs.) shout with glee

Juchzer *der;* **~s, ~** (ugs.) shout of glee; **einen ~ ausstoßen** shout with glee

jucken /'jʊkn̩/
A *tr., itr. V.* 1) **mir juckt die Haut** I itch; **es juckt mir** *od.* **mich auf dem Kopf** my head itches; **es juckt mich am ganzen Körper** I itch all over; **es juckt mich hier** I've got an itch here; **wens juckt, der kratze sich** (fig.) anybody who does not like it should say something 2) (Juckreiz verursachen) irritate; **die Wolle juckt ihn** *od.* **ihm auf der Haut** the wool makes him itch; the wool irritates his skin; **ein ~der Hautausschlag** an itching rash 3) (bes. nordd. salopp) **lass ~!** get a move on! (coll.)
B *tr. V.* (reizen, verlocken) **es juckt mich, das zu tun** I am itching *or* dying to do it; **ihn juckt das Geld** he is tempted by the money; **das juckt mich nicht** (ugs.) I couldn't care less (coll.)
C *refl. V.* (ugs.: sich kratzen) scratch

Jucken *das;* **~s** itching; **ein ~ verspüren** feel an itch

Juck-: ~pulver *das* itching powder; **~reiz** *der* itch

Judäa /ju'dɛ:a/ *(das);* **~s** Jud[a]ea

Judaika /ju'da:ika/ *Pl.* Judaica

Judaist *der;* **~en, ~en, Judaistin** *die;* **~, ~nen** specialist in Jewish studies; (Student) student of Jewish studies

Judaistik *die;* **~:** Jewish studies *pl., no art.*

Judas /'ju:das/
A *(der);* **Judas'** Judas; **~ Ischariot** Judas Iscariot
B *der;* **~, ~se** (fig.) Judas

Jude /'ju:də/ *der;* **~n, ~n** Jew; **er ist ~:** he is a Jew; he is Jewish

jüdeln /'jy:dl̩n/ *itr. V.* speak half Yiddish

Juden-: ~frage *die* (ns. verhüll.) Jewish question; **~hass**, ***~haß** *der* anti-Semitism; hatred of [the] Jews; **~hetze** *die* Jew-baiting; **~pogrom** *der od. das* pogrom against the Jews; **~stern** *der* (ns.) Star of David

Judentum *das;* **~s** 1) (Volk) Jewry; Jews *pl.*; **das gesamte ~:** the whole of Jewry 2) (Kultur u. Religion) Judaism 3) (jüdisches Wesen) Jewishness

Juden-: ~verfolgung *die* persecution of [the] Jews; **~viertel** *das* Jewish quarter; (hist.) Jewry

Judikative /judika'ti:və/ *die;* **~, ~n** (Rechtsw., Politik) judiciary

Judikatur /judika'tu:ɐ/ *die;* **~, ~en** (Rechtsw.) judicature

Jüdin /'jy:dɪn/ *die;* **~, ~nen** Jewess; **sie ist ~:** she is Jewish *or* a Jewess

jüdisch *Adj.* Jewish; **~ fühlen/denken** feel/think like a Jew

judizieren /judi'tsi:rən/ *itr. V.* (Rechtsspr.) administer justice

Judo /'ju:do/ *das;* **~[s]** judo *no art.*

Judo·griff *der* judo throw; (Haltegriff) judo hold

Judoka /ju'do:ka/ *der;* **~[s], ~[s]** judoka; judoist

Jugend /'ju:gn̩t/ *die;* **~** 1) youth; **in ihrer ~:** in her youth; when she was young; **schon in früher ~:** at an early age; **seit früher ~, schon von ~ auf** from an early age; from his/her *etc.* youth 2) (Jugendliche) young people; **die ~ der Welt** the youth *or* the young people of the world; **die weibliche/männliche ~:** girls *pl.*/boys *pl.*; **er spielt in der ~** (Sport) he plays in the youth side *or* team; **die reifere ~** (scherzh.) the over-forties *pl.* 3) (Biol., Med.) immature stage [of development]

jugend-, Jugend-: ~alkoholismus *der* alcoholism among young people; **~alter** *das* adolescence; **~amt** *das* youth office *(agency responsible for education and welfare of young people)*; **~arbeit** *die* 1) (Bildung und Erziehung) youth work; 2) (Erwerbstätigkeit) youth employment; employment of young people; **~arbeitslosigkeit** *die* youth unemployment; **~arbeits·schutz** *der* protection of young people at work; **~arrest** *der* detention in a community home; **zu vier Wochen ~arrest verurteilt werden** be sentenced to four weeks in a community home; **~bewegt** *Adj.* (meist scherzh.) boyscoutish; **~bewegung** *die* (hist.) [German] Youth Movement; **~bild** *das:* **ein ~bild seines Vaters/seiner Mutter** a picture of his father/mother as a young man/woman; **~brigade** *die* (DDR) youth brigade; **~buch** *das* book for young people; **~erinnerung** *die* memory of one's youth; (Foto usw.) memento of one's youth; **~film** *der* film for young people; **~frei** *Adj.* ‹film, book, etc.› suitable for persons under 18; **nicht ~frei** ‹film› 18 certificate *pred.*; (scherzh.) ‹joke, story, etc.› not for young ears *pred.*; **~freund** *der,* **~freundin** *die* 1) friend of [the days of] one's youth; **er ist ein ~freund von ihr** he used to be a friend of hers when she was young; 2) (DDR) FDJ member; **~frische** *die* youthfulness; **~funk** *der* programmes *pl.* for young people; **~gefährdend** *Adj.* liable to have an undesirable influence on the moral development of young people *postpos.*; **~gericht** *das* juvenile court; **~gruppe** *die* youth group; **~heim** *das* youth centre; **~herberge** *die* youth hostel; **~klub** *der* youth club; **~kriminalität** *die* juvenile delinquency; **~kultur** *die* youth culture

jugendlich /'ju:gn̩tlɪç/
A *Adj.* 1) young ‹offender, customer, etc.›; **noch in ~em Alter sein** still be a youngster; still be young 2) (für Jugendliche charakteristisch) youthful; **in ~er Begeisterung** fired by the spirit of youth *or* by youthful enthusiasm 3) (jung wirkend) youthful ‹person, appearance›; **sie ist/wirkt noch sehr ~:** she still is/looks very young 4) (bes. Werbespr.) young ‹fashions, dress, hairstyle, etc.›
B *adv.* **sich ~ kleiden** dress young

Jugendliche /'ju:gn̩tlɪçə/ *der/die; adj. Dekl.* 1) young person; **die ~n** the young people

2 (Rechtsspr.) juvenile; young person; **zwei ~:** two juveniles; two young persons; **ein 16-jähriger ~r/eine 16-jährige ~:** a 16-year-old youth/girl

Jugendlichkeit *die* youth; (jugendliche Wirkung) youthfulness

Jugend-: ~liebe *die* love *or* sweetheart of one's youth; **seine/ihre [alte] ~liebe** the love *or* sweetheart of his/her youth; **~mannschaft** *die* (Sport) youth team *or* side; **~meister** *der,* **~meisterin** *die* youth champion; (Mannschaft) youth champions; **~meisterschaft** *die* youth championship; **~objekt** *das* (DDR) youth project; **~pfleger** *der,* **~pflegerin** *die* youth worker; **~psychologie** *die* psychology of adolescence; adolescent psychology *no art.;* **~recht** *das* laws *pl.* relating to young persons; **~schutz** *der* protection of young people; **~schutz·gesetz** *das* laws *pl.* protecting young people; **~sprache** *die* young people's language *no art.;* **~stil** *der* art nouveau; (in Deutschland) Jugendstil; **Möbel im ~stil** art nouveau/Jugendstil furniture; **~strafanstalt** *die* detention centre; **~strafe** *die* youth custody sentence; **sechs Monate ~strafe bekommen** get six months in a detention centre; **~sünde** *die,* **~torheit** *die* youthful folly; **~traum** *der* youthful dream; **es war sein ~traum gewesen, zu ...** when he was young, it had been his ambition to ...; **~verband** *der* youth organization; **~vorstellung** *die* performance for young people; **~weihe** *die* **1** (bes. DDR) *ceremony in which fourteen-year-olds are given adult social status;* **2** *Freechurch ceremony for child of primary school leaving age, in place of confirmation;* **~werk** *das* early *or* youthful work; (gesamtes) early *or* youthful works *pl.;* juvenilia *pl.;* **~zeit** *die* youth; younger days *pl.;* **~zeitschrift** *die* magazine for young people; **~zentrum** *das* youth centre

Jugo·slawe /jugo-/ *der* ▸❶ **S. 520** Yugoslav

Jugo·slawien *(das);* **~s** Yugoslavia

Jugo·slawin *die* ▸❶ **S. 520** Yugoslav; *s. auch* **-in**

jugo·slawisch *Adj.* ▸❶ **S. 520** Yugoslav[ian]

juhu *Interj.* **1** /ju'hu:/ (Ausruf des Jubels) yippee; hooray **2** /'ju'hu:/ (Zuruf) yoo-hoo

Juice /dʒu:s/ *der od. das;* **~, ~s** /'dʒu:sɪs/ (bes. österr., DDR: Fruchtsaft) (esp. citrus) [fruit] juice; (DDR: Gemüsesaft) vegetable juice

Julei /ju:'lai/ *der;* **~[s], ~s** ▸ **Juli**

Jul·fest /'ju:l-/ *das* Yuletide festival

Juli /'ju:li/ *der;* **~[s], ~s** ▸❶ **S. 165** July; *s. auch* **April**

Jumbo·jet, Jumbo-Jet /'jʊmbo-/ *der* jumbo jet

Jumelage /ʒym'la:ʒ/ *die;* **~, ~n zwischen Bonn und Oxford besteht eine ~:** Bonn and Oxford are twinned (Brit.) *or* (Amer.) are sister cities

Jumper /'dʒampɐ/ *der;* **~s, ~:** jumper (Brit.); pullover

jun. *Abk.* **= junior** Jr.

jung /jʊŋ/ *Adj.;* **jünger** /'jʏŋɐ/, **jüngst...** /'jʏŋst.../ **1** ▸❶ **S. 29** young; **in ~en Jahren** at an early age; **er ist ~ gestorben** he died young; **in seinen ~en Jahren** in the days of his youth; **~ an Jahren sein** be young [in years]; **der jüngere Bruder** the younger brother; **die jüngste Tochter** the youngest daughter; **der ~e Meier** (ugs.) Meier junior; **Sport erhält ~:** sport keeps you young **2** (neu) young ‹*state, country, firm, foliage*›; new ‹*project, undertaking, sport, marriage, etc.*›; **die Nacht ist noch ~:** the night is young; **der ~e Tag** (geh.) the new day **3** (letzt...) recent; **in jüngster Zeit** recently; lately; **ein Ereignis der jüngeren/jüngsten Geschichte** an event in recent/very recent history; **die jüngsten Geschehnisse** the latest *or* [most] recent happenings **4** (ugs. scherzh.) **er ist ganze 30 Jahre ~:** he's 30 years young **5** **der Jüngste Tag** doomsday; *s. auch* **Gericht¹ 4; jünger**

Jung-: ~akademiker *der,* **~akademikerin** *die* newly-qualified [university] graduate; **~arbeiter** *der,* **~arbeiterin** *die* young worker; **~bauer** *der;* **~~n, ~~n** young farmer; **~bäuerin** *die* young farmer's wife; **~brunnen** *der* Fountain of Youth; **das ist ein wahrer ~brunnen** (fig.) that's a real tonic; **~bürger** *der,* **~bürgerin** *die* (bes. österr.) first-time voter; new voter

Jungchen *das;* **~s, ~** (bes. ostd.) little boy; little lad; **mein ~:** my boy *or* lad

Jung·demokrat *der,* **Jung·demokratin** *die* Young Democrat

Junge¹ /'jʊŋə/ *der;* **~n, ~n** *od.* (ugs.) **Jung[en]s** **1** boy; (Lauf~, Lehr~) boy; lad; **Tag, alter ~!** (ugs.) hello, old pal! (coll.); **jmdn. wie einen dummen ~n behandeln** (ugs.) treat sb. like a child; **~, ~!** (ugs.) [boy], oh boy!; *s. auch* **schwer A 5** **2** (ugs.: beim Kartenspiel) jack; knave

Junge² *das; adj. Dekl.* **ein ~s** one of the young; **~ kriegen** give birth to young; **eine Löwin und ihr ~s** a lioness and her cub

Jüngelchen /'jʏŋlçən/ *das;* **~s, ~** (ugs. abwertend) young puppy *or* cub

jungen *itr. V.* give birth; produce young; ‹*cat*› have kittens; ‹*dog*› have pups

jungenhaft

A *Adj.* boyish

B *adv.* **seine Stimme klang ~ hell** his voice was high and clear like a boy's; **sie kleidet sich ~:** she dresses boyishly

Jungen-: ~klasse *die* boys' class; **wir waren eine reine ~klasse** our class was all boys; **~schule** *die* boy's school; school for boys; **~streich** *der* boyish prank

jünger /'jʏŋɐ/ *Adj.* youngish; **sie ist noch ~:** she is still quite young; *s. auch* **jung**

Jünger *der;* **~s, ~:** follower; disciple; (der Kunst, Literatur) devotee; **Jesus und seine ~:** Jesus and his disciples

Jüngere *der/die; adj. Dekl.* **die ~n unter Ihnen** the younger ones amongst you; **die ~n werden das nicht mehr wissen** younger people won't remember it; **Lucas Cranach der ~:** Lucas Cranach the younger

Jüngerin *die;* **~, ~nen** ▸ **Jünger**

Jungfer /'jʊŋfɐ/ *die;* **~, ~n** **1** (veralt.) (Fräulein) young lady; (als Anrede) Mistress **2** (abwertend: ältere ledige Frau) spinster; **eine alte ~:** an old maid

Jungfern-: ~fahrt *die* maiden voyage; **~flug** *der* maiden flight; **~häutchen** *das* hymen; **~kranz** *der* (veralt.) ▸ **Brautkranz;** **~rede** *die* maiden speech; **~zeugung** *die* (Biol.) parthenogenesis

Jung·frau *die* **1** virgin; **sie ist noch ~:** she is still a virgin; **die Heilige ~:** the Holy Virgin; **die ~ Maria** the Virgin Mary; **die eiserne ~:** the iron maiden; **zu etw. kommen wie die ~ zum Kind[e]** get sth. by sheer chance or luck; **wir sind zu den Büchern gekommen wie die ~ zum Kind[e]** we have no idea how the books got here **2** (Astrol.) Virgo; *s. auch* **Fisch 3** **3** (veralt.: junges Mädchen) young maid *or* maiden (arch.)

jung·fräulich /-frɔylɪç/ *Adj.* (geh., auch fig.) virgin; virginal ‹*innocence, appearance*›; **~ in die Ehe gehen** be a virgin bride; **ihr ~er Leib** (dichter.) her chaste body

Jungfräulichkeit *die* (geh.) virginity; (fig.: von Wald, Erde usw.) virgin state

Jung·geselle *der* bachelor; **~ bleiben** remain a bachelor

Jung·gesellen-: ~bude *die* (ugs.) bachelor pad (coll.); **~leben** *das* bachelor['s] life; **~wirtschaft** *die* (ugs., oft scherzh.) **ich habe die ~wirtschaft satt** I've had enough of looking after myself; **~wohnung** *die* bachelor flat (esp. Brit.); **~zeit** *die* bachelor days *pl.;* bachelorhood

Jung-: ~gesellin *die* bachelor girl; **sie ist ~gesellin geblieben** she never married; **~lehrer** *der,* **~lehrerin** *die* probationary teacher (teaching before second Staatsexamen)

Jüngling /'jʏŋlɪŋ/ *der;* **~s, ~e** (geh./spött.) youth; boy; **ein grüner** *od.* **unreifer ~** (spött.) a raw youth

Jünglings-: ~alter *das* (geh.) youth; **im zarten ~alter** as a tender youth; **~jahre** *Pl.* (geh.) years of one's youth; young years

Jung-: ~mädel *das* (ns.): *girl member of the Hitler Youth, aged 10-14;* **~mann** *der* (veralt.) young man; **~sozialist** *der,* **~sozialistin** *die* Young Socialist

jüngst /'jʏŋst/ *Adv.* (geh.) recently

jüngst... ▸ **jung**

Jüngste *der/die; adj. Dekl.* youngest [one]; **die ~n** the youngest ones

Jung-: ~steinzeit *die* Neolithic period; New Stone Age; **~tier** *das* young animal; **~trieb** *der* new growth; **~verheiratete** *der/die; adj. Dekl.,* **~vermählte** *der/die; adj. Dekl.* (geh.) young married man/woman; **die ~verheirateten** the newly-weds; **~volk** *das* **1** (veralt.) young folk; **2** (ns.) *10-14- year-old members of the Hitler Youth;* **~wähler** *der,* **~wählerin** *die* first-time voter; new voter; **~wald** *der* (Forstw.) young forest/wood

Juni /'ju:ni/ *der;* **~[s], ~s** ▸❶ **S. 165** June; *s. auch* **April**

Juni·käfer *der* summer chafer

junior /'ju:njɔr/ *indekl. Adj.; nach Personennamen* junior

Junior *der;* **~s, ~en** /-'nio:rən/ **1** (oft scherzh.) junior (joc.); **mit seinem ~:** with junior **2** (Kaufmannsspr.) junior partner **3** (Sport) junior

Junior·chef *der,* **Junior·chefin** *die* owner's *or* (coll.) boss's son/daughter

Junioren-: ~mannschaft *die* youth team; **~meister** *der,* **~meisterin** *die* junior champion; (Mannschaft) junior champions; **~meisterschaft** *die* junior championship

Juniorin *die;* **~, ~nen** junior partner

Junior-: ~partner *der,* **~partnerin** *die* (Kaufmannsspr.) junior partner; **~professor** *der,* **~professorin** *die* (Hochschulw.) Junior Professor; ≈ Assistant Professor (Amer.); **~professur** *die* (Hochschulw.) Junior Professorship; ≈ Assistant Professorship (Amer.)

Junker /'jʊŋkɐ/ *der;* **~s, ~** **1** (hist.) junker; young nobleman; (als Anrede) young sir **2** (oft abwertend: Landadliger) junker; squire

Junkertum *das;* **~s** (hist.) junkerdom; squirearchy

Junkie /dʒaŋki/ *der;* **~s, ~s** (Drogenjargon) junkie (sl.)

Junktim *das;* **~s, ~s** package [deal]; **zwischen den beiden Abkommen besteht ein ~:** the two agreements form one package

Juno /ju'no:/ *der;* **~[s], ~s** ▸ **Juni**

Junta /'xʊnta/ *die;* **~, Junten** junta

Jupiter¹ /'ju:pitɐ/ *der;* **~s** (Astron.), **Jupiter²** *(der)* **~s** (Myth.) Jupiter

Jupiter·mond *der* (Astron.) moon of Jupiter

Jupon /ʒy'põ:/ *der;* **~[s], ~s** (schweiz.) petticoat; slip

Jura¹ /'ju:ra/ *Pl.* law *sing.;* **~ studieren** read *or* study Law

Jura² *der;* **~s** (Geol.) Jurassic [period/system]

juridisch /ju'ri:dɪʃ/ *Adj.* (österr./veralt.) ▸ **juristisch**

Jurisdiktion /jurɪsdɪk'tsio:n/ *die;* **~, ~en** (Rechtsw., kath. Kirche) jurisdiction

Jurisprudenz /jurɪspru'dɛnts/ *die;* **~** (geh.) jurisprudence *no art.*

Jurist *der;* **~en, ~en** ▸❶ **S. 113** lawyer; jurist

Juristen·deutsch *das* (oft abwertend) legal jargon

Juristerei *die;* **~** (abwertend, oft scherzh.) law *no art.*

Juristin *die;* **~, ~nen** ▸❶ **S. 113** lawyer; jurist; *s. auch* **-in**

juristisch

A *Adj.* legal ‹*wrangle, term, training, career*›; **eine ~e Staatsprüfung** a state law examination; **die Juristische Fakultät** the Law Faculty

B *adv.* **~ denken** think in legal terms; **~ argumentieren** use legal arguments

Juror /'ju:rɔr/ *der;* **~s, ~en** /-'ro:ren/, **Jurorin** *die;* **~, ~nen** judge

Jurte /'jʊrtə/ *die;* **~, ~n** yurt

Jury /ʒy'ri:/ *die;* ~, ~**s** 1▸ (Preisrichter) panel [of judges]; jury 2▸ (Sachverständige) panel [of experts]

Jus¹ /ju:s/ *das;* ~ (österr., schweiz.) ▸**Jura¹**

Jus² /ʒy:/ *die od. das od. der;* ~ 1▸ (Fleischsaft) meat juices *pl.*; meat stock 2▸ (schweiz.) (Fruchtsaft) fruit juice; (Gemüsesaft) vegetable juice

Juso /'ju:zo/ *der;* ~**s,** ~**s** Young Socialist

just /jʊst/ *Adv.* (veralt., noch scherzh.) just; ~ **in diesem Augenblick** just at that moment; at that very moment; ~ **an jenem Tag** on that very day

justieren *tr. V.* adjust

Justierung *die;* ~, ~**en** adjustment

Justitia /jʊs'ti:tsi̯a/ *die;* ~: Justice *no art.;* (Statue) statue of Justice

justitiabel ▸**justiziabel**

Justitiar ▸**Justiziar**

Justiz /jʊs'ti:ts/ *die;* ~ 1▸ justice 2▸ (Behörden) judiciary; **ein Vertreter der** ~: a representative of justice *or* of the law

Justiz-: ~**beamte** *der,* ~**beamtin** *die* court official; ~**behörde** *die* judicial authority

justiziabel /jʊsti'tsi̯a:bl/ *Adj.* (geh.) justiciable

Justiziar /jʊsti'tsi̯a:ɐ/ *der;* ~**s,** ~**e, Justiziarin** *die;* ~, ~**nen** company lawyer

Justiz-: ~**irrtum** *der* miscarriage of justice; ~**minister** *der,* ~**ministerin** *die* Minister of Justice; ~**ministerium** *das* Ministry of Justice; ~**mord** *der* judicial murder; ~**vollzugsanstalt** *die* (Amtsspr.) penal institution (formal); prison; ~**wachtmeister** *der,* ~**wachtmeisterin** *die* court usher

Jute /'ju:tə/ *die;* ~: jute

Jute·sack *der* jute *or* gunny sack

Jütland /'jy:t-/ *(das);* ~**s** Jutland

Juwel¹ /ju've:l/ *das od. der;* ~**s,** ~**en** piece *or* item of jewellery; (Edelstein) jewel; gem; **Schmuck und** ~**en** jewellery

Juwel² *das;* ~**s,** ~**e** (Kostbarkeit) gem; **ein** ~ **gotischer Baukunst** a gem *or* jewel of Gothic architecture

Juwelen-: ~**händler** *der,* ~**händlerin** *die* dealer in precious stones; ~**raub** *der* jewel robbery *or* theft

Juwelier /juvə'li:ɐ̯/ *der;* ~**s,** ~**e, Juwelierin** *die;* ~, ~**nen** ▸❶ **S. 113** jeweller; *s. auch* **Bäcker**

Juwelier·geschäft *das* jeweller's shop

Jux /jʊks/ *der;* ~**es,** ~**e** (ugs.) joke; **aus** ~: as a joke; for fun; **sie machten sich** *(Dat.)* **einen** ~ **daraus, das zu tun** they did it as a joke *or* for a lark; **sich** *(Dat.)* **einen** ~ **mit jmdm. machen** play a [practical] joke on sb.; **aus [lauter]** ~ **und Tollerei** just for the fun *or* (coll.) hell of it

Juxta·position /'juksta-/ *die* (Sprachw.) juxtaposition

jwd /jɔtve:'de:/ *Adv.* (ugs. scherzh.) in *or* at the back of beyond; miles out

Kk

k, K /ka:/ *das;* ∼, ∼: k/K; *s. auch* **a, A**

K *Abk.* (Physik) = **Kelvin** K

Kabale /ka'ba:lə/ *die;* ∼, ∼**n** (veralt.) cabal

Kabarett /kaba'rɛt/ *das;* ∼**s**, ∼**s** *od.* ∼**e** 1 satirical cabaret [show]; satirical revue; **ein politisches** ∼: a satirical political revue 2 (Ensemble) cabaret act 3 (Speiseplatte) [revolvable] partitioned dish

Kabarettist *der;* ∼**en**, ∼**en**, **Kabarettistin** *die;* ∼, ∼**nen** revue performer

kabarettistisch *Adj.* [satirical] revue *attrib.*; ∼**e Szenen** scenes in the style of a [satirical] revue

Kabäuschen /ka'bɔysçən/ *das;* ∼**s**, ∼ (ugs.) (Zimmer) cubbyhole; (Häuschen) little hut

Kabbala /'kabala/ *die;* ∼: cabbala

Kabbalistik *die;* ∼: cabbalism *no art.*

Kabbelei *die;* ∼, ∼**en** squabble

kabbelig *Adj.* (Seemannsspr.) choppy

kabbeln /'kabl̩n/ *refl. V.* (ugs.) squabble, bicker (**mit** with)

Kabel /'ka:bl̩/ *das;* ∼**s**, ∼ 1 (elektrische Leitung) cable; (für kleineres Gerät) flex 2 (Stahltrosse) cable 3 (veralt.: Telegramm) cable

Kabel-: ∼**bericht** *der* (veralt.) cabled dispatch; ∼**fernsehen** *das* cable television

Kabeljau /'ka:bl̩jau/ *der;* ∼**s**, ∼**e** *od.* ∼**s** cod

kabel-, Kabel-: ∼**länge** *die* (Seew.) cable['s length]; ∼**leger** *der;* ∼∼**s**, ∼∼: cable ship; ∼**los** A *Adj.* wireless; B *adv.* ⟨*communicate*⟩ in wireless format; ⟨*install*⟩ without wires; ∼**mantel** *der* cable sheath

kabeln *tr., itr. V.* (veralt.) cable

Kabel-: ∼**rolle** *die* cable drum; ∼**schacht** *der* cable duct; (in der Straße) cable pit

Kabine /ka'bi:nə/ *die;* ∼, ∼**en** 1 (auf Schiffen, in Flugzeugen) cabin 2 (Umkleideraum, abgeteilter Raum) cubicle; **in die** ∼**n gehen** (Fußball) go back into the dressing rooms 3 (einer Seilbahn) [cable] car

Kabinen-: ∼**bahn** *die* cableway; ∼**roller** *der* bubble car

Kabinett /kabi'nɛt/ *das;* ∼**s**, ∼**e** 1 (Gesamtheit der Minister) Cabinet 2 (veralt.: Arbeitszimmer) cabinet (arch.) 3 (österr.: kleines Zimmer) small room with one window; boxroom (Brit.)

Kabinetts-: ∼**beschluss**, *∼**beschluß** *der* Cabinet decision; ∼**bildung** *die* formation of a/the Cabinet; ∼**justiz** *die: interference by ruler or government in the process of law;* ∼**krise** *die* Cabinet crisis; ∼**liste** *die* list of Cabinet members; ∼**sitzung** *die* Cabinet meeting

Kabinett-: ∼**stück[chen]** *das* tour de force; ∼**wein** *der* Kabinett wine

Kabis /'ka:bɪs/ *der;* ∼ (südd., schweiz.) cabbage

Kabrio /'ka:brio/ *das;* ∼**s**, ∼**s**, **Kabriolett** /kabrio'lɛt/ *das;* ∼**s**, ∼**s** 1 convertible 2 (veralt.: Kutsche) cabriolet

Kabuff /ka'bʊf/ *das;* ∼**s**, ∼**s** (ugs., oft abwertend) [poky little] cubbyhole

Kachel /'kaxl̩/ *die;* ∼, ∼**n** [glazed] tile; **etw. mit** ∼**n auslegen** tile sth.

Kachel·bad *das* tiled bathroom

kacheln *tr. V.* tile; **eine grün gekachelte Wand** a wall covered with green tiles

Kachel·ofen *der* tiled stove

kack·braun *Adj.* (derb) dirty brown; shit-coloured (coarse)

Kacke /'kakə/ *die;* ∼ (derb; auch fig.) shit (coarse); crap (coarse); **so eine** ∼**!** shit! (coarse); **dann/jetzt ist die** ∼ **am Dampfen** then/now there'll be hell to pay (coll.)

kacken /'kakn̩/ *itr. V.* (derb) shit (coarse); crap (coarse)

Kacker *der;* ∼**s**, ∼, **Kackerin** *die;* ∼, ∼**nen** (derb) shit (coarse)

Kadaver /ka'da:vɐ/ *der;* ∼**s**, ∼ (auch fig., abwertend) carcass

Kadaver·gehorsam *der* (abwertend) blind obedience

Kadenz /ka'dɛnts/ *die;* ∼, ∼**en** 1 (Musik) cadence; (solistische Paraphrasierung) cadenza 2 (Verslehre) cadence

Kader /'ka:dɐ/ *der od.* (schweiz.) *das;* ∼**s**, ∼ 1 cadre 2 (Sport) squad

kader-, Kader-: ∼**abteilung** *die* (DDR) personnel department; ∼**akte** *die* (DDR) personal file; ∼**arbeit** *die* (DDR) cadre work; ∼**armee** *die* cadre army; ∼**leiter** *der,* ∼**leiterin** *die* (DDR) [chief] personnel officer; ∼**partei** *die* cadre party; ∼**politisch** *Adj.* (DDR) ⟨*matters, problems, measures, etc.*⟩ relating to the political development and function of the cadres; ∼**schmiede** *die* (ugs.) training ground for new cadres

Kadett /ka'dɛt/ *der;* ∼**en**, ∼**en** 1 (hist., Milit.) cadet 2 (ugs.: Bursche) lad

Kadetten·anstalt *die* (hist.) cadet school

Kadi /'ka:di/ *der;* ∼**s**, ∼**s** 1 (islam. Richter) cadi 2 (ugs.: Gericht) **jmdn. vor den** ∼ **schleppen** haul sb. up before a judge *or* (Brit. coll.) the beak; **zum** ∼ **laufen** go to court

Kadmium /'katmiʊm/ *das;* ∼**s** (Chemie) cadmium

Käfer /'kɛ:fɐ/ *der;* ∼**s**, ∼ 1 (Insekt; auch ugs.: VW) beetle 2 (ugs.: junges Mädchen) lass; girl; **ein flotter** ∼: a nice bit of fluff (coll.)

Kaff /kaf/ *das;* ∼**s**, ∼**s** *od.* **Käffer** /'kɛfɐ/ (ugs. abwertend) dump (coll.); [dead-and-alive] hole (coll.)

Kaffee /'kafe *od.* (österr.) ka'fe:/ *der;* ∼**s**, ∼**s** 1 coffee; ∼ **kochen** make coffee; ∼ **mit Milch** white coffee (Brit.); coffee with milk/cream; **mir kam der** ∼ **hoch** (ugs.) I felt like puking (coarse); **dir haben sie wohl was in den** ∼ **getan?** (ugs.) have you gone soft in the head? (coll.); **das ist kalter** ∼ (ugs.) (ist längst bekannt) that's old hat (coll.); (ist Unsinn) that's a load of old rubbish (coll.) 2 (Nachmittags∼) afternoon coffee; ∼ **trinken** have afternoon coffee; **jmdn. zum** ∼ **einladen** invite sb. round for afternoon coffee

> **Kaffee**
>
> This refers not only to coffee as a drink but also to the small meal taken at about four in the afternoon, consisting of coffee and cakes or biscuits. It is often a social occasion, as it is common to invite family or friends for *Kaffee und Kuchen* (rather than for tea or dinner), especially on birthdays and other family occasions.

kaffee-, Kaffee-: ∼**automat** *der* coffee maker; ∼**bohne** *die* coffee bean; ∼**braun** *Adj.* coffee-coloured; ∼**durst** *der:* ∼**durst haben** feel like a [cup of] coffee; ∼**ersatz**, ∼**Ersatz** *der* coffee substitute; ∼**extrakt**, ∼**Extrakt** *der* coffee essence; ∼**fahrt** *die* 1 (Fahrt) trip [out] for afternoon coffee; 2 (Werbefahrt) *free trip for afternoon coffee during which goods are offered for sale to participants by sponsoring firm;* ∼**filter** *der* coffee filter; (Filtertüte) filter [paper]; ∼**geschirr** *das* coffee service *or* set (*including small plates*); ∼**haube** *die* ▸∼**wärmer**

Kaffee·haus *das* (bes. österr.) coffee house

Kaffee·haus-: ∼**atmosphäre** *die* coffee house atmosphere; ∼**musik** *die* (oft abwertend) palm-court music

Kaffee-: ∼**kanne** *die* coffee pot; ∼**kirsche** *die* coffee cherry; ∼**klatsch** *der* (ugs. scherzh.) get-together and a chat over coffee; coffee klatsch (Amer.); **heute ist bei ihr** ∼**klatsch** she's having people round today for coffee and a chat; ∼**kränzchen** *das* (veralt.) 1 (Zusammentreffen) coffee afternoon; 2 (Gruppe) coffee circle; ∼**löffel** *der* coffee spoon; ∼**maschine** *die* coffee maker; ∼**mühle** *die* coffee grinder; ∼**pause** *die* coffee break; ∼**pflanze** *die* coffee plant; ∼**plantage** *die* coffee plantation; ∼**pulver** *das* coffee powder; ∼**rösterei** *die* coffee-roasting establishment; ∼**sahne** *die* coffee cream; ∼**satz** *der* coffee grounds *pl.*; **sich aus dem** ∼**satz wahrsagen lassen** have one's fortune told from the coffee cup; ∼**schale** *die* (österr.) coffee cup; ∼**service** *das* coffee service *or* set; ∼**sieb** *das* coffee strainer; ∼**strauch** *der* coffee tree *or* plant; ∼**stube** *die* coffee shop; ∼**tafel** *die: table laid with coffee and cakes;* ∼**tante** *die* (ugs. scherzh.) coffee addict; ∼**tasse** *die* coffee cup; ∼**tisch** *der:* **sie saßen gerade am** ∼**tisch** they were [sitting] having coffee and cakes; **den** ∼**tisch decken** lay the table for coffee and cakes; ∼**trinker** *der,* ∼**trinkerin** *die* coffee drinker; ∼**wärmer** *der;* ∼∼**s**, ∼∼: coffee pot cosy *or* cover; ∼**wasser** *das* water for the coffee; **ich werde** ∼**wasser/das** ∼**wasser aufsetzen** I'll put on some water for coffee/the water for the coffee

Kaffer /'kafɐ/ *der;* ∼**s**, ∼**n** Xhosa

Kaffern·büffel *der;* ∼**s**, ∼: African *or* Cape buffalo

Käfig /'kɛ:fɪç/ *der;* ∼**s**, ∼**e** cage; **in einem goldenen** ∼ **sitzen** (fig.) be a bird in a gilded cage

Käfig-: ∼**haltung** *die* battery farming *no art.*; ∼**vogel** *der* cage bird

kafkaesk /kafka'ɛsk/ *Adj.* (geh.) Kafkaesque

Kaftan /'kaftan/ *der;* ∼**s**, ∼**e** caftan

kahl /ka:l/ *Adj.* 1 (ohne Haare) bald; (ohne Federn) bald; featherless; ∼ **werden** go bald; **jmdn.** ∼ **scheren** shave sb.'s hair off; shave sb.'s head; **ein Schaf** ∼ **scheren** shear a sheep completely bald; **sein** ∼ **geschorener Kopf** his shaven head 2 (ohne Grün, schmucklos) bare; **etw.** ∼ **fressen** strip sth. bare; **eine Fläche** ∼ **schlagen** clear-fell or clear-cut an area

Kahl·fraß *der* [complete] defoliation [by insects]

*__kahl|fressen__ ▸**kahl 2**

Kahlheit *die;* ∼ ▸**kahl 1, 2**: baldness; bareness

kahl-, Kahl-: ∼**hieb** *der* ▸**Kahlschlag 1**; ∼**kopf** *der* 1 bald head; 2 (ugs.: Person) baldhead; ∼**köpfig** *Adj.* bald[-headed]; ∼**köpfig werden** go bald; ∼**köpfigkeit** *die;*

~~: baldness; bald-headedness; ***~|scheren** ▸**kahl 1**; **~schlag** *der* [1] clear-felling *no indef. art.*; clear-cutting *no indef. art.*; [2] (Waldfläche) clear-felled area; [3] (fig.) (Beseitigung) clearance; (Kürzung) massive cutbacks *pl.*; ***~|schlagen** ▸**kahl 2**

Kahm·haut /ˈka:m-/ *die* (Biol.) film of mould

Kahn /ka:n/ *der;* **~[e]s, Kähne** /ˈkɛ:nə/ [1] (Ruder~) rowing boat; (Stech~) punt; **~ fahren** go rowing/punting [2] (Lastschiff) barge [3] (ugs., oft abwertend: Schiff) tub [4] *Pl.* (ugs.: ausgetretene Schuhe) old, worn-out shoes [5] (Soldatenspr.: Gefängnis) glasshouse (Mil. sl.) [6] (ugs. scherzh.: Bett) bed; **in den ~ gehen** hit the hay (coll.)

Kahn·fahrt *die* trip in a rowing boat/punt

Kai /kai/ *der;* **~s, ~s** quay

Kai·anlage *die* quays *pl.*

Kaiman /ˈkaiman/ *der;* **~s, ~e** (Zool.) cayman

Kai·mauer *die* quay wall

Kains·mal /ˈkains-/ *das; Pl.* **~e, Kains·zeichen** *das* mark of Cain

Kairo /ˈkairo/ *(das);* **~s** ▸ⓘ **S. 675** Cairo

Kaiser-: ~adler *der* imperial eagle; **~haus** *das* imperial house *or* family

Kaiserin *die;* **~, ~nen** empress

Kaiser-: ~krone *die* [1] imperial crown; [2] (Zierpflanze) crown imperial; **~krönung** *die* imperial coronation

kaiserlich

[A] *Adj.* imperial; **der ~e Hof** the imperial court

[B] *adv.* **~ gesinnt sein** be loyal to the emperor; (monarchistisch sein) be monarchistic *or* imperialistic

kaiserlich-königlich *Adj.* imperial and royal; **die ~e Monarchie** the Austro-Hungarian monarchy

Kaiser: ~pinguin *der* emperor penguin; **~reich** *das* empire; **~schmarren** *der* (österr., südd.): *pancake pulled to pieces and sprinkled with powdered sugar and raisins;* **~schnitt** *der* Caesarean section

Kaisertum *das;* **~s** empire

Kaiser·wetter *das* (scherzh.) glorious, sunny weather (*for an event*)

Kajak /ˈka:jak/ *der;* **~s, ~s** kayak

Kajüt·boot *das* cabin cruiser

Kajüte /kaˈjy:tə/ *die;* **~, ~n** (Seemannsspr.) cabin

Kakadu /ˈkakadu/ *der;* **~s, ~s** cockatoo

Kakao /kaˈkau/ *der;* **~s, ~s** cocoa; **jmdn./etw. durch den ~ ziehen** (ugs.) make fun of sb./sth.; take the mickey out of sb./sth. (Brit. sl.)

Kakao-: ~baum *der* cacao tree; **~bohne** *die* cocoa bean; **~pulver** *das* cocoa powder

kakeln /ˈka:kl̩n/ *itr. V.* (nordd.) [1] (gackern) cluck [2] (schwatzen) chat; natter (sl.)

Kakerlak /ˈka:kɐlak/ *der;* **~s** *od.* **~en, ~en** cockroach; black beetle

kakophon /kakoˈfo:n/, **kakophonisch**

[A] *Adj.* cacophonous

[B] *adv.* cacophonously; creating a cacophony

Kakophonie /kakofoˈni:/ *die;* **~, ~n** cacophony

Kaktee /kakˈte:ə/ *die;* **~, ~n, Kaktus** /ˈkaktʊs/ *der;* **~, ~n** cactus

Kalamität /kalamiˈtɛ:t/ *die;* **~, ~en** calamity; **sich in einer ~/in ~en befinden** be in [serious] difficulties *pl.*

Kalander /kaˈlandɐ/ *der;* **~s, ~** (Technik) calender

Kalauer /ˈka:lauɐ/ *der;* **~s, ~:** laboured *or* (coll.) corny joke; (Wortspiel) atrocious *or* (coll.) corny pun

kalauern *itr. V.* tell laboured *or* (coll.) corny jokes; (mit Wortspielen) make atrocious *or* (coll.) corny puns

Kalb /kalp/ *das;* **~[e]s, Kälber** /ˈkɛlbɐ/ [1] calf; (Hirschkalb) fawn; **glotzen** *od.* **Augen machen wie ein [ab]gestochenes ~** (ugs.) look pop-eyed; **das Goldene ~ anbeten/um das Goldene ~ tanzen** (geh.) worship the golden calf [2] (ugs.: ~fleisch) veal [3] (dummer, alberner Mensch) [silly] idiot

Kälbchen /ˈkɛlpçən/ *das;* **~s, ~:** little calf; (Hirsch~) little fawn

kalben *itr. V.* [1] (ein Kalb gebären) calve [2] (Geogr.) ‹*glacier, iceberg*› calve

Kalberei *die;* **~, ~en** (ugs.) messing *or* fooling about *or* around *no pl.*

kalbern /ˈkalbɐn/ *itr. V.* (ugs.) mess *or* fool about *or* around

Kalb-: ~fell *das* ▸**Kalbsfell**; **~fleisch** *das* veal; **~leder** *das* ▸**Kalbsleder**

Kalbs-: ~braten *der* (Kochk.) roast veal *no indef. art.*; (Gericht) roast of veal; **~brust** *die* breast of veal; **~fell** *das* calfskin; **~frikassee** *das* (Kochk.) fricassee of veal; **~hachse,** (südd.:) **~haxe** *die* (Kochk.) knuckle of veal; **~kotelett** *das* veal cutlet (*with bone*); **~leder** *das* calfskin; calf leather; **~nieren·braten** *der* (Kochk.) loin of veal with kidneys; **~schnitzel** *das* veal escalope

Kaldaune /kalˈdaunə/ *die;* **~, ~n** entrails *pl.*

Kalebasse /kaleˈbasə/ *die;* **~, ~n** calabash

Kaleidoskop /kalaidoˈsko:p/ *das;* **~s, ~e** (auch fig.) kaleidoscope

kalendarisch /kalɛnˈda:rɪʃ/ *Adj.* ‹*age etc.*› according to the calendar; **der ~e Beginn einer Jahreszeit** the beginning of a season according to the calendar

Kalender /kaˈlɛndɐ/ *der;* **~s, ~** [1] calendar; **sich** (*Dat.*) **etw./einen Tag im ~ [rot] anstreichen** (oft iron.) mark sth. in red on the calendar/mark a day as a red-letter day; **der julianische ~:** the Julian calendar; *s. auch* **gregorianisch** [2] (Taschen~) diary

Kalender-: ~blatt *das* calendar sheet; **~geschichte** *die: edifying story or fable published on a calendar;* **~jahr** *das* calendar year; **~uhr** *die* calendar watch

Kalesche /kaˈlɛʃə/ *die;* **~, ~n** (hist.) barouche

Kalfaktor /kalˈfaktɔr/ *der;* **~s, ~en** (veralt., oft abwertend) [1] general factotum; general dogsbody (coll. derog.) [2] (Strafgefangener) trusty

kalfatern /kalˈfa:tɐn/ *tr., itr. V.* (Seemannsspr.) caulk

Kali /ˈka:li/ *das;* **~s, ~s** potash

Kaliber /kaˈli:bɐ/ *das;* **~s, ~** [1] (Technik, Waffenkunde) calibre [2] (ugs., oft abwertend) sort; kind; **älteren/jüngeren ~s sein** be older/younger

Kali·dünger *der* potash fertilizer

Kalif /kaˈli:f/ *der;* **~en, ~en** (hist.) caliph

Kalifat /kaliˈfa:t/ *das;* **~[e]s, ~e** (hist.) caliphate

Kalifornien /kaliˈfɔrni̯ən/ *(das);* **~s** California

kalifornisch *Adj.* Californian

Kaliko /ˈkaliko/ *der;* **~s, ~s** calico

Kali-: ~lauge *die* caustic potash solution; **~salpeter** *der* saltpetre; potassium nitrate; **~salz** *das* potassium *or* potash salt

Kalium /ˈka:li̯ʊm/ (Chemie) *das;* **~s** potassium

Kali·werk *das* potash works *sing. or. pl.*

Kalk /kalk/ *der;* **~[e]s, ~e** [1] (Kalziumkarbonat) calcium carbonate [2] (Baustoff) lime; quicklime; burnt lime; **die Wände mit ~ streichen** whitewash *or* limewash the walls; **bei ihm rieselt schon der ~** (salopp) he's going a bit senile [3] (Knochensubstanz) calcium

Kalk-: ~ablagerung *die* deposit of calcium carbonate; **~boden** *der* limy soil; lime soil; **~bruch** *der* ▸**~steinbruch**

kalken /ˈkalkn̩/ *tr. V.* [1] (tünchen) whitewash [2] (Kalk zuführen) lime

kalk-, Kalk-: ~erde *die* [1] (gebrannter ~) lime; quicklime; burnt lime; [2] (~haltige Erde) lime *or* limy soil; **~grube** *die* lime pit; **~haltig** *Adj.* (bes. Geol., Mineral.) limy ‹*soil*›; calcareous ‹*soil, rock*› (Geol., Min.); ‹*water*› containing calcium carbonate; **das Wasser ist sehr ~haltig** the water is high in calcium carbonate; **~mangel** *der* [1] (Mangel an Kalzium) calcium deficiency; [2] (Mangel an ~) deficiency of lime; **~milch** *die* limewash; **~sandstein** *der* sand-lime brick; **~spat** *der* calcite; **~stein** *der* limestone; **~steinbruch** *der* limestone quarry

Kalkül[1] /kalˈky:l/ *das od. der;* **~s, ~e** (geh.) calculation

Kalkül[2] *der;* **~s, ~e** (Math.) calculus

Kalkulation /kalkulaˈtsi̯o:n/ *die;* **~, ~en** (auch Wirtsch.) calculation; **die ~ der Herstellungskosten eines Buches** the costing of a book; **in der ~ liegt ein Fehler** there's an error in the costings *pl.*; **nach meiner ~:** according to my calculations *pl.*

Kalkulator /kalkuˈla:tɔr/ *der;* **~s, ~en** /-laˈto:rən/, **Kalkulatorin** *die;* **~, ~nen** cost accountant

kalkulieren

[A] *tr. V.* [1] (Kaufmannsspr.: veranschlagen) calculate ‹*cost, price*›; cost ‹*product, article*›; **die Herstellungskosten eines Buches ~:** cost a book [2] (abschätzen) calculate [3] (ugs.: annehmen) reckon

[B] *itr. V.* calculate; **falsch ~:** miscalculate

Kalkutta /kalˈkʊta/ *(das);* **~s** ▸ⓘ **S. 675** Calcutta

kalk·weiß *Adj.* [1] (weiß wie Kalk) chalk-white [2] (sehr bleich) deathly pale; chalky white; **~ sein** be as white as a sheet

Kalligraphie /kaligraˈfi:/ *die;* **~:** calligraphy *no art.*

Kalme /ˈkalmə/ *die;* **~, ~n** (Met.) calm

Kalmen·gürtel *der* (Met.) calm belt

Kalorie /kaloˈri:/ *die;* **~, ~n** calorie

kalorien-, Kalorien-: ~arm [A] *Adj.* low-calorie *attrib.*; **~arm sein** be low in calories; [B] *adv.* **~arm kochen/essen** cook low-calorie meals/eat low-calorie foods; **~bewusst,** ***~bewußt** [A] *Adj.* calorie-conscious; [B] *adv.* in a calorie-conscious way; **~bombe** *die* (ugs.) mountain of calories (coll.); **~gehalt** *der* calorie content; **~reich** [A] *Adj.* high-calorie *attrib.*; **~reich sein** be high in calories; [B] *adv.* **~reich kochen/essen** cook high-calorie meals/eat high-calorie foods

Kalori·meter /kalori-/ *das;* **~s, ~** (Physik) calorimeter

kalt /kalt/; **kälter** /ˈkɛltɐ/, **kältest...** /ˈkɛltəst.../

[A] *Adj.* cold; chilly, frosty ‹*atmosphere, smile*›; **ein ~es Buffet** a cold buffet; **mir ist/wird ~:** I am/am getting cold; **das Essen wird ~:** the food is getting cold; **im Kalten sitzen** sit in the cold; **~ und berechnend sein** be cold and calculating; **es packte uns das ~e Grausen/Entsetzen** our blood ran cold; **jmdm. die ~e Schulter zeigen** give sb. the cold shoulder; cold-shoulder sb.; **jmdn. ~ lassen** (ugs.) leave sb. unmoved; (nicht interessieren) leave sb. cold (coll.); **~ bleiben** remain unmoved

[B] *adv.* [1] **~ duschen** have *or* take a cold shower; **~ schlafen** sleep in a cold room; **Getränke/Sekt ~ stellen** cool drinks/chill champagne; **~ Zigarre/Pfeife rauchen** (ugs.) have an unlit cigar/pipe in one's mouth; **jmdn. ~ erwischen** (bes. Sportjargon) catch sb. on the hop [2] (nüchtern) coldly [3] (abweisend, unfreundlich) coldly; frostily; **jmdn. ~ anblicken** look at sb. coldly; **~ lächeln** smile coldly *or* frostily; **etw. ~ lächelnd tun** (fig. ugs. abwertend) take callous pleasure in doing sth. [4] **mich überlief** *od.* **durchrieselte es ~:** cold shivers ran down my spine

kalt-, Kalt-: *~|bleiben ▸**kalt A**; **~blut** *das* heavy draught horse; **~blüter** /-bly:tɐ/ *der;* **~~s, ~~** (Zool.) cold-blooded animal; **~blütig** [A] *Adj.* [1] (beherrscht) cool-headed; [2] (abwertend: skrupellos) cold-blooded; [3] (Zool.) cold-blooded; [B] *adv.* [1] (beherrscht) coolly; calmly; **einer Gefahr ~blütig ins Auge sehen** face a danger coolly *or* calmly; [2] (abwertend: skrupellos) cold-bloodedly; **~blütigkeit** *die;* **~~** ▸▸**blütig 1, 2**: cool-headedness; cold-bloodedness

Kälte /ˈkɛltə/ *die;* **~** [1] cold; **10 Grad ~:** 10 degrees of frost; 10 degrees below freezing; **vor ~ zittern** *od.* (ugs.) **bibbern** shiver with cold; **bei dieser ~:** in this cold; when it's as cold as this [2] (Teilnahmslosigkeit, Unbehaglichkeit) coldness

kälte-, Kälte-: ~beständig *Adj.* cold-resistant; **~beständig sein** be resistant to cold; **~ein·bruch** *der* (Met.) sudden onset of cold weather; **~empfindlich** *Adj.* sensitive to cold *pred.*; **~empfindliche Pflanzen** plants which are sensitive to cold; **~gefühl** *das* sensation *or* feeling of cold; chill; **~grad** *das* (ugs.) degree of frost; **~maschine** *die* (Technik) refrigerating machine; **~pol** *der* cold pole

kälter ▸ **kalt**

kältest... ▸ **kalt**

Kälte-: ~sturz *der* (Met.) sudden drop in temperature; **~technik** *die* refrigeration engineering *no art.*; **~tod** *der*: **den ~tod erleiden** freeze to death; die of cold; **~welle** *die* cold wave *or* spell

kalt-, Kalt-: ~front *die* (Met.) cold front; **~gepresst**, ***~gepreßt** *Adj.* cold-pressed; **~haus** *das* (Gartenbau) cold house; **~herzig** *Adj.* cold-hearted; **~lächelnd** ▸ **kalt B3**; ***~|lassen** ▸ **kalt A**; **~leim** *der* [cold] woodworking adhesive; **~luft** *die* (Met.) cold air; **polare ~luft** cold polar air; **~|machen** *tr. V.* (salopp) **jmdn. ~machen** do sb. in (sl.); **~mamsell** *die* ▸ⓘ **S. 113** girl/woman who prepares and serves cold dishes in a restaurant, hotel, etc.; **~miete** *die* rent exclusive of heating; **~schale** *die: cold sweet soup made with fruit, beer, wine, or milk;* **~schnäuzig** /-ʃnɔytsɪç/ (ugs.) **A** *Adj.* cold and insensitive; (frech) insolent; **B** *adv.* coldly and insensitively; (frech) insolently; **~schnäuzigkeit** *die*; **~~** (ugs.) coldness and insensitivity; (Frechheit) insolence; **~start** *der* (Kfz-W.) cold start; **beim ~start** when starting from cold; **~|stellen** *tr. V.* (ugs.) **jmdn. ~stellen** put sb. out of the way (coll. joc.); **den Mittelstürmer ~stellen** cut the centre forward out of the game

Kalvarien·berg /kal'va:ri̯ən-/ *der:* [Mount] Calvary

Kalvinismus /kalvi'nɪsmʊs/ *der;* **~:** Calvinism *no art.*

Kalvinist *der;* **~en, ~en, Kalvinistin** *die;* **~, ~nen** Calvinist

kalvinistisch *Adj.* Calvinist

Kalzium /'kaltsi̯ʊm/ *das;* **~s** calcium

kam /ka:m/ *1. u. 3. Pers. Prät. v.* **kommen**

Kamarilla /kama'rɪlja/ *die;* **~, Kamarillen** (geh.) camarilla

Kambodscha /kam'bɔdʒa/ *(das);* **~s** Cambodia

Kambodschaner /kambo'dʒa:nɐ/ *der;* **~s, ~, Kambodschanerin** *die;* **~, ~nen** Cambodian

käme /'kɛ:mə/ *1. u. 3. Pers. Konjunktiv II v.* **kommen**

Kamel /ka'me:l/ *das;* **~s, ~e** **1** camel; **eher geht ein ~ durch ein Nadelöhr, als dass das geschieht** that will never happen in a million years **2** (salopp: dummer Mensch) clot (Brit. coll.); twit (Brit. coll.); fathead

Kamel-: ~haar *das* camel['s] hair; **~haar·mantel** *der* camel-hair coat

Kamelie /ka'me:li̯ə/ *die;* **~, ~n** camellia

Kamellen /ka'mɛlən/ *Pl.* (ugs.) *in* **das sind alte** *od.* **olle ~:** that's old hat (coll.); **es wurden nur alte** *od.* **olle ~ aufgewärmt** the same old stuff was dished up (coll.)

Kamel·treiber *der* **1** camel driver **2** (salopp abwertend) smelly Arab (sl. derog.)

Kamera /'kaməra/ *die;* **~, ~s** camera; **vor der ~ stehen** appear in front of the cameras *pl.*

Kamera·assistent *der,* **Kamera·assistentin** *die* camera assistant; assistant cameraman

Kamerad /kamə'ra:t/ *der;* **~en, ~en** (Lebens~, Gefährte) companion; (Freund) friend; (Mitschüler) mate; friend; (Soldat) comrade; (Sport) teammate

Kameraderie /kamərada'ri:/ *die;* **~** (meist abwertend) loyalty to a/the clique; **falsch verstandene ~:** mistaken sense of comradeship and loyalty

Kameradin *die;* **~, ~nen** ▸ **Kamerad**

Kameradschaft *die;* **~, ~en** **1** comradeship; **die ~ zwischen ihnen** the sense of comradeship between them **2** (Gruppe) association

kameradschaftlich
A *Adj.* comradely
B *adv.* in a comradely way

Kameradschaftlichkeit *die;* **~:** comradeliness

Kameradschafts-: ~abend *der* social evening *(of youth group, ex-servicemen's association, etc.)*; **~ehe** *die: marriage based on feelings of companionship;* **~geist** *der* spirit of comradeship

Kamera-: ~frau *die* ▸ⓘ **S. 113** camerawoman; **~führung** *die* (Film) camerawork *no indef. art.*; **~mann** *der Pl.* **~männer** *od.* **~leute** ▸ⓘ **S. 113** cameraman; **~recorder, ~rekorder** *der* camcorder; **~team** *das* camera crew

Kamerun /'kaməru:n/ *(das);* **~s** Cameroon; the Cameroons *pl.*

Kameruner *der;* **~s, ~, Kamerunerin** *die;* **~, ~nen** native of Cameroon *or* the Cameroons; Cameroonian

Kamille /ka'mɪlə/ *die;* **~, ~n** camomile

Kamillen·tee *der* camomile tea

Kamin /ka'mi:n/ *der, schweiz.: das;* **~s, ~e** **1** (Feuerstelle) fireplace; **sie saßen am ~:** they sat by the hearth *or* the fireside **2** (bes. südd.: Schornstein) chimney; **er kann/muss das in den ~ schreiben** (ugs.) he can/will have to kiss goodbye to that (coll.) **3** (Bergsteigen: Felsspalt) chimney

Kamin-: ~feger *der,* **~fegerin** *die;* **~~, ~~nen** ▸ⓘ **S. 113** (bes. südd.) ▸ **Schornsteinfeger**; **~feuer** *das* [open] fire; **~kehrer** *der;* **~~s, ~~, ~kehrerin** *die;* **~~, ~~nen** (bes. südd.) ▸ **Schornsteinfeger**; **~sims** *der* mantelpiece; mantelshelf

Kamm /kam/ *der;* **~[e]s, Kämme** /'kɛmə/ **1** comb; **alle/alles über einen ~ scheren** lump everyone/everything together **2** (bei Hühnern usw.) comb; (bei Reptilien, Amphibien) crest; **ihm schwillt der ~** (ugs.) his hackles rise; (er wird überheblich) he gets cocky and big-headed (coll.) **3** (Gebirgs~) ridge; crest **4** (Wellen~) crest **5** (Rinder~) neck; (Schweine~) spare rib **6** (beim Pferd) crest

kämmen /'kɛmən/ *tr. V.* **1** comb; **jmdm./sich die Haare ~, jmdn./sich ~:** comb sb.'s/one's hair; **jmdm. einen Scheitel/Pony ~:** put a parting in sb.'s hair/comb sb.'s hair into a fringe **2** (Textilind.) comb

Kammer /'kamɐ/ *die;* **~, ~n** **1** storeroom; (veralt.: Schlafraum) chamber **2** (Biol., Med., Technik, Waffenkunde) chamber **3** (Parl.) chamber; House; **die erste/zweite ~:** the upper/lower chamber *or* House **4** (Rechtsw.) court *(dealing with a particular branch of judicial business)* **5** (gewerbliche Vereinigung) professional association **6** (Milit.) stores *pl.*

Kämmerchen /'kɛmɐçən/ *das;* **~s, ~:** small room; (Abstellkammer) [small] storeroom

Kammer·chor *der* chamber choir

Kammer·diener *der* (veralt.) valet

Kämmerer /'kɛmərɐ/ *der;* **~s, ~** (veralt.) [town/city] treasurer

Kammer-: ~frau *die* (veralt.) lady's maid; **die ~frau der Fürstin** the princess's maid; **~gericht** *das* (hist.) Supreme Court; **~herr** *der* (hist.) chamberlain

Kämmerin /'kɛmərɪn/ *die;* **~, ~nen** ▸ **Kämmerer**

Kammer-: ~jäger *der,* **~jägerin** *die* pest controller; **~konzert** *das* chamber concert

Kämmerlein /'kɛmɐlai̯n/ *das;* **~s, ~** (oft scherzh.) *in* **ich muss mal im stillen ~ darüber nachdenken** I must [go away by myself and] think about that in peace and quiet; **das hat er sich im stillen ~ ausgedacht** he thought that up all by himself without anyone realizing

Kammer-: ~musik *die* chamber music; **~orchester** *das* chamber orchestra; **~sänger** *der,* **~sängerin** *die: title awarded to singer of outstanding merit;* **~spiel** *das* **1** (kleines Theaterstück) intimate chamber-drama; **2** *Pl.* (kleines Theater) studio theatre *sing.*; **~ton** *der; Pl.* **~töne** (Musik) standard pitch; **~zofe** *die* (veralt.) lady's maid

Kamm-: ~garn *das* worsted; **~griff** *der* (Turnen) undergrasp; **~muschel** *die* scallop

***Kammuschel** ▸ **Kammmuschel**

Kamm·wolle *die* (Textilw.) worsted

Kamp /kamp/ *der;* **~s, Kämpe** /'kɛmpə/ (Forstw.) [small] tree nursery

Kampagne /kam'panjə/ *die;* **~, ~n** **1** (größere Aktion) campaign (**für** for, on behalf of; **gegen** against) **2** (bestimmte Zeitspanne) busy season **3** (Archäol.) phase *(of an excavation)*

Kampanile /kampa'ni:lə/ *der;* **~, ~:** campanile

Kämpe /'kɛmpə/ *der;* **~n, ~n** (veralt.) [brave] warrior *or* fighter; **ein alter ~** (scherzh.) an old campaigner; a seasoned veteran

Kampf /kampf/ *der;* **~[e]s, Kämpfe** **1** (militärisch) battle (**um** for); **nach wochenlangen erbitterten Kämpfen** after weeks of bitter fighting; **den ~ einstellen** stop fighting; **er ist im ~ gefallen** he fell *or* was killed in action *or* combat **2** (zwischen persönlichen Gegnern) fight; (fig.) struggle; **ein ~ aller gegen alle** a free-for-all; **ein ~ Mann gegen Mann** a hand-to-hand fight; **ein ~ auf Leben und Tod** a fight to the death; **den ~ aufgeben** *od.* **verloren geben** give up the fight; **aus einem ~ als Sieger/Verlierer hervorgehen** emerge as victor *or* winner/loser from a fight; **sich dem ~ stellen** be prepared to fight **3** (Wett~) contest; (Boxen) contest; fight; bout; **sich einen spannenden ~ liefern** produce an exciting contest **4** (Einsatz aller Mittel) struggle, fight (**um, für** for; **gegen** against); **der ~ ums Dasein** the struggle for existence; **jmdm./einer Sache den ~ ansagen** declare war on sb./sth.; **~ dem Faschismus/Atomtod!** fight fascism/the nuclear menace! **5** (heftig ausgetragene Kontroverse) battle; **der ~ zwischen den Geschlechtern** the battle of the sexes; **auf in den ~!** (scherzh.) into the fray! **6** (innerer Zwiespalt) **ein ~ mit sich selbst** a struggle *or* battle with oneself

kampf-, Kampf-: ~abschnitt *der* (Milit.) combat *or* battle sector; **~abstimmung** *die* (Politik) crucial vote; **~ansage** *die* declaration of war; **~anzug** *der* combat uniform; **~bahn** *die* (für Gladiatoren) arena; (für Stiere) ring; (veralt.: Sportstadion) stadium; **~bereit** *Adj.* willing to fight *postpos.*; (fertig) ready to fight *postpos.*; ‹*army*› ready for battle; ‹*troops*› ready for battle *or* action; **~bereitschaft** *die* willingness to fight; (eines Heeres) readiness for battle; (einer Truppe) readiness for battle *or* action; **~boot** *das* fighting ship; warship; **~bündnis** *das* alliance; **~einheit** *die* (Milit.) combat unit

kämpfen /'kɛmpfn̩/
A *itr. V.* **1** fight; **mit jmdm. ~:** fight [with] sb.; **gegen jmdn. ~:** fight [against] sb.; **um die Vorherrschaft/eine Stadt/Frau ~:** fight for supremacy/a town/over a woman; **um einen Titel ~:** compete for a title; **um seine Existenz ~:** fight *or* struggle for one's existence; **für jmdn./etw. ~:** fight for sb./sth.; **mit den Tränen ~** (fig.) fight back one's tears; **mit dem Schlaf ~** (fig.) struggle to keep awake; **mit dem Tod ~** (fig.) fight for one's life *or* to stay alive; **mit etw. zu ~ haben** (fig.) have to contend with sth.; **[lange] mit sich** *(Dat.)* **~:** have a [long] struggle with oneself **2** (Sport: sich messen) ‹*team*› play; ‹*wrestler, boxer*› fight; **gegen jmdn. ~:** play/fight sb.
B *refl. V.* (auch fig.) fight one's way
C *tr. V.* **einen Kampf ~** (auch fig.) fight a battle

Kampfer /'kampfɐ/ *der;* **~s** camphor

Kämpfer[1] /'kɛmpfɐ/ *der;* **~s, ~:** fighter

Kämpfer[2] *der;* **~s, ~** **1** (Archit.) impost **2** (Bauw.) transom

Kämpferin *die;* **~, ~nen** fighter

kämpferisch
A *Adj.* **1** fighting ‹*spirit, mood*›; ‹*person*› full of fighting spirit; **eine ~e Natur sein** be full of fighting spirit **2** (Sport: mit großem Einsatz) spirited
B *adv.* **1** (voller Kampfgeist) in a fighting spirit

k

2 (Sport: mit großem Einsatz) spiritedly

Kämpfer·natur *die* fighter

kampf·erprobt *Adj.* battle-tried; battle-tested ‹*equipment*›

Kampfes·lust *die* eagerness for the fray; **in wilder ~:** lusting for battle

kampf-, Kampf-: ~fähig *Adj.* ‹*troops*› fit for action *or* battle; ‹*boxer etc.*› fit to fight; **~fahrzeug** *das* (Milit.) combat vehicle; **~flieger** *der* (Milit.) bomber pilot; **~flugzeug** *das* bomber; **~gas** *das* war gas; **~gebiet** *das* battle area; combat zone; **~gefährte** *der*, **~gefährtin** *die* (im militärischen ~) comrade in arms; (im politischen ~) comrade in the struggle; **~geist** *der* fighting spirit; **~gemeinschaft** *die* action group; **~gericht** *das* (Sport) [panel of] judges *pl.*; **~geschehen** *das* fighting *no indef. art.*; **~gruppe** *die* (Milit.) task force; **~hahn** *der*; *Pl.* **~hähne** 1 (Hahn für Kämpfe) fighting cock; 2 (ugs.) fighter; brawler; **~handlungen** *Pl.* fighting *sing.*; **die ~handlungen einstellen** cease hostilities *or* fighting; **~hubschrauber** *der* (Milit.) helicopter gunship; **~kraft** *die* fighting power *or* strength; (einer Mannschaft) strength; **~lied** *das* battle song; (einer Bewegung) battle anthem; **~los** A *Adj.* peaceful; **an eine ~lose Übergabe der Stadt war nicht zu denken** to hand over the town without a fight was unthinkable; B *adv.* without a fight; **~lustig** A *Adj.* belligerent; B *adv.* belligerently; **~maschine** *die* (ugs., oft abwertend) fighting machine; **~maßnahme** *die* active measure; **~maßnahmen ergreifen** take action *sing.*; **~moral** *die* morale; **~panzer** *der* [battle] tank; **~platz** *der* battlefield; **~preis** *der* (Wirtsch.) cut price; **~richter** *der*, **~richterin** *die* (Sport) judge; **~schiff** *das* fighting ship; warship; **~schrift** *die* polemical document; **~spiel** *das* (Sport) contact sport; **~stark** *Adj.* powerful ‹*army*›; efficient ‹*troops*›; strong, powerful ‹*team*›; **~stärke** *die* (eines Feindes, Heeres) fighting strength *or* power; (einer Mannschaft) strength; **~stier** *der* fighting bull; **~stoff** *der* warfare agent; **~tag** *der* day of action; **~truppe** *die* (Milit.) fighting *or* combat unit; **~truppen** fighting *or* combat troops; **~unfähig** *Adj.* ‹*troops*› unfit for action *or* battle; ‹*boxer etc.*› unfit to fight; **jmdn./etw. ~unfähig machen** put sb./sth. out of action; **der Boxer schlug seinen Gegner ~unfähig** the boxer put his opponent out of the fight; **~verband** *der* (Milit.) combat unit; **~wagen** *der* chariot; **~ziel** *das* objective; **~zone** *die* (Milit.) battle zone; combat zone

kampieren /kam'pi:rən/ *itr. V.* camp; (ugs.: wohnen) camp down *or* out; **du kannst bei uns im Wohnzimmer ~:** you can bed down *or* (Brit. sl.) doss down in our living room

Kamputschea /kampʊ'tʃe:a/ *(das)*; **~s** Kampuchea

Kamuffel /ka'mʊfl/ *das*; **~s, ~** (Schimpfwort) [silly] fool

Kanada /'kanada/ *(das)*; **~s** Canada

Kanadier /ka'na:di̯ɐ/ *der*; **~s, ~** ▸ⓘ **S. 520** 1 (Einwohner Kanadas) Canadian 2 (Boot) Canadian canoe

Kanadierin *die*; **~, ~nen** ▸ⓘ **S. 520** Canadian; *s. auch* **-in**

kanadisch /ka'na:dɪʃ/ *Adj.* ▸ⓘ **S. 520** Canadian

Kanaille /ka'nalj̯ə/ *die*; **~, ~n** (abwertend) 1 (gemeiner Mensch) scoundrel; villain 2 (Mob, Pöbel) rabble; mob

Kanake /ka'na:kə/ *der*; **~n, ~n** 1 (Polynesier) kanaka 2 (derb abwertend: Südländer, Orientale) dago (sl. derog.)

Kanal /ka'na:l/ *der*; **~s, Kanäle** /ka'nɛ:lə/ 1 (künstlicher Wasserlauf) canal 2 (Geogr.) **der ~:** the [English] Channel 3 (für Abwässer) sewer 4 (zur Entwässerung, Bewässerung) channel; (Graben) ditch 5 (Rundf., Ferns., Weg der Information) channel 6 (salopp) **den ~ voll haben** (betrunken sein) be canned *or* plastered (sl.); (überdrüssig sein) have had a bellyful *or* as much as one can take

Kanal-: ~arbeiter *der*, **~arbeiterin** *die* 1 sewerage worker; 2 (Politik Jargon) backroom boy; **~bau** *der* canal/sewer building *or* construction; **~deckel** *der* manhole cover; **~gebühr** *die* canal toll; canal dues *pl.*; **~inseln** *Pl.* Channel Islands

Kanalisation /kanaliza'tsi̯o:n/ *die*; **~, ~en** 1 (System der Abwasserkanäle) sewerage system; sewers *pl.* 2 (Bau der Abwasserkanäle) installation of a/the sewerage system 3 (Ausbau eines Flusses) canalization

Kanalisations·system *das* sewerage system; [system of] sewers *pl.*

kanalisieren *tr. V.* 1 (mit Kanalisation versehen) install a sewerage system in ‹*area, village, etc.*› 2 (lenken) channel ‹*energies, goods, etc.*› 3 (schiffbar machen) canalize

Kanalisierung *die*; **~, ~en** 1 installation of a/the sewerage system; **die ~ des Dorfes** the installation of a/the sewerage system in the village 2 (Lenkung) channelling 3 (Schiffbarmachen) canalization

Kanal-: ~tunnel *der* Channel Tunnel; **~zone** *die* Canal Zone

Kanapee /'kanape/ *das*; **~s, ~s** 1 (veralt., noch scherzh.: Sofa) sofa; settee 2 (belegtes Weißbrotschnittchen) canapé

Kanaren /ka'na:rən/ *Pl.* Canaries

Kanari /ka'na:ri/ *der*; **~s, ~** (südd., österr. ugs.), **Kanarien·vogel** /ka'na:ri̯ən-/ *der* canary

kanarien·gelb *Adj.* canary yellow

Kanarische Inseln *Pl.* Canary Islands

Kandare /kan'da:rə/ *die*; **~, ~n** curb bit; **jmdn. an die ~ nehmen** (fig.) take sb. in hand; **jmdn. an der ~ haben** (fig.) keep sb. on a tight rein

Kandelaber /kande'la:bɐ/ *der*; **~s, ~:** candelabrum

Kandidat /kandi'da:t/ *der*; **~en, ~en** 1 candidate; **jmdn. als ~en aufstellen** nominate sb. *or* put sb. forward as a candidate 2 (beim Quiz usw.) contestant 3 (an Hochschulen) *person studying for the final examination for a doctorate*; **~ der Medizin/Philosophie** *usw.* 'Kandidat' in medicine/philosophy *etc.*

Kandidaten-: ~land *das* (EU) candidate country; **~liste** *die* list of candidates

Kandidatin *die*; **~, ~nen** ▸**Kandidat**; *s. auch* **-in**

Kandidatur /kandida'tu:ɐ̯/ *die*; **~, ~en** candidature (**auf** + *Akk.* for)

kandidieren *itr. V.* stand [as a candidate] (**für** for)

kandieren /kan'di:rən/ *tr. V.* candy; **kandiert** crystallized ‹*orange, petal*›; glacé ‹*cherry, pear*›; candied ‹*peel*›

Kandis /'kandɪs/ *der*; **~, Kandis·zucker** *der* rock candy

Kaneel /ka'ne:l/ *der*; **~s, ~e** cinnamon

Känguru, *Känguruh /'kɛŋguru/ *das*; **~s, ~s** kangaroo

Kanin /ka'ni:n/ *das*; **~s, ~e** (fachspr.) rabbit [fur]

Kaninchen /ka'ni:nçən/ *das*; **~s, ~:** rabbit

Kaninchen-: ~bau *der*; *Pl.* **~e** rabbit burrow; rabbit hole; **~fell** *das* rabbit fur; **~fleisch** *das* rabbit [meat]; **~stall** *der* rabbit hutch

Kanister /ka'nɪstɐ/ *der*; **~s, ~:** can; [metal/plastic] container

kann /kan/ *1. u. 3. Pers. Sg. Präsens v.* **können**

Kann·bestimmung, Kann-Bestimmung *die* authorization

Kännchen /'kɛnçən/ *das*; **~s, ~:** [small] pot; (für Milch) [small] jug; **ein ~ Kaffee/Milch** a [small] pot of coffee/jug of milk

Kanne /'kanə/ *die*; **~, ~n** 1 (Krug) (Tee~, Kaffee~) pot; (Milch~, Wein~, Wasser~) jug 2 (Henkel~) can; (für Milch) pail; (beim Melken) churn; (für Essen) container; (Gieß~) watering can 3 (Jazzjargon: Saxophon) sax (coll.)

Kannelierung *die*; **~, ~en** (Archit.) fluting

kannen·weise *Adv.* by the jugful

Kannibale /kani'ba:lə/ *der*; **~n, ~n**, **Kannibalin** *die*; **~, ~nen** cannibal

kannibalisch *Adj.* cannibalistic

kannibalisieren *tr. V.* 1 (Zool.) induce cannibalism in ‹*animal*› 2 (Jargon: ruinieren) cannibalize

Kannibalismus *der*; **~** (auch Zool.) cannibalism *no art.*

kannst /kanst/ *2. Pers. Sg. Präsens v.* **können**

kannste /'kanstə/ (ugs.) **= kannst du;** *s. auch* **haste**

kannte /'kantə/ *1. u. 3. Pers. Sg. Prät. v.* **kennen**

Kanon /'ka:nɔn/ *der*; **~s, ~s** (Musik, Lit., Theol., geh.) canon

Kanonade /kano'na:də/ *die*; **~, ~n** (Milit.) cannonade; **eine ~ aufs Tor** (fig.) a barrage of shots [at goal]; **eine ~ von Flüchen** *usw.* (fig. ugs.) a barrage of curses *or* oaths *etc.*

Kanone /ka'no:nə/ *die*; **~, ~n** 1 (Geschütz) cannon; big gun; **mit ~n auf Spatzen** (*Akk.*) **schießen** (fig.) take a sledgehammer to crack a nut; **das ist unter aller ~** (ugs.) it's appallingly bad *or* indescribably dreadful (coll.); **unter aller ~ spielen** (ugs.) play appallingly badly (coll.) 2 (ugs.: Könner) ace 3 (salopp: Revolver) shooting iron (coll.); rod (Amer. sl.)

Kanonen·boot *das* gunboat

Kanonenboot-: ~diplomatie *die*, **~politik** *die* gunboat diplomacy

Kanonen-: ~donner *der* [rumble of] gunfire; **~futter** *das* (ugs.) cannon fodder; **~kugel** *die* cannon ball; **~ofen** *der* cylindrical [iron] stove; **~rohr** *das* gun barrel; **[ach du] heiliges ~rohr!** (ugs.) good grief!; **~schlag** *der* thunderflash; cannon cracker

Kanonier /kano'ni:ɐ̯/ *der*; **~s, ~e** (Milit.) gunner; artilleryman

Kanoniker /ka'no:nikɐ/ *der*; **~s, ~, Kanonikus** /ka'no:nikʊs/ *der*; **~, ~** (christl. Kirche) canon

kanonisch
A *Adj.* 1 (kath. Kirche) canonical; **~es Recht** canon law 2 (mustergültig, klassisch) canonical
B *adv.* canonically

kanonisieren *tr. V.* canonize

Kanossa /ka'nɔsa/ *das*; **~s** (geh.) humiliation; **nach ~ gehen** eat humble pie; go to Canossa (literary)

Kanossa·gang *der* (geh.) humiliation; **einen ~ antreten/machen** eat humble pie; go to Canossa (literary)

Kantate /kan'ta:tə/ *die*; **~, ~n** (Musik) cantata

Kante /'kantə/ *die*; **~, ~n** 1 (Schnittlinie zweier Flächen, Rand) edge; (bei Stoffen) selvedge; **etw. auf die hohe ~ legen** (ugs.) put sth. away *or* by; **etw. auf der hohen ~ haben** (ugs.) have sth. put away *or* by; *s. auch* **Ecke 1**; **sich die ~ geben** (ugs.) get plastered (coll.) 2 (landsch.: Gegend) part

kanten
A *tr. V.* 1 tilt; (auf die Kante stellen) stand on edge; **„Nicht ~!"** 'do not tilt!' 2 (Skisport) edge ‹*ski*›
B *itr. V.* (Skisport) edge

Kanten *der*; **~s, ~** (nordd.) (Anfangs- oder Endstück von Brot) crust

Kanter *der*; **~s, ~** (Reiten) canter

Kanter·sieg *der* (Sport) runaway *or* easy victory

Kant-: ~haken *der* 1 **jmdn. beim ~haken nehmen** *od.* **kriegen** (salopp) give sb. what for (coll.); **jetzt haben wir ihn beim ~haken** (salopp) now we've got him (coll.); 2 cant hook; **~holz** *das* squared timber; (Stück) piece of squared timber

Kantianer /kan'ti̯a:nɐ/ *der*; **~s, ~, Kantianerin** *die*; **~, ~nen** (Philos.) Kantian

kantig *Adj.* square-cut ‹*timber, stone*›; rough-edged ‹*rock*›; angular ‹*face, figure, etc.*›; sharp ‹*nose*›; square ‹*chin*›; jerky, awkward ‹*movement*›

Kantine /kan'ti:nə/ *die*; **~, ~n** canteen

Kantinen·essen *das* canteen food *no indef. art.*

kantisch *Adj.* Kantian

Kanton /kan'to:n/ *der*; **~s, ~e** canton

k

Kanton

The name for the individual autonomous states that make up Switzerland. There are 26 *Kantone*, each with its own government and constitution. The Swiss cantons are: Aargau; Appenzell Außerrhoden; Appenzell Innerrhoden; Basel-Stadt (Basle, urban); Basel-Landschaft (Basle, rural); Bern (Berne); Freiburg; Genf (Geneva); Glarus; Graubünden; Jura; Luzern (Lucerne); Neuenburg (Neuchatel); Sankt Gallen (St Gall); Schaffhausen; Schwyz; Solothurn; Tessin; Thurgau; Unterwalden nid dem Wald (Nidwalden); Unterwalden ob dem Wald (Obwalden); Uri; Waadt; Wallis; Zug; Zürich.

kantonal /kanto'na:l/
A *Adj.* cantonal
B *adv.* on a cantonal basis

Kantonist /kanto'nɪst/ *der;* **~en, ~en** *in* **ein unsicherer ~ sein** (ugs.) be an unreliable type; be unreliable

Kantons-: ~rat *der* (schweiz.) cantonal great council; **~regierung** *die* (schweiz.) cantonal government

Kantor /'kantɔr/ *der;* **~s, ~en** /-'to:rən/ ▸❶ **S. 113** choirmaster and organist

Kantorei *die;* **~, ~en** [church] choir

Kantorin *die;* **~, ~nen** ▸❶ **S. 113** choir mistress and organist

Kant·stein *der* kerb

Kanu /'ka:nu/ *das;* **~s, ~s** canoe

Kanu·fahrer *der,* **Kanu·fahrerin** *die* canoeist

Kanüle /ka'ny:lə/ *die;* **~, ~n** (Med.) cannula; (einer Injektionsspritze) [hypodermic] needle

Kanu·sport *der* canoeing *no art.*

Kanute /ka'nu:tə/ *der;* **~n, ~n, Kanutin,** *die;* **~, ~nen** (Sport) canoeist

Kanzel /'kantsl̩/ *die;* **~, ~n** 1 pulpit; **auf der ~:** in the pulpit; **von der ~ herab** from the pulpit 2 (Flugw.) cockpit 3 (Bergsteigen) spur 4 (Jägerspr.) raised hide; high seat

Kanzel-: ~missbrauch, ***~mißbrauch** *der* abuse *or* misuse of the pulpit [for political ends]; **~redner** *der,* **~rednerin** *die* preacher

kanzerogen /kantsero'ge:n/ *Adj.* (Med.) carcinogenic

kanzerös /kantse'rø:s/ *Adj.* (Med.) cancerous

Kanzlei /kants'lai/ *die;* **~, ~en** 1 (veralt.: Büro) office 2 (Anwalts~) chambers *pl.* (*of barrister*); office (*of lawyer*) 3 ▸ **Staatskanzlei**

Kanzlei-: ~diener *der,* **~dienerin** *die* (veralt.) messenger; **~kraft** *die* (österr.) ▸ **Bürokraft**; **~sprache** *die* language of officialdom; officialese; **~stil** *der* (abwertend) officialese

Kanzler /'kantslɐ/ *der;* **~s, ~** 1 chancellor 2 (an Hochschulen) vice-chancellor 3 (in diplomatischen Vertretungen) chief secretary

Kanzler·amt *das* 1 (Kanzlerbüro) chancellor's office 2 (Amt des Kanzlers) chancellorship; office of chancellor

Kanzlerin *die;* **~, ~nen** ▸ **Kanzler**

Kanzler-: ~kandidat *der,* **~kandidatin** *die* candidate for the chancellorship; **~mehrheit** *die* (Jargon) majority of one

Kanzlerschaft *die;* **~, ~en** chancellorship

Kaolin /kao'li:n/ *das,* (fachspr.:) *der;* **~s, ~e** kaolin

Kap /kap/ *das;* **~s, ~s** cape; **~ der Guten Hoffnung** Cape of Good Hope; **~ Hoorn** Cape Horn

Kapaun /ka'paun/ *der;* **~s, ~e** capon

Kapazität /kapatsi'tɛ:t/ *die;* **~, ~en** 1 (Wirtsch.: Leistung) capacity 2 (Wirtsch.: Gesamtheit der Einrichtungen) capacity *no pl.* 3 (Fassungsvermögen) capacity 4 (Experte) expert 5 (Physik) capacitance

Kapazitäts·auslastung *die* (Wirtsch.) use *or* utilization of capacity

Kapee /ka'pe/ *in* **schwer von ~ sein** (salopp) be slow on the uptake

Kapelle¹ /ka'pɛlə/ *die;* **~, ~n** (Archit.) chapel

Kapelle² *die;* **~, ~n** (Musik~) band; [light] orchestra

Kapell·meister *der,* **Kapell·meisterin** *die* bandleader; bandmaster; (im Orchester) conductor; (im Theater usw.) musical director

Kaper¹ /'ka:pɐ/ *die;* **~, ~n** caper *usu. in pl.*

Kaper² *der;* **~s, ~** (hist.: Schiff, Freibeuter) privateer

Kaper·brief *der* (hist.) letter[s *pl.*] of marque

Kaperei *die;* **~, ~en** (hist.) privateering *no art.*

kapern *tr. V.* 1 (hist.) capture; seize 2 (ugs.) **jmdn. [für etw.] ~:** rope sb. in[to sth.]; **sich** (*Dat.*) **eine Frau/einen Mann ~:** hook [oneself] a wife/husband

Kapern·soße *die* caper sauce

Kaper·schiff *das* (hist.) privateer

kapieren /ka'pi:rən/ (ugs.)
A *tr. V.* (ugs.) get (coll.); understand; **kapier das endlich!** get that into your thick skull! (coll.)
B *itr. V.* **kapiert?** got it? (coll.); **sie hat schnell kapiert** she was quick to catch on (coll.)

Kapillare /kapɪ'la:rə/ *die;* **~, ~n** ▸❶ **S. 435** (Biol., Med.) capillary

Kapillar·gefäß *das* ▸❶ **S. 435** (Biol., Med.) capillary vessel

kapital /kapi'ta:l/ *Adj.* 1 (außergewöhnlich) major ‹*error, blunder, etc.*›; **eine ~e Dummheit begehen** do something exceedingly foolish 2 (Jägerspr.: sehr groß und stark) large and powerful; royal ‹*stag*› 3 (schwerwiegend) serious, bad ‹*accident etc.*›

Kapital *das;* **~s, ~e** *od.* **~ien** 1 capital 2 (fig.) asset; **seine Hände sind sein einziges ~:** his capable hands are his only asset; **~ aus etw. schlagen** make capital out of sth.; capitalize on sth. 3 (Kapitalisten) capital

Kapital-: ~abwanderung *die* (Wirtsch.) exodus of capital; **~anlage** *die* (Wirtsch.) capital investment; **~anteil** *der* (Wirtsch.) share; stake

Kapitale *die;* **~, ~n** (geh.) capital [city]

kapital-, Kapital-: ~eigner *der,* **~eignerin** *die* (Wirtsch.) share owner; **~ertrag** *der* (Wirtsch.) return on capital; **~ertrag[s]steuer** *die* (Steuerw.) tax on capital income; **~flucht** *die* flight of capital; **~geber** *der,* **~geberin** *die* investor; **~gedeckt** *Adj.* secured by capital *postpos.*; **~gesellschaft** *die* joint-stock company

kapitalisieren *tr. V.* (Wirtsch.) capitalize

Kapitalismus *der;* **~:** capitalism *no art.*

Kapitalist *der;* **~en, ~en, Kapitalistin** *die;* **~, ~nen** capitalist

kapitalistisch
A *Adj.* capitalistic
B *adv.* capitalistically

kapital-, Kapital-: ~konto *das* (Wirtsch.) capital account; **~kräftig** *Adj.* (Wirtsch.) financially strong; **~markt** *der* (Wirtsch.) capital market; **~verbrechen** *das* serious offence *or* crime; (mit Todesstrafe bedroht) capital offence *or* crime; **~verbrecher** *der,* **~verbrecherin** *die* serious/capital offender; **~verflechtung** *die* interlacing of capital interests

Kapitän /kapi'tɛ:n/ *der;* **~s, ~e, Kapitänin** *die;* **~, ~nen** ▸❶ **S. 44** 1 (Seew.) captain; (auf einem Handelsschiff) master; captain; (auf einem kleineren Schiff) skipper; captain; **~ der Landstraße** (ugs.) knight of the road; [long-distance] truck driver *or* (Brit.) lorry driver 2 (Flugw.) captain 3 (Sport) captain; skipper

Kapitän·leutnant *der* (Marine) lieutenant commander

Kapitäns·patent *das* master's certificate

Kapitel /ka'pɪtl̩/ *das;* **~s, ~** 1 (Abschnitt, auch fig.) chapter; **das ist ein anderes ~** (fig.) that's another story; **ein dunkles ~ in jmds. Geschichte** (fig.) a black period in sb.'s history; **das ist ein ~ für sich** (fig.) that's an awkward subject; (etwas Unklares) that's a complicated subject 2 (Geistliche einer Dom- oder Stiftskirche) chapter

Kapitell /kapi'tɛl/ *das;* **~s, ~e** capital

Kapitulation /kapitula'tsio:n/ *die;* **~, ~en** 1 surrender; capitulation; **seine ~ erklären** admit defeat 2 (fig.: das Aufgeben) giving up 3 (Vertrag) surrender *or* capitulation document

kapitulieren *itr. V.* 1 surrender; capitulate; **vor dem Feind ~:** surrender to the enemy 2 (fig.: aufgeben) give up; **vor etw.** (*Dat.*) **~:** give up in the face of sth.

Kaplan /ka'pla:n/ *der;* **~s, Kapläne** (kath. Kirche) 1 (Hilfsgeistlicher) curate 2 (Geistlicher mit besonderen Aufgaben) chaplain

Kapo /'kapo/ *der;* **~s, ~s** 1 (Soldatenspr.) NCO 2 (Lagerjargon) prisoner acting as an overseer

Kapok /'kapɔk/ *der;* **~s** kapok

Kapott·hut /ka'pɔt-/ *der* capote; (ugs. abwertend) (*old or old-fashioned*) hat

Kappe /'kapə/ *die;* **~, ~n** 1 (Kopfbedeckung) cap; (Flieger~) helmet; **etw. auf seine [eigene] ~ nehmen** (ugs.) take the responsibility for sth. 2 (Abdeckung) cover; (eines Rades) hubcap 3 (Verschluss) cap; top; (eines Füllers) cap 4 (am Schuh) (vorn) [toe]cap; (hinten) counter

kappen *tr. V.* 1 (Seemannsspr.) cut 2 (beschneiden) cut back ‹*hedge etc.*›; (fig.) cut 3 (abschneiden) cut off ‹*branches, shoots, crown, etc.*› 4 (kastrieren) caponize, castrate ‹*cockerel*›

Kappen·abend *der* (landsch.) carnival party (*at which funny hats are worn*)

Kappes /'kapəs/ *der;* **~** (bes. westd.) 1 (Weißkohl) cabbage 2 (ugs.: Unsinn) rubbish; nonsense

Käppi /'kɛpi/ *das;* **~s, ~s** overseas cap; garrison cap

Kapp·naht *die* (Schneiderei) flat-fell seam

Kaprice /ka'pri:sə/ *die;* **~, ~n** (geh.) caprice; whim

Kapriole /kapri'o:lə/ *die;* **~, ~n** 1 (Luftsprung) caper; capriole; **~n schlagen** cut capers 2 (Streich) trick 3 (Reiten) capriole

Kaprize /ka'pri:tsə/ *die;* **~, ~n** (österr.) ▸ **Kaprice**

kaprizieren *refl. V.* **sich darauf ~, etw. zu tun** be intent on doing sth.; **sich auf ein Land ~:** be utterly committed to a country

kapriziös /kapri'tsiø:s/
A *Adj.* capricious
B *adv.* capriciously

Kapsel /'kapsl̩/ *die;* **~, ~n** capsule

kapseln *tr. V.* (Technik) encapsulate

Kapstadt /'kapʃtat/ (*das*); **~s** Cape Town

kaputt /ka'pʊt/ *Adj.* 1 (entzwei) broken ‹*toy, cup, plate, arm, leg, etc.*›; **die Maschine/das Auto ist ~:** the machine/car has broken down; (ganz und gar) the machine/car has had it (coll.); **irgendetwas ist am Auto ~:** there's something wrong with the car; **diese Jacke ist ~:** this jacket needs mending; (ist zerrissen) this jacket's torn; **die Birne ist ~:** the bulb has gone; (ist zerbrochen) the bulb is smashed; **das Telefon ist ~:** the phone is not working *or* is out of order; **der Fernseher ist ~:** the television has gone wrong; **sein Leben ist ~:** his life is in ruins; **eine ~e Ehe** (ugs.) a marriage that has broken up; **ein ~er Typ** (fig. ugs.) a down-and-out; **eine ~e Lunge/ein ~es Herz haben** (ugs.) have bad lungs/a bad heart; **die Ehe ist ~:** the marriage has failed *or* (coll.) is on the rocks; **was ist denn jetzt ~?** (salopp) what's wrong *or* the matter now?; **bei dir ist was ~** (salopp) there must be something wrong with you (coll.) 2 (ugs.: erschöpft) shattered (coll.); whacked (Brit. coll.); pooped (coll.) 3 (salopp: krankhaft, abartig) sick

kaputt-: ~|arbeiten *refl. V.* (ugs.) work oneself into the ground (coll.); **~|fahren** *unr. tr. V.* (ugs.) run over ‹*animal*›; smash up ‹*car etc.*›; **~|gehen** *unr. itr. V.; mit sein* (ugs.) 1 (entzweigehen) break; ‹*machine*› break down, (coll.) pack up; ‹*clothes, shoes*› fall to pieces; ‹*lightbulb*› go; (zerbrechen) be smashed; (eingehen) ‹*plant*› die; (verderben) ‹*fish, fruit, etc.*› go off; (fig.) ‹*marriage*› fail; ‹*community, relationship, etc.*› break up; 2 (zugrunde gehen) ‹*firm*› go bust (coll.); ‹*person*› go to pieces; **er ist an Drogen ~gegangen** he was destroyed by drugs; **~|kriegen** *tr. V.* (ugs.) break; **wie hast du das ~gekriegt?** how did you [manage to] break it?; **~|lachen** *refl. V.* (ugs.) kill oneself [laughing] (coll.); **das ist ja zum Kaputtlachen!** that's a laugh!;

~|**machen** (ugs.) A *tr. V.* 1) (zerstören) break ‹*watch, spectacles, plate, etc.*›; spoil ‹*sth. made with effort*›; ruin ‹*clothes, furniture, etc.*›; burst ‹*balloon*›; 2) (ruinieren) drive ‹*business, company*› to the wall; destroy ‹*political party*›; finish ‹*person*› off; B *refl. V.* wear oneself out; ~|**schlagen** *unr. tr. V.* (ugs.) smash; ~|**schmeißen** *unr. tr. V.* (ugs.) smash

Kapuze /ka'pu:tsə/ *die;* ~, ~n hood; (bei Mönchen) cowl; hood

Kapuzen·mantel *der* coat with a hood

Kapuziner /kapu'tsi:nɐ/ *der;* ~s, ~ 1) (Mönch) Capuchin [friar] 2) (österr.: Kaffee) cappuccino

Kapuziner·kresse *die* nasturtium

Kar /ka:ɐ̯/ (Geol.) *das;* ~[e]s, ~e cirque; corrie; kar

Karabiner /kara'bi:nɐ/ *der;* ~s, ~ 1) (Gewehr) carbine 2) (österr.) ▸ **Karabinerhaken**

Karabiner·haken *der* snap hook; spring hook; (Bergsteigen) karabiner

Karacho /ka'raxo/ *das;* ~s *in* **mit ~** *od.* **in vollem ~** (ugs.) hell for leather (coll.)

Karaffe /ka'rafə/ *die;* ~, ~n carafe; (mit Glasstöpsel) decanter

Karakul·schaf /kara'kʊl-/ *das* caracul [sheep]

Karambolage /karambo'la:ʒə/ *die;* ~, ~n 1) (ugs.) crash; collision 2) (Billard) cannon

Karambole /karam'bo:lə/ *die;* ~, ~n (Billard) red [ball]

karambolieren *itr. V.* 1) (Billard) cannon 2) *mit haben od. sein* (zusammenstoßen) crash; **mit etw. ~:** crash into sth.; collide with sth.

***Karamel** *usw.:* ▸ **Karamell** *usw.*

Karamell /kara'mɛl/ *der (schweiz.: das);* ~s caramel

Karamell-: ~**bonbon** *der od. das* caramel [toffee]; ~**creme** *die* crème caramel

Karamelle /kara'mɛlə/ *die;* ~, ~n caramel [toffee]

Karaoke *das;* ~[s] karaoke

Karaoke·bar *die* karaoke bar

Karat /ka'ra:t/ *das;* ~[e]s, ~e carat; **ein Diamant von 5 ~:** a 5-carat diamond; **reines Gold hat 24 ~:** pure gold is 24 carats

Karate /ka'ra:tə/ *das;* ~[s] karate

-karäter /-karɛ:tɐ/ *der;* ~s, ~: **Zehn~/Fünf~:** ten-carat/five-carat diamond/stone

Karate·schlag *der* karate chop

-karätig /-karɛ:tɪç/ *Adj.* -carat; **zehn~/fünf~:** ten-carat/five-carat

Karavelle /kara'vɛlə/ *die;* ~, ~n (hist.) caravel

Karawane /kara'va:nə/ *die;* ~, ~n caravan; **~n von Autos** (fig.) long lines of cars

Karawanen·straße *die* caravan route

Karawanserei /karavanzə'rai̯/ *die;* ~, ~en caravanserai

Karbid /kar'bi:t/ *das;* ~[e]s, ~e (Chem.) carbide

Karbid·lampe *die* carbide lamp

Karbol /kar'bo:l/ *das;* ~s, **Karbol·säure** *die* carbolic acid

Karbol·seife *die* carbolic soap

Karbonat /karbo'na:t/ *das;* ~[e]s, ~e (Chem.) carbonate

Karbunkel /kar'bʊŋkl̩/ *der;* ~s, ~ ▸ⓘ **S. 439** (Med.) carbuncle

Kardamom /karda'mo:m/ *der od. das;* ~s, ~e[n] cardamom

Kardan- /kar'da:n-/: ~**antrieb** *der* (Technik) cardan drive; ~**aufhängung** *die* (Technik) cardanic suspension; ~**gelenk** *das* (Technik) cardan joint

kardanisch *Adj.: in* **~e Aufhängung** cardanic suspension

Kardan-: ~**tunnel** *der* (Kfz-W.) cardan tunnel; cardan-shaft housing; ~**welle** *die* (Technik) cardan shaft

Kardätsche /kar'dɛ:tʃə/ *die;* ~, ~n dandy brush; body brush

kardinal /kardi'na:l/ *Adj.* cardinal

Kardinal *der;* ~s, **Kardinäle** /kardi'nɛ:lə/ 1) (kath. Kirche) cardinal 2) (Vogel) cardinal [bird]

Kardinal-: ~**bischof** *der* cardinal bishop; ~**fehler** *der* cardinal error

Kardinals·kollegium *das* college of cardinals; Sacred College

Kardinal-: ~**tugend** *die* cardinal virtue; ~**zahl** *die* cardinal [number]

Kardiogramm /kardio'gram/ *das;* ~s, ~e (Med.) 1) ▸ **Elektrokardiogramm** 2) (Bild der Herzstoßkurven) cardiogram

Kardiologe *der;* ~n, ~n ▸ⓘ **S. 113** cardiologist

Kardiologie *die;* ~ (Med.) cardiology *no art.*

Kardiologin *die;* ~, ~nen ▸ⓘ **S. 113** cardiologist

Karditis /kar'di:tɪs/ *die;* ~, **Karditiden** /kardi'ti:dn̩/ ▸ⓘ **S. 439** (Med.) carditis

Karenz /ka'rɛnts/ *die;* ~, ~en, **Karenz·zeit** *die* waiting period

Karfiol /kar'fi̯o:l/ *der;* ~s (südd., österr.) cauliflower

Kar·freitag /ka:ɐ̯-/ *der* Good Friday

Karfunkel /kar'fʊŋkl̩/ *der;* ~s, ~ (Edelstein; volkst.: Geschwür) carbuncle

karg /kark/
A *Adj.* meagre ‹*wages, pay, etc.*›; frugal ‹*meal etc.*›; poor ‹*light, accommodation*›; scanty ‹*supply*›; meagre, scant ‹*applause*›; sketchy ‹*report*›; sparse ‹*furnishings*›; (wenig fruchtbar) barren, poor ‹*soil*›; barren ‹*desert, land*›; **~ mit Lob sein** be grudging *or* sparing in one's praise
B *adv.* **~ bemessen sein** ‹*helping*› be mingy (Brit. coll.); ‹*supply*› be scanty; **~ leben** live frugally; **~ möbliert** sparsely furnished; **~ ausgestattet** scantily equipped

kargen *itr. V.* **mit Geld ~:** be mean with one's money; **mit seinen Worten ~:** be a person of few words

Kargheit *die;* ~ (geh.) ▸ **karg** A: meagreness; frugality; poorness; scantiness; sketchiness; sparseness; barrenness

kärglich /'kɛrklɪç/
A *Adj.* meagre, poor ‹*wages, pension, etc.*›; poor ‹*light*›; frugal ‹*meal*›; scanty ‹*supply*›; meagre ‹*existence*›; meagre, scant ‹*applause*›; sparse ‹*furnishing*›
B *adv.* sparsely ‹*furnished*›; poorly ‹*lit, paid, rewarded*›

Kargo /'kargo/ *der;* ~s, ~s (Seemannsspr.) cargo

Karibik /ka'ri:bɪk/ *die;* ~: Caribbean; **in die ~:** to the Caribbean

karibisch *Adj.* Caribbean; **die ~en Inseln** the Caribbean Islands

kariert /ka'ri:ɐ̯t/
A *Adj.* check, checked ‹*material, pattern*›; check ‹*jacket etc.*›; squared ‹*paper*›
B *adv.* (ugs.) **~ reden** *od.* **quatschen** talk rubbish

Karies /'ka:ri̯ɛs/ *die;* ~ ▸ⓘ **S. 439** (Zahnmed.) caries

Karikatur /karika'tu:ɐ̯/ *die;* ~, ~en 1) cartoon; (Porträt) caricature 2) (abwertend: Zerrbild) caricature

Karikaturist *der;* ~en, ~en, **Karikaturistin** *die;* ~, ~nen ▸ⓘ **S. 113** cartoonist; (Porträtist) caricaturist

karikaturistisch
A *Adj.* caricatural; **der Film gibt eine ~e Darstellung des Familienlebens** the film is a caricature of family life
B *adv.* **etw. ~ überzeichnen** caricature sth.

karikieren /kari'ki:rən/ *tr. V.* caricature

kariös /ka'ri̯ø:s/ *Adj.* (Zahnmed.) carious

Karitas /'ka:ritas/ *die;* ~ (geh.) charity

karitativ /karita'ti:f/
A *Adj.* charitable
B *adv.* **sich ~ betätigen** do work for charity

Karkasse /kar'kasə/ *die;* ~, ~n (Technik, Kochk.) carcass

Karl /karl/ *(der)* Charles; **~ der Große** Charlemagne

Karmeliter /karme'li:tɐ/ *der;* ~s, ~: Carmelite [friar]

Karmelit[er]in *die;* ~, ~nen Carmelite [nun]

Karmesin /karme'zi:n/ *das;* ~s ▸ **Karmin**

karmesin·rot *Adj.* ▸ **karminrot**

Karmin /kar'mi:n/ *das;* ~s carmine

karmin·rot *Adj.* carmine

Karneol /karne'o:l/ *der;* ~s, ~e carnelian

Karneval /'karnəval/ *der;* ~s, ~e *od.* ~s carnival; **im ~:** at carnival time; **~ feiern** join in the carnival festivities

> **Karneval**
>
> ▸ **Fasching, Fastnachtszeit.**

Karnevalist *der;* ~en, ~en, **Karnevalistin** *die;* ~, ~nen carnival reveller; (Vortragende[r] bei Karnevalssitzungen) carnival performer

karnevalistisch
A *Adj.* carnival *attrib.* ‹*time, festivities, etc.*›
B *adv.* **sich ~ verkleiden** dress up in a carnival costume/carnival costumes

Karnevals-: ~**kostüm** *das* carnival costume; ~**sitzung** *die* carnival convention (*variety show organized by carnival society*); ~**verein** *der* carnival society; ~**zug** *der* carnival procession

Karnickel /kar'nɪkl̩/ *das;* ~s, ~ 1) (landsch.) rabbit 2) (ugs.: Sündenbock) **immer bin ich das ~!** I always get the blame!

Karnickel-: ~**bock** *der* (bes. nordd.) buck rabbit; ~**stall** *der* (bes. nordd.) rabbit hutch

karnivor /karni'vo:ɐ̯/ *Adj.* (Biol.) carnivorous

Kärnten /'kɛrntn̩/ *(das);* ~s Carinthia

Kärnt[e]ner *der;* ~s, ~, **Kärntnerin** *die;* ~, ~nen Carinthian

Karo /'ka:ro/ *das;* ~s, ~s 1) (Viereck) square; (auf der Spitze stehend) diamond 2) (~muster) check 3) (Kartenspiel: Farbe) diamonds *pl.* 4) (Kartenspiel: Karte) diamond; *s. auch* **Pik²**

Karo-: *~**as**, ~**ass** *das* ace of diamonds; ~**bube** *der* jack of diamonds; ~**dame** *die* queen of diamonds; ~**könig** *der* king of diamonds; ~**muster** *das* check; check[ed] pattern

Karolinger /'ka:rolɪŋɐ/ *der;* ~s, ~, **Karolingerin** *die;* ~, ~nen (hist.) Carolingian

Karosse /ka'rɔsə/ *die;* ~, ~n 1) (Prunkwagen) [state] coach 2) (scherzh. iron.: Auto) limousine

Karosserie /karɔsə'ri:/ *die;* ~, ~n bodywork; coachwork

Karosserie·bauer *der;* ~s, ~: ▸ⓘ **S. 113** coachbuilder

Karotin /karo'ti:n/ *das;* ~s carotene

Karotte /ka'rɔtə/ *die;* ~, ~n small carrot

Karpaten /kar'pa:tn̩/ *Pl.* Carpathians; Carpathian Mountains

Karpfen /'karpfn̩/ *der;* ~s, ~: carp

Karpfen·teich *der* carp pond; *s. auch* **Hecht 1**

Karre /'karə/ *die;* ~, ~n (bes. nordd.) 1) ▸ **Karren** 2) (abwertend: Fahrzeug) [old] heap (coll.)

Karree /ka're:/ *das;* ~s, ~s 1) (Viereck) rectangle; (Quadrat) square; (bes. Milit.: Formation) square 2) (Häuserblock) **ums ~ gehen/fahren** walk/drive round the block

karren
A *tr. V.* 1) (mit einer Karre) cart; **etw./jmdn. nach Hause ~:** bring/take sth./sb. home in a cart 2) (salopp: mit einem Auto) run (coll.)
B *itr. V.; mit sein* (ugs.) drive [around]

Karren *der;* ~s, ~ (bes. südd., österr.) cart; (zweirädrig) barrow; (Schubkarren) [wheel]barrow; (für Gepäck usw.) trolley; **ein ~ voll Sand** a cartload/barrowload of sand; (fig.) **den ~ in den Dreck fahren** (ugs.) get things into a mess; mess things up; **den ~ [für jmdn.] aus dem Dreck ziehen** (ugs.) sort out the mess [for sb.]; **jmdm. an den ~ fahren** (ugs.) tell sb. where he/she gets off (coll.)

Karrette /ka'rɛtə/ *die;* ~, ~n (schweiz.) 1) handcart; (Schubkarren) [wheel]barrow 2) (Einkaufswagen) [shopping] trolley

Karriere /ka'ri̯e:rə/ *die;* ~, ~**n** 1 career; ~ **machen** make a [successful] career for oneself 2 (Reiten) [full *or* extended] gallop

Karriere-: ~**frau** *die* career woman/girl; ~**knick** *der* career break; ~**macher** *der,* ~**macherin** *die* (abwertend) careerist

Karrierist *der;* ~**en,** ~**en, Karrieristin** *die;* ~, ~**nen** (abwertend) careerist

karriolen *itr. V.; mit sein* (ugs.) ride around

Kärrner /'kɛrnɐ/ *der;* ~**s,** ~ (veralt.) labourer

Kärrner·arbeit *die* donkey work

Kar·samstag /ka:ɐ̯-/ *der* Easter Saturday; Holy Saturday

Karst[1] /karst/ *der;* ~**[e]s,** ~**e** (landsch.) [two-pronged] hoe

Karst[2] *der;* ~**[e]s,** ~**e** (Geol.) karst

karstig *Adj.* karstic

Karst·landschaft *die* karst landscape

Kartätsche /kar'tɛ:tʃə/ *die;* ~, ~**n** (hist.) case-shot

Kartäuser /kar'tɔyzɐ/ *der;* ~**s,** ~ 1 (Mönch) Carthusian [monk] 2 (Likör) chartreuse

Kartäuserin *die;* ~, ~**nen** Carthusian [nun]

Karte /'kartə/ *die;* ~, ~**n** 1 (Kartei~, Loch~ usw.) card; **die gelbe/rote** ~ (Fußball) the yellow/red card; **die grüne** ~ (Verkehrsw.) the green card 2 (Ansichts~, Post~, Glückwunsch~, Visiten~) card; (Einladungs~) invitation [card] 3 (Speise~) menu; (Wein~) wine list; **nach der** ~ **essen** eat à la carte 4 (Fahr~, Flug~, Eintritts~) ticket 5 (Lebensmittel~) ration card; **auf** ~**n** on coupons 6 (Land~) map; (See~) chart; ~**n lesen** map-read 7 (Spiel~) card; **jmdm. die** ~**n legen** read sb.'s fortune from the cards; (fig.) **diese** ~ **sticht nicht [mehr]** that won't work [any more]; **die** *od.* **seine** ~**n aufdecken** *od.* **[offen] auf den Tisch legen** *od.* **offen legen** put one's cards on the table; **alles auf eine** ~ **setzen** stake everything on one chance; **auf die falsche** ~ **setzen** back the wrong horse; **jmdm. in die** ~**n sehen** *od.* (ugs.) **gucken** find out *or* see what sb. is up to; **sich** (*Dat.*) **nicht in die** ~**n sehen** *od.* (ugs.) **gucken lassen** play one's cards close to one's chest; not show one's hand; **mit offenen/verdeckten** ~**n spielen** put one's cards on the table/play one's cards close to one's chest 8 (Anzahl von Spielkarten) hand; **eine schlechte** ~ **[auf der Hand] haben** have a poor hand

Kartei /kar'tai̯/ *die;* ~, ~**en** card file *or* index

Kartei-: ~**karte** *die* file *or* index card; ~**kasten** *der* file-card *or* index-card box; ~**leiche** *die* (scherzh.) 1 dead card; 2 (ugs.: passives Mitglied) inactive member

Kartell /kar'tɛl/ *das;* ~**s,** ~**e** (Wirtsch., Politik) cartel

kartell-, Kartell-: ~**amt** *das,* ~**behörde** *die: government body concerned with the control and supervision of cartels;* ≈ Monopolies and Mergers Commission (Brit.); ~**gesetz** *das,* ~**recht** *das* law relating to cartels; ≈ monopolies law (Brit.); ~**rechtlich** **A** *Adj.* relating to cartel law; ‹*proceedings*› under cartel law; **B** *adv.* in cartel law

Karten-: ~**bestellung** *die* [ticket] reservation; booking; ~**brief** *der* letter-card; ~**gruß** *der* greeting *or* short message on a [post]card; **an jmdn. einen** ~**gruß verschicken** send sb. a card; ~**haus** *das* house of cards; ~**kunststück** *das* card trick; ~**legen** *das;* ~~**s** reading the cards *no art.;* cartomancy; ~**leger** *der;* ~~**s,** ~~, ~**legerin** *die;* ~~, ~~**nen** fortune teller (*who tells fortunes by reading the cards*); ~**lesen** *das;* ~~**s** map-reading; ~**spiel** *das* 1 (Spiel mit ~) card game; 2 (Satz Spiel~) pack *or* (Amer.) deck [of cards]; 3 (das ~spielen) card playing *no art.;* ~**spieler** *der,* ~**spielerin** *die* card player; ~**ständer** *der* map stand; ~**telefon** *das* cardphone; ~**tisch** *der* 1 (bes. Milit.) map table; (Seew.) chart table; 2 (Spieltisch) card table; ~**verkauf** *der* sale of tickets; ~**vorverkauf** *der* advance booking; **im** ~**vorverkauf sind die Karten billiger** the tickets are cheaper if you buy them in advance

kartesianisch /karte'zi̯a:nɪʃ/, **kartesisch** /kar'te:zɪʃ/ *Adj.* Cartesian

Karthager /kar'ta:gɐ/ *der;* ~**s,** ~, **Karthagerin** *die;* ~, ~**nen** ▸ⓘ **S. 520** Carthaginian

Karthago /kar'ta:go/ *(das);* ~**s** ▸ⓘ **S. 675** Carthage

Kartoffel /kar'tɔfl̩/ *die;* ~, ~**n** 1 potato; **rin in die** ~**n, raus aus die** ~**n** (salopp scherzh.) it's 'do this' one minute and 'do that' the next; **jmdn. wie eine heiße** ~ **fallen lassen** (ugs.) drop sb. just like that (coll.) 2 (ugs. scherzh.: Nase) conk (coll.); hooter (Brit. coll.) 3 (ugs. scherzh.: Loch im Strumpf) large hole; potato (coll.)

Kartoffel-: ~**acker** *der* potato field; ~**brei** *der* mashed *or* creamed potatoes *pl.;* mash (coll.); ~**chips** *Pl.* [potato] crisps (Brit.) *or* (Amer.) chips; ~**ernte** *die* potato harvest; ~**ferien** *Pl.* (ugs.) autumn [school] holiday *sing.;* ~**feuer** *das* fire to dispose of potato leaves (*after the potato harvest*); ~**käfer** *der* Colorado beetle; potato beetle; ~**kloß** *der,* ~**knödel** *der* (südd.) potato dumpling; ~**mehl** *das* potato flour; ~**puffer** *der* potato pancake (*made from grated raw potatoes*); ~**püree** *das* ▸~**brei;** ~**sack** *der* potato sack; ~**salat** *der* potato salad; ~**schale** *die* potato skin; (abgeschält) potato peel *or* peelings *pl.;* ~**suppe** *die* potato soup

Kartograph /karto'gra:f/ *der;* ~**en,** ~**en** ▸ⓘ **S. 113** cartographer

Kartographie *die;* ~: cartography *no art.*

kartographieren *tr. V.* map

Kartographin *die;* ~, ~**nen** ▸ⓘ **S. 113** cartographer

kartographisch *Adj.* cartographic

Karton /kar'tɔŋ/ *der;* ~**s,** ~**s** 1 (Pappe) card[board] 2 (Behälter) cardboard box; (kleiner und dünner) carton; **zwei** ~**[s] Seife/Batterien** two boxes *or* packs of soap/batteries 3 (Kunstwiss.) cartoon

Kartonage /karto'na:ʒə/ *die;* ~, ~**n** cardboard boxes [and cartons] *pl.;* cardboard packaging

kartonieren /karto'ni:rən/ *tr. V.* (Buchw.) bind in [paper] boards

Kartothek /karto'te:k/ *die;* ~, ~**en** ▸**Kartei**

Kartusche /kar'tʊʃə/ *die;* ~, ~**n** 1 (Metallhülse) cartridge 2 (Kunstwiss.) cartouche

Karussell /karʊ'sɛl/ *das;* ~**s,** ~**s** *od.* ~**e** merry-go-round; carousel (Amer.); (kleineres) roundabout; ~ **fahren** have a ride on *or* go on the merry-go-round/roundabout; **mit jmdm.** ~ **fahren** (fig. ugs.) give sb. a good telling-off

Kar·woche /'ka:ɐ̯vɔxə/ *die* Holy Week; Passion Week

Karyatide /karya'ti:də/ *die;* ~, ~**n** (bild. Kunst) caryatid

Karzer /'kartsɐ/ *der;* ~**s,** ~ (hist.) 1 (Arrestraum) detention room (in university, school) 2 (Strafe) detention (*often lasting several days*)

karzinogen /kartsino'ge:n/ *Adj.* (Med.) carcinogenic

Karzinologie *die* (Med.) oncology *no art.*

Karzinom /kartsi'no:m/ *das;* ~**s,** ~**e** ▸ⓘ **S. 439** (Med.) carcinoma

Kasack /'ka:zak/ *der;* ~**s,** ~**s** (*österr.: die;* ~, ~**s**) tunic

Kaschemme /ka'ʃɛmə/ *die;* ~, ~**n** (abwertend) [low] dive (coll.)

kaschen /'kaʃn̩/ *tr. V.* (salopp) 1 (verhaften) nab (coll.); nick (coll.) 2 (sich aneignen) pinch (coll.); nick (Brit. coll.)

kaschieren /ka'ʃi:rən/ *tr. V.* 1 (verhüllen) conceal; hide; disguise ‹*fault*› 2 (Buchw.) laminate ‹*jacket etc.*›; line ‹*cover etc.*› [with paper] 3 (Textilw.) bond [together]

Kaschmir[1] /'kaʃmi:ɐ̯/ *(das);* ~**s** Kashmir

Kaschmir[2] *der;* ~**s,** ~**e** (Textilw.) cashmere; **ein Pullover/Kleid aus** ~: a cashmere sweater/dress

Käse /'kɛ:zə/ *der;* ~**s,** ~ 1 cheese 2 (ugs. abwertend: Unsinn) rubbish; nonsense; codswallop (Brit. coll.)

Käse-: ~**blatt** *das* (salopp abwertend) rag; ~**brot** *das* slice of bread and cheese; (zugeklappt) cheese sandwich; ~**fondue** *das* cheese fondue; ~**fuß** *der* (salopp abwertend) cheesy *or* smelly foot; ~**gebäck** *das* cheese savouries *pl.;* ~**glocke** *die* cheese dome

Kasein /kaze'i:n/ *das;* ~**s,** (Chemie:) **Casein** *das;* ~**s** casein

Käse·kuchen *der* cheesecake

Kasematte /kazə'matə/ *die;* ~, ~**n** (Milit., Marine) casemate

Käse·platte *die* (Platte) cheeseboard; (Gericht) [selection of] assorted cheeses *pl.*

Käserei /kɛ:zə'rai̯/ *die;* ~, ~**en** 1 (Herstellung von Käse) cheesemaking *no art.* 2 (Betrieb) cheese factory

Kaserne /ka'zɛrnə/ *die;* ~, ~**n** barracks *sing. or pl.*

Kasernen-: ~**hof** *der* barrack square; ~**sprache** *die* (abwertend) army lingo

kasernieren *tr. V.* quarter in barracks; (fig.) keep in isolation

Kasernierung *die;* ~, ~**en** quartering in barracks *no art.;* (fig.) keeping in isolation *no art.*

käse-, Käse-: ~**stange** *die* cheese straw; ~**torte** *die* cheesecake; ~**weiß** *Adj.* (ugs.) [as] white as a sheet; **sie war** ~**weiß im Gesicht** her face was as white as a sheet

käsig *Adj.* 1 (ugs.: bleich) pasty; pale; (vor Schreck) as white as a sheet 2 (wie Käse) cheesy; cheeselike

Kasino /ka'zi:no/ *das;* ~**s,** ~**s** 1 (Spiel~) casino 2 (Offiziers~) [officers'] mess 3 (Speiseraum) canteen

Kaskade /kas'ka:də/ *die;* ~, ~**n** 1 (Wasserfall, auch fig.) cascade; **in** ~**n fallen** cascade [down]; **eine** ~ **von Verwünschungen/Flüchen** (fig.) a barrage of curses 2 (Sprung) acrobatic leap (in which the acrobat pretends to fall) 3 (Elektrot.) cascade

kasko·versichern *tr. V.; nur im Inf. u. 2. Part. gebr.* (mit Vollkasko) insure comprehensively; (mit Teilkasko) insure against theft, fire, or act of God

Kasko·versicherung *die* (Voll~) comprehensive insurance; (Teil~) insurance against theft, fire, or act of God

Kasper /'kaspɐ/ *der;* ~**s,** ~ 1 ≈ Punch 2 (ugs.: alberner Mensch) clown; fool

Kasperl /'kaspɐl/ *das;* ~**s,** ~**[n]** (österr.), **Kasperle** /'kaspɐlə/ *das od. der;* ~**s,** ~ ▸**Kasper**

Kasperle-: ~**puppe** *die* ≈ Punch and Judy puppet; ~**theater** *das* ≈ Punch and Judy show; (Puppenbühne) ≈ Punch and Judy theatre

kaspern *itr. V.* (ugs.) clown *or* fool around

Kasper·theater *das* ▸**Kasperletheater**

Kaspische Meer /'kaspɪʃə/ *das* Caspian Sea

Kassa /'kasa/ *die;* ~, **Kassen** (österr.) ▸**Kasse**

Kassa-: ~**geschäft** *das* 1 (Börsenw.) spot transaction; 2 (Wirtsch.) cash transaction; ~**kurs** *der* (Börsenw.) spot price; ~**markt** *der* (Börsenw.) spot market

Kassandra·ruf /ka'sandra-/ *der* (geh.) prophecy of doom

Kassation /kasa'tsi̯o:n/ *die;* ~, ~**en** 1 (von Urkunden) annulment 2 (von Urteilen) quashing; setting aside 3 (veralt.: unehrenhafte Entlassung) cashiering

Kassations·gericht *das* (schweiz. Rechtsw.) court of appeal (*in a canton*)

Kasse /'kasə/ *die;* ~, ~**n** 1 (Kassette) cash box; (Registrier~) till; cash register; **in die** ~ **greifen** *od.* **einen Griff in die** ~ **tun** (ugs.; auch fig.) help oneself from the till; **er wurde beim Griff in die** ~ **ertappt** (auch fig.) he was caught with his fingers in the till; **die** ~ **klingelt** (fig.) the tills are ringing merrily 2 (Ort zum Bezahlen) cash *or* pay desk; (im Supermarkt) checkout; (in einer Bank) counter; ~ **machen** (Kaufmannsspr.) cash up; **jmdn. zur** ~ **bitten** (ugs.) ask sb. to pay up 3 (Bargeld) cash; **gemeinsame** ~ **führen** *od.* **machen** share expenses; **getrennte**

k

~ **haben** pay separately; **gut/knapp bei ~ sein** be well-off *or* flush/be short of cash *or* money; **bei ~ sein** be in the money; **etw. reißt ein Loch in die ~** (ugs.) sth. makes a hole in sb.'s pocket *or* a dent in sb.'s finances; **die ~ führen** be in charge of the money *or* finances *pl.* 4 (in Behörde, Unternehmen) cashier's office 5 (Kassenraum) cashier's office; (in einer Bank) counter hall 6 (Theater~, Kino~, Stadion~) box office 7 (Spar~) [savings] bank 8 ▸**Krankenkasse** 9 (Kaufmannsspr.: Barzahlung) [payment in] cash; **wir liefern nur gegen ~:** we deliver only if payment is made in cash

Kasseler /'kasəlɐ/ *das;* ~**s** smoked loin of pork; *s. auch* **Rippenspeer**

kassen-, Kassen-: ~**arzt** *der,* ~**ärztin** *die: doctor who treats members of health insurance schemes;* ~**ärztlich** *Adj.* ~**ärztliche Behandlung** treatment under a health insurance scheme; ~**bericht** *der* (Wirtsch.) financial report *or* statement; ~**bestand** *der* cash [in hand]; ~**bon** *der* sales slip; receipt; ~**brille** *die* (ugs.) *glasses provided under a health insurance scheme;* ≈ National Health glasses *pl.* (Brit.); ~**buch** *das* cash book; ~**erfolg** *der* box office success; ~**führer** *der,* ~**führerin** *die* treasurer; ~**gestell** *das* (ugs.) *spectacle frame provided under a health insurance scheme;* ≈ National Health frame (Brit.); ~**lage** *die* financial situation; **nach ~lage** according to available finances; **Politik nach ~lage** finance-driven policy; ~**magnet** *der* (ugs.) box office draw; ~**patient** *der,* ~**patientin** *die: patient who is a member of a health insurance scheme;* ~**raum** *der* counter hall; ~**schlager** *der* (ugs.) 1 (Film, Theater) box office hit; 2 (von Waren) top seller; ~**schrank** *der* safe; ~**stunden** *Pl.* hours of business, business hours (*of bank, cashier's office, etc.*); ~**sturz** *der* (ugs.) ~**sturz machen** check up on one's ready cash; ~**wart** *der;* ~~**s**, ~~**e**, ~**wartin** *die;* ~~, ~~**nen** ▸❶ **S. 113** treasurer; ~**zettel** *der* 1 (Quittung) receipt; 2 (Kassenbon) sales slip

Kasserolle /kasə'rɔlə/ *die;* ~, ~**n** saucepan

Kassette /ka'sɛtə/ *die;* ~, ~**n** 1 (für Geld u. Wertsachen) box; case 2 (mit Büchern, Schallplatten) boxed set 3 (Tonband~) cassette; **etw. auf ~ aufnehmen** record *or* tape sth. on cassette 4 (Filmrolle) cassette 5 (Behälter für Filmrollen) can 6 (Archit.) coffer; lacunar

Kassetten-: ~**deck** *das* cassette deck; ~**film** *der* film cassette; cassette of film; ~**recorder**, ~**rekorder** *der* cassette recorder *or* player

Kassiber /ka'si:bɐ/ *der;* ~**s**, ~ (Gaunerspr.) [secret] message

Kassier /ka'si:ɐ̯/ *der;* ~**s**, ~**e** (südd., österr., schweiz.) ▸**Kassierer**

kassieren[1]

A *tr. V.* 1 (einziehen) collect ‹*rent etc.*› 2 (ugs.: einnehmen) collect ‹*money, fee, etc.*›; (fig.) receive, get ‹*recognition, praise, etc.*›; **dafür hat er viel Geld kassiert** he got a lot of money for it *or* made a lot of money out of it; **bei der Transaktion hat er 100 000 Euro kassiert** he made 100,000 euros on the deal 3 (ugs.: hinnehmen müssen) receive, get ‹*penalty points, scorn, ingratitude, etc.*› 4 (ugs.: wegnehmen) confiscate; take away ‹*driving licence*›; **er hat das Erbteil seiner Schwester kassiert** he appropriated his sister's share of the inheritance 5 (ugs.: verhaften/gefangen nehmen) pick up; nab (coll.); nick (Brit. coll.)

B *itr. V.* 1 (ab~) **bei jmdm. ~:** give sb. his/her bill *or* (Amer.) check; (ohne Rechnung) settle up with sb.; **darf ich bei Ihnen ~?** would you like your bill?/can I settle up with you? 2 (ugs.: Geld einnehmen) collect the money; (bezahlt werden) make money; **[bei einem Geschäft] ganz schön ~:** make a packet *or* a bomb [on a deal] (coll.)

kassieren[2] *tr. V.* (Rechtsw.) quash ‹*judgement etc.*›

Kassierer *der;* ~**s**, ~, **Kassiererin** *die;* ~, ~**nen** ▸❶ **S. 113** 1 (in Geschäften, Banken) cashier; teller 2 (bei einem Verein) treasurer

Kastagnette /kastan'jɛtə/ *die;* ~, ~**n** castanet

Kastanie /kas'ta:ni̯ə/ *die;* ~, ~**n** chestnut; **[für jmdn.] die ~n aus dem Feuer holen** (ugs.) pull the chestnuts out of the fire [for sb.]

kastanien-, Kastanien-: ~**baum** *der* chestnut tree; ~**braun** *Adj.* chestnut

Kästchen /'kɛstçən/ *das;* ~**s**, ~ 1 small box 2 (vorgedrucktes Quadrat) square; (auf Fragebögen) box

Kaste /'kastə/ *die;* ~, ~**n** caste

kasteien /kas'tai̯ən/ *refl. V.* 1 (als Bußübung) chastise oneself 2 (sich Entbehrungen auferlegen) deny oneself

Kasteiung *die;* ~, ~**en** 1 (als Bußübung) self-chastisement 2 (Auferlegung von Entbehrungen) self-denial

Kastell /kas'tɛl/ *das;* ~**s**, ~**e** 1 (hist.: röm. Lager) fort 2 (Burg) castle

Kastellan /kastɛ'la:n/ *der;* ~**s**, ~**e** (hist.) castellan

Kasten /'kastn̩/ *der;* ~**s**, **Kästen** /'kɛstn̩/ 1 box 2 (für Flaschen) crate 3 (ugs.: Briefkasten) postbox; letter box 4 (ugs. abwertend: Gebäude) barracks *sing. or pl.*; **das ist ja ein furchtbarer alter ~:** that's a terrible old barracks of a place 5 (ugs. abwertend) (Flugzeug) crate (sl.); (Schiff) tub; (Auto) heap (coll.); (Fernseher, Radio) box (coll.) 6 (ugs.: Kamera) **ein Bild im ~ haben** have got a picture; **eine Szene im ~ haben** have a picture in the can 7 *in* **etw. auf dem ~ haben** (ugs.) have got it up top (coll.); have plenty of grey matter 8 (Schaukasten) showcase; display case 9 (Soldatenspr.) glasshouse (Milit. sl.); **vier Tage ~:** four days in the glasshouse *or* the cooler 10 (Turnen) box 11 (Ballspiele Jargon) goal 12 (bes. nordd.: Schublade) drawer 13 (südd., österr., schweiz.: Schrank) cupboard

Kasten-: ~**brot** *das* tin [loaf]; ~**form** *die* [rectangular] tin; ~**geist** *der* caste spirit; ~**wagen** *der* cart; (Lieferwagen) van; ~**wesen** *das* caste system

Kastilien /kas'ti:li̯ən/ *(das);* ~**s** Castile

kastilisch *Adj.* Castilian

Kastrat /kas'tra:t/ *der;* ~**en**, ~**en** 1 (Eunuch) eunuch 2 (Musik hist.) castrato

Kastraten·stimme *die* 1 (Musik) castrato voice 2 (abwertend) falsetto voice

Kastration /kastra'tsi̯o:n/ *die;* ~, ~**en** castration

Kastrations-: ~**angst** *die* (Psych.) castration anxiety; ~**komplex** *der* (Psych.) castration complex

kastrieren *tr. V.* castrate; **eine Kastrierte** (salopp scherzh.) a filter cigarette

Kasuistik /ka'zu̯ɪstɪk/ *die;* ~ (Philos., geh.) casuistry

kasuistisch *Adj.* (Philos., geh.) casuistic

Kasus /'ka:zʊs/ *der;* ~, ~ /'ka:zu:s/ (Sprachw.) case

Kasus-: ~**bildung** *die* (Sprachw.) case formation; ~**endung** *die* (Sprachw.) case ending

Kat /kat/ *der;* ~**s**, ~**s** (ugs.) ▸**Katalysator 2**

Katafalk /kata'falk/ *der;* ~**s**, ~**e** catafalque

Katakombe /kata'kɔmbə/ *die;* ~, ~**n** catacomb

katalanisch /kata'la:nɪʃ/ *Adj.* ▸❶ **S. 670** Catalan

Katalog /kata'lo:k/ *der;* ~**[e]s**, ~**e** (auch fig.) catalogue

katalogisieren *tr. V.* catalogue

Katalonien /kata'lo:ni̯ən/ *(das);* ~**s** Catalonia

Katalysator /kataly'za:tɔr/ *der;* ~**s**, ~**en** /-za'to:rən/ 1 (Chemie, fig. geh.) catalyst 2 (Kfz-W.) catalytic converter; *s. auch* **geregelt B**

Katalyse /kata'ly:zə/ *die;* ~, ~**n** (Chemie) catalysis

katalytisch /kata'ly:tɪʃ/ *Adj.* (Chemie) catalytic

Katamaran /katama'ra:n/ *der od. das;* ~**s**, ~**e** catamaran

Katapult /kata'pʊlt/ *das od. der;* ~**[e]s**, ~**e** catapult

katapultieren *tr. V.* (auch fig.) catapult; eject ‹*pilot*›

Katapult-: ~**sitz** *der* ejector seat; ~**start** *der* catapult launch

Katarakt /kata'rakt/ *der;* ~**[e]s**, ~**e** (Stromschnelle) rapids *pl.*; (Wasserfall) cataract

Katarrh /ka'tar/ *der;* ~**s**, ~**e** ▸❶ **S. 439** (Med.) catarrh; **einen ~ haben** have catarrh

Kataster /ka'tastɐ/ *der od. das;* ~**s**, ~: land register

Kataster·amt *das* land registry

katastrophal /katastro'fa:l/

A *Adj.* disastrous; (stärker) catastrophic; (entsetzlich) appalling; atrocious

B *adv.* disastrously; (stärker) catastrophically; **sich ~ auswirken** have a disastrous/catastrophic effect; **~ enden** end in disaster/catastrophe

Katastrophe /katas'tro:fə/ *die;* ~, ~**n** 1 (Unglück) disaster; (stärker) catastrophe; **jmd. ist eine ~** (ugs.) sb. is a disaster 2 (Literaturw.) catastrophe

Katastrophen-: ~**alarm** *der* emergency *or* disaster alert; ~**dienst** *der* emergency services *pl.*; ~**einsatz** *der:* **den ~einsatz üben** practise procedures in case of a disaster; ~**fall** *der* disaster [situation]; ~**gebiet** *das* disaster area; ~**meldung** *die* report of a disaster; ~**meldungen** reports of disasters; ~**schutz** *der* 1 (Organisation) emergency services *pl.*; 2 (Maßnahmen) disaster procedures *pl.*; **dem ~schutz dienen** be useful in the event of a disaster

Kate /'ka:tə/ *die;* ~, ~**n** (bes. nordd.) small cottage

Katechese /katɛ'çe:zə/ *die;* ~, ~**n** (christl. Kirche) catechesis

Katechet /katɛ'çe:t/ *der;* ~**en**, ~**en**, **Katechetin** *die;* ~, ~**nen** (christl. Kirche) catechist

Katechismus /katɛ'çɪsmʊs/ *der;* ~, **Katechismen** (christl. Kirche) catechism

Katechist *der;* ~**en**, ~**en**, **Katechistin** *die;* ~, ~**nen** catechist

kategorial /katego'ri̯a:l/ *Adj.* (geh.) categorial

Kategorie /katego'ri:/ *die;* ~, ~**n** /-i:ən/ category; **diese ~ Mensch** that sort of person

kategorisch

A *Adj.* categorical; *s. auch* **Imperativ 2**

B *adv.* categorically

kategorisieren *tr. V.* categorize

Kater /'ka:tɐ/ *der;* ~**s**, ~ 1 tom cat; **wie ein verliebter ~:** like an amorous tom cat; *s. auch* **gestiefelt** 2 (ugs.: schlechte Verfassung) hangover; **einen ~ haben** have a hangover; be hung-over

Kater-: ~**frühstück** *das: breakfast, usually of pickled herrings and gherkins, supposed to cure a hangover;* ~**stimmung** *die* morning-after feeling; **er ist in der fürchterlichsten ~stimmung** he's got a terrible hangover

Katharina /kata'ri:na/ *(die)* Catherine; Katherine

Katharsis /'ka(:)tarzɪs/ *die;* ~ (Literaturw.) catharsis

kathartisch /ka'tartɪʃ/ (geh.)

A *Adj.* cathartic

B *adv.* cathartically

Katheder /ka'te:dɐ/ *das od. der;* ~**s**, ~: lectern; (Pult des Lehrers) teacher's desk

Katheder·weisheit *die* theoretical *or* academic knowledge *no pl., no indef. art.*

Kathedrale /kate'dra:lə/ *die;* ~, ~**n** cathedral

Kathete /ka'te:tə/ *die;* ~, ~**n** (Math.) leg (*of a right-angled triangle*)

Katheter /ka'te:tɐ/ *der;* ~**s**, ~ (Med.) catheter

Kathode /ka'to:də/ *die;* ~, ~**n** (Physik) cathode

Katholik /kato'li:k/ *der;* ~**en**, ~**en**, **Katholikin** *die;* ~, ~**nen** [Roman] Catholic

katholisch *Adj.* [Roman] Catholic; **die Katholischen** (ugs.) the Catholics; *s. auch* **taufen 1**

Katholizismus /katoli'tsɪsmʊs/ *der;* ~: [Roman] Catholicism *no art.*

Katholizität /katolitsi'tɛ:t/ *die;* ~: Catholicism

Katode /ka'to:də/ *die;* ~, ~**n** ▸**Kathode**

Kattun /ka'tu:n/ *der;* ~**s**, ~**e** calico

Kattun·kleid *das* calico dress

Katz /kats/ *die: in* ~ **und Maus [mit jmdm.] spielen** (ugs.) play cat and mouse [with sb.]; **für die ~ sein** (salopp) be a waste of time

katzbalgen *refl. V.* (ugs.) scrap; fight

katzbuckeln *itr. V.* (abwertend) bow and scrape; **vor jmdm. ~:** bow and scrape to sb.

Kätzchen /ˈkɛtsçən/ *das;* ~**s,** ~ **1** (kleine Katze) little cat; (liebkosend) pussy; (junge Katze) kitten **2** (Blüte der Birke, Erle u. a.) catkin **3** (ugs.: Mädchen) kitten

Kätzchen·zweig *der* catkin twig

Katze /ˈkatsə/ *die;* ~, ~**n** **1** cat; **die ~ lässt das Mausen nicht** (Spr.) a leopard cannot change its spots (prov.); **bei Nacht** *od.* **nachts sind alle ~n grau** it's impossible to see any details in the dark; **wenn die ~ aus dem Haus ist, tanzen die Mäuse [auf dem Tisch]** (Spr.) when the cat's away the mice will play (prov.); **da beißt sich die ~ in den Schwanz** (fig.) we've come round in a circle; **die ~ aus dem Sack lassen** (ugs.) let the cat out of the bag; **die ~ im Sack kaufen** (ugs.) buy a pig in a poke; **um etw. herumgehen wie die ~ um den heißen Brei** (ugs.) beat about the bush; *s. auch* **Katz** **2** (Jägerspr.) female **3** (temperamentvolle Frau) cat

Katzelmacher *der;* ~**s,** ~ (südd., österr.: salopp abwertend) wop (sl. derog.)

katzen-, Katzen-: ~**auge** *das* **1** (ugs.: Rückstrahler) reflector; **2** (Mineral.) cat's-eye; ~**buckel** *der* hunched back; **einen ~buckel machen** hunch one's back; ~**fell** *das* cat's skin; ~**freundlich** *Adj.* ingratiatingly friendly; ~**haft** *Adj.* catlike; ~**jammer** *der* **1** (Kater) hangover; **2** (fig.) mood of depression; ~**klo** *das* (ugs.) cat's [litter] tray; ~**kopf** *der* (ugs.) cobble[stone]; ~**musik** *die* (ugs. abwertend) terrible row (coll.); cacophony; ~**sprung** *der* ▸ℹ **S. 224** stone's throw; **bis zum Strand ist es nur ein ~sprung** the beach is only a stone's throw away; ~**tisch** *der* (ugs. scherzh.) children's table; ~**wäsche** *die* (ugs.) lick and a promise (coll.); catlick (coll.); **~wäsche machen** have a lick and a promise *or* a catlick; ~**zunge** *die* langue de chat

Kau·bewegung *die* chewing movement

Kauderwelsch /ˈkaudɐvɛlʃ/ *das;* ~**[s]** gibberish *no indef. art.;* double Dutch *no indef. art.;* **juristisches/medizinisches ~:** legal/medical jargon; **ein ~ aus Deutsch, Englisch und Französisch** an incomprehensible hotchpotch of German, English, and French

kauderwelschen *itr. V.* talk gibberish *or* double Dutch

kauen /ˈkauən/

A *tr. V.* chew; masticate (Med., formal); **[die] Nägel ~:** bite *or* chew one's nails

B *itr. V.* **1** chew; **an etw.** (*Dat.*) **~:** chew [on] sth.; **an einem Problem ~** (fig.) wrestle *or* struggle with a problem; **an dieser Niederlage wird er noch einige Zeit zu ~ haben** (fig.) it will take him some time to get over this defeat; **mit vollen Backen ~** (ugs.) chew with one's mouth [stuffed] full **2** (nagen, knabbern) chew; bite; **an einem Bleistift/den Fingernägeln ~:** chew a pencil/bite *or* chew one's nails

kauern /ˈkauɐn/

A *itr. V.* crouch [down]; (ängstlich) cower

B *refl. V.* crouch [down]; (ängstlich) cower; **sich an jmdn. ~:** huddle up to sb.

Kauf /kauf/ *der;* ~**[e]s, Käufe** /ˈkɔyfə/ **1** (das ~en) buying; purchasing (formal); **den ~ vermitteln** arrange the purchase; **einen ~ abschließen/tätigen** complete/make a purchase; **jmdn. zum ~ ermuntern/veranlassen** encourage/induce sb. to buy; **jmdm. etw. zum ~ anbieten** offer sb. sth. for sale; **etw. in ~ nehmen** (fig.) accept sth.; **jmdn. in ~ nehmen** (fig. ugs.) put up with sb. **2** (das käuflich Erworbene) purchase

Kauf-: ~**auftrag** *der* order to buy *or* purchase; ~**brief** *der* bill of sale; (beim Hauskauf) title deed

kaufen

A *tr. V.* **1** (erwerben) buy; purchase; **etw. billig/zu teuer ~:** buy sth. cheaply/pay too much for sth.; **sich/jmdm. etw. ~:** buy sth. for oneself/sb.; buy oneself/sb. sth.; **etw. auf Raten** *od.* **Abzahlung ~:** buy sth. on hire purchase (Brit.) *or* (Amer.) the installment plan; **etw. auf Stottern** *od.* **Pump ~** (ugs.) buy sth. on the never-never (Brit. coll.) *or* (Amer. coll.) on time; **etw. für viel** *od.* **teures Geld ~:** pay a lot of money for sth.; **das wird viel** *od.* **gern gekauft** it sells well; **dafür kann ich mir nichts ~** (ugs.) a [fat] lot of use that is to me (coll.); **sich** (*Dat.*) **jmdn. ~** (ugs.) give sb. what for (coll.); let sb. have *or* give sb. a piece of one's mind **2** (ugs.: bestechen) buy

B *itr. V.* (ein~) shop; **in diesem Laden kaufe ich nicht mehr** I'm not getting anything in that shop again

Käufer /ˈkɔyfɐ/ *der;* ~**s,** ~, **Käuferin** *die;* ~, ~**nen** buyer; purchaser; (Kunde/Kundin) customer; *s. auch* **-in**

Käufer·schicht *die* class of customer *or* consumer

kauf-, Kauf-: ~**fahrer** *der* (veralt.), ~**fahrtei·schiff** /-faːɐ̯ˈtai-/ *das* (veralt.) merchantman; ~**frau** *die* businesswoman; (Händlerin) trader; merchant; ~**haus** *das* department store; ~**haus·detektiv** *der,* ~**haus·detektivin** *die* ▸ℹ **S. 113** store detective; ~**kassette** *die* [commercially produced] video; **den Film/die Reihe gibt es auch als ~kassette** you can buy that film/series on video too; ~**kraft** *die* (Wirtsch.) **1** (Wert des Geldes) purchasing power; **2** (Zahlungsfähigkeit) spending power; ~**kräftig** *Adj.* **ein ~kräftiger Kunde/Interessent** a customer with money to spend/a wealthy potential buyer; **~kräftig sein** have money to spend; ~**laden** *der; Pl.* ~**läden** **1** (veralt.) (kleiner Laden) [small] shop; (Lebensmittelladen) [small] grocer's shop; **2** (Kinderspielzeug) toy shop

käuflich /ˈkɔyflɪç/

A *Adj.* **1** (gegen Bezahlung erhältlich) for sale *postpos.;* **~e Liebe** (fig.) prostitution; **ein ~es Mädchen** (fig.) a woman/girl of easy virtue **2** (bestechlich) venal; **~ sein** be easily bought

B *adv.* **etw. ~ erwerben/erstehen** buy *or* purchase sth.; **~ zu erwerben sein** be for sale

kauf-, Kauf-: ~**lust** *die* inclination *or* desire to buy; ~**lustig** *Adj.* eager to buy *pred.;* **die ~lustigen** the eager shoppers

Kauf·mann *der; Pl.* **Kaufleute** **1** (Geschäftsmann) businessman; (Händler) trader; merchant; **gelernter ~:** *person who has completed a course of training in some branch of business* **2** (Besitzer eines Kaufladens) shopkeeper; (Besitzer eines Lebensmittelladens) grocer; **zum ~ gehen** go to the shop/grocer's

kaufmännisch

A *Adj.* commercial; business *attrib.;* commercial ⟨*bookkeeping*⟩; **~er Angestellter** clerk; employee in business; **einen ~en Beruf ergreifen/erlernen** go into business/receive a business training; **~es Geschick/~e Erfahrung haben** possess business skill/experience

B *adv.* **~ tätig sein** be in business; **~ denken** think along commercial lines

Kaufmanns-: ~**sprache** *die* business parlance; ~**stand** *der* (veralt.) merchant class

kauf-, Kauf-: ~**objekt** *das* article for sale; (Haus usw.) property for sale; ~**preis** *der* purchase price; ~**rausch** *der* frantic urge to spend; ~**summe** *die* purchase price; ~**vertrag** *der* contract of sale; (beim Hauskauf) title deed; ~**willig** *Adj.* ⟨*person*⟩ who wants to buy; **~willig sein** want to buy; ~**zurückhaltung** *die* reluctance to buy; ~**zwang** *der* obligation to buy *or* purchase; **ohne ~zwang** without obligation [to buy *or* purchase]

Kau·gummi *der od. das;* ~**s,** ~**s** chewing gum

Kaukasien /kauˈkaːzi̯ən/ *(das);* ~**s** Caucasia

Kaukasier *der;* ~**s,** ~, **Kaukasierin** *die;* ~, ~**nen** Caucasian

kaukasisch *Adj.* Caucasian

Kaukasus /ˈkaukazʊs/ *der;* **~:** the Caucasus

Kaulquappe /ˈkaulkvapə/ *die;* ~, ~**n** tadpole

kaum /kaum/ *Adv.* **1** (fast gar nicht) hardly; scarcely; **~ jemand/etwas** hardly anybody *or* anyone/anything; **~ älter/größer/besser** hardly *or* scarcely any older/bigger/better; **wir haben ~ noch Zeit** we really haven't the time; **das war ~ noch zu erwarten** it was really too late to expect that **2** (nur mit Mühe) hardly; scarcely; barely; **ich kann es ~ glauben/erwarten** I can hardly believe it/wait; **ich konnte ~ rechtzeitig damit fertig werden** I could hardly *or* barely finish it in time; **diese Schrift ist ~ zu entziffern** this writing is barely decipherable **3** (vermutlich nicht) hardly; scarcely; **er wird [wohl] ~ zustimmen** he is hardly likely to agree; **ich glaube ~:** I hardly *or* scarcely think so; **es wird sich ~ lohnen** it is unlikely to be profitable **4** (in dem Augenblick) **~ hatte er Platz genommen, als ...** no sooner had he sat down than ... **5** (nicht lange nachdem) **~ dass er aus dem Gefängnis gekommen war ...** hardly *or* scarcely had he left prison when ...; **der Regen war, ~ dass er angefangen hatte, auch schon wieder vorüber** the rain had stopped almost as soon as it had started **6** (geh.) **~ dass ich mich an die Landschaft erinnere** I can hardly even remember the scenery

Kau·muskel *der* ▸ℹ **S. 435** (Anat.) masticatory muscle; **[äußerer] ~:** masseter

kausal /kauˈzaːl/ *Adj.* (geh., Sprachw.) causal

Kausal·gesetz *das* (bes. Philos., Logik) law of causality

Kausalität /kauzaliˈtɛːt/ *die;* ~, ~**en** causality

Kausalitäts·gesetz *das* ▸**Kausalgesetz**

Kausal-: ~**kette** *die* (bes. Philos., Logik) causal chain; ~**satz** *der* (Sprachw.) causal clause; ~**zusammenhang** *der* (bes. Philos., Logik) causal connection

Kausativ /ˈkauzatiːf/ *das;* ~**s,** ~**e** /-iːvə/ (Sprachw.) causative verb

Kau·tabak *der* chewing tobacco

Kautel /kauˈteːl/ *die;* ~, ~**en** (Rechtsw.) proviso

Kaution /kauˈtsi̯oːn/ *die;* ~, ~**en** **1** (bei Freilassung eines Gefangenen) bail; **eine ~ für jmdn. stellen** stand bail *or* surety for sb.; **gegen ~:** on bail; **jmdn. gegen ~ freibekommen** bail sb. out **2** (beim Mieten einer Wohnung) deposit

Kautschuk /ˈkautʃʊk/ *der;* ~**s,** ~**e** [india] rubber

Kautschuk-: ~**milch** *die* rubber latex; ~**paragraph** *der* (ugs.) ▸**Gummiparagraph**

Kauz /kauts/ *der;* ~**es, Käuze** /ˈkɔytsə/ **1** (Wald~) tawny owl; (Stein~) little owl **2** (Sonderling) odd *or* strange fellow; oddball (coll.); **ein komischer ~:** an odd *or* a queer bird (coll.)

Käuzchen /ˈkɔytsçən/ *das;* ~**s,** ~ ▸**Kauz 1**

kauzig *Adj.* odd; queer; funny (coll.)

Kavalier /kavaˈliːɐ̯/ *der;* ~**s,** ~**e** **1** (höflicher Mann) gentleman; **der ~ genießt und schweigt** a gentleman never talks about his amours **2** (veralt., noch scherzh.: Freund) beau (dated); young man **3** (hist.: Edelmann) cavalier; nobleman

kavaliers-, Kavaliers-: ~**delikt** *das* trifling offence; peccadillo; ~**mäßig** **A** *Adj.* gentlemanly; **B** *adv.* like a gentleman; in a gentlemanly manner; ~**start** *der* racing start

Kavalkade /kavalˈkaːdə/ *die;* ~, ~**n** (veralt.) cavalcade

Kavallerie /kavaləˈriː/ *die;* ~, ~**n** (Milit. hist.) cavalry

Kavallerie·pferd *das* cavalry horse

Kavallerist *der;* ~**en,** ~**en** cavalryman; trooper

Kavents·mann /kaˈvɛnts-/ *der* (bes. nordd.) (übergroßes Exemplar) monster

Kaverne /kaˈvɛrnə/ *die;* ~, ~**n** **1** (unterirdischer Hohlraum) [artificial] cavern **2** (Med.) cavern

Kaviar /ˈkaːvi̯ar/ *der;* ~**s,** ~**e** caviare

Kaviar·brot *das* French bread; **ein ~:** a French loaf

kcal *Abk.* = **Kilo[gramm]kalorie** kcal

KdF *Abk.* (ns.) = **Kraft durch Freude** Strength through Joy [movement]

Kebse /ˈkeːpsə/ *die;* ~, ~n (hist.), **Kebs·weib** *das* (hist.) concubine

keck /kɛk/

A *Adj.* **1** (respektlos) impertinent; cheeky; saucy (Brit.) **2** (veralt.: verwegen) bold **3** (flott) jaunty, pert ‹hat etc.›

B *adv.* **1** (respektlos) impertinently; cheekily; saucily (Brit.) **2** (veralt.: verwegen) boldly **3** (flott) jauntily

Keckheit *die;* ~, ~en **1** (Respektlosigkeit) impertinence; cheek; sauce (Brit.) **2** (veralt.: Kühnheit) boldness

Keeper /ˈkiːpɐ/ *der;* ~s, ~, **Keeperin** *die;* ~, ~nen (Fußball, bes. österr.) [goal]keeper

Kefir /ˈkeːfɪr/ *der;* ~s kefir

Kegel /ˈkeːgl̩/ *der;* ~s, ~ **1** (geometrischer Körper) cone **2** (Spielfigur) skittle; (beim Bowling) pin; ~ **schieben** play skittles *or* ninepins **3** (Berg~) peak **4** (Licht~) beam **5** (Druckw.) body size; point size

kegel-, Kegel-: ~**abend** *der* skittles night; ~**bahn** *die* skittle alley; ~**bruder** *der* skittle-club friend; ~**förmig** *Adj.* conical; cone-shaped; ~**klub** *der* skittle club; ~**kugel** *die* [skittle] ball; ~**mantel** *der* (Geom.) lateral surface of a/the cone

kegeln

A *itr. V.* **1** (eine Kegelpartie machen) play skittles *or* ninepins; (beim Bowling) bowl **2** *mit sein* (ugs.: hinfallen) tumble

B *tr. V.* **1** (durch Kegeln ausführen) play **2** (durch Kegeln erzielen) bowl; score

kegel-, Kegel-: ~**rad** *das* (Technik) bevel wheel; *~|**schieben** ▸ **Kegel 2**; ~**schieben** *das;* ~~s skittles *sing.*; ninepins *sing.*; ~**schnitt** *der* (Geom.) conic section; ~**schwester** *die* ▸ ~**bruder**; ~**sport** *der* skittles *sing.*; ninepins *sing.*; ~**stumpf** *der* truncated cone; frustum of a cone

Kegler *der;* ~s, ~, **Keglerin** *die;* ~, ~nen skittle player; (bei Bowling) [tenpin] bowler

Kehle /ˈkeːlə/ *die;* ~, ~n **1** ▸ ❶ **S. 435** throat; **jmdm. an die** ~ **springen/fahren** leap at sb.'s throat; **sich** (*Dat.*) **die** ~ **schmieren** *od.* **ölen** *od.* **anfeuchten** wet one's whistle (coll.); **sich** (*Dat.*) **die** ~ **aus dem Hals schreien** (ugs.) shout *or* yell one's head off; **aus voller** ~: at the top of one's voice; **sein ganzes Geld durch die** ~ **jagen** pour all one's money down one's throat; **etw. bleibt jmdm. in der** ~ **stecken** sth. sticks in sb.'s throat *or* gullet; **etw. in die falsche** ~ **bekommen** (ugs.) (fig.: etw. missverstehen) take sth. the wrong way; (sich an etw. verschlucken) have sth. go down the wrong way; *s. auch* **Messer 1 2** (Archit.) hollow moulding; (Dach~) [roof] valley

kehlig

A *Adj.* guttural ‹language, speech, sound, etc.›; throaty, guttural ‹voice, laugh, etc.›

B *adv.* throatily; gutturally; in a throaty *or* guttural voice

Kehl·kopf *der* ▸ ❶ **S. 435** (Anat.) larynx

Kehlkopf-: ~**entzündung** *die* laryngitis *no indef. art.*; ~**krebs** *der* ▸ ❶ **S. 439** (Med.) cancer of the larynx; ~**mikrofon**, ~**mikrophon** *das* throat microphone; ~**spiegel** *der* (Med.) laryngoscope

Kehl·laut *der* **1** guttural sound **2** (Sprachw.) guttural

Kehr-: ~**aus** *der;* ~~ **1** (letzter Tanz) last dance; **2** (Schluss einer Veranstaltung) **den** ~**aus machen** finish; call it a day (coll.); (zumachen) close; ~**besen** *der* broom; (Handfeger) brush; ~**blech** *das* (bes. südd.) small shovel (*used as dustpan*)

Kehre /ˈkeːrə/ *die;* ~, ~n **1** (scharfe Kurve) sharp bend *or* turn; (Haarnadelkurve) hairpin bend **2** (geh.: Wende) [abrupt] change of direction **3** (Turnen) back *or* rear vault

kehren¹

A *tr. V.* turn; **die Innenseite von etw. nach außen** ~: turn sth. inside out; **jmdm. den Rücken** ~: turn one's back on sb.; **die Augen zum Himmel** ~: raise one's eyes to the sky *or* heavenwards; **etw./alles zum Besten** ~: make sure sth./everything turns out for the best

B *refl. V.* turn; **sich gegen jmdn./etw.** ~: turn against sb./sth.; **etw./alles wird sich zum Besten** ~: sth./everything will turn out all right; **sich an etw.** (*Dat.*) **nicht** ~: pay no attention to *or* not care about sth.

C *itr. V.* **1** (selten: um~) turn [round]; **Abteilung kehrt!** (Milit.) squad, about turn *or* (Amer.) face!; **rechtsum/linksum kehrt!** right/left turn *or* (Amer.) face! **2** *mit sein* (geh.: zurück~/ein~) return; **in sich** (*Akk.*) **gekehrt** lost in thought; in a brown study; **ein in sich** (*Akk.*) **gekehrter Mensch** an introverted person

kehren²

A *itr. V.* (bes. südd.) sweep; do the sweeping

B *tr. V.* sweep; (mit einem Handfeger) brush; **den Staub von etw./auf etw.** (*Akk.*) ~: sweep/brush the dust off sth./on to sth.

Kehricht /ˈkeːrɪçt/ *der od. das;* ~s **1** (geh.: Schmutz, Unrat) rubbish; **das geht dich einen feuchten** ~ **an!** (salopp) mind your own damned business! **2** (schweiz.: Müll) refuse; garbage (Amer.)

Kehricht-: ~**eimer** *der* dustbin; garbage can (Amer.); ~**haufen** *der* pile *or* heap of rubbish; ~**schaufel** *die* ▸ **Kehrschaufel**

Kehr-: ~**maschine** *die* [mechanical] road sweeper; ~**reim** *der* refrain; ~**schaufel** *die* dustpan; ~**seite** *die* **1** (Rückseite) back; (einer Münze, Medaille) reverse; (eines Stoffes) back; wrong side; **die** ~**seite der Medaille** (fig.) the other side of the coin; **2** (scherzh.) (Gesäß) backside; (Rücken) back; **3** (nachteiliger Aspekt) drawback; disadvantage

kehrt|machen *itr. V.* (ugs.) (sich umdrehen) do an about-turn; (umkehren) turn [round and go] back; (plötzlich) turn in one's tracks; **auf dem Absatz** ~: turn on one's heel

Kehrt·wende *die* ▸ **Kehrtwendung**

Kehrt·wendung *die* (bes. Milit. od. fig.) about-turn; about-face (Amer.); **eine** ~ **machen** make *or* do an about-turn *or* (Amer.) about-face

Kehr·wert *der* (Math.) reciprocal

keifen /ˈkaifn̩/ *itr. V.* (abwertend) nag; scold; **das Keifen der Marktfrauen** the squabbling *or* bickering of the market women

Keiferei /kaifəˈrai/ *die;* ~, ~en (abwertend) nagging; scolding

Keil /kail/ *der;* ~[e]s, ~e **1** (zum Spalten) wedge; **einen** ~ **in etw.** (*Akk.*) **treiben** drive a wedge into sth.; **einen** ~ **zwischen die beiden Freunde treiben** (fig.) drive a wedge between the two friends **2** (zum Festklemmen) chock; (unter einer Tür) wedge **3** (bes. Milit.: keilförmige Formation) wedge **4** (Schneiderei) [wedge-shaped] gusset

Keil·absatz *der* wedge [heel]

Keile /ˈkailə/ *die;* ~ (nordd.) walloping (coll.); thrashing; ~ **bekommen** *od.* **kriegen** get a walloping (coll.) *or* thrashing

keilen

A *refl. V.* (ugs.: sich prügeln) fight; scrap; **sich um etw.** ~: fight over sth.

B *tr. V.* **1** (fachspr.: mit einem Keil spalten) split with a wedge **2** (fachspr.: als Keil hineinschlagen) **etw. in etw.** (*Akk.*) ~: drive sth. into sth. **3** (ugs.: anwerben) rope in (coll.); recruit

C *itr. V.* (ausschlagen) kick

Keiler *der;* ~s, ~ (Jägerspr.) wild boar

Keilerei *die;* ~, ~en (ugs.) punch-up (coll.); brawl; fight; **eine allgemeine** ~: a free-for-all

keil-, Keil-: ~**förmig** wedge-shaped; cuneiform ‹lettering, script›; ~**hose** *die* tapering trousers; (Skihose) tapering ski pants; ~**kissen** *das* wedge-shaped bolster; ~**riemen** *der* (Technik) V-belt; ~**schrift** *die* cuneiform script

Keim /kaim/ *der;* ~[e]s, ~e **1** (Bot.: erster Trieb) shoot **2** (Biol.: befruchtete Eizelle) embryo **3** (Ursprung, Ausgangspunkt) seed[s *pl.*]; **etw. im** ~ **ersticken** nip sth. in the bud; **den** ~ **zu etw. legen** sow the seeds *pl.* of sth. **4** (Biol., Med.: Krankheitserreger) germ **5** (Physik) nucleus

Keim-: ~**bahn** *die* (Biol.) germ line; ~**bahn·therapie** *die* (Med.) germ-line therapy; ~**blatt** *das* **1** (Bot.) cotyledon; seed leaf; **2** (Biol., Med.) germ layer; ~**drüse** *die* ▸ ❶ **S. 435** (Zool., Med.) gonad; ~**drüsen·hormon** *das* sex hormone

keimen *itr. V.* **1** (zu sprießen beginnen) germinate; sprout **2** (innerlich entstehen) ‹hope› stir; ‹thought, belief, decision› form; ‹love, yearning› awaken

keim-, Keim-: ~**fähig** *Adj.* viable; capable of germinating *postpos.*; ~**fähigkeit** *die* viability; ability to germinate; ~**frei** *Adj.* germ-free; sterile; **etw.** ~**frei machen** sterilize sth.; ~**freie Milch** sterilized milk; ~**frei verpackt/gelagert** packed in sterile containers/stored in sterile conditions

keimhaft

A *Adj.* (geh.) incipient; (noch nicht ausgeprägt) embryonic

B *adv.* ~ **angelegt** embryonically present

Keimling /ˈkaimlɪŋ/ *der;* ~s, ~e **1** (Bot.) seedling **2** (Biol., Med.) embryo

keim-, Keim-: ~**scheibe** *die* (Biol.) blastodisc; germinal disc; ~**tötend** *Adj.* germicidal; ~**träger** *der*, ~**trägerin** *die* (Med.) carrier

Keimung *die;* ~, ~en germination

Keim·zelle *die* **1** (Ausgangspunkt) nucleus **2** (Bot.) germ cell **3** ▸ **Gamet**

kein /kain/ *Indefinitpron.* **1** no; (bei abstrakten Begriffen) no; not any; **er hat** ~ **Wort gesagt** he didn't say a word; he said not a word; **er konnte** ~**e Arbeit finden** he could find no work; he could not find any work; **ich habe** ~ **Geld/**~**e Zeit** I have no money/time; I don't have any money/time; **hat er** ~**e Kinder?** has he no children?; **kennst du** ~**e Deutschen/**~**en Deutschen, der ...?** don't you know any Germans/a German who ...?; ~ **Mensch/**~ **einziger** nobody *or* no one/not a single one; **in** ~**er Weise/unter** ~**en Umständen** in no way/in *or* under no circumstances; **das ist** ~ **dummer Vorschlag** that's not a bad suggestion; **er ist** ~ **Dichter** he is not a poet; (er dichtet schlecht) he is no poet; **zwischen den beiden Vorgängen besteht** ~ **großer Unterschied** there's no great difference between the two processes; ~ **anderer als er kann es gewesen sein** it can't have been anybody else but him **2** (ugs.: nicht ganz, nicht einmal) less than; **es ist** ~**e drei Tage her, dass ich zuletzt dort war** it's not *or* it's less than three days since I was last there; **sie ist noch** ~**e zehn Jahre alt** she's not ten years old yet; **es dauert** ~**e fünf Minuten** it won't take five minutes **3** *allein stehend* (niemand/nichts) nobody; no one; ~**er von uns** not one of us; none of us; **ich kenne** ~**en, der dir helfen kann** I don't know anyone who can help you; ~**s von beiden** neither [of them]; **ich wollte** ~**es von beiden** I didn't want either of them; **mir kann** ~**er!** (salopp) I can look after myself!; **Kannst du mir Geld geben? — Ich habe selbst** ~**[e]s mehr** Can you give me some money? — No, I haven't any left either **4** *allein stehend* (überhaupt nicht) **Post kam** ~**e** there was no *or* wasn't any post *or* mail; **Lust habe ich** ~**e** I don't feel like it

keinerlei *indekl. unbest. Gattungsz.* no ... at all; no ... what[so]ever

keiner·seits *Adv.* (selten) **ihr Vorschlag fand** ~ **Zustimmung** her suggestion met with no support anywhere *or* from any side

keines·falls *Adv.* on no account; **die Aufgabe ist schwer, aber** ~ **unlösbar** the problem is difficult but by no means insoluble

keines·wegs *Adv.* by no means; not by any means; not at all; **sein Einfluss darf** ~ **unterschätzt werden** his influence must in no way be underestimated; **ich nehme euch eure Offenheit** ~ **übel** I'm not in any way *or* not in the least offended by your frankness

kein·mal *Adv.* not [even] once; *s. auch* **einmal 1**

Keks /keːks/ *der;* ~ *od.* ~**es**, ~ *od.* ~**e** (*österr.:* ~, ~[e]) biscuit (Brit.); cookie (Amer.); ~**[e] essen/backen** eat/bake biscuits/cookies; **das/er geht mir auf den** ~ (salopp) it/he gets up my nose (coll.)

Kelch /kɛlç/ *der;* ~[e]s, ~e **1** (Trinkgefäß) goblet; **den [bitteren]** ~ **bis auf den Grund** *od.*

bis zur Neige leeren [müssen] (geh.) [have to] drain the [bitter] cup to the dregs; **der ~ ist an uns/ihm vorübergegangen** (geh.) we were/he was spared that ordeal **2** (Rel.) chalice; communion cup **3** (Bot.) calyx

kelch-, Kelch-: ~blatt *das* (Bot.) sepal; **~förmig** *Adj.* goblet-shaped; **~glas** *das* goblet

Kelim /ˈkeːlɪm/ *der;* **~s, ~s** Kilim

Kelle /ˈkɛlə/ *die;* **~, ~n** **1** (Schöpflöffel) ladle **2** (Signalstab) signalling disc **3** (Maurer~) trowel **4** (ugs.) (Tischtennisschläger) bat; (Tennisschläger) racket

Keller /ˈkɛlɐ/ *der;* **~s, ~** **1** cellar; (einer Burg usw.) cellars *pl.*; (~geschoss) basement; **der Dollar/der Kurs des Dollars ist in den ~ gefallen** (fig.) the dollar has gone through the floor (fig.); **im ~ sein** (Skatjargon) have a minus score *or* minus points **2** (~raum) cellar **3** (ugs.: Weinvorrat) cellar **4** (Luftschutz) [air-raid] shelter **5** ▸ **Kellerlokal**

Keller·assel *die* woodlouse

Kellerei *die;* **~, ~en** **1** (Betrieb) winery; wine producer's **2** (Kellerräume) [wine] cellars *pl.*

Keller-: ~fenster *das* cellar window; (von ~geschoss) basement window; **~geschoss**, ***~geschoß** *das* basement; **~gewölbe** *das* underground vault; **~kind** *das* (ugs.) slum child *or* (sl.) kid; **~lokal** *das* cellar bar/disco *etc.*; (Restaurant) cellar restaurant; **~meister** *der*, **~meisterin** *die* cellarmaster; maître de chai; **~treppe** *die* cellar stairs *pl.*; (zum ~geschoss) basement stairs *pl.*; **~wohnung** *die* basement flat (esp. Brit.) *or* (esp. Amer.) apartment

Kellner /ˈkɛlnɐ/ *der;* **~s, ~** ▸ⓘ **S. 113** waiter

Kellnerin *die;* **~, ~nen** ▸ⓘ **S. 113** waitress

kellnern *itr. V.* (ugs.) work as a waiter/waitress

Kelte /ˈkɛltə/ *der;* **~n, ~n** Celt

Kelter /ˈkɛltɐ/ *die;* **~, ~n** (für Weintrauben) wine press; (für andere Obstarten) fruit press

Kelterei *die;* **~, ~en** (für Weintrauben) grape crushing and pressing plant; (für andere Obstarten) fruit crushing and pressing plant

keltern *tr. V.* press ‹*grapes etc.*›

Keltin *die;* **~, ~nen** ▸ **Kelte**

keltisch *Adj.* ▸ⓘ **S. 670** Celtic

Keltisch *das;* **~[s]** ▸ⓘ **S. 670** Celtic; *s. auch* **Deutsch**

Kelvin /ˈkɛlvɪn/ *das;* **~s, ~** (Phys.) kelvin

Kemenate /kemeˈnaːtə/ *die;* **~, ~n** [ladies'] heated apartments *pl.* (*in a medieval castle*)

Kenia /ˈkeːni̯a/ *(das);* **~s** Kenya

Kenianer /keˈni̯aːnɐ/ *der;* **~s, ~, Kenianerin** *die;* **~, ~nen** ▸ⓘ **S. 520** Kenyan; *s. auch* **-in**

Kenn·daten /ˈkɛn-/ *Pl.* (fachspr.) personal data *or* details

kennen /ˈkɛnən/ *unr. tr. V.* **1** know; **jmdn./etw. [näher] ~ lernen** get to know sb./sth. [better]; become [better] acquainted with sb./sth.; **jmdn. als etw. ~ lernen** come to know sb. as sth.; **jmdn. von einer bestimmten Seite ~ lernen** see a particular side of sb.; **du wirst mich noch ~ lernen!** you'll find out I don't stand for any nonsense; **das Leben ~:** know about life; know the ways of the world; **das ~ wir gar nicht anders** (haben es nie anders gemacht) we've always done it that way; (haben es erfahren) it's always been like that; **jmdn. als Schriftsteller/Feigling ~:** know sb. as a writer/know sb. to be a coward; **kennst du den?** (diesen Mann) do you know who he is?; (bist du mit ihm bekannt) are you acquainted with him?; (diesen Witz) have you heard this one?; **jmds. Bücher/Werk ~:** know *or* be acquainted with sb.'s books/work; **da kennst du mich aber schlecht** (ugs.) that just shows you don't know me very well; **das ~ wir [schon]** (ugs. abwertend) (das ist nichts Neues) we've heard all that before; (diese Ausrede ~ wir) we've heard that one before; **sich nicht mehr ~ [vor ...]** be beside oneself [with ...]; **einen guten Arzt/ein gutes Restaurant ~:** know [of] a good doctor/restaurant; **da kenne ich/da kennt er nichts** (ugs.) and to hell with everything else (coll.) **2** (bekannt sein mit) know; be acquainted with; **jmdn. flüchtig/persönlich ~:** know sb. slightly/personally; **jmdn. ~ lernen** (jmdm. erstmals begegnen) meet sb.; **freut mich, Sie ~ zu lernen** pleased to meet you; pleased to make your acquaintance (formal); **die beiden ~ sich nicht mehr** the two are no longer on speaking terms; **ich glaube, wir beide ~ uns noch nicht** I don't think we've been introduced; **er will mich nicht mehr ~:** he doesn't want to know me any more **3** (haben) have; **keinen Winter/Sommer ~:** have no winter/summer; **er kennt keine Kopfschmerzen** he never gets a headache; **kein Mitleid ~:** know *or* have no pity **4** (wiedererkennen) know; recognize; **na, kennst du mich noch?** well, do you remember me?; **jmdn. am Gang/an der Stimme ~:** know *or* recognize sb. by his/her walk/voice

***kennen|lernen** ▸ **kennen 1, 2**

Kenner *der;* **~s, ~** **1** (Fachmann) expert, authority (+ *Gen.* on) **2** (von Wein, Speisen) connoisseur; **dieser Wein ist etwas für den ~:** this is a wine for the connoisseur

Kennerblick *der* expert eye; **mit ~:** with an expert eye; **er warf ~e auf die Ausstellungsstücke** he cast an expert eye over the exhibits

Kennerin *die;* **~, ~nen** ▸ **Kenner**

Kenner·miene *die* air of an expert/connoisseur; **mit ~:** with the air of an expert/connoisseur

Kennerschaft *die;* **~:** connoisseurship; (Sachkenntnis) expertise

Kenn-: ~karte *die* identity card; **~marke** *die* [police] identification badge; ≈ [police] warrant card *or* (Amer.) ID card; **~melodie** *die* (Rundf.) signature tune; **~nummer** *die* reference number; code number

kenntlich /ˈkɛntlɪç/ *Adj.* **~ sein** be recognizable *or* distinguishable **(an** by); **etw./jmdn. ~ machen** mark sth./make sb. [easily] identifiable; **etw. als Gift ~ machen** mark *or* label sth. as a poison

Kenntnis /ˈkɛntnɪs/ *die;* **~, ~se** **1** (das Kennen, Wissen) knowledge; **von etw. ~ haben/erhalten** be informed on sth. *or* have knowledge of sth./learn *or* hear about sth.; **das entzieht sich meiner ~** (geh.) I have no knowledge of that; **von etw. ~ nehmen, etw. zur ~ nehmen** take note of sth.; **jmdn. von etw. in ~ setzen** inform *or* notify sb. of sth.; **jmdn. zur ~ nehmen** take notice of sb. **2** *Pl.* (Sach- und Erfahrungswissen) knowledge *sing.*; **oberflächliche/gründliche ~se von etw. haben** have a superficial/thorough knowledge of sth.; **~se in Mathematik** *od.* **auf dem Gebiet der Mathematik** a knowledge of mathematics

Kenntnisnahme *die;* **~** (Papierdt.) **jmdm. etw. zur ~ vorlegen** submit sth. to sb. for his/her attention; **wir bitten um gefällige ~ der Akten** please give these documents your kind attention; **nach ~ der Akten** after giving the documents my/his *etc.* attention

kenntnis·reich *Adj.* well-informed; knowledgeable

***Kennummer** ▸ **Kennnummer**

kenn-, Kenn-: ~wort *das; Pl.* **~wörter** **1** (Erkennungszeichen) code word; reference; **2** (Parole) password; code word; **~zahl** *die* **1** (charakteristischer Zahlenwert) index; **2** (Fernspr.) code; **~zeichen** *das* **1** (Merkmal) sign; mark; **ein ~zeichen für einen Witterungsumschlag** a sign of a change in the weather; **ein ~zeichen eines Genies** a [hall]mark of a genius; **besondere ~zeichen** distinguishing marks; **2** (Erkennungszeichen) badge; (auf einem Behälter, einer Ware usw.) label; **etw. als ~zeichen tragen** carry/wear sth. as a means of identification; (einer Gruppe) carry/wear sth. as an indication of membership; **3** (am Fahrzeug) registration number; **~zeichnen** *tr. V.* **1** (mit einem ~zeichen versehen) mark; label ‹*container, goods, etc.*›; mark, signpost ‹*way*›; tag ‹*bird, animal*›; **etw. als ... ~zeichnen** mark *or* identify sth. as ...; **2** (charakterisieren) characterize; **jmdn. als ... ~zeichnen** characterize sb. as ...; **3** (in seiner Eigenart erkennen lassen) typify; **jmdn. als ... ~zeichnen** mark sb. out as ...; **~zeichnend** *Adj.* typical, characteristic **(für** of); **~zeichnung** *die* **1** marking; (von Behältern, Waren) labelling; (von Vögeln, Tieren) tagging; **2** (Charakterisierung) characterization; **3** (~zeichen) label; **eine auffällige ~zeichnung von Fußgängerüberwegen** a conspicuous means of marking pedestrian crossings; **4** (Logik) definite description; **~zeichnungspflicht** *die* requirement to label *or* mark goods; labelling requirement; **~zeichnungspflichtig** *Adj.* that has/have to be labelled *postpos.*; **~zeichnungspflichtig sein** have to be labelled; **~ziffer** *die* **1** (Ziffer zur Unterscheidung) reference number; (bei einem Zeitungsinserat) box number; **2** (Math.) characteristic

Kenotaph /kenoˈtaːf/ *das;* **~s, ~e** cenotaph

Kentaur /kɛnˈtau̯ɐ/ *der;* **~en, ~en** ▸ **Zentaur**

kentern /ˈkɛntɐn/ *itr. V.* **1** *mit sein* ‹*boat, ship, etc.*› capsize **2** (Seemannsspr.) ‹*tide, wind*› turn

Keramik /keˈraːmɪk/ *die;* **~, ~en** **1** (gebrannter Ton) ceramics *pl.*; pottery **2** (Keramikgegenstand) ceramic; piece of pottery **3** (Material) fired clay **4** (Technik) ceramics *sing.*; pottery

keramisch *Adj.* ceramic

Kerbe /ˈkɛrbə/ *die;* **~, ~n** notch; **in dieselbe** *od.* **die gleiche ~ hauen** *od.* **schlagen** (ugs.) take the same line

Kerbel /ˈkɛrbl̩/ *der;* **~s** chervil

kerben *tr. V.* **1** (mit Kerben versehen) notch; cut a notch/notches in **2** carve ‹*pattern etc.*›

Kerb-: ~holz *das: in* **etwas/einiges auf dem ~holz haben** (ugs.) have done a job/a job or two (sl.); **~tier** *das* insect

Kerker /ˈkɛrkɐ/ *der;* **~s, ~** **1** (hist.: Gefängnis) dungeons *pl.*; (einzelne Zelle) dungeon **2** (österr., hist.: Freiheitsstrafe) imprisonment

Kerker-: ~haft *die* (hist.) imprisonment; **~meister** *der* (hist.) jailer; **~strafe** *die* (österr., hist.) ▸ **Gefängnisstrafe**

Kerl /kɛrl/ *der;* **~s, ~e** (*nordd., md. auch:* **Kerls**) **1** (ugs.: männliche Person) fellow (coll.); chap (coll.); bloke (Brit. sl.); **ein ganzer** *od.* **richtiger ~:** a splendid fellow (coll.) *or* chap (coll.); **ein gemeiner/frecher ~** (abwertend) a nasty so-and-so (coll.)/an impudent fellow (coll.) **2** (ugs.: sympathischer Mensch) **er ist ein feiner ~:** he's a fine chap (coll.) *or* (sl.) a good bloke; **sie ist ein netter/feiner ~:** she's a nice/fine woman

Kern /kɛrn/ *der;* **~[e]s, ~e** **1** (Fruchtsamen) pip; (von Steinobst) stone; (von Nüssen, Mandeln usw.) kernel; **der ~ eines Problems/Vorschlags** (fig.) the crux *or* gist of a problem/gist of a suggestion; **er hat einen guten** *od.* **in ihm steckt ein guter ~** (fig.) he is good at heart; **das birgt einen wahren ~** (fig.) it contains a core of truth; **zum ~ einer Sache** (*Gen.*) **kommen** (fig.) get to the heart of a matter **2** (wichtigster Teil einer Gruppe) core; nucleus; **der harte ~:** the hard core **3** (Physik: Atom~) nucleus **4** (einer elektrischen Spule, eines Reaktors) core **5** (Gießerei) core **6** (Biol.: Zell~) nucleus; (Anat., Biol.: Nerven~) centre **7** (Zentrum) city/town centre **8** (Met.) **mit seinem ~ über Schottland liegend** ‹*depression etc.*› centred over Scotland

kern-, Kern-: ~aufgabe *die* central task; **~aussage** *die* central message; **~beißer** *der* hawfinch; **~brenn·stoff** *der* nuclear fuel; **~chemie** *die* nuclear chemistry; **~energie** *die* nuclear energy *no art.*; **~explosion** *die* **1** (von atomaren Sprengkörpern) nuclear explosion; **2** (Physik) [complete] fragmentation of the nucleus; **~fach** *das* (Schulw.) core subject; **~fäule** *die* (Forstw.) heart rot; **~forschung** *die* nuclear research; **~frage** *die* central question; **~frucht** *die* (Bot.) pome; **~fusion** *die* (Phys., Biol.) nuclear fusion *no art.*; **~gedanke** *der* central idea; **~gehäuse** *das* core; **~geschäft** *das* core business; **~gesund** *Adj.* fit as a fiddle *pred.*; sound as a bell *pred.*; **~haus** *das* ▸ **~gehäuse**; **~holz** *das* (Holzverarb.) heartwood

kernig

A *Adj.* **1** (urwüchsig, markig) robust, earthy ‹*language*›; down-to-earth ‹*remarks*›; (kraftvoll)

k

powerful, forceful ‹speech›; pithy ‹saying›; **ein ~er Mann/Typ** (ugs.) a robust and athletic man/type 2) (fest, haltbar) robust, stout, sturdy ‹boots, shoes›; sound ‹wood›; robust ‹leather› 3) (gehaltvoll, kräftig) full-bodied ‹wine› 4) (ugs.: vortrefflich) great (coll.) 5) (voller Kerne) full of pips *pred.*

B *adv.* 1) (urwüchsig, markig) robustly; (kraftvoll) forcefully; (knapp) pithily ‹expressed› 2) (ugs.: vortrefflich) **wir haben ~ gezecht und geschwoft** we had a whale of a time drinking and dancing (coll.)

Kern·kompetenz *die* 1) (Fähigkeit) essential skill; core skill; (einer Firma od. Organisation) core competence; 2) (Zuständigkeit) main area of authority *or* competence

Kern·kraft *die* 1) *Pl.* (Physik) nuclear forces 2) nuclear power *no art.*

Kernkraft-: ~gegner *der*, **~gegnerin** *die* opponent of nuclear power; **~werk** *das* nuclear power station *or* plant

kern-, Kern-: ~ladungszahl *die* atomic number; **~land** *das* heartland; **~los** *Adj.* seedless; **~obst** *das* pomaceous fruit; pomes *pl.*; **~pflichtfach** *das* (Schulw.) core-curriculum subject; **~physik** *die* nuclear physics *sing., no art.*; **~physiker** *der*, **~physikerin** *die* nuclear physicist; **~punkt** *der* central point; **~reaktion** *die* (Physik) nuclear reaction; **~reaktor** *der* nuclear reactor; **~satz** *der* 1) (wesentlicher Satz) key sentence *or* statement; 2) (Sprachw.) *basic structural form of the sentence, with the finite verb as the second idea;* kernel sentence; **~schatten** *der* (Optik, Astron.) umbra; total shadow; **~schmelze** *die* (Physik) core meltdown; **~seife** *die* washing soap; hard soap; **~spaltung** *die* (Physik) nuclear fission *no art.*; **~spin·tomographie** /ˈkɛrnspɪn----/ *die* (Med.) [nuclear] magnetic resonance imaging; **~spruch** *der* wise saw *or* saying; **~stück** *das* centrepiece; (einer Diskussion, eines Programms) central *or* main item; (eines Plans) main point; **~technik** *die* nuclear engineering *no art.*; **~truppe** *die* crack unit; **~verschmelzung** *die* (Physik, Biol.) nuclear fusion *no art.*; **~waffe** *die* nuclear weapon; **~waffen·frei** *Adj.* nuclear-free; **~waffen·versuch** *der* nuclear [weapons] test; **~zeit** *die* core time

Kerosin /keroˈziːn/ *das;* **~s** kerosene

Kerze /ˈkɛrt͡sə/ *die;* **~, ~n** 1) candle; **elektrische ~:** candle bulb 2) (Zünd~) spark plug; sparking plug 3) (Turnen Jargon) shoulder stand 4) (Physik veralt.) candela

kerzen-, Kerzen-: ~beleuchtung *die* candlelight *no indef. art.*; **~docht** *der* [candle] wick; **~gerade,** (ugs.) **~grade** A *Adj.* dead straight ‹tree, post, etc.›; very stiff ‹bow›; B *adv.* bolt upright; ‹rise› straight upwards; **~halter** *der* candle holder; **~leuchter** *der* candlestick; (für mehrere ~) candelabrum; **~licht** *das* the light of a candle/of candles; **bei ~licht** by candlelight; **~schein** *der* candlelight *no pl.*; **~schlüssel** *der* (Kfz-W.) plug spanner; **~stummel** *der*, **~stumpf** *der* stump of a/the candle

Kescher /ˈkɛʃɐ/ *der;* **~s, ~** (für Fische) hand net; fishing net; (für Schmetterlinge) butterfly net

kess, *keß /kɛs/

A *Adj.* 1) (hübsch, flott) pert; pert, jaunty ‹hat, dress, etc.›; *s. auch* **Sohle 1** 2) (frech, vorlaut) cheeky 3) (salopp) **kesser Vater** [bull]dyke (sl.); butch (sl.)

B *adv.* 1) (hübsch, flott) jauntily 2) (frech, vorlaut) cheekily

Kessel /ˈkɛsl̩/ *der;* **~s, ~** 1) (Tee~) kettle 2) (zum Kochen) pot; (für offenes Feuer) cauldron; (in einer Brauerei) vat; (Wasch~) copper; wash boiler 3) (Berg~) basin-shaped valley 4) (Milit.) encircled area; (kleiner) pocket 5) (Jägerspr.) ring of hunters and beaters 6) (Dampf~, Heiz~) boiler 7) (schweiz.: Eimer) bucket

Kessel-: ~fleisch *das* ▸**Wellfleisch**; **~haus** *das* boilerhouse; **~jagd** *die* ▸**~treiben 1**; **~pauke** *die* kettledrum; **~raum** *der* boiler room; **~schlacht** *die* battle of encirclement; **~schmied** *der*, **~schmiedin** *die* boilermaker; **~schmiede** *die* boiler shop; **~stein** *der* fur; scale; **~treiben** *das* 1) (Jägerspr.: Treibjagd) battue (*using a circle of hunters and beaters*); 2) (Hetzkampagne) witch-hunt; **~wagen** *der* (Kfz-W.) road tanker; tanker lorry (Brit.); tank truck (Amer.); (Eisenbahn) tank wagon; tank car

Kessheit, *Keßheit *die;* **~, ~en** ▸**kess** A: pertness; jauntiness; cheekiness

Ketchup ▸**Ketschup**

Ketsch /kɛt͡ʃ/ *die;* **~, ~en** (Segeln) ketch

Ketschup /ˈkɛt͡ʃap/ *der od. das;* **~s, ~s** ketchup

Kettchen /ˈkɛtçən/ *das;* **~s, ~:** [neck] chain (*with cross etc. attached*); (Fuß~) anklet; (Arm~) bracelet

Kette /ˈkɛtə/ *die;* **~, ~n** 1) chain; (von Kettenfahrzeugen) track; **die ~ [an der Tür] vorlegen** put the chain across [the door]; **an der ~ liegen** ‹dog› be chained up; **jmdn. in ~n legen** put sb. in chains; **die ~n abwerfen/sprengen** *od.* **zerreißen** (fig. geh.) cast off *or* throw off/break one's chains *or* shackles; **jmdn. an die ~ legen** (fig.) keep sb. on a [tight *or* short] leash 2) (Halsschmuck) necklace; (eines Bürgermeisters usw.) chain 3) (Reihe) chain; (von Autos) line; **eine ~ bilden** form a chain; **eine ~ von Beweisen** a chain of evidence; **die ~ der Berge** the chain of mountains; **~ rauchen** (ugs.) chain-smoke 4) (von Ereignissen) string; series 5) (Weberei) warp

Kettel·maschine /ˈkɛtl̩-/ *die* (Textilw.) looper

ketten *tr. V.* 1) (mit einer Kette anbinden) chain (**an** + *Akk.* to) 2) (unauflösbar binden) bind; **jmdn. an sich** (*Akk.*) **~:** bind sb. to oneself; **sich an jmdn. ~:** tie oneself to sb.

Ketten-: ~antrieb *der* chain drive; chain transmission; **~armband** *das* (für eine Armbanduhr) [mesh-link/open-link] bracelet; (Schmuck) [chain] bracelet; **~blatt** *das* chain wheel; front sprocket; **~brücke** *die* chain bridge; **~fahrzeug** *das* ▸**Raupenfahrzeug**; **~glied** *das* [chain] link; **~hemd** *das* (hist.) coat of chain mail; **~hund** *der* 1) watchdog *or* guard dog (kept on a chain); 2) (Milit. Jargon) Military Policeman; **~laden** *der; Pl.* **~läden** chain store; **~panzer** *der* chain mail; chain armour; **~rad** *das* sprocket [wheel]; **~rauchen** *das;* **~~s** chain-smoking *no art.*; **~raucher** *der*, **~raucherin** *die* chain-smoker; **~reaktion** *die* chain reaction; **eine ~reaktion auslösen** trigger a chain reaction; **~ritzel** *das* [rear] sprocket; [rear] sprocket wheel; **~säge** *die* chain saw; **~schaltung** *die* derailleur gears *pl.*; **~schluss, *~schluß** *der* (Logik) chain syllogism; sorites; **~schutz** *der* chain guard; **~stich** *der* (Handarb.) chain stitch **~werfer** *der* ▸**Umwerfer**

Ketzer /ˈkɛt͡sɐ/ *der;* **~s, ~** (auch fig.) heretic

Ketzerei *die;* **~, ~en** (auch fig.) heresy

Ketzer·gericht *das* (hist.) Inquisition

Ketzerin *die;* **~, ~nen** (auch fig.) heretic

ketzerisch (auch fig.)

A *Adj.* heretical

B *adv.* heretically

keuchen /ˈkɔyçn̩/ *itr. V.* 1) (schwer atmen) pant; gasp for breath; (fig.) ‹locomotive› chug; **mit ~dem Atem** gasping *or* panting for breath 2) *mit sein* (sich ~d fortbewegen) puff *or* pant one's way; come/go puffing *or* panting along

Keuch·husten *der* ▸ⓘ **S. 439** whooping cough *no art.*

Keule /ˈkɔylə/ *die;* **~, ~n** 1) (Schlagwaffe) club; cudgel; **chemische ~:** Chemical Mace ® 2) (Gymnastik) [Indian] club 3) (Kochk.) leg; (Reh~, Hasen~) haunch; (Gänse~, Hühner~) drumstick; leg

keulen *tr. (auch. itr.) V.* (Tiermed.) cull

Keulen-: ~hieb *der*, **~schlag** *der* blow with a club *or* cudgel; (fig.) terrible blow; **~schwingen** *das* (Gymnastik) club swinging; swinging [Indian] clubs

Keulung *die;* **~, ~en** (Tiermed.) culling; **~en** culls

keusch /kɔyʃ/

A *Adj.* 1) (sexuell enthaltsam) chaste; pure 2) (geh. veralt.) (sittsam) modest; demure; (sittlich und moralisch rein) pure

B *adv.* 1) (sexuell enthaltsam) **~ leben** lead a chaste life 2) (sittsam) modestly; demurely; (sittlich und moralisch rein) in a pure manner

Keuschheit *die;* **~** 1) (sexuelle Enthaltsamkeit) chastity 2) (geh. veralt.) (Sittsamkeit) modesty; (sittliche und moralische Reinheit) purity

Keuschheits-: ~gelübde *das* vow of chastity; **~gürtel** *der* chastity belt

Kfz *Abk.* **= Kraftfahrzeug**

> **Kfz-Kennzeichen**
>
> This is the number plate on German motor vehicles, which have to be licensed by the *Zulassungsstelle* (vehicle registration office) for the owner's registered place of residence. You can easily tell from the first, or first two or three, letters on the *Kfz-Kennzeichen* where the car comes from.

kg *Abk.* ▸ⓘ **S. 315 = Kilogramm** kg

KG *Abk.* **= Kommanditgesellschaft**

K-Gruppe /ˈkaː-/ *die* (Politik) [*anti-Soviet*] *Communist organization*

Khaki[1] /ˈkaːki/ *der;* **~[s]** (Stoff) khaki

Khaki[2] *das;* **~[s]** (Farbe) khaki

khaki·farben *Adj.* khaki[-coloured]

kHz *Abk.* **= Kilohertz** kHz

Kibbuz /kɪˈbuːt͡s/ *der;* **~, ~im** /kɪbuˈt͡siːm/ *od.* **~e** kibbutz

Kibbuznik /kɪˈbuːt͡snɪk/ *der;* **~s, ~s** kibbutznik

Kicher·erbse *die* chickpea

kichern /ˈkɪçɐn/ *itr. V.* giggle; **in sich hinein/vor sich hin ~:** giggle to oneself; **dass ich nicht kichere!** (iron.) don't make me laugh!

Kick /kɪk/ *der;* **~[s], ~s** (Fußball, ugs.) kick

Kick-: ~board /ˈkɪkbɔːd/ *das;* **~~s, ~~s** kickboard [scooter]; **~down, ~-down** /kɪkˈdaun/ *das;* **~~s, ~~s** (Kfz-W.) kick-down

kicken (ugs.)

A *itr. V.* play football

B *tr. V.* kick

Kicker *der;* **~s, ~, Kickerin** *die;* **~, ~nen** (ugs.) footballer; [football] player

Kick·starter *der* (Kfz-W.) kick-starter; kick-start

kidnappen /ˈkɪtnɛpn̩/ *tr. V.* kidnap

Kidnapper /ˈkɪtnɛpɐ/ *der;* **~s, ~, Kidnapperin** *die;* **~, ~nen** kidnapper

Kidnapping /ˈkɪtnɛpɪŋ/ *das;* **~s, ~s** kidnapping

kiebig /ˈkiːbɪç/ *Adj.* (bes. nordd.) (frech) cheeky; impertinent; (gereizt) touchy

Kiebitz /ˈkiːbɪt͡s/ *der;* **~es, ~e** 1) (Vogel) lapwing; peewit 2) (ugs.: Zuschauer beim Spiel) kibitzer (coll.)

kiebitzen *itr. V.* (ugs. scherzh.) 1) (bei einem Spiel zuschauen) kibitz (coll.) 2) (neugierig beobachten) look on

Kiefer[1] /ˈkiːfɐ/ *der;* **~s, ~** ▸ⓘ **S. 435** jaw; (Kieferknochen) jawbone

Kiefer[2] *die;* **~, ~n** 1) (Baum) pine [tree] 2) (Holz) pine [wood]

Kiefer-: ~bruch *der* ▸ⓘ **S. 439** (Med.) fracture of the jaw; fractured jaw; **~chirurgie** *die* oral surgery *no art.*; **~höhle** *die* ▸ⓘ **S. 435** (Anat.) maxillary sinus; **~höhlen·entzündung** *die* maxillary sinusitis *no art.*; **~klemme** *die* (Med.) lockjaw; trismus (Med.); **~knochen** *der* ▸ⓘ **S. 435** jawbone

Kiefern-: ~holz *das* pine [wood]; **~nadel** *die* pine needle; **~wald** *der* pinewood; (größer) pine forest; **~zapfen** *der* pine cone

Kiefer-: ~orthopäde *der*, **~orthopädin**, *die* ▸ⓘ **S. 113** orthodontist; **~orthopädie** *die* orthodontics *sing., no art.*

kieken /ˈkiːkn̩/ *itr. V.* (nordd.) look

Kieker /ˈkiːkɐ/ *der;* **~s, ~** 1) (Seemannsspr.) (Fernglas) binoculars *pl.*; (Fernrohr) telescope 2) *in* **jmdn. auf dem ~ haben** (ugs.) have it in for sb. (coll.); (misstrauisch beobachten) keep a careful eye *or* watch on sb.

kieksen /ˈkiːksn̩/ ▸**gicksen**

Kiel[1] /kiːl/ *der;* ~[e]s, ~e keel; **ein Schiff auf ~ legen** (Schiffsbau) lay down a ship; lay the keel of a ship

Kiel[2] *der;* ~[e]s, ~e [1] (Teil einer Vogelfeder) quill [2] (hist.: Schreibfeder) quill [pen]

kiel-, Kiel-: ~**feder** *die* quill feather; ~**holen** *tr. V.* (Seemannsspr.) [1] (auf die Seite legen) careen ‹*ship*›; [2] (unter dem Schiff hindurchziehen) keelhaul; ~**oben** /-'--/ *Adv.* bottom up; ~**raum** *der* bilge; ~**wasser** *das* wake; **in jmds. ~wasser segeln** *od.* **schwimmen** (fig.) follow in sb.'s wake

Kieme /'kiːmə/ *die;* ~, ~n gill

Kiemen-: ~**atmer** /-|aːtmɐ/ *der;* ~~s, ~~ (Zool.) gill-breathing animal; gill-breather; ~**spalte** *die* (Zool.) gill slit

Kien /kiːn/ *der;* ~[e]s resinous wood; (Kiefernholz) resinous pine wood

Kien-: ~**apfel** *der* ▸**Kiefernzapfen**; ~**fackel** *die* pine [wood] torch; ~**span** *der* pine wood chip; (zum Anzünden) pine wood spill

Kiepe /'kiːpə/ *die;* ~, ~n (nordd., md.) dosser; pannier

Kies /kiːs/ *der;* ~es, ~e [1] (kleine, runde Steine) gravel; (auf dem Strand) shingle [2] (Mineral.) pyrites *sing.* [3] (salopp: Geld) dough (coll.); bread (coll.)

Kiesel /'kiːzl̩/ *der;* ~s, ~: pebble

Kiesel-: ~**erde** *die* siliceous earth; ~**säure** *die* (Chemie) silicic acid; ~**stein** *der* pebble

kiesen /'kiːzn̩/ *unr., auch regelm. tr. V.* (dichter. veralt.) choose; select

Kies·grube *die* gravel pit

Kies·weg *der* gravel path

Kiez /kiːts/ *der;* ~es, ~e [1] (nordostd., bes. berlin.) (Stadtteil) neighbourhood [2] (Jargon: Bordellgegend) red-light district

Kif /kɪf/ *der;* ~[s] (ugs.) pot (sl.); grass (sl.)

kiffen /'kɪfn̩/ *itr. V.* (ugs.) smoke pot (sl.) *or* grass (sl.)

Kiffer *der;* ~s, ~, **Kifferin** *die;* ~, ~nen (ugs.) pothead (sl.)

kikeriki /kikəri'kiː/ *Interj.* (Kinderspr.) cock-a-doodle-doo

Kikeriki *das;* ~s, ~s cock-a-doodle-doo

Kilbi /'kɪlbi/ *die;* ~, **Kilbenen** /'kɪlbənən/ (schweiz.) ▸**Kirchweih**

killekille /'kɪlə'kɪlə/ *Interj.* (Kinderspr.) tickle-tickle; **bei jmdm. ~ machen** tickle sb.

killen[1] /'kɪlən/ *tr. V.* (salopp) do in (sl.); bump off (coll.)

killen[2] *itr. V.* (Seemannsspr.) ‹*sail*› shiver

Killer *der;* ~s, ~, **Killerin** *die;* ~, ~nen (salopp) killer; (gegen Bezahlung) hit man/hit woman (coll.)

Killer-: ~**satellit** *der* (ugs.) hunter-killer satellite; ~**zelle** *die* (Jargon) killer cell

Kilo /'kiːlo/ *das;* ~s, ~[s] ▸ⓘ **S. 315** kilo

Kilo-: ~**gramm** *das* ▸ⓘ **S. 315** kilogram; ~**hertz** *das;* ~, ~ (Physik) kilohertz; ~**kalorie** *die* (Physik veralt.) kilocalorie

Kilometer *der;* ~s, ~ ▸ⓘ **S. 224**, ▸ⓘ **S. 310** kilometre; **75 ~ in der Stunde** 75 kilometres per hour

kilometer-, Kilometer-: ~**fresser** *der,* ~**fresserin** *die* (ugs. scherzh. od. abwertend) **er ist ein ~fresser** he really burns up the miles (coll.); ~**geld** *das* mileage allowance; ~**lang** [A] *Adj.* miles long *pred.;* **eine ~lange Autoschlange** a traffic jam stretching [back] for miles; [B] *adv.* for miles [and miles]; ~**pauschale** *die* (Steuerw.) mileage allowance (*to taxpayer driving to and from work*); ~**stand** *der* mileage reading; ~**stein** *der* milestone; ~**weit** [A] *Adj.* **in ~weiter Entfernung** miles away in the distance; **eine ~weite Aussicht** a view for miles; [B] *adv.* for miles [and miles]

Kilo-: ~**preis** *der* price per kilo; ~**watt** *das* (Physik, Elektrot.) kilowatt

Kilowatt·stunde *die* (Physik; bes. Elektrot.) kilowatt-hour

kilo·weise *Adv.* [1] by the kilo; [2] (ugs.: in großen Mengen) **~ Bücher lesen** read tons of books (coll.)

Kimbern /'kɪmbɐn/ *Pl.* Cimbri

Kimm /kɪm/ *die;* ~ (Seemannsspr.) [1] (Horizontlinie) apparent *or* visible horizon [2] (von Schiffen) bilge

Kimme /'kɪmə/ *die;* ~, ~n [1] (Einschnitt im Visier) sighting notch [2] (salopp: Gesäßspalte) cleft between the buttocks

Kimmung *die;* ~ (Seemannsspr.) mirage

Kimono /ki'moːno/ *der;* ~s, ~s kimono

Kind /kɪnt/ *das;* ~[e]s, ~er [1] child; (Klein~) child; infant; (Baby) child; baby; **ein ~ erwarten/bekommen** *od.* (ugs.) **kriegen** be expecting/have a baby; **ich glaube, ihre Tochter kriegt ein ~:** I think her daughter's going to have a baby; **ein ~ zur Welt bringen** (geh.) give birth to a child; **ein ~/~er in die Welt setzen** bring a child/children into the world; **von einem ~ entbunden werden** be delivered of a child; **das ~ beim [rechten] Namen nennen** (fig.) call a spade a spade; **das ~ muss doch einen Namen haben** (ugs.) we need a good name for it; (wir müssen einen Vorwand dafür finden) we've got to dress it up somehow; **wir werden das ~ schon [richtig] schaukeln** (ugs.) we'll soon sort things out *or* have things sorted out; **unschuldig wie ein neugeborenes ~ sein** be as innocent as a newborn babe; **jmdm. ein ~ machen** *od.* **andrehen** (ugs.) put sb. in the family way (coll.) *or* in the club (sl.); **das ~ mit dem Bade ausschütten** (fig.) throw the baby out with the bathwater; **jmdn. wie ein [kleines] ~ behandeln** treat sb. like a [small] child; **das weiß/kann doch jedes ~:** any child *or* five-year old knows/can do that; **von ~ an** *od.* **auf** from childhood; **er ist ein großes ~:** he is a big baby; **sich wie ein ~ freuen** be [as] pleased as Punch; **über schöne Dinge kann er sich wie ein ~ freuen** he takes a childlike pleasure in beautiful things; **du bist als ~ [wohl] zu heiß gebadet worden** (ugs.) you [must] have a screw loose (coll.); **wie sag ichs meinem ~e?** I don't know the best way to put it; (bei einer unangenehmen Nachricht) how do I break the news?; **aus ~ern werden Leute** childhood passes [all too soon]; **dann kommt bei ihm das ~ im Manne durch** (scherzh.) then he shows that he is [still] a child at heart; **[seine/deine** *usw.***] ~er und ~eskinder** [his/your *etc.*] children and [his/your *etc.*] children's children; **bei jmdm. lieb ~ sein** (ugs.) be a favourite with sb.; **sich bei jmdm. lieb ~ machen** (ugs.) get on the right side of sb.; **ein ziges ~ sein** be an only child; **armer/reicher Leute ~ sein** be the child of poor/wealthy parents; come from a poor/wealthy family; **ein ~ seiner Zeit** (fig.) a child of one's times; **~er Gottes** (fig.) God's children; **ein ~ des Todes sein** (fig. geh.) be as good as dead; **ein [echtes] Wiener/Berliner ~:** a [true] Viennese/Berliner; **ein ~ der Liebe** (geh. verhüll.) a love child; **er ist/du bist** *usw.* **kein ~ von Traurigkeit** (ugs.) he knows/you know *etc.* how to enjoy himself/yourself *etc.*; **jmds. liebstes ~ sein** ‹*person*› be sb.'s pet; **das Auto/die Oberstufenreform ist sein liebstes ~:** the car is his first love/reform of the sixth form is his pet project; **jmdn. an ~es statt annehmen** (veralt.) adopt sb.; *s. auch* **tot 1** [2] (ugs.: als Anrede) **mein [liebes] ~:** my [dear] child; **~er, hört mal alle her!** listen to this, all of you (coll.); **[~er,] ~er!** my goodness!

Kind·bett *das* (veralt.) ▸**Wochenbett**

Kindbett·fieber *das* childbed *or* puerperal fever

Kindchen /'kɪntçən/ [1] (kleines Kind) [small *or* little] child [2] (Anrede) dear child

kinder-, Kinder-: ~**arbeit** *die* child labour; ~**arm** *Adj.* with few children *postpos., not pred.;* ~**armut** *die* [1] (Armut unter Kindern) child poverty; [2] (Mangel an Kindern) lack of children; ~**arzt** *der,* ~**ärztin** *die* ▸ⓘ **S. 113** paediatrician; ~**auge** *das:* **mit sehnsüchtigen ~augen auf etw.** (*Akk.*) **blicken** look at sth. with the wistful eyes of a child; ~**beihilfe** *die* (österr.) ▸~**geld**; ~**bekleidung** *die* children's wear; ~**besteck** *das* children's cutlery; **ein ~besteck** a set of children's cutlery; ~**bett** *das* cot; (für größeres Kind) child's bed; ~**bewahr·anstalt** *die* (veralt.) children's home; ~**bild** *das* (Foto) photograph of a child; (Malerei usw.) portrait of a child; ~**buch** *das* children's book; ~**chor** *der* children's choir; ~**dorf** *das* children's village; ~**ehe** *die* child marriage

Kinderei *die;* ~, ~en childishness *no indef. art., no pl.;* **eine ~:** a childish prank; **~en** childishness *sing.;* childish behaviour *sing.*

kinder-, Kinder-: ~**ermäßigung** *die* reduction for children; ~**erziehung** *die* bringing up of children; ~**fahrrad** *das* child's bicycle; ~**feindlich** [A] *Adj.* hostile to children *pred.;* anti-children *pred.;* (für Kinder nicht förderlich) ‹*planning, policy*› which does not cater for the needs of children; [B] *adv.* **sich ~feindlich verhalten** act in a manner hostile to children; ~**feindlichkeit** *die* hostility to children; (von Planung, Politik) failure to cater for children; ~**fernsehen** *das* children's television; children's TV; ~**fest** *das* children's party; children's fête; ~**film** *der* children's film; ~**fräulein** *das* ▸**Gouvernante**; ~**freund** *der,* ~**freundin** *die:* **ein [großer] ~freund/[große] ~freunde sein** be [very] fond of children; ~**freundlich** [A] *Adj.* fond of children *pred.;* ‹*town, resort*› which caters for children; child-friendly ‹*planning, policy*›; ‹*planning, policy*› which caters for the needs of children; [B] *adv.* in a child-friendly way; ~**freundlichkeit** *die* fondness for children; (of planning, policy etc.) child-friendliness; ~**funk** *der* children's programme; (Abteilung) Children's Programmes *sing., no art.;* ~**garten** *der* kindergarten; nursery school; ~**gärtnerin** *die* ▸ⓘ **S. 113** kindergarten teacher; nursery-school teacher; ~**geld** *das* child benefit; ~**geschrei** *das* (oft abwertend) screaming *or* shouting of children; noise of children screaming *or* shouting; ~**gesicht** *das* child's face; (eines Erwachsenen) childlike face; baby face; ~**glaube** *der* childlike belief *or* faith; (abwertend) childish belief *or* faith; ~**gottesdienst** *der* children's service; ~**heilkunde** *die* paediatrics *sing., no art.;* ~**heim** *das* children's home; ~**hort** *der* day home for schoolchildren; ~**jahre** *Pl.* childhood years; ~**karussell** *das* children's roundabout; ~**kleidung** *die* children's clothes *pl.;* children's wear; ~**klinik** *die* children's hospital; ~**kram** *der* (ugs.) [1] (Aufziehen von Kindern) business of bringing up kids (coll.); [2] (Unbedeutendes, Unproblematisches) kids' stuff (coll.); ~**krankenhaus** *das* ▸~**klinik**; ~**krankheit** *die* [1] (Infektionskrankheit bei ~n) children's disease *or* illness; **welche ~krankheiten hatten Sie?** what childhood diseases have you had?; [2] *Pl.* (Anfangsschwierigkeiten) teething troubles; ~**kreuzzug** *der* (hist.) Children's Crusade; ~**kriegen** *das;* ~~s (ugs.) having children; ~**krippe** *die* crèche; day nursey; ~**lähmung** *die* ▸ⓘ **S. 439** poliomyelitis; infantile paralysis *no art.;* ~**leicht** (ugs.) [A] *Adj.* childishly simple *or* easy; dead easy; **das ist ~leicht** it's child's play *or* (coll.) kid's stuff; [B] *adv.* **das kann ~leicht bedient werden** it's childishly simple to use; ~**lieb** *Adj.* fond of children *pred.;* ~**liebe** *die* love of children; ~**lied** *das* nursery rhyme; ~**los** *Adj.* childless; ~**losigkeit** *die;* ~~: childlessness; ~**mädchen** *das* nursemaid; nanny; ~**märchen** *das* [children's] fairy tale; ~**mord** *der* child murder; ~**mund** *der* child's mouth; **~mund tut Wahrheit kund** (Prov.) it takes a child to point out the truth; ~**narr** *der:* **er ist ein ~narr** he adores children; ~**närrin** *die:* **sie ist eine ~närrin** she adores children; ~**pflegerin** *die* children's nurse; ~**popo** *der* (ugs.) [baby's] bottom; **glatt wie ein ~popo** [as] smooth as a baby's bottom; ~**porno** *der* (ugs.) child-porn *or* kiddy-porn film/video (coll); ~**pornographie** *die* child pornography; ~**psychologie** *die* child psychology *no art.;* ~**puder** *der* baby powder; ~**reich** *Adj.* with many children *postpos., not pred.;* **eine ~reiche Familie** a large family; ~**reichtum** *der* large number of children; ~**reim** *der* nursery rhyme; ~**schänder** *der;* ~~s, ~~, ~**schänderin** *die;* ~~, ~~nen child abuser; ~**schar** *die* crowd of children; ~**schreck** *der* bogyman; ~**schuh** *der*

k

child's shoe; **ich bin/du bist den ~schuhen entwachsen** (fig.) I'm/you're not a child any more; **noch in den ~schuhen stecken** ‹*process, technique, etc.*› be still in its infancy; **~schutz** *der* child protection legislation; **~schwester** *die* children's nurse; **~segen** *der* (oft scherzh.) **eine Familie mit reichem ~segen** a family blessed with a large number of children; **~sitz** *der* child's seat; (an einem Fahrrad) child-carrier [seat]; (im Auto) child's safety seat; **~soldat** *der*, **~soldatin** *die* child soldier; **~spiel** *das* children's game; **[für jmdn.] ein ~spiel sein** be child's play [to sb.]; **~spielplatz** *der* [children's] playground; **~spiel·zeug** *das* [children's] toys *pl. or* playthings *pl.*; (einzeln) [child's] toy *or* plaything; **~sprache** *die* [1] (Sprache eines Kindes) child language; children's language; [2] (kindliche Sprechweise Erwachsener) nursery language; **~sterblichkeit** *die* child mortality; **~stimme** *die* child's voice; **~stube** *die*: **eine gute/schlechte ~stube gehabt** *od.* **genossen haben** have been well/badly brought up; **hast du gar keine ~stube?** didn't you ever learn any manners?; **~stuhl** *der* child's chair; (Hochstuhl) high chair; **~tages·heim** *das*, **~tages·stätte** *die* day nursery; **~teller** *der* [1] child's plate; [2] (auf der Speisekarte) children's menu; **~trommel** *die* toy drum; **~wagen** *der* pram (Brit.); baby carriage (Amer.); (Sportwagen) pushchair (Brit.); stroller (Amer.); **~wäsche** *die* [children's] underwear; (für Neugeborene) baby linen; **~wunsch** *der* [1] (Wunsch nach einem Kind, nach Kindern) desire to have a child/children; [2] (Wunsch eines Kindes) childhood wish; **~zahl** *die* number of children per family; **~zeit** *die* childhood; **~zimmer** *das* [1] children's room; (für Kleinkinder) nursery; [2] (Einrichtung) furniture for the children's room/nursery; **~zuschlag** *der* child benefit

Kindergarten

Every German pre-school child has the right to attend *Kindergarten* (nursery or play school) between the ages of three and six. *Kindergarten* concentrates on play, crafts, singing, etc., and aims to foster the child's social and emotional development. There is no formal teaching at all, this being reserved for the **Grundschule**.

Kindertagesstätte

Often called *Kita* for short, this is a day nursery intended for the children of working parents. The age range is usually from babies to six, although some *Kitas* also offer after-school care for older children.

Kinder- und Hausmärchen

Jakob Grimm (1785-1863) and his brother Wilhelm (1786-1859) collected fairy tales for their famous book of *Kinder- und Hausmärchen*. In 1852 they started compiling a comprehensive German dictionary. The work was so vast that it was only completed with the 32nd volume in 1961.

Kindes-: **~alter** *das* childhood; **im ~alter** at an early age; **~annahme** *die* ▸ **Adoption**; **~aussetzung** *die* abandonment of [newborn] children; **~beine** *Pl.*: *in* **von ~beinen an** from *or* since childhood; from an early age; **~entführung** *die* kidnapping [of a child]; child abduction; **~kind** *das* (veralt.) grandchild; *s. auch* **Kind 1**; **~liebe** *die* (geh.) filial love *or* affection; **~missbrauch**, ***~mißbrauch** *der* child abuse; **~misshandlung**, ***~mißhandlung** *die* (Rechtsw.) child abuse; **~mord** *der* child murder; (Mord am eigenen Kind) infanticide; **~mörderin** *die* infanticide; **~nöte** *Pl.* (veralt.) labour pains; **in ~nöten liegen** *od.* **sein** be in labour *sing.*; **~pflicht** *die* filial duty; **~raub** *der* ▸ **~entführung**; **~tötung** *die* (Rechtsw.) infanticide

Kind·frau *die* [1] (frühreifes Mädchen) precocious young lady [2] (kindliche Frau) childlike woman

kind·gemäß *Adj.* suitable for children *postpos.*

kindhaft *Adj.* childlike

Kindheit *die*; ~: childhood; **seit frühester ~:** from earliest childhood; from infancy

Kindheits·erinnerung *die* childhood memory

kindisch

A *Adj.* childish, infantile ‹*behaviour, enjoyment*›; naïve ‹*ideas*›; **~ werden** become childish; **werd nicht ~!** do behave sensibly

B *adv.* childishly; **sich ~ über etw.** (*Akk.*) **freuen** be absurdly pleased about sth.; **sich ~ an etw.** (*Dat.*) **freuen** take childish pleasure in sth.

kindlich

A *Adj.* childlike; **~er Gehorsam** filial obedience; **im ~en Alter** at an early age

B *adv.* ‹*behave*› in a childlike way *or* manner; **sich ~ über etw.** (*Akk.*) **freuen** take a childlike pleasure in sth.

Kindlichkeit *die*; ~: childlike quality

Kinds·kopf *der* overgrown child; **sei doch kein ~!** don't be so childish!; act your age!

Kind·taufe *die* christening

Kinematographie /kinematogra'fi:/ *die*; ~: cinematography *no art.*

Kinetik /ki'ne:tɪk/ *die*; ~ [1] (Physik) kinetics *sing., no art.* [2] (bild. Kunst) kinetic art

kinetisch *Adj.* (Physik, bild. Kunst) kinetic

King /kɪŋ/ *der*; **~s, ~s** (ugs.) boss (coll.); top dog (coll.)

Kinkerlitzchen /'kɪŋkɐlɪtsçən/ *Pl.* (ugs.) trifles

Kinn /kɪn/ *das*; **~[e]s, ~e** ▸ ❶ **S. 435** chin

Kinn-: **~backe** *die*, **~backen** *der*; **~~s, ~~** (südd.) cheek; **~bart** *der* chin-beard; chin-tuft; **~haken** *der* hook to the chin; **~lade** *die* jaw; **~riemen** *der* chinstrap

Kino /'ki:no/ *das*; **~s, ~s** [1] (Filmtheater) cinema (Brit.); movie theatre *or* house (Amer.); **in die [deutschen] ~s kommen** go on general release [in Germany] [2] (Filmvorstellung) film; movie (Amer.); **ins ~ gehen** go to the cinema (Brit.) *or* pictures (Brit.) *or* (Amer.) movies *pl.* [3] (Film als Medium) cinema

Kino-: **~besuch** *der* visit to the cinema (Brit.) *or* (Amer.) movies; **~besucher** *der*, **~besucherin** *die* cinema-goer (Brit.); movie-goer (Amer.); **~film** *der* cinema film (Brit.); movie film (Amer.); **~gänger** *der*; **~~s, ~~**, **~gängerin** *die*; **~~, ~~nen** cinema-goer (Brit.); movie-goer (Amer.); **~karte** *die* cinema ticket (Brit.); movie ticket (Amer.); **~kasse** *die* cinema (Brit.) *or* (Amer.) movie box office; **~programm** *das* [1] (Programm zu einem Film) film programme; [2] (Programmvorschau) cinema guide; **~reklame** *die* [1] (Reklame für einen Film) publicity *no indef. art.* for the/a film; [2] (Werbung vor einer Vorstellung) cinema advertisements *pl.*; screen commercials *pl.*; **~start** *der* [first] release; **~vorstellung** *die* ▸ **Filmvorstellung**

Kintopp /'ki:ntɔp/ *der od. das*; **~s, ~s** *od.* **Kintöppe** /'ki:ntœpə/ (ugs.) cinema

Kiosk /kiɔsk/ *der*; **~[e]s, ~e** kiosk

Kipf /kɪpf/ *der*; **~[e]s, ~e** (südd.) long loaf

Kipfel /'kɪpfl̩/ *das*; **~s, ~**, **Kipferl** /'kɪpfɐl/ *das*; **Kipferls, Kipferln** (bayr., österr.) ▸ **Hörnchen 2**

Kippe[1] /'kɪpə/ *die*; **~, ~n** (ugs.) cigarette end; fag end (coll.); dog-end (coll.)

Kippe[2] *die*; **~, ~n** [1] (Bergmannsspr.: Abraumhalde) slag heap [2] *in* **auf der ~ stehen** (ugs.) be balanced precariously; **etw. steht auf der ~** (fig.) (etw. befindet sich in einer kritischen Lage) it's touch and go with sth.; (etw. ist noch nicht entschieden) sth. hangs in the balance [3] (Turnen) upstart; kip (Amer.) [4] (Müll~) tip; dump

kippelig /'kɪpəlɪç/ *Adj.* (ugs.) wobbly; rickety, wobbly ‹*chair, table*›

kippeln /'kɪpl̩n/ *itr. V.* (ugs.) [1] (leicht wackeln) wobble; ‹*chair, table*› wobble; be wobbly *or* rickety [2] (mit dem Stuhl wackeln) **[mit seinem Stuhl] ~:** rock one's chair backwards and forwards

kippen

A *tr. V.* [1] (schräg stellen, neigen) tip [up]; tilt [2] (ausschütten) tip [out] [3] (ugs.: trinken) knock back (sl.); **einen ~:** have a quick one (coll.) *or* a drink [4] (ugs.: abbrechen) give ‹*project, series*› the chop (coll.)

B *itr. V.*; *mit sein* tip over; ‹*top-heavy object*› topple over; ‹*person*› fall, topple; ‹*boat*› overturn; ‹*car*› roll over; **von etw. ~:** topple *or* fall off sth.

Kipper *der*; **~s, ~:** tipper lorry *or* truck; dump truck; (Eisenb.) tipper *or* tipping wagon; dump car (Amer.)

Kipp-: **~fenster** *das* horizontally pivoted window; **~lore** *die* tipper *or* tipping wagon; **~schalter** *der* tumbler *or* toggle switch; **~wagen** *der* ▸ **~lore**

Kirche /'kɪrçə/ *die*; **~, ~n** [1] (Gebäude) church; **die ~ im Dorf lassen** (fig.) keep a sense of proportion; **mit der ~ ums Dorf laufen** (einen unnötigen Umweg machen) go all round the houses; (unnötig kompliziert vorgehen) do things in a roundabout way [2] (Gottesdienst) church *no art.*; **in der ~ sein** be at church; **in die ~ gehen** go to church [3] (Institution) Church

kirchen-, Kirchen-: **~älteste** *der* (ev. Kirche) [church] elder; **~amt** *das* [1] (Stellung) ecclesiastical office; [2] (Verwaltungsstelle) Church administrative offices *pl.*; **~austritt** *der* secession from the Church; **die Zahl der ~austritte** the number of people seceding from *or* leaving the Church; **~bank** *die*; *Pl.* **~bänke** [church] pew; **~bann** *der* (kath. Kirche) excommunication; **~besuch** *der* attendance at church; **~besucher** *der*, **~besucherin** *die* churchgoer; worshipper; **~blatt** *das* parish magazine; **~buch** *das* parish register; **~chor** *der* church choir; **~diebstahl** *der* theft from a/the church; **~diener** *der*, **~dienerin** *die* sexton; **~feindlich** *Adj.* hostile to the Church *postpos.*; **~fenster** *das* church window; **~fest** *das* religious festival; church festival; **~fürst** *der* (geh.) high ecclesiastical dignitary; high dignitary of the Church; (kath. Kirche: Kardinal) Prince of the Church; **~gebet** *das* (veralt.) collect; **~gemeinde** *die* parish; (beim Gottesdienst) congregation; **~geschichte** *die* ecclesiastical history *no art.*; Church history *no art.*; **~gestühl** *das* [church] pews *pl.*; **~glocke** *die* church bell; **~jahr** *das* ecclesiastical year; Church year; **~kampf** *der* struggle between the Church and the State (*e.g. in the period of Nazi rule*); **~leitung** *die* governing body of the Church; **~licht** *das*; *Pl.* **~~er:** *in* **kein** *od.* **nicht gerade ein [großes] ~licht sein** (ugs. scherzh.) be not too *or* not all that bright; **~lied** *das* hymn; **~maus** *die*: *in* **arm sein wie eine ~maus** (ugs. scherzh.) be as poor as a church mouse; **~musik** *die* church music; sacred music; **~politik** *die* policy of the State towards the Church; **~portal** *das* portal *or* main door of the/a church; **~rat** *der* (ev. Kirche) [1] (Verwaltungsorgan) ecclesiastical council; [2] (Mitglied) member of the/an ecclesiastical council; **~rätin** *die* ▸ **~rat 2**; **~raub** *der* ▸ **~diebstahl**; **~räuber** *der*, **~räuberin** *die* church-robber; **~recht** *das* ecclesiastical law; **~schändung** *die* sacrilege *no indef. art.*; profanation of a/the church; **~schiff** *das* (Archit.) nave; **~spaltung** *die* schism; **~staat** *der* (hist.) Papal States *pl.*; **~steuer** *die* church tax; **~tag** *der* Church congress; **~ton·art** *die* (Musik) ecclesiastical *or* church mode; **~tür** *die* church door; **~vater** *der* Father of the Church; **~vor·stand** *der* parochial church council

Kirchensteuer

Any taxpayer who is a member of one of the established churches in Germany (mainly Catholic and Protestant) has to pay *Kirchensteuer* (church tax). It is calculated as a proportion of income tax and is collected at source by the tax office, which then passes on the money to the relevant church.

Kirch-: **~gang** *der*: **der sonntägliche ~gang** going to church on Sunday; **~gänger** *der*; **~~s, ~~**, **~gängerin** *die*; **~~, ~~nen** churchgoer; **~hof** *der* (veralt.) churchyard; graveyard

kirchlich
A *Adj.* **1** (die Kirche betreffend) ecclesiastical; Church *attrib.*; ecclesiastical ‹*law, building*›; religious, church ‹*music, festival*› **2** (den Riten der Kirche entsprechend) church *attrib.* ‹*wedding, funeral*›
B *adv.* ~ **getraut/begraben werden** have a church wedding *or* be married in church/have a church funeral

Kirch·spiel *das* (veralt.) parish

Kirch·turm *der* (mit Turmspitze) [church] steeple; (ohne Turmspitze) church tower

Kirchturm-: ~politik *die* parish-pump politics *sing.*; **~spitze** *die* church spire; **~uhr** *die* church clock

Kirch-: ~weih *die*; **~~**, **~~en** fair (*held on the anniversary of the consecration of a church*); **~weihe** *die* consecration of a/the church

Kirmes /ˈkɪrməs/ *die*; **~**, **~sen** /ˈkɪrmɛsn̩/ (bes. md., niederd.) ▸ **Kirchweih**

kirre /ˈkɪrə/ *Adj.* (ugs.) compliant; obedient; **jmdn. ~ machen/kriegen** bring sb. to heel

Kirsch /kɪrʃ/ *der*; **~[e]s**, **~** ▸ **Kirschwasser**

Kirsch-: ~baum *der* **1** cherry [tree]; **2** (Holz) cherry[wood]; **~blüte** *die* **1** (Blüte des ~baums) cherry blossom; **2** (Zeit der ~blüte) cherry blossom time

Kirsche /ˈkɪrʃə/ *die*; **~**, **~n** **1** cherry; **mit ihm ist nicht gut ~n essen** (ugs.) it's best not to tangle with him **2** ▸ **Kirschbaum**

kirsch-, Kirsch-: ~kern *der* cherry stone; **~kuchen** *der* cake with cherry topping; **~likör** *der* cherry liqueur; (Weinbrand) cherry brandy; **~rot** *Adj.* cherry[-red]; **~saft** *der* cherry juice; **~stein** *der* ▸ **~kern**; **~torte** *die* cherry gateau; (mit Tortenboden) cherry flan; **Schwarzwälder ~torte** Black Forest gateau; **~wasser** *das* kirsch

Kissen /ˈkɪsn̩/ *das*; **~s**, **~**: cushion; (Kopf~) pillow

Kissen-: ~bezug *der* cushion cover; (für Kopfkissen) pillowcase; pillowslip; **~schlacht** *die* (ugs.) pillow fight

Kiste /ˈkɪstə/ *die*; **~**, **~n** **1** (Behälter) box; (Truhe) chest; (Latten~) crate; (für Obst) case; box; **eine ~ Wein/ Zigarren** a case of wine/box of cigars; **in die ~ gehen** (fig. ugs.) hit the hay (coll.); go to bed **2** (salopp) (Flugzeug, Auto) bus (coll.); (Boot) tub **3** (ugs., bes. berlin.: Sache, Angelegenheit) affair; business

kisten·weise *Adv.* **Wein/Obst ~ kaufen** buy wine by the case/fruit by the case *or* box; **Obst ~ wegwerfen** throw away fruit by the caseful *or* boxful

Kita /ˈkiːta/ *die*; **~**, **~s** day nursery; crèche

> **Kita**
> ▸ **Kindertagesstätte.**

Kite-: /ˈkait-/ **~surfen** *das*; **~~s** kite surfing; **~surfer** *der*, **~surferin** *die* kite surfer

Kitsch /kɪtʃ/ *der*; **~[e]s** kitsch

kitschig *Adj.* kitschy

Kitsch: ~postkarte *die* kitschy *or* tacky postcard; **~roman** *der* kitschy *or* tacky novel

Kitt /kɪt/ *der*; **~[e]s**, (Arten:) **~e** (Fensterkitt) putty; (für Porzellan, Kacheln usw.) cement; (Füllmasse) filler

Kittchen *das*; **~s**, **~** (ugs.) clink (sl.); jug (sl.); jail; **im ~ sitzen** be inside (coll.); be in clink *or* jug (sl.)

Kittel /ˈkɪtl̩/ *der*; **~s**, **~** **1** overall; (eines Arztes, Krankenpflegers, Laboranten) white coat **2** (hemdartige Bluse) smock **3** (südd.: Jackett) jacket

Kittel-: ~kleid *das* [simple] button-through dress; **~schürze** *die* sleeveless overall

kitten *tr. V.* cement [together]; stick [together] with cement; (fig.) mend ‹*breach*›; patch up ‹*broken marriage, friendship*›

Kitz /kɪts/ *das*; **~es**, **~e** (Reh~) fawn; (Ziegen~, Gämsen~) kid

Kitzel /ˈkɪtsl̩/ *der*; **~s**, **~** **1** (Juckreiz) tickle; tickling feeling *or* sensation **2** (Reiz, Antrieb) itch; urge; (freudige Erregung) thrill

kitzelig ▸ **kitzlig**

kitzeln
A *tr. V.* **1** tickle; **es kitzelt mich in der Nase** my nose tickles **2** (einen Sinnenreiz hervorrufen) tickle; **der Duft kitzelte sie in der Nase** the aroma tickled her nose; **jmds. Eitelkeit ~:** tickle sb.'s vanity **3** (reizen) prompt; (in freudige Erregung versetzen) thrill; **es kitzelt jmdn., etw. zu tun** sb. is itching to do sth.; sb. feels an urge to do sth.
B *itr. V.* tickle; **auf der Haut ~:** tickle [the skin]

Kitzler *der*; **~s**, **~** ▸ **ⓘ S. 435** (Anat.) clitoris

kitzlig *Adj.* **1** (empfindlich gegen Kitzeln) ticklish **2** (empfindlich reagierend) touchy (**in** + *Dat.* about) **3** (schwierig, heikel) ticklish

Kiwi /ˈkiːvi/ *die*; **~**, **~s** kiwi [fruit]

KKW *Abk.* = **Kernkraftwerk**

Kl. *Abk.* = **Klasse**

Klabauter·mann /klaˈbautɐ-/ *der* (nordd.) *protective spirit of a/the ship*

klack /klak/ *Interj.* **1** click **2** (von Tropfen) tap

klacken *itr. V.* (ugs.) click

klackern /ˈklakɐn/ *itr. V.* (landsch.) clatter

Klacks /klaks/ *der*; **~es**, **~e** (ugs.) (~ Schlagsahne, Kartoffelbrei) dollop (coll.); (~ Senf) blob; dab; **etw. ist nur ein ~ [für jmdn.]** (fig.) sth. is no trouble at all [for sb.]

Kladde /ˈkladə/ *die*; **~**, **~n** **1** (Heft für erste Niederschrift) rough book; **etw. in ~ schreiben** write sth. in rough **2** (dickes Schreibheft) thick notebook

kladderadatsch /kladəraˈdaːtʃ/ *Interj.* crash bang wallop

Kladderadatsch *der*; **~[e]s**, **~e** (ugs.) **1** (Chaos, Durcheinander) unholy mess (coll.) **2** (Skandal) scandal

klaffen /ˈklafn̩/ *itr. V.* gape; yawn; ‹*hole, wound*› gape; ‹*gap*› yawn; **in der Mauer klaffte ein großes Loch** there was a gaping hole in the wall

kläffen /ˈklɛfn̩/ *itr. V.* (abwertend) yap

klaffend *Adj.* gaping; yawning; gaping ‹*hole, wound*›; yawning ‹*gap*›

Kläffer *der*; **~s**, **~** (ugs. abwertend) yapping dog; yapper

Klafter /ˈklaftɐ/ *der od. das*; **~s**, **~** **1** (frühere Längeneinheit) fathom **2** (Raummaß für Holz) cord

klafter·tief *Adj.* six feet deep; ‹*water*› a fathom deep; (fig.) very deep

klagbar *Adj.* (Rechtsw.) actionable ‹*matter*›; enforceable ‹*claim*›

Klage /ˈklaːgə/ *die*; **~**, **~n** **1** (Äußerung der Trauer) lamentation; lament; (Äußerung des Schmerzes) complaint; **die ~n um jmdn./über den Verlust von etw.** the lamentations *pl.* for sb./over the loss of sth. **2** (Beschwerde, Äußerung des Unmuts) complaint; **~n werden laut** complaints are being voiced; **keinen Grund zur ~ geben/haben** give/have no grounds *pl. or* reason for complaint; **bei jmdm. über jmdn./etw. ~ führen** make a complaint to sb. *or* lodge a complaint with sb. about sb./sth. **3** (Rechtsw.) (im Zivilrecht) action; suit; (im Strafrecht) charge; **eine ~ auf etw.** (*Akk.*) an action for sth.; **eine ~ auf Scheidung** a petition for divorce; **[öffentliche] ~ gegen jmdn. einreichen/erheben** bring an action against sb.; institute [criminal] proceedings against sb.

Klage-: ~ab·weisung *die* (Rechtsw.) dismissal of the action *or* suit; **~erhebung** *die* (Rechtsw.) institution of [legal] proceedings; bringing of an action *or* a suit; **~frau** *die* ▸ **~weib**; **~laut** *der* plaintive cry; (von Schmerzen verursacht) cry of pain; (stöhnend) moan; **~lied** *das* lament; **ein ~lied [über jmdn./etw.] anstimmen/singen** start to moan/moan [about sb./sth.]; **~mauer** *die* Wailing Wall

klagen
A *itr. V.* **1** (geh.: jammern) wail; (stöhnend) moan; ‹*animal*› cry plaintively; **der ~de Ruf des Käuzchens** the plaintive cry of the little owl **2** (sich beschweren) complain; **über etw.** (*Akk.*) **~:** complain about sth.; **über Rückenschmerzen/Kopfschmerzen ~:** complain of backache *sing.*/a headache; **[ich] kann nicht ~:** [I] can't complain; [I] mustn't grumble **3** (geh.) **um jmdn./jmds. Tod ~:** mourn sb./sb.'s death; **über den Verlust seines Vermögens ~:** lament *or* bewail the loss of one's fortune **4** (bei Gericht) sue; take legal action; **auf Schadenersatz ~:** sue for damages; bring an action for damages; **auf Scheidung ~:** petition for divorce; **gegen jmdn. ~:** sue sb.; take legal action against sb.
B *tr. V.* **1** **jmdm. sein Leid/seine Not/sein Missgeschick ~:** pour out one's sorrows *pl.*/troubles *pl.*/tale of misfortune to sb.; **Gott seis geklagt** (veralt.) alas, alack (arch.) **2** (österr.: verklagen) sue; take legal action against

Klage·punkt *der* (Rechtsw.) (im Zivilrecht) particular of the/a claim; (im Strafrecht) count of the/a charge

Kläger /ˈklɛːgɐ/ *der*; **~s**, **~**, **Klägerin** *die*; **~**, **~nen** (im Zivilrecht) plaintiff; (im Strafrecht) prosecuting party; (bei einer Scheidung) petitioner; **wo kein ~ ist, ist auch kein Richter** (Spr.) if there's no law against it/if nobody complains, he/we *etc.* needn't worry

Klage-: ~ruf *der* plaintive cry; (von Schmerz verursacht) cry of pain; (stöhnend) moan; **~schrift** *die* (Rechtsw.) (im Zivilrecht) statement of claim; (im Strafrecht) charge/list of charges; (bei einer Scheidung) petition; **~weg** *der* (Rechtsw.) **auf dem ~weg** *od.* **im ~weg** by [taking] legal action *or* proceedings; through the courts; **~weib** *das* [professional] mourner

kläglich /ˈklɛːklɪç/
A *Adj.* **1** (mitleiderregend) pitiful ‹*expression, voice, cry*›; pitiful, wretched ‹*condition, appearance*›; **ein ~es Ende nehmen** come to a miserable end **2** (minderwertig) pathetic ‹*achievement, result, etc.*›; **ein ~er Rest** a few pathetic remains *pl.* **3** (erbärmlich) despicable, wretched ‹*behaviour, role, compromise*›; pathetic ‹*result, defeat*›
B *adv.* **1** ‹*weep, sob*› pitifully **2** (erbärmlich) ‹*behave*› wretchedly, despicably; ‹*fail*› miserably

Kläglichkeit *die*; **~** ▸ **kläglich A 1-3**: pitifulness; wretchedness; patheticness; despicableness

klaglos
A *Adj.* uncomplaining
B *adv.* uncomplainingly; without complaint

Klamauk /klaˈmauk/ *der*; **~s** (ugs. abwertend) fuss; to-do; (Lärm, Krach) row (coll.); racket; (Reklamewirbel) fuss; hullabaloo; (im Theater) slapstick

klamaukig (ugs., oft abwertend)
A *Adj.* full of commotion *pred.*; (laut) noisy; (im Theater) slapstick *attrib.* ‹*scene etc.*›
B *adv.* with a lot of commotion/(im Theater) slapstick

klamm /klam/ *Adj.* **1** (feucht) cold and damp **2** (steif) numb; **~ vor Kälte** numb with cold **3** **~ sein** (salopp) be hard up

Klamm *die*; **~**, **~en** [deep and narrow] gorge; ravine

Klammer *die*; **~**, **~n** **1** (Wäsche~) peg **2** (Haar~) [hair]grip **3** (Zahn~) brace **4** (Wund~) clip **5** (Büro~) paper clip; (Heft~) staple **6** (Bau~) cramp[-iron]; [timber-]dog **7** (Schriftzeichen) bracket; **runde ~n** round brackets; parentheses; **eckige/spitze ~n** square/angle *or* pointed brackets; **geschweifte ~n** braces; **~ auf/zu** open/close brackets **8** (Text in Klammern) bracketed material; material in [the] brackets; (Math.) bracket; bracketed expression; **die ~n auflösen** remove the brackets **9** (Griff) grip **10** (fig.) (Verbindung) bond; link; (Fessel) shackle; tie

Klammer-: ~affe *der* (Zool.) spider monkey; (ugs.: At-Zeichen) at sign; **~ausdruck** *der*; *Pl.* **~ausdrücke** (Math.) bracket; bracketed expression; **~beutel** *der* peg bag; **dich haben sie wohl mit dem ~beutel gepudert!** (berlin. salopp) you must be off your rocker! (coll.); **~griff** *der* iron grip (also fig.); (Umschlingung) clinch; **im ~griff** in an iron grip/in a clinch

klammern
A *refl. V.* **sich an jmdn./etw. ~** (auch fig.) cling to sb./sth.; **sich an Worte ~:** be pedantic about the words used
B *tr. V.* **1** **er klammerte seine Hände um das Geländer** he grasped the railing [with both

hands] **2** (zusammenhalten) **eine Wunde ~:** close a wound with a clip/clips **3** (befestigen) (mit einer Büroklammer) clip; (mit einer Heftmaschine) staple; (mit einer Wäscheklammer) peg
C *itr. V.* (Boxen) clinch

klamm·heimlich
A *Adj.* (ugs.) on the quiet *postpos.*; ‹*meeting*› held on the quiet
B *adv.* on the quiet

Klamotte /kla'mɔtə/ *die;* ~, ~**n** **1** *Pl.* (salopp: Kleidung) clobber *sing.* (coll.); gear *sing.* (coll.) **2** *Pl.* (salopp: Kram) junk *sing.*; stuff *sing.* **3** (ugs. abwertend: Schwank) rubbishy play/film *etc.*

Klamotten·kiste *die* (ugs.) **in etw. aus der ~ hervorholen** dig sth. up again; **ein Witz/eine Anekdote aus der ~:** an old chestnut

Klampfe /'klampfə/ *die;* ~, ~**n** **1** (volkst.: Gitarre) guitar **2** (österr.) ▸**Klammer 6**

Klan /kla:n/ *der;* ~**s,** ~**e** ▸**Clan**

klang /klaŋ/ *1. u. 3. Pers. Sg. Prät. v.* **klingen**

Klang *der;* ~**[e]s, Klänge** /'klɛŋə/ **1** (Ton) sound **2** (~farbe) tone; **der Name dieser Familie/Firma hat einen guten/schlechten ~** (fig.) this family/firm has a good/bad name; **ihre Worte hatten einen bitteren ~** (fig.) there was a bitter note in *or* edge to her words **3** *Pl.* (Melodie) **das Orchester spielte alte, wohl bekannte Klänge** the orchestra played old familiar tunes; **nach den Klängen eines Walzers tanzen** dance to the strains of a waltz

Klang-: ~bild *das* (fachspr.) sound; **~effekt** *der* sound effect; **~farbe** *die* tone colour *or* quality; (einer Stimme) tone; **~fülle** *die* (eines Instruments) richness *or* fullness of tone; (eines Orchesters) richness *or* fullness of sound; (einer Stimme) sonority

klanglich
A *Adj.* tonal ‹*beauty, quality, etc.*›; tonal, tone *attr.* ‹*characteristics*›
B *adv.* tonally

klanglos
A *Adj.* toneless; **mit ~er Stimme** in a toneless voice; tonelessly
B *adv.* tonelessly; *s. auch* **sanglos**

klang-, Klang-: ~regler *der* (Technik) ▸**Tonblende**; **~rein** **A** *Adj.* **~rein sein** have a pure tone *or* sound; **B** *adv.* **er spielte so ~rein, dass ...:** he played with such [a] purity of tone that ...; **~schön** *Adj.* **ein ~schönes Instrument** an instrument with a beautiful tone *or* sound; **~teppich** *der* carpet of sound; **~treu** *Adj.* faithful ‹*reproduction*›; high-fidelity ‹*receiver, reception*›; **~voll** *Adj.* **1** sonorous ‹*voice, language*›; **2** (berühmt) illustrious ‹*name, title*›

klapp /klap/ *Interj.* click

Klapp-: ~bett *das* folding bed; **~brücke** *die* bascule bridge; **~deckel** *der* hinged lid

Klappe *die;* ~, ~**n** **1** [hinged] lid; (am Fenster) [hinged] vent; (am Briefkasten) flap; (am Tisch) leaf; **~ zu, Affe tot** (salopp) there's an end to it **2** (am LKW) tailboard; tailgate; (seitlich) side gate; (am Kombiwagen) tailgate **3** (am Kleidertaschen) flap **4** (am Ofen) [drop-]door **5** (an Musikinstrumenten) key; (an einer Trompete) valve **6** (Herz~) valve **7** (Augen~) [eye]patch **8** (Achselstück) shoulder strap **9** (Filmjargon) clapperboard; **das war die letzte ~:** that was the last take **10** (salopp: Mund) trap (sl.); **die** *od.* **seine ~ halten** shut one's trap (sl.); **eine große** *od.* **freche ~ haben** (abwertend) have a big mouth **11** (ugs.: Bett) **sich in die ~ hauen** hit the hay (coll.); get one's head down

klappen
A *tr. V.* **nach oben/unten ~:** turn up/down ‹*collar, hat brim*›; lift up/put down *or* lower ‹*lid*›; **nach vorne/hinten ~:** fold forward/back ‹*seat*›
B *itr. V.* **1** ‹*door, shutter*› bang; **mit der Tür ~:** bang the door **2** (stoßen) bang **3** (ugs.: gelingen) work out all right; ‹*rehearsal, performance, etc.*› go [off] all right; **die Sache wird schon ~:** it *or* things will work out all right; **hat es mit den Karten geklappt?** did you get the tickets all right?

Klappen-: ~fehler *der* ▸**Herzklappenfehler**; **~text** *der* (Buchw.) blurb

Klapper *die;* ~, ~**n** rattle

klapper-, Klapper-: ~dürr (ugs.) all skin and bone *pred.*; **~gestell** *das* (ugs.) **1** (dünner Mensch) bag of bones; **2** (scherzh.: Fahrzeug) rattletrap; **~kasten** *der,* **~kiste** *die* (ugs.) rattletrap

klappern *itr. V.* **1** rattle; ‹*heels, knitting needles*› click; **vor Kälte ~ ihr die Zähne** her teeth are chattering with cold **2** (ein Klappern erzeugen) make a clatter; **vor Angst/Kälte klapperte er mit den Zähnen** his teeth were chattering with fear/cold; **auf der Schreibmaschine ~** (ugs.) clatter away on the typewriter; **mit den Augen ~** (ugs.) keep blinking; (kokettieren) flutter one's eyelashes **3** *mit sein* (sich ~d fortbewegen) ‹*car*› rattle along; ‹*person*› clatter along

Klapper-: ~schlange *die* rattlesnake; **~storch** *der* (Kinderspr.) stork; **glaubst du noch an den ~storch?** do you still believe that babies are brought by the stork?

Klapp-: ~fahrrad *das* folding bicycle; **~fenster** *das* top-hung window; **~handy** *das* flip phone; clamshell phone; **~laden,** *der; Pl.* **~läden,** *auch* **~~:** folding shutter; **~liege** *die* [folding] lounger *or* sunbed; **~messer** *das* clasp knife; **~rad** *das* folding bicycle

klapprig *Adj.* **1** (alt) rickety; ramshackle **2** (wenig stabil) rickety; wobbly **3** (ugs.: hinfällig) decrepit; **er ist noch etwas ~:** he's still a bit shaky

Klapp-: ~sitz *der* folding seat; tip-up seat; **~stuhl** *der* folding chair; **~stulle** *die* (berlin.) sandwich; **~tisch** *der* folding table; **~tür** *die* hinged door; **~verdeck** *das* collapsible *or* folding hood *or* top; **~zylinder** *der* opera hat; crush hat

Klaps /klaps/ *der;* ~**es,** ~**e** **1** (ugs.: leichter Schlag) smack; slap; **jmdm. einen ~ geben** give sb. a slap *or* smack **2** (salopp) **einen ~ haben** have a screw loose (coll.); be a bit bonkers (coll.)

Klaps·mühle *die* (salopp) loony bin (sl.); nuthouse (sl.)

klar /kla:ɐ̯/
A *Adj.* **1** clear; **~e Brühe** clear soup; **mit ~en Augen** clear-eyed; **bei ~er Sicht** when it's clear; on a clear day; **einen ~en Moment haben** (fig.) have a lucid moment; **ein ~er Verstand** clear judgement *no art.*; **er ist nicht bei ~em Verstand** he's not in his right mind; he's not in full possession of his faculties; **~ [im Kopf] sein** have a clear head; be able to think clearly *or* straight; **er ist nicht ganz ~ im Kopf** (salopp) he's not quite right in the head (sl.) **2** (eindeutig) clear ‹*decision*›; straight ‹*question, answer*›; **ein ~es Ziel vor Augen haben** have a clear aim *or* objective; **~e Verhältnisse schaffen** set things straight; **[ist] alles ~?** [is] everything clear?; **jetzt ist mir alles ~:** now I understand; **jmdm. wird etw. ~:** sth. becomes clear to sb.; **sich** (*Dat.*) **über etw.** (*Akk.*) **~ werden** realize *or* grasp sth.; **ich muss mir über meine Pläne für die Zukunft erst ~ werden** I must first get my plans for the future clear in my own mind; **na ~!** (ugs.), **aber ~!** (ugs.) of course!; **~, dass ...** naturally, ...; **Das werdet ihr nicht tun. Ist das ~?** You must not do that. Is that clear *or* Do I make myself clear?; **ist dir ~, dass ...?** are you aware that ...?; **das ist ~ wie Klärchen** *od.* **Kloßbrühe** *od.* **dicke Tinte** (ugs.) it's as plain as a pikestaff (Brit.) *or* as the nose on your face; **sich** (*Dat.*) **über etw.** (*Akk.*) **im Klaren sein** realize *or* be aware of sth. **3** (fertig) ready; **~ zum Auslaufen** ready to sail
B *adv.* clearly; **sie haben die gegnerische Mannschaft ~ besiegt** they won a clear[-cut] victory over the opposing team; **nicht ~ denken können** be unable to think clearly *or* straight; **~ auf der Hand liegen** (ugs.) be blindingly obvious; **etw. ~ und deutlich sagen** say sth. clearly and unambiguously; **ein ~ denkender Mann** a clear-thinking man; **~ sehen** (fig.) understand the matter

Klar *das;* ~**s,** ~ (österr.) ▸**Eiweiß 1**

Klär·anlage *die* sewage treatment plant; (einer Fabrik) waste-water treatment plant

klar-, Klar-: ~apfel *der: type of early dessert apple;* ≈ White/Yellow Transparent; **~blick** *der* clear-sightedness; **~blickend** *Adj.* clear-sighted; **~denkend** ▸**klar B**

Klare *der;* ~**n,** ~**n** schnapps

klären /'klɛ:rən/
A *tr. V.* **1** (auf~) settle, resolve ‹*question, issue, matter*›; clarify ‹*situation*›; clear up ‹*case, affair, misunderstanding*› **2** (reinigen) purify; treat ‹*effluent, sewage*›; clear ‹*beer, wine*›
B *refl. V.* **1** (klar werden) ‹*situation*› become clear; ‹*question, issue, matter*› be settled *or* resolved **2** (rein werden) ‹*liquid, sky*› clear; ‹*weather*› clear [up]
C *itr. V.* (Ballspiele) clear [the ball]; **auf der Linie ~:** clear [the ball] off the line

klar|gehen *unr. itr. V.; mit sein* (ugs.) go OK (coll.); **geht das klar mit dem Antrag?** is the application going OK? (coll.); **es wird schon ~:** it'll be OK (coll.)

Klarheit *die;* ~, ~**en** **1** clarity **2** (Eindeutigkeit) clarity; (von Ausführungen, Rede usw.) clarity; lucidity **3** (Gewissheit) **sich** (*Dat.*) **über etw.** (*Akk.*) **~ verschaffen** clarify sth.; **völlige ~ verlangen** demand full information *or* all the facts (**über** + *Akk.* about) **4** (ugs. scherzh.) **jetzt sind alle ~en beseitigt** now I'm/everyone's *etc.* totally confused

klarieren *tr. V.* (Seemannsspr.) **etw. ~:** clear sth. [through customs]

Klarinette /klari'nɛtə/ *die;* ~, ~**n** clarinet

Klarinettist *der;* ~**en,** ~**en, Klarinettistin** *die;* ~, ~**nen** ▸❶ **S. 113** clarinettist

Klarisse /kla'rɪsə/ *die;* ~, ~**n, Klarissin** *die;* ~, ~**nen** nun of the order of St. Clare; **die Klariss[inn]en** the poor Clares

klar-, Klar-: ~|kommen *unr. itr. V.; mit sein* (ugs.) manage; cope; **mit jmdm. ~kommen** get on with sb.; **ich komme mit der neuen Waschmaschine/der Matheaufgabe nicht ~:** I can't get on with my new washing machine/sort out this maths exercise; **~lack** *der* clear varnish; **~|legen** *tr. V.* (ugs.) make clear; explain; **~|machen** *tr. V.* **1** (ugs.: erklären) make clear; **jmdm./sich etw. ~machen** make sth. clear to sb./realize sth.; **2** (Seemannsspr.) get ready; prepare; **~name** *der* real name

klaro /'kla:ro/ *Adv.* clearly; obviously; (versteht sich) of course; **~?** is that clear?

Klär·schlamm *der* (Technik) sludge

Klar·schrift·leser *der* (DV) optical character reader

***klar|sehen** ▸**klar B**

Klarsicht-: ~folie *die* transparent film; **~packung** *die* transparent pack; **~umschlag** *der* transparent cover

klar-, Klar-: ~|spülen *itr. V.* rinse; **~spüler** *der,* **~spülmittel** *das* rinse aid; **~|stellen** *tr. V.* clear up; clarify; **ich möchte ~stellen, dass ...** I should like to make it clear that ...; **~stellung** *die* clarification; **~text** *der* (auch DV) clear *or* plain text; **im ~text** (fig.) in plain language; **[mit jmdm.] ~text reden** (fig. ugs.) talk turkey [to *or* with sb.] (coll.)

Klärung *die;* ~, ~**en** **1** (Beseitigung von Missverständnissen) clarification **2** (Reinigung) purification; (von Abwässern) treatment

Klärungs·bedarf *der* need for clarification

***klar|werden** ▸**klar A 2**

Klär·werk *das* sewage works *sing. or pl.*; (einer Fabrik) wastewater treatment works *sing. or pl.*

klass, *klaß /klas/ (südd., österr.) ▸**klasse**

klasse /'klasə/ (ugs.)
A *indekl. Adj.* great (coll.); marvellous
B *adv.* marvellously

Klasse *die;* ~, ~**n** **1** (Schul~) class; form (esp. Brit.); (Raum) classroom; (Stufe) year; grade (Amer.); **die vierte ~ besuchen** be in the fourth year *or* (Amer.) grade **2** (Bevölkerungsgruppe) class; **die ~ der Werktätigen/der Besitzlosen** the working/propertyless class **3** (Sport) league; (Boxen) division; class **4** (Fahrzeug~) class; **PKWs der gehobenen ~:** upmarket cars; **ein Führerschein der ~ 1/2/3/4/5** ≈ a driving licence for a motorcycle/a heavy goods vehicle/a private car/a moped/a motor-assisted bicycle 5 (Boots~) class 6 (Qualitätsstufe) class; **ein Wagen/eine Fahrkarte erster ~:** a first-class carriage/ticket; **zweiter ~ liegen** occupy a second-class hospital bed; **er ist ein Künstler erster ~** (ugs.) he is a first-class *or* first-rate artist; **das ist [einsame** *od.* **ganz große] ~!** (ugs.) that's [just] great (coll.) *or* marvellous!; **der Verdienstorden erster ~:** the Order of Merit first-class 7 (Biol.) class

Klasse-: ~frau *die* (ugs.) [real] stunner (coll.); **~mann** *der* 1 (ugs.) marvellous man; fantastic guy (coll.); 2 (Sportjargon) top-class *or* first-rate player; **~mannschaft** *die* (Sportjargon) top-class *or* first-rate team

Klassement /klasə'mã:/ *das;* **~s, ~s** (Sport) [list *sing.* of] rankings *pl.*

klassen-, Klassen-: ~arbeit *die* (Schulw.) [written] class test; **~aufsatz** *der* (Schulw.) essay written in class; class essay; **~ausflug** *der* (Schulw.) class outing; **~beste** *der/die; adj. Dekl.* top pupil in the class; **wer ist denn bei euch der oder die ~beste?** who is top of your class?; **~bewusstsein, *~bewußtsein** *das* (Soziol.) class consciousness; **~buch** *das* (Schulw.) *book recording details of pupils' attendance, behaviour, and of topics covered in each lesson* ≈ [class] register; **~clown** *der* (Schulw.) classroom clown; **den ~clown spielen** play the clown in class; **~durchschnitt** *der* (Schulw.) class average; **~erhalt** *der* (Sport) **um den ~erhalt kämpfen** struggle *or* battle to avoid relegation; **~fahrt** *die* (Schulw.) class outing; **~feind** *der* (marx.) class enemy; **~gegensatz** *der* class difference; **~geist** *der* (Schulw.) class spirit; **~gemeinschaft** *die* (Schulw.) (~kollektiv) class; (~geist) class spirit; **~gesellschaft** *die* (Soziol.) class society; **~hass, *~haß** *der* (Sozialpsych.) class hatred *no art.*; **~herrschaft** *die* (Soziol.) class rule *no art.*; **~justiz** *die* (Soziol.) legal system with a built-in class bias; **~kamerad** *der,* **~kameradin** *die* (Schulw.) class fellow; classmate; **~kampf** *der* (marx.) class struggle; **~kämpferisch** *Adj.* (marx.) **~kämpferische Parolen** slogans supporting the class struggle; **~keile** *die* (Schülerspr.) **~keile beziehen** *od.* **bekommen** be punched and pushed by the rest of the class; **~lehrer** *der,* **~lehrerin** *die,* **~leiter** *der,* **~leiterin** *die* (Schulw.) class *or* form teacher; form master/mistress; **~los** *Adj.* (Soziol.) classless; **~lotterie** *die: lottery in which draws are made on a number of different days and for which tickets can be bought for each individual draw;* **~raum** *der* ▸**~zimmer**; **~reise** *die* class trip; **~schranke** *die* (Soziol.) class barrier; **~sprecher** *der,* **~sprecherin** *die* (Schulw.) class spokesman; ≈ form leader *or* captain; **~stärke** *die* (Schulw.) size of the/a class/of classes; **~treffen** *das* (Schulw.) class reunion; **~unterschied** *der* 1 (Soziol.) class difference; 2 (Sport) difference in class; **~wahlrecht** *das* (hist.) class-based electoral system; class[-based] system of franchise; **~weise** *Adv.* (Schulw.) class by class; **~ziel** *das* (Schulw.) required standard (*for pupils in a particular class*); **das ~ziel erreichen** reach the required standard; (fig.) make the grade; come up to scratch; **~zimmer** *das* (Schulw.) classroom

Klasse-: ~spieler *der,* **~spielerin** *die* (Sport Jargon) [top-]class *or* first-rate player; **~weib** *das* (ugs.) [real] stunner (coll.)

Klassifikation /klasifika'tsio:n/ *die;* **~, ~en** classification

klassifizieren /klasifi'tsi:rən/ *tr. V.* classify (**als** as)

Klassifizierung *die;* **~, ~en** classification

-klassig *Adj.* -class; **mehr~/zwei~:** with a number of/two classes

Klassik /'klasɪk/ *die;* **~** 1 (Antike) classical antiquity *no art.* 2 (Zeit kultureller Höchstleistung) classical period *or* age

Klassiker *der;* **~s, ~, Klassikerin** *die;* **~, ~nen** 1 (der antiken Klassik) classic; classical writer 2 (einer Epoche) classic; classical writer/composer *etc.* 3 (jmd., dessen Werk als mustergültig gilt) classical exponent; classic

klassisch *Adj.* 1 classical 2 (vollendet, zeitlos; auch iron.) classic 3 (herkömmlich) classical; conventional ‹*warfare*›

Klassizismus /klasi'tsɪsmʊs/ *der;* **~, Klassizismen** 1 (Stilform) classicism 2 (Stilmerkmal) feature of the classical style

klassizistisch *Adj.* classical

-klässler, *-kläßler /-klɛslɐ/ *der;* **-~s, -~, -klässlerin, *-kläßlerin** *die;* **~, ~nen** -former; **Erst~/Zweit~:** first-former/second-former

klatsch *Interj.* smack; (wenn etw. Weiches auf den Boden fällt) splosh

Klatsch /klatʃ/ *der;* **~[e]s, ~e** 1 (ugs. abwertend: Gerede) gossip; tittle-tattle 2 (Geräusch) smack; **es gab einen lauten ~, als er auf dem Wasser aufschlug** there was a loud splash *or* (lauter und schärfer) smack as he hit the water

Klatsch·base *die* (ugs. abwertend) gossip

Klatsche *die;* **~, ~n** 1 (Fliegen~) fly swatter 2 (Schülerspr.: Übersetzung) crib 3 (abwertend) ▸**Klatschbase**

klatschen

A *itr. V.* 1 *auch mit sein* ‹*waves, wet sails*› slap (**gegen** against); **der Regen klatscht gegen die Scheiben** the rain beats against the windows; **sie gab ihm eine Ohrfeige, dass es nur so klatschte** she gave him a resounding smack *or* slap round the face 2 (mit den Händen; applaudieren) clap; **in die Hände ~:** clap one's hands; **lautes Klatschen** loud applause 3 (schlagen) slap; **sich** (*Dat.*) **auf die Schenkel/gegen die Stirn ~:** slap one's thighs/clap one's hand to one's forehead 4 (ugs. abwertend: reden) gossip (**über** + *Akk.* about)

B *tr. V.* 1 (ugs.: werfen) slap; chuck (coll.) ‹*book etc.*› 2 **den Takt ~** ‹*teacher*› clap time; ‹*audience*› clap in time; **jmdm. Beifall ~:** clap *or* applaud sb. 3 (ugs.: schlagen) **jmdm. eine ~:** slap sb. across the face; give sb. a slap across the face

Klatscherei *die;* **~, ~en** (ugs. abwertend) gossiping

Klatsch·geschichte *die* (abwertend) piece of gossip; **~n** gossip *sing.*

klatschhaft *Adj.* gossipy; fond of gossip *pred.*

Klatschhaftigkeit *die;* **~:** fondness for gossip

klatsch-, Klatsch-: ~kolumnist *der,* **~kolumnistin** *die* (abwertend) gossip columnist; **~maul** *das* (ugs. abwertend) gossip; **~mohn** *der* corn poppy; field poppy; **~nass, *~naß** *Adj.* (ugs.) soaking *or* sopping wet ‹*clothes*›; dripping wet ‹*hair*›; **wir sind ~nass geworden** we got soaked [to the skin] *or* drenched; **~reporter** *der,* **~reporterin** *die* (abwertend) society reporter; (mit Klatschspalte) gossip columnist; **~spalte** *die* (ugs. abwertend) gossip column; **~sucht** *die* (abwertend) passion for gossip *or* tittle-tattle; **~süchtig** *Adj.* extremely gossipy; **~süchtig sein** be a compulsive gossip/compulsive gossips; **~tante** *die* (ugs. abwertend), **~weib** *das* (ugs. abwertend) ▸**Klatschbase**

klauben /'klaubn̩/ *tr. V.* (landsch.) 1 (entfernen) **die Flusen vom Teppich/die Rosinen aus dem Kuchen ~:** pick the fluff *sing.* off the carpet/the raisins out of the cake 2 (auslesen) pick over 3 (bes. südd., österr. ugs.: sammeln) pick ‹*berries*›; gather, collect ‹*wood*›; dig ‹*potatoes*›

Klaue /'klauə/ *die;* **~, ~n** 1 claw; (von Raubvögeln) talon; (fig. geh.) **in den ~n eines Erpressers** in the clutches of a blackmailer; **jmdn. den ~n des Todes entreißen** snatch sb. from the jaws of death 2 (Huf) hoof 3 (salopp: Hand) mitt (coll.); paw (coll.) 4 (salopp abwertend: Handschrift) handwriting; **seine ~ kann ich nicht entziffern** I can't decipher his scrawl

klauen (ugs.)

A *tr. V.* pinch (coll.), nick (Brit. coll.); (fig.) pinch (coll.), nick (Brit. coll.), crib ‹*idea*›; **jmdm. etw. ~:** pinch *or* (Brit.) nick/crib sth. from sb.

B *itr. V.* pinch (coll.) *or* nick (Brit. coll.) things

Klauen·seuche *die* ▸**Maul- und Klauenseuche**

Klause /'klauzə/ *die;* **~, ~n** 1 (Einsiedelei) hermitage 2 (Klosterzelle) cell; (fig.) den 3 ▸**Klus**

Klausel /'klauzl̩/ *die;* **~, ~n** clause; (Bedingung) stipulation; condition; (Vorbehalt) proviso

Klausner /'klausnɐ/ *der;* **~s, ~:** hermit; recluse

Klaustrophobie /klaustrofo'bi:/ *die;* **~, ~n** (Psych.) claustrophobia

klaustrophobisch

A *Adj.* claustrophobic.

B *adv.* claustrophobically

Klausur /klau'zu:ɐ̯/ *die;* **~, ~en** 1 (Abgeschlossenheit) **in ~ leben/tagen** live in seclusion/meet in private 2 (~arbeit) [examination] paper; (Examen) examination; **eine ~ schreiben** take a[n examination] paper/an examination 3 (Klosterbereich) enclosure

Klausur-: ~arbeit *die* [examination] paper; **~tagung** *die* private meeting

Klaviatur /klavia'tu:ɐ̯/ *die;* **~, ~en** 1 keyboard 2 (Vielfalt) [whole] gamut *or* range

Klavichord /klavi'kɔrt/ *das;* **~[e]s, ~s** clavichord

Klavier /kla'vi:ɐ̯/ *das;* **~s, ~e** piano

Klavier-: ~auszug *der* piano score; **~bauer** *der;* **~~s, ~~, ~bauerin** *die;* **~~, ~~nen** piano maker; **~bearbeitung** *die* piano arrangement; arrangement for the piano; **~begleitung** *die* piano accompaniment; **~hocker** *der* piano stool; **~konzert** *das* 1 (Musikstück) piano concerto; 2 (Veranstaltung) piano recital; **~lehrer** *der,* **~lehrerin** *die* piano teacher; **~schemel** *der* piano stool; **~schule** *die* piano tutor; **~sonate** *die* piano sonata; **~spiel** *das* piano playing; **~spieler** *der,* **~spielerin** *die* pianist; piano player; **~stimmer** *der;* **~~s, ~~, ~stimmerin** *die;* **~~, ~~nen** ▸ⓘ **S. 113** piano tuner; **~stunde** *die* piano lesson; **~unterricht** *der* piano lessons *pl.*

k

Klebe /'kle:bə/ *die;* **~** (ugs.) glue

Klebe-: ~band *das; Pl.* **~bänder** adhesive *or* sticky tape; **~bindung** *die* (Buchw.) adhesive *or* perfect binding; **~folie** *die* adhesive film; (für Regale) self-adhesive plastic sheeting

kleben

A *itr. V.* 1 stick (**an** + *Dat.* to); **~ bleiben** stick, remain stuck (**an** +*Dat.* to); **an allen Hauswänden klebten riesige Plakate** there were huge posters stuck on the walls of all the houses; **das Hemd klebte ihm am Körper** his shirt stuck *or* clung to his body; **an seinen Händen klebt Blut** (fig.) he has blood on his hands (fig.); his hands are stained with blood (fig.); **am Berghang ~** ‹*hut etc.*› cling to the mountainside; **jmdm. an der Stoßstange ~** (fig. salopp) ‹*driver, vehicle*› hang on sb.'s tail; **an jmdm. ~** (salopp) cling to sb. 2 (ugs.: klebrig sein) be sticky (**von, vor** + *Dat.* with) 3 (ugs.: an sich hängen haben) **voller Fliegen/Kletten** *usw.* **~:** be covered in flies/burrs 4 (ugs.: sich klammern) **an seinem Stuhl/an der Theke ~:** stay put in one's chair (coll.)/prop the bar up (coll.); **klebt nicht so an der Textvorlage** (fig.) don't stick so closely to the original text 5 (verbunden sein) **daran klebt ein Makel** there's a stigma attached to it; **diese Schande wird an ihr ~ bleiben** this disgrace will remain with her 6 (ugs.: Sozialversicherungsbeiträge entrichten) pay stamps 7 **~ bleiben** (ugs.: in der Schule nicht versetzt werden) stay down; have to repeat a year

B *tr. V.* 1 (befestigen) stick; (mit Klebstoff) stick; glue; (mit Leim) stick; paste; **jmdm. eine ~** (salopp) belt sb. one (coll.) 2 (mit Klebstoff reparieren) stick *or* glue ‹*vase etc.*› back together 3 (zusammenfügen) splice ‹*tape, film*›

***kleben|bleiben** ▸**kleben A1, 5, 7**

Klebe·pflaster *das* adhesive plaster; sticking plaster

Kleber *der;* **~s, ~:** adhesive; glue

Klebe-: ~streifen *der* ▸**Klebstreifen**; **~verband** *der* (Med.) adhesive bandage

Kleb-: ~fläche *die* adhesive surface; sticky side; **~kraft** *die* adhesive strength; **~pflaster** *das* ▸**Klebepflaster**

klebrig *Adj.* 1 (klebend) sticky; (von Schweiß) clammy ‹*hands etc.*› 2 (abwertend: schmierig) slimy

Klebrigkeit *die;* ~ ▸**klebrig**: stickiness; clamminess; sliminess

Kleb-: **~stelle** *die* join; (eines Films, Tonbandes) splice; **~stoff** *der* adhesive; glue; **~streifen** *der* adhesive *or* sticky tape; (zum Befeuchten auch) gummed tape

Kleckerei *die;* ~, **~en** (ugs.) mess

Klecker·kram *der* (ugs. abwertend) peanuts (coll.)

kleckern /ˈklɛkɐn/ (ugs.)

A *itr. V.* **1** (Flecken machen) make a mess; **oje, jetzt habe ich gekleckert** oh dear, now I've gone and spilled something (coll.) **2** *mit sein* (heruntertropfen) drip; spill **3** (zögernd verlaufen) ‹*orders*› come in dribs and drabs **4** (ugs.: halbherzig handeln) mess about with half measures; **nicht ~, sondern klotzen** stop messing about with half measures, and do the thing properly, whatever the cost

B *tr. V.* spill; splash ‹*paint*›

kleckerweise *Adv.* (ugs.) in dribs and drabs; **der Umzug ging nur ~ vonstatten** the move went ahead in fits and starts

Klecks /klɛks/ *der;* **~es, ~e** **1** stain; (nicht aufgesogen) blob; (Tintenfleck) [ink] blot **2** (ugs.: kleine Menge) spot; (von Senf, Mayonnaise) dab

klecksen

A *itr. V.* **1** (Klecks[e] machen) make a stain/stains; (mit Tinte) make a blot/blots; ‹*pen*› blot; **er hat auf den Teppich gekleckst** he has made a stain/stains on the carpet **2** (ugs. abwertend: schlecht malen) daub

B *tr. V.* (ugs.) daub ‹*paint*›; **Marmelade aufs Brot ~:** smear blobs of jam on the bread

Kleckser *der;* **~s,** ~ (ugs.) **1** (abwertend) (Maler) dauber; (Schriftsteller) scribbler **2** ▸**Klecks**

Kleckserei *die;* ~, **~en** (ugs. abwertend) **1** (dauerndes Klecksen) making stains *no art.*; (mit Tinte) making blots *no art.* **2** (Hingeschmiertes) scribble; scrawl; (schlecht gemaltes Bild) daub; daubing

Kledage /kleˈdaːʒə/ *die;* ~, **Kledasche** /kleˈdaːʃə/ *die;* ~ (nordd., md. salopp) clobber (sl.) *no indef. art.*

Klee /kleː/ *der;* **~s** clover; **jmdn./etw. über den grünen ~ loben** (ugs.) praise sb./sth. to the skies

Klee·blatt *das* **1** (Blatt des Klees) cloverleaf; (als Symbol Irlands) shamrock; **ein vierblättriges ~:** a four-leaf *or* four-leaved clover **2** (ugs.: drei Personen) trio; threesome **3** (Verkehrsw.: Straßenkreuz) cloverleaf [intersection *or* junction]

Kleiber /ˈklaibɐ/ *der;* **~s,** ~: nuthatch

Kleid /klait/ *das;* **~es, ~er** **1** dress; **ein zweiteiliges ~:** a two-piece [suit]; **die Natur trägt ein weißes ~** (fig. geh.) Nature is dressed *or* covered in a mantle of white (literary) **2** *Pl.* (Kleidung) clothes; **in den ~ern schlafen** sleep in one's clothes; **~er machen Leute** (Spr.) clothes make the man; the apparel oft proclaims the man (literary) **3** (geh.) (Gefieder) plumage; (Fell) coat **4** (veralt. geh.: Uniform) uniform **5** (schweiz.: Anzug) suit

Kleidchen *das;* **~s,** ~ **1** little dress **2** (ugs.: leichtes Kleid) plain little dress

kleiden

A *refl. V.* dress

B *tr. V.* **1** dress; **die Armen ~:** clothe the poor **2** suit; look well on; **die Farbe kleidet dich gut** the colour suits you *or* looks well on you **3** **etw. in Worte ~:** express sth. in words; put sth. into words; **etw. in schöne Worte ~:** clothe sth. in fine language

Kleider-: **~ab·lage** *die* **1** (Ablage) coat rack; **2** (Raum) cloakroom; checkroom (Amer.); **~bad** *das: dry-cleaning process in which the article is simply dipped in the cleaning fluid and not given any finishing treatment;* **~bügel** *der* clothes hanger; coat hanger; **~bürste** *die* clothes brush; **~größe** *die* size; **~haken** *der* coat hook; **~kammer** *die* (bes. Milit.) clothing store; **~kasten** *der* (südd., österr., schweiz.) ▸**~schrank**; **~macher** *der,* **~macherin** *die* (österr./veralt.) ▸**Schneider**; **~ordnung** *die* (hist.) laws *pl.* governing dress; **~puppe** *die* tailor's dummy; **~rock** *der* pinafore dress; **~sack** *der* (bes. Milit.) kitbag; **~schrank** *der* wardrobe; **er ist ein ~schrank** (fig. ugs.) he is a great hulk *or* a giant of a man; **~ständer** *der* coat stand; **~stange** *die* clothes rail; **~stoff** *der* (Stoff für ein Kleid) dress material; (Stoff für Kleidungsstücke) clothes material

kleidsam *Adj.* becoming

Kleidung *die;* ~**:** clothes *pl.*; **leichte/warme ~:** light/warm clothes *pl. or* clothing

Kleidungs·stück *das* garment; article of clothing; **~e** clothes

Kleie /ˈklaiə/ *die;* **~:** bran

klein /klain/

A *Adj.* **1** ▸❶ **S. 374** little; small; small ‹*format, letter*›; little ‹*finger, toe*›; **das Kleid ist mir zu ~:** the dress is too small for me; **ein ~es Bier** a small beer; ≈ a half[-pint]; **ein ~es Export** ≈ a half[-pint] of Export; **eine ~e Terz/Sekunde** (Musik) a minor third/second; **~e Schritte machen** take small *or* short steps; **sich ~ machen** make oneself small; **auf ~stem Raum** in the minimum of space; **sie ist ~ [von Gestalt/für ihr Alter]** she is small [in stature/for her age]; **er ist [einen Kopf] ~er als ich** he is [a head] shorter than me *or* shorter than I am [by a head]; **im Kleinen** in miniature; on a small scale; **Pippin der Kleine** (hist.) Pippin the Short; **~, aber oho** he/she may be small, but he/she certainly makes up for it; **~, aber fein** little, but very nice; **etw. ~ hacken** chop sth. up; **etw. ~ schneiden** cut sth. up small *or* in small pieces; **Zwiebeln ~ hacken/schneiden** chop up onions [small]; **etw. ~ machen** cut sth. up small; (ugs.: aufbrauchen) get through *or* (sl.) blow sth.

2 (jung) little; **sein ~er Bruder** his little brother; **als ich [noch] ~ war** when I was small *or* little; **unsere Kleine/unser Kleiner** our little girl/boy; **für die Kleinen** for the little ones; **von ~ auf** from an early age

3 (von kurzer Dauer) little, short ‹*while*›; short ‹*walk, break, holiday*›; short, brief ‹*delay, introduction*›; brief ‹*moment*›

4 (von geringer Menge) small ‹*family, amount, audience, staff*›; small, low ‹*salary*›; low ‹*price*›; **das Gas auf ~ stellen** turn the gas down [low]; **~es Geld haben** have some [small] change; **haben Sie es ~?** (ugs.) do you have the right money?; **~er habe ich es nicht** I don't have anything smaller; **einen Schein ~ machen** (ugs.: wechseln) change a note; **kann mir jemand ein 5-Franken-Stück ~ machen?** can anyone give me change for a five-franc piece?

5 (von geringem Ausmaß) light ‹*refreshment*›; small ‹*party, gift*›; scant, little ‹*attention*›; slight ‹*cold, indisposition*›; slight, small ‹*mistake, irregularity*›; minor ‹*event, error*›; **die ~en Dinge des Alltags** the little everyday things; **einen ~en Schreck bekommen** get a bit of a shock; **das ~ere Übel** the lesser evil; the lesser of the two evils; **das ist meine ~ste Sorge** that's the least of my worries; **du ~er Schwindler!** you little twister!; **ein ~es Spielchen** a little game; **ein ~[es] bisschen** a little *or* tiny bit; **ein ~ wenig** a little bit; **ein ~ wenig Rücksichtnahme** a little bit of consideration; **im Kleinen wie im Großen** in little things as well as in big ones; **bis ins Kleinste** down to the smallest *or* tiniest detail

6 (unbedeutend) lowly ‹*employee, sales assistant*›; minor ‹*official*›; **der ~e Mann** the ordinary citizen; the man in the street; **die ~en Leute** ordinary people; the man *sing.* in the street; **in ~en Verhältnissen leben** live in humble *or* modest circumstances; **~ anfangen** (ugs.) start off in a small way; **die Kleinen hängt man, die Großen lässt man laufen** it's always the small fry that get caught, while the big fish get away

7 **ganz ~ [und hässlich] werden** become meek and subdued; **den mache ich so ~ mit Hut!** (ugs.) I'll bring him down a peg or two; **jetzt ist sie so ~:** she's come down a peg or two

8 **ein ~er Geist** (engstirnig) a narrow-minded person; (beschränkt) a person of limited intellect

B *adv.* **1** **die Heizung ~/~er einstellen** turn the heating down low/lower; **~ gedruckt** in small print (postpos.); **das klein Gedruckte** the small print; **~ gemustert** small-patterned; **~ kariert** with a small check or a small-checkered pattern (postpos.); **~ geblümt** with a small floral pattern (postpos.); **~ geschrieben werden** (fig. ugs.) count for [very] little (**bei** with); **~ machen** (Kindersprache) do number one (child lang.)

2 (engstirnig) **~ von jmdm./etw. denken** think little *or* have a low opinion of sb./sth.; *s. auch* **beigeben B**

Klein *das;* **~s** (Kochk.) (von Geflügel) giblets *pl.*; (von Hasen) trimmings *pl.*

klein-, Klein-: **~aktie** *die* (Wirtsch.) *minimum par-value (50-mark) share;* **~aktionär** *der,* **~aktionärin** *die* (Wirtsch.) small shareholder; **~anzeige** *die* (Zeitungsw.) small *or* classified advertisement *or* (coll.) ad; **~arbeit** *die* painstaking and detailed work; **~asien** *(das)* Asia Minor; **~bahn** *die* light [narrow-gauge] railway; **~bauer** *der;* **~~n, ~~n** small farmer; smallholder; **~|bekommen** *unr. tr. V.:* ▸**~kriegen**; **~betrieb** *der* **1** (Industrie) small business; **ein industrieller/handwerklicher ~betrieb** a small factory/small workshop; **2** (Landw.) small farm; smallholding; **~bild·kamera** *die* (Fot.) miniature camera; 35 mm camera; **~buchstabe** *der* small letter; lower-case letter (Printing); **~bürger** *der,* **~bürgerin** *die* lower middle-class person; (abwertend: Spießbürger) petit bourgeois; **die ~bürger** lower middle-class people; **~bürgerlich** **A** *Adj.* **1** (das ~bürgertum betreffend) lower middle class; **2** (abwertend: spießbürgerlich) petit bourgeois; **B** *adv.* (abwertend: spießbürgerlich) **~bürgerlich denken** have a petit bourgeois way of thinking; **~bürgerlichkeit** *die* (abwertend) petit bourgeois nature; **~bürgertum** *das* lower middle class; petite bourgeoisie; **~bus** *der* minibus; **~darsteller** *der,* **~darstellerin** *die* small-part *or* (coll.) bit-part actor/actress

Kleine[1] *der; adj. Dekl.* **1** (kleiner Junge) little boy **2** (ugs. Anrede) little man; **na, ~r** (Prostituierte zum Passanten) hello, dearie

Kleine[2] *die; adj. Dekl.* **1** (kleines Mädchen) little girl **2** (ugs. Anrede) love; (abwertend) little madam **3** (ugs.: Freundin) girl[friend]

Kleine[3] *das; adj. Dekl.* **1** (ugs. scherzh.) little boy/girl (joc.); **das ~ der Familie** the baby of the family **2** (von Tieren) baby; little one

Kleine·leute·milieu *das* world of simple, ordinary people

Klein-: **~familie** *die* (Soziol.) nuclear family; **~format** *das* small size; (bei Büchern) small format *or* size

Klein·garten *der* ≈ allotment (*cultivated primarily as a garden*); **in ihrem ~:** on her allotment

Kleingarten·anlage *die* ≈ allotments *pl.*

klein-, Klein-: **~gärtner** *der,* **~gärtnerin** *die* ≈ allotment holder; **~gebäck** *das* biscuits (Brit.) *or* (Amer.) cookies and small pastries; **~geblümt** ▸**klein B 1**; **~gedruckt** ▸**klein B 1**; **~gedruckte** *das; adj. Dekl.* small print; **~geist** *der* (abwertend) small-minded person; **~geistig** *Adj.* small-minded; petty-minded ‹*official*›; **~geld** *das* ▸❶ **S. 299** [small] change; **würden Sie mir für 10 Euro ~geld geben?** can you change a *or* give me change for a ten-euro note?; **über das nötige ~geld verfügen** (iron.) have the wherewithal (coll.); **~gemustert** ▸**klein B 1**; **~gläubig** *Adj.* (unfähig zum festen Glauben) of little faith *postpos.*; sceptical; (ängstlich-zweifelnd) faint-hearted; **o ihr Kleingläubigen!** (bibl.) o ye of little faith!; **die Kleingläubigen** the doubters/faint-hearts; **~gläubigkeit** *die* ▸**~gläubig**: lack of faith; scepticism; faint-heartedness; ***~|hacken** ▸**klein A 1**

Kleinheit *die;* ~ **1** (geringe Größe) smallness; small size **2** (selten: Beschränktheit) limitedness; restrictedness

Klein-: **~hirn** *das* (Anat.) cerebellum; little brain; **~holz** *das* chopped wood; **~holz machen** chop wood; **~holz aus etw. machen, etw. zu ~holz machen** (ugs.) smash sth. to pieces; **~holz aus jmdm. machen, jmdn. zu ~holz machen** (ugs.) make mincemeat of sb.

Kleinigkeit *die;* ~, ~en 1 (kleine Sache) small thing; (Einzelheit) [small] detail; minor point; **bis auf einige ~en habe ich alle Einkäufe gemacht** apart from a few small items *or* a few odds and ends I've done all the shopping; **ich habe noch eine ~ zu erledigen** I still have a small matter to attend to; **jmdm. eine ~ schenken** give sb. a small *or* little gift *or* present; **eine ~ essen** have a [small] bite to eat; **das kostet eine ~** (ugs. iron.) that costs a bob *or* two (Brit. coll.) *or* a tidy sum (coll.); **die ~ von 50 000 Euro** (ugs. iron.) the small *or* little matter of 50,000 euros; **sich nicht mit ~en abgeben** not concern oneself with details *or* trifles 2 (leichte Aufgabe) **eine ~ für jmdn. sein[, etw. zu tun]** be no trouble for sb. [to do sth.]; be a simple matter for sb. [to do sth.]; **es war eine ~ für sie, ihren Mann zu überreden** she had no trouble in persuading her husband; **es war keine ~ für ihn** it was no small matter for him; **das war eine ~:** it was nothing 3 (ugs.: ein Stückchen) a little bit; (noch kleiner) a fraction; a shade

Kleinigkeits·krämer *der* (abwertend) pettifogger; pettifogging individual

Kleinigkeits·krämerei *die* (abwertend) pettifoggery; pettifogging

Kleinigkeits·krämerin *die* ▸ Kleinigkeitskrämer

klein-, Klein-: ~kaliber·gewehr *das* small-bore rifle; **~kalibrig** *Adj.* small-bore *attrib.*; **~kariert** A *Adj.* (ugs. abwertend: engstirnig) narrow-minded; *s. auch* **klein B 1**; B *adv.* narrow-mindedly; in a narrow-minded way; **~kind** *das* small child; **~kleckersdorf** /-'klɛkɐs-/ *(das)* **~~s** (ugs. spött.) somewhere in the back of beyond (coll.); some tiny little place way out in the sticks (coll.)

Klein-Klein *das;* ~s (Sport Jargon) pretty-pretty stuff

klein-, Klein-: ~klima *das* (Met.) microclimate; **~kram** *der* (ugs.) 1 (~e Dinge) odds and ends *pl.*; 2 (unbedeutende Dinge) trivial matters *pl.*; (Einzelheiten) trivial details; (~ere Arbeiten) trivial little jobs; **der tägliche ~kram** the trivial concerns *pl.* of everyday life; **~kredit** *der* (Bankw.) personal loan *(repayable within two years)*; **~krieg** *der* 1 (Guerillakrieg) guerrilla warfare; **ein ~krieg** a guerrilla war; 2 (ständiger Streit) running battle; **~|kriegen** *tr. V.* (ugs.) 1 (zerkleinern) crush [to pieces]; get one's teeth through ‹*tough meat*›; 2 (zerstören) smash; break; **nicht ~zukriegen sein** be indestructible; 3 (aufbrauchen) get through, (sl.) blow ‹*money*›; get through, (joc.) demolish ‹*sweets, cakes, etc.*›; 4 (entmutigen) **jmdn. ~kriegen** get sb. down; (durch Drohungen) intimidate sb.; (gefügig machen) bring sb. into line; **sich nicht ~kriegen lassen** not allow oneself to be got down/intimidated

Klein·kunst *die* 1 cabaret 2 (Kunsthandwerk) craftwork

Kleinkunst·bühne *die* cabaret ensemble

klein·laut
A *Adj.* subdued; (verlegen) sheepish
B *adv.* in a subdued fashion; (verlegen) sheepishly

kleinlich (abwertend)
A *Adj.* pernickety; (ohne Großzügigkeit) mean; (engstirnig) small-minded; petty; (in Bezug auf Sauberkeit und Ordnung) pernickety; fussy; petty ‹*regulations*›
B *adv.* meticulously; punctiliously; **~ denken** have a mean and petty cast of mind

Kleinlichkeit *die;* ~ (abwertend) ▸ **kleinlich:** pernicketiness; meanness; small-mindedness; pettiness; fussiness

klein-, Klein-: *~|machen ▸ **klein A 1**; **~möbel** *das* smaller item of furniture; **teure ~möbel** expensive smaller furniture *sing.*; **~mut** *der* (geh.) faint-heartedness; timidity; **~mütig** *Adj.* (geh.) faint-hearted; timid

Kleinod /'klaino:t/ *das;* ~[e]s, ~e *od.* ~ien /-'no:di̯ən/ (geh.) 1 (Schmuckstück) piece of jewellery; (Edelstein) jewel 2 (Kostbarkeit) gem

klein-, Klein-: ~rentner *der,* **~rentnerin** *die* person living on a small pension; ***~|schneiden** ▸ **klein A 1**; **~|schreiben** *unr. tr. V* write ‹*word etc.*› with a small initial letter; *s. auch* **klein B 1**; **~schreibung** *die* use of small initial letters; **~sparer** *der,* **~sparerin** *die* (Finanzw.) small saver; **~staat** *der* small state; **~stadt** *die* small town; **~städter** *der,* **~städterin** *die* small-town dweller; **~städtisch** *Adj.* small-town *attrib.*

Kleinst·betrag *der* minimum *or* smallest sum *or* amount

Kleinst·bild·kamera *die* subminiature camera

Kleinste *der/die/das; adj. Dekl.* smallest *or* youngest boy/girl/child

klein|stellen *tr. V.* turn down [low]

kleinst-, Kleinst-: ~kind *das* very small child (up to two years old); **~lebewesen** *das* micro-organism; **~möglich** *Adj.* smallest possible

kleinteilig
A *Adj.* made up of many small elements; detailed ‹*painting*›; **zu ~:** made up of too many small elements; ‹*painting*› with too much detail
B *adv.* in many small elements; ‹*paint*› in detail

Klein·tier *das* pet; (Nutztier) small domestic animal

Kleintier-: ~halter *der,* **~halterin** *die* breeder of small animals; **~haltung** *die* breeding of small animals; **~zucht** *die* [professional] breeding of small animals; (Betrieb) establishment for breeding small animals

Klein·verdiener *der,* **Klein·verdienerin** *die* person on a low income

Klein·vieh *das* small farm *or* domestic animals *pl.*; small livestock; **~ macht auch Mist** (ugs.) many a mickle makes a muckle (prov.); every little helps

Kleinvieh·zucht *die* breeding of small farm *or* domestic animals

Klein·wagen *der* small car

klein·wüchsig /-vy:ksɪç/ *Adj.* ‹*person*› of small stature; small, short ‹*person, race*›; small ‹*variety, species*›

Kleister /'klaistɐ/ *der;* ~s, ~: paste; (ugs. abwertend: Brei) goo (coll.)

kleist[e]rig *Adj.* (ugs.) gooey (coll.)

kleistern *tr. V.* (ugs.) 1 (kleben) paste, stick (**an** + *Akk.* on) 2 (reparieren) stick 3 (dick auftragen) plaster (**auf** + *Akk.* on) 4 **jmdm. eine ~:** belt sb. one (coll.)

Klementine /klemɛn'ti:nə/ *die;* ~, ~n clementine

***Klemmappe** ▸ **Klemmmappe**

Klemm·brett *das* clipboard

Klemme /'klɛmə/ *die;* ~, ~n 1 (Haar~) [hair] clip; (Papier~) paper clip; (Technik) clip; (Elektrot.) terminal; (Med.) clip 2 (ugs.: schwierige Lage) **in der ~ sein** *od.* **sitzen** be in a fix *or* jam (coll.); **jmdm. aus der ~ helfen** help sb. out of a fix *or* jam (coll.)

klemmen
A *tr. V.* 1 (befestigen) tuck; stick (coll.); **etw. unter den Arm ~:** tuck *or* (coll.) stick sth. under one's arm 2 (quetschen) **sich** *(Dat.)* **den Fuß/die Hand ~:** get one's foot/hand caught *or* trapped; catch *or* trap one's foot/hand 3 (salopp: stehlen) swipe (coll.); pinch (coll.); nick (Brit. coll.)
B *refl. V.* **sich hinter etw.** *(Akk.)* **~:** wedge oneself behind sth.; (fig. ugs.: sich einsetzen) put some hard work into sth.; **sich hinter jmdn. ~:** squeeze in behind sb.; (fig. ugs.: antreiben) get to work on sb. (coll.); **sich hinters Lenkrad ~** (ugs.) get behind the wheel
C *itr. V.* ‹*door, drawer, etc.*› stick

Klemm·mappe *die* spring *or* springback binder

Klempner /'klɛmpnɐ/ *der;* ~s, ~, **Klempnerin** *die;* ~, ~nen ▸ ℹ S. 113 tinsmith; (~ und Installateur) plumber

Klepper /'klɛpɐ/ *der;* ~s, ~ (abwertend) broken-down nag

Kleptokrat /klɛpto'kra:t/ *der;* ~en, ~en kleptocrat

Kleptokratie /klɛptokra'ti:/ *die;* ~, ~n kleptocracy

Kleptokratin *die;* ~, ~nen kleptocrat

Kleptomane /klɛpto'ma:nə/ *der;* ~n, ~n (Psych.) kleptomaniac; **~ sein** be a kleptomaniac

Kleptomanie /klɛptoma'ni:/ *die;* ~ (Psych.) kleptomania *no art.*

Kleptomanin *die;* ~, ~nen kleptomaniac

kleptomanisch *Adj.* (Psych.) kleptomaniac

klerikal /kleri'ka:l/ *Adj.* (auch abwertend) clerical; church ‹*property*›

Klerikale *der/die; adj. Dekl.* (auch abwertend) cleric; **die ~n** the clergy *sing.*

Klerikalismus *der;* ~ (oft abwertend) clericalism

Kleriker /'kle:rikɐ/ *der;* ~s, ~: cleric

Klerus /'kle:rʊs/ *der;* ~: clergy

Klett /klɛt/ *der;* ~s, ~s Velcro ®

Klette /'klɛtə/ *die;* ~, ~n burr; (Pflanze) burdock; **sich wie eine ~ an jmdn. hängen** (ugs.) stick like a burr to sb.

Kletter·affe *der:* **ein ~ sein** be able to climb like a monkey

Kletterei *die;* ~, ~en (ugs.) 1 (Herumklettern) climbing [about] 2 (Bergsteigen) climbing

Kletterer *der;* ~s, ~: climber

Kletter·gerüst *das* climbing frame

Kletterin *die;* ~, ~nen ▸ **Kletterer**

Klettermaxe *der;* ~n, ~n (ugs. scherzh.) 1 (Kind, das gerne klettert) climbing-mad child 2 (Fassadenkletterer) cat burglar

klettern /'klɛtɐn/ *itr. V.; mit sein* (auch fig.) climb; (mit Mühe) clamber; **auf einen Baum ~:** climb a tree; **aus dem Bett/Auto ~** (ugs.) climb out of bed/the car (coll.)

Kletter-: ~partie *die* 1 (Bergsteigen) climb; 2 (ugs.: anstrengende Wanderung) climbing expedition; **~pflanze** *die* creeper; (Bot.) climbing plant; climber; **~rose** *die* climbing *or* rambling rose; **~seil** *das* climbing rope; **~stange** *die* (Turnen) climbing pole; **~tau** *das* ▸ **~seil**; **~tour** *die* ▸ **~partie**; **~wand** *die* (Turnen) climbing wall

Klett·verschluss, *Klett·verschluß *der* Velcro ® fastening

Kletze /'klɛtsə/ *die;* ~, ~n (österr.) dried pear

klick /klɪk/ *Interj.* click; **~ machen** click; go click; **da machte es bei ihm ~** (fig. ugs.) and then the penny dropped (coll.)

klicken *itr. V.* 1 click; **es klickte** there was a click 2 (DV) click

Klicker *der;* ~s, ~ (westmd.) marble

klickern *itr. V.* (westmd.) play marbles

Klient /kli'ɛnt/ *der;* ~en, ~en client

Klientel /kliɛn'te:l/ *die;* ~, ~en clientele

Klientin *die;* ~, ~nen client

klieren /'kli:rən/ *tr., itr. V.* (nordd.) scrawl

Kliff /klɪf/ *das;* ~[e]s, ~e cliff

Kliff·küste *die* cliffed coast; cliffs *pl.*

Klima /'kli:ma/ *das;* ~s, ~s *od.* ~te /kli'ma:tə/ climate; **das politische/soziale ~** (fig.) the political/social climate; **im Büro herrscht ein angenehmes ~** (fig.) there's a pleasant atmosphere in the office

Klima-: ~an·lage *die* air conditioning *no indef. art.*; air-conditioning system; **mit ~anlage** air-conditioned; **~kammer** *die* (Med., Biol.) climatic chamber; **~karte** *die* climatic map

Klimakterium /klimak'te:ri̯ʊm/ *das;* ~s (Med.) menopause; change of life

Klima-: ~kunde *die* climatology *no art.*; **~schutz** *der* climate protection; **~technik** *die* air-conditioning engineering *no art.*

klimatisch /kli'ma:tɪʃ/
A *Adj.* climatic
B *adv.* climatically

klimatisieren *tr. V.* air-condition

Klimatologie /klimatolo'gi:/ *die;* ~: climatology *no art.*

Klima-: ~wandel *der* climate change; **~wechsel** *der* (Med.) change of climate

Klimax /'kli:maks/ *die;* ~: climax

Klima·zone *die* climatic zone

Klimbim /klɪm'bɪm/ *der;* ~s (ugs.) 1 (Kram) junk; odds and ends *pl.* 2 (Wirbel) fuss; **~ um**

etw. machen make a fuss about sth.

klimmen /ˈklɪmən/ *unr. itr. V.; mit sein* (geh.) clamber; climb

Klịmm·zug *der* (Turnen) pull-up; **geistige Klimmzüge machen** (fig. ugs.) do mental gymnastics

Klimper̲ei *die;* ~, ~**en** (ugs. abwertend) [awful] plunking

Klịmper·kasten *der* (ugs. abwertend) joanna (sl.); piano

klimpern /ˈklɪmpɐn/

A *itr. V.* jingle; tinkle; ‹*coins, keys*› jingle; **mit den Geldstücken/Schlüsseln ~:** jingle the coins/keys; **mit den Wimpern ~** (scherzh.) flutter one's eyelashes [seductively]; **auf dem Klavier/der Gitarre/dem Banjo ~** (ugs.) plunk away on the piano/guitar/banjo

B *tr. V.* (ugs. abwertend) plunk out ‹*tune etc.*›

kling /klɪŋ/ *Interj.* (einer Glocke) ding; (von Gläsern) chink; clink; **~ machen** ding/chink *or* clink

Klịnge *die;* ~, ~**n** **1** blade **2** (geh. veralt.: Waffe) blade (literary); **mit jmdm. die ~n kreuzen** (geh.) cross swords with sb.; **eine [gute] ~ schlagen** (geh.) be a good swordsman; **eine scharfe ~ führen** (fig. geh.) be hard-hitting in debate; **jmdn. über die ~ springen lassen** (fig.) (töten) dispose of *or* kill sb.; (ugs.: ruinieren) ruin sb.; (beruflich) put paid to sb.'s career (coll.)

Klingel /ˈklɪŋl̩/ *die;* ~, ~**n** **1** bell **2** (kleine Glocke) small bell

Klịngel-: ~**beutel** *der* offertory bag; collection bag; ~**draht** *der* bell wire

klinge[linge]ling /klɪŋə(lɪŋə)ˈlɪŋ/ *Interj.* ting-a-ling

Klịngel·knopf *der* bell button; bell push

klịngeln *itr. V.* **1** ring; ‹*alarm clock*› go off; ring; **es klingelt** (an der Tür) somebody is ringing the doorbell; there is a ring at the door; (Telefon) the telephone is ringing; **es hat bei ihm/ihr** *usw.* **geklingelt** (ugs.) the penny's dropped (coll.); *s. auch* **Kasse 1** **2** (die Klingel betätigen) ring [the bell]; **nach jmdm. ~:** ring for sb.; **der Radfahrer klingelte** the cyclist rang his/her bell; **es klingelte zur Pause** the bell went for the break; **jmdn. aus dem Schlaf ~:** ring [the bell] and wake sb. up **3** (Kfz-W.) ‹*engine*› pink

Klịngel-: ~**putzen** *das;* ~~**s** (ugs.) ringing doorbells [and running away]; ~**schnur** *die* bell pull; ~**ton** *der* ringtone; ~**zeichen** *das* ring; **das ist das ~zeichen für das Ende der Pause** that is the bell for the end of break/the interval (Brit.) *or* (Amer.) intermission; ~**zug** *der* bell pull

klịngen *unr. itr. V.* **1** **die Glocken klangen** the bells were ringing; **aus dem Haus klangen fröhliche Stimmen** the sound of merry voices came from the house; **aus dem Wald klang der Ruf des Kuckucks** from the forest could be heard the call of the cuckoo; **die Gläser ~ lassen** clink glasses [in a toast] **2** (einen bestimmten Klang haben) sound; **seine Worte klangen wie ein Vorwurf** his words sounded like a reproach; **es klang, als ob geschossen wurde** it sounded as if a shot had been fired

klịngend

A ▸**klingen**

B *Adj.* **ein ~er Reim** (Verslehre) a feminine rhyme; **~e Münze** [hard] cash; **mit ~em Spiel** with the band playing

klingling /klɪŋˈlɪŋ/ *Interj.* ting-a-ling

Klinik /ˈkliːnɪk/ *die;* ~, ~**en** **1** hospital; (spezialisiert) clinic **2** (Med.: klinisches Studium) clinical training

Klịniker *der;* ~**s**, ~ (Med.) **1** (Arzt) clinician; doctor teaching at a university hospital **2** (Student) medical student doing his/her clinical training

Klinikum /ˈkliːnikʊm/ *das;* ~**s**, **Klịnika** *od.* **Klịniken** **1** (Med.: Ausbildung) clinical training **2** (Zusammenschluss mehrerer Kliniken) hospital complex (*usually teaching hospitals and clinics, with central administration*)

klịnisch

A *Adj.* (Med.) clinical; **sie ist jetzt im 5. ~en Semester** she is now in the fifth term of her clinical training

B *adv.* **~ tot** clinically dead

Klinke /ˈklɪŋkə/ *die;* ~, ~**n** **1** (an der Tür) door handle; **sich** (*Dat.*) **die ~ in die Hand geben** (ugs.) come and go in a continuous stream; **~n putzen** (ugs. abwertend) (als Vertreter) peddle one's goods from door to door; (betteln) go begging from door to door **2** (Technik) catch; pawl

Klịnken·putzer *der* (ugs. abwertend) (Vertreter) door-to-door salesman; (Bettler) beggar

Klịnker *der;* ~**s**, ~: [Dutch] clinker

Klịnker-: ~**bau** *der* building of clinker brick; ~**stein** *der* ▸**Klinker**

klipp /klɪp/ *Adv.* **~ und klar** (ugs.) quite plainly *or* clearly

Klịppe *die;* ~, ~**n** rock; **alle ~n umschiffen** (fig.) negotiate every obstacle [successfully]

Klịpper *der;* ~**s**, ~ (hist.) clipper

Klịpp·fisch *der: cod etc. split open, salted, and partly dried;* klipfish

Klịpp·schule *die* (nordd. abwertend) second-rate school

klirren /ˈklɪrən/ *itr. V.* ‹*glasses, ice cubes*› clink; ‹*weapons in fight*› clash; ‹*window pane*› rattle; ‹*chains, spurs*› clank, rattle; ‹*harness*› jingle; **mit der Kette/den Sporen ~:** clank *or* rattle the chain/one's spurs; **~der Frost** (fig.) sharp frost

Klịrr·faktor *der* (Elektrot.) distortion factor

Klischee /kliˈʃeː/ *das;* ~**s**, ~**s** **1** cliché; **das ~ vom braven Hausmütterchen** the conventional picture *or* stereotype of the good little housewife **2** (Druckw.) block; plate

klisch̲ee̲haft

A *Adj.* stereotyped, hackneyed ‹*picture, description*›; cliché-ridden ‹*style*›

B *adv.* in a stereotyped *or* hackneyed way *or* manner

Klisch̲ee̲·vorstellung *die* stereotyped idea

klischi̲e̲ren *tr. V.* (Druckw.) stereotype

Klistier /klɪsˈtiːɐ̯/ *das;* ~**s**, ~**e** (Med.) enema

Klitoris /ˈkliːtorɪs/ *die;* ~, ~ *od.* **Klitorides** /kliˈtoːrideːs/ ▸ⓘ **S. 435** (Anat.) clitoris

klịtsch, klạtsch *Interj.* smack; ~, ~, **schlug der Regen gegen die Scheiben** pitter-patter went the rain on the window panes

Klitsch /klɪtʃ/ *der;* ~**[e]s**, ~**e** (landsch.) **1** (Brei) soggy mass; mush **2** (Schlag) slap; smack

Klịtsche *die;* ~, ~**n** (ugs.) **1** (ärmlicher Bauernhof) poor, run-down farm **2** (armseliges Dorf) wretched little village *or* place **3** (kleiner Betrieb) little shoestring outfit (coll.) **4** (Schmierentheater) third-rate little theatre

klịtsch·nass, *klịtsch·naß *Adj.* (ugs.) soaking *or* sopping wet; (tropfnass) dripping wet; **wir sind ~ geworden** we got soaked [to the skin] *or* drenched

klitze·kl̲e̲i̲n /ˈklɪtsə-/ *Adj.* (ugs.) teeny[-weeny] (coll.)

Klivie /ˈkliːvi̯ə/ *die;* ~, ~**n** (Bot.) clivia

Klo /kloː/ *das;* ~**s**, ~**s** (ugs.) loo (Brit. coll.); john (Amer. coll.); **aufs ~ müssen** have to go to the loo; **etw. ins ~ schütten** tip sth. down the loo

Kloake /kloˈaːkə/ *die;* ~, ~**n** (Senkgrube, auch fig.) cesspit; (Kanal) sewer

Kloben /ˈkloːbn̩/ *der;* ~**s**, ~ (Holz~) log

kl̲o̲big *Adj.* **1** (kantig) heavy and clumsy[-looking] ‹*shoes, furniture*›; heavily-built, bulky ‹*figure*› **2** (plump) clumsy; boorish; boorish ‹*behaviour*›

Kl̲o̲-: ~**brille** *die* (ugs.) loo seat (Brit. coll.); toilet seat; ~**bürste** *die* (ugs.) loo brush (Brit. coll.); toilet brush; ~**frau** *die* (ugs.) loo attendant (Brit. coll.); bathroom attendant (Amer.)

klomm /klɔm/ *1. u. 3. Pers. Sg. Prät. v.* **klimmen**

Klon /kloːn/ *der;* ~**s**, ~**e** (Biol.) clone

kl̲o̲nen *tr. V.* clone

klönen /ˈkløːnən/ *itr. V.* (nordd.) chat

kloni̲e̲ren *tr. V.:* ▸**klonen**

Kl̲o̲nung *die;* ~, ~**en** cloning

Kl̲o̲·papier *das* (ugs.) loo paper (Brit. coll.); toilet paper

klopfen /ˈklɔpfn̩/

A *itr. V.* **1** (schlagen) knock; **an die Tür ~:** knock at the door; **es hat geklopft** there's somebody knocking at the door; **jmdm.** *od.* **jmdn. auf die Schulter ~:** slap sb. on the shoulder; **„bitte ~!"** 'please knock'; **„bitte zweimal ~!"** 'please give two knocks' **2** (pulsieren) ‹*heart*› beat; ‹*pulse*› throb; **sein Herz schien ihm bis zum Hals zu ~:** his heart was in his mouth *or* was pounding wildly; **mit ~dem Herzen** with pounding *or* beating heart; **ein ~der Schmerz** a throbbing pain **3** (Kfz-W.) ‹*engine*› knock

B *tr. V.* beat ‹*carpet*›; **Beifall ~:** applaud by banging *or* rapping on the desk/table with one's fist; **den Takt [zur Musik] ~:** beat time [to the music]; **Fleisch ~:** beat *or* tenderize meat; **Steine ~:** break stones; (pflastern) lay cobbles; **Staub vom Mantel ~:** beat dust from one's coat; **die Asche aus der Pfeife ~:** knock *or* tap the ash out of one's pipe; **einen Nagel in die Wand ~:** knock *or* hammer a nail into the wall; **jmdn. aus dem Schlaf ~:** knock sb. up (Brit.); awaken sb. by knocking

Klopfer *der;* ~**s**, ~ **1** (Teppich~) carpet beater **2** (Tür~) [door] knocker **3** (Fleisch~) meat mallet *or* tenderizer

klopf-, Klopf-: ~**fest** *Adj.* antiknock ‹*petrol, fuel*›; ~**festigkeit** *die* antiknock properties *pl.*; ~**zeichen** *das* knock; (leiser) tap

Kloppe /ˈklɔpə/ *die;* ~ (nordd., md.) [good] hiding (coll.) *or* thrashing; **~ kriegen** get a [good] hiding (coll.) *or* thrashing

Klöppel /ˈklœpl̩/ *der;* ~**s**, ~ **1** (Glocken~) clapper **2** (Musik) beater **3** (Handarbeiten: Spule) bobbin

Klọ̈ppel·arbeit *die* **1** bobbin-lace *or* pillow-lace making *no art.* **2** (Erzeugnis) piece of pillow lace *or* bobbin lace

klöppeln *tr., itr. V.* **[etw.] ~:** make *or* work [sth. in] pillow lace *or* bobbin lace

Klọ̈ppel·spitze *die* pillow lace; bobbin lace

klọppen (nordd., md.)

A *tr. V.* hit

B *refl. V.* fight; scrap (coll.)

Klopper̲ei *die;* ~, ~**en** (nordd., md.) fight; scrap (coll.)

Klọ̈ppler *der;* ~**s**, ~, **Klọ̈pplerin** *die;* ~, ~**nen** pillow-lace *or* bobbin-lace maker

Klops /klɔps/ *der;* ~**es**, ~**e** (nordostd.) meat ball

Klosett /kloˈzɛt/ *das;* ~**s**, ~**s** *od.* ~**e** lavatory; **etw. ins ~ schütten** tip sth. down the lavatory

Klosẹtt-: ~**becken** *das* lavatory pan; toilet bowl; ~**brille** *die* toilet seat; ~**bürste** *die* lavatory brush; toilet brush; ~**deckel** *der* toilet lid; ~**frau** *die* lavatory attendant; ~**papier** *das* toilet paper; lavatory paper; ~**sitz** *der* toilet seat; lavatory seat

Kloß /kloːs/ *der;* ~**es**, **Klöße** /ˈkløːsə/ dumpling; (Fleisch~) meat ball; **ihm sitzt ein ~ im Hals, er hat einen ~ im Hals** (ugs.) he has a lump in his throat

Kloster /ˈkloːstɐ/ *das;* ~**s**, **Klöster** /ˈkløːstɐ/ (Mönchs~) monastery; (Nonnen~) convent; nunnery; **ins ~ gehen** enter a monastery/convent

Kl̲o̲ster-: ~**bruder** *der* lay brother; (veralt.: Mönch) monk; ~**frau** *die* (geh. veralt.) nun; ~**kirche** *die* monastery/convent church

kl̲ö̲sterlich

A *Adj.* **1** monastic; monastic/convent ‹*life*› **2** (zum Kloster gehörend) of the monastery/convent *postpos., not pred.*; monastery/convent *attrib.*

B *adv.* **~ abgeschieden leben** live in monastic seclusion

Kl̲o̲ster-: ~**regel** *die* rules *pl.* of the monastery/convent; ~**schule** *die* monastery-school/convent-school; ~**schüler** *der*, ~**schülerin** *die* monastery-school/convent-school pupil

Klotz /klɔts/ *der;* ~**es**, **Klötze** /ˈklœtsə/ **1** (Stück Holz) block [of wood]; (Stück eines Baumstamms) log; **schlafen wie ein ~** (fig.) sleep like a log; **ein ~ aus Beton [und Glas]** (fig.) a concrete [and glass] monstrosity; **jmdm. ein ~ am Bein sein** (ugs.) be a millstone round sb.'s neck; **mit ihm hast du dir einen ~ ans Bein gebunden** (ugs.) you have tied a millstone round your neck by getting involved with him; **auf einen groben ~ gehört ein grober Keil** (Spr.) rudeness can only be answered with rudeness **2** (salopp abwertend) (ungehobelter Mensch) clod; oaf; (roher Mensch) lout

Klötzchen /ˈklœtsçən/ *das;* **~s, ~:** small block of wood

klotzen (ugs.)
A *itr. V.* **1** (großzügig vorgehen) lash out in a big way (coll.); *s. auch* **kleckern A 4 2** (hart arbeiten) graft (sl.)
B *tr. V.* stick up (coll.) ‹*building, town*›

klotzig *Adj.* **1** (abwertend: unförmig) large and ugly[-looking] ‹*building*›; large and clumsy[-looking] ‹*furniture*› **2** (ugs.: gewaltig) massive great (coll.) ‹*car, villa, etc.*›

Klub /klʊp/ *der;* **~s, ~s 1** (Vereinigung) club **2** (Gebäude) club; **im ~:** at the club **3** (Clique) crowd

klub-, Klub-: ~eigen *Adj.* club's *attrib.*; the club's *pred.*; **~garnitur** *die* thickly upholstered three-piece suite; **~haus** *das* clubhouse; **~jacke** *die* blazer; **~mitglied** *das* club member; **~sessel** *der* club chair; **~zwang** *der* (österr.) ▸ **Fraktionszwang**

Kluft¹ /klʊft/ *die;* **~, ~en** (ugs.) rig-out (coll.); gear (coll.); (Uniform) uniform; garb; **sich in seine beste ~ werfen** put on one's Sunday best *or* one's best things

Kluft² *die;* **~, Klüfte** /ˈklʏftə/ **1** (veralt.) (Spalte) cleft; fissure; (im Gletscher) crevasse; (Abgrund) chasm **2** (Gegensatz) gulf

klug /klu:k/; **klüger** /ˈkly:gɐ/, **klügst...** /ˈkly:kst.../
A *Adj.* **1** (intelligent) clever; intelligent; clever, bright ‹*child, pupil*›; intelligent ‹*eyes*›; **er ist ein ~er Kopf** he's clever *or* bright; he's got brains **2** (gelehrt, weise) wise; **so ~ wie vorher** *od.* **zuvor sein** be none the wiser; **so ~ waren wir auch!** we know that as well as you do; **hinterher ist man immer klüger** it's easy to be wise after the event; **daraus werde ich nicht ~, daraus soll ein Mensch ~ werden** I can't make head or tail of it; **aus jmdm. nicht ~ werden** not know what to make of sb. **3** (vernünftig) wise; wise, sound ‹*advice*›; wise, prudent ‹*remark, course of action*›; (geschickt) clever, shrewd ‹*politician, negotiator, question*›; shrewd, astute ‹*businessman*›; great ‹*foresight*›; **es wäre das Klügste, wenn wir ...** the wisest course *or* thing would be for us to ...; **der Klügere gibt nach** (Spr.) discretion is the better part of valour (prov.); **der ~e Mann baut vor** it pays to be prepared
B *adv.* **1** (intelligent) cleverly; intelligently; **~ [daher]reden** talk as if one knows it all; **~ daherreden kann jeder!** anyone can talk! **2** (vernünftig) wisely; (geschickt) cleverly; shrewdly

Klügelei *die;* **~, ~en** (abwertend) **~[en** *Pl.***]** oversubtle reasoning *no pl.*

klügeln /ˈkly:gl̩n/ *itr. V.* **an etw.** (*Dat.*) **~:** ponder [over] sth.

klüger ▸ **klug**

klugerweise *Adv.* wisely

Klugheit *die;* **~, ~en 1** ▸ **klug 1, 2, 3**: cleverness; intelligence; brightness; wisdom; soundness; prudence; shrewdness; astuteness **2** (iron.: weiser Spruch) clever remark

klüglich *Adv.* (geh.) wisely

klug|reden ▸ **klug B 1**

Klug·scheißer *der,* **Klug·scheißerin** *die* (salopp abwertend) know-it-all (coll.); smart aleck (coll.)

klügst... ▸ **klug**

Klump /klʊmp/ *der;* **~s** *in* **einen Wagen zu** *od.* **in ~ fahren** (salopp) smash up *or* write off a car; **jmdn. zu ~ schlagen** (salopp) beat the living daylights out of sb. (coll.)

Klumpatsch /ˈklʊmpatʃ/ *der;* **~[e]s** (salopp abwertend) junk

klumpen /ˈklʊmpn̩/ *itr. V.* go lumpy

Klumpen *der;* **~s, ~ 1** lump; **ein ~ Erde** a lump *or* clod of earth; **ein ~ Gold** a gold nugget **2** (rhein.: Holzschuh) clog

Klump·fuß *der* club foot

klumpig *Adj.* lumpy

Klüngel /ˈklʏŋl̩/ *der;* **~s, ~** (abwertend) **1** (Clique) clique **2** (Cliquenwesen) cliquism *no indef. art.*

Klüngelei *die;* **~, ~en** (abwertend) cliquism *no pl.*; (Vetternwirtschaft) nepotism *no pl.*

klüngeln *itr. V.* (ugs.) ▸ **Klüngelei**: indulge in cliquism/nepotism

Klunker /ˈklʊŋkɐ/ *die;* **~, ~n** *od. der;* **~s, ~** (ugs.) rock (sl.)

Klus /klu:s/ *die;* **~, ~en** (schweiz.) narrow gorge; cluse (Geol.)

Klüse /ˈkly:zə/ *die;* **~, ~n** ▸ **Ankerklüse**

Klüver /ˈkly:vɐ/ *der;* **~s, ~** (Seemannsspr.) jib

Klüver·baum *der* (Seemannsspr.) jib boom

km *Abk.* **= Kilometer** km.

knabbern /ˈknabɐn/
A *tr. V.* nibble; **etw. zum Knabbern** sth. to nibble; **nichts mehr zu ~ haben** (ugs. verhüll.) be broke (coll.) *or* skint (sl.)
B *itr. V.* **an etw.** (*Dat.*) **~:** nibble *or* gnaw [at] sth.; **an etw.** (*Dat.*) **[noch lange] zu ~ haben** (ugs.) (sich anstrengen müssen) have sth. to think about *or* chew on; (leiden müssen) take a long time to get over sth.; **an dieser Übersetzung hatten die Schüler ganz schön zu ~:** this translation really gave the pupils something to think about *or* chew on

Knabe /ˈkna:bə/ *der;* **~n, ~n 1** (geh. veralt./südd., österr., schweiz.) boy **2** (ugs.: Bursche) chap (coll.); **Na, alter ~! Wie gehts?** well, old boy *or* old chap, how are you? (coll.)

Knaben-: ~alter *das* (geh.) boyhood; **~chor** *der* boys' choir

knabenhaft
A *Adj.* boyish
B *adv.* boyishly

Knaben-: ~kraut *das* orchis; wild orchid; **~liebe** *die* (geh.) pederasty; **~schule** *die* (veralt.) boys' school; **~stimme** *die* boy's voice; **~streich** *der* (geh.) boyish prank

knack /knak/ *Interj.* crack

Knack *der;* **~[e]s, ~e** crack

Knäcke /ˈknɛkə/ *das;* **~s, ~, Knäcke·brot** *das* crispbread; (Scheibe) slice of crispbread

knacken
A *itr. V.* **1** (krachen) ‹*bed, floor, etc.*› creak; **es knackt im Telefon** the [telephone] line is crackling; **es knackte im Gebälk** the beams creaked; **mit den Fingern ~:** crack one's fingers **2** *mit sein* (ugs.: zerbrechen) snap; ‹*window*› crack **3** **an etw.** (*Dat.*) **zu ~ haben** (ugs.) take a long time to get over sth.
B *tr. V.* **1** (zerbrechen) crack ‹*nut, shell*› **2** (salopp: zerquetschen) squash **3** (aufbrechen) crack ‹*safe*› [open]; break into ‹*car, bank, vending machine, etc.*›; crack, break ‹*code*›

Knacker *der;* **~s, ~ 1** **alter ~** (salopp) old fogey **2** (ugs.: Geldschrankknacker) safe-cracker **3** ▸ **Knackwurst**

knack·frisch *Adj.* (ugs.) crispy fresh ‹*rolls, crisps, etc.*›; crisp fresh ‹*fruit, vegetables*›

Knacki /ˈknaki/ *der;* **~s, ~s** (salopp) con (coll.); jailbird

knackig *Adj.* **1** (knusprig) crisp; crisp, crunchy ‹*apple*› **2** (ugs.: attraktiv) luscious, delectable ‹*girl*›

Knack·laut *der* (Phon.) glottal stop

knacks *Interj.* crack

Knacks *der;* **~es, ~e** (ugs.) **1** (Ton) crack **2** (Sprung) crack **3** (fig.: Defekt) **einen ~ bekommen** ‹*person*› have *or* suffer a breakdown; ‹*health*› suffer; **die Ehe hatte einen ~:** the marriage was in difficulties

Knack·wurst *die: type of frankfurter, made with beef and pork, the tight skin of which makes a cracking sound when bitten;* knackwurst

Knall /knal/ *der;* **~[e]s, ~e** bang; (fig.) big row; **einen ~ haben** (salopp) be barmy (sl.) *or* off one's rocker (coll.); **auf ~ und Fall, ~ auf Fall** (ugs.) without warning

knall-, Knall-: ~bonbon *der od. das* cracker; **~bunt** *Adj.* gaudy; ‹*car*› painted in gaudy colours; **~effekt** *der* (ugs.) (Überraschendes) astonishing part; (Sensation) sensational part

knallen
A *itr. V.* **1** (einen Knall verursachen) ‹*shot*› ring out; ‹*firework*› go bang; ‹*cork*› pop; ‹*door*› bang, slam; ‹*whip, rifle*› crack; **die Peitsche ~ lassen** crack the whip; **mit der Tür ~:** bang *or* slam the door; **an der Kreuzung hat es geknallt** (ugs.) there was a crash at the crossroads; **sei ruhig, oder es knallt!** (fig. ugs.) be quiet, or you'll get a good hiding **2** (ugs.: schießen) shoot, fire (**auf** + *Akk.* at); (mehrere Male) blaze *or* (coll.) bang away (**auf** + *Akk.* at); **Hände hoch, oder es knallt!** hands up, or I'll shoot! **3** (Ballspiele ugs.) **aufs Tor ~:** belt the ball/puck at the goal (coll.) **4** *mit sein* (ugs.: prallen) **die Tür knallte ins Schloss** the door slammed *or* banged shut; **sie knallte mit dem Fahrrad gegen einen Laternenpfahl** she crashed into a lamp post on her bicycle; **mit dem Kopf gegen die Windschutzscheibe ~:** bang one's head against the windscreen; **der Ball knallte gegen die Latte** the ball slammed against the crossbar **5** (ugs.: scheinen) blaze *or* beat down
B *tr. V.* **1** (ugs.) (hart aufsetzen) slam *or* bang down; (werfen) sling (coll.); **den Hörer auf die Gabel ~:** slam *or* bang down the receiver **2** (ugs.: schlagen) **du kriegst gleich eine geknallt!** you're going to get a clout any minute (coll.); **jmdm. eine ~** (salopp) belt *or* clout sb. one (coll.) **3** (Ballspiele ugs.) belt ‹*ball*›

knall·eng *Adj.* (ugs.) skintight

Knaller *der;* **~s, ~:** banger

Knall·erbse *die* ≈ cap bomb

Knallerei *die;* **~, ~en** (ugs.) (von Korken) popping; (einer Peitsche) cracking; (von Gewehren) banging, shooting; (von Feuerwerk) banging

knall-, Knall-: ~frosch *der* jumping jack; **~gas** *das* (Chemie) oxyhydrogen; **~gelb** *Adj.* (ugs.) bright *or* vivid yellow; **~grün** *Adj.* (ugs.) bright *or* vivid green; **~hart** (ugs.) **A** *Adj.* **1** very tough ‹*job, demands, action, measures, etc.*›; ‹*person*› as hard as nails; hard [core] ‹*pornography*›; very sharp ‹*criticism*›; **ein ~harter Bursche** a thug; **2** (kraftvoll) fierce ‹*serve*›; crashing ‹*blow*›; **B** *adv.* **1** (rücksichtslos, brutal) brutally; **gegen etw. ~hart vorgehen** take very tough action against sth.; **jmdm. etw. ~hart sagen** say sth. to sb. quite brutally; **2** (kraftvoll) ‹*serve, hit*› really hard; **~heiß** *Adj.* (ugs.) boiling *or* baking hot (coll.)

knallig *Adj.* (ugs.) loud; gaudy

knall-, Knall-: ~kopf, ~kopp *der* (salopp) [stupid] berk (Brit. coll.) *or* (Amer. coll.) jerk; **~körper** *der* banger; (bei Aufprall explodierend) ≈ cap bomb; **~rot** *Adj.* bright *or* vivid red; **sie bekam einen ~roten Kopf** she *or* her face turned [bright] scarlet *or* as red as a beetroot; **~tüte** *die* (ugs.) nitwit (coll.); clot (Brit. sl.)

knapp /knap/
A *Adj.* **1** (kaum ausreichend) meagre, low ‹*pension, wage, salary*›; meagre ‹*pocket money*›; **Kaffee war ~:** coffee was scarce *or* in short supply; **das Geld wird ~:** money is getting tight; **die Vorräte wurden ~:** supplies ran short; **etw. ~ halten** keep sth. in short supply; **sie bekam nur ein sehr ~es Haushaltsgeld** she received very little housekeeping money; **~ mit etw. sein** be short of sth.; **..., und nicht zu ~!** ... and how! **2** (gerade ausreichend) narrow ‹*victory, lead*›; narrow, bare ‹*majority*›; close ‹*result*› **3** (nicht ganz) **vor einer ~en Stunde** almost *or* just under an hour ago **4** (eng) tight-fitting ‹*garment*›; (zu eng) tight ‹*garment*› **5** (kurz) terse ‹*reply, greeting*›; concise, succinct ‹*description, account, report*›; **mit ~en Worten** in a few brief words
B *adv.* **1** (kaum ausreichend) **~ bemessen sein** be meagre; **seine Zeit war ~ bemessen** his time was limited; **~ gerechnet** at the lowest estimate; **jmdn. ~ halten** (ugs.) keep sb. short (**mit** of) **2** (gerade ausreichend) **~ gewinnen/verlieren** win/lose narrowly *or* by a narrow margin; **eine Prüfung ~ bestehen** just pass an examination **3** (sehr nahe) just; **~ über dem Knie enden** come to just above the knee **4** (nicht

ganz) just under; not quite; **vor ~ einer Stunde** just under *or* not quite an hour ago; **er ist ~ fünfzig** he is not quite fifty *or* just this side of fifty 5 (eng) **~ sitzen** fit tightly; (zu eng) be a tight fit; **~ geschnitten/sitzend** tight-fitting 6 (kurz) ‹*reply*› tersely; ‹*describe, summarize*› concisely, succinctly

Knạppe *der;* **~n, ~n** 1 (Bergmann) miner (*who has completed his apprenticeship*) 2 (hist.) squire

***knapp|halten** ▸ **knapp A 1, B 1**

Knạppheit *die;* ~ 1 (Mangel) shortage, scarcity (**an** + *Dat.* of); (von Geld, Zeit) shortage 2 (Kürze) (einer Antwort, eines Grußes) terseness; (einer Beschreibung, eines Berichts) conciseness, succinctness

Knạppschaft *die;* **~, ~en** (Bergmannsspr.) 1 (Gesamtheit der Knappen) miners *pl.* 2 (Organisation) miners' guild

knapsen /ˈknapsn̩/ *itr. V.* (ugs.) skimp; scrimp

Knarre /ˈknarə/ *die;* **~, ~n** 1 (Rassel) rattle 2 (salopp: Gewehr) shooting iron (coll.)

knạrren *itr. V.* creak; **mit ~der Stimme** in a rasping *or* grating voice

knarzen /ˈknartsn̩/ *itr. V.* (landsch.) creak

knạrzig

A *Adj.* rough ‹*voice*›

B *adv.* (mit **~er** Stimme) in a rough voice; **~ schnarrend** rasping

Knast /knast/ *der;* **~[e]s, Knäste** /ˈknɛstə/ *od.* **~e** (ugs.) 1 (Strafe) bird (sl.); time; **man hat ihm zwei Jahre ~ gegeben** he got two years' bird (sl.); **~ schieben** (salopp) do bird (sl.) *or* time 2 (Gefängnis) clink (sl.); jug (sl.); prison; **im ~ sitzen** be in clink *or* jug (sl.)

Knạst·bruder *der* (ugs.) 1 jailbird; old lag (sl.) 2 (Mitgefangener) fellow jailbird

Knạster *der;* **~s, ~** 1 (veralt.: Tabak) weed (arch.) 2 (ugs. abwertend: schlechter Tabak) evil-smelling tobacco

Knastologe /knastoˈloːɡə/ *der;* **~n, ~n, Knastologin** *die;* **~, ~nen** (ugs. scherzh.) jailbird; old lag (sl.)

Knatsch /knaːtʃ/ *der;* **~[e]s** (ugs.: Ärger) trouble; **die beiden haben schon wieder ~ miteinander** the two of them are already rowing again

knạtschig *Adj.* (ugs.) grumpy; (weinerlich) fretful

knattern /ˈknatɐn/ *itr. V.* 1 ‹*machine gun*› rattle, clatter; ‹*sail*› flap; ‹*radio*› crackle; ‹*motor vehicle, engine*› clatter 2 *mit sein* (knatternd fahren) clatter

Knäuel /ˈknɔyəl/ *der od. das;* **~s, ~** 1 ball; (wirres **~**) tangle; **er knüllte den Brief zu einem ~ zusammen** he screwed the letter into a ball 2 (fig.) (von Menschen) knot; (größer) [milling] crowd; (von Widersprüchen, Ereignissen) tangle

Knauf /knauf/ *der;* **~[e]s, Knäufe** /ˈknɔyfə/ (einer Tür, eines Gehstocks) knob; (eines Schwertes, Dolches) pommel

Knauser *der;* **~s, ~** (ugs. abwertend) Scrooge; skinflint; miser

Knauserei *die;* **~, ~en** (ugs. abwertend) 1 (knauseriges Wirtschaften) stinginess; penny-pinching; miserliness 2 (Fall von **~**) piece of stinginess *or* miserliness

knauserig *Adj.* (ugs. abwertend) stingy; tight-fisted; close-fisted

Knauserigkeit *die;* **~, ~en** ▸ **Knauserei**

knausern /ˈknauzɐn/ *itr. V.* (ugs. abwertend) be stingy; skimp; scrimp; **mit etw. ~:** be stingy with sth.

Knaus-Ogino-Methode /ˈknaus|oˈɡiːno-/ *die* rhythm method (*with calendar-marking*)

knautschen /ˈknautʃn̩/ (ugs.)

A *tr. V.* crumple, crease ‹*dress*›

B *itr. V.* ‹*dress, material*› crease, get creased

knautschig *Adj.* (ugs.) crumpled ‹*suit, dress, etc.*›

Knautsch-: ~lack *der,* **~lack·leder** *das,* **~leder** *das* patterned patent leather; (Imitat) imitation patterned patent leather; **~zone** *die* (Kfz-W.) crumple zone

Knebel /ˈkneːbl̩/ *der;* **~s, ~** 1 (zum **~n**) gag 2 (Griff) toggle; (am Schraubstock) handle

Knebel-: ~bart *der* Vandyke beard; (Schnurrbart) twisted moustache; **~knopf** *der* toggle

knebeln *tr. V.* gag; (fig.) gag, muzzle ‹*the press, a people*›

Knecht /knɛçt/ *der;* **~[e]s, ~e** 1 farm labourer; farmhand; (fig.) slave; vassal 2 **~ Ruprecht** *helper to St. Nicholas* [≈ *to Santa Claus*]

knechten *tr. V.* (geh.) (versklaven) reduce to servitude *or* slavery; enslave; (unterdrücken) oppress ‹*people, nation*›

knechtisch (geh.)

A *Adj.* servile, slavish ‹*obedience, submissiveness*›; servile, submissive ‹*person, character*›

B *adv.* servilely; submissively

Knechtschaft *die;* **~, ~en** (geh.) bondage; servitude; slavery

Knechtung *die;* **~, ~en** (geh.) ▸ **knechten**: enslavement; oppression

kneifen /ˈknaifn̩/

A *unr. tr., itr. V.* pinch; **jmdm.** *od.* **jmdn. in den Arm ~:** pinch sb.'s arm

B *unr. itr. V.* 1 (drücken) ‹*clothes*› be too tight 2 (ugs. abwertend: sich drücken) chicken (coll.) *or* back out (**vor** + *Dat.* of); **vor einer Prüfung/ Verantwortung ~:** funk an examination (coll.)/(coll.) duck [out of] a responsibility

Kneifer *der;* **~s, ~:** pince-nez

Kneif·zange *die* pincers *pl.*; **eine ~:** a pair of pincers

Kneip·abend *der* [students'] drinking evening

Kneipe /ˈknaipə/ *die;* **~, ~n** 1 (ugs.) pub (Brit.); bar (Amer.) 2 (Studentenspr. veralt.) [students'] drinking evening

Kneipen·wirt *der* (salopp) [pub] landlord (Brit.); barkeeper (Amer.)

Kneipen·wirtin *die* (salopp) [pub] landlady (Brit.); barkeeper (Amer.)

Kneipier /knaiˈpieː/ *der;* **~s, ~s** (salopp) ▸ **Kneipenwirt**

kneippen /ˈknaipn̩/ *itr. V.* (ugs.) take *or* undergo a Kneipp cure

Kneipp·kur *die* Kneipp cure

knetbar *Adj.* workable; kneadable ‹*dough*›

Knete *die;* **~** 1 (ugs.) ▸ **Knetmasse** 2 (salopp: Geld) dough (coll.)

kneten /ˈkneːtn̩/ *tr. V.* 1 (bearbeiten) knead ‹*dough, muscles*›; work ‹*clay*› 2 (formen) model ‹*figure*›; **eine Figur aus Ton ~:** mould *or* fashion a figure in clay

Knet-: ~maschine *die* kneading machine; **~masse** *die* plastic modelling material; Plasticine ®

Knick /knɪk/ *der;* **~[e]s, ~e/~s** 1 *Pl.* **~e** (Biegung) sharp bend; (in einem Draht) kink; **du hast wohl einen ~ in der Optik!** (ugs. scherzh.) are you blind? 2 *Pl.* **~e** (Falz) crease 3 *Pl.* **~s** (nordd.: Hecke) boundary hedge [with ditches and rampart]

Knickebein /ˈknɪkəbain/ *der;* **~s** *egg liqueur used as a filling in sweets, Easter eggs, etc.*

Knick·ei *das* cracked egg

knicken

A *tr. V.* 1 (brechen) snap 2 (falten) crease ‹*page, paper, etc.*›; **„Bitte nicht ~!"** (auf einem Umschlag) 'please do not bend'; (auf einem Formular) 'please do not fold'

B *itr. V.*; *mit sein* snap

Knicker *der;* **~s, ~** 1 (ugs. abwertend) Scrooge; skinflint; miser 2 (niederd.: Murmel) marble

Knickerbocker /-bɔkɐ/ *Pl.* knickerbockers; (länger und breiter) plus-fours

knick[e]rig *Adj.* (ugs. abwertend) stingy; tight-fisted

Knick[e]rigkeit *die;* **~** (ugs. abwertend) stinginess; tight-fistedness

Knick·fuß *der* club foot

Knicks /knɪks/ *der;* **~es, ~e** curtsy; **einen ~ machen** make *or* drop a curtsy (**vor** + *Dat.* to)

knicksen *itr. V.* curtsy (**vor** + *Dat.* to)

Knie /kniː/ *das;* **~s, ~** /ˈkniː(ə)/ 1 ▸ ❶ **S. 435** knee; **jmdm. auf [den] ~n danken** go down on one's knees and thank sb.; **jmdn. auf ~n bitten** beg sb. on bended knees; **vor jmdm. auf die ~ fallen** go down on one's knees before sb.; **er hatte/bekam weiche ~** (ugs.) his knees trembled/started to tremble; **vor lauter Aufregung hatte ich ganz weiche ~:** I was weak at the knees with sheer excitement; **jmdn. auf** *od.* **in die ~ zwingen** (geh.) force sb. to his knees; **in die ~ gehen** (umfallen) sink to one's knees; (eine **~beuge** machen) bend one's knees; (sich unterordnen) submit, bow (**vor** + *Dat.* to); **jmdn. übers ~ legen** (ugs.) put sb. across one's knee; **etw. übers ~ brechen** (ugs.) rush sth. 2 (an Hosen, Strümpfen) knee 3 (Biegung) sharp bend; (eines Rohres) elbow

Knie·beuge *die* ▸ ❶ **S. 435** knee bend

Knie·bund·hose *die* knee breeches *pl.*; **eine ~:** a pair of knee breeches

knie-, Knie-: ~fall *der:* **einen ~fall tun** *od.* **machen** (auch fig.) go down on one's knees (**vor** + *Dat.* before); **~fällig** A *Adj.* **sein ~fälliges Bitten** his pleading on bended knee; B *adv.* on bended knees; on one's knees; **~frei** *Adj.* ‹*skirt*› worn above the knee; **wird die Mode wieder ~frei?** is the above-the-knee look coming back again?; **~gelenk** *das* ▸ ❶ **S. 435** knee joint; **~hoch** *Adj.* knee-deep ‹*water, snow*›; knee-high ‹*grass*›; knee-length ‹*boots*›; **~hose** *die* knee breeches *pl.*; **~kehle** *die* ▸ ❶ **S. 435** hollow of the knee; popliteal space (Anat.); **~lang** *Adj.* knee-length

knien /ˈkniː(ə)n/

A *itr. V.* kneel; **diese Arbeit muss man ~d verrichten** this work has to be done on one's knees *or* kneeling

B *refl. V.* kneel [down]; get down on one's knees; **sich in die Arbeit/die Akten ~** (fig. ugs.) get stuck into one's work/the files (sl.)

Knies /kniːs/ *der;* **~es** (ugs.) 1 (Schmutzschicht) layer of muck (coll.) *or* dirt 2 (Unstimmigkeit) quarrel; **ständig ~ mit jmdm. haben** always be quarrelling with sb.

knie-, Knie-: ~scheibe *die* ▸ ❶ **S. 435** kneecap; patella (Anat.); **~schützer** *der* (Sport) knee pad; **~strumpf** *der* knee-length sock; knee sock; **~tief** *Adj.* knee-deep

Kniff /knɪf/ *der;* **~[e]s, ~e** 1 (das Kneifen) pinch 2 (Falte) crease; (in Papier) crease; fold 3 (Kunstgriff) trick; dodge; **den ~ [bei etw.] heraushaben** have got the knack [of sth.]

Kniffelei *die;* **~, ~en** (ugs.) fiddly job

kniff[e]lig *Adj.* 1 (schwierig) fiddly; tricky ‹*problem, crossword puzzle*› 2 (heikel) tricky

Knigge /ˈknɪɡə/ *der;* **~[s], ~:** book on etiquette

Knilch /knɪlç/ *der;* **~s, ~e** (salopp abwertend) bastard (coll.)

knipsen /ˈknɪpsn̩/

A *tr. V.* 1 (entwerten) clip; punch 2 (fotografieren) snap; take a snap[shot] of 3 (wegschnellen) flick

B *itr. V.* 1 (fotografieren) take snapshots 2 **mit den Fingern ~:** snap one's fingers

Knipser *der;* **~s, ~, Knips·schalter** *der* (ugs.) snap switch

Knirps /knɪrps/ *der;* **~es, ~e** 1 (Wz) *Taschenschirm*) telescopic umbrella 2 (ugs.: Junge) nipper (coll.) 3 (ugs. abwertend: kleiner Mann) [little] squirt (coll.)

knirschen /ˈknɪrʃn̩/ *itr. V.* 1 crunch 2 **mit den Zähnen ~:** grind one's teeth; (fig.) gnash one's teeth

knistern /ˈknɪstɐn/ *itr. V.* rustle; ‹*wood, fire*› crackle; **mit etw. ~:** rustle sth.; **eine ~de Atmosphäre** (fig.) a tense *or* charged atmosphere; *s. auch* **Gebälk**

Knittel·vers /ˈknɪtl̩-/ *der* (Metrik) rhyming couplets of four-stress lines

Knitter /ˈknɪtɐ/ *der;* **~s, ~:** crease

knitter·frei *Adj.* non-crease; **[vollkommen] ~ sein** not crease [at all]

knitt[e]rig *Adj.* creased; crumpled; (fig.) wrinkled ‹*face*›

knittern *tr., itr. V.* crease; crumple

Knobel·becher *der* 1 (Würfelbecher) dice cup 2 (Soldatenspr.: Stiefel) army boot

knobeln *itr. V.* 1 (mit Würfeln) play dice; (mit Streichhölzern) play spoof; (mit Handzeichen) play scissors, paper, stone; **um etw. ~:** play dice *etc.* to decide sth. 2) (ugs.: nachdenken) puzzle (**an** + *Dat.* over)

Knob·lauch /ˈknoːp-/ *der* garlic

Knoblauch-: ~butter *die* (Kochk.) garlic butter; **~zehe** *die* clove of garlic; **~zwiebel** *die* garlic bulb

Knöchel /ˈknœçl̩/ *der;* **~s, ~** ▸ⓘ **S. 435** 1) (am Fuß) ankle; **bis an/über die ~:** up to the *or* one's ankles/to above ankle level; **das Kleid reicht bis an die ~:** the dress reaches [down] to the ankles 2) (am Finger) knuckle

knöchel-, Knöchel-: ~bruch *der* broken ankle; **~lang** *Adj.* ankle-length; **~tief** *Adj.* ankle-deep

Knochen /ˈknɔxn̩/ *der;* **~s, ~** 1) ▸ⓘ **S. 435** bone; **Fleisch mit/ohne ~:** meat on/off the bone; **jmdm. alle ~ [einzeln] brechen** (salopp) break every [single] bone in sb.'s body; **die Wunde geht bis auf den ~:** the wound reaches to the bone; **mir tun sämtliche ~ weh** (ugs.) every bone in my body aches; **der Schreck fuhr ihm in die ~** (ugs.) he was shaken to the core; **eine Grippe in den ~ haben** (ugs.) feel the flu coming on (coll.); **keinen Mumm in den ~ haben** (ugs.) be a weed; **sich** (*Dat.*) **die ~ brechen** break something; **seine ~ für etw. hinhalten [müssen]** (ugs.) [have to] risk one's neck fighting for sth.; **die ~ zusammenreißen** (Soldatenspr.) stand up straight; **das geht auf die ~** (salopp) it's knackering (Brit. sl.); it burns you out (Amer. coll.); **sie hat mich bis auf die ~ blamiert** (ugs.) she made a complete *or* proper fool of me 2) (ugs. abwertend: Kerl) so-and-so (coll.) 3) (ugs.: Schraubenschlüssel) double-ended ring spanner

knochen-, Knochen-: ~arbeit *die* (ugs.) back-breaking work; **~bau** *der* bone structure; **ein sehr kräftiger ~bau** a very powerful frame; **~bruch** *der* ▸ⓘ **S. 439** fracture; **sich** (*Dat.*) **einen ~bruch zuziehen** sustain a fracture; **~erweichung** *die* ▸ⓘ **S. 439** (Med.) softening of the bones; osteomalacia (Med.); **~gerüst** *das* 1) skeleton; 2) (ugs. abwertend: magere Person) bag of bones (coll.); **~hart** *Adj.* (ugs.) rock-hard; **der Kuchen ist ja ~hart** the cake is as hard as a rock; **~haut** *die* ▸ⓘ **S. 435** (Anat.) periosteum; **~hautentzündung** *die* ▸ⓘ **S. 439** (Med.) periostitis; **~job** *der* (ugs. abwertend) really tough *or* hard job; (körperliche Arbeit) back-breaking job; **~mann** *der* (veralt.) Death; **~mark** *das* ▸ⓘ **S. 435** bone marrow; **~mark[s]transplantation** *die* (Med.) bone marrow transplant; **~mehl** *das* bonemeal; **~mühle** *die* (ugs.) **diese Fabrik ist die reinste ~mühle** working in this factory is worse than the chain gang! (joc.); **~schinken** *der* ham on the bone; **~schwund** *der* ▸ⓘ **S. 439** (Med.) bone atrophy; osteoporosis (Med.); **~trocken** *Adj.* (ugs.) bone dry; **~tuberkulose** *die* (Med.) tuberculosis of the bones

knöchern /ˈknœçɐn/ *Adj.* bony, (formal) osseous ‹*material etc.*›; bone *attrib.* ‹*handle, tool, etc.*›

knochig
A *Adj.* bony
B *adv.* **sehr ~ gebaut sein** be very bony

Knockdown /nɔkˈdaʊn/ *der;* **~[s], ~** (Boxen) knock-down

Knockout, Knock-out /nɔkˈaʊt/ *der;* **~s, ~s** (Boxen) knockout

Knödel /ˈknøːdl̩/ *der;* **~s, ~** (bes. südd., österr.) dumpling

knödeln /ˈknøːdl̩n/ (ugs.)
A *itr. V.* sing in a strangled voice; (leise) croon
B *tr. V.* sing in a strangled voice; (leise) croon

Knöllchen /ˈknœlçən/ *das;* **~s, ~** 1) ▸**Knolle**; **Knollen** 2) (ugs.: Strafzettel) [parking] ticket

Knolle /ˈknɔlə/ *die;* **~, ~n** 1) (einer Pflanze) tuber 2) (ugs.: Auswuchs) large round lump; (Nase) big fat conk (coll.) *or* (Amer.) schnozzle

Knollen *der;* **~s, ~** 1) (Klumpen) lump; clod 2) (ugs.: Strafzettel) [parking] ticket

Knollen-: ~begonie *die* tuberous begonia; **~blätter·pilz** *der* amanita; **~nase** *die* large bulbous nose

knollig *Adj.* bulbous

Knopf /knɔpf/ *der;* **~[e]s, Knöpfe** /ˈknœpfə/ 1) (an Kleidungsstücken, Geräten, Anlagen) button; **[sich** (*Dat.*)**] etw. an den Knöpfen abzählen** (ugs. scherzh.) decide sth. by counting off one's buttons 2) (Knauf) knob; (eines Schwertes, Dolches) pommel 3) (ugs. abwertend: kleiner Mann) [little] squirt (coll.) 4) (ugs.: Kind) little thing (coll.) 5) (südd., österr., schweiz.: Knoten) knot 6) (südd., österr., schweiz.: Knospe) bud

Knopf-: ~auge *das* [boot-]button eye; **~druck** *der; Pl.* **~drücke** touch of a/the button; **auf ~druck** at the touch of a/the button

knöpfen /ˈknœpfn̩/ *tr. V.* button [up]; **der Rock wird seitlich/vorn/hinten geknöpft** the skirt buttons up at the side/in front/at the back

Knopf-: ~leiste *die* button-facing; **ein Mantel mit verdeckter ~leiste** a coat with a fly front; **~loch** *das* buttonhole; **aus allen** *od.* **sämtlichen ~löchern platzen** (ugs.) be bursting at the seams; **aus allen** *od.* **sämtlichen ~löchern stinken** (salopp) stink *or* smell to high heaven (coll.); stink *or* smell something terrible (sl.)

knorke /ˈknɔrkə/ *Adj.* (berlin. veralt.) super (coll.); terrific (coll.)

Knorpel /ˈknɔrpl̩/ *der;* **~s, ~** 1) ▸ⓘ **S. 435** (Anat.) cartilage 2) (im Steak o. Ä.) gristle

knorpelig, knorplig *Adj.* 1) (Anat.) cartilaginous 2) gristly ‹*meat*›

Knorren /ˈknɔrən/ *der;* **~s, ~** 1) (Teil eines Astes) gnarl; knot 2) (Baumstumpf) [tree] stump 3) (im Holz) knot

knorrig *Adj.* 1) (krumm gewachsen) gnarled ‹*tree, branch*› 2) (wenig umgänglich) gruff

Knospe /ˈknɔspə/ *die;* **~, ~n** bud; **~n ansetzen** put forth buds; bud; **eine zarte ~** (fig.) a tender young bloom (literary)

knospen *itr. V.* bud; (fig.) burgeon

Knötchen /ˈknøːtçən/ *das;* **~s, ~** 1) (scherzh.: Haartracht) [little] bun *or* knot 2) ▸ⓘ **S. 439** (Med.) nodule; tubercle

knoten /ˈknoːtn̩/ *tr. V.* 1) (zu einem Knoten schlingen) knot; tie a knot in; **sich** (*Dat.*) **ein Tuch um den Hals ~:** tie a scarf round one's neck 2) (durch einen Knoten verknüpfen) knot together; do *or* tie up ‹*shoelace*›

Knoten *der;* **~s, ~** 1) knot; **sich** (*Dat.*) **einen ~ ins Taschentuch machen** tie a knot in one's handkerchief; **der ~ der Handlung schürzt sich** (fig.) the plot thickens; *s. auch* **gordisch** 2) (Haartracht) bun; knot 3) (Maßeinheit) knot 4) (Bot.) node 5) ▸ⓘ **S. 439** (Med.) node (Med.); lump; (Gicht~) tophus (Med.) 6) (Astron., Physik, Elektrot., Anat., Math., Sprachw.) node 7) ▸ **~punkt 1**

Knoten-: ~punkt *der* 1) (Verkehrsknotenpunkt) junction; intersection; 2) ▸**Knoten 6**; **~stock** *der* knobby *or* knobbly *or* gnarled [walking] stick

Knöterich /ˈknøːtərɪç/ *der;* **~s, ~e** (Gattung) Polygonum; (Vogel~) knotgrass; (Wiesen~) bistort

knotig *Adj.* 1) (Knoten aufweisend) knobby; knobbly; gnarled; knobbly ‹*fabric*› 2) (knotenförmig) nodular

Know-how /noʊˈhaʊ/ *das;* **~[s]** know-how

Knubbel /ˈknʊbl̩/ *der;* **~s, ~** (bes. nordd.) (Verdickung) small lump

knubbelig *Adj.* (bes. nordd.) podgy (coll.)

knuddeln /ˈknʊdl̩n/ *tr. V.* (bes. nordd.) hug and squeeze

Knuff /knʊf/ *der;* **~[e]s, Knüffe** /ˈknʏfə/ (ugs.) poke

knuffen /ˈknʊfn̩/ *tr. V.* poke; **jmdn. in den Arm/in die Rippen ~:** poke sb. in the arm/in the ribs

knuffig /ˈknʊfɪç/
A *Adj.* 1) (putzig) cute; 2) (gemütlich) cosy
B *adv.* 1) **~ klein** cute and small; 2) **~ warm/weich** warm/soft and cosy

knülle /ˈknʏlə/ *Adj.* (ugs.) tight (coll.); pie-eyed (coll.)

knüllen
A *tr. V.* crumple [up] ‹*paper*›; crease, crumple ‹*clothes, fabrics*›
B *itr. V.* crease; crumple

Knüller *der;* **~s, ~** (ugs.) sensation; (Film, Buch usw.) sensation; sensational success; (Angebot, Verkaufsartikel) sensational offer

knüpfen /ˈknʏpfn̩/
A *tr. V.* 1) tie (**an** + *Akk.* to); **Bande der Freundschaft ~** (fig.) establish ties *or* bonds of friendship 2) (durch Knoten herstellen) knot; make ‹*net*› 3) (gedanklich verbinden) **große Erwartungen/Hoffnungen an etw.** (*Akk.*) **~:** have great expectations/hopes of sth.; **Bedingungen an etw.** (*Akk.*) **~:** attach conditions to sth.
B *refl. V.* **sich an etw.** (*Akk.*) **~:** be connected with sth.; **an dieses Haus ~ sich nette Erinnerungen für mich** this house has pleasant memories for me

Knüppel /ˈknʏpl̩/ *der;* **~s, ~** 1) cudgel; club; (Polizei~) truncheon; **da möchte man doch gleich mit dem ~ dreinschlagen** (ugs.) sb. ought to bang *or* knock their heads together; *s. auch* **Bein** 2) ▸**Steuerknüppel** 3) ▸**Schaltknüppel**

knüppel-, Knüppel-: ~damm *der* log road; corduroy road; **~dick** *Adv.* (ugs.) **es kam ~dick** it was one disaster after the other; **~dick voll** full to bursting; **~hart** *Adj.:* ▸**knochenhart**

knüppeln
A *tr. V.* cudgel; club; beat with a cudgel *or* club/(Polizeiknüppel) truncheon
B *itr. V.* 1) use a/one's cudgel *or* club/truncheon 2) (Sport Jargon) play rough 3) (unpers.) (ugs.) **heute knüppelt es wieder** things are hectic again today

Knüppel·schaltung *die* (Kfz-W.) floor[-type] gear change

knurren /ˈknʊrən/
A *itr. V.* 1) ‹*animal*› growl; (wütend) snarl; **jmdm. knurrt der Magen** (fig.) sb.'s stomach is rumbling; **mit ~dem Magen** (fig.) with one's stomach rumbling 2) (murren) grumble (**über** + *Akk.* about) 3) (verärgert reden) growl
B *tr. V.* (verärgert sagen) growl

Knurr·hahn *der; Pl.* **Knurr·hähne** (Zool.) gurnard

knurrig
A *Adj.* grumpy
B *adv.* grumpily

Knusper·häuschen *das* gingerbread house

knusperig ▸**knusprig**

knuspern /ˈknʊspɐn/ *tr., itr. V.* nibble; (geräuschvoll) crunch; **an etw.** (*Dat.*) **~:** nibble [at] sth.

knusprig
A *Adj.* 1) crisp; crisp, crusty ‹*roll*›; crusty ‹*bread*›; **etw. ~ braten** roast/fry sth. crisp and brown 2) (ugs.: frisch u. adrett) delightfully fresh and attractive
B *adv.* **~-frisch** crunchy fresh ‹*crisps, nuts*›; crispy fresh ‹*rolls*›

Knust /knuːst/ *der;* **~[e]s, ~e** *od.* **Knüste** /ˈknyːstə/ (bes. nordd.) crust

Knute /ˈknuːtə/ *die;* **~, ~n** knout; **unter jmds. ~ [stehen]** (fig.) [be] under sb.'s heel

knutschen /ˈknuːtʃn̩/ (ugs.)
A *tr. V.* smooch with (coll.); neck with (coll.); (sexuell berühren) pet; **sich ~:** smooch (coll.) *or* neck (coll.)/pet
B *itr. V.* smooch (coll.), neck (coll.) (**mit** with); (sich sexuell berühren) pet

Knutscherei *die;* **~, ~en** (ugs.) **~[en]** smooching (coll.); necking (coll.); (sexuelle Berührung) petting

Knutsch·fleck *der* (ugs.) love bite

Knüttel /ˈknʏtl̩/ *der;* **~s, ~** ▸**Knüppel**

Knüttel·vers *der* ▸**Knittelvers**

k. o. /kaːˈloː/ *Adj.* 1) (Boxen) **jmdn. ~ schlagen** knock sb. out; **stehend ~ sein** be counted out on one's feet; **~ gehen** be knocked out 2) (ugs.: übermüdet) all in (coll.); whacked (coll.)

K. o. *der;* **~, ~** (Boxen) knockout; **[Sieger] durch ~:** [the winner] by a knockout

koagulieren /koˌlaguˈliːrən/ (Chemie)
A *itr. V.; auch mit sein* coagulate
B *tr. V.* coagulate

Koala /koˈaːla/ *der;* **~s, ~s** koala [bear]

k

koalieren /koǀaˈliːrən/ *itr. V.* (Politik) form a coalition (**mit** with)

Koalition /koǀaliˈt̮si̯oːn/ *die;* ~, **~en** coalition; **die große/kleine ~:** the grand/little coalition

Koalitions-: **~freiheit** *die* freedom of association (*of workers or employers*); **~partner** *der* coalition partner; **~recht** *das* right of freedom of association (*of workers or employers*); **~regierung** *die* coalition government; **~vertrag** *der* coalition agreement

Ko·autor *der,* **Ko·autorin** *die* co-author

Koaxial·kabel /koǀaˈksi̯aːl-/ *das* (Technik) coaxial cable

Kob /kɔp/ *der;* **~s,** **~s** (ugs.) ▸**Kontaktbereichsbeamte**

Kobalt /ˈkoːbalt/ *das;* **~s** (Chemie) cobalt

kobalt·blau *Adj.* cobalt blue

Kobalt·bombe *die* cobalt bomb

Koben /ˈkoːbn̩/ *der;* **~s,** ~ (Schweinestall) pigsty; (Verschlag) pen

Kober /ˈkoːbɐ/ *der;* **~s,** ~ (ostmd.) food basket

Kobold /ˈkoːbɔlt/ *der;* **~[e]s,** **~e** goblin; kobold; (fig.) imp

Kobolz /koˈbɔlt̮s/ *der:* in ~ **schießen** *od.* **schlagen** (bes. nordd.) turn *or* do a somersault/somersaults

Kobra /ˈkoːbra/ *die;* ~, **~s** cobra

Koch /kɔx/ *der;* **~[e]s, Köche** ▸❶ **S. 113** /ˈkœçə/ cook; (Küchenchef) chef; **viele Köche verderben den Brei** (Spr.) too many cooks spoil the broth (prov.)

koch-, Koch-: **~an·leitung** *die* cooking instructions *pl.;* **~apfel** *der* cooking apple; **~buch** *das* cookery book; cookbook; **~echt** *Adj.* ‹*fabric, garment*› that is washable in boiling water; ‹*colour, dye*› that is fast in boiling water

Köchel·verzeichnis /ˈkœçl̩-/ *das* (Musik) Köchel Catalogue

kochen

A *tr. V.* **1** boil; (zubereiten) cook ‹*meal*›; make ‹*purée, jam*›; **Suppe/Kaffee/Tee/Kakao ~:** make some soup/coffee/tea/cocoa; **sich** (*Dat.*) **Tee ~:** make some tea; **die Eier hart/weich ~:** hard-/soft-boil the eggs; **etw. weich/gar ~:** cook sth. until it is soft/[properly] done; **gar gekocht sein** be done; *s. auch* **Flamme 1** **2** (waschen) boil **3** (verflüssigen) heat ‹*tar, glue, etc.*› (*till it melts*)

B *itr. V.* **1** (Speisen zubereiten) cook; (das K~ übernehmen) do the cooking; **gerne/gut ~:** like cooking/be a good cook; **fett/fettarm ~:** use a lot of fat/little fat in cooking **2** (sieden) ‹*water, milk, etc.*› boil; (fig.) ‹*sea*› boil, seethe; **das Wasser/die Milch kocht** the water/the milk is boiling; **~d heiß** boiling hot; piping hot ‹*soup etc.*›; **am Kochen sein** (landsch.) be on the boil; be boiling; **etw. zum Kochen bringen** bring sth. to the boil **3** (in ~dem Wasser liegen) be boiled **4** (ugs.: wütend sein) **vor Wut/innerlich ~:** be boiling *or* seething with rage/inwardly

***kochend·heiß** ▸**kochen B 2**

Kocher *der;* **~s,** ~ **1** [small] stove; (Kochplatte) hotplate **2** (Technik) boiler

Köcher /ˈkœçɐ/ *der;* **~s,** ~ **1** (für Pfeile) quiver **2** (für Fernglas o. Ä.) case

Kocherei *die;* ~ (ugs.) cookery

koch-, Koch-: **~feld** *das* hob; **~fertig** *Adj.* ready-to-cook *attrib.;* ready to cook *pred.;* **~fest** *Adj.:* ▸**~echt**; **~fleisch** *das* stewing meat; **~gelegenheit** *die* cooking facilities *pl.;* **~geschirr** *das* (Milit.) mess tin; **~herd** *der* ▸**Herd 1**

Köchin /ˈkœçɪn/ *die;* ~, **~nen** ▸❶ **S. 113** cook

Koch-: **~käse** *der* (type of) processed curd cheese; **~kunst** *die* **1** culinary art; **2** *Pl.* **~künste** (ugs.: Fertigkeit im ~en) culinary skill[s *pl.*]; **~kurs[us]** *der* cookery course; **~löffel** *der* wooden spoon; **den ~löffel schwingen** (scherzh.) do the cooking; **~nische** *die* kitchenette; **~platte** *die* **1** hotplate; **2** (Kocher) [small] stove; **~rezept** *das* recipe

Koch·salz *das* common salt; sodium chloride (Chem.)

Kochsalz·lösung *die* salt solution; sodium chloride solution (Chem.)

Koch-: **~schinken** *der* boiled ham; **~topf** *der* [cooking] pot; **~wäsche** *die* washing that is to be boiled; **~zeit** *die* cooking time

kodderig /ˈkɔd(ə)rɪç/ *Adj.* (nordd.) **1** *in* **jmdm. ist ~:** sb. feels sick **2** (frech) impertinent; impudent

Kode /koːt/ *der;* **~s,** **~s** code

Kodein /kodeˈiːn/ *das;* **~s** (Pharm.) codeine

Köder /ˈkøːdɐ/ *der;* **~s,** **~:** bait; (fig.) bait; lure; **einen/mehrere ~ auslegen** put out bait/a number of baits

ködern *tr. V.* lure; **jmdn. für eine Show ~** (fig. ugs.) entice sb. to appear on a show; **sich von jmdm./etw. nicht ~ lassen** (fig. ugs.) not be tempted by sb.'s offer/by sth.

Kodex /ˈkoːdɛks/ *der;* **~es** *od.* ~, **~e** *od.* **Kodizes** /ˈkoːdit̮seːs/ **1** (Handschrift) codex **2** (hist.: Gesetzbuch) code; codex **3** (Verhaltensregel) code

kodieren *tr. V.* code; encode

kodifizieren /kodifiˈt̮siːrən/ *tr. V.* (bes. Rechtsw.) codify

Kodizes ▸**Kodex**

Koedukation /koǀedukaˈt̮si̯oːn/ *die;* **~:** coeducation

Koeffizient /koǀɛfiˈt̮si̯ɛnt/ *der;* **~en,** **~en** (Math., Physik) coefficient

Koexistenz *die;* **~:** coexistence

Koffein /kɔfeˈiːn/ *das;* **~s** caffeine

koffein·frei *Adj.* decaffeinated

Koffer /ˈkɔfɐ/ *der;* **~s,** ~ **1** [suit]case; (Schrank~) wardrobe trunk; **die ~ packen** pack one's bags [and leave]; **aus dem ~ leben** live out of a suitcase **2** (Soldatenspr.) heavy shell **3** (Straßenbau) roadbed

Koffer·anhänger *der* luggage tag *or* label

Köfferchen /ˈkœfɐçən/ *das;* **~s,** **~:** small [suit]case

Koffer-: **~gerät** *das* portable [radio/record player *etc.*]; **~kuli** *der* luggage trolley; **~radio** *das* portable radio; **~raum** *der* boot (Brit.); trunk (Amer.); **~schreibmaschine** *die* portable typewriter

Kogel /ˈkoːgl̩/ *der;* **~s,** ~ (südd., österr.) rounded, wooded mountain top

Kogge /ˈkɔgə/ *die;* ~, **~n** cog

Kognak /ˈkɔnjak/ *der;* **~s,** **~s** brandy; *s. auch* **Cognac**

Kognak-: **~bohne** *die: bean-shaped brandy-filled chocolate;* **~schwenker** *der* brandy glass

kognitiv /kɔgniˈtiːf/ *Adj.* (bes. Psych., Päd.) cognitive

kohärent /kohɛˈrɛnt/ *Adj.* (Phys.) coherent

Kohäsion /kohɛˈzi̯oːn/ *die;* ~ (geh., Physik) cohesion

Kohäsions·fonds *der* (EU) Cohesion Fund

Kohl /koːl/ *der;* **~[e]s** **1** cabbage; **das macht den ~ [auch] nicht fett** (ugs.) that doesn't help a lot **2** (ugs. abwertend: Unsinn) rubbish; rot (coll.); **red/mach keinen ~!** don't talk rot! (coll.)/stop messing around (coll.)

Kohl·dampf *der* (salopp) **~ haben** be ravenously hungry; **~ schieben [müssen]** [have to] go hungry

Kohle /ˈkoːlə/ *die;* ~, **~n** **1** (Brennstoff) coal; **glühende ~n** live coals; embers; **wir haben keine ~n mehr** we have run out of coal; **[wie] auf [glühenden] ~n sitzen** (gespannt warten) be on tenterhooks; (ungeduldig warten) suffer agonies of impatience; **feurige ~n auf jmds. Haupt** (*Akk.*) **sammeln** (geh.) heap coals of fire upon sb.'s head **2** *Pl.* (salopp: Geld) dough *sing.* (coll.); **Hauptsache, die ~n stimmen!** as long as the money's right **3** (Elektrot.) ▸**Bürste 3** **4** (Chemie) ▸**Aktivkohle** **5** ▸**Zeichenkohle**

Kohle-: **~filter** *der,* (fachspr. meist) *das* charcoal filter; **~hydrat** ▸**Kohlenhydrat**; **~kraft·werk** *das* coal-fired power station

kohlen[1] *itr. V.* smoulder; ‹*wick*› smoke

kohlen[2] *itr. V.* (fam.) (lügen) tell fibs; (übertreiben) exaggerate; (prahlen) boast

kohlen-, Kohlen-: **~bergbau** *der* coal mining *no art.;* **~bergwerk** *das* coal mine; colliery; **~bunker** *der* coal bunker; **~dioxid, ~dioxyd** /-ˈ--ˈ--/ *das* (Chemie) carbon dioxide; **~eimer** *der* coal scuttle; **~grube** *die* coal mine; [coal] pit; **~grus** *der* breeze; slack; **~halde** *die* coal heap; **~händler** *der,* **~händlerin** *die* ▸❶ **S. 113** coal merchant; **~handlung** *die* coal merchant's; **~heizung** *die* coal-fired central heating *no indef. art.;* **~hydrat** *das* (Chemie) carbohydrate; **~kasten** *der* coal box; **~keller** *der* coal cellar; **~monoxid, ~monoxyd** /-ˈ--ˈ--/ *das* (Chemie) carbon monoxide; **~monoxid·vergiftung, ~monoxyd·vergiftung** /-ˈ--ˈ------/ *die* carbon monoxide poisoning; **~ofen** *der* coal-burning stove; **~pott** *der* (abwertend) Ruhr [area]; **~sauer** *Adj.* (Chemie) carbonic; **~saures Natron/Kalzium** sodium/calcium carbonate; **~säure** *die* **1** (Chem.) carbonic acid; **2** (ugs.: in Getränken) fizz; **Mineralwasser mit ~säure** sparkling mineral water; **~säure·haltig** *Adj.* carbonated; **~schaufel** *die* coal shovel; **~staub** *der* coal dust; **~stoff** *der* carbon; **~wasserstoff** /-ˈ--ˈ--/ *der* (Chemie) hydrocarbon; **~zange** *die* coal tongs *pl.*

Kohle-: **~ofen** ▸**Kohlenofen**; **~papier** *das* carbon paper

Köhler /ˈkøːlɐ/ *der;* **~s,** **~:** charcoal burner

Köhlerei *die;* **~:** charcoal burning *no art.*

Köhler·glaube *der* (geh. abwertend) blind faith

Kohle-: **~stift** *der* **1** (Elektrot.) carbon rod; **2** (zum Zeichnen) charcoal stick; **~tablette** *die* charcoal tablet; **~zeichnung** *die* charcoal drawing

kohl-, Kohl-: **~kopf** *der* [head of] cabbage; **~meise** *die* great tit; **~räbchen** /-ˈ-/ *das;* **~~s,** **~~:** young kohlrabi; **~raben·schwarz** *Adj.* raven *attrib.*, raven-black, jet-black ‹*hair*›; jet-black ‹*eyes*›; ‹*face, hands, etc.*› as black as soot; **~rabi** /-ˈraːbi/ *der;* **~~[s],** **~~[s]** kohlrabi; **~roulade** *die* (Kochk.) stuffed cabbage; **~rübe** *die* swede; **~sprosse** *die* (österr.) [Brussels] sprout; **~weißling** *der;* **~~s,** **~~e** cabbage white; cabbage butterfly

Kohorte /koˈhɔrtə/ *die;* ~, **~n** cohort

Koinzidenz /koǀɪnt̮siˈdɛnt̮s/ *die;* ~ (geh.) coincidence

koitieren /koiˈtiːrən/ *itr. V.* (geh.) engage in *or* have sexual intercourse

Koitus /ˈkoːitʊs/ *der;* ~, **Koitus** (geh.) sexual intercourse; coitus (formal)

Koje /ˈkoːjə/ *die;* ~, **~n** **1** (Seemannsspr.) bunk; berth **2** (Ausstellungsstand) stand **3** (ugs. scherzh.: Bett) bed

Kojote /koˈjoːtə/ *der;* **~n,** **~n** coyote

Kokain /kokaˈiːn/ *das;* **~s** cocaine

kokain·süchtig *Adj.* addicted to cocaine *postpos.*

Kokarde /koˈkardə/ *die;* ~, **~n** cockade

Koka·strauch /ˈkoːka-/ *der* coca

kokeln /ˈkoːkl̩n/ *itr. V.* (ugs.) play with fire

Kokerei /koːkəˈrai̯/ *die;* ~, **~en** coking plant

kokett /koˈkɛt/

A *Adj.* coquettish

B *adv.* coquettishly

Koketterie /kokɛtəˈriː/ *die;* **~:** coquetry; coquettishness

kokettieren *itr. V.* **1** play the coquette; flirt **2** (kokett erwähnen) **mit etw. ~:** make much play with sth. **3** (fig.) **mit der Gefahr ~:** flirt with danger

Kokke /ˈkɔkə/ *die;* ~, **~n** (Biol.) coccus

Kokolores /kokoˈloːrɛs/ *der;* ~ (ugs.) **1** (Unsinn) rubbish; nonsense; rot (coll.) **2** (Getue) fuss

Kokon /koˈkõː/ *der;* **~s,** **~s** cocoon

Kokos- /ˈkoːkɔs-/: **~fett** *das* coconut oil; **~faser** *die* coconut fibre; **~flocken** *Pl.* coconut ice *sing.;* (als Füllung) desiccated coconut *sing.;* **~läufer** *der* runner made of coconut matting; **~milch** *die* coconut milk; **~nuss,** ***~nuß** *die* coconut; **~palme** *die* coconut palm; coconut tree

k

Kokotte /ko'kɔtə/ *die;* ~, ~**n** (geh. veralt.) cocotte (arch.)

Koks¹ /ko:ks/ *der;* ~**es** 1 coke 2 (salopp scherzh.: Geld) dough (coll.)

Koks² *der;* ~**es** (Drogenjargon: Kokain) coke (coll.); snow (sl.)

Koks³ *der;* ~**es** (salopp: Unsinn) rubbish; nonsense; rot (coll.)

koksen *itr. V.* (Jargon) take coke (sl.)

Kokser *der;* ~**s**, ~, **Kokserin** *die;* ~, ~**nen** (Drogenjargon) [cocaine-]sniffer; snowbird (Amer. sl.)

Koks-: ~**heizung** *die* coke-fired heating; ~**ofen** *der* 1 (mit ~ geheizt) coke-burning stove; 2 (für die ~herstellung) coke oven

Kola ▸ **Kolon**

Kola·baum /'ko:la-/ *der* cola *or* kola [tree]

Kolben /'kɔlbn̩/ *der;* ~**s**, ~ 1 (Technik) piston 2 (Chemie: Glasgefäß) flask 3 (Teil des Gewehrs) butt 4 (Bot.) spadix; (Mais~) cob 5 (salopp: dicke Nase) hooter (Brit. coll.); conk (coll.) 6 (der Glühlampe) glass

Kolben-: ~**fresser** *der* (ugs.) piston seize-up; **einen** ~**fresser haben** have piston seizure *or* a seized[-up] piston; ~**hub** *der* (Technik) piston stroke; ~**ring** *der* (Technik) piston ring

Kolchos·bauer /'kɔlçɔs-/ *der;* ~**n**, ~**n** kolkhoznik; worker on a Soviet collective farm

Kolchose /kɔl'ço:zə/ *die;* ~, ~**n** kolkhoz; Soviet collective farm

Kolibri /'ko:libri/ *der;* ~**s**, ~**s** hummingbird

Kolik /'ko:lɪk/ *die;* ~, ~**en** colic

Kolk·rabe /'kɔlk-/ *der* (Zool.) raven

kollabieren /kɔla'bi:rən/ *itr. V.; mit sein* (Med.) collapse

Kollaborateur /kɔlabora'tø:ɐ̯/ *der;* ~**s**, ~**e**, **Kollaborateurin** *die;* ~, ~**nen** collaborator

Kollaboration /kɔlabora'tsi̯o:n/ *die;* ~: collaboration

kollaborieren *itr. V.* collaborate (**mit** with)

Kollagen /kɔla'ge:n/ *das;* ~**s**, ~**e** (Med., Biol.) collagen

Kollaps /'kɔlaps/ *der;* ~**es**, ~**e** ▸ℹ S. 439 (Med., fig.) collapse; **einen** ~ **erleiden** collapse

kollationieren /kɔlatsi̯o'ni:rən/ *tr. V.* 1 (vergleichen) collate, compare (**mit** with); (Druckw.) read (**mit** against) 2 (bes. Buchbinderei) collate

Kolleg /kɔ'le:k/ *das;* ~**s**, ~**s** 1 (Vorlesung) lecture; (Vorlesungsreihe) course of lectures 2 (Institut) *college offering full-time courses to prepare qualified adults for university entrance* 3 (kath. Kirche) theological college

Kollege /kɔ'le:gə/ *der;* ~**n**, ~**n** ▸ℹ S. 44 1 colleague; (Arbeiter) workmate; **die** ~**n vom Fach** professional colleagues; ~ **kommt gleich!** (im Restaurant) somebody [else] will be with you in a moment; **Herr** ~**!** Mr. Smith/ Jones *etc.!*; **Herr** ~ **[Müller** *usw.***]** (Abgeordneter) ≈ the Honourable Gentleman; (als Anrede) **Herr** ~ **[Müller], Sie müssen ...** ≈ the Honourable Gentleman must ... 2 (Gewerkschaftsmitglied) [union] member 3 (DDR: Werktätiger) worker; **der** ~ **Werkleiter/Ober** the works manager/ the waiter 4 (salopp: Freund) mate (coll.)

Kollegen-: ~**kreis** *der:* **im** ~**kreis** among colleagues; ~**rabatt** *der* trade discount (in the publishing trade)

Kolleg-: ~**geld** *das* (Hochschulw.) lecture fee; ~**heft** *das* lecture notebook

kollegial /kɔle'gi̯a:l/

A *Adj.* helpful and considerate

B *adv.* ‹*act etc.*› like a good colleague/good colleagues

Kollegialität /kɔlegi̯ali'tɛ:t/ *die;* ~: helpfulness and consideration

Kollegin *die;* ~, ~**nen** ▸ **Kollege 1, 2, 3**; *s. auch* **-in**

Kollegium /kɔ'le:gi̯ʊm/ *das;* ~**s**, **Kollegien** 1 (Gruppe) group; (unmittelbar zusammenarbeitend) team 2 (Lehrkörper) [teaching] staff 3 (Komitee) committee

Kolleg-: ~**mappe** *die* document case; ~**stufe** *die* (Schulw.) sixth-form college (offering academic and vocational courses)

Kollekte /kɔ'lɛktə/ *die;* ~, ~**n** collection

Kollektion /kɔlɛk'tsi̯o:n/ *die;* ~, ~**en** 1 (Sortiment) range; (Mode) collection 2 (Sammlung, Zusammenstellung) collection

kollektiv /kɔlɛk'ti:f/

A *Adj.* collective; joint ‹*collaboration*›

B *adv.* collectively

Kollektiv *das;* ~**s**, ~**e** *od.* ~**s** 1 group; **als** ~ **auftreten** put up a united front 2 (Arbeitsgruppe) collective 3 (Statistik) population

Kollektiv-: ~**arbeit** *die* joint work; ~**bewusstsein**, *~**bewußtsein** *das* collective consciousness; ~**geist** *der* collective spirit; ~**gesellschaft** *die* (schweiz. Wirtsch.) general partnership

kollektivieren *tr. V.* collectivize

Kollektivismus *der;* ~: collectivism *no art.*

kollektivistisch *Adj.* collectivist

Kollektiv-: ~**schuld** *die* collective guilt; ~**strafe** *die* collective punishment

Kollektivum /kɔlɛk'ti:vʊm/ *das;* ~**s**, **Kollektiva** (Sprachw.) collective noun; collective

Kollektiv·wirtschaft *die* collective farm

Kollektor /kɔ'lɛktɔr/ *der;* ~**s**, ~**en** /-'to:rən/ (Elektrot., Physik) collector

Koller¹ /'kɔlɐ/ *der;* ~**s**, ~ (ugs.) rage; **einen** ~ **haben/bekommen** be in/fly *or* get into a rage

Koller² *das;* ~**s**, ~ (hist.) cape collar

kollern¹ *itr. V.; mit sein* roll

kollern² *itr. V.* ‹*turkey etc.*› gobble; ‹*stomach*› rumble

kollidieren /kɔli'di:rən/ *itr. V.* 1 *mit sein* (zusammenstoßen) collide, be in collision (**mit** with) 2 (im Widerspruch stehen) clash, conflict (**mit** with); **miteinander** ~ ‹*meetings etc.*› clash

Kollier /kɔ'li̯e:/ *das;* ~**s**, ~**s** 1 (Halskette) necklace 2 (schmaler Pelz) necklet

Kollision /kɔli'zi̯o:n/ *die;* ~, ~**en** 1 (Zusammenstoß) collision 2 (Widerstreit) conflict, clash (+ *Gen.* between); **mit etw. in** ~ **geraten** come into conflict with sth.

Kollisions·kurs *der* collision course; **gegen jmdn./etw. auf** ~ **gehen** (fig.) be heading for a confrontation with sb./sth.

Kolloid /kɔlo'i:t/ *das;* ~**[e]s**, ~**e** (Chemie) colloid

Kolloquium /kɔ'lɔkvi̯ʊm/ *das;* ~**s**, **Kolloquien** 1 (Hochschulw.) seminar 2 (Zusammenkunft) colloquium 3 (österr.: Prüfung) test

Köln /kœln/ *(das);* ~**s** ▸ℹ **S. 675** Cologne

Kölner ▸ℹ **S. 675**

A *indekl. Adj.* Cologne *attrib.*; (in Köln) in Cologne *postpos., not pred.*; ‹*suburb, archbishop, mayor, speciality*› of Cologne; ‹*car factory, river bank*› at Cologne; **der** ~ **Dom/Karneval** Cologne Cathedral/the Cologne carnival; **meine** ~ **Freunde** (in Köln) my friends in Cologne; (aus Köln) my friends from Cologne; **seine** ~ **Heimat** his native Cologne; **meine** ~ **Zeit** my time in Cologne; **die** ~ **Innenstadt** Central Cologne; **alle** ~ **Bahnhöfe** every station in Cologne; **die 2000 jährige** ~ **Geschichte** Cologne's 2000-year history

B *der;* ~**s**, ~: inhabitant of Cologne; (von Geburt) native of Cologne; **er ist** ~: he is a native of Cologne; he comes from Cologne; **ein echter** ~: someone born and bred in Cologne; (dem Naturell nach) a true native of Cologne; **der** ~ (bestimmter Mann) the man from Cologne; that chap from Cologne (coll.); (das Kölner Auto usw.) the car/bus *etc.* with the Cologne number plate; (ugs.: die Kölner) people *pl.* from Cologne; **wir** ~: we citizens of Cologne; **die** ~: the people of Cologne; (die Kölner Mannschaft usw.) Cologne *pl.*; (die Kölner Fans usw.) the Cologne supporters; (die Kölner Firma usw.) the Cologne works *sing. or pl.*/group *etc. sing.*; **die** ~ **haben einen Oberbürgermeister gewählt** Cologne has elected a mayor; ~ *Pl.* Cologne people; (außerhalb Kölns) people from Cologne; **das sind** ~: they are from Cologne; **er hatte als** ~ **eine tiefe Abneigung gegen Düsseldorf** coming from Cologne, he had a great dislike for Düsseldorf; **Sie als** ~ **mögen den Karneval nicht?** you come from Cologne, and you don't like the carnival?

Kölnerin *die;* ~, ~**nen** ▸ **Kölner B**; *s. auch* **-in**

kölnisch *Adj.* ▸ℹ **S. 675** Cologne *attrib.*; of Cologne *postpos., not pred.*; **kölnisch Wasser** eau de Cologne

Kolombine /kolɔm'bi:nə/ *die;* ~, ~**n** Columbine

Kolon /'ko:lɔn/ *das;* ~**s**, ~**s** *od.* **Kola** (antike Metrik, Rhet. veralt.: Doppelpunkt) colon

Kolonel /kolo'nɛl/ *die;* ~ (Druckw.) minion

kolonial /kolo'ni̯a:l/ *Adj.* colonial

kolonialisieren *tr. V.* colonialize

Kolonialisierung *die;* ~, ~**en** colonialization

Kolonialismus *der;* ~: colonialism *no art.*

kolonialistisch *Adj.* colonialist

Kolonial-: ~**macht** *die* colonial power; ~**politik** *die* colonial policy; ~**stil** *der* colonial style; ~**waren** *Pl.* (veralt.) groceries *pl.*; ~**waren·händler** *der*, ~**waren·händlerin** *die* (veralt.) grocer; ~**zeit** *die* colonial era *or* period

Kolonie /kolo'ni:/ *die;* ~, ~**n** 1 (auch Gruppe von Ausländern, Biol.) colony 2 (Siedlung) colony; settlement

Kolonisation /koloniza'tsi̯o:n/ *die;* ~, ~**en** colonization

kolonisieren *tr. V.* 1 (zur Kolonie machen) colonize 2 (besiedeln, erschließen) settle and develop; (urbar machen) clear and cultivate ‹*land*›; reclaim ‹*swampland*›

Kolonisierung *die;* ~, ~**en** colonization

Kolonist *der;* ~**en**, ~**en**, **Kolonistin** *die;* ~, ~**nen** colonist; (früher Siedler) settler

Kolonnade /kolɔ'na:də/ *die;* ~, ~**n** colonnade

Kolonne /ko'lɔnə/ *die;* ~, ~**n** 1 (Truppe, Gruppe von Menschen, Zahlenreihe) column; **die fünfte** ~: the fifth column 2 (Fahrzeuge) column; (Schlange) [long] line of traffic; (Konvoi) convoy; ~ **fahren** drive in a [long] line of traffic 3 (Arbeits~) gang

Kolonnen-: ~**fahren** *das;* ~**s** driving in a [long] line of traffic; ~**springer** *der*, ~**springerin** *die* (ugs.) *motorist who dodges in and out of a line of traffic in order to overtake*

Kolophonium /kolo'fo:ni̯ʊm/ *das;* ~**s** colophony; rosin

Koloratur /kolora'tu:ɐ̯/ *die;* ~, ~**en** (Musik) coloratura

Koloratur·sängerin *die* (Musik) coloratura

kolorieren /kolo'ri:rən/ *tr. V.* 1 (ausmalen) colour 2 (Musik) decorate; embellish

Kolorit /kolo'ri:t/ *das;* ~**[e]s**, ~**e** *od.* ~**s** 1 (Farbgebung) colouring 2 (Musik: Klangfarbe) [tone] colour 3 (Atmosphäre) colour

Koloss, ***Koloß** /ko'lɔs/ *der;* **Kolosses**, **Kolosse** 1 (Standbild) colossus; **der** ~ **von Rhodos** the Colossus of Rhodes 2 (riesiges Gebilde, ugs. scherzh.: große Person) colossus; giant

kolossal /kolɔ'sa:l/

A *Adj.* 1 (riesenhaft) colossal; gigantic; enormous 2 (ugs.: sehr groß) tremendous (coll.); incredible (coll.) ‹*rubbish, nonsense*›; **eine** ~**e Dummheit begehen** do something incredibly stupid; ~**es Glück haben** be incredibly lucky (coll.)

B *adv.* (ugs.) tremendously (coll.); ~ **viel Geld** a tremendous *or* vast amount of money (coll.)

Kolossal-: ~**film** *der* [film] epic; ~**gemälde** *das* huge painting; ~**schinken** *der* (salopp abwertend) 1 (Film) massive great epic (coll.); 2 (Gemälde) whacking great painting (coll.)

Kolportage /kɔlpɔr'ta:ʒə/ *die;* ~, ~**n** 1 (minderwertiger Bericht) trashy writing; trash 2 (Verbreitung von Gerüchten) rumour-mongering

Kolportage-: ~**literatur** *die* trashy literature; ~**roman** *der* trashy novel

Kolporteur /kɔlpɔr'tø:ɐ̯/ *der;* ~**s**, ~**e**, **Kolporteurin** *die;* ~, ~**nen** (geh.) rumourmonger

kolportieren *tr. V.* (geh.) spread, circulate ‹*rumour, story*›

kölsch /kœlʃ/ ▸ **kölnisch**

Kölsch *das;* **~[s]** 1 *strong very pale beer brewed in Cologne* 2 Cologne dialect; *s. auch* **Deutsch 1**

Kolumbianer /kolʊmˈbi̯aːnɐ/ *der;* **~s, ~, Kolumbianerin** *die;* **~, ~nen** Colombian

kolumbianisch *Adj.* Colombian

Kolumbien /koˈlʊmbi̯ən/ *(das);* **~s** Colombia

Kolumbus /koˈlʊmbʊs/ *(der)* Columbus; *s. auch* **Ei 1**

Kolumne /koˈlʊmnə/ *die;* **~, ~n** (Druckw., Meinungsbeitrag) column

Kolumnen·titel *der* (Druckw.) running title *or* head

Kolumnist *der;* **~en, ~en, Kolumnistin** *die;* **~, ~nen** columnist

Koma /ˈkoːma/ *das;* **~s, ~s** *od.* **~ta** ▸ⓘ **S. 439** (Med.) coma

Kombattant /kɔmbaˈtant/ *der;* **~en, ~en** (Völkerr.; geh. veralt.) combatant

Kombi[1] /ˈkɔmbi/ *der;* **~[s], ~s** ▸ **Kombiwagen**

Kombi[2] *die;* **~, ~s** combination (**aus** of)

Kombi·lohn *der: wage supplemented by a state allowance*

Kombinat /kɔmbiˈnaːt/ *das;* **~[e]s, ~e** (bes. DDR) combine

Kombination /kɔmbinaˈt͡si̯oːn/ *die;* **~, ~en** 1 (Verbindung) combination 2 (gedankliche Verknüpfung) deduction; piece of reasoning; **unsere ~en** our reasoning *sing. or* deductions 3 (Kleidungsstücke) ensemble; suit; (Herren~) suit; (Flieger~) flying suit 4 (Ballspiele) combined move 5 (Schach) combination 6 (Ski) ▸ **alpin; nordisch**

Kombinations-: ~gabe *die* powers *pl.* of deduction *or* reasoning; **~schloss,** ***~schloß** *das* combination lock; **~sprung·lauf** *der* (Ski) jumping event (*of Nordic combination*)

Kombinatorik /kɔmbinaˈtoːrɪk/ *die;* **~** (Math.) combinatorial analysis *no art.*

kombinatorisch *Adj.* deductive; **~e Fähigkeiten** powers of deduction *or* reasoning; deductive powers

kombinieren /kɔmbiˈniːrən/
A *tr. V.* combine; **zwei Dinge zu etw. ~:** combine two things into sth.; **etw. mit etw. ~:** combine sth. with sth.
B *itr. V.* 1 (Zusammenhänge herstellen) deduce; reason; **falsch/richtig ~:** come to the wrong/right conclusion 2 (Ballspiele) combine

Kombi-: ~wagen *der* estate [car]; station wagon (Amer.); **~zange** *die* combination pliers *pl.*; **eine ~zange** a pair of combination pliers

Kombüse /kɔmˈbyːzə/ *die;* **~, ~n** (Seemannsspr.) galley

Komet /koˈmeːt/ *der;* **~en, ~en** comet

kometen·haft *Adj.* meteoric ‹*rise, career*›; extremely rapid ‹*upturn, development*›

Komfort /kɔmˈfoːɐ̯/ *der;* **~s** comfort; **mit allem ~** ‹*flat, house*› with all modern conveniences *pl.*; ‹*car*› with all the latest luxury features *pl.*

komfortabel /kɔmfɔrˈtaːbl̩/
A *Adj.* comfortable
B *adv.* comfortably

Komfort·wohnung *die* [comfortable] flat (esp. Brit.) *or* (esp. Amer.) apartment with all modern conveniences

Komik /ˈkoːmɪk/ *die;* **~:** comic effect; (komisches Element) comic element *or* aspect; **die ~ der Situation** the funny side of the situation; **Sinn für ~ haben** have a sense of the comic; **etw. entbehrt nicht einer gewissen ~:** sth. is not without an element of comedy; **~ und Tragik** comedy and tragedy; the comic and the tragic

Komiker *der;* **~s, ~, Komikerin** *die;* **~, ~nen** ▸ⓘ **S. 113** 1 (Vortragskünstler[in]) comedian/comedienne; comic (coll.) 2 (Darsteller[in]) comic actor/actress 3 (salopp abwertend) clown

Kominform /komɪnˈfɔrm/ *das;* **~s** (hist.) Cominform

Komintern /komɪnˈtɛrn/ *die;* **~** (hist.) Comintern

komisch /ˈkoːmɪʃ/ *Adj.* 1 (lustig) comical; funny; **ich finde das gar nicht ~** (ugs.) I don't think that's at all funny 2 (seltsam) funny; strange; odd; **~, was?** (ugs.) [it's] funny *or* strange *or* odd, isn't it?; **~ [zu jmdm.] sein** act *or* behave strangely [towards sb.]; **~ [ist nur], dass ...** it's [just] funny *or* strange *or* odd that ...; **mir ist/wird so ~:** I'm feeling funny *or* peculiar 3 (Theater) comic ‹*part*›

komischer·weise *Adv.* (ugs.) strangely enough

Komitee /komiˈteː/ *das;* **~s, ~s** committee

Komma /ˈkɔma/ *das;* **~s, ~s** *od.* **~ta** 1 (Satzzeichen) comma 2 (Math.) ▸ⓘ **S. 826** decimal point; **zwei ~ acht** two point eight; **zwei Stellen hinter dem ~:** two decimal places

Komma·fehler *der* mistake involving the use of the comma

Kommandant /kɔmanˈdant/ *der;* **~en, ~en** (einer Stadt, Festung) commandant; (eines Panzers, Raumschiffs) commander; (einer Militäreinheit) commander; commanding officer; (eines Flugzeugs, Schiffs) captain

Kommandantur /kɔmandanˈtuːɐ̯/ *die;* **~, ~en** commandant's headquarters *sing. or pl.*

Kommandeur /kɔmanˈdøːɐ̯/ *der;* **~s, ~e** (Milit.) commander; commanding officer

kommandieren
A *tr. V.* 1 (befehligen) command; be in command of 2 (ab~) **jmdn. an die Front ~:** order sb. to the front 3 order ‹*retreat, advance*› 4 (ugs.: herum~) **jmdn. ~:** order *or* (sl.) boss sb. about
B *itr. V.* 1 (Milit.) **Kommandierender General** Corps commander 2 (ugs.) order *or* (sl.) boss people about

Kommandit·gesellschaft /kɔmanˈdiːt-/ *die* (Wirtsch.) limited partnership

Kommanditist *der;* **~en, ~en, Kommanditistin** *die;* **~, ~nen** (Wirtsch.) limited partner

Kommando /kɔˈmando/ *das;* **~s, ~s,** *österr. auch:* **Kommanden** 1 (Befehl) command; **das ~ zum Schießen geben** give the command *or* order to shoot; **auf ~ gehorchen** obey [immediately] on command; **wie auf ~:** as if by command; *s. auch* **hören B 4** 2 (Befehlsgewalt) command; **das ~ haben** *od.* **führen/übernehmen** be in/assume *or* take command 3 (Milit.) (Einheit) detachment; (Stoßtrupp) commando; (Dienststelle) headquarters *sing. or pl.*

Kommando-: ~brücke *die* bridge; **~sache** *die:* **in geheime ~sache** (bes. Milit.) military secret; **~stab** *der* (Milit.) headquarters *or* command staff; **~stand** *der* (Milit.) command post; **~stelle** *die* (Milit.) command post; **~stimme** *die* commanding [tone of] voice; **~ton** *der* peremptory tone

Komma·stelle *die* decimal place; **auf die ~ [genau]** [correct] to the last decimal place; (fig.) ‹*know, calculate*› with complete accuracy; ‹*fulfil*› down to the last detail

Kommata ▸ **Komma**

kommen /ˈkɔmən/ *unr. itr. V.; mit sein* 1 come; (eintreffen) come; arrive; **der Kellner kommt sofort** the waiter will be with you directly; **zu spät ~:** be late; **zu Fuß/mit dem Auto ~:** come on foot/by car; **in einer halben Stunde/zwei Monaten ~:** come in half an hour/two months' time; **durch eine Gegend ~:** pass through a region; **von der Arbeit ~:** come [back] from work; **nach Hause ~:** come *or* get home; **ins Zimmer ~:** come into the room; **ich komme schon!** I'm coming!; **ich komme, Sie abzuholen** I've come to fetch you; **komm ich heut nicht, komm ich morgen** (spött.) you'll/he'll *etc.* get there eventually!
2 (gelangen) get; **ans Ufer/Ziel ~:** reach the bank/finishing line; **komme ich hier zum Bahnhof?** can I get to the station this way?; **wie komme ich nach Paris?** how do I get to Paris?; **kaum noch aus dem Haus/ins Kino ~:** hardly ever get out of the house/to the cinema; **auf etw.** (Akk.) **zu sprechen ~** (fig.) turn to the discussion of sth.; **zum Schluss seiner Ausführungen ~** (fig.) come to the end of one's remarks
3 **+** *Bewegungsverb im 2. Part.* **angelaufen/angebraust ~:** come running/roaring along; (auf jmdn. zu) come running/roaring up; **angekrochen ~** (fig.) come crawling up
4 (teilnehmen) come; attend; **zu einer Tagung ~:** come to/attend a meeting
5 (besuchen) come; **zu jmdm. ~:** come and see sb.; **er kommt zu uns zum Abendbrot** he's coming [to us] for supper
6 (gebracht werden) come; **die Post/ein Paket ist ge~:** the post/a parcel has come; **ist keine Post für mich ge~?** is/was there no post for me?
7 **~ lassen** (bestellen) order ‹*taxi*›; **den Arzt/die Polizei ~ lassen** send for *or* call a doctor/the police; **Getränke** *usw.* **aufs Zimmer ~ lassen** have drinks *etc.* sent up to one's room
8 (aufgenommen werden) **zur Schule/aufs Gymnasium ~:** go to *or* start school/grammar school; **ins Krankenhaus/Gefängnis ~:** go into hospital/to prison; **in die Lehre ~:** start an apprenticeship; **in den Himmel/in die Hölle ~** (fig.) go to heaven/hell
9 (auftauchen) ‹*seeds, plants*› come up; ‹*buds, flowers*› come out; ‹*peas, beans*› form; ‹*teeth*› come through; **zur Welt ~:** be born; **ihr ist ein Gedanke/eine Idee ge~:** she had a thought/an idea; a thought/an idea came to her; **die Tränen ~ jmdm. in die Augen** tears come to sb.'s eyes; *s. auch* **Herz 2**
10 (seinen festen Platz haben) go; belong; **in die Schublade/ins Regal ~:** go *or* belong in the drawer/on the shelf
11 (seinen Platz erhalten) **in die Mannschaft ~:** get into the team; **auf den ersten Platz ~:** go into first place
12 (geraten) get; **in Gefahr/Not/Verlegenheit ~:** get into danger/serious difficulties/get *or* become embarrassed; **unter ein Auto/zu Tode ~:** be knocked down by a car/be *or* get killed; **ins Schleudern ~:** go into a skid; *s. auch* **Schwung; Stimmung**
13 (Gelegenheit haben) **dazu ~, etw. zu tun** get round to doing sth.; **zum Einkaufen/Waschen ~:** get round to doing the shopping/washing; **kaum noch zum Schlafen ~:** hardly be able to find time to sleep
14 (nahen) **ein Gewitter/die Flut kommt** a storm is approaching/the tide's coming in; **den Zeitpunkt für ge~ halten** think *or* consider the moment has come; **der Tag/die Nacht kommt** (geh.) day is breaking/night is falling; **dieses Unglück habe ich schon lange ~ sehen** I saw this disaster coming a long time ago; **im Kommen sein** ‹*fashion etc.*› be coming in; ‹*person*› be on the way up
15 (sich ereignen) come about; happen; **was auch immer ~ mag** come what may; **das durfte [jetzt] nicht ~** (ugs. spött.) that's hardly the thing to say now; **es kam, wie es ~ musste** the inevitable happened; **es kam zum Streit/Kampf** there was a quarrel/fight; **es kam alles ganz anders** it all *or* everything turned out quite differently; **wies kommt, so kommts** *od.* **wies kommt, so wirds genommen** (ugs.) what will be will be; **so weit kommt es noch[, dass ich euern Dreck wieder wegräume]!** (ugs. iron.) that really is the limit[, expecting me to clear up your rubbish after you]!
16 (ugs.: erreicht werden) **wann kommt der nächste Bahnhof?** when do we get to the next station? (coll.); **jetzt kommt gleich Mannheim** we'll be at Mannheim any moment; **da vorn kommt eine Tankstelle** there's a petrol station coming up (coll.)
17 **zu Geld ~:** become wealthy; **zu Erfolg/Ruhm** *usw.* **~:** gain success/fame *etc.*; **nie zu etwas ~** (ugs.) never get anywhere; **wieder zu Kräften ~:** regain one's strength; **[wieder] zu sich ~:** regain consciousness; come round; **zu sich ~** (sich fassen) become one's normal self again
18 **jmdm. auf die Spur/Schliche ~:** get on sb.'s trail/get wise to sb.'s tricks; **wie kommst du darauf?** what gives you that idea?; **hinter jmds. Geheimnis/Pläne ~:** find out sb.'s secret/plans

19 (an der Reihe sein; folgen) **zuerst/zuletzt kam ...** first/last came ...; **als Erster/Letzter ~:** come first/last; **jetzt komme ich an die Reihe** it is my turn now; **wann ~ wir an die Reihe?** when do we get a turn?
20 (sich darstellen) **gelegen/ungelegen ~** ‹*offer, opportunity*› come/not come at the right moment; ‹*visit*› be/not be convenient; **überraschend [für jmdn.] ~:** come as a surprise [to sb.]
21 (ugs.: sich verhalten) **jmdm. frech/unverschämt/grob ~:** be cheeky/impertinent/rude to sb.; **so lasse ich mir nicht ~!** I don't stand for that sort of thing!; **so können Sie mir nicht ~!** don't take that line with me! (coll.)
22 (ugs.: sich an jmdn. wenden) **komm mir nicht mit ...!** don't give me ...; **da könnte ja jeder ~!** who do you think you are?/who does he think he is? *etc.*; **komm mir nicht damit, du hättest keine Zeit!** don't try and tell me you don't have the time!; **mit so etw. darfst du mir nicht ~:** don't try that sort of thing on with me (coll.)
23 **ich lasse auf ihn** *usw.* **nichts ~:** I won't hear anything said against him *etc.*
24 + *Inf. mit* **zu** (in eine Lage geraten) **neben jmdn. zu sitzen ~:** get to sit next to sb.
25 **über jmdn. ~** (erfassen) ‹*feeling*› come over sb.
26 (verlieren) **um etw. ~:** lose sth.; **ums Leben ~:** lose one's life; **wir sind um unseren Theaterbesuch ge~:** we missed out on our visit to the theatre
27 (entfallen) **auf hundert Berufstätige ~ vier Arbeitslose** for every hundred people in employment, there are four people unemployed
28 **woher ~ diese Sachen?** where do these things come from?; **seine Eltern ~ aus Sachsen** his parents come *or* are from Saxony
29 **daher kommt es, dass ...** that's [the reason] why ...; **das kommt davon, dass ...** that's because ...; **vom vielen Rauchen/vom Vitaminmangel ~:** be due to smoking/vitamin deficiency; **wie kommt es, dass du/er** *usw.* **...** how is it that you/he *etc.* ...; how come that you/he *etc.* ... (coll.); **das kommt davon!** see what happens!; **das kommt davon, wenn du nicht aufpasst!** that's what happens when you don't pay attention; that's what comes of not paying attention
30 (ugs.: kosten) **auf 100 Euro ~:** cost 100 euros; **alles zusammen kam auf ...** altogether it came to ...; **wie teuer kommt der Stoff?** how much *or* dear is that material?; **etw. kommt [jmdn.] teuer** sth. comes expensive [for sb.]
31 (ugs.: starten) start
32 (salopp: Orgasmus haben) come (sl.); **es kommt jmdm.** sb. is coming (sl.)
33 (im Funkverkehr) **[bitte] ~!** come in[, please]
34 (ugs.: als Aufforderung, Ermahnung) **komm/kommt/~ Sie** come on, now; **komm, komm** oh, come on
35 (Sportjargon: gelingen) **[gut] ~/nicht ~** ‹*serve, backhand, forehand, etc.*› be going/not be going well
36 *in festen Wendungen* ▸**Ausbruch 2**; **Einsatz 3**; **Entfaltung 1**; **Fall¹ 1**; **Gesicht¹ 3** *usw.*

kommend *Adj.* 1 ▸❶ **S. 165**, ▸❶ **S. 816** (bevorstehend) next; **das ~e Wochenende/am ~en Sonntag** next weekend/Sunday; **in der ~en Saison/Woche** next season/week; **~e Generationen** generations to come; future generations; **in den ~en Jahren** in years to come 2 (mit großer Zukunft) **der ~e Mann/Meister** the coming man/future champion

kommensurabel /kɔmɛnzu'ra:bl̩/ *Adj.* (Physik, Math.) commensurable

Komment /kɔ'mã:/ *der;* **~s, ~s** (Studentenspr.) code of conduct (in student fraternities)

Kommentar /kɔmɛn'ta:ɐ̯/ *der;* **~s, ~e** 1 (Erläuterung) commentary 2 (Stellungnahme) commentary; comment; **kein ~!** no comment! 3 (oft abwertend: Anmerkung) comment; **~ überflüssig** no comment needed; **sich** (*Dat.*) **jedes ~s enthalten** refrain from commenting; **seinen ~ zu etw. geben** comment on sth.

kommentarlos
A *Adj.* without comment *postpos.*
B *adv.* without comment

Kommentator /kɔmɛn'ta:tɔr/ *der;* **~s, ~en** /-ta'to:rən/, **Kommentatorin** *die;* **~, ~nen** commentator

kommentieren *tr. V.* 1 (erläutern) furnish with a commentary, annotate ‹*text, work*›; **eine kommentierte Ausgabe** an annotated edition 2 (Stellung nehmen zu; ugs.: Anmerkungen machen zu) comment on

Kommers /kɔ'mɛrs/ *der;* **~es, ~e** (Studentenspr.) students' drinking evening (*to celebrate a particular occasion*)

Kommers·buch *das* book of students' drinking songs

Kommerz /kɔ'mɛrts/ *der;* **~es** (abwertend) business interests *pl.*

kommerzialisieren /kɔmɛrtsiali'zi:rən/ *tr. V.* commercialize

Kommerzial·rat /kɔmɛr'tsia:l-/ *der* (österr.) ▸**Kommerzienrat**

kommerziell /kɔmɛr'tsiɛl/
A *Adj.* commercial
B *adv.* commercially

Kommerzien·rat /kɔ'mɛrtsiən-/ *der* (hist.) *honorary title conferred on business magnates and financiers*

Kommilitone /kɔmili'to:nə/ *der;* **~n, ~n**, **Kommilitonin** *die;* **~, ~nen** [one's] fellow student; **der Kommilitone/die Kommilitonin Meyer** ≈ Mr/Ms Meyer

Kommis /kɔ'mi:/ *der;* **~** /kɔ'mi:(s)/, **~** /kɔ'mi:s/ (veralt.) *employee on the business side of a commercial firm;* (in einem Laden) [shop] assistant

Kommiss, ***Kommiß** /kɔ'mɪs/ *der;* **Kommisses** (Soldatenspr.) army; **beim ~ sein** be in the army

Kommissar /kɔmɪ'sa:ɐ̯/ *der;* **~s, ~e** 1 (Beamter der Polizei) detective superintendent 2 ▸❶ **S. 44** (staatlicher Beauftragter) commissioner; **der Hohe ~:** the High Commissioner

Kommissariat /kɔmɪsa'ria:t/ *das;* **~s, ~e** 1 (Dienststelle) (der Polizei) detective superintendent's office; (allgemein) commissioner's office 2 (Amt) (der Polizei) rank of detective superintendent; (allgemein) commissionership 3 (österr.: Polizeistation) police station

Kommissarin *die;* **~, ~nen** 1 (Beamte der Polizei) detective superintendent 2 ▸❶ **S. 44** (staatliche Beauftragte) commissioner; **die Hohe ~:** the High Commissioner

kommissarisch
A *Adj.* acting
B *adv.* in an acting capacity

Kommiss·brot, ***Kommiß·brot** *das* [coarse] wholemeal bread

Kommission /kɔmɪ'sio:n/ *die;* **~, ~en** 1 (Gremium) committee; (Prüfungs~) commission 2 (Kaufmannsspr. veralt.: Bestellung) order 3 **etw. in ~ nehmen/haben/geben** (Wirtsch.) take/have sth. on commission/give sth. to a dealer for sale on commission 4 (veralt.: Einkauf) **~en machen** *od.* **tätigen** do some shopping

Kommissionär /kɔmɪsio'nɛ:ɐ̯/ *der;* **~s, ~e**, **Kommissionärin** *die;* **~, ~nen** 1 (Wirtsch.) commission agent *or* merchant 2 (Buchhändler) wholesale bookseller

Kommissions-: ~buch·handel *der* (Wirtsch.) wholesale book trade; **~geschäft** *das* (Wirtsch.) commission business

Kommiss-, ***Kommiß-: ~stiefel** *der* army boot; **~ton** *der* (abwertend) peremptory tone [of voice]

kommod /kɔ'mo:t/ *Adj.* (bes. österr.) ▸**bequem A 1, B 1**

Kommode /kɔ'mo:də/ *die;* **~, ~n** chest of drawers

Kommodore /kɔmo'do:rə/ *der;* **~s, ~n** *od.* **~s** (Marine, Handelsmarine) commodore; (Luftwaffe) wing commander

kommunal /kɔmu'na:l/
A *Adj.* local; (bei einer städtischen Gemeinde) municipal; local
B *adv.* **etw. wird ~ verwaltet** sth. comes under local government

Kommunal-: ~abgaben *Pl.* rates [and local taxes]; **~anleihe** *die* municipal bond; **~politik** *die* local politics *sing.*; **~verwaltung** *die* local government; **~wahl** *die* local [government] elections *pl.*

Kommunarde /kɔmu'nardə/ *der;* **~n, ~n**, **Kommunardin** *die;* **~, ~nen** 1 (hist.) Communard 2 (einer Wohngemeinschaft) member of a/the commune

Kommune /kɔ'mu:nə/ *die;* **~, ~n** 1 (politische Gemeinde) local authority area; (städtische Gemeinde) municipality 2 **die Pariser ~** (hist.) the Paris Commune 3 (Wohngemeinschaft) commune

Kommunikant /kɔmuni'kant/ *der;* **~en, ~en**, **Kommunikantin** *die;* **~, ~nen** 1 (kath. Kirche) communicant 2 (Sprachw., Soziol.) participant in the communicative process

Kommunikation /kɔmunika'tsio:n/ *die;* **~, ~en** (Sprachw., Soziol.) communication

Kommunikations-: ~mittel *das* communication medium; **~satellit** *der* communications satellite; **~schwierigkeit** *die* difficulty in communicating; **~wissenschaft** *die* communication science *no art.*; **~zentrum** *das* central meeting place (*for social and cultural activities*)

kommunikativ /kɔmunika'ti:f/ *Adj.* communicative

Kommunikator /kɔmuni'ka:to:ɐ̯/ *der;* **~s, ...oren** /-'to:rən/, **Kommunikatorin** *die;* **~, ~nen** communicator

Kommunikee /kɔmuni'ke:/ ▸**Kommuniqué**

Kommunion /kɔmu'nio:n/ *die;* **~, ~en** (kath. Kirche) [Holy] Communion

Kommunion-: ~bank *die:* **auf der ~bank knien** ≈ kneel at the Communion rail; **~kleid** *das: dress worn to first Communion;* **~unterricht** *der: preparation for first Communion*

Kommuniqué /kɔmyni'ke:/ *das;* **~s, ~s** communiqué

Kommunismus *der;* **~:** communism; (Bewegung) Communism *no art.*

Kommunist *der;* **~en, ~en**, **Kommunistin** *die;* **~, ~nen** communist; (Parteimitglied) Communist

kommunistisch
A *Adj.* communist; (die ~e Partei betreffend) Communist; **das Kommunistische Manifest** the Communist Manifesto
B *adv.* Communist-‹*influenced, led, ruled, etc.*›

kommunizieren /kɔmuni'tsi:rən/ *itr. V.* 1 (geh.) communicate; **~de Röhren** (Physik) communicating tubes 2 (kath. Kirche) receive [Holy] Communion

Kommutation /kɔmuta'tsio:n/ *die;* **~, ~en** (Math., Sprachw., Astron.) commutation

kommutativ /kɔmuta'ti:f/ *Adj.* (Math., Sprachw.) commutative

Komödiant /komø'diant/ *der;* **~en, ~en** 1 (veralt.: Schauspieler) actor; player 2 (abwertend: Heuchler) play-actor

komödiantenhaft *Adj.* theatrical

Komödiantin *die;* **~, ~nen** 1 (veralt.: Schauspielerin) actress 2 (abwertend: Heuchlerin) play-actor

komödiantisch *Adj.* theatrical; acting ‹*talent*›

Komödie /ko'mø:diə/ *die;* **~, ~n** 1 comedy; (fig.) farce 2 (Theater) comedy theatre 3 (Heuchelei) play-acting; **~ spielen** put on an act

Kompagnon /kɔmpan'jõ:/ *der;* **~s, ~s** (Wirtsch.) partner; associate

kompakt /kɔm'pakt/ *Adj.* 1 (massiv) solid 2 (ugs.: gedrungen) stocky

Kompakt-: ~an·lage *die* music centre; (bei übereinander angeordneten Geräten) compact stereo system; **~bau·weise** *die* compact design

Kompanie /kɔmpa'ni:/ *die;* **~, ~n** (Milit., veralt.: Handelsgesellschaft) company

k

Kompanie·chef *der*, **Kompanie·führer** *der* (Milit.) company commander

Komparation /kɔmpara'tsi̯o:n/ *die*; ~, ~en (Sprachw.) comparison

Komparatistik /kɔmpara'tɪstɪk/ *die*; ~: comparative literature *no art.*

Komparativ /'kɔmparati:f/ *der*; ~s, ~e (Sprachw.) comparative

Komparse /kɔm'parzə/ *der*; ~n, ~n (Theater) supernumerary; super (coll.); (Film) extra

Komparserie /kɔmparzə'ri:/ *die*; ~, ~n (Theater) supernumeraries *pl.*; supers *pl.* (*coll.*); (Film) extras *pl.*

Komparsin *die*; ~, ~nen ▸ **Komparse**

Kompass, *Kompaß /'kɔmpas/ *der*; **Kompasses, Kompasse** compass; **nach dem ~ marschieren** march by the compass

Kompass-, ***Kompaß-**: **~häuschen** *das* (Seew. hist.) binnacle; **~nadel** *die* compass needle; **~rose** *die* compass card

kompatibel /kɔmpa'ti:bl̩/ *Adj.* (Nachrichtenw., Sprachw.) compatible

Kompendium /kɔm'pɛndi̯ʊm/ *das*; ~s, **Kompendien** (geh.) compendium

Kompensation /kɔmpɛnza'tsi̯o:n/ *die*; ~, ~en (Wirtsch., Physik, geh.) compensation

kompensatorisch *Adj.* (Päd., Psych.) compensatory

kompensieren *tr. V.* 1 (ausgleichen) **etw. mit etw.** *od.* **durch etw.** ~: compensate for *or* make up for sth. by sth. 2 (Wirtsch.: gegeneinander aufrechnen) offset; **etw. durch etw.** ~: offset sth. against sth.

kompetent /kɔmpe'tɛnt/ *Adj.* 1 (sachverständig) competent; **ein ~er Sprecher** (Sprachw.) a person with native-speaker competence; **für diese Probleme/Fragen ist er nicht ~**: he's not competent to deal with these problems/answer these questions 2 (bes. Rechtsw.: zuständig) competent, responsible ‹*authority*›; **das dafür ~e Gericht/der dafür ~e Kollege** the court which has jurisdiction in/the colleague who deals with these matters

Kompetenz /kɔmpe'tɛnts/ *die*; ~, ~en 1 (Sachverstand) competence 2 (bes. Rechtsw.: Zuständigkeit) authority; powers *pl.*; (eines Gerichts) jurisdiction; competence; **in jmds.** ~ (*Dat.*) **liegen/in jmds.** ~ (*Akk.*) **fallen** be/come within sb.'s authority *or* powers; **das liegt außerhalb meiner ~**: that doesn't lie within my authority *or* powers; **seine ~ überschreiten** exceed one's authority *or* powers; **die ~ haben/erhalten, etw. zu tun** have/receive the authority to do sth. 3 (Sprachw.) competence

Kompetenz-: **~bereich** *der* area of authority *or* responsibility/jurisdiction; **~konflikt** *der*, **~streitigkeit** *die* dispute over respective areas of authority *or* responsibility/jurisdiction

Kompilation /kɔmpila'tsi̯o:n/ *die*; ~, ~en (geh., meist abwertend) [mere] compilation

kompilieren *tr. V.* (geh., meist abwertend) [merely] compile

Komplement /kɔmple'mɛnt/ *das*; ~[e]s, ~e (Math.) complement

komplementär /kɔmplemɛn'tɛ:ɐ̯/

A *Adj.* complementary

B *adv.* **sich ~ verhalten/~ zueinander stehen** complement one another; be complementary

Komplementär *der*; ~s, ~e, **Komplementärin** *die*; ~, ~nen (Wirtsch.) general partner

Komplementär·farbe *die* (Optik) complementary colour

Komplement·winkel *der* (Math.) complementary angle

Komplet[1] /kõ'ple:/ *das*; ~s, ~s dress and matching jacket/coat

Komplet[2] /kɔm'ple:t/ *die*; ~, ~e (kath. Kirche) compline

komplett /kɔm'plɛt/

A *Adj.* 1 (vollständig) complete; **das kostet ~ 1 500 Euro** it costs 1,500 euros complete; **heute sind wir ~** (ugs.) today we are all here 2 (ugs.: ganz und gar) complete; utter 3 (österr.: voll) full ‹*hotel, tram, etc.*›

B *adv.* 1 (vollständig) **~ möbliert/ausgerüstet** fully furnished/equipped 2 (ugs.: ganz und gar) completely; totally

komplettieren *tr. V.* complete

komplex /kɔm'plɛks/ (geh.)

A *Adj.* 1 complex; **~e Zahl** (Math.) complex number 2 (allseitig) full, complete ‹*automation*›; comprehensive ‹*reconstruction, planning, provision*›; ‹*analysis, treatment*› by several methods

B *adv.* **etw. ~ vorbereiten** make comprehensive preparations for sth.

Komplex *der*; ~es, ~e 1 (Bereich) complex; **Fragen im ~ lösen** solve questions as parts of an integrated whole 2 (Gebäudeblock) complex; **in diesem ~ des Schlosses** in this complex of buildings in the castle 3 (Psych.) complex

Komplexität /kɔmplɛksi'tɛ:t/ *die*; ~: complexity

Komplikation /kɔmplika'tsi̯o:n/ *die*; ~, ~en (auch Med.) complication

Kompliment /kɔmpli'mɛnt/ *das*; ~[e]s, ~e 1 compliment; **jmdm. ein ~ machen** pay sb. a compliment (**über** + *Akk.* on); **mein ~!** permit me to compliment you; my compliments!; **nicht gerade ein ~ für jmdn. sein** (fig.) not exactly do sb. credit 2 (veralt.: Gruß) **meine ~e an die gnädige Frau** give my respects to your good wife

komplimentieren *tr. V.* (geh.) **jmdn. ins Haus/in den Sessel ~**: usher *or* show sb. into the house/help sb. into his/her seat with a great show of courtesy; **jmdn. aus dem Zimmer ~** (verhüll.) usher sb. out of the room

Komplize /kɔm'pli:tsə/ *der*; ~n, ~n (abwertend) accomplice

komplizieren *tr. V.* complicate; **sich ~**: become more complicated

kompliziert

A *Adj.* complicated; complicated, intricate ‹*device, piece of apparatus*›; complicated, involved ‹*problem, procedure*›; **ein ~er Bruch** (Med.) a compound fracture

B *adv.* **~ aufgebaut sein** have a complicated *or* complex structure; **sich ~ ausdrücken** express oneself in a complicated *or* an involved way *or* manner; *s. auch* **einfach A 2**

Kompliziertheit *die*; ~: complexity; complicatedness

Komplizin *die*; ~, ~nen ▸ **Komplize**

Komplott /kɔm'plɔt/ *das*; ~[e]s, ~e plot; conspiracy; **ein ~ zur Ermordung des Diktators** a plot *or* conspiracy to assassinate the dictator; **ein ~ schmieden** hatch a plot

Komponente /kɔmpo'nɛntə/ *die*; ~, ~n 1 (Bestandteil) component 2 (Aspekt) component; element

komponieren

A *tr. V.* (auch geh.: gestalten) compose

B *itr. V.* compose

Komponist *der*; ~en, ~en, **Komponistin** *die*; ~, ~nen ▸ **i S. 113** composer

Komposition /kɔmpozi'tsi̯o:n/ *die*; ~, ~en (Musik, geh.) composition; **eine ~ kostbarer Essenzen** (geh.) a fusion *or* blend of expensive essential oils

Kompositions·lehre *die* (Musik) [theory of] composition

kompositorisch /kɔmpozi'to:rɪʃ/ *Adj.* compositional

Kompositum /kɔm'po:zitʊm/ *das*; ~s, **Komposita** (Sprachw.) compound [word]

Kompost /kɔm'pɔst/ *der*; ~[e]s, ~e compost

Kompost-: **~erde** *die* [well-rotted] compost; **~haufen** *der* compost heap

kompostieren *tr. V.* compost

Kompott /kɔm'pɔt/ *das*; ~[e]s, ~e stewed fruit; compote; **~ aus Pflaumen/Himbeeren** stewed plums/raspberries *pl.*

Kompott·schale *die* fruit dish *or* bowl

kompress, *kompreß /kɔm'prɛs/ (Druckw.)

A *Adj.* solid

B *adv.* ‹*set*› in solid type

Kompresse /kɔm'prɛsə/ *die*; ~, ~n (Med.) 1 (Umschlag) [wet] compress 2 (Mull) [gauze] pad

Kompression /kɔm'prɛ'si̯o:n/ *die*; ~, ~en (Physik, Technik, Med.) compression

Kompressions·verband *der* (Med.) ▸ **Druckverband**

Kompressor /kɔm'prɛso:ɐ̯/ *der*; ~s, ~en /-'so:rən/ 1 (Technik) compressor 2 (Kfz.-W.) supercharger

komprimieren /kɔmpri'mi:rən/ *tr. V.* (auch Physik, Technik, DV) compress; (fig.) condense ‹*book, text*›

komprimiert

A *Adj.* 1 condensed ‹*account etc.*› 2 (DV) compresssed

B *adv.* **etw. ~ darstellen** present sth. in a condensed form

Komprimierung *die* ▸ **komprimieren:** compression; condensation

Kompromiss, *Kompromiß /kɔmpro'mɪs/ *der*; **Kompromisses, Kompromisse** compromise; **einen ~ schließen** make a compromise; compromise; **zu einem/keinem ~ bereit sein** be/not be ready to compromise; **ein fauler ~** (ugs.) a poor sort of compromise (coll.)

kompromiss-, ***kompromiß-**, **Kompromiss-**, ***Kompromiß-**: **~bereit** *Adj.* ready *or* willing to compromise *pred.*; **~bereitschaft** *die* readiness *or* willingness to compromise; **~fähig** *Adj.* able to compromise *postpos.*; capable of compromise *postpos.*; ‹*version, offer, etc.*› allowing a compromise; **~fähigkeit** *die* ability to compromise; **~los** **A** *Adj.* uncompromising; **B** *adv.* uncompromisingly; **~losigkeit** *die*; ~~, ~~: inability to compromise; **~lösung** *die* compromise solution; **~vorschlag** *der* compromise proposal *or* suggestion

kompromittieren /kɔmpromɪ'ti:rən/ *tr. V.* compromise; **sich ~**: compromise oneself

Komsomolze /kɔmzo'mɔltsə/ *der*; ~n, ~n, **Komsomolzin**, *die*; ~, ~nen Komsomol member

Komtess, *Komteß, Komtesse /kɔm'tɛs(ə)/ *die*; ~, **Komtessen** (veralt.) count's [unmarried] daughter

Komtur /kɔm'tu:ɐ̯/ *der*; ~s, ~e (hist.) commander (*of an honorary or a religious military order*)

Kondensat /kɔndɛn'za:t/ *das*; ~[e]s, ~e (Physik, Chemie) condensate

Kondensation /kɔndɛnza'tsi̯o:n/ *die*; ~, ~en (Physik, Chemie) condensation

Kondensations·punkt *der* (Physik, Chemie) condensation point

Kondensator /kɔndɛn'za:tɔr/ *der*; ~s, ~en /-za'to:rən/ 1 (Elektrot.) capacitor; condenser 2 (Technik) condenser

kondensieren *tr., itr. V.* (itr. auch mit sein) (Physik, Chemie) condense

Kondens-: **~milch** *die* condensed milk; **~streifen** *der* condensation trail; vapour trail; **~wasser** *das* condensation

Kondition /kɔndi'tsi̯o:n/ *die*; ~, ~en 1 (bes. Kaufmannsspr., Finanzw.) condition; **die ~en** the terms *or* conditions; **zu günstigen ~en** on favourable terms 2 (körperlich-seelische Verfassung, Leistungsfähigkeit) condition; **eine gute/schlechte ~ haben** be/not be in good condition *or* shape; **keine ~ haben** be out of condition; (fig.) have no stamina

konditional /kɔnditsi̯o'na:l/ *Adj.* (bes. Sprachw.) conditional

Konditional·satz *der* (Sprachw.) conditional clause

konditionieren *tr. V.* (Technik, Psych.) condition

Konditions-: **~mangel** *der*, **~schwäche** *die* lack of condition *or* fitness; **~training** *das* fitness training

Konditor /kɔn'di:tɔr/ *der*; ~s, ~en /-di'to:rən/ ▸ **i S. 113** confectioner; pastry cook; **beim ~**: at the cake shop

Konditorei *die*; ~, ~en 1 cake shop; (Lokal) café 2 (Herstellung) confectionery

Konditorin, *die;* ~, ~nen ▸ⓘ S. 113 ▸**Konditor**

Konditor·waren *Pl.* cakes and pastries

Kondolenz- /kɔndo'lɛnts-/: **~besuch** *der* visit of condolence; **~buch** *das* book of condolence

kondolieren /kɔndo'li:rən/ *itr. V.* offer one's condolences; **jmdm. [zu jmds. Tod] ~:** offer one's condolences to sb. *or* condole with sb. [on sb.'s death]

Kondom /kɔn'do:m/ *das od. der;* **~s, ~e** condom; [contraceptive] sheath

Kondominium /kɔndo'mi:niʊm/ *das;* **~s, Kondominien** (Völkerr.) condominium

Kondor /'kɔndɔr/ *der;* **~s, ~e** condor

Kondukteur /kɔndʊk'tø:ɐ̯/ *der;* **~s, ~e** ▸ⓘ S. 113 (schweiz.) (in der Straßenbahn) conductor; (in der Eisenbahn) ticket collector

Kondukteurin *die;* **~, ~nen** ▸ⓘ S. 113 (schweiz.) ▸**Kondukteur**: conductress/ticket collector

Konen ▸**Konus**

Konfekt /kɔn'fɛkt/ *das;* **~[e]s** 1 (Süßigkeiten) confectionery; sweets *pl.* (Brit.); candies *pl.* (Amer.) 2 (bes. südd., österr., schweiz.: Teegebäck) [small] fancy biscuits *pl.* (Brit.) *or* (Amer.) cookies *pl.*

Konfektion /kɔnfɛk'tsio:n/ *die;* **~, ~en** 1 (Anfertigung) manufacture of ready-made *or* off-the-peg (Brit.) *or* (Amer.) off-the-rack clothes *or* garments 2 (Kleidung) ready-made *or* off-the-peg (Brit.) *or* (Amer.) off-the-rack clothes *pl. or* garments *pl.* 3 (Industrie) clothing industry

Konfektionär /kɔnfɛktsio'nɛ:ɐ̯/ *der;* **~s, ~e** manufacturer of ready-made *or* off-the-peg (Brit.) *or* (Amer.) off-the-rack clothing; clothing manufacturer; (Angestellter) employee in a clothing factory

Konfektions-: **~anzug** *der* ready-made *or* off-the-peg (Brit.) *or* (Amer.) off-the-rack suit; **~geschäft** *das* [ready-made *or* off-the-peg (Brit.) *or* (Amer.) off-the-rack] clothes shop; **~größe** *die* size; **~ware** *die* ready-made *or* off-the-peg (Brit.) *or* (Amer.) off-the-rack clothes *pl. or* garments *pl.*

Konferenz /kɔnfe'rɛnts/ *die;* **~, ~en** conference; (Besprechung) meeting

Konferenz-: **~saal** *der* conference hall; **~schaltung** *die* (Rundf., Ferns., Fernspr.) conference circuit; **~teilnehmer** *der,* **~teilnehmerin** *die* conference participant; **~tisch** *der* conference table

konferieren /kɔnfe'ri:rən/

A *itr. V.* 1 (beraten) confer (**über** + *Akk.* on, about) 2 (ansagen) act as compère

B *tr. V.* (ansagen) compère

Konfession /kɔnfɛ'sio:n/ *die;* **~, ~en** 1 denomination; religion; **die katholische ~:** the Catholic religion; **welche ~ haben Sie?** what denomination *or* religion are you? 2 (geh.: Geständnis) confession

Konfessionalismus /kɔnfɛsiona'lɪsmʊs/ *der;* **~** (geh.) denominationalism *no art.*

konfessionell /kɔnfɛsio'nɛl/

A *Adj.* denominational

B *adv.* as regards denomination; **~ [un]gebunden sein/sich ~ [un]gebunden fühlen** have/feel [no] denominational ties

konfessions·los *Adj.* not belonging to any denomination *or* religion *postpos., not pred.*

Konfessions·schule *die* denominational school

Konfetti /kɔn'fɛti/ *das;* **~[s]** confetti

Konfident /kɔnfi'dɛnt/ *der;* **~en, ~en, Konfidentin** *die;* **~, ~nen** (österr.: Spitzel) [police] informer

Konfiguration /kɔnfigura'tsio:n/ *die;* **~, ~en** (Physik, Chemie, Sprachw.) configuration

Konfirmand /kɔnfɪr'mant/ *der;* **~en, ~en** (ev. Rel.) confirmand

Konfirmanden·unterricht *der* confirmation classes *pl.*

Konfirmandin *die;* **~, ~nen** ▸**Konfirmand**

Konfirmation /kɔnfɪrma'tsio:n/ *die;* **~, ~en** (ev. Rel.) confirmation

konfirmieren *tr. V.* (ev. Rel.) confirm

Konfiserie /kɔnfizə'ri:/ *die;* **~, ~n** (schweiz.) ▸**Konditorei**

Konfiskation /kɔnfɪska'tsio:n/ *die;* **~, ~en** (Rechtsw.) confiscation

konfiszieren /kɔnfɪs'tsi:rən/ *tr. V.* (bes. Rechtsw.) confiscate

Konfitüre /kɔnfi'ty:rə/ *die;* **~, ~n** jam (made from whole fruit)

Konflikt /kɔn'flɪkt/ *der;* **~[e]s, ~e** conflict; **ein offener/bewaffneter ~:** open/armed conflict; **mit etw. in ~ geraten** *od.* **kommen** come into conflict with sth.

konflikt-, Konflikt-: **~fähig** *Adj.* able to deal with conflict *postpos.;* **~fähigkeit** *die* ability to deal with conflict; **~fall** *der:* **im ~fall** in the event of conflict; **~forschung** *die* conflict studies *pl.;* **~los** *Adj.* conflict-free; **~scheu** *Adj.* ‹*person*› who shies away from conflict; **~scheu sein** shy away from conflict; **seine ~scheue Art** his aversion to *or* distaste for conflict; **~scheu** *die* aversion to conflict; **~situation** *die* conflict situation; **~stoff** *der* cause for conflict *or* dispute; **~trächtig** *Adj.* full of conflict[s] *postpos.;* conflict-ridden; **~trächtigkeit** *die* conflict-ridden nature

Konföderation /kɔnfødera'tsio:n/ *die;* **~, ~en** confederation; (von kürzerer Dauer) confederacy

Konföderierte *der/die; adj. Dekl.* confederate; **die ~n** (hist.) the Confederates

konform /kɔn'fɔrm/ *Adj.* concurring *attrib.* ‹*views*›; **mit jmdm./etw. ~ gehen** be in agreement with sb./sth.; **in etw.** (*Dat.*) **~ sein** agree *or* be in agreement on sth.

Konformismus *der;* **~:** conformism

Konformist *der;* **~en, ~en, Konformistin** *die;* **~, ~nen** (auch Rel.) conformist

konformistisch

A *Adj.* conformist

B *adv.* in a conformist way

Konformität /kɔnfɔrmi'tɛ:t/ *die;* **~:** conformity

Konfrater /kɔn'fra:tɐ/ *der;* **~s, Konfratres** (kath. Kirche) fellow clergyman; brother-priest

Konfrontation /kɔnfrɔnta'tsio:n/ *die;* **~, ~en** confrontation

konfrontieren *tr. V.* confront; **sich mit etw. konfrontiert sehen** be confronted with sth.

konfus /kɔn'fu:s/

A *Adj.* confused; muddled; **jmdn. ~ machen** confuse *or* muddle sb.

B *adv.* in a confused *or* muddled fashion; confusedly

Konfusion /kɔnfu'zio:n/ *die;* **~, ~en** confusion

konfuzianisch /kɔnfu'tsia:nɪʃ/ *Adj.* Confucian

Konfuzianismus *der;* **~:** Confucianism *no art.*

kongenial /kɔnge'nia:l/ *Adj.* (geh.) congenial, kindred ‹*spirits*›; ideally matched ‹*translation*›

Kongenialität /kɔngeniali'tɛ:t/ *die;* **~** (der Geister) congeniality; (einer Übersetzung) well-matched quality

Konglomerat /kɔnglome'ra:t/ *das;* **~[e]s, ~e** 1 conglomeration 2 (Geol.) conglomerate

Kongo[1] /'kɔŋgo/ *der;* **~[s]** ▸ⓘ S. 267 (Fluss) Congo

Kongo[2] /'kɔŋgo/ *(das);* **~s** *od. der;* **~[s]** (Staat) the Congo

Kongolese /kɔŋgo'le:zə/ *der;* **~n, ~n, Kongolesin** *die;* **~, ~nen** Congolese

Kongregation /kɔngrega'tsio:n/ *die;* **~, ~en** (kath. Kirche) congregation

Kongress, *Kongreß /kɔn'grɛs/ *der;* **Kongresses, Kongresse** 1 (Tagung) congress; conference 2 (USA) **der ~:** Congress

Kongress-, *Kongreß-: **~halle** *die* conference hall; **~mit·glied** *das* (USA) Congressman/Congresswoman; **~teilnehmer** *der,* **~teilnehmerin** *die* congress *or* conference participant; **~zentrum** *das* conference centre

kongruent /kɔngru'ɛnt/ *Adj.* 1 (geh.) identical 2 (Math.) congruent

Kongruenz /kɔngru'ɛnts/ *die;* **~, ~en** 1 (geh.) identity 2 (Math.) congruence 3 (Sprachw.) agreement; concord

kongruieren *itr. V.* 1 (geh.) coincide 2 (Math.) be congruent 3 (Sprachw.) agree

K.-o.-Nieder·lage *die* (Boxen) defeat by a knockout; **durch eine ~:** by a knockout

Konifere /koni'fe:rə/ *die;* **~, ~n** (Bot.) conifer

König /'kø:nɪç/ *der;* **~s, ~e** (auch Schach, Kartenspiele, fig.) king; **der ~ der Wüste/Lüfte** (dicht.)/**des Jazz** the king of beasts/birds/jazz; **der Kunde ist ~:** the customer is always right

Königin *die;* **~, ~nen** (auch Bienen~) queen; **die ~ des Festes/Balles** (geh.) the belle of the ball; **~ der Nacht** (Bot.) queen of the night

Königin·mutter *die; Pl.* **Königinmütter** queen mother

königlich

A *Adj.* 1 royal 2 (vornehm) regal 3 (reichlich) princely ‹*gift, salary, wage*›; lavish ‹*hospitality*› 4 (ugs.: außerordentlich) tremendous (coll.) ‹*fun*›

B *adv.* 1 (reichlich) ‹*entertain*› lavishly; ‹*pay*› handsomely; **~ beschenkt werden** be showered with lavish presents 2 (ugs.: außerordentlich) ‹*enjoy oneself*› immensely (coll.); **sich über etw.** (*Akk.*) **~ freuen** be as pleased as Punch about sth.

König·reich *das* kingdom

königs-, Königs-: **~blau** *Adj.* royal blue; **~disziplin** *die* premier *or* supreme discipline; **~haus** *das* royal house; **~hof** *der* royal court; king's court; **~kerze** *die* (Bot.) mullein; **~kind** *das* prince/princess; king's son/daughter; **~krone** *die* royal crown; **~macher** *der,* **~macherin** *die* (ugs.) kingmaker; **~paar** *das* royal couple; **~sohn** *der* prince; king's son; **~thron** *der* royal throne; **~tiger** *der* Bengal tiger; **~tochter** *die* princess; king's daughter; **~treu** *Adj.* loyal to the king *postpos.;* (der Monarchie treu) royalist; **~wasser** *das* (Chemie, Technik) aqua regia; **~weg** *der* (geh.) ideal way

Königtum *das;* **~s, Königtümer** 1 (Monarchie) monarchy 2 (veralt.: Reich) kingdom

konisch /'ko:nɪʃ/

A *Adj.* conical

B *adv.* conically; **~ zugespitzt sein** taper to a point

Konjektur /kɔnjɛk'tu:ɐ̯/ *die;* **~, ~en** (Literaturw.) conjecture

Konjugation /kɔnjuga'tsio:n/ *die;* **~, ~en** (Sprachw.) conjugation

konjugieren *tr. V.* (Sprachw.) conjugate

Konjunktion /kɔnjʊŋk'tsio:n/ *die;* **~, ~en** (Sprachw.) conjunction

Konjunktional·satz *der* (Sprachw.) conjunctional clause

Konjunktiv /'kɔnjʊŋkti:f/ *der;* **~s, ~e** (Sprachw.) subjunctive; **~ I/II** present/imperfect subjunctive

konjunktivisch

A *Adj.* (Sprachw.) subjunctive

B *adv.* in the subjunctive

Konjunktur /kɔnjʊŋk'tu:ɐ̯/ *die;* **~, ~en** (Wirtsch.) 1 (wirtschaftliche Lage) [level of] economic activity; economy; (Tendenz) economic trend; **eine rückläufige/steigende ~:** declining/increasing economic activity; **die ~ beleben/bremsen** stimulate/slow down the economy 2 (Hoch~) boom; (Aufschwung) upturn [in the economy]; **~ haben** (fig.) be in great demand

konjunktur-, Konjunktur-: **~abhängig** *Adj.* (Wirtsch.) dependent on economic trends *postpos.;* **~abschwächung** *die* (Wirtsch.) economic downturn; **~aufschwung** *der* (Wirtsch.) economic upturn; upturn in the economy; **~barometer** *das* (Wirtsch.) graph of leading economic indicators; (fig.) economic barometer; **~bedingt** *Adj.* (Wirtsch.) due to economic trends *postpos.;* cyclical; **~bericht** *der* (Wirtsch.) report on the economy

konjunkturell /kɔnjʊŋktu'rɛl/

A *Adj.* economic; **die ~e Entwicklung** the devel-

k

ℹ können

Es kommen hauptsächlich zwei Übersetzungen in Betracht: **be able to** (die einzige Möglichkeit im Infinitiv und im Futur und den anderen zusammengesetzten Zeiten) und **can/could.** Im Präsens ist **can** fast immer möglich und in vielen Fällen vorzuziehen. In der Vergangenheit dagegen ist **was able to** manchmal vorzuziehen, da **could** auch konditional sein kann (= *könnte*).

Es ist wichtig, kochen zu können
= It is important to be able to cook

Wenn sie frei bekommt, wird sie hingehen können
= If she gets time off she will be able to go there

Er kann sie oft durch einen Freund bekommen
= He can often get them *od.* is often able to get them through a friend

Ich kann es nur mit einer Brille lesen
= I can only read it with spectacles

Er kann sie nicht leiden
= He can't stand her

Sie können (= dürfen) rauchen, wenn Sie wollen
= You can smoke if you wish

Ich konnte mit vier Jahren lesen
= I could *od.* was able to read at the age of four

Sie konnten nicht früher kommen
= They couldn't *od.* were unable to come any earlier

In den beiden letzten Beispielen ist keine Verwechslung möglich.

Er konnte sie durch einen Freund bekommen
= He was able to get them through a friend

Aber

Er könnte sie durch einen Freund bekommen
= He could get them through a friend

Im Perfekt, auch konditional:

Glücklicherweise habe ich umbuchen können
= Fortunately I was able/have been able to change the booking

Sie hätten uns Bescheid sagen können
= You could have let us know

Und schließlich im Plusquamperfekt:

Sie hatte das Buch nicht finden können
= She had been unable to find the book

Bitten und Vorschläge

Könntest du mir helfen?
= Could you help me?

Könnten Sie vielleicht Freitag kommen?
= Perhaps you could come on Friday?

Unpersönlicher Gebrauch: *may, might*

Es kann sein, dass er es vergessen hat
= It may be that he has forgotten it, He may have forgotten it

Es könnte sein, dass wir es noch brauchen
= We might still need it

Es könnte ratsam sein, sie anzurufen
= It might be advisable to telephone her

Das kann nicht sein
= That's not possible, It can't be

opment of the economy
B *adv.* **~ bedingt** due to economic trends *postpos.*

konjunktur-, Konjunktur-: ~entwicklung *die* (Wirtsch.) economic trends *pl.*; **~flaute** *die* (Wirtsch.) [economic] downturn; (Rezession) recession; **~gerecht** *Adj.* (Wirtsch.) in keeping with the needs of the economy *postpos.*; **~politik** *die* (Wirtsch.) stabilization policy; measures *pl.* aimed at avoiding violent fluctuations in the economy; **~ritter** *der* (Wirtsch. abwertend) opportunist; **~rückgang** *der* (Wirtsch.) [economic] recession; decline in economic activity; **~schwankung** *die* (Wirtsch.) fluctuation in the level of economic activity; **~spritze** *die* (Wirtsch. ugs.) boost to the economy; **~zyklus** *der* (Wirtsch.) trade cycle

konkav /kɔn'ka:f/ (Optik)
A *Adj.* concave
B *adv.* concavely

Konkav·spiegel *der* (Optik) concave mirror

Konklave /kɔn'kla:və/ *das;* **~s, ~n** (kath. Kirche) conclave

Konklusion /kɔnklu'zi̯o:n/ *die;* **~, ~en** (bes. Philos.) conclusion

Konkordanz /kɔnkɔr'dants/ *die;* **~, ~en** (Wissensch.) concordance

Konkordat /kɔnkɔr'da:t/ *das;* **~[e]s, ~e** concordat

konkret /kɔn'kre:t/
A *Adj.* concrete; **~e Literatur/Musik** concrete poetry/music
B *adv.* **1** (nicht abstrakt) in concrete terms; **kannst du mal ~ sagen, was du damit meinst?** could you tell me exactly what you mean by that?; **kannst du dich etwas ~er ausdrücken?** could you be a bit move specific [about that]? **2** (in der Praxis) in practice

konkretisieren *tr. V.* **etw. ~:** put sth. in concrete terms

Konkubinat /kɔnkubi'na:t/ *das;* **~[e]s, ~e** (Rechtsw.) concubinage; **mit jmdm. im ~ leben** live in concubinage with sb.

Konkubine /kɔnku'bi:nə/ *die;* **~, ~n** **1** (hist.) concubine **2** (abwertend: Geliebte) mistress

Konkurrent /kɔnku'rɛnt/ *der;* **~en, ~en, Konkurrentin** *die;* **~, ~nen** rival; (Sport, Wirtsch.) competitor

Konkurrenz /kɔnku'rɛnts/ *die;* **~, ~en** **1** (Rivalität) rivalry *no indef. art.*; (Sport, Wirtsch.) competition *no indef. art.*; **jmdm. ~ machen** compete with sb.; **mit jmdm. in ~ treten/stehen** enter into/be in competition with sb. **2** (Wettbewerb) competition; **außer ~ starten/teilnehmen** take part as an unofficial competitor **3** (die Konkurrenten) competition

konkurrenz-, Konkurrenz-: ~druck *der* pressure of competition; **~fähig** *Adj.* competitive; **~kampf** *der* competition; (zwischen zwei Menschen) rivalry; **~los** *Adj.* ‹*product, firm, etc.*› that has no competition *or* competitors; (unvergleichlich) unrivalled; **~los sein** have no competition *or* competitors; **~unternehmen** *das* rival company *or* concern; **zwei ~unternehmen** two rival *or* competing companies *or* concerns

konkurrieren *itr. V.* compete; **mit jmdm./etw. [um etw.] ~:** compete with sb./sth. [for sth.]

Konkurs /kɔn'kʊrs/ *der;* **~es, ~e** **1** (Bankrott) bankruptcy; **~ machen** *od.* **in ~ gehen** go bankrupt; **[den] ~ anmelden** file for bankruptcy; have oneself declared bankrupt **2** (gerichtliches Verfahren) bankruptcy proceedings *pl.*

Konkurs-: ~masse *die* (Wirtsch.) bankrupt's assets *pl.*; **~verfahren** *das* (Wirtsch.) bankruptcy proceedings *pl.*; **~verwalter** *der,* **~verwalterin** *die* (Wirtsch.) receiver

können /'kœnən/
A *unr. Modalverb; 2. Part.* **~** ▸ ℹ S. 430 **1** (vermögen) be able to; **er hat/hätte es machen ~:** he was able to *or* he could do it/he could have done it; **er kann es machen/nicht machen** he can do it *or* is able to do it/cannot *or* (coll.) can't do it *or* is unable to do it; **er kann gut reden/tanzen** he can talk/dance well; he is a good talker/dancer; **Auto fahren/Klavier spielen ~:** be able to drive [a car]/play the piano; **er kann Auto fahren** he can drive; **ich kann nicht schlafen** I cannot *or* (coll.) can't sleep; **er konnte das genau hören/sehen** he could hear/see everything; **er konnte nicht bleiben** he couldn't stay; **ich kann das nicht mehr hören/sehen** I can't stand *or* bear to hear it/can't stand *or* bear the sight of it any longer (coll.); **ich kann dir sagen!** (ugs.) I can tell you; **nirgends kann man besser jagen als in ...** nowhere is the hunting *or* shooting better than in ...
2 (die Möglichkeit haben) **kann das explodieren?** could it explode?; **er kann jeden Moment kommen** he may come at any moment; **wer kann es sein/gewesen sein?** who can it be/could it have been?; **man kann nie wissen** you never know; one never knows; **es kann sein, dass ...** it may be that ...; **das könnte [gut] sein** that could [well] be the case; **das kann nicht sein** that's not possible; **kann ich Ihnen helfen?** can I help you?; **~ Sie mir sagen, ...?** can you tell me ...?; **~ Sie nicht grüßen?** don't you know how to salute?; **kannst du nicht aufpassen?** can't you be more careful?; **kann sein** (ugs.) could be (coll.); **kann sein, kann nicht sein** (ugs.) might be, might not be (coll.); **Kommst du morgen? — Kann sein** Are you coming tomorrow? — Might do
3 (Grund haben) **du kannst ganz ruhig sein** you don't have to worry; **wir ~ uns/er kann sich freuen, dass ...** we can/he should be glad that ...; **er kann sie/es nicht leiden** he can't stand her/it; **er kann einem Leid tun** (ugs.) you have to feel sorry for him; **das kann man wohl sagen!** you could well say that
4 (dürfen) **kann ich gehen?** can I go?; **~ wir mitkommen?** can we come too?; **du kannst mich [mal]!** (salopp verhüll.) you can get stuffed (sl.); you know what you can do (coll.)
B *unr. tr. V.* **1** (beherrschen) know ‹*language*›; be able to play, know how to play ‹*game*›; **sie kann das [gut]** she can do that [well]; **sie kann Mathe/kann keine Mathe** she can/can't do maths; **er kann etwas auf seinem Gebiet** he has quite a lot of know-how in his field; **hast du die Hausaufgabe gekonnt?** could you do the homework?; **ein Gedicht ~:** know a poem [by heart]; **er lief, was er konnte** he ran as fast as he could; **etwas/nichts für etwas ~:** be/not be responsible for sth.; **was kann ich dafür?** what am I supposed to do about it?
C *unr. itr. V.* **1** (fähig sein) **er kann nicht anders** there's nothing else he can do; (es ist seine Art) he can't help it (coll.); **~ vor Lachen** (ugs.) I would if I could
2 (Zeit haben) **ich kann heute nicht** I can't today (coll.)
3 (ugs.: Kraft haben) **kannst du noch?** can you go on?; **der Läufer konnte nicht mehr** the runner could not go on
4 (ugs.: essen ~) **für mich keinen Nachtisch, ich kann nicht mehr** no dessert for me, I couldn't manage any more
5 (ugs.: umgehen ~) **[gut] mit jmdm. ~:** get on *or* along [well] with sb.

Können *das;* **~s** ability; (Kunstfertigkeit) skill

Könner *der;* **~s, ~, Könnerin** *die;* **~, ~nen** expert

Konnex /kɔ'nɛks/ *der;* **~es, ~e** (geh.) **1** (Zusammenhang) connection; link **2** (Kontakt) contact

Konnossement /kɔnɔsə'mɛnt/ *das;* **~[e]s, ~e** (Seew.) bill of lading

Konnotation /kɔnota'tsi̯o:n/ *die;* **~, ~en** (Sprachw.) connotation

konnte /'kɔntə/ *1. u. 3. Pers. Sg. Prät. v.* **können**

könnte /'kœntə/ *1. u. 3. Pers. Sg. Konjunktiv II v.* **können**

Konrektor /'kɔnrɛktɔr/ *der;* **~s, ~en** /-'to:rən/, **Konrektorin** *die;* **~, ~nen** (Schulw.) deputy head[master]

Konsekration /kɔnzekraˈtsi̯oːn/ *die;* ~, ~**en** (kath. Kirche) consecration

konsekutiv /kɔnzekuˈtiːf/ *Adj.* (auch Sprachw.) consecutive; ~**es Dolmetschen** consecutive interpreting

Konsekutiv·satz *der* (Sprachw.) consecutive clause

Konsens /kɔnˈzɛns/ *der;* ~**es,** ~**e** **1** (Übereinstimmung) consensus **2** (veralt.: Zustimmung) consent

konsequent /kɔnzeˈkvɛnt/

A *Adj.* **1** (folgerichtig) logical; logically consistent, logical ‹*thinking, argumentation*› **2** (unbeirrbar) consistent **3** (Sport) close, tight ‹*marking*›

B *adv.* **1** (folgerichtig) logically **2** (unbeirrbar) consistently; **ein Ziel ~ verfolgen** resolutely and single-mindedly pursue a goal; **~ durchgreifen** take rigorous action **3** (Sport) ‹*mark*› closely, tightly

konsequenter·maßen, konsequenter·weise *Adv.* to be consistent

Konsequenz /kɔnzeˈkvɛnts/ *die;* ~, ~**en** **1** (Folge) consequence; **die ~en tragen** take the consequences; **[aus etw.] die ~en ziehen** draw the obvious conclusion [from sth.]; (gezwungenermaßen) accept the obvious consequences [of sth.] **2** (Unbeirrbarkeit) resolution; determination; **einer Sache** (*Dat.*) **mit ~ nachgehen** investigate sth. rigorously **3** (Folgerichtigkeit) logicality; (eines Gedankenganges, einer Argumentation) logical consistency; logicality

konservativ /kɔnzɛrvaˈtiːf/

A *Adj.* (auch Med.) conservative; (die ~e Partei betreffend) Conservative

B *adv.* (althergebracht) conservatively

Konservative *der/die; adj. Dekl.* conservative; **die ~n** (Politik) the Conservatives

Konservativismus *der;* ~: conservatism

Konservator /kɔnzɛrˈvaːtɔr/ *der;* ~**s,** ~**en** /-ˈtoːrən/, **Konservatorin** *die;* ~, ~**nen** curator; keeper

Konservatorium /kɔnzɛrvaˈtoːri̯ʊm/ *das;* ~**s, Konservatorien** conservatoire; conservatory (Amer.)

Konserve /kɔnˈzɛrvə/ *die;* ~, ~**n** **1** (Büchse) can; tin (Brit.); **Musik aus der ~** (fig. ugs.) canned music (coll.) **2** (konservierte Lebensmittel) preserved food; (in Dosen) canned *or* (Brit.) tinned food; **von ~n leben** eat out of cans *or* (Brit.) tins; live on canned *or* (Brit.) tinned food **3** (Med.: Blut~) stored blood

Konserven-: ~büchse *die,* **~dose** *die* can; tin (Brit.); **~fabrik** *die* canning factory; cannery; **~nahrung** *die* canned *or* (Brit.) tinned food

konservierbar *Adv.* preservable

konservieren *tr. V.* preserve; conserve, preserve ‹*building, work of art*›

Konservierung *die;* ~, ~**en** preservation; (von Gebäuden, Kunstwerken usw.) conservation; preservation

Konservierungs-: ~mittel *das,* **~stoff** *der* preservative

konsistent /kɔnzɪsˈtɛnt/ *Adj.* **1** (zähflüssig) stiff **2** (beständig) stable **3** (widerspruchsfrei) consistent

Konsistenz /kɔnzɪsˈtɛnts/ *die;* ~, ~**en** **1** (Beschaffenheit) consistency **2** (Stabilität) stability

Konsistorium /kɔnzɪsˈtoːri̯ʊm/ (kath. Kirche) *das;* ~**s, Konsistorien** consistory

Konsole /kɔnˈzoːlə/ *die;* ~, ~**n** **1** (Archit.) console **2** (Brett) shelf; (Tischchen) console [table] **3** (im Auto, Spiel~) console

konsolidieren /kɔnzoliˈdiːrən/

A *tr. V.* **1** (festigen) consolidate **2** (Wirtsch.) (in Anleihen umwandeln) fund ‹*debts*›; (vereinigen) consolidate ‹*debts*›

B *refl. V.* become consolidated

Konsolidierung *die;* ~, ~**en** **1** (Festigung) consolidation **2** (Wirtsch.) (Umwandlung in Anleihen) funding; (Vereinigung) consolidation

Konsonant /kɔnzoˈnant/ *der;* ~**en,** ~**en** consonant

konsonantisch (Sprachw.)

A *Adj.* consonantal

B *adv.* ‹*pronounce*› as a consonant

Konsorten /kɔnˈzɔrtn̩/ *Pl.* (abwertend) **Meier und ~:** Meier and his lot *or* crowd (coll.); Meier and Co. (coll.)

Konsortium /kɔnˈzɔrtsi̯ʊm/ *das;* ~**s, Konsortien** (Wirtsch.) consortium

Konspekt /kɔnˈspɛkt/ *der;* ~**[e]s,** ~**e** (DDR) synopsis; summary

Konspiration /kɔnspiraˈtsi̯oːn/ *die;* ~, ~**en** conspiracy

konspirativ /kɔnspiraˈtiːf/

A *Adj.* conspiratorial; **eine ~e Wohnung** a flat (esp. Brit.) *or* (esp. Amer.) an apartment used by persons engaged in subversive activities

B *adv.* **sich ~ zusammenschließen** form a conspiracy

konspirieren *itr. V.* conspire, plot (**gegen** against)

konstant /kɔnˈstant/

A *Adj.* **1** (gleich bleibend, ständig) constant; **eine ~e Größe** (Math.) a constant quantity; **eine ~e Leistung zeigen** maintain a constant standard **2** (beharrlich) consistent; persistent

B *adv.* **1** (gleich bleibend) constantly; **wir hatten ~ schlechtes Wetter** we had consistently bad weather **2** (beharrlich) consistently; persistently

Konstante *die;* ~**[n],** ~**n** (Math., Physik) constant; (fig.) constant factor (+ *Gen.* in)

Konstantin /ˈkɔnstantiːn/ (*der*) Constantine

Konstantinopel /kɔnstantiˈnoːpl̩/ (*das*); ~**s** (hist.) Constantinople

Konstanz /kɔnˈstants/ *die;* ~: constancy

konstatieren /kɔnstaˈtiːrən/ *tr. V.* **1** (feststellen) establish ‹*facts*›; (wahrnehmen) detect ‹*changes etc.*› **2** (erklären) state

Konstellation /kɔnstɛlaˈtsi̯oːn/ *die;* ~, ~**en** **1** (von Parteien usw.) grouping; (von Umständen) combination; **die gesamte ~:** the whole situation **2** (Astron., Astrol.) constellation

konsternieren /kɔnstɛrˈniːrən/ *tr. V.* **jmdn. ~:** fill sb. with consternation

konsterniert

A ▸ **konsternieren**

B *Adj.* filled with consternation *pred.*

C *adv.* with consternation; **sie blickte ihn ~ an** she looked at him in consternation

Konstituente /kɔnstiˈtu̯ɛntə/ *die;* ~, ~**n** (Sprachw.) constituent

konstituieren /kɔnstituˈiːrən/

A *tr. V.* (gründen) constitute; set up; (für etw. konstitutiv sein) constitute; **die ~de Versammlung** the constituent assembly

B *refl. V.* be constituted

Konstitution /kɔnstituˈtsi̯oːn/ *die;* ~, ~**en** (auch Politik, Chemie) constitution

konstitutionell /kɔnstitutsi̯oˈnɛl/ (Politik, Med.)

A *Adj.* constitutional

B *adv.* constitutionally

konstitutiv /kɔnstituˈtiːf/ *Adj.* (geh.) constitutive; **für etw. ~ sein** be a[n essential] constitutive element of sth.

konstruieren /kɔnstruˈiːrən/ *tr. V.* **1** (entwerfen) design; (entwerfen und zusammenbauen) design and construct **2** (aufbauen, Geom.) construct **3** (Sprachw.) construct; **dieses Verb wird mit dem Dativ konstruiert** this verb takes the dative *or* is construed with the dative **4** (abwertend: künstlich aufbauen) fabricate; **ein konstruierter Fall** a hypothetical *or* fictitious case; **die Handlung/seine Begründung wirkt sehr konstruiert** the plot seems/his reasons *pl.* seem very contrived

Konstrukteur /kɔnstrʊkˈtøːɐ̯/ *der;* ~**s,** ~**e, Konstrukteurin** *die;* ~, ~**nen** ▸ⓘ **S. 113** designer; design engineer

Konstruktion /kɔnstrʊkˈtsi̯oːn/ *die;* ~, ~**en** **1** (Aufbau, Geom., Sprachw.) construction; (das Entwerfen) designing; (das Entwerfen und Zusammenbauen) designing and construction **2** (Entwurf) design; (Bau) construction; structure

Konstruktions-: ~büro *das* drawing office; **~fehler** *der* design fault

konstruktiv /kɔnstrʊkˈtiːf/

A *Adj.* **1** constructive; **ein ~es Misstrauensvotum** (Parl.) a constructive vote of no confidence **2** (Technik) constructional

B *adv.* **1** constructively **2** (Technik) with regard to construction

Konstruktivismus *der;* ~ (bild. Kunst) constructivism *no art.*

Konsul /ˈkɔnzʊl/ *der;* ~**s,** ~**n** ▸ⓘ **S. 44,** ▸ⓘ **S. 113** (Dipl., hist.) consul

konsularisch *Adj.* (Dipl.) consular

Konsulat /kɔnzuˈlaːt/ *das;* ~**[e]s,** ~**e** (Dipl., hist.: Amt) consulate

Konsulin *die;* ~, ~**nen** ▸ **Konsul**

Konsultation /kɔnzʊltaˈtsi̯oːn/ *die;* ~, ~**en** consultation; **sich zu ~en treffen** meet for consultations

konsultieren *tr. V.* (auch fig.) consult

-konsum *der;* **-~s** ... consumption

Konsum[1] /kɔnˈzuːm/ *der;* ~**s** consumption (**an** + *Dat.* of); **der ~ von Alkohol steigt** alcohol consumption is on the increase

Konsum[2] /ˈkɔnzuːm/ *der;* ~**s,** ~**s** **1** (Genossenschaft) cooperative society **2** (Laden) cooperative shop *or* store; co-op (coll.)

Konsum·artikel *der* (Wirtsch.) consumer item *or* article; ~ *Pl.* consumer goods

Konsumation /kɔnzumaˈtsi̯oːn/ *die;* ~, ~**en** (österr., schweiz.) consumption

Konsument /kɔnzuˈmɛnt/ *der;* ~**en,** ~**en, Konsumentin** *die;* ~, ~**nen** consumer

Konsum-: ~freudig *Adj.* eager to consume *postpos.*; (kauflustig) eager to buy *postpos.*; **~genossenschaft** *die* (Wirtsch.) cooperative society; **~gesellschaft** *die* consumer society; **~gewohnheiten** *Pl.* (Wirtsch.) consumer habits

Konsum·gut *das* (Wirtsch.) ▸ **Konsumartikel**

Konsumgüter·industrie *die* (Wirtsch.) consumer goods industry

konsumierbar *Adj.* (verfügbar) available; (zugänglich) accessible (**für** to); **leicht/schnell ~:** readily available; (zugänglich) easily/readily accessible; **ein schwer ~er Film** a film that is not easily accessible

konsumieren *tr. V.* consume; (fig.) devour ‹*book*›

Konsum-: ~tempel *der* (abwertend) temple to consumerism; **~terror** *der* (abwertend) pressure to buy (*generated in a consumer society*); **~verzicht** *der* reduction in consumption; **~zwang** *der* pressure to buy (*generated in a consumer society*)

Kontakt /kɔnˈtakt/ *der;* ~**[e]s,** ~**e** **1** (auch fachspr.) contact; **mit** *od.* **zu jmdm. ~ haben/halten** be/remain in contact *or* touch with sb.; **mit jmdm. [keinen] ~ bekommen** [not] get to know sb.; **[den] ~ mit jmdm./etw. finden/suchen** establish/try to establish contact with sb./sth.; **er findet keinen ~ zu seinen Zuhörern** he cannot establish a rapport with his audience; **in ~ mit jmdm. stehen** be in contact *or* touch with sb.; **den ~ zu jmdm. abbrechen/verlieren** break off contact/lose contact *or* touch with sb.; **mit jmdm. ~ aufnehmen** get into contact with sb.; contact sb. **2** (Elektrot.) contact; **die Klingel hat/die Drähte haben keinen ~:** the bell is not connected up properly/the wires are not making contact

kontakt-, Kontakt-: ~abzug *der* (Fot.) contact print; **~anzeige** *die* contact advertisement; **~arm** *Adj.* **~arm sein** not make friends easily; find it difficult to make friends; **~aufnahme** *die:* **unsere erste ~aufnahme mit dieser Firma** our first approach to this firm; **~bereichs·beamte** *der* community policeman

kontakten

A *tr. V.* contact

B *itr. V.* make contacts

kontakt-, Kontakt-: ~fähig *Adj.* **ein ~fähiger Mensch** a good mixer; **ein ~fähiger Mitarbeiter** a colleague who is able to communicate easily with people; **~feder** *die* (Elektrot.) contact spring; **~freudig** *Adj.* sociable; **~freudig sein** make friends easily; **~hof** *der:* [*inner*] *courtyard of an eros centre etc. where prostitutes wait for clients*

kontaktieren *tr. V.* contact

kontakt-, Kontakt-: ~linse *die* contact lens; **~los** *Adj.* friendless; lonely; **~mangel** *der* lack of social contact; **~mann** *der; Pl.:* **~männer** *od.* **~leute** (Agent) contact; **~nahme** *die; ~~, ~~n* ▸ **~aufnahme**; **~person** *die* (Med.) contact; **~pflege** *die:* **~pflege betreiben** be sociable; mix socially; **~schale** *die* ▸ **~linse**; **~schwelle** *die* (Verkehrsw.) vehicle detector pad; **~schwierigkeiten** *Pl.* problems in mixing with others; **~sperre** *die* (Rechtsw.) ban on visits and letters; **~sperre über jmdn. verhängen** ban all sb.'s visits and letters; **~studium** *das* (Hochschulw.) *in-service study undertaken to keep up with the latest developments in one's field*

Kontamination /kɔntamina'tsi̯o:n/ *die; ~, ~en* **1** (bes. Med., Biol., Milit.) contamination **2** (Sprachw.) contamination; blending; (Wort) blend

kontaminieren *tr. V.* **1** (bes. Med., Biol., Milit.) contaminate **2** (Sprachw.) blend

Kontemplation /kɔntɛmpla'tsi̯o:n/ *die; ~, ~en* (geh.) contemplation

kontemplativ /kɔntɛmpla'ti:f/ (geh.)
A *Adj.* contemplative
B *adv.* contemplatively

Konten ▸ **Konto**

Kontenance ▸ **Contenance**

Konten·bewegung *die* (Bankw.) change in the state of the/an account

Konter /'kɔntɐ/ *der; ~s, ~* **1** (Boxen) counter **2** (Ballspiele) counter-attack

Konter-: ~admiral *der* (Marine) rear admiral; **~bande** *die* **1** (Völkerrecht) contraband [of war]; **2** (veralt.: Schmuggelware) contraband

Konterfei /'kɔntɐfai/ *das; ~s, ~s od. ~e* (veralt., noch scherzh.) likeness

konterfeien *tr. V.* (veralt., noch scherzh.) paint/draw a likeness of

kontern *tr., itr. V.* (Boxen) counter; (Ballspiele) counter-attack; (fig.) counter (**mit** with)

konter-, Konter-: ~part *der* counterpart; **~revolution** *die* counter-revolution; **~revolutionär** *Adj.* counter-revolutionary; **~revolutionär** *der,* **~revolutionärin** *die* counter-revolutionary; **~schlag** *der* (Boxen) counter; (Ballspiele, fig.) counter-attack

Kontext /kɔn'tɛkst/ *der; ~[e]s, ~e* (auch Sprachw.) context

Konti ▸ **Konto**

Kontinent /kɔnti'nɛnt/ *der; ~[e]s, ~e* continent

kontinental /kɔntinɛn'ta:l/ *Adj.* continental

Kontinental-: ~klima *das* (Geogr.) continental climate; **~sockel** *der* (Geogr.) continental shelf; **~sperre** *die* (hist.) Continental System; **~verschiebung** *die* (Geol.) continental drift

Kontingent /kɔntɪŋ'gɛnt/ *das; ~[e]s, ~e* **1** (Menge) quota; (fig.) contingent **2** (Truppen~) contingent

kontingentieren *tr. V.* (bes. Wirtsch.) limit by quotas; impose quotas on; (rationieren) ration

Kontingentierung *die; ~, ~en* (bes. Wirtsch.) imposition of quotas (*Gen.* on)

kontinuierlich /kɔntinu'i:ɐ̯lɪç/
A *Adj.* steady; continuous; **eine ~e Außenpolitik** a consistent foreign policy
B *adv.* steadily

Kontinuität /kɔntinui̯'tɛ:t/ *die; ~:* continuity

Kontinuum /kɔn'ti:nuʊm/ *das; ~s, Kontinua od. Kontinuen* continuum

Konto /'kɔnto/ *das; ~s, Konten od. Konti* account; **ein laufendes ~:** a current account; **die nächste Runde geht auf mein ~** (ugs.) the next round is on me (coll.); **etw. geht auf jmds. ~** (ugs.: jmd. ist schuld an etw.) sb. is to blame *or* is responsible for sth.

Konto-: ~aus·zug *der* (Bankw.) [bank] statement; statement of account; **~auszugs·drucker** *der* (Bankw.) statement machine *or* printer; **~buch** *das* (Buchf.) account book; **~führungsgebühr** *die* (Bankw.) bank charges *pl.*; **~inhaber** *der,* **~inhaberin** *die* (Bankw.) account holder; holder of an/the account; **~korrent** /-kɔ'rɛnt/ *das; ~~s, ~~e* **1** (Wirtsch.) open account; **2** (Buchf.) open accounting *no art.*; **~nummer** *die* account number

Kontor /kɔn'to:ɐ̯/ *das; ~s, ~e* **1** (Niederlassung) (eines Handelsunternehmens) branch; (einer Reederei) office **2** (DDR: Handelszentrale) wholesale organization **3** (veralt.: Büro) office; *s. auch* **Schlag 1**

Kontorist *der; ~en, ~en,* **Kontoristin** *die; ~, ~nen* [office] clerk; *s. auch* **-in**

Konto·stand *der* (Bankw.) balance; state of an/one's account

kontra /'kɔntra/
A *Präp. mit Akk.* (Rechtsspr., auch fig.) versus
B *Adv.* against; **ich bin dazu ~ eingestellt** I am against it

Kontra *das; ~s, ~s* (Kartenspiele) double; **~ sagen** *od.* **geben** double; **jmdm. ~ geben** (fig. ugs.) flatly contradict sb.

Kontra·bass, *Kontra·baß *der* (Musik) double bass

kontradiktorisch /kɔntradɪkˈto:rɪʃ/
A *Adj.* contradictory
B *adv.* in a contradictory way

Kontra·fagott *das* (Musik) double bassoon; contrabassoon

Kontrahent /kɔntra'hɛnt/ *der; ~en, ~en,* **Kontrahentin** *die; ~, ~nen* **1** (Gegner[in]) adversary; opponent **2** (Rechtsw., Kaufmannsspr.: Vertragspartner[in]) contracting party

kontrahieren
A *itr., refl. V.* (Biol., Med.) contract
B *tr. V.* **1** (Biol., Med.) contract **2** (Rechtsw., Kaufmannsspr.) **Erdgaslieferungen ~:** contract to supply natural gas

Kontrakt /kɔn'trakt/ *der; ~[e]s, ~e* contract

Kontraktion /kɔntrak'tsi̯o:n/ *die; ~, ~en* (Med., Sprachw.) contraction

kontraktlich
A *Adj.* contractual
B *adv.* contractually; by contract

Kontra·punkt *der* (Musik, fig.) counterpoint

kontrapunktisch (Musik, fig.)
A *Adj.* contrapuntal
B *adv.* contrapuntally

konträr /kɔn'trɛ:ɐ̯/
A contrary; opposite
B *adv.* **zwei so ~ gesinnte Politiker** two politicians with such opposing views; **sich ~ entwickeln** develop in contrary *or* opposite ways

Kontrast /kɔn'trast/ *der; ~[e]s, ~e* (auch Fot., Film, Fernsehen) contrast; **etw. steht im/in ~ zu etw. anderem** sth. is in contrast with sth. else

Kontrast-: ~brei *der* (Med.) opaque *or* test meal; **~farbe** *die* contrasting colour; **~filter** *der* (Fot.) contrast filter

kontrastieren *tr., itr. V.* contrast

kontrastiv /kɔntras'ti:f/ *Adj.* (Sprachw.) constrastive

kontrast-, Kontrast-: ~mittel *das* (Med.) contrast medium; **~programm** *das* (Rundf., Fernsehen) alternative programme; **~reich** *Adj.* rich in *or* full of contrasts *pred.*; richly varied

Kontrazeptivum /kɔntratsɛp'ti:vʊm/ *das; ~s,* **Kontrazeptiva** (Med.) contraceptive

Kontribution /kɔntribu'tsi̯o:n/ *die; ~, ~en* (hist.) contribution

Kontroll·abschnitt *der* stub

***Kontrollampe** ▸ **Kontrolllampe**

Kontroll-: ~anruf *der* check-up call (+ *Gen.* from); **~apparat** *der* supervisory apparatus; (Polizei, Geheimdienst o. Ä.) surveillance and control apparatus; **~beamte** *der,* **~beamtin** *die* inspector; (an der Pass-/Zollkontrolle) passport/customs officer; **~behörde** *die* monitoring authority

Kontrolle /kɔn'trɔlə/ *die; ~, ~n* **1** (Überwachung) surveillance; **unter ~ stehen** be under surveillance; **der ~ durch das Parlament unterliegen** be under the scrutiny of Parliament; **eine gegenseitige ~ ausüben** keep a check on each other **2** (Überprüfung) check; (bei Waren) check; inspection; (bei Lebensmitteln) inspection; **~n durchführen** carry out checks/inspections; **jmdn./etw. einer ~ unterziehen** check sb./sth.; **Anwärter auf eine Stelle einer ~ unterziehen** screen candidates for a post; **in eine ~ kommen** be stopped at a police check; **zur ~:** as a check **3** (Herrschaft) control; **die ~ über etw.** (*Akk.*) **verlieren** lose control of sth.; **die ~ über sich** (*Akk.*) **verlieren** lose control of oneself; **außer ~ geraten** get out of control; **etw. unter ~** (*Akk.*) **bringen/halten** get *or* bring/keep sth. under control **4** (~punkt) checkpoint; (an der Pass~/Zoll~) passport control/customs

Kontrolleur /kɔntrɔ'lø:ɐ̯/ *der; ~s, ~e,* **Kontrolleurin** *die; ~, ~nen* inspector

Kontroll-: ~funktion *die* monitoring function; **~gang** *der* tour of inspection; (eines Nachtwächters) round; (eines Polizisten) patrol; **~gruppe** *die* (Med., Psych., Soziol.) control group

kontrollierbar *Adj.* ‹*authority, body, decision, etc.*› that is open to scrutiny; ‹*statement, statistic, etc.*› that is verifiable *or* checkable; demonstrable ‹*progress*›

kontrollieren
A *tr. V.* **1** (überwachen) check; monitor; **die Regierung ~:** scrutinize the actions of the government; **die Lebensmittelproduktion wird streng kontrolliert** strict checks are kept *or* made on the production of food **2** (überprüfen) check; check, inspect ‹*goods*›; inspect ‹*food*›; **jmdn. auf etw.** (*Akk.*) **[hin] ~:** check sb. for sth.; **etw. auf etw.** (*Akk.*) **[hin] ~:** check/inspect sth. for sth. **3** (beherrschen) control
B *itr. V.* carry out a check/checks

***Kontrolliste** ▸ **Kontrollliste**

Kontroll-: ~lampe *die* pilot light; indicator light; (Warnleuchte) warning light; **~liste** *die* checklist; **~organ** *das* monitoring body; **~punkt** *der* checkpoint; (bei einer Rallye) control [point]; **~rat** *der:* **Alliierter ~rat** Allied Control Commission; **~raum** *der* control room; **~stempel** *der* (auf Waren, Lebensmitteln) inspection stamp; (bei einer Rallye) control stamp; **~turm** *der* control tower; **~uhr** *die* time clock; (für Wächter) telltale clock

kontrovers /kɔntro'vɛrs/
A *Adj.* conflicting; (strittig) controversial
B *adv.* **sich ~ zu etw. äußern** express conflicting opinions on sth.; **etw. ~ schildern** give conflicting accounts of sth.

Kontroverse *die; ~, ~n* controversy (**um, über** + *Akk.* about)

Kontur /kɔn'tu:ɐ̯/ *die; ~, ~en* contour; outline; **~ gewinnen/an ~ verlieren** (fig.) become clearer/fade

Konturen·stift *der* lip pencil

konturieren *tr. V.* (auch fig.) outline

Konus /'ko:nʊs/ *der; ~, ~se od.* **Konen** (Math., Technik) cone

Konvektor /kɔn'vɛktɔr/ *der; ~s, ~en* /-'to:rən/ convector [heater]

konvenieren /kɔnve'ni:rən/ *itr. V.* (österr.) **jmdm. ~:** be convenient for sb.; suit sb.

Konvent /kɔn'vɛnt/ *der; ~es, ~e* **1** (kath. Kirche) (von Nonnen) convent; (von Mönchen) monastery **2** (Hochschulw.) *qualified academic staff of a university*

Konvention /kɔnvɛn'tsi̯o:n/ *die; ~, ~en* (Verhaltensnorm, Völkerr.) convention

Konventional·strafe *die* (Rechtsw.) liquidated damages *pl.*

konventionell
A *Adj.* **1** (herkömmlich) conventional; **~e Waffen** (Milit.) conventional weapons **2** (förmlich) formal
B *adv.* **1** (herkömmlich, Milit.) conventionally; in a conventional way **2** (förmlich) formally; **hier geht es sehr ~ zu** things are very formal here

konvergent /kɔnvɛr'gɛnt/ (geh., Math.)
A *Adj.* convergent
B *adv.* convergently

Konvergenz /kɔnvɛr'gɛnts/ *die; ~, ~en* (geh., Math., EU) convergence

Konvergenz-: ~kriterium *das* (EU) convergence criterion; **~theorie** *die* (Politik) theory of convergence

konvergieren *tr. V.* (geh., Math.) converge

Konversation /kɔnvɛrza'tsi̯o:n/ *die;* **~, ~en** conversation; **~ in Französisch treiben** hold a conversation in French; **~ machen** make conversation

Konversations·lexikon *das* encyclopedia

Konversion *die;* **~, ~en** (Kirche, Sprachw., Psych., Kerntechnik, Börsenw.) conversion

Konverter /kɔn'vɛrtɐ/ *der;* **~s, ~** 1▸ (Hüttenw., Rundfunk) converter 2▸ (Fot.) converter [lens]

konvertibel /kɔnvɛr'ti:bl̩/, **konvertierbar** *Adj.* (Wirtsch.) convertible

Konvertierbarkeit *die;* **~** (Wirtsch.) convertibility

konvertieren
A *itr. V.; auch mit sein* (Rel.) be converted
B *tr. V.* 1▸ (Wirtsch.) convert; **sein Geld in Franken ~:** convert one's money into francs 2▸ (DV) convert

Konvertit /kɔnvɛr'ti:t/ *der;* **~en, ~en, Konvertitin** *die;* **~, ~nen** convert

konvex /kɔn'vɛks/ (Optik)
A *Adj.* convex
B *adv.* convexly

Konvex·spiegel *der* (Optik) convex mirror

Konvikt /kɔn'vɪkt/ *das;* **~[e]s, ~e** 1▸ (Stift) seminary; (Wohnheim) hall of residence (*for theology students*) 2▸ (österr.: kath. Internat) [Roman Catholic] boarding school

Konvoi /kɔn'vo̯y/ *der;* **~s, ~s** (bes. Milit.) convoy; **im ~ fahren** travel in convoy

Konvolut /kɔnvo'lu:t/ *das;* **~[e]s, ~e** bundle (*of letters, papers, etc.*)

Konvulsion /kɔnvʊl'zi̯o:n/ *die;* **~, ~en** (Med.) convulsion

konvulsiv /kɔnvʊl'zi:f/, **konvulsivisch** (Med.)
A *Adj.* convulsive
B *adv.* convulsively

konzedieren /kɔntse'di:rən/ *tr. V.* (geh.) concede; **jmdm. etw. ~:** concede sb. sth.

Konzentrat /kɔntsɛn'tra:t/ *das;* **~[e]s, ~e** (bes. Chemie) concentrate; **ein ~ seiner früheren Werke** (fig.) a collection of his most important writings, chosen from his earlier works

Konzentration /kɔntsɛntra'tsi̯o:n/ *die;* **~, ~en** (auch Chemie) concentration

Konzentrations-: ~fähigkeit *die* ability to concentrate; powers *pl.* of concentration; **~lager** *das* (bes. ns.) concentration camp; **~mangel** *der* (Med., Psych.) lack of concentration; **~schwäche** *die* (Med., Psych.) poor powers *pl.* of concentration

konzentrieren
A *refl. V.* 1▸ concentrate; **sich auf etw.** (*Akk.*) **~:** concentrate on sth. 2▸ (richten) be concentrated
B *tr. V.* concentrate; **seine Gedanken auf etw.** (*Akk.*) **~:** concentrate one's thoughts on sth.

konzentriert
A ▸**konzentrieren**
B *Adj.* (auch Chemie) concentrated
C *adv.* with concentration; **sehr ~ arbeiten** work with great concentration

konzentrisch (Math., fig.)
A *Adj.* concentric
B *adv.* concentrically

Konzept /kɔn'tsɛpt/ *das;* **~[e]s, ~e** 1▸ (Rohfassung) [rough] draft; **es ist im ~ fertig** the [rough] draft is finished; **aus dem ~ kommen** *od.* **geraten** lose one's thread; **jmdn. aus dem ~ bringen** put sb. off his/her stroke 2▸ (Programm) programme; (Plan) plan; **jmdm. das ~ verderben** (ugs.) ruin sb.'s plans; **jmdm. nicht ins ~ passen** (ugs.) not suit sb.'s plans

Konzeption /kɔntsɛp'tsi̯o:n/ *die;* **~, ~en** 1▸ central idea; (Entwurf) conception 2▸ (Med.) conception

konzeptionslos
A *Adj.* haphazard
B *adv.* haphazardly; with no clear plan

Konzeptionslosigkeit *die;* **~:** haphazardness; lack of any clear plan

Konzept-: ~kunst *die* conceptual art; **~papier** *das* rough paper

-konzern *der;* **~~[e]s, ~~e** ... group

Konzern /kɔn'tsɛrn/ *der;* **~[e]s, ~e** (Wirtsch.) group [of companies]

Konzert /kɔn'tsɛrt/ *das;* **~[e]s, ~e** 1▸ (Komposition) concerto 2▸ (Veranstaltung) concert; **ins ~ gehen** go to a concert 3▸ (geh.: Zusammenspiel) concert

Konzert-: ~abend *der* concert evening; **~agentur** *die* concert artists' agency

konzertant /kɔntsɛr'tant/ *Adj.* (Musik) concert ‹*performance etc.*›; **~e Sinfonie** [sinfonia] concertante

Konzert-: ~direktion *die* concert promotion agency; **~flügel** *der* concert grand; **~führer** *der* concert guide

konzertieren *itr. V.* (geh.) give a concert

konzertiert
A ▸**konzertieren**
B *Adj.* concerted; **die ~e Aktion** concerted action

Konzertina /kɔntsɛr'ti:na/ *die;* **~, ~s** concertina

Konzert-: ~meister *der,* **~meisterin** *die* ▸❶ **S. 113** leader [of a/the orchestra]; concertmaster (esp. Amer.); **~pavillon** *der* bandstand; **~pianist** *der,* **~pianistin** *die* ▸❶ **S. 113** concert pianist; **~reise** *die* concert tour; **~saal** *der* concert hall; **~sänger** *der,* **~sängerin** *die* concert singer

Konzession /kɔntse'si̯o:n/ *die;* **~, ~en** 1▸ (Amtsspr.) licence 2▸ (Zugeständnis) concession; **~en [an jmdn./etw.] machen** make concessions [to sb./sth.]

Konzessionär /kɔntsesi̯o'nɛ:ɐ̯/ *der;* **~s, ~e, Konzessionärin** *die;* **~, ~nen** (Amtsspr.) licensee

konzessions·bereit *Adj.* ready *or* willing or prepared to make concessions *pred.*

konzessiv /kɔntse'si:f/ *Adj.* (Sprachw.) concessive

Konzessiv·satz *der* (Sprachw.) concessive clause

Konzil /kɔn'tsi:l/ *das;* **~s, ~e** *od.* **~ien** 1▸ (kath. Kirche) council 2▸ (Hochschulw.) ≈ senate

konziliant /kɔntsi'li̯ant/ (geh.)
A *Adj.* accommodating; obliging
B *adv.* accommodatingly; obligingly

Konzilianz /kɔntsi'li̯ants/ *die;* **~** (geh.) obligingness

konzipieren /kɔntsi'pi:rən/
A *tr. V.* draft ‹*speech, essay*›; draw up, draft ‹*plan, policy, etc.*›; design ‹*device, car, etc.*›
B *itr. V.* (Med.) conceive

konzis /kɔn'tsi:s/
A *Adj.* concise
B *adv.* concisely

Koog /ko:k/ *der;* **~[e]s, Köge** /'kø:gə/ (niederd.) polder

Kooperation *die;* **~, ~en** cooperation *no indef. art.*

kooperations·bereit *Adj.* ready *or* willing *or* prepared to cooperate *pred.*

kooperativ
A *Adj.* cooperative
B *adv.* cooperatively

Kooperativ *das;* **~s, ~e, Kooperative** *die;* **~e, ~en** cooperative

kooperieren *tr. V.* cooperate

Koordinate *die;* **~, ~n** 1▸ (Geogr.) coordinate 2▸ (Math.) coordinate

Koordinaten-: ~achse *die* (Math.) coordinate axis; **~kreuz** *das* (Math.) coordinate axes *pl.*; **~system** *das* (Math.) system of coordinates

Koordination *die;* **~, ~en** coordination

Koordinations·störung *die* (Med.) impaired coordination *no indef. art., no pl.*

Koordinator /ko|ɔrdi'na:tɔr/ *der;* **~s, ~en** /-'to:rən/, **Koordinatorin** *die;* **~, ~nen** coordinator

koordinieren *tr. V.* coordinate

Koordinierung *die;* **~, ~en** coordination

Kopeke /ko'pe:kə/ *die;* **~, ~n** copeck

Kopenhagen /ko:pn̩'ha:gn̩/ (*das*); **~s** ▸❶ **S. 675** Copenhagen

Köpenickiade /kø:pənɪ'ki̯a:də/ *die;* **~, ~n** hoax (involving impersonation of a uniformed official or military officer)

Köper /'kø:pɐ/ *der;* **~s, ~:** twill

kopernikanisch /kopɛrni'ka:nɪʃ/ *Adj.* Copernican

Kopernikus /ko'pɛrnikʊs/ (*der*) Copernicus

Kopf /kɔpf/ *der;* **~[e]s, Köpfe** /'kœpfə/ 1▸ ▸❶ **S. 435** head; **jmdm. den ~ waschen** wash sb.'s hair; (fig. ugs.: jmdn. zurechtweisen) give sb. a good talking-to (coll.); give sb. what for (coll.); **[um] einen ganzen/halben ~ größer sein** be a good head/a few inches taller; **die Köpfe zusammenstecken** go into a huddle; **sie haben sich die Köpfe heiß geredet** the conversation/debate became heated; **~ an ~** (dicht gedrängt) shoulder to shoulder; (im Wettlauf) neck and neck; **~ weg!** (ugs.) mind your head!; **den ~ einziehen** duck; (fig.: sich einschüchtern lassen) be intimidated; **und wenn du dich auf den ~ stellst** you can talk until you're blue in the face; **~ ab!** off with his head!; **ich werde/er wird dir nicht gleich den ~ abreißen** (ugs.) I'm/he's not going to bite your head off; **auf dem ~ stehen** (Kopfstand machen) stand on one's head; (ugs.: umgedreht sein) be upside down; **~ stehen** (Kopfstand machen) stand on one's head; (ugs.: überrascht sein) be bowled over; (fig.) **auf seinen ~ ist eine Belohnung ausgesetzt** there is a price on his head; **jmdm. schwirrt/** (ugs.) **raucht der ~:** sb.'s head is spinning; **nicht wissen, wo einem der ~ steht** not know whether one is coming or going; **einen dicken** *od.* **schweren ~ haben** have a headache; (vom Alkohol) have a thick head (coll.) *or* a hangover; **jmdm.** *od.* **jmdn. den ~ kosten** cost sb. dearly; (jmdn. das Leben kosten) cost sb. his/her life; **~ hoch!** chin up!; **den ~ hängen lassen** become disheartened; **~ und Kragen riskieren** risk one's neck; **den ~ hinhalten [müssen]** (ugs.) [have to] face the music; [have to] take the blame *or* (coll.) rap; **sich** (*Dat.*) **[an etw.** (*Dat.*)**] den ~ einrennen** beat *or* run one's head against a brick wall [with sth.]; **den ~ aus der Schlinge ziehen** avoid any adverse consequences *or* (sl.) the rap; **den ~ in den Sand stecken** bury one's head in the sand; **den ~ hoch tragen** hold one's head high; **es gibt keinen Grund dafür, dass er den ~ so hoch trägt** (überheblich ist) there is no reason for him to act so superior; **jmdm. den ~ zurechtrücken** (ugs.) bring sb. to his/her senses; **sich [gegenseitig]** *od.* **einander die Köpfe einschlagen** be at each other's throats; **jmdn. [um] einen ~ kürzer** *od.* **kleiner machen** (ugs.) chop sb.'s head off; **sich** (*Dat.*) **an den ~ fassen** *od.* **greifen** (ugs.) throw up one's hands in despair; **jmdm. Beleidigungen an den ~ werfen** hurl insults at sb.; **sein Geld auf den ~ hauen** (ugs.) blow one's money (coll.); **etw. auf den ~ stellen** (ugs.) turn sth. upside down; **die Tatsachen/den Ablauf der Ereignisse auf den ~ stellen** get the facts/the order of events completely *or* entirely wrong; **jmdm. auf dem ~ herumtanzen** (ugs.) treat sb. just as one likes; do what one likes with sb.; **sich** (*Dat.*) **nicht auf den ~ spucken lassen** (salopp) not let people walk all over one (coll.); **jmdm. auf den ~ spucken können** (salopp scherzh.) be head and shoulders taller than sb.; **er ist nicht auf den ~ gefallen** (ugs.) there are no flies on him (coll.); **jmdm. etw. auf den ~ zusagen** say sth. to sb.'s face; **das hältst du im ~ nicht aus!** (ugs.) he/she/it really is the limit! (coll.); **jmdm. in den** *od.* **zu ~ steigen** go to sb.'s head; **mit dem ~ durch die Wand wollen** (ugs.) beat *or* run one's head against a brick wall; **etw. über jmds. ~ [hin]weg entscheiden** decide sth. over sb.'s head; **über die Köpfe der Zuhörer** *usw.* **hinwegreden** talk over the heads of the audience *etc.*; **jmdm.**

über den ~ wachsen (ugs.) outgrow sb.; (überfordern) become too much for sb.; **bis über den ~ in etw. stecken** (ugs.) be up to one's ears in sth.; **es geht um ~ und Kragen** (ugs.) it's a matter of life and death; **sich um ~ und Kragen reden** (ugs.) risk one's neck with careless talk; (sich belasten) incriminate oneself as soon as one opens one's mouth; **von ~ bis Fuß** from head to toe *or* foot; **jmdn. vor den ~ stoßen** (ugs.) offend sb.; **wie vor den ~ geschlagen sein** (ugs.) be stunned; *s. auch* **Hand 6**

2 (Person) person; **ein kluger/fähiger ~ sein** be a clever/able man/woman; **pro ~:** per head *or* person; **eine Familie mit acht Köpfen** a family of eight

3 (geistige Leitung) **er ist der ~ der Firma** he's the brains of the firm; **die führenden Köpfe der Wirtschaft** the leading minds in the field of economics

4 (Wille) **seinen ~ durchsetzen** make sb. do what one wants; **einen dicken ~ haben** have a mind of one's own; **muss es immer nach deinem ~ gehen?** why must 'you always decide?

5 (Verstand) mind; head; **hast du noch im ~, wie ...?** can you still remember how ...?; **er hat die Zahlen im ~** (ugs.) he has the figures in his head; **er hat nur Autos im ~** (ugs.) all he ever thinks about is cars; **was wohl in ihrem ~ vorgeht?** what's going on in her mind?; **sie ist nicht ganz richtig im ~** (ugs.) she's not quite right in the head; **einen klaren/kühlen ~ bewahren** *od.* **behalten** keep a cool head; keep one's head; **ich habe den ~ voll mit anderen Dingen** I've got a lot of other things on my mind; **den ~ verlieren** lose one's head; **jmdm. den ~ verdrehen** (ugs.) steal sb.'s heart [away]; **sich** (*Dat.*) **den ~ zerbrechen** (ugs.) rack one's brains (**über** + *Akk.* over); (sich Sorgen machen) worry (**über** + *Akk.* about); **aus dem ~:** off the top of one's head; **das geht** *od.* **will ihm nicht aus dem ~:** he can't get it out of his mind; **sich** (*Dat.*) **etw. aus dem ~ schlagen** put sth. out of one's head; **sich** (*Dat.*) **etw. durch den ~ gehen lassen** think sth. over; **der Gedanke geht mir gerade durch den ~:** it just occurs to me; **jmdm. [plötzlich] durch den ~ schießen** [suddenly] occur to sb.; **jmdm. im ~ herumgehen** (ugs.) go round and round in sb.'s mind; **jmdm./sich etw. in den ~ setzen** put sth. into sb.'s head/get sth. into one's head; **etw. im ~ [aus]rechnen** work sth. out in one's head; **was man nicht im ~ hat, muss man in den Beinen haben** a short memory makes work for the legs; **jmdm. geht** *od.* **will etw. nicht in den ~ [hinein]** (ugs.) sb. can't get sth. into his/her head

6 (von Nadeln, Nägeln, Blumen) head; (von Pfeifen) bowl

7 **ein ~ Salat/Blumenkohl/Rotkohl** a lettuce/cauliflower/red cabbage

8 (oberer Teil) (eines Briefes, einer Tafel) head; (einer Zeitung) heading; head

9 (auf Münzen) **~ [oder Zahl?]** heads [or tails?]

kopf-, Kopf-: ~-an-~-Rennen *das* (Sport, auch fig.) neck-and-neck race (+ *Gen.* between); **~arbeit** *die* brainwork; intellectual work; **~arbeiter** *der,* **~arbeiterin** *die* brainworker; **~bahn·hof** *der* terminal station; **~ball** *der* (Fußball) header; **durch ~ball** with a header; **~ball·spiel** *das* (Fußball) heading; **~ball·stark** *Adj.* (Fußball) good at heading *pred.*; **der einzige ~ballstarke Spieler** the only good header of the ball; **~ball·tor** *das* (Fußball) headed goal; **ein ~balltor von Fischer** a goal headed by Fischer; **~bedeckung** *die* headgear; **ohne ~bedeckung** without anything on one's head; without a hat

Köpfchen /ˈkœpfçən/ *das;* **~s, ~** 1 little head 2 (Findigkeit) brains *pl.*; **~ muss man haben** you've got to have it up here (coll.); **~ haben** have brains *pl.*; **~, ~!** clever, eh? (coll.)

köpfeln /ˈkœpfl̩n/ (südd., österr., schweiz.)
A *tr. V.:* ▸ **köpfen 2**
B *itr. V.* dive head first

köpfen /ˈkœpfn̩/ *tr. V.* 1 decapitate; (hinrichten) behead; (fig.) break *or* crack open ‹*bottle*›; slice the top off ‹*egg*› 2 (Fußball) head; **das 2:0 ~:** head [in] the goal to make it 2-0

Kopf-: ~ende *das* head end; **~form** *die* head shape; shape of the head; **~freiheit** *die* headroom; **~füßer** *der;* **~~s, ~~** (Zool.) cephalopod; **~geld** *das* reward; bounty; **~grippe** *die* (volkst.) headachy cold; **~haar** *das* hair on the head; **~haltung** *die:* **die/eine ~haltung** the way one holds one's head; **~haut** *die* ▸ ❶ **S. 435** [skin of the] scalp; **~höhe** *die:* **in ~höhe** at head height; **~hörer** *der* headphones *pl.*

-köpfig *Adj.* -headed; **drei~/fünf~:** three-headed/five-headed ‹*monster*›; **eine dreiköpfige/fünfköpfige Familie** a family of three/five

kopf-, Kopf-: ~jäger *der,* **~jägerin** *die* headhunter; **~kissen** *das* pillow; **~kissen·bezug** *der* pillow case; **~lage** *die* (Med.) cephalic *or* head presentation; **~länge** *die* head; **mit einer ~länge Vorsprung** by a head; **~lastig** *Adj.* down by the head *pred.*; nose-heavy ‹*aircraft*›; (fig.) top-heavy; **~laus** *die* head louse; **~los** A *Adj.* 1 rash; (in Panik) panic-stricken; **seine ~lose Flucht** his headlong *or* panic-stricken flight; 2 (ohne ~) headless; B *adv.* rashly; **~los davonrennen/umherrennen** flee in panic/run round in a panic; **~losigkeit** *die;* **~~:** rashness; (Panik) panic; **~nicken** *das;* **~~s** nod [of the head]; **durch ~nicken** by nodding [one's head]; **~nuss,** ***~nuß** *die* (ugs.) rap on the head with one's *or* the knuckles; **~rechnen** *itr. V.; nur im Inf. gebr.* do mental arithmetic; **gut ~rechnen können** be good at mental arithmetic; **~rechnen** *das* mental arithmetic; **~salat** *der* cabbage *or* head lettuce; **~scheu** *Adj.* in **jmdn. ~scheu machen** (ugs.) unnerve sb.; **~scheu werden** lose one's nerve; **~schmerz** *der* ▸ ❶ **S. 439** headache; **~schmerzen haben** have a headache *sing.*; **sich** (*Dat.*) **über etw.** (*Akk.*) *od.* **wegen etw. keine ~schmerzen machen** (ugs.) not worry about *or* concern oneself about sth.; **etw. bereitet** *od.* **macht jmdm. ~schmerzen** (ugs.) sth. weighs on sb.'s mind; **~schmerz·tablette** *die* headache pill; **~schmuck** *der* headdress; **~schuppe** *die* flake of dandruff; **~schuppen** dandruff; **~schuss,** ***~schuß** *der* bullet wound in the head; **er wurde durch einen ~schuss getötet** he was killed by a bullet in the head; **~schütteln** *das;* **~~s** shake of the head; **ein allgemeines ~schütteln auslösen** cause everyone to shake their heads; **durch ~schütteln** by shaking one's head; **nicht ohne ~schütteln** not without some head-shaking; **~schüttelnd** *Adj.* **sich ~schüttelnd abwenden** turn away, shaking one's head; **~schutz** *der* (Sport) protective headgear; **~sprung** *der* header; **einen ~sprung machen** dive head first; **~stand** *der* headstand; ***~|stehen** ▸ **Kopf 1**; **~stein·pflaster** *das* cobblestones *pl.*; **~steuer** *die* (hist.) poll tax; **~stimme** *die* head voice; (Falsett) falsetto [voice]; **~stoß** *der* 1 (Fußball) header; 2 (Boxen) butt; **~stück** *das* (Kochk.) head end; **~stütze** *die* headrest; **~tuch** *das; Pl.* **~tücher** headscarf; **~über** /-ˈ-ˈ-/ *Adv.* head first; (fig.) (voller Tatendrang) with a will; (ohne Zögern) headlong; **~verband** *der* head bandage; **~verletzung** *die* head injury; **~wäsche** *die* 1 hair wash; shampoo; 2 (fig. ugs.) dressing down; **~weh** *das* (ugs.) headache; **~weh haben** have a headache; **~weide** *die* pollarded willow; **~zerbrechen** *das;* **~~s: etw. bereitet** *od.* **macht jmdm. ~zerbrechen** sb. has to rack his/her brains about sth.; (etw. macht jmdm. Sorgen) sth. is a worry to sb.; **sich** (*Dat.*) **über etw.** (*Akk.*) **[kein] ~zerbrechen machen** [not] worry about sth.

Kopie /koˈpiː/ *die;* **~, ~n** 1 copy; (Durchschrift) carbon copy; (Fotokopie) photocopy 2 (Fot., Film) print 3 (Nachbildung) copy 4 (Abklatsch) (Werk) pastiche; (Person) likeness

Kopier·anstalt *die* (Fot.) [photographic] processing laboratory

kopieren *tr. V.* 1 copy; (foto~) photocopy; **etw. mit Blaupapier ~:** take a carbon copy of sth. 2 (Fot., Film) print 3 (nachbilden) copy; (imitieren) imitate

Kopierer *der;* **~s, ~:** [photo]copier

kopier-, Kopier-: ~gerät *das* photocopier; photocopying machine; **~geschützt** *Adj* (DV) copy-protected; **~papier** *das* 1 (Fot.) printing paper; 2 (zum Fotokopieren) photocopying paper; **~schutz** *der* (DV) copy protection; **~stift** *der* indelible pencil

Kopilot *der;* **~en, ~en, Kopilotin** *die;* **~, ~nen** (Flugw.) co-pilot; (Motorsport) co-driver

Kopist *der;* **~en, ~en, Kopistin** *die;* **~, ~nen** 1 (Kunst) copier; copyist 2 (Vervielfältiger[in]) photocopying-machine operator; photocopier; (Fot.) [darkroom] printer

Koppel[1] /ˈkɔpl̩/ *das;* **~s, ~,** *österr.: die;* **~, ~n** (Gürtel) [leather] belt (*as part of a uniform*)

Koppel[2] *die;* **~, ~n** 1 (Weide) paddock; **auf** *od.* **in der ~:** in the paddock 2 (Hunde~) pack; (Pferde~) string 3 (Musik) coupler

koppeln *tr. V.* 1 (aneinander binden) string together ‹*horses*›; leash together ‹*dogs*›; couple ‹*hounds*› 2 (aneinander hängen) dock ‹*spacecraft*›; couple [up] ‹*railway carriage, trailers, etc.*› (**an** + *Akk.* to) 3 (verbinden) link; couple ‹*circuits, systems, etc.*›; **etw. an etw.** (*Dat.*) **~:** link sth. to sth.; **mit etw. gekoppelt sein** be associated with sth. 4 (Sprachw.) link

Koppel-: ~rick *das;* **~~s, ~~e** 1 (Zaun) paddock fence; 2 (Hindernis) post and rails; **~schloss,** ***~schloß** *das* belt buckle (*as part of a uniform*)

Koppelung ▸ **Kopplung**

Köpper /ˈkœpɐ/ *der;* **~s, ~** (ugs.) header

kopphelster /kɔpˈhaistɐ/ *Adv.* (nordd.) ▸ **kopfüber**

Kopplung *die;* **~, ~en** 1 (Raumf.) docking; (von Eisenbahnwagen, Anhängern usw.) coupling [up] 2 (Verbindung) linking; (von Schaltungen, Systemen) coupling 3 (Sprachw.) linking

Kopplungs-: ~geschäft *das* (Wirtsch.) package deal; tie-in deal (Amer.); **~manöver** *das* (Raumf.) docking manoeuvre

Kopra /ˈkoːpra/ *die;* **~:** copra

Koproduktion *die;* **~, ~en** co-production; joint production

Koproduzent *der;* **~en, ~en, Koproduzentin** *die;* **~, ~nen** co-producer

Kopte /ˈkɔptə/ *der;* **~n, ~n** Copt

Koptin *die;* **~, ~nen** ▸ **Kopte**

koptisch *Adj.* Coptic

Kopula /ˈkoːpula/ *die;* **~, ~s** *od.* **Kopulae** /ˈkoːpulɛ/ (Sprachw.) copula

Kopulation /kopulaˈtsi̯oːn/ *die;* **~, ~en** 1 (Biol.) copulation 2 (Gartenbau) splice graft

kopulativ /kopulaˈtiːf/ *Adj.* (Sprachw.) copulative

Kopulativum /kopulaˈtiːvʊm/ *das;* **~s, Kopulativa** (Sprachw.) copulative conjunction; copulative

kopulieren
A *itr. V.* copulate
B *tr. V.* (Gartenbau) splice-graft

kor /koːɐ̯/ ▸ **küren; kiesen**

Koralle /koˈralə/ *die;* **~, ~n** coral

korallen-, Korallen-: ~bank *die; Pl.* **~bänke** coral reef; **~bäumchen** *das* (Bot.) Jerusalem cherry; **~fischer** *der* coral fisherman; **~insel** *die* coral island; **~riff** *das* coral reef; **~rot** *Adj.* coral-red; **~schmuck** *der* coral jewellery

Koran /koˈraːn/ *der;* **~s, ~e** Koran

Koran·schule *die* Koranic school

Korb /kɔrp/ *der;* **~es, Körbe** /ˈkœrbə/ 1 basket; (für ein Baby) wicker cradle; (Last~ auf einem Tier) pannier; (Bienen~) hive; (Förder~) cage; **ein ~ Kartoffeln** a basket[ful] of potatoes 2 (Gondel) basket 3 (~ball) net; (Basketball) basket; (Treffer) goal 4 (Flechtwerk) wicker[work] 5 (Ablehnung) **jmdm. einen ~ geben** turn sb. down; **einen ~ bekommen, sich** (*Dat.*) **einen ~ holen** be turned down

Korb-: ~ball *der* netball; **~blütler** *der;* **~~s, ~~** (Bot.) composite flower; composite

ℹ Körperteile

Im Englischen verwendet man ein Possessivum (**my, his, your** usw.) für Körperteile viel häufiger, auch zum Beispiel für die, die zum Subjekt des Satzes gehören:

Er hob die Hand
= He raised his hand

Sie schloss die Augen
= She closed her eyes

Ebenso in Fällen, wo man im Deutschen einen Dativ der Person (auch ein Reflexivum), gefolgt von einem Akkusativobjekt, verwendet:

Sie schloss ihm die Augen
= She closed his eyes

Du hast ihm fast den Arm ausgerenkt
= You nearly dislocated his arm

Kannst du mir den Rücken eincremen?
= Can you put some cream on my back [for me]?

Ich habe mir das Bein gebrochen
= I've broken my leg

Er hat sich den Arm ausgerenkt
= He dislocated his arm

Sie hat sich den Kopf am Balken angestoßen
= She hit her head on the beam

Sie fuhr mir/sich mit der Hand über die Stirn
= She passed her hand over my/her forehead

Verwendet man diese Konstruktion mit einem Substantiv statt dem Personalpronomen im Dativ, so hat man im Englischen einen entsprechenden Genitiv:

Sie massierte ihrem Sohn den Rücken
= She massaged her son's back

Die deutsche unpersönliche Konstruktion hat keine direkte Entsprechung im Englischen. Auch hier verwendet man ein Possessivum:

Mir dreht sich der Kopf
= My head is spinning

Es kribbelte mir in den Füßen
= My feet were tingling

Siehe auch ◻ **Krankheiten und Schmerzen**

Körbchen /ˈkœrpçən/ *das;* ~s, ~ **1** [little] basket; **husch, husch ins ~** (fam.) time for bye-bye[s] *or* beddy-byes (child lang.) **2** (des Büstenhalters) cup

Körbchen·größe *die* cup size

körbeweise /ˈkœrbə-/ *Adv.* by the basketful

Korb-: **~flasche** *die* wicker bottle; **~geflecht** *das* wicker[work]; **~macher** *der*, **~macherin** *die* ▸ℹ **S. 113** basket-maker; **~möbel** *das* piece of wicker[work] furniture; **teure ~möbel** expensive wicker[work] furniture *sing.*; **~wagen** *der* wicker pram; **~waren** *Pl.* wickerwork *sing.*; basketry *sing.*; wickerwork articles; **~weide** *die* osier; basket willow; **~wurf** *der* (Basketball) throw *or* shot at goal *or* the basket

Kord /kɔrt/ *der;* **~[e]s** **1** corduroy; cord **2** ▸ **Kordsamt**

Kord·anzug *der* corduroy suit

Kordel /ˈkɔrdl/ *die;* ~, ~n **1** cord **2** (landsch.: Bindfaden) string

Kord-: **~hose** *die* corduroy *or* cord trousers *pl.*; **~jeans** *Pl.* corduroy *or* cord jeans

Kordon /kɔrˈdõ, *österr.:* -ˈdoːn/ *der;* **~s, ~s** *od. österr.:* **~e** **1** (Absperrung) cordon **2** (Ordensband) cordon; ribbon

Kord·samt *der* cord velvet

Korea /koˈreːa/ *(das);* **~s** Korea

Korea·krieg *der* Korean War

Koreaner /koreˈaːnɐ/ *der;* **~s, ~, Koreanerin** *die;* **~, ~nen** ▸ℹ **S. 520** Korean; *s. auch* **-in**

koreanisch *Adj.* ▸ℹ **S. 520**, ▸ℹ **S. 670** Korean; *s. auch* **deutsch**; **Deutsch**; **Deutsche²**

Koreferat ▸ **Korreferat**

kören /ˈkøːrən/ *tr. V.* (Landw.) rank *or* classify ‹*males*› for breeding

Korfu /ˈkɔrfu/ *(das);* **~s** Corfu

Koriander /koˈri̯andɐ/ *der;* **~s, ~:** coriander

Korinth /koˈrɪnt/ *(das);* **~s** ▸ℹ **S. 675** Corinth

Korinthe /koˈrɪntə/ *die;* ~, **~n** currant

Korinthen-: **~brot** *das* currant bread; **~kacker** *der*, **~kackerin** *die* (derb abwertend) stupid rule-bound bastard (sl.)

Korinther *der;* **~s, ~, Korintherin** *die;* **~, ~nen** Corinthian

korinthisch *Adj.* (Kunstwiss.) Corinthian ‹*column, order, etc.*›

Kork /kɔrk/ *der;* **~s, ~e** cork

Kork·eiche *die* cork oak

Korken *der;* **~s, ~:** cork

Korken·zieher *der* corkscrew

Korkenzieher·locke *die* corkscrew *or* spiral curl

korkig *Adj.* corked, corky ‹*wine*›

Kork·sohle *die* cork sole

Kormoran /kɔrmoˈraːn/ *der;* **~s, ~e** cormorant

Korn¹ /kɔrn/ *das;* **~[e]s, Körner** /ˈkœrnɐ/ **1** (Frucht) seed; grain; (Getreide~) grain [of corn]; (Pfeffer~) corn **2** (Getreide) corn; grain; **das ~ steht gut** the grain harvest looks promising **3** (Salz~, Sand~) grain; (Hagel~) stone **4** *Pl.* **~e** (an Handfeuerwaffen) front sight; foresight; **etw. aufs ~ nehmen** take aim at *or* draw a bead on sth.; (fig. ugs.) attack sth.; **jmdn. aufs ~ nehmen** take aim at *or* draw a bead on sb.; (fig. ugs.) start to keep close tabs on sb. (coll.) **5** (Fot.; von Papier, Stoff) grain

Korn² *der;* **~[e]s, ~** (ugs.) corn schnapps; corn liquor (Amer.)

korn-, Korn-: **~ähre** *die* ear of corn; **~blume** *die* cornflower; **~blumen·blau** *Adj.* cornflower [blue]; (fig. salopp) paralytic (coll.); **~branntwein** *der* corn schnapps; corn liquor (Amer.)

Körnchen /ˈkœrnçən/ *das;* **~s, ~** (Frucht) tiny seed *or* grain; (von Sand usw.) [tiny] grain; granule; **an etw.** *(Dat.)* **ist ein ~ Wahrheit** (fig.) there's a grain of truth in sth.

körnen /ˈkœrnən/ *tr. V.* **1** (zerkleinern, körnig machen) granulate; **gekörnte Brühe** stock granules *pl.* (*for soup*) **2** (Handw.: markieren) punch

Körner ▸ **Korn**

Körner-: **~fresser** *der* (Ornith.) seedeater; granivore; **~futter** *das* grain [feed]; (für Vögel) seed

Kornett /kɔrˈnɛt/ *das;* **~[e]s, ~e** *od.* **~s** (Musik) cornet

Korn·feld *das* cornfield

körnig /ˈkœrnɪç/ *Adj.* granular; (Fot.) grainy

-körnig *Adj.* -grained

Korn-: **~kammer** *die* granary; **~rade** *die;* **~~, ~~n** corn cockle; corn campion; **~silo** *der od. das* grain silo

Körnung *die;* **~, ~en** **1** (Korngröße) grain size; (von Papier) grain **2** (Jägerspr.) ▸ **Körnerfutter**

Korona /koˈroːna/ *die;* ~, **Koronen** **1** (Astron.) corona **2** (fig.) crowd (coll.)

Koronar·insuffizienz /koroˈnaːɐ̯-/ *die* ▸ℹ **S. 439** (Med.) coronary insufficiency

Körper /ˈkœrpɐ/ *der;* **~s, ~** **1** body; **~ und Geist** body and mind; **am ganzen ~ frieren/zittern** be [freezing] cold/shake all over **2** (Rumpf) trunk; body **3** (Gegenstand) object **4** (Physik, Chemie) body **5** (Geom.) solid body; solid **6** (von Wein, Farbe) body **7** ▸ **Körperschaft**

körper-, Körper-: **~bau** *der* physique; **~behaarung** *die* body hair *no indef. art.*; **~beherrschung** *die* body control; **~behindert** *Adj.* physically handicapped *or* disabled; **~behinderte** *der/die* physically handicapped *or* disabled person; **~behinderte** *Pl.* physically handicapped *or* disabled people; **die ~behinderten** (als Kategorie) the physically handicapped *or* disabled; **~behinderung** *die* physical handicap *or* disability; **~beschädigte** *der/die* (Amtsspr.) disabled person; **~betont** **A** *Adj.* figure-hugging ‹*clothes*›; ‹*clothes*› that emphasize the figure; **B** *adv.* **~betont geschnitten** cut to emphasize the figure; **~bewegung** *die* body movement; **~eigen** *Adj.* (Biol.) endogenous; **~ertüchtigung** *die* physical training; **~erzieher** *der* (bes. DDR) physical education teacher; **~flüssigkeit** *die* body fluid; **~fremd** *Adj.* (Biol.) foreign; **~fülle** *die* corpulence; **~funktion** *die* bodily function; **~gerecht** *Adj.* shaped to fit the contours of the body *postpos.*; **~geruch** *der* body odour; BO (coll.); **~gewicht** *das* ▸ℹ **S. 315** body weight; **~größe** *die* ▸ℹ **S. 374** height; **~hälfte** *die* side of the body; **~haltung** *die* posture; **~hygiene** *die* ▸ **~pflege**; **~kontakt** *der* (Psych.) physical contact; **~kraft** *die* physical strength; **~kultur** *die* (bes. DDR) physical education *no art.*; **~länge** *die* (bei Menschen) height; (bei Tieren) length

körperlich
A *Adj.* physical; **~e Ertüchtigung** physical training; **~e Züchtigung** corporal punishment; **~e Liebe** carnal love
B *adv.* physically; **~ [hart] arbeiten** do [hard] physical work

körper-, Körper-: **~los** *Adj.* incorporeal; **~maße** *Pl.* measurements; **~öffnung** *die* orifice of the body; **~pflege** *die* body care *no art.*; (Reinigung) personal hygiene; **~saft** *der* body fluid

Körperschaft *die;* **~, ~en** **1** (Rechtsw.) corporation; corporate body; **~ des öffentlichen Rechts** public corporation **2** (Politik) body

Körperschaft[s]·steuer *die* (Steuerw.) corporation tax

Körper-: **~schwäche** *die* physical weakness; **~sprache** *die* body language; **~spray** *der od. das* aerosol deodorant; deodorant spray; **~stärke** *die* physical strength; **~teil** *der* ▸ℹ **S. 435** part of the/one's body; **~temperatur** *die* body temperature; **~verletzung** *die* (Rechtsw.) bodily harm *no indef. art.*; **schwere/leichte ~verletzung** grievous/actual bodily harm; **~verletzung mit Todesfolge** *bodily harm resulting in death*; **~verletzung im Amt** bodily harm caused by a public servant when executing his/her duty; **~wärme** *die* body heat

Korpora ▸ **Korpus²**

Korporal /kɔrpoˈraːl/ *der;* **~s, ~e** *od.* **Korporäle** /kɔrpoˈrɛːlə/ (Milit. veralt.) corporal

Korporation /kɔrporaˈtsi̯oːn/ *die;* **~, ~en** **1** (veralt.: Körperschaft) corporation **2** (Studentenverbindung) student society

korporiert /kɔrpoˈriːɐ̯t/ *Adj.* ‹*student*› belonging to a student society

Korporierte *der; adj. Dekl.* member of a student society

Korps /koːɐ̯/ *das;* **~** /koːɐ̯(s)/, **~** /koːɐ̯s/ **1** (Milit.) corps **2** (Studentenverbindung) student duelling society

Korps-: **~bruder** *der* (Studentenspr.) fellow member of a student duelling society; **~geist** *der* (geh.) esprit de corps; **~student** *der* student belonging to a duelling society

korpulent /kɔrpuˈlɛnt/ *Adj.* corpulent

Korpulenz /kɔrpuˈlɛnts/ *die;* **~:** corpulence

Korpus¹ /ˈkɔrpʊs/ *der;* **~, ~se** **1** (scherzh.) body **2** (bild. Kunst) figure of Christ (*on crucifix*) **3** (fachspr.) carcass

Korpus² *das;* **~, Korpora** /ˈkɔrpora/ **1** (Sprachw.) corpus **2** (Musik) body

Korpus³ *die;* **~** (Druckw.) long primer

Korpuskel /kɔrˈpʊskl/ *das;* **~s, ~n** *od. die;* **~, ~n** (Physik) corpuscle; particle

Korreferat /kɔrefeˈraːt/ *das;* ~s, ~e *scholarly paper which supplements the main paper;* supplementary paper (*to a paper read at a seminar etc.*)

Korreferent /kɔrefeˈrɛnt/ *der;* ~en, ~en, **Korreferentin** *die;* ~, ~nen [1] (Redner) reader of a/the supplementary paper [2] (Prüfer) second examiner

korrekt /kɔˈrɛkt/
[A] *Adj.* correct; **es wäre ~ gewesen, ...** the correct thing would have been to ...; **ein ~er Beamter** a very correct civil servant
[B] *adv.* correctly

korrekter·weise *Adv.* to be [strictly] correct

Korrektheit *die;* ~: correctness

Korrektiv /kɔrɛkˈtiːf/ *das;* ~s, ~e corrective (**gegen** to)

Korrektor /kɔˈrɛktɔr/ *der;* ~s, ~en /-ˈtoːrən/, **Korrektorin** *die;* ~, ~nen ▸ S. 113 proof-reader

Korrektur /kɔrɛkˈtuːɐ̯/ *die;* ~, ~en [1] correction; (von Ansichten usw.) revision [2] (Druckw.) proof-reading; (Verbesserung) proof correction; **~ lesen** read/correct the proofs

Korrektur-: **~ab·zug** *der,* **~fahne** *die* galley [proof]; **~zeichen** *das* proof-correction mark

Korrelat /kɔreˈlaːt/ *das;* ~[e]s, ~e correlate

Korrelation /kɔrelaˈt̮si̯oːn/ *die;* ~, ~en (auch Math.) correlation

korrelieren *itr. V.* correlate (**mit** with, to)

Korrepetitor /kɔrepeˈtiːtɔr/ *der;* ~s, ~en /-tiˈtoːrən/, **Korrepetitorin** *die;* ~, ~nen (Musik) répétiteur

Korrespondent /kɔrɛspɔnˈdɛnt/ *der;* ~en, ~en, **Korrespondentin** *die;* ~, ~nen ▸ S. 113 [1] (Zeitungsw., veralt.: Briefpartner) correspondent [2] (Wirtsch.) correspondence clerk

Korrespondenz /kɔrɛspɔnˈdɛnt̮s/ *die;* ~, ~en [1] correspondence; **die ~ erledigen** deal with the correspondence; **in ~ mit jmdm. stehen** correspond with sb. [2] (Brief) letter; **~en** correspondence *sing.*

Korrespondenz-: **~büro** *das* press agency; **~karte** *die* (österr., schweiz.) *prestamped postcard*

korrespondieren *itr. V.* [1] (schreiben) correspond (**mit** with) [2] (geh.: übereinstimmen) **mit etw. ~:** correspond to *or* with sth.; ‹*colour*› match sth.

Korridor /ˈkɔridoːɐ̯/ *der;* ~s, ~e corridor; **der Polnische ~:** the Polish Corridor

korrigierbar *Adj.* correctable

korrigieren /kɔriˈgiːrən/ *tr. V.* correct; revise ‹*opinion, view*›

korrodieren /kɔroˈdiːrən/ (bes. Chemie, Geol.) *tr., itr. V.* (itr. mit sein) corrode

Korrosion /kɔroˈzi̯oːn/ *die;* ~, ~en (auch Geol., Med.) corrosion

korrosions-, Korrosions-: **~beständig** *Adj.,* **~fest** *Adj.* corrosion-resistant; **~schutz** *der* protection against corrosion

korrosiv /kɔroˈziːf/ *Adj.* [1] corrosive [2] (korrosionsbedingt) ‹*damage etc.*› caused by corrosion

korrumpieren /kɔrʊmˈpiːrən/ *tr. V.* corrupt

Korrumpierung *die;* ~, ~en corruption

korrupt /kɔˈrʊpt/ *Adj.* corrupt

Korruption /kɔrʊpˈt̮si̯oːn/ *die;* ~, ~en corruption

Korsage /kɔrˈzaːʒə/ *die;* ~, ~n strapless, tight-fitting corsage *or* bodice

Korsar /kɔrˈzaːɐ̯/ *der;* ~en, ~en [1] (hist.) corsair [2] (Segeln) Korsar

Korse /ˈkɔrzə/ *der;* ~n, ~n Corsican

Korselett /kɔrzəˈlɛt/ *das;* ~s, ~s *od.* ~e corselette

Korsett /kɔrˈzɛt/ *das;* ~s, ~s *od.* ~e corset; (fig.) straitjacket

Korsett·stange *die* corset bone

Korsika /ˈkɔrzika/ *(das);* ~s Corsica

Korsin *die;* ~, ~nen ▸ **Korse**

korsisch *Adj.* ▸ S. 670 Corsican

Korso /ˈkɔrzo/ *der;* ~s, ~s procession

Kortison /kɔrtiˈzoːn/ *das;* ~s (Med.) cortisone

Korund /koˈrʊnt/ *der;* ~[e]s, ~e corundum

Körung *die;* ~, ~en (Landw.) ranking *or* classification for breeding

Korvette /kɔrˈvɛtə/ *die;* ~, ~n (auch hist.) corvette

Korvetten·kapitän *der* lieutenant commander

Koryphäe /koryˈfɛːə/ *die;* ~, ~n eminent authority; distinguished expert

Kosak /koˈzak/ *der;* ~en, ~en (hist.) Cossack

Kosaken·mütze *die* Cossack hat

Koschenille /kɔʃəˈnɪljə/ *die;* ~: cochineal

koscher /ˈkoːʃɐ/ *Adj.* [1] kosher [2] (ugs.: einwandfrei) kosher (coll.)

K.-o.-Schlag *der* (Boxen) knockout punch

Kose·form *die* familiar form

Kosekans /ˈkoːzekans/ *der;* ~, ~ (Math.) cosecant

kosen /ˈkoːzn̩/ (dichter. veralt.)
[A] *tr. V.* caress
[B] *itr. V.* **mit jmdm. ~:** caress sb.

Kose·name *der* pet name

Kose·wort *das; Pl.* **Kosewörter** term of endearment; **jmdm. Kosewörter ins Ohr flüstern** whisper endearments in sb.'s ear

K.-o.-Sieg *der* (Boxen) knockout victory; victory by a knockout

Kosinus /ˈkoːzinʊs/ *der;* ~, ~ *od.* ~se (Math.) cosine

Kosmetik /kɔsˈmeːtɪk/ *die;* ~ [1] beauty culture *no art.* [2] (fig.) cosmetic procedures *pl.*

Kosmetika ▸ **Kosmetikum**

Kosmetik·abteilung *die* cosmetics department

Kosmetiker *der;* ~s, ~, **Kosmetikerin** *die;* ~, ~nen ▸ S. 113 [1] cosmetician; beautician [2] (Chemiker/Chemikerin) cosmetics chemist

Kosmetik-: **~salon** *der* beauty salon; **~tasche** *die* make-up bag; (groß) vanity case

Kosmetikum /kɔsˈmeːtikʊm/ *das;* ~s, **Kosmetika** cosmetic

kosmetisch
[A] *Adj.* (auch fig.) cosmetic
[B] *adv.* **jmdn. ~ beraten** give sb. advice on beauty care; **sich ~ behandeln lassen** have beauty treatment

kosmisch /ˈkɔsmɪʃ/ *Adj.* cosmic ‹*ray, dust, etc.*›; space ‹*age, station, research, etc.*›; meteoric ‹*iron*›

Kosmodrom /kɔsmoˈdroːm/ *das;* ~s, ~e cosmodrome

Kosmologie /kɔsmoloˈgiː/ *die;* ~, ~n cosmology

Kosmonaut /kɔsmoˈnau̯t/ *der;* ~en, ~en, **Kosmonautin** *die;* ~, ~nen ▸ S. 113 cosmonaut

Kosmopolit /kɔsmopoˈliːt/ *der;* ~en, ~en, **Kosmopolitin** *die;* ~, ~nen (geh.) cosmopolitan

kosmopolitisch *Adj.* cosmopolitan

Kosmos /ˈkɔsmɔs/ *der;* ~ [1] (Weltall) cosmos [2] (geh.: Welt) world

Kosovare *der;* ~n, ~n, **Kosovarin** *die;* ~, ~nen Kosovar; Kosovan

kosovarisch *Adj.* Kosovar, Kosovan

Kosovo /ˈkɔsovo/ *(das);* ~s *od. der;* ~[s] Kosovo

Kosovo·albaner /ˈkɔsovo.../ *der* Kosovo Albanian

Kost /kɔst/ *die;* ~ [1] (Nahrung) food; **vegetarische ~:** vegetarian food; a vegetarian diet; **geistige ~** (fig.) intellectual nourishment; **leichte/schwere ~** (fig.) easy/heavy going [2] (Verpflegung) **~ und Logis** board and lodging

kostbar
[A] *Adj.* [1] (erlesen) valuable [2] (wichtig) precious; **die Zeit ist ~:** time is precious
[B] *adv.* expensively ‹*dressed*›; luxuriously ‹*decorated*›

Kostbarkeit *die;* ~, ~en [1] (Sache) treasure; precious object [2] (Eigenschaft) value

kosten[1]
[A] *tr. V.* [1] (probieren) taste; try; sample; **jmdm. etw. zum Kosten geben** give sb. sth. to taste *or* try *or* sample [2] (geh.: empfinden) taste; (fig. iron.) have a taste of
[B] *itr. V.* (probieren) have a taste; **von etw. ~:** have a taste of *or* taste sth.

kosten[2]
[A] *tr. V.* [1] ▸ S. 299 cost; **wie viel kostet .../was kostet ...?** how much/what does ... cost?; how much is ...?; **koste es** *od.* **es koste, was es wolle** whatever the cost; **sich** (*Akk. od. Dat.*) **eine Sache etwas ~ lassen** (ugs.) spend a fair bit of money on sth. [2] (erfordern) take; cost ‹*lives*›; **es kostet mich nur ein Wort** it would only take a word from me; **viel Arbeit ~:** take a great deal of work [3] (Verlust nach sich ziehen) **jmdn.** *od.* **jmdm. etw. ~:** cost sb. sth.; **jmdn. den Sieg ~:** cost sb. victory
[B] *itr. V.* (Geld ~) **das kostet!** that will cost a bit!

Kosten *Pl.* cost *sing.*; costs; (Auslagen) expenses; (Rechtsw.) costs; **die ~ tragen, für die ~ aufkommen** bear the cost[s]; **keine ~ scheuen** spare no expense; **laufende ~:** running costs; **auf seine ~ kommen** cover one's costs; (fig.) get one's money's worth; **auf jmds. ~:** at sb.'s expense; **auf ~ von jmdm./etw.** at the expense of sb./sth.

kosten-, Kosten-: **~aufwand** *der* expense; cost; **mit einem ~aufwand von ...** at a cost of ...; **~berechnung** *die* costing; **~beteiligung** *die* sharing of expenses; **~bewusst** [A] *Adj.* cost-conscious; [B] *adv.* in a cost-conscious manner; **~bewusstsein** *das* cost-consciousness; **~dämpfung** *die* reducing costs *no art.*; cost-cutting; **~deckend** [A] *Adj.* that covers/cover [one's] costs *postpos., not pred.*; [B] *adv.* **~deckend kalkulieren** ensure that the estimates cover the true costs; **~druck** *der* (Wirtsch.) pressure of costs; **~ersparnis** *die* cost saving; **~erstattung** *die* reimbursement of costs; **~explosion** *die* cost explosion; **~frage** *die* question of cost; **~intensiv** *Adj.* (Wirtsch.) cost-intensive; **~lawine** *die* (Wirtsch., Jargon) huge increase in costs; **~los** [A] *Adj.* free; [B] *adv.* free of charge; **~pflichtig** (Rechtsw.) [A] *Adj.* **eine ~pflichtige Verwarnung** a fine and a caution; [B] *adv.* **eine Klage ~pflichtig abweisen** dismiss a case with costs; **ein Auto ~pflichtig abschleppen** tow a car away at the owner's expense; **~punkt** *der* (ugs.) **~punkt?** how much is it/are they?; **~punkt 25 Euro** it costs/they cost 25 euros; **~rechnung** *die* (Wirtsch.) cost accounting; **~senkung** *die* reducing costs *no art.*; cost-cutting; **~sparend** *Adj.* (Wirtsch.) cost-saving; **~stelle** *die* (Wirtsch.) cost centre; **~träger** *der* (Wirtsch.) cost unit; **~vor·an·schlag** *der* estimate

Kost-: **~gänger** *der;* ~~s, ~~, **~gängerin** *die;* ~~, ~~nen (veralt.) boarder; **~geld** *das* payment for [one's] board; **er gab seinen Eltern ~geld** he paid his parents for his board

köstlich /ˈkœstlɪç/
[A] *Adj.* [1] delicious [2] (unterhaltsam) delightful; **der Witz war einfach zu ~:** the joke was simply priceless (coll.)
[B] *adv.* [1] ‹*taste*› delicious [2] **sich ~ amüsieren/unterhalten** enjoy oneself enormously (coll.)

Köstlichkeit *die;* ~, ~en [1] (Sache) delicacy; **eine literarische ~:** a literary gem [2] (geh.: Eigenschaft) deliciousness

Kost·probe *die;* ~, ~n taste; (fig.) sample

kost·spielig /-ʃpiːlɪç/
[A] *Adj.* expensive; costly
[B] *adv.* expensively

Kostüm /kɔsˈtyːm/ *das;* ~s, ~e [1] suit [2] (historisches ~, Theater~, Verkleidung) costume

Kostüm-: **~ball** *der* fancy-dress ball; **~bildner** *der;* ~~s, ~~, **~bildnerin** *die;* ~~, ~~nen (Theater, Film) costume designer; **~film** *der* period picture *or* film

kostümieren *tr. V.* [1] (verkleiden) **jmdn./sich ~:** dress sb. up/dress [oneself] up; **wie hatte er sich kostümiert?** what was he dressed [up] as?; **alle erschienen kostümiert** they all came in fancy dress **2** (ugs. abwertend: unpassend anziehen) **jmdn./sich ~:** get sb./oneself up

Kostüm-: ~jacke *die* jacket; **~probe** *die* (Theater) dress rehearsal; **~rock** *der* skirt; **~schneider** *der,* **~schneiderin** *die* ▸ S. 113 costumier; **~verleih** *der* [theatrical] costume agency

Kost·verächter *der: in* **kein ~ sein** (scherzh.) be fond of one's food; (die Frauen lieben) be one for the ladies

Kost·verächterin *die:* **keine ~ sein** be fond of one's food

K.-o.-System *das* (Sport) knockout system

Kot /ko:t/ *der;* **~[e]s, ~e 1** (Exkrement) excrement **2** (veralt.: Schmutz) mud; dirt

Kotangens /ˈko:taŋgɛns/ *der;* **~, ~** (Math.) cotangent

Kotau /koˈtau̯/ *der;* **~s, ~s** kowtow; **[vor jmdm.] einen** *od.* **seinen ~ machen** kowtow [to sb.]

Kotelett /kɔtˈlɛt/ *das;* **~s, ~s 1** chop; (vom Nacken) cutlet **2** (Teil des Tieres) (eines Schweins) loin; (eines Kalbs) loin and rib

Koteletten *Pl.* side whiskers

koten /ˈko:tn̩/ *itr. V.* (Zool.) defecate

Köter /ˈkø:tɐ/ *der;* **~s, ~** (abwertend) cur; tyke

Kot·flügel *der* (Kfz-W.) wing

Kothurn /koˈtʊrn/ *der;* **~s, ~e** cothurnus

kotig /ˈko:tɪç/ *Adj.* **1** dirty ‹*nappy, underpants*› **2** (schmutzig) muddy; filthy

Kotz·brocken *der* (derb) shit (coarse); turd (coarse)

Kotze[1] /ˈkɔtsə/ *die;* **~** (derb) vomit; puke (coarse)

Kotze[2] *die;* **~, ~n** (südd., österr.) **1** coarse woollen blanket **2** (Umhang) cape

kotzen *itr. V.* (derb) puke (coarse); throw up (coll.); **das ist/ich finde ihn zum Kotzen** it/he makes me sick; it/he makes me want to puke (coarse); **da kann man das [große] Kotzen kriegen** *od.* **bekommen** it makes you want to puke (coarse)

kotz-: ~langweilig *Adj.* (derb abwertend) bleeding boring (coarse); **~übel** *Adj.* (derb) **mir ist ~übel** I feel as if I'm going to throw up (coll.) *or* (coarse) puke

KP *Abk.* **= Kommunistische Partei** CP

Krabbe /ˈkrabə/ *die;* **~, ~n 1** (Zool.) crab **2** (ugs.: Garnele) shrimp; (größer) prawn **3** (ugs. scherzh.: Kind) [little] mite; (älter) kid (coll.) **4** (bild. Kunst) crochet

Krabbel·alter *das* (ugs.) crawling stage

krabbeln /ˈkrabl̩n/
A *itr. V.; mit sein* crawl
B *tr. V.* (ugs.: kraulen) tickle

krach *Interj.* crash; bang; (wenn etw. zerbricht, einstürzt) crash

Krach /krax/ *der;* **~[e]s, Kräche** /ˈkrɛçə/ **1** (Lärm) noise; row; **~ machen** make a noise *or* (coll.) a row; be noisy **2** (lautes Geräusch) crash; bang; (wenn etw. zerbricht, einstürzt) crash; **mit** *od.* **unter lautem ~:** with a loud crash *or* bang/crash **3** (ugs.: Streit) row; **mit jmdm. ~ anfangen/kriegen** start/have a row with sb. (coll.); **~ machen** *od.* **schlagen** (ugs.) kick up *or* make a fuss; **es gibt oft ~:** there are frequent rows **4** (ugs.: Börsen~) crash

krachen
A *itr. V.* **1** (Krach auslösen) ‹*thunder*› crash; ‹*shot*› ring out; ‹*floorboard*› creak; **in allen Fugen ~:** creak at the joints; **~de Kälte/~der Frost** (fig.) bitter cold/heavy frost **2** *mit sein* (ugs.: bersten) ‹*ice*› crack; ‹*bed*› collapse; ‹*trousers, dress, etc.*› split **3** *mit sein* (ugs.: mit Krach auftreffen) crash; **die Tür krachte ins Schloss** the door banged *or* slammed shut **4** (ugs.: Bankrott machen) crash **5** (unpers.) **an der Kreuzung kracht es dauernd** there are frequent crashes at that junction; **sonst krachts!** (fig. ugs.) or there'll be trouble; (es gibt Schläge) or you'll get a beating; **etw. tun, dass es nur so kracht** (ugs.) do sth. with a vengeance
B *refl. V.* (ugs.) row (coll.); have a row (coll.)

Kracher *der;* **~s, ~** (ugs.: Knallkörper) banger

Kracherl /ˈkraxɐl/ *das;* **~s, ~n** (südd., österr.) fizzy lemonade; pop (coll.)

krach·ledern *Adj.* rustic

Krach·lederne *die;* **~n, ~n** (südd.) Lederhosen *pl.*; leather shorts *pl.*

Krach·macher *der* (ugs.) (Person) noisy so-and-so (coll.); (Gerät) noise-maker

Krach·macherin *die* noisy so-and-so

krächzen /ˈkrɛçtsn̩/ *itr. V.* ‹*raven, crow*› caw; ‹*parrot*› squawk; ‹*person*› croak; (fig.) ‹*loudspeaker etc.*› crackle and splutter

kracken /ˈkrakn̩/ *tr. V.* (Chemie) crack

Kräcker /ˈkrɛkɐ/ *der;* **~s, ~** ▸ **Cracker**

Krad /kra:t/ *das;* **~[e]s, Kräder** /ˈkrɛ:dɐ/ (bes. Milit.) ▸ **Kraftrad**

Krad-: ~fahrer *der* (bes. Milit.) motorcyclist; motorcycle rider; **~melder** *der* (Milit.) [motorcycle] despatch rider

kraft /kraft/ *Präp. + Gen.* (Amtsspr.) **~ [meines] Amtes** by virtue of my office; **~ Gesetzes** by law; **~ [des] Gesetzes hat der Richter ihn zum Tode verurteilt** as empowered by the law, the judge sentenced him to death

Kraft *die;* **~, Kräfte** /ˈkrɛftə/ **1** strength; **geistige/schöpferische Kräfte** mental/creative powers; **unter Aufbietung aller Kräfte** applying all one's energies; **jmds. Kräfte übersteigen** be too much for sb.; **wieder bei Kräften sein** have [got] one's strength back; **bei Kräften bleiben** keep one's strength up; **mit letzter ~:** with one's last ounce of strength; **mit frischer ~:** with renewed energy; **aus eigener ~:** by oneself *or* one's own efforts; **ich werde tun, was in meinen Kräften steht** I shall do everything [with]in my power; **mit vereinten Kräften sollte es gelingen** if we join forces *or* combine our efforts we should succeed; **nach [besten] Kräften** to the best of one's ability; **die militärische/wirtschaftliche ~ eines Landes** (fig.) the military/economic strength of a country **2** (Wirksamkeit) power; **die treibende ~:** the driving force **3** (Arbeits~) employee; (in einer Fabrik) employee; worker; **Kräfte** employees/workers; personnel *pl.;* (Angestellte auch) staff *pl.* **4** *Pl.* (Gruppe) forces **5** (Physik) force **6** (Seemannsspr.) **mit voller/halber ~:** at full/half speed; **volle/halbe ~ voraus!** full/half speed ahead! **7** *in* **außer ~ setzen** repeal ‹*law*›; countermand ‹*order*›; **außer ~ sein/treten** no longer be/cease to be in force; **in ~ treten/sein/bleiben** come into/be in/remain in force

Kraft-: ~akt *der* feat of strength; (im Zirkus usw.) strongman act; (fig.) show of strength; **~arm** *der* (Physik) [lever] arm to which force is applied; **~aufwand** *der* effort; **~ausdruck** *der; Pl.* **~ausdrücke** swear word; **~brühe** *die* strong meat broth; **~droschke** *die* (veralt.) hackney carriage; taxi

kräfte-, Kräfte-: ~messen *das;* **~~s** trial of strength; **~parallelogramm** *das* (Physik) parallelogram of forces; **~sparend** ▸ **kraftsparend**; **~verhältnis** *das* (bes. Politik) balance of power; **~verschleiß** *der* loss of strength

Kraft·fahrer *der* ▸ **S. 113** (bes. Amtsspr.) driver; motorist; (Beruf) driver

Kraftfahrer·gruß *der* ▸ **Autofahrergruß**

Kraft·fahrerin *die* ▸ **S. 113** ▸ **Kraftfahrer**

Kraft·fahrzeug *das;* **~[e]s, ~e** (bes. Amtsspr.) motor vehicle

Kraftfahrzeug-: ~bau *der* automobile construction; **~brief** *der* vehicle registration document; logbook (Brit.); **~industrie** *die* motor industry; **~mechaniker** *der,* **~mechanikerin** *die* ▸ **S. 113** motor mechanic; **~schein** *der* vehicle registration document (*containing detailed technical description of the vehicle and details of the owner*); **~steuer** *die* vehicle *or* road tax; **~zulassungs·stelle** *die* vehicle registration office

Kraft-: ~feld *das* (Physik) force field; **~futter** *das* concentrated feed

kräftig /ˈkrɛftɪç/
A *Adj.* **1** (stark) strong ‹*person*›; strong, powerful ‹*arms, voice*›; vigorous ‹*plant, shoot*› **2** (fest) powerful, hefty, hard ‹*blow, kick, etc.*›; firm ‹*handshake*› **3** (ausgeprägt) strong ‹*breeze, high-pressure area*›; deep ‹*depression*›; considerable ‹*increase*›; **einen ~en Schluck nehmen** take a deep drink *or* (coll.) good swig; **eine ~e Tracht [Prügel]** a good hiding (coll.); a sound beating **4** (intensiv) strong, powerful ‹*smell, taste, etc.*›; bold ‹*pattern*›; strong ‹*colour*› **5** (~end) nourishing ‹*soup, bread, meal, etc.*›; **etw. Kräftiges essen** eat a good nourishing meal **6** (grob) strong ‹*language*›; coarse ‹*expression, oath, etc.*›
B *adv.* **1** strongly, powerfully ‹*built*›; ‹*hit, kick, press, push*› hard; ‹*sneeze*› loudly; **~ entwickelt** strong, vigorous ‹*plant*›; sturdy ‹*child*› **2** (tüchtig) ‹*rain, snow*› heavily; ‹*eat*› heartily; ‹*sing*› lustily; **etw. ~ schütteln** shake sth. vigorously; give sth. a good shake; **die Preise sind ~ gestiegen** prices have risen steeply; **der Flasche/dem Alkohol ~ zusprechen** hit the bottle in a big way (coll.) **3** (mit Nachdruck) **jmdm. ~ die** *od.* **seine Meinung sagen** give sb. a piece of one's mind

kräftigen *tr. V.* ‹*holiday, air, etc.*› invigorate; ‹*food etc.*› fortify; **sich ~:** build up one's strength; **~de Nahrung/Luft** nourishing food/bracing air

Kräftigung *die;* **~, ~en** strengthening

Kräftigungs·mittel *das* tonic

kraft-, Kraft-: ~linien *Pl.* (Physik) lines of force; **~los** *Adj.* weak; feeble; (fig.) weak ‹*sun*›; **~losigkeit** *die;* **~~:** weakness; feebleness; **~maschine** *die* (Technik) engine; prime mover; **~meier** *der;* **~~s, ~~** (ugs. abwertend) muscleman; **~meierei** *die;* **~~** (ugs. abwertend) playing the muscleman; **~meierisch** (ugs. abwertend) **A** *Adj.* pugnacious; strong-arm ‹*methods, tactics*›; **~meierisches Auftreten** great show of strength; **~meierische Töne** *od.* **Sprache** aggressive language; **B** *adv.* with a great show of strength; **~mensch** *der* strongman; muscleman; **~messer** *der;* **~~s, ~~ 1** (Physik) dynamometer; **2** (auf dem Jahrmarkt) try-your-strength machine; **~paket** *das* (Spieler) powerhouse; (Pferd) powerful animal; (Auto) powerful machine; **ein ~paket von Spieler** a powerhouse of a player; **~post** *die* post-bus service; **~probe** *die* trial of strength; **~protz** *der* (abwertend) muscleman; **~rad** *das* (Amtsspr.) motorcycle; **~reserven** *Pl.* reserves of strength; **~sparend** (bes. Sport) **A** *Adj.* energy-saving; **B** *adv.* without overexerting oneself; **~sport** *der* ▸ **Schwerathletik**; **~stoff** *der* (Kfz-W.) fuel; **~stoff·anzeiger** *der* (Kfz-W.) fuel gauge; **~stoff-Luft-Gemisch** *das* (Kfz-W.) air-fuel mixture; **~stoff·verbrauch** *der* fuel consumption; **~strotzend** *Adj.* vigorous; bursting with vigour *postpos.*; **~training** *das* power training; **~vergeudung** *die* waste of energy; **~verkehr** *der* (Amtsspr.) [motor] traffic; **~verschwendung** *die* ▸ **~vergeudung**; **~voll A** *Adj.* powerful; **B** *adv.* powerfully; **~wagen** *der* motor vehicle; **~werk** *das* power station; **~wort** *das; Pl.* **~wörter** *od.* **~~e** ▸ **~ausdruck**

Kragen /ˈkra:gn̩/ *der;* **~s, ~,** *südd., österr. u. schweiz. auch:* **Krägen** /ˈkrɛ:gn̩/ **1** collar **2 ihm platzte der ~** (salopp) he blew his top (coll.); **jetzt platzt mir aber der ~!** (salopp) that's the last straw!; **es geht ihm an den ~** (ugs.) he's in for it now; **jmdn. am** *od.* **beim ~ packen** *od.* **nehmen** (ugs.) collar sb.; **jmdm. an den ~ wollen** (ugs.) get at *or* be after sb.; (jmdn. verantwortlich machen) try to hang something on sb. (coll.); *s. auch* **Kopf 1 3** (Jägerspr.) collar

Kragen-: ~bär *der* [Himalayan] black bear; **~knopf** *der* collar stud (Brit.); (oberster Knopf am Hemd) top button; **~weite** *die* collar size; **[nicht] jmds. ~weite sein** (salopp) [not] be sb.'s cup of tea (coll.)

Krag·stein *der* (Archit.) bracket; (Konsole) console

Krähe /ˈkrɛ:ə/ *die;* **~, ~n** crow; **eine ~ hackt der anderen kein Auge aus** (Spr.) dog does not eat dog (prov.)

krähen *itr. V.* (auch fig.) crow; *s. auch* **Hahn**

Krähen-: ~füße *Pl.* (ugs.) **1** (Hautfalten) crow's feet; **2** (aus Eisen) *devices with many sharp points scattered on the road to burst the tyres*

k

of a vehicle; ≈ [tin] tacks; **~nest** *das* (auch Seemannsspr.) crow's nest

Kräh·winkel *(das);* **~s** (spött.) provincial backwater

Krakau /ˈkraːkau̯/ *(das);* **~s** ▸❶ **S. 675** Cracow; Krakow

Krakauer¹ *der;* **~s, ~:** Cracovian

Krakauer² *die;* **~, ~** (Wurst) *highly spiced, smoked beef and pork sausage*

Krake /ˈkraːkə/ *der;* **~n, ~n** 1 (Tintenfisch) octopus 2 (Meeresungeheuer) kraken

Krakeel /kraˈkeːl/ *der;* **~s** (ugs. abwertend) row (coll.)

krakeelen

A *itr. V.* (ugs. abwertend) kick up a row (coll.)

B *tr. V.* scream

Krakeeler *der;* **~s, ~, Krakeelerin** *die;* **~, ~nen** (ugs. abwertend) rowdy

Krakel /ˈkraːkl/ *der;* **~s, ~** (ugs. abwertend) scrawl; scribble

krakelig ▸ **kraklig**

krakeln *tr., itr. V.* (ugs. abwertend) scrawl; scribble

Krakel·schrift *die* (ugs. abwertend) scrawl

kraklig *Adj.* (ugs. abwertend) scrawly

Kral /kraːl/ *der;* **~s, ~e** *od.* **~s** kraal

Kralle /ˈkralə/ *die;* **~, ~n** claw; (von Raubvögeln) claw; talon; **die ~n des Todes** (fig.) the jaws of death; **jmdm. die ~n zeigen** (ugs.) show sb. one's claws; **etw. in die ~n bekommen** *od.* **kriegen** (ugs.) get sth. in one's clutches

krallen

A *refl. V.* **sich an etw.** *(Akk.)* **~** ‹*cat*› dig its claws into sth.; ‹*bird*› dig its claws *or* talons into sth.; ‹*person*› clutch sth. [tightly]; **sich in/um etw.** *(Akk.)* **~:** dig into/clutch sth.

B *tr. V.* 1 (fest greifen) **die Finger in/um etw.** *(Akk.)* **~:** dig one's fingers into sth./clutch sth. [tightly] with one's fingers 2 (krümmen) **er krallte seine Finger/seine Hand** he bent his fingers into [the shape of] a claw 3 (salopp: stehlen) pinch (coll.); nick (Brit. coll.) 4 (salopp: ergreifen) collar; (verhaften) nab (coll.)

Kram /kraːm/ *der;* **~[e]s** (ugs.) 1 stuff; (Gerümpel) junk; **den ganzen ~ hinschmeißen** (fig. ugs.) chuck the whole thing in (coll.) 2 (Angelegenheit) business; affair; **mach deinen ~ alleine!** do it yourself!; **jmdm. [genau] in den ~ passen** suit sb. [down to the ground (coll.)]

kramen

A *itr. V.* 1 (ugs.: herumwühlen) **in etw.** *(Dat.)* **~:** rummage about in *or* rummage through sth.; **nach etw. ~:** rummage about looking for sth. 2 (schweiz.: einkaufen) do some *or* a bit of shopping

B *tr. V.* (ugs.) **etw. aus etw. ~:** fish (coll.) *or* get sth. out of sth.

Krämer /ˈkrɛːmɐ/ *der;* **~s, ~, Krämerin** *die;* **~, ~nen** 1 (veralt.: Lebensmittelhändler[in]) grocer 2 (abwertend) (geiziger Mensch) skinflint; stingy person; (engstirniger Mensch) petty-minded *or* small-minded person

Krämer·seele *die* (abwertend) 1 (Geiz) stingy nature; (Engstirnigkeit) petty-mindedness; small-mindedness 2 (geiziger Mensch) skinflint; (engstirniger Mensch) petty-minded *or* small-minded person

Kramladen *der; Pl.* **Kramläden** (ugs. abwertend) junk shop

Krampe /ˈkrampə/ *die;* **~, ~n** staple

Krampen *der;* **~s, ~** 1 ▸ **Krampe** 2 (bayr., österr.: Spitzhacke) pick[axe]

Krampf /krampf/ *der;* **~[e]s, Krämpfe** /ˈkrɛmpfə/ 1 ▸❶ **S. 439** cramp; (Zuckung) spasm; (bei Anfällen) convulsion; **sich in Krämpfen winden** curl up in convulsions; **einen ~ bekommen** *od.* (ugs.) **kriegen** get cramp; **einen ~** *od.* **Krämpfe kriegen** (fig. ugs.) have a fit 2 (gequältes Tun) painful strain; (sinnloses Tun) senseless waste of effort; **das ist doch alles ~:** it's all a senseless waste of effort

Krampf·ader *die* ▸❶ **S. 439** varicose vein

krampf·artig

A *Adj.* convulsive

B *adv.* convulsively

krampfen

A *itr. V.* 1 be affected with cramp; (bei Anfällen) be convulsed; **sein Magen krampfte** he got stomach cramp 2 (schweiz.: sich anstrengen) slave away

B *refl. V.* 1 be affected with cramp; (bei Anfällen) be convulsed 2 (umklammern) **sich um/in etw.** *(Akk.)* **~:** clench sth./dig into sth.

C *tr. V.* 1 (schließen) **die Fäuste/Finger um/in etw.** *(Akk.)* **~:** clench sth./dig one's hands/fingers into sth. 2 (ugs.: an sich bringen) **sich** *(Dat.)* **etw. ~:** grab sth.

krampfhaft

A *Adj.* 1 convulsive 2 (verbissen) desperate; forced ‹*cheerfulness*›

B *adv.* 1 convulsively 2 (verbissen) desperately

krampf-, Krampf-: ~husten *der* ▸❶ **S. 439** (Med.) whooping cough; **~lösend** *Adj.,* **~stillend** *Adj.* antispasmodic

> **Krampus - Knecht Ruprecht**
>
> The legendary figure known as *Krampus* in Austria and Bavaria and *Knecht Ruprecht* in other regions is St Nicholas' helper, who carries the sack and a birch for punishing disobedient children. Most children are frightened of *Krampus* when he visits them in his furs on St Nicholas' Day. He is also believed to help the **Christkind** carry Christmas presents.

Kran /kraːn/ *der;* **~[e]s, Kräne** /ˈkrɛːnə/ 1 crane 2 *Pl. auch* **~en** (südwestd.: Wasserhahn) tap; faucet (Amer.)

Kran-: ~brücke *die* (Technik) gantry; **~führer** *der,* **~führerin** *die* ▸❶ **S. 113** crane operator; (~fahrer[in]) crane driver

Kranich /ˈkraːnɪç/ *der;* **~s, ~e** crane

krank /kraŋk/, **kränker** /ˈkrɛŋkɐ/, **kränkst...** /ˈkrɛŋkst.../ *Adj.* 1 ▸❶ **S. 439** ill *usu. pred.;* sick; bad ‹*leg, tooth*›; diseased ‹*plant, organ*›; (fig.) sick, ailing ‹*economy, business*›; **ein ~es Herz/eine ~e Leber haben** have a bad heart/a liver complaint; **[schwer] ~ werden** be taken *or* fall [seriously *or* very] ill; **er wurde immer kränker** he got steadily worse; **du siehst ~ aus** you don't look well; **sie liegt ~ zu/im Bett** she is ill in bed; **auf den Tod ~ sein** be critically *or* dangerously ill; **jmdn. ~ machen** make sb. ill; (fig.) get on sb.'s nerves; **vor Heimweh/Liebe ~ sein** be homesick/lovesick; ***sich ~ melden** let the office/boss *etc.* know that one is off sick; ***jmdn. ~ schreiben** give sb. a medical certificate 2 (Jägerspr.: angeschossen) wounded

Kranke /ˈkraŋkə/ *der/die; adj. Dekl.* sick man/woman; (Patient) patient; **die ~n** the sick *pl.;* the patients

kränkeln /ˈkrɛŋkl̩n/ *itr. V.* be in poor health; not be well; (fig.) be in poor shape; **er kränkelt leicht** he is always ailing

kranken *itr. V.* (leiden) **an etw.** *(Dat.)* **~** ‹*firm, project, etc.*› suffer from sth.

kränken /ˈkrɛŋkn̩/

A *tr. V.* **jmdn. ~:** hurt *or* wound sb. *or* sb.'s feelings; **jmdn. in seiner Ehre/seinem Stolz/seiner Eitelkeit ~:** wound sb.'s honour/injure *or* wound sb.'s pride/vanity; **~d sein** be hurtful; **tief/schwer gekränkt sein** be deeply hurt

B *refl. V.* (geh. veralt.) **sich über jmdn./etw. ~:** be *or* feel hurt by sb./sth.

kranken-, Kranken-: ~anstalten *Pl.* (Amtsspr.) hospital complex *sing.;* **~auto** *das* ▸ **~wagen; ~bericht** *der* case report; **~besuch** *der* visit to a sick person; **~bett** *das* sickbed; **~blatt** *das* medical report [card]; **~fahrstuhl** *der* (Amtsspr.) wheelchair; **~geld** *das* sickness benefit; **~geschichte** *die* case history; **~gymnastik** *die* remedial *or* medical gymnastics *sing.;* physiotherapy; **~gymnastin** *die;* **~, ~nen** ▸❶ **S. 113** remedial gymnast; medical gymnast; physiotherapist; **~haus** *das* hospital; **jmdn. ins ~haus einliefern/aus dem ~haus entlassen** take sb. to hospital/discharge sb. from hospital; **im ~haus liegen** be in hospital; **ins ~haus [gehen] müssen** have to go [in]to hospital; **~haus·arzt** *der,* **~haus·ärztin** *die* hospital doctor; **~haus·aufenthalt** *der* stay in hospital; **~haus·reif** *Adj.* (salopp) **~hausreif aussehen** look like a hospital case; **jmdn. ~hausreif schlagen** make a real mess of sb. (coll.); **~kassa** *die* (österr.), **~kasse** *die* health insurance scheme; (Körperschaft) health insurance institution; (privat) health insurance company; **~kassen·beitrag** *der* health insurance contribution; **~lager** *das* (geh.) 1 (Zeit des Krankseins) illness; 2 (~bett) sickbed; **~pflege** *die* nursing; **in der ~pflege tätig sein** be a nurse; **~pfleger** *der* ▸❶ **S. 113** male nurse; **~saal** *der* ward; **~salbung** *die* (kath. Kirche) extreme unction *no art.;* **~schein** *der* health insurance certificate; **~schwester** *die* ▸❶ **S. 113** nurse; **~stand** *der* number of staff away sick; **im ~stand sein** (österr.) be away sick; **~stuhl** *der* ▸ **~fahrstuhl; ~transport** *der* transportation of sick/injured persons; **~versicherung** *die* 1 (Versicherung) health insurance; 2 (Unternehmen) health insurance company; **~versicherungs·pflichtig** *Adj.* ‹*person*› who is required to join a health insurance scheme; **~wagen** *der* ambulance; **~zimmer** *das* sickroom; (im ~haus) patients' room

> **Krankenkasse**
>
> There are many different health insurance organizations in Germany with the **AOK** being the largest. Contributions are high, due to the high standard (and cost) of health care in Germany. The *Krankenkassen* issue their members with plastic cards which entitle them to treatment by the doctor of their choice.

kränker ▸ **krank**

krank|feiern *itr. V.* (ugs.) skive off work (coll.) [pretending to be ill]; **ich glaube, ich feiere mal krank** I think I might just [have to] go sick (joc.)

krankhaft

A *Adj.* 1 (pathologisch) pathological ‹*change etc.*›; morbid ‹*growth, state, swelling, etc.*› 2 (abnorm gesteigert) pathological; pathological, morbid ‹*fear, obsession*›

B *adv.* 1 (pathologisch) pathologically; morbidly ‹*swollen*› 2 (abnorm gesteigert) pathologically; pathologically, morbidly ‹*obsessed, sensitive*›

Krankheit *die;* **~, ~en** ▸❶ **S. 439** 1 illness; (bestimmte Art, von Pflanzen, Organen) disease; **von einer ~ befallen werden** contract *or* catch an illness/a disease; **an einer ~ leiden/sterben** suffer from/die of an illness/a disease; **eine ~ heilen/einer ~ vorbeugen** cure/prevent an illness/a disease; **das ist doch kein Auto, das ist eine ~** (fig. ugs. scherzh.) that's just an apology for a car 2 (Zeit des Krankseins) illness; **nach langer/schwerer ~:** after a long/serious illness

krankheits-, Krankheits-: ~bild *das* clinical picture; **~erreger** *der* pathogen; disease-causing agent; **~fall** *der* case of illness; **im ~fall** in the event of illness; **~halber** *Adv.* due to illness; **~herd** *der* seat of a/the disease; **~keim** *der* germ [causing the/a disease]

krank|lachen *refl. V.* (ugs.) laugh one's head off; laugh oneself silly

kränklich /ˈkrɛŋklɪç/ *Adj.* sickly; ailing

krank-, Krank-: ~|machen *itr. V.* (ugs.) ▸ **~feiern;** *s. auch* **krank 1; ~|melden** *refl. V.* let the office/boss *etc.* know that one is sick; **~meldung** *die* notification of absence through illness; **~|schreiben** *unr. tr. V.* give ‹*person*› a medical certificate

kränkste ▸ **krank**

Kränkung *die;* **~, ~en eine ~:** an injury to one's/sb.'s feelings; **etw. als ~ empfinden** be hurt by sth.; take offence at sth.

Kranz /krants/ *der;* **~es, Kränze** /ˈkrɛntsə/ 1 wreath; garland; (auf einem Grab, Sarg, an einem Denkmal) wreath; **einen ~ niederlegen** lay a wreath 2 (Haar~) chaplet (*of plaited hair*) 3 (Kuchen) ring cake 4 (geh.: Kreis) circle; **ein ~ von Sagen** a cycle of legends

Kränzchen /ˈkrɛntsçən/ *das;* **~s, ~** 1 (zum Kaffeetrinken) coffee circle; coffee klatch (Amer.);

Krankheiten und Schmerzen

Verletzungen

Wo haben Sie Schmerzen?, Wo tut es weh?
= Where does it hurt?
Mir tut der Arm weh
= My arm is hurting
Sie hat sich am Fuß weh getan/verletzt
= She has hurt her foot
Ich habe mir den Fuß verstaucht/die Hand verbrannt
= I have sprained my ankle/burnt my hand
Er hat sich das Bein gebrochen
= He has broken his leg
Sie hat einen Kieferbruch/Schädelbruch/Beckenbruch
= She has a fractured jaw/skull/pelvis

Man sieht, dass das Possessivum im Englischen verwendet wird, wo im Deutschen der bestimmte Artikel mit dem Dativ der Person steht. Siehe auch □ **Körperteile**

Schmerzen

Ich habe Zahnschmerzen/Kopfschmerzen/Magenschmerzen od. Zahnweh/Kopfweh/Magenweh
= I've got toothache/a headache/a stomach ache *od.* a pain in my stomach
Sie hat Schmerzen im Rücken
= (*allgemein*) She has back pain/(*dumpf*) backache;
(*an verschiedenen Stellen*) She has pains in her back
Sie hat Schmerzen
= She is in pain
ein stechender/bohrender Schmerz
= a stab of pain/a gnawing pain

Ein starker Schmerz kann also nur **pain** sein, **ache** ist immer dumpf und anhaltend. Und *Schmerzen* sind auch meist **pain**; nur bei Schmerzen an verschiedenen Stellen sagt man **pains**.

Das Kranksein

Ich fühle mich krank/elend
= I feel ill/wretched
***Mir ist schlecht/sauschlecht* (ugs.)**
= I don't feel well/I feel awful (*ugs.*)
Ihnen war/wurde bei der Überfahrt übel
= They felt/were sick on the crossing
Sie ist schwer/unheilbar krank
= She is seriously/terminally ill
Er ist an Grippe erkrankt
= He is ill with flu *od.* has [got] flu
Sie hat sich erkältet/ist erkältet
= She has caught a cold/has a cold
Du holst dir eine Lungenentzündung
= You'll catch pneumonia
Sie leiden an Asthma/Bronchitis
= They suffer from asthma/bronchitis

Mit Ausnahme von **cold** wird der unbestimmte Artikel bei Krankheiten nicht verwendet, auch dann nicht, wenn ein Adjektiv vor dem Substantiv steht:

Ich habe eine schlimme Gelenkarthrose
= I have bad arthritis
Er bekommt immer eine leichte Bronchitis
= He always gets slight bronchitis

Allerdings:

eine schlimme Grippe
= a nasty bout of flu
ein schwerer Fall von Kehlkopfkrebs
= a serious case of throat cancer
eine hartnäckige Halsinfektion
= a persistent throat infection
ein Asthmaanfall
= an attack of asthma

Leiden und Leidende

Er hat ein Herzleiden/ein Magenleiden/eine Hautkrankheit
= He has a heart condition/a stomach complaint/a skin complaint
Sie hat Rückenprobleme od. hats mit dem Rücken
= She suffers from back trouble
Herzbeschwerden/Magenbeschwerden
= heart/stomach trouble

In Zusammensetzungen wird *-kranke(r)* meist mit **sufferer** bzw. **patient** übersetzt:

ein Aidskranker = an Aids sufferer
Krebskranke = cancer patients
ein Asthmakranker = an asthma sufferer

Aber:

ein Epileptiker = an epileptic
ein Diabetiker = a diabetic

Behandlung

Sie ist [bei einem Facharzt] in Behandlung
= She is having *od.* receiving treatment [from a specialist]
Er wird wegen Krebs/eines Magengeschwürs behandelt
= He is being treated for cancer/a stomach ulcer
Sie haben ihn auf ein Magengeschwür behandelt, aber es stellte sich heraus, dass er Krebs hatte
= They treated him for a stomach ulcer, but it turned out he had cancer
Ich bin wegen Gallensteinen operiert worden
= I was operated on for gallstones
mit Vollnarkose/Lokalanästhesie
= under a general/local anaesthetic
Sind Sie gegen Cholera geimpft [worden]?
= Have you been vaccinated against cholera *od.* had a cholera vaccination?

Heilmittel

Haben Sie etwas gegen Verstopfung?
= Have you got anything for constipation?
Was kann ich gegen Heuschnupfen nehmen?
= What can I take for hay fever?
Dreimal täglich einzunehmen
= To be taken three times a day
Vor Gebrauch schütteln
= Shake the bottle
Es gibt kein Mittel gegen Aids
= There is no cure for Aids

Erholung

Er ist auf dem Wege der Besserung
= He is getting better *od.* is on the mend
Es geht ihr od. Sie fühlt sich viel besser
= She is [feeling] much better
Ich habe mich vollständig erholt
= I am fully recovered

(zum Handarbeiten) sewing circle **2▸** (kleiner Kranz) small wreath *or* garland

Kranz-: ~gefäß *das* ▸**Herzkranzgefäß**; **~geld** *das* (Rechtsw.) *damages for loss of virginity awarded against a woman's fiancé if he breaks off the engagement without good cause*; **~kuchen** *der* ▸**Kranz 3**; **~niederlegung** *die* laying of a wreath; **~spende** *die* wreath; **„von ~spenden bitten wir abzusehen"** 'no flowers please'

Krapfen /ˈkrapfn̩/ *der;* **~s, ~** **1▸** (Berliner) doughnut **2▸** (Kochkunst) fritter

krass, *kraß /kras/
A *Adj.* **1▸** blatant ‹*case*›; gross, flagrant ‹*injustice*›; glaring, stark ‹*contrast, contradiction*›; sharp ‹*difference*›; gross ‹*discrepancy, imbalance*› **2▸** rank, complete ‹*outsider*›; out-and-out ‹*egoist*›
B *adv.* **sich ~ ausdrücken** put sth. bluntly; **sich von etw. ~ unterscheiden** be in stark contrast to sth.

Krassheit, *Kraßheit *die;* **~, ~en** ▸**krass 1**: blatancy; grossness, flagrancy; starkness; sharpness

Krater /ˈkraːtɐ/ *der;* **~s, ~**: crater

Krater-: ~landschaft *die* cratered landscape; **~see** *der* crater lake

Kratz·bürste *die* (ugs. scherzh.) stroppy (Brit. coll.) *or* prickly so-and-so

kratzbürstig *Adj.* (ugs. scherzh.) stroppy (Brit. coll.); prickly

Kratze *die;* **~, ~n** scraper

Krätze /ˈkrɛtsə/ *die;* **~** ▸**ⓘ S. 439** scabies *sing.*

kratzen /ˈkratsn̩/
A *tr. V.* **1▸** scratch; **jmdm./sich den Arm blutig ~**: scratch sb.'s/one's arm and make it bleed **2▸** (scharren) scratch; **seinen Namen in die Wand ~**: scratch one's name on the wall **3▸** (entfernen) scrape; **etw. aus/von etw. ~**: scrape sth. out of/off sth. **4▸** (ugs.: stören) bother; **jmdn. wenig ~**: not bother sb. all that much; **wen kratzt das schon?** who cares *or* who's bothered [about that]?
B *itr. V.* **1▸** scratch; (aus~) scrape; **das Kratzen** scratching; **an jmds. Ehre/Vormachtstellung** (*Dat.*) **~** (fig.) chip away at sb.'s honour/supremacy **2▸** (jucken) itch; be scratchy *or* itchy **3▸** (brennen) **im Hals ~** ‹*wine*› taste rough; ‹*tobacco*› be rough on the throat; ‹*smoke*› irritate the throat
C *refl. V.* scratch [oneself]; **sich hinter dem Ohr/am Kopf ~**: scratch oneself behind the ear/scratch one's head

Kratzer *der;* **~s, ~** **1▸** (ugs.) scratch **2▸** (Schaber) scraper

Krätzer /ˈkrɛtsɐ/ *der;* **~s, ~** (abwertend) rough wine; plonk (Brit. coll.)

kratz·fest *Adj.* scratch-proof; non-scratch

Kratz·fuß *der* (veralt.) leg (arch.); **einen ~ machen** make a leg (arch.)

kratzig *Adj.* scratchy, itchy ‹*material, pullover, etc.*›; scratchy, rough ‹*voice*›

krätzig /ˈkrɛtsɪç/ *Adj.* scabious ‹*skin*›; mangy ‹*dog*›

Krätz·milbe *die* (Zool.) itch mite

Kratz-: ~putz *der* sgraffito; **~spur** *die* scratch [mark]; **~wunde** *die* scratch

krauchen /ˈkrauxn̩/ *itr. V.; mit sein* (md.) ▸**kriechen**

krauen /ˈkrauən/ *tr. V.* ▸**kraulen²**

Kraul /kraul/ *das;* **~s** (Sport) crawl

kraulen¹
A *itr. V.* **1▸** do *or* swim the crawl **2▸** *mit sein* **über den See/ans Ufer ~**: swim across the lake/to the bank using the crawl
B *tr. V.; auch mit sein* **eine Strecke ~**: cover a distance using the crawl

kraulen² *tr. V.* **jmdm. das Kinn ~**: tickle sb. under the chin; **jmdn. in den Haaren ~**: run

k

one's fingers through sb.'s hair; **seinen Bart ~:** finger one's beard

Kraul·schwimmen *das* crawl; **beim ~:** when doing the crawl

kraus /kraus/ *Adj.* 1 frizzy ‹*hair, beard*›; creased ‹*skirt etc.*›; wavy ‹*sea*›; wrinkled ‹*brow*›; **die Stirn ~ ziehen** wrinkle one's brow; (unmutig) frown; **die Nase ~ ziehen** wrinkle one's nose 2 (abwertend: verworren) muddled; confused

Krause *die;* **~, ~n** 1 (Kragen) ruff; (am Ärmel) ruffle; frill 2 (im Haar) frizziness; **eine [starke] ~ haben/bekommen** ‹*hair*› be/go [very] frizzy; ‹*person*› be/go [very] frizzy-haired

Kräusel-: ~band *das; Pl.* **~bänder** Rufflette [tape] ®; **~krepp** *der* crêpe

kräuseln /'krɔyzl̩n/

A *tr. V.* ruffle ‹*water, surface*›; gather ‹*material etc.*›; frizz ‹*hair*›; pucker [up] ‹*lips*›

B *refl. V.* ‹*hair*› go frizzy; ‹*water*› ripple; ‹*smoke*› curl up; ‹*material*› pucker up

krausen

A *tr. V.* gather ‹*material etc.*›; frizz ‹*hair*›; wrinkle [up] ‹*forehead, nose*›

B *itr. V.* ‹*material, clothes*› crease

kraus·haarig *Adj.* frizzy-haired ‹*person*›; curly-coated ‹*dog etc.*›

Kraus·kopf *der* frizzy hair; **einen ~ haben** have frizzy hair; be frizzy-haired; *s. auch* **Wuschelkopf**

Kraut /kraut/ *das;* **~[e]s, Kräuter** /'krɔytɐ/ 1 herb; **dagegen ist kein ~ gewachsen** (ugs.) there's nothing anyone can do about it 2 (Blätter) foliage; stems and leaves *pl.*; (von Kartoffeln, Bohnen usw.) haulm; (von Möhren, Rüben) tops *pl.*; **ins ~ schießen** put on too much foliage; bolt; (fig.) run wild; **wie ~ und Rüben** (ugs.) all over the place; in a complete muddle 3 (bes. südd., österr.: Kohl) cabbage 4 (ugs. abwertend: Tabak) tobacco; **er raucht ein ganz elendes ~:** he is smoking some really foul stuff

Kräutchen /'krɔytçən/ *das;* **~s, ~:** [small] herb; **ein ~ Rührmichnichtan sein** (veralt.) be oversensitive and easily upset

Kräuter-: ~buch *das* herbal; **~butter** *die* herb butter; **~essig** *der* herb vinegar; **~frau** *die* herbwoman; **~garten** *der* herb garden; **~käse** *der* cheese flavoured with herbs; **~kissen** *das* herb pillow; **~likör** *der* herb liqueur; **~sammler** *der,* **~sammlerin** *die* herbalist; **~tee** *der* herb tea; **~weib** *das* (veralt.) ▸ **~frau**

krautig *Adj.* herbaceous

Kraut-: ~junker *der* (hist. abwertend) large landowner; **~kopf** *der* ▸ **Kohlkopf**

Kräutlein *das;* **~s, ~** ▸ **Kräutchen**

Kraut-: ~rock *der* (Jargon) Kraut rock; German rock [music]; **~salat** *der* coleslaw; **~wickel** *der* (südd., österr.) ▸ **Kohlroulade**

Krawall /kra'val/ *der;* **~s, ~e** 1 (Tumult) riot 2 (ugs.: Lärm) row (coll.); racket; **es gab ~:** there was a row (coll.) *or* racket; **~ machen** kick up *or* make a row (coll.) *or* racket; **~ schlagen** kick up *or* make a fuss

Krawall·macher *der,* **Krawall·macherin** *die* rowdy

Krawatte /kra'vatə/ *die;* **~, ~n** 1 tie 2 (Catchen) headlock; chancery

Krawatten-: ~halter *der* tie clip; **~knoten** *der* knot [of the/a/one's tie]; **~muffel** *der* (ugs.) stick-in-the-mud where ties are concerned; **~nadel** *die* tiepin; **~zwang** *der:* **hier herrscht [kein] ~zwang** you [do not] have to wear a tie here

kraxeln /'kraksl̩n/ *itr. V.; mit sein* (bes. südd., österr. ugs.) climb; (mit Mühe) clamber; **auf etw.** (*Akk.*) **~:** climb [up] sth.; (mit Mühe) clamber up sth.

Kreation /krea'tsi̯o:n/ *die;* **~, ~en** (bes. Mode) creation

kreativ /krea'ti:f/

A *Adj.* creative

B *adv.* **~ veranlagt sein** have a creative bent

Kreative *der/die; adj. Dekl.* creative

Kreativität /kreativi'tɛ:t/ *die;* **~:** creativity

Kreativ·urlaub *der* [arts and crafts] activity holiday

Kreatur /krea'tu:ɐ̯/ *die;* **~, ~en** 1 (Geschöpf) creature 2 (alle Lebewesen) creation; **alle ~:** all creation; **Gott schuf alle ~:** God made all creatures *pl.* 3 (Mensch) creature; wretch 4 (abwertend: willenloser Mensch) minion; creature

kreatürlich /krea'ty:ɐ̯lɪç/ *Adj.* (geh.) creaturely, natural ‹*feeling, love, etc.*›; animal *attrib.* ‹*fear*›

Krebs /kre:ps/ *der;* **~es, ~e** 1 crustacean; (Fluss~) crayfish; (Krabbe) crab; **rot wie ein ~:** as red as a lobster; **einen ~ fangen** (Ruderersjargon) catch a crab 2 ▸ ❶ S. 439 (Krankheit) cancer 3 (Astrol.) Cancer; the Crab; *s. auch* **Fisch**

krebs·artig

A *Adj.* cancerous

B *adv.* cancerously; in the manner of a cancer

krebsen *itr. V.* 1 (Flusskrebse fangen) catch crayfish; (Krabben fangen) catch crabs 2 (ugs.: sich abmühen) **mit etw. zu ~ haben** find sth. a real *or* uphill struggle

krebs-, Krebs-: ~erregend, ~erzeugend *Adj.* carcinogenic; cancer-producing *usu. attrib.*; **das Rauchen kann ~erregend** *od.* **~erzeugend sein** smoking can cause cancer; **~forschung** *die* cancer research; **~gang** *der* 1 (rückläufige Entwicklung) retrogression; **den ~gang gehen** ‹*business*› go downhill; **im ~gang gehen** go backwards; 2 (Musik) retrograde movement; retrogression; **~geschwulst** *die* cancerous growth *or* tumour; **~geschwür** *das* (volkst.) cancerous ulcer; (fig. geh.) cancer; **~krank** *Adj.* cancer *attrib.* ‹*patient etc.*›; **~krank sein** suffer from *or* have cancer; **~kranke** *der/die* person suffering from cancer; (Patient) cancer patient; **~leiden** *das* cancer *no def. art.*; **~risiko** *das* cancer risk; risk of cancer; **~rot** *Adj.* as red as a lobster *postpos.*; (aus Verlegenheit) as red as a beetroot *postpos.*; **~rot werden** *od.* **anlaufen** go *or* turn as red as a beetroot; **~suppe** *die* crab soup; (aus Flusskrebsen) crayfish soup; **~tier** *das* (Zool.) crustacean; **~vorsorge** *die* (bes. Amtsspr.) **[Maßnahmen zur] ~vorsorge** precautions *pl.* against cancer; **~zelle** *die* cancer cell

Kredenz /kre'dɛnt̮s/ *die;* **~, ~en** (veralt.) sideboard

kredenzen *tr. V.* (geh.) **[jmdm.] etw. ~:** serve [sb. with] sth.

Kredit[1] /kre'di:t/ *der;* **~[e]s, ~e** ▸ ❶ S. 299 1 (Darlehen) loan; credit; **jmdm. einen ~ gewähren** *od.* **einräumen** *od.* **geben** give *or* grant sb. a loan *or* a credit; **einen ~ kündigen** call in a loan 2 (Zahlungsaufschub) credit; **er hat bei uns ~:** his credit is good with us; **jmdm. ~ geben** give *or* grant sb. credit; **auf ~:** on credit 3 (Kaufmannsspr.: Vertrauenswürdigkeit) good reputation *or* name; **jmdm. großen politischen ~ verschaffen** give sb. considerable political standing

Kredit[2] /'kre:dɪt/ *das;* **~s, ~s** (Finanzw.) credit side

kredit-, Kredit-: ~abteilung *die* credit department; **~anstalt** *die* credit institution; **~aufnahme** *die:* **durch ~aufnahme** by means of a loan/loans; **~brief** *der* (Finanzw.) letter of credit; **~fähig** *Adj.* (Finanzw.) creditworthy; **~geber** *der,* **~geberin** *die* lender; **~geschäft** *das* credit transaction; **~hai** *der* (ugs. abwertend) loan shark (coll.)

kreditieren *tr. V.* (Kaufmannsspr.) **jmdm. einen Betrag ~/jmdn. für einen Betrag ~:** advance sb. an amount *or* give sb. an amount on credit/credit sb. with an amount

kredit-, Kredit-: ~institut *das* credit institution; **~karte** *die* ▸ ❶ S. 299 credit card; **mit ~karte bezahlen** pay by credit card; **~kauf** *der* credit purchase; **~linie** *die* (Finanzw.) credit limit; **~nehmer** *der;* **~~s, ~~, ~nehmerin** *die;* **~~, ~~nen** borrower; **~schutz** *der* (Finanzw.) credit protection; **~würdig** *Adj.* (Finanzw.) creditworthy

Kredo /'kre:do/ *das;* **~s, ~s** 1 (kath. Kirche) creed; credo 2 (fig. geh.) credo

kregel /'kre:gl̩/ *Adj.* (bes. nordd., md.) lively

Kreide /'krai̯də/ *die;* **~, ~n** 1 (Kalkstein) chalk 2 (zum Schreiben) chalk; **mit ~ zeichnen/schreiben** draw/write in *or* with chalk; **ein Stück ~:** a piece of chalk; **bei jmdm. [tief] in der ~ stehen** *od.* **sitzen** *od.* **sein** be [deep] in debt to sb.; owe sb. [a lot of] money 3 (Geol.) Cretaceous [period]

kreide-, Kreide-: ~bleich *Adj.* as white as a sheet *postpos.*; **~felsen** *der* chalk cliff; **~haltig** *Adj.* chalky; cretaceous (Geol.); **~stift** *der* [piece of] chalk; (bild. Kunst) chalk; crayon; **~weiß** *Adj.:* ▸ **~bleich**; **~zeichnung** *die* chalk drawing; **~zeit** *die* ▸ **Kreide 3**

kreidig *Adj.* 1 (voller Kreide) chalky 2 (kreidehaltig) chalky; cretaceous (Geol.) 3 (geh.: bleich) deathly pale ‹*face*›

kreieren /kre'i:rən/ *tr. V.* (auch Theater) create

Kreis /krai̯s/ *der;* **~es, ~e** 1 circle; **einen ~ schlagen** *od.* **beschreiben** describe a circle; **jmds. ~e stören** (geh.) disturb sb. 2 (Handball: Wurf~) goal area 3 (Ring) circle; **einen ~ bilden** *od.* **schließen** form *or* make a circle; **in einem** *od.* **im ~ stehen/sitzen** stand/sit in a circle; **sich im ~ drehen** *od.* **bewegen** go *or* turn round in a circle; (fig.) go round in circles; **mir dreht sich alles im ~:** everything's going round and round; **der ~ hat sich geschlossen** the last piece has fallen into place; **~e ziehen** ‹*court case*› have [wide] repercussions; ‹*movement*› grow in size and influence 4 (Gruppe) circle; **der ~ meiner Freunde** my circle of friends; **im ~e der Freunde/Familie** among *or* with friends/within the family; **im kleinen** *od.* **engsten ~:** with a few close friends [and relatives]; **der ~ seiner Leser/Anhänger** his readers *pl.*/followers *pl.* 5 (Teil der Gesellschaft) circle; **in seinen ~en** in the circles in which he moves/moved; **in weiten** *od.* **breiten ~en der Bevölkerung** amongst wide sections of the population; **die besseren/besten ~e** the best circles 6 (von Problemen, Lösungen usw.) range 7 (Verwaltungsbezirk) district; (Wahl~) ward; **der ~ Heidelberg** the Heidelberg district *or* district of Heidelberg 8 (Elektrot.) circuit

Kreis-: ~abschnitt *der* (Geom.) segment [of a/the circle]; **~arzt** *der,* **~ärztin** *die* district medical officer; **~ausschnitt** *der* (Geom.) sector [of a/the circle]; **~bahn** *die* orbit; **~bewegung** *die* circular movement; **~bogen** *der* (Geom.) arc [of a/the circle]

kreischen /'krai̯ʃn̩/ *regelm.* (*veralt. auch unr.*) *itr. V.* ‹*person*› screech, shriek; ‹*bird*› screech; ‹*brakes*› squeal, screech; ‹*door*› creak; ‹*saw*› screech; **mit ~den Bremsen** with a squeal *or* screech of brakes

Kreisel /'krai̯zl̩/ *der;* **~s, ~** 1 (Technik) gyroscope 2 (Kinderspielzeug) top; **den ~ schlagen** spin *or* whip the top 3 (ugs.: Kreisverkehr) roundabout

Kreisel-: ~bewegung *die* gyration; spinning movement; **~kompass,** ***~kompaß** *der* (Schifffahrt) gyrocompass

kreiseln *itr. V.* 1 *auch mit sein* (sich drehen) spin [round]; gyrate 2 (mit einem Kreisel spielen) play with a top; spin a top

Kreisel·pumpe *die* (Technik) centrifugal pump

kreisen *itr. V.* 1 *auch mit sein* ‹*planet*› revolve (**um** around); ‹*satellite etc.*› orbit; ‹*aircraft, bird*› circle; **der Satellit kreist um die Erde** the satellite orbits the Earth; **das Blut kreiste schneller in seinen Adern** (fig.) the blood coursed faster in his veins; **die Flasche [in der Runde] ~ lassen** (fig.) pass the bottle round; **seine Gedanken kreisten immer um dasselbe Thema** (fig.) his thoughts always revolved around the same subject 2 (Sport) **die Arme ~ lassen** swing one's arms round [in a circle]

kreis-, Kreis-: ~fläche *die* (Geom.) area of a/the circle; **~förmig** A *Adj.* circular; B *adv.* **ein ~förmig gebogenes Stück Draht** a piece of wire bent into a circle; **~frei** *Adj.* (Amtsspr.) **eine ~freie Stadt** a town that is administered as a district in its own right; **~klasse** *die* (Sport) district league; **~kolben·motor** *der* ▸ **Wankelmotor**; **~lauf** *der* 1 (der Natur, der

Wirtschaft, des Lebens usw.) cycle; (des Geldes; Technik) circulation; [2] (Physiol.) circulation; **~läufer** *der*, **~läuferin** *die* (Hallenhandball) ▸**~spieler**; **~lauf·kollaps** *der* ▸❶ **S. 439** (Med.) circulatory collapse; **~lauf·mittel** *das* [1] remedy to prevent faintness; [2] (Med.) circulatory preparation; (den ~lauf anregend) circulatory stimulant; **~lauf·störung** *die* ▸❶ **S. 439** [1] *bes. im Pl.* faintness; [2] (Med.) cardio-vascular disorder; circulatory disturbance; **~laufstörungen** *Pl.* circulatory trouble *sing.*; **~leitung** *die* (DDR) district committee; **~linie** *die* (Geom.) circumference [of a/the circle]; **~ring** *der* (Geom.) annulus; **~rund** **A** *Adj.* [perfectly] circular *or* round; **B** *adv.* ‹*bent etc.*› in[to] a [perfect] circle; **~säge** *die* [1] (Werkzeug) circular saw; [2] (ugs. scherzh.: Strohhut) boater

kreißen /ˈkraisn̩/ *itr. V.* (veralt.) be in labour

Kreis·spieler *der*, **Kreis·spielerin** *die* (Hallenhandball) pivot player

Kreiß·saal *der* (Med.) delivery room

Kreis-: ~stadt *die* chief town of a/the district; **~tag** *der* district assembly; **~verkehr** *der* traffic on *or* going round a/the roundabout; (Platz) roundabout; **~verwaltung** *die* administration of a/the district; (Behörde) district authority; **~wehrersatz·amt** *das* district recruiting office; **~zahl** *die* (Math.) pi *no art.*

Krem /kreːm/ *die*; **~, ~s** ▸**Creme**

Krematorium /kremaˈtoːri̯ʊm/ *das*; **~s, Krematorien** crematorium

kremig ▸**cremig**

Kreml /ˈkrɛml̩/ *der*; **~s** Kremlin

Krempe /ˈkrɛmpə/ *die*; **~, ~n** brim

Krempel[1] /ˈkrɛmpl̩/ *der*; **~s** (ugs. abwertend) stuff; (Gerümpel) junk; **den ganzen ~ hinwerfen** (fig.) chuck the whole thing in (coll.)

Krempel[2] *die*; **~, ~n** (Textilind.) carding machine

krempeln[1] *tr. V.* roll

krempeln[2] *tr. V.* (Textilind.) card

Kremser /ˈkrɛmzɐ/ *der*; **~s, ~** (veralt.) [covered] charabanc (Brit. dated)

Kren /kreːn/ *der*; **~[e]s** (südd., bes. österr.) ▸**Meerrettich**

Kreole /kreˈoːlə/ *der*; **~n, ~n, Kreolin** *die*; **~, ~nen** Creole

kreolisch *Adj.* ▸❶ **S. 670** Creole

krepieren /kreˈpiːrən/ *itr. V.*; *mit sein* [1] (zerplatzen) explode; go off [2] (salopp: sterben) ‹*animal*› die; ‹*person*› snuff it (sl.)

Krepp /krɛp/ *der*; **~s, ~s** *od.* **~e** crêpe

***Kreppapier** ▸**Krepppapier**

Krepp-: ~papier *das* crêpe paper; **~sohle** *die* crêpe sole

Kresse /ˈkrɛsə/ *die*; **~, ~n** (Bot.) cress

Kreta /ˈkreːta/ *(das)*; **~s** Crete

Kreter /ˈkreːtɐ/ *der*; **~s, ~, Kreterin** *die*; **~, ~nen** Cretan

Krethi und Plethi *Pl., auch Sg.* (abwertend) every Tom, Dick and Harry *sing.*

Kretin /kreˈtɛ̃ː/ *der*; **~s, ~s** [1] (Med.) cretin [2] (fig. abwertend) imbecile

Kretinismus /kretiˈnɪsmʊs/ *der*; **~** (Med.) cretinism *no art.*

kreucht /krɔyçt/ *in* **alles, was da ~ und fleucht** all living creatures *or* things

kreuz: **~ und quer durch die Stadt fahren** drive all over/round the town; **in die Kreuz und [in die] Quere fahren** drive all over the place

Kreuz /krɔyts/ *das*; **~es, ~e** [1] cross; (Symbol) cross; crucifix; **etw. über ~ legen/falten** lay sth. down/fold sth. crosswise; **das ~ des Südens** (Astron.) the Southern Cross; **mit jmdm. über ~ sein** *od.* **liegen** (ugs.) be at loggerheads with sb.; **zu ~e kriechen** humble oneself; *s. auch* **eisern A 1**; **rot A** [2] (hist.) cross; **jmdn. ans ~ schlagen** *od.* **nageln** nail sb. to the cross [3] (**~zeichen**) sign of the cross; **das/ein ~ schlagen** make the sign of the cross; (sich bekreuzigen) cross oneself; **drei ~e machen** (ugs.) heave a sigh of relief [4] (Leid) cross; **sein ~ auf sich nehmen/tragen** take up/bear one's cross; **es ist ein ~ mit jmdm./etw.** (ugs.) sb. is a real strain *or* is really trying/sth. is a real problem [5] (Teil des Rückens) small of the back; **ein steifes ~ haben** have a stiff back; **Schmerzen im ~**: pain in the small of the back; **ich habs im ~** (ugs.) I've got back trouble *or* a bad back; **jmdn. aufs ~ legen** (salopp) take sb. for a ride (coll.); **eine Frau aufs ~ legen** (salopp: mit ihr schlafen) lay a woman (sl.); **fast** *od.* **beinahe aufs ~ fallen** (fig.) almost fall through the floor; **jmdm. etw. aus dem ~ leiern** (salopp) talk sb. into handing sth. over [6] (Kartenspiel) (Farbe) clubs *pl.*; (Karte) club; *s. auch* **Pik**[2] [7] (Autobahn) interchange [8] (Musik) sharp

kreuz-, Kreuz-: ~abnahme *die* (bild. Kunst) Descent *or* Deposition from the Cross; ***~as, ~ass** *das* ace of clubs; **~band** *das*; *Pl.* **~bänder** ▸❶ **S. 435** (Anat.) cruciate ligament; **~bein** *das* ▸❶ **S. 435** (Anat.) sacrum; **~blume** *die* [1] (Bot.) milkwort; [2] (Archit.) finial; **~blütler** *der*; **~~s, ~~** (Bot.) cruciferous plant; crucifer; **~brav** *Adj.* thoroughly good and honest ‹*person*›; very good *or* well-behaved ‹*child*›; **~bube** *der* jack of clubs; **~dame** *die* queen of clubs

kreuzen

A *tr. V.* (auch Biol.) cross; **die Arme/Beine [übereinander] ~**: cross *or* fold one's arms/cross one's legs; *s. auch* **Klinge 2**

B *refl. V.* [1] (überschneiden) cross; intersect; **ihre Wege ~ sich** (fig.) their paths cross; **ihre Blicke ~ sich** (fig.) their eyes meet [2] (zuwiderlaufen) clash (**mit** with)

C *itr. V.* [1] *mit haben od. sein* (hin und her fahren) cruise [2] (Seemannsspr.) tack

Kreuzer *der*; **~s, ~** [1] (Milit.: Kriegsschiff) cruiser [2] (Segelsport) cruising yacht; cruiser [3] (hist.: Münze) kreuzer

Kreuzes·tod *der* [death by] crucifixion; **den ~ sterben** die on the cross

kreuz-, Kreuz-: ~fahrer *der* (hist.) crusader; **~fahrt** *die* [1] (Seereise) cruise; **eine ~fahrt machen** go on a cruise; [2] (hist.) ▸**~zug**; **~fahrt·schiff** *das* cruise ship; **~feuer** *das* (Milit., auch fig.) crossfire; **etw. unter ~feuer nehmen** direct crossfire at sth.; **im ~feuer stehen** be under fire from all sides; **ins ~feuer geraten** come under fire from all sides; **~fidel** *Adj.* (ugs.) (sehr gut gelaunt) very cheerful; (sehr lustig) very jolly; **~förmig** **A** *Adj.* cross-shaped; cruciform; **B** *adv.* ‹*built, arranged, etc.*› in the shape of a cross; **~gang** *der* cloister; **~gelenk** *das* ▸**Kardangelenk**; **~gewölbe** *das* (Archit.) cross vault; **~griff** *der* (Turnen) cross grip; **~hacke** *die* pickaxe

kreuzigen /ˈkrɔytsɪgn̩/ *tr. V.* crucify; **der Gekreuzigte** Christ crucified

Kreuzigung *die*; **~, ~en** [1] (das Kreuzigen) crucifixion [2] (bild. Kunst) Crucifixion

kreuz-, Kreuz-: ~knoten *der* (Seemannsspr.) reef knot; **~könig** *der* king of clubs; **~lahm** *Adj.* broken-backed ‹*horse etc.*›; **ich bin ganz ~lahm** (ugs.) my back is killing me (coll.); **~mast** *der* (Seemannsspr.) mizzen-mast; **~otter** *die* adder; [common] viper; **~reim** *der* (Verslehre) alternate rhyme; **~rippen·gewölbe** *das* (Archit.) ribbed vault; **~ritter** *der* (hist.) [1] crusader; [2] (vom deutschen Ritterorden) Teutonic Knight; knight of the Teutonic Order; **~schlitz·schraube** *die* Phillips screw ®; **~schlitz·schrauben·dreher** *der* Phillips screwdriver ®; **~schlüssel** *der* four-way wheel brace; **~schmerzen** *Pl.* pain *sing.* in the small of the back; **~schnabel** *der* (Zool.) crossbill; **~spinne** *die* cross spider; garden spider; **~stich** *der* (Handarb.) cross stitch

Kreuzung *die*; **~, ~en** [1] ▸❶ **S. 800** junction; crossroads *sing.* [2] (Biol.) crossing; cross-breeding; (Ergebnis) cross; cross-breed; **eine ~ aus** *od.* **von ... und ...** a cross between ... and ...

kreuz·unglücklich *Adj.* (ugs.) terribly miserable (coll.)

kreuzungs·frei *Adj.* (Verkehrsw.) without [any] junctions *postpos.*

Kreuzungs·punkt *der* junction; (von Autobahnen) intersection

kreuz-, Kreuz-: ~verband *der* (Bauw.) English cross bond; **~verhör** *das* cross-examination; **jmdn. ins ~verhör nehmen** (fig.) cross-examine sb.; **~weg** *der* [1] (Wegkreuzung) crossroads *sing.*; **am ~weg stehen/an einen ~weg gekommen sein** (geh.) stand *or* be at/have reached a crossroads; [2] (kath. Kirche: Darstellung, Gebete) stations of the Cross, way of the Cross; **~weise** *Adv.* crosswise; crossways; **du kannst mich mal ~weise!** (derb) [you can] get stuffed! (sl.); **~wort·rätsel** *das* crossword [puzzle]; **~zeichen** *das* (bes. kath. Kirche) sign of the cross; **das ~zeichen machen** make the sign of the cross; (sich bekreuzigen) cross oneself; **~zug** *der* [1] (hist.) crusade; [2] (Kampagne) crusade

Krevette /kreˈvɛtə/ *die*; **~, ~n** palaemon prawn; leander

kribbelig *Adj.* (ugs.) [1] (vor Ungeduld) fidgety; (nervös) edgy [2] (kribbelnd) **ein ~es Gefühl in der Hand** pins and needles in one's hand

kribbeln /ˈkrɪbl̩n/ *itr. V.* [1] (jucken) tickle; (prickeln) tingle; **es kribbelt mir** *od.* **mich in der Nase/in den Füßen/unter der Haut** I've got a tickle in my nose/my feet are tingling *or* I've got pins and needles in my feet/my skin is itching *or* prickling; **es kribbelt mir in den Fingern, es zu tun** (fig.) I'm just itching to do it [2] (wimmeln) swarm [about]; **in dem Ameisenhaufen kribbelte und krabbelte es** the ants were swarming about in the anthill

kribblig ▸**kribbelig**

Krickelkrakel /ˈkrɪkl̩krakl̩/ *das*; **~s** (ugs.) scribble; scrawl

Kricket /ˈkrɪkət/ *das*; **~s** cricket

Krida /ˈkriːda/ *die*; **~** (österr. Rechtsw.) fraudulent bankruptcy; (fahrlässig) bankruptcy through negligence

kriechen /ˈkriːçn̩/ *unr. itr. V.* [1] *mit sein* ‹*insect, baby*› crawl; ‹*plant*› creep; ‹*person, animal*› creep, crawl; ‹*car, train, etc.*› crawl *or* creep [along]; **aus dem Ei/der Puppe ~**: hatch [out]/emerge from the chrysalis; **~de Pflanzen** creepers; **erschöpft ins Bett ~**: crawl exhausted into bed; **auf allen vieren/auf dem Bauch ~**: crawl on all fours/crawl [along] on one's stomach; **die Zeit/der Zeiger kriecht** (fig.) time creeps by/the hand creeps [around the dial]; *s. auch* **Kreuz 1** [2] *mit sein* (ugs.: sich fortbewegen) walk; get about; **kaum noch ~ können** hardly be able to get about *or* walk; (alt und gebrechlich sein) be old and decrepit [3] *auch mit sein* (abwertend: sich unterwürfig verhalten) crawl, grovel (**vor** + *Dat.* to)

Kriecher *der*; **~s, ~, Kriecherin** *die*; **~, ~nen** (abwertend) crawler; groveller

kriecherisch *Adj.* (abwertend) crawling; grovelling

Kriech-: ~spur *die* (Verkehrsw.) crawler lane; **~strom** *der* (Elektrot.) leakage current; **~tempo** *das* (abwertend) **im ~tempo** at a snail's pace; **~tier** *das* (Zool.) reptile

Krieg /kriːk/ *der*; **~[e]s, ~e** war; (Kriegführung) warfare; **[gegen jmdn.] ~ führen** wage war [on sb.]; **~ führend** warring; belligerent; **einem Land den ~ erklären** declare war on a country; **sich im ~ befinden** *od.* **im ~ stehen [mit ...]** be at war [with ...]; **in den ~ ziehen** go to war; **im ~ bleiben** *od.* **fallen** be killed in the war; **der kalte ~**: the cold war

kriegen *tr. V.* (ugs.) [1] (bekommen) get; **noch Geld von jmdm. ~**: be owed money by sb.; **Bescheid ~**: be told; **Schläge** *od.* **sie ~**: get a good hiding (coll.) *or* beating; **du kriegst gleich eine/ein paar!** I'll clout you in a moment!; **ein Jahr [Gefängnis] ~**: get a *or* one year [in prison]; **einen Schnupfen ~**: catch [a] cold; **Besuch ~**: have a visitor/visitors; **seinen Willen ~**: get one's own way; **ich kriege keine Verbindung** *od.* **keinen Anschluss** I can't get through; **am Ende des Films ~ sie sich** at the end of the film boy gets girl; **was ~ Sie?** what can I get you?; **ein Baby/Kind ~**: have a baby/child; **Junge ~**: have puppies/kittens *etc.*; **jmdn. dazu ~, etw. zu tun** get sb. to do sth.; **er ist nicht aus dem Haus** *od.* **vor die**

k

Tür zu ~: nothing will get him out of the house *or* front door; **jmdn. satt/frei ~:** feed sb./get sb. free; **wir werden das** *od.* **es schon ~:** we'll soon sort it out; **zu viel ~** (ugs.) blow one's top (coll.); (bei jmds. Worten) see red; *s. auch* **genug; Motte 1; zu viel A 1** 2▸ (befallen werden) get; **die Wut/Angst/einen Schrecken ~:** get angry scared/have *or* get a shock; **Hunger/Durst ~:** get hungry/thirsty; **Heimweh/Fernweh ~:** get homesick/start suffering from wanderlust; **einen roten Kopf ~:** go red; blush; **Falten/eine Glatze ~:** get wrinkles/go bald 3▸ (erreichen) catch ‹*train, bus, etc.*› 4▸ (fangen) catch 5▸ + *Inf. mit „zu"* (die Möglichkeit haben) **etw. zu essen ~:** get sth. to eat; **er kriegte den Ast zu fassen** he was able to *or* he managed to grab hold of the branch 6▸ + *Inf. mit „zu"* (ertragen müssen) **etw. zu spüren/hören ~:** feel the force of sth./get a good talking-to; **es mit jmdm. zu tun ~:** have sb. to reckon with 7▸ + *2. Part.* **etw. geschenkt ~:** get sth. as a present; **ein gutes Essen vorgesetzt ~:** get served with a good meal 8▸ *in* **es nicht über sich ~, etw. zu tun** (ugs.) not be able to bring oneself to do sth.

Krieger *der;* **~s, ~:** warrior; (nordamerikanischer Indianer) brave; **die alten ~:** the veterans; **ein müder ~** (fig.) a tired old thing

Krieger·denkmal *das* (veralt.) war memorial

Kriegerin *die;* **~, ~nen** warrior

kriegerisch *Adj.* 1▸ (kampflustig) warlike 2▸ (militärisch) military; **eine ~e Auseinandersetzung** an armed conflict

Krieger·witwe *die* war widow

krieg·führend ▸**Krieg**

Krieg·führung *die* warfare *no art.;* (Leitung) conduct of the war

kriegs-, Kriegs-: ~anleihe *die* war loan; **~aus·bruch** *der* outbreak of war; **bei/vor ~ausbruch** at/before the outbreak of war; **~bedingt** *Adj.* caused by the war *postpos.;* **~beginn** *der* beginning *or* start of the war; **~beil** *das* tomahawk; **das ~beil ausgraben/begraben** (scherzh.) start fighting/bury the hatchet; **~bemalung** *die* (Völkerk.) warpaint; **in voller ~bemalung** (scherzh.) in full warpaint; **~berichterstatter** *der,* **~berichterstatterin** *die* war correspondent; **~bericht·erstattung** *die* war reporting *no art.;* **~beschädigt** *Adj.* war-disabled; **~beschädigte** *der/die* war-disabled person; war invalid; **~beute** *die* spoils *pl.* of war; **~blinde** *der/die* person blinded in the war; **~dienst** *der* 1▸ (im Krieg) active service; 2▸ (Wehrdienst) military service; **den ~dienst verweigern** be a conscientious objector; **~dienst·verweigerer** *der* conscientious objector; **~dienst·verweigerung** *die* conscientious objection; **~einwirkung** *die:* **infolge von ~einwirkungen** as a result of the war; **~ende** *das* end of the war; **bei/vor ~ende** at/before the end of the war; **~entschädigung** *die* reparations *pl.;* **~entscheidend** *Adj.* decisive for the outcome of the war *postpos.;* **~erklärung** *die* declaration of war; **~erlebnis** *das* wartime experience; **~fall** *der:* **im ~fall[e]** in the event of war; **~film** *der* war film; **~flagge** *die* naval ensign; **~flotte** *die* navy; fleet; **~freiwillige** *der* [war] volunteer; **~führung** *die* ▸**Kriegführung; ~fuß** *der: in* **mit jmdm. auf [dem] ~fuß stehen** *od.* **leben** (scherzh.) be at loggerheads with sb.; **mit etw. auf [dem] ~fuß stehen** (scherzh.) be totally lost when it comes to sth.; **~gebiet** *das* war zone; **~gefahr** *die* danger of war; **~gefangen** *Adj.* captured; **~gefangene** *der/die* prisoner of war; POW; **~gefangenschaft** *die* captivity; **in ~gefangenschaft sein/geraten** be a prisoner of war/be taken prisoner; **aus der ~gefangenschaft entlassen werden** be released from captivity; **~gegner** *der* 1▸ (Gegner im Krieg) enemy; 2▸ (Gegner des Krieges) opponent of the/a war; (Pazifist) opponent of war; **~gegnerin** *die* ▸**~gegner 2; ~gericht** *das* court martial; **jmdn. vor ein ~gericht stellen** court-martial sb.; **~geschrei** *das* war cries *pl.;* **~gewinnler** /-gəvɪnlɐ/ *der;* **~~s, ~~, ~gewinnlerin** *die;* **~~, ~~nen** (abwertend) war profiteer; **~glück** *das* (geh.) fortune *or* luck in war; **~gott** *der* (Myth.) god of war; **~gräber·fürsorge** *die* 1▸ care of war graves; 2▸ (Institution) war graves commission; **~gräuel,** ***~greuel** *der* wartime atrocity; **~hafen** *der* naval port; **~handwerk** *das* (geh. veralt.) art of warfare; **~held** *der* (geh.) war hero; **~herr** *der* (geh. veralt.) commander; **oberster ~herr** supreme commander; commander-in-chief; **~hetze** *die* (abwertend) warmongering; **~hetze betreiben** stir up war; **~hinterbliebene** *der/die* war orphan/widow; **die ~hinterbliebenen** war widows and orphans; **~industrie** *die* armaments industry; **~invalide** *der* war-disabled person; war invalid; **~jahr** *das:* **im ersten/dritten ~jahr** in the first/third year of the war; **während der ~jahre/der letzten ~jahre** during the war years/the last years of the war; **~kamerad** *der* wartime comrade; **~knecht** *der* (veralt.) soldier; (Söldner) mercenary; **~kunst** *die* (geh., veralt.) art of war *or* warfare; **~list** *die* military stratagem; (fig. scherzh.) ruse; **~lüstern** *Adj.* bellicose; warlike; **~marine** *die* navy; **~maschine** *die* (hist.) engine [of war]; **~maschinerie** *die* (abwertend) machinery of war; **~minister** *der* (hist.) minister of *or* for war; **~ministerium** *das* (hist.) war ministry; (in Großbritannien) War Office (Hist.); **~müde** *Adj.* war-weary; **~opfer** *das* war victim; **~pfad** *der: in* **auf dem ~pfad** (auch fig.) on the warpath; **~propaganda** *die* wartime propaganda; **~rat** *der: in* **~rat [ab]halten** (scherzh.) have a powwow; **~recht** *das* 1▸ laws *pl.* of war; 2▸ **das ~recht verhängen** impose martial law; **~schaden** *der* (bes. Amtsspr.) war damage *no art.;* **~schäden** *Pl.* war damage *sing., no art.;* **~schauplatz** *der* theatre of war; **~schiff** *das* warship; **~schuld** *die* war guilt; **~schulden** *Pl.* war debts; **~spiel** *das* 1▸ (Milit.) war game; 2▸ (Kinderspiel) [game of] soldiers *sing.;* **~spiel·zeug** *das* war toys *pl.;* (einzelnes) war toy; **~stärke** *die* wartime strength; **~tanz** *der* (Völkerk.) war dance; **~tauglich** *Adj.* fit for active service *postpos.;* **~teilnehmer** *der* combatant; (ehemaliger Soldat) ex-serviceman; war veteran (Amer.); **~trauung** *die* war-marriage; **~treiber** *der,* **~treiberin** *die* (abwertend) warmonger; **~untauglich** *Adj.* unfit for active service *postpos.;* **~verbrechen** *das* (Rechtsw.) war crime; **~verbrecher** *der,* **~verbrecherin** *die* war criminal; **~verbrecher·prozess,** ***~verbrecher·prozeß** *der* war crimes trial; **~verbündet** *Adj.* co-belligerent; **~verbündete** *der* co-belligerent; **~verletzung** *die* war wound *or* injury; **~versehrt** *Adj.:* ▸**~beschädigt; ~versehrte** *der/die* ▸**~beschädigte; ~verwendungs·fähig** *Adj.* (Amtsspr.) fit for active service *postpos.;* **~waise** *die* war orphan; **~wichtig** *Adj.* essential to the war effort *postpos.;* **~wirren** *Pl.* chaos *sing.* of war; **~wirtschaft** *die* war[time] economy; **~zeit** *die* wartime; **in ~zeiten** *Pl.* in wartime; **~ziel** *das* war aim; aim of a/the war; **~zustand** *der* state of war; **sich im ~zustand befinden** be at war

Krill /krɪl/ *der;* **~[e]s** krill

Krim /krɪm/ *die;* **~ die ~:** the Crimea

Krimi /ˈkriːmi/ *der;* **~[s], ~[s]** (ugs.) 1▸ (Film, Stück) crime thriller; whodunnit (coll.); (fig.: Fußballspiel, Quizsendung usw.) thriller; cliffhanger 2▸ (Roman) crime thriller; whodunnit (coll.); (mit Detektiv als Held) detective story

Kriminal·beamte /krimiˈnaːl-/ *der,* **Kriminal·beamtin** *die* ▸❶ **S. 113** [plain-clothes] detective

Kriminale *der; adj. Dekl.,* **Kriminaler** *der;* **~s, ~** (ugs.) detective

Kriminal-: ~fall *der* criminal case; crime; **~film** *der* crime film *or* thriller; **~gericht** *das* (veralt.) ▸**Strafgericht; ~hörspiel** *das* radio crime thriller

kriminalisieren *tr. V.* 1▸ (kriminell machen) **jmdn. ~:** make sb. turn to crime 2▸ (als kriminell hinstellen) **jmdn./etw. ~:** present sb. as a criminal/sth. as [being] criminal *or* a criminal act

Kriminalisierung *die;* **~, ~en** 1▸ (das Kriminellmachen) **die ~ von jmdm.** making sb. turn to crime; 2▸ (Hinstellen als kriminell) (einer Person/Organisation) presentation as a criminal/a criminal organization; (einer Aktivität) presentation as a criminal act

Kriminalist *der;* **~en, ~en, Kriminalistin** *die* detective

Kriminalistik *die;* **~:** criminalistics *sing., no art.*

kriminalistisch

A *Adj.* ‹*methods, practice*› of criminalistics; ‹*abilities*› in the field of criminalistics

B *adv.* ‹*proceed etc.*› using the methods of criminalistics

Kriminalität /kriminaliˈtɛːt/ *die;* **~** 1▸ crime *no art.;* **ein Absinken der ~:** a drop in the level of crime *or* in the crime rate 2▸ (Straffälligkeit) criminality

Kriminal-: ~kommissar *der,* **~kommissarin** *die* ▸❶ **S. 113** ≈ detective superintendent; **~komödie** *die* comedy thriller; **~polizei** *die* criminal investigation department; **~roman** *der* crime novel *or* thriller; (mit Detektiv als Held) detective novel

> **Kriminalpolizei - Kripo**
>
> The criminal investigation department deals with serious offences, including murder and organized crime. It has special units to fight terrorism and for observation and searches.

kriminell /krimiˈnɛl/

A *Adj.* (auch ugs.: rücksichtslos) criminal; **~ werden/sein** become a criminal *or* turn to crime/be a criminal

B *adv.* 1▸ **~ veranlagt sein** have criminal tendencies; **~ handeln** act illegally; break the law 2▸ (ugs.: rücksichtslos) criminally; ‹*drive*› with criminal recklessness

Kriminelle *der/die; adj. Dekl.* criminal

Kriminologe *der;* **~n, ~n** ▸❶ **S. 113** criminologist

Kriminologie /kriminoloˈgiː/ *die* criminology *no art.*

Kriminologin *die;* **~, ~nen** ▸❶ **S. 113** criminologist

Krim·krieg /ˈkrɪm-/ *der;* **~[e]s** Crimean War

Krimskrams /ˈkrɪmskrams/ *der;* **~[es]** (ugs.) stuff; **einigen ~ kaufen** buy a few bits and pieces

Kringel /ˈkrɪŋl̩/ *der;* **~s, ~** 1▸ (Kreis) [small] ring; (Kritzelei) round squiggle 2▸ (Gebäck) [ring-shaped] biscuit; ring

kringelig *Adj.* crinkly ‹*hair*›; squiggly ‹*shape, line, etc.*›; **sich ~ lachen** (ugs.) laugh one's head off; kill oneself [laughing] (coll.)

kringeln

A *tr. V.* curl [up] ‹*tail*›; **jmds. Haar ~:** curl sb.'s hair; ‹*wind, rain*› make sb.'s hair go curly

B *refl. V.* curl [up]; ‹*hair*› go curly; **sich [vor Lachen] ~** (ugs.) laugh one's head off; kill oneself [laughing] (coll.)

Krinoline /krinoˈliːnə/ *die;* **~, ~n** (hist.) crinoline

Kripo /ˈkriːpo/ *die;* **~** (ugs.) **die ~:** ≈ the CID

Krippe /ˈkrɪpə/ *die;* **~, ~n** 1▸ (Futtertrog) manger; crib; *s. auch* **Futter~** 2▸ (Weihnachten) model of a nativity scene; crib 3▸ (Kinder~) crèche; day nursery

Krippen·spiel *das* nativity play

Kris /kriːs/ *der;* **~es, ~e** kris

Krise /ˈkriːzə/ *die;* **~, ~n** (auch Med.) crisis; **eine ~ durchmachen/überwinden** go through/overcome a crisis; **in eine ~ geraten** enter a state of crisis; **wenn sie das hört, kriegt sie die ~** (ugs.) she'll have a fit when she hears that (coll.)

kriseln /ˈkriːzl̩n/ *itr. V.* (unpers.) **es kriselt in ihrer Ehe/in der Partei** (eine Krise droht) their marriage is running into trouble/there is a

k

crisis looming in the party; (eine Krise ist vorhanden) their marriage is in trouble/the party is in a state of crisis

krisen-, Krisen-: ~anfällig *Adj.* crisis-prone; **~fest** *Adj.* that is/are unaffected by crises *postpos., not pred.*; **~fest sein** be unaffected by crises; **~gebeutelt** *Adj.* crisis-torn; **~gebiet** *das* crisis area; **~geplagt** *Adj.* crisis-ridden; **~geschüttelt** *Adj.* crisis-torn; (krisengeplagt) crisis-ridden; **~herd** *der* trouble spot; **~management** *das* crisis management; **~stab** *der* crisis team

Krisis /ˈkriːzɪs/ *die;* ~, **Krisen** (veralt., Med.) ▸**Krise**

Kristall¹ /krɪsˈtal/ *der;* **~s, ~e** crystal

Kristall² *das;* **~s** **1** (Material) crystal *no indef. art.*; **Gläser aus ~:** crystal glasses **2** (Gegenstände) crystal *no indef. art.*

Kristall·bildung *die* ▸**Kristallisation**

kristallen *Adj.* crystal

***Kristalleuchter** ▸**Kristallleuchter**

Kristall-: ~gitter *das* (Chemie) crystal lattice; **~glas** *das* **1** crystal glass; **2** (Bleikristall) crystal

kristallin /krɪstaˈliːn/ *Adj.* (bes. Mineral.) crystalline

Kristallisation /krɪstalizaˈtsi̯oːn/ *die;* ~, **~en** (bes. Chemie) crystallization

kristallisieren (bes. Chemie)

A *itr. V.* crystallize

B *refl. V.* (auch fig.) crystallize

kristall-, Kristall-: ~klar *Adj.* (auch fig.) crystal clear; **~kugel** *die* crystal ball; **~leuchter** *der*, **~lüster** *der* (veralt.) crystal chandelier; **~nacht** *die* (ns.) crystal night; Kristallnacht; *National Socialist pogrom against Jews in November 1938*; **~schale** *die* crystal bowl

***Kristallüster** ▸**Kristalllüster**

Kristall-: ~waren *Pl.* crystal [glass] *sing.*; **~zucker** *der* (bes. fachspr.) refined sugar in crystals

Kriterium /kriˈteːri̯ʊm/ *das;* **~s, Kriterien** **1** criterion **2** (bes. Skisport) race **3** (Radsport) criterium

Kritik /kriˈtiːk/ *die;* ~, **~en** **1** criticism *no indef. art.* (**an** + *Dat.* of); **an jmdm./etw. ~ üben** criticize sb./sth.; **auf ~ stoßen** meet with *or* come in for criticism; **unter aller** *od.* **jeder ~ sein** (ugs.) be absolutely hopeless **2** (Besprechung) review; notice; **eine gute/schlechte ~** *od.* **gute/schlechte ~en bekommen** get good/bad reviews *or* notices **3** (die ~er) critics *pl.*; reviewers *pl.* **4** (Philos., Analyse) critique

Kritikaster /kritiˈkastɐ/ *der;* **~s, ~, Kritikasterin** *die;* ~, **~nen** (geh. abwertend) criticaster; caviller

Kritiker /ˈkriːtikɐ/ *der;* **~s, ~, Kritikerin** *die;* ~, **~nen** ▸❶ **S. 113** critic

Kritik·fähigkeit *die* critical faculties *pl.*

kritik·los

A *Adj.* uncritical;

B *adv.* uncritically; **etw. ~ hinnehmen** accept sth. without criticism

kritisch /ˈkriːtɪʃ/

A *Adj.* **1** (auch Kernphysik) critical; **ein ~er Apparat** (Wissensch.) critical apparatus; **eine ~e Ausgabe** (Wissensch.) a critical edition **2** (entscheidend) critical; **~er Punkt** (Skisport) critical point; **~e Temperatur** (Physik, Chemie) critical temperature

B *adv.* critically; **sich mit etw. ~ auseinander setzen** make a critical study of sth.; **jmdm./etw. ~ gegenüberstehen** be critical of sb./sth.

kritisierbar *Adj.* criticizable; open to criticism *pred.*

kritisieren /kritiˈziːrən/ *tr. V.* criticize; review ‹*book, play, etc.*›; **immer etwas zu ~ haben** always find something to criticize

Kritizismus /kritiˈtsɪsmʊs/ *der;* ~ (Philos.) critical philosophy

Krittelei *die;* ~, **~en** (abwertend) fault-finding; carping

kritteln /ˈkrɪtl̩n/ *itr. V.* (abwertend) find fault (**an** + *Dat.*, **über** + *Akk.* with); carp (**an** + *Dat.*, **über** + *Akk.* at)

Kritzelei *die;* ~, **~en** **1** (das Schreiben) scribbling; (das Zeichnen) doodling **2** (Schrift) scribble; (Zeichnung) doodle; (an Wänden) graffiti *sing. or pl.*

kritzeln /ˈkrɪts̩ln/

A *itr. V.* (schreiben) scribble; (zeichnen) doodle

B *tr. V.* scribble; **etw. auf/in etw.** (*Akk.*) **~:** scribble sth. on/in sth.

Kroate /kroˈaːtə/ *der;* **~n, ~n** Croat; Croatian

Kroatien /kroˈaːtsi̯ən/ (*das*) Croatia

Kroatin *die;* ~, **~nen** ▸**Kroate**; *s. auch* **-in**

kroatisch *Adj.* ▸❶ **S. 670** Croatian

Kroatz·beere /kroˈats-/ *die;* ~, **~n** (ostmd.) ▸**Brombeere**

kroch *1. u. 3. Pers. Sg. Prät. v.* **kriechen**

Krocket /ˈkrɔkət/ *das;* **~s** croquet

Krokant /kroˈkant/ *der;* **~s** praline

Krokette /kroˈkɛtə/ *die;* ~, **~n** (Kochk.) croquette

Kroki /kroˈkiː/ *das;* **~s, ~s** sketch map; (künstlerische Skizze) sketch

Kroko /ˈkroːko/ *das;* **~[s]** crocodile [leather]

Krokodil /krokoˈdiːl/ *das;* **~s, ~e** crocodile

Krokodil·leder *das* crocodile skin *or* leather

Krokodils·tränen *Pl.* (ugs.) crocodile tears

Kroko·tasche *die* crocodile[-skin] [hand]bag

Krokus /ˈkroːkʊs/ *der;* ~, ~ *od.* **~se** crocus

Krönchen /ˈkrøːnçən/ *das;* **~s, ~:** small crown; (einer Welle) small crest

Krone /ˈkroːnə/ *die;* ~, **~n** **1** crown; (kleinere, eines Herzogs, eines Grafen) coronet; **einer Sache** (*Dat.*)**/allem die ~ aufsetzen** cap sth./cap it all; **das setzt doch allem die ~ auf** that beats everything; **jmdm. in die ~ steigen** (ugs.) go to sb.'s head; **einen in der ~ haben** (ugs.) have had a drop too much (coll.); **die ~** (fig.: Herrscherhaus) the Crown; **dir wird keine Perle** *od.* **kein Stein aus der ~ fallen, wenn du uns mal hilfst** (ugs.) it won't hurt you to help us occasionally **2** (Spitze) (eines Baumes) top; crown; (einer Welle) crest **3** (das Beste) **die ~ der Schöpfung/meiner Sammlung** the pride of creation/my collection; **die ~ der Literatur** the highest form of literature **4** (Zahnmed.) crown **5** (Jägerspr.) (beim Hirsch) surroyals *pl.*; surroyal antlers *pl.*; (beim Rehbock) antlers *pl.* **6** (Rad an Uhren) winder; [winding] crown **7** (Währungseinheit) (hist.) crown; (in Schweden, Island) krona; (in Dänemark, Norwegen) krone; (in der Tschechischen Republik und der Slowakei) koruna

krönen /ˈkrøːnən/ *tr. V.* **1** crown; **jmdn. zum König/Kaiser ~:** crown sb. king/emperor; **gekrönte Häupter** crowned heads **2** (den Höhepunkt bilden) crown; **von Erfolg gekrönt sein** *od.* **werden** be crowned with success; **der ~de Abschluss** the culmination **3** (oben abschließen) crown

Kronen-: ~korken *der* crown cap *or* cork; **~mutter** *die; Pl.* **~~n** castle nut; castellated nut

Kron-: ~erbe *der*, **~erbin** *die* ▸**Thronfolger**; **~gut** *das* royal demesne; **~juwel** *das od. der* **1** **die ~juwelen** the crown jewels; **2** (fig.) gem; **~kolonie** *die* crown colony; **~land** *das* (österr. hist.) crownland; **~leuchter** *der* chandelier; **~prinz** *der* crown prince; **~prinzessin** *die* crown princess

Krönung *die;* ~, **~en** **1** coronation **2** (Höhepunkt) culmination

Kron·zeuge *der*, **Kron·zeugin** *die* (Rechtsw.) person who turns Queen's/King's evidence; **als ~ auftreten** turn Queen's/King's evidence

Kropf /krɔpf/ *der;* **~[e]s, Kröpfe** /ˈkrœpfə/ **1** ▸❶ **S. 439** (Med.) goitre **2** (von Vögeln) crop

Kropf·taube *die* pouter

Kroppzeug /ˈkrɔp-/ *das;* **~s** (ugs. abwertend) **1** (Gesindel) rabble; riff-raff **2** (unnützes Zeug) junk

kross, *kroß /krɔs/ *Adj.* (nordd.) ▸**knusprig**

Krösus /ˈkrøːzʊs/ *der;* ~ *od.* **~ses, ~se** (oft scherzh.) Croesus; **ich bin doch kein ~:** I'm not made of money

Kröte /ˈkrøːtə/ *die;* ~, **~n** **1** toad **2** *Pl.* (salopp: Geld) **ein paar/eine ganze Menge ~n verdienen** earn a few bob (Brit. sl.)/a fair old whack (coll.); **meine letzten paar ~n** my last few bob (Brit. sl.)/bucks (Amer. sl.) **3** (ugs. scherzh.: Kind) **du kleine ~:** you little rascal; **eine süße kleine ~:** a sweet little thing **4** (abwertend: Mensch) creature

Kröten·test *der* (Med.) ▸**Froschtest**

Krücke /ˈkrʏkə/ *die;* ~, **~n** **1** (Stock) crutch; **an** *od.* **auf ~n** (*Dat.*) **gehen** walk on crutches **2** (Griff) crook; handle **3** (ugs. abwertend) (Versager) dead loss (coll.); washout (coll.); (Gegenstand) dead loss (coll.); **meine ~ von Auto** my old junk heap of a car (coll.)

Krück·stock *der* walking stick; *s. auch* **Blinde**

krude /ˈkruːdə/

A *Adj.* rude

B *adv.* rudely

Krug /kruːk/ *der;* **~[e]s, Krüge** /ˈkryːgə/ **1** (Gefäß für Flüssigkeiten) jug; (größer) pitcher; (Bier~) mug; (aus Ton) mug; stein; (Honig~) jar; pot; **der ~ geht so lange zum Brunnen, bis er bricht** (Spr.) one day you'll come unstuck; you'll try it once too often **2** (bes. nordd.: Wirtshaus) inn

Kruke /ˈkruːkə/ *die;* ~, **~n** (bes. nordd.) **1** (Krug) [earthenware] jug; (zum Einlegen usw.) [earthenware] jar; (größer) [earthenware] pitcher **2** (kauziger Mensch) **eine seltsame** *od.* **schrullige ~:** a queer fish

Krüll·schnitt /ˈkrʏl-/ *der* shag

Krümchen /ˈkryːmçən/ *das;* **~s, ~:** [tiny] crumb; **ein ~ Erde** a grain of soil

Krume /ˈkruːmə/ *die;* ~, **~n** **1** crumb **2** ▸**Ackerkrume**

Krümel /ˈkryːml̩/ *der;* **~s, ~** **1** crumb; **ein ~ Zucker** a grain of sugar **2** (scherzh.: kleines Kind) little one

krümelig *Adj.* **1** crumbly **2** (voller Krümel) covered in crumbs *postpos.*

krümeln *itr. V.* **1** (zerfallen) crumble; be crumbly **2** (Krümel machen) make crumbs

krumm /krʊm/

A *Adj.* **1** bent ‹*nail etc.*›; crooked ‹*stick, branch, etc.*›; bandy ‹*legs*›; bent ‹*back*›; **eine ~e Nase** a crooked nose; (Hakennase) a hooked nose; **~ sein/werden** ‹*person*› stoop/develop a stoop; **etw. ~ biegen** bend sth.; **mach nicht so einen ~en Buckel** *od.* **Rücken** don't sit/stand with such a bent back; **~e Beine haben** have bandy legs; be bow-legged; **jmdn. ~ und lahm schlagen** beat sb. black and blue; *s. auch* **krummlachen** **2** (ugs.: unrechtmäßig) crooked; **ein ~es Ding drehen** get up to sth. crooked; **auf die ~e Tour versuchen, etw. zu tun** try to do sth. by crooked means **3** **etw. ~ nehmen** (ugs.) take offence at sth.; take sth. the wrong way; **sich ~ legen** (ugs.) scrimp *or* pinch and scrape

B *adv.* crookedly; **~ gewachsen** crooked ‹*tree etc.*›; **~ dasitzen/gehen** slouch/walk with a stoop; **sitz nicht so ~ da!** sit up straight!; *s. auch* **Finger 2**

krumm·beinig *Adj.* bandy[-legged]; bow-legged

Krumm·darm *der* ▸❶ **S. 435** (Anat.) ileum

krümmen /ˈkrʏmən/

A *tr. V.* bend; **in gekrümmter Haltung** stooping

B *refl. V.* **1** (sich winden) writhe; **sich vor Schmerzen/in Krämpfen ~:** double up with pain/cramp; **sich vor Lachen ~:** double up with laughter; **sich ~ wie ein Wurm** wriggle like a worm; **das Blech krümmte sich in der Hitze** the metal warped *or* buckled in the heat **2** (krumm verlaufen) ‹*road, path, river*› bend, curve; **eine gekrümmte Fläche** a curved surface

krumm-, Krumm-: ~horn *das* (Musik) krummhorn; **~|lachen** *refl. V.* (ugs.) **sich über etw.** (*Akk.*) **~lachen** *od.* **~- und schieflachen** fall about laughing (Brit.) *or* laugh one's head off over sth.; ***~|legen** ▸**krumm A3**; **~nasig** *Adj.* crooked-nosed; (mit Hakennase)

k

hook-nosed; *~|**nehmen** ▸**krumm A3**; ~**säbel** *der* scimitar; ~**stab** *der* ▸**Bischofsstab**

Krümmung *die;* ~, ~**en** **1** (Biegung) (der Wirbelsäule) curvature; (der Nase usw.) curve; (eines Weges, Flusses usw.) bend; turn **2** (Geom.) curvature

krumpelig /ˈkrʊmpəlɪç/ *Adj.* (westmd.) creased

krumpfen /ˈkrʊmpfn̩/ *tr. V.* (Textilind.) pre-shrink

Kruppe /ˈkrʊpə/ *die;* ~, ~**n** croup

Krüppel /ˈkrʏpl̩/ *der;* ~**s**, ~: cripple; **zum ~ werden** be crippled; **jmdn. zum ~ schlagen** beat sb. and leave him/her a cripple

krüppelig *Adj.* crippled ‹*person*›; stunted ‹*tree, growth, etc.*›

Kruste /ˈkrʊstə/ *die;* ~, ~**n** **1** crust; (vom Braten) crisp; (vom Schweinebraten) crackling **2** (Überzug) coating; **mit ~:** with a coating; **eine ~ aus** *od.* **von Blut und Dreck/Blut** a crust of blood and dirt/a scab

Krux ▸**Crux**

Kruzifix /ˈkruːtsifɪks/ *das;* ~**es**, ~**e** crucifix

Krypta /ˈkrʏpta/ *die;* ~, **Krypten** (Archit.) crypt

krypto-, Krypto- /ˈkrʏpto-/ crypto-

Krypton /ˈkrʏptɔn/ *das;* ~**s** (Chemie) krypton

KSZE *Abk.* = **Konferenz für Sicherheit und Zusammenarbeit in Europa** CSCE

Kuba /ˈkuːba/ *(das);* ~**s** Cuba

Kubaner /kuˈbaːnɐ/ *der;* ~**s**, ~, **Kubanerin** *die;* ~, ~**nen** ▸🛈 **S. 520** Cuban; *s. auch* **-in**

kubanisch *Adj.* ▸🛈 **S. 520** Cuban

Kübel /ˈkyːbl̩/ *der;* ~**s**, ~ **1** pail; (Wasser~, Abfall~) pail; bucket; (Pflanzen~) tub; **Palmen in ~n** potted palms; ~ **voll** *od.* **von Bosheit über jmdn. ausgießen** (fig.) pour torrents of abuse over sb.; **es gießt wie aus ~n** (ugs.) it's bucketing down **2** (Toiletteneimer) [latrine] bucket

kübeln *itr. V.* (salopp: trinken) booze (coll.)

kübel·weise *Adv.* (in Kübeln) in buckets; (in großen Mengen) by the bucketful; in bucketfuls

Kuben ▸**Kubus**

Kubik- /kuˈbiːk-/ ▸🛈 **S. 582** cubic ‹*metre, foot, etc.*›

Kubik-: ~**meter·preis** *der* price per cubic metre; ~**wurzel** *die* (Math.) cube root; ~**zahl** *die* (Math.) cube number

kubisch /ˈkuːbɪʃ/ *Adj.* **1** (würfelförmig) cubical; cube-shaped **2** (Math.) cubic ‹*equation etc.*›

Kubismus *der;* ~ (Kunstw.) cubism *no art.*

Kubist *der;* ~**en**, ~**en** (Kunstw.) cubist

kubistisch *Adj.* (Kunstw.) cubist

Kubus /ˈkuːbʊs/ *der;* ~, **Kuben** cube

Küche /ˈkʏçə/ *die;* ~, ~**n** **1** (Raum) kitchen; (klein) kitchenette; **was ~ und Keller zu bieten haben** the best food and drink in the house **2** (Einrichtung) kitchen furniture *no indef. art.;* ~**n** kitchen furniture *sing.* **3** (Kochk.) cooking; cuisine; **die chinesische/französische** *usw.* ~: Chinese/French *etc.* cooking; **kalte/warme ~:** cold/hot meals *pl. or* food; *s. auch* **gutbürgerlich**

Kuchen /ˈkuːxn̩/ *der;* ~**s**, ~: cake; (Obst~) flan; (Torte) gateau; cake

Küchen-: ~**abfälle** *Pl.* kitchen scraps; ~**bank** *die; Pl.* ~**bänke** kitchen bench-seat; ~**benutzung** *die:* **Zimmer mit ~benutzung** room and shared kitchen *or* use of kitchen

Kuchen·blech *das* baking sheet *or* -tray; (mit höherem Rand) baking tin

Küchen-: ~**bulle** *der* (Soldatenspr. salopp) cookhouse wallah (Mil. coll.); ~**chef** *der*, ~**chefin** *die* ▸🛈 **S. 113** chef; ~**dienst** *der* kitchen duty; ~**dienst haben** be on kitchen duty; ~**fee** *die* (ugs. scherzh.) cook

Kuchen-: ~**form** *die* cake tin; ~**gabel** *die* pastry fork

Küchen-: ~**gerät** *das* kitchen utensil; (als Kollektivum) kitchen utensils *pl.;* ~**geschirr** *das* kitchen crockery; ~**handtuch** *das* kitchen towel; ~**herd** *der* cooker; (mit Holz- od. Kohlefeuer) kitchen range; ~**hilfe** *die* kitchen help; ~**junge** *der* (veralt.) apprentice cook; ~**latein** *das* (iron.) dog Latin; ~**maschine** *die* food processor; ~**meister** *der*, ~**meisterin** *die* chef; *s. auch* **Schmalhans**; ~**messer** *das* kitchen knife; ~**möbel** *das* piece of kitchen furniture; **teure ~möbel** expensive kitchen furniture *sing.;* ~**personal** *das* kitchen staff; ~**schabe** *die* cockroach; ~**schrank** *der* kitchen cupboard; ~**schürze** *die* kitchen apron

Kuchen-: ~**teig** *der* cake mixture; ~**teller** *der* **1** (mit ~) plate of cakes; **2** (für ~) cake plate

Küchen-: ~**tisch** *der* kitchen table; ~**uhr** *die* kitchen clock; ~**waage** *die* kitchen scales *pl.;* ~**zeile** *die: kitchen fittings along one wall of a room;* ~**zettel** *der* menu

Küchlein[1] *das;* ~**s**, ~ (veralt.: Küken) chick

Küchlein[2] *das;* ~**s**, ~ (kleiner Kuchen) small cake

kucken /ˈkʊkn̩/ (nordd.) ▸**gucken**

Kücken /ˈkʏkn̩/ (österr.) ▸**Küken**

kuckuck /ˈkʊkʊk/ *Interj.* cuckoo; (beim Versteckspiel mit Kindern) yoo-hoo

Kuckuck *der;* ~**s**, ~**e** **1** cuckoo; **[das] weiß der ~** (salopp) heaven [only] knows; it's anybody's guess; **hol dich der ~!, der ~ soll dich holen!** (salopp) go to blazes! (coll.); **zum ~ [noch mal]!** (salopp) for crying out loud! (coll.); **wo, zum ~, hast du nur die Zeitung hingelegt?** (salopp) where the hell did you put the newspaper? (coll.); **das Geld ist zum ~** (salopp) the money's all gone **2** (scherzh.: Siegel des Gerichtsvollziehers) bailiff's seal (*placed on distrained goods*)

Kuckucks-: ~**ei** *das* **1** cuckoo's egg; **2** (ugs.: zweifelhafte Gabe) **sich als ~ei erweisen** turn out to be more of a liability than an asset; **jmdm./sich ein ~ei ins Nest legen** do sb./oneself a dubious service; **3** (salopp: Kind eines anderen Vaters) **ein ~ei** somebody else's *or* another man's child; ~**uhr** *die* cuckoo clock

Kuddelmuddel /ˈkʊdl̩mʊdl̩/ *der od. das;* ~**s** (ugs.) muddle; confusion

Kufe[1] /ˈkuːfə/ *die;* ~, ~**n** **1** (von Schlitten, Schlittschuhen) runner **2** (von Flugzeugen, Hubschraubern) skid

Kufe[2] (landsch.) *die;* ~, ~**n** tub; (zum Keltern, Brauen) tun; vat

Küfer /ˈkyːfɐ/ *der;* ~**s**, ~, **Küferin** *die;* ~, ~**nen** **1** (südwestd., schweiz.) cooper **2** (Wein~) cellarman

Kugel /ˈkuːgl̩/ *die;* ~, ~**n** **1** ball; (Geom.) sphere; (Kegeln) bowl; (beim ~stoßen) shot; (eines ~lagers) ball [bearing]; **die Erde ist eine ~:** the Earth is a sphere; **der Croupier ließ die ~ rollen** the croupier spun the wheel; **eine ruhige ~ schieben** (ugs.) take it *or* things easy; (keine anstrengende Stellung haben) have a cushy number (coll.) **2** (ugs.: Geschoss) bullet; (Kanonen~) [cannon]ball; (Luftgewehr~) pellet; **sich** (*Dat.*) **eine ~ durch** *od.* **in den Kopf schießen** *od.* (ugs.) **jagen** blow one's brains out

Kugel-: ~**abschnitt** *der* (Geom.) spherical segment [of one base]; ~**ausschnitt** *der* (Geom.) spherical sector; ~**blitz** *der* ball lightning

Kügelchen /ˈkyːgl̩çən/ *das;* ~**s**, ~: small ball; (aus Papier) pellet

kugel-, Kugel-: ~**fang** *der* butt; **ein Kind/eine Frau als ~fang benutzen** (fig.) use a child/woman as a shield; ~**fest** *Adj.* bulletproof; ~**förmig** *Adj.* spherical; ~**gelenk** *das* (Anat., Technik) ball-and-socket joint; ~**hagel** *der* hail of bullets

kugelig *Adj.* spherical; ‹*head*› as round as a football; (fig. scherzh.: dick) rotund; plump; tubby; **sich ~ lachen** (ugs.) double *or* roll up [laughing *or* with laughter]; **ich hätte mich ~ lachen können** (ugs.) I could have died laughing

Kugel-: ~**kopf** *der* golf ball; ~**kopfmaschine** *die* golf-ball typewriter; ~**lager** *das* (Technik) ball bearing

kugeln

A *tr. V.* roll

B *refl. V.* roll [about]; **sich [vor Lachen] ~** (ugs.) double *or* roll up [laughing *or* with laughter]

C *itr. V.; mit sein* roll

kugel-, Kugel-: ~**oberfläche** *die* (Geom.) surface of a sphere; (Flächeninhalt) surface area of a sphere; ~**regen** *der* ▸~**hagel**; ~**rund** /-ˈ-ˈ-/ *Adj.* **1** round as a ball *postpos.;* **2** (scherzh.: dick) rotund; plump; tubby; ~**schreiber** *der* ballpoint [pen]; ball pen; Biro ®; ~**schreiber·mine** *die* refill for a ballpoint [pen]; ~**sicher** *Adj.* bulletproof; ~**stoßen** *das;* ~~**s** shot[-put]; (Disziplin) shot-putting *no art.;* putting the shot *no art.;* ~**stoßer** *der;* ~~**s**, ~~, (schweiz.) ~**stößer** /-ʃtøːsɐ/ *der;* ~~**s**, ~~, ~**stoßerin** *die;* ~~, ~~**nen**, (schweiz.) ~**stößerin** *die;* ~~, ~~**nen** shot-putter; ~**wechsel** *der* exchange of shots

Kuh /kuː/ *die;* ~, **Kühe** /ˈkyːə/ **1** cow; **heilige ~** (ugs.) sacred cow; **ich bin doch keine ~, die man melken kann** (ugs.) I am not made of money; *s. auch* **dastehen 1** **2** (Elefanten~, Giraffen~, Flusspferd~) cow; (Hirsch~) hind **3** (salopp abwertend: Frau) cow (sl. derog.)

kuh-, Kuh-: ~**augen** *Pl.* (salopp) cow-eyes; ~**dorf** *das* (salopp abwertend) one-horse town (coll.); ~**fladen** *der* cowpat; ~**fuß** *der* (Technik) crowbar; ~**glocke** *die* cow bell; ~**handel** *der* (ugs. abwertend) shady horse-trading *no indef. art.;* **ein ~handel** a bit of shady horse-trading; ~**haut** *die* cowhide; **das geht auf keine ~haut** (fig. salopp) it's absolutely staggering *or* beyond belief; ~**herde** *die* herd of cows; ~**hirt** *der* cowherd

kühl /kyːl/

A *Adj.* **1** cool; **mir ist/wird ~:** I feel/I'm getting chilly; **etw. ~ lagern** *od.* **aufbewahren** keep sth. in a cool place **2** (abweisend, nüchtern) cool; **ein ~er Rechner** a cool, calculating person; **aus diesem ~en Grunde** (scherzh.) for this simple reason

B *adv.* (abweisend, nüchtern) coolly

Kühl-: ~**aggregat** *das* refrigeration unit; ~**an·lage** *die* refrigeration plant; cold-storage plant; ~**box** *die* cool box

Kuhle /ˈkuːlə/ *die;* ~, ~**n** (ugs.) hollow

Kühle /ˈkyːlə/ *die;* ~ **1** (Frische) coolness; **die ~ des Morgens/Abends** the cool of the morning/evening **2** (Nüchternheit) coolness

kühlen

A *tr. V.* cool; chill, cool ‹*wine*›; **seinen Zorn/seine Rache [an jmdm.] ~:** vent one's rage/revenge oneself [on sb.]

B *itr. V.* ‹*cold compress, ointment, breeze, etc.*› have a cooling effect

Kühler *der;* ~**s**, ~ **1** (am Auto) radiator; (~haube) bonnet (Brit.); hood (Amer.); **jmdn. auf den ~ nehmen** (ugs.) drive *or* run into *or* hit sb. **2** (Sekt~) ice bucket **3** (Chem.) condenser

Kühler-: ~**figur** *die* radiator mascot; ~**haube** *die* bonnet (Brit.); hood (Amer.)

Kühl-: ~**fach** *das* frozen food compartment; ~**haus** *das* cold store; ~**kette** *die* (Wirtsch.) cold chain; ~**mittel** *das* (Technik) coolant; ~**raum** *der* cold store; cold-storage room; ~**rippe** *die* cooling fin *or* rib; ~**schiff** *das* refrigerator ship; refrigerated ship; ~**schlange** *die* (Technik) cooling coil; ~**schrank** *der* refrigerator; fridge (Brit. coll.); icebox (Amer.); ~**tasche** *die* cool bag; ~**theke** *die* cold shelves *pl.;* ~**truhe** *die* [chest] freezer; deep-freeze; (im Lebensmittelgeschäft) freezer [cabinet]; ~**turm** *der* (Technik) cooling tower

Kühlung *die;* ~, ~**en** **1** cooling; **zur ~ der entzündeten Stellen** to cool the inflamed areas; **auch bei ~ sind die Waren nur begrenzt haltbar** even when refrigerated, the goods will keep only for a limited time **2** (Vorrichtung) cooling system; (für Lebensmittel) refrigeration system **3** (Frische) coolness; **sich** (*Dat.*) **~ verschaffen** cool down *or* off

Kühl-: ~**wagen** *der* **1** (Eisenb.) refrigerated *or* refrigerator car *or* (Brit.) wagon; **2** (Lastwagen) refrigerated *or* refrigerator truck *or* (Brit.) lorry; ~**wasser** *das* cooling water

Kuh-: ~**milch** *die* cow's milk; ~**mist** *der* cow dung

kühn /ky:n/
A *Adj.* 1 (mutig, eigenwillig) bold; (gewagt) daring; brave, fearless ‹*warrior*›; **das übertraf meine** ~**sten Träume** that exceeded my wildest dreams 2 (dreist) audacious; impudent
B *adv.* 1 (mutig, eigenwillig) boldly; (gewagt) daringly; **eine** ~ **geschwungene Nase** an aquiline nose 2 (dreist) audaciously; impudently

Kühnheit *die;* ~ 1 (Mut, Eigenwilligkeit) boldness; (Gewagtheit) daringness 2 (Dreistigkeit) audacity; impudence

kuh-, Kuh-: ~**pocken** *Pl.* cowpox *sing., no art.;* ~**schelle** *die* (Bot.) pasque flower; ~**stall** *der* cowshed; ~**warm** *Adj.* ‹*milk*› warm *or* fresh from the cow

Kujon /ku'jo:n/ *der;* ~**s,** ~**e** (veralt. abwertend) scoundrel; rogue

kujonieren *tr. V.* (veralt. abwertend) bully; harass

k. u. k. /'ka:|ʊnt'ka:/ *Abk.* (österr. hist.) = **kaiserlich und königlich** imperial and royal

Küken /'ky:kn̩/ *das;* ~**s,** ~ 1 (von Hühnern) chick 2 (ugs.) (kleines Kind) kiddie (sl.); (junges Mädchen) young girl

Ku-Klux-Klan /kuklʊks'kla:n/ *der;* ~**[s]** Ku-Klux-Klan

kulant /ku'lant/
A *Adj.* obliging; accommodating; fair ‹*terms*›
B *adv.* **sich** ~ **verhalten** be obliging *or* accommodating

Kulanz /ku'lants/ *die;* ~: readiness *or* willingness to oblige; **aus** ~: out of good will; **eine Reparatur auf** ~: repair done free of charge out of good will

Kuli /'ku:li/ *der;* ~**s,** ~**s** 1 coolie; (fig.) slave 2 (ugs.: Kugelschreiber) ballpoint; Biro ®

kulinarisch /kuli'na:rɪʃ/ *Adj.* culinary; **ein rein** ~**es Interesse an der Musik haben** (fig.) be interested in music purely as entertainment

Kulisse /ku'lɪsə/ *die;* ~, ~**n** piece of scenery; flat; wing; (Hintergrund) backdrop; **die** ~**n** the scenery *sing.;* ~**n schieben** be a scene-shifter; **aus der** ~ **treten** step out from the wings *pl.;* **die** ~ **für etw. bilden** (fig.) form the backdrop to sth.; **hinter den** ~**n** (fig.) behind the scenes

kulissenhaft *Adj.* like a stage setting *pred.*

Kulissen-: ~**schieber** *der* (ugs. scherzh.) scene-shifter; ~**wechsel** *der* scene change

Kuller *die;* ~, ~**n** (ostmd.: Murmel) marble

Kuller·augen *Pl.* (ugs. scherzh.) big, round eyes; **er machte** ~: his eyes nearly popped out of his head

kullern /'kʊlɐn/ (ugs.)
A *itr. V.* 1 *mit sein* roll 2 **mit den Augen** ~: roll one's eyes
B *tr. V.* roll

Kuller·pfirsich *der* (ugs.) peach served in a glass of champagne

Kulmination /kʊlmina'tsi̯o:n/ *die;* ~, ~**en** (auch Astron.) culmination

Kulminations·punkt *der* 1 culmination; culminating point 2 (Astron.) point of culmination

kulminieren /kʊlmi'ni:rən/ *itr. V.* (auch Astron.) culminate (**in** + *Dat.* in)

-kult *der:* **Motorrad~/Star~/Wagner~** *usw.* motorcycle/star/Wagner *etc.* cult

Kult /kʊlt/ *der;* ~**[e]s,** ~**e** 1 cult; **der** ~ **der Ahnen** ancestor worship 2 (fig.) cult (**mit** of); **mit jmdm./etw. einen** ~ **treiben** make a cult [figure] out of sb./make a cult out of sth.

Kult-: ~**bild** *das* devotional image; ~**buch** *das* cult book; ~**figur** *die* cult figure; ~**film** *der* cult film; ~**handlung** *die* ritual; ritualistic act

kultig
A *Adj.* trendy
B *adv.* trendily

kultisch
A *Adj.* cultic; ritual, cultic ‹*object*›
B *adv.* ‹*worship*› cultically

Kultivator /kʊlti'va:tɔr/ *der;* ~**s,** ~**en** /-va'to:rən/ (Landw.) cultivator

kultivierbar *Adj.* 1 cultivable; cultivatable; **leicht/schwer** ~: easy/hard to cultivate

kultivieren /kʊlti'vi:rən/ *tr. V.* (auch fig.) cultivate

kultiviert
A ▸**kultivieren**
B *Adj.* 1 (gepflegt) cultivated; cultured 2 (vornehm) refined
C *adv.* in a cultivated *or* cultured manner; (vornehm) in a refined manner; with refinement; ~ **essen** get a civilized meal

Kultiviertheit *die;* ~: refinement

Kultivierung *die;* ~, ~**en** (auch fig.) cultivation; improvement

Kult-: ~**objekt** *das* cult object; ~**serie** *die* cult series; (Fortsetzungsgeschichte) cult serial; ~**stätte** *die* centre of cult worship; ~**status** *der* cult status

Kultur /kʊl'tu:ɐ̯/ *die;* ~, ~**en** 1 (geistiger und moralischer Überbau) culture 2 (Zivilisation, Lebensform) civilization 3 (Kultiviertheit, geistiges Niveau) **ein Mensch von** ~: a cultured person; **sie hat [keine]** ~: she is [un]cultured 4 (kultivierte Lebensart, Verfeinerung) refinement; ~ **haben** be refined 5 (Landw., Gartenbau) young crop; (Forstw.) young plantation 6 (Biol., Med.) culture 7 (Landw., Gartenbau: Kultivierung) cultivation

Kultur-: ~**abkommen** *das* cultural agreement; ~**anthropologie** *die* cultural anthropology *no art.;* ~**arbeit** *die* cultural activity *or* activities; ~**attaché** *der* cultural attaché; ~**aus·tausch** *der* cultural exchange; ~**banause** *der* (abwertend, oft scherzh.) philistine; ~**bei·lage** *die* arts supplement; ~**betrieb** *der* culture industry; ~**beutel** *der* sponge bag (Brit.); toilet bag; ~**boden** *der* 1 (bearbeiteter Boden) cultivated land; 2 (Gebiet mit bedeutendem ~boden) **[ur]alter** ~**boden** the site of an ancient civilization; ~**denkmal** *das* cultural monument

kulturell /kʊltu'rɛl/
A *Adj.* cultural
B *adv.* culturally; **die ehemals** ~ **führende Metropole** the metropolis, once cultural centre

kultur-, Kultur-: ~**epoche** *die* cultural epoch; ~**erbe** *das* cultural heritage; ~**feindlich** *Adj.* ‹*atmosphere, policy, etc.*› that is hostile to culture; ~**feindlich sein** be hostile to culture; ~**film** *der* documentary film; ~**flüchter** *der;* ~~**s,** ~~ (Biol.) plant/animal that does not survive in areas developed by man; ~**föderalismus** *der: system of separate ministries for education and cultural affairs;* ~**folger** *der;* ~~**s,** ~~ (Biol.) plant/animal that survives in areas developed by man; ~**geschichte** *die* 1 history of civilization; (einer bestimmten ~) cultural history; **die** ~**geschichte des Menschen** the history of human civilization; 2 (Buch) cultural history; ~**geschichtlich** A *Adj.* ‹*importance*› for *or* in the history of civilization/cultural history; ‹*question, factor*› connected with the history of civilization/cultural history; ‹*essay, reflections*› on the history of civilization/cultural history; (die ~geschichte eines bestimmten Landes betreffend) historico-cultural ‹*law, phenomenon, standpoint, study, etc.*›; B *adv.* from the standpoint of the history of civilization/of cultural history; ~**gut** *das* cultural possessions *pl.;* ~**haupt·stadt** *die* cultural capital; ~**haus** *das* arts and leisure centre; ~**historisch** *Adj., adv.:* ▸~**geschichtlich**; ~**hoheit** *die* autonomy *or* independence in cultural and educational matters; ~**industrie** *die* (meist abwertend) culture industry; ~**kampf** *der* (hist.) kulturkampf (struggle between the Prussian state and the Church 1872-87); ~**kanal** *der* cultural channel; ~**kreis** *der* 1 (~raum) cultural area; 2 (Verein) arts society; ~**kritik** *die* critique of contemporary civilization *or* culture; ~**kritiker** *der,* ~**kritikerin** *die* critic of contemporary civilization *or* culture; ~**landschaft** *die* 1 (Agrargebiet) cultivated area; area cultivated by man; (Industrie-, Bergbaugebiet) area developed by man; 2 (kulturelles Leben) cultural scene; ~**leben** *das* cultural life; ~**los** *Adj.* uncultured; lacking in culture *postpos.;* ~**magazin** *das* (Ferns.) arts magazine; ~**minister** *der,* ~**ministerin** *die* minister for the arts; ~**ministerium** *das* ministry for the arts; ~**palast** *der* (bes. DDR) palace of culture; ~**pessimismus** *der* cultural pessimism; ~**pessimist** *der,* ~**pessimistin** *die* cultural pessimist; ~**pflanze** *die* cultivated plant; ~**politik** *die* cultural and educational policy; ~**politisch** A *Adj.* ‹*area, questions, aims, principles*› of cultural and educational policy; ‹*programme*› of cultural and educational policies; ‹*periodical*› devoted to matters of cultural and educational policy; B *adv.* in regard to cultural and educational policy; ~**preis** *der* arts prize; ~**psychologie** *die* psychology of culture; ~**raum** *der* cultural area; ~**revolution** *die* cultural revolution; ~**schaffende** *der/die; adj. Dekl.* (DDR) creative artist; (Intellektueller) intellectual; ~**schande** *die* (abwertend) disgrace in a civilized society; ~**schock** *der* (Soziol.) culture shock; ~**soziologie** *die* cultural sociology; ~**sprache** *die* language of a civilized people; **in fast alle** ~**sprachen übersetzt** translated into nearly every civilized language; ~**stätte** *die* (geh.) site of archaeological and cultural interest; ~**steppe** *die* (Geogr.) cultivated steppe land; steppe [land] created by excessive cultivation of the soil; ~**stufe** *die* level of civilization; ~**szene** *die* (ugs.) cultural scene; ~**träger** *der* vehicle of culture; ~**volk** *das* civilized people *sing.;* ~**voll** *Adj.* rich in culture *postpos.;* (niveauvoll) sophisticated; ~**wissenschaften** *Pl.* ▸**Geisteswissenschaften**; ~**zentrum** *das* 1 cultural centre; centre of cultural life; 2 (Anlage) arts centre

Kulturstadt Weimar

Weimar in Thuringia was chosen as the European city of culture in 1999. This 1000-year-old city has played an important role in Germany's cultural history. The composer Johann Sebastian Bach (1685-1750) and the artist Lucas Cranach (1472-1553) lived and worked there. Other important writers and poets such as Johann Wolfgang von Goethe (1749-1832), Johann Gottfried von Herder (1744-1803) and Christoph Martin Wieland (1733-1813) - who translated Shakespeare's plays - made the city their home. Friedrich von Schiller (1759-1805) wrote many of his plays in Weimar. The composer Franz Liszt (1811-86) composed and gave concerts in the city. In 1919 the **Bauhaus** was founded in Weimar. 1919 was also the year that the constitution of the first German republic - the Weimar Republic - was drafted there.

Kultus /'kʊltʊs/ *der;* ~ 1 (geh.) ▸**Kult 1** 2 (Amtsspr.) **Ministerium für Unterricht und** ~ ▸**Kultusministerium**

Kultus-: ~**minister** *der,* ~**ministerin** *die* minister for education and cultural affairs; ~**ministerium** *das* ministry of education and cultural affairs; ~**senator** *der,* ~**senatorin** *die* minister for education and cultural affairs (in Bremen, Hamburg, and West Berlin)

Kumarin /kuma'ri:n/ *das;* ~**s** coumarin

Kumaron /kuma'ro:n/ *das;* ~**s** (Chemie) coumarone

Kumme /'kʊmə/ *die;* ~, ~**n** (nordd.) bowl

Kümmel /'kʏml̩/ *der;* ~**s,** ~ 1 (Pflanze) caraway 2 (Gewürz) caraway [seed] 3 (Branntwein) kümmel

Kümmel-: ~**brannt·wein** *der* caraway brandy; ~**brötchen** *das* caraway[-seed] roll; ~**käse** *der* caraway-seed[-flavoured] cheese; ~**öl** *das* caraway oil; ~**schnaps** *der* ▸~**branntwein**; ~**türke** *der,* ~**türkin** *die* 1 (salopp abwertend: Türke/Türkin) Turkish bastard (derog.); 2 **schuften wie ein** ~**türke/die** ~**türken** (ugs.) work like a slave/like slaves

Kummer /'kʊmɐ/ *der;* ~**s** sorrow; grief; (Ärger, Sorgen) trouble; ~ **um** *od.* **über jmdn.** grief for *or* over sb.; **hast du** ~**?** is there a problem?; **viel** *od.* **großen** ~ **haben** have a lot of trouble; **was hast du denn für** ~**?** what's bothering *or* troubling you?; **jmdm.** ~ **machen** give sb. trouble *or* bother; **ich bin** ~ **gewohnt** (ugs.) it

happens all the time; I'm used to it
Kummer·falte *die* wrinkle [caused by worry]; **~n** lines of worry
Kümmer·form *die* (Biol.) degenerate form
Kummer-: ~kasten *der* (scherzh.) complaints box; **~kasten·tante** *die* (scherzh.) agony columnist *or* aunt (coll.)
kümmerlich
A *Adj.* **1** (schwächlich) puny; stunted ‹*vegetation, plants*› **2** (ärmlich) wretched; miserable **3** (abwertend: gering) miserable; meagre, scanty ‹*knowledge, leftovers*›; very poor ‹*effort*›
B *adv.* **sich ~ ernähren** live on a poor *or* meagre diet; **sich ~ durchschlagen** eke out a bare/miserable existence
Kümmerling *der;* **~s, ~e** stunted plant/animal
kümmern /ˈkʏmɐn/
A *refl. V.* **1** **sich um jmdn./etw. ~:** take care of *or* look after sb./sth.; **du solltest dich mal darum ~, dass ...** you should see to it that ...; **du kümmerst dich aber auch um gar nichts!** you don't bother to do anything! **2** (sich befassen mit) **sich nicht um das Geschwätz** *usw.* **~:** not worry *or* mind about the gossip *etc.*; **sich nicht um Politik ~:** not care about *or* be interested in politics; **kümmere dich um deine eigenen Angelegenheiten** mind your own business
B *tr. V.* concern; **was kümmert dich das?** what concern *or* business is it of yours?; what's it to you?; **Mach doch, was du willst! Was kümmerts mich?** Do what you like! What do I care?
C *itr. V.* (ver~) become stunted
Kümmernis *die;* **~, ~se** (geh.) trouble; worry
Kummer·speck *der* (ugs.) overweight caused by overeating as a result of emotional stress; **sie hat ~ angesetzt** all the worrying has made her eat too much, and she's [really] put on weight
kummer·voll
A *Adj.* sorrowful; sad; sad ‹*face*›
B *adv.* sorrowfully; sadly
Kummet /ˈkʊmət/ *das, schweiz. auch der;* **~s, ~e** [horse] collar
Kümo /ˈkyːmo/ *das;* **~s, ~s** [motor-]coaster
Kumpan /kʊmˈpaːn/ *der;* **~s, ~e** (ugs.) **1** pal (coll.); mate; buddy (coll.) **2** (abwertend: Mittäter) accomplice
Kumpanei *die;* **~** (ugs.) chumminess (coll.)
Kumpanin *die;* **~, ~nen** ▸**Kumpan**
Kumpel /ˈkʊmpl̩/ *der;* **~s, ~,** *ugs. auch:* **~s** **1** (Bergmannsspr.) miner; collier **2** (salopp: Kamerad) pal; mate; buddy (coll.)
kumpelhaft
A *Adj.* matey; chummy (coll.)
B *adv.* matily; chummily (coll.)
Kumpen /ˈkʊmpn̩/ *der;* **~s, ~** (nordd.) bowl; basin
Kumt /kʊmt/ *das;* **~[e]s, ~e** ▸**Kummet**
Kumulation /kumulaˈt͡si̯oːn/ *die;* **~, ~en** cumulation; (von Ämtern) plurality
kumulativ /kumulaˈtiːf/ *Adj.* cumulative
kumulieren /kumuˈliːrən/ *tr. V.* cumulate; **eine ~de Bibliographie** a cumulative bibliography
Kumulierung *die;* **~, ~en** cumulation
Kumulus /ˈkuːmulʊs/ *der;* **~, Kumuli** (Met.) cumulus [cloud]
Kumulus·wolke *die* (Met.) cumulus cloud
kund /kʊnt/ *Adj.* in **jmdm. etw. ~ und zu wissen tun** (veralt.) make sth. known to sb.
kündbar *Adj.* terminable ‹*contract*›; redeemable ‹*loan, mortgage*›; **er hat eine nicht ~e Stellung** his employment cannot be terminated; **Beamte sind nicht ~:** established civil servants cannot be dismissed *or* given their notice
Kündbarkeit *die;* **~** (von Verträgen) terminability; (von Anleihen, Hypotheken) redeemability
-kunde *die* science of ...; **Metall~/Vogel~:** metallurgy/ornithology
Kunde¹ /ˈkʊndə/ *der;* **~n, ~n** **1** customer; (eines Architekten-, Anwaltbüros, einer Versicherung usw.) client; **Dienst am ~n sein** be a service to the customer; *s. auch* **König** **2** (ugs.: Kerl) customer (coll.)
Kunde² *die;* **~** **1** (geh.) tidings *pl.* (literary); **jmdm. von etw. ~ geben** (veralt.) bring sb. tidings of sth. **2** (Lehre) science
Kunde³ *die;* **~** (österr.) ▸**Kundschaft 1**
künden /ˈkʏndn̩/
A *tr. V.* (geh.: ver~) proclaim; **diese Zeichen ~ Unglück** these omens herald misfortune
B *itr. V.* (geh.) **von etw. ~:** bear witness to *or* tell of sth.
Kunden-: ~beratung *die* **1** customer advisory service; **~beratungen durchführen** advise customers; **2** (Stelle) customer advisory department; **~besuch** *der* call on a/the customer/client; **~bindung** *die* the achieving and maintaining customer loyalty; **~dienst** *der* **1** service to customers; (Wartung) after-sales service; **2** (Abteilung) service department; **~fang** *der* (abwertend) touting for custom *or* customers; **auf ~fang gehen** go touting for custom *or* customers; **~kredit** *der* (Wirtsch.) credit terms *pl.*; **einen ~kredit in Anspruch nehmen** use the credit facilities which are available; **~kreis** *der* customers *pl.*; (eines Architekten-, Anwaltbüros, einer Versicherung usw.) clientele; **~service** *der* customer service; **~stamm** *der* regular clientele *or* trade; **~werbung** *die* advertising aimed at attracting customers; **zu Zwecken der ~werbung** to attract custom *or* customers
Künder *der;* **~s, ~, Künderin** *die;* **~, ~nen** (geh.) herald
Kund·gabe *die* (geh.) announcement; (von Gefühlen, Erfahrungen) expression
kund|geben *unr. tr. V.* (geh.) declare; announce; express, make known ‹*opinion, feelings*›
Kundgebung *die;* **~, ~en** **1** rally **2** (geh.: Äußerung) expression
kundig
A *Adj.* (kenntnisreich) knowledgeable; well-informed; (sachverständig) expert; **mit ~er Hand** with an expert hand; **sich über etw.** (*Akk.*) **~ machen** (Amtsspr.) inform oneself about sth.; **einer Sache** (*Gen.*) **~/nicht ~ sein** (geh.) know about sth./have no knowledge of sth.
B *adv.* expertly
kündigen /ˈkʏndɪɡn̩/
A *tr. V.* call in, cancel ‹*loan*›; foreclose ‹*mortgage*›; cancel, discontinue ‹*magazine subscription, membership*›; terminate ‹*contract, agreement*›; denounce ‹*treaty*›; **seine Stellung ~:** give in *or* hand in one's notice (**bei** to); **jmdm. die Stellung** *od.* **jmds. Arbeitsverhältnis ~:** give sb. his/her notice; **ich bin gekündigt worden** (ugs.) I've been given my notice; **der Vermieter hat ihm die Wohnung gekündigt** the landlord gave him notice to quit the flat (esp. Brit.) *or* (esp. Amer.) apartment; **er hat seine Wohnung gekündigt** he's given notice that he's leaving his flat (esp. Brit.) *or* (esp. Amer.) apartment; **jmdm. die Freundschaft ~** (fig.) break off a friendship with sb.
B *itr. V.* **1** (ein Mietverhältnis beenden) ‹*tenant*› give notice [that one is leaving]; **jmdm. ~** ‹*landlord*› give sb. notice to quit; **zum 1. Juli ~:** give notice for 1 July **2** (ein Arbeitsverhältnis beenden) ‹*employee*› give in *or* hand in one's notice (**bei** to); **jmdm. ~** ‹*employer*› give sb. his/her notice
Kündigung *die;* **~, ~en** **1** (eines Kredits) calling-in; cancellation; (einer Hypothek) foreclosure; (der Mitgliedschaft, eines Abonnements) cancellation; discontinuation; (eines Vertrags) termination; **die Bank droht mit der ~ der Kredite** the bank is threatening to call in *or* cancel the loans **2** (eines Arbeitsverhältnisses) **jmdm. die ~ aussprechen** give sb. his/her notice; dismiss sb.; **mit ~ drohen** ‹*employee*› threaten to give in *or* hand in one's notice *or* to quit; ‹*employer*› threaten dismissal; **ihm droht die ~:** he is threatened with dismissal; **eine fristlose ~:** dismissal without notice **3** (eines Mietverhältnisses) **sie musste mit ~ rechnen** she had to reckon on being given notice to quit; **ich sah mich zur ~ gezwungen** I felt compelled to give notice **4** ▸**Kündigungsschreiben** **5** (~sfrist) [period *or* term of] notice; **bei jährlicher ~ betragen die Zinsen 9,5%** with one year's notice of withdrawal, interest is at 9.5%
Kündigungs-: ~frist *die* period of notice; **~grund** *der* (Arbeitsrecht) grounds *pl.* for dismissal; grounds *pl.* for giving sb. his/her notice; (Mietrecht) grounds *pl.* for giving sb. notice to quit; **~schreiben** *das* written notice; notice in writing; **~schutz** *der* protection against wrongful dismissal
Kundin *die;* **~, ~nen** customer/client; *s. auch* **Kunde¹ 1**
kund|machen *tr. V.* (österr. Amtsspr.) announce; make known; (feierlich) proclaim; promulgate ‹*law*›
Kundschaft *die;* **~, ~en** **1** ▸**Kunde¹ 1**: customers *pl.*; clientele; **~!** service!; **ich habe gerade ~:** I've got a customer/customers at the moment **2** (veralt.: Erkundung) **auf ~ ausgehen/jmdn. auf ~ ausschicken** go out on/send sb. out on reconnaissance *or* to reconnoitre **3** (veralt.: Nachricht) news *sing.*; tidings *pl.* (literary)
Kundschafter *der;* **~s, ~, Kundschafterin** *die;* **~, ~nen** scout
kund|tun (geh.)
A *unr. tr. V.* announce; make known
B *unr. refl. V.* be revealed; show itself
kund|werden *unr itr. V.*; *mit sein* (veralt.) become known; **ihm wurde der Verrat kund** he learned of the betrayal
künftig /ˈkʏnftɪç/
A *Adj.* future; **ihr ~er Mann** her future husband; her husband-to-be; **am 15. ~en Monats** (geh.) on the 15th of next month
B *adv.* in future
künftig·hin *Adv.* (geh.) henceforth; henceforward; in future
Kungelei *die;* **~, ~en** (abwertend) wheeling and dealing; **eine ~ um etw.** bargaining over sth.; **große ~en** a great deal *sing.* of wheeling and dealing
kungeln /ˈkʊŋl̩n/ *itr. V.* **[mit jmdm.] um etw. ~:** bargain [with sb.] over sth.; **dort wird viel gekungelt** there is a lot of wheeling and dealing there
Kunst /kʊnst/ *die;* **~, Künste** /ˈkʏnstə/ **1** art; **die schwarze ~** (Magie) the black art; (Buchdruck) [the art of] printing; **die schönen Künste** [the] fine arts; fine art *sing.*; **was macht die ~?** (ugs.) how are things?; how's tricks? (sl.); *s. auch* **bilden 1**; **darstellen A 1**; **sieben² 2** (das Können) skill; **die ärztliche ~:** medical skill; **die ~ des Reitens/der Selbstverteidigung** the art of riding/self-defence; **nach einer Vorlage zu stricken ist keine ~:** it's easy enough *or* it doesn't take anything to knit from a pattern; **~ kommt von können** (meist iron.) either you've got it or you haven't; **das ist keine/die ganze ~!** (ugs.) there's nothing 'to it/nothing more to it than that; **mit seiner ~ am Ende sein** be at a complete loss; *s. auch* **brotlos**; **Regel 1**
Kunst-: ~akademie *die* ▸**~hochschule**; **~ausstellung** *die* art exhibition; **~banause** *der* (abwertend) philistine; **~band** *der:* (*high-quality*) art book; **~besitz** *der* art collection; **~blatt** *das* art print; **~buch** *das* art book; **~darm** *der* artificial *or* synthetic sausage skin; **~denkmal** *das* artistic and cultural monument; **~denkmäler der Kelten/Griechen** *usw.* monuments of Celtic/Greek *etc.* art; **~diebstahl** *der* art theft; **~druck** *der; Pl.* **~~e** **1** [fine] art print; **2** (Druckw.) fine-art printing; **etw. im ~druck herstellen** produce sth. by fine-art printing methods; **~druck·papier** *das* art paper; **~dünger** *der* chemical *or* artificial fertilizer; **~eis·bahn** *die* artificial ice rink
Künstelei *die;* **~** (abwertend) affectation
künsteln ▸**gekünstelt**
kunst-, Kunst-: ~erzieher *der*, **~erzieherin** *die* ▸ⓘ **S. 113** art teacher; **~erziehung** *die* art education; (Schulfach) art; **~fälschung** *die* art forgery; **~faser** *die* man-made *or* synthetic fibre; **~fehler** *der*

professional error; (fig. scherzh.: Versehen) mistake; **ein ärztlicher ~fehler** a professional error on the part of a doctor; **~fertig** A *Adj.* skilful; B *adv.* skilfully; **~fertigkeit** *die* skill; skilfulness; **~figur** *die* fictitious character; **~flieger** *der*, **~fliegerin** *die* aerobatic pilot; stunt pilot (coll.); **~flug** *der* aerobatics *sing.*; stunt-flying (coll.); **ein ~flug** a piece of aerobatic flying *or* (coll.) stunt-flying; **~form** *die* art form; **~freund** *der*, **~freundin** *die* art lover; lover of the arts; **~führer** *der* guide to cultural and artistic monuments [of an/the area]; **~galerie** *die* art gallery; **~gattung** *die* art form; **~gegenstand** *der* work of art; **~genuss**, ***~genuß** *der* enjoyment of art; (Ereignis) artistic treat; **~gerecht** A *Adj.* expert; skilful; B *adv.* expertly; skilfully; **~geschichte** *die* 1 art history; history of art; 2 (Buch) art history book; book on the history of art; **~geschichtlich** A *Adj.* art historical ‹*studies, evidence, expertise, etc.*›; ‹*work*› on art history *or* the history of art; ‹*interest*› in art history *or* the history of art; **~geschichtliches Museum** art-history museum; museum of art history; B *adv.* **~geschichtlich interessiert/versiert** interested/well versed in art history *or* the history of art; **~geschichtlich bedeutsam** significant from an art-historical point of view; **~gewerbe** *das* arts and crafts *pl.*; **~gewerblich** A *Adj.* craft *attrib.* ‹*objects, skills, etc.*›; **~gewerbliche Arbeiten** craftwork *sing.*; B *adv.* **~gewerblich hergestellte Produkte** craft products; **~glied** *das* artificial limb; **~griff** *der* move; (fig.) trick; dodge; **~halle** *die* art gallery; **~handel** *der* [fine-]art trade; **~händler** *der*, **~händlerin** *die* [fine-]art dealer; **~handwerk** *das* craftwork; **Erzeugnisse des ~handwerks** craft products; craftwork *sing.*; **~harz** *das* (Chemie) synthetic resin; **~herz** *das* artificial heart; **~historiker** *der*, **~historikerin** *die* ▸ⓘ S. 113 art historian; **~historisch** ▸**~geschichtlich**; **~hochschule** *die* art college; college of art; **~honig** *der* artifical honey; honey substitute; **~kalender** *der* art calendar; **~kenner** *der*, **~kennerin** *die* art connoisseur *or* expert; **~kopf** *der* (Tontechnik) dummy head; **~kraftsport** *der* sports acrobatics *sing.*; **~kritik** *die* art criticism; (die Kritiker) art critics *pl.*; **~kritiker** *der*, **~kritikerin** *die* ▸ⓘ S. 113 art critic; **~lauf** *der* (Sport) figure skating; **~leder** *das* artificial *or* imitation leather

Künstler /ˈkʏnstlɐ/ *der*; **~s**, **~**, **Künstlerin** *die*; **~**, **~nen** ▸ⓘ S. 113 1 artist; (Zirkus~, Varieté~) artiste; **ein bildender ~**: a visual artist 2 (Könner) genius (**in** + *Dat.* at); **ein ~ in seinem Fach** a genius in one's field/at one's trade

Künstler-: ~atelier *das* studio; **~beruf** *der* artistic career; **~hand** *die*: *in* **von ~hand** by the artist's hand

künstlerisch
A *Adj.* artistic
B *adv.* artistically; **etw. ~ darstellen** express sth. in artistic form; **ein ~ wertvoller Film** a film of great artistic worth

Künstler-: ~kneipe *die* pub (Brit.) *or* (Amer.) bar frequented by artists; **~kolonie** *die* artists' colony; colony of artists; **~mähne** *die* (ugs. veralt. scherzh.) mane of hair; **~name** *der* stage name; **~pech** *das* (ugs. scherzh.) hard luck

Künstlertum *das*; **~s** artistic genius

künstlich /ˈkʏnstlɪç/
A *Adj.* 1 artificial; artificial, glass ‹*eye*›; false ‹*teeth, eyelashes, hair*›; synthetic, man-made ‹*fibre*›; imitation, synthetic ‹*diamond*› 2 (gezwungen) forced ‹*laugh, cheerfulness, etc.*›; enforced ‹*rest*›
B *adv.* 1 artificially; **jmdn. ~ ernähren** feed sb. artificially 2 (gezwungen) **sich ~ aufregen** (ugs.) get worked up *or* excited about nothing

Künstlichkeit *die*; **~**: artificiality

kunst-, Kunst-: ~licht *das* artificial light; **bei ~licht** in artificial light; **~liebhaber** *der*, **~liebhaberin** *die* art lover; lover of the arts; **~lied** *das* art song; Kunstlied; **~los** A *Adj.* plain; B *adv.* plainly; **~maler** *der*, **~malerin** *die* ▸ⓘ S. 113 artist; painter; **~märchen** *das* (Literaturw.) literary fairy tale; **~pause** *die* pause for effect; (iron.: Stockung) awkward pause; **eine ~pause machen** pause for effect/pause awkwardly; **~post·karte** *die* art postcard; **~rasen** *der* artificial turf; **~raub** *der* art theft; **~reich** ▸**~voll**; **~reiter** *der*, **~reiterin** *die* circus rider; bareback rider; **~richtung** *die* trend in art; **neue ~richtungen** new directions in art; **~sammler** *der*, **~sammlerin** *die* art collector; **~sammlung** *die* art collection; **~schaffende** *der/die*; *adj. Dekl.* artist; **~schatz** *der* art treasure; **~schmied** *der*, **~schmiedin** *die* wrought-iron craftsman; **~schnee** *der* artificial snow; **~schwimmen** *das* (Sport) synchronized swimming *no art.*; **~seide** *die* artificial silk; rayon; **~sinn** *der* artistic sense; feeling for art; **~sprache** *die* artificial language; **~springen** *das*; **~~s** (Sport) springboard diving; **~stein** *der* artificial stone

Kunst·stoff *der* synthetic material; plastic

***Kunststoffaser** ▸**Kunststofffaser**

Kunststoff-: ~bahn *die* (Sport) synthetic track; **~faser** *die* synthetic fibre; **~karosserie** *die* plastic body

kunst-, Kunst-: ~stopfen *tr. V.* (*nur im Inf. u. 2. Part. gebr.*) repair by invisible mending; invisibly mend; **~stück** *das* trick; **das ist kein ~stück** (ugs.) it's no great feat *or* achievement; **~stück!** (ugs. iron.) that's no great achievement; (ist nicht verwunderlich) it's hardly surprising; **~szene** *die* art scene; art world; **~turnen** *das* gymnastics *sing.*; **~verstand** *der* artistic sense; feeling for art; **~voll** A *Adj.* ornate *or* elaborate and artistic; (kompliziert) elaborate; B *adv.* 1 ornately *or* elaborately and artistically; 2 (geschickt) skilfully; **~werk** *das* (auch fig.) work of art; **~wissenschaft** *die* aesthetics and art history; **~wort** *das*; *Pl.* **~wörter** (Sprachw.) made-up *or* invented word

kunter·bunt /ˈkʊntɐ-/
A *Adj.* 1 (vielfarbig) multicoloured 2 (abwechslungsreich) varied; **wir laden Sie zu unserem ~en Abend mit ... ein** you are invited to our evening of varied entertainment with ... 3 (ungeordnet) jumbled ‹*confusion, muddle, rows, etc.*›
B *adv.* 1 ‹*painted, printed*› in many colours 2 (abwechslungsreich) **ein ~ gestalteter Abend** an evening of varied entertainment; **sein Leben verlief recht ~**: he had a very varied life 3 (ungeordnet) **~ durcheinander sein** be higgledy-piggledy *or* all jumbled up; **es ging ~ durcheinander** it was completely chaotic

Kunterbunt *das*; **~s** 1 (von Farben) riotous profusion of colour 2 (Gemisch) potpourri 3 (Durcheinander) muddle

Kunz /kʊnts/ ▸**Hinz**

Kupfer /ˈkʊpfɐ/ *das*; **~s** 1 copper; **etw. in ~** (*Akk.*) **stechen** engrave *or* etch sth. on copper 2 (~geschirr) copperware; (~geld) coppers *pl.* 3 ▸**Kupferstich 2**

kupfer-, Kupfer-: ~blech *das* copper sheeting; **ein ~blech** a copper sheet; **~draht** *der* copper wire; **~druck** *der*; *Pl.* **~~e** 1 copperplate printing *no art.*; **etw. in ~druck herstellen** produce sth. by copperplate printing; 2 (Abbildung) copperplate [print]; **~erz** *das* copper ore; **~geld** *das* coppers *pl.*; **~haltig** *Adj.* containing copper *postpos., not pred.*; cupriferous; **~kessel** *der* copper kettle; (zum Bierbrauen) copper vat; **~legierung** *die* copper alloy; **~münze** *die* copper coin; copper

kupfern *Adj.* (geh.) 1 copper; **die ~e Hochzeit** the seventh wedding anniversary 2 (wie Kupfer) coppery

kupfer-, Kupfer-: ~rot *Adj.* copper-red; copper-coloured; **~schmied** *der*, **~schmiedin** *die* coppersmith; **~stecher** *der*, **~stecherin** *die*; **~~**, **~~nen** copper[plate] engraver; **mein lieber Freund und ~stecher** (ugs. scherzh.) now then, my friend; **~stich** *der* 1 copperplate engraving *no art.*; 2 (Blatt) copperplate print *or* engraving; **~sulfat** *das* (Chemie) copper sulphate; **~vitriol** *das* (Chemie) blue vitriol

kupieren /kuˈpiːrən/ *tr. V.* 1 crop, dock ‹*tail*›; crop ‹*ears, hedge*›; clip ‹*wings*›; prune ‹*bush etc.*› 2 (Med.) arrest; check

Kupon ▸**Coupon**

Kuppe /ˈkʊpə/ *die*; **~**, **~n** 1 [rounded] hilltop 2 (Finger~) tip; end

Kuppel /ˈkʊpl̩/ *die*; **~**, **~n** dome; (kleiner) cupola; **die ~ der Bäume** the domed canopy of trees

Kuppel-: ~bau *der*; *Pl.* **~~ten** domed building; **~dach** *das* domed *or* dome-shaped roof

Kuppelei *die*; **~**, **~en** 1 (veralt. abwertend) matchmaking 2 (Rechtsspr.) procuring; procuration

Kuppel·mutter *die*; *Pl.* **Kuppel·mütter** (abwertend) procuress

kuppeln
A *itr. V.* 1 (bei einem Kfz) operate the clutch; **hier muss man viel ~**: you have to use the clutch a great deal here 2 (veralt.: Kuppelei betreiben) matchmake; play the matchmaker
B *tr. V.* 1 (koppeln) couple (**an** + *Akk.*, **zu** [on] to) 2 (Technik) couple; **gekuppelt** coupled ‹*exposure meter, rangefinder*›; **mit etw. gekuppelt sein** (fig.) be linked with sth.

Kuppel·pelz *der*: *in* **sich** (*Dat.*) **den ~ verdienen** (abwertend) arrange a/the match; play the matchmaker

Kuppelung ▸**Kupplung**

Kuppler *der*; **~s**, **~** (abwertend) procurer

Kupplerin *die*; **~**, **~nen** (abwertend) procuress

Kupplung *die*; **~**, **~en** 1 (Kfz-W.) clutch 2 (Technik: Vorrichtung zum Verbinden) coupling 3 (das Verbinden) coupling; (fig.) linking

Kupplungs-: ~pedal *das* (Kfz-W.) clutch pedal; **~scheibe** *die* (Kfz-W.) clutch plate; **~seil** *das* (Kfz-W.) clutch cable

Kur /kuːɐ̯/ *die*; **~**, **~en** [health] cure; (ohne Aufenthalt im Badeort) course of treatment; **eine ~ machen** take a cure/a course of treatment; **in ~ gehen** go to a health resort *or* spa [to take a cure]

Kür /kyːɐ̯/ *die*; **~**, **~en** 1 (Eiskunstlauf) free programme; (Turnen) optional exercises *pl.*; **eine ~ laufen/tanzen** skate/dance one's free programme; **eine ~ turnen** perform one's optional exercises; **die beste ~ laufen** skate the best free programme 2 (veralt.: Wahl) choosing

Kurant /kuˈrant/ *das*; **~[e]s**, **~e** (veralt.) *coin whose face value is equal to the value of its constituent metals*

Kürass, ***Küraß** /ˈkyːras/ *der*; **Kürasses**, **Kürasse** (hist.) cuirass

Kürassier /kyraˈsiːɐ̯/ *der*; **~s**, **~e** (Milit. hist.) cuirassier

Kurat /kuˈraːt/ *der*; **~en**, **~en** (kath. Kirche) curate

Kuratel /kuraˈteːl/ *die*; **~**, **~en** (Rechtsspr. veralt.) guardianship; **unter ~ stehen** be under the care of a guardian; **jmdn. unter ~ stellen** place sb. under the care of a guardian; (jmdn. stärker kontrollieren) place sb. under closer supervision

Kurator /kuˈraːtɔr/ *der*; **~s**, **~en**, /kuraˈtoːrən/ **Kuratorin** *die*; **~**, **~nen** 1 (einer Stiftung) trustee 2 (einer Universität) *university officer dealing with financial and legal matters* 3 (veralt.: Vormund) guardian

Kuratorium /kuraˈtoːri̯ʊm/ *das*; **~s**, **Kuratorien** board of trustees

> **Kuratorium Junger Deutscher Film**
>
> Young creative directors are given financial support by the *Länder*. The Young German Film Board awards prizes for first films (sometimes also second films) of artistic value. The *Filmförderungsanstalt - FFA* (German Film Board) provides financial assistance for film productions and cinemas.

Kur-: ~aufenthalt *der* stay at a health resort *or* spa; **ein ~aufenthalt am Meer** a stay at a seaside health resort; **~bad** *das* health resort; spa

Kurbel /ˈkʊrbl̩/ *die;* ~, ~**n** (bei Autos, Maschinen) crank [handle]; (an Fenstern, Spieldosen, Grammophonen) winder; (an einem Brunnen) [winding] handle

kurbeln
A *tr. V.* **1** **etw. nach oben/unten ~:** wind sth. up/down; **den Eimer aus dem Brunnen ~:** wind the bucket up out of the well; **sie kurbelte den Tisch so tief es ging** she wound the table down as far as it would go **2** (ugs.: filmen) film; shoot ‹*film*›
B *itr. V.* turn *or* wind a/the handle; (bei Autos) turn a/the crank [handle]; crank; **er musste ziemlich ~, um aus der Parklücke herauszukommen** (fig. ugs.) he had to use a lot of lock (Brit.) to get out of the parking space

Kurbel·welle *die* (Technik) crankshaft

Kürbis /ˈkʏrbɪs/ *der;* ~**ses,** ~**se** **1** pumpkin **2** (salopp: Kopf) nut (coll.); bonce (Brit. coll.)

Kürbis-: ~**flasche** *die* gourd; ~**kern** *der* pumpkin seed; ~**suppe** *die* pumpkin soup

Kurde /ˈkʊrdə/ *der;* ~**n,** ~**n, Kurdin** *die;* ~, ~**nen** Kurd

kurdisch *Adj.* ▸ⓘ **S. 670** Kurdish; **das Kurdische** Kurdish; *s. auch* **deutsch**; **Deutsch**

Kurdistan /ˈkʊrdɪstaːn/ *(das);* ~**s** Kurdistan

kuren *itr. V.* (ugs.) take a cure

küren *regelm. (veralt. auch unr.) tr. V.* choose (**zu** as)

Kürettage /kyrɛˈtaːʒə/ *die;* ~, ~**n** (Med.) curettage

Kürette /kyˈrɛtə/ *die;* ~, ~**n** (Med.) curette

kur-, Kur-: ~**fürst** *der* (hist.) Elector; ~**fürstentum** *das* (hist.) electorate; ~**fürstlich** *Adj.* (hist.) electoral; ~**gast** *der* visitor to a/the health resort *or* spa; (Patient) patient at a/the health resort *or* spa; ~**haus** *das* assembly rooms [at a health resort *or* spa]; ~**heim** *das* sanatorium

Kurie /ˈkuːri̯ə/ *die;* ~, ~**n** (kath. Kirche) Curia

Kurien·kardinal *der* (kath. Kirche) cardinal of the Roman Curia

Kurier /kuˈriːɐ̯/ *der;* ~**s,** ~**e** courier; messenger

Kurier·dienst *der* courier *or* messenger service; ~**e leisten** act as a courier/as couriers

kurieren *tr. V.* (auch fig.) cure (**von** of)

Kurier·gepäck *das* diplomatic bags *pl.*

Kurierin *die;* ~, ~**nen** ▸ **Kurier**

kurios /kuˈri̯oːs/
A *Adj.* curious; strange; odd
B *adv.* curiously; strangely; oddly

Kuriosa ▸ **Kuriosum**

kurioser·weise *Adv.* curiously *or* strangely *or* oddly enough

Kuriosität /kuri̯oziˈtɛːt/ *die;* ~, ~**en** **1** strangeness; oddity; peculiarity **2** (Gegenstand) curiosity; curio; (Ereignis) curious occurrence

Kuriositäten·kabinett *das* gallery of curios

Kuriosum /kuˈri̯oːzʊm/ *das;* ~**s, Kuriosa** (Gegenstand) curiosity; curio; oddity; (Situation) curious *or* odd *or* strange situation

Kur-: ~**kapelle** *die* spa orchestra; ~**karte** *die* [visitor's] pass *or* season ticket (allowing use of the facilities of a health resort *or* spa); ~**klinik** *die* health clinic; ~**konzert** *das* concert [at a health resort *or* spa]; spa concert

Kurkuma /ˈkʊrkuma/ *das;* ~**[s]** turmeric

Kurlaub /ˈkuːɐ̯laup/ *der;* ~**[e]s,** ~**e** holiday [combined with cure] at a health resort *or* spa

Kür·lauf *der* (Eiskunstlauf) free programme; **er zeigte einen hervorragenden ~:** he gave an excellent display of free skating

kur-, Kur-: ~**mittel** *das* spa treatment; ~**mittel·haus** *das* spa house; ~**ort** *der* health resort; spa; ~**park** *der* gardens *pl.* [of a/the health resort *or* spa]; ~**pfalz** *die* (hist.) Electoral Palatinate; ~**pfälzisch** *Adj.* (hist.) of the Electoral Palatinate *postpos., not pred.;* ~**pfuscher** *der* (ugs. abwertend) quack; doctor; ~**pfuscherei** *die* (ugs. abwertend) quackery; ~**pfuscherin** *die* ▸ ~**pfuscher**; ~**promenade** *die* [spa] promenade

Kurrende /kʊˈrɛndə/ *die;* ~, ~**n** (ev. Kirche) young people's choir

Kurrent·schrift /kʊˈrɛnt-/ *die* **1** (österr.) Gothic handwriting *or* script **2** (veralt.: Schreibschrift) cursive writing *or* script; running hand

Kurrikulum ▸ **Curriculum**

Kurs /kʊrs/ *der;* ~**es,** ~**e** **1** (Richtung) course; **auf [nördlichen] ~ gehen** set [a northerly] course; **ein harter/weicher ~** (fig.) a hard/soft line; **den ~ ändern** (auch fig.) change *or* alter course; **seinen ~ beibehalten** (auch fig.) maintain course; **vom ~ abkommen** deviate from one's/its course; **den ~ halten** hold *or* maintain course; **~ auf Hamburg** (*Akk.*) **nehmen** set course for *or* head for Hamburg; **~ haben auf** (+ *Akk.*) be heading for; *s. auch* **einschlagen A 4** **2** (von Wertpapieren) price; (von Devisen) rate of exchange; exchange rate; **zum ~ von ...** at a rate of ...; **die ~e steigen/fallen** prices/rates are rising/falling; **der ~ des Dollars** the dollar rate; **hoch im ~ stehen** ‹*securities*› be high; (fig.) be very popular (**bei** with); **er steht hoch im ~ bei seinem Chef** his boss thinks very highly of him; **etw. außer ~ setzen** withdraw sth. from circulation **3** (Lehrgang) course; **ein ~ in Spanisch** (*Dat.*) a course in Spanish; a Spanish course **4** (die Teilnehmer eines ~es) class **5** (Sport: Rennstrecke) course

Kurs-: ~**änderung** *die* (auch fig.) change of course; ~**anstieg** *der* (Börsenw.) rise in prices/price; price rise; (an Devisenbörsen) rise in exchange rates/the exchange rate

Kursant /kʊrˈzant/ *der;* ~**en,** ~**en** ▸ **Kursteilnehmer**

Kurs-: ~**bericht** *der* (Börsenw.) ▸ ~**zettel**; ~**buch** *das* (Eisenb.) timetable

Kur·schatten *der* (ugs. scherzh.) lady friend/boyfriend at/from the spa

Kürschner /ˈkʏrʃnɐ/ *der;* ~**s,** ~ ▸ⓘ **S. 113** furrier

Kürschnerei *die;* ~, ~**en** **1** furriery **2** (Werkstatt) furrier's workroom

Kürschnerin *die;* ~, ~**nen** furrier

Kurs-: ~**einbruch** *der* (Börsenw.) sharp fall in prices; ~**einbuße** *die* (Börsenw.) fall in prices/price; price fall; (bes. bei Devisen) fall *or* decline in value; ~**gewinn** *der* (Börsenw.) **1** market profit; (bei Devisen) profit on the foreign exchange market; **2** (Wertzuwachs) market gain

kursieren *itr. V.; auch mit sein* circulate

Kursist *der;* ~**en,** ~**en, Kursistin** *die;* ~, ~**nen** ▸ **Kursteilnehmer**

kursiv /kʊrˈziːf/ (Druckw.)
A *Adj.* italic
B *adv.* **etw. ~ drucken** print sth. in italics; (zur Hervorhebung) italicize sth.

Kursive *die;* ~, ~**n, Kursiv·schrift** *die* (Druckw.) italics *pl.*; **in ~schrift** in italics

Kurs-: ~**korrektur** *die* (auch fig.) course correction; ~**leiter** *der* course leader

kursorisch /kʊrˈzoːrɪʃ/
A *Adj.* cursory
B *adv.* cursorily

Kurs-: ~**rallye** *die od. schweiz. das* (Börsenw.) price rally; ~**rückgang** *der* (Börsenw.) fall in prices/price; price fall; (bei Devisen) fall in exchange rates/the exchange rate; ~**schwankung** *die* (Börsenw.) fluctuation in prices/price; (bei Devisen) fluctuation in exchange rates/the exchange rate; ~**system** *das* (Schulw.) course system; ~**teilnehmer** *der,* ~**teilnehmerin** *die* course participant

Kursus /ˈkʊrzʊs/ *der;* ~, **Kurse** ▸ **Kurs 3, 4**

Kurs-: ~**verlust** *der* (Börsenw.) market loss; (bei Devisen) loss on the foreign exchange market; ~**wagen** *der* (Eisenb.) through carriage *or* coach; ~**wechsel** *der* (auch fig.) change of course; ~**wert** *der* (Börsenw.) market value *or* price; ~**zettel** *der* (Börsenw.) stock exchange list; list of [market] quotations; (bei Devisen) list of foreign exchange rates

Kur·taxe *die* visitors' tax (*at a health resort*)

Kurtisane /kʊrtiˈzaːnə/ *die;* ~, ~**n** (hist.) courtesan

Kurve /ˈkʊrvə/ *die;* ~, ~**n** **1** (einer Straße) bend; curve; (sehr scharf) corner; **in dieser ~:** on this bend *or* curve; **die Straße macht eine [scharfe] ~:** the road bends *or* curves [sharply]; **die ~ kratzen** (ugs.) quickly make oneself scarce (coll.); **die ~ kriegen** (ugs.) manage to do it; (etw. überwinden) manage to do something decisive about it; *s. auch* **schneiden** **2** (Geom.) curve **3** (in der Statistik, Temperatur~ usw.) graph; curve **4** (Bogenlinie) curve; **eine ~ fliegen** do a banking turn **5** *Pl.* (ugs.: Körperformen) curves

kurven *itr. V.; mit sein* **1** ‹*aircraft*› circle; ‹*tanks etc.*› circle [round]; **um die Ecke ~:** turn the corner **2** (ugs.: fahren) drive around; (mit dem Motorrad, Fahrrad) ride around; **durch ganz Frankreich ~:** drive/ride all round France

kurven-, Kurven-: ~**diskussion** *die* (Math.) curve-tracing; ~**lineal** *das* French curve; ~**reich** *Adj.* **1** winding; twisting; **„~reiche Strecke"** 'series of bends'; **2** (ugs. scherzh.) curvaceous; ~**schreiber** *der* (Technik) graphic recording instrument; (DV) plotter; ~**verhalten** *das* (Kfz-W.) cornering characteristics *pl.*; ~**vorgabe** *die* (Leichtathletik) stagger

Kur·verwaltung *die* administrative office/offices of a/the health resort *or* spa

kurvig *Adj.* curved; winding, twisting ‹*path, road, etc.*›

kurz /kʊrt͜s/; **kürzer** /ˈkʏrt͜sɐ/, **kürzest...** /ˈkʏrt͜səst.../
A *Adj.* **1** (räumlich) short; **~e Hosen** short trousers; shorts; **etw. kürzer machen** make sth. shorter; shorten sth.; **~ geschnitten** cropped short *postpos.*; **ein kürzerer Weg** a shorter *or* quicker way; **die Hundeleine ~ halten** keep the dog on a short lead; **etw./alles ~ und klein schlagen** *od.* **hauen** (ugs.) smash sth./everything to bits *or* pieces; **den Kürzeren ziehen** come off worst *or* second-best; get the worst of it; **nicht zu ~/zu ~ kommen** get one's/less than one's fair share **2** (zeitlich) short, brief ‹*trip, journey, visit, reply*›; short ‹*life, break, time*›; quick ‹*look*›; **nach einer ~en Weile** after a short *or* little while; **es ~ machen** make *or* keep it short; be brief **3** (knapp) short, brief ‹*outline, note, report, summary, introduction*›; **etw. in ~en Worten sagen** say sth. in a few brief words; **~ und bündig** *od.* **knapp** brief and succinct
B *adv.* **1** (zeitlich) briefly; for a short time *or* while; **~ gebratenes Fleisch** meat fried on high heat for a very short time; **die Freude währte nur ~** (geh.) his/her *etc.* joy was short-lived; **binnen ~em** *od.* **Kurzem** shortly; soon; **er hatte binnen ~em** *od.* **Kurzem das ganze Vermögen verjubelt** before long he had frittered away the entire fortune; **über ~ oder lang** sooner or later; **vor ~em** *od.* **Kurzem** a short time *or* while ago; recently; **sie lebt erst seit ~em** *od.* **Kurzem in Bonn** she's only been living in Bonn [for] a short time *or* while **2** (knapp) **~ gesagt** in a word; **~ angebunden sein** be curt *or* brusque (**mit** with); **sich ~ fassen** be brief; **~ gefasst** terse; succinct; briefly worded; **~ und bündig** *od.* **knapp** briefly and succinctly; **~ und gut** in a word **3** (rasch) **ich muss mal ~ weg** I must leave you for a few minutes; **er schaute ~ herein** he looked *or* dropped in for a short while; **kann ich Sie ~ sprechen?** can I speak to you *or* have a word with you for a moment?; **ich muss ~ etwas in der Stadt erledigen** I've just got something to do in town. I won't be long; **~ und schmerzlos** (ugs.) quickly and smoothly *or* without any hitches; *s. auch* **entschlossen C 4** (in geringer Entfernung) **~ vor/hinter der Kreuzung** just before/past the crossroads; **~ vor Bremen hatten wir eine Panne** just before we reached Bremen, we broke down **5** (mit geringem zeitlichem Abstand) **~ vor/nach Pfingsten** just *or* shortly before/after Whitsun; **~ bevor .../nachdem ...** just *or* shortly before .../after ... **6** **jmdn. ~ halten** (jmdm. wenig Geld geben) keep sb. short of money; (jmdm. wenig erlauben) keep sb. on a tight rein; **~ treten** (sich schonen) take things *or* it easy; (sparsam sein) retrench; cut back; **kürzer treten** (sich mehr schonen) take things *or* it easier; (sparsam

k

sein) cut back; spend less; s. auch **Atem**; **Kopf 1**; **Prozess 3**

kurz-, Kurz-: **~arbeit** die short time; short-time working; **~|arbeiten** itr. V. work short time; **~arbeiter** der, **~arbeiterin** die short-time worker; worker on short time; **~ärm[e]lig** /-ɛrm(ə)lɪç/ Adj. short-sleeved; **~arm·hemd** das short-sleeved shirt; **~atmig** /-a:tmɪç/ **A** Adj. (auch fig.) short-winded; **~atmig sein** be short of breath; be short-winded; **B** adv. ‹speak› breathlessly; **~atmigkeit** die; **~~:** short-windedness; **~beinig** Adj. short-legged ‹breed, dog, etc.›; ‹person› with short legs; **~bericht** der brief or short report; **~biographie** die short or potted biography

Kurze der; adj. Dekl. (ugs.) 1 (Kurzschluss) short (coll.) 2 (Schnaps) schnapps

Kürze /ˈkʏrtsə/ die; ~, ~n 1 shortness 2 (geringe Dauer) shortness; short duration; brevity; **in ~:** shortly; soon 3 (Knappheit) brevity; **in aller/gebotener ~:** very briefly/with due brevity; **in der ~ liegt die Würze** (Spr.) brevity is the soul of wit (prov.) 4 (Verslehre) short syllable; short

Kürzel /ˈkʏrtsl̩/ das; ~s, ~ 1 shorthand symbol 2 (Abkürzung) abbreviation

kürzen tr. V. 1 shorten; shorten, take up ‹garment›; **ein Kleid um 5 cm ~:** shorten a dress by 5 cm; take a dress up 5 cm 2 (verringern) shorten ‹speech›; shorten, abridge ‹article, book›; reduce, cut ‹pension, budget, etc.›; **jmdm. das Gehalt ~:** reduce or cut sb.'s salary; **eine gekürzte Fassung** a shortened or an abridged version 3 (Math.) cancel

Kurzentschlossene der/die; adj. Dekl.: person who takes decisions on the spur of the moment

kürzer ▸ **kurz**

kurzer·hand Adv. without more ado; **jmdn. ~ vor die Tür setzen** (ugs.) unceremoniously throw sb. out; **etw. ~ ablehnen** flatly reject sth.; reject sth. out of hand; **sich ~ entschließen, etw. zu tun** decide there and then to do sth.

***kürzer|treten** ▸ **kurz B 6**

kürzest... ▸ **kurz**

kurz-, Kurz-: **~fassung** die shortened or abridged version; **~film** der short; short film; **~form** die (Sprachw.) shortened or abbreviated form; **~fristig** **A** Adj. 1 (plötzlich) ‹refusal, resignation, etc.› at short notice; 2 (für ~e Zeit) short-term; **eine ~fristige Freiheitsstrafe** a short period of imprisonment; 3 (rasch) quick ‹solution›; **B** adv. 1 (plötzlich) at short notice; **sich ~fristig entschließen, etw. zu tun** make up one's mind within a short time to do sth.; 2 (für ~e Zeit) for a short time or period; (auf ~e Sicht) in the short term; **~fristig gesehen** looked at or viewed in the short term; 3 (in ~er Zeit) without delay; **~gebraten** ▸ **kurz B 1**; ***~gefasst**, **~gefaßt** ▸ **kurz B 2**; **~geschichte** die (Literaturw.) short story; **~geschnitten** ▸ **kurz A 1**; **~haar·frisur** die bob; bobbed hairstyle; **~haar·dackel** der short-haired dachshund; **~haarig** Adj. short-haired ‹dog, breed, etc.›; ‹person› with short hair; ***~|halten** ▸ **kurz B 6**; **~lebig** /-le:bɪç/ Adj. (auch fig.) short-lived; (wenig haltbar) non-durable ‹goods, materials›; with a short life postpos.; **~lebigkeit** die short-livedness; (von Gebrauchsgütern) lack of durability; **~lehrgang** der short course

kürzlich Adv. recently; not long ago; **erst ~:** just or only recently; only a short time ago

kurz-, Kurz-: **~meldung** die brief report; (während einer anderen Sendung) news flash; **~mitteilung** die SMS message; text message; **~nachrichten** Pl. news sing. in brief; news summary sing.; **~parker** der; **~~s, ~~,** **~parkerin** die; **~~, ~~nen** short-stay (Brit.) or short-term parker; **„nur für ~parker“** 'short-stay (Brit.) or short-term parking only'; **~referat** das short paper; **~|schließen** **A** unr. tr. V. short-circuit; **ein Auto ~schließen** short-circuit a car's ignition; **B** unr. refl. V. **sich mit jmdm./etw. ~schließen** contact sb./sth. directly; **~schluss**, ***~schluß** der 1 (Elektrot.) short-circuit; 2 (fig. ugs.) brainstorm; 3 (falscher Schluss) fallacy; **~schluss·handlung**, ***~schluß·handlung** die sudden irrational act; **~schrift** die shorthand; **~sichtig** (auch fig.) **A** Adj. short-sighted; **B** adv. short-sightedly; **~sichtigkeit** die; **~~** (auch fig.) short-sightedness; **~ski** der short ski; **~stielig** Adj. short-stemmed ‹glass, flower›; short-handled ‹axe, hammer, etc.›; **~strecke** die 1 short haul or distance; **auf ~strecken** over short distances; 2 (Sport) sprint distance; sprint; **auf [den] ~strecken** over sprint distances; in sprinting

Kurzstrecken-: **~flug** der short-haul flight; **~lauf** der (Sport) short-distance race; sprint; (Disziplin) sprinting no art.; **~läufer** der, **~läuferin** die (Sport) sprinter; **~rakete** die short-range missile

kurz-: ***~|treten** ▸ **kurz B6**; **~um** /-ˈ-/ Adv. in short; in a word

Kürzung die; ~, ~en 1 cut; reduction; **eine ~ des Gehaltes** a cut or reduction in salary; a salary cut 2 (Streichung) cut; (das Streichen) abridgement

kurz-, Kurz-: **~urlaub** der short holiday; (Milit.) short leave; **~wahl** die (Fernspr.) abbreviated dialling; **~waren** Pl. haberdashery sing. (Brit.); notions (Amer.); **~waren·abteilung** die haberdashery department (Brit.); notions department (Amer.); **~weg** /-ˈ-/ Adv. ▸ **kurzer·hand**; **~weil** die; **~~** (veralt.) amusement; **allerlei ~weil treiben** have fun; amuse oneself; **~weilig** Adj. entertaining; **~welle** die (Physik, Rundf.) short wave; **auf** od. **über ~welle** on short wave; **~wellen·empfänger** der (Funkt., Rundf.) short-wave receiver; **~wellen·sender** der (Funkt., Rundf.) short-wave transmitter; **~wort** das; Pl. **~wörter** (Sprachw.) abbreviation; **~zeit·gedächtnis** das (Psych.) short-term memory; **~zeitig** **A** Adj. brief; **B** adv. briefly; for a short time

kusch Interj. [lie] down; (sei still) quiet

Kuschel·ecke die cosy corner

kuschelig Adj. cosy

kuscheln /ˈkʊʃl̩n/ refl. V. **sich an jmdn. ~:** snuggle up or cuddle up to sb.; ‹cat etc.› snuggle up to sb.; **sich in etw.** (Akk.) **~:** snuggle up in sth.

Kuschel·tier das cuddly toy

kuschel·weich Adj. beautifully soft

kuschen /ˈkʊʃn̩/ itr. V. 1 knuckle under (**vor** + Dat. to) 2 ‹dog› lie down

Kusine /kuˈzi:nə/ die; ~, ~n ▸ **Cousine**

Kuss, ***Kuß** /kʊs/ der; **Kusses, Küsse** /ˈkʏsə/ kiss; **Gruß und ~ [dein ...]** love and kisses [from ...]

Küsschen, ***Küßchen** /ˈkʏsçən/ das; ~s, ~: little kiss; **ein ~ in Ehren kann niemand verwehren** (Spr.) a friendly kiss can do no harm

kuss·echt, ***kuß·echt** Adj. kissproof

küssen /ˈkʏsn̩/ tr., itr. V. kiss; **jmdm. die Hand ~:** kiss sb.'s hand; **küss die Hand** (südd., österr.) (beim Kommen) how do you do?; good day; (beim Gehen) goodbye; **sich** od. (geh.) **einander ~:** kiss [each other]

kuss·fest, ***kuß·fest** Adj.: ▸ **~echt**

Kuss·hand, ***Kuß·hand** die: **jmdm. eine ~ zuwerfen** blow sb. a kiss; **mit ~** (ugs.) gladly; with [the greatest] pleasure; **jmdn./etw. mit ~ nehmen** (ugs.) be only too glad or pleased to take sb./sth.

Küste /ˈkʏstə/ die; ~, ~n coast

Küsten-: **~bewohner** der, **~bewohnerin** die coastal inhabitant; **die deutschen ~bewohner** those living on the German coast; **~fischerei** die inshore fishing; **~gewässer** das, **~meer** das coastal waters pl.; ***~schiffahrt**, **~schifffahrt** die coastal shipping no art.; **~straße** die coast road; **~strich** der stretch of coast; coastal strip; **~wache** die coastguard [service]

Küster /ˈkʏstɐ/ der; ~s, ~, **Küsterin** die; ~, ~nen ▸ⓘ S. 113 sexton

Kustos /ˈkʊstɔs/ der; ~, **Kustoden** /kʊsˈto:dn̩/ ▸ⓘ S. 113 curator

Kutsch·bock der coach box

Kutsche /ˈkʊtʃə/ die; ~, ~n 1 coach; carriage 2 (salopp: Auto) jalopy (coll.)

kutschen ▸ **kutschieren**

Kutschen·schlag der coach door; carriage door

Kutscher der; ~s, ~: coachman; coach driver

Kutscherin die; ~, ~nen coachwoman; coach driver

kutschieren
A itr. V.; mit sein 1 drive, ride [in a coach or carriage] 2 (ugs.) **durch die Gegend/durch Europa ~:** drive around/drive around Europe
B tr. V. 1 **jmdn. ~:** drive sb. [in a coach or carriage] 2 (ugs.) **jmdn. nach Hause ~:** run sb. home 3 (ugs.: lenken) drive ‹car, lorry›

Kutsch·pferd das coach horse; carriage horse

Kutte /ˈkʊtə/ die; ~, ~n 1 [monk's/nun's] habit 2 (Jugendspr.) (Jacke) jacket; (Mantel) coat

Kutteln /ˈkʊtl̩n/ Pl. (südd., österr., schweiz.) tripe sing.

Kutter /ˈkʊtɐ/ der; ~s, ~: cutter

Kuvert /kuˈve:ɐ̯/ das; ~s, ~s 1 (landsch., veralt.: Umschlag) envelope 2 (geh.: Gedeck) cover

kuvertieren /kuvɛrˈti:rən/ tr. V. **etw. ~:** put sth. into an envelope

Kuvertüre /kuvɛrˈty:rə/ die; ~, ~n chocolate coating

Kuwait /kuˈvait/ (das); ~s Kuwait

Kuwaiter der; ~s, ~, **Kuwaiterin** die; ~, ~nen Kuwaiti

kuwaitisch Adj. ▸ⓘ S. 520 Kuwaiti

kV Abk. (Physik) = **Kilovolt** kV

kW Abk. (Physik) = **Kilowatt** kW

KW Abk. = **Kurzwelle** SW

Kwass, ***Kwaß** /kvas/ der; ~ od. **Kwasses** kvass

kWh Abk. (Physik) = **Kilowattstunde** kWh

Kybernetik /kybɛrˈne:tɪk/ die; ~: cybernetics sing.

Kybernetiker der; ~s, ~, **Kybernetikerin** die; ~, ~nen cybernetician; cyberneticist

kybernetisch Adj. cybernetic

Kyrie /ˈky:ri̯ə/ das; ~, ~s kyrie; **~ eleison!** /eˈlaizɔn/ kyrie eleison

kyrillisch /kyˈrɪlɪʃ/ Adj. Cyrillic

KZ Abk. = **Konzentrationslager**

KZ-Häftling der, **KZler** der; ~s, ~, **KZlerin** die; ~, ~nen concentration-camp prisoner

L l

l, L /ɛl/ *das;* ~, ~: l/L; *s. auch* **a, A**

l *Abk.* = **Liter** l

la /la:/ la; **etw. auf la la singen** la-la sth.

Lab /la:p/ *das;* **~[e]s, ~e** 1 (Enzym) rennin 2 (zur Käseherstellung) rennet

labberig /ˈlabərɪç/ *Adj.* (ugs. abwertend) 1 (fade) wishy-washy; **~ schmecken** taste of nothing 2 (weich) floppy, limp ‹*material*›; floppy ‹*trousers, dress, etc.*›; slack ‹*elastic*› 3 (flau) queasy

labbern /ˈlabɐn/ (nordd. abwertend)
A *tr. V.* slurp
B *itr. V.* ‹*sail*› flap [about]

labbrig ▸ **labberig**

Labe *die;* ~ (dichter. veralt.) refreshment *no indef. art.;* (~trunk) refreshing draught

Label /ˈle:bl̩/ *das;* **~s, ~s** label

laben /ˈla:bn̩/ (geh.)
A *tr. V.* **jmdn. ~:** give sb. refreshment; **ein ~der Trunk** a refreshing drink; **das Auge ~** (fig.) delight the eye
B *refl. V.* refresh oneself (**an** + *Dat.*, **mit** with)

labern /ˈla:bɐn/ (ugs. abwertend)
A *tr. V.* talk; **was laberst du da?** what are you rabbiting (Brit. coll.) *or* babbling on about?
B *itr. V.* rabbit (Brit. coll.) *or* babble on

labial /laˈbi̯a:l/ (Phon.)
A *Adj.* labial
B *adv.* labially

Labial *der;* **~s, ~e, Labial·laut** *der* (Sprachw.) labial [sound]

labil /laˈbi:l/ *Adj.* 1 (Med.) delicate, frail ‹*constitution, health*›; poor ‹*circulation*› 2 (auch Psych.) unstable ‹*person, character, situation, equilibrium, etc.*›

Labilität /labiliˈtɛ:t/ *die;* **~, ~en** ▸ **labil 1, 2**: delicateness; frailness; poorness; instability

Labiodental /labi̯o-/ *der* (Sprachw.) labiodental

Lab-: ~kraut *das* (Bot.) bedstraw; **~magen** *der* (Zool.) abomasum; rennet stomach

Labor /laˈbo:ɐ̯/ *das;* **~s, ~s,** *auch:* **~e** laboratory

Laborant /laboˈrant/ *der;* **~en, ~en, Laborantin** *die;* **~, ~nen** ▸ **S. 113** laboratory *or* (coll.) lab assistant *or* technician

Laboratorium /laboraˈto:ri̯ʊm/ *das;* **~s, Laboratorien** laboratory

laborieren *itr. V.* (ugs.) 1 (leiden) suffer (**an** + *Dat.* from); **er laboriert schon seit Wochen an einer Grippe** he's been trying to shake off the flu for weeks (coll.) 2 (sich abmühen) **an etw.** (*Dat.*) **~:** labour *or* toil away at sth.

Labor-: ~platz *der* place in a/the laboratory; **~test** *der* laboratory test (**an** + *Dat.* of; **auf** + *Akk.* for); **~versuch** *der* laboratory experiment

Labsal /ˈla:pza:l/ *das;* **~[e]s, ~e** *od.* (südd., österr.) *die;* **~, ~e** (geh.) refreshment; **ein ~ für jmdn. sein** refresh sb.

Labskaus /ˈlapskaus/ *das;* ~ (Kochk.) ≈ lobscouse; *stew made with beef, potatoes, onions, gherkins, and beetroot, eaten with a fried egg*

Labung *die;* **~, ~en** (geh.) refreshment

Labyrinth /labyˈrɪnt/ *das;* **~[e]s, ~e** 1 maze; labyrinth 2 (Anat.) labyrinth

labyrinthisch
A *Adj.* labyrinthine
B *adv.* **~ verschlungene Wege** a maze of winding paths

Lach·anfall *der* laughing fit; fit of laughing

Lache[1] /ˈlaxə/ *die;* **~, ~n** (ugs.) laugh

Lache[2] /ˈla(:)xə/ *die;* **~, ~n** puddle; (von Blut, Öl) pool

lächeln /ˈlɛçl̩n/ *itr. V.* smile (**über** + *Akk.* at); **freundlich/verlegen ~:** give a friendly/an embarrassed smile

Lächeln *das;* **~s** smile

lachen
A *itr. V.* 1 laugh; **da kann man** *od.* **ich doch nur ~:** that's a laugh; **jmdn. zum Lachen bringen** make sb. laugh; **die Clowns waren zum Lachen** the clowns were very amusing; **platzen/sterben vor Lachen** (fig.) split one's sides laughing/die laughing; **die Sonne** *od.* **der Himmel lacht** (fig.) the sun is shining brightly; **ihm lacht das Glück** (dichter.) Fortune smiled upon *or* favoured him; **wer zuletzt lacht, lacht am besten** (Spr.) he who laughs last, laughs longest; **zum Lachen sein** (ugs. abwertend) be laughable *or* ridiculous; **dass ich nicht lache!** (ugs.) don't make me laugh (coll.) 2 (sich lustig machen) laugh, make *or* poke fun (**über** + *Akk.* at); *s. auch* **dritt...; Erbe**[2]
B *tr. V.* **was gibt es denn zu ~?** what's so funny?; **es** *od.* **das wäre ja** *od.* **doch gelacht, wenn ...** (ugs.) it would be ridiculous if ...; **wenn dein Vater das erfährt, hast du nichts zu ~:** you won't think it funny if your father finds out about it; **da gibt es gar nichts zu ~:** it's no laughing matter; **nichts zu ~ haben** (ugs.) have a hard time of it (**bei** with); *s. auch* **scheckig**

Lachen *das;* **~s** laughter; **ein lautes ~:** a loud laugh; **sie konnte sich das ~ kaum verbeißen** she could hardly stop herself laughing; **ihm wird das ~ noch vergehen** he'll be laughing on the other side of his face

Lacher *der;* **~s, ~** 1 laugher; **die ~:** those who are/were laughing; **die ~ auf seiner Seite haben** score by making everybody laugh 2 (kurzes Lachen) laugh

Lach·erfolg *der:* **einen ~ haben, ein ~ sein** make everybody laugh; **einen großen ~ haben, ein großer ~ sein** bring the house down

Lacherin *die;* **~, ~nen** ▸ **Lacher 1**

lächerlich /ˈlɛçɐlɪç/ (abwertend)
A *Adj.* 1 (komisch) ridiculous; **jmdn./sich [vor jmdm.] ~ machen** make a fool of sb./oneself *or* make sb./oneself look silly [in front of sb.]; **sich** (*Dat.*) **~ vorkommen** feel ridiculous; **etw. ins Lächerliche ziehen** make a joke out of sth. 2 (töricht) ridiculous; ludicrous ‹*argument, statement*› 3 (gering) derisory, ridiculously *or* ludicrously small ‹*sum, amount*›; ridiculously low ‹*price, payment*› 4 (geringfügig) ridiculously trivial *or* trifling; **~e Kleinigkeiten** ridiculous trivialities
B *adv.* ridiculously; **~ wenig** ridiculously *or* ludicrously little

lächerlicher·weise *Adv.* (abwertend) ridiculously enough

Lächerlichkeit *die;* **~, ~en** (abwertend) 1 ridiculousness; (von Argumenten, Behauptungen usw.) ridiculousness; ludicrousness; **jmdn. der ~ preisgeben** make a laughing stock of sb.; make sb. look ridiculous 2 ridiculous triviality

Lach-: ~fältchen *das* laughter line; **~gas** *das* laughing gas

lachhaft (abwertend)
A *Adj.* ridiculous; laughable
B *adv.* ridiculously

Lach-: ~krampf *der* paroxysm of laughter; violent fit of laughter; **einen ~krampf bekommen** go [off] into fits of laughter; **einen ~krampf haben** be in fits of laughter; be convulsed with laughter; **~möwe** *die* laughing gull; peewit gull; **~nummer** *die* (ugs.) **eine ~nummer sein** be just a joke

Lachs /laks/ *der;* **~es, ~e** salmon

Lach·salve *die* roar *or* peal of laughter

lachs-, Lachs-: ~ersatz *der* rock salmon; **~farben** *Adj.* salmon pink; salmon-coloured; **~schinken** *der* lachsschinken; *rolled, smoked, and cured loin of pork*

Lach·träne *die* tear of laughter

Lack /lak/ *der;* **~[e]s, ~e** varnish; (für Metall, ~arbeiten) lacquer; (Auto~) paint; (transparent) lacquer; (Nagel~) varnish; **der ~ ist ab** (salopp: etw. hat seinen Reiz verloren) the novelty has worn off; (salopp: jmd. ist nicht mehr ganz jung) he/she's no spring chicken any more; *s. auch* **fertig**

Lack-: ~affe *der* (ugs. abwertend) dandy; **~arbeit** *die* piece of lacquerwork

Lackel /ˈlakl̩/ *der;* **~s, ~** (bes. südd., österr. abwertend) oaf; **so ein ~!** stupid oaf!

lacken *tr. V.:* ▸ **lackieren 1**

Lack·farbe *die* lacquer paint; (für Autos) paint; (Emaillelack) enamel paint

lackieren *tr. V.* 1 varnish ‹*wood*›; varnish, paint ‹*fingernails*›; spray ‹*car*›; (mit Emaillelack) paint ‹*metal*›; **einen Wagen neu ~:** respray a car 2 (ugs.: täuschen) **jmdn. ~:** take sb. for a ride (coll.); dupe sb.; **der Lackierte sein** have to carry the can (Brit. coll.)

Lackierer *der;* **~s, ~** (Möbel~) varnisher; (Metall~) painter; (Auto~) [paint] sprayer

Lackiererei *die;* **~, ~en** varnisher's; (für Autos) paint shop

Lackiererin *die;* **~, ~nen** ▸ **Lackierer**

Lackierung *die;* **~, ~en** 1 (von Holz) varnishing; (von Autos) [paint-]spraying 2 (Lackschicht) (auf Holz) varnish; (auf Metall, Autos) paintwork; (auf Lackarbeiten) lacquer; **die zweite ~:** the second coat [of varnish/paint/lacquer]

Lack·leder *das* patent leather

lackmeiern ▸ **gelackmeiert**

Lackmus /ˈlakmʊs/ *das od. der;* ~ (Chemie) litmus

Lackmus·papier *das* (Chemie) litmus paper

Lack-: ~reiniger *der,* **~~s, ~~:** original-colour restorer; **~schaden** *der* damage to the paintwork; **~schuh** *der* patent-leather shoe

Lade /ˈla:də/ *die;* **~, ~n** (landsch.) 1 (Schub~) drawer 2 (veralt.: Truhe) chest

Lade-: ~baum *der* derrick boom; cargo boom; **~bühne** *die* ▸ **~rampe**; **~fläche** *die* payload area; **~gerät** *das* (Elektrot.) charger; **~gewicht** *das* carrying capacity; maximum [permitted] load; **~hemmung** *die* jam; stoppage; **[eine] ~hemmung haben** (fig. scherzh.) have a mental block; **~klappe** *die* (an einem LKW) tailboard; tailgate; (an einem Flugzeug) taildoor; **~kran** *der* loading crane; **~luke** *die* cargo hatch; loading hatch; **~mast** *der* derrick mast

laden¹
A *unr. tr. V.* **1** (ver~, be~) load **2** (aufnehmen) **die Schiffe ~ Getreide** the ships are taking on *or* are being loaded with grain; **der LKW hat Sand ge~:** the truck is loaded up with sand; **der Tanker hat Flüssiggas ge~:** the tanker has a cargo of *or* is carrying liquid gas **3** (legen) load; **sich** (*Dat.*) **einen Sack auf die Schultern ~:** load a sack on one's shoulders; **schwere Schuld auf sich ~** (fig.) incur a heavy burden of guilt; **eine ziemliche Verantwortung auf sich ~:** shoulder quite a bit of responsibility **4** (Munition einlegen) load ‹*gun, pistol, etc.*› **5** (Physik) charge; **er ist ge~** (ugs.) he's livid (coll.); he's hopping mad (coll.) **6** (aus~) unload (**aus** from)
B *unr. itr. V.* load [up]; **der LKW hat schwer ge~:** the truck is heavily loaded; **schwer** *od.* **ganz schön ge~ haben** (ugs. scherzh.) be well tanked up (sl.); have had a skinful

laden² *unr. tr. V.* **1** (Rechtsspr.) summon **2** (geh.: ein~) invite

Laden *der;* **~s, Läden** /ˈlɛːdn̩/, **~ 1** *Pl.* **Läden** shop; store (Amer.) **2** *Pl.* **Läden** (ugs.: Unternehmung) **der ~ läuft** business is good; **wie ich den ~ kenne** (fig.) if I know how things go in this outfit (coll.); **den ~ dichtmachen** shut up shop; **den ~ schmeißen** manage *or* handle everything with no problem; **den ~ hinwerfen** *od.* **hinschmeißen** chuck the whole thing in (coll.) **3** *Pl.* **Läden,** *auch* **~** (Fenster~) shutter

Laden-: ~besitzer *der,* **~besitzerin** *die* shopkeeper; storekeeper (Amer.); **~dieb** *der,* **~diebin** *die* shoplifter; **~diebstahl** *der* shoplifting; **[die] ~diebstähle** shoplifting offences; **~front** *die* shopfront; **~glocke** *die* shop bell; **~hüter** *der* (abwertend) (sich schlecht verkaufend) slow seller; slow-moving article/line; (sich nicht verkaufend) non-seller; article/line which isn't/wasn't selling; **~inhaber** *der,* **~inhaberin** *die* ▸**~besitzer**; **~kasse** *die* till; **~öffnungszeiten** *Pl.* shop *or* (Amer.) store opening times; **~preis** *der* shop price; **~schild** *das* shop sign

Laden·schluss, *Laden·schluß *der* shop *or* (Amer.) store closing time; **kurz vor/nach ~:** shortly before/after the shops *or* (Amer.) stores close/closed; **samstags ist um 14 Uhr ~:** the shops *or* (Amer.) stores close at two o'clock on Saturdays

Ladenschluss-, *Ladenschluß-: ~gesetz *das* law regulating shop *or* (Amer.) store closing times; **~zeit** *die* shop *or* (Amer.) store closing time

> **Ladenschlusszeit**
>
> The strict regulations governing shop closing times in Germany were relaxed in 1996. Shops are allowed to stay open until 8 p.m. on weekdays and 4 p.m. on Saturdays, and bakeries may open for 3 hours on Sundays. However, the actual opening times vary, depending on the location and size of the shop.

Laden-: ~schwengel *der* (ugs. abwertend) shop boy; **~straße** *die* shopping street; **~tisch** *der* [shop] counter; **unterm ~tisch** (ugs.) under the counter; **~tochter** *die* (schweiz.) salesgirl; shop *or* sales assistant

Lade-: ~platz *der* loading area; **~rampe** *die* loading ramp; **~raum** *der* **1** (beim Auto) luggage space; **2** (beim Flugzeug, Schiff) hold; **3** (bei LKWs) payload space; **~station** *die* (Elektrot.) charging unit; charger; charging station; **~stock** *der; Pl.* **~stöcke** (hist.) ramrod

lädieren /lɛˈdiːrən/ *tr. V.* damage; (fig.) damage, harm ‹*reputation etc.*›; undermine ‹*confidence*›; **lädiert aussehen** (ugs. scherzh.) look battered

lädst /lɛːtst/ *2. Pers. Sg. Präsens v.* **laden**

lädt /lɛːt/ *3. Pers. Sg. Präsens v.* **laden**

Ladung *die;* **~, ~en 1** (Schiffs~, Flugzeug~) cargo; (LKW~) load; **eine ~ Kohle** a cargo/load of coal **2** (beim Sprengen, Schießen) charge; **eine ~ Dynamit/Schrot** a charge of dynamite/shot **3** (ugs.: Menge) load (coll.); **eine ganze ~ Sand** a whole load of sand **4** (Physik) charge **5** (Rechtsspr.: Vor~) summons *sing.*

Lady /ˈleɪdɪ/ *die;* **~, ~s 1** (Adlige) Lady **2** (Dame) lady

Lafette /laˈfɛtə/ *die;* **~, ~n** gun carriage

Laffe /ˈlafə/ *der;* **~n, ~n** (veralt. abwertend) fop; dandy

lag /laːk/ *1. u. 3. Pers. Sg. Prät. v.* **liegen**

Lage /ˈlaːgə/ *die;* **~, ~n 1** situation; location; **in ruhiger ~:** in a quiet location; **eine gute ~ haben** be peacefully/well situated; be in a good/peaceful location; **in höheren/tieferen ~n** (Met.) on high/low ground **2** (Art des Liegens) position; **jetzt habe ich eine bequeme ~:** now I'm lying comfortably; now I'm [lying] in a comfortable position **3** (Situation) situation; **jmdn./sich in eine dumme ~ bringen** get sb./get [oneself] into a stupid situation; **er war nicht in der ~, das zu tun** he was not in a position to do that; **versetzen Sie sich in meine ~:** put yourself in my position *or* place; **jmdn. in die ~ versetzen, etw. zu tun** put somebody in a position to do sth.; **nach ~ der Dinge** as matters stand/stood; **die ~ der Dinge erfordert es, dass ...** the situation requires that ...; **die ~ peilen** *od.* **spannen** (ugs.) see how the land lies; find out the lie of the land; *s. auch* **Herr 4** (Schwimmen) **die 400 m ~n** the 400 m. individual medley; **die 4×100 m ~n** the 4×100 m. medley relay **5** (Schicht) layer **6** (Stimm~) register **7** (Musik: Stellung der Hand) position **8** (ugs.: Runde) round; **eine ~ ausgeben** (ugs.) *od.* **schmeißen** (salopp) get *or* stand a round

Lage-: ~bericht *der* report; (Milit.) situation report; **~besprechung** *die* discussion of the situation; **eine ~besprechung abhalten** discuss the situation

Lagen-: ~schwimmen *das* (Schwimmen) individual medley; **~staffel** *die* (Schwimmen) **1** (Wettbewerb) medley relay; **2** (Mannschaft) medley relay team

Lage·plan *der* map of the area

Lager /ˈlaːgɐ/ *das;* **~s, ~ 1** camp; **ein ~ aufschlagen** set up *or* pitch camp **2** (Gruppe, politischer Block) camp; **ins andere ~ überwechseln** change camps *or* sides; join the other side **3** (Raum) storeroom; (in Geschäften, Betrieben) stockroom; **etw. auf** *od.* **am ~ haben** have sth. in stock; **am ~ sein** be in stock; **etw. auf ~ haben** (fig. ugs.) be ready with sth. **4** (Warenbestand) stock; **wir müssen das ~ auffüllen** we must replenish our stocks **5** (geh.) bed; **jmdn. aufs ~ werfen** force sb. to take to his/her bed; put sb. in bed; **an jmds. ~ treten** step up to sb.'s bedside **6** (Geol.) bed **7** (Technik) bearing

lager-, Lager-: ~bestand *der* (Wirtsch.) stock; **den ~bestand aufnehmen** do a stocktaking; **die ~bestände räumen** clear stocks; **~bier** *das* lager [beer]; **~fähig** *Adj.* suitable for storage *or* storing *postpos.*; **~feuer** *das* campfire; **~feuer·romantik** *die* romance of the great outdoors; **~gebühr** *die* (Wirtsch.) storage charge; **~halle** *die* warehouse; **~haltung** *die* **1** storage; **2** (Wirtsch.) holding stocks *no art.*; **~haus** *das* warehouse

Lagerist *der;* **~en, ~en** ▸ⓘ **S. 113** storeman; storekeeper

Lageristin *die* ▸ⓘ **S. 113** storekeeper

Lager-: ~koller *der:* **einen ~koller bekommen** *od.* **kriegen** be driven to a frenzy by life in the camp; **~leben** *das* camp life *no art.*; (im Straf~, KZ usw.) life in the camp; **~leiter** *der,* **~leiterin** *die* (im Jugend~, Ferien~) camp leader; (im Straf~, KZ usw.) camp director

lagern
A *tr. V.* **1** store; **etw. kühl/trocken ~:** keep *or* store sth. in a cool/dry place **2** (hinlegen) lay down; **jmdn. flach/bequem ~:** lay sb. flat/in a comfortable position; **die Beine hoch ~:** rest one's legs in a raised position **3** (Technik) support; mount ‹*machine part, workpiece*›; **drehbar gelagert sein** be mounted on a pivot
B *itr. V.* **1** camp; be encamped; **auf Luftmatratzen ~:** use air mattresses **2** (liegen) lie; ‹*foodstuffs, medicines, etc.*› be stored *or* kept; (sich ab~) have settled; (fig.) ‹*mist, fog, stillness, heat, etc.*› lie, hang; **ein guter Wein muss mehrere Jahre ~:** a good wine must be kept for several years **3** (Geol.) **hier ~ Eisenerze/Ölvorräte** there are deposits of iron ore/oil here **4** (Technik) be supported; ‹*machine part, workpiece*› be mounted **5** (beschaffen sein, sich verhalten) **ganz ähnlich/anders gelagert sein** be quite similar/different [in nature]
C *refl. V.* settle oneself/itself down; (fig.) ‹*mist, fog*› lie, hang

Lager-: ~obst *das* fruit for storing; **gutes ~obst sein** be good [fruit] for storing; [be fruit that] keep well; **~platz** *der* campsite; **~raum 1** storeroom; (im Geschäft, Betrieb) stockroom; **2** (Fläche) storage space; (in ~hallen) warehouse space; **~schein** *der* (Wirtsch.) warehouse receipt; **~statt** *die* (geh.) bed; couch (literary); **~stätte** *die* **1** (Geol.) deposit; **2** ▸**~statt**

Lagerung *die;* **~, ~en 1** storage; **bei ~ im Tiefkühlfach** if *or* when stored in a deep-freeze **2** (von Kranken) **bei richtiger/falscher ~ des Verletzten** if the injured person is placed in the correct/wrong position

Lager·verwalter *der,* **Lager·verwalterin** *die* storekeeper; stores supervisor

Lagune /laˈguːnə/ *die;* **~, ~n** lagoon

Lagunen·stadt *die:* **die ~ Venedig** Venice with its lagoons and islands

lahm /laːm/
A *Adj.* **1** (gelähmt) lame; crippled, useless ‹*wing*›; **ein ~es Bein haben** be lame in one leg; **auf dem linken Bein ~ sein** be lame in the *or* one's left leg **2** (ugs.: unbeweglich) stiff; **ihm wurde der Arm ~:** his arm became *or* got stiff **3** (ugs. abwertend: unzureichend) lame, feeble ‹*excuse, explanation, etc.*› **4** (ugs. abwertend: matt) dreary; dull; feeble ‹*protest*›; dull, dreary, lifeless ‹*discussion*›; **ein ~er Typ** a dull, lethargic [sort of] bloke (Brit. coll.) *or* (coll.) guy **5 ~ legen** (+ *Akk.*) bring ‹*traffic, production, industry*› to a standstill; paralyse ‹*industry*› *s. auch* **Ente 1**
B *adv.* **1** (kraftlos) feebly **2** (ugs. abwertend) lethargically

lahm-, Lahm-: ~arsch *der* (derb) boring, lethargic old sod (Brit. coarse) *or* (coll.) bastard; **~arschig** (derb) **A** *Adj.* bloody (Brit. sl.) *or* damned lethargic; **B** *adv.* bloody (Brit. sl.) *or* damned lethargically; **~arschigkeit** *die;* **~~:** bloody (Brit. sl.) *or* damned lethargy

Lahme *der/die; adj. Dekl.* cripple

lahmen *itr. V.* be lame; **auf der rechten Hinterhand ~:** be lame in the right hind leg

lähmen /ˈlɛːmən/ *tr. V.* **1** paralyse; **an beiden Beinen gelähmt sein** be paralysed in both legs; **er ist durch einen Unfall gelähmt** he was paralysed in an accident; **einseitig gelähmt sein** be paralysed down one side of one's body; **vor Angst wie gelähmt sein** be paralysed with fear **2** (fig.) cripple, paralyse ‹*economy, industry*›; bring ‹*traffic*› to a standstill; deaden ‹*enthusiasm*›; numb ‹*will*›; **die Angst lähmte seine Schritte** (geh.) he was rooted to the spot with fear; **von ~der Müdigkeit/~dem Entsetzen befallen werden** be completely numbed with fatigue/paralysed with horror

***lahm|legen** ▸**lahm A 5**

Lahmlegung *die;* **~: eine ~ des Verkehrs/der Wirtschaft zur Folge haben** bring traffic to a standstill/paralyse the economy

Lähmung *die;* **~, ~en 1** ▸ⓘ **S. 439** paralysis; **eine halbseitige ~:** paralysis down one side of the body **2** (fig.) (der Wirtschaft, Industrie) paralysis; (der Begeisterung) deadening; (des Willens) numbing; **zu einer ~ des Verkehrs führen** bring traffic to a standstill

Lähmungs·erscheinung *die* symptom *or* sign of paralysis

Lahn /laːn/ *die;* **~, ~en** (bayr., österr.) ▸**Lawine**

Laib /laip/ *der;* **~[e]s, ~e** loaf; **ein [halber] ~ Brot** [half] a loaf of bread; **ein ~ Käse** a whole cheese

Laibung *die;* **~, ~en** (Archit., Bauw.) reveal; (eines Bogens) intrados; soffit

Laich /laiç/ *der;* **~[e]s, ~e** spawn

laichen *itr. V.* spawn

Laich-: **~platz** *der* spawning ground; **~zeit** *die* spawning time

Laie /ˈlaiə/ *der;* **~n, ~n** [1] (Mann) layman; (Frau) laywoman; **da staunt der ~ [und der Fachmann wundert sich]** it's incredible [2] (Kirche) (Mann) layman; (Frau) laywoman; **die ~n** the laity *pl.*

Laien-: **~bruder** *der* (kath. Kirche) lay brother; **~bühne** *die* amateur theatre group; **~darsteller** *der* amateur actor; **~darstellerin** *die* amateur actress

laienhaft
A *Adj.* amateurish; unprofessional; inexpert
B *adv.* amateurishly; unprofessionally; inexpertly

Laien-: **~investitur** *die* (MA.) lay investiture; **~prediger** *der,* **~predigerin** *die* (Rel.) lay preacher; **~richter** *der,* **~richterin** *die* lay judge; **~schauspieler** *der,* **~schauspielerin** *die* amateur actor; **~schwester** *die* (kath. Kirche) lay sister; **~spiel** *das* amateur performance; **~spieler** *der* amateur actor; **~spielerin** *die* amateur actress; **~stand** *der* (Rel.) laity *pl.;* **~theater** *das* [1] (Ensemble) amateur theatre group; [2] ▸**~spiel**

Laiin *die;* **~, ~nen** laywoman

laisieren /laiˈziːrən/ *tr. V.* (kath. Kirche) unfrock; defrock

Laisierung *die;* **~, ~en** unfrocking; defrocking

Laisser-faire /lɛseˈfɛːr/ *das;* **~:** laisser-faire *no art.*

Laizismus /laiˈt͡sɪsmʊs/ *der;* **~** (Politik, Geschichte) laicism *no art.*

Lakai /laˈkai/ *der;* **~en, ~en** [1] lackey; liveried footman [2] (abwertend) lackey

lakaienhaft (abwertend)
A *Adj.* servile
B *adv.* servilely

Lake /ˈlaːkə/ *die;* **~, ~n** brine

Laken /ˈlaːkn̩/ *das;* **~s, ~** (bes. nordd.) sheet

Lakonie /lakoˈniː/ *die;* **~:** laconicism

lakonisch /laˈkoːnɪʃ/
A *Adj.* laconic
B *adv.* laconically

Lakritz /laˈkrɪt͡s/ *der od. das;* **~es, ~e,** **Lakritze** *die;* **~, ~n** liquorice

Laktation /laktaˈt͡si̯oːn/ *die;* **~, ~en** (Biol.) lactation

Laktose /lakˈtoːzə/ *die;* **~** (Biochemie) lactose

Lakto·vegetarier /ˈlakto-/ *der,* **Lakto·vegetarierin** *die* lacto-vegetarian

lala /laˈla/ *in* **so ~** (ugs.) so-so; **es geht ihm so ~:** he's so-so *or* not too bad

lallen /ˈlalən/ *tr., itr. V.* ‹*baby*› babble; ‹*drunk/drowsy person*› mumble

Lama[1] /ˈlaːma/ *das;* **~s, ~s** (Zool.) llama

Lama[2] *der;* **~[s], ~s** (Rel.) lama

Lamaismus *der;* **~:** lamaism

Lama·kloster *das* lamasery

Lamäng /laˈmɛŋ/ *die: in* **aus der ~** (ugs.) just like that; off the top of one's head (sl.); (ohne Besteck) with one's fingers

Lama·wolle *die* llama [wool]

Lambda·sonde /ˈlambda-/ *die* (Technik) lambda probe

Lambris /lãˈbriː/ *der;* **~, ~:** wainscoting

Lamé, Lamee /laˈmeː/ *der;* **~s, ~s** lamé

Lamelle /laˈmɛlə/ *die;* **~, ~n** [1] (einer Jalousie) slat [2] (eines Heizkörpers) rib [3] (eines Pilzes) lamella (Bot.); gill

Lamellen·kupplung *die* (Technik) multiplate clutch; multiple-disc clutch

lamentieren /lamɛnˈtiːrən/ *itr. V.* (ugs.) moan, complain (**über** + *Akk.* about)

Lamento /laˈmɛnto/ *das;* **~s, ~s** (ugs. abwertend) loud regrets *pl.;* **ein [lautes** *od.* **großes] ~ [über etw.** (*Akk.*) *od.* **um etw.** *od.* **wegen etw.] anstimmen** kick up *or* make a [great] fuss [about sth.]

Lametta /laˈmɛta/ *das;* **~s** [1] lametta [2] (ugs. iron.: Orden) gongs *pl.* (coll.)

Laminat /lamiˈnaːt/ *das;* **~[e]s, ~e** laminate

Laminat·boden *der* laminated floor

laminieren /lamiˈniːrən/ *tr. V.* [1] (Buchw.) laminate ‹*material, book cover*› [2] (Textilw.) draw ‹*fibres*›

Lamm /lam/ *das;* **~[e]s, Lämmer** /ˈlɛmɐ/ [1] lamb; **das ~ Gottes** the Lamb of God [2] (**~fell**) lambskin

Lamm·braten *der* roast lamb *no indef. art.;* (Gericht) roast of lamb

Lämmchen /ˈlɛmçən/ *das;* **~s, ~:** little lamb

lammen *itr. V.* lamb

Lämmer-: **~geier** *der* bearded vulture; **~wolke** *die* [light] fleecy cloud; cotton-wool cloud

lamm-, Lamm-: **~fell** *das* lambskin; **~fleisch** *das* lamb; **~fromm** **A** *Adj.* ‹*horse*› as gentle as a [little] lamb; ‹*person*› as meek as a [little] lamb; **B** *adv.* **~fromm antworten** answer like a lamb; **~kotelett** *das* lamb chop

Lämpchen /ˈlɛmpçən/ *das;* **~s, ~:** small *or* little light; **ein rotes ~:** a little red light

Lampe /ˈlampə/ *die;* **~, ~n** [1] light; (Tisch~, Öl~, Signal~) lamp; (Straßen~) lamp; light; **[sich** (*Dat.*)**] einen auf die ~ gießen** (fig. ugs.) wet one's whistle (coll.) [2] (bes. fachspr.: Glüh~) bulb; *s. auch* **Meister**

Lampen-: **~fieber** *das* stage fright; **~licht** *das* lamplight; **bei ~licht** by lamplight; by the light of a lamp/lamps; **~schirm** *der* [lamp]shade

Lampion /lamˈpi̯ɔŋ/ *der;* **~s, ~s** Chinese lantern

Lampion·blume *die* Chinese-lantern plant; winter cherry

lancieren /lãˈsiːrən/ *tr. V.* [1] [deliberately] spread ‹*report, rumour, etc.*›; **eine Nachricht in die Presse ~:** get a report into the papers [2] **jmdn. in eine Stellung ~:** get sb. into a position by pulling strings [3] (bes. Wirtsch., Werbung) launch

-land *das;* **~es** (geh.) **[das] Bayern~:** Bavaria's fair land; **das große Sowjet~:** the mighty Soviet nation; **das schöne Schweizer~:** the lovely country of Switzerland

Land /lant/ *das;* **~es, Länder** /ˈlɛndɐ/ [1] (Festland) land *no indef. art.;* **an ~:** ashore; **~ in Sicht!** (Seemannsspr.) land [ahead]!; **„~ unter!" melden** report that the land is flooded *or* under water; **auf dem ~ leben** live on [dry] land; **festes ~ unter den Füßen haben** be on dry land *or* terra firma; **[wieder] ~ sehen** (fig.) be able to see light at the end of the tunnel (fig.); **kein ~ mehr sehen** (fig.) be getting deeper and deeper into the mire (fig.); **[sich** (*Dat.*)**] eine Millionärin/antike Truhe/einen fetten Auftrag an ~ ziehen** (ugs., oft scherzh.) hook a millionairess/get one's hands on an antique chest/land a fat contract [2] (Ackerboden, Gelände) land; **ein Stück/5 Hektar ~:** a plot *or* piece of land *or* ground/five hectares of land; **das ~ bebauen/bestellen** farm/till the land [3] *Pl. auch* **~e** (Gegend) country; land; **dies ist das ~ van Goghs** this is van Gogh country; **in deutschen ~en** (veralt.) in Germany; **durch die ~e ziehen** travel around *or* about; **Wochen/Jahre waren ins ~ gegangen** *od.* **gezogen** weeks/years had passed *or* gone by [4] (dörfliche Gegend) country *no indef. art.;* **auf dem ~ wohnen** live in the country; **aufs ~ ziehen** move into the country; **über ~ fahren** (veralt.) travel from village to village [5] (Staat) country; **andere Länder, andere Sitten** (Spr.) every nation has its own ways of behaving; **~ und Leute kennen lernen** get to know the country and its people *or* inhabitants; **außer ~es gehen/sich außer ~es befinden** leave the country/be out of the country; **das ~ der unbegrenzten Möglichkeiten** the land of opportunity; **das ~ der aufgehenden Sonne** the land of the rising sun; **das ~ der tausend Seen** the land of a thousand lakes; **wieder im ~e sein** (ugs.) be back again; **das ~ meiner/seiner Väter** (geh.) the land of my/his fathers (literary); **hier/dort zu ~e** ▸**hierzulande**; **dortzulande**; **bei jmdm. zu ~e** where sb. comes from; in sb.'s country [6] (Bundesland) Land; state; (österr.) province; **das ~ Bayern/Kärnten** the Land *or* state of Bavaria/the province of Carinthia

> **Land**
>
> Germany is a federal republic consisting of 16 member states called *Länder* or *Bundesländer*. Five so-called *neue Bundesländer* were added after reunification in 1990. The *Land* has a degree of autonomy and is responsible for all educational and cultural affairs, the police, the environment, and local government. The German *Länder*, including three city-states, and their state capitals are: Baden-Württemberg, capital: Stuttgart; Bayern (Bavaria), capital: München (Munich); Berlin; Brandenburg, capital: Potsdam; Bremen; Hamburg; Hessen (Hesse), capital: Wiesbaden; Mecklenburg-Vorpommern (Mecklenburg-Western Pomerania), capital: Schwerin; Niedersachsen (Lower Saxony), capital: Hannover (Hanover); Nordrhein-Westfalen (North Rhine-Westphalia), capital: Düsseldorf; Rheinland-Pfalz (Rhineland-Palatinate), capital: Mainz; Saarland, capital: Saarbrücken; Sachsen (Saxony), capital: Dresden; Sachsen-Anhalt (Saxony-Anhalt), capital: Magdeburg; Schleswig-Holstein, capital: Kiel; Thüringen (Thuringia), capital: Erfurt. Austria is a federal state consisting of 9 *Länder*: Burgenland; Kärnten (Carinthia); Niederösterreich (Lower Austria); Oberösterreich (Upper Austria); Salzburg; Steiermark (Styria); Tirol (Tyrol); Vorarlberg; Wien (Vienna). The Swiss equivalent of a German or Austrian *Land* is a **Kanton**.

land-, Land-: **~ab** /-ˈ-/ ▸**~auf**; **~adel** *der* (hist.) landed aristocracy; **~arbeit** *die* agricultural work; farm work; **~arbeiter** *der,* **~arbeiterin** *die* ▸**i** S. 113 agricultural worker; farm worker; **~arzt** *der,* **~ärztin** *die* country doctor

Landauer /ˈlandau̯ɐ/ *der;* **~s, ~** (hist.) landau

land-, Land-: **~auf** /-ˈ-/ *Adv. in* **~auf, ~ab** (geh.) throughout the land; far and wide; **~aus** /-ˈ-/ *Adv. in* **~aus, ~ein** throughout the [length and breadth of the] country; **~bau** *der* ▸**Ackerbau**; **~besitz** *der* ▸**Grundbesitz**; **~bevölkerung** *die* rural population; **~brot** *das* farm-baked bread; (Laib) *round loaf of farm-baked type;* **~brücke** *die* (Geogr.) land bridge; **~butter** *die* farm butter

Lande-: **~anflug** *der* (Flugw.) [landing] approach; **~bahn** *die* (Flugw.) [landing] runway; **~erlaubnis** *die* (Flugw.) permission to land *no art.*

land-, Land-: **~ei** *das* [1] farm egg; [2] (ugs. abwertend od. scherzh.) country bumpkin; yokel; **~ein** /-ˈ-/ ▸**~aus**; **~einwärts** /-ˈ--/ *Adv.* inland

Lande·klappe *die* (Flugw.) landing flap

landen
A *itr. V.; mit sein* [1] land; (im Hafen) ‹*ship:*› arrive; **weich ~:** make a soft landing; **bei jmdm. nicht ~ [können]** (fig. ugs.) not get anywhere *or* very far with sb. [2] (ugs.: ankommen) **zu Hause/in Paris ~:** get home/to Paris [3] (ugs.: gelangen) land *or* end up; **im Krankenhaus/Zuchthaus/Papierkorb ~:** land up in hospital/end up in prison/the waste-paper basket
B *tr. V.* [1] land ‹*aircraft, troops, passengers, fish, etc.*› [2] (ugs.: zustande bringen) pull off ‹*victory, coup*›; have ‹*smash hit*› [3] (Boxen) land ‹*punch*›

länden /ˈlɛndn̩/ *tr. V.* recover ‹*corpse, wreck, etc.*›

Land·enge *die* (Geogr.) isthmus

Lande-: **~piste** *die* landing strip; **~platz** *der* [1] (Flugw.) landing strip; airstrip; (für Hubschrauber) landing pad; (nicht ausgebaut) place to land; [2] ▸**Landungsplatz**

Ländereien /lɛndəˈrai̯ən/ *Pl.* estates

Länder-: **~kammer** *die* second *or* upper chamber (*composed of representatives of the member states of a federation*); **~kampf** *der* (Sport) international match; **~kunde** *die* regional geography *no art.;* **~spiel** *das* (Sport) international [match]

landes-, Landes-: **~bank** *die; Pl.* **~banken** regional bank; **~behörde** *die* regional authority; **~brauch** *der* custom of the country; national custom; **~ebene** *die:* **auf [hessischer] ~ebene** at regional level [in Hessen]; at the level of the Land [of Hessen]; **~farben** *Pl.* national colours; (eines Bundeslandes) colours of a Land/province; **~fürst** *der* (hist.) ▸ **~herr**; **~fürstin** *die* ▸ **~herrin**; **~gericht** *das* (österr.) district court (*at a provincial capital*); **~grenze** *die* national border *or* frontier; **die ~grenzen** the borders of the country; **~haupt·frau** *die,* **~hauptmann** *der; Pl.* **~hauptleute** *od.* **~hauptmänner** (österr.) prime minister of a province; **~hauptstadt** *die* capital; **~herr** *der* (hist.) sovereign prince; **~herrin** *die* (hist.) sovereign princess; **~innere** *das* interior [of the country]; **~kind** *das* (veralt., noch scherzh.) citizen [of the country]; **~kirche** *die* Land church; **~kunde** *die* regional studies *pl., no art.; study of the geography, history, and civilization of a country/region;* **~kundig** *Adj.* knowledgeable about the country *postpos.;* **~kundlich** *Adj.* **~kundliche Forschungen** research into the geography, history, and civilization of a/the country/region; **~liste** *die* (Politik) regional list; **~mutter** *die; Pl.* **~mütter** (geh. veralt.) sovereign lady; **~recht** *das* (Rechtsw.) law of a/the Land/province; **~regierung** *die* government of a/the Land/province; **~rekord** *der* (Sport) national record; **~sprache** *die* language of the country; **die drei belgischen ~sprachen** the three national languages of Belgium

Lande·steg *der* landing stage; jetty

landes-, Landes-: ~tracht *die* national costume *or* dress; **~üblich** *Adj.* usual *or* customary in a/the country; **die ~übliche Kleidung** the costume of the country; **~vater** *der* (veralt.) sovereign lord; **~verrat** *der* (Rechtsw.) treason; **~verteidigung** *die* national defence; **~verweisung** *die* (bes. österr.) ▸ **Ausweisung**; **~währung** *die* currency of a/the country; **~wappen** *das* national coat of arms; **~weit** **A** *Adj.* countrywide; nationwide; **B** *adv.* throughout the country; ‹*highest etc.*› in the whole country; **~weit einmalig** unique for the whole country

land-, Land-: ~fahrer *der,* **~fahrerin** *die* vagrant; **~fahrzeug** *das* land vehicle; **~fein** *in* **sich ~fein machen** (Seemannsspr.) get spruced up *or* dressed up to go ashore; **~flucht** *die* migration from the land *or* countryside [to the towns]; **~frau** *die* countrywoman

Land·friede[n] *der* (hist.) general peace

Landfriedens·bruch *der* (Rechtsw.) breach of the peace

land-, Land-: ~funk *der* farming programme [on the radio]; (Sendefolge) farming programmes *pl.* [on the radio]; **~gang** *der* (Seemannsspr.) shore leave; **~gericht** *das* regional court; Land court; **~gestützt** *Adj.* (Milit.) land-based; **~gewinnung** *die* reclamation of land; **~graf** *der* (hist.) landgrave; **~gräfin** *die* (hist.) landgravine; **~gut** *das* country estate; **~haus** *das* country house; **~jäger** *der* 1▸ (veralt.: Polizist) country policeman; 2▸ (Wurst) *small, highly seasoned, smoked, hard, flat sausage;* **~karte** *die* map; **~klima** *das* continental climate; **~kreis** *der* district; **~krieg** *der* land warfare; **~läufig** *Adj.* widely held *or* accepted; (nicht fachlich) popular; **nach ~läufiger Meinung/Auffassung** according to popular belief; **~leben** *das* country life

Ländler /ˈlɛntlɐ/ *der;* **~s, ~:** ländler

Land·leute *Pl.* 1▸ (veralt.) country folk *or* people 2▸ ▸ **Landmann**

ländlich /ˈlɛntlɪç/ *Adj.* rural; country *attrib.* ‹*life*›; **die ~e Ruhe** the quiet of the countryside

ländlich-sittlich *Adj.* (scherzh.) countrified; rustic; **hier herrschen noch ~e Zustände** people are still very countrified in their ways around here

Land-: ~luft *die* country air; **~macht** *die* land power; **~mann** *der; Pl.* **~leute** (geh. veralt.) husbandman (arch.); farmer; **~maschine** *die* agricultural machine; farm machine; **~maschinen** agricultural machinery; farm machinery; **~messer** *der;* **~~s, ~~, ~messerin** *die;* **~~, ~~nen** ▸ S. 113 [land] surveyor; **~mine** *die* landmine; **~nahme** *die;* **~~:** occupation and settlement of land; **~partie** *die* (veralt.) outing into the country; **~pfarrer** *der,* **~pfarrerin** *die* country parson *or* priest; **~pfleger** *der* (bibl.) governor; **~plage** *die* plague [on the country]; (fig.) pest; nuisance; **dieses Jahr sind die Wespen eine wahre ~plage** there is an absolute plague of wasps all over the country this year; **~pomeranze** *die* (ugs. abwertend) country cousin (derog.); **~rat** *der* 1▸ chief administrative officer of a/the district; 2▸ (schweiz.) parliament of a/the canton; **~rätin** *die* ▸ **~rat 1**; **~ratte** *die* (ugs., oft scherzh.) landlubber; **~recht** *das* (hist.) common law; **~regen** *der* steady rain; **~rücken** *der* (Geogr.) ridge of land

-landschaft *die* (fig.) scene; **in der Banken~:** on the banking scene

Landschaft *die;* **~, ~en** 1▸ landscape; (ländliche Gegend) countryside; **in die politische ~ passen** (fig.) fit in with the political mood; **in der ~ herumstehen** (ugs.) stand around; **die politische ~** (fig.) the political scene 2▸ (Gemälde) landscape 3▸ (Gegend) region

landschaftlich

A *Adj.* regional ‹*accent, speech, expression, custom, usage, etc.*›; **die ~en Gegebenheiten** the nature *sing.* of the landscape; the topography *sing*

B *adv.* **~ herrlich gelegen sein** be in a glorious natural setting; **die Umgebung der Stadt ist ~ sehr schön** the town is in *or* has a beautiful natural setting; **eine ~ gefärbte Aussprache** an accent with a regional tinge; **~ verschieden sein** differ from one part of the country to another

Landschafts-: ~bild *das* 1▸ (Gemälde) landscape [painting]; 2▸ (Aussehen) landscape; **~gärtner** *der,* **~gärtnerin** *die* ▸ S. 113 landscape gardener; **~maler** *der* landscape painter; **~malerei** *die* landscape painting; **~malerin** *die* ▸ **~maler**; **~pflege** *die* landscape conservation *no art.;* **~schutz·gebiet** *das* conservation area

Land·schildkröte *die* land tortoise

Landser /ˈlantsɐ/ *der;* **~s, ~** (veralt.) [ordinary] soldier

Land·sitz *der* country seat

Lands-: ~knecht *der* (hist.) lansquenet; **~mann** *der; Pl.* **~leute** fellow countryman; compatriot; **~männin** *die;* **~~, ~~nen** fellow countrywoman; compatriot; **~mannschaft** *die* 1▸ (studentische Verbindung) *association of students from the same country or region;* 2▸ (von Heimatvertriebenen) *association of refugees and displaced Persons from a particular region*

Land-: ~straße *die* country road; (im Gegensatz zur Autobahn) ordinary road; **~streicher** *der* tramp; vagrant; **~streicherei** *die* vagrancy *no art.;* **~streicherin** *die* tramp; vagrant; **~streitkräfte** *Pl.* land forces; **~strich** *der* area; **ein bewaldeter ~strich** a wooded tract of land; a wooded area; **~sturm** *der* 1▸ (hist.) landsturm; territorial reserve; 2▸ (schweiz.) *territorial reserve consisting of men between the ages of 49 and 60;* **~tag** *der* Landtag; state parliament; (österr.) provincial parliament

> **Landtag**
>
> The parliament of a **Land**, which is elected every 4 to 5 years using a similar mixed system of voting as for the **Bundestag** elections.

Landung *die;* **~, ~en** landing; **zur ~ ansetzen** begin one's/its landing approach; **den Piloten/das Flugzeug zur ~ zwingen** force the pilot/aircraft to land

Landungs-: ~boot *das* landing craft; **~brücke** *die* [floating] landing stage; **~platz** *der* landing place; **~steg** *der* landing stage

land-, Land-: ~urlaub *der* shore leave; **~vermesser** *der,* **~vermesserin** *die* ▸ **~messer**; **~vermessung** *die* [land] surveying; **~vogt** *der* governor (*of an imperial province*); landvogt; **~wärts** *Adv.* landward; towards the land; **~weg** *der* 1▸ (über das Fest~) overland route; **auf dem ~weg** overland; by the overland route; 2▸ (Feldweg) track across the fields; **~wehr** *die* (hist.: Reserveeinheit) territorial reserve; **~wein** *der* ordinary local wine; vin du pays; **~wind** *der* land *or* offshore breeze; **~wirt** *der,* **~wirtin** *die* ▸ S. 113 farmer

Land·wirtschaft *die* 1▸ agriculture *no art.;* farming *no art.* 2▸ (Betrieb) [small] farm

land·wirtschaftlich

A *Adj.* agricultural; agricultural, farm *attrib.* ‹*machinery*›

B *adv.* **~ genutzt werden** be used for agricultural *or* farming purposes

Landwirtschafts-: ~ministerium *das* ministry of agriculture; **~schule** *die* agricultural college

Land·zunge *die* (Geogr.) tongue of land

lang[1] /laŋ/; **länger** /ˈlɛŋɐ/, **längst...** /ˈlɛŋst.../

A *Adj.* 1▸ ▸ S. 454 (räumlich) long; **eine Bluse mit ~en Ärmeln** a long-sleeved blouse; **etw. länger machen** make sth. longer; lengthen sth. 2▸ (von bestimmter Länge) **ein fünf Meter ~es Seil** a rope five metres long *or* in length 3▸ (ugs.: groß) tall; **komm mal her, Langer** come here, lofty (coll.); *s. auch* **Latte 1**; **Lulatsch** 4▸ (ausführlich) long; **des Langen und Breiten** (geh.) at great length; in great detail 5▸ (zeitlich) long; long, lengthy ‹*speech, lecture, etc.*›; prolonged ‹*thought*›; **seit ~er Zeit, seit ~em** *od.* **Langem** for a long time 6▸ **ein vier Wochen ~es Seminar** a four-week seminar; **sein sechs Jahre ~es Studium** his six years of study

B *adv.* 1▸ (zeitlich) [for] a long time; **der ~ anhaltende Beifall** the lengthy *or* prolonged applause; **ein ~ gehegter Wunsch** a long-cherished wish; **~ ersehnt** long-awaited; longed-for; **etw. nicht länger ertragen können** be unable to bear *or* stand sth. any longer; **~ und breit** at great length; in great detail 2▸ (von bestimmter Dauer) **eine Sekunde/einen Augenblick/mehrere Stunden ~:** for a second/a moment/several hours; **den ganzen Winter ~:** all through the winter; **sein Leben ~:** all one's life; **ich werde das mein Leben ~ nicht vergessen** I won't forget it as long as I live 3▸ **~ gestreckt** long; **~ gezogen** long drawn-out; *s. auch* **länger B, C**

lang[2] (bes. nordd.)

A *Präp.:* ▸ **entlang**

B *Adv.* **[nicht] wissen, wo ~ es geht** (fig.) [not] know what it's all about; *s. auch* **entlang**

lang-, Lang-: ~ärm[e]lig /-ɛrm(ə)lɪç/ *Adj.* long-sleeved; **~atmig** /-a:tmɪç/ **A** *Adj.* long-winded; **B** *adv.* long-windedly; **etw. ~atmig erzählen** relate sth. at great length; **~atmigkeit** *die;* **~~:** long-windedness; **~beinig** *Adj.* long-legged

lange; länger, am längsten *Adv.* 1▸ a long time; **er ist schon ~ fertig** he finished long ago; **~ schlafen/arbeiten** sleep/work late; **bist du schon ~ hier?** have you been here long?; **es ist schon ~/länger her, dass ...** it's a long time/some time since ...; **es ist noch gar nicht ~ her, dass ich ihn gesehen habe** it's not long since I saw him; I saw him not long ago; **[es dauert] nicht mehr ~, und es gibt Ärger** it won't be long before there's trouble; **da kannst du ~ warten** you can wait for ever; **sie wird es nicht mehr ~ machen** (ugs.) she won't last much longer; **was fragst du noch ~?** why do you keep asking questions?; *s. auch* **länger C** 2▸ (bei weitem) **das ist [noch] ~ nicht alles** that's not all by any means; that's not all, not by a long chalk *or* shot (coll.); **er spielt ~ nicht so gut Tennis wie du** he doesn't play tennis nearly *or* anything like as well as you; **er ist noch ~ nicht so weit** he's got a long time to go till then

Länge /ˈlɛŋə/ *die;* **~, ~n** 1▸ ▸ S. 454 (räumliche Ausdehnung) length; **eine ~ von zwei Metern haben** be two metres in length; **auf einer ~ von zwei Kilometern** for two kilometres; **etw. der ~ nach falten** fold sth. lengthways; **der ~ nach hinschlagen** fall flat

L

ℹ Länge und Breite

1 Millimeter = one millimetre* (1 mm) = 0.039 inch (in.)
1 Zentimeter = one centimetre* (1 cm) = 0.394 inch (in.)
1 Meter = one metre* (1 m) = 39.4 inches (ins), 3 feet (ft) 3.4 inches†
1 Kilometer = one kilometre* (1 km) = 1094 yards (yds) *od.* 0.6214 mile

*Die amerikanische Schreibweise hat **-er** am Ende (**millimeter, centimeter, meter, kilometer**).
†Kann auch so geschrieben werden: 3' 3.4". Vergessen Sie nicht, dass bei Dezimalbrüchen ein Punkt gesetzt wird, und kein Komma.

Wie breit/lang ist es?
= How wide/long is it?, What width/length is it?
Das Zimmer ist vier mal fünf Meter [groß]
= The room is four metres [wide] by five metres [long],
≈ The room is 12 feet [wide] by 15 feet [long]
A hat die gleiche Länge/Breite wie B
= A is the same length/width as B
Sie haben die gleiche Länge* od. *sind gleich lang
= They are the same length *od.* are equal in length
Sie sind nicht gleich breit* od. *sind verschieden breit
= They are not the same width *od.* are different widths
eine 100 Meter lange Einfahrt
= a drive 100 metres long *od.* in length
ein fünf Zentimeter breites Brett
= a plank five centimetres wide
Der Stoff wird meterweise verkauft
= The material is sold by the metre
drei Meter Stoff zu 10 Euro das* od. *der Meter
= three metres of material at 10 euros a *od.* the metre
ein vier Meter langes Stück Seide
= a four-metre length of silk

on one's face; measure one's length on the ground/floor; **sich der ~ nach hinwerfen** throw oneself flat on the ground/floor **2** (hoher Wuchs) tallness; **sich zu seiner ganzen ~ aufrichten** draw oneself up to one's full height **3** (Ausführlichkeit) length **4** (Geogr.) longitude; **die Insel liegt auf** *od.* **unter 15° östlicher ~:** the longitude of the island is 15° east **5** (zeitliche Ausdehnung) length; **ein Film von einer Stunde ~:** a film one hour in length; an hour-long film; **etw. in die ~ ziehen** drag sth. out; **sich in die ~ ziehen** drag on; go on and on **6** (Sport) length; **mit einer ~ [Vorsprung] siegen** win by a length; **um ~n gewinnen** (ugs.) win easily **7** *Pl.* (in einem Film, Theaterstück usw.) long drawn-out *or* tedious scene; (in einem Buch) long drawn-out *or* tedious passage **8** (Verslehre) long syllable; long

länge·lang *Adv.* at full length

langen (ugs.)
A *itr. V.* **1** (ausreichen) be enough; **das Geld langt nicht** I/we *etc.* haven't got enough money; **das langt mir** that's enough to do for me; **jetzt langts mir aber!** now I've had enough!; that's enough of that! **2** (greifen) reach (**in** + *Akk.* into; **auf** + *Akk.* on to; **nach** for) **3** (sich erstrecken) **bis zu etw. ~:** reach sth. **4** (erreichen) reach; **bis zu etw. ~:** reach sth.
B *tr. V.* **jdmm. etw. ~:** pass *or* hand sb. sth.; **jdmm. eine ~:** give sb. a clout [around the ear] (coll.)

längen *tr. V.* **1** lengthen ‹*garment*› **2** (strecken) thin ‹*soup, sauce*›

Längen-: ~grad *der* (Geogr.) degree of longitude; **dieser Ort liegt auf dem 20. ~grad der östlichen Halbkugel** the longitude of this place is 20° east; **~kreis** *der* ▸ **Meridian**; **~maß** *das* unit of length

länger /ˈlɛŋɐ/
A ▸ **lang¹, lange**
B *Adj.* **eine ~e Abwesenheit/Behandlung** a fairly long *or* prolonged absence/period of treatment; **seit ~er Zeit** for quite some time; **es ist doch eine ~e Strecke** it's quite a long way; it's a longish way
C *adv.* for some time; **es hat etwas ~ gedauert** it took/has taken some time

länger·fristig /-frɪstɪç/
A *Adj.* fairly long-term
B *adv.* on a fairly long-term basis

Lange·weile *die;* ~ *od.* **Langenweile** boredom; **~ haben** be bored; **aus ~** *od.* **Langerweile** out of boredom

lang-, Lang-: ~fädig /-fɛːdɪç/ *Adj.* (schweiz.) long-winded; **~finger** *der* (oft scherzh.) (Dieb) thief; (Taschendieb) pickpocket; **~fristig** /-frɪstɪç/ **A** *Adj.* long-term; long-dated ‹*loan*›; **B** *adv.* on a long-term basis; **~fristig gesehen** in the long term; **~gehegt** ▸ **lang B 1**; **~|gehen** *unr. itr. V.; mit sein* (ugs.) **an etw.** (*Dat.*) **~gehen** go along sth.; *s. auch* **lang²**; **~gestreckt** ▸ **lang B 3**; **~gezogen** ▸ **lang B 3**; **~haar·dackel** *der* long-haired dachshund; **~haarig** *Adj.* long-haired; **~haus** *das* nave; (mit Seitenschiffen) nave and side aisles; **~holz** *das* (Forstw.) long timber; **~jährig** *Adj.* ‹*customer, friend*› of many years' standing; long-standing ‹*friendship*›; **~jährige Erfahrung** many years of experience; many years' experience; **eine ~jährige Strafe** a long sentence; **einer unserer ~jährigen Mitarbeiter** a colleague who has been with us for many years; **~lauf** *der* (Skisport) cross-country; **~läufer** *der,* **~läuferin** *die* cross-country skier

Langlauf·ski *der* cross-country ski

lang-, Lang-: ~lebig /-leːbɪç/ *Adj.* long-lived ‹*animals, organisms*›; durable ‹*goods, materials*›; **~lebige Gebrauchsgüter** consumer durables; **~lebigkeit** *die;* ~~ (von Organismen) longevity; long-livedness; (von Gebrauchsgütern) durability; **~|legen** *refl. V.* (ugs.) **1** **sich eine Stunde/etwas ~legen** lie down *or* have a lie down for an hour/a bit; **2** (salopp: hinfallen) fall flat [on one's face/back]

länglich /ˈlɛŋlɪç/
A *Adj.* oblong; long narrow ‹*opening*›; long [narrow] ‹*envelope*›; long ‹*box*›; oval ‹*roll*›
B *adv.* **~ rund** oval

***länglich·rund** ▸ **länglich B**

lang-, Lang-: ~mähnig /-mɛːnɪç/ *Adj.* long-maned ‹*animal*›; long-haired ‹*person*›; **~mut** *die;* **~~:** forbearance; **~mütig** /-myːtɪç/ *Adj.* forbearing; **~mütigkeit** *die;* **~~:** forbearance

Langobarde /laŋgoˈbardə/ *der;* **~n, ~n, Langobardin** *die;* **~, ~nen** Lombard

langobardisch *Adj.* Lombardic

Lang-: ~ohr *das* (scherzh.) **1** (Hase) hare; (Kaninchen) rabbit; bunny (child lang.); **2** (Esel) donkey; **~pferd** *das* (Turnen) long horse

längs /lɛŋs/
A *Präp.* + *Gen. od.* (*selten*) *Dat.* along; **~ des Flusses** *od.* **dem Fluss** along the river [bank]; **~ der Straße standen Apfelbäume** the road was lined with apple trees
B *Adv.* **1** lengthways; **stellt das Sofa hier ~ an die Wand** put the sofa along here against the wall **2** (nordd.) ▸ **entlang**

Längs·achse *die* longitudinal axis

langsam
A *Adj.* **1** slow; low ‹*speed*› **2** (allmählich) gradual
B *adv.* **1** slowly; **geh [etwas] ~er!** go [a bit] more slowly; slow down [a bit]!; **~, aber sicher** (ugs.) slowly but surely **2** (allmählich) gradually; **es wird ~ Zeit, dass du gehst** it's about time you left *or* went

Langsamkeit *die;* **~:** slowness

Lang-: ~schäfter /-ʃɛftɐ/ *der;* **~~s, ~~:** high boot; **~schläfer** *der,* **~schläferin** *die* late riser; **~seite** *die* long side

längs·gestreift ▸ **gestreift B**

Lang·spiel·platte *die* long-playing record; LP

längs-, Längs-: ~richtung *die* longitudinal direction; **in der ~richtung** lengthways; **~schnitt** *der* longitudinal section; **~seite** *die* long side; **~seits** (Seemannsspr.) **A** *Präp.* + *Gen.* alongside; **B** *Adv.* alongside; **~seits am Kai** alongside the quay

längst /lɛŋst/ *Adv.* **1** (schon lange) a long time ago; long since; **ich wusste das ~:** I've known that for a long time; I knew that long ago; **er ist ~ gestorben** he's been dead for a long time; he is long since dead; **seine ~ fälligen Schulden** his long overdue debts **2** (bei weitem) **hier ist es ~ nicht so schön** it isn't nearly as nice here; **sie singt ~ nicht so gut wie du** she doesn't sing anything like as well as you; **ich bin ~ noch nicht fertig** I'm nowhere near finished

längst... ▸ **lang¹**

längstens /ˈlɛŋstn̩s/ *Adv.* (ugs.) **1** (höchstens) at [the] most; **~ eine Woche** a week at the most **2** (spätestens) at the latest

lang·stielig *Adj.* long-stemmed ‹*glass, flower*›; long-handled ‹*axe, hammer, etc.*›

Lang·strecke *die* **1** long haul *or* distance; **auf ~n** over long distances **2** (Sport) long distance; **auf [den] ~n** over long distances; in long-distance running

Langstrecken-: ~flug *der* long-haul flight; **~lauf** *der* (Sport) long-distance race; (Disziplin) long-distance running *no art.*; **~läufer** *der,* **~läuferin** *die* (Sport) long-distance runner; **~rakete** *die* long-range missile

Languste /laŋˈgʊstə/ *die;* **~, ~n** spiny lobster; langouste

lang-, Lang-: ~weile *die:* ▸ **Langeweile**; **~weilen** **A** *tr. V.* bore; **er sah gelangweilt aus dem Fenster** he gazed out of the window, feeling bored. **B** *refl. V.* be bored; **sich tödlich** *od.* **zu Tode ~weilen** be bored to death; **~weiler** *der,* **~weilerin** *die;* **~~, ~~nen** (ugs. abwertend) **1** bore; **2** (schwerfälliger Mensch) slowcoach; **~weilig** **A** *Adj.* **1** boring; dull ‹*place*›; **2** (ugs.: schleppend) slow ‹*person*›; tedious ‹*business*›; **ein ~weiliger Kerl** a slowcoach; **B** *adv.* boringly; **~weiligkeit** *die;* **~~** **1** boringness; **2** (**~**samkeit) slowness; **~welle** *die* (Physik, Rundf.) long wave; **auf** *od.* **über ~welle** on long wave; **~wierig** /-viːrɪç/ *Adj.* lengthy; prolonged ‹*search*›; protracted, lengthy, long ‹*negotiations, treatment*›; **~wierigkeit** *die;* **~~:** lengthiness; **~zeile** *die* (Verslehre) long line; **~zeit·arbeitslos** *Adj.* long-term unemployed; **~zeit·gedächtnis** *das* long-term memory; **~zeit·programm** *das* long-term programme

Lanolin /lanoˈliːn/ *das;* **~s** lanolin

Lanze /ˈlant͡sə/ *die;* **~, ~n** lance; (zum Werfen) spear; **für jmdn. eine ~ brechen** (fig.) take up the cudgels on sb.'s behalf

Lanzen-: ~spitze *die* lance head; (der Wurflanze) spearhead; **~stoß** *der* lance thrust; (mit der Wurflanze) spear thrust

Lanzette /lanˈt͡sɛtə/ *die;* **~, ~n** (Med.) lancet

Lanzett·fischchen *das* (Zool.) lancelet

Laos /ˈlaːɔs/ (*das*) Laos

Laote /laˈoːtə/ *der;* **~n, ~n, Laotin** *die;* **~, ~nen** Laotian

laotisch *Adj.* Laotian

lapidar /lapiˈdaːɐ̯/
A *Adj.* (kurz, aber wirkungsvoll) succinct; (knapp) terse; **in ∼er Kürze** succinctly/tersely
B *adv.* succinctly/tersely

Lapislazuli /lapɪsˈlaːt͜suli/ *der;* **∼, ∼:** lapis lazuli

Lappalie /laˈpaːli̯ə/ *die;* **∼, ∼n** trifle

Lappe /ˈlapə/ *der;* **∼n, ∼n** Lapp; Laplander

läppen /ˈlɛpn̩/ *tr. V.* (Technik) lap

Lappen *der;* **∼s, ∼** **1** cloth; (Fetzen) rag; (Wasch∼) flannel **2** (salopp: Geldschein) [large] note; **ein blauer ∼:** a hundred-mark note **3** (Zool.) flap of skin; (eines Hahns) wattle **4** *in* **jmdm. durch die ∼ gehen** (ugs.) slip through sb.'s fingers **5** (Anat.) lobe

läppern /ˈlɛpɐn/ *tr. V.* (ugs.) *in* **es läppert jmdn. nach etw.** (landsch.) sb. has a sudden craving for sth.; **es läppert sich** it's mounting up

lappig *Adj.* (ugs.) limp; loosely sagging ‹*skin*›

Lappin *die;* **∼, ∼nen** ▸**Lappe**

läppisch /ˈlɛpɪʃ/ *Adj.* silly

Lappland (*das*); **∼s** Lapland

lappländisch *Adj.* Lapp

Läpp·maschine *die* (Technik) lapping machine

Lapsus /ˈlapsʊs/ *der;* **∼, ∼** (geh.) slip; (gesellschaftlich) faux pas; **mir ist ein ∼ unterlaufen** I made a slip/committed a faux pas

Laptop /ˈlɛptɔp/ *der;* **∼s, ∼s** (DV) laptop

Lärche /ˈlɛrçə/ *die;* **∼, ∼n** larch

Largo /ˈlargo/ *das;* **∼[s], ∼s** *od.* **Larghi** /ˈlargi/ (Musik) largo

larifari /lariˈfaːri/ (ugs.)
A *Interj.* nonsense; rubbish; fiddlesticks
B *Adj.* slipshod
C *adv.* sloppily

Larifari *das;* **∼s** (ugs.) nonsense; rubbish

Lärm /lɛrm/ *der;* **∼[e]s** noise; (Krach) din; row (coll.); (fig.) fuss; to-do; **um jmdn./etw. ∼ machen** (fig.) make a fuss about sb./sth.; **„Viel ∼ um Nichts"** 'Much Ado about Nothing'; **viel ∼ um nichts machen** (fig.) make a big fuss *or* to-do about nothing; **∼ schlagen** kick up *or* make a fuss

lärm-, Lärm-: ∼bekämpfung *die* noise abatement; **∼belästigung** *die* disturbance caused by noise; **∼belastung** *die* noise pollution; **∼empfindlich** *Adj.* sensitive to noise *postpos.*

lärmen *itr. V.* make a noise *or* (coll.) row; ‹*radio*› blare; **die ∼de Menge** the noisy crowd; **∼d vorbeigehen** go noisily past

larmoyant /larmo̯aˈjant/ (geh.)
A *Adj.* maudlin; tearfully sentimental
B *adv.* in a maudlin way; in a tearful and sentimental manner

Larmoyanz /larmo̯aˈjant͜s/ *die;* **∼** (geh.) maudlin *or* tearful sentimentality

Lärm-: ∼pegel *der* noise level; **∼quelle** *die* source of noise; **∼schutz** *der* **1** protection against noise; **2** (Vorrichtung) noise barrier; noise *or* sound insulation *no indef. art.*; **∼schutz·wand** *die* sound-insulating wall

Larve /ˈlarfə/ *die;* **∼, ∼n** **1** grub; larva **2** (veralt.: Maske) mask **3** (abwertend veralt.: Gesicht) mask

las /laːs/ *1. u. 3. Pers. Sg. Prät. v.* **lesen**

lasch /laʃ/
A *Adj.* limp ‹*handshake*›; feeble ‹*action, measure*›; listless ‹*movement, gait*›; lax ‹*upbringing*›
B *adv. s. Adj.:* limply; feebly; listlessly; laxly; **∼ gewürzt sein** be insipid *or* tasteless

Lasche *die;* **∼, ∼n** **1** (Gürtel∼) loop; (eines Briefumschlags) flap; (Schuh∼) tongue **2** (Technik) (von Eisenbahnschienen) fish plate; (Stoßplatte) butt strap

Laschheit *die;* **∼** ▸**lasch A:** limpness; feebleness; listlessness; laxness

Laser /ˈleɪzɐ/ *der;* **∼s, ∼** (Physik) laser

Laser-: ∼drucker *der* (DV) laser printer; **∼licht** *das* laser light

lasern /ˈleɪzɐn/
A *tr. V.* **1** treat ‹*eye etc.*› using a laser beam/laser beams **2** (die Geschwindigkeit messen) clock ‹*driver, vehicle*› with a laser gun
B *itr. V.* (Med.) use laser beam treatment

Laser-: ∼pistole *die* laser gun; **∼pointer** *der;* **∼∼s, ∼∼** (DV) laser pointer; **∼strahl** *der* (Physik) laser beam; **∼ziel·gerät** *das* laser sight

lasieren /laˈziːrən/ *tr. V.* varnish

lass, *laß /las/ *Imperativ Sg. v.* **lassen**

lassen /ˈlasn̩/
A *unr. tr. V.* **1** *mit Inf. + Akk.* (*2. Part.* **∼**) (veran∼) **etw. tun/machen/bauen/waschen ∼:** have *or* get sth. done/made/built/washed; **von welcher Baufirma haben Sie Ihr Haus bauen ∼?** which builder did you get to build your house?; **Essen kommen ∼:** have some food sent in; **Wasser in die Wanne laufen ∼:** run water into the bath; **das Licht über Nacht brennen ∼:** keep the light on overnight; **sie ließ mir eine Nachricht zukommen** she sent me a message; **jmdn. warten/erschießen ∼:** keep sb. waiting/have sb. shot; **jmdn. grüßen ∼:** send one's regards to sb.; **jmdn. kommen/rufen ∼:** send for sb.; **jmdm. etw. mitteilen/jmdn. etw. wissen ∼:** let sb. know sth.
2 *mit Inf. + Akk.* (*2. Part.* **∼**) (erlauben) **jmdn. etw. tun ∼:** let sb. do sth.; allow sb. to do sth.; **jmdn. ausreden ∼:** let sb. finish speaking; allow sb. to finish speaking; **er lässt sich** (*Dat.*) **nichts sagen** you can't tell him anything; **ich lasse mich nicht beleidigen/einschüchtern** I won't be insulted/intimidated; **das lasse ich mir nicht gefallen** I'm not standing for that; **alles mit sich geschehen ∼:** put up with anything and everything
3 (zugestehen, be∼) **lass den Kindern den Spaß** let the children enjoy themselves; **jmdn. in Frieden ∼:** leave sb. in peace; **lass ihn in seinem Glauben** don't disillusion him; **nichts unversucht ∼:** try everything; **etw. ungesagt ∼:** leave sth. unsaid; **jmdn. kalt/unbeeindruckt ∼:** leave sb. cold/unimpressed; **das muss man ihm/ihr ∼:** one must grant *or* give him/her that
4 (hinein∼/heraus∼) let *or* allow (**in** + *Akk.* into, **aus** out of); **jmdn. in die Wohnung ∼:** let *or* allow sb. into the flat (esp. Brit.) *or* (esp. Amer.) apartment
5 (unter∼) stop; (Begonnenes) put aside; **lass das!** stop that *or* it!; **etw. nicht ∼ können** be unable to stop sth.; **es nicht ∼ können, etw. zu tun** be unable to stop doing sth.; **tu, was du nicht ∼ kannst** go ahead and do what you want to do; **die Arbeit Arbeit sein ∼** (ugs.) forget about work (coll.); **lass das Grübeln!** stop brooding!
6 (zurücklassen; bleiben ∼) leave; **jmdn. allein ∼:** leave sb. alone *or* on his/her own
7 (über∼) **jmdm. etw. ∼:** let sb. have sth.; **jmdm. etw. als** *od.* **zum Pfand ∼:** leave sb. sth. as security; **jmdm. etw. billig/für 10 Euro ∼:** let sb. have sth. cheaply/for ten euros
8 (als Aufforderung) **lass/lasst uns gehen/fahren!** let's go!
9 (verlieren) lose; (ausgeben) spend; **sein Leben für eine Idee ∼:** lay down one's life for an idea; **er hat zwei Söhne im Krieg ∼ müssen** he lost two sons in the war; **er hat im Kasino viel Geld ge∼:** he lost/(langfristig) has lost a lot of money at the casino
10 (abwarten, bis ...) **lass sie nur erst einmal erwachsen sein** wait till she's grown up
B *unr. refl. V.* **1** **die Tür lässt sich leicht öffnen** the door opens easily; **dieses Material lässt sich gut verarbeiten** this material is easy to work with; **das lässt sich nicht beweisen** it can't be proved; **das lässt sich machen** that can be done; *s. auch* **hören A 2, 3**
2 (unpers.) **es lässt sich nicht leugnen/verschweigen, dass ...** it cannot be denied *or* there's no denying that .../we/you *etc.* cannot hide the fact that ...; **hier lässt es sich leben/wohl sein** it's a good life here
C *unr. itr. V.* **1** (ugs.) **Lass mal. Ich mache das schon** Leave it. I'll do it; **Lass doch! Du kannst mir das Geld später zurückgeben** That's all right. You can pay me back later
2 (veran∼) **ich lasse bitten** would you ask him/her/them to come in; **einspannen ∼:** have the horses harnessed; **ich habe mir sagen ∼, dass ...** I've been told *or* informed that ...
3 (veralt.: aufgeben) **von jmdm./etw. ∼:** part from sb./sth.; **vom Alkohol nicht ∼ können** be unable to give up alcohol

lässig /ˈlɛsɪç/
A *Adj.* casual
B *adv.* **1** (ungezwungen) casually **2** (ugs.: leicht) easily; effortlessly

Lässigkeit *die;* **∼** **1** casualness **2** (ugs.: Leichtigkeit) effortlessness

lässlich, *läßlich /ˈlɛslɪç/ *Adj.* (kath. Kirche, auch fig.) venial, pardonable ‹*sin*›

Lasso /ˈlaso/ *das od. der;* **∼s, ∼s** lasso

lässt, *läßt /lɛst/ *3. Pers. Sg. Präsens v.* **lassen**

Last /last/ *die;* **∼, ∼en** **1** load; (Trag∼) load; burden **2** (belastendes Gewicht) weight **3** (Bürde) burden; **die ∼ des Amtes/der Verantwortung** the burden of office/responsibility; **die ∼ auf andere abwälzen** shift the burden on to others; **jmdm. zur ∼ fallen/werden** be/become a burden on sb.; **jmdm. etw. zur ∼ legen** charge sb. with sth.; accuse sb. of sth. **4** *Pl.* (Abgaben) charges; (Kosten) costs; **die steuerlichen ∼en** the tax burden *sing.* **5** **zu ∼en** ▸**zulasten**

Last-: ∼arm *der* (Physik) load arm; weight arm; **∼auto** *das* ▸▸**∼kraftwagen**

lasten *itr. V.* **1** be a burden; **auf jmdm./etw. ∼:** weigh heavily [up]on sb./sth.; **das Amt lastet auf seinen Schultern** (fig.) the burden of office rests on his shoulders; **auf seinen Schultern lastet die ganze Arbeit** (fig.) all the work falls on his shoulders; **eine ∼de Stille/Hitze** (fig.) an oppressive silence/heat **2** (liegen) **auf dem Haus ∼ zwei Hypotheken** the house is encumbered with two mortgages

Lasten-: ∼aufzug *der* goods lift (Brit.); freight elevator (Amer.); **∼ausgleich** *der* (Bundesrepublik Deutschland): *compensation paid to individuals for damage and losses during and immediately after the Second World War*

Laster[1] *der;* **∼s, ∼** (ugs.: Lkw) truck; lorry (Brit.)

Laster[2] *das;* **∼s, ∼:** vice; **ein langes ∼** (fig. ugs.) a beanpole

Lästerer *der;* **∼s, ∼** **1** **ein ∼ sein** have a malicious tongue; be constantly making malicious remarks **2** (veralt.: Gottes∼) blasphemer

lasterhaft *Adj.* (abwertend) depraved

Lasterhaftigkeit *die;* **∼:** depravity

Laster·höhle *die* (ugs. abwertend) den of vice *or* iniquity

Lästerin *die;* **∼, ∼nen** ▸**Lästerer**

Laster·leben *das* (oft scherzh.) life of depravity

lästerlich
A *Adj.* malicious ‹*remark*›; malevolent ‹*curse, oath*›
B *adv.* ‹*curse*› malevolently; ‹*speak*› maliciously

Läster·maul *das* (abwertend salopp) **ein ∼ sein/haben** have a malicious tongue; be constantly making malicious remarks; **halt dein ∼!** keep your malicious remarks to yourself!

lästern /ˈlɛstɐn/
A *itr. V.* (abwertend) **über jmdn./etw. ∼:** make malicious remarks about sb./sth.
B *tr. V.* (veralt.: schmähen) blaspheme against ‹*God, God's law, etc.*›

Lästerung *die;* **∼, ∼en** malicious remark; (gegen Gott) blasphemy

Lästerzunge *die* (abwertend) malicious tongue

Last·esel *der* pack donkey

Lastex Ⓦⓩ /ˈlastɛks/ *das;* **∼:** Lastex ®; stretch fabric

Lastex·hose *die* stretch trousers *or* pants *pl.*

lästig /ˈlɛstɪç/ *Adj.* tiresome ‹*person*›; tiresome, irksome ‹*task, duty, etc.*›; troublesome ‹*illness, cough, etc.*›; **jmdm. ∼ sein** *od.* **fallen/werden** be/become a nuisance to sb.

Last-: ∼kahn *der* [cargo] barge; **∼kraftwagen** *der* (bes. Amtsspr.) heavy goods (Brit.) *or* (Amer.) freight vehicle

Lästling /ˈlɛstlɪŋ/ *der;* **∼s, ∼e** pest

Last-: ∼pferd *das* pack horse; **∼schiff** *das* cargo ship; freighter; **∼schrift** *die* **1** (Betrag) debit; **2** (Bescheinigung) debit advice; **3** (Vorgang) debiting; **4** (Verkehr) direct debit; **~tier** *das* pack animal; **~träger** *der,* **~trägerin** *die* porter; bearer; **~wagen** *der* truck; lorry (Brit.); **~wagen·fahrer** *der,* **~wagen·fahrerin** *die* ▸ⓘ **S. 113** truck driver; lorry driver (Brit.); **~zug** *der* truck *or* (Brit.) lorry and trailer/trailers

Lasur /la'zu:ɐ̯/ *die;* **~, ~en** varnish; (farbig) glaze

lasziv /las'tsi:f/ *Adj.* lascivious

Laszivität /lastsivi'tɛ:t/ *die;* **~:** lasciviousness

Latein /la'tain/ *das;* **~s** ▸ⓘ **S. 670** Latin; **mit seinem ~ am Ende sein** be at one's wit's end; *s. auch* **Deutsch**

latein-, Latein-: ~amerika *(das)* Latin America; **~amerikaner** *der,* **~amerikanerin** *die* Latin American; **~amerikanisch** *Adj.* Latin American

Lateiner /la'tainɐ/ *der;* **~s, ~, Lateinerin** *die;* **~, ~nen** Latin scholar; Latinist; (Schüler) Latin pupil

lateinisch *Adj.* ▸ⓘ **S. 670** Latin; *s. auch* **deutsch**; **Deutsche²**

Latein-: ~schule *die* (hist.) grammar school; **~unterricht** *der* Latin teaching; *s. auch* **Englischunterricht**

latent /la'tɛnt/

A *Adj.* latent

B *adv.* **~ vorhanden sein** be latent

Latenz /la'tɛnts/ *die* (geh.) latency

Latenz·periode *die* (Psych.) latency period

Laterna magica /la'tɛrna 'ma:gika/ *die;* **~, Laternae magicae** /-nɛ -tsɛ/ magic lantern

Laterne /la'tɛrnə/ *die;* **~, ~n** **1** (Leuchte) lamp; lantern (Naut.); **gute Handwerker/so ein Auto kann man mit der ~ suchen** (fig.) good craftsmen/cars like that are few and far between **2** (Straßen~) street light; street lamp **3** **die rote ~ übernehmen/an eine andere Elf abgeben** (Sport Jargon) drop to/move off the bottom of the table **4** (Bauw.) lantern

Laternen-: ~licht *das* light of the street lamp/lamps; **~parker** *der;* **~s, ~, ~parkerin** *die;* **~, ~nen** (scherzh.) driver who regularly parks in the road; **~pfahl** *der* lamp post

Latex /'la:tɛks/ *der;* **~, Latizes** /'la:titse:s/ latex

Latifundium /lati'fʊndiʊm/ *das;* **~s, Latifundien** (hist.) latifundium

Latina /la'ti:na/ *die;* **~, ~s** Latina

latinisieren /latini'zi:rən/ *tr. V.* Latinize

Latinismus *der;* **~, Latinismen** (Sprachw.) Latinism

Latinist *der;* **~en, ~en, Latinistin** *die;* **~, ~nen** Latinist; Latin scholar

Latino /la'ti:no/ *der;* **~s, ~s** Latino

Latinum /la'ti:nʊm/ *das;* **~s: das kleine/große ~:** ≈ GCSE/'A' level Latin [examination]

Latizes ▸ **Latex**

Latrine /la'tri:nə/ *die;* **~, ~n** latrine

Latrinen·parole *die* (ugs. abwertend) empty rumour

Latsche¹ /'latʃə/ *die;* **~, ~n** (variety of) [Swiss] mountain pine

Latsche² /'la:tʃə/ *die;* **~, ~n** ▸ **Latschen**

latschen /'la:tʃn/ *itr. V.; mit sein* (salopp) trudge; (schlurfend) slouch

Latschen *der;* **~s, ~** (ugs.) old worn-out shoe; (Hausschuh) old worn-out slipper; **wenn ich nicht bald etwas zu essen kriege, kippe ich noch aus den ~** (salopp) if I don't get something to eat soon, I shall keel over; **er ist bald aus den ~ gekippt, als er hörte, dass ich im Lotto gewonnen hatte** (salopp) he was flabbergasted when he heard I'd got a prize in the lottery

Latschen·kiefer *die:* ▸ **Latsche¹**

Latte /'latə/ *die;* **~, ~n** **1** lath; slat; (Zaun~) pale; **eine lange ~** (ugs.) a beanpole **2** (Sport: Quer~ des Tores) [cross]bar **3** (Leichtathletik) bar **4** *in* **eine [lange] ~ von Schulden/Vorstrafen** (ugs.) a [large] pile of debts/a [long] list *or* string of previous convictions

Latten-: ~kiste *die* crate; **~kreuz** *das* (Fuß-, Handball) angle of the [cross]bar and the post; **im ~kreuz** in the top corner of the net; **~rost** *der* (auf dem Boden) duckboards *pl.*; (eines Bettes) slatted frame; **~schuss, *~schuß** *der* (Ballspiele) **es war nur ein ~schuss** the shot only hit the [cross]bar; **~zaun** *der* paling fence

Lattich /'latɪç/ *der;* **~s, ~e** lettuce

Latüchte /la'tʏçtə/ *die;* **~, ~n** (ugs. scherzh.) lamp; **geh mir aus der ~!** (salopp) get out of the light!

Latwerge /lat'vɛrgə/ *die;* **~, ~n** **1** (Med. veralt.) confection **2** (bes. südwestd.: Mus) [fruit] purée

Latz /lats/ *der;* **~es, Lätze** /'lɛtsə/ **1** bib; **jmdm. eine[n] vor den ~ knallen** *od.* **ballern** (salopp) sock (sl.) *or* thump sb. **2** ▸ **Hosenlatz**

Lätzchen /'lɛtsçən/ *das;* **~s, ~:** bib

Latz-: ~hose *die* bib and brace; (für Kinder) dungarees *pl.*; **~rock** *der* bib-top pinafore dress

lau /lau/ *Adj.* **1** (mäßig warm) tepid, lukewarm ‹*water etc.*›; (nicht mehr kalt) warm ‹*beer etc.*› **2** (mild) mild ‹*wind, air, evening, etc.*›; mild and gentle ‹*rain*› **3** (unentschlossen) lukewarm; half-hearted

Laub /laup/ *das;* **~[e]s** leaves *pl.*; **dichtes/neues ~:** thick/new foliage; **~ tragende Bäume** trees bearing [broad] leaves

Laub-: ~baum *der* broad-leaved tree; **~blatt** *das* [broad] leaf; **~dach** *das* (dicht.) leafy canopy (poet.); canopy of leaves

Laube *die;* **~, ~n** **1** summer house; (überdeckter Sitzplatz) bower; arbour; *s. auch* **fertig** **2** (Archit.) porch

Lauben-: ~kolonie *die* group of allotment gardens; **~pieper** *der;* **~~s, ~~, ~pieperin** *die;* **~~, ~~nen** (berlin. scherzh.) allotment gardener

Laub-: ~frosch *der* tree frog; **~hölzer** *Pl.* broad-leaved trees and shrubs; **~hütten·fest** *das* (jüd. Rel.) Feast of Tabernacles; Succoth; **~krone** *die* **1** (geh.: Wipfel) treetop; **2** (Krone) crest coronet

Laub·säge *die* fretsaw

Laubsäge·arbeit *die* fretsaw work; **eine ~:** a piece of fretsaw work

laub-, Laub-: ~sänger *der* (Zool.) leaf warbler; **~tragend** ▸ **Laub**; **~wald** *der* deciduous wood/forest; **~werk** *das* **1** (Archit., Kunst) foliage; **2** (geh.) ▸ **Belaubung 2**

Lauch /laux/ *der;* **~[e]s, ~e** (Bot.) allium; (Porree) leek

Laudatio /lau'da:tsio/ *die;* **~, ~nes** /-'tsio:ne:s/ *od.* **~nen** /-'tsio:nən/ eulogy; encomium

Laudator /lau'da:tɔr/*der;* **~s, Laudatoren** /-'to:rən/, **Laudatorin** *die;* **~, ~nen** eulogizer

Laue[ne] /'lauə(nə)/ *die;* **~, ~n** (schweiz.) ▸ **Lawine**

Lauer /'lauɐ/ *die;* **~** *in* **auf der ~ liegen** *od.* **sein** (ugs.) (jmdm. auflauern) lie in wait; (etw. erfahren wollen) be on the lookout; (um zu hören) be listening out; **sich auf die ~ legen** settle down to lie in wait

lauern *itr. V.* **1** (auch fig.) lurk; **auf jmdn./etw. ~:** lie in wait for sb./sth.; **er wartete ~d auf unsere Antwort** he slyly awaited our reply; **ein ~der Blick** a sly look **2** (ugs.: ungeduldig warten) **auf jmdn./etw. ~:** wait [impatiently] for sb./sth.

Lauf /lauf/ *der;* **~[e]s, Läufe** /'lɔyfə/ **1** running **2** (Sport: Wettrennen) heat **3** (Ver~, Entwicklung) course; **im ~[e] der Zeit** in the course of time; **im ~[e] der Jahre** over the years; as the years go/went by; **im ~[e] des Tages** during the day; **[irgendwann] im ~[e] des Sommers** [some time] during the summer; **im ~[e] seines Lebens** in the course of *or* during his life; **einer Sache** *(Dat.)* **ihren** *od.* **freien ~ lassen** give free rein to sth.; **seinem Zorn freien ~ lassen** give vent to one's anger; **seiner Fantasie freien ~ lassen** give free rein to one's imagination; (zu sehr) indulge in flights of fancy; **lass doch den Dingen ihren ~!** let matters *or* things take their course; **der ~ der Geschichte/Welt** the course of history/the way of the world; **seinen ~ nehmen** take its course **4** (von Schusswaffen) barrel; **etw. vor den ~ bekommen** get a shot at sth. **5** (eines Flusses, einer Straße) course; **der obere/untere ~ eines Flusses** the upper/lower reaches *pl.* of a river; **der ~ der Straße** the route followed by the road; **dem ~ der Straße/Bahnschienen folgen** follow the road/railway lines **6** (Musik) run **7** (Jägerspr.) leg **8** (von Maschinen) running

Lauf-: ~bahn *die* **1** (Werdegang) career; **eine wissenschaftliche/künstlerische ~bahn einschlagen** take up a career in the sciences/as an artist; **2** (Leichtathletik) running track; **~band** *das* **1** conveyer belt; (für Personen) moving pavement; travelator; moving sidewalk (Amer.); (im Fitnesscenter) treadmill; **2** (Streifen mit Lauftext) text crawl; **~buchse** *die* (Technik) cylinder liner; **~bursche** *der* errand boy; messenger boy

laufen

A *unr. itr. V.; mit sein* **1** run; **ge~ kommen** come running up; **er lief, was er konnte** (ugs.) he ran as fast as he could; **jmdn. ~ lassen** (ugs.) let sb. go

2 (gehen) go; (zu Fuß gehen) walk; **auf und ab/hin und her ~:** walk up and down/back and forth; **wir sind im Urlaub viel ge~:** we did a lot of walking while on holiday; **es sind noch/nur fünf Minuten zu ~:** it's another/only five minutes' walk; **das Kind lernt ~:** the child is learning to walk

3 (stoßen) **in** (+ *Akk.*)/**gegen etw. ~:** walk into sth.

4 (ugs.: ständig hingehen) **dauernd zum Arzt/ins Kino/in die Kirche ~:** keep running to the doctor/be always going to the cinema (Brit.) *or* (Amer.) the movies/to church; **in jede Veranstaltung der Partei ~:** go to every event organized by the party

5 (in einem Wettkampf) run; (beim Eislauf) skate; (beim Ski~) ski; **ein Pferd ~ lassen** run a horse

6 (in Gang sein) ‹*machine*› be running; ‹*radio, television, etc.*› be on; (funktionieren) ‹*machine*› run; ‹*radio, television, etc.*› work; **ruhig/auf Hochtouren ~:** be running quietly/at full speed

7 (sich bewegen, [aus]fließen; auch fig.) **auf Schienen/über Rollen ~:** run on rails/over pulleys; **von den Fließbändern ~:** come off the conveyor belts; **es lief mir eiskalt über den Rücken** a chill ran down my spine; **ihm lief der Schweiß über das Gesicht** the sweat ran down his face; **Wasser in die Wanne ~ lassen** run the bathwater; **deine Nase läuft** your nose is running; you've got a runny nose; **der Käse läuft** the cheese has gone runny (coll.)

8 (gelten) ‹*contract, agreement, engagement, etc.*› run; **der Vertrag läuft noch bis ...** the contract runs until ...

9 (gespielt werden) ‹*programme, play*› be on; ‹*film*› be on *or* showing; ‹*show*› be on *or* playing; **im dritten Programm ~:** be on the regional programme; **der Hauptfilm läuft schon** the main film has already started

10 (fahren) run; **auf Grund ~:** run aground

11 (vonstatten gehen) **parallel mit etw. ~:** run in parallel with sth.; **ich möchte wissen, wie der Prozess ge~ ist** I'd like to know the outcome of the trial; **der Laden läuft/die Geschäfte ~ gut/schlecht** (ugs.) the shop is doing well/badly/business is good/bad; **wie geplant/nach Wunsch ~:** go as planned *or* according to plan; **die Sache ist ge~** (ugs.: daran ist nichts mehr zu ändern) it's too late now; **schief ~** (ugs.) go wrong

12 (eingeleitet sein) ‹*negotiations, investigations*› be in progress *or* under way; ‹*application*› be under consideration

13 (registriert sein) **auf jmds. Namen** *(Akk.)* **~:** be in sb.'s name

14 (ugs.: gut verkäuflich sein) go *or* sell well

15 (ver~) run

B *unr. tr. u. itr. V.* **1** *mit sein (zurücklegen)* (zu Fuß gehen) walk; (rennen) run; **die 800 m/einige**

Runden/sechs Rennen ~ (Sport) run the 800 m./a few laps/[in] six races [2] *mit sein* (erzielen) **einen Rekord ~:** set up a record; **über die 100 m 9,9 Sekunden ~:** run the 100 m. in 9.9 seconds [3] *mit haben od. sein* **Ski/Schlittschuh/Rollschuh ~:** ski/skate/roller skate [4] **sich** (*Dat.*) **die Füße wund ~:** get sore feet from running/walking; **sich** (*Dat.*) **ein Loch in die Schuhsohle ~:** wear a hole in one's shoe *or* sole

C *unr. refl. V.* [1] **sich warm ~:** warm up; *s. auch* **müde** [2] (unpers.) **in diesen Schuhen läuft es sich sehr bequem** these shoes are very comfortable for running/walking *or* to run/walk in; **auf dem steinigen Weg lief es sich nicht gut** the stony path was not good for walking/running on

laufend
A *Adj.* [1] (ständig) regular ‹*interest, income*›; recurring ‹*costs*›; **die ~en Arbeiten/Geschäfte** the day-to-day *or* routine work *sing.* /business *sing.* [2] (gegenwärtig) current ‹*issue, year, month, etc.*› [3] (aufeinander folgend) **zehn Euro der ~e Meter** ten euros a *or* per metre [4] **auf dem Laufenden sein/bleiben** be/keep *or* stay up-to-date *or* fully informed; **jmdn. auf dem Laufenden halten** keep sb. up-to-date *or* informed; **mit etw. auf dem Laufenden sein** be up-to-date with sth.
B *adv.* constantly; continually; ‹*increase*› steadily

***laufen|lassen** ▸ **laufen A 1**

Läufer /ˈlɔyfɐ/ *der;* **~s, ~** [1] (Sport) runner; (Handball) halfback [2] (Fußball veralt.) halfback [3] (Teppich) (long narrow) carpet [4] (Schach) bishop [5] (Landw.: junges Schwein) young pig [6] (Bauw.: Mauerstein) stretcher

Lauferei *die;* **~, ~en** (ugs.) running around *no pl.*; **die ~ zu den Ärzten kostet viel Zeit** it takes a lot of time to go the rounds of all the doctors

Läuferin *die;* **~, ~nen** runner

läuferisch
A *Adj.* athletic; (beim Eislaufen) skating *attrib*
B *adv.* as regards the skating

Läufer·reihe *die* (Fußball veralt.) halfback line

Lauf-: ~feuer *das* brush fire; **wie ein ~feuer** like wildfire; **~fläche** *die* (am Reifen) tread; (am Ski) sole [of the ski]; **~gewicht** *das* sliding weight; **~graben** *der* (Milit.) communications trench

läufig /ˈlɔyfɪç/ *Adj.* on heat *postpos.*; in season *postpos.*

Lauf-: ~junge *der:* ▸ **~bursche**; **~katze** *die* (Technik) crab; **~kran** *der* (Technik) travelling crane; **~kundschaft** *die* passing trade; **~kundschaft haben** have a passing trade; **~masche** *die* ladder; **~pass**, ***~paß** *der:* **der Präsident gab seinem Berater den ~pass** (ugs.) the president gave his adviser his marching orders (coll.); **er hat seiner Freundin den ~pass gegeben** (ugs.) he finished with his girlfriend (coll.); **~pensum** *das* (Sport) **der Verteidiger bewältigte** *od.* **absolvierte ein ungeheures ~pensum** the defender never stopped running; **~planke** *die* gangplank; gangway; **~rad** *das* (Technik) [1] (des Fahrrads) wheel; [2] (an Turbinen) runner; **~richtung** *die* direction [of movement]; **die ~richtung ändern** change direction; **~rolle** *die* (Technik) (von Toren, Türen) roller; (von Panzern) road wheel; (von Möbeln) castor; **~schiene** *die* (Technik) track; rail; **~schrift** *die* newscaster; **~schritt** *der* [1] **wir haben die ganze Strecke im ~schritt zurückgelegt** we ran all the way; **im ~schritt, marsch, marsch!** at the double, quick march!; [2] (Leichtathletik) running step

läufst /lɔyfst/ *2. Pers. Sg. Präsens v.* **laufen**

Lauf-: ~stall *der* playpen; **~steg** *der* catwalk

läuft /lɔyft/ *3. Pers. Sg. Präsens v.* **laufen**

Lauf-: ~text *der* crawling text; **~vogel** *der* (Zool.) ratite (Zool.); flightless bird; **~werk** *das* (Technik) [1] mechanism; [2] (Uhrwerk) clockwork; mechanism; [3] (Eisenb.) running gear; [4] (DV) drive; **~zeit** *die* [1] term; **der Vertrag hatte eine ~zeit von zwei Jahren** the agreement ran for two years; **ein Kredit mit befristeter ~zeit** a limited-term loan; [2] (Film, Theater) run; [3] (Sport) time; **~zettel** *der* (Bürow., Verwaltung) [1] (Rundschreiben) circular; [2] (Empfangsbestätigung) distribution slip; circulation slip; [3] (Passierschein) pass; permit; [4] (an Werkstücken) work progress slip; control tag

Lauge /ˈlau̯gə/ *die;* **~, ~n** [1] soapy water; soapsuds [2] (Chemie) alkaline solution

Laugen·brezel *die* (südd.) pretzel

Lauheit *die;* **~:** half-heartedness

Lau·mann *der* (ugs. abwertend) shilly-shallyer

Laune /ˈlau̯nə/ *die;* **~, ~n** [1] (momentane Stimmung) mood; **schlechte/gute ~ haben** be in a bad/good mood *or* temper; **[nicht] in** *od.* **bei ~ sein** [not] be in a good mood; **jmdn. bei guter ~ halten** keep sb. in a good mood; keep sb. happy (coll.); **bringt gute ~ mit!** come ready to enjoy yourselves [2] (wechselnde Stimmung) mood; **sie hat nur selten ~n** she is rarely moody; **die ~n des Wetters/Zufalls** (fig.) the vagaries of the weather/of chance [3] (spontane Idee) whim; **aus einer ~ heraus** on a whim; on the spur of the moment

launenhaft *Adj.* temperamental; (unberechenbar) capricious

Launenhaftigkeit *die;* **~:** moodiness; (Unberechenbarkeit) capriciousness

launig
A *Adj.* witty
B *adv.* wittily

launisch *Adj.:* ▸ **launenhaft**

Laus /lau̯s/ *die;* **~, Läuse** /ˈlɔyzə/ louse; **ihm ist eine ~ über die Leber gelaufen** (ugs.) he has got out of bed on the wrong side; **was ist ihm für eine ~ über die Leber gelaufen?** (ugs.) what's eating him? (coll.); **jmdm./sich eine ~ in den Pelz setzen** (ugs.) land sb./oneself in it

Laus·bub *der* little rascal *or* devil; scamp

Lausbuben·streich *der* prank

laus·bübisch
A *Adj.* impish
B *adv.* impishly

Lausch·aktion *die,* **Lausch·angriff** *der* bugging operation (coll.)

lauschen /ˈlau̯ʃn̩/ *itr. V.* [1] (horchen) listen (*so as to overhear sth.*); **an der Tür ~:** eavesdrop at the door [2] (zuhören) listen [attentively]; **jmds. Worten** *usw.* **~:** listen [attentively] to sb.'s words *etc.*

Lauscher *der;* **~s, ~** [1] eavesdropper; **der ~ an der Wand hört seine eigene Schand** (Spr.) eavesdroppers never hear any good of themselves [2] (Jägerspr.: Ohr) ear

Lauscherin *die;* **~, ~nen** ▸ **Lauscher 1**

lauschig *Adj.* cosy, snug ‹*corner*›; **ein ~es Plätzchen im Grünen** a quiet *or* secluded spot in the country

Lause-: ~bengel, ~junge, ~lümmel *der* (salopp) little rascal *or* devil; scamp

lausen *tr. V.* delouse; **ich denk, mich laust der Affe!** (salopp) well, I'll be damned *or* blowed!

Lauser *der;* **~s, ~** (landsch. ugs.) little rascal *or* devil; scamp

lausig
A *Adj.* (ugs.) [1] (abwertend: unangenehm, schäbig) lousy (coll.); rotten (coll.); **~e Zeiten** hard times [2] (sehr groß) perishing (Brit. sl.), freezing ‹*cold*›; terrible (coll.), awful ‹*heat*›
B *adv.* terribly (coll.); awfully; **draußen ist es ~ kalt** it's perishing cold outside (Brit. sl.)

laut¹ /lau̯t/
A *Adj.* [1] loud; (fig.) loud, garish ‹*colour*›; garish ‹*advertisement*›; **der Motor ist zu ~:** the engine is too noisy; **spreche ich jetzt ~ genug?** can you hear me now?; **er wusste sich ohne ein ~es Wort Respekt zu verschaffen** he was able to gain respect without raising his voice; **werden Sie bitte nicht ~!** there's no need to shout; **~ werden** (fig.: bekannt werden) be made known; **es sind Zweifel an der Gültigkeit dieser Aussage ~ geworden** doubts have been raised *or* expressed *or* voiced as to the validity of this statement [2] (geräuschvoll) noisy
B *adv.* [1] loudly; **~er sprechen** speak louder; speak up; **~ lachen** laugh out loud; **etw. nicht ~ sagen dürfen** not be allowed to say sth. out loud; **~ denken** think aloud; **das kannst du aber ~ sagen** (ugs.) you can say 'that again [2] (geräuschvoll) noisily; **geht es hier immer so ~ zu?** is it always this noisy here?

laut² *Präp. + Gen. od. Dat.* (Amtsspr.) according to; (gemäß) in accordance with; **~ Vertrag** according to/in accordance with the contract

Laut *der;* **~[e]s, ~e** [1] (Geräusch) sound; **keinen ~ von sich geben** not make a sound; **~ geben** ‹*dog, hound*› give tongue [2] (sprachliche Einheit) sound; **fremde/heimatliche ~e** sounds of a foreign/familiar tongue

Laut·bildung *die* (Sprachw.) articulation; formation of sounds

Laute *die;* **~, ~n** lute

lauten
A *itr. V.* ‹*answer, instruction, slogan*› be, run; ‹*letter, passage, etc.*› read, go; ‹*law*› state; **die Anklage/das Urteil lautet auf ...** the charge/sentence is ...; **auf jmds. Namen** (*Akk.*) **~:** be in sb.'s name
B *tr. V.* (Sprachw.: aussprechen) pronounce

läuten /lɔytn̩/
A *tr., itr. V.* ring; ‹*alarm clock*› go off; **12 Uhr/Mittag ~:** strike 12 o'clock/midday; **Feuer/Sturm ~** (hist.) ring the fire bell/storm bell; **ich habe davon ~ gehört** *od.* **hören, dass ...** I have heard rumours that ...
B *itr. V.* (bes. südd.: klingeln) ring; **nach jmdm. ~:** ring for sb.; **es läutete** the bell rang *or* went **(zu** for)

Lautenist /lau̯təˈnɪst/ *der;* **~en, ~en, Lautenistin** *die;* **~, ~nen** ▸ **ⓘ S. 113** lutenist

Lauten·spieler *der,* **Lauten·spielerin** *die* lute player

lauter¹ *Adj.* (geh.) [1] honourable ‹*person, intentions, etc.*›; honest ‹*truth*› [2] (rein) pure ‹*gold, silver, etc.*›; clear ‹*water*›

lauter² *indekl. Adj.* nothing but; sheer, pure ‹*nonsense, joy, etc.*›; **das sind ~ Lügen** that's nothing but lies; that's a pack of lies; **das sind ~ Kunden unserer Firma** they are all customers of our firm; **aus ~ kleinen Quadraten zusammengesetzt** made up entirely of little squares; **vor ~ Arbeit komme ich nicht ins Theater** I can't go to the theatre because of all the work I've got

Lauterkeit *die;* **~:** honourableness

läutern /ˈlɔytɐn/ *tr. V.* (geh.) [1] reform ‹*character*›; purify ‹*soul*› [2] (reinigen) purify **(von** of)

Läuterung *die;* **~, ~en** (geh.) [1] (des Charakters) reformation; (der Seele) purification [2] (Reinigung) purification

laut-, Laut-: ~gesetz *das* (Sprachw.) phonetic law; **~getreu** **A** *Adj.* phonetically accurate; **B** *adv.* with phonetic accuracy; **~hals** *Adv.* ‹*sing, shout, etc.*› at the top of one's voice; **~hals lachen** roar with laughter

Laut·lehre *die* (Sprachw.) phonetics and phonology *no art.*

lautlich
A *Adj.* phonetic
B *adv.* phonetically

laut-, Laut-: ~los **A** *Adj.* silent; soundless; (wortlos) silent; **~lose Stille** utter *or* complete silence; **B** *adv.* silently; soundlessly; **~losigkeit** *die;* **~~:** silence; soundlessness; (Wortlosigkeit) silence; **~malend** *Adj.* (Sprachw.) onomatopoeic; **~schrift** *die* (Phon.) phonetic alphabet; (Umschrift) phonetic transcription

Laut·sprecher *der* loudspeaker; loudhailer (esp. Naut.); (einer Stereoanlage usw.) speaker; **über ~:** over the loudspeaker[s]

Lautsprecher-: ~anlage *die* public address *or* PA system; loudspeaker system; **~box** *die* speaker cabinet; **~wagen** *der* loudspeaker car/van

laut-, Laut-: ~stark **A** *Adj.* loud; vociferous, loud ‹*protest*›; **B** *adv.* loudly; ‹*protest*› vociferously, loudly; **~stärke** *die* [1] volume; **in/bei voller ~stärke** at full volume; **das Radio auf volle ~stärke drehen**

turn the radio right up; [2] (Lärm) **die ~stärke in diesem Raum** the volume of noise in this room; **~stärke·regler** *der* volume control

Lautung *die;* ~, ~**en** (Sprachw.) pronunciation

Laut-: ~verschiebung *die* (Sprachw.) sound shift; **die erste** *od.* **germanische/zweite** *od.* **hochdeutsche ~verschiebung** the first *or* Germanic/second *or* High German sound shift; **~wandel** *der* (Sprachw.) sound change

Läut·werk *das* [1] (Eisenb.) bell [2] (des Weckers) alarm

lau·warm *Adj.* lukewarm ‹*food*›; lukewarm, tepid ‹*drink*›; (nicht mehr kalt) warm ‹*beer etc.*›

Lava /ˈlaːva/ *die;* ~, **Laven** (Geol.) lava

Lavabo /laˈvaːbo/ *das;* ~**[s]**, ~**s** (schweiz.) ▸**Waschbecken**

Lava·strom *der* lava stream; (ausströmende Lava) lava flow

Lavendel /laˈvɛndl̩/ *der;* ~**s**, ~**:** lavender

Lavendel·öl *das* lavender oil

lavieren¹ /laˈviːrən/ *tr. V., itr. V.* manoeuvre

lavieren² *tr. V.* (bild. Kunst) wash; **eine lavierte Zeichnung** a wash drawing

Lavoir /laˈvo̯aːɐ̯/ *das;* ~**s**, ~**s** (österr.) ▸**Waschbecken**

Lawine /laˈviːnə/ *die;* ~, ~**n** (auch fig.) avalanche; **eine ~ von Protesten** (fig.) a storm of protest

lawinen-, Lawinen-: ~artig *Adv.* like an avalanche; **~artig anschwellen** ‹*political etc. movement, number of accidents etc.*› snowball; **~gefahr** *die* danger of avalanches; **~[such]hund** *der* avalanche dog

lax /laks/

A *Adj.* lax

B *adv.* laxly

Laxativ /laksaˈtiːf/ *das;* ~**s**, ~**e** (Med.) laxative

Laxheit *die;* ~**:** laxness; laxity

Lay-out /leɪˈaut/ *das;* ~**s**, ~**s** (Druckw., Elektronik) layout

Layouter /ˈleːlautɐ/ *der;* ~**s**, ~, **Layouterin** *die;* ~, ~**nen** layout artist

Lazarett /latsaˈrɛt/ *das;* ~**[e]s** military hospital

Lazarett·schiff *das* hospital ship

leasen /ˈliːzn̩/ *tr. V.* rent; (für längere Zeit mieten) lease ‹*car etc.*›

Leasing /ˈliːzɪŋ/ *das;* ~**s**, ~**s** (Wirtsch.) leasing

Lebe-: ~dame *die* (abwertend) good-time girl; **~hoch** /--ˈ-/ *das* cheer; **ein dreifaches ~hoch** three cheers *pl.*; **~mann** *der* playboy

leben /ˈleːbn̩/

A *itr. V.* live; (~dig sein) be alive; **anständig/sorgenfrei ~:** live a respectable/carefree life; **auf dem Land/im Wasser ~de Tiere** animals which live on land/in water; **für jmdn./etw. ~** *od.* (geh.) **jmdm./einer Sache ~:** live for sb./sth.; **leb[e] wohl!** farewell!; **so [et]was lebt, und Schiller musste sterben!** (scherzh.) why do we have to put up with people like that?; **nicht mehr ~ wollen** not want to go on living; have lost the will to live; **er wird nicht mehr lange zu ~ haben** he will not live much longer; **lebst du noch?** (ugs. scherzh.) are you still in the land of the living? (joc.); **lang lebe der König!** long live the king!; **von seiner Rente/seinem Gehalt ~:** live on one's pension/salary; **von seiner Hände Arbeit ~:** live by the work of one's hands; **Wie geht es dir? — Man lebt!** (ugs.) How are you? — Oh, surviving (coll.); **~ und ~ lassen** live and let live; **davon kann ich/sie/er** *usw.* **nicht ~ und nicht sterben** it's hardly enough to keep body and soul together; **fleischlos ~:** not eat meat; **von Kartoffeln ~:** live on potatoes; **er lebt in seinen Werken** he lives on in his works; *s. auch* **Brot**; **Diät**

B *tr. V.* live; **ein glückliches Leben ~:** live a happy life

Leben *das;* ~**s**, ~ [1] life; **das ~:** life; **jmdm. das ~ retten** save sb.'s life; **sein ~ für etw. wagen/** (geh.) **hingeben** risk/give one's life for sth.; **sich** (*Dat.*) **das ~ nehmen,** (geh.) **[freiwillig] aus dem ~ scheiden** take one's [own] life; **am ~ sein/bleiben** be/stay alive; **seines ~s nicht [mehr] sicher sein** not be safe [any more]; **um sein ~ rennen** run for one's life; **ums ~ kommen** lose one's life; **das nackte ~ retten** barely escape with one's life; **sein ~ teuer verkaufen** sell one's life dearly; **seinem ~ ein Ende setzen** *od.* **machen** (verhüll.) take one's [own] life; **auf Tod und ~ kämpfen** be engaged in a life-and-death struggle; **etw. für sein ~ gern tun** love doing sth.; **etw. für sein ~ gern essen** love sth.; **etw. ins ~ rufen** bring sth. into being; **mit dem ~ davonkommen** escape with one's life; **jmdm. nach dem ~ trachten** try to kill sb.; **wie das blühende ~ aussehen** (ugs.) look the picture of health; **ein/sein [ganzes] ~ lang** one's whole life long; **zeit seines ~s** all his life; **noch nie im ~/zum ersten Mal im ~:** never in/for the first time in one's life; **jmdm. das ~ sauer machen** make sb.'s life a misery; **sich durchs ~ schlagen** struggle through life; **mit beiden Beinen** *od.* **Füßen im ~ stehen** have one's feet firmly on the ground; **nie im ~, im ~ nicht!** (ugs.) not on your life! (coll.); never in your life! (coll.); **ein ~ in Wohlstand/Armut** a life of affluence/poverty; **das süße ~:** la dolce vita; **wie das ~ so spielt** it's funny the way things turn out; **im öffentlichen ~ stehen** be in public life; **so ist das ~:** such is life; that's the way things go; **die Musik ist ihr ~:** music is her [whole] life [2] (Betriebsamkeit) **auf dem Markt herrschte ein reges ~:** the market was bustling with activity; **das ~ auf der Straße** the comings and goings in the street; **~ ins Haus bringen** bring some life into the house

lebend *Adj.* living; live ‹*animal*›; **~e Sprachen** living languages; **tot oder ~:** dead or alive; **nicht mehr unter den Lebenden weilen** (geh.) have passed away

lebend·gebärend *Adj.* (Zool.) viviparous

Lebend·gewicht *das* [1] live weight [2] (scherzh.: Gewicht eines Menschen) **100 kg ~ auf die Waage bringen** turn the scales at 100 kg

lebendig /leˈbɛndɪç/

A *Adj.* [1] (lebend) living; **jmdn. ~** *od.* **bei ~em Leibe verbrennen** burn sb. alive; **man fühlt sich hier wie ~ begraben** being stuck here is like being buried alive (coll.); **ich kann ihn nicht wieder ~ machen** I can't bring him back to life [again]; **mehr tot als ~:** more dead than alive; **es von den Lebendigen nehmen** be unduly grasping [2] (wirksam) living ‹*tradition etc.*›; **die Erinnerung daran wurde in ihm wieder ~:** the memory of it came back to him vividly [3] (lebhaft) lively ‹*account, imagination, child, etc.*›; gay, bright ‹*colours*›; **auf der Straße wurde es allmählich ~:** the street began to fill with life

B *adv.* (lebhaft) in a lively fashion *or* way; **etw. ~ schildern** give a lively description of sth.

Lebendigkeit *die;* ~**:** liveliness

lebens-, Lebens-: ~abend *der* (geh.) evening *or* autumn of one's life (literary); **~abschnitt** *der* stage of *or* chapter in one's life; **~ader** *die* vital line of communication; **~alter** *das* age; **ein hohes ~alter erreichen** live to a considerable age *or* (coll.) a ripe old age; **~angst** *die* unwillingness to face life's problems; (Angst um die Existenz) worry about one's ability to survive; **~art** *die* [1] way of life; [2] (Umgangsformen) manners *pl.*; **keine ~art haben** have no manners; be ill-mannered; **~aufgabe** *die* life's work; **sich** (*Dat.*) **etw. zur ~aufgabe machen** make sth. one's life's work; **~baum** *der* [1] arbor vitae; [2] (Rel., Kunstwiss.) tree of life; **~bedingungen** *Pl.* conditions of life; **~bejahend** *Adj.* ‹*person*› with a positive attitude *or* approach to life; **~bejahung** *die* positive attitude *or* approach to life; affirmation of life; **~beratung** *die* advice on everyday problems; **~bereich** *der* area of life; **~beschreibung** *die* biography; (Buch) biography; life; **~dauer** *die* [1] lifespan; [2] (von Maschinen) [useful] life; **~echt A** *Adj.* true-to-life; **B** *adv.* in a true-to-life way; **~elixier** *das* (Volksk.; auch fig.) elixir of life; **~ende** *das* end [of one's life]; **bis an sein** *od.* **bis ans ~ende** to the end of one's life *or* days; **~erfahrung** *die* experience *no indef. art.* of life; **~erinnerungen** *Pl.* memories of one's life; (aufgezeichnet) memoirs; **~erwartung** *die* life expectancy; **~fähig** *Adj.* (auch fig.) viable; **~fähigkeit** *die* viability; **~form** *die* [1] (Biol.) life form; [2] (~weise) way of life; **~frage** *die* vital matter *or* question; **~fremd** *Adj.* out of touch with *or* remote from everyday life *postpos.*; **~freude** *die* zest for life; joie de vivre; **~froh** *Adj.* full of zest for life *or* joie de vivre *postpos.*; **~führung** *die* lifestyle; **eine moralisch einwandfreie ~führung** a completely blameless life; **~gefahr** *die* mortal danger; **für jmdn. besteht [keine] ~gefahr** sb.'s life is [not] in danger; **„Achtung, ~gefahr!"** 'danger'; **sie schwebt in ~gefahr** she is in danger of dying; (von einer Kranken) her condition is critical; **außer ~gefahr sein** be out of danger; **etw. unter ~gefahr** (*Dat.*) **tun** risk one's life to do sth.; **~gefährlich A** *Adj.* highly *or* extremely dangerous; critical ‹*injury*›; **B** *adv.* critically ‹*injured, ill*›; **jmdn. ~gefährlich verletzen** cause sb. critical injuries; **~gefährte** *der,* **~gefährtin** *die* (geh.) companion through life (literary); **~gefühl** *das* awareness of life; **~geister** *Pl.* **jmds. ~geister [wieder] wecken** put new life into sb.; **~gemeinschaft** *die* [1] (von Menschen) long-term relationship; [2] (Biol.: von Tieren, Pflanzen) biocoenosis; **~geschichte** *die* life story; **~groß** *Adj.* life-size; **~größe** *die:* **eine Statue in ~größe** a life-size statue; **ein Porträt von jmdm. in ~größe malen** paint a life-size portrait of sb.

Lebens·haltung *die* [1] (~skosten) cost of living; **die ~ ist teurer geworden** the cost of living has risen [2] (Lebensführung) lifestyle

Lebenshaltungs-: ~index *der* (Wirtsch.) cost-of-living index; **~kosten** *Pl.* cost of living *sing.*

lebens-, Lebens-: ~hilfe *die* counselling; **~hunger** *der* desire to live life to the full; **~hungrig** *Adj.* ‹*person*› who is eager to live life to the full; **~inhalt** *der* purpose in life; **die Musik/ihre Familie ist ihr ~inhalt** music/her family is her whole life; **~jahr** *das* year of [one's] life; **die letzten ~jahre** the last years of one's life; one's last years; **in seinem 12. ~jahr** in his twelfth year; **mit dem vollendeten 18. ~jahr** on reaching the age of eighteen; **~kampf** *der* struggle for existence *or* life; **~klug A** *Adj.* worldly-wise; **B** *adv.* with worldly wisdom; **~klugheit** *die* worldly wisdom; **~kraft** *die* vitality; vital energy; **~kreis** *der:* **in jmds. ~kreis** (*Akk.*) **treten** come into *or* enter sb.'s life; **~künstler** *der,* **~künstlerin** *die:* **ein [echter/wahrer] ~künstler** a person who always knows how to make the best of things; **~lage** *die* situation [in life]; **in allen ~lagen** in any situation; **~lang A** *Adj.* lifelong; **B** *adv.* all one's life; **~länglich A** *Adj.* **~länglicher Freiheitsentzug** life imprisonment; **„~länglich" bekommen** *od.* (ugs.) **kriegen** get life imprisonment *or* (coll.) life; **B** *adv.* **jmdn. ~länglich gefangen halten** keep sb. imprisoned for life; **~längliche** *der/die; adj. Dekl.* (salopp) lifer (coll.); **~lauf** *der* [1] curriculum vitae; c.v.; [2] (Verlauf eines ~) life; **~leistung** *die* lifetime achievement; **~licht** *das; Pl.* **~~er** (geh.) flame of life (literary); **jmdm. das ~licht ausblasen** *od.* **auspusten** (ugs.) send sb. to kingdom come (coll.); **~linie** *die* life line; **~lüge** *die* lifelong illusion; **~lust** *die* ▸**~freude**; **~lustig** *Adj.* ‹*person*› full of the joys of life; **~mitte** *die* middle years *pl.* of one's life; **die Krise in der ~mitte** midlife crisis

Lebens·mittel *das* food[stuff]; **~** *Pl.* food *sing.*; foods (formal); foodstuffs (formal); (als Ware) food *sing.*

Lebensmittel-: ~abteilung *die* food department; **~chemie** *die* food chemistry *no art.*; **~geschäft** *das* food shop; **~karte** *die* food ration card

Lebens·mittelpunkt *der* place where he/she *etc.* lives and works; **ihr ∼punkt ist Deutschland** they have their work and all their family and social ties in Germany

Lebensmittel·vergiftung *die* ▸ⓘ S. 439 (Med.) food poisoning

lebens-, Lebens-: ∼motto *das* motto [by which he/she *etc.* lives]; **∼müde** *Adj.* weary of life *pred.*; **du bist wohl ∼müde?** (scherzh.) you must be tired of living; **∼müdigkeit** *die* weariness of life; **∼mut** *der* courage to go on living; **∼nah** A *Adj.* true-to-life ‹*film, description, etc.*›; **∼naher Unterricht** teaching that is closely related to life; B *adv.* **etw. ∼nah schildern** describe sth. in a true-to-life way; **∼nerv** *der*: **eine Industrie/Firma in ihrem ∼nerv treffen** hit a vital nerve of an industry/a firm; **∼notwendig** *Adj.* essential; vital; vital ‹*organ*›; essential ‹*foodstuff*›

Lebens-: ∼partner *der*, **∼partnerin** *die* partner; **∼partnerschaft** *die* partnership; **eingetragene ∼partnerschaft** registered same-sex partnership; civil partnership

leben·spendend ▸ **spenden 2**

lebens-, Lebens-: ∼plan *der* life plan; **so etwas wie einen ∼plan hat sie nie gehabt** she has never planned her life; **∼philosophie** *die* philosophy of life; (Lehre) life philosophy *no art.*; Lebensphilosophie *no art.*; **∼qualität** *die* quality of life; **∼raum** *der* 1 (Umkreis) Lebensraum; 2 (Biol.) ▸ **Biotop**; **∼regel** *die* rule [of life]; maxim; **sich** (*Dat.*) **etw. zur ∼regel machen** make sth. a rule [in life] *or* a maxim; **∼retter** *der*, **∼retterin** *die* rescuer; **sein ∼retter** the person who saved his life; **du bist meine ∼retterin** you saved my life; **∼rhythmus** *der* rhythm of life; **sein ∼rhythmus** the rhythm of his life; **∼standard** *der* standard of living; **∼stellung** *die* permanent position *or* job; job for life; **∼stil** *der* lifestyle; **∼traum** *der* dream of a lifetime; ultimate dream; **∼tüchtig** *Adj.* able to cope with life *postpos.*; **∼überdruss**, ***∼überdruß** *der* weariness of life; world-weariness; **∼umstände** *Pl.* circumstances; **∼unfähig** *Adj.* non-viable; **∼unterhalt** *der*: **seinen ∼unterhalt verdienen/bestreiten** earn one's living/support oneself; **für jmds. ∼unterhalt sorgen** support sb.; **∼untüchtig** *Adj.* unable to cope with life *postpos.*; **∼versicherung** *die* life insurance; life assurance; **eine ∼versicherung abschließen** take out a life insurance *or* assurance policy; **∼wandel** *der* way of life; **einen zweifelhaften/einwandfreien ∼wandel führen** lead a dubious/an irreproachable life; **∼weg** *der* [journey through] life; **jmdm. etw. mit auf den ∼weg geben** give sb. sth. to take with him/her on his/her journey through life; **alles Gute für den weiteren ∼weg** all the best for the future; **∼weise** *die* way of life; **die sitzende ∼weise** the sedentary life; **∼weisheit** *die* 1 (Erfahrung) wisdom; 2 (weiser Ausspruch) wise saying *or* maxim; **∼welt** *die* everyday world; **unsere ∼welt** the world in which we live; **∼werk** *das* life's work; **∼wert** *Adj.* **ein ∼wertes Leben** a life worth living; **das ist kein ∼wertes Dasein mehr** that's no kind of life any more; **das Leben ist ∼wert** life is worth living; **∼wert** *der* basic human value; **∼wichtig** ▸ **∼notwendig**; **∼wille** *der* will to live; **∼zeichen** *das* sign of life; **kein ∼zeichen [von sich] geben** show no sign of life; **kein ∼zeichen von jmdm. bekommen** (fig.) have no sign of life from sb.; **∼zeit** *die* life[span]; **auf ∼zeit** for life; **ein Beamter auf ∼zeit** an established civil servant; **∼ziel** *das* aim in life; **∼zweck** *der* purpose in life; **∼zyklus** *der* life cycle

Leber /ˈleːbɐ/ *die*; **∼**, **∼n** ▸ⓘ S. 435 liver; **es an der ∼ haben** (ugs.) have [got] liver trouble; **frisch** *od.* **frei von der ∼ weg sprechen** *od.* **reden** (ugs.) speak one's mind; **sich** (*Dat.*) **etw. von der ∼ reden** (ugs.) get sth. off one's chest (coll.); *s. auch* **Laus**

leber-, Leber-: ∼blümchen *das* liverwort; **∼entzündung** *die* ▸ⓘ S. 439 inflammation of the liver; hepatitis (Med.); **∼fleck** *der* liver spot; **∼haken** *der* (Boxen) hook to the liver; **∼käse** *der*: *meat loaf made with mincemeat,* [*minced liver,*] *eggs, and spices*; **∼knödel** *der* (südd., österr.) *meat ball made from minced liver, onions, eggs, and flour*; **∼krank** *Adj.* ‹*patient etc.*› suffering from a liver complaint *or* disorder; **∼krank sein** have a liver complaint *or* disorder; **∼krebs** *der* ▸ⓘ S. 439 (Med.) cancer of the liver; **∼leiden** *das* ▸ⓘ S. 439 (Med.) liver complaint *or* disorder; **∼pastete** *die* (Kochk.) liver pâté; **∼schaden** *der* liver damage; damage to the liver; **∼schrumpfung** *die*; **∼**, **∼en** ▸ **∼zirrhose**; **∼tran** *der* fish-liver oil; (des Kabeljaus) cod-liver oil; **∼wurst** *die* liver sausage; **die gekränkte** *od.* **beleidigte ∼wurst spielen** (ugs.) get all huffy (coll.); **∼zirrhose** *die* ▸ⓘ S. 439 (Med.) cirrhosis of the liver

Lebe-: ∼welt *die* playboy set; **∼wesen** *das* living being *or* thing *or* creature; **einzellige ∼wesen** single-celled creatures; unicellular organisms (Biol.); **∼wohl** /-ˈ-/ *das*; **∼[e]s**, **∼** *od.* **∼e** (geh.) farewell; **jmdm. ∼wohl sagen** bid sb. farewell

lebhaft

A *Adj.* 1 (lebendig) lively ‹*person, gesture, imagination, bustle, etc.*›; lively, animated ‹*conversation, discussion*›; lively, brisk ‹*activity*›; busy ‹*traffic*›; brisk ‹*business*› 2 (deutlich) vivid ‹*idea, picture, etc.*›; **etw. in ∼er Erinnerung haben** remember sth. vividly 3 (kräftig) lively ‹*interest*›; lively, gay ‹*pattern*›; bright, gay ‹*colour*›; vigorous ‹*applause, opposition*›

B *adv.* 1 (lebendig) in a lively way *or* fashion; **sich ∼ unterhalten/∼ diskutieren** have a lively *or* animated conversation/discussion 2 (deutlich) vividly; **sich ∼ an etw.** (*Akk.*) **erinnern können** be able to remember sth. vividly; **sich** (*Dat.*) **etw. ∼ vorstellen können** have a vivid picture of sth. 3 (kräftig) brightly, gaily ‹*coloured*›; gaily ‹*patterned*›; **etw. ∼ bedauern** deeply regret sth.; **sich ∼ für etw. interessieren** take a lively *or* keen interest in sth.

Lebhaftigkeit *die*; **∼** 1 (reges Wesen) liveliness; (einer Unterhaltung, Diskussion) liveliness; animation 2 (Intensität) liveliness; (eines Musters) liveliness; gaiety; (von Farben) brightness; gaiety

Leb·kuchen *der* ≈ gingerbread

leb-, Leb-: ∼los *Adj.* lifeless ‹*body, eyes*›; **[wie] ∼los daliegen** lie there as if dead; **∼losigkeit** *die*; **∼**: lifelessness; **∼tag** *der*: *in* **[all] mein/dein** *usw.* **∼tag** (ugs.) all my/your *etc.* life; **so was habe ich mein ∼tag nicht erlebt** (ugs.) I've never seen anything like it in all my life *or* in all my born days; **∼zeiten** *Pl.*: *in* **bei** *od.* **zu ∼zeiten** while still alive; **bei** *od.* **zu jmds. ∼zeiten** while sb. is/was still alive; during sb.'s lifetime

lechzen /ˈlɛçtsn̩/ *itr. V.* (geh.) **nach einem Trunk/nach Kühlung ∼**: long for a drink/to be able to cool off; **nach Rache/Macht** *usw.* **∼**: thirst for revenge/power *etc.*

Lecithin /letsiˈtiːn/ ▸ **Lezithin**

leck /lɛk/ *Adj.* leaky; **∼ sein** leak

Leck *das*; **∼[e]s**, **∼s** leak

Lecke /ˈlɛkə/ ▸ **Salzlecke**

lecken[1]

A *tr. V.* lick; **sich** (*Dat.*) **die Wunden/Lippen** *usw.* **∼**: lick one's wounds/lips *etc.*; **jmdm. die Hand** *usw.* **∼**: lick sb.'s hand *etc.*; **sich** (*Dat.*) **etw. von etw. ∼**: lick sth. off sth.; **leck mich [doch]!** (derb) [why don't you] piss off! (sl.); *s. auch* **Arsch 1**; **Finger 2**

B *itr. V.* **an etw.** (*Dat.*) **∼**: lick sth.

lecken[2] *itr. V.* (leck sein) leak

lecker *Adj.* tasty ‹*meal*›; delicious ‹*cake etc.*›; good ‹*smell, taste*›; (fig.: ansprechend) lovely ‹*girl*›; **hier riecht es aber ∼**: there's a delicious smell around here

Lecker·bissen *der* delicacy; **ein musikalischer ∼** (fig.) a musical treat

Leckerei *die*; **∼**, **∼en** (ugs.) dainty; (Süßigkeit) sweet [meat]

Lecker-: ∼maul *das*, **∼mäulchen** *das*; **∼∼s**, **∼∼**: **ein ∼maul** *od.* **∼mäulchen sein** have a sweet tooth

leck|schlagen *unr. itr. V.*; *mit sein* (Seemannsspr.) be holed

led. *Abk.* = **ledig**

Leder /ˈleːdɐ/ *das*; **∼s**, **∼** 1 leather; **in ∼ [gebunden]** leather-bound; **ein Gürtel aus ∼**: a leather belt; **zäh wie ∼ sein** be as tough as leather; ‹*person*› be as hard as nails; **jmdm. ans ∼ gehen/wollen** (ugs.) go for sb./be out to get sb.; **gegen jmdn./etw. vom ∼ ziehen** (ugs.) speak one's mind about sb./sth. 2 (Fenster∼) leather; chamois *or* chammy [leather] 3 (Fußballjargon: Ball) ball; leather (dated sl.)

leder-, Leder-: ∼artig *Adj.* leathery; leather-like ‹*material*›; **∼band** *der* leather-bound volume; **∼fetischist** *der*, **∼fetischistin** *die* leather fetishist; **∼garnitur** *die* leather-upholstered suite; **∼handschuh** *der* leather glove; **∼haut** *die* ▸ⓘ S. 435 (Anat., Zool.) dermis; **∼hose** *die* leather shorts *pl.*; lederhosen *pl.*; (lang) leather trousers; **∼jacke** *die* leather jacket; **∼mantel** *der* leather [over]coat

ledern[1] *tr. V.* leather

ledern[2] *Adj.* 1 (aus Leder) leather 2 (wie Leder) leathery

Leder-: ∼nacken *der* leatherneck (sl.); **∼riemen** *der* [leather] strap; **∼schuh** *der* leather shoe; **∼schurz** *der* leather apron; **∼sessel** *der* leather[-upholstered] armchair; **∼sitz** *der* leather seat; **∼sofa** *das* leather sofa; **∼sohle** *die* leather sole; **∼waren** *Pl.* leather goods

ledig /ˈleːdɪç/ *Adj.* 1 (nicht verheiratet) unmarried; single; **eine ∼e Mutter** an unmarried mother 2 *in* **einer Sache** (*Gen.*) **∼ sein** (geh.) be free of sth.

Ledige *der/die*; *adj. Dekl.* single person

lediglich *Adv.* only; merely; simply

Lee /leː/ *die od. das*; **∼** (Seemannsspr.) **nach ∼ drehen** turn to leeward; **in ∼ liegen** lie to leeward

leer /leːɐ̯/ *Adj.* 1 empty; blank, clean ‹*sheet of paper*›; **die Kasse ist ∼** (ugs.) there's no money left; **sein Glas ∼ trinken** empty *or* drain one's glass; **seinen Teller ∼ essen** clear one's plate; **die Schachtel ∼ machen** (ugs.) finish the box; **den Laden/die Regale ∼ kaufen** strip every shelf in the shop/strip the shelves bare; **die Warnungen gingen ins Leere** the warnings fell on deaf ears; **∼ ausgehen** come away empty-handed; **∼ laufen** ‹*machine*› idle; ‹*business*› be at a standstill; ‹*barrel etc.*› run dry; **die Badewanne läuft ∼**: the bathwater is running out: **der Tank lief ∼**: the oil/wine *etc.* was running *or* draining out of the tank; **jmdn. ∼ laufen lassen** (Ballspiele) send sb. the wrong way; sell sb. a dummy (coll.) 2 (menschenleer) empty; empty, deserted ‹*streets*›; **vor ∼en Bänken spielen** play to an empty house/empty houses; **die Wohnung steht ∼**: the house is standing empty *or* is unoccupied; **∼ stehend** empty, unoccupied ‹*house, flat*›; **[wie] ∼ gefegt** deserted; 3 (abwertend: oberflächlich) empty ‹*words, promise, talk, display*›; vacant ‹*expression*›; **mit ∼en Augen/∼em Blick starren** stare vacantly

Leere *die*; **∼** (auch fig.) emptiness; **eine gähnende ∼**: a gaping void; **im Restaurant/Theatersaal herrschte ∼**: the restaurant/theatre was completely empty; **eine innere ∼** (fig.) a feeling of emptiness inside

leeren

A *tr. V.* 1 empty; empty, clear ‹*postbox*› 2 (österr.: gießen) pour ‹*water, milk, etc.*›; empty ‹*bucket*›

B *refl. V.* ‹*hall, theatre, etc.*› empty

leer-, Leer-: ∼formel *die* (geh.) empty formula; ***∼gefegt** ▸ **leer 2**; **∼gewicht** *das* unladen weight; **∼gut** *das* empties *pl.*; **∼lauf** *der* 1 **im ∼lauf den Berg hinunterfahren** ‹*driver*› coast down the hill in neutral; ‹*cyclist*› freewheel *or* coast down the hill; **eine Maschine auf ∼lauf stellen** let a machine idle; 2 (fig.) **es gab [viel] ∼lauf im Büro** there were [long] slack periods in the office; **zwischen den Hauptdarbietungen gab es viel ∼lauf** between the main acts there were long periods when nothing happened;

*~|**laufen** ▸**leer 1**; ~**packung** *die* dummy; display package; ~**stehend** ▸**leer 2**; ~**taste** *die* space bar

Leerung *die;* ~, ~**en** emptying; **die ~ der Mülltonnen erfolgt einmal wöchentlich** the dustbins are emptied once a week; **nächste ~ um 12 Uhr** (auf Briefkästen) next collection at 12.00

Leer·zeichen *das* (Druckw.) space; **geschütztes ~:** indivisible space

Lefze /ˈlɛftsə/ *die;* ~, ~**n** lip; **die ~n eines Jagdhundes** the flews of a hound

legal /leˈɡaːl/
A *Adj.* legal; **auf ~em Wege** by legal means; legally
B *adv.* legally

legalisieren *tr. V.* legalize

Legalität /legaliˈtɛːt/ *die;* ~: legality; **außerhalb der ~:** outside the law; **am Rande der ~:** just within the bounds of legality

Legalitäts·prinzip *das* (Rechtsw.): *principle that all complaints must be investigated and that, where an offence appears to have been committed, a charge must be brought*

Legasthenie /legasteˈniː/ *die;* ~, ~**n** (Psych., Med.) dyslexia

Legastheniker /legasˈteːnikɐ/ *der;* ~**s**, ~, **Legasthenikerin** *die;* ~, ~**nen** (Psych., Med.) dyslexic

Legat¹ /leˈɡaːt/ *der;* ~**en**, ~**en** (kath. Kirche) legate

Legat² *das;* ~**[e]s**, ~**e** (Rechtsw.) legacy

Legations·rat /legaˈtsjoːns-/ *der*, **Legations·rätin** *die* counsellor

legato /leˈɡaːto/ *Adv.* (Musik) legato

Lege-: ~**batterie** *die* laying battery; ~**henne** *die* laying hen

Legel /ˈleːɡl̩/ *der od. das;* ~**s**, ~ (Seemannsspr.) **1** (aus Tauwerk) cringle **2** (aus Holz) mast hoop

legen /ˈleːɡn̩/
A *tr. V.* **1** lay [down]; **jmdn. auf den Rücken ~:** lay sb. on his/her back; **einen Gegenspieler ~** (Sportjargon) bring down an opposing player; **etw. auf den Tisch/Boden ~:** lay sth. on the table/floor; **etw. aus der Hand ~:** put sth. down; **etw. in Spiritus ~:** preserve sth. in alcohol; **etw. beiseite ~:** put sth. aside *or* down; **das Fleisch in den Kühlschrank ~:** put the meat in the refrigerator; **die Hand an die Mütze ~:** raise one's hand to one's cap; **die Füße auf den Tisch ~:** put one's feet on the table; **etw. auf den Abend ~:** arrange sth. for the evening **2** (ver~) lay ‹*pipe, cable, railway track, carpet, tiles, etc.*›; plant ‹*potatoes*›; *s. auch* **Fundament 1**; **Grundstein**; **Karte 7** **3** (in eine bestimmte Form bringen) **etw. in Falten ~:** fold sth.; **sich** (*Dat.*) **die Haare ~ lassen** have one's hair set; *s. auch* **Falte 3** **4** (schräg hinstellen) lean; **etw. an etw.** (*Akk.*) **~:** lean sth. [up] against sth.
B *tr., itr. V.* ‹*hen*› lay; **die Hühner ~ fleißig/schlecht** the hens are laying/not laying well
C *refl. V.* **1** lie down; **sich auf etw.** (*Akk.*) **~:** lie down on sth.; **sich in die Sonne ~:** lie in the sun; **das Schiff/Flugzeug legte sich auf die Seite** the ship keeled over/the aircraft banked steeply; **sich in die Kurve ~:** lean into the bend; *s. auch* **Bett 1**; **Ohr 2** **2** (nachlassen) ‹*wind, storm*› die down, abate, subside; ‹*noise*› die down, abate; ‹*enthusiasm*› wear off, subside, fade; ‹*anger*› abate, subside; ‹*excitement*› die down, subside **3** (sich herabsenken) **sich auf** *od.* **über etw.** (*Akk.*) **~** ‹*mist, fog*› descend *or* settle on sth., [come down and] blanket sth.

legendär /legenˈdɛːɐ̯/ *Adj.* legendary

Legende /leˈɡɛndə/ *die;* ~, ~**n** **1** legend; **zur ~ werden** (fig.) ‹*event, incident, etc.*› become legendary; **[schon zu Lebzeiten] zur ~ werden** (fig.) ‹*person*› become a legend [in one's own lifetime] **2** (Zeichenerklärung) legend; key

legenden·umwoben *Adj.* ‹*person, figure, etc.*› surrounded by legends

leger /leˈʒeːɐ̯/
A *Adj.* **1** (ungezwungen) casual; relaxed; (oberflächlich) casual **2** (bequem) casual ‹*jacket etc.*›
B *adv.* **1** (ungezwungen) casually; in a casual *or* relaxed manner; (oberflächlich) casually **2** (bequem) ‹*dress*› casually

Leg·henne /ˈleːk-/ *die* ▸**Legehenne**

legieren /leˈɡiːrən/ *tr. V.* **1** alloy; **Kupfer mit Zinn ~:** alloy copper and tin **2** (Kochk.) thicken

Legierung *die;* ~, ~**en** alloy

Legion /leˈɡjoːn/ *die;* ~, ~**en** **1** (Milit.) legion; (Fremden~) Legion **2** (Menge) horde (**von** of); **~ sein** (geh.) be legion

Legionär /legjoˈnɛːɐ̯/ *der;* ~**s**, ~**e** legionary

Legionärs·krankheit *die* ▸ⓘ **S. 439** (Med.) legionnaire's disease

legislativ /legɪslaˈtiːf/
A *Adj.* (Politik) legislative
B *adv.* by legislation

Legislative /legɪslaˈtiːvə/ *die;* ~, ~**n** (Politik) legislature

Legislatur /legɪslaˈtuːɐ̯/ *die;* ~, ~**en** **1** legislature **2** ▸**Legislaturperiode**

Legislatur·periode *die* (Politik) parliamentary term; legislative period; (Amtsdauer einer Regierung) term of office

legitim /legiˈtiːm/
A *Adj.* legitimate
B *adv.* legitimately

Legitimation /legitimaˈtsjoːn/ *die;* ~, ~**en** **1** (auch Rechtsw.: Ehelicherklärung) legitimation **2** (Ausweis) proof of identity; (Bevollmächtigung) authorization

legitimieren
A *tr. V.* **1** (rechtfertigen) justify **2** (bevollmächtigen) authorize **3** (für legitim erklären) legitimize ‹*child, relationship*›
B *refl. V.* show proof of one's identity

Legitimität /legitimiˈtɛːt/ *die;* ~: legitimacy; (Rechtfertigung) justification

Leguan /leˈɡu̯aːn/ *der;* ~**s**, ~**e** (Zool.) iguana

Lehen /ˈleːən/ *das;* ~**s**, ~ (hist.) fief; **jmdm. etw. zu ~ geben** grant sb. sth. in fee

Lehm /leːm/ *der;* ~**s** loam; (Ton) clay

lehm-, Lehm-: ~**bau** *der; Pl.* ~~**ten** clay *or* mud building; ~**bau·weise** *die* building with clay; (~flechtwerk) wattle and daub construction; ~**boden** *der* loamy soil; (Tonerde) clay soil; ~**farben**, ~**farbig** *Adj.* clay-coloured; ~**grube** *die* clay pit; ~**haltig** *Adj.* loamy; (tonartig) clayey; ~**hütte** *die* mud hut

lehmig *Adj.* loamy ‹*soil, earth*›; (tonartig) clayey ‹*soil, shoes, etc.*›

Lehm·ziegel *der* clay brick

Lehn /leːn/ ▸**Lehen**

Lehn-: ~**bedeutung** *die* loan-meaning; ~**bildung** *die* loan-formation

Lehne /ˈleːnə/ *die;* ~, ~**n** **1** (Rücken~) back; (Arm~) arm **2** (südd., österr., schweiz.: Abhang) slope

lehnen
A *tr. V.* lean (**an** + *Akk.*, **gegen** against); **den Kopf/Arm an etw.** (*Akk.*) **~:** lean one's head/arm on sth.
B *refl. V.* lean (**an** + *Akk.*, **gegen** against; **über** + *Akk.* over); **sich aus dem Fenster ~:** lean out of the window; **sich zu weit aus dem Fenster ~** (fig.) stick one's neck out (coll.); go too far
C *itr. V.* be leaning (**an** + *Dat.* against)

Lehns·dienst *der* (hist.) feudal service *no pl., no art.*

Lehn·sessel *der* armchair

Lehns-: ~**frau** *die* vassal; ~**herr** *der* feudal lord; ~**herrin** *die* feudal lady; ~**mann** *der; Pl.* ~**männer** *od.* ~**leute** vassal; ~**pflicht** *die* feudal duty

Lehn·stuhl *der* armchair

Lehns·wesen *das* (hist.) system of feudal tenure; feudal system

Lehn-: ~**übersetzung** *die* loan translation; ~**wort** *das; Pl.* ~**wörter** loanword

Lehr-: ~**amt** *das* (Schulw.) teaching post; (Beruf) **das ~amt** the teaching profession; **das höhere ~amt** *teaching at Gymnasien or vocational schools;* ~**amts·anwärter** *der*, ~**amts·anwärterin** *die* (Schulw.) trainee primary-school teacher; ~**amts·kandidat** *der*, ~**amts·kandidatin** *die* trainee grammar-school teacher/vocational school teacher; ~**anstalt** *die* (Amtsspr.) educational establishment; **höhere ~anstalt** (veralt.) secondary education establishment; ~**auftrag** *der* lectureship (*not giving full status as member of a department or as a permanent civil servant*); ~**beauftragte** *der/die* lecturer (*not having full status as member of a department or as a permanent civil servant*); ~**befähigung** *die* (Amtsspr.) teaching qualification; ~**behelf** *der* (österr.) ▸~**mittel**; ~**berechtigung** *die* teaching qualification; ~**beruf** *der* **1** ▸**Ausbildungsberuf**; **2** (Lehrerberuf) **der ~beruf** the teaching profession; **den ~beruf ausüben** teach; be a teacher/teachers; ~**betrieb** *der* teaching programme; ~**bub** *der* (südd., österr., schweiz.) ▸~**junge**; ~**buch** *das* textbook; ~**dichtung** *die* (Literaturw.) **1** didactic poetry; **2** (Gedicht) didactic poem

Lehre¹ /ˈleːrə/ *die;* ~, ~**n** **1** (Berufsausbildung) apprenticeship; **eine ~ machen** serve an apprenticeship (**als** as); **bei einem Handwerker in die ~ gehen** be apprenticed to a craftsman; **bei jmdm. in die ~ gegangen sein** (fig.) have learnt a lot from sb. **2** (Weltanschauung) doctrine; **die christliche ~:** Christian doctrine; **die ~ Kants/Hegels/Buddhas** the teachings *pl.* of Kant/Hegel/Buddha **3** (Theorie, Wissenschaft) theory; **die ~ vom Schall** the science of sound *or* acoustics **4** (Erfahrung) lesson; **lass dir das eine ~ sein!** let that be a lesson to you; **jmdm. eine [heilsame] ~ erteilen** teach sb. a [salutary] lesson; **aus etw. seine ~ ziehen** learn one's lesson from sth. **5** (Verhaltensregel) precept

> **Lehre**
>
> This type of apprenticeship is still the normal way to learn a trade or train for a practical career in Germany. A *Hauptschulabschluss* is the minimum requirement, although many young people with a *Realschulabschluss* or *Abitur* opt to train in this way. A *Lehre* takes about 2 to 3 years and involves practical training by a **Meister(in)** backed up by lessons at a **Berufsschule**, with an exam at the end.

Lehre² *die;* ~, ~**n** (Bauw., Technik) gauge

lehren *tr., itr. V.* teach; **jmdn. lesen/schreiben ~:** teach sb. to read/write; **ich bin das gelehrt worden** I was taught that; **ich werde dich ~, so bockig zu sein!** (ugs.) I'll teach you to be so contrary (coll.); **die Geschichte lehrt, dass ...** history teaches *or* shows us that ...; **erst die Zukunft wird uns ~, ...** time alone will tell ...

Lehrende *der/die; adj. Dekl.* (Hochschulw.) **~ und Lernende** teaching staff and students

-lehrer *der;* ~**s**, ~**: Türkisch~/Ski~:** teacher of Turkish/skiing instructor; **unser Französisch~:** our French teacher

Lehrer *der;* ~**s**, ~ ▸ⓘ **S. 113** **1** (auch fig.) teacher; **er ist ~ für Geschichte** he teaches history; he is a history teacher **2** (Ausbilder) instructor

lehrer-, Lehrer-: ~**ausbildung** *die* teacher training *no art.;* ~**ausflug** *der* staff outing; ~**haft** *Adj.* (abwertend) schoolmasterly; (von Frauen) schoolmarmish (coll.)

Lehrerin *die;* ~, ~**nen** ▸ⓘ **S. 113** teacher; *s. auch* **-in**; **Lehrer**; **-lehrer**

Lehrer-: ~**kollegium** *das* teaching staff; faculty (Amer.); ~**mangel** *der* shortage of teachers

Lehrerschaft *die;* ~, ~**en** teachers *pl.;* (einer Schule) teaching staff; faculty (Amer.)

Lehrer-: ~**schwemme** *die* (ugs.) glut of teachers; ~**zimmer** *das* staffroom

Lehr-: ~**fach** *das* **1** subject; **2** (Beruf des Lehrens) teaching profession; **im ~fach tätig sein** be a teacher; be in teaching; ~**film** *der* educational film; ~**freiheit** *die* academic freedom *no art.;* ~**gang** *der* course (**für, in** + *Dat.* in); **einen ~gang machen, an einem ~gang teilnehmen** take a course; ~**gebäude** *das* (geh.) **das hegelsche ~gebäude** the edifice of Hegelian teachings; ~**gegenstand** *der* (österr.) ▸~**fach 1**; ~**geld** *das*

1 (hist.) apprenticeship premium; 2 (fig.) **du kannst dir dein ~geld zurückgeben lassen!** your education was wasted on you; **~geld geben** *od.* **[be]zahlen [müssen]** learn the hard way

lehrhaft *Adj.* (belehrend) instructive; didactic ‹*intention*›

Lehr-: ~herr *der* (geh. veralt.) master (*of an apprentice*); **~jahr** *das* year as an apprentice; **sie ist im zweiten ~jahr** she is in the second year of her apprenticeship; **~jahre sind keine Herrenjahre** (Spr.) we all have to start at the bottom of the ladder; **~junge** *der* apprentice; **~kanzel** *die* (österr.) ▸**~stuhl**; **~körper** *der* (Amtsspr.) teaching staff; faculty (Amer.); **~kraft** *die* teacher

Lehrling /ˈleːɐ̯lɪŋ/ *der;* **~s, ~e** ▸ⓘ **S. 113** apprentice; (in kaufmännischen Berufen) trainee

Lehrlings-: ~ausbildung *die* training of apprentices; **~heim** *das* apprentices' hostel

lehr-, Lehr-: ~mädchen *das* [girl] apprentice; (in kaufmännischen Berufen) [girl] trainee; **~meinung** *die* (geh.) [expert] opinion; **~meister** *der,* **~meisterin** *die* teacher; (Vorbild) mentor; **~methode** *die* teaching method; **~mittel** *das* (Schulw.) teaching aid; **~mittel** *Pl.* teaching materials; **~mittelfreiheit** *die* (Schulw.) free provision of teaching materials; **~pfad** *der* trail; (Naturpfad) nature trail; **~plan** *der* (Schulw.) syllabus; (Gesamtlehrgang) curriculum; **~probe** *die* (Schulw.) teaching practice; **eine ~probe geben** *od.* **machen** do a teaching practice; **~reich** *Adj.* instructive, informative ‹*book, film, etc.*›; **es war eine ~reiche Erfahrung für ihn** the experience taught him a lot; **~satz** *der* proposition; (in der Geometrie, Logik) theorem; **die euklidischen ~sätze** the propositions of Euclid; **~schwimmbecken** *das* learners' [swimming] pool; **~stelle** *die* apprenticeship; (in kaufmännischen Berufen) trainee post; **~stoff** *der* (Schulw.) syllabus; **~stück** *das* (Literaturw.) didactic play; **~stuhl** *der* (Hochschulw.) chair (**für** of); **~stuhl·inhaber** *der,* **~stuhl·inhaberin** *die* holder of a/the chair; **~veranstaltung** *die* (Hochschulw.) class; (Vorlesung) lecture; **~vertrag** *der* indentures *pl.*; **~werk** *das* course; (Buch) textbook; **~werkstatt** *die* apprentices' *or* training workshop; **~zeit** *die* [period of] apprenticeship

Leib /laip/ *der;* **~[e]s, ~er** (geh.) 1 body; **ich hatte keinen trockenen Faden mehr am ~[e]** I was wet through *or* soaked to the skin; **am ganzen ~ zittern** shiver all over; **bleib mir vom ~[e]!** keep away from me!; keep your distance!; **der ~ Christi/des Herrn** (christl. Rel.) the Body of Christ; **etw. am eigenen ~ erfahren** *od.* **erleben** experience sth. for oneself; **er hat sich mit ~ und Seele der Musik verschrieben** he dedicated himself heart and soul to music; **mit ~ und Seele Arzt/Krankenschwester** *usw.* **sein** be a dedicated doctor/nurse *etc.*; **mit ~ und Seele dabei sein** put one's whole heart into it; **jmdm. auf den ~** *od.* **zu ~e rücken** (ugs.) chiv[v]y sb.; (mit Kritik) get at sb. (coll.); **jmdm. so zu ~e rücken, dass ...** go on at sb. until ...(coll.); **sich** (*Dat.*) **jmdn. vom ~e halten** (ugs.) keep sb. at arm's length; **jmdm. mit einer Sache vom ~e bleiben** (ugs.) not pester sb. with sth.; **einer Sache** (*Dat.*) **zu ~e gehen** *od.* **rücken** tackle sth.; set about sth.; **jmdm. auf den ~ geschnitten sein** be tailor-made for sb.; suit sb. down to the ground; **die Rolle ist ihm [wie] auf den ~ geschrieben** the part could have been written for him; (fig.) the role fits him like a glove; **was hast du für einen Ton am ~?** (salopp) what a way to talk!; *s. auch* **lebendig A 1** 2 (geh., fachspr.: Bauch) belly; (Magen) stomach; **gesegneten ~es sein** (veralt.) be with child (dated) 3 (veralt.) **~ und Gut wagen/hingeben** risk/give one's all; **eine Gefahr für ~ und Leben** a danger to life and limb; **~ und Leben opfern** sacrifice one's life

Leib-: ~arzt *der,* **~ärztin** *die* personal physician; **~binde** *die* [warm] body belt

Leibchen /ˈlaipçən/ *das;* **~s, ~** 1 (Trachten~) bodice 2 (landsch.: Unterhemd) vest (Brit.); undershirt (Amer.)

leib-, Leib-: ~diener *der* valet; **~dienerin** *die* personal servant; **~eigen** *Adj.* (hist.) in serfdom *postpos.*; **~eigene** *der/die; adj. Dekl.* (hist.) serf; (fig.) slave; **~eigenschaft** *die* (hist.) serfdom *no def. art.*

leiben *itr. V. in* **wie er/sie** *usw.* **leibt und lebt** to a T

Leibes-: ~ertüchtigung *die* (veralt.) keeping fit *or* in trim *no art.*; physical training *no art.*; **~erziehung** *die* (Schulw.) physical education; PE; **~frucht** *die* (Med.) embryo; (nach 8 Wochen) fetus; (Rechtsspr.) unborn child; **~fülle** *die* (geh.) corpulence; (Umfang) girth; **~kräfte** *Pl. in* **aus** *od.* **nach ~kräften** with all one's might; **aus ~kräften schreien** shout for all one is worth; **~übungen** *Pl.* (Schulw.) physical education *sing.*; PE; **~visitation** /-vizitatsio:n/ *die;* **~~, ~en** body search

Leib-: ~garde *die* bodyguard; **die ~garde der Königin** (in Großbritannien) the Queen's Life Guards *pl.*; **~gardist** *der* [member of the/a] bodyguard; (der britischen Monarchen) Life Guard; **~gericht** *das* favourite dish

leibhaftig /laipˈhaftɪç/

A *Adj.* 1 (persönlich) in person *postpos.*; **da stand er ~ vor uns** there he was, as large as life; **der ~e Beweis dafür, dass ...** the living proof that ... 2 (echt) real; **ein ~er Herzog** a real live duke; **der ~e Teufel,** (scherzh.) **der Leibhaftige** the devil incarnate

B *adv.* (ugs.) actually; believe it or not

leiblich *Adj.* 1 physical ‹*well-being*› 2 (blutsverwandt) real ‹*mother, parents, etc.*›; **er liebte ihn wie seinen ~en Sohn** he loved him like his own son

Leib-: ~rente *die* life annuity; **~riemen** *der* (veralt.) belt; **~schmerzen** *Pl.* abdominal pain *sing.*; **~speise** *die* ▸**~gericht**; **~wache** *die* bodyguard; **~wächter** *der,* **~wächterin** *die* bodyguard; **~wäsche** *die* underwear; underclothes *pl.*

Leiche /ˈlaiçə/ *die;* **~, ~n** 1 [dead] body; (bes. eines Unbekannten) corpse; **er sieht aus wie eine lebende** *od.* **wandelnde ~** (salopp) he looks like death warmed up (coll.); **nur über meine ~!** over my dead body!; **über ~n gehen** (abwertend) be utterly ruthless *or* unscrupulous; **um seine Interessen durchzusetzen, geht er über ~n** he will stick at nothing to attain his own ends; **eine ~ im Keller haben** (fig. ugs.) have a skeleton in the cupboard 2 (landsch. veralt.: Begräbnis) funeral 3 (Druckw.) out (Printing); omission

leichen-, Leichen-: ~begängnis *das;* **~~ses, ~~se** (geh.) funeral; **~beschauer** *der,* **~beschauerin** *die* ▸ⓘ **S. 113** *doctor who performs a postmortem;* autopsist (Amer.); **~bestatter** *der,* **~bestatterin** *die* ▸ⓘ **S. 113** undertaker; mortician (Amer.); **~bitter·miene** *die* (iron.) doleful expression; **~blass,** ***~blaß** *Adj.* deathly pale; white as a sheet *postpos.*; **~fledderei** *die;* **~~, ~~en** (Rechtsw.) *robbery of a dead or unconscious person;* **~fledderer** *der;* **~~s, ~~, ~fledderin** *die;* **~~, ~~nen** (Rechtsw.) *one who robs a dead or unconscious person;* **~frau** *die* layer-out; **~halle** *die* mortuary; **~hemd** *das* burial garment; **~öffnung** *die* postmortem *or* autopsy (*with dissection*); **~rede** *die* (geh.) funeral oration; **~schänder** *der;* **~~s, ~~, ~schänderin** *die;* **~~, ~~nen** desecrator of a/the corpse; (sexuell) necrophiliac; **~schändung** *die* desecration of a corpse; (sexuell) necrophilia *no art.*; **der zweite Schlag ist ~schändung** (salopp, scherzh.) these fists are lethal weapons (joc.); **~schau** *die* postmortem; autopsy; **~schau·haus** *das* morgue; **~schmaus** *der* (scherzh.) funeral meal; **~starre** *die* rigor mortis; **~tuch** *das; Pl.* **~tücher** (veralt.) winding sheet; shroud; **~verbrennung** *die* cremation; **~wagen** *der* hearse; **~wäscher** *der;* **~~s, ~~, ~wäscherin** *die: person who washes corpses for burial;* **~zug** *der* (geh.) cortège; funeral procession

Leichnam /ˈlaiçnaːm/ *der;* **~s, ~e** (geh.) body; **jmds. ~:** sb.'s body *or* mortal remains *pl.*

leicht /laiçt/

A *Adj.* 1 light; lightweight ‹*suit, material*›; **~e Waffen** small-calibre arms; **~e Kleidung** thin clothes; (luftig) light *or* cool clothes; **gewogen und zu ~ befunden** tried and found wanting; **jmdn. um etw. ~er machen** (ugs.) relieve sb. of sth.; **mit ~er Hand** with ease; **etw. auf die ~e Schulter** *od.* **Achsel nehmen** (ugs.) take sth. casually; make light of sth.

2 (einfach) easy ‹*task, question, job, etc.*›; (nicht anstrengend) light ‹*work, duties, etc.*›; **ein ~es Leben haben** have an easy life; **es ~/nicht ~ haben** have/not have it easy *or* an easy time of it; **nichts ~er als das** nothing could be simpler *or* easier; **du machst dir die Sache zu ~:** you're making it too easy for yourself *or* not taking it seriously enough; **es wäre ihm ein Leichtes zu helfen** it would be an easy *or* simple matter for him to help; **keinen ~en Stand haben** not have an easy time of it; **mit jmdm. [kein] ~es Spiel haben** find sb. is [not] easy meat; **man hats nicht ~, aber leicht hats einen** (salopp) it's a hard *or* tough life; **~ fallen** be easy; **das fällt mir ~:** it is easy for me; I find it easy; **jmdm./sich etw. ~ machen** make sth. easy for sb./oneself; **es sich** (*Dat.*) *od.* **sich** (*Dat.*) **die Sache zu ~ machen** make it *or* things easy for oneself; **etw. ~ nehmen** make light of sth.; **seine Aufgabe nicht ~ nehmen** take one's task seriously; **nimms ~:** don't worry about it; **sich mit etw. ~/nicht ~ tun** manage sth. easily/have a hard time with sth.

3 (schwach) slight ‹*accent, illness, wound, doubt, etc.*›; light ‹*wind, rain, sleep, perfume*›; **ein ~er Stoß [in die Rippen]** a gentle nudge [in the ribs]; **eine ~e Grippe** a mild attack of flu (coll.)

4 (bekömmlich) light ‹*food, wine*›; mild ‹*cigar, cigarette*›

5 (heiter) light-hearted; **ihr wurde ~ ums Herz** (geh.) a weight was lifted from her heart; **ihr wurde es etwas/viel ~er** she felt somewhat/much easier *or* relieved

6 (unterhaltend) light ‹*music, reading, etc.*›

7 (veralt. abwertend) **ein ~es Mädchen** a loose-living girl

B *adv.* 1 lightly ‹*built*›; **~ bewaffnet** lightly armed; **~ geschürzt** scantily clad; **~ bekleidet** lightly *or* thinly dressed; (fast nackt) scantily clad

2 (einfach, schnell, spielend) easily; **~ verdaulich** [easily] digestible; **~ verkäuflich** fast-selling; **~ verständlich** *od.* **zu verstehen sein** be easy to understand; be easily understood; **~ zerbrechlich** very fragile; **~ entzündlich** highly inflammable; **sie hat ~ reden** it's easy *or* all very well for her to talk; **das ist ~er gesagt als getan** that's easier said than done; **jemanden wie ihn werden Sie nicht so ~ wieder finden** you won't find someone like him again in a hurry (coll.); **sie wird ~ böse** she has a quick temper; **das ist ~ möglich** that is perfectly possible; **ihr wird ~ schlecht** the slightest thing makes her sick

3 (geringfügig) slightly; **~ gewürzt** lightly seasoned; **es regnete ~:** there was a light rain falling; **es hat ~ gefroren** there was a slight frost; **~ verletzt/verwundet** slightly injured/wounded

4 (bekömmlich) **~ essen** eat light food

leicht-, Leicht-: ~athlet *der* [track/field] athlete; **~athletik** *die* [track and field] athletics *sing.*; **~athletin** *die* ▸**~athlet**; **~bauplatte** *die* (Bauw.) lightweight building board; **~bauweise** *die* lightweight construction; **etw. in ~bauweise herstellen** *od.* **produzieren** make sth. with lightweight materials; **~bekleidet** ▸**leicht B1**; **~benzin** *das* benzine; **~beschwingt** *Adj.* carefree; ‹*music*› with a gay lilt; **~bewaffnet** ▸**leicht B1**; **~blütig** *Adj.* (geh.) happy-go-lucky; (**~sinnig**) frivolous; ***~entzündlich** ▸**leicht B2**

Leichter *der;* **~s, ~** (Seew.) lighter

leichterhand *Adv.* (ohne Überlegung) unthinkingly; without thinking; (ohne Schwierigkeit) easily; effortlessly

l

leicht-, Leicht-: *~|fallen ▸leicht A2; **~fertig** A *Adj.* 1 careless ‹*behaviour, person*›; rash ‹*promise*›; ill-considered, slapdash ‹*plan*›; 2 (veralt.: moralisch bedenkenlos) promiscuous; loose ‹*woman*›; B *adv.* carelessly; **~fertigkeit** *die* carelessness; **~fuß** *der* (abwertend) Casanova; ladykiller; **~füßig** (geh.) A *Adj.* nimble; B *adv.* with light *or* nimble steps; **~füßigkeit** *die;* ~~: lightness *or* nimbleness of foot; **~geschürzt** ▸**leicht B1**; **~gewicht** *das* (Schwerathletik) 1 lightweight; *s. auch* **Fliegengewicht**; 2 ▸**~gewichtler**; 3 (ugs. scherzh.) (Mädchen) sylph; (Mann) featherweight; **~gewichtler** /-gəvɪçtlɐ/ *der;* **~~s, ~~** (Schwerathletik) lightweight; **~gläubig** *Adj.* gullible; credulous; **~gläubigkeit** *die* gullibility; credulity; **~hin** *Adv.* 1 (ohne Überlegung) without [really] thinking; (lässig) casually; **etw. ~hin sagen** say sth. casually *or* unthinkingly; 2 (nebenbei) in an offhand *or* casual manner

Leichtigkeit /ˈlaiçtɪçkait/ *die;* ~ 1 (geringes Gewicht, Schwerelosigkeit) lightness 2 (Mühelosigkeit) ease; **es ist eine ~ [für ihn], das zu tun** it is a simple matter [for him] to do it; **mit ~:** with ease; easily

leicht-, Leicht-: **~industrie** *die* light industry; **~lebig** *Adj.* happy-go-lucky; **~lebigkeit** *die;* **~~:** happy-go-lucky attitude; **~lohn·gruppe** *die* (verhüll.) low-wage group; ***~|machen** ▸**leicht A2**; **~matrose** *der* ordinary seaman; **~metall** *das* light metal; (Legierung) [light] alloy; ***~|nehmen** ▸**leicht A2**; **~öl** *das* light oil; **~schwer·gewicht** *das* (Schwerathletik) light heavyweight; **Weltmeister im ~schwergewicht** world light heavyweight champion; **~sinn** *der* carelessness *no indef. art.*; (mit Gefahr verbunden) recklessness *no indef. art.*; (Fahrlässigkeit) negligence *no indef. art.*; **das sagst du so in deinem jugendlichen ~sinn** (ugs.) that's easier said than done; **~sinnig** A *Adj.* careless; (sich, andere gefährdend) reckless; (fahrlässig) negligent; B *adv.* carelessly; (gefährlich) recklessly; ‹*promise*› rashly; **~sinnig mit seinem Geld umgehen** be careless with one's money; **~sinnigerweise** *Adv.* carelessly; (gefährlicherweise) recklessly; ‹*promise*› rashly; **~sinnigkeit** *die;* **~~:** ▸**Leichtsinn**; ***~|tun** ▸**leicht A2**; ***~verdaulich** ▸**leicht B2**; ***~verkäuflich** ▸**leicht B2**; **~verletzt** ▸**leicht B3**; **~verletzte** *der/die* slightly injured man/woman/person; **200 ~verletzte** two hundred slightly injured; **~verwundet** ▸**leicht B3**; **~verwundete** *der/die* slightly wounded man/woman/person; **die ~verwundeten** those with slight wounds

leid /lait/ *Adj.* **etw./jmdn. ~ sein/werden** (ugs.) be/get fed up with (coll.) *or* tired of sth./sb.; **wird sie es nie ~, das zu tun?** will she never tire of doing this?; **jmdm. ~ sein/werden** (veralt.) be/become wearisome to sb.; **die Arbeit ist ihm längst ~:** he wearied of the work long ago; *s. auch* **Leid²**

Leid¹ *das;* **~[e]s** 1 (Schmerz) suffering; (Kummer) grief; sorrow; **großes** *od.* **schweres ~ erfahren** suffer greatly; (Kummer) suffer great sorrow; **geteiltes ~ ist halbes ~** (Spr.) a sorrow shared is a sorrow halved; **jmdm. sein ~ klagen** tell sb. all one's woes 2 (Unrecht) wrong; (Böses) harm; **jmdm. ein ~ zufügen** wrong/harm sb.; do sb. wrong/harm; **ihm soll kein ~** *od.* (veralt.) **~s geschehen** he shall come to no harm; **sich** (*Dat.*) **ein ~s antun** (ugs. veralt.) take one's own life

Leid² ▸ⓘ **S. 227** *in* **es tut mir ~[, dass...]** I'm sorry [that...]; **das braucht dir nicht ~ zu tun** you needn't feel sorry *or* (coll.) bad about that; **so ~ es mir tut, aber...** I'm very sorry, but...; **er tut mir ~:** I feel sorry for him; **es tut mir ~ darum/um ihn** I feel sorry *or* (coll.) bad about it/sorry for him

Leide·form *die* (Sprachw.) ▸**Passiv**

leiden ▸ⓘ **S. 439**

A *unr. itr. V.* 1 suffer (**an, unter** + *Dat.* from); **unter jmdm. ~:** suffer because of sb. 2 (Schaden nehmen) suffer (**durch, unter** + *Dat.* from); **durch den Frost ~:** suffer from *or* be harmed by the frost

B *unr. tr. V.* 1 **jmdn. [gut] ~ können** *od.* **mögen** like sb.; **ich kann sie/das nicht ~:** I can't stand her/it 2 (geh.: ertragen müssen) suffer ‹*hunger, thirst, want, torment, etc.*› 3 (dulden) tolerate; **sie ist überall/bei ihren Vorgesetzten wohl gelitten** (geh.) she is liked by everybody/by her superiors 4 (veralt.: aushalten) **sie litt es nicht mehr zu Hause** she could endure it no longer at home

-leiden *das;* **~s, ~:** **ein Asthma~/Herz~ haben** have an asthmatic condition/a heart condition

Leiden *das;* **~s, ~** 1 ▸ⓘ **S. 439** (Krankheit) illness; (Gebrechen) complaint; **nach langem, schwerem ~ sterben** die after a long and painful illness; **[es ist] immer das alte ~** [it's] the same old story 2 (Qual) suffering; **Freud[en] und ~[en]** joy[s] and sorrow[s]; **das** *od.* **die ~ Christi** Christ's Passion 3 **ein langes ~ [von Sohn]** (ugs. scherzh.) a beanpole [of a son]

leidend *Adj.* 1 (krank) ailing; in poor health *postpos.*; **~ aussehen** look sickly *or* poorly 2 (schmerzvoll) strained ‹*voice*›; martyred ‹*expression*›; ‹*look*› full of suffering

Leidenschaft *die;* **~, ~en** passion (**zu, für** for); **mit ~:** fervently; passionately; **Reiten ist seine [ganze] ~:** riding is his great love; **seine ~ für etw. entdecken** realize one's great love for sth.; **er ist Sammler aus ~:** he is a dedicated collector; **ein Thema frei von jeder ~ diskutieren** discuss a subject dispassionately

leidenschaftlich

A *Adj.* passionate; ardent, passionate ‹*lover*›; passionate[ly keen] ‹*skier, collector, etc.*›; violent, passionate ‹*hatred, quarrel*›; vehement ‹*protest*›

B *adv.* 1 passionately; (eifrig) dedicatedly; **~ diskutiert werden** be discussed heatedly; **etw. ~ ablehnen/verneinen** reject/deny sth. vehemently; **er treibt ~ Sport/sammelt ~ Briefmarken** he is a passionately keen sportsman/stamp collector 2 (intensivierend) **etw. ~ gern tun** adore doing sth.; **sie isst ~ gerne Schokolade** she adores *or* has a passion for chocolate

Leidenschaftlichkeit *die;* ~ 1 passion; (in der Liebe) ardour; (bei einer Diskussion) heat; (bei der Darlegung eines Standpunkts) vehemence 2 (Begeisterung) passionate dedication; **mit ungeheurer ~:** with tremendous enthusiasm

leidenschaftslos

A *Adj.* dispassionate; detached

B *adv.* dispassionately; in a detached way

Leidenschaftslosigkeit *die;* **~:** detachment; **mit völliger ~:** in an entirely detached manner; (ohne Nachdruck) without any expression

leidens-, Leidens-: **~druck** *der* (Psych.) strain imposed by suffering; psychological strain (+ *Gen.* on); **~fähig** *Adj.* with a great capacity for suffering *postpos., not pred.*; **~fähigkeit** *die* capacity for suffering; **~gefährte** *der,* **~gefährtin** *die;* **~genosse** *der,* **~genossin** *die* fellow sufferer; **~geschichte** *die* (christl. Rel.) **die ~geschichte Christi** Christ's Passion; **seine ~geschichte** (fig.) his tale of woe; **~miene** *die* woeful *or* martyred expression; **~weg** *der* (geh.) life of suffering *or* hardship

leider *Adv.* ▸ⓘ **S. 227** unfortunately; **ich habe ~ keine Zeit** unfortunately *or* I'm afraid I haven't any time; **~ ja/nein** I'm afraid so/afraid not; **~ Gottes ist es nun einmal so** (ugs.) that's how it is, I'm afraid *or* worse luck; (in förmlichen Briefen) **wir müssen Ihnen ~ mitteilen ...** we regret to inform you ...

leid-: **~erfüllt** *Adj.* full of suffering *postpos.*; wretched; ‹*look*› of suffering; **~geprüft** *Adj.* sorely tried; long-suffering

leidig *Adj.* tiresome; wretched; **das ist ein ~er Trost** that's not much comfort

leidlich

A *Adj.* reasonable; passable

B *adv.* reasonably; fairly; **es geht mir [ganz] ~** (ugs.) I'm quite well *or* not too bad; **sie kann ~ Klavier spielen** she can play the piano reasonably well

leid-, Leid-: **~tragende** *der/die; adj. Dekl.* victim; **der** *od.* **die ~tragende/die ~tragenden [dabei] sein** be the one/ones to suffer [in this]; **~|tun** ▸ **Leid²**; **~voll** *Adj.* (geh.) ‹*life, youth, look*› full of suffering; painful ‹*experience*›; **in der langen, ~vollen Geschichte Afrikas** in the long history of Africa with all its suffering; **~wesen** *das: in* **zu jmds. ~wesen** to sb.'s regret; **ja, sehr zu meinem ~wesen** yes, much to my regret

Leier /ˈlaiɐ/ *die;* **~, ~n** lyre; **[es ist] immer die alte/dieselbe ~** (ugs. abwertend) [it's] always the same old story

Leier·kasten *der* (ugs.) barrel organ; hurdy-gurdy (coll.)

Leierkasten·mann *der* organ-grinder; hurdy-gurdy man (coll.)

leiern (ugs.)

A *tr. V.* 1 (kurbeln) wind; *s. auch* **Kreuz 5** 2 (auf der Drehorgel spielen) grind out ‹*tune*› 3 (monoton aufsagen) drone through; (schnell) reel *or* rattle off

B *itr. V.* 1 **an etw.** (*Dat.*) **~:** wind away at sth. 2 (monoton sprechen) drone [on]

Leih-: **~arbeit** *die* (Wirtsch.) subcontracted labour; **~arbeiter** *der,* **~arbeiterin** *die* subcontracted worker; **~bibliothek** *die,* **~bücherei** *die* lending library

leihen /ˈlaiən/ *unr. tr. V.* 1 **jmdm. etw. ~:** lend sb. sth.; lend sth. to sb.; **leihst du es mir?** will you lend it to me? 2 (ent~) borrow; **[sich** (*Dat.*)**] [von** *od.* **bei jmdm.] etw. ~:** borrow sth. [from sb.]; **ein geliehener Wagen** a borrowed car 3 (geh.: gewähren) lend, give ‹*support*›; give ‹*attention*›

Leih-: **~frist** *die* loan period; (bei Wagen, Frack usw.) hire period; rental period (Amer.); **~gabe** *die* loan (*Gen.* from); **~gebühr** *die* hire *or* (Amer.) rental charge; (bei Büchern) lending charge; borrowing fee; **~haus** *das* pawnbroker's; pawnshop; **im ~haus sein** ‹*possession*› be at the pawnbroker's; be pawned; **~mutter** *die; Pl.* **~mütter** surrogate mother; **~mutterschaft** *die* surrogate motherhood; **~schein** *der* 1 (im ~haus) pawn ticket; 2 (in der Bibliothek) borrowing slip; **~verkehr** *der* [inter-library] loan service; **~wagen** *der* hire *or* (Amer.) rental car; **[sich** (*Dat.*)**] einen ~wagen nehmen** hire *or* (Amer.) rent a car; **~weise** A *Adv.* on loan; **das hat er mir ~weise überlassen** he has lent it to me; **hier hast du das Buch, aber nur ~weise** I'll give you the book, but only to borrow; B *adj.* **„~weise Überlassung durch die Nationalgalerie"** 'on loan from the National Gallery'

Leim /laim/ *der;* **~[e]s** glue; **aus dem ~ gehen** (ugs.) (entzweigehen) come apart; ‹*marriage, friendship*› break up; (dick werden) put on a lot of weight; ‹*woman*› lose one's figure; **jmdm. auf den ~ gehen** *od.* **kriechen** (ugs.) be taken in by sb.; fall for sb.'s trick/tricks; **jmdn. auf den ~ führen** (ugs.) take sb. in

leimen *tr. V.* 1 glue (**an** + *Akk.* to); (zusammen~) glue [together] 2 (ugs.: hereinlegen) **jmdn. ~:** take sb. in

Leim·farbe *die* distemper

leimig *Adj.* gluey; (noch nicht trocken) tacky

Leim·rute *die* [bird]lime twig

-lein *das;* **~s, ~:** little ...; **sein schwarzes Büch~:** his little black book

Lein /lain/ *der;* **~[e]s, ~e** (Bot.) flax

Leine /ˈlainə/ *die;* **~, ~n** 1 rope; (Zelt~) guy rope; **die ~n losmachen** (Seemannsspr.) cast off; **~ ziehen** (ugs.) clear off 2 (Wäsche~, Angel~) line; **einen Fisch an die ~ kriegen** hook a fish 3 (Hunde~) lead (esp. Brit.); leash; **den Hund an die ~ nehmen** put the dog on the lead/leash; **„Hunde sind an der ~ zu führen"** 'dogs must be kept on a lead/leash'; **jmdm. ~/mehr ~ lassen** (ugs.) give sb. plenty of/more leeway; **jmdn. an der [kurzen] ~ haben** *od.* **halten** (ugs.) keep sb. on a tight rein; **jmdn. an die ~ legen** (ugs.) get sb. under one's thumb

leinen *Adj.* linen ‹*tablecloth, sheet, etc.*›; cloth[-covered] ‹*cushion etc.*›; **~es Verdeck** canvas [car] hood

Leinen *das;* **~s** 1 (Gewebe) linen 2 (Buchw.) cloth; **Ausgabe in ~:** cloth edition

Leinen-: ~band *der* cloth-bound volume; **~einband** *der* cloth binding; **~kleid** *das* linen dress **~tuch** *das; Pl.* **~tücher** linen sheet; (Tischtuch) linen [table]cloth; **~zeug** *das* linen

Leine·weber *der,* **Leine·weberin** *die* linen weaver

Lein-: ~kraut *das* toadflax; **~öl** *das* linseed oil; **~pfad** *der* towpath; **~samen** *der* linseed

Lein·wand *die* 1 linen; (grob) canvas 2 (des Malers) canvas 3 (für Filme und Dias) screen; **einen Roman** *usw.* **auf die ~ bringen** (fig.) film a novel *etc.*; **jmdn. von der ~ kennen** (fig.) know sb. from films

Leinwand-: ~bindung *die* (Textilind.) plain weave; **~größe** *die* (scherzh.) famous film star; film great; **~held** *der* (iron.) hero of the silver screen

Lein·zeug *das* ▸**Leinenzeug**

leis ▸**leise**

leise /ˈlaizə/

A *Adj.* 1 quiet; soft ‹*steps, music, etc.*›; faint ‹*noise*›; **sei ~!** be quiet!; **könnt ihr nicht ~r sein?** can't you make less noise?; **das Radio/die Musik ~[r] stellen** turn the radio/music down 2 (leicht, kaum merklich) faint; slight; slight, gentle ‹*touch*›; light ‹*rain*›; **ich habe ~ Bedenken** I have my doubts; **eine ~ Andeutung machen** give a gentle hint; **nicht die ~ste Ahnung haben, nicht im Leisesten ahnen** not have the faintest *or* slightest idea; **ich zweifle nicht im Leisesten daran, dass …** I haven't the slightest doubt that …

B *adv.* 1 quietly; **sprich doch etwas ~r** lower your voice; **~ weinend** crying softly 2 (leicht, kaum merklich) slightly; ‹*touch, rain*› gently; **~ kochen** simmer gently; **~ zweifeln/hoffen/ahnen** have a slight doubt/hope/suspicion

Leise-: ~treter *der* (abwertend) pussyfooter; **~treterei** *die;* **~~** (abwertend) pussyfooting; **~treterin** *die;* **~~, ~~nen** ▸**~treter**

Leiste /ˈlaistə/ *die;* **~, ~n** 1 strip; (Holz~) batten; (profiliert) moulding; (halbrund) beading; (am Auto) trim; (Tapeten~) [picture] rail; picture moulding (Amer.); (eines Bilderrahmens) frame wood; **eine ~:** a piece *or* strip of moulding/beading/trim/frame wood; (Holz~) a batten 2 (Knopf~) facing 3 ▸❶ **S. 435** (Anat.) groin 4 (Weberei) selvage

leisten

A *tr. V.* 1 do ‹*work*›; (schaffen) achieve ‹*a lot, nothing*›; **gute** *od.* **ganze Arbeit ~:** do good work *or* a good job; (gründlich arbeiten) do a thorough job; **der Motor leistet 80 PS** the engine develops *or* produces 80 b.h.p.; **der Wagen leistet 220 km/h** the car will do 220 k.p.h.; **die Produktionsstraße leistet 30 Einheiten pro Stunde** the production line has an output of 30 units per hour 2 (verblasst od. als Funktionsverb) **jmdm. Hilfe ~:** help sb.; **einen Eid ~:** swear *or* take an oath; *s. auch* **Abbitte**; **Beistand 1**; **Beitrag 1**; **Folge 3**; **Gehorsam**; **Gewähr**; **Widerstand 1** *usw.*

B *refl. V.* (ugs.) 1 **sich** (*Dat.*) **etw. ~:** treat oneself to sth.; **wer leistet sich** (*Dat.*) **denn heute noch diesen Luxus?** who nowadays is prepared to spend the money on such a luxury? 2 (mit „können") **sich** (*Dat.*) **etw. [nicht] ~ können** [not] be able to afford sth.; **er kann es sich** (*Dat.*) **~, das zu tun** he can afford to do it; (etw. Riskantes) he can get away with doing it 3 (wagen) **sich** (*Dat.*) **etw. ~:** get up to sth.; **was der sich** (*Dat.*) **leistet!** the things he gets away with!; **sich** (*Dat.*) **einen groben Schnitzer ~:** make a great blunder; **wer hat sich** (*Dat.*) **diese Frechheit geleistet?** who was it who had the cheek to do/say *etc.* that?; **ich habe mir heute vielleicht was [Schönes] geleistet** (ugs.) I really excelled myself today (iron.); I did something really brilliant today (iron.)

Leisten *der;* **~s, ~:** last; **alles/alle über einen ~ schlagen** (ugs.) lump everybody/everything together

Leisten-: ~bruch *der* rupture; **~gegend** *die* ▸❶ **S. 435** (Anat.) [area of the] groin

Leistung *die;* **~, ~en** 1 (Qualität bzw. Quantität der Arbeit) performance; **Bezahlung nach ~:** payment according to performance *or* results; (in der Industrie) payment according to productivity 2 (Errungenschaft) achievement; (im Sport) performance; **reife ~!** (Jugendspr.) not bad!; **gute / hervorragende / außergewöhnliche ~en vollbringen** achieve good/outstanding/exceptional results; **eine große sportliche/technische ~:** a great sporting/technical feat; **die schulischen ~en** results at school 3 (Leistungsvermögen, Physik: Arbeits~) power; (Ausstoß) output; **die ~ einer Fabrik** the output *or* [production] capacity of a factory 4 (Zahlung, Zuwendung) payment; (Versicherungsw.) benefit; **die sozialen ~en der Firma** the firm's fringe benefits 5 (Dienst~) service 6 (das Leisten) carrying out; (Eides~) swearing; **jmdn. auf ~ verklagen** (Rechtsspr.) sue sb. for specific performance

leistungs-, Leistungs-: ~berechtigt *Adj.* (Amtsspr.) entitled to benefits *postpos.;* **~bilanz** *die* (Wirtsch.) balance of trade; **~druck** *der* (bei Arbeitnehmern) pressure to work harder; (bei Sportlern, Schülern) pressure to achieve *or* to do well; **~fähig** *Adj.* 1 capable ‹*person*›; (körperlich) able-bodied; (gute Arbeit leistend) efficient ‹*worker, factory, industry, etc.*›; powerful ‹*engine, computer, etc.*›; (konkurrenzfähig) competitive ‹*firm, industry*›; 2 (zahlungsfähig) capable of paying *postpos.;* solvent; **~fähigkeit** *die* (eines Menschen) capability; (bei guter Arbeitsleistung) efficiency; (eines Betriebs, der Industrie) productivity; (Wirtschaftlichkeit) efficiency; (eines Motors, eines Computers usw.) power; performance; **die Grenze seiner ~fähigkeit erreicht haben** have reached the limit of what one can do; **~fördend** *Adj.* performance-enhancing; **~gerecht** A *Adj.* ‹*salary, income*› based on performance *or* results; (in der Industrie) based on productivity; B *adv.* **~gerecht bezahlt werden** receive a performance-related salary; **~gesellschaft** *die* [highly] competitive society; performance-oriented society; **~grenze** *die* maximum potential; (eines Sportlers) performance limit; (von Maschinen, Fabriken) maximum output; **seine ~grenze erreichen** reach the limit of one's/its capacity; **~klage** *die* (Rechtsw.) action for specific performance; **~kontrolle** *die* (Schulw.) 1 **der ~kontrolle dienen** be used as a check on the standard reached; 2 (Test) [performance] test; **~kraft** *die* ▸**~fähigkeit**; **~kurs** *der* (Schulw.) extension course (going beyond the basic course, based on a university form of study); **~kurve** *die* performance curve; (eines Motors) power curve; **~lohn** *der* pay based on productivity; **~motivation** *die* (Psych.) achievement motivation; **~nachweis** *der* evidence of [academic] achievement; **~niveau** *das* (Schulw.) level of achievement; (Sport) standard of performance; **~orientiert** *Adj.* 1 achievement-oriented; [highly] competitive ‹*society*›; 2 ▸**~gerecht**; **~prämie** *die* (Arbeitswelt) productivity bonus; **~prinzip** *das* achievement principle; competitive principle; **~prüfung** *die* 1 (Schulw.) achievement test; 2 (Sport) trial; test [of performance]; **~schau** *die* (Wirtsch., Landw.) [product] exhibition; **~schwach** *Adj.* not performing well *pred.;* low-achieving *attrib.* ‹*worker, pupil*›; (minderbegabt) less able, lower-ability *attrib.* ‹*pupil*›; weak ‹*team*›; low-powered ‹*engine*›; **~schwächer** lower-achieving *attrib.* ‹*worker, pupil*›; lower-ability *attrib.* ‹*pupil*›; less powerful ‹*engine*›; **~schwäche** *die* poor performance; (Schulw.) low achievement; (eines Motors) low power; **~sport** *der* competitive sport *no art.;* **~sportler** *der* competitive sportsman; **~sportlerin** *die* competitive sportswoman; **~stand** *der* level of performance; (Schulw.) standard of work; (Ausstoß) level of output; **~stark** *Adj.* high-performing *attrib.* ‹*athlete*›; able ‹*pupil, athlete, etc.*›; high-performance *attrib.*, powerful ‹*engine, car*›; highly efficient ‹*business, power station*›; (sehr konkurrenzfähig) highly competitive ‹*business, athlete*›; **~stärke** *die* level of performance; (Schulw.) standard of work; (Ausstoß) level of output; **~steigernd** *Adj.* performance-enhancing; **~steigerung** *die* improvement in performance; (eines Schülers) improvement [in his/her work]; (eines Unternehmens) improvement in efficiency; (in der Produktion) improvement in output; **~test** *der* (bei Motoren, Maschinen) performance test; (bei Schülern) achievement test; **~träger** *der,* **~trägerin** *die* main contributor; (Sport) key player; **~vergleich** *der* competition; **~vermögen** *das* ▸**~fähigkeit**; **~verweigerung** *die* (bes. Soziol., Päd.) refusal to work; (allgemein) refusal to be part of competitive society; **~wettbewerb** *der* (Wirtsch.) competition [for high output and efficiency]; **~zentrum** *das* (Sport) intensive training centre; **~zulage** *die,* **~zuschlag** *der* bonus (*for additional work, responsibility, etc.*); **~zwang** *der* (Soziol.) (bei Arbeitnehmern) compulsion to work hard; (bei Sportlern/Schülern) compulsion to achieve *or* to do well

Leit-: ~antrag *der* (Politik) motion put forward by the party leadership; **~artikel** *der* (Zeitungsw.) leading article; leader; **~artikler** *der;* **~~s, ~~, ~artiklerin** *die;* **~~, ~~nen** (Zeitungsw.) leader writer; **~bild** *das* model; **~bilder der Mode** leaders of fashion

leiten /ˈlaitn̩/ *tr. V.* 1 (anführen) lead, head ‹*expedition, team, discussion, etc.*›; be head of ‹*school*›; (verantwortlich sein für) be in charge of ‹*project, expedition, etc.*›; manage ‹*factory, enterprise*›; (den Vorsitz führen bei) chair ‹*meeting, discussion, etc.*›; (Musik: dirigieren) conduct ‹*orchestra, choir*›; direct ‹*small orchestra etc.*›; (Sport: als Schiedsrichter) referee ‹*game, match*›; **~der Angestellter** executive; manager; **~de Angestellte** senior *or* managerial staff; **~der Beamter** senior civil servant; **eine ~de Position** a position in [senior] management; a managerial position 2 (beg~, führen) lead; **jmdn. auf die richtige Spur ~:** put sb. on the right track; **sich von etw. ~ lassen** [let oneself] be guided by sth.; **er lässt sich nur von seinen Gefühlen ~:** he is governed solely by his feelings; **sich schwer/leicht ~ lassen** be hard/easy to manage; **die ~de Hand/der ~de Gedanke** the guiding hand/principle 3 (lenken) direct; route ‹*traffic*›; (um~) divert ‹*traffic, stream*›; **Erdöl durch Rohre ~:** pipe oil; **den Verkehr über eine Umgehungsstraße ~:** route/divert traffic along a bypass; **etw. an die zuständige Stelle ~:** pass on *or* forward sth. to the competent authority 4 *auch itr.* (Physik) conduct ‹*heat, current, sound*›; **etw. leitet gut/schlecht** sth. is a good/bad conductor; **nicht ~de Materialien** non-conducting materials

Leiter[1] *der;* **~s, ~** 1 (einer Delegation, Gruppe) leader; head; (einer Abteilung) head; manager; (eines Instituts) director; (einer Schule) head teacher; headmaster (Brit.); principal (esp. Amer.); (einer Diskussion) leader; (Vorsitz) chair[man]; (eines Chors) choirmaster; (Dirigent) conductor; **kaufmännischer ~:** marketing manager; (Verkaufs~) sales manager; **technischer/künstlerischer ~:** technical/artistic director 2 (Physik) conductor

Leiter[2] *die;* **~, ~n** ladder; (Steh~) stepladder; **die ~ des Erfolgs** (fig.) the ladder of success

Leiterin *die;* **~, ~nen** ▸**Leiter**[1]; (einer Schule) head teacher; headmistress (Brit.); principal (esp. Amer.); (eines Chors) choirmistress

Leiter-: ~sprosse *die* rung [of a/the ladder]; **~wagen** *der* open-frame wooden handcart

leit-, Leit-: ~faden *der* 1 [basic] textbook; **~faden der Physik** basic course in physics; introduction to physics; 2 (~gedanke) main idea *or* theme; **das durchzieht sein Werk wie ein ~faden** it runs through his works like a connecting thread; **~fähig** *Adj.* (Physik) conductive; **~fähigkeit** *die* (Physik) conductivity; **~feuer** *das* (Schifffahrt) leading light; **~fossil** *das* (Geol.) index fossil; **~gedanke** *der* dominant *or* central theme; **~hammel** *der* 1 bellwether; 2 (abwertend:

Führer) leader [of the herd]; boss-figure; **~linie** *die* [1] (Richtlinie) guideline; [2] (Verkehrsw.) lane marking; [3] (Geom.) directrix; **~medium** *das* chief medium; **~motiv** *das* (Musik, Literaturw., fig.) [1] leitmotiv; [2] (~gedanke) dominant *or* central theme; **~planke** *die* crash barrier; guardrail (Amer.); **~satz** *der* guiding principle; **~spruch** *der* motto; **~stelle** *die* control room; (Büro) central office; **~stern** *der* (auch fig. geh.) lodestar; **~strahl** *der* [1] (Flugw., Milit.) radio guidance beam; [2] (Geom.) radius vector; **~tier** *das* (Zool.) leader [of the herd]; **~ton** *der; Pl.* **~töne** (Musik) leading note

Leitung *die;* **~, ~en** [1] ▶ **leiten 1**: leading; heading; being in charge; management; chairing; (Schulw.) working as a/the head; (Musik) conducting; directing; (Sport) refereeing [2] (einer Expedition usw.) leadership; (Verantwortung) responsibility (*Gen.* for); (eines Betriebes, Unternehmens) management; (einer Sitzung, Diskussion) chairmanship; (Schulw.) headship; (Musik) conductorship; (Sport) [task of] refereeing; **unter der ~ eines Managers stehen** be headed by a manager; **unter jmds. ~** (*Dat.*) **arbeiten** work under sb. *or* under sb.'s direction; (Musik) **unter der ~ von X/des Komponisten** conducted by X/the composer; **die ~ hatte Otto Klemperer** the conductor was Otto Klemperer; **die ~ der Sendung/Diskussion hat X** the programme is presented/the discussion is chaired by X; **bei einem Spiel die ~ haben** referee a match [3] (leitende Personen) management; (einer Schule) head and senior staff [4] (Rohr~) pipe; (Haupt~) main; **Wasser aus der ~ trinken** drink tap water [5] (Draht, Kabel) cable; (für ein Gerät) lead; (einzelne od. ohne Isolierung) wire; **die ~en [im Haus/Auto** *usw.*] the wiring *sing.* [of the house/car *etc.*] [6] (Telefon~) line; **es ist jemand in der ~** (ugs.) there's somebody on the line; **gehen Sie aus der ~!** get off the line!; **auf einer anderen ~ sprechen** be [talking] on another line; **eine lange ~ haben** (ugs.) be slow on the uptake; **er steht** *od.* **sitzt auf der ~** (salopp) he's not really with it (coll.)

Leitungs-: ~draht *der* [electrical] wire; (größer) [electrical] cable; **~gremium** *das* [executive] committee; **~mast** *der* (für Strom) pylon; (Telefonmast) telegraph pole; **~netz** *das* [1] (für Wasser, Gas) mains network; mains *pl.*; (für Fernwärme usw.) network of pipes; [2] (Elektrizität) mains network *or* grid; [3] (Telefonnetz) telephone network; **~rohr** *das* [water/gas] pipe; (Hauptleitungsrohr) main; **~wasser** *das* tap water

Leit-: ~währung *die* (Wirtsch.) base *or* key currency; **~werk** *das* [1] (Flugw., Waffent.) control surfaces *pl.*; (am Heck) tail unit; [2] (Seew.) approach pier; [3] (DV) control unit; **~wert** (Physik, Elektrot.) conductance; **~wolf** *der,* **~wölfin** *die* leader of the pack; **~wort** *das* [1] *Pl.* **~wörter** catchword; motto; [2] *Pl.* **~~e** ▶ **Leitspruch**; **~zahl** *die* (Fot.) guide number; **~zins[satz]** *der* (Finanzw.) [1] (Diskontsatz) discount rate; ≈ base rate; [2] ▶ **Eckzins**

Lektion /lɛk'tsi̯o:n/ *die;* **~, ~en** lesson; **jmdm. eine ~ erteilen** (fig.) teach sb. a lesson

Lektor /'lɛktɔr/ *der;* **~s, ~en** /lɛk'to:rən/ [1] ▶ ❶ **S. 113** (Hochschulw.) *junior university teacher in charge of practical or supplementary classes etc.* [2] ▶ ❶ **S. 113** (Verlags~) [publisher's] editor

Lektorat /lɛkto'ra:t/ *das;* **~[e]s, ~e** [1] (Hochschulw.) post of 'Lektor' [2] (im Verlag) editorial department

Lektorin *die;* **~, ~nen** ▶ **Lektor**

Lektüre /lɛk'ty:rə/ *die;* **~, ~n** [1] reading; **bei der ~ des Romans** when reading the novel [2] (Lesestoff) reading [matter]; **etw. als ~/als leichte ~ empfehlen** recommend sth. as a good read/as light reading; **nicht die richtige ~ für den Urlaub** not the right thing to read while on holiday; **das ist keine passende ~ für dich** that is not suitable reading for you

Lemma /'lɛma/ *das;* **~s, ~ta** (Sprachw.) lemma; headword

Lemming /'lɛmɪŋ/ *der;* **~s, ~e** (Zool.) lemming

Lemure /le'mu:rə/ *der;* **~n, ~n** [1] (Myth.) **die ~n** the lemures [2] (Zool.) lemur

Lende /'lɛndə/ *die;* **~, ~n** ▶ ❶ **S. 435** loin

lenden-, Lenden-: ~braten *der* (Kochk.) roast loin; (vom Rind) sirloin steak; **~gegend** *die* ▶ ❶ **S. 435** loins *pl.*; lumbar region (Anat.); **~lahm** *Adj.* [1] (kreuzlahm) **[furchtbar] ~lahm sein** be bent double with backache; [2] (fig.) crippled; feeble, lame ‹*excuse*›; **~schurz** *der* loincloth; **~stück** *das* (Kochk.) piece of loin; **~wirbel** *der* ▶ ❶ **S. 435** (Anat.) lumbar vertebra

Leninismus /leni'nɪsmʊs/ *der;* **~:** Leninism *no art.*

Leninist *der;* **~en, ~en, Leninistin** *die;* **~, ~nen** Leninist

leninistisch *Adj.* Leninist

Lenk·achse *die* (Eisenb.) pivot axle

lenkbar *Adj.* [1] (Technik) **leicht/schwer ~ sein** be easy/difficult to steer; (kontrollierbar) be easy/difficult to control [2] (von Menschen) acquiescent; obedient; manageable, controllable ‹*child*›

Lenk·drachen *der* guided kite

lenken /'lɛŋkn̩/ *tr. V.* [1] *auch itr.* steer ‹*car, bicycle, etc.*›; be at the controls of ‹*aircraft*›; guide ‹*missile*›; (fahren) drive ‹*car etc.*›; **wenn du geschickt lenkst** if you do some crafty steering [2] direct, guide ‹*thoughts etc.*› (**auf** + *Akk.* to); turn ‹*attention*› (**auf** + *Akk.* to); steer ‹*conversation*›; **die Diskussion auf etw./jmdn. ~:** steer *or* bring the discussion round to sth./sb.; **den Verdacht auf jmdn. ~:** throw suspicion on sb.; **seine Blicke auf jmdn. ~:** turn one's gaze on sb.; **seine Schritte gen Bahnhof/heimwärts ~** (geh., scherzh.) direct one's steps towards the station/wend one's way homewards [3] (kontrollieren) control ‹*person, press, economy*›; rule, govern ‹*state*›; **die ~de Hand** the guiding hand; **eine gelenkte Wirtschaft** a planned economy

Lenker *der;* **~s, ~** [1] (Lenkstange) handlebars *pl.*; (Lenkrad) steering wheel; **sich** (*Dat.*) **den goldenen ~ verdienen** (ugs. spött.) win the prize for bootlicking [2] (Fahrer) driver [3] (fig. geh.) director; controller; (eines Staates) captain

Lenker-: ~band *das* handlebar tape; **~hörnchen** *das* bar end

Lenkerin *die;* **~, ~nen** ▶ **Lenker 2, 3**

Lenker·vorbau *der* stem

Lenk-: ~flug·körper *der* (Waffent.) guided missile; **~rad** *das* steering wheel; **jmdm. ins ~rad greifen** grab the steering wheel from sb.; **~rad·schaltung** *die* (Kfz-W.) steering column gear change (Brit.) *or* (Amer.) gearshift; **~rad·schloss, *~rad·schloß** *das* (Kfz-W.) steering [wheel] lock; **~säule** *die* (Kfz-W.) steering column; **~stange** *die* handlebars *pl.*

Lenkung *die;* **~, ~en** [1] (Leitung) control; (eines Staates) ruling *no indef. art.*; governing *no indef. art.* [2] (Kfz-W.) steering

Lenz /lɛnts/ *der;* **~es, ~e** (dichter. veralt.) spring; **der ~ ist da!** spring is here!; **der ~ des Lebens** (fig.) the springtime of life; **einen sonnigen** *od.* **ruhigen** *od.* **faulen ~ haben** *od.* **schieben** (salopp) have an easy time of it; (eine leichte Arbeit haben) have a cushy job (coll.); **sich** (*Dat.*) **einen schönen ~ machen** (salopp) take it easy; **sie zählt erst 15 ~e** she is a girl of only 15 summers (literary)

lenzen (Seemannsspr.)

A *tr. V.* bail out ‹*boat, water*›; (mit Pumpe) pump out ‹*water, bilge*›

B *itr. V.* scud [under light sail]

Lenz·pumpe *die* (Seemannsspr.) bilge pump

Leopard /leo'part/ *der;* **~en, ~en** leopard

Lepra /'le:pra/ *die;* **~:** leprosy *no art.*

Lepra·kranke *der/die* leper

leprös /le'prø:s/ *Adj.* leprous

leptosom /lɛpto'zo:m/ *Adj.* (Med., Anthrop.) leptosome; leptosomatic

Lerche /'lɛrçə/ *die;* **~, ~n** lark

lernbar *Adj.* learnable; **das ist [für jeden] ~:** that can be learnt [by anybody]; **leicht ~:** easy to learn *pred.*

lern-, Lern-: ~begier *die,* **~begierde** *die* eagerness to learn; **~begierig** *Adj.* eager to learn *postpos.*; **~behindert** *Adj.* (Päd.) with learning difficulties *postpos., not pred.*; **~behinderte** *der/die* slow learner; child with learning difficulties; **~eifer** *der* eagerness to learn

lernen /'lɛrnən/

A *itr. V.* study; (als Berufsausbildung) train; **gut/schlecht ~:** be a good/poor learner *or* pupil; (fleißig/nicht fleißig sein) work hard/not work hard [at school]; **leicht ~:** find it easy to learn; find school work easy; **mit jmdm. ~** (ugs.) help sb. with his/her [school] work; **auf etw.** (*Akk.*) **~** (ugs.) train to be sth.

B *tr. V.* [1] learn (**aus** from); **schwimmen/sprechen ~:** learn to swim/talk; **Trompete/Klavier ~:** learn to play the trumpet/piano; **er/mancher lernt es nie** (ugs.) he/some people [will] never learn; **von ihm kann man noch was ~:** you can learn a thing or two from him; **das will gelernt sein** that is something one has to learn; **gelernt ist gelernt** once learnt, never forgotten; **das Fürchten ~:** find out what it is to be afraid [2] **einen Beruf ~:** learn a trade; **Maurer/Bäcker** *usw.* **~:** train to be *or* as a bricklayer/baker *etc.*; **sie hat Friseurin gelernt** she trained as a hairdresser

Lernende *der/die; adj. Dekl.* ▶ **Lehrende**

Lerner *der;* **~s, ~, Lernerin** *die;* **~, ~nen** (Sprachw.) learner

lern-, Lern-: ~fabrik *die* (abwertend) swotting factory (Brit.); cramming mill (Amer.); **~fähig** *Adj.* able to learn *pred.*; capable of learning *pred.*; **~hilfe** *die* aid to learning; **~mittel** *das* learning aid; (Lehrmittel) teaching aid; **~mittel** *Pl.* teaching materials; **~mittel·freiheit** *die* free provision of teaching materials; **~prozess, *~prozeß** *der* learning process; **~psychologie** *die* psychology of learning; **~schwester** *die* student nurse; **~software** *die* educational software; **~ziel** *das* [educational] aim

Les·art /'le:s-/ *die* [1] (Fassung) variant [2] (Deutung) interpretation; reading

lesbar *Adj.* [1] legible [2] (klar) lucid ‹*style*›; (verständlich) comprehensible; **gut ~:** easy to read; very readable

Lesbe /'lɛsbə/ *die;* **~, ~n** (ugs.) Lesbian; dyke (sl.)

Lesben·bewegung *die* gay women's movement

Lesbierin /'lɛsbi̯ərɪn/ *die;* **~, ~nen** Lesbian

lesbisch *Adj.* Lesbian; **~ sein** be a Lesbian/Lesbians

Lese /'le:zə/ *die;* **~, ~n** [1] (Weinernte) grape harvest [2] (geh.: Auswahl) selection

Lese-: reading …

Lese-: ~abend *der* [evening] reading; **einen ~abend geben** read from one's works; **~automat** *der* ▶ **~gerät**; **~brille** *die* reading glasses *pl.*; **~buch** *das* reader; **~exemplar** *das* reading copy; (noch ungebunden) proof copy; **~gerät** *das* (DV) reader; **~hunger** *der* appetite for reading matter; **~lampe** *die* reading lamp; **~maschine** *die* ▶ **~gerät**

lesen[1]

A *unr. tr., itr. V.* [1] read; **sie las in der Zeitung/in einem Buch** she was reading the paper/a book; **er hat wochenlang an dem Buch ge~:** he has been reading the book for weeks; **er liest aus seinem neuesten Werk** he is reading from his latest work; **ein Gesetz [zum ersten Mal] ~** (Parl.) give a bill a [first] reading; **die/eine Messe ~:** say Mass/a Mass; **hier ist zu ~, dass …** it says here that …; **der Text ist so zu ~, dass …** the text is to be taken as meaning that …; *s. auch* **Leviten** [2] (entnehmen) tell (**in** + *Dat.*, **aus** from); **in seiner Miene war Verbitterung zu ~:** there were signs of bitterness in his expression; **aus den Zeilen konnte man gewisse Zweifel ~:** reading between the lines, one could make out certain doubts; **Gedanken ~ können** be a mind-reader; **jmds. Gedanken ~:** read sb.'s mind *or* thoughts; **aus der Hand ~:** read palms; **sich**

(Dat.) **aus der Hand ~ lassen** have one's palm *or* hand read **3** (Hochschulw.) lecture (**über** + *Akk.* on); **er liest neue Geschichte/Völkerrecht** he lectures on modern history/international law

B *unr. refl. V.* read; **es liest sich leicht/schnell** it is easy/quick to read; **es liest sich sehr unterhaltsam** it's a very entertaining read

lesen² *unr. tr. V.* **1** (sammeln, pflücken) pick ‹*grapes, berries, fruit*›; gather ‹*firewood*›; **Ähren ~:** glean [ears of corn] **2** (aussondern) pick over

lesens·wert *Adj.* worth reading *postpos.*

Leser *der;* **~s, ~:** reader

Leser·analyse *die* readership survey

Lese·ratte *die* (ugs. scherzh.) bookworm; voracious reader

Leser·brief *der* reader's letter; **~e** readers' letters; **„~e"** (Zeitungsrubrik) 'Letters to the editor'

Leserin *die;* **~, ~nen** reader

Leser·kreis *der* readership

leserlich

A *Adj.* legible

B *adv.* legibly

Leserschaft *die;* **~:** readership

Leser-: ~wunsch *der* reader's request; **~wünsche** readers' requests; **~zahl** *die* circulation; (**~kreis**) readership; **~zuschrift** *die* reader's letter; **~zuschriften** readers' letters (**zu** in response to)

Lese-: ~saal *der* reading room; **~stoff** *der* reading matter; **~wut** *die* craving to read; **~zeichen** *das* (auch DV) bookmark; **~zirkel** *der: commercial enterprise which supplies a selection of magazines on a regular loan basis to subscribers*

Lesung *die;* **~, ~en** **1** (auch Parl.) reading **2** (christl. Kirche) lesson

Lethargie /letar'gi:/ *die;* **~:** lethargy

lethargisch

A *Adj.* lethargic

B *adv.* lethargically

Lette /'lɛtə/ *der;* **~n, ~n** Latvian; Lett

Letter *die;* **~, ~n** **1** letter **2** (Druckw.) character; sort (as tech. term)

Lettin *die;* **~, ~nen** ▸**Lette**

lettisch *Adj.* ▸ⓘ **S. 670** Latvian; Lettish ‹*language*›

Lettland (*das*); **~s** Latvia

Lettner /'lɛtnɐ/ *der;* **~s, ~** (Archit.) choir screen

Letzt /'lɛtst/ *in* **zu guter ~:** in the end; (endlich) at long last

letzt... *Adj.* **1** ▸ⓘ **S. 165,** ▸ⓘ **S. 816** last; **die ~e Reihe** the back row; **auf dem ~en Platz sein** be [placed] last; (während des Rennens) be in last place; (in einer Tabelle) be in bottom place; **er war** *od.* **wurde Letzter, er ging als Letzter durchs Ziel** he came last; **~er Mann** (bes. Fußball) back; **der/die Letzte sein** be the last; **als Letzter aussteigen** be the last [one] to get off; **er ist der Letzte, dem ich das sagen würde** he's the last person I would tell [about it]; **am Letzten [des Monats]** on the last day of the month; **im ~en Moment** at the last moment; **die Letzten werden die Ersten sein** (Spr.) the last shall be first; **das ist mein ~es Wort/Angebot** that is my last word [on the subject]/my final offer; **mein ~es Geld** the last of my money; **ist das dein ~es Geld?** is that all the money you have left?; **mit ~er Kraft** gathering all his/her remaining strength; **~en Endes** in the end; when all is said and done; **jmds./die ~e Rettung sein** (fig.) be sb.'s/the last hope; *s. auch* **Ölung; Wille** **2** (äußerst...) ultimate; **jmdm. das Letzte an ...** (*Dat.*) **abverlangen** demand of sb. the utmost *or* maximum ...; **das Letzte hergeben** give one's all; **bis aufs Letzte** totally; (finanziell) down to the last penny; **bis ins Letzte** down to the last detail; **bis zum Letzten** to the utmost **3** (gerade vergangen) last; (neuest...) latest ‹*news*›; **in den ~en Wochen/Jahren** in the last few weeks/in recent years; **in der ~en Zeit** recently; *s. auch* **Schrei** **4** (ugs. abwertend) (schlechtest...) worst; (entsetzlichst...) most dreadful; **er ist der ~e Mensch** he is the lowest of the low; **die Show war das Letzte** (ugs.) the show was the end (coll.) *or* the pits (coll.); **das ist doch das Letzte!** (ugs.) that really is the limit!; *s. auch* **Dreck 2**

***letzte·mal** ▸**Mal¹**

letzt·endlich *Adv.* in the end; (schließlich doch) ultimately

***letzten·mal** ▸**Mal¹**

letztens /'lɛtstn̩s/ *Adv.* **1** (kürzlich) recently **2** **drittens/viertens und ~:** thirdly/fourthly and lastly

letzter... *Adj.* latter; **Letzteres** *od.* **das Letztere trifft hier zu** the latter is the case here

letzt·genannt *Adj.* last-mentioned; last-named ‹*person*›

letzt·hin *Adv.* **1** (kürzlich) recently **2** (schließlich doch) ultimately

letztlich *Adv.* ultimately; in the end

letzt-: ~mals *Adv.* the last time; **er hat ~mals vor fünf Jahren teilgenommen** the last time he took part was five years ago; **~möglich** *Adj.* latest possible; **~willig** **A** *Adj.* in his/her/the will *postpos.*; **~willige Verfügung** last will and testament; **B** *adv.* in his/her/the will

Leu /lɔy/ *der;* **~en, ~en** (dichter. veralt.) lion

Leucht-: ~boje *die* (Seew.) light buoy; **~bombe** *die* parachute flare; **~buchstabe** *der* neon-sign letter; **~diode** *die* light-emitting diode; LED

Leuchte /'lɔyçtə/ *die;* **~, ~n** **1** light; **hast du eine ~?** have you got a torch? **2** (fig. ugs.) **[in Mathe** *usw.***] eine ~ sein** be brilliant *or* shine [at maths *etc.*]; **er ist eine ~ auf diesem Gebiet** he is a leading light in this field

leuchten *itr. V.* **1** ‹*moon, sun, star, etc.*› be shining; ‹*fire, face*› glow; **grell ~:** give a glaring light; glare; **in der Sonne ~:** ‹*hair, sea, snow*› gleam in the sun; ‹*mountains etc.*› glow in the sun; **golden ~:** have a golden glow; **seine Augen leuchteten vor Freude** (fig.) his eyes were shining *or* sparkling with joy **2** shine a/the light; **jmdm. ~:** light the way for sb.; **mit etw. in etw.** (*Akk.*) **~:** shine sth. into sth.; **jmdm. mit etw. ins Gesicht ~:** shine sth. into sb.'s face

leuchtend *Adj.* **1** shining ‹*eyes*›; brilliant, luminous ‹*colours*›; bright ‹*blue, red, etc.*›; **grell ~:** glaring; **sanft ~:** softly glowing; **etw. in den ~sten Farben schildern** (fig.) paint sth. in glowing colours **2** (großartig) shining ‹*example*›

Leuchter *der;* **~s, ~:** candelabrum; (für eine Kerze) candlestick; (Kron~) chandelier

Leucht-: ~erscheinung *die* (bes. Astron.) luminous phenomenon; **~farbe** *die* luminous paint; **~feuer** *das* (Seew.) beacon; light; (Flugw.) runway light; **~gas** *das* ▸**Stadtgas**; **~geschoss, *~geschoß** *das* ▸**~kugel**; **~käfer** *der* firefly; (Glühwürmchen) glow-worm; **~kraft** *die* **1** brilliance; **2** (Astron.) luminosity; **~kugel** *die* flare; **~pistole** *die* flare pistol; **~rakete** *die* rocket flare; **~reklame** *die* neon [advertising] sign; **~röhre** *die* neon tube; **~schrift** *die* neon letters *pl.*; (Schild) neon sign; **~spur·geschoss, *~spur·geschoß** *das* tracer bullet; **~stoff** *der* (Physik) fluorescent substance; (nachleuchtend) luminous substance; **~stoff·lampe** *die* fluorescent light *or* lamp; **~stoff·röhre** *die* fluorescent tube; (für **~reklame**) neon tube; **~tonne** *die* light buoy; **~turm** *der* lighthouse; **~turm·wärter** *der*, **~turm·wärterin** *die* lighthouse keeper; **~zeiger** *der* luminous hand; **~ziffer** *die* luminous numeral; **~ziffer·blatt** *das* luminous dial

leugnen /'lɔygnən/

A *tr. V.* deny; **er leugnete die Tat/das Verbrechen** he denied doing the deed/committing the crime; **er leugnet, daran beteiligt zu sein** *od.* **dass er daran beteiligt ist** he denies being involved *or* that he is involved in it; **es ist nicht zu ~:** it is undeniable

B *itr. V.* deny it; (alles ~) deny everything; **er leugnet noch** he still denies doing it *or* that he did it

Leugnung *die;* **~, ~en** denial

Leukämie /lɔykɛ'mi:/ *die;* **~, ~n** ▸ⓘ **S. 439** (Med.) leukaemia

leukämisch *Adj.* (Med.) leukaemic; ‹*symptoms*› of leukaemia

Leukoplast Ⓦⓩ /lɔyko'plast/ *das* sticking plaster (*containing zinc oxide*)

Leukozyt /lɔyko'tsy:t/ *der;* **~en, ~en** ▸ⓘ **S. 435** (Anat.) leucocyte

Leumund /'lɔymʊnt/ *der;* **~[e]s** (geh.) reputation; **den guten ~ verlieren** lose one's good name; **jmdm. einen guten ~ bescheinigen** vouch for sb.'s good character

Leumunds·zeugnis *das* **1** (geh.) character reference (**über** + *Akk.* for) **2** (schweiz. Rechtsspr.) ▸**Führungszeugnis**

Leutchen /'lɔytçən/ *Pl.* (ugs.) people; *s. auch* **Leute 2**

Leute /'lɔytə/ *Pl.* **1** people; **die reichen/alten ~:** the rich/the old; **wir sind hier bei feinen ~n** we are in a respectable household; **die kleinen ~:** the ordinary people; the man *sing.* in the street; **was werden die ~ sagen?** (ugs.) what will people say?; **wir sind geschiedene ~:** our ways have parted; we have parted company; (in Zukunft) I will have no more to do with you/him *etc.*; **unter ~ gehen** mix with people; **vor allen ~n** in front of everybody; **hier ist es ja nicht wie bei armen ~n** (scherzh.) we're not in the poorhouse *or* (Amer.) on the breadline yet; **unter die ~ bringen** (ugs.) spread ‹*rumour*›; tell everybody about ‹*suspicions etc.*›; *s. auch* **Kind** **2** (ugs.: als Anrede) **auf, [ihr] ~!** come on, everybody! (coll.); c'mon, folks! (Amer.); **~, ~!** oh dear! **3** (ugs.: Arbeiter) people; (Milit.: Soldaten) men; **die Hälfte der ~:** half the staff **4** (landsch. ugs.: Familie) **meine ~:** my family *sing. or* (coll.) folks **5** (veralt.: Gesinde) servants

Leute·schinder *der*, **Leute·schinderin** *die* (abwertend) slave driver

Leutnant /'lɔytnant/ *der;* **~s, ~s** *od. selten:* **~e** ▸ⓘ **S. 44** second lieutenant (Milit.); **~ zur See** sub lieutenant (Brit.); lieutenant junior grade (Amer.)

leut·selig

A *Adj.* affable

B *adv.* affably

Leut·seligkeit *die* affability

Levante /le'vantə/ *die;* **~** (geh.) the Levant

Levantiner /levan'ti:nɐ/ *der;* **~s, ~, Levantinerin** *die;* **~, ~nen** ≈ Levantine (arch.) (*person from the middle east with a European father and Middle Eastern mother*)

levantinisch /levan'ti:nɪʃ/

A *Adj.* Levantine (arch.); (des Nahen Ostens) Middle Eastern

B *adv.* in Levantine (arch.)/Middle Eastern fashion

Leviat[h]an /le'vja:tan/ *der;* **~s, ~e** (Myth.) leviathan

Leviten /le'vi:tn̩/ *Pl. in* **jmdm. die ~ lesen** (ugs.) read sb. the Riot Act (coll.)

Levkoje /lɛf'ko:jə/ *die;* **~, ~n** (Bot.) stock

Lex /lɛks/ *die;* **~, Leges** /'le:ge:s/ (Parl.) **die ~ Heinze** the Heinze Act

Lexem /lɛ'kse:m/ *das;* **~s, ~e** (Sprachw.) lexeme

Lexik /'lɛksɪk/ *die;* **~** (Sprachw.) lexicon

lexikalisch /lɛksi'ka:lɪʃ/ (auch Sprachw.)

A *Adj.* lexical

B *adv.* lexically

lexikalisieren *tr. V.* (Sprachw.) lexicalize

Lexikograph /lɛksiko'gra:f/ *der;* **~en, ~en** ▸ⓘ **S. 113** lexicographer

Lexikographie /lɛksikogra'fi:/ *die;* **~:** lexicography *no art.*

Lexikographin *die;* **~, ~nen** ▸ⓘ **S. 113** lexicographer; *s. auch* **-in**

lexikographisch

A *Adj.* lexicographical

B *adv.* lexicographically; **~ gesehen** looked at from a lexicographical point of view; **~ arbeiten** work as a lexicographer

l

Lexikologie /lɛksikoloˈgiː/ *die;* ∼: lexicology *no art.*

Lexikon /ˈlɛksikɔn/ *das;* **∼s, Lexika** *od.* **Lexiken** 1 encyclopedia (+ *Gen.*, **für** of); **ein wandelndes ∼ sein** (ugs. scherzh.) be a walking encyclopedia 2 (veralt.: Wörterbuch) dictionary 3 (Sprachw.) lexicon

Lezithin, (fachspr.:) **Lecithin** /letsiˈtiːn/ *das;* **∼s, ∼e** (Chemie, Biol.) lecithin

lfd. *Abk.* = **laufend**

Lfg. *Abk.* = **Lieferung**

Liaison /liɛˈzõː/ *die;* **∼, ∼s** (geh.) liaison; (fig.: zwischen Staaten, Firmen) link; tie-up; **eine ∼ eingehen** enter into a liaison

Liane /ˈliaːnə/ *die;* **∼, ∼n** (Bot.) liana

Libanese /libaˈneːzə/ *der;* **∼n, ∼n** Lebanese; **roter ∼** (Drogenjargon) Lebanese red

Libanesin *die;* **∼, ∼nen** Lebanese; *s. auch* **-in**

libanesisch *Adj.* Lebanese

Libanon[1] /ˈliːbanɔn/ *(das) od. der;* **∼s** Lebanon

Libanon[2] *der;* **∼s** (Gebirge) Lebanon Mountains *pl.*

Libelle /liˈbɛlə/ *die;* **∼, ∼n** 1 dragonfly 2 (Haarspange) winged hairslide 3 (an Messinstrumenten) bubble tube; (Wasserwaage) spirit level

liberal /libəˈraːl/

A *Adj.* liberal; **∼ wählen** vote liberal

B *adv.* liberally; **jmdn. ∼ erziehen** give sb. a liberal education; **∼ ausgerichtet** following liberal principles *postpos., not pred.*

Liberale *der/die; adj. Dekl.* liberal

liberalisieren *tr. V.* liberalize; relax ‹*import controls*›

Liberalisierung *die;* **∼, ∼en** liberalization; (von Kontrollen) relaxation

Liberalismus /libəraˈlɪsmʊs/ *der;* **∼:** liberalism

Liberalität /liberaliˈtɛːt/ *die;* **∼** 1 liberalism; liberality 2 (Großzügigkeit) liberality

Liberia /liˈbeːria/ *(das);* **∼s** Liberia

Liberianer *der;* **∼s, ∼, Liberianerin** *die;* **∼, ∼nen** Liberian; *s. auch* **-in**

liberianisch *Adj.* Liberian

Libero /ˈliːbəro/ *der;* **∼s, ∼s** (Fußball) sweeper

libidinös /libidiˈnøːs/ *Adj.* (Psych.) libidinal

Libido /ˈliːbido/ *die;* **∼** (Psych.) libido

Librettist /librɛˈtɪst/ *der;* **∼en, ∼en, Librettistin** *die;* **∼, ∼nen** librettist; *s. auch* **-in**

Libretto /liˈbrɛto/ *das;* **∼s, ∼s** *od.* **Libretti** libretto

Libyen /ˈliːbyən/ *(das);* **∼s** Libya

Libyer /ˈliːbyɐ/ *der;* **∼s, ∼, Libyerin** *die;* **∼, ∼nen** Libyan

libysch /ˈliːbʏʃ/ *Adj.* Libyan

licht /lɪçt/ *Adj.* 1 (geh.) light; light, pale ‹*colour*›; **es war ∼er Tag** it was broad daylight; **einen ∼en Moment** *od.* **Augenblick/∼e Momente haben** (fig.) have a lucid moment/lucid moments; (scherzh.) have a bright moment/bright moments 2 (dünn bewachsen) sparse; thin; **∼es Haar haben** be thin on top; **die Reihen der alten Kameraden/der Zuschauer werden ∼er** (fig.) the ranks of old comrades are dwindling/the rows of spectators are emptying 3 (bes. Technik) **die ∼e Höhe/Weite** the [overall] internal height/width; **die ∼e Höhe/Weite einer Brücke** the headroom/span of a bridge

Licht *das;* **∼[e]s, ∼er/∼e** 1 light; **das ∼ des Tages** the light of day; **etw. gegen das ∼ halten** hold sth. up to the light; **etw. bei ∼ sehen** see sth. in daylight; **bei ∼ besehen** (fig.) seen in the light of day; **jmdm. das [ganze] ∼ [weg]nehmen** take [all] sb.'s light; **jmdm. im ∼ stehen** stand in sb.'s light; **das ∼ der Welt erblicken** (geh.) see the light of day; **ein zweifelhaftes/ungünstiges ∼ auf jmdn. werfen** (fig.) throw a dubious/unfavourable light on sb.; **∼ in etw.** (*Akk.*) **bringen** (fig.) shed some light on sth.; **jmdn. hinters ∼ führen** (fig.) fool sb.; pull the wool over sb.'s eyes; **jmdn./etw./sich ins rechte ∼ rücken** *od.* **setzen** *od.* **stellen** (fig.) show sb./sth. in the correct light/appear in the correct light; **in einem guten** *od.* **günstigen/schlechten ∼ erscheinen** (fig.) appear in a good *or* a favourable/a bad *or* an unfavourable light; **etw. in einem besseren ∼ erscheinen lassen** (fig.) put a better complexion on sth.; **etw. in einem milderen ∼ sehen** (fig.) take a more lenient view of sth.; **in ein falsches ∼ geraten** (fig.) give the wrong impression; **das ∼ scheuen** (fig.) shun the light; **ans ∼ kommen** (fig.) come to light; be revealed 2 *Pl.* **∼er** (elektrisches ∼) light; **das ∼ anmachen/ausmachen** switch *or* turn the light on/off; **mach doch ∼!** turn the light on[, will you]! 3 *Pl.* **∼er,** *auch* **∼e** (Kerze) candle; **kein** *od.* **nicht gerade ein großes ∼ sein** (ugs.) be no genius; be not exactly brilliant; **mir ging ein ∼ auf** (ugs.) it dawned on me; I realized what was going on; **sein ∼ [nicht] unter den Scheffel stellen** [not] hide one's light under a bushel; **jmdm. ein ∼ aufstecken** (ugs.) enlighten sb.; put sb. wise 4 (ugs.: Strom) electricity 5 *Pl.* **∼er** (Jägerspr.) eye

licht-, Licht-: **∼allergie** *die* (Med.) photoallergy; **∼anlage** *die* lighting installation; **∼behandlung** *die* (Med.) phototherapy; (mit Sonnen∼) sunlight treatment; **∼beständig** *Adj.* light-fast; **∼bild** *das* 1 [small] photograph (*for passport etc.*); 2 (veralt.) (Diapositiv) slide; (Fotografie) photograph; **∼bilder·vortrag** *der* slide lecture; **∼blick** *der* bright spot; **∼bogen** *der* (Elektrot.) arc; **∼brechung** *die* (Optik) refraction of light; **∼bündel** *das* beam [of light]; **∼druck** *der; Pl.* **∼∼e** (Druckw.) 1 collotype; 2 (Bild) collotype [print]; **∼durchflutet** *Adj.* (geh.) flooded with light *postpos.*; **∼durchlässig** *Adj.* translucent; **∼echt** *Adj.* light-fast; **∼echtheit** *die* light-fastness; **∼effekt** *der* light effect; **∼einwirkung** *die* effects *pl.* of light; **∼elektrisch** *Adj.* (Physik) photoelectric; **∼empfindlich** *Adj.* sensitive to light; (Chemie) photosensitive ‹*film, solution, etc.*›; **∼empfindlichkeit** *die* sensitivity to light; (Chemie) photosensitivity

lichten[1]

A *tr. V.* thin out ‹*trees etc.*›; (fig.) reduce ‹*number*›

B *refl. V.* 1 ‹*trees*› thin out; ‹*hair*› grow thin; ‹*fog, mist*› clear, lift; **die Reihen ∼ sich** (fig.) the numbers are dwindling; (im Theater usw.) the rows are emptying 2 (geh.) (heller werden) become lighter; lighten; (fig.) ‹*mystery etc.*› be cleared up

lichten[2] *tr. V.* (Seemannsspr.) **den/die Anker ∼:** weigh anchor

Lichtenergie *die* light energy

Lichter-: **∼baum** *der* Christmas tree; **∼fest** *das* (jüd. Rel.) Hanukkah; Festival of Lights; **∼glanz** *der* blaze of lights; *s. auch* **erstrahlen; ∼kette** *die* chain of lights

lichterloh /ˈlɪçtɐˈloː/

A *Adj.* blazing ‹*fire*›; fierce, leaping ‹*flames*›

B *adv.* **∼ brennen** be blazing fiercely; (fig.) ‹*heart*› be aflame

Lichter-: **∼meer** *das* sea of lights; **das ∼meer der Stadt** the sea of lights formed by the city; **∼stadt** *die* city of light

licht-, Licht-: **∼filter** *der od. das* light filter; **∼geschwindigkeit** *die* speed of light; **∼hof** *der* 1 (Bauw.) light well; 2 (Fot.) halation; **∼hupe** *die* headlight flasher; **die ∼hupe betätigen** flash [one's lights]; **∼jahr** *das* (Astron.) light year; **∼kegel** *der* beam; (Physik) cone of light; **∼leitung** *die* (ugs.) lighting wire; **die ∼leitungen** the wiring for the lights; **∼los** *Adj.* dark; poorly lit; **∼mangel** *der* lack of light; **∼maschine** *die* (Kfz-W.) (mit Gleichstrom) dynamo; (mit Wechselstrom) alternator; generator (esp. Amer.); **∼mast** *der* lamp standard; **∼mess,** ***∼meß** *(das);* **∼∼** (kath. Kirche) Candlemas; **[das Fest] Mariä ∼mess** [the Feast of the] Purification of the Virgin Mary; **∼nelke** *die* campion; **∼orgel** *die* colour organ; clavilux; **∼pause** *die* photostat (*Brit.* ®) (*of transparent original*); **∼punkt** *der* spot of light; **∼quant** *das* (Physik) light quantum; **∼quelle** *die* light source; **∼reklame** *die* neon [advertising] sign; **∼satz** *der* (Druckw.) filmsetting; **∼schacht** *der* light shaft; **∼schalter** *der* light switch; **∼schein** *der* gleam [of light]; (∼strahl) beam of light; **∼scheu** *Adj.* 1 shade-loving ‹*plant*›; ‹*animal*› that shuns the light; 2 (fig.) shady ‹*riff-raff*›; **∼schranke** *die* photoelectric beam; **∼schutzfaktor** *der* protection factor (*against sunburn*); **∼seite** *die* bright *or* good side; **alles hat seine ∼- und Schattenseiten** everything has its good and bad sides; **∼setz·maschine** *die* (Druckw.) filmsetting machine; **∼spielhaus** *das,* **∼spiel·theater** *das* (geh.) cinema; picture theatre (dated); movie house (Amer.); **∼stark** *Adj.* (Fot.) fast ‹*lens*›; **∼stärke** *die* 1 (Physik) luminous intensity; 2 (Fot.) speed (of a lens); **∼strahl** *der* beam [of light]; **∼undurchlässig** *Adj.* lightproof

Lichtung *die;* **∼, ∼en** clearing; **auf dieser ∼:** in this clearing

Licht-: **∼verhältnisse** *Pl.* light conditions; **∼wechsel** *der* (Astron.) light-variation; **∼zeichen** *das* light signal

Lid /liːt/ *das;* **∼[e]s, ∼er ▸❶ S. 435** eyelid

Lid-: **∼schatten** *der* eyeshadow; **∼strich** *der* line drawn with eyeliner pencil; eyelining *no indef. art.*

lieb /liːp/

A *Adj.* 1 (∼evoll) kind ‹*words, gesture*›; **viele ∼e Grüße [an …** (*Akk.*)**]** much love [to …] (coll.); **sei so ∼ und hilf mir beim Aufräumen** be a dear and help me clear up; **das ist ∼ von dir** it's sweet of you

2 (∼enswert) likeable; nice; (stärker) lovable, sweet ‹*child, girl, pet*›; **seine Frau/ihr Mann ist sehr ∼:** his wife/her husband is a dear; **sie hat ein ∼es Gesicht** she has a sweet *or* charming face; **∼ aussehen** look sweet *or* (Amer.) cute

3 (artig) good, nice ‹*child, dog*›; **die Kinder könnten etwas ∼er sein** the children could be a little better behaved; **sei schön ∼!** be a good girl/boy!; **sich bei jmdm. ∼ Kind machen** (ugs. abwertend) get on the right side of sb.; **bei jmdm. ∼ Kind sein** (ugs. abwertend) be sb.'s pet *or* favourite

4 (geschätzt) dear; **sein ∼stes Spielzeug** his favourite toy; **∼er Hans/∼e Else/∼e Oma!** (am Briefanfang) dear Hans/Else/Grandma; **∼e Karola, ∼er Ernst!** (am Briefanfang) dear Karola and Ernst; **∼er Gott** dear God; **der ∼e Gott** the Good Lord; **die ∼e Verwandtschaft** (iron.) my/our/your/their *etc.* dear relations (iron.); **sie ist mir ∼ und teuer** *od.* **wert** she is very dear to me; **wenn dir dein Leben ∼ ist, …** if you value your life …; **eine ∼ gewordene Gewohnheit ablegen** give up a habit of which one has grown very fond; **ein ∼ gewordener Gegenstand** a much loved object; **das ∼e Geld** (iron.) the wretched money; **den ∼en langen Tag** (ugs.) all the livelong day; **so manches ∼e Mal, so manch ∼es Mal** (veralt.) many a time; **meine Lieben** (Familie) my people; my nearest and dearest (joc.); (als Anrede) [you] good people; (an Familie usw.) my dears; **meine Liebe** my dear; (herablassend) my dear woman/girl; **mein Lieber** (Mann an Mann) my dear fellow; (Frau/Mann an Jungen) my dear boy; (Frau an Mann) my dear man; (als Publikumsanrede) **∼e Mitbürgerinnen und Mitbürger** fellow citizens; **∼e Kinder/Freunde/Genossen!** children/friends/comrades; **∼e Hörerinnen und Hörer/∼e Zuschauer!** *Anreden dieser Art sind im Englischen ungebräuchlich und werden deshalb nicht übersetzt;* **∼e Gemeinde, ∼e Schwestern und Brüder!** (christl. Kirche) dearly beloved; **[ach] du ∼e Güte** *od.* **∼e Zeit** *od.* **∼er Himmel** *od.* **∼es Lieschen** *od.* **∼es bisschen** (ugs.) (erstaunt) good grief!; good heavens!; [good] gracious!; (entsetzt) good grief!; heavens above!; **mit jmdm./etw. seine ∼e Not haben** have no end of trouble with sb./sth.

5 (angenehm) welcome; **er ist uns** (*Dat.*) **ein ∼er Gast** he is a welcome visitor [with us]; **unser Besuch war ihr nicht ∼:** our visit was unwelcome [to her]; **es wäre mir ∼/∼er, wenn …** I should be glad *or* should like it/should prefer it if …; **am ∼sten wäre mir, ich könnte heute noch abreisen** I should like it best if I could leave today; **wir hatten mehr**

Schnee, als mir ~ war we had too much snow for my liking; **das wirst du noch früher erfahren, als dir ~ ist** you'll hear about it sooner than you've bargained for
6 **jmdn. ~ haben** love sb.; (jmdn. gern haben) be fond of sb.; **jmdn./etw. ~ gewinnen** grow fond of sb./sth.; **jmdn. ~ behalten** [continue to] be fond of sb.; (jmdn. weiter lieben) go on loving sb.
B *adv.* **1** (liebenswert) kindly; **das hast du aber ~ gesagt** you 'did put that nicely; **sie hat sich sehr ~ um die alten Leute gekümmert** it was very sweet the way she looked after the old people
2 (artig) nicely; **er ist ganz ~ ins Bett gegangen** he went off to bed as good as gold

lieb·äugeln *itr. V.* **1** **mit etw. ~:** have one's eye on sth.; fancy sth.; **er liebäugelt mit dem Gedanken, das zu tun** he's toying *or* flirting with the idea of doing it **2** (geh.: flirten) **mit jmdm. ~:** make eyes at sb.

***lieb|behalten** ▸ **lieb A6**

Liebchen /ˈliːpçən/ *das;* **~s, ~** (veralt.) **1** **[mein] ~:** my darling; my sweet[heart] **2** (abwertend) lady-love

Liebe /ˈliːbə/ *die;* **~, ~n** **1** love (**zu** for); **~ zu Gott** love of God; **aus ~ zu jmdm.** for love of sb.; **aus ~ heiraten** marry for love; **was macht die ~?** how's your love life?; **bei aller ~, aber das geht zu weit** much as I sympathize, that's going too far; **bei aller ~, aber ich kann das nicht** much as I'd like to, I can't do it; (Briefschluss) **in ~ dein Egon** [with] all my love, yours, Egon; **~ geht durch den Magen** (scherzh.) the way to a man's heart is through his stomach; **~ macht blind** (Spr.) love is blind (prov.); **wo die ~ hinfällt!** (ugs.) the ways of love are strange indeed; **~ auf den ersten Blick** love at first sight **2** **~ zu etw.** love of sth.; **seine ganze ~ gehört dem Meer** he adores the sea; **mit ~:** lovingly; with loving care **3** (ugs.: geliebter Mensch) love; **seine große ~:** his great love; the [great] love of his life **4** (Gefälligkeit) favour; **tu mir die ~ und warte noch** do me a favour and wait a while

liebe-, Liebe-: **~bedürftig** *Adj.* in need of love *or* affection *postpos.*; **~dienerei** /-diːnəˈrai/ *die* (abwertend) toadying; sycophancy; **~dienern** *itr. V.* toady (**bei, vor** + *Dat.* to)

Liebelei /liːbəˈlai/ *die;* **~, ~en** (abwertend) flirtation

liebeln *itr. V.* (veralt.) flirt

lieben
A *tr. V.* **1** **jmdn. ~:** love sb.; (verliebt sein) be in love with *or* love sb.; (sexuell) make love to sb.; **sich ~:** be in love; (sexuell) make love; **was sich liebt, das neckt sich** (Spr.) lovers always tease each other **2** **etw. ~:** be fond of sth.; like sth.; (stärker) love sth.; **es ~, etw. zu tun** like *or* enjoy doing sth.; (stärker) love doing sth.; **diese Pflanzen ~ Schatten** these plants like shade **3** **jmdn./etw. ~ lernen** learn to love sb./sth.
B *itr. V.* be in love; (sexuell) make love; **er ist unfähig zu ~:** he is incapable of love

liebend
A *Adj.* loving; **der/die Liebende** the lover; **eine Liebende** a woman in love; **Liebende** *pl.* lovers
B *adv.* **etw. ~ gerne tun** [simply] love doing sth.

***lieben|lernen** ▸ **lieben A 3**

liebens-, Liebens-: **~wert** *Adj.* likeable ‹*person*›; (stärker) loveable ‹*person*›; attractive, endearing ‹*trait*›; **~würdig** *Adj.* kind; charming ‹*smile*›; **seien Sie doch so ~würdig und öffnen Sie das Fenster** would you be so kind as to open the window?; **~würdigerweise** *Adv.* kindly; **~würdigkeit** *die;* **~~, ~~en** **1** kindness; **würden Sie die ~würdigkeit haben, das Fenster zu schließen?** would you be so kind as to shut the window?; **2** (Handlung, Äußerung) kindness; **jmdm. einige ~würdigkeiten sagen** (iron.) say a few choice words to sb. (iron.)

lieber
A *Adj.:* ▸ **lieb**
B *Adv.:* ▸ **gern**

liebes-, Liebes-: **~abenteuer** *das* amorous adventure; **~affäre** *die* love affair; amour; **~akt** *der* (geh.) act of love; **ein Paar beim ~akt** a couple engaged in sexual intercourse; **~bande** *Pl.* (dichter. veralt.) bonds of love; **~bedürfnis** *das* need for love; **~beweis** *der* proof *or* token of love; **~beziehung** *die* [love] affair (**zu, mit** with); **~brief** *der* love letter; **~dichtung** *die* love poetry; **~dienerin** *die* (verhüll. scherzh.) lady of pleasure; **~dienst** *der* [act of] kindness; favour; **jmdm. einen ~dienst erweisen** do sb. a kindness *or* favour; **~entzug** *der* (Psych.) withdrawal of love; **~erklärung** *die* declaration of love; **~fähig** *Adj.* capable of love *postpos.*; **~fähigkeit** *die* capacity for love; **~film** *der* romantic film; **~gabe** *die* charitable gift; (Spende) donation; **~gedicht** *das* love poem; **~geschichte** *die* **1** love story; **2** (**~affäre**) [love] affair; **~gott** *der* god of love; **~göttin** *die* goddess of love; **~heirat** *die* love match; **~hungrig** **A** *Adj.* ‹*person*› who is/was hungry for love; hungry for love *pred.*; **B** *adv.* hungry for love; **~knochen** *der* (landsch.) eclair; **~krank** *Adj.* lovesick; **~kummer** *der* lovesickness; **~kummer haben** be lovesick; be unhappily in love; **sich aus ~kummer umbringen** kill oneself for love; **~kunst** *die* art of love; **~laube** *die* (scherzh.) love nest; **~leben** *das* love life; **~lied** *das* love song; **~müh[e]** *die:* in **das ist vergebliche** *od.* **verlorene ~müh[e]** that is a waste of effort; **~nacht** *die* night of love; **~nest** *das* love nest; **~paar** *das* courting couple; [pair of] lovers; **~perlen** *Pl.* hundreds and thousands; **~roman** *der* romantic novel; **~schwur** *der* pledge of love; **~spiel** *das* love play; **~szene** *die* love scene; **~toll** *Adj.* lovecrazed; **~töter** *Pl.* (ugs. scherzh.) passion killers (sl. joc.); **~trank** *der;* **~~[e]s, ~tränke** love potion; **~trunken** *Adj.* (dichter.) intoxicated with love *postpos.*; **~verhältnis** *das* [love] affair; **~verlust** *der* (Psych.) loss of love

liebe·voll
A *Adj.* loving *attrib.* ‹*care*›; affectionate ‹*embrace, gesture, person*›
B *adv.* **1** lovingly; affectionately **2** (mit Sorgfalt) lovingly; with loving care; **sehr ~ dekoriert** decorated with much loving care

***lieb|gewinnen** ▸ **lieb A 6**

lieb·geworden ▸ **lieb A 4**

***lieb|haben** ▸ **lieb A 6**

Liebhaber /ˈliːphaːbɐ/ *der;* **~s, ~** **1** lover **2** (Interessierter, Anhänger) enthusiast (+ *Gen.* for); (Sammler) collector; **ein ~ von schönen Teppichen/Oldtimern** a lover of beautiful carpets/a vintage-car enthusiast; **ein Stück für ~:** a collector's item

Liebhaber·ausgabe *die* collector's edition; bibliophile edition

Liebhaberei *die;* **~, ~en** hobby

Liebhaberin *die;* **~, ~nen** ▸ **Liebhaber**

Liebhaber-: **~preis** *der* collector's price; **~stück** *das* collector's item; **~wert** *die* **~wert haben** be valuable as a collector's item/collectors' items

lieb·kosen *tr. V.* (geh.) caress

Liebkosung *die;* **~, ~en** (geh.) caress

lieblich
A *Adj.* **1** charming; appealing; (friedlich) peaceful; gentle ‹*landscape*› **2** (angenehm) sweet ‹*scent, sound*›; fragrant ‹*flower*›; melodious ‹*sound*›; mellow ‹*red wine*›; [medium] sweet ‹*white wine*› **3** (ugs. iron: unangenehm) **das kann ja ~ werden** this is going to be just great (coll. iron.)
B *adv.* **1** charmingly; sweetly **2** (angenehm) pleasingly; **eine ~ klingende Stimme** a sweet and melodious voice

Lieblichkeit *die;* **~** **1** charm; sweetness; (einer Landschaft) gentleness **2** (angenehme Wirkung) sweetness; (des Klangs) melodiousness; (des Dufts) fragrance; (des Rotweins) mellowness **3** (Karnevalsprinzessin) **Ihre ~:** *title given to carnival queen*

Liebling *der;* **~s, ~e** **1** (geliebte Person; bes. als Anrede) darling **2** (bevorzugte Person) favourite; (des Publikums) darling; **der ~ des Lehrers** teacher's pet; **der ~ der Nation** the nation's favourite; **ein ~ der Götter** (fig.) a darling of the gods

Lieblings- favourite

lieb·los
A *Adj.* loveless; (grausam) heartless, unfeeling ‹*treatment, behaviour*›
B *adv.* **1** without affection; **~ von jmdm. sprechen** speak unkindly of sb. **2** (ohne Sorgfalt) carelessly; without proper care

Lieblosigkeit *die;* **~, ~en** **1** (Handlung/Äußerung) unkind *or* unfeeling act/word **2** (lieblose Art) unkindness; lack of feeling; (Mangel an Sorgfalt) lack of care

Lieb·reiz *der* (geh.) beguiling charm

Liebschaft *die;* **~, ~en** [casual] affair; (Flirt) flirtation

liebst... /liːpst.../
A *Adj.:* ▸ **lieb**
B *Adv.* **am ~en** ▸ **gern**

Liebste *der/die; adj. Dekl.* (veralt.) loved one; sweetheart; **meine ~:** my dearest

Liebstöckel /ˈliːpʃtœkl/ *das od. der;* **~s, ~** (Bot.) lovage

Liechtenstein /ˈlɪçtn̩ʃtain/ *(das);* **~s:** Liechtenstein; *s. auch* **Fürstentum**

Lied /liːt/ *das;* **~[e]s, ~er** song; (Kirchen~) hymn; (deutsches Kunst~) lied; **und das Ende vom ~ ist dann, dass ...** (ugs.) and the upshot *or* net result is that...; **es ist immer das alte** *od.* **gleiche** *od.* **dasselbe ~** (ugs.) it's always the same old story; **davon kann ich ein ~ singen** I can tell you a thing or two about that; **das Hohe ~** *od.* **der ~er** (bibl.) the Song of Songs

Lieder-: **~abend** *der* [evening] song recital; (mit deutschen Kunstliedern) [evening] lieder recital; **~buch** *das* songbook; **~handschrift** *die* [medieval] song manuscript

Liederjan /ˈliːdɐjaːn/ *der;* **~[e]s, ~e** (ugs.) messy devil

liederlich /ˈliːdɐlɪç/
A *Adj.* **1** (schlampig) slovenly; messy ‹*hairstyle, person*›; slipshod, slovenly ‹*work*› **2** (verwerflich) dissolute; **ein ~es Weibsstück** (salopp abwertend) a floozie (coll.)
B *adv.* sloppily; messily; **~ angezogen sein** be slovenly dressed; **~ geschrieben** written in a slipshod manner

Liederlichkeit *die;* **~** **1** (Schlampigkeit) slovenliness **2** (Verwerflichkeit) dissoluteness

Lieder-: **~macher** *der,* **~macherin** *die* singer-songwriter (writing satirical songs mainly on topical/political subjects); **~zyklus** *der* song cycle

lief /liːf/ *1. u. 3. Pers. Sg. Prät. v.* **laufen**

Lieferant /lifəˈrant/ *der;* **~en, ~en** (Firma) supplier; (Auslieferer) delivery man; **~en werden gebeten, den Eingang im Hof zu benutzen** all deliveries via the entrance in the yard

Lieferanten·eingang *der* goods entrance; (bei Wohnhäusern) tradesmen's entrance

Lieferantin *die;* **~, ~nen** ▸ **Lieferant**: supplier; delivery woman

lieferbar *Adj.* available; (vorrätig) in stock; **sofort ~:** available for immediate delivery; **~ zum 1. 10. 2005** for delivery by 1. 10. 2005

Liefer-: **~bedingungen** *Pl.* terms of delivery; **~betrieb** *der,* **~firma** *die* supplier; **~frist** *die* delivery time; **bei Möbeln besteht eine ~frist von 6 bis 8 Wochen** there is 6-8 weeks delivery on furniture

liefern /ˈliːfɐn/ *tr. V.* **1** (bringen) deliver (**an** + *Akk.* to); (zur Verfügung stellen) supply; **wir ~ auch ins Ausland** we also supply our goods abroad *or* deliver to foreign destinations; **wir ~ nicht an Privat** we do not supply private individuals; **jmdm. etw. ~:** supply sb. with sth.; deliver sth. to sb. **2** (hervorbringen) produce; (geben) provide ‹*eggs, honey, examples, raw material, etc.*›; **den Nachweis** *od.* **Beweis für etw. ~:** provide proof of sth. **3** (austragen) **sich** (*Dat.*) **eine Schlacht ~:** fight a battle [with each other]; **jmdm. ein gutes Spiel ~:** give sb. a good game *or* match **4** (ugs.:) **geliefert sein**

be sunk (coll.); have had it (coll.)

Liefer-: ~schein *der* acknowledgement of delivery; delivery note; **~termin** *der* delivery date **~umfang** *der* (Kaufmannsspr.) scope of supply; **die Batterien gehören zum ~umfang** batteries are included [in the price]

Lieferung *die;* **~, ~en** 1 (das Liefern) delivery; **Zahlung bei ~:** payment on delivery 2 (Ware) consignment [of goods]; delivery 3 (Buchw.) instalment; (eines Wörterbuchs usw.) fascicle

Liefer-: ~vertrag *der* supply contract; **~wagen** *der* [delivery] van; (offen) pick-up; **~zeit** *die* delivery time

Liege /'liːgə/ *die;* **~, ~n** daybed; (zum Ausklappen) bed settee; sofa bed; (als Gartenmöbel) sunlounger

Liege·geld *das* (Schifffahrt) demurrage

liegen *unr. itr. V.;* (südd., österr., schweiz. mit sein) 1 lie; ‹*person*› be lying down; (sich hinlegen) lie down; **~ bleiben** ‹*person*› stay [lying]; **[im Bett] ~ bleiben** stay in bed; **bewusstlos/bewegungslos ~ bleiben** lie unconscious/motionless; **verletzt ~ bleiben** end up lying on the ground injured; **während der Krankheit musste er ~:** while he was ill he had to lie down all the time; **Weinflaschen sollen ~:** wine bottles should lie flat *or* on their sides; **die Beine sollen höher ~ als der Kopf** your legs should be [placed] higher than your head; **auf dem Boden ~:** lie on the floor; ‹*carpet*› be on the floor; **im Bett ~:** lie in bed; (das Bett hüten) be *or* stay in bed; **auf den Knien ~:** be prostrate on one's knees; **im Krankenhaus/auf Station 6 ~:** be in hospital/in ward 6; **krank im Bett ~:** be ill in bed; **der Wagen liegt gut auf der Straße** the car holds the road well; **richtig ~:** be in the right position; ‹*hair*› stay in place; **die Säge liegt gut/fest in der Hand** the saw rests comfortably/firmly in the hand
2 (vorhanden sein) lie; **es liegt Schnee auf den Bergen** there is snow [lying] on the hills; **der Schnee liegt meterhoch** the snow is more than a metre deep; **der Schnee bleibt ~:** the snow lies; **der Stoff liegt 80 cm breit** the material is 80 cm wide
3 (sich befinden) be; ‹*object*› be [lying]; ‹*town, house, etc.*› be [situated]; **etw. im Keller** *usw.* **~ haben** have sth. [lying] in the cellar *etc.*; **die Preise ~ höher** prices are higher; **die Verhältnisse ~/die Sache liegt anders** circumstances are/the situation is different; **wie die Dinge ~:** as things are or stand [at the moment]; **die Stadt liegt an der Küste** the town is *or* lies on the coast; **das Dorf liegt sehr hoch** the village is very high up; **das liegt an meinem Weg** it is on my way; **schön ~:** be beautifully situated; **ein einsam ~der Hof** an isolated farm; **verkehrsgünstig ~:** be well placed for transport; ‹*town, city*› have good communications; **etw. rechts/links ~ lassen** leave sth. on one's right/left; **das Fenster liegt nach vorn/nach Süden/zum Garten** the window is at the front/faces south/faces the garden; **es liegt nicht in meiner Absicht, das zu tun** it is not my intention to do that; **nichts liegt uns ferner, als ...** nothing could be further from our intentions than ...; **die Betonung liegt auf der ersten Silbe** the stress is on the first syllable; **das Essen lag mir schwer im Magen** the food/meal lay heavy on my stomach; **auf ihm liegt eine große Verantwortung** a heavy responsibility rests on his shoulders
4 (zeitlich) be; **das liegt noch vor mir/schon hinter mir** I still have that to come/that's all behind me now; **die Stunden, die zwischen den Prüfungen lagen** the hours between the examinations; **das liegt so weit** *od.* **lange zurück** it is so long ago
5 **das liegt an ihm** *od.* **bei ihm** it is up to him; (ist seine Schuld) it is his fault; **die Verantwortung/Schuld liegt bei ihm** it is his responsibility/fault; **an mir soll es nicht ~:** don't let me stop you; I won't stand in your way; (ich werde mich beteiligen) I'm easy (coll.); **es liegt daran, dass ...** it is because ...; **ich weiß nicht, woran es liegt** I don't know what the reason is; **woran mag es nur ~, dass ...?** why ever is it that ...?
6 (gemäß sein) **es liegt mir nicht** it doesn't suit me; it isn't right for me; (es spricht mich nicht an) it doesn't appeal to me; (ich mag es nicht) I don't like it *or* care for it; **Physik liegt ihr sehr** physics is right up her street (coll.); **solche Tätigkeiten ~ ihm [sehr]** this kind of activity suits him [down to the ground]; **es liegt ihm nicht, das zu tun** he does not like doing that; (so etwas tut er nicht) it is not his way to do that; **mit Kindern umzugehen scheint ihr nicht zu ~:** handling children doesn't seem to be her cup of tea (coll.)
7 **daran liegt ihm viel/wenig/nichts** he sets great/little/no store by that; it means a lot/little/nothing to him; **ihr liegt [einiges] daran, anerkannt zu werden** it is of [some] importance to her to be recognized; **an ihm liegt mir schon etwas** I do care about him [a bit]
8 (bedeckt sein) **der Tisch liegt voller Bücher** the desk is covered with books
9 (bes. Milit.: verweilen) be; ‹*troops*› be stationed; ‹*ship*› lie; **vor Verdun ~:** be stationed *or* positioned outside Verdun; **irgendwo [in Quartier] ~:** be quartered *or* billeted somewhere
10 **~ bleiben** ‹*thing*› stay, be left; (vergessen werden) be left behind; (nicht verkauft werden) remain unsold; (nicht erledigt werden) be left undone; **diese Briefe können bis morgen ~ bleiben** these letters can wait until tomorrow; **etw. ~ lassen** leave sth.; (vergessen) leave sth. [behind]; (unerledigt lassen) leave sth. undone; **er ließ die Papiere auf dem Tisch ~:** he left the papers [lying] on the desk; **sie hat die Briefe ~ lassen** she left the letters unopened/unposted *etc.*; **alles stehen und ~ lassen** drop everything
11 **~ bleiben** (eine Panne haben) break down; *s. auch* **Straße**

***liegen|bleiben** ▸ **liegen 1, 2, 10, 11**

liegend reclining, recumbent ‹*figure, posture*›; prone ‹*position*›; horizontal ‹*position, engine*›; **etw. ~ aufbewahren** store sth. flat/on its side

***liegen|lassen** ▸ **liegen 10**

Liegenschaft *die;* **~, ~en** (bes. Rechtsspr.) land holding; (Gebäude) property

Liege-: ~platz *der* mooring; **~rad** *das* recumbent bicycle; **~sitz** *der* reclining seat; **~statt** *die* (geh.) resting place; (Bett) bed; **~stuhl** *der* (einfach, mit Holzgestell) deckchair; (Luxusausstattung, mit Metallgestell) lounger; **~stütz** *der;* **~~es, ~~e** press-up; **~stütz machen** do press-ups; **in den ~stütz gehen** get into a press-up position; **~wagen** *der* couchette car; **wollen Sie Schlafwagen oder ~wagen?** do you want a sleeper or a couchette?; **der ~wagen ist hinten** the couchettes are at the back of the train; **~wiese** *die* sunbathing lawn

lieh /liː/ *1. u. 3. Pers. Sg. Prät. v.* **leihen**

lies /liːs/ *Imperativ Sg. v.* **lesen**

Lieschen /'liːsçən/ **~ Müller** (ugs.) the average girl/woman (coll.); **Fleißiges ~** (Bot.) busy Lizzie; *s. auch* **lieb 4**

Liese *die;* **~, ~n** (ugs. abwertend) **eine dumme ~:** a stupid cow (sl.); **eine liederliche ~:** a slovenly Sue; a messy Jessie

ließ /liːs/ *1. u. 3. Pers. Sg. Prät. v.* **lassen**

liest /liːst/ *3. Pers. Sg. Präsens v.* **lesen**

Lift /lɪft/ *der;* **~[e]s, ~e** *od.* **~s** 1 lift (Brit.); elevator (Amer.) 2 *Pl.:* **~e** (Ski~, Sessel~) lift

Lift·boy *der* lift boy (Brit.); elevator boy (Amer.)

liften[1] /'lɪftn̩/ *itr. V.; mit sein* take the [ski] lift

liften[2] *tr. V.* **die Gesichtshaut ~:** tighten the skin of the face; **sich ~ lassen** (ugs.) have a facelift

Lifting /'lɪftɪŋ/ *das;* **~s, ~s** 1 cosmetic operation; (an Gesicht) facelift; **etw. einem ~ unterziehen** (fig.) give sth. a facelift 2 (Sport: Übung) rising on tiptoe

Liga /'liːga/ *die;* **~, Ligen** league; (Sport) division; **~ für Menschenrechte** League of Human Rights

Ligament /liga'mɛnt/ *das;* **~[e], ~e** ▸ⓘ **S. 435** (Anat.) ligament

Ligatur /liga'tuːɐ̯/ *die;* **~, ~en** (Druckw., Musik, Med.) ligature; (Musik: in der modernen Notenschrift) ligature; tie

Liguster /li'gʊstɐ/ *der;* **~s, ~** (Bot.) privet

liieren /li'iːrən/
A *refl. V.* 1 **sich mit jmdm. ~:** start an affair with sb.; **mit jmdm. liiert sein** be having an affair with sb. 2 (bes. Wirtsch., Politik) ‹*firm*› form links (**mit** with); **sich [miteinander] ~** ‹*firms, countries*› form links; **mit einer Firma liiert sein** have links with a firm
B *tr. V.* (bes. Wirtsch.) **zwei Betriebe miteinander ~:** establish links between two businesses

Likör /li'køːɐ̯/ *der;* **~s, ~e** liqueur

lila /'liːla/ *indekl. Adj.* mauve; (dunkel~) purple

Lila *das;* **~s, ~** *od.* (ugs.) **~s** mauve; (Dunkel~) purple

Lilie /'liːli̯ə/ *die;* **~, ~n** 1 lily 2 (Her.) fleur-de-lis

Liliput- /'liːlipʊt-/ miniature ‹*railway, format*›; tiny ‹*house, country*›

Liliputaner /lilipu'taːnɐ/ *der;* **~s, ~, Liliputanerin** *die;* **~, ~nen** dwarf; midget

limbisch /'lɪmbɪʃ/ *Adj.* (Anat.) **~es System** limbic system

Limburger /'lɪmbʊrgɐ/ *der;* **~s, ~, Limburger Käse** *der* Limburger [cheese]

Limerick /'lɪmərɪk/ *der;* **~[s], ~s** limerick

Limes /'liːmɛs/ *der;* **~, ~** 1 (hist.) limes 2 (Math.) limit

Limit /'lɪmɪt/ *das;* **~s, ~s** limit; **das äußerste ~:** the top limit; (Termin) the latest possible date; **das ~ überschreiten** exceed the limit; (fig.) go too far; **dieses ~ kann nicht unterschritten werden** one cannot go below this minimum; **jmdm. ein ~ [bis Ende der Woche** *usw.***] setzen** set sb. a limit [of the end of the week *etc.*]

limitieren *tr. V.* limit; restrict

Limo /'lɪmo/ *die, auch: das;* **~, ~[s]** (ugs.) fizzy drink; **die Kinder kriegen ~:** the children can have pop (coll.)

Limonade /limo'naːdə/ *die;* **~, ~n** fizzy drink; mineral; (Zitronen~) lemonade

Limone /li'moːnə/ *die;* **~, ~n** lime

Limousine /limu'ziːnə/ *die;* **~, ~n** [large] saloon (Brit.) *or* (Amer.) sedan; (mit Trennwand) limousine

lind /lɪnt/ *Adj.* (dichter.) 1 (mild) balmy ‹*night, air*› 2 (sanft) gentle ‹*wind, voice*›

Linde /'lɪndə/ *die;* **~, ~n** 1 (Baum) lime [tree] 2 (Holz) limewood

Linden-: ~baum *der* lime tree; **~blüten·honig** *der* lime-blossom honey; **~blüten·tee** *der* lime-blossom tea

lindern /'lɪndɐn/ *tr. V.* alleviate, relieve ‹*suffering*›; ease, relieve ‹*pain*›; quench, slake ‹*thirst*›

Linderung *die;* **~** (der Not) relief; alleviation; (des Schmerzes) relief; **jmdm. [vorübergehend/sofort] ~ bringen** bring sb. [temporary/immediate] relief

lind·grün *Adj.* lime green

Lind·wurm /'lɪnt-/ *der* (Myth.) lindworm

Lineal /line'aːl/ *das;* **~s, ~e** ruler; **Striche mit einem ~ ziehen** rule lines; **er ging, als ob er ein ~ verschluckt hätte** he walked as stiff as a poker

linear /line'aːɐ̯/
A *Adj.* 1 (Math., Physik; auch geh.: geradlinig) linear 2 (Arbeitswelt) **~e Lohnerhöhung** phased pay rise in a series of equal steps; **~e Abschreibung** straight-line depreciation
B *adv.* 1 (Phys., geh.) linearly; in a linear manner 2 (Arbeitswelt) **die Gehälter ~ erhöhen/eine Lohnerhöhung ~ vornehmen** increase salaries/implement a pay increase in a series of equal steps

Linguist /lɪŋ'gʊɪst/ *der;* **~en, ~en** linguist

Linguistik *die;* **~:** linguistics *sing., no art.*

Linguistin *die;* **~, ~nen** linguist

linguistisch
A *Adj.* linguistic
B *adv.* linguistically

Linie /ˈliːni̯ə/ *die;* ~, ~n [1] line; **ein Kleid in modischer/strenger ~:** a dress in a fashionable/severe style *or* with fashionable/severe lines; **auf die [schlanke] ~ achten** (ugs. scherzh.) watch one's figure; **in einer ~ stehen/sich in einer ~ aufstellen** stand in line/line up; **die feindliche[n] ~[n]** (Milit.) [the] enemy lines *pl.*; **in der vordersten** *od.* **in vorderster ~ kämpfen** (Milit.) fight in the front line; **in vorderster ~ stehen** (fig.) be in the front line; **in ~ antreten** (Milit.) fall in; (Sport) line up [2] ▸ⓘ **S. 800** (Verkehrsstrecke) route; (Eisenbahn~, Straßenbahn~) line; route; **die ~ Frankfurt-London** the Frankfurt-London route; **eine ~ stilllegen** stop a service [3] (Verkehrsmittel) **fahren Sie mit der ~ 4** take a *or* the number 4; **die ~ 12** the number 12 [4] (allgemeine Richtung) line; policy; **eine ~ vertreten** take a line; **die große ~ wahren** stick to the broad principle; **eine/keine klare ~ erkennen lassen** reveal a/no clear policy; **sich auf der gleichen ~ bewegen** be on *or* along the same lines *pl.* [5] (Verwandtschaftszweig) line; **in direkter ~ von jmdm. abstammen** be directly descended from *or* a direct descendant of sb. [6] *in* **in erster ~ geht es darum, dass das Projekt beschleunigt wird** the first priority is to speed up the project; **in erster ~ kommt sein Stellvertreter infrage** his deputy is first in line; **wir müssen in erster ~ darauf bedacht sein, dass ...** our prime concern must be that ...; **Geld spielt in dieser Sache erst in zweiter ~ eine Rolle** money is only of secondary importance *or* plays only a secondary role in this matter; **auf der ganzen ~:** all along the line [7] (Seemannsspr.: Äquator) **die ~ passieren** *od.* **kreuzen** cross the line

linien-, Linien-: ~**blatt** *das* line guide; guide sheet; ~**bus** *der* regular bus; ~**dienst** *der* regular service; (Flugw.) scheduled *or* regular service; **im ~dienst fahren/fliegen** ‹bus, coach/aircraft› be used on regular routes; ~**flug** *der* scheduled flight; ~**flugzeug** *das* scheduled plane *or* aircraft; ~**führung** *die* [1] (Art des Zeichnens) linework; [2] (Gestaltung der Umriss~) lines *pl.*; ~**maschine** *die* ▸~**flugzeug**; ~**netz** *das* route network; ~**papier** *das* ruled *or* lined paper; ~**richter** *der* (Fußball usw.) linesman; (Tennis) line judge; (Rugby) touch judge; ~**richterin** *die* (Fußball usw.) lineswoman; (Tennis) line judge; (Rugby) touch judge; ~**schiff** *das* [1] liner; [2] (hist.) ship of the line; ~**treu** (abwertend) [A] *Adj.* loyal to the party line *postpos.*; [B] *adv.* ‹act› in accordance with the party line; ~**verkehr** *der* regular services *pl.*; (Flugw.) scheduled *or* regular services *pl.*; **im ~verkehr fahren/fliegen** ‹aircraft› be used on regular *or* scheduled routes

linieren /liˈniːrən/, **liniieren** /liniˈiːrən/ *tr. V.* rule; rule lines on; **lini[i]ertes Papier** ruled *or* lined paper

Linierung, Liniierung *die;* ~, ~en [1] (Vorgang) ruling [2] (Linien) [ruled] lines *pl.*

link /lɪŋk/ (salopp)
[A] *Adj.* underhand; shady, underhand ‹deal›; **ein ~er Vogel** a shady customer (coll.) *or* character; **komm mir bloß nicht auf die ~e Tour!** just don't try and pull a fast one on me (coll.)
[B] *adv.* in an underhand way

Link *der;* ~s, ~s (DV) link

link... *Adj.* [1] left; left[-hand] ‹edge›; **die ~e Spur** the left-hand lane; **~er Hand, zur ~en Hand** on the left-hand side; on the left; **auf der ~en Seite** on the left-hand side; **auf der ~en Seite gehen** walk on the left; **der ~e Außenstürmer/Verteidiger** (Ballspiele) the outside left/the left back; **mit dem ~en Fuß** *od.* **Bein zuerst aufgestanden sein** (fig. ugs.) have got out of bed on the wrong side; *s. auch* **Ehe** [2] (außen, sichtbar) wrong, reverse ‹side›; **~e Maschen** (Handarb.) purl stitches; **eine ~e Masche stricken** purl one [3] (in der Politik) left-wing; leftist (derog.); **der ~e Flügel einer Partei** the left wing of a party

Linke[1] *der/die; adj. Dekl.* left-winger; leftist (derog.); **von den ~n organisiert sein** be organized by the left

Linke[2] *die;* ~n, ~n [1] (Hand) left hand; **seine ~ einsetzen** (Boxen) use one's left; **zur ~n des Königs** on *or* to the left of the king; on the king's left; **jmdm. zur ~n** on sb.'s left; to the left of sb.; **zur ~n** on the left [2] (Politik) left

linker·seits *Adv.* on the left[-hand side]

linkisch
[A] *Adj.* awkward
[B] *adv.* awkwardly

links /lɪŋks/
[A] *Adv.* [1] ▸ⓘ **S. 800** (auf der linken Seite) on the left; (Theater) stage right; **die zweite Straße ~:** the second street *or* turning on the left; **~ von jmdm/etw.** on sb.'s left *or* to the left of sb./on *or* to the left of sth.; **von ~ kommen** come from the left; **nach ~ gehen/sich nach ~ wenden** go/turn to the left; **er wandte sich nach ~:** he turned to his *or* the left; **sich ~ halten** keep to the left; **weder nach ~ noch nach rechts schauend verließ sie den Saal** looking neither [to the] left nor [to the] right she walked out of the room; **er blickte weder nach ~ noch nach rechts, sondern rannte einfach über die Straße** he didn't look left or right, but just ran straight across the road; **sich ~ einordnen** move *or* get into the left-hand lane; **~ außen** (Ballspiele) ‹run, break through› down the left wing; **[den Ball] nach ~ außen spielen** play the ball out to the left wing; **jmdn./etw. ~ liegen lassen** (fig.) ignore sb./sth.; **ich weiß/sie wissen** *usw.* **nicht [mehr], was ~ und [was] rechts ist** (fig.) I don't know 'where I am/they don't know 'where they are *etc.* [2] (Politik) on the left wing; **~ stehen** *od.* **sein** be left-wing *or* on the left; **~ eingestellt sein** have left-wing leanings; **weit ~ stehen** be on the far left; **ganz ~ außen stehen** be on the extreme left [wing]; **nach ~ außen** to the extreme left; **~ stehend** left-wing [3] (ugs.: ~händig) left-handed; **mit ~** (fig.) easily; with no trouble [4] (Handarb.) **zwei ~, zwei rechts** two purl, two plain; purl two, knit two; **ein ~ gestrickter Pullover** a purl[-knit] pullover [5] (~seitig) **etw. von ~ bügeln** iron sth. on the wrong side *or* reverse side; **nach ~ wenden** turn ‹dress, skirt, etc.› inside out
[B] ▸ⓘ **S. 800** *Präp. mit Gen.* **~ des Rheins/der Straße** on the left side *or* bank of the Rhine/on the left-hand side of the road *or* to the left of the road

links-, Links-: ~**abbieger** *der,* ~**abbiegerin** *die* (Verkehrsw.) motorist/cyclist/car *etc.* turning left; **die ~abbieger** the traffic *sing.* turning left; **als ~abbieger musste er ...** since he was turning left he had to ...; ~**abbieger·spur** *die* (Verkehrsw.) left-hand turn lane; ~**abweichler** *der,* ~**abweichlerin** *die* (Politik) left deviationist; *~**außen** ▸**links A1, 2**; ~**außen** *der;* ~~s, ~~ [1] (Ballspiele) left wing; outside left; [2] (Politik ugs.) extreme left-winger; ~**drall** *der* [1] pull to the left; **der Tennisspieler gab dem Ball einen ~drall** the tennis player swerved the ball to the left; [2] (Waffent.) left-handed twist; [3] (Politik ugs.) tendency to the left; left-wing tendency; ~**drehend** *Adj.* [1] (bes. Technik) left-hand ‹thread›; [2] (Chemie, Physik) laevorotatory; ~**drehung** *die* (Chemie, Physik) laevorotation; ~**extremismus** *der* (Politik) left-wing extremism; ~**extremist** *der,* ~**extremistin** *die* (Politik) left-wing extremist; ~**gängig** *Adj.* ▸~**drehend 1**; ~**gerichtet** *Adj.* (Politik) left-wing orientated; ~**gewinde** *das* (Technik) left-hand thread; ~**händer** /-hɛndɐ/ *der;* ~~s, ~~, ~**händerin** *die;* ~~, ~~nen left-hander; **~händer[in] sein** be left-handed; ~**händig** [A] *Adj.* left-handed; [B] *adv.* with one's left hand; ~**händigkeit** *die;* ~~: left-handedness; ~**herum** *Adv.* [round] to the left; **etw. ~herum drehen** turn sth. anticlockwise *or* [round] to the left; ~**intellektuelle** *der/die* left-wing intellectual; ~**kurve** *die* left-hand bend; ~**lastig** *Adj.* [1] ‹ship› listing to the left; ‹car› down at the left, leaning to the left; **~lastig sein** ‹ship› list to the left, have a list to the left; ‹car› be down at the left, lean to the left; [2] (Politik ugs.) leftist; ~**läufig** *Adj.* running from right to left *postpos., not pred.*; ~**liberal** *Adj.* left-wing liberal; ~**liberale** *der/die* left-wing liberal; ~**partei** *die* (Politik) left-wing party; ~**radikal** (Politik) [A] *Adj.* radical left-wing; [B] *adv.* **eine ~radikal orientierte Gruppe** a group with a radical left-wing orientation; ~**radikale** *der/die* left-wing radical; ~**radikalismus** *der* left-wing radicalism; ~**rheinisch** [A] *Adj.* on *or* to the left of the Rhine *postpos.*; **auf der ~rheinischen Seite** on the left side of the Rhine; [B] *adv.* on *or* to the left of the Rhine; ~**ruck** *der* (Politik ugs.) shift to the left; ~**rum** *Adv.* (ugs.) ▸~**herum**; ~**seitig** [A] *Adj.* ‹paralysis› of the left side; [B] *adv.* on the left [side]; **~seitig gelähmt sein** be paralysed on *or* down the *or* one's left side; ~**stehend** ▸**links A2**; ~**steuerung** *die* left-hand drive; ~**um** /*auch:* -ˈ-/ *Adv.* (bes. Milit.) to the left; **~um kehrt!** to the left about turn!; **~um machen** do a left turn; ~**verkehr** *der* driving *no art.* on the left

linnen /ˈlɪnən/ *Adj.* (veralt.) linen

Linnen *das;* ~s, ~ (veralt.) linen

Linoleum /liˈnoːleʊm/ *das;* ~s linoleum; lino

Linol·schnitt *der* linocut

Linse /ˈlɪnzə/ *die;* ~, ~n [1] (Bot., Kochk.) lentil [2] (Med., Optik) lens [3] (ugs.: Objektiv) lens; **jmdn. vor die ~ bekommen** get sb. in front of the camera

linsen *itr. V.* (ugs.) peep; peek

Linsen-: ~**gericht** *das* lentil dish; **für ein ~gericht** (geh.) for a mess of pottage; ~**suppe** *die* lentil soup

Lipid /liˈpiːt/ *das;* ~[e]s, ~e (Chem.) lipid

Lippe /ˈlɪpə/ *die;* ~, ~n ▸ⓘ **S. 435** lip; **jmdm. nicht über die ~n kommen, nicht über jmds. ~n** (Akk.) **kommen** not pass sb.'s lips; **sie brachte es nicht über die ~n** she couldn't bring herself to say it; **jmdm. glatt von den ~n gehen** come easily to sb.'s lips; **ein fröhliches Lied auf den ~n** singing merrily; **an jmds. ~n** (Dat.) **hängen** hang on sb.'s every word; **eine [dicke** *od.* **große] ~ riskieren** (salopp) shoot one's mouth off (sl.)

Lippen-: ~**bekenntnis** *das* (abwertend) empty talk *no pl.*; **~bekenntnisse für etw. ablegen** pay lip service to sth.; ~**blütler** *der;* ~~s, ~~ (Bot.) labiate; ~**laut** *der* (Phon.) labial; ~**stift** *der* lipstick

liquid /liˈkviːt/ *Adj.* (Wirtsch.) liquid ‹funds, resources›; solvent ‹business›; **ich bin zur Zeit nicht ~:** I'm out of funds at the moment

Liquida /ˈliːkvida/ *die;* ~, **Liquidä** *od.* **Liquiden** (Phon.) liquid

Liquidation /likvidaˈt͜si̯oːn/ *die;* ~, ~en [1] (verhüll.: Tötung) liquidation [2] (Wirtsch.) liquidation *no indef. art.* [3] (Rechnung) account [4] (geh.: Tilgung) elimination; (eines Systems) abolition

liquide ▸**liquid**

liquidieren /likviˈdiːrən/
[A] *tr. V.* [1] (verhüll.: töten) liquidate [2] (Wirtsch.) liquidate [3] (Rechnung ausstellen) charge [4] (geh.: tilgen) eliminate; abolish ‹system of government›
[B] *itr. V.* (Wirtsch.) go into liquidation

Liquidierung *die;* ~, ~en ▸**Liquidation**

Liquidität /likvidiˈtɛːt/ *die;* ~, ~en (Wirtsch.) liquidity; solvency; (flüssige Mittel) liquid assets *pl.*

Liquiditäts·schwierigkeiten *Pl.* **in ~ sein** (Wirtsch.) have liquidity problems

lispeln /ˈlɪspl̩n/ *itr. V.* [1] lisp; **er hat schon immer gelispelt** he's always had a lisp [2] *auch tr.* (flüstern) whisper

Lissabon /ˈlɪsabɔn/ *(das);* ~s ▸ⓘ **S. 675** Lisbon

Lissabonner /ˈlɪsabɔnɐ/ ▸ⓘ **S. 675**
[A] *indekl. Adj.* Lisbon; *s. auch* **Kölner A**
[B] *der;* ~s, ~: inhabitant/native of Lisbon; *s. auch* **Kölner B**

Lissabonnerin *die;* ~, ~nen ▸**Lissabonner B**

List /lɪst/ *die;* ~, ~en [1] [cunning] trick *or* ruse; **zu einer ~ greifen** resort to a [cunning] trick *or* ruse; use a little cunning [2] (listige Art)

l

cunning; **mit ~ und Tücke** (ugs.) by cunning and trickery

Liste *die;* ~, ~n list; **eine ~ über etw.** (*Akk.*) **anlegen/führen** draw up/keep a list of sth.; **jmdn./etw. auf eine ~ setzen** put sb./sth. on a list; **jmdn./etw. von einer ~ streichen** take *or* cross sb./sth. off a list; **eine schwarze ~:** a blacklist

Listen-: ~platz *der* (Politik) place on the [party] list; **~preis** *der* list price; **~wahl** *die* (Parl.) list system

listig
A *Adj.* cunning; crafty
B *adv.* cunningly; craftily; **jmdn. ~ ansehen/angrinsen** look/grin at sb. slyly.

Litanei /lita'nai/ *die;* ~, ~en (Rel., auch fig. abwertend) litany; **eine ~ beten**/(abwertend) **herbeten** recite a litany

Litauen /'lɪtauən/ (*das*); ~s Lithuania

Litauer *der;* ~s, ~, **Litauerin** *die;* ~, ~nen Lithuanian

litauisch *Adj.* ▸❶ **S. 670** Lithuanian

Liter /'li:tɐ/ *der, auch: das;* ~s, ~ ▸❶ **S. 582** litre

literar·historisch ▸**literaturgeschichtlich**

literarisch /lɪtə'ra:rɪʃ/
A *Adj.* literary
B *adv.* ~ **hervortreten** emerge as a writer; **sich ~ betätigen** write; do some writing; **~ interessiert/gebildet sein** be interested in literature/be well-read

Literat /lɪtə'ra:t/ *der;* ~en, ~en, **Literatin** *die;* ~, ~nen writer; literary figure

Literatur /lɪtəra'tu:ɐ/ *die;* ~, ~en literature; **belletristische ~:** belles-lettres *pl.*; **in die ~ eingehen** find one's place in literature

literatur-, Literatur-: ~angabe *die* [bibliographical] reference; **~denkmal** *das* literary monument; **~gattung** *die* literary genre; **~geschichte** *die* literary history; history of literature; **~geschichtlich** **A** *Adj.* literary-historical; **B** *adv.* **~geschichtlich interessiert/beschlagen sein** interested/versed in literary history; **~geschichtlich gesehen** from the point of view of literary history; **~hinweis** *der* reference to further reading; **~historiker** *der,* **~historikerin** *die* literary historian; **~kritik** *die* literary criticism; **~kritiker** *der,* **~kritikerin** *die* literary critic; **~papst** *der* (iron.) leading literary pundit; **~preis** *der* prize for literature; literary prize; **~verfilmung** *die* film of the book; **~verzeichnis** *das* list of references; **~wissenschaft** *die* literary studies *pl., no art.*; study of literature; **vergleichende ~wissenschaft** comparative literature; **~zeitschrift** *die* literary magazine; (Fachzeitschrift) literary journal

liter-, Liter-: ~flasche *die* litre bottle; **~preis** *der* price per litre; **~weise** *Adv.* by the litre; in litres

Litfaß·säule /'lɪtfas-/ *die* advertising column *or* pillar

> **Litfaßsäule**
>
> The *Litfaßsäule* is an advertising column named after the printer E. Litfaß (1816-74), who gained official approval to set up the first column in Berlin in 1855. It copied the French and English idea of advertising cultural and other events in public.

Lithograph /lito'gra:f/ *der;* ~en, ~en lithographer

Lithographie /litogra'fi:/ *die;* ~, ~n **1** (Verfahren) lithography *no art.* **2** (Druck) lithograph

Lithographin *die;* ~, ~nen ▸**Lithograph**

lithographisch *Adj.* lithographic

Litotes /'li:to:tɛs/ *die;* ~, ~ (Rhet.) litotes

litt /lɪt/ *1. u. 3. Pers. Sg. Prät. v.* **leiden**

Liturgie /litʊr'gi:/ *die;* ~, ~n (christl. Kirche) liturgy

liturgisch
A *Adj.* liturgical
B *adv.* liturgically

Litze /'lɪtsə/ *die;* ~, ~n **1** braid **2** (Elektrot.) flex (Brit.); cord (Amer.)

live /laif/ (Rundf., Ferns.)
A *Adj.* live
B *adv.* live; **in dieser Sendung wird nur ~ gesungen** in this programme all the singing is live

Live-: ~bild, ~-Bild *das* live picture; **~sendung, ~-Sendung** *die* (Rundf., Ferns.) live programme; (Übertragung) live broadcast; **~show, ~-Show** *die* live show; **~übertragung, ~-Übertragung** *die* live transmission

Livius /'li:viʊs/ (*der*) Livy

Livree /li'vre:/ *die;* ~, ~n livery; **ein Diener in ~:** a liveried servant

livriert *Adj.* liveried

Lizentiat, Lizentiatin ▸**Lizenziat**[1,2], **Lizenziatin**

Lizenz /li'tsɛnts/ *die;* ~, ~en licence; **etw. in ~ herstellen** manufacture sth. under licence

Lizenz-: ~ausgabe *die* (Buchw.) licensed edition; **~gebühr** *die* licence fee; (Verlagsw.) royalty

Lizenziat[1] /litsɛn'tsia:t/ *der;* ~en, ~en (schweiz.) licentiate

Lizenziat[2] *das;* ~s, ~e (schweiz.) licentiate

Lizenziatin *die;* ~, ~nen ▸**Lizenziat**[1]

lizenzieren /litsɛn'tsi:rən/ *tr. V.* license

Lizenz-: ~spieler *der,* **~spielerin** *die* (Sport) licensed professional; **~träger** *der,* **~trägerin** *die* licensee; **~vertrag** *der* licence agreement

Lkw, LKW *Abk.* = **Lastkraftwagen** truck; lorry (Brit.)

Lkw-Fahrer *der,* **Lkw-Fahrerin** *die* truck *or* (Brit.) lorry driver; trucker (Amer.)

Lkw-Maut, LKW-Maut *die* truck toll

Lob[1] /lo:p/ *das;* ~[e]s, ~e praise *no indef. art.*; **ein ~ bekommen** receive praise; come in for praise; **[ein] ~ für etw. verdienen** deserve praise for sth.; **jmdm. ~ spenden** (geh.) bestow praise on sb.; **über jedes ~ erhaben sein** be beyond praise; **voll des ~es** *od.* **des ~es voll über jmdn./etw. sein** (geh.) be full of praise for sb./sth.; **Gott sei ~ und Dank!** (geh.) praise and thanks be to God; **ein ~ dem Küchenchef/der Hausfrau** my compliments to the chef/the hostess

Lob[2] /lɔp/ *der;* ~s, ~s (Tennis) lob

Lobby /'lɔbi/ *die;* ~, ~s lobby

Lobbyismus *der;* ~: lobbyism *no art.*

Lobbyist *der;* ~en, ~en, **Lobbyistin** *die;* ~, ~nen lobbyist

loben *tr., auch itr. V.* praise; **jmdn. für** *od.* **wegen etw. ~:** praise sb. for sth.; **jmdn./etw. ~d erwähnen** commend sb./sth.; **da lob ich mir ...** give me ... any day; what I like is ...; **das lob ich mir** good for you/him *etc.* (coll.); **„Bravo", lobte er [seinen Sohn]** 'Bravo', he said approvingly [to his son]; **er lobt gern** he is generous with his praise

lobens·wert
A *Adj.* praiseworthy; laudable; commendable
B *adv.* laudably; commendably

lobesam *Adj.* (veralt.) **Kaiser Rotbart ~:** the good Emperor Redbeard *or* Barbarossa

Lobes·hymne *die* (oft iron.) hymn of praise; **~n auf jmdn./etw. singen** *od.* **anstimmen** (fig.) sing sb.'s praises/the praises of sth.; praise sb./sth. to the skies

Lob-: ~gesang *der* song *or* hymn of praise; **~hudelei** *die* (abwertend) extravagant praise *no pl.* (**auf** + *Akk.* of)

löblich /'lø:plɪç/ *Adj.* (oft iron.) laudable; commendable

lob-, Lob-: ~lied *das* song of praise; **ein ~lied auf jmdn./etw. anstimmen** (fig.) sing sb.'s praises/the praises of sth.; **~preisen** *unr. od. regelm. tr. V.* (dichter.) praise; **~preisung** *die;* ~, ~en (dichter.) praise; **zur ~preisung Gottes** in praise of God; **~rede** *die* eulogy; panegyric; **eine ~rede auf jmdn. halten** make a speech in praise of sb.; eulogize sb.

Loch /lɔx/ *das;* ~[e]s, **Löcher** /'lœçɐ/ **1** ▸❶ **S. 374** hole; **ein ~ im Zahn/Kopf haben** have a hole *or* cavity in one's tooth/gash on one's *or* the head; **sich** (*Dat.*) **ein ~ in den Kopf** *usw.* **stoßen** gash one's head *etc.*; **das ~ in etw.** (*Dat.*) **stopfen** (fig.) plug the gap in sth.; **ein großes ~ in jmds. Geldbeutel reißen** (fig.) make a big hole in sb.'s pocket; **jmdm. ein ~** *od.* **Löcher in den Bauch fragen** (salopp) drive sb. up the wall with [all] one's questions (coll.); **Löcher in die Luft gucken** *od.* **starren** (ugs.) gaze into space; **ein ~** *od.* **Löcher in die Luft schießen** (ugs.) shoot wide; miss completely; **auf** *od.* **aus dem letzten ~ pfeifen** be on one's/its last legs; *s. auch* **saufen A 2** **2** (salopp abwertend: Wohnraum) hole **3** (salopp: Gefängnis) nick (sl.); clink (sl.); **ins ~ kommen/im ~ sitzen** be put in/be in the nick *or* clink **4** (derb: Vagina) cunt (coarse); hole (coarse) **5** (ugs.: im Billardtisch) pocket

Loch-: ~beitel *der* mortise chisel; **~billard** *das* pocket billiards; pool; **~eisen** *das* punch

lochen *tr. V.* **1** punch holes/a hole in; punch, clip ‹*ticket*›; punch [holes in] ‹*invoice, copy, bill*› (*for filing*); (perforieren) perforate **2** (DV) punch

Locher *der;* ~s, ~ **1** (auch DV) punch **2** (Beruf) keypunch operator

löcherig *Adj.* holey; full of holes *pred.*; **die Abwehr war ~** (fig.) the defence was full of gaps *or* was wide open; **sein Alibi/seine Argumentation war recht ~** (fig.) his alibi/argument was full of holes

Locherin *die;* ~, ~nen keypunch operator

löchern *tr. V.* (ugs.) **jmdn. ~:** pester sb. to death; **jmdn. ~, etw. zu tun** pester sb. to do sth.

Loch-: ~kamera *die* pinhole camera; **~karte** *die* (Technik, DV) punch[ed] card

Lochkarten·verfahren *das* punch[ed]-card system

löchrig *Adj.* ▸**löcherig**

Loch-: ~säge *die* compass saw; keyhole saw; **~stickerei** *die* broderie anglaise; **~streifen** *der* (Technik, DV) punch[ed] tape; **~zange** *die* [ticket] punch; **~ziegel** *der* (Bauw.) perforated brick

Locke /'lɔkə/ *die;* ~, ~n curl; **~n haben** have curly-hair

locken[1] *tr. V.* **1** lure; (fig.) entice (**aus** out of, **in** + *Akk.* into); **die Henne lockte die Küken** the hen called her chicks; **ein Tier aus dem Bau/in den Käfig ~:** lure an animal out of its hole/into its cage; **jmdn. in einen Hinterhalt/auf eine falsche Fährte ~:** lure sb. into an ambush/put sb. on the wrong track **2** (reizen) tempt; **es lockt mich sehr** I am very tempted; **ein ~des Angebot/Abenteuer** a tempting offer/alluring adventure

locken[2]
A *tr. V.* curl; **jmdm. das Haar ~:** curl sb.'s hair; **gelocktes Haar** curly hair
B *refl. V.* ‹*hair*› curl

löcken /'lœkn̩/ *itr. V.* **wider** *od.* **gegen den Stachel ~** (geh.) kick against the pricks

locken-, Locken-: ~haar *das* curly hair; **~kopf** *der* **1** curly hair; **2** (Mensch) curly head; **~köpfig** *Adj.* curly-haired; **~pracht** *die* (scherzh.) magnificent head of curls; **~wickler** *der;* **~~s, ~~:** [hair] curler *or* roller; **sich** (*Dat.*) **~wickler ins Haar drehen** put one's hair in curlers

locker
A *Adj.* **1** loose ‹*tooth, nail, chair leg, etc.*›; **etw. ~ machen** loosen sth.; *s. auch* **Schraube** **2** (durchlässig, leicht) loose ‹*soil, snow, fabric*›; light ‹*mixture, cake*› **3** (entspannt) relaxed ‹*position, muscles*›; slack ‹*rope, rein*›; (fig.: unverbindlich) loose ‹*relationship, connection, etc.*›; **das Seil/die Zügel ~ lassen** slacken the rope [off]/slacken the reins; **~ werden** ‹*person*› loosen up **4** (leichtfertig) loose ‹*morals, life*›; frivolous ‹*jokes, remarks*›; **sein ~es Mundwerk** (salopp) his big mouth (coll.); **ein ~er Vogel** (ugs.) a bit of a lad (coll.); *s. auch* **Hand 6**
B *adv.* **1** **~ sitzen** ‹*tooth, screw, nail*› be loose; **ein ~ sitzender Zahn** a loose tooth; **bei ihm sitzt das Geld ~ [in der Tasche]** (fig.) money

burns a hole in his pocket 2 (durchlässig) loosely; ‹bake› lightly 3 (entspannt, ungezwungen) loosely; **etw. ganz ~ machen** (ugs.) do sth. without any trouble; **sich ~ geben** be relaxed; **~ vom Hocker** (ugs.) coolly; **dieses Gesetz wird ~ gehandhabt** this law is not strictly enforced

locker-: ~|lassen *unr. itr. V.* (ugs.) **nicht ~lassen** not give *or* let up; **~|machen** *tr. V.* (ugs.) fork up *or* out (coll.); shell out (coll.); **bei jmdm. etw. ~machen** get sb. to fork up *or* fork out sth.

lockern

A *tr. V.* 1 loosen ‹screw, tie, collar, etc.›; slacken [off] ‹rope, dog leash, etc.›; (fig.) relax ‹regulation, law, etc.›; **seinen Griff ~:** loosen or relax one's grip 2 (entspannen) loosen up, relax ‹muscles, limbs›; (fig.) relax ‹attitude› 3 (auf~) loosen, break up ‹soil›

B *refl. V.* 1 ‹brick, tooth, etc.› work itself loose; **bei mir hat sich ein Zahn gelockert** one of my teeth has worked itself loose; **sein Griff lockerte sich** his grip loosened 2 (entspannen) ‹person› loosen up; (vor Spielbeginn) loosen *or* limber up; (fig.) ‹tenseness, tension› ease; **die Sitten haben sich gelockert** (fig.) morals have become *or* grown lax

Lockerung *die; ~, ~en* 1 loosening; (fig.: von Bestimmung, Gesetz usw.) relaxation 2 (Entspannung) loosening up; relaxation

Lockerungs·übung *die* loosening-up *or* limbering-up exercise

lockig *Adj.* curly

Lock-: ~mittel *das* enticement; **~ruf** *der* call; **~speise** *die* (geh.) bait; **~spitzel** *der* (abwertend) agent provocateur; **~stoff** *der* (Biol.) attractant

Lockung *die; ~, ~en* (geh.) temptation; **die ~ der Ferne** the lure of distant lands; **jmds. ~en (*Dat.*) widerstehen** resist sb.'s enticements

Lock·vogel *der* decoy; (fig.) lure; decoy

Loden /ˈloːdn̩/ *der; ~s, ~:* loden

Loden·mantel *der* loden coat

lodern *itr. V.* (geh., auch fig.) blaze; **die Flammen loderten zum Himmel** the flames leapt up to the sky; **ihre Augen loderten vor Zorn** (fig.) her eyes blazed with anger

Löffel /ˈlœfl̩/ *der; ~s, ~* 1 spoon; (als Maßangabe) spoonful; **ein ~ Zucker** a spoonful of sugar; **den ~ abgeben** (fig. salopp) kick the bucket (coll.); **mit einem goldenen** *od.* **silbernen ~ im Mund geboren sein** (fig. ugs.) be born with a silver spoon in one's mouth; **jmdn. über den ~ barbieren** *od.* **balbieren** (fig. ugs.) do (sl.) *or* swindle sb. 2 (Jägerspr.) ear; (fig.) **sperr doch die ~ auf!** (ugs.) pin your lugholes (Brit.) *or* ears back! (coll.); **jmdm. eins** *od.* **ein paar hinter die ~ geben** (ugs.) give sb. a clout round the ear; **sich (*Dat.*) etw. hinter die ~ schreiben** (ugs.) get sth. into one's head

Löffel·bagger *der* mechanical shovel; excavator

löffeln *tr. V.* spoon [up]; **sie löffelte Suppe aus der Terrine** she ladled soup from the tureen

Löffel·stiel *der* [spoon] handle

löffel·weise *Adv.* by the spoonful

Loft *das od. der; ~s, ~s* loft

log /loːk/ *1. u. 3. Pers. Sg. Prät. v.* **lügen**

Log /lɔk/ *das; ~s, ~e* (Seew.) log

Logarithmen·tafel *die* (Math.) log[arithmic] table

logarithmieren (Math.)

A *tr. V.* find the log[arithm] of

B *itr. V.* do logs *or* logarithms

logarithmisch *Adj.* (Math.) logarithmic

Logarithmus /logaˈrɪtmʊs/ *der; ~, Logarithmen* (Math.) logarithm; log

Log·buch *das* (Seew.) log [book]

Loge /ˈloːʒə/ *die; ~, ~n* 1 (Theater) box 2 (Freimaurer~, Pförtner~) lodge

Logen-: ~bruder *der* brother mason; **~platz** *der* (Theater) seat in a box; **~schließer** *der,* **~schließerin** *die* box attendant

Logger /ˈlɔɡɐ/ *der; ~s, ~* (Seew.) lugger

Loggia /ˈlɔdʒia/ *die; ~, Loggien* 1 (Balkon) balcony 2 (Archit.) loggia

Logier·besuch *der* (veralt.) house guest/guests

logieren /loˈʒiːrən/ (veralt.)

A *itr. V.* stay

B *tr. V.* (schweiz.) **jmdn. bei sich ~:** put sb. up [at one's house/flat (esp. Brit.) *or* (esp. Amer.) apartment *etc.*]

Logier·gast *der* (veralt.) house guest

Logik /ˈloːɡɪk/ *die; ~:* logic; **in der ~:** in logic

Logiker /ˈloːɡikɐ/ *der; ~s, ~,* **Logikerin** *die; ~, ~nen* 1 (Philos.) logician 2 (logisch Denkende/Denkender) logical thinker

Log-in /lɔkˈɪn/*das; ~s, ~s* (DV) login

Logis /loˈʒiː/ *das; ~* /loˈʒiː(s)/, *~* /loˈʒiːs/ 1 lodgings *pl.*; room/rooms *pl.*; *s. auch* **Kost** 2 */auch:* ˈloːɡɪs/ (Seemannsspr.) **das ~ [der Matrosen]** the crew's quarters *pl.*

logisch /ˈloːɡɪʃ/

A *Adj.* logical; **in keinem ~en Zusammenhang stehen** have no logical connection; **[ist doch] ~** (ugs.) yes, of course

B *adv.* logically

logischerweise *Adv.* logically; (selbstverständlich) naturally

Logistik *die; ~* 1 (Math.) mathematical *or* symbolic logic *no art.* 2 (Milit., Wirtsch.) logistics *pl.*; (als Fachbereich) logistics *sing.*

logistisch (Milit., Wirtsch.)

A *Adj.* logistic[al]

B *adv.* logistically

Log·leine *die* (Seew.) log line

logo /ˈloːɡo/ *Adj.* (salopp) **[ist doch] ~!** you bet! (coll.); of course!

Logo *der od. das; ~s, ~s* logo

Logopäde /loɡoˈpɛːdə/ *der; ~n, ~n* speech therapist

Logopädie /loɡopɛˈdiː/ *die; ~:* speech therapy *no art.*

Logopädin *die; ~, ~nen* speech therapist

Lohe[1] /ˈloːə/ *die; ~, ~n* (dichter.: Flamme) blaze; **die ~n** the raging flames

Lohe[2] *die; ~, ~n* tan [bark]

lohen[1] *itr. V.* (dichter.) blaze

lohen[2] *tr. V.* tan ‹hides etc.› [with tanbark]

Loh-: ~gerber *der* [vegetable] tanner; **~gerberei** *die* 1 (Betrieb) [vegetable] tannery; 2 (~gerbung) [vegetable] tanning; **~gerberin** *die* ▸**~gerber**

Lohn /loːn/ *der; ~[e]s,* **Löhne** /ˈløːnə/ 1 wage[s *pl.*]; pay *no indef. art., no pl.*; **die Löhne drücken/einfrieren** (ugs.) lower/freeze wages; **bei jmdm./einer Firma in ~ und Brot stehen** be employed by sb./a firm; work for sb./a firm; **jmdn. um ~ und Brot bringen** deprive sb. of his/her livelihood 2 (Belohnung, auch fig.) reward; **als** *od.* **zum ~ für ...** as a reward for ...; **der Verbrecher hat seinen ~ bekommen** (fig.) the criminal got his deserts *pl.*

lohn-, Lohn-: ~abbau *der* reduction in wages; **~abhängig** *Adj.* wage-earning *attrib.*; **~abhängig sein** be a wage earner; **~abhängige** *der/die* wage earner; **~abrechnung** *die* wage slip; payslip; **~arbeit** *die* (Soziol.) wage labour; **~ausfall** *der* loss of earnings; **~ausgleich** *der* making-up of wages; **[eine] kürzere Arbeitszeit bei vollem ~ausgleich** shorter working hours with no loss of pay; **~buchhalter** *der,* **~buchhalterin** *die* payroll clerk; **~buchhaltung** *die* 1 payroll accounting; 2 (Abteilung) payroll office; **~büro** *das* payroll office; **~dumping** *das* wage dumping; **~empfänger** *der,* **~empfängerin** *die* wage earner

lohnen

A *refl., itr. V.* be worth it; be worthwhile; **die Anstrengung hat sich gelohnt** it was worth the effort; **das lohnt [sich] nicht** it's not worth it; **es lohnt [sich], den Versuch zu machen** it's worth making the attempt; **das lohnt sich nicht für mich** it's not worth my while; **die Mühe hat [sich] gelohnt** it was worth the trouble *or* effort; **lohnt [sich] das?** is it worth it?; **der Film lohnt sich sehr** the film is well worth seeing

B *tr. V.* 1 (rechtfertigen) be worth; **die Ausstellung lohnt einen Besuch** the exhibition is worth a visit *or* is worth visiting; **das lohnt die Mühe nicht** it is not worth the trouble 2 **jmdm. etw. ~:** reward sb. for sth.; (vergelten) repay sb. for sth.; **Gott wird dir deine Hilfe ~** (geh.) God will reward you for your help

löhnen *tr., itr. V.* 1 (Lohn auszahlen) pay 2 (salopp: bezahlen) pay; fork out *or* up (coll.)

lohnend *Adj.* rewarding ‹task›; worthwhile, rewarding ‹occupation›; worthwhile ‹aim›; (einträglich) financially rewarding; lucrative; **das Studium dieses Buches ist wirklich ~:** this book is really worth studying; it is really worth studying this book; **die Ausstellung ist wirklich ~:** the exhibition is really worth seeing

lohnens·wert *Adj.* worthwhile *attrib.*; worth while *pred.*

lohn-, Lohn-: ~erhöhung *die* wage *or* pay increase *or* (Brit.) rise; **~forderung** *die* wage demand *or* claim; **~fort·zahlung** *die* continued payment of wages; **~gruppe** *die* wage group; **~intensiv** *Adj.* (Wirtsch.) wage-intensive; **~kampf** *der* wage dispute; **~kosten** *Pl.* wage costs; **~kürzung** *die* wage cut *or* reduction; **~liste** *die* payroll; **~nebenkosten** *Pl.* non-wage [labour] costs *pl.*; **~pause** *die* pay pause; **~pfändung** *die* garnishment [of wages]; **~politik** *die* (Politik, Wirtsch.) pay policy; policy on wages; **~-Preis-Spirale** *die* wage-price spiral; **~raub** *der* (abwertend) wage exploitation; **~runde** *die* wage *or* pay round; **~skala** *die* wage *or* pay scale

Lohn·steuer *die* income tax

Lohnsteuer-: ~jahres·ausgleich *der* annual adjustment of income tax; **~karte** *die* income-tax card

Lohn-: ~stopp *der* wage *or* pay freeze; **~streifen** *der* payslip; **~tarif** *der* wage rate; **~tüte** *die* pay packet (Brit.); wage packet

Löhnung *die; ~, ~en* 1 (Auszahlung) payment of wages 2 (Lohn) pay

Lohn-: ~zettel *der* payslip; **~zuwachs** *der* pay increase

Loipe /ˈlɔypə/ *die; ~, ~n* (Skisport) [cross-country] course

Lok /lɔk/ *die; ~, ~s* engine; locomotive

lokal /loˈkaːl/

A *Adj.* 1 (örtlich) local; **Lokales** (Zeitungsw.) local news *sing.* 2 (Gram.) of place *postpos.*

B *adv.* **jmdn. ~ betäuben** give sb. a local anaesthetic

Lokal *das; ~s, ~e* pub (Brit.); bar (Amer.); (Speise~) restaurant

Lokal-: ~anästhesie *die* (Med.) local anaesthesia; **~augenschein** *der* (österr.) ▸**Lokaltermin**; **~blatt** *das* (Zeitungsw.) local paper

lokalisieren *tr. V.* locate; (eingrenzen, Med.) localize; limit, contain ‹fire›

Lokalisierung *die; ~, ~en* location; (Eingrenzung, Med.) localization

Lokalität /lokaliˈtɛːt/ *die; ~, ~en* locality; **die ~en kennen** know the locality *or* district *or* area; **wo sind hier die ~en?** (verhüll.) where is the cloakroom? (Brit. euphem.); where's the restroom? (esp. Amer. euphem.)

Lokal-: ~kolorit *das* local colour; **~matador** *der,* **~matadorin** *die* (bes. Sport) local hero *or* favourite; **~patriotismus** *der* local patriotism; **~politik** *die* local politics *sing., no art.*; **~politiker** *der,* **~politikerin** *die* local politician; **~presse** *die* local press; **~redakteur** *der,* **~redakteurin** *die* (Zeitungsw.) local-news editor; editor of the local[-news] section; **~redaktion** *die* (Rundf., Ferns., Zeitungsw.) local-news section; **~runde** *die* round for everyone [in the pub (Brit.) *or* (Amer.) bar]; **eine ~runde ausgeben** *od.* (salopp) **schmeißen** buy a round *or* drink for everyone in the pub (Brit.) *or* (Amer.) bar; **~seite** *die* (Zeitungsw.) local page; **~teil** *der* (Zeitungsw.) local section; **~termin** *der* (Rechtsspr.) visit to the scene [of the crime]; **~verbot** *das:* **[in einer Gaststätte] ~verbot haben/bekommen** be/get banned [from a pub (Brit.) *or* (Amer.) bar]; **jmdm. ~verbot erteilen** ban sb. [from the/a pub (Brit.) *or* (Amer.) bar]; **~zeitung** *die* local [news]paper

Lok·führer *der,* **Lok·führerin** *die* ▸❶ **S. 113** ▸**Lokomotivführer**

Lokomotive /lokomo'ti:və/ *die;* **~, ~n** locomotive; [railway] engine

Lokomotiv·führer *der,* **Lokomotiv·führerin** *die* ▸❶ **S. 113** engine driver (Brit.); engineer (Amer.)

Lokus /'lo:kʊs/ *der;* **~** *od.* **~ses, ~** *od.* **~se** (salopp) loo (Brit. coll.); john (Amer. coll.)

Lokus·papier *das* (salopp) loo paper (Brit. coll.); toilet paper

Lombardei /lɔmbar'dai/ *die;* **~:** Lombardy

lombardisch *Adj.* Lombardic

Lombard·satz *der* (Bankw.) Lombard rate

London /'lɔndɔn/ *(das);* **~s** ▸❶ **S. 675** London

Londoner ▸❶ **S. 675**

A *indekl. Adj.* London

B *der;* **~s, ~:** Londoner; *s. auch* **Kölner**

Londonerin *die;* **~, ~nen** ▸**Londoner B**

Long·drink /'lɔŋdrɪŋk/ *der* long drink

Longe /'lõ:ʒə/ *die;* **~, ~n** 1 (Reiten) lunge 2 (Turnen, Schwimmen) harness

Look /lʊk/ *der;* **~s, ~s** look

Looping /'lu:pɪŋ/ *der;* **~s, ~s** (Fliegerspr.) loop; **einen ~ drehen** loop the loop

Lorbeer /'lɔrbe:ɐ̯/ *der;* **~s, ~en** 1 (Baum) laurel 2 (Gewürz) bayleaf 3 (**~kranz**) laurel wreath; **mit etw. keine ~en ernten können** (fig.) get no credit for sth.; **[sich] auf seinen ~en ausruhen** (fig. ugs.) rest on one's laurels

Lorbeer-: ~baum *der* laurel [tree]; **~blatt** *das* bayleaf; **~kranz** *der* laurel wreath

Lord /lɔrt/ *der;* **~s, ~s** lord

Lord·kanzler *der* Lord Chancellor

Lordschaft *die:* **Eure ~:** Your Lordship

Lord·siegel·bewahrer *der;* **~s, ~:** Lord Privy Seal

Lore /'lo:rə/ *die;* **~, ~n** car; (kleiner) tub

Lorenz /'lo:rɛnts/ *(der)* Lawrence; Laurence

Lorgnette /lɔrn'jɛtə/ *die;* **~, ~n** lorgnette

Lorgnon /lɔrn'jõ:/ *das;* **~s, ~s** lorgnon

los /lo:s/

A *Adj.* 1 (abgetrennt) **der Knopf ist ~:** the button has come off; **der Hund ist [von der Leine] ~:** the dog is off the leash; **jmdn./etw. ~ sein** (befreit sein von) be rid *or* (coll.) shot of sb./sth.; (verloren haben) have lost sth.; **einer Sache** *(Gen.)* **~ und ledig sein** (geh.) be totally free *or* well and truly rid of sth. 2 **es ist etwas ~:** something is *or* there is something going on; **hier ist viel/wenig/immer etw. ~:** there is a lot/not much/always sth. going on here; **was ist hier ~?** (was geschieht?) what's going on here?; (was ist nicht in Ordnung?) what's the matter here?; what's up here? (coll.); **mit jmdm./etw. ist nichts/nicht viel ~** (ugs.) sb./sth. isn't up to much (coll.); **was ist denn mit dir ~?** what's up *or* wrong *or* the matter with you?

B *Adv.* 1 come on!; (geh schon!) go on!; **auf die Plätze** *od.* **Achtung, fertig, ~!** on your marks, get set, go; **~ doch!** go on!; **nun aber ~!** [come on,] let's get moving *or* going!; **nichts wie ~!** (ugs.) let's scarper (Brit. coll.); let's beat it (coll.) 2 (ugs.: ~gehen, ~fahren usw.); **er ist mit dem Wagen ~:** he's gone off in the car; *s. auch* **losmüssen**; **lossollen**; **loswollen** 3 (ugs.: gelöst) **ich habe die Schraube/das Brett/das Rad ~:** I have got the screw out/the board/wheel off; *s. auch* **loshaben**; **loskriegen** *usw.*

-los *Adj.* -less

Los *das;* **~es, ~e** 1 lot; **etw. durch [das] ~ entscheiden** decide sth. by drawing lots; **das ~ soll entscheiden** it shall be decided by drawing lots; **das ~ hat mich getroffen** it has fallen to my lot 2 (Lotterie~) ticket; **ein halbes/ganzes ~:** a half ticket/full ticket; **das große ~:** [the] first prize; **mit jmdm./etw. das große ~ ziehen** (fig.) hit the jackpot with sb./sth. 3 (geh.: Schicksal) lot; **ihm war ein schweres ~ beschieden** his was a hard lot 4 (Wirtsch.: Maßeinheit) batch; lot; (bei Versteigerungen) lot 5 (Bau~) section

los|ballern *itr. V.* (salopp) start blazing away

lösbar *Adj.* 1 soluble, solvable *‹problem, equation, etc.›* 2 (löslich) soluble *‹substance, gas›*

los-: ~|bekommen *unr. tr. V.* get *‹string, tape, ribbon, etc.›* off; get *‹screw, nail, etc.›* out; **die Hände ~bekommen** get one's hands free; **~|binden** *unr. tr. V.* untie; **~|brechen** A *unr. itr. V.; mit sein* 1 (beginnen) *‹storm›* break; *‹cheering, laughter, etc.›* break out; 2 (abbrechen) break off. B *unr. tr. V.* break off

Lösch-: ~arbeit *die* firefighting operations *pl.;* **wir halfen bei den ~arbeiten** we helped to fight *or* to put out the fire; **~blatt** *das* piece of blotting paper; **~boot** *das* fire boat; **~eimer** *der* fire bucket; **~einsatz** *der* fire-fighting operation

löschen¹ /'lœʃn̩/ *tr. V.* 1 (aus~) put out, extinguish *‹fire, candle, flames, etc.›*; **seinen Durst ~** (fig.) quench one's thirst 2 (tilgen) close *‹bank account›*; delete, strike out *‹entry›*; extinguish, wipe out, pay off *‹debt›*; erase, wipe out *‹recording, memory, etc.›*; **die Schrift auf der Tafel ~:** clean *or* (Amer.) erase the blackboard; **im Register gelöscht werden** *‹firm, name, etc.›* be removed from the register 3 (geh.: ausschalten) switch off, turn off *or* out *‹light, lamp›* 4 (trocknen) blot *‹ink etc.›* 5 (vermischen) slake *‹lime›*

löschen² *tr. V.* (Seemannsspr.) unload

Löscher *der;* **~s, ~** 1 (Tinten~) blotter 2 (Feuer~) [fire] extinguisher

Lösch-: ~fahrzeug *das* fire engine; **~kalk** *der* slaked lime; **~kopf** *der* (Elektronik) erase head; **~mannschaft** *die* firefighting team; **~papier** *das* blotting paper; **~taste** *die* erase button; **~trupp** *der* ▸**~mannschaft**

Löschung¹ *die;* **~, ~en** (eines Kontos) closing; (einer Eintragung) deletion; striking out; (einer Schuld) extinguishing; wiping out; paying off

Löschung² (Seemannsspr.) *die;* **~:** unloading

Lösch·zug *der* set of firefighting appliances

los|donnern (ugs.)

A *itr. V.; mit sein* roar off

B *tr. V.* **„...", donnerte er los** '...', he bellowed

lose

A *Adj.* 1 (nicht fest, auch fig.) loose; **zwischen ihnen besteht nur eine ~ Bekanntschaft** (fig.) they are not closely acquainted 2 (nicht verpackt) loose *‹sugar, cigarettes, sweets, sheets of paper, nails, etc.›*; unbottled *‹drink›*; **etw. ~ verkaufen** sell sth. loose/unbottled 3 (locker) loose[-fitting] *‹clothes›* 4 (ugs.: leichtfertig) **ein ~s Mädchen** (veralt.) a loose woman; **er ist ein ~r Vogel** he is a bit of a lad 5 (ugs.: vorlaut, frech) cheeky; impudent; **einen ~n Mund haben** be a cheeky *or* impudent so-and-so (coll.); **~ Reden führen** be cheeky 6 (geh.: aufgelockert) loose *‹group, line, etc.›*

B *adv.* 1 (nicht fest, auch fig.) loosely; **~ herunterhängen** hang down loosely *or* loose 2 (locker) *‹hang, drape, etc.›* loosely

Loseblatt·sammlung *die:* **als ~** *od.* **in Form einer ~ herauskommen** be published in loose-leaf form

Löse·geld *das* ransom; **1 Million Pfund ~:** a ransom of one million pounds; **das ~ wurde in einer Telefonzelle hinterlegt** the ransom money was left in a telephone kiosk

Lösegeld·forderung *die* ransom demand

los|eisen *tr. V.* (ugs.) **jmdn./etw. von jmdm./etw. ~:** prise *or* get sb./sth. away from sb./sth.; **sich von jmdm./etw. ~:** get away from sb./sth.; **etw. bei jmdm. ~:** get sth. out of sb.

losen *itr. V.* draw lots (**um** for); **~, wer anfangen soll** draw lots to decide who will start

lösen /'lø:zn̩/

A *tr. V.* 1 remove, take *or* get off *‹stamp, wallpaper›*; **etw. von etw. ~:** remove sth. from sth.; **das Fleisch von den Knochen ~:** take the meat off the bones; **den Blick von etw. nicht ~ können** (fig.) not be able to take one's eyes off sth. 2 (lockern) take *or* let *‹handbrake›* off; release *‹handbrake›*; undo *‹screw, belt, tie›*; let *‹hair›* down; remove, untie *‹string, rope, knot, bonds›*; loosen *‹phlegm›*; ease *‹cramp›*; (fig.) ease, relieve *‹[mental] pain, tension, etc.›*; remove *‹inhibitions›*; **jmds. Zunge ~** (fig.) loosen sb.'s tongue 3 (klären) solve *‹problem, puzzle, equation, etc.›*; resolve *‹contradiction, conflict›*; solve, resolve *‹difficulty›* 4 (annullieren) break off *‹engagement›*; cancel *‹contract›*; sever *‹connection, relationship›*; **sein Arbeitsverhältnis ~:** terminate one's employment (formal) 5 (zergehen lassen) **etw. in etw.** *(Dat.)* **~:** dissolve sth. in sth. 6 (kaufen) buy; obtain *‹ticket›*

B *refl. V.* 1 (lose werden) come off; *‹avalanche›* start; **sich von etw. ~:** come off sth. 2 (sich trennen) **sich aus etw. ~:** free oneself from sth.; **das Flugzeug löste sich vom Boden** the plane left the ground; **ein Läufer hat sich vom Feld gelöst** a runner broke away from the field; **sich von seinem Elternhaus ~** (fig.) break away from one's parental home; **sich aus einer Verpflichtung ~:** free *or* rid oneself of an obligation 3 (sich lockern) *‹wallpaper, plaster›* come off *or* away; *‹packing, screw›* come loose *or* undone; *‹paint, book cover›* come off; *‹phlegm, cough›* get looser; *‹cramp›* ease; *‹muscle›* loosen up 4 (sich klären, entwirren) *‹puzzle, problem›* be solved; **sich von selbst ~** *‹problem›* solve *or* resolve itself 5 (zergehen) **sich in etw.** *(Dat.)* **~:** dissolve in sth. 6 **aus seiner Pistole löste sich ein Schuss** (geh.) his pistol went off

Los·entscheid *der:* **durch ~:** by drawing lots; (bei einem Preisausschreiben) by [making *or* having] a draw

los-: ~|fahren *unr. itr. V.; mit sein* 1 (starten) set off; (wegfahren) move off; 2 (zufahren) **auf jmdn./etw. ~fahren** drive/ride towards sb./sth.; **direkt auf jmdn./etw. ~fahren** drive/ride straight at sb./sth.; **~|gehen** *unr. itr. V.; mit sein* 1 (aufbrechen) set off; **auf ein Ziel ~gehen** (fig.) go straight for a goal; **~ gehts** let's be off; 2 (ugs.: beginnen) start; **es geht ~:** it's starting; (fangen wir an) let's go; **~ gehts** let's get started; **gleich geht es wieder ~ mit dem Lärm** the noise will soon start up again; **ich glaube, es geht ~!** (salopp) you/he, *etc.* must be kidding (coll.); 3 (ugs.: abgehen) *‹button, handle, etc.›* come off; 4 (angreifen) **auf jmdn. ~gehen** go for sb.; 5 (abgefeuert werden) *‹gun, mine, firework, etc.›* go off; **~|haben** *unr. tr. V.* (ugs.) **in seinem Beruf hat er was ~:** he's very good at his job; **~|heulen** *itr. V.* (ugs.) burst out crying; burst into tears; **~|kaufen** *tr. V.* **jmdn. ~kaufen** buy sb.'s freedom *or* release; **~|kommen** *unr. itr. V.; mit sein* (ugs.) 1 (fortkommen) get away; 2 (freikommen) get free; free oneself; (freigelassen werden) be freed; **von jmdm./etw. ~kommen** (fig.) get away from sb./get rid of sth.; **vom Alkohol ~kommen** (fig.) get off *or* give up alcohol; **er kam von dem Gedanken nicht ~:** he couldn't get the thought out of his mind; **~|kriegen** *tr. V.* (ugs.) 1 (lösen können) get *‹screw, nail, etc.›* out; get *‹lid›* off; 2 (~werden) get rid *or* (coll.) shot of; 3 (verkaufen können) get rid of; **~|lachen** *itr. V.* burst out laughing; **~|lassen** *unr. tr. V.* 1 (nicht festhalten) let go of; **der Gedanke/das Bild ließ sie nicht mehr ~** (fig.) she could not get the thought/image out of her mind; 2 (freilassen) let *‹person, animal›* go; 3 (ugs. abwertend: hetzen) **jmdn. auf jmdn./etw. ~lassen** let sb. loose on sb./sth.; 4 (ugs.: äußern) come out with *‹remark, joke, etc.›*; let out *‹curse›*; 5 (abschicken) send off *‹letter, telegram, etc.›*; **~|laufen** *unr. itr. V.; mit sein* (weglaufen) run off; (anfangen zu laufen) start running; **lauf schnell ~ und hol Brot** run out and get some bread; **~|legen** *itr. V.* (ugs.) 1 (sich stürmisch äußern) let rip; **mit Fragen ~legen** start firing questions; **wenn er ~legt** (zu reden anfängt) when *or* once he gets going *or* started; 2 (anfangen) get going *or* started; **mit der Arbeit ~legen** get down to work

löslich *Adj.* soluble; **leicht/schwer ~:** readily/not readily *or* only slightly soluble

Löslichkeit *die;* **~:** solubility

los-: ~|lösen A *tr. V.* remove; take off; B *refl. V.* *‹wallpaper›* come off; *‹trailer›* become uncoupled *or* detached; **~|machen** A *tr. V.* (ugs.) let ‹*animal*› loose; untie, undo ‹*string, line, rope*›; take out ‹*plank*›; unhitch ‹*trailer*›; **das Boot ~machen** cast off; B *refl. V.* (ugs.: sich befreien, auch fig.) free oneself (**von** from); C *itr. V.* 1 (Seemannsspr.: ablegen) cast off; 2 (ugs.: sich beeilen) get a move on (coll.); **nun mach ~, dass du fertig wirst** hurry up and get ready; **~|müssen** *unr. itr. V.* (ugs.) have to be off; have to go; **ich muss ~:** I must be off

Los·nummer *die* [lottery-]ticket number

los-: ~|platzen *itr. V.; mit sein* (ugs.) 1 burst out; **sofort platzte sie damit ~:** she blurted it out immediately; 2 (plötzlich lachen) burst out laughing; **~|prusten** *itr. V.* (ugs.) burst out laughing; **~|rasen** *itr. V.; mit sein* race *or* tear off; **auf etw.** (*Akk.*) **~rasen** race towards sth.; **~|reißen** A *unr. tr. V.* tear off; (schneller, gewaltsamer) rip off; pull ‹*plank*› off; ‹*wind*› rip ‹*tile*› off; **er konnte seine Augen nicht von der Statue ~reißen** (fig.) he couldn't take his eyes off the statue; B *unr. refl. V.* break free *or* loose; **sich von etw.** (*Dat.*) **~reißen** break free *or* loose from sth.; (fig.) tear oneself away from sth.

Löss, *Löß /lœs/ *der;* **Lösses, Lösse** (Geol.) loess

los-, Los-: ~|sagen *refl. V.* **sich von jmdm./etw. ~sagen** renounce sb./sth.; break with sb./sth.; **~sagung** *die;* **~~, ~~en** renunciation (**von** of); break (**von** with)

Löss·boden, *Löß·boden *der* loess soil; loessial soil

los-: ~|schicken *tr. V.* (ugs.) send off ‹*letter, telegram, etc.*›; **jmdn. ~schicken, um etw. zu holen** send sb. out to get sth.; **~|schießen** *unr. itr. V.* (ugs.) 1 start shooting; 2 *mit sein* (sich schnell bewegen) shoot *or* race off; **auf jmdn./etw. ~schießen** race towards sb./sth.; (direkt) race up to sb./sth.; **~|schlagen** A *unr. tr. V.* 1 (abschlagen) knock off; knock ‹*board, plank*› out; **den Verputz von der Wand ~schlagen** knock the rendering off the wall; 2 (ugs.: verkaufen) get rid of; flog (Brit. sl.); B *unr. itr. V.* 1 (einschlagen) **auf jmdn. ~schlagen** let fly at sb.; 2 (bes. Milit.) attack; launch one's attack; **~|schnallen** *tr. V.* unfasten; **~|sollen** *unr. itr. V.* **wann sollen wir ~?** what time should we be off?; **~|sprechen** *unr. tr. V.* (bes. Rel.) absolve (**von** from); **jmdn. von aller Schuld ~sprechen** absolve sb. of all guilt; **~|steuern** *itr. V.; mit sein* **auf etw.** (*Akk.*) **~steuern** head *or* make for sth.; **auf ein Ziel ~steuern** (fig.) aim for a goal; **~|tigern** *itr. V.; mit sein* (ugs.) march off; **~|trennen** *tr. V.* undo; unpick ‹*seam, hem*›; **~|treten** *unr. tr. V.* set in motion; start [up] ‹*campaign, discussion*›; start ‹*avalanche*›

Los·trommel *die* [lottery] drum

Losung[1] *die;* **~, ~en** 1 (Wahlspruch) slogan 2 (Milit.: Kennwort) password; **die ~ nennen** give the password

Losung[2] *die;* **~, ~en** (Jägerspr.) droppings *pl.*

Lösung *die;* **~, ~en** 1 (Bewältigung) solution (*Gen.* to); (eines Konflikts, Widerspruchs) resolution; (einer Aufgabe, eines Problems, usw.) solution (*Gen.*, **für** to); **des Rätsels ~:** the answer to the mystery; **das also ist des Rätsels ~:** so 'that's it *or* the answer 2 (Annullierung) (einer Verlobung) breaking off; (eines Vertrags) cancellation; (einer Verbindung, eines Verhältnisses) severing; (eines Arbeitsverhältnisses) termination 3 (Physik, Chemie) (Flüssigkeit) solution; (das Auflösen) dissolution; dissolving

Lösungs-: ~mittel *das* (Physik, Chemie) solvent; **~vorschlag** *der* proposed solution (**für** to); **ich hätte einen ~vorschlag für euer Problem** I think I might have a solution to your problem; I've got a suggestion as to how you might solve your problem

Losungs·wort *das; Pl.* **~e** *od.* **Losungs·wörter** password

Los·verkäufer *der,* **Los·verkäuferin** *die* [lottery-]ticket seller

los-: ~|werden *unr. tr. V.; mit sein* 1 (sich befreien können von) get rid of; **ich werde den Gedanken/Verdacht nicht ~, dass ...** I can't get the thought/suspicion/impression out of my mind that ...; 2 (ugs.: aussprechen, mitteilen) tell; **er wollte etwas ~werden** he wanted to tell me/us *etc.* something; **... konnte ich endlich meine Frage ~werden** ... I finally got the chance to put my question; 3 (ugs.: verkaufen) get rid of; flog (Brit. sl.); 4 (ugs.: verlieren) lose; **~|wollen** *unr. itr. V.* (ugs.) want to be off; **~|ziehen** *unr. itr. V.; mit sein* (ugs.) 1 (~gehen) set off; 2 (abwertend: herziehen) **über jmdn. ~ziehen** pull sb. to pieces

Los·ziehung *die* draw

Lot /lo:t/ *das;* **~[e]s, ~e** 1 (Bauw.) plumb [bob] 2 (Bauw.: Senkrechte) **im ~ stehen** be plumb; **nicht im ~ sein, außer ~ sein** be out of plumb; **nicht im ~ sein** (fig.) not be straightened *or* sorted out; **[wieder] ins ~ kommen** (fig.) be all right [again] 3 (Seew.) sounding line; lead line 4 (Geom.) perpendicular; **das ~ fällen** drop a perpendicular 5 (veralt.: Maßeinheit) *measure varying between 15.5 g and 16.6 g*

loten *tr. V.* 1 (Bauw.) plumb 2 (Seew.) sound; take soundings of; plumb

löten /'lø:tn̩/ *tr. V.* (Technik) solder

Lothringen /'lo:trɪŋən/ *(das);* **~s** Lorraine

Lothringer *indekl. Adj.*

A Lorraine *attrib.;* **das ~ Kreuz** the Cross of Lorraine

B *der;* **~s, ~:** Lorrainer

Lothringerin *die;* **~, ~nen** Lorrainer

lothringisch *Adj.* Lorraine *attrib.;* Lorrainese

Lotion /lo'tsi̯o:n/ *die;* **~, ~en** *od.* **~s** lotion

Löt-: ~kolben *der* soldering iron; **~lampe** *die* blowlamp

Lot·leine *die* (Seew.) sounding line; lead line

Löt·mittel *das* [soldering] flux

Lotos /'lo:tɔs/ *der;* **~, ~:** lotus

Lotos-: ~blume *die* lotus flower; **~sitz** *der* (Yoga) lotus position

lot·recht

A *Adj.* perpendicular; vertical

B *adv.* perpendicularly; vertically

Lot·rechte *die; adj. Dekl.* perpendicular; vertical

Lotse /'lo:tsə/ *der;* **~n, ~n** ▸ⓘ **S. 113** (Seew.) pilot; (fig.) guide; **ich mache den ~n** (fig.) I'll guide you; I'll show you the way

lotsen *tr. V.* 1 (Seew.) pilot; (Flugw.) guide 2 (leiten) guide 3 (ugs.: führen, leiten) drag

Lotsen-: ~boot *das* pilot boat; **~dienst** *der* 1 pilot service; 2 (Verkehrsw.) driver-guide service; **~zwang** *der* compulsory pilotage *no art.*

Lotsin *die;* **~, ~nen** ▸**Lotse**

Löt·stelle *die* soldered joint

Lotterie /lɔtə'ri:/ *die;* **~, ~n** lottery; **[in der] ~ spielen** take part in *or* do the lottery

Lotterie-: ~einnehmer *der;* **~~s, ~~, ~einnehmerin** *die;* **~~, ~~nen** lottery-ticket seller; **~gewinn** *der* win in the lottery; (gewonnenes Geld) lottery winnings *pl.;* **~los** *das* lottery ticket; **~spiel** *das* (auch fig.) lottery

lotterig /'lɔtərɪç/ *Adj.* (ugs. abwertend) slovenly, sloppy ‹*work*›; scruffy ‹*appearance, house, clothes, etc.*›

Lotter·leben *das* (abwertend) dissolute life

Lotter·wirtschaft *die* (abwertend) [slovenly] mess *or* muddle; shambles (coll.)

Lotto /'lɔto/ *das;* **~s, ~s** 1 national lottery; **4 Richtige im ~ haben** have four correct numbers in the national lottery; **~ spielen** do the [national] lottery 2 (Gesellschaftsspiel) lotto

Lotto-: ~annahmestelle *die* acceptance point for national-lottery coupons; (Stand) national-lottery kiosk; **~gewinn** *der* win in the national lottery; (gewonnenes Geld) winnings *pl.* in the national lottery; **~schein** *der* national-lottery coupon; **~zahlen** *Pl.* winning national-lottery numbers

Lotung *die;* **~, ~en** 1 (Bauw.) plumbing 2 (Seew.) sounding; plumbing; **die ~ der Wassertiefe** sounding *or* plumbing the depth of the water

Lotus /'lo:tʊs/ *der;* **~, ~:** lotus

Löt·zinn *der* [tin-lead] solder

Louis /'lu:i/ *der;* **~** /'lu:i(:s)/, **~** /'lu:i:s/ (ugs.) pimp

Louisdor /lui̯'do:ɐ̯/ *der;* **~s, ~e** louis-d'or

Loveparade /'lʌvpereɪd/ *die;* **~, ~s** Love Parade

> **Loveparade**
>
> A techno music and dance festival which takes place in Berlin every summer, with hundreds of thousands of mainly young people attending. Originally a celebration of youth culture, it has become a major tourist attraction.

Lover /'lavɐ/ *der;* **~s, ~** (ugs.) boyfriend

Löwe /'lø:və/ *der;* **~n, ~n** 1 lion 2 (Astrol.) Leo; the Lion; *s. auch* **Fisch**

Löwen-: ~anteil *der* lion's share; **sich den ~anteil [von etw.** (*Dat.*)**] sichern** get the lion's share [of sth.]; **~bändiger** *der;* **~~s, ~~, ~bändigerin** *die;* **~~, ~~nen** (veralt.) lion tamer; **~jagd** *die* lion hunting; (Veranstaltung) lion hunt; **~mähne** *die* 1 lion's mane; 2 (ugs.: fülliges Haar) [flowing] mane; **~maul, ~mäulchen** *das;* **~~s, ~~** (Bot.) snapdragon; antirrhinum; **~mut** *der* courage of a lion; **~zahn** *der* (Bot.) dandelion; (Herbstlöwenzahn) hawkbit

Löwin /'lø:vɪn/ *die;* **~, ~nen** lioness

loyal /lo̯a'ja:l/

A *Adj.* loyal (**gegenüber** to)

B *adv.* loyally; **einen Vertrag ~ erfüllen/einhalten** faithfully fulfil/keep to an agreement

Loyalität /lo̯ajali'tɛ:t/ *die;* **~:** loyalty (**gegenüber** to)

LP *Abk.* **= Langspielplatte** LP

LPG *Abk.* (DDR) **= Landwirtschaftliche Produktionsgenossenschaft;** ▸**Produktionsgenossenschaft**

LSD /ɛlǀɛs'de:/ *das;* **~[s]** LSD

lt. *Abk.* **= laut**[2]

Luchs /lʊks/ *der;* **~es, ~e** (auch **~fell**) lynx; **wie ein ~ aufpassen** watch like a hawk

Luchs·auge *das* (fig.) eagle eye; **den ~n meiner Wirtin entgeht nichts** my hawk-eyed landlady misses nothing

Lücke /'lʏkə/ *die;* **~, ~n** 1 gap; (Park~, auf einem Formular, in einem Text) space; **eine ~ füllen/schließen** fill/close a gap 2 (Mangel) gap; (in der Versorgung) break; (im Gesetz) loophole

Lücken·büßer *der,* **Lücken·büßerin** *die* stopgap; **den Lückenbüßer spielen** act as a stopgap

Lücken·füller *der,* **Lücken·füllerin** *die;* ▸**Lückenbüßer, Lückenbüßerin**

lückenhaft

A *Adj.* ‹*teeth*› full of gaps; gappy ‹*teeth*›; sketchy ‹*knowledge*›; sketchy, vague ‹*memory*›; incomplete, sketchy ‹*report, account, etc.*›; incomplete ‹*statement*›; ‹*alibi*› full of holes; **sein Wissen/seine Erinnerung ist ~:** there are gaps in his knowledge/memory

B *adv.* ‹*remember*› vaguely, sketchily; **einen Fragebogen [sehr] ~ ausfüllen** fill in a questionnaire leaving [many] gaps

Lückenhaftigkeit *die;* **~** (von Wissen, Kenntnissen) sketchiness; (eines Berichts) incompleteness; sketchiness

lücken-, Lücken-: ~los A *Adj.* unbroken ‹*line, row, etc.*›; complete ‹*account, report, curriculum vitae*›; solid, cast-iron ‹*alibi*›; comprehensive, perfect ‹*knowledge*›; **sie hat ein strahlend weißes, ~loses Gebiss** she has gleaming white teeth without any gaps; **eine ~lose Beweiskette** a solid chain of evidence. B *adv.* without any gaps; **ein ~los nachgewiesenes Alibi** a cast-iron alibi; **~losigkeit** *die;* **~~** (einer Darstellung) completeness; (eines Alibis) solidness

lud /lu:t/ *1. u. 3. Pers. Sg. Prät. v.* **laden**

Lude /'lu:də/ *der;* **~n, ~n** (salopp) pimp; ponce

Luder *das;* **~s, ~** (salopp) so-and-so (coll.); **ein armes/freches ~:** a poor/cheeky so-and-so (coll.)

Luft /lʊft/ *die;* **~, Lüfte** /'lʏftə/ 1 air; **an die frische ~ gehen/in der frischen ~ sein** get out in[to]/be out in the fresh air; **jmdn. an die**

[frische] ~ setzen *od.* **befördern** (ugs.) (hinauswerfen) show sb. the door; (entlassen) give sb. the sack (coll.) *or* push (coll.); **etw. mit ~ kühlen** air-cool sth.; **die ~ anhalten** hold one's breath; **halt die ~ an!** (ugs.) (hör auf zu reden!) pipe down (coll.); put a sock in it (Brit. sl.); (übertreib nicht so!) come off it! (coll.); **tief ~ holen** take a deep breath; **~ schnappen** (ugs.) get some fresh air; **nach ~ schnappen** (fig. ugs.) struggle to keep one's head above water (fig.); **er kriegte keine/kaum ~:** he couldn't breathe/could hardly breathe; **die ~ ist rein** (fig.) the coast is clear; **hier/im Büro ist dicke ~** (fig. ugs.) there's a bad atmosphere here/in the office (fig.); **aus der Sache ist die ~ raus** (fig. ugs.) it's/the whole thing has gone flat; **sich in ~ auflösen** (ugs.) vanish into thin air; ‹*plans*› go up in smoke (fig.); **er ist ~ für mich** (ugs.) I ignore him completely; **jmdn. wie ~ behandeln** (ugs.) treat sb. as if he/she didn't exist; **die ~ aus jmds. Glas lassen** (ugs. scherzh.) fill sb. up; **da bleibt einem die ~ weg** (ugs.) it takes your breath away; **ihm/der Firma geht die ~ aus** (fig. ugs.) he's/the firm's going broke (coll.); **von ~ und Liebe kann man nicht leben** (ugs.) you can't live on nothing at all **2** (Himmelsraum) air; **Aufnahmen aus der ~ machen** take pictures from the air; **in die ~ ragen** soar *or* rise up into the sky; **sich in die Lüfte schwingen** (geh.) soar into the air; **etw. in die ~ sprengen** *od.* **jagen** (ugs.) blow sth. up; **aus der ~ gegriffen sein** (fig.) ‹*story, accusation, etc.*› be pure invention; **in der ~ liegen** (fig.) ‹*crisis, ideas, etc.*› be in the air; **in der ~ hängen** *od.* **schweben** (fig. ugs.) ‹*plans, etc.*› be up in the air; ‹*person*› be left dangling (fig.); **in die ~ gehen** (fig. ugs.) blow one's top (coll.); **etw. in der ~ zerreißen** (fig. ugs.) tear sth. to pieces; **ich könnte ihn in der ~ zerreißen** (ugs.) I could murder him (coll.) **3** (fig.: Spielraum) space; room; **~ schaffen** *od.* **machen** create *or* make space *or* room; **sich** (*Dat.*) **~ [ver]schaffen** take the pressure off oneself; **deine 300 Euro haben mir erst mal ~ verschafft** your 300 euros have given me a breathing space; **in den Preisen ist noch ~ [drin]** (ugs.) there's some leeway in the prices; **sich** (*Dat.*) *od.* **seinem Herzen ~ machen** get it off one's chest (coll.); **ich hatte eine solche Wut, ich musste mir einmal ~ machen** I was so angry I had to give vent to my feelings; **seinem Zorn/Ärger** *usw.* **~ machen** (ugs.) give vent to one's anger *etc.* **4** (Brise) breeze; **sich** (*Dat.*) **~ zufächeln** fan oneself

Luft-: ~abwehr *die* (Milit.) air defence; anti-aircraft defence; **~akrobat** *der,* **~akrobatin** *die* trapeze artist; **~angriff** *der* (Milit.) air raid; **~armee** *die* (DDR) air force unit; **~aufklärung** *die* (Milit.) air reconnaissance; aerial reconnaissance; **~aufnahme** *die* aerial photograph; **~ballon** *der* balloon; **~befeuchter** *der;* **~~s, ~~:** humidifier; **~bild** *das* aerial photograph; **~blase** *die* air bubble; **~-Boden-Rakete** *die* air-to-ground missile; **~brücke** *die* airlift

Lüftchen /ˈlʏftçən/ *das;* **~s, ~:** breeze; **kein ~ regte sich** there was not the slightest breath of wind

luft-, Luft-: ~dicht *Adj.* airtight; **etw. ~dicht abpacken/abschließen** pack sth. in an airtight container/put an airtight seal around sth.; **~dichte** *die* (Physik., Met.) air density; **~druck** *der; Pl.* **~drücke** **1** (Physik) air pressure; atmospheric pressure; **2** (Druckwelle) blast; **~druck·messer** *der;* **~~s, ~~:** barometer; **~durchlässig** *Adj.* pervious *or* permeable to air *postpos.*; well-ventilated ‹*shoes*›; **~durchlässigkeit** *die* perviousness *or* permeability to air

lüften

A *tr. V.* **1** air; (ständig; mit Klimaanlage usw.) ventilate; **das L~:** airing/ventilation **2** (aus~) air ‹*clothes, bed. etc.*› **3** (hochheben) raise, lift ‹*hat, lid, veil, etc.*› **4** (enthüllen) reveal; disclose ‹*secret*›; **jmds. Inkognito ~:** reveal sb.'s identity

B *itr. V.* air the room/house/flat (esp. Brit.) *or* (esp. Amer.) apartment *etc.*; **wir müssen hier mal ~:** we must let some [fresh] air in here

Lüfter *der;* **~s, ~:** fan

Luft·fahrt *die* aeronautics *sing., no art.*; (mit Flugzeugen) aviation *no art.*

Luftfahrt·gesellschaft *die* airline

luft-, Luft-: ~fahrzeug *das* aircraft; **~feuchte, ~feuchtigkeit** *die* [atmospheric] humidity; **~filter** *der od. das* (Technik) air filter; **~flotte** *die* (Milit.) air fleet; **~fracht** *die* air freight; **~geist** *der* (Myth.) spirit of the air; **~gekühlt** *Adj.* air-cooled; **~getrocknet** *Adj.* air-dried; **~gewehr** *das* air rifle; airgun; **~gitarre** *die* air guitar; **~hauch** *der* (geh.) breath of air; **~herrschaft** *die* (Milit.) air supremacy; **~hoheit** *die* air sovereignty; **~hülle** *die* atmosphere

luftig

A *Adj.* airy ‹*room, building, etc.*›; well ventilated ‹*cellar, store*›; light, cool ‹*clothes*›; **auf der Terrasse ist es etwas ~er** there's more air out on the terrace

B *adv.* **~/zu ~ angezogen sein** be lightly/not warmly enough dressed

Luftikus /ˈlʊftikʊs/ *der;* **~[ses], ~se** (ugs. abwertend) careless and unreliable sort (coll.)

Luft-: ~kampf *der* air battle; aerial battle; **~kissen** *das* (Technik) air cushion

Luftkissen-: ~boot *das* hovercraft; **~fahrzeug** *das* hovercraft; air cushion vehicle

luft-, Luft-: ~klappe *die* ventilation flap; **~korridor** *der* (Flugw.) air corridor; **~krieg** *der* air warfare *no art.*; aerial warfare *no art.*; **~kühlung** *die* (Technik) air cooling; **ein Motor mit ~kühlung** an air-cooled engine; **~kurort** *der* climatic health resort; **~lande·truppe** *die* (Milit.) airborne troops *pl.*; **~leer** *Adj.* **ein ~leerer Raum** a vacuum; **im ~leeren Raum** (fig.) in a vacuum; **~linie** *die:* **1 000 km ~linie** 1,000 km as the crow flies; **~loch** *das* **1** (Öffnung) air hole; **2** (ugs.: Windbö) air pocket; **~-~-Rakete** *die* (Milit.) air-to-air missile; **~mangel** *der* **1** lack of air; **2** (Atembeschwerden) shortness of breath; **~masche** *die* (Handarb.) chain stitch; **~massen** *Pl.* (Met.) air masses; **~matratze** *die* airbed; air mattress; Lilo ®; **~mine** *die* aerial mine; air mine; **~pirat** *der,* **~piratin** *die* [aircraft] hijacker

Luft·post *die* airmail; **etw. per** *od.* **mit ~ schicken** send sth. [by] airmail

Luftpost-: ~brief *der* airmail letter; **~leicht·brief** *der* aerogramme; **~papier** *das* airmail paper

Luft-: ~pumpe *die* air pump; (für Fahrrad) [bicycle] pump; **~qualität** *die* air quality; **~raum** *der* airspace; **~röhre** *die* ▸**ⓘ S. 435** (Anat.) windpipe; trachea (Anat.); **~sack** *der* **1** (Kfz-W.) airbag; **2** (Zool.) air sac; **~schacht** *der* ventilation shaft; (einer Klimaanlage) ventilation duct; **~schadstoff** *der* air pollutant; atmospheric pollutant; **~schaukel** *die* swingboat; **~schiff** *das* airship; ***~schiffahrt, ~schifffahrt** *die* airship travel; **~schlacht** *die* air battle; aerial battle; **die ~schlacht um England** the Battle of Britain; **~schlag** *der* air strike; **~schlange** *die* [paper] streamer; **~schleuse** *die* (Technik) airlock; **~schloss,** ***~schloß** *das* castle in the air; **~schlösser bauen** build castles in the air; **~schraube** *die* (Technik) airscrew; propeller

Luft·schutz *der* air-raid protection *no art.*

Luftschutz-: ~bunker *der,* **~keller** *der,* **~raum** *der* air-raid shelter; **~sirene** *die* air-raid siren; **~übung** *die* air-raid drill; **~wart** *der* (hist.) air-raid warden

Luft-: ~sieg *der* air victory; **~spiegelung** *die* mirage; **~sprung** *der* jump in the air; **vor Freude ~sprünge/einen ~sprung machen** *od.* **vollführen** jump for joy; **~streitkräfte** *Pl.* (Milit.) air force *sing.*; **~strom** *der* stream of air; **~strömung** *die* (Met.) airstream; air current; **~stützpunkt** *der* (Milit.) air base; **~taxe** *die,* **~taxi** *das* air taxi; **~temperatur** *die* (Met.) air temperature; **~überlegenheit** *die* (Milit.) air superiority; **~-und-Raumfahrt** *die* aerospace

Lüftung *die;* **~, ~en** **1** (das Lüften) ventilation **2** (Anlage) ventilation system

Lüftungs-: ~anlage *die* ventilation system; **~klappe** *die* ventilation flap

Luft-: ~veränderung *die* change of air; **~verflüssigung** *die* (Physik) liquefaction of air; **~verkehr** *der* air traffic; **~verpestung** *die* (abwertend), **~verschmutzung** *die* air pollution; **~verteidigung** *die* (Milit.) air defence; **~waffe** *die* air force; **bei der ~waffe** in the air force; **~weg** *der* **1** **etw. auf dem ~weg verschicken/befördern** send/transport sth. by air; **auf dem ~weg reisen** travel by air; **2** *Pl.* ▸**ⓘ S. 435** (Anat.: Atemwege) airways; air passages; respiratory tract *sing.*; **~widerstand** *der* (Physik) air resistance; **~wurzel** *die* (Bot.) aerial root; **~zufuhr** *die* air supply; **~zug** *der* [gentle] breeze; (in Zimmern, Gebäuden) draught

Lug /luːk/ *in* **~ und Trug** lies *pl.* and deception

Luganer See, (schweiz.) **Luganersee** *der;* **~s** Lake Lugano

Lüge /ˈlyːɡə/ *die;* **~, ~n** lie; **eine barmherzige ~:** a compassionate falsehood; **jmdn. der ~ bezichtigen** accuse sb. of lying; call sb. a liar; **jmdm. ~n auftischen** (ugs.) serve sb. up a lot *or* load of lies (coll.); **~n haben kurze Beine** (Spr.) [the] truth will out; **jmdn./etw. ~n strafen** prove sb. a liar/give the lie to sth.; *s. auch* **fromm A 3**

lugen *itr. V.* (südwestd.) (auch fig.) peep; (hervorgucken) **aus etw. ~:** poke out of sth.

lügen

A *itr. V.* lie; **hier wird nur gelogen und betrogen** there's nothing but lies and deception here; **~ wie gedruckt** lie like mad (coll.); be a terrible liar (coll.); **ich müsste ~, wenn ...** I should be lying if ...; **das Lügen** lying; **die Sterne ~ nicht** (fig.) the stars never lie; **wer einmal lügt, dem glaubt man nicht, und wenn er auch die Wahrheit spricht** (Spr.) a liar is never believed, even when he's telling the truth; *s. auch* **Tasche**

B *tr. V.* **er hat das alles gelogen** that was all a lie *or* all lies; **das ist gelogen!** that's a lie!

Lügen-: ~bold /-bɔlt/ *der;* **~~[e]s, ~~e** liar; **~detektor** *der* lie detector; **~gebäude** *das* tissue of lies; **~gespinst** *das* (geh.) web *or* tissue of lies

lügenhaft (abwertend)

A *Adj.* untruthful, mendacious ‹*statement, account, report, etc*›

B *adv.* untruthfully; mendaciously

Lügen-: ~kampagne *die* campaign of lies; **~märchen** *das* tall story; cock and bull story; **~maul** *das* (derb) filthy liar

Lügner *der;* **~s, ~, Lügnerin** *die;* **~, ~nen** liar

lügnerisch *Adj.* untruthful; mendacious; lying *attrib.* ‹*scoundrel*›

Lukas[1] /ˈluːkas/ *(der)* (Evangelist) Luke

Lukas[2] *der;* **~, ~** (Maschine) try-your-strength machine; **hau den ~!** try your strength!

Lukas·evangelium *das* St Luke's Gospel; Gospel according to St Luke

Luke /ˈluːkə/ *die;* **~, ~n** **1** (Dach~) skylight **2** (bei Schiffen) hatch; (Keller~) trapdoor

lukrativ /lukraˈtiːf/

A *Adj.* lucrative

B *adv.* lucratively

lukullisch /luˈkʊlɪʃ/ (geh.)

A *Adj.* Lucullan; epicurean

B *adv.* **~ essen** *od.* **speisen** eat *or* have a Lucullan *or* an epicurean meal/meals

Lulatsch /ˈluːla(ː)tʃ/ *der;* **~[e]s, ~e** (ugs.) [long] lanky fellow; **ein langer ~:** a beanpole

Lulle /ˈlʊlə/ *die;* **~, ~n** (ugs.) cig (coll.); fag (Brit. coll.)

lullen *tr. V.* lull; **ein Kind in den Schlaf ~:** lull a child to sleep

Lumme /ˈlʊmə/ *die;* **~, ~n** (Zool.) guillemot

Lümmel /ˈlʏml̩/ *der;* **~s, ~** **1** (abwertend: Flegel) lout **2** (ugs., fam.: Bengel) rascal **3** (salopp: Penis) willy (coll.)

Lümmelei *die;* **~, ~en** (abwertend) ▸**Flegelei**

lümmelhaft (abwertend) ▸**flegelhaft**

lümmeln *refl. V.* (ugs. abwertend) ▸**flegeln**

Lump /lʊmp/ *der;* **~en, ~en** scoundrel; rogue

lumpen (ugs.)
A *tr. V. in* **sich nicht ~ lassen** splash out (coll.)
B *itr. V.* be out on the tiles (coll.)

Lumpen *der;* **~s, ~** (auch fig. abwertend) rag

Lumpen-: ~gesindel *das* (abwertend) rabble; riff-raff; **~händler** *der* rag-and-bone man; **~händlerin** *die* rag-and-bone woman; **~hund** *der,* **~kerl** *der* (abwertend) scoundrel; bastard (coll.); **~pack** *das* (abwertend) ▸**~gesindel**; **~proletariat** *das* (Soziol.) lumpenproletariat; **~sammler** *der* **1** rag-and-bone man; **2** (scherzh.: letztes Verkehrsmittel) last bus/tram (Brit.) *or* (Amer.) streetcar/train; **~sammlerin** *die* rag-and-bone woman

Lumperei *die;* **~, ~en** (abwertend) dirty *or* mean trick; **eine große ~:** a very dirty *or* mean trick

lumpig (abwertend)
A *Adj.* **1** (kümmerlich) paltry, miserable ‹*pay, wages, etc.*› **2** (niederträchtig) mean, shabby ‹*behaviour, attitude*›; mean ‹*person*›
B *adv.* ‹*act, behave*› shabbily

lunar /luˈnaːɐ̯/ *Adj.* lunar

Lunch /lanʃ/ *der;* **~[e]s** *od.* **~, ~[e]s** *od.* **~e** lunch; luncheon (formal)

lunchen /ˈlanʃn̩/ *itr. V.* have lunch *or* (formal) luncheon; lunch

Lüneburger Heide /ˈlyːnəbʊrgɐ ˈ--/ *die;* **~:** Lüneburg Heath

Lunge /ˈlʊŋə/ *die;* **~, ~n** ▸**i S. 435** lungs *pl.;* (**~nflügel**) lung; **er hat es auf der ~** (ugs.) he has got lung trouble (coll.); **auf ~** *od.* **über die ~ rauchen** inhale; **die grüne ~ einer Großstadt** (fig.) the lungs *pl.* of a city; **sich** (*Dat.*) **die ~ aus dem Hals** *od.* **Leib schreien** (ugs.) yell one's head off (coll.)

lungen-, Lungen-: ~bläschen *das* ▸**i S. 435** (Anat.) pulmonary alveolus; **~braten** *der* (österr.) ▸**Lendenbraten**; **~embolie** *die* ▸**i S. 439** (Med.) pulmonary embolism; **~entzündung** *die* ▸**i S. 439** pneumonia *no indef. art.;* **~flügel** *der* ▸**i S. 435** lung; **~haschee** *das* (Kochk.) chopped lights *pl.* in sauce; **~krank** *Adj.* suffering from a lung disease *postpos.;* (an Tuberkulose leidend) suffering from tuberculosis *postpos.;* **~kranke** *der/die* person with *or* suffering from a lung disease; (an Tuberkulose leidend) tuberculosis sufferer; **~krebs** *der* ▸**i S. 439** lung cancer; **~tuberkulose** *die* tuberculosis [of the lung]; pulmonary tuberculosis; **~zug** *der* inhalation; **einen tiefen ~zug machen** inhale deeply

lungern *itr. V.* ▸**herumlungern**

Lunte /ˈlʊntə/ *die;* **~, ~n** **1** (veralt.: Zündschnur) fuse; match; **~ riechen** (ugs.) smell a rat **2** (Jägerspr.: Schwanz) brush

Lupe /ˈluːpə/ *die;* **~, ~n** magnifying glass; **jmdn./etw. unter die ~ nehmen** (ugs.) examine sb./sth. closely; take a close look at sb./sth.; **so etwas/solche Leute kann man mit der ~ suchen** (ugs.) things/people like that are very hard to find *or* are few and far between

lupen·rein *Adj.* **1** flawless ‹*diamond, stone, etc.*›; ‹*diamond*› of the first water **2** (musterhaft) genuine ‹*amateur*›; unimpeachable ‹*record, reputation*›; perfect ‹*forgery, gentleman*›

lupfen /ˈlʊpfn̩/ (südd., schweiz., österr.), **lüpfen** /ˈlʏpfn̩/ *tr. V.* raise; lift

Lupine /luˈpiːnə/ *die;* **~, ~n** (Bot.) lupin

Lurch /lʊrç/ *der;* **~[e]s, ~e** (Zool.) amphibian

Lure /ˈluːrə/ *die;* **~, ~n** (hist.) lur

Lusche /ˈlʊʃə/ *die;* **~, ~n** (ugs.) low card

Lust /lʊst/ *die;* **~, Lüste** /ˈlʏstə/ **1** (Bedürfnis) **~ haben** *od.* **verspüren, etw. zu tun** feel like doing sth.; **große/keine ~ haben, etw. zu tun** really/not feel like doing sth.; **wir hatten nicht die geringste ~, das zu tun** we didn't feel in the least *or* slightest like doing it; **plötzlich ~ bekommen, etw. zu tun** suddenly feel like doing sth.; **auf etw.** (*Akk.*) **~ haben** fancy sth.; **ich hätte große ~ auf ...** (*Akk.*) I could really fancy ...; **ich habe jetzt keine ~:** I'm not in the mood at the moment; **das kannst du machen, wie du ~ hast** you can do it however you like *or* whatever way you like; **mir ist die ~ dazu vergangen** I've lost [all] enthusiasm for it; **ich mache das nach ~ und Laune** I do it when I feel like it; **ich hätte ~ dazu** I'd like to **2** (Vergnügen) pleasure; joy; **~ an etw.** (*Dat.*) **haben** take great pleasure in *or* really enjoy sth.; **die ~ an etw.** (*Dat.*) **verlieren** lose interest in *or* stop enjoying sth.; **aus purer ~ am Töten** out of sheer pleasure in killing; **er hat an allem die ~ verloren** he no longer takes pleasure in anything; **etw. mit ~ und Liebe tun** love doing sth. **3** (Begierde) desire; (geschlechtlich) desire; lust (usu. derog.); **die ~ des Fleisches** (geh.) the desires *pl.* *or* lusts *pl.* of the flesh

Lustbarkeit *die;* **~, ~en** (geh. veralt.) entertainment; festivity

lust·betont *Adj.* pleasure-orientated ‹*behaviour*›; fun-loving, pleasure-loving ‹*person*›; **~es Spielen** fun-orientated play

Luster /ˈlʊstɐ/ *der;* **~s, ~** (österr.) ▸**Lüster 1**

Lüster /ˈlʏstɐ/ *der;* **~s, ~** **1** (veralt.: Kronleuchter) chandelier **2** (Überzug) lustre

Lüster·klemme *die* (Elektrot.) terminal block

lüstern
A *Adj.* **1** lecherous; lascivious; **nach jmdm. ~ sein** lust after sb. **2** (begierig) **mit ~en Augen/Blicken** with greedy eyes
B *adv.* **1** lecherously; lasciviously **2** (begierig) greedily

Lust-: ~fahrt *die* (veralt.) excursion; **~garten** *der* (hist.) pleasance (arch.); pleasure ground; **~gefühl** *das* feeling of pleasure; **~gewinn** *der* pleasure; **~greis** *der* (abwertend) [old] lecher; **~haus** *das* (hist.) summer house

lustig
A *Adj.* **1** (vergnügt) merry; jolly; merry, jolly, jovial ‹*person*›; happy, enjoyable ‹*time*›; **dort war es immer sehr ~:** it was always a lot of fun there; **das kann ja ~ werden!** (ugs. iron.) this/that is going to be fun! **sich über jmdn./etw. ~ machen** make fun of sb./sth. **2** (komisch) funny; amusing; **etw. Lustiges** sth. funny **3** (ugs.) *in* **wie du ~ bist** (ugs.) however you fancy; whatever way you fancy; **solange du ~ bist** (ugs.) for as long as you like
B *adv.* **1** (vergnügt) ‹*laugh, play*› merrily, happily; **bei euch scheint es sehr ~ zuzugehen** you seem to be really enjoying yourselves *or* having a lot of fun; **~ brennen/flattern** (fig.) burn/flutter merrily **2** (komisch) funnily; amusingly; **sie kann so ~ erzählen** she can tell such funny *or* amusing stories **3** (unbekümmert) gaily

-lustig *adj.* **[sehr] tanz~/sanges~/lese~ sein** be very fond of *or* keen on dancing/singing/reading; **der wanderlustige Urlauber** the holidaymaker who is keen on hiking

Lustigkeit *die;* **~** **1** (Fröhlichkeit) merriness; jolliness; (Frohsinn auch) joviality **2** (Komik) funniness

Lust·knabe *der* (veralt., scherzh.) catamite

Lüstling /ˈlʏstlɪŋ/ *der;* **~s, ~e** (veralt. abwertend, scherzh.) lecher

lust-, Lust-: ~los **A** *Adj.* **1** (unlustig) listless; (ohne Begeisterung) unenthusiastic [and uninterested]; **2** (Börsenw.) slack; dull; **B** *adv.* listlessly; (ohne Begeisterung) without enthusiasm [or interest]; **sie stocherte ~los in ihrem Essen herum** she picked at her food with no real [interest or] enthusiasm; **~losigkeit** *die;* **~~:** **1** (Un~) listlessness; (mangelnde Begeisterung) lack of [interest and] enthusiasm; **2** (Börsenw.) slackness; dullness; **~molch** *der* (ugs. scherzh.) sex maniac; **ein alter ~molch** an old lecher; **~mord** *der* sex murder; **~mörder** *der* sex killer; **~objekt** *das* sex object; **~prinzip** *das* (Psych.) pleasure principle; **~schloss, *~schloß** *das* summer residence; **~schrei** *der* cry of pleasure; **~seuche** *die* **1** (veralt.: Syphilis) syphilis *no art.;* **2** (geh.: Geschlechtskrankheit) sexual scourge; **~spiel** *das* comedy; **~spiel·dichter** *der,* **~spiel·dichterin** *die* comic dramatist; **~wandeln** *itr. V.;* *mit sein od. haben* (geh. veralt.) stroll; take a stroll

Lutheraner /lʊtəˈraːnɐ/ *der;* **~s, ~, Lutheranerin** *die;* **~, ~nen** Lutheran

Luther·bibel *die* Luther's Bible; Lutheran Bible

lutherisch, *Lutherisch
A *Adj.* Lutheran; **das berühmte ~e Wort** Luther's famous words *pl*
B *adv.* ‹*think etc.*› as a Lutheran; **jmdn. ~ erziehen** bring sb. up in the Lutheran religion

luthersch, *Luthersch /ˈlʊtɐʃ/ *Adj.* Luther's; **das berühmete ~e Wort** Luther's famous words *pl.*

Luthertum *das;* **~s** Lutheranism *no art.*

lutschen /ˈlʊtʃn̩/
A *tr. V.* suck
B *itr. V.* suck **an etw.** (*Dat.*) **~:** suck sth.; **am Daumen ~:** suck one's thumb

Lutscher *der;* **~s, ~** **1** lollipop **2** (Schnuller) dummy (Brit.); pacifier (Amer.)

Lutsch·tablette *die* lozenge

Lüttich /ˈlʏtɪç/ *(das);* **~s** Liège

Luv /luːf/ *die, auch das;* **~** (Seemannsspr.) *in* **in/nach ~:** to windward

luven /ˈluːfn̩/ *itr. V.* (Seemannsspr.) luff

Lux /lʊks/ *das;* **~, ~** (Physik) lux

Luxation /lʊksaˈtsi̯oːn/ *die;* **~, ~en** ▸**i S. 439** (Med.) luxation (Med.); dislocation

Luxemburg /ˈlʊksm̩bʊrk/ *(das);* **~s** ▸**i S. 675** Luxembourg; *s. auch* **Großherzogtum**

Luxemburger ▸**i S. 675**
A *indekl. Adj.* Luxembourg; **die ~ EG-Behörden** the EEC authorities in Luxembourg
B *der;* **~s, ~:** Luxembourger; *s. auch* **Kölner**

Luxemburgerin *die;* **~, ~nen** Luxembourger; *s. auch* **-in**

luxemburgisch *Adj.* Luxembourgian

luxuriös /lʊksuˈri̯øːs/
A *Adj.* luxurious; **ein ~es Leben führen** lead a life of luxury
B *adv.* luxuriously; **[sehr] ~ leben/wohnen** live in [great] luxury

Luxus /ˈlʊksʊs/ *der;* **~** (auch fig.) luxury; **etw. ist reiner ~:** sth. is sheer extravagance; **den ~ lieben** love luxury; **im ~ leben** live in [the lap of] luxury; **sich** (*Dat.*) **den ~ leisten, etw. zu tun** (fig.) allow oneself the luxury of doing sth.

Luxus-: ~artikel *der* luxury article; **dieses Geschäft führt nur ~artikel** this shop sells only luxury goods; **~ausführung** *die* de luxe version; **~ausgabe** *die* de luxe edition; **~dampfer** *der* luxury cruiser; **~hotel** *das* luxury hotel; **~jacht** *die* luxury yacht; **~kabine** *die* luxury cabin; **~klasse** *die* luxury class; **Automobile der ~klasse** luxury cars; **~limousine** *die* luxury saloon; **~schlitten** *der* (ugs.) classy car *or* job (sl.); **~weibchen** *das* (abwertend) woman who expects to live in luxury

Luzern /luˈtsɛrn/ *(das);* **~s** ▸**i S. 675** Lucerne

Luzerne /luˈtsɛrnə/ *die;* **~, ~n** (Bot.) alfalfa; lucerne (Brit.)

luzid /luˈtsiːt/ *Adj.* lucid

Luzidität /lutsidiˈtɛːt/ *die;* **~:** lucidity

Luzifer /ˈluːtsifɛr/ *(der)* Lucifer

luziferisch *Adj.* (geh.) diabolical; vicious ‹*sarcasm*›

LW *Abk.* = **Langwelle** LW

Lymph·drüse *die* (veralt.) ▸**Lymphknoten**

L

Lymphe /ˈlʏmfə/ *die;* ~, ~**n** (Physiol.) lymph

Lymph·knoten *der* (Anat.) lymph node *or* gland

lynchen /ˈlʏnçn̩/ *tr. V.* lynch; (scherzh.) lynch; kill

Lynch-: ~justiz *die* lynch law; **~mord** *der* lynching

Lyoner [Wurst] /ˈli̯oːnɐ (-)/ *die;* ~, **Lyoner [Würste]** bologna [sausage]

Lyra /ˈlyːra/ *die;* ~, **Lyren** **1** (Mus.) lyre **2** (Astron.) Lyra; the lyre

Lyrik /ˈlyːrɪk/ *die;* ~: lyric poetry

Lyriker *der;* ~**s**, ~, **Lyrikerin** *die;* ~, ~**nen** lyric poet; lyricist

lyrisch

A *Adj.* **1** lyric ‹*poem, poetry, epic, drama*›; lyrical ‹*passage, style, description, etc.*› **2** (gefühlvoll) lyrical **3** (Mus.) lyric

B *adv.* lyrically

Lyzeum /lyˈtseːʊm/ *das;* ~**s**, **Lyzeen** /lyˈtseːən/ girls' high school

m, M /ɛm/ *das;* ~, ~: m/M; *s. auch* **a, A**

m *Abk.* ▸ℹ **S. 454 = Meter** m

M *Abk.* (DDR) **= Mark¹**

MA *Abk.* **= Mittelalter**

Mäander /mɛˈandɐ/ *der;* **~s, ~** (Geogr., Kunstwiss.) meander

Maar /maːɐ̯/ *das;* **~[e]s, ~e** (Geogr.) maar; (See) crater lake

Maas /maːs/ *die;* ~: Meuse

Maat /maːt/ *der;* **~[e]s, ~e[n]** ▸ℹ **S. 44** **1** (Seemannsspr.) [ship's] mate **2** (Dienstgrad) petty officer

Mach /max/ *das;* **~[s], ~** (Physik) Mach

Machandel /maˈxandl̩/ *der;* **~s, ~** (nordd.) ▸**Wacholder**

Mach·art *die* style; (Schnitt) cut

machbar *Adj.* feasible

Mache *die;* ~ (ugs.) **1** (abwertend) sham; **das ist reine** *od.* **nichts als ~:** it's pure sham; it's all put on **2** **etw. in der ~ haben** have sth. on the stocks; be working on sth.; **jmdn. in der ~ haben/in die ~ nehmen** (salopp) (jmdn. zusetzen) be working/work on sb.; (jmdn. verprügeln) be working/work sb. over (coll.)

machen /ˈmaxn̩/

A *tr. V.* **1** (herstellen) make; **aus Plastik/Holz** *usw.* **gemacht** made of plastic/wood *etc.;* **aus diesen Äpfeln ~ wir Saft** we will make juice from these apples; **aus diesem Zimmer ~ wir gerade ein Büro** we are making *or* turning this room into an office; **sich** *(Dat.)* **etw. ~ lassen** have sth. made; **Geld/ein Vermögen/einen Gewinn ~:** make money/a fortune/a profit; **dafür ist er wie gemacht/nicht gemacht** (fig.) that's just his line/that's not his line; **etw. aus jmdm. ~:** make sb. into sth.; (verwandeln) turn sb. into sth.; **jmdn. zum Präsidenten** *usw.* **~:** make sb. president *etc.;* **er machte sie zu seiner Frau** (geh. veralt.) he made her his wife

2 (geben) **jmdm. einen Kostenvoranschlag ~:** let sb. have *or* give sb. an estimate; **jmdm. einen guten Preis ~** (ugs.) (beim Kauf) make sb. a good offer; (beim Verkauf) name a good price

3 (zubereiten) get, prepare ‹*meal*›; **den Salat ~** (ugs.) do the salad (coll.); **was machst du heute zum Abendessen?** what are you getting/doing for supper tonight?; **jmdm./sich [einen] Kaffee ~:** make [some] coffee for sb./oneself; **jmdm. einen Cocktail ~:** get *or* mix sb. a cocktail

4 (verursachen) **jmdm. Arbeit ~:** cause *or* make [extra] work for sb.; **jmdm. Sorgen ~:** cause sb. anxiety; worry sb.; **jmdm. Mut/Hoffnung ~:** give sb. courage/hope; **das macht Durst/Hunger** *od.* **Appetit** this makes one thirsty/hungry; this gives one a thirst/an appetite; **das macht das Wetter** that's [because of] the weather; **das macht das viele Rauchen** that comes from smoking a lot; **mach, dass er gesund wird!** make him get well!; **mach, dass du nach Hause kommst!** (ugs.) off home with you!; **ich muss ~, dass ich zum Bahnhof komme** (ugs.) I must see that I get to the station

5 (ausführen) do ‹*job, repair, etc.*›; **seine Hausaufgaben ~:** do one's homework; **ein Foto** *od.* **eine Aufnahme ~:** take a photograph; **ein Examen ~:** take an exam; **einen Spaziergang ~:** go for *or* take a walk; **eine Reise ~:** go on a journey *or* trip; **einen Besuch [bei jmdm.] ~:** pay [sb.] a visit; **wie mans macht, macht mans falsch** *od.* **verkehrt** (ugs.) [however you do it,] there's always something wrong; (jmdm. ist nichts recht) there's no pleasing some people; **er macht es nicht unter 100 Euro** he won't do it for under *or* less than 100 euros

6 (+ *Adj. od. V.: Zustand verändern*) **jmdn. glücklich/eifersüchtig** *usw.* **~:** make sb. happy/jealous *etc.;* **etw. größer/länger/kürzer ~:** make sth. bigger/longer/shorter; **mach es dir gemütlich** *od.* **bequem!** make yourself comfortable *or* at home; **das Kleid macht sie älter** the dress makes her look older; **jmdn. lachen/weinen/leiden ~** (geh.) make sb. laugh/cry/suffer

7 (tun) do; **was machst du da?** what are you doing?; **musst du noch viel ~?** do you still have a lot to do?; **mach doch etwas!** 'do something!; **mach ich, wird gemacht!** (ugs.) will do!; **was ~ Sie [beruflich]?** what do you do [for a living]?; **da ist nichts zu ~, dagegen kann man nichts ~:** there's nothing one can do [about it]; **was soll ich nur ~?** what am I to do?; **was macht der Fußball in der Küche?** what is the football doing in the kitchen?; **was hat er nur wieder gemacht [, dass alle so wütend sind]?** what has he been up to this time [to make everyone so angry]?; **so etwas macht man nicht** that [just] isn't done; **mach was dran!** (ugs.) what can you do?; **mit mir könnt ihr es ja ~** (ugs.) you can get away with it with me; **sie lässt alles mit sich ~:** she is very long-suffering

8 **was macht ...?** (wie ist um ... bestellt?) how is ...?; **was macht die Arbeit?** how is the job [getting on]?; how are things at work?; **was macht die Gesundheit?** how are you keeping?

9 (ergeben) (beim Rechnen) be; (bei Geldbeträgen) come to; **zwei mal zwei macht vier** two times two is four; **was** *od.* **wie viel macht das [alles zusammen]?** how much does that come to?; **das macht 12 Euro** that is *or* costs 12 euros; (Endsumme) that comes to 12 euros

10 (schaden) **was macht das schon?** what does it matter?; **macht das was?** does it matter?; do you mind?; **macht nichts!** (ugs.) never mind!; it doesn't matter

11 (teilnehmen an) **einen Kursus** *od.* **Lehrgang ~:** take a course; **ein Seminar ~** (ugs.) take part in a seminar

12 (ugs.: veranstalten) organize, (coll.) do ‹*trips, meals, bookings, etc.*›; **ein Fest ~:** give a party

13 **machs gut!** (ugs.) look after yourself!; (auf Wiedersehen) so long!; **er macht es nicht mehr lange** (ugs.) he won't last much longer

14 (ugs.: ordnen, sauber ~, renovieren); do ‹*room, stairs, washing, etc.*›; **das Bett ~:** make the bed; **die Haare/Fingernägel ~:** do one's hair/nails; **den Garten ~:** do the garden (coll.)

15 (ugs. verhüll.: seine Notdurft verrichten) **sein Geschäft ~:** relieve oneself; **groß/klein ~:** do big jobs/small jobs (child language)

16 (ugs.: spielen, sein) play, act ‹*part, the clown, etc.*› **wer macht hier den Vorarbeiter?** who is the foreman here?

17 **es [mit jmdm.] ~** (ugs. verhüll.) have it off [with sb.] (sl.); **es jmdm. ~** (derb) give it to sb. (sl.)

B *refl. V.* **1** *mit Adj.* **sich ... ~:** make oneself ...; **sich hübsch ~:** smarten [oneself] up; **sich schmutzig ~:** get [oneself] dirty; **sich verständlich ~:** make oneself clear; **das macht sich bezahlt!** it's worth it!; **sie macht sich besser, als sie ist** she pretends to be better than she is

2 (beginnen) **sich an etw.** *(Akk.)* **~:** get down to sth.; **mach dich ans Werk/an die Arbeit** get down to work; get on with it

3 (ugs.: sich entwickeln) do well; get on; **du hast dich aber gemacht!** you've made great strides!

4 (passen) **das macht sich gut hier** this fits in well; this looks good here

5 **mach dir nichts daraus!** (ugs.) don't let it bother you; **ich mache mir nichts daraus** it doesn't bother me; **sich** *(Dat.)* **nichts/wenig aus jmdm./etw. ~** (ugs.) not care at all/much for sb./sth.

6 (gestalten) **wir wollen uns** *(Dat.)* **einen schönen Abend ~:** we want to have an enjoyable evening; **macht euch ein paar schöne Stunden** enjoy yourselves for a few hours

7 **sich** *(Dat.)* **Feinde ~:** make enemies; **sich** *(Dat.)* **jmdn. zum Freund/Feind ~:** make a friend/an enemy of sb.; **sich** *(Dat.)* **etw. zum Grundsatz/zur Aufgabe ~:** make sth. a principle/one's task

8 **das macht sich von selbst** it takes care of itself; **wenn es sich [irgendwie] ~ lässt** if it can [somehow] be done; if it is [at all] possible

C *itr. V.* **1** (ugs.: sich beeilen) **mach schon!** get a move on! (coll.); look snappy! (coll.); **mach schneller!** hurry up!

2 **das macht müde** it makes you tired; it is tiring; **das macht hungrig** it makes you hungry; **das macht durstig** it makes you thirsty; **das Kleid macht dick** the dress makes one look fat

3 (tun) **lass mich nur ~** (ugs.) leave it to me

4 (ugs. verhüll.) ‹*child, pet*› perform (coll.); **ins Bett/in die Hose ~:** wet one's bed/pants

5 (salopp: tätig sein) **er macht in Lederwaren** he is in leather goods; **der Konzern macht auch in Versicherungen** the group also does insurance

6 (salopp abwertend: mimen) **auf naiv** *usw.* **~:** pretend to be naïve *etc.;* act naïve *etc.;* **auf feine Dame/großen Geschäftsmann ~:** act the fine lady/big business man; **auf vornehm ~:** give oneself airs

7 *mit sein* (landsch. ugs.: sich begeben) go; **in den Westen ~:** go to the west

Machenschaften *Pl.* (abwertend) machinations; wheeling and dealing *sing.*

-macher *der;* **~s, ~, -macherin** *die;* **~, ~nen** ...-maker; **Filme~/Besen~/Bücher~:** film-maker/broom-maker/maker of books

Macher *der;* **~s, ~, Macherin** *die;* **~, ~nen** (ugs.) doer; **der Typ des Machers** the dynamic type who just gets on with things

Macher·lohn *der* (Schneiderei) making-up charge

Machete /maˈxeːtə/ *die;* **~, ~n** machete

Machiavellismus /makiaveˈlɪsmʊs/ *der;* **~** (Philos., Politik) Machiavellianism *no art.*

machiavellistisch *Adj.* (Philos., Politik) Machiavellian

Machismo /maˈtʃɪsmo/ *der;* **~[s]** (abwertend) machismo

Macho /ˈmatʃo/ *der;* **~s, ~s** (abwertend) macho

machohaft (abwertend)
A *Adj.* macho
B *adv.* in a macho manner

Macht /maxt/ *die;* **~, Mächte** /ˈmɛçtə/ **1)** (Kraft, Einfluss) power; (Stärke) strength; (Befugnis) authority; power; **mit aller ~:** with all one's might; **alles, was in seiner ~ steht, tun** do everything in one's power; **seine ~ ausspielen** use one's authority *or* power; **das liegt nicht in ihrer ~:** that is not within her power; that is outside her authority; **~ über jmdn. haben** have a hold over sb.; **eine unwiderstehliche ~ auf** *od.* **über jmdn. ausüben** exert an irresistible influence over sb.; **die ~ der Gewohnheit/der Verhältnisse** the force of habit/circumstances; **der Frühling kommt mit ~:** spring is coming with a vengeance **2)** (Herrschaft) power *no art.*; **die ~ ergreifen** *od.* **an sich reißen** seize power; **an die ~ kommen** come to power **3)** (Staat) power **4)** (Machtgruppe; geheimnisvolle Kraft) power; force; **die Mächte der Reaktion** the forces of reaction; **die Mächte der Finsternis** the powers of darkness; **böse Mächte** evil forces **5)** (geh., veralt.: Heer) forces *pl.*; **mit großer ~:** with a large force *or* army

macht-, Macht-: ~anspruch *der* claim *or* pretension to power; **~apparat** *der* power structure; **~ausübung** *die* exercise of power (*Gen.* by); **~befugnis** *die* authority *no pl., no art.*; power *no art.*; **~bereich** *der* sphere of influence; **~besessen A** *Adj.* power-crazed; **B** *adv.* in a power-crazed manner; **~block** *der; Pl.* **~blöcke** power bloc

Mächte·gruppierung *die* (Politik) power grouping

macht-, Macht-: ~entfaltung *die* expansion of power; **~ergreifung** *die* (Politik) seizure of power (*Gen.* by); **~erhalt** *der* retention of power; holding on to power; **~gier** *die* (abwertend) craving for power; **~gierig** *Adj.* with a craving for power *postpos., not pred.*; **~gierig sein** crave power; **~haber** /-haːbɐ/ *der;* **~~s, ~~, ~haberin** *die;* **~~, ~~nen** ruler; **die gegenwärtigen ~haber** those at present in power; **~hunger** *der* hunger for power; **~hungrig** *Adj.* power-hungry

mächtig /ˈmɛçtɪç/
A *Adj.* **1)** powerful; **die Mächtigen dieser Welt** the high and mighty; the wielders of power **2) seiner Sinne** *od* **seiner selbst** (*Gen.*) **[nicht] ~ sein** [not] be in control of oneself; **einer Sprache** (*Gen.*) **/des Lesens und Schreibens ~ sein** (geh.) have a command of a language/be capable of reading and writing **3)** (beeindruckend groß) mighty; powerful, mighty ‹*voice, blow*›; tremendous, powerful ‹*effect*›; (ugs.) terrific (coll.) ‹*luck*›; terrible (coll.) ‹*fright*›; **~en Hunger/~e Angst haben** be terribly hungry/afraid **4)** (landsch.: schwer) heavy ‹*food*›; (sättigend) filling ‹*food*›
B *adv.* (ugs.) terribly (coll.); extremely; **~ viel** an awful lot (coll.); **~ groß** tremendously large (coll.); **er ist ~ gewachsen** he has grown a lot; **ihr müsst euch ~ beeilen** you'll really have to step on it (coll.)

Mächtigkeit *die;* **~ 1)** (Einfluss) power **2)** (Größe) massive size; (Gewalt) force

macht-, Macht-: ~instrument *das* (Politik) instrument of power; **~kampf** *der* (bes. Politik) power struggle; **~los** *Adj.* powerless; impotent; **gegen etw. ~los sein, einer Sache** (*Dat.*) **~los gegenüberstehen** be powerless in the face of sth.; **gegenüber jmdm. ~los sein** be powerless against sb.; **gegen so viel Frechheit/Dummheit bin ich/ist man einfach ~los** there is nothing one can do in the face of such impudence/stupidity; **~losigkeit** *die;* **~~:** impotence (**gegen, gegenüber** in the face of); **~missbrauch,** ***~mißbrauch** *der* abuse of power; **~mittel** *das* instrument of power; **~politik** *die* power politics *sing., no art.*; **~position** *die* (bes. Politik) position of power; **~probe** *die* trial of strength; **~spiel** *das* power game; **~stellung** *die* ▸ **~position**; **~streben** *das* ambition for power; **~übernahme** *die* (Politik) takeover [of power] (*Gen.* by); **~verhältnisse** *Pl.* balance of power *sing.*; (innerhalb einer Organisation) power structure *sing.*; **~voll A** *Adj.* powerful; (imponierend) impressive ‹*demonstration, appearance*›; **B** *adv.* powerfully; (imponierend) impressively; **~vollkommenheit** *die* absolute power; **aus eigener ~vollkommenheit** on one's own authority *or* initiative; **~wechsel** *der* (Politik) change of government; **~wort** *das;* **~~e** word of command; decree; **ein ~wort sprechen** put one's foot down; lay down the law

Mach·werk *das* (abwertend) shoddy effort

Macke /ˈmakə/ *die;* **~, ~n 1)** (salopp: Tick) fad; **'ne ~ haben** have a fad; (verrückt sein) be off one's rocker (coll.) **2)** (ugs.: Defekt) defect; (optisch) mark; blemish

Macker *der;* **~s, ~ 1)** (Jugendspr.: Freund, Kerl) guy (coll.); bloke (Brit. sl.) **2)** (abwertend) macho

MAD *Abk.* **= Militärischer Abschirmdienst** Military Counter Intelligence [Service]

Madagaskar /madaˈgaskar/ *(das);* **~s** Madagascar

Madagasse /madaˈgasə/ *der;* **~n, ~n, Madagassin** *die;* **~, ~nen** Madagascan; Malagasy

madagassisch *Adj.* Malagascan; Malagasy

Madam /maˈdam/ *die;* **~, ~s 1)** (ugs. scherzh.) [portly] matron **2)** (landsch. scherzh.: Ehefrau) better half (joc.)

Mädchen /ˈmɛːtçən/ *das;* **~s, ~ 1)** girl; (ugs. veralt.: Freundin) girl[friend]; **für kleine ~ müssen** (fam. scherzh. verhüll.) need to spend a penny (Brit. coll.) **2)** (Haus~) maid; **~ für alles** (ugs.) maid of all work; (im Büro usw.) girl Friday; (Mann) man Friday

Mädchen·alter *das* girlhood years *pl.*; **im [zarten] ~alter** when still a [young] girl

mädchenhaft
A *Adj.* girlish; **~ aussehen** ‹*boy*› have a girlish look; look like a girl; ‹*girl*› look childlike
B *adv.* **sich ~ kleiden** dress in a girlish manner; ‹*older woman*› wear young clothes, dress like a young girl

Mädchen-: ~handel *der* white-slave traffic; **~händler** *der,* **~händlerin** *die* white-slave trader; **~klasse** *die* girls' class; **~kleidung** *die* girls' clothes *pl.*; **~name** *der* **1)** (Vorname) girl's name; **2)** (Name vor der Ehe) maiden name; **~pensionat** *das* girls' boarding school; **~schule** *die* girls' school; school for girls; **~zimmer** *das* **1)** (für ein ~zimmer) girl's room; (für mehrere) girls' room; **2)** (für Hausmädchen) maid's room

Made /ˈmaːdə/ *die;* **~, ~n** maggot; (Larve) larva; **leben wie die ~ im Speck** be living in the lap of luxury *or* off the fat of the land

Madeira /maˈdeːra/ *der;* **~s, ~s, Madeira·wein** *der* Madeira

Madel /maːdl̩/ *das;* **~s, ~n,** (südd., österr. mundartl.), **Mädel** /ˈmɛːdl̩/ *das;* **Mädels, Mädel,** *od. nordd.:* **Mädels** ▸ **Mädchen 1**

Maderl, Mäderl /ˈmɛːdɐl̩ /,/ *das;* **~s, ~n** (österr. ugs.) ▸ **Mädchen 1**

madig *Adj.* maggoty; **jmdm. etw./ein Vergnügen ~ machen** (ugs.) spoil sb.'s pleasure in sth./spoil a pleasure for sb.; **jmdn./etw. ~ machen** (ugs.) run sb./sth. down

Madonna /maˈdɔna/ *die;* **~, Madonnen 1)** (christl. Rel.) **die ~:** Our Lady; the Virgin Mary **2)** (Kunst) madonna

madonnen-, Madonnen-: ~gesicht *das* madonna-like features *pl.*; **~haft A** *Adj.* madonna-like; **B** *adv.* in a madonna-like manner; **~scheitel** *der* centre parting

Madrigal /madriˈgaːl/ *das;* **~s, ~e** (Literaturw., Musik) madrigal

Maestro /maˈɛstro/ *der;* **~s, ~s** *od.* **Maestri** maestro

Maf[f]ia /ˈmafi̯a/ *die;* **~, ~s 1)** Mafia **2)** (fig.) mafia

mafios /maˈfi̯oːs/, **mafiös** /maˈfi̯øːs/
A *Adj.* Mafia *attrib.*; (nach Art der Mafia) Mafia-like
B *adv.* ‹*organized, controlled*› along Mafia lines

Mafioso /maˈfi̯oːzo/ *der;* **~s, Mafiosi** Mafioso

mag /maˈk/ *1. u. 3. Pers. Sg. Präsens v.* **mögen**

Magazin /magaˈtsiːn/ *das;* **~s, ~e 1)** (Lager) store; (für Waren) stockroom; (für Waffen u. Munition) magazine; (in der Bibliothek) stack [room]; stacks *pl.* **2)** (für Patronen, Dias, Film usw.) magazine; (an Werkzeugmaschinen) feeder **3)** (Zeitschrift) magazine; (Rundf., Ferns.) magazine programme

Magazineur /magatsiˈnøːɐ̯/ *der;* **~s, ~e** (österr.) storekeeper; stores supervisor

magazinieren *tr. V.* [put in] store; put ‹*explosives, weapons*› in a/the magazine

Magd /maːkt/ *die;* **~, Mägde** /ˈmɛːkdə/ **1)** (veralt.) (Landarbeiterin) [female] farmhand; (Vieh~) milkmaid; (Dienst~) maidservant **2)** (dichter. veralt.: Jungfrau) maid; damsel; **Maria, die reine ~** (christl. Rel.) Mary, the pure Virgin

Mägdelein /ˈmɛːkdəlai̯n/ *das;* **~s, ~, Mägdlein** /ˈmɛːktlai̯n/ *das;* **~s, ~** (dichter. veralt.) maiden

Magellan·straße /mageˈlaːn-/ *die* Straits *pl.* of Magellan

Magen /ˈmaːgn̩/ *der;* **~s, Mägen** /ˈmɛːgn̩/ *od.* **~** ▸ ❶ **S. 435** stomach; **mir knurrt der ~** (ugs.) my tummy is rumbling (coll.); **sich** (*Dat.*) **den ~ verderben** get an upset stomach; **etw. auf nüchternen** *od.* **leeren ~ essen/trinken** eat/drink sth. on an empty stomach; **etwas/nichts im ~ haben** have had something/nothing to eat; **jmdm. auf den ~ schlagen** upset sb.'s stomach; **jmdm. schwer im ~ liegen** lie heavy on sb.'s stomach; **diese Sache liegt mir schwer auf dem** *od.* **im ~** (fig. ugs.) this business is preying on my mind; **mit leerem ~:** with an empty stomach; **da dreht sich einem/mir der ~ um** (ugs.) it's enough to make *or* it makes one's/my stomach turn; (fig.) it makes you/me sick; *s. auch* **Liebe 1**

magen-, Magen-: ~ausheberung *die;* **~~, ~~en** (Med.) pumping-out of the stomach; **~beschwerden** *Pl.* stomach trouble *sing.*; **~bitter** *der;* **~~, ~~s** bitters *pl.*; **~blutung** *die* gastric haemorrhage; **~-Darm-Kanal** *der* ▸ ❶ **S. 435** (Anat.) gastro-intestinal tract; **~-Darm-Katarr[h]** *der* ▸ ❶ **S. 439** (Med.) gastro-enteritis; **~drücken** *das;* **~~s** feeling of pressure in the stomach; (~schmerzen) stomach ache; **~durchbruch** *der* ▸ ❶ **S. 439** (Med.) ▸ **~perforation**; **~fahrplan** *der* (ugs. scherzh.) menu; eating schedule; **~freundlich** *adj.* kind to the stomach *pred.*; **~gegend** *die* the region of the stomach; **ein unangenehmes Gefühl in der ~gegend** an unpleasant feeling in the [pit of the] stomach; **~geschwür** *das* ▸ ❶ **S. 439** stomach ulcer; **~grube** *die* pit of the stomach; **~inhalt** *der* contents *pl.* of the stomach; **~katarr[h]** *der* ▸ ❶ **S. 439** (Med.) gastritis; **~knurren** *das;* **~~s** (ugs.) tummy rumbles *pl.* (coll.); **~krampf** *der* stomach cramp; **~krämpfe** stomach spasms; **~krank** *Adj.* ‹*person*› suffering from a stomach disorder *or* complaint; **~krank sein/werden** have/get a stomach disorder *or* complaint; **~krankheit** *die* stomach complaint; **~krebs** *der* ▸ ❶ **S. 439** cancer of the stomach; **~leiden** *das* ▸ ❶ **S. 439** ▸ **~krankheit**; **~leidend** *Adj.:* ▸ **~krank**; **~mittel** *das* medicine for the stomach; stomachic (Pharm.); **~perforation** *die* ▸ ❶ **S. 439** (Med.) perforation of the stomach; **~saft** *der* gastric juice; **~säure** *die* gastric acid; **~schleimhaut** *die* ▸ ❶ **S. 435** lining of the stomach; **~schleimhaut·entzündung** *die* gastritis; **~schmerzen** *Pl.* ▸ ❶ **S. 439** stomach ache *sing.*; **~spiegelung** *die* (Med.) gastroscopy; **~spülung** *die* (Med.) gastric irrigation; **~verstimmung** *die* stomach upset

mager /ˈmaːgɐ/
A *Adj.* **1)** (dünn) thin **2)** (fettarm) low-fat; low in fat *pred.*; lean ‹*meat*›; **ein ~es Benzingemisch** (Kfz-W.) a lean mixture **3)** (nicht ertragreich) poor ‹*soil, harvest*›; infertile ‹*field*›; lean ‹*years*›; (fig.: dürftig) meagre ‹*profit, increase, success, report, etc.*›; thin ‹*programme*› **4)** (Druckw.) light-face ‹*type, characters*›
B *adv.* **~ essen** follow a low-fat diet; eat low-fat foods

Mager·käse *der* low-fat cheese

Magerkeit *die;* ~ 1 thinness 2 (Ertragsarmut) poorness; (fig.: Dürftigkeit) meagreness

Mager-: **~milch** *die* skim[med] milk; **~quark** *der* low-fat curd cheese; **~sucht** *die* ▸ⓘ S. 439 (Med.) wasting disease; (Anorexie) anorexia

Magie /maˈgiː/ *die;* ~: magic; **schwarze/weiße ~:** black/white magic

Magier /ˈmaːgi̯ɐ/ *der;* **~s,** ~, **Magierin** *die* (auch fig.) magician; **die drei Magier** (bibl.); the Three Magi

magisch
A *Adj.* 1 magic ‹*powers*›; **~es Quadrat** magic square 2 (geheimnisvoll) magical ‹*attraction, light, force, etc.*›; (unwirklich) eerie ‹*light, half-light*›
B *adv.* (durch Zauber) by magic; (wie durch Zauber) as if by magic; magically; (unwirklich) eerily; **~ beleuchtet** with magical/eerie lighting *post-pos., not pred.*

Magister /maˈgɪstɐ/ *der;* **~s,** ~ 1 ≈ Master's degree (*first degree at a German university*); **den ~ haben/machen** have/work for an MA *or* (Amer.) a Master's; **~ Artium** /- ˈartsi̯ʊm/ Master of Arts 2 (Inhaber des Titels) ≈ person holding a Master's degree; **~ sein** ≈ have a Master's degree

Magistrat[1] /magɪsˈtraːt/ *der;* **~[e]s, ~e** City Council

Magistrat[2] *der;* **~en, ~en** (schweiz.) Federal Councillor

Magma /ˈmagma/ *das;* **~s, Magmen** (Geol.) magma

Magna Charta /ˈmagna ˈkarta/ *die;* ~ (hist.) Magna Carta

magna cum laude /ˈmagna kʊm ˈlaudə/ (Hochschulw.) with great distinction; *second of four grades of successful doctoral examination*

Magnat /maˈgnaːt/ *der;* **~en, ~en** 1 magnate 2 (hist.) great nobleman

Magnesia /maˈgneːzi̯a/ *die;* ~ 1 (Chemie, Med.) magnesia 2 (Turnen) chalk

Magnesium /maˈgneːzi̯ʊm/ *das;* **~s** (Chemie) magnesium

Magnet /maˈgneːt/ *der;* **~en** *od.* **~[e]s, ~e** (auch fig.) magnet

Magnet-: **~auf·zeichnung** *die* [magnetic] tape recording; **~band** *das Pl.* **~bänder** magnetic tape; **~berg** *der* Magnetic Mountain; **~bild·verfahren** *das* (Technik) videotape technique; **~eisen·stein** *der* (Mineral.) magnetite; **~feld** *das* (Physik) magnetic field

magnetisch
A *Adj.* (auch fig.) magnetic
B *adv.* magnetically; **~ gespeichert/aufgezeichnet** stored/recorded on magnetic tape; **jmdn. ~ anziehen** (fig.) have a magnetic attraction for sb.

Magnetiseur /magnetiˈzøːɐ̯/ *der;* **~s, ~e** mesmerist

magnetisieren *tr. V.* 1 (Physik) magnetize 2 (Psych. veralt.) treat ‹*patient*› by mesmerism

Magnetisierung *die;* **~, ~en** (Physik) magnetization

Magnetismus *der;* ~ 1 (Physik) magnetism 2 (Psych. veralt.) mesmerism *no art.*

Magnet-: **~kern** *der* (Physik) core [of a/the magnet]; **~kompass,** ***~kompaß** *der* magnetic compass; **~nadel** *die* [compass] needle

Magneton /ˈmagnetɔn/ *das;* **~s, ~[s]** (Kernphysik) magneton

Magnetophon ⓌⓏ /magnetoˈfoːn/ *das;* **~s, ~e** tape recorder

Magnetosphäre *die;* ~: magnetosphere

Magnetron /ˈmagnetrɔn/ *das;* **~s, ~e** /-ˈtroːnə/ (Physik) magnetron

Magnet-: **~schalter** *der* (Kfz-W.) solenoid switch; (im Spannungsregler) [magnetic] cut-out; **~schwebebahn** *die* maglev [system]; (Zug) maglev train; **~spule** *die* 1 coil [of an/the electromagnet]; 2 (Solenoid) solenoid; **~zündung** *die* (Kfz-W.) magneto ignition

Magnifikat /maˈgniːfikat/ *das;* **~s** (kath. Kirche) Magnificat

Magnifizenz /magnifiˈtsɛnts/ *die;* **~, ~en** (Hochschulw.) **Seine/Eure ~:** His/Your Magnificence (mode of address or title of German university rector); **die ~en** the rectors

Magnolie /maˈgnoːli̯ə/ *die;* **~, ~n** magnolia

mäh /mɛː/ *Interj.* baa

Mahagoni /mahaˈgoːni/ *das;* **~s** mahogany

Maharadscha /mahaˈratʃa/ *der;* **~s, ~s** maharaja

Maharani /mahaˈraːni/ *die;* **~, ~s** maharanee

Mäh·binder *der* harvester[-binder]

Mahd[1] /maːt/ *die;* **~, ~en** (landsch.) 1 (Mähen) mowing 2 (das Gemähte) mown grass; (Heu) [new-mown] hay

Mahd[2] *das;* **~[e]s, Mähder** /ˈmɛːdɐ/ (österr., schweiz.) high pasture

Mäh·drescher *der* combine harvester

mähen[1] /ˈmɛːən/
A *tr. V.* mow ‹*grass, lawn, meadow*›; cut, reap ‹*corn*›
B *itr. V.* mow; (Getreide ernten) reap

mähen[2] *itr. V.* ‹*sheep*› bleat

Mäher *der;* **~s,** ~ 1 mower; (von Getreide) reaper 2 (ugs.) ▸**Mähmaschine**

Mäherin *die;* **~, ~nen** ▸**Mäher 1**

Mahl /maːl/ *das;* **~[e]s, Mähler** /mɛːlɐ/ (geh.) meal; repast (formal); **beim ~ sitzen** sit at table

mahlen *unr. tr., itr. V.* grind; **etw. fein/grob ~:** grind sth. fine/coarsely; **wer zuerst kommt, mahlt zuerst** (Spr.) the early bird catches the worm (prov.)

Mahl-: **~gang** *der* (Technik) grinding-machine; (**~steine**) set of millstones; **~gut** *das* grist

mählich /ˈmɛːlɪç/ (geh. veralt.)
A *Adj.* gradual
B *adv.* gradually

Mahl-: **~stein** *der* 1 grinding stone; 2 (Mühlstein) millstone; **~strom** *der* (geh.) maelstrom; **~zahn** *der* molar; **~zeit** meal; **sich an die ~en halten** eat meals at regular times; **~zeit!** (ugs.) have a good lunch; bon appetit; **[na dann] prost ~zeit!** (ugs.) what a delightful prospect! (iron.); (an einen anderen) [in that case] the best of British! (Brit. coll.)

Mäh·maschine *die* [power] mower; (für Getreide) reaper

Mahn-: **~bescheid** *der* writ for payment; **~brief** *der* ▸**~schreiben**

Mähne /ˈmɛːnə/ *die;* **~, ~n** mane; (scherzh.: Haarschopf) mane [of hair]

mahnen /ˈmaːnən/
A *tr., itr. V.* 1 (auffordern) urge; **zur Eile/Vorsicht ~:** urge haste/caution; **jmdn. zur Eile/Vorsicht ~:** urge sb. to hurry/to be careful; **jmdn. eindringlich ~:** give sb. an urgent warning; **jmdn. ~d ansehen** look admonishingly at sb. 2 (erinnern) remind (**an** + *Akk.* of); **einen Schuldner [schriftlich] ~:** send a debtor a [written] demand for payment *or* a reminder
B *itr. V.* (geh.) **an etw.** (*Akk.*) **~:** be reminiscent of sth.

Mahner *der;* **~s,** ~, **Mahnerin** *die;* **~, ~nen** (geh.) admonisher; (Unheilsprophet) Cassandra

Mahn-: **~gebühr** *die* reminder fee; **~mal** *das; Pl.* **~~e** *od.* **~mäler** memorial (erected as a warning to future generations); **~ruf** *der* (geh.) warning cry; admonition; **~schreiben** *das* reminder (+ *Gen.* from); (an einen Schuldner) demand [for payment]; reminder

Mahnung *die;* **~, ~en** 1 (Aufforderung) exhortation; (Warnung) admonition 2 (Erinnerung) reminder 3 ▸**Mahnschreiben**

Mahn·verfahren *das* summary proceedings *pl.* [for the payment of a debt]

Mähre /ˈmɛːrə/ *die;* **~, ~n** (veralt. abwertend) jade (dated)

Mähren (*das*); **~s** Moravia

mährisch *Adj.* Moravian

Mai /mai̯/ *der;* **~[e]s** *od.* ~, *dichter.:* **~en, ~e** ▸ⓘ **S. 165** May; **der Erste ~:** the first of May; May Day; **Kundgebungen zum Ersten ~:** May Day rallies; **im ~ des Lebens** (geh.) in the springtime of life; **wie einst im ~:** as in the days of my/their *etc.* youth

Mai-: **~andacht** *die* (kath. Kirche) May devotion; **~baum** *der* 1 maypole; 2 (Birkenbäumchen) *small birch tree traditionally tied to doorpost for May festival;* **~blume** *die* 1 mayflower; 2 (**~glöckchen**) lily of the valley; **~bowle** *die: cup made of white wine and champagne with fresh woodruff*

Maid /mai̯t/ *die;* **~, ~en** (veralt.) maiden

Mai·demonstration *die* May Day demonstration

Maie *die;* **~, ~n** (veralt.): *young birch tree or birch leaves traditionally tied to doorpost for May celebrations*

Maien·nacht *die* (dichter. veralt.) May night

Mai-: **~feier** *die* May Day celebration; **~feier·tag** *der* May Day *no def. art.;* **~glöckchen** *das* lily of the valley; **~käfer** *der* May bug; **~königin** *die* (Volksk.) Queen of the May; **~kundgebung** *die* May Day rally

Mail /meɪl/ *die;* **~, ~s** e-mail

Mailand (*das*); **~s** ▸ⓘ **S. 675** Milan

Mailänder /ˈmailɛndɐ/ ▸ⓘ **S. 675**
A *indekl. Adj.* Milan; Milanese ‹*climate, spring, etc.*› **die ~ Scala** La Scala, Milan
B *der;* **~s, ~:** Milanese; *s. auch* **Kölner**

Mailänderin *die;* **~, ~nen** Milanese

mailändisch *Adj.* Milanese

Mail·box /ˈmeɪlbɔks/ *die* mailbox

mailen /meɪlən/ *tr. V.* e-mail

Mai·parade *die* May Day parade

Mais /mai̯s/ *der;* **~es** maize; corn (esp. Amer.); (als Gericht) sweetcorn

Mais-: **~birne** *die* (Sport) [suspended] punchball (Brit.) *or* (Amer.) punching bag; **~brei** *der* maize *or* (Amer.) corn [meal] porridge; **~brot** *das* corn bread

Maische /ˈmai̯ʃə/ *die;* **~, ~n** (bei Bier, Spiritus) mash; (bei Wein) must

maischen *tr. V.* mash ‹*malt*›; crush ‹*grapes*›

Mais-: **~kolben** *der* corn cob; (als Gericht) corn on the cob; **~korn** *das* grain of maize *or* (Amer.) corn; **~mehl** *das* maize *or* (Amer.) corn flour

Maison[n]ette /mɛzoˈnɛt/ *die;* **~, ~s, Maison[n]ette·wohnung** *die* maisonette

Mais·stärke *die* cornflour (Brit.); cornstarch (esp. Amer.)

Maître de Plaisir /mɛtrə de plɛˈziːr/ *der;* **~ ~ ~, ~s** /mɛtrə-/ **~ ~** (veralt., noch scherzhaft) Master of Ceremonies

Majestät /majɛsˈtɛːt/ *die;* **~, ~en** 1 ▸ⓘ **S. 44** (Titel) Majesty; **Seine/Ihre/Eure** *od.* **Euer ~:** His/Her/Your Majesty 2 (geh.: Erhabenheit) majesty

majestätisch
A *Adj.* majestic
B *adv.* majestically

Majestäts·beleidigung *die* lèse-majesté

Majo /ˈmaːjo/ *die;* **~, ~s** (ugs.) mayo (coll.)

Majolika /maˈjoːlika/ *die;* **~, Majoliken** majolica; **Majoliken** pieces of majolica

Majonäse /majɔˈnɛːzə/ *die;* **~, ~n** mayonnaise

Major /maˈjoːɐ̯/ *der;* **~s, ~e** ▸ⓘ **S. 44** (Milit.) major; (der Luftwaffe) squadron leader (Brit.); major (Amer.)

Majoran /ˈmaːjoran/ *der;* **~s, ~e** marjoram

Majorette /majɔˈrɛt/ *die;* **~, ~s** *od.* **~n** majorette

Majorin *die;* **~, ~nen** 1 (in der Heilsarmee) major 2 (veralt.) major's wife

majorisieren *tr. V.* (geh.) outvote

Majorität /majoriˈtɛːt/ *die;* **~, ~en** majority; **die ~ haben** have a majority

Majoritäts-: **~beschluss,** ***~beschluß** *der* majority decision; **~prinzip** *das* principle of a majority vote; majority principle

Majuskel /maˈjʊskl̩/ *die;* **~, ~n** (Druckw.) capital [letter]

makaber /ma'ka:bɐ/ *Adj.* macabre

Makedonien /make'do:ni̯ən/ *(das);* **~s** Macedonia

Makedonier *der;* **~s, ~, Makedonierin** *die;* **~, ~nen** Macedonian

makedonisch *Adj.* Macedonian

Makel /'ma:kl̩/ *der;* **~s, ~** (geh.) **1** (Schmach) stigma; taint; **an ihm haftet ein ~:** a stain *or* taint clings to him **2** (Fehler) blemish; flaw; **ohne ~:** without a [single] flaw

Mäkelei *die;* **~** (abwertend) carping

mäkelig *Adj.* (abwertend) carping; (beim Essen) fussy; particular

makel·los
A *Adj.* flawless, perfect ‹*skin, teeth, figure, stone*›; spotless, immaculate ‹*white, cleanness, clothes*›; impeccable ‹*accent*›; (fig.) spotless, unblemished ‹*reputation, character*›
B *adv.* immaculately; spotlessly ‹*clean*›; (fehlerfrei) flawlessly

Makellosigkeit *die;* **~** ▸**makellos**: flawlessness; perfection; spotlessness; immaculateness; impeccability; (fig.) spotlessness

makeln *tr. V.* (ugs.) be a broker for ‹*stocks, shares*›; be an agent for ‹*houses, building sites, etc.*›

mäkeln /'mɛ:kl̩n/ *itr. V.* (abwertend) carp; **an etw.** *(Dat.)* *od.* **über etw.** *(Akk.)* **~:** carp at *or* find fault with sth.

Make-up /me:k'|ap/ *das;* **~s, ~s 1** make-up **2** (Präparate) make-up; **die ~s** the make-up products **3** (Tönungscreme) liquid make-up; foundation

Makkaroni /maka'ro:ni/ *Pl.* macaroni *sing.*

Makkaroni·fresser *der,* **Makkaroni·fresserin** *die* (derb abwertend) Eyetie (sl. derog.); wop (sl. derog.)

Makler /'ma:klɐ/ *der;* **~s, ~ 1** ▸**❶ S. 113** (Häuser~) estate agent (Brit.); realtor (Amer.) **2** ▸**❶ S. 113** (Börsen~) broker

Makler-: ~firma *die* estate agents *pl.* (Brit.); (Amer.) realtors *pl.*; **~gebühr** *die* ▸**Maklerprovision**; **Maklerin** *die;* **~, ~nen** ▸**Makler**; **~provision** *die* agent's fee *or* commission; (eines Börsenmaklers) brokerage charges *pl.*

Mako /'mako/ *die;* **~, ~s** *od. der od. das;* **~[s], ~s** Egyptian cotton

Makramee /makra'me:/ *das;* **~[s]** macramé

Makrele /ma'kre:lə/ *die;* **~, ~n** mackerel

Makro *der od. das;* **~s, ~s** (DV) macro

makro-, Makro- /makro-/: **~biotik** /-'bi̯o:tɪk/ *die;* **~~:** macrobiotics *sing., no art.*; **~biotisch A** *Adj.* macrobiotic; **B** *adv.* on macrobiotic principles; **~klima** *das* (Met.) macroclimate; **~kosmos** *der* macrocosm; **~molekül** *das* macromolecule

Makrone /ma'kro:nə/ *die;* **~, ~n** macaroon

Makulatur /makula'tu:ɐ̯/ *die;* **~, ~en 1** (Druckw.) spoilt sheets *pl.*; spoilage *no pl.* **2** (Altpapier) waste paper; **~ reden** (ugs. abwertend) talk rubbish

mal /ma:l/
A *Adv.* ▸**❶ S. 826** (Math.) times; (bei Flächen) by; **zwei ~ zwei** twice two; two times two; **der Raum ist 5 ~ 6 Meter groß** the room is five metres by six
B *Partikel* (ugs.) **komm ~ her!** come here!; **hör ~ zu!** listen!; *s. auch* **einmal B**

Mal[1] *das;* **~[e]s, ~e** *od.* (nach Zahlwörtern) **~:** time; **ein anderes ~:** another time; **nur dies eine ~:** just this once; **kein einziges ~:** not once; not a single time; **jedes ~:** every time; **das achte/dritte** *usw.* **~:** the eighth/third *etc.* time; (zum achten/dritten usw. Mal) for the eighth/third *etc.* time; **beim achten/dritten** *usw.* **~:** the eighth/third *etc.* time; **zum achten/dritten** *usw.* **~:** for the eighth/third *etc.* time; **das letzte ~** (beim letzten Mal) last time; (zum letzten Mal) for the last time; **das x-te ~:** the umpteenth time; (zum x-ten Mal) for the umpteenth time; **mit einem ~[e]** all at once; all of a sudden; **von ~ zu ~ heftiger werden** become more and more violent [each time]; **beide ~[e]** both times; **einige ~[e]** a few times; on a few occasions; **etliche ~[e]** several times; a number of times; **unzählige ~[e]** countless times; over and over again; **verschiedene ~[e]** on various occasions; **Dutzende** *od.* **dutzende/Millionen ~[e]** dozens/millions of times; **ein/ein halbes/zwei/viel Dutzend ~:** a/half a/two/many dozen times; **eine Million/acht Millionen ~:** a/eight million times

Mal[2] *das;* **~[e]s, ~e** *od.* **Mäler** /'mɛ:lɐ/ **1** mark; (Mutter~) birthmark; (braun) mole **2** (geh.: Denk~, Mahn~) memorial **3** (Baseball) base **4** (Rugby) goal; (~feld) in-goal

Malachit /mala'xi:t/ *der;* **~s, ~e** malachite

malad[e] /ma'la:d(ə)/ *Adj.* (veralt., landsch.) ill; sick (esp. Amer.)

Malaga /'malaga/ *der;* **~s, ~s, Malaga·wein** *der* Malaga [wine]

Malaie /ma'lai̯ə/ *der;* **~n, ~n, Malaiin** *die;* **~, ~nen** ▸**❶ S. 520** Malay

malaiisch *Adj.* ▸**❶ S. 520**, ▸**❶ S. 670** Malayan

Malaise /ma'lɛ:zə/ *die;* **~, ~n,** *schweiz.: das;* **~s, ~s 1** malaise; sense of unease **2** (Misere) unhappy situation

Malaria /ma'la:ri̯a/ *die;* **~** ▸**❶ S. 439** malaria

malaria·krank *Adj.* suffering from malaria *postpos.*

Malaria·mücke *die* malaria mosquito

Malawi /ma'la:vi/ *(das);* **~s** Malawi

Malawier *der;* **~s, ~, Malawierin** *die;* **~, ~nen** Malawian

malawisch *Adj.* Malawian

Malaysia /ma'lai̯zi̯a/ *(das);* **~s** Malaysia

malaysisch *Adj.* Malaysian

Mal·buch *das* colouring book

malen
A *tr., itr. V.* **1** paint ‹*picture, portrait, person, etc.*›; (mit Farbstiften) draw with crayons; (aus~) colour; **sich ~ lassen** have one's portrait painted; **etw. in düsteren Farben ~** (fig.) paint *or* portray sth. in gloomy colours; **etw. allzu rosig/schwarz ~** (fig.) paint far too rosy/black a picture of sth. **2** (sauber schreiben) write carefully **3** (anstreichen) paint ‹*door, window, etc.*›; decorate ‹*flat, room, walls*›
B *refl. V.* **1** paint one's self-portrait **2** (geh.) **auf seinem Gesicht malte sich Erstaunen/Entsetzen** astonishment/horror was mirrored in his face

Maler /'ma:lɐ/ *der;* **~s, ~** ▸**❶ S. 113** painter

Maler·arbeit *die* painting and decorating *no pl.*

Malerei *die;* **~, ~en 1** painting *no art.* **2** (Gemälde) painting

Malerin *die;* **~, ~nen** ▸**❶ S. 113** [woman] painter

malerisch
A *Adj.* **1** picturesque ‹*village, house, etc.*›; **einen ~en Anblick bieten** look as pretty as a picture **2** (zur Malerei gehörend) artistic ‹*skill, talent*›; ‹*skill, talent*› as a painter; ‹*motif, subject*› for painters; **sein ~es Werk** his paintings *pl*
B *adv.* **1** picturesquely ‹*situated*› **2** ‹*train*› as a painter; **ihr ~ geschultes Auge** her trained artist's eye

Maler-: ~lein·wand *die* [artist's] canvas; **~meister** *der,* **~meisterin** *die* master painter [and decorator]

Malesche /ma'lɛʃə/ *die;* **~, ~n** (nordd. ugs.) mess; **in der ~ sitzen/in ~n kommen** be/land in the soup (coll.)

Mal·feld *das* (Rugby) in-goal

Malheur /ma'lø:ɐ̯/ *das;* **~s, ~e** *od.* **~s** mishap; **das ist doch kein ~!** it's not the end of the world!

Mali /'ma:li/ *(das);* **~s** Mali

maligne /ma'lɪgnə/ *Adj.* (Med.) malignant

maliziös /mali'tsi̯ø:s/ (geh.)
A *Adj.* malicious
B *adv.* maliciously

Mal·kasten *der* paintbox

mall /mal/ *Adj.* (ugs., bes. nordd.) barmy (Brit. coll.); crazy

Mallorca /ma'lɔrka/ *(das);* **~s** Majorca

mallorquinisch /malɔr'ki:nɪʃ/ *Adj.* Majorcan

mal|nehmen *unr. tr., itr. V.* multiply (**mit** by); **das Malnehmen:** multiplication

Maloche /ma'lo:xə/ *die;* **~** (salopp) drudgery *no indef. art.*; slog; **auf ~ sein** be at work; (schwer arbeiten) slog away

malochen *itr. V.* (salopp) slog *or* slave [away]

Mal-: ~pinsel *der* paintbrush; **~stift** *der* crayon; **~strom** *der* ▸**Mahlstrom**

Malta /malta/ *(das);* **~s** Malta

Mal·technik *die* painting technique

Malteser /mal'te:zɐ/
A *indekl. Adj.* Maltese
B *der;* **~s, ~ 1** Maltese; *s. auch* **Kölner B 2** ▸**Malteserritter**

Malteser-: ~hilfsdienst *der* ≈ St John Ambulance Brigade; **~kreuz** *das* (auch Technik) Maltese cross; **~orden** *der* Order of the Knights of St John; **~ritter** *der* Knight of St John

maltesisch *Adj.* ▸**❶ S. 670** Maltese

Maltesisch *das;* **~** ▸**❶ S. 670** (Sprachw.) Maltese

Maltose /mal'to:zə/ *die;* **~** (Biochemie) maltose

malträtieren /maltrɛ'ti:rən/ *tr. V.* maltreat; ill-treat

Malus /'ma:lʊs/ *der;* **~** *od.* **~ses, ~** *od.* **~se 1** (Versicherungsw.) supplementary premium (imposed after a number of claims) **2** (Schulw.) negative weighting; handicap; **einen ~ von ... bekommen** be marked down by ...

Mal·utensilien *Pl.* painting equipment *sing. or* (coll.) things

Malve /'malvə/ *die;* **~, ~n** mallow

malven-: ~farben, ~farbig *Adj.* [pale] mauve

Malwinen /mal'vi:nən/ *Pl.* **die ~:** the Falkland Islands

Malz /malt͜s/ *das;* **~es** malt

Malz-: ~bier *das* malt beer; **~bonbon** *das* malted cough lozenge

Mal·zeichen *das* multiplication sign

mälzen /'mɛlt͜sn̩/ *tr., itr. V.* (Brauereiwesen) malt

Mälzerei *die;* **~, ~en** (Brauereiwesen) **1** (Gebäude) malthouse; malting **2** (Malzbereitung) malting

Malz-: ~extrakt *der* malt extract; **~kaffee** *der: coffee substitute made from germinated, dried, and roasted barley;* **~zucker** *der* (Biochemie) maltose

Mama /'mama, *geh. veralt.:* ma'ma:/ *die;* **~, ~s** (fam.) mamma

Mama-: ~puppe *die* talking doll (*saying 'Mama'*); **~söhnchen** *das* (abwertend) mummy's boy (coll.)

Mameluck /mamə'lʊk/ *der;* **~en, ~en** (hist.) Mameluke

Mami /'mami/ *die;* **~, ~s** (fam.) mummy (Brit. coll.); mommy (Amer. coll.)

Mammographie /mamogra'fi:/ *die;* **~, ~n** (Med.) mammography *no art.*

Mammon /'mamɔn/ *der;* **~s** (abwertend) Mammon; **dem ~ nachjagen** devote oneself to the pursuit of Mammon *or* of riches; **der schnöde ~:** filthy lucre

Mammut /'mamʊt/ *das;* **~s, ~e** *od.* **~s** mammoth

Mammut- mammoth; (sehr lange dauernd) marathon

Mammut-: ~baum *der* mammoth tree; sequoia; **~film** *der* mammoth [screen] epic; blockbuster; **~konzern** *der* mammoth concern; **~projekt** *das* mammoth project; **~prozess, *~prozeß** *der* marathon trial; **~sitzung** *die* marathon session

mampfen /'mampfn̩/ *tr., itr. V.* (salopp) munch; nosh (coll.)

Mamsell /mam'zɛl/ *die;* **~, ~en** *od.* **~s** (veralt.: Hauswirtschafterin) housekeeper

man[1] /man/ *Indefinitpron. im Nom.* **1** one; you; **~ hat von dort eine herrliche Aussicht** one has *or* there is a magnificent view from there; **~ kann nie wissen** one *or* you never can tell; **dagegen muss ~ etwas unternehmen** something has to be done about it; **~ nehme 250 g**

m

Butter take 250 grams of butter; **für weitere Auskünfte wende ~ sich an ...** for further information apply to ... **2** (irgendjemand) somebody; (die Behörden; die Leute dort) they; **~ hat mir gesagt ...** I was told ...; they told me ...; **hat ~ dir das nicht mitgeteilt?** didn't anybody/they tell you that?; **~ vermutet/hat herausgefunden, dass ...** it is thought/has been discovered that ...; they think/have discovered that ... **3** (die Menschen im Allgemeinen) people *pl.*; **das trägt ~ heute** that's what people wear *or* what is worn nowadays; **so etwas tut ~ [einfach] nicht** that's [just] not done **4** (ich) one; **~ versteht sein eigenes Wort nicht** you can't hear yourself speak

man[2] *Adv.* (bes. nordd.) **lass ~ gut sein!** forget it!; **na, denn ~ los** let's be off then

Management /ˈmɛnɪdʒmənt/ *das;* **~s, ~s** management

Management-Buy-out *das* (Wirtsch.) management buyout

managen /ˈmɛnɪdʒn̩/ *tr. V.* **1** (ugs.) fix; organize; **ich manage das schon** I'll fix it; (durch Tricks) I'll fiddle it (coll.) **2** (betreuen) manage, act as manager for ‹*singer, artist, player*›; **von seiner Frau gemanagt werden** have one's wife as one's manager

Manager /ˈmɛnɪdʒɐ/ *der;* **~s, ~, Managerin** *die;* **~, ~nen** ▸**i** **S. 113** manager; (eines Fußballvereins) club secretary

Manager·krankheit *die* ▸**i** **S. 439** (volkst.) stress disease *no def. art.*

manch /manç/ *Indefinitpron.* **1** many a; **[so] ~er Beamte, ~ ein Beamter** many an official; **in [so] ~er Beziehung** in many respects; **[so] ~ schöne[n] Stunden** many a happy hour; **~ einer** *od.* **~er** many a person/man; **~ eine** *od.* **~e** many a woman **2** *substantivisch* **~e** some; (viele) many; **[so] ~er musste das erleben** many people had to go through this; **[so] ~es** a number of things; (allerhand Verschiedenes) all kinds of things; **[so] ~es von dem, was wir lernten** much of what we learnt

manchenorts ▸**mancherorts**

mancherlei *unbest. Gattungsz.; indekl.* **1** various; a number of; **~ Käse** various kinds of cheese **2** (Verschiedenes) various things; a number of things

mancherorten, mancherorts *Adv.* (geh.) in some places; (an verschiedenen Orten) in various places

Manchester /ˈmɛntʃɛstɐ/ *der;* **~s** [heavy] corduroy

manch·mal *Adv.* sometimes

Mandant /manˈdant/ *der;* **~en, ~en, Mandantin** *die;* **~, ~nen** (Rechtsw.) client

Mandarin /mandaˈriːn/ *der;* **~s, ~e** (hist.) mandarin

Mandarine /mandaˈriːnə/ *die;* **~, ~n** mandarin [orange]; tangerine

Mandat /manˈdaːt/ *das;* **~[e]s, ~e** **1** (Parlamentssitz) [parliamentary] seat; **sein ~ niederlegen** resign one's seat **2** (Auftrag) (eines Abgeordneten) mandate; (eines Anwalts) brief; **das politische ~ der Studentenausschüsse** the right of student committees to make political statements on behalf of members **3** (Treuhandgebiet) mandate; mandated territory

Mandatar /mandaˈtaːɐ̯/ *der;* **~s, ~e, Mandatarin** *die;* **~, ~nen** **1** mandatary **2** (österr.: Abgeordneter) member [of parliament]; deputy

Mandats-: ~gebiet *das* mandated territory; mandate; **~träger** *der,* **~trägerin** *die* (Politik) member of parliament; deputy

Mandel /ˈmandl̩/ *die;* **~, ~n** **1** almond **2** ▸**i** **S. 435** (Anat.) tonsil

mandel-, Mandel-: ~augen *Pl.* (geh.) almond eyes; **~äugig** *Adj.* (geh.) almond-eyed; **~baum** *der* almond [tree]; **~entzündung** *die* ▸**i** **S. 439** tonsillitis *no indef. art.*; **~förmig** *Adj.* almond-shaped; **~operation** *die* tonsillectomy

Mandoline /mandoˈliːnə/ *die;* **~, ~n** mandolin

Mandrill /manˈdrɪl/ *der;* **~s, ~e** (Zool.) mandrill

Mandschure /manˈdʒuːrə/ *der;* **~n, ~n** Manchu; Manchurian

Mandschurei *die;* **~:** Manchuria *no art.*

Mandschurin *die;* **~, ~nen** ▸**Mandschure**

mandschurisch *Adj.* Manchurian

Manege /maˈneːʒə/ *die;* **~, ~n** (im Zirkus) ring; (in der Reitschule) arena

mang /maŋ(k)/ *Präp. mit Dat. od. Akk.* (nordd., berlin.) among

Mangan /maŋˈgaːn/ *das;* **~s** (Chemie) manganese

Mangan-: ~erz *das* manganese ore; **~säure** *die* manganic acid

Mangel[1] /ˈmaŋl̩/ *der;* **~s, Mängel** /ˈmɛŋl̩/ **1** (Fehlen) lack (**an** + *Dat.* of); (Knappheit) shortage, lack (**an** + *Dat.* of); **es herrscht** *od.* **besteht ~ an etw.** (*Dat.*) there is a lack *or* shortage of sth.; sth. is in short supply; **~ an Vitaminen** vitamin deficiency; **aus ~** *od.* **wegen ~s an Beweisen** for lack of evidence; **aus ~ an Erfahrung** from *or* owing to lack of experience; **keinen ~ leiden** not go short [of anything]; not want for anything **2** (Fehler) defect; **geringfügige Mängel** minor flaws *or* imperfections; **die Mängel eines Nachschlagewerkes/Drehbuchs** the shortcomings *or* deficiencies of a reference work/film script

Mangel[2] *die;* **~, ~n** (Wäsche~) [large] mangle; **jmdn. durch die ~ drehen** *od.* **in die ~ nehmen** *od.* **in der ~ haben** (fig. salopp) put sb. through the hoop

Mängel·bericht *der* (Technik) defect report (+ *Gen.* on); list of faults

Mangel-: ~beruf *der* understaffed profession; **~erscheinung** *die* ▸**i** **S. 439** (Med.) deficiency symptom

mangelhaft

A *Adj.* (fehlerhaft) defective ‹*goods, memory*›; faulty ‹*goods, German, English, etc.*›; (schlecht) poor ‹*memory, lighting*›; bad ‹*road conditions, German*›; (unzulänglich) inadequate ‹*knowledge, lighting*›; incomplete ‹*reports*›; (Schulw.) **die Note „~"** the mark 'unsatisfactory'; (bei Prüfungen) the fail mark

B *adv.* (fehlerhaft) defectively; faultily; (schlecht) poorly; (unzulänglich) inadequately; **~ befestigte Straßen** badly made roads; **Französisch beherrsche ich nur ~:** I have only an imperfect command of French

Mängel·haftung *die* (Rechtsw.) liability for defects

Mangel·krankheit *die* ▸**i** **S. 439** (Med.) deficiency disease

mangeln[1] *itr. V.* **es mangelt an etw.** (*Dat.*) (ist nicht vorhanden) there is a lack of sth.; (ist unzureichend vorhanden) there is a shortage of sth.; sth. is in short supply; **jmdm./einer Sache mangelt etw.** *od.* **es an etw.** (*Dat.*) sb./sth. lacks sth.; **es mangelt mir an Platz** I am short of space; **seine ~de Menschenkenntnis** his inadequate understanding of people; **die ~de Kompromissbereitschaft** the unwillingness to compromise

mangeln[2]

A *tr. V.* mangle

B *itr. V.* do the mangling

Mängel·rüge *die* (Rechtsw.) complaint (*about quality, service, etc.*)

mangels /ˈmaŋls/ *Präp. mit Gen.* in the absence of; **~ eines eigenen Büros** having no office of his *etc.* own; **~ Beweisen** (*Dat.*) owing to lack of evidence

Mangel·ware *die:* **~ sein** be scarce *or* in short supply; ‹*article*› be a scarce commodity; **erfahrene Fachkräfte sind ~** (fig. ugs.) experienced skilled workers are thin on the ground (coll.)

Mangel·wäsche *die* [laundry for] mangling

Mango /ˈmaŋgo/ *die;* **~, ~s** mango

Mangold /ˈmaŋgɔlt/ *der;* **~[e]s** [Swiss] chard

Mangrove /maŋˈgroːvə/ *die;* **~, ~n** mangrove forest

Mangrove[n]-: ~baum *der* mangrove [tree]; **~küste** *die* mangrove coastline

Manichäismus /maniçɛˈɪsmʊs/ *der;* **~:** Manichaeism *no art.*

Manie /maˈniː/ *die;* **~, ~n** mania; **bei jmdm. zur ~ werden** become an obsession with sb.

Manier /maˈniːɐ̯/ *die;* **~, ~en** **1** manner; **in gewohnter ~:** in his/her usual way *or* manner; **auf eine bravouröse ~:** brilliantly; in a masterly fashion; **in der ~ Dalís** in Dalí's manner *or* style; in the manner of Dalí **2** *Pl.* (Umgangsformen) manners; **keine ~en haben** have no manners; **ich werde dir ~en beibringen!** I'll teach you some manners! **3** (veralt.) **das ist doch keine ~!** that's no way to behave

manieriert /maniˈriːɐ̯t/ (geh.)

A *Adj.* mannered

B *adv.* in a mannered fashion

Manieriertheit *die;* **~, ~en** (geh.) mannerism

Manierismus *der;* **~** (Kunstwiss., Literaturw.) mannerism

manierlich

A *Adj.* **1** (fam.) well-mannered; well-behaved ‹*child*› **2** (ugs.: einigermaßen gut) reasonable; decent

B *adv.* **1** (fam.) properly; nicely **2** (ugs.: einigermaßen gut) **ganz/recht ~:** quite/really nicely *or* decently

manifest /maniˈfɛst/ *Adj.* (geh.) manifest; **es wird an diesem Beispiel ~:** it is made manifest by this example

Manifest *das;* **~[e]s, ~e** manifesto

Manifestant /manifɛsˈtant/ *der;* **~en, ~en, Manifestantin** *die;* **~, ~nen** (schweiz.) demonstrator

Manifestation /manifɛstaˈtsi̯oːn/ *die;* **~, ~en** **1** (Med., Psych. usw.) manifestation **2** (schweiz.: Kundgebung) demonstration

manifestieren (geh.)

A *refl. V.* be manifested; manifest itself

B *tr. V.* demonstrate

C *itr. V.* (veralt.) demonstrate

Maniküre /maniˈkyːrə/ *die;* **~, ~n** **1** manicure; **~ machen** manicure oneself **2** (Person) manicurist

Maniküre·etui *das* manicure set

maniküren *tr. V.* manicure

Manila·faser /maˈniːla-/ *die,* **Manila·hanf** *der* Manila [hemp]

Maniok /maˈni̯ɔk/ *der;* **~s, ~s** manioc; cassava

Manipulant /manipuˈlant/ *der;* **~en, ~en, Manipulantin** *die;* **~, ~nen** (geh.) manipulator

Manipulation /manipulaˈtsi̯oːn/ *die;* **~, ~en** (geh.) manipulation

manipulativ /manipulaˈtiːf/ (geh.)

A *Adj.* manipulative

B *adv.* by manipulation

Manipulator /manipuˈlaːtɔr/ *der;* **~s, ~en** /-toːrən/ **1** (Person, Gerät) manipulator **2** (Zauberkünstler) sleight-of-hand performer; (Jongleur) conjuror

Manipulatorin *die;* **~, ~nen** ▸**Manipulator**

manipulierbar *Adj.* (geh.) manipulable; susceptible to manipulation *postpos.*; **leicht ~:** easy to manipulate

Manipulierbarkeit *die;* **~** (geh.) manipulability; susceptibility to manipulation; **die ~ der öffentlichen Meinung** the extent to which public opinion can be manipulated

manipulieren /manipuˈliːrən/ *tr. V.* manipulate; rig ‹*election result, composition of a committee*›

Manipulierung *die;* **~, ~en** manipulation

manisch /ˈmaːnɪʃ/ (geh., Psych.)

A *Adj.* manic

B *adv.* maniacally

manisch-depressiv *Adj.* (Psych.; Med.) manic-depressive; **~es Irresein** (veralt.) manic depression

Manitu /ˈmaːnitu/ *der;* **~s** manitou

Manko /ˈmaŋko/ *das;* **~s, ~s** **1** (Mangel) shortcoming; deficiency; (Nachteil) handicap **2** (Fehlbetrag) deficit; **ein ~ von 1 200 Euro haben** be 1,200 euros short

m

Mann /man/ *der;* **~[e]s, Männer** /ˈmɛnɐ/; *s. auch* **Mannen** 1 man; **alle erwachsenen Männer wurden festgenommen** all adult males were arrested; **ein ~, ein Wort** a man's word is his bond; **ein ~ der Tat** a man of action; **ein ~ des Todes** (geh.) a doomed man; **ein ~ der Feder/der Wissenschaft** (geh.) a man of letters/of science; **ein ~ aus dem Volk** a man of humble origins; **ein ~ des Volkes** a man of the people; **der ~ am Klavier** the pianist; the man at the piano; **der geeignete** *od.* **richtige ~ sein** be the right man; **der böse** *od.* **schwarze ~:** the bogy man; **der ~ des Tages/Jahres** the man of the moment/year; **der ~ auf der Straße** the man in the street; **auf den ~ dressiert sein** ‹*dog*› be trained to attack people; **der ~ im Mond** the man in the moon; ; **[mein lieber] ~!** (ugs.) (überrascht, bewundernd) my goodness!; (verärgert) for goodness sake!; **~ [Gottes]!** (ugs.) my God!; **wie ein ~:** to a man; with one voice; **der Geschäftsleitung wie ein ~ entgegentreten** approach the management like one man *or* with a united front; **[nicht] ~s genug sein, etw. zu tun** [not] be man enough to do sth.; **[nicht] der ~ sein, etw. zu tun** [not] be the right man to do sth.; **er ist nicht der ~, der kurz entschlossen eine Entscheidung treffen kann** he is not the sort who can make a decision at the drop of a hat; **seinen ~ stehen** (seine Pflicht tun) do one's duty; (selbstständig sein) stand on one's own two feet; (sich durchsetzen) stand up for oneself; **seinen ~ gefunden haben** have met one's match; **dieser Beruf ernährt seinen ~:** you can make a good living in that job; **du hast wohl einen kleinen ~ im Ohr** (salopp) you must be out of your tiny mind (sl.); **etw. an den ~ bringen** (ugs.) (verkaufen) flog sth. (Brit. coll.); push sth. (Amer.); find a taker/takers for sth.; **seine Ansicht/seine Witze an den ~ bringen** (ugs.) find an audience for one's view/one's jokes; **seine Tochter an den ~ bringen** (ugs. scherzh.) find a taker for *or* marry off one's daughter; **~ für ~:** one by one; **Kämpfe** *od.* **der Kampf ~ gegen ~:** hand-to-hand fighting; **von ~ zu ~:** [from] man to man; **lass dir mal von ~ zu ~ sagen, ...** let me tell you straight, ...; *s. auch* **Welt 1**
2 (Besatzungsmitglied) man; **mit 1 000 ~ Besatzung** with a crew of 1,000 [men]; **an Bord des Düsenjägers waren 4 ~:** there were four men on board the jet fighter; **bis zum letzten ~:** to the last man; **alle ~ an Deck!** (Seemannsspr.) all hands on deck!; **~ über Bord!** (Seemannsspr.) man overboard!; **mit ~ und Maus untergehen** (Seemannsspr.) go down with all on board
3 (Teilnehmer) **pro ~** (ugs.) per person; per head; **alle ~ [hoch]** (ugs.) in force; all together; **wir gingen noch alle ~ [hoch] in eine Kneipe** (ugs.) afterwards the whole lot of us went into a pub (Brit) *or* (Amer.) bar; **uns fehlt der dritte/vierte ~ zum Skatspielen** we need a third/fourth person *or* player for a game of skat; **~ decken** mark [an/one's opponent]; **an** *od.* **in den ~ gehen** (bes. Fußball) go in hard; *s. auch* **frei A 15**; **Gott 1**; **letzt... 1**; **Not 6**
4 (Ehemann) husband; **als** *od.* **wie ~ und Frau leben** (geh.) live as man and wife; **~ und Frau werden** (geh.) become man and wife

Manna /ˈmana/ *das;* **~[s]**, *auch: die;* **~** (bibl.) manna

mannbar *Adj.* (geh. veralt.) 1 marriageable ‹*daughter, girl*›; **~ werden** become of marriageable age 2 (geschlechtsreif) sexually mature ‹*youth*›; **das ~e Alter** sexual maturity

Männchen /ˈmɛnçən/ *das;* **~s, ~** 1 little man; **ein altes, verhutzeltes ~:** a little wizened old man; **~ malen** draw matchstick men
2 (Tier~) male; (Vogel~) male; cock; **~ machen** ‹*animal*› sit up and beg; (fig. ugs.: salutieren) ‹*soldier*› salute smartly

Mann·deckung *die* (Ballspiele) man-to-man marking

Männe /ˈmɛnə/ *der;* **~, ~s** (ugs.) hubby (coll.)

Männeken /ˈmɛnəkn̩/ *das;* **~s, ~s** (niederd., bes. berlin.) little chap; **kleines ~:** tiny fellow

Mannen *Pl.* (dichter. veralt.) vassals; **der Trainer und seine ~** (scherzh.) the manager and his troops

Mannequin /ˈmanəkɛ̃/ *das;* **~s, ~s** mannequin; [fashion] model

männer-, Männer-: ~arbeit *die* a man's work; work for a man; **~bekanntschaft** *die* male *or* gentleman friend; **von ~bekanntschaften leben** earn one's living from prostitution; **~beruf** *der* all-male profession; (überwiegend von ~n ausgeübt) male-dominated profession; **~bund** *der* male society; **~chor** *der* male voice choir; **~domäne** *die* male preserve; **~fang** *der: in* **auf ~fang gehen/aus sein** (ugs.) go/be after the men; **~feindlich** A *Adj.* anti-male; B *adv.* in an anti-male way; **~freundschaft** *die* friendship between men; **~gesangverein** *der* male choral society; **~gesellschaft** *die* male-dominated society; **~geschichten** *Pl.* (ugs.) affairs with men; **~haus** *das* (Völkerk.) men's house; **~herz** *das* man's heart; **~herzen** men's hearts; **~kleider** *Pl.* men's clothes; **~mordend** *Adj.* (ugs. scherzh.) man-eating (fig.); **~sache** *die: in* **das ist ~sache** that's men's business; **~station** *die* men's ward; **~stimme** *die* man's voice; male voice; **~treu** *die;* **~~, ~~** (Bot.) (Veronica) speedwell; veronica; (Eryngium) eryngo; sea holly; **~überschuss**, ***~überschuß** *der* surplus of men; **~welt** *die* (scherzh.) men *pl.;* **~wirtschaft** *die* (scherzh.) male housekeeping *no art.;* **~wohnheim** *das* men's hostel

Mannes-: ~alter *das* manhood *no art.;* **im besten ~alter sein** be in the prime of life *or* in one's prime; **~jahre** *Pl.* [years of] manhood *sing.;* **~kraft** *die* (geh.) virility; **~tugend** *die* (geh. veralt.) manly virtue; **~wort** *das; Pl.* **~~e** (geh.) word as a gentleman; **~würde** *die* (geh.) honour as a gentleman; **~zucht** *die* (geh. veralt.) manly self-control *or* discipline

mannhaft
A *Adj.* manful; (tapfer) courageous ‹*decision etc.*›; (entschlossen) resolute ‹*behaviour*›; stout ‹*resistance*›
B *adv.* manfully; (tapfer) courageously; (entschlossen) resolutely; **~ Widerstand leisten** offer stout resistance

Mannhaftigkeit *die;* **~:** manfulness; (Mut) [manly] courage

mannig·fach
A *Adj.* multifarious; manifold (literary)
B *adv.* in a whole variety of ways; **etw. ~ gestalten** give sth. many different forms

mannig·faltig (geh.)
A *Adj.* multifarious; manifold (literary); (verschiedener Art) diverse
B *adv.* in a large variety of different ways; **das ~ gestaltete Programm** the programme with its diversity of different items

Mannig·faltigkeit *die;* **~:** [great] diversity

Männin /ˈmɛnɪn/ *die;* **~** (bibl., dichter.) woman; (Gefährtin) spouse

Männlein /ˈmɛnlain/ *das;* **~s, ~** 1 **[kleines] ~:** little man 2 (ugs. scherzh.) **~ und/oder Weiblein** men and/or women; (bei jüngeren) boys and/or girls

männlich
A *Adj.* 1 male ‹*sex, line, descendant, flower, etc.*›; **~er Vorname** boy's *or* man's name; **das ~e Tier** the male [animal] 2 (für den Mann typisch) masculine ‹*behaviour, characteristic, etc.*›; male ‹*vanity*›; **ausgesprochen ~ wirken** have a decidedly masculine appearance; **eine ~e Haltung** a manly attitude; **~e Stärke/Energie** the strength/energy of a man 3 (Sprachw.) masculine; (Verslehre) male ‹*rhyme*›
B *adv.* in a masculine way

Männlichkeit *die;* **~** 1 masculinity; manliness 2 (Potenz) virility 3 (scherzh.: Geschlechtsteile) privates *pl.;* private parts *pl.*

Männlichkeits·wahn *der* obsession with masculinity

Mann·loch *das* (Technik) manhole

Mannomann /ˈmanoˈman/ *Interj.* (salopp) boy, oh boy!

Manns·bild *das* (ugs., bes. südd., österr.) man

Mannschaft *die;* **~, ~en** 1 (Sport, auch fig.) team; **die erste/zweite ~** (Fußball) the first/second eleven 2 (Schiffs-, Flugzeugbesatzung) crew 3 (Milit.: Einheit) unit; **vor versammelter ~:** in front of all the men; (fig.) in front of everybody 4 *Pl.* (Milit.: einfache Soldaten) other ranks

mannschaftlich (Sport)
A *Adj.* as a team *postpos.;* **das ~e Zusammenwirken** the teamwork
B *adv.* as a team

Mannschafts-: ~auf·stellung *die* (Sport) 1 [composition of the] team; team line-up; 2 (das Aufstellen) selection of the team; **~dienst·grad** *der* (Milit.) [lower] non-commissioned rank; **~führer** *der,* **~führerin** *die* (Sport) team captain; **~geist** *der* (Sport) team spirit; **~kampf** *der* (Sport) team contest *or* event; **~kapitän** *der,* **~kapitänin** *die* (Sport) team captain; **~meisterschaft** *die* (Sport) team championship; **~raum** *der* (Seew.) crew's quarters *pl.;* **~spiel** *das* (Sport) 1 team game; 2 (Zusammenspiel) team play; teamwork; **~sport** *der* team sport; **~stärke** *die* 1 (Sport) team strength; 2 (Milit.) personnel; **~wagen** *der* personnel carrier; **~wertung** *die* (Sport) team placings *pl. or* classification

manns-, Manns-: ~hoch *Adj.* as tall as a man *postpos.;* six-foot-high; **~leute** *Pl.* (veralt.) menfolk; **~person** *die* (veralt.) male personage; **~toll** *Adj.* (ugs. abwertend) man-mad (coll.); nymphomaniac; **~tollheit** *die* (ugs. abwertend) nymphomania *no art.;* **~volk** *das* (veralt.) menfolk *pl.*

Mann·weib *das* (abwertend) amazon

Manometer /manoˈmeːtɐ/ *das;* **~s, ~**
1 (Physik) manometer; pressure gauge
2 *Interj.* (salopp) **~!** boy, oh boy!

Manöver /maˈnøːvɐ/ *das;* **~s, ~** 1 (Milit.) exercise; **~** *Pl.* manoeuvres; **ins ~ gehen** *od.* **ziehen** go on manoeuvres 2 (Bewegung; fig. abwertend: Trick) manoeuvre

Manöver-: ~gelände *das* manoeuvre area; **~gelände der amerikanischen Truppen** area used for manoeuvres by the American troops; **~kritik** *die* (Milit.) exercise evaluation; (fig.) post-mortem (coll.); **~kritik üben** (fig.) hold a post-mortem; **~schaden** *der* damage *no pl.* caused by manoeuvres/an exercise

manövrieren
A *itr. V.* manoeuvre; **politisch klug/unklug ~** (fig.) perform clever/imprudent political manoeuvres
B *tr. V.* manoeuvre ‹*vehicle*›; **jmdn. in eine einflussreiche Position ~** (fig.) wangle sb. into an influential position (sl.)

manövrier-, Manövrier-: ~fähig *Adj.* manoeuvrable; **~fähigkeit** *die* manoeuvrability; **~unfähig** *Adj.* unmanoeuvrable

Mansarde /manˈzardə/ *die;* **~, ~n** attic; (Zimmer) attic room

Mansarden-: ~dach *das* mansard roof; **~fenster** *das* mansard dormer window; **~wohnung** *die* attic flat (esp. Brit.) *or* (esp. Amer.) apartment

Mansch /manʃ/ *der;* **~[e]s** (ugs.) sloshy mess (coll.); (Schneematsch) slush

manschen *itr. V.* (ugs.) slosh about (coll.)

Manschette /manˈʃɛtə/ *die;* **~, ~n** 1 cuff; **[vor etw.** (*Dat.*)**] ~n haben** (fig. ugs.) have got the willies (coll.) *or* have got the wind up (Brit. coll.) [about sth.]; **jetzt, wo es ernst wird, hat sie ~n** (fig. ugs.) now it's serious she's got cold feet; **sag bloß, du hast ~n vor ihm!** (fig. ugs.) don't say you're scared of him! 2 (Umhüllung) paper frill 3 (Ringen: Würgegriff) stranglehold 4 (Technik: Dichtungsring) sealing ring; ring seal

Manschetten·knopf *der* cuff link

Mantel /ˈmantl̩/ *der;* **~s, Mäntel** /ˈmɛntl̩/ 1 coat; (schwerer) overcoat; **der ~ des Schweigens/Vergessens** (fig.) the cloak *or* mantle of silence/oblivion; **den ~ des Schweigens über etw.** (*Akk.*) **breiten** *od.* **decken** (fig.) observe a strict silence about sth. 2 (Technik) (Isolier~, Kühl~) jacket; (Ofen~) casing; (Rohr~) sleeve; (Kabel~) sheath;

(Geschoss~) [bullet] casing; (einer Granate) [shell] case; (Glocken~) cope; (Reifen~) [outer] cover; casing 3 (Geom.: Zylinder~, Kegel~) curved surface 4 (Finanzw.) share *or* (Amer.) stock certificate 5 (Arbeitswelt ugs.) ▸ **~tarifvertrag**

Mäntelchen /ˈmɛntl̩çən/ *das;* **~s, ~:** little coat; (für Kinder) [child's] coat; **einer Sache** (*Dat.*) **ein ~ umhängen** cover up sth.; (etw. beschönigen) gloss over sth.; *s. auch* **Wind**

Mantel-: ~futter *das* [over]coat lining; **~kleid** *das* coat dress; **~pavian** *der* hamadryas baboon; **~sack** *der* (veralt.) saddlebag; **~tarif** *der* (Arbeitswelt) terms of the **Manteltarifvertrag**; **~tarifvertrag** *der* (Wirtsch.) framework collective agreement [on working conditions]; **~tiere** *Pl.* (Zool.) tunicates

Mantisse /manˈtɪsə/ *die;* **~, ~n** (Math.) mantissa

Mantra /ˈmantra/ *das;* **~[s], ~s** mantra (also fig.)

Mantsch /mantʃ/ *der;* **~[e]s** ▸ **Mansch**

mantschen *itr. V.* ▸ **manschen**

Manual /maˈnu̯aːl/ *das;* **~s, ~e, Manuale** *das;* **~e[s], ~e[n]** (Musik) keyboard; manual

manuell /maˈnu̯ɛl/
A *Adj.* manual
B *adv.* manually; by hand

Manufaktur /manufakˈtuːɐ̯/ *die;* **~, ~en** 1 [small] factory (*where goods are produced largely by hand*) 2 (veralt.: handgearbeitete Ware) hand-made *or* handcrafted article

Manus /ˈmaːnʊs/ *das;* **~, ~** (österr., schweiz.), **Manuskript** /manuˈskrɪpt/ *das;* **~[e]s, ~e** 1 (auch hist.) manuscript; (Typoskript) typescript; (zu einem Film/Fernsehspiel/Hörspiel) script; **als ~ gedruckt** printed for private circulation 2 (Notizen eines Redners usw.) notes *pl.*

Maoismus /maoˈɪsmʊs/ *der;* **~:** Maoism *no art.*

Maoist *der;* **~en, ~en, Maoistin** *die;* **~, ~nen** Maoist

maoistisch
A *Adj.* Maoist
B *adv.* on Maoist lines

Mäppchen /ˈmɛpçən/ *das;* **~s, ~:** pencil case

Mappe /ˈmapə/ *die;* **~, ~n** 1 folder; (größer, für Zeichnungen usw.) portfolio 2 (Aktentasche) briefcase; (Schul~) schoolbag

Mär /mɛːɐ̯/ *die;* **~, ~en** (dichter.) fable; (fig.) myth

Marabu /ˈmaːrabu/ *der;* **~s, ~s** (Zool.) marabou

-marathon *das;* **-~s, -~s** (ugs.) **Verhandlungs~/Sitzungs~:** marathon negotiations *pl.* /session

Marathon- /ˈma(ː)ratɔn/: **~lauf** *der* marathon; **~läufer** *der,* **~läuferin** *die* marathon runner; **~sitzung** *die* marathon session

Märchen /ˈmɛːɐ̯çən/ *das;* **~s, ~** 1 fairy story; fairy tale 2 (ugs.: Lüge) [tall] story (coll.); **erzähl doch keine ~!** don't give me that story! (coll.)

Märchen-: ~buch *das* book of fairy stories; **~dichtung** *die* fairy tale literature; **~erzähler** *der,* **~erzählerin** *die* teller of fairy stories; **~figur** *die* fairy tale figure; **~film** *der* film of a fairy story

märchenhaft
A *Adj.* 1 fairy-story *attrib.*; (wie ein Märchen) fairy-story-like; as in a fairy story *postpos.* 2 (zauberhaft) magical; (feenhaft) fairy-like; **~ sein** be sheer magic; be like a dream 3 (ugs.) (großartig) fabulous; (sehr groß) fantastic (coll.), incredible (coll.) ‹*speed, wealth*›
B *adv. s. Adj.:* 1 as in a fairy story; **~ gestaltet** in the form of a fairy story 2 magically; **~ schön** bewitchingly beautiful 3 (ugs.) fantastically (coll.); incredibly (coll.); **~ spielen** play like a dream *or* fabulously

Märchen-: ~land *das:* **das ~land** the world of fairy tale; fairyland; **~onkel** *der* (fam.) story-hour presenter; **~prinz** *der* fairy tale prince; (fig.) Prince Charming; **~prinzessin** *die* fairy tale princess; **~schloss, *~schloß** *das* fairy tale castle; **~stunde** *die* [children's] story hour; **~tante** *die* (fam.) [female] story-hour presenter

Marder /ˈmardɐ/ *der;* **~s, ~:** marten

Mare /ˈmaːrə/ *das;* **~, ~** *od.* **Maria** (Astron.) mare

Margarete /margaˈreːtə/ (*die*) Margaret

Margarine /margaˈriːnə/ *die;* **~:** margarine

Marge /ˈmarʒə/ *die;* **~, ~n** (Wirtsch.) margin; (Preisdifferenz) difference in price; (bei Aktien) increase in price (*over issue price*)

Margerite /margəˈriːtə/ *die;* **~, ~n** ox-eye daisy; (als Zierpflanze) marguerite

marginal /margiˈnaːl/ (geh.)
A *Adj.* marginal
B *adv.* marginally

Marginalie /margiˈnaːli̯ə/ *die;* **~, ~n** marginal note; **~n** marginalia

marginalisieren /marginaliˈziːrən/ *tr. V.* marginalize

Marginalisierung *die;* **~, ~en** marginalization

Maria /maˈriːa/ (*die*); **~s** *od.* **Mariens** *od.* (Rel.) **Mariä** Mary; **Mariä Empfängnis/Geburt** Conception/Nativity of the Blessed Virgin Mary; **Mariä Himmelfahrt** Assumption

marianisch /maˈri̯aːnɪʃ/ *Adj.* (kath. Kirche) Marian

Marianne /maˈri̯anə/ (*die*) Marianne; (fig.: Frankreich) France; the French *pl.*

Marie /maˈriː/ *die;* **~** (salopp: Geld) dough (coll.); lolly (Brit. coll.)

Marien-: ~altar *der* Lady altar; **~bild** *das* madonna; **~dichtung** *die* (Literaturw.) Marian literature; **~käfer** *der* ladybird; **~kult** *der* Marian cult; Mariolatry; **~leben** *das* (Literaturw., Kunstw.) life of our Lady; **~legende** *die* legend of the Virgin Mary; Marian legend; **~verehrung** *die* worship of the Virgin Mary; Mariolatry

Marihuana /mariˈhu̯aːna/ *das;* **~s** marijuana

Marille /maˈrɪlə/ *die;* **~, ~n** (bes. österr.) apricot

marin /maˈriːn/ *Adj.* marine

Marinade /mariˈnaːdə/ *die;* **~, ~n** 1 (Beize) marinade 2 (Salatsauce) [marinade] dressing 3 (Fischkonserve) marinaded fish

Marine /maˈriːnə/ *die;* **~, ~n** 1 (Flotte) fleet 2 (Kriegs~) navy

marine-, Marine-: ~blau *Adj.* navy [blue]; **~flieger** *der* naval airman; **~infanterie** *die* marines *pl.*; **~infanterist** *der* marine; **~luft·waffe** *die* Fleet Air Arm (Brit.); Navy Air Force (Amer.); **~maler** *der,* **~malerin** *die* (Kunst) marine painter

Mariner *der;* **~s, ~** (ugs.) sailor

Marine-: ~schule *die* naval academy; **~soldat** *der,* **~soldatin** *die* marine; **~stütz·punkt** *der* naval base; **~truppen** *Pl.* marines; **~uniform** *die* naval uniform

marinieren *tr. V.* marinade; **marinierte Heringe** soused herrings

Marionette /mari̯oˈnɛtə/ *die;* **~, ~n** puppet; marionette; (fig. abwertend) puppet

Marionetten-: ~regierung *die* (abwertend) puppet government; **~spieler** *der* puppet master; puppeteer; **~spielerin** *die* puppeteer; **~theater** *das* puppet theatre

maritim /mariˈtiːm/ *Adj.* maritime

Mark[1] /mark/ *die;* **~, ~** *od.* (ugs. scherzh.:) **Märker** /ˈmɛrkɐ/ mark; **Deutsche ~:** Deutschmark; German mark; **~ der DDR** GDR *or* East German mark; **die paar Märker** (ugs.) those few measly marks (sl.)

Mark[2] *das;* **~[e]s** 1 (Knochen~) marrow; medulla (Anat.); **jmdm. das ~ aus den Knochen saugen** (fig. ugs.) (finanziell) bleed sb. white; (arbeitsmäßig) work sb. to death; **das ging mir durch ~ und Bein** *od.* (scherzh.) **durch ~ und Pfennig** (fig.) it put my teeth on edge; it went right through me; **jmdn. bis ins ~ treffen** (fig.) cut *or* sting sb. to the quick 2 (Bot.) (Frucht~) pulp; (inneres Gewebe) medulla (as tech. term); pith

Mark[3] *die;* **~, ~en** (hist.) march; **die ~ Brandenburg** the Mark [of] Brandenburg

markant /marˈkant/ *Adj.* striking; distinctive; prominent ‹*figure, nose, chin*›; clear-cut, distinctive ‹*features, profile*›; **ein ~er Punkt in der Stadt** a landmark in the town

mark·durch·dringend
A *Adj.* spine-chilling; blood-curdling
B *adv.* **~ schreien** utter a spine-chilling scream

Marke *die;* **~, ~n** 1 (Waren~) brand; (Fabrikat) make; **Tabak der ~ Erinmore** the Erinmore brand of tobacco 2 (Brief~, Rabatt~, Beitrags~) stamp; **zehn ~n zu 60 Cent** ten 60-cent stamps 3 (Garderoben~) [cloakroom *or* (Amer.) checkroom] counter *or* tag; (Zettel) [cloakroom *or* (Amer.) checkroom] ticket; (Essen~) meal ticket 4 (Erkennungs~) [identification] disc; (Dienst~) [police] identification badge; ≈ warrant card (Brit.) *or* (Amer.) ID card 5 (Lebensmittel~) coupon; **auf ~n verkauft werden** be on coupons 6 (Markierung) mark; (Sport: Rekord) record [height/distance] 7 (salopp) **du bist mir vielleicht eine ~!** you are a fine one! (iron.)

Märke /ˈmɛrkə/ *die;* **~, ~n** (österr.) monogram

marken-, Marken-: ~artikel *der* proprietary *or* (Brit.) branded article; **~artikel** *Pl.* proprietary *or* (Brit.) branded goods; **~bewusst**
A *Adj.* brand-aware; B *adv.* ‹*buy, shop*› with brand awareness; **~bewusstsein** *das* brand awareness; **~butter** *die* best butter (*legally defined first grade of butter*); **~erzeugnis** *das,* **~fabrikat** *das* proprietary *or* (Brit.) branded product; **~image** *das* brand image; **~name** *der* brand name; **~piraterie** *die* brand piracy; **~produkt** *das* branded product; **~schutz** *der* protection of trade marks; **~treue** *die* brand loyalty; **~zeichen** *das* trade mark

mark·erschütternd
A *Adj.* heart-rending
B *adv.* heart-rendingly

Marketender /markəˈtɛndɐ/ *der;* **~s, ~, Marketenderin** *die;* **~, ~nen** (hist.) sutler

Marketender·ware *die* troops' personal supplies *pl.*; ≈ NAAFI (Brit.) *or* (Amer.) PX goods *pl.*

Marketing /ˈmarkətɪŋ/ *das;* **~s** (Wirtsch.) marketing

mark-, Mark-: ~graf *der* margrave; **~gräfin** *die* margravine; **~gräflich** *Adj.* margrave's; of the margrave *postpos.*

markieren
A *tr. V.* 1 (auch fig.) mark; (Sport) mark out ‹*course*› 2 (ugs.) sham ‹*illness, breakdown, etc.*›; **den Dummen ~:** act stupid 3 (Sport) mark ‹*player*›
B *itr. V.* (ugs.) sham; put it on (coll.)

Markierung *die;* **~, ~en** 1 (Zeichen) marking; **ein Flugzeug mit fremder ~:** an aircraft with foreign markings *pl.* 2 marking [out]

Markierungs-: ~fähnchen *das* course marker; marker flag; **~linie** *die* line

markig
A *Adj.* (kernig) pithy ‹*saying, style*›; (kraftvoll) vigorous, breezy ‹*commands, manner*›; powerful ‹*voice*›; **~e Worte** strong words; (iron.: große Reden) big words
B *adv.* pithily

märkisch *Adj.* of the Mark [of] Brandenburg *postpos.*; ‹*food, produce, etc.*› from the Mark [of] Brandenburg; *s. auch* **badisch**

Markise /marˈkiːzə/ *die;* **~, ~n** awning

Mark-: ~klößchen *das;* **~~s, ~~** (Kochk.) bone-marrow dumpling; **~knochen** *der* marrowbone; **~scheide** *die* (Bergmannsspr.) boundary (*of a mining area*); **~stein** *der* (fig.) milestone

Markt /markt/ *der;* **~[e]s, Märkte** /ˈmɛrktə/ 1 market; **heute/freitags ist ~:** today/Friday is market day; **zum** *od.* **auf den ~ gehen** go to the market; **auf dem ~:** at the market 2 ▸ **~platz** 3 (Super~) supermarket 4 (Warenverkehr, Absatzgebiet) market; **der ~ für Gebrauchtwagen** the used-car market; **eine Ware auf den ~ bringen** *od.* **werfen** market a product; (mit viel Werbung) launch a product; **auf dem** *od.* **am ~ sein** ‹*firm*› be in the market;

‹article› be on the market; s. auch **gemeinsam A 1**; **grau 3**; **schwarz A 3**

Markt

Weekly markets are still held in most German cities and towns, usually laid out very attractively in the picturesque market squares. Fresh fruit and vegetables, flowers, eggs, cheese and other dairy products, bread, meat and fish are available direct from the producer. Many Germans still buy most of their provisions *auf dem Markt*.

markt-, Markt-: ~absprache *die* (Wirtsch.) marketing agreement; **~analyse** *die* (Wirtsch.) market analysis; **~anteil** *der* share of the market; **~anteile zurückgewinnen** regain parts of the market; **~beherrschend** *Adj.* market-dominating *attrib.*; **eine ~beherrschende Stellung** a dominant market position; **~beherrschend sein** have a dominant market position; **~bewusst**, ***~bewußt** **A** *Adj.* aware of products and prices *postpos.*; **B** *adv.* with a knowledge of products and prices; **~fähig** *Adj.* (Wirtsch.) marketable; **~fähig werden** become a marketable proposition; **~flecken** *der* (veralt.) small market town; **~forschung** *die* market research *no def. art.*; **~frau** *die* market woman; **~gängig** *Adj.* (Wirtsch.) with a ready sale *postpos., not pred.*; (fig.: üblich) customary; usual; **~gerecht** **A** *Adj.* ‹product› geared to market requirements; ‹price› in line with market conditions; **B** *adv.* in accordance with market conditions; **~halle** *die* covered market; **~lage** *die* market situation; state of the market; **~leiter** *der*, **~leiterin** *die* supermarket manager; **~lücke** *die* gap in the market; **in eine ~lücke [vor]stoßen** fill a gap in the market; **~macht** *die* market power; **~ordnung** *die* **1** (Wirtsch.) [Common] Market regulations *pl.*; **2** (bei Wochenmärkten) market regulations *pl.*; **~platz** *der* market place *or* square; **~recht** *das* (hist.) right to hold a market; market right; **~reif** *Adj.* market-ready; **~reife** *die* market-readiness; **etw. zur ~reife bringen** bring sth. to market-readiness; **~schreier** *der*, **~schreierin** *die* barker; stallholder who cries his wares; (fig. abwertend) vociferous propagandist; **~schreierisch** (abwertend, auch fig.) **A** *Adj.* vociferous; **B** *adv.* vociferously; **~segment** *das* market segment; **~stand** *der* market stall; **~tag** *der* market day; **~üblich** *Adj.* customary [in the market] *postpos.*; **~übliche Zinsen** customary market rates; **~weib** *das* (salopp) market woman; **wie ein ~weib** like a fishwife; **~wert** *der* market value; **~wirtschaft** *die*: **[freie] ~wirtschaft** [free] market economy; **die soziale ~wirtschaft** the social market economy (*with State intervention safeguarding social justice and free competition*); **~wirtschaftlich** **A** *Adj.* market economy; free market; **B** *adv.* on market economy lines

Markus·evangelium /ˈmarkʊs-/ *das* St Mark's Gospel; Gospel according to St Mark

Marmara·meer /ˈmarmara-/ *das* Sea of Marmara

Marmelade /marməˈlaːdə/ *die*; **~**, **~n** jam; (Orangen~) marmalade

Marmelade[n]-: ~brot [piece of] bread and jam; (zugeklappt) jam sandwich; **~glas** *das* jam jar

Marmor /ˈmarmɔr/ *der*; **~s** marble

Marmor-: ~bild *das* (veralt.) marble statue; **~block** *der*; *Pl.* **~blöcke** block of marble; marble block; **~bruch** *der* marble quarry; **~büste** *die* marble bust

marmorieren *tr. V.* **etw. ~:** give sth. a marbled effect; marble sth.; **eine marmorierte Platte** a marbled slab

Marmorierung *die*; **~**, **~en** marbling; marbled effect

Marmor·kuchen *der* marble cake

marmorn *Adj.* marble; (fig.) pale as marble *postpos.*; ashen ‹pallor›

marode /maˈroːdə/ *Adj.* (ugs. abwertend) clapped-out (Brit. sl.)

Marodeur /maroˈdøːɐ̯/ *der*; **~s**, **~e** (Soldatenspr.) looter

Marokkaner /marɔˈkaːnɐ/ *der*; **~s**, **~**, **Marokkanerin** *die*; **~**, **~nen** Moroccan

marokkanisch *Adj.* Moroccan

Marokko /maˈrɔko/ *(das)*; **~s** Morocco

Marone /maˈroːnə/ *die*; **~**, **~n** **1** [sweet] chestnut **2** ▸ **Maronenpilz**

Maronen·pilz *der* chestnut boletus

Maronit /maroˈniːt/ *der*; **~en**, **~en**, **Maronitin** *die*; **~**, **~nen** (Rel.) Maronite

Marotte /maˈrɔtə/ *die*; **~**, **~n** fad

Marquis /marˈkiː/ *der*; **~** /marˈkiː(s)/, **~** /marˈkiːs/ marquis

Marquise /marˈkiːzə/ *die*; **~**, **~n** marquise

Mars¹ /mars/ *der*; **~** (Astron.), **Mars²** *(der)* (Myth.) Mars *no def. art.*

Mars³ *der*; **~**, **~e** *od. die*; **~**, **~en** (Seemannsspr.) crow's nest

Marsala /marˈzaːla/ *der*; **~s**, **~s**, **Marsalawein** *der* Marsala

Mars·bewohner *der*, **Mars·bewohnerin** *die* Martian

marsch /marʃ/ *Interj.* **1** (Milit.) [forward] march; **kehrt — ~!** about turn *or* (Amer.) face! forward march!; *s. auch* **Gleichschritt** **2** (ugs.) **~ ~!** off with you!; (beeil dich!) move it! (coll.); look snappy! (coll.); **~ ins Bett!** off to bed [with you]!; **~ an die Arbeit!** get down to work!

Marsch¹ *der*; **~[e]s**, **Märsche** /ˈmɛrʃə/ **1** (Milit.) march; (Wanderung) [long] walk; hike; **ein ~ von einer Stunde** an hour's march/walk; **einen ~ [von einer Stunde] machen** go for *or* take a long walk [lasting an hour]; **jmdn. in ~ setzen** (Milit.) march sb. off; (fig.) mobilize sb.; **sich in ~ setzen** make a move; get moving; (Milit.) march off **2** (Musikstück) march; **jmdm. [gehörig] den ~ blasen** (fig. salopp) give sb. a real rocket (Brit. coll.) *or* (coll.) bawling out

Marsch² *die*; **~**, **~en** fertile marshland

Marschall /ˈmarʃal/ *der*; **~s**, **Marschälle** /ˈmarʃɛlə/ (hist.) marshal

Marschall[s]·stab *der* marshal's baton; **den ~ im Tornister tragen** (fig.) have what it takes to achieve high rank

marsch-, Marsch-: ~befehl *der* (Milit.) marching orders *pl.*; **der ~befehl** one's marching orders; **~bereit** *Adj.* (Milit.) ready to march *or* move *pred.*; (ugs.) ready to go *pred.*; **~boden** *der* [fertile] marshy soil; **~flug·körper** *der* cruise missile; **~gepäck** *das* (Milit.) marching pack; **unser ~gepäck** our marching packs *pl.*

marschieren *itr. V.*; *mit sein* **1** march **2** (ugs.: mit großen Schritten gehen) march; stalk; (wandern) walk; hike **3** (ugs.: vorankommen) **[richtig] ~:** progress smoothly; **der Fortschritt marschiert** the march of progress is inexorable

Marsch-: ~kolonne *die* (Milit.) marching column; **~land** *das* [fertile] marshland; **~lied** *das* marching song; **~musik** *die* march music; **~ordnung** *die* (Milit.) marching order; **~pause** *die* halt [on the march]; **eine ~pause einlegen** make a halt; **~richtung** *die* (Milit.) direction of march; **~route** *die* (Milit.) route; (fig.) line [of approach]; **die ~route für die Verhandlungen** (fig.) the line to be taken in the negotiations; **~säule** *die* column of marchers; **~tempo** *das* marching pace; (Musik) march tempo; **im ~tempo** at a quick march; (Musik) in march tempo; **~verpflegung** *die* (Milit.) marching rations *pl.*; (fig. ugs.) rations *pl.* [for the journey]

Marseillaise /marzɛˈjɛːzə/ *die*; **~:** Marseillaise

Marseille /marˈzɛːj/ *(das)*; **~s** Marseilles

Marshall·plan /ˈmarʃal-/ *der* (hist.) Marshall Plan

Mars-: ~mensch *der* Martian; **~segel** *das* (Seemannsspr.) main topsail; **~sonde** *die* (Raumfahrt) Mars probe

Mar·stall /ˈmar-/ *der* (hist.) [royal *or* princely] stables *pl.*

Marter /ˈmartɐ/ *die*; **~**, **~n** (geh.) (Folter) torture; (fig.: seelisch) torment; **jmdm. ~n bereiten** *od.* **zufügen** (körperlich) subject sb. to torture; (seelisch) inflict torment on sb.

Marter·instrument *das* instrument of torture

Marterl /ˈmartɐl/ *das*; **~s**, **~n** (bayr., österr.) wayside shrine

martern *tr. V.* (geh.) torture; (fig.: seelisch) torment; **jmdn. zu Tode ~:** torture sb. to death

Marter-: ~pfahl *der* stake; **~tod** *der* (geh.) death by torture; (Märtyrertod) death of a martyr

Marterung *die*; **~**, **~en** (geh.) torture; (seelisch) torment

martialisch /marˈtsi̯aːlɪʃ/ (geh.)
A *Adj.* warlike ‹appearance, figure, etc.›; martial ‹music›
B *adv.* in a warlike manner; (drohend) threateningly; aggressively

Martin-Horn Ⓦⓩ *das* ▸ **Martinshorn**

Martini /marˈtiːni/ *(das)*; *indekl.* **zu ~:** on St Martin's Day; at Martinmas

Martins-: ~gans *die* Martinmas goose; **~horn** *das* (volkstümlich) siren (*of emergency vehicle*); **mit ~horn** sounding its siren; **~tag** *der* St Martin's Day

Märtyrer /ˈmɛrtyrɐ/ *der*; **~s**, **~**, **Märtyrerin** *die*; **~**, **~nen** martyr

Märtyrer-: ~krone *die* martyr's crown; **die ~krone tragen** be a martyr/martyrs; **~tod** *der* death of a martyr; **den ~tod sterben** die a martyr's death

Märtyrin /ˈmɛrtyrɪn/ *die*; **~**, **~nen** ▸ **Märtyrerin**

Martyrium /marˈtyːri̯ʊm/ *das*; **~s**, **Martyrien** martyrdom; **das war ein ~** (fig.) it was sheer martyrdom

Marxismus /marˈksɪsmʊs/ *der*; **~:** Marxism *no art.*

Marxismus-Leninismus *der* Marxism-Leninism *no art.*

Marxist *der*; **~en**, **~en**, **Marxistin** *die*; **~**, **~nen** Marxist

marxistisch
A *Adj.* Marxist
B *adv.* ‹view, interpret› from a Marxist point of view; ‹think, act› in line with Marxism

marxistisch-leninistisch
A *Adj.* Marxist-Leninist
B *adv.* ‹view, interpret› from a Marxist-Leninist point of view; ‹think, act› in line with Marxism-Leninism

März /mɛrts/ *der*; **~[es]**, *dichter.*: **~en** ▸ **ⓘ S. 165** March; *s. auch* **April**

März[en]-: ~becher *der* **1** Spring Snowflake; **2** (volkstümlich: Narzisse) daffodil; **~bier** *das: kind of dark bock beer*

Marzipan /martsiˈpaːn, *österr.* ˈ---/ *das*; **~s**, *österr.*: *der*; **~s** marzipan

Marzipan-: ~kartoffel *die* marzipan ball; **~schwein** *das* marzipan pig

Mascara /masˈkaːra/ *der*; **~**, **~s** mascara brush/pencil

Masche /ˈmaʃə/ *die*; **~**, **~n** **1** stitch; (Lauf~) run; ladder (Brit.); (beim Netz) mesh; **die ~n eines Netzes** the mesh *sing.* of a net; **durch die ~n des Gesetzes schlüpfen** (fig.) slip through a loophole in the law **2** (ugs.: Trick) trick; **das ist die ~:** that's the way *or* trick **3** (ugs.: Mode, Gag) **die neueste ~:** the latest fad *or* craze **4** (österr.: Schleife) bow

Maschen-: ~draht *der* wire netting; **~draht·zaun** *der* wire-netting fence; **~probe** *die* (Handarb.) tension check

Maschine /maˈʃiːnə/ *die*; **~**, **~n** **1** machine; (Näh~/Wasch~) [sewing/washing] machine; **ich bin doch keine ~:** I'm not a machine **2** (ugs.: Automotor) engine **3** (Flugzeug) [aero]plane; **die erste ~ nach Zürich** the first plane *or* flight to Zurich **4** (ugs.: Motorrad) machine **5** (Schreib~) typewriter; **einen Brief in die ~ diktieren** dictate a letter straight on to the typewriter; **~ schreiben** type **6** (ugs. abwertend: dicke Frau) great hulk of a woman

maschine·geschrieben *Adj.* typed; typewritten

maschinell /maʃiˈnɛl/

A *Adj.* 1 machine *attrib.*; by machine *postpos.*; **~e Herstellung** machine production 2 (wie eine Maschine) mechanical

B *adv.* 1 by machine; **~ hergestellt** machine-made 2 (wie eine Maschine) mechanically

maschinen-, Maschinen-: ~bau *der* 1 machine construction *no art.*; mechanical engineering *no art.*; 2 (Lehrfach) mechanical engineering *no art.*; **~bauer** *der*; **~~s, ~~, ~bauerin** *die*; **~~, ~~nen** ▸ S. 113 machine builder; **~bau·ingenieur** *der*, **~bau·ingenieurin** *die* mechanical engineer; **~fabrik** *die* engineering works *sing. or pl.*; **~geschrieben** *Adj.* ▸ **maschinegeschrieben B**; **~gewehr** *das* machine gun; **~halle** *die* machine shop; **~haus** *das* power house; (auf Schiffen) engine room; **~kraft** *die* mechanical power; engine power; **mit ~kraft** by mechanical *or* engine power; **~lesbar A** *Adj.* machine-readable; **B** *adv.* in machine-readable form; **~park** *der* plant; **~pistole** *die* sub-machine gun; **~raum** *der* engine room; **~satz** *der* (Druckw.) machine composition; **~schaden** *der* engine trouble *no indef. art.*; **~schlosser** *der*, **~schlosserin** *die* ▸ S. 113 fitter; **~schreiben** *das* typing; **das ~schreiben lernen** learn to type; **~schreiber** *der*, **~schreiberin** *die* typist; **~schrift** *die* typing; (Schriftart) typeface; type; **in ~schrift** typed; **~schriftlich** *Adj.* typewritten; typed; **~stürmer** *der* (hist.) machine breaker; machine wrecker; **~stürmerei** *die*; **~~:** machine breaking; machine wrecking; **~stürmerin** *die* ▸ **~stürmer**; **~zeitalter** *das* machine age

Maschinerie /maʃinəˈriː/ *die*; **~, ~n** machinery; **die gnadenlose ~ der Justiz** (fig. geh.) the merciless wheels *pl.* of justice

***maschine·schreiben** ▸ **Maschine 5**

Maschinist *der*; **~en, ~en, Maschinistin** *die*; **~, ~nen** 1 machinist 2 (Schiffs~) engineer

Maser /ˈmaːzɐ/ *die*; **~, ~n** figure

maserig *Adj.* figured

masern *tr. V.* grain ‹*wood*›

Masern *Pl.* ▸ S. 439 measles *sing. or pl.*

Maserung *die*; **~, ~en** (in Holz, Leder) [wavy] grain; (in Marmor) vein; (in Fell) patterning

Maske /ˈmaskə/ *die*; **~, ~n** 1 (auch fig.) mask; **ihr Gesicht erstarrte zur ~:** her features froze into a mask; **die ~ fallen lassen** *od.* **abwerfen** (fig.) drop one's mask; **jmdm. die ~ vom Gesicht reißen** (fig.) unmask sb. 2 (Theater) make-up; **~ machen** make up 3 (Mensch) masker

Masken-: ~ball *der* masked ball; masquerade; **~bildner** *der*; **~~s, ~~, ~bildnerin** *die*; **~~, ~~nen** ▸ S. 113 make-up artist

maskenhaft

A *Adj.* mask-like

B *adv.* like a mask; **ein ~ starres Gesicht** a face frozen into a mask

Maskerade /maskəˈraːdə/ *die*; **~, ~n** 1 [fancy-dress] costume; **~ sein** (fig.) be a masquerade 2 (veralt.: Maskenball) masquerade; (Kostümfest) fancy-dress ball

maskieren

A *tr. V.* 1 mask 2 (verkleiden) dress up

B *refl. V.* 1 put on a mask/masks 2 (sich verkleiden) dress up

Maskierung *die*; **~, ~en** 1 (das Verkleiden) dressing up 2 (Verkleidung) disguise; (beim Kostümball) [fancy-dress] costume 3 (Tarnung) masking; disguising

Maskottchen /masˈkɔtçən/ *das*; **~s, ~:** [lucky] mascot

maskulin /maskuˈliːn, *auch* ˈ---/

A *Adj.* (auch Sprachw.) masculine

B *adv.* in a masculine way

Maskulinum /ˈmaskuliːnʊm/ *das*; **~s, Maskulina** (Sprachw.) masculine noun

Masochismus /mazɔˈxɪsmʊs/ *der*; **~** (Psych.) masochism *no art.*

Masochist /mazɔˈxɪst/ *der*; **~en, ~en, Masochistin** *die*; **~, ~nen** (Psych.) masochist

masochistisch (Psych.)

A *Adj.* masochistic

B *adv.* masochistically; **~ veranlagt sein** have masochistic tendencies

maß *1. u. 3. Pers. Sg. Prät. v.* **messen**

Maß[1] /maːs/ *das*; **~es, ~e** 1 measure (**für** of); **~e und Gewichte** weights and measures 2 (fig.) **ein gerüttelt ~ [an** (*Dat.*) *od.* **von etw.]** (geh.) a good measure [of sth.]; **das ~ ist voll** enough is enough; **das ~ voll machen** go too far; **mit zweierlei ~ messen** apply different [sets of] standards 3 (Größe) measurement; (von Räumen, Möbeln) dimension; measurement; **ihre ~e sind ...** her measurements *or* vital statistics are ...; **[bei] jmdm. ~ nehmen** take sb.'s measurements; measure sb. [up] 4 (Grad) measure, degree (**an** + *Dat.* of); **in solchem ~e** *od.* **in einem ~e, dass ...** to such an extent that ...; **in großem/gewissem ~e** to a great/certain extent; **im höchsten ~[e]** extremely; exceedingly; **in vollem ~e** fully; **im gleichen ~[e]** to the same extent 5 (Mäßigung) **weder ~ noch Ziel kennen** know no restraint; **ohne ~ und Ziel** immoderately; **in** *od.* **mit ~en** in moderation; **über die** *od.* **alle ~en** (geh.) beyond [all] measure 6 **~ halten** exercise moderation

Maß[2] *die*; **~, ~[e]** (bayr., österr.) litre [of beer]; **zwei ~ Bier** two litres of beer

Massage /maˈsaːʒə/ *die*; **~, ~n** massage; **zur ~ gehen** go for a massage

Massage-: ~gerät *das* massager; **~institut** *das* (auch verhüll.) massage parlour; **~öl** *das* massage oil; **~salon** *der* (verhüll.) massage parlour (euphem.); **~stab** *der* vibrator

Massaker /maˈsaːkɐ/ *das*; **~s, ~:** massacre

massakrieren *tr. V.* massacre

Maß-: ~analyse *die* (Chemie) volumetric analysis; **~angabe** *die* stated dimensions *pl. or* measurements *pl.*; (bei Hohlmaßen) stated capacity; **~anzug** *der* made-to-measure suit; tailor-made suit; **~arbeit** *die* 1 custom-made item; (Kleidungsstück) made-to-measure item; **[eine] ~arbeit sein** be custom-made/made-to-measure; 2 (genaue Arbeit) neat work

Masse /ˈmasə/ *die*; **~, ~n** 1 mass; (Kochk.) mixture 2 (Menge) mass; **~n an** (*Dat.*) *od.* **von Autos** masses of cars; **riesige ~n Papier** huge piles *or* heaps of paper; **die ~ der Befragten** the bulk of those questioned; **die ~ machts** (ugs.) it's quantity that's important; **sie kamen in ~n** they came in their masses *or* in droves; **das ist eine ganze ~:** that's a lot (coll.) *or* a great deal 3 (Menschen~) **eine große ~ [an] Menschen** (*Dat.*) a great mass of people; **die namenlose ~:** the anonymous masses *pl.*; **die breite ~:** the bulk *or* broad mass of the population; **die [werktätigen] ~n** the [working] masses 4 (Physik) mass 5 (Wirtsch.) assets *pl.*; (Erb~) estate; **mangels ~:** for lack of assets

Maß-: ~einheit *die* unit of measurement; **~einteilung** *die* calibrations *pl.*

Massel /ˈmasl̩/ *der*; **~s** (ugs.) **~ haben** be dead lucky (coll.)

Massen-: ~abfertigung *die* (oft abwertend) mass processing *no indef. art.*; **~absatz** *der* mass sale; **für den ~absatz gefertigt** produced for mass sale; **~andrang** *der* crush; **~anziehung** *die* (Physik) gravitation; **~arbeitslosigkeit** *die* mass unemployment; **~artikel** *der* mass-produced article; **~aufgebot** *das* large body *or* contingent; **~bedarf** *der* mass demand; **~bedarfsartikel** *der* mass consumer commodity; **~bewegung** *die* mass movement; **~blatt** *das* mass-circulation paper; **~demonstration** *die* mass demonstration; **~entlassungen** *Pl.* mass redundancies *pl.*; **~fabrikation** *die* mass production; **~geschmack** *der* popular taste; **~gesellschaft** *die* (Soziol.) mass society; **~grab** *das* mass grave; **~güter** *Pl.* 1 mass-produced goods; 2 (Frachtgut) bulk goods

massenhaft

A *Adj.* in huge numbers *postpos.*; **das ~e Auftreten dieser Schädlinge** the appearance of huge numbers of these pests

B *adv.* on a huge *or* massive scale; **~ kommen** come in vast *or* huge numbers; **~ Geld haben** (ugs.) have pots of money (coll.); **~ Schulden haben** have a pile of debts (coll.)

massen-, Massen-: ~herstellung *die* ▸ **~produktion**; **~hinrichtung** *die* mass execution; **~hysterie** *die* mass hysteria; **~karambolage** *die* multiple crash; [multiple] pile-up; **~kommunikationsmittel** *das* medium of mass communication; mass medium; **~kundgebung** *die* mass rally; **~medium** *das* mass medium; **~mord** *der* mass murder; **~mörder** *der*, **~mörderin** *die* mass murderer; **~organisation** *die* mass organization; **~produktion** *die* mass production; **etw. in ~produktion herstellen** mass-produce sth.; **~psychologie** *die* mass psychology *no art.*; **~psychose** *die* mass psychosis *no indef. art.*; **~quartier** *das* (abwertend) mass accommodation *no indef. art.*; **~schlägerei** *die* [grand] free-for-all; pitched battle (fig.); **~sport** *der* mass sport; **~sterben** *das*; **~~s, ~~: das ~sterben von ...** the death of huge numbers of ...; **ein ~sterben begann** people/animals *etc.* began to die in huge numbers; **~szene** *die* crowd scene; **~tourismus** *der* mass tourism *no art.*; **~verhaftung** *die* mass arrest; **~verkehrsmittel** *das* means *sing.* of mass transportation; **~vernichtung** *die* mass extermination; **~vernichtungs·waffen** *Pl.* weapons of mass destruction; **~wahn** *der* mass hysteria; **~ware** *die* mass-produced goods *pl.*; **~waren** mass-produced goods; **~weise** *Adv.* in huge numbers *or* quantities; **~wirksam** *Adj.* with mass impact *postpos., not pred.*; **~wirksam sein** have mass impact; **~wirkung** *die* mass impact

Masseur /maˈsøːɐ̯/ *der*; **~s, ~e** ▸ S. 113 masseur

Masseurin *die*; **~, ~nen** ▸ S. 113 masseuse

Masseuse /maˈsøːzə/ *die*; **~, ~n** ▸ S. 113 (auch verhüll.) masseuse

Maß·gabe *die*: *in* **nach ~** (+ *Gen.*) (geh.) in accordance with; **mit der ~, etw. zu tun** with instructions to do sth.

maß·gearbeitet *Adj.* custom-made; made-to-measure ‹*clothes*›

maß·gebend, maß·geblich

A *Adj.* authoritative ‹*book, expert, opinion*›; definitive ‹*text*›; important, influential ‹*person, circles, etc.*›; decisive ‹*factor, influence, etc.*›; (zuständig) competent ‹*authority, person, etc.*›; **sein Urteil ist nicht ~:** his opinion carries no weight

B *adv.* ‹*influence*› considerably, to a considerable extent; (entscheidend) decisively; **~ an etw.** (*Dat.*) **beteiligt sein** play a leading role in sth.

maßgefertigt *Adj.* ▸ **maßgearbeitet**

maß-, Maß-: ~gerecht A accurate; **genau ~gerecht für etw. sein** be just the right size for sth.; **B** *adv.* accurately; **~gerecht zugeschnittene Regalbretter** shelves cut to size; **~geschneidert** *Adj.* made-to-measure; (fig.) tailor-made; **~halte·appell** *der* call *or* appeal for moderation; ***~|halten** ▸ **Maß**[1] **6**

massieren[1]

A *tr. V.* massage

B *itr. V.* **gut ~ können** be a good masseur/masseuse

massieren[2]

A *tr. V.* mass ‹*troops etc.*›

B *refl. V.* ‹*troops etc.*› mass

massig

A *Adj.* massive; bulky, massive ‹*figure*›

B *adv.* (ugs.) **~ Geld verdienen** earn pots of money (coll.); **~ zu tun haben** have loads *or* tons to do (coll.)

mäßig /ˈmɛːsɪç/

A *Adj.* 1 moderate; **im Essen ~ sein** eat in moderation; be a moderate eater 2 (gering) moderate, modest ‹*interest, income, talent,*

m

attendance› 3› (mittel~) mediocre; indifferent; indifferent ‹*health*›; **seine Leistungen sind mehr als ~:** his performance is worse than mediocre
B *adv.* 1› in moderation; **~, aber regelmäßig** (scherzh.) in moderation but regularly 2› (gering) moderately ‹*gifted, talented*›; **nur ~ verkauft worden sein** have had only a modest sale 3› (mittel~) indifferently

mäßigen (geh.)
A *tr. V.* moderate ‹*language, demands*›; curb, check ‹*anger, impatience*›; slacken, reduce ‹*speed*›
B *refl. V.* 1› practise *or* exercise moderation (**bei** in); (sich beherrschen) control *or* restrain oneself 2› (nachlassen) ‹*storm*› abate; ‹*heat*› grow less intense

Mäßigkeit *die;* ~ 1› moderation; **jmdm. ~ empfehlen** advise sb. to exercise moderation 2› (Mittel~) mediocrity

Mäßigung *die;* ~: moderation; restraint; **jmdn. zur ~ mahnen** urge sb. to control *or* restrain himself/herself

massiv /ma'si:f/
A *Adj.* 1› solid; **~ bauen** build solidly 2› (heftig) massive ‹*demand*›; crude ‹*accusation, threat*›; heavy, strong ‹*attack, criticism, pressure*›; **~ werden** (ugs.) get tough
B *adv.* ‹*attack*› heavily, strongly; ‹*accuse, threaten*› crudely

Massiv *das;* **~s, ~e** massif

Massiv-: ~bau *der,* **~bau·weise** *die* massive construction; **in ~bauweise errichtet sein** be of massive construction

Massivität /masivi'tɛ:t/ *die;* ~ ▸**massiv 2**: massiveness; crudeness; heaviness; strength

Maß·krug *der* (südd., österr.) litre tankard *or* beer mug; (aus Steingut) stein

Maß·liebchen *das* daisy

maß·los
A *Adj.* (äußerst) extreme; (übermäßig) inordinate; gross ‹*exaggeration, insult*›; excessive ‹*demand, claim*›; (grenzenlos) boundless ‹*ambition, greed, sorrow, joy*›; extravagant ‹*spendthrift*›; **~ im Essen/Trinken sein** eat/drink to excess; **~ in seinen Ansprüchen sein** be excessive in one's demands
B *adv.* (äußerst) extremely; (übermäßig) inordinately; ‹*exaggerate*› grossly; **sie ist ~ ehrgeizig** her ambition knows no bounds

Maßlosigkeit *die;* ~ ▸**maßlos**: extremeness; inordinateness; grossness; excessiveness; boundlessness

Maßnahme *die;* **~, ~n** measure; **~n gegen etw. einleiten/treffen** introduce/take measures against sth.; **~n zur Verhütung von Unfällen treffen** take measures *or* steps to prevent accidents; **eine abschreckende ~:** a deterrent

Maß·regel *die* regulation; (Maßnahme) measure

maßregeln *tr. V.* (zurechtweisen) reprimand; (bestrafen) discipline

Maß·reg[e]lung *die* (Zurechtweisung) reprimand; (Bestrafung) disciplinary measure

Maß·schneider *der,* **Maß·schneiderin** *die* bespoke tailor (Brit.); custom tailor (Amer.)

Maß·stab *der* 1› standard; **einen hohen ~ anlegen/setzen** apply/set a high standard; **sich** (*Dat.*) **jmdn./etw. zum ~ nehmen** take sb./sth. as one's model 2› (Geogr.) scale; **diese Karte hat einen großen/kleinen ~:** this is a large-/small-scale map; **den ~ 1:150 000 haben** be drawn to a scale of 1:150,000; **im ~ 1:100** to a scale of 1:100 3› (Zollstock) rule; (Lineal) ruler

maßstäblich /-ʃtɛ:plɪç/, **maßstab[s]·gerecht, maßstab[s]·getreu**
A *Adj.* scale *attrib.* ‹*model, drawing, etc.*›; [true] to scale *pred.*;
B *adv.* to scale

maß-, Maß-: ~system *das* system of measuring units; **~voll A** *Adj.* moderate; **B** *adv.* in moderation; **~voll urteilen** be moderate in one's judgements; **~vorlage** *die* (Fußballjargon) accurate pass; **~werk** *das* (Archit.) tracery

Mast¹ /mast/ *der;* **~[e]s, ~en,** *auch:* **~e** (Schiffs~, Antennen~) mast; (Stange, Fahnen~) pole; (Hochspannungs~) pylon

Mast² *die;* **~, ~en** (Landw.) fattening; **für die ~ geeignet** suitable for fattening

Mast-: ~baum *der* mast; **~bulle** *der* (gemästet) fattened bull; (für die ~ vorgesehen) fattening bull; **~darm** *der* ▸ⓘ **S. 435** (Anat.) rectum

mästen /'mɛstn̩/ *tr. V.* fatten; (fig. ugs.) overfeed; **sich ~** (ugs.) fatten oneself up

Mast·futter *das* fattening feed[stuff]

Mastiff /'mastɪf/ *der;* **~s, ~s** (Zool.) mastiff

Mast-: ~korb *der* crow's-nest; **~schwein** *das* (gemästet) fattened pig; (für die ~ vorgesehen) fattening pig

Mästung *die;* ~: fattening

Masturbation /masturba'tsi̯o:n/ *die;* **~, ~en** masturbation

masturbieren /mastur'bi:rən/ *itr., tr. V.* masturbate

Matador /mata'do:ɐ̯/ *der;* **~s, ~e, Matadorin** *die;* **~, ~nen** 1› matador 2› (fig.) star

Match /mɛtʃ/ *das od. der;* **~[e]s, ~s** *od.* **~e** match

Match-: ~ball *der* ([Tisch]tennis) match point; **~beutel** *der,* **~sack** *der* duffle bag

Mate /'ma:tə/ *der;* **~, Mate·tee** *der* maté

Mater /'ma:tɐ/ *die;* **~, ~n** (Druckw.) ▸**Matrize**

material *Adj.* (Philos.) material

Material /mate'ri̯a:l/ *das;* **~s, ~ien** 1› material; (Bau~) materials *pl.* 2› (Hilfsmittel, Utensilien) materials *pl.*; (für den Bau) equipment; **das rollende ~** (Eisenb.) the rolling stock 3› (Beweis~) evidence

Material-: ~ausgabe *die* 1› issue of materials; 2› (Raum) stores *pl.*; storeroom; **~beschaffung** *die* obtaining of materials; (Kauf) purchasing of materials; **~fehler** *der* material defect

Materialisation /materializa'tsi̯o:n/ *die;* **~, ~en** (Parapsych., Physik) materialization

materialisieren *tr., refl. V.* (Parapsych., Physik) materialize

Materialismus *der;* ~ (auch abwertend) materialism

Materialist *der;* **~en, ~en, Materialistin** *die;* **~, ~nen** (auch abwertend) materialist

materialistisch (auch abwertend)
A *Adj.* materialistic
B *adv.* materialistically

Materialität /materi̯ali'tɛ:t/ *die;* ~ (Philos.) materiality

Material-: ~kosten *Pl.* cost *sing.* of materials; **~prüfung** *die* materials testing; **~prüfungen** tests on materials; **~sammlung** *die* collection *or* gathering of material; **~schlacht** *die* (Milit.) battle of matériel

Materie /ma'te:ri̯ə/ *die;* **~, ~n** 1› (geh.) subject 2› (Physik, Philos.) matter

materiell /mate'ri̯ɛl/
A *Adj.* 1› (stofflich) material; physical 2› (wirtschaftlich) material ‹*value, damage*›; (finanziell) financial 3› (abwertend: materialistisch) materialistic
B *adv.* 1› (wirtschaftlich) materially; (finanziell) financially 2› (abwertend) materialistically; **~ eingestellt sein** be materialistic

Mate·tee *der* ▸**Mate**

Mathe /'matə/ *die;* ~ (ugs.) maths *sing.* (Brit. coll.); math (Amer. coll.)

Mathe·arbeit *die* (ugs.) maths test (coll.)

Mathematik /matəma'ti:k/ *die;* ~: mathematics *sing., no art.*

Mathematiker *der;* **~s, ~, Mathematikerin** *die;* **~, ~nen** ▸ⓘ **S. 113** mathematician

Mathematik·unterricht *der* mathematics teaching/lesson; *s. auch* **Englischunterricht**

mathematisch
A *Adj.* mathematical
B *adv.* mathematically

Matinee /mati'ne:/ *die;* **~, ~n** morning performance

Matjes /'matjəs/ *der;* **~, ~:** matie [herring]

Matjes-: ~filet *das* filleted matie [herring]; **~hering** *der* salted matie [herring]

Matratze /ma'tratsə/ *die;* **~, ~n** mattress; **er horcht an der ~** (fig. scherzh.) he's [in bed] having a kip (Brit. coll.) *or* (coll.) snooze

Matratzen·lager *das* mattress/mattresses on the floor

Mätresse /mɛ'trɛsə/ *die;* **~, ~n** (geh. veralt.) mistress

matriarchalisch /matriar'ça:lɪʃ/ *Adj.* matriarchal

Matriarchat /matriar'ça:t/ *das;* **~[e]s, ~e** matriarchy

Matriarchin *die;* **~, ~nen** matriarch

Matrikel /ma'tri:kl̩/ *die;* **~, ~n** 1› (Hochschulw.) student register 2› (österr.: Personenstandsregister) register of births, deaths, and marriages

Matrix /'ma:trɪks/ *die;* **~, Matrizes** /ma'tri:tse:s/ (Biol., Math., Sprachw.) matrix

Matrize /ma'tri:tsə/ *die;* **~, ~n** (Druckw.) 1› matrix 2› (Folie) stencil; **einen Text auf ~** (*Akk.*) **schreiben** make a stencil of a text

Matrone /ma'tro:nə/ *die;* **~, ~n** matron

matronenhaft (abwertend)
A *Adj.* matronly
B *adv.* in a matronly manner *or* fashion

Matrose /ma'tro:zə/ *der;* **~n, ~n** ▸ⓘ **S. 113** 1› sailor; seaman 2› (Dienstgrad) ordinary seaman

Matrosen-: ~anzug *der* sailor suit; **~mütze** *die* sailor's cap

Matsch *der;* **~[e]s** (ugs.), **Matsche** /'matʃə/ *die;* **~e** (nordd.) 1› (aufgeweichter Boden) mud; (breiiger Schmutz) sludge; (Schnee~) slush 2› (Brei) mush

matschen *itr. V.* (ugs.) **in etw.** (*Dat.*) **~:** splash about in sth.; **im Essen ~:** mess about with one's food

matschig *Adj.* (ugs.) 1› muddy; slushy ‹*snow*› 2› (weich) mushy; squashy ‹*fruit*›

Matsch·wetter *das* (ugs.) **bei diesem ~:** when it's muddy like this; (bei Schneematsch) when it's slushy like this; **dieses widerliche ~:** this revolting weather, when there's mud/slush everywhere

matt /mat/
A *Adj.* 1› weak; weary ‹*limbs, spirit, etc.*›; weak, faint ‹*voice, smile, pulse*›; feeble ‹*applause, reaction*›; limp, feeble ‹*handshake*›; faint ‹*echo*›; **vor Hunger/Durst ~ sein** be faint *or* weak with hunger/thirst; **sich ~ fühlen** feel weak and listless; **ein ~es Echo finden** find a lukewarm response 2› (glanzlos) matt ‹*paper, polish, etc.*›; dull ‹*metal, mirror, etc.*›; dull, lustreless ‹*eyes, look*› 3› (undurchsichtig) frosted ‹*glass*›; pearl ‹*lightbulb*› 4› (gedämpft) soft, subdued ‹*light*›; soft, pale ‹*colour*› 5› (unbeherzt, nicht überzeugend) feeble; weak; feeble, lame ‹*excuse, joke*› 6› (beim Schachspiel) **[Schach und] ~!** checkmate!; **~ sein** be checkmated; **jmdn. ~ setzen** (auch fig.) checkmate sb.
B *adv.* 1› (kraftlos) weakly; ‹*smile*› weakly, faintly; ‹*applaud, react*› feebly 2› (gedämpft) softly ‹*lit*›; **der Mond schien ~ durch die Bäume** the moon shone wanly through the trees 3› (mäßig) ‹*protest, contradict*› feebly, weakly

Matt *das;* **~s** (Schach) [check]mate

matt·blau *Adj.* pale blue

Matte¹ /'matə/ *die;* **~, ~n** (auch Sport) mat; **um 7 Uhr hier/dort auf der ~ stehen** (fig. ugs.) be here/there at 7 o'clock; **bei jmdm. auf der ~ stehen** (fig. ugs.) turn up on sb.'s doorstep

Matte² *die;* **~, ~n** (schweiz., dichter. veralt.) meadow

Matt-: ~glas *das* frosted glass; (Fot.) ground glass; **~gold** *das* dull gold

Matthäi /ma'tɛ:i/ *in* **bei ihm ist ~ am Letzten** (ugs.) it's all up with him; (finanziell) he hasn't got a penny to his name

Matthäus /ma'tɛ:ʊs/ *(der);* **Matthäus'** Matthew

Matthäus·evangelium *das* St Matthew's Gospel; the Gospel according to St Matthew

mattieren *tr. V.* give a matt finish to; matt; frost ‹*glass*›

Mattigkeit *die;* ~ (Schwäche) weakness; (Erschöpfung) weariness

Matt-: ~lack *der* matt varnish; **~scheibe** *die* [1] (ugs.) telly (Brit. coll.); box (coll.); [2] (Fot.) matt screen; ground-glass screen; **ich habe ~scheibe** (fig. ugs.) I'm not with it (coll.)

Matur /ma'tu:ɐ̯/ *die;* ~ (schweiz.), **Matura** *die;* **~a** (österr., schweiz.) ▸**Abitur**

Matura

▸ Abitur

Maturand /matu'rant/ *der;* **~en, ~en, Maturandin** *die;* **~, ~nen** (schweiz.) ▸**Abiturient, Abiturientin**

Maturant /matu'rant/ *der;* **~en, ~en, Maturantin** *die;* **~, ~nen** (österr.) ▸**Abiturient, Abiturientin**

Maturität /maturi'tɛ:t/ *die;* ~ [1] (veralt.: Reife) maturity [2] (schweiz.) ▸**Abitur**

Matz /mat͜s/ *der;* **~es, ~e** *od.* **Mätze** /'mɛt͜sə/ (fam.) **kleiner ~:** little man

Mätzchen /'mɛt͜sçən/ *das;* **~s, ~** (ugs.) (Posse) antic; (Kniff) trick; **lasst die ~:** stop fooling about *or* around; stop your antics; **~ machen** fool about *or* around; **Hände hoch, und keine ~!** (salopp) stick 'em up, and no tricks! (coll.)

Matze /'mat͜sə/ *die;* **~, ~n, Matzen** /'mat͜sn̩/ *der;* **~s, ~:** matzo

mau /mau̯/ (ugs.)

A *Adj.* (flau) queasy; (unwohl) poorly

B *adv.* badly; **die Geschäfte gehen ~:** business is bad

mauen *itr. V.* (südwestd., schweiz.) miaow

Mauer /'mau̯ɐ/ *die;* **~, ~n** (auch Sport) wall; **in den ~n einer Stadt** (geh.) in a town/city; **die [Berliner] ~** (hist.) the [Berlin] Wall; **die Chinesische ~:** the Great Wall of China; **eine ~ des Schweigens** (fig.) a wall of silence

Mauer

Die Mauer, the Berlin Wall, was opened on November 9 1989. It had been put up by the GDR to stop East Germans leaving for the West. The 42-kilometre structure of concrete blocks, put up almost overnight in 1961, divided the city into West and East Berlin, splitting up families and friends. Numerous attempts to escape to the West ended in gunfire and death. The announcement by the East German Government that border checkpoints in the city had been abandoned meant that everyone was now free to travel without restrictions. It resulted in an exodus and finally the **Wiedervereinigung**. Parts of the Berlin Wall were sold to museums and private collectors. A few small sections remain as a memorial and tourist attraction.

Mauer-: ~absatz *der* offset; **~arbeit** *die* ▸**Maurerarbeit**; **~bau** *der* construction *or* building of the wall/walls; (Bau der Berliner Mauer) building of the Wall; **~blümchen** *das* (ugs.) (beim Tanz) wallflower (coll.); (unscheinbares Mädchen, auch fig.) Cinderella; **~brecher** *der* (hist.) battering ram; **~kelle** *die* ▸**Maurerkelle**; **~krone** *die* coping [of a/the wall]

mauern

A *tr. V.* build; **ein gemauerter Schornstein** a brick chimney

B *itr. V.* [1] lay bricks [2] (Sportjargon) (Ballspiele) play defensively; (Kricket, fig.) stonewall [3] (Kartenspiele) hold back one's good cards

Mauer-: ~schwalbe *die,* **~segler** *der* swift; **~stein** *der* building brick; **~verband** *der* (Bauw.) masonry bond; **~vorsprung** *der* projecting section of a/the wall; **~werk** *das* [1] (aus Stein) stonework; masonry; (aus Ziegeln) brickwork; [2] (~n) walls *pl.;* **~ziegel** *der* [building] brick

Mauke /'maukə/ *die;* **~, ~n** (Tiermed.) mallenders *pl.*

Mauken *Pl.* (berlin. salopp) hooves (coll.); feet

Maul /mau̯l/ *das;* **~[e]s, Mäuler** /'mɔy̯lɐ/ [1] (von Tieren) mouth [2] (derb: Mund) gob (sl.); **ein freches** *od.* **loses ~ haben** have a cheeky tongue; **ein gottloses ~ haben** have an insolent tongue; **jmdn. aufs ~ hauen** smack sb. in the gob (sl.); **er hat fünf hungrige Mäuler zu stopfen** (fig.) he's got five hungry mouths to feed; **das** *od.* **sein ~ aufmachen** (fig.) say something; **dein/sein** *usw.* **ungewaschenes ~** (fig.) your/his *etc.* filthy trap (sl.) *or* mouth; **das ~ aufreißen** *od.* **voll nehmen, ein großes ~ haben** (fig.) shoot one's mouth off (fig. sl.); **sich** (*Dat.*) **das ~ [über jmdn.] zerreißen** (fig.) gossip maliciously [about sb.]; **ein schiefes ~ ziehen** (fig.) pull a long face; **das ~ halten** keep one's trap shut (sl.); **halts** *od.* **halt dein ~:** shut your trap (sl.); shut up (coll.); **das** *od.* **sein ~ nicht aufkriegen** (fig.) not dare [to] open one's mouth; **jmdm. übers ~ fahren** (fig.) cut sb. short; *s. auch* **stopfen A 4; verbrennen B 2**

Maul-: ~affe *der* [1] *in* **~affen feilhalten** (abwertend) stand gaping *or* (coll.) gawping; [2] (veralt.) gaping fool; **~beer·baum** *der* mulberry tree; **~beere** *die* mulberry

maulen *itr. V.* (salopp) grouse (coll.); moan; grumble

maul-, Maul-: ~esel *der* mule; (Zool.) hinny; **~faul** *Adj.* (ugs. abwertend) uncommunicative; taciturn; **sei doch nicht so ~faul!** come on, haven't you got any more to say for yourself than that?; **~held** *der* (ugs. abwertend) loudmouth; braggart

Maul·korb *der* (auch fig.) muzzle; **einem Hund/** (fig.) **jmdm. einen ~ anlegen** muzzle a dog/ sb.; **einen ~ tragen** (auch fig.) be muzzled

Maulkorb·erlass, *Maulkorb·erlaß *der* (ugs.) decree muzzling freedom of speech

Maul-: ~schelle *die* (ugs. veralt.) slap round the face; **~schlüssel** *der* open-ended spanner; **~sperre** *die* (salopp) **die ~sperre kriegen** *od.* **bekommen** (fig.) gape in surprise; **~tasche** *die* (Kochk.) *filled pasta case served in soup;* **~tier** *das* mule; **~trommel** *die* Jew's harp; **~- und Klauen·seuche** *die* (Tiermed.) foot-and-mouth disease

Maul·wurf *der* mole

Maulwurfs-: ~haufen *der,* **~hügel** *der* molehill

Mau-Mau /mau̯'mau̯/ *das;* **~[s]** (Kartenspiele) Mau-Mau

maunzen /'mau̯nt͜sn̩/ *itr. V.* (ugs.) ‹*cat*› miaow plaintively; ‹*baby*› mewl

Maure /'mau̯rə/ *der;* **~n, ~n** Moor

Maurer /'mau̯rɐ/ *der;* **~s, ~** ▸ⓘ **S. 113** bricklayer; **pünktlich wie die ~** (ugs. scherzh.) bang on time (coll.)

Maurer-: ~arbeit *die* bricklaying [work] *no pl.;* **~geselle** *der* journeyman bricklayer; **~handwerk** *das* bricklaying [trade]

Maurerin *die;* **~, ~nen** ▸ⓘ **S. 113** ▸**Maurer**

Maurer-: ~kelle *die* brick/layer's/ trowel; **~kolonne** *die* bricklaying gang; **~meister** *der* master bricklayer; **~polier** *der* foreman bricklayer

Mauretanien /mau̯re'ta:ni̯ən/ *(das);* **~s** Mauritania

Mauretanier /mau̯re'ta:ni̯ɐ/ *der;* **~s, ~, Mauretanierin** *die;* **~, ~nen** Mauritanian

Maurin *die;* **~, ~nen** ▸**Maure**

Mauritius /mau̯'ri:t͜si̯ʊs/ *(das);* **~'** Mauritius

Maus /mau̯s/ *die;* **~, Mäuse** /'mɔy̯zə/ [1] mouse; **da beißt die ~ keinen Faden ab** (ugs.) there's nothing to be done about it; **die weißen Mäuse** (fig. ugs. scherzh.) the traffic police; **weiße Mäuse sehen** (fig. ugs.) see pink elephants; **eine graue ~** (fig. ugs. abwertend) a colourless nondescript sort of [a] person; *s. auch* **Katze** [2] *Pl.* (salopp: Geld) bread *sing.* (coll.); dough *sing.* (coll.); **ein paar Mäuse** a few marks/quid (Brit. coll.)/bucks (Amer. sl.) *etc.*

Mauschelei *die;* **~, ~en** (ugs. abwertend) shady wheeling and dealing *no indef. art.*

mauscheln /'mau̯ʃl̩n/ *itr. V.* (ugs. abwertend) engage in shady wheeling and dealing; **da wird viel gemauschelt** a lot of shady wheeling and dealing goes on there

Mauscheln *das;* **~s** *card game similar to four-card loo*

Mäuschen /'mɔy̯sçən/ *das;* **~s, ~** [1] little mouse; **~ sein** *od.* **spielen** (fig. ugs.) be a fly on the wall (coll.) [2] (fig. ugs.) **mein ~:** my sweet

mäuschen·still

A *Adj.* **~ sein** ‹*person*› be as quiet as a mouse; **es war ~:** it was so quiet you could have heard a pin drop

B *adv.* **~ dort sitzen bleiben/sich ~ verhalten** sit there/keep as quiet as a mouse

Mäuse·bussard *der* (Zool.) [common] buzzard

Mause-: ~falle *die* mousetrap; (fig.) trap; **~loch** *das* mousehole; **ich hätte mich am liebsten in ein ~loch verkrochen** (ugs.) I wished the ground would open and swallow me up

Mäuse·melken *das:* in **es ist zum ~** (ugs.) it's enough to send *or* drive you up the wall (coll.)

mausen

A *tr. V.* (ugs. veralt.) pinch (coll.)

B *itr. V.* (veralt.: Mäuse fangen) catch mice; mouse

Mauser *die;* **~:** moult; **in der ~ sein** be moulting

Mäuserich /'mɔy̯zərɪç/ *der;* **~s, ~e** (ugs.) [male] mouse

mausern *refl. V.* moult; **sich zur Dame ~** (fig. ugs.) blossom into a lady

Mauser·pistole *die* Mauser [pistol]

mause·tot *Adj.* (ugs.) [as] dead as a doornail *pred.;* stone dead

Mause·zähnchen *Pl.* (Handarb.) picot edging *sing.*

maus·grau *Adj.* mouse-grey

mausig *Adj.* in **sich ~ machen** (salopp) be cheeky and make a nuisance of oneself

Mausklick *der;* **~s, ~s** (DV) mouse click

Mäuslein /'mɔy̯slai̯n/ *das;* **~s, ~** ▸**Mäuschen**

Mausoleum /mau̯zo'le:ʊm/ *das;* **~s, Mausoleen** mausoleum

maus, Maus: ~pad/-pɛt/ *das;* **~~s, ~~s** (DV) mouse mat; **~taste** *die* (DV) mouse button; **~tot** *Adj.* (österr.) ▸**mausetot**; **~zeiger** *der* (DV) mouse pointer

Maut /mau̯t/ *die;* **~, ~en** toll; **~ bezahlen/ erheben** pay/levy a toll

Maut-: ~gebühr *die* toll; **~straße** *die* toll road

m.a.W. *Abk.* **= mit anderen Worten** in other words

Max /maks/ *in* **strammer ~** (Kochk.) fried egg on ham and bread

Maxi *das;* **~s, ~s** (Mode) maxi (coll.); **im ~:** in a maxi (coll.); **ein Rock in ~:** a maxi-length skirt; **~ tragen** wear a maxi (coll.)

maximal /maksi'ma:l/

A *Adj.* maximum

B *adv.* **~ zulässige Geschwindigkeit** maximum permitted speed; **bis zu ~ 85 °C/20 t** up to a maximum of 85 °C/20 t; **dieses Boot ist für ~ vier Personen zugelassen** this boat is licensed to carry a maximum of four people

Maximal-: ~forderung *die* maximum demand; **~wert** *der* maximum value

Maxime /ma'ksi:mə/ *die;* **~, ~n** maxim

maximieren *tr. V.* maximize

Maximierung *die;* **~, ~en** maximization

Maximum /'maksimʊm/ *das;* **~s, Maxima** maximum (**an** + *Dat.* of)

Maxi·single *die* maxi-single

Mayo /'ma:jo/ *die;* **~, ~s** (ugs.) mayo

Mayonnaise /majo'nɛ:zə/ *die;* **~, ~n** mayonnaise

MAZ /mat͜s/ *die;* **~** (Ferns.) VTR

Mazedonien /mat͜se'do:ni̯ən/ ▸**Makedonien**

Mäzen /mɛ't͜se:n/ *der;* **~s, ~e** (geh.) patron

Mäzenatentum /mɛt͜sena'ta:ntu:m/ *das;* **~s** (geh.) patronage

Mäzenin *die;* **~, ~nen** (geh.) patron[ess]

Mazurka /ma'zʊrka/ *die;* **~, Mazurken** *u.* **~s** mazurka

MdB, M.d.B. *Abk.* **= Mitglied des Bundestages** Member of the Bundestag

MdEP *Abk.* (EU) **= Mitglied des Europäischen Parlaments** MEP

MdL, M.d.L. *Abk.* **= Mitglied des Landtages** Member of the Landtag

MdNR *Abk.* = **Mitglied des Nationalrates** (Österr.) Member of the Nationalrat

MDR *Abk.* = **Mitteldeutscher Rundfunk**

MdV, M.d.V. *Abk.* = **Mitglied der Volkskammer** (DDR) Member of the Volkskammer

m.E. *Abk.* = **meines Erachtens**

Mechanik /meˈça:nɪk/ *die;* ~ [1] (Physik) mechanics *sing., no art.* [2] (Bauelement) mechanism; (eines Klaviers) action [3] (Funktion) mechanics *sing. or pl.*

Mechaniker *der;* **~s, ~, Mechanikerin** *die;* **~, ~nen** ▸ⓘ **S. 113** mechanic

mechanisch

[A] *Adj.* mechanical; power *attrib.* ‹*loom, press*›

[B] *adv.* mechanically

mechanisieren *tr. V.* mechanize

Mechanisierung *die;* **~:** mechanization

Mechanismus *der;* **~, Mechanismen** (auch fig.) mechanism; (fig.: einer Organisation, Bürokratie) machinery

Mechatronik /meçaˈtro:nɪk/ *die;* **~:** mechatronics *sing.*

meck /mɛk/ (Interj.) me-e-eh (*of goat*)

Mecker·ecke *die* (ugs.) grumbles section (Brit. coll.); complaints column

Meckerei *die;* **~, ~en** (ugs. abwertend) moaning; grousing (sl.); grumbling

Meckerer *der;* **~s, ~** (ugs. abwertend) moaner; grouser (sl.); grumbler

Mecker·fritze *der* (salopp abwertend) grouser (sl.); moaner; grumbler

Meckerin *die;* **~, ~nen** ▸**Meckerer**

Mecker·liese *die* (salopp abwertend) moaning Minnie (Brit. coll.); grouser (sl.); grouch (coll.)

meckern /ˈmɛkɐn/ *itr. V.* [1] (auch fig.) bleat [2] (ugs. abwertend: nörgeln) grumble; moan; grouse (sl.); **etw. zu ~ haben** have sth. to grumble *etc.* about

Mecklenburg /ˈme:klənbʊrk/ *(das);* **~s** Mecklenburg

mecklenburgisch *Adj.* Mecklenburg *attrib.; s. auch* **badisch**

Mecklenburg-Vorpommer *der;* **~n, ~n, Mecklenburg-Vorpommerin** *die;* **~, ~nen** Mecklenburg-West Pomeranian

mecklenburg-vorpommerisch *Adj.* Mecklenburg-West Pomeranian

Mecklenburg-Vorpommern *(das);* **~s** Mecklenburg-West Pomerania

med. *Abk.* = **medizinisch** med.

Medaille /meˈdaljə/ *die;* **~, ~n** medal; *s. auch* **Kehrseite 1**

Medaillen-: ~gewinner *der,* **~gewinnerin** *die* medallist; medal winner; **~spiegel** *der* medal table

Medaillon /medalˈjõ:/ *das;* **~s, ~s** [1] locket [2] (Kochk., bild. Kunst) medallion

Media- /ˈmɛ:di̯a-/ (Werbespr.) ▸**Medien-**

medial /meˈdi̯a:l/ *Adj.* (Parapsych.) mediumistic

Mediävist /medi̯ɛˈvɪst/ *der;* **~en, ~en** medievalist

Mediävistik *die;* **~:** medieval studies *pl., no art.*

Mediävistin *die;* **~, ~nen** medievalist

medien-, Medien-: ~fachfrau *die,* **~fachmann** *der* media expert; **~forschung** *die* media research; **~gerecht** *Adj.* adapted to the needs of the media *postpos.*; media-friendly; **~haus** *das* media company; **~kompetenz** *die* media competence; **~konzern** *der* media concern; **~landschaft** *die* media scene; **~politik** *die* media policy; **~politisch** *Adj.* media-policy *attrib.* ‹*spokesman, measure, etc.*›; **~präsenz** *die* media presence; **~rummel** *der* (ugs.) media excitement *no indef. art.*; excitement *no indef. art.* in the media; **~verbund** *der* [1] (für den Unterricht) multimedia system; **im ~verbund** using the multimedia system; [2] (kommerziell) media syndicate; (Ergebnis einer Fusion) media group; **~vielfalt** *die* variety in the media; **~wirksam** [A] *Adj.* media-effective; creating an effect *or* (coll.) making a splash in the media *postpos.*; [B] *adv.* in a media-effective way

Medikament /medikaˈmɛnt/ *das;* **~[e]s, ~e** medicine; (Droge) drug; **ein ~ gegen Kopfschmerzen** a remedy for headaches

Medikamenten·schrank *der* medicine cabinet

medikamentös /medikamɛnˈtø:s/

[A] *Adj.* ‹*treatment*› with drugs

[B] *adv.* ‹*treat, cure*› with drugs

Medikus /ˈme:dikʊs/ *der;* **~, Medizi** /ˈme:ditsi/ (scherzh.) doctor; doc (coll.)

medioker /meˈdi̯o:kɐ/ *Adj.* (geh.) mediocre

Mediothek /medi̯oˈte:k/ *die;* **~, ~en** audio-visual library

Meditation /meditaˈtsi̯o:n/ *die;* **~, ~en** meditation

Meditations·übung *die* meditation exercise

meditativ /meditaˈti:f/ (geh.)

[A] *Adj.* meditative

[B] *adv.* through meditation

mediterran /mediteˈra:n/ *Adj.* Mediterranean

meditieren /mediˈti:rən/ *itr. V.* meditate (**über** + *Akk.* [up]on)

Medium /ˈme:di̯ʊm/ *das;* **~s, Medien** medium; **das ~ Presse** the medium of the press

Medizin /mediˈtsi:n/ *die;* **~, ~en** [1] medicine *no art.* [2] (Heilmittel) medicine (**gegen** for); **eine bittere ~ für jmdn. sein** (fig.) be a bitter pill for sb. to swallow

Medizinal- /meditsiˈna:l-/: **~assistent** *der* house officer (Brit.); houseman (Brit.); intern (Amer.); **~assistentin** *die* house officer (Brit.); intern (Amer.); **~rat** *der,* **~rätin** *die* ≈ medical officer

Medizin·ball *der* (Sport) medicine ball

Mediziner /mediˈtsi:nɐ/ *der;* **~s, ~, Medizinerin** *die;* **~, ~nen** ▸ⓘ **S. 113** doctor; (Student) medical student; **seine Brüder sind alle ~:** his brothers are all medical men

medizinisch

[A] *Adj.* [1] medical ‹*journal, problem, etc.*›; **~e Fakultät** faculty of medicine [2] (heilend) medicinal ‹*bath etc.*›; medicated ‹*toothpaste, soap, etc.*›

[B] *adv.* medically

medizinisch-technisch *Adj.* **~e Assistentin** medical laboratory assistant

Medizin-: ~mann *der* medicine man; **~schränkchen** *das* medicine cabinet; **~student** *der,* **~studentin** *die* medical student

Meduse /meˈdu:zə/ *die;* **~, ~n** [1] (Myth.) Medusa [2] (Zool.) medusa (Zool.); jellyfish

Medusen·haupt *das* [1] (geh.) head of Medusa [2] ▸ⓘ **S. 439** (Med.) caput medusae; cirsomphalos

Meer /me:ɐ̯/ *das;* **~[e]s, ~e** [1] (auch fig.) sea; (Weltmeer) ocean; **die sieben ~e** the seven seas; **ans ~ fahren** go to the seaside; **am ~:** by the sea; **im ~:** in the sea; **aufs ~ hinausfahren** go out to sea; **übers ~ fahren** cross the sea; **1000 m über dem ~:** 1000 m above sea-level

Meer-: ~busen *der* gulf; **der Finnische/Bottnische ~busen** the Gulf of Finland/Bothnia; **~enge** *die* straits *pl.*; strait

Meeres-: ~algen *Pl.* marine algae; **~biologe** *der,* **~biologin** *die* ▸ⓘ **S. 113** marine biologist; **~biologie** *die* marine biology *no art.*; **~boden** *der* sea bed *or* bottom *or* floor; **~bucht** *die* bay; **~fauna** *die* marine fauna; **~flora** *die* marine flora; **~forschung** *die* marine research; **~früchte** *Pl.* (Kochk.) seafood *sing.*; **ein Salat mit ~früchten** a seafood salad; **~grund** *der* ▸**~boden**; **~klima** *das* maritime climate; **~kunde** *die* oceanography *no art.*; **~luft** *die* (Met.) maritime air; **~oberfläche** *die* surface of the sea; **~rauschen** *das;* **~~s** sound of the sea; **~säuger** *der,* **~säugetier** *das* marine mammal; **~spiegel** *der* sea-level; **200 m über/unter dem ~spiegel** 200 m above/below sea-level; **~strand** *der* (geh., dichter.) seashore; strand (poet.); **~straße** *die* straits *pl.*; strait; **~strömung** *die* current; (im Weltmeer) ocean current; **~tiefe** *die* depth of the sea; (im Weltmeer) depth of the ocean; **~ufer** *das* shore

meer-, Meer-: ~forelle *die* salmon *or* sea trout; **~gott** *der* sea god; **~göttin** *die* sea goddess; **~grün** *Adj.* sea-green; **~jungfrau** *die* mermaid; **~katze** *die* guenon; **~rettich** *der* horseradish; **~salz** *das* sea salt; **~schaum** *der* meerschaum; **~schaum·pfeife** *die* meerschaum [pipe]; **~schweinchen** *das* guinea pig; **~ungeheuer** *das* (Myth.) sea monster; **~wasser** *das* sea water

Meeting /ˈmi:tɪŋ/ *das;* **~s, ~s** meeting

mega- /ˈme:ga/ mega- (coll.); **~cool** mega cool (coll.); ultra cool (coll.); **~geil** really awesome (coll.)

Mega- mega-; **~star** megastar; **~event** mega event

Mega·hertz *das* (Phys.) megahertz

Megalith /megaˈli:t/ *der;* **~s** *od.* **~en, ~e[n]** megalith

Megalith·grab *das* megalithic tomb

megaloman /megaloˈma:n/ *Adj.* (Psych.) megalomaniac[al]; **~ sein** be a megalomaniac

Megalomanie *die* (Psych.) megalomania *no art.*

Megaphon *das;* **~s, ~e** megaphone; loudhailer

Megäre /meˈgɛ:rə/ *die;* **~, ~n** (geh.) fury

Mega-: ~tonne *die* megaton[ne]; **~tote** *der* (milit. Jargon) mega death; **~watt** *das* (Physik) megawatt

Mehl /me:l/ *das;* **~[e]s** [1] flour; (gröber) meal [2] (Pulver) powder; (Knochen~, Fisch~) meal

Mehl-: ~beere *die* whitebeam; **~brei** *der* flour [and water/milk] paste

mehlig *Adj.* [1] floury [2] (wie Mehl) powdery ‹*sand etc.*› [3] (nicht saftig) mealy ‹*potato, apple, etc.*›

Mehl-: ~sack *der* (Sack für ~) flour sack; (Sack voll ~) sack of flour; **wie ein ~sack hinfallen** fall like a sack of potatoes; **~schwalbe** *die* house martin; **~schwitze** *die* (Kochk.) roux; **~speise** *die* [1] *dish with flour as the main ingredient;* [2] (österr.) sweet; dessert; (Kuchen) cake; **~tau** *der* mildew; **~wurm** *der* mealworm

mehr /me:ɐ̯/

[A] *Indefinitpron.* more; **~ als genug** more than enough; **~ als die Hälfte** more than half; **ein Grund ~, es zu tun** one more *or* an additional reason for doing it; **das war ~ als unverschämt** that was impertinent, to say the very least; **das schmeckt nach ~** (ugs.) it's very moreish (coll.); **~ nicht?** is that all?; **~ und ~:** more and more; **~ oder minder** *od.* **weniger** more or less

[B] *adv.* [1] (in größerem Maße) more; **das sagt ihr ~ zu** it appeals to her more; she likes it better [2] (eher) **~ tot als lebendig** more dead than alive; **~ schlecht als recht** after a fashion; **er ist ~ Künstler als Gelehrter** he is more of an artist than a scholar [3] (+ *Negation*) **es war niemand ~ da** there was no one left; **es hat sich keiner ~ gemeldet** there was not another word from anyone; **ich erinnere mich nicht ~:** I no longer remember; **nicht ~ über etw.** (*Akk.*) **sprechen** not discuss sth. any more *or* further; **das wird nie ~ vorkommen** it will never happen again; **davon will ich nichts ~ hören** I don't want to hear any more about it; **da ist nichts ~ zu machen** there is nothing more to be done; **ich habe keine Lust/kein Interesse ~:** I have lost all desire/interest; **du bist doch kein Kind ~:** you're no longer a child; you're not a child any more; **er musste nicht ~ an die Front** he never had to go to the front; **sie hat ihren Großvater nicht ~ gekannt** she never had the chance to know her grandfather [4] (südd.) **nur ~ 5 Euro** only 5 euros

Mehr *das;* **~s** increase (**an** + *Dat.* in); **mit einem ~ an Zeit** with more time

mehr-, Mehr-: ~arbeit *die* extra *or* additional work; (Überstunden) overtime; **das bedeutet ~arbeit für mich** that means more *or* extra work for me; **~aufwand** *der* additional expenditure *no pl.*; **~ausgabe** *die*

m

additional expenditure *no pl.*; **~bändig** *Adj.* in several volumes *postpos.*; **~bedarf** *der* (Wirtsch.) increased demand (**an** + *Dat.* for); **~belastung** *die* extra *or* additional burden (*Gen.* on); **~bereichs·öl** *das* (Technik) multi-purpose oil; **~betrag** *der* extra *or* additional amount; (Überschuss) surplus; **~deutig** **A** *Adj.* ambiguous; **B** *adv.* ambiguously; **~deutig·keit** *die*; **~~**, **~~en** ambiguity; **~dimen·sional** *Adj.* multidimensional; **~ein·nahme** *die* additional revenue

mehren (geh.)
A *tr. V.* increase
B *refl. V.* **1** increase; **diese Vorfälle ~ sich** these incidents are increasing in number **2** (veralt.) **seid fruchtbar und mehret euch** (bibl.) be fruitful and multiply

mehrer... *Indefinitpron.* **1** *attr.* several; a number of; (verschieden) various; several; **~e hundert/Hundert Bücher** several hundred[s of] books **2** *allein stehend* **~e** several people; **~es** several things *pl.*; **sie kamen zu ~en** several of them came

mehrerlei *indekl. unbest. Gattungsz.* (ugs.) several [different]; various; *allein stehend* several *or* various things

Mehr-: ~erlös *der* extra *or* additional proceeds *pl.*; **~ertrag** *der* additional profit

mehr·fach
A *Adj.* multiple; (wiederholt) repeated; **ein Bericht in ~er Ausfertigung** several copies *pl.* of a report; **der ~e deutsche Meister** the player/sprinter *etc.* who has been German champion several times; **ein ~er Millionär** a multimillionaire; **er verdient ein Mehrfaches von dem, was ich bekomme** he earns several times as much as I do
B *adv.* several times; (wiederholt) repeatedly; **~ vorbestraft sein** have several previous convictions

Mehrfach-: ~impfstoff *der* polyvalent *or* mixed vaccine; **~sprengkopf** *der* multiple warhead

mehr-, Mehr-: ~familien·haus *das* multiple dwelling (formal); large house with several flats (esp. Brit.) *or* (esp. Amer.) apartments; **~farben·druck** *der* [multi]colour printing; **~farbig** *Adj.* multicoloured; [multi]colour *attrib.*; **~gebot** *das* higher bid; **~geschossig** *Adj.* ▸ **~stöckig**; **~gewicht** *das* additional weight; (Übergewicht) excess weight

Mehrheit *die*; **~**, **~en** majority; **in der ~ sein** be in the majority; **die ~ haben/erringen** have/win a majority; **die ~ verlieren** lose one's majority; **er wurde mit großer ~ gewählt** he was elected by a large majority; **die ~ der Stimmen auf sich vereinigen** secure a majority of votes; **die/eine absolute ~** (Politik) an absolute majority; **die einfache/relative ~** (Politik) a simple/relative majority; **eine qualifizierte ~** (Politik) a qualified majority

mehrheitlich
A *Adj.* majority; of the majority *postpos.*
B *adv.* by a majority

mehrheits-, Mehrheits-: ~be·schluss, ***~beschluß** *der*, **~ent·scheidung** *die* majority decision; **~fähig** *Adj.* **~fähig sein** ‹*law*› be capable of securing a majority; ‹*party*› be capable of forming a majority; **~partei** *die* majority party; **~prinzip** *das* principle of majority rule; **~wahlrecht** *das* first-past-the-post electoral system

mehr-, Mehr-: ~jährig *Adj.* **1** lasting several years *postpos.*; **eine ~jährige Erfahrung** several years' experience; several years of experience; **eine ~jährige Freundschaft** a friendship of several years' standing; **2** (Bot.) perennial; **~kampf** *der* (Sport) multi-discipline event; **~klassig** *Adj.* (Schulw.) ‹*school*› with several classes; **~kosten** *Pl.* additional *or* extra costs; **~malig** *Adj.* repeated; **~mals** *Adv.* several times; (wiederholt) repeatedly; **~parteien·system** *das* multi-party system; **~produktion** *die* increased production; (Überproduktion) surplus *or* excess production; **~seitig** *Adj.* consisting of several pages *postpos., not pred.*; several pages long *postpos.*; **~silbig** *Adj.* polysyllabic; **~sprachig** *Adj.* multilingual; **~sprachig aufwachsen** grow up speaking several languages; **~sprachigkeit** *die*; **~~**: multilingualism; **~spurig** **A** *Adj.* multi-lane ‹*highway, motorway*›; **~spuriges Abbiegen** turning off from several lanes; **B** *adv.* in several lanes; **~spurig ausbauen** widen ‹*road*› by several lanes; rebuild ‹*railway*› with several tracks; **~stim·mig** (Musik) **A** *Adj.* for several voices *postpos.*; **ein ~stimmiges Lied** a part-song; **B** *adv.* **~stimmig singen** sing in harmony; **etwas ~stimmig singen** sing sth. as a part-song; **~stöckig** **A** *Adj.* several storeys high *postpos.*; (vielstöckig) multi-storey; **B** *adv.* **~stöckig bauen** erect multi-storey buildings/a multi-storey building; **~stufig** *Adj.* consisting of several steps *postpos., not pred.*; multi-stage ‹*rocket*›; **~stündig** *Adj.* lasting several hours *postpos., not pred.*; ‹*delay*› of several hours; **~stündige Verhandlungen** several hours of negotiations; **~tägig** *Adj.* lasting several days *postpos., not pred.*; **~teiler** *der* serial; (Dokumentarfilm etc.) series; **~teilig** *Adj.* in several parts *postpos.*

Mehrung *die*; **~** (geh.) increase

Mehrweg-: ~flasche *die* returnable *or* reusable bottle; **~verpackung** *die* reusable packaging

mehr-, Mehr-: ~wert *der* (Wirtsch.) surplus value; **~wert·steuer** *die* ▸❶ **S. 299** (Wirtsch.) value added tax (Brit.); VAT (Brit.); sales tax (Amer.); **~wöchig** *Adj.* lasting several weeks *postpos., not pred.*; ‹*absence*› of several weeks; **~zahl** *die* **1** (Sprachw.) plural; **2** (~heit) majority; **~zeilig** *Adj.* of several lines *postpos.*

Mehr·zweck-: multi-purpose ...

meiden /ˈmaidn̩/ *unr. tr. V.* (geh.) avoid

Meierei *die*; **~**, **~en** **1** (hist.) feudal estate **2** (Molkerei) dairy

Meile /ˈmailə/ *die*; **~**, **~n** ▸❶ **S. 224**, ▸❶ **S. 310** mile; **das riecht man drei ~n gegen den Wind** (abwertend) you can smell it a mile off; (fig.) you can tell that a mile off; it stands out a mile

Meilen·stein *der* (auch fig.) milestone

meilen·weit
A *Adj.* ‹*distance*› of many miles
B *adv.* for miles; **~ entfernt** (auch fig.) miles away (**von** from)

Meiler *der*; **~s**, **~** **1** (Kohlen~) charcoal kiln **2** (Atom~) [atomic] pile

mein[1] /main/ *Possessivpron.* my; **ich trinke so ~e acht Tassen Kaffee am Tag** I drink my eight cups of coffee a day; **~e Damen und Herren** ladies and gentlemen; **das Buch dort, ist das ~[e]s?** that book over there, is it mine?; **das ist nicht ihr Vater, sondern ~er** that's not her father but mine; **was Mein ist, ist auch Dein** what's mine is yours; **das ist nicht sein Auto, sondern das ~e** that's not his car but mine; **der/die Meine** (geh.) my husband/wife; **die Meinen** (geh.) my family *sing.*; **das Meine** (geh.: Eigentum) my possessions *pl. or* property; **ich habe das Meine getan** (was ich konnte) I have done what I could; (meinen Teil) I have done my share; **sie kann Mein und Dein nicht unterscheiden** (scherzh.) she doesn't understand that some things don't belong to her

mein[2] *Gen. des Personalpronomens* **ich** (dichter. veralt.) ▸ **meiner**

Mein·eid *der* perjury *no indef. art.*; **einen ~ schwören** perjure oneself; commit perjury

meineidig *Adj.* perjured; **~ werden** perjure oneself; commit perjury

Meineidige *der/die*; *adj. Dekl.* perjurer

meinen
A *itr. V.* think; **[ganz] wie Sie ~!** whatever you think; (wie Sie möchten) [just] as you wish; **~ Sie?** do you think so?; **wie ~ Sie?** I beg your pardon?; **wie ~?** (scherzh.) beg your pardon?; **ich meine ja nur [so]** (ugs.) it was just an idea or a thought
B *tr. V.* **1** (denken, glauben) think; **meinst du, das weiß ich nicht?** do you think I don't know that?; **man könnte ~, ...** one might [almost] think ...; **man sollte ~, ...** one would think *or* would have thought ...; **das meine ich auch** I think so too **2** (sagen wollen, im Sinn haben) mean; **was meint er damit?** what does he mean by that?; **das habe ich nicht gemeint** that's not what I meant; **was ~ Sie?** what do you mean? **3** (beabsichtigen) mean; intend; **er meint es gut/ehrlich** he means well *or* his intentions are good/his intentions are honest; **es gut mit jmdm. ~**: mean well by sb.; **etw. wörtlich/ironisch ~**: mean sth. literally/ironically; **es war nicht böse gemeint** no harm was meant *or* intended; **er hat es nicht so gemeint** (ugs.) he didn't mean it like that; **das Wetter/die Sonne meint es gut mit uns** (fig. ugs.) the weather is [being] kind to us/the sun is certainly doing its best for us **4** (sagen) say **5** (geh.) **sie meinte zu träumen** she thought she was dreaming

meiner *Gen. des Personalpronomens* **ich** (geh.) **gedenke ~**: remember me; **erbarme dich ~**: have mercy upon me

meinerseits *Adv.* for my part; **ganz ~**: the pleasure is [all] mine

meinesgleichen *indekl. Pron.* people *pl.* like me *or* myself; (abwertend) the likes *pl.* of me; my sort *or* kind

meinesteils *Adv.* for my part

meinethalben *Adv.* (veralt.), **meinetwe·gen** *Adv.* **1** because of me; (für mich) on my behalf; (mir zuliebe) for my sake; (um mich) about me **2** /*auch* -ˈ--/ (ugs.) as far as I'm concerned; **meinetwegen!** if you like; **meinetwegen soll er sich den Hals brechen** he can break his neck for all I care; **also gut, meinetwegen!** fair enough!; **Darf ich heute Abend ausgehen? — Meinetwegen!** May I go out tonight? — It's all right with me **3** (zum Beispiel) for instance

meinetwillen *Adv.* in **um ~**: for my sake

meinige /ˈmainɪgə/ *Possessivpron.*; *adj. Dekl.* (geh. veralt.) **der/die/das ~**: mine; **ich habe das ~** *od.* **Meinige getan** (was ich konnte) I have done what I could; (meinen Teil getan) I have done my share; **die ~n** *od.* **Meinigen** my family *sing.*

Meinung *die*; **~**, **~en** opinion; (Ansicht, Auffassung) opinion; view; **eine vorgefasste/gegenteilige ~ haben** have preconceived ideas *pl.*/hold an opposite opinion; **eine ~ zu etw./über jmdn./etw. haben** have an opinion on/about sb./sth.; **was ist deine** *od.* **was hast du für eine ~?** what is your opinion?; **die ~en sind geteilt** *od.* **gehen auseinander** opinions are divided; **anderer/geteilter ~ sein** be of a different opinion/differing opinions *pl.*; hold a different view/differing views *pl.*; **seine ~ ändern** change one's opinion *or* mind; **er ist der ~, dass ...** he is of the opinion *or* takes the view that ...; **nach meiner ~, meiner ~ nach** in my opinion *or* view; **ganz meine ~:** I agree entirely; **einer ~ sein** be of *or* share the same opinion; **eine hohe ~ von jmdm. haben** have a high opinion of sb.; think highly of sb.; **die öffentliche ~**: public opinion; **jmdm. [gehörig] die ~ sagen** give sb. a [good] piece of one's mind

meinungs-, Meinungs-: ~äußerung *die* [expression of] opinion; **das Recht auf freie ~äußerung** the right of free speech; **~austausch** *der* exchange of views; **in einem ~austausch mit jmdm. stehen** exchange views with sb.; **~bildend** *Adj.* opinion-forming; **~bildung** *die*: **die öffentliche ~bildung** the shaping of public opinion; **der Prozess der ~bildung ist bei uns noch im Gange** we have not yet formed an opinion; **~forscher** *der*, **~forscherin** *die* ▸❶ **S. 113** opinion pollster *or* researcher; **~forschung** *die* opinion research; **~forschungs·institut** *das* opinion research institute; **~freiheit** *die* freedom to form and express one's own opinions; (Redefreiheit) freedom of speech; **~mache** *die* (abwertend) attempted manipulation of people's opinions; **~macher** *der*, **~macherin** *die* opinion-maker; **~monopol** *das* (abwertend) monopolizing influence over public opinion;

m

~seite *die* opinions page; (mit Leitartikeln) editorial page; **~stark** **A** *Adj.* ‹*person*› with strong opinions; ‹*article etc.*› expressing strong opinions; **~stark sein** ‹*person*› hold strong opinions; ‹*article etc.*› express strong opinions; **B** *adv.* expressing strong opinions; **~umfrage** *die* [public] opinion poll; **~umschwung** *der* swing of opinion; **~verschiedenheit** *die* (auch verhüll.: Streit) difference of opinion

Meise /ˈmaizə/ *die;* ~, ~n tit[mouse]; **eine ~ haben** (salopp) be nuts (coll.); be off one's head (coll.)

Meißel /ˈmaisl̩/ *der;* ~s, ~: chisel

meißeln

A *tr. V.* chisel; carve ‹*statue, sculpture*› with a chisel

B *itr. V.* chisel; work with a chisel; carve; **an einer Statue ~:** be working on *or* carving a statue with a chisel

Meiß[e]ner /ˈmaisənɐ/ *Adj.* **~ Porzellan** Meissen china *or* porcelain

meist /maist/ *Adv.* mostly; usually; (zum größten Teil) mostly; for the most part; **er hat ~ keine Zeit** he doesn't usually have any time; **er ist ~ betrunken** he's drunk most of the time

meist... *Indefinitpron. u. unbest. Zahlw.* most; **das ~e Geld haben** have [the] most money; **die ~e Angst haben** be [the] most afraid; **seine ~e Zeit** most of his time; **am ~en arbeiten** work [the] most; **die ~en Leute haben ...** most people have ...; **die ~en Leute, die da waren** most of the people who were there; **darüber habe ich mich am ~en gefreut** that pleased me [the] most; **die ~e Zeit des Jahres** most of the year; **die ~en meiner Kollegen** most of my colleagues; **er hat das ~e vergessen** he has forgotten most of it; **die am ~en befahrene Straße** the most used road; **das am ~en verkaufte Buch** the best-selling book

meist·bietend

A *Adj.* highest-bidding; **der ~e Käufer** the highest bidder

B *adv.* **etw. ~ versteigern/verkaufen** *usw.* auction sth. off/sell sth. *etc.* to the highest bidder

Meist·bietende *der/die; adj. Dekl.* highest bidder

meistens /ˈmaistn̩s/ *Adv.* ▸ **meist**

meistenteils *Adv.* for the most part

Meister /ˈmaistɐ/ *der;* ~s, ~ **1** master craftsman; **~ im Kürschnerhandwerk sein** be a master furrier; **seinen ~ machen** (ugs.) get one's master craftsman's diploma *or* certificate **2** (Vorgesetzter) (in der Fabrik, auf der Baustelle) foreman; (in anderen Betrieben) boss (coll.); **in Ordnung, ~!** OK, chief *or* boss (coll.) **3** (geh.: Könner) master; **es ist noch kein ~ vom Himmel gefallen** (Spr.) you can't always expect to get it right first time; **früh übt sich, was ein ~ werden will** (Spr.) there's nothing like starting young; **[in jmdm.] seinen ~ gefunden haben** have met one's match [in sb.] **4** (Künstler, geh.: Lehrer) master; **die alten ~:** the old masters **5** (Sport) champion; (Mannschaft) champions *pl.* **6** (salopp: Anrede) chief (coll.); guv (Brit. coll.) **7** (in Märchen) **~ Lampe** Master Hare; **~ Petz** Bruin the Bear; (Anrede) Master Bruin; **~ Grimbart** Brock the Badger; (Anrede) Master Brock; **~ Urian** Old Nick

> **Meister(in)**
>
> A master craftsman or craftswoman who has completed rigorous training in his/her trade or vocation and has passed a final exam after several years' experience in a job. A *Meister(in)* is allowed to set up in business and train young people who are doing their **Lehre**.

Meister-: **~brief** *der* master craftsman's diploma *or* certificate; **~dieb** *der,* **~diebin** *die* master thief; **~elf** *die* (Fußball) **die ~elf aus München/die Münchner ~elf** the champions Munich; **~gesang** *der* Meistergesang; art and music of the Meistersingers

meisterhaft

A *Adj.* masterly

B *adv.* in a masterly manner; **es ~ verstehen, etw. zu tun** be a [past] master *or* an expert at doing sth.; **die Gitarre ~ beherrschen** be a masterly guitar player

Meister·hand *die* master hand; **von ~:** by a master hand

Meisterin *die;* ~, ~nen **1** master craftswoman **2** (geh.: Könnerin) master; **im Erfinden von Ausreden ist sie eine ~:** she is a [past] master *or* an expert at inventing excuses **3** (Sport) [women's] champion

Meister-: **~klasse** *die* **1** (Sport) championship class; **2** (Musik, Kunst) master class; **~leistung** *die* masterly performance; (~stück) masterpiece; (geniale Tat) master stroke

meisterlich (geh. veralt.) ▸ **meisterhaft**

Meister-: **~macher** *der,* **~macherin** *die* (Sportjargon) champion maker; **~mannschaft** *die* champions *pl.;* title-holders *pl.*

meistern *tr. V.* master; master, overcome ‹*problem, difficulty*›; control ‹*anger, excitement, etc.*›; **sein Schicksal/Leben ~:** cope with one's fate/with life

Meister·prüfung *die* examination for the/one's master craftsman's diploma *or* certificate

Meisterschaft *die;* ~, ~en **1** mastery **2** (Sport) championship; (Veranstaltung) championships *pl.;* **die ~ erringen** take the championship

Meisterschafts-: **~kampf** *der* (Sport) championship; **~spiel** *das* (Sport) championship match *or* game

Meister-: **~schüler** *der,* **~schülerin** *die* (Musik, Kunst) master-class student; **~singer** *der;* ~~s, ~~: Meistersinger; mastersinger; **~stück** *das* **1** *piece of work executed to qualify as a master craftsman;* **2** (~leistung) masterpiece (**an** + *Dat.* of); (geniale Tat) master stroke; **~titel** *der* **1** (Sport) championship [title]; **2** (im Handwerksberuf) title of master craftsman

Meisterung *die;* ~: mastering

Meister-: **~werk** *das* masterpiece (**an** + *Dat.* of); **~würde** *die* title of master craftsman

Meist·gebot *das* highest bid

meistverbreitet *Adj.* most common ‹*disease etc.*›; most widely distributed ‹*writings etc.*›; most widely used ‹*language*›

Mekka /ˈmɛka/ *(das);* ~s ▸ **ⓘ S. 675** Mecca; (fig.) Mecca (+ *Gen.* for)

Melamin·harz /melaˈmiːn-/ *das* melamine resin

Melancholie /melaŋkoːˈliː/ *die;* ~, (Psych.:) ~n (Gemütszustand) melancholy; (Psych.) melancholia

Melancholiker /melaŋˈkoːlikɐ/ *der;* ~s, ~, **Melancholikerin** *die;* ~, ~nen melancholic

melancholisch

A *Adj.* melancholy; melancholy, melancholic ‹*person, temperament*›

B *adv.* melancholically

Melanesien /melaˈneːzi̯ən/ *(das);* ~s Melanesia

Melange /meˈlãːʒ(ə)/ *die;* ~, ~n **1** (österr.) ▸ **Milchkaffee** **2** (Gemisch) blend

Melanom /melaˈnoːm/ *das;* ~s, ~e ▸ **ⓘ S. 439** (Med.) melanoma

Melasse /meˈlasə/ *die;* ~: molasses *sing.*

Melde-: **~amt** *das* registration office (*for registering with the authorities on changing one's place of residence*); **~fahrer** *der* (Milit.) dispatch rider; **~frist** *die* (bei der Anmeldung, Abmeldung) registration period; (Versicherungsw.) notification period; **~gänger** *der;* ~~s, ~~ (Milit.) runner; messenger

melden /ˈmɛldn̩/

A *tr. V.* **1** report; (registrieren lassen) register ‹*birth, death, etc.*› (*Dat.* with); **wie soeben gemeldet wird** (Fernseh., Rundf.) according to reports just coming in; **etw. den Behörden ~:** report sth. to the authorities; **jmdn. als vermisst ~:** report sb. missing; **melde gehorsamst, ...** (Milit. veralt.) beg to report ...; **nichts/nicht viel zu ~ haben** (ugs.) have no/little say **2** (ankündigen) announce; **wen darf ich ~?** what name shall I say?; who shall I say is here? **3** (Schülerspr.) **jmdn. ~:** tell on sb; **das wird gemeldet!** I'll tell!

B *refl. V.* **1** report; **sich polizeilich ~:** register with the police; **sich auf dem Polizeipräsidium ~:** report to police headquarters; **sich zum Militär ~:** enlist [in the armed forces]; **sich freiwillig ~:** volunteer (**zu** for); **sich auf eine Anzeige ~:** reply to *or* answer an advertisement; **sich zu einem Lehrgang ~:** sign on *or* enrol for a course; **sich zu einer Prüfung ~:** enter for an examination; **sich zum Dienst ~:** report for duty; *s. auch* **krank 1** **2** (am Telefon) answer; **der Teilnehmer meldet sich nicht/es meldet sich niemand** there is no answer *or* reply **3** (ums Wort bitten) put one's hand up **4** (von sich hören lassen) get in touch (**bei** with); **wenn du etwas brauchst, melde dich** if you need anything let me/us know; **Otto 2, bitte ~!** Otto 2, come in please! **5** (sich ankündigen) ‹*old age, rheumatism, etc.*› make itself *or* its presence felt

C *itr. V.* ‹*dog*› start barking

Melde·pflicht *die* **1** (Gesundheitsw.) obligation (*on doctor*) to notify the authorities; **Thypus unterliegt der ~:** cases of typhoid must be notified to the authorities **2** (Verwaltung) obligation to register with the authorities; **polizeiliche ~:** obligation to register with the police

> **Meldepflicht**
>
> This obligation to register applies to all German residents, regardless of nationality. Residents must inform the **Einwohnermeldeamt** every time they change their address. The applicant is issued with an *Abmeldebestätigung* and must then register the new address. The system means that every resident can quickly be traced.

melde·pflichtig *Adj.* **1** (Gesundheitsw.) notifiable ‹*disease*› **2** (Verwaltung) ‹*accident*› which must be reported

Melder *der;* ~s, ~ (Milit.) runner; messenger

Melde-: **~schluss,** ***~schluß** *der* closing date; **~wesen** *das* system of registration; **~zettel** *der* registration form

Meldung *die;* ~, ~en **1** report; (Nachricht) piece of news; (Ankündigung) announcement; **~en aus dem Ausland** news from abroad; **~en vom Sport** sports news *sing.;* **~en in Kürze** news headlines **2** **~ machen** *od.* **erstatten** (Milit.) report; make a report **3** (Anzeige) report; **über etw.** (*Akk.*) **~ machen** report sth. **4** (An~) (bei einem Wettbewerb, Examen) entry; (bei einem Kurs) enrolment; **wir bitten um freiwillige ~en** we are asking *or* calling for volunteers; **seine ~ [zu etw.] zurückziehen** withdraw [from sth.] **5** (Wort~) request to speak; **gibt es noch weitere ~en?** does anyone else wish to speak?

meliert /meˈliːɐt/ *Adj.* mottled; **grün/braun ~:** mottled green/brown; **[grau] ~es Haar** hair streaked with grey

Melioration /meli̯oraˈtsi̯oːn/ *die;* ~, ~en (Landw.) melioration; land improvement

Melisse /meˈlɪsə/ *die;* ~, ~n melissa; balm

Melk-: **~anlage** *die* (Landw.) milking equipment *no indef. art.;* **~eimer** *der* (Landw.) milking pail

melken /ˈmɛlkn̩/

A *regelm. (auch unr.) tr. V.* (auch fig. salopp) milk

B *regelm. (auch unr.) itr. V.* (veralt.: Milch geben) give milk; **eine ~de Kuh** a cow in milk; a milch cow

Melker *der;* ~s, ~ ▸ **ⓘ S. 113** milker

Melkerin *die;* ~, ~nen ▸ **ⓘ S. 113** milkmaid

Melk-: **~maschine** *die* milking machine; **~schemel** *der* milking stool

Melodei /meloˈdai̯/ *die;* ~, ~en (dichter. veralt.) ▸ **Melodie 1**

Melodie /meloˈdiː/ *die;* ~, ~n **1** melody; (Weise) tune; melody; **nach einer ~:** to a melody/tune **2** (Satz~) intonation

Melodien-: **~folge** *die,* **~reigen** *der* medley [of tunes]; musical medley

Melodik /meˈloːdɪk/ *die;* ~ (Musik) **1** (Lehre) theory of melody **2** (melodische Merkmale) melodic characteristics *pl.*

melodiös /meloˈdi̯øːs/

A *Adj.* melodious

B *adv.* melodiously

melodisch
A *Adj.* melodic; melodious
B *adv.* melodically; melodiously; **~ sprechen** speak in a melodic *or* melodious voice

Melodram /melo'dra:m/ *das;* **~s, Melodramen, Melodrama** *das;* **~as, Melodramen** melodrama

melodramatisch
A *Adj.* melodramatic
B *adv.* melodramatically

Melone /me'lo:nə/ *die;* **~, ~n** 1▸ melon 2▸ (ugs. scherzh.) bowler [hat]

Membran /mɛm'bra:n/ *die;* **~, ~en, Membrane** *die;* **~, ~n** 1▸ (Technik) diaphragm 2▸ (Biol., Chemie) membrane

Memento /me'mɛnto/ *das;* **~s, ~s** 1▸ (kath. Rel.) Memento 2▸ (geh.: Mahnung) warning reminder

Memme /'mɛmə/ *die;* **~, ~n** (veralt. abwertend) [craven] coward

Memoiren /me'mo̯a:rən/ *Pl.* memoirs

Memorandum /memo'randʊm/ *das;* **~s, Memoranden** *od.* **Memoranda** memorandum

Memorial /memo'ri̯a:l/ *das;* **~s, ~s** (geh.) memorial event; (Rennen) memorial race

memorieren /memo'ri:rən/ *tr. V.* (geh. veralt.) memorize

Menage /me'na:ʒə/ *die;* **~, ~n** cruet [stand]

Menagerie /menaʒə'ri:/ *die;* **~, ~n** (veralt.) menagerie

menagieren /mena'ʒi:rən/ *itr. V.* (österr. Milit.) draw rations

mendeln /'mɛndl̩n/ *itr. V.* (Biol.) Mendelize

mendelsche Gesetze /'mɛndl̩ʃə-/ *Pl.* (Biol.) Mendel's laws

Menetekel /mene'te:kl̩/ *das;* **~s, ~** (geh.) warning sign *or* portent

Menge /'mɛŋə/ *die;* **~, ~n** 1▸ (Quantum) quantity; amount; **die dreifache ~:** three times *or* triple the amount; three times as much; **in ausreichender ~:** in sufficient quantities *pl.*; **in ~n zu ...** in quantities of ... 2▸ (große Anzahl) large number; lot (coll.); **eine ~ Leute** a lot *or* lots *pl.* of people (coll.); **eine ~** (ugs.) a lot *or* lots [of it/them] (coll.); **eine ~ Zeit** (ugs.) a lot *or* lots of time; plenty of time; **Kuchen/Blumen in ~n** cakes/flowers in abundance; lots of cakes/flowers (coll.); **er weiß eine [ganze] ~** (ugs.) he knows [quite] a lot (coll.) *or* a great deal; **sie bildet sich eine ~ ein** (ugs.) she is very conceited (**auf** + *Akk.* about); **eine ~ trinken/essen** (ugs.) drink/eat a hell of a lot (coll.); **jede ~ Arbeit/Alkohol** *usw.* (ugs.) masses *pl. or* loads *pl.* of work/alcohol *etc.* (coll.); *s. auch* **rau A 8** 3▸ (Menschen~) crowd; throng 4▸ (Math.) set

mengen (veralt.)
A *tr. V.* mix; **Rosinen unter den Teig ~:** mix raisins into the dough
B *refl. V.* (ugs.) mingle (**unter** + *Akk.* with)

mengen-, Mengen-: ~angabe *die* indication of quantity/quantities; **~lehre** *die* (Math., Logik) set theory *no art.*; **~mäßig** **A** *Adj.* quantitative; **B** *adv.* quantitatively; as far as quantity is/was concerned; **~rabatt** *der* (Wirtsch.) bulk discount

Menhir /'mɛnhɪr/ *der;* **~s, ~e** menhir

Meningitis /menɪŋ'gi:tɪs/ *die;* **~, Meningitiden** ▸ⓘ **S. 439** (Med.) meningitis

Meniskus /me'nɪskʊs/ *der;* **~, Menisken** ▸ⓘ **S. 435** (Anat., Optik) meniscus

Meniskus·riss, *Meniskus·riß *der* ▸ⓘ **S. 439** (Med.) torn meniscus

Menkenke /mɛŋ'kɛŋkə/ *die;* **~** (md. ugs.) fuss; **mach keine ~:** don't make a fuss

Mennige /'mɛnɪgə/ *die;* **~:** red lead

Menopause /meno'pau̯zə/ *die;* **~, ~n** (Physiol.) menopause

Menora /mɛno'ra:/ *die;* **~, ~:** menorah

Mensa /'mɛnza/ *die;* **~, ~s** *od.* **Mensen** refectory, canteen (*of university, college*)

Mensa·essen *das* refectory *or* canteen food

Mensch¹ /mɛnʃ/ *der;* **~en, ~en** 1▸ (Gattung) **der ~:** man; **die ~en** man *sing.*; human beings; **das Gute im ~en** the good in man; **das sind starrköpfige ~en** they are stubborn people; **alle ~en müssen sterben** we are all mortal; **der ~ lebt nicht vom Brot allein** (Spr.) man does not live by bread alone (prov.); **ich bin auch nur ein ~:** I'm only human; **der ~ denkt, Gott lenkt** (Spr.) man proposes, God disposes (prov.); **das sind doch keine ~en mehr!** they are a pack of animals; **nur noch ein halber ~ sein** be just about all in; **wieder ein ~ sein** (ugs.) feel like a human being again; **~en fressend** man-eating 2▸ (Person) person; man/woman; **~en** people; **kein ~:** no one; **es war kein ~ da** there was no one *or* not a soul there; **unter die ~en gehen** mix with people; **des ~en Wille ist sein Himmelreich** you/he *etc.* must do whatever makes you/him *etc.* happy; **wie der erste ~/die ersten ~en** extremely awkwardly; **ein neuer ~ werden** become a new man/woman; **von ~ zu ~:** man to man/woman to woman; **~, ärgere dich nicht** (Gesellschaftsspiel) ludo 3▸ *Pl.* (~heit) mankind *sing., no art.*; man *sing., no art.* 4▸ (salopp: Anrede) (bewundernd) wow; (erstaunt) wow; good grief; (vorwurfsvoll) for heaven's sake; **~, war das ein Glück!** boy, that was a piece of luck!; **~, hast du dich verändert!** good Lord, haven't you changed!; **~, das habe ich ganz vergessen!** damn *or* (Brit.) blast, I completely forgot!; **~ Meier!** good grief!

Mensch² *das;* **~[e]s, ~er** (abwertend: Frau) slut; trollop

menschen-, Menschen-: ~affe *der* anthropoid [ape]; **~ähnlich** *Adj.* manlike; like a human being/human beings *postpos.*; **~alter** *das* lifetime; **~ansammlung** *die* gathering [of people]; (~menge) crowd [of people]; **~arm** *Adj.* sparsely populated; **~auflauf** *der* crowd [of people]; **~bild** *das* conception of man; **~feind** *der,* **~feindin** *die* misanthropist; **~feindlich** **A** *Adj.* 1▸ misanthropic; 2▸ (unmenschlich) inhuman ‹*system, policy etc.*›; ‹*environment*› hostile to man; **B** *adv.* 1▸ misanthropically; 2▸ (unmenschlich) inhumanly; **~feindlich konzipierte Trabantenstädte** satellite towns designed in a way that creates an environment hostile to man; **~feindlichkeit** *die* ▸**menschenfeindlich A:** misanthropy; inhumanity; hostility to man; **~fleisch** *das* human flesh; **~fressend** ▸**Mensch 1**; **~fresser** *der,* **~fresserin** *die* (ugs.) cannibal; (Mythol.) maneater; **er ist doch kein ~fresser** (scherzh.) he won't eat *or* bite you; **~freund** *der,* **~freundin** *die* philanthropist; **~freundlich** **A** *Adj.* 1▸ philanthropic; 2▸ (human) ‹*environment*› catering for human needs; ‹*architecture*› designed with [the needs of] people in mind; **B** *adv.* 1▸ philanthropically; 2▸ **~freundlich gestaltet/konstruiert** designed with [the needs of] people in mind; **~freundlichkeit** *die* philanthropy; **aus reiner ~freundlichkeit** out of the sheer goodness of one's heart; **~führung** *die* leadership; **~gedenken** *das:* **das wird seit ~gedenken so gemacht** it has been done that way for as long as anyone can remember; **der heißeste Sommer seit ~gedenken** the hottest summer in living memory; **~geschlecht** *das* (geh.) human race; **~gestalt** *die* human form; **ein Engel/Teufel** *od.* **Satan in ~gestalt sein** be an angel in human form/the devil incarnate; **~gewühl** *das* milling crowd; **~haar** *das* human hair; **~hand** *die* (geh.) hand of man; human hand; **von ~hand geschaffen** created by the hand of man *or* by human hand; **~handel** *der* trade *or* traffic in human beings; (Sklavenhandel) slave trade; **~händler** *der,* **~händlerin** *die* trafficker [in human beings]; (Sklavenhändler) slave trader; **~hass, *~haß** *der* misanthropy; **~hasser** *der;* **~~s, ~~, ~hasserin** *die;* **~~, ~~nen** ▸**~feind**; **~jagd** *die* (abwertend) manhunting; manhunts *pl.*; (Verfolgung) persecution; **eine ~jagd** a manhunt; **~kenner** *der,* **~kennerin** *die* judge of character *or* human nature; **~kenntnis** *die* ability to judge character *or* human nature; **~kette** *die* human chain; **~kind** *das* creature; soul; **~leben** *das* life; **ein ~leben lang währen** (geh.) last a whole lifetime; **der Unfall forderte vier ~leben** (geh.) the accident claimed four lives; **~leben waren nicht zu beklagen** (geh.) there was no loss of life; **~leer** *Adj.* deserted; **~liebe** *die* philanthropy; love of humanity *or* mankind; **~masse** *die* crowd [of people]; **~material** *das* (Militärjargon) [human] material; **~menge** *die* crowd [of people]; **~möglich** *Adj.* humanly possible; **das ist doch nicht ~möglich!** but that's impossible!; **alles Menschenmögliche tun** do all that is/was humanly possible; **~opfer** *das* 1▸ human sacrifice; 2▸ (~leben) **es waren Hunderte von ~opfern zu beklagen** hundreds of lives were lost; **~raub** *der* kidnapping; abduction; **~recht** *das* human right; **~rechtler** *der;* **~~s, ~~, ~rechtlerin** *die;* **~~, ~~nen** human rights campaigner; **~rechts·konvention** *die* Human Rights Convention; **~rechts·verletzung** *die* human rights violation; **~scheu** *Adj.* afraid of people; (ungesellig) unsociable; **~scheu** *die* fear of people; **~schinder** *der,* **~schinderin** *die* (abwertend) cruel and ruthless slave driver; **~schlag** *der* race *or* breed [of people]; **~seele** *die* human soul; **keine ~seele** not a [living] soul

Menschens·kind *Interj.* (salopp) (erstaunt) good heavens; good grief; (vorwurfsvoll) for heaven's sake

Menschen·sohn *der* (christl. Rel.) Son of Man

menschen-, Menschen-: ~unwürdig **A** *Adj.* degrading and inhumane ‹*treatment*›; ‹*accommodation*› unfit for human habitation; ‹*conditions*› unfit for human beings; ‹*behaviour*› unworthy of a human being; **B** *adv.* ‹*treat*› in a degrading and inhumane way; ‹*live, be housed*› in conditions unfit for human beings; **~verächter** *der* despiser of humanity *or* mankind; **~verachtung** *die* contempt for humanity *or* mankind; **~verstand** *der* human intelligence *or* intellect; *s. auch* **gesund**; **~werk** *das* (geh.) work of man; **alles ~werk ist vergänglich** the works *pl.* of men are ephemeral; **~würde** *die* human dignity *no art.*; **~würdig** **A** *Adj.* humane ‹*treatment*›; ‹*accommodation*› fit for human habitation; ‹*conditions*› fit for human beings; ‹*behaviour*› worthy of a human being; **B** *adv.* ‹*treat*› humanely; ‹*live, be housed*› in conditions fit for human beings

Menschewik /mɛnʃe'vɪk/ *der;* **~en, ~en** *u.* **~i, Menschewikin** *die;* **~, ~nen** (hist.) Menshevik

Menschheit *die;* **~:** mankind *no art.*; humanity *no art.*; human race

Menschheits-: ~entwicklung *die* evolution of man; **~geschichte** *die* history of mankind *or* of the human race; **~traum** *der* dream of mankind

menschlich
A *Adj.* 1▸ human; **~es Versagen** human error; **das ~e Leben** human life; *s. auch* **irren 1** 2▸ (annehmbar) civilized; **wieder ganz ~ aussehen** (ugs.) look quite presentable again 3▸ (human) humane ‹*person, treatment, etc.*›; human ‹*trait, emotion, etc.*›; **sich von der ~en Seite zeigen** show one's human side
B *adv.* 1▸ **er ist ~ sympathisch** I like him as a person; **sich ~ näher kommen** get on closer [personal] terms [with one another] 2▸ (human) humanely; in a humane manner

Menschliche *das; adj. Dekl.* **nichts ~s war ihr fremd** she was familiar with every aspect of human experience; **er hat nichts ~s an sich** he shows no human traits; there's nothing human about him

Menschlichkeit *die* humanity *no art.*; **etw. aus reiner ~ tun** do sth. for purely humanitarian reasons

Mensch·werdung /-ve:ɐdʊŋ/ *die;* **~** (christl. Rel.) incarnation

Mensen ▸**Mensa**

Menses /'mɛnze:s/ *Pl.* (Med.) [monthly] period; menses *pl.*

Menstruation /mɛnstrua'tsi̯o:n/ *die;* **~, ~en** (Physiol.) menstruation; (Periode) [menstrual] period

m

menstruieren *itr. V.* (Physiol.) menstruate
Mensur /mɛnˈzuːɐ̯/ *die;* ~, ~**en** 1) students' duel; **eine ~ schlagen** fight a duel 2) (Fechten) [fencing] measure *or* distance
mental /mɛnˈtaːl/ (geh.)
A *Adj.* mental
B *adv.* mentally
Mentalität /mɛntaliˈtɛːt/ *die;* ~, ~**en** mentality
Menthol /mɛnˈtoːl/ *das;* ~**s** menthol
Mentor /ˈmɛntɔr/ *der;* ~**s**, ~**en** /-ˈtoːrən/, **Mentorin** *die;* ~, ~**nen** 1) (geh.) mentor 2) (veralt.: Lehrer[in]) tutor 3) (Schulw.) supervisor
Menu /meˈnyː/ *das;* ~**s**, ~**s** (schweiz.), **Menü** /meˈnyː/ *das;* ~**s**, ~**s** (auch DV) menu; (im Restaurant) set meal *or* menu
Menuett /meˈnu̯ɛt/ *das;* ~**s**, ~**e** *od.* ~**s** minuet
Menü-: ~**führung** *die* (DV) menu design; ~**leiste** *die* (DV) menu bar
mephistophelisch /mefɪstoˈfeːlɪʃ/ (geh.) Mephistophelian
Mercator·projektion /mɛrˈkaːtɔr-/ *die* (Geogr.) Mercator's projection
Mergel /ˈmɛrgl̩/ *der;* ~**s** (Geol.) marl
Meridian /meriˈdi̯aːn/ *der;* ~**s**, ~**e** (Geogr., Astron.) meridian
Meridian·kreis *der* (Astron.) meridian circle
Meringe /meˈrɪŋə/ *die;* ~, ~**n** meringue
Merino /meˈriːno/ *der;* ~**s**, ~**s** 1) (Schaf) merino [sheep] 2) (Stoff) merino
Merino-: ~**schaf** *das* merino [sheep]; ~**wolle** *die* merino wool
Meriten /meˈriːtn̩/ *Pl.* (geh. veralt.) merits
merkantil /mɛrkanˈtiːl/ *Adj.* (geh.) mercantile
Merkantilismus *der;* ~ (hist.) mercantilism *no art.*
merkantilistisch *Adj.* (hist.) mercantilist
merkbar
A *Adj.* 1) perceptible; noticeable; (deutlich) noticeable 2) (leicht zu behalten) **eine gut** *od.* **leicht ~e Nummer** an easily remembered number; **leicht/schwer ~ sein** be easy/difficult to remember
B *adv.* perceptibly; noticeably; (deutlich) noticeably
Merk-: ~**blatt** leaflet; (mit Anweisungen) instruction leaflet; ~**buch** *das* notebook
merken /ˈmɛrkn̩/
A *tr. V.* notice; **deutlich zu ~ sein** be plain to see; be obvious; **er hat [davon] nichts gemerkt** he didn't notice anything [of that]; **davon merkt man nicht viel** it's hardly noticeable; **an seinem Benehmen merkt man, dass ...** you can tell by his behaviour that ...; **das merkt doch jeder/keiner** everybody/nobody will notice; **jmdn. etw. ~ lassen** let sb. see sth.; **du merkst aber auch alles!** (ugs. iron.) how very observant of you!; **merkst du was?** (ugs.) have you noticed something?
B *refl. V.* **sich** (*Dat.*) **etw. ~:** remember sth.; **hast du dir die Adresse gemerkt?** have you made a mental note of the address?; **diesen Mann muss man sich** (*Dat.*) **~:** this is a man to take note of; **ich werd mirs** *od.* **werds mir ~** (ugs.) I won't forget that; I'll remember that; **merk dir das** just remember that
Merk-: ~**heft** *das* notebook; ~**hilfe** *die* mnemonic; memory aid
merklich
A *Adj.* perceptible; noticeable; (deutlich) noticeable
B *adv.* perceptibly; noticeably; (deutlich) noticeably
Merkmal *das;* ~**s**, ~**e** feature; characteristic; **besondere ~e** distinguishing features *or* marks
Merk-: ~**satz** *der* mnemonic sentence/phrase; mnemonic; ~**spruch** *der* 1) pithy maxim *or* saying; 2) (~hilfe) mnemonic verse/sentence/phrase mnemonic
Merkur[1] /mɛrˈkuːɐ̯/ *der;* ~**s** (Astron.), **Merkur**[2] (*der*) (Myth.) Mercury
merkwürdig
A *Adj.* strange; odd; peculiar
B *adv.* strangely; oddly; peculiarly
merkwürdiger·weise *Adv.* strangely *or* oddly *or* curiously enough
Merkwürdigkeit *die;* ~, ~**en** 1) strangeness; oddness; peculiarity 2) (Erscheinung) curiosity
Merk-: ~**zeichen** *das* mark; marker; ~**zettel** *der* note; (Liste) list
Merowinger *der;* ~**s**, ~, **Merowingerin** *die;* ~, ~**nen** (hist.) Merovingian
merzerisieren /mɛrtsəriˈziːrən/ *tr. V.* (Textilind.) mercerize
Mesalliance /mezaˈli̯ãːs/ *die;* ~, ~**n** (geh.) mésalliance
meschugge /meˈʃʊgə/ *Adj.; nicht attrib.* (salopp) barmy (Brit. coll.); nuts *pred.* (coll.); off one's rocker *pred.* (coll.)
Meskalin /mɛskaˈliːn/ *das;* ~**s** mescaline
Mesmerismus /mɛsməˈrɪsmʊs/ *der;* ~ *Mesmer's theory of biomagnetic effects*
Mesner /ˈmɛsnɐ/ *der;* ~**s**, ~, **Mesnerin** *die;* ~, ~**nen** sexton
Mesolithikum /mezoˈliːtikʊm/ *das;* ~**s** (Geol.) Mesolithic period
mesolithisch *Adj.* (Geol.) Mesolithic
Mesopotamien /mezopoˈtaːmi̯ən/ *(das);* ~**s** Mesopotamia
Mesozoikum /mezoˈtsoːikʊm/ *das;* ~**s** (Geol.) Mesozoic era
mesozoisch *Adj.* (Geol.) Mesozoic
Mess·band, *Meß·band *das; Pl.* **Mess·bänder** measuring tape
messbar, *meßbar /ˈmɛsbaːɐ̯/ *Adj.* measurable; **schwer ~:** difficult to measure
Mess-, *Meß-: ~**becher** *der* measuring jug; ~**bild** *das* (Kartographie) photogrammetric photograph; ~**buch** *das* missal; mass book; ~**diener** *der*, ~**dienerin** *die* (kath. Kirche) server
Messe[1] /ˈmɛsə/ *die;* ~, ~**n** (Gottesdienst, Musik) mass; **die ~ halten** *od.* (geh.) **zelebrieren** say *or* celebrate mass; **für jmdn. eine ~ lesen** say a mass for sb.
Messe[2] *die;* ~, ~**n** 1) (Ausstellung) [trade] fair; **auf der ~:** at the [trade] fair 2) (landsch.: Jahrmarkt, Volksfest) fair
Messe[3] *die;* ~, ~**n** (Seew., Milit.) mess; (Raum) mess room
Messe-: ~**besucher** *der*, ~**besucherin** *die* visitor to a/the [trade] fair; ~**gelände** *das* site of a/the [trade] fair; (mit festen ~hallen) exhibition centre; ~**halle** *die* exhibition hall
messen
A *unr. tr. V.* 1) measure; **[jmdm.] den** *od.* **jmds. Blutdruck/Puls ~:** take sb.'s blood pressure/pulse; **jmds. Temperatur ~:** take sb.'s temperature; **die Zeit eines Sprinters ~:** time a sprinter; **am Morgen wurden schon 20° ge~:** the temperature was already 20° in the morning; **etw. nach Litern/Metern ~:** measure sth. in litres/metres; *s. auch* **Fieber** 2) (beurteilen) judge (**nach** by); **etw. an etw.** (*Dat.*) **~:** judge sth. by sth.; **jmdn. an jmdm. ~:** judge sb. by comparison with sb.; compare sb. with sb.; **ge~ an** (+ *Dat.*) having regard to 3) (geh.) **jmdn. mit den Augen** *od.* **Blicken ~:** look sb. up and down
B *unr. itr. V.* measure; **er misst 1,85 m** he's 1.85 m [tall]; **genau ~:** make an exact measurement/exact measurements
C *unr. refl. V.* (geh.) compete (**mit** with); **sich mit jmdm./etw. [in etw.** (*Dat.*)**] [nicht] ~ können** [not] be as good as sb./sth. [in sth.]
Messer *das;* ~**s**, ~ 1) knife; (Hack~) chopper; (Rasier~) [cut-throat] razor; **mit ~ und Gabel essen** eat with a knife and fork; **jmdm. das ~ an die Kehle setzen** (fig. ugs.) hold sb. at gunpoint; **auf des ~s Schneide stehen** (fig.) hang in the balance; be balanced on a knife-edge; **es steht auf des ~s Schneide, ob ...** it's touch and go whether ...; **jmdn. ans ~ liefern** (fig. ugs.) inform on sb.; **bis aufs ~** (fig. ugs.) ‹*fight etc.*› to the bitter end; **jmdm. ins [offene] ~ laufen** (fig. ugs.) play right into sb.'s hands; **da geht mir das ~ in der Tasche auf** (fig. ugs.) I see red 2) (ugs.: Skalpell) **jmdn. unter dem ~ haben** have sb. under the knife (coll.); **unters ~ müssen** have to go under the knife (coll.) 3) (Technik) cutter; (Klinge) blade
messer-, Messer-: ~**bänkchen** *das* (individual eater's) knife rest; ~**griff** *der*, ~**heft** *das* knife handle; handle of a/the knife; ~**held** *der* (abwertend) thug with a knife; ~**klinge** *die* knife blade; blade of a/the knife; ~**rücken** *der* back of a/the knife; ~**scharf** **A** *Adj.* razor-sharp; (fig.) trenchant ‹*criticism*›; incisive ‹*logic*›; razor-sharp ‹*wit, intellect*›; **B** *adv.* (fig. ugs.) ‹*think*› with penetrating insight; ‹*argue*› incisively; ~**schmied** *der*, ~**schmiedin** *die* ▸ℹ **S. 113** *maker of saws, knives, and other cutting tools;* ~**spitze** *die* 1) point of a/the knife; 2) (Mengenangabe) **eine ~spitze** just a trace; **eine ~spitze Salz** a large pinch of salt; ~**stecher** *der;* ~~**s**, ~~**:** knifeman; ~**stecherei** /-ʃtɛçəˈrai̯/ *die;* ~~, ~~**en** knife fight; fight with knives; ~**stecherin** *die;* ~~, ~~**nen:** knifewoman; ~**stich** *der* knife thrust; (Wunde) knife wound; stab wound; ~**werfer** *der*, ~**werferin** *die* knife-thrower
Messe-: ~**stadt** *die* town well known for its trade fairs; **die ~stadt Leipzig** Leipzig with its trade fairs; ~**stand** *der* stand [at a/the trade fair]
Mess-, *Meß-: ~**fühler** *der* (Technik) sensor; ~**gerät** *das* measuring device *or* instrument; (Zähler) meter; ~**glas** *das* measuring glass; graduated measure; ~**gewand** *das* chasuble
messianisch /mɛˈsi̯aːnɪʃ/ *Adj.* Messianic
Messianismus *der;* ~**:** Messianism *no art.*
Messias /mɛˈsiːas/ *der;* ~**:** Messiah
Messing /ˈmɛsɪŋ/ *das;* ~**s** brass; **mit ~ beschlagen sein** have brass fittings *pl.*
messingen *Adj.* brass
Messing·waren *Pl.* brassware *sing.*
Mess-, *Meß-: ~**instrument** *das* measuring instrument; ~**latte** *die* surveyor's wooden rod *or* staff
Messner, Messnerin ▸ Mesner, Mesnerin
Mess-, *Meß-: ~**opfer** *das* (kath. Kirche) sacrifice of the mass; ~**stab** *der* measuring rod; ~**technik** *die* technology of measurement; ~**tisch** *der* plane table; ~**tisch·blatt** *das* large-scale map (*1:25,000*); ~**uhr** *die* dial flowmeter
Messung *die;* ~, ~**en** (das Messen, Messergebnis) measurement; (das Ablesen, Ableseergebnis) reading
Mess-, *Meß-: ~**wein** *der* (kath. Kirche) Communion wine; altar wine; ~**wert** *der* measured value; (Ableseergebnis) reading; ~**zylinder** *der* measuring cylinder
Mestize /mɛsˈtiːtsə/ *der;* ~**n**, ~**n** mestizo
Mestizin *die;* ~, ~**nen** mestiza
Met /meːt/ *der;* ~**[e]s** mead
Metabolismus /metaboˈlɪsmʊs/ *der;* ~**:** (Physiol.) metabolism
Metall /meˈtal/ *das;* ~**s**, ~**e** metal; **die ~ verarbeitende Industrie** the metalworking industry
Metall-: ~**arbeiter** *der*, ~**arbeiterin** *die* metalworker; ~**bearbeitung** *die* metalworking
metallen
A *Adj.* 1) (aus Metall) metal 2) (geh.: metallisch) metallic
B *adv.* (geh.) **ihr Haar glänzte/die Becken klirrten ~:** her hair gleamed/the cymbals sounded metallically
Metaller *der;* ~**s**, ~, **Metallerin** *die;* ~, ~**nen** (ugs.) metalworker
Metall·geld *das* metal money; specie (as tech. term)
metall·haltig *Adj.* metalliferous
metallic /meˈtalɪk/ *indekl. Adj.* metallic [grey/blue/*etc.*]
Metallic·lackierung *die* metallic finish
Metall·industrie *die* metal-processing and metal-working industries *pl.*

metallisch
A *Adj.* metallic; metal *attrib.*, metallic ‹*conductor, coating*›
B *adv.* metallically

metallisieren *tr. V.* (Technik) metallize

Metall-: ~kunde *die* [physical] metallurgy *no art.*; **~säge** *die* hacksaw; **~überzug** *der* metal *or* metallic coating

Metallurg /meta'lʊrk/ *der;* **~en, ~en, Metallurge** *der;* **~en, ~en, Metallurgin** *die;* **~, ~nen** ▸ℹ **S. 113** metallurgist

Metallurgie /metalʊr'gi:/ *die;* **~:** [extractive] metallurgy *no art.*

metallurgisch *Adj.* metallurgical

metall·verarbeitend ▸**Metall**

Metall·waren *Pl.* metalware *sing.*

Metamorphose /metamɔr'fo:zə/ *die;* **~, ~n** metamorphosis

Metapher /me'tafɐ/ *die;* **~, ~n** (Stilk.) metaphor; **Gebrauch von ~n** use of metaphor

Metaphorik /meta'fo:rɪk/ *die;* **~** (Stilk.) **1** (Gebrauch von Metaphern) use of metaphor **2** (Metaphern) imagery; metaphors *pl.*

metaphorisch (Stilk.)
A *Adj.* metaphorical
B *adv.* metaphorically

meta-, Meta-: ~physik *die;* **~~, ~~en** **1** metaphysics *sing., no art.*; **2** (darstellendes Werk) metaphysical work; **~physiker** *der,* **~physikerin** *die* metaphysicist; **~physisch** **A** *Adj.* metaphysical; **B** *adv.* metaphysically; **~physisch denken** think in metaphysical terms; **~sprache** *die* (Sprachw., Math.) metalanguage; **~stase** /-'sta:zə/ *die;* **~~, ~~n** ▸ℹ **S. 439** (Med.) metastasis

Meteor /mete'o:ɐ̯/ *der;* **~s, ~e** (Astron.) meteor

Meteorit /meteo'ri:t/ *der;* **~en** *od.* **~s, ~e[n]** (Astron.) meteorite

Meteorologe /meteoro'lo:gə/ *der;* **~n, ~n** ▸ℹ **S. 113** meteorologist; (im Fernsehen) weatherman

Meteorologie *die;* **~:** meteorology *no art.*

Meteorologin *die;* **~, ~nen** ▸ℹ **S. 113** meteorologist; (im Fernsehen) weather lady

meteorologisch
A *Adj.* meteorological
B *adv.* meteorologically

Meter /'me:tɐ/ *der od. das;* **~s, ~** ▸ℹ **S. 224,** ▸ℹ **S. 374,** ▸ℹ **S. 454** metre; **drei ~ hoch/breit/tief/lang** three metres high/wide/deep/long; **[ungefähr] in 100 ~ Höhe/Entfernung** at a height/distance of [about] 100 metres; **nach ~n** by the metre; **auf den letzten ~n** in the last few metres; *s. auch* **laufend A 3**

meter-, Meter-: ~dick *Adj.* a metre thick *postpos.*; (sehr dick) metres thick *postpos.*; **~hoch** *Adj.* a metre high *postpos.*; (sehr hoch) metres high *postpos.*; ‹*snow*› a metre/metres deep; **der Schnee lag ~hoch** the snow was a metre/metres deep; **~lang** *Adj.* a metre long *postpos.*; (sehr lang) metres long *postpos.*; **~maß** *das* tape measure; (Stab) [metre] rule; **~preis** *der* price per metre; **~ware** *die* fabric/material *etc.* sold by the metre; **etw. als ~ware kaufen/verkaufen** buy/sell sth. by the metre; **~weise** *Adv.* by the metre; **ich habe den Stoff gleich ~weise gekauft** I bought yards of the material straight away; **~weit** **A** *Adj.* (in der Länge) a metre long *postpos.*; (sehr lang) metres long *postpos.*; (in der Breite) a metre wide *postpos.*; (sehr breit) metres wide *postpos.*; **B** *adv.* **das Ziel ~weit verfehlen** be yards off [the] target; **einen Baumstamm ~weit schleudern** hurl a tree trunk several yards

Methan /me'ta:n/ *das;* **~s** methane

Methan·gas *das* methane gas

Methanol /meta'no:l/ *das;* **~s** (Chemie) methanol

Methode /me'to:də/ *die;* **~, ~n** method; **~ haben** be quite deliberate

Methoden·lehre *die* ▸**Methodologie**

Methodik /me'to:dɪk/ *die;* **~, ~en** methodology; **~ zeigen** be methodical

methodisch
A *Adj.* methodological; (nach einer Methode vorgehend) methodical
B *adv.* methodologically; (nach einer Methode) methodically; **~ vorgehen** proceed methodically

Methodist /meto'dɪst/ *der;* **~en, ~en** Methodist

Methodisten·kirche *die* Methodist church

Methodistin *die;* **~, ~nen** Methodist

methodistisch *Adj.* Methodist

Methodologie /metodolo'gi:/ *die;* **~, ~n** methodology

methodologisch *Adj.* methodological

Methusalem /me'tu:zalɛm/ *der;* **~s, ~s** Methuselah; **[so] alt wie ~ sein** be as old as Methuselah; **als ~:** when a very old man

Methyl·alkohol *der* methyl alcohol

Methylen /metʏ'le:n/ *das;* **~s** (Chemie) methylene

Metier /me'tie:/ *das;* **~s, ~s** profession; **sein ~ beherrschen, sich auf sein ~ verstehen** know one's job; **Langstreckenlauf war sein ~:** long-distance running was his métier

Metonymie /metonʏ'mi:/ *die;* **~, ~n** (Rhet., Stilk.) metonymy

Metren ▸**Metrum**

Metrik /'me:trɪk/ *die;* **~, ~en** **1** (Verslehre) metrics **2** (Musik) study of rhythm and tempo *or* of metre

metrisch
A *Adj.* **1** (Verslehre, Musik) metrical **2** (auf den Meter bezogen) metric
B *adv.* metrically

Metro /'me:tro/ *die;* **~, ~s** Metro

Metronom /metro'no:m/ *das;* **~s, ~e** (Musik) metronome

-metropole *die* capital; metropolis; **die deutsche Bier~:** the German beer capital; **die Schwarzwald~:** the chief city of the Black Forest

Metropole /metro'po:lə/ *die;* **~, ~n** (größte Stadt) metropolis; (Zentrum für etw.) capital; metropolis

Metropolit /metropo'li:t/ *der;* **~en, ~en** (kath. u. orthodoxe Kirche) metropolitan

Metrum /'me:trʊm/ *das;* **~s, Metren** (Verslehre, Musik) metre

Mett /mɛt/ *das;* **~[e]s** (landsch.) minced meat, mince (*pork*)

Mettage /mɛ'ta:ʒə/ *die;* **~, ~n** (Zeitungsw.) page make-up

Mette /'mɛtə/ *die;* **~, ~n** (kath. u. ev. Kirche) midnight mass; (am frühen Morgen) early [morning] mass

Metteur /mɛ'tø:ɐ̯/ *der;* **~s, ~e, Metteurin** *die;* **~, ~nen** (Zeitungsw.) make-up arranger

Mett·wurst *die: soft smoked sausage made of minced pork and beef*

Metze /'mɛtsə/ *die;* **~, ~n** (veralt.) strumpet (arch.); whore

Metzelei /mɛtsə'lai/ *die;* **~, ~en** (abwertend) slaughter; butchery

metzeln *tr. V.* ▸**niedermetzeln**

Metzger /'mɛtsgɐ/ *der;* **~s, ~** ▸ℹ **S. 113** (bes. westmd., südd., schweiz.) butcher; (im Schlachthof) slaughterman; *s. auch* **Bäcker**

Metzger- ▸**Fleischer-**

Metzgerei *die;* **~, ~en** (bes. westmd., südd., schweiz.) butcher's [shop]

Meuchel- /'mɔyçl-/: **~mord** *der* (abwertend) [cowardly/treacherous] murder; **~mörder** *der,* **~mörderin** *die* (abwertend) [cowardly/treacherous] murderer

meucheln *tr. V.* (geh. abwertend) murder [in a cowardly/treacherous manner]; assassinate ‹*king, ruler, etc.*›

meuchlerisch (abwertend)
A *Adj.* cowardly; (heimtückisch) treacherous
B *adv.* in a cowardly/treacherous manner

meuchlings /'mɔyçlɪŋs/ *Adv.* (geh. abwertend) treacherously

Meute /'mɔytə/ *die;* **~, ~n** **1** (Jägerspr.) pack **2** (ugs. abwertend: Menschengruppe) mob

Meuterei /mɔytə'rai/ *die;* **~, ~en** mutiny; (fig.) revolt; mutiny

Meuterer /'mɔytərɐ/ *der;* **~s, ~, Meuterin** *die;* **~, ~nen** mutineer; (fig.) rebel

meutern *itr. V.* **1** mutiny (**gegen** against); ‹*prisoners*› riot **2** (ugs.: Unwillen äußern) moan (**gegen** about)

Mexikaner /mɛksi'ka:nɐ/ *der;* **~s, ~, Mexikanerin** *die;* **~, ~nen** ▸ℹ **S. 520** Mexican

mexikanisch *Adj.* ▸ℹ **S. 520** Mexican

Mexiko /'mɛksiko/ *(das);* **~s** ▸ℹ **S. 675** Mexico

MEZ *Abk.* **= mitteleuropäische Zeit** CET

Mezzo·sopran /'mɛtso-/ *der,* **Mezzo·sopranistin** (Musik) mezzo-soprano

Mfg. *Abk.* **= Mitfahrgelegenheit**

MfS *Abk.* (DDR) **= Ministerium für Staatssicherheit**

mg *Abk.* ▸ℹ **S. 315 = Milligramm** mg

MG *Abk.* **= Maschinengewehr**

mhd. *Abk.* **= mittelhochdeutsch** MHG

MHz *Abk.* (Physik) **= Megahertz** MHz

Mi. *Abk.* **= Mittwoch** Wed.

Mia. *Abk.* **= Milliarde[n]** bn.

miau /mi'au/ *Interj.* miaow

miauen *itr. V.* miaow

mich /mɪç/
A *Akk. des Personalpron.* **ich** me
B *Akk. des Reflexivpron. der 1. Pers.* myself; **Was tust du im Badezimmer? — Ich wasche ~:** What are you doing in the bathroom? — I'm washing [myself]; **ich möchte ~ entschuldigen** I'd like to apologize

Michael /'mɪçae:l/ *(der)* Michael

Michaeli[s] *(das);* **~, Michael[i]stag** *der* Michaelmas

Michel /'mɪçl/ *der;* **~s, ~** *in* **der deutsche ~:** *proverbial figure representing the blinkered, simple-minded German, uninterested in politics and the world at large*

Michigan·see /'mɪʃɪgən-/ *der;* **~s** Lake Michigan

mick[e]rig /'mɪk(ə)rɪç/ *Adj.* (ugs.) miserable; measly (sl.); miserable, paltry, (sl.) measly ‹*amount*›; puny ‹*person*›; puny, stunted ‹*plant, tree*›

Mickymaus /'mɪki-/ *die;* **~:** Mickey Mouse *no art.*

Midi /'mi:di/ *das;* **~s, ~s** (Mode) midi (coll.); **im ~:** in a midi; **~ tragen/gehen** wear a midi[-skirt/dress/coat]

Midlife·krise /'mɪtlaif-/ *die* midlife crisis

mied /mi:t/ *1. u. 3. Pers. Sg. Prät. v.* **meiden**

Mieder /'mi:dɐ/ *das;* **~s, ~** **1** (Korsage) girdle **2** (Leibchen) bodice

Mieder-: ~hose *die* pantie-girdle; **~waren** *Pl.* corsetry *sing.*

Mief /mi:f/ *der;* **~[e]s** (salopp abwertend) fug (coll.); **der ~ der Kleinstadt** (fig.) the claustrophobic small-town atmosphere

miefen *itr. V.* (ugs. abwertend) pong (coll.); stink

Miene /'mi:nə/ *die;* **~, ~n** expression; face; **mit unbewegter ~:** with an impassive expression; impassively; **keine ~ verziehen** not turn a hair; **er schluckte die Medizin, ohne eine ~ zu verziehen** he swallowed the medicine without turning a hair; **~ machen, etw. zu tun** make as if to do sth.; **gute ~ zum bösen Spiel machen** grin and bear it

Mienen·spiel *das* facial expressions *pl.*

mies /mi:s/ (ugs.)
A *Adj.* (abwertend) terrible (coll.); lousy (coll.); rotten (coll.); lousy (coll.), foul ‹*mood*›; **jmdn./etw. ~ machen** (ugs.) run sb./sth. down; **jmdm. etw. ~ machen** spoil sth. for sb.
B *adv.* **1** (abwertend: schlecht) terribly badly (coll.); lousily (coll.); rottenly (coll.); **das ist aber ~ gearbeitet** the workmanship on this is terrible (coll.) *or* lousy (coll.) *or* rotten (coll.) **2** (unwohl) **ihm geht es ~:** he's in a terrible state (coll.)

Miese /'mi:zə/ *Pl.; adj. Dekl.* (salopp) **2 000 ~ auf dem Konto haben** be 2,000 marks in the red at the bank; **in den ~n sein** be in the red;

m

(beim Kartenspiel) be down on points

Miese·peter *der;* **~s, ~** (ugs. abwertend) misery guts (coll.)

miesepet[e]rig *Adj.* (ugs. abwertend) grumpy

Miesling /ˈmiːslɪŋ/ *der;* **~s, ~e** (ugs. abwertend) slimeball (coll.)

mies-, Mies-: *~|machen ▸mies A; **~macher** *der,* **~macherin** *die* (ugs. abwertend) carping critic; (Spielverderber) killjoy; **~muschel** *die* [common] mussel

Miet·ausfall *der* loss of rent

Miete[1] /ˈmiːtə/ *die;* **~, ~n** ① rent; (für ein Auto, Boot) hire charge; (für Fernsehgeräte usw.) rental; **das ist schon die halbe ~** (fig. ugs.) I'm/you're *etc.* halfway there ② (das Mieten) renting; **zur ~ wohnen** live in rented accommodation; rent a house/flat (esp. Brit.) *or* (esp. Amer.) apartment/room/rooms; **bei jmdm. zur ~ wohnen** lodge with sb.

Miete[2] *die;* **~, ~n** (Landw.) pit

Miet·einnahmen *Pl.* income *sing.* from rents

mieten *tr. V.* ① rent; (für kürzere Zeit) hire ② (veralt.: in Dienst nehmen) hire ‹*servant*›

Mieter /ˈmiːtɐ/ *der;* **~s, ~:** tenant

Miet·erhöhung *die* rent increase

Mieterin *die;* **~, ~nen** tenant

Mieter·schutz *der* protection of tenants; tenants' protection

miet·frei *Adj., adv.* rent-free

Miet·kauf *der* (Wirtsch.) ≈ hire purchase (Brit.) *or* (Amer.) installment plan (*with option to buy outright or terminate the agreement at a specified date*)

Mietling /ˈmiːtlɪŋ/ *der;* **~s, ~e** (veralt. abwertend) hireling

Miet-: ~partei *die* tenant; **~preis** *der* rent; (für ein Auto, Boot) hire charge; (für Fernsehgeräte usw.) rental; **~recht** *das* law of landlord and tenant

Miets-: ~haus *das* block of rented flats (esp. Brit.) *or* (esp. Amer.) apartments; **~kaserne** *die* (abwertend) tenement block

Miet-: ~verhältnis *das* (Amtsspr.) tenancy; **~vertrag** *der* tenancy agreement; **~wagen** *der* hire car; **~wohnung** *die* rented flat (esp. Brit.) *or* (esp. Amer.) apartment; **~wucher** *der* charging of exorbitant rents; **~zahlung** *die:* **mit seiner ~zahlung im Rückstand sein** be behind with the rent; **~zins** *der; Pl.* **~e** (südd., österr., schweiz., Amtsspr.) rent; **~zuschuss**, ***~zuschuß** *der* assistance with the rent

Mieze /ˈmiːtsə/ *die;* **~, ~n** ① (fam.: Katze) puss; pussy (child lang.) ② (salopp: Mädchen) chick (sl.); (als Anrede) sweetie

Mieze·katze *die* (fam.) puss; pussy cat (child lang.)

Migräne /miˈɡrɛːnə/ *die;* **~, ~n** ▸❶ **S. 439** migraine

Migräne·anfall *der* attack of migraine

Migrant *der;* **~en, ~en**, **Migrantin** *die;* **~, ~nen** migrant

Mikado /miˈkaːdo/ *das;* **~s** spillikins *sing.;* jackstraws *sing.*

mikro-, Mikro- micro-

Mikro /ˈmiːkro/ *das;* **~s, ~s** (ugs.) mike (coll.)

Mikrobe /miˈkroːbə/ *die;* **~, ~n** microbe

Mikro-: ~elektronik *die* microelectronics *sing., no art.;* **~faser** *die* (Textilw.) microfibre; **~fiche** /-fiːʃ/ *das od. der;* **~~s, ~~s** (Informationst.) microfiche; **~film** *der* (Informationst.) microfilm; **~fon** /--ˈ-/ *das;* **~~s, ~~e** microphone; **~klima** *das* microclimate; **~kosmos** *der* (Philos.) microcosm; **~meter** *der od. das* micron

Mikronesien /mikroˈneːzi̯ən/ *(das);* **~s** Micronesia

mikro-, Mikro-: ~organismus *der* (Biol.) micro-organism; **~phon ▸ ~fon**; **~prozessor** /-proˈtsɛsɔr/ *der* microprocessor; **~skop** /-ˈskoːp/ *das;* **~~s, ~~e** microscope; **~skopie** /-skoˈpiː/ *die;* **~~:** microscopy *no art.;* **~skopisch** A *Adj.* microscopic; B *adv.* microscopically; **etw. ~skopisch untersuchen** examine sth. under the microscope; **~welle** *die* (ugs.) microwave [oven]; **~wellen** *Pl.* microwaves; **~wellen·herd** *der* microwave oven

Milan /ˈmiːlan/ *der;* **~s, ~e** (Zool.) kite

Milbe /ˈmɪlbə/ *die;* **~, ~n** mite; (Zecke) tick

Milch /mɪlç/ *die;* **~** ① milk; **~ geben** give *or* yield milk; **aussehen wie ~ und Blut** have a lilies-and-roses complexion; **das Land, wo ~ und Honig fließt** (bibl.) the land flowing with milk and honey ② (Fischsamen) milt; soft roe

milch-, Milch-: ~bar *die* milk bar; **~bart** *der* (abwertend) callow youth; **~bärtig** *Adj.* (abwertend) callow; **~becher** *der* milk mug; **~brötchen** *das* milk roll; **~drüse** *die* ▸❶ **S. 435** mammary gland; **~eiweiß** *das* (Biol.) milk protein; **~flasche** *die* ① (für Säuglinge) feeding bottle; baby's bottle; ② (Flasche für ~) milk bottle; **~frau** *die* (ugs.) dairywoman; **~gebiss**, ***~gebiß** *das* ▸❶ **S. 435** milk teeth *pl.;* **~geschäft** *das* dairy; **~gesicht** *das* (abwertend) callow youth; **~glas** *das* ① milk glass; (aufgeraut) frosted glass; ② (Trinkglas) milk glass

milchig

A *Adj.* milky

B *adv.* **~ weiß** milky-white; **die ~trübe Färbung des Wassers** the milky cloudiness of the water

Milch-: ~kaffee *der* coffee with plenty of milk; **~kännchen** *das* milk jug; **~kanne** *die* milk can; (zum Transportieren von Milch) [milk] churn; **~kuh** *die* dairy *or* milk *or* milch cow; **~mädchen** *das* dairymaid; **~mädchen·rechnung** *die* (ugs.) naïve miscalculation; **~mann** *der* ▸❶ **S. 113** (ugs.) milkman; **~mix·getränk** *das* milk shake

Milchner /ˈmɪlçnɐ/ *der;* **~s, ~** (Zool.) milter

Milch-: ~pumpe *die* breast pump; **~reis** *der* rice pudding; **~säure** *die* (Chemie) lactic acid; **~schokolade** *die* milk chocolate; **~schorf** *der* ▸❶ **S. 439** milk crust; crusta lactea (Med.); **~straße** *die* Milky Way; Galaxy; (System) Galaxy; **~straßen·system** *das* (Astron.) galaxy; **~suppe** *die* milk soup; **~vieh** *das* dairy cattle; **~wirt·schaft** *die* dairying *no art.;* **~zahn** *der* milk tooth; **~zucker** *der* (Chemie) lactose

mild /mɪlt/, **milde**

A *Adj.* ① (gütig) lenient ‹*judge, judgement*›; benevolent ‹*ruler*›; mild, lenient, light ‹*punishment*›; mild ‹*words, accusation*›; mild, gentle ‹*reproach*›; gentle ‹*smile, voice*›; **jmdn. ~[e] stimmen** induce sb. to take a lenient attitude ② (nicht rau) mild ‹*climate, air, winter, etc.*› ③ (gedämpft) soft ‹*light, glow*› ④ (nicht scharf) mild ‹*spice, coffee, tobacco, cheese, etc.*›; smooth ‹*brandy*›; **~ schmecken** be mild/smooth ⑤ (schonend) mild ‹*soap, shampoo, detergent*› ⑥ (veralt.: mildtätig) charitable; **eine ~e Gabe** alms *pl*

B *adv.* ① (gütig) leniently; ‹*smile, say*› gently ② (nicht rau) **der Wind wehte/die Sonne schien ~:** the wind blew gently/a gentle sun shone down ③ (sanft) **~ schimmern/leuchten** shimmer softly/shine gently ④ (gelinde) mildly; **~e ausgedrückt** to put it mildly; putting it mildly

Milde *die;* **~** ① (Gnade, Güte) leniency; **[jmdm. gegenüber] ~ walten lassen** be lenient [with sb.]; **väterliche/christliche ~:** fatherly/Christian kindness ② (des Klimas usw.) mildness ③ (milder Geschmack) (von Tabak, Gewürzen usw.) mildness; (von Weinbrand) smoothness ④ (Gedämpftheit) softness ⑤ (veralt.: Wohltätigkeit) charity

mildern

A *tr. V.* ① (herabmindern) moderate ‹*criticism, judgement*›; mitigate ‹*punishment*›; **~de Umstände** mitigating circumstances ② (dämpfen) moderate ‹*language*›; soothe ‹*anger*›; lessen ‹*agitation*› ③ (abschwächen) reduce ‹*intensity, strength, effect*›; modify ‹*impression*›; ease, soothe, relieve ‹*pain*›; alleviate ‹*poverty, need*›; ease ‹*sorrow*›

B *refl. V.* ① (geringer werden) ‹*anger, rage, agitation*› abate ② (abschwächen) ‹*effect*› be reduced; ‹*impression*› be modified ③ (wärmer werden) ‹*weather*› become milder

Milderung *die;* **~** ① (eines Tadels, Urteils) moderation; (einer Strafe) mitigation ② (Linderung) (von Schmerz) easing; soothing; relief; (von Armut, Not) alleviation

Milderungs·grund *der* mitigating circumstance

mild·tätig

A *Adj.* charitable; **für ~tätige Zwecke sammeln** collect for charity

B *adv.* **~ wirken** perform charitable acts

Mild·tätigkeit *die* charity

Milieu /miˈli̯øː/ *das;* **~s, ~s** ① (soziales Umfeld) milieu; environment; (fig.: Prostitution usw.) world of pimps and prostitutes; **das ~ der Berliner Kneipen** the world of Berlin pubs (Brit.) *or* (Amer.) bars; **er stammt aus kleinbürgerlichem ~:** his background is petit bourgeois ② (Biol.: Lebensraum) environment

milieu-, Milieu-: ~geschädigt *Adj.* (Psych.) maladjusted (*as a result of adverse environmental influences*); **~schilderung** *die* description of the physical and social environment; **~studie** *die* study of an environment; **~theorie** *die* (Psych.) environmentalism *no art.*

militant /miliˈtant/ *Adj.* militant

Militanz *die;* **~:** militancy

Militär[1] /miliˈtɛːɐ̯/ *das;* **~s** ① armed forces *pl.;* military; **beim ~ sein/vom ~ entlassen werden** be in/be discharged from the forces; **zum ~ müssen** have to join the forces; **zum ~ einberufen werden** be called up ② (Soldaten) soldiers *pl.;* army; **~ gegen jmdn. einsetzen** use the army against sb.

Militär[2] *der;* **~s, ~s** [high-ranking military] officer

Militär-: ~akademie *die* military academy; **~aktion** *die* military action; (einzelner Schlag) military strike; **~arzt** *der* medical officer; **~attaché** *der* military attaché; **~basis** *die* military base; **~block** *der; Pl.* **~blöcke** military [alliance-]bloc; **~dienst** *der* military service; **seinen ~dienst ableisten** do one's military *or* national service; **~diktatur** *die* military dictatorship; **~fahrzeug** *das* military vehicle; **~flugplatz** *der* military airfield; **~flugzeug** *das* military aircraft; **~geistliche** *der* army chaplain; **~gericht** *das* military court; court martial; **vor ein ~gericht gestellt werden** be brought before *or* tried by a military court; be court-martialled; **~gerichtsbarkeit** *die* military jurisdiction *no art.;* **~hilfe** *die* military aid *no art.;* **~hubschrauber** *der* military helicopter

Militaria /miliˈtaːri̯a/ *Pl.* military objects; militaria

militärisch

A *Adj.* military; **jmdm. ~e Ehren erweisen** award *or* give sb. military honours; **mit allen ~en Ehren** with full military honours

B *adv.* **gegen jmdn. ~ vorgehen** take military action against sb.; **jmdn. ~ grüßen** salute sb.; **~ strammstehen** stand to attention

militarisieren /militariˈziːrən/ *tr. V.* militarize

Militarisierung *die;* **~:** militarization

Militarismus *der;* **~** (abwertend) militarism

Militarist *der;* **~en, ~en**, **Militaristin** *die;* **~, ~nen** (abwertend) militarist

militaristisch *Adj.* (abwertend) militarist; militaristic

Militär-: ~junta *die* military junta; **~kapelle** *die* (Musik) military band; **~marsch** *der* military march; **~musik** *die* military music; **~parade** *die* military parade; **~polizei** *die* military police; **~putsch** *der* military putsch; **~regierung** *die* military government; **~schlag** *der* military strike; **~seelsorge** *die* pastoral care of military personnel; **in der ~seelsorge tätig sein** look after the spiritual welfare of military personnel; **~streife** *die* military patrol; **~stützpunkt** *der* military base; **~wesen** *das* military affairs *pl., no art.;* **~wissenschaft** *die* military science

Military /ˈmɪlɪtərɪ/ *die;* **~, ~s** (Reiten) three-day event

Militär·zeit *die* time in the forces *or* services

Miliz /miˈliːts/ *die;* ~, ~**en** militia; (Polizei) police

Milizionär /militsi̯oˈnɛːɐ̯/ *der;* ~**s,** ~**e** 1 militiaman 2 (Polizist) policeman

milk /mɪlk/, **milkst, milkt** (veralt.) *Imperativ Sg., 2. u. 3. Pers. Sg. Präsens v.* **melken**

Mill. *Abk.* = **Million** m.

Mille /ˈmɪlə/ *die;* ~, ~ (salopp) grand (coll.); thousand marks/pounds *etc.;* **zwei** ~: two grand (coll.)

Millennium /mɪˈlɛni̯ʊm/ *das;* ~**s, Millennien** millennium

milli- /ˈmɪli-/, **Milli-** milli-

Milliardär /mɪli̯arˈdɛːɐ̯/ *der;* ~**s,** ~**e, Milliardärin** *die;* ~, ~**nen** multi-millionaire (possessing at least a thousand million marks etc.); billionaire; *s. auch* **Millionär**

Milliarde /mɪˈli̯ardə/ *die;* ~, ~**n** ▸ⓘ **S. 826** thousand million; billion; **mehrere** ~**n Euro/Einwohner** several thousand million *or* several billion euros/inhabitants; *s. auch* **Million**

Milliarden-: ~**höhe** *die: in* **in** ~**höhe** of the order of a thousand million *or* a billion; ~**kredit** *der* credit of the order of a thousand million *or* a billion; *s. auch* **millionen-, Millionen-**

milliardst... *Ordinalz.* ▸ⓘ **S. 826** thousand millionth; billionth; *s. auch* **hundertst...**

milliardstel *Bruchz.* thousand millionth; billionth; *s. auch* **hundertstel**

Milliardstel *das, schweiz. der;* ~**s,** ~: part in a billion *or* thousand million; *s. auch* **Hundertstel**

Milli-: ~**bar** *das* (Met.) millibar; ~**gramm** *das* ▸ⓘ **S. 315** milligram; ~**liter** *der od. das* ▸ⓘ **S. 582** millilitre

Milli·meter *der od. das* ▸ⓘ **S. 454** millimetre

millimeter-, Millimeter-: ~**arbeit** *die* (ugs.) (am Steuer) delicate piece of manoeuvring; (bei Ballspielen) [neat] piece of precision play; ~**genau** **A** *Adj.* accurate to the last millimetre *postpos.;* (fig.) minutely accurate ‹*analysis*›; perfect ‹*precision*›; **B** *adv.* to the last millimetre; (fig.) with complete accuracy; ~**genau treffen** hit home with deadly accuracy; ~**papier** *das* [graph] paper ruled in millimetre squares

Million /mɪˈli̯oːn/ *die;* ~, ~**en** ▸ⓘ **S. 826** 1 million; **eine** ~ **Menschen war** *od.* **waren ...** a million people were ...; **zwei** ~**en [Einwohner]** two million [inhabitants] 2 *Pl.* (unbestimmte Anzahl od. Summe) millions; ~**en von Menschen** millions of people; **in die** ~**en gehen** run into millions

Millionär /mɪli̯oˈnɛːɐ̯/ *der;* ~**s,** ~**e, Millionärin** *die;* ~, ~**nen** millionaire

millionen-, Millionen-: ~**auf·lage** *die* (Buchw.) **dieses Buch erschien in** ~**auflage** *od.* **erlebte eine** ~**auflage** [over] a million copies of this book were printed; ~**auftrag** *der* contract worth a million/worth millions; ~**fach** **A** *Adj.* millionfold ‹*increase etc.*›; **in** ~**fachen Tests** in a million tests; ~**fache Zustimmung finden** meet with the approval of millions of people; **es kam zu** ~**fachen Protesten** there were millions of protests; **B** *adv.* a million times; ~**geschäft** *das* deal worth a million/worth millions; ~**gewinn** *der* 1 (Ertrag) profit of a million/of millions; ~**gewinne** profits running into millions; 2 (Lotteriegewinn) prize of a million/of millions; ~**heer** *das* millions *pl.;* ~**höhe** *die: in* **in** ~**höhe** of the order of a million; ~**kredit** *der* credit of the order of a million; *~**mal** ▸**Mal**[1]; ~**schaden** *der* damage *no pl., no indef. art.* running into millions; ~**schwer** *Adj.* (ugs.) worth millions *pred.;* ~**stadt** *die* town with over a million inhabitants; ~**vermögen** *das* fortune of millions

millionst... *Ordinalz.* ▸ⓘ **S. 826** millionth; *s. auch* **hundertst...**

million[s]tel *Bruchz.* ▸ⓘ **S. 826** millionth; *s. auch* **hundertstel**

Million[s]tel *das od.* (schweiz.) *der;* ~**s,** ~ ▸ⓘ **S. 826** millionth; (Teilmenge) part in a million; ppm

Milz /mɪlts/ *die;* ~ ▸ⓘ **S. 435** (Anat.) spleen

Milz·brand *der* ▸ⓘ **S. 439** (Tiermed.) anthrax

Milzbrand·erreger *der* (Med.) anthrax pathogen

Mime /ˈmiːmə/ *der;* ~**n,** ~**n** (geh.) Thespian

mimen

A *tr. V.* 1 (ugs. abwertend) put on a show of ‹*admiration, efficiency*›; **Trauer/Besorgnis** ~: act sad/concerned (coll.); **den Kranken/Unschuldigen** ~: pretend to be ill/act the innocent; **den starken Mann** ~: act tough 2 (darstellen) play; act; **den Tell** ~: play Tell

B *itr. V.* (ugs. abwertend) **auf Millionär/krank** *usw.* ~: pretend to be a millionaire/to be ill *etc.*

Mimesis /ˈmiːmezɪs/ *die;* ~, **Mimesen** (Liter., Philos.) mimesis; imitation

Mimik /ˈmiːmɪk/ *die;* ~: gestures and facial expressions *pl.*

Mimikry /ˈmɪmikri/ *die;* ~ (Zool.) mimicry; (fig.) camouflage

Mimin *die;* ~, ~**nen** ▸**Mime**

mimisch

A *Adj.* mimic; **seine** ~**e Ausdruckskraft** the expressive power of his gestures and facial movements; **eine** ~**e Begabung** a gift for mimic expression

B *adv.* ‹*show*› by means of gestures and facial expressions; ~ **begabt sein** have a gift for mimic expression

Mimose /miˈmoːzə/ *die;* ~, ~**n** 1 mimosa; (volkst.: Akazie) silver wattle 2 (empfindsamer Mensch) oversensitive person; **die reinste** ~ **sein** be extraordinarily sensitive

mimosenhaft

A *Adj.* oversensitive

B *adv.* oversensitively

Min. *Abk.* = **Minute[n]** min.

Minarett /minaˈrɛt/ *das;* ~**s,** ~**e** *od.* ~**s** minaret

mind. *Abk.* = **mindestens**

minder /ˈmɪndɐ/ *Adv.* (geh.) less; **[nicht]** ~ **angenehm sein** be [no] less pleasant; *s. auch* **mehr**

minder... *Adj.* inferior ‹*goods, brand*›; **von** ~**er Bedeutung/Qualität sein** be of less importance/inferior *or* lower quality

minder-, Minder-: ~**begabt** *Adj.* less gifted *or* able; ~**begütert** *Adj.* less well-off; ~**bemittelt** *Adj.* without much money *postpos., not pred.;* ~**bemittelt sein** not have much money; **er ist doch geistig** ~**bemittelt** (fig. salopp abwertend) he isn't all that bright (coll.); ~**bemittelte** *der/die; adj. Dekl.* needy person; ~**einnahme** *die* decrease in revenue; (geringere Einnahme, als kalkuliert) shortfall in revenue

Minderheit *die;* ~, ~**en** minority

Minderheiten·recht *das* right of a/the minority

Minderheits·regierung *die* minority government

minder-, Minder-: ~**jährig** *Adj.* (Rechtsw.) ‹*child etc.*› who is/was a minor *or* under age; ~**jährig sein** be a minor *or* under age; ~**jährige** *der/die; adj. Dekl.* (Rechtsw.) minor; person under age; ~**jährigkeit** *die;* ~~ (Rechtsw.) minority; **bis zum Ende der** ~**jährigkeit** until he/she comes/came of age

mindern (geh.)

A *tr. V.* reduce ‹*income, price, number of staff, tension, etc.*›; impair ‹*performance, abilities*›; diminish, reduce ‹*value, quality, dignity, pleasure, influence*›; detract from ‹*reputation*›

B *refl. V.* diminish; ‹*vehemence*› lessen

Minderung *die;* ~, ~**en** ▸**mindern A**: reduction (*Gen.* in); impairment (*Gen.* of); diminution (*Gen.* of); detraction (*Gen.* from)

minder·wertig *Adj.* (abwertend) inferior, low-quality ‹*goods, material*›; low-quality, low-grade ‹*meat*›; (fig.) inferior; **ein moralisch** ~**wertiger Mensch** (abwertend) a person of questionable character

Minder·wertigkeit *die* ▸**minderwertig**: inferiority; low quality; low grade; (fig.) inferiority

Minderwertigkeits-: ~**gefühl** *das* (Psych.) feeling of inferiority; ~**komplex** *der* (Psych.) inferiority complex

Minder·zahl *die* minority

mindest... /ˈmɪndəst.../ *Adj.* slightest; least; **ohne die** ~**e Angst** without the slightest *or* least trace of fear; **ich habe nicht die** ~**e Ahnung** I haven't the slightest idea; **das ist das Mindeste, was du tun kannst** it is the least you can do; **sie versteht nicht das Mindeste vom Kochen** she doesn't know the slightest *or* first thing about cooking; **nicht im Mindesten** *od.* ~**en** not in the least; **zum Mindesten** *od.* ~**en** at least

Mindest-: ~**alter** *das* minimum age; ~**anforderung** *die* minimum requirement; ~**betrag** *der* minimum amount

mindestens /ˈmɪndəstn̩s/ *Adv.* at least

Mindest-: ~**gebot** *das* reserve price; ~**geschwindigkeit** *die* minimum speed; ~**größe** *die* minimum size; ~**haltbarkeits·datum** *das* best-before date; ~**lohn** *der* minimum wage; ~**maß** *das* minimum (**an** + *Dat.*, **von** of); ~**preis** *der* minimum [legal] price; ~**strafe** *die* (Rechtsw.) minimum penalty; ~**urlaub** *der* minimum holiday entitlement; ~**zahl** *die* minimum

Mine /ˈmiːnə/ *die;* ~, ~**n** 1 (Erzbergwerk) mine 2 (Sprengkörper) mine; **auf eine** ~ **laufen** strike a mine 3 (Bleistift~) lead; (Kugelschreiber~, Filzschreibe~) refill

Minen-: ~**feld** *das* minefield; ~**leger** *der;* ~~**s,** ~~ (Milit.) minelayer; ~**such·boot** *das* (Milit.) minesweeper; ~**such·gerät** *das* (Milit.) mine-detector; ~**werfer** *der* (Milit. Hist.) trench mortar

Mineral /mineˈraːl/ *das;* ~**s,** ~**e** *od.* **Mineralien** mineral

Mineral-: ~**bad** *das* spa; ~**brunnen** *der* ▸~**quelle**; ~**dünger** *der* inorganic fertilizer

Mineraloge /mineraˈloːgə/ *der;* ~**n,** ~**n** mineralogist

Mineralogie *die;* ~: mineralogy *no art.*

Mineralogin *die;* ~, ~**nen** ▸**Mineraloge**

mineralogisch *Adj.* mineralogical

Mineral·öl *das* mineral oil

Mineralöl-: ~**gesellschaft** *die* oil company; ~**industrie** *die* oil industry; ~**steuer** *die* tax on oil

Mineral-: ~**quelle** *die* mineral spring; ~**salz** *das,* ~**stoff** *der* mineral salt; ~**wasser** *das; Pl.* ~**wässer** mineral water

mini-, Mini- mini-

Mini *das;* ~**s,** ~**s** (Mode) mini (coll.); **im** ~: in a mini (coll.); **diese Kleider sind alle in** ~: all these dresses are mini-length *or* (coll.) minis *pl.;* ~ **tragen** wear a mini (coll.)

Miniatur /mini̯aˈtuːɐ̯/ *die;* ~, ~**en** miniature

Miniatur-: ~**ausgabe** *die* (Buchw.) abridged edition; ~**maler** *der* miniaturist; ~**malerei** *die* miniature painting; ~**malerin** *die* ▸~**maler**

Mini: ~**golf** *das* minigolf; crazy golf; ~**job** *der* short-term job (*esp. for unemployed people*)

minimal /miniˈmaːl/

A *Adj.* minimal; marginal ‹*advantage, lead*›; very slight ‹*benefit, profit*›

B *adv.* minimally; **sie unterscheiden sich nur** ~: the differences between them are minimal

Minimal-: ~**forderung** *die* minimum demand; ~**gewicht** *das* minimum weight; ~**wert** *der* minimum value

Minimalismus /minimaˈlɪsmʊs/ *der;* ~: minimalism

Minimalist /minimaˈlɪst/ *der;* ~**en,** ~**en, Minimalistin** *die;* ~, ~**nen** minimalist

minimalistisch

A *Adj.* minimalist

B *adv.* minimalistically

minimieren *tr. V.* (bes. Math.) minimize

Minimierung *die;* ~, ~**en** (bes. Math.) minimization

Minimum /ˈmiːnimʊm/ *das;* ~**s, Minima** minimum (**an** + *Dat.* of); **ein** ~ **an Vertrauen** a certain minimum degree of trust; **etw. unter dem ~ verkaufen** sell sth. below the minimum [legal] price

Mini-: ~rock *der* miniskirt; **~spion** *der* miniaturized listening *or* (coll.) bugging device

Minister /mi'nɪstɐ/ *der;* **~s,** ~ ▸ⓘ **S. 44,** ▸ⓘ **S. 113** minister (**für** for); (eines britischen Hauptministeriums) Secretary of State (**für** for); (eines amerikanischen Hauptministeriums) Secretary (**für** of)

Minister-: ~amt *das* ministerial office; **~ebene** *die: in* **auf ~ebene** at ministerial level

Ministerial-: ~beamte *der,* **~beamtin** *die* ministry official; **~direktor** *der,* **~direktorin** *die* head of a ministry department; **~dirigent** *der,* **~dirigentin** *die* head of a section within a ministry department

Ministeriale /minɪste'ri̯a:lə/ *der/die; adj. Dekl.* ▸**Ministerialbeamte**

Ministerial·rat *der,* **Ministerial·rätin** *die* ▸**Ministerialdirigent**

ministeriell /minɪste'ri̯ɛl/

A *Adj.* ministerial

B *adv.* by the minister

Ministerin *die;* **~, ~nen** ▸ⓘ **S. 44,** ▸ⓘ **S. 113** ▸**Minister**

Ministerium /minɪs'te:ri̯ʊm/ *das;* **~s, Ministerien** Ministry; Department (Amer.)

Minister-: ~präsident *der,* **~präsidentin** *die* **1** (eines deutschen Bundeslandes) minister-president; prime minister (Brit.); governor (Amer.); **2** (Premierminister[in]) Prime Minister; **~rat** *der* (EU) Council of Ministers; **~sessel** *der* (ugs.) ministerial post

ministrabel /minɪs'tra:bl̩/ *Adj.* capable of holding ministerial office *pred.*

Ministrant /minɪs'trant/ *der;* **~en, ~en, Ministrantin** *die* (kath. Kirche) server

ministrieren *itr. V.* (kath. Kirche) serve [at the altar]; act as server

Mini·van *der* compact MPV

Minna /'mɪna/ *die;* **~, ~s** (ugs. veralt.) maid; **jmdn. zur ~ machen** (ugs.) tear sb. off a strip (Brit. coll.); bawl out (coll.); **eine grüne ~** (ugs.) a Black Maria; a patrol wagon (Amer.)

Minne /'mɪnə/ *die;* ~ (MA.) courtly love

Minne-: ~dienst *der* (MA.) knight's homage to his lady; **~sang** *der* (Literaturw.) Minnesong; **~sänger** *der,* **~singer** *der;* **~~s, ~~** (MA.) Minnesinger

Minorität /minori'tɛ:t/ *die;* **~, ~en** ▸**Minderheit**

Minuend /mi'nu̯ɛnt/ *der;* **~en, ~en** (Math.) minuend

minus /'mi:nʊs/

A *Konj.* ▸ⓘ **S. 826** (Math.) minus

B *Adv.* **1** ▸ⓘ **S. 703** (bes. Math.) minus; **~ fünf Grad, fünf Grad ~:** minus five degrees; five degrees below [zero] **2** (Elektrot.) negative

C *Präp. mit Gen.* (Kaufmannsspr.) less; minus

Minus *das;* ~ **1** (Fehlbetrag) deficit; (auf einem Konto) overdraft; **~ machen** make a loss; **im ~ sein** be in debit; be in the red **2** (Nachteil) minus; drawback; (im Beruf) disadvantage

Minus·betrag *der* deficit

Minuskel /mi'nʊskl̩/ *die;* **~, ~n** (Druckw.) minuscule

Minus-: ~pol *der* (Physik) negative pole; (einer Batterie) negative terminal; **~punkt** *der* **1** minus *or* penalty point; **2** (Nachteil) disadvantage; **~zeichen** *das* minus sign

Minute /mi'nu:tə/ *die;* **~, ~n** **1** ▸ⓘ **S. 224,** ▸ⓘ **S. 729** minute; **6 ~n nach/vor zwei** six minutes to/past two; **es ist neun Uhr [und] sieben ~n** it is seven minutes past nine *or* nine seven; **~ um ~ verging** *od.* **verstrich** minutes went by *or* passed **2** (Moment) minute; moment; **hast du ein paar ~n Zeit für mich?** can you spare me a few minutes *or* moments?; **in letzter ~:** at the last minute *or* moment; **auf die ~ pünktlich sein** *od.* **kommen** be punctual to the minute

minuten·lang

A *Adj.* ‹*applause, silence, etc.*› lasting [for] several minutes; **sein ~es Schweigen** his silence, which lasted for several minutes

B *adv.* for several minutes

Minuten·zeiger *der* minute hand

-minütig *Adj.* **ein fünf~er Heulton** a wail lasting five minutes; **eine fünfzehn~e Verspätung** a fifteen-minute delay; a delay of fifteen minutes

minütlich /mi'ny:tlɪç/

A *Adj.* **in ~en Abständen** at intervals of a minute

B *adv.* every minute

minuziös /minu'tsi̯ø:s/ (geh.)

A *Adj.* minutely *or* meticulously precise *or* detailed ‹*account, description*›; minute ‹*detail*›; ‹*manoeuvre*› requiring minute precision

B *adv.* meticulously

Minze /'mɪnt͜sə/ *die;* **~, ~n** mint

Mio. *Abk.* **= Million[en]** m.

mir /mi:ɐ̯/

A *Dat. Sg. des Personalpron.* **ich** **1** to me; (nach Präpositionen) me; **gib es ~:** give it to me; give me it; **gib ~ das Buch** give me the book; **Freunde von ~:** friends of mine; **gehen wir zu ~:** let's got to my place; **~ nichts, dir nichts** (ugs.) just like that; without so much as a 'by your leave'; **von ~ aus** as far as I'm concerned; **Kann ich das Radio abstellen? — Von ~ aus** Can I turn the radio off? — As far as I'm concerned you can **2** (Dativus ethicus) **geht ~ nicht an meinen Schreibtisch!** keep away from my desk!; **und grüß ~ alle Verwandten!** and give my regards to all the relatives; **du bist ~ vielleicht einer!** (ugs.) a fine one you are!; **wie du ~, so ich dir** tit for tat; (drohend) I'll get my own back

B *Dat. des Reflexivpron. der 1. Pers. Sg.* myself; **ich habe ~ deine Vorschläge genau überlegt** I have given careful thought to your suggestions; **ich habe ~ gedacht, dass ...** I thought that ...; **ich will ~ ein neues Kleid kaufen** I want to buy myself a new dress; **ich nehme ~ noch von dem Braten** I'll help myself to some more roast

Mirabelle /mira'bɛlə/ *die;* **~, ~n** mirabelle

Mirakel /mi'ra:kl̩/ *das;* **~s, ~** (geh. veralt.) miracle

Misanthrop /mizan'tro:p/ *der;* **~en, ~en, Misanthropin** *die;* **~, ~nen** (geh.) misanthrope

Misch-: ~batterie *die* mixer tap; mixing faucet (Amer.); **~blut** *das* (geh.) ▸**Mischling 1**; **~brot** *das* bread made from wheat and rye flour; **~ehe** *die* mixed marriage

mischen /'mɪʃn̩/

A *tr. V.* mix; **etw. in etw.** (*Akk.*) **~:** put sth. into sth.; **Wasser und Wein ~:** mix water with wine; **[sich** (*Dat.*)**] Tees/Tabake ~:** blend [one's own] teas/tobaccos; **die Karten ~:** shuffle the cards

B *refl. V.* **1** (sich ver~) mix (**mit** with); ‹*smell, scent*› blend (**mit** with); **in meine Freude mischte sich Angst** my joy was mingled with fear **2** (sich ein~) **sich in etw.** (*Akk.*) **~:** interfere *or* meddle in sth.; **sich in das Gespräch ~:** butt into the conversation **3** (sich begeben) **sich unters Publikum** *usw.* **~:** mingle with the audience *etc.*

C *itr. V.* **1** (Kartenspiel) shuffle; **wer muss ~?** whose shuffle is it? **2** (Film, Rundf., Ferns.) mix; *s. auch* **gemischt**

Mischer *der;* **~s, ~** (Bauw.) [cement] mixer

Misch-: ~farbe *die* non-primary colour; **~form** *die* mixture; (Kunstform) fusion; **~futter** *das* mixed feed; **~gewebe** *das* mixture; **~kultur** *die* **1** (Landw.) mixed cultivation; **2** (Soziol.) mixed culture

Mischling /'mɪʃlɪŋ/ *der;* **~s, ~e** **1** half-caste; half-breed **2** (Biol.) hybrid

Mischmasch /'mɪʃmaʃ/ *der;* **~[e]s, ~e** (ugs., meist abwertend) hotchpotch; mishmash; (Essen) concoction

Misch·maschine *die* (Bauw.) cement mixer

Mischpoke /mɪʃ'po:kə/ *die;* ~ (salopp abwertend) **1** (Verwandtschaft) tribe (derog.) **2** (Gesellschaft) mob (coll.); shower (Brit. coll.)

Misch-: ~pult *das* (Film, Rundf., Ferns.) mixing desk *or* console; **~sprache** *die* hybrid language; **~trommel** *die* mixing drum

Mischung *die;* **~, ~en** **1** (Gemisch, auch fig.) mixture; (Tee~, Kaffee~, Tabak~) blend; (Pralinen~) assortment **2** (das Mischen) mixing; (von Tee, Kaffee, Tabak) blending

Mischungs·verhältnis *das* proportion in the mixture

Misch·wald *der* mixed [deciduous and coniferous] forest

miserabel /mizə'ra:bl̩/ (ugs.)

A *Adj.* **1** (schlecht) dreadful (coll.), atrocious ‹*film, wine, food*›; pathetic, miserable ‹*achievement*›; miserable, dreadful (coll.), atrocious ‹*weather*› **2** (elend) miserable; wretched; **mir ist ~ zumute, ich fühle mich ~:** I feel dreadful **3** (niederträchtig) abominable ‹*behaviour*›

B *adv.* **1** (schlecht) dreadfully (coll.); atrociously; ‹*sleep*› dreadfully badly (coll.); **~ bezahlt werden** be very badly *or* poorly paid **2** (elend) **ihm geht es gesundheitlich ~:** he's in a bad way **3** (niederträchtig) **sich ~ benehmen** *od.* **verhalten** behave abominably

Misere /mi'ze:rə/ *die;* **~, ~n** (geh.) wretched *or* dreadful state; (Elend) misery; (Not) distress; **seine finanzielle ~:** his wretched *or* dreadful financial state

Miserere /mize're:rə/ *das;* **~s** (bibl.) miserere

Mispel /'mɪspl̩/ *die;* **~, ~n** medlar

miss, *miß /mɪs/ *Imperativ Sg. v.* **messen**

Miss, *Miß /mɪs/ *die;* **~, ~es** /'mɪsɪz/ Miss

miss·achten, *miß·achten *tr. V.* **1** (ignorieren) disregard; ignore **2** (gering schätzen) disdain; be contemptuous of; **sich missachtet fühlen** feel scorned

Miss·achtung, *Miß·achtung *die* **1** (Nichtbeachtung) disregard (+ *Gen.* of, for); **die ~ der Vorschriften/meines Rates** disregarding *or* ignoring the regulations/my advice **2** (Verachtung) disdain, contempt (+ *Gen.* for)

Miss·behagen, *Miß·behagen *das* [feeling of] unease; uncomfortable feeling; **bei dem Gedanken daran befiel sie ein tiefes ~:** she did not at all like the thought of it

Miss·bildung, *Miß·bildung *die* deformity

miss·billigen, *miß·billigen *tr. V.* disapprove of

Miss·billigung, *Miß·billigung *die* disapproval

Miss·brauch, *Miß·brauch *der* **1** (das ~en) abuse; misuse; (falsche Anwendung) misuse; (von Feuerlöscher, Notbremse) improper use; **mit seiner Stellung/Macht ~ treiben** abuse *or* misuse one's position/power; **unter ~ seines Amtes** by misusing his position **2** (übermäßiger Gebrauch) misuse **3** (geh.: Vergewaltigung) rape

miss·brauchen, *miß·brauchen *tr. V.* **1** abuse; misuse; abuse ‹*trust*›; **jmdn. für** *od.* **zu etw. ~:** use sb. for sth. **2** (übermäßig gebrauchen) misuse ‹*drugs, medicines*› **3** (geh.: vergewaltigen) rape

missbräuchlich, *mißbräuchlich /-brɔyçlɪç/

A *Adj.* **~e Verwendung/Anwendung** misuse

B *adv.* **etw. ~ verwenden/handhaben** misuse sth.

miss·deuten, *miß·deuten *tr. V.* misinterpret

Miss·deutung, *Miß·deutung *die* misinterpretation

missen *tr. V.* (geh.) **1** (entbehren) do *or* go without; do without ‹*person*›; **jmdn./etw. nicht ~ können/mögen** be unable to do without/not want to be without sb./sth. **2** (selten) ▸**vermissen A**

Miss·erfolg, *Miß·erfolg *der* failure

Miss·ernte, *Miß·ernte *die* crop failure

Misse·tat /'mɪsə-/ *die* (geh. veralt.) misdeed

Misse·täter *der,* **Misse·täterin** *die* (geh. veralt.) malefactor

miss·fallen, *miß·fallen *unr. itr. V.* **etw. missfällt jmdm.** sb. dislikes *or* does not like sth.; **es missfiel mir, wie unfreundlich sie ...** I

m

disliked *or* did not like the unkind way she ...

Missfallen, *Mißfallen *das;* **~s** displeasure (**über** + *Akk.* at); (Missbilligung) disapproval (**über** + *Akk.* of); **~ erregen** arouse displeasure/disapproval; **jmds. ~ erregen** incur sb.'s displeasure/disapproval

Missfallens·äußerung, *Mißfallens·äußerung *die* expression of displeasure/disapproval

miss·fällig, *miß·fällig (veralt.)
A *Adj.* disapproving
B *adv.* disapprovingly

miss·gebildet, *miß·gebildet *Adj.* deformed

Miss·geburt, *Miß·geburt *die* (Med.) monster; monstrosity; **diese ~ von [einem] Krämer!** (fig. abwertend) that misbegotten scoundrel of a shopkeeper

miss·gelaunt, *miß·gelaunt (geh.)
A *Adj.* ill-humoured
B *adv.* ill-humouredly

Miss·geschick, *Miß·geschick *das* (ärgerlicher Vorfall) mishap; (Pech) bad luck; (Unglück) misfortune; **jmdm. passiert** *od.* **widerfährt ein ~:** sb. has a mishap/a piece *or* stroke of bad luck/a misfortune; **vom ~ verfolgt sein** be dogged by bad luck/misfortune

Miss·gestalt, *Miß·gestalt *die* (geh.) misshapen figure

miss·gestaltet, *miß·gestaltet *Adj.* misshapen; deformed ‹*person, child*›

miss·gestimmt, *miß·gestimmt
A *Adj.* (geh.) ill-humoured; **~ sein** be in a bad mood
B *adv.* ill-humouredly

miss·glücken, *miß·glücken *itr. V.; mit sein* fail; be unsuccessful; **der Kuchen/Plan ist mir missglückt** the cake I made turned out a failure/my plan failed *or* was a failure; **ein missglückter Versuch** a failed *or* unsuccessful attempt

miss·gönnen, *miß·gönnen *tr. V.* **jmdm. etw. ~:** begrudge sb. sth.; **er missgönnte ihr, dass sie ...** he begrudged the fact that she ...

Miss·griff, *Miß·griff *der* error of judgement; **einen ~ tun** *od.* **machen** make an error of judgement

Miss·gunst, *Miß·gunst *die* [envy and] resentment (**gegenüber** of); (fig.: des Schicksals) malevolence

miss·günstig, *miß·günstig
A *Adj.* resentful; (fig.) malevolent ‹*fate*›
B *adv.* resentfully; (fig.) malevolently

miss·handeln, *miß·handeln *tr. V.* maltreat; ill-treat; **misshandelte Frauen/Kinder** battered wives/children

Miss·handlung, *Miß·handlung *die* maltreatment; ill-treatment; **~en** maltreatment *sing.*; ill-treatment *sing.*

Miss·helligkeiten, *Miß·helligkeiten *Pl.* (geh.) differences

missingsch /ˈmɪsɪŋʃ/ *Adv.* **~ sprechen** speak Missingsch

Missingsch *das;* **~:** Missingsch (Hamburg dialect made up of High German and some Low German elements)

Mission /mɪˈsi̯oːn/ *die;* **~, ~en** **1** (geh.: Auftrag) mission; **in geheimer ~:** on a secret mission **2** (geh.: Personengruppe) mission; (Delegation) delegation **3** (Rel.) mission; **in der [äußeren/inneren] ~ tätig sein** do missionary work [abroad/in one's own country] **4** (geh.: diplomatische Vertretung) mission

Missionar /mɪsi̯oˈnaːɐ̯/ *der;* **~s, ~e,** (österr.) **Missionär** /mɪsi̯oˈnɛːɐ̯/ *der;* **~s, ~e, Missionarin** *die;* **~, ~nen,** (österr.) **Missionärin** *die;* **~, ~nen** ▸ **S. 113** missionary

missionarisch
A *Adj.* missionary
B *adv.* **~ tätig sein** do missionary work

Missionar·stellung *die* (ugs.) missionary position

missionieren
A *itr. V.* do missionary work
B *tr. V.* convert by missionary work; (fig.) convert to one's own ideas

Missionierung *die;* **~: die ~ eines Landes/eines Volkes** missionary work in a country/among a people; (als Ergebnis) the conversion of a country/people [by missionary work]

Missions-: ~chef *der,* **~chefin** *die* (Politik) head of a/the mission; **~gesellschaft** *die* missionary society; **~station** *die* mission station; **~wissenschaft** *die* missiology *no art.*; study of the Christian mission

Miss·klang, *Miß·klang *der* discord; dissonance; (fig.) discord; **mit einem ~ enden** (fig.) end on a note of discord; **es gab einige Missklänge** (fig.) there was a certain amount of discord

Miss·kredit, *Miß·kredit *der: in* **jmdn./etw. in ~ bringen** bring sb./sth. into discredit; bring discredit on sb./sth.; **bei jmdm. in ~ geraten** get a bad name with sb.

misslang, *mißlang *1. u. 3. Pers. Sg. Prät. v.* **misslingen**

miss·launig, *miß·launig *Adj.* (geh.) ▸ **missgelaunt**

misslich, *mißlich *Adj.* (geh.) awkward, difficult ‹*situation*›; difficult ‹*conditions*›; unfortunate ‹*consequences, incident*›; **es steht ~ um die [Finanzkraft der] Firma** the firm is not doing very well [financially]

Misslichkeit, *Mißlichkeit *die;* **~, ~en** (geh.) (missliche Situation) awkward *or* difficult situation; (misslicher Vorfall) unfortunate incident

missliebig, *mißliebig /ˈmɪsliːbɪç/ *Adj.* unpopular; **~e Ausländer** unwanted foreigners; **sich ~ machen** make oneself persona non grata (**bei** with)

misslingen, *mißlingen /mɪsˈlɪŋən/ *unr. itr. V.; mit sein* fail; be unsuccessful; be a failure; **ein misslungener Kuchen** an unsuccessful attempt at a cake; **ein misslungener Versuch** a failed *or* unsuccessful attempt

Misslingen, *Mißlingen *das;* **~s** failure

misslungen, *mißlungen /mɪsˈlʊŋən/ *2. Part. v.* **misslingen**

Miss·mut, *Miß·mut *der* ill humour *no indef. art.*; **mit leichtem ~:** somewhat in a bad temper; **jmds. ~ (Akk.) erregen** put sb. in a bad mood

miss·mutig, *miß·mutig
A *Adj.* bad-tempered; sullen ‹*face*›; **warum bist du heute so ~?** why are you in such a bad mood today?
B *adv.* bad-temperedly

miss·raten, *miß·raten *unr. itr. V.; mit sein* ‹*cake, photo, etc.*› turn out badly; **gänzlich ~:** be a complete failure; **das Bild/der Kuchen ist ihr ~/nicht ~:** her picture/cake turned out badly/well; **ein ~es Kind** a child who has turned out badly

Miss·stand, *Miß·stand *der:* **die vorhandenen Missstände** the serious shortcomings that exist; **das ist ein ~:** it is deplorable; **Missstände in der Verwaltung** serious irregularities in the administration; **soziale Missstände** social evils; **einen ~ beseitigen** put an end to a deplorable state of affairs

Miss·stimmung, *Miß·stimmung *die* (gedrückte Stimmung) ill humour *no indef. art.*; (gereizte Stimmung) discord *no indef. art.*

misst, *mißt *2. u. 3. Pers. Sg. Präsens v.* **messen**

Miss·ton, *Miß·ton *der; Pl.* **Miss·töne** discordant note; (fig.) note of discord; discordant note; **mit einem ~ enden** (fig.) end on a note of discord

misstönend, *mißtönend, misstönig, *mißtönig
A *Adj.* discordant
B *adv.* discordantly

miss·trauen, *miß·trauen *itr. V.* **jmdm./einer Sache ~:** mistrust *or* distrust sb./sth.; **sich (Dat.) selbst ~:** have no confidence in oneself

Misstrauen, *Mißtrauen *das;* **~s** mistrust, distrust (**gegen** of); **voll[er] ~:** extremely mistrustful *or* distrustful (**gegen** of); **~ gegen jmdn./etw. haben, jmdm./einer Sache ~ entgegenbringen** mistrust *or* distrust sb./sth.

Misstrauens-, *Mißtrauens-: ~antrag *der* motion of no confidence; **~votum** *das* vote of no confidence (**gegen [über]** in)

misstrauisch, *mißtrauisch /ˈmɪstrau̯ɪʃ/
A *Adj.* mistrustful; distrustful; (argwöhnisch) suspicious
B *adv.* mistrustfully; distrustfully; (argwöhnisch) suspiciously

Miss·vergnügen, *Miß·vergnügen *das* (geh.) (Ärger) annoyance; (Unzufriedenheit) discontentment; **jmdm. ~ bereiten** make sb. annoyed/discontented

miss·vergnügt, *miß·vergnügt (geh.)
A *Adj.* (verärgert) annoyed; (unzufrieden) discontented; (verdrießlich) ill-humoured
B *adv. s. Adj.*: in an annoyed way; discontentedly; ill-humouredly

Miss·verhältnis, *Miß·verhältnis *das* disparity; (an Größe) disproportion

miss·verständlich, *miß·verständlich
A *Adj.* unclear; ‹*formulation, concept, etc.*› that could be misunderstood; **~ sein** be liable to be misunderstood
B *adv.* ‹*express oneself, describe*› in a way that could be misunderstood

Miss·verständnis, *Miß·verständnis *das* **1** misunderstanding **2** (Meinungsverschiedenheit) misunderstanding; disagreement

miss·verstehen, *miß·verstehen *unr. tr. V.;* **ich missverstehe, missverstanden, misszuverstehen** misunderstand

Miss·wahl, *Miß·wahl *die: contest for the title of 'Miss Europe', 'Miss World' etc.*

Miss·weisung, *Miß·weisung *die* (Physik) declination

Miss·wirtschaft, *Miß·wirtschaft *die* mismanagement

Mist /mɪst/ *der;* **~[e]s** **1** dung; (Dünger) manure; (mit Stroh usw. gemischt) muck; **das ist nicht auf ihrem ~ gewachsen** (fig. ugs.) that didn't come out of her own head **2** (**~haufen**) dung/manure/muck heap **3** (ugs. abwertend) (Schund) rubbish, junk, trash *all no indef. art.*; (Unsinn) rubbish, nonsense, (coll.) rot *all no indef. art.*; (lästige, dumme Angelegenheit) nonsense; **mach deinen ~ doch alleine!** bloody (Brit. sl.) *or* damn well do it yourself!; **~ bauen** make a mess of things; mess things up; **mach bloß keinen ~!** just don't do anything stupid!; **so ein ~!** what a damned *or* blasted nuisance!; damn *or* blast it!

Mist·beet *das* hotbed; forcing bed

Mistel /ˈmɪstl̩/ *die;* **~, ~n** mistletoe

Mistel·zweig *der* piece of mistletoe

misten
A *tr. V.* **1** (düngen) manure **2** ▸ **ausmisten**
B *itr. V.* (Landw.) dung

Mist-: ~fink *der* (derb) dirty *or* (coll.) mucky so-and-so; **~forke** *die* (nordd.), **~gabel** *die* dung fork; **~haufen** *der* dung/manure/muck heap

mistig (salopp)
A *Adj.* rotten (coll.)
B *adv.* in a rotten way (coll.)

Mist·käfer *der* dung beetle

Mistral /mɪsˈtraːl/ *der;* **~s** mistral

Mist-: ~stück *das* (derb) lousy good-for-nothing bastard (sl.); (Frau) lousy good-for-nothing bitch (sl.); **~vieh** *das* (derb) **1** (Tier) bloody (Brit. sl.) *or* damn animal; **dieses ~vieh von Katze** that bloody (Brit. sl.) *or* damn cat; **2** ▸ **~stück**; **~wagen** *der* dung cart; **~wetter** *das* (salopp) lousy weather (coll.); **bei so einem ~wetter** in lousy weather like this (coll.)

Miszellen /mɪsˈtsɛlən/ *Pl.* (geh.) miscellany *sing.*

mit /mɪt/
A *Präp. mit Dat.* **1** (Gemeinsamkeit, Beteiligung) with; **~ jdm. spielen/essen/streiten** play/eat/quarrel with sb.; **ein Fest ~ Damen** a celebration

at which ladies are/were present; **Verkehrsunfälle ~ Kindern** traffic accidents involving children 2) (Zugehörigkeit) with; **ein Haus ~ Garten** a house with a garden; **Herr Müller ~ Frau** Herr Müller and his wife 3) (einschließlich) with; including; **ein Zimmer ~ Frühstück** a room with breakfast included; **~ mir waren ...** including me *or* myself there were ...; **~ mir nicht!** (ugs.) count me out! (coll.) 4) (Inhalt) **ein Sack ~ Kartoffeln/Glas ~ Marmelade** a sack of potatoes/pot of jam 5) (Begleitumstände) with; **etw. ~ Absicht tun/~ Nachdruck fordern** do sth. deliberately/demand sth. forcefully; **~ 50 [km/h] fahren** drive at 50 [k.p.h]; **~ dem Auftrag, etw. zu tun** with the task of doing sth. 6) (Hilfsmittel) with; **~ Maschine geschrieben sein** be typed; **~ der Bahn/dem Auto fahren** go by train/car; **~ der Fähre/„Hamburg"** on the ferry/the 'Hamburg' 7) (allgemeiner Bezug) with; **~ der Arbeit ging es recht langsam voran** the work went very slowly; **~ Zustimmung seiner Eltern** with the consent of his parents; **~ einer Tätigkeit beginnen/aufhören** take up/give up an occupation; **was ist ~ ihm?** (ugs.) what's up with him? (coll.); **raus/fort ~ dir!** out/off you go! 8) (zeitlich) **~ Einbruch der Dunkelheit/Nacht** when darkness/night falls/fell; **~ dem Einsetzen des Nachtfrostes** when we/they *etc.* start/started to get frosts at night; **~ 20 [Jahren]** at [the age of] twenty; **~ dem heutigen Tag bist du volljährig** today you have reached your majority; **~ der Zeit/den Jahren** in time/as the years go/went by 9) (gleiche Richtung) with; **~ dem Strom/Wind** with the tide/wind

B *Adv.* 1) (auch) too; as well; **~ dabei sein** be there too; **er ist beim letzten Ausflug nicht ~ gewesen** he didn't come [with us] on our last trip; **waren eure Kinder im Urlaub ~?** did your children go on holiday with you?; **warst du auch ~ im Konzert?** were you at the concert too?; *s. auch* **Partie 6** 2) (neben anderen) also; too; as well; **es lag ~ an ihm** it was partly his doing; **das musst du ~ berücksichtigen** you must also take that into account; you must take that into account too *or* as well 3) (~ Sup.) (ugs.) **dieses ist ~ das wichtigste der Bücher** this is one of the most important of the books; **seine Arbeit war ~ am besten** his work was among the best; **~ der Beste** one of the best 4) (vorübergehende Beteiligung) **er ist bereit, heute ~ zu helfen** he's willing to help [just for] today; **ihr könntet ruhig einmal ~ anfassen** it wouldn't hurt you to lend a hand just for once 5) *s. auch* **damit A 3; womit 2**

Mit·angeklagte *der/die* co-defendant; (mit geringerer Strafandrohung) defendant to a lesser charge

Mit·arbeit *die* 1) (das Tätigsein) collaboration (**bei, an** + *Dat.* on); **die ~ in der Praxis ihres Mannes** working in her husband's practice; **unter ~** (*Dat.*) **von** in collaboration with 2) (Mithilfe) assistance (**bei, in** + *Dat.* in); **seine zwanzigjährige ~ in der Organisation** his twenty years of service to the organization; **unter ~ von** with the assistance of 3) (Beteiligung) participation (**in** + *Dat.* in)

mit|arbeiten *itr. V.* 1) (mithelfen) **bei einem Projekt/an einem Buch ~:** collaborate on a project/book; **im elterlichen Geschäft ~:** work in one's parents' shop; **ich arbeite bei einem Projekt mit, das ...** I'm working [with others] on a project that ... 2) (sich beteiligen) participate (**in** + *Dat.* in); **im Unterricht besser ~:** take a more active part in lessons 3) (ugs.: auch arbeiten) **seine Frau arbeitet mit** his wife works too

Mit·arbeiter *der,* **Mit·arbeiterin** *die* 1) (Betriebsangehörige[r]) employee 2) (bei einem Projekt, an einem Buch) collaborator; **ein freier Mitarbeiter** a freelance; a freelance worker; **ein freier/ständiger Mitarbeiter bei einer Zeitung** a freelance contributor to a newspaper/a writer on the permanent staff of a newspaper

Mitarbeiter·stab *der* staff; **zu jmds. engstem ~ gehören** be one of sb.'s closest assistants

Mit·begründer *der,* **Mit·begründerin** *die* co-founder

mit|bekommen *unr. tr. V.* 1) **etw. ~:** be given *or* get sth. to take with one; (fig.) inherit sth.; **etw. bei der Heirat ~:** be given sth. on marriage 2) (wahrnehmen) be aware of; (durch Hören, Sehen) hear/see; **es war so laut, dass ich nur die Hälfte mitbekam** it was so noisy that I only caught half of it; **hast du das ~?** (ugs.) did you know? 3) (miterleben) **etw. ~:** manage to hear/see sth.; **etwas von etw. ~:** hear/see something of sth.; **nicht viel/nichts von etw. ~:** not be able to hear/see much/anything of sth. 4) (verstehen) **ich war so müde, dass ich nicht viel ~ habe** I was so tired that I did not grasp very much; **ich habe gar nicht ~, wie er das meinte** I did not realize at all how he meant it

mit|benutzen, (bes. südd.) **mit|benützen** *tr. V.* share; have the use of

Mit·benutzung, (südd.) **Mit·benützung** *die* use

Mit·besitz *der* share [of the ownership]; **an etw.** (*Dat.*) **[einen] ~ haben** have a share in sth.

Mit·besitzer *der,* **Mit·besitzerin** *die* joint owner; co-owner

mit|bestimmen

A *itr. V.* have a say (**in** + *Dat.* in); **mehr ~ können** *od* **dürfen** have a greater say

B *tr. V.* have an influence on; **etw. maßgeblich ~:** have a determining influence on

Mit·bestimmung *die* participation (**bei** in); (der Arbeitnehmer) co-determination; **betriebliche ~, ~ am Arbeitsplatz** involvement of employees in management decisions

Mit·bestimmungs-: ~gesetz *das* law of co-determination; **~recht** *das* right of co-determination

Mit·bewerber *der,* **Mit·bewerberin** *die* competitor; **ich hatte nur einen Mitbewerber für** *od.* **um diese Stelle** there was only one other applicant for the job [besides me]; **alle Mitbewerber hatten bessere Qualifikationen** all the other applicants had better qualifications; **seine Mitbewerber** the other competitors/applicants

Mit·bewohner *der,* **Mit·bewohnerin** *die* other occupant; **seine Mitbewohner** his fellow occupants; the other occupants

mit|bringen *unr. tr. V.* 1) **etw. ~:** bring sth. with one; **etw. aus der Stadt/dem Urlaub/von dem Markt/der Reise ~:** bring sth. back from town/holiday/the market/one's trip; **jmdm./sich etw. ~:** bring sth. with one for sb./bring sth. back for oneself; **Gäste ~:** bring guests home; **eine Grippe/großen Hunger ~** (fig.) come back with influenza/feeling very hungry 2) (einbringen) have, possess ‹*ability, gift, etc.*› (**für** for); **genügend Zeit ~:** come with enough time at one's disposal

Mitbringsel /-brɪŋzl̩/ *das;* **~s, ~:** [small] present; (Andenken) [small] souvenir

Mit·bürger *der,* **Mit·bürgerin** *die* fellow citizen; **ältere Mitbürger** (Amtsspr.) senior citizens

mit|denken *unr. itr. V.* follow [the argument/explanation/what is being said *etc.*]; **ein Schüler, der mitdenkt** a pupil who follows the lesson; **die Fähigkeit zum Mitdenken** the ability to think for oneself

mit|dürfen *unr. itr. V.* (ugs.) (mitkommen dürfen) be allowed to come along *or* too; (mitgehen, mitfahren dürfen) be allowed to go along *or* too

Mit·eigentum *das* ▸ **Mitbesitz**

Mit·eigentümer *der,* **Mit·eigentümerin** *die* ▸ **Mitbesitzer**

mit·einander *Adv.* 1) with each other *or* one another; **~ sprechen/kämpfen** talk to each other *or* one another/fight with each other *or* one another 2) (gemeinsam) together; **~ gegen jmdn. kämpfen** fight together against sb.; **alle ~:** all together; **ihr seid Gauner, alle ~!** you are all a pack of rogues!; you're all rogues, the lot of you!

Mit·einander *das;* **~[s]** living and working together *no art.;* **im ~:** by mutual cooperation

mit|empfinden

A *unr. tr. V.* **jmds. Schmerz/Leid ~:** know the pain/sorrow sb. is/was feeling

B *unr. itr. V.* **mit jmdm. ~:** sympathize with sb.

Mit·empfinden *das* sympathy

Mit·erbe *der,* **Mit·erbin** *die* (Rechtsw.) joint heir; co-heir

mit|erleben *tr. V.* 1) (dabei sein bei) witness ‹*events etc.*›; **sie hat das Unglück miterlebt** she was involved in the accident; **eine Premiere ~:** be present at a première 2) (mitmachen) be alive during

mit|essen

A *unr. tr. V.* eat ‹*skin etc.*› as well; **bei dem Apfel habe ich einen Wurm mitgegessen** I've swallowed a grub along with the apple

B *unr. itr. V.* **jmdn. einladen mitzuessen** invite sb. to eat with one *or* have a meal; **bei jmdm. ~:** eat *or* have a meal with sb.

Mit·esser *der* 1) blackhead 2) (ugs. scherzh.) **einen [zusätzlichen] ~ haben** have one more to dinner/lunch/*etc.*

Mit·esserin *die* ▸ **Mitesser 2**

mit|fahren *unr. itr. V.; mit sein* **bei jmdm. [im Auto] ~:** go with sb. [in his/her car]; (auf einer Reise) travel with sb. [in his/her car]; (mitgenommen werden) get *or* have a lift with sb. [in his/her car]; **jmdn. ~ lassen** let sb. go; (jmdn. mitnehmen) give sb. a lift

Mit·fahrer *der,* **Mit·fahrerin** *die* fellow passenger; (vom Fahrer aus gesehen) passenger

Mitfahrer·zentrale *die* ▸ **Mitfahrzentrale**

Mitfahr-: ~gelegenheit *die* lift; **~zentrale** *die: office for putting those wanting lifts in touch with those who can offer them*

> **Mitfahrzentrale**
>
> An agency that puts drivers and passengers in contact with each other (including via the Internet) to save petrol costs and reduce pollution. The *Mitfahrzentrale* charges a small fee, complies with particular requests (non-smoking, female drivers, etc.), and is popular throughout Germany for long-distance travel.

mit|feiern *itr. V.* join in the celebrations

mit|fiebern *itr. V.* share *or* join in the excitement (**bei** of); **mit jmdm. ~:** share sb.'s excitement

mit|fühlen *tr., itr. V.* ▸ **mitempfinden**

mit·fühlend

A *Adj.* sympathetic

B *adv.* sympathetically

mit|führen *tr. V.* 1) (Amtsspr.: bei sich tragen) **etw. ~:** carry sth. [with one]; **führen Sie zollpflichtige Waren mit?** have you anything to declare? 2) (transportieren) ‹*river, stream*› carry along

mit|geben *unr. tr. V.* **jmdm. etw. ~:** give sb. sth. to take with him/her; **er gab mir einen Brief an seine Eltern mit** he gave me a letter for *or* to give to his parents; **ich werde Ihnen eine Begleitung ~:** I'll get somebody to accompany you; **jmdm. eine gute Erziehung/Ausbildung ~** (fig.) provide sb. with a good training/education

Mit·gefangene *der/die* fellow prisoner

Mit·gefühl *das* sympathy

mit|gehen *unr. itr. V.; mit sein* 1) (mitkommen) go too; **mit jmdm. ~:** go with sb.; **sie ist bis zur Bushaltestelle mitgegangen** she went with him/her *etc.* to the bus stop; **etw. ~ lassen** (fig. ugs.) walk off with sth. (coll.); pinch sth. (coll.) 2) (sich mitreißen lassen) **begeistert/enthusiastisch ~:** respond enthusiastically (**bei, mit** to) 3) (weggerissen werden) be carried away

mit·genommen *Adj.*

A ▸ **mitnehmen**

B (beschädigt) worn-out ‹*furniture, carpet*›; **~ sein/aussehen** ‹*book etc.*› be/look to be in a sorry state; (fig.) ‹*person*› be/look worn out

Mit·gesellschafter *der,* **Mit·gesellschafterin** *die* (Wirtsch.) [fellow] partner; co-partner

Mit·gift *die;* **~, ~en** (veralt.) dowry

Mitgift·jäger *der* (veralt. abwertend) dowry hunter

Mit·glied *das* member (+ *Gen.*, **in** + *Dat.* of); **~ im Finanzausschuss sein** be a member of *or* sit on the finance committee; **„Zutritt nur für ~er"** 'members only'; **~ des Europäischen Parlaments** Member of the European Parliament

mitglieder-, Mitglieder-: ~liste *die* list of members; **~stark** *Adj.* with a large membership *postpos.*; **~stark sein** have a large membership; **~versammlung** *die* general meeting; **~zahl** *die* number of members; membership

Mitglieds-: ~ausweis *der* membership card; **~beitrag** *der* membership subscription

Mitgliedschaft *die;* **~:** membership (+ *Gen.*, **in** + *Dat.*) of

Mitglied[s]·staat *der* member state *or* country

mit|haben *unr. tr. V.* (ugs.) **etw./jmdn. ~:** have got sth./sb. with one

mit|halten *unr. itr. V.* **1** (Schritt halten) keep up (**bei** in, **mit** with); **keiner konnte [mit ihm] ~** (in einer Diskussion, auf einem Fachgebiet usw.) nobody could touch him **2** (beim Essen, Trinken) eat/drink one's share

mit|helfen *unr. itr. V.* help (**bei, in** + *Dat.* with); **ein bisschen ~:** lend a hand for a bit; **bei dem Bau der Garage ~:** help to build the garage

Mit·helfer *der,* **Mit·helferin** *die* (abwertend) accomplice

Mit·herausgeber *der,* **Mit·herausgeberin** *die* joint editor; co-editor; (Verlag) co-publisher

mit·hilfe
A *Präp. mit Gen.* with the help *or* aid of
B *Adv.* **~ von** with the help *or* aid of

Mit·hilfe *die* help; assistance

mit·hin *Adv.* therefore

mit|hören
A *tr. V.* listen to; (zufällig) overhear ‹*conversation, argument, etc.*›; (abhören) listen in on
B *itr. V.* listen; (zufällig) overhear; **fürchten, dass mitgehört wird** be afraid that somebody is listening in; *s. auch* **Feind**

Mit·inhaber *der,* **Mit·inhaberin** *die* joint owner; co-owner; (einer Firma, eines Restaurants auch) joint proprietor

mit|kämpfen *itr. V.* take part in the fighting

Mit·kämpfer *der,* **Mit·kämpferin** *die* comrade-in-arms; (Sport) teammate

mit|klingen *unr. itr. V.:* ▸ **mitschwingen**

mit|kommen *unr. itr. V.; mit sein* **1** come too; **kommst du mit?** are you coming [with me/us]?; **ich kann nicht ~:** I can't come; **bis zur Tür ~:** come with sb. to the door **2** (Schritt halten) keep up; **in der Schule/im Unterricht gut/schlecht ~:** get on well/badly at school/with one's lessons; **da komme ich nicht mehr mit!** (fig. ugs.) I can't understand it at all!

mit|können *unr. itr. V.* (ugs.) **er kann mit** he can come too; (darf mitgehen, mitfahren) he can go too

mit|kriegen *tr. V.* (ugs.) ▸ **mitbekommen**

mit|laufen
A *unr. itr. V.; mit sein* **1** **mit jmdm. ~:** run with sb. **2** (Sport) **beim 100-m-Lauf** *usw.* **~:** run in the 100 m. *etc.* **3** **ein Tonband ~ lassen** have a tape recorder running **4** (ugs.: nebenbei erledigt werden) **die Reparaturen müssen nebenher ~:** the repairs have to be fitted in along with everything else *or* as we go along
B *unr. tr. V.; mit sein* **ein Rennen ~:** run in a race

Mit·läufer *der,* **Mit·läuferin** *die* (abwertend) [mere] supporter; (Schmarotzer) hanger-on

Mit·laut *der* consonant

Mit·leid *das* pity, compassion (**mit** for); (Mitgefühl) sympathy (**mit** for); **mit jmdm. ~ haben** *od.* **empfinden** feel pity *or* compassion/have *or* feel sympathy for sb.; **jmds. ~ erregen** arouse sb.'s sympathy; **ein Sympathie und ~ erregendes Schicksal** a fate arousing compassion and sympathy

Mit·leidenschaft *die:* in **jmdn./etw. in ~ ziehen** affect sb./sth.

mitleid·erregend *Adj.* pitiful

mit·leidig
A *Adj.* compassionate; (mitfühlend) sympathetic
B *adv.* compassionately; (mitfühlend) sympathetically; (iron.) pityingly

mitleid[s]-: ~los **A** *Adj.* pitiless; (herzlos) unfeeling; **B** *adv.* without pity; (herzlos) unfeelingly; **~voll** **A** *Adj.* compassionate; **B** *adv.* compassionately

mit|lesen *unr. tr. V.* **1** (zur Kenntnis nehmen) **etw. ~:** read sth. (*as well as sth. else*) **2** (zugleich lesen) **etw. [mit jmdm.] ~:** read sth. at the same time as sb.; **mein Gegenüber las meine Zeitung mit** the person opposite me was also reading my newspaper

mit|machen
A *tr. V.* **1** (teilnehmen an) go on ‹*trip*›; join in ‹*joke*›; follow ‹*fashion*›; fight in ‹*war*›; do ‹*course, seminar*› **2** (ugs.: billigen) **das mache ich nicht mit** I can't go along with it; **ich mache das nicht länger mit!** I'm not standing for it any longer! **3** (ugs.: zusätzlich erledigen) **jmds. Arbeit ~:** do sb.'s work as well as one's own **4** (ugs.: erleiden) **zwei Weltkriege/viele Bombenangriffe mitgemacht haben** have been through two world wars/many bomb attacks; **er hat viel mitgemacht** he has been through a great deal
B *itr. V.* **1** (sich beteiligen) join in; **bei einem Wettbewerb/einer Aktion ~:** take part in a competition/take part in *or* join in a campaign; **willst du ~?** do you want to join in?; **da[bei] mache ich nicht mit** I'm not joining in; you can count me out (coll.) **2** (ugs.: funktionieren) **meine Beine machen nicht mehr mit** my legs are giving up on me (coll.); **mein Herz/Kreislauf macht nicht mit** my heart/circulation can't take it

Mit·mensch *der* fellow man; fellow human being; **urteile nicht so hart über deine ~en** don't be so harsh in your judgements of other people

mit·menschlich *Adj.* human, interpersonal ‹*relations, relationships*›; interpersonal ‹*contacts, communication*›

mit|mischen *itr. V.* (ugs.) **1** (sich einmischen) interfere (**bei** in); (sich beteiligen) get involved (**bei** in) **2** (Sportjargon) (mit vollem Einsatz kämpfen) give everything one's got; (dem Gegner Paroli bieten) give as good as one gets

mit|müssen *unr. itr. V.* (mitkommen müssen) have [got] to come with sb.; (mitgehen, mitfahren müssen) have [got] to go with sb.

Mitnahme *die;* **~, ~n** (Amtsspr.) **die ~ von Taschen in das Museum ist nicht erlaubt** it is forbidden *or* visitors are not allowed to take bags into the museum; **die Diebe verschwanden unter ~ des gesamten Schmucks** the thieves vanished with all the jewelry *or* vanished, taking all the jewelry with them

Mitnahme-: ~markt *der* (*retail*) cash and carry [store]; **~preis** *der* (Kaufmannsspr.) takeaway price

mit|nehmen *unr. tr. V.* **1** **jmdn. ~:** take sb. with one; **etw. ~:** take sth. with one; (verhüll.: stehlen) walk off with sth. (coll.); (kaufen) take sth.; **etw. wieder ~:** take sth. away [with one] again; **das Frachtschiff nimmt auch Passagiere mit** the cargo ship also carries passengers; **Essen/Getränke zum Mitnehmen** food/drinks to take away *or* (Amer.) to go; **könntest du einen Brief für mich ~?** could you take a letter for me?; **jmdn. im Auto ~:** give sb. a lift [in one's car] **2** (ugs.: streifen) **der LKW hat die Hecke mitgenommen** the truck *or* (Brit.) lorry took the hedge with it **3** (ugs.: wahrnehmen) do (coll.) ‹*sights etc.*›; **auch Soho ~:** take in Soho as well; **sie nimmt alles mit, was sich ihr bietet** she makes the most of everything life has to offer her **4** (in Mitleidenschaft ziehen) **jmdn. ~:** take it out of sb.; **von etw. mitgenommen sein** be worn out by sth.; (traurig gemacht) be grieved by sth. **5** (lernen) **etw. aus einem Vortrag/einer Predigt ~:** get sth. out of *or* from a lecture/sermon

Mitnehm·preis *der* ▸ **Mitnahmepreis**

mitnichten *Adv.* (veralt.) in no way; not at all; by no means; **er gehorchte ~:** he wouldn't obey at all

Mitochondrium /mitoˈxɔndrium/ *das;* **~s, Mitochondrien** (Biol.) mitochondrion

Mitra /ˈmiːtra/ *die;* **~, Mitren** (kath. Kirche) mitre

mit|rauchen
A *tr. V.* **eine [Zigarette] ~:** have a cigarette with sb.
B *itr. V.* inhale other people's tobacco smoke

mit|rechnen
A *itr. V.* work the sum out at the same time; **ich habe bei deiner Addition mitgerechnet** I did the addition at the same time as you
B *tr. V.* **etw. ~:** include sth. [in the calculation]

mit|reden *itr. V.* **1** (Sinnvolles beisteuern) join in the conversation; **die einzige Kunstart, bei der sie ~ kann** the only art form she knows enough about to hold a conversation **2** (mitbestimmen) have a say

mit|regieren *itr. V.* share power

mit|reisen *itr. V.* **[mit jmdm.] ~:** travel with sb.

Mit·reisende *der/die* fellow passenger; **einer der ~n** one of the other passengers

mit|reißen *unr. tr. V.* **1** (wegreißen) ‹*avalanche, flood*› sweep away; **der Abstürzende hat die ganze Seilschaft mitgerissen** the falling climber dragged the whole of the roped party down with him **2** (begeistern) **die Begeisterung/seine Rede hat alle Zuhörer mitgerissen** the audience was carried away with enthusiasm/by his speech; **nicht gerade ~d** not exactly thrilling; **sein ~des Spiel** his exciting playing; **die ~de Musik** the rousing music

mitsammen /mɪtˈzamən/ *Adv.* (österr.) together

mit·samt *Präp. mit Dat.* together with; **die ganze Familie ~ Hund und Katze** the whole family, complete with cat and dog

mit|schicken *tr. V.* **ich schicke dir [im Brief] sein Foto mit** I'll send you his photo [with the letter]; **jmdm. einen Führer ~:** send a guide [along] with sb.

mit|schleifen *tr. V.* (auch fig. ugs.) **jmdn./etw. ~:** drag sb./sth. along

mit|schleppen *tr. V.* (ugs.) **1** (tragen) **etw. ~:** lug *or* (coll.) cart sth. with one **2** ▸ **mitschleifen**

mit|schneiden *unr. tr. V.* (Rundf., Ferns.) record [live]

Mit·schnitt *der* (Rundf., Ferns.) [live] recording

mit|schreiben
A *unr. tr. V.* **etw. ~:** take sth. down
B *unr. itr. V.* write *or* take down what is/was said; (in Vorlesungen usw.) take notes

Mit·schuld *die* share of the blame *or* responsibility (**an** + *Dat.* for); (an Verbrechen) complicity (**an** + *Dat.* in)

mit·schuldig *Adj.* **an etw.** (*Dat.*) **~ sein/werden** be/become partly to blame *or* partly responsible for sth.; (an Verbrechen) be/become guilty of complicity in sth.; **sich ~ machen** put oneself in the position of being partly to blame *or* partly responsible for sth.; (an Verbrechen) become guilty of complicity as a result of one's own actions

Mit·schuldige *der/die* one who is/was partly to blame *or* partly responsible (**an** + *Dat.* for); (an Verbrechen) accomplice (**an** + *Dat.* in)

Mit·schüler *der,* **Mit·schülerin** *die* schoolfellow

mit|schwingen *unr. itr. V.* **in seinen Worten/seiner Stimme schwang Triumph/Freude mit** there was a note of triumph/joy in his words/voice

***mit|sein** ▸ **mit B 1**

mit|singen
A *unr. tr. V.* join in ‹*song etc.*›
B *unr. itr. V.* join in [the singing]; sing along; **im Chor ~:** be a member of the choir

mit|sollen *itr. V.* (ugs.) **soll der Koffer auch mit?** is this case to go too?; **wenn ich mitsoll, musst du es nur sagen** just say if you want me to go with you

mit|spielen *itr. V.* [1] (sich beteiligen) join in the game; **wenn das Wetter mitspielt** (fig.) if the weather is kind [2] (mitwirken) **in einem Film/bei einem Theaterstück ~:** be *or* act in a film/play; **in einem Orchester/in** *od.* **bei einem Fußballverein ~:** play in an orchestra/for a football club [3] (sich auswirken) play a part (**bei** in); **viele Gründe haben bei der Entscheidung mitgespielt** there were many reasons for this decision [4] (zusetzen) **jmdm. übel** *od.* **böse ~** ‹*authorities*› treat sb. badly; ‹*opponent*› give sb. a rough time

Mit·spieler *der,* **Mit·spielerin** *die* player; (in derselben Mannschaft) teammate; **seine ~** (Sport) his teammates; (bei Kartenspielen usw.) the other players

Mit·sprache *die* say; **ein Recht auf ~:** the right to a share in decisions

Mitsprache·recht *das:* **ein/kein ~ bei etw. haben** have a say/no say in sth.; **ein ~ bekommen** gain the right to a share in decisions

mit|sprechen
A *unr. tr. V.* (gemeinsam sprechen) join in [saying]
B *unr. itr. V.:* ► **mitreden**

Mit·streiter *der,* **Mit·streiterin** *die* (geh.) comrade-in-arms; **er fand viele Mitstreiter** (fig.) he found many people who were willing to join his campaign

Mitt-: **~achtziger** *der* man in his mid-eighties; **~achtzigerin** *die* woman in her mid-eighties

***mittag** /ˈmɪtaːk/ ► **Mittag¹ 1**

Mittag¹ *der;* **~s, ~e** [1] midday *no art.*; **gegen ~:** around midday *or* noon; **jeden/diesen ~:** every day at lunchtime/at lunchtime today; **heute/morgen/gestern ~:** at midday *or* lunchtime today/tomorrow/yesterday; **über ~:** at midday *or* lunchtime; **zu ~ essen** have lunch; **was essen wir zu ~?** what is there for lunch?; **was gibts zu ~?** what's for lunch?; **was gibt es heute ~ zu essen?** what's for lunch today? [2] (ugs.: ~spause) lunch hour; lunch break; **~ machen** (ugs.) take one's lunch hour *or* lunch break [3] (dichter. veralt.: Süden) south

Mittag² *das;* **~s** (ugs.) lunch; **~ essen** have lunch

Mittag-: **~brot** *das* (landsch.), **~essen** *das* lunch; midday meal; **beim ~essen sitzen** be having [one's] lunch *or* one's midday meal; **nach dem ~essen** after lunch

> **Mittagessen**
>
> This is a cooked meal eaten in the middle of the day and is the main meal of the day for most Germans. Schoolchildren come home from school in time for *Mittagessen*, and most large companies have canteens where hot meals are served at lunchtime. On a Sunday, *Mittagessen* might consist of a starter such as clear broth, followed by a roast with gravy, boiled potatoes and vegetables, and a dessert.

mittäglich /ˈmɪtɛːklɪç/
A *Adj.* midday; lunchtime ‹*invitation*›
B *adv.* at midday *or* lunchtime; **es war ~ heiß auf der Straße** the street was baking in the noonday heat

mittags /ˈmɪtaːks/ *Adv.* ► S. 729 at midday *or* lunchtime; **bis ~:** until midday *or* lunchtime; **12 Uhr ~:** 12 noon; 12 o'clock midday; **dienstags ~:** Tuesday lunchtime; **von morgens bis ~:** in the morning until midday

Mittags-: **~glut** *die,* **~hitze** *die* midday *or* noonday heat; heat of midday; **~linie** *die* (Astron.) meridian; **~mahl** *das* (geh.) luncheon; **~pause** *die* lunch hour; lunch break; **~pause haben** have one's lunch hour *or* lunch break; **nach der ~pause** after lunch; **in der ~pause sein** (ugs.) have gone to lunch; **~ruhe** *die* period of quiet after lunch; **~ruhe halten** have one's after-lunch rest; **~schlaf** *der* after-lunch sleep; **[seinen] ~schlaf halten** have an after-lunch sleep; **~schläfchen** *das* (ugs.) after-lunch nap; **[s]ein ~schläfchen halten** have an after-lunch nap; **~sonne** *die* midday *or* noonday sun; **~sonne haben** get the midday sun; **~stunde** *die* midday; **um die ~stunde** at midday; **~tisch** *der* [1] lunch table; **der ~tisch ist gedeckt** the table is laid for lunch; **am ~tisch sitzen** be sitting at the table having lunch; [2] (veralt.: im Restaurant) lunch; midday meal; **einen ~tisch für Studenten anbieten** do student lunches; **~zeit** *die* [1] (Zeit gegen 12 Uhr) lunchtime *no art.*; midday *no art.*; **in der ~zeit** at lunchtime; **um die ~zeit** at lunchtime; around midday; [2] (~pause) lunch hour; lunch break

Mit·täter *der,* **Mit·täterin** *die* accomplice

Mit·täterschaft *die* complicity; **jmdn. der ~** (*Gen.*) **bei etw. anklagen** accuse sb. of complicity in sth.

Mitte /ˈmɪtə/ *die;* **~, ~n** [1] (Teil) middle; (Punkt) middle; centre; (eines Kreises, einer Kugel, Stadt) centre; **bis zur ~ gekommen sein** (beim Lesen) be halfway through; **wir nahmen sie in die ~:** we had her between us; **eine Politik der ~** (fig.) a middle-of-the-road policy; **die goldene ~** (fig.) the golden mean; **ab durch die ~!** (fig. ugs.) off you go [2] ► S. 29, ► S. 165 (Zeitpunkt) middle; **~ des Monats/Jahres** in the middle of the month/year; **~ Februar** in mid-February; in the middle of February; **er ist ~ dreißig** he's in his mid-thirties [3] (Politik) (Gruppierung) centre; **eine Partei der ~:** a centrist party [4] (Kreis von Menschen) **wir haben sie wieder in unserer ~ begrüßt** we welcomed her back into our midst *or* amongst us; **der Tod hat ihn aus unserer ~ gerissen** (geh.) death has taken him from our midst [5] (veralt.: Taille) middle; waist

mit|teilen
A *tr. V.* **jmdm. etw. ~:** tell sb. sth.; (informieren) inform sb. of *or* about sth.; communicate sth. to sb. (formal); (amtlich) notify *or* inform sb. of sth.; **er teilte mit, dass ...** he announced that ...; **teile ihr die schlechte Nachricht schonend mit** break the news to her gently
B *refl. V.* (geh.) [1] (sich anvertrauen) **sich jmdm. ~:** confide in sb. [2] (sich übertragen auf) **sich jmdm. ~:** communicate itself to sb.

mitteilsam *Adj.* communicative; (gesprächig) talkative

Mitteilsamkeit *die;* **~:** communicativeness; (Gesprächigkeit) talkativeness

Mit·teilung *die* communication; (Bekanntgabe) announcement; **jmdm. eine vertrauliche ~ machen** give sb. confidential information; **ich muss dir eine traurige ~ machen** I have some sad news for you; **zweckdienliche ~en** useful information *sing.*

Mitteilungs·bedürfnis *das* need to communicate

Mittel /ˈmɪtl̩/ *das;* **~s, ~** [1] means *sing.*; (Methode) way; method; (Werbe~, Propaganda~, zur Verkehrskontrolle) device (+ *Gen.* for); **mit allen ~n versuchen, etw. zu tun** try by every means to do sth.; **kein ~ unversucht lassen** try every means; **zum letzten** *od.* **äußersten ~ greifen, und das Kind in ein Erziehungsheim bringen** as a last resort put the child in a community home; **[nur] ~ zum Zweck sein** be [just] a means to an end; **~ und Wege suchen/finden** look for/find ways and means [2] (Arznei) **ein ~ gegen Grippe/Husten/Schuppen** *usw.* a remedy *or* cure for influenza/coughs *pl.*/dandruff *sing. etc.*; **ein ~ gegen Schmerzen** a pain-reliever; **ein ~ zum Einreiben** a cream/ointment *etc.* to be rubbed in; *s. auch* **schmerzstillend** [3] (Substanz) **ein ~ gegen Ungeziefer/Insekten** a pesticide/an insect repellent; **ein ~ zur Reinigung von Teppichböden/zum Entfernen von Flecken** a cleaning agent for carpets/a stain remover [4] *Pl.* (Geld~) funds; [financial] resources; (Privat~) means; resources; **mit** *od.* **aus öffentlichen ~n** from public funds; **von seinen bescheidenen ~n** with his modest means; **meine ~ sind erschöpft** my funds are exhausted; **etw. aus eigenen ~n bezahlen** pay for sth. out of one's own resources [5] (Durchschnittswert) average; **im ~:** on [the] average; **das arithmetische/geometrische ~** (Math.) the arithmetic/geometric mean

mittel-, Mittel-: **~achse** *die* central axis; **~alter** *das* Middle Ages *pl.*; **das finstere ~alter** the Dark Ages *pl.*; **das sind Zustände wie im ~alter** (ugs.) it's positively medieval; **~alterlich** *Adj.* medieval; **~amerika** (*das*) Central America [and the West Indies]

mittelbar
A *Adj.* indirect
B *adv.* indirectly

mittel-, Mittel-: **~bau** *der; Pl.* **~~ten** [1] (Gebäudeteil) central *or* main part [of a/the building]; [2] (Hochschulw.) non-professorial teaching staff; **~deck** *das* (Schiffbau) middle deck; **~deutsch** *Adj.* [1] (Geogr.) of central Germany *postpos., not pred.*; [2] (Sprachw.) middle German; [3] (Politik veralt.) East German; **~deutschland** (*das*) [1] (Geogr.) central Germany; [2] (Politik veralt.) East Germany; **~ding** *das:* **ein ~ding sein** be something in between; **ein ~ding zwischen Moped und Fahrrad** something between a moped and a bicycle; **~europa** (*das*) Central Europe; **~europäer** *der,* **~europäerin** *die* Central European; **~europäisch** *Adj.* Central European; **~fein** A *Adj.* medium-fine ‹*thread*›; medium-grade ‹*peas, sandpaper*›; medium-ground ‹*coffee*›; ‹*paper*› containing 40-50% mechanical wood; B *adv.* **~fein gemahlen** medium ground; **~feld** *das* [1] (Fußball: Spielfeldteil, Spieler) midfield; [2] (Sport: im Wettbewerb) **im ~feld sein** be in the pack; (in der Tabelle) be in mid-table; **~feld·spieler** *der,* **~feld·spielerin** *die* (Fußball) midfield player; **~finger** *der* middle finger; **~fristig** /-frɪstɪç/ (Finanzw.) A *Adj.* medium-term ‹*solution, financial planning*›; B *adv.* **[etw.] ~fristig planen** plan [sth.] on a medium-term basis; **~fuß** *der* (Anat., Zool.) metatarsus; **~gang** *der* (eines Eisenbahnwagens, Schiffes) central gangway; (einer Kirche, eines Flugzeugs) central *or* centre aisle; **~gebirge** *das* low-mountain region; low mountains *pl.*; **~gebirgs·landschaft** *die* low-mountain landscape; **~gewicht** *das* (Schwerathletik) [1] middleweight; *s. auch* **Fliegengewicht**; [2] (Sportler) ► **~gewichtler**; **~gewichtler** /-gəvɪçtlɐ/ *der;* **~~s, ~~:** middleweight; **~groß** *Adj.* medium-sized; ‹*person*› of medium height; **~hand** *die* (Anat.) metacarpus; **~hand·knochen** *der* (Anat.) metacarpal [bone]; **~hochdeutsch** *Adj.* Middle High German; **~hochdeutsch** *das* Middle High German; **~klasse** *die* [1] (Güteklasse) middle range; (Größenklasse) middle [size-]range; **ein Wagen der ~klasse** a car in the middle range/a medium-sized car; [2] (~schicht) middle class; **~klasse·wagen** *der* car in the middle range; (hinsichtlich der Größe) medium-sized car; **~konsole** *die* (Kfz.-W.) centre console; **~kreis** *der* (Ballspiele) centre circle; **~latein** *das* medieval Latin; **~lateinisch** *Adj.* medieval Latin; **~linie** *die* centre line; (Fußball) halfway line; **~los** *Adj.* without means *postpos.*; penniless; (arm) poor; (verarmt) impoverished; **~los dastehen** be left without means; **~losigkeit** *die;* **~~:** lack of means; (Armut) poverty; **~maß** *das:* **gutes ~maß sein** be a good average; **das gesunde ~maß** the happy medium; **~mäßig** (oft abwertend) A *Adj.* mediocre; indifferent; indifferent ‹*weather*›; B *adv.* indifferently; **~mäßigkeit** *die* (oft abwertend) mediocrity; **~meer** *das* Mediterranean [Sea]; **~meerisch** *Adj.* Mediterranean

Mittelmeer-: **~länder** *Pl.* Mediterranean countries; **~raum** *der* Mediterranean [area]

mitteln /ˈmɪtl̩n/ *tr. V.* average [out]; **gemittelte Werte** average *or* mean values

mittel-, Mittel-: **~ohr** *das* (Anat.) middle ear; **~ohr·entzündung** *die* ► S. 439 (Med.) inflammation of the middle ear; **~prächtig** (ugs. scherzh.) A *Adj.* **[nur] ~prächtig** not particularly marvellous; B *adv.* **Wie gehts? — ~prächtig** How are you? — Fair to middling (coll.); **~punkt** *der* [1] (Geom.) centre; (einer Strecke) midpoint; [2] (Mensch/Sache im Zentrum) centre *or* focus of attention; **ein kultureller ~punkt** a cultural

m

centre; **im ∼punkt stehen** be the centre *or* focus of attention; **im ∼punkt der Diskussion stehen** be the main topic of the discussion; **etw. in den ∼punkt [seiner Rede] stellen** focus on sth. [in one's speech]; **∼punkt·schule** *die: school centrally situated in a wide rural catchment area*

mittels *Präp. mit Gen.* (Papierdt.) by means of

mittel-, Mittel-: ∼scheitel *der* centre parting; **∼schicht** *die* (Soziol.) ▸ **∼klasse 2**; **∼schiff** *das* (Archit.) nave; **∼schule** *die* 1 ▸ **Realschule**; 2 (österr. veralt., schweiz.) secondary school; high school (Amer.); **∼schul·lehrer** *der*, **∼schul·lehrerin** *die* 1 ▸ **Realschullehrer**; 2 (österr. veralt., schweiz.) secondary school *or* (Amer.) high school teacher; **∼schwer** *Adj.* ‹*climb, problem, etc.*› of medium *or* moderate difficulty; moderately difficult ‹*climb, problem, etc.*›; moderately heavy ‹*suitcase etc.*›

Mittels-: ∼mann *der Pl.* **∼männer** *od.* **∼leute**, **∼person** *die* intermediary; go-between

mittel-, Mittel-: ∼stadt *die* medium-sized town; **∼stand** *der* middle class; **∼ständisch** *Adj.* middle-class; medium-sized ‹*firm*› (in private ownership); **∼ständler** /-ʃtɛntlɐ/ *der*; **∼∼s**, **∼∼**, **∼ständlerin** *die*; **∼∼**, **∼∼nen** (ugs.) middle-class person; member of the middle class; **∼steinzeit** *die* Mesolithic period; **∼stellung** *die* intermediate *or* midway position; **etw. nimmt eine ∼stellung zwischen A und B ein** sth. is intermediate between A and B; **∼stimme** *die* (Musik) middle part *or* voice

Mittel·strecke *die* 1 medium haul *or* distance; **auf ∼n** over medium distances 2 (Sport) middle distance; **auf [den] ∼n** in middle-distance running

Mittelstrecken-: ∼flug *der* medium-haul flight; **∼lauf** *der* (Sport) middle-distance race; (Disziplin) middle-distance running *no art.*; **∼läufer** *der*, **∼läuferin** *die* (Sport) middle-distance runner; **∼rakete** *die* medium-range missile

Mittel-: ∼streifen *der* central reservation; median strip (Amer.); **∼stufe** *die* (Schulw.) middle school; **∼stürmer** *der*, **∼stürmerin** *die* (Sport) centre forward; **∼teil** *der od. das* middle section; (eines Buches) middle [part]; **∼weg** *der* middle course; **der goldene ∼weg** the happy medium; **∼welle** *die* (Physik, Rundf.) medium wave; **auf** *od.* **über ∼welle** on [the] medium wave; **∼wert** *der* mean [value]; **∼wort** *das; Pl.* **∼wörter** participle

mitten *Adv.* **∼ an/auf etw.** (*Akk. od. Dat.*) in the middle of sth.; **der Teller brach ∼ durch** the plate broke in half; **∼ in etw.** (*Akk./Dat.*) into/in the middle of sth.; **∼ durch die Stadt** right through the town; **∼ durch die Menge** through the middle of the crowd; **∼ aus etw.** from the middle of sth.; **∼ darin** ▸ **∼drin**; **mitten unter uns** (*Dat.*) in our midst; **der Schuss traf ihn ∼ ins Herz** the shot hit him right in the heart; **∼ in der Luft/im Pazifik** in mid-air/mid-Pacific; **∼ in der Aufregung** in the midst of the excitement

mitten-: ∼drin *Adv.* 1 (zwischen anderen) [right] in the middle; 2 (gerade dabei) **∼drin sein, etw. zu tun** be [right] in the middle of doing sth.; **∼durch** *Adv.* [right] through the middle; **sie schnitt den Kuchen ∼durch** she cut the cake in half *or* into two equal pieces; **∼mang** *Adv.* (nordd., berlin.) [right] in/into the middle of it/them

Mitter·nacht /ˈmɪtɐ-/ *die* ▸ⓘ **S. 729** midnight *no art.*

mitter·nächtlich *Adj.* midnight; **zu ∼er Stunde** at midnight; at the midnight hour (literary)

Mitternachts-: ∼sonne *die* midnight sun; **∼stunde** *die* midnight hour; **zur/bis zur ∼stunde** at/by around midnight

mittig (Technik)

A *Adj.* aligned

B *adv.* ‹*arranged*› in line; ‹*divided*› centrally

Mittler /ˈmɪtlɐ/ *der*; **∼s**, **∼**: mediator

mittler... /ˈmɪtlər.../ *Adj.* 1 (zwischen anderen befindlich) middle; **der/die/das ∼e** the middle one; **die ∼e Reife** (Schulw.) *standard of achievement for school-leaving certificate at a Realschule or for entry to the sixth form in a Gymnasium; s. auch* **Osten 3** 2 (einen Mittelwert darstellend) average ‹*temperature*›; moderate ‹*speed*›; medium-sized ‹*company, town*›; medium ‹*quality, size*›; **ein Mann ∼en Alters** a middle-aged man

Mittler·amt *das* role of mediator

> **Mittlerer Schulabschluss**
>
> Students who have achieved the *Realschulabschluss* at a **Realschule** or the *Hauptschulabschluss* at a **Hauptschule** are awarded an intermediate school certificate. A *mittlerer Schulabschluss* qualifies the recipient to continue their education at a full-time vocational **Berufsfachschule**.

Mittlerin *die*; **∼**, **∼nen** mediator

Mittler·rolle *die* mediating role

mittler·weile /ˈmɪtlɐˈvailə/ *Adv.* 1 (seitdem, allmählich) since then; (bis jetzt) by now 2 (unterdessen) in the mean time

mit|tragen *unr. tr. V.* bear part of, share ‹*responsibility, cost*›; take part of, share ‹*blame*›; give one's support to ‹*aims, proposal*›

mit|trinken

A *unr. tr. V.* **etw. ∼**: drink sth. with me/us *etc.*; **trinkst du einen mit?** are you going to have a drink with me/us *etc.?*

B *unr. itr. V.* **mit jmdm. ∼**: have a drink with sb.

mitt-, Mitt-: ∼schiffs *Adv.* (Seemannsspr.) amidships; **∼sommer** *der* midsummer; **∼sommer·nacht** *die* midsummer's night; (Nacht der Sommersonnenwende) Midsummer Night

mit|tun *unr. itr. V.* (landsch.) join in

Mittwoch /ˈmɪtvɔx/ *der*; **∼[e]s**, **∼e** ▸ⓘ **S. 165**, ▸ⓘ **S. 816** Wednesday; *s. auch* **Dienstag**; **Dienstag-**

mittwochs *Adv.* ▸ⓘ **S. 816** on Wednesday[s]; *s. auch* **dienstags**

mit·unter *Adv.* now and then; from time to time; sometimes

mit·verantwortlich *Adj.* partly responsible *pred.*; (beide/alle zusammen) jointly responsible *pred.*

Mit·verantwortung *die* share of the responsibility; **∼ übernehmen** take one's share of the responsibility

mit|verdienen *itr. V.* go out to work as well; **der ältere Sohn verdient jetzt mit** the eldest son is earning now too

Mit·verfasser *der*, **Mit·verfasserin** *die* co-author; joint author

mit|verfolgen *tr. V.* follow

Mit·verschulden *das*: **ihn trifft ein ∼ an seinem Unfall** he was partly to blame for his accident

mit|versichern *tr. V.* include in one's insurance

mit|wachsen *unr. itr. V.*; *mit sein* grow too; grow at the same time; **mit etw. ∼**: grow along with sth.

Mit·welt *die* fellow men *pl.*; **die ∼**: sb.'s fellow men

mit·wirken *itr. V.* 1 (tätig sein) **an etw.** (*Dat.*)/**bei etw. ∼**: collaborate on/be involved in sth.; **an der Aufklärung eines Verbrechens ∼**: help to solve a crime; **ohne jmds. Mitwirken** without sb.'s help *or* assistance 2 (mitspielen) **in einem Orchester/Theaterstück ∼wirken** play in an orchestra/act *or* appear in a play 3 (Bedeutung haben) **[bei etw.] ∼**: play a role [in sth.]

Mitwirkende *der/die; adj. Dekl.* (an einer Sendung) participant; (in einer Show) performer; (in einem Theaterstück) actor; **die ∼n** (in einem Theaterstück) the cast *sing.*

Mit·wirkung *die* **jmds. ∼ an etw.** (*Dat.*)/**bei etw.** sb.'s collaboration on/involvement in sth.; **unter ∼ vieler Fachwissenschaftler** in collaboration with many experts; **die Veranstaltung findet unter ∼ bekannter Künstler statt** some famous artists are taking part in the event

Mit·wisser *der*; **∼s**, **∼**, **Mit·wisserin** *die*; **∼**, **∼nen**: **∼ einer Sache** (*Gen.*) **sein** know about sth.; (einer Straftat) be an accessory to sth.; **er hatte zu viele Mitwisser** there were too many people who knew about what he'd done; **zum Mitwisser gemacht werden** be told about it; (bei einer Straftat) be made an accessory

Mitwisserschaft *die*; **∼**: knowledge of the matter/crime; **seine ∼ leugnen** deny all knowledge [of the matter]

mit|wollen *unr. itr. V.* (ugs.) (mitkommen wollen) want to come with sb.; (mitgehen, mitfahren wollen) want to go with sb.

mit|zählen

A *itr. V.* 1 count; **die Sonntage zählen bei den Urlaubstagen nicht mit** Sundays don't count as holidays 2 (gelten) ‹*objection*› be valid; ‹*factor*› be relevant

B *tr. V.* count in; include

mit|ziehen *unr. itr. V.*; *mit sein* 1 (mitgehen) go with him/them *etc.*; **mit der Kapelle ∼**: march along with the band; **mit dem Zirkus ∼**: travel round with the circus 2 (ugs.: mitmachen) go along with it; (bei einer Klage, Initiative) give it one's backing 3 (Sport) go with him/her *etc.*

Mix /mɪks/ *der*; **∼es**, **∼e** mixture (**aus** of)

Mix·becher /ˈmɪks-/ *der* [cocktail] shaker

Mixed /mɪkst/ *das*; **∼[s]**, **∼[s]** (Sport) mixed doubles

Mixedpickles /mɪkstˈpɪkl̩s/ *Pl.* mixed pickles

mixen /ˈmɪksn̩/ *tr. V.* (auch Rundf., Ferns., Film) mix; **sich** (*Dat.*) **einen Drink ∼**: fix oneself a drink; **etw. unter etw.** (*Akk.*) **∼** (Kochk.) mix sth. into sth.

Mixer *der*; **∼s**, **∼** 1 (Bar∼) barman; bartender (Amer.) 2 (Gerät) blender and liquidizer

Mixerin *die*; **∼**, **∼nen** barmaid

Mix·getränk *das* mixed drink; cocktail

Mixtur /mɪksˈtuːɐ̯/ *die*; **∼**, **∼en** 1 (Pharm., fig.) mixture 2 (Musik) mixture [stop]

mm *Abk.* ▸ⓘ **S. 454 = Millimeter** mm.

Mnemo·technik /mnemo-/ *die* (Psych.) mnemonics *sing., no art.*

Mo. *Abk.* **= Montag** Mon.

Mob /mɔp/ *der*; **∼s** (abwertend) mob

mobben /ˈmɔbn̩/ *tr. V.* (ugs.) hassle and bully

Mobbing /ˈmɔbɪŋ/ *das*; **∼s** (ugs.) hassling and bullying

Möbel /ˈmøːbl̩/ *das*; **∼s**, **∼**: piece of furniture; **neue ∼**: new furniture *sing.*

Möbel-: ∼geschäft *das* furniture shop; **∼haus** *das* furniture store; **∼industrie** *die* furniture industry; **∼lager** *das* furniture warehouse; (zur Einlagerung) furniture repository; **∼packer** *der* removal man; **∼politur** *die* furniture polish; **∼schreiner** *der*, **∼schreinerin** *die* ▸ **Möbeltischler**; **∼spedition** *die* furniture-removal firm; **∼stück** *das* piece of furniture; **∼tischler** *der*, **∼tischlerin** *die* cabinetmaker; **∼wagen** *der* furniture van; removal van

mobil /moˈbiːl/ *Adj.* 1 (auch Milit.) mobile; (einsatzbereit) mobilized; **∼ machen** mobilize; rope in (coll.) ‹*person*› 2 (ugs.) (lebendig) lively; (rüstig) sprightly 3 (Rechtsw., Wirtsch.) movable ‹*property*›; floating ‹*capital*›

Mobil·box *die* mobile mailbox

Mobile /ˈmoːbilə/ *das*; **∼s**, **∼s** mobile

Mobil·funk *der* mobile telephony

Mobilfunk·netz *das* mobile phone network; cell *or* cellular phone network (esp. Amer.)

Mobiliar /mobiˈli̯aːɐ̯/ *das*; **∼s** furnishings *pl.*

Mobilisation /mobilizaˈt͜si̯oːn/ *die*; **∼**, **∼en** (Milit., Politik) mobilization

mobilisieren *tr. V.* 1 (Milit., fig.) mobilize; **die Massen ∼** (fig.) stir the masses into action 2 (aktivieren) activate ‹*circulation etc.*›; summon up ‹*energy etc.*› 3 (Wirtsch.) make ‹*capital*› available; realize ‹*capital*›

m

Mobilisierung *die;* ~, ~**en** 1 (Milit., fig.) mobilization 2 (Aktivierung) (des Kreislaufs) activation; (von Energie) summoning up 3 (Wirtsch.: von Kapital) realization

Mobilität /mobili'tɛːt/ *die;* ~ (Soziol.) mobility; **geistige** ~ (fig.) mental agility

Mobilmachung *die;* ~, ~**en** mobilization; **die allgemeine** ~ **ausrufen** order a general mobilization

Mobil·telefon *das* cellular phone

möbl. *Abk.* = **möbliert** furn.

möblieren *tr. V.* furnish; **ein möbliertes Zimmer** a furnished room; **möbliert wohnen** live in furnished accommodation; **ein möblierter Herr** (ugs. veralt.) a lodger

Möblierung *die;* ~, ~**en** 1 (das Möblieren) furnishing 2 (Einrichtung) furnishings and furniture (+ *Gen.* in)

Moçambique /mosam'biːk/ *(das);* ~**s** ▸**Mosambik**

Mocca /'mɔka/ ▸**Mokka**

mochte /'mɔxtə/ *1. u. 3. Pers. Sg. Prät. v.* **mögen**

möchte /'mœçtə/ *1. u. 3. Pers. Sg. Konjunktiv II v.* **mögen**

Möchte·gern-: ~**dichter**/~**casanova**/~**politiker** would-be poet/Casanova/politician

modal /mo'daːl/ *Adj.* (Sprachw.) modal

Modalität /modali'tɛːt/ *die;* ~, ~**en** 1 (geh.) (Bedingung) provision; condition; (Umstand) circumstance 2 (Sprachw., Philos.) modality

Modal-: ~**satz** *der* (Sprachw.) modal sentence/phrase; ~**verb** *das* (Sprachw.) modal verb

Modder /'mɔdɐ/ *der;* ~**s** (nordd. ugs.) mud

modd[e]rig /'mɔd(ə)rɪç/ *Adj.* (nordd. ugs.) muddy

Mode /'moːdə/ *die;* ~, ~**n** 1 fashion; **die** ~ **verlangt, dass ...** fashion dictates that ...; **jede** ~ **mitmachen** follow fashion's every whim; **mit der** ~ **gehen** follow the fashion; **etw. ist [in]** ~: sth. is in *or* the fashion; **[ganz] groß in** ~ *od.* **große** ~ **sein** be all the rage *or* very fashionable; **nach der neuesten** ~: in the latest style; **in** ~/**aus der** ~ **kommen** come into/go out of fashion; **neue** ~**n** (abwertend) newfangled ideas; **was sind denn das für neue** ~**n?** (ugs.) what do you think you're/does he think he's *etc.* doing? 2 *Pl.* (~kleidung) fashions

mode-, Mode-: ~**artikel** *der* 1 (modisches Zubehör) [fashion] accessory; 2 (viel gekaufter Artikel) fashionable novelty; in thing; ~**arzt** *der,* ~**ärztin** *die* (ugs.) fashionable doctor; ~**ausdruck** *der; Pl.* ~**ausdrücke** vogue word; 'in' expression (coll.); ~**beruf** *der* fashionable occupation; ~**bewusst**, *~**bewußt** **A** *Adj.* fashion-conscious; **B** *adv.* fashionably; ~**branche** *die* fashion *or* (Brit. coll.) rag trade; ~**designer** *der,* ~**designerin** *die* fashion designer; ~**droge** *die* fashion drug; ~**farbe** *die* fashionable colour; ~**geschäft** *das* fashion store; (kleiner) boutique; ~**haus** *das* 1 fashion house; 2 (Geschäft) fashion store; ~**journal** *das* fashion magazine; ~**krankheit** *die* fashionable disease *or* complaint

Modell /mo'dɛl/ *das;* ~**s**, ~**e** (auch fig.) model; (Technik: Entwurf) [design] model; pattern; (in Originalgröße) mock-up; **jmdm.** ~ **sitzen** *od.* **stehen** model *or* sit for sb.

Modell-: ~**bahn** *die* ▸**Modelleisenbahn**; ~**bauer** *der;* ~~**s**, ~~, ~**bauerin** *die;* ~~, ~~**nen** model-maker; ~**charakter** *der:* **etw. hat** ~**charakter** sth. can act as a model; **etw. hat** ~**character für etw.** sth. acts as *or* provides a model for sth.; ~**eisenbahn** *die* model railway

Modelleur /modɛ'løːɐ̯/ *der;* ~**s**, ~**e** modeller

Modell-: ~**fall** *der* 1 model; perfect example; 2 (klassisches Beispiel) textbook case; ~**flugzeug** *das* model aircraft

modellhaft *Adj.* exemplary; model *attrib.;* pilot ‹*scheme*›; **etw. hat** ~**en Charakter** sth. can act as a model

modellieren
A *tr. V.* 1 model, mould ‹*figures, objects*›; mould ‹*clay, wax*›; **jmdn./etw. in Ton** ~: model sb./sth. in clay; **etw. nach etw.** ~ (fig.) model sth. on sth. 2 (gestalten) design ‹*clothes*› 3 (Wissensch.) model ‹*processes*›
B *itr. V.* model (*esp. in clay or wax*)

Modellier·masse *die* modelling material (*esp. clay or wax*)

Modell-: ~**kleid** *das* model dress; ~**pflege** *die* (Kfz-W.) improving the specification; ~**projekt** *das* pilot scheme; ~**reihe** *die* (Wirtsch.) range [of models]; ~**versuch** *der* pilot scheme; ~**zeichnung** *die* drawing [of a model/mock-up]

modeln /'moːdl̩n/ *tr. V.* **etw. nach dem Vorbild von etw.** ~: model sth. on sth.

Modem /'moːdem/ *der od. das;* ~**s**, ~**s** (DV) modem

Mode·macher *der,* **Mode·macherin** *die* ▸**i** **S. 113** fashion designer

Moden-: ~**schau** *die* fashion show *or* parade; ~**zeit·schrift** *die* ▸**Modezeitschrift**

Mode-: ~**püppchen** *das,* ~**puppe** *die* fashion-crazy bird (Brit. sl.) *or* (Amer. coll.) dame

Moder /'moːdɐ/ *der;* ~**s** 1 mould; (~geruch) mustiness; (Verwesung, auch fig.) decay; **es riecht nach** ~: there is a musty smell 2 ▸**Modder**

moderat /mode'raːt/ *Adj.* moderate

Moderation /modera'tsi̯oːn/ *die;* ~, ~**en** (Rundf., Ferns.) presentation; **die** ~ **haben** be the presenter

Moderator /mode'raːtɔr/ *der;* ~**s**, ~**en** /-'toːrən/, **Moderatorin** *die;* ~, ~**nen** ▸**i** **S. 113** (Rundf., Ferns.) presenter

moderieren /mode'riːrən/
A *tr. V.* (Rundf., Ferns.) present ‹*programme*›
B *itr. V.* be the presenter

moderig *Adj.* musty

modern[1] /'moːdɐn/ *itr. V.;* auch mit *sein* go mouldy; (verwesen) decay; ~**de Gebeine** mouldering skeletons

modern[2] /mo'dɛrn/
A *Adj.* modern; (modisch) fashionable
B *adv.* in a modern manner *or* style; (modisch) fashionably; (aufgeschlossen) progressively; ~ **denken** have modern/progressive ideas; ~ **eingestellt** *od.* **denkend** with modern/progressive ideas *postpos., not pred.*

Moderne *die;* ~ 1 **die** ~, **das Zeitalter der** ~: the modern age; modern times 2 (Kunstrichtung) **die** ~: modern arts *pl.*; **typisch für die** ~: typical of modern writing/painting/music *etc.*

modernisieren
A *tr. V.* modernize; (modisch gestalten) bring ‹*clothes*› in line with the current fashion
B *itr. V.* introduce modern methods

Modernisierer *der;* ~**s**, ~, **Modernisiererin** *die;* ~, ~**nen** modernizer

Modernisierung *die;* ~, ~**en** modernization

Modernismus *der;* ~, **Modernismen** 1 modernism 2 (Stilelement) modernism; modernistic element

modernistisch (abwertend)
A *Adj.* modernistic
B *adv.* in a modernistic style *or* manner

Modernität *die;* ~: modernity

Mode-: ~**sache** *die:* in **[eine]** ~**sache sein** be a [passing] fashion; ~**salon** *der* [smart] fashion boutique; ~**schau** *die* ▸**Modenschau**; ~**schmuck** *der* costume jewellery; ~**schöpfer** *der* ▸**i** **S. 113** couturier; ~**schöpferin** *die* ▸**i** **S. 113** couturière; ~**schriftsteller** *der,* ~**schriftstellerin** *die* fashionable author; ~**tanz** *der* dance [briefly] in vogue; ~**torheit** *die* crazy fashion; ~**trend** *der* fashion trend; ~**wort** *das; Pl.* ~**wörter** vogue word; 'in' expression (coll.); ~**zar** *der,* ~**zarin** *die* (ugs.) fashion mogul; ~**zeichner** *der* (veralt.), ~**zeichnerin** *die* (veralt.) dress designer; ~**zeitschrift** *die* fashion magazine

Modi ▸**Modus**

Modifikation /modifika'tsi̯oːn/ *die;* ~, ~**en** modification

modifizierbar *Adj.* modifiable

modifizieren /modifi'tsiːrən/ *tr. V.* (geh.) modify

Modifizierung *die;* ~, ~**en** (geh.) modification

modisch /'moːdɪʃ/
A *Adj.* fashionable; trendy (coll. derog.)
B *adv.* fashionably; trendily (coll. derog.)

Modistin /mo'dɪstɪn/ *die;* ~, ~**nen** milliner

Modul[1] /'moːdʊl/ *der;* ~**s**, ~**n** (Math.) modulus

Modul[2] /mo'duːl/ *das;* ~**s**, ~**e** (DV, Elektronik) module

Modulation /modula'tsi̯oːn/ (auch Musik, Technik) *die;* ~, ~**en** modulation

modulieren *tr., itr. V.* (auch Musik, Technik) modulate

Modus /'mɔdʊs/ *der;* ~, **Modi** 1 (geh.) procedure (+ *Gen.* for); method; **nach diesem** ~: by this method 2 (Sprachw.) mood

Modus Vivendi /- vi'vɛndi/ *der;* ~ ~, **Modi Vivendi** (geh.) modus vivendi

Mofa /'moːfa/ *das;* ~**s**, ~**s** [low-powered] moped

Mofa·fahrer *der,* **Mofa·fahrerin** *die* moped rider

Mogelei *die;* ~, ~**en** (ugs.) cheating *no pl.*

mogeln (ugs.)
A *itr. V.* cheat; (lügen) fib; **beim Kartenspiel/bei der Klassenarbeit** ~: cheat at cards/in the class test
B *tr. V.* **etw. in etw.** (*Akk.*) ~: slip sth. into sth.
C *refl. V.* **sich in/zwischen etw.** (*Akk.*) ~ ‹*error*› slip into/in among sth.

Mogel·packung *die* (abwertend) deceptive packaging

mögen /'møːgn̩/
A *unr. Modalverb; 2. Part.* ~: 1 (wollen) want to; **das hätte ich sehen** ~: I would have liked to see that; **sie mochte nicht länger bleiben** she didn't want to stay any longer 2 (geh.: sollen) **das mag genügen** that should be *or* ought to be enough; **bitte ihn** *od.* **sag ihm, er möge kommen** (veralt.) ask/tell him to come 3 (geh.: Wunschform) **möge er bald kommen!** I do hope he'll come soon!; **möge es so bleiben** may it stay like that; **das möge der Himmel verhüten!** Heaven forbid! 4 (Vermutung, Möglichkeit) **sie mag/mochte vierzig sein** she must be/must have been [about] forty; **wie alt sie wohl sein mag?** I wonder how old she is; **Meier, Müller, Koch — und wie sie alle heißen** ~: Meier, Müller, Koch and [the rest,] whatever they're called; **wie viele Personen** ~ **das sein?** how many people would you say there are?; **was mag sie damit gemeint haben?** what can she have meant by that?; **[das] mag sein** maybe; **es mag sein, dass ...** it may be *or* it is possible that ... 5 (geh.: Einräumung) **er mag tun, was er will** no matter what he does; **es mag kommen, was will** come what may; **mag er nur warten** let him wait; he can wait; **wer er auch sein mag** whoever he may be; **wie dem auch sein mag** be that as it may; **mag das Wetter auch noch so schlecht sein, ...** however bad the weather may be, ...; *s. auch* **hingehen 4** 6 *Konjunktiv II + Inf.* (den Wunsch haben) **ich/sie möchte gern wissen ...** I would *or* should/she would like to know ...; **ich möchte ihn [gerne] sprechen** I should like to speak to him; **möchten Sie etwas essen/trinken?** would you like something to eat/drink?; **ich möchte nicht stören, aber ...** I don't want to interrupt, but ...; **ich möchte zu gerne wissen** I'd love to know ...; **ich möchte sagen, ...** (in zögernder Aussage) I'd say ...; **man möchte meinen, er sei der Chef** one would [really] think he was the boss
B *unr. tr. V.* **[gern]** ~: like; **sie mag keine Rosen** she does not like roses; **er mag mich nicht** he does not like me; **sie mag ihn sehr [gern]** she likes him very much; (hat ihn sehr gern) she is very fond of him; **sie** ~ **sich** they're fond of one another; **möchten Sie ein Glas Wein?** would you like a glass of wine?; **ich mag lieber/am liebsten Bier** I like beer better/best [of all]; **ich möchte lieber Tee** I would prefer tea *or* rather have tea; **ich möchte nicht, dass**

er heute kommt I would not like him to come today

C *unr. itr. V.* [1] (es wollen) like to; **ich mag nicht** I don't want to; **magst du?** do you want to?; (bei einem Angebot) would you like one/some?; **magst du noch?** do you want any more?; **ich möchte schon, aber ...** I should like to, but ... [2] (fahren, gehen usw. wollen) **ich möchte nach Hause/in die Stadt/auf die Schaukel** I want *or* I'd like to go home/into town/on the swing; **er möchte zu Herrn A** he would like to see Mr A

Mogler /ˈmoːglɐ/ *der;* **~s, ~, Moglerin** *die;* **~, ~nen** (ugs.) cheat

möglich /ˈmøːklɪç/ *Adj.* possible; **es war ihm nicht ~ [zu kommen]** he was unable [to come]; it was not possible for him [to come]; **sobald/so gut es mir ~ ist** as soon/as well as I can; **das ist schon eher ~:** that is more likely [to be possible]; **[jmdm.] etw. ~ machen** ‹*thing*› make sth. possible [for sb.]; ‹*person*› arrange sth. [for sb.]; **das** *od.* **alles Mögliche tun** do everything possible; do one's utmost; **dort kann man alles Mögliche kaufen** (ugs.) you can get all sorts of things there; **sie hatte alles Mögliche zu kritisieren** she criticized everything; **alle ~en Entschuldigungen** (ugs.) every excuse you can think of; **alle ~en Leute** (ugs.) all sorts of people; **das ist gut/leicht/durchaus ~:** that is very/wholly/entirely possible; **bei ihm ist alles ~:** he is capable of anything; **man sollte es nicht für ~ halten** one would not believe it possible; **[das ist doch] nicht ~!** impossible!; I don't believe it!; **ist das ~!** [that's] incredible!; whatever next!

möglicherweise *Adv.* possibly; **~ hat er Glück/Glück gehabt** he may be/may have been lucky; **wir werden ~ versetzt** we may [possibly] be transferred; **~ hast du es nur geträumt** it's possible that you just dreamt it

Möglichkeit *die;* **~, ~en** [1] (möglicher Weg) possibility; (Methode) way; **nach ~:** if possible [2] (Möglichsein) possibility; **es besteht die ~, dass ...** there is a chance *or* possibility that ...; **es besteht die ~, eine Zusatzversicherung abzuschließen** it is possible to arrange additional insurance; **ist es die** *od.* **ist [denn] das die ~!** (ugs.) well, I'll be damned! (coll.); whatever next! [3] (Gelegenheit) opportunity; chance; **die ~ haben, etw. zu tun** have an opportunity of doing sth. *or* to do sth. [4] *Pl.* (Mittel) [*esp.* financial] means *or* resources; **künstlerische ~en** artistic resources *or* potential *sing.*

Möglichkeits·form *die* (Sprachw.) subjunctive

möglichst

A *Adv.* [1] (so weit wie möglich) as much *or* far as possible; **sich ~ zurückhalten** restrain oneself as far as possible [2] (wenn möglich) if [at all] possible; **macht ~ keinen Lärm** don't make any noise if you can possibly help it [3] (so ... wie möglich) **~ groß/schnell/oft** as big/fast/often as possible; **mit ~ großer Sorgfalt** with the greatest possible care

B *adj. in* **sein Möglichstes tun** do one's utmost; do everything possible

Mogul /ˈmoːgʊl/ *der;* **~s, ~n** (hist.) Mogul

Mohair /moˈhɛːɐ̯/ *der;* **~s** mohair

Mohammed /ˈmoːhamɛt/ (*der*) Muhammad

Mohammedaner *der;* **~s, ~, Mohammedanerin,** *die;* **~, ~nen** Muslim; Muhammadan

mohammedanisch

A *Adj.* Muslim, Muhammadan

B *adv.* **~ geprägt** imbued with Muslim *or* Muhammadan characteristics *postpos.*

Mohikaner /mohiˈkaːnɐ/ *der;* **~s, ~, Mohikanerin** *die;* **~, ~nen** Mohican; **der letzte Mohikaner, der Letzte der Mohikaner** (ugs. scherzh.) the last one; the last survivor (joc.)

Mohn /moːn/ *der;* **~s** [1] (Pflanze) poppy [2] (Samen) poppy seed; (auf Brot, Kuchen) poppy seeds *pl.*

Mohn-: ~blume *die* poppy; **~brötchen** *das* poppy-seed roll; **~feld** *das* field of poppies; **~kuchen** *der* poppy-seed cake

Mohr /moːɐ̯/ *der;* **~en, ~en** (veralt.) Moor; **schwarz wie ein ~:** as black as the ace of spades; **der ~ hat seine Schuldigkeit getan, der ~ kann gehen** (fig.) when one has served one's purpose one is simply discarded

Möhre /ˈmøːrə/ *die;* **~, ~n** carrot

Mohren·kopf *der* [1] chocolate marshmallow [2] (Gebäck) *small cream-filled spherical sponge cake covered with chocolate*

Möhren·saft *der* carrot juice

Mohren·wäsche *die* [attempt at] whitewashing (fig.)

Mohrin *die;* **~, ~nen** ▸ **Mohr**

Mohr·rübe *die* carrot

Moiré /mo̯aˈreː/ *der;* **~s, ~s** moiré

mokant /moˈkant/ (geh.)

A *Adj.* mocking

B *adv.* mockingly

Mokassin /mokaˈsiːn/ *der;* **~s, ~s** moccasin

Mokick /ˈmoːkɪk/ *das;* **~s, ~s** light motorcycle (*with kick-starter*)

mokieren /moˈkiːrən/ *refl. V.* (geh.) **sich über etw.** (*Akk.*) **~:** mock *or* scoff at sth.; **sich über jmdn. ~:** mock sb.

Mokka /ˈmɔka/ *der;* **~s** [1] (Bohnen) mocha [coffee] [2] (Getränk) strong black coffee

Mokka-: ~löffel *der* [small] coffee spoon; **~tasse** *die* small coffee cup

Mol /moːl/ *das;* **~s, ~e** (Chemie) mole

Molar /moˈlaːɐ̯/ *der;* **~s, ~en, Molar·zahn** *der* molar

Molch /mɔlç/ *der;* **~[e]s, ~e** newt

Moldau¹ /ˈmɔldau̯/ *die;* **~:** [river] Vltava

Moldau² *die;* **~** (Sowjetrepublik) Moldavia

Mole /ˈmoːlə/ *die;* **~, ~n** [harbour] mole

Molekül /moleˈkyːl/ *das;* **~s, ~e** (Chemie) molecule

molekular /molekuˈlaːɐ̯/ *Adj.* molecular

Molekular-: molecular

Molesten /moˈlɛstn̩/ *Pl.* (veralt.) minor ailments

molk /mɔlk/ *1. u. 3. Pers. Sg. Prät. v.* **melken**

Molke *die;* **~:** whey

Molkerei *die;* **~, ~en** dairy

Molkerei-: ~butter *die* dairy butter; **~genossenschaft** *die* cooperative dairy; **~produkt** *das* dairy product

Moll /mɔl/ *das;* **~** (Musik) minor [key]; **in ~ enden** finish in a minor key

Moll-: ~akkord *der* (Musik) minor chord; **~drei·klang** *der* minor triad

Molle *die;* **~, ~n** (berlin.) [glass of] beer; **eine ~ zischen** have a jar (coll.)

Mollen·friedhof *der* (berlin. scherzh.) beer belly (coll.)

Molli /ˈmɔli/ *der;* **~s, ~s** (salopp) Molotov cocktail

mollig /ˈmɔlɪç/

A *Adj.* [1] (rundlich) plump [2] (warm) cosy; snug; **ein ~er Wintermantel** a warm and cosy winter coat

B *adv.* cosily; snugly; **~ warm** warm and cosy

Moll-: ~ton·art *die* (Musik) minor key; **~ton·leiter** *die* (Musik) minor scale

Molluske /mɔˈlʊskə/ *die;* **~, ~n** (Biol.) mollusc

Moloch /ˈmoːlɔx/ *der;* **~s, ~e** (geh.) Moloch; voracious giant

Molotow·cocktail /ˈmɔlotɔf-/ *der* Molotov cocktail

Molybdän /molʏpˈdɛːn/ *das;* **~s** (Chemie) molybdenum

Moment¹ /moˈmɛnt/ *der;* **~[e]s, ~e** moment; **einen ~ zögern** hesitate [for] a moment; **einen ~ bitte!** just a moment, please!; **~ [mal]!** [hey!] just a moment!; wait a mo! (coll.); **im nächsten/gleichen ~:** the next/at the same moment; **jeden ~** (ugs.) [at] any moment; **im ~:** at the moment; *s. auch* **licht 1**

Moment² *das;* **~[e]s, ~e** [1] (Umstand) factor, element (**für** in); **das auslösende ~ für etw. sein** be the trigger for sth. [2] (Physik) moment

momentan /momɛnˈtaːn/

A *Adj.* [1] present; current [2] (vorübergehend) temporary; (flüchtig) momentary; **eine ~e Besserung** a short-lived improvement

B *adv.* [1] at the moment; at present [2] (vorübergehend) temporarily; (flüchtig) momentarily; for a moment

Moment·aufnahme *die* (Fot.) snapshot

Monaco /ˈmoːnako/ (*das*); **~s** Monaco

Monade /moˈnaːdə/ *die;* **~, ~n** (Philos.) monad

Monarch /moˈnarç/ *der;* **~en, ~en** monarch

Monarchie *die;* **~, ~n** monarchy

Monarchin *die;* **~, ~nen** monarch

monarchisch

A *Adj.* monarchical

B *adv.* monarchically; **~ regiert** ruled by a monarch/monarchs

Monarchismus *der;* **~:** monarchism *no art.*

Monarchist *der;* **~en, ~en, Monarchistin** *die;* **~, ~nen** monarchist

monarchistisch

A *Adj.* monarchist ‹*party, group*›; monarchistic ‹*tendency, views*›

B *adv.* monarchistically

Monat /ˈmoːnat/ *der;* **~s, ~e** ▸ⓘ **S. 165** month; **letzten ~:** last month; **im ~ April** in the month of April; **am 10. dieses ~s** on the tenth [of this month]; **Ihr Schreiben vom 22. dieses ~s** your letter of the 22nd [inst.]; **sie ist im vierten ~ [schwanger]** she is four months pregnant; **er war drei ~e [lang] hier** he was here for three months; **er ist seit drei ~en hier** he has been here for three months; **was verdienst du im ~?** how much do you earn per month?; **ich bezahle 250 Euro im ~:** I pay 250 euros a month *or* per month; *s. auch* **hinaus**

monatelang

A *Adj.* lasting for months *postpos., not pred.;* **die ~en Verhandlungen** the negotiations, which lasted for several months; **nach ~er Krankheit** after months of illness; **mit ~er Verspätung** months late

B *adv.* for months [on end]

-monatig [1] (... Monate alt) ...-month-old; **ein achtmonatiges Kind** an eight-month-old baby [2] (... Monate dauernd) ... month's/months'; ...-month; **eine viermonatige Kur** a four-month course of treatment; **mit dreimonatiger Verspätung** three months late

monatlich

A *Adj.* monthly

B *adv.* monthly; every month; (im Monat) per month; **etw. ~ überweisen** pay sth. monthly; **sich ~ treffen** meet every month

-monatlich

A *Adj.* ...-monthly; **acht~/drei~:** eight-monthly/three-monthly

B *adv.* every ... months

Monats-: ~abrechnung *die* monthly accounts *pl.;* (Abrechnungsblatt) monthly [statement of] account; **~anfang** *der,* **~beginn** *der* beginning of the month; **zu/am ~anfang** *od.* **~beginn** at the beginning of the month; **~beitrag** *der* monthly subscription; **~binde** *die* sanitary towel (Brit.); sanitary napkin (Amer.); **~blutung** *die* [monthly] period; **~einkommen** *das* monthly income; **~ende** *das* end of the month; **~erste** *der; adj. Dekl.* first [day] of the month; **~frist** *die:* **in** *od.* **innerhalb** *od.* **binnen ~frist** within [a period of] a *or* one month; **nach ~frist** after [a period of] a *or* one month; **vor ~frist** in less than a month; within [a period of] a *or* one month; (vor einem Monat) a month ago; **~gehalt** *das* month's salary; **vier ~gehälter** four months' salary *sing.;* **ein dreizehntes ~gehalt** an extra month's salary; **ein ~gehalt von 3 000 Euro** a monthly salary of 3,000 euros; **~hälfte** *die* half of the month; **~karte** *die* monthly season ticket; **~letzte** *der; adj. Dekl.* last day of the month; **~lohn** *der* month's wages; **vier ~löhne** four months' wages *pl.;* **ein ~lohn von 2 000 Euro** a monthly wage of 2,000 euros; **~miete** *die* month's rent; **zwei ~mieten** two months' rent; **eine ~miete von 1 000 Euro** a monthly rent of 1,000 euros; **~mitte** *die* middle of the month; **~rate** *die* monthly instalment; **~wechsel** *der* (veralt.) monthly allowance (*esp. for a student*)

monat[s]weise *Adv.* by the month

Mönch /mœnç/ *der;* **~[e]s, ~e** monk

mönchisch *Adj.* monkish; of a monk *postpos., not pred.*

Mönchs-: ~kloster *das* monastery; **~kutte** *die* monk's habit *or* cowl; **~latein** *das* monkish Latin; dog Latin (derog.); **~leben** *das* monastic life; life of a monk; **~orden** *der* monastic order

Mönch[s]tum *das;* **~s** [1] monasticism [2] (das Mönchsein) monkhood

Mönchs·zelle *die* monk's cell

Mond /mo:nt/ *der;* **~[e]s, ~e** [1] moon; **den ~ anbellen** (fig. ugs.) talk to a brick wall; **ich könnte** *od.* **möchte ihn auf den** *od.* **zum ~ schießen** (salopp) I wish he'd get lost (coll.); **auf** *od.* **hinter dem ~ leben** (fig. ugs.) be a bit behind the times *or* not quite with it (coll.); **lebst du auf dem ~?** (ugs.) where have you been?; **wir leben auch nicht hinter dem ~** (ugs.) we're not fuddy-duddies (sl.); we do have some idea of what's going on; **in den ~ gucken** (fig. ugs.) be left empty-handed *or* (coll.) out in the cold; **etw. in den ~ schreiben** (ugs.) write sth. off; **nach dem ~ gehen** (ugs.) ‹*clock, watch*› be hopelessly wrong [2] (dichter. veralt.) month; **viele ~e waren ins Land gegangen** many moons had passed

Mondamin Ⓦᶻ /mɔnda'mi:n/ *das;* **~s** (*a proprietary brand of*) cornflour

mondän /mɔn'dɛ:n/

[A] *Adj.* [highly] fashionable; smart; **die ~e Welt** the smart set

[B] *adv.* fashionably; in a fashionable style

mond-, Mond-: ~aufgang *der* moonrise; **~auto** *das* (Raumf.) moon buggy; **~bahn** *die* orbit of a satellite; (des Erdmondes) lunar orbit; **~beschienen** *Adj.* moonlit

Monden·schein *der* (dichter.) moonlight

Mondes·finsternis *die* (österr.) ▸ **Mondfinsternis**

mond-, Mond-: ~fähre *die* (Raumf.) lunar module; **~finsternis** *die* (Astron.) lunar eclipse; eclipse of the moon; **~flug** *der* lunar expedition; **~gebirge** *das* lunar mountain range *or* mountains *pl.*; **~gesicht** *das* moon face; **~gestein** *das* moon rock; **~hell** *Adj.* (geh.) moonlit; **~jahr** *das* lunar year; **~kalb** *das* (salopp) dimwit (coll.); dope (coll.); **~krater** *der* lunar crater; **~lande·fähre** *die* (Raumf.) lunar module; **~landschaft** *die* (auch fig.) lunar landscape; **~landung** *die* moon landing; **~licht** *das* moonlight; **~los** *Adj.* moonless; **~oberfläche** *die* lunar surface; **~phase** *die* moon's phase; **~preis** *der* (Wirtsch. Jargon) artificially high price (*from which the actual asking price is 'reduced'*); (Wucherpreis) exorbitant price; **~rakete** *die* moon rocket; **~schein** *der* moonlight; **der kann mir mal im ~schein begegnen** (salopp) he can get lost (coll.); **~sichel** *die* crescent moon; **~sonde** *die* lunar probe; **~stein** *der* moonstone; **~süchtig** *Adj.* sleepwalking *attrib.* (esp. by moonlight); **~süchtig sein** be a sleepwalker; **~süchtigkeit** *die;* **~~:** sleepwalking (esp. by moonlight); **~umkreisung** *die* orbiting of the moon; **~umlaufbahn** *die* lunar orbit; **~untergang** *der* moonset; **~wechsel** *der* change of the moon

Monegasse /mone'gasə/ *der;* **~n, ~n, Monegassin** *die;* **~, ~nen** Monégasque

monegassisch *Adj.* Monégasque

monetär /mone'tɛ:ɐ̯/

[A] *Adj.* monetary

[B] *adv.* on a monetary basis

Monetarismus /moneta'rɪsmʊs/ *der;* **~** (Wirtsch.) monetarism *no art.*

Moneten /mo'ne:tn̩/ *Pl.* (ugs.) cash *sing.*; dough *sing.* (coll.)

Mongole /mɔŋ'go:lə/ *der;* **~n, ~n** [1] Mongol [2] (Bewohner der Mongolei) Mongolian

Mongolei /mɔŋgo'lai/ *die;* **~:** Mongolia; **in der Inneren/Äußeren ~:** in Inner/Outer Mongolia

Mongolen-: ~falte *die* (Anthrop.) Mongolian fold; **~fleck** *der* (Anthrop.) Mongolian spot

mongolid /mɔŋgo'li:t/ *Adj.* (Anthrop.) Mongoloid

Mongolide *der/die; adj. Dekl.* (Anthrop.) Mongoloid

Mongolin *die;* **~, ~nen** [1] Mongol [2] (Bewohnerin der Mongolei) Mongolian

mongolisch *Adj.* ▸ⓘ **S. 670** Mongolian

Mongolismus *der;* **~** ▸ⓘ **S. 439** (Med.) mongolism *no art.*

mongoloid *Adj.* (Med.) mongoloid

Mongoloide *der/die; adj. Dekl.* (Med.) Mongoloid

monieren /mo'ni:rən/ *tr. V.* criticize; (beanstanden) find fault with

Monismus /mo'nɪsmʊs/ *der;* **~** (Philos.) monism *no art.*

Monitor /'mo:nitɔr/ *der;* **~s, ~en** /-'to:rən/ (Ferns., Technik, Physik) monitor

mono /'mo:no/ *Adv.* (ugs.) ‹*hear, play, etc.*› in mono (coll.)

mono-, Mono-: mono-

monochrom /mono'kro:m/ *Adj.* (Malerei, Fot.) monochrome; monochromatic ‹*light*›

monocolor /monoko'lo:ɐ̯/ *Adj.* (österr. Politik) one-party

monogam /mono'ga:m/

[A] *Adj.* monogamous

[B] *adv.* monogamously

Monogamie *die;* **~:** monogamy

Mono·gramm *das;* **~s, ~e** monogram

Monographie /monogra'fi:/ *die;* **~, ~n** monograph

Monokel /mo'nɔkl̩/ *das;* **~s, ~:** monocle

Mono·kultur *die* (Landw.) monoculture

Monolith /mono'li:t/ *der;* **~s** *od.* **~en, ~en** monolith

Monolog /mono'lo:k/ *der;* **~s, ~e** monologue; **einen ~ halten** hold a monologue

monologisch

[A] *Adj.* monologic[al]; ‹*form*› of a monologue; ‹*statement*› in the form of a monologue

[B] *adv.* in monologue

monologisieren *itr. V.* talk in monologue

monoman /mono'ma:n/ (Psych.)

[A] *Adj.* monomaniacal

[B] *adv.* monomaniacally

Monomanie /monoma'ni:/ *die;* **~, ~n** (Psych.) monomania

Monophthong /mono'ftɔŋ/ *der;* **~s, ~e** (Sprachw.) monophthong

Monopol /mono'po:l/ *das;* **~s, ~e** monopoly (**auf** + *Akk.*, **für** in, of)

monopolisieren *tr. V.* monopolize

Monopolisierung *die;* **~, ~en** monopolization

Monopolist *der;* **~en, ~en, Monopolistin** *die;* **~, ~nen** monopolist

monopol-, Monopol-: ~kapital *das* monopoly capital; **~kapitalismus** *der* monopoly capitalism; **~kapitalistisch** [A] *Adj.* monopoly capitalist; [B] *adv.* ‹*structured, organized*› on the principles of monopoly capitalism; **~stellung** *die* [position of] monopoly

Monopoly Ⓦᶻ /mo'no:poli/ *das;* **~:** Monopoly ® (game)

Monotheismus /monote'ɪsmʊs/ *der;* **~** (Rel.) monotheism

monotheistisch (Rel.)

[A] *Adj.* monotheistic

[B] *adv.* monotheistically

monoton /mono'to:n/

[A] *Adj.* monotonous

[B] *adv.* monotonously

Monotonie *die;* **~, ~n** monotony

Monotype Ⓦᶻ /'mɔnotaip/ *die;* **~, ~s** (Druckw.) Monotype ® [composing machine]

Mon·oxid, Mon·oxyd *das* (Chemie) monoxide

Mono·zelle *die* (Elektrot.) [single-cell] battery

Monster /'mɔnstɐ/ *das;* **~s, ~:** monster; (hässlich) [hideous] brute

Monster- mammoth; (sehr lange dauernd) marathon

Monster-: ~film *der* [1] (ugs.) mammoth [screen] epic; blockbuster (sl.); [2] (Film mit ~n) horror film [with a monster/monsters]; **~prozess, *~prozeß** *der* marathon trial; **~veranstaltung** *die* giant spectacular; (sehr lange dauernd) marathon [event]

Monstranz /mɔn'strants/ *die;* **~, ~en** (kath. Kirche) monstrance

Monstren ▸ **Monstrum**

monströs /mɔn'strø:s/ (geh.)

[A] *Adj.* [1] (auch fig.) monstrous; [huge and] hideous [2] (gigantisch) massive, overpowering ‹*building, monument*›

[B] *adv.* monstrously

Monstrosität /mɔnstrozi'tɛ:t/ *die;* **~, ~en** monstrosity; (fig.: monströse Tat) monstrous action; atrocity

Monstrum /'mɔnstrʊm/ *das;* **~s, Monstren** [1] (auch fig.: Mensch) monster [2] (Ungetüm) hulking great thing (coll.); **das/ein ~ von ...** the/a giant [of a] ...

Monsun /mɔn'zu:n/ *der;* **~s, ~e** (Geogr.) monsoon

Monsun-: ~regen *der* (Geog.) monsoon rains *pl.*; **~wald** *der* (Geog.) monsoon forest

Montag /'mo:nta:k/ *der* ▸ⓘ **S. 165**, ▸ⓘ **S. 816** Monday; *s. auch* **blau**; **Dienstag**; **Dienstag-**

Montag- Monday; *s. auch* **Dienstag-**

Montage /mɔn'ta:ʒə/ *die;* **~, ~n** [1] (Bauw., Technik) (Zusammenbau) assembly; (Einbau) installation; (Aufstellen) erection; (Anbringen) fitting (**an** + *Akk. od. Dat.* to); mounting (**auf** + *Akk. od. Dat.* on); **auf ~** (ugs.) away on a job [2] (Film, bild. Kunst, Literaturw.) montage [3] (Druckw.) make-up

Montage-: ~band *das; Pl.* **~bänder** assembly line; **~halle** *die* assembly shop

montags *Adv.* ▸ⓘ **S. 816** on Monday[s]; *s. auch* **dienstags**

Montags·wagen *der* (ugs.) Friday car

Montan-: ~industrie *die* coal and steel industry; **~union** *die* European Coal and Steel Community

Monteur /mɔn'tø:ɐ̯/ *der;* **~s, ~e** ▸ⓘ **S. 113** mechanic; (Installateur) fitter; (Elektro~) electrician

Monteur·anzug *der* [mechanic's] overalls *pl.*

Monteurin *die;* **~, ~nen** ▸ⓘ **S. 113** ▸ **Monteur**

montieren /mɔn'ti:rən/ *tr. V.* [1] (zusammenbauen) assemble (**aus** from); erect ‹*building*› [2] (anbringen) fit (**an** + *Akk. od. Dat.* to; **auf** + *Akk. od. Dat.* on); (einbauen) install (**in** + *Akk.* in); (befestigen) fix (**an** + *Akk. od. Dat.* to); **eine Lampe an die** *od.* **der Decke ~:** put up *or* fix a light on the ceiling; **eine Antenne auf das** *od.* **dem Dach ~:** put up *or* mount an aerial on the roof [3] (Film, bild. Kunst) put together; (Druckw.) make up

Montierer *der;* **~s, ~, Montiererin** *die;* **~, ~nen** assembly worker

Montur /mɔn'tu:ɐ̯/ *die;* **~, ~en** [1] (ugs.) outfit (coll.); gear *no pl.* (coll.) [2] (veralt.: Uniform) uniform

Monument /monu'mɛnt/ *das;* **~[e]s, ~e** (auch fig.) monument

monumental

[A] *Adj.* (auch fig.) monumental; (massiv) massive

[B] *adv.* in a monumental style; (überdimensional) on a monumental scale

Monumental-: monumental

Moor /mo:ɐ̯/ *das;* **~[e]s, ~e** bog; (Bruch) marsh; (Flach~) fen; (Hoch~) high moor

Moor-: ~bad *das* mudbath; **~boden** *der* bog soil; (Torfboden) peaty soil

moorig *Adj.* boggy

Moor-: ~kultur *die* bogland/fenland [reclamation and] cultivation; **~leiche** *die* [well-preserved] body found in a bog

Moos /mo:s/ *das;* **~es, ~e** [1] moss; **~ ansetzen** gather moss; (fig. ugs.) become old hat (coll.)

2 (salopp) cash; dough (coll.) **3** *Pl. auch:* **Möser** (südd., österr., schweiz.) bog; (Bruch) marsh

moos-: **~bedeckt**, **~bewachsen** *Adj.* moss-covered; **~grün** *Adj.* moss-green

moosig *Adj.* **1** mossy; (moosbedeckt) moss-covered **2** (südd., österr., schweiz.: sumpfig) marshy

Moos-: **~rose** *die,* **~röschen** *das* moss rose

***Mop** ▸**Mopp**

Moped /'mo:pɛt/ *das;* **~s, ~s** moped

Moped·fahrer *der,* **Moped·fahrerin** *die* moped rider

Mopp /mɔp/ *der;* **~s, ~s** mop

Moppel /'mɔpl̩/ *der;* **~s, ~** (fam. scherzh.) podge (coll.)

moppen /'mɔpn̩/ *tr., itr. V.* mop; mop the floor in ‹room›

Mops /mɔps/ *der;* **~es, Möpse** /'mœpsə/ **1** (Hund) pug [dog] **2** (salopp: dicke Person) podge (coll.); fatty (derog.) **3** *Pl.* (salopp: Geld) bread (sl.); lolly (Brit. coll.); **die paar Möpse** such a piffling sum (coll.); such peanuts (sl.) **4** *Pl.* (derb: Busen) knockers (sl.); tits (coarse)

mopsen
A *tr. V.* (fam.) pinch (coll.)
B *refl. V.* (ugs.) be bored

mops·fidel *Adj.* (ugs.) very jolly *or* cheerful

mopsig *Adj.* (ugs.) **1** podgy; tubby **2** **sich ~ machen, ~ werden** get fresh

Moral /mo'ra:l/ *die;* **~** **1** (Norm) morality; **gegen die ~ verstoßen** offend against morality *or* the code of conduct; **die herrschende ~:** [currently] accepted standards *pl.* **2** (Sittlichkeit) morals *pl.*; **keine ~ haben** have no sense of morals; **[eine] doppelte ~:** double standards *pl.*; **[jmdm.] ~ predigen** (abwertend) moralize [to sb.] **3** (Selbstvertrauen) morale; **die ~ ist gut/schlecht** morale is high/low **4** (Lehre) moral **5** (Philos.) ethics *sing.*

Moral-: **~apostel** *der* (abwertend) upholder of moral standards; **~begriff** *der* [personal] moral code; sense of morals

Moralin *das;* **~s** (abwertend, scherzh.) [hypocritical] moral indignation; (rechthaberisch) [priggish] self-righteousness

moralin·sauer (abwertend, scherzh.)
A *Adj.* [priggishly] indignant; (rechthaberisch) [priggishly] self-righteous; holier-than-thou (coll.)
B *adv.* with [priggish] indignation

moralisch /mo'ra:lɪʃ/
A *Adj.* **1** moral; **das war [für ihn] eine ~e Ohrfeige** that was a slap in the face [for him]; **[s]einen Moralischen haben** (ugs.) (Gewissensbisse haben) have a fit of remorse; (niedergeschlagen sein) be down in the dumps (coll.) (*as the result of a failure*) **2** (sittlich einwandfrei) moral; morally upright; (tugendhaft) virtuous **3** (diszipliniert) **eine gute ~e Verfassung** good morale; **~er Zusammenbruch** breakdown of *or* in morale
B *adv.* **1** morally; **ein ~ hoch stehender Mensch** a person of unimpeachable morals *or* high moral standing **2** (tugendhaft) morally; virtuously; **jmdm. ~ kommen** (ugs.) adopt a high moral tone with sb.

moralisieren *itr. V.* (geh.) moralize

Moralismus *der;* **~** **1** (Moralität) sense of morality **2** (abwertend: das Moralisieren) moralizing

Moralist *der;* **~en, ~en, Moralistin** *die;* **~, ~nen** moralist

moralistisch
A *Adj.* moralistic
B *adv.* moralistically; from a moralistic viewpoint

Moralität *die;* **~, ~en** **1** (geh.) morality **2** (Literaturw.) morality [play]

Moral-: **~kodex** *der* moral code; **~philosophie** *die* moral philosophy; **~prediger** *der,* **~predigerin** *die* (abwertend) moralizing prig; **~predigt** *die* (abwertend) [moralizing] lecture; homily; **[jmdm.] eine ~predigt halten** deliver a homily [to sb.]; **~theologie** *die* moral theology *no art.*; **~vorstellung** *die* ideas *pl.* on *or* attitude to morality

Moräne /mo'rɛ:nə/ *die;* **~, ~n** (Geol.) moraine

Morast /mo'rast/ *der;* **~[e]s, ~e** *od.* **Moräste** /mo'rɛstə/ **1** bog; swamp **2** (Schlamm) mud; (auch fig.) mire; **im ~ versinken** sink into the mire

morastig *Adj.* muddy

Moratorium /mora'to:ri̯ʊm/ *das;* **~s, Moratorien** (Wirtsch., Politik) moratorium (**für** on)

morbid /mɔr'bi:t/ *Adj.* (geh.) (kränklich) sickly; (todgeweiht) deathly pale; (fig.) moribund, degenerate ‹*society, institution, etc.*›

Morbidität /mɔrbidi'tɛ:t/ *die;* **~** **1** (geh.) sickliness; (fig.) moribund *or* degenerate state **2** (Med.) morbidity

Morchel /'mɔrçl̩/ *die;* **~, ~n** morel

Mord /mɔrt/ *der;* **~[e]s, ~e** murder (**an** + *Dat.* of); (durch ein Attentat) assassination; **einen ~ begehen** commit murder; **einen ~ an jmdm. begehen** murder sb.; **ein versuchter ~:** an attempted murder; **wegen ~es angeklagt/verurteilt** accused of *or* charged with murder/condemned for murder; (in Schlagzeilen) **~ aus Eifersucht** jealousy killing; **~ an Außenminister** foreign minister murdered/assassinated; **dann gibt es ~ und Totschlag** (fig. ugs.) all hell is/will be let loose; **das ist [glatter** *od.* **der reinste] ~** (fig. ugs.) it's sheer murder; (unverantwortlich) it's sheer lunacy

Mord-: **~anklage** *die* charge of murder; **unter ~anklage stehen** be charged with murder; **~anschlag** *der* attempted murder (**auf** + *Akk.* of); (Attentat) assassination attempt (**auf** + *Akk.* on); **einen ~anschlag auf jmdn. verüben** make an attempt on sb.'s life; **einem ~anschlag zum Opfer fallen** be murdered/assassinated; **~brenner** *der,* **~brennerin** *die;* **~~, ~~nen** murdering fire-raiser; **~bube** *der* (veralt.) murdering thug; **~drohung** *die* murder threat

morden *tr., itr. V.* murder; **das sinnlose Morden** the senseless killing

Mörder /'mœrdɐ/ *der;* **~s, ~:** murderer (esp. Law); killer; (politischer ~) assassin; **vierfacher ~ sein** have committed four murders

Mörder-: **~bande** *die* gang of murderers *or* killers; **~grube** *die* ▸**Herz 2**; **~hand** *in* **durch** *od.* **von ~hand sterben** (geh.) die at the hand of a murderer

Mörderin *die;* **~, ~nen** murderer; murderess; (politische ~) assassin

mörderisch
A *Adj.* **1** (ugs.: furchtbar, mächtig) murderous; fiendish ‹*cold*›; dreadful (coll.) ‹*crowd, clamour, weather, storm*›; cutthroat ‹*competition*› **2** (todbringend) murderous
B *adv.* **1** (ugs.) dreadfully (coll.); frightfully (coll.); **~ fluchen/toben** curse/rage like blazes (sl.) **2** (todbringend) murderously

mord-, Mord-: **~fall** *der* murder case; **der ~fall Dr. Crippen** [the case of] the Dr Crippen murders; **~gierig** *Adj.* intent on murder *postpos.*; (blutgierig) bloodthirsty; **~instrument** *das* **1** murder weapon; **2** (fig. scherzh.) murderous[-looking] weapon or device

Mordio /'mɔrdi̯o/ ▸**Zeter**

Mord-: **~kommission** *die* murder *or* (Amer.) homicide squad; **~prozess**, ***~prozeß** *der* murder trial; **~sache** *die* murder case; **die ~sache Müller** the Müller murder [case]

mords-, Mords- (ugs.) terrific (coll.); tremendous (coll.)

mords-, Mords-: **~arbeit** *die* (ugs.) **eine ~arbeit** a hell of a job (coll.); **sich** (*Dat.*) **eine ~arbeit machen** take a tremendous amount of trouble (coll.) (**mit** over); **~ding** *das; Pl.* **~~er** (ugs.) whopper (coll.); **~dusel** *der* (ugs.) ▸**~glück**; **~gaudi** *die* (bayr., österr. ugs.) ▸**~spaß**; **~geschrei** *das* (ugs.) terrific hubbub (coll.); (Lärm) frightful racket (coll.); (furchtbares Theater) terrible fuss (coll.) (**um** over); **~glück** *das* (ugs.) **ein ~glück** incredible luck (coll.); **ein ~glück haben** be incredibly lucky (coll.); **~hunger** *der* (ugs.) terrific hunger (coll.); **einen ~hunger haben** be ravenous *or* famished; **~kerl** *der* (ugs.) **1** (Riese) enormous bloke (Brit. coll.); huge guy (coll.); **2** (tüchtiger Kerl) really good sort (coll.); great guy (Amer.); (Kamerad) real pal (coll.); **~krach** *der* (ugs.) **1** terrible din *or* racket (coll.); **2** (Streit) terrific row (coll.); **~mäßig** (ugs.) **A** *Adj.* terrific (coll.); tremendous (coll.); (entsetzlich) terrible (coll.); infernal (coll.) ‹*din, racket*›; **~mäßiges Glück** incredible luck (coll.); **B** *adv.* tremendously (coll.); incredibly (coll.); (entsetzlich) terribly (coll.); **~schreck** *der,* **~schrecken** *der* (ugs.) hell of a fright (coll.); terrible fright (coll.); **~spaß** *der* (ugs.) **ein ~spaß** tremendous fun (coll.); **einen ~spaß haben** have a whale of a time (coll.); **~stimmung** *die* (ugs.) terrific atmosphere (coll.); **~wut** *die* (ugs.) towering rage; **eine ~wut [im Bauch] haben** be fuming with rage

Mord-: **~tat** *die* (geh.) murder; **~verdacht** *der* suspicion of murder; **~versuch** *der* attempted murder; (Attentat) assassination attempt; **~waffe** *die* murder weapon

Mores /'mo:re:s/ *Pl. in* **jmdn. ~ lehren** (ugs.) tell sb. what's what *or* where he/she gets off (coll.); **dich werde ich ~ lehren!** I'll give you a piece of my mind!

morganatisch /mɔrga'na:tɪʃ/ *Adj. in* **~e Ehe** (hist.) morganatic marriage

morgen /'mɔrgn̩/ *Adv.* ▸**❶ S. 816** tomorrow; **~ früh/Mittag/Abend** tomorrow morning/lunchtime/evening; **~ in einer Woche/in vierzehn Tagen** tomorrow week/fortnight; a week/fortnight tomorrow; **~ um diese** *od.* **die gleiche Zeit** this time tomorrow; **bis ~!** until tomorrow!; see you tomorrow!; **~ ist auch [noch] ein Tag** tomorrow is another day; **~, ~, nur nicht heute, sagen alle faulen Leute** (Spr.) ≈ never put off till tomorrow what you can do today; **die Mode/Technik von ~** (fig.) tomorrow's fashions *pl.*/technology; *s. auch* **Morgen² 1**

Morgen¹ *das;* **~:** **das ~:** the future

Morgen² *der;* **~s, ~** **1** ▸**❶ S. 331** morning; **am ~,** (geh.) **des ~s** in the morning; **am folgenden** *od.* **nächsten ~:** next *or* the following morning; **heute/gestern ~:** this/yesterday morning; **früh am ~, am frühen ~:** early in the morning; **am ~ seiner Abreise** on the morning of his departure; **eines [schönen] ~s** one [fine] morning; **bis in den [frühen] ~ feiern/arbeiten** celebrate/work until the early hours; **gegen ~:** towards morning; **~ für ~:** every single morning; morning after morning; **es wird ~:** day *or* dawn is breaking; **sie gingen erst, als es bereits ~ wurde** they didn't go until it was already becoming daylight; **den ganzen ~:** all morning; **guten ~!** good morning!; **~!** (ugs.) morning! (coll.); **[jmdm.] guten ~ sagen** *od.* **wünschen** say good morning [to sb.]; wish [sb.] good morning; (grüßen) say hello [to sb.]; **schön** *od.* **frisch wie der junge ~** (scherzh.) fresh as a daisy **2** (fig. geh.) **der ~ des Lebens** the springtide of life (literary); **der ~ der Freiheit/eines neuen Zeitalters** the dawn of liberty/of a new age **3** (geh. veralt.) east; **gen ~:** towards the east **4** ▸**❶ S. 262** (veralt.: Feldmaß) ≈ acre; **fünf ~ Land** five acres of land

Morgen-: **~andacht** *die* morning service; **~ausgabe** *die* morning edition; **~dämmerung** *die* dawn; daybreak; **in der ~dämmerung** at daybreak

morgendlich *Adj.* morning; **die ~e Kühle/Stille** the cool/peace of [early] morning; **der ~e Sturm aufs Badezimmer** (scherzh.) the fight for the bathroom every morning

Morgen-: **~frühe** *die* early morning; **~gabe** *die* (hist.) *husband's present to wife on morning after wedding night;* **~gebet** *das* morning prayer; **~grauen** *das* daybreak; **im** *od.* **beim ~grauen** in the first light of day; **~gymnastik** *die* morning exercises *pl.*; daily dozen (coll.); **~kaffee** *der* **1** (Mahlzeit) light breakfast with coffee; **2** (Kaffee) breakfast coffee;

Morgenland *das;* **~[e]s** (veralt.) East; Orient

morgenländisch (veralt.)
A *Adj.* oriental; eastern
B *adv.* in an oriental style *or* fashion

Morgen-: **~licht** *das* morning light; **beim ersten ~licht** in the first light of day; **~luft** *die* morning air; **~luft wittern** (fig. scherzh.) see one's chance; **~mantel** *der* dressing gown;

m

~muffel der (ugs.) **ein ~muffel sein** be grumpy in the mornings; **~nebel** der morning fog; (weniger dicht) morning mist; **~post** die morning post; **~rock** der dressing gown; **~rot** das, **~röte** die (geh.) rosy dawn; (tiefer) red dawn; (fig.) dawn

morgens Adv. ▸ S. 729 in the morning; (jeden Morgen) every morning; **~ um 7 Uhr, um 7 Uhr ~:** at 7 in the morning/every morning; **Dienstag** od. **dienstags ~:** on Tuesday morning[s]; **von ~ bis abends** all day long; from morning to evening

Morgen-: ~sonne die morning sun; **~sonne haben** get the morning sun; **~spaziergang** der (esp. early) morning walk; **~stern** der 1) morning star; 2) (hist.) spiked mace; (mit Kette) nail-studded flail; **~stunde** die hour of the morning; **die frühen ~stunden** the early or small hours [of the morning]; **~stunde hat Gold im Munde** (Spr.) the early bird catches the worm (prov.); **~zeitung** die morning paper

morgig Adj. tomorrow's; **der ~e Tag** tomorrow

moribund /mori'bʊnt/ Adj. (Med., auch fig.) moribund

Moritat /'mo:rita:t/ die; ~, ~en (usually gruesome) street ballad

Moritz /'mo:rɪts/ in **wie sich der kleine ~ das vorstellt** (ugs. scherzh.) as some Simple Simon might imagine it

Mormone /mɔr'mo:nə/ der; ~n, ~n, **Mormonin** die; ~, ~nen Mormon

Morph /mɔrf/ das; ~s, ~e (Sprachw.) morph

Morphem /mɔr'fe:m/ das; ~s, ~e (Sprachw.) morpheme

Morpheus /'mɔrfɔys/ (der) (Myth.) Morpheus

Morphin /mɔr'fi:n/ das; ~s (Chemie, Med.) ▸ **Morphium**

Morphing /'mɔrfɪŋ/ das; ~s morphing

Morphinismus der; ~ (Med.) morphinism no art.; morphine addiction no art.

Morphinist der; ~en, ~en, **Morphinistin** die; ~, ~nen morphine addict

Morphium /'mɔrfiʊm/ das; ~s morphine

Morphium·sucht die ▸ **Morphinismus**

morphium·süchtig Adj. addicted to morphine pred.

Morphologie /mɔrfolo'gi:/ die; ~ (Biol., Sprachw.) morphology

morphologisch (Biol., Sprachw.)
A Adj. morphological
B adv. morphologically

morsch /mɔrʃ/ Adj. (auch fig.) rotten; brittle ‹bones›; crumbling ‹rock, masonry›

Morse-: ~alphabet das Morse code or alphabet; **~apparat** der Morse telegraph

morsen /'mɔrzn̩/
A itr. V. send a message/messages in Morse
B tr. V. send ‹signal, message› in Morse

Mörser /'mœrzɐ/ der; ~s, ~ (auch Milit.) mortar

Morse·zeichen das Morse symbol

Mortadella /mɔrta'dɛla/ die; ~, ~s mortadella

Mortalität /mɔrtali'tɛ:t/ die; ~: mortality [rate]

Mörtel /'mœrtl̩/ der; ~s mortar

Mosaik /moza'i:k/ das; ~s, ~en od. ~e (auch fig.) mosaic; **mit ~en ausgelegt** covered in mosaics

Mosaik-: ~[fuß]boden der mosaic floor; **~stein** der tessera; (fig.) piece of a jigsaw

mosaisch /mo'za:ɪʃ/ (Rel.)
A Adj. Mosaic ‹Law›; Jewish ‹faith›
B adv. in the Jewish faith

Mosambik /mozam'bi:k/ (das); ~s Mozambique

Moschee /mɔ'ʃe:/ die; ~, ~n mosque

Moschus /'mɔʃʊs/ der; ~: musk

Moschus·ochse der musk ox

Mose /'mo:zə/ (der); ~[s] (Rel.) Moses; **die fünf Bücher ~:** the Pentateuch

Möse /'mø:zə/ die; ~, ~n (vulg.) cunt (coarse)

Mosel /'mo:zl̩/ die; ~ ▸ S. 267 Moselle

Möser /'mø:zɐ/ ▸ **Moos 3**

mosern /'mo:zɐn/ itr. V. (ugs.) gripe (coll.) (**über** + Akk. about); **du findest aber auch an allem etwas zu ~:** you always manage to find something to complain about (coll.)

Moses[1] der; ~, ~ (Seemannsspr.) ship's boy

Moses[2] (der) Moses; **die fünf Bücher Mosis** (Rel.) the Pentateuch

Moskau /'mɔskaʊ/ (das); ~s ▸ S. 675 Moscow

Moskauer ▸ S. 675
A indekl. Adj. Moscow attrib.
B der; ~s, ~: Muscovite; s. auch **Kölner**

Moskauerin die; ~, ~en Muscovite

Moskito /mɔs'ki:to/ der; ~s, ~s mosquito

Moskito·netz das mosquito net

Moskowiter /mɔsko'vi:tɐ/ der; ~s, ~, **Moskowiterin** die; ~, ~nen (veralt.) Muscovite

moskowitisch /mɔsko'vi:tɪʃ/ Adj. (veralt.) Muscovite

Moslem /'mɔslɛm/ der; ~s, ~s ▸ **Muslim**

moslemisch ▸ **muslimisch**

Most /mɔst/ der; ~[e]s, ~e 1) (südd.: junger Wein) new wine 2) (Weinbasis) must 3) (südd.: Obstsaft) [cloudy fermented] fruit juice 4) (südd., schweiz., österr.: Obstwein) fruit wine; (Apfel~) [rough] cider

Most·apfel der [sour] cider apple

Mostert /'mɔstɐt/ der; ~s (nordwestd.), **Mostrich** /'mɔstrɪç/ der; ~s (nordostd.) mustard

Motel /'mo:tl̩/ das; ~s, ~s motel

Motette /mo'tɛtə/ die; ~, ~n (Musik) motet

Motherboard /'maðɐbɔ:d/ das; ~s, ~s (DV) motherboard

Motion /mo'tsio:n/ die; ~, ~en 1) (schweiz.) motion (Gen. by) 2) (Sprachw.) change of form determined by gender

Motiv /mo'ti:f/ das; ~s, ~e 1) motive; **das ~ einer Tat** the motive for an action 2) (Literaturw., Musik usw.: Thema) motif; theme; (bild. Kunst: Gegenstand) subject

Motivation /motiva'tsio:n/ die; ~, ~en (Psych., Päd.) motivation

Motiv·forschung die motivation research

motivieren tr. V. (geh.) 1) (begründen) give a [sufficient] reason for; **eine Entscheidung/sein Verhalten ~:** account for a decision/one's behaviour 2) (anregen) motivate; **[hoch] motiviert** [highly] motivated

Motivierung die; ~, ~en (geh.) motivation

Motocross /moto'krɔs/ das; ~, ~e 1) (Sport) motocross no pl. 2) (Veranstaltung) motocross event or meeting

Motodrom /moto'dro:m/ das; ~s, ~e autodrome; speedway (Amer.)

Motor /'mo:tɔr/ der; ~s, ~en (Verbrennungs~) engine; (Elektro~) motor; (fig.) driving force (Gen. behind)

Motor-: ~block der; Pl. **~blöcke** (Kfz-W.) engine block; cylinder block; **~boot** das motor boat; (im Gegensatz zum Segelboot) power boat

Motoren-: ~geräusch das sound of the engine/engines; **~lärm** der engine noise

Motor-: ~fahrzeug das motor vehicle; **~flug** der [powered] flying (as a sport); **~haube** die (Kfz-W.) bonnet (Brit.); hood (Amer.)

-motorig adj. -engined; **ein~/zwei~:** single-engined/twin-engined

Motorik /mo'to:rɪk/ die; ~ 1) (bes. Med.) motor functions pl. 2) (Lehre) study of motor functions

motorisch Adj. 1) (Psych.) motor attrib. 2) (Kfz-W.) with regard to the engine postpos., not pred.

motorisieren
A tr. V. motorize; (mit Maschinen ausrüsten) mechanize; **ein Boot ~:** fit a boat with an engine; **motorisierte Besucher** visitors with cars; **sind Sie motorisiert?** (ugs.) have you got any wheels? (coll.)
B refl. V. get a car/motorcycle; get oneself wheels (coll.)

Motorisierung die; ~ ▸ **motorisieren A:** motorization; mechanization

Motor-: ~jacht die motor yacht; **~leistung** die (Kfz-W.) engine performance; (PS) power output; **~öl** das (Kfz-W.) engine oil; **~rad** das motorcycle

Motorrad-: ~brille die motorcycling goggles; **~fahrer** der, **~fahrerin** die motorcyclist; **~rennen** das motorcycle race; (Sport) motorcycle racing; **~sport** motorcycling

Motor-: ~raum der (Kfz-W.) engine compartment; **~roller** der motor scooter; **~säge** die power saw; **~schaden** der engine trouble no indef. art.; (Panne) mechanical breakdown; **~schiff** das motor ship or vessel; **~schlitten** der motorized sledge; **~sport** der motor sport no art.; **~wäsche** die engine wash-down

Motte /'mɔtə/ die; ~, ~n 1) moth; **von etw. angezogen werden wie die ~n vom Licht** be attracted by sth. as moths to the light; **[ach,] du kriegst die ~n!** (ugs.) my godfathers!; **die ~n haben** (salopp veralt.) have TB 2) (salopp veralt.: Mädchen) chick (sl.); **flotte** od. **tolle ~:** smasher (sl.); **kesse ~:** saucy or pert little miss (coll.)

motten-, Motten-: ~echt, ~fest Adj. mothproof; **~fraß** der moth [damage]; **~kiste** die 1) (veralt.) mothproof chest; 2) (fig.) **Filme/Geschichten/Gags aus der ~kiste** ancient films/stories/gags; **~kugel** die mothball; **~pulver** das moth powder; **~zerfressen** Adj. moth-eaten

Motto /'mɔto/ das; ~s, ~s motto; (Schlagwort) slogan; **der Kirchentag stand unter dem ~: ...** the motto of the church assembly was ...; **nach dem ~: ... leben** live according to the maxim: ...

motzen /'mɔtsn̩/ itr. V. (ugs.) grouch (coll.), bellyache (coll.) (**über** + Akk. about); **was hast du schon wieder zu ~?** what are you bellyaching about now? (coll.)

Motzerei die; ~, ~en (ugs.) bellyaching (coll.); **~en** moans and complaints

motzig (ugs.)
A Adj. grouchy (coll.); grumpy
B adv. grouchily (coll.); grumpily

Mountain·bike /'maʊntɪnbaɪk/ das mountain bike

Mousse /mʊs/ die; ~, ~s (Kochk.) mousse

Mousse au Chocolat /'mʊs o ʃoko'la/ die; ~ ~ ~, ~s ~ ~ /'mʊs o ʃoko'la/ (Gastr.) mousse au chocolat; chocolate mousse

moussieren /mʊ'si:rən/ itr. V. sparkle; (als Eigenschaft) be sparkling; **~der Wein** sparkling wine

Möwe /'mø:və/ die; ~, ~n gull

Mozart·zopf /'mo:tsart-/ der bag wig

MPi /ɛm'pi:/die; ~, ~s sub-machine gun

Mrd. Abk. = **Milliarde** bn.

m.s., MS Abk. = **multiple Sklerose** MS

Ms., MS Abk. = **Manuskript** MS

MS Abk. = **Motorschiff** MV; MS (Amer.)

MTA Abk. = **medizinisch-technische Assistentin** medical-laboratory assistant

MTB Abk. = **Mountainbike** MTB

mtl. Abk. = **monatlich** mthly.

Mücke /'mʏkə/ die; ~, ~n 1) midge; gnat; (größer) mosquito; **aus einer ~ einen Elefanten machen** (ugs.) make a mountain out of a molehill; **die ~ machen** (salopp) push off (coll.) 2) Pl. (salopp: Geld) bread (sl.); lolly (Brit. coll.)

Muckefuck /'mʊkəfʊk/ der; ~s (ugs.) coffee substitute

mucken /'mʊkn̩/ itr. V. (ugs.) grumble; mutter; **ohne zu ~:** without a murmur

Mucken Pl. (ugs.) whims; (Eigenarten) little ways or peculiarities; (Launen) moods; **[seine] ~ haben** ‹person› have one's little ways/one's moods; ‹car, machine› be a little unpredictable or temperamental; **jmdm. seine ~ austreiben** sort sb. out (coll.)

Mücken·stich der midge/mosquito bite

Mucker *der;* **~s, ~** (ugs. abwertend) yes-man

Muckerin *die;* **~, ~nen** (ugs. abwertend) yes-woman

Muckertum *das* (ugs. abwertend) being *no art.* a yes-man (coll.)

Muckis /'mʊkis/ *Pl.* (ugs., meist scherzh.) muscles

Mucks /mʊks/ *der;* **~es, ~e** (ugs.) murmur [of protest]; slight[est] sound; **keinen ~ sagen** *od.* **von sich geben** not utter a [single] word *or* sound; **die Kinder gaben keinen ~ von sich** there was not the slightest sound/murmur out of the children

mucksen *refl. V.* (ugs.) 1 (meist negativ) make a sound; (sich rühren) stir; budge; **sie wagten nicht, sich zu ~:** they didn't dare to budge [an inch]/make a sound 2 (aufbegehren) object; make noises (coll.)

Muckser *der;* **~s, ~** (ugs.) ▸ **Mucks**

mucks·mäuschen·still (ugs.)

A *Adj.* utterly silent; ‹*person*› as quiet as a mouse *postpos.*; **es wurde ~:** you could have heard a pin drop

B *adv.* in total silence; without making a sound

Mud[d] /mʊt/ *der;* **~s** (nordd.) mud

müde /'my:də/

A *Adj.* tired; (ermattet) weary; (schläfrig) sleepy; **mit ~n Schritten** with weary steps; **ich war zum Umfallen ~:** I was out on my feet; **Bier macht ~:** beer makes you feel sleepy; **sich ~ laufen/weinen** tire oneself out with walking/crying; **ein ~s Lächeln** (auch fig.) a weary smile; **jmdn./etw.** *od.* **jmds./einer Sache ~ sein** (geh.) be tired of sb./sth.; **jmds./einer Sache** (*Gen.*) **~ werden** (geh.) tire *or* grow tired of sb./sth.; **nicht ~ werden, etw. zu tun** never tire of doing sth.; (bei unangenehmer Tätigkeit) never stop doing sth.; **kein ~r Euro/keine ~ Mark** (ugs.) not a penny; not a cent (Amer)

B *adv.* wearily; (schläfrig) sleepily

-müde *adj.* tired of ...; **amts~/kino~/stadt~:** tired of [holding] office/[going to] the cinema/city life *postpos.*

-müdigkeit *die* weariness of ...; **Zivilisations~:** weariness of civilized living; culture fatigue; **Kriegs~:** war-weariness

Müdigkeit *die;* **~:** tiredness; **~/eine tiefe ~ kam über ihn** he began to feel tired/a great weariness come over him; **von ~ übermannt werden** be overcome by fatigue; **ich könnte vor ~ umfallen** I'm so tired I can hardly stand; **[nur] keine ~ vorschützen!** (ugs.) it's no use saying you're tired!

Müesli /'my:ɛsli/ *das;* **~s** (schweiz.) ▸ **Müsli**

Muff[1] /mʊf/ *der;* **~[e]s** (nordd.) musty smell; (Gestank) fug

Muff[2] *der;* **~[e]s, ~e** muff

Muffe *die;* **~, ~n** 1 (Technik) sleeve; (Verbindungsstück) sleeve [coupling] 2 (fig.) **jmdm. geht die ~** (salopp) sb. is shaking in his shoes; **~ haben** (salopp) be in a funk (coll.) (**vor** + *Dat.* about)

-muffel *der;* **-~s, -~** (ugs.) person indifferent to ...

Muffel /'mʊfl/ *der;* **~s, ~** (ugs.) 1 sourpuss (coll.); grouch (coll.) 2 (desinteressierter Mensch) **was ... betrifft, ist er ein [richtiger] ~:** as far as ... is concerned he's just not interested

muffelig (ugs.)

A *Adj.* grumpy; surly; **du bist aber ~ heute!** you are in a bad mood today!

B *adv.* grumpily

muffeln[1] (ugs.)

A *itr. V.* be grumpy *or* in a huff

B *tr., itr. V.* mutter [grumpily]; grunt

muffeln[2] *itr. V.* (südd., österr.: muffig riechen) smell musty

Muffen-sausen *das* (salopp) **~ haben/kriegen** be/get in a funk (coll.) (**vor** + *Dat.* about)

muffig[1] *Adj.* (modrig riechend) musty; (stickig; auch fig.) stuffy

muffig[2] (ugs.) ▸ **muffelig**

Muffigkeit *die;* **~** (ugs.) grumpiness; surliness

Mufflon /'mʊflɔn/ *der;* **~s, ~s** (Zool.) mouflon

Mufti /'mʊfti/ *der;* **~s, ~s** mufti

Mugel /'mu:gl/ *der;* **~s, ~[n]** (österr.) hillock; (auf der Skipiste) mogul

muh /mu:/ *Interj.* (Kinderspr.) moo

Müh /my:/ ▸ **Mühe**

Mühe /'my:ə/ *die;* **~, ~n** trouble; **alle ~ haben, etw. zu tun** be hard put to do sth.; **mit jmdm./etw. seine ~ haben** have a lot of trouble *or* a hard time with sb./sth.; **die ~ hat sich gelohnt** it was worth the trouble *or* effort; **keine ~ scheuen** spare no pains *or* effort; **sich** (*Dat.*) **viel ~ machen** go to *or* take a lot of trouble (**mit** over); **machen Sie sich [bitte] keine ~!** (tun Sie es nicht) [please] don't put yourself out!; [please] don't bother!; **wenn es dir keine ~ macht, ...** if it's no trouble *or* bother, ...; **es hat viel ~ gekostet** it took much time and effort; **die ~ kannst du dir sparen** you can save yourself the trouble; **sich** (*Dat.*) **~ geben[, etw. zu tun]** make an effort *or* take pains [to do sth.]; **sich** (*Dat.*) **mit jmdm./etw. ~ geben** take [great] pains *or* trouble over sb./sth.; **wenn du dir mehr ~ geben würdest** if you would take more trouble/try harder; **gib dir doch etwas ~!** do make some sort of an effort!; **gib dir keine ~!** you needn't bother; **mit Müh und Not** with great difficulty; only just; **der** (*Gen.*) *od.* **die ~ wert sein** be worth the trouble *or* worth it; **wäre es der ~ wert, nach X zu fahren?** would it be worth [while] going to X?

mühelos

A *Adj.* effortless

B *adv.* effortlessly; without the slightest difficulty

Mühelosigkeit *die;* **~:** effortlessness

muhen *itr. V.* moo

mühen *refl. V.* (geh.) strive; **sich mit etw. ~:** take pains over sth.; **sosehr er sich auch mühte** hard though he tried

mühe·voll *Adj.* laborious; painstaking ‹*work*›; **ein ~er Weg** an arduous path

Mühewaltung /-valtʊŋ/ *die;* **~** (Papierdt.) efforts *pl.*; (im Brief) **für Ihre ~ dankend** thanking you for your trouble

Muh-kuh *die* (Kinderspr.) moo-cow (child lang.)

Mühl-bach *der* millstream

Mühle /'my:lə/ *die;* **~, ~n** 1 mill; **in die ~ der Justiz geraten** (fig.) become enmeshed in the wheels *or* machinery of justice; **das ist Wasser auf seine ~** (ugs.) it's [all] grist to his mill; it just confirms what he has always thought; *s. auch* **Gott** 2 (Kaffee~) [coffee] grinder 3 (Spiel) nine men's morris 4 (Figur beim Mühlespiel) mill 5 (ugs. abwertend) (Auto, Motorrad) heap (coll.); (Auto, Flugzeug) crate (coll.); (Fahrrad) rattletrap; boneshaker

Mühle-spiel *das* nine men's morris

Mühl-: ~rad *das* mill wheel; **~stein** *der* millstone

Muhme /'mu:mə/ *die;* **~, ~n** (veralt.) aunt

Mühsal /'my:za:l/ *die;* **~, ~e** (geh.) tribulation; (Strapaze) hardship; (Arbeit) toil *no pl.*

mühsam

A *Adj.* laborious; **ein ~es Lächeln** a forced smile

B *adv.* laboriously; (schwierig) with difficulty; **~ verdientes Geld** hard-earned money

müh·selig (geh.)

A *Adj.* laborious; arduous ‹*journey, life*›; **... alle, die ihr ~ und beladen seid** (bibl.) ... all ye that labour and are heavy laden

B *adv.* with [great] difficulty

Müh·seligkeit *die* (geh.) laboriousness; (einer Reise, des Lebens) arduousness

Mulatte /mu'latə/ *der;* **~n, ~n, Mulattin** *die;* **~, ~nen** mulatto

Mulde /'mʊldə/ *die;* **~, ~n** 1 hollow 2 (Trog) trough

Muli /'mu:li/ *das;* **~s, ~s** mule

Mull[1] /mʊl/ *der;* **~[e]s** (Stoff) muslin; (Verband~) gauze

Mull[2] *der;* **~[e]s, ~e** (nordd.: Humus) mull

Müll /mʏl/ *der;* **~s** 1 refuse; rubbish; garbage (Amer.); trash (Amer.); (Industrie~) [industrial] waste; **etw. in den ~ werfen** throw sth. in the dustbin (Brit.) *or* (Amer.) garbage can; **„~ abladen verboten"** 'no dumping'; 'no tipping' (Brit.) 2 (alte Sachen) rubbish; junk

Müll-: ~abfuhr *die* 1 refuse *or* (Amer.) garbage collection; 2 (Unternehmen) refuse *or* (Amer.) garbage collection [service]; **~ablade·platz** *der* [refuse] dump *or* (Brit.) tip; **~auto** *das* ▸ **~wagen**; **~beutel** *der* dustbin (Brit.) *or* (Amer.) garbage can liner

Mull·binde *die* gauze bandage

Müll-: ~deponie *die* (Amtsspr.) refuse disposal site; **~eimer** *der* rubbish *or* waste bin; **~entsorgung** *die* refuse disposal

Müller /'mʏlɐ/ *der;* **~s, ~** ▸ **i S. 113** miller

Müller·bursche *der* (veralt.) miller's lad

Müllerin *die;* **~, ~nen** (veralt.) miller's wife

Müll-: ~fahrer *der,* **~fahrerin** *die* ▸ **i S. 113** dustcart (Brit.) *or* (Amer.) garbage truck driver; **~halde** *die* refuse dump; **~haufen** *der* heap of rubbish *or* (Amer.) garbage; **~kippe** *die* ▸ **Müllabladeplatz**; **~mann** *der* (ugs.) dustman (Brit.); garbage man (Amer.); **~sack** *der* refuse bag; **~schippe** *die* dustpan; **~schlucker** *der* rubbish *or* (Amer.) garbage chute; **~tonne** *die* dustbin (Brit.); garbage *or* trash can (Amer.); **~trennung** *die* waste separation; **~tüte** *die* bin bag; **~verbrennung** *die* refuse *or* (Amer.) garbage incineration; **~verbrennungs·anlage** *die* refuse *or* (Amer.) garbage incinerator; **~verwertung** *die* refuse *or* (Amer.) garbage recycling; **~wagen** *der* dustcart (Brit.); garbage truck (Amer.); **~werker** *der;* **~~s, ~~, ~werkerin** *die;* **~~, ~~nen** ▸ **i S. 113** refuse *or* (Amer.) garbage operative

Mull·windel *die* muslin nappy (Brit.) *or* (Amer.) diaper

mulmig /'mʊlmɪç/ *Adj.* 1 (ugs.: bedenklich) ticklish; tricky; (unbehaglich) uncomfortable; **als es ~ wurde** when things began to look nasty 2 (ugs.: übel) (im Magen) queasy; (unbehaglich) uneasy; **ein ~es Gefühl haben** feel queasy/uneasy; **mir war ganz ~ zumute** I felt quite weak at the knees 3 (faulig) rotten

multi-, Multi-: multi‹*lateral, -lingual, -millionaire, -national*›

Multi /'mʊlti/ *der;* **~s, ~s** (ugs.) multinational

Multifunktions·taste *die* multi-function button

Multi·halle *die* multi-purpose hall

Multikulti *das;* **~s** multicultural mix

Multikulturalismus *der;* **~:** multiculturalism

multikulturell *Adj.* multicultural

Multimedia·computer *der* multimedia computer

multi·medial

A *Adj.* multimedia *attrib.*; **~er Unterricht** teaching with multimedia material

B *adv.* on a multimedia basis

Multimedia- /-'me:dia/: **~show** *die* multimedia presentation; **~system** *das* (Päd.) multimedia method; **~technik** *die* (DV) multimedia technology

multipel /mʊl'ti:pl/ *Adj.* (bes. Fachspr.) multiple; **multiple Sklerose** (Med.) multiple sclerosis

Multiplechoice·verfahren /'maltɪpl 'tʃɔɪs.../ *das* (Psych., Päd.) multiple-choice method; **Prüfungen nach dem ~:** examinations using multiple-choice tests

Multiplex *das;* **~[es], ~e** multiplex

Multiplikand /mʊltipli'kant/ *der;* **~en, ~en** (Math.) multiplicand

Multiplikation /mʊltiplika'tsio:n/ *die;* **~, ~en** (Math.) multiplication

Multiplikator /mʊltipli'ka:tɔr/ *der;* **~s, ~en** /-'to:rən/ 1 (Math.) multiplier 2 (fig.) disseminator (*of information, opinions*)

multiplizieren /mʊltipli'tsi:rən/

A *tr. V.* (Math., fig.) multiply (**mit** by)

B *refl. V.* (fig.) multiply [several times]

Multi·talent *das* all-round talent; multi-talent (esp. Amer.); (fig.: Sache) multi-purpose *or* versatile item/product *etc.*

Mumie /'mu:miə/ *die;* **~, ~n** mummy

mumienhaft

A *Adj.* mummy-like

B *adv.* like a mummy; as though mummified

Mumifikation /mumifika'tsio:n/ *die;* **~, ~en** mummification

mumifizieren /mumifiˈtsiːrən/ *tr. V.* mummify

Mumifizierung *die;* ~, ~**en** mummification

Mumm /mʊm/ *der;* ~**s** (ugs.) (Mut) guts *pl.* (coll.); spunk (coll.); (Tatkraft) drive; zap (coll.); (Kraft) muscle-power; *s. auch* **Knochen 1**

Mummel·greis /ˈmʊml̩-/ *der* (ugs. abwertend) old dodderer; doddery old man

Mümmel·mann /ˈmʏml̩-/ *der* (fam. scherzh.) hare

mummeln[1] *tr., refl. V.* (fam.) **jmdn./sich in eine Decke ~:** wrap sb./oneself [up] snugly in a blanket

mummeln[2] (nordd.), **mümmeln** *tr., itr. V.* (fam.) (kauen) chew; (knabbern) nibble

Mummenschanz /ˈmʊmənʃants/ *der;* ~**es** (veralt.) [1] (Fest) fancy-dress party *or* ball [2] (Verkleidung) fancy dress

Mumpf /mʊmpf/ *der;* ~**s** (schweiz.) mumps *sing.*

Mumpitz /ˈmʊmpɪts/ *der;* ~**es** (ugs. abwertend) rubbish; tripe (coll.)

Mumps /mʊmps/ *der od. die;* ~ ▸ⓘ **S. 439** mumps *sing.*

München /ˈmʏnçn̩/ *(das);* ~**s** ▸ⓘ **S. 675** Munich

Münch[e]ner /ˈmʏnçnɐ/

A *indekl. Adj.* Munich *attrib.*

B *der;* ~**s,** ~: inhabitant/native of Munich; *s. auch* **Kölner**

Münch[e]nerin *die;* ~, ~**nen** inhabitant/native of Munich

Mund /mʊnt/ *der;* ~**[e]s, Münder** /ˈmʏndɐ/ mouth; **seinen/den ~ verziehen** make a face; **seinen/den ~ spitzen** purse one's lips; **vor Staunen blieb ihm der ~ offen stehen** he gaped in astonishment; **er küsste ihren ~** *od.* **küsste sie auf den ~:** he kissed her on the lips; **den Finger auf den ~ legen** put one's finger to one's lips; **von ~ zu ~ beatmet werden** be given mouth-to-mouth resuscitation *or* the kiss of life; **aus dem ~ riechen** have bad breath; **mit vollem ~ sprechen** speak with one's mouth full; **etw. aus jmds. ~ hören** hear *or* have sth. from sb.'s [own] lips; **sein ~ steht nicht** *od.* **nie still** (ugs.) he never stops talking; **den ~ nicht aufbekommen** *od.* **aufkriegen** (fig. ugs.) not open one's mouth; have nothing to say for oneself; **den ~ aufmachen/nicht aufmachen** (fig. ugs.) say something/not say anything; **den ~ voll nehmen** (fig. ugs.) talk big (coll.); **nimm doch den ~ nicht so voll!** don't be such a bighead!; **~ und Augen** *od.* **Nase aufreißen** *od.* **aufsperren** (ugs.) gape in astonishment; **einen großen ~ haben** (fig. ugs.) talk big (coll.); **den** *od.* **seinen ~ halten** (ugs.) (schweigen) shut up (coll.); (nichts sagen) not say anything; (nichts verraten) keep quiet (**über** + *Akk.* about); **jmdm. den ~ verbieten** silence sb.; **jmdm. den ~ [ganz] wässrig machen** (ugs.) [really] make sb.'s mouth water; **er/sie ist nicht auf den ~ gefallen** (fig. ugs.) he's/she's never at a loss for words; **... ist in aller ~e** everybody's talking about ...; **etw./ein Wort in den ~ nehmen** utter sth./use a word; **jmdm. nach dem ~ reden** echo what sb. says; (schmeichelnd) butter sb. up; tell sb. what he/she wants to hear; **jmdm. über den ~ fahren** (ugs.) cut sb. short; **von ~ zu ~ gehen** be passed on from mouth to mouth; **sich** *(Dat.)* **etw. vom ~e absparen** scrimp and save for sth.; **ein ~ voll Wein** a mouthful of wine; *s. auch* **berufen**[2] **1; fusselig; Hand 6; stopfen A 2; verbrennen B 2**

Mund·art *die* dialect

Mundart-: ~**dichter** *der,* ~**dichterin** *die* dialect author; (Lyriker[in]) dialect poet; ~**dichtung** *die* [1] dialect literature; [2] (Werk) work [written] in dialect; ~**forschung** *die* dialectology; dialect research

mundartlich

A *Adj.* dialectal ‹*forms, expressions, words*›; ‹*texts, poems, etc.*› in dialect

B *adv.* in dialect; **stark ~ gefärbt** strongly coloured by dialect

Mundart-: ~**sprecher** *der,* ~**sprecherin** *die* dialect speaker; ~**wörterbuch** *das* dialect dictionary

Mund·dusche *die* water pick

Mündel /ˈmʏndl̩/ *das;* ~**s,** ~: ward

mündel·sicher (Bankw.)

A *Adj.* gilt-edged; trustee *attrib.* (Amer.)

B *adv.* in gilt-edged *or* (Amer.) trustee securities

munden *itr. V.* (geh.) taste good; **es mundete ihm nicht** he did not enjoy it; he did not like the taste of it; **das wird dir ~:** this will tickle your palate

münden /ˈmʏndn̩/ *itr. V.; mit sein* ▸ⓘ **S. 267** ‹*river*› flow (**in** + *Akk.* into); ‹*corridor, street, road*› lead (**in** + *Akk. od. Dat.,* **auf** + *Akk. od. Dat.* into); **in eine/einer Frage** *usw.* ~ (fig.) ‹*discussion*› lead to a question *etc.*

mund-, Mund-: ~**falte** *die* line at the corner of the mouth; ~**faul** (ugs.) **A** *Adj.* uncommunicative; **B** *adv.* uncommunicatively; ~**fäule** *die* ▸ⓘ **S. 439** (Med.) ulcerative stomatitis; ~**gerecht A** *Adj.* bite-sized; (fig.) easily digestible ‹*information*›; **B** *adv.* ‹*serve*› in bite-sized pieces; ‹*divided*› into small mouthfuls; (fig.) in an easily digestible form; ~**geruch** *der* bad breath *no indef. art.;* ~**harmonika** *die* mouth organ; ~**höhle** *die* ▸ⓘ **S. 435** oral cavity

mündig *Adj.* [1] of age *pred.;* **drei ~e Töchter** three daughters who are of age; **~ werden** come of age; **jmdn. ~ sprechen** *od.* **für ~ erklären** declare sb. of age [2] (urteilsfähig) responsible adult *attrib.;* **~ werden** become capable of mature judgement

***mündig|sprechen** ▸ **mündig 1**

Mündig·sprechung *die;* ~, ~**en jmds. ~:** the declaration that sb. is/was of age

mündlich

A *Adj.* oral; **~e Zusage** verbal agreement; **~e Verhandlung** (Rechtsw.) hearing

B *adv.* orally; ‹*agree*› verbally; **alles Weitere ~** (im Brief) I'll tell you the rest when we meet

Mund-: ~**öffnung** *die* (Zool.) oral aperture; ~**partie** *die* lower part of one's face; ~**pflege** *die* oral hygiene; ~**raub** *der* petty theft [of food/consumables]; ~**schenk** /-ʃɛŋk/ *der;* ~~**en,** ~~**en** (hist.) cupbearer; ~**schutz** *der* [1] (Med.) face mask; [2] (Boxen) gumshield

M-und-S-Reifen /ˈɛm ʊnt ˈɛs-/ *der* snow tyre

mund-, Mund-: ~**stellung** *die* position of the mouth; ~**stück** *das* [1] (bei Instrumenten, Pfeifen usw.) mouthpiece; [2] (bei Zigaretten) tip; [3] (beim Zaumzeug) bit; ~**tot** *Adj.* in **jmdn./eine Organisation ~tot machen** silence sb./an organization; ~**tuch** *das; Pl.* ~**tücher** (geh. veralt.) [table] napkin

Mündung *die;* ~, ~**en** [1] ▸ⓘ **S. 267** mouth; (größer) estuary [2] (bei Straßen) end [3] (bei Feuerwaffen) muzzle

Mündungs·feuer *das* muzzle flash

Mund-: ~**verkehr** *der* oral sex; *~**voll** *der;* ~~, ~~: mouthful; ~**vorrat** *der* (veralt.) victuals *pl.;* ~**wasser** *das; Pl.* ~**wässer** mouthwash; ~**werk** *das* (ugs.) **ein flinkes ~werk haben** talk nineteen to the dozen (Brit.); **ein loses ~werk [haben]** [have] a loose tongue; ~**winkel** *der* corner of one's mouth; ~**-zu-~-Beatmung** *die* mouth-to-mouth resuscitation; kiss of life; ~**-zu-Nase-Beatmung** *die* mouth-to-nose resuscitation

Munition /muniˈtsi̯oːn/ *die;* ~ (auch fig.) ammunition; **seine ~ verschossen haben** (auch fig.) have run out of ammunition

Munitions-: ~**depot** *das* ammunition dump; ~**fabrik** *die* munitions factory; ~**lager** *das* ammunition dump

Munkelei *die;* ~, ~**en** (ugs.) [1] rumour-mongering [2] (Gerücht[e]) rumour[s]

munkeln /ˈmʊŋkl̩n/ *tr., itr. V.* (ugs.) **man munkelt so allerlei, es wird so allerlei gemunkelt** there are all kinds of rumours [flying about]; **es wird gemunkelt** *od.* **man munkelt, dass ...** there is a rumour that ...

Münster /ˈmʏnstɐ/ *das;* ~**s,** ~: minster; (Dom) cathedral; **das Straßburger ~:** Strasbourg Cathedral

munter /ˈmʊntɐ/

A *Adj.* [1] cheerful; merry; (lebhaft) lively ‹*eyes, game*›; **~ werden** cheer up; liven up; **[gesund und] ~ sein** be as fit as a fiddle; ‹*elderly person*› be hale and hearty [2] (wach) awake; **~ werden** wake up; come round (joc.); **jmdn. ~ machen** wake sb. up

B *adv.* [1] cheerfully; merrily [2] (unbekümmert) gaily; cheerfully

Munterkeit *die;* ~: cheerfulness; gaiety

Münz-: ~**anstalt** *die* mint; ~**automat** *der* slot machine; (Telefon) payphone; pay station (Amer.)

Münze /ˈmʏntsə/ *die;* ~, ~**n** [1] ▸ⓘ **S. 299** coin; **klingende** *od.* **bare ~** (geh.) cash; **etw. für bare ~ nehmen** (fig.) take sth. literally; **jmdm. [etw.] in** *od.* **mit gleicher ~ heimzahlen** pay sb. back in the same coin [for sth.] [2] (Münzanstalt) mint

Münz·einwurf *der* [coin] slot

münzen *tr. V.* coin; **auf jmdn./etw. gemünzt sein** (fig.) ‹*remark etc.*› be aimed at sb./sth.

Münzen·sammlung *die* coin collection

Münz-: ~**fälscher** *der,* ~**fälscherin** *die* counterfeiter [of coins]; ~**fälschung** *die* counterfeiting [of coins]; ~**fernsprecher** *der* coin-box telephone; payphone; pay station (Amer.); ~**fuß** *der* standard [for content] of coinage; ~**gewicht** *das* standard weight (*of a coin*); ~**hoheit** *die* coining prerogative (*of the State*); ~**kunde** *die* numismatics *sing.;* ~**recht** *das* [1] ▸ ~**hoheit;** [2] (~gesetze) coinage laws *pl.;* ~**sammlung** *die* coin collection; ~**tankstelle** *die* coin-in-the-slot petrol (Brit.) *or* (Amer.) gas station; ~**wechsler** *der* change machine; ~**wesen** *das* coinage [system]; ~**zähler** *der* [slot] meter

Muräne /muˈrɛːnə/ *die* moray eel

mürb /mʏrp/ (südd., österr.), **mürbe** /ˈmʏrbə/ *Adj.* [1] crumbly ‹*biscuit, cake, etc.*›; tender ‹*meat*›; soft ‹*fruit*›; mealy ‹*apple*›; **das Fleisch ~e machen** tenderize the meat [2] (brüchig) crumbling; (morsch) rotten; ‹*leather*› worn soft; **~e werden/sein** (fig.: zermürbt) get/be worn out; **jmdn. ~e machen** (fig.) wear sb. down

Mürbe·teig, (südd., österr.) **Mürb·teig** *der* short pastry

Murks /mʊrks/ *der;* ~**es** (salopp abwertend) botch; mess; **das ist doch ~!** this is a right botch-up!; **~ machen** make a botch *or* mess [of it]

murksen *itr. V.* (salopp abwertend) mess about (**an** + *Dat.* with); **bei einer Arbeit ~:** make a botch *or* mess of a job

Murmel /ˈmʊrml̩/ *die;* ~, ~**n** marble; **~n spielen** play [with] marbles

murmeln[1] *tr., itr. V.* [1] mumble; mutter; (sehr leise) murmur; **etw. vor sich hin ~:** mutter *or* mumble/murmur sth. to oneself [2] (dichter.) ‹*stream, fountain*› murmur

murmeln[2] *itr. V.* (M~ spielen) play [with] marbles

Murmel·tier *das* marmot; *s. auch* **schlafen A 1**

murren /ˈmʊrən/ *itr. V.* grumble (**über** + *Akk.* about); **was hast du nun schon wieder zu ~?** what are you grumbling about now?; **ohne zu ~:** without a murmur

mürrisch /ˈmʏrɪʃ/

A *Adj.* grumpy; (wortkarg) surly; surly, sullen ‹*expression*›

B *adv.* grumpily; (wortkarg) sullenly

Mus /muːs/ *das od. der;* ~**es,** ~**e** purée; **zu ~ kochen** cook to a pulp; **jmdn./etw. zu ~ machen** *od.* **schlagen** (salopp) beat sb./sth. to a pulp

Muschel /ˈmʊʃl̩/ *die;* ~, ~**n** [1] mussel [2] (Schale) [mussel] shell [3] (am Telefon) (Hör~) earpiece; (Sprech~) mouthpiece [4] (Ohr~) [outer] ear

Muschel-: ~**bank** *die; Pl.* ~**bänke** mussel bed; ~**kalk** *der* (Geol.) Muschelkalk

Muschi /ˈmʊʃi/ *die;* ~, ~**s** [1] (Kinderspr.: Katze) pussy [cat] [2] (salopp: Vulva) pussy (coarse)

Muschkote /mʊʃˈkoːtə/ *der;* ~**n,** ~**n** (Soldatenspr. veralt., abwertend) common soldier; squaddy (Brit. sl.)

Muse /ˈmuːzə/ *die;* ~, ~**n** muse; **die leichte ~:** light [musical] entertainment; **von der ~**

m

geküsst werden (scherzh.) get some inspiration

museal /muzeˈaːl/ (geh.)
A *Adj.* 1 museum *attrib.*; of the museum *postpos.* 2 (wie ein Museum, wie im Museum) museum-like ‹*building, appearance*›
B *adv.* like a museum; in the style of a museum

Museen ▸ **Museum**

Muselman /ˈmuːzl̩man/ *der;* ~en, ~en, **Muselmanin** *die;* ~, ~nen, **Muselmann** *der; Pl.* **Muselmänner** (veralt., noch scherzh.) Muslim

Musen-: ~**almanach** *der* (hist.): *18th/19th century annual anthology of mainly unpublished poetry;* ~**sohn** *der* (veralt., noch scherzh.) son of the Muses; ~**tempel** *der* (veralt., noch scherzh.) temple of the Muses

Museum /muˈzeːʊm/ *das;* ~s, **Museen** museum; **ins ~ gehen** go to a/the museum

museums-, Museums-: ~**aufseher** *der,* ~**aufseherin** *die* ▸❶ **S. 113** museum attendant; ~**führer** *der,* ~**führerin** *die* ▸❶ **S. 113** museum guide; ~**pädagogik** *die* museum education; ~**reif** *Adj.* (ugs. iron.) fit for a museum *postpos.*; **das ist wirklich ~reif** it's a real museum piece *or* positively antiquated; ~**stück** *das* (auch fig. ugs. iron.) museum piece; ~**wärter** *der,* ~**wärterin** *die* ▸❶ **S. 113** museum attendant; ~**wert** *der:* ~**wert haben** (ugs.) be a valuable museum piece; (abwertend) be positively antiquated *or* a museum piece

Musical /ˈmjuːzɪkl̩/ *das;* ~s, ~s musical

Music·box /ˈmjuːzɪk-/ *die;* ~, ~en ▸ **Musikbox**

Musik /muˈziːk/ *die;* ~, ~en 1 music; **einen Text in ~ setzen** set a text to music; **die ~ lieben** like music; **~ im Blut haben** have music in one's blood; **~ in jmds. Ohren** *(Dat.)* **sein** (fig. ugs.) be music to sb.'s ears; **dahinter** *od.* **darin sitzt** *od.* **steckt ~** (fig. ugs.) there is real power in it 2 (Werk) *Pl.:* ~**en** piece [of music]; (Partitur) score (**zu** for); **die ~ zu diesem Stück** the [incidental] music for this play 3 (ugs.: Kapelle) band 4 (Gastr.) ▸ **Handkäse**

Musikalien /muziˈkaːli̯ən/ *Pl.* sheet music *sing.*

Musikalien·handlung *die* music shop

musikalisch /muziˈkaːlɪʃ/
A *Adj.* musical; **die ~e Leitung haben** be the musical director; (als Dirigent) be the conductor; **~e Leitung: ...** conducted by ...
B *adv.* musically; **er ist ~ veranlagt** he is musical

Musikalität /muzikaliˈtɛːt/ *die;* ~: musicality

Musikant /muziˈkant/ *der;* ~en, ~en musician

Musikanten·knochen *der* ▸❶ **S. 435** funny bone

Musikantin *die;* ~, ~nen ▸ **Musikant**

musikantisch (ugs.)
A *Adj.* full of brio *postpos.*; with a swing to it *postpos.*
B *adv.* with brio

Musik-: ~**automat** *der* 1 (Spieluhr o. Ä.) mechanical instrument; 2 ▸ ~**box**; ~**box** *die* jukebox; ~**-CD** *die* audio CD; music CD; ~**direktor** *der,* ~**direktorin** *die;* ~~, ~~**nen** musical director; ~**drama** *das* music drama

Musiker *der;* ~s, ~, **Musikerin** *die;* ~, ~nen ▸❶ **S. 113** musician; **die ~ stimmten ihre Instrumente** the players were tuning their instruments

musik-, Musik-: ~**erziehung** *die* musical education; ~**festspiele** *Pl.* music festival *sing.*; ~**freund** *der,* ~**freundin** *die* music lover; ~**geschichte** *die* history of music; **in die ~geschichte eingehen** find a place in musical history; ~**geschichtlich,** ~**historisch** A *Adj.* musico-historical; B *adv.* in terms of the history of music; from the point of view of musical history; ~**hochschule** *die* academy *or* college of music; ~**instrument** *das* musical instrument; ~**kapelle** *die* band; ~**korps** *das* military band (forming a separate unit); ~**kritik** *die* 1 music criticism; 2 (Artikel) music review; ~**kritiker** *der,* ~**kritikerin** *die* music critic; ~**leben** *das* musical life; ~**lehre** *die* 1 musical theory *no art.*; 2 (Buch) manual of musical theory; music textbook; ~**lehrer** *der,* ~**lehrerin** *die* music teacher; ~**lexikon** *das* musical encyclopedia; encyclopedia of music; ~**pädagogik** *die* [theory of] music teaching; ~**saal** *der* 1 (in der Schule) music room; 2 (Konzertsaal) concert hall; ~**schule** *die* school of music; ~**stück** *das* piece of music; **ein ~stück Chopins/von Chopin** a piece by Chopin; ~**stunde** *die* music lesson; ~**theater** *das* music theatre (*where text and production are as important as the music*); ~**theorie** *die* 1 (theoretische Erfassung) theory of music; 2 (Lehrfach) musical theory *no art.*; ~**therapie** *die* music therapy; ~**truhe** *die* radiogram (*in a large cabinet*); ~**unterricht** *der* 1 (das Unterrichten) music teaching; 2 (Stunde) music lesson; (Stunden) music lessons *pl.*; 3 (als Schulfach) music; *s. auch* **Englischunterricht**

Musikus /ˈmuːzikʊs/ *der;* ~, **Musizi** /ˈmuːzit͡si/ *od.* ~**se** (scherzh.) musician

Musik-: ~**verlag** *der* music publishers *pl.*; music publishing house; ~**video** *das* music video; ~**werk** *das* musical work; composition; ~**wissenschaft** *die* musicology; ~**wissenschaftler** *der,* ~**wissenschaftlerin** *die* ▸❶ **S. 113** musicologist

musisch
A *Adj.* artistic ‹*talent, person, family, etc.*›; ‹*talent*› for the arts; ‹*education*› in the arts; **die ~en Fächer** art and music; **ein ~es Gymnasium** *a* **Gymnasium** *specializing in teaching art and music*
B *adv.* artistically; **~ veranlagt sein** have an artistic disposition

musizieren /muziˈt͡siːrən/ *itr. V.* play music; (bes. unter Laien) make music; **früher wurde viel mehr musiziert** there used to be a lot more music-making

Muskat /mʊsˈkaːt/ *der;* ~[e]s, ~e nutmeg

Muskateller /mʊskaˈtɛlɐ/ *der;* ~s, ~: muscatel [wine]

Muskat-nuss, *Muskat-nuß *die* nutmeg

Muskel /ˈmʊskl̩/ *der;* ~s, ~n ▸❶ **S. 435** muscle; **der hat vielleicht ~n!** (ugs.) he has quite some muscles (coll.); he's really muscular; **~n bekommen** develop muscles; **seine ~n spielen lassen** flex one's muscles

Muskel-: ~**atrophie** *die* ▸❶ **S. 439** (Med.) muscular atrophy; ~**faser** *die* ▸❶ **S. 435** muscle fibre; ~**kater** *der* stiff muscles *pl.*; **~kater haben** be stiff and aching; **~kater in den Waden haben** have stiff calves; be stiff in one's calves; ~**kraft** *die* muscle-power; ~**krampf** *der* cramp; **~krämpfe/einen ~krampf bekommen** get cramp; ~**mann** *der* (ugs.) muscleman; ~**paket** *das* (ugs.) 1 (~n) bulging muscles *pl.* 2 ▸ **Muskelmann**; ~**protz** *der* (ugs.) muscleman; Tarzan (joc.); ~**riss, *~riß** *der* ▸❶ **S. 439** torn muscle; ~**schwund** *der* ▸❶ **S. 439** (Med.) muscular atrophy; ~**shirt** *das* muscle shirt; ~**zerrung** *die* ▸❶ **S. 439** (Med.) pulled muscle; **sich** *(Dat.)* **eine ~zerrung zuziehen** pull a muscle

Muskete /mʊsˈkeːtə/ *die;* ~, ~n (hist.) musket

Musketier /mʊskeˈtiːɐ̯/ *der;* ~s, ~e (hist.) musketeer

Muskulatur /mʊskulaˈtuːɐ̯/ *die;* ~, ~en ▸❶ **S. 435** musculature; muscular system

muskulös /mʊskuˈløːs/ *Adj.* muscular

Müsli /ˈmyːsli/ *das;* ~s, ~s muesli

Muslim /ˈmʊslɪm/ *der;* ~s, ~e *od.* ~s Muslim

Muslimin *die;* ~, ~nen Muslim [woman]

muslimisch
A *Adj.* Muslim
B *adv.* on Muslim principles; **~ erzogen werden** be brought up in the Muslim faith

muss, *muß /mʊs/ *1. u. 3. Pers. Sg. Präsens v.* **müssen**

Muss, *Muß *das;* ~: necessity; must (coll.); **es ist kein ~:** it's not essential

Muss-Bestimmung, *Muß-Bestimmung *die* absolute *or* fixed rule

Muße /ˈmuːsə/ *die;* ~: leisure; **dazu fehlt mir die ~:** I have no time to spare for it; **etw. in** *od.* **mit ~ tun** do sth. at one's leisure; take one's time over sth.

Muss·ehe, *Muß·ehe *die* (ugs.) shotgun marriage

Musselin /mʊsəˈliːn/ *der;* ~s, ~e muslin

müssen /ˈmʏsn̩/
A *unr. Modalverb; 2. Part.* ~ 1 (gezwungen, verpflichtet, notwendig sein) have to; **er muss es tun** he must do it; he has to *or* (coll.) has got to do it; **er muss es nicht tun** he does not have to do it; he has not got to do it (coll.); **er musste es tun** *od.* **hat es tun ~:** he had to do it; **du musstest nicht kommen** you did not have to come; **muss er es tun?** must he do it?; does he have to *or* (coll.) has he got to do it?; **irgendwann muss es ja doch mal gemacht werden** after all, it's got to be done some time; **wir werden zurückkommen ~:** we shall have to come back; **heiraten ~** (ugs.) have to get married; **muss das jetzt sein?** does it have to be now?; **muss das sein?** it is really necessary?; (Ärger über jmds. Verhalten ausdrückend) do you have to?; **es muss nicht sein** it is not essential; **es muss ja nicht stimmen** it is not necessarily true; **so musste es ja kommen** it was inevitable that it should come to this; it had to happen; **warum muss das ausgerechnet mir passieren?** why does it have to happen to me, of all people?; **das muss man gesehen haben!** you mustn't miss ist!; it's not to be missed!; (iron.) it's a sight not to be missed!; **wir ~ Ihnen leider mitteilen, dass ...** we regret to have to inform you that ...; **das muss man sich** *(Dat.)* **mal vorstellen!** just imagine!; **das muss 1980 gewesen sein** it must have been in 1980; **er muss gleich hier sein** he will be here *or* he is bound to be here at any moment 2 *im 2. Konjunktiv* **es müsste doch möglich sein** it ought to be possible; **das müsstest du eigentlich schon wissen** you really ought to *or* should know that by now; **so müsste es immer sein** it ought to be like this all the time; this is how it should always be; **reich müsste man sein!** how nice it would be to be rich!; all one needs is [plenty of] money!; **man müsste nochmals zwanzig sein** oh to be twenty again! 3 *verneint* (nordd.: dürfen) **du musst nicht alles glauben, was er sagt** you must not believe everything he says
B *unr. itr. V.* 1 (irgendwohin gehen ~) have to go; **ich muss zur Arbeit/nach Hause** I have to *or* must go to work/go home; **der Brief muss zur Post** the letter needs posting *or* taking to the post; **muss der Antrag heute zum Amt?** does the application have to be taken to the office today?; **ich muss mal** (fam.) I've got to *or* need to spend a penny (Brit. coll.) *or* (Amer. coll.) go to the john 2 (gezwungen, verpflichtet sein) **muss er?** does he have to?; has he got to? (coll.); **er muss nicht** he doesn't have to *or* (coll.) hasn't got to; **kein Mensch muss ~:** nobody 'has to do 'anything 3 (ugs.: an der Reihe sein) **heute muss Peter** it's Peter's turn today

Muße-stunde *die* free hour; hour of leisure

müßig /ˈmyːsɪç/
A *Adj.* 1 idle ‹*person*›; ‹*hours, weeks, life*› of leisure 2 (zwecklos) pointless
B *adv.* idly

Müßig-: ~**gang** *der* leisure; (Untätigkeit) idleness; **~gang ist aller Laster Anfang** (Spr.) the devil finds work for idle hands; ~**gänger** *der;* ~~s, ~~, ~**gängerin** *die;* ~~, ~~**nen** idler; **~gänger** *Pl.* people with time on their hands

Müßigkeit *die;* ~ (geh.) 1 idleness 2 (Zwecklosigkeit) pointlessness

musste, *mußte /ˈmʊstə/ *1. u. 3. Pers. Sg. Prät. v.* **müssen**

Mustang /ˈmʊstaŋ/ *der;* ~s, ~s mustang

Muster /ˈmʊstɐ/ *das;* ~s, ~ 1 (Vorlage) pattern; **nach einem ~ stricken** knit from a pattern; **das ausgefüllte Formular dient als ~ für den Antragsteller** the form that is filled in is intended as a specimen for the applicant to follow; **nach diesem ~ arbeiten** (fig.) operate on these lines *or* on this model 2 (Vorbild) model (**an** + *Dat.* of); **er ist ein ~ an Fleiß** he is a model of industry; **er ist ein ~ von einem Ehemann** (ugs.) he is a model husband 3 (Verzierung) pattern; **~ entwerfen** produce designs; **in welchem ~ strickst du die Jacke?** which stitch are you using to knit the jacket? 4 (Warenprobe) sample; **unverkäufliches ~:** sample not for sale; (veralt.: auf einer Warensendung) **~ ohne Wert** sample with no commercial value

muster-, Muster-: ~beispiel *das* perfect example; (Vorbild) model; **ein ~beispiel dafür sein, wie ...** be a perfect example of how ...; **~betrieb** *der* model enterprise; (Fabrik) model factory; **~brief** *der* sample letter; **~buch** *das* 1 (Kunstwiss.: Motivsammlung) pattern book; 2 (mit Proben) book of samples; pattern book; **~ehe** *die* perfect *or* ideal marriage; **~exemplar** *das* 1 (oft iron.: Vorbild) perfect specimen; **ein ~exemplar von [einem] Sohn** a model son; 2 (Probeexemplar) specimen copy; **~gültig** A *Adj.* exemplary; perfect, impeccable ‹*order*›; B *adv.* in an exemplary fashion

musterhaft
A *Adj.* exemplary; perfect, impeccable ‹*order, condition*›; model ‹*pupil*›
B *adv.* in an exemplary fashion; **~ geführt** perfectly *or* impeccably run

Muster-: ~haus *das* show house; **~knabe** *der* (oft abwertend) model child; **~koffer** *der* case of samples; **~ländle** /-lɛndlə/ *das;* **~~s** (scherzh.): *Baden-Württemberg, the 'model state' of the FRG*

mustern *tr. V.* 1 (betrachten) eye; (gründlich) scrutinize; (Milit.: inspizieren) inspect ‹*troops*›; **jmdn. von Kopf bis Fuß** *od.* **von oben bis unten ~:** look sb. up and down 2 (Milit.: ärztlich untersuchen) **einen Wehrpflichtigen/den Jahrgang 1962 ~:** give somebody liable for military service his medical/give those born in 1962 their medicals

Muster-: ~prozess, *~prozeß *der* test case; **~schüler** *der,* **~schülerin** *die* model pupil; **~sendung** *die* consignment of samples

Musterung *die;* **~, ~en** 1 (das Betrachten) scrutiny; (Milit.: Inspektion) inspection 2 (Milit.: von Wehrpflichtigen) medical examination; medical 3 (Verzierung) pattern

Musterungs·bescheid *der* summons to attend one's medical examination

Mut /muːt/ *der;* **~[e]s** 1 courage; **es gehört viel ~ dazu** it takes a lot of courage [to do it]; **allen** *od.* **all seinen ~ zusammennehmen** take one's courage in both hands; screw up one's courage; **sich** (*Dat.*) **~ antrinken** give oneself Dutch courage; **mit dem ~ der Verzweiflung** with courage born of desperation; **jmdm. ~ zusprechen** [try to] bolster up sb.'s courage; **sich gegenseitig ~ machen** keep each other's spirits up; **das gab** *od.* **machte ihr neuen ~:** that gave her new heart; **den ~ [nicht] sinken lassen** *od.* **verlieren** [not] lose heart; **[neuen] ~ fassen** take [new] heart; **nur ~!** don't lose heart!; (trau dich) be brave! 2 (veralt.) *in* **guten** *od.* **frohen ~es sein** be in good spirits; **mit frischem ~:** full of cheer (dated); with a cheerful countenance; **zu ~e** ▸**zumute**

Mutation /mutaˈt͜sioːn/ *die;* **~, ~en** (Biol.) mutation

Mütchen /ˈmyːtçən/ *in* **sein ~ [an jmdm.] kühlen** (ugs. [scherzh.]) vent one's wrath [on sb.]

mutieren *itr. V.* (Biol.) mutate

mutig
A *Adj.* brave; courageous, brave ‹*words, decision, speech*›; **dem Mutigen gehört die Welt** fortune favours the brave
B *adv.* bravely; courageously

mut·los *Adj.* (niedergeschlagen) dejected; despondent; (entmutigt) disheartened; dispirited

Mut·losigkeit *die;* **~:** dejection; despondency

mutmaßen /ˈmuːtmaːsn̩/ *tr., itr. V.* conjecture; **~, dass ...** suppose *or* surmise that ...; **darüber ist schon viel gemutmaßt worden** there has been much conjecture *or* speculation about that

mutmaßlich
A *Adj.* supposed; presumed; suspected ‹*terrorist etc.*›
B *adv.* (geh.) **es wird sich ~ noch verschlechtern** it is presumed it will get worse; **sie sind ~ ertrunken** they are presumed drowned

Mutmaßung *die;* **~, ~en** conjecture

Mut-probe *die* test of courage

Muttchen /ˈmʊtçən/ *das;* **~s, ~** (ugs.) 1 (Koseform) mama 2 **[altes] ~:** little old lady 3 (abwertend: biedere Frau) good little housewife; (mütterlicher Typ) matronly sort (coll.); motherly soul

Mutter[1] /ˈmʊtɐ/ *die;* **~, Mütter** /ˈmʏtɐ/ 1 mother; **sie wird ~** (ist schwanger) she is expecting a baby; **eine werdende ~:** an expectant mother; **eine ~ von drei Kindern** a mother of three; **~ sein** be a mother; **grüßen Sie Ihre Frau ~!** remember me to your mother; **wie bei ~n** just like at home; ‹*food*› like mother makes/used to make; **die ~ Gottes** (kath. Rel.) the Mother of God; **~ Erde/Natur** (dichter.) Mother Earth/Nature; **bei ~ Grün schlafen** (ugs.) sleep out in the open; **die ~ der Kompanie** (Soldatenspr.) the company sergeant major 2 (Wirtsch.: **~gesellschaft**) parent company

Mutter[2] *die;* **~, ~n** (Schrauben~) nut

Mütter·beratungs·stelle *die* advisory centre for [pregnant or nursing] mothers

Mutter-: ~bindung *die* (Psych.) attachment to the/one's mother; **~boden** *der* topsoil; **~brust** *die* mother's breast

Mütterchen /ˈmʏtɐçən/ *das;* **~s, ~** 1 (Koseform) mummy (Brit. coll.); mommy (Amer. coll.) 2 **[altes] ~:** little old lady 3 *in* **~ Russland** Mother Russia

Mutter-: ~erde *die* ▸**~boden; ~freuden** *Pl. in* **~freuden entgegensehen** (geh.) be expecting a child

Mütter·genesungs·heim *das* convalescent home for mothers

Mutter-: ~gesellschaft *die* (Wirtsch.) parent company; **~glück** *das* joys *pl.* of motherhood; **~gottes** /-ˈ--/ *die;* **~~** (kath. Rel.) Mother of God; (Bild) Madonna

Mütter·heim *das* [residential] home for [unmarried] mothers and their children

Mutter-: ~herz *das* mother's heart; (scherzh. Anrede) mother [dear]; **~instinkt** *der* maternal instinct; **~komplex** *der* (Psych.) 1 (**~bindung**) mother fixation; 2 (**~instinkt**) [excessive] maternal instinct; mothering instinct; **~korn** *das; Pl.* **~~e** (Bot.) ergot; **~kreuz** *das* (ns.) *medal awarded to prolific mothers* (in the Nazi period); **~kuchen** *der* (Med.) placenta; **~land** *das* 1 (Kolonialstaat) mother country; 2 (Heimat) original home; motherland; **~leib** *der* womb; (Zool.) uterus

mütterlich
A *Adj.* 1 (von der Mutter) his/her *etc.* mother's; (verallgemeinernd) the mother's; (einer Mutter) maternal ‹*line, love, instincts, etc.*›; **die ~en Pflichten** the duties of a mother 2 (fürsorglich) motherly ‹*woman, care*›
B *adv.* in a motherly way

mütterlicher·seits *Adv.* on the/his/her *etc.* mother's side; **sein Großvater ~:** his maternal grandfather; his grandfather on his mother's side

Mütterlichkeit *die;* **~:** motherliness; (mütterliche Gefühle) motherly feeling

mutter-, Mutter-: ~liebe *die* motherly love *no art.*; **~los** *Adj.* motherless; **~mal** *das; Pl.* **~~e** birthmark; **~milch** *die* mother's milk; **etw. mit der ~milch einsaugen** (fig.) imbibe sth. with one's mother's milk; **~mord** *der* matricide; **~mund** *der* ▸**i S. 435** neck of the womb; cervix

Mütter-pass, *Mütter·paß *der: document carried by pregnant woman which gives details of her medical history, blood group, etc.*

Mutter-: ~pflicht *die* duty as a mother; maternal duty; **~schaf** *das* mother ewe

Mutterschaft *die;* **~:** motherhood

Mutterschafts-: ~geld *das* maternity benefit; **~urlaub** *der* maternity leave

mutter-, Mutter-: ~schiff *das* mother ship; (im Weltraum) parent ship; **~schutz** *der* 1 (Rechtsw.) *laws pl. protecting working pregnant women and mothers of newborn babies;* 2 (ugs.: Urlaub) maternity leave; **~schwein** *das* mother sow; **~seelen·allein** *Adj.* all alone; all on my *etc.* own; **~söhnchen** *das* (abwertend) mummy's *or* (Amer.) mama's boy; **~sprache** *die* native language; mother tongue; **~sprachler** /-ʃpraːxlɐ/ *der;* **~~s, ~~,** **~sprachlerin** *die;* **~~, ~~nen** (Sprachw.) native speaker; **~stelle** *die:* **bei** *od.* **an jmdm. ~stelle vertreten** take the place of a mother to sb.

Mütter·sterblichkeit *die* childbirth mortality

Mutter-: ~stolz *der* motherly pride; maternal pride; **~stute** *die* dam; **~tag** *der* Mother's Day *no def. art.*; **~tier** *das* 1 (Tier, das Junge hat) mother [animal]; dam; 2 (Zuchttier) brood animal; **~witz** *der* 1 (Humor) natural wit; 2 (Schläue) native cunning

Mutti /ˈmʊti/ *die;* **~, ~s** mummy (Brit. coll.); mum (Brit. coll.); mommy (Amer. coll.); mom (Amer. coll.)

mut-, Mut-: ~wille *der* wilfulness; (Über~) devilment; **aus [bloßem] ~willen** from [sheer] devilment; **~willig** A *Adj.* wilful; wanton ‹*destruction*›; (übermütig) high-spirited; B *adv.* wilfully; wantonly; (aus Über~) from devilment; **~willigkeit** *die;* **~~:** ▸**~wille**

Mützchen *das;* **~s, ~s** little cap

Mütze /ˈmʏt͜sə/ *die;* **~, ~n** cap; **etwas** *od.* **eins auf die ~ kriegen** (fig. ugs.) get told off; get a telling off; **eine ~ voll Schlaf** (ugs.) a nap; forty winks *pl.*

Mützen·schirm *der* peak of the/one's cap

MW *Abk.* 1 (Rundf.) = **Mittelwelle** MW 2 (Physik) = **Megawatt** MW

Mw.-St., MwSt. *Abk.* ▸**i S. 299 = Mehrwertsteuer** VAT

mykenisch /myˈkeːnɪʃ/ *Adj.* Mycenaean

Mykologie /mykoloˈgiː/ *die;* **~:** mycology *no art.*

Mykose /myˈkoːzə/ *die;* **~, ~n** mycosis

Myom /myˈoːm/ *das;* **~s, ~e** ▸**i S. 439** (Med.) myoma

Myriade /myˈri̯aːdə/ *die;* **~, ~n** (geh.) myriad

Myrrhe /ˈmʏrə/ *die;* **~, ~n** myrrh

Myrte /ˈmʏrtə/ *die;* **~, ~n** myrtle

Myrten·kranz *der* myrtle wreath

Mysterien·spiel *das* miracle play

mysteriös /mysteˈri̯øːs/
A *Adj.* mysterious
B *adv.* mysteriously

Mysterium /mʏsˈteːri̯ʊm/ *das;* **~s, Mysterien** mystery

Mystifikation /mʏstifikaˈt͜si̯oːn/ *die;* **~, ~en** shrouding *no indef. art.* in mystery

mystifizieren /mʏstifiˈt͜siːrən/ *tr. V.* shroud in mystery; (unklar machen) obfuscate

Mystifizierung *die;* **~, ~en** ▸**Mystifikation**

Mystik /ˈmʏstɪk/ *die;* **~:** mysticism

Mystiker *der;* **~s, ~, Mystikerin** *die;* **~, ~nen** mystic

mystisch
A *Adj.* mystical
B *adv.* mystically

Mystizismus /mʏstiˈt͜sɪsmʊs/ *der;* **~:** mysticism

mythisch /ˈmyːtɪʃ/ *Adj.* 1 mythical; ‹*heroes, traditions*› of myth [and legend], of mythology 2 (legendär) legendary

Mythologie /mytoloˈgiː/ *die;* **~, ~n** mythology

mythologisch *Adj.* mythological

mythologisieren *tr. V.* mythologize

Mythos /ˈmyːtɔs/ *der;* **~, Mythen** 1 (Sage, auch fig.: Unwahrheit) myth 2 (glorifizierte Person od. Sache) legend

Nn

ℹ nach

Wohin? = to

Ich fuhr mit dem Zug nach Wien
= I went to Vienna by train, I took the train to Vienna

Aber (die Richtung angebend):

Der Zug nach Wien hält nicht in Wels
= The train for *od.* to Vienna does not stop in Wels

Passagiere nach Zürich
= passengers [bound] for Zurich

Das Schiff ist unterwegs od. auf dem Wege nach Bombay
= The ship is on its way to *od.* is bound for Bombay

Sie sind nach Australien abgereist
= They have left for Australia

Die Maschine flog nach Osten
= The aircraft flew east[wards] *od.* towards the east

nach dem Meer zu
= towards the sea

nach allen Richtungen
= in all directions

Wann? = after

Nach dem Rennen gab er ein Interview
= He gave an interview after the race

nach Erhalt der Rechnung
= after receiving the invoice

Nach fünf Minuten trafen die ersten Läufer ein
= After five minutes *od.* Five minutes later the first runners arrived

Nach 22.00 Uhr verkehren die Züge stündlich
= After 10 p.m. trains run every hour

Aber bei Uhrzeitangaben:

um viertel/fünfundzwanzig nach sieben
= at a quarter/twenty-five past seven

Auch in der Reihenfolge:

Nach Ihnen!
= After you

eins nach dem andern
= one thing after another

Nach „für" steht der Akkusativ
= 'Für' is followed by the accusative

B kommt nach A in der Weltrangliste
= B comes after *od.* below A in the world rankings

Gemäß = according to, in accordance with

Diesem Bericht nach soll sie ein Kind bekommen
= According to this report she is expecting a child

nach deutschem Recht
= in accordance with German law

nach der neuesten Mode gekleidet
= dressed in [accordance with] the latest fashion

nach italienischer Art
= in the Italian manner

meiner Ansicht od. Meinung nach
= in my opinion

aller Wahrscheinlichkeit nach
= in all probability

nach etwas urteilen
= to judge by sth.

Seiner Sprache nach ist er Norddeutscher
= Going *od.* Judging by the way he speaks, he's North German

---

n, N /ɛn/ *das;* **~, ~:** n/N; *s. auch* **a, A**

N *Abk.* **= Nord[en]** ▸ℹ **S. 363** N

'n ▸**ein**; **einen**

na /na/ *Interj.* (ugs.) 1▸ (als Frage, Anrede, Aufforderung) well; **na, wie gehts?** well, how are you?; **na, du?** oh, it's you?; **na los!** come on then!; **na, wirds bald?/wo bleibst du denn?** come on, aren't you ready yet?/what's happened to you?; **na und?** (wennschon) so what? 2▸ (beschwichtigend) **na, na, na!** now, now, come along 3▸ ([zögernd] zustimmend) **na schön!, na gut!** oh, OK (coll.); well, all right; **na ja, wenn du meinst** well [all right], if you think so; **na, dann bis später** right, see you later then 4▸ (bekräftigend) **na und ob!** and how! (coll.); I'll say! (coll.); **na, der wird schauen!** gosh, he'll get a surprise!; **na und wie!** and how! (coll.); **na eben!** exactly!; **na dann!** oh, in 'that case!; **na endlich!** at last! 5▸ (triumphierend) **Na also! Ich hatte doch recht!** There you are! I was right! 6▸ (zweifelnd, besorgt) **na, wenn das mal gut geht** *od.* **klappt** well, let's hope it'll be OK (coll.); **na, wenn das dein Vater merkt!** oh dear, what if your father notices? 7▸ (ablehnend) **na, ich danke** you can keep it 8▸ (unsicher) **na, ich weiß nicht** hmm, I'm not sure; (staunend) **na so [et]was!** well I never! 9▸ (konsterniert) **na, was soll das denn?** now what's all this about? 10▸ (drohend) **na warte!** just [you] wait!; (auf einen nicht Anwesenden bezogen) just let him wait!

Nabe /'na:bə/ *die;* **~, ~n** hub

Nabel /'na:bl̩/ *der;* **~s, ~** ▸ℹ **S. 435** navel; **der ~ der Welt** (geh.) the hub of the universe

nabel-, Nabel-: ~binde *die* umbilical bandage; **~bruch** *der* ▸ℹ **S. 439** (Med.) umbilical hernia; **~frei** *Adj.* **ein ~freies Top** a crop top; **~frei gehen** wear a crop top; **~piercing** *das* navel piercing; belly-button piercing; (Schmuck) navel stud; belly-button stud; **~schau** *die* (salopp) **~schau halten** bare one's soul; **das Buch ist nichts als eine egozentrische ~schau** the book is nothing but a self-indulgent ego trip (coll.); **~schnur** *die Pl.* **~schnüre** umbilical cord

Naben-: ~dynamo *der* hub dynamo; **~schaltung** *die* hub gear

nach /na:x/

A *Präp. mit Dat.* 1▸ (räumlich) to; **~ Rom fahren** travel to Rome; **ist das der Zug ~ Köln?** is that the train for Cologne *or* the Cologne train?; **ja, der Zug fährt ~ Köln** yes, this train goes to Cologne; **~ Hause gehen** go home; **~ ... abreisen** leave for ...; **sich ~ vorn/hinten beugen** bend forwards/backwards; **stell den Schrank weiter ~ hinten** put the cupboard further back; **komm ganz ~ vorn** come right to the front; **~ links/rechts** to the left/right; **~ der Seite** to the side; **~ allen Richtungen** in all directions; **~ Osten [zu]** eastwards; [towards the] east; **~ ... zu** towards ...; **~ außen/innen** outwards/inwards; **ich bringe den Abfall ~ draußen** I am taking the rubbish outside; **ein Zimmer ~ der Straße** a room looking out on to *or* facing the street 2▸ ▸ℹ **S. 729** (zeitlich) after; **~ fünf Minuten** after five minutes; five minutes later; **zehn [Minuten] ~ zwei** ten [minutes] past two; **wird man noch ~ 100 Jahren daran denken?** will anyone remember it in a hundred years' time?; **im Jahre 1500 ~ Christus** *od.* **Christi Geburt** in AD 1500; **vier Wochen ~ Erhalt der Rechnung** four weeks after receipt of *or* after receiving the invoice; **gleich ~ Erhalt der Rechnung** immediately upon *or* after receiving the invoice 3▸ (mit bestimmten Verben, bezeichnet das Ziel der Handlung) for; **greifen/streben/schicken ~:** grasp/strive/send for 4▸ (bezeichnet [räumliche und zeitliche] Reihenfolge) after; **~ Ihnen/dir!** after you; **die Post kommt ~ dem Rathaus** the post office is after *or* past the town hall; **~ „für" steht der Akkusativ** 'für' is followed by the accusative; 'für' takes the accusative; **der Bundestagspräsident kommt ~ dem Bundespräsidenten** (im gesellschaftlichen Rang) the president of the Federal Parliament is lower in rank than the Federal President; *s. auch* **ander... B 2** 5▸ (gemäß) according to; (in Übereinstimmung mit) in accordance with; **~ meiner Ansicht** *od.* **Meinung, meiner Ansicht** *od.* **Meinung ~:** in my view *or* opinion; **~ menschlichem Ermessen** as far as anyone can judge; **aller Wahrscheinlichkeit ~:** in all probability; **~ Lage der Dinge wird es kaum möglich sein** as matters stand it will hardly be possible; **je** *od.* **ganz ~ Wunsch** just as you/they *etc.* wish; however you/they *etc.* like; **Variationen ~ einem Thema von Händel** variations on a theme of Handel; **[frei] ~ Goethe** [freely] adapted from Goethe; **~ einer Vorlage zeichnen** draw from an original; **eine Suppe ~ Art des Hauses** (Kochk.) a soup à la maison; **~ rheinischer Art** (Kochk.) in the Rhenish style; **~ altem Brauch** in accordance with *or* by ancient custom; **~ der neuesten Mode gekleidet** dressed in [accordance with] the latest fashion; **~ etw. schmecken/riechen** taste/smell of sth.; **seinem Wesen ~:** by nature; **sie kommt eher ~ dem Vater** (ugs.) she takes more after her father; **~ dem [zu urteilen], was er gesagt hat** going *or* judging by what he said; from what he said; **jmdn. nur dem Namen ~**

kennen know sb. by name only; **~ jmdm. genannt werden** be named after sb.; **Dienst ~ Vorschrift** work to rule; **dem Gesetz ~:** in accordance with the law; by law; **~ Paragraph 5, Artikel 4** in accordance with *or* under paragraph 5, clause 4; **der Größe ~/~ dem Gewicht** according to *or* by size/weight; **~ Stunden/Umsatz bezahlt werden** be paid by the hour/according to turnover; **15 Pfund sind etwa 21 Euro ~ unserem Geld** 15 pounds are about 21 euros in our money
B *Adv.* **1** (räumlich) **[alle] mir ~!** [everybody] follow me!
2 (zeitlich) **~ und ~:** little by little; gradually; **~ wie vor** still; as always

nach|äffen /-ɛfn̩/ *tr. V.* (abwertend) mimic

Nachäfferei *die;* ~ (abwertend) mimicry; mimicking

nach|ahmen /-a:mən/ *tr. V.* **1** (kopieren) imitate **2** (nacheifern) emulate

nachahmens·wert *Adj.* worthy of imitation *postpos.;* exemplary; **nicht ~:** not to be imitated *postpos.*

Nachahmer *der;* **~s, ~, Nachahmerin** *die;* **~, ~nen** imitator

Nachahmung *die;* **~, ~en** **1** imitation **2** (das Nacheifern) emulation

Nachahmungs-: ~täter *der,* **~täterin** *die* copycat criminal; copycat offender; **~trieb** *der* (Verhaltensf., Psych.) imitative instinct

nach|arbeiten
A *tr. V.* **1** (nachholen) **eine Stunde ~:** work an extra hour to make up; **sie muss die versäumten Stunden ~:** she has to make up for the hours she missed **2** (überarbeiten) go over, finish off ‹*workpiece*›; (retuschieren) retouch ‹*picture*› **3** (nachbilden) copy (+ *Dat.* from)
B *itr. V.* do extra work to make up

Nachbar /'naxba:ɐ̯/ *der;* **~n** *od. selten* **~s, ~n** neighbour; **Herr ~:** neighbour; **die lieben ~n** (iron.) the nice people next door (iron.); **~s Hund** the neighbours'/neighbour's dog; **mein ~ im Kino** the man [sitting] next to me in the cinema

Nachbar-: ~dorf *das* neighbouring village; **~haus** *das* house next door; **unser ~haus** the house next door to us

Nachbarin *die;* **~, ~nen** neighbour; **meine ~ im Kino** the woman [sitting] next to me in the cinema

Nachbar·land *das* neighbouring country; **unser westliches ~:** our western neighbour

nachbarlich
A *Adj.* **1** (dem Nachbarn/den Nachbarn gehörend) neighbour's/neighbours'; (benachbart) neighbouring; next-door **2** (unter Nachbarn üblich) neighbourly; **in gutem ~em Einvernehmen leben** be good neighbours
B *adv.* (freundschaftlich) in a neighbourly way

Nachbarschaft *die;* ~ **1** (die Nachbarn) **die [ganze] ~:** all the neighbours *pl.;* the whole neighbourhood; **es hat sich in der ganzen ~ herumgesprochen** everybody in the neighbourhood has heard about it **2** (Beziehungen) **gute ~:** good neighbourliness; **wir halten** *od.* **pflegen eine gute ~:** we try to be good neighbours **3** (Gegend) neighbourhood; (Nähe) vicinity

nachbarschaftlich
A *Adj.* neighbourly
B *adv.* ▸**nachbarlich B**

Nachbarschafts-: ~haus *das* (Sozialwesen) neighbourhood [social] centre; **~hilfe** *die* **1** (gegenseitige Hilfe) neighbourly help; **mit ~hilfe gebaut** built with the assistance of the neighbours; **2** (Sozialwesen) neighbourhood social welfare organization (*run by independent welfare organizations*)

Nachbars-: ~familie *die* family next door; **~frau** *die* woman next door

Nachbar-: ~tisch *der* next *or* neighbouring table; **~wissenschaft** *die* allied *or* related science

Nach·bau *der;* **~[e]s, ~ten** **1** (das Nachbauen) reproduction; (von etw., was nicht mehr existiert) reconstruction **2** (das Nachgebaute) ▸**1:** reproduction; reconstruction

nach|bauen *tr. V.* reproduce; (wenn etw. nicht mehr existiert) reconstruct ‹*building, vehicle, etc.*›

Nach·beben *das* aftershock

nach|behandeln *tr. V.* **1** (nochmals behandeln) treat again **2** (nach ärztlicher Behandlung) **jmdn./etw. ~:** give sb./sth. follow-up treatment

Nach·behandlung *die* follow-up treatment; aftercare

nach|bekommen *unr. tr. V.* **1** (mehr bekommen) **[noch] etw. ~:** have some more of sth.; (bei Tisch) have seconds of sth. **2** (mehr kaufen können) get more of

nach|bereiten *tr. V.* (bes. Päd.) **1** (analysieren) assess the effectiveness of ‹*lesson*› **2** (vertiefen) go over [again] (in order to internalize the material)

Nachbereitung *die;* **~, ~en** (bes. Päd.) **1** (Analyse) assessment **2** (Vertiefung) further study (*for internalization*)

nach|bessern *tr. V.* repair; make good, put right ‹*defects*›

nach|bestellen *tr. V.* **[noch] etw. ~:** order more of sth.; ‹*shop*› order further stock of sth., reorder sth.; **die Teile des Geschirrs ~:** order more [parts] of the service

Nach·bestellung *die;* **~, ~en** further order (+ *Gen.* for); (vom Händler aufgegeben) repeat order (+ *Gen.* for)

nach|beten *tr. V.* (ugs. abwertend) repeat parrot-fashion; regurgitate

nach|bezahlen ▸**nachzahlen**

nach|bilden *tr. V.* reproduce, copy (+ *Dat.* from); **einem ägyptischen Original nachgebildet sein** be a reproduction *or* copy of an Egyptian original

Nach·bildung *die* **1** (das Nachbilden) copying **2** (Gegenstand) copy; replica

nach|bleiben *unr. tr. V.; mit sein* (landsch.) be left (*from an injury etc.*); **wenn da bloß nichts nachbleibt!** let's hope there's no lasting damage *or* after-effects!

nach|blicken *tr. V.* (geh.) **jmdm./einer Sache ~:** look *or* gaze after sb./sth.

Nach·blutung *die* (Med.) secondary haemorrhage

nach|bringen *unr. tr. V.* bring along ‹*sth. left behind*›; **sie hat ihm den Schirm nachgebracht** she brought the umbrella he left behind

nach·christlich *Adj.:* **im ersten ~en Jahrhundert** in the first century AD

nach|datieren *tr. V.* backdate

nachdem *Konj.* **1** (zeitlich) after; **ich ging erst, ~ ich mich vergewissert hatte** I only left when I had made sure; I did not leave until I had made sure; **~ ich das Buch gelesen hatte** after *or* when I had read the book **2** (südd.: kausal) since **3** ▸**je¹ C 2**

nach|denken *unr. itr. V.* think (**über** + *Akk.* about); (lange u. erwägend) reflect (**über** + *Akk.* on); **darüber darf man gar nicht ~!** it doesn't bear thinking about; **denk mal [gut** *od.* **scharf] nach** have a [good] think; think carefully; **er dachte darüber nach, wie er sich entscheiden sollte** he considered how he should decide; **ohne nachzudenken** without stopping to think

Nach·denken *das* thought; **Zeit zum ~:** time to think; **nach langem ~:** after thinking about it for a long time; after mature consideration (formal); **in tiefes ~ versunken** sunk in thought

nachdenklich
A *Adj.* thoughtful; pensive; **jmdn. [sehr] ~ machen** *od.* **stimmen** [really] make sb. think; give sb. [much] cause for thought
B *adv.* thoughtfully; pensively

Nach·dichtung *die* adaptation/recreation (in another language)

nach|drängen *itr. V.; mit sein* (nach vorn schieben) push forwards; (von hinten) push from behind; **einige liefen auf das Spielfeld, andere drängten nach** some ran on to the pitch and others crowded after them

Nach·druck *der; Pl.* **~e** **1** **mit ~:** emphatically; **etw. mit ~/mit größtem ~ fordern** demand sth. vigorously *or* forcefully/with the utmost vigour; **seinen Worten ~ verleihen** give one's words emphasis; **auf etw.** (*Akk.*) **[besonderen] ~ legen** place [particular] emphasis on sth.; stress sth. [particularly] **2** (Druckw.) reprint; (beim Copyrightvermerk) **~[, auch auszugsweise,] verboten** not to be reproduced [in part or in whole]

nach|drucken *tr. V.* reprint ‹*book*›; print more ‹*invoices, letterheads, etc.*›

nachdrücklich
A *Adj.* emphatic ‹*warning, confirmation, advice*›; insistent ‹*demand*›; urgent ‹*request, appeal*›
B *adv.* emphatically; **ich muss Sie ~ bitten, zu ...** I must urgently request you to ...; **etw. ~ verlangen** demand sth. vigorously; **~ darauf hinweisen, dass ...** emphasize that ...:

Nachdrücklichkeit *die;* ~ ▸**nachdrücklich:** emphatic nature; insistent nature; urgency

nach|dunkeln *itr. V.; mit sein* get darker

Nach·durst *der* morning-after thirst

nach|eifern *itr. V.* **jmdm. ~:** emulate sb.

nach|eilen *itr. V.; mit sein* **jmdm. ~:** hurry after sb.

nach·einander *Adv.* **1** (räumlich, zeitlich) one after the other; **kurz/unmittelbar ~:** one shortly/immediately after the other; **fünfmal/drei Tage ~:** five times/three days in a row **2** *in Verbindung mit best. Verben* **~ sehen** keep an eye on each other; **sich ~ richten** coordinate with one another; **sich ~ sehnen** long for one another

nach|empfinden *unr. tr. V.* **1** (nachfühlen) empathize with ‹*feeling*›; share ‹*delight, sorrow*›; **ich kann [dir] deinen Ärger gut ~:** I can well understand *or* appreciate your feeling of anger **2** (nachmachen) recreate ‹*expression, atmosphere, event*›; take ‹*work of art*› as a model; **einer Sache** (*Dat.*) **nachempfunden sein** take its inspiration from sth.; be modelled on sth.

Nachen /'naxn̩/ *der;* **~s, ~** (dichter.) shallop

nach|erzählen *tr. V.* retell

Nach·erzählung *die* retelling [of a story]; (Schulw.) reproduction

Nachfahr /-fa:ɐ̯/ *der;* **~en** *od. selten* **~s, ~en** (geh.) descendant; (fig.: Nachfolger) successor

nach|fahren *unr. itr. V.; mit sein* follow [on]; **jmdm. ~:** follow sb.

Nachfahrin *die;* **~, ~nen** (geh.) descendant; (fig.: Nachfolgerin) successor

nach|fassen
A *itr. V.* **1** (noch einmal zufassen) change one's grip (**an** + *Dat.* on); (beim Fangen des Balls) make a second attempt to gather the ball **2** (ugs.: nachfragen) ask a supplementary question **3** (bes. Soldatenspr.) **[noch einmal** *od.* **noch mal] ~:** have seconds
B *tr. V.* (bes. Soldatenspr.) have seconds of ‹*soup etc.*›

Nach·feier *die* belated celebration

nach|feiern
A *tr. V.* celebrate ‹*birthday, Christmas*› at a later date
B *itr. V.* have a belated celebration

Nach·folge *die* succession; **die ~ B.s regeln** settle who is to be B's successor; **jmds. ~ antreten** succeed sb.; **die ~ Christi** the discipleship of Christ

nach|folgen *itr. V.; mit sein* follow; **jmdm./einer Sache ~:** follow sb./sth.; **jmdm. im Amt ~:** succeed sb. in office

nach·folgend *Adj.* following; subsequent ‹*chapter, issue*›; **im Nachfolgenden** below; in the text that follows

Nachfolge·organisation *die* successor organization (*Gen.* to)

Nachfolger *der;* **~s, ~, Nachfolgerin** *die;* **~, ~nen** successor

Nachfolge·staat *der* succession *or* successor state

nach|fordern *tr. V.* **[noch] 500 Euro ~:** demand an additional 500 euros

Nach·forderung *die* additional demand (*Gen.,* **von** for)

nach|forschen *itr. V.* make inquiries; investigate [the matter]; **~, ob .../wer .../welcher ...**

n

try to find out *or* investigate whether .../who .../which ...; **einer Sache** (*Dat.*) **~** (geh.) investigate a matter

Nach·forschung *die* investigation; inquiry; **~en [nach etw.] anstellen** make inquiries [into sth.]; **die ~en, wohin ...** the inquiries as to where ...

Nach·frage *die* **1** (Kaufmannsspr.) demand (**nach** for); **es herrscht keine ~ mehr danach** there is no longer any demand for it; *s. auch* **Angebot** **2** (veralt.: Frage) inquiry; question; **danke der [gütigen] ~/für die [gütige] ~** (meist scherzh.) how kind of you to inquire

nach|fragen *itr. V.* ask; inquire; **bei jmdm. ~:** ask sb.; **ob ich mal ~ soll?** should I ask about it *or* make inquiries?; **um etw. ~:** ask for *or* request sth.

Nach·frist *die* (Rechtsw.): *additional time given for performance of a contract*

nach|fühlen *tr. V.* empathize with; **jmdm. seine Wut ~:** understand sb.'s anger; **das kann ich dir ~!** I know how you feel!

nach|füllen *tr. V.* refill ‹*glass, vessel, etc.*›; (wenn nicht leer) fill up; top up; **jmdm. das Glas** *od.* **jmds. Glas ~:** refill/fill up sb.'s glass; **Salz/Wein ~:** put [some] more salt/wine in

Nach·gang *in* **im ~** (Amtsspr.) subsequently

nach|geben
A *unr. itr. V.* **1** give way; (aus Schwäche) give in; **jmdm. zu viel ~:** give in to sb. *or* let sb. have his/her way too often; **seiner Verzweiflung/Müdigkeit ~:** give in to one's despair/tiredness **2** (sich dehnen) stretch; **das Material gibt ein wenig nach** there is some give in the material **3** (Bankw., Wirtsch.: sinken) ‹*prices, currency*› weaken
B *unr. tr. V.* **1** (mehr geben) **jmdm. [etwas] Fleisch/Suppe** *usw.* **~:** give sb. [some] more meat/soup *etc.* **2** *in* **jmdm. nichts/nicht viel** *od.* **wenig ~:** be sb.'s equal/almost sb.'s equal (**an** + *Dat.* in)

nach·geboren *Adj.* **1** posthumous ‹*son, daughter*› **2** (viel jünger) much younger; born much later *postpos.*

Nach·gebühr *die* excess postage

Nach·geburt *die* **1** (Vorgang) expulsion of the afterbirth **2** (Gewebe) afterbirth

nach|gehen *unr. itr. V.; mit sein* **1** (folgen) **jmdm./einer Sache ~:** follow sb./sth.; **gehen Sie der Musik nach** follow the sound of the music; **einer Sache/einer Frage/einem Problem** *usw.* **~** (fig.) look into a matter/question/problem *etc.* **2** (nicht aus dem Kopf gehen) **jmdm. ~:** remain on sb.'s mind; occupy sb.'s thoughts **3** **seinen Geschäften** *od.* **Beschäftigungen/seinem Tagewerk ~:** go about one's business/daily work; **seinen Interessen/seinem Studium ~:** pursue one's interests/one's studies; **einem Beruf ~:** practise a profession **4** ‹*clock, watch*› be slow; **[um] eine Stunde ~:** be an hour slow; **eine Stunde am Tag ~:** lose an hour a day

nach·gelassen
A *2. Part. v.* **nachlassen**
B *Adj.*; unpublished (*at the author's/composer's death*); **die ~en Schriften des Autors** the unpublished writings left by the author

nach·gemacht
A *2. Part. v.* **nachmachen**
B *Adj.* imitation ‹*leather, gold*›; **~ aussehen** look like an imitation

nach·geordnet *Adj.* (Amtsspr.) inferior ‹*authority*›; subordinate ‹*person*›

nach·gerade *Adv.* **1** (allmählich) in time; by and by **2** (geradezu) positively; **das ist ~ eine Unverschämtheit** it's an absolute cheek

nach|geraten *unr. itr. V.; mit sein* **jmdm. ~:** take after sb.

Nach·geschmack *der* aftertaste; **einen üblen** *od.* **unguten ~ hinterlassen** (fig.) leave a nasty taste in the mouth

nach·gewiesener·maßen *Adv.* as has been proved

nach·giebig /-giːbɪç/ *Adj.* **1** (nicht streng) indulgent; yielding; **seinen Kindern gegenüber zu ~ sein** be too indulgent to *or* (coll.) soft with one's children **2** (weich) soft; yielding

Nach·giebigkeit *die; ~* **1** (gütige Art) indulgence **2** (Weichheit) softness

nach|gießen
A *unr. tr. V.* pour [in] some more; **darf ich Ihnen [noch] Wein ~?** may I top up your wine?
B *unr. itr. V.* (die Gläser nachfüllen) top up the drinks; **jmdm. ~:** pour sb. some more; top sb. up (coll.)

nach|grübeln *itr. V.* ponder (**über** + *Akk.* over)

nach|gucken (ugs.) ▸**nachsehen A 1, 2, 3, B 1, 2**

nach|haken *itr. V.* **1** (ugs.: noch einmal fragen) raise another question; **an einem Punkt muss ich ~:** I must come back on one point **2** (ugs.: nachgehen) make further inquiries **3** (Fußball) tackle from behind

Nach·hall *der; ~[e]s, ~e* reverberation; (fig. geh.: Nachwirkung) reverberations *pl.*; (in der Literatur o. Ä.) lingering echo

nach|hallen *itr. V.* reverberate; **seine Schritte hallten in dem leeren Haus nach** his footsteps echoed in the empty house

Nachhall·zeit *die* (Physik) reverberation period

nach·haltig
A *Adj.* **1** lasting; **jmdm. einen ~en Schreck versetzen** give sb. a fright that he/she will not forget [for a long time] **2** (Ökologie) sustainable
B *adv.* **1** (auf längere Zeit) for a long time; (nachdrücklich) persistently; **jmdn. ~ prägen** have a lasting effect on sb.; **~ geschädigt werden** sustain lasting damage **2** (Ökologie) sustainably

nach|hängen *unr. itr. V.* **1** (in Gedanken) dwell on; **seinen Gedanken ~:** lose oneself in one's thoughts; give oneself up to one's thoughts **2** (anhaften) **jmdm. ~:** stick to sb. **3** (ugs.: in der Schule zurück sein) lag behind

nach·hause *Adv.* (österr., schweiz.) home

Nach·hause·weg *der* way home

nach|helfen *unr. itr. V.* help; **jmdm. ~:** help sb. along; lend sb. a hand; **der Schönheit ~:** improve on Mother Nature; **dem Glück ~:** assist one's chances

nach·her /*auch:* '--/ *Adv.* **1** afterwards; (später) later [on]; **bis ~!** see you later!; **ich kann mich erst ~ darum kümmern** I can't deal with it until after that *or* later **2** (ugs.: womöglich) then perhaps; (sonst) otherwise; **erzählen Sie die Geschichte nicht weiter, ~ ist sie nicht wahr** don't tell this story to anyone — it might turn out to be untrue

Nach·hilfe *die* coaching

Nachhilfe-: ~lehrer *der,* **~lehrerin** *die* coach; **~schüler** *der:* **mein ~schüler** the boy I am coaching; **sie hat drei ~schüler** she is coaching three boys; **~schülerin** *die:* **meine ~schülerin** the girl I am coaching; **sie hat drei ~schülerinnen** she is coaching three girls; **~stunde** *die* private lesson; **~unterricht** *der* coaching

***nach·hinein, Nachhinein** *in* **im ~** (nachträglich) afterwards; later; (zurückblickend) with hindsight; **im ~ ist man immer klüger** one is always wiser after the event

Nachhol·bedarf *der* need to catch up; **ein ~ an etw.** (*Dat.*) a need to make up for the shortage of sth.

nach|holen *tr. V.* **1** (nachträglich erledigen) catch up on ‹*work, sleep*›; make up for ‹*working hours missed*›; **er hat viel/einiges nachzuholen** he has a lot of/some catching up to do; **den Schulabschluss ~:** take one's final school examination as a mature student; **ich habe ihr nicht gratuliert — ich muss es morgen ~:** I didn't congratulate her — I shall have to do it tomorrow instead **2** (zu sich holen) fetch; **seine Familie ~:** bring one's family to join one

Nach·hut *die; ~, ~en* (Milit.; auch fig.) rearguard

Nach·impfung *die* booster injection

nach|jagen *itr. V.; mit sein* **jmdm./einer Sache ~:** chase after sb./sth.; **dem Erfolg/Geld ~** (fig.) devote oneself to the pursuit of success/money

Nach·klang *der* reverberation

nach|klingen *unr. itr. V.; mit sein* go on sounding; **in jmdm. ~** (fig. geh.) linger on in sb.'s mind; stay with sb.

nach|kochen *tr. V.* cook ‹*dish, meal*› [following a/the recipe]

Nach·komma·stelle *die* decimal place; **auf die ~ genau** correct to the last decimal place

Nachkomme *der; ~n, ~n* descendant; (eines Tieres) offspring; **ohne ~n sterben** die without issue

nach|kommen *unr. itr. V.; mit sein* **1** follow [later]; come [on] later; **seine Familie wird [später] ~:** his family will join him later; **da kann noch etwas ~** (ugs.) something could still turn up; **die ~den Truppen** the cars/troops following behind **2** **seinen Pflichten ~:** fulfil one's duties; **seinen Verpflichtungen ~:** meet one's commitments; **einem Wunsch/Befehl/einer Bitte ~:** comply with a wish/an order/grant a request **3** (Schritt halten können) be able to keep up; **ich komme mit dem Abtrocknen nicht nach** I can't dry [the dishes] fast enough

Nachkommenschaft *die; ~:* descendants *pl.*; (eines Tieres) offspring

Nachkömmling /-kœmlɪŋ/ *der; ~s, ~e* much younger child (*than the rest*); afterthought (joc.); **Christoph, unser ~:** Christoph, much the youngest child in our family

Nach·kriegs-: ~generation *die* post-war generation; **~zeit** *die* post-war period; **in der [ersten] ~zeit** [immediately] after the war

Nach·kur *die* [period of] convalescence (*after a health cure*)

nach|laden *unr. itr. V.* reload

Nach·lass, *Nach·laß *der;* **Nachlasses, Nachlasse** *od.* **Nachlässe** **1** estate; (hinterlassene Gegenstände) personal effects *pl.* (*left by the deceased*); **literarischer/künstlerischer ~:** unpublished/unexhibited works *pl.* (*left by a writer/an artist*); **aus dem ~ veröffentlichen** publish posthumously **2** (Kaufmannsspr.: Rabatt) discount; reduction; **ein hoher ~:** a high discount *or* big reduction

nach|lassen
A *unr. itr. V.* **1** (schwächer/weniger werden) let up; ‹*rain, wind*› ease, let up; ‹*storm, heat*› abate, die down; ‹*anger*› subside, die down; ‹*pain, stress, pressure*› ease, lessen; ‹*noise*› lessen; ‹*fever*› go down; ‹*speed, demand*› decrease, drop; ‹*effect*› wear off; ‹*interest, enthusiasm, strength, courage*› flag, wane; ‹*resistance*› weaken; (schlechter werden) ‹*health, hearing, memory*› get worse, deteriorate; ‹*reactions*› become slower; ‹*performance*› deteriorate, fall off; ‹*business*› drop off, fall off; **meine Augen haben stark nachgelassen** my eyesight has deteriorated considerably **2** (landsch.: aufhören) **mit etw. nicht ~:** keep on with sth.; **du sollst damit jetzt ~!** stop that at once!; *s. auch* **Schreck**
B *unr. tr. V.* **1** (Kaufmannsspr.) give *or* allow a discount of; **man hat mir 30% des Preises nachgelassen** they gave me 30% off [the price] *or* a discount of 30% **2** (erlassen) **jmdm. seine Schulden ~:** let sb. off his/her debts **3** (lockern) slacken ‹*rope*›

Nachlass·gericht, *Nachlaß·gericht *das* (Rechtsw.) ≈ probate court

nach·lässig
A *Adj.* **1** (unordentlich) careless; untidy ‹*dress*›; negligent ‹*staff*›; lax, casual ‹*behaviour, way of talking*› **2** (unbeteiligt) indifferent; apathetic
B *adv.* **1** (unordentlich) carelessly; untidily ‹*dressed*› **2** (unbeteiligt) indifferently; apathetically

nachlässiger·weise *Adv.* carelessly

Nach·lässigkeit *die; ~, ~en* **1** ▸**nachlässig A 1**: carelessness; untidiness; negligence; laxness; casualness **2** (Fehler) careless mistake; **die kleinste ~:** the slightest mistake

Nachlass-, *Nachlaß-: ~pfleger *der,* **~pflegerin** *die* (Rechtsw.) administrator [of an/the estate] (*appointed by the court until the*

n

estate is settled); **~verwalter** *der*, **~verwalterin** *die* (Rechtsw.) executor

Nach·lauf *der* (Kfz-W.) castor angle

nach|laufen *unr. itr. V.; mit sein* **jmdm./einer Sache ~:** run *or* chase after sb./sth.; **einem Mädchen ~** (ugs.) chase a girl; **einer Illusion** (*Dat.*) **~** (fig.) chase after *or* pursue an illusion; **diese Kleider laufen sich nach** (fig. ugs.) these dresses are everywhere

nach|legen *tr., itr. V.* **[Holz/Kohlen] ~:** put some more wood/coal on

Nach·lese *die* **1** gleaning; (Ertrag) gleanings *pl.* **2** (geh.: Auswahl) further selection

nach|lesen *unr. tr. V.* look up; (überprüfen) check; **in den Statistiken ist nachzulesen, dass ...** the statistics show that ...

nach|liefern *tr. V.* (später liefern) supply later; (zusätzlich liefern) supply additionally; **der Rest wird nächste Woche nachgeliefert** the rest of the delivery will follow next week

Nach·lieferung *die* **1** (das Nachliefern) [subsequent] delivery **2** (Ware) further consignment

nach|lösen
A *tr. V.* **eine Fahrkarte ~:** buy a ticket [on the train/tram (Brit.) *or* (Amer.) streetcar]
B *itr. V.* pay the excess [fare]; (für die 1. Klasse) pay the extra [fare]

nachm. *Abk.* **nachmittags** p.m.

nach|machen *tr. V.* **1** (auch tun) copy; (imitieren) imitate; do an impersonation of ‹*politician etc.*›; (genauso herstellen) reproduce ‹*period furniture etc.*›; forge ‹*signature*›; forge, counterfeit ‹*money*›; **jmdm. alles ~:** copy everything sb. does; **das soll mir einer ~!** follow that!; **das macht ihm so schnell keiner nach** nobody is going to equal that in a hurry; *s. auch* **nachgemacht 2** (ugs.: später machen) do later; take ‹*exam*› later; **Hausaufgaben ~:** catch up on one's homework

nach|malen *tr. V.* go over [with fresh paint]

nach·malig *Adj.* (veralt.) future; **X, der ~e US-Präsident** X, who was to become President of the USA

nach|messen
A *unr. tr. V.* check the measurements of; check ‹*distance, length, etc.*›
B *itr. V.* check the measurements

Nach·mieter *der*, **Nach·mieterin** *die* next tenant; **einen Nachmieter stellen** find a tenant to take over the lease

***nach·mittag** ▸ **Nachmittag 1**

Nach·mittag *der* **1** afternoon; **zwei ~e in der Woche arbeiten** work two afternoons a week; **den ganzen ~:** all afternoon; **am ~,** (geh.) **des ~s** in the afternoon; (heute) this afternoon; **am frühen/späten ~:** early/late in the afternoon; **am selben ~:** the same afternoon; **am ~ des 8. März** on the afternoon of 8 March; **an einem sonnigen ~ im Juli** one sunny afternoon in July; **heute/morgen/gestern ~:** this/tomorrow/yesterday afternoon **2** (Veranstaltung) social afternoon

nachmittäglich /-mɪtɛːklɪç/ *Adj.* afternoon ‹*walk, nap*›

nach·mittags *Adv.* ▸ **❶ S. 729** in the afternoon; (heute) this afternoon; **dienstags ~:** on Tuesday afternoons; **um vier Uhr ~:** at four in the afternoon; at 4 p.m.

Nach·mittags-: **~kaffee** *der* afternoon coffee [and cakes]; **~vor·stellung** *die* afternoon performance; [afternoon] matinée

Nachnahme *die;* **~, ~n 1** **per ~:** cash on delivery; COD **2** (Sendung) COD parcel

Nachnahme-: **~gebühr** *die* (Postw.) cash on delivery fee; **~sendung** *die* (Postw.) COD parcel

Nach·name *der* surname; **wie heißt du mit ~n?** what is your surname?

nach|nutzen *tr. V.* (DDR) take over ‹*sb. else's innovation/method*›; make use of ‹*sb. else's experience*›

nach|plappern *tr. V.* (oft abwertend) repeat parrot-fashion; **jmdm. alles ~:** repeat everything sb. says

Nach·porto *das* excess postage

nach|prägen *tr. V.* **1** mint more, re-mint ‹*coins, medals*›; **[noch] 100 Stück wurden nachgeprägt** another 100 copies were minted **2** (fälschen) forge; counterfeit

Nach·prägung *die* **1** (Vorgang) re-minting **2** (Münze) copy; (Fälschung) forgery; counterfeit [coin]

nachprüfbar *Adj.* verifiable

Nachprüfbarkeit *die;* **~:** verifiability

nach|prüfen
A *tr. V.* **1** check ‹*document, statement, weight, alibi*›; verify ‹*correctness*› **2** (später prüfen) examine ‹*candidate*› later; (bei der Fahrprüfung) test ‹*learner driver*› later
B *itr. V.* check

Nach·prüfung *die* **1** checking **2** (spätere Prüfung) postponed examination

nachrangig *Adj.* of lower status *postpos.*; (weniger wichtig) less important; ‹*question*› of lower priority

Nachrangigkeit *die;* **~, ~en** ▸ **nachrangig:** lower status; lesser importance; lower priority

nach|rechnen
A *tr. V.* check ‹*figures*›
B *itr. V.* **1** (zur Kontrolle) check [the figures] **2** (zurückverfolgen) [think back and] work it out

Nach·rede *die:* **üble ~:** malicious gossip; (Rechtsw.) defamation [of character]

nach|reden *tr. V.* **1** (wiederholen) repeat **2** ▸ **nachsagen 2**

nach|reichen *tr. V.* hand in subsequently

nach|reifen *itr. V.; mit sein* ripen further (*after picking*)

nach|reisen *itr. V.; mit sein* **jmdm. ~:** travel after sb.; (losfahren) set off after sb.

nach|rennen *unr. itr. V.:* ▸ **nachlaufen**

Nachricht /ˈnaːxrɪçt/ *die;* **~, ~en 1** (Mitteilung) news *no pl.*; **das ist eine gute ~:** that is [a piece of] good news; **gute/schlechte ~en** good/bad news; **eine ~ hinterlassen** leave a message; **ich habe keine ~ von ihm** (Brief usw.) I haven't heard *or* had any word from him; **wir warten auf ~** *od.* **sind noch ohne ~** (Bestätigung) we are waiting to hear *or* have not heard yet; **jmdm. ~ geben** inform sb. **2** *Pl.* (Ferns., Rundf.) news *sing.*; **~en hören** listen to the news; **Sie hören ~en** here is the news; **das kam in den ~en** it was on the news

Nachrichten-: **~agentur** *die* news agency; **~dienst** *der* **1** (Geheimdienst) intelligence service; **2** ▸ **~agentur**; **~magazin** *das* news magazine; **~satellit** *der* communications satellite; **~sendung** *die* news broadcast; **~sperre** *die* news embargo *or* blackout; **~sprecher** *der*, **~sprecherin** *die* ▸ **❶ S. 113** newsreader; **~technik** *die* telecommunications [technology] *no art.*; **~übermittlung** *die* news transmission *no art.*

nach|rücken *itr. V.; mit sein* (aufrücken) move up; **[auf den Posten] ~:** be promoted [to the post]; take over [the post]; **dem Feind ~** (Mil.) move up behind the enemy

Nach·ruf *der;* **~[e]s, ~e** obituary (**auf** + *Akk.* of)

nach|rufen *unr. tr., itr. V.* **jmdm. [etw.] ~:** call [sth.] after sb.

Nach·ruhm *der;* **~[e]s** posthumous reputation

nach|rühmen *tr. V.* **jmdm. etw. ~:** credit sb. with sth.; **ihm rühmt man nach, dass er ...** he is famous for the fact that he ...

nach|rüsten
A *itr. V.* counter-arm
B *tr. V.* (Technik: zusätzlich ausstatten) **mit etw. ~:** equip additionally with sth.; upgrade ‹*television, hi-fi, etc.*› with sth.

Nach·rüstung *die;* **~ 1** (Waffen) counter-arming **2** (Technik) [additional] equipment; (von Stereoanlagen usw.) upgrading

Nachrüstungs·beschluss, ***Nachrüstungs·beschluß** *der* (Politik) decision to counter-arm

nach|sagen *tr. V.* **1** (wiederholen) repeat; **sag mir Folgendes nach** repeat the following after me **2** (über jmdn. sagen) **jmdm. Schlechtes ~:** speak ill of sb.; **man sagt ihm nach, er verstehe etwas davon** he is said to know something about it; **du darfst dir nicht ~ lassen, dass ...** you mustn't let it be said of you that ...; **wir wollen uns doch nichts ~ lassen!** we don't want anything said against us!; we don't want to get a bad reputation!

Nach·saison *die* late season

nach|salzen *unr.* (*auch regelm.*) *tr., itr. V.* **[etw.] ~:** put more salt in/on [sth.]

Nach·satz *der* **1** (letzte Bemerkung) postscript; (gesprochen) final remark **2** (Sprachw.) postponed clause

Nach·schau *in:* **~ halten** (geh.) investigate; look into it

nach|schauen (bes. südd., österr., schweiz.) ▸ **nachsehen A 1, 2, 3, B 1, 2**

nach|schenken *tr., itr. V.* top up one's/sb.'s glass; **jmdm. [Wein] ~:** top up sb.'s glass [with wine]

nach|schicken *tr. V.* **1** (durch die Post o. Ä.) forward; send on **2** (folgen lassen) **jmdm. jmdn. ~:** send sb. after sb.

Nach·schlag *der* **1** (ugs.: zusätzliche Portion) second helping; seconds *pl.* **2** (Musik: verzierender Ton) grace note (*after another note*); (Abschluss eines Trillers) two-note termination (*of a trill*)

nach|schlagen
A *unr. tr. V.* look up ‹*word, reference, text*›; (ugs.) consult, look at ‹*dictionary, book*›; **schlag mal nach, was X heißt** look up to see what X means
B *unr. itr. V.* **1** **im Lexikon/Wörterbuch ~:** consult the encyclopedia/dictionary **2** *mit sein* (geh.: ähnlich werden) **jmdm. ~:** take after sb.

Nachschlage·werk *das* work of reference

nach|schleichen *unr. itr. V.; mit sein* **jmdm. ~:** creep *or* steal after sb.

nach|schleifen[1] *unr. tr. V.* resharpen ‹*knife, blade*›; repolish ‹*lens*›

nach|schleifen[2] *tr. V.* (ugs.) drag [along] behind one/it

Nach·schlüssel *der* duplicate key

nach|schmeißen *unr. tr. V.* (ugs.) **1** (billig o. ä. geben) give away; **man bekommt sie nachgeschmissen** you get them for next to nothing; **sie haben ihm das Abitur nachgeschmissen** his school-leaving exam was handed to him on a plate (coll.) **2** ▸ **nachwerfen 1**

Nach·schrift *die* **1** notes *pl.* (+ *Gen.* on) **2** (Postskriptum) postscript (+ *Gen.* to)

Nach·schub *der* (Milit.) **1** supply (**an** + *Dat.* of); (fig.) [provision of] further *or* fresh supplies *pl.* (**an** + *Dat.* of); **der ~ ist schlecht organisiert** the supply services *or* supplies are badly organized **2** (~material) supplies *pl.* (**an** + *Dat.* of); (fig.) further supplies *pl.*

Nachschub·weg *der* (Milit.) supply line

Nach·schuss, ***Nach·schuß** *der* **1** (Wirtsch.) contribution in excess of one's original share; further call **2** (Ballspiele) shot on the rebound

nach|schütten *tr. V.* put on more ‹*coal, coke, etc.*›; pour in more ‹*water*›

nach|schwatzen, (bes. südd., österr.) **nach|schwätzen** *tr. V.* (abwertend) repeat [parrot-fashion]

nach|sehen
A *unr. itr. V.* **1** (hintersehen) **jmdm./einer Sache ~:** look *or* gaze after sb./sth. **2** (kontrollieren) check *or* have a look [to see]; **~, wer da ist** go and see *or* have a look who's there **3** (nachschlagen) look it up; have a look
B *unr. tr. V.* **1** (nachlesen) look up ‹*word, passage*› **2** (überprüfen) check [over]; look over **3** ▸ **❶ S. 227** (nicht verübeln) overlook, let pass ‹*remark*›; **jmdm. etw./zu viel ~:** let sb. get away with sth./too much

Nach·sehen *das: in* **das ~ haben** not get a look-in; (nichts abbekommen) be left with nothing; **jmdm. bleibt das ~:** sb. does not get a look-in; (bekommt nichts ab) sb. is left with nothing

nach|senden *unr. od. regelm. tr. V.:* ▸ **nachschicken**

Nach·sendung *die* (Postw.) forwarding

nach|setzen *itr. V.* **jmdm./einem Tier ~:** pursue sb./an animal

Nach·sicht *die* leniency; forbearance; **mit jmdm. ~ haben** *od.* **üben** be lenient with sb.; make allowances for sb.; **ich muss um ~ bitten, dass ich so spät komme** please forgive me *or* I must apologize for coming so late; **keine ~ kennen** make no allowances; (bei Strafen) show no mercy

nachsichtig
A *Adj.* lenient, forbearing (**gegen, mit** towards); (verständnisvoll) understanding
B *adv.* leniently; (verständnisvoll) understandingly

Nachsichtigkeit *die;* **~:** leniency; forbearance

nachsichts·voll ▸ **nachsichtig**

Nach·silbe *die* (Sprachw.) suffix

nach|sinnen *unr. itr. V.* (geh.) ponder; **einer Sache** (*Dat.*) **~:** think back to sth.

nach|sitzen *unr. itr. V.* be in detention; **[eine Stunde] ~ müssen** have [an hour's] detention

Nach·sommer *der* Indian summer

Nach·sorge *die* (Med.) aftercare *no indef. art.*

Nach·spann *der;* **~[e]s, ~e** (Film, Ferns.) [final] credits *pl.*

Nach·speise *die* dessert; sweet

Nach·spiel *das* **1** **die Sache wird noch ein ~ haben!** this affair will have repercussions; **ein gerichtliches ~ haben** result in court proceedings **2** (Theater o. Ä.) epilogue; (Musik) postlude **3** (beim Geschlechtsverkehr) afterplay

nach|spielen
A *tr. V.* **1** (Kartenspiel) **den Buben** *usw.* **~:** follow up with the jack *etc.* **2** (auch spielen) **er hat es mir vorgespielt, ich musste es ~:** he played it over to me, and I then had to play it myself **3** (nachahmen) imitate, mimic ‹*person*›; re-enact ‹*scene*› **4** (anderswo aufführen) take up, put on ‹*new play etc.*›
B *itr. V.* (Ballspiele, bes. Fußball) **[einige Minuten] ~:** play [a few minutes of] time added on; **der Schiedsrichter lässt ~:** the referee has added on time [for stoppages]

nach|spionieren *itr. V.* **jmdm. ~:** spy on sb.

nach|sprechen *unr. tr. V.* **[jmdm.] etw. ~:** repeat sth. [after sb.]

nach|spülen
A *tr. V.* rewash; wash again; (mit klarem Wasser) rinse
B *itr. V.* **1** (ausspülen) give it/them a rinse; **mit viel Wasser ~:** rinse out with plenty of water **2** (ugs.: trinken) **mit einem Bierchen ~:** have a beer as a chaser (coll.) *or* to wash it down

nach|spüren *itr. V.* **jmdm./einer Bande ~:** track down sb./a gang; **einer Sache** (*Dat.*) **~** (fig.) follow up *or* investigate sth.

nächst /nɛːçst/ *Präp. mit Dat.* (geh.) next to

nächst...
A *Sup. zu* **nahe**
B *Adj.* **1** ▸ **S. 800 der ~e Weg zum Bahnhof** the shortest way to the station; **in ~er Nähe** very near **2** ▸ **S. 800** (unmittelbar danach) next; **die ~e Straße links** the next street on the left; **beim ~en Bäcker** at the next baker's we come to; *s. auch* **best... 2 3** ▸ **S. 165**, ▸ **S. 816** (zeitlich) next; **am ~en Tag** the next day; **am ~en Ersten** on the first of next month; **bei ~er Gelegenheit** at the next opportunity; **in ~er Zukunft** in the very near future; **in den ~en Tagen/Jahren** in the next few days/years; **beim ~en Mal, das ~e Mal** the next time; **der Nächste, bitte!** next [one], please; **wer kommt als Nächster dran?** whose turn is it next?; **als Nächstes räume ich den Boden auf** the next thing I do *or* my next job will be to tidy the loft

nächst·beste *Adj.* ▸ **erstbeste**

Nächst·beste *der/die/das; adj. Dekl.* the first one [to turn up]; **das ~, was ich finde** the first thing I find

Nächste *der;* **~n, ~n** (geh.) neighbour; **jeder ist sich selbst der ~:** one has to look after one's own interests

nach|stehen *unr. itr. V.* **jmdm. an etw.** (*Dat.*) **nicht ~:** be sb.'s match in sth.; **jmdm./einer Sache in nichts ~:** be in no way inferior to sb./sth.

nach·stehend
A *Adj.* following
B *adv.* below

nach|steigen *unr. itr. V.; mit sein* (ugs.) **einem Mädchen ~:** try to get off with (Brit. coll.) *or* (Amer. coll.) make it with a girl

nach|stellen
A *tr. V.* **1** (Sprachw.) **A wird B** (*Dat.*) **nachgestellt** A is placed after B; **nachgestellte Präposition** postpositive preposition; **nachgestellter Satz** postponed clause **2** (zurückstellen) put back ‹*clock, watch*› **3** (neu/genauer einstellen) [re]adjust; take up the adjustment on ‹*brakes, clutch*› **4** (darstellen) portray; represent
B *itr. V.* (geh.) **einem Tier/einem Flüchtling ~:** hunt an animal/hunt *or* pursue a fugitive; **Hühnern** *usw.* **~** ‹*dog*› chase chickens *etc.*; **einem Mädchen ~** (ugs.) chase a girl

Nach·stellung *die* **1** (Sprachw.) postposition **2** *Pl.* (Verfolgung) pursuit *sing.*; (ugs.: Umwerbung) advances

Nächsten·liebe *die* charity [to one's neighbour]; brotherly love

nächstens /ˈnɛːçstn̩s/ *Adv.* **1** (demnächst) shortly; in the near future; **passen Sie ~ besser auf!** be more careful next time **2** (ugs.: wenn es so weitergeht) if it goes on like this

nächst-: **~folgend** *Adj.* next; **~gelegen** *Adj.* nearest; **~höher** *Adj.* next higher; **die ~höhere Klasse** the next class [up]; **~jährig** *Adj.* next year's; **~liegend** *Adj.* first, immediate ‹*problem*›; [most] obvious ‹*explanation etc.*›; **das Nächstliegende** the [most] obvious thing; **~möglich** *Adj.* earliest possible

nach|stoßen *unr. itr. V.* **1** *mit sein* (Milit.: vordringen) move up *or* advance [behind them] **2** (im Gespräch) follow up [with another thrust]

nach|suchen *itr. V.* **1** (geh.: bitten) **um etw. ~:** request sth.; (bes. schriftlich) apply for sth. **2** (intensiv suchen) search

***nacht** /naxt/ ▸ **Nacht**

Nacht *die;* **~, Nächte** /ˈnɛçtə/ night; **es wird/ist ~:** it is getting dark/it is dark; night is falling/has fallen; **die ~ brach herein** night fell; **bei ~, in der ~,** (geh.) **des ~s** at night[-time]; **eines ~s** one night; **~ für ~:** night after night; **letzte ~:** last night; **die halbe ~:** half the night; **die ganze ~ [hindurch]** all night long; **diese ~:** tonight; **mitten in der ~:** in the middle of the night; **bis tief in die ~ hinein, bis spät in der ~:** until late at night; (bis in die Morgenstunden) into the small hours; **in der ~ vom 12. auf den 13. Mai** on the night of 12 May; **in der ~ auf Montag** on Sunday night; **über ~ bleiben** stay overnight; **über ~ berühmt werden** (fig.) become famous overnight; **zu[r] ~ essen** (südd., österr.) have one's evening meal; **gute ~!** good night!; **[na,] dann gute ~!** (iron.) [well,] that's that!; **die ~ zum Tage machen, sich** (*Dat.*) **die ~ um die Ohren schlagen** (ugs.) stay up all night; **bei ~ und Nebel** under cover of darkness; (heimlich) furtively; like a thief in the night; **~ der langen Messer** (salopp) night of the long knives; **die ~ des Wahnsinns/Krieges/der Tyrannei** (dichter.) the dark night of madness/war/tyranny; **gestern/morgen ~:** last/tomorrow night; **heute ~:** tonight; (letzte Nacht) last night; *s. auch* **hässlich A 1**; **heilig 2**; **schwarz A 1**

nacht·aktiv *Adj.* (Zool.) nocturnal

nach|tanken *tr., itr. V.* fill up; ‹*aircraft*› refuel; **20 Liter ~:** put in another 20 litres

nacht-, Nacht-: **~arbeit** *die* night work *no art.*; **~aufnahme** *die* night photograph *or* shot; **~bar** *die* night spot (coll.); **~blau** *Adj.* (geh., dichter.) midnight blue; **~blind** *Adj.* night-blind; **~blindheit** *die* night blindness; **~creme** *die* night cream; **~dienst** *der* night duty; **~dienst haben** be on night duty; ‹*chemist's shop*› be open late

Nach·teil *der* disadvantage; **der ~, allein zu reisen** the disadvantage *or* drawback of travelling alone; **aus etw. entsteht** *od.* **erwächst jmdm. ein ~:** sth. puts sb. at a disadvantage; **im ~ sein, sich im ~ befinden** be at a disadvantage; **ich hatte nur ~e davon** I had nothing but disadvantages as a result; **der Prozess ging zu seinem ~ aus** the trial went against him; **sich zu seinem ~ verändern** change for the worse; **jmdm. zum ~ gereichen, zu jmds. ~ gereichen** (geh.) be to sb.'s detriment

nachteilig
A *Adj.* detrimental; harmful; **über sie ist nichts Nachteiliges bekannt** nothing to her disadvantage is known about her
B *adv.* detrimentally; harmfully; **sich ~ auswirken** have a detrimental *or* harmful effect

nächte·lang
A *Adj.*; lasting several nights *postpos.*; (ganze Nächte dauernd) all-night
B *adv.* night after night

nachten /ˈnaxtn̩/ *itr. V.* (unpers.) (schweiz., sonst dichter.) **es nachtet** night *or* darkness is falling

Nacht-: **~essen** *das* (bes. südd., schweiz.) evening meal; supper; (formell) dinner; **~eule** *die* (ugs. scherzh.) night owl (coll.); **~falter** *der* moth; **~flug** *der* night flight; **~flugverbot** *das* ban on night flying; **~frost** *der* night frost; **~gebet** *das* bedtime prayer; **~geschirr** *das* chamber pot; **~gespenst** *das* [nocturnal] ghost; **~gewand** *das* (geh.) nightdress; **~hemd** *das* nightshirt; **~himmel** *der* night sky

Nachtigall /ˈnaxtɪgal/ *die;* **~, ~en** nightingale; **~, ich hör dir trapsen** (salopp) I can see which way the wind blows *or* what he/she's after

Nachtigallen·schlag *der* song of the nightingale

nächtigen /ˈnɛçtɪgn̩/ (österr., sonst geh.) spend the night

Nächtigung *die;* **~, ~en** (österr.) overnight stay; **drei ~en ab 150 Euro** three nights from 150 euros

Nach·tisch *der* dessert; sweet; **zum** *od.* **als ~:** as a *or* for dessert; **was gibts zum ~?** what's for pudding *or* (coll.) afters?

Nacht-: **~kästchen** *das* (südd., österr.) bedside table; **~klub** *der* nightclub; **~lager** *das* **1** (geh.: Schlafstätte) resting place for the night; **2** (Biwak) bivouac; **~leben** *das* nightlife

nächtlich /ˈnɛçtlɪç/ *Adj.* nocturnal; night ‹*sky*›; ‹*darkness, stillness*› of the night; **durch den ~en Wald gehen** go through the dark woods [at night-time]; **~e Ruhestörung** (Rechtsspr.) *causing a disturbance at night*

Nacht-: **~lokal** *das* night spot (coll.); **~luft** *die* night air; **~mahl** *das* (österr., auch südd.) evening meal; supper; (formell) dinner; **~mahr** /-maːɐ̯/ *der;* **~~[e]s, ~~e** **1** (Gespenst) [nocturnal] ghost *or* spectre; **2** (Albtraum) nightmare; **~mensch** *der* night owl (coll.); **~mütze** *die* nightcap; **~portier** *der* night porter; **~quartier** *das* accommodation *no indef. art.* for the night

Nachtrag /-traːk/ *der;* **~[e]s, Nachträge** /-trɛːgə/ appendix; (als weiteres Buch/Heft) supplement

nach|tragen *unr. tr. V.* **1** (hinterhertragen) **jmdm. etw. ~:** follow sb. carrying sth. **2** (schriftlich ergänzen) insert, add; (noch sagen) add; **nachzutragen wäre noch, dass ...** I should add that ...; it should be added that ... **3** (übel nehmen) **jmdm. etw. ~:** hold sth. against sb.

nach·tragend *Adj.* unforgiving; (rachsüchtig) vindictive; **ich bin nicht ~:** I don't bear grudges

nachträglich /-trɛːklɪç/
A *Adj.* later; subsequent ‹*apology*›; (verspätet) belated ‹*greetings, apology*›; (zusätzlich) additional; **eine ~e Gratifikation** a retrospective bonus
B *adv.* afterwards; subsequently; (verspätet) belatedly; **~ feiern** have a belated celebration

n

Nachtrags·haushalt *der* supplementary budget

nach|trauern *itr. V.* **jmdm./einer Sache ~:** bemoan *or* lament the passing of sb./sth.; (sich sehnen nach) pine for sb./sth.

nach|treten *unr. itr. V.* (Fußball) [1] (Fußball: sich revanchieren) retaliate [with a kick] [2] (Fußball: absichtlich treten) lash out with one's foot (**gegen** at) [3] (noch einmal treten) lash out again with one's foot [4] (fig.) put the boot in

Nacht·ruhe *die* night's sleep; **angenehme ~!** sleep well!; **er wünschte ihnen eine angenehme ~:** he [said he] hoped they would sleep well

nachts *Adv.* ▸❶ **S. 729** at night; **montag~** *od.* **montags ~:** on Monday nights; **um 3 Uhr ~, ~ um 3 [Uhr]** at 3 o'clock in the morning

nacht-, Nacht-: ~schatten·gewächs *das* (Bot.) plant of the Solanaceae family; **~schattengewächse** Solanaceae; **~schicht** *die* night shift; **~schicht haben** be on night shift; work nights; **~schlafend** *Adj.* *in* **bei/zu ~schlafender Zeit** *od.* **Stunde** (ugs.) at a time when all good people are in their beds; **~schwärmer** *der* (scherzh.) nocturnal reveller; **~schwarz** *Adj.* (geh.) jet-black; **~schwester** *die* night nurse; **~speicher·ofen** *der* night storage heater; **~strom** *der* off-peak electricity; **~stuhl** *der* commode

nachts·über *Adv.* overnight; during the night

Nacht-: ~tarif *der* night rate; (für Strom) off-peak rate; **~tisch** *der* bedside table; **~tisch·lampe** *die* bedside light; **~topf** *der* chamber pot; **auf den ~topf gehen** use the chamber pot; **~tresor** *der* night safe

nach|tun *unr. tr. V.* (ugs.) copy; **es jmdm. ~:** copy sb.

Nacht-und-Nebel-Aktion *die* hush-hush [*esp.* night-time] operation

nacht-, Nacht-: ~vorstellung *die* late-night show; **~wache** *die* [1] (Wachdienst) night watch; (im Krankenhaus) night duty; (eines Soldaten) night guard-duty; **bei einem Kranken ~wache halten** sit up [at night] with a sick person; [2] (Person) night guard; (für Fabrik, Büro o. Ä.) nightwatchman; **~wächter** *der* ▸❶ **S. 113** [1] nightwatchman; [2] (salopp: Dummkopf) dimwit (coll.); thickhead (coll.); **~wächter·staat** *der* laissez-faire state providing for security only; **~wandeln** *itr. V.*; *auch mit sein* sleepwalk; **~wanderung** *die* nocturnal ramble; **~wandler** /-vandlɐ/ *der;* **~~s, ~~, ~wandlerin** *die;* **~~, ~~nen** sleepwalker; somnambulist (formal); **~wandlerisch** *Adj.* *in* **mit ~wandlerischer Sicherheit** with the sureness of a sleepwalker; with instinctive sureness; **~zeit** *die:* *in* **zu später** *od.* **vorgerückter ~zeit** at a late hour [of the night]; **~zeug** *das* (ugs.) overnight things *pl.* (coll.); **~zug** *der* night train; **~zuschlag** *der* night work supplement

nach|untersuchen *tr. V.* **jmdn./etw. ~:** give sb. a follow-up examination/check sth.

Nach·untersuchung *die* follow-up examination; check-up

Nach·versicherung *die* [1] (Rentenversicherung) retrospective state pension contributions *pl.* ‹*for previously uninsured employee*› [2] (von Sachwerten o. Ä.) additional insurance cover

nachvollziehbar *Adj.* comprehensible; **leicht/schwer ~:** easy/difficult to comprehend; **das ist für mich nicht ~:** I find this impossible to understand *or* comprehend

nach|vollziehen *unr. tr. V.* reconstruct; re-enact ‹*event*›; (innerlich) relive; (begreifen) comprehend

Nach·vollzug *der* ▸**nachvollziehen**: reconstruction; re-enactment; reliving; comprehension

nach|wachsen *unr. itr. V.*; *mit sein* **[wieder] ~:** grow again

Nach·wahl *die* (Politik) postponed election; (nach dem Tod o. Ä. eines Abgeordneten) by-election

Nach·wehen *Pl.* (Med.) afterpains; (fig. geh.) unpleasant after-effects

nach|weinen *itr. V.* **jmdm./einer Sache ~:** bemoan the loss of sb./sth.; **einer Sache** (*Dat.*) **nicht ~:** have no regrets about sth.; *s. auch* **Träne**

Nachweis /-vais/ *der;* **~es, ~e** proof *no indef. art.* (*Gen.*, **über** + *Akk.* of); (Zeugnis) certificate (**über** + *Akk.* of); **den ~ für etw. erbringen** *od.* **führen** produce *or* furnish proof of sth.; **als** *od.* **zum ~:** as proof; **es gelang ihm der ~, dass ...** he managed to prove that ...

nachweisbar

A *Adj.* demonstrable ‹*fact, truth, error, defect, guilt*›; provable ‹*fact, guilt*›; detectable ‹*substance, chemical*›; **die Siedlung ist bis ins 7. Jahrhundert ~:** the settlement can be shown to have existed up to the 7th century

B *adv.* demonstrably

nach|weisen *unr. tr. V.* [1] prove; **jmdm. einen Fehler/Diebstahl ~:** prove sb. made a mistake/committed a theft; **man konnte ihm nichts ~:** they could not prove anything against him; **im Körper wurden Spuren des Giftes nachgewiesen** traces of the poison were detected in the body [2] (Amtsspr.) (vermitteln) arrange ‹*hotel room*›; (informieren über) provide information on ‹*hotel room, job*›

nachweislich

A *Adj.* demonstrable; **eine ~e Falschmeldung** a demonstrably wrong report

B *adv.* demonstrably; as can be proved

Nach·welt *die* posterity *no art.*; future generations *pl., no art.*

nach|werfen *unr. tr. V.* [1] **jmdm. etw. ~:** throw sth. after sb.; **jmdm. einen wütenden Blick ~** (fig.) cast a furious glance in sb.'s direction; **eine Münze ~:** put in another coin [2] ▸**nachschmeißen 1**

nach|winken *itr. V.* **jmdm./einer Sache ~:** wave after sb./sth.

nach|wirken *itr. V.* have a lasting effect (**bei** on); ‹*medicine*› continue to have an effect; ‹*literary work*› continue to have an influence

Nach·wirkung *die* after-effect; (fig.: Einfluss) influence

nach|wollen *itr. V.* (ugs.) **jmdm. ~:** want to follow sb.

Nach·wort *das; Pl.* **~e** afterword, postface (**zu** to)

Nach·wuchs *der; o. Pl* [1] (fam.: Kind[er]) offspring; **sie erwartet ~:** she's expecting [a baby] [2] (junge Kräfte) new blood; (für eine Branche usw.) new recruits *pl.*; (in der Ausbildung) trainees *pl.*; **der musikalische ~:** the rising generation of musicians

Nachwuchs-: ~autor *der,* **~autorin** *die* up-and-coming author; **~kraft** *die* new recruit; (in der Ausbildung) trainee; **~kräfte** junior staff; **~mangel** *der* lack of new blood *or* new recruits; **~sorgen** *Pl.* recruitment problems; **~spieler** *der,* **~spielerin** *die* (Sport) up-and-coming player; **~star** *der* up-and-coming star; star in the making

nach|zahlen *tr., itr. V.* [1] pay later; pay ‹*salary*› in arrears; **1 000 Euro Steuern ~:** pay 1,000 euros back tax [2] (zusätzlich zahlen) **25 Euro ~:** pay another 25 euros

nach|zählen *tr., itr. V.* [re]count; check

Nach·zahlung *die* additional payment; (spätere Zahlung) deferred payment; (Steuerzahlung) back tax

nach|zeichnen *tr. V.* copy ‹*picture*›; draw ‹*tree, horse*›; (mit Pauspapier o. Ä.) trace ‹*picture, tree, horse*›; (fig.: schildern) portray

Nach·zeitigkeit *die;* **~** (Sprachw.) future sense of the subordinate clause

nach|ziehen

A *unr. itr. V.* [1] (ugs.: ebenso handeln) do likewise; follow suit [2] *mit sein* (hinterhergehen) **jmdm./einer Sache ~:** follow sb./sth. [3] *mit sein* (nachträglich übersiedeln) **jmdm. ~:** [go to] join sb.

B *unr. tr. V.* [1] (hinter sich herziehen) drag ‹*foot, leg*› [2] (verstärkend) retrace, go over ‹*line*›; pencil ‹*eyebrows*›; **die Lippen ~:** put on more lipstick [3] (festziehen) tighten [up] ‹*nut, bolt*›

nach|züchten *tr. V.* (klonen) clone

Nach·zug *der* (Eisenb.) relief train

Nachzügler /-tsy:klɐ/ *der;* **~s, ~:** straggler; (spät Ankommender) latecomer

Nackedei /'nakədai/ *der;* **~s, ~s** [1] (fam. scherzh.: Kind) **[kleiner] ~:** naked little thing *or* monkey; little bare-bum (Brit. coll.) [2] (ugs. scherzh.: Person) person in the buff; (im Bild, Film usw.) nude

Nacken /'nakn̩/ *der;* **~s, ~** ▸❶ **S. 435** back *or* nape of the neck; (Hals) neck; **den Hut in den ~ schieben** push one's hat right back; **den Kopf in den ~ werfen** throw one's head right back; **das Haar fiel ihm bis in den ~:** his hair hung down the back of his neck; **die Arme im ~ verschränken** fold one's arms behind one's neck; **den ~ steif halten** (fig. ugs.) keep one's chin up; **jmdm. im ~ sitzen** (fig.) be breathing down sb.'s neck; **die Furcht/Angst sitzt ihm im ~:** he is gripped by fear

nackend (veralt., noch landsch.) ▸**nackt 1**

Nacken-: ~haar *das* hair on the back of one's neck; neck hair; **~rolle** *die* bolster; **~schutz** *der* neck guard

nackert /'nakɐt/ (südd., österr. ugs.), **nackig** (bes. md.) ▸**nackt 1**

nackt /nakt/ *Adj.* [1] (unbekleidet) naked; bare ‹*feet, legs, arms, skin, fists*›; **mit ~em Oberkörper** stripped to the waist; **~ und bloß** completely naked; **sich ~ ausziehen** strip naked; strip off completely; **~ baden** bathe in the nude [2] (kahl) bald ‹*head*›; hairless ‹*chin*›; featherless ‹*bird*›; bare ‹*rocks, island, tree, branch, walls, bulb*›; **auf dem ~en Boden schlafen** sleep on the bare floor [3] (unverhüllt) stark ‹*poverty, misery, horror*›; naked ‹*greed*›; plain ‹*fact, words*›; plain, unvarnished ‹*truth*›; **~e Angst** sheer *or* stark terror [4] bare ‹*existence*›; **das ~e Leben retten** barely manage to escape with one's life; save one's skin [and nothing more]

Nackt-: ~arsch *der* (salopp scherzh.) bare-bum (Brit. coll.); bare-bottom; **~baden** *das;* **~~s** nude bathing; **~bade·strand** *der* nudist beach

Nackte *der/die; adj. Dekl.* naked man/woman; (im Bild, Film usw.) nude; **die ~n am Strand** the naked people *or* people in the nude on the beach

Nackt-: ~foto *das* nude photo; **~frosch** *der* (fam. scherzh.) **[kleiner] ~frosch** naked little thing *or* monkey; litte bare-bum (Brit. coll.)

Nacktheit *die;* **~:** nakedness; nudity; (fig.: der Landschaft usw.) bareness

Nackt-: ~kultur *die;* (ugs.) nudism *no art.*; **~samer** /-za:mɐ/ *der;* **~~s, ~~** (Bot.) gymnosperm; **~tänzerin** *die* nude dancer

Nadel /'na:dl̩/ *die;* **~, ~n** needle; (Steck~, Hut~, Haar~) pin; (Häkel~) hook; (für Tonabnehmer) stylus; **etw. mit heißer/mit der heißen ~ nähen** (fig. ugs.) sew sth. in a great hurry; **an der ~ hängen** (fig. ugs.) be on the needle (sl.); **man konnte eine ~ fallen hören** you could have heard a pin drop

nadel-, Nadel-: ~baum *der* conifer; coniferous tree; **~drucker** *der* (DV) dot-matrix printer; **~filz** *der* needle felt; **~förmig** *Adj.* needle-shaped; needle-like ‹*point etc.*›; **~geld** *das* (veralt.) pin money *no indef. art.*; **~holz** *das* [1] softwood; pinewood; [2] (Baum) conifer; **~kissen** *das* pincushion

nadeln *itr. V.* ‹*tree*› shed its needles

nadel-, Nadel-: ~öhr *das* eye of a/the needle; **~spitz** *Adj.* needle-sharp; as sharp as a needle/as needles *postpos.*; **~spitze** *die* point of a/the needle; **~stärke** *die* needle size; size of needle; **~stich** *der* [1] (Stich) needle prick; (einer Stecknadel usw.) pinprick; (fig.: Bosheit) barbed *or* (coll.) snide remark; **jmdm. ~stiche versetzen** aim barbed *or* (coll.) snide remarks at sb.; [2] (Nähstich) stitch; **~streifen** *der* pinstripe; **~streifen·anzug** *der* pinstripe suit; **~wald** *der* coniferous forest

Nadir /na'di:ɐ̯/ *der;* **~s** (Astron.) nadir

Nagel /'na:gl̩/ *der;* **~s, Nägel** /'nɛ:gl̩/ [1] nail; (Med.: für Bruchstellen) pin [2] (fig.) **ein ~ zu jmds. Sarg sein** (salopp) be a nail in sb.'s coffin; **den ~ auf den Kopf treffen** (ugs.) hit the nail on the head (coll.); **Nägel mit Köpfen machen** (ugs.) do things properly; make a real job of it;

den Sport usw./den Beruf an den ~ hängen (ugs.) give up sport etc./(coll.) chuck in one's job; seine Boxhandschuhe an den ~ hängen (ugs.) hang up one's boxing gloves 3 ▸❶ S. 435 (Finger~, Zehen~) nail; das brennt mir auf od. unter den Nägeln (fig. ugs.) it's so urgent I just have to get on with it or it just won't wait; sich (Dat.) etw. unter den ~ reißen (fig. salopp) make off with sth.; s. auch Schwarze[3] 2

nagel-, Nagel-: ~bett das ▸❶ S. 435 nail bed; ~brett das bed of nails; ~bürste die nail brush; ~feile die nail file; ~fest ▸niet- und nagelfest; ~haut die ▸❶ S. 435 cuticle; ~hautentferner der; ~~s, ~~: cuticle remover

Nägel·kauen das; ~s nail-biting no art.

Nagel-: ~kopf der nail head; ~lack der nail varnish (Brit.); nail polish; ~lackentferner der; ~~s, ~~: nail-varnish (Brit.) or nail-polish remover

nageln tr. V. nail (an + Akk. to, auf + Akk. on); (Med.) pin ‹bone, leg, etc.›; aus Brettern Kisten ~: nail planks together to make crates

nagel-, Nagel-: ~neu Adj. (ugs.) brand-new; ~pflege die care of the nails; nail care; ~probe die (fig.) acid test (auf + Akk. of); die ~probe machen try the acid test; ~reiniger der; ~~s, ~~: nail-cleaner; ~schere die nail scissors pl.; ~schuh der hobnailed boot; ~zange die nail clippers pl.

nagen /ˈna:gn̩/

A itr. V. gnaw; an etw. (Dat.) ~: gnaw [at] sth.; an der Unterlippe ~: chew one's lower lip; an jmdm. ~ (fig.) prey on sb.; an jmds. Gesundheit ~ (fig.) undermine sb.'s health

B tr. V. gnaw off; ein Loch ins Holz ~: gnaw a hole in the wood

C refl. V. sich durch etw. ~: gnaw through sth.

nagend Adj. gnawing ‹pain, hunger, fear›; nagging ‹pain, doubts, uncertainty, etc.›

Nage·tier das rodent

nah /na:/ ▸nahe

Näh·arbeit die [piece of] sewing; ~en sewing jobs; sewing sing.

Nah-: ~aufnahme die (Fot.) close-up [photograph]; ~bereich der 1 (Fot.) foreground; 2 (nähere Umgebung) [immediate] surrounding area; locality; (Fernspr.) local area

nah[e] /ˈna:(ə)/

A Adj. näher /ˈnɛ:ɐ/, nächst... /nɛ:çst.../ 1 ▸❶ S. 224 (räumlich) near pred.; close pred.; nearby attrib.; es ist ganz nah bis zum Bahnhof it's not far to the station; ich bin dir in Gedanken ~ (geh.) I am close to you or with you in my thoughts; in der näheren Umgebung in the neighbourhood; around here/there; in der nächsten Umgebung von Köln in the immediate neighbourhood of Cologne; s. auch Osten 3 2 (zeitlich) imminent; near pred.; in ~r Zukunft in the near future; Weihnachten ist/die Ferien sind ~: Christmas is/the holidays are nearly here; die Rettung ist ~: help is imminent or at hand; das nahe Wochenende the fast approaching weekend 3 (eng) close ‹relationship, relative, friend›; seine nähere/nächste Verwandtschaft his close/closest relatives pl

B adv. näher, am nächsten 1 ▸❶ S. 224 (räumlich) ~ an (+ Dat./Akk.), ~ bei close to; ~ gelegen nearby; komm mir nicht zu ~! don't come too close!; keep your distance!; ~ beieinander close together; von nahem od. Nahem from close up; at close quarters; aus od. von nah und fern (geh.) from near and far; (fig.) jmdm. zu nahe treten offend sb.; jmdm. die moderne Kunst usw. nahe bringen make modern art etc. accessible to sb.; (lebendig machen) bring modern art etc. to life for sb.; jmdm. etw. näher bringen make sth. more real or more accessible to sb.; das brachte sie einander nahe that brought them closer together; jmdm. nahe gehen affect sb. deeply; einer Sache (Dat.) nahe kommen come close to sth.; jmdm. [menschlich] nahe kommen get to know sb. well; jmdm. [menschlich] näher kommen get on closer terms with sb.; sich (Dat.) näher kommen become closer; nahe legen (+ Akk.) suggest; give rise to ‹suspicion, supposition, thought›; jmdm. etw. nahe legen suggest sth. to sb.; jmdm. den Rücktritt nahe legen, jmdm. nahe legen zurückzutreten put it to sb. that he/she should resign; nahe liegen ‹thought› suggest itself; ‹suspicion, question› arise; näher liegen be more obvious; was liegt da näher, als ... what can be more obvious or natural than ...; nahe liegend ‹question, idea› which [immediately] suggests itself; natural ‹suspicion›; obvious ‹reason, solution›; das nahe Liegende the obvious thing [to do]; jmdm. nahe stehen be on close or intimate terms with sb.; jmdm. näher stehen be closer to sb.; einer Partei nahe stehen sympathize with a party; eine der Witwe nahe stehende Cousine a cousin who is/was on close terms with the widow; die ihm nahe Stehenden those close to him 2 (zeitlich) ~ an Mittag nearly midday; ~ an die achtzig (ugs.) pushing eighty (coll.); ~ bevorstehen be in the offing; be fast approaching; ~ daran sein, etw. zu tun be on the point of doing sth. 3 (eng) closely; nah befreundet sein be close friends; s. auch näher

C Präp. mit Dat. (geh.) near; close to; den Tränen/dem Wahnsinn ~ sein be on the brink of tears/on the verge of madness; dem Tode ~ sein be close to death

Nähe /ˈnɛ:ə/ die; ~ ▸❶ S. 800 closeness; proximity; (Nachbarschaft) vicinity; in der ~ der Stadt near the town; in nächster od. unmittelbarer ~ des Sees right next to the lake; in meiner ~: near me; (um mich herum) around me; (in der Nachbarschaft) in my neighbourhood; near where I live; ich traue mich nicht in seine ~: I dare not go anywhere near him; seine ~ stört mich having him around puts me off; jmds. ~ suchen seek sb.'s company; menschliche Wärme und ~ spüren feel the warmth of human friendship around one; er wohnt in der ~/ganz in der ~: he lives in the vicinity or nearby/very near; irgendwo hier/dort [ganz] in der ~: somewhere [very] near here/there; bleibt in der ~! stay nearby; don't go too far away; etw. aus der ~ betrachten take a closer look at sth.; aus der ~ betrachtet (auch fig.) viewed more closely; in unmittelbare ~ rücken ‹events› become imminent; die zeitliche ~ zu den Ereignissen erlaubt noch keine distanzierte Analyse the closeness or recentness of the events does not yet permit a detached analysis; s. auch greifbar A 1

nahe-: ~bei Adv. nearby; close by; *~|bringen ▸nah[e] B 1; *~|gehen ▸nah[e] B 1

Nah·einstellung die (Fot.) close focusing

nahe-: *~|kommen ▸nah[e] B 1; *~|legen ▸nah[e] B 1; *~|liegen ▸nah[e] B 1; ~liegend Adj. ‹question, idea› which [immediately] suggests itself; natural ‹suspicion›; obvious ‹reason, solution›; das Naheliegende the obvious thing [to do]; ~ sein ‹thought› suggest itself; ‹suspicion, question› arise

nahen (geh.)

A refl. V.; mit sein (veralt.: sich nähern) approach; draw near or (arch.) nigh; sich jmdm. ~: approach sb.

B itr. V.; mit sein draw near; sein/ihr Ende nahte the end was near; eine ~de Katastrophe imminent disaster

nähen

A itr. V. sew; (Kleider machen) make clothes; an einem Mantel ~: work on [the sewing of] a coat

B tr. V. 1 sew ‹seam, hem›; (mit der Maschine) machine ‹seam, hem›; (herstellen) make ‹dress, coat, curtains, etc.›; etw. an od. auf etw. (Akk.) ~: sew sth. on to sth. 2 (Med.) stitch ‹wound etc.›; der Patient musste genäht werden (ugs.) the patient had to have stitches; s. auch doppelt B 1

näher

A Komp. zu nahe

B Adj. 1 ▸❶ S. 224 (kürzer) shorter ‹way, road› 2 (genauer) further, more precise ‹information›; closer ‹investigation, inspection›; die ~en Umstände the precise circumstances; bei ~em Hinsehen on closer examination; wissen Sie Näheres [darüber]? do you know any more [about it]?; do you know any details?; Näheres hierzu siehe unten for further information on this see below; des ~en (geh.) in detail

C adv. 1 bitte treten Sie ~! please come in/nearer/this way; es bringt uns unserem Ziel nicht ~: it does not bring us any closer to our goal 2 (genauer) more closely; (im Einzelnen) in [more] detail; etw. ~ ansehen have a closer look at sth.; examine sth. more closely; ~ auf etw. (Akk.) eingehen, sich ~ mit etw. befassen go into sth. in [more] detail; jmdn./etw. ~ kennen lernen get to know sb./sth. better; ich kenne ihn nicht ~: I don't know him well; allmählich kommen wir der Sache ~: we're gradually getting to the point

***näher|bringen** ▸nah[e] B 1

Nah·erholungs·gebiet das nearby recreational area

Näherin die; ~, ~nen needlewoman; (hist.) seamstress

näher-: *~|kommen ▸nah[e] B 1; *~|liegen ▸nah[e] B 1

nähern

A refl. V. 1 (herankommen) approach; die Tiere näherten sich bis auf wenige Meter the animals came up to within a few metres; sich jmdm./einer Sache (Dat.) ~: approach sb./sth.; draw nearer to sb./sth.; sich dem Ende ~ ‹stay, summer› near its end, draw to an end; sich dem Ziel der Reise ~: near one's destination 2 (Kontakt aufnehmen) sich jmdm. ~: approach sb. 3 (sich angleichen) sich einem Ideal ~: come close to an ideal; approximate to an ideal

B tr. V. (heranbringen) etw. einer Sache (Dat.) ~: bring sth. closer to sth.

***näher|stehen** ▸nah[e] B 1

Näherung die; ~, ~en approximation

Näherungs·wert der (Math.) approximate value

nahe-: *~|stehen ▸nah[e] B 1; ~stehend ▸nah[e] B 1; ~zu Adv. (mit Adjektiven) almost; nearly; well-nigh ‹impossible, superhuman›; all but ‹exhausted, impossible›; (mit Zahlenangabe) close on

Näh-: ~faden der sewing thread; ~garn das [sewing] cotton

Nah·kampf der 1 (Milit.) close combat 2 (Boxen) infighting

Näh-: ~kästchen das 1 ▸~kasten; 2 aus dem ~kästchen plaudern (ugs. scherzh.) tell all; (als Kenner, Fachmann) tell the inside story; ~kasten der sewing box; workbox; ~korb der sewing basket

nahm /na:m/ 1. u. 3. Pers. Sg. Prät. v. nehmen

Näh-: ~maschine die sewing machine; ~nadel die sewing needle

Nah·ost in in/aus usw. ~: in/from etc. the Middle East

nah·östlich Adj. Middle Eastern

Nähr-: ~boden der culture medium; (fig.) breeding ground; ~creme die skin food

nähren /ˈnɛ:rən/

A tr. V. 1 (ernähren) feed ‹animal, child› (mit on); gut/schlecht genährt well-fed/underfed 2 (geh.: entstehen lassen) nurture ‹hope, suspicion, hatred›; cherish ‹desire, hope›; foster ‹plan, hatred› 3 (geh.: Lebensunterhalt geben) provide a [good] living for; dieser Beruf nährt seinen Mann you can make a good living in this job

B itr. V. (nahrhaft sein) be nourishing

C refl. V. (geh.) sich von etw. ~: live on sth.; ‹animal› feed on sth.

nahrhaft Adj. nourishing; nutritious; ein ~es Essen od. (geh.) Mahl a square meal

Nähr-: ~lösung die 1 fluid culture medium; 2 (für Hydrokultur, künstliche Ernährung) nutrient solution; ~salze Pl. nutrient salts; ~stoffe Pl. nutrients

Nahrung /ˈna:rʊŋ/ die; ~: food; flüssige/feste ~: liquids pl./solids pl.; die ~ verweigern refuse food; geistige ~ (fig.) intellectual nourishment; dem Verdacht/den Gerüchten usw. ~ geben od. bieten (fig.) help to nurture or foster the suspicion/the rumours *etc.*; **es gab seinem Zorn neue ~** (fig.) it gave fresh fuel to his anger; it rekindled his anger

Nahrungs-: ~aufnahme *die* intake of food; **die ~aufnahme verweigern** refuse food; **~mittel** *das* food [item]; **~mittel** *Pl.* foodstuffs; **~mittel·chemie** *die* food chemistry *no art.*; **~mittel·industrie** *die* food *or* foodstuffs industry; **~quelle** *die* source of food; **~suche** *die* search for food; **auf ~suche gehen** search for food; (jagen) hunt for food

Nähr·wert *der* nutritional value; **keinen [sittlichen** *od.* **geistigen] ~ haben** (fig. salopp) be completely and utterly pointless

Näh·seide *die* sewing silk

Nah·sicht *die* close[-up] [vision]; (fig.) close-up view

Naht /na:t/ *die;* **~, Nähte** /'nɛ:tə/ **1** seam; **aus den** *od.* **allen Nähten platzen** (fig. ugs.) ‹*person, fig.: institution etc.*› be bursting at the seams **2** (Med., Anat.) suture

Näh·tisch *der* sewing table

naht·los

A *Adj.* seamless; (fig.) perfectly smooth ‹*transition*›

B *adv.* **Studium und Beruf gehen nicht ~ ineinander über** there is not a perfectly smooth transition from study to work

Naht·stelle *die* **1** (Schweißnaht) seam **2** (Berührungsstelle) point of contact, interface (**von** between); (Grenzlinie) borderline

Nah-: ~verkehr *der* local traffic; **nur im ~verkehr eingesetzt werden** be used only for local services; **~verkehrs·mittel** *das* form of local transport; **~verkehrs·zug** *der* local train

Näh·zeug *das* sewing things *pl.*

Nah·ziel *das* short-term *or* immediate aim

naiv /na'i:f/

A *Adj.* naïve; ingenuous ‹*look, child*›; unaffected ‹*pleasure*›; **ein ~er Zugang zur Musik** an unsophisticated approach to music; **die Naive/den Naiven spielen** act naïve

B *adv.* naïvely; **sich ~ an etw.** (*Dat.*) **freuen** take an unaffected pleasure in sth.

Naive *die; adj. Dekl.* (Theater) ingénue

Naivität /naivi'tɛ:t/ *die;* **~:** naïvety; (eines Blickes, Kindes) ingenuousness; (von Vergnügen) unaffectedness

Naivling *der;* **~s, ~e** (ugs. abwertend) [naïve] simpleton

Name /'na:mə/ *der;* **~ns, ~n,** (seltener) **Namen** /'na:mən/ *der;* **~s, ~:** name; **wie ist der ~ dieser Tiere/Leute?** what are these animals/people called?; **die Dinge/das Unrecht beim ~n nennen** call a spade a spade/acknowledge injustice as such; **[gestatten,] mein ~ ist Maier** [allow me to introduce myself,] my name is Maier; **wie war gleich Ihr ~?** what was your name again?; **ich kenne ihn/es nur dem ~n nach** I know him/it only by name; **der Hund hört auf den ~n Fifi** the dog answers to the name of Fifi; **unter jmds. ~n** (*Dat.*) under sb.'s name; **das Konto läuft auf meinen ~n/das Auto ist auf meinen ~n gemeldet** the account is in/the car is registered in my name; **ein Mann mit ~n Emil** a man by the name of Emil; **er rief mich bei** *od.* **mit meinem ~n** he called me by my name; **in jmds./einer Sache ~n, im ~n von jmdm./etw.** on behalf of sb./sth.; **im eigenen ~n handeln** act on one's own account; **im ~n des Volkes/Gesetzes** (Rechtsspr.) in the name of the people/the law; **in Gottes ~n!** (ugs.) for God's sake; **sich** (*Dat.*) **einen ~n machen** make a name for oneself; *s. auch* **daher 2; Hase 1; hergeben 1; Kind 1**

namen-, Namen-: ~forschung *die* ▸ **~kunde; ~gebung** *die;* **~~, ~~en** (allgemein) giving of names; (in einem bes. Fall) choice of name; **~gedächtnis** *das* memory for names; **~kunde** *die* onomastics *sing., no art.*; **~liste** *die* list of names; **~los A** *Adj.* **1** nameless; (unbekannt) unknown; anonymous ‹*author, poet*›; **2** (geh.: unbeschreiblich) unspeakable, indescribable ‹*misery*›; inexpressible ‹*joy*›; **B** *adv.* (geh.) unspeakably; unutterably; **~register** *das* ▸ **~liste**

namens

A *Adv.* by the name of; called

B *Präp. mit Gen.* (Amtsspr.) on behalf of

Namens-: ~änderung *die* change of name; **~gebung** *die;* **~~, ~~en** ▸ **Namengebung; ~nennung** *die* mention of a name/of names; (Nennung des eigenen Namens) giving of one's name; **~patron** *der,* **~patronin,** *die* patron saint; **~schild** *das* **1** (an Türen usw.) nameplate; **2** (zum Anstecken) name badge; **~tag** *der* name day; **sie hat am ... ~tag** it is her name day on the ...; **~vetter** *der* namesake; **~zug** *der* **1** (Unterschrift) signature; **2** (veralt.: Monogramm) monogram

> **Namenstag**
>
> This day is celebrated by many Germans, especially Catholics, in the same way as a birthday. It is the day dedicated to the saint whose name the person carries, so someone called Martin, for example, would celebrate their *Namenstag* on *Martinstag* (November 11).

namentlich /'na:məntlɪç/

A *Adj.* by name *postpos.*; **eine ~e Liste** a list of names; **eine ~e Abstimmung** a roll-call vote

B *Adv.* **1** (mit Namen) by name; **jmdn. ~ nennen** mention sb. by name; name sb. **2** (besonders) particularly; especially

namhaft

A *Adj.* **1** (berühmt) noted; of note *postpos.* **2** (ansehnlich) noteworthy ‹*sum, difference*›; notable ‹*contribution, opportunity*› **3** **in jmdn./etw. ~ machen** (Papierdt.) name sb./sth.

B *adv.* (beträchtlich) considerably

Namibia /na'mi:bi̯a/ *(das);* **~s** Namibia

Namibier *der;* **~s, ~, Namibierin** *die;* **~, ~nen** Namibian

nämlich /'nɛ:mlɪç/

A *Adv.* **1** **er kann nicht kommen, er ist ~ krank** he cannot come, as he is ill; he can't come — he's ill[, you see] (coll.) **2** (und zwar) namely; (als Füllwort) **das war ~ ganz anders** it was quite different in fact *or* actually

B *Adj.* (geh. veralt.) same; (steigernd) selfsame

nannte /'nantə/ *1. u. 3. Pers. Sg. Prät. v.* **nennen**

Nano·technologie /'nano.../ *die* nanotechnology

nanu /na'nu:/ *Interj.* **~, was machst du denn hier?** hello, what are you doing here?; **~, wo ist denn der ganze Käse geblieben?** that's funny, what's happened to all that cheese?; **~, Sie gehen schon?** what, you're going already?

Napalm /'na:palm/ *das;* **~s** napalm

Napalm·bombe *die* napalm bomb

Napf /napf/ *der;* **~[e]s, Näpfe** /'nɛpfə/ bowl (*esp. for animal's food*)

Napf·kuchen *der* gugelhupf; ring cake

Naphthalin /nafta'li:n/ *das;* **~s** naphthalene

Nappa /'napa/ *das;* **~[s], ~s, Nappa·leder** *das* nappa [leather]

Narbe /'narbə/ *die;* **~, ~n** **1** scar; **von dieser Verletzung werden ~n zurückbleiben** this wound will leave scars; **tiefe ~n bei jmdm. hinterlassen** (fig.) leave sb. deeply scarred **2** (Bot.) stigma

Narben-: ~bildung *die* scar formation; **~leder** *das* (Gerberei) grained leather; **~seite** *die* (Gerberei) hair *or* grain side

narbig *Adj.* scarred; (von Pocken o. Ä.) pitted; pockmarked

Narbung *die;* **~, ~en** (Gerberei) grain[ing]

Narkose /nar'ko:zə/ *die;* **~, ~n** (Med.) narcosis; **mit** *od.* **in/ohne ~:** under anaesthesia/without an anaesthetic; **dem Patienten eine ~ geben** give the patient a general anaesthetic; **aus der ~ aufwachen** come round from the anaesthetic; **jmdn. aus der ~ holen** awaken sb. from the anaesthetic

Narkose-: ~arzt *der,* **~ärztin** *die* anaesthetist; **~gewehr** *das* tranquillizer gun; **~mittel** *das* anaesthetic

Narkotikum /nar'ko:tikʊm/ *das;* **~s, Narkotika** (Med.) narcotic

narkotisch

A *Adj.* (Med., auch fig.) narcotic; overpowering ‹*scent*›

B *adv.* **auf jmdn. ~ wirken** have a narcotic effect on sb.

narkotisieren *tr. V.* (Med.) anaesthetize ‹*patient*›; put ‹*patient*› under a general anaesthetic

Narr /nar/ *der;* **~en, ~en** fool; (Hof~) jester; fool; (Fastnachts~) carnival jester *or* reveller; **sich zum ~en machen** let oneself be fooled; **jmdn. zum ~en haben** *od.* **halten** play tricks on sb.; (täuschen) pull the wool over sb.'s eyes; **einen ~en an jmdm. gefressen haben** (ugs.) be dotty about sb. (coll.)

narren /'narən/ *tr. V.* (geh.) **jmdn. ~:** make a fool of sb.; (täuschen) deceive sb.

narren-, Narren-: ~freiheit *die* freedom to do as one pleases; **jmdn. ~freiheit gewähren** let sb. do as he/she pleases; **~hände** *Pl.* **in ~hände beschmieren Tisch und Wände** (Spr.) little vandals scribble on everything; **~kappe** *die* (hist.) jester's cap and bells; **~possen** *Pl.* (geh. veralt.) tomfoolery *sing.*; **~sicher** (ugs.) **A** *Adj.* foolproof; **B** *adv.* in a foolproof way; **~zepter** *das* jester's sceptre *or* bauble

Narretei /narə'tai̯/ *die;* **~, ~en** (geh.) **1** (Scherz) prank; **~en** fooling about *sing.* **2** (Torheit) folly; stupidity

Narrheit *die;* **~, ~en** **1** (Art) foolishness **2** (Handlung) foolish prank

Närrin /'nɛrɪn/ *die;* **~, ~nen** fool; **liebe ~nen und Narren!** my dear she-asses and jackasses! (*form of address used by speakers at carnival time*)

narrisch (südd.) ▸ **närrisch A 1, 2, B 1, 2**

närrisch /'nɛrɪʃ/

A *Adj.* **1** (verrückt) crazy; (wirr im Kopf) scatter-brained; dotty (coll.); **[ein] ~es Zeug reden** talk gibberish; **halb/ganz ~ [vor Glück]** be almost/quite beside oneself [with joy]; **auf etw.** (*Akk.*) *od.* **nach etw. ganz ~ sein** be mad keen on sth. (coll.) **2** (ugs.: sehr viel, groß) terrific (coll.); **ein ~es Geld** a fantastic amount of money (coll.) **3** (karnevalistisch) carnival-crazy ‹*season*›; **das ~e Treiben [beim Karneval** *od.* **Fasching]** the mad *or* crazy carnival antics *pl*

B *adv.* **1** (verrückt) crazily; **sich ~ benehmen** carry on like a madman/madwoman; act crazy **2** (ugs.: sehr) terrifically (coll.); **~ verliebt sein** be madly in love (coll.)

Narziss, *Narziß /nar'tsɪs/ *der;* **~** *od.* **Narzisses, Narzisse** Narcissus

Narzisse /nar'tsɪsə/ *die;* **~, ~n** narcissus; **gelbe ~:** daffodil

Narzissmus, *Narzißmus *der;* **~** (Psych.) narcissism

narzisstisch, *narzißtisch *Adj.* (Psych.) narcissistic

nasal /na'za:l/

A *Adj.* nasal

B *adv.* nasally

Nasal *der;* **~s, ~e** (Sprachw.) nasal

nasalieren *tr. V.* (Sprachw.) nasalize

Nasal·laut *der* (Sprachw.) nasal

naschen /'naʃn̩/

A *itr. V.* **1** (Süßes essen) eat sweet things; (Bonbons essen) eat sweets (Brit.) *or* (Amer.) candy; **[so] gern ~:** have [such] a sweet tooth **2** (heimlich essen) have a nibble; **er hat vom Pudding genascht** he's been at the pudding

B *tr. V.* **1** (essen) eat ‹*sweets, chocolate, etc.*› **2** (heimlich essen) **er/sie hat Milch genascht** he/she has been at the milk

Näschen /'nɛ:sçən/ *das;* **~s, ~:** little nose

Nascherei *die;* **~, ~en** **1** [continually] eating sweet things; **hör auf mit der ~!** don't keep eating sweet things all the time! **2** (Süßigkeit) **~en** sweets

naschhaft *Adj.* fond of sweet things *postpos.*; sweet-toothed; **[so] ~ sein** have [such] a sweet tooth

Naschhaftigkeit *die;* **~:** fondness for sweet things; **ihre ~ kostet viel Geld** her sweet tooth comes expensive

Nasch-: ~katze *die* (fam.) compulsive nibbler; (Süßigkeiten naschend) compulsive sweet (Brit.) *or* (Amer.) candy eater; **~sucht** *die* addiction to sweet things; **~werk** *das* (veralt.) sweet titbits

Nase /ˈnaːzə/ *die;* **~, ~n** [1] ▸ S. 435 nose; **mir blutet die ~:** my nose is bleeding; I've got a nosebleed; **mir läuft die ~, meine ~ läuft** I've got a runny nose [2] (fig.) **direkt vor deiner ~** (ugs.) right under your nose; **der Bus ist mir vor der ~ weggefahren** (ugs.) I missed the bus by a whisker; **jmdm. die Tür vor der ~ zuschlagen** (ugs.) shut the door in sb.'s face; **jmdm. etw. vor der ~ wegschnappen** (ugs.) snatch sth. from under sb.'s nose; **man hat ihm einen jungen Manager vor die ~ gesetzt** (ugs.) they have appointed a young manager over his head; **die ~ voll haben** (ugs.) have had enough; **von jmdm./etw. die ~ [gestrichen] voll haben** (ugs.) be sick [to death] of sb./sth.; **seine ~ in etw./alles stecken** (ugs.) stick one's nose into sth./everything (coll.); **nicht weiter sehen als seine ~** (ugs.) see no further than the end of one's nose; **ihm passt** *od.* **gefällt deine ~ nicht** (ugs.) he doesn't like your face; **sich** (*Dat.*) **die ~ begießen** (ugs.) have a drink or two; **die** *od.* **seine ~ in die Bücher stecken** (ugs.) get down to one's studies; **jmdm. eine lange ~ machen** *od.* **eine ~ drehen** (ugs.) cock a snook at sb.; **immer der ~ nach** (ugs.) just follow your nose; **fass dich an die eigene ~!** (ugs.) you're a fine one to talk!; **jmdn. an der ~ herumführen** (ugs.) pull the wool over sb.'s eyes; **auf der ~ liegen** (ugs.) be laid up; **auf die ~ fallen** (ugs.) come a cropper (sl.); **jmdm. etw. auf die ~ binden** (ugs.) let sb. in on sth.; **jmdm. auf der ~ herumtanzen** (ugs.) play sb. up; **jmdm. eins** *od.* **was auf die ~ geben** (ugs.) put sb. in his/her place; **jmdm. etw. aus der ~ ziehen** (ugs.) worm sth. out of sb.; **das sticht mir schon lange in die ~** (ugs.) I've had my eye on that for a long time; **jmdn. mit der ~ auf etw.** (*Akk.*) **stoßen** (ugs.) spell sth. out to sb.; **pro ~** (ugs.) per head; **jmdm. unter die ~ reiben, dass ...** (ugs.) rub it in that ...; **das brauchst du mir nicht unter die ~ zu reiben** (ugs.) you don't have to rub my nose in it; *s. auch* **Mund; rümpfen** [3] (Geruchssinn, Gespür) nose; **eine gute ~ für etw. haben** have a good nose for sth.; (etw. intuitiv wissen) have a sixth sense for sth. [4] (geh.: Bug) bow; (eines Flugzeugs) nose [5] (Felsvorsprung) spur [6] (ugs.: Farbtropfen) run

nase·lang ▸ **nasenlang**

näseln /ˈnɛːzl̩n/ *itr. V.* talk through one's nose

näselnd

A *Adj.* nasal

B *adv.* nasally; **~ sprechen** speak in a nasal tone

nasen-, Nasen-: ~bär *der* coati; **~bein** *das* ▸ S. 435 nasal bone; **~bluten** *das;* **~~s** bleeding from the nose; **~bluten haben/bekommen** have/get a nosebleed; **~flügel** *der* ▸ S. 435 side of the nose; (einschl. ~loch) nostril; **~höhle** *die* ▸ S. 435 (Anat.) nasal cavity; **~lang** *in* **alle ~lang** constantly; all the time; **~länge** *die:* **mit einer ~länge** (Pferdesport), **um eine ~länge** (fig.) by a head; **er war mir um eine ~länge voraus** he was fractionally ahead of me; **~loch** *das* ▸ S. 435 nostril; **~pflaster** *das* nasal strip; **~ring** *der* nosering; **~rücken** *der* ▸ S. 435 ridge of the/one's nose; **~scheide·wand** *die* ▸ S. 435 nasal septum; **~schleim** *der* nasal mucus; **~schleim·haut** *die* ▸ S. 435 nasal mucous membrane; **~spitze** *die* ▸ S. 435 tip of the/one's nose; **nicht weiter sehen, als die ~spitze reicht** (fig. ugs.) not be able to see further than the end of one's nose; **jmdm. etw. an der ~spitze ansehen** (fig. ugs.) tell sth. by sb.'s face; **~spray** *der od. das* nasal spray; **~stüber** *der;* **~~s, ~~:** swat on the nose; **~tropfen** *Pl.* nose drops; **~wurzel** *die* ▸ S. 435 root of the nose

nase-, Nase-: ~rümpfen *das;* **~~s: mit ~rümpfen** with a look of disgust *or* disdain; **dafür hat sie nur ein ~rümpfen übrig** she only turns up her nose at that; **~rümpfend**

A *Adj.* disapproving; **B** *adv.* disdainfully; **~weis A** *Adj.* precocious; pert ‹*remark, reply*›; **sei nicht so ~weis!** don't be such a little know-all!; **B** *adv.* precociously; **~weis** *der;* **~~es, ~~e** (fam.) [little] know-all; [little] clever Dick (coll.)

nas-, Nas-: ~führen *tr. V.* lead up the garden path; **sich genasführt fühlen** feel one has been led up the garden path; **~horn** *das* rhinoceros; **~lang** ▸ **nasenlang**

-nasig *adj.* -nosed

nass, *naß /nas/, **nasser** *od.* **nässer** /ˈnɛsɐ/, **nassest...** *od.* **nässest...** /ˈnɛsəst.../

A *Adj.* [1] wet; **~ machen** + *Akk.* make wet; sprinkle ‹*washing*›; **sich/das Bett ~ machen** wet oneself/one's bed; **mit nassen Augen** with tears in one's eyes; **durch und durch** *od.* **bis auf die Haut ~:** wet through; soaked to the skin; **~ geschwitzt** soaked in sweat *postpos.;* **wie ein nasser Sack** (ugs.) as limp as a wet sack; **ein nasses Grab** (dichter.) a watery grave; **mach dich bloß nicht ~!** (fig. salopp) don't overdo it! (iron.); **jmdn. ~ machen** (Sportjargon) trounce sb.; beat sb. hollow (coll.) [2] **für ~** (bes. berlin. u. ostmd.) for free; for nothing

B *adv.* **sich ~ rasieren** have a wet shave; (immer) use a razor and shaving cream

Nass, *Naß *das;* **Nasses** (dichter. od. scherzh.) [1] (Wasser) water; (Regen) wetness (esp. joc.); **hinein ins kühle ~!** in[to the water] we go! [2] (Getränk) **das edle** *od.* **kostbare ~:** the precious liquid

Nassauer /ˈnasaʊ̯ɐ/ *der;* **~s, ~, Nassauerin** *die;* **~, ~nen** (ugs. abwertend) sponger; (Schnorrer[in]) scrounger (coll.)

nassauern (ugs. abwertend)

A *tr. V.* **etw. bei jmdm. ~:** scrounge sth. from sb. (coll.)

B *itr. V.* scrounge (coll.)

Nässe /ˈnɛsə/ *die;* **~:** wetness; (an Wänden usw.) dampness; **bei ~:** in the wet; in wet weather; **„vor ~ schützen"** 'protect from damp'

nässen

A *itr. V.* ‹*wound, eczema*› suppurate

B *tr. V.* (geh.) make wet; wet ‹*bed, feet, etc.*›

nass, *naß-, Naß, *Naß-: ~forsch A *Adj.* brash. **B** *adv.* brashly; **~geschwitzt** ▸ **nass A 1**; **~kalt** *Adj.* cold and wet; raw; **~rasur** *die* wet shaving *no art.;* **zur ~rasur braucht man ...** for a wet shave one needs ...; **~wäsche** *die: washing not dried by the laundry;* wet washing

Nas·tuch *das; Pl.* **Nastücher** (schweiz.) handkerchief

Nation /naˈtsi̯oːn/ *die;* **~, ~en** nation; **die Vereinten ~en** the United Nations *sing.;* **der Liebling der ~ sein** (ugs.) be a national hero

national /natsi̯oˈnaːl/

A *Adj.* [1] national; **~e und internationale Märkte** domestic and international markets [2] (patriotisch) nationalist

B *adv.* [1] (innerstaatlich) at a national level; nationally [2] (patriotisch) ‹*think, feel*› nationalistically

national-, National-: ~bewusst, *~bewußt *Adj.* nationally conscious; **~bewusst sein** be conscious of one's national identity; have a sense of national identity; **~bewusst·sein, *~bewußt·sein** *das* [sense of] national consciousness; sense of national identity; **~charakter** *der* national character; **~china** (*das*) (veralt.) Nationalist China

Nationale *das;* **~s, ~** (österr.) [1] personal details *or* particulars *pl.* [2] (Fragebogen) form *or* questionnaire asking for personal details

National-: ~elf *die* (Fußball) national team *or* side; **~epos** *das* national epic; **~farben** *Pl.* national colours; **~feier·tag** *der* national holiday; **~flagge** *die* national flag; **~gefühl** *das* national feeling; feeling for one's country; **~gericht** *das* national dish; **~getränk** *das* national drink; **~held** *der* national hero; **~heldin** *die* national heroine; **~hymne** *die* national anthem

nationalisieren *tr. V.* nationalize

Nationalisierung *die;* **~, ~en** nationalization

Nationalismus *der;* **~:** nationalism *usu. no art.*

Nationalist *der;* **~en, ~en, Nationalistin** *die;* **~, ~nen** nationalist

nationalistisch

A *Adj.* nationalist; nationalistic

B *adv.* nationalistically

Nationalität /natsi̯onaliˈtɛːt/ *die;* **~, ~en** ▸ S. 520 nationality; **welcher ~ sind Sie?** what nationality are you?

Nationalitäten-: ~frage *die* problem of different nationalities within one state; **~staat** *der* multinational state

national-, National-: ~literatur *die* national literature; **~mannschaft** *die* national team; **~ökonomie** *die* political economy *no art.;* **~park** *der* national park; **~preis** *der:* (DDR) *annual award for achievement in science, technology, and the arts;* **~rat** *der* [1] (österr., schweiz.) National Council; [2] (Mitglied) member of the National Council; [3] (DDR) *highest governing body of the 'Nationale Front';* **~rätin** *die* ▸ **~rat 2**; **~sozialismus** *der* National Socialism; **~sozialist** *der,* **~sozialistin** *die* National Socialist; **~sozialistisch A** *Adj.* National Socialist; **B** *adv.* **eindeutig ~sozialistisch geprägt sein** bear all the marks of National Socialism; **~spieler** *der,* **~spielerin** *die* (Sport) national player; international; **~sprache** *die* national language; **~staat** *der* nation state; **~staatlich** *Adj.* **~staatliche Bestrebungen** efforts towards the creation of a nation state; **~staatliches Denken** thinking in nationalistic terms; **~stolz** *der* national pride; **~straße** *die* (schweiz.) national highway; **~tracht** *die* national costume; **~versammlung** *die* National Assembly

> **Nationalrat**
>
> In Austria the *Nationalrat* is the Federal Assembly's lower house, whose 183 members are elected for four years under a system of proportional representation. The **Bundeskanzler** commands the majority in the *Nationalrat*. The **Bundesrat**, the 64-member upper house, is elected by provincial assemblies. In Switzerland the National Council is made up of 200 representatives. Together with the **Ständerat** it forms the Federal Assembly.

nativ *Adj.* virgin ‹*olive oil*›

NATO, Nato /ˈnaːto/ *die;* **~:** NATO; Nato *no art.*

nato·grün *Adj.* dark olive green

NATO-Staat *der* NATO state *or* country

Natrium /ˈnaːtri̯ʊm/ *das;* **~s** (Chemie) sodium

Natron /ˈnaːtrɔn/ *das;* **~s; [doppeltkohlensaures] ~:** sodium bicarbonate; bicarbonate of soda; bicarb (coll.); **[kohlensaures] ~:** sodium carbonate; soda

Natron·lauge *die* caustic soda [solution]

Natter /ˈnatɐ/ *die;* **~, ~n** colubrid; **eine ~ am Busen nähren** (fig. geh.) nurture a viper in one's bosom (literary)

Nattern·gezücht *das* (veralt. abwertend) nest of vipers

Natur /naˈtuːɐ̯/ *die;* **~, ~en** [1] nature *no art.;* **die Wunder der ~:** the wonders of nature; **wider die ~:** unnatural; **zurück zur ~:** back to nature; **die unberührte ~:** unspoilt nature; **die freie ~:** [the] open countryside; **Tiere in freier ~ sehen** see animals in the wild; **nach der ~ zeichnen/malen** draw/paint from nature [2] (Art, Eigentümlichkeit) nature; **eine gesunde/eiserne/labile ~ haben** (ugs.) have a healthy/cast-iron/delicate constitution; **das widerspricht ihrer ~:** it is not in her nature; **jmdm. gegen** *od.* **wider die ~ gehen** go against sb.'s nature; **jmdm. zur zweiten ~ werden** become second nature to sb.; **die Verletzung war nur leichter ~:** the injury was only slight; **in der ~ der Sache/der Dinge liegen** be in the nature of things [3] (Mensch) sort *or* type of person; sort (coll.); type (coll.) [4] (natürlicher Zustand) **Möbel in Kiefer ~:** natural pine furniture; **sie ist von ~ aus blond/ein gutmütiger Mensch** she is naturally fair/good-natured; **Hat sie eine Dauerwelle?**

n

ℹ Nationalität

1. Adjektive

Alle Nationalitätsbezeichnungen im Englischen werden großgeschrieben:

die italienische Sprache
= the Italian language
ein indischer Brauch
= an Indian custom
Diese Haltung ist typisch deutsch
= This attitude is typically German

Wenn man bloß die Nationalität einer Person angeben will, verwendet man im Englischen oft das prädikative Adjektiv, wo man im Deutschen das Substantiv verwendet:

Seine Frau ist Schottin
= His wife is Scottish
Der Lehrer ist Franzose
= The teacher is French

Diese Adjektive werden von den Ländernamen abgeleitet. Bei Ländernamen, die auf **-a** enden, werden sie durch Hinzufügen eines **-n** gebildet, und bei denen, die auf **-y** enden, wird das **-y** durch **-ian** ersetzt. (Ausnahmen: China→Chinese; Germany→German; Canada→Canadian).

America→American
Austria→Austrian
Australia→Australian
Russia→Russian
Romania→Romanian
India→Indian
Italy→Italian
Burgundy→Burgundian usw.

Andere Ableitungen sind nicht regelmäßig gebildet. Mehrere enden auf **-ish**, den deutschen Formen entsprechend:

England→English
Britain→British
Scotland→Scottish
Spain→Spanish
Turkey→Turkish
Denmark→Danish
Finland→Finnish

Sonstige Beispiele:

France→French
Greece→Greek
Iceland→Icelandic

2. Substantive

Die Bezeichnungen der Einwohner haben die gleiche Form wie das Adjektiv, sofern dieses auf **-an** oder **-ese** endet. Die substantivierte Einwohnerbezeichnung erfordert im Singular einen Artikel:

ein reicher Amerikaner
= a rich American
die Inder
= the Indians
Sie heiratet einen Italiener
= She is marrying an Italian
Als Japanerin fühlt sie sich benachteiligt
= As a Japanese she feels disadvantaged

Die Substantive, die auf **-ese** und **-ss** enden, lauten im Singular und Plural gleich:

die Chinesen
= the Chinese
die Schweizer
= the Swiss

In den Fällen, wo das entsprechende Adjektiv auf **-[i]sh** oder **-ch** endet, wird oft **-man** bzw. **-woman** angefügt (im Plural **-men** bzw. **-women**). Nur wenn das Volk gemeint ist, verwendet man oft die Form des Adjektivs. Andere Formen sind unregelmäßig, aber meist ihren deutschen Entsprechungen sehr ähnlich:

English→Englishman/Englishwoman→Englishmen/Englishwomen; the English
Scottish, Scots→Scot, Scotsman/Scotswoman→Scotsmen/Scotswomen; the Scots
Welsh→Welshman/Welshwoman→Welshmen/Welshwomen; the Welsh
Irish→Irishman/Irishwoman→Irishmen/Irishwomen; the Irish
French→Frenchman/Frenchwoman→Frenchmen/Frenchwomen; the French
Dutch→Dutchman/Dutchwoman→Dutchmen/Dutchwomen; the Dutch
British→Briton→Britons; the British
Swedish→Swede→Swedes; the Swedish
Finnish→Finn→Finns; the Finnish
Danish→Dane→Danes; the Danish
Spanish→Spaniard→Spaniards; the Spanish
Polish→Pole→Poles; the Polish
Turkish→Turk→Turks; the Turkish

eine Britin/Schwedin/Finnin/Dänin/Spanierin/Polin/ Türkin kann nur als 'a British/Swedish/Finnish/Danish/Spanish/Polish/Turkish woman/girl' übersetzt werden.

Sonstige Ausdrücke

Sie ist von Geburt Spanierin
= She is Spanish by birth
Er ist deutscher Abstammung
= He is of German extraction
Ich stamme aus Norddeutschland
= I come from North Germany
Er ist belgischer Staatsbürger
= He is a Belgian national
ein eingebürgerter Schweizer
= a naturalized Swiss [citizen]

n

— **Nein, das ist alles ~:** Is her hair permed? — No, it's naturally curly

Natural·abgaben *Pl.* taxes [paid] in kind

Naturalien /natu'ra:li̯ən/ *Pl.* natural produce *sing.* (*used as payment*); **in ~** (*Dat.*) **bezahlen** pay in kind

Naturalien·kabinett *das* (veralt.) natural-history collection

naturalisieren *tr. V.* (auch Biol.) naturalize; **sich ~:** become naturalized

Naturalisierung *die;* **~, ~en** (auch Biol.) naturalization

Naturalismus *der;* **~:** naturalism

Naturalist *der;* **~en, ~en, Naturalistin** *die;* **~, ~nen** naturalist

naturalistisch
A *Adj.* **1** naturalistic **2** (den Naturalismus betreffend) naturalist
B *adv.* **1** ‹*paint, describe*› naturalistically **2** (den Naturalismus betreffend) naturalistically; ‹*influenced*› by naturalism

Natural-: ~lohn *der* wages *pl.* [paid] in kind; **~wirtschaft** *die* barter economy

natur-, Natur-: ~apostel *der* (iron.) back-to-nature freak (coll.); **~belassen** *Adj.* natural ‹*oils, foods, etc.*›; **~beobachtung** *die* observation of nature; **~beschreibung** *die* description of nature; **~blond** *Adj.* naturally fair *or* blond; **~bursche** *der* child of nature; **~darm** *der* natural [animal] intestine (*used as sausage-casing*); **~denkmal** *das* natural monument; **~dünger** *der* natural fertilizer

nature /na'ty:ɐ̯/ *indekl. Adj.* (Gastr.) ‹*steak, escalope, etc.*› au naturel

Naturell *das;* **~s, ~e** disposition; temperament; **das widerspricht seinem ~:** it's not in his nature

natur-, Natur-: ~ereignis *das* natural phenomenon; (Versicherungsw.) act of God; **~erscheinung** *die* natural phenomenon; **~erzeugnis** *das* ▸ **~produkt**; **~farbe** *die* **1** natural colour; **2** (Farbstoff) natural dye; **~farben** *Adj.* natural-coloured ‹*leather, wool, wood, etc.*›; **~faser** *die* natural fibre; **~film** *der* nature film; **~forscher** *der,* **~forscherin** *die* naturalist; **~forschung** *die* natural-history research; **~freund** *der,* **~freundin** *die* nature lover; **~gegeben** *Adj.* natural and inevitable ‹*state of affairs*›; **etw. als ~gegeben ansehen** regard sth. as part of the natural order [of things]; **~gemäß A** *Adv.* naturally; **B** *adj.* **1** natural; ‹*forest management*› in keeping with the natural environment; **~geschichte** *die* **1** natural history; **2** (veralt.) ▸ **~kunde**; **~geschichtlich A** *Adj.* natural history; ‹*teaching*› of natural history; **die ~geschichtliche Entwicklung des Menschen** the natural history of mankind; **B** *adv.* from the point of view of natural history; **~gesetz** *das* law of nature; **~getreu A** *Adj.;* lifelike ‹*portrait, imitation*›; faithful ‹*reproduction*›; **B** *adv.* ‹*draw*› true to life; ‹*reproduce*› faithfully; **etw. ~getreu darstellen** portray sth. in a true-to-life way; **~gewalt** *die* force of nature; **~gottheit** *die* (Rel.) nature deity; **~haft** *Adj.* (geh.) natural; **~heilkunde** *die* naturopathy *no art.;* **~heilverfahren** *das* naturopathic treatment; **~identisch** *Adj.* nature-identical; **~katastrophe** *die* natural disaster; **~kind** *das* child of nature; **~kraft** *die* force of nature; **~krause** *die* naturally frizzy hair *no indef. art.;* **~kunde** *die* (veralt.) nature study *no art.;* **~kundlich** *Adj.* natural-history ‹*museum, field trip, etc.*›; **~landschaft** *die* natural *or* unspoilt landscape; **~lehr·pfad** *der* nature trail

natürlich /na'ty:ɐ̯lɪç/
A *Adj.* natural; **eines ~en Todes sterben** die a natural death; die of natural causes; **ein Bild in ~er Größe** a life-size portrait; **das ist die ~ste Sache der Welt** it is the most natural thing in the world; *s. auch* **Person**
B *adv.* ‹*laugh, behave*› naturally
C *Adv.* **1** (selbstverständlich, wie erwartet) naturally; of course **2** (zwar) of course; **er wird natürlich zustimmen, aber ...** of course he is bound to agree, but ...

natürlicher·weise *Adv.* naturally; of course

Natürlichkeit *die;* **~:** naturalness

natur-, Natur-: ~locken *Pl.* natural curls; **~nah[e]** *Adj.* ‹*life, existence*› close to nature; semi-natural; **~notwendigkeit** *die* objective necessity; **~park** *der* ≈ national park; **~phänomen** *das* natural phenomenon; **~philosophie** *die* philosophy of nature; **~produkt** *das* natural product; **~produkte** natural produce *sing.;* **~recht** *das* natural law; **~rein** *Adj.* pure ‹*honey, jam, fruit, juice, etc.*›; ‹*wine*› free of additives; **~religion** *die* nature religion; **~schauspiel** *das* natural spectacle; **~schönheit** *die* site of natural beauty; **~schutz** *der* [nature] conservation; **unter ~schutz** (*Dat.*) **stehen** be protected by law; be a protected species/variety/area *etc.;* **etw. unter ~schutz** (*Akk.*) **stellen** protect sth. by law; **~schutz·gebiet** *das* nature reserve; **~seide** *die* real *or* natural silk; **~stein** *der* natural stone; **~stoff** *der* natural substance; **~talent** *das* [great] natural talent *or* gift; (begabter Mensch) naturally talented *or* gifted person; **ein ~talent sein** have a [great] natural gift *or* talent; **~ton** *der; Pl.* **~töne** (Musik) natural note; **~trieb** *der* (veralt.) [natural] instinct; **~trüb** *Adj.* unfiltered, naturally cloudy ‹*fruit juice*›; **~verbunden** *Adj.* ‹*person*› in tune with nature; **~volk** *das* primitive people; **~widrig** *Adj.* unnatural; against nature *postpos.;* **~wissenschaft** *die* natural science *no art.;* **die**

~wissenschaften the [natural] sciences; **~wissenschaftler** *der*, **~wissenschaftlerin** *die* [natural] scientist; **~wissenschaftlich** **A** *Adj.* scientific; **B** *adv.* scientifically; **~wüchsig** (Philos.) **A** *Adj.* natural; organic; **B** *adv.* naturally; organically; **~wunder** *das* miracle *or* wonder of nature

nauf /nauf/ (südd.) ▸**hinauf**

naus /naus/ (südd.) ▸**hinaus**

Nautik /'nautɪk/ *die;* ~ **1** nautical science *no art.* **2** (Navigation) navigation *no art.*

nautisch /'nautɪʃ/ *Adj.* (Seew.) naval ‹*officer*›; navigational ‹*instrument, calculation*›

Navel·orange /'na:vl̩-/ *die* navel orange

Navigation /naviga'tsio:n/ *die;* ~ (Seew., Flugw.) navigation *no art.*

Navigations-: **~fehler** *der* (Seew., Flugw.) navigational error; **~instrument** *das* (Seew., Flugw.) navigational instrument; **~karte** *die* (Seew., Flugw.) navigational chart; **~offizier** *der* (Seew., Flugw.) navigating officer; **~system** *das* navigation system

Navigator /naviga'to̞r/ *der;* **~s, ~en**, **Navigatorin** *die;* **~, ~nen** (Seew., Flugw.) navigator

navigieren *tr., itr. V.* navigate

Nazarener /natsa're:nɐ/ *der;* **~s, ~**, **Nazarenerin** *die;* **~, ~nen** Nazarene

Nazareth /'na:tsarɛt/ *(das);* **~s** Nazareth

Nazi /'na:tsi/ *der;* **~s, ~s** Nazi

Nazi·deutschland *(das)* Nazi Germany

Nazismus *der;* **~:** Nazi[i]sm *no art.*

nazistisch *Adj.* Nazi

Nazi-: **~vergangenheit** *die* Nazi past; **~zeit** *die* Nazi period

NB, N.B. *Abk.* = **notabene** NB

n.Br. *Abk.* = **nördliche[r] Breite; 60° n.Br.** lat. 60°N

n.Chr. *Abk.* ▸❶ **S. 165** = **nach Christus** AD

NDR *Abk.* **Norddeutscher Rundfunk** North German Radio

ne /nə/ (ugs.) ▸**nicht 3**

'ne /nə/ (ugs.) ▸**eine**

Neandertaler /ne'andəta:lɐ/ *der;* **~s, ~** (Anthrop.) Neanderthal man; **[die] Neandertaler lebten in ...** Neanderthal man *sing.* lived in ...

Neapel /ne'a:pl̩/ *(das);* **~s** ▸❶ **S. 675** Naples

Neapolitaner /neapoli'ta:nɐ/ *der;* **~s, ~** **1** Neapolitan **2** (österr.: Gebäck) wafer biscuit with chocolate cream filling

Neapolitanerin *die;* **~, ~nen** ▸**Neapolitaner 1**

nebbich /'nɛbɪç/ *Interj.* (salopp) so what?

Nebel /'ne:bl̩/ *der;* **~s, ~** **1** fog; (weniger dicht) mist; **bei ~:** in fog/mist; when it is foggy/misty; **im ~ der Vergessenheit versinken** (fig.) sink into the mists *pl.* of oblivion; **ein ~ von Tabakrauch** a thick haze of tobacco smoke; **ausfallen wegen ~[s]** (ugs. scherzh.) be cancelled; *s. auch* **Nacht** **2** (Astron.) nebula

Nebel-: **~bank** *die; Pl.:* **~bänke** (über dem Meer) fog bank; (über dem Land) large patch of fog; **~bildung** *die* formation of fog; **stellenweise ~bildung** local mist or fog patches; **~feld** *das* mist/fog patch; patch of mist/fog

nebelhaft *Adj.* hazy ‹*idea, recollection, etc.*›; **das liegt in ~er Ferne** that's in the distant future

Nebel·horn *das* foghorn

nebelig ▸**neblig**

Nebel-: **~kammer** *die* (Atomphysik) cloud chamber; **~krähe** *die* hooded crow

nebeln

A *itr. V.* (unpers.) (geh.) **es nebelt** it is foggy; (weniger dicht) it is misty; **es begann zu ~:** it began to grow foggy/misty

B *tr. V.* spray ‹*pesticide, insecticide*›

nebel-, Nebel-: **~schein·werfer** *der* fog lamp; **~schleier** *der* (geh. dichter.) veil of mist; **~schluss·leuchte**, ***~schluß·leuchte** *die* rear fog lamp; **~schwaden** *Pl.* swathes of mist; **~verhangen** *Adj.* (geh.) shrouded in mist *postpos.*; **~wand** *die* wall of fog; **~werfer** *der* (Milit.) six-barrelled rocket mortar; nebelwerfer

neben /'ne:bn̩/

A *Präp. mit Dat.* **1** (Lage) next to; beside; **sie fuhren ~ dem Zug her** they kept pace with the train; **dicht ~ jmdm./etw. sitzen** sit close *or* right beside sb./sth.; **er duldet keinen Konkurrenten ~ sich** (fig.) he brooks no competition; **ihr sollt keine anderen Götter ~ mir haben!** (bibl.) thou shalt have no other gods before me **2** (außer) apart from; aside from (Amer.); **wir brauchen ~ Schere und Papier auch Leim** as well as scissors and paper we need glue

B *Präp. mit Akk.* **1** (Richtung) next to; beside; **sich dicht ~ jmdn./etw. setzen** sit down close *or* right beside sb./sth. **2** (verglichen mit) beside; compared to *or* with

neben-, Neben-: **~absicht** *die* secondary aim; **~akzent** *der* (Phon.) secondary accent *or* stress; **~amtlich** **A** *Adj.* ‹*activity*› relating to a secondary office/occupation; **B** *adv.* **etw. ~amtlich machen** do sth. as a secondary office/occupation

neben·an *Adv.* next door; **die Kinder von ~** (ugs.) the children from next door; **nach ~ gehen** go next door

Neben-: **~anschluss**, ***~anschluß** *der* extension; **~arbeit** *die* **1** second job; **2** (unwichtige Arbeit) less important job; **~arbeiten** less important work *sing. or* jobs; **~arm** *der* branch; **~ausgabe** *die* additional expense; **[eventuelle] ~ausgaben** incidental expenses; **~ausgang** *der* side exit; **~bedeutung** *die* secondary meaning

neben·bei *Adv.* **1** ‹*work*› on the side, as a sideline; (zusätzlich) as well; in addition; **sie versorgt ihren Haushalt und hilft ~ im Geschäft** she looks after the house and helps in the shop as well; **für Geologie interessiert er sich nur ~:** his interest in geology is only secondary **2** (beiläufig) ‹*remark*› incidentally, by the way; ‹*ask*› by the way; ‹*inform*› by the by; ‹*mention*› in passing; **~ gesagt** *od.* **bemerkt** incidentally; by the way; **dies nur ~:** that is only by the way

neben-, Neben-: **~bemerkung** *die* incidental remark; **~beruf** *der* second job; sideline; **er ist im ~beruf Fotograf** he has a second job *or* sideline as a photographer; **~beruflich** **A** *Adj.* **eine ~berufliche Tätigkeit** a second job; **er musste ~berufliche Tätigkeiten annehmen** he had to take on extra work *sing. or* jobs; **B** *adv.* on the side; **er arbeitet ~beruflich als Übersetzer** he translates as a sideline; **~beschäftigung** *die* second job; sideline; **seine zahlreichen ~beschäftigungen** his many sidelines; **~buhler** *der*, **~buhlerin** *die* rival; **~effekt** *der* side effect

neben·einander *Adv.* **1** next to one another *or* each other; ‹*be sitting, standing*› next to one another, side by side; (fig.: zusammen) ‹*live, exist*› side by side; **~ wohnen** live next door to one another *or* each other; **~ legen** (+ *Akk.*) lay *or* place ‹*objects*› next to each other *or* side by side; **~ schalten** (+ *Akk.*) (Elektrot.) connect *or* wire ‹*devices, lamps, etc.*› in parallel; **sich zu zweit ~ aufstellen** line up two abreast **2** (gleichzeitig) together

Nebeneinander *das;* **~s** juxtaposition

nebeneinander·her *Adv.* alongside each other *or* one another; ‹*walk*› side by side

***nebeneinander|legen** *usw.* ▸**nebeneinander 1**

Neben-: **~eingang** *der* side entrance; **~einkünfte** *Pl.* additional *or* supplementary income *sing.*; **~einnahme** *die:* **~einnahme[n]** additional or supplementary income; **~erwerb** *der* second job; secondary occupation; **~erwerbs·betrieb** *der:* (Landw.) *smallholding, market stall, etc. run to supplement a person's main income;* **~fach** *das* subsidiary subject; minor (Amer.); **etw. im ~fach studieren** study sth. as a subsidiary subject; minor in sth. (Amer.); **~fluss**, ***~fluß** *der* ▸❶ **S. 267** tributary; **~form** *die* variant; **~frage** *die* side issue; secondary issue; **~frau** *die* concubine; **~gebäude** *das* **1** annexe; outbuilding; **2** (Nachbargebäude) adjacent *or* neighbouring building; **~geordnet** *Adj.* (Sprachw.) coordinate ‹*clause*›; **~geräusch** *das* background noise; **~geräusche** (Funkw., Fernspr.) interference *sing.*; noise *sing.*; (bei Tonband, Plattenspieler) [background] noise *sing.*; **~gleis** *das* (Eisenb.) siding; **jmdn. auf ein ~gleis [ab]schieben** (fig.) put sb. out of harm's way; **~handlung** *die* subplot; **~haus** *das* house next door; neighbouring house

neben·her *Adv.* ▸**nebenbei**

nebenher-: **~|fahren** *unr. itr. V.; mit sein* drive alongside; (mit dem Rad, Motorrad) ride alongside; **~|gehen** *unr. itr. V.; mit sein* walk alongside; **~|laufen** *unr. itr. V.; mit sein* **1** run alongside; **2** (zugleich ablaufen) proceed at the same time

neben·hin *Adv.* ‹*ask*› by the way; ‹*mention, say*› in passing

neben-, Neben-: **~höhle** *die* ▸❶ **S. 435** (Anat.) paranasal sinus; **~kläger** *der*, **~klägerin** *die* (Rechtsw.) accessory prosecutor; **~kosten** *Pl.* **1** additional costs; **2** (bei Mieten) heating, lighting, and services; **~kriegs·schauplatz** *der* secondary theatre of war; (fig.) secondary area of conflict; **~linie** *die* **1** (Eisenb.) ▸**~strecke**; **2** (Genealogie) collateral branch; **~mann** *der; Pl.:* **~männer** *od.* **~leute** neighbour; **sein ~mann** the person sitting/standing/walking next to him; his neighbour; **~niere** *die* ▸❶ **S. 435** (Anat.) adrenal *or* suprarenal gland; **~nieren·rinde** *die* ▸❶ **S. 435** (Anat.) adrenal *or* suprarenal cortex; **~ordnend** *Adj.* (Sprachw.) coordinating ‹*conjunction*›; **~produkt** *das* (auch fig.) by-product; **~raum** *der* next *or* adjoining room; room next door; (kleiner, unwichtiger) side room; **~rolle** *die* supporting role; **eine ~rolle [in etw. (*Dat.*)] spielen** (fig.) play a secondary *or* minor role [in sth.]; **~sache** *die* minor *or* inessential matter; **~sachen** inessentials; minor *or* inessential matters; **das ist ~sache** (ugs.) that's beside the point; **~sächlich** *Adj.* of minor importance *postpos.*; unimportant; minor, trivial ‹*detail*›; **etw. als ~sächlich abtun** reject sth. as irrelevant *or* beside the point; **sich über ~sächliche Dinge aufregen** get worked up about trivial things *or* matters; **~sächlichkeit** *die;* **~~, ~~en** **1** unimportance; (fehlender Bezug zur Sache) irrelevance; **2** (Unwichtiges) matter of minor importance; unimportant matter; (nicht zur Sache Gehörendes) irrelevancy; **~satz** *der* (Sprachw.) ▸**Gliedsatz**; **~stehend** *Adj.* accompanying ‹*text, illustration, table, etc.*›; (auf der Seite gegenüber) ‹*text, illustration, table, etc.*› opposite; **~stelle** *die* **1** extension; **2** (Filiale) branch; **~straße** *die* side street; (außerhalb der Stadt) minor road; **~strecke** *die* **1** (Eisenb.) branch *or* local line; **2** (Entlastungsstraße) minor road running parallel to the main road; **~tätigkeit** *die* second job; sideline; **~tisch** *der* next *or* neighbouring table; **~tür** *die* **1** side door; **2** (benachbarte Tür) next *or* neighbouring door; **~verdienst** *der* additional earnings *pl. or* income; **~winkel** *der* (Geom.) adjacent angle; **~wirkung** *die* side effect; **~zimmer** *das* next room; **sie gingen in ein ~zimmer** they went into an adjoining room; **~zweck** *der* secondary aim

neblig *Adj.* foggy; (weniger dicht) misty

nebst /ne:pst/ *Präp. mit Dat.* (veralt.) together with; plus; (zusätzlich zu) in addition to

nebst·bei (österr.) ▸**nebenbei**

nebst·dem (schweiz.) ▸**außerdem**

nebulos /nebu'lo:s/, **nebulös** /nebu'lø:s/ (geh.)

A *Adj.* nebulous ‹*idea, concept*›; obscure, vague ‹*hint*›

B *adv.* ‹*talk, hint*› vaguely

Necessaire /nesɛ'sɛ:ɐ̯/ *das;* **~s, ~s** **1** sponge bag (Brit.); toilet bag (Amer.) **2** (Behälter für Nähzeug) sewing bag

necken /'nɛkn̩/ *tr. V.* tease; **jmdn. mit jmdm./etw. ~:** tease sb. about sb./sth.; **sich ~:** tease each other *or* one another; *s. auch* **lieben**

Neckerei *die;* **~:** teasing

n

neckisch
A *Adj.* [1] teasing; (verspielt) playful; (schelmisch) mischievous [2] (kess) jaunty, saucy ‹*cap*›; saucy, provocative ‹*dress, blouse, etc.*›
B *adv.* ‹*smile, say*› saucily, cheekily

nee /neː/ (ugs.) no; nope (Amer. coll.)

Neer /neːɐ̯/ *die;* ~, ~**en** (nordd.) eddy

Neffe /ˈnɛfə/ *der;* ~**n**, ~**n** nephew

neg. *Abk.* = **negativ** neg.

Negation /negaˈtsi̯oːn/ *die;* ~, ~**en** negation

negativ /ˈneːgatiːf/
A *Adj.* negative; ~**e Zahlen** (Math.) negative *or* minus numbers
B *adv.* ‹*answer*› in the negative; **einen Antrag ~ bescheiden** reject an application; **einer Sache** (*Dat.*) **~ gegenüberstehen** take a negative view of a matter; **etw. ~ beeinflussen** have a negative influence on sth.; **etw. ~ bewerten** judge sth. unfavourably; **sich ~ äußern** comment negatively (**zu** on); **der Test/die Testbohrung verlief ~:** the test proved unsuccessful/the test well yielded nothing; **~ geladen** (Physik) negatively charged

Negativ *das;* ~**s**, ~**e** (Fot.) negative

Negativ-: ~**beispiel** *das* negative example; **das ~beispiel Stalin** the negative example of Stalin; ~**bilanz** *die* generally negative picture; (Ergebnis) generally negative outcome; ~**bild** *das* (Fot.) negative image; ~**film** *der* negative film

Negativität /negativiˈtɛːt/ *die;* ~: negativity; negativeness

Negativum /ˈneːgativʊm/ *das;* ~**s**, **Negativa** (Faktor) negative factor; (Eigenschaft) negative characteristic

neger (österr. ugs.) *in:* **~ sein** be broke (coll.)

Neger /ˈneːgɐ/ *der;* ~**s**, ~ [1] (oft als diskriminierend empfunden) Negro (dated/offensive) [2] (Fernsehen: schwarze Tafel) gobo; (Texttafel) cue card

Negerin *die;* ~, ~**nen** (oft als diskriminierend empfunden) Negress (dated/offensive)

Neger-: ~**krause** *die* (ugs. veralt.) frizzy hair *no art.*; ~**kuss**, *~**kuß** *der* ▸**Mohrenkopf 1**

Negerlein *das;* ~**s**, ~: (oft als diskriminierend empfunden) little Negro (dated/offensive)

Neger·sklave *der* Negro slave

negieren *tr. V.* [1] deny ‹*fact, assertion, guilt, etc.*› [2] (ablehnen) reject ‹*opinion, suggestion*› [3] (Sprachw.) negate

Negligee, Negligé /negliˈʒeː/ *das;* ~**s**, ~**s** négligé; negligee

negrid /neˈgriːt/ *Adj.* (Anthrop.) Negrid

negroid /negroˈiːt/ *Adj.* (Anthrop.) Negroid

nehmen /ˈneːmən/ *unr. tr. V.* [1] (ergreifen, an sich bringen, an~, als Beispiel ~) take; **etw. in die Hand/unter den Arm ~:** take sth. in one's hand/take *or* put sth. under one's arm; **etw. an sich** (*Akk.*) **~:** pick sth. up; (und aufbewahren) take charge of sth.; **sich** (*Dat.*) **etw. ~:** take sth.; (sich bedienen) help oneself to sth.; **sich** (*Dat.*) **einen Mann/eine Frau ~:** take a husband/wife; **woher ~ und nicht stehlen?** (scherzh.) where on earth am I going to get hold of that/them *etc.?*; **zu sich ~:** take in ‹*orphan*›; **sie nahm ihren Vater zu sich** she had her father come and live with her; **Gott hat ihn zu sich genommen** (geh.) God has taken him unto Himself ; **auf sich** (*Akk.*) **~:** take on ‹*responsibility, burden*›; take ‹*blame*›; **es auf sich** (*Akk.*) **~, etw. zu tun** take on the responsibility of doing sth.; **die Dinge ~, wie sie kommen** take things as they come; **jmdn. ~, wie er ist** take sb. as he is; **nimm doch mal den Fall, dass man dir einen Vertrag anböte** let's assume [that] they offered you a contract [2] (weg~) **jmdm./einer Sache etw. ~:** deprive sb./sth. of sth.; **jmdm. die Sicht/den Ausblick ~:** block sb.'s view; **jmdm. den Glauben/alle Illusionen ~** (fig.) deprive *or* rob sb. of his/her belief/all his/her illusions; **die Angst/die Sorgen von jmdm. ~:** relieve sb. of his/her fear/worries; **es sich** (*Dat.*) **nicht ~ lassen, etw. zu tun** not let anything stop one from doing sth.; **das nimmt der Sache den ganzen Reiz** it takes all the fun out of it [3] (benutzen) use ‹*ingredients, washing powder, wool, brush, knitting needles, etc.*›; **man nehme ...** (in Rezepten) take ...; **den Zug/das Auto/ein Taxi** *usw.* **~:** take the train/the car/a taxi *etc.*; **[sich** (*Dat.*)**] einen Anwalt/Privatlehrer** *usw.* **~:** get a lawyer/private tutor *etc.* [4] (aussuchen) take; **ich nehme die Pastete/die broschierte Ausgabe** I'll have the pâté/the paperback [5] (in Anspruch ~) take ‹*lessons, holiday, etc.*›; **einen Tag frei ~:** take a day off [6] (verlangen) charge; **was ~ Sie dafür?** what *or* how much do you charge for it? [7] (ein~, essen) take ‹*medicines, tablets, etc.*›; **etwas [Richtiges] zu sich ~:** have something [decent] to eat; **sie nimmt die Pille** she's taking *or* she's on the pill (coll.); **das Frühstück/einen Imbiss ~** (geh.) take breakfast/a snack; **den Kaffee ~** (geh.) have [one's] coffee [8] (auffassen) take (**als** as); **etw. ernst/leicht ~:** take sth. seriously/lightly; **jmdn. ernst ~:** take sb. seriously; **gleichgültig/je nachdem, wie mans nimmt** (ugs.) however you look at it/depending on how you look at it; **jmdn. nicht für voll ~** (ugs.) not take sb. seriously [9] (behandeln) treat ‹*person*›; **wissen, wie man jmdn. zu ~ hat** know how to treat sb. [10] (überwinden, militärisch ein~) take ‹*obstacle, bend, incline, village, bridgehead, etc.*›; (fig.) take ‹*woman*› [11] (auf~) **etw. auf Videokassette/Band ~:** record sth. on video cassette/record *or* tape sth. [12] (Sport) take ‹*ball, punch*›; **einen Spieler hart ~:** foul a player blatantly

Nehrung /ˈneːrʊŋ/ *die;* ~, ~**en** sand bar

Neid /nai̯t/ *der;* ~**[e]s** envy; jealousy; **aus ~:** out of envy; **von ~ erfüllt [sein]** [be] filled with envy; **vor ~ platzen** (ugs.) die of envy (coll.); **gelb** *od.* **grün vor ~ werden, vor ~ erblassen** turn *or* go green with envy; **das muss der ~ ihr lassen** (ugs.) you've got to give her that; you've got to say that much for her; **das ist der ~ der Besitzlosen** (ugs.) that's just sour grapes; **nur kein ~!** don't be envious!

neiden *tr. V.* (geh.) **jmdm. etw. ~:** envy sb. [for] sth.

Neider *der;* ~**s**, ~: envious person; **seine ~:** those who are/were envious of him; **erfolgreiche Leute haben immer viele ~:** successful people are always much *or* greatly envied

neid·erfüllt *Adj.* filled with *or* full of envy *postpos.*

Neiderin *die;* ~, ~**nen** ▸**Neider**

Neid·hammel *der* (salopp abwertend) envious sod (sl.)

neidisch
A *Adj.* envious; **auf jmdn./etw. ~ sein** be envious of sb./sth.
B *adv.* enviously

neid-: ~**los** **A** *Adj.* ungrudging ‹*admiration*›; ‹*joy*› without envy; **B** *adv.* ‹*acknowledge, admire*› without envy; ~**voll** **A** *Adj.* envious ‹*glance*›; ‹*person*› filled with *or* full of envy; ‹*admiration*› mixed with envy; **B** *adv.* ‹*watch*› full of envy

Neige /ˈnai̯gə/ *die;* ~ (geh.) dregs *pl.*; lees *pl.*; **ein Glas bis zur ~ leeren** drain a glass to the dregs; **etw. bis zur ~ auskosten** (fig.) enjoy sth. to the full; **etw. bis zur bitteren ~ durchstehen** (fig.) see sth. through to the bitter end; **zur ~ gehen** (aufgebraucht sein) ‹*money, supplies, etc.*› run low; (zu Ende gehen) ‹*year, day, holiday*› draw to its close

neigen
A *tr. V.* tip, tilt ‹*bottle, glass, barrel, etc.*›; incline ‹*head, upper part of body*›; **den Kopf zum Gruß ~:** incline one's head in greeting
B *refl. V.* [1] ‹*person*› lean, bend; ‹*ship*› heel over, list; ‹*scales*› tip; ‹*sun*› sink; ‹*branches*› bow down; **sich nach vorne/zur Seite ~:** bend *or* lean over *or* forward/lean to one side [2] (schräg abfallen) ‹*meadows*› slope down; **eine geneigte Fläche** a sloping surface [3] (geh.: zu Ende gehen) ‹*day, year, holiday*› draw to its close
C *itr. V.* [1] **zu Erkältungen/Krankheiten ~:** be susceptible *or* prone to colds/illnesses; **zur** *od.* **zu Korpulenz/Schwermut ~:** have a tendency to put on weight/tend to be melancholy; **ein zum** *od.* **zu Jähzorn ~der Mensch** a person who is prone to violent outbursts of temper [2] (tendieren) tend; **zu der Ansicht** *od.* **der Auffassung ~, dass ...** tend towards the view or opinion that ...; *s. auch* **geneigt B**

Neigung *die;* ~, ~**en** [1] (des Kopfes) nod [2] (Geneigtsein) inclination; (eines Geländes) slope; **die Straße weist eine leichte ~ auf** the street has a slight incline *or* gradient [3] (Vorliebe) inclination; **seine politischen/künstlerischen ~en** his political/artistic leanings; **eine ~ für etw.** a penchant *or* fondness for sth. [4] (Anfälligsein) tendency; **eine ~ zur Korpulenz/zum Faulsein haben** have a tendency to put on weight/to be lazy [5] (Lust) inclination [6] (Liebe) affection; fondness; liking; **jmds. ~ gewinnen/erwidern** win/return sb.'s affection

Neigungs-: ~**ehe** *die* love match; ~**messer** *der;* ~~**s**, ~~: clinometer; inclinometer; ~**winkel** *der* angle of inclination

nein /nai̯n/ *Partikel* no; **~ danke** no, thank you; **sie kann nicht Nein sagen** she can't say no; **da sage ich nicht Nein** I wouldn't say no; **man muss auch Nein sagen können** one must be able to say no; **~, nicht!** no, don't!; **~, so was!** well I never!; **~ und abermals ~!** no, and that's final!; **aber ~!** good heavens no!; **du gehst doch jetzt noch nicht, ~?** you're not going now, are you?; **das wird dir doch nicht zu viel, ~?** that's not too much for you, is it?; **~, dass ich das noch erleben durfte!** simply wonderful, that I should live to see this!; **~, wie schön Sie das gesagt haben!** gosh, you really put that beautifully! (coll.)

'nein (südd.) ▸**hinein**

Nein *das;* ~**[s]**, ~**[s]** no; **bei seinem ~ bleiben** stick by one's refusal; **mit ~ stimmen** vote no

Nein-: ~**sager** *der;* ~~**s**, ~~, ~**sagerin** *die;* ~~, ~~**nen** (abwertend) person who always says no *or* who says no to everything; ~**stimme** *die* no-vote; vote against

Nekrolog /nekroˈloːk/ *der;* ~**[e]s**, ~**e** (geh.) obituary; necrology (rare)

Nekrophilie /nekrofiˈliː/ *die;* ~: necrophilia *no art.*

Nektar /ˈnɛktar/ *der;* ~**s**, ~**e** [1] (Bot., Myth.) nectar [2] (Getränk) *drink made from crushed fruit, sugar, and water*

Nektarine /nektaˈriːnə/ *die;* ~, ~**n** nectarine

Nelke /ˈnɛlkə/ *die;* ~, ~**n** [1] pink; (Dianthus caryophyllus) carnation [2] (Gewürz) clove

Nelken·öl *das* oil of cloves

Nelson /ˈnɛlzɔn/ *der;* ~**[s]**, ~**s** (Ringen) nelson

Nemesis /ˈneːmezɪs/ *die;* ~: nemesis

'nen /nən/ ▸**einen**

nennbar *Adj.* specifiable ‹*change, problem*›; nameable ‹*feeling*›; **nicht ~:** unspecifiable/unnameable

Nenn·betrag *der* ▸**Nennwert**

nennen /ˈnɛnən/
A *unr. tr. V.* [1] call; **jmdn. nach jmdm. ~:** call *or* name sb. after sb.; **sie nannten das Kind Günther** they called *or* named the child Günther; **jmdn. beim Vornamen ~:** call sb. by his/her first *or* Christian name; **jmdn. einen Lügner ~:** call sb. a liar; **wenn du es so ~ willst** if you want to call it that; **das nenne ich Mut/eine Überraschung** that's what I call courage/well, that 'is a surprise; **Max Müller, genannt „der weiße Würger"** Max Müller, known as the 'White Strangler' [2] (mitteilen) give ‹*name, date of birth, address, reason, price, etc.*›; **jmdm. ein gutes Hotel/einen Arzt ~:** give sb. the name of a good hotel/a doctor [3] (anführen) give, cite ‹*example*›; (erwähnen) mention ‹*person, name*›; **das oben Genannte** the item[s] mentioned above; **die im folgenden genannten Punkte** the points mentioned below
B *unr. refl. V.* ‹*person, thing*› be called; **er nennt sich Maler/Dichter** *usw.* (behauptet Maler/Dichter usw. zu sein) he calls himself a painter/poet *etc.*; **und so was nennt sich nun ein Freund/tolerant** (ugs.) and he/she has the nerve to call himself/herself a friend/tolerant; **und das nennt sich ein gutes Hotel** and that's supposed to be a good hotel

nẹnnens·wert *Adj.* considerable ‹*influence, changes, delays, damage*›; **kaum ~e Veränderungen** changes scarcely worth mentioning; **es ist nichts Nennenswertes passiert** nothing worth mentioning *or* nothing of note has happened

Nẹnner *der;* **~s, ~** (Math.) denominator; **der gemeinsame ~:** the common denominator; **etw. auf einen [gemeinsamen] ~ bringen** (fig.) reduce sth. to a common denominator

Nẹnn-: **~fall** *der* ▸**Nominativ**; **~form** *die* ▸**Infinitiv**; **~leistung** *die* (Technik) rated output; (Elektrot.) rated power; (eines Motors) rated horsepower; **~onkel** *der* uncle only in name; **er ist nicht mein richtiger Onkel, sondern nur ein ~onkel** he's not my real uncle, I just call him that; **~tante** *die* aunt only in name; *s. auch* **~onkel**

Nẹnnung *die;* **~, ~en** [1] ▸**nennen A 2, 3**: giving; citing; mentioning [2] (Sport) entry (**zu, für** for)

Nẹnn-: **~wert** *der* (Wirtsch.) nominal *or* face value; (von Aktien) par *or* nominal *or* face value; **~wort** *das; Pl.* **~wörter** ▸**Substantiv**

neo-, Neo-: neo-

neo-: **~konservativ** [A] *Adj.* neo-conservative; neo-con (coll.); [B] *adv.* in a neo-conservative manner **~liberal** [A] *Adj.* neo-liberal; [B] *adv.* in a neo-liberal manner

Neolithikum /neo'li:tikʊm/ *das;* **~s** (Archäol.) Neolithic period

Neologismus /neolo'gɪsmʊs/ *der;* **~, Neologismen** (Sprachw.) neologism

Neon /'ne:ɔn/ *das;* **~s** (Chemie) neon

Neo·nazi *der* neo-Nazi

Neon-: **~licht** *das; Pl.* **~~er** neon light; **~reklame** *die* neon sign; **~röhre** *die* neon tube; [neon] strip light

Neopren Ⓦⓩ /neo'pre:n/ *das;* **~s, ~e** neoprene

Neopren-anzug *der* neoprene suit

Nepal /'ne:pal/ *(das);* **~s** Nepal

Nepalese /nepa'le:zə/ *der;* **~n, ~n, Nepalesin** *die;* **~, ~nen** Nepali; Nepalese

Nepotismus /nepo'tɪsmʊs/ *der;* **~:** nepotism *no art.*

Nepp /nɛp/ *der;* **~s** (ugs. abwertend) daylight robbery *no art.*; rip-off (coll.)

nẹppen *tr. V.* (ugs. abwertend) rook; rip ‹*tourist, customer, etc.*› off (sl.)

Nẹpper *der;* **~s, ~, Nẹpperin** *die;* **~, ~nen** (ugs. abwertend) shark; rip-off merchant (coll.)

Nẹpp·lokal *das* (ugs. abwertend) clip joint (coll. derog.)

Neptun[1] /nɛp'tu:n/ *der;* **~s** (Astron.), **Neptun**[2] *(der);* **~s** (Myth.) Neptune

Nerv /nɛrf/ *der;* **~s, ~en** [1] ▸ⓘ **S. 435** nerve; **an den ~ der Sache rühren** (fig.) get to the heart of the matter; **das Buch trifft den ~ der Zeit** (fig.) the book taps the pulse of the age; **den ~ haben, etw. zu tun** (fig. ugs.) have the nerve to do sth.; **jmdm. den ~ töten** (fig. ugs.) drive sb. up the wall (coll.) [2] *Pl.* (nervliche Konstitution) nerves; **gute/schwache ~en haben** have strong/bad nerves; **meine ~en halten das nicht aus** my nerves won't stand it; **die ~en [dazu] haben, etw. zu tun** have the nerve to do sth.; **die ~en bewahren** *od.* **behalten** keep calm; **die ~en verlieren** lose control [of oneself]; lose one's cool (sl.); **ich bin mit den ~en fertig** *od.* **am Ende** my nerves cannot take any more; **du hast vielleicht ~en!** (ugs.) you've got a nerve!; **~en haben wie Drahtseile** *od.* **Stricke** (ugs.) have nerves of steel; **jmdm. auf die ~en gehen** *od.* **fallen** get on sb.'s nerves [3] (in Blättern, Insektenflügeln) vein; nerve

nẹrven (salopp)
[A] *tr. V.* **jmdn. ~:** get on sb.'s nerves
[B] *itr. V.* be wearing on the nerves

nẹrven-, Nẹrven-: **~an·spannung** *die* nervous strain; nervous tension *no indef. art.*; **~arzt** *der,* **~ärztin** *die* neurologist; **~aufreibend** *Adj.* nerve-racking; **~belastung** *die* strain on the nerves; **~beruhigend** *Adj.* sedative ‹*effect, drug*›; **~beruhigend wirken** have a calming effect on the nerves; ‹*drug*› act as a sedative/tranquillizer; **~beruhigungsmittel** *das* sedative; (gegen Depressionen, Angstzustände) tranquillizer; **~bündel** *das* [1] (ugs.) bundle of nerves (coll.); [2] ▸ⓘ **S. 435** (Anat.) bundle of nerve fibres; **~entzündung** *die* ▸ⓘ **S. 439** (Med.) neuritis; **~faser** *die* ▸ⓘ **S. 435** (Anat.) nerve fibre; **~gas** *das* nerve gas; **~gift** *das* neurotoxin; **~heilanstalt** *die* (veralt.) mental *or* psychiatric hospital; **~kitzel** *der* (ugs.) kick (coll.); **~klinik** *die* [1] clinic for nervous diseases; [2] (ugs.) mental *or* psychiatric hospital; **~kostüm** *das* (ugs. scherzh.) nerves *pl.*; **ein schwaches ~kostüm haben** have bad nerves; **~kraft** *die* nervous strength; **~krank** *Adj.* [1] ‹*person*› suffering from a nervous disease *or* disorder; [2] (psychisch krank) mentally ill; **~kranke** *der/die* [1] person suffering from a nervous disease *or* disorder; [2] (psychisch Kranke) mentally ill person; **~kranke sind ...** the mentally ill are ...; **~krankheit** *die* ▸ⓘ **S. 439** [1] nervous disease *or* disorder; [2] (psychische Krankheit) mental illness; **~krieg** *der* (ugs.) war of nerves; **~leiden** *das* ▸ⓘ **S. 439** nervous complaint *or* disorder; **~nahrung** *die:* **~nahrung sein** be good for the *or* one's nerves; **~probe** *die* mental trial; **~sache** *die:* in **das ist reine ~sache** (ugs.) it's a matter *or* question of nerves; **~säge** *die* (salopp) pain in the neck (coll.); **~schmerz** *der* ▸ⓘ **S. 439** (Med.) neuralgia; **~schock** *der* nervous *or* psychic shock; **~schwach** *Adj.* ‹*person*› with bad nerves *not pred.*; neurasthenic ‹*person*› (Med.); **~schwäche** *die* ▸ⓘ **S. 439** [1] neurasthenia (Med.); [2] (psychische Schwäche) bad nerves *pl.*; **~stärkend** *Adj.* nerve-strengthening; **ein ~stärkendes Mittel** a nerve tonic; **~strang** *der* ▸**~bündel 2**; **~system** *das* ▸ⓘ **S. 435** (Anat.) nervous system; **~zelle** *die* ▸ⓘ **S. 435** (Anat.) nerve cell; **~zusammenbruch** *der* ▸ⓘ **S. 439** nervous breakdown

nẹrvig *Adj.* (auch fig.) sinewy

nẹrvlich
[A] *Adj.* nervous ‹*strain*›; **eine ~e Belastung für jmdn. sein** be a strain on sb.'s nerves
[B] *adv.* **dieser ständigen Spannung war er ~ nicht gewachsen** his nerves were not up to this constant tension

nervös /nɛr'vø:s/
[A] *Adj.* [1] nervy, jittery ‹*person*›; nervous ‹*haste, movement*›; **~ sein** be jittery (coll.) *or* on edge; **das macht mich ganz ~:** it really gets on my nerves; (das beunruhigt mich) it makes me really nervous [2] (Med.) nervous ‹*twitch, gastric disorder, etc.*›
[B] *adv.* [1] nervously [2] (Med.) **~ bedingt sein** be caused by nerves

Nervosität /nɛrvozi'tɛ:t/ *die;* **~:** nervousness; **voller ~:** nervously

nẹrv·tötend *Adj.* nerve-racking ‹*wait*›; nerve-shattering ‹*sound, noise*›; soul-destroying ‹*activity, work*›

Nẹrz /nɛrts/ *der;* **~es, ~e** mink

Nẹrz·mantel *der* mink coat

Nẹssel[1] /'nɛsl̩/ *die;* **~, ~n** nettle; **sich in die ~n setzen** (fig. ugs.) get [oneself] into hot water (coll.)

Nẹssel[2] *der;* **~s, ~** (Stoff) coarse, untreated cotton cloth

Nẹssel-: **~fieber** *das* nettle rash accompanied by fever; **~sucht** *die* nettle rash; hives

Nest /nɛst/ *das;* **~[e]s, ~er** [1] nest; **sich (Dat.) gemeinsam ein ~ einrichten** (fig.) set up home together; **das eigene** *od.* **sein eigenes ~ beschmutzen** (fig.) foul one's own nest; **er hat sich ins warme** *od.* **gemachte ~ gesetzt** (fig. ugs.) he had his future made for him [2] (fam.: Bett) bed; **raus aus dem ~!** show a leg! (coll.) [3] (ugs. abwertend: kleiner Ort) little place; **ein winziges ~:** a tiny little place; **ein gottverlassenes/armseliges ~:** a godforsaken/miserable hole [4] (Schlupfwinkel) hideout; den [5] (Haartracht) plaited bun

Nẹst-: **~bau** *der* nest-building *no art.*; **~beschmutzer** *der;* **~~s, ~~, ~beschmutzerin** *die;* **~~, ~~nen** (abwertend) person who is/was guilty of fouling his/her own nest

nesteln /'nɛstl̩n/ *itr. V.* fiddle, (ungeschickt) fumble (**an** + *Dat.* with)

nẹst-, Nẹst-: **~flüchter** *der;* **~~s, ~~** (Zool.) (bird) precocial *or* nidifugous bird; (animal) precocial animal; **~häkchen** *das* (fam.) [spoilt] baby of the family; **~hocker** *der* (Zool.) nidicolous bird/animal; **~warm** *Adj.* ‹*eggs*› warm from the nest; **~wärme** *die* warmth of a [happy] family upbringing *or* of [happy] family life

nett /nɛt/
[A] *Adj.* [1] nice; (freundlich) nice; kind; **sei so ~ und hilf mir!** would you be so good *or* kind as to help me?; **sie war so ~, uns einen Kaffee anzubieten** she very kindly offered us a coffee; **das war [nicht] ~ von dir** that was[n't very] nice of you; **~, dass du anrufst** it's nice *or* kind of you to ring; **etwas Nettes erleben/sagen** have a pleasant experience/say something nice [2] (hübsch) pretty ‹*girl, town, dress, etc.*›; nice, pleasant ‹*pub, house, town, etc.*› [3] (ugs.: beträchtlich) nice little (coll.) ‹*profit, extra earnings, income*›; **sie hat eine ganz ~e Oberweite** she's very well endowed (coll.); **eine ~e Summe/eine ~e Stange Geld** a tidy sum (coll.) [4] (ugs. iron.: unerfreulich) nice (coll.) ‹*affair*›; nice (coll.), fine ‹*state of affairs, mess*›; **das sind ja ~e Aussichten** that's a nice *or* charming prospect (coll.); **das kann ja ~ werden!** that'll be fun (coll.)
[B] *adv.* (angenehm) nicely; (freundlich) nicely; kindly; **sich ~ mit jmdm. unterhalten** have a pleasant conversation with sb.; **hier sitzt man sehr ~:** it's very nice *or* pleasant sitting here

nẹtter·weise *Adv.* (ugs.) kindly; **würden Sie mir ~ diesen Platz überlassen?** would you be so kind as to let me have your seat?

Nẹttigkeit *die;* **~, ~en** [1] kindness; goodness [2] (Äußerung) **jmdm. ein paar ~en sagen** say a few nice *or* kind things to sb.; (iron.) say a few choice words to sb.

netto /'nɛto/ *Adv.* ▸ⓘ **S. 315** ‹*weigh, earn, etc.*› net

Nẹtto-: **~einkommen** *das* net income; **~ertrag** *der* net return; **~gehalt** *das* net salary; **~gewicht** *das* net weight; **~lohn** *der* net wage; **~preis** *der* net price; **~raum·zahl** *die* net register tonnage; **~register·tonne** *die* (Seew.) net register ton; **~sozial-produkt** *das* (Wirtsch.) net national product

Netz /nɛts/ *das;* **~es, ~e** [1] (auch Fischer~, Tennis~, Ballspiele) net; (Haar~) [hair] net; (Einkaufs~) string bag; (Gepäck~) [luggage] rack; (Sicherheits~) safety net; **sich in einem ~ von Lügen verstricken** (fig.) become entangled in a web of lies; **jmdm. ins ~ gehen** (fig.) fall into sb.'s trap; **jmdm. durchs ~ gehen** (fig.) slip through sb.'s net; **seine ~e überall auswerfen** (fig.) put out feelers in all directions; **ans ~ gehen** (Tennis) go to the net [2] (Spinnen~) web [3] (Verteiler~, Verkehrs~, System von Einrichtungen, DV, Fernspr.) network; (für Strom, Wasser, Gas) mains *pl.*; **ans ~ gehen** ‹*power station*› go on stream; **das soziale ~:** the social security system [4] (Math.) net

nẹtz-, Nẹtz-: **~anbieter** *der* (DV, Fernspr.) network provider; **~anschluss**, ***~anschluß** *der* mains connection; **~artig** *Adj.* netlike ‹*material, pattern, etc.*›; **~auge** *das* (Zool.) compound eye; **~ball** *der* (Tennis, Volleyball) net ball

nẹtzen *tr. V.* (geh.) moisten ‹*soil, plant, one's lips*›; wet ‹*hair, cheeks*›

Nẹtz-: **~frequenz** *die* (Elektrot.) mains frequency; **~gerät** *das* (Elektrot.) power pack; **~gewölbe** *das* (Kunstwiss.) net vault; **~haut** *die* ▸ⓘ **S. 435** (Anat.) retina

Nẹtzhaut-: **~ablösung** *die* (Med.) detachment of the retina; retinal detachment; **~entzündung** *die* (Med.) retinitis

Nẹtz-: **~hemd** *das* string vest; **~karte** *die* area season ticket; (Eisenb.) unlimited travel ticket; **~magen** *der* (Zool.) reticulum; honeycomb stomach; **~roller** *der* (Tennis) net cord [stroke]; **~spannung** *die* (Elektrot.) mains

n

voltage; **~stecker** *der* mains plug; **~strumpf** *der* net stocking

Netz·werk *das* (auch Elektrot.) network

netzwerk-, Netzwerk-: ~betreiber *der;* ~~s, ~~, **~betreiberin** *die;* ~~, ~~nen (DV) network operator; **~fähig** *Adj.* (DV) networkable; **~kabel** *das* (DV) network cable; **~karte** *die* (DV) network card

neu /nɔy/

A *Adj.* **1** ▸ **i S. 331** new; **ein ganz ~es Fahrrad** a brand new bicycle; **die Neue Welt** the New World; **das Neue Testament** the New Testament; **die ~este Mode/die ~esten Schlager/der ~este Witz** the latest fashion/hits/joke; **die ~e Literatur/Physik** modern literature/physics; **die ~esten Nachrichten/Ereignisse** the latest news/most recent events; **viel Glück im ~en Jahr** best wishes for the New Year; Happy New Year; **er brachte eine ~e Flasche** he fetched another bottle; **das sieht aus wie ~**: that looks like new *or* as good as new; **das ist mir ~**: that is news to me; **ich bin ~ in dieser Gegend/in diesem Beruf** I am new to this area/job; **das Neue daran ist ...** what's new about it is ...; **den Reiz des Neuen haben** have novelty value; **das Neueste auf dem Markt** the latest thing on the market; **der/die Neue** the new man/woman/boy/girl; **etw./nichts Neues wissen/berichten** know/report something/nothing new; **was gibt es Neues?** what's new?; **weißt du schon das Neueste?** (ugs.) have you heard the latest?; **etw. Neues unternehmen/anfangen** do/start something new *or* different; **eine ~e Flasche aufmachen** open another bottle; **eine ~e Seite/Zeile beginnen** start a new *or* fresh page/line; **aufs Neue** anew; afresh; again; **auf ein Neues!** let's try again!; **von ~em** *od.* **Neuem** all over again; (noch einmal) [once] again; **von ~em** *od.* **Neuem beginnen** start *or* begin all over again; make a fresh start; **seit ~estem** *od.* **Neuestem werden dort keine Kreditkarten mehr akzeptiert** just recently they've started refusing to accept credit cards; **in ~erer/~ester Zeit** quite/just *or* very recently; **das ist ~eren Datums** that is of a more recent date; **die ~en** *od.* **~eren Sprachen** modern languages **2** (kürzlich geerntet) new ‹*wine, potatoes*› **3** (sauber) clean ‹*shirt, socks, underwear, etc.*›

B *adv.* **1** **~ tapeziert/gespritzt/gestrichen/möbliert/eröffnet** repapered/resprayed/repainted/refurnished/reopened; **einen Sessel ~ beziehen** re-cover an armchair; **ein Geschäft ~ eröffnen** reopen a shop; **sich ~ einkleiden/einrichten** provide oneself with a new set of clothes/refurnish one's home; **noch einmal ~ beginnen** start again from scratch; **sich ~ formieren** ‹*party, organization, etc.*› re-form; **~ bearbeitet** [newly] revised ‹*edition*›; newly adapted ‹*version*› **2** (gerade erst) **diese Ware ist ~ eingetroffen** this item has just come in *or* arrived; **das Geschäft ist ~ eröffnet** the shop has only just been opened; **ein ~ eröffneter Laden** a newly-opened shop; **~ erschienene Bücher** newly published books; books that have just come out *or* appeared; **3 000 Wörter sind ~ hinzugekommen** 3,000 new words have been added; **~ vermählt** newly wed *or* married; **die neu Vermählten** the newly-weds

neu-, Neu-: ~anfang *der* new beginning; fresh start; **einen ~anfang machen** make a fresh start; **~anfertigung** *die* **1** making; (serienweise) manufacture; **2** (Angefertigtes) **eine ~anfertigung sein** be new; **~ankömmling** *der* new arrival; **~anschaffung** *die* **1** **die ~anschaffung von Produktionsanlagen** the acquisition of new production plant; **~anschaffungen machen** buy new items; **2** (Artikel, Gegenstand) new acquisition; **~apostolisch** *Adj.* (christl. Rel.) New Apostolic; **die ~apostolische Gemeinde** the New Apostolic Church

neu·artig *Adj.* new; **ein ~er Staubsauger** a new type of vacuum cleaner; **das Neuartige an diesem Gerät** the novel feature of this device

Neuartigkeit *die;* ~: novelty

Neu-: ~auflage *die* reprint [with alterations]; (mit umfangreichen Veränderungen) new edition; **eine ~auflage des vorjährigen Endspiels** (fig.) a repeat of last years's final; **~ausgabe** *die* new edition

Neu·bau *der; Pl.* **~ten** **1** new house/building **2** (Wiedererrichtung) rebuilding

Neubau-: ~gebiet *das* new [housing] development; **~viertel** *das* new district; **~wohnung** *die* flat (esp. Brit.) *or* (esp. Amer.) apartment in a new building; new flat *or* (esp. Amer.) apartment

neu-, Neu-: ~bearbeitet ▸ **neu B1**; **~bearbeitung** *die* **1** (eines Buches, Textes) revision; (eines Theaterstücks) adaptation; **2** (~e Fassung) new version; **~bedeutung** *die* (Sprachw.) new meaning; **~beginn** *der* new beginning; **~besetzung** *die:* **die ~besetzung einer Stelle** the refilling of a post; **eine ~besetzung ihrer Rolle wurde notwendig** it became necessary to cast someone else in her part; **~bildung** *die* **1** **die ~bildung der Regierung/des Kabinetts** the formation of a new government/cabinet; **2** (von Gewebe) regeneration; (~ Gebildetes) new growth; **die ~bildung von Geschwülsten** the growth of new tumours; (wiederholt) the regrowth of tumours; **3** (eines Wortes) coining; (~es Wort) neologism; **~bürger** *der,* **~bürgerin** *die* new citizen

Neu-Delhi /nɔyˈdeːli/ *(das);* **~s** ▸ **i S. 675** New Delhi

neu-, Neu-: ~deutsch *Adj.* (meist abwertend) modern West German ‹*society*›; typical West German ‹*arrogance, smugness, customs*›; **~druck** *der; Pl.* ~~e reprint [with corrections]; **~einstellung** *die:* **eine ~einstellung vornehmen** take on a new employee; (von Angestellten) make a new appointment; **~einstellungen notwendig machen** make it necessary to take on new staff; **~einstudierung** *die* (Theater) new production

> **Neue Kronen Zeitung**
>
> An Austrian tabloid that is published in Vienna and is read by half the population. It is considered to be right-wing, as is the *Kurier*, Austria's other tabloid.

Neu·england *(das)* New England

neu·englisch *Adj.* modern English

Neu-: ~entdeckung *die* **1** (auch fig.) new discovery; **2** (Wiederentdeckung) rediscovery; **~entwicklung** *die* **1** **die ~entwicklung von Heilmitteln/Maschinen** the development of new medicines/machines; **2** (neu Entwickeltes) new development

neuerdings /ˈnɔyɐˈdɪŋs/ *Adv.* **1** recently; **Fahrkarten gibt es ~ nur noch am Automaten** as of a short while ago one can only get tickets from a machine; **~ kann man direkt dorthin fliegen** it has recently become possible to fly there direct; **er trägt ~ eine Perücke** he has recently started wearing a wig **2** (südd., österr., schweiz.: erneut) again

Neuerer *der;* **~s,** ~, **Neuerin** *die;* ~, **~nen** innovator

neuerlich

A *Adj.* further

B *adv.* again

neu-, Neu-: ~eröffnet ▸ **neu B 1, 2**; **~eröffnung** *die* **1** opening; **2** (Wiedereröffnung) reopening; **~erscheinung** *die* new publication; (Schallplatte) new release

Neuerung *die;* ~, **~en** innovation

Neu·erwerbung *die* **1** **die ~ von Büchern/Möbeln** *usw.* the acquisition of new books/furniture *etc.* **2** (Gegenstand) new acquisition **3** (Sport) new signing

neuestens /ˈnɔyəstn̩s/ *Adv.* ▸ **neuerdings 1**

> **Neue Zürcher Zeitung**
>
> A Swiss quality daily which is held in high esteem at home and abroad.

Neu·fassung *die* revised version; (eines Films) remake

Neufundland *(das);* **~s** Newfoundland

Neufundländer *der;* **~s,** ~ (Hunderasse) Newfoundland [dog]

neu-, Neu-: ~geboren *Adj.* newborn; **sich wie ~geboren fühlen** feel a new man/woman; **~geborene** *das; adj. Dekl.* newborn child; **~geburt** *die* (geh.) rebirth; **~gestaltung** *die* (einer Gemeinschaft, Gesellschaft) reorganization; reshaping; (der Politik, eines Programms) reshaping; (einer Titelseite, einer Einrichtung) redesigning; (eines Stadtviertels, einer Parkanlage) replanning; **~gewürz** *das* (österr.) allspice; pimento

Neu·gier, Neugierde /-ɡiːɐ̯də/ *die;* ~: curiosity; (Wissbegierde) inquisitiveness; **aus [reiner] ~**: out of [sheer] curiosity; **vor ~ platzen** be bursting with curiosity

neu·gierig

A *Adj.* curious; inquisitive; prying (derog.), nosy (coll. derog.) ‹*person*›; **sei nicht so ~!** don't be so inquisitive *or* (coll. derog.) nosy!; **da bin ich aber ~!** (iron.) I'll believe it when I see it; I can hardly wait! (iron.); **auf etw.** (*Akk.*) **~ sein** be curious about sth.; **viele Neugierige** many inquisitive people *or* spectators; **ich bin ~, was er dazu sagt** I'm curious to know what he'll say about it; **ich bin ~, ob er kommt** I wonder whether he'll come; **er war ~ [zu hören], was passiert war** he was curious to know what had happened

B *adv.* ‹*ask*› inquisitively; ‹*peer*› nosily (coll. derog.); **jmdn. ~ mustern** eye sb. curiously; **~ lehnten die Nachbarn aus dem Fenster** the neighbours leaned out of the window full of curiosity

neu-, Neu-: ~gliederung *die* reorganization; restructuring; **~gotik** *die* Gothic Revival; **~gotisch** *Adj.* neo-Gothic; **~gründung** *die* **1** **die ~gründung eines Vereins/einer Partei/Universität** *usw.* the founding *or* establishment of a new club/party/university *etc.*; **2** (~ Gegründetes) **eine ~gründung sein** have recently been founded *or* established; **3** (erneute Gründung) refoundation; re-establishment

Neu·guinea *(das)* New Guinea

Neuheit *die;* ~, **~en** **1** novelty; **den Reiz der ~ haben** have novelty value **2** (Neues) new product/gadget/article *etc.*

neu·hoch·deutsch *adj.* New High German

Neu·hoch·deutsch *das* New High German

Neuigkeit *die;* ~, **~en** piece of news; **~en** news *sing.*

Neu·inszenierung *die* (Theater) new production

Neu·jahr *das* ▸ **i S. 331** New Year's Day; **~ feiern** celebrate New Year; *s. auch* **prosit**

Neujahrs-: ~abend *der* New Year's Eve; **~ansprache** *die* New Year address; **~fest** *das* New Year's Day; (Feier) New Year celebration; **das jüdische/chinesische ~fest** the Jewish/Chinese New Year; **das ~fest begehen** celebrate New Year; **~gruß** *der* New Year greetings *pl.*; **~karte** *die* New Year card; **~konzert** *das* New Year concert; **~nacht** *die* New Year's night; **~tag** *der* New Year's Day

neu-, Neu-: ~land *das* **1** newly reclaimed *or* new land; **2** (unerforschtes Land) new *or* virgin territory; **wissenschaftliches/medizinisches ~land betreten** (fig.) break new ground in science/medicine; **~latein** *das* New Latin; Neo-Latin; **~lateinisch** *Adj.* Neo-Latin

neulich *Adv.* recently; the other day; **~ morgens/abends** the other morning/evening; **der Mann von ~, der in unserem Zugabteil saß** (ugs.) the man who was sitting in our compartment on the train the other day

Neuling /ˈnɔylɪŋ/ *der;* **~s, ~e** newcomer (**in** + *Dat.* to); new man/woman/girl/boy; (auf einem Gebiet) novice

neu·modisch (abwertend)

A *Adj.* newfangled (derog.)

B *adv.* ‹*dress*› in a newfangled way

Neu·mond *der* new moon; **heute ist/haben wir ~**: there's a new moon today; **zwei Tage nach ~**: two days after the new moon

neun /nɔyn/ *Kardinalz.* ▸ⓘ **S. 29**, ▸ⓘ **S. 729**, ▸ⓘ **S. 826** nine; **alle ~[e]** (Kegeln) a floorer; *s. auch* **acht**

Neun *die;* **~, ~en** nine; **ach, du grüne ~e** (ugs.) oh, my goodness!; good grief!; *s. auch* **Acht**[1] **1, 2, 4, 5, 7**

neun-, Neun- (*s. auch* **acht-, Acht-**): **~eck** *das* nonagon; **~eckig** *Adj.* nonagonal; *s. auch* **achteckig**; **~einhalb** *Bruchz.* nine and a half

Neuner *der;* **~s, ~** (ugs.) nine *s. auch* **Acht**[1] **1, 2, 5; Achter 4**

neunerlei *indekl. Gattungsz.* ① *attr.* nine kinds *or* sorts of; nine different ‹*sorts, kinds, sizes, possibilities*› ② *subst.* nine [different] things

Neuner·probe *die* (Math.) casting out nines [check]

neun-, Neun- (*s. auch* **acht-, Acht-**): **~fach** *Vervielfältigungsz.* ninefold; *s. auch* **achtfach**; **~fache** *das; adj. Dekl.* **das ~fache von 4 ist 36** nine fours are *or* nine times four makes thirty-six; *s. auch* **Achtfache**; **~hundert** *Kardinalz.* ▸ⓘ **S. 826** nine hundred; **~jährig** *Adj.* (9 Jahre alt) nine-year-old *attrib.*; (9 Jahre dauernd) nine-year *attrib.*; *s. auch* **achtjährig**; **~köpfig** *Adj.* nine-headed ‹*monster*›; ‹*family, committee*› of nine; **~mal** *Adv.* nine times; *s. auch* **achtmal**; **~mal·gescheit**, **~mal·klug** (spöttisch) **A** *Adj.* smart-aleck *attrib.* (coll.); **du bist immer so ~malgescheit** *od.* **~malklug** you're such a smart aleck (coll.); **ein ~malgescheiter** *od.* **~malkluger** a smart aleck (coll.); **B** *adv.* in a smart-aleck way (coll.); **~schwänzig** /-ʃvɛntsɪç/ *Adj. in* **~schwänzige Katze** (Seemannsspr.) cat-o'-nine-tails; **~stellig** *Adj.* nine-figure *attrib.*; *s. auch* **achtstellig**; **~stöckig** *Adj.* nine-storey *attrib.*; *s. auch* **achtstöckig**; **~stündig** *Adj.* nine-hour *attrib.*; lasting nine hours *postpos., not pred.*; *s. auch* **achtstündig**

neunt /nɔynt/ *in* **wir waren zu ~**: there were nine of us; *s. auch* **acht**[2]

neunt... *Ordinalz.* ▸ⓘ **S. 165**, ▸ⓘ **S. 826** ninth; *s. auch* **acht...**

neun- (*s. auch* **acht-, Acht-**): **~tägig** *Adj.* (9 Tage alt) nine-day-old *attrib.*; (9 Tage dauernd) nine-day-long *attrib.*; *s. auch* **achttägig**; **~tausend** *Kardinalz.* ▸ⓘ **S. 826** nine thousand

Neuntel *das* (schweiz. *meist der*); **~s, ~**: ▸ⓘ **S. 826** ninth

***neunte·mal, *neunten·mal** ▸**Mal**[1]

neuntens *Adv.* ninthly

Neun·töter *der* (Zool.) red-backed shrike

neun·zehn *Kardinalz.* ▸ⓘ **S. 29**, ▸ⓘ **S. 729**, ▸ⓘ **S. 826** nineteen; *s. auch* **achtzehn**

neunzehnt... *Ordinalz.* ▸ⓘ **S. 165** nineteenth; *s. auch* **acht...**

neunzig /ˈnɔyntsɪç/ *Kardinalz.* ▸ⓘ **S. 29**, ▸ⓘ **S. 826** ninety; *s. auch* **achtzig**

Neunzig *die;* **~, ~en** ninety; *s. auch* **Achtzig**

neunziger *indekl. Adj.* **die ~ Jahre** the nineties; *s. auch* **achtziger**

Neunziger·jahre *Pl.* ▸ⓘ **S. 29**, ▸ⓘ **S. 165** nineties *pl.*

neunzigst... /ˈnɔyntsɪçst.../ *Ordinalz.* ▸ⓘ **S. 826** ninetieth; *s. auch* **acht...**, **achtzigst...**

Neu-: **~ordnung** *die* reorganization; **~orientierung** *die* reorientation; **~philologe** *der* modern linguist; **~philologie** *die* modern languages [and literature] *sing.; no art.*; **~philologin** *die* ▸**~philologe**; **~prägung** *die* ① (Münzk.) new minting; **die ~prägung von Münzen** the minting of new coins; ② (Sprachw.) new coinage; neologism; **die ~prägung von Wörtern/Wendungen** *usw.* the coining of new words/expressions *etc.*

Neuralgie /nɔyralˈgiː/ *die;* **~, ~n** ▸ⓘ **S. 439** (Med.) neuralgia

neuralgisch

A *Adj.* ① (Med.) neuralgic ② (empfindlich) **das ist mein ~er Punkt** it's a sore *or* touchy point with me

B *adv.* (empfindlich) ‹*react*› touchily

neu-, Neu-: **~reg[e]lung** *die* ① **die ~regelung der Arbeitszeit/der Zulassung zu den Universitäten** *usw.* the revision of regulations governing working hours/admission to university *etc.*; ② (Bestimmung) new regulation; **~reich** *Adj.* (abwertend) nouveau riche; **Familie ~reich** (ugs.) the typical nouveau riche family; **~reiche** *der/die* nouveau riche; **die ~reichen** the nouveaux riches; the new rich

Neuritis /nɔyˈriːtɪs/ *die;* **~, Neuritiden** (Med.) neuritis

Neuro·chirurgie *die;* **~** (Med.) neurosurgery

Neurodermitis *die;* **~, Neurodermitiden** ▸ⓘ **S. 439** (Med.) neurodermatitis

Neurologe *der;* **~n, ~n** ▸ⓘ **S. 113** neurologist

Neurologie *die;* **~** ① neurology ② (Abteilung) neurology department; (Station) neurology ward; (ugs.: Klinik) neurology clinic

Neurologin *die;* **~, ~nen** ▸ⓘ **S. 113** neurologist

neurologisch *Adj.* neurological

Neuron /ˈnɔyrɔn/ *das;* **~s, ~e** *od.* **~en** ▸ⓘ **S. 435** (Anat.) neuron

Neurose /nɔyˈroːzə/ *die;* **~, ~n** ▸ⓘ **S. 439** (Med., Psych.) neurosis

Neurotiker /nɔyˈroːtikɐ/ *der;* **~s, ~, Neurotikerin** *die;* **~, ~nen** (Med., Psych., auch ugs.) neurotic

neurotisch *Adj.* (Med., Psych., auch ugs.) neurotic

Neurotransmitter /nɔyrotransˈmɪtɐ/ *der;* **~s, ~** (Med.) neurotransmitter

Neu-: **~satz** *der* (Druckw.) new setting; **~schnee** *der* fresh snow

Neuseeland *(das);* **~s** New Zealand

Neuseeländer *der;* **~s, ~**: New Zealander

Neuseeländerin *die;* **~, ~nen** New Zealander; New Zealand lady/woman/girl; *s. auch* **-in**

neuseeländisch *Adj.* New Zealand

neu-, Neu-: **~silber** *das* German silver; nickel silver; **~sprachler** /-ʃpraːxlɐ/ *der;* **~~s, ~~, ~sprachlerin** *die;* **~~, ~~nen** modern linguist; **~sprachlich** *Adj.* modern languages *attrib.* ‹*teaching*›; **der ~sprachliche Zweig** (Schulw.) the modern languages side; **ein ~sprachliches Gymnasium** a grammar school with emphasis on modern languages; **~sprech** /-ʃprɛç/ *der;* **~~s, ~~e** newspeak; **~start** *der* fresh start; (einer Firma, eines Projektes) relaunch

neustens /ˈnɔystn̩s/ ▸**neuerdings 1**

neutestamentlich *Adj.* New Testament *attrib.*

neutral /nɔyˈtraːl/

A *Adj.* ① (auch Völkerr., Phys., Chem.) neutral ② (Sprachw.) neuter

B *adv.* **sich ~ verhalten** remain neutral; **ich kann das nicht ~ entscheiden/beurteilen** I cannot give an impartial decision/judgement

-neutral *adj.* **kosten~/erfolgs~**: not affecting costs/profits *postpos., not pred.*; **geschmacks~/geruchs~**: neutral-tasting/neutral-smelling

Neutralisation /nɔytralizaˈtsi̯oːn/ *die;* **~, ~en** (auch Chemie) neutralization

neutralisieren *tr. V.* (auch Völkerr., Chem., Elektrot.) neutralize; (Rennsport) stop ‹*race*›

Neutralisierung *die;* **~, ~en** (auch Völkerr., Chem., Elektrot.) neutralization; (Rennsport) stopping

Neutralität /nɔytraliˈtɛːt/ *die;* **~, ~en** (auch Völkerr., Chem., Elektrot.) neutrality

Neutralitäts-: **~abkommen** *das* (Völkerr.) treaty of neutrality; **~verletzung** *die* (Völkerr.) violation of neutrality

Neutron /ˈnɔytrɔn/ *das;* **~s, ~en** /-ˈtroːnən/ (Kernphysik) neutron

Neutronen-: **~bombe** *die* neutron bomb; **~waffe** *die* neutron weapon; **~zahl** *die* (Kernphysik) neutron number

Neutrum /ˈnɔytrʊm/ *das;* **~s, Neutra** (österr. nur so) *od.* **Neutren** ① (Sprachw.) neuter ② (abwertend: Mensch ohne erotische Ausstrahlung) sexless individual

neu-, Neu-: **~vermählt** ▸**neu B 2**; **~vermählte** *Pl.; adj. Dekl.* (geh.) newly-weds; **~wagen** *der* new car; **~wahl** *die* new election; **die ~wahl des Bundespräsidenten** the election of a new Federal President; **~wahlen ansetzen/ausschreiben** call new elections; **~wert** *der* ① value when new; original value; (Versicherungsw.) replacement value; ② (marx.: ~ geschaffener Wert) new value; **~wertig** *Adj.* as new; **~wertiger Kühlschrank für 150 € zu verkaufen** for sale, refrigerator, as new — 150 €; **~wort** *das; Pl.* **~wörter** (Sprachw.) new word; neologism; **~zeit** *die* (Zeit nach 1500) modern era *or* age; (Gegenwart) modern times *pl.*; modern age; **~zeitlich** **A** *Adj.* modern; since the Middle Ages *postpos., not pred.*; (modern) modern ‹*device, equipment, methods, etc.*›; **B** *adv.* (modern) ‹*equip, fit*› with all modern conveniences; **~zugang** *der* (im Krankenhaus) new admission; (im Gefängnis) new inmate; (bei Militär, bei einer Firma, einem Verein) new recruit; (Buch für eine Bibliothek) new accession; **~zulassung** *die* (Amtsspr.) ① **die ~zulassung von Kraftfahrzeugen** the registration of new vehicles; ② (Fahrzeug) new registration

Nexus /ˈnɛksʊs/ *der;* **~, ~**: nexus

Niagara·fall /ni̯aˈgaːra-/ *der,* **Niagarafälle** *Pl.* Niagara Falls

Nibelungen·treue /ˈniːbəlʊŋən-/ *die;* **~** (oft abwertend) unquestioning loyalty [unto death]

Nicaragua /nikaˈraːgu̯a/ *(das);* **~s** Nicaragua

Nicaraguaner *der;* **~s, ~, Nicaraguanerin** *die;* **~, ~nen** Nicaraguan; *s. auch* **-in**

nicaraguanisch *Adj.* Nicaraguan

nicht /nɪçt/ *Adv.* ① not; **sie raucht ~** (im Moment) she is not smoking; (gewöhnlich) she does not *or* doesn't smoke; **alle klatschten, nur sie ~**: they all applauded except for her; **Wer hat das getan? — Sie ~!** Who did that? — It wasn't her; **Gehst du hin? — Nein, ich gehe ~!** Are you going? — No, I'm not; **Ich mag ihn ~. — Ich auch ~**: I don't like him. — Neither do I; **ich kann das ~ mehr** *od.* **länger sehen** I can't stand the sight of it any more *or* longer; **~ einmal** *od.* (ugs.) **mal** not even; **~ mehr als** no more than; **~ ihn kenne ich, sondern sie** I don't know him, but I know her; **~ einer** not one; **~ dass ich ~ wollte, ich habe bloß keine Zeit** [it's] not that I don't want to, I just don't have the time; **das ist wirklich/absolut/gewiss/gar ~ schlimm!** it's not as bad as all that! ② (Bitte, Verbot o. Ä. ausdrückend) **~!** [no,] don't!; **„~ hinauslehnen!"** (im Zug) 'do not lean out of the window'; **bitte ~!** please don't!; **~ doch!** not at all!; (bitte aufhören) stop that!; **~ doch, ärgere dich doch ~!** come, come *or* come on, there's no need to get so worked up; **nur das ~!** anything but that!; **ärgere dich doch ~, das ist die Sache gar ~ wert** don't get so angry, it just isn't worth it ③ (Zustimmung erwartend) **er ist dein Bruder, ~?** he's your brother, isn't he?; **du magst das, ~ [wahr]?** you like that, don't you?; **kommst du [etwa] ~?** aren't you coming[, then]?; **willst du ~ mitkommen?** won't you come too?; **ist es ~ herrlich hier?** isn't it glorious here? ④ (verwundert) **was du ~ sagst!** you don't say!; **was ich mir ~ alles bieten lassen muss!** the things I have to put up with! ⑤ ([bedingte] Anerkennung ausdrückend) **~ übel!** not bad!; **sie ist ~ dumm!** she's not stupid

nicht-, Nicht-: non-; **~beteiligung/~demokratisch/~akademiker** non-participation/non-democratic/non-graduate

nicht-, Nicht-: **~achtung** *die* ① *in* **jmdn. mit ~achtung strafen** punish sb. by ignoring him/her; send sb. to Coventry; ② (Geringschätzung) lack of regard *or* respect; **~achtung des Gerichts** contempt of court; **~amtlich** *Adj.* unofficial; **~anerkennung** *die* non-recognition; **~angriffs·pakt** *der* non-aggression pact; **~beachtung** *die* non-observance; **~beachtung einer roten Ampel** failure to observe a red light; **~befolgung** *die:* **~befolgung der Anweisungen/eines Befehls** failure to follow the instructions/to obey an order; **~befolgung der Bestimmungen/Vorschriften** non-compliance *or* failure to comply with the instructions/regulations; **~berufstätig** *Adj.*

n

non-employed ‹*housewives*›

Nịchte *die;* ~, ~**n** niece

nịcht-, Nịcht-: ~**ehelich** (bes. Rechtsspr.) **A** *Adj.* illegitimate ‹*child, birth*›; **aus ~ehelichen Beziehungen geborene Kinder** children born out of wedlock; **B** *adv.* ‹*born*› out of wedlock; ~**einhaltung** *die* non-compliance, failure to comply (*Gen.* with); non-observance; ~**ein·mischung** *die* (Politik) non-intervention; non-interference; ~**eisen·metall** *das* non-ferrous metal; ~**erfüllung** *die* non-fulfilment; ~**erscheinen** *das;* ~~**s** non-appearance; failure to appear; ~**fachmann** *der* non-expert; layman; ~**flektierbar** *Adj.* (Sprachw.) non-inflected; ~**gefallen** *das:* *in* **bei ~gefallen** (Kaufmannsspr.) if not satisfied

nịchtig *Adj.* **1** (geh.: wertlos, belanglos) vain ‹*things, pleasures, etc.*›; paltry ‹*desire*›; trivial ‹*reason*›; petty ‹*quarrel*›; idle ‹*chatter, thoughts*›; empty ‹*pretext*› **2** (Rechtsspr.: ungültig) invalid, void ‹*contract, will, marriage, etc.*›; **für ~ erklären** (Rechtsspr.) declare ‹*contract, will, etc.*› invalid *or* void; annul ‹*marriage*›; *s. auch* **null**

Nịchtigkeit *die;* ~, ~**en** **1** (geh.) ▸**nichtig 1**: vanity; paltriness; pettiness, triviality; idleness; emptiness **2** (geh.: belanglose Sache) trifle **3** (Rechtsspr.) invalidity; voidness; (einer Ehe) nullity

Nịchtigkeits·klage *die* (Rechtsw.) nullity suit

nịcht-, Nịcht-: ~**inanspruchnahme** *die* (Amtsspr.) failure to take advantage; ~**kapitalistisch** *Adj.* non-capitalist ‹*country, state*›; ~**leitend** ▸**leiten 4**; ~**leiter** *der* (Physik) non-conductor; ~**metall** *das* non-metal; ~**mitglied** *das* non-member; ~**öffentlich** *Adj.* not open to the public *pred.*; closed, private ‹*meeting*›; **die ~ öffentliche Beweisaufnahme** the hearing of the evidence in camera; ~**organisiert** ▸**organisiert**; ~**raucher** *der* non-smoker; **ich bin ~raucher** I don't smoke; I'm a non-smoker; '**~raucher**' 'no smoking'; ~**raucher·abteil** *das* non-smoking *or* no-smoking compartment; ~**raucherin** *die* ▸~**raucher**; ~**regierungs·organisation** *die* non-governmental organization; NGO; ~**rostend** ▸**rosten**

nichts /nɪçt̬s/ *Indefinitpron.* nothing; **er sieht ~:** he sees nothing; he doesn't see anything; **hast du ~ gegessen?** haven't you eaten anything?; **ich möchte ~:** I don't want anything; **das ist ~ für mich** it's not for me; it isn't my cup of tea (coll.); **für ~ und wieder ~** (ugs.) for nothing at all; **sich in ~ von jmdm./etw. unterscheiden** be no different from sb./sth.; **~ zu machen!** (ugs.) nothing doing (coll.); **er ist durch ~ zu überzeugen** nothing will convince him; **von mir bekommst du ~ mehr** you'll get nothing more from me; you won't get anything more from me; **ich will ~ mehr davon hören** I don't want to hear any more about it; **die Ärzte konnten ~ mehr für ihn tun** the doctors could do nothing more *or* could not do any more for him; **~ anderes** nothing else; **jetzt interessiert er sich für ~ anderes mehr** he's now no longer interested in anything else; **haben Sie ~ anderes als Hamburger?** haven't you got anything else besides hamburgers?; **~ als** nothing but; **das/er ist zu ~ zu gebrauchen** it's/he's no use; it's/he's useless; **das war wohl ~** (salopp) that wasn't exactly brilliant; **wir wissen ~ Näheres/Genaues** we don't know any more/any details; **~ wie ins Bett/weg!** quick into bed/let's go!; **~ wie hinterher!** put your skates on, after him/her/them! (sl.); **~ weiter** nothing else; **von ~ kommt ~:** you don't get anything without effort; **~ da!** (ugs.) nothing doing! (coll.); **wie ~:** in a trice *or* flash; **die Angelegenheit ist ~ weniger als schön** it's not at all a nice business; *s. auch* **danken B 1**

Nịchts *das;* ~, ~**e** **1** (Philos.: das Nicht-sein) nothingness *no art.* **2** (leerer Raum) void; **er war wie aus dem ~ aufgetaucht** he appeared from nowhere **3** (wenig von etw.) **er hat die Fabrik aus dem ~ aufgebaut** he built the factory up from nothing; **vor dem ~ stehen** be left with nothing; be faced with ruin; **ein ~ von einem Bikini** *usw.* **[sein]** [be] a scrap of a bikini *etc.* **4** (abwertend: Mensch) nobody; nonentity

nịchts·ahnend *Adj.* unsuspecting

Nịcht-: ~**schwimmer** *der* non-swimmer; **er war ~schwimmer** he could not swim; ~**schwimmer·becken** *das* non-swimmers' *or* learners' pool ~**schwimmerin** *die* ▸~**schwimmer**

nịchts-: ~**desto·mịnder**, ~**desto·trọtz** (ugs. scherzh.), ~**desto·wẹniger** *Adv.* nevertheless; nonetheless

Nịcht-: ~**sein** *das* (Philos.) non-existence *no art.*; non-being *no art.*; ~**sesshafte**, *~**seßhafte** *der/die; adj. Dekl.* (Amtsspr.) person of no fixed abode (Admin. Lang.)

nịchts-, Nịchts-: ~**könner** *der,* ~**könnerin** *die* (abwertend) incompetent; bungler; ~**nutz** *der;* ~~**es,** ~~**e** (veralt. abwertend) good-for-nothing; **mein ~nutz von Bruder** my good-for-nothing [of a] brother; ~**nutzig** *Adj.* (veralt. abwertend) good-for-nothing *attrib.*; worthless ‹*existence*›; ~**sagend** **A** *Adj.* meaningless, empty ‹*talk, phrases, etc.*›; (fig.: ausdruckslos) vacant ‹*smile*›; expressionless ‹*face*›; **ein ~sagender Typ** a nonentity; **B** *adv.* meaninglessly ‹*formulated*›; ‹*smile*› vacantly; ~**tuer** /-tuːɐ/ *der;* ~~**s,** ~~ (abwertend) layabout; loafer; **die reichen ~tuer** the idle rich; ~**tuerei** /---'-/ *die;* ~~ (abwertend) idle loafing; ~**tuerin** *die;* ~~, ~~**nen** ▸~**tuer**; ~**tun** *das* **1** (Untätigkeit) inactivity; doing nothing *no art.*; **2** (Müßiggang) idleness *no art.*; lazing about *no art.*; **das süße ~tun** being gloriously idle; ~**würdig** (geh. abwertend) **A** *Adj.* worthless, despicable ‹*person*›; base, unworthy, despicable ‹*deed*›; **~würdiger!** worthless *or* despicable wretch!; **B** *adv.* ‹*betray, deceive*› basely; ‹*act*› unworthily; ~**würdigkeit** *die;* ~~ (geh. veralt.) ▸~**würdig**: worthlessness; despicableness; baseness; unworthiness

nịcht-, Nịcht-: ~**tänzer** *der,* ~**tänzerin** *die* non-dancer; **ich bin ~tänzer[in]** I don't dance; ~**wähler** *der,* ~**wählerin** *die* non-voter; abstainer; ~**zielend** *Adj.* (Sprachw.) intransitive; ~**zustandekommen** *das;* ~~**s** (eines Vertrags) non-conclusion; **das ~zustandekommen der Konferenz** the failure of the conference to take place; ~**zutreffende** *das; adj. Dekl.* **~zutreffendes streichen** delete as applicable

Nịckel¹ /'nɪkl̩/ *das;* ~**s** nickel

Nịckel² *der;* ~**s,** ~ (ugs. veralt.: Münze) 10-pfennig piece

Nịckel-: ~**allergie** *die* nickel allergy; ~**brille** *die* metal-rimmed glasses *or* spectacles; ~**legierung** *die* nickel alloy

nicken /'nɪkn̩/
A *itr. V.* **1** nod; **befriedigt/zustimmend ~:** nod one's satisfaction/agreement; **mit dem Kopf ~:** nod one's head **2** (fam.: schlafen) doze; snooze (coll.)
B *tr. V.* (geh.: ~d ausdrücken) nod; **Zustimmung/Beifall ~:** nod one's agreement/approval

Nịckerchen *das;* ~**s,** ~ (fam.) nap; snooze (coll.); **ein ~ halten** *od.* **machen** take *or* have forty winks *or* a nap

Nịcki /'nɪki/ *der;* ~**[s],** ~**s** velour pullover *or* sweater

Nicotin ▸**Nikotin**

nie /niː/ *Adv.* never; **mich besucht ~ jemand** nobody ever visits me; **fast ~:** hardly ever; **~ mehr!** never again!; **[einmal und] ~ wieder** [only once and] never again; **~ und nimmer!** never!; **~ im Leben!** not on your life!; **das werde ich ~ im Leben vergessen** I shall never forget it as long as I live

nieder /'niːdɐ/
A *Adj.* **1** (von minderem Rang) lower ‹*class, intelligence*›; petty, minor ‹*official*›; lowly ‹*family, origins, birth*›; menial ‹*task*›; **das ~e Volk** the common people; **der ~e Klerus/Adel** the lower clergy/aristocracy **2** (bes. südd.) ▸**niedrig 1** **3** (Biol.: nicht hoch entwickelt) lower ‹*plant, animal, organism*›; *s. auch* **Jagd 1**
B *Adv.* (hinunter) down; **die Waffen ~!** lay down your arms!; **~ mit dem Militarismus!** down with militarism!

niẹder-, Niẹder-: ~**|beugen** (geh.) **A** *tr. V.* bend ‹*knee*› downwards; bow ‹*head*›; **B** *refl. V.* bend down; ~**|brennen** **A** *unr. itr. V.*; *mit sein* (herunterbrennen) ‹*fire*› burn low; ‹*building*› burn down; **B** *unr. tr. V.* burn down ‹*building, village, etc.*›; ~**|brüllen** *tr. V.* (ugs.) **jmdn. ~brüllen** shout sb. down; ~**deutsch** *Adj.* Low German ‹*dialect*›; North German ‹*custom, farmhouse, landscape*›; ~**|donnern** *itr. V.*; *mit sein* ‹*avalanche*› thunder down; ‹*roof*› come crashing down; ~**druck** *der; Pl.* ~**drücke** (Technik) low pressure; ~**|drücken** *tr. V.* **1** (herunterdrücken) press down; press *or* push down, (formal) depress ‹*handle, lever*›; **2** (bedrücken) depress; ‹*memory*› weigh on, oppress ‹*person*›; *s. auch* **niedergedrückt**; ~**|fallen** *unr. itr. V.*; *mit sein* (geh.) ‹*snow*› fall; **vor jmdm. ~fallen** fall down [on one's knees] before sb.; ~**frequenz** *die* (Physik) low frequency; ~**gang** *der* **1** (Verfall) fall; decline; **2** (Seemannsspr.: Treppe) companionway; companion ladder; ~**gedrückt** **A** *2. Part. v.* ~**drücken;** **B** *Adj.* depressed; dejected; ~**|gehen** *unr. itr. V.*; *mit sein* **1** (landen) ‹*plane, spacecraft, balloonist*› come down; ‹*parachutist*› drop; ‹*birds, flock*› land; **2** (fallen) ‹*rain, satellite, avalanche*› come down; ‹*meteor*› come to earth; **3** (Boxen: zu Boden fallen) go down; **4** (sich senken) ‹*theatre curtain*› fall; **5** (untergehen) ‹*sun, moon*› go down; ‹*epoch*› decline; ~**geschlagen** **A** *2. Part. v.* ~**schlagen;** **B** *Adj.* despondent; dejected; ~**geschlagenheit** *die;* ~**geschlagenheit** despondency; dejection; ~**|halten** *unr. tr. V.* **1** (unterdrücken) oppress ‹*nation, people, class*›; keep ‹*nation, people, class*› in subjection; keep ‹*person*› down; **2** (kontrollieren) keep down ‹*resistance*›; **3** (unten halten) hold down; ~**|holen** *tr. V.* haul down, lower ‹*sail, flag*›; ~**|kämpfen** *tr. V.* **1** (besiegen) overcome ‹*enemy, opponent*›; **2** (zurückhalten) suppress ‹*rage, excitement*›; fight back ‹*tears*›; fight ‹*tiredness*›; ~**|knien** *itr. V.* (*auch mit sein*), *refl. V.* kneel down; (unterwürfig, demütig) go down on one's knees; ~**|knüppeln** *tr. V.* **jmdn. ~knüppeln** beat *or* club sb. to the ground with a truncheon; ~**|kommen** *unr. itr. V.*; *mit sein* (geh. veralt.) be delivered (**mit** of); give birth (**mit** to); ~**kunft** /-kʊnft/ *die;* ~~, ~**künfte** /-kʏnftə/ (geh. veralt.) confinement; ~**lage** *die* **1** (das Besiegtwerden) defeat; **eine ~lage einstecken müssen** suffer a defeat; **jmdm. eine ~lage beibringen** inflict a defeat on sb.; **2** (Zweiggeschäft) branch; (Lager) warehouse; depot

Niẹder·lande *Pl.*: **die ~:** the Netherlands

Niẹderländer *der;* ~**s,** ~ ▸**❶ S. 520** Dutchman; Netherlander; **die ~:** the Dutch

Niẹderländerin *die;* ~, ~**nen** ▸**❶ S. 520** Dutchwoman; Netherlander; *s. auch* **-in**

niẹderländisch *Adj.* ▸**❶ S. 520**, ▸**❶ S. 670** Dutch; Netherlands *attrib.* ‹*government, embassy, etc.*›; **das Niederländische** Dutch

niẹder-, Niẹder-: ~**|lassen** **A** *unr. refl. V.* **1** (ein Geschäft, eine Praxis eröffnen) set up *or* establish oneself in business; ‹*doctor, lawyer*› set up a practice *or* in practice; **sich als Fotograf ~lassen** set up as a photographer; **~gelassene Ärzte** *registered doctors/specialists having their own independent practices;* **2** (seinen Wohnsitz nehmen) settle; **3** (geh.: sich setzen) sit down; seat oneself; ‹*bird*› settle, alight; **B** *unr. tr. V.* lower ‹*theatre curtain, blind, etc.*›; ~**lassung** *die;* ~~, ~~**en** **1** ▸~**lassen 1**: setting up in business; setting up of a practice *or* in practice; **2** (Ort) settlement; **3** (Wirtsch.: Zweigstelle) branch; ~**|legen** *tr. V.* **1** (geh.: hinlegen) lay *or* put *or* set down; lay ‹*wreath*›; **die Waffen ~legen** lay down one's arms; **2** (nicht weitermachen) lay down, resign [from] ‹*office*›; relinquish ‹*command*›; discontinue ‹*course of treatment*›; **das Mandat ~legen** ‹*member of parliament*› resign one's seat; ‹*lawyer*› give up the brief; *s. auch* **Arbeit 1**; **3** (geh.: aufschreiben) set down; ~**legung** *die;* ~~, ~~**en** **1** (geh.: eines Kranzes) laying; **2** (eines Amtes) resignation (+ *Gen.* from); (eines Kommandos) relinquishing; **die ~legung der Arbeit** stopping work; **3** (geh.: ~schrift) setting down;

n

~|machen *tr. V.* (ugs.) butcher; **~|mähen** *tr. V.* mow down ‹*prisoners, soldiers, etc.*›; **~|metzeln** *tr. V.* butcher

Nieder·österreich *(das)* Lower Austria

nieder-: ~|prasseln *itr. V.; mit sein* ‹*rain, hail*› beat down; ‹*blows, rebukes, questions, etc.*› rain down; **~|reißen** *unr. tr. V.* **1** (abreißen) pull down ‹*building, wall*›; **2** (zu Boden reißen) **jmdn. ~reißen** knock sb. over; **~rheinisch** *Adj.* in the Lower Rhine valley *postpos.*

Nieder·sachse *der* inhabitant of Lower Saxony; (von Geburt) native of Lower Saxony; *s. auch* **Kölner B**

Nieder·sachsen *(das)* Lower Saxony

Nieder·sächsin *die* ▸ **Niedersachse**

niedersächsisch *Adj.* Lower Saxon

nieder-, Nieder-: ~|schießen A *unr. tr. V.* gun down; **der ~geschossene** the victim of the shooting; **B** *unr. itr. V.; mit sein* (herabfliegen) ‹*bird*› stoop, swoop down; ‹*aircraft*› hurtle down; **~schlag** *der* **1** (Met.) precipitation; **es sind zeitweise ~schläge, teils Regen, teils Schnee, zu erwarten** occasional showers can be expected, some falling as snow; **2** (Boxen) knock-down; **3** (Ausdruck) expression; **[seinen] ~schlag in etw.** *(Dat.)* **finden** find expression in sth.; **4** (Chemie) precipitate; **5** **radioaktiver ~schlag** [radioactive] fallout; **~|schlagen A** *unr. tr. V.* **1** (zu Boden schlagen) **jmdn. ~schlagen** knock sb. down; **2** (umschlagen) turn down ‹*hat brim, collar*›; **3** (beenden) suppress, put down ‹*revolt, uprising, etc.*›; put an end to ‹*strike*›; **4** (senken) lower ‹*eyes, eyelids*›; **den Blick ~schlagen** lower one's eyes; **5** (Rechtsspr.: einstellen) abandon ‹*proceedings*›; dismiss ‹*claim*›; **ein Verfahren ~schlagen** dismiss a case; **6** (Rechtsspr.: erlassen) waive ‹*costs*›; remit ‹*punishment*›; *s. auch* **niedergeschlagen**; **B** *unr. refl. V.* **1** **sich in etw.** *(Dat.)* **~schlagen** ‹*experience, emotion*› find expression in sth.; ‹*performance, hard work*› be reflected in sth.; **2** ‹*steam*› condense; **~schlags·arm** *Adj.* ‹*climate, area, period*› with low precipitation *not pred.*; **~schlags·frei** *Adj.* ‹*period*› without [any] precipitation *not pred.*; **die Aussichten: heiter bis wolkig und ~schlagsfrei** the outlook: dry with variable amounts of cloud; **~schlagung** *die;* **~~, ~~en** **1** (einer Revolte, eines Aufstands) suppression; putting down; **2** (Rechtsspr.) ▸ **~schlagen A 5, 6**: abandonment; dismissal; waiving; remission; **~|schmettern** *tr. V.* **1** (~schlagen) **jmdn. ~schmettern** send sb. crashing to the ground/floor; **2** (erschüttern) ‹*bad news*› shatter; ‹*rejection, result*› devastate; **~schmetternd** *Adj.* shattering ‹*experience, news*›; devastating ‹*result, review*›; **~|schreiben** *unr. tr. V.* write down; write ‹*essay, novel*›; **~|schreien** *unr. tr. V.* **jmdn. ~schreien** shout sb. down; **~schrift** *die* **1** (das Schreiben) writing down; **etw. zur ~schrift erklären** (Rechtsspr.) dictate a statement on sth.; **2** (Schriftstück) document; (Protokoll) minutes *pl.*; **~|setzen A** *refl. V.* sit down; **B** *tr. V.* put *or* set down; **~|sinken** *unr. itr. V.; mit sein* sink down; **ohnmächtig ~sinken** sink unconscious to the ground/floor; **~spannung** *die* (Elektrot.) low voltage *or* tension; **~|stechen** *unr. tr. V.* stab; (erstechen) stab to death; **~|stimmen** *tr. V.* vote ‹*proposal, person, etc.*› down; **~|stoßen A** *unr. tr. V.* (geh.: zu Boden stoßen) **jmdn. ~stoßen** knock sb. down; **B** *unr. itr. V.; mit sein* ‹*hawk, etc.*› stoop, swoop down; ‹*aircraft*› hurtle down; **~|strecken** (geh.) **A** *tr. V.* **jmdn. ~strecken** knock sb. down; (mit einem Schuss) shoot sb. down; **einen Tiger/Hirsch ~strecken** bring down a tiger/stag; **B** *refl. V.* (sich hinlegen) lie down; **auf das** *od.* **dem Sofa ~gestreckt** stretched out on the sofa; **~|stürzen** *itr. V.; mit sein* (geh.) **1** (zu Boden fallen) fall down; **ohnmächtig ~stürzen** fall unconscious to the ground/floor; **2** (herabfallen) ‹*rocks*› fall; ‹*avalanche*› sweep down; **~tourig** /-tu:rɪç/ (Technik) **A** *Adj.* **im ~tourigen Bereich** at low revs (coll.); **B** *adv.* at low revs (coll.); **~tracht** *die;* **~tracht** (geh.) malice; (als Charaktereigenschaft) vileness; despicableness; **etw. aus ~tracht tun** do sth. out of malice; **~trächtig A** *Adj.* malicious ‹*person, slander, lie, etc.*›; (verachtenswert) vile, despicable ‹*person*›; base, vile ‹*misrepresentation, slander, lie*›; **B** *adv.* ‹*betray, lie, treat*› in a vile *or* despicable way; ‹*smile*› maliciously; **~trächtigkeit** *die* **1** ▸ **~trächtig A**: maliciousness; vileness; despicableness; baseness; **2** (gemeine Handlung) vile *or* despicable act; **~|trampeln** *tr. V.* (ugs.), **~|treten** *unr. tr. V.* tread ‹*grass, flowers, carpet pile, etc.*›; (fig.) trample ‹*person*› underfoot

Niederung *die;* **~, ~en** low-lying area; (an Flussläufen, Küsten) flats *pl.*; (Tal) valley; **sumpfige ~en** marshes; **die ~en des [alltäglichen] Lebens** (fig.) the lowly spheres of everyday life

nieder-, Nieder-: ~wald *der* (Forstw.) coppice; **~|walzen** *tr. V.* flatten; **jmdn. mit Argumenten ~walzen** (fig.) overwhelm sb. with arguments; **~|werfen A** *unr. tr. V.* **1** (geh.: besiegen) overcome, defeat ‹*enemy, rebels, etc.*›; **2** (geh.: beenden) ▸ **~schlagen A 3**; **3** (geh.: schwächen) ‹*illness, fever*› lay ‹*person*› low; **4** (geh.: erschüttern) ‹*bad news*› shake ‹*person*› profoundly; **der Tod seiner Frau hat ihn ~geworfen** he took the death of his wife very badly; **B** *unr. refl. V.* throw oneself down; **sich vor jmdm. ~werfen** prostrate oneself before sb.; **~werfung** *die;* **~~, ~~en** (geh.) (von Feinden, Aufständischen) overthrow; defeat; (einer Revolte, eines Aufstands) suppression; putting down; **~wild** *das* (Jägerspr.) *smaller game animals, e.g. roe-deer, hare, fox, badger*; **~|zwingen** *unr. tr. V.* (geh.) force ‹*opponent*› to the ground *or* down; (fig.) suppress ‹*anger, excitement*›

niedlich /'ni:tlɪç/

A *Adj.* sweet; cute (Amer. coll.); sweet little *attrib.*; dear little *attrib*

B *adv.* ‹*dance, nibble*› sweetly, prettily; ‹*babble, play*› sweetly, cutely (Amer. coll.); **auf dem Foto guckt die Kleine so ~**: in the photo the little girl has such a sweet expression

niedrig

A *Adj.* **1** ▸ **S. 374** (von geringer Höhe) low; short ‹*grass*› **2** (von geringem Rang) lowly ‹*origins, birth*›; low ‹*rank, status, intellectual level*› **3** (sittlich tief stehend) base ‹*instinct, desire, emotion, person*›; vile ‹*motive*›; **von ~er Gesinnung** low-minded

B *adv.* ‹*hang, fly*› low

Niedrig·energie·haus *das* low-energy house

Niedrigkeit *die;* **~, ~en** **1** (geringe Höhe) lowness **2** (niedrige Gesinnung) baseness **3** (gemeine Tat) base deed

Niedrig-: ~lohn *der* low wages *pl.*; **~lohnland** *das* country with a low-wage economy; **etw. im ~lohnland Taiwan produzieren** produce sth. in Taiwan, with its low wages *or* low-wage economy; **~preis** *der* low price; **~wasser** *das* **1** (von Seen/Flüssen) **bei ~wasser** when the [level of the] lake/river is low; **2** (bei Ebbe) low tide; low water; **bei ~wasser** at low tide *or* low water

niemals /'ni:ma:ls/ *Adv.* never

niemand /'ni:mant/ *Indefinitpron.* nobody; no one; **~ war im Büro** there was nobody *or* no one in the office; there wasn't anybody *or* any one in the office; **wir haben ~[en] gesehen** we saw nobody *or* no one; we didn't see anybody *or* any one; **~ anders** *od.* **anderer** nobody *or* no one else; **es kann ~ anders** *od.* **anderer als du gewesen sein** it can't have been anybody *or* any one [else] but you; **das war ~ anders als der Kaiser** it was none other than the emperor himself; **er hat mit ~[em] von uns reden wollen** he didn't want to talk to any of us; **das darfst du ~[em] sagen!** you mustn't tell anybody that!; **~ Bekanntes** nobody I know/he knows *etc.*; (keine prominenten Leute) nobody famous; **lass ~ Fremdes herein** don't let anybody *or* anyone in you don't know; don't let any strangers in; **er ist ~[e]s Feind** he has no enemies; **ein N~ sein** be a nobody

Niemands·land *das* **1** (auch fig.) no man's land **2** (unerforschtes Gebiet, auch fig.) unknown *or* unexplored territory

Niere /'ni:rə/ *die;* **~, ~n** ▸ⓘ **S. 435** kidney; **künstliche ~**: kidney machine; artificial kidney; **jmdm. an die ~n gehen** (fig. ugs.) get to sb. (coll.)

nieren-, Nieren-: ~becken·entzündung *die* ▸ⓘ **S. 439** pyelitis; **~entzündung** *die* ▸ⓘ **S. 439** nephritis; **~förmig** *Adj.* kidney-shaped; **~kolik** *die* ▸ⓘ **S. 439** renal colic; **~leiden** *das* ▸ⓘ **S. 439** kidney disease; **~stein** *der* ▸ⓘ **S. 439** kidney stone; renal calculus (Med.); **~tisch** *der* kidney-shaped table

nieseln /'ni:zl̩n/ *unpers. V.* drizzle

Niesel-: ~priem *der* (veralt. scherzh.) misery [guts] (coll.); **~regen** *der* drizzle

niesen /'ni:zn̩/ *itr. V.* sneeze

Nies-: ~pulver *das* sneezing powder; **~reiz** *der* urge to sneeze

Nieß·brauch /'ni:sbraux/ *der* (Rechtsw.) usufruct

Nies·wurz *die* (Bot.) hellebore

Niet /ni:t/ *der,* (auch:) *das;* **~[e]s, ~e** (fachspr.) ▸ **Niete²**

Niete¹ /'ni:tə/ *die;* **~, ~n** **1** (Los) blank; **eine ~ ziehen** draw a blank **2** (ugs.: Mensch) dead loss (coll.) (**in** + *Dat.* at)

Niete² *die;* **~, ~n** rivet

nieten /'ni:tn̩/ *tr. V.* rivet

Nieten·hose *die* [pair of] studded jeans

niet- und nagelfest *in* **[alles] was nicht ~ ist** (ugs.) [everything] that's not nailed *or* screwed down

nigel·nagel·neu *Adj.* (schweiz. ugs.) brand-new

Niger¹ /'ni:gɐ/ *(das);* **~s** (Staat) Niger

Niger² *der;* **~[s]** ▸ⓘ **S. 267** (Fluss) Niger

Nigeria /ni'ge:ri̯a/ *(das);* **~s** Nigeria

Nigerianer *der;* **~s, ~, Nigerianerin** *die;* **~, ~nen** Nigerian; *s. auch* **-in**

nigerianisch *Adj.* Nigerian

Nigger /'nɪgɐ/ *der;* **~s, ~** (abwertend, oft als Schimpfwort) nigger (derog.)

Nihilismus /nihi'lɪsmʊs/ *der;* **~**: nihilism

Nihilist *der;* **~en, ~en, Nihilistin** *die;* **~, ~nen** nihilist

nihilistisch *Adj.* nihilistic

Nikolaus¹ /'nɪkolaus/ *der;* **~, ~e** **1** St Nicholas **2** (Tag) St Nicholas' Day

Nikolaus² *(der)* (hist. Name) Nicholas

Nikolaus·tag *der* St Nicholas' Day

Nikotin /niko'ti:n/ *das;* **~s** nicotine

nikotin-, Nikotin-: ~arm *Adj.* low-nicotine *attrib.*; low in nicotine *pred.*; **~frei** *Adj.* nicotine-free; **~gehalt** *der* nicotine content; **~haltig** *Adj.* containing nicotine *postpos., not pred.*; **~haltig sein** contain nicotine; **~vergiftung** *die* nicotine poisoning

Nil /ni:l/ *der;* **~[s]** ▸ⓘ **S. 267** Nile

Nil·pferd *das* hippopotamus; hippo (coll.)

Nimbus /'nɪmbʊs/ *der;* **~, ~se** **1** (geh.: Ruhm) aura; **sein ~ als großer Dichter** his reputation as a great poet **2** (Kunstwiss.) nimbus

nimm /nɪm/ *Imperativ Sg. v.* **nehmen**

nimmer /'nɪmɐ/ *Adv.* **1** (geh. veralt.: niemals) never **2** (südd., österr.) never again; **das kann ich ~ aushalten** I can't endure it any longer; *s. auch* **nie**

Nimmerleinstag /'nɪmɐlainsta:k/ *in* **am ~** (ugs. scherzh.) never; **etw. auf den** *od.* **bis zum ~ verschieben** (ugs. scherzh.) put sth. off indefinitely

nimmer-, Nimmer-: ~mehr *Adv.* **1** (veralt.: nie) never; **2** (südd., österr.: nie wieder) never again; **~müde** (geh.) **A** *Adj.* tireless, untiring ‹*helper, worker, etc.*›; **in ~müder Arbeit** working tirelessly *or* untiringly; **B** *adv.* tirelessly; untiringly; **~satt** *Adj.* (fam.) insatiable; **~satt** *der;* **~~[e]s, ~~e** (fam.) gannet (coll.); **~wieder·sehen** *in* **auf ~wiedersehen verschwinden** (ugs., oft scherzh.) vanish never to be seen again

Nimrod /'nɪmrɔt/ *der;* **~s, ~e** (geh., oft scherzh.) Nimrod

Nippel /'nɪpl̩/ *der;* **~s, ~** **1** (Technik; ugs.: Brustwarze) nipple **2** (am Wasserball) valve

nippen /ˈnɪpn̩/ *itr. V.* (trinken) sip; take a sip/sips; (essen) nibble (**von** at); **vom Wein ~:** sip [at] the wine; take a sip/sips of the wine; **am Glas ~:** sip from *or* take a sip/sips from the glass

Nippes /ˈnɪpəs/, **Nipp·sachen** *Pl.* [porcelain] knick-knacks; small [porcelain] ornaments

Nipp·tide *die* neap tide

nirgend-: ~her *Adv.* ▸ **nirgendwoher**; **~hin** *Adv.* ▸ **nirgendwohin**

nirgends /ˈnɪrgn̩ts/ *Adv.* nowhere; **er war ~ zu finden** he was nowhere *or* wasn't anywhere to be found; **ich fühle mich ~ so wohl wie hier** there is nowhere *or* isn't anywhere I feel as happy as here; **sonst ~:** nowhere else; **er hält es ~ lange aus** he doesn't stay anywhere for long

nirgend-: ~wo *Adv.* ▸ **nirgends**; **~woher** *Adv.* from nowhere; **sie konnten die Medikamente ~woher bekommen** they couldn't get the medicines from anywhere; **~wohin** *Adv.* **der Weg führt ~wohin** the path doesn't go anywhere; **wir gehen ~wohin** we're not going anywhere

Nirwana /nɪrˈva:na/ *das;* **~[s]** nirvana

Nische /ˈni:ʃə/ *die;* **~, ~n** [1] (Einbuchtung) niche [2] (Erweiterung eines Raumes) recess

Nischen·produkt *das* niche product

Niss, *Niß /nɪs/ *die;* **~, Nisse** (veralt.), **Nisse** /ˈnɪsə/ *die;* **~, ~n** nit

nisten /ˈnɪstn̩/ *itr. V.* nest; **eine tiefe Traurigkeit nistete in ihrem Herzen** (fig. geh.) a deep sadness dwelt in her heart

Nist-: ~kasten *der* nest box; nesting box; **~platz** *der* nesting site; **~zeit** *die* nesting time *or* season

Nitrat /niˈtra:t/ *das;* **~[e]s, ~e** (Chemie) nitrate

Nitrid /niˈtri:t/ *das;* **~s, ~e** (Chemie) nitride

nitrieren *tr. V.* [1] (Chemie) nitrate [2] (Technik) nitride ‹*steel*›

Nitrit /niˈtri:t/ *das;* **~s, ~e** (Chemie) nitrite

Nitrofen /nitroˈfe:n/ *das;* **~s** (Chem.) nitrofen

Nitro·glyzerin /ni:tro-/ *das* nitroglycerine

Niveau /niˈvo:/ *das;* **~s, ~s** [1] level; **auf dem geistigen ~ eines Fünfjährigen stehen** have the mental age of a five-year-old; **überhaupt kein ~ haben** ‹*programme, article, etc.*› be totally undistinguished, lack any distinction whatever; **eine Zeitung mit ~:** a quality newspaper; **er hat wenig ~:** he is not very cultured *or* knowledgeable; **der Unterricht dieses Lehrers hat ein sehr hohes ~:** this teacher's lessons are intellectually very demanding [2] (Qualitäts~) standard

niveau-, Niveau-: ~los *Adj.* intellectually undemanding ‹*lesson*›; mediocre ‹*performance, programme, exhibition*›; [intellectually] dull ‹*person*›; **~unterschied** *der* ▸ **Niveau 1, 2:** difference in level/standard; **~voll** *Adj.* intellectually demanding ‹*lecture*›; cultured and intelligent ‹*person*›; ‹*entertainment, programme*› of quality *postpos., not pred.*; [high-]quality ‹*goods*›

nivellieren /niveˈli:rən/ *tr. V.* [1] (ausgleichen) level *or* even out ‹*difference*›; (nach unten) level down [2] (Vermessungsw.) level

Nivellier·instrument *das;* **~[e]s, ~en** [surveyor's] level

Nivellierung *die;* **~, ~en** levelling out; evening out; (nach unten) levelling down

nix /nɪks/ *Indefinitpron.* (ugs.) ▸ **nichts**

Nix *der;* **~es, ~e** (germ. Myth.) nix; (mit Fischschwanz) merman

Nixe *die;* **~, ~n** (germ. Myth.) nixie; (mit Fischschwanz) mermaid

Nizza /ˈnɪtsa/ *(das);* **~s** Nice

NN *Abk.* **= Normallnull[punkt]; unter/über NN** below/above sea level

N.N. *Abk.* **= nomen nescio** n.n.; (vorläufig unbekannt) A. N. Other

NNO *Abk.* ▸ ℹ **S. 363 = Nordnordost[en]** NNE

NNW *Abk.* ▸ ℹ **S. 363 = Nordnordwest[en]** NNW

nö /nø:/ *Partikel* (ugs.) no

NO *Abk.* ▸ ℹ **S. 363 = Nordost[en]** NE

nobel /ˈno:bl̩/

A *Adj.* [1] (geh.: edel) noble; noble[-minded] ‹*person*› [2] (oft spött.: luxuriös) elegant, (coll.) posh ‹*boutique, house, hotel*›; fine ‹*cigar*›; **~, ~!** very posh (coll.); **~ geht die Welt zugrunde** (iron.) one has to make a splash even if it's the last one (coll.) [3] (ugs.: freigebig) lavish, generous ‹*tip, present*›; generous ‹*person*›

B *adv.* [1] (geh.: edel) nobly [2] (oft spött.: luxuriös) ‹*dress, live, eat*› in the grand style

Nobel-: ~marke luxury brand; **~hotel/~restaurant/~boutique** posh hotel/restaurant/boutique (coll.); **~herberge/~kutsche** (salopp) posh *or* swish hotel/car (coll.)

Nobel·karosse *die* (ugs.) prestige car

Nobel- /noˈbɛl-/: **~preis** *der* Nobel Prize; **~preis·träger** *der,* **~preis·trägerin** *die* Nobel Prizewinner

Noblesse /noˈblɛsə/ *die;* **~** (geh.) [1] (edle Art) nobility; noble-mindedness [2] (Eleganz) elegance

noch /nɔx/

A *Adv.* [1] ([wie] bisher, derzeit) still; **~ nicht** not yet; **~ regnet es nicht** it's not raining yet; it hasn't started raining yet; **sie sind immer ~ nicht da** they're still not here; **ich sehe ihn kaum ~:** I hardly ever see him any more; **ich habe ~ nie Pizza gegessen** I've never eaten a pizza before; **ich bleibe ~ ein Weilchen** I'll stay a little bit longer; **~ nach Jahren** even years later; **er hat [bis jetzt] ~ immer/nie gewonnen** he's won every time up until now/never won yet

[2] (als Rest einer Menge) **ich habe [nur] ~ zehn Euro** I've [only] ten euros left; **es dauert ~ fünf Minuten** it'll be another five minutes; **Beuteltiere gibt es ~/nur ~ in Australien** marsupials still exist/now only exist in Australia; **es sind ~ 10 km bis zur Grenze** it's another 10 km. to the border; **es fehlt [mir/dir *usw.*] ~ ein Euro** I/you *etc.* need another euro

[3] (bevor etw. anderes geschieht) just; **ich will ~ [schnell] duschen** I just want to have a [quick] shower; **ich mache das [jetzt/dann] ~ fertig** I'll just get this finished

[4] (irgendwann einmal) some time; one day; **du wirst ihn [schon] ~ kennen lernen** you'll get to know him yet; **er wird ~ anrufen/kommen** he will still call/come

[5] (womöglich) if you're/he's *etc.* not careful; **du kommst ~ zu spät!** you'll be late if you're not careful; **er endet ~ im Gefängnis** he'll land up in prison if he doesn't watch out *or* isn't careful

[6] (drückt eine geringe zeitliche Distanz aus) only; **gestern habe ich ihn ~ gesehen/~ mit ihm gesprochen** I saw him only yesterday/I was speaking to him only yesterday; **~ Ende des 19. Jahrhunderts** as late as the end of the 19th century; **sie war eben** *od.* **gerade ~ hier** she was here only a moment ago; **es ist ~ keine Woche her, dass ...** it was less than a week ago that ...

[7] (nicht später als) **das muss ~ diese Woche/vor Monatsende geschehen** that's got to happen this week/by the end of the month; **~ am selben Abend** the [very] same evening; **~ ehe er antworten konnte, legte sie auf** even before he could reply she hung up; **er wurde ~ am Unfallort operiert** he was operated on at the scene of the accident

[8] (drückt aus, dass etw. unwiederholbar ist) **ich habe Großvater ~ gekannt** I'm old enough to have known grandfather; **dass er das ~ erleben durfte!** and to think that he lived long enough to experience that!

[9] (drückt aus, dass sich etw. im Rahmen hält) **das lasse ich mir gerade ~ gefallen** I'll put up with it; **Er hat ~ Glück gehabt. Es hätte weit schlimmer kommen können** He was lucky. It could have been much worse; **das ist [im Vergleich] ~ billig** that's [still] cheap in comparison; **es ist immer ~ teuer genug** it's still expensive enough; **der Koffer geht ~ zu** the case will still close; **das geht ~:** that's [still] all right *or* (coll.) OK; **das ist ~ lange kein Grund** that still isn't any sort of reason; **wenn er sich [wenigstens] ~ entschuldigt hätte** if he had apologized at least; **das ist ja ~ [ein]mal gut gegangen** (ugs.) it was just about all right

[10] (außerdem, zusätzlich) **wer war ~ da?** who else was there?; **er hat [auch/außerdem] ~ ein Fahrrad** he has a bicycle as well; **~ etwas Kaffee?** [would you like] some more coffee?; **wenn man alt ist und [dann auch] ~ allein** when you're old and [also] on your own; **hinzu kommt ~, dass ...** on top of that there's the fact that ...; **~ ein/zwei Bier, bitte!** another beer/two more beers, please!; **und ~ eins** *od.* **etwas** and another thing; **ich habe das ~ einmal/~ einige Male gemacht** I did it again/several times more; **da möchte ich ~ einmal/einige Male hin** (ugs.) I'd like to go there again; **~ einmal so lang** as long again; **Spanien? Und ~ dazu im Juli?** Spain, and in July too?; **er ist frech und ~ dazu dumm** *od.* **dumm dazu** he's cheeky and stupid with it; **und es schneite ~ dazu** *od.* **auch ~:** and what's more, it was snowing; **Geld/Kleider** *usw.* **~ und ~** *od.* (ugs. scherzh.) **~ und nöcher** heaps and heaps of money/clothes *etc.* (coll.)

[11] (bei Vergleichen) **er ist ~ größer [als Karl]** he is even taller [than Karl]; **das ist ~ viel wichtiger** that's far *or* much more important still; **er will ~ mehr haben** he wants even *or* still more; **das ist ~ besser** that's even better *or* better still; **es war ~ anders** it was different again; **darüber hat er sich ~ mehr gefreut** he was even more pleased about that; **jeder ~ so dumme Mensch versteht das** anyone, however stupid, can understand that; **und wenn er auch ~ so bittet** however much he pleads; **du kannst ~ so sehr bitten** you can plead as much as you like

[12] (nach etw. Vergessenem fragend) **wie heißt/hieß sie [doch] ~?** [now] what's/what was her name again?

B *Partikel* **das ist ~ Qualität!** that's what I call quality; **auf ihn kann man sich wenigstens ~ verlassen** one can rely on 'him at least; **du wirst es ~ bereuen!** you'll regret it!; **der wird sich ~ wundern** (ugs.) he's in for a surprise; **das dauert ~ keine zehn Minuten** it won't even take ten minutes; **er kann ~ nicht einmal lesen** he can't even read; **~ in der größten Hitze trägt er seinen Pullover** however hot it is he still wears his pullover

C *Konj.* (und auch nicht) nor; **weder ... ~:** neither ... nor; **weder er ~ die Mutter ~ der Vater** neither he nor his mother nor his father; **er hat keine Verwandten** *od.* **nicht Verwandte ~ Freunde** he has no relatives or friends

nochmalig /ˈnɔxma:lɪç/ *Adj.* further

noch·mals *Adv.* again; (einige Minuten später) after another few minutes; **~: wo waren Sie zwischen ...?** once again: where were you between ...?

Nocken /ˈnɔkn̩/ *der;* **~s, ~** (Technik) cam

Nocken·welle *die* (Technik) camshaft

Nockerl /ˈnɔkɐl/ *das;* **~s, ~n** (österr., bayr. Kochk.) [semolina] dumpling; **Salzburger ~n** Salzburg dumpling soufflé *sing.*

NOK *Abk.* **= Nationales Olympisches Komitee** NOC

nölen /ˈnø:lən/ *itr. V.* (bes. nordd. abwertend) [1] (trödeln) dawdle [2] (sprechen) speak in a slow drawl

Nom. *Abk.* **= Nominativ** Nom.

Nomade /noˈma:də/ *der;* **~n, ~n** nomad

nomadenhaft *Adj.* (auch fig.) nomadic

Nomadentum *das;* **~s** (Völkerk.) nomadism

Nomadin *die;* **~, ~nen** nomad

nomadisieren *itr. V.* lead a nomadic existence; **~de Stämme** nomadic tribes

Nomen /ˈno:mən/ *das;* **~s, Nomina** [1] (Substantiv) noun; substantive [2] (deklinierbares Wort) declinable word (*including nouns, adjectives, and numerals*)

nomen est omen /ˈno:mən ˈɛst ˈo:mən/ (geh.) true to his/its *etc.* name

Nomenklatur /nomɛnklaˈtu:ɐ̯/ *die;* **~, ~en** (Wissensch.) nomenclature

Nomina ▸ **Nomen**

nominal /nomiˈna:l/ *Adj.* (Sprachw., Wirtsch.) nominal

n

Nominal-: **~einkommen** *das* (Wirtsch.) nominal income; **~lohn** *der* (Wirtsch.) nominal wages *pl.*; **~stil** *der* (Sprachw.) style in which there is a preponderance of nominal constructions; **~wert** *der* (Wirtsch.) ▸**Nennwert**

Nominativ /'no:minati:f/ *der*; **~s**, **~e** (Sprachw.) nominative [case]; (Wort im ~) nominative [form]; **im ~ stehen** be in the nominative [case]

nominell /nomi'nɛl/
A *Adj.* nominal ‹*member, leader*›; ‹*Christian*› in name only
B *adv.* **er ist nur ~ Präsident** he is President in name only; **~ ist er nur Berater des Präsidenten** nominally he is just an adviser to the President

nominieren /nomi'ni:rən/ *tr. V.* **1** (zur Wahl vorschlagen) nominate **2** (Sport: aufstellen) name ‹*player, team*›

Nominierung *die*; **~, ~en** **1** (für eine Wahl) nomination **2** (Sport: Aufstellung) selection

Nonchalance /nõʃa'lã:s/ *die*; **~**: nonchalance

nonchalant /nõʃa'lã:/
A *Adj.* nonchalant
B *adv.* nonchalantly

None /'no:nə/ *die*; **~, ~n** **1** (kath. Kirche) nones **2** (Musik) ninth

Nonius /'no:niʊs/ *der*; **~**, **Nonien** /...iən/ (Technik) vernier

Nonkonformismus /nɔnkɔnfɔr'mɪsmʊs/ *der*; **~**: nonconformism

nonkonformistisch
A *Adj.* nonconformist; unconventional ‹*dress*›
B *adv.* ‹*think, behave, argue, etc.*› in an unconventional way

Nonne /'nɔnə/ *die*; **~, ~n** **1** nun **2** (Zool.) nun [moth]

Nonnen-: **~kloster** *das* convent; nunnery; **~schule** *die* (ugs.) convent school

Non·plus·ultra /nɔnplʊs'ʊltra/ *das*; **~** (geh., oft scherzh.) ultimate (**an** + *Dat.* in); non plus ultra; **das/ein ~ an Handlichkeit** *usw.* the ultimate in handiness *etc.*

Nonsens /'nɔnzɛns/ *der*; **~[es]** nonsense

nonstop /nɔn'stɔp/ *adv.* non-stop

Nonstop-: **~flug** *der* non-stop flight; **~kino** *das* 24-hour cinema

Noppe /'nɔpə/ *die*; **~, ~n** **1** (in einem Faden, Gewebe) knop; nub **2** (auf einer Oberfläche) bump; (auf einem Tischtennisschläger) pimple

Nord[1] /nɔrt/ ▸**i** S. 363 **1** (Seemannsspr., Met.: Richtung) north; **nach ~**: northwards; **aus** *od.* **von ~**: from the north **2** (nördliches Gebiet, Politik) North; **~ und Süd** North and South; **aus ~ und Süd** from the North and [from] the South; **zwischen ~ und Süd** between [the] North and [the] South **3** *einem Subst. nachgestellt* (nördlicher Teil, nördliche Lage) **Autobahnkreuz Köln ~**: motorway intersection Cologne North; **Europa ~** (Milit.) Northern Europe

Nord[2] *der*; **~[e]s, ~e** (Seemannsspr.) northerly; (dichter.) north wind

nord-, Nord-: **~afrika** (*das*) North Africa; **~amerika** (*das*) North America; **~amerikaner** *der*, **~amerikanerin** *die* North American; **~amerikanisch** *Adj.* North American; **~atlantik·pakt** *der* North Atlantic alliance; **~deutsch** **A** *Adj.* North German; **B** *adv.* **etw. ~deutsch aussprechen** pronounce sth. with a North German accent; **~deutschland** (*das*) North Germany

norden *tr. V.* ▸**i** S. 363 **etw. ~**: orient sth. to the north

Norden *der*; **~s** **1** (Richtung) north; **im ~**: in the north; **aus dem** *od.* **von ~**: from the north; **nach ~**: northwards; **die Grenze nach ~**: the northern border; **gegen** *od.* (geh.) **gen ~**: northwards **2** (Gegend) northern part; **aus dem ~**: from the north **3** (Geogr.) North; **der hohe/höchste ~**: the far North

nord-, Nord-: **~england** (*das*) the North of England; **~europa** (*das*) Northern Europe; **~europäer** *der*, **~europäerin** *die* Northern European; **~europäisch** *Adj.* Northern European; **~flanke** *die* (Milit., Geogr.) northern flank; (Met.) northern edge; **~hang** *der* northern slope; **~insel** *die* North Island; **~irland** (*das*) Northern Ireland

nordisch *Adj.* (auch Völkerk.) Nordic; **~e Kombination** (Skisport) Nordic combined

Nordistik /nɔr'dɪstɪk/ *die*; **~**: Scandinavian Studies *pl.*, *no art.*

Nord-: **~kap** *das* North Cape; **~korea** (*das*) North Korea; **~küste** *die* north *or* northern coast; **~länder** *der*; **~~s, ~~**, **~länderin** *die*; **~~, ~~nen** native/inhabitant of [a country of] the North (esp. Scandinavia)

nördlich /'nœrtlɪç/ ▸**i** S. 363
A *Adj.* **1** (im Norden gelegen) northern; **15° ~er Breite** 15 degrees north; **das ~e Frankreich** northern France; **der ~ste Punkt** the most northerly point; *s. auch* **Eismeer**; **Polarkreis**; **Wendekreis 1** **2** (nach, aus dem Norden) northerly **3** (aus dem Norden kommend, für den Norden typisch) Northern
B *adv.* northwards; **~ von ...** [to the] north of ...; **sehr [weit] ~ sein** be a long way north
C *Präp. mit Gen.* [to the] north of

nord-, Nord-: **~licht** /'--/ *das*; *Pl.* **~~er** **1** Northern Lights *pl.*; aurora borealis; **ein ~licht/~lichter** the Northern Lights; **2** (scherzh.) Northerner; **~nord·ost**[1] (Seemannsspr., Met.) north-north-east; *s. auch* **~**[1] **1**; **~nord·ost**[2] *der* (Seemannsspr.) north-north-easter[ly]; **~nord·osten** *der* ▸**i** S. 363 north-north-east; *s. auch* **Norden 1**; **~nord·west**[1] (Seemannsspr., Met.) north-north-west; *s. auch* **~**[1] **1**; **~nord·west**[2] *der* (Seemannsspr.) north-north-wester[ly]; **~nord·westen** *der* north-north-west; *s. auch* **Norden 1**; **~ost**[1] (Seemannsspr., Met.) north-east; **nach ~ost** north-eastwards; **aus** *od.* **von ~ost** from the north-east; **~ost**[2] *der* (Seemannsspr.) north-easter[ly]; (dichter.) north-east[erly] wind; **~osten** *der* **1** (Richtung, Gegend) north-east; *s. auch* **Norden 1**; **~östlich** ▸**i** S. 363 **A** *Adj.* **1** (im ~osten gelegen) north-eastern; *s. auch* **nördlich A 1**; **2** (nach ~osten gerichtet, aus ~osten kommend) north-easterly; **B** *adv.* north-eastwards; **~östlich von ...** [to the] north-east of ...; *s. auch* **nördlich B**; **C** *Präp. mit Gen.* [to the] north-east of; **~-Ostsee-Kanal** *der* Kiel Canal; **~ost·wind** *der* north-east[erly] wind; **~pol** /'--/ *der* **1** North Pole; **2** (eines Magneten) north pole

Nordpolar-: **~gebiet** *das* North Polar Region; **~meer** *das* Arctic Ocean

Nord-: **~pol·expedition** *die* expedition to the North Pole; **~rand** *der* northern edge

Nordrhein-Westfale *der*; **~n, ~n** North Rhine-Westphalian

Nord·rhein-Westfalen (*das*) North Rhine-Westphalia

nordrhein-westfälisch *Adj.* North Rhine-Westphalian

Nord·see *die* North Sea

nord-, Nord-: **~seite** /'---/ *die* northern side; (eines Gebäudes, Geländes) north side; **~stern** /'--/ *der* North Star; Polaris; **~-Süd-Dialog** *der* (Politik) North-South dialogue; **~-Süd-Gefälle** *das* (Politik) North-South gap; **~südlich** ▸**i** S. 363 **A** *Adj.* **in ~südlicher Richtung** from north to south; **B** *adv.* **~südlich verlaufen** run from north to south; **~wand** /'--/ *die* (Felswand) north face; **~wärts** /'--/ *Adv.* ▸**i** S. 363 **1** (nach ~en) northwards; **2** (im ~en) to the north; **~west**[1] **1** (Seemannsspr., Met.) north-west; **nach ~west** north-westwards; **aus** *od.* **von ~west** from the north-west; **2** *einem Subst. nachgestellt* **Autobahnkreuz Frankfurt-~west** motorway intersection Frankfurt North-West; **~west**[2] *der* (Seemannsspr.) north-wester[ly]; (dichter.) north-west[erly] wind; **~westen** *der* ▸**i** S. 363 **1** (Richtung, Gegend) north-west; *s. auch* **Norden 1**; **~westlich** ▸**i** S. 363 **A** *Adj.* **1** (im ~westen gelegen) north-western; *s. auch* **nördlich A 1**; **2** (nach ~westen gerichtet, aus ~westen kommend) north-westerly; **B** *adv.* (nach ~westen) north-westwards; **~westlich von ...** [to the] north-west of ...; *s. auch* **nördlich B**; **C** *Präp. mit Gen.* [to the] north-west of; **~west-wind** *der* north-west[erly] wind; **~wind** /'--/ *der* north *or* northerly wind

Nörgelei *die*; **~, ~en** (abwertend) **1** (das Nörgeln) moaning; grumbling; (das Kritteln) carping **2** (Äußerung) moan; grumble; **deine ewigen ~en** your constant moaning *sing.* *or* grumbling *sing.*

nörgelig *Adj.* (abwertend) moaning *attrib.*; grumbling *attrib.*; grumbly (coll.); **ein ~er Kerl** a moaner *or* grumbler; **müde und ~**: tired and niggly

nörgeln /'nœrgl̩n/ *itr. V.* (abwertend) moan, grumble (**an** + *Dat.* about); (kritteln) carp (**an** + *Dat.* about)

Nörgler *der*; **~s, ~**, **Nörglerin** *die*; **~, ~nen** (abwertend) moaner; grumbler; (Krittler) carper; fault-finder

nörglerisch *Adj.* (abwertend) moaning *attrib.*; grumbling *attrib.*; grumbly (coll.); (krittelig) carping *attrib.*

nörglig ▸**nörgelig**

Norm /nɔrm/ *die*; **~, ~en** **1** norm; **zur ~ werden/als ~ gelten** become the norm/count as the norm **2** (geforderte Arbeitsleistung) quota; target; **die ~ erfüllen** fulfil one's/its quota; meet *or* achieve one's/its target **3** (Sport) qualifying standard **4** (technische, industrielle ~) standard; standard specifications *pl.*; **der ~ entsprechen** conform to the standard **5** (Buchw.) signature (*at foot of page*)

normal /nɔr'ma:l/
A *Adj.* **1** normal; **du bist doch nicht ~!** (ugs.) there must be something wrong with you! **2** (ugs.: gewöhnlich) ordinary
B *adv.* **1** normally **2** (ugs.: gewöhnlich) in the normal *or* ordinary way **3** (ugs.: ~erweise) normally; usually

Normal *das*; **~s** (ugs.) ≈ regular (esp. Amer.)

Normal·benzin *das* ≈ two-star petrol (Brit.); regular (Amer.)

Normale *die*; **~[n], ~n** (Math.) normal

normalerweise *Adv.* normally; usually

Normal-: **~fall** *der* normal case; **im ~fall** normally, usually; **~form** *die* **1** (Math.) standard *or* normal form; **2** (Sport) usual form; **~gewicht** *das* normal weight

normalisieren
A *tr. V.* normalize
B *refl. V.* return to normal

Normalisierung *die*; **~, ~en** normalization

Normalität /nɔrmali'tɛ:t/ *die*; **~**: normality *no def. art.*

Normal-: **~maß** *das* **1** (normales Maß) normal size; (normales Niveau) normal level; **~maße haben** be [of] a normal size; **2** (Messwesen) standard measure; **~null** *das*; **~s** (Geodäsie) national datum level; **~spur** *die* (Eisenb.) standard gauge; **~sterbliche** *der/die*; normal mortal; **~ton** *der*; *Pl.* **~töne** **1** (Akustik) reference tone; **2** (Musik) standard pitch; **~uhr** *die* **1** (genau gehende Uhr) regulator; **2** (öffentliche Uhr) public clock; **~verbraucher** *der*, **~verbraucherin** *die* **1** ordinary *or* average consumer; **2** (ugs.: Durchschnittsmensch) average punter (coll.); **Otto ~verbraucher** (scherzh.) the average punter (coll.); **~zeit** *die* standard time; **~zustand** *der* **1** normal state; **im ~zustand** in its/his normal state; **2** ▸**Normzustand**

Normandie /nɔrman'di:/ *die*; **~**: Normandy; **in/aus der ~**: in/from Normandy

Normanne /nɔr'manə/ *der*; **~n, ~n**, **Normannin** *die*; **~, ~nen** Norman

normannisch *Adj.* Norman

normativ /nɔrma'ti:f/ *Adj.* normative

Norm·blatt *das* list of standard specifications

normen *tr. V.* standardize

Normen-: **~ausschuss**, ***~ausschuß** *der* standards committee; **~kontroll·verfahren** *das*: (Rechtsw.) *suit brought before the constitutional court relating to the constitutionality of a law*

Norm·erhöhung *die* raising of production targets

normieren *tr. V.* standardize

Normierung *die*; **~, ~en**, **Normung** *die*; **~, ~en** standardization

n

Norm·zustand *der* (Physik, Technik) standard state

Norne /'nɔrnə/ *die;* ~, ~**n** (nord. Myth.) Norn

Norwegen /'nɔrve:gn̩/ *(das);* ~**s** Norway

Norweger *der;* ~**s**, ~, **Norwegerin** *die;* ~, ~**nen** ▸ⓘ **S. 520** Norwegian; *s. auch* **-in**

Norweger·muster *das* (Handarb.) ≈ Fair Isle design

norwegisch *Adj.* ▸ⓘ **S. 520**, ▸ⓘ **S. 670** Norwegian; *s. auch* **deutsch**; **Deutsch**; **Deutsche²**

Nostalgie /nɔstal'gi:/ *die;* ~: nostalgia

nostalgisch
A *Adj.* nostalgic
B *adv.* nostalgically; ~ **gestimmt** in a nostalgic mood

***not** ▸**Not 5**

Not /no:t/ *die;* ~, **Nöte** /'nø:tə/ **1** (Bedrohung, Gefahr) **in seiner** ~: at that perilous juncture; **jmdm. in der Stunde der** ~ **helfen** help sb. in his/her hour of need; **in höchster** *od.* **äußerster** ~: in extremis; **Rettung in** *od.* **aus höchster** ~: rescue from extreme difficulties; **in** ~ **sein** be in desperate straits; ~ **bricht Eisen** desperation gives you strength; ~ **lehrt beten** adversity teaches you to pray; **in** ~ **und Tod** (geh.) through thick and thin **2** (Mangel, Armut) need; poverty [and hardship]; ~ **leiden** suffer poverty *or* want [and hardship]; ~ **leidende Menschen** needy *or* impoverished people; **etw. aus** ~ **tun** do sth. from sheer need; **in** ~ **geraten/sein** encounter hard times/be suffering want [and deprivation]; **in diesem Land herrscht große** ~: there is great poverty and hardship in this country; **er kennt keine** ~: he's doing all right for himself; ~ **macht erfinderisch** necessity is the mother of invention (prov.); ~ **kennt kein Gebot** [when] needs must; **in der** ~ **frisst der Teufel Fliegen** beggars can't be choosers (prov.) **3** (Verzweiflung) anguish; distress **4** (Sorge, Mühe) trouble; **in Nöten sein** have many troubles; **seine [liebe]** ~ **haben, etw. zu tun** have great difficulty in doing sth.; **seine [liebe]** ~ **mit jmdm./etw. haben** have a lot of trouble *or* a lot of problems with sb./sth.; **mit knapper** ~: by the skin of one's teeth **5** (veralt.: Notwendigkeit) necessity; **ohne** ~ (geh.) without pressing cause; **zur** ~: if need be; if necessary; **wenn** ~ **am Mann ist** when the need arises; **aus der** ~ **eine Tugend machen** make a virtue of necessity; ~ **tun** *od.* **sein** (geh., landsch.) be necessary

Notabeln /no'ta:bl̩n/ *Pl.* (hist.) Notables

notabene /nota'be:nə/ *Adv.* (geh. veralt.) nota bene (arch. literary); please note

Not-: ~**abitur** *das: early* **Abitur** *taken in wartime by students about to be conscripted;* ~**anker** *der* (Seew., auch fig.) sheet anchor

Notar /no'ta:ɐ̯/ *der;* ~**s**, ~**e** notary

Notariat /notar'i̯a:t/ *das;* ~**[e]s**, ~**e** **1** (Amt) notaryship **2** (Kanzlei) notary's office

notariell /nota'ri̯ɛl/
A *Adj.* notarial
B *adv.* ~ **beglaubigt** attested by a notary

Notarin *die;* ~, ~**nen** notary

Not-: ~**arzt** *der,* ~**ärztin** *die* doctor on [emergency] call; emergency doctor; ~**arzt·wagen** *der* doctor's car for emergency calls

Notation /nota'tsi̯o:n/ *die;* ~, ~**en** (Musik, Schach) notation

Not-: ~**aufnahme** *die* (Gesundheitswesen) casualty department; casualty *no art.;* ~**aus·gabe** *die* (Zeitungsw.) emergency edition; ~**aus·gang** *der* emergency exit; ~**behelf** *der* makeshift; ~**beleuchtung** *die* emergency lighting *no indef. art.;* ~**bremse** *die* emergency brake; **die** ~**bremse ziehen** pull the emergency brake; pull the communication cord (Brit. Railw.); (Sportjargon) bring the attacker down; ~**brücke** *die* temporary bridge; ~**dienst** *der* ▸**Bereitschaftsdienst**

Notdurft /-dʊrft/ *die;* ~ **1** (geh.) **seine [große/kleine]** ~ **verrichten** relieve oneself **2** (geh. veralt.: das Nötige) need; **mehr als seine knappe** ~ **verdienen** earn more than one needs to buy the bare necessities of life

not·dürftig
A *Adj.* meagre ‹*payment, pension*›; rough and ready, makeshift ‹*shelter, repair*›; scanty ‹*cover, clothing*›
B *adv.* scantily ‹*clothed*›; **etw.** ~ **reparieren** repair sth. in a rough and ready *or* makeshift way; **sich** ~ **verständigen** manage to communicate after a fashion

Note /'no:tə/ *die;* ~, ~**n** **1** (Zeichen) note; **eine ganze/halbe** ~: a crotchet/quaver (Brit.); a whole note/half note (Amer.); **etw. in** ~**n setzen** (veralt.) set sth. to music **2** *Pl.* (Text) music *sing.;* **nach/ohne** ~**n spielen** play from/without music **3** (Schul~) mark **4** (Eislauf, Turnen) score **5** (Dipl.) note **6** (Flair) touch; **einer Sache eine persönliche** ~ **geben** give sth. a personal touch **7** ▸ⓘ **S. 299** (Bank~) note

Notebook /'noʊtbʊk/ *das;* ~**s**, ~**s** (DV) notebook [computer]

Noten-: ~**austausch** *der* (Dipl.) exchange of notes; ~**bank** *die; Pl.* ~~**en** bank of issue; ~**blatt** *das* sheet of music; ~**druck** *der* **1** (Druck von Banknoten) printing of [bank]notes; **2** (Druck von Musikalien) music printing; printing of music; **3** (Leistungsdruck) pressure to achieve high marks; ~**durchschnitt** *der* average mark; ~**heft** *das* **1** (Publikation) book of music; **2** (Heft mit ~papier) manuscript book; ~**linie** *die* (Musik) line [of the staff]; ~**papier** *das* music paper; ~**presse** *die* (Bankw.) printing press for banknotes; **die** ~**presse in Gang setzen/anwerfen**/(salopp) **anschmeißen** [start up the printing presses and] print money; ~**pult** *das* music rest; music stand; ~**schlüssel** *der* clef; ~**schrift** *die* [musical] notation; ~**ständer** *der* music stand

not-, Not-: ~**fall** *der* **1** (Gefahr) emergency; **im** ~**fall** in an emergency; **für den** ~**fall** in case of emergency; **in** *od.* **bei** ~**fällen** in emergencies; **2** (Schwierigkeiten) case of need; **im** ~**fall** if need be; **für den** ~**fall habe ich immer einen Reservekanister im Kofferraum** I always have a spare can of petrol (Brit.) *or* (Amer.) gasoline in the boot (Brit.) *or* (Amer.) trunk, just in case; ~**falls** *Adv.* if need be; if necessary; ~**gedrungen** *Adv.* of necessity; **ich habe** ~**gedrungen eine neue gekauft** I had no choice but to *or* I was forced to buy a new one; ~**geil** *Adj.* (oft abwertend) desperately horny (sl.); ~**geld** *das* (Finanzw.) necessity money; emergency money; ~**gemein·schaft** *die* **1** (Interessengemeinschaft) emergency action organization; **2** (durch gemeinsame ~lage Verbundene) union born of necessity; ~**groschen** *der* nest egg; **die 500 Euro lege ich als** ~**groschen zurück** I'll put that 500 euros away for a rainy day; ~**hilfe** *die* (Rechtsw.) assistance in an emergency (*as required by law*); **in** ~**hilfe schießen** shoot in defence of a third person

notieren /no'ti:rən/
A *tr. V.* **1** **[sich** *(Dat.)*] **etw.** ~: note sth. down; make a note of sth.; **die Polizei hat den Fahrer notiert** the police took [down] the driver's particulars; **jmdn. für etw.** ~: put sb.'s name down for sth.; ~ **Sie bitte: ...** please note that down: ...; **ein Musikstück** ~: write a piece of music down [in musical notation] **2** (Börsenw., Wirtsch.) quote (**mit** at)
B *itr. V.* (Börsenw., Wirtsch.) be quoted (**mit** at); **die meisten Rohstoffe** ~ **unverändert** most commodity prices are unchanged

Notierung *die;* ~, ~**en** **1** ▸**Notation** **2** (Börsenw., Wirtsch.) quotation; (Preis) quoted [price] (**für** of); (von Devisen) rate (**für** for)

nötig /'nø:tɪç/
A *Adj.* necessary; **dafür** *od.* **dazu fehlt mir die** ~**e Geduld/das** ~**e Geld** I don't have the patience/money necessary *or* needed for that; **es ist nicht** ~**, dass du dabei bist** there's no need for you to be there; you don't have to be there; **etw./jmdn.** ~ **haben** need sth./sb.; **Hilfe dringend** ~ **haben** be in urgent need of help; need help urgently; **es** ~ **haben, etw. zu tun** need to do sth.; **er hat es manchmal** ~**, dass man ihn zurechtweist** he sometimes needs reprimanding; **das habe ich nicht** ~ (das lasse ich mir nicht gefallen) I won't have that; **sich zu entschuldigen, hat er natürlich nicht** ~ (iron.) of course he does not feel the need to apologize; **du hast/er hat** *usw.* **es gerade** ~ (ugs.) you're/he's a fine one to talk (coll.); **das wäre [doch] nicht** ~ **gewesen!** (ugs.) you shouldn't have!; **das Nötige veranlassen** do all that is necessary; **das Nötigste** the bare essentials *pl*
B *adv.* **er braucht** ~ **Hilfe** he is in urgent need of *or* urgently needs help; **was er am** ~**sten braucht, ist ...** what he most urgently needs is ...; **ich muss** ~ **aufs Klo** (ugs.) I'm dying to go to the loo (Brit. coll.) *or* (Amer. coll.) the john

nötigen
A *tr. V.* **1** (zwingen) compel; force; (Rechtsspr.) intimidate; coerce; **jmdn. zur Unterschrift** ~: compel *or* force sb. to sign; **sich genötigt sehen, etw. zu tun** feel compelled to do sth. **2** (geh.: auffordern) press; urge; **lass dich nicht [lange]** ~: don't wait to be asked
B *itr. V.* (geh.) **zur Wachsamkeit/zu einer vorsichtigen Fahrweise** ~: compel one to be vigilant/drive carefully

nötigenfalls *Adv.* if necessary; if need be

Nötigung *die;* ~, ~**en** **1** (bes. Rechtsspr.) intimidation; coercion **2** (geh.: Notwendigkeit) necessity **3** (geh.: das Nötigen) urging

Notiz /no'ti:ts/ *die;* ~, ~**en** **1** note; **sich** *(Dat.)* **eine** ~ **machen** make a note **2** (Zeitungs~) **eine [kurze]** ~: a brief report **3** *in* **von jmdm./etw. [keine]** ~ **nehmen** take [no] notice of sb./sth. **4** (Börsenw.) ▸**Notierung 2**

Notiz-: ~**block** *der; Pl.* ~~**s** *od.* ~**blöcke** notepad; ~**buch** *das* notebook; ~**zettel** *der* note; **etw. als** ~**zettel benutzen** use sth. to write a note/notes on

not-, Not-: ~**lage** *die* serious difficulties *pl.;* **jmds.** ~**lage ausnutzen** exploit sb.'s plight; ~**lager** *das* makeshift bed; ~**landen: ich** ~**lande,** ~**gelandet,** ~**zulanden** **A** *itr. V.; mit sein* do an emergency landing; **B** *tr. V.* **er konnte/musste die Maschine** ~**landen** he was able to do/had to do an emergency landing; ~**landung** *die* emergency landing; ~**leidend** *Adj.* needy; impoverished; (fig.) ailing ‹*industry*›; (Finanzw.) ‹*loan*› in default; unsecured ‹*credit*›; **die** ~**leidenden** the [poor and] needy; ~**lösung** *die* stopgap; ~**lüge** *die* evasive lie; (aus Rücksichtnahme) white lie; **um der Bestrafung zu entgehen, griff er zu einer** ~**lüge** he resorted to a lie to avoid punishment; ~**maßnahme** *die* emergency measure; ~**opfer** *das* (Steuerw.) emergency levy

notorisch /no'to:rɪʃ/
A *Adj.* notorious
B *adv.* notoriously; ~ **lügen** be a notorious liar

not-, Not-: ~**pfennig** *der* ▸~**groschen**; ~**quartier** *das* emergency quarters *pl.;* ~**ruf** *der* **1** (Hilferuf) emergency call; (eines Schiffes) Mayday call; distress call; **2** (Nummer) emergency number; **3** (eines Tieres) alarm call; ~**ruf·nummer** *die* emergency number; ~**ruf·säule** *die* emergency telephone (*mounted in a piller*); ~**schlachten** *tr., itr. V.;* **ich** ~**schlachte,** ~**geschlachtet,** ~**zuschlachten** slaughter ‹*sick or injured animal*›; ~**schlachtung** *die* slaughtering (*of sick or injured animal*); ~**schrei** *der* **1** (geh. veralt.) cry of distress; **2** ▸~**ruf 3**; ~**situation** *die* emergency; ~**sitz** *der* extra seat; (ausklappbar) tip-up seat; fold-away seat; ~**stand** *der* **1** (Krise, Übelstand) crisis; **2** (Staatsrecht) state of emergency; **den** ~**stand erklären** *od.* **verkünden** *od.* **ausrufen** declare a state of emergency; **äußerer** ~**stand** threat of attack; **innerer/ziviler** ~**stand** internal/civil emergency; **3** (bes. Rechtsw.) necessity; **rechtfertigender** ~**stand** *necessity which justifies a normally illegal act;* ~**stands·gebiet** *das* **1** (auch fig.) disaster area; **2** (Wirtsch.) depressed area; ~**stands·gesetz** *das* emergency law; ~**stands·gesetzgebung** *die* emergency legislation; ~**taufe** *die* emergency baptism (*by a layman*); ~**unterkunft** *die* emergency accommodation *no pl., no indef. art.;* ~**unterkünfte** emergency accommodation *sing.;* ~**verband** *der* emergency dressing; **~verordnung** *die* emergency decree; **~vorrat** *der* emergency supply; **~wassern** *itr. V.; mit sein, tr. V.;* **ich ~wassere, ~gewassert, ~zuwassern** ditch; **~wehr** *die* (Rechtsw.) self-defence; **in** *od.* **aus ~wehr** in self-defence

not·wendig
A *Adj.* 1 necessary; **es ist ~, dass wir etwas tun** we must do something; **das Notwendigste** the bare essentials *pl.* 2 (zwangsläufig) necessary; (unvermeidlich) inevitable; *s. auch* **Übel**
B *adv.* 1 ▸**nötig B** 2 (zwangsläufig, unbedingt) necessarily

notwendiger·weise *Adv.* necessarily

Notwendigkeit *die;* **~, ~en** necessity

not-, Not-: ~zeichen *das* distress signal; **~zeit** *die* time of emergency; (Zeit des Mangels) time of need; **~zucht** *die* (Rechtsw. veralt.) rape; **~zucht [an jmdm.] begehen** *od.* **verüben** commit rape [on sb.]; **~züchtigen** *tr. V.;* **ich ~züchtige, genotzüchtigt, ~zuzüchtigen** (Rechtsw. veralt.) rape; **~zucht·verbrechen** *das* (Rechtsw. veralt.) rape

Nougat /ˈnuːɡat/ *der; auch das;* **~s** nougat

Nov. *Abk.* **= November** Nov.

Nova ▸**Novum**

Novelle /noˈvɛlə/ *die;* **~, ~n** 1 (Literaturw.) novella 2 (Gesetzes~) amendment

novellieren *tr. V.* (Politik, Rechtsw.) amend

Novellierung *die;* **~, ~en** (Politik, Rechtsw.) amendment

novellistisch
A *Adj.* **die ~e Literatur** literature in novella form; the novella; **das ~e Werk Kellers** Keller's novellas
B *adv.* **etw. ~ gestalten/bearbeiten** put sth. into/treat sth. in novella form

November /noˈvɛmbɐ/ *der;* **~[s], ~** ▸❶ **S. 165** November; *s. auch* **April**

novemberlich
A *Adj.* Novemberish
B *adv.* **~ unfreundlich/trüb sein** be as dreary/grey as in November

Novität /noviˈtɛːt/ *die;* **~, ~en** 1 novelty; (neue Erfindung) innovation; (neue Schallplatte) new release; (neues Buch) new publication 2 (veralt.: Nachricht) piece of news; **~en** news *sing.*

Novize /noˈviːtsə/ *der;* **~n, ~n, Novize** *die;* **~, ~n** novice

Noviziat /noviˈtsiaːt/ *das;* **~[e]s, ~e** noviciate

Novizin *die;* **~, ~nen** novice

Novum /ˈnoːvʊm/ *das;* **~s, Nova** novelty; (neue Erfindung) innovation; **ein ~ in der Geschichte der Partei** an unprecedented event in the history of the party

NPD *Abk.* **= Nationaldemokratische Partei Deutschlands** National Democratic Party of Germany

Nr. *Abk.* **= Nummer** No

NRW *Abk.* **= Nordrhein-Westfalen**

NSDAP *Abk.* **= Nationalsozialistische Deutsche Arbeiterpartei** National Socialist German Workers' Party

N.T. *Abk.* **= Neues Testament** NT

nu /nuː/ *Adv.* (bes. nordd.) ▸**nun**

Nu *der: in* **im Nu, in einem Nu** in no time

Nuance /ˈnỹãːsə/ *die;* **~, ~n** 1 (Unterschied, Feinheit) nuance 2 (Grad) shade; **[um] eine ~ dunkler/schneller** a shade darker/faster

nuancenreich
A *Adj.* full of nuances *postpos.;* finely *or* subtly nuanced
B *adv.* with subtlety of nuance

nuancieren *tr., itr. V.* **etw. ~:** give sth. subtle nuances; **farblich stärker ~:** give more definite nuances of colour

nuanciert
A *Adj.* finely *or* subtly nuanced
B *adv.* **[sehr] ~:** with [great] subtlety of nuance

'nüber /ˈnyːbɐ/ *Adv.* (südd.) ▸**hinüber**

nüchtern /ˈnʏçtɐn/
A *Adj.* 1 (nicht betrunken) sober; **mit ~em Kopf** with a clear head; **wieder ~ werden** sober up 2 (mit leerem Magen) **der Patient muss ~ sein** the patient's stomach must be empty; **auf ~en Magen rauchen** smoke on an empty stomach; **das war ein Schreck auf ~en Magen** (scherzh.) that's just what I needed at that time of the morning (iron.) 3 (realistisch) sober; sober, matter-of-fact ‹*account, assessment, question, etc.*›; bare ‹*figures*› 4 (schmucklos, streng) austere; bare ‹*room*›; unadorned, bare ‹*walls*›; (ungeschminkt) bare, plain ‹*fact*› 5 (bes. nordostd.: ungewürzt, ungesalzen) bland; (fade) insipid
B *adv.* 1 (realistisch) soberly; **wir sollten einmal ganz ~ darüber sprechen** we ought to have a down-to-earth talk about this sometime 2 (schmucklos, streng) austerely

Nüchternheit *die;* **~** 1 sobriety 2 (Realitätsbezogenheit) sobriety; soberness 3 (Schmucklosigkeit) austerity

Nuckel /ˈnʊkl/ *der;* **~s, ~** (ugs.) ▸**Schnuller**

nuckeln (ugs.)
A *itr. V.* suck (**an** + *Dat.* at); **am Daumen/Schnuller ~:** suck one's thumb/a *or* one's dummy
B *tr. V.* suck

Nuckel·pinne *die* (salopp) old banger (Brit. coll.) *or* (coll.) crate

Nudel /ˈnuːdl/ *die;* **~, ~n** 1 piece of spaghetti/vermicelli/tortellini *etc.;* (als Suppeneinlage) noodle; **~n** (Teigwaren) pasta *sing.;* (als Suppeneinlage, Reisnudeln) noodles; **Spaghetti und andere ~n** spaghetti and other types of pasta 2 (ugs.) **eine dicke ~:** a fatty (coll.); **eine giftige ~:** a nasty piece of work (coll.); **eine komische ~:** a real character

Nudel-: ~brett *das* board (*for rolling out pasta dough*); pastry board; **~holz** *das* rolling pin

nudeln *tr. V.* cram ‹*geese*›; (fig. ugs.) stuff

Nudel-: ~salat *der* pasta salad; **~suppe** *die* soup with noodles; **~teig** *der* pasta dough

Nudismus /nuˈdɪsmʊs/ *der;* **~:** nudism *no art.;* naturism *no art.*

Nudist /nuˈdɪst/ *der;* **~en, ~en, Nudistin** *die;* **~, ~nen** nudist; naturist

Nugat ▸**Nougat**

nuklear /nukleˈaːɐ̯/
A *Adj.* nuclear
B *adv.* **~ angetrieben** nuclear-powered; **~ bewaffnet** possessing nuclear weapons *postpos.*

Nuklear-: ~krieg *der* nuclear war; **~macht** *die* nuclear power; **~medizin** *die* nuclear medicine *no art.;* **~physik** *die* nuclear physics *sing., no art.;* **~waffe** *die* nuclear weapon

Nukleus /ˈnuːkleʊs/ *der;* **~, Nuklei** /...ei/ (Biol., Anat., Sprachw.) nucleus

null /nʊl/
A *Kardinalz.* ▸❶ **S. 703,** ▸❶ **S. 729,** ▸❶ **S. 826** nought; **~ Komma sechs** [nought] point six; **sieben, ~, ~, sechs, ~, vier** (Fernspr.) seven double-O, six O four (Brit.); seven zero zero, six zero four (Amer.); **~ Grad Celsius** nought *or* zero degrees Celsius; **bei ~ Fehlern** if there are no mistakes; **fünf zu ~ Tore** five goals to nil; **fünf zu ~:** five-nil; **das Spiel endete ~ zu ~:** the game was a goalless draw; **fünfzehn ~** (Tennis) fifteen-love; **gegen ~ Uhr** around twelve midnight; **es ist ~ Uhr dreißig** it is twelve-thirty a.m.; **elf Uhr, ~ Minuten und fünfzehn Sekunden** eleven, no minutes, and fifteen seconds; **etw. für ~ und nichtig erklären** declare sth. null and void; **in ~ Komma nichts** (ugs.) in less than no time; **gleich ~ sein** (fig.) be practically zero; **auf ~ stehen** ‹*indicator, needle, etc.*› be at zero; **fünf Grad unter/über ~:** five degrees below/above zero *or* freezing; **die Augen auf ~ gestellt haben** (salopp) have snuffed it (sl.); **jmdn. auf ~ bringen** (salopp) destroy sb. (fig.)
B *indekl. Adj.* (ugs.) **~ Ahnung/Interesse** no idea/interest at all; **auf etw.** (*Akk.*) **~ Bock haben** not fancy sth. at all

Null¹ *die;* **~, ~en** 1 (Ziffer) nought; zero; **eine schwarze Null schreiben** make *or* show a small profit 2 (abwertend) (Versager) failure; dead loss (coll.); (unbedeutender Mensch) nonentity

Null² *der* (*auch: das*); **~[s], ~s** (Skat) null; **~ Hand** null from hand

Null- zero

null·acht·fünfzehn, null·acht·fuffzehn (ugs. abwertend)
A *indekl. Adj.* run-of-the-mill; **das Essen war eher ~:** the meal really wasn't anything to write home about
B *adv.* **~ gekleidet/eingerichtet** dressed/furnished in a run-of-the-mill way

Null·acht·fünfzehn-, Null·acht·fuffzehn- (ugs. abwertend) run-of-the-mill

Null-: ~-Bock-Generation *die* (ugs.) switched-off generation; **~diät** *die* absolute diet

***Nulleiter** ▸**Nullleiter**

Null-: ~leiter *der* (Elektrot.) neutral conductor; **~lösung** *die* (Politik) zero option; **~menge** *die* (Math.) empty set; **~meridian** *der* (Geogr.) Greenwich meridian; **~nummer** *die: free first issue (of magazine etc.)*

***Nullösung** ▸**Nulllösung**

Null ouvert /nʊl|uˈveːɐ̯/ *der;* (auch:) *das;* **~[s], ~s** (Skat) open null

Null-: ~punkt *der* zero; **die Temperatur ist auf den ~punkt abgesunken** the temperature has dropped to zero *or* to freezing point; **die Stimmung war auf dem ~punkt angelangt** *od.* **hatte den ~punkt erreicht** (fig.) we/they were in very low spirits; **~spiel** *das* (Skat) null; **beim ~spiel** when playing null *or* a null game; **~tarif** *der:* **die Rentner haben ~tarif im Nahverkehr/Schwimmbad** *usw.* pensioners can use local public transport/the swimming pool *etc.* free of charge; **zum ~tarif** free of charge; **zum ~tarif einkaufen/fernsehen** (scherzh.) go shoplifting/watch television without a licence; **~wachstum** *das* zero growth

Nulpe /ˈnʊlpə/ *die;* **~, ~n** (ugs. abwertend) drip (coll.)

Numerale /numəˈraːlə/ *das;* **~s, Numeralien** *od.* **Numeralia** (Sprachw.) ▸numeral

Numeri ▸**Numerus**

***numerieren** ▸**nummerieren**

***Numerierung** ▸**Nummerierung**

numerisch /nuˈmeːrɪʃ/
A *Adj.* numerical
B *adv.* numerically; **~ überlegen sein** be superior in numbers

Numero /ˈnʊməro/ *in Verbindung mit einer Zahl* (veralt.) number

Numerus /ˈnʊmərʊs/ *der;* **~, Numeri** 1 (Sprachw.) number 2 (Math.) antilogarithm; antilog (coll.)

Numerus clausus /- ˈklaʊzʊs/ *der;* **~** *fixed number of students admissible to a university to study a particular subject;* numerus clausus

> **Numerus clausus**
> The *Numerus clausus* system is used to limit the number of students studying certain oversubscribed subjects such as medicine at German universities. It means that only those students who have achieved a minimum average mark in their **Abitur** are admitted.

Numismatik /numɪsˈmaːtɪk/ *die;* **~:** numismatics *sing., no art.*

Nummer /ˈnʊmɐ/ *die;* **~, ~n** 1 number; **ein Wagen mit [einer] Münchner ~:** a car with a Munich registration; **ich bin unter der ~ 242679 zu erreichen** I can be reached on 242679; **bloß eine ~ sein** (fig.) be just a *or* nothing but a number; **[die] ~ eins** [the] number one; **Thema ~ eins sein** be the number-one topic of conversation; **ich muss auf ~ null** (ugs. verhüll.) I must go to the loo (Brit. coll.) *or* (Amer. coll.) the john; **er sitzt auf ~ sicher** (ugs.) he's doing time (coll.); **auf ~ sicher gehen** (ugs.) play safe; not take any chances; **bei jmdm. eine gute** *od.* **große** *od.* **dicke ~ haben** (ugs.) be well in with sb. (coll.) 2 (Ausgabe) number; issue 3 (Größe) size; **diese Sache ist eine ~/ein paar ~n zu groß für dich** (ugs.) this business is in a different league from anything you could cope with 4 (Darbietung) turn 5 (ugs.: Musikstück) number

n

6 (ugs.: Person) character; **er ist eine ~ [für sich]** he is a real character *or* quite a character; **er ist eine große ~ im Verkaufen** he's quite a *or* (coll.) some salesman 7 (derb: Koitus) screw (coarse)

nummerieren /numəˈriːrən/ *tr. V.* number

Nummerierung *die;* ~, ~**en** numbering

Nummern-: ~konto *das* (Bankw.) numbered account; **~oper** *die* (Musik) number opera; **~scheibe** *die* dial; **~schild** *das* 1 (eines Fahrzeugs) number plate; license plate (Amer.); 2 (an Häusern, Straßen) number; **~schlüssel** *der* (DV) numerical code

nun /nuːn/

A *Adv.* now; **von ~ an** from now on; **~, wo sie krank ist** now [that] she's ill; **~ erst, erst ~:** only now; **gestern ist er ~ endlich wiedergekommen** he finally came back yesterday

B *Partikel* now; **so wichtig ist es ~ auch wieder nicht** it's not all 'that important; **~ ist es in der Tat zutreffend, dass ...** now it is indeed quite correct that ...; **und bei dem Lärm soll man ~ schlafen können!** and people are supposed to sleep with that noise going on; **und so was nennt sich ~ Diplomübersetzer** and he calls himself a qualified translator; **das hast du ~ davon!** it serves you right!; **hat sich das ~ gelohnt?** was it really worth it?; **~ gib schon her!** now hand it over!; **~ mach dir deswegen mal keine Sorgen!** now don't you worry; **kommst du ~ mit oder nicht?** now are you coming or not?; **er muss es tun, ob er ~ will oder nicht** he has to do it, whether he wants to or not; **so ist das ~ [einmal/mal]** that's just the way it is *or* things are; **er braucht ~ einmal viel Schlaf** he happens to need a lot of sleep; **~ gut** *od.* **schön** [well,] all right; **~, ~!** now, come on; **ja ~!** oh, well!; **~?** well?; **Das Brett ist etwas zu lang — Nun, das lässt sich ändern** The board is a bit too long — Well, that can be altered; **~ ja ... well, yes ...; ~ denn!** (also gut) well, all right!; (also los) well then;

C *Konj.* (veralt. geh.) now that

nun·mehr *Adv.* (geh.) 1 now; **er ist ~ seit zehn Jahren Kanzler** he has been Chancellor now for ten years; **seine ~ 80-jährige Mutter** his mother, [who is] now 80 years old 2 (von ~ an) from now on; henceforth

'nunter /ˈnʊntɐ/ *Adv.* (südd.) ▸**hinunter**

Nuntius /ˈnʊntsi̯ʊs/ *der;* ~, **Nuntien** nuncio; *s. auch* **apostolisch**

nur /nuːɐ̯/

A *Adv.* 1 (nicht mehr als) only; just; **ich habe ~ eine Stunde Zeit/zehn Euro** I only have an hour/ten euros; **ich habe es für ~ fünf Euro gekauft** I bought it for just five euros; **er hat ~ einen einzigen Fehler gemacht** he made just a single mistake; **um eines ~ möchte ich dich bitten** I'd ask just one thing of you; **er tat es ~ ungern** he did it only reluctantly; **das ist ~ recht und billig** it is only right and proper; **ohne auch ~ zu lächeln** without so much as smiling; **eine ~ mittelmäßige Leistung** only a mediocre performance

2 (ausschließlich) only; **~ er darf das** only he is allowed to do that; **alle durften mitfahren, ~ ich nicht** everyone was allowed to go, all except me; **er will dir doch ~ helfen** he only wants to help you; **~ darauf will ich mich beschränken** I want to restrict myself to just this; **ich frage mich ~, warum** I just want to know why; **er tut das mit Absicht, ~ um dich zu provozieren** he does it deliberately, just to provoke you; **nicht ~ ..., sondern auch ...** not only ..., but also ...; **ich tue es nicht nur wegen des Geldes, sondern auch, weil ...** I'm not doing it just for the money, but also because ...; **nicht ~, dass ...** it's not just that ...; **[alles,] ~ das nicht** anything but that; **~ gut, dass ...** it's a good thing that ...; **~ schade, dass ...** it's just a pity that ...; **ich male ~ so zum Spaß** I paint just for fun; **Warum fragst du? — Ach, ~ so** Why do you ask? — Oh, no particular reason; **das hat er ~ so gesagt[, ohne sich dabei etwas zu denken]** he just said it without thinking; **~ dass ...** except that ...; **das weiß ich ~ zu gut** I know that only too well; **das ist ~ zu wahr!** it's only too true!

B *Partikel* 1 (in Wünschen) **wenn das ~ gut geht!** let's [just] hope it goes well; **dass ihm ~ nichts zustößt!** let's [just] hope nothing happens to him; **wenn er ~ käme/hier wäre** if only he would come/he were here

2 (ermunternd, tadelnd) **sag ihm ~ deine Meinung** just tell him what you think; **~ keine Hemmungen!** don't be inhibited!; **Lass ~! Ich schaffe das schon allein** Don't bother! I can do it by myself; **wehr dich ~!** stand up for yourself!; **~ her damit!** hand it over!; **~ weiter!** keep going; **~ zu!** go ahead; **sieh ~, was du gemacht hast!** just look what you've done!

3 (warnend) **lass dich ~ nicht erwischen** just don't let me/him/her/them catch you; **er soll es ~ wagen** just let him try; **glaub ~ nicht, dass ich das nicht merke** don't think I don't notice; **~ vorsichtig/langsam** just be careful/take it easy; **~ Geduld** just be patient; **~ nicht!** don't, for goodness' sake!

4 (fragend) just; **wie soll ich ihm das ~ erklären?** just how am I supposed to explain it to him?; **was sollen wir ~ tun?** what on earth are we going to do?; **was hat er ~?** whatever's the matter with him?; **wie kann ich das ~ wieder gutmachen?** however can I make amends?

5 (verallgemeinernd) just; **er lief, so schnell er ~ konnte** he ran just as fast as he could; **alles, was man sich ~ vorstellen kann** everything one could imagine

6 (sogar) only; just; **davon werden die Schmerzen ~ [noch] schlimmer** that only *or* just makes the pain [even] worse

7 **es wimmelte ~ so von Insekten** it was just teeming with insects; **er schlug auf den Tisch, dass es ~ so krachte** he crashed his fist [down] on the table

C *Konj.* but; **ich kann dir das Buch leihen, ~ nicht heute** I can lend you the book, but *or* only not today; **das Wetter ist schön, ~ noch etwas kalt** the weather is fine, though still somewhat cold

Nur·haus·frau *die* full-time housewife; **sie ist ~:** she is only *or* just a housewife

Nürnberg /ˈnʏrnbɛrk/ *(das);* ~s ▸ℹ **S. 675** Nuremberg

Nürnberger *indekl. Adj.* Nuremberg *attrib.*; **bei ihm hilft nur der ~ Trichter** you really have to drum things into him; *s. auch* **Kölner**

nuschelig /ˈnʊʃəlɪç/

A *Adj.* mumbling

B *adv.* in a mumble

nuscheln /ˈnʊʃl̩n/ *tr., itr. V.* (ugs.) mumble

Nuss, *Nuß /nʊs/ *die;* ~, **Nüsse** /ˈnʏsə/ 1 nut; **eine taube ~** (fig.) a useless article *or* item (coll.); **eine harte ~ [für jmdn.]** (fig.) a hard *or* tough nut [for sb. to crack] 2 (salopp abwertend: Mensch) so-and-so (coll.) 3 (Kochk.: Fleischstück) eye 4 (Technik) socket 5 *in* **jmdm. eins** *od.* **eine auf/vor die ~ geben** (ugs.) belt sb. [one] in the head/face (coll.)

Nuss·baum, *Nuß·baum *der* 1 walnut tree 2 (Holz) walnut

nuss·braun, *nuß·braun *Adj.* nut-brown

Nüsschen, *Nüßchen /ˈnʏsçən/ *das;* ~s, ~: 1 little nut 2 (Kochk.) eye

Nuss-, *Nuß-: ~kern *der* [nut] kernel; **~knacker** *der* nutcrackers *pl.*; **~schale** *die* nutshell; (fig.: Boot) cockleshell; **das Boot wurde wie eine ~schale umhergeworfen** the boat was tossed about like a cork; **~schokolade** *die* nut chocolate

Nüster /ˈnʏstɐ/ *die;* ~, ~**n** nostril

Nut /nuːt/ *die;* ~, ~**en, Nute** /ˈnuːtə/ *die;* ~**e,** ~**en** (Technik) groove

nuten (Technik)

A *tr. V.* groove

B *itr. V.* cut grooves

Nutria[1] /ˈnuːtria/ *die;* ~, ~**s** (Tier) coypu

Nutria[2] *der;* ~**s,** ~**s** (Pelz) nutria [fur]; coypu fur

Nutsche /ˈnuːtʃə/ *die;* ~, ~**n** (Technik) vacuum filter

Nutte /ˈnʊtə/ *die;* ~, ~**n** (derb abwertend) tart (sl.); pro (Brit. coll.); hooker (Amer. sl.)

nutz /nʊts/ (südd., österr.) ▸**nütze**

Nutz *in* **jmdm. zu** *od.* **zu jmds. ~ und Frommen [dienen]** (veralt.) [be] for the benefit of sb.; **zu ~e** ▸**zunutze**

nutz-, Nutz-: ~an·wendung *die* 1 practical application; 2 (praktische Lehre) moral; practical lesson; **~bar** *Adj.* usable; exploitable, utilizable ‹*mineral resources, invention*›; cultivatable ‹*land, soil*›; **etw. praktisch ~bar machen** turn sth. to practical use; **landwirtschaftlich ~bar** usable for agriculture *postpos.*; **die Sonnenenergie ~bar machen** harness solar energy (**für** for)

Nutzbarkeit *die;* ~: usability; (von Bodenschätzen) exploitability; utilizability

Nutzbarmachung /-maxʊŋ/ *die;* ~, ~**en** utilization; (von Bodenschätzen) exploitation; utilization; (von Forschungsergebnissen) application

nutz·bringend

A *Adj.* (nützlich) useful; (gewinnbringend) profitable

B *adv.* profitably; **die Reserven so ~ wie möglich einsetzen** use the reserves to maximum advantage

nütze /ˈnʏtsə/ *in* **zu etw. ~ sein** be good for sth.; **[jmdm.] zu nichts ~ sein** be no use *or* good [to sb.]; **du bist zu gar nichts ~:** you're totally useless; **wozu ist das ~?** what's the good of that?

Nutz·effekt *der* 1 useful effect 2 (Technik) ▸**Wirkungsgrad**

nutzen /ˈnʊtsn̩/

A *tr. V.* 1 use; exploit, utilize ‹*natural resources*›; cultivate ‹*land, soil*›; use, harness ‹*energy source*›; exploit ‹*advantage*›; **eine Fläche landwirtschaftlich ~:** use an area for agriculture; **eine Erfindung industriell ~:** give an invention an industrial application 2 (be~, aus~) use; make use of; **wir müssen das herrliche Wetter ~:** we must take advantage of the marvellous weather; **eine Gelegenheit ~, etw. zu tun** take [advantage of] an opportunity to do sth.; **seine Chance ~:** take one's chance; **~ wir die Zeit!** let's make the most of the time

B *itr. V.* ▸**nützen A**

nützen /ˈnʏtsn̩/

A *itr. V.* be of use (+ *Dat.* to); **nichts ~:** be useless *or* no use; **seine Bitten nützten nichts** his pleas were to no avail *or* were in vain; **jmdm. sehr ~:** be very useful *or* of great use to sb.; **wem soll das ~?** who is supposed to gain from that?; **was hat ihm das genützt?** what good did it do him?; **wozu nützt das alles jetzt noch?** what's the point of all that now?; **es würde nichts/wenig ~:** it wouldn't be any/much use *or* wouldn't do any/much good; **dein Leugnen nützt jetzt auch nichts mehr** and it's no use your denying it any longer; **da nützt alles nichts** there's nothing to be done; **es nützt alles nichts, wir müssen jetzt anfangen** (ugs.) it's no good, we've got to start now

B *tr. V.* ▸**nutzen A**

Nutzen *der;* ~**s** 1 benefit; **der ~ des Kanals für die Schifffahrt** the usefulness *or* benefits *pl.* of the canal to shipping; **die Maßnahme hat großen/wenig/keinen ~:** the measure is very useful/of little/no use; **den ~ [von etw.] haben** benefit *or* gain [from sth.]; **~ aus etw. ziehen** benefit from sth.; exploit sth.; **er hätte dem Land großen ~ gebracht** he would have been of great service to the country; **ich habe das Buch mit großem ~ gelesen** I profited greatly from reading the book; **[jmdm.] von ~ sein** be of use [to sb.] 2 (Profit) profit; **etw. mit ~ verkaufen** sell sth. at a profit

Nutzer *der;* ~**s,** ~ (Amtsspr.) user

Nutz-: ~fahrzeug *das* (Lastwagen, Lieferwagen usw.) commercial vehicle; goods vehicle; (Bus, Straßenbahn usw.) public-service vehicle; **~fläche** *die* 1 (von Gebäuden) usable floor space; 2 (Landw.) **landwirtschaftliche ~flächen** land *sing.* available for agriculture; **~garten** *der* kitchen garden; **~holz** *das* timber; **~land** *das* ▸▸**~fläche 2**; **~last** *die* (Kfz-W.) maximum permitted load; **~leis-**

tung *die* (Technik) effective *or* useful output *or* power

nützlich /ˈnʏt͜slɪç/

A *Adj.* useful; **jmdm. ~ sein** be useful *or* of use to sb.; **kann ich Ihnen ~ sein?** can I do anything for you?; **sich ~ machen** make oneself useful; *s. auch* **angenehm A**

B *adv.* usefully

Nützlichkeit *die;* **~:** usefulness

Nützlichkeits·denken *das* utilitarian thinking

nutzlos

A *Adj.* useless; (vergeblich) futile; vain *attrib.;* in vain *pred.;* **es wäre ~, das zu tun** it would be useless *or* pointless *or* futile doing that; **all sein Flehen war ~:** all his pleading was in vain *or* of no avail

B *adv.* uselessly; (vergeblich) futilely; in vain; **er hat das Geld ~ vergeudet** he squandered the money on useless items

Nutz·losigkeit *die;* **~:** uselessness; (Vergeblichkeit) futility; vainness

nutznießen /-ni:sn̩/ *itr. V.* (geh.) **von etw. ~:** benefit *or* profit from sth.

Nutznießer *der;* **~s, ~, Nutznießerin** *die;* **~, ~nen** **1** beneficiary **2** (Rechtsw.) usufructuary

Nutz·pflanze *die* economically useful plant

Nutz·tier *das* economically useful animal

Nutzung *die;* **~, ~en** use; (des Landes, des Bodens) cultivation; (von Bodenschätzen) exploitation; utilization; (einer Energiequelle) use; harnessing; **die wirtschaftliche/landwirtschaftliche ~ einer Fläche** the use of an area for financial benefit/for agriculture; **jmdm. etw. zur ~ überlassen** give sb. the use of sth.

Nutzungs-: ~gebühr *die* charge [for use]; **die ~ gebühr für die Toiletten** the charge for using the toilets; **~recht** *das* (Rechtsw.) right of use; **das ~recht an etw.** (*Dat.*) the right to use sth.

NVA *Abk.* **= Nationale Volksarmee** (DDR) National People's Army

NW *Abk.* **= Nordwest[en]** ▸**i S. 363** NW

Nylon (Wz) /ˈnailɔn/ *das;* **~s** nylon

Nylon·strumpf *der* nylon stocking

Nymphe /ˈnʏmfə/ *die;* **~, ~n** (Myth., Zool.) nymph

nymphoman /nʏmfoˈma:n/ *Adj.* (Psych.) nymphomaniac; **~ sein** be a nymphomaniac

Nymphomanie *die;* **~** (Psych.) nymphomania *no art.*

Nymphomanin *die;* **~, ~nen** (Psych.) nymphomaniac

nymphomanisch *Adj.* (Psych.) ▸**nymphoman**

n

o, O /oː/ *das;* ~, (ugs.) ~**s**, ~, (ugs.) ~**s** o/O; *s. auch* **a, A**
o /oː/ *Interj.* oh; *s. auch* **oh**
O *Abk.* = **Ost[en]** E
ö, Ö /øː/ *das;* ~, (ugs.) ~**s**, ~, (ugs.) ~**s** o/O umlaut; *s. auch* **a, A**
o.ä. *Abk.* = **oder ähnlich...** or similar...
o.Ä. *Abk.* = **oder Ähnliche[s]**
ÖAMTC *Abk.* = **Österreichischer Automobil-, Motorrad- und Touring Club** Austrian Automobile, Motorcycle, and Touring Club
Oase /oˈaːzə/ *die;* ~, ~**n** (auch fig.) oasis
ob¹ /ɔp/ *Konj.* **1** whether; **ob du ihn anrufst?** would you give him a ring?; **ob wir es schaffen?** will we manage it?; **ob ich doch lieber zu Hause bleibe?** hadn't I better stay at home?; **ob ... oder ...** whether ... or ...; **ob er will oder nicht** whether he wants to or not; **ob arm, ob reich** whether rich or poor **2** (veralt.) *in* **ob ... auch** *od.* **gleich** even though **3** *in* **und ob!** of course!; you bet! (coll.); **Hast du keinen Hunger mehr? — Und ob!** Don't you want any more? — You bet I do! (coll.); *s. auch* **als**
ob² *Präp.* **1** *mit Gen., selten Dativ* (veralt. geh.: wegen) on account of **2** *mit Dativ* (schweiz., veralt.: über) above
o.B. *Abk.* = **ohne Befund**
OB *Abk.* = **Oberbürgermeister[in]**
Obacht /ˈoːbaxt/ *die;* ~ (bes. südd.) caution; ~, **da kommt ein Auto!** watch out! *or* look out! *or* careful!, there's a car coming; ~ **auf jmdn./etw. geben** look after *or* take care of sb./sth.; (aufmerksam sein) pay attention to sb./sth.; ~ **geben, dass ...** take care that ...
ÖBB *Abk.* = **Österreichische Bundesbahnen** Austrian Federal Railways
Obdach /ˈɔpdax/ *das;* ~**[e]s** (geh.) shelter; **kein** ~ **haben** be without shelter
obdach·los *Adj.* homeless; ~ **werden** be made homeless
Obdachlose *der/die; adj. Dekl.* homeless person/man/woman; **die** ~**n** the homeless
Obdachlosen: ~**asyl** *das,* ~**heim** *das* hostel for the homeless; ~**zeitung** *die* magazine sold in aid of the homeless
Obdachlosigkeit *die;* ~: homelessness
Obduktion /ɔpdukˈtsi̯oːn/ *die;* ~, ~**en** (Med., Rechtsw.) post-mortem [examination]; autopsy
Obduktions·befund *der* (Med., Rechtsw.) findings *pl. or* results *pl.* of a/the post-mortem [examination] *or* autopsy
obduzieren /ɔpduˈtsiːrən/
A *tr. V.* carry out *or* perform a/the post-mortem [examination] *or* autopsy on
B *itr. V.* carry out *or* perform a/the post-mortem [examination] *or* autopsy
O-Beine *Pl.* bandy legs; bow legs
o-beinig, O-beinig *Adj.* bandy-legged; bow-legged
Obelisk /obeˈlɪsk/ *der;* ~**en**, ~**en** obelisk
oben /ˈoːbn̩/ *Adv.* **1** (an hoch/höher gelegenem Ort) **hier/dort** ~: up here/there; **[hoch]** ~ **am Himmel** [high] up in the sky; ~ **bleiben** stay up; **weiter** ~: further up; **nach** ~: upwards; **der Weg nach** ~: the way up; **warme Luft steigt nach** ~: warm air rises; **das Auto blieb mit den Rädern nach** ~ **liegen** the car came to rest upside down; ~ **auf dem Dach** up on the roof; **Wo ist er? — Da** ~. Where is he? — Up there; **[im Bett]** ~ **schlafen** sleep in the upper bunk; **von** ~: from above; **von** ~ **herab** (fig.) condescendingly
2 (im Gebäude) upstairs; **du bleibst heute besser** ~ (in der Wohnung) you had better stay at home today; **nach** ~: upstairs; **ich komme gerade von** ~: I have just come down; **der Aufzug fährt nach** ~**/kommt von** ~: the lift (Brit.) *or* (Amer.) elevator is going up/coming down; **hier** ~: up here
3 (am oberen Ende, zum oberen Ende hin) at the top; ~ **im Schrank** at the top of the cupboard; **ein** ~ **offener Zylinder** a cylinder open at the top; **nach** ~ **[hin]** towards the top; **weiter** ~ **[im Tal/am Berg]** further *or* higher up [the valley/mountain]; **von** ~: from the top; ~ **links/rechts** at the top on the left/right; ~ **rechts in der Ecke** in the top right-hand corner; ~ **[rechts] auf der Seite** on the top [right] of the page; ~ **[links/rechts]** (in Bildunterschriften) above [left/right]; **auf Seite 25** ~: at the top of page 25; **die fünfte Zeile von** ~: the fifth line from the top; the fifth line down; ~ **auf dem Bücherschrank** up on top of the bookcase; **der Weisheitszahn** ~ **links** the upper left wisdom tooth; **nach** ~ **kommen** (an die Oberfläche) come up; **Fett schwimmt** ~: fat floats on the top *or* the surface; (fig.) there are always some people who do all right; „~" 'this side up'; **wo** *od.* **was ist [bei dem Bild]** ~: which is the right way up [on the picture]?; which is the top [of the picture]?; **bis** ~ **hin** (ugs.) up to the top; **bis** ~ **hin voll sein** (ugs.) be full to the top; **der Keller steht bis** ~ **hin unter Wasser** (ugs.) the cellar is full up with water; **von** ~ **bis unten** from top to bottom; **er musterte sie von** ~ **bis unten** he looked her up and down; **er ist** ~ **nicht ganz richtig** (ugs.) he's not quite right in the head (coll.) *or* up top (coll.); ~ **ohne** topless; **hier wird** ~ **ohne bedient** there are topless waitresses here; ~ **herum** (im Bereich der Brust) round the top; **es steht mir bis hier** ~ (ugs.) I'm fed up to the back teeth with it (coll.); ~ **an der Tafel** at the head of the table; **er saß weiter** ~ **als ich** (fig.) he sat further up the table than me
4 (an der Oberseite) on top
5 (in einer Hierarchie, Rangfolge) at the top; **weit/ganz** ~: near the top/right at the top; **der Befehl kam von** ~: the order came from above; **etw. nach** ~ **weitergeben** pass sth. on up; **die da** ~ (ugs.) the high-ups (coll.); **der Weg nach** ~: the road to the top; **er wollte nach** ~: he wanted to get to *or* make it to the top; **sich** ~ **halten** stay at the top; **die Band ist jetzt ganz** ~: the group is now riding high [in the charts]
6 ([weiter] vorn im Text) above; ~ **erwähnt** *od.* **genannt** *od.* **stehend** above-mentioned; **von dem Obengenannten ...** of the above-mentioned ...; **das Obenstehende** the above; **der** ~ **[schon] erwähnte Fall** the case [already] referred to above
7 (im Norden) up north; **hier/dort** ~: up here/there [in the north]; ~ **in Dänemark/im Norden** up in Denmark/up [in the] north; **weiter** ~: further up [north]
oben-, Oben-: ~**an** *Adv.* at the top; **diese Frage steht für mich immer** ~**an** this question will always have top priority for me; ~**auf** *Adv.* **1** (zuoberst) on [the] top; **2** (guter Dinge) on top of the world; **3** (gesund) fit and well; ~**drauf** *Adv.* (ugs.) on top; ~**drein** *Adv.* (ugs.) on top of that; ~**drüber** *Adv.* (ugs.) above it/them; (darauf) on it/them; ~**erwähnt**, ~**genannt** ▸**oben 6**; ~**hinaus** *in* ~**hinaus wollen** (ugs.) be aiming at big things; ~**stehend** ▸**oben 6**; ~**stehende** *das; adj. Dekl.* **das** ~**stehende:** the above
ober /ˈoːbɐ/ *Adj.* **1** upper *attrib.*; top *attrib.*; (ganz oben liegend) top *attrib.*; **die** ~**e rechte Ecke** the top right-hand corner; **am** ~**en Ende der Tafel/der Straße** at the top [end] of the table/street; **das Oberste zuunterst kehren** turn everything upside down; **das** ~**ste Stockwerk/die** ~**ste Stufe** the top[most] storey/step **2** (der Quelle näher gelegen) upper **3** (in der Rangfolge o. Ä.) higher ‹*authority*›; upper ‹*[social] class, storey, floor*›; **die** ~**en Klassen der Schule** the senior classes *or* forms of the school; **das** ~**ste Gericht des Landes** the highest court in the land; **der Oberste Sowjet** the Supreme Soviet; **das Oberste Gericht** (DDR) the Supreme Court; *s. auch* **Obere**; **zehntausend**
Ober *der;* ~**s**, ~ **1** waiter; **Herr** ~! waiter! **2** (Spielkarte) ≈ queen
ober-, Ober-: ~**arm** *der* ▸❶ **S. 435** upper arm; ~**arzt** *der,* ~**ärztin** *die* (Vertreter[in] des Chefarztes) assistant medical director; (Leiter[in] einer Spezialabteilung) consultant; ~**aufseher** *der,* ~**aufseherin** *die* senior supervisor; ~**aufsicht** *die* overall supervision; **die** ~**aufsicht über etw.** (*Akk.*) **haben** have overall supervisory responsibility for sth.; ~**bau** *der; Pl.* ~~**ten** **1** (eines Gebäudes) superstructure; **2** (Straßenbau) pavement; **3** (Eisenb.) permanent way; superstructure and roadbed; ~**bauch** *der* ▸❶ **S. 435** (Anat.) upper abdomen; ~**bayern** (*das*) Upper Bavaria; ~**befehl** *der* (Milit.) supreme command *no art.*; **den** ~**befehl über etw.** (*Akk.*) **haben** be in supreme command of sth.; ~**befehlshaber** *der* (Milit.) supreme commander; commander-in-chief; ~**begriff** *der* generic term; ~**bekleidung** *die* outer clothing; ~**bett** *das* duvet (Brit.); continental quilt (Brit.); stuffed quilt (Amer.); ~**bürgermeister** *der* ▸❶ **S. 44** mayor; (von bestimmten englischen/schottischen Großstädten) Lord Mayor/Provost; ~**bürgermeisterin** *die* mayor[ess]; ~**cool** (ugs.) **A** *Adj.* **1** (sehr gelassen) ultra-cool; **2** (fabelhaft) really cool (coll.); **B** *adv.* **1** (sehr gelassen) ‹*appear etc.*› looking ultra-cool; ~**cool tun** play it dead cool (coll.); **2** (fabelhaft) quite fabulously (coll.); ~**deck** *der* upper deck; (eines Busses) upper *or* top deck; ~**deutsch** **A** *Adj.* Upper German; **B** *adv.* **etw.** ~**deutsch aussprechen** pronounce sth. with an Upper German accent
Obere *der; adj. Dekl.* **1** (geh.) **die** ~**n [des Landes]** those in high places [in the country]; **seine** ~**n** his superiors **2** (eines Klosters o. Ä.) superior
ober-, Ober-: ~**faul** *Adj.* (ugs.) very fishy (coll.); ~**feldwebel** *der* (beim Heer) staff sergeant (Brit.); sergeant first class (Amer.); platoon sergeant (Amer.); (bei der Luftwaffe) flight sergeant (Brit.); master sergeant (Amer.); ~**fläche** *die* surface; (Flächeninhalt) surface area; **an die** ~**fläche kommen** come to the surface; surface; **wieder an die** ~**fläche kommen** resurface; **die Diskussion blieb zu sehr an der**

~fläche (fig.) the discussion remained far too superficial; **~flächen·struktur** *die* (auch Sprachw.) surface structure

oberflächlich

A *Adj.* superficial; **eine ~e Düngung des Bodens kann …** top-dressing the soil can …; **eine erste, ~ Berechnung/Schätzung** a first, rough calculation/estimate

B *adv.* superficially; **etw. nur ~ kennen** have only a superficial knowledge of sth.; **etw. ~ lesen** read sth. cursorily; **er arbeitet zu ~:** he is too superficial in the way he works

Oberflächlichkeit *die;* **~:** superficiality

ober-, Ober-: ~förster *der* (veralt.) *senior forestry official;* **~gärig** /-gɛːrɪç/ *Adj.* top-fermented ‹*beer*›; top-fermenting ‹*yeast*›; **~gefreite** *der* (beim Heer) lance corporal (Brit.); private first class (Amer.); (bei der Luftwaffe) leading aircraftman (Brit.); airman first class (Amer.); (bei der Marine) able rating (Brit.); seaman (Amer.); **~geschoss, *~geschoß** *das* upper storey; **das Haus hat zwei ~geschosse** the house has three storeys; **er wohnt im fünften ~geschoss** he lives on the fifth floor (Brit.) *or* (Amer.) the sixth floor; **~grenze** *die* upper limit

ober·halb

A *Adv.* above; **weiter ~:** further up; **~ von** above

B *Präp. mit Gen.* above

Ober-: ~hand *die:* in **die ~hand [über jmdn./etw.] haben** have the upper hand [over sb./sth.]; **die ~hand [über jmdn./etw.] gewinnen/bekommen** gain *or* get the upper hand [over sb./sth.]; **~haupt** *das* head; (einer Verschwörung) leader; **~haus** *das* (Parl.) upper house *or* chamber; (in Großbritannien) House of Lords; Upper House; **~hemd** *das* shirt; **~herrschaft** *die* sovereignty; supreme power; **~hirte** *der* (geh.) spiritual leader *or* head; **~hoheit** *die* sovereignty; supreme power

Oberin *die;* **~, ~nen** **1** (christliche Kirche) Mother Superior **2** ▸ **Oberschwester**

ober-, Ober-: ~inspektor *der,* **~inspektorin** *die* senior inspector; (bei der Polizei) detective chief inspector; **~irdisch** **A** *Adj.* surface *attrib.* ‹*pipes, cables*›; ‹*pipes, cables*› laid above ground; **~irdische Lagerung** above-ground storage; storage above ground; **~irdische Pflanzenteile** parts of a/the plant above the ground; **B** *adv.* **die U-Bahn fährt hier ~irdisch** the underground [system] runs above ground here; **~italien** (*das*) Northern Italy; **~kante** *die* top edge; **es steht mir bis ~kante Unterlippe** (salopp) I'm sick to death of it (coll.); **~kellner** *der* head waiter; **~kiefer** *der* upper jaw; **~kirchenrat** *der* **1** (Gremium) *highest administrative body of some evangelical Land churches;* **2** (Person) *member of an Oberkirchenrat a;* **~kirchenrätin** *die* ▸ **~kirchenrat 2;** **~klasse** *die* **1** (Soziol.) upper class; **2** (Schulw.) senior class *or* form; **3** (bei Autos) luxury class; **ein Wagen der ~klasse** a large luxury car; **~kommandierende** *der; adj. Dekl.* (Milit.) supreme commander; commander-in-chief; **~kommando** *das* supreme command (**über** + *Akk.* of); **jmds. ~kommando** (*Dat.*) **unterstehen** be under the supreme command of sb.; **~körper** *der* upper part of the body; **mit nacktem ~körper** stripped to the waist; **den ~körper frei machen** strip to the waist; **~land** *das* uplands *pl.;* **das Berner ~land** the Bernese Oberland; **~landes·gericht** *das* Higher Regional Court; ≈ *high court and court of appeal of a Land;* **~länge** *die* ascender; **~lastig** *Adj.* (Seemannsspr.) top-heavy; **~lauf** *der* ▸ ❶ **S. 267** upper reaches *pl.;* **~leder** *das* [leather] upper; **~lehrer** *der* (fig.) schoolmaster; **~lehrerhaft** *Adj.* (abwertend) schoolmasterish; **~lehrerin** *die* (fig.) schoolmistress; **~leitung** *die* **1** (elektrische Leitung) overhead cable; **2** (Kontrolle) overall control; **~leitungs·bus** *der* trolley bus (Brit.); **~leutnant** *der* ▸ ❶ **S. 44** (beim Heer) lieutenant (Brit.); first lieutenant (Amer.); (bei der Luftwaffe) flying officer (Brit.); first lieutenant (Amer.); **~leutnant zur See** sub lieutenant (Brit.); lieutenant junior grade (Amer.); **~licht** *das; Pl.* **~~er** **1** light from above; **2** (Deckenlampe) ceiling light; overhead light; **3** high window; (über einer Tür) fanlight; (Klappfenster) transom; **~lid** *das* upper [eye] lid; **~liga** *die* (Sport) **1** second division; **2** (DDR) first division; **~lippe** *die* ▸ ❶ **S. 435** upper lip; **~lippenbart** *der* moustache; **~maat** *der* (Marine) petty officer; **~material** *das:* **„~material Leder"** 'leather uppers'; **~österreich** (*das*) Upper Austria; **~post·direktion** *die: regional postal administration;* **~prima** *die* (Schulw. veralt.) top form (*of a Gymnasium*); ≈ upper sixth [form] (Brit.); **~primaner** *der,* **~primanerin** *die* (Schulw. veralt.) pupil in the top form (*of a Gymnasium*); **~regierungsrat** *der,* **~regierungsrätin** *die: senior civil servant;* **~rheinisch** *Adj.* in the Upper Rhine valley *postpos.;* **Oberrheinische Tiefebene** Upper Rhine valley

Obers /ˈoːbɐs/ *das;* **~** (österr.) ▸ **Sahne**

Ober-: ~schenkel *der* ▸ ❶ **S. 435** thigh; **~schenkel·hals·bruch** *der* ▸ ❶ **S. 439** (Med.) fracture of the neck of the femur; **~schicht** *die* (Soziol.) upper class; **der ~schicht angehören** be a member of the upper classes *pl.;* **~schlesien** (*das*) Upper Silesia; **~schule** *die* **1** secondary school; **2** (DDR) unified comprehensive school; **[allgemeinbildende] polytechnische ~schule** *unified comprehensive school for children aged 7-17;* **erweiterte ~schule** *unified comprehensive school providing a further two years' preparation for university entrance qualification;* **~schulrat** *der,* **~schulrätin** *die* local education officer; **~schwester** *die* senior nursing officer; (Stationsschwester) ward sister; matron; **~seite** *die* top[side]; upper side; (eines Stoffes) right side; **~sekunda** *die* (Schulw. veralt.) seventh year (*of a Gymnasium*); **~sekundaner** *der,* **~sekundanerin** *die* (Schulw. veralt.) pupil in the seventh year (*of a Gymnasium*); **~seminar** *das* (Hochschulw.) graduate class

Oberst *der;* **~en** *od.* **~s, ~en** *od.* **~e** ▸ ❶ **S. 44** (beim Heer) colonel; (bei der Luftwaffe) group captain (Brit.); colonel (Amer.)

oberst… ▸ **ober…**

Ober-: ~staatsanwalt *der,* **~staatsanwältin** *die* ▸ ❶ **S. 44** (*senior public prosecutor at a regional court*); **~stadt** *die* upper part of the town; upper town; **~stadtdirektor** *der,* **~stadtdirektorin** *die* chief executive [of a/the town council]; **~steiger** *der* (Bergbau) undermanager; **~stimme** *die* (Musik) treble; (Sopran) soprano; (Diskant) descant

Oberst·leutnant *der* ▸ ❶ **S. 44** (beim Heer) lieutenant colonel; (bei der Luftwaffe) wing commander; lieutenant colonel (Amer.)

Ober-: ~stübchen *das* ▸ **richtig A 2;** **~studiendirektor** *der* ▸ ❶ **S. 44** headmaster (Brit.); principal; **~studiendirektorin** *die* ▸ ❶ **S. 44** headmistress (Brit.); principal; **~studienrat** *der,* **~studienrätin** *die* ▸ ❶ **S. 44** senior teacher; **~stufe** *die* (Schulw.) upper school; **~teil** *das od. der* top [part]; (eines Bikinis, Anzugs, Kleids usw.) top [half]; **~tertia** *die* (Schulw. veralt.) fifth year (*of a Gymnasium*); **~tertianer** *der,* **~tertianerin** *die* (Schulw. veralt.) pupil in the fifth year (*of a Gymnasium*); **~ton** *der; Pl.* **~töne** (Musik, Physik) overtone; **~wasser** *das* headwater; (fig.) **~wasser haben** feel in a strong position; **~wasser bekommen/kriegen** have one's hand strengthened; **~weite** *die* bust measurement; **sie hat ~weite 91** she has a 36-inch bust; **eine beachtliche ~weite haben** (ugs.) be well-endowed (joc.)

Ob·frau *die* ▸ **Obmännin**

ob·gleich *Konj.* ▸ **obwohl**

Ob·hut *die;* **~** (geh.) care; **jmdn./etw. in seine ~ nehmen** take sb./sth. into one's care; **jmdn./etw. jmds. ~** (*Dat.*) **anvertrauen** entrust sb./sth. to sb.'s care; **unter jmds. ~** (*Dat.*) **stehen** be in sb.'s care

obig /ˈoːbɪç/ *Adj.* above; **die ~e Tabelle** the above table; the table above

Objekt /ɔpˈjɛkt/ *das;* **~s, ~e** **1** (auch Sprachw., Kunstwiss.) object; (Fot., bei einem Experiment) subject **2** (Kaufmannsspr.: Immobilie) property **3** (bes. DDR: Projekt) project **4** (österr. Amtsspr.: Gebäude) building **5** (DDR: staatliche Einrichtung) (Fabrik) factory; (Gaststätte, Verkaufsstelle) establishment

objektiv /ɔpjɛkˈtiːf/

A *Adj.* objective; real, actual ‹*cause, danger*›

B *adv.* objectively; **er hat uns ~ geschadet** he did in fact do us harm

Objektiv *das;* **~s, ~e** **1** (Optik) objective **2** (Fot.) lens

objektivieren *tr. V.* objectify; objectivize

Objektivismus *der;* **~** (Philos.) objectivism *no def. art.*

Objektivität /ɔpjɛktiviˈtɛːt/ *die;* **~:** objectivity

Objekt-: ~satz *der* (Sprachw.) object clause; **~schutz** *der* (Amtsspr.) protection of property; **für etw. ~schutz beantragen** apply to have sth. protected; **~träger** *der* (Optik) [specimen] slide

Oblate /oˈblaːtə/ *die;* **~, ~n** wafer

Ob·leute *Pl.* ▸ **Obmann**

ob|liegen, ob·liegen *unr. itr. V.* (geh.) **etw. liegt jmdm. ob** *od.* **obliegt jmdm.** sth. is sb.'s responsibility

Obliegenheit *die;* **~, ~en** (geh.) duty; **seine dienstlichen ~en erfüllen** carry out one's duties; **zu jmds. ~en gehören** be one of sb.'s duties

obligat /obliˈgaːt/ *Adj.* **1** (geh.) ▸ **obligatorisch A 1** **2** (iron.: unvermeidlich) obligatory **3** (Musik) obbligato

Obligation /obligaˈtsi̯oːn/ *die;* **~, ~en** (Wirtsch.) bond; debenture

obligatorisch /obligaˈtoːrɪʃ/

A *Adj.* **1** obligatory; compulsory ‹*subject, lecture, etc.*›; necessary ‹*qualification*› **2** ▸ **obligat 2**

B *adv.* obligatorily; compulsorily

Obligatorium /obligaˈtoːri̯ʊm/ *das;* **~s, Obligatorien** (schweiz.) (Verpflichtung) compulsory duty; (Beitrag) compulsory contribution

Obligo /ˈoːbligo/ *das;* **~s, ~s** (Wirtsch.) liability; **ohne ~:** without recourse

Ob·mann *der;* **~[e]s, Obmänner** *od.* **Obleute, Obmännin** /ˈɔpmɛnɪn/ *die;* **~, ~nen** (bes. österr.) chairman; (einer Delegation) head; (einer Gruppe) representative

Oboe /oˈboːə/ *die;* **~, ~en** oboe

Oboist /oboˈɪst/ *der;* **~en, ~en, Oboistin** *die;* **~, ~nen** ▸ ❶ **S. 113** oboist; oboe player

Obolus /ˈoːbolʊs/ *der;* **~, ~** *od.* **~se** (geh. scherzh.) small sum; (Spende) small contribution

Obrigkeit /ˈoːbrɪçkai̯t/ *die;* **~, ~en** authorities *pl.*

obrigkeitlich *Adj.* **1** official ‹*decree, approval, etc.*› **2** (autoritär) authoritarian

obrigkeits-, Obrigkeits-: ~denken *das* (abwertend) attitude of obedience to authority; **~hörig** **A** *Adj.* subservient [to authority *pred.*]; **B** *adv.* subserviently; **~staat** *der* authoritarian state

Obrist /oˈbrɪst/ *der;* **~en, ~en** (veralt., noch abwertend) colonel

ob·schon *Konj.* (geh.) although; though

Observanz /ɔpzɛrˈvants/ *die;* **~, ~en** **1** kind; type **2** (Rel.) observance

Observation /ɔpzɛrvaˈtsi̯oːn/ *die;* **~, ~en** **1** (Überwachung) surveillance *no pl.;* **~en** surveillance operations **2** (wissenschaftlich) observation

Observatorium /ɔpzɛrvaˈtoːri̯ʊm/ *das;* **~s, Observatorien** observatory

observieren *tr. V.* **1** **jmdn./etw. ~:** keep sb./sth. under surveillance **2** (wissenschaftlich) observe; **einen Patienten ~:** keep a patient under observation

Obsession /ɔpzɛˈsi̯oːn/ *die;* **~, ~en** (Psych., geh.) obsession

obsessiv /ɔpzɛˈsiːf/ (Psych.)

A *Adj.* obsessive

B *adv.* obsessively

ob·siegen, *auch:* **ob|siegen** *itr. V.* (geh. veralt.) be victorious

obskur /ɔps'ku:ɐ/ *Adj.* (geh.) **1** (unbekannt, unklar) obscure **2** (dubios) dubious

Obskurantismus /ɔpskuran'tɪsmʊs/ *der;* ~ (geh.) obscurantism

obsolet /ɔpzo'le:t/ *Adj.* (geh.) obsolete

Obst /o:pst/ *das;* **~[e]s** fruit

Obst-: **~anbau** *der*, **~bau** *der* fruit-growing; **~anbau betreiben** grow fruit; **~baum** *der* fruit tree; **~garten** *der* orchard; **~händler** *der*, **~händlerin** *die* ▸ℹ **S. 113** fruiterer

obstinat /ɔpsti'na:t/ (geh.)
A *Adj.* obstinate
B *adv.* obstinately

Obst·kuchen *der* fruit flan

Obstler /'o:pstlɐ/ *der;* **~s**, ~ (bes. südd.) fruit brandy

Obst·messer *das* fruit knife

Obstruktion /ɔpstrʊk'tsio:n/ *die;* **~**, **~en** (auch Parl., Med.) obstruction; (Pol.: durch Dauerreden) filibustering

Obstruktions·politik *die* (Parl.) policy of obstruction; (durch Dauerreden) filibustering policy

Obst-: **~saft** *der* fruit juice; **~salat** *der* fruit salad; **~tag** *der* day for eating only fruit; **~torte** *die* fruit flan; **~wasser** *das; Pl.* **~wässer** fruit brandy; **~wein** *der* fruit wine

obszön /ɔps'tsø:n/
A *Adj.* obscene
B *adv.* obscenely

Obszönität /ɔpstsøni'tɛ:t/ *die;* **~**, **~en** obscenity

O·bus *der* trolley bus (Brit.)

ob|walten, **ob·walten** *itr. V.* (geh. veralt.) prevail

ob·wohl
A *Konj.* although; though
B *Adv.* (ugs.) although

ob·zwar *Konj.* (geh.) **~ [dass]** although

Occasion (österr., schweiz.) ▸**Okkasion**

och /ɔx/ *Interj.* (ugs.) oh

Ochs /ɔks/ *der;* **~en**, **~en** (südd., österr., schweiz., ugs.), **Ochse** /'ɔksə/ *der;* **~en**, **~en** **1** ox; bullock; **~ am Spieß** roast ox; **du sollst dem ~en, der da drischt, nicht das Maul verbinden** you shouldn't be too strict with those who have to work hard; *s. auch* **dastehen 1** **2** (salopp) numskull (coll.); **ich ~!** what a numskull I am!

ochsen *tr., itr. V.* ▸**büffeln**

Ochsen-: **~brust** *die* (Kochk.) brisket of beef; **~frosch** *der* bullfrog; **~gespann** *das* **1** team *or* span of oxen; **2** (Wagen) ox cart; **~maul·salat** *der* (Kochk.) ox-cheek salad; **~schwanz·suppe** *die* (Kochk.) oxtail soup; **~tour** *die* (ugs. scherzh.) **1** long, hard climb; **2** (Schinderei) hard slog; **~ziemer** *der* [bull's] pizzle; **~zunge** *die* (Kochk.) ox-tongue

Öchsle·grad *der* degree Öchsle

ocker /'ɔkɐ/ *indekl. Adj.* ochre

Ocker *das;* **~s**, **~:** ochre

ocker-: **~braun** *Adj.* ochre-brown; **~gelb** *Adj.* ochre-yellow

od. *Abk.* **= oder**

öd /ø:t/ (geh.) ▸**öde**

öde /'ø:də/ *Adj.* **1** (verlassen) deserted ‹*beach, village, house, street, etc.*›; (unbewohnt) desolate ‹*area, landscape*› **2** (unfruchtbar) barren **3** (langweilig) tedious; dreary; dreary ‹*life, time*›; barren, tedious, dreary ‹*existence*›

Öde *die;* **~**, **~n** **1** ▸**öde 1-3**: desertedness; desolateness; barrenness **2** (öde Gegend) wasteland; waste **3** (Langeweile) tediousness; dreariness

Ode /'o:də/ *die;* **~**, **~n** ode (**an** + *Akk.* to, **auf** + *Akk.* on)

Ödem /ø'de:m/ *das;* **~s**, **~e** ▸ℹ **S. 439** (Med.) oedema

Odem /'o:dəm/ *der;* **~s** (dichter. veralt.) breath

oder /'o:dɐ/ *Konj.* **1** or; **~ auch** or; **~ aber** or else; *s. auch* **entweder** **2** (in Fragen) **du kommst doch mit, ~?** you will come, won't you?; **er ist doch hier, ~?** he is here, isn't he? (zweifelnd) he is here — or isn't he?; **das ist doch erlaubt, ~ [nicht** *od.* **etwa nicht]?** that is allowed, isn't it?; **das ist doch nicht erlaubt, ~ [doch** *od.* **etwa doch]?** that isn't allowed, is it?; **das hört sich gut an, ~?** it sounds good, don't you think *or* agree?

Odermennig /'o:dɐmɛnɪç/ *der;* **~[e]s**, **~e** (Bot.) agrimony

Oder-Neiße-[Friedens]grenze (DDR), **Oder-Neiße-Linie** *die* Oder-Neisse Line

Ödipus·komplex /'ø:dipʊs-/ *der* (Psych.) Oedipus complex

Odium /'o:diʊm/ *das;* **~s** (geh.) odium

Öd·land *das* uncultivated land (*and land exploited for raw materials, e. g. gravel pits*); **Ödländer** uncultivated land *sing. or* areas

Ödnis *die;* ~ (geh.) ▸**Öde**

Odyssee /ody'se:/ *die;* **~**, **~n** odyssey; **Homers ~:** Homer's Odyssey

Odysseus /o'dysɔʏs/ *(der);* **~:** Odysseus

OECD /o:|e:tse:'de:/ *Abk.* **= Organization for Economic Cooperation and Development** OECD

Œuvre /'ø:vrə/ *das;* **~**, **~s** (geh.) oeuvre

OEZ *Abk.* **= osteuropäische Zeit** EET

Öfchen /'ø:fçən/ *das;* **~s**, **~:** small stove *etc.;* ▸**Ofen 1-4**

Ofen /'o:fn̩/ *der;* **~s**, **Öfen** **1** heater; (Kohle~) stove; (Öl~, Petroleum~) stove; heater; (elektrischer ~) heater; fire; **wenn sie uns erwischen, ist der ~ aus** (ugs.) if they catch us, it's all over; **jetzt ist bei mir der ~ aus** (ugs.: jetzt habe ich aber genug) that does it! **2** (Back~) oven **3** (Industrie~) furnace; (Brenn~, Trocken~) kiln **4** (landsch.: Herd) cooker **5** *in* **heißer ~** (salopp) fast set of wheels (coll.)

ofen-, Ofen-: **~bank** *die; Pl.* **~bänke** bench round a/the stove; **~frisch** *Adj.* oven-fresh; freshly baked; **~heizung** *die* heating *no art.* by stoves; **das Haus hat ~heizung** the house is heated by stoves; **~klappe** *die* **1** damper; **2** (~tür) stove door; **~rohr** *das* [stove] flue; **~schirm** *der* fire screen; **~setzer** *der*, **~setzerin** *die* (der/die Öfen baut) stove builder; (der/die Öfen instand setzt) stove fitter; **~warm** *Adj.* oven-hot

Off *das;* **~s** (Film) **aus dem ~:** from off camera

offen /'ɔfn̩/
A *Adj.* **1** open; **mit ~em Mund/~en Augen** with one's mouth/eyes open; **der Knopf/Schlitz/Schuh ist ~:** the button is/one's flies/shoelaces are undone; **ein ~es Hemd** a shirt with the collar unfastened; **sie trägt ihr Haar ~:** she wears her hair loose; **ein ~es Haus führen** *od.* **haben** keep open house; **eine ~e Anstalt** an open prison; **~ bleiben** remain *or* stay open; **etw. ~ halten/lassen** keep/have sth. open; **~ stehen** be open; **der Mund stand ihm vor Staunen ~:** his mouth hung open in astonishment; **~ haben** *od.* **sein** be open; **ein ~er Umschlag** an unsealed envelope; **ein ~er Brief** an open letter; **Tag der ~en Tür** open day; **~e Beine** ulcerated legs; **die Tür ist ~** (nicht abgeschlossen) the door is unlocked; **mit ~en Karten spielen** play with the cards face up on the table; (fig.) put one's cards on the table; **~es Licht/Feuer** a naked light/an open fire; **eine ~e Bauweise** an open layout; **das ~e Meer, die ~e See** the open sea; **~es Gelände** open terrain; **die Jagd ist ~:** it's open season; **Beifall auf ~er Szene** spontaneous applause; **unter ~em Himmel** in the open; **~e Türen einrennen** (fig.) fight a battle that's/battles that are already won; **bei ihm rennst du ~e Türen ein** (fig.) you're preaching to the converted with him; **mit ~en Augen** *od.* **Sinnen durch die Welt** *od.* **durchs Leben gehen** go about/go through life with one's eyes open; **mit ~en Augen in sein Verderben/Unglück rennen** be heading for disaster with one's eyes open; **ein ~es Geheimnis** an open secret; **für neue Ideen** *od.* **gegenüber neuen Ideen ~ sein** be receptive *or* open to new ideas; **etw. ~ legen** reveal sth.; (bekannt geben) disclose sth.; **jmdm. ~ stehen** be open to sb.; **es steht dir ~ teilzunehmen** you are free to attend; *s. auch* **Arm 1**; **Handelsgesellschaft**; **Karte 7**; **Ohr 2**; **Straße 1**; **Strecke 2**; **Visier 1**
2 (lose) loose ‹*sugar, flour, oats, etc.*›; **~er Wein** wine on tap *or* draught; **ein Glas von dem ~en Rotwein** a glass of the draught red wine
3 (frei) vacant ‹*job, post*›; **~e Stellen** vacancies; (als Rubrik) 'Situations Vacant'; **lassen Sie die Zeile ~:** leave the line blank
4 (ungewiss, ungeklärt) open, unsettled ‹*question*›; uncertain ‹*result*›; **~ bleiben** remain open; ‹*decision*› be left open **~ lassen, ob ...:** leave it open whether ...; **der Ausgang des Spiels ist noch völlig ~:** the result of the match is still wide open; **wann es stattfindet, ist immer noch ~:** it's not yet been decided when it will take place
5 (noch nicht bezahlt) outstanding ‹*bill*›; **der ~e Betrag** the amount outstanding; **~ stehen** be outstanding; **~ stehende Rechnungen** outstanding bills
6 (freimütig, aufrichtig) frank [and open] ‹*person*›; frank, candid ‹*look, opinion, reply*›; open, frank ‹*confession, manner*›; frank ‹*talk*›; honest ‹*character, face*›; **~ zu jmdm. sein** be open *or* frank with sb.
7 (unverhohlen) open ‹*threat, mutiny, hostility, opponent, etc.*›; **in ~em Kampf** in an open fight
8 (Sprachw.) open ‹*vowel, syllable*›
B *adv.* **1** (frei zugänglich, sichtbar, unverhohlen) openly; *s. auch* **zutage**
2 (freimütig, aufrichtig) openly; frankly; **~ gesagt** frankly; to be frank *or* honest; **~ gestanden** to tell you the truth; **darf ich ~ reden?** can I be frank?; can I speak frankly?
3 (Sprachw.); **das e ~ aussprechen** pronounce 'e' as an open vowel

offen·bar
A *Adj.* obvious; **seine Absicht war allen ~:** his intention was obvious *or* apparent to all
B *adv.* **1** (offensichtlich) obviously; clearly **2** (anscheinend) evidently

offenbaren (geh.)
A *tr. V.* reveal
B *refl. V.* **1** (sich erweisen) **sich als etw. ~** ‹*person*› show *or* reveal oneself to be sth.; **seine Worte offenbarten sich als Lüge** his words were revealed as a lie *or* to be a lie **2** (sich mitteilen) **sich jmdm. ~:** confide in sb.

Offenbarung *die;* **~**, **~en** **1** revelation **2** (Rel.) revelation; **die ~ [des Johannes]** [the Book of] Revelations

Offenbarungs·eid *der* (Rechtsw.) oath of disclosure

offen-: ***~|bleiben** ▸**offen A 1, 4**; ***~|halten** ▸**offen A 1**

Offen·heit *die;* ~ ▸**offen 6**: frankness [and openness]; candidness; candour; openness; honesty; **~ gegenüber den Problemen anderer zeigen** be responsive to other people's problems

offen-, Offen-: **~herzig** **A** *Adj.* **1** frank, candid ‹*conversation, remark*›; frank and open ‹*person*›; **2** (iron.: dekolletiert) revealing, low-cut ‹*dress*›; **B** *adv.* frankly; openly; **~herzigkeit** *die;* **~~:** frankness; candidness; candour; **~kundig** **A** *Adj.* obvious, evident (**für** to); obvious, patent, manifest ‹*lie, betrayal, misuse*›; **~kundig werden** become apparent; **B** *adv.* obviously; clearly; ***~|lassen** ▸**offen A 1, 4**; ***~|legen** ▸**offenA 1**; **~sichtlich** **A** *Adj.* obvious; evident; **B** *adv.* obviously; evidently; (anscheinend) evidently

offensiv /ɔfən'zi:f/
A *Adj.* **1** offensive; aggressive ‹*marketing strategy*› **2** (Sport) attacking
B *adv.* **1** offensively; ‹*speak, argue, behave*› aggressively **2** (Sport) **~ spielen** play an attacking game

Offensive *die;* **~**, **~n** (auch Sport) offensive; **in der ~:** on the offensive; **die ~ ergreifen, in die ~ gehen** go on to the offensive

Offensiv-: **~krieg** *der* offensive war; **~spiel** *das* (Sport) attacking game

***offen|stehen** ▸**offen A 1, 5**

öffentlich /'œfn̩tlɪç/
A *Adj.* public; state *attrib.*, [state-]maintained

‹school›; **alle Teilnehmer am ~en Straßenverkehr** all road users; **etw. in ~er Sitzung beraten** debate sth. in open session; **die ~e Ordnung/Sicherheit** public order/security; **Erregung ~en Ärgernisses** (Rechtsw.) creating a public nuisance; **~es Ärgernis erregen** create a public nuisance; **die ~e Meinung** public opinion; **das ~e Recht** (Rechtsw.) public law; **Anstalt des ~en Rechts** institution incorporated under public law; **Körperschaft des ~en Rechts** public corporation; **der ~e Dienst** the civil service; **die Ausgaben der ~en Hand** public spending *sing.*; **von der ~en Hand finanziert** financed out of public funds; **die ~en Hände** local authorities and the state; **ein ~es Haus** (veralt. verhüll.) a house of ill repute; **ein ~es Geheimnis** an open secret; **eine Persönlichkeit des ~en Lebens** a public figure

B *adv.* **1** publicly; ‹*perform, appear*› in public; **~ tagen** meet in open session; **~ auftreten** appear in public; **etw. ~ versteigern** sell sth. by public auction **2** (vom Staat usw.) publicly ‹*funded etc.*›

Öffentlichkeit *die;* ~ **1** public; **unter Ausschluss der ~:** in private *or* secret; (Rechtsw.) in camera; **etw. an die ~ bringen** bring sth. to public attention; make sth. public; **mit etw. an die ~ gehen** make sth. public; **vor die ~ treten** appear in public; **in aller ~:** [quite openly] in public; *s. auch* **Flucht**[1] **2** **2** (das Öffentlichsein) **das Prinzip der ~ in der Rechtsprechung** the principle that justice be administered in open court; **die ~ einer Versammlung herstellen** throw a meeting open to the public

Öffentlichkeits·arbeit *die* public relations work *no art.*

öffentlichkeits·wirksam

A *Adj.* effective ‹*presentation, campaign, etc.*› in PR terms

B *adv.* effectively in PR terms

öffentlich-rechtlich *Adj.* under public law *postpos., not pred.*; **~es Fernsehen** state-owned television; **~e Körperschaften** bodies incorporated under public law

offerieren /ɔfəˈriːrən/ *tr. V.* (bes. Kaufmannsspr.) offer

Offerte /ɔˈfɛrtə/ *die;* **~, ~n** (Kaufmannsspr.) offer

Offizial·verteidiger /ɔfiˈtsi̯aːl-/ *der,* **Offizial·verteidigerin** *die* (Rechtsw.) ▸ **Pflichtverteidiger**

offiziell /ɔfiˈtsi̯ɛl/

A *Adj.* **1** official **2** (förmlich) formal

B *adv.* **1** officially **2** (förmlich) **bei der Feier ging es furchtbar ~ zu** the celebration was terribly formal

Offizier /ɔfiˈtsiːɐ̯/ *der;* **~s, ~e** **1** ▸ⓘ **S. 113** officer; **~ werden** become an officer; gain a commission **2** (Schach) piece (*other than a pawn*)

Offizierin *die;* **~, ~nen** ▸ⓘ **S. 113** ▸ **Offizier 1**

Offiziers-: ~an·wärter *der,* **~an·wärterin** *die* officer cadet; **~kasino** *das* officers' mess; **~korps** *das* officer corps; **~lauf·bahn** *die* officer's career; **~messe** *die* (Seemannsspr.) wardroom; **~rang** *der* officer's rank

Offizin /ɔfiˈtsiːn/ *die;* **~, ~en** **1** (Pharm.) dispensary **2** (veralt.: Apotheke) chemist's [shop] (Brit.); drugstore (Amer.) **3** (veralt.: Druckerei) printing works *sing. or pl.*

offiziös /ɔfiˈtsi̯øːs/

A *Adj.* semi-official

B *adv.* semi-officially; **wie ~ verlautet wurde** according to semi-official sources

Offizium /ɔˈfiːtsi̯ʊm/ *das;* **~s, Offizien** (kath. Kirche) **1** ▸ **Chorgebet** **2** (hist.) **das Heilige ~:** the Holy Office

offline /ˈɔflai̯n/ *Adv.* (DV) offline

öffnen /ˈœfnən/

A *tr.* (*auch itr.*) *V.* open; turn on ‹*tap*›; undo ‹*coat, blouse, button, zip*›; **die Grenzen ~:** open [up] the borders; **die Bank ist** *od.* **hat über Mittag geöffnet** the bank is open at lunchtime; **der Zoo wird um 9 Uhr geöffnet** the zoo opens at 9 a.m.; **sich** (*Dat.*) **die Pulsadern ~:** slash one's wrists; **„hier ~"** 'open here'; **jmdm. den Blick für etw. ~:** open sb.'s eyes to sth.; **mit geöffnetem Mund atmen** breathe with one's mouth open *or* through one's mouth; **eine Leiche ~:** carry out a postmortem *or* an autopsy on a body; *s. auch* **Auge**

B *itr. V.* **1** **[jmdm.] ~:** open the door [to sb.]; **wenn es klingelt, musst du ~:** if there's a ring at the door, you must go and answer it **2** (geöffnet werden) ‹*shop, bank, etc.*› open **3** (sich ~) ‹*door*› open

C *refl. V.* **1** open; **die Erde öffnete sich** the ground opened up **2** (sich erweitern) ‹*valley, lane, forest, etc.*› open out (**auf** + *Akk.*, **zu** on to); ‹*view*› open up **3** (sich aufschließen) **sich einer Sache** (*Dat.*) **~:** become receptive to sth. **4** (sich ergeben) ‹*opportunity etc.*› open up **5** (seine Verschlossenheit aufgeben) open up (+ *Dat.* to) **6** (offen sein) ‹*plain, clearing, etc.*› open up; **sich nach Süden/Norden ~** ‹*room etc.*› be open to the south/north

Öffner *der;* **~s, ~:** opener

Öffnung *die;* **~, ~en** **1** (offene Stelle) opening; (Fot., Optik) aperture **2** (das Öffnen) opening; **die ~ der Grenzen** the opening [up] of the borders; **eine ~ der Leiche** a post-mortem on the body **3** (das Aufgeschlossensein) openness (**für** to); **eine ~ nach links anstreben** (Pol.) strive to open the party up to left-wing ideas

Öffnungs·zeiten *Pl.* (eines Geschäfts, einer Bank) opening times; hours of business; (eines Museums, Zoos usw.) opening times

Offset·druck /ˈɔfsɛt-/ *der; Pl.* **~e** **1** offset printing **2** (Produkt) offset print

Off·sprecher *der,* **Off·sprecherin** *die* (Film) off-screen narrator

Off·stimme *die* (Film) off-screen voice

o-förmig, O-förmig *Adj.* circular

oft /ɔft/ *Adv.* **öfter** /ˈœftɐ/; (selten) **öftest** /ˈœftəst/ often; **wie oft fährt der Bus?** how often does the bus go *or* run?; **wie ~ soll ich dir noch sagen, dass ...?** how many [more] times do I have to tell you that ...?

öfter /ˈœftɐ/ *Adv.* now and then; [every] once in a while; **des Öfteren** (geh.) on many occasions

öfters /ˈœftɐs/ *Adv.* (österr. ugs.) ▸ **öfter**

oftmals *Adv.* often; frequently

o.g. *Abk.* = **oben genannt**

o.G. *Abk.* = **ohne Gewähr**

OG *Abk.* = **Obergeschoss**

ÖGB *Abk.* = **Österreichischer Gewerkschaftsbund** Austrian Trade Union Federation

ogottogott /ˈoɡɔtoɡɔt/ *Interj.* goodness me; oh dear, oh dear

oh /oː/ *Interj.* oh

Oheim /ˈoːhai̯m/ *der;* **~s, ~e** (veralt.) uncle

OHG *Abk.* = **Offene Handelsgesellschaft** general partnership

Ohm /oːm/ *das;* **~[s], ~** (Physik) ohm

ohmsch /oːmʃ/ *Adj.* (Physik) **das ~e Gesetz** Ohm's Law; **der ~e Widerstand** ohmic resistance

ohne /ˈoːnə/

A *Präp. mit Akk.* **1** without; **~ mich!** [you can] count me out!; **der Versuch blieb ~ Erfolg** the attempt was unsuccessful; **sie ist ~ Jacke gekommen** she came without a jacket; **~ Appetit sein** have no appetite; **ein Mann ~ jeglichen Humor** a man totally lacking in humour *or* without any sense of humour **2** (mit Auslassung des Akkusativs) **ich rauche nur ~:** I only smoke untipped *or* filterless cigarettes; **wir baden am liebsten ~:** we prefer to bathe in the nude; **wenn du keinen Zucker hast, trinke ich den Tee auch ~:** if you haven't got any sugar, I can have my tea without; **du brauchst ein Visum, ~ lassen sie dich nicht einreisen** you need a visa, they won't let you in without one; **er/sie ist [gar] nicht [so] ~** (ugs.) he's/she's quite something; **der Vorschlag ist [gar] nicht [so] ~** (ugs.) it's not such a bad *or* daft suggestion; *s. auch* **oben 3** **3** **~ weiteres** *od.* **Weiteres** (leicht, einfach) easily; (~ Einwand) readily; **das würde ich nicht so ~ weiteres** *od.* **Weiteres glauben** I wouldn't believe it just like that; **die Genehmigung kriegst du ~ weiteres** *od.* **Weiteres** you won't have any problem *or* difficulty getting approval; **das traue ich ihm ~ weiteres** *od.* **Weiteres zu** I can quite *or* easily believe he's capable of that **4** excluding; **~ mich sind es 10 Teilnehmer** there are ten participants excluding *or* not counting *or* not including me

B *Konj.* **er nahm Platz, ~ dass er gefragt hätte** he sat down without asking; **~ zu zögern** without hesitating; without hesitation

ohne-: ~dies *Adv.* (geh.) in any case; **die, die ~dies schon [am meisten] Geld haben** those who already have [the most] money in any case; **~einander** *Adv.* without each other; **~gleichen** *Adv., nachgestellt* **mit einer Hartnäckigkeit ~gleichen** with unparalleled obstinacy; **ein Skandal/eine Frechheit ~gleichen** an unprecedented scandal/impertinence; **das ist ein Unsinn ~gleichen** I've never heard such nonsense; **~hin** *Adv.* anyway; **er war ~hin schon überlastet** he was already overburdened as it was; **das hat ~hin keinen Zweck** there is really no point in it

Ohnmacht /ˈoːnmaxt/ *die;* **~, ~en** **1** faint; swoon (literary); **in ~ fallen** *od.* (geh.) **sinken** faint *or* pass out/swoon; **sich einer ~ nahe fühlen** feel faint; **aus der** *od.* **seiner ~ erwachen** come to; **von** *od.* **aus einer ~ in die andere fallen** (ugs. scherzh.) constantly be having fits (coll.) **2** (Machtlosigkeit) powerlessness; impotence

ohnmächtig

A *Adj.* **1** unconscious; **~ werden** faint; pass out; **~ sein** have fainted *or* passed out; be in a dead faint; **~ zusammenbrechen** collapse unconscious; **halb ~:** half fainting **2** (machtlos) powerless; impotent; impotent, helpless ‹*fury, rage*›; helpless ‹*bitterness, despair*›

B *adv.* impotently; **~ zusehen** watch powerlessly *or* helplessly

Ohnmachts·anfall *der* fainting fit

oho /oˈhoː/

A *Interj.* oho; (protestierend) oh no

B ▸ **klein A 1**

Öhr /øːɐ̯/ *das;* **~[e]s, ~e** eye

Ohr /oːɐ̯/ *das;* **~[e]s, ~en** **1** ▸ⓘ **S. 435** ear; **auf dem linken ~ taub sein** be deaf in one's left ear; **jmdm. etw. ins ~ flüstern** whisper sth. in sb.'s ear; **gute/schlechte ~en haben** have good/poor hearing *sing.*; **er hört nur auf einem ~:** he only has one good ear; **ein geschultes ~:** a trained ear; **mit den ~en wackeln** wiggle one's/its ears; **das war nicht für deine/fremde ~en [bestimmt]** that wasn't for your/everbody's ears; **ich habe seine Worte/die Melodie noch im ~:** his words are still ringing in my ears/the tune is still going around my head; **die Melodie geht einem gleich/leicht ins ~:** the tune is very catchy

2 (fig.) **wo hast du bloß deine ~en?** (ugs.), **du sitzt wohl auf den** *od.* **deinen ~en!** (ugs.) are you deaf or something? (coll.); **wasch dir mal die ~en!** (ugs.) get your ears seen to! (coll.); **die ~en aufmachen** *od.* **aufsperren** (ugs.) pin back one's ears; **tauben ~en predigen** (geh.) preach to deaf ears; **ich bin ganz ~:** I'm all ears; **mir klingen die ~en** my ears are burning; **die Wände haben ~en** the walls have ears; **ein offenes ~ für jmdn./etw. haben** be ready to listen to sb./be open to *or* ready to listen to sth.; **jmdm. sein ~ leihen** lend sb. one's ear[s]; **bei jmdm. ein offenes ~ finden** (geh.) find a sympathetic *or* ready listener in sb.; **[vor jmdm./etw.] die ~en verschließen** (geh.) close one's ears to sb./sth.; **die ~en spitzen** (ugs.) prick up one's ears; **spitz mal die ~en!** (ugs.) pin back your ears (coll.); **jmdm. die ~en lang ziehen** (ugs.) take sb. by the ear and give him/her a good talking-to (coll.); **halt die ~en steif!** (ugs.) keep smiling!; **die ~en hängen lassen** (ugs.) lose heart; get downhearted; **sich** (*Dat.*) **[fast] die ~en brechen** (salopp scherzh.) bite off [almost] more than one can chew; **auf dem** *od.* **diesem ~ hört er schlecht/nicht** (ugs.) he doesn't want to hear anything about that; **sich**

aufs ~ legen *od.* (ugs.) **hauen** get one's head down (coll.); **noch feucht/nicht [ganz] trocken hinter den ~en sein** (ugs.) be still wet behind the ears; **schreib dir das mal hinter die ~en!** (ugs.) just you remember that!; **eine** *od.* **eins/ein paar hinter die ~en kriegen** (ugs.) get a thick ear (coll.); **jmdm. [mit etw.] in den ~en liegen** (ugs.) pester sb. the whole time [with sth.]; **mit den ~en schlackern** (ugs.) be staggered; **da kannst du/kann man nur mit den ~en schlackern** (ugs.) it's just staggering; **bis über beide ~en verliebt [in jmdn.]** (ugs.) head over heels in love [with sb.]; **bis über beide** *od.* **die ~en in etw. stecken** (ugs.) be up to one's ears in sth. (coll.); **jmdn. übers ~ hauen** (ugs.) take sb. for a ride (coll.); put one over on sb. (coll.); **viel** *od.* **eine Menge um die ~en haben** (ugs.) have a lot on one's plate (coll.); **jmdm. etw. um die ~en hauen** *od.* **schlagen** (ugs.) throw sth. back at sb.; **jmdm. um die ~en fliegen** (ugs.) blow up in sb.'s face; **von einem ~ zum anderen strahlen** (ugs.) grin from ear to ear; **etw. kommt jmdm. zu den ~en heraus** (ugs.) sb. has got sth. coming out of his/her ears; **zum einen ~ rein- und zum anderen wieder rausgehen** (ugs.) go in one ear and out the other (coll.); *s. auch* **Durchzug 1**; **faustdick B**; **Fell 1**; **Floh 1**; **Mann 1**; **Nacht**

ohren-, Ohren-: ~arzt *der*, **~ärztin** *die* otologist; ear specialist; **~beichte** *die* (kath. Rel.) auricular confession; **~betäubend** **A** *Adj.* ear-splitting; deafening; deafening ‹*applause*›; **B** *adv.* deafeningly; **~betäubend lärmen** make a deafening noise; **~klappe** *die* ear flap; **~leiden** *das* ear complaint; **~sausen** *das*; **~~s** ▸ⓘ **S. 439** ringing in the *or* one's ears; tinnitus (Med.); **~schmalz** *das* earwax; **~schmaus** *der* (ugs.) **ein ~schmaus sein** be a joy to hear; **~schmerz** *der* earache; **~schmerzen haben** have [an] earache *sing.*; **~schützer** *der*; **~~s**, **~~:** earmuff; **~sessel** *der* wing chair; **~zeuge** *der*, **~zeugin** *die*: **ich wurde ~zeuge des Gesprächs** I heard the conversation myself

ohr-, Ohr-: ~feige *die* box on the ears; **~feigen bekommen** *od.* (ugs.) **einstecken** get one's ears boxed; **jmdm. eine ~feige geben** *od.* (ugs.) **verpassen** box sb.'s ears; give sb. a box on the ears; **~feigen** /-faign/ *tr. V.* **jmdn. ~feigen** box sb.'s ears; **ich könnte mich [selbst] ~feigen!** (ugs.) I could kick myself!; **~feigen·gesicht** *das* (salopp abwertend) **er hat ein richtiges ~feigengesicht** he's got the sort of face you'd like to clout; **~hörer** *der* earphone; **~klipp** /-klɪp/ *der*; **~~s**, **~~s** ear clip; **~läppchen** *das*; **~~s**, **~~** ▸ⓘ **S. 435** earlobe; **~muschel** *die* ▸ⓘ **S. 435** external ear; auricle

Ohropax ⓦ /oro'paks/ *das*; **~:** earplugs *pl.*

Ohr-: ~ring *der* earring; **~stecker** *der* ear stud; **~wurm** der **1** earwig; **2** (ugs.: Melodie) catchy tune; **ein ~wurm sein** be really catchy

o.J. *Abk.* **= ohne Jahr** n.d.

oje /o'je:/ *Interj.* (veralt.), **ojemine** /o'je:mine/, **ojerum** /o'je:rʊm/ *Interj.* (veralt.) oh dear; dear me

Okarina /oka'ri:na/ *die*; **~**, **~s** *od.* **Okarinen** ocarina

okay /o'ke/ *Interj.*, *Adj.*, *adv.* (ugs.) OK (coll.); okay (coll.); **das geht ~:** that's OK *or* okay

Okay *das*; **~[s]**, **~s** (ugs.) OK (coll.); okay (coll.)

Okkasion /ɔka'zi̯o:n/ *die*; **~**, **~en** (veralt.) opportunity

okkult /ɔ'kʊlt/ *Adj.* occult

Okkultismus *der*; **~:** occultism *no art.*

Okkupant /ɔku'pant/ *der*; **~en**, **~en**, **Okkupantin** *die*; **~**, **~nen** (abwertend) occupier

Okkupation /ɔkupa'ts̮i̯o:n/ *die*; **~**, **~en** (abwertend) occupation

okkupieren *tr. V.* **1** (abwertend) occupy **2** (sich aneignen) **jmds. Stuhl ~:** occupy sb.'s chair

öko /'ø:ko/ *Adj.* (ugs.) ecologically sound; green

öko-, Öko- /øko-/ eco-

Öko *der*; **~s**, **~s** (ugs.) environmentalist

Ökoaudit /'ø:ko:ɔ:dɪt/ *das*; **~s**, **~s** eco-audit; environmental audit

Ökologe /øko'lo:gə/ *der*; **~n**, **~n** ecologist

Ökologie *die*; **~:** ecology

Ökologin *die*; **~**, **~nen** ecologist

ökologisch
A *Adj.* ecological
B *adv.* ecologically

Ökonom /øko'no:m/ *der*; **~en**, **~en** economist

Ökonomie *die*; **~**, **~n** **1** economics *sing.*; **politische ~:** political economy **2** (Wirtschaft, Wirtschaftlichkeit) economy

Ökonomik *die*; **~:** economics *pl.*

Ökonomin *die*; **~**, **~nen** economist

ökonomisch
A *Adj.* **1** economic; **eine ~e Abhandlung** a treatise on economics **2** (sparsam) economical
B *adv.* economically

Öko-: ~steuer *die* eco-tax; **~strom** *der* green electricity; **~system** *das* ecosystem; **~tourismus** *der* ecotourism

Ökotrophologie /økotrofolo'gi:/ *die*; **~:** home economics *sing.*, *no art.*

Okt. *Abk.* **= Oktober** Oct.

Oktaeder /ɔkta'ǀe:dɐ/ *das*; **~s**, **~** (Math.) octahedron

Oktan·zahl /ɔk'ta:n-/ *die* octane rating *or* number

Oktav /ɔk'ta:f/ *das*; **~s** octavo

Oktav-: ~band *der* octavo volume; **~heft** *das* octavo notebook

Oktave /ɔk'ta:və/ *die*; **~**, **~n** octave

Oktett /ɔk'tɛt/ *das*; **~[e]s**, **~e** octet

Oktober /ɔk'to:bɐ/ *der*; **~[s]**, **~** ▸ⓘ **S. 165** October; *s. auch* **April**

Oktober-: ~fest *das* Munich October festival; **~revolution** *die* (hist.) October Revolution

Oktoberfest

Germany's most famous beer festival (the Munich October festival) actually starts each year in September. Over five million litres of beer are drunk over a period of 16 days. The *Oktoberfest* goes back to the year 1810, when the Bavarian crown prince and later King Ludwig I married Therese of Saxony-Hildburghausen. A horse race was organized in honour of the couple on the *Theresienwiese* (Therese's meadow, named after the bride), and almost the entire population of Munich joined in the celebrations. The party was such a success that it became an annual event. Today the *Wies'n* (meadow), as the locals call the *Oktoberfest*, looks more like a giant fairground with huge marquees in which the big breweries set up beer halls for visitors to drink many a *Maß*, eat *Weißwurst*, *Schweinshaxe* (pork knuckles) and giant *Brezen* while listening and singing along to Bavarian music.

oktroyieren /ɔktro̯a'ji:rən/ *tr. V.* (geh.) impose; force; **jmdm. etw. ~:** impose *or* force sth. on sb.

Okular /oku'la:ɐ̯/ *das*; **~s**, **~e** eyepiece

okulieren *tr. V.* (Gartenbau) bud

Ökumene /øku'me:nə/ *die*; **~** (christl. Rel.) **1** ecumenical Christianity **2** (Bewegung) ecumenical movement

ökumenisch
A *Adj.* (christl. Rel.) ecumenical; **Ökumenischer Rat der Kirchen** World Council of Churches
B *adv.* ecumenically

Okzident /'ɔkts̮idɛnt/ *der*; **~s** (veralt., geh.) Occident

Öl /ø:l/ *das*; **~[e]s**, **~e** oil; **auf ~ stoßen** strike oil; **~ exportierende Länder** oil-exporting countries; **in ~ malen** paint in oils; **eine Landschaft in ~:** a landscape in oils; **~ auf die Wogen gießen** (fig.) pour oil on troubled waters; **~ ins Feuer gießen** (fig.) add fuel to the flames; **das ging ihm runter wie ~** (fig. ugs.) he lapped it up

OLAF *Abk.* **= Office Européen de Lutte Anti-Fraude** OLAF

Öl-: ~baum *der* olive tree; **~berg** *der* Mount of Olives; **~bild** *das* oil painting; **~bohrung** *die* drilling *no art.* for oil; **eine ~bohrung/~bohrungen durchführen** drill for oil; **~druck** *der*; *Pl.* **~drücke** (Technik) oil pressure; **~druck·bremse** *die* hydraulic brake

Oldtimer /'oʊldtaɪmɐ/ *der*; **~s**, **~:** vintage car; (vor 1905 gebaut) veteran car

Oleander /ole'andɐ/ *der*; **~s**, **~** (Bot.) oleander

ölen *tr. V.* oil; oil, lubricate ‹*shaft, engine, etc.*›; **wie geölt** (fig. ugs.) like clockwork; *s. auch* **Blitz 1**

öl-, Öl-: ~exportierend ▸**Öl**; **~farbe** *die* **1** oil-based paint; **2** (zum Malen) oil paint; **mit ~farben malen** paint in oils; **~feld** *das* oilfield; **~film** *der* film of oil

OLG *Abk.* **= Oberlandesgericht**

öl-, Öl-: ~gemälde *das* oil painting; **~götze** *der*: *in* **wie ein ~götze/wie die ~götzen** (ugs.) like a zombie/zombies; **~hahn** *der*: *in* **den ~hahn zudrehen** (fig.) stop the supply of oil; **~haltig** *Adj.* containing oil *postpos.*, *not pred.*; oil-bearing ‹*rock, shale, etc.*›; **~heizung** *die* oil-fired heating *no indef. art.*

ölig
A *Adj.* (auch fig. abwertend) oily
B *adv.* **1** **~ glänzen** have an oily sheen **2** (fig. abwertend) in an oily way

Oligarchie /oligar'çi:/ *die*; **~**, **~n** oligarchy

oliv /o'li:f/ *Adj.* olive[-green]

Oliv *das*; **~s**, **~** *od.* **~s** olive[-green]

Olive /o'li:və/ *die*; **~**, **~n** olive

Oliven-: ~baum *der* olive tree; **~öl** *das* olive oil

oliv·grün *Adj.* olive-green

Öl-: ~kanister *der* oilcan; **~jacke** *die* oilskin jacket; **~kanne** *die* oilcan; **~krise** *die* oil crisis; **~kuchen** *der* (Landw.) oilcake

oll /ɔl/ *Adj.* (ugs., bes. nordd.) old; **je ~er, je doller** (ugs. scherzh.) the older they get, the more they want to live it up

Öl·lampe *die* oil lamp

Olle[1] *der*; *adj. Dekl.* (ugs., bes. nordd.) **1** (alter Mann) old boy (coll.) **2** (Vater, Ehemann) old man (coll.); **meine ~n** my old man and old lady (coll.) **3** (Chef) old man (coll.); boss (coll.)

Olle[2] *die*; *adj. Dekl.* (ugs., bes. nordd.) **1** (alte Frau) old dear (coll.) **2** (Mutter, Ehefrau) old lady (coll.) **3** (Chefin) boss (coll.)

Öl-: ~leitung *die* oil pipe; (größer) oil pipeline; **~malerei** *die* oil painting *no art.*; **~messtab**, ***~meßstab** *der* (bes. Kfz-W.) dipstick; **~mühle** *die* oil mill; **~multi** *der* oil multinational; **~ofen** *der* oil heater; **~papier** *das* oiled paper; **~pest** *die* oil pollution *no indef. art.*; **~preis** *der* oil price; **~pumpe** *die* oil pump; **~quelle** *die* oil well; **~raffinerie** *die* oil refinery; **~sardine** *die* sardine in oil; **eine Dose ~sardinen** a tin of sardines; **~scheich** *der* (ugs.) oil sheikh; **~schiefer** *der* oil shale; **~schinken** *der* (ugs. abwertend) large pretentious oil painting; **~spur** *die* trail of oil; **~stand** *der* oil level; **~tank** *der* oil tank; **~tanker** *der* oil tanker; **~teppich** *der* oil slick

Ölung *die*; **~**, **~en** oiling; lubrication; **Letzte ~** (kath. u. orthodoxe Kirche) extreme unction

öl-, Öl-: ~verschmiert *Adj.* covered in oil *postpos.*; oily ‹*hands*›; **~wanne** *die* (bes. Kfz-W.) sump; **~wechsel** *der* (bes. Kfz-W.) oil change

Olymp /o'lʏmp/ *der*; **~s** **1** Mount Olympus **2** (ugs. scherzh.: im Theater) **der ~:** the gods *pl.*; **auf dem ~:** [up] in the gods

Olympia[1] /o'lʏmpi̯a/ *(das)*; **~s** (Geogr.) Olympia

Olympia[2] *das*; **~[s]** ▸**Olympiade 1**

Olympiade /olʏm'pi̯a:də/ *die*; **~**, **~n** **1** Olympic Games *pl.*; Olympics *pl.*; **die ~ 1980** the 1980 Olympic Games *or* Olympics

O

[2] (Wettbewerb) Olympiad [3] (Zeitraum) Olympiad

olympia-, Olympia-: ~dorf *das* Olympic village; **~mannschaft** *die* Olympic team *or* squad; **~sieger** *der,* **~siegerin** *die;* Olympic champion; **~stadion** *das* Olympic stadium; **~teilnehmer** *der,* **~teilnehmerin** *die* Olympic competitor; **~verdächtig** *Adj.* (ugs.) Olympic-standard; **~verdächtig sein** be of Olympic standard

Olympier /oˈlʏmpi̯ɐ/ *der;* **~s,** ~ (geh. veralt.) Olympian

Olympionike /olympi̯oˈniːkə/ *der;* **~n, ~n, Olympionikin** *die;* **~, ~nen** (geh.) [1] (Sieger[in]) Olympic champion [2] (Teilnehmer[in]) Olympic competitor

olympisch *Adj.* [1] Olympic; **die Olympischen Spiele** the Olympic Games; the Olympics [2] (zum Olymp gehörend, auch fig. geh.) Olympian

Öl-: ~zeug *das* oilskins *pl.*; **~zweig** *der* olive branch

Oma /ˈoːma/ *die;* **~, ~s** (fam.) gran[ny] (coll./child lang.); grandma (coll./child lang.)

Ombuds- /ˈɔmbʊt͡s-/: **~frau** *die* ombudswoman; **~mann** *der; Pl.* **~männer** *od.* **~leute** ombudsman

Omega /ˈoːmega/ *das;* **~[s], ~s** omega

Omelett *das;* **~[e]s, ~e** *od.* **~s,** (österr., schweiz.) **Omelette** /ɔm(ə)ˈlɛt/ *die;* **~, ~en** (Kochk.) omelette

Omen /ˈoːmən/ *das;* **~s,** ~ *od.* **Omina** /ˈoːmina/ omen

Omi /ˈoːmi/ *die;* **~, ~s** (fam.) granny (coll./child lang.)

Omikron /ˈoːmikrɔn/ *das;* **~[s], ~s** omicron

ominös /omiˈnøːs/
[A] *Adj.* [1] ominous [2] (bedenklich, zweifelhaft) sinister; (berüchtigt) unsavoury
[B] *adv.* ominously

Omnibus /ˈɔmnibʊs/ *der;* **~ses, ~se** omnibus (formal); (Privat- und Reisebus auch) coach

Omnibus- ▸ **Bus-**

omnipotent /ɔmnipoˈtɛnt/ *Adj.* (geh.) omnipotent

Omnipotenz /ɔmnipoˈtɛnt͡s/ *die;* ~ (geh.) omnipotence

Onanie /onaˈniː/ *die;* **~:** onanism *no art.*; masturbation *no art.*

onanieren *itr. V.* masturbate

Ondit /õˈdiː/ *das;* **~[s], ~s** (geh.) on dit; rumour

ondulieren /ɔnduˈliːrən/ *tr. V.* (veralt.) crimp; wave

Onkel[1] /ˈɔŋkl̩/ *der;* **~s,** ~ *od.* (ugs.) **~s** [1] uncle [2] (Kinderspr.: Mann) **der ~ dort** that man there; **sag dem ~ guten Tag!** say hello to the nice man; **der ~ Doktor** the nice doctor [3] (ugs. abwertend) bloke (Brit. coll.); guy (coll.)

Onkel[2] *der;* **~s, ~s** in **großer** *od.* **dicker ~:** big toe; **über den großen ~ gehen** walk pigeon-toed

Onkel·ehe *die* (ugs.): *cohabitation of a widow with a man who (in order to retain benefits due to her from the first marriage) is not married to her*

onkel·haft
[A] *Adj.* avuncular
[B] *adv.* in an avuncular manner

online /ˈɔnlai̯n/ (DV)
[A] *Adj.* online; **~ gehen** go online
[B] *Adv.* online

Online-: ~banking /-bɛŋkɪŋ/ *das;* **~~s** (DV) online banking; **~betrieb** *der* (DV) online operation; **~dienst** *der* (DV) online service; **~shop** *der* (DV) online shop; **~zeit** *die* (DV) connection *or* usage time

ONO *Abk.* = **Ostnordost[en]** ▸❶ **S. 363** ENE

onomato·poetisch *Adj.* (Sprachw.) onomatopoeic

ontisch /ˈɔntɪʃ/ (Philos.)
[A] *Adj.* ontic
[B] *adv.* ontically

Onto·genese /ɔnto-/ *die* (Biol.) ontogeny; ontogenesis

onto·genetisch (Biol.)
[A] *Adj.* ontogenetic
[B] *adv.* ontogenetically

onto·logisch (Philos.)
[A] *Adv.* ontological
[B] *adv.* ontologically

Onyx /ˈoːnʏks/ *der;* **~[e]s, ~e** (Mineral., Med.) onyx

o.O. *Abk.* = **ohne Ort** n.p.

Op. *Abk.* = **Opus** op.

OP /oːˈpeː/ *der;* **~[s], ~[s]** *Abk.* = **Operationssaal**

Opa /ˈoːpa/ *der;* **~s, ~s** (fam.) grandad (coll./child lang.); grandpa (coll./child lang.)

opak /oˈpaːk/ *Adj.* opaque

Opal /oˈpaːl/ *der;* **~s, ~e** opal

opalisieren *itr. V.* opalesce; **~d** opalescent

Op-Art /ˈɔplaːɐ̯t/ *die;* **~:** op art

OPEC /ˈoːpɛk/*die;* **~** *Abk.* OPEC

Oper /ˈoːpɐ/ *die;* **~, ~n** opera; (Institution, Ensemble) Opera; (**~nhaus**) Opera; opera house; **in die ~ gehen** go to the opera; **an die/zur ~ gehen** (als Sänger) become an opera singer; **quatsch keine ~n!** (salopp) don't talk rot! (coll.)

Opera ▸ **Opus**

Operateur /operaˈtøːɐ̯/ *der;* **~s, ~e** [1] (Arzt) [operating] surgeon [2] (Filmvorführer) projectionist

Operation /operaˈt͡si̯oːn/ *die;* **~, ~en** ▸❶ **S. 439** operation; **~ gelungen, Patient tot** (ugs.) [it was] a brilliant idea, but it hasn't done the trick (coll.)

operationalisieren /operat͡si̯onaliˈziːrən/ *tr. V.* (Wissensch., Päd.) operationalize

Operations-: ~basis *die* (bes. Milit.) base of operations; **~gebiet** *das* (Milit., auch fig.) area of operations; **~narbe** *die* operation scar; **~saal** *der* operating theatre (Brit.) *or* -room; **~schwester** *die* theatre sister (Brit.); operating-room nurse (Amer.); **~tisch** *der* operating table

operativ /operaˈtiːf/
[A] *Adj.* [1] (Med.) operative [2] (Milit.) operational
[B] *adv.* [1] (Med.) by operative surgery; **etw. ~ entfernen** operate to remove sth. [2] (Milit.) operationally

Operator /opəˈraːtɔr/ *der;* **~s, ~en, Operatorin** *die;* **~, ~nen** (DV) [computer] operator

Operette /opəˈrɛtə/ *die;* **~, ~n** operetta

operettenhaft
[A] *Adj.* reminiscent of operetta *postpos.*
[B] *adv.* in a way reminiscent of operetta

Operetten·staat *der* (abwertend) little tinpot state (derog.)

operieren
[A] ▸❶ **S. 439** *tr. V.* operate on ‹*patient*›; **jmdn. am Magen ~:** operate on sb.'s stomach; **sich ~ lassen** have an operation
[B] *itr. V.* operate; **vorsichtig ~** (vorgehen) proceed carefully

Opern-: ~arie *die* [operatic] aria; **~bühne** *die* opera house; **~führer** *der* opera guide; **~glas** *das* opera glass[es *pl.*]; **~haus** *das* opera house; **~sänger** *der,* **~sängerin** *die* ▸❶ **S. 113** opera singer

Opfer /ˈɔpfɐ/ *das;* **~s,** ~ [1] (Verzicht) sacrifice; **ein ~ [für etw.] bringen** make a sacrifice [for sth.]; **kein ~ scheuen** consider no sacrifice too great; **unter großen ~n** by making great sacrifices; **manches ~ auf sich** (*Akk.*) **nehmen** make quite a few sacrifices [2] (Geschädigter) victim; **das Haus wurde ein ~ der Flammen** (geh.) the house fell victim to the flames; **jmdm./einer Sache zum ~ fallen** fall victim to sb./sth.; be the victim of sb./sth. [3] (**~gabe**) sacrifice; **jmdm./einer Sache etw. zum ~ bringen** sacrifice sth. to sb./sth.

opfer-, Opfer-: ~bereit *Adj.* ‹*person*› who is ready *or* willing to make sacrifices; **~bereitschaft** *die* readiness *or* willingness to make sacrifices; **~gabe** *die* [sacrificial] offering; **~gang** *der* [1] (kath. Kirche) offertory procession; [2] (geh.) **seinen ~gang antreten** sacrifice oneself; **~lamm** *das* sacrificial lamb; **wie ein ~lamm** (fig. ugs.) like a lamb to the slaughter; **~mut** *der* (geh.) readiness *or* willingness to make sacrifices

opfern
[A] *tr. V.* [1] (darbringen) sacrifice; make a sacrifice of; offer up ‹*fruit, produce, etc.*› [2] (fig.: hingeben) sacrifice, give up ‹*time, holiday, money, life*›
[B] *itr. V.* **[den Göttern] ~:** offer sacrifice [to the gods]
[C] *refl. V.* [1] **sich für jmdn./etw. ~:** sacrifice oneself for sb./sth. [2] (ugs. scherzh.) be the martyr; **wer opfert sich denn und isst den Nachtisch auf?** who's going to volunteer to finish off the dessert?

Opfer-: ~stock *der; Pl.* **~stöcke** offertory box; **~tier** *das* sacrificial animal; **~tod** *der* (geh.) **den ~tod sterben** sacrifice one's life

Opferung *die;* **~, ~en** [1] sacrifice [2] (kath. Kirche) offertory

Opfer·wille *der* ▸ **Opfermut**

opfer·willig *Adj.* ▸ **opferbereit**

Opiat /oˈpi̯aːt/ *das;* **~[e]s, ~e** opiate

Opium /ˈoːpi̯ʊm/ *das;* **~s** (auch fig.) opium

Opium-: ~höhle *die* (ugs.) opium den; **~krieg** *der* (hist.) Opium War; **~raucher** *der,* **~raucherin** *die* opium smoker; **~rausch** *der* opium dream; **~sucht** *die* opium addiction

ÖPNV *Abk.* = **öffentlicher Personennahverkehr** local public transport

Opossum /oˈpɔsʊm/ *das;* **~s, ~s** opossum

Opponent /ɔpoˈnɛnt/ *der;* **~en, ~en, Opponentin** *die;* **~, ~nen** opponent

opponieren *itr. V.* take the opposite side; **gegen jmdn./etw. ~:** oppose sb./sth.

opportun /ɔpɔrˈtuːn/ *Adj.* (geh.) appropriate; (günstig) advantageous

Opportunismus *der;* **~:** opportunism

Opportunist *der;* **~en, ~en, Opportunistin** *die;* **~, ~nen** opportunist

opportunistisch
[A] *Adj.* opportunist; opportunistic
[B] *adv.* opportunistically; **~ handeln** be opportunistic; (im Einzelfall) act in an opportunistic fashion

Opportunität /ɔpɔrtuniˈtɛːt/ *die;* **~, ~en** (geh.) appropriateness

Opportunitäts·prinzip *das:* (Rechtsw.) *principle that the public prosecutor has the power to decide whether or not to institute proceedings*

Opposition /ɔpoziˈt͡si̯oːn/ *die;* **~, ~en** (auch Politik, Sprachw., Astron., Schach, Fechten) opposition; **etw. aus [reiner** *od.* **lauter] ~ tun** do sth. just to be contrary; **~ gegen jmdn./etw. machen** (ugs.) oppose sb./sth.; **in die ~ gehen** (Politik) go into opposition; **Jupiter und Mars stehen in ~:** Jupiter and Mars are in opposition

oppositionell /ɔpozit͡si̯oˈnɛl/
[A] *Adj.* opposition *attrib.* ‹*group, movement, circle, etc.*›; ‹*newspaper, writer, artist, etc.*› opposed to the government; ‹*feelings*› of opposition; ‹*attempts*› at opposition; opposing ‹*trend, tendency*›; **~es Verhalten** opposition; **die seit 1982 ~e SPD** the SPD, in opposition since 1982
[B] *adv.* **~ eingestellt sein** hold opposing views

Oppositionelle *der/die; adj. Dekl.* member of the opposition; (Regimekritiker) dissident

Oppositions-: ~führer *der,* **~führerin** *die* opposition leader; (in Großbritannien) Leader of the Opposition; **~partei** *die* opposition party

Optativ /ˈɔptatiːf/ *der;* **~s, ~e** (Sprachw.) optative

optieren /ɔpˈtiːrən/ *itr. V.* [1] (Völkerr.) opt; **für Polen ~:** opt for Polish citizenship [2] (Rechtsw.) **auf etw.** (*Akk.*) **~:** take an option on sth.

Optik *die;* **~, ~en** [1] (Wissenschaft) optics *sing., no art.* [2] (Fot. ugs.) (Linse) lens; (Linsen) optics *pl.*; lens system; **das ist eine Frage der ~** (fig.) it depends on your point of view [3] (Erscheinungsbild) appearance; **der ~ wegen** for visual effect

Optiker *der;* **~s, ~, Optikerin** *die;* **~, ~nen** ▸❶ **S. 113** optician

Optima ▸**Optimum**

optimal /ɔpti'ma:l/
A *Adj.* optimal; optimum *attrib*
B *adv.* **jmdn. ~ beraten** give sb. the best possible advice; **ein Problem ~ lösen** find the optimal *or* optimum solution to a problem

optimieren *tr. V.* optimize

Optimierung *die;* **~, ~en** optimization

Optimismus *der;* **~:** optimism

Optimist *der;* **~en, ~en, Optimistin** *die;* **~, ~nen** optimist; **~ sein** be an optimist

optimistisch
A *Adj.* optimistic
B *adv.* optimistically

Optimum /'ɔptimʊm/ *das;* **~s, Optima** (auch Biol.) optimum

Option /ɔp'tsi̯o:n/ *die;* **~, ~en** [1] (Völkerr.) opting [2] (Rechtsw.) option (**auf** + *Akk.* on)

optisch
A *Adj.* optical; visual ‹*impression*›; **eine ~e Täuschung** an optical illusion; **aus ~en Gründen** for [the sake of] optical *or* visual effect; (fig.) for [the sake of] effect
B *adv.* optically; visually ‹*impressive, successful, effective*›; **~ wahrnehmbar sein** be perceivable with the eye

Opto·elektronik *die* optoelectronics *sing.*

opto·elektronisch *Adj.* optoelectronic

Opt-out /ɔpt'aut/ *das;* **~[s], ~s** opt-out

Opt-out-Klausel *die* opt-out clause

opulent /opu'lɛnt/
A *Adj.* [1] sumptuous ‹*meal, banquet, etc.*› [2] (aufwendig [gestaltet]) opulent; lavish ‹*theatrical production*›
B *adv.* opulently ‹*dressed*›; **~ essen** eat a sumptuous meal

Opus /'o:pʊs/ *das;* **~, Opera** /'o:pəra/ opus; (Gesamtwerk) oeuvre

Orakel /o'ra:kl̩/ *das;* **~s, ~** (auch fig.) oracle; **in ~n reden** *od.* **sprechen** (fig.) talk *or* speak in riddles

orakel·haft *Adj.* oracular

orakeln
A *tr. V.* **~, dass ...** make mysterious prophecies that ...
B *itr. V.* make mysterious prophecies

oral /o'ra:l/
A *Adj.* oral
B *adv.* orally; **~ verkehren** have oral intercourse *or* sex

Oral-: ~sex *der* oral sex; **~verkehr** *der* oral intercourse

orange /o'rã:ʒ(ə)/ *indekl. Adj.* orange

Orange[1] *das;* **~s, ~** *od.* (ugs.) **~s** orange

Orange[2] *die;* **~, ~n** (bes. südd., österr., schweiz.: Apfelsine) orange

Orangeade /orã'ʒa:də/ *die;* **~, ~n** orangeade

Orangeat /orã'ʒa:t/ *das;* **~s, ~e** candied orange peel

orange·farben, orange·farbig *Adj.* orange[-coloured]

orangen /o'rã:ʒn̩/ *Adj.* orange

orangen-, Orangen-: ~baum orange tree; **~farben, ~farbig** *Adj.* ▸**orangefarben**; **~haut** *die* (Med.) orange-peel skin; (Zellulitis) cellulitis; **~marmelade** *die* orange marmalade; **~saft** *der* orange juice; **~schale** *die* orange peel *no pl.*

Orangerie /orãʒə'ri:/ *die;* **~, ~n** orangery

Orang-Utan /'o:raŋ|u:tan/ *der;* **~s, ~s** orang-utan

Oranien /o'ra:ni̯ən/ *(das);* **~s** Orange; **Wilhelm von ~:** William of Orange

Oranier *der;* **~s, ~, Oranierin** *die;* **~, ~nen** member of the House of Orange

Oratorium /ora'to:ri̯ʊm/ *das;* **~s, Oratorien** oratorio

Orbiter /'ɔrbitɐ/ *der;* **~s, ~** (Raumf.) orbiter

Orchester /ɔr'kɛstɐ/ *das;* **~s, ~:** orchestra; (~graben) orchestra [pit]

Orchester-: ~begleitung *die* orchestral accompaniment; **~graben** *der* orchestra pit; **~musiker** *der,* **~musikerin** *die* orchestral musician

orchestral /ɔrkɛs'tra:l/
A *Adj.* orchestral
B *adv.* **~ begleitet** accompanied by an orchestra

orchestrieren *tr. V.* (Musik, auch fig.) orchestrate

Orchestrierung *die;* **~, ~en** (Musik, auch fig.) orchestration

Orchidee /ɔrçi'de:(ə)/ *die;* **~, ~n** orchid

Orden /'ɔrdn̩/ *der;* **~s, ~** [1] (Gemeinschaft) order; **in einen ~ eintreten, einem ~ beitreten** join an order; become a member of an order [2] (Ehrenzeichen) decoration; (Milit.) decoration; (in runder Form) medal; **jmdm. einen ~ [für etw.] verleihen** decorate sb. [for sth.]; **ihm wurde der ~ pour le Mérite verliehen** he was given the Ordre pour le Mérite; **einen ~ bekommen** receive a decoration/medal

orden·geschmückt *Adj.* bemedalled and beribboned

Ordens-: ~band *das; Pl.* **~bänder** ribbon; **~bruder** *der* brother [of an/the order]; monk; **~regel** *die* rule [of an/the order]; **~schwester** *die* sister [of an/the order]; nun; **~tracht** *die* habit [of an/the order]; **~verleihung** *die* awarding of a/the decoration; **die jährliche ~verleihung** the annual award of decorations

ordentlich /'ɔrdn̩tlɪç/
A *Adj.* [1] (ordnungsliebend) [neat and] tidy; (methodisch) orderly [2] (geordnet) [neat and] tidy ‹*room, house, desk, etc.*›; neat ‹*handwriting, clothes*› [3] (anständig) respectable; proper ‹*manners*›; **etwas Ordentliches lernen** learn a proper trade [4] (planmäßig) regular, ordinary ‹*meeting*›; **~es Mitglied** full member; **~es Gericht** court exercising civil and criminal jurisdiction; *s. auch* **Professor 1** [5] (ugs.: richtig) proper; real; **etwas Ordentliches essen** have some proper food; **eine ~e Tracht Prügel** a real good hiding (coll.) [6] (ugs.: tüchtig) **ein ~es Stück Kuchen** a nice big piece of cake; **ein ~es Stück Arbeit/Weg** a fair old bit of work (coll.) /a fair old way (coll.); **die haben ja ~e Preise** their prices are steep (coll.) [7] (ugs.: recht gut) decent ‹*wine, flat, marks, etc.*›; **ganz ~:** pretty good
B *adv.* (geordnet) [1] tidily; neatly; ‹*write*› neatly; **~ aufgeräumt** neatly tidied [2] (anständig) properly [3] (ugs.: gehörig) **~ feiern** have a real good celebration (coll.); **~ einen heben** (ugs.) have a fair few drinks (coll.); **greift ~ zu!** tuck in!; **sich ~ ausschlafen** have a really good sleep; **letzte Nacht hat es ~ geschneit** it really snowed last night; **es jmdm. ~ geben** give sb. a piece of one's mind [4] (ugs.: recht gut) ‹*ski, speak, etc.*› really well; **ganz ~ verdienen** earn a pretty good wage

Ordentlichkeit *die;* **~:** [neatness and] tidiness; (der Schrift, Kleidung) neatness; (methodische Veranlagung) orderliness

Order /'ɔrdɐ/ *die;* **~, ~s** *od.* **~n** [1] (Befehl) order; **~ haben, etw. zu tun** have orders to do sth.; **sich an seine ~ halten** obey one's orders [2] *Pl.* **~s** (Kaufmannsspr.: Auftrag) order; **einer Firma eine ~ erteilen** place an order with a firm

ordern *tr., itr. V.* (Kaufmannsspr.) order

Order·papier *das* (Bankw.) instrument made out to order (*and transferable by endorsement*)

Ordinal·zahl *die* ordinal [number]

ordinär /ɔrdi'nɛ:ɐ̯/
A *Adj.* [1] (abwertend) vulgar; common; vulgar ‹*joke, song, expression, language*›; cheap and obtrusive ‹*perfume*› [2] (alltäglich) ordinary
B *adv.* vulgarly; in a vulgar manner

Ordinariat /ɔrdinaˈri̯a:t/ *das;* **~[e]s, ~e** [1] (kath. Kirche) ordinariate [2] (Hochschulw.) chair

Ordinarius /ɔrdi'na:ri̯ʊs/ *der;* **~, Ordinarien** [1] (Professor) [full] professor (holding a chair) (**für** of) [2] (kath. Kirche) ordinary

Ordinate /ɔrdi'na:tə/ *die;* **~, ~n** (Math.) ordinate

Ordinaten·achse *die* (Math.) axis of ordinates

Ordination /ɔrdina'tsi̯o:n/ *die;* **~, ~en** [1] (ev., kath. Kirche) ordination [2] (Med.: Verordnung) prescription [3] (Med. veralt.: Sprechstunde) surgery

ordinieren *tr. V.* [1] (ev., kath. Kirche) ordain [2] (Med.) prescribe

ordnen /'ɔrdnən/
A *tr. V.* [1] arrange; (systematisieren) arrange, organize ‹*ideas, thoughts, material, etc.*› [2] (regeln) regulate ‹*traffic*›; **sein Leben/seine Finanzen ~:** straighten out one's life/put one's finances in order; **seine Angelegenheiten ~:** settle one's affairs; *s. auch* **geordnet**
B *refl. V.* form up; **ihre Gedanken ordneten sich** (fig.) her thoughts became more collected

Ordner *der;* **~s, ~** [1] (Hefter) file [2] (Aufsichtsperson) steward; (bei Demonstrationen) marshal; steward

Ordnerin *die;* **~, ~nen** ▸**Ordner 2**

Ordnung *die;* **~, ~en** [1] (ordentlicher Zustand) order; tidiness; **~ halten** keep things tidy; **durch sie kam etwas mehr ~ ins Haus** she made the house a little tidier; **~ in die Papiere bringen** put the papers into order; **hier herrscht ~:** everything is neat and tidy here; **hier herrscht ja eine schöne ~!** (iron.) a nice mess we've got here!; **der ~ halber** *od.* **wegen** (weil es sich so gehört) for the sake of form; **~ schaffen, für ~ sorgen** sort things out; **sehr auf ~ halten** set great store by tidiness; **~ ist das halbe Leben** (Spr.) muddle makes trouble; **etw. in ~ bringen** sort sth. out; **in ~ kommen** sort itself out; **in ~ sein** (ugs.) be OK (coll.) *or* all right; **ist dein Pass in ~?** is your passport in order?; **das Fleisch ist nicht ganz in ~:** the meat has started to go bad; **hier ist etw. nicht in ~:** there's something wrong here; **mit ihr ist etwas nicht in ~, sie ist nicht in ~** (ugs.) there's something wrong *or* the matter with her; **jetzt bin ich wieder in ~** (ugs.) I'm better *or* all right now; **sie ist in ~** (ugs.: ist nett, verlässlich o. Ä.) she's OK (coll.); **alles [ist] in schönster** *od.* **bester ~:** everything's [just] fine; [things] couldn't be better; **[das] geht [schon] in ~** (ugs.) that'll be OK (coll.) *or* all right; **ich finde es nicht in ~, dass ...** I don't think it's right that ...; **sie scheint es ganz in [der] ~ zu finden, wenn ...** she doesn't seem to mind at all if ...; **in ~!** (ugs.) OK! (coll.); all right! [2] (geregelter Ablauf) routine; **hier muss alles seine ~ haben** we/they *etc.* like to keep to a routine here [3] (System von Normen) order; **die ~ einer Gemeinschaft** the rules *pl.* of a community; *s. auch* **öffentlich A** [4] (Disziplin) order; **hier/da herrscht ~:** we have some discipline here/they have some discipline there; **sich an ~ gewöhnen** get used to discipline; **~ halten** ‹*teacher etc.*› keep order; **sehr auf ~ halten** be a great disciplinarian [5] (System) order; (Struktur) structure [6] (Formation) formation [7] (Biol.) order [8] (Rang) **eine Straße zweiter ~:** a second-class road; **ein Stern vierter ~:** a fourth-magnitude star; **ein Reinfall/Fehlschlag** *usw.* **erster ~** (fig. ugs.) a disaster/failure *etc.* of the first order *or* water [9] (Math.) order [10] (Mengenlehre) ordered set [11] (Gesellschafts~) order

ordnungs-, Ordnungs-: ~amt *das:* [*offices of*] *municipal authority responsible for registering residents, regulating public events such as demonstrations and galas, supervising trading standards, and licensing street traders, street musicians, etc.;* **~gemäß** **A** *Adj.* ‹*conduct etc.*› in accordance with the regulations; **alles ging seinen ~gemäßen Gang** everything took its proper course; **B** *adv.* in accordance with the regulations; **~halber** *Adv.* as a matter of form; **~hüter** *der* (scherzh.) custodian of the law (joc.); **~kraft** *die* law enforcement officer; **~liebe** *die* liking for neatness and tidiness; **~liebend** *Adj.* ‹*person*› who likes to see things neat and tidy; **~ruf** *der* call to order; **jmdm. einen ~ruf erteilen** call sb. to order; **~sinn** *der* liking for neatness and tidiness; **~strafe** *die* (Rechtsw.) penalty for contempt of court; **~widrig** (Rechtsw.) **A** *Adj.* ‹*actions, behaviour, etc.*› contravening the regulations; illegal ‹*parking*›; **~widriges Verhalten im Verkehr** an infringement of traffic regulations; **B** *adv.* **~widrig parken** park illegally;

O

~widrig handeln act in contravention of the regulations; contravene *or* infringe the regulations; **~widrigkeit** *die* (Rechtsw.) infringement of the regulations; **~zahl** *die* ordinal [number]; (Physik) atomic number

Ordonnanz /ɔrdɔˈnants/ *die;* ~, **~en** (Milit.) orderly

Ordonnanz·offizier *der* (Milit.) aide[-de-camp]

Oregano /oˈreːgano/ *der;* ~: oregano

ORF *Abk.* **= Österreichischer Rundfunk** Austrian Radio

Organ /ɔrˈgaːn/ *das;* **~s, ~e** [1] ▸ℹ **S. 435** (Anat., Biol.) organ; **ein/kein ~ für etw. haben** (fig.) have a feeling/no feeling for sth. [2] (ugs.: Stimme) voice; **er hat ein furchtbar lautes ~:** his voice is awfully loud [3] (Zeitung) organ (formal) [4] (Institution) organ; (Mensch) agent; **die Polizei ist nur ausführendes ~:** the police act only as an executive agency; **staatliche ~e** organs of state; **bewaffnete ~e der DDR** armed defensive forces of the GDR

Organ·bank *die; Pl.* **~en** (Med.) organ bank

Organdy /ɔrˈgandi/ *der;* **~s** organdie

Organ·empfänger *der,* **Organ·empfängerin** *die* (Med.) organ recipient; recipient of an/the organ

Organisation /ɔrganizaˈtsjoːn/ *die;* ~, **~en** organization; **~ für wirtschaftliche Zusammenarbeit und Entwicklung** Organization for Economic Cooperation and Development

Organisations-: ~büro *das* organizational headquarters *sing. or pl.;* **~grad** *der* level of *(trade union etc.)* membership; **gewerkschaftlicher ~grad** degree of unionization; **~talent** *das* [1] (Fähigkeit) talent for organization; [2] (Mensch) person with a talent for organization; **ein [ausgesprochenes] ~talent sein** have a [marked] talent for organization

Organisator /ɔrganiˈzaːtɔr/ *der;* **~s, ~en** /-ˈtoːrən/. **Organisatorin** *die;* **~, ~nen** organizer

organisatorisch
A *Adj.* organizational
B *adv.* organizationally; **~ begabt sein** have a talent for organization

organisch
A *Adj.* [1] (auch Chemie) organic; **~e Chemie** organic chemistry [2] (Med.) organic; physical
B *adv.* [1] organically; **sich ~ in etw.** *(Akk.)* **einfügen** form an organic part of sth. [2] (Med.) organically; physically

organisierbar *Adj.* organizable; **etw. ist ~:** sth. can be organized

organisieren
A *tr. V.* [1] (vorbereiten, aufbauen) organize [2] (ugs.: beschaffen) get [hold of]
B *itr. V.* **gut ~ können** be a good organizer
C *refl. V.* organize (**zu** into); **er will sich ~:** he wants to join the union *etc.*

organisiert *Adj.* organized ‹*system etc.*›; **gewerkschaftlich ~e/nicht ~e Arbeiter** unionized/non-unionized workers; **sind Sie politisch/gewerkschaftlich ~?** are you a member of a political party/trade union?

Organismus *der;* **Organismen** organism

Organist *der;* **~en, ~en, Organistin** *die;* **~, ~nen** ▸ℹ **S. 113** organist; *s. auch* **-in**

Organ-: ~spender *der,* **~spenderin** *die* organ donor; **~transplantation** *die,* **~verpflanzung** *die* organ transplantation

Organza /ɔrˈgantsa/ *der;* **~s** organza

Orgasmus /ɔrˈgasmʊs/ *der;* ~, **Orgasmen** orgasm

orgastisch *Adj.* orgastic; orgasmic

Orgel /ˈɔrgl̩/ *die;* ~, **~n** organ; **~ spielen** play the organ

Orgel-: ~bauer *der;* **~~s, ~~, ~baue·rin** *die;* **~~, ~~nen** organ builder; **~konzert** *das* organ concerto; (Solo) organ recital; **~musik** *die* organ music

orgeln *itr. V.* [1] (Drehorgel spielen) grind the organ [2] (ugs.: tönen) ‹*barrel organ, song*› grind on [3] (Jägerspr.: schreien) bell

Orgel-: ~pfeife *die* organ pipe; **[dastehen] wie die ~pfeifen** (scherzh.) [stand in a row] from the tallest to the shortest; **~punkt** *der* (Musik) pedal *or* organ point; **~werk** *das* work for the organ

orgiastisch
A *Adj.* orgiastic
B *adv.* orgiastically

Orgie /ˈɔrgi̯ə/ *die;* ~, **~n** (auch fig.) orgy; **eine ~ feiern** have an orgy

Orient /ˈoːri̯ɛnt/ *der;* **~s** [1] (Vorder- u. Mittelasien) Middle East and south-western Asia (*including Afghanistan and Nepal*); **der Vordere ~:** the Middle East [2] (veralt.: Osten) Orient

Orientale /ori̯ɛnˈtaːlə/ *der;* **~n, ~n** ▸ **Orient 1**: *man from the Middle East [or south-western Asia]*

Orientalin *die;* **~, ~nen** ▸ **Orient 1**: *woman from the Middle East [or south-western Asia]*; *s. auch* **-in**

orientalisch *Adj.* oriental

Orientalist *der;* **~en, ~en, Orientalistin** *die;* **~, ~nen** orientalist; *s. auch* **-in**

Orientalistik *die;* **~:** [Middle Eastern and] oriental studies

orientieren
A *refl. V.* [1] (sich zurechtfinden) get one's bearings; **ich muss mich zuerst ~, wo ich eigentlich bin** first I must get my bearings [and find out where I am]; **sich an etw.** *(Dat.)*/**nach einer Karte ~:** get one's bearings by sth./using a map [2] **sich über etw.** *(Akk.)* **~:** inform oneself about sth. [3] **sich an etw.** *(Dat.)* **~:** be oriented towards sth.; ‹*policy, advertising*› be geared towards sth.; **politisch links/rechts orientiert sein** lean towards the left/right politically; **sich an bestimmten Leitbildern ~:** follow certain models [4] **sich auf jmdn./etw. ~:** concentrate [one's attention] on sb./sth.
B *tr. V.* [1] (unterrichten) inform (**über** + *Akk.* about); **die Gespräche haben nur ~den Charakter** the talks are only for the purposes of exchanging information [2] **sein Ziel nach etw. ~:** base one's aims on sth.; **gewerkschaftlich orientierte Interessen** interests centred on the trade unions [3] **jmdn. auf etw.** *(Akk.)* **~:** direct sb.'s attention to sth.; **alle Kräfte auf eine Politik des Friedens ~:** concentrate every effort on a policy of promoting peace
C *itr. V.* [1] **über etw.** *(Akk.)* **~:** report on sth. [2] **auf etw.** *(Akk.)* **~:** concentrate [one's/its attention] on sth.

-orientiert *adj.* orientated towards …

Orientierung *die;* **~** [1] (das Sichorientieren) **hier ist die ~ schwer** it's difficult to get your bearings here; **die ~ verlieren** lose one's bearings [2] (Unterrichtung) **zu Ihrer ~:** for your information; **die ~ der Bevölkerung** informing the population (**über** + *Akk.* about) [3] (das Sichausrichten) orientation (**auf** + *Akk.* towards, **an** + *Dat.* according to) [4] (Konzentration, Hinwendung) **die ~ auf etw.** *(Akk.)* concentration on sth.; **jmdm. die ~ auf etw.** *(Akk.)* **geben** direct sb.'s attention to sth.

orientierungs-, Orientierungs-: ~hilfe *die* aid to orientation; **als ~hilfe legen wir Ihnen eine Karte bei** we enclose a map to help you find your way; **~lauf** *der* orienteering event; (Disziplin) orienteering *no art.;* **~los** *Adj.* (auch fig.) disoriented; **~los umherirren** wander around in a state of disorientation; **~punkt** *der* landmark by which one can/could find one's bearings; (fig.) point of reference; **~sinn** *der* sense of direction; **~stufe** *die* (Schulw.) ▸ **Förderstufe**

> **Orientierungsstufe**
>
> The name given to the first two years at a **Hauptschule**, a **Realschule**, or a **Gymnasium**. During this time pupils can find out if they are suited to the type of school they are attending, and at the end of the two years they may transfer to a different school.

Orient- /ˈoːri̯ɛnt-/: **~tabak** *der* Oriental tobacco; **~teppich** *der* oriental carpet; (Läufer) oriental rug

orig. *Abk.* **= original** genuine

Origano /oˈriːgano/ *der;* **~:** oregano

original /origiˈnaːl/
A *Adj.* original; (echt) genuine; authentic
B *adv.* **~ indische Seide** genuine Indian silk; **etw. ~ übertragen** broadcast sth. live

Original *das;* **~s, ~e** [1] (Urschrift o. Ä.) original [2] (eigenwilliger Mensch) character

original-, Original-: ~aus·gabe *die* original *or* first edition; **~fassung** *die* original version; **in der spanischen ~fassung** in the original Spanish version; **~getreu A** *Adj.* faithful *or* true [to the original] *postpos.;* **B** *adv.* in a manner faithful *or* true to the original

Originalität /originaliˈtɛːt/ *die;* **~** [1] (Echtheit) genuineness; authenticity [2] (Einmaligkeit) originality

Original-: ~rezept *das* original recipe; **~titel** *der* original-language title; **~ton** *der; Pl.* **~töne** (Film, Ferns.) direct sound; original sound; **Reportageausschnitte im ~ton von 1936** excerpts from news reports with the original 1936 soundtrack; **„~ton DDR-Fernsehen"** 'GDR television commentary'

originär /origiˈnɛːɐ̯/ *Adj.; adv.* original

originell /origiˈnɛl/
A *Adj.* (ursprünglich) original; (neu) novel; (ugs.: witzig) witty, funny, comical ‹*story*›; comical, funny ‹*costume*›; **ein ~er Kopf sein** have an original mind
B *adv.* (ursprünglich) ‹*write, argue*› with originality; (ugs.: witzig) ‹*write, argue*› wittily

Orkan /ɔrˈkaːn/ *der;* **~[e]s, ~e** hurricane; (fig.) thunderous storm; **der Sturm schwoll zum ~ an** the storm rose to hurricane force

orkan·artig *Adj.* ‹*winds, gusts*› of almost hurricane force; **~er Beifall** (fig.) thunderous applause

Orkney·inseln /ˈɔːknɪ-/ *Pl.* Orkney Islands; Orkneys

Orkus /ˈɔrkʊs/ *der;* **~** (geh.) Orcus; Hades

Ornament /ɔrnaˈmɛnt/ *das;* **~[e]s, ~e** (Kunstw.) ornament

ornamental /ɔrnamɛnˈtaːl/ *Adj.* (Kunstw.) ornamental; decorative

Ornat /ɔrˈnaːt/ *der;* **~[e]s, ~e** (eines Priesters) vestments *pl.;* (eines Hochschullehrers) academic dress; (eines Richters) official robes *pl.;* **in vollem ~** (ugs. scherzh.) dressed [up] to the nines

Ornithologe /ɔrnitoˈloːgə/ *der;* **~n, ~n** ornithologist

Ornithologie *die;* **~:** ornithology *no art.*

Ornithologin *die;* **~, ~nen** ornithologist

ornithologisch *Adj.* ornithological

Ort[1] /ɔrt/ *der;* **~[e]s, ~e** [1] (Platz) place; **an öffentlichen ~en** in public places; **etw. an seinem ~ lassen** leave sth. where it is/was; **ein ~ des Schreckens/der Stille** a place of terror/quiet; **~ der Handlung: …** the scene of the action is …; **an den ~ des Verbrechens zurückkehren** return to the scene of the crime; **an ~ und Stelle** there and then; **an ~ und Stelle sein/ankommen** (an der gewünschten Stelle) be/arrive there; **höheren ~[e]s** higher up; **am angegebenen ~** (Schrift u. Druckw.) in the same work; **der gewisse** *od.* **stille** *od.* **bewusste ~** (ugs. verhüll.) the smallest room (coll. euphem.); *s. auch* **Örtchen** [2] (~schaft) (Dorf) village; (Stadt) town; **am ~ wohnen** live in the village/town; **von ~ zu ~:** from place to place; **das beste Hotel am ~:** the best hotel in the place

Ort[2] *in* **vor ~:** on the spot; (Bergmannsspr.) at the [coal]face

Örtchen /ˈœrtçən/ *das;* **~s, ~** (ugs. verhüll.) **das ~:** the smallest room (coll. euphem.); **aufs ~ müssen** have to pay a visit (coll. euphem.)

orten *tr. V.* (bes. Flugw., Seew.) find the position of

orthodox /ɔrtoˈdɔks/ *Adj.* [1] (Rel.) orthodox; **die ~en Kirchen** the Orthodox Churches [2] (starr) rigid [3] (strenggläubig) strict [4] (fig.: traditionell) orthodox

Orthodoxie /ɔrtodɔˈksiː/ *die;* **~** (Rel.) orthodoxy

Orthographie *die;* **~, ~n** orthography

orthographisch
A *Adj.* orthographic; **~e Fehler** spelling mistakes

B *adv.* orthographically; **~ richtig schreiben** spell correctly

Orthopäde /ɔrtoˈpɛːdə/ *der;* **~n, ~n** ▸ℹ **S. 113** orthopaedist; orthopaedic specialist

Orthopädie /ɔrtopɛˈdiː/ *die;* **~, ~n** 1 orthopaedics *sing., no art.;* **Facharzt für ~** ▸**Orthopäde** 2 (ugs.: Abteilung) orthopaedic department; **auf/in der ~ liegen** be a patient in the orthopaedic department

Orthopädin *die;* **~, ~nen** ▸ℹ **S. 113** ▸**Orthopäde**

orthopädisch
A *Adj.* orthopaedic
B *adv.* orthopaedically

örtlich /ˈœrtlɪç/
A *Adj.* 1 (Med.) local ‹*anaesthetic etc.*› 2 (begrenzt) local
B *adv.* 1 (Med.) locally; **~ betäubt werden** be given a local anaesthetic 2 (begrenzt) **~ begrenzte Kampfhandlungen** [limited] local encounters; **~ verschieden sein** vary from place to place

Örtlichkeit *die;* **~, ~en** 1 (Gebiet) locality; **sich mit den ~en vertraut machen** get to know the area 2 (Stelle) place 3 ▸**Örtchen**

orts-, Orts-: ~angabe *die* indication of place; **~ansässig** *Adj.* local; **seine Familie ist schon lange ~ansässig** his family has lived locally for a long time; **die ~ansässigen** the local residents; **~ausgang** *der* end of the village/town; **~bestimmung** *die* (Geogr.) determination of the latitude and longitude of a place

Ortschaft *die;* **~, ~en** (Dorf) village; (Stadt) town; **geschlossene ~:** built-up area

orts-, Orts-: ~eingang *der* entrance to the village/town; **~fremd** *Adj.* 1 (nicht ~ansässig) **~fremde Personen** visitors to the village/town; **die ~fremden Besucher** visitors from outside the village/town; 2 (nicht ~kundig) **~fremd sein** be a stranger [to the village/town]; **~fremde** *Pl.* strangers [to the village/town]; **~gebunden** *Adj.* tied to the locality *postpos.;* **~gespräch** *das* (Fernspr.) local call; **~gruppe** *die* local branch; **~kenntnis** *die* knowledge of the place; **[gute] ~kenntnisse haben** know the place [well]; **~krankenkasse** *die* compulsory medical *or* health insurance scheme (organized at district level); **~kundig** *Adj.* **ein ~kundiger Führer** a guide who knows the place well; **ein ~kundiger** someone who knows the place well; **~name** *der* place name; **~netz** *das* 1 (Fernspr.) local exchange network; 2 (Energiewirtsch.) local distribution network; **~netzkennzahl** *die* (Fernspr.) dialling code; area code (Amer.); **~schild** *das* place name sign; **~sinn** *der* sense of direction; **~tarif** *der* local rate; **~teil** *der* area [of the village/town]; **~üblich** *Adj.* local ‹*customs, practices*›; **die ~übliche Miete** the rents *pl.* here/there; **~unkundig** *Adj.* ‹*person*› who does not know the place; **~verkehr** *der* 1 (Straßenverkehr) local traffic; 2 (Post) local postal service; 3 (Telefon) local telephone service; **~wechsel** *der* change of locality; **ein ~wechsel wird dir gut tun** a change of environment will do you good; **~zeit** *die* local time; **~zulage** *die,* **~zuschlag** *der: salary weighting allowance for employees in the public services*

Ortung *die;* **~, ~en** (bes. Flugw., Seew.) **die ~ von feindlichen Schiffen/Flugzeugen** finding the position of enemy ships/aircraft

Oscar /ˈɔskar/ *der;* **~[s], ~s** Oscar

Öse /ˈøːzə/ *die;* **~, ~n** eye; (an Schuh, Stiefel) eyelet

osmanisch /ɔsˈmaːnɪʃ/ *Adj.* (hist.) **das Osmanische Reich** the Ottoman Empire

Osmose /ɔsˈmoːzə/ *die;* **~, ~n** (chem., Bot.) osmosis

OSO *Abk.* **= Ostsüdost[en]** ▸ℹ **S. 363** ESE

Ossi¹ /ˈɔsi/ *der;* **~s, ~s** (ugs.) Easterner; East German

Ossi² *die;* **~, ~s** (ugs.) Easterner; East German [woman]

> **Ossi**
>
> A colloquial and sometimes derogatory term for someone from East Germany, as opposed to a **Wessi** (someone from West Germany).

Ost¹ /ɔst/ ▸ℹ **S. 363** 1 (bes. Seemannsspr., Met.: Richtung) east; **nach ~:** eastwards; **aus** *od.* **von ~:** from the east 2 (östliches Gebiet, Politik) East; **in ~ und West** in the East and [in] the West; **aus ~ und West** from East and West; **~ und West** the East and the West; **zwischen ~ und West** between [the] East and [the] West 3 *einem Substantiv nachgestellt* East; **Berlin (~)** East Berlin

Ost² *der;* **~[e]s, ~e** (Seemannsspr.) easterly; (dichter.) east wind

ost-, Ost-: ~afrika *(das)* East Africa; **~asien** *(das)* East *or* Eastern Asia; **~asiatisch** *Adj.* East Asian

Ost·berlin *(das)* East Berlin

Ost·berliner
A *der* East Berliner
B *indekl. Adj.* East Berlin

Ost·berlinerin *die* ▸**Ostberliner**

ost-, Ost-: ~besuch *der* (ugs.) visitor/visitors from East Germany; **~block** *der* Eastern bloc; **~block·staat** *der* Eastern-bloc state; **~deutsch A** *Adj.* 1 Eastern German; 2 (politisch) East German; **B** *adv.* in an Eastern German manner; **~deutsche** *der/die* 1 (Politik) East German; 2 (Geogr.) Eastern German; **~deutschland** *(das)* 1 (Politik) East Germany; 2 (Geogr.) Eastern Germany; **~elbisch** *Adj.* from east of the Elbe *postpos.* (*usu. referring to the conservative landowners in 19th-century Prussia*)

Osten *der;* **~s** ▸ℹ **S. 363** 1 (Richtung) east; **nach ~:** eastwards; **aus** *od.* **von ~:** from the east; *s. auch* **Norden 1** 2 (Gegend) eastern part; **aus dem ~:** from the east 3 (Geogr.) **der ~:** the East; **der Ferne ~:** the Far East; **der Mittlere ~:** south-western Asia (*including Afghanistan and Nepal*); **der Nahe ~:** the Middle East 4 (Politik) **der ~** (der Ostblock) the East; (die DDR, Ostdeutschland) the East; East Germany

Ost·ende /ɔstˈɛndə/ *(das);* **~s** ▸ℹ **S. 675** Ostend

ostentativ /ɔstɛntaˈtiːf/ (geh.)
A *Adj.* pointed ‹*absence, silence*›; overt ‹*hostility*›; exaggerated ‹*heartiness*›; studied ‹*calm, casualness*›; ostentatious ‹*gesture*›
B *adv.* pointedly; ‹*embrace*› ostentatiously

Oster-: ~ei *das* Easter egg; **~feier·tag** *der: in* **über die ~feiertage** over Easter; on Easter Sunday and [Easter] Monday; **der erste/zweite ~feiertag** Easter Sunday/Monday; **~fest** *das* Easter [holiday]; **~glocke** *die* daffodil; **~hase** *der* Easter hare (said to bring children their Easter Eggs); **~insel** *die* Easter Island; **~kerze** *die* (kath. Rel.) paschal *or* Easter candle; **~lamm** *das* Paschal lamb

österlich /ˈøːstɐlɪç/
A *Adj.* Easter *attrib*
B *adv.* **~ geschmückt** decorated for Easter

Oster-: ~marsch *der* Easter march (*against war and nuclear weapons*); **~montag** *der* Easter Monday *no def. art.; s. auch* **Dienstag**

Ostern /ˈoːstɐn/ *das;* **~, ~** ▸ℹ **S. 331** Easter; **Frohe** *od.* **Fröhliche ~:** Happy Easter!; **diese/letzte/nächste ~:** this/last/next Easter; **zu** *od.* (bes. südd.) **an ~:** at Easter; **[zu/über] ~ Besuch bekommen** have people to stay at/over Easter; **zu ~ einen Kuchen backen** bake a cake for Easter; **wenn ~ und Pfingsten** *od.* **Weihnachten zusammenfallen** *od.* **auf einen Tag fallen** (ugs.) not this side of doomsday (coll.)

> **Ostern**
>
> German Easter traditions include hiding Easter eggs (often dyed hardboiled eggs or the chocolate variety) in the garden for children. The *Osterhase* (Easter hare) is supposed to have brought them. *Ostermontag* (Easter Monday) is also a public holiday.

Österreich /ˈøːstəraiç/ *(das);* **~s** Austria; **~-Ungarn** (hist.) Austria-Hungary

Österreicher *der;* **~s, ~, Österreicherin** *die;* **~, ~nen** Austrian; **er/sie ist ~/~in** he/she is Austrian; *s. auch* **-in**

österreichisch *Adj.* Austrian; **das Österreichische** what is Austrian; (Sprache) Austrian German; **~-ungarisch** (hist.) Austro-Hungarian; *s. auch* **deutsch; Deutsch**

Oster-: ~sonntag *der* Easter Sunday *no def. art.; s. auch* **Dienstag**; **~spiel** *das* Easter play

Ost·erweiterung *die* (Politik) Eastward expansion

Oster-: ~woche *die* week before Easter; **~zeit** *die:* **in der ~zeit** at Easter time

ost-, Ost-: ~europa *(das)* Eastern Europe; **~europäisch** *Adj.* East[ern] European; **~europäische Zeit** Eastern European Time; **~flanke** *die* (Milit., Geogr.) eastern flank; (Met.) eastern edge

Ost·friesische Inseln *Pl.* East Frisian Islands

Ost·friesland *(das);* **~s** East Friesland; Ostfriesland

ost-, Ost-: ~gebiet *das* 1 (**~en**) eastern part; 2 *Pl. former German territories east of the Oder-Neisse line;* **~geld** *das* (ugs.) East German money; **~germanisch** *Adj.* East Germanic; **~gote** *der,* **~gotin** *die* Ostrogoth; **~hang** *der* eastern slope

Ostinato /ɔstiˈnaːto/ *der od. das;* **~s, ~s** *od.* **Ostinati** (Mus.) ostinato

Ost-: ~jude *der,* **~jüdin** *die* East[ern] European Jew; **~kirche** *die* Eastern Church; **~kolonisation** *die* (hist.) *German colonization of Eastern Europe in the Middle Ages;* **~küste** *die* east[ern] coast

Ostler /ˈɔstlɐ/ *der;* **~s, ~** (ugs.) Easterner; East German; **Ostlerin** *die;* **~, ~nen** (ugs.) Easterner; East German [woman]

östlich /ˈœstlɪç/
A *Adj.* ▸ℹ **S. 363** 1 (im Osten) eastern; **15 Grad ~er Länge** 15 degrees east [longitude]; **~st** easternmost; **das ~e Ufer** the east bank; **der ~ste Punkt** the most easterly point 2 (nach, aus dem Osten) easterly 3 (aus dem Osten kommend, für den Osten typisch) Eastern 4 (politisch) Eastern; ‹*delegates, spies, etc.*› from the East; ‹*infiltration*› by the East; ‹*influence, policies*› of the East
B *adv.* eastwards; **~ von ...** [to the] east of ...
C *Präp. mit Gen.* [to the] east of

ost-, Ost-: ~mark¹ *die; Pl.* **~ ~** (ugs.) East German mark; **~mark²** *die* (hist.) East March; **~nord·ost¹** /-ˈ-ˈ-/ (Seemannsspr., Met.) east-north-east; *s. auch* **Nord¹ 1**; **~nord·ost²** /-ˈ-ˈ-/ *der* (Seemannsspr.) east-north-easter[ly]; **~nord·osten** /-ˈ-ˈ--/ *der* east-north-east; *s. auch* **Norden 1**; **~politik** *die* Ostpolitik (West German policy towards Eastern Europe, and towards East Germany in particular); **~preuße** *der* East Prussian; **~preußen** *(das)* East Prussia; **~preußin** *die* East Prussian; **~preußisch** *Adj.* East Prussian

Östrogen /œstroˈgeːn/ *das;* **~s, ~e** (Physiol.) oestrogen

Ost·see *die* Baltic [Sea]

Ostsee- Baltic

ost-, Ost-: ~seite *die* eastern side; **~süd·ost¹** /-ˈ-ˈ-/ (Seemannsspr., Met.) east-south-east; *s. auch* **Nord¹ 1**; **~süd·ost²** /-ˈ-ˈ-/ *der* (Seemannsspr.) east-south-easter[ly]; **~südosten** /-ˈ-ˈ--/ *der* east-south-east; *s. auch* **Norden 1**; **~teil** *der* eastern part; **~timor** *(das);* **~s** East Timor; **~verträge** *Pl.* (Politik) treaties with the Eastern bloc; **~wärts** *Adv.* ▸ℹ **S. 363** 1 (nach **~en**) eastwards; 2 (im **~en**) to the east; **~-West-Dialog** *der* (Politik) East-West dialogue; **~-West-Konflikt** *der* (Politik) East-West conflict; **~westlich** **A** *Adj.* east-west *attrib.*; from east to west *postpos.;* **B** *adv.* east-west; [from] east to west; **~wind** *der* east[erly] wind; **~zone** *die* Eastern zone; **die ~zone** (ugs.: die DDR) the East

Oszillation /ɔstsɪlaˈtsi̯oːn/ *die;* **~, ~en** (Physik, auch fig.) oscillation

oszillieren /ɔstsɪˈliːrən/ *itr. V.* (Physik, auch fig.) oscillate

Oszillograph *der;* **~en, ~en** (Physik) oscillograph

O-Ton *der; Pl.* **O-Töne** ▸**Originalton**

Otter[1] /ˈɔtɐ/ *der;* **~s, ~** (Fisch~) otter

Otter[2] *die;* **~, ~n** (Viper) adder; viper

Ottern·gezücht *das* (veralt. abwertend) brood of vipers

Otto /ˈɔto/ *der;* **~s, ~s** (salopp) whopper (coll.); *s. auch* **flott**; **Normalverbraucher**

Ottomane /ɔtoˈmaːnə/ *die;* **~, ~n** (veralt.) ottoman

Otto·motor *der* Otto engine

Ottone /ɔˈtoːnə/ *der;* **~n, ~n** (hist.) Ottonian (*Saxon emperor, esp. Otto I, II, or III*)

ÖTV *Abk.* **= Gewerkschaft öffentliche Dienste, Transport und Verkehr** union of transport and public-service workers

out /aut/ *Adj.* **~ sein** (ugs.) be out

outen /ˈautn/ *tr. V.* (ugs.) out (coll.)

Output /ˈautput/ *der od. das;* **~s, ~s** output

outrieren /uˈtriːrən/ *itr. V.* (geh.) exaggerate; ‹*Schauspieler*› overact; **outriert** exaggerated; over the top (coll.)

Ouvertüre /uvɛrˈtyːrə/ *die;* **~, ~n** (auch fig.) overture (+ *Gen.* to)

oval /oˈvaːl/ *Adj.* oval

Oval *das;* **~s, ~e** oval

Ovation /ovaˈtsi̯oːn/ *die;* **~, ~en** ovation; **jmdm. ~en darbringen** give sb. an ovation

Overall /ˈouvərɔːl/ *der;* **~s, ~s** overalls *pl.*

Ovid /oˈviːt/ (*der*) Ovid

Ovolakto·vegetarier /ovoˈlakto-/ *der,* **Ovolakto·vegetarierin** *die* ovolacto-vegetarian

ÖVP *Abk.* **= Österreichische Volkspartei** Austrian People's Party

> **ÖVP – Österreichische Volkspartei**
>
> The conservative People's Party is Austria's centrist party. It was founded in 1945 and is the second largest party.

Ovulation /ovulaˈtsi̯oːn/ *die;* **~, ~en** (Zool., Physiol.) ovulation

Ovulations·hemmer *der;* **~s, ~** (Med.) anovulant

Oxid /ɔˈksiːt/ *das;* **~[e]s, ~e** (Chemie) oxide

Oxidation /ɔksidaˈtsi̯oːn/ *die;* **~, ~en** (Chemie) oxidation

oxidieren (Chemie)
A *itr. V.; auch mit sein* oxidize
B *tr. V.* oxidize

Oxyd /ɔˈksyːt/ *usw.* ▸**Oxid** *usw.*

Ozean /ˈoːtseaːn/ *der;* **~s, ~e** (auch fig.) ocean

Ozean·dampfer *der* ocean-going steamer; (für Passagiere) ocean liner

Ozeanien /otseˈaːni̯ən/ (*das*); **~s** Oceania

ozeanisch *Adj.* oceanic; (Ozeanien betreffend) Oceanic

Ozeanographie /otseanograˈfiː/ *die;* **~:** oceanography *no art.*

Ozeanologe *der;* **~n, ~n** oceanologist

Ozeanologie *die;* **~:** oceanology

Ozeanologin *die;* **~, ~nen** oceanologist

ozeanologisch
A *Adj.* oceanological
B *adv.* **~ interessiert sein** be interested in oceanology

Ozelot /ˈoːtselɔt/ *der;* **~s, ~e** *od.* **~s** **1** (Tier, Fell) ocelot **2** (Kleidungsstück) ocelot coat/jacket *etc.*

Ozon /oˈtsoːn/ *der od. das;* **~s** ozone; **lieber warmer Mief als kalter ~!** (ugs. scherzh.) I'd rather be breathing a warm fug than cold fresh air

Ozon-: ~alarm *der* ozone alert; **bei ~alarm** when there is/was an ozone alert; **~alarm geben** issue an ozone alert; **~killer** *der* (ugs.) ozone killer; **~konzentration** *die;* ozone concentration; **~loch** *das* hole in the ozone layer; **~schicht** *die* ozone layer; **~wert** *der* ozone value

O

Pp

p, P /pe/ *das;* **~, ~:** p/P; *s. auch* **a, A**

p.A. *Abk.* (österr.) **= per Adresse** c/o

Pa /pa/ *der;* **~s, ~s** (fam. veralt.) dad (coll.)

paar /paːɐ̯/ *indekl. Indefinitpron.* **ein ~ ...** a few ...; (zwei od. drei) a couple of ...; a few ...; **ein ~ Hundert Bücher** *usw.* a few hundred/a couple of hundred books *etc.*; **ein ~ waren dagegen** a few [people]/a couple [of people] were against [it]; **in ein ~ Tagen** in a few/a couple of days[' time]; **ein ~ Mal[e]** a few times/a couple of times; **deine ~ Euro** the few/couple of euros you've got; **die ~ Mal[e], die ich dort war** the few times I've been there; **alle ~ Minuten** every few minutes/every couple of minutes; **du kriegst gleich ein ~ [gelangt]** (ugs.) I'll stick one on you (coll.); *s. auch* **Zeile 1**

Paar *das;* **~[e]s, ~e** **1** pair; (Mann und Frau, Tanz~) couple; **sich in** *od.* **zu ~en aufstellen** line up in pairs **2** (Tiere, Dinge) pair; **ein ~ Würstchen** two sausages; a couple of sausages; **ein ~ Schuhe** a pair of shoes; **zwei ~ Socken** two pairs of socks; **ein ~ Hosen** (ugs.) a pair of trousers

Paar·beziehung *die* relationship [as a couple]

paaren

A *refl. V.* **1** (sich begatten) ‹*animals*› mate; ‹*people*› couple, copulate **2** (sich verbinden) **sich mit etw. ~:** be combined with sth.

B *tr. V.* **1** (kreuzen) mate **2** (zusammenstellen) pair **3** (verbinden) combine (**mit** with)

Paarhufer *der;* **~s, ~** (Zool.) even-toed ungulate (Zool.); cloven-hoofed animal

paarig (bes. Biol., Anat.)

A *Adj.* paired *attrib.*; **~ sein** occur in pairs

B *adv.* **~ angeordnet** arranged in pairs *postpos.*

paar-, Paar-: ~lauf *der,* **~laufen** *das;* **~~s** pairs skating; pairs *pl.*; ***~mal** ▸**paar**; **~reim** *der* (Verslehre) rhyming couplets *pl.*

Paarung *die;* **~, ~en** **1** (Zool.) mating **2** (das Zusammenstellen) pairing; **die ~ der Mannschaften für das Endturnier** deciding which teams will/would play each other in the finals **3** (das Verbinden) combination

paarungs-, Paarungs-: ~verhalten *das* (Zool.) mating behaviour; **~willig** *Adj.* (Zool.) wanting to mate *postpos.*; **~zeit** *die* (Zool.) mating season

paar·weise

A *Adv.* in pairs

B *adj.* ‹*arrangement etc.*› in pairs

Paar·zeher *der;* **~s, ~** (Zool.) ▸**Paarhufer**

Pacht /paxt/ *die;* **~, ~en** **1** (Nutzung) **etw. in ~ nehmen** lease sth.; take sth. on lease; **etw. in ~ haben** have sth. on lease; **etw. in ~ geben** lease sth.; let sth. on lease **2** (Vertrag) lease **3** (Miete) rent

Pacht·brief *der* lease

pachten *tr. V.* lease; take a lease on; **jmdn./etw. [für sich] gepachtet haben** (fig. ugs.) have got a monopoly on sb./sth. (coll.)

Pächter /ˈpɛçtɐ/ *der;* **~s, ~, Pächterin** *die;* **~, ~nen** leaseholder; lessee; (eines Hofes) tenant

Pacht·geld *das* rent

Pachtung *die;* **~, ~en** leasing

Pacht-: ~vertrag *der* lease; **~zins** *der; Pl.* **~~e** rent

Pack¹ /pak/ *der;* **~[e]s, ~e** *od.* **Päcke** /ˈpɛkə/ pile; (zusammengeschnürt) bundle; (Packung) pack; (Kartenspiel) pack (Brit.); deck (Amer.)

Pack² *das;* **~[e]s** (ugs. abwertend) rabble; riff-raff; **~ schlägt sich, ~ verträgt sich** (ugs.) rabble *or* riff-raff like that are at each other's throats one minute and the best of friends [again] the next

Package /ˈpɛkɪtʃ/ *das;* **~, ~s** (Werbespr. Jargon) package

Päckchen /ˈpɛkçən/ *das;* **~s, ~** **1** (kleines Paket) package; small parcel; (Bündel) packet; bundle; (Postw.) small parcel (below a specified weight); **sein ~ zu tragen haben** (fig. ugs.) have one's troubles **2** ▸**Packung 1**

Pack·eis *das* pack ice

packeln /ˈpakl̩n/ *itr. V.* (österr. abwertend) make *or* do a deal/deals

packen

A *tr. V.* **1** pack; **etw. in einen Koffer/ein Paket ~:** pack *or* put sth. in[to] a suitcase/put sth. in[to] a parcel; **etw. aus etw. ~:** unpack sth. from sth.; **sich/jmdn. ins Bett ~** (ugs.) go to bed/put sb. to bed; **der Bus war gepackt voll** (fig. ugs.) the bus was jam-packed (coll.) **2** (fassen) grab [hold of]; seize; **jmdn. am** *od.* **beim Kragen ~:** grab [hold of] *or* seize sb. by the collar; **eine Windbö packte das Auto** a gust of wind caught the car; *s. auch* **Ehre** **3** (überkommen) **Furcht/Angst** *usw.* **packte ihn/er wurde von Furcht/Angst** *usw.* **gepackt** he was seized with fear *etc.*; **es hat ihn gepackt** (ugs.) he's got it bad (coll.) **4** (fesseln) enthral; ‹*thriller, crime story, etc.*› grip; **ein ~des Rennen** a thrilling race **5** (ugs.: schaffen) **ein Examen ~:** manage to get through an exam (coll.); **es ~:** make a go of it; **~ wir's noch?** are we going to make it?; **einen Gegner ~** (Sportjargon: besiegen) get the better of an opponent **6** (ugs.: begreifen) get (coll.) **7** (salopp: weggehen) **~ wir's?** shall we push off? (coll.) **8** (DV) pack; zip

B *itr. V.* (Koffer usw. ~) pack

C *refl. V.* (ugs. veralt.) beat it (coll.); clear off (coll.)

Packen *der;* **~s, ~:** pile; (von Büchern, Zeitungen) pile; stack; (zusammengeschnürt) bundle; (von Geldscheinen) wad

Packer *der;* **~s, ~:** packer; (Möbel~) [packer and] removal man (Brit.) *or* (Amer.) moving man

Packerei *die;* **~, ~en** **1** (ugs. abwertend) packing and unpacking **2** (eines Betriebs) packing department

Packerin *die;* **~, ~nen** packer

Pack-: ~esel *der* (ugs.) pack donkey; (fig.) packhorse; **~papier** *das* [stout] wrapping paper; **~pferd** *das* packhorse; **~tisch** *der* packing table

Packung *die;* **~, ~en** **1** packet; pack (esp. Amer.); **eine ~ Zigaretten** a packet *or* (Amer.) pack of cigarettes; **eine ~ Pralinen** a box of chocolates **2** (Med., Kosmetik) pack **3** (Technik) packing

Pack-: ~wagen *der* **1** luggage van (Brit.); baggage car (Amer.); **2** (hist.: Fuhrwerk) baggage wagon; **~zettel** *der* packing slip

Pädagoge /pɛdaˈgoːgə/ *der;* **~n, ~n** ▸ⓘ **S. 113** **1** (Erzieher, Lehrer) teacher **2** (Wissenschaftler) educationalist; educational theorist

Pädagogik *die;* **~:** [theory and methodology of] education

Pädagogin *die;* **~, ~nen** ▸ⓘ **S. 113** ▸**Pädagoge**

pädagogisch

A *Adj.* **1** (erzieherisch) educational; **seine ~en Fähigkeiten** his teaching ability *sing.* **2** (die Pädagogik betreffend) ‹*lecture, dissertation, etc.*› on education; **Pädagogische Hochschule** College of Education; **eine ~e Ausbildung** a training in education

B *adv.* **1** (erzieherisch) educationally ‹*sound, wrong*›; **~ wirken** have an educational effect **2** (die Pädagogik betreffend) **~ nicht auf dem neuesten Stand sein** not be up with the latest developments in educational theory [and methodology]

pädagogisieren *tr. V.* (oft abwertend) **etw. ~:** look at sth. through the eyes of an educational theorist

Paddel /ˈpadl̩/ *das;* **~s, ~:** paddle

Paddel·boot *das* canoe

paddeln *itr. V.; mit sein; ohne Richtungsangabe auch mit haben* **1** (Paddelboot fahren) paddle; canoe; (als Sport) canoe **2** (ugs.: schlecht schwimmen) dog-paddle

Paddel·sport *der* canoeing *no art.*

Paddler *der;* **~s, ~, Paddlerin** *die;* **~, ~nen** canoeist

Päderast /pedeˈrast/ *der;* **~en, ~en** pederast

Päderastie /pɛderasˈtiː/ *die;* **~:** pederasty *no art.*

Pädiater /pɛˈdiaːtɐ/ *der;* **~s, ~, Pädiaterin** *die;* **~, ~nen** (Med.) paediatrician

Pädiatrie /pɛdiaˈtriː/ *die;* **~** (Med.) paediatrics *sing., no art.*

pädiatrisch *Adj.* (Med.) paediatric

pädophil *Adj.* (Med., Psych.) paedophile

Pädophile *der; adj. Dekl.* (Med., Psych.) paedophile

paff /paf/ *Interj.* bang

paffen

A *tr. V.* puff at ‹*pipe etc.*›; puff out ‹*smoke*›; **vierzig Zigaretten am Tag ~:** puff one's way through forty cigarettes a day

B *itr. V.* puff away; **er pafft nur** he's just puffing at it

Page /ˈpaːʒə/ *der;* **~n, ~n** ▸ⓘ **S. 113** **1** (Hotel~) page; bellboy **2** (hist.) page

Pagen·kopf *der* pageboy cut *or* style

Pager /ˈpeɪdʒɐ/ *der;* **~s, ~:** pager

paginieren /pagiˈniːrən/ *tr. V.* (Schrift- und Buchw.) paginate

Pagode /paˈgoːdə/ *die;* **~, ~n** **1** (Gebäude) pagoda **2** (österr., sonst veralt.: Figur) mandarin

pah /paː/ *Interj.* huh

Paillette /paiˈjɛtə/ *die;* **~, ~n** (Mode) paillette; sequin; spangle

Pak /pak/ *die;* **~, ~** *od.* **~s** (Milit.) **1** (Panzerabwehrkanone) anti-tank gun **2** (Artillerie) anti-tank force

Paket /paˈkeːt/ *das;* **~[e]s, ~e** **1** pile; (zusammengeschnürt) bundle; (Eingepacktes, Post~, Schachtel) parcel; (Packung) packet; pack (esp. Amer.) **2** (fig.: Gesamtheit) package

Paket-: ~annahme *die* **1** acceptance of parcels; **2** (Stelle) parcels office; (Schalter) parcels counter; **~ausgabe** *die* **1** issue of parcels; **2** ▸**~annahme 2**; **~boot** *das*

P

(veralt.) packet [boat]; **~dienst** *der* parcel service; **~karte** *die* parcel dispatch form; **~post** *die* **1** (Beförderung) parcel post; **2** (Fahrzeug) parcel *or* post office delivery van; **~schalter** *der* parcels counter; **~sendung** *die* parcel

Pakistan /ˈpaːkɪstaːn/ *(das)*; **~s** Pakistan

Pakistaner *der*; **~s, ~, Pakistanerin** *die*; **~, ~nen, Pakistani** /pakɪsˈtaːni/ *der*; **~[s], ~[s]**/*die*; **~, ~[s]** ▸**i S. 520** Pakistani

pakistanisch *Adj.* ▸**i S. 520** Pakistani

Pakt /pakt/ *der*; **~[e]s, ~e** pact; **einen ~ [ab]schließen** make *or* conclude a pact

paktieren *itr. V.* (oft abwertend) make *or* do a deal/deals (**mit** with)

Paladin /palaˈdiːn/ *der*; **~s, ~e** **1** (Myth.) paladin **2** (Gefolgsmann) henchman

Palais /paˈlɛː/ *das*; **~** /...ɛː(s)/, **~** /...ɛːs/ palace

Paläolithikum /paleoˈliːtikʊm/ *das*; **~s** Palaeolithic

Paläontologie /paleɔntoloˈgiː/ *die*; **~:** palaeontology *no art.*

Paläozän /paleoˈtsɛːn/ *das*; **~s** (Geol.) Palaeocene

Paläozoikum /paleoˈtsoːikʊm/ *das*; **~s** palaeozoic era

Palast /paˈlast/ *der*; **~[e]s, Paläste** /paˈlɛstə/ palace

palast·artig *Adj.* palatial

Palästina /paleˈstiːna/ *(das)*; **~s** Palestine

Palästinenser *der*; **~s, ~, Palästinenserin** *die*; **~, ~nen** ▸**i S. 520** Palestinian

palästinensisch *Adj.* ▸**i S. 520** Palestinian

Palast·revolution *die* (Politik, auch fig.) palace revolution

Palatschinke /palaˈtʃɪŋkə/ *die*; **~, ~n** (österr.) pancake with sweet filling

Palaver /paˈlaːvɐ/ *das*; **~s, ~** (ugs. abwertend) palaver; **ein ~ abhalten** palaver

palavern *itr. V.* (ugs. abwertend) palaver

Paletot /ˈpaləto/ *der*; **~s, ~s** (man's double-breasted) overcoat [*with high velvet collar*]

Palette /paˈlɛtə/ *die*; **~, ~n** **1** (Malerei) palette **2** (bes. Werbespr.: Vielfalt) diverse range; **die ganze ~:** the whole range **3** (Technik, Wirtsch.: Untersatz) pallet

paletten·weise *Adv.* **1** (auf Paletten) on pallets **2** (ugs.: in großer Menge) by the pallet-load

paletti *Adj.*: *in* **alles ~** (ugs.) everything's OK (coll.) *or* all right

Palimpsest /palɪmˈpsɛst/ *der od. das*; **~[e]s, ~e** palimpsest

Palindrom /palɪnˈdroːm/ *das*; **~s, ~e** palindrome

Palisade /paliˈzaːdə/ *die*; **~, ~n** **1** (Pfahl) pale; stake **2** (Anlage) palisade

Palisander /paliˈsandɐ/ *der*; **~s, ~, Palisander·holz** *das* (Dalbergia nigra) Brazilian rosewood; (Dalbergia latifolia) blackwood

palliativ /paljaˈtiːf/ (Med.)

A *Adj.* palliative

B *adv.* **jmdn. ~ behandeln** give sb. palliative treatment

Palme /ˈpalmə/ *die*; **~, ~n** palm [tree]; **jmdn. auf die ~ bringen** (ugs.) ‹*person*› rile sb. (coll.); ‹*situation*› make sb. wild; **auf die ~ gehen** (ugs.) go off the deep end (coll.); **die ~ [des Sieges]** (fig. geh.) the palm [of victory]

Palmen-: ▸**Palm-**

Palm-: **~kätzchen** *das* [willow] catkin; **~öl** *das* palm oil; **~sonntag** [*auch*: ˈ-ˈ--] *der* (christl. Kirche) Palm Sunday; *s. auch* **Dienstag**

Palmtop (Wz) /ˈpaːmtɔp/ *der*; **~s, ~s** palmtop

Palm-: **~wedel** *der* palm frond; **~zweig** *der* **1** palm branch; **2** (christl. Kirche) palm; **~wein** *der* palm wine

Pamp /pamp/ *der*; **~s** (nordd., ostd.) mush

Pampa /ˈpampa/ *die*; **~, ~s** pampa *usu. in pl.*; **[mitten] in der ~** (Jugendspr.) out in the wilds (coll.)

Pampe /ˈpampə/ *die*; **~** (bes. nordd. u. md.) **1** (Matsch) mud; mire **2** (Brei) mush

Pampelmuse /ˈpampl̩muːzə/ *die*; **~, ~n** grapefruit

Pampf /pampf/ *der*; **~s** (südd.) mush

Pamphlet /pamˈfleːt/ *das*; **~[e]s, ~e** (Streitschrift) polemical pamphlet; (Schmähschrift) defamatory pamphlet

pampig

A *Adj.* **1** (ugs. abwertend: frech) insolent **2** (bes. nordd., ostd.: breiig) mushy

B *adv.* (ugs. abwertend: frech) insolently

Pamps ▸**Pamp**

pan-, Pan- /pan-/: *in Zus.* pan-

Panade /paˈnaːdə/ *die*; **~, ~n** (Kochk.) bread-crumb coating

Panama[1] /ˈpanama/ *(das)* Panama

Panama[2] *der*; **~s, ~s** **1** (Textilind.) Panama fabric **2** (Hut) panama [hat]

Panamaer *der*; **~s, ~, Panamaerin** *die*; **~, ~nen** Panamanian

panamaisch *Adj.* Panamanian

Panama·kanal *der*; **~s** Panama Canal

Panda /ˈpanda/ *der*; **~s, ~s** panda

Pandekten /panˈdɛktn̩/ *Pl.* pandects; (fig.) jurisprudence *sing.*

Pandschab /panˈdʒaːp/ *das*; **~s** Punjab

Paneel /paˈneːl/ *das*; **~s, ~e** **1** (einzelnes Feld) panel **2** (Täfelung) panelling

paneelieren *tr. V.* panel

Pan·flöte *die* pan pipes *pl.*

pan·germanisch *Adj.* pan-German

pan·hellenisch *Adj.* pan-Hellenic

Panier[1] /paˈniːɐ̯/ *das*; **~s, ~e** (veralt.) banner; (Motto) motto

Panier[2] *die*; **~** (österr. Kochk.) ▸**Panade**

panieren *tr. V.* (Kochk.) **etw. ~:** bread sth.; coat sth. with breadcrumbs

Panier·mehl *das* breadcrumbs *pl.*

Panik /ˈpaːnɪk/ *die*; **~, ~en** panic; **[eine] ~ brach aus** panic broke out; **jmdn. in ~** (*Akk.*) **versetzen** throw sb. into a state of panic; **von ~ ergriffen** panic-stricken; **nur keine ~!** don't panic!

Panik-: **~mache** *die* (abwertend) panic-mongering; **~macher** *der*, **~macherin** *die* (abwertend) panic-monger

panisch

A *Adj.* panic *attrib.* ‹*fear, terror*›; panic-stricken ‹*voice, flight*›; **~e Angst vor etw.** (*Dat.*) **haben** have a panic fear of sth.

B *adv.* **sich ~ vor etw.** (*Dat.*) **fürchten** have a panic fear of sth.

Panje·wagen /ˈpanjə-/ *der*: *small wooden cart drawn by a horse* (in Eastern Europe)

Pankreas /ˈpankreas/ *das*; **~, Pankreaten** ▸**i S. 435** (Anat.) pancreas

Panne /ˈpanə/ *die*; **~, ~n** **1** (Auto~) breakdown; (Reifen~) puncture; flat [tyre]; **ich hatte eine ~** (mit dem Auto) my car broke down/my car *or* I had a puncture; (mit dem Fahrrad) I had some trouble with my bicycle/my bicycle *or* I had a puncture **2** (Betriebsstörung) breakdown **3** (Missgeschick) slip-up; mishap; **mit unserem Urlaub haben wir eine ganz schöne ~ erlebt** our holiday this year was a real disaster; **bei der Organisation gab es viele ~n** there were many organizational hitches

Pannen·dienst *der* breakdown service

Panoptikum /paˈnɔptikʊm/ *das*; **~s, Panoptiken** **1** (Kuriositätenkabinett) collection of curios **2** (Wachsfiguren) waxworks *sing. or pl.*

Panorama /panoˈraːma/ *das*; **~s, Panoramen** panorama

Panorama-: **~aufnahme** *die* panorama; **~bus** *der* coach with panoramic windows; **~scheibe** *die* panoramic window; (an Autos) wraparound windscreen; **~spiegel** *der* (Kfz-W.) panoramic mirror

panschen /ˈpanʃn̩/

A *tr. V.* (ugs. abwertend) water down; adulterate; **Whisky mit Wasser ~:** adulterate whisky with water

B *itr. V.* **1** (ugs. abwertend: mischen) water down *or* adulterate the wine/beer *etc.* **2** (ugs.: planschen) splash about

Panscher *der*; **~s, ~** (ugs.) adulterator

Panscherei *die*; **~, ~en** **1** (ugs. abwertend: das Mischen) watering-down; adulteration **2** (ugs.: das Planschen) splashing [about]

Panscherin *die*; **~, ~nen** ▸**Panscher**

Pansen /ˈpanzn̩/ *der*; **~s, ~** **1** (Magen der Wiederkäuer) rumen **2** (nordd.: Magen) stomach; belly

Panter ▸**Panther**

Pan·theismus *der* (Philos., Rel.) pantheism *no art.*

pan·theistisch *Adj.* (Philos., Rel.) pantheistic

Panther /ˈpantɐ/ *der*; **~s, ~:** panther

Pantine /panˈtiːnə/ *die*; **~, ~n** (nordd.) clog; *s. auch* **Latschen**

Pantoffel /panˈtɔfl̩/ *der*; **~s, ~n** **1** backless slipper **2** (mit Absatz) mule **3** (fig.) **unterm ~ stehen** (ugs.) be henpecked

Pantoffel-: **~held** *der* (ugs. abwertend) henpecked husband; **~kino** *das* (ugs.) telly (coll.); **~tierchen** *das* (Biol.) slipper animalcule

Panto·graph /panto-/ *der*; **~en, ~en** pantograph

Pantolette /pantoˈlɛtə/ *die*; **~, ~en** backless slipper

Pantomime[1] /pantoˈmiːmə/ *die*; **~, ~n** mime

Pantomime[2] *der*; **~n, ~n** mime

Panto·mimik *die* mime

panto·mimisch

A *Adj.* ‹*presentation, depiction*› in mime

B *adv.* **etw. ~ darstellen/zeigen** present/show sth. in mime; mime sth.

pantschen *usw.* /ˈpantʃn̩/ ▸**panschen** *usw.*

Panzer /ˈpantsɐ/ *der*; **~s, ~** **1** (Milit.) tank; **die schwedischen ~:** the Swedish tanks *or* armour *sing.* **2** (Zool.) armour *no indef. art.*; (von Schildkröten, Krebsen) shell **3** (hist.: Rüstung) armour *no indef. art.*; **ein ~:** a suit of armour; **ein ~ der Gleichgültigkeit** (fig.) a defensive barrier of indifference **4** (Panzerung) armour-plating *or* -plate *no indef. art.*; (eines Reaktors) shielding

Panzer-: **~abwehr** *die* (Milit.) **1** (Verteidigung) anti-tank defence; **2** (Truppe) anti-tank force; **~abwehr·kanone** *die* (Milit.) anti-tank gun; **~abwehr·rakete** *die* (Milit.) anti-tank rocket; **~division** *die* (Milit.) tank division; armoured division; **~faust** *die* (Milit.) anti-tank rocket launcher; bazooka; **~glas** *das* bulletproof glass; **~grenadier** *der* (Milit.) soldier in the armoured infantry; **~hemd** *das* (hist.) coat of [chain] mail; **~kette** *die* tank track; **~kreuzer** *der* (Marine hist.) armoured cruiser; **„~kreuzer Potemkin"** 'The Battleship Potemkin'; **~mine** *die* anti-tank mine

panzern

A *tr. V.* armour[-plate]

B *refl. V.* (hist.) put on one's armour

Panzer-: **~platte** *die* armour-plate; **~schlacht** *die* (Milit.) tank battle; **~schrank** *der* safe; **~späh·wagen** *der* (Milit.) armoured scout car; **~sperre** *die* (Milit.) anti-tank obstacle; **~truppe** *die* (Milit.) tank force

Panzer·wagen *der* (Milit.) **1** ▸**Panzer 1** **2** (Waggon) armoured wagon

Papa /ˈpapa, *geh., veralt.* paˈpaː/ *der*; **~s, ~** (ugs.) daddy (coll.); **der Herr ~** /-ˈ-/ your/my/his *etc.* [dear] father

Papagallo /papaˈgalo/ *der*; **~[s], ~s** *od.* **Papagalli** Latin Romeo

Papagei /papaˈgai̯/ *der*; **~en** *od.* **~s, ~e[n]** parrot; **alles wie ein ~ nachplappern** repeat everything parrot-fashion

Papageien·krankheit *die* ▸**i S. 439** (Med.) parrot disease; psittacosis *no art.*

Paparazzo *der*; **~s, Paparazzi** paparazzo

Paper /ˈpeɪpə/ *das*; **~s, ~s** paper

Paperback /ˈpeɪpəbɛk/ *das*; **~s, ~s** paperback

Papeterie /papɛtəˈriː/ *die*; **~, ~n** (schweiz.) stationer's

Papi /ˈpapi/ *der*; **~s, ~s** (ugs.) daddy (coll.)

P

Papier /pa'piːɐ̯/ *das;* ~s, ~e [1] paper; **ein Blatt/Fetzen/eine Rolle ~:** a sheet/scrap/roll of paper; **[nur] auf dem ~** (fig.) [only] on paper; **etw. aufs ~ werfen** (fig. geh.) jot sth. down; **etw. zu ~ bringen** get *or* put sth. down on paper; **~ ist geduldig** (Spr.) what's written down in black and white isn't necessarily true; **die ~ verarbeitende Industrie** the paper-processing industry [2] *Pl.* (Ausweis[e]) [identity] papers; **dann können Sie sich Ihre ~e holen** (ugs.) then you might as well collect your cards on the way out [3] (Finanzw.: Wert~) security

Papier-: **~abzug** *der* (Fot.) [paper] print; (Druckw.) paper proof; **~blume** *die* paper flower; **~deutsch** *das* (abwertend) officialese

papieren
[A] *Adj.* [1] (aus Papier) paper [2] (fig.) wooden ‹*style etc.*› [3] (wie Papier) papery
[B] *adv.* (fig.) ‹*speak*› woodenly; ‹*write*› in a wooden style

Papier-: **~fabrik** *die* paper mill; **~fähnchen** *das* paper pennant; **~fetzen** *der* scrap of [torn] paper; **~flieger** *der* paper dart; **~format** *das* paper size; **~geld** *das* paper money; **~geschäft** *das* stationer's; **~handtuch** *das* paper towel; **~korb** *der* waste-paper basket; (an öffentlichen Orten) litter bin; **~kram** *der* (ugs. abwertend) [tedious] paperwork; **~krieg** *der* (ugs. abwertend) tedious form-filling; (Korrespondenz) tiresome exchange of letters

Papiermaché /papiema'ʃe/ *das;* ~s, ~s papier mâché

papier-, Papier-: **~mühle** *die* [1] (Maschine) [paper-pulp] beater; [2] (Fabrik) paper mill; **~rolle** *die* roll of paper; (in Registrierkassen) paper roll; **~schere** *die* paper scissors *pl.*; **~schlange** *die* [paper] streamer; **~schnitzel** *der od. das* bit *or* scrap of paper; **~serviette** *die* paper serviette *or* napkin; **~stau** *der* paper jam; **~taschentuch** *das* paper handkerchief; **~tiger** *der* paper tiger; **~tonne** *die* waste-paper bin; **~tüte** *die* paper bag; **~verarbeitend** ▸**Papier 1**; **~währung** *die* paper currency; **~waren** *Pl.* stationery *sing.*; **~warenhandlung** *die* stationer's

> **Papiertonne**
> ▸ Recycling

Papist /pa'pɪst/ *der;* ~en, ~en, **Papistin** *die;* ~, ~nen (abwertend) papist

papistisch *Adj.* (abwertend) papist

papp /pap/ *in* **ich kann nicht mehr ~ sagen** (ugs.) I'm full to bursting point (coll.)

Papp *der;* ~s, ~s (bes. südd.) mush

Papp-: **~band** *der* book bound in boards; **~becher** *der* paper cup; **~deckel** *der* cardboard; **ein ~deckel** a piece of cardboard

Pappe /'papə/ *die;* ~, ~n [1] (Karton) cardboard; **eine ~:** a piece of cardboard [2] (ugs.: Brei) mush; **er ist nicht von** *od.* **aus ~** (ugs.) he's not to be trifled with; **5 000 Euro sind nicht von** *od.* **aus ~** (ugs.) 5,000 euros isn't chicken feed (coll.)

Pappel /'papl̩/ *die;* ~, ~n poplar

Pappel·allee *die* avenue of poplars

päppeln /'pɛpl̩n/ *tr. V.* feed up; **eine Industrie ~** (fig. ugs.) featherbed an industry

pappen (ugs.)
[A] *tr. V.* stick (**an, auf** + *Akk.* on)
[B] *itr. V.* (haften bleiben) stick (**an** + *Dat.* to); (klebrig sein) be sticky

Pappen-: **~deckel** *der* (bes. südd.) ▸**Pappdeckel**; **~heimer** /-haimɐ/ *Pl.: in* **ich kenne meine/wir kennen unsere ~heimer** (ugs.) I/we know them well (coll.); **~stiel** *der: in* **das ist kein ~stiel** (ugs.) it's not chicken feed (coll.); **etw. für einen ~stiel kaufen/kriegen** (ugs.) buy/get sth. for a song *or* for next to nothing

papperlapapp /papɐla'pap/ *Interj.* rubbish

pappig *Adj.* [1] sticky [2] doughy ‹*bread etc.*› [3] (breiig) mushy

papp-, Papp-: **~kamerad** *der* (ugs., auch fig.) cardboard figure; **~karton** *der* cardboard box; **~maschee** /-ma'ʃeː/ *das;* ~~s, ~~s papier mâché; **~nase** *die* false nose (made of cardboard); **~satt** *Adj.* (ugs.) completely stuffed; (fig.) completely fed up; **~schnee** *der* sticky snow; **~teller** *der* paper *or* cardboard plate

Paprika /'paprika/ *der;* ~s, ~[s] [1] pepper [2] (Gewürz) paprika

Paprika-: **~schnitzel** *das* cutlet with paprika sauce; **~schote** *die* pepper; **gefüllte ~schoten** stuffed peppers

Paps /paps/ *der;* ~ (ugs.) dad (coll.)

-papst *der* (fig. iron.) high priest of ...

Papst /paːpst/ *der;* ~[e]s, **Päpste** /'pɛːpstə/ pope; (fig. iron.) high priest

-päpstin *die* (fig. iron.) high priestess of...

Päpstin *die;* ~, ~nen pope; (fig. iron.) high priestess

päpstlich /'pɛːpstlɪç/ *Adj.* papal; (fig. abwertend) pontifical; **~er Gesandter** nuncio; **nicht ~er sein als der Papst** (fig.) not be a stickler for the regulations

Papsttum *das;* ~s papacy

Papua-Neu·guinea /'paːpu̯a-/ (*das*); ~s Papua New Guinea

Papyrus /pa'pyːrʊs/ *der;* ~, **Papyri** papyrus

Papyrus·rolle *die* papyrus scroll

para-, Para- /'paːra/ para-

Parabel /pa'raːbl̩/ *die;* ~, ~n [1] (bes. Literaturw.) parable [2] (Math.) parabola

Parabol·antenne *die* parabolic antenna

parabolisch /para'boːlɪʃ/ *Adj.* parabolic

Parabol·spiegel *der* (Technik) parabolic mirror

Parade /pa'raːdə/ *die;* ~, ~n [1] (Milit.) parade; **eine ~ abnehmen** take the salute at a parade [2] (Ballspiele) save; **jmdm. in die ~ fahren** (fig. ugs.) cut sb. short [3] (Fechten) parry [4] (Pferdesport) **ganze ~:** halt; **halbe ~:** half-halt; **in ~** (*Dat.*) **stehen** halt

Parade-: **~beispiel** *das* perfect example; **~bett** *das* (veralt.) large imposing bed

Paradeiser /para'daizɐ/ *der;* ~s, ~ (österr.) tomato

Parade-: **~kissen** *das* (veralt.) decorative pillow; **~marsch** *der* (Milit.) marching in parade step; (Stechschritt) goose-stepping; **~pferd** *das* [1] (Pferd) parade horse; [2] (ugs.: Musterexemplar) showpiece; (Person) star; **~platz** *der* (hist.) parade ground; **~schritt** *der* (Milit.) parade step; (Stechschritt) goose step; **~stück** *das* showpiece; **~uniform** *die* (Milit.) full-dress uniform

paradieren *itr. V.* (Milit.) parade

Paradies /para'diːs/ *das;* ~es, ~e (auch fig.) paradise; **die Vertreibung aus dem ~:** the expulsion from paradise; **das ~ auf Erden** heaven on earth

paradiesisch
[A] *Adj.* [1] (Rel.) paradisical [2] (herrlich) heavenly; magnificent ‹*view*›
[B] *adv.* (herrlich) **~ ruhig gelegen** in a wonderfully peaceful situation; **dort ist es ~ schön** it's beautiful there, a real paradise

Paradies·vogel *der* bird of paradise; (fig.) strange and beautiful creature

Paradigma /para'dɪgma/ *das;* ~s, **Paradigmen** *od.* **Paradigmata** (bes. Sprachw.) paradigm

paradigmatisch (bes. Sprachw.)
[A] *Adj.* paradigmatic
[B] *adv.* paradigmatically

Paradigmen·wechsel *der* paradigm shift

paradox /para'dɔks/ *Adj.* [1] paradoxical [2] (ugs.: merkwürdig) odd; strange

Paradox *das;* ~es, ~e (bes. Philos., Rhet.) paradox

paradoxer·weise *Adv.* [1] paradoxically [2] (ugs.: merkwürdigerweise) strangely *or* oddly enough

Paradoxie /paradɔ'ksiː/ *die;* ~, ~n [1] paradox [2] (Eigenschaft) paradoxicalness

Paradoxon /pa'raːdɔksɔn/ *das;* ~s, **Paradoxa** (Philos., Rhet.) paradox

Paraffin /para'fiːn/ *das;* ~s, ~e (Chemie) paraffin; (für Kerzen) paraffin wax

Paragraph /para'graːf/ *der;* ~en, ~en section; (im Vertrag) clause

Paragraphen-: **~dickicht** *das,* **~gestrüpp** *das* (abwertend) jungle of regulations; **~hengst** *der* (salopp abwertend) lawyer; **~reiter** *der,* **~reiterin** *die* (abwertend) [1] (Jurist[in]) lawyer; [2] (Pedant[in]) stickler for the rules

Paraguay /'paragvai̯/ (*das*); ~s Paraguay

Paraguayer *der;* ~s, ~, **Paraguayerin** *die;* ~, ~nen Paraguayan

paraguayisch *Adj.* Paraguayan

Parallaxe /para'laksə/ *die;* ~, ~n (Physik, Astron.) parallax

parallel /para'leːl/
[A] *Adj.* (auch fig.) parallel
[B] *adv.* **~ verlaufen** (auch fig.) run parallel (**mit, zu** to); **~ zu etw.** (fig.) in parallel with sth.

Parallele *die;* ~, ~n [1] (Math.) parallel [line]; **eine ~ zu etw. ziehen** draw a line parallel to sth. [2] (fig.) parallel; **jmdn./etw. mit jmdm./etw. in ~ setzen** *od.* **stellen** draw a parallel between sb./sth. and sb./sth.

Parallel-fall *der* parallel case

Parallelität /paraleli'tɛːt/ *die;* ~, ~en (auch Math.) parallelism

Parallel·klasse *die* (Schulw.) parallel class

Parallelogramm /paralelo'gram/ *das;* ~s, ~e (Math.) parallelogram

Parallel-: **~schaltung** *die* (Elektrot.) parallel connection; **~schwung** *der* (Skisport) parallel swing; **~straße** *die* street running parallel (**von** to); **~ton·art** *die* (Musik) relative key

Paralyse /para'lyːzə/ *die;* ~, ~n ▸❶ **S. 439** (Med., fig.) paralysis

paralysieren *tr. V.* (Med., fig.) paralyse

Paralytiker *der;* ~s, ~, **Paralytikerin** *die;* ~, ~nen paralytic

paralytisch *Adj.* (Med.) paralytic

Parameter /pa'raːmetɐ/ *der;* ~s, ~(Wirtsch., Technik, Math.) parameter; (beim Kegelschnitt) principal parameter

para·militärisch
[A] *Adj.* paramilitary
[B] *adv.* ‹*operate, be organized*› along paramilitary lines

Paranoia /para'nɔya/ *die;* ~ ▸❶ **S. 439** (Med.) paranoia

paranoid /parano'iːt/ *Adj.* (Med.) paranoid

Paranoiker /para'noːikɐ/ *der;* ~s, ~, **Paranoikerin** *die;* ~, ~nen (Med.) paranoiac

paranoisch *Adj.* (Med.) paranoiac

Para·nuss, *Para·nuß *die* Brazil nut

Paraphe /pa'raːfə/ *die;* ~, ~n [1] (geh.: Namenszug) signature [2] (Dipl.) initials *pl.*

paraphieren *tr. V.* (Dipl.) initial

Paraphierung *die;* ~, ~en (Dipl.) initialling

Para·phrase *die* (Sprachw., Musik) paraphrase

paraphrasieren *tr. V.* [1] (Sprachw.) paraphrase [2] (Musik) compose a paraphrase on

Para·psychologie *die* parapsychology *no art.*

Parasit /para'ziːt/ *der;* ~en, ~en (Biol., fig. abwertend) parasite

parasitär /parazi'tɛːɐ̯/, **parasitisch** (Biol., fig. abwertend)
[A] *Adj.* parasitic
[B] *adv.* parasitically; **~** *od.* **parasitisch leben** (Biol.) be parasitic; (fig.) be a parasite

Parasol /para'zoːl/ *der;* ~s, ~e *od.* ~s, **Parasol-pilz** *der* parasol mushroom

Parasympathikus /parazʏm'paːtikʊs/ *der;* ~ ▸❶ **S. 435** (Anat., Physiol.) parasympathetic nervous system

parat /pa'raːt/ *Adj.* ready; **eine Ausrede/Antwort ~ haben** be ready with an excuse/answer; **ich habe kein passendes Beispiel ~:** I can't think of a suitable example

Para·typhus *der* ▸❶ **S. 439** (Med.) paratyphoid [fever]

Paravent /para'vãː/ *der od. das;* ~s, ~s (österr., sonst veralt.) screen

Pärchen /'pɛːɐ̯çən/ *das;* ~s, ~: pair; (Liebespaar) couple

pärchen·weise *Adv.* in pairs

Parcours /par'ku:ɐ̯/ *der;* ~ /...ɐ̯(s)/, ~ /...ɐ̯s/ (Pferdesport) course

Pardon /par'dõ/ *der od. das;* ~**s** pardon; **jmdn. um ~ bitten** (veralt.) ask sb.'s pardon; **jmdm. ~ gewähren** (veralt.) pardon sb.; **kein[en] ~ kennen** be completely ruthless; **~!** I beg your pardon

Parenthese /parɛn'te:zə/ *die;* ~, ~**n** (Sprachw.) **1** (Satzteil) parenthesis **2** (Klammern o. Ä.) parenthesis; parentheses *pl.*; **in ~**: in parenthesis

par excellence /parɛksɛ'lã:s/ *Adj.; nachgestellt* par excellence; **ein Gentleman ~**: an outstanding example of a gentleman

Parforce- /par'fɔrs-/: **~jagd** *die* (Jagdw. veralt.) hunt with horses and hounds; (Art des Jagens) riding to hounds; **~ritt** *der* (geh.) feat of concentrated effort

Parfum /par'fœ̃:/ *das;* ~**s,** ~**s, Parfüm** /par'fy:m/ *das;* ~**s,** ~**s** perfume; scent

Parfümerie /parfymə'ri:/ *die;* ~, ~**en** perfumery

Parfüm-: ~fläschchen *das,* **~flasche** *die* perfume bottle; scent bottle

parfümieren *tr. V.* perfume; scent; **sich [viel zu stark] ~**: put [too much] perfume *or* scent on

Parfüm-: ~wolke *die* cloud of perfume *or* scent; **~zerstäuber** *der* perfume spray; perfume atomizer

pari /'pa:ri/ **1** *in* **zu/über/unter ~** (Börsenw.) at/above/below par **2** *in* **die/ihre Chancen stehen ~**: the odds are even/they have the same *or* an equal chance

Paria /'pa:ri̯a/ *der;* ~**s,** ~**s** (auch fig.) pariah

parieren¹ /pa'ri:rən/ *itr. V.* (ugs.) do what one is told; **jmdm. ~**: do what sb. tells one; **aufs Wort ~**: jump to it (coll.)

parieren² *tr. V.* **1** (Fechten, Boxen, fig.) parry **2** (Fußball) save ‹*shot*›; parry ‹*attack*› **3** (Pferdesport) hold ‹*horse*› at half-halt; (zum Stehen bringen) halt

Pari·kurs *der* (Wirtsch.) par value; (bei Devisen) par rate of exchange

Pariser /pa'ri:zɐ/

A *indekl. Adj.* ▸ S. 675 Parisian; Paris *attrib.*; **die ~ Metro** the Paris Metro

B *der;* ~**s,** ~ **1** (Einwohner) ▸ S. 675 Parisian **2** (ugs.: Kondom) French letter (coll.)

Pariserin *die;* ~, ~**nen** Parisian

pariserisch *Adj.* Parisian

Parität /pari'tɛ:t/ *die;* ~, ~**en** **1** (Gleichheit) parity; equality **2** (Wirtsch.) parity

paritätisch

A *Adj.* equal; **~e Mitbestimmung** co-determination based on equal representation

B *adv.* equally; **Ausschüsse müssen ~ besetzt werden** there must be equal representation on committees

Park /park/ *der;* ~**s,** ~**s** park; (Schloss~ usw.) grounds *pl.*

Parka *der;* ~**s,** ~**s** parka

Park-: ~anlage *die* park; (bei Schlössern usw.) grounds *pl.*; **~bahn** *die* (Raumf.) parking orbit; **~bank** *die; Pl.* **~bänke** park bench

parken

A *tr. V.* park

B *itr. V.* **1** park; **„P~ verboten!"** 'No Parking' **2** (stehen) be parked; **ein ~des Auto** a parked car

Parkett /par'kɛt/ *das;* ~**[e]s,** ~**e** **1** (Bodenbelag) parquet floor; **~ legen** lay parquet flooring; **sich auf jedem ~ bewegen können** (fig.) be able to move in any circles **2** (Theater) [front] stalls *pl.*; parquet (Amer.); **das ~ applaudierte** there was applause from the stalls **3** *in* **etw. aufs ~ legen** (ugs.) dance sth.; *s. auch* **Sohle 1**

Parkett·[fuß]boden *der* parquet floor; **~ haben** have parquet flooring

Parkett·handel *der* (Börsenw.) floor trading

parkettieren *tr. V.* lay parquet flooring; parquet

Parkett·platz *der* seat in the [front] stalls

Park-: ~gebühr *die* parking fee; **~haus** *das* multi-storey car park

parkieren (schweiz.) ▸ **parken**

Parkinson·krankheit /'parkɪnzɔn'--/ *die* Parkinson's disease

Park-: ~kralle *die* wheel clamp; **~landschaft** *die* parkland; **~leit·system** *das* (Verkehrsw.) parking guidance system; *traffic-control system providing information on the location of available parking spaces;* **~leuchte** *die,* **~licht** *das* parking light; **~lücke** *die* parking space; **~möglichkeit** *die* parking; (Parklücke) parking space; **keine ~möglichkeit** nowhere to park; **~platz** *der* **1** car park; parking lot (Amer.); **2** (für ein einzelnes Fahrzeug) parking space; place to park; **~platz·not** *die* lack of parking space[s]; **~scheibe** *die* parking disc; **~schein** *der* car park ticket; **~uhr** *die* parking meter; **~verbot** *das* ban on parking; **hier ist ~verbot** you are not allowed to park here; **im ~verbot stehen** be parked illegally; **aus dem ~verbot wegfahren** move one's car from where it is/was parked illegally; **~verbots·schild** *das* no-parking sign

> **Parkscheibe**
>
> When parking your car in Germany in an area where parking time is limited, you have to display a *Parkscheibe* (parking disc) on your windscreen, with the hands of its clock set to your arrival time. These blue cardboard or plastic discs are available at newsagents and department stores.

Parlament /parla'mɛnt/ *das;* ~**[e]s,** ~**e** parliament; (eines bestimmten Landes) Parliament *no def. art.*

Parlamentär /parlamɛn'tɛ:ɐ̯/ *der;* ~**s,** ~**e, Parlamentärin** *die;* ~, ~**nen** peace negotiator

Parlamentarier /parlamɛn'ta:ri̯ɐ/ *der;* ~**s,** ~, **Parlamentarierin** *die;* ~, ~**nen** member of parliament; (in Großbritannien) Member of Parliament; MP; (in den Vereinigten Staaten) Congressman/Congresswoman; **die Berliner ~**: the members of the Berlin Parliament; **die dem Europarat angehörenden ~**: the MPs *or* deputies in the Council of Europe

parlamentarisch

A *Adj.* parliamentary; **~er Staatssekretär [im Bundesministerium für ...]** parliamentary secretary [to the Federal Ministry of ...]

B *adv.* **etw. ~ diskutieren** discuss sth. in parliament

Parlamentarismus *der;* ~: parliamentarianism *no art.*; parliamentary system

Parlaments-: ~ausschuss, ***~ausschuß** *der* parliamentary committee; **~ferien** *Pl.* [parliamentary] recess *sing.*; **~gebäude** *das* parliament building[s *pl.*]; **die ~gebäude** (in London) the Houses of Parliament; **~mitglied** *das* member of parliament; (in Großbritannien) Member of Parliament; MP; (in den Vereinigten Staaten) member of Congress; **~reform** *die* parliamentary reform; **~sitzung** *die* sitting [of parliament]; **~wahl** *die* parliamentary election

parlieren /par'li:rən/ *itr. V.* (geh.; oft iron.) make conversation; (plaudern) chat (**über** + *Akk.* about); (reden) talk ‹*French etc.*›

Parmesan /parme'za:n/ *der;* ~**[s]** Parmesan

Parnass, ***Parnaß** /par'nas/ *der;* ~ *od.* **Parnasses** (dichter.) Parnassus *no def. art.* (poet.)

Parodie /paro'di:/ *die;* ~, ~**n** parody; **eine ~ auf etw./jmdn.** a parody of sth./take-off of sb.

parodieren *tr. V.* parody ‹*literary work, manner*›; take off ‹*person*›; satirize ‹*event*›

Parodist *der;* ~**en,** ~**en, Parodistin** *die;* ~, ~**nen** parodist

parodistisch *Adj.* parodistic; ‹*ability*› as a parodist

Parodontose /parodɔn'to:zə/ *die;* ~, ~**n** periodontosis *no art.* (Dent.); receding gums *pl.*, *no art.*

Parole /pa'ro:lə/ *die;* ~, ~**n** **1** (Wahlspruch) motto; (Schlagwort) slogan **2** (bes. Milit.: Kennwort) password **3** (Gerücht) rumour

Paroli /pa'ro:li/ *in* **jmdm./einer Sache ~ bieten** give sb. as good as one gets/pit oneself against sth.

Part /part/ *der;* ~**s,** ~**s** *od.* ~**e** **1** (Musik: Stimme, Partie) part **2** (Theater, Film: Rolle) part; role; **einen/den [entscheidenden] ~ in** *od.* **bei etw.** (*Dat.*) **spielen** (auch fig.) play a/the [crucial] part *or* role in sth.

Parte /'partə/ *die;* ~, ~**n** (österr.: Todesanzeige) death announcement

Partei /par'tai̯/ *die;* ~, ~**en** **1** (Politik) party; **in** *od.* **bei der ~ sein** be a party member; **die ~ wechseln** change parties **2** (Rechtsw.) party **3** (Gruppe, Mannschaft) side; **es mit beiden ~en halten** run with the hare and hunt with the hounds (fig.); **~ sein** be an interested party; **jmds.** *od.* **für jmdn./für etw. ~ ergreifen** *od.* **nehmen** side with sb./take a stand for sth.; **gegen jmdn./etw. ~ nehmen** *od.* **ergreifen** side against sb./take a stand against sth.; **über den ~en stehen** be impartial **4** (Miets~) tenant; (mehrere Personen) tenants *pl.*

partei-, Partei-: ~abzeichen *das* party badge; **~amtlich** *Adj.* official party ‹*regulations etc.*›; **~apparat** *der* party machine *or* organization; **~basis** *die* [party] rank and file; grass roots *pl.* of the party; **~bonze** *der* (abwertend) party bigwig (coll.); **~buch** *das* party membership book; **das falsche/richtige ~buch haben** belong to the wrong/right party; **~chef** *der,* **~chefin** *die* party leader; **~chinesisch** *das* (ugs. scherzh.) party gobbledegook; **~disziplin** *die* party discipline

Parteien-: ~landschaft *die* party political scene *or* set-up; **~verkehr** *der* (österr.) **„~verkehr von 9 bis 14 Uhr"** 'open to the public from 9 till 2'

partei-, Partei-: ~freund *der,* **~freundin** *die* fellow party member; party colleague; **~führer** *der,* **~führerin** *die* party leader; **~führung** *die* party leadership; **der ~führung angehören** be one of the party leaders *pl. or* executive; **~gänger** *der;* ~~**s,** ~~, **~gängerin** *die;* ~~, ~~**nen** (oft abwertend) [loyal] party supporter; **Mussolini und seine ~gänger** Mussolini and his party faithful; **~genosse** *der,* **~genossin** *die* (hist.: Mitglied der NSDAP) party member; (einer Arbeiter~) **~genosse X** Comrade X; **~intern** **A** *Adj.* internal [party] ‹*conflict, matters, material, etc.*›; **B** *adv.* within the party

parteiisch

A *Adj.* biased

B *adv.* in a biased manner

Partei·leitung *die* ▸ **~führung**

parteilich

A *Adj.* **1** (eine Partei betreffend) party ‹*matter, work, principles, etc.*› **2** (parteiisch) biased ‹*judgement, view, etc.*› **3** (der Parteilinie folgend) in accordance with the party line *postpos*

B *adv.* **1** (von der Partei) by the party **2** (parteiisch) in a biased manner **3** (der Parteilinie folgend) ‹*think, behave, act*› in accordance with the party line

Parteilichkeit *die;* ~ **1** (Linientreue) adherence to the party line **2** (einseitige Parteinahme) bias, partiality (**für** towards)

partei-, Partei-: ~linie *die* party line; **~los** *Adj.* (Politik) independent ‹*MP*›; **er ist ~los** he is not attached to *or* aligned with any party; **~lose** *der/die; adj. Dekl.* (Politik) independent; person not attached to a party; **~losigkeit** *die;* ~~ (Politik) independence; **~mitglied** *das* party member; **~nahme** *die;* ~~, ~~**n** partisanship; taking sides *no art.*; **~organ** *das* **1** party representative; (Gruppe) group of persons representing a party; **2** (Zeitung) party organ; **~politik** *die* party politics *sing.*; **~politisch** **A** *Adj.* party political; **B** *adv.* from a party political point of view; **~programm** *das* party manifesto *or* programme; **~tag** *der* party conference *or* (Amer.) convention; **~übergreifend** **A** *Adj.* cross-party; **B** *adv.* on a cross-party basis; **wir sind uns ~übergreifend einig in der Ablehnung der Pläne** we have cross-party agreement on the rejection of the plans;

P

~unabhängig **A** *Adj.* non-party; independent; **B** *adv.* on a non-party basis

Parteiung *die; ~, ~en* ‹*political, religious*› group

Partei-: ~verfahren *das: proceedings instituted by the party against a member;* **~vorsitz** *der* party leadership; **~vorsitzende** *der/die* party leader; **~vorstand** *der* party executive; **~zugehörigkeit** *die* party membership

parterre /par'tɛr/ *Adv.* on the ground *or* (Amer.) first floor

Parterre /par'tɛr/ *das* **~s, ~s** **[1]** (Erdgeschoss) ground floor; first floor (Amer.); **im ~:** on the ground *or* (Amer.) first floor **[2]** (Theater veralt.) stalls *pl.* (Brit.); parterre (Amer.); parquet (Amer.)

Parterre·wohnung *die* ground-floor flat (esp. Brit.); first-floor apartment (esp. Amer.)

Partie /par'ti:/ *die;* **~, ~n** **[1]** (Teil) part **[2]** (Spiel, Sport: Runde) game; (Golf) round; **eine ~ Schach spielen** play a game of chess **[3]** (Musik) part **[4]** (Ehepartner) **eine gute ~ [für jmdn.] sein** be a good match [for sb.]; **sie hat eine gute/glänzende ~ gemacht** she has married well/extremely well **[5]** (veralt.: Ausflug) **eine ~ aufs Land machen** go on *or* for an outing *or* a trip into the country **[6]** **mit von der ~ sein** join in; (bei einer Reise usw.) go along too; **da bin ich mit von der ~!** count me in! **[7]** (Kaufmannsspr.) batch **[8]** (österr.: Gruppe von Arbeitern) gang

Partie-: ~führer *der* (österr.: Vorarbeiter) foreman; **~führerin** *die* (österr.: Vorarbeiterin) forewoman

partiell /par'tsiɛl/
A *Adj.* partial
B *adv.* partially

Partikel[1] /par'ti:kl/ *die;* **~, ~n** (Sprachw.) particle

Partikel[2] *das;* **~s, ~** *od. die;* **~, ~n** (bes. Physik, Chemie, Technik) particle

partikular /partiku'la:ɐ̯/, **partikulär** /partiku'lɛ:ɐ̯/ *Adj.* (geh.) minority *attrib.* ‹*interest, viewpoint*›

Partikularismus *der;* **~** (meist abwertend) particularism *no art.*

partikularistisch *Adj.* (meist abwertend) particularistic

Partisan /parti'za:n/ *der;* **~s** *od.* **~en, ~en** guerrilla; (gegen Besatzungstruppen im Krieg) partisan

Partisanen·krieg *der* guerilla war; (Kriegführung) guerilla warfare

Partisanin *die;* **~, ~nen** ▸ **Partisan**

Partita /par'ti:ta/ *die;* **~, Partiten** (Musik) partita

Partitur /parti'tu:ɐ̯/ *die;* **~, ~en** (Musik) score

Partizip /parti'tsi:p/ *das;* **~s, ~ien** /-'tsi:pjən/ (Sprachw.) participle; **das 1. ~** *od.* **~ Präsens/das 2. ~** *od.* **~ Perfekt** the present/past participle

Partizipation /partitsipa'tsio:n/ *die;* **~, ~en** participation (**an** + *Dat.* in)

Partizipations·geschäft *das* (Wirtsch.) joint venture

Partizipial- (Sprachw.) participial

partizipieren *itr. V.* **an etw.** (*Dat.*) **~:** have a share in sth.

Partner /'partnɐ/ *der;* **~s, ~, Partnerin** *die;* **~, ~nen** partner; (Bündnis~) ally; (im Film/Theater) co-star

Partner·look *der* coordinated fashion (in which man and woman wear matching clothes); **~ tragen** wear matching his-and-hers outfits

Partnerschaft *die;* **~, ~en** partnership

partnerschaftlich
A *Adj.* ‹*cooperation etc.*› on a partnership basis; **wir haben ein ~es Verhältnis** ours is a relationship between equal partners; **sein Führungsstil ist [sehr] ~:** his style of leadership involves treating people [very much] as equal partners
B *adv.* in a spirit of partnership; (als Partnerschaft) as a partnership; **sich jmdm. gegenüber** *od.* **zu jmdm. ~ verhalten** treat sb. as an equal [partner]

Partner-: ~stadt *die* twin town (Brit.); sister city *or* town (Amer.); **~tausch** *der* partner-swapping (coll.); **~wahl** *die* choice of mate *or* partner

partout /par'tu:/ *Adv.* (ugs.) at all costs; **er will es ~ nicht einsehen** but he absolutely refuses to see it

Party /'pa:ɐ̯ti/ *die;* **~, ~s** *od.* **Parties** party; **eine ~ [zu ihrem bestandenen Examen/zu seinem Geburtstag] geben** give a party [to celebrate her passing the exam/for his birthday]; **auf** *od.* **bei ~s** at parties; **auf eine** *od.* **zu einer ~ gehen** go to a party

Party-: ~keller *der: basement room equipped for parties;* **~löwe** *der* (ugs.) [male] partygoer (*who is the centre of attraction*); social lion

Parvenü /parve'ny:/ *der;* **~s, ~s** (österr.:) **Parvenu** /parve'ny:/ *der;* **~s, ~s** (geh.) parvenu

Parze /'partsə/ *die;* **~, ~n** (röm. Myth.) **die drei ~n** the Three Fates

Parzelle /par'tsɛlə/ *die;* **~, ~n** [small] plot [of land]

parzellieren *tr. V.* divide into [small] plots

Pascal /pas'kal/ *das;* **~s, ~:** (Physik) pascal

Pasch /paʃ/ *der;* **~[e]s, ~e** *u.* **Päsche** **[1]** (beim Würfelspiel) **einen ~ werfen** (bei zwei Würfeln) throw doubles *pl.*; (bei drei Würfeln) throw triplets **[2]** (beim Domino) double

Pascha /'paʃa/ *der;* **~s, ~s** **[1]** (hist.) pasha **[2]** (fig. abwertend) male chauvinist; **den ~ spielen** act the lord and master

Paspel /'paspl/ *die;* **~, ~n** *od. der;* **~s, ~:** piping *no pl.*

paspelieren *tr. V.* pipe ‹*pocket, collar, hem, seam*›

Pass, *Paß /pas/ *der;* **Passes, Pässe** /'pɛsə/ **[1]** (Reise~) passport; **der diplomatischen Vertretung die Pässe zustellen** break off diplomatic relations **[2]** (Gebirgs~) pass **[3]** (Ballspiele) pass

passabel /pa'sa:bl/
A *Adj.* reasonable; tolerable; fair ‹*report*›; presentable ‹*appearance*›
B *adv.* reasonably *or* tolerably well

Passage /pa'sa:ʒə/ *die;* **~, ~n** **[1]** (Ladenstraße) [shopping] arcade **[2]** (Abschnitt) (im Text) passage; (im Film) sequence; (beim Eistanz, bei Turnübungen) routine; (Musik) [virtuoso] passage **[3]** (Stelle zum Passieren, Schiffs~, Reiten) passage

Passagier /pasa'ʒi:ɐ̯/ *der;* **~s, ~e** passenger; **~e der Lufthansa nach London** Lufthansa passengers [bound] for London; **blinder ~:** stowaway

Passagier-: ~dampfer *der* passenger steamer; **~flugzeug** *das* passenger aircraft

Passagierin *die;* **~, ~nen** ▸ **Passagier**

Passagier-: ~liste *die* passenger list; **~schiff** *das* passenger ship

Passah /'pasa/ *das;* **~s** (jüd. Rel.) Passover

Passah·fest *das* (jüd. Rel.) Feast of the Passover

Pass·amt, *Paß·amt *das* passport office

Passant /pa'sant/ *der;* **~en, ~en, Passantin** *die;* **~, ~nen** **[1]** (Fußgänger[in]) passer-by **[2]** (schweiz.: Durchreisende[r]) traveller [passing through]

Passat /pa'sa:t/ *der;* **~[e]s, ~e, Passat·wind** *der* trade wind

Pass·bild, *Paß·bild *das* passport photograph

passé /pa'se:/ *indekl. Adj.* (ugs.) (überholt) passé; out of date; (vorüber) over [and done with]; **er ist als Politiker ~:** as a politician he has had his day

Passe /'pasə/ *die;* **~, ~n** (Schneiderei) yoke

Pässe /'pɛsə/ ▸ **Pass**

passee ▸ **passé**

passen
A *itr. V.* **[1]** (die richtige Größe/Form haben) fit; **etw. passt [jmdm.] gut/nicht** sth. fits [sb.] well/does not fit [sb.]; **etw. passt [nicht] in/auf/unter etw.** (*Akk.*)/**zwischen zwei Sachen** sth. fits/does not fit into/on [to]/underneath sth./between two things; **der Schlüssel passt nicht ins Schloss** the key does not fit the lock; **das Buch passt nicht in den Karton** the book won't go in the box; **ein Kleidungsstück ~d machen** make an article of clothing fit **[2]** (geeignet sein) be suitable, be appropriate (**auf** + *Akk.,* **zu** for); (harmonieren) ‹*colour etc.*› match; **dieses Bild passt besser in die Diele** this picture goes better in the hall; **zu etw./jmdm. ~:** go well with sth./be well suited to sb.; **zueinander ~** ‹*things*› go well together; ‹*two people*› be suited to each other; **das** *od.* **dieses Benehmen passt zu ihm/passt nicht zu ihm** (ugs.) that's just like him (coll.)/that's not like him; **diese Beschreibung passt [genau] auf sie/[absolut] nicht auf sie** this description fits her [exactly]/does not fit her [at all]; **sie passt nicht hierher/nach X** she does not fit in here/in X; **nicht in die Welt ~:** be unsuited to this life; **sie passt nicht zu uns** *od.* **in unseren Kreis** she is out of place in our circle; *s. auch* **Faust**; **Konzept**; **Kram**; **passend** **[3]** (genehm sein) **jmdm. ~** ‹*time*› be convenient for sb., suit sb.; **jmdm. passt etw. nicht** sth. is inconvenient for sb.; (jmd. mag etw. nicht) sb. does not like sth.; **das könnte dir so ~!** (ugs.) you'd just love that, wouldn't you? **[4]** (Kartenspiel) pass; **bei dieser Frage muss ich ~** (fig.) I'll have to pass on that question **[5]** (österr.: warten, lauern) wait (**auf** + *Akk.* for)
B *tr. V.* **[1]** (auch itr.) *V.* (Ballspiele) pass ‹*ball*› **[2]** (passgerecht einfügen) **etw. in etw.** (*Akk.*) **~:** fit sth. into sth.
C *refl. V.* (ugs.: sich schicken) be proper *or* (coll.) done; **das/es passt sich einfach nicht** it simply isn't done *or* the done thing (coll.)

passend *Adj.* **[1]** (geeignet) suitable ‹*dress, present, etc.*›; appropriate, right ‹*words, expression*›; right ‹*moment*›; **bei einer ~en Gelegenheit** at an opportune moment; **haben Sie es ~?** (ugs.) have you got the right money? **[2]** (harmonierend) matching ‹*shoes etc.*›; **die zum Kleid ~en Schuhe** the shoes to go with *or* match the dress

passender·weise *Adv.* appropriately

Passepartout /paspar'tu/ *das;* (schweiz.:) *der;* **~s, ~s** **[1]** (Umrahmung) mount **[2]** (bes. schweiz.) ▸ **Hauptschlüssel**

pass-, *paß-, Pass-, *Paß-: ~form *die* fit; **eine gute ~form haben** be a good fit; **~foto** *das* ▸ **~bild**; **~gang** *der* amble; **im ~gang gehen** amble; **~genau, ~gerecht** *Adj.* that fits/fit exactly *or* perfectly *postpos., not pred.*; **die Schuhe sind ~genau** *od.* **~gerecht** the shoes fit exactly *or* are a perfect fit

passierbar *Adj.* passable ‹*road*›; navigable ‹*river*›; negotiable ‹*path*›

passieren
A *tr. V.* **[1]** pass; **die Grenze ~:** cross the border; **eine Brücke/einen Tunnel ~:** pass over a bridge/through a tunnel; **die Zensur ~** (fig.) be passed by the censor; get past the censor; *s. auch* **Revue 4** **[2]** pass through a sieve; strain ‹*curd cheese etc.*›
B *itr. V.*; *mit sein* happen; ‹*murder, event*› take place; **es ist ein Unglück/etwas Schreckliches passiert** there has been an accident/something dreadful has happened; **gib es ihm sofort zurück, sonst passiert was!** give it back to him straight away, or there'll be trouble!; **jmdm. ist etwas/nichts passiert** something/nothing happened to sb.; (jmd. ist verletzt/nicht verletzt) sb. was/was not hurt; **mir ist eine Panne/ein Versehen passiert** I [have] had a breakdown/made a mistake; **das kann doch jedem mal ~!** that can happen to anybody!

Passier-: ~schein *der* pass; permit; **~schlag** *der* (Tennis) passing shot

Passion /pa'sio:n/ *die;* **~, ~en** **[1]** passion **[2]** (christl. Rel., Kunst, Musik) Passion

passioniert *Adj.* ardent, passionate ‹*collector, card player, huntsman*›

Passions-: ~spiel *das* Passion play; **~zeit** *die* (christl. Rel.) Passiontide

Passionsspiel

The famous Passion Play is held every ten years in the small Bavarian mountain village of Oberammergau. It has its origin in a vow sworn by the villagers in 1633 that they would perform the passion of Jesus if God delivered them from the plague.

passiv /ˈpasiːf/
A *Adj.* passive; non-active ‹*member*›; **~e Handelsbilanz** balance of trade deficit; **das ~e Wahlrecht** eligibility [for political office]; **das ~e Wahlrecht haben** be eligible to stand as a candidate; *s. auch* **Bestechung**
B *adv.* passively; **sich [bei** *od.* **in etw.** (*Dat.*)**] ~ verhalten** take a passive stance [in sth.]; take no active part [in sth.]

Passiv *das;* **~s, ~e** (Sprachw.) passive; **im ~ stehen** be in the passive

Passiva /paˈsiːva/ *Pl.* (Wirtsch.) liabilities

Passiv·bildung *die* (Sprachw.) formation of the passive

Passiven ▸ **Passiva**

Passiv·haus *das* (Archit. Jargon) passive house

passivisch (Sprachw.)
A *Adj.* passive
B *adv.* passively; in the passive form

Passivität /pasiviˈtɛːt/ *die;* **~:** passivity

Passiv-: ~posten *der* (Kaufmannsspr.) liability; **~rauchen** *das;* **~~s** passive smoking; **~raucher** *der,* **~raucherin** *die* passive smoker; **~saldo** *der* (Kaufmannsspr.) debit balance; **~seite** *die* (Kaufmannsspr.) liabilities side

Pass-, *Paß-: ~kontrolle *die* **1** (das Kontrollieren) passport inspection *or* check; **2** (Stelle) passport control; **~stelle** *die* ▸ **~amt**; **~straße** *die* [mountain] pass road

Passung *die;* **~, ~en** (Technik) fit; tolerance [for mating parts]

Passus /ˈpasʊs/ *der;* **~, ~** /ˈpasuːs/ passage

Pass-, *Paß-: ~wort *das* (DV) password; **~zwang** *der* obligation to carry a passport

passwort·geschützt (DV)
A *Adj.* password-protected
B *adv.* with password protection

Paste /ˈpastə/ *die;* **~, ~n** (auch Pharm.) paste

Pastell /pasˈtɛl/ *das;* **~[e]s, ~e** **1** (Farbton) pastel shade **2** (Maltechnik) pastel *no art.*; **in ~:** in pastel **3** (Bild) pastel [drawing]

pastell-, Pastell-: ~farbe *die* pastel colour; **~farben** *Adj.* pastel-coloured; **~malerei** *die* pastel drawing; **~ton** *der* pastel shade

Pastetchen *das;* **~s, ~:** [small] vol-au-vent; (Hülle) [small] vol-au-vent case

Pastete /pasˈteːtə/ *die;* **~, ~n** **1** (gefüllte ~) vol-au-vent; (Hülle) vol-au-vent case **2** (in einer Schüssel o. Ä. gegart) pâté; (in einer Hülle aus Teig gebacken) pie

pasteurisieren /pastøriˈziːrən/ *tr. V.* pasteurize

Pasteurisierung *die;* **~, ~en** pasteurization

Pastille /pasˈtɪlə/ *die;* **~, ~n** pastille

Pastinake /pastiˈnaːkə/ *die;* **~, ~n** parsnip

Past·milch *die* (schweiz.) pasteurized milk

Pastor /ˈpastɔr/ *der;* **~s, ~en** ▸ⓘ **S. 44** pastor; *s. auch* **Pfarrer**

pastoral /pastoˈraːl/ *Adj.* **1** (seelsorgerlich) pastoral **2** (salbungsvoll) unctuous **3** (idyllisch) pastoral ‹*literature*›

Pastorale *das;* **~s, ~s** *od. die;* **~, ~n** **1** (Musik) pastorale **2** (Literaturw., Kunst) pastoral

Pastorin *die;* **~, ~nen** ▸ⓘ **S. 44** pastor

Pate /ˈpaːtə/ *der;* **~n, ~n** (Taufzeuge) godparent; (Patenonkel; in der Mafia) godfather; (DDR) sponsor (*responsible for the child's socialist upbringing*); **bei etw. ~ stehen** (fig.) be [the influence/influences] behind sth.; (als Vorbild dienen) act as the model for sth.

Patene /paˈteːnə/ *die;* **~, ~n** (christl. Kirche) paten

Paten-: ~kind *das* godchild; (DDR) sponsored child; **~onkel** *der* godfather; (DDR) [male] sponsor

Patenschaft *die;* **~, ~en** (christl. Rel.) godparenthood; (DDR, fig.) sponsorship (**für, über** + *Akk.* of)

Paten-: ~sohn *der* godson; (DDR) sponsored boy; **~stadt** *die* twin town (Brit.); sister city *or* town (Amer.)

patent /paˈtɛnt/ (ugs.)
A *Adj.* **1** (tüchtig) capable; **ein ~er Kerl** a great guy (coll.) **2** (zweckmäßig) ingenious ‹*device, method, idea*›; clever ‹*slogan etc.*›
B *adv.* ingeniously; cleverly; neatly ‹*solved*›

Patent *das;* **~[e]s, ~e** **1** (Schutz) patent; **ein ~ auf etw.** (*Akk.*) **haben** have a patent for sth.; **etw. zum** *od.* **als ~ anmelden, auf** *od.* **für etw. ein ~ anmelden** apply for a patent for sth.; **„als ~ angemeldet"** 'patent pending'; 'patent applied for' **2** (Erfindung) [patented] invention; (fig.: Konstruktion/Verfahren) [patent] design/method **3** (Ernennungsurkunde) certificate [of appointment]; (eines Kapitäns) master's certificate; (eines Offiziers) commission

Patent-: ~amt *das* Patent Office; **~anmeldung** *die* patent application

Paten·tante *die* godmother; (DDR) [female] sponsor

patent-, Patent-: ~anwalt *der,* **~anwältin** *die* ▸ⓘ **S. 113** patent agent *or* (Amer.) attorney; **~fähig** *Adj.* patentable; **~gesetz** *das* Patents Act; **~geschützt** *Adj.* protected by a patent/by patents *postpos.*

patentierbar *Adj.* patentable

patentieren *tr. V.* patent; **jmdm. etw. ~:** grant sb. a patent for sth.; **sich** (*Dat.*) **eine Erfindung ~ lassen** have an invention patented

Patent-: ~inhaber *der,* **~inhaberin** *die* patentee; **~lösung** *die* patent remedy (**für, zu** for)

Paten·tochter *die* god-daughter; (DDR) sponsored girl

Patent-: ~recht *das* **1** (Rechtsnormen) patent law *no art.*; **2** (berechtigter Anspruch) patent rights *pl.*; **~register** *das* (österr., schweiz.) ▸ **~rolle**; **~rezept** *das* patent remedy (**gegen, für** for); **kein ~rezept dafür haben, wie man etw. tut** have no magic recipe for doing sth.; **~rolle** *die* ≈ Register of Patents (Brit.); **~schrift** *die* patent specification; **~schutz** *der* patent protection

Pater /ˈpaːtɐ/ *der;* **~s, ~** *od.* **Patres** /ˈpaːtreːs/ (kath. Kirche) Father

Paternoster[1] /paːtɐˈnɔstɐ/ *der;* **~s, ~** (Aufzug) paternoster [lift]

Paternoster[2] *das;* **~s, ~** (Gebet) Lord's Prayer

pathetisch /paˈteːtɪʃ/
A *Adj.* emotional, impassioned ‹*speech, manner*›; melodramatic ‹*gesture*›; emotive ‹*style*›; pompous ‹*voice*›
B *adv.* emotionally; with much emotion; (dramatisch) [melo]dramatically

Pathologe /patoˈloːgə/ *der;* **~n, ~n** ▸ⓘ **S. 113** pathologist

Pathologie /patoloˈgiː/ *die;* **~, ~n** **1** (Gebiet) pathology *no art.* **2** (Abteilung/Institut) pathology department/institute

Pathologin *die;* **~, ~nen** ▸ⓘ **S. 113** pathologist

pathologisch
A *Adj.* (Med.; auch fig.) pathological
B *adv.* pathologically

Pathos /ˈpaːtɔs/ *das;* **~:** emotionalism; **ein unechtes/hohles ~:** false/empty pathos; **eine Rede voller ~:** a speech full of emotion; **etw. mit ~ vortragen** recite sth. with much feeling

Patience /paˈsi̯ãːs/ *die;* **~, ~n** [game of] patience; **~n/eine ~ legen** play patience/a game of patience

Patient /paˈtsi̯ɛnt/ *der;* **~en, ~en, Patientin** *die;* **~, ~nen** ▸ⓘ **S. 439** patient; **~ von** *od.* **bei Dr. X sein** be a patient of Dr X

Patin *die;* **~, ~nen** (Taufzeugin) godmother; (DDR) sponsor (*responsible for the child's socialist upbringing*); *s. auch* **Pate**

Patina /ˈpaːtina/ *die;* **~:** patina; **~ ansetzen** become covered with a patina; (fig.) begin to show its age; become dated

patinieren *tr. V.* patinate

Patisserie /patɪsəˈriː/ *die;* **~, ~n** (schweiz.) patisserie

Patres ▸ **Pater**

Patriarch /patriˈarç/ *der;* **~en, ~en** patriarch

patriarchalisch
A *Adj.* patriarchal; (fig.: autoritär) authoritarian
B *adv.* in a patriarchal *or* (fig.) authoritarian manner

Patriarchat *das;* **~[e]s, ~e** **1** (Gesellschaftsordnung) patriarchy **2** (kath. u. orthodoxe Kirche) patriarchate

Patriot /patriˈoːt/ *der;* **~en, ~en, Patriotin** *die;* **~, ~nen** patriot

patriotisch
A *Adj.* patriotic
B *adv.* patriotically; **~ erzogen werden** be brought up to be a patriot

Patriotismus *der;* **~:** patriotism *usu. no def. art.*

Patrize /paˈtriːtsə/ *die;* **~, ~n** (Druckw.) steel punch *or* die

Patriziat /patriˈtsi̯aːt/ *das;* **~[e]s, ~e** (hist.) patriciate

Patrizier /paˈtriːtsi̯ɐ/ *der;* **~s, ~, Patrizierin** *die;* **~, ~nen** (hist.) patrician

Patron /paˈtroːn/ *der;* **~s, ~e** **1** (Schutzheiliger) patron saint **2** (Stifter einer Kirche) patron; founder **3** (ugs. abwertend: Kerl) type (coll.); **ein übler ~:** a nasty piece of work (coll.) **4** (hist.: Schutzherr; veralt.: Gönner) patron

Patronage /patroˈnaːʒə/ *die;* **~, ~n** favouritism *no art.*; (im Staatsapparat) patronage *no art.*

Patronat /patroˈnaːt/ *das;* **~[e]s, ~e** **1** (hist.; Würde, Amt) patronate **2** (Schirmherrschaft; Kirchenrecht: Rechtsstellung) patronage

Patrone /paˈtroːnə/ *die;* **~, ~n** **1** (für das Gewehr, den Füller) cartridge; (für die Kleinbildkamera) cassette **2** (Textilind.) point paper plan; draft

Patronen-: ~gurt *der* cartridge belt; (über der Schulter getragen) bandolier; **~hülse** *die* cartridge case; **~tasche** *die* cartridge pouch

Patronin *die;* **~, ~nen** **1** (Schutzheilige) patron saint **2** (veralt.: Gönnerin) patroness

Patrouille /paˈtrʊljə/ *die;* **~, ~n** patrol

Patrouillen-: ~boot *das* patrol boat; **~gang** *der* patrol

patrouillieren /patrʊlˈjiːrən/ *itr. V.; auch mit sein* be on patrol; **durch die Straßen ~:** patrol the streets

patsch /patʃ/ *Interj.* splat; slap; (auf Wasser usw.) splash

Patsche *die;* **~, ~n** **1** (ugs.) ▸ **Klemme 2** **2** (ugs.: Hand) paw (coll.); **kleine ~n** (eines Kindes) little hands **3** (Feuer~) fire beater

patschen *itr. V.* (ugs.) **1** (klatschen) slap; **sich** (*Dat.*) **auf die Schenkel ~:** slap one's thighs; **das Kind patschte in die Hände** the child clapped its hands **2** *mit sein* (**~d** gehen/fallen) splash; **über die Fliesen ~** (mit nassen Stiefeln usw.) go flip-flop over the tiles; (unbeholfen) lollop over the tiles; **durch die Pfützen ~:** splash *or* go splashing through the puddles **3** (**~des** Geräusch hervorbringen) ‹*slush, wet shoes*› squelch

patsch-, Patsch-: ~hand *die;* **~händchen** *das* (fam.) [little] hand; handy-pandy (child lang.); **~nass, *~naß** *Adj.* (ugs.) sopping wet; **~nass geschwitzt** soaked in sweat

patt /pat/ (Schach) **~ sein** be stalemated

Patt *das;* **~s, ~s** (Schach; auch fig.) stalemate; **mit einem ~ enden** *od.* **ausgehen** end in stalemate

Patte *die;* **~, ~n** [pocket] flap

Patt·situation *die* [position of] stalemate

patzen /ˈpatsn̩/ *itr. V.* **1** (ugs.: Fehler machen) slip up (coll.); boob (coll.); **der Pianist hat ziemlich/erheblich gepatzt** the pianist came rather/well and truly unstuck (coll.) **2** (österr.: klecksen) make a blot/blots

Patzer der; ∼s, ∼ (ugs.) slip (coll.); boob (coll.); **ein dicker ∼:** a real howler (coll.)

patzig (ugs. abwertend)
A *Adj.* snotty (coll.); (frech) cheeky
B *adv.* snottily (coll.); (frech) cheekily

Paukant /paʊ̯'kant/ *der;* **∼en, ∼en** (Studentenspr.) duellist

Pauke /'paʊ̯kə/ *die;* **∼, ∼n** kettledrum; **∼n** (im Orchester) timpani; **die ∼ schlagen** beat the drum/drums; **auf die ∼ hauen** (ugs.) (feiern) paint the town red (coll.); (großtun) blow one's own trumpet; (sich lautstark äußern) come right out with it; **mit ∼n und Trompeten durchfallen** (ugs.) ‹*candidate*› fail resoundingly; ‹*broadcast, film, etc.*› be a resounding failure; **jmdn. mit ∼n und Trompeten empfangen** (fig.) give sb. the red-carpet treatment

pauken
A *tr. V.* (ugs.) swot up (Brit. sl.), bone up on (Amer. coll.) ‹*facts, figures, etc.*›; **Latein/Mathe ∼:** swot up one's Latin/maths
B *itr. V.* **1** (ugs.: lernen) swot (Brit. sl.); (fürs Examen) cram (coll.) **2** (Musik) (in einer Band o. Ä.) play the big drum[s]; (im Orchester) play the timpani **3** (Studentenspr.) duel

Pauken-: ∼schlag *der* **1** drumbeat; **Haydns Sinfonie mit dem ∼schlag** Haydn's Surprise Symphony; **2** (fig. Eklat) sensation; bombshell; **∼schlägel, *∼schlegel** *der* drumstick

Pauker *der;* **∼s, ∼** **1** (Musik) (im Orchester) timpanist; (in einer Band) big-drum player **2** (Schülerspr.: Lehrer) teacher; teach (school sl.)

Paukerei *die;* **∼** (ugs. abwertend) swotting (Brit. sl.); boning up (Amer. coll.); (fürs Examen) cramming

Paukerin *die;* **∼, ∼nen** ▸ **Pauker**

Paukist *der;* **∼en, ∼en, Paukistin** *die;* **∼, ∼nen** ▸ ❶ **S. 113** ▸ **Pauker 1**

Paulus /'paʊ̯lʊs/ *(der);* **∼'** Paul

Pauperismus /paʊ̯pə'rɪsmʊs/ *der;* **∼** (Soziol.) pauperism *usu. no art.*

Paus·backen *Pl.* (fam.) chubby cheeks

pausbäckig /'paʊ̯sbɛkɪç/ *Adj.* chubby-cheeked; chubby-faced; chubby ‹*face*›

pauschal /paʊ̯'ʃa:l/
A *Adj.* **1** (rund gerechnet) all-inclusive ‹*price, settlement*›; **eine ∼e Summe/Bezahlung** a lump sum/payment **2** (verallgemeinernd) sweeping ‹*judgement, criticism, statement*›; indiscriminate ‹*prejudice*›; wholesale ‹*discrimination*›
B *adv.* **1** (alles zusammengenommen) ‹*cost*› overall, all in all; ‹*pay*› in a lump sum; **das Angebot gilt ∼ für 10 Tage** the offer covers all costs *or* is inclusive for 10 days; **eine Frage ∼ beantworten** answer a question in general terms **2** (ohne zu differenzieren) wholesale

Pauschal-angebot *das* package deal

Pauschale *die;* **∼, ∼n** *od. das;* **∼s, Pauschalien** /-'ʃa:li̯ən/ flat-rate payment; (Pauschalsumme) lump sum; **monatliche ∼:** flat monthly rate

Pauschal-gebühr *die* flat-rate [charge]

pauschalieren /paʊ̯ʃa'li:rən/
A *itr. V.* [bring together small amounts to] form a lump sum; (fig.) lump things together
B *tr. V.* lump together

Pauschal-: ∼preis *der* (Einheitspreis) flat rate; (Inklusivpreis) inclusive *or* all-in price; **∼reise** *die* package holiday; (mit mehreren Reisezielen) package tour; **∼summe** *die* lump sum; **∼urteil** *das* (abwertend) sweeping judgement *or* statement

Pausch·betrag /'paʊ̯ʃ-/ *der* lump sum

Pause[1] /'paʊ̯zə/ *die;* **∼, ∼n** **1** (Unterbrechung) break; (Ruhe∼) rest; (Theater) interval (Brit.); intermission (Amer.); (Kino) intermission; (Sport) half-time interval; **kleine/große ∼** (Schule) short/[long] break; (Theater) short/main interval (Brit.) *or* (Amer.) intermission; **in** *od.* **während der ∼** (Schule) in *or* during break; (Theater) in *or* during the interval (Brit.) *or* (Amer.) intermission; (Sport) at half-time; **wann haben wir [große] ∼?** (Schule) when is [the long] break?; **es klingelt zur ∼** (Schule) the bell is ringing for break; **[eine] ∼ machen** take *or* have a break; (zum Ausruhen) have a rest; **wir machen kurz/eine Viertelstunde ∼:** we'll take a short break/a quarter of an hour's break; **eine ∼ einlegen** *od.* **einschieben** have a rest; **mach mal ∼!** take a break! **2** (in der Unterhaltung o. Ä.) pause; (verlegenes Schweigen) silence **3** (Musik) rest; **eine ganze/halbe ∼:** a semibreve/minim rest; a whole [note]/half [note] rest (Amer.)

Pause[2] *die;* **∼, ∼n** (Kopie) tracing; (Licht∼) Photostat (*Brit.* ®)

pausen *tr. V.* trace; (eine Lichtpause machen) Photostat (*Brit.* ®)

Pausen-: ∼brot *das* sandwich (eaten during break); **∼füller** *der* (ugs.) interval material *no art.;* **∼gong** *der* (Boxen, Ringen) bell [for the end of the round]; (Schulw.) bell [for the start/end of break]; **∼hof** *der* school yard

pausen·los
A *Adj.* incessant ‹*noise, moaning, questioning*›; continuous, uninterrupted ‹*work, operation*›
B *adv.* incessantly; ceaselessly; ‹*work*› non-stop

Pausen·zeichen *das* **1** (Musik) rest **2** (Rundfunk, Ferns.) interval signal

pausieren *itr. V.* **1** (innehalten) pause **2** (aussetzen) have *or* take a rest; **acht Wochen ∼ müssen** (Sport) ‹*player*› be out of the game for eight weeks

Paus·papier *das* (durchsichtig) tracing paper; (Kohlepapier) carbon paper

Pavian /'pa:vi̯a:n/ *der;* **∼s, ∼e** baboon

Pavillon /'pavɪljɔŋ/ *der;* **∼s, ∼s** (Archit.) pavilion; (einer Schule o. Ä.) annexe

Payback·karte /'peɪbɛk-/ *die* Payback card (*type of loyalty card*)

Paycard /'peɪka:d/ *die;* **∼, ∼s** [charge] card

Pazifik /pa'tsi:fɪk/ *der;* **∼s** Pacific

pazifisch *Adj.* Pacific ‹*area*›; **der Pazifische Ozean** the Pacific Ocean

Pazifismus *der;* **∼:** pacifism *no art.*

Pazifist *der;* **∼en, ∼en, Pazifistin** *die;* **∼, ∼nen** pacifist

pazifistisch
A *Adj.* pacifist
B *adv.* in a pacifist way

PC /pe:'tse:/ *der;* **∼[s], ∼[s]** (DV) PC

PDF-Datei *die* (DV) PDF file

PDS *Abk.* **= Partei des Demokratischen Sozialismus** Party of Democratic Socialism

PDS — Partei des Demokratischen Sozialismus

A party formed in 1990 from the old East German SED, the Communist party which ruled in the former GDR. The ultra left-wing *PDS* is against a free-market economy and advocates social justice. It is not a major political force in Germany but has acquired the status of a parliamentary party.

Pech /pɛç/ *das;* **∼[e]s, ∼e** **1** pitch; **schwarz wie ∼ sein** be pitch-black; ‹*hair*› be jet-black; **zusammenhalten wie ∼ und Schwefel** (ugs.) be inseparable; ‹*friends*› be as thick as thieves (coll.) **2** (Missgeschick) bad luck; **großes/unerhörtes ∼:** rotten (coll.)/(coll.) terrible luck; **bei** *od.* **mit etw./mit jmdm. ∼ haben** have bad luck with sth./sb.; be unlucky with sth./sb.; **im Leben/in der Liebe/bei den Frauen/beim Examen ∼ haben** have no luck in life/in love/with women/in the exam; **∼ gehabt!** (ugs.) tough luck! (coll.); **dein ∼, wenn du nicht aufpasst** (ugs.) that's just your hard luck if you don't pay attention; **sein ∼!** (ugs.) that's his lookout; **∼ für dich** (ugs.) that's just too bad (coll.); **vom ∼ verfolgt sein** be dogged by bad luck

pech-, Pech-: ∼blende *die* (Mineral.) pitchblende; **∼[raben]schwarz** *Adj.* (ugs.) pitch-black ‹*night, darkness, coffee*›; jet-black ‹*eyes*›; raven[-black] ‹*hair*›; **∼strähne** *die* run of bad luck; **∼vogel** *der* unlucky devil (coll.); (Opfer vieler Unfälle) walking disaster area (coll.)

Pedal /pe'da:l/ *das;* **∼s, ∼e** pedal; (bei der Orgel) pedals *pl.;* **mit/ohne ∼ spielen** (beim Klavier) use/not use pedal; **[kräftig] in die ∼e treten** (beim Fahrrad) pedal [really] hard

Pedale *die;* **∼, ∼n** (landsch.) ▸ **Pedal**

pedant (österr.) ▸ **pedantisch**

Pedant /pe'dant/ *der;* **∼en, ∼en** pedant

Pedanterie /pedantə'ri:/ *die;* **∼, ∼n** pedantry; **seine ∼n** his pedantic ways

Pedantin *die;* **∼, ∼nen** ▸ **Pedant**

pedantisch
A *Adj.* pedantic
B *adv.* pedantically

Peddig·rohr /'pɛdɪç-/ *das* rattan [cane]

Pedell /pe'dɛl/ *der;* **∼s, ∼e,** (österr. meist:) **∼en, ∼en** (veralt.) caretaker (Brit.); janitor (esp. Amer.)

Pediküre /pedi'ky:rə/ *die;* **∼, ∼n** **1** ▸ **Fußpflege** **2** (Fußpflegerin) chiropodist

pediküren *tr. V.* pedicure ‹*feet, nails*›

Peep·show /'pi:p-/ *die;* **∼, ∼s** peep show

Peergroup /'pi:ɐ̯gru:p/ *die;* **∼, ∼s** (Soziol.) peer group

Pegel /'pe:gl̩/ *der;* **∼s, ∼** **1** (Gerät) water level indicator; (für die Gezeiten am Meer) tide gauge **2** (Wasserstand) water level; (Technik, Physik; auch fig.) level (*of noise, alcohol consumption, etc.*)

Pegel·stand *der* water level

Peil·antenne *die* (Funkw., Seew.) direction-finding antenna

peilen /'paɪ̯lən/
A *tr. V.* **1** take a bearing on ‹*transmitter, fixed point*›; *s. auch* **Daumen; Lage 3** **2** (Wassertiefe messen) sound ‹*depth*›; take soundings in ‹*bay etc.*›
B *itr. V.* **1** take one's bearings; get a fix **2** (Wassertiefe messen) take a sounding/soundings **3** (ugs.: spähen) peek

Peilung *die;* **∼, ∼en** (Seew.) **1** (das Peilen) taking a bearing; (des eigenen Standorts) plotting one's position; (Resultat) fix; bearing **2** (der Wassertiefe) sounding

Pein /paɪ̯n/ *die;* **∼** (geh.) torment; **körperliche/seelische ∼:** physical/mental anguish; **jmdm. [viel** *od.* **große] ∼ bereiten** cause sb. [much] anguish

peinigen /'paɪ̯nɪgn̩/ *tr. V.* (geh.) torment; (foltern) torture; **von Durst/Kälte gepeinigt werden** suffer agonies from thirst/cold; **von Schmerzen gepeinigt werden** be tormented by *or* racked with pain; *s. auch* **Blut**

Peiniger *der;* **∼s, ∼, Peinigerin** *die;* **∼, ∼nen** (geh.) tormentor; (Folterer) torturer

Peinigung *die;* **∼, ∼en** (geh.) torment; (Folterung) torture

peinlich
A *Adj.* **1** embarrassing; awkward ‹*question, position, pause*›; **es ist mir sehr ∼:** I feel very bad (coll.) *or* embarrassed about it; **es ist mir sehr ∼, Ihnen das mitteilen zu müssen** I feel terrible about having to tell you this (coll.); **es ist mir sehr ∼, aber ich wollte Sie fragen, …** I don't know quite how to put this, but I wanted to ask you … **2** (äußerst genau) meticulous; scrupulous; **er hielt sich mit ∼ster Genauigkeit an diese Vorschrift** he was most punctilious in observing this regulation **3** (Rechtsspr. veralt.) **das ∼e Gericht** the criminal *or* penal court; **ein ∼es Verhör** an interrogation under torture
B *adv.* **1** unpleasantly ‹*surprised*›; **[von etw.] ∼ berührt** *od.* **betroffen sein** be painfully embarrassed [by sth.] **2** (überaus [genau]) scrupulously; meticulously; **er vermied es ∼[st], dieses heikle Thema zu berühren** he took [the utmost] pains to avoid touching on this delicate subject; **∼ genau registriert** listed down to the last detail

peinlicher·weise *Adv.* embarrassingly

Peinlichkeit *die;* **∼, ∼en** **1** embarrassment; **die ∼ der Situation** the awkwardness of the situation **2** (Genauigkeit) scrupulousness; meticulousness **3** (peinliche Situation) embarrassing situation; (heikle Situation) awkward situation; (Fehler) embarrassing blunder

peinsam *Adj.* (meist scherzh.) ▸ **peinlich A 1**

pein·voll *Adj.* (geh.) painful; agonizing ‹*uncertainty*›; ‹*period*› full of anguish

Peitsche /'paɪ̯tʃə/ *die;* **∼, ∼n** whip; **er knallte mit der ∼:** he cracked the whip; *s. auch* **Zuckerbrot**

peitschen
A *tr. V.* whip; (fig.) ‹*storm, waves, rain*› lash

P

B *itr. V.; mit sein* ‹*rain*› lash (**an, gegen** + *Akk.* against, **in** + *Akk.* into); ‹*shot*› ring out

Peitschen-: ~hieb *der* lash [of the whip]; **wie ein ~hieb** like a whiplash; **~knall** *der* crack of the whip; **~lampe** *die* street lamp (hanging over the street from a curved standard); **~stiel** *der* whip handle; whipstock

pejorativ /pejora'ti:f/ (Sprachw.)

A *Adj.* pejorative

B *adv.* pejoratively

Pekinese /peki'ne:zə/ *der;* **~n, ~n** Pekinese

Peking·mensch /'pe:kiŋ-/ *der* Peking Man

Pektin /pɛk'ti:n/ *das;* **~s, ~e** (Biol.) pectin

pekuniär /pɛku'ni̯ɛ:ɐ̯/

A *Adj.* pecuniary; financial

B *adv.* financially

Pelerine /pelə'ri:nə/ *die;* **~, ~n** cape

Pelikan /'pe:lika:n/ *der;* **~s, ~e** pelican

Pelle /'pɛlə/ *die;* **~, ~n** (bes. nordd.) skin; (abgeschält) peel; **Kartoffeln in** *od.* **mit der ~ kochen** boil potatoes in their skins; **sie hocken sich** (*Dat.*) **[dauernd] auf der ~** (salopp) they never leave each other alone; **jmdm. nicht von der ~ gehen** (salopp) refuse to leave sb. alone *or* in peace; *s. auch* **rücken B 1**; **sitzen 1**

pellen (bes. nordd.)

A *tr. V.* peel ‹*potato, egg, etc.*›; **sie pellte sich/das Kind aus dem warmen Winterzeug** (fig.) she peeled off her/the child's warm winter things; *s. auch* **Ei 1**

B *refl. V.* ‹*person, skin*› peel

Pell·kartoffel *die* potato boiled in its skin

Pelz /pɛlts/ *der;* **~es, ~e** **1** fur; coat; (des toten Tieres) skin; pelt; **einen weichen ~ haben** have a soft coat; have soft fur; **einem Tier den ~ abziehen** skin an animal **2** (gegerbt; als Material) fur; **aus ~:** made of fur; **mit ~ gefüttert** fur-lined **3** fur; (~mantel) fur coat; (~jacke) fur jacket **4** (ugs.: Haut) **sich** (*Dat.*) **die Sonne auf den ~ brennen** *od.* **scheinen lassen** soak up the sun; **jmdm./einem Tier eins auf den ~ brennen** take a potshot at sb./an animal; *s. auch* **Laus**; **rücken B 1**; **sitzen 1**

pelz-, Pelz-: ~besatz *der* fur trimming; **~besetzt** *Adj.* fur-trimmed; **~futter** *das* fur lining; **~gefüttert** *Adj.* fur-lined; **~händler** *der,* **~händlerin** *die* furrier; **~hand·schuh** *der* fur glove; (~gefüttert) fur-lined glove

pelzig *Adj.* **1** (wie Pelz, mit Flaum) furry; downy ‹*peach*› **2** (bes. westd.: mehlig) mealy ‹*apple*›; (holzig) woody ‹*radish*› **3** (belegt) furred, coated ‹*tongue, mouth*›

Pelz-: ~imitation *die* imitation fur; **~jacke** *die* fur jacket; **~kragen** *der* fur collar; **~mantel** *der* fur coat; **~mütze** *die* fur hat; **~stiefel** *der* fur boot; (pelzgefüttert) fur-lined boot; **~tier** *das* animal prized for its fur; **~tier·farm** *die* fur farm; **~tier·jäger** *der,* **~tier·jägerin** *die* fur-hunter; trapper; **~tier·zucht** *die* fur farming *no def. art.*; **~waren** *Pl.* furs; fur goods; **~werk** *das* fur

Pence /'pɛns/ *Pl. von* **Penny**

Pendant /pã'dã:/ *das;* **~s, ~s** (Gegenstück) counterpart (**zu** of); (ein Stück von einem Paar) companion piece (**zu** of); (Entsprechung) equivalent (**zu** of)

Pendel /'pɛndl̩/ *das;* **~s, ~:** pendulum

pendeln *itr. V.* **1** (hin- u. herschwingen) swing [to and fro] (**an** + *Dat.* by); (mit weniger Bewegung) dangle **2** *mit sein* (hin- u. herfahren) **zwischen X und Y ~** ‹*bus, ferry, etc.*› operate a shuttle service between X and Y; ‹*person*› commute between X and Y **3** (Boxen) weave

Pendel-: ~tür *die* swing door; **~uhr** *die* pendulum clock; **~verkehr** *der* **1** (Berufsverkehr) commuter traffic; **2** (mit ~zug o. Ä.) shuttle service; **~zug** *der* shuttle[-service] train

Pendler *der;* **~s, ~, Pendlerin** *die;* **~, ~nen** commuter

Penes ▸ **Penis**

penetrant /pene'trant/ (abwertend)

A *Adj.* **1** (durchdringend) penetrating, pungent ‹*smell, taste*›; overpowering ‹*stink, perfume*› **2** (aufdringlich) pushing, (coll.) pushy ‹*person*›; overbearing ‹*tone, manner*›; aggressive, pointed ‹*question*›

B *adv.* **1** (durchdringend) overpoweringly; **es riecht/schmeckt ~ nach ...** there is an overpowering smell/an overpowering *or* pungent taste of ... **2** (aufdringlich) overbearingly; in an overbearing manner

Penetranz /pene'trants/ *die;* **~** **1** (von Geruch, Geschmack) overpowering nature **2** (Aufdringlichkeit) overbearing nature

Penetration /penetra'tsi̯o:n/ *die;* **~, ~en** **1** (Technik) penetration; **2** (Wirtsch.) penetration [of the market] **3** (Med.) perforation

penetrieren *tr. V.* (geh.) penetrate

peng /pɛŋ/ *Interj.* bang

penibel /pe'ni:bl̩/

A *Adj.* over-meticulous ‹*person*›; (pedantisch) pedantic; **penible Kleinarbeit** painstakingly detailed work

B *adv.* painstakingly; over-meticulously ‹*dressed*›

Penicillin ▸ **Penizillin**

Penis /'pe:nɪs/ *der;* **~, ~se** *od.* **Penes** /'pe:ne:s/ ▸ **S. 435** penis

Penis·neid *der* (Psych.) penis envy

Penizillin /penitsɪ'li:n/ *das;* **~s, ~e** penicillin

Pennäler /pɛ'nɛ:lɐ/ *der;* **~s, ~** (ugs.) [secondary] schoolboy

Pennälerin *die;* **~, ~nen** (ugs.) [secondary] schoolgirl

Penn·bruder *der* (ugs. abwertend) tramp (Brit.); hobo (Amer.)

Penne /'pɛnə/ *die;* **~, ~n** **1** (Schülerspr.: Schule) [secondary] school; swot-shop (Brit. sl.) **2** (ugs. abwertend: Nachtquartier) dosshouse (Brit. coll.); flophouse (sl.)

pennen *itr. V.* (salopp) **1** (schlafen) kip (coll.); **auf einer Bank ~:** doss down on a bench (sl.) **2** (fig.: nicht aufpassen) be half asleep; **du hast im Unterricht wohl mal wieder gepennt?** (fig.) I suppose you were dreaming again during the lesson? **3** (koitieren) **mit jmdm. ~:** sleep with sb.

Penner *der;* **~s, ~, Pennerin** *die;* **~, ~nen** (salopp abwertend) **1** (Stadtstreicher) tramp (Brit.); hobo (Amer.) **2** (jmd., der viel schläft) sleepyhead

Penny /'pɛni/ *der;* **~s, ~s** ▸ **S. 299** penny; **20 Pence** 20 pence

Pensa, Pensen ▸ **Pensum**

Pension /pã'zi̯o:n/ *die;* **~, ~en** **1** (Ruhestand) **[vorzeitig] in ~ gehen** retire [early]; **in ~ sein** be retired *or* in retirement; **einen Beamten in ~** (*Akk.*) **schicken** retire a civil servant **2** (Ruhegehalt) [retirement] pension **3** (Haus für [Ferien]gäste) guest house; (auf dem Kontinent) pension **4** (Unterkunft u. Verpflegung) board; **[die] halbe/volle ~:** half/full board; **bei jmdm. in ~ sein** board with sb.

Pensionär /pãzi̯o'nɛ:ɐ̯/ *der;* **~s, ~e, Pensionärin** *die;* **~, ~nen** **1** (Beamter in Ruhestand) retired civil servant; (ugs.: Rentner) [old-age] pensioner; **~ sein** be retired *or* in retirement **2** (schweiz., sonst veralt.: Bewohner einer Pension) boarder; [paying] guest

Pensionat /pãzi̯o'na:t/ *das;* **~[e]s, ~e** (veralt.) boarding school (*esp. for girls*)

pensionieren *tr. V.* pension off; retire; **sich [vorzeitig] ~ lassen** retire [early]; take [early] retirement

Pensionierung *die;* **~, ~en** retirement; **bis zur ~:** up to [his, her, *etc.*] retirement

Pensionist, *der;* **~en, ~en, Pensionistin** *die;* **~, ~nen** (südd., österr., schweiz.) ▸ **Pensionär 1**

pensions-, Pensions-: ~alter *das* retirement age; **~anspruch** *der* pension entitlement; **~ansprüche** pension rights; **~berechtigt** *Adj.* entitled to a pension *postpos.*; **~berechtigung** *die* pension entitlement; **~gast** *der* patron [of a/the guest house]; **~kasse** *die* (Versicherungsw.) [staff] pension fund; **~reif** *Adj.* (ugs.) ripe for retirement *pred.*; **~rückstellungen** *Pl.* (Wirtsch.) pension reserves

Pensum /'pɛnzʊm/ *das;* **~s, Pensen** *od.* **Pensa** **1** (Arbeit) amount of work; work quota; **sein tägliches ~ [an Arbeit] erledigen** do one's daily stint [of work] **2** (Päd. veralt.: Lehrstoff) syllabus

Pentagon /pɛnta'go:n/ *das;* **~s, ~e** **1** (Geom.) pentagon **2** (amerikan. Verteidigungsministerium) Pentagon

Penta-: ~gramm *das* pentagram; **~meter** /-'---/ *der* (Verslehre) pentameter

Pentatonik /pɛnta'to:nɪk/ *die;* **~** (Musik) pentatonic scale

Pent·haus /'pɛnt-/ *das,* **Penthouse** /'pɛnthaʊs/ *das;* **~, ~s** penthouse

Penunse /pe'nʊnzə/ *die;* **~, ~n, Penunze** /pe'nʊntsə/ *die;* **~, ~n** (ugs.) **~[n]** cash; dough (coll.)

Pep /pɛp/ *der;* **~[s]** (ugs.) pep (sl.); zip; **~ haben** be dynamic *or* full of zip

Peperoni /pepe'ro:ni/ *die;* **~, ~:** chilli

Pepita /pe'pi:ta/ *der od. das;* **~s, ~s** shepherd's check

Pepsin /pɛ'psi:n/ *das;* **~s, ~e** (Med.) pepsin

per /pɛr/ *Präp. mit Akk.* **1** (mittels) by; **~ Post** by post; **~ Adresse X** care of X; c/o X; *s. auch* **Anhalter**; **du**; **Eilbote**; **Einschreiben**; **Nachnahme** **2** (Kaufmannsspr.: [bis] zum) by; (am) on; **~ Jahresende** by the end of the year; **~ sofort** immediately; as of now **3** (Kaufmannsspr.: pro) per; **etw. ~ Kilo/Stück verkaufen** sell sth. by the kilo/by the piece *or* separately

per definitionem /- defini'tsi̯o:nɛm/ *Adv.* (geh.) by definition

perennierend /pɛrɛ'ni:rənt/ *Adj.* (Biol., Geogr., fig.) perennial

Perf. *Abk.* **= Perfekt** perf.

perfekt /pɛr'fɛkt/

A *Adj.* **1** (hervorragend) outstanding; first-rate; (vollkommen) perfect ‹*crime, host*›; faultless ‹*English, French, etc.*›; **eine ~e Sekretärin** a fully accomplished secretary **2** (ugs.: endgültig, abgeschlossen) finalized; concluded; **~ sein/werden** ‹*contract, deal*› be concluded *or* finalized; ‹*scandal, defeat*› be complete; **~ machen** finalize ‹*contract, date, booking, deal*›; complete ‹*disaster*›

B *adv.* **1** (hervorragend) outstandingly well; (vollkommen) ‹*fit, work, etc.*› perfectly; **~ beherrschen** have a complete mastery of ‹*language, material*›; play ‹*game*› with complete mastery; **er spricht ~ Englisch** he speaks faultless *or* perfect English **2** (ugs.: vollständig) good and proper (coll.); **er hat sich ~ blamiert** he made a complete fool of himself

Perfekt /'pɛrfɛkt/ *das;* **~s, ~e** (Sprachw.) perfect [tense]

Perfektion /pɛrfɛk'tsi̯o:n/ *die;* **~:** perfection; **handwerkliche/technische ~:** mastery of a craft/technical mastery; **etw. mit [großer] ~ ausführen/spielen** do/play sth. to perfection; do/play sth. with great mastery; **Reitkunst in höchster** *od.* **absoluter ~:** the art of riding at its most perfect

perfektionieren *tr. V.* perfect

Perfektionismus *der;* **~:** perfectionism

Perfektionist *der;* **~en, ~en, Perfektionistin** *die;* **~, ~nen** perfectionist

perfektionistisch

A *Adj.* perfectionist ‹*standards etc.*›

B *adv.* in a perfectionist manner

perfektiv /'pɛrfɛkti:f/ *Adj.* (Sprachw.) perfective

perfid /pɛr'fi:t/, **perfide** (geh.)

A *Adj.* perfidious

B *adv.* perfidiously

Perfidie /pɛrfi'di:/ *die;* **~, ~n** (geh.) perfidy

Perforation /pɛrfora'tsi̯o:n/ *die;* **~, ~en** (Technik, Med.) perforation

perforieren *tr. V.* (Technik, Med.) perforate

Pergament /pɛrga'mɛnt/ *das;* **~[e]s, ~e** parchment; (bes. für Bucheinbände) vellum

Pergament·band *der* vellum-bound volume

pergamenten *Adj.* **1** parchment; vellum ‹*binding*›; vellum-bound ‹*book*› **2** (wie aus Pergament) ‹*skin, face*› like parchment

P

Pergament-: **~papier** *das* greaseproof paper; **~rolle** *die* parchment scroll

Pergola /ˈpɛrgola/ *die;* ~, **Pergolen** pergola

Periode /peˈri̯o:də/ *die;* ~, **~n** [1] (auch Chemie, Physik, Technik, Astron., Met., Sprachw., Musik) period; (Geol.) era; **sie hat ihre ~ nicht bekommen** she didn't get *or* have her period [2] (Math.) repetend; period; **3,3 ~:** 3.3 recurring

Perioden·system *das* (Chemie) periodic system; (grafische Darstellung) periodic table

Periodikum /peˈri̯o:dikʊm/ *das;* **~s, Periodika** periodical

periodisch

A *Adj.* [1] (regelmäßig) regular; ‹*meeting, statement of account*› at regular intervals; (Chemie) periodic ‹*system*›; **eine ~e Dezimalzahl** (Math.) a recurring decimal [2] (zeitweilig) sporadic ‹*moods etc.*›

B *adv.* [1] (regelmäßig) regularly; at regular intervals [2] (zeitweilig) periodically; from time to time

peripher /periˈfe:ɐ̯/

A *Adj.* (auch Anat., fig.) peripheral; **~e Stadtteile** districts on the outskirts of the town

B *adv.* (auch Anat., fig.) peripherally; **die Siedlung liegt ~:** the estate is on the outskirts; **ein Thema nur ~ behandeln** just touch on a subject

Peripherie /perifeˈri:/ *die;* ~, **~n** [1] periphery; (einer Stadt) outskirts *pl.*; fringe; (Geom.: Begrenzungslinie) circumference; **die ~ des Körpers** the peripheral areas of the body [2] (DV: periphere Geräte) peripherals *pl.*

Peripherie·gerät *das* (DV) peripheral device; peripheral

Periskop /periˈsko:p/ *das;* **~s, ~e** periscope

Peristaltik /periˈstaltɪk/ *die;* ~ (Physiol.) peristalsis

Perkussion *die;* ~, **~nen** percussion

Perkussionist *der;* **~en, ~en, Perkussionistin** *die;* ~, **~nen** percussionist

perkussiv /pɛrkʊˈsi:f/ (Mus.)

A *Adj.* percussive

B *adv.* percussively

perkutan /pɛrkuˈta:n/ *Adj.* (Med.) percutaneous

Perlator Ⓦⓩ /pɛrˈla:to:ɐ̯/ *der;* **~s, Perlatoren** /-laˈto:rən/ *tap attachment with fine rose*

Perle /ˈpɛrlə/ *die;* ~, **~n** [1] (auch fig.) pearl; **~n vor die Säue werfen** (fig. ugs.) cast pearls before swine; *s. auch* **Krone 1** [2] (aus Holz, Glas o. Ä.) bead; (Tröpfchen) drop; (Bläschen beim Sekt usw.) bubble [3] (ugs. scherzh.: Hausgehilfin) [invaluable] home help

perlen *itr. V.* [1] *auch mit sein* **auf etw.** (*Dat.*) **~:** form pearls on sth.; ‹*dew*› form droplets on sth.; **der Schweiß perlte ihm auf der Stirn** beads of perspiration stood out on his brow [2] *mit sein* **von etw. ~** ‹*dew, sweat*› trickle *or* drip from sth.; **Tränen perlten über ihre Wangen** tears trickled *or* rolled down her cheeks [3] (Bläschen bilden) ‹*champagne etc.*› sparkle, bubble [4] (melodisch ertönen) ‹*laughter, music*› ripple

perlen-, Perlen-: **~bestickt** *Adj.* embroidered *or* decorated with pearls *postpos.*; **~fischer** *der* pearl fisher; **~fischerei** *die* pearl fishing; **~fischerin** *die* ▸ **~fischer**; **~kette** *die* string of pearls; pearl necklace; (mit Holz~ usw.) string of beads; bead necklace; **~kollier** *das* pearl necklace; **~schnur** *die* string of pearls; (mit Holz~ usw.) string of beads; **~stickerei** *die* pearl embroidery; (mit Holz~ usw.) bead embroidery; **~taucher** *der,* **~taucherin** *die* pearl diver

perl-, Perl-: **~garn** *das* pearl cotton; **~grau** *Adj.* pearl-grey; **~huhn** *das* guineafowl; **~muschel** *die* pearl oyster; **~muster** *das* moss stitch; **~mutt** /-mʊt/ *das;* **~~s, ~mutter** *die;* ~~ *od. das;* **~~s** mother-of-pearl; **~muttern** *Adj.* mother-of-pearl; (fig.: wie Perlmutter) like mother-of-pearl *postpos.*

Perlon Ⓦⓩ *das;* **~s** ≈ nylon

Perlon·strumpf *der* ≈ nylon stocking

Perl-: **~schrift** *die* elite; **~wein** *der* sparkling wine; **~zwiebel** *die* pearl *or* cocktail onion

permanent /pɛrmaˈnɛnt/

A *Adj.* permanent ‹*institution, deficit, crisis*›; constant ‹*danger, threat, squabble*›

B *adv.* constantly

Permanenz /pɛrmaˈnɛnts/ *die;* **~:** permanence; **in ~:** permanently; **in ~ tagen** sit continuously; be in permanent session

permissiv /pɛrmɪˈsi:f/ *Adj.* (Soziol., Psych.) permissive

per pedes *Adv.* (ugs.) on Shank's pony

Perpendikel /pɛrpɛnˈdi:kl̩/ *der od. das;* **~s,** ~ [1] (veralt.: einer Uhr) pendulum [2] (Schiffbau) perpendicular

perpetuieren /pɛrpetuˈi:rən/ *tr. V.* (geh.) perpetuate

Perpetuum mobile /pɛrˈpɛ:tuʊm ˈmo:bilə/ *das;* ~ **~[s],** ~ **~[s]** *od.* **Perpetua mobilia** [1] (utopische Maschine) perpetual-motion machine [2] (Musik) perpetuum mobile

perplex /pɛrˈplɛks/ (ugs.)

A *Adj.* (verblüfft) baffled, puzzled (**über** + *Akk.* by); (verwirrt) bewildered

B *adv.* **~ dreinschauen** look baffled/bewildered

Perron /peˈrõ:/ *der;* **~s, ~s** (österr., schweiz.) platform

per saldo /-ˈsaldo/ (Kaufmannsspr.) net; (fig.: im Endeffekt) on balance; **~ rund 4 Millionen Verlust/Gewinn** a net loss/gain of about four million

Persenning /pɛrˈzɛnɪŋ/ *die;* **~, ~e[n]** *od.* **~s** [1] (bes. Seemannsspr.: Bezug) tarpaulin [2] (Textilind.: Segeltuch) [waterproof] canvas

Perser /ˈpɛrzɐ/ *der;* **~s,** ~ [1] ▸ⓘ **S. 520** Persian [2] ▸ **Perserteppich**

Perserin *die;* **~, ~nen** ▸ⓘ **S. 520** Persian

Perser-: **~katze** *die* Persian [cat]; **~teppich** *der* Persian carpet; (kleiner) Persian rug

Persianer /pɛrˈzi̯a:nɐ/ *der;* **~s, ~:** Persian lamb; (**~mantel**) Persian lamb coat

Persianer·mantel *der* Persian lamb coat

Persien /ˈpɛrzi̯ən/ *(das);* **~s** Persia

Persiflage /pɛrziˈfla:ʒə/ *die;* **~, ~n** [gentle] mocking *no indef. art.*; **eine ~ auf jmdn./etw.** a [gentle] satire of sb./sth.

persiflieren *tr. V.* satirize

Persil·schein /pɛrˈzi:l-/ *der* (ugs. scherzh.) certificate of blamelessness

persisch *Adj.* ▸ⓘ **S. 520,** ▸ⓘ **S. 670** Persian; *s. auch* **deutsch; Deutsch; Deutsche**[2]

Person /pɛrˈzo:n/ *die;* **~, ~en** [1] person; **eine männliche/weibliche ~:** a male/female; **~en** (als Gruppe) people; **die Familie besteht aus fünf ~en** it is a family of five; **~en sind bei dem Brand nicht umgekommen** there was no loss of life in the fire; **pro ~:** per person; **seine** *od.* **die eigene ~ zu wichtig nehmen** take oneself too seriously; **deine ~/die ~ des Kanzlers soll nicht erwähnt werden** you are/the Chancellor is not to be mentioned in person; **ich für meine ~ ...** I for my part ...; **sich in der ~ irren** get the wrong person; **der Minister in [eigener] ~:** the minister in person; **sie ist die Güte/Geduld in ~:** she is kindness/patience personified *or* itself; **Politiker und Lyriker in einer ~ sein** be a politician and a lyric poet rolled into one; **Fragen zur ~:** questions to sb. on his/her identity; **Angaben zur ~ machen** give one's personal details; **jmdn. zur ~ vernehmen** *od.* **befragen** (Rechtsw.) examine *or* question sb. concerning his/her identity; **eine natürliche/juristische ~** (Rechtsw.) a natural/juristic person; *s. auch* **Ansehen 2** [2] (in der Dichtung, im Film) character; **die ~en der Handlung** the characters [in the action]; (im Theater) the dramatis personae; **komische** *od.* **lustige ~** (Literaturw.) [stock] comic figure [3] (emotional: Frau) female (derog./joc.) [4] (Sprachw.) person; **in der dritten ~ Singular/Plural** in the third person singular/plural

Personal /pɛrzoˈna:l/ *das;* **~s** [1] (in einem Betrieb o. Ä.) staff; (hinsichtlich der Verwaltung) personnel; **ungenügend/ausreichend mit ~ versehen** inadequately/adequately staffed; **das fliegende ~:** the flight personnel; the aircrews *pl.* [2] (im Haushalt) servants *pl.*; [domestic] staff *pl.*

Personal-: **~abbau** *der* reduction in staff; (in mehreren Abteilungen/Betrieben) staff cuts *pl.*; **~abteilung** *die* personnel department; **~akte** *die* personal file *or* dossier; **~angaben** *Pl.* personal details *or* particulars; **~ausweis** *der* identity card; **~bedarf** *der* staffing requirements *pl.*; **~bestand** *der* number of staff *or* employees (+ *Gen.* in); **~büro** *das* personnel office; **~chef** *der,* **~chefin** *die* ▸ⓘ **S. 113** personnel manager; **~einsparung** *die* saving in staff

> **Personalausweis**
>
> The standard German identity card, with the holder's photograph and particulars, should in theory be carried at all times. If you are stopped by the police without any ID you might be taken to a police station and kept there for up to six hours. The *Personalausweis* acts as a passport for Germans and Austrians travelling within the EU.

Personalien /pɛrzoˈna:li̯ən/ *Pl.* personal details *or* particulars; **die ~ angeben** give one's [personal] particulars

personalisieren *tr. V.* personalize; reduce ‹*quarrel, relations, etc.*› to a personal level

Personal-: **~karussell** *das* (ugs.) [game of] musical chairs *no art.*; *reallocation of jobs amongst the existing staff*; **~kosten** *Pl.* (Wirtsch., Verwaltung) staff costs; **~mangel** *der* staff shortage; **~planung** *die* (bes. Wirtsch.) personnel planning; **~politik** *die* staff *or* personnel policy; (bei der Einstellung) staffing policy; **~pronomen** *das* (Sprachw.) personal pronoun; **~rat** *der* [1] (Ausschuss) staff council (*for civil servants*); [2] (einzelnes Mitglied) staff council representative; **~rätin** *die* ▸ **~rat 2**; **~union** *die* [1] (im Staatsrecht) personal union; [2] (Vereinigung von Ämtern) combination of the functions (**zwischen** + *Dat.* of)

Persönchen /pɛrˈzø:nçən/ *das;* **~s, ~:** little lady

personell /pɛrzoˈnɛl/

A *Adj.* staff ‹*changes, difficulties*›; ‹*savings*› in staff; ‹*questions, decisions*› regarding staff *or* personnel

B *adv.* with regard to staff *or* personnel

personen-, Personen-: **~aufzug** *der* passenger lift (Brit.) *or* (Amer.) elevator; **~beförderung** *die* (Verkehrsw.) passenger transport *no art.*; **~beförderung mit der Bahn** carrying passengers by rail; **~beschreibung** *die* personal description; **~bezogen** **A** *Adj.* personal; **B** *adv.* on a personal basis; **~gedächtnis** *das* memory for faces; **~gesellschaft** *die* (Wirtsch.) general partnership; **~kontrolle** *die* identity check; (von Passagieren) passenger check; **~kraftwagen** *der* (bes. Amtsspr.) private car *or* (Amer.) automobile; **~kreis** *der* group [of people]; **~kult** *der* (abwertend) personality cult; **~nahverkehr** *der* local public transport; **~name** *der* personal name; **~register** *das* index of names; **~schaden** *der* (Versicherungsw.) physical *or* personal injury; **bei dem Unfall entstand kein ~schaden** nobody was injured in the accident; **Unfälle mit ~schaden** accidents in which injuries are/were sustained; **~stands·register** *das* register of births, marriages, and deaths; **~verkehr** *der* (Verkehrsw.) passenger transport *no art.*; **~verzeichnis** *das* [1] (~register) index of names; [2] (im Drama) list of characters; **~waage** *die* scales *pl.*; **~wagen** *der* [1] (Auto) [private] car; automobile (Amer.); (im Unterschied zum Lastwagen) passenger car *or* (Amer.) automobile; [2] (bei Zügen) passenger coach; **~zug** *der* slow *or* stopping train; (im Unterschied zum Güterzug) passenger train

Personifikation /pɛrzonifikaˈtsi̯o:n/ *die;* **~, ~en** personification

personifizieren /pɛrzonifiˈtsi:rən/ *tr. V.* personify; **das personifizierte schlechte Gewissen** the very picture *or* personification of a guilty conscience

Personifizierung *die;* **~, ~en** personification

P

persönlich /pɛr'zøːnlɪç/
A *Adj.* personal; **er findet für jeden ein ~es Wort** he has a friendly word for everyone; **etw. steht jmdm. zur ~en Verfügung** sth. is available to sb. for his/her own *or* personal use; **eine ~e Bemerkung** an observation from one's personal point of view; **eine ~e Frage/Bemerkung** (zur anderen Person) a personal question/observation; **~ werden** get personal; **~es Fürwort** (Sprachw.) personal pronoun
B *adv.* personally; (auf Briefen) 'private [and confidential]'; **sich um alles ~ kümmern** see to everything personally *or* oneself; **~ erscheinen/gehen/kommen** appear/go/come in person; **nimm doch nicht gleich alles [so] ~!** don't take everything so personally!

Persönlichkeit *die;* **~, ~en** 1 (Wesensart) personality 2 (Mensch) person of character; **eine/keine ~ sein** have a strong personality/lack personality 3 (herausragende Person) personality; **~en des öffentlichen Lebens** public figures

Persönlichkeits-: ~recht *das* (Rechtsw.) right to live one's own life; **~spaltung** *die* (Psych.) split personality; **~störung** *die* (Psych., Med.) personality disorder; **~wahl** *die* (Politik) 1 *electoral system in which votes are cast for a candidate rather than a party;* 2 (Wahl mit starken Persönlichkeiten) personality contest; **diese Wahl war eine reine ~wahl** this election was fought purely on the basis of personalities

Perspektiv /pɛrspɛk'tiːf/ *das;* **~s, ~e** [hand-held] telescope

Perspektive /pɛrspɛk'tiːvə/ *die;* **~, ~n** (Optik, bild. Kunst, auch fig.) perspective; (Blickwinkel) angle; viewpoint; (Zukunftsaussicht) prospect; **aus soziologischer ~/aus der ~ des Soziologen** (fig.) from a sociological viewpoint/the viewpoint of a sociologist; **aus dieser ~ [gesehen]** (fig.) [seen] from this point of view; **eine neue ~ gewinnen** (fig.) gain a new perspective *or* aspect

perspektivisch
A *Adj.* ‹*drawing etc.*› in perspective; ‹*effect, narrowing, etc.*› of perspective; **~e Verkürzung** foreshortening
B *adv.* in perspective; **~ verkürzen** foreshorten

perspektiv·los
A *Adj.* with no prospects *postpos.*; hopeless ‹*situation*›
B *adv.* with no prospects

Peru /pe'ruː/ *(das);* **~s** Peru

Peruaner /pe'ru̯aːnɐ/ *der;* **~s, ~, Peruanerin** *die;* **~, ~nen** Peruvian

peruanisch *Adj.* Peruvian

Perücke /pɛ'rʏkə/ *die;* **~, ~n** wig

pervers /pɛr'vɛrs/ (abwertend)
A *Adj.* 1 (bes. in sexueller Hinsicht) perverted; (fig.: gegen jede Vernunft) perverse; **ein ~er Mensch** a pervert 2 (ugs.: empörend, schändlich) outrageous; scandalous
B *adv.* in a perverted manner; **~ veranlagt sein** be of a perverted disposition

Perversion /pɛrvɛr'zi̯oːn/ *die;* **~, ~en** perversion

Perversität /pɛrvɛrzi'tɛːt/ *die;* **~, ~en** 1 (Eigenschaft) perversion 2 (Handlung) perversity; (sexuell) perverted act

pervertieren /pɛrvɛr'tiːrən/ (geh.)
A *tr. V.* pervert; (verderben) corrupt
B *itr. V.; mit sein* become perverted (**zu** into)

perzentuell /pɛrt͜sɛn'tu̯ɛl/ (österr.) ▸**prozentual**

Perzeption /pɛrt͜sɛp'tsi̯oːn/ *die;* **~, ~en** (Philos., Psych., Physiol.) perception

perzeptiv /pɛrt͜sɛp'tiːf/ *Adj.* (Philos., Psych., Physiol.) perceptive

pesen /'peːzn̩/ *itr. V.; mit sein* (ugs.) dash; (mit Fahrzeug) race

Pessar /pɛ'saːɐ̯/ *das;* **~s, ~e** (Med.) pessary

Pessimismus /pɛsi'mɪsmʊs/ *der;* **~:** pessimism

Pessimist *der;* **~en, ~en, Pessimistin** *die;* **~, ~nen** pessimist

pessimistisch
A *Adj.* pessimistic
B *adv.* pessimistically; **etw. ~ sehen** *od.* **betrachten** take a pessimistic view of sth.; **sich zu etw. ~ äußern** express a pessimistic view on sth.

Pest /pɛst/ *die;* **~** ▸❶ **S. 439** plague; (fig.: Mensch, Ungeziefer) pest; menace; **ich hasse ihn/es wie die ~** (ugs.) I hate his guts/can't stand it (coll.); **wie die ~ stinken** (salopp) stink to high heaven (coll.)

Pest-: ~beule *die* [pestilential] bubo; **~gestank** *der* (abwertend) foul stench; **~hauch** *der* (geh.) miasma

Pestilenz /pɛsti'lɛnts/ *die;* **~, ~en** (veralt.) pestilence (arch.); plague (lit. or fig.)

Pestizid /pɛsti't͜siːt/ *das;* **~s, ~e** pesticide

Pest·kranke *der/die* person stricken with the plague

Peter[1] /'peːtɐ/ *(der)* Peter

Peter[2] *der;* **~s, ~** (ugs.) fellow; **ein vergesslicher/dummer ~:** a forgetful/silly old thing (coll.); **Schwarzer ~** (Kartenspiel) ≈ old maid (*with a black cat card instead of an old maid*); **jmdm. den Schwarzen ~ zuschieben** *od.* **zuspielen** (fig.) pass the buck to sb. (coll.)

Petersilie /petɐ'ziːli̯ə/ *die;* **~:** parsley; **ihm ist die ~ verhagelt** (ugs.) he's down in the dumps

Peters·kirche *die:* **die ~:** St Peter's

Peter·wagen *der* (ugs.) [police] patrol car; panda car (Brit.)

PET-Flasche *die* PET bottle

Petition /peti'tsi̯oːn/ *die;* **~, ~en** (Amtsspr.) petition

Petitions-: ~aus·schuss, *~aus·schuß *der* petitions committee (in W. German parliaments); **~recht** *das* right of petition

Petrarca /pe'trarka/ *(der)* Petrarch

Petri Heil /'peːtri-/ (Gruß der Angler) good fishing!; make a good catch!

Petri·jünger *der,* **Petri·jüngerin** *die* (ugs. scherzh.) angling buff (coll.)

Petri·schale /'peːtri-/ *die* Petri dish

Petro- /'petro:-/: **~chemie** *die* 1 (Wissenschaft) petrochemistry; 2 (Erdölindustrie) petrochemicals industry; **~dollar** *der* (Wirtsch.) petrodollar

Petrol /pe'troːl/ *das;* **~s** (schweiz.), **Petroleum** /pe'troːleʊm/ *das;* **~s** 1 paraffin (Brit.); kerosene (Amer.) 2 (veralt.) ▸**Erdöl**

Petroleum-: ~kocher *der* paraffin (Brit.) *or* (Amer.) kerosene stove; **~lampe** *die* paraffin (Brit.) *or* (Amer.) kerosene lamp

Petrus /'peːtrʊs/ *(der);* **Petrus** *od.* **Petri** 1 (christl. Rel.: Apostel) St Peter 2 (Patron des Wetters) the clerk of the weather; **wenn ~ mitspielt** if [the clerk of] the weather doesn't let us down

Petschaft /'pɛtʃaft/ *das;* **~s, ~e** seal; (zur Beglaubigung od. als Unterschrift) signet

Petticoat /'pɛtɪkoʊt/ *der;* **~s, ~s** [stiffened] petticoat

Petting /'pɛtɪŋ/ *das;* **~[s], ~s** petting; **[mit jmdm.] ~ machen** have a petting session [with sb.]

Petunie /pe'tuːni̯ə/ *die;* **~, ~n** (Bot.) petunia

Petze *die;* **~, ~n** (Schülerspr. abwertend) telltale; sneak (Brit. school coll.)

petzen (Schülerspr.)
A *itr. V.* tell tales; sneak (Brit. school coll.)
B *tr. V.* **~, dass ...** tell teacher/sb.'s parents that ...

Petzer *der;* **~s, ~** (Schülerspr. abwertend) telltale; sneak (Brit. school coll.); tattletale (Amer. school sl.)

Petz·liese *die* (Schülerspr. abwertend) [girl who is a] telltale

peu à peu /pøa'pø/ *Adv.* bit by bit

Pf *Abk.* **= Pfennig**

Pfad /pfaːt/ *der;* **~[e]s, ~e** 1 path; **krumme ~e** *od.* **auf krummen ~en wandeln** (fig. geh.) deviate from the straight and narrow; **vom ~ der Tugend abweichen** (fig. geh.) stray from the path of virtue; *s. auch* **austreten A 2** 2 (DV) path

Pfad-: ~finder *der* Scout; **er ist bei den ~n** he is in the Scouts; **~finderin** *die* Guide (Brit.); girl scout (Amer.); **sie ist bei den ~nen** she is in the Guides (Brit.) *or* (Amer.) girl scouts

Pfaffe /'pfafə/ *der;* **~n, ~n** (abwertend) cleric; Holy Joe (coll. derog.)

pfäffisch /'pfɛfɪʃ/ *Adj.* (abwertend) priestly; (frömmelnd) sanctimonious

Pfahl /pfaːl/ *der;* **~[e]s, Pfähle** /'pfɛːlə/ post; stake; (Bauw.: Stütze für Gebäude) pile; **[jmdm.] ein ~ im Fleisch[e] sein** be a thorn in sb.'s flesh

Pfahl-: ~bau *der; Pl.* **~~ten** pile dwelling; **~dorf** *das* pile-village

pfählen /'pfɛːlən/ *tr. V.* 1 (Landw.) stake ‹*trees etc.*› 2 (hist.: hinrichten) impale

Pfahl-: ~werk *das* pilework; piling; **~wurzel** *die* (Bot.) taproot

Pfalz /pfalts/ *die;* **~, ~en** 1 (Gebiet) **die ~:** the Palatinate 2 (hist.: Palast) [imperial *or* royal] palace

Pfälzer /'pfɛlt͜sɐ/
A *der;* **~s, ~** 1 (Person) inhabitant/native of the Palatinate 2 (Wein) wine from the Palatinate
B *indekl. Adj.* ‹*wine etc.*› from the Palatinate

Pfälzerin *die;* **~, ~nen** ▸**Pfälzer A 1**

Pfalz·graf *der* (hist.) Count Palatine

Pfand /pfant/ *das;* **~[e]s, Pfänder** /'pfɛndɐ/ 1 security; pledge (esp. fig.); **etw. auf ~ leihen** lend sth. against a security; **etw. als** *od.* **in ~ nehmen/etw. als** *od.* **zum** *od.* **in ~ geben** take/give sth. as [a] security; **ich gebe** *od.* **setze meine Ehre/mein Leben dafür zum ~, dass ...** (fig. geh.) I pledge my honour/stake my life on it that ...; **als ~ seiner Liebe** (geh.) as a token of his love 2 (für leere Flaschen usw.) deposit (**auf** + *Dat.* on); **[ein] ~ für etw. bezahlen** pay a deposit on sth.; **kostet die Flasche ~?** is there a deposit on the bottle? 3 (beim Pfänderspiel) forfeit

pfändbar *Adj.* distrainable (Law) ‹*goods, chattels*›; attachable (Law) ‹*wages etc.*›

Pfand·brief *der* (Wirtsch., Bankw.) mortgage bond

pfänden /'pfɛndn̩/ *tr.* (*auch itr.*) *V.* impound, seize [under distress] (Law) ‹*goods, chattels*›; attach ‹*wages etc.*› (Law); **bei ihm wurde gepfändet, er ist gepfändet worden** the bailiffs have been on to him; execution was levied against him (Law.)

Pfänder ▸**Pfand**

Pfänder·spiel *das* [game of] forfeits

pfand-, Pfand-: ~flasche *die* returnable bottle (*on which a deposit is payable*); **~haus** *das* (veralt.), **~leihe** *die;* **~~, ~~n** pawnshop; pawnbroker's; **etw. auf die** *od.* **in die** *od.* **zur ~leihe bringen** take sth. to the pawnbroker's; **~leiher** *der;* **~~s, ~~, ~leiherin** *die;* **~~, ~~nen** ▸❶ **S. 113** pawnbroker; **~pflicht** *die* obligation to pay a deposit; **~pflichtig** *Adj.* ‹*container*› on which a deposit is payable; **sie sollen ~pflichtig werden** a deposit is to become payable on them; **~recht** *das* (Rechtsw.) [right of] lien (**an** + *Dat.* on, upon); **~schein** *der* pawn ticket

Pfändung *die;* **~, ~en** seizure; distraint (Law); (von Geldsummen, Vermögensrechten) attachment (Law); **der Gerichtsvollzieher kam zur ~:** the bailiff came to seize *or* impound possessions

Pfändungs·verfügung *die* (Rechtsw.) garnishee *or* attachment order (Law)

Pfand·verkauf *der* sale of property put up as security; distress sale (Law)

Pfanne /'pfanə/ *die;* **~, ~n** 1 (zum Braten, Backen) [frying] pan; **sich** (*Dat.*) **ein paar Eier in die ~ schlagen** fry [up] some eggs; **jmdn. in die ~ hauen** (ugs.) (kritisieren) take sb. to pieces; (ruinieren) land sb. in trouble; (vernichtend schlagen) beat sb. hollow (coll.) 2 (hist.: Zünd~) [priming] pan; **etw. auf der ~ haben** (ugs. fig.) have sth. at the ready 3 (Geogr.: Senke) pan; (Salz~) salt pan 4 (Hüttenw.) [foundry] ladle 5 (Bett~) bedpan 6 (Bauw.: Dach~) pantile 7 (Anat.: Gelenk~) socket

Pfannen·gericht *das* (Kochk.) fried dish

Pfann·kuchen *der* 1 (bes. südd.: Eierkuchen) pancake 2 (Berliner ~) doughnut; **aufgehen wie ein ~** (ugs.) turn into a real dumpling

Pfarr-: ~amt *das* 1 parish office; 2 (Stellung) pastorate; **~bezirk** *der* parish

P

Pfarre /ˈpfarə/ *die;* ~, ~n (veralt.), **Pfarrei** /pfaˈrai/ *die;* ~, ~en **1** (Bezirk) parish **2** (Dienststelle) parish office **3** ▸**Pfarrhaus**

Pfarrer /ˈpfarɐ/ *der;* ~s, ~ ▸ⓘ **S. 44**, ▸ⓘ **S. 113** (katholisch) parish priest; (evangelisch) pastor; (anglikanisch) vicar; (von Freikirchen) minister; (Militär~) chaplain; padre; (in der Anschrift) **Herrn ~ Meyer** [the] Revd. Meyer; **Frau ~ Meyer** (~in) [the] Revd. Meyer; (~sfrau) Mrs Meyer

Pfarrerin *die;* ~, ~nen [woman] pastor; (in Freikirchen) [woman] minister; **Frau ~ Schmidt** Pastor *or* [the] Revd. Schmidt

Pfarrers·frau *die* pastor's wife; (in Freikirchen) minister's wife; (anglikanisch) vicar's wife

Pfarr-: **~haus** *das* vicarage; (katholisch) presbytery; (in Schottland) manse; **~kirche** *die* parish church

Pfau /pfau/ *der;* ~[e]s, ~en (österr. auch:) ~en, ~e peacock; **er ist ein [eitler] ~** (fig.) he is as vain as a peacock

Pfauen-: **~auge** *das* peacock butterfly; (Nachtpfauenauge) peacock moth; **~feder** *die* peacock feather

Pfd. *Abk.* = **Pfund** lb.

Pfeffer /ˈpfɛfɐ/ *der;* ~s, ~ **1** pepper; **roter ~:** cayenne [pepper]; red pepper; **spanischer ~:** paprika; **hingehen** *od.* **bleiben, wo der ~ wächst** (ugs.) go to hell (coll.); get lost (coll.); *s. auch* **Hase 1**; **Hintern** **2** (Textilw.) **~ und Salz** pepper-and-salt **3** (ugs.: Schwung) punch (coll.); zap (coll.); **dahinter steckt ~:** it's got plenty of zap (coll.) *or* (coll.) zing

Pfeffer-: **~fresser** *der* (Zool.) toucan; **~gurke** *die* pickled gherkin; **~korn** *das* peppercorn; **~kuchen** *der* ≈ gingerbread

Pfefferminz·bonbon *der od. das* peppermint [sweet]

Pfeffer·minze *die* peppermint [plant]

Pfefferminz-: **~likör** *der* peppermint liqueur; **~plätzchen** *das* peppermint drop; (weich) peppermint cream; **~tee** *der* peppermint tea

Pfeffer·mühle *die* pepper mill

pfeffern *tr. V.* **1** (würzen) season with pepper; **stark gepfeffert** very peppery **2** (ugs.: werfen) chuck (coll.); (mit Wucht) fling; hurl; **jmdm. eine ~** (salopp) sock *or* biff sb. one (coll.); **eine gepfeffert kriegen** (salopp) get a clout *or* (coll.) biff; *s. auch* **gepfeffert**

Pfeffer-: **~nuss**, ***~nuß** *die* [small round] gingerbread biscuit; **~spray** *das* pepper spray; **~steak** *das* steak au poivre; pepper steak; **~strauch** *der* pepper plant; **~streuer** *der;* ~~s, ~~: pepper pot; **~-und-Salz-Muster** *das* pepper-and-salt pattern

pfeffrig /ˈpfɛfrɪç/ *Adj.* peppery

Pfeifchen /ˈpfaifçən/ *das;* ~s, ~ (fam.: Tabakpfeife) pipe

Pfeife /ˈpfaifə/ *die;* ~, ~n **1** (Tabak~) pipe; **~ rauchen** smoke a pipe; be a pipe smoker; **eine ~ rauchen** smoke *or* have a pipe **2** (Musikinstrument) pipe; (aus Zinn) penny whistle; tin whistle; (der Militärkapelle) fife; (Triller~, an einer Maschine usw.) whistle; (Orgel~) [organ] pipe; **nach jmds. ~ tanzen** (fig.) dance to sb.'s tune **3** (salopp abwertend: Versager) washout (sl.)

pfeifen

A *unr. itr. V.* **1** whistle; ‹*bird*› sing; pipe; ‹*mouse*› squeak; **dreimal kurz ~:** give three short whistles; **er pfiff vor Bewunderung** he gave a whistle of admiration; he whistled in admiration; **sie pfiff [nach] ihrem Hund/einem Taxi** she whistled her dog/for a taxi; **von den Rängen wurde laut gepfiffen und gebuht** there were loud catcalls and boos from the auditorium; **etwas** *od.* **es pfiff in der Leitung** there was a whistle *or* a whistling noise on the telephone line; **seine Lungen ~/es pfeift in seiner Brust** he wheezes in his lungs/chest; **~der Atem** wheezing [breath]; *s. auch* **Loch 1** **2** *mit sein* **die Kugeln pfiffen ihm um die Ohren** the bullets whistled around him **3** (auf einer Trillerpfeife o. Ä.) ‹*policeman, referee, etc.*› blow one's whistle; (Sport: als Schiedsrichter fungieren) act as referee; **er pfeift beim Endspiel** he is refereeing the final **4** (salopp) **auf jmdn./etw. ~:** not give a damn about sb./sth.; **ich pfeife auf dein Geld** you can keep your money (coll.) **5** (salopp: geständig sein) squeal (sl.)

B *unr. tr. V.* **1** whistle ‹*tune etc.*›; ‹*bird*› pipe, sing ‹*song*›; (auf einer Pfeife) pipe, play ‹*tune etc.*›; (auf einer Trillerpfeife o. Ä.) blow ‹*signal etc.*› on one's whistle; **einen Elfmeter ~** (Sport) blow [the whistle] for a penalty; **sich** (*Dat.*) **eins ~** (ugs.) whistle [nonchalantly] to oneself; (fig.: sich nichts daraus machen) shrug one's shoulders; **ich pfeif dir was** (salopp spött.) go and get knotted (coll.) **2** (Sport: als Schiedsrichter leiten) referee ‹*match*› **3** (salopp: verraten) let out ‹*secret*›; **wer hat dir das gepfiffen?** who let on to you about that? (coll.) **4** (salopp: trinken) **einen ~:** knock one back (sl.)

Pfeifen-: **~deckel** *der* [pipe-]bowl lid; **~deckel!** (ugs.) no way! (coll.); **~kopf** *der* pipe bowl; **~raucher** *der,* **~raucherin** *die* pipe smoker; **~reiniger** *der;* ~~s, ~~: pipe-cleaner; **~ständer** *der* pipe rack; **~stopfer** *der;* ~~s, ~~: tobacco-stopper; **~tabak** *der* pipe tobacco; **~werk** *das* (Musik) [organ] pipes *pl.;* pipework

Pfeifer *der;* ~s, ~ **1** (Musik) (bes. hist.) piper; (in einer Militärkapelle) fife player **2** (jmd., der pfeift) whistler

Pfeiferei *die;* ~, ~en (abwertend) whistling

Pfeiferin *die;* ~, ~nen ▸**Pfeifer**

Pfeif-: **~kessel** *der* whistling kettle; **~konzert** *das* chorus of catcalls; **~ton** *der; Pl.* **~töne** whistling sound

Pfeil /pfail/ *der;* ~[e]s, ~e arrow; (Wurfpfeil) dart; **~ und Bogen** bow and arrow; **wie ein ~ davonschießen** be off like a shot *or* like lightning; **schnell wie ein ~:** as quick as lightning; **alle [seine] ~e verschossen haben** (fig.) have run out of arguments; *s. auch* **Amor**

Pfeiler *der;* ~s, ~ (Bauw., Bergbau; auch fig.) pillar; (Brücken~) pier

pfeil-, Pfeil-: **~flügel** *der* (Flugzeugtechnik) swept-back wing; **~förmig** **A** *Adj.* arrow-shaped; sagittate ‹*leaf*›; **B** *adv.* **~förmig angeordnet** arranged in the shape of an arrow *postpos.;* **~gerade** **A** *Adj.* [as] straight as an arrow *postpos.;* dead straight; **B** *adv.* [as] straight as an arrow; **~gift** *das* arrow poison; **~richtung** *die:* **in ~richtung** in the direction of the arrow; **~schnell** **A** *Adj.* lightning-swift; **B** *adv.* like a shot; **~spitze** *die* arrowhead

Pfennig /ˈpfɛnɪç/ *der;* ~s, ~e pfennig; **er hat keinen ~ [Geld]** he hasn't a penny *or* (Amer.) cent; **nicht für fünf ~ Anstand/Verstand/Geschmack/Humor** *usw.* **haben** (ugs.) have not an ounce of respectability/common sense/have no taste/sense of humour whatsoever; **das interessiert mich nicht für fünf ~** (ugs.) that doesn't interest me in the slightest; **wer den ~ nicht ehrt, ist des Talers nicht wert** (Spr.) take care of the pennies and the pounds will look after themselves (prov.); *s. auch* **Heller**; **Mark² 1**

Pfennig-: **~absatz** *der* stiletto heel; **~fuchser** /-fʊksɐ/ *der;* ~~s, ~~, **~fuchserin** *die;* ~~, ~~nen (ugs.) penny-pincher

Pferch /pfɛrç/ *der;* ~[e]s, ~e pen

pferchen *tr. V.* cram; pack

Pferd /pfeːɐ̯t/ *das;* ~[e]s, ~e **1** horse; **zu ~[e]** on horseback; **aufs/vom ~ steigen** mount/dismount; **zu ~:** by horse; on horseback; **das hält ja kein ~ aus** (ugs.) that's more than flesh and blood can stand; **ich denk, mich tritt ein ~** (salopp) I'm absolutely flabbergasted; **man hat schon ~e kotzen sehen** (salopp) [you never know,] anything can happen; **immer sachte mit den jungen ~en** (fig. ugs.) not so fast! (coll.); **er ist das beste ~ im Stall** (ugs.) he is their/our number one man; **wie ein ~ arbeiten** (ugs.) work like a Trojan; **keine zehn ~e bringen mich dahin/dazu, es zu tun** (ugs.) wild horses would not drag me there/make me do it; **ihm gehen die ~e durch** (ugs.) he flies off the handle (coll.); **auf das falsche ~ setzen** (fig.) back the wrong horse; **die ~e scheu machen** (ugs.) put people off; **das ~ am** *od.* **beim Schwanze aufzäumen** (ugs.) put the cart before the horse; **mit ihr kann man ~e stehlen** (ugs.) she's game for anything; *s. auch* **trojanisch** **2** (Turngerät) horse **3** (Schachfigur) knight

Pferdchen *das;* ~s, ~ **1** (kleines Pferd) little horse **2** (salopp: Prostituierte) tart (sl.); hooker (Amer. sl.) (*working for a pimp*)

Pferde-: **~anhänger** *der* ▸**~transportwagen**; **~apfel** *der* (ugs.) piece of horse dung; **~äpfel** horse droppings; horse dung; **~bremse** *die* (Zool.) horsefly; **~decke** *die* horse blanket; **~fleisch** *das* horsemeat; **~fuhrwerk** *das* horse and cart; **~fuhrwerke** horse-drawn carts; **~fuß** *der* **1** (fig.: Mangel, Nachteil) snag; drawback; **2** (eines ~s) horse's foot; (des Teufels) cloven hoof; **~gebiss**, ***~gebiß** *das* **1** (fig. ugs.) **er hat ein ~gebiss** he has teeth *pl.* like a horse; **2** (eines ~s) horse's teeth *pl.;* **~gesicht** *das* (ugs.) horsy face; **er hat ein ~gesicht** he has a face like a horse; **~händler** *der,* **~händlerin** *die* horse dealer; **~knecht** *der* (veralt.) groom; **~kopf** *der* horse's head; **~koppel** *die* paddock; **~länge** *die* length; **mit zwei ~längen Vorsprung siegen** win by two lengths (**vor** + *Dat.* from); **~metzger** *der* (landsch.) ▸**~schlachter**; **~mist** *der* horse manure; **~pfleger** *der,* **~pflegerin** *die* groom; **~rasse** *die* breed of horse; **~rennbahn** *die* racecourse; **~rennen** *das* horse race; (Sportart) horseracing; **beim ~rennen sein** be at the races *pl.;* **~schlachter**, **~schlächter** *der* (bes. nordd.) horse butcher; **~schlitten** *der* horse[-drawn] sleigh; **~schwanz** *der* horse's tail; (fig.: Frisur) ponytail; **~sport** *der* equestrian sport *no art.;* (~rennen) horseracing *no art.;* **~stall** *der* stable; **~stärke** *die* horsepower; **~transport·wagen** *der* horsebox; **~wagen** *der* (für Güter) cart; (für Personen) carriage; (der amerikanischen Pioniere usw.) wagon; **~wirt** *der,* **~wirtin** *die* fully qualified groom (*with veterinary training*); **~zucht** *die* horse breeding *no art.*

pfiff /pfɪf/ *1. u. 3. Pers. Sg. Prät. v.* **pfeifen**

Pfiff *der;* ~[e]s, ~e **1** whistle **2** (ugs.: besonderer Reiz) style; **mit ~:** stylish; with style; (adv.) stylishly; ‹*cook*› with flair; **der letzte** *od.* **richtige ~:** the finishing touch; that extra something **3** (ugs.) ▸**Dreh 1**

Pfifferling /ˈpfɪfɐlɪŋ/ *der;* ~s, ~e chanterelle; **keinen** *od.* **nicht einen ~ wert sein** (ugs.) be not worth a bean (coll.)

pfiffig

A *Adj.* smart; bright, clever ‹*idea*›; artful, knowing ‹*smile, expression*›

B *adv.* artfully; cleverly; **jmdn. ~ ansehen/anlächeln** look/smile knowingly *or* artfully at sb.

Pfiffikus /ˈpfɪfikʊs/ *der;* ~[ses], ~se (ugs.) smart lad

Pfingsten /ˈpfɪŋstn̩/ *das;* ~, ~: Whitsun; **zu** *od.* (bes. südd.) **an ~:** at Whitsun; **habt ihr schöne ~ gehabt?** did you have a nice Whitsun?; *s. auch* **Ostern**

Pfingst-: **~feier·tag** *der:* **über die ~feiertage** over Whitsun; **an den ~feiertagen** on Whit Sunday and Whit Monday; **der erste/zweite ~feiertag** Whit Sunday/Monday; **~fest** *das* Whitsun [holiday]; (Rel.) Whitsun festival

pfingstlich

A *Adj.* Whitsuntide *attrib.;* (Rel.) Pentecostal ‹*miracle*›

B *adv.* **~ geschmückt** decorated for Whitsun *postpos.*

Pfingst-: **~montag** *der* Whit Monday *no def. art.;* **~ochse** *der:* in **er sah aus/hatte sich herausgeputzt wie ein ~ochse** (ugs.) he looked like/was dressed up like a dog's dinner (coll.); **~rose** *die* peony; **~sonntag** *der* Whit Sunday *no def. art.;* **~woche** *die* week before Whitsun

Pfirsich /ˈpfɪrzɪç/ *der;* ~s, ~e peach

Pfirsich-: **~baum** *der* peach tree; **~blüte** *die* peach blossom; **~haut** *die* **1** peach skin; **2** (fig.: Gesichtshaut) peaches-and-cream complexion

Pflänzchen /ˈpflɛntsçən/ *das;* **~s, ~** 1 little plant 2 (fig.: Mensch) **ein [zartes] ~:** a delicate creature

Pflanze /ˈpflantsə/ *die;* **~, ~n** 1 plant; **~n fressend** (Biol.) herbivorous 2 (ugs.: Mensch) **du bist mir vielleicht eine ~!** you're a right one! (coll.); **eine echte Berliner ~** (veralt.) a genuine Berlin type

pflanzen
A *tr. V.* plant (**in** + *Akk.* in); (fig.) plant, stick ‹*flag*›
B *refl. V.* (ugs.) plant oneself

pflanzen-, Pflanzen-: ~farbstoff *der* 1 (pflanzlicher Farbstoff) vegetable dye; 2 (Bot.: Pigment) plant *or* vegetable pigment; **~fett** *das* vegetable fat; **~fressend** ▸**Pflanze 1**; **~fresser** *der* herbivore; **~kunde** *die* botany *no def. art.*; **~öl** *das* vegetable oil; **~reich** *das* plant kingdom; **~schutz·mittel** *das* [crop] pesticide; (für den Garten) garden pesticide; **~welt** *die* flora

Pflanzer *der;* **~s, ~, Pflanzerin** *die;* **~, ~nen** planter; plantation owner

Pflanz-: ~gut *das* seed stock; **~holz** *das* dibble; **~kartoffel** *die* seed potato

pflanzlich *Adj.* plant *attrib.* ‹*life, motif*›; vegetable ‹*dye, fat*›; (vegetarisch) vegetarian

Pflänzling /ˈpflɛntslɪŋ/ *der;* **~s, ~e** seedling

Pflanzung *die;* **~, ~en** 1 plantation 2 (das Pflanzen) planting

Pflaster /ˈpflastɐ/ *das;* **~s, ~** 1 (Straßen~) road surface; (auf dem Gehsteig) pavement; **~ treten** (ugs.) trail through the streets 2 (ugs.: Ort) **ein teures/gefährliches** *od.* **heißes ~:** an expensive/dangerous place *or* spot to be; **mir wird das ~ hier zu heiß** this place is getting too hot for me 3 (Wund~) sticking plaster

Pflaster·maler *der,* **Pflaster·malerin** *die* pavement artist

pflastern *tr.* (*auch itr.*) *V.* surface ‹*road, path*›; (mit Kopfsteinpflaster, Steinplatten) pave ‹*street, path*›; *s. auch* **Vorsatz**

Pflaster·stein *der* paving stone; (Kopfstein) cobblestone

Pflaume /ˈpflaumə/ *die;* **~, ~n** 1 plum; **getrocknete ~n** [dried] prunes 2 (ugs. abwertend: Versager) dead loss (coll.); (Feigling) baby 3 (derb: Vulva) pussy (coarse)

pflaumen-, Pflaumen-: ~baum *der* plum tree; **~kuchen** *der* plum flan; **~mus** *das* plum purée; **~saft** *der* plum juice; **~schnaps** *der* plum brandy; **~weich** *Adj.* (ugs. abwertend) weak-kneed; spineless

Pflege /ˈpfle:gə/ *die;* **~:** care; (Maschinenpflege, Fahrzeugpflege) maintenance; (fig.: von Beziehungen, Kunst, Sprache) cultivation; fostering; **die ~ des Körpers** personal hygiene; **die Blumen brauchen viel/kaum ~:** the flowers need a lot of/hardly any attention; **jmdn./etw. in ~** (*Akk.*) **nehmen** look after sb./sth.; **jmdm. etw.** *od.* **etw. bei jmdm. in ~** (*Akk.*) **geben** give sb. sth. to look after; entrust sth. to sb.'s care; **ein Kind in ~** (*Akk.*) **nehmen** look after a child; (als ~eltern) foster a child; **jmdm. ein Kind** *od.* **ein Kind bei jmdm. in ~** (*Akk.*) **geben** give sb. a child to look after; (bei ~eltern) have a child fostered by sb.; **bei jmdm. in ~** (*Dat.*) **sein** be looked after by sb.

pflege-, Pflege-: ~bedürftig *Adj.* needing care *or* attention *postpos.*; ‹*person*› in need of care; **~bedürftig sein** need looking after; need attention; **~eltern** *Pl.* foster-parents; **~fall** *der* person in [permanent] need of nursing; **ein ~fall sein/zum ~fall werden** be/become in [permanent] need of nursing; **~heim** *das* nursing home (esp. Brit.); **~kind** *das* foster-child; **~leicht** *Adj.* easy-care *attrib.* ‹*textiles, flooring*›; minimum-care *attrib.* ‹*plant, pan*›; **~leicht sein** require little attention *or* care; ‹*cloth, clothing*› be made of easy-care material; **~mutter** *die; Pl.* **~mütter** foster-mother

pflegen
A *tr. V.* look after; care for; care for, nurse ‹*sick person*›; care for, take care of ‹*skin, teeth, floor*›; look after, maintain ‹*bicycle, car, machine*›; look after, tend ‹*garden, plants*›; cultivate ‹*relations, arts, interests*›; foster ‹*contacts, cooperation*›; keep up, pursue ‹*hobby*›; **jmdn./ein Tier gesund ~:** nurse sb./an animal back to health; **Kontakt/den Umgang mit jmdm. ~:** keep in touch with/associate with sb.
B *itr. V.; mit Inf. + zu* **etw. zu tun ~:** be in the habit of doing sth.; usually do sth.; **..., wie er zu sagen pflegt/pflegte** ..., as he is wont to say/as he used to say; **er pflegte jeden Morgen um sieben Uhr aufzustehen** he used to get up every morning at seven
C *refl. V.* take care of oneself; (gesundheitlich) look after oneself; **sie sollte sich mehr ~:** she should take more care of herself
D *regelm. (veralt. auch unr.) itr. V.* (geh.) **einer Sache** (*Gen.*) **~:** indulge in sth.; **der Ruhe ~:** rest; take one's ease; *s. auch* **gepflegt**

Pflege·notstand *der* health-care crisis

Pfleger *der;* **~s, ~** 1 ▸❶ **S. 113** (Kranken~) [male] nurse 2 ▸❶ **S. 113** (Tier~) keeper

Pflegerin *die;* **~, ~nen** 1 ▸❶ **S. 113** (Kranken~) nurse 2 ▸❶ **S. 113** (Tier~) keeper

pflegerisch *Adj.* nursing *attrib.*

Pflege-: ~satz *der* hospital [daily] rate; charge for a hospital bed [per day]; **~sohn** *der* foster-son; **~tochter** *die* foster-daughter; **~vater** *der* foster-father; **~versicherung** *die* (*long-term*) [nursing-]care insurance

> **Pflegeversicherung**
>
> Compulsory nursing-care insurance which all employees have to pay into as part of their **Sozialabgaben.** It was introduced in Germany in 1995 and pays for the long-term nursing care of the elderly and the severely disabled. Employers and employees make equal contributions to the scheme.

pfleglich
A *Adj.* careful
B *adv.* with care

Pflegling /ˈpfle:klɪŋ/ *der;* **~s, ~e** charge; (Pflegekind) foster-child; **unsere ~e** the children/animals in our care

Pflegschaft *die;* **~, ~en** (Rechtsw.) (durch Pflegeeltern) foster care; (eines Vermögens) trusteeship

Pflicht /pflɪçt/ *die;* **~, ~en** 1 duty; **seine alltäglichen [kleinen] ~en** his everyday chores; **die ~ ruft** duty calls; **~ sein** be obligatory; **es ist seine [(salopp) verdammte** *od.* **verfluchte] ~ und Schuldigkeit** [damn it all,] it's his bounden duty; **jmdn. in die ~ nehmen** (geh.) make sb. discharge his/her duties 2 (Sport) compulsory exercises *pl.*

pflicht-, Pflicht-: ~bewusst, ***~bewußt** A *Adj.* conscientious; **~bewusst sein** have a sense of duty; B *adv.* conscientiously; with a sense of duty; **~bewusstsein,** ***~bewußtsein** *das* sense of duty; **~eifer** *der* zeal; **~eifrig** A *Adj.* zealous; B *adv.* zealously; full of zeal; **~erfüllung** *die* performance of one's duty; **in treuer/gewissenhafter ~erfüllung** faithfully/conscientiously following the path of duty; **~exemplar** *das* (Verlagsw.) deposit copy; **~fach** *das* compulsory subject; **es ist ~fach** it is a compulsory subject; **~gefühl** *das* sense of duty; **aus [bloßem] ~gefühl** [simply] from a sense of duty; **~gemäß** A *Adj.* in accordance with one's duty *postpos.;* B *adv.* in accordance with one's duty; **ich teile Ihnen ~gemäß mit, dass ...** it is my duty to inform you that ...

-pflichtig *Adj.* subject to ...; **beitrags~e Beschäftigung** occupation entailing the payment of insurance contributions; *s. auch* **abgaben~; zuschlags~**

pflicht-, Pflicht-: ~lektüre *die* required reading; (Schulw.) set books *pl.;* **zur ~lektüre gehören, ~lektüre sein** be required reading; (in der Schule) be a set book/be set books; **~schuldig** A *Adj.* dutiful; (höflich) polite; B *adv.* dutifully; (höflich) politely; **~teil** *der od. das:* (Rechtsw.) *portion of an estate that must go to the closest relation regardless of testator's dispositions;* legitimate portion; **jmdn. auf den** *od.* **das ~teil setzen** leave sb. nothing but the legal minimum; **~übung** *die* 1 (Sport) compulsory exercise; 2 (fig.) ritual exercise; (Buch, Film usw.) obligatory effort; **~umtausch** *der* compulsory exchange of currency; **~vergessen** A *Adj.* neglectful of one's duty *postpos.*; negligent ‹*behaviour*›; B *adv.* negligently; **~verletzung** *die* breach of duty; **~versichert** *Adj.* compulsorily insured; **~versicherung** *die* compulsory insurance; **~verteidiger** *der,* **~verteidigerin** *die:* (Rechtsw.) *defence counsel appointed by the court;* assigned counsel; **~widrig** *Adj., adv.* in breach of one's duty *postpos.*

Pflock /pflɔk/ *der;* **~[e]s, Pflöcke** /ˈpflœkə/ peg; (für Tiere) stake

pflog /pflo:k/ (veralt.) *1. u. 3. Pers. Sg. Prät. v.* **pflegen D**

pflücken /ˈpflʏkn̩/ *tr. V.* pick ‹*flowers, fruit, hops*›; **Kirschen in einen Korb ~:** pick cherries and put them in a basket

Pflücker *der;* **~s, ~, Pflückerin** *die;* **~, ~nen** ▸❶ **S. 113** picker

Pflück·maschine *die* [mechanical] picker

Pflug /pflu:k/ *der;* **~[e]s, Pflüge** /ˈpfly:gə/ plough; **Land unter den ~ nehmen** (geh.) put land to the plough

pflügen /ˈpfly:gn̩/ *tr., itr. V.* plough; (fig. geh.) ‹*ship*› plough *or* carve a way through ‹*waves, sea*›

Pflug·schar *die* ploughshare

Pforte /ˈpfɔrtə/ *die;* **~, ~n** 1 (Tor) gate; (Tür) door; (Eingang) entrance; **seine ~n öffnen/schließen** (fig. geh.) open/close its doors; **Pforzheim, die ~ zum Schwarzwald** (fig.) Pforzheim, the gateway to the Black Forest 2 (Geogr.) **die Westfälische ~:** the Minden Gap; the Porta Westfalica; **die Burgundische ~:** the Belfort Gap

Pförtner /ˈpfœrtnɐ/ *der;* **~s, ~** 1 ▸❶ **S. 113** porter; (eines Wohnblocks, Büros) doorkeeper; (am Tor) gatekeeper 2 ▸❶ **S. 435** (Anat.) pylorus

Pförtner·haus *das* gatehouse; porter's lodge

Pförtnerin *die;* **~, ~nen** ▸❶ **S. 113** ▸**Pförtner 1**

Pförtner·loge *die* porter's lodge

Pfosten /ˈpfɔstn̩/ *der;* **~s, ~** 1 post; (Tür~) jamb 2 (Sport: Tor~) [goal]post

Pfosten·schuss, ***Pfosten·schuß** *der* (Ballspiele) shot hitting the [goal]post

Pfötchen /ˈpfø:tçən/ *das;* **~s, ~:** [little] paw; **~ geben** hold out a paw; **[gib] ~!** [give us a] paw!

Pfote /ˈpfo:tə/ *die;* **~, ~n** 1 paw; **die ~ geben** hold out a paw; **[gib die] ~!** [give us a] paw! 2 (ugs.: Hand) paw (coll.); mitt (sl.); **sich** (*Dat.*) **die ~n verbrennen** (fig.) burn one's fingers (fig.); **seine ~n in etw.** (*Dat.*)**/überall [drin] haben** (fig. salopp) have a hand in sth./everything; be mixed up in sth./everything 3 (salopp abwertend: Schrift) ▸**Klaue 4**

Pfriem /pfri:m/ *der;* **~[e]s, ~e** awl

Pfropf /pfrɔpf/ *der;* **~[e]s, ~e** blockage; (in der Vene) clot; **ein ~ aus Haaren** a plug *or* (Brit. coll.) wodge of hair

pfropfen[1] *tr. V.* (ugs.) cram; stuff; **gepfropft voll** crammed [full]; packed

pfropfen[2] *tr. V.* (Gartenbau) graft ‹*scion*› (**auf** + *Akk.* on); improve ‹*tree, vine*› by grafting

Pfropfen *der* (für Flaschen) stopper; (Korken) cork; (für Fässer) bung

Pfröpfling /ˈpfrœpflɪŋ/ *der;* **~s, ~e** scion

Pfropf-: ~messer *das* grafting knife; **~reis** *das* scion

Pfründe /ˈpfrʏndə/ *die;* **~, ~n** 1 (kath. Kirche) living; benefice; **auf einer ~ sitzen** hold a living 2 (fig.) sinecure

Pfuhl /pfu:l/ *der;* **~[e]s, Pfühle** /ˈpfy:lə/ muddy pool; (fig.) murky waters *pl.*; **ein ~ der Sünde** *od.* **Sittenlosigkeit** (fig.) a sink of iniquity

pfui /pfʊi/ *Interj.* 1 (Ekel ausdrückend) ugh; yuck (sl.); (zu Kindern, Hunden) [ugh,] you mucky pup; (hör auf) stop that; **~ Teufel** *od.* **Deibel** *od.* **Spinne!** (ugs.) ugh *or* (sl.) yuck, how disgusting!; **das ist ~:** that's yucky (sl.) *or* disgusting 2 (Missbilligung, Empörung ausdrückend) ugh; really; (Ruf) boo; **~, schäm dich!** shame on you!; **Pfui** *od.* **~ rufen** boo

P

Pfui·ruf *der* boo

Pfund /pfʊnt/ *das;* ~[e]s, ~e (bei Maßangaben ungebeugt) **1** ▸ⓘ **S. 315** (Gewicht) pound (= *500 grams in German-speaking countries*); **zwei ~ Kartoffeln** two pounds of potatoes; **überflüssige ~e loswerden** ‹*person*› get rid of unwanted pounds **2** ▸ⓘ **S. 299** (Währungseinheit) pound; **100 ~:** £100; one hundred pounds; **wie viel ist das in ~ [Sterling]?** how much is that in pounds [sterling]?; **mit seinem ~[e] wuchern** (geh.) make the most of one's capabilities

pfundig (ugs.)
A *Adj.* great (coll.); fantastic (coll.)
B *adv.* fantastically (coll.)

Pfunds-: **~kerl** *der* (ugs.) great bloke (Brit. coll.); great guy (coll.); **~stimmung** *die* (ugs.) terrific atmosphere (coll.)

pfund·weise *Adv.* by the pound; **die könnte ich ~ essen** I could eat pounds of them

Pfund·zeichen *das* pound sign

Pfusch /pfʊʃ/ *der;* ~[e]s **1** (ugs. abwertend) **das ist ~:** it's a botch-up; **[großen] ~ machen** botch it [in a big way] **2** (österr.: Schwarzarbeit) work done on the side (*and not declared for tax*); (nach Feierabend) moonlighting (coll.); **etw. im ~ machen** do sth. on the side

Pfusch·arbeit *die* (ugs. abwertend) botch; botched-up job

pfuschen *itr. V.* **1** (ugs. abwertend) botch it; do a botched-up job **2** (österr.: schwarzarbeiten) do work on the side (*not declared for tax*); (nach Feierabend) moonlight (coll.)

Pfuscher *der;* ~s, ~ **1** (ugs. abwertend) botcher; bungler **2** (österr.: Schwarzarbeiter) person doing work on the side; (nach Feierabend) moonlighter (coll.)

Pfuscherei *die;* ~, ~en botching *no pl.;* (Pfuscharbeit) botched-up job

Pfuscherin *die;* ~, ~nen ▸**Pfuscher**

Pfütze /ˈpfʏtsə/ *die;* ~, ~n puddle

PH *Abk.* = **Pädagogische Hochschule**

Phalanx /ˈfa:laŋks/ *die;* ~, **Phalangen** (hist., fig.) phalanx

phallisch /ˈfalɪʃ/ (geh.)
A *Adj.* phallic
B *adv.* like a phallus

Phallus /ˈfalʊs/ *der;* ~, **Phalli** *od.* **Phallen,** (auch:) **~se** (geh.) phallus

Phallus-: **~kult** *der* phallic cult; **~symbol** *das* phallic symbol

Phänomen /fenoˈme:n/ *das;* ~s, ~e phenomenon; **er ist ein ~** (ugs.) he is phenomenal

phänomenal /fenomeˈna:l/
A *Adj.* phenomenal
B *adv.* phenomenally

Phänomenologie *die* (Philos.) phenomenology

Phantasie *usw.* ▸**Fantasie** *usw.*

Phantast *usw.* ▸**Fantast** *usw.*

Phantom /fanˈto:m/ *das;* ~s, ~e phantom; illusion; **einem ~ nachjagen** (fig.) chase [after] an illusion *or* a shadow

Phantom-: **~bild** *das* **1** (Kriminalistik) Identikit [picture] ®; (aus Fotos) photofit picture; **2** (Fot.) see-through *or* cut-away picture; **~schmerz** *der* phantom limb [pain]

Pharao /ˈfa:rao/ *der;* ~s, ~nen /faraˈo:nən/ Pharaoh

Pharisäer /fariˈzɛ:ɐ/ *der;* ~s, ~ (auch fig.) Pharisee

pharisäerhaft *Adj.* (geh.) holier-than-thou

Pharisäerin *die;* ~, ~nen Pharisee

Pharisäertum *das;* ~s (geh.) Pharisaism; hypocrisy

Pharma-: **~berater** *der,* **~beraterin** *die* ▸**~referent;** **~industrie** *die* pharmaceutical industry

Pharmakologe /farmakoˈlo:gə/ *der;* ~n, ~n pharmacologist

Pharmakologie /farmakoloˈgi:/ *die;* ~: pharmacology *no art.*

Pharmakologin *die;* ~, ~nen pharmacologist

pharmakologisch
A *Adj.* pharmacological
B *adv.* pharmacologically; **~ ausgebildet** trained in pharmacology *postpos.*

Pharma·referent *der,* **Pharma·referentin** *die* pharmaceutical representative

Pharmazeut /farmaˈtsɔyt/ *der;* ~en, ~en pharmacist

Pharmazeutik /farmaˈtsɔytɪk/ *die;* ~ ▸**Pharmazie**

Pharmazeutin *die;* ~, ~nen pharmacist

pharmazeutisch
A *Adj.* pharmaceutical
B *adv.* pharmaceutically; **~ ausgebildet** with pharmaceutical training *postpos.*

Pharmazie /farmaˈtsi:/ *die;* ~: pharmaceutics *sing., no art.;* pharmaceutical chemistry *no art.*

Phase /ˈfa:zə/ *die;* ~, ~n phase

Phasen·verschiebung *die* (Physik) phase difference

phasen·weise
A *Adj.* phased ‹*introduction, development, withdrawal, etc.*›
B *Adv.* in phases; (zeitweilig) intermittently; at times

-phasig *Adj.* -phase

Phenacetin /fenatseˈti:n/ *das;* ~s (Pharm.) phenacetin

Pheromon /feroˈmo:n/ *das;* ~s, ~e (Biol.) pheromone

Philanthrop /filanˈtro:p/ *der;* ~en, ~en, **Philanthropin** *die;* ~, ~nen (geh.) philanthropist

philanthropisch (geh.)
A *Adj.* philanthropic
B *adv.* philanthropically

Philatelie /filateˈli:/ *die;* ~: philately *no art.*

Philatelist *der;* ~en, ~en, **Philatelistin** *die;* ~, ~nen philatelist

Philharmonie /fɪlharmoˈni:/ *die;* ~, ~n **1** (Orchester) philharmonic [orchestra] **2** (Gebäude, Saal) philharmonic hall

Philharmoniker /fɪlharˈmo:nikɐ/ *der;* ~s, ~, **Philharmonikerin** *die;* ~, ~nen member of a/the philharmonic orchestra; **die Wiener Philharmoniker** the Vienna Philharmonic Orchestra

philharmonisch *Adj.* philharmonic

Philipp /ˈfi:lɪp/ (*der*) Philip

Philippika /fiˈlɪpika/ *die;* ~, **Philippiken** (geh.) philippic; diatribe

Philippinen /filɪˈpi:nən/ *Pl.* Philippines

Philister /fiˈlɪstɐ/ *der;* ~s, ~, **Philisterin** *die;* ~, ~nen (geh.) Philistine

philister·haft, philiströs (geh.)
A *Adj.* Philistine
B *adv.* in a Philistine manner

Philologe /filoˈlo:gə/ *der;* ~n, ~n teacher/student of language and literature; philologist (Amer.)

Philologie *die;* ~, ~n study of language and literature; philology *no art.* (Amer.)

Philologin *die;* ~, ~nen ▸**Philologe**

philologisch
A *Adj.* literary and linguistic; philological (Amer.)
B *adv.* from a literary and linguistic viewpoint; philologically (Amer.)

Philo·semit *der,* **Philo·semitin** *die* [keen] supporter of the Jewish/Israeli cause

Philosoph /filoˈzo:f/ *der;* ~en, ~en ▸ⓘ **S. 113** philosopher

Philosophie *die;* ~, ~n philosophy

philosophieren *itr.* (*auch tr.*) *V.* philosophize

Philosophin *die;* ~, ~nen ▸ⓘ **S. 113** philosopher

philosophisch
A *Adj.* philosophical; ‹*dictionary, principles*› of philosophy; **~e Fakultät** (Hochschulw.) ≈ arts faculty
B *adv.* philosophically

Phiole /ˈfjo:lə/ *die;* ~, ~n pear-shaped flask (*with long neck*)

Phlegma /ˈflɛgma/ *das;* ~s *od.* (österr. meist:) ~: phlegmatic disposition; (Trägheit) lethargy; (Apathie) apathy

Phlegmatiker /flɛˈgma:tikɐ/ *der;* ~s, ~: phlegmatic person; (träger Mensch) lethargic person

phlegmatisch
A *Adj.* phlegmatic; (träge) lethargic; (apathisch) apathetic
B *adv.* ▸**A:** phlegmatically; lethargically; apathetically

Phobie /foˈbi:/ *die;* ~, ~n (Psych.) phobia

Phon /fo:n/ *das;* ~s, ~s phon; **50 ~:** 50 phons

Phonem /foˈne:m/ *das;* ~s, ~e (Sprachw.) phoneme

Phonetik /foˈne:tɪk/ *die;* ~: phonetics *sing.*

phonetisch
A *Adj.* phonetic
B *adv.* phonetically

Phönix /ˈfø:nɪks/ *der;* ~[es], ~e phoenix; **wie ein ~ aus der Asche** like a phoenix from the ashes

Phönizier /føˈni:tsiɐ/ *der;* ~s, ~, **Phönizierin** *die;* ~, ~nen (hist.) Phoenician

Phono- /ˈfo:no-/ phono ‹*socket, input*›; **~geschäft/~abteilung** audio and record store/department

Phono·gerät *das* record player

Phono·graph *der* (veralt.) [cylinder] phonograph

Phono·koffer *der* portable record player

Phonologie *die;* ~ (Sprachw.) phonology

phonologisch (Sprachw.)
A *Adj.* phonological
B *adv.* phonologically

Phono·typistin /-tyˈpɪstɪn/ *die;* ~, ~nen audio typist

phon·stark *Adj.* loud; noisy; high-volume ‹*reproduction*›

Phon·zahl *die* phon count; ≈ decibel level

Phosphat /fɔsˈfa:t/ *das;* ~[e]s, ~e (Chemie) phosphate

Phosphor /ˈfɔsfɔr/ *der;* ~s phosphorus

Phosphor·bombe *die* phosphorus [incendiary] bomb

Phosphoreszenz /fɔsforɛsˈtsɛnts/ *die;* ~: phosphorescence

phosphoreszieren *itr. V.* phosphoresce; be phosphorescent; **~d** phosphorescent

phosphor·haltig *Adj.* containing phosphorus *postpos., not pred.;* **stark ~:** with a high phosphorus content; **[stark] ~ sein** contain [a high level of] phosphorus

Phosphor·säure *die* phosphoric acid

photo-, Photo- *s. auch* **foto-, Foto-**

Photo /ˈfo:to/ *das;* ~s, ~s ▸**Foto**

Photo-: **~chemie** *die* photochemistry *no art.;* **~element** *das* (Elektrot.) photoelement; photovoltaic cell; **~metrie** *die;* ~~ (Physik) photometry *no art.*

Photon /ˈfo:tɔn/ *das;* ~s, ~en /foˈto:nən/ (Physik) photon

photo-, Photo-: **~synthese** *die* photosynthesis; **~voltaik** /-vɔlˈta:ɪk/ *die;* ~~: photovoltaics *sing., no art.;* **~voltaik·anlage** *die* photovoltaic array; **~voltaisch** /-vɔlˈta:ɪʃ/ **A** *Adj.* photovoltaic; **B** *adv.* by a photovoltaic process; by photovoltaic means; **~zelle** *die* photo[-electric] cell

Phrase /ˈfra:zə/ *die;* ~, ~n **1** (abwertend) [empty] phrase; cliché; **leere ~n** empty phrases; waffle *sing.;* **~n dreschen** (ugs.) spout clichés; dole out catchphrases **2** (Musik, Sprachw.) phrase

phrasen-, Phrasen-: **~drescher** *der* (ugs. abwertend) phrase-monger; cliché-monger; **~drescherei** /-drɛʃəˈrai/ *die;* ~~, ~~en (ugs. abwertend) phrase-mongering; cliché-mongering; **~drescherin** *die* ▸**~drescher;** **~haft** (abwertend) **A** *Adj.* empty; trite; (voller Klischees) cliché-ridden; **B** *adv.* in an empty *or* trite manner

Phraseologie /frazeoloˈgi:/ *die;* ~, ~n (Sprachw.) idiomatic usage *no art.;* (Buch) dictionary of idioms

P

phraseologisch *Adj.* (Sprachw.) idiomatic; phrasal ‹*unit*›; **~es Wörterbuch** dictionary of idioms

phrasieren *itr., tr. V.* (Musik) phrase

Phrasierung *die;* ~, ~en (Musik) phrasing

pH-Wert /pe:ˈha:-/ *der* (Chemie) pH [value]

phylogenetisch /fylogeˈne:tɪʃ/ (Biol.)
A *Adj.* phylogenetic
B *adv.* phylogenetically

Phylogenie /fylogeˈni:/ *die* (Biol.) phylogeny

Physik /fyˈzi:k/ *die;* ~: physics *sing., no art.*; **ein Lehrbuch der ~:** a physics textbook

physikalisch /fyziˈka:lɪʃ/
A *Adj.* physics *attrib.* ‹*experiment, formula, research, institute*›; physical ‹*map, chemistry, therapy, process*›; **~e Gesetze** laws of physics; physical laws
B *adv.* in terms of physics

Physiker *der;* ~s, ~, **Physikerin** *die;* ~, ~nen ▸ⓘ S. 113 physicist

Physik·saal *der* (Schulw.) physics laboratory

Physikum /ˈfy:zikʊm/ *das;* ~s, **Physika** (Hochschulw.) *examination ending the pre-clinical stage*

Physiognomie /fyzi̯ognoˈmi:/ *die;* ~, ~n physiognomy

Physiologe /fyzi̯oˈlo:gə/ *der;* ~n, ~n ▸ⓘ S. 113 physiologist

Physiologie /fyzi̯oloˈgi:/ *die;* ~: physiology

Physiologin *die;* ~, ~nen ▸ⓘ S. 113 physiologist

physiologisch
A *Adj.* physiological
B *adv.* physiologically

Physio·therapeut *der,* **Physio·therapeutin** *die* ▸ⓘ S. 113 physiotherapist

Physio·therapie /fyzi̯o-/ *die* physiotherapy

physisch
A *Adj.* physical
B *adv.* physically

Pi /pi:/ *das;* ~[s], ~s pi

Pianist /pi̯aˈnɪst/ *der;* ~en, ~en, **Pianistin** *die;* ~, ~nen ▸ⓘ S. 113 pianist

Piano /ˈpi̯a:no/ *das;* ~s, ~s piano

Piano·bar *die* piano bar

Pianoforte /pi̯anoˈfɔrtə/ *das;* ~s, ~s (veralt.) pianoforte (formal/arch.)

picheln /ˈpɪçl̩n/ (ugs.)
A *itr. V.* booze (coll.)
B *tr. V.* **einen ~ gehen** go out for a jar (Brit. coll.)

Pickel /ˈpɪkl̩/ *der;* ~s, ~ 1 (auf der Haut) pimple 2 (Spitzhacke) pickaxe; (Eis~) ice axe

Pickel·haube *die* spiked helmet

pickelig *Adj.* pimply; **~ [im Gesicht] sein** have a spotty *or* pimply face

picken /ˈpɪkn̩/
A *itr. V.* peck (**nach** at; **an** + *Akk.*, **gegen** on, against)
B *tr. V.* 1 ‹*bird*› peck; (ugs.) ‹*person*› pick; (aufheben) pick up 2 (österr. ugs.: kleben) stick

picklig ▸ **pickelig**

Picknick /ˈpɪknɪk/ *das;* ~s, ~e *od.* ~s picnic; **~ machen** *od.* **halten** have a picnic

picknicken *itr. V.* picnic

picobello /ˈpi:koˈbɛlo/ (ugs.)
A *indekl. Adj.* super-duper (sl.); (makellos) immaculate
B *adv.* immaculately; **~ in Ordnung** in immaculate order; spick and span

Pidgin·englisch /ˈpɪdʒɪn-/ *das* pidgin English

piefig /ˈpi:fɪç/ (ugs. abwertend)
A *Adj.* tacky ‹*thing, appearance*›; (kleinkariert) small-minded; narrow-minded ‹*person*›
B *adv.* in a small-minded *or* narrow-minded way; **es geht ~ zu** attitudes are narrow-minded

Piefke /ˈpi:fkə/ *der;* ~s, ~s 1 (bes. nordd. abwertend) bumptious lout 2 (österr. abwertend: Deutscher) bloody (Brit. sl.) *or* damn German

pieken ▸ **piken**

piek·fein /ˈpi:kˈfai̯n/ (ugs.)
A *Adj.* posh (coll.)
B *adv.* poshly (coll.); **~ angezogen** wearing posh clothes (coll.); dressed to the nines

pienzen /ˈpi:nt͜sn̩/ *itr. V.* (landsch.) moan

piep /pi:p/ *Interj.* ~, ~! cheep, cheep!; **nicht ~ sagen** (ugs.) not say a word; **er kann nicht mehr ~ sagen** (ugs.) he's been silenced

Piep *der;* ~s, ~e (ugs.) 1 (Ton) peep; **keinen ~ [davon] sagen** not say a thing [about it] 2 *in* **einen [kleinen] ~ haben** have a [bit of a] screw loose (coll.)

piepe /ˈpi:pə/, **piep·egal** *Adj: in* **[jmdm.] ~ sein** (ugs.) not matter at all [to sb.]; **es ist mir ~!** (ugs.) I don't give a damn!

piepen *itr. V.* (ugs.) squeak; ‹*small bird*› cheep; chirp; ‹*paging device*› bleep; **bei dir piepts wohl!** (salopp) you must be off your rocker (coll.); **zum P~ sein** (ugs.) be a hoot *or* a scream (coll.)

Piepen *Pl.* (salopp: Geld) dough *sing.* (coll.); **50 ~:** 50 marks/francs *etc.*

Piep-: **~hahn** *der; Pl.* **~hähne** (Kinderspr.) willy (coll.); **~matz** *der* (Kinderspr.) dicky bird (coll.)

pieps /pi:ps/ ▸ **piep**

Pieps *der;* ~es, ~e (ugs.) ▸ **Piep 1**

piepsen (ugs.)
A *itr. V.* ▸ **piepen**
B *itr., tr. V.* (mit hoher Stimme sprechen) pipe; (aufgeregt) squeal

Piepser *der;* ~s, ~ (ugs.) 1 (Piepsen) chirp; tweet 2 (kleiner Empfänger) bleeper

piepsig *Adj.* (ugs.) squeaky

Pieps·ton *der* ▸ **Piepton**

Piep·ton *der* bleep

Pier /pi:ɐ̯/ *der;* ~s, ~e *od.* ~s *od.* (Seemannsspr.) *die;* ~, ~s jetty

Piercing /ˈpi:ɐ̯sɪŋ/ *das;* ~s [body] piercing; (Schmuck) stud

piesacken /ˈpi:zakn̩/ *tr. V.* (ugs.) pester; **hör endlich auf, mich damit zu ~!** stop pestering me about that!

pieseln /ˈpi:zl̩n/ *itr.* (*auch tr.*) *V.* (salopp) ▸ **pinkeln**

Pietät /pi̯eˈtɛ:t/ *die;* ~, ~en 1 respect; (Ehrfurcht) reverence 2 (Bestattungsinstitut) [firm of] funeral directors *or* (Amer.) morticians

pietät-, Pietät-: **~los** A *Adj.* irreverent; (gefühllos) unfeeling; (respektlos) disrespectful; lacking in respect *postpos.*; B *adv.* irreverently; **~losigkeit** *die;* ~, ~~en irreverence; (Gefühllosigkeit) lack of feeling; (Respektlosigkeit) lack of respect; (Handlung) act of irreverence; **~voll** A *Adj.* respectful; (ehrfurchtsvoll) reverent; B *adv.* respectfully; (ehrfurchtsvoll) reverently

Pietismus /pi̯eˈtɪsmʊs/ *der;* ~: pietism *no art.*

Pietist *der;* ~en, ~en, **Pietistin** *die;* ~, ~nen pietist

pietistisch
A *Adj.* pietistic
B *adv.* in a pietistic manner

piff, paff /ˈpɪf ˈpaf/ *Interj.* (Kinderspr.) bang, bang

Pigment /pɪˈgmɛnt/ *das;* ~[e]s, ~e pigment

Pigmentation /pɪgmɛntaˈt͜si̯o:n/ *die;* ~, ~en pigmentation

Pigment·fleck *der* pigmentation mark

Pik[1] /pi:k/ *der: in* **einen ~ auf jmdn. haben** (ugs.) have it in for sb.

Pik[2] *das;* ~[s], ~[s], *österr. auch die;* ~, ~ (Kartenspiel) 1 (Farbe) spades *pl.*; **von ~ habe ich nur noch die Sieben** the only spade I have left is the seven; **~ ziehen/ausspielen** draw/play spades 2 (Karte) spade

pikant /piˈkant/
A *Adj.* 1 piquant; (würzig) spicy; well-seasoned; (appetitanregend) appetizing; **ich möchte lieber etwas Pikantes** I'd rather have something savoury 2 (fig.: witzig) piquant; ironical 3 (verhüll.: schlüpfrig) racy ‹*joke, story*›; titillating ‹*pictures*›
B *adv.* spicily; **etw. ~ zubereiten** season sth. well; **~ gewürzt** piquantly *or* appetizingly seasoned

Pikanterie /pikantəˈri:/ *die;* ~, ~n 1 (fig.) piquancy; (Witzigkeit) irony 2 (verhüll.: schlüpfrige Geschichte) racy story

pikanter·weise *Adv.* (geh.) ironically [enough]

Pik-: ***~as**, **~ass** *das* ace of spades; **~bube** *der* jack of spades; **~dame** *die* queen of spades

Pike /ˈpi:kə/ *die;* ~, ~n pike; **etw. von der ~ auf [er]lernen** learn sth. by working one's way up from the bottom

Pikee /piˈke:/ *der; österr. auch das;* ~s, ~s (Textilw.) piqué

piken *tr., itr. V.* (ugs.) prick; **etw. in etw.** (*Akk.*) **~:** poke sth. into sth.; **jmdm. eine Nadel in den Arm ~:** poke a needle into sb.'s arm

pikieren *tr. V.* (Gartenbau) prick out ‹*seedlings*›

pikiert /piˈki:ɐ̯t/
A *Adj.* piqued; nettled; **ein ~es Gesicht machen** look aggrieved
B *adv.* ‹*reply, say*› in an aggrieved tone *or* voice

Pikkolo[1] /ˈpɪkolo/ *der;* ~s, ~s [trainee] waiter

Pikkolo[2] *das;* ~s, ~s (Flöte) piccolo

Pikkolo[3] *die;* ~, ~[s] (Fläschchen) miniature bottle of champagne (*for one person*)

Pikkolo·flöte *die* piccolo

Pik·könig *der* king of spades

piksen /ˈpi:ksn̩/ *tr., itr. V.* (ugs.) ▸ **piken**

Pik·sieben *die* (Kartenspiel) seven of spades; **dastehen wie ~** (ugs.) stand there looking stupid

-pilger *der:* **Mekka~/Rom~:** pilgrim on his/her way to Rome/Mecca

Pilger /ˈpɪlgɐ/ *der;* ~s, ~: pilgrim

Pilger·fahrt *die* pilgrimage

Pilgerin *die;* ~, ~nen pilgrim

pilgern *itr. V.; mit sein* 1 (auch fig.) go on *or* make a pilgrimage 2 (ugs.: gehen) traipse (coll.)

Pilgerschaft *die;* ~, ~en pilgrimage

Pilger-: **~stab** *der* pilgrim's staff; **~väter** *Pl.* (hist.) Pilgrim Fathers

Pille /ˈpɪlə/ *die;* ~, ~n pill; **sie nimmt schon seit Jahren die ~:** she's been on the pill for years (coll.); **eine bittere ~ [für jmdn.] sein** (fig.) be a bitter pill [for sb.] to swallow; **jmdm. die bittere ~ versüßen** *od.* **verzuckern** (fig.) sugar the pill for sb.; (es jmdm. erleichtern) make it easier for sb.

Pillen-: **~dreher** *der* 1 (Käfer) scarab [beetle]; 2 (ugs. scherzh.: Apotheker) pill peddler (coll.); **~dreherin** *die* ▸ **~dreher 2**; **~knick** *der;* ~~[e]s decline in the birth rate [due to the pill]

Pilot /piˈlo:t/ *der;* ~en, ~en, **Pilotin** *die;* ~, ~nen 1 ▸ⓘ S. 113 pilot 2 (Motorsport) [racing] driver

Pilot-: **~phase** *die* pilot phase; **~projekt** *das* pilot project; **~studie** *die* pilot study

Pils /pɪls/ *das;* ~, ~: Pils; Pils[e]ner [beer]

Pilz /pɪlt͜s/ *der;* ~es, ~e 1 fungus; (Speise~, auch fig.) mushroom; **essbare, giftige und ungenießbare ~e** mushrooms, poisonous and inedible fungi; **in die ~e gehen** (ugs.) go mushrooming; **wie ~e aus dem Boden** *od.* **der Erde schießen** be springing up like mushrooms 2 (ugs.: ~infektion) fungus [infection]

pilz-, Pilz-: **~förmig** *Adj.* mushroom-shaped; **~infektion** *die* (Med.) fungal infection; **~krankheit** *die* 1 ▸ⓘ S. 439 (Mykose) mycosis; 2 (bei Pflanzen) fungus [disease]; **~kultur** *die* fungus culture; **~kunde** *die* mycology

Pilzling /ˈpɪlt͜slɪŋ/ *der;* ~s, ~e (österr.) ▸ **Steinpilz**

Pilz-: **~sammler** *der,* **~sammlerin** *die* mushroom picker; **~vergiftung** *die* ▸ⓘ S. 439 fungus poisoning *no art.*; (durch verdorbene Pilze) mushroom poisoning *no art.*

Piment /piˈmɛnt/ *der od. das;* ~[e]s, ~e pimento; allspice

Pimmel /ˈpɪml̩/ *der;* ~s, ~ (salopp) willy (coll.)

pimpern /ˈpɪmpɐn/ (salopp)
A *itr. V.* have it off (sl.)

P

B *tr. V.* have it off with (sl.)
Pimpf /pɪmpf/ *der;* **~[e]s, ~e** **1** (ugs.: Junge) kid (coll.) **2** (ns.) *member of the* **Jungvolk**
PIN /pɪn/ *die;* **~, ~s** PIN
pingelig /ˈpɪŋəlɪç/ (ugs.)
A finicky; pernickety (coll.); (wählerisch) fussy; choosy (coll.)
B *adv.* in a pernickety way (coll.); (pedantisch) pedantically
Pingpong /ˈpɪŋpɔŋ/ *das;* **~s** (ugs.) ping-pong
Pinguin /ˈpɪŋguiːn/ *der;* **~s, ~e** penguin
Pinie /ˈpiːni̯ə/ *die;* **~, ~n** [stone *or* umbrella] pine
Pinien·kern *der* pine nut; pine kernel
Pinke /ˈpɪŋkə/ *die;* **~** (ugs. veralt.) dough (coll.); lolly (Brit. coll.)
Pinkel /ˈpɪŋkl̩/ *der;* **~s, ~** (ugs. abwertend) **ein [feiner] ~:** a stuck-up prig
pinkeln *itr. (auch tr.) V.* (salopp) **1** pee (coll.); ‹*esp. child*› wee (sl.); **~ [gehen]** [go and] have a pee (coll.) **2** (unpers.: regnen) **es pinkelt** it's spitting
Pinkel·pause *die* (ugs.) stop for a pee (coll.); comfort stop (Amer.)
Pinke·pinke ▸**Pinke**
pink·farben /ˈpɪŋk-/ *Adj.* [shocking] pink
Pinne /ˈpɪnə/ *die;* **~, ~n** (Seemannsspr.) tiller
pinnen *tr. V.* (ugs.) pin (**auf, an** + *Akk.* on)
PIN-Nummer *die* PIN number
Pinn·wand *die* pinboard
Pinscher /ˈpɪnʃɐ/ *der;* **~s, ~** **1** pinscher **2** (ugs. abwertend: Mensch) pipsqueak (coll.)
Pinsel /ˈpɪnzl̩/ *der;* **~s, ~** **1** brush; (Mal~) paintbrush; **mit leichtem/kühnem ~:** with light/bold brush strokes **2** (ugs. abwertend: Dummkopf) nitwit (coll.); idiot (coll.)
Pinsel·führung *die* brushwork *no indef. art.*
pinseln *tr. V.* **1** (ugs.: anstreichen) paint ‹*room, house, etc.*› **2** (malen) paint ‹*landscape, picture*›; daub ‹*slogans*› **3** (ugs.: schreiben) write ‹*letters, homework*› in one's best writing **4** (streichen) brush [on] ‹*paint*›, put on ‹*paint*› with a brush; apply ‹*liquid*› [with a brush] (**auf** + *Akk.* to) **5** (Med.: ein~) paint ‹*wound, gums, throat, etc.*›
Pinsel·strich *der* **1** brush stroke **2** (Pinselführung) brushwork *no indef. art.*
Pinte /ˈpɪntə/ *die;* **~, ~n** **1** (ugs.) ▸**Kneipe 1** **2** (hist.: Hohlmaß) [*former*] *measure of capacity for liquids*
Pin-up /pɪnˈlap-/ *das;* **~s, ~s** pin-up
Pin-up-Girl /pɪnˈlap-/ *das;* **~s, ~s** pin-up girl
Pinzette /pɪnˈt̮sɛtə/ *die;* **~, ~n** tweezers *pl.*; **chirurgische ~:** surgical forceps *pl.*
Pionier /pi̯oˈniːɐ̯/ *der;* **~s, ~e** **1** (Milit.) sapper; engineer **2** (fig.: Wegbereiter) pioneer **3** (DDR) **[Junger] ~:** [Young] Pioneer
Pionier·arbeit *die* pioneering work
Pionierin *die;* **~, ~nen** pioneer
Pionier-: ~tat *die* pioneering achievement; **~truppe** *die* (Milit.) corps of engineers
Pipapo /pipaˈpoː/ *das;* **~s** (salopp) **das ganze ~:** all the frills; **mit allem ~:** with all the frills
Pipeline /ˈpaiplain/ *die;* **~, ~s** pipeline
Pipette /piˈpɛtə/ *die;* **~, ~n** (Chemie) pipette
Pipi /piˈpiː/ *das;* **~s** (Kinderspr.) **~ machen** do wee-wees (sl.); **~ müssen** have to do wee-wees *or* have a wee (sl.)
Pipifax /ˈpipifaks/ *der;* **~** (salopp) piffling trifles *pl.* (sl.)
Piranha /piˈranja/ *der;* **~[s], ~s** piranha
Pirat /piˈraːt/ *der;* **~en, ~en** pirate
Piraten-: ~schiff *das* pirate ship; **~sender** *der* pirate radio station
Piraterie /piratəˈriː/ *die;* **~, ~n** piracy *no art.*
Piratin *die;* **~, ~nen** ▸**Pirat**
Pirol /piˈroːl/ *der;* **~s, ~e** oriole
Pirouette /piˈru̯ɛtə/ *die;* **~, ~n** pirouette
Pirsch /pɪrʃ/ *die;* **~** (Jägerspr.) [deer-]stalking; **auf die ~ gehen** go [deer-]stalking
pirschen
A *itr. V.* **1** (Jägerspr.) stalk; go stalking; **auf Rehwild** (*Akk.*) **~:** stalk roe deer **2** (ugs.: schleichen) creep [silently]; steal
B *refl. V.* (ugs.) creep [silently]; steal
Pisse /ˈpɪsə/ *die;* **~** (derb) piss (coarse)
pissen *itr. (auch tr.) V.* (derb) **1** piss (coarse); **ich muss ~ [gehen]** I must have a piss **2** (unpers.: regnen) piss down (sl.)
Pissoir /pɪˈsoa̯ːɐ̯/ *das;* **~s, ~e** *od.* **~s** [public] urinal
Piss·pott, *Piß·pott *der* (salopp) piss-pot (coarse)
Pistazie /pɪsˈtaːt̮si̯ə/ *die;* **~, ~n** pistachio
Piste /ˈpɪstə/ *die;* **~, ~n** **1** (Skisport) piste; ski run; (Renn~) course **2** (Rennstrecke) track **3** (Flugw.) runway; **auf der ~ aufsetzen** touch down **4** (Straße) dirt road
Pistole /pɪsˈtoːlə/ *die;* **~, ~n** pistol; **wie aus der ~ geschossen** like a shot *or* a flash; **jmdm. die ~ auf die Brust setzen** (fig.) hold a pistol to sb.'s head
Pistolen-: ~schuss, *~schuß *der* pistol shot; **~tasche** *die* holster
pitsch·nass, *pitsch·naß /ˈpɪtʃˈnas/ *Adj.* (ugs.) dripping wet; wet through
pittoresk /pɪtoˈrɛsk/ (geh.)
A *Adj.* picturesque
B *adv.* picturesquely
Pizza /ˈpɪt̮sa/ *die;* **~, ~s** *od.* **Pizzen** pizza
Pizza-: ~bäcker *der,* **~bäckerin** *die* pizza cook; **~service** *der* pizza delivery service
Pizzeria /pɪt̮seˈriːa/ *die;* **~, ~s** *od.* **Pizzerien** pizzeria
Pkw, PKW *Abk.* = **Personenkraftwagen** [private] car; automobile (Amer.)
Placebo /plaˈt̮seːbo/ *das;* **~s, ~s** (Med.) placebo
Placebo·effekt *der* placebo effect
***placieren** ▸**platzieren**
placken /ˈplakn̩/ *refl. V.* (ugs.) slave away
Plackerei *die;* **~, ~en** (ugs.) drudgery *no indef. art.*; [hard] grind
pladdern /ˈpladɐn/ *itr. V.* (unpers.) **es pladdert** (nordd.) it's pouring [down]
plädieren /plɛˈdiːrən/ *itr. V.* (Rechtsw.) plead (**auf** + *Akk.*, **für** for); (das Plädoyer halten) ‹*counsel*› make one's final speech, sum up; (fig.) argue (**für** for, in favour of); **auf Freispruch/auf schuldig ~:** plead for acquittal/for a verdict of guilty; **er plädiert dafür, dass ...** he argues *or* advocates that ...
Plädoyer /plɛdo̯aˈjeː/ *das;* **~s, ~s** (Rechtsw.) final speech, summing up (*for the defence/prosecution*); (fig.) plea; **sein ~ halten** make one's final speech; sum up
Plafond /plaˈfõː/ *der;* **~s, ~s** (südd., österr., auch fig.) ceiling
Plage /ˈplaːgə/ *die;* **~, ~n** **1** [cursed *or* (coll.) pestilential] nuisance; **das macht ihm das Leben zur ~:** it makes his life a misery; **die ägyptischen ~n** (bibl.) the plagues of Egypt **2** (ugs.: Mühe) bother; trouble; **seine ~ mit jmdm./etw. haben** find sb./sth. a real handful
Plage·geist *der* (fam.) pest
plagen
A *tr. V.* **1** torment; plague; **Zweifel ~ ihn** he is plagued *or* beset with doubts; **von Kopfschmerzen/Träumen geplagt** plagued with headaches/dreams; **er ist ein geplagter Mensch** he has a hard time of it **2** (ugs.: bedrängen) harass; (mit Bitten, Fragen) pester
B *refl. V.* **1** (sich abmühen) slave away; **sie musste sich ~, um die Arbeit zu bewältigen** she had to struggle to get through all the work **2** (leiden) **sich mit etw. ~:** be troubled *or* bothered by sth.
Plagiat /plaˈgi̯aːt/ *das;* **~[e]s, ~e** plagiarism *no art.*; **ein [eindeutiges] ~:** a [clear] case of plagiarism
Plagiator /plaˈgi̯aːtɔr/ *der;* **~s, ~en**, **Plagiatorin** *die;* **~, ~nen** (geh.) plagiarist
plagiieren /plagiˈiːrən/ *tr. (auch itr.) V.* (geh.) plagiarize
Plaid /pleːt/ *das od. der;* **~s, ~s** **1** (Decke) tartan [travelling] rug (Brit.) *or* (Amer.) lap robe **2** (Tuch) plaid
Plakat /plaˈkaːt/ *das;* **~[e]s, ~e** poster; (zum Tragen) placard; **„~e ankleben verboten"** 'post no bills'
plakatieren
A *tr. V.* announce by poster
B *itr. V.* put up posters
plakativ /plakaˈtiːf/
A *Adj.* bold and simple, eye-catching ‹*design, representation*›; bold ‹*colours*›
B *adv.* eye-catchingly; in a bold and simple style
Plakat-: ~kunst *die* poster art *no art.*; **~maler** *der,* **~malerin** *die* poster artist; **~wand** *die* [poster] hoarding; billboard
Plakette /plaˈkɛtə/ *die;* **~, ~n** **1** (Schildchen) badge; (Scheibe) disc **2** (an einem Gebäude) plaque
plan /plaːn/ *Adj.* (Technik) flat; plane ‹*surface*›; **~ liegen** lie flat
Plan[1] *der;* **~[e]s, Pläne** /ˈplɛːnə/ **1** plan; **nach ~ verlaufen** go according to plan; **auf dem ~ stehen** be on the agenda; be planned; **wir sind im ~** (Zeit~) we are on schedule **2** (Karte) map; plan; (Stadt~) [street] plan
Plan[2] *der:* in **auf den ~ treten, auf dem ~ erscheinen** (geh.) appear on the scene; **auf den ~ rufen** (geh.) bring ‹*person*› on to the scene; bring ‹*opponent*› into the arena; arouse ‹*curiosity*›
planbar *Adj.* plannable
Plane *die;* **~, ~n** tarpaulin
planen *tr., itr. V.* plan
Planer *der;* **~s, ~, Planerin** *die;* **~, ~nen** planner
Plan·erfüllung *die* (bes. DDR) attainment of the planned [production] target
planerisch *Adj.* planning ‹*measures, genius, ability*›; **eine ~e Meisterleistung** a masterpiece of planning
Pläne·schmieden *das;* **~s** planning; making plans
Planet /plaˈneːt/ *der;* **~en, ~en** planet
Planetarium /planeˈtaːri̯ʊm/ *das;* **~s, Planetarien** planetarium
Planeten-: ~bahn *die* planetary orbit; **~system** *das* planetary system
Planetoid *der;* **~en, ~en** asteroid, planetoid
planieren *tr. V.* level; grade (as tech. term)
Planier·raupe *die* bulldozer
Plan·jahr *das* (bes. DDR) planning year
Planke /ˈplaŋkə/ *die;* **~, ~n** **1** plank; board **2** (Zaun) [close-boarded] wooden fence
Plänkelei *die;* **~, ~en** ▸**Geplänkel 1**
plänkeln /ˈplɛŋkl̩n/ *itr. V.* have a rough and tumble; fight playfully
Plankton /ˈplaŋktɔn/ *das;* **~s** (Biol.) plankton
plan-, Plan-: ~los **A** *Adj.* aimless; (ohne System) unsystematic; **B** *adv.* ▸**A:** aimlessly; unsystematically; **~losigkeit** *die;* **~~:** aimlessness; (Mangel an System) lack of system; **~mäßig** **A** *Adj.* **1** regular, scheduled ‹*service, steamer*›; **~mäßige Ankunft/Abfahrt** scheduled time of arrival/departure; **2** (systematisch) systematic; **B** *adv.* **1** (wie geplant) according to plan; as planned; (pünktlich) on schedule; **2** (systematisch) systematically; **~mäßigkeit** *die;* **~:** methodicalness; (Vorgehen) systematic procedure; **~quadrat** *das* grid square
Plansch·becken /ˈplanʃ-/ *das* paddling pool
planschen *itr. V.* splash [about]
Plan-: ~soll *das* planned [production] target; **~spiel** *das* simulation; (Kriegsspiel) war game; **~stelle** *die* established post
Plantage /planˈtaːʒə/ *die;* **~, ~n** plantation
Planung *die;* **~, ~en** **1** (das Planen) planning; **in** (*Dat.*) **~ sein** be planned; **bei der ~:** at the planning stage **2** (Plan) plan
Planungs·stadium *das* planning stage; **im ~:** at the planning stage
plan-, Plan-: ~voll **A** *Adj.* methodical; systematic; **B** *adv.* methodically; systematically; **~wagen** *der* covered wagon; **~wirtschaft** *die* planned economy

Plapperei *die;* ~, ~**en** (ugs. abwertend) chatter

Plapper·maul *das* (ugs. abwertend) chatterbox

plappern /ˈplapɐn/ (ugs.)
A *itr. V.* **1** (schwätzen) chatter **2** (ausplaudern) blab
B *tr. V.* babble ‹*nonsense*›

plärren /ˈplɛrən/
A *tr. V.* bawl [out] ‹*song*›; ‹*radio etc.*› blare out
B *itr. V.* **1** bawl; yell; ‹*radio etc.*› blare **2** (ugs.: weinen) wail; (sehr laut) howl

Pläsier /plɛˈziːɐ̯/ *das;* ~**s**, ~**e** (veralt.) pleasure (**an** + *Dat.* in); **lass ihm doch sein** ~: let him have his fun

Plasma /ˈplasma/ *das;* ~**s**, **Plasmen** (Med., Physik) plasma; (Proto~) protoplasm

Plasma·bildschirm *der* (DV) plasma screen

Plast /plast/ *der;* ~**[e]s**, ~**e** (regional) plastic

Plaste /ˈplastə/ *die;* ~, ~**n** (regional ugs.) plastic

Plastik[1] /ˈplastɪk/ *die;* ~, ~**en** **1** (Werk, Kunst) sculpture **2** (Med.) plastic surgery operation; **jmdm. eine** ~ **machen** perform plastic surgery on sb.

Plastik[2] *das;* ~**s** plastic

Plastik-: ~**beutel** *der* plastic bag; ~**bombe** *die* plastic bomb; ~**folie** *die* plastic film; ~**geld** *das* (ugs.) plastic money (coll.); ~**sprengstoff** *der* plastic explosive; ~**tüte** *die* plastic bag

Plastilin /plastiˈliːn/ *das;* ~**s** ≈ Plasticine ®

Plastinat /plastiˈnaːt/ *das;* ~**[e]s**, ~**e** plastinate

Plastination /plastinaˈt͜sioːn/ *die;* ~, ~**en** plastination

plastinieren /plastiˈniːrən/ *tr. V.* plastinate

plastisch
A *Adj.* **1** (knetbar) plastic; workable **2** (bildhauerisch) sculptural; ‹*ability*› as a sculptor **3** (dreidimensional) three-dimensional ‹*effect, formation, vision*›; sculptural ‹*decoration*› **4** (fig.: anschaulich) vivid ‹*description, picture*› **5** (Med.) plastic ‹*surgery, surgeon*›
B *adv.* **1** (bildhauerisch) sculpturally; **etw.** ~ **ausarbeiten** *od.* **gestalten** sculpture sth. **2** (dreidimensional) three-dimensionally **3** (fig.: anschaulich) vividly; **sich** (*Dat.*) **etw.** ~ **vorstellen können** have a clear picture of sth. [in one's mind]

Plastizität /plastit͜siˈtɛːt/ *die;* ~ **1** plasticity **2** (fig.: Anschaulichkeit) vividness; (von Prosa usw.) graphic quality; (eines Bildes) three-dimensional quality

Platane /plaˈtaːnə/ *die;* ~, ~**n** plane tree

Plateau /plaˈtoː/ *das;* ~**s**, ~**s** plateau

Plateau-: ~**schuh** *der* platform shoe; ~**sohle** *die* platform sole

Platin /ˈplaːtiːn/ *das;* ~**s** platinum

platin·blond *Adj.* platinum blonde

***Platitüde** ► **Plattitüde**

Platon /ˈplaːtɔn/ (*der*) Plato

platonisch /plaˈtoːnɪʃ/
A *Adj.* **1** Platonic ‹*philosophy, state*› **2** (nicht sinnlich) platonic ‹*love, relationship*›
B *adv.* platonically

platsch /platʃ/ *Interj.* splash

platschen *itr. V.* **1** splash **2** *mit sein* (~d schlagen) splash (**an** + *Akk.*, **gegen** against) **3** (planschen) splash about

plätschern /ˈplɛtʃɐn/ *itr. V.* **1** splash; ‹*rain*› patter; ‹*stream*› burble; (fig.) ~**de Unterhaltung** casual *or* desultory conversation **2** (planschen) splash about **3** *mit sein* ‹*stream*› burble along

platsch·nass, ***platsch·naß** *Adj.* (ugs.) ► **klatschnass**

platt /plat/
A *Adj.* **1** (flach) flat; **sich** (*Dat.*) **die Nase** ~ **drücken** flatten one's nose; **ein Platter** (ugs.) a flat (coll.); a flat tyre; (mit Loch) a puncture; **etw.** ~ **machen** (salopp abwertend) close sth. down; **das** ~**e Land** (ugs.) the countryside; the rural areas *pl.*; **sie ist** ~ **wie ein [Bügel]brett** (salopp) she is flat-chested **2** (geistlos) dull, vapid ‹*conversation, book*›; vacuous, feeble ‹*poem, joke*›; shallow, empty ‹*materialism, argument, imitation*› **3** (ausgesprochen) downright ‹*lie, swindle, slander*›; sheer ‹*cynicism*›; absolute ‹*matter of course*› **4** (ugs., bes. nordd.: erstaunt) dumbfounded; flabbergasted
B *adv.* **1** (flach) **sich** ~ **legen** lie down flat **2** (geistlos) feebly
C *Adv.* ~ **sprechen** talk Low German dialect

Platt *das;* ~**[s]** **1** [local] Low German dialect; (allgemein: Niederdeutsch) Low German **2** (ugs.: Dialekt) patois

Plätt·brett *das* (nordd., md.) ► **Bügelbrett**

Plättchen /ˈplɛtçən/ *das;* ~**s**, ~: small plate *or* disc

platt·deutsch *Adj.*: ► **niederdeutsch**

Platte *die;* ~, ~**n** **1** (Stein~) slab; (Metall~) plate; sheet; (Mikroskopie usw.: Glas~) slide; (Elektronik) board; (Paneel) panel; (Span~, Hartfaser~ usw.) board; (Styropor~ usw.) sheet; (Tisch~) [table] top; (Grab~) [memorial] slab; (fotografische ~) [photographic] plate; (Druck~) [pressure] plate; (Kachel, Fliese) tile; (zum Pflastern) flagstone; paving stone; **etw./jmdn. auf die** ~ **bannen** (scherzh.) immortalize sb./sth. [in a photograph] (joc.) **2** (Koch~) hotplate **3** (Schall~) record; **eine** ~ **mit Gitarrenmusik** a record of guitar music; **etw. auf** ~ (*Akk.*) **aufnehmen** make a record of sth.; **die** ~ **kenne ich [schon]** (fig. ugs.) I've heard that one before **leg [doch endlich mal] 'ne neue/andere** ~ **auf!** (fig. ugs.) can't you talk about sth. else for a change?; **immer dieselbe** ~! (fig. ugs.) always the same old tune **4** (Teller) plate; (zum Servieren, aus Metall) dish **5** (Speise) dish; **kalte** ~: selection of cold meats [and cheese] **6** (ugs.: Glatze) bald pate **7** (Gaumen~) [dental] plate **8** **die** ~ **putzen** (salopp) make oneself scarce (coll.); ~ **machen** (salopp) doss *or* kip down (Brit. coll.); bed down **9** (österr. ugs.: Bande) gang

Plätte /ˈplɛtə/ *die;* ~, ~**n** (österr.) flat-bottomed barge (*with pointed prow*)

Plätt·eisen /ˈplɛt-/ *das* (nordd., md.) iron; (hist.) flat iron

plätten *tr., itr. V.* (nordd., md.) iron

Platten-: ~**album** *das* record album; ~**cover** *das* record sleeve; ~**firma** *die* record company; ~**hülle** *die* record sleeve; ~**label** /-leɪbl̩/ *das* record label; ~**laden** *der* record shop *or* (esp. Amer.) store; ~**sammlung** *die* record collection

Plattensee *der;* ~**s** (Geogr.) Lake Balaton

Platten-: ~**spieler** *der* (als Baustein) record deck; (komplettes Gerät) record player; ~**teller** *der* turntable; ~**wechsler** *der* record changer

platter·dings *Adv.* (ugs.) absolutely

platt-, Platt-: ~**fisch** *der* flatfish; ~**form** *die* **1** platform; **2** (fig.: Basis) basic programme; (Wahlplattform) platform; [election] programme; **eine gemeinsame** ~**form** common ground; (bei Wahlen) a common platform; ~**fuß** *der* **1** flat foot; **2** (ugs.: Reifenpanne) flat (coll.); flat tyre; ~**füßig** *Adj.* flat-footed

Plattheit *die;* ~, ~**en** **1** flatness **2** (fig.) dullness **3** (Plattitüde) platitude

Plattitüde /platiˈtyːdə/ *die;* ~, ~**n** (geh.) platitude

Plätt·wäsche *die* (nordd., md.) laundry to be ironed; ironing

Platz /plat͜s/ *der;* ~**es**, **Plätze** /ˈplɛt͜sə/ **1** (freie Fläche) space; area; (Bau~, Ausstellungsgelände usw.) site; (umbaute Fläche) square; **ein freier** ~: an open space **2** (Park~) car park; [parking] lot (Amer.); (Camping~) [camp]site; [camp]ground (Amer.); (Schrott~, Lager~) yard **3** (Sport~) (ganze Anlage) ground; (Spielfeld) field; (Tennis~, Volleyball~ usw.) court; (Golf~) course; **der** ~ **ist nicht bespielbar** the ground is not playable; **einen Spieler vom** ~ **stellen/tragen** send/carry a player off [the field]; **auf eigenem/gegnerischem** ~ **spielen** play at home/away **4** (Stelle) place; spot; (Position) location; position; (wo jmd., etw. hingehört) place; **ein** ~ **an der Sonne** (fig.) a place in the sun; **auf die Plätze, fertig, los!** on your marks, get set, go!; **sich** (*Dat.*) **einen festen** ~ **in der Literatur erobern** become firmly established in literature; **am** *od.* **an seinem** ~: in its/his place; **nicht** *od.* **fehl am** ~**[e] sein** (fig.) be out of place; be inappropriate; **am** ~**[e] sein** (fig.) be appropriate; be called for **5** (Sitz~) seat; (am Tisch, Steh~ usw.; fig.: im Kurs, Krankenhaus, Kindergarten usw.) place; **der Bus/Saal hat 60 Plätze** the bus/hall will take 60 *or* has room for 60; **erster/zweiter** ~ (im Kino usw.) seat at the front/back; ~ **nehmen** sit down; **nehmen Sie** ~! take a seat; ~ **behalten** (geh.) remain seated **6** (bes. Sport: Platzierung) place; **auf** ~ **drei** *od.* **dem dritten** ~: in third place; **den dritten** ~ **belegen** come third; **der Song ist auf** ~ **eins/neun der Hitparade** the song is number one/nine in the hit parade **7** (Ort) place; locality; **am** ~: in the town/village; **das größte Hotel am** ~: the largest hotel in the place; **die Bedeutung des** ~**es Frankfurt** (bes. Wirtsch.) the importance of Frankfurt as a location **8** (Raum) space; room; **im Kofferraum ist kein** ~ **mehr** there is no room left in the boot (Brit.) *or* (Amer.) trunk; **er/es hat [noch]** ~/**keinen** ~: there is enough space *or* room [left] for him/it/no room for him/it; **es nimmt viel** ~ **weg** it takes up a lot of space; **drei Familien/500 Autos** (*Dat.*) ~ **bieten** have room for three families/500 cars; **der Saal bietet** ~ *od.* **hat** ~ **für 3 000 Personen** the hall takes *or* holds 3,000 people; **im Viktoriasee hätte ganz Irland** ~: the whole of Ireland could fit into Lake Victoria; **[jmdm./einer Sache]** ~ **machen** make room [for sb./sth.]; **macht doch mal ein bisschen** ~: clear a bit of space; (aufrücken) move up a bit; **einem neuen System** ~ **machen** give way to a new system; ~ **da!** make way!; out of the way!; ~ **greifen** (fig.) spread

Platz-: ~**angst** *die* **1** (volkst.: Klaustrophobie) claustrophobia; **2** (Med.) agoraphobia; ~**anweiser** *der;* ~~**s**, ~~: ► **❶ S. 113** usher; ~**anweiserin** *die;* ~~, ~~**nen** ► **❶ S. 113** usherette

Plätzchen /ˈplɛt͜sçən/ *das;* ~**s**, ~ **1** little place *or* spot; (kleiner Raum) little space **2** (Keks) biscuit (Brit.); cookie (Amer.); (Schokoladen~) [chocolate] pastille

platzen *itr. V.; mit sein* **1** burst; (explodieren) explode; **dem Boxer war eine Augenbraue geplatzt** one of the boxer's eyebrows had split open; **vor Wut/Spannung** (*Dat.*) ~ (fig.) be bursting with rage/excitement; **er ist vor Lachen fast geplatzt** he nearly died with laughter; *s. auch* **Neid** **2** (ugs.: scheitern) fall through; **geplatzt sein** ‹*concert, meeting, performance, holiday, engagement*› be off; **der Wechsel ist geplatzt** the bill has bounced (sl.); **etw.** ~ **lassen** put the kibosh on sth. (coll.); **der Betrug platzte** (ugs.) the plot collapsed; **einen Spionagering/eine Bande** ~ **lassen** bust a spy ring/a gang (coll.) **3** (ugs.: hinein~) **in eine Versammlung** ~: burst into a meeting

Platz·hirsch *der* (Jägerspr.) dominant stag; (fig. ugs.: beherrschende Figur) boss-type (coll.); **er ist hier der** ~: he's the big noise around here (coll.)

platzieren /plaˈt͜siːrən/
A *tr. V.* **1** place; position ‹*loudspeakers*›; **Polizisten an den Ausgängen** ~: post policemen by the exits **2** (Sport: gezielt werfen, schlagen usw.) place ‹*shot, ball*›; (Boxen, Fechten) land ‹*blow, hit*›; **ein platzierter Schuss** a well-aimed shot **3** (Wirtsch.: unterbringen, anlegen) place ‹*money*›
B *refl. V.* **1** (sich setzen) place *or* seat oneself (**auf** + *Akk. od. Dat.* on); (sich stellen) take up position (**an** + *Akk. od. Dat.* at, by) **2** (Sport) be placed; **er konnte sich nicht** ~: he was unplaced

Platzierung *die;* ~, ~**en** **1** (das Platzieren) placing; (auf Sitzplätze) seating; (das Aufstellen) positioning; (von Polizisten usw.) posting **2** (Sport) placing; place; **eine gute** ~/**gute** ~**en erreichen** be well placed

platz-, Platz-: ~**karte** *die* reserved-seat ticket; **sich** (*Dat.*) **eine** ~**karte bestellen** reserve a seat; ~**konzert** *das* open-air concert (*by a military or brass band*); ~**mangel** *der* lack of space; ~**miete** *die* **1** (auf Märkten, Messen usw.) pitch rent; **2** (Theater) [cost of a] season ticket (*for a particular seat*); **3** (Sport) ground hire charge; (Tennis) court hire charge; court fees *pl.*; ~**patrone** *die* blank [cartridge]; ~**raubend** *Adj.* wasting space *postpos., not pred.*; bulky; ~**raubend sein** take up a lot of space; **~regen** *der* downpour; cloudburst; **~sparend** **A** *Adj.* space-saving; **möglichst ~sparend** saving as much space as possible *postpos., not pred.*; **B** *adv.* economically; in a space-saving manner; **~verweis** *der* (Sport) sending-off; **einen ~verweis gegen jmdn. verhängen** order sb. off the field; **~vorteil** *der* (Sport) home advantage; **~wart** *der*; **~~[e]s, ~~e** (Sport) groundsman; **~wartin** *die*; **~~, ~~nen** groundswoman; **~wunde** *die* lacerated wound

Plauderei *die*; **~, ~en** chat

Plauderer *der*; **~s, ~, Plauderin** *die*; **~, ~nen** talker; conversationalist

plaudern /ˈplaudɐn/ *itr. V.* **1** chat (**über** + *Akk.*, **von** about); **nett ~:** have a nice chat **2** (etw. aus~) let on (coll.); **er plaudert** he doesn't keep his mouth shut (sl.)

Plauder·ton *der* conversational *or* chatty tone; **im ~:** in a conversational tone

Plausch /plauʃ/ *der*; **~[e]s, ~e** (bes. südd., österr.) cosy chat

plauschen *itr. V.* (bes. südd., österr.) chat; **miteinander ~:** have a chat

plausibel /plauˈziːbl/

A *Adj.* plausible; **jmdm. etw. ~ machen** make sth. seem convincing to sb.

B *adv.* plausibly

Plauze /ˈplautsə/ *die*; **~, ~n** (salopp, bes. ostmd.) **1** (Lunge) lung **2** (Bauch) belly; **auf der ~ liegen** (fig.) be laid up

Playback /ˈpleɪbɛk/ *das*; **~s, ~s** (Tontechnik) **1** (Aufnahme) pre-recorded version; recording; (Begleitung) [pre-recorded] backing **2** (Verfahren) (beim Fernsehen) miming to a recording; (bei Schallplatten) double-tracking

Play·boy /ˈpleɪbɔɪ/ *der* playboy

Plazenta /plaˈtsɛnta/ *die*; **~, ~s** *od.* **Plazenten** ▸ⓘ **S. 435** (Med.) placenta

Plazet /ˈplaːtsɛt/ *das*; **~s, ~s** (geh.) approval

***plazieren** *usw.* ▸**platzieren** *usw.*

Plebejer /pleˈbeːjɐ/ *der*; **~s, ~, Plebejerin** *die*; **~, ~nen** **1** (hist.) plebeian **2** (abwertend) common type

plebejisch

A *Adj.* **1** (hist.) plebeian **2** (abwertend) common

B *adv.* (abwertend) in a common manner

Plebiszit /plebɪsˈtsiːt/ *das*; **~[e]s, ~e** plebiscite

plebiszitär /plebɪstsiˈtɛːɐ/

A *Adj.* plebiscitary; ‹*decision, legislation, election*› by plebiscite

B *adv.* by plebiscite

Plebs¹ /plɛps/ *die*; **~** (hist.) plebs *pl.* (*of ancient Rome*)

Plebs² *der*; **~es** *od. österr.*: *die*; **~** (abwertend) **der ~:** common herd; the masses *pl.*

pleite /ˈplaitə/ (ugs.) *in* **~ sein** ‹*person*› be broke (coll.); ‹*company*› have gone bust (coll.); *s. auch* **Pleite 1**

Pleite *die*; **~, ~n** (ugs.) **1** (Bankrott) bankruptcy *no def. art.*; **vor der ~ stehen** be faced with bankruptcy; **~ machen** *od.* **gehen** go bust (coll.) **2** (Misserfolg) flop (sl.); washout (coll.)

Pleite·geier *der* (ugs.) spectre of bankruptcy; **den ~ vertreiben** chase the wolf from the door

Plejaden /pleˈjaːdn̩/ *Pl.* (Astron.) Pleiades

Plektron /ˈplɛktrɔn/ *das*; **~s, Plektren, Plektrum** /ˈplɛktrʊm/ *das*; **~s, Plektren** plectrum

plempern /ˈplɛmpɐn/ (ugs.)

A *tr. V.* sprinkle; spatter

B *itr. V.* potter

plemplem /plɛmˈplɛm/ *in* **~ sein** (ugs.) be nuts (coll.) *or* cuckoo (sl.); **ich bin doch nicht ~:** I'm not crazy

Plenar- /pleˈnaːɐ-/: **~saal** *der* plenary chamber; **~sitzung** *die* plenary session

Plenum /ˈpleːnʊm/ *das*; **~s** (Versammlung) plenary meeting; (Sitzung) plenary session

Pleonasmus /pleoˈnasmʊs/ *der*; **~, Pleonasmen** (Stilk.) pleonasm

pleonastisch /pleoˈnastɪʃ/ (Stilk.)

A *Adj.* pleonastic

B *adv.* pleonastically

Pleuel·stange /ˈplɔyəl-/ *die* (Technik) connecting rod

Plexi·glas Ⓦⓩ /ˈplɛksiglaːs/ *das* ≈ Perspex ®

plieren /ˈpliːrən/ *itr. V.* (nordd.) squint

plinkern /ˈplɪŋkɐn/ *itr. V.* (nordd.) blink

Plissee /plɪˈseː/ *das*; **~s, ~s** **1** (Falten) accordion pleats *pl.* **2** (Stoff) accordion-pleated material

Plissee·rock *der* accordion-pleated skirt

plissieren *tr. V.* pleat

PLO *Abk.* = **Palästinensische Befreiungsorganisation** PLO

Plombe /ˈplɔmbə/ *die*; **~, ~n** **1** (Siegel) [lead] seal **2** (veralt.: Zahnfüllung) filling

plombieren *tr. V.* **1** (versiegeln) seal **2** (veralt.) fill ‹*tooth*›

Plombierung *die*; **~, ~en** **1** (Versiegelung) sealing **2** (veralt.: das Füllen) filling

Plörre /ˈplœrə/ *die*; **~, ~n** (nordd. abwertend) dishwater (coll.)

Plot /plɔt/ *der*; **~s, ~s** (Literaturw.) plot

plötzlich /ˈplœtslɪç/

A *Adj.* sudden

B *adv.* suddenly; **~ aufragen** rise up abruptly; **..., aber etwas** *od.* **ein bisschen ~** (salopp) ..., and jump to it; ..., and make it snappy (coll.)

Plötzlichkeit *die*; **~:** suddenness

Pluder·hose /ˈpluːdɐ-/ *die* pantaloons *pl.*; (orientalischer Art) Turkish trousers *pl.*; (hist.) slops *pl.*

Plumeau /plyˈmoː/ *das*; **~s, ~s** duvet

plump /plʊmp/

A *Adj.* **1** (dick) plump; podgy; massive ‹*stone, lump*›; (unförmig) ungainly, clumsy ‹*shape*›; (rundlich) bulbous **2** (schwerfällig) awkward, clumsy ‹*movements, style*› **3** (abwertend: dreist) crude, blatant ‹*lie, deception, trick*›; (leicht durchschaubar) blatantly obvious; (unbeholfen) clumsy ‹*excuse, advances*›; crude ‹*joke, forgery*›; **~e Vertraulichkeit** embarrassing overfamiliarity

B *adv.* **1** (schwerfällig) clumsily; awkwardly **2** (abwertend: dreist) in a blatantly obvious manner; **~ gefälscht** crudely *or* clumsily forged

Plumpheit *die*; **~, ~en** **1** (Dicke) plumpness; podginess; (Unförmigkeit) ungainliness; clumsiness; (Rundlichkeit) bulbousness **2** (Schwerfälligkeit) clumsiness; awkwardness; (eines dicken Menschen) ponderousness **3** (abwertend: Dreistigkeit) blatant nature; (primitive Art) crudity; clumsiness

plumps *Interj.* bump; thud; (ins Wasser) splash; **~ machen** go bump

Plumps *der*; **~es, ~e** (ugs.) bump; thud; (ins Wasser) splash

plumpsen **1** *itr. V.* fall with a bump; thud; (ins Wasser) splash **2** *unpers.* **es plumpste** there was a thud *or* bump; (ins Wasser) there was a splash

Plumps·klo[sett] *das* (ugs.) earth closet

plump·vertraulich, plump·vertraulich

A *Adj.* overfamiliar; (bei Männern) hail-fellow-well-met

B *adv.* with excessive familiarity

Plunder /ˈplʊndɐ/ *der*; **~s** (ugs. abwertend) junk; rubbish

Plünderei *die*; **~, ~en** ▸**Plünderung**

Plünderer *der*; **~s, ~, Plünderin** *die*; **~, ~nen** looter

plündern /ˈplʏndɐn/ *itr., tr. V.* **1** loot; plunder, pillage ‹*town*› **2** (scherzh.: [fast] leeren) raid ‹*larder, fridge, account*›; ‹*bird, animal*› strip ‹*tree, border*›

Plünderung *die*; **~, ~en** looting; (einer Stadt) plundering; **~en** cases of looting/plundering

Plünnen *Pl.* (bes. nordd. ugs.: Kleider) gear *sing.* (coll.)

Plural /ˈpluːraːl/ *der*; **~s, ~e** **1** plural; **„Atlanten" ist [der] ~ von** *od.* **zu „Atlas"** 'Atlanten' is the plural of 'Atlas' **2** (Wort) word in the plural; plural form; **im ~ stehen** be [in the] plural

Pluraletantum /pluraleˈtantʊm/ *das*; **~s, Pluraliatantum** /pluraljaˈtantʊm/ plural-only noun

pluralisch (Sprachw.)

A *Adj.* plural ‹*form, ending*›; ‹*word, clause*› in the plural

B *adv.* in the plural

Pluralismus *der*; **~:** pluralism

pluralistisch

A *Adj.* pluralistic

B *adv.* pluralistically; along pluralistic lines

plus /plʊs/

A *Konj.* ▸ⓘ **S. 826** (Math.) plus

B *Adv.* **1** ▸ⓘ **S. 703** (bes. Math.) plus **2** (Elektrot.) positive

C *Präp. mit Dat.* (Kaufmannsspr.) plus

Plus *das*; **~** **1** (Überschuss) surplus; (auf einem Konto) credit balance; **~ machen** make a profit; **im ~ sein** be in credit **2** (Vorteil) advantage; [extra] asset; **das ist ein ~ für dich** it's a point in your favour

Plüsch /plyːʃ/ *der*; **~[e]s, ~e** plush

Plüsch-: ~sessel *der* plush chair; **~sofa** *das* plush sofa; **~tier** *das* cuddly toy

Plus-: ~pol *der* (Physik) positive pole; (einer Batterie) positive terminal; **~punkt** *der* **1** [plus] point; **2** ▸**Plus 2**; **~punkte sammeln** strengthen one's/its position; (sich beliebt machen) gain brownie points

Plusquam·perfekt /ˈplʊskvampɛrfɛkt/ *das* pluperfect [tense]

plustern /ˈpluːstɐn/

A *tr. V.* ruffle [up] ‹*feathers*›

B *refl. V.* ‹*bird*› ruffle [up] its feathers

Plus·zeichen *das* plus sign

Pluto¹ /ˈpluːto/ *der*; **~** (Astron.), **Pluto²** (*der*) (Myth.) Pluto

Plutokrat /plutoˈkraːt/ *der*; **~en, ~en** (geh. abwertend) plutocrat

Plutokratie /plutokraˈtiː/ *die*; **~, ~n** (geh. abwertend) plutocracy

Plutokratin *die*; **~, ~nen** ▸**Plutokrat**

Plutonium /pluˈtoːni̯ʊm/ *das*; **~s** (Physik) plutonium

PLZ *Abk.* = **Postleitzahl**

Pneu /pnɔy/ *der*; **~s, ~s** (bes. österr., schweiz.) tyre

Pneumatik¹ /pnɔyˈmaːtɪk/ *die*; **~, ~en** **1** pneumatics *sing., no art.* **2** (Anlage) pneumatic system

Pneumatik² *der*; **~s, ~s,** (österr.:) *die*; **~, ~en** (österr., schweiz., veralt.) tyre

pneumatisch (Technik)

A *Adj.* pneumatic

B *adv.* pneumatically

Po /poː/ *der*; **~s, ~s** (ugs.) bottom

Po·backe *die* (ugs.) buttock

Pöbel /ˈpøːbl̩/ *der*; **~s** (abwertend) rabble

pöbelhaft (abwertend)

A *Adj.* loutish; uncouth

B *adv.* in a loutish manner

Pöbel·herrschaft *die* mob rule

pöbeln *itr. V.* make rude *or* coarse remarks

pochen /ˈpɔxn̩/ *itr. V.* **1** (meist geh.: klopfen) knock (**gegen** at, on); (kräftig) rap; thump; **an die Tür ~:** knock at *or* on the door; **es pocht** somebody is knocking at *or* on the door **2** (geh.: sich berufen) **auf etw.** (*Akk.*) **~:** insist on sth. **3** (geh.: pulsieren) ‹*heart*› pound, thump; ‹*blood*› pound, throb

pochieren /pɔˈʃiːrən/ *tr. V.* (Kochk.) poach

Pocke /ˈpɔkə/ *die*; **~, ~n** pock

Pocken *Pl.* ▸ⓘ **S. 439** smallpox *sing.*

pocken-, Pocken-: ~narbe *die* pockmark; **~narbig** *Adj.* pockmarked; **~schutz·impfung** *die* smallpox vaccination

pockig *Adj.* pockmarked ‹*face, surface*›; pimpled ‹*leather*›

Podest /poˈdɛst/ *das od. der*; **~[e]s, ~e** **1** rostrum **2** (bes. nordd.: Treppenabsatz) landing

Podex *der*; **~[es], ~e** (fam.) bottom; behind

Podium /'po:dịum/ *das;* **~s, Podien** 1 (Plattform) platform; (Bühne) stage 2 (trittartige Erhöhung) rostrum; podium

Podiums·diskussion *die,* **Podiums·gespräch** *das* panel discussion

Po·ebene *die* (Geogr.) plain of the River Po

Poem /po'e:m/ *das;* **~s, ~e** (veralt.) poem

Poesie /poe'zi:/ *die;* **~, ~n** 1 poetry; **ein Abend voller ~:** an evening full of magic 2 (Gedicht) poem

Poesie·album *das* autograph album (*with verses or sayings contributed by friends*)

Poet /po'e:t/ *der;* **~en, ~en** (veralt.) poet; bard (literary)

Poetik /po'e:tɪk/ *die;* **~, ~en** 1 poetics *sing.* 2 (Lehrbuch) treatise on poetry

Poetin *die;* **~, ~nen** poetess; poet; bard (literary)

poetisch
A *Adj.* poetic[al]
B *adv.* poetically

pofen /'po:fn̩/ *itr. V.* (nordd. salopp) kip (Brit. coll.); snooze (coll.)

Pogo /'po:go/ *der;* **~s, ~s** pogo; **~ tanzen** pogo-dance

Pogrom /po'gro:m/ *das od. der;* **~s, ~e** pogrom

Pogrom-: **~hetze** *die* hate campaign (leading up to a pogrom); **~stimmung** *die* bloodthirsty mood

Pointe /'pọɛ̃:tə/ *die;* **~, ~n** (eines Witzes) punch line; (einer Geschichte) point; (eines Sketches) curtain line; **die ~ verderben** spoil the effect of the story/joke; **eine überraschende ~:** a surprising twist

pointiert /pọɛ̃'ti:ɐ̯t/
A *Adj.* pointed ‹*remark*›
B *adv.* pointedly

Pokal /po'ka:l/ *der;* **~s, ~e** 1 (Trinkgefäß) goblet 2 (Siegestrophäe, ~wettbewerb) cup

Pokal-: **~sieger** *der,* **~siegerin** *die* (Sport) cup winner; (Mannschaft) cup winners *pl.* **~spiel** *das* (Sport) cup tie; **~wettbewerb** *der* (Sport) cup competition

Pökel-: **~fleisch** *das* salt meat; **~hering** *der* salt herring

pökeln /'pø:kl̩n/ *tr. V.* salt

Poker /'po:kɐ/ *das od. der;* **~s** poker; (fig.) manoeuvrings *pl.*

Poker-: **~gesicht** *das* poker face; **ein ~gesicht machen** put on a poker-faced expression; **~miene** *die* poker face

pokern *itr. V.* 1 (Poker spielen) play poker 2 (fig.) **um etw. ~:** bid for sth.

Pol /po:l/ *der;* **~s, ~e** pole; **der ruhende ~** (fig.) the calming influence

Polack /po'lak/ *der;* **~en, ~en, Polacke** *der;* **~n, ~n** (ugs. abwertend) [dirty (derog.)] Pole

polar /po'la:ɐ̯/ *Adj.* 1 polar 2 (gegensätzlich) diametrically opposed; **~e Gegensätze** complete *or* polar opposites

Polar-: **~eis** *das* polar ice; **~expedition** *die* polar expedition; **~front** *die* (Met.) polar front; **~fuchs** *der* Arctic fox

Polarisation /polariza'tsi̯o:n/ *die;* **~, ~en** polarization

polarisieren
A *tr. V.* (Chemie, Physik) polarize
B *refl. V.* (in Gegensätzen hervortreten) become polarized

Polarisierung *die;* **~, ~en** (auch Chemie, Physik) polarization

Polarität *die;* **~, ~en** (auch Geogr., Astron., Physik) polarity

Polar-: **~kreis** *der* polar circle; **nördlicher/südlicher ~kreis** Arctic/Antarctic Circle; **~licht** *das; Pl.* **~er** aurora; polar lights *pl.*

Polaroid·kamera Ⓦ /polaro'i:t-/ *die* Polaroid camera ®

Polar-: **~station** *die* polar [research] station; **~stern** *der* polar star; pole star; **~zone** *die* frigid zone; polar region

Polder *der;* **~s, ~:** polder

Pole *der;* **~n, ~n** ▸ **S. 520** Pole

Polemik /po'le:mɪk/ *die;* **~, ~en** polemic; **ein Pamphlet voller ~:** a pamphlet full of polemics

polemisch
A *Adj.* polemic[al]
B *adv.* polemically

polemisieren *itr. V.* polemize

polen *tr. V.* (Physik, Elektrot.) connect; **auf diesem Sektor sind Paris und Bonn nicht gleich gepolt** (fig.) in this area Paris and Bonn hold different views

Polen (*das*); **~s** Poland; **noch ist ~ nicht verloren** (fig.) all is not [yet] lost; **da/dann ist ~ offen** (fig.) all hell is/will be let loose

Polente /po'lɛntə/ *die;* **~** (salopp) cops *pl.* (coll.)

Poleposition, *Pole-position /'poul pəzɪʃən/ *die;* **~:** pole position

Police /po'li:sə/ *die;* **~, ~n** (Versicherungsw.) policy

Polier /po'li:ɐ̯/ *der;* **~s, ~e** [site] foreman

polieren *tr. V.* polish; (fig.) polish up; **jmdm. die Fresse ~** (derb) smash sb.'s face in

Polier-: **~mittel** *das* polish; **~tuch** *das; Pl.* **~tücher** polishing cloth

-polig /'po:lɪç/ *adj.* **ein~/drei~/mehr~:** single-/three-/multi-pin

Poli·klinik *die* outpatients' department *or* clinic

Polin *die;* **~, ~nen** ▸ **S. 520** Pole; *s. auch* **-in**

Polio /'po:li̯o/ *die;* **~:** polio

Polit- political; **~blatt** politically oriented publication

Polit·büro *das* politburo

Politesse /poli'tɛsə/ *die;* **~, ~n** [woman] traffic warden

Politik /poli'ti:k/ *die;* **~, ~en** 1 politics *sing., no art.*; **eine gemeinsame/neue ~:** a common/new policy 2 (eine spezielle ~) policy; **eine ~ der kleinen Schritte** a gradualist policy 3 (Taktik) tactics *pl.*

Politika ▸ **Politikum**

Politiker /po'li:tikɐ/ *der;* **~s, ~, Politikerin** *die;* **~, ~nen** ▸ **S. 113** politician

Politikum /po'li:tikum/ *das;* **~s, Politika** political issue; (Ereignis) political event

politik-, Politik-: **~verdrossen** *Adj.* disenchanted with politics *postpos.*; tired of politics *postpos.*; **~verdrossenheit** *die* disenchantment with politics; **~wissenschaft** *die* political science *no art.*

politisch
A *Adj.* 1 political 2 (klug u. berechnend) politic
B *adv.* 1 politically 2 (klug u. berechnend) politicly; judiciously

-politisch *adj., adv.* concerning … policy

Politische *der/die; adj. Dekl.* (ugs.) political prisoner

politisieren
A *itr. V.* talk politics; politicize; **es wurde viel politisiert** there was a great deal of political discussion
B *tr. V.* 1 (politisch aktivieren) make politically active 2 (politisch behandeln) politicize

Politisierung *die;* **~:** politicization

Politologe /polito'lo:gə/ *der;* **~n, ~n** political scientist

Politologie *die;* **~:** political science *no art.*

Politologin *die;* **~, ~nen** political scientist

politologisch *Adj.* ‹*analysis*› in terms of political science; ‹*sense*› of political science; **~es Studium** political studies *pl.*

Politur /poli'tu:ɐ̯/ *die;* **~, ~en** polish

Polizei /poli'tsai̯/ *die;* **~, ~en** 1 police *pl.*; **er ist** *od.* **arbeitet bei der ~:** he is in the police force 2 (Dienststelle) police station

Polizei-: **~angabe** *die:* **nach** *od.* **laut ~angabe[n]/~angaben zufolge** according to police reports; **~apparat** *der* police force; **~aufgebot** *das* police contingent; **trotz überdurchschnittlichen ~aufgebots** despite the larger than average police presence; **~auto** *das* police car; **~beamte** *der,* **~beamtin** *die* ▸ **S. 113** police officer; **~behörde** *die* police authority; **~chef** *der,* **~chefin** *die* chief of police; chief constable (Brit.); **~direktion** *die* police authority; **~einsatz** *der* police operation; **~eskorte** *die* police escort; **~funk** *der* police radio; **~gewahrsam** *der* [police] custody; **~gewalt** *die* 1 (Machtbefugnis) police powers *pl.*; 2 (ausgeübte Gewalt) use of force by the police; **~gewerkschaft** *die* police trade union; **~griff** *der* [police] arm hold *or* lock; **er wurde im ~griff abgeführt** he was frogmarched away; **~hund** *der* police dog; **~knüppel** *der* [policeman's] truncheon; **~kommissar,** (südd., österr., schweiz.) **~kommissär** *der,* **~kommissarin,** (südd., österr., schweiz.) **~kommissärin** *die* ≈ [police] superintendent; **~kontrolle** *die* police check; (Kontrollpunkt) police checkpoint; **~kräfte** *Pl.* police *pl.*

polizeilich
A *Adj.* police; **~e Meldepflicht** obligation to register with the police
B *adv.* by the police; **~ verboten** prohibited by order of the police

polizei-, Polizei-: **~methoden** *Pl.* (abwertend) **das sind ja ~methoden!** that is sheer brutality *sing.*; **~präsident** *der,* **~präsidentin** *die* chief of police; chief constable (Brit.); **~präsidium** *das* police headquarters *sing. or pl.*; **~revier** *das* 1 (~dienststelle) police station; **sich auf dem ~revier melden** report to the police; 2 (Bezirk) police district; **~schutz** *der* police protection; **~sirene** *die* [police car] siren; **~spitzel** *der* police informer; **~staat** *der* police state; **~streife** *die* police patrol; **~stunde** *die* closing time; **die ~stunde verlängern** extend the opening hours *pl.*; **die ~stunde aufheben** waive the restrictions on opening hours *pl.*; **~verordnung** *die* police regulation; **~wache** *die* police station; **~widrig** A *Adj.* against police regulations *postpos.*; illegal; B *adv.* against police regulations; illegally

Polizist /poli'tsɪst/ *der;* **~en, ~en** ▸ **S. 113** policeman

Polizistin *die;* **~, ~nen** ▸ **S. 113** policewoman

Polka /'pɔlka/ *die;* **~, ~s** polka

Pollen /'pɔlən/ *der;* **~s, ~** (Bot.) pollen

Pollen·flug *der:* **bei ~:** when the pollen level is high/when pollen levels are high; **hier herrscht so gut wie kein ~:** pollen levels here are very low; **ein schwacher/starker ~:** a low/high pollen count *or* level

Poller *der;* **~s, ~:** bollard

Pollution /pɔlu'tsi̯o:n/ *die;* **~, ~en** (Med.) [nocturnal] emission

polnisch /'pɔlnɪʃ/ *Adj.* ▸ **S. 520,** ▸ **S. 670** Polish; **eine ~e Wirtschaft** (ugs. abwertend) a shambles; *s. auch* **deutsch; Deutsch; Deutsche**[2]

Polo /'po:lo/ *das;* **~s** polo

Polo·hemd *das,* **Polo·shirt** *das* polo shirt

Polonaise, Polonäse /polo'nɛ:zə/ *die;* **~, ~n** polonaise

Polster /'pɔlstɐ/ *das od.* (österr.) *der;* **~s, ~** *od.* (österr.) **Pölster** /'pœlstɐ/ 1 (~ung) upholstery *no pl., no indef. art.* 2 (Schulter~) [shoulder] pad 3 (Rücklage) reserves *pl.* 4 (Bot.) cushion 5 (österr.: Kissen) cushion; (Kopfkissen) pillow

Pölsterchen *das;* **~s, ~:** bulge of fat

Polsterer *der;* **~s, ~** ▸ **S. 113** upholsterer

Polster·garnitur *die* suite

Polsterin *die;* **~, ~nen** ▸ **Polsterer**

Polster·möbel *das* piece of upholstered furniture; **teure ~:** expensive upholstered furniture *sing.*

polstern *tr. V.* upholster ‹*furniture*›; pad ‹*door*›; **sie ist gut gepolstert** (fig. ugs. scherzh.) she is well-upholstered (joc.); **finanziell gut gepolstert sein** (fig. ugs. scherzh.) be comfortably off

Polster-: **~sessel** *der* [upholstered] armchair; easy chair; **~stuhl** *der* upholstered chair; **~tür** *die* padded door

Polsterung *die;* **~, ~en** 1 (Polster) upholstery *no pl.; no indef. art.* 2 (das Polstern) upholstering

P

Polter·abend *der; party on the eve of a wedding (at which crockery is smashed to bring good luck)*

Polterabend

This is Germany's equivalent of stag and hen nights. The *Polterabend* usually takes place a few days before the wedding and takes the form of a large party for the family and friends of both bride and groom. Traditionally, the guests smash some crockery, as this is supposed to bring good luck to the couple.

Polter·geist *der* poltergeist

poltern /'pɔltɐn/
A *itr. V.* **1** (lärmen) crash *or* thump about; **es polterte** there is a bang *or* crash; **ein ~der Lärm** a din *or* racket **2** *mit sein* (sich laut bewegen) **der Karren polterte über das Pflaster** the cart clattered over the cobblestones; **er kam ins Zimmer gepoltert** he came clumping into the room **3** (schimpfen) rant [and rave] **4** (ugs.: Polterabend feiern) hold a *Polterabend*
B *tr. V.* **„Ruhe!", polterte er** 'Be quiet!' he bawled

poly-, Poly- /poly-/ poly-

poly-, Poly-: ~eder /-'|eːdɐ/ *das; ~~s, ~~* (Geom.) polyhedron; **~ester** /-'|ɛstɐ/ *der* (Chemie) polyester; **~gam** /-'gaːm/ **A** *Adj.* polygamous; **B** *adv.* polygamously; **~gamie** /-ga'miː/ *die; ~~:* polygamy; **~glott** /-'glɔt/ *Adj.* polyglot

Polynesien /poly'neːzi̯ən/ *(das);* **~s** Polynesia

polynesisch *Adj.* Polynesian

Polyp /po'lyːp/ *der;* **~en, ~en 1** ▸ **S. 439** (Zool., Med.) polyp **2** (salopp: Polizist) cop (coll.); copper (Brit. coll.) **3** (veralt.: Krake) octopus

poly-, Poly-: ~phonie /-fo'niː/ *die; ~~* (Musik) polyphony; **~technik** *die* (DDR), **~technikum** *das* polytechnic; **~technisch A** *Adj.* polytechnic; **B** *adv.* **er war ~technisch ausgebildet** he had a polytechnic training

Pomade /po'maːdə/ *die;* **~, ~n** pomade; hair cream

pomadig
A *Adj.* **1** pomaded; greased down; (fig.) overslick **2** (bes. nordd.: blasiert) blasé **3** (ugs.: langsam) sluggish
B *adv.* **1** (bes. nordd.: blasiert) in a blasé way **2** (ugs.: langsam) sluggishly

Pomeranze /pomə'rant͜sə/ *die;* **~, ~n** Seville *or* sour *or* bitter orange

Pommer *der;* **~n, ~n, Pommerin** *die;* **~, ~nen** Pomeranian

Pommern *(das);* **~s** Pomerania

Pommes frites /pɔm'frit/ *Pl.* chips *pl.* (Brit.); French fries *pl.* (Amer.)

Pomp /pɔmp/ *der;* **~[e]s** pomp

Pompeji /pɔm'peːji/ *(das);* **~s** ▸ **S. 675** Pompeii

pomphaft, pompös /pɔm'pøːs/
A *Adj.* grandiose; ostentatious
B *adv.* grandiosely; ostentatiously

Poncho /'pɔnt͜ʃo/ *der;* **~s, ~s** poncho

Pond /pɔnt/ *das;* **~s, ~** (Physik) gram-force

Pontifikal- /pɔntifi'kaːl-/: **~amt** *das,* **~messe** *die* (kath. Kirche) Pontifical Mass

Pontifikat /pɔntifi'kaːt/ *das od. der;* **~[e]s, ~e** (kath. Kirche) pontificate

Pontius /'pɔnt͜si̯ʊs/ *in* **von ~ zu Pilatus laufen** (ugs.) rush from pillar to post

Ponton /põ'tõː/ *der;* **~s, ~s** pontoon

Pony[1] /'pɔni/ *das;* **~s, ~s** pony

Pony[2] *der;* **~s, ~s** (Frisur) fringe

Pony·frisur *die* [hairstyle with a] fringe

Pool /puːl/ *der;* **~s, ~s** (Wirtsch.) pool

Pool·billard *das* pool

Pop /pɔp/ *der;* **~[s]** pop

Popanz *der;* **~es, ~e 1** (abwertend) bogey; bugbear; (willenloser Mensch) puppet **2** (veralt.: Schreckgestalt) scarecrow

Pop-Art /'pɔp|aːɐ̯t/ *die;* **~:** pop art

Popcorn /'pɔpkɔrn/ *das;* **~s** popcorn

Pope *der;* **~n, ~n** (abwertend) cleric

Popel /'poːpl̩/ *der;* **~s, ~** (ugs.) **1** bogey (sl.) **2** (abwertend: Mensch) nobody

popelig (ugs. abwertend)
A *Adj.* crummy (coll.); lousy (coll.); (durchschnittlich) second-rate
B *adv.* crummily (sl.)

Popelin /popə'liːn/ *der;* **~s, ~e, Popeline** *der;* **~s, ~** *od. die;* **~, ~** poplin

Popeline·mantel *der* poplin coat

popeln *itr. V.* (ugs.) **[in der Nase] ~:** pick one's nose

Pop-: ~farbe *die* brilliant colour; **~festival** *das* pop festival; **~gruppe** *die* pop group; **~konzert** *das* pop concert; **~kultur** *die* pop culture

poplig ▸ **popelig**

Pop·musik *die* pop music

Popo /po'poː/ *der;* **~s, ~s** (fam.) bottom

Popo·scheitel *der* (ugs. scherzh.) straight middle *or* centre parting

Popper /'pɔpɐ/ *der;* **~s, ~, Popperin** *die;* **~, ~nen** *fashion-conscious, apolitical young person*

poppig /'pɔpɪç/
A *Adj.* trendy
B *adv.* trendily

Pop·star *der* pop star

populär /popu'lɛːɐ̯/
A *Adj.* popular (**bei** with); **in ~em Deutsch** in German which is comprehensible to the layman
B *adv.* popularly; **etw. ~ ausdrücken** express sth. in layman's language

popularisieren *tr. V.* popularize

Popularisierung *die;* **~, ~en** popularization

Popularität *die;* **~:** popularity

populär·wissenschaftlich
A *Adj.* popular science *attrib.;* **zu ~ sein** be too much on the popular-science level
B *adv.* in a popular scientific way

Population *die;* **~, ~en** population

Populismus *der;* **~:** populism *no art.*

Populist *der;* **~en, ~en, Populistin** *die;* **~, ~nen** populist

Pop-up- /-|ap-/: **~-Fenster** *das* (DV) pop-up window; **~-Menü** *das* (DV) pop-up menu

Pore /'poːrə/ *die;* **~, ~n** pore

poren·tief (Werbespr.)
A *Adj.* deep-down
B *adv.* pore-deep

porig *Adj.* porous

Porno /'pɔrno/ *der;* **~s, ~s** (ugs.) **1** (~graphie) porn[o] (coll.) **2** (~film, ~heft usw.) porn[o] film/magazine *etc.*

porno-, Porno-: ~film *der* (ugs.) porn[o] film (coll.); **~graphie** /--'-/ *die* pornography; **~graphisch** /-'--/ **A** *Adj.* pornographic; **B** *adv.* pornographically

porös /po'røːs/ porous

Porosität /porozi'tɛːt/ *die;* **~:** porousness

Porphyr /'pɔrfyːɐ̯/ *der;* **~s, ~e** /pɔr'fyːrə/ (Geol.) porphyry

Porree /'pɔre/ *der;* **~s, ~s** leek; **ich mag ~:** I like leeks

Portal /pɔr'taːl/ *das;* **~s, ~e** (auch DV) portal

Portefeuille /pɔrt(ə)'føːj/ *das;* **~s, ~s** (geh. veralt.) wallet

Portemonnaie /pɔrtmɔ'neː/ *das;* **~s, ~s** purse

Porti *Pl.* ▸ **Porto**

Portier /pɔr'ti̯eː/ *der;* **~s, ~s,** *österr.:* /pɔr'tiːɐ̯/ *der;* **~s, ~e** ▸ **S. 113 1** (Pförtner) porter. **2** (veralt.: Hausmeister) caretaker; **stiller ~** (bes. berlin.) list of tenants' names

portieren *tr. V.* (schweiz.) put up; nominate

Portiers·frau *die* **1** porter **2** (Frau des Portiers) porter's wife

Portier[s]·loge *die* porter's lodge

Portion /pɔr'tsi̯oːn/ *die;* **~, ~en 1** (beim Essen) portion; helping; **eine halbe ~** (fig. ugs. spött.) a feeble little titch (coll.); **eine ~ Eis** one ice cream; **eine zweite ~:** a second helping **2** (ugs.: Anteil) amount; **eine große ~ Geduld** a fair amount of patience

portionieren *tr. V.* divide into portions

portions·weise *Adv.* in portions

Porto /'pɔrto/ *das;* **~s, ~s** *od.* **Porti** postage (**für** on, for); **„~ zahlt Empfänger"** 'postage will be paid by licensee'

porto-, Porto-: ~frei *Adj.* post-free; **~kasse** *die* (Wirtsch.) cash box (*for postal expenses*); **~pflichtig** *Adj.* liable *or* subject to postage *postpos.*

Porträt /pɔr'trɛː/ *das;* **~s, ~s** portrait; **jmdm. ~ sitzen** sit for sb. [for a portrait]

Porträt: ~aufnahme *die* portrait [photograph]; **~fotograf** *der,* **~fotografin** *die* portrait photographer

porträtieren /pɔrtrɛ'tiːrən/ *tr. V.* paint a portrait of/take a portrait [photograph] of; (fig.) portray

Porträtist *der;* **~en, ~en, Porträtistin** *die;* **~, ~nen** portrait painter/portrait photographer; portraitist

Portugal /'pɔrtugal/ *(das);* **~s** Portugal

Portugiese /pɔrtu'giːzə/ *der;* **~n, ~n, Portugiesin** *die;* **~, ~nen** ▸ **S. 520** Portuguese; *s. auch* **-in**

portugiesisch *Adj.* ▸ **S. 520,** ▸ **S. 670** Portuguese; *s. auch* **deutsch; Deutsch; Deutsche**[2]

Portwein /'pɔrtvai̯n/ *der* port

Porzellan /pɔrt͜sɛ'laːn/ *das;* **~s, ~e 1** porcelain; china; **~ zerschlagen** (fig. ugs.) cause a lot of harm *or* trouble **2** (Gegenstand aus ~) piece of porcelain *or* china

Porzellan-: ~erde *die* china clay; kaolin; **~geschirr** *das* china [crockery]; **~laden** *der; Pl.* **~läden** china shop; *s. auch* **Elefant**

pos. *Abk.* = **positiv** pos.

Posaune /po'zau̯nə/ *die;* **~, ~n** trombone; **die ~n von Jericho** the trumpets of Jericho

posaunen
A *itr. V.* (musizieren) play the trombone
B *tr. V.* (ugs. abwertend) **1** (hinaus~) **etw. in die** *od.* **alle Welt ~:** tell the whole world about sth. **2** (laut sprechen) bellow; bawl

Posaunen-: ~chor *der* brass ensemble; **~engel** *der* **1** (Kunst) angel with a trumpet; **2** (ugs. scherzh.) chubby-cheeks *sing.*

Posaunist *der;* **~en, ~en, Posaunistin** *die;* **~, ~nen** ▸ **S. 113** trombonist

Pose /'poːzə/ *die;* **~, ~n** pose

Posemuckel /poːzə'mʊkl̩/ *(das);* **~s** (salopp abwertend) the back of beyond

posieren *itr. V.* pose

Position /pozi'tsi̯oːn/ *die;* **~, ~en 1** position; **in gesicherter ~ sein** have a secure position **2** (Wirtsch.: einzelner Posten) item

Positions-: ~lampe *die,* **~licht** *das* (Seew., Flugw.) navigation light; **~wechsel** *der* change of position *or* attitude

positiv /'poːzitiːf/
A *Adj.* positive; **~e Zahlen** (Math.) positive *or* plus numbers; **ist es schon ~, dass ...?** (ugs.) is it definite *or* certain that ...?
B *adv.* positively; **einen Antrag ~ bescheiden** accept an application; **einer Sache** (*Dat.*) **~ gegenüberstehen** take a positive view of a matter; **etw. ~ beeinflussen** have a positive influence on sth.; **etw. ~ bewerten** judge sth. favourably; **der Test verlief ~:** the test proved successful; **ich weiß das ~** (ugs.) I know that for certain *or* for sure; **sich ~ verändern** change for the better

Positiv[1] *der;* **~s, ~e** (Sprachw.) positive

Positiv[2] *das;* **~s, ~e 1** (Fot.) positive **2** (kleine Orgel) positive organ

Positiva ▸ **Positivum**

Positivismus *der;* **~:** positivism *no art.*

positivistisch *Adj.* positivist[ic]

Positivum /'poːzitiːvʊm/ *das;* **~s, Positiva** (geh.) positive aspect

Positron /'poːzitrɔn/ *das;* **~s, Positronen** (Physik) positron

Positur /pozi'tuːɐ̯/ *die;* **~, ~en 1** pose; posture; **sich in ~ setzen** *od.* **stellen** *od.* **werfen**

(ugs. leicht spött.) strike a pose; take up a posture 2 (Sport) stance; **in ~ gehen/sein** take up/have taken up one's stance

Posse /ˈpɔsə/ *die;* ~, ~n farce

Possen *der;* ~s, ~ (veralt.) 1 *Pl.* pranks; tricks; ~ **reißen** play tricks 2 **jmdm. einen ~ spielen** play a prank *or* trick on sb.

Possen·reißer *der,* **Possen·reißerin** *die;* ~, ~nen clown; buffoon

possessiv /ˈpɔsɛsiːf/ *Adj.* (Sprachw.) possessive

Possessiv *das;* ~s, ~e, **Possessiv·pronomen** *das,* **Possessivum** /pɔseˈsiːvʊm/ *das;* ~s, **Possessiva** (Sprachw.) possessive pronoun

possierlich /pɔˈsiːɐ̯lɪç/

A *Adj.* sweet; cute (Amer.)

B *adv.* sweetly; cutely (Amer.)

Post /pɔst/ *die;* ~, ~en 1 post (Brit.); mail; **er ist** *od.* **arbeitet bei der** ~: he works for the Post Office; **etw. mit der** *od.* **per ~ schicken** send sth. by post *or* mail; **ist ~ für mich da?** is there any post *or* mail for me?; **sonntags kommt** *od.* **gibt es keine ~**: there is no post *or* delivery on Sundays; **mit gleicher ~**: by the same post; **mit getrennter ~**: under separate cover; **auf [die] ~ warten** (ugs.) wait for [the] post; *s. auch* **ab B 2** 2 (~amt) post office; **auf die** *od.* **zur ~ gehen** go to the post office 3 (veralt.: ~kutsche) mail [coach] 4 (~bus) post [office] bus 5 (veralt.: Botschaft) news *sing.*

Post

▸ Deutsche Post

postalisch /pɔsˈtaːlɪʃ/ *Adj.* postal; **auf ~em Wege** by post

Postament /pɔstaˈmɛnt/ *das;* ~[e]s, ~e pedestal

Post-: ~**amt** *das* post office; ~**anschrift** *die* postal address; ~**anweisung** *die* 1 (Geldsendung) *remittance paid in at a post office and delivered to the addressee by a postman;* 2 (Formular) postal remittance form; ~**auto** *das* post office *or* mail van; ~**beamte** *der,* ~**beamtin** *die* ▸ⓘ **S. 113** post office official; ~**bote** *der* (ugs.) postman (Brit.); mailman (Amer.); ~**botin** *die* (ugs.) postwoman (Brit.); mailwoman (Amer.); ~**bus** *der* post [office] bus

Pöstchen /ˈpœstçən/ *das;* ~s, ~ (abwertend) little job *or* number (coll.)

Post·dienst *der* 1 post office; **ein Beamter im ~**: a post office official 2 (die Post) postal service 3 (Service der Post) postal service

Posten /ˈpɔstn̩/ *der;* ~s, ~ 1 (bes. Milit.: Wach~) post; **auf dem ~ sein** (ugs.) (in guter körperlicher Verfassung sein) be in good form; (wachsam sein) be on one's guard; **sich nicht [ganz] auf dem ~ fühlen** (ugs.) be a bit under the weather (coll.); **auf verlorenem ~ stehen** *od.* **kämpfen** be fighting a losing battle 2 (bes. Milit.: Wachmann) sentry; guard; ~ **stehen** *od.* (Soldatenspr.:) **schieben** stand guard *or* sentry 3 (Anstellung) post; position; job 4 (Funktion) position 5 (bes. Kaufmannsspr.: Rechnungs~) item 6 (bes. Kaufmannsspr.: Waren~) quantity

Posten-: ~**dienst** *der* (bes. Milit.) guard duty; ~**jäger** *der,* ~**jägerin** *die* (salopp) careerist

Poster /ˈpoːstɐ/ *das od. der;* ~s, ~[s] poster

post-, Post-: ~**fach** *das* 1 ▸ⓘ **S. 143** (im ~amt) post office *or* PO box; 2 (im Büro, Hotel o. Ä.) pigeon-hole; ~**flugzeug** *das* mail plane; ~**frisch** *Adj.* (Philat.) in mint condition *postpos.;* ~**gebühr** *die* [postal] charge *or* rate; ~**geheimnis** *das* secrecy of the post; ~**gewerkschaft** *die* post office workers' union; ~**giro·amt** *das* post office giro office; ≈ National Giro[bank] centre (Brit.); ~**giro·konto** *das* post office giro account; ≈ National Giro[bank] account (Brit.); ~**horn** *das* post horn

posthum /pɔstˈhuːm/ ▸ **postum**

postieren *tr. V.* 1 (aufstellen) post; station; **sich ~**: station *or* position oneself 2 (stellen) position

Postille /pɔsˈtɪlə/ *die;* ~, ~n (spött. abwertend) (Zeitschrift) mag (coll.); (Zeitung) rag (derog.)

Postillion /pɔstɪlˈjoːn/ *der;* ~s, ~e (veralt.) mail coach driver

Postillon d'Amour /pɔstijõdaˈmuːr/ *der;* ~ ~, ~s ~ (scherzh.) go-between

post-, Post-: ~**karte** *die* postcard; ~**karten·größe** *die* postcard size; **in ~kartengröße** postcard-sized; ~**kasten** *der* (bes. nordd.) postbox; mail box (Amer.); pillar box (Brit.); ~**kunde** *der,* ~**kundin** *die* post office user; ~**kutsche** *die* mail coach; ~**lagernd** *Adj., adv.* poste restante; general delivery (Amer.); ~**leit·zahl** *die* ▸ⓘ **S. 143** postcode; postal code; Zip code (Amer.); ~**minister** *der,* ~**ministerin** *die* Postmaster General; ~**modern** A *Adj.* postmodern[ist] ‹*architecture, style*›; B *adv.* **etw. ~modern stylen/bauen** design/build sth. in the postmodern[ist] style; ~**moderne** *die* 1 (Stil) postmodernism; 2 (Epoche) postmodern age; ~**paket** *das* parcel; **per ~paket** [by] parcel post; ~**sache** *die* (Amtsspr.) item of post office mail; ~**schalter** *der* post office counter; ~**scheck** *der* post office giro cheque; ≈ National Giro[bank] cheque (Brit.); ~**scheck·amt** *das* (veralt.) ▸ ~**giroamt**; ~**scheck·konto** *das* (veralt.) ▸ ~**girokonto**; ~**sendung** *die* postal item

Post·skriptum /-ˈskrɪptʊm/ *das;* ~s, **Post·skripta** postscript

Post-: ~**spar·buch** *das* post office savings book (Brit.); ~**spar·kasse** *die* post office savings bank (Brit.); ~**stelle** *die* 1 (kleines ~amt) sub-post office; 2 (in einem Betrieb) post room; ~**stempel** *der* 1 (Gerät) stamp [for cancelling mail]; 2 (Abdruck) postmark

Postulat /pɔstuˈlaːt/ *das;* ~[e]s, ~e 1 (Forderung) demand 2 (Gebot) decree

postulieren *tr. V.* 1 (fordern) postulate; demand 2 (behaupten) assert

postum /pɔsˈtuːm/

A *Adj.* posthumous

B *adv.* posthumously

post-, Post-: ~**wagen** *der* (Eisenb.) mail van (Brit.); mail car (Amer.); ~**weg** *der:* **auf dem ~weg** by post *or* mail; ~**wendend** *Adv.* by return [of post]; (fig.) immediately; ~**wert·zeichen** *das* (Amtsspr.) postage stamp; ~**wesen** *das* postal operations *pl.;* ~**wurf·sendung** *die* direct-mail item; ~**zug** *der* mail train; ~**zustellung** *die* postal delivery *no def. art.*

Pot /pɔt/ *das;* ~s (Drogenjargon) pot (sl.)

potemkinsch /poˈtɛmkiːnʃ/ *Adj.* **in ~e Dörfer** facade *sing.;* sham *sing.*

potent /poˈtɛnt/ *Adj.* 1 (zeugungsfähig) potent 2 (finanzstark) [financially] strong 3 (fähig) capable; able

Potentat /potɛnˈtaːt/ *der;* ~en, ~en, **Potentatin** *die;* ~, ~nen (abwertend) potentate

Potential *usw.* ▸ **Potenzial** *usw.*

Potenz /poˈtɛnʦ/ *die;* ~, ~en 1 potency 2 (Stärke) power 3 ▸ⓘ **S. 826** (Math.) power; **mit ~en rechnen** do calculations involving powers; **eine Zahl in die sechste ~ erheben** raise a number to the power [of] six; **das ist Blödsinn in [höchster] ~** (fig.) that is complete *or* utter nonsense 4 (Med.: Grad der Verdünnung) potency

Potenz·angst *die* impotence anxiety

Potenzial /potɛnˈʦi̯aːl/ *das;* ~s, ~e 1 (Mittel, Möglichkeit) potential; **das ~ an Energie/Aggression** energy resources *pl.*/aggressive capacity 2 (Physik) potential

potenziell /potɛnˈʦi̯ɛl/

A *Adj.* potential

B *adv.* potentially

potenzieren

A *tr. V.* 1 (verstärken) increase 2 (Math.) **mit 5 ~**: raise to the power [of] 5; **mit diesem Rechner kann man auch ~**: you can calculate *or* work out powers on this calculator

B *refl. V.* (sich steigern) increase

potenz·steigernd *Adj.* potency *attrib.;* to increase potency *postpos.*

Potpourri /ˈpɔtpʊri/ *das;* ~s, ~s *od. österr.:* *die;* ~, ~s (auch fig.) potpourri, medley (**aus, von** of)

Pott /pɔt/ *der;* ~[e]s, **Pötte** /ˈpœtə/ (ugs., bes. nordd.) 1 (Topf) pot 2 (Nachttopf) chamber pot; po (coll.); potty (coll.); **zu ~[e] kommen** (fig.) get the job over and done with 3 (Schiff) tub (derog./joc.)

pott-, Pott-: ~**asche** *die* potash; ~**hässlich,** *~**häßlich** *Adj.* (ugs.) dead ugly (coll.); ‹*person, face*› [as] ugly as sin (coll.); ~**wal** *der* (Zool.) physeterid; (Spermwal) sperm whale

potz·tausend *Interj.* (veralt.) 1 (überrascht) upon my soul (dated) 2 (unwillig) damn it [all]

poussieren /puˈsiːrən/

A *itr. V.* (ugs. veralt.: flirten) flirt

B *tr. V.* (veralt.: umwerben) curry favour with

power /ˈpoːvɐ/ *Adj.* (veralt.) miserable; **eine ~e Gegend** a poor area

Powidl /ˈpɔvidl̩/ *der;* ~s (österr.) ▸ **Pflaumenmus**

PR *Abk.* = **Public Relations** PR

Prä /prɛː/ *das;* ~s: **[das] ~ haben** have priority

Präambel /prɛˈambl̩/ *die;* ~, ~n preamble

Pracht /praxt/ *die;* ~: splendour; magnificence; **eine [wahre] ~ sein** (ugs.) be [really] marvellous *or* (coll.) great; **in voller ~**: in all its/their splendour

Pracht-: ~**ausgabe** *die* de luxe edition; ~**bau** *der; Pl.* ~~**ten** splendid *or* magnificent building; ~**exemplar** *das* (ugs.) magnificent specimen; beauty

prächtig /ˈprɛçtɪç/

A *Adj.* 1 (prunkvoll) splendid; magnificent 2 (großartig) splendid; marvellous; **ein ~er Muskelriss** (iron.) a terrific example of a torn muscle (coll.)

B *adv.* 1 (prunkvoll) splendidly; magnificently 2 (großartig) splendidly; marvellously

pracht-, Pracht-: ~**kerl** *der* (ugs.) great chap *or* (Brit. coll.) bloke *or* (coll.) guy; **ein ~kerl [von einem Kind]** a great kid (sl.); ~**straße** *die* boulevard; ~**stück** *das* (ugs.) magnificent specimen; beauty; **ein ~stück von [einem] Karpfen** a beautiful specimen of a carp; **sie/er ist ein ~stück** (Kind) she/he is a really splendid girl/boy; (Frau) she is a magnificent *or* splendid woman; (Mann) he is a great chap *or* (Brit. coll.) bloke *or* (coll.) guy; ~**villa** *die* luxurious mansion; ~**voll** *Adj., adv.* ▸ **prächtig**; ~**weib** *das* (ugs.) magnificent *or* splendid woman; (gut aussehend) gorgeous female (coll.)

Prädestination /prɛdɛstinaˈʦi̯oːn/ *die;* ~: predestination

prädestinieren *tr. V.* predestine

prädestiniert *Adj.* predestined; **etw. ist für ein Ziel ~**: sth. is just right for a purpose; **er ist für diese Rolle einfach ~**: he is just the man for this part

Prädikat /prɛdiˈkaːt/ *das;* ~[e]s, ~e 1 (Auszeichnung) rating; **das ~ „gut"** the rating of 'good'; **Qualitätswein mit ~** = *wine made from selected grapes of specified maturity* 2 (Sprachw.) predicate

prädikativ /prɛdikaˈtiːf/ (Sprachw.)

A *Adj.* predicative

B *adv.* predicatively

Prädikativ *das;* ~s, ~e ▸ **Prädikatsnomen**

Prädikativ·satz *der* (Sprachw.) predicate *or* predicative clause

Prädikats·nomen *das* (Sprachw.) predicate nominative *or* complement

prä·disponieren *tr. V.* (Med.) predispose (**für** to)

Präferenz /prɛfeˈrɛnʦ/ *die;* ~, ~en preference

Präferenz-: ~**liste** *die* priority list; ~**stellung** *die* (Wirtsch.) privileged status

Präfix /prɛˈfɪks/ *das;* ~es, ~e (Sprachw.) prefix

Prag /praːk/ *(das);* ~s ▸ⓘ **S. 675** Prague

Präge *die;* ~, ~n mint

Präge-: ~**druck** *der* embossing; ~**form** *die* (Münzwesen) coining die

P

prägen /'prɛːgn̩/ *tr. V.* **1** emboss ‹*metal, paper, leather*› **2** (herstellen) mint, strike ‹*coin*› **3** (auf~) (vertieft) impress; (erhaben) emboss **4** (fig.: beeinflussen) shape; mould; **Tempo und Wagemut ~ seinen Stil** his style is characterized by speed and daring; **eine männlich geprägte Arbeitswelt** a male-oriented work environment **5** (fig.: erfinden) coin ‹*word, expression, concept*›

Präge-: ~stempel *der* (Druckw.) die; **~stock** *der* (Druckw.) punch

Pragmatik /pra'gmaːtɪk/ *die;* ~ **1** pragmatism **2** (Sprachw.) pragmatics *sing., no art.*

Pragmatiker *der;* **~s, ~, Pragmatikerin** *die;* **~, ~nen** pragmatist

pragmatisch
A *Adj.* pragmatic
B *adv.* pragmatically

Pragmatismus *der;* **~:** pragmatism

prägnant /prɛ'gnant/
A *Adj.* concise; succinct
B *adv.* concisely; succinctly

Prägnanz /prɛ'gnants/ *die;* **~:** conciseness; succinctness

Prägung *die;* **~, ~en** **1** (von Papier, Leder, Metall) embossing; (von Münzen) minting; striking **2** (auf Metall, Papier) (vertieft) impression; (erhaben) embossing **3** (Eigenart) character **4** (eines sprachlichen Ausdrucks) coining **5** (geprägter Ausdruck) coinage

prä·historisch *Adj.* prehistoric

prahlen /'praːlən/ *itr. V.* boast, brag (**mit** about)

Prahler *der;* **~s, ~:** boaster; braggart

Prahlerei *die;* **~, ~en** (abwertend) boasting; bragging; **~en** boasts

Prahlerin *die;* **~, ~nen** boaster; braggart

Prahl·hans *der;* **~es, Prahlhänse** /-hɛnzə/ (ugs.) show-off

Prahm /praːm/ *der;* **~[e]s, ~e** *od.* **Prähme** /'prɛːmə/ pra[a]m

Präjudiz /prɛju'diːts/ *das;* **~es, ~e** (Rechtsw., Politik) precedent

präjudizieren *tr. V.* (Rechtsw., Politik) prejudge

Praktik /'praktɪk/ *die;* **~, ~en** practice

Praktika ▸ **Praktikum**

praktikabel /prakti'kaːbl̩/ *Adj.* practicable; practical

Praktikant /prakti'kant/ *der;* **~en, ~en, Praktikantin** *die;* **~, ~nen** **1** (in einem Betrieb) student trainee; trainee student **2** (an der Hochschule) physics/chemistry student (doing a period of practical training)

Praktiker *der;* **~s, ~, Praktikerin** *die;* **~, ~nen** **1** practical person **2** (ugs.: Arzt/Ärztin) general practitioner; GP

Praktikum /'praktikʊm/ *das;* **~s, Praktika** period of practical instruction *or* training

praktisch /'praktɪʃ/
A *Adj.* **1** (auf die Praxis bezogen) practical; **~es Jahr** year of practical training; **~er Arzt** general practitioner **2** (wirklich) practical ‹*result, problem, matter, etc.*›; concrete ‹*example*› **3** (nützlich) practical ‹*furniture, clothes, etc.*›; useful ‹*present*› **4** (geschickt, realistisch) practical; **er hat einen ~en Verstand** he is practically minded
B *adv.* **1** (auf die Praxis bezogen) in practice; **~ experimentieren/arbeiten** do practical experiments/work **2** (wirklich) in practice **3** (nützlich) practically **4** (geschickt, realistisch) practically; **~ veranlagt** practically minded; practical **5** (ugs.: so gut wie) practically; virtually

praktizieren /prakti'tsiːrən/
A *tr. V.* **1** (anwenden) practise; **~de Katholiken** practising Catholics **2** (ugs.: irgendwohin bringen) conjure; **jmdm. etw. in die Tasche/ins Essen ~:** slip sth. into sb.'s pocket/food
B *itr. V.* (als Arzt) practise

Prälat /prɛ'laːt/ *der;* **~en, ~en, Prälatin** *die;* **~, ~nen** (Kirche) prelate

Präliminarien /prelimi'naːri̯ən/ *Pl.* preliminaries

Praline /pra'liːnə/ *die;* **~, ~n, Praliné, Pralinee** (österr., schweiz., sonst veralt.) /prali'neː/ *das;* **~s, ~s** [filled] chocolate

prall /pral/
A *Adj.* **1** (fest und straff) hard ‹*ball*›; firm ‹*tomato, grape*›; bulging ‹*sack, wallet, bag*›; big strong *attrib.* ‹*thighs, muscles, calves*›; well-rounded ‹*buttocks*›; full, well-rounded ‹*breasts*›; full, swollen ‹*udder*›; full, chubby ‹*cheeks*›; taut, full ‹*sail*›; firm ‹*pillow, bed*›; (fig.) intense ‹*life*›; vivid ‹*picture*›; full, rich ‹*laughter*›; fully inflated ‹*balloon*› **2** (intensiv) blazing ‹*sun*›; strong ‹*light*›
B *adv.* **1** (fest und straff) fully ‹*inflated*›; **ein ~ gestopfter Rucksack** a rucksack filled to bursting; **eine ~ gefüllte Brieftasche** a wallet bulging with banknotes **2** (intensiv) **die Sonne scheint ~:** the sun is blazing [down]

prallen *itr. V.* **1** *mit sein* (hart auftreffen) crash (**gegen/auf/an** + *Akk.* into); collide (**gegen/auf/an** + *Akk.* with); **der Ball prallte an den Pfosten** the ball hit the post **2** (scheinen) blaze

prall·voll *Adj.* (ugs.) ‹*suitcase, rucksack*› full to bursting; packed ‹*room*›; bulging ‹*wallet*›; very full ‹*diary*›

Präludium /prɛ'luːdi̯ʊm/ *das;* **~s, Präludien** /...i̯ən/ prelude

Prämie /'prɛːmi̯ə/ *die;* **~, ~n** **1** (Leistungs~; Wirtschaft: ~ zum Grundlohn) bonus; (Belohnung) reward; (Spar~, Versicherungs~) premium **2** (einer Lotterie) [extra] prize

prämien-, Prämien-: ~begünstigt
A *Adj.* ≈ premium[-account] *attrib.*; **~begünstigtes Bausparen** ≈ saving with a building society premium account **B** *adv.* **~begünstigt sparen** ≈ save with a premium account; **~los** *das* ≈ Premium [Savings] Bond (Brit.); **~sparen** *das;* **~~s** ≈ Premium Bond saving (Brit.)

prämieren /prɛ'miːrən/, **prämiieren** /prɛmi'iːrən/ *tr. V.* award a prize to ‹*person, film*›; give an award for ‹*best essay etc.*›

Prämierung, Prämiierung *die;* **~, ~en** **1** (Auszeichnung) **er/der Film wurde zur ~ vorgeschlagen** it was proposed that he should be given a prize/that a prize should be given for the film **2** (Preisverleihung) **die ~ der besten Schüler/Filme** the presentation of prizes to the best pupils/for the best films

Prämisse /prɛ'mɪsə/ *die;* **~, ~n** (auch Philos.) premise; **unter der ~, dass ...** on the premise that ...

pränatal /prɛna'taːl/ *Adj.* (Med.) pre-natal

prangen /'praŋən/ *itr. V.* **1** be prominently displayed; **auf dem Sofa prangte ein großes Kissen** a large cushion was placed eye-catchingly on the sofa **2** (geh.: auffallen) be resplendent; **Sterne ~ am Himmel** stars are glittering in the sky

Pranger *der;* **~s, ~** (hist.) pillory; **jmdn./etw. an den ~ stellen** (fig.) pillory sb./sth.

Pranke /'praŋkə/ *die;* **~, ~n** **1** (Pfote) paw **2** (salopp: große Hand) paw (coll.)

Präparat /prɛpa'raːt/ *das;* **~[e]s, ~e** **1** (Mittel, Substanz) preparation **2** (Biol., Med.: präpariertes Objekt) specimen

Präparation /prɛpara'tsi̯oːn/ *die;* **~, ~en** preparation

präparieren
A *tr. V.* **1** (Biol., Med.: konservieren) preserve **2** (Biol., Anat.: zerlegen) dissect **3** (vorbereitend bearbeiten, geh.: vorbereiten) prepare
B *refl. V.* (geh.: sich vorbereiten) prepare oneself

Präposition /prɛpozi'tsi̯oːn/ *die;* **~, ~en** (Sprachw.) preposition

präpositional /prɛpozitsi̯o'naːl/ *Adj.* (Sprachw.) prepositional

Präpositional- (Sprachw.) prepositional

präpotent /prɛpo'tɛnt/ *Adj.* (österr.) officiously impertinent

Prärie /prɛ'riː/ *die;* **~, ~n** prairie

Prärie·wolf *der* prairie wolf; coyote

Präsens /'prɛːzɛns/ *das;* **~, Präsentia** /prɛ'zɛntsi̯a/ *od.* **Präsenzien** /prɛ'zɛntsi̯ən/ (Sprachw.) present [tense]

präsent /prɛ'zɛnt/ *Adj.* present; **Forderungen/Fragen ~ haben** have one's demands/questions ready; **ich habe den Vorfall** *od.* **der Vorfall ist mir im Augenblick nicht ~:** I do not recall the incident at the moment

Präsent *das;* **~[e]s, ~e** (geh.) present; **jmdm. ein ~ machen** give sb. a present

präsentabel /prɛzɛn'taːbl̩/ (veralt.) presentable

Präsentation /prɛzɛnta'tsi̯oːn/ *die;* **~, ~en** **1** (Vorstellung) presentation **2** (Wirtsch.) presentment

präsentieren
A *tr. V.* **1** (anbieten; überreichen) offer **2** (vorlegen) present; **jmdm. die Rechnung [für etw.] ~:** present sb. with the bill [for sth.] **3** (Milit.) **präsentiert das Gewehr!** present arms!
B *refl. V.* (sich zeigen) present oneself; appear
C *itr. V.* (Milit.) present arms

Präsentier·teller *der:* **auf dem ~ sitzen** (ugs. abwertend) be on show *or* display

Präsent·korb *der* gift hamper

Präsenz /prɛ'zɛnts/ *die;* **~:** presence

Präsenz-: ~bibliothek *die* reference library; **~liste** *die* [attendance] register; **~pflicht** *die* duty to attend

Präser /'prɛzɐ/ *der;* **~s, ~** (salopp), **Präservativ** /prɛzɛrva'tiːf/ *das;* **~s, ~e** condom

Präses /'prɛːzɛs/ *der;* **~, Präsides** /'prɛːzideːs/ **1** (kath. Kirche) chairman **2** (ev. Kirche) president (*of a synod*)

Präsident /prɛzi'dɛnt/ *der;* **~en, ~en** ▸❶ **S. 44** president; **~ der Europäischen Kommission** President of the European Commission

Präsidenten·wahl *die* presidential election

Präsidentin *die;* **~, ~nen** ▸❶ **S. 44** president

Präsidentschaft *die;* **~, ~en** presidency

Präsidentschafts-: ~kandidat *der,* **~kandidatin** *die* candidate for the presidency: **~wahl** *die* presidential election

präsidial /prɛzi'di̯aːl/ *Adj.* (Politik) presidential

Präsidial·demokratie *die* presidential democracy

Präsidien *Pl.* ▸ **Präsidium**

präsidieren
A *itr. V.* preside
B *tr. V.* (schweiz.) **einen Verein** *usw.* **~:** be president of a society *etc.*

Präsidium /prɛ'ziːdi̯ʊm/ *das;* **~s, Präsidien** **1** (Führungsgruppe) committee; **im ~ sitzen** be on the committee **2** (Vorsitz) chairmanship **3** (Polizei~) police headquarters *sing. or pl.*

prasseln /'prasl̩n/ *itr. V.* ‹*rain, hail*› pelt down; ‹*shots*› clatter; ‹*fire*› crackle; **Kies prasselte gegen das Auto** gravel rattled against the car; **~der Beifall** thunderous applause

prassen /'prasn̩/ *itr. V.* live extravagantly; (schlemmen) feast

Prasser *der;* **~s, ~:** spendthrift; extravagant person; (Schlemmer) glutton

Prasserei *die;* **~, ~en** **1** extravagant living *no pl.* **2** (das Schlemmen) gluttony *no pl.*; (Gelage) feasting *no pl.*

Prasserin *die;* **~, ~nen** ▸ **Prasser**

präsumtiv /prɛzʊm'tiːf/ *Adj.* **1** prospective **2** (Rechtsw.) presumptive

Prätendent /prɛtɛn'dɛnt/ *der;* **~en, ~en, Prätendentin** *die;* **~, ~nen** pretender

prätentiös /prɛtɛn'tsi̯øːs/ *Adj.* pretentious

> **Prater**
>
> Vienna's largest and most popular amusement park. In 1766 Joseph II, the son of Empress Maria Theresa, decreed that *der Prater* should be open to everyone. Earlier it had been forbidden to enter forests and meadows reserved for imperial hunts. The *Prater* has old-fashioned swings, skittle alleys, and merry-go-rounds, including the oldest carousel in Europe. A *Riesenrad* (big wheel) with a diameter of 67 metres was put up for the World Exhibition of 1897 and is a famous Viennese landmark.

Präteritum /prɛ'teːritʊm/ *das;* **~s, Präterita** (Sprachw.) preterite [tense]

Pratze /ˈpratsə/ *die;* **~, ~n** (bes. südd.) ▸**Pranke**

präventiv /prɛvɛnˈtiːf/
A *Adj.* preventive
B *adv.* preventively; **~ vorgehen** take preventive measures

Präventiv-: ~krieg *der* preventive war; **~maßnahme** *die* preventive measure

Praxis /ˈpraksɪs/ *die;* **~, Praxen** **1** (im Unterschied zur Theorie) practice *no art.*; **in der ~:** in practice; **etw. in die ~ umsetzen** put sth. into practice; **Beispiele aus der ~:** practical examples; **er ist ein Mann der ~:** he is a practical man **2** (Erfahrung) [practical] experience **3** (eines Arztes, Anwalts, Psychologen, Therapeuten usw.) practice **4** (~räume) (eines Arztes) surgery (Brit.); office (Amer.); (eines Anwalts, Psychologen, Therapeuten usw.) office **5** (Handhabung) procedure

praxis-, Praxis-: ~bezogen **A** *Adj.* practical ‹*experience, training*›; ‹*project*› based on practical work; **B** *adv.* practically; **~nah, ~orientiert** **A** *Adj.* practical; **B** *adv.* practically; **~tauglich** *Adj.* practical; ‹*regulation*› that will work in practice; **~tauglichkeit** *die;* **~~** practicality

Präzedenz·fall /prɛtseˈdɛnts-/ *der* precedent

präzis (österr.), **präzise** /prɛˈtsiːzə/
A *Adj.* precise ‹*definition, answer*›; specific ‹*wishes, suspicion*›
B *adv.* precisely

präzisieren *tr. V.* make more precise; state more precisely; **ein Angebot näher ~:** give more precise details of an offer; **seine Wünsche ~:** specify one's wishes

Präzision /prɛtsiˈzi̯oːn/ *die;* **~:** precision

Präzisions-: ~arbeit *die* precision work; (genau nach Zeitplan) precise timing; **~instrument** *das* precision instrument; **~uhr** *die* precision [stop]watch/clock

predigen /ˈpreːdɪɡn̩/
A *itr. V.* (Predigt halten) deliver *or* give a/the sermon; **gegen etw. ~:** preach against sth.
B *tr. V.* **1** (verkündigen) preach **2** (ugs.: auffordern zu) preach **3** (ugs.: belehrend sagen) **wie oft habe ich dir das schon gepredigt!** how often have I told you that!

Prediger *der;* **~s, ~, Predigerin** *die;* **~, ~nen** preacher; **ein ~ in der Wüste** (fig.) a voice [crying] in the wilderness

Predigt /ˈpreːdɪçt/ *die;* **~, ~en** **1** sermon; **eine ~ halten** deliver *or* give a sermon **2** (ugs.: Ermahnung) lecture; **jmdm. eine ~ halten** lecture sb.; **ich bin deine endlosen ~en leid** I am tired of your endless lecturing

Predigt·text *der* text (*for a sermon*)

-preis *der* price of …

Preis /prai̯s/ *der;* **~es, ~e** **1** ▸**i** **S. 299** (Kauf~) price (**für** of); **das hat seinen ~:** it costs money; (fig.) there is a price to be paid for it; **im ~ steigen** rise in price; **jeden ~ für etw. zahlen** pay any price for sth.; **jmdm. einen guten ~ machen** give sb. a good price; **nach dem ~ fragen** ask the price; **eine Ware unter[m] ~ verkaufen** sell an article at a reduced *or* cut price; **etw. zum halben ~ erwerben** buy sth. at half-price; **hoch/gut im ~ stehen** fetch a high/good price; **diese Ausstellung möchte ich um jeden ~ besuchen** (fig.) I should like to go to this exhibition at all costs; **diese Einladung möchte ich um keinen ~ annehmen** (fig.) I wouldn't accept this invitation at any price **2** (Belohnung) prize; **einen ~ auf jmds. Kopf aussetzen** put a price on sb.'s head; **der Große ~ von Frankreich** (Rennsport) the French Grand Prix; **der ~ der Nationen** (Reitsport) Prix des Nations **3** (geh.: Lob) praise; **ein Gedicht zum ~e der Natur** a poem in praise of nature

preis-, Preis-: ~abschlag *der* (Kaufmannsspr.) ▸**~nachlass**; **~absprache** *die* (Wirtsch.) price-fixing agreement; **~änderung** *die* price change *or* variation; **~angabe** *die* (displayed or listed) price; **~anstieg** *der* rise *or* increase in prices; **~aufgabe** *die* [prize] competition; **eine ~aufgabe lösen** solve a puzzle (*in a prize competition*); **~aufschlag** *der* (Kaufmannsspr.) additional *or* extra charge; **~auftrieb** *der* (Wirtsch.) rise *or* increase in prices; **~ausschreiben** *das* [prize] competition; **~auszeichnung** *die* labelling with a price/prices; **~bewegung** *die* movement of prices; **~bewusst, *~bewußt** **A** *Adj.* price-conscious; **B** *adv.* price-consciously; **~bewusst tanken** be conscious of petrol (Brit.) *or* (Amer.) gasoline prices [when filling up]; **~bindung** *die* (Wirtsch.) price-fixing; **~bindung der zweiten Hand** resale price maintenance; **~boxer** *der* (ugs. veralt.) prizefighter; **~brecher** *der,* **~brecherin** *die* cut-price operator; **~einbruch** *der* (Wirtsch.) [massive] drop in prices

Preisel·beere /ˈprai̯zl̩beːrə/ *die* cowberry; cranberry (Gastr.)

Preis·empfehlung *die* (Kaufmannsspr.) recommended price

preisen *unr. tr. V.* (geh.) praise; **man pries ihn als den besten Kenner auf diesem Gebiet** he was acclaimed as the leading authority in this field; **sich glücklich ~ [können]** [be able to] count *or* consider oneself lucky

Preis-: ~entwicklung *die* price trend; **~erhöhung** *die* price increase *or* rise

-preis·erhöhung *die* increase in the price of …

preis-, Preis-: ~ermäßigung *die* price reduction; **~explosion** *die* snowballing prices *pl.*; **~frage** *die* **1** (bei einem ~ausschreiben) [prize] question; (fig.) big question; sixty-four thousand dollar question; **2** (Geldfrage) question of price; **~gabe** *die* (geh.) **1** (Verzicht) abandonment; **2** (von Geheimnissen) revelation; giving away; **~|geben** *unr. tr. V.* (geh.) **1** (ausliefern) **jmdn. einer Sache** (*Dat.*) **~geben** expose sb. to *or* leave sb. to be the victim of sth.; **die Bauten waren dem Verfall ~gegeben** the buildings were left to fall into ruin; **2** (aufgeben) relinquish ‹*ideal, independence*›; surrender ‹*territory*›; **3** (verraten) betray; give away; **~gebunden** *Adj.* (Wirtsch.) subject to price maintenance *postpos.*; **~gefälle** *das* difference *or* variation in prices; **~gefüge** *das* (Wirtsch.) price structure; **~gekrönt** *Adj.* prize *or* awardwinning; **er/sein Werk ist ~gekrönt** he has been given/his work has won a prize *or* an award; **~gericht** *das* jury; panel of judges; **~gestaltung** *die* pricing; **~grenze** *die* price limit; **obere/untere ~grenze** ceiling *or* maximum/floor *or* minimum price; **~günstig** **A** *Adj.* ‹*goods*› available at unusually low prices; ‹*purchases*› at favourable prices; inexpensive ‹*holiday*›; **das ~günstigste Angebot** the best bargain *or* value; **das ist [sehr] ~günstig** that is [very] good value; **B** *adv.* **etw. ~günstig herstellen/verkaufen/bekommen** produce/sell/get sth. at a low price; **hier kann man ~günstig einkaufen** their prices are very reasonable here; **~index** *der* (Wirtsch.) price index; **~kampf** *der* price war; **sich** (*Dat.*) **einen scharfen** *od.* **erbitterten ~kampf liefern** fight *or* wage a bitter price war; **~klasse** *die* price range; **~kontrolle** *die* price control; **~lage** *die* price range; **in jeder ~lage** at prices to suit every pocket; **~lawine** *die* (ugs.) snowballing prices *pl.*; **~-Leistungs-Verhältnis** *das* cost effectiveness; **ein gutes ~-Leistungs-Verhältnis bieten** give good value for money

preislich *Adj.* price; in price *postpos.*; **in ~er Hinsicht** as regards price

preis-, Preis-: ~liste *die* price list; **~nachlass, *~nachlaß** *der* price reduction; discount; **mit erheblichem ~nachlass** at a greatly reduced price; **~niveau** *das* (Wirtsch.) price level; **~politik** *die* policy on prices; **~rätsel** *das* [prize] competition; **~reduziert** **A** *Adj.* reduced in price *pred.*; reduced-price *attrib.*; **B** *adv.* ‹*offer, sell, etc.*› at a reduced price; **~richter** *der,* **~richterin** *die* judge; **~schießen** *das;* **~~s, ~~:** shooting competition *or* contest; **~schild** *das* price tag; **~schlager** *der* (ugs.) bargain [offer]; **~schlager der Saison** best bargain of the season; **~schraube** *die* (Wirtschaftsjargon) **an der ~schraube drehen** put [one's] prices up; **~schwankung** *die* price fluctuation; **~senkung** *die* price reduction *or* cut; **~skat** *der* skat competition; **~steigerung** *die* rise *or* increase in prices; **~steigerungs·rate** *die* (Wirtsch.) rate of increase in prices; **~stopp** *der* price freeze; **~sturz** *der* sharp drop *or* fall in prices; **~träger** *der,* **~trägerin** *die* prizewinner; **~treiber** *der* (abwertend) *person who/company which forces prices up*; **dieses Reiseunternehmen gilt als ~treiber** this tour operator is known for forcing prices up; **~treiberei** *die;* **~~** (abwertend) forcing up of prices; **~treiberin** *die* ▸**~treiber**; **~unterschied** *der* price difference (**zu** compared with); **~vergleich** *der* price comparison; **~vergleiche anstellen** compare prices; **~verleihung** *die* presentation [of prizes/awards]; award ceremony; **~vor·teil** *der* price benefit; **~wert** **A** *Adj.* good value *pred.*; **ein ~wertes Angebot** a bargain [offer]; **haben Sie ~wertere Schuhe?** do you have any shoes which are less expensive?; **B** *adv.* **sie hat ~wert eingekauft** she bought things at reasonable prices; **dort kann man ~wert einkaufen** you get good value for money there; **hier kann man ~wert essen** you can eat at a reasonable price here; **~würdig** *Adj.* (geh.) praiseworthy

prekär /preˈkɛːɐ̯/ *Adj.* precarious

Prell-: ~ball *der:* (Sport) *game similar to volleyball;* **~bock** *der* (Eisenb.) buffer

prellen /ˈprɛlən/
A *tr. V.* **1** (betrügen) cheat (**um** out of); **die Zeche ~:** avoid paying the bill **2** (verletzen) bash; bruise **3** (Ballsport) bounce
B *refl. V.* (sich verletzen) bruise oneself; **ich habe mich an der Schulter geprellt** I have bruised *or* bashed my shoulder

Prellung *die;* **~, ~en** bruise

Premier /prəˈmi̯eː/ *der;* **~s, ~s** premier

Premiere /prəˈmi̯eːrə/ *die;* **~, ~n** opening night; first night; (Uraufführung) première; (fig.) first appearance; **das Stück hat morgen ~:** the play has its opening night/première tomorrow

> **Premiere**
>
> Germany's main pay-TV channel was introduced in 1991 and can be received via satellite or cable. *Premiere* subscribers can watch the latest feature films, sports events, cultural programmes and documentaries uninterrupted by advertising.

Premieren-: ~abend *der* opening night; first night; (eines neuen Stückes) première; **~publikum** *das* audience at a/the première/opening *or* first night

Premier- /prəˈmi̯eː-/: **~minister** *der,* **~ministerin** *die* prime minister

Premium·marke /ˈpreːmi̯ʊm-/ *die* (Werbespr. Wirtsch.) premium brand; (Auto) prestige make

Presbyter /ˈprɛsbytɐ/ *der;* **~s, ~, Presbyterin,** *die;* **~, ~nen** (ev. Kirche) presbyter; elder

Presbyterianer /prɛsbyteˈri̯aːnɐ/ *der;* **~s, ~, Presbyterianerin** *die;* **~, ~nen** Presbyterian

presbyterianisch *Adj.* Presbyterian

preschen /ˈprɛʃn̩/ *itr. V.; mit sein* tear; **sie kam ins Zimmer geprescht** she came dashing into the room

Presse /ˈprɛsə/ *die;* **~, ~n** **1** (zum Zusammenpressen) press **2** (zum Auspressen) (von Obst, Knoblauch) press; (von Zitronen) squeezer **3** (Zeitungen) press **4** (Druckw. veralt.: Druckmaschine) press **5** (ugs., abwertend: Schule) crammer

Presse-: ~agentur *die* press agency; news agency; **~amt** *das* press office; **~ausweis** *der* press card; **~ball** *der: celebrity dance held by a national or provincial journalists' association;* **~bericht** *der* press report; **~chef** *der,* **~chefin** *die* [chief] press officer; **~dienst** *der* regular press release; **~empfang** *der* press reception; **~erklärung** *die* press statement; **~fotograf** *der,* **~fotografin** *die* press photographer; **~freiheit** *die* freedom of the press; **~gesetz** *das* press law; **~kampagne** *die* press campaign; **~karte** *die* press ticket; **~kommentar**

P

der press commentary; **~konferenz** die press conference; **~konzentration** die concentration of the press; **~meldung** die press report

pressen tr. V. **1** (zusammendrücken) press **2** (aus~) press ‹fruit, garlic›; squeeze ‹lemon› **3** (drücken) press; **Kleider in einen Koffer ~:** squash or squeeze clothes into a suitcase; **jmdm. die Hand auf den Mund ~:** press one's hand over sb.'s mouth; **mit gepresster Stimme** (fig.) in a strained voice **4** (herstellen) press ‹record›; mould ‹plastic object› **5** (zwingen) force **6** (veralt.: unterdrücken) oppress

Presse-: ~notiz die news item; **etw. in einer kurzen ~notiz erwähnen** give sth. a mention in the press; **~organ** das (Zeitung) newspaper; (Zeitschrift) journal; magazine; **die ~organe** the press; **~recht** das press legislation; **~referent** der, **~referentin** die press officer; **~sprecher** der, **~sprecherin** die ▸ⓘ S. 113 spokesman/spokeswoman; spokesperson; press officer; **~stelle** die press office; **~stimmen** Pl. press commentaries or reviews; **~text** der press release; **~tribüne** die press box; **auf der ~tribüne** in the press box; **~vertreter** der, **~vertreterin** die representative of the press; **~zentrum** das press centre

Press-, *Preß-: ~glas das pressed glass; **~holz** das compressed wood

pressieren itr. V. (bes. südd.) ‹matter› be urgent; **er ist sehr pressiert/mir pressierts sehr** he is/I am in a great hurry

Pression /prɛˈsi̯oːn/ die; ~, ~en pressure

Press-, *Preß-: ~kohle die compressed coal no pl.; **~kopf** der brawn; head cheese (Amer.); **~luft** die compressed air

Press·luft-, *Preß·luft-: ~bohrer der pneumatic drill; **~hammer** der (Bauw.) pneumatic or air hammer

Press·sack, *Preß·sack der ▸**Presskopf**

Pressung die; ~, ~en (das Pressen) pressure; (das Gepresstwerden) compression

Press·wehe, *Preß·wehe die (Med.) contraction (in second stage of labour)

Prestige /prɛsˈtiːʒə/ das; ~s prestige

Prestige-: ~denken das desire to establish one's prestige; **~frage** die question or matter of prestige; **~verlust** der loss of prestige

pretiös ▸**preziös**

Pretiosen ▸**Preziosen**

Preuße /ˈprɔysə/ der; ~n, ~n Prussian; **so schnell schießen die ~n nicht** (fig.) these things take time

Preußen (das); ~s Prussia

Preußentum das; ~s **1** (preußische Wesensart) Prussian character **2** (Volkszugehörigkeit) Prussianness **3** (die Preußen) Prussian people pl.; Prussians pl.

Preußin die; ~, ~nen ▸**Preuße**

preußisch /ˈprɔysɪʃ/ Adj. Prussian; s. auch **deutsch**; **Deutsch**; **Deutsche²**

preußisch·blau Adj., **Preußisch·blau** das Prussian blue

Preview /ˈpriːvjuː/ die; ~, ~s preview

preziös /preˈtsi̯øːs/ Adj. (geh.) precious

Preziosen /preˈtsi̯oːzn̩/ Pl. valuables

Pricke /ˈprɪkə/ die; ~, ~n (Seew.) perch

prickelig Adj. tingling

prickeln /ˈprɪkl̩n/ itr. V. **1** (kribbeln, kitzeln) tingle; **es prickelte ihm in den Fingerspitzen** his fingertips were tingling **2** (perlen) sparkle **3** (reizen) **eine ~de Spannung** a tingling atmosphere; **der ~de Reiz des Unbekannten** the thrill of the unknown

pricklig Adj. ▸**prickelig**

Priel /priːl/ der; ~[e]s, ~e narrow channel (in mudflats)

Priem /priːm/ der; ~[e]s, ~e **1** (Kautabak) chewing tobacco; **~ kauen** chew tobacco **2** (Stück Kautabak) quid [of tobacco]

priemen itr. V. chew tobacco

pries /priːs/ 1. u. 3. Pers. Sg. Prät. v. **preisen**

Priester /ˈpriːstɐ/ der; ~s, ~: priest; **Hoher ~** (bibl.) high priest

Priester·amt das priesthood

Priesterin die; ~, ~nen priestess

priesterlich Adj. priestly ‹function›; clerical ‹robe, collar›; priest's ‹blessing›

Priester·rock der cassock

Priesterschaft die; ~: priests pl.

Priester·seminar das seminary

Priestertum das; ~s priesthood

Priester·weihe die ordination [to the priesthood]

prima /ˈpriːma/
A indekl. Adj. **1** (ugs.) great (coll.); fantastic (coll.) **2** (Kaufmannsspr. veralt.) first-class; top-quality
B adv. (ugs.) ‹taste› great (coll.), fantastic (coll.); ‹sleep› fantastically (coll.) or really well; **es geht mir ~:** I feel great (coll.); **es lief alles ~:** everything went really well; **das finde ich ~:** that's fantastic or great (coll.); **das hast du ~ gemacht** well done indeed

Prima die; ~, **Primen** (Schulw.) **1** (veralt.) eighth and ninth years (of a Gymnasium) **2** (österr.) first year (of a Gymnasium)

Prima-: ~ballerina die (Theater) prima ballerina; **~donna** /-ˈdɔna/ die; ~, **~donnen** prima donna

Primaner /priˈmaːnɐ/ der; ~s, ~ (Schulw.) **1** (veralt.) pupil in the eighth and ninth years (of a Gymnasium); **wie ein ~** (fig.) like a schoolboy **2** (österr.) pupil in the first year (of a Gymnasium)

primanerhaft
A Adj. schoolboyish/schoolgirlish
B adv. like a schoolboy/schoolgirl

Primanerin die; ~, ~nen ▸**Primaner**

primär /priˈmɛːɐ̯/
A Adj. primary
B adv. primarily

Primar·lehrer /priˈmaːɐ̯-/ der, **Primar·lehrerin** die (schweiz.) primary school teacher

Primär·literatur die primary literature

Primar-: ~schule die (schweiz.) primary school; **~stufe** die primary stage (of education)

Primas /ˈpriːmas/ der; ~, ~se od. **Primaten** **1** (kath. Kirche) primate **2** Pl. nur **~se** (Geiger) leading fiddle player

Primat¹ /priˈmaːt/ der od. das; ~[e]s, ~e **1** (Vorrang) primacy, priority (**vor** + Dat., **über** + Akk. over) **2** (kath. Kirche) primacy

Primat² der; ~en, ~en (Zool.) primate

Prime /ˈpriːmə/ die; ~, ~n (Musik) **1** (Einklang) unison **2** (Ton) keynote; tone

Primel /ˈpriːml̩/ die; ~, ~n primula; primrose; (Schlüsselblume) cowslip; **eingehen wie eine ~** (salopp) go completely to pot (coll.)

Primi Pl. ▸**Primus**

primitiv /primiˈtiːf/
A Adj. **1** (einfach, schlicht) simple; crude (derog.); **die ~sten Regeln des Anstands** the most basic rules of behaviour **2** (oft abwertend: dürftig) primitive **3** (abwertend: niveaulos, ungebildet) primitive ‹person, behaviour›; crude ‹expression, view, idea, speech› **4** (urtümlich, ursprünglich, naiv) primitive
B adv. **1** (einfach, schlicht) in a simple manner; crudely (derog.) **2** (oft abwertend: dürftig) primitively **3** (abwertend: niveaulos, ungebildet) ‹argue› primitively; ‹talk› crudely **4** (urtümlich) primitively

Primitivität /primitiviˈtɛːt/ die; ~ ▸**primitiv A 2-4**: primitiveness; crudeness

Primitivling der; ~s, ~e (abwertend) peasant (fig.)

Primus /ˈpriːmʊs/ der; ~, **Primi** od. ~se (veralt.) top of the class

Prim·zahl die (Math.) prime [number]

Printe /ˈprɪntə/ die; ~, ~n kind of oblong sweet spiced cake

Prinz /prɪnts/ der; ~en, ~en prince

Prinzessin die; ~, ~nen princess

Prinz·gemahl der prince consort

Prinzip /prɪnˈtsiːp/ das; ~s, ~ien /-ˈtsiːpi̯ən/ principle; **aus ~:** on principle; **er hat es aus ~ getan** he did it as a matter of principle; **im ~:** in principle; **ein Mensch von** od. **mit ~ien sein** be a man/woman of principle

Prinzipal /prɪntsiˈpaːl/ der; ~s, ~e (veralt.) **1** (eines Theaters) [theatre] manager; (einer Theatergruppe) leader **2** (Leiter eines Privatbetriebs) proprietor; (Lehrherr) master

Prinzipalin die; ~, ~nen (veralt.) **1** (eines Theaters) [theatre] manager[ess]; (einer Theatergruppe) leader **2** (Leiterin eines Privatbetriebs) proprietress; (Lehrherrin) mistress

prinzipiell /prɪntsiˈpi̯ɛl/
A Adj. in principle postpos., not pred.; ‹rejection› on principle; **eine ~e Frage/Frage von ~er Bedeutung** a question of principle/of fundamental importance
B adv. **1** (im Prinzip) in principle **2** (aus Prinzip) on principle; as a matter of principle

prinzipien-, Prinzipien-: ~los Adj. unprincipled; **~losigkeit** die; ~~: lack of principles; **~reiter** der (abwertend) person who sticks rigidly to his/her principles; **~reiterei** die (abwertend) rigid adherence to principles; **~reiterin** die ▸**~reiter**

prinzlich Adj. prince's

Prinz·regent der Prince Regent

Prion das; ~s, ~en (Biol.) prion

Prior /ˈpriːɔr/ der; ~s, ~en /priˈoːrən/ (kath. Kirche) prior

Priorin die; ~, ~nen (kath. Kirche) prioress

priorisieren /prioriˈziːrən/ tr. V. prioritize; **etw. richtig ~:** give sth. the right priority

Priorisierung die; ~, ~en prioritization; **entsprechend der ~ von ...** according to the [degree of] priority given to ...

Priorität /prioriˈtɛːt/ die; ~, ~en **1** (Vorrang) priority; precedence; **~ vor etw.** (Dat.) **haben** have or take precedence over sth. **2** Pl. (Rangfolge) priorities; **~en setzen** establish priorities; **die richtigen ~en setzen** get one's priorities right

Prise /ˈpriːzə/ die; ~, ~n **1** pinch; **eine ~ Salz** a pinch of salt; **eine ~ Sarkasmus/Ironie** (fig.) a hint or touch of sarcasm/irony **2** (Seew.) prize; **eine ~ machen** take a prize

Prisma /ˈprɪsma/ das; ~s, **Prismen** (Math., Optik) prism

prismatisch /prɪsˈmaːtɪʃ/
A Adj. prismatic
B adv. prismatically

Prismen ▸**Prisma**

Pritsche /ˈprɪtʃə/ die; ~, ~n **1** (Liegestatt) plank bed **2** (Ladefläche) platform **3** (Narren~) slapstick

Pritschen·wagen der platform truck

privat /priˈvaːt/
A Adj. private; personal ‹opinion, happiness, etc.›; **eine Feier im ~en Kreis** a celebration restricted to one's intimate circle; **an/von ~:** to/from private individuals pl
B adv. privately; **~ ist er ganz anders** he's completely different in private; **jmdn. ~ sprechen** speak to sb. in private or privately; **der Patient liegt ~:** the patient is in a/the private ward; **~ versichert** privately insured; covered by private insurance (postpos.)

Privat-: ~adresse die private or home address; **~angelegenheit** die private affair or matter; **das ist seine ~angelegenheit** that's his own business or his own private affair; **~armee** die private army; **~audienz** die private audience; **~besitz** der private property; **das Gemälde befindet sich im ~besitz** the painting is privately owned or in private ownership; **~detektiv** der, **~detektivin** die ▸ⓘ S. 113 private detective or investigator; **~dozent** der, **~dozentin** die: lecturer who is not a member of the salaried university staff; **~druck** der; Pl. **~~e** privately published edition; **als ~druck erscheinen** be published privately; **~eigentum** das private property; **das ~eigentum**

an den Produktionsmitteln private ownership of the means of production; **~fernsehen** *das* privately operated television; ≈ commercial television; **~frau** *die* ▸**~person; ~gelehrte** *der/die* (veralt.) scholar [working] on his/her own account; **~gespräch** *das* private conversation; (Telefongespräch) private call

Privatheit *die;* **~, ~en** 1 (das Privatsein) privacy; (Privatsphäre) private world 2 *Pl.* (private Angelegenheiten, Dinge) private matters

Privatier /priva'tie:/ *der;* **~s, ~s** (veralt.) man of private *or* independent means

privatim /pri'va:tım/ *adv.* (geh.) privately

Privat-: ~initiative *die* private initiative; **~interesse** *das* private interest

privatisieren

A *tr. V.* (Wirtsch.) privatize; transfer into private ownership

B *itr. V.* (geh.: als Privatier leben) live on a private income

Privatisierung *die;* **~, ~en** (Wirtsch.) privatization; transfer into private ownership

privat-, Privat-: ~klage *die* (Rechtsw.) private action *or* prosecution; **~kläger** *der,* **~klägerin** *die* (Rechtsw.) plaintiff [in a/the private action]; **~klinik** *die* private clinic *or* hospital; **~kunde** *der,* **~kundin** *die* private customer; **~leben** *das* private life; **sich ins ~leben zurückziehen** return to private life; **~lehrer** *der,* **~lehrerin** *die* private tutor; **~mann** *der; Pl.* **~leute** ▸**~person; ~patient** *der,* **~patientin** *die* private patient; **~person** *die* private individual; **als ~person auftreten** appear in a private capacity; **~quartier** *das* private accommodation *no pl.;* **zahlreiche ~quartiere** plentiful private accommodation *sing.;* **~recht** *das* (Rechtsw.) private *or* civil law; **~rechtlich** (Rechtsw.) **A** *Adj.* civil-law *attrib.;* under private *or* civil law *postpos.;* **B** *adv.* in private *or* civil law; **~sache** *die* ▸**~angelegenheit; ~sammlung** *die* private collection; **~schule** *die* private school; (Eliteschule in Großbritannien) public school; **~sekretär** *der,* **~sekretärin** *die* private secretary (**von,** *Gen.* to); **~sender** *der* private broadcaster; (Radiosender) commercial station; (TV) commercial channel; **~sphäre** *die* privacy; (~leben) private life; **~station** *die* private ward; **~stunde** *die* private lesson; **~unternehmen** *das* private concern *or* enterprise; **~unterricht** *der* private tuition; private lessons *pl.;* **~vergnügen** *das* (ugs.) **eine Dienstreise ist kein ~vergnügen** you don't go on business trips for your own enjoyment; **das ist doch mein ~vergnügen** that's my own business *or* affair; **~vermögen** *das* private fortune; **~vermögen/kein ~vermögen haben** have a/no private fortune; **~versichert** ▸**privat B; ~versicherung** *die* private insurance; **in einer ~versicherung sein** be privately insured; be in a private insurance scheme; **~weg** *der* private way; **~wirtschaft** *die* private sector; **~wirtschaftlich A** *Adj.* private-sector *attrib.;* ‹*enterprise, company, firm*› in the private sector; **auf ~wirtschaftlicher Basis** on a private-enterprise basis; **B** *adv.* **~wirtschaftlich orientiert/gesehen** orientated towards/from the point of view of the private sector; **~wirtschaftlich geführt** run as a private enterprise; **~wohnung** *die* private flat (esp. Brit.) *or* (esp. Amer.) apartment

Privileg /privi'le:k/ *das;* **~[e]s, ~ien** /-'le:giən/ privilege

privilegieren *tr. V.* grant privileges to

privilegiert *Adj.* privileged

pro /pro:/ *Präp. mit Akk.* per; **~ Jahr/Monat** per year *or* annum/month; **~ Person** per person; **~ Kopf** per head; **~ Stück** each; apiece; **~ Nase** (ugs.) each; a head

pro-: pro-; **~westlich/~kommunistisch** pro-western/pro-communist

Pro *das; in* **[das] ~ und [das] Kontra** the pros and cons *pl.*

> **Pro 7**
>
> Germany's third largest private television channel, *Pro 7* is financed entirely by advertising and offers films, documentaries, and news programmes.

Proband /pro'bant/ *der;* **~en, ~en, Probandin** *die;* **~, ~nen** 1 (Psych., Med.: Testperson) subject 2 (Strafentlassener) offender on probation

probat /pro'ba:t/ *Adj.* tried and tested; (wirksam) effective

Probe /'pro:bə/ *die;* **~, ~n** 1 (Prüfung) test; **die ~ aufs Exempel machen** put it to the test; **auf ~ sein** be on probation; **ein Beamter/eine Ehe auf ~:** a probationary civil servant/a trial marriage; **jmdn./etw. auf die ~ stellen** put sb./sth. to the test; **jmds. Geduld/Liebe/Freundschaft auf eine harte ~ stellen** sorely try *or* test sb.'s patience/sorely test sb.'s love/friendship; **jmdn. auf ~ einstellen** employ sb. on a trial basis; **~ laufen** test-run; **etw. ~ laufen lassen** test-run sth.; **ein Auto ~ fahren** test-drive a car; **ein Boot ~ fahren** test a boat out on the water 2 (Muster, Teststück) sample; **eine ~ seines Könnens zeigen** *od.* **geben** (fig.) show what one can do 3 (Theater~, Orchester~) rehearsal

probe-, Probe-: ~abzug *der* (Druckw., Fot.) proof; **~alarm** *der* practice alarm; (Feueralarm) fire drill *or* -practice; **~aufnahme** *die* 1 test take; 2 (bei der Auswahl von Filmschauspielern) screen test; **mit jmdm. ~aufnahmen machen** screen-test sb.; **~bohrung** *die* test drilling *no indef. art., no pl.;* **~bohrungen/eine ~bohrung durchführen** drill test wells/a test well; **~druck** *der; Pl.* **~~e** (Druckw.) proof; **~exemplar** *das* specimen copy; ***~|fahren** ▸**Probe; ~fahrt** *die* trial run; (vor dem Kauf, nach einer Reparatur) test drive; **eine ~fahrt machen** go for a trial run/test drive *or* test run; **hast du mit deinem neuen Boot schon eine ~fahrt gemacht?** have you tried out your new boat yet?; **~flug** *der* test flight; **~halber** *adv.* as a test; **jmdn. ~halber beschäftigen** employ sb. on a trial basis; **~jahr** *das* probationary year; **~lauf** *der* (Technik) test run

proben *tr., itr. V.* rehearse

Proben·arbeit *die* rehearsals *pl.* (**zu** for)

probe-, Probe-: ~nummer *die* specimen copy; **~weise A** *Adv.* ‹*employ*› on a trial basis; **den Motor ~weise laufen lassen** test[-run] the engine; **B** *adj.* trial; **~zeit** *die* 1 probationary *or* trial period; 2 (schweiz. Rechtsspr.: Bewährungsfrist) period of probation; **eine ~zeit von drei Jahren** three years' probation

probieren

A *tr. V.* 1 (versuchen) try; have a go *or* try at; **~, ob der Schlüssel passt** try the key to see whether it fits 2 (kosten) taste; try; sample 3 (aus~) try out; (an~) try on ‹*clothes, shoes*› 4 (Theaterjargon: proben) rehearse

B *itr. V.* 1 (versuchen) try; have a go *or* try; **Probieren geht über Studieren** the proof of the pudding is in the eating (prov.) 2 (kosten) have a taste; **willst du ~?** do you want a taste?; **probier mal!** have a taste!; try some! 3 (Theaterjargon) rehearse

Problem /pro'ble:m/ *das;* **~s, ~e** problem; **vor einem ~ stehen** be faced *or* confronted with a problem

Problem- problem; **ihr Kind war eine ~geburt** she had a difficult time with the birth of her child

Problematik /proble'ma:tık/ *die;* **~** (Schwierigkeit) problematic nature; (Probleme) problems *pl.*

problematisch *Adj.* problematic[al]

problematisieren *tr. V.* **etw. ~:** expound the problems of sth.

problem-, Problem-: ~bewusstsein, *~bewußtsein *das* awareness of the problem/problems (**für** of); **~fall** *der* problem case; **~film** *der* serious film; **~kind** *das* problem child; **~los A** *Adj.* problem-free; **B** *adv.* without any problems; **~stellung** *die* way of looking at *or* posing a problem/problems; (zu erörterndes Thema) problem; **~stück** *das* problem play

Produkt /pro'dʊkt/ *das;* **~[e]s, ~e** (auch Math., fig.) product; **~e der Landwirtschaft** agricultural produce *sing. or* products; **das ~ aus fünf mal zwei** the product of five times two

Produkten-: ~börse *die* (Wirtsch.) ▸**Warenbörse; ~handel** *der* (Kaufmannsspr.) trade in agricultural commodities

Produktion /prodʊk'tsio:n/ *die;* **~, ~en** production; **die ~ steigern/stoppen** increase/stop production

Produktions-: ~ablauf *der* production process; **~abteilung** *die* production department; **~anlage** *die* production unit; **~anlagen** production plant *sing.;* **~ausfall** *der* loss of production; **~fehler** *der* production fault; manufacturing fault; **~firma** *die* production company; **~genossenschaft** *die* (DDR) cooperative; **eine landwirtschaftliche ~genossenschaft** a collective farm; **~güter** *Pl.* (Wirtsch.) producer goods; **~kosten** *Pl.* production costs; **~leistung** *die* output; **~leiter** *der,* **~leiterin** *die* production manager; **~mittel** *Pl.* (marx.) means of production; **~prozess, *~prozeß** *der* production process; **~verfahren** *das* production process; **~verhältnisse** *Pl.* (marx.) relations of production; **~weise** *die* production methods *pl.;* **~ziffern** *Pl.* production figures; **~zweig** *der* branch of production

produktiv /prodʊk'ti:f/

A *Adj.* productive; prolific ‹*writer, artist, etc.*›

B *adv.* ‹*work, cooperate*› productively

Produktivität /prodʊktivi'tɛ:t/ *die;* **~:** productivity

Produktiv·kraft *die* (marx.) productive force; force of production

Produkt-: ~linie *die* product line; **~palette** *die* product range

Produzent /produ'tsɛnt/ *der;* **~en, ~en, Produzentin** *die;* **~, ~nen** ▸ⓘ **S. 113** producer

produzieren

A *tr. V.* 1 *auch itr.* (herstellen) produce 2 (ugs.: hervorbringen) make ‹*bow, noise*›; come up with ‹*excuse, report*›

B *refl. V.* (ugs.: großtun) show off

Prof[1] /prɔf/ *der;* **~s, ~s** (ugs.) prof

Prof[2] *die;* **~, ~s** (ugs.) prof

Prof. *Abk.* **= Professor** Prof.

profan /pro'fa:n/

A *Adj.* 1 (weltlich) profane; secular; secular ‹*building*› 2 (alltäglich) mundane

B *adv.* (alltäglich) mundanely; in a mundane way

Profan·bau *der; Pl.* **~ten** (Archit., Kunstwiss.) secular building

profanieren *tr. V.* (geh.) 1 (entweihen) profane 2 (säkularisieren) secularize

Profession /profɛ'sio:n/ *die;* **~, ~en** (österr., sonst veralt.) occupation; (akademische, wissenschaftliche, medizinische ~) profession; (handwerkliche ~) trade

Professionalismus /profɛsiona'lısmʊs/ *der;* **~:** professionalism

professionell /profɛsio'nɛl/

A *Adj.* professional

B *adv.* professionally

-professor *der;* **~s, ~en** 1 professor of ‹*history, mathematics, etc.*› 2 (österr., sonst veralt.: -lehrer) ‹*history, mathematics, etc.*› teacher (*at a Gymnasium*)

Professor /pro'fɛsɔr/ *der;* **~s, ~en** /-'so:rən/ ▸ⓘ **S. 44,** ▸ⓘ **S. 113** 1 (Hochschul~) professor; **ordentlicher ~:** [full] professor (holding a chair); **außerordentlicher ~:** extraordinary professor (*not holding a chair*); **außerplanmäßiger ~:** supernumerary professor; *s. auch* **zerstreut A** 2 (österr., sonst veralt.: Gymnasial~) [grammar school] teacher; **Herr ~!** sir!

professoral /profɛso'ra:l/ *Adj.* (auch abwertend) professorial

Professorenschaft *die;* **~:** professoriate

Professorin /profe'so:rın/ *die;* **~, ~nen** ▸ⓘ **S. 44;** ▸ⓘ **S. 113** 1 (Hochschul~) professor; *s. auch* **-in** 2 (österr.: Studienrätin) mistress

P

Professur /profɛ'su:ɐ/ *die;* ~, ~**en** professorship, chair (**für** in)

Profi *der;* ~**s,** ~**s** (ugs.) pro (coll.)

Profi·fußball *der* professional football

profihaft
A *Adj.* professional
B *adv.* professionally

Profil /pro'fi:l/ *das;* ~**s,** ~**e** 1 (Seitenansicht) profile; **im** ~: in profile 2 (von Reifen, Schuhsohlen) tread 3 (ausgeprägte Eigenart) image; **kein** ~ **haben** *od.* **besitzen** lack a distinctive image 4 (Geol.) profile

> **profil**
> An Austrian news and current affairs magazine, with a circulation of over 100,000. It has a reputation for hard-hitting journalism.

Profi·lager *das* (Sportjargon) **ins** ~ **überwechseln** turn professional

profilieren
A *refl. V.* make one's name *or* mark; (sich unterscheiden) give oneself a clearer image
B *tr. V.* profile ‹*moulding, frame, etc.*›; put a tread on ‹*tyre, shoe*›

profiliert *Adj.* 1 (markant, bedeutend) prominent 2 **eine grob** ~**e Gummisohle** a rubber sole with a heavy tread

Profilierung *die;* ~, ~**en** 1 ▸ **Profil 1** 2 (Unterscheidung) image; **die politische** ~ **einer Gruppe** the political complexion of a group

profil-, Profil-: ~**los** *Adj.* ‹*politican, writer*› lacking any distinctive image; ~**neurose** *die* neurosis about one's image; ~**sohle** *die* treaded sole; ~**stahl** *der* (Technik) sectional steel; ~**träger** *der* (Technik) sectional beam

Profi-: ~**spieler** *der,* ~**spielerin** *die* professional player; ~**sport** *der* professional sport

Profit /pro'fi:t/ *der;* ~**[e]s,** ~**e** profit; **etw. mit** ~ **verkaufen** sell sth. at a profit; **aus etw.** ~ **ziehen** *od.* **herausschlagen** turn sth. to one's profit *or* advantage; ~ **machen** make a profit; **mit/ohne** ~ **arbeiten** run/not run at a profit

profitabel /profi'ta:bl̩/
A *Adj.* profitable
B *adv.* profitably

profit-, Profit-: ~**bringend** ▸ **profitabel**; ~**gier** *die* (abwertend) greed for profit; ~**gierig** *Adj.* (abwertend) greedy for profit *postpos.*; profit-seeking

profitieren
A *itr. V.* profit (**von, bei** by); (fig.) profit, gain (**von, bei, an** + *Dat.* from, by); **ich kann dabei nur** ~: I can't lose
B *tr. V.* **er hat bei diesem Geschäft nichts/wenig profitiert** he did not make a profit/much of a profit on the deal

Profit-: ~**jäger** *der,* ~**jägerin** *die* profiteer; ~**maximierung** *die* maximization of profits; ~**rate** *die* (Wirtsch., marx.) rate of profit; ~**streben** *das* (abwertend) profit-seeking

pro forma /pro: 'fɔrma/ *Adv.* 1 (der Form halber) as a matter of form 2 (zum Schein) for the sake of appearances

profund /pro'fʊnt/ *Adj.* (geh.) profound; deep

Prognose /pro'gno:zə/ *die;* ~, ~**n** (auch Med.) prognosis; (Wetter~, Wirtschafts~) forecast; **eine** ~ **stellen** make a prognosis/give *or* make a forecast

prognostizieren /prognɔsti'tsi:rən/ *tr. V.* (geh.) forecast; predict

-programm *das;* ~**s,** ~**e** programme; program (Amer., Computing); **Besuchs**~: programme of visits

Programm /pro'gram/ *das;* ~**s,** ~**e** 1 programme; program (Amer., Computing); (Theater~ auch) bill; (bei Pferderennen) card; (Verlags~) list; (Ferns.: Sender) channel; **das** ~ **für die kommende Woche** (Ferns., Rundfunk) the programmes *pl.* for the coming week; **etw. passt jmdm. nicht ins** *od.* **in sein** ~: sth. doesn't fit in with sb.'s plans; **nach** ~ (fig.) according to plan; **auf jmds./dem** ~ **stehen** (fig.) be on sb.'s/the programme *or* agenda; **auf dem** ~ **stehen** (bei einer Sitzung, Versammlung) be on the agenda 2 (Kaufmannsspr.: Sortiment) range

Programm·änderung *die* change of programme

Programmatik /progra'ma:tɪk/ *die;* ~, ~**en** (Politik) [political] objectives *pl.*

programmatisch
A *Adj.* programmatic ‹*speech, statement*›; **die** ~**en Ziele/Absichten der Regierung** the aims of the government's programme
B *adv.* **die** ~ **festgelegten Ziele der Partei** the aims laid down in the party's programme

programm-, Programm-: ~**datei** *die* (DV) program file; ~**direktor** *der,* ~**direktorin** *die* (Ferns.) director of programmes; ~**folge** *die* (Ferns.) order of programmes; (einer Show) order of acts; running order; ~**gemäß** A *Adj.* **die** ~**gemäße Abfolge der Darbietungen** the order of acts as stated in the programme; B *adv.* according to programme *or* plan; ~**gestaltung** *die* programme planning; ~**heft** *das* programme; ~**hinweis** *der* programme announcement

programmieren *tr. V.* 1 (DV) program 2 (auf etw. festlegen) programme; condition; **auf Erfolg programmiert sein** be geared to achieving success 3 (nach einem Programm ansetzen) schedule

Programmierer *der;* ~**s,** ~, **Programmiererin** *die;* ~, ~**nen** ▸ ❶ **S. 113** (DV) programmer

Programmier·sprache *die* (DV) programming language

Programmierung *die;* ~, ~**en** ▸ **programmieren 1-3**: programming; conditioning; scheduling

Programm-: ~**kino** *das* art-house [cinema]; ~**musik** *die* programme music; ~**punkt** *der* item on the programme; (bei einer Sitzung) item on the agenda

***Programmusik** ▸ **Programmmusik**

Programm-: ~**vor·schau** *die* (im Fernsehen) preview [of the week's/evening's *etc.* viewing]; (im Kino) trailers *pl.*; ~**zeitschrift** *die* radio and television magazine; ~**zettel** *der* programme

Progression /progrɛ'sio:n/ *die;* ~, ~**en** (Steuerw.) progressive tax system; **in die** ~ **kommen** move into a higher tax bracket

progressiv /progrɛ'si:f/
A *Adj.* progressive
B *adv.* progressively; **er schreibt sehr** ~: he's a very progressive writer; **sie erziehen ihre Kinder sehr** ~: they are giving their children a very modern upbringing

Progressiv·steuer *die* (Steuerw.) progressive tax

Prohibition /prohibi'tsio:n/ *die;* ~: prohibition

Projekt /pro'jɛkt/ *das;* ~**[e]s,** ~**e** project

Projekt·gruppe *die* project team *or* group

projektieren *tr. V.* (entwerfen) draw up the plans for; plan; (planen) project; plan

Projektil /projɛk'ti:l/ *das;* ~**s,** ~**e** projectile

Projektion /projɛk'tsio:n/ *die;* ~, ~**en** (Optik, Math., Geogr., Psych.) projection

Projektions-: ~**apparat** *der* projector; ~**ebene** *die* (Math.) plane of projection; ~**wand** *die* projection screen

Projekt·leiter *der,* **Projekt·leiterin** *die* project leader

Projektor /pro'jɛktɔr/ *der;* ~**s,** ~**en** /-'to:rən/ projector

Projekt·planung *die* project planning

projizieren /proji'tsi:rən/ *tr. V.* (Optik, Math., Psych.) project

Proklamation /proklama'tsio:n/ *die;* ~, ~**en** proclamation

proklamieren *tr. V.* proclaim

Pro-Kopf- per head *or* capita *postpos.*

Prokrustes·bett /pro'krʊstɛs-/ *das* (geh.) Procrustean bed

Prokura /pro'ku:ra/ *die;* ~, **Prokuren** (Kaufmannsspr.) [full] power of attorney; procuration (formal)

Prokurist /proku'rɪst/ *der;* ~**en,** ~**en, Prokuristin** *die;* ~, ~**nen** ≈ authorized signatory; ~ **bei einer Firma sein** ≈ have [full] signing powers in a firm

Prolet /pro'le:t/ *der;* ~**en,** ~**en** 1 (abwertend: ungebildeter Mensch) peasant; boor 2 (ugs. veralt.: Proletarier) prole (coll.)

Proletariat /proleta'ria:t/ *das;* ~**[e]s** proletariat

Proletarier /prole'ta:riɐ/ *der;* ~**s,** ~, **Proletarierin** *die;* ~, ~**nen** proletarian

proletarisch
A *Adj.* proletarian
B *adv.* ‹*think, behave*› like a proletarian

proletarisieren *tr. V.* proletarianize

proletenhaft (abwertend)
A *Adj.* boorish
B *adv.* boorishly

Proletin *die;* ~, ~**nen** ▸ **Prolet**

Prolog /pro'lo:k/ *der;* ~**[e]s,** ~**e** (auch Radsport) prologue

Prolongation /prolɔŋga'tsio:n/ *die;* ~, ~**en** 1 (Wirtsch.) renewal 2 (bes. österr.) prolonging; (eines Vertrages) extension

prolongieren *tr. V.* 1 (Wirtsch.: stunden) renew 2 (bes. österr.: verlängern) extend ‹*contract, engagement*›

Promenade /promə'na:də/ *die;* ~, ~**n** promenade

Promenaden-: ~**deck** *das* promenade deck; ~**konzert** *das* promenade concert; ~**mischung** *die* (scherzh.) mongrel

promenieren *itr. V.; auch mit sein* (geh.) promenade

prometheisch /prome'te:ɪʃ/ (geh.)
A *Adj.* Promethean
B *adv.* like Prometheus

Promi[1] *der;* ~**s,** ~**s** (ugs. scherzh.) celebrity

Promi[2] *die;* ~, ~**s** (ugs. scherzh.) celebrity

Promille /pro'mɪlə/ *das;* ~**s,** ~ 1 (Tausendstel) **ein Blutalkoholgehalt von zwei** ~: a blood alcohol level of two parts per thousand; **bei 0,4/unter einem** ~ **liegen** be 0.4/less than one in a *or* per thousand 2 (ugs.: Blutalkohol) alcohol level; **Ich fahre! Du hast zu viel** ~: I'll drive. You're over the limit; **er fährt nur ohne** ~: he never drinks and drives

Promille·grenze *die* legal [alcohol] limit

prominent /promi'nɛnt/ *Adj.* prominent

Prominente *der/die; adj. Dekl.* prominent figure

Prominenz /promi'nɛnts/ *die;* ~: prominent figures *pl.*; (das Prominentsein) prominence; **er gehört zur politischen** ~: he is a prominent political figure

Promiskuität /promiskui'tɛ:t/ *die;* ~: promiscuity

Promotion[1] /promo'tsio:n/ *die;* ~, ~**en** 1 (Erlangung der Doktorwürde) gaining of a/one's doctorate; **er schloss sein Studium mit der** ~ **ab** he completed his studies by gaining *or* obtaining his doctorate; **jmds.** ~ **[zum Doktor der Philosophie] feiern** celebrate the award of a doctorate *or* Ph.D. to sb. 2 (österr.: offizielle Feier) [doctoral] degree ceremony; **seine** ~ **zum Doktor der Philosophie** his Ph.D. ceremony

Promotion[2] /prə'moʊʃən/ *die;* ~ (Wirtsch.) promotion; **für etw.** ~ **machen** promote sth.

promovieren /promo'vi:rən/
A *itr. V.* 1 (die Doktorwürde erlangen) gain *or* obtain a/one's doctorate 2 (eine Dissertation schreiben) do a doctorate (**über** + *Akk.* on)
B *tr. V.* confer a doctorate *or* the degree of doctor on

prompt /prɔmpt/
A *Adj.* prompt
B *adv.* 1 (umgehend) promptly 2 (ugs., meist iron.: wie erwartet) [and] sure enough; **er ist auf den Trick** ~ **hereingefallen** and sure enough he fell for the trick; **„Gleich fällt er", dachte ich, und** ~ **fiel er** 'He's going to fall,' I thought and sure enough he did; **er wird** ~ **in die Falle hineinlaufen** as sure as fate he'll fall into the trap

Promptheit *die;* ~: promptness

Pronomen /pro'no:mən/ *das;* ~**s,** ~ *od.* **Pronomina** /pro'no:mina/ (Sprachw.) pronoun

pronominal /pronomi'na:l/ (Sprachw.)
A *Adj.* pronominal
B *adv.* pronominally

Pronominal- (Sprachw.) pronominal

prononciert /pronõ'si:ɐ̯t/ (geh.)
A *Adj.* pronounced, definite, decided ‹*opinion, views*›; staunch, determined ‹*supporter, advocate, etc.*›
B *adv.* (entschieden) clearly; **sich ~ über etw.** (*Akk.*) **äußern** express a definite opinion on sth.

Propädeutik /propɛ'dɔy̆tɪk/ *die;* ~, ~**en** (Wissensch.) **1** preparatory instruction *no indef. art.*; **die philosophische ~:** philosophical propaedeutics *pl.* **2** (Lehrbuch) introductory textbook (**zu** on)

propädeutisch *Adj.* (Wissensch.) propaedeutic

Propaganda /propa'ganda/ *die;* ~ **1** (auch fig. ugs.) propaganda **2** (Reklame) publicity

Propaganda-: ~**apparat** *der* propaganda machine; ~**feld·zug** *der* propaganda campaign; ~**minister** *der,* ~**ministerin** *die* minister of propaganda; ~**sender** *der* (abwertend) (Rundf.) propaganda station; (Ferns.) propaganda channel

Propagandist *der;* ~**en,** ~**en, Propagandistin** *die;* ~, ~**nen** **1** propagandist **2** (Wirtsch.: Werbefachmann/-frau) demonstrator; (Vertreter) representative

propagandistisch
A *Adj.* propagandist; propaganda *attrib.* ‹*purposes, measures, success, effort*›
B *adv.* ‹*use, distort, etc.*› for propaganda purposes

propagieren *tr. V.* (geh.) propagate ‹*idea, view, belief, etc.*›; **ein vereinigtes Europa ~:** propagate the idea of a united Europe

Propan /pro'pa:n/ *das;* ~**s, Propan·gas** *das* propane

Propeller /pro'pɛlɐ/ *der;* ~**s,** ~ **1** propeller; airscrew; prop (coll.) **2** (Seew.: Schiffsschraube) propeller; screw

Propeller-: ~**antrieb** *der* propeller drive; **mit ~antrieb** propeller-driven; ~**flugzeug** *das* propeller-driven aircraft

proper /'prɔpɐ/
A *Adj.* **1** (adrett) smart **2** (ordentlich und sauber) neat and tidy **3** (sorgfältig, genau) meticulous
B *adv.* **1** (ordentlich und sauber) neatly and tidily **2** (sorgfältig, genau) meticulously

Prophet /pro'fe:t/ *der;* ~**en,** ~**en** prophet; **ich bin doch kein ~!** (ugs.) I can't see into the future!; **der ~ gilt nichts in seinem Vaterland[e]** (Spr.) a prophet is without honour in his own country; *s. auch* **Bart 1**; **Berg 1**

Prophetin *die;* ~, ~**nen** prophetess

prophetisch
A *Adj.* prophetic
B *adv.* prophetically

prophezeien /profe'tsa̯iən/ *tr. V.* prophesy (*Dat.* for); predict ‹*result, weather*›; **das kann ich dir ~!** I can promise you that!

Prophezeiung *die;* ~, ~**en** ▸**prophezeien**: prophecy; prediction

prophylaktisch /profy'laktɪʃ/ (Med.)
A *Adj.* prophylactic
B *adv.* prophylactically; as a prophylactic measure

Prophylaxe /profy'laksə/ *die;* ~, ~**n** (Med.) prophylaxis

Proportion /propɔr'tsi̯o:n/ *die;* ~, ~**en** (auch Math., Musik) proportion

proportional /propɔrtsi̯o'na:l/ (auch Math.)
A *Adj.* proportional; **umgekehrt ~ zu ...** in inverse proportion to ...; (Math. auch) inversely proportional to ...
B *adv.* proportionally; in proportion; **~ [zu** *od.* **mit] einer Sache** (*Dat.*) in proportion to sth.

proportioniert /propɔrtsi̯o'ni:ɐ̯t/ *Adj.* proportioned

Proporz /pro'pɔrts/ *der;* ~**es,** ~**e** (Politik) proportional representation *no art.*; **Ämter im** *od.* **nach dem ~ besetzen** fill posts in proportion to the number of votes received

Proporz·wahl *die* (bes. österr. u. schweiz.) ▸**Verhältniswahl**

Proppen /'prɔpn̩/ *der;* ~**s,** ~ **1** (nordd.) ▸**Pfropfen 2** (ugs.: Kind) podge (coll.)

proppen·voll *Adj.* (ugs.) jam-packed (coll.)

Propst /pro:pst/ *der;* ~**[e]s, Pröpste** /prø:pstə/, **Pröpstin** *die;* ~, ~**nen** (kath., ev. Kirche) provost

Pro·rektor *der,* **Pro·rektorin** *die* (Hochschulw.) ≈ pro-vice-chancellor

Prosa /'pro:za/ *die;* ~**:** prose

prosaisch
A *Adj.* **1** (geh., oft abwertend: nüchtern) prosaic; plain ‹*building*› **2** (veralt.: in Prosa abgefasst) prose *attrib.*
B *adv.* (geh., oft abwertend) prosaically

Prosaist *der;* ~**en,** ~**en, Prosaistin** *die;* ~, ~**nen** prose writer

Proselyt /proze'ly:t/ *der;* ~**en,** ~**en, Proselytin** *die;* ~, ~**nen** proselyte; **Proselyten machen** (geh. abwertend) proselytize

Pro·seminar *das* (Hochschulw.) introductory seminar course (*for students in their first and second year*)

prosit /'pro:zɪt/ *Interj.* ▸**❶ S. 331** your [very good] health; **~ Neujahr!** happy New Year!

Prosit *das;* ~**s,** ~**s** ▸**❶ S. 331** toast; **ein ~ dem Geburtstagskind!** here's to the birthday boy/girl!

Prosodie /prozo'di:/ *die;* ~, ~**n** (Verslehre) prosody

Prospekt /pro'spɛkt/ *der od.* (bes. österr.) *das;* ~**[e]s,** ~**e** **1** (Werbeschrift) brochure; (Werbezettel) leaflet; (Verlags~) illustrated catalogue; (nur mit Neuerscheinungen) seasonal list **2** (Theater: Bühnenbild) backdrop; backcloth **3** (bild. Kunst: Ansicht) perspective view **4** (Wirtsch.) prospectus

prospektiv /prospɛk'ti:f/ *Adj.* prospective

prosperieren /prospe'ri:rən/ *itr. V.* (geh.) prosper; ‹*art, science*› prosper, flourish

Prosperität /prosperi'tɛ:t/ *die;* ~ (geh.) prosperity

prost /pro:st/ *Interj.* (ugs.) cheers (Brit. coll.); **na denn** *od.* **dann ~!** (ugs. iron.) that's brilliant! (coll. iron.); *s. auch* **Mahlzeit**

Prost *das;* ~**[e]s,** ~**e** (ugs.) ▸**Prosit**

Prostata /'prɔstata/ *die;* ~, ~**e** /'prɔstatɛ/ ▸**❶ S. 435** (Anat.) prostate [gland]

Prostata·krebs *der* (Med.) prostate cancer

prosten *itr. V.* say cheers (Brit. coll.)

Prösterchen /'prø:stɐçən/ *Interj.* (fam.) cheers (Brit. coll.)

prostituieren /prostitu'i:rən/
A *tr. V.* (geh.) prostitute
B *refl. V.* (auch fig., geh.) prostitute oneself; **sich als Künstler ~** (fig. geh.) prostitute one's artistic talent

Prostituierte *die/der; adj. Dekl.* ▸**❶ S. 113** prostitute

Prostitution /prostitu'tsi̯o:n/ *die;* ~ (auch fig. geh.) prostitution *no art.*

Proszenium /pro'stse:ni̯ʊm/ *das;* ~**s, Proszenien** (Theater) proscenium

Protagonist /protago'nɪst/ *der;* ~**en,** ~**en, Protagonistin** *die;* ~, ~**nen** (geh.) protagonist

Protegé /prote'ʒe:/ *der;* ~**s,** ~**s** (geh.) protégé

protegieren /prote'ʒi:rən/ *tr. V.* (geh.) sponsor; patronize ‹*artist, composer, etc.*›

Protein /prote'i:n/ *das;* ~**s,** ~**e** (Biochemie) protein

Protektion /protɛk'tsi̯o:n/ *die;* ~, ~**en** (geh.) patronage *no indef. art.*

Protektionismus *der;* ~ (Wirtsch.) protectionism *no art.*

Protektorat /protɛkto'ra:t/ *das;* ~**[e]s,** ~**e** **1** (geh.: Schirmherrschaft) patronage **2** (Völkerr.: Schutzherrschaft, Schutzgebiet) protectorate

Protest /pro'tɛst/ *der;* ~**[e]s,** ~**e** **1** protest; **[bei jmdm.] ~ gegen jmdn./etw. erheben** *od.* **einlegen** make a protest [to sb.] against sb./sth.; **etw. aus ~ tun** do sth. as a *or* in protest; **unter [lautem] ~:** protesting [loudly] **2** (Finanzw.) protest; **der Wechsel ist zu ~ gegangen** the bill has been protested **3** (DDR Rechtsw.) protest

Protest·aktion *die* protest campaign

Protestant /protɛs'tant/ *der;* ~**en,** ~**en, Protestantin** *die;* ~, ~**nen** Protestant

protestantisch
A *Adj.* Protestant
B *adv.* **[streng] ~ erzogen sein** have had a [strict] Protestant upbringing

Protestantismus *der;* ~**:** Protestantism *no art.*

Protest-: ~**bewegung** *die* protest movement; ~**demonstration** *die* protest demonstration

protestieren
A *itr. V.* protest, make a protest (**gegen** against, about)
B *tr. V.* (Finanzw.) protest

Protest-: ~**kundgebung** *die* protest rally; ~**marsch** *der* protest march; ~**note** *die* (Dipl.) protest note; ~**ruf** *der* shout of protest; ~**sänger** *der,* ~**sängerin** *die* protest singer; ~**song** *der* protest song; ~**streik** *der* protest strike; ~**sturm** *der* storm of protest; ~**versammlung** *die* protest meeting; ~**welle** *die* wave of protest

Prothese /pro'te:zə/ *die;* ~, ~**n** **1** artificial limb; prosthesis (Med.) **2** (Zahn~) set of dentures; dentures *pl.*; prosthesis (Med.)

Protokoll /proto'kɔl/ *das;* ~**s,** ~**e** **1** (wörtlich mitgeschrieben) transcript; (Ergebnis~) minutes *pl.*; (bei Gericht) record; records *pl.*; (einer Verhandlung auf diplomatischer Ebene) protocol; **[das] ~ führen** make a transcript [of the proceedings]; (bei einer Sitzung Notizen machen) take *or* keep the minutes; **etw. zu ~ geben/zu ~ geben, dass ...** make a statement about sth./to the effect that ...; **zu ~ nehmen** take down ‹*statement etc.*›; (bei Gericht) enter ‹*objection, statement*› in the record **2** (diplomatisches Zeremoniell) protocol **3** (Strafzettel) ticket

Protokollant /protokɔ'lant/ *der;* ~**en,** ~**en, Protokollantin** *die;* ~, ~**nen** transcript writer; (eines Ergebnisprotokolls) keeper of the minutes; (bei Gericht) court reporter

protokollarisch /protokɔ'la:rɪʃ/
A *Adj.* **1** (in Form, aufgrund eines Protokolls) on record *postpos.*; (bei einer Sitzung) minuted **2** (das diplomatische Zeremoniell betreffend) **die ~en Vorschriften** the rules of protocol
B *adv.* **1** (in Form, aufgrund eines Protokolls) **etw. ~ niederschreiben** (bei einer Sitzung) take sth. down in the minutes; (bei Gericht) enter sth. in the *or* place sth. on record **2** (das diplomatische Zeremoniell betreffend) from the point of view of protocol

Protokoll-: ~**chef** *der,* ~**chefin** *die* Chief of Protocol; ~**führer** *der,* ~**führerin** *die* ▸**Protokollant**

protokollieren
A *tr. V.* take down; minute, take the minutes of ‹*meeting*›; minute, record in the minutes ‹*remark*›
B *itr. V.* (bei einer Sitzung) take *or* keep the minutes; (bei Gericht) keep the record; (bei polizeilicher Vernehmung) keep a record

Proton /'pro:tɔn/ *das;* ~**s,** ~**en** /-'to:nən/ (Physik) proton

Proto·plasma /proto'plasma/ *das* (Biol.) protoplasm

Proto·typ /'pro:toty:p/ *der* **1** (geh.: Inbegriff) archetype; epitome **2** (Urform, erste Ausführung, Motorsport) prototype

Protozoon /proto'tso:ɔn/ *das;* ~**s, zoen** (Biol.) protozoan

-protz *der;* ~**es** *od.* ~**en,** ~**e** *od.* ~**en** (ugs.) **Bildungs~/Sex[ual]~** *usw.* swank[pot] (coll.) when it comes to education/sex *etc.*; **Muskel~:** muscleman

Protz /prɔts/ *der;* ~**es** *od.* ~**en,** ~**e** *od.* ~**en** (ugs.) **1** (Angeber) swank[pot] (coll.); show-off **2** (Prunk) swank (coll.); show

protzen *itr. V.* (ugs.) swank (coll.); show off; **mit etw. ~:** show sth. off

P

Protzerei *die;* ~, ~**en** (ugs.) [1] (das Protzen) swanking (coll.); showing off [2] (protzige Äußerung) swanky remark (coll.)

protzig (ugs. abwertend)
A *Adj.* swanky (coll.); showy
B *adv.* swankily (coll.)

Provenienz /prove'ni̯ɛnts/ *die;* ~, ~**en** (geh.) provenance

provenzalisch /provɛn'tsa:lɪʃ/ *Adj.* Provençal

Proviant /pro'vi̯ant/ *der;* ~**s,** ~**e** provisions *pl.;* ~ **[für die Reise] mitnehmen** take some food for the journey

Provider /prɔ'vaidɐ/ *der;* ~**s,** ~ (DV) [service] provider

Provinz /pro'vɪnts/ *die;* ~, ~**en** [1] (Verwaltungsbezirk) province [2] (oft abwertend: kulturell rückständige Gegend) **aus der** ~ **kommen/in der** ~ **leben** come from/live in the provinces *pl.;* **finsterste** *od.* **hinterste** ~ **sein** be terribly provincial

Provinz-: ~**bewohner** *der,* ~**bewohnerin** *die* (oft abwertend) provincial; ~**blatt** *das* (abwertend) provincial [news]paper; local rag (derog.)

Provinzialismus /provɪntsi̯a'lɪsmʊs/ *der;* ~, **Provinzialismen** [1] (Sprachw.) provincialism [2] (abwertend) provincialism

provinziell /provɪn'tsi̯ɛl/ (meist abwertend)
A *Adj.* provincial; parochial ‹views›
B *adv.* provincially

Provinzler /pro'vɪntslɐ/ *der;* ~**s,** ~, **Provinzlerin** *die;* ~, ~**nen** (ugs. abwertend) [narrow-minded] provincial

Provinz-: ~**nest** *das* (ugs. abwertend) [tiny] provincial backwater; ~**stadt** *die* provincial town

Provision /provi'zi̯o:n/ *die;* ~, ~**en** (Kaufmannsspr.) commission; **auf** *od.* **gegen** ~ **arbeiten** work on a commission basis

provisorisch /provi'zo:rɪʃ/
A *Adj.* temporary ‹*accommodation, filling, bridge, etc.*›; provisional ‹*status, capital, etc.*›; provisional, caretaker *attrib.* ‹*government*›; provisional, temporary ‹*measure, regulation, etc.*›; **bei uns ist alles noch sehr** ~: everything's still very makeshift in our house/flat *etc*
B *adv.* temporarily; **etw.** ~ **reparieren** do *or* effect a temporary repair on sth.

Provisorium /provi'zo:ri̯ʊm/ *das;* ~**s, Provisorien** (geh.) temporary measure

provokant /provo'kant/ (geh.) ▸ **provokativ**

Provokateur /provoka'tø:ɐ̯/ *der;* ~**s,** ~**e, Provokateurin** *die;* ~, ~**nen** agent provocateur; agitator

Provokation /provoka'tsi̯o:n/ *die;* ~, ~**en** provocation

provokativ /provoka'ti:f/, **provokatorisch** /provoka'to:rɪʃ/ (geh.)
A *Adj.* provocative
B *adv.* provocatively

provozieren /provo'tsi:rən/
A *tr. V.* [1] (herausfordern) provoke [2] (auslösen) provoke; cause ‹*accident, fight*›
B *itr. V.* be provocative; **zum Nachdenken [über etw.** (*Akk.*)**]** ~: provoke people into thinking [about sth.]

Prozedur /protse'du:ɐ̯/ *die;* ~, ~**en** (auch DV) procedure

Prozent /pro'tsɛnt/ *das;* ~**[e]s,** ~**e** [1] *nach Zahlenangaben Pl. ungebeugt* (Hundertstel) per cent *sing.;* **fünf** ~: five per cent; **ich bin mir zu 90** ~ **sicher** I'm 90 per cent certain; **der Plan wurde zu 90** ~ **erfüllt** 90 per cent of the plan was fulfilled; **etw. in** ~**en ausdrücken** express sth. as a percentage; **60** ~ **Alkohol enthalten** contain 60 per cent alcohol by volume; be 105 per cent proof [2] *Pl.* (ugs.: Gewinnanteil) share *sing.* of the profits; (Rabatt) discount *sing.;* **auf etw.** (*Akk.*) ~**e bekommen** get a discount on sth.

-prozentig *adj.* -per-cent

Prozent-: ~**punkt** *der* percentage point; ~**rechnung** *die* percentage calculation; ~**satz** *der* percentage; **zu einem beträchtlichen** ~**satz** be to a considerable extent

prozentual /protsɛn'tu̯a:l/
A *Adj.* percentage; **der** ~**e Anteil der Autobesitzer an der Bevölkerung** the percentage of car owners in the population
B *adv.* ~ **am Gewinn beteiligt sein** have a percentage share in the profits

Prozess, *Prozeß /pro'tsɛs/ *der;* ~**es,** ~**e** [1] trial; (Fall) [court] case; **jmdm. den** ~ **machen** take sb. to court; **es wurde ihm wegen der Ermordung von X der** ~ **gemacht** he stood trial charged with the murder of X; **der** ~ **Meyer gegen Schulze** the case of Meyer versus Schulze; **einen** ~ **gewinnen/verlieren** win/lose a case *or* lawsuit; *s. auch* **anstrengen B 3; führen A 3** [2] (Entwicklung, Ablauf) process [3] (fig.) **mit jmdm./etw. kurzen** ~ **machen** (ugs.) make short work of sb./sth.; **jetzt wird kurzer** ~ **gemacht** (ugs.) we're going to sort this out once and for all

prozess-, *prozeß-, Prozess-, *Prozeß-: ~**beobachter** *der,* ~**beobachterin** *die* trial observer; ~**bevollmächtigte** *der/die* (Rechtsspr.) person with power of attorney in legal proceedings; ~**führend** *Adj.* (Rechtsspr.) **die** ~**führenden Parteien** the litigants; ~**gegner** *der,* ~**gegnerin** *die* (Rechtsspr.) opposing party

prozessieren *itr. V.* go to court; **mit jmdm. um etw.** *od.* **wegen etw.** ~: be engaged in a court action *or* lawsuit with sb. about sth.; **gegen jmdn.** ~: bring an action *or* a lawsuit against sb.; (seit längerer Zeit) be engaged in an action *or* a lawsuit against sb.

Prozession /protse'si̯o:n/ *die;* ~, ~**en** procession

Prozess-kosten, *Prozeß-kosten *Pl.* legal costs

Prozessor /pro'tsɛsɔr/ *der;* ~**s,** ~**en** /-'so:rən/ (DV) [central] processor

Prozess-, *Prozeß-: ~**ordnung** *die* (Rechtsw.) code of procedure; ~**rechner** *der* (DV) process-control computer; ~**recht** *das* (Rechtsw.) procedural law; ~**vollmacht** *die* (Rechtsw.) power of attorney in legal proceedings; ~**wärme** *die* (Kerntechnik) process heat

prüde /'pry:də/ (abwertend)
A *Adj.* prudish
B *adv.* prudishly; ~ **erzogen worden sein** have had a prudish upbringing

Prüderie /pry:də'ri:/ *die;* ~ (abwertend) prudery; prudishness

prüfen /'pry:fn̩/
A *tr. V.* [1] *auch itr.* test ‹*pupil*› (**in** + *Dat.* in); (beim Examen) examine ‹*pupil, student, etc.*› (**in** + *Dat.* in); **ein geprüfter Elektrotechniker** a qualified electrician; **mündlich/schriftlich geprüft werden** have an oral/a written test/examination; **Latein/Anatomie** ~: be the examiner for Latin/Anatomy; **jmds. Kenntnisse** ~: test sb.'s knowledge [2] (untersuchen) examine (**auf** + *Akk.* for); check, examine ‹*device, machine, calculation*› (**auf** + *Akk.* for); investigate, look into ‹*complaint*›; (testen) test (**auf** + *Akk.* for); test, inspect ‹*goods, materials, food*›; test, check ‹*temperature*›; **einen Fall nochmals** ~: re-examine a case [3] (kontrollieren) check ‹*papers, passport, application, calculation, information, correctness, etc.*›; audit, check, examine ‹*accounts, books*› [4] (vor einer Entscheidung) check ‹*price*›; examine ‹*offer*›; consider ‹*applica tion*›; **drum prüfe, wer sich ewig bindet** (Spr.) marry in haste, repent at leisure (prov.) [5] (forschend ansehen) scrutinize; **jmdn.** ~**d** *od.* **mit** ~**den Blicken ansehen** scrutinize sb. [6] (geh.: großen Belastungen aussetzen) try; **sie ist vom Leben schwer geprüft worden** her life has been a hard trial [7] (Sport: stark fordern) test
B *refl. V.* search one's heart

Prüfer *der;* ~**s,** ~, **Prüferin** *die;* ~, ~**nen** [1] tester; inspector; (Buch~) auditor [2] (im Examen) examiner

Prüf-gerät *das* (Technik) piece of test equipment; test instrument

Prüfling /'pry:flɪŋ/ *der;* ~**s,** ~**e** examinee; [examination] candidate

Prüf-: ~**stand** *der* (Technik) test bed; test stand; **auf dem** ~**stand** (fig.) under the microscope (fig.); ~**stein** *der* touchstone (**für** for, of); measure (**für** of); ~**stück** *das* test-piece; [test] specimen

Prüfung *die;* ~, ~**en** [1] ▸ⓘ **S. 331** (Examen) examination; exam (coll.); **eine** ~ **machen** *od.* **ablegen** take *or* do an examination [2] (das [Über]prüfen) ▸ **prüfen 2-4:** examination; investigation; inspection; (Kontrolle) check; (das Kontrollieren) checking *no indef. art.;* (Test) test; (das Testen) testing *no indef. art.;* **klinische** ~**en** clinical trials; **nach/bei** ~ **Ihrer Beschwerde** after/on examining *or* investigating your complaint; **nach nochmaliger** ~ **Ihres Antrags** on reconsidering your application [3] (geh.: schicksalhafte Belastung) trial

Prüfungs-: ~**angst** *die* examination phobia; (im Einzelfall) examination nerves *pl.;* ~**arbeit** *die* examination; exam (coll.); ~**aufgabe** *die* problem set in an/the examination; ~**ausschuss, *~ausschuß** *der* board of examiners; ~**ergebnis** *das* examination result; ~**kandidat** *der,* ~**kandidatin** *die* [examination] candidate; ~**ordnung** *die* examination regulations *pl.;* ~**termin** *der* date of an/the examination; ~**unterlagen** *Pl.* documents required on entering for an/the examination

Prüf-verfahren *das* test procedure

Prügel /'pry:gl̩/ *der;* ~**s,** ~ [1] (Knüppel) stick; cudgel [2] *Pl.* (Schläge) beating *sing.;* (als Strafe für Kinder) hiding (coll.); ~ **bekommen** *od.* **beziehen** get a hiding (coll.) *or* beating

Prügelei *die;* ~, ~**en** (ugs.) punch-up (coll.); fight

Prügel-knabe *der* whipping boy

prügeln
A *tr.* (*auch itr.*) *V.* beat; **musst du immer gleich** ~**?** do you have to resort to beatings straight away?
B *refl. V.* **sich** ~: fight; **sich mit jmdm. [um etw.]** ~: fight sb. [over *or* for sth.]

Prügel-: ~**strafe** *die* corporal punishment *no art.;* ~**szene** *die* [1] (im Film, Theaterstück) fight scene; [2] (Prügelei) fight

Prunk /prʊŋk/ *der;* ~**[e]s** splendour; magnificence; (einer Ausstattung, eines Saales usw. auch) sumptuousness; (eines Gebäudes, einer Architektur usw.) magnificence; grandeur; (einer Zeremonie) splendour; pageantry; ~ **entfalten** put on a display of splendour

Prunk-bau *der; Pl.* ~**ten** magnificent building

prunken *itr. V.* [1] be resplendent; ~**d** magnificent [2] (prahlen, sich hervortun) show off; **mit etw.** ~: flaunt *or* make a great show of sth.

prunk-, Prunk-: ~**stück** *das* showpiece; ~**süchtig** *Adj.* ‹*person*› with a passion for splendour [and grandeur]; ~**voll** **A** *Adj.* magnificent; splendid; **B** *adv.* magnificently; splendidly; magnificently, splendidly, sumptuously ‹*furnished, decorated*›

prusten /'pru:stn̩/ *itr. V.* (ugs.) (schnauben) snort; (keuchen) puff and blow; **vor Lachen** ~: snort with laughter

PS *Abk.* [1] = **Pferdestärke** h.p. [2] = **Postskript[um]** PS

Psalm /psalm/ *der;* ~**s,** ~**en** psalm

Psalmist *der;* ~**en,** ~**en** (Rel.) psalmist

Psalter /'psaltɐ/ *der;* ~**s,** ~ [1] (Musik) psaltery [2] (Rel.) psalter

PSchA *Abk.* = **Postscheckamt**

pscht /pʃt/ ▸ **pst**

pseudo-, Pseudo- /psɔydo-/ (abwertend) pseudo-

Pseudonym /psɔydo'ny:m/ *das;* ~**s,** ~**e** pseudonym; (eines Schriftstellers) pseudonym; nom de plume; pen name

pst /pst/ *Interj.* sh; hush

Psyche /'psy:çə/ *die;* ~, ~**n** [1] psyche [2] (österr.: Frisiertoilette) dressing table

psychedelisch /psyçe'de:lɪʃ/
A *Adj.* psychedelic
B *adv.* psychedelically

Psychiater /psy'çi̯a:tɐ/ *der;* ~**s,** ~, **Psychiaterin** *die;* ~, ~**nen** ▸ⓘ **S. 113** psychiatrist

P

Psychiatrie /psyçi̯a'tri:/ *die;* ~, ~n 1) psychiatry *no art.* 2) (ugs.) (Abteilung) psychiatric department; (Klinik) psychiatric clinic

psychiatrisch
A *Adj.* psychiatric
B *adv.* **jmdn. ~ untersuchen/behandeln** give sb. a psychiatric examination/give sb. psychiatric treatment

psychisch
A *Adj.* psychological; psychological, mental ‹*strain, disturbance, process*›; mental ‹*illness*›
B *adv.* psychologically; **~ gesund/krank sein** be mentally fit/ill; **ein ~ bedingtes Leiden** an illness of psychological origin

psycho-, Psycho- /psy:ço-/: **~analyse** *die* psychoanalysis *no art.*; **~analytiker** *der,* **~analytikerin** *die* ▸ℹ S. 113 psychoanalyst; **~analytisch** A *Adj.* psychoanalytical; B *adv.* psychoanalytically; **~diagnostik** *die* psychodiagnostics *sing., no art.*; **~drama** *das* 1) (Literaturw.) psychological drama; 2) (Psych.) psychodrama; **~gen** /-'ge:n/ *Adj.* (Med., Psych.) psychogenic; **~gramm** *das* (Psych.) psychograph; **~krimi** /'----/ *der* (ugs.) psychological thriller; **~loge** /-'lo:gə/ *der;* **~~n, ~~n** ▸ℹ S. 113 psychologist; **~logie** /-lo'gi:/ *die;* **~~:** psychology; **~login** *die;* **~, ~~nen** ▸ℹ S. 113 psychologist; **~logisch** A *Adj.* 1) psychological; 2) (ugs.: ~logisch geschickt) **das war nicht sehr ~logisch von dir** that wasn't very good psychology on your part; B *adv.* psychologically; **~logisch geschult** trained in psychology; **~logisieren** *itr.* (*auch tr.*) *V.* (abwertend) psychologize; **~path** /-'pa:t/ *der;* **~~en, ~~en, ~pathin** *die;* **~~,~~nen** psychopath; **~pathie** /-pa'ti:/ *die;* **~~, ~~n** psychopathy *no art.*; **~pathisch** A *Adj.* psychopathic; B *adv.* psychopathically; **~pathologie** *die* psychopathology *no art.*; **~pharmakon** /-'farmakɔn/ *das;* **~~s, ~pharmaka** psychotropic drug

Psychose /psy'ço:zə/ *die;* ~, ~n psychosis

psycho-, Psycho-: **~somatisch** (Med.) A *Adj.* psychosomatic; B *adv.* **~somatisch bedingt** of psychosomatic origin *postpos.*; **~terror** /'----/ *der* psychological intimidation; **~therapeut** *der,* **~therapeutin** *die* ▸ℹ S. 113 psychotherapist; **~therapeutisch** A *Adj.* psychotherapeutic; B *adv.* **jmdn. ~therapeutisch behandeln** give sb. psychotherapeutic treatment; **~therapie** *die* psychotherapy *no art.*; **~thriller** /'----/ *der* psychological thriller

Psychotiker /psy'ço:tikɐ/ *der;* **~s, ~, Psychotikerin** *die;* ~, **~nen** psychotic

psychotisch *Adj.* psychotic

PTA *Abk.* **= pharmazeutisch-technische Assistentin** pharmaceutical-laboratory assistant

ptolemäisch /ptole'mɛ:ɪʃ/ *Adj.* Ptolemaic

Ptolemäus /ptole'mɛ:ʊs/ *(der)* Ptolemy

PTT *Abk.* **= Schweizerische Post-, Telefon- und Telegrafenbetriebe** *Swiss postal, telephone, and telegraph services*

pubertär /puber'tɛ:ɐ̯/
A *Adj.* pubertal; **sein Benehmen ist typisch ~:** his behaviour is typical for the age of puberty
B *adv.* **~ bedingt** caused by puberty *postpos.*

Pubertät /puber'tɛ:t/ *die;* **~:** puberty; **in die ~ kommen** reach puberty

pubertieren *itr. V.* reach puberty; **~d** pubescent

Publicity /pa'blɪsɪtɪ/ *die;* **~:** publicity

publicity-: **~scheu** *Adj.* publicity-shy; **~trächtig** A *Adj.* with good publicity potential *postpos.* B *adv.* with plenty of publicity

Publicrelations, Public Relations /'pablɪk rɪ'leɪʃənz/ *Pl.* public relations

publik /pu'bli:k/ *Adj.*; **in ~ sein/werden** be/become public knowledge; **die Sache ist längst ~:** that's long been common knowledge; **etw. ~ machen** make sth. public

Publikation /publika'tsi̯o:n/ *die;* **~, ~en** publication

Publikum /'pu:blikʊm/ *das;* **~s** 1) (Zuschauer, Zuhörer) audience; (bei Sportveranstaltungen) crowd 2) (Kreis von Interessierten) public; (eines Schriftstellers) readership 3) (Besucher) clientele

publikums-, Publikums-: **~erfolg** *der* success with the public; **~liebling** *der* idol of the public; **~magnet** *der* crowd-puller; **~verkehr** *der:* **„heute kein ~verkehr!"** 'closed to the public [today]'; **~wirksam** *Adj.* with public appeal *postpos., not pred.*; punchy ‹*headline*›; ‹*headline*› with a strong appeal; effective, compelling ‹*broadcast*›; **~wirksam sein** have public appeal

publizieren /publi'tsi:rən/ *tr.* (*auch itr.*) *V.* publish; **in verschiedenen Fachzeitschriften ~:** have articles *or* work published in various journals

Publizist *der;* **~en, ~en** commentator on politics and current affairs; publicist

Publizistik *die;* **~:** mass communications *pl., no art.*; (Journalismus) journalism *no art.*

Publizistin *die;* **~, ~nen** ▸ **Publizist**

publizistisch
A *Adj.* **seine ~e Aktivität** his journalistic activities *pl.*; **die Reise war ein ~er Misserfolg** the trip failed to get the media's attention
B *adv.* **etw. ~ verbreiten** disseminate sth. via the media; **~ tätig sein** work in mass communications/as a journalist

Publizität /publitsi'tɛ:t/ *die;* **~:** publicity

Puck /pʊk/ *der;* **~s, ~s** (Eishockey) puck

puckern /'pʊkɐn/ *itr. V.* (ugs.) throb

Pudding /'pʊdɪŋ/ *der;* **~s, ~e** *od.* **~s** *thick, usually flavoured, milk-based dessert;* ≈ blancmange; *s. auch* **hauen B 3**

Pudding·pulver *das* ≈ blancmange powder

Pudel /'pu:dl̩/ *der;* **~s, ~** 1) (Hund) poodle; **das war also des ~s Kern** (fig.) so 'that's what was behind it; **wie ein begossener ~ dastehen** (ugs.) stand there crestfallen; (nach einer Zurechtweisung) stand there sheepishly 2) (ugs.: beim Kegeln) miss; **einen ~ werfen** *od.* **schießen** miss

pudel-, Pudel-: **~mütze** *die* bobble *or* pompom hat; **~nass, *~naß** *Adj.* (ugs.) drenched; soaked to the skin; **~wohl** *Adv.* (ugs.) **sich ~wohl fühlen** feel on top of the world

Puder /'pu:dɐ/ *der;* **~s, ~:** powder

Puder·dose *die* powder compact

pudern *tr. V.* powder; **sich** (*Dat.*) **die Nase ~:** powder one's nose

Puder-: **~quaste** *die* powder puff; **~zucker** *der* icing sugar (Brit.); confectioners' sugar (Amer.)

Puertoricaner /pu̯ertori'ka:nɐ/ *der;* **~s, ~, Puertoricanerin** *die;* **~, ~nen** Puerto Rican; *s. auch* **-in**

puertoricanisch *Adj.* Puerto Rican

puff /pʊf/ *Interj.* bang

Puff[1] *der;* **~[e]s, Püffe** /'pʏfə/ (ugs.) 1) (Stoß) thump; (leichter/kräftiger Stoß mit dem Ellenbogen) nudge/dig; **einen ~** *od.* **einige Püffe vertragen [können]** (fig.) be able to take a few knocks 2) (Knall) bang

Puff[2] *der od. das;* **~s, ~s** (salopp: Bordell) knocking shop (Brit. sl.); brothel

Puff[3] *der;* **~[e]s, ~e** *od.* **~s** 1) (Wäsche~) linen basket 2) (Sitzkissen) pouffe 3) (veralt.: Bausch) puff

Puff·ärmel *der* puff *or* puffed sleeve

puffen (ugs.)
A *tr.* (*auch itr.*) *V.* 1) (stoßen) thump; (mit dem Ellenbogen) nudge; dig; **~ und schubsen** push and shove 2) (irgendwohin befördern) push; shove; (mit dem Ellenbogen) elbow; **jmdn. zur Seite ~:** push *or* shove/elbow sb. aside
B *itr. V.* ‹*locomotive*› puff

Puffer *der;* **~s, ~** 1) (Vorrichtung) buffer 2) ▸ **Kartoffel~**

Puffer-: **~staat** *der* buffer state; **~zone** *die* buffer zone

Puff-: **~mutter** *die; Pl.* **~mütter** (salopp) madam; **~reis** *der* puffed rice

puh /pu:/ *Interj.* ugh; (erleichtert) phew

pulen /'pu:lən/ (nordd. ugs.)
A *itr. V.* pick (**an** + *Dat.* at); **[sich** (*Dat.*)**] in der Nase ~:** pick one's nose
B *tr. V.* pick (**aus** out of); **etw. von etw. ~:** pick sth. off sth.

Pulk /pʊlk/ *der;* **~[e]s, ~s** *od.* **~e** 1) (Milit.: Verband) group 2) (Menge) crowd; (Sport: Hauptfeld) pack; bunch

Pulle /'pʊlə/ *die;* **~, ~n** (salopp) bottle; **volle ~** (fig. salopp) flat out

pullen
A *itr. V.* (Seemannsspr.) row
B *itr. V.* (Pferdesport) pull

pullern /'pʊlɐn/ *itr. V.* (fam., bes. ostmd.) pee (coll.)

Pulli /'pʊli/ *der;* **~s, ~s** (ugs.), **Pullover** /pʊ'lo:vɐ/ *der;* **~s, ~:** pullover; sweater

Pullunder /pʊ'lʊndɐ/ *der;* **~s, ~:** slipover

Puls /pʊls/ *der;* **~es, ~e** 1) pulse; **jmds. ~ fühlen/messen** feel/take sb.'s pulse 2) (Elektrot., Nachrichtent.) pulse

Puls·ader *die* artery; **sich** (*Dat.*) **die ~n aufschneiden** slash one's wrists

pulsen *itr. V.* (auch fig.) pulse

pulsieren *itr. V.* (auch fig.) pulsate; ‹*blood*› pulse

Puls-: **~schlag** *der* (auch fig.) pulse; (einzelner ~schlag) beat; **~wärmer** *der;* **~~s, ~~:** wristlet; **~zahl** *die* (Med.) pulse rate

Pult /pʊlt/ *das;* **~[e]s, ~e** 1) desk; (Lese~) lectern; desk 2) (Schalt~) control desk; console

Pulver /'pʊlfɐ/ *das;* **~s, ~** 1) powder 2) (Schieß~) [gun]powder; **das ~ hat er [auch] nicht [gerade] erfunden** (ugs.) he'll never set the world *or* (Brit.) the Thames on fire; **sein ~ verschossen haben** (fig. ugs.) have shot one's bolt 3) (salopp: Geld) dough (coll.)

Pülverchen /'pʏlfɐçən/ *das;* **~s, ~** (spött.) [medicinal] powder

Pulver-: **~dampf** *der* gun smoke; **~fass, *~faß** *das* barrel of gunpowder; (kleiner) powder keg; **auf einem** *od.* **dem ~fass sitzen** (fig.) be sitting on a powder keg *or* on top of a volcano; **~form** *die:* **in ~form** in powder form

pulverisieren *tr. V.* pulverize; powder

Pulver-: **~kaffee** *der* instant coffee; **~kammer** *die* 1) (Schiffbau) powder magazine; 2) (Milit. veralt.) chamber

pulvern *tr. V.* **zu viel Geld in die Rüstung ~:** throw money away on arms

Pulver·schnee *der* powder snow

Puma /'pu:ma/ *der;* **~s, ~s** puma

Pummel /'pʊml̩/ *der;* **~s, ~** (ugs.), **Pummelchen** *das;* **~s, ~** (ugs.) podge

pumm[e]lig /'pʊm(ə)lɪç/ *Adj.* (ugs.) chubby

Pump /pʊmp/ *der;* **~s** (salopp) **auf ~:** on tick (coll.)

Pumpe /'pʊmpə/ *die;* **~, ~n** 1) pump 2) (salopp: Herz) ticker (joc.)

pumpen *tr., itr. V.* 1) (auch fig.) pump 2) (salopp: verleihen) lend; **jmdm. etw. ~:** lend sb. sth. 3) (entleihen) borrow; **sich** (*Dat.*) **[bei** *od.* **von jmdm.] etw. ~:** borrow sth. from *or* (coll.) off sb.

Pumpen·schwengel *der* pump handle

pumpern /'pʊmpɐn/ *itr. V.* (südd., österr. ugs.) thump; ‹*heart*› thump, pound; ‹*heavy artillery*› thud

Pumper·nickel *der* pumpernickel

Pump·hose *die* harem trousers *pl.*; (veralt.: Knickerbocker) knickerbockers *pl.*

Pumps /pœmps/ *der;* **~, ~:** court shoe

Pump·station *die* pumping station

Punier /'pu:ni̯ɐ/ *der;* **~s, ~, Punierin** *die;* **~, ~nen** Phoenician

punisch *Adj.* Punic

Punk /paŋk/ *der;* **~[s], ~s** punk

Punker /'paŋkɐ/ *der;* **~s, ~, Punkerin** *die;* **~, ~nen** 1) (Musiker[in]) punk rocker 2) (Anhänger[in]) punk

Punk·rock *der* punk rock

Punkt /pʊŋkt/ *der;* **~[e]s, ~e** 1) (Tupfen) dot; (größer) spot; **ein Stoff mit blauen ~en** a fabric with blue spots; **das ist [nicht] der springende ~** (fig.) that's [not] the point; **ein dunkler ~**

[in jmds. Vergangenheit] a dark chapter [in sb.'s past] 2 (Satzzeichen) full stop; period; **drei ~e bedeuten eine Auslassung im Zitat** three dots mean an omission in the quotation; **einen ~ machen** *od.* **setzen** put a full stop; **nun mach [aber] mal einen ~!** (fig. ugs.) come off it! (coll.); **ohne ~ und Komma reden** (ugs.) talk nineteen to the dozen (Brit.); rabbit (Brit. coll.) *or* talk on and on 3 (i-~) dot; **den ~ auf dem i vergessen** forget to dot the i; **etw. auf den ~ genau wissen** know sth. quite precisely; *s. auch* **i, I** 4 (Stelle) point; **an einem ~ sein, wo ...** (fig.) have reached the point *or* stage where ...; **ein schwacher/wunder/neuralgischer ~** (fig.) a weak/sore/vulnerable *or* sensitive point; **die Unterhaltung war/die Verhandlungen waren an einem toten ~ angelangt** the conversation had come to a dead stop/the talks had reached deadlock *or* an impasse; **ein starker Kaffee half ihm über den toten ~ hinweg** a strong coffee helped him to get his second wind; **nachmittags um zwei Uhr habe ich meinen toten ~:** I'm at my lowest ebb at two o'clock in the afternoon 5 (Gegenstand, Thema, Abschnitt) point; (einer Tagesordnung) item; point; **in diesem/über diesen ~:** on this point; **sich in allen ~en einig sein** agree on all points; **~ für ~:** point by point; **etw. auf den ~ bringen** sum sth. up; put sth. in a nutshell; **jmdn. in allen ~en der Anklage freisprechen** acquit sb. on all counts 6 (Bewertungs~) point; (bei einer Prüfung) mark; **nach ~en siegen** win on points; **~e sammeln** (fig.) score points (**bei** with) 7 (Musik) dot 8 (Math.) point 9 ▸ⓘ S. 729 (Zeit~) point; **jetzt ist der ~ gekommen, wo ich ...** the moment *or* time has now arrived when I ...; **~ 12 Uhr** at 12 o'clock on the dot 10 *nach Zahlenangaben ungebeugt* (Druckw.) point

Punkt·abzug *der* (Sport) points deduction; deduction of points

Pünktchen /'pʏŋktçən/ *das;* **~s, ~:** little dot *or* spot; **rote ~:** little red dots *or* spots

punkten *itr. V.* (bes. Boxen) pick up points; score [points]

punkt-, Punkt-: ~feuer *das* (Milit.) precision fire; **~förmig** *Adj.* **eine ~förmige Lichtquelle** a point source of light; **~gewinn** *der* (Sport, bes. Ballspiele) **sie blieben im Turnier ohne ~gewinn** they failed to win any points in the competition; **~gleich** *Adj.* (Sport) level on points *pred.*; **~gleich stehen** be level on points; **die ~gleichen Teams** the teams on equal points; **~gleichheit** *die* (Sport) **bei ~gleichheit** if the same number of points have been scored

punktieren *tr. V.* 1 (mit Punkten darstellen) dot 2 (Med.) puncture 3 (Musik) **eine Rolle ~:** transpose individual notes in a vocal part 4 *auch itr.* (Musik: verlängern) dot ‹*note*›

Punktion /pʊŋk'tsi̯o:n/ *die;* **~, ~en** (Med.) puncture

pünktlich /'pʏŋktlɪç/

A *Adj.* 1 punctual; **er ist immer ~:** he's always punctual *or* on time; **der Zug ist ~/nicht ~:** the train is on time/is late 2 (veralt.: gewissenhaft genau) meticulous

B *adv.* 1 punctually; on time; **das Konzert beginnt ~ um 20 Uhr** the concert will begin at 8 o'clock sharp; **~ auf die Minute** punctually to the minute 2 (veralt.: gewissenhaft, genau) meticulously

Pünktlichkeit *die;* **~:** punctuality

punkt-, Punkt-: ~nieder·lage *die* (Sport) defeat on points; points defeat; **~richter** *der,* **~richterin** *die* (Sport) judge; **~schweißen** *tr., itr. V.; nur Inf. u. 2. Part. gebr.* spot weld; **~sieg** *der* (Sport) win on points; points win; **~spiel** *das* (Mannschaftssport) league game

punktuell /pʊŋk'tu̯ɛl/

A *Adj.* isolated ‹*interventions, checks, approaches, initiatives, etc.*›; **einige ~e Verbesserungen** improvements in a few matters of detail

B *adv.* **sich mit einem Thema nur ~ befassen** deal only with certain *or* particular points relating to a topic; **Kontrollen wurden nur ~ durchgeführt** only spot checks were carried out

Punktum *Interj.* (veralt.) *in* **[und damit] ~:** and that's that; and that's final *or* flat

Punkt-: ~wertung *die* points system; **~zahl** *die* score; number of points; (beim Eiskunstlauf) score; [number of] marks

Punsch /pʊnʃ/ *der;* **~[e]s, ~e** *od.* **Pünsche** /'pʏnʃə/ punch

Punze /'pʊntsə/ *die;* **~, ~n** 1 (Werkzeug) punch; (zum Gravieren) burin 2 (Gütezeichen) hallmark

Pupille /pu'pɪlə/ *die;* **~, ~n** pupil

Püppchen /'pʏpçən/ *das;* **~s, ~** 1 ([kleine] Puppe) little doll *or* (child lang.) dolly 2 (Kosewort) pet; (niedliches Mädchen) little sweetie (coll.); (hübsches, aber nichts sagendes Mädchen) dolly bird (Brit. sl.)

Puppe /'pʊpə/ *die;* **~, ~n** 1 doll[y] 2 (Marionette) puppet; marionette; (fig.) puppet; **die ~n tanzen lassen** (fig. ugs.) pull the strings; (es hoch hergehen lassen) paint the town red (coll.) 3 (salopp: Mädchen) bird (sl.); (als Anrede) sweetie (coll.) 4 (Zool.) pupa 5 (ostmd.: aus Getreidegarben) stook; shock 6 *in* **bis in die ~n** (ugs.) till all hours

Puppen-: ~doktor *der* (ugs.) doll repairer; **etw. zum ~doktor bringen** take sth. to the dolls' hospital; **~gesicht** *das* baby-doll face; **~haus** *das* doll's house; dollhouse (Amer.); **~spiel** *das* 1 puppet theatre; 2 (Stück) puppet show; **~spieler** *der,* **~spielerin** *die* puppeteer; **~stube** *die* doll's house; dollhouse (Amer.); **~theater** *das* puppet theatre; **~wagen** *der* doll's pram

puppig *Adj.* (ugs.) 1 ▸**niedlich** 2 (kinderleicht) dead easy

pur /pu:ɐ̯/ *Adj.* 1 (rein) pure 2 (unvermischt) neat; straight; **bitte einen Whisky ~!** a neat whisky, please 3 (bloß) sheer; pure; **das ist ~er Wahnsinn** that's sheer *or* pure *or* absolute madness

Püree /py're:/ *das;* **~s, ~s** 1 purée 2 ▸**Kartoffelbrei**

pürieren /py'ri:rən/ *tr. V.* (Kochk.) purée ‹*potatoes, apples, etc.*›; (zerstampfen) mash

Purismus *der;* **~** (Sprachw., Kunstw.) purism

Purist *der;* **~en, ~en, Puristin** *die;* **~, ~nen** purist

puristisch

A *Adj.* purist; puristic

B *adv.* puristically

Puritaner /puri'ta:nɐ/ *der;* **~s, ~, Puritanerin** *die;* **~, ~nen** 1 Puritan 2 (fig.) puritan

puritanisch *Adj.* 1 Puritan 2 (fig.) puritanical

Puritanismus *der;* **~:** Puritanism *no art.*

Purpur /'pʊrpʊr/ *der;* **~s** 1 (Farbton) crimson 2 (Gewand) purple

purpur-, Purpur-: ~farben, ~farbig *Adj.* crimson; **~mantel** *der* crimson *or* purple robe

purpurn, purpur·rot *Adj.* crimson

Purzel·baum *der* (ugs.) somersault; **einen ~ machen** *od.* **schlagen** do *or* turn a somersault

purzeln /'pʊrtsl̩n/ *itr. V.; mit sein* (fam.) tumble; **auf dem Eis ~:** fall over on the ice

puschen *usw.* ▸**pushen** *usw.*

Puschen /'pu:ʃn̩/ *der;* **~s, ~** (nordd.) slipper

pushen /'pʊʃn̩/

A *tr. V.* 1 (Drogenjargon) push 2 (Journalistenjargon) push

B *itr. V.* (Drogenjargon) be a pusher

Pusher *der;* **~s, ~, Pusherin** *die;* **~, ~nen** (Drogenjargon) pusher

pusselig *Adj.* (ugs., bes. nordd.) 1 (Geduld fordernd) fiddly ‹*work, task*› 2 (übergenau) pernickety (coll.); (umständlich) fussy

pusseln /'pʊsl̩n/ *itr. V.* (ugs.) potter about; mess about (**an** + *Dat.* with)

Puste /'pu:stə/ *die;* **~** (salopp) puff; breath; **ganz aus der** *od.* **außer ~ sein** be out of puff; be puffed [out]; *s. auch* **ausgehen A 2**

Puste-: ~blume *die* (ugs.) dandelion clock; **~kuchen** *in* **[ja** *od.* **aber] ~kuchen** (ugs.) (es ist/war nicht der Fall) not a bit of it!; (es hat nicht geklappt) nothing doing!

Pustel /'pʊstl̩/ *die;* **~, ~n** ▸ⓘ **S. 439** pimple; spot; pustule (Med.)

pusten (ugs.)

A *itr. V.* 1 (blasen) ‹*person, wind*› blow; **es pustet draußen ganz schön** (ugs.) there's a fair old wind blowing out there (coll.); **~ müssen** (ugs.: bei einer Verkehrskontrolle) have to blow into the bag 2 (keuchen) puff [and pant *or* blow]

B *tr. V.* (blasen) blow; **jmdm. was** *od.* **eins ~** (salopp) tell sb. where to get off (coll.)

Puste·rohr *das* (ugs.) pea-shooter

Puszta /'pʊsta/ *die;* **~, Puszten,** ***Pußta** *die;* **~, Pußten** puszta; *steppeland in Hungary*

putativ /puta'ti:f/ *Adj.* (Rechtsspr.) putative

Putativ·notwehr *die* (Rechtsw.) **in ~ handeln** act in the mistaken belief that one is being attacked

Pute /'pu:tə/ *die;* **~, ~n** 1 (Truthenne) turkey hen; (als Braten) turkey 2 (salopp abwertend: Mädchen, Frau) **eine dumme/extravagante ~:** a silly goose *or* creature/an extravagant creature; **eine eingebildete ~:** a stuck-up little madam

Puter *der;* **~s, ~:** turkeycock; (als Braten) turkey

puter·rot *Adj.* scarlet; bright red

Putsch /pʊtʃ/ *der;* **~[e]s, ~e** putsch; coup [d'état]

putschen *itr. V.* organize a putsch *or* coup

Putschist *der;* **~en, ~en, Putschistin** *die;* **~, ~nen** putschist; rebel

Putsch·versuch *der* attempted putsch *or* coup

Pütt /pʏt/ *der;* **~s, ~e** *od.* **~s** (rhein., westfäl. Bergmannsspr.) pit; mine; **auf dem ~ sein** work in the mine

Putte /'pʊtə/ *die;* **~, ~n** (Kunstwiss.) putto

Putz /pʊts/ *der;* **~es** 1 (Baumaterial) plaster; (für Außenmauern) rendering; (Rau~) roughcast; **eine Wand mit ~ bewerfen** *od.* **verkleiden** plaster/render/roughcast a wall; **die Rohre liegen über ~:** the pipes are exposed; **auf den ~ hauen** (fig. salopp) (angeben) boast; brag; (ausgelassen feiern) have a rave-up (Brit. coll.) 2 (salopp: Streit) row (coll.); **wenn er spät nach Hause kommt, kriegt er ~ mit seiner Frau** when he gets home late, his wife starts rowing with him; **~ machen** (salopp) cause aggro (Brit. sl.) 3 (veralt.: Kleidung) finery

Putze *die;* **~, ~n** (salopp) char (Brit. coll.); cleaner

putzen *tr. V.* 1 (blank reiben) polish; clean; **Schuhe/die Fenster ~:** polish *or* clean one's shoes/clean the windows; **den Teller blank ~** (fig.) clear one's plate; *s. auch* **Klinke 1** 2 (säubern) clean; groom ‹*horse*›; **[sich** (*Dat.*)**] die Zähne/die Nase ~:** clean *or* brush one's teeth/blow one's nose; **er putzte seinem Kind die Nase** he wiped his child's nose; **sich ~** ‹*cat*› wash itself; ‹*bird*› preen itself 3 *auch itr.* (bes. rhein., südd., schweiz.: sauber machen) clean ‹*room, shop, etc.*›; **~ gehen** work as a cleaner *or* (Brit.) char[woman] 4 (zum Essen, Kochen vorbereiten) wash and prepare ‹*vegetables*› 5 (Sportjargon: besiegen) beat 6 (beschneiden) trim ‹*wick, lamp, candle*› 7 (österr.: chemisch reinigen) [dry-]clean; **etw. ~ lassen** take sth. to the [dry-]cleaners 8 (veralt.: schmücken) dress ‹*person*› up; decorate ‹*Christmas tree etc.*›; **sich ~:** dress [oneself] up 9 *auch itr.* (veralt.: zieren) decorate; adorn; **deine Schleife putzt aber ungemein!** your ribbon makes you look really pretty!

Putzerei *die;* **~, ~en** 1 (ugs. abwertend: das Putzen) [obsessive] cleaning 2 (österr.: Reinigungsanstalt) dry-cleaner's

Putz-: ~fimmel *der* (ugs. abwertend) mania for cleaning; **~frau** *die* ▸ⓘ **S. 113** cleaner; char[lady] (Brit.)

putzig (ugs.)

A *Adj.* 1 (entzückend) sweet; cute (Amer.); (possierlich) funny; comical 2 (seltsam) funny; peculiar

B *adv.* 1 (entzückend) sweetly; cutely (Amer.); (possierlich) comically 2 (seltsam) peculiarly

putz-, Putz-: ~lappen *der* [cleaning] rag; cloth; **~leute** *Pl.* cleaners; **~lumpen** *der* (südd.) [cleaning] rag; **~macherin** *die*

P

▸❶ S. 113 milliner; **~mann** *der;* ▸❶ S. 113 cleaner; **~mittel** *das* cleaning agent; **~munter** (ugs.) **A** *Adj.* chirpy (coll.); perky; **~munter sein** be as bright as a button; **B** *adv.* chirpily (coll.); perkily; **~tuch** *das; Pl.* **~tücher** cloth; (Lappen) [cleaning] rag; **~wolle** *die* cotton waste

puzzeln /ˈpazl̩n/ *itr. V.* do jigsaw puzzles/a jigsaw [puzzle]

Puzzle /ˈpazl̩/ *das;* **~s, ~s, Puzzle·spiel** *das* jigsaw [puzzle]

PVC *Abk.* **= Polyvinylchlorid** PVC

Pygmäe /pʏˈgmɛːə/ *der;* **~n, ~n** pygmy

pygmäenhaft *Adj.* pygmy-like

Pyjama /pʏˈdʒaːma/ *der* (*österr., schweiz. auch: das*); **~s, ~s** pyjamas *pl.*

Pyjama·hose *die* pyjama trousers *pl.*

Pykniker /ˈpʏknikɐ/ *der;* **~s, ~, Pyknikerin** *die;* **~, ~nen** (Med., Anthrop.) stocky person; pyknic *as tech. term*

pyknisch *Adj.* (Med., Anthrop.) stocky; pyknic *as tech. term*

Pylon /pʏˈloːn/ *der;* **~en, ~en, Pylone** *die;* **~, ~n** **1** (Tempeleingang) pylon **2** (bei Brücken) [suspension-bridge] tower **3** (Straßenmarkierung) traffic cone

Pyramide /pyraˈmiːdə/ *die;* **~, ~n** pyramid

pyramiden·förmig *Adj.* pyramidal; pyramid-shaped

Pyrenäen /pyreˈnɛːən/ *Pl.* Pyrenees

Pyrenäen·halb·insel *die* Iberian Peninsula

Pyrolyse /pyroˈlyːzə/ *die;* **~, ~n** (Chemie) pyrolysis

Pyro- /pyro-/: **~mane** /-ˈmaːnə/ *der;* **~~n, ~~n** (Med., Psych.) pyromaniac; **~manie** *die* (Med., Psych.) pyromania; **~manin** *die;* **~~, ~~nen** ▸**~mane**; **~techniker** *der,* **~technikerin** *die* fireworks expert; pyrotechnist

Pyrrhus·sieg /ˈpʏrʊs-/ *der* (geh.) Pyrrhic victory

pythagoräisch /pʏtagoˈrɛːɪʃ/ ▸**pythagoreisch**

Pythagoras /pyˈtaːgoras/ (*der*) Pythagoras

pythagoreisch /pʏtagoˈreːɪʃ/ *Adj.* Pythagorean; **der ~e Lehrsatz** (Geom.) Pythagoras' theorem

Python /ˈpyːtɔn/ *der;* **~s, ~s** *od.* **~en** /pyˈtoːnən/, **Python·schlange** *die* python

P

q, Q /kuː/ *das;* ~, ~: q/Q; **das Gütezeichen Q** (DDR) the grade A marking; *s. auch* **a, A**

qm *Abk.* ▸ⓘ **S. 262 = Quadratmeter** sq. m.

QMV *Abk.* **= Qualified Majority Voting** QMV

qua /kva/ (geh.)

A *Präp., meist mit ungebeugtem Substantiv* **1** *auch mit Gen.* (mittels) by means of **2** (gemäß) in accordance with; (kraft) by virtue of; ~ **Herkunft** by virtue of its/their *etc.* origins

B *Konj.* (als) ~ **Beamter** [in his function] as an official

quabbelig /ˈkvabəlɪç/, **quabblig** *Adj.* (nordd.) jelly-like ‹*frogspawn*›; (weich und dick) flabby, podgy ‹*face*›

quackeln /ˈkvakl̩n/ (bes. nordd. ugs.)

A *itr. V.* chatter; (dauernd) natter on (Brit. coll.)

B *tr. V.* **dummes Zeug** ~: talk drivel

Quacksalber /ˈkvakzalbɐ/ *der;* ~**s,** ~ (abwertend) quack [doctor]

Quacksalberei *die;* ~, ~**en** (abwertend) quackery

Quacksalberin *die;* ~, ~**nen** ▸**Quacksalber**

Quaddel /ˈkvadl̩/ *die;* ~, ~**n** [irritating] spot

Quader /ˈkvaːdɐ/ *der;* ~**s,** ~ *od.* (österr.:) ~**n** **1** (Steinblock) ashlar block; [rectangular] block of stone **2** (Geom.) rectangular parallelepiped; cuboid

Quader·stein *der* ▸**Quader 1**

Quadrant /kvaˈdrant/ *der;* ~**en,** ~**en** (Geom., Geogr., Astron., Math.) quadrant

quadrat-, Quadrat- ▸ⓘ **S. 262** square ‹*kilometre etc.*›

Quadrat[1] /kvaˈdraːt/ *das;* ~**[e]s,** ~**e** **1** (Geom.) square; **6 cm im** ~: 6 cm. square **2** (Math.: zweite Potenz) square; **eine Zahl ins** ~ **erheben** square a number; **drei im** *od.* **zum** ~: three squared; **Pech/Glück im** ~ (ugs.) terrible [bad] luck/terrific luck (coll.) **3** (bebaute Fläche) block [of houses]; **ums** ~ **gehen** walk round the block

Quadrat[2] *das;* ~**[e]s,** ~**en** (Druckw.) quadrat

quadratisch *Adj.* **1** square **2** (Math.) quadratic

Quadrat-: ~**latschen** *der* (salopp) **1** (Schuh) dirty great shoe (sl.); **2** (Pl.: Füße) dirty great feet (sl.); ~**meter** *der od. das* ▸ⓘ **S. 262** square metre; **unsere Wohnung hat 92** ~**meter** our flat (esp. Brit.) *or* (esp. Amer.) apartment has 92 square metres of floor space; ~**meter·preis** *der* price per square metre; ~**schädel** *der* **1** (ugs.: Kopf) dirty great nut (sl.); **2** (ugs. abwertend: sturer Mensch) mule; pig-headed type

Quadratur /kvadraˈtuːɐ̯/ *die;* ~, ~**en** (Math., Astron.) quadrature; **die** ~ **des Zirkels** (geh.) the achievement of the impossible

Quadrat-: ~**wurzel** *die* (Math.) square root (**aus** of); ~**zahl** *die* square number

quadrieren (Math.)

A *tr. V.* square

B *itr. V.* square numbers

Quadriga /kvaˈdriːga/ *die;* ~, **Quadrigen** quadriga

Quadrille /kaˈdrɪljə/ *die;* ~, ~**n** (Tanz, Musik) quadrille

Quadrillion /kvadrɪˈli̯oːn/ *die;* ~, ~**en** quadrillion (Brit.); septillion (esp. Amer.)

quadro-, Quadro- /ˈkvaːdro-/ quadraphonic ‹*system, effect, sound, etc.*›

quadro·phon (Akustik)

A quadraphonic

B *adv.* in quad[raphony]

Quadro·phonie *die;* ~ (Akustik) quadraphony

Quai /ke/ *der od. das;* ~**s,** ~**s** (schweiz.) **1** ▸**Kai** **2** (Uferstraße) embankment [road]

quak *Interj.* ~**!** (von Enten) quack!; (von Fröschen) croak!

quaken /ˈkvaːkn̩/ *itr. V.* ‹*duck*› quack; ‹*frog*› croak; (fig. abwertend) ‹*person, radio*› squawk

quäken /ˈkvɛːkn̩/

A *tr. V.* squawk; bawl out ‹*song*›

B *itr. V.* **1** (unangenehm tönen) ‹*voice*› squawk; (kreischen) screech; ‹*radio*› blare **2** (klagen) ‹*child*› whine, whinge

Quäker /ˈkvɛːkɐ/ *der;* ~**s,** ~, **Quäkerin** *die;* ~, ~**nen** Quaker

Qual /kvaːl/ *die;* ~, ~**en** **1** torment; agony *no indef. art.;* **[für jmdn.] eine** ~**/eine einzige** ~ **sein** be agony *or* torment/one long torment for sb.; **er macht uns** (*Dat.*) **das Leben/den Aufenthalt zur** ~: he's making our lives *pl.*/our stay a misery; **er hat die** ~ **der Wahl** (scherzh.) he is spoilt for choice **2** (Schmerzen) agony; ~**en** pain *sing.;* agony *sing.;* (seelisch) torment *sing.;* **jmds.** ~**en lindern** ease sb.'s pain *or* suffering; **jmdn. von seinen** ~**en erlösen** put sb. out of his/her agony; **unter [schlimmsten]** ~**en sterben** die in [the most terrible] agony; **jmdm. [große]** ~**en bereiten** cause sb. [great] pain; torment sb.; **er konnte sein letztes Werk nur unter** ~**en vollenden** he could only complete his last work in great pain *or* suffering

quälen /ˈkvɛːlən/

A *tr. V.* **1** (körperlich, seelisch) torment ‹*person, animal*›; maltreat, be cruel to ‹*animal*›; (foltern) torture; ~**de Schmerzen** agonizing *or* excruciating pain *sing.;* **ihn quälte der Gedanke[, dass ...]** he was tormented by the thought [that ...]; ~**de Ungewissheit** agonizing uncertainty **2** (plagen) ‹*cough etc.*› plague; (belästigen) pester; *s. auch* **gequält**

B *refl. V.* **1** (leiden) suffer; **sich sehr** ~: suffer greatly; suffer agonies **2** (sich abmühen) struggle; **sich durch ein Buch** ~: struggle through a book

Quälerei *die;* ~, ~**en** **1** torment; (Folter) torture; (Grausamkeit) cruelty; **Tierversuche sind [eine] reine** ~: animal experiments are simply cruel **2** (das Belästigen) pestering **3** (ugs.: große Anstrengung) **das Treppensteigen ist eine** ~ **für ihn** climbing stairs is a terrible struggle for him

quälerisch *Adj.* (geh.) agonizing

Quäl·geist *der; Pl.* ~**er** (fam.) pest

Qualifikation /kvalifikaˈtsi̯oːn/ *die;* ~, ~**en** **1** ▸**Qualifizierung 1** **2** (Befähigung) capability **3** (Sport) qualification; (Wettkampf zur ~) qualifier; qualifying round; **sie schafften die** ~ **für die Endrunde** they managed to qualify for the final round

Qualifikations-: ~**runde** *die* (Sport) qualifying round; ~**spiel** *das* (Sport) qualifier, qualifying match (**zu, für** for)

qualifizieren /kvalifiˈtsiːrən/

A *refl. V.* **1** (sich bilden) gain qualifications; **sich für einen Posten/zum Facharbeiter** ~: gain the qualifications needed for a post/to be a skilled worker **2** (Sport) qualify

B *tr. V.* **1** (ausbilden) **jmdn. [zu etw.]** ~: train sb. [to be sth.]; (weiterbilden) give sb. further training [for sth.] **2** (befähigen) qualify; **seine Berufserfahrung qualifiziert ihn zum** *od.* **als Abteilungsleiter** his experience gives him the necessary qualifications for the post of departmental manager

qualifiziert

A *2. Part. v.* **qualifizieren**

B *Adj.* **1** ‹*work, post*› requiring particular qualifications **2** (sachkundig) competent; skilled ‹*work*›; **hoch** ~: highly qualified **3** ~**e Mitbestimmung** (Wirtsch.) full participation by employees in decision-making; **Abstimmung mit** ~**er Mehrheit** (Politik) Qualified Majority Voting; ~**e Straftat** (Rechtsw.) aggravated offence; *s. auch* **Mehrheit**

C *adv.* (sachkundig) competently

Qualifizierung *die;* ~, ~**en** **1** (Ausbildung) training; (erworbene Qualifikation) qualifications *pl.* **2** (Weiterbildung) further training

Qualität /kvaliˈtɛːt/ *die;* ~, ~**en** **1** quality; **Waren guter/schlechter/erster** ~: goods of high/low/prime quality; ~ **kaufen** buy quality goods **2** (Textilw.) material *no pl.;* **schwere** ~**en** heavy fabrics **3** (Schach) **die** ~ **gewinnen** win the exchange

qualitativ /kvalitaˈtiːf/

A *Adj.* qualitative; ‹*difference, change*› in quality

B *adv.* with regard to quality; ~ **gut** good-quality; of good quality *postpos.;* ~ **besser werden** improve in quality

qualitäts-, Qualitäts-: ~**arbeit** *die* high-quality workmanship; ~**bewusst,** *~**bewußt** *Adj.* quality-conscious; ~**erzeugnis** *das* quality product; ~**kontrolle** *die* quality control; ~**sicherung** *die* quality assurance; ~**standard** *der* quality standard; standard of quality; ~**unterschied** *der* difference in quality

qualitätsvoll, qualitätvoll

A *Adj.* high-quality; **wirklich** ~ **sein** be of really high quality;

B *adv.* to a high standard [of quality]

Qualitäts- ~**ware** *die* quality goods *pl.;* ~**waren** quality goods; ~**wein** *der* [high-]quality wine (*from a recognized growing area, and made with a permitted type of grape*)

Qualle /ˈkvalə/ *die;* ~, ~**n** jellyfish; ~**n** jellyfish

quallig *Adj.* ▸**quabbelig**

Qualm /kvalm/ *der;* ~**[e]s** **1** [thick] smoke; (~wolken) clouds of [thick] smoke **2** (bes. nordd.: Dampf) steam

qualmen

A *itr. V.* **1** give off clouds of [thick] smoke; **aus dem Kamin qualmt es** clouds of [thick] smoke are coming from the fireplace; ~**de Schornsteine** chimneys belching [thick] smoke **2** (ugs.: rauchen) puff away

B *tr. V.* (ugs.: rauchen) puff away at ‹*cigarette etc.*›

qualmig *Adj.* (ugs.) thick with smoke *postpos.;* smoke-filled

qual·voll

A *Adj.* agonizing; **einen** ~**en Tod sterben** die in great pain

B *adv.* agonizingly; ~ **sterben** die in great pain

Quant /kvant/ *das;* ~**s,** ~**en** (Physik) quantum

Quäntchen /ˈkvɛntçən/ *das;* ~**s,** ~ (veralt.) scrap; **ein** ~ **Salz** a pinch of salt; **kein** ~: not

q

an iota; **ein ~ Glück** (fig. geh.) a little bit of luck; **dieses ~ Hoffnung** (fig. geh.) this glimmer of hope

quanteln /ˈkvantl̩n/ *tr. V.* (Physik) quantize

Quanten¹ ▸ **Quant, Quantum**

Quanten² *Pl.* (salopp) dirty great feet (sl.)

Quanten-: **~mechanik** *die* (Physik) quantum mechanics *sing., no art.*; **~sprung** *der* (Physik, fig.) quantum leap; **~theorie** *die* (Physik) quantum theory *no art.*

quantifizierbar *Adj.* quantifiable

quantifizieren /kvantifiˈtsiːrən/ quantify

Quantität /kvantiˈtɛːt/ *die;* **~, ~en** quantity; (Zahl) number

quantitativ /kvantitaˈtiːf/
A *Adj.* quantitative
B *adv.* quantitatively

Quantum /ˈkvantʊm/ *das;* **~s, Quanten** quota (**an** + *Dat.* of); (Dosis) dose; **mein tägliches ~ Kaffee** my daily quota *or* (joc.) dose of coffee; **ein gehöriges ~ Glück** (fig.) a good helping *or* big slice of luck

Quappe /ˈkvapə/ *die;* **~, ~n** 1 (Fisch) burbot 2 (Kaul~) tadpole

Quarantäne /karanˈtɛːnə/ *die;* **~, ~n** quarantine; **über jmdn./etw. ~ verhängen** put sb./sth. under quarantine; **unter ~ stellen** put into quarantine; **unter ~ stehen** be in quarantine

Quarantäne·station *die* isolation ward

Quargel /ˈkvargl̩/ *der od. das;* **~s, ~** (österr.) *soft, smelly sour-milk cheese*

Quark¹ /kvark/ *der;* **~s** 1 quark; [sour skim milk] curd cheese 2 (ugs. abwertend: Quatsch) twaddle; piffle (sl.); **so ein ~!** what a load of rubbish!; **sich über jeden ~ aufregen** make a fuss about every tiny *or* (sl.) piffling detail; **seine Nase in jeden ~ stecken** poke one's nose in everywhere

Quark² /kwɔːk/ *das;* **~s, ~s** (Physik) quark

Quark·speise *die* quark dish

Quart¹ /kvart/ *die;* **~, ~en** 1 (Musik) ▸ **Quarte** 2 (Fechten) quart

Quart² *das;* **~s, ~e** 1 (hist.: Hohlmaß) (in Preußen) quart; (in Bayern) ≈ half-pint 2 (Buchw.) quarto

Quarta /ˈkvarta/ *die;* **~, Quarten** (Schulw.) 1 (veralt.) third year (*of a Gymnasium*) 2 (österr.) fourth year (*of a Gymnasium*)

Quartal /kvarˈtaːl/ *das;* **~s, ~e** quarter [of the year]; **in diesem/im nächsten ~:** this quarter/next quarter

quartal[s]-, Quartal[s]-: **~ende** *das* end of a/the quarter; **~säufer** *der*, **~säuferin** *die* (ugs.) periodic boozer (coll.); **~weise** *Adv.* quarterly

Quartaner /kvarˈtaːnɐ/ *der;* **~s, ~, Quartanerin** *die;* **~, ~nen** (Schulw.) 1 (veralt.) pupil in the third year (*of a Gymnasium*) 2 (österr.) pupil in the fourth year (*of a Gymnasium*)

Quartär /kvarˈtɛːɐ̯/ *das;* **~s** (Geol.) Quaternary [Period]

Quart·band *der* quarto volume

Quarte *die;* **~, ~n** (Musik) fourth

Quarten ▸ **Quart¹, Quarta, Quarte**

Quartett /kvarˈtɛt/ *das;* **~[e]s, ~e** 1 quartet; **ein kriminelles ~:** a quartet of criminals; [a gang of] four criminals 2 (*Spiel*) *card game in which one tries to get sets of four;* ≈ Happy Families 3 (Spielkarten) pack (Brit.) *or* (Amer.) deck of cards for **~**; (Satz von vier Spielkarten) set of four *Quartett* cards 4 (Verslehre) quatrain

Quart·format *das* (Buchw.) quarto

Quartier /kvarˈtiːɐ̯/ *das;* **~s, ~e** 1 (Unterkunft) accommodation *no indef. art.*; accommodations *pl.* (Amer.); place to stay; (Mil.) quarters *pl.*; **die ~e der Truppen/der Athleten** the troops'/athletes' quarters; **ein billiges ~:** somewhere cheap to stay; **bei jmdm. ~ beziehen** put up *or* move in with sb.; **in einer Schule in ~ liegen** (Milit. veralt.) be quartered *or* billeted in a school 2 (bes. schweiz., österr.: Stadtviertel) quarter; district

Quartier·macher *der* (Milit. veralt.) billeting officer

Quart·sext·akkord *der* (Musik) six-four chord

Quarz /kvaːɐ̯ts/ *der;* **~es, ~e** 1 (Mineral) quartz 2 (~kristall) quartz crystal

quarzen
A *itr. V.* (ugs.) puff away; (Haschisch rauchen) smoke a joint (coll.)
B *tr. V.* puff away at ‹*cigar, cigarette, joint*›; **einen/was ~:** smoke a joint

quarz·gesteuert *Adj.* quartz ‹*clock, watch*›; crystal-controlled ‹*transmitter*›

Quarz·glas *das* quartz glass

Quarzit /kvarˈtsiːt/ *der;* **~s, ~e** (Geol., Mineral.) quartzite

Quarz-: **~kristall** *der* quartz crystal; **~lampe** *die* quartz lamp; **~steuerung** *die* (Elektrot.) [quartz-]crystal control; **~uhr** *die* quartz clock; (Armbanduhr) quartz watch

Quasar /kvaˈzaːɐ̯/ *der;* **~s, ~e** (Astron.) quasar

quasi /ˈkvaːzi/ *Adv.* **[so] ~:** more or less; (so gut wie) as good as; (fast) almost

quasi-, Quasi- quasi-‹*military, religious, philosopher*›; (fast) semi-‹*automatic, official*›

Quasselei *die;* **~, ~en** (ugs.) [constant] prattling *or* jabbering

quasseln /ˈkvasl̩n/ (ugs.)
A *itr. V.* chatter; rabbit on (Brit. coll.) (**von** about)
B *tr. V.* spout, babble ‹*nonsense*›; **hör nicht auf sein Quasseln:** don't listen to his blather *or* waffle

Quassel·strippe *die* 1 (ugs. scherzh.: Telefon) blower (Brit. coll.) 2 (ugs. abwertend: Schwätzer) chatterbox

Quaste *die;* **~, ~n** 1 (Troddel; auch fig.) tassel 2 (nordd.) ▸ **Quast 1**

Quästur /kvɛsˈtuːɐ̯/ *die;* **~, ~en** (bes. Hochschulw.) bursar's office

Quatsch /kvatʃ/ *der;* **~[e]s** 1 (ugs. abwertend: dumme Äußerung) rubbish; **~ mit Soße** (salopp) absolute rubbish; stuff and nonsense (coll.); **so ein ~!** what rubbish! 2 (ugs. abwertend: dumme Handlung) nonsense; (ugs.: Unfug) messing about; **lass den ~:** stop that nonsense; stop messing about; **mach keinen ~:** don't do anything stupid 3 (ugs.: Jux) lark (coll.); **die Kinder haben nur ~ gemacht** the children were just larking about (coll.) *or* fooling around; **das habe ich aus ~ gesagt** I said it for a laugh 4 (ugs.: wertloser Gegenstand) trashy thing; (wertloses Zeug) trash *no indef. art.*

quatschen
A *itr. V.* 1 (ugs.: dumm reden) rabbit on (Brit. coll.); blather; (viel reden) chatter; natter (Brit. coll.); **im Unterricht ~:** chatter in class 2 (ugs.: klatschen) gossip; **es wird so viel gequatscht** there is so much gossip 3 (ugs.: klatschen, berichten) blab; open one's mouth 4 (ugs.: sich unterhalten) [have a] chat *or* (coll.) natter (**mit** with); (ugs.: reden) talk (**mit** to); **lass ihn erst mal ~:** let him say his bit (coll.) 5 (landsch.: ein klatschendes Geräusch verursachen) squelch
B *tr. V.* 1 (ugs.: äußern) spout ‹*nonsense, rubbish*›; **was hast du da wieder gequatscht?** what sort of rubbish have you been talking? 2 (salopp) **jmdn. dämlich ~:** talk sb.'s head off

Quatsch·kopf *der* (salopp) stupid chatterbox; (Schwätzer, Schwafler) windbag

quatsch·nass, *quatsch·naß *Adj.* (ugs.) sopping wet

Queck·silber /ˈkvɛk-/ *das* mercury; (fig.) quicksilver; **~ im Leib** *od.* **im Hintern haben** (fig. ugs.) have ants in one's pants (coll.)

quecksilber-, Quecksilber-: **~haltig** *Adj.* containing mercury *postpos., not pred.*; **~haltig sein** contain mercury; **~säule** *die* [column of] mercury; **~vergiftung** *die* mercury poisoning

queck·silbrig *Adj.* 1 silvery 2 (fig.: unruhig) fidgety

Quell /kvɛl/ *der;* **~[e]s, ~e** (geh.) spring; (fig.: Ursprung) source; fount (poet.)

Quell-: **~bewölkung** *die* (Met.) cumulus clouds *pl.*; **~code** *der* (DV) source code

Quelle /ˈkvɛlə/ *die;* **~, ~n** 1 spring; (eines Baches, eines Flusses) source 2 (fig.) source; **die ~ der Weisheit** the fount of wisdom (poet.); **eine Mitteilung aus zuverlässiger ~:** a piece of information from a reliable source; **an der ~ sitzen** (ugs.) (für Informationen) have access to inside information; (für günstigen Erwerb) be at the source of supply

quellen¹ *unr. itr. V.; mit sein* 1 (hervordringen) ‹*liquid*› gush, stream; (aus der Erde) well up; ‹*smoke*› billow; ‹*crowd*› stream, pour; (fig.) ‹*tears*› well up 2 (sich wölben) bulge; **die Augen quollen ihm [fast] aus dem Kopf** his eyes nearly popped out [of his head] 3 (sich ausdehnen) swell [up]

quellen² *tr. V.* (~ lassen) soak ‹*peas, beans*›; steep ‹*barley*›

Quellen-: **~angabe** *die* reference; **~forschung** *die* source research; **~nachweis** *der* ▸ **~angabe**; **~sammlung** *die* collection of source materials; **~steuer** *die* (Finanzw.) tax deducted at source; **~studium** *das* study of [the] sources; **~verzeichnis** *das* list of references

Quell-: **~fluss, *~fluß** *der* (Geogr.) headstream; **~gebiet** *das* (Geogr.) headwater region; **~text** *der* (DV) ▸ **~code**; **~wasser** *das; Pl.* **~~** *od.* **~wässer** spring water

Quengelei *die;* **~** (ugs.) nagging; pestering

quengelig (ugs.)
A *Adj.* whining; fretful; **~ werden** start whining *or* (coll.) grizzling
B *adv.* in a whining voice; fretfully

quengeln /ˈkvɛŋl̩n/ *itr.* (*auch tr.*) *V.* (ugs.) 1 (weinen) ‹*baby*› whimper, (coll.) grizzle 2 (drängen) nag 3 (nörgeln) carp

***Quentchen** ▸ **Quäntchen**

quer /kveːɐ̯/ *Adv.* sideways; crosswise; (schräg) diagonally; at an angle; **~ zu etw.** at an angle to sth.; (rechtwinklig) at right angles to sth.; **der Wagen steht ~ auf der** *od.* **zur Fahrbahn** the car is standing sideways across the road; **das Blatt/den Stoff ~ legen** lay the sheet/material crosswise; **die Streifen verlaufen ~:** the stripes are diagonal/(horizontal) horizontal; **~ auf dem Bett liegen** lie across the bed; **~ durch/über** (+ *Akk.*) straight through/across; **~ über die Straße gehen** go straight across the road; (schräg) cross the road at an angle; **~ durch Amerika fahren** travel right across America; **~ durch die Parteien** (fig.) across all party boundaries; **sich ~ legen** (fig. ugs.) make difficulties; (hartnäckig) dig in one's heels; **~ schießen** (fig. ugs.) put a spanner in the works (coll.)

quer-, Quer-: **~achse** *die* transverse axis; **~balken** *der* 1 cross-beam; (kleiner) crosspiece; 2 (Musik) stroke; **~beet** *Adv.* ugs. (~feldein) across country; (ohne Ziel) at random; (fig.: überall) everywhere and anywhere; **~denker** *der*, **~denkerin** *die* lateral thinker; **~durch** /-ˈ-/ *Adv.* straight through [the middle of] it/them

Quere *die:* *in* **jmdm./sich in die ~ kommen** *od.* **geraten** (jmdm./sich begegnen) bump into sb./one another (coll.); **jmdm. in die ~ kommen** *od.* **geraten** (fig.: jmdn. behindern) get in sb.'s way (coll.); **jmdm./einem Auto/einem Flugzeug in die ~ geraten** cross sb.'s path/the path of a car/an aircraft

Quer·einsteiger *der;* **~s, ~, Quer·einsteigerin** *die;* **~, ~nen** (Jargon) *person from a different professional or educational background;* **er ist [ein] ~:** he has come from a different professional/educational background

Querele /kveˈreːlə/ *die;* **~, ~n** (geh.) squabble, wrangle (**um** about, over)

queren *tr. V.* (geh.) cross

quer·feld·ein *Adv.* across country

Querfeldein-: **~lauf** *der* (Wettbewerb) cross-country [race]; (Sportart) cross-country running; **~rennen** *das* (Wettbewerb) cross-country [cycle] race; (Sportart) cyclo-cross *no def. art.*

quer-, Quer-: **~flöte** *die* transverse flute; **~format** *das* landscape format; (Bild/Buch) picture/book in landscape format; **~gestreift** ▸ **gestreift B**; **~kopf** *der* (ugs.) awkward cuss (coll.); (komischer Kauz) oddball (coll.); **~köpfig** *Adj.* awkward; perverse;

q

~lage *die* (Med.) transverse presentation; **~latte** *die* horizontal slat; (Fuß-, Handball) crossbar; ***~|legen** ▸**quer**; **~pass**, ***~paß** *der* (Fuß-, Handball) cross-field pass; cross; lateral pass (Amer.); **~richtung** *die* transverse direction; **in [der] ~richtung** transversely; crosswise; (schräg) diagonally; **~ruder** *das* (Flugw.) aileron; ***~|schießen** ▸**quer**; **~schiff** *das* (Archit.) transept; **~schläger** *der* (Geschoss) deflected shot; ricochet; **~schnitt** *der* **1** cross section; **im ~schnitt** in cross section; **2** (Auswahl) selection (**durch** from); **ein repräsentativer ~schnitt der Wähler** a representative cross section of voters; **~schnitt[s]·gelähmt** *Adj.* (Med.) paraplegic; **~schnitt[s]·gelähmte** *der/die* ▸**i S. 439** (Med.) paraplegic; **~schnitt[s]·lähmung** *die* ▸**i S. 439** (Med.) paraplegia *no indef. art.*; paraplegic condition; **~schuss**, ***~schuß** *der* (ugs.) spanner in the works (coll.); **~schüsse gegen jmds. Politik** attempts at obstructing sb.'s policies; **~straße** *die* (Abzweigung) turning; (Nebenstraße) side street; **die zweite ~straße links** the second turning on the left; **~streifen** *der* diagonal stripe; (horizontal) horizontal stripe; **~summe** *die* (Math.) sum of the digits (**von, aus** of); **eine Zahl, deren ~summe 19 ergibt** a number the sum of whose digits is 19; **~treiber** *der*, **~treiberin** *die* (ugs. abwertend) troublemaker

Querulant /kveru'lant/ *der;* **~en, ~en, Querulantin** *die;* **~, ~nen** (abwertend) malcontent

Quer-: ~verbindung *die* connection, link (**zu** with); (Verkehrsw.) cross-country route; (direkte Verbindung) direct connection; **~verweis** *der* (Buchw.) cross reference

Quetsche[1] /'kvɛtʃə/ *die;* **~, ~n** (bes. südd., westmd.) ▸**Zwetsche**

Quetsche[2] *die;* **~, ~n** **1** (bes. nordd.) potato crusher **2** (ugs. abwertend: Ort, Betrieb) miserable hole

quetschen

A *tr. V.* **1** crush ‹*person, limb, thorax*›; **sich** (*Dat.*) **den Arm/die Hand ~:** get one's arm/hand caught; **sich** (*Dat.*) **den Finger/die Zehe ~:** pinch one's finger/toe **2** (drücken, pressen) squeeze, squash (**gegen, an** + *Akk.* against, **in** + *Akk.* into); (bes. nordd.: auspressen) squeeze ‹*juice*› (**aus** out of); **ein paar Zeilen an den Rand ~** (ugs.) squeeze a few lines into the margin **3** (bes. nordd.: zerdrücken) mash ‹*potatoes*›

B *refl. V.* **sich in/durch etw.** (*Akk.*) **~:** squeeze [one's way] into/through sth.

Quetsch-: ~kartoffeln *Pl.* (bes. berlin.) mashed potatoes; **~kommode** *die* (salopp scherzh.: Akkordeon) squeeze box (sl.)

Quetschung *die;* **~, ~en** ▸**i S. 439** (Med.) bruise; contusion

Quetsch·wunde *die* ▸**i S. 439** (Med.) contusion

Queue /kø:/ *das od.* (österr.) *der;* **~s, ~s** cue

quick /kvɪk/ (bes. nordd.)

A *Adj.* lively

B *adv.* in a lively way; animatedly

quick·lebendig

A *Adj.* [very] lively; active; (bes. im Alter) sprightly; spry; vivacious ‹*personality*›; frisky ‹*small animal*›; **~ sein** be full of [the joys of] life; be bright as a button; ‹*child*› be full of beans (coll.)

B *adv.* bright as a button; ‹*talk*› animatedly

quiek[s]en /'kvi:k(s)n̩/

A *itr. V.* squeak; ‹*piglet, fig.: person*› squeal (**vor** with); **zum Quiek[s]en sein** be a hoot (coll.)

B *tr. V.* squawk

Quietismus /kvie'tɪsmʊs/ *der;* **~:** quietism *no def. art.*

quietsch·bunt /'kvi:tʃ-/ (ugs.)

A *Adj.* **1** brightly coloured; jazzy ‹*colours*› **2** (bunt gemischt) full of variety *postpos*

B *adv.* ‹*paint*› in jazzy colours/a jazzy colour; **~ gemustert** with a jazzy pattern

quietschen /'kvi:tʃn̩/ *itr. V.* ‹*thing*› squeak; ‹*brakes, tyres, crane*› squeal, screech; (ugs.) ‹*person*› squeal, shriek (**vor** + *Dat.* with)

quietsch-, Quietsch-: ~fidel (ugs.) **A** *Adj.* [really] chirpy (coll.) *or* (esp. Amer.) chipper; (gesund und munter) bright-eyed and bushy-tailed *pred.* (coll.); **B** *adv.* [really] chirpy (coll.); **~lebendig** *Adj.* (ugs.) bright-eyed and bushy-tailed *pred.* (*coll.*); (sehr aktiv) full of beans *pred.* (*coll.*); (hellwach) wide awake; **~ton** *der; Pl.* **~töne** (ugs.) screeching noise; (bes. durch Reibung) squeal; **~vergnügt** (ugs.) **A** *Adj.* [really] chirpy (coll.) *or* (esp. Amer.) chipper **B** *adv.* as happily *or* (coll.) chirpily as could be

Quinta /'kvɪnta/ *die;* **~, Quinten** (Schulw.) **1** (veralt.) second year (*of a Gymnasium*) **2** (österr.) fifth year (*of a Gymnasium*)

Quintaner /kvɪn'ta:nɐ/ *der;* **~s, ~, Quintanerin** *die;* **~, ~nen** (Schulw.) **1** (veralt.) pupil in the second year (*of a Gymnasium*) **2** (österr.) pupil in the fifth year (*of a Gymnasium*)

Quinte /'kvɪntə/ *die;* **~, ~n** (Musik) fifth

Quinten·zirkel *der* (Musik) circle of fifths

Quint·essenz *die* (geh.) substance; (wesentlicher Punkt) essential point; (Schlussfolgerung) conclusion; **als ~ bleibt festzuhalten, dass ...** the essential point *or* conclusion to be drawn is that ...

Quintett /kvɪn'tɛt/ *das;* **~[e]s, ~e** (Musik) quintet

Quint·sext·akkord *der* (Musik) six-five chord

Quirl /kvɪrl/ *der;* **~[e]s, ~e** **1** (Küchengerät) *long-handled blender with a star-shaped head* **2** (Mensch) live wire

quirlen

A *tr. V.* ≈ whisk

B *itr. V.* swirl [about]

quirlig *Adj.* lively; (flink) nimble

quitt /kvɪt/ *Adj.* (ugs.) quits; **mit jmdm. ~ sein** be quits with sb.; **damit sind wir ~:** that makes us quits

Quitte /'kvɪtə/ *die;* **~, ~n** quince

quitte[n]·gelb *Adj.* pale greenish-yellow

quittieren *tr. V.* **1** *auch itr.* (bescheinigen) acknowledge, confirm ‹*receipt, condition*›; receipt, give a receipt for ‹*sum, invoice*›; **würden Sie bitte auf der Rückseite der Rechnung ~?** could you please receipt the bill on the back? **2** (reagieren auf) **etw. mit etw. ~:** react *or* respond to sth. with sth.; **ein Urteil mit Pfiffen ~:** greet a decision with catcalls **3** **den Dienst ~** (veralt.) resign one's position; ‹*officer*› resign one's commission

Quittung *die;* **~, ~en** **1** receipt (**für, über** + *Akk.* for) **2** (fig.) comeuppance (coll.); deserts *pl.*; **nun hast du die ~ für deine Faulheit** you've got what you deserve for being lazy

Quittungs·block *der; Pl.* **~s** *od.* **Quittungsblöcke** receipt pad

Quivive /ki'vi:f/ *das: in* **auf dem ~ sein** (ugs.) be on the alert *or* (coll.) watch it

Quiz /kvɪs/ *das;* **~, ~:** quiz

Quiz-: ~sendung *die* quiz programme; **~show** *die* quiz show

quoll /kvɔl/ *1. u. 3. Pers. Sg. Prät. v.* **quellen**

Quorum /'kvo:rʊm/ *das;* **~s , Quoren** (bes. Politik) quorum

Quote /'kvo:tə/ *die;* **~, ~n** **1** (Anteil) proportion; (Zahl) number **2** (Rundf., Ferns.) ▸**Einschaltquote**

Quoten-: ~bringer *der;* **~~s, ~~, ~bringerin** *die;* **~~, ~~nen** (Rundf., Ferns. Jargon) ratings winner; **~regelung** *die: requirement that women should be adequately represented*

Quotient /kvo'tsi̯ɛnt/ *der;* **~en, ~en** (Math.) quotient (**aus** of)

quotieren *tr., itr. V.* (Börsenw.) quote

q

Rr

r, R /ɛr/ *das;* ~, ~: r/R; **er rollt das R** he rolls his r's; *s. auch* **a, A**

R *Abk.* (Physik) **= Reaumur** Réaum.

Rabatt /ra'bat/ *der;* **~[e]s, ~e** discount; **~ gewähren** give a discount

Rabatte /ra'batə/ *die;* **~, ~n** border

rabattieren *tr. V.* (Kaufmannsspr.) **[jmdm.] einen Auftrag mit 30 Prozent ~:** give [sb.] a discount of 30 per cent on an order

Rabatt·marke *die* trading stamp

Rabatz /ra'bats/ *der;* **~es** (ugs.) [1] (Lärm) racket; din [2] (Protest) **~ machen** kick up a fuss, (coll.) raise a stink (**bei** with)

Rabauke /ra'baukə/ *der;* **~n, ~n** (ugs.) roughneck (coll.); (Rowdy) hooligan

Rabbi /'rabi/ *der;* **~[s], ~nen** /ra'bi:nən/ *od.* **~s** ▸❶ **S. 44** [1] (Titel) Rabbi [2] (Person) rabbi

Rabbinat *das* rabbinate

Rabbiner /ra'bi:nɐ/ *der;* **~s, ~:** rabbi

Rabbinerin *die;* **~, ~nen** [female] rabbi

rabbinisch *Adj.* rabbinical

Rabe /'ra:bə/ *der;* **~n, ~n** raven; **ein weißer ~** (fig.) a great rarity; **schwarz wie ein ~/wie die ~n** (ugs.) as black as pitch; (schmutzig) as black as soot; **stehlen** *od.* (salopp) **klauen wie ein ~/wie die ~n** (ugs.) pinch everything one can lay one's hands on (coll.)

raben-, Raben-: ~aas *das* (salopp abwertend) beast; wretch; **~eltern** *Pl.* (abwertend) uncaring [brutes of] parents; **~krähe** *die* carrion crow; **~mutter** *die; Pl.* **~mütter** (abwertend) uncaring [brute of a] mother; **~schwarz** *Adj.* [1] jet-black; raven-black ‹*beard, hair*›; coal-black ‹*man, woman*›; pitch-black ‹*night*›; [2] (unheilvoll) black ‹*thoughts, soul, day*›; disastrous ‹*day, year*›

rabiat /ra'bia:t/

[A] *Adj.* [1] (gewalttätig) violent; brutal; savage ‹*kick*›; ruthless ‹*methods*› [2] (wütend) furious; blistering, savage ‹*attack*›; rabid ‹*opponent*›

[B] *adv.* [1] (gewalttätig) violently; brutally [2] (wütend) furiously

Rabulist /rabu'lɪst/ *der;* **~en, ~en** (geh.) sophist; quibbler

Rabulistik *die;* ~ (geh.) sophistry

Rabulistin *die;* **~, ~nen** ▸**Rabulist**

rabulistisch (geh.)

[A] *Adj.* sophistical

[B] *adv.* sophistically

Rache /'raxə/ *die;* **~:** revenge; **[an jmdm.] ~ nehmen** take revenge [on sb.]; **~ üben** take revenge; wreak vengeance (literary); **aus ~:** in revenge; **~ ist süß** *od.* (ugs. scherzh.) **Blutwurst** revenge is sweet; **das ist die ~ des kleinen Mannes** (ugs., oft scherzh.) that's how ordinary mortals get their own back [on the powers that be] (coll.); **die ~ ist mein** (bibl.) vengeance is mine

Rache-: ~akt *der* (geh.) act of revenge, reprisal (*Gen.* by, on the part of); **~durst** *der* (geh.) thirst for revenge *or* (literary) vengeance; **~engel** *der* avenging angel; **~feldzug** *der* campaign of retaliation; **~gefühl** *das* desire *no pl.* for revenge

rächen /'rɛçn/

[A] *tr. V.* avenge ‹*person, crime*›; take revenge for ‹*insult, crime*›; **jmds. Mord an jmdm. ~:** take revenge on sb. for sb.'s murder

[B] *refl. V.* [1] take one's revenge; **sich an jmdm. [für etw.] ~:** take one's revenge on sb. [for sth.]; get even with sb. [for sth.] [2] (sich übel auswirken) ‹*mistake[s], bad behaviour*› take its/their toll; **dein Leichtsinn wird sich noch ~/es wird sich noch ~, dass du das tust** you will have to pay [the penalty] for your recklessness/for doing that

Rachen /'raxn/ *der;* **~s, ~** [1] ▸❶ **S. 435** (Schlund) pharynx (Anat.); **jmdm. den ~ pinseln** paint sb.'s throat [2] (Maul) mouth; maw (literary); (fig.) jaws *pl.*; **jmdm. den ~ stopfen** (salopp) shut sb. up (coll.); **jmdm. etwas in den ~ werfen** *od.* **schmeißen** (salopp) give sb. sth. to keep him/her happy

Rachen-: ~höhle *die* ▸❶ **S. 435** (Anat.) pharyngeal cavity; **~mandel** *die* ▸❶ **S. 435** (Anat.) [pharyngeal] tonsil

Rache·plan *der* plan for revenge

Rächer *der;* **~s, ~, Rächerin** *die;* **~, ~nen** (geh.) avenger

Rache·schwur *der* (geh.) oath of revenge

Rach·gier *die* lust for revenge

rach·gierig (geh.) ▸**rachsüchtig**

Rachitis /ra'xi:tɪs/ *die;* **~** ▸❶ **S. 439** (Med.) rickets *sing.*

rachitisch *Adj.* with rickets *postpos., not pred.*; rachitic (Med.)

Rach·sucht *die* (geh.) lust for revenge

rach·süchtig (geh.)

[A] *Adj.* vengeful; **~ sein** ‹*person*› be out for revenge

[B] *adv.* vengefully; seeking to exact revenge

Racker *der;* **~s, ~** (fam.) rogue; rascal

rackern /'rakɐn/ *itr. V.* (ugs.) slave [away (coll.)

Racket /'rɛkət/ *das;* **~s, ~s** (Tennis) racket

Raclette /'raklɛt/ *die;* **~, ~s** *od. das;* **~s, ~s** (Kochk.) raclette

Rad[1] /ra:t/ *das;* **~es, Räder** /'rɛ:dɐ/ [1] wheel; (Zahn~) gear; (kleines Zahn~) cog; (einer Uhr) [toothed] wheel; (für Riemen) pulley; **das ~ der Zeit/der Geschichte lässt sich nicht anhalten** (fig.) the march of time/of history cannot be halted; **fünftes** *od.* **das fünfte ~ am Wagen sein** (fig. ugs.) be superfluous; (die Harmonie stören) be in the way; **er kam unter die Räder des Lkws** he was run over by the lorry (Brit.) *or* truck; **unter die Räder kommen** (fig. ugs.) fall into bad ways; (total verkommen) go to the dogs (coll.); **nur** *od.* **bloß ein ~ im Getriebe sein** be just a small cog in the machine [2] (Fahr~) bicycle; bike (coll.); **mit dem ~ fahren** go by bicycle *or* (coll.) bike; **~ fahren** cycle; ride a bicycle *or* (coll.) bike; (fig. ugs. abwertend: unterwürfig sein) suck up to people (coll.); **er fährt gern ~:** he likes cycling [3] (Turnen) cartwheel; **ein ~ schlagen** *od.* **ausführen** do *or* perform a cartwheel; **~ schlagen** do a cartwheel; (mehrmals) do cartwheels [4] (hist.: Foltergerät) wheel; **jmdn. aufs ~ flechten** break sb. on the wheel [5] (bei Vögeln: Schwanzfedern) fan; **ein ~ schlagen** ‹*peacock*› fan out its tail

Rad[2] *das;* **~[s], ~** (Physik) rad

Rad·achse *die* (Technik) axle

Radar /ra'da:ɐ/ *der od. das;* **~s** (Technik) radar

Radar-: ~anlage *die* radar installation; **~astronomie** *die* radar astronomy *no art.*; **~falle** *die* (ugs.) [radar] speed trap; **~gerät** *das* radar [system]; **~geräte** radar [equipment] *sing.*; **~kontrolle** *die* (Verkehrsw.) [radar] speed check; **~schirm** *der* radar screen

Radau /ra'dau/ *der;* **~s** (ugs.) row (coll.); racket

Radau·bruder *der* (ugs. abwertend) rowdy

Rad·aufhängung *die* (Kfz-W.) suspension

Rädchen /'rɛ:tçən/ *das;* **~s, ~** [1] [little] wheel; (Zahnrad) [small] cog; *s. auch* **Rad 1** [2] (Fahrrad) [little] bicycle *or* (coll.) bike [3] (für Schnittmuster) tracing wheel; (für Gebäckteig) pastry wheel

Rad·dampfer *der* paddle steamer

radebrechen

[A] *tr. V.* **Französisch/Deutsch** *usw.* **~:** speak broken French/German *etc*

[B] *itr. V.* speak pidgin

radeln /'ra:dln/ *itr.* (*auch tr.*) *V.; mit sein* (ugs., bes. südd.) cycle; **irgendwohin ~:** go somewhere by bike (coll.); bike it somewhere (coll.); **50 km ~:** cycle 50 km

Rädels·führer /'rɛ:dls-/ *der,* **Rädels·führerin** *die* (abwertend) ringleader

-räderig ▸**-rädrig**

rädern /'rɛ:dɐn/ *tr. V.* **jmdn. ~** (hist.) break sb. on the wheel; *s. auch* **gerädert**

Räder·werk *das* (Mechanik) mechanism; works *pl.*; (Räder) wheels *pl.*; (Zahnräder) gears *pl.*; cogs *pl.*; **das ~ der Justiz** (fig.) the wheels *pl. or* machinery of justice

rad-, Rad-: *~|fahren ▸**Rad 2**; **~fahrer** *der,* **~fahrerin** *die* [1] cyclist; [2] (ugs. abwertend: Schmeichler) toady; crawler (coll.); **~fahr·streifen** *der* bicycle lane; **~fahr·weg** *der* cycle path; cycle track

Radi /'ra:di/ *der;* **~s, ~** (bayr., österr. ugs.) [large white] radish

radial /ra'dia:l/

[A] *Adj.* radial

[B] *adv.* radially; **~ verlaufend** radiating

Radiator /ra'dia:tɔr/ *der;* **~s, ~en** /-'to:rən/ [central-heating] radiator

Radicchio /ra'dɪkio/ *der;* **~s** radicchio

Radien ▸**Radius**

radieren /ra'di:rən/ *tr.* (*auch itr.*) *V.* [1] (tilgen) erase [2] (Grafik) etch

Radierer *der;* **~s, ~** [1] (ugs.) ▸**Radiergummi** [2] (Künstler) etcher

Radiererin *die;* **~, ~nen** ▸**Radierer 2**

Radier-: ~gummi *der* rubber [eraser]; **~kunst** *die* etching; **~nadel** *die* (Grafik) [dry-point] etching needle

Radierung *die;* **~, ~en** (Grafik) etching

Radieschen /ra'di:sçən/ *das;* **~s, ~:** radish; **sich** (*Dat.*) **die ~ von unten betrachten** (salopp) be pushing up the daisies (sl.)

radikal /radi'ka:l/

[A] *Adj.* radical; drastic ‹*measure, method, cure*›; (rücksichtslos) ruthless ‹*measure, method, hardness*›; **ein ~er Bruch mit der Vergangenheit** a complete break with the past

[B] *adv.* radically; (rücksichtslos) ruthlessly; (vollständig) ‹*abolish, eradicate*› totally, completely; **~ gegen jmdn. vorgehen** adopt drastic *or* ruthless methods against sb.; **~ [links/rechts] denken/eingestellt sein** have radical [left-wing/right-wing] views

Radikal *das;* **~s, ~e** [1] (Chemie) [free] radical [2] (Math., Sprachw.) radical

Radikale *der/die; adj. Dekl.* radical

r

Radikalen·erlass, *Radikalen·erlaß *der: decree excluding members of extremist organizations from civil-service employment*

radikalisieren
A *tr. V.* make [more] radical
B *refl. V.* become more radical (**durch** owing to, as a result of)

Radikalisierung *die;* ~, **~en** radicalization; (das Radikalwerden) growing radicalism, trend to radicalism (*Gen.* among)

Radikalismus *der;* ~, **Radikalismen** radicalism; (Haltung) radical attitude; (Unnachgiebigkeit) rigid attitude

Radikalität /radikali'tɛːt/ *die;* ~: radicalness; radical nature; (Härte) ruthlessness; (Vollständigkeit) completeness

Radikal·kur *die* (auch fig.) drastic remedy (**gegen** for)

Radio /'raːdio/ *das* (*südd., schweiz. auch: der*); **~s, ~s** radio; **sie haben nicht einmal ~:** they don't even have a radio; **im ~:** on the radio; **~ hören** listen to the radio

radio-, Radio-: ~aktiv A *Adj.* radioactive; **B** *adv.* radioactively; **~aktiv verseucht** contaminated by radioactivity *postpos.*; **~aktivität** *die* radioactivity; **~apparat** /'-----/ *der* radio set; **~astronomie** *die* radio astronomy *no art.*; **~biologie** *die* ▸**Strahlenbiologie**; **~gerät** /'---/ *das* radio set; **~isotop** *das* (Physik) radioisotope; **~loge** /-'loːgə/ *der;* **~~n, ~~n** ▸❶ **S. 113** radiologist; **~logie** *die;* **~~:** radiology *no art.*; **~login** *die;* **~~, ~~nen** ▸❶ **S. 113** radiologist; **~moderator** /'-------/ *der,* **~moderatorin** /'--------/ *die* ▸❶ **S. 113** (Rundf.) radio presenter; **~musik** /'----/ *die* music on the radio; **~quelle** /'------/ *die* (Astron., Physik) radio source; **~sender** /'---/ *der* radio station; **~spot** /'----/ *der* radio commercial; **~strahlung** /'-----/ *die* (Astron., Physik) radio-frequency radiation; **~therapie** *die* (Med.) radiotherapy; **~wecker** /'----/ *der* radio alarm clock; **~welle** /'----/ *die* (Technik, Physik) radio wave

Radium /'raːdiʊm/ *das;* **~s** radium

Radius /'raːdiʊs/ *der;* ~, **Radien** /'raːdiən/ (Math.) radius

Rad-: ~kappe *die* hubcap; **~kranz** *der* (Technik) **1** (beim Fahrrad) wheel rim; **2** (beim Zahnrad) toothed rim; **~lager** *das* wheel bearing

Radler *der;* **~s,** ~ **1** cyclist **2** (bes. südd.: Getränk) shandy

Radler·hose *die* cycle shorts *pl.*

Radlerin *die;* ~, **~nen** cyclist

Rad·nabe *die* [wheel] hub

Radon /'raːdɔn/ *das;* **~s** (Chemie) radon

Rad-: ~renn·bahn *die* cycle racing track; (Stadion) velodrome; **~rennen** *das* cycle race; (Sport) cycle racing; **~rennfahrer** *der,* **~rennfahrerin** *die* racing cyclist

-rädrig /-rɛːdrɪç/ *Adj.* -wheeled; **drei/vier~:** three-/four-wheeled

rad-, Rad-: *~|schlagen ▸**Rad 3**; **~sport** *der* cycling *no def. art.*; **~stand** *der* wheelbase; **~tour** *die* bicycle ride; (länger) cycling tour; **eine ~tour machen** go for a bicycle ride/on a cycling tour; **~wanderung** *die* cycling tour; **~wechsel** *der* wheel change; **~weg** *der* cycle path *or* -track

RAF *Abk.* = **Rote-Armee-Fraktion** Red Army Faction

raffen /'rafn̩/ *tr. V.* **1** (an sich reißen) snatch; grab; rake in (coll.) ‹*money*›; (abwertend: in seinen Besitz bringen) **etw. [an sich] ~:** seize sth.; (eilig) snatch *or* grab sth. **2** (zusammenhalten) gather ‹*material, curtain*› **3** (gekürzt wiedergeben) condense ‹*text*›; (kürzen) shorten ‹*text, play, film*›

Raff·gier *die* rapacity; acquisitive greed

raff·gierig
A *Adj.* greedy
B *adv.* greedily

Raffinement /rafinə'mãː/ *das;* **~s, ~s** (geh.) **1** (Feinheit) refinement **2** ▸**Raffinesse 1**

Raffinerie /rafinə'riː/ *die;* ~, **~n** refinery

Raffinesse /rafi'nɛsə/ *die;* ~, **~n 1** (Schlauheit) guile; ingenuity **2** (Finesse) refinement

raffinieren /rafi'niːrən/ *tr. V.* (bes. Chemie, Geol.) refine

raffiniert
A *Adj.* **1** ingenious ‹*plan, design*›; (verfeinert) refined, subtle ‹*colour, scheme, effect*›; sophisticated ‹*dish, cut (of clothes)*› **2** (gerissen) cunning, artful ‹*person, trick*›
B *adv.* **1** ingeniously; cleverly; (verfeinert) with great refinement/sophistication; **eine ~ geschnittene Bluse** a blouse with a sophisticated cut **2** (gerissen) cunningly; artfully

Raffiniertheit *die;* ~ **1** (Klugheit) ingenuity; (Verfeinerung) refinement; sophistication; (der Kleidung) stylishness; (von Speisen) subtle flavour **2** (Gerissenheit) cunning; artfulness

Raffke /'rafkə/ *der;* **~s, ~s** (ugs. abwertend) money-grubber

Rage /'raːʒə/ *die;* ~ (ugs.) fury; rage; **in [blinder] ~:** in a [blind] fury; **in ~ sein** be livid (Brit. coll.) *or* furious; **jmdn. in ~ bringen** make sb. hopping mad (coll.) *or* absolutely furious; **in ~ kommen** *od.* **geraten** fly into a rage; **immer mehr in ~ kommen** become more and more furious

ragen /'raːgn̩/ *itr. V.* **1** (vertikal) rise [up]; ‹*mountains*› tower up; **aus dem Wasser ~:** stick *or* jut right out of the water; **in die Höhe** *od.* **in den Himmel ~:** tower *or* soar into the sky; **er ragte aus der Menge** he towered above the rest of the crowd **2** (horizontal) project, stick out (**in** + *Akk.* into; **über** + *Akk.* over)

Raglan·ärmel /'raglan-/ *der* raglan sleeve

Ragout /ra'guː/ *das;* **~s, ~s** (Kochk.) ragout

Ragtime /'rɛgtaim/ *der;* ~ (Musik) **1** (Stil, Musik) ragtime *no art.* **2** (Musikstück) rag

Rah[e] /'raː(ə)/ *die;* ~, **Rahen** (Seemannsspr.) yard

Rahm /raːm/ *der;* **~[e]s** (bes. südd., österr., schweiz.) cream; *s. auch* **abschöpfen**

rahmen[1] *tr. V.* frame

rahmen[2] *tr. V.* (bes. südd., österr., schweiz.) skim ‹*milk*›

Rahmen *der;* **~s,** ~ **1** frame; (Kfz-W.: Fahrgestell) chassis **2** (fig.: Bereich, Literaturw.: ~erzählung) framework; (szenischer Hintergrund) setting; (Zusammenhang) context; (Grenzen) bounds *pl.*; limits *pl.*; **in großem/bescheidenem ~ feiern** celebrate on a grand/modest scale; **aus dem ~ fallen** be out of place; stick out; ‹*behaviour*› be unsuited to the occasion; **im ~ einer Sache** (*Gen.*) (in den Grenzen) within the bounds of sth.; (im Zusammenhang) within the context of sth.; (im Verlauf) in the course of sth.; **im ~ des Möglichen** within the bounds of possibility; **im ~ der Wiener Festwochen** as part of the Vienna Festival; **im ~ bleiben** stay within reasonable bounds; ‹*person*› not overdo it, not go too far; ‹*prices*› not be too high; **den ~ sprengen** be out of proportion; **den ~ einer Sache** (*Gen.*) **sprengen** go beyond the scope of sth.

Rahmen-: ~abkommen *das* basic agreement; **~antenne** *die* (Funkw.) frame aerial *or* (Amer.) antenna; **~bedingung** *die* prevailing condition *or* circumstance; (Soziol.) structural condition; **~erzählung** *die* (Literaturw.) framework story; **~gesetz** *das* (Rechtsw.) *law providing framework for more specific legislation*; **~gesetze** *Pl.* outline legislation *sing.*; **~handlung** *die* (Literaturw.) framework plot; subplot (framing the main plot); **~programm** *das* supporting programme; **~richtlinie** *die* overall guideline; **~vertrag** *der* outline agreement

rahmig *Adj.* (bes. südd., österr., schweiz.) creamy

Rahm-: ~käse *der* cream cheese; **~soße** *die* (bes. südd., österr., schweiz.) cream sauce

Rah·segel *das* (Seemannsspr.) square sail

Rain /rain/ *der;* **~[e]s, ~e 1** (geh.: Ackergrenze) margin of a/the field **2** (südd., schweiz.: Abhang) slope

räkeln /'rɛːkl̩n/ ▸**rekeln**

Rakete /ra'keːtə/ *die;* ~, **~n** rocket; (Milit.) missile

raketen-, Raketen-: ~abschussbasis, *~abschußbasis *die* missile [launching] base; **~abwehr·system** *das* (Milit.) anti-missile defence system; **~antrieb** *der* rocket propulsion; **~basis** *die* ▸**~abschussbasis**; **~flugzeug** *das* rocket plane; **~getrieben** *Adj.* rocket-propelled; **~schlitten** *der* (Technik) rocket sled; **~startrampe** *die* rocket launching pad; **~stufe** *die* (Technik) rocket stage; **~träger** *der* missile-carrier; **~triebwerk** *das* (Technik) rocket engine; **~werfer** *der* (Milit.) rocket launcher

Raki /'raːki/ *der;* **~[s], ~s** raki

Ralle /'ralə/ *die;* ~, **~n** (Zool.) rail

Rallye /'rali/ *die;* **~, ~s** *od. schweiz. das;* **~s, ~s** (Motorsport) rally; **die ~ Monte Carlo** the Monte Carlo Rally; **eine ~ fahren** take part in a rally

Rambazamba /ramba'tsamba/ *der od. das;* **~s, ~s** (ugs.) racket; row; (Auseinandersetzung) row; (Rummel) razzmatazz; **~ machen** make a racket; (Rabatz machen) kick up a fuss; raise a stink (coll.)

ramm-, Ramm-: ~bär *der* (Bauw.) [piledriver] ram; **~bock** *der* **1** (hist.) battering ram; **2** ▸**~bär**; **3** ▸**Ramme**; **~dösig** *Adj.* (salopp) **1** (benommen) dizzy; **2** (dumm) dopey (coll.)

Ramme /'ramə/ *die;* ~, **~n** (Bauw.) (Pfahl~) piledriver; (für Erde, Steine) rammer

rammeln /'raml̩n/
A *itr. V.* **1** (Jägerspr.) mate **2** (derb: koitieren) have a screw (coarse)
B *tr. V.* **1** (Jägerspr.) serve; mount **2** (derb: koitieren mit) screw (coarse)

rammel·voll *Adj.* (ugs.) jam-packed (coll.), chock-full (coll.)

rammen
A *tr. V.* ram; **etw. in etw.** (*Akk.*) **~:** ram *or* jam sth. into sth.
B *itr. V.* (stoßen) ram, crash (**gegen, auf** + *Akk.* into)

Rammler *der;* **~s,** ~ (Jägerspr.) buck [rabbit]

Rampe /'rampə/ *die;* ~, **~n 1** (waagrechte Fläche) [loading] platform **2** (schiefe Fläche) ramp; (Auffahrt) [sloping] drive; (Bergsteigen) sloping slab of rock **3** ▸**Startrampe 4** (Theater) apron; forestage; **an** *od.* **vor die ~ treten** come to the front of the stage; **[nicht] über die ~ kommen** (Theaterjargon) [not] come across

Rampen-: ~licht *das; Pl.* **~er** (Theater) **1** (Licht) [light *sing.* from the] footlights *pl.*; **im ~ [der Öffentlichkeit] stehen** be in the limelight; **2** (Lichtquelle) footlight; **~sau** *die* (Theater Jargon) ham actor

ramponieren /rampo'niːrən/ *tr. V.* (ugs.) batter; **ramponiert** battered, knocked-about ‹*furniture, phone-box*›; run-down, down-at-heel ‹*dwelling, room*›; shabby ‹*suit*›; dented ‹*confidence*›

Ramsch[1] /ramʃ/ *der;* **~[e]s, ~e** (ugs. abwertend) **1** (Ware) trashy goods *pl.* **2** (Kram) junk

Ramsch[2] *der;* **~[e]s, ~e** (Kartenspiel) ramsch

ramschen *tr., auch itr. V.* (ugs.) grab; **[Sachen] beim Schlussverkauf ~:** get masses of things cheap in a sale/the sales

Ramsch-: ~laden *der; Pl.* **~läden** (ugs. abwertend) shop selling trashy goods; **~ware** *die* (ugs. abwertend) trashy goods *pl.*; **~waren** trashy goods

ran /ran/ *Adv.* (ugs.) **1** ▸**heran 2** (fang an) off you go; get going; (fangen wir an) let's go; **los, ~ an die Arbeit!** come on, get down to work! **3** (greif[t] an) go at him/them!; (beim Boxen) let him/them have it!; *s. auch* **rangehen**; **ranhalten**; **rankommen** *usw.*

Ranch /rɛntʃ/ *die;* ~, **~[e]s** ranch

Rancher /'rɛntʃɐ/ *der;* **~s, ~:** rancher

Rand /rant/ *der;* **~[e]s, Ränder** /'rɛndɐ/ **1** edge; (Einfassung) border; (Hut~) brim; (Brillen~, Gefäß~, Krater~) rim; (eines Abgrunds) brink; (auf einem Schriftstück) margin; (Weg~) verge; (Stadt~) edge; outskirts *pl.*; **voll bis zum ~:** full to the brim; **etwas an den ~ schreiben** write sth. in the margin; (fig.) **etw. am ~e erwähnen** mention sth. in passing; **am ~e liegen** ‹*problem etc.*› be of marginal importance; **außer ~ und Band geraten/sein** (ugs.) go/be wild (**vor** with); (rasen) go/be berserk (**vor**

with); **das versteht sich am ~e** it goes without saying; **am ~e der Pleite sein** be on the verge of bankruptcy; **jmdn. an den ~ des Wahnsinns/Ruins bringen** bring sb. to the verge *or* brink of insanity/ruin; **zu ~e** ▸**zurande**; *s. auch* **Grab** [2] (Schmutz~) mark; (rund) ring; (in der Wanne) tidemark (coll.); **dunkle Ränder unter den/um die Augen haben** have dark lines under/dark rings round one's eyes [3] (salopp: Mund) gob (sl.); trap (sl.)

Randale /ranˈdaːlə/ *die* (salopp) riot; **~ machen/beginnen** riot/start to riot

randalieren *itr. V.* riot; rampage; (Radau machen) create an uproar; **~de Halbstarke** young hooligans on the rampage

Randalierer *der;* **~s, ~, Randaliererin** *die;* **~, ~nen** hooligan

Rand-: ~bedingung *die* peripheral feature; **~bemerkung** *die* marginal note *or* comment; (mündlich) incidental remark; aside; **~bereich** *der* [1] fringe; [2] (fig.) fringe area; **im ~bereich** on the fringe

Rande /ˈrandə/ *die;* **~, ~n** (schweiz.) beetroot

Rändel /ˈrɛndl̩/ *das;* **~s, ~** (Mech.) knurl

rändeln *tr. V.* (Mech.) knurl; mill ‹*coins*›

Ränder ▸**Rand**

rand-, Rand-: ~erscheinung *die* peripheral phenomenon; **~figur** *die* minor figure; (Nebenrolle) minor part; **~gebiet** *das* outlying district; (Grenzgebiet) frontier area *or* district; **die ~gebiete einer Stadt** the outskirts of a town; **ein ~gebiet der Medizin** a fringe area of medicine; **~gruppe** *die* (Soziol.) fringe *or* marginal group; **~los** *Adj.* rimless ‹*spectacles*›; brimless ‹*hat*›; ‹*paper*› with no margin; **~notiz** *die* marginal note; **~problem** *das* secondary problem; **~sportart** *die* minority sport; **~ständig** *Adj.* (Soziol.) marginal; **~stein** *der* kerb; **~streifen** *der* verge; (auf Autobahnen) hard shoulder

rand·voll
[A] *Adj.* ‹*glass etc.*› full to the brim (**mit** with); brimfull ‹*glass, cup, bowl*› (**mit** of); **~ mit Notizen** crammed full of notes
[B] *adv.* **~ gefüllt** jam-packed (coll.); chock-full (coll.); (mit Flüssigkeit) full to the brim

Rand·zone *die* outlying area; (einer Stadt) outskirts *pl.*; (fig.) fringe area

rang /raŋ/ *1. u. 3. Pers. Sg. Prät. v.* **ringen**

Rang *der;* **~[e]s, Ränge** /ˈrɛŋə/ [1] (Stellung, Stufe) rank; (in der Gesellschaft) status; (in Bezug auf Bedeutung, Qualität) standing; **im ~ eines Generals stehen** hold the rank of general; **jmdm. den ~ streitig machen** try to step [up] into sb.'s shoes; **jmdm./einer Sache den ~ ablaufen** leave sb./sth. far behind; **alles, was ~ und Namen hat** everybody who is anybody; **ein Physiker von ~:** an eminent physicist; **einen außerordentlichen künstlerischen ~ haben** be of exceptional artistic importance; **ersten ~es** of the greatest significance; (qualitätsmäßig) of the first order [2] (im Theater) circle; **erster ~:** dress circle; **zweiter ~:** upper circle; **dritter ~:** gallery; **die Zuschauer auf den Rängen** the audience in the circle [and gallery] seats; **vor überfüllten/fast leeren Rängen spielen** play to a packed/a nearly empty house [3] (Sport) ▸**Platz 6** [4] (Gewinnklasse in Lotterien) prize category

Rang-: ~abzeichen *das* insignia [of rank]; **~älteste** *der/die; adj. Dekl.* senior officer (holding a particular rank)

Range /ˈraŋə/ *die;* **~, ~n** (bes. md.) [young] tearaway; **freche** *od.* **kesse ~n** cheeky brats

ran|gehen *unr. itr. V.* (ugs.) [1] ▸**herangehen** [2] (erotisch) **bei den Mädchen ~:** be a fast worker with the girls (coll.)

Rangelei *die;* **~, ~en** (ugs.) ▸**Gerangel**

rangeln /ˈraŋl̩n/ *itr. V.* (ugs.) wrestle; struggle; (kämpfen) ‹*children*› scrap; **um etw. ~:** scramble *or* tussle for sth.; (fig.: argumentieren) wrangle over sth.

rang-, Rang-: ~folge *die* order of precedence; (finanziell) order of merit; **~hoch**
[A] *Adj.* high-ranking; senior ‹*manager*›; [B] *adv.* **eine ~hoch besetzte Veranstaltung** an event with high-ranking participants; **~höchste** *der/die; adj. Dekl.* most senior person; (Tier) dominant animal

Rangier-bahn·hof *der* marshalling yard

rangieren /raŋˈʒiːrən/
[A] *tr. V.* shunt ‹*trucks, coaches*›; switch ‹*cars*› (Amer.)
[B] *itr. V.* be placed; **an letzter Stelle/auf Platz zwei ~:** be placed last/second; **hinter/vor jmdm. ~** (bei der Arbeit usw.) be junior/senior to sb.

Rangierer *der;* **~s, ~:** shunter (Brit.); switchman (Amer.)

Rangiererin *die;* **~, ~nen** shunter (Brit.)

Rangier-: ~lok *die* (ugs.), **~lokomotive** *die* shunting *or* (Amer.) switch engine

rang-, Rang-: ~liste *die* [1] (Sport) ranking list; **Nummer eins der internationalen ~liste** number one in the world rankings; [2] (von Offizieren, Beamten) army/navy/civil service list; **~mäßig** [A] *Adj.* according to rank *postpos.*; ‹*equality etc.*› with regard to rank; **~mäßige Unterschiede** differences of rank; [B] *adv.* according to *or* with regard to rank; **~ordnung** *die* order of precedence; (Verhaltensf.) pecking order; **der ~ordnung nach unter/über jmdm. stehen** be below/above sb. in the pecking order *or* hierarchy; **~skala** *die* hierarchy; (Rangliste) ranking list; **in der ~skala der Beliebtheit** on the scale of popularity; **~unterschied** *der* difference in [social] status; (Milit.) difference in rank

ran|halten *unr. refl. V.* (ugs.) get a move on (coll.); (bei der Arbeit) get stuck in (coll.)

rank *Adj.* (geh.) lissom; **~ und schlank** lithe and lissom

Ranke /ˈraŋkə/ *die;* **~, ~n** (Bot.) tendril

Ränke /ˈrɛŋkə/ *Pl.* (geh. veralt.) intrigues; **~ schmieden** (geh.) scheme; hatch plots

ranken
[A] *refl. V.* climb, grow (**an** + *Dat.* up, **über** + *Akk.* over); **sich um etw. ~:** entwine itself around sth.; (fig. geh.) ‹*legends, mysteries*› be woven around sth.
[B] *itr. V.* [1] *mit sein* ▸**ranken A** [2] (Ranken treiben) put out tendrils

Ranken-: ~gewächs *das* creeper; **~werk** *das* [1] (verschlungene Ranken) mass of entwined tendrils; [2] (Verzierung) plant arabesques *pl.*

Ränke-: ~schmied *der* (veralt.) intriguer; schemer; **~spiel** *das* (veralt.) intrigues *pl.*

ran-: ~|klotzen *itr. V.* (salopp) get stuck in (coll.); pull one's finger out (coll.); (auf Dauer) keep hard at it; **~|kommen** *unr. itr. V.; mit sein* (ugs.) ▸**herankommen 1, 3; ~|können** *unr. itr. V.* (ugs.) **an etw.** (*Akk.*) **nicht ~können** be unable to get at sth.; **ich kann nicht ~:** I can't get at it/them

Rankune /raŋˈkyːnə/ *die;* **~** (geh. veralt.) [sense of] rancour; acrimony

ran-: ~|lassen *unr. tr. V.* [1] (ugs.: herankommen lassen) **jmdn. ~lassen** let sb. get up close; (salopp: sexuell) **sie lässt ihn nicht ~:** she won't let him do it (coll.); **sie lässt jeden ~:** she's anybody's; **jmdn. an etw.** (*Akk.*) **nicht ~lassen** not let sb. anywhere near sth.; [2] (ugs.: tätig werden lassen) **jmdn. an etw.** (*Akk.*) **~lassen** let sb. have a go at sth.; **lass mich mal ~!** let me have a go!; **~|machen** *refl. V.* (ugs.) ▸**heranmachen 1, 2; ~|müssen** *unr. itr. V.* (ugs.: arbeiten müssen) have to get stuck in (coll.)

rann /ran/ *1. u. 3. Pers. Sg. Prät. v.* **rinnen**

rannte /ˈrantə/ *1. u. 3. Pers. Sg. Prät. v.* **rennen**

ran-: ~|schaffen *tr. V.* (ugs.) get hold of; **~|schmeißen** *unr. refl. V.* **sich an jmdn. ~schmeißen** (ugs.) throw oneself at sb.; **~|wollen** *unr. itr. V.* (ugs.) want to get down to work; **an etw.** (*Akk.*) **nicht ~wollen** not feel like getting on with sth.

Ranzen /ˈrantsn̩/ *der;* **~s, ~** [1] (Schul~) satchel; (veralt.: Rucksack) rucksack [2] (salopp: Bauch) [fat] belly

ranzig *Adj.* rancid

Rap /rɛp/ *der;* **~[s], ~s** rap

rapid /raˈpiːt/ (südd., österr., schweiz.), **rapide**
[A] *Adj.* rapid
[B] *adv.* rapidly

Rap·musik /ˈrɛp-/ *die* rap music

Rappe /ˈrapə/ *der;* **~n, ~n** black horse

Rappel /ˈrapl̩/ *der;* **~s, ~** (ugs.) crazy turn (coll.); **du hast wohl einen ~?** are you crazy?

rappelig *Adj.* (ugs.) nervy; **das macht mich ganz ~:** it really irritates me

rappeln *itr. V.* [1] (ugs.: klappern, rütteln) rattle (**an** + *Dat.* at); ‹*alarm, telephone*› jangle; **es rappelt an der Tür** there's a rattling at the door; **bei ihm rappelts** (salopp) he's got one of his crazy turns (coll.) [2] *mit sein* (ugs.: sich fortbewegen) clatter [along] [3] (österr. ugs.: verrückt sein) be a bit crackers (Brit. coll.)

rappel·voll *Adj.* (ugs.) jam-packed (coll.) (**mit** with); chock-full (coll.) (**mit** of)

rappen /ˈrɛpn̩/ *itr. V.* rap

Rappen *der;* **~s, ~:** [Swiss] centime

Rappen·spalter *der;* **~s, ~, Rappen·spalterin** *die;* **~, ~nen** (schweiz. ugs.) penny-pincher

Rapper /ˈrɛpɐ/ *der;* **~s, ~, Rapperin** *die;* **~, ~nen** rapper

rapplig *Adj.* ▸**rappelig**

Rapport /raˈpɔrt/ *der;* **~s, ~e** [1] (veralt.) report; **jmdm. ~ erstatten** report to sb.; **sich zum ~ melden** report; **jmdn. zum ~ bestellen** ask sb. to give a report [2] (Psych.) rapport

Raps /raps/ *der;* **~es** (Bot., Landwirtsch.) rape

Raps·öl *das* rape oil

Rapunzel /raˈpʊntsl̩/ *die;* **~, ~n** [1] (Märchengestalt) Rapunzel [2] ▸**Feldsalat**

rar /raːɐ̯/ *Adj.* (knapp) scarce; (selten vorkommend; begehrt) rare ‹*case, opportunity, stamp, etc.*›; **sich ~ machen** (ugs.) not be around much (coll.); (selten erscheinen) make only rare appearances; **sie machten sich ~, als wir ihre Hilfe brauchten** they made themselves scarce when we needed their help; **du hast dich in letzter Zeit bei uns ~ gemacht** we haven't seen much of you at our place recently

Rarität /rariˈtɛːt/ *die;* **~, ~en** rarity

Raritäten-: ~kabinett *das:* room housing a display of rare specimens; **~sammlung** *die* collection of rare specimens

rasant /raˈzant/
[A] *Adj.* [1] (ugs.) (sehr schnell) tremendously fast (coll.) ‹*car, horse, runner, etc.*›; tremendous (coll.), lightning *attrib.* ‹*speed, acceleration*›; meteoric, lightning *attrib.* ‹*development, progress, growth*›; hairy (coll.) ‹*driving*›; (schnittig) racy ‹*car, styling*›; **in ~em Tempo, in ~er Fahrt** at a terrific speed (coll.) [2] (ugs.) (schwungvoll) dynamic, lively ‹*show*›; action-packed, exciting ‹*film, story*›; (fabelhaft) terrific (coll.) ‹*film, show, dress, song, etc.*›; (rassig) classy (sl.) ‹*woman*›; dashing ‹*style, dress*›; **eine ~e Kür laufen** skate an exciting programme [3] (Ballistik: flach) flat ‹*trajectory*›
[B] *adv.* [1] (ugs.) (sehr schnell) at terrific speed (coll.); ‹*increase*› by leaps and bounds; **~ beschleunigen** ‹*car*› have terrific acceleration (coll.); ‹*car, driver*› accelerate like a mad thing (coll.); **~ gestylt** *od.* **geschnitten** (schnittig) racily styled; with racy lines [2] (ugs.) (schwungvoll) dashingly; (rassig) stylishly [3] (Ballistik: flach) **~ verlaufen** ‹*trajectory*› be flat

Rasanz /raˈzants/ *die;* **~** [1] (ugs.: Schnelligkeit) terrific speed (coll.); **die ~ der Beschleunigung** the terrific [rate of] acceleration (coll.) [2] (ugs.: Dynamik) verve; excitement

rasch /raʃ/
[A] *Adj.* quick; quick, rapid ‹*step, progress, decision, action*›; speedy, swift ‹*end, action, decision, progress*›; fast, quick ‹*service, work, pace, tempo, progress*›; **ein ~es Tempo** a fast pace; (eines Fahrzeugs) a high speed; **in ~er Folge** in rapid *or* swift succession
[B] *adv.* quickly; ‹*drive, act*› quickly, fast; ‹*decide, end, proceed*› swiftly, rapidly; **das geht mir zu ~:** that's too quick for me; **notieren Sie das ~!** make a quick note of that!

rascheln /ˈraʃl̩n/ *itr. V.* rustle; **die Maus raschelte** the mouse made a rustling noise; **es raschelte im Stroh** there was a rustling in the straw; **mit der Zeitung ~:** rustle the newspaper

rasen /ˈraːzn̩/ *itr. V.* [1] *mit sein* (ugs.: eilen) dash *or* rush [along]; (fahren) tear *or* race along; (fig.)

r

‹*pulse*› race; **gegen einen Baum ~:** crash [at full speed] into a tree; **ein Auto kam um die Ecke gerast** a car came tearing *or* racing round the corner; **die Zeit raste** (fig.) the time simply flew past [2] (toben) ‹*person*› rage; (wie wahnsinnig) rave; (fig.) ‹*storm, sea, war*› rage; **[vor Begeisterung] ~:** go wild [with enthusiasm]

Rasen *der;* **~s, ~:** grass *no indef. art.;* (gepflegte ~fläche) lawn; (eines Spielfeldes usw., Grassode) turf; **in unserem Garten ist hauptsächlich ~:** our garden is mainly grass *or* lawn; **ihn deckt der kühle** *od.* **grüne ~** (geh. verhüll.) he has been laid to rest; **er musste den ~ verlassen** (Sportjargon) he was sent off [the field *or* (coll.) park]

rasend
[A] *Adj.* [1] (sehr schnell) **in ~er Fahrt, mit ~er Geschwindigkeit** at breakneck speed [2] (tobend) raging; (wie wahnsinnig) raving; (verrückt) mad; **[vor Wut** *usw.*] **~ werden** be beside oneself [with rage *etc.*]; **die Schmerzen machen mich ~:** the pain is driving me mad [3] (heftig) violent ‹*jealousy, rage*›; violent, excruciating ‹*pain*›; tumultuous ‹*applause*›; **~e Kopfschmerzen haben** have a splitting headache
[B] *adv.* (ugs.) incredibly (coll.) ‹*fast, funny, expensive*›; madly (coll.) ‹*in love*›; insanely ‹*jealous*›; **ich täte es ~ gern** I'd really love to do it

Rasen-: ~fläche *die* lawn; (kleiner) patch of grass; **~mäher** /-mɛːɐ/ *der;* **~~s, ~~:** lawnmower; **~platz** [1] ▸ **~fläche;** [2] (Fußball usw.) pitch; (Tennis) grass court; **~schere** *die* grass shears *pl.;* **~sprenger** *der;* **~~s, ~~:** lawn sprinkler; **~stück** *das* area of lawn

Raser *der;* **~s, ~** (ugs. abwertend) speed merchant (coll.); (rücksichtslos) road hog

Raserei *die;* **~, ~en** [1] (ugs.: schnelles Fahren) tearing along *no art.* [2] (das Toben) [insane] frenzy; (Wut) rage; **jmdn. zur ~ bringen** drive sb. mad *or* to distraction

Raserin *die;* **~, ~nen** ▸ **Raser**

Rasier-: ~apparat *der* [safety] razor; (elektrisch) electric shaver *or* razor; **~creme** *die* shaving cream

rasieren /raˈziːrən/ *tr. V.* [1] shave; **sich ~:** shave; **sich nass/trocken/elektrisch ~:** have a wet/dry shave/use an electric shaver; **sich** (*Dat.*)/**jmdm. die Beine** *usw.* **~:** shave one's/sb.'s legs; (ab~) **sich** (*Dat.*)/**jmdm. die Haare/den Bart ~:** shave off one's/sb.'s hair/beard [2] (zerstören) raze to the ground

Rasierer *der;* **~s, ~** (ugs.) [electric] shaver

Rasier-: ~klinge *die* razor blade; **~messer** *das* cutthroat razor; **~pinsel** *der* shaving brush; **~schaum** *der* [1] (in der Sprühdose) shaving foam; [2] (der ~seife) shaving lather; **~seife** *die* shaving soap; **~wasser** *das; Pl.* **~wässer** (nach der Rasur) aftershave; (vor der Rasur) pre-shave lotion; **~zeug** *das* shaving things *pl.*

Räson /rɛˈzɔŋ/ *die:* in **zur ~ kommen,** (veralt.) **~ annehmen** come to one's senses; **jmdn. zur ~ bringen** make sb. see reason

räsonieren /rɛzoˈniːrən/ *itr. V.* (veralt. abwertend) [1] (sich wortreich äußern) reason [at length]; expatiate [2] (nörgeln) grumble (**über** + *Akk.* about)

Raspel /ˈraspl̩/ *die;* **~, ~n** [1] (grobe Feile) rasp [2] (Küchengerät) grater

raspeln *tr. V.* [1] *auch itr.* (mit einer Feile) rasp; **an etw.** (*Dat.*) **~:** work away at sth. with a rasp [2] (Kochk.) grate

raß /raːs/, **räß** /rɛːs/ *Adj.* (südd., österr., schweiz.) highly-seasoned; hot ‹*curry, goulash*›

Rasse /ˈrasə/ *die;* **~, ~n** [1] (Biol.) breed; **ein Pferd von edler ~:** a horse of noble pedigree [2] (Anthrop.: Menschen~) race [3] **~ haben** *od.* **sein** (ugs.) be terrific (coll.); (Temperament haben) have plenty of spirit *or* mettle; **von** *od.* **mit ~** (ugs.) terrific (coll.); (temperamentvoll) [high-] spirited

Rasse·hund *der* pedigree dog

Rassel /ˈrasl̩/ *die;* **~, ~n** [1] (Musikinstrument) rattle, *esp.* maraca [2] (Spielzeug) rattle

Rassel·bande *die* (ugs. scherzh.) [gang of] little rascals *pl.*

rasseln *itr. V.* [1] rattle; **mit seinen Ketten/seinem Schlüsselbund ~:** rattle one's chains/jangle one's bunch of keys; **der Wecker rasselt** the alarm goes off with a jangling sound; **~d atmen** (fig.) breathe stertorously; **seine Lunge rasselt** (fig.) he has a rattle in his lung; *s. auch* **Säbel** [2] *mit sein* (sich ~d fortbewegen) clatter; **gegen einen Baum ~** (ugs.) go smash into a tree (coll.) [3] *mit sein* (salopp: durchfallen) **durch eine Prüfung ~:** come unstuck in *or* (Amer.) flunk an exam (coll.)

Rassen-: ~diskriminierung *die* racial discrimination *no art.;* **~frage** *die* race issue; race question; **~gesetze** *Pl.* race laws; **~hass,** ***~haß** *der* racial hatred *no art.;* **~ideologie** *die* racial ideology; **~konflikt** *der* racial conflict; **~krawall** *der* race riot; **~problem** *das* racial problem; **das ~problem** the race problem; **~schranke** *die* racial barrier; **~trennung** *die* racial segregation *no art.;* **~unruhen** *Pl.* racial unrest *sing;* **~vorurteil** *das* racial prejudice; **~wahn** *der* racial fanaticism

Rasse·pferd *das* thoroughbred [horse]

rasse·rein *Adj.* ▸ **reinrassig**

rassig *Adj.* spirited, mettlesome ‹*horse*›; spirited, vivacious ‹*woman*›; sporty ‹*car*›; tangy ‹*wine, perfume*›; (markant) striking ‹*face, features, beauty*›

rassisch
[A] *Adj.* racial; **aus ~en Gründen** for reasons of race
[B] *adv.* racially

Rassismus *der;* **~:** racism; racialism

Rassist *der;* **~en, ~en, Rassistin** *die;* **~, ~nen** racist; racialist

rassistisch
[A] *Adj.* racist; racialist
[B] *adv.* racialistically; **~ begründet** for racialist reasons *postpos.;* ‹*policy*› based on race; **~ gefärbt** with a racialist slant

Rast /rast/ *die;* **~, ~en** rest; **~ machen** stop for a break; **ohne ~ und Ruh** (geh.) without respite

Rasta /ˈrasta/ *der;* **~s, ~s** Rasta[farian]

Rasta·locken *Pl.* dreadlocks

Raste *die;* **~, ~n** (Technik) notch

rasten *itr. V.* rest; take a rest *or* break; **eine Stunde ~:** have an hour's rest; **wer rastet, der rostet** (Spr.) if you don't keep at it, you get rusty; *s. auch* **ruhen 4**

Raster *der;* **~s, ~** [1] (Druckw.) (Platte, Linien) screen [2] (fig.) [conceptual] framework; set pattern

Raster-: ~ätzung *die* (Druckw.) half-tone engraving; **~fahndung** *die* (Kriminologie) *pinpointing of suspects by means of computer analysis of data on many people*

rastern *tr. V.* screen; (Ferns.) scan

Raster·punkt *der* (Druckw.) half-tone dot

Raster·schaltung *die* ▸ **Indexschaltung**

Rasterung *die;* **~, ~en** [1] (das Rastern) screening; (Ferns.) scanning [2] (Struktur) screen

rast-, Rast-: ~haus *das* roadside café; (mit Hotelbetrieb) roadside hotel; motel; (an der Autobahn) motorway restaurant; **~hof** *der* [motorway] motel [and service area]; **~los** [A] *Adj.* restless ‹*person, spirit*›; restless, unsettled ‹*life*›; (ununterbrochen) unremitting, ceaseless ‹*work, search*›; (unermüdlich) tireless, unflagging ‹*work, enthusiasm*›; [B] *adv. s. Adj.:* restlessly; unremittingly; ceaselessly; tirelessly; unflaggingly; **~losigkeit** *die;* **~~:** restlessness; **~platz** *der* [1] place to rest; [2] (an Autobahnen) parking place (*with benches and WCs*); picnic area; **~stätte** *die* service area

Rasur /raˈzuːɐ̯/ *die;* **~, ~en** [1] (das Rasieren) shave; **nach der ~:** after shaving [2] (ausradierte Stelle) erasure

rät /rɛːt/ *3. Pers. Sg. Präsens v.* **raten**

Rat /raːt/ *der;* **~[e]s, Räte** /ˈrɛːtə/ [1] (Empfehlung) advice; **ein ~:** a piece *or* word of advice; **gib mir einen ~, was ich tun soll!** please tell me what I should do; **ich gab ihm den ~ zu …** I advised him to …; **jmds. ~ einholen, sich** (*Dat.*) **bei jmdm. ~ holen** take advice from sb.; **bei jmdm. ~ suchen** seek sb.'s advice; **da ist guter ~ teuer** I/we *etc.* hardly know which way to turn; **jmdm. mit ~ und Tat zur Seite stehen** *od.* **beistehen** stand by sb. with moral and practical support; **mit sich zu ~[e] gehen** give the matter a lot of thought; **jmdn./etw. zu ~[e] ziehen** consult sb./sth. [2] (Ausweg) way out; solution; **[sich** (*Dat.*)**] keinen ~ wissen** not know what to do; **ich wusste [mir] keinen ~ mehr** I was at my wit's end *or* completely at a loss; **weiß jemand ~?** has anybody any ideas? [3] (Gremium) council; (Sowjet) soviet; **der ~ der Stadt** the town council; **~ für Gegenseitige Wirtschaftshilfe** Council for Mutual Economic Aid; COMECON [4] (Ratsmitglied) councillor; council member [5] (Titel) Councillor

Rate /ˈraːtə/ *die;* **~, ~n** [1] (Teilbetrag) instalment; **etw. auf ~n kaufen** buy sth. by instalments *or* (Brit.) on hire purchase *or* (Amer.) on the installment plan [2] (Statistik: Verhältnis) rate

Räte·demokratie *die* government by soviets *no art.;* sovietism *no art.*

Rate·fuchs *der* (ugs.) quiz show ace

raten
[A] *unr. itr. V.* [1] (einen Rat, Ratschläge geben) **jmdm. ~:** advise sb.; **lass dir von einem Freund ~:** take the advice of a friend; **er lässt sich von niemandem ~:** he won't listen to anybody; **wem nicht zu ~ ist, dem ist [auch] nicht zu helfen** (Spr.) you can't help some people — they just won't listen; ≈ you can take a horse to the water, but you can't make him drink (prov.); **sich** (*Dat.*) **nicht zu ~ wissen** be quite at a loss; **wozu rätst du mir?** what do you advise me to do?; **ich würde zu diesem Bewerber ~:** my advice would be to choose this applicant [2] (schätzen) guess; **richtig/falsch ~:** guess right/wrong; **dreimal darfst du ~** (ugs. iron.) I'll give you three guesses
[B] *tr. V.* [1] (an~) **jmdm. ~, etw. zu tun** advise sb. to do sth.; **was rätst du mir?** what do you advise [me to do]?; **lass dir das ge~ sein!** you better had [do that]!; (tu das nicht) don't you dare do that!; **das möchte ich dir auch ge~ haben!** I should hope so! [2] (er~) guess

Raten-: ~kauf *der* purchase by instalments *or* (Amer.) on the installment plan; **~zahlung** *die* [1] payment by instalments; [2] (das Zahlen des Teilbetrags) hire purchase (Brit.) *or* (Amer.) installment plan payment; **die dritte ~zahlung ist fällig** the third instalment is due

Räte·republik *die* (hist.) soviet republic

Rate-: ~show *die* quiz show; **~spiel** *das* guessing-game

Rat-: ~geber *der* adviser; (Buch) guide; **~geberin** *die* adviser; **~haus** *das* town hall; **jmdn. ins ~haus wählen** elect sb. to the town council; **die FDP ist wieder ins ~haus eingezogen** the FDP is again represented on the town council; **~haus·saal** *der* town-hall council chamber

Ratifikation /ratifikaˈtsi̯oːn/ *die;* **~, ~en** ratification

ratifizieren /ratifiˈtsiːrən/ *tr. V.* ratify

Ratifizierung *die;* **~, ~en** ratification

Rätin /ˈrɛːtɪn/ *die;* **~, ~nen** councillor

Ratio /ˈraːtsi̯o/ *die;* **~** (geh.) [pure] reason *no art.;* rational logic *no art.*

Ration /raˈtsi̯oːn/ *die;* **~, ~en** ration; **jmdn. auf halbe/doppelte ~ setzen** (ugs.) put sb. on half/double rations; *s. auch* **eisern A 4**

rational /ratsi̯oˈnaːl/
[A] *Adj.* rational; **~e Zahlen** rational numbers
[B] *adv.* rationally

rationalisieren *tr., itr. V.* rationalize

Rationalisierung *die;* **~, ~en** rationalization; **~en** rationalization measures

Rationalisierungs·maßnahme *die* rationalization measure

Rationalismus *der;* **~:** rationalism *no art.*

Rationalist *der;* **~en, ~en, Rationalistin** *die;* **~, ~nen** rationalist

rationalistisch
[A] *Adj.* rationalistic; rationalist ‹*principles*›; **das**

r

~e Zeitalter the age of reason
B *adv.* rationalistically
Rationalität /ratsi̯onali'tɛ:t/ *die;* **~:** rationality
rationell /ratsi̯o'nɛl/
A *Adj.* efficient; (wirtschaftlich) economic
B *adv.* efficiently; (wirtschaftlich, kräftesparend) economically
rationieren *tr. V.* ration
Rationierung *die;* **~, ~en** rationing *no indef. art.*; **~en vornehmen** introduce rationing [measures]
rat·los
A *Adj.* baffled; at a loss *pred.*; helpless ‹*look*›; **einer Sache** (*Dat.*) **~ gegenüberstehen** not know what to do about sth.
B *adv.* helplessly; in a baffled way
Rat·losigkeit *die;* **~:** perplexity; helplessness; **in meiner ~:** not knowing what to do
Rätoromanisch /rɛtoro'ma:nɪʃ/ *das;* **~[s]** Rhaeto-Romanic; Rhaeto-Romance
ratsam /'ra:tza:m/ *Adj.* advisable; (weise) prudent
ratsch /ratʃ/ *Interj.* zip; (beim Zerreißen) rip; **es machte ~:** there was a ripping sound; *s. auch* **ritsch**
Ratsche /'ra:tʃə/ *die;* **~, ~n** (bes. südd., österr.), **Rätsche** /'rɛ:tʃə/ *die;* **~, ~n** (südd.) **1** (Geräuschinstrument) [football fan's] rattle **2** (Technik: Sperre) ratchet
ratschen¹ (ugs.)
A *itr. V.* (Geräusch erzeugen) rip
B *refl. V.* (landsch.: kratzen) scratch oneself
ratschen² (bes. südd., österr.), **rätschen** (südd.) *itr. V.* **1** (Ratsche drehen) swing a/one's rattle; (fig.) make a rasping noise **2** (ugs.: schwatzen) gossip
Rat-: **~schlag** *der* [piece of] advice; (Hinweis) tip; **auf meinen ~schlag hin** acting on my advice; **~schläge** advice/tips; **kluge ~schläge** (iron.) brilliant advice *sing.* (iron.); **~schluss, *~schluß** *der* (geh.) counsel (formal); **nach Gottes unerforschlichem ~schluss** in accordance with the unfathomable will of God
Rätsel /'rɛ:tsl̩/ *das;* **~s, ~** **1** (Denkaufgabe) riddle; (Bilder~, Kreuzwort~ usw.) puzzle; **das ist des ~s Lösung** (fig.) [so] that is the explanation; **jmdm. ~/ein ~ aufgeben** ask *or* set sb. riddles/a riddle; (fig.: vor Probleme stellen) puzzle *or* baffle sb. **2** (Geheimnis) mystery; enigma; **jmdm.** *od.* **für jmdn. ein ~ sein/bleiben** be/remain a mystery to sb.; **vor einem ~ stehen** be baffled
Rätsel·ecke *die* (ugs.) puzzle corner (*in a magazine/newspaper*)
rätselhaft
A *Adj.* mysterious; (unergründlich) enigmatic ‹*smile, expression, person*›; baffling ‹*problem*›; **es blieb/es ist [mir] ~, warum ...** it remained/is a mystery [to me] why ...
B *adv.* mysteriously; (unergründlich) enigmatically
Rätselhaftigkeit *die;* **~:** enigmatic nature; mysteriousness
Rätsel·heft *das* puzzle magazine
rätseln *itr. V.* puzzle, rack one's brains (**über +** *Akk.* over); **~, wer .../ob ...** try to work out who .../whether ...
Rätsel·raten *das* **1** ▸**Rätsel 1**: solving puzzles/riddles *no art.* **2** (das Rätseln) puzzling; (das Raten) guessing; **das ~, wer sein Nachfolger werden soll** the guessing game as to who is to be his successor
rätsel·voll
A *Adj.* mysterious; enigmatic ‹*person*›
B *adv.* mysteriously; ‹*smile*› enigmatically
Rats-: **~herr** *der,* **~herrin** *die* [town/city] councillor; **~keller** *der* [restaurant in the] town-hall cellar; **~präsident** *der,* **~präsidentin** *die* (EU) President of the Council; **~präsidentschaft** *die* (EU) Presidency of the Council; **~stube** *die* (veralt.) [town hall] council chamber
Rattan /'ratan/ *das;* **~s** rattan [cane]
Ratte /'ratə/ *die;* **~, ~n** (auch fig.) rat; **die ~n verlassen das sinkende Schiff** the rats are leaving the sinking ship
ratten-, Ratten-: **~bekämpfung** *die* rat control; **~fänger** *der,* **~fängerin** *die* **1** rat-catcher; **der ~fänger von Hameln** (Lit.) the Pied Piper of Hamelin; **2** (abwertend: Volksverführer) pied piper; **~gift** *das* rat poison; **~scharf** (Jugendspr.) *Adj.* **1** (großartig) wicked (coll.); fantastic (coll.); **2** (sexy) red-hot (coll.); (geil) red-hot; horny as hell *pred.* (sl.); **~schwanz** *der* **1** (fig.: große Anzahl) **ein ~schwanz von Änderungen/Gerüchten** a whole welter *or* string of changes/rumours; **2** (scherzh.: Zopf) pigtail; **3** (Schwanz der Ratte) rat's tail
rattern /'ratɐn/ *itr. V.* **1** (knattern) clatter; ‹*sewing machine, machine gun*› chatter; ‹*engine*› rattle **2** *mit sein* (sich **~d** fortbewegen) clatter [along]
Ratz /rats/ *der;* **~es, ~e** **1** (südd., österr., schweiz.) rat **2** (volkst.: Siebenschläfer) [edible] dormouse; **schlafen wie ein ~:** sleep like a log
ratze·kahl *Adv.* (ugs.) totally; completely
ratzen *itr. V.* (ugs.) [have a] kip (Brit. coll.)
ratzeputz /'ratsə'pʊts/ *Adv.* (ugs.) completely; **die Kuchen waren ~ weg** the cakes had completely vanished *or* were all gone; **~ leer sein** be completely empty; ‹*table, buffet*› be stripped bare
rau /rau̯/
A *Adj.* **1** (nicht glatt) rough; **in einer ~en Schale steckt oft ein weicher Kern** (Spr.) behind a rough exterior there often beats a heart of gold **2** (nicht mild) harsh, raw ‹*climate, winter*›; raw ‹*wind*› **3** (unwirtlich) bleak, inhospitable ‹*region, mountains, etc.*›; rough ‹*weather*› **4** (kratzig) husky, hoarse ‹*voice*› **5** (entzündet) sore ‹*throat*› **6** (grob, nicht feinfühlig) rough; harsh ‹*words, tone*›; **er ist ~, aber herzlich** he is a rough diamond **7** (Ballspiele) rough ‹*play*› **8** (ugs.) **in ~en Mengen** in huge *or* vast quantities
B *adv.* **1** (kratzig) ‹*speak etc.*› huskily, hoarsely **2** (grob, nicht feinfühlig) roughly **3** (Ballspiele) roughly; **~ spielen** play rough
Raub /raup/ *der;* **~[e]s** **1** robbery; (Entführung) kidnapping; **jmdn. wegen ~es anklagen/verurteilen** accuse/convict sb. of robbery *or* (jur.) larceny [from the person]; **der ~ der Sabinerinnen** (Myth.) the rape of the Sabine women **2** (Beute) [robber's] loot; stolen goods *pl.*; **ein ~ der Flammen werden** (geh.) be consumed by the flames (literary)
rau-, Rau-: **~bauz** /-bauts/ *der;* **~~es, ~~e** (ugs.) ▸**~bein**; **~bauzig** *Adj.* (ugs.) ▸**~beinig**; **~bein** *das* (ugs.) rough diamond; **~beinig** *Adj.* (ugs.) gruff; rough and ready
Raub·bau *der* over-exploitation (**an +** *Dat.* of); (beim Fischfang) overfishing; (beim Bergbau) overworking; **~ an etw.** (*Dat.*) **treiben** over-exploit sth.; **~ mit seiner Gesundheit treiben** (fig.) ruin one's health by overdoing things; **~ an seinen Kräften** (fig.) overtaxing one's strength
Raub·druck *der;* *Pl.* **~e** pirated edition
rauben
A *tr. V.* steal; kidnap ‹*person*›; **jmdm. etw. ~:** rob sb. of sth.; (geh.: wegnehmen) deprive sb. of sth.; **jmdm. den Atem/die Sprache ~:** take sb.'s breath away/render sb. speechless; **er hat ihr die Unschuld geraubt** (veralt.) he deprived her of her virginity; he deflowered her (dated)
B *itr. V.* rob; (plündern) plunder
Räuber /'rɔybɐ/ *der;* **~s, ~** **1** robber; (Entführer) kidnapper; (fig. scherzh.) rascal; **~ und Gendarm** cops and robbers; **anscheinend bin ich unter die ~ gefallen** (ugs.) it seems I'm being fleeced (coll.) **2** (Zool.: Tier) predator
Räuber-: **~bande** *die* (veralt.) band of robbers; **~geschichte** *die* **1** story about robbers; **2** (ugs.: erlogene Geschichte) tall story; **~hauptmann** *der* (veralt.) robber chief; **~höhle** *die* (veralt.) robber's den; **hier sieht es aus wie in einer ~höhle** it's a frightful mess in here (coll.)
Räuberin *die;* **~, ~nen** ▸**Räuber 1**
räuberisch
A *Adj.* **1** rapacious, predatory ‹*gang, horde, etc.*›; **~e Erpressung** (Rechtsw.) extortion by means of force *or* under threat of force **2** (Zool.) predatory ‹*animal, fish, etc.*›
B *adv.* (Zool.) **~ lebend** living as a predator/as predators; predatory
räubern *itr. V.* go robbing; (plündern) loot
Räuber-: **~pistole** *die* (ugs. scherzh.) tall story; **~zivil** *das* (ugs. scherzh.) scruffy clothes *pl.*
raub-, Raub-: **~fisch** *der* predatory fish; **~gier** *die* rapacity; **~gierig** *Adj.* rapacious; **~gut** *das* stolen goods *or* property; **~katze** *die* wild cat; **~kopie** *die* pirated copy; **~mord** *der* (Rechtsw.) murder (**an +** *Dat.* of) in the course of a robbery *or* with robbery as motive; **~mörder** *der,* **~mörderin** *die* robber and murderer; **~ritter** *der* (hist.) robber baron; **~tier** *das* predator; beast of prey; **~tier·käfig** *der* predators' cage; (für Löwen und Tiger) lions' and tigers' cage; **~überfall** *der* robbery (**auf +** *Akk.* of); (von einer Bande auf eine Bank od. dergl.) raid (**auf +** *Akk.* on); **~vogel** *der* bird of prey; **~wild** *das* (Jägerspr.) predators *pl.* (*hunted as game*); **~zug** *der* plundering raid
Rauch /raux/ *der;* **~[e]s** smoke; **kein ~ ohne Flammen** (Spr.) there's no smoke without fire (prov.); **in ~ [und Flammen] aufgehen** go up in smoke *or* flames; **sich in ~ auflösen, in ~ aufgehen** (fig.) go up in smoke
Rauch-: **~abzug** *der* smoke outlet; (Rohr, Schacht) flue; **~bombe** *die* smoke bomb
rauchen
A *itr. V.* smoke; **es rauchte in der Küche** there was smoke in the kitchen; **sonst raucht es!** (ugs.) or there'll be trouble
B *tr.* (*auch itr.*) *V.* smoke ‹*cigarette, pipe, etc.*›; **~ Sie?** do you smoke?; **eine ~:** have a smoke; **stark** *od.* **viel ~:** be a heavy smoker; **„Rauchen verboten"** 'No smoking'
Rauch·entwicklung *die* build-up of smoke
Raucher *der;* **~s, ~:** smoker; **möchten Sie ~ oder Nichtraucher [fliegen]?** would you like smoking or no smoking?
Räucher·aal *der* smoked eel
Raucher-: **~abteil** *das* smoking compartment; smoker; **~bein** *das* ▸ℹ **S. 439** (Med.) *narrowing of the arteries of the leg as a result of heavy smoking*
Räucher·hering *der* smoked herring
Raucher·husten *der* smoker's cough
Raucherin *die;* **~, ~nen** smoker
Räucher-: **~kammer** *die* smokehouse; **~lachs** *der* smoked salmon
Raucher·lunge *die* (volkst.) smoker's lung
räuchern /'rɔyçɐn/
A *tr. V.* smoke ‹*meat, fish*›
B *itr. V.* burn incense/joss sticks *etc.*
Räucher-: **~schinken** *der* smoked ham; **~speck** *der* smoked [streaky] bacon; **~stäbchen** *das* joss stick
Raucher·zimmer *das* smoking room
rauch-, Rauch-: **~fahne** *die* plume of smoke; **~fang** *der* **1** (**~abzug**) chimney hood; **2** (österr.: Schornstein) chimney; **~fang·kehrer** *der,* **~fang·kehrerin** *die* (österr.) chimney sweep; **~farben, ~farbig** *Adj.* smoke-coloured; smoke-grey; **~fass, *~faß** *das* (kath. Kirche) censer; **~frei** *Adj.* smoke-free; **~gas** *das* flue gas; **~gasentschwefelung** *die;* **~~:** flue gas desulphurization; **~geschwängert** *Adj.* smoke-filled; **die Luft war ~geschwängert** the air was heavy with smoke; **~geschwärzt** *Adj.* smoke-blackened; **~glas** *das* smoked glass
rauchig *Adj.* smoky; husky ‹*voice*›
rauch-, Rauch-: **~los** *Adj.* smokeless; **~melder** *der* smoke detector; **~pilz** *der* mushroom cloud; **~ring** *der* smoke ring; **~salon** *der* smoking room; **~säule** *die* column *or* pillar of smoke; **~schwaden** *der* cloud of smoke; **~signal** *das* smoke signal; **~tisch** *der* smoker's table; **~verbot** *das* ban on smoking; **aus Sicherheitsgründen herrscht ~verbot** smoking is prohibited for safety reasons; **~vergiftung** *die* poisoning *no art.* by smoke inhalation; **~verzehrer** *der;* **~~s, ~~:** air cleaner

r

ℹ Rauminhalt

Raummaße

1 Kubikzentimeter	=	one cubic centimetre (cc)	=	0.06 cubic inch (cu. in.)
1 Kubikmeter	=	one cubic metre (cu. m)	=	35.714 cubic feet (cu. ft) *od.* 1.307 cubic yards (cu. yds)

Hohlmaße

1 Zentiliter	=	one centilitre (cl)	=	0.0176 pints (*brit.*), 0.021 pints (*amerik.*)
1 Liter	=	one litre (l)	=	1.76 pints (*brit.*), 2.1 pints (*amerik.*) *od.* 0.22 gallons (*brit.*), 0.264 gallons (*amerik.*)

Wie viel* od. *Welches Volumen hat es?
= What is its volume?

Es hat ein Volumen von 6 m³
= Its volume is 6 cubic metres,
≈ the volume is 200 cubic feet

Wie viel fasst der Tank?
= How much does the tank hold? What is the capacity of the tank?

Der Tank fasst 45 Liter
= The tank holds 45 litres,
≈ the tank holds 10 gallons (*brit.*)/12 gallons (*amerik.*)

Die beiden Tanks haben das gleiche Fassungsvermögen
= The two tanks have the same capacity *od.* hold the same amount

Mein Wagen verbraucht 10 Liter auf 100 Kilometer
≈ My car does 28 (*UK*) *od.* 23 (*USA*) miles per gallon (mpg).

[Um Liter auf 100 Kilometer in miles per gallon umzurechnen (oder auch umgekehrt), dividiert man 280 (bei britischen gallons) bzw. 230 (bei US gallons) durch die bekannte Zahl].

Benzin wird literweise verkauft
= Petrol is sold by the litre

Der Hubraum eines Motors wird im britischen Einflussbereich in Kubikzentimeter (cc) bzw. Liter angegeben, dagegen in den USA und Kanada in cubic inches (cu. in.):

Wie viel Hubraum hat der Motor?
= What is the capacity of the engine *od.* (*amerik.*) motor?

Der Motor hat 1 600 cm³* od. *1,6 Liter Hubraum
= It's a 1600 cc *od.* 1.6 litre engine (*brit.*) *od.* a 96 cu. in. motor (*amerik.*)

[and freshener]; **~waren** *Pl.* (fachspr.) ▸**Pelzwaren**; **~wolke** *die* cloud of smoke; **~zeichen** *das* smoke signal

Räude /'rɔydə/ *die;* **~, ~n** mange *no art.*

räudig *Adj.* mangy; **ein ~es Schaf** (fig.) a bad apple (fig.); **du ~er Hund!** (derb) you dirty rat! (sl.)

rauf /rauf/ *Adv.* (ugs.) up; **~ mit euch!** up you go!; *s. auch* **herauf**; **hinauf**

rauf- (ugs.) up; **~brüllen/~klettern** shout/climb

Rau·faser·tapete *die* woodchip wallpaper

Raufbold /-bɔlt/ *der;* **~[e]s, ~e** (veralt.) ruffian

rauf|bringen *unr. tr. V.* (ugs.) (her) bring up; (hin) take up

Raufe *die;* **~, ~n** hay rack

raufen

A *itr., refl. V.* fight; **[sich] wegen** *od.* **um etw. ~:** fight [each other] over sth.

B *tr. V.* pull up ‹*weeds, plants, etc.*›; pull ‹*flax*›; **sich** (*Dat.*) **die Haare/den Bart ~:** tear one's hair/at one's beard

Rauferei *die;* **~, ~en** fight

rauf|fahren *unr. itr. V.; mit sein* (ugs.) drive up; **jmdm. hinten ~:** drive into the back of sb.['s car]

rauf|gehen *unr. itr. V.; mit sein* (ugs.) go up

Rauf·handel *der;* **~s, Raufhändel** (veralt.) brawl; fight

rauf-: ~|holen *tr. V.* (ugs.) fetch *or* bring up; **~|kommen** *unr. itr. V.; mit sein* (ugs.) come up

rauf·lustig *Adj.* (veralt.) pugnacious; **er ist ein ~er Bursche** he is always spoiling for a fight

Rau·frost *der* rime

***rauh** *usw.* ▸**rau** *usw.*

Rau·haar·dackel *der* wire-haired dachshund

Rauheit *die;* **~, ~en** ▸**rau 1-4**: roughness; harshness; rawness; bleakness; inhospitableness; huskiness; hoarseness

***Rauh·faser·tapete** *usw.* ▸**Raufasertapete** *usw.*

raum /raum/ *Adj.* (Seemannsspr.) **1** (weit) open ‹*sea*› **2** (von hinten) quartering, following ‹*sea, current, wind*›

Raum *der;* **~[e]s, Räume** /'rɔymə/ **1** (Wohn~, Nutz~) room; **im ~ stehen** (fig.) be in the air; ‹*threat*› be hanging in the air; **etw. im ~ stehen lassen** (fig.) leave sth. hanging in the air; **eine Anschuldigung im ~ stehen lassen** leave an accusation unanswered **2** (nicht fest eingegrenztes Gebiet) expanse; **~ und Zeit** (Philos.) space and time **3** (Platz) room; space; **5 m ~:** a space of 5 m; **auf engstem ~ leben** live in a very confined space; **einen zu breiten ~ einnehmen** (fig.) be given too much attention **4** (Welt~) space *no art.* **5** (Gebiet) area; region; **im ~ Hamburg** in the Hamburg area *or* region **6** (Wirkungsfeld) sphere **7** (Math.) space

Raum-: ~akustik *die* (Physik) room acoustics *sing., no art.*; **~angabe** *die* (Sprachw.) adverbial expression of place; **~anzug** *der* spacesuit; **~ausstatter** *der;* **~~s, ~~** **1** (Beruf) interior decorator; **2** (Geschäft) [firm of] interior decorators *pl.*; **~ausstatterin** *die;* **~~, ~~nen** ▸**~ausstatter 1**; **~bild** *das* (Optik) stereoscopic picture; 3-D picture; **~deckung** *die* (Ballspiele) zonal defence

räumen /'rɔymən/

A *tr. V.* **1** (entfernen) clear [away]; clear ‹*snow*›; **Minen ~:** clear mines; (auf See) sweep *or* clear mines; **etw. vom Tisch ~:** clear sth. off the table; **etw. aus dem Weg ~:** clear sth. out [of] the way **2** (an einen Ort) clear; move; **seine Sachen auf die Seite ~:** clear *or* move one's things to one side; **etw. in Schubfächer** (*Akk.*) **~:** put sth. away in drawers **3** (frei machen) clear ‹*street, building, warehouse, stocks, etc.*› **4** (verlassen) vacate ‹*hotel room*›; vacate, clear ‹*hall, cinema, etc.*›; vacate, move out of ‹*house, flat*›; evacuate, vacate ‹*military position, area*› **5** (durch die Polizei usw. frei machen) clear ‹*room, hall, street, etc.*›

B *itr. V.* clear up

Raum-: ~ersparnis *die* saving of space; **~fähre** *die* space shuttle; **~fahrer** *der,* **~fahrerin** *die* astronaut; (Kosmonaut) cosmonaut; **~fahrt** *die* **1** space flight; space travel; **2** (~flug) space flight

Raumfahrt-: ~behörde *die* space agency; **~medizin** *die* space medicine *no art.*; **~technik** *die* space technology *no art.*

Raum·fahrzeug *das* spacecraft

Räum·fahrzeug *das* bulldozer; (für Schnee) snowplough

Raum-: ~flug *der* space flight; **~forschung** *die* space research *no art.*

Räum·gerät *das* clearing equipment

raum-, Raum-: ~gestalter *der,* **~gestalterin** *die* interior designer; **~gleiter** *der;* **~s, ~** (Raumf.) space shuttle; **~greifend** *Adj.* (Sport) long ‹*pass, stride, etc.*›; **~inhalt** *der* ▸ℹ **S. 582** (Math.) volume; **~kapsel** *die* space capsule; **~klang** *der* stereophonic sound; **~klima** *das* room climate

räumlich

A *Adj.* **1** (den Raum betreffend) spatial; **aus ~en Gründen** for reasons of space; **wir sind ~ sehr beschränkt** we are cramped for space; **~e Nähe** physical proximity **2** (dreidimensional) three-dimensional; stereophonic ‹*sound*›; stereoscopic ‹*vision*›; **~ wirken** have a three-dimensional effect; **~es Vorstellungsvermögen** ability to visualize things in three dimensions

B *adv.* **1** spatially; **in zeitlich und ~ enger Nachbarschaft** in close temporal and spatial proximity **2** (dreidimensional) three-dimensionally

Räumlichkeit *die;* **~, ~en** **1** *Pl.* rooms; **uns** (*Dat.*) **fehlen die ~en** we don't have enough space; **die ~en des Museums** the museum's premises **2** (räumliche Wirkung) three-dimensionality

raum-, Raum-: ~maß *das* ▸ℹ **S. 582** measure of capacity; **~meter** *der od. das* cubic metre (*of stacked wood, logs*); **~not** *die* shortage *or* lack of space (*Gen.* in); **~ordnung** *die* (Amtsspr.) regional planning; **~ordnungs·plan** *der* (Amtsspr.) regional development plan; **~pfleger** *der* cleaner; **~pflegerin** *die* cleaning lady; cleaner; **~schiff** *das* spaceship; **~sonde** *die* space probe; **~sparend** *Adj.* ▸**platzsparend**; **~station** *die* space station; **~teiler** *der* room divider; **~transporter** *der* space shuttle

Räumung *die;* **~, ~en** **1** clearing **2** (einer Wohnung, eines Hotelzimmers) vacation; vacating **3** (wegen Gefahr) evacuation **4** (von Vorräten, eines Geschäfts) clearance

Räumungs-: ~klage *die* (Rechtsw.) action for eviction; **~klage erheben** ≈ apply for an eviction order; **~verkauf** *der* (Kaufmannsspr.) clearance sale

raunen /'raunən/ *tr., itr. V.* (geh.) whisper; **ein Raunen ging durch die Reihen** a murmur went through the ranks

raunzen /'rauntsn̩/ *itr. V.* (bes. südd., österr.) grumble; grouse (coll.)

Raupe /'raupə/ *die;* **~, ~n** **1** (Larve) caterpillar **2** ▸**Planierraupe** **3** ▸**~nkette**

Raupen-: ~fahrzeug *das* Caterpillar vehicle; Caterpillar ®; **~kette** *die* Caterpillar track; **~schlepper** *der* Caterpillar tractor

Rau-: ~putz *der* roughcast; **~reif** *der* hoar frost

raus /raus/ *Adv.* (ugs.) out; **~ mit euch!** out you go!; **Nazis ~!** Nazis out!; *s. auch* **heraus**; **hinaus 1**

raus|bekommen *unr. tr. V.* (ugs.) ▸**herausbekommen**

Rausch /rauʃ/ *der;* **~[e]s, Räusche** /'rɔyʃə/ **1** (durch Alkohol) state of drunkenness; **sich** (*Dat.*) **einen ~ antrinken** get drunk; **einen [leichten/schweren] ~ haben** be [slightly/very] drunk; **seinen ~ ausschlafen** sleep off the effects of drink; sleep it off (coll.); **etw. im ~ tun** do sth. while drunk **2** (durch Drogen) drugged state; **einen ~ haben** be drugged; be high (coll.) [on drugs]; **etw. im ~ tun** do sth. while drugged **3** (starkes Gefühl) transport; **der ~ des Erfolgs/Sieges** the exhilaration *or* intoxication of success/victory; **ein wilder/blinder ~:** a wild/blind frenzy; **der ~ der**

r

Geschwindigkeit the exhilaration *or* thrill of speed

rausch·arm
A *Adj.* low-noise
B *adv.* with a low noise level

Rausche·bart *der* (scherzh.) 1 full beard 2 (Mann) bearded [old] gentleman

rauschen *itr. V.* 1 ‹*water, wind, torrent*› rush; ‹*trees, leaves*› rustle; ‹*skirt, curtains, silk*› swish; ‹*waterfall, strong wind*› roar; ‹*rain*› pour down; **ich hörte das Wasser ~:** I heard the sound of rushing water; **es rauscht im Radio** there's a hiss coming from the radio; **das Rauschen der Brandung/des Meeres** the roar of the surf/sea; **~der Beifall** (fig.) resounding applause; **~de Feste** (fig.) glittering parties 2 *mit sein* (sich bewegen) ‹*water, river, etc.*› rush; ‹*bird, bullet, etc.*› whoosh; **der Ball rauschte ins Tor** (Sport ugs.) the ball slammed into the back of the net; **sie rauschte aus dem Zimmer** she swept out of the room

Rausch·gift *das* drug; narcotic; **~ nehmen** take drugs; be on drugs

rausch·gift-, Rausch·gift-: ~handel *der* drug trafficking; **~händler** *der*, **~händlerin** *die* drug trafficker; **~süchtig** *Adj.* drug-addicted; addicted to drugs *postpos.*; **sie war ~süchtig** she was addicted to drugs *or* a drug addict; **~süchtige Jugendliche** young drug addicts; **~süchtige** *der/die* drug addict; **~tote** *der/die* person who dies/died as a result of drug abuse; **im vergangenen Jahr gab es 400 ~tote** last year 400 people died as a result of drug abuse

Rausch·gold *das* Dutch metal

Rauschgold·engel *der* angel (made of Dutch metal)

rausch·haft *Adj.* ecstatic

Rausch·mittel *das* ▸ **Rauschgift**

raus-: ~|dürfen *unr. itr. V.* (ugs.) ▸ **heraus-, hinausdürfen**; **~|ekeln** *tr. V.* (ugs.) ▸ **hinausekeln**; **~|fahren** *unr. tr. V.*; *mit sein* (ugs.) ▸ **heraus-, hinausfahren**; **~|fallen** *unr. itr. V.*: *mit sein* (ugs.) fall out (**aus** of); (ausscheiden) drop out, be eliminated (**aus** from); **~|feuern** *tr. V.* (ugs.) chuck out (coll.); **~|finden** (ugs.) A *unr. tr. V.* ▸ **herausfinden**; B *unr. itr. V.* ▸ **herausfinden, hinausfinden**; **~|fischen** *tr. V.* (ugs.) ▸ **herausfischen**; **~|fliegen** *unr. itr. V.*; *mit sein* (ugs.) ▸ **heraus-, hinausfliegen**; **~|gehen** *unr. itr. V.*; *mit sein* (ugs.) ▸ **heraus-, hinausgehen**; **~hängen**[1] *unr. itr. V.* (ugs.) ▸ **heraushängen**[1], **hinaushängen**[1]; **~|hängen**[2] *tr. V.* (ugs.) ▸ **heraushängen**[2], **hinaushängen**[2]; **~|hauen** *unr. tr. V.* (ugs.) ▸ **heraushauen**; **~|kommen** *unr. itr. V.*; *mit sein* (ugs.) ▸ **heraus-, hinauskommen**; **~|können** *unr. itr. V.* (ugs.) be able to go/come out; (sich befreien können) be able to get out; **~|kriegen** *tr. V.* (ugs.) get out (**aus** of); **ich habe das Rätsel/die Aufgabe nicht ~gekriegt** I couldn't do the puzzle/exercise; **~|müssen** *unr. itr. V.* (ugs.) have got to go/come out; **wir müssen aus unserer Wohnung ~:** we have got to get out of our flat (esp. Brit.) *or* (esp. Amer.) apartment; **~|nehmen** *unr. tr. V.* (ugs.) ▸ **heraus-, hinausnehmen**; **~|pauken** *tr. V.* (ugs.) **jmdn. ~pauken** get sb. off the hook (coll.)

räuspern /'rɔyspɐn/ *refl. V.* clear one's throat

raus-, Raus-: ~|posaunen *tr. V.* (ugs.) ▸ **hinausposaunen**; **~|rutschen** *itr. V.*; *mit sein* (ugs.) ▸ **herausrutschen**; **~|schicken** *tr. V.* (ugs.) ▸ **hinausschicken**; **~|schmeißen** *unr. tr. V.* (ugs.) chuck (coll.) *or* sling (coll.) ‹*objects*› out *or* away; give ‹*employee*› the push (coll.) *or* sack (coll.) *or* boot (sl.); chuck (coll.) *or* throw ‹*customer, drunk, tenant*› out (**aus** of); **das ist ~geschmissenes Geld** that's money down the drain (coll.); **~schmeißer** *der*; **~~s, ~~** (ugs.) 1 (Person) chucker-out (coll.); bouncer (coll.); 2 (Tanz) last dance; **~schmeißerin** *die*; **~~, ~~nen** ▸ **~schmeißer 1**; **~schmiss**, ***~schmiß** *der* (ugs.) ▸ **~schmeißen**: chucking out (coll.); slinging out (coll.); sacking (coll.); chucking out (coll.); throwing out; **nach dem ~schmiss des Angetrunkenen ...** after the drunk had been chucked out; **nach unserem ~schmiss aus der Wohnung** after we were chucked (coll.) *or* thrown out of our flat; **~|schmuggeln** *tr. V.* (ugs.) ▸ **herausschmuggeln, hinausschmuggeln**; **~|schreien** *unr. tr. V.* (ugs.) ▸ **herausschreien, hinausschreien**; **~|sollen** *itr. V.* (ugs.) **der Zahn/Blinddarm soll ~:** the tooth/appendix is to come out; **wir sollen zum Jahresende aus unserer Wohnung ~:** we're to be out of our flat by the end of the year; **~|springen** *unr. itr. V.*; *mit sein* (ugs.) ▸ **herausspringen**; **~|strecken** *tr. V.* (ugs.) ▸ **herausstrecken, hinausstrecken**; **~|wollen** *unr. itr. V.* (ugs.) want to go/come out; **ich will ~!** I want to get out!; **~wurf** *der* (ugs.) ▸ **Hinauswurf**; **~|ziehen** (ugs.) A *unr. tr. V.* ▸ **herausziehen A, hinausziehen A**; B *unr. itr. V.*; *mit sein* ▸ **herausziehen B, hinausziehen B**; C *unr. refl. V.* ▸ **hinausziehen C**; **~|zögern** (ugs.) A *tr. V.* ▸ **hinauszögern A**; B *refl. V.* ▸ **hinauszögern B**

Raute /'rautə/ *die*; **~, ~n** 1 (Pflanze) rue 2 (Geom.) rhombus

rauten·förmig *Adj.* rhombic; diamond-shaped

rautiert /rau'ti:ɐt/ *Adj.* squared ‹*paper*›

Rave /reɪv/ *der*; **~s, ~s** rave

raven /'reɪvn̩/ *itr. V.* rave

Raver /'reɪvɐ/ *der*; **~s, ~:** raver

Ravioli /ra'vi̯o:li/ *Pl.* (Kochk.) ravioli *sing.*

Rayon /rɛ'jõ:/ *der*; **~s, ~s** *od.* (österr.) **~e** 1 (Warenhausabteilung) department 2 (österr., schweiz.: Bezirk) district

Rayons·inspektor *der*, **Rayons·inspektorin** *die* (österr. schweiz.) district inspector

Razzia /'ratsi̯a/ *die*; **~, Razzien** raid; **in dieser Kneipe führte die Polizei oft Razzien durch** the police has often raided this bar

RB *Abk.* = **Radio Bremen**

RBB *Abk.* = **Rundfunk Berlin-Brandenburg** Berlin-Brandenburg Radio

Re *das*; **~s, ~s** (Skat) redouble

Reagens *das*; **~, Reagenzien** /rea'gɛntsi̯ən/, **Reagenz** /rea'gɛnts/ *das*; **~es, ~ien** (Chemie) reagent

Reagenz-: ~glas *das* test tube; **~papier** *das* test paper

reagieren *itr. V.* 1 react (**auf** + *Akk.* to) 2 (Chemie) react; **miteinander ~:** react together

Reaktanz /reak'tants/ *die*; **~, ~en** (Elektrot.) reactance

Reaktion /reak'tsi̯o:n/ *die*; **~, ~en** (auch Politik abwertend, Chemie) reaction (**auf** + *Akk.* to)

reaktionär /reaktsi̯o'nɛ:ɐ/ *Adj.* (Politik abwertend) reactionary

Reaktionär *der*; **~s, ~e, Reaktionärin** *die*; **~, ~nen** (Politik abwertend) reactionary

reaktions-, Reaktions-: ~fähig *Adj.* 1 capable of reacting *postpos.*; **durch den Alkoholgenuss war er nicht mehr voll ~fähig** his alcohol intake had impaired his reactions 2 (Chemie) reactive; **~fähigkeit** *die* 1 ability to react; **jmds. ~fähigkeit überprüfen** test sb.'s reactions 2 (Chemie) reactivity; **~geschwindigkeit** *die* (Chemie) reaction rate; **~schnell** A *Adj.* ‹*person*› with quick reactions; **~schnell sein** have quick reactions; **durch sein ~schnelles Abbremsen** through his quick reaction in braking; B *adv.* **sie schrieb ~schnell die Autonummer auf** she reacted quickly and wrote down the car's number; **~schnelligkeit** *die* speed of reaction; **~vermögen** *das* ▸ **~fähigkeit**; **~wärme** *die* (Chemie) heat of reaction; **~weg** *der* reaction distance; **~zeit** *die* (Physiol.) reaction time

reaktiv /reak'ti:f/
A *Adj.* reactive
B *adv.* reactively

reaktivieren *tr. V.* 1 (wieder anstellen) recall [to duty] 2 (wieder in Gebrauch nehmen) bring ‹*vehicle, machine, etc.*› back into service; (fig.) brush *or* polish up ‹*knowledge, skill, etc.*› 3 (Chemie) reactivate ‹*catalyst, serum*›

Reaktivierung *die* 1 (Wiedereinstellung) recalling [to duty] 2 (Wiederinbetriebnahme) **die ~ einer Sache** (*Gen.*) **beschließen** decide to bring sth. back into service 3 (Chemie) reactivation

Reaktor /re'aktɔr/ *der*; **~s, ~en** /-'to:rən/ reactor

Reaktor-: ~katastrophe *die* [nuclear] reactor disaster; **~sicherheit** *die* reactor safety

real /re'a:l/
A *Adj.* 1 real 2 (wirklichkeitsbezogen) realistic
B *adv.* 1 actually 2 (wirklichkeitsbezogen) realistically 3 (Wirtsch.) in real terms

Reala /re'a:la/ *die*; **~, ~s** (Jargon) [Green Party] realist

Real-: ~einkommen *das* real income; **~enzyklopädie** *die* (veralt.) ▸ **~lexikon**

Realien /re'a:li̯ən/ *Pl.* 1 (Tatsachen) realities *pl.*; facts *pl.* 2 (veralt.: Naturwissenschaften) natural sciences

Real·injurie *die* (Rechtsw.) assault and battery

Realisation /realiza'tsi̯o:n/ *die*; **~, ~en** 1 ▸ **realisieren 1**: realization; implementation 2 (Film, Ferns.) production

realisierbar *Adj.* ▸ **realisieren 1, 3**: realizable; implementable; sellable

Realisierbarkeit *die*; **~:** practicability; feasibility

realisieren /reali'zi:rən/ *tr. V.* 1 (geh.: verwirklichen) realize ‹*plan, idea, proposals, aim, project, wish*›; implement ‹*plan, programme, decision*› 2 (geh.: verstehen) realize 3 (Wirtsch.) realize ‹*profit, assets, etc.*›; sell ‹*property*›

Realisierung *die*; **~, ~en** ▸ **realisieren 1, 3**: realization; implementation; selling

Realismus *der*; **~, Realismen** realism

Realist *der*; **~en, ~en** realist

Realistik *die*; **~:** realism

Realistin *die*; **~, ~nen** realist

realistisch
A *Adj.* realistic
B *adv.* realistically

Realität *die*; **~, ~en** 1 reality 2 *Pl.* (österr.) ▸ **Immobilien**

Realitäten-: ~händler *der*, **~händlerin** *die*, **~vermittler** *der*, **~vermittlerin** *die* (österr.) estate agent (Brit.); real estate agent (Amer.)

realitäts-, Realitäts-: ~bezogen *Adj.*, *adv.* ▸ **~nah**; **~bezug** *der* contact with reality; **~fern** A *Adj.* unrealistic; B *adv.* unrealistically; **~ferne** *die* lack of contact with reality; lack of realism; **~nah** A *Adj.* realistic; B *adv.* realistically; **~nähe** *die* realism; **einer Behauptung etwas ~nähe verschaffen** make a remark correspond more closely to reality; **~sinn** *der* sense of reality

realiter /re'a:litɐ/ *Adv.* (geh.) in reality

Reality·show /ri'ɛlɪti-/ *die* (Ferns.) reality TV show

Real-: ~kanzlei *die* (österr.) estate agency (Brit.); real estate office (Amer.); **~katalog** *der* (Bibliothekswesen) subject catalogue; **~konkurrenz** *die* (Rechtsw.) accumulation of offences (*dealt with at the same trial*); **~lexikon** *das* specialist encyclopedia; **~lohn** *der* (Wirtsch.) real wages *pl.*

Realo /re'a:lo/ *der*; **~s, ~s** (Jargon) [Green Party] realist

real-, Real-: ~politik *die* realpolitik; practical politics *sing.*; **~politiker** *der*, **~politikerin** *die* practical politician; **~politisch** A *Adj.* ‹*advantages, interests, etc.*› in terms of realpolitik; ‹*decision*› based on realpolitik; B *adv.* in terms of realpolitik; **~satire** *die* reality parodying itself; **~schule** *die* ▸ **BOX Realschule**; **~schüler** *der*, **~schülerin** *die* pupil at a *Realschule*; **~schullehrer** *der*, **~schul·lehrerin** *die* teacher at a *Realschule*

r

> **Realschule**
>
> The secondary school which prepares pupils for the *Realschulabschluss* (*Mittlere Reife*) (school-leaving certificate). This type of school is in between **Hauptschule** and **Gymnasium**, catering for less academic children who will probably train for a practical career. Pupils stay at the *Realschule* for 6 years after the **Grundschule**. See also **Schule, Lehre.**

Reanimation *die* (Med.) resuscitation

reanimieren *tr. V.* (Med.) resuscitate

Reaumur /'re:omy:ɐ/ Réaumur; *s. auch* **Grad 3**

Rebbe /'rɛbə/ *der;* **∼[s], ∼s** (jidd.) ▸**Rabbi**

Rebe /'re:bə/ *die;* **∼, ∼n** **1** (Wein∼) vine shoot **2** (geh.: Weinstock) [grape] vine

Rebell /re'bɛl/ *der;* **∼en, ∼en** rebel; (Aufständischer) rebel; insurgent

rebellieren *itr. V.* rebel (**gegen** against)

Rebellin *die;* **∼, ∼nen** ▸**Rebell**

Rebellion /rebe'li̯o:n/ *die;* **∼, ∼en** rebellion; (Aufstand) rebellion; insurrection

rebellisch

A *Adj.* rebellious

B *adv.* rebelliously

Reben·saft *der* (geh.) juice of the grape

Reb-: ∼huhn *das* partridge; **∼laus** *die* phylloxera; **∼sorte** *die* type of grape; **∼stock** *der* vine

Receiver /ri'si:vɐ/ *der;* **∼s, ∼:** receiver

Rechaud /re'ʃo:/ *der od. das;* **∼s, ∼s** **1** (Gastr.) food/tea/coffee warmer; réchaud **2** (südd., österr., schweiz.) gas cooker

rechen /'rɛçn̩/ *tr. V.* (bes. südd.) rake

Rechen *der;* **∼s, ∼** **1** (bes. südd.: Harke) rake **2** (Gitter an Gewässern) grating

Rechen-: ∼anlage *die* computer; **∼art** *die* type of arithmetical operation; **∼aufgabe** *die* arithmetical problem; **∼automat** *der* calculator; **∼brett** *das* abacus; **∼buch** *das* (veralt.) arithmetic book; **∼exempel** *das:* **das ist doch ein ganz einfaches ∼exempel** that's a matter of simple arithmetic; **∼fehler** *der* arithmetical error; **∼heft** *das* arithmetic book; **∼knecht** *der* (DV Jargon) basic computer; **∼künstler** *der,* **∼künstlerin** *die* mathematical genius *or* wizard; **∼lehrer** *der,* **∼lehrerin** *die* (veralt.) arithmetic teacher; **∼maschine** *die* calculator; **∼operation** *die* arithmetical operation; **∼papier** *das* arithmetic paper

Rechenschaft *die;* **∼:** account; **jmdm. über etw.** (*Akk.*) **∼ geben** *od.* **ablegen** account to sb. for sth.; **von jmdm. ∼ über etw.** (*Akk.*) **verlangen** demand an explanation *or* account from sb. about sth.; **jmdm. über etw.** (*Akk.*) **∼ schuldig sein** *od.* **schulden** have to account to sb. for sth.; **ich bin Ihnen keine ∼ schuldig** I am not answerable to you; I owe you no explanation; **jmdn. für etw. zur ∼ ziehen** call *or* bring sb. to account for sth.

Rechenschafts-: ∼bericht *der* report; **∼legung** *die;* **∼∼, ∼∼en** report; **zur öffentlichen ∼legung verpflichtet sein** be obliged to render public account

Rechen-: ∼schieber *der,* **∼stab** *der* slide rule; **∼stunde** *die* arithmetic lesson; **∼unterricht** *der* teaching of arithmetic; (Fach) arithmetic *no art.;* **∼zentrum** *das* computer centre

Recherche /re'ʃɛrʃə/ *die;* **∼, ∼n** **1** (geh.) investigation; enquiry; **∼n über jmdn./etw. anstellen** make investigations *or* enquiries about sb./into sth. **2** (DV) search

recherchieren (geh.)

A *itr. V.* investigate; make investigations *or* enquiries

B *tr. V.* investigate

rechnen /'rɛçnən/

A *tr. V.* **1** **eine Aufgabe ∼:** work out a problem **2** (veranschlagen) reckon; estimate; **wir ∼ pro Person drei Flaschen Bier** we are reckoning on three bottles of beer per person; **wir müssen zwei Stunden ∼:** we must reckon on two hours; **alles in allem gerechnet** all in all; altogether; **gut/rund gerechnet** at a generous/rough estimate; **das ist zu hoch/niedrig gerechnet** that's an overestimate/underestimate **3** (berücksichtigen) take into account; **ich rechne es mir zur Ehre** (geh.) I consider it *or* count it an honour **4** (einbeziehen) count; **jmdn. zu seinen Freunden ∼:** count sb. among *or* as one of one's friends; **jmdn. zu den Fachleuten ∼:** rate sb. as an expert

B *itr. V.* **1** (addieren) do *or* make a calculation/calculations; **an einer Aufgabe/auf der Tafel ∼:** do *or* make calculations on a problem/the blackboard; **der Lehrer rechnet mit den Kindern** the teacher is doing arithmetic with the children; **gut/schlecht ∼ können** be good/bad at figures *or* arithmetic **2** (zählen) reckon; **vom 1. April an gerechnet** reckoning from 1 April; **in Schillingen/nach Lichtjahren ∼:** reckon in shillings/light years **3** (ugs.: be∼) calculate; estimate; **das ist zu viel gerechnet** that's too high an estimate; **er ist ein klug ∼der Kopf** he is a shrewdly calculating person **4** (wirtschaften) budget carefully; **mit jedem Euro** *od.* **jedem Cent ∼ müssen** have to count *or* watch every penny **5** (sich verlassen) **auf jmdn./etw.** *od.* **mit jmdm./etw. ∼:** reckon *or* count on sb./sth. **6** (etw. einkalkulieren) **mit etw. ∼:** reckon with sth.; **mit einer Antwort ∼:** expect an answer; **wir haben mit mehr Besuchern gerechnet** we reckoned on *or* expected more visitors; **man muss mit allem/mit dem Schlimmsten ∼:** one has to be prepared for anything/for the worst

C *refl. V.* (sich rentieren) **das rechnet sich nicht** it doesn't pay

Rechnen *das;* **∼s** arithmetic

Rechner *der;* **∼s, ∼** **1** (Mensch) **ein guter/schlechter ∼ sein** be good/bad at figures *or* arithmetic; **ein nüchterner ∼ sein** (fig.) be shrewdly calculating **2** (Gerät) calculator; (Computer) computer

Rechner·architektur *die* (DV) computer architecture

Rechnerei *die;* **∼, ∼en** (ugs.) **1** (das Rechnen) **das war eine komplizierte ∼:** that was a complicated piece of figurework; **dazu war eine ewige ∼ nötig** it involved [some] endless calculations **2** (Rechnung) calculation

rechner·gesteuert *Adj.* (Elektronik) computer-controlled

Rechnerin *die* ▸**Rechner 1**

rechnerisch

A *Adj.* arithmetical; ‹*value*› in figures; **die ∼e Ermittlung des Schadens** calculating the damage in figures

B *adv.* ‹*determine*› by calculation, mathematically; **diese Ergebnisse sind ∼ falsch** the figurework in these results is wrong

rechner·unterstützt *Adj.* computer-aided

Rechnung *die;* **∼, ∼en** **1** (Aus∼) calculation; **[jmdm.] eine ∼ aufmachen** work it out [for sb.]; **seine ∼ geht [nicht] auf** (fig.) his plans [do not] work out **2** (schriftliche Kosten∼) bill; invoice (Commerc.); **eine hohe/niedrige ∼:** a large/small bill; **eine ∼ über 500 Euro** a bill for 500 euros; **die ∼ beträgt** *od.* **macht ...** the bill is for ...; **die ∼ ist überfällig** the account is overdue; **etw. [mit] auf die ∼ setzen** put sth. on *or* add sth. to the bill; **das geht auf meine ∼:** I'm paying for that; **diese Runde** *od.* **Lage geht auf meine ∼:** this round's on me; this is my round; **etw. auf ∼ bestellen/kaufen** order/buy sth. on account; **er hatte aber die ∼ ohne den Wirt gemacht** (fig.) there was one thing he hadn't reckoned with; **[mit jmdm.] eine [alte] ∼ begleichen** (fig.) settle a[n old] score [with sb.]; **auf seine** *od.* (schweiz.) **die ∼ kommen** get one's money's worth; **auf eigene ∼:** on one's own account; (auf eigenes Risiko) at one's own risk; **[jmdm.] etw. in ∼ stellen** charge [sb.] for sth. **3** (Be∼, Überlegung) calculation; **nach meiner ∼:** according to my calculations; **einer Sache** (*Dat.*) **∼ tragen, etw. in ∼ stellen** *od.* **setzen** take sth. into account; *s. auch* **begleichen**

Rechnungs-: ∼art *die* type of calculation; **∼betrag** *der* amount of a/the bill/invoice; **∼block** *der; Pl.* **∼∼s** *od.* **∼blöcke** receipt pad; **∼buch** *das* **1** accounts book *or* ledger **2** (schweiz.) ▸**Rechenbuch**; **∼einheit** *die* (Geldw.) unit of account; **∼fehler** *der* (schweiz.) ▸**Rechenfehler**; **∼führung** *die* ▸**Buchführung**; **∼hof** *der* audit office; **∼jahr** *das* financial *or* fiscal year; **∼prüfer** *der,* **∼prüferin** *die* auditor; **∼prüfung** *die* (Wirtsch., Politik) audit; **∼wesen** *das* (Wirtsch.) accountancy *no art.*

recht /rɛçt/

A *Adj.* **1** (geeignet) right **2** (richtig) right; **ganz ∼!** quite right!; **das ist ∼, so ist es ∼,** (ugs.) **∼ so** that's fine; **bin ich hier ∼?** am I in the right place? **3** (gesetzmäßig, anständig) right; proper; **was dem einen ∼ ist, ist dem anderen billig** (Spr.) what's sauce for the goose is sauce for the gander (prov.); **∼ und billig** right and proper; **alles, was ∼ ist** (das kann man nicht leugnen) you've got to give him/it *etc.* his/its *etc.* due; (das geht zu weit) there is a limit **4** (wunschgemäß) **jmdm. ∼ sein** be all right with sb.; **es war ihr nicht ∼, dass ...** she was not pleased that ...; **wenn es dir ∼ ist** if it's all right with you **5** (wirklich, echt) real; **keine ∼e Lust haben, etw. zu tun** not particularly *or* really feel like doing sth. **6** (ziemlich) **er hat sich ∼e Mühe gegeben** he made quite an effort; **er ist noch ein ∼es Kind** (veralt.) he is still a child

B *adv.* **1** (geeignet) **du kommst gerade ∼, um zu ...** you are just in time *or* you've come just at the right time to ...; **du kommst mir gerade ∼** (auch iron.) you're just the person I needed **2** (richtig) correctly; **wenn ich es mir ∼ überlege, dann ...** if I really stop and think about it; **verstehen Sie mich bitte ∼:** please don't misunderstand me; **habe ich ∼ gehört?** did I hear right *or* correctly?; **ich denke, ich höre nicht ∼** (ugs.) I think I must be hearing things; **gehe ich ∼ in der Annahme, dass ...?** am I right in assuming that ...? **3** (gesetzmäßig, anständig) **∼ handeln/leben** act/live properly; **tue ∼ und scheue niemand** (Spr.) do what's right and fear no one; *s. auch* **Recht 4; geschehen 3** **4** (wunschgemäß) **man kann ihm nichts ∼ machen** there's no pleasing him; **man kann es nicht allen ∼ machen** you can't please everyone **5** (wirklich, echt) really; rightly; **er kann sich nicht ∼ entscheiden** he cannot really *or* rightly decide; **die Wunde will nicht ∼ heilen** the wound is not healing properly; *s. auch* **erst B** **6** (ziemlich) quite; rather; **„∼ herzliche Grüße, Dein Peter"** 'best wishes, Peter'

Recht *das;* **∼[e]s, ∼e** **1** (∼sordnung) law; **das ∼ brechen/beugen** break/bend the law; **∼ sprechen** administer the law; administer justice; **von ∼s wegen** by law; (ugs.: eigentlich) by rights; **gegen ∼ und Gesetz verstoßen** infringe *or* violate the law **2** (∼sanspruch) right; **das ∼ haben, etw. zu tun** have the right to do sth.; **das ∼ des Stärkeren** the law of the jungle; **das ist sein gutes ∼:** that is his right; **alle ∼e vorbehalten** all rights reserved; **mit welchem ∼ hat er das getan?** by what right did he do that?; **gleiche ∼e, gleiche Pflichten** (Spr.) equal rights mean equal obligations; **sein ∼ fordern** *od.* **verlangen** demand one's rights; **der Körper verlangt sein ∼:** the body demands its due; **zu seinem ∼ kommen** (fig.) be given due attention; **auf sein ∼ pochen** insist *or* stand on one's rights **3** (Berechtigung) right (**auf** + *Akk.* to); **gleiches ∼ für alle!** equal rights for all!; **das ∼ war auf seiner Seite** he had right on his side; **etw. mit [gutem] ∼ tun** be [quite] right to do sth.; **das Gericht hat für ∼ erkannt, dass ...** the court has decided *or* has reached the verdict that ...; **im ∼ sein** be in the right; **zu ∼:** rightly; with justification **4** **∼ haben** be right; **∼ behalten** be proved right; **jmdm. ∼ geben** concede *or* admit that sb. is right; **∼ bekommen** win one's case **5** *Pl.* (veralt.: Jura) jurisprudence; **Doktor beider ∼e** Doctor of Laws

recht... *Adj.* **1** right; right[-hand] ‹*edge*›; **die ∼e Spur** the right-hand lane; **∼er Hand, zur ∼en Hand, auf der ∼en Seite** on the right-hand side; **auf der ∼en Seite gehen** walk on the right; **der ∼e Außenstürmer/Verteidiger** (Ballspiele) the outside right/the right back **2** (außen, sichtbar) right ‹*side*›; **∼e Maschen**

(Handarb.) knit stitches; **eine ~e Masche stricken** knit one 3) (in der Politik) right-wing; rightist (derog.); **der ~e Flügel einer Partei** the right wing of a party 4) (Geom.) **ein ~er Winkel** a right angle

Rechte[1] *der/die; adj. Dekl.* right-winger; rightist (derog.); **die ~n** the right *sing.*

Rechte[2] *die; adj. Dekl.* 1) (Hand) right hand; **seine ~ einsetzen** (Boxen) use one's right; **zur ~n des Königs** on *or* to the right of the king; **jmdm. zur ~n** to the right of sb.; **zur ~n** on the right 2) (Politik) right

Recht·eck *das* rectangle

recht·eckig *Adj.* rectangular

Rechte·hand·regel *die* (Physik) right-hand rule

rechten *itr. V.* (geh.) argue; dispute

rechtens, *Rechtens *Adv.* (von Rechts wegen) legally; by law; (zu od. mit Recht) rightly; **~ sein** be legal

rechter·seits *Adv.* on the right[-hand side]

recht·fertigen
A *tr. V.* justify; **sein Handeln ist durch nichts zu ~:** nothing can justify his behaviour; **etw. vor jmdm. ~:** justify sth. to sb.; **er hat sich bemüht, das in ihn gesetzte Vertrauen zu ~:** he tried to live up to the trust placed in him
B *refl. V.* justify oneself (**vor** + *Dat.* to)

Recht·fertigung *die* justification; **er konnte nichts zu seiner ~ vorbringen** he could not say anything to justify himself

Rechtfertigungs·grund *der* justification

recht-, Recht-: ~gläubig *Adj.* orthodox; **~gläubigkeit** *die* orthodoxy; **~haber** *der;* **~~s, ~~** (abwertend) self-opinionated person; **er ist ein ~haber** he's self-opinionated; he always thinks he's right; **~haberei** *die;* **~~** (abwertend) self-opinionatedness; **~haberin** *die;* **~~, ~~nen** ▸ **~haber**; **~haberisch** (abwertend) A *Adj.* self-opinionated; B *adv.* in a self-opinionated manner

rechtlich
A *Adj.* 1) legal 2) (veralt.: rechtschaffen) upright; honest
B *adv.* 1) legally; **~ nicht zulässig** not permissible in law; illegal; **etw. ~ verankern** establish sth. in law 2) (veralt.: rechtschaffen) uprightly; honestly; **ein ~ denkender Mensch** an honest-minded person

Rechtlichkeit *die;* **~** ▸ **Rechtmäßigkeit**

recht·los *Adj.* without rights *postpos.*; **jmdn. ~ machen** deprive sb. of his/her *etc.* rights; **die ~e Stellung der Sklaven** the slaves' position without rights

Rechtlosigkeit *die;* **~:** lack of rights

rechtmäßig
A *Adj.* lawful; rightful; legitimate ⟨*claim*⟩
B *adv.* lawfully; rightfully; **das steht ihm ~ zu** that is his by right *or* rightfully his; **etw. ~ beanspruchen** have a legal *or* rightful claim to sth.

Rechtmäßigkeit *die;* **~:** legality; lawfulness; (eines Anspruchs) legitimacy

rechts
A *Adv.* 1) ▸❶ **S. 800** (auf der rechten Seite) on the right; (Theater) stage left; **die zweite Straße ~:** the second street *or* turning on the right; **~ von jmdm./etw.** on sb.'s right *or* the right of sb./on *or* to the right of sth.; **von ~ kommen** come from the right; **nach ~ gehen/sich nach ~ wenden** go/turn to the right; **sich ~ halten** keep to the right; **sich ~ einordnen** move *or* get into the right-hand lane; **~ außen** (Ballspiele) ⟨*run, break through*⟩ down the right wing; **[den Ball] nach ~ außen spielen** play the ball out to the right wing; *s. auch* **links 1** 2) (Politik) on the right wing; **~ stehen** *od.* **sein** be right-wing *or* on the right; **~ eingestellt sein** have right-wing leanings; **weit ~ stehen** be on the far right; **ganz ~ außen stehen** be on the extreme right [wing]; **nach ~ außen** to the extreme right; **~ stehend** right-wing 3) (ugs.: ~händig) right-handed; **alles mit ~ machen** do everything right-handed *or* with the right hand 4) (Handarb.) **ein glatt ~ gestrickter Pullover** a pullover in stocking stitch; *s. auch* **links A 4** 5) (~seitig) on the right [side]; **etw. von ~ bügeln** iron sth. on the right side; **nach ~ wenden** turn ⟨*dress, skirt, etc.*⟩ right side out
B ▸❶ **S. 800** *Präp. mit Gen.* **~ des Rheins/der Straße** on the right side *or* bank of the Rhine/on the right-hand side of the road *or* to the right of the road

Rechts-: ~abbieger *der,* **~abbiegerin** *die* (Verkehrsw.) motorist/cyclist/car *etc.* turning right; **die ~abbieger** the traffic *sing.* turning right; *s. auch* **Linksabbieger**; **~abbieger·spur** *die* (Verkehrsw.) right-turn lane; **~ab·teilung** *die* legal department; **~abweichler** *der,* **~abweichlerin** *die* (Politik) right deviationist; **~angelegenheit** *die* legal matter; **~anspruch** *der* legal right *or* entitlement; **einen ~anspruch auf etw.** (*Akk.*) **haben** have a legal right to *or* be legally entitled to sth.; **~anwalt** *der,* **~anwältin** *die* ▸❶ **S. 113** lawyer; solicitor (Brit.); attorney (Amer.); (vor Gericht) barrister (Brit.); attorney[-at-law] (Amer.); advocate (Scot.); **sich** (*Dat.*) **einen ~anwalt nehmen** get a lawyer *or* (Amer.) an attorney

Rechtsanwalts-: ~büro *das,* **~kanzlei** *die* ▸ **Anwaltsbüro**

rechts-, Rechts-: ~auffassung *die* (Rechtsw.) conception of legality; **~aufsicht** *die: state supervision of the legality of administrative acts;* **~auskunft** *die* piece of legal advice; **~auskünfte** legal advice *sing.*; **~aus·schuss, *~ausschuß** *der* legal affairs committee; ***~außen** ▸ **rechts A1, 2**; **~außen** *der;* **~~, ~~** 1) (Ballspiele) right wing; outside right; 2) (Politik ugs.) extreme right-winger; **~beistand** *der* ▸❶ **S. 113** legal adviser; **~beratung** *die* legal advice; **~beugung** *die* (Rechtsw.) perversion of justice *or* the law; **~bewusst·sein, *~bewußt·sein** *das,* sense of [what is] right and wrong; **~brecher** *der,* **~brecherin** *die;* **~~, ~~nen** lawbreaker

recht-, Recht-: ~schaffen A *Adj.* honest; upright; honest, decent ⟨*work*⟩; B *adv.* 1) (ehrlich, redlich) honestly; uprightly; **~schaffen leben** live an honest[, decent] life; 2) (intensivierend) really ⟨*tired, full, etc.*⟩; **~schaffenheit** *die;* **~:** honesty, uprightness; **~schreib[e]·buch** *das* spelling book; speller; (Wörterbuch) spelling dictionary; **~schreiben** *itr. V.; nur im Inf. gebr.* spell; **sie ist im ~schreiben schwach** she's poor at spelling; **~schreibfehler** *der* spelling mistake; **~schreibung** *die* orthography; **~schreib·wörter·buch** *das* spelling dictionary

> **Rechtschreibreform**
>
> After much controversy, a reform aiming to simplify the strict rules governing German spelling and punctuation was implemented in 1998. The old spellings were officially acceptable for a transitional period until 2005. The new spellings are still controversial, however, and since they are only binding for schools and public authorities and since some well-known and respected newspapers have retained the old spellings, it remains to be seen whether or how quickly they will gain general acceptance.

rechts-, Rechts-: ~drall *der* 1) pull to the right; **der Wagen hatte einen ~drall** the car was pulling to the right; **der Tennisspieler gab dem Ball einen ~drall** the tennis player swerved the ball to the right; 2) (Waffent.) right-handed twist; 3) (Politik ugs.) tendency to the right; right-wing tendency; **~drehend** *Adj.* 1) (bes. Technik) right-hand ⟨*thread*⟩ 2) (Chemie, Physik) dextrorotatory; **~drehung** *die* (Chemie, Physik) dextrorotation; **~empfinden** *das* sense of [what is] right and wrong; **~experte** *der,* **~expertin** *die* legal expert; **~extremismus** *der* (Politik) right-wing extremism; **~extremist** *der,* **~extremistin** *die* (Politik) right-wing extremist; **~fähig** *Adj.* (Rechtsw.) having legal capacity *postpos., not pred.*; **~fähigkeit** *die* legal capacity; **~fall** *der* (Rechtsw.) legal case; court case; **~findung** *die;* **~~** (Rechtsw.) legal finding; **~form** *die* (Rechtsspr.) legal form; **~frage** *die* (Rechtsw.) legal question *or* issue; **~gängig** *Adj.* ▸ **~drehend 1**; **~gefühl** *das* sense of [what is] right and wrong; **~gelehrte** *der/die* jurist; **~gerichtet** *Adj.* (Politik) right-wing orientated; **~geschäft** *das* legal transaction; **~geschichte** *die* legal history; **~gewinde** *das* (Technik) right-hand thread; **~grund** *der* (Rechtsw.) cause in law; **~grundsatz** *der* (Rechtsw.) legal principle; **~gültig** (Rechtsw.) A *Adj.* legally valid; B *adv.* **etw. ~gültig abschließen** conclude sth. in legally valid form; **~gut** *das* (Rechtsw.) object/interest protected by law; **~handel** *der; Pl.* **~händel** (geh.) lawsuit; court case; **~händer** /-hɛndɐ/ *der;* **~~s, ~~, ~händerin** *die;* **~~, ~~nen** right-hander; **~händer[in] sein** be right-handed; **~händig** A *Adj.* right-handed; B *adv.* right-handed; with one's right hand; **~händigkeit** *die;* **~~:** righthandedness; **~handlung** *die* (Rechtsw.) legal act; **~hängigkeit** *die;* **~~** (Rechtsw.) pendency; **~herum** *Adv.* [round] to the right; **etw. ~herum drehen** turn sth. clockwise *or* [round] to the right; **~hilfe** *die* (Rechtsw.) [official] assistance between courts; **~hilfe·ersuchen** *das* (Rechtsw.) request for assistance with a case; **~konservativ** A *Adj.* right-wing conservative; B *adv.* ⟨*vote*⟩ along right-wing conservative lines; **~konservativ eingestellt sein** have right-wing conservative views; **~kraft** *die* (Rechtsw.) legal force; **einer Sache** (*Dat.*) **~kraft verleihen** make sth. law; give legal effect to sth.; **~kräfte** *Pl.* (Politik) right-wing forces; **~kräftig** (Rechtsw.) A *Adj.* final [and absolute] ⟨*decision, verdict, etc.*⟩; **~kräftig sein/werden** ⟨*contract, agreement*⟩ be in/come into force; B *adv.* **jmdn. ~kräftig verurteilen** pass a final sentence on sb.; **die Ehe wurde ~kräftig geschieden** the divorce became absolute; **~kundig** *Adj.* versed in the law *postpos.*; **~kurve** *die* right-hand bend; **~lage** *die* (Rechtsw.) legal situation; **~lastig** *Adj.* 1) ⟨*ship*⟩ listing to the right; ⟨*car*⟩ down at the right, leaning to the right; 2) (Politik ugs.) rightist; **~läufig** *Adj.* (bes. Technik) running from left to right; **~lehre** *die* ▸ **~wissenschaft**; **~liberal** *Adj.* right-wing liberal; **~liberale** *der/die* right-wing liberal; **~mediziner** *der,* **~medizinerin** *die* ▸❶ **S. 113** specialist in forensic medicine; **~missbrauch, *~mißbrauch** *der* (Rechtsw.) abuse of a/one's right; **~mittel** *das* (Rechtsw.) appeal; **es ist kein ~mittel zulässig** there is no right of appeal; **~mittel einlegen** lodge an appeal; appeal; **~mittelbelehrung** *die* (Rechtsw.) information *no pl., no indef. art.* on one's right to appeal; **~nachfolge** *die* 1) (Rechtsw.) succession [to rights and obligations]; 2) (Staatensukzession) succession; **~norm** *die* (Rechtsw.) legal norm; **~ordnung** *die* legal system; **~partei** *die* (Politik) right-wing party; **~pflege** *die* (Rechtsw.) administration of justice; **~pfleger** *der,* **~pflegerin** *die: official with certain administrative and judicial powers;* **~philosophie** *die* philosophy of law; **~politik** *die* judicial policy; **~politiker** *der,* **~politikerin** *die* expert on judicial policy; **~politisch** A *Adj.* judicial policy *attrib.*; B *adv.* in terms of judicial policy; **~populismus** *der* (Politik) right-wing populism; **~populist** *der,* **~populistin** *die* (Politik) right-wing populist; **~praxis** *die* legal practice

Rechtsprechung *die;* **~, ~en** administration of justice; (eines Gerichts) jurisdiction

rechts-, Rechts-: ~radikal (Politik) A *Adj.* radical right-wing; B *adv.* **eine ~radikal orientierte Gruppe** a group with a radical right-wing orientation; **~radikale** *der/die* right-wing radical; **~radikalismus** *der* right-wing radicalism; **~rheinisch** A *Adj.* on *or* to the right of the Rhine *postpos.*; **auf der ~rheinischen Seite** on the right side of the Rhine; B *adv.* on *or* to the right of the Rhine; **~ruck** *der* (Politik ugs.) shift to the right; **~rum** *Adv.* (ugs.) ▸ **~herum**; **~sache** *die* (Rechtsw.) legal matter; (Streitsache) case;

r

~schutz *der* (Rechtsw.) legal protection; **~schutz·versicherung** *die* insurance for legal costs; **~seitig** A *Adj.* ‹*paralysis*› of the right side; **die ~seitige Uferbefestigung** the reinforcement of the right bank; B *adv.* on the right [side]; **~seitig gelähmt sein** be paralysed on *or* down the *or* one's right side; **~sicherheit** *die* (Rechtsw.) certainty of the law; **~sprache** *die* (Sprachw.) legal terminology; **~spruch** *der* judgement; **~staat** *der* [constitutional] state founded on the rule of law; **~staatlich** A *Adj.* founded on the rule of law *postpos.;* B *adv.* **~staatlich orientiert** oriented towards maintaining and promoting the rule of law *postpos.;* **~staatlich einwandfrei** legally correct; **~staatlich·keit** *die;* **~~:** rule of law; **~stehend** ▸**rechts A2**; **~steuerung** *die* right-hand drive; **~streit** *der* lawsuit; **~titel** *der* (Rechtsw.) legal title; **~um** *Adv.* (bes. Milit.) to the right; **~um kehrt!** to the right about turn!; **~um machen** do a right turn; **~unsicher·heit** *die* (Rechtsw.) uncertainty regarding the law; **~verbindlich** *Adj.* (Rechtsw.) legally binding; **~verdreher** *der;* **~~s, ~~,** **~verdreherin** *die;* **~~, ~~nen** 1▸ (abwertend) person who twists the law; shyster (Amer. sl.); 2▸ (ugs. scherzh.: ~anwalt) legal eagle (coll.); **~verkehr** *der* driving *no art.* on the right; **in Frankreich ist ~verkehr** they drive on the right in France; **~verletzung** *die* (Rechtsw.) infringement *or* violation of the law; **~verordnung** *die* (Rechtsw.) statutory instrument; **~vertreter** *der,* **~vertreterin** *die* (Rechtsw.) legal representative; **~weg** *der* (Rechtsw.) recourse to legal action *or* the courts *or* the law; **den ~weg beschreiten** (geh.) take legal proceedings *or* action; go to the courts *or* to court; **unter Ausschluss des ~wegs** without the possibility of recourse to legal action *or* the courts *or* the law; **~wesen** *das* legal system; **~widrig** A *Adj.* unlawful; illegal; B *adv.* unlawfully; illegally; **~widrigkeit** *die* 1▸ unlawfulness; illegality; 2▸ (Handlung) unlawful act; **~wirksam** *Adj.* ▸**~gültig**; **~wissenschaft** *die* jurisprudence; **Professor für ~wissenschaft** Professor of Law; **~wissenschaftler** *der,* **~wissenschaftlerin** *die* ▸**ℹ S. 113** jurist

recht-: **~wink[e]lig** *Adj.* right-angled; **~zeitig** A *Adj.* (früh genug) timely; (pünktlich) punctual; **wir bitten um ~zeitige Lieferung** please deliver in good time; B *adv.* (früh genug) in time; (pünktlich) on time; **~zeitig zu/zum/zur** in [good] time for; **sagen Sie mir bitte ~zeitig Bescheid** please let me know in good time; **~zeitig zu Bett gehen** go to bed early

Reck /rɛk/ *das;* **~[e]s, ~e** *od.* **~s** horizontal bar; high bar

Recke /ˈrɛkə/ *der;* **~n, ~n** (geh.) warrior

recken

A *tr. V.* 1▸ stretch; **den Hals/Kopf ~:** crane one's neck; **die Faust ~:** raise one's fist 2▸ (bes. nordd.: in Form ziehen) **etw ~:** pull sth. back into shape

B *refl. V.* stretch oneself; **sich ~ und strecken** have a good stretch

Reck-: **~stange** *die* horizontal *or* high bar; **~turnen** *das* horizontal-bar exercises *pl.*

Recorder /reˈkɔrdɐ/ *der;* **~s, ~:** recorder

recycelbar /riˈsaikl̩baːɐ̯/ *Adj.* recyclable

recyceln /riˈsaikl̩n/ *tr. V.* recycle

recyclebar /riˈsaikl̩baːɐ̯/ *Adj.* ▸**recycelbar**

Recycling /riˈsaiklɪŋ/ *das;* **~s** recycling

Recycling

All *Hausmüll* (domestic waste) in Germany is collected in at least three bins, and waste materials are recycled and reused. The **Biotonne** is for biodegradable kitchen waste (vegetable and fruit peel, meat, cheese, nutshells, tea leaves and coffee filters, etc.). The **Wertstofftonne** can be used for plastic containers, metal objects, cans, aluminium, ▸▸▸

▸▸▸ textiles, etc., and anything with a **Grüner Punkt**. A separate **Papiertonne** is used for paper and cardboard, although most wrapping is discarded at source or is re-used - German supermarkets don't hand out a free supply of plastic bags. The **Restmüll** is for sweepings and general household rubbish. Bottles and glass are taken to the **Glascontainer** (bottle bank). A deposit on drinks bottles encourages returning empties to the shop. There are also collection points for fridges, freezers, and bulky items. See also **Duales System**.

recycling·fähig /riˈsaiklɪŋ-/ *Adj.* recyclable

Recycling·material /riˈsaiklɪŋ-/ *das* recycled material

Redakteur /redakˈtøːɐ̯/ *der;* **~s, ~e,** **Redakteurin** *die;* **~, ~nen** ▸**ℹ S. 113** editor; **~ für Politik/Wirtschaft** political/economics editor; **~ vom Dienst** duty editor

Redaktion /redakˈtsi̯oːn/ *die;* **~, ~en** 1▸ (Redakteure) editorial staff 2▸ (Büro) editorial department *or* office/offices *pl.* 3▸ (Fach~) editorial department 4▸ (das Redigieren) editing; **bei der ~ des Textes** when the text is/was being edited

redaktionell /redaktsi̯oˈnɛl/

A *Adj.* editorial; **die ~e Verantwortung tragen** be responsible for the editing

B *adv.* editorially; **etw. ~ bearbeiten** edit sth.

Redaktions·schluss, ***Redaktions·schluß** *der* time of going to press; **nach ~:** after going to press

Redaktor /reˈdaktɔr/ *der;* **~s, ~en** /-ˈtoːrən/, **Redaktorin** *die;* **~, ~nen** (bes. schweiz.) editor

Rede /ˈreːdə/ *die;* **~, ~n** 1▸ speech; (Ansprache) address; speech; **eine ~ halten** give *or* make a speech; **die ~ des Betriebsleiters** the manager's speech; *s. auch* **schwingen** 2▸ (Vortrag) rhetoric; **die Kunst/Gabe der ~:** the art/gift of rhetoric; **etw. in freier ~ vortragen** make a speech *or* speak about sth. without notes 3▸ (Äußerung, Ansicht) **~ und Gegenrede** dialogue; **„...", das war seine stehende** *od.* **ständige ~:** '...' was one of his favourite sayings; **der langen ~ kurzer Sinn ist, dass ...** the long and the short of it is that ...; **das war schon immer meine ~** (ugs.) that is what I've always said; **lockere/kluge ~n** loose/clever talk *sing.;* **dumme ~n führen** talk nonsense; **die ~ auf ein anderes Thema bringen** turn the conversation to another subject; **von jmdm./etw. ist die ~:** there is some talk about sb./sth.; **es ist die ~ davon, dass ...** it is being said *or* people are saying that ...; **davon kann keine ~ sein** it's out of the question; **nicht der ~ wert sein** be not worth mentioning; **jmdm. ~ und Antwort stehen** give a full explanation [of one's actions] to sb.; **jmdn. zur ~ stellen** make someone explain himself/herself; **die in ~ stehende Person/der in ~ stehende Fall** (Papierdt.) the person/case in question 4▸ (Gerücht) **es geht die ~, dass ...** (geh.) there is a rumour *or* it is rumoured that ... 5▸ (Sprachw.) **[direkte** *od.* **wörtliche/indirekte] ~:** [direct/indirect] speech; **gebundene/ungebundene ~:** verse/prose

rede-, Rede-: **~duell** *das* duel of words; **~figur** *die* (Rhet., Stilk.) figure of speech; **~fluss,** ***~fluß** *der* (abwertend) flow of words; **~freiheit** *die* freedom of speech; **~gewandt** *Adj.* eloquent; **~gewandt·heit** *die* eloquence; **~kunst** *die* rhetoric

reden

A *tr. V.* 1▸ (sagen) say; speak; **kein Wort ~:** not say *or* speak a word 2▸ (sprechen) talk; **Unsinn/viel ~:** talk nonsense/(coll.) a lot; **es wird immer viel geredet** there is always a lot of talk (coll.); **es kann dir doch egal sein, was über dich geredet wird** it should not matter to you what people say about you; **etw. zu ~ haben** have sth. to talk about 3▸ **jmdn. besoffen ~** (salopp) drive sb. round the bend with one's nattering (Brit. coll.) *or* chattering

B *itr. V.* 1▸ (sprechen) talk; speak; **viel/wenig ~:** talk a lot (coll.)/not talk much; **er redete vor sich hin** he was talking to himself; **darüber ließe sich ~:** that's a possibility 2▸ (sich äußern, eine Rede halten) speak; **er lässt mich nicht zu Ende ~:** he doesn't let me finish what I'm saying; **wer redet heute Abend?** who is to speak this evening?; **gut ~ können** be a good speaker; *s. auch* **gut B 2** 3▸ (sich unterhalten) talk; **mit jmdm./über jmdn. ~:** talk to/about sb.; **darüber wird noch zu ~ sein** we shall have to come back to that; **miteinander ~:** have a talk [with one another]; **mit ihm kann man nicht ~:** you just can't talk to him; **sie ~ nicht mehr miteinander** they are no longer on speaking terms; **so lasse ich nicht mit mir ~:** I won't be spoken to like that; **~ wir nicht mehr darüber!** let's not talk about it any more; **was gibt es da groß zu ~?** so what?; **nicht zu ~ von ...** not to mention ...; **mit sich ~ lassen** (bei Geschäften) be open to offers; (bei Meinungsverschiedenheiten) be willing to discuss the matter; **von sich ~ machen** make a name for oneself

C *refl. V.* **sich heiser/in Wut ~:** talk oneself hoarse/into a rage

Redens·art *die* 1▸ expression; (Sprichwort) saying 2▸ *Pl.* (Phrase) empty *or* meaningless words; **allgemeine ~en** empty generalizations; **jmdn. mit ~en abspeisen** put sb. off with [fine] words

Reden·schreiber *der,* **Reden·schreiberin** *die* speechwriter

Rederei *die;* **~, ~en** 1▸ talking; talk 2▸ (Pl.: Gerücht) **die ~en über seine Vergangenheit** the gossip *sing.* about his past

Rede-: **~schwall** *der* (abwertend) torrent of words; **~strom** *der* ▸**~fluss**; **~verbot** *das* ban on speaking; **~verbot haben/erhalten** be banned from speaking; **~weise** *die* manner of speaking; **~wendung** *die* 1▸ (Sprachw.) idiom; idiomatic expression; 2▸ (Floskel) expression; phrase; **~zeit** *die:* **die ~zeit auf zehn Minuten begrenzen** restrict speakers to ten minutes; **er musste aufhören, seine ~zeit war abgelaufen** he had to stop speaking because he had run out of time

redigieren /rediˈgiːrən/ *tr. V.* edit

redlich

A *Adj.* 1▸ (rechtschaffen, aufrichtig) honest; honest, upright ‹*person*› 2▸ (intensivierend) real ‹*effort*›

B *adv.* 1▸ (rechtschaffen, aufrichtig) honestly; **sich ~ durchs Leben schlagen** make an honest living; **bleibe im Lande und nähre dich ~** (Spr.) stay here where you can earn a decent living 2▸ (intensivierend) really

Redlichkeit *die;* **~:** honesty

Redner *der;* **~s, ~** 1▸ (Vortragender) speaker 2▸ (Rhetoriker) orator; **er ist kein ~:** he is no orator; he is not a good speaker

Redner·bühne *die* [speaker's] platform *or* rostrum

Rednerin *die;* **~, ~nen** ▸**Redner**

rednerisch

A *Adj.* oratorical; **eine ~e Glanzleistung** a masterpiece of oratory

B *adv.* oratorically

Redner-: **~liste** *die* list of speakers; **~pult** *das* lectern

Redoute /reˈduːtə/ *die;* **~, ~n** 1▸ (veralt.: Festsaal) ballroom 2▸ (österr.) ▸**Maskenball**

red·selig *Adj.* talkative

Red·seligkeit *die* talkativeness

Reduktion /redukˈtsi̯oːn/ *die;* **~, ~en** reduction

redundant /redʊnˈdant/ *Adj.* (Sprachw., Kommunikationsf.) redundant

Redundanz /redʊnˈdants/ *die;* **~, ~en** (Sprachw., Kommunikationsf.) redundancy

reduzieren /reduˈtsiːrən/

A *tr. V.* (auch Chemie, Physik) reduce (**auf** + *Akk.* to)

B *refl. V.* decrease; diminish

Reduzierung *die;* **~, ~en** ▸**Reduktion**

Reede /ˈreːdə/ *die;* **~, ~n** (Seew.) roads *pl.;* roadstead; **das Schiff liegt auf der ~:** the ship is [lying] in the roads

Reeder *der;* **~s, ~:** shipowner

Reederei *die;* **~, ~en** shipping firm *or* company

Reederei·flagge *die* house flag

Reederin *die;* ~, ~nen ▸**Reeder**

reell /re'ɛl/

A *Adj.* **1** (anständig) honest, straight ‹*person, deal, etc.*›; sound, solid ‹*business, firm, etc.*›; straight ‹*offer*› **2** (wirklich) real **3** (ugs.: den Erwartungen entsprechend) decent; realistic ‹*price*›; **ein ~es Mittagessen** a solid *or* decent lunch

B *adv.* **1** (anständig) honestly **2** (wirklich) actually; really **3** (ugs.: den Erwartungen entsprechend) **der Wirt hat ~ eingeschenkt** the landlord poured [out] a decent measure/decent measures

Reep /re:p/ *das;* **~[e]s, ~e** (Seemannsspr.) rope

Reet /re:t/ *das;* **~s** (nordd.) reeds *pl.*

Reet·dach *das* thatched roof (*with reeds*)

reet·gedeckt *adj.* thatched

REFA /'re:fa/ *der;* **~s** *Abk.* = **Reichsausschuss für Arbeitszeitermittlung** (*heute:* = **Verband für Arbeitsstudien**) *work-study organization*

REFA-Fachfrau *die,* **REFA-Fachmann** *der: work-study expert*

Refektorium /refɛk'to:ri̯ʊm/ *das;* **~s, Refektorien** refectory

Referat /refe'ra:t/ *das;* **~[e]s, ~e** **1** (umfangreichere Abhandlung) paper; **ein ~ halten** give *or* present a paper **2** (kurzer schriftlicher Bericht) report (+ *Gen.* on) **3** (Abteilung, Fachgebiet) department

Referendar /referɛn'da:ɐ̯/ *der;* **~s, ~e, Referendarin** *die;* **~, ~nen** *candidate for a higher civil-service post who has passed the first state examination and is undergoing in-service training*

Referendum /refe'rɛndʊm/ *das;* **~s, Referenden** *od.* **Referenda** referendum

Referent /refe'rɛnt/ *der;* **~en, ~en** **1** (Vortragender) person presenting a/the paper; (Redner) speaker **2** (Gutachter) examiner **3** (Sachbearbeiter) expert (**für** on); (eines Ministers) adviser (**für** on)

Referentin *die;* **~, ~nen** ▸**Referent**

Referenz /refe'rɛnt͜s/ *die;* **~, ~en** **1** (Empfehlung) reference **2** (Person, Stelle) referee; **jmdn. als ~ angeben** give sb.'s name *or* give sb. as a reference

referieren /refe'ri:rən/

A *itr. V.* **über etw.** (*Akk.*) **~:** give *or* present a paper on sth.; (zusammenfassend) give a report on sth.

B *tr. V.* **etw. ~:** give *or* present a paper on sth.; (zusammenfassend) give a report on sth.

Reff[1] /rɛf/ *das;* **~s, ~s** (Seemannsspr.) reef

Reff[2] *das;* **~[e]s, ~e** (ugs. abwertend) old hag

reffen *tr.* (*auch itr.*) *V.* (Seemannsspr.) reef ‹*sail*›; **wir müssen ~:** we must reef sail

Refinanzierung *die* (Geldw.) procurement of funds to provide credit

reflektieren /reflɛk'ti:rən/

A *tr. V.* (zurückstrahlen) reflect

B *itr. V.* **1** (nachdenken) reflect, ponder (**über** + *Akk.* [up]on) **2** (ugs.: streben nach) **auf etw.** (*Akk.*) **~:** have [got] one's eye on sth.

C *tr. V.* (nachdenken über) reflect [up]on; ponder

reflektiert

A *Adj.* reflective

B *adv.* reflectively; in a reflective manner

Reflektor /re'flɛktɔr/ *der;* **~s, ~en** /-'to:rən/ reflector

reflektorisch *Adj.* (Physiol.) reflex *attrib.*

Reflex /re'flɛks/ *der;* **~es, ~e** **1** (Physiol.) reflex **2** (Licht~) reflection

reflex-, Reflex-: ~artig **A** *Adj.* reflex-like; **B** *adv.* as if by reflex; **~bewegung** *die* reflex movement; **~handlung** *die* reflex action

Reflexion /reflɛ'ksi̯o:n/ *die;* **~, ~en** reflection

Reflexions·winkel *der* (Physik) angle of reflection

reflexiv /reflɛ'ksi:f/

A *Adj.* **1** (Sprachw.) reflexive **2** (geh.: reflektiert) reflective

B *adv.* **1** (Sprachw.) reflexively **2** (geh.: reflektiert) through reflection

Reflexiv *das;* **~s, ~e, Reflexiv·pronomen** *das* (Sprachw.) reflexive pronoun

Reform /re'fɔrm/ *die;* **~, ~en** reform

Reformation *die;* **~** (hist.) Reformation

Reformations·fest *das* Reformation Day

Reformator /refɔr'ma:tɔr/ *der;* **~s, ~en** /-ma'to:rən/ **1** reformer **2** (hist.) Reformer

reformatorisch *Adj.* reformational; reformatory, reformative ‹*zeal, attempts*›

reform-, Reform-: ~bedürftig *Adj.* in need of reform *postpos.*; **~bestrebungen** *Pl.* efforts towards reform; **~bewegung** *die* reform movement; **~eifer** *der* reforming zeal

Reformer *der;* **~s, ~, Reformerin** *die;* **~, ~nen** reformer

reformerisch *Adj.* reforming *attrib.* ‹*government*›; ‹*idea, policy, party, etc.*› of reform; ‹*efforts*› towards reform

reform·freudig *Adj.* ‹*person*› eager for reform

Reform·haus *das* health food shop

reformierbar *Adj.* reformable; amenable to reform *pred.*; **schwer ~:** difficult to reform *pred.*

reformieren *tr. V.* reform; **die reformierte Kirche** the Reformed Church

Reformierte *der/die; adj. Dekl.* member of the Reformed Church

Reformismus *der;* **~** (bes. Politik) reformism

Reformist *der;* **~en, ~en, Reformistin** *die;* **~, ~nen** (bes. Politik) reformist

reformistisch *Adj.* (Politik) reformist

Reform-: ~kost *die* health food; **~kurs** *der* policy of reform; **auf ~kurs** (*Akk.*) **gehen** embark on a policy of reform; **~plan** *der* plan for reform; **~politik** *die* policy of reform; **~werk** *das* reform package

Refrain /rə'frɛ̃:/ *der;* **~s, ~s** (eines Lieds) chorus; refrain; (eines Gedichts) refrain

Refraktor /re'fraktɔr/ *der;* **~s, ~en** /-'to:rən/ (Astron.) refractor

Refugium /re'fu:gi̯ʊm/ *das;* **~s, Refugien** (geh.) refuge

Regal[1] /re'ga:l/ *das;* **~s, ~e** [set *sing.* of] shelves *pl.*; **ein Buch aus dem ~ nehmen/ins ~ zurückstellen** take a book from/put a book back on the shelf

Regal[2] *das;* **~s, ~e** (Musik) regal

Regal[3] *das;* **~s, ~ien** /...li̯ən/ (hist.) [royal] prerogative

Regal·brett *das* shelf

Regatta /re'gata/ *die;* **~, Regatten** (Sport) regatta

Reg.-Bez. *Abk.* = **Regierungsbezirk**

rege /'re:gə/

A *Adj.* **1** (betriebsam) busy ‹*traffic*›; brisk ‹*demand, trade, business, etc.*›; **[ein] ~s Treiben** bustling activity; hustle and bustle; **~ Beteiligung** *od.* **Teilnahme** good participation *or* attendance; **~r Briefwechsel** lively correspondence **2** (lebhaft) lively; lively, animated ‹*discussion, conversation*›; keen ‹*interest*›; **geistig noch sehr ~ sein** be still mentally alert *or* active; **eine ~ Fantasie** a lively *or* vivid imagination

B *adv.* **1** (betriebsam) actively; **~ an etw.** (*Akk.*) **teilnehmen** take an active part in sth. **2** (lebhaft) actively; **für sein Alter bewegt er sich noch sehr ~:** he is still very active for his age; **~ plaudern** chat animatedly

Regel /'re:gl̩/ *die;* **~, ~n** **1** (Vorschrift) rule; **die ~n eines Spiels/der Rechtschreibung** the rules of a game/of spelling; **die ~n des Anstands** the rules of decency; **die ~n des Verkehrs** traffic regulations; **nach allen ~n der Kunst** (fig.) well and truly **2** (Gewohnheit) rule; custom; **die ~ sein** be the rule; **das ist bei ihm die ~:** that is his rule *or* custom; **sich** (*Dat.*) **etw. zur ~ machen** make a habit *or* rule of sth.; **[bei jmdm.] zur ~ werden** become a rule *or* habit [with sb.]; **in der** *od.* **aller ~:** as a rule **3** (Menstruation) period; **die ~ ihre ~ haben/bekommen** have a *or* her period; **sie hat mit 13 ihre ~ bekommen** her periods started when she was 13

regelbar *Adj.* adjustable

regel-, Regel-: ~fall *der* rule; **im ~fall** as a rule; **~haft** **A** *Adj.* in accordance with rules *postpos.*; **B** *adv.* in accordance with rules; **~los** **A** *Adj.* disorderly; (ungeregelt) irregular; **ein ~loses Durcheinander** a confused muddle; **sie stürmten in ~loser Flucht davon** they fled pell-mell; **B** *adv.* in a disorderly manner; (ungeregelt) irregularly; **~losigkeit** *die;* **~~, ~~en** disorderliness; irregularity; **~mäßig** **A** *Adj.* regular; **B** *adv.* regularly; **sie schreibt ~mäßig** she has even *or* regular handwriting; **~mäßigkeit** *die* regularity

regeln

A *tr. V.* **1** (festsetzen, einrichten) settle ‹*matter, question, etc.*›; put ‹*finances, affairs, etc.*› in order; **etw. durch Gesetz ~:** regulate sth. by law; **wir haben die Sache so geregelt, dass ...** we've arranged things so that …; **er wird die Sache schon ~** *od.* (nordd. ugs.) **geregelt kriegen** he will see to it; **kriegst du das geregelt?** (nordd. ugs.) can you manage it/that? **2** (einstellen, regulieren) regulate; (steuern) control

B *refl. V.* take care of itself; **die Sache hat sich [von selbst] geregelt** the matter has sorted itself out *or* resolved itself

regel-, Regel-: ~recht **A** *Adj.* **1** (ugs.: richtiggehend) proper (coll.); real; real ‹*shock*›, absolute ‹*scandal*›; complete, utter ‹*flop, disaster*›; real, downright ‹*impertinence, insult*›; **eine ~rechte Schlägerei** a regular fight *or* brawl (coll.); **ich hatte ~rechte Angst** I was really afraid; **2** (ordnungsgemäß) proper; **B** *adv.* (ugs.: richtiggehend) really; **ich habe mich ~recht mit ihm angefreundet** I became quite friendly with him; **jmdn. ~recht hinauswerfen** throw sb. out good and proper (coll.); **~studien·zeit** *die* (Hochschulw.) *period within which a course must be completed;* **~technik** *die* control engineering

Regelung *die;* **~, ~en** **1** ▸**regeln A 1, 2:** settlement; putting in order; regulation; control **2** (Vorschrift) regulation

Regelungs·technik *die* control engineering

Regel-: ~verstoß *der* infringement *or* breach [of the rules/(Vorschriften) regulations]; **~werk** *das* set of rules/(Vorschriften) regulations; (größer) body of rules/(Vorschriften) regulations

regel·widrig

A *Adj.* that is against the rules *postpos.*; (gegen die Vorschriften) that is against the regulations *postpos.*; (Ballspiele) improperly taken ‹*penalty kick, throw-in, etc.*›; **~ sein** be against the rules/regulations; **~es Verhalten im Verkehr** breaking traffic regulations

B *adv.* **sich [im Verkehr] ~ verhalten** break [traffic] regulations; **den Stürmer ~ attackieren** (Ballspiele) foul the forward

Regel·widrigkeit *die* breach of the rules/regulations

regen /'re:gn̩/

A *tr. V.* (geh.) move

B *refl. V.* **1** (sich bewegen) move; **kein Lüftchen/kein Blatt regte sich** not a breath of air/not a leaf stirred **2** (geh.: sich bemerkbar machen) ‹*hope, doubt, desire, conscience*› stir

Regen *der;* **~s, ~** **1** rain; **bei strömendem ~:** in pouring rain; **bei ~ wird in der Halle gespielt** if it's raining the match will be played inside; **es wird ~ geben** it will rain; it is going to rain; **es sieht nach ~ aus** it looks like rain; **auf ~ folgt Sonnenschein** (Spr.) good times always follow bad; **ein warmer ~** (fig.) a windfall; **vom** *od.* **aus dem ~ in die Traufe kommen** (fig.) jump out of the frying pan into the fire; **jmdn. im ~ stehen lassen** *od.* **in den ~ stellen** (fig. ugs.) leave sb. in the lurch **2** (fig.) shower; **ein ~ von Schimpfwörtern ging auf ihn nieder** curses rained down upon him

regen·arm *Adj.* ‹*period, region, etc.*› with little rain[fall], with low rainfall; **der letzte Sommer war so ~, dass ...** there was so little rain last summer that …

Regen·bogen *der* rainbow

regen·bogen-, Regen·bogen-: ~farben, ~farbig *Adj.* rainbow-coloured; **~haut** *die* ▸ℹ **S. 435** (Anat.) iris; **~presse** *die* (abwertend) gossip magazines *pl.*; **~trikot**

r

das (Radsport) rainbow jersey

regen-, Regen-: ~cape *das* rain cape; **~dach** *das* rain canopy; **~dicht** *Adj.* rainproof

Regeneration *die* 1 regeneration 2 (Technik: Rückgewinnung) reclamation

regenerations·fähig *Adj.* (Biol., Med.) capable of regeneration *postpos.*

regenerativ /regenəra'ti:f/
A *Adj.* (Biol., Med. Technik) regenerative
B *adv.* (Technik) ~ **erzeugt/gewonnen** produced from regenerative sources

Regenerator *der* (Technik) regenerator

regenerieren /regene'ri:rən/
A *refl. V.* (Biol., Med.) regenerate
B *tr. V.* 1 (erneuern) regenerate; **sich ~** ‹*person*› recuperate; ‹*group, organization, etc.*› regenerate itself 2 (Technik: wiedergewinnen) reclaim

regen-, Regen-: ~fall *der* fall of rain; **heftige/anhaltende ~fälle** heavy rains *or* heavy [falls *pl.* of] rain *sing.*/continuous rain *sing.*; **~frei** *Adj.* without rain *postpos.*; rainless; **~guss, *~guß** *der* downpour; **~haut** *die* [light] plastic mackintosh *or* (coll.) mac; **~macher** *der,* **~macherin** *die* rainmaker; rain doctor; **~mantel** *der* raincoat; mackintosh; mac (coll.); **~nass, *~naß** *Adj.* that is/are wet from the rain *postpos., not pred.*; **~nass sein** be wet from the rain; **~pfeifer** *der* (Zool.) plover; **~pfütze** *die* [rain] puddle; **~reich** *Adj.* ‹*period, region, etc.*› with high rainfall; **der letzte Frühling war so ~reich, dass ...** there was so much rain last spring that ...; **~rinne** *die* gutter; **~schauer** *der* shower [of rain]; rain shower; **~schirm** *der* umbrella

Regent /re'gɛnt/ *der;* **~en, ~en** 1 (Herrscher) ruler; (Monarch) monarch 2 (Stellvertreter) regent

Regen·tag *der* rainy day

Regentin *die;* **~, ~nen** ▸**Regent**

Regen·tonne *die* water butt

Regentschaft *die;* **~, ~en** regency

Regen-: ~umhang *der* rain cape; **~wald** *der* (Geogr.) rainforest; **~wasser** *das* rainwater; **~wetter** *das* rainy *or* wet weather; **er macht ein Gesicht wie drei Tage ~wetter** (ugs.) he looks as miserable as sin; **~wolke** *die* rain cloud; **~wurm** *der* earthworm; **~zeit** *die* rainy season

Reggae /'rɛgeɪ/ *der;* **~[s]** reggae

Regie /re'ʒi:/ *die;* **~** 1 (Theater, Film, Ferns., Rundf.) direction; **die ~ bei etw. haben** *od.* **führen** direct sth.; **unter der ~ von ...** directed by ... 2 (Leitung, Verwaltung) management; **etw. in eigene ~ bekommen** *od.* **nehmen** take over control of sth.; **unter staatlicher ~:** under state control; **etw. in eigener ~ tun** (ugs.) do sth. oneself

Regie-: ~anweisung *die* stage direction; **~arbeit** *die* work as director; **die ~arbeit lernen** learn directing; **~assistent** *der,* **~assistentin** *die* assistant director; **~debüt** *das* directing debut; **~fehler** *der* (fig. scherzh.) slip-up

regieren /re'gi:rən/
A *itr. V.* rule (**über** + *Akk.* over); ‹*monarch*› reign, rule (**über** + *Akk.* over); ‹*party, administration*› govern; (fig.) ‹*peace, corruption, terror, etc.*› reign; **der Regierende Bürgermeister von Berlin** the Governing Mayor of Berlin
B *tr. V.* 1 rule; govern; ‹*monarch*› reign over, rule; **ein demokratisch regierter Staat** a democratically governed state 2 (Sprachw.) govern, take ‹*case*›

Regierung *die;* **~, ~en** 1 (Herrschaft) rule; (eines Monarchen) reign; **die ~ übernehmen** *od.* **antreten** take over; come to power 2 (eines Staates) government

regierungs-, Regierungs-: ~amtlich
A *Adj.* [official] governmental *attrib.*; government's [official] *attrib.* ‹*decision, announcement, etc.*›; **B** *adv.* by the government; **~antritt** *der:* **bei ~antritt der Sozialisten** when the Socialists come/came to power; (nach der Wahl auch) when the Socialists take/took office; **~auftrag** *der* 1 government order; **im ~auftrag** on orders from the government; ‹*research*› commissioned by the government; 2 (Wählerauftrag) mandate to form a government; **~bank** *die; Pl.* **~bänke** government bench; **~beamte** *der,* **~beamtin** *die* government official; **~beteiligung** *die* share in government; **~bezirk** *der: largest administrative division of a Land;* **~bildung** *die* formation of a/the government; **mit der ~bildung betraut werden** be asked to form a government; **~chef** *der,* **~chefin** *die* head of a government; **~erklärung** *die* government statement; (in Großbritannien) Queen's/King's Speech; **~feindlich** *Adj.* anti-government; **~form** *die* form of government; **~freundlich** *Adj.* pro-government; **~gebäude** *das* government building; **~gewalt** *die* government power *no art.*; **~konferenz** *die* (EU) intergovernmental conference; **~kreise** *Pl.* government circles; **~krise** *die* government crisis; **~lager** *das* government camp; **~macht** *die* [government] power; **~mannschaft** *die* government team; **~partei** *die* ruling *or* governing party; party in power; **~präsident** *der,* **~präsidentin** *die: head of a Regierungsbezirk;* **~rat** *der* 1 (Amtstitel) senior civil servant; 2 (schweiz.: Kantonsregierung) canton government; **~rätin** *die* ▸**~rat 1**; **~sitz** *der* seat of government; **~sprecher** *der* government spokesman; **~sprecherin** *die* government spokeswoman; **~treu** *Adj.* loyal to the government *postpos.*; **~truppe** *die* government troops *pl.*; **~umbildung** *die* government reshuffle; **~vorlage** *die* government bill; **~wechsel** *der* change of government; **~zeit** *die* rule; (eines Monarchen) reign; (einer Regierung, eines Regierungschefs) period *or* term of office; **nach 12-jähriger ~zeit** after 12 years in power *or* in office; **~zentrale** *die* government headquarters

Regie·stuhl *der* director's chair

Regime /re'ʒi:m/ *das;* **~s, ~** /re'ʒi:mə/ (abwertend) regime

regime-, Regime-: ~gegner *der,* **~gegnerin** *die* opponent of a/the regime; **~kritiker** *der,* **~kritikerin** *die* critic of a/the regime; dissident; **~kritisch** **A** *Adj.* critical of the regime *postpos.*; **B** *adv.* ‹*speak*› critically of the regime

Regiment /regi'mɛnt/ *das;* **~[e]s, ~e** *od.* **~er** 1 *Pl.* **~e** (Herrschaft) rule; **das ~ antreten/an sich reißen** come to/seize power; **das ~ führen** (fig.) give the orders; **ein strenges/straffes ~ führen** (fig.) be strict/run a tight ship (coll.) 2 *Pl.* **~er** (Milit.) regiment

Regiments·kommandeur *der* regimental commander

Regime·wechsel *der* regime change

Region /re'gio:n/ *die;* **~, ~en** 1 region 2 (geh.: Bereich, Sphäre) sphere; **in höheren ~en schweben** have one's head in the clouds

regional /regio'na:l/
A *Adj.* regional
B *adv.* regionally; **~ verschieden sein** differ from region to region

Regional·ausgabe *die* regional edition

Regional-: ~bahn *die* local railway *or* (Amer.) railroad; **~beihilfe** *die* (EU) regional aid; **~fürst** *der* regional overlord; local overlord

regionalisieren *tr. V.* regionalize

Regionalisierung *die* regionalization

Regionalismus *der;* **~:** regionalism *no art.*

Regional-: ~küche *die* regional cuisine; **~liga** *die* regional league; **~ligist** *der;* **~~en, ~~en** (Sport) regional league team; **~programm** *das* regional programme; **~zug** *der* ▸**~bahn**

Regisseur /reʒɪ'sø:ɐ̯/ *der;* **~s, ~e, Regisseurin** *die;* **~, ~nen** (Theater, Film) director; (Ferns., Rundf.) director; producer

Register /re'gɪstɐ/ *das;* **~s, ~** 1 index 2 (Daumen~) thumb index 3 (amtliche Liste) register 4 (Musik) (bei Instrumenten) register; (Orgel~) stop; (Tonbereich) register; **alle ~ ziehen** (fig.) pull out all the stops 5 (hist.: Urkundensammlung) file 6 (Druckw.) register; **~ halten** be in register

Register·tonne *die* register tonne

Registrator /regɪs'tra:tɔr/ *der;* **~s, ~en** /-stra'to:rən/ (veralt.) registrar

Registratur /regɪstra'tu:ɐ̯/ *die;* **~, ~en** 1 (das Registrieren) registration 2 (Büro) filing room 3 (Schrank, Regal) filing cabinet 4 (Musik: Orgel~) stop mechanism

registrieren /regɪs'tri:rən/ *tr. V.* 1 (eintragen, verzeichnen) register 2 (aufzeichnen) register 3 (bemerken) note; register 4 (feststellen) note; **alle Zeitungen registrierten den Fall** all the papers mentioned the case; **es wurde sehr wohl registriert, dass er häufig unpünktlich war** it did not pass unnoticed that he often arrived late

Registrier·kasse *die* cash register

Registrierung *die;* **~, ~en** 1 (Eintragung, Aufzeichnung) registration 2 (Feststellung) **sich auf die ~ der Tatsachen beschränken** restrict oneself/itself to noting the facts

Reglement /reglə'mã:, *schweiz.:* reglə'mɛnt/ *das;* **~s, ~s** *od.* (schweiz.) **~e** (Vorschriften) regulations *pl.*; (Sport) rules *pl.*

reglementieren *tr. V.* regulate; regiment ‹*people, life*›

Reglementierung *die;* **~, ~en** regulation; (Bevormundung) regimentation

Regler *der;* **~s, ~** (Technik) regulator; (Kybernetik) control

Reglette /re'glɛtə/ *die;* **~, ~n** (Druckw.) lead; reglet

reg·los *Adj.* ▸**regungslos**

Reglosigkeit *die;* **~** ▸**Regungslosigkeit**

regnen /'re:gnən/
A *itr., tr. V.* (unpers.) rain; **es regnet** it is raining; **es regnet/regnete jeden Tag** it rains/rained every day; *s. auch* **Strom 1**
B *itr. V.; mit sein* (fig.) rain down; **es regnete Steine** (fig.) stones rained down; **es regnete Briefe/Anfragen** *usw.* (fig.) there was a flood *or* deluge of letters/enquiries *etc.*

Regner *der;* **~s, ~:** sprinkler

regnerisch *Adj.* rainy; **~-trüb** dull and rainy *or* wet

regredieren /regre'di:rən/ *itr. V.* (Psych.) regress

Regress, *Regreß /re'grɛs/ *der;* **~es, ~e** 1 (Rechtsw.) recourse; **~ auf jmdn. nehmen** have recourse against sb. 2 (Philos.) regress

Regress-, *Regreß-: ~anspruch *der* (Rechtsw.) right to compensation; **~forderung** *die* (Rechtsw.) demand *or* claim for compensation; **~forderungen stellen** demand *or* claim compensation

Regression /regrɛ'sio:n/ *die;* **~, ~en** 1 **wirtschaftliche ~:** economic recession 2 (Psych., Geol., Statistik, Biol.) regression

regressiv /regrɛ'si:f/ *Adj.* (Psych., Geol., Statistik, Biol.) regressive

regress·pflichtig, *regreß·pflichtig *Adj.* liable for compensation *postpos.*

regsam *Adj.* (geh.) lively; active; **geistig ~ sein** have a lively *or* active mind

Regsamkeit *die;* **~** (geh.) liveliness; activeness

regulär /regu'lɛ:ɐ̯/ *Adj.* 1 (vorschriftsmäßig) in accordance with the regulations *postpos.*; (richtig, gesetzlich) proper; regular ‹*troops*›; normal, regular ‹*working hours*›; **die ~e Spielzeit** (Sport) normal time 2 (normal, üblich) normal; regular ‹*flight*› 3 (ugs.: regelrecht) proper (coll.); regular (coll.)

Regularität /regulari'tɛ:t/ *die;* **~, ~en** (auch Sprachw.) regularity

Regulation /regula'tsio:n/ *die;* **~, ~en** 1 ▸**Regulierung** 2 (Biol., Med.) regulation

Regulativ /regula'ti:f/ *das;* **~s, ~e** 1 (regulierendes Element) regulative; regulator; **Angebot und Nachfrage sind ~e des Marktes** supply and demand have a regulating effect on the market 2 (regelnde Vorschrift) regulation

Regulator /regu'la:tɔr/ *der;* **~s, ~en** /-la'to:rən/ 1 (regulierende Kraft, Technik) regulator 2 (veralt.: Pendeluhr) pendulum clock

regulierbar *Adj.* regulable; adjustable ‹*backrest*›

regulieren /regu'li:rən/ **A** *tr. V.* regulate; (einstellen) adjust; regulate; set ‹*clock, watch*›; **automatisch regulierte Türen** automatically controlled doors **B** *refl. V.* regulate itself; **sich selbst ~d** self-regulating

Regulierung *die;* **~, ~en** ▸**regulieren**: regulation; adjustment; setting

Regulierungs·behörde *die* regulatory authority

Regung *die;* **~, ~en** (geh.) **1** (Bewegung) movement **2** (Gefühl) stirring; **seine erste ~ war Unmut** his first emotion was displeasure; **sie folgte einer ~ ihres Herzens** she followed the promptings of her heart **3** (Bestrebung) striving

regungs·los *Adj.* motionless

Regungslosigkeit *die;* **~:** motionlessness; **in voller ~ verharren** stay completely motionless

Reh /re:/ *das;* **~[e]s, ~e** roe deer

Reha /'re:ha/ *die;* **~, ~s** rehab; **in ~ sein/gehen** be in/go into rehab

Rehabilitand *der;* **~en, ~en**, **Rehabilitandin** *die;* **~, ~nen** (Med.) person undergoing rehabilitation

Rehabilitation *die;* **~, ~en** rehabilitation

Rehabilitations-: ~maßnahme *die* rehabilitation; (Programm) rehabilitation programme; **~zentrum** *das* rehabilitation centre

rehabilitieren *tr. V.* rehabilitate

Rehabilitierung *die* rehabilitation

Reha-: ~klinik *die* rehab clinic; **~zentrum** *das* rehab centre

reh-, Reh-: ~bock *der* roebuck; **~braten** *der* (Kochk.) roast venison; **~braun** *Adj.* light reddish brown; **~keule** *die* (Kochk.) haunch of venison; **~kitz** *das* fawn *or* kid [of a/the roe deer]; **~rücken** *der* (Kochk.) saddle of venison; **~wild** *das* (Jägerspr.) roe deer *pl.*

Reibach /'raibax/ *der;* **~s** (ugs.) profits *pl.*; **einen [kräftigen] ~ machen** make a killing (coll.)

Reib·ahle *die* (Technik) reamer

Reibe /'raibə/ *die;* **~, ~n** grater

Reib·eisen *das* grater; **rau wie ein ~:** as rough as sandpaper; **eine Stimme wie ein ~:** a voice like a rasp

Reibe-: ~kuchen *der* (Kochk.) *grated raw potatoes fried into a pancake;* **~laut** *der* (Sprachw.) fricative

reiben
A *unr. tr. V.* **1** rub; **jmdm./sich die Backen ~:** rub sb.'s/one's cheeks; **das Pferd rieb sich an der Mauer** the horse rubbed itself against the wall; **etw. sauber ~:** rub sth. clean; **etw. blank ~:** rub sth. until it shines; **einen Fleck aus einem Kleid ~:** rub a mark off a dress; **sich** (*Dat.*) **den Schlaf aus den Augen ~:** rub the sleep from one's eyes; **sich** (*Dat.*) **die Haut/die Hand wund ~:** chafe one's skin/hand **2** (zerkleinern) grate
B *unr. itr. V.* **1** rub; **mit einem Tuch über die Schuhe ~:** rub one's/sb.'s shoes with a cloth **2** (scheuern) ‹*collar, shoes, etc.*› rub (**an** + *Dat.* on)
C *unr. refl. V.* **sich an einem Problem ~:** come up against a problem; **sich mit jmdm. ~:** be at loggerheads with sb.; **sich [aneinander] ~:** rub each other up the wrong way

Reiberei *die;* **~, ~en** friction *no pl.*; **er hatte ständig ~en mit seinen Eltern** there was constant friction between him and his parents

Reib·fläche *die* striking surface (*of matchbox*)

Reibung *die;* **~, ~en** **1** (das Reiben) rubbing **2** ▸**Reiberei** **3** (Physik) friction

reibungs-, Reibungs-: ~elektrizität *die* (Physik) frictional electricity; **~fläche** *die* (fig.) source of friction; **~los** **A** *Adj.* smooth; **B** *adv.* smoothly; **~wärme** *die* (Physik) frictional heat; **~wider·stand** *der* (Physik) frictional resistance

reich /raiç/
A *Adj.* **1** (vermögend) rich; **~ heiraten** marry [into] money **2** (prächtig) costly ‹*goods, gifts*›; rich ‹*décor, ornamentation, finery, furnishings*› **3** (üppig) rich; rich, abundant ‹*harvest*›; lavish, sumptuous ‹*meal*›; abundant ‹*mineral resources*›; productive ‹*oil well*›; **~ an etw.** (*Dat.*) **sein** be rich in sth.; **in ~em Maße** (geh.) in abundance **4** (vielfältig) rich ‹*collection, possibilities, field of activity*›; wide, large, extensive ‹*selection, choice*›; wide ‹*knowledge, experience*›; full ‹*life*›
B *adv.* richly; **~ geschmückt** richly decorated; richly adorned ‹*façade, building*›; **~ verziert** highly ornate

-reich rich in …; **variations~/kontrast~:** rich in variation/contrast; **wasser~ sein** have abundant water

Reich *das;* **~[e]s, ~e** **1** empire; (König~) kingdom; realm; **das [Deutsche] ~** (hist.) the German Reich *or* Empire; **das Russische ~** (hist.) the Russian Empire; **das Dritte ~** (hist.) the Third Reich **2** (fig.) realm; **ins ~ der Fabel gehören** belong to the realm[s] of fantasy; **das ~ der Pflanzen/Tiere** the plant/animal kingdom; **Dein ~ komme** (bibl.) thy Kingdom come

Reiche *der/die; adj. Dekl.* rich man/woman; **die ~n** the rich

reichen
A *itr. V.* **1** (aus~) be enough; **das Geld reicht nicht** I/we *etc.* haven't got enough money; **der Stoff reicht für ein** *od.* **zu einem Kostüm** there's enough material to make a suit; **das Brot muss noch bis Montag ~:** the bread must last till Monday; **die Farbe hat gerade gereicht** there was just enough paint; **das Seil reicht nicht** the rope's not long enough; **jetzt reichts mir aber!** now I've had enough!; **danke, es reicht** that's enough, thank you; *s. auch* **langen** **2** (sich erstrecken) reach; ‹*forest, fields, etc.*› extend; **bis zu etw. ~:** extend as far as sth.; **er reicht mit dem Kopf bis zur Decke** his head touches the ceiling; **bis zum Horizont ~:** extend *or* stretch to the horizon; **sein Einfluss reicht sehr weit** his influence extends a long way; **soweit das Auge reicht** (geh.) as far as the eye can see; **jmdm. bis an die Schultern ~:** come up to sb.'s shoulder; **an die Grenze des Pathologischen ~:** verge on the pathological **3** **mit dem Geld/Brot** *usw.* **[nicht] ~:** [not] have enough money/bread *etc.*; **damit müssen wir ~:** we'll have to make it last
B *tr. V.* **1** (geh.: entgegenhalten) hand; (herüber~, hinüber~) pass; hand; **jmdm. die Hand ~:** hold out one's hand to sb.; **das Abendmahl ~:** administer *or* give Communion; **sich** (*Dat.*) **die Hand ~:** shake hands; **jmdm. Feuer ~:** give sb. a light **2** (servieren) serve ‹*food, drink*›

reich-, Reich-: ~geschmückt ▸**reich B**; **~haltig** *Adj.* extensive; wide, large, extensive ‹*range, selection*›; varied ‹*programme*›; substantial ‹*meal*›; **~haltigkeit** *die;* **~~:** extensiveness; (eines Programms) varied content; (einer Mahlzeit) substantialness; **die ~haltigkeit des Materials** the wealth of material

reichlich
A *Adj.* large; substantial; ample ‹*space, time, reward*›; plenty of ‹*time, space*›; good ‹*hour, year*›; generous ‹*tip*›; **~e Niederschläge** heavy rain/hail/snow; **der Mantel ist ein bisschen ~** (ugs.) the coat is a bit on the large side
B *adv.* amply; **~ Trinkgeld geben** tip generously; **Fleisch ist noch ~ vorhanden** there is still plenty of meat left; **~ Zeit/Platz/Gelegenheit haben** have plenty of *or* ample time/room/opportunity; **das ist ~ gerechnet** that's a generous estimate; **~ spenden** give *or* donate generously; **~ zu leben haben** live well
C *Adv.* **1** (mehr als) over; more than; **nach ~ einer Stunde** a good hour later; **~ vier Wochen** a good month; **~ 5 000 Euro** a good 5,000 euros **2** (ugs.: ziemlich, sehr) **~ frech/teuer/spät** a bit too cheeky/dear/late

reichs-, Reichs-: ~acht *die* (hist.) imperial ban; **~adel** *der* (hist.) nobility of the Empire; **~adler** *der* (hist.) Imperial Eagle; **~apfel** *der* (hist.) imperial orb; **~arbeitsdienst** *der* (ns.) Reich Labour Service; **~bahn** *die* **1** (DDR) **Deutsche ~bahn** [East German] State Railway; **2** (hist.) German National Railway; **3** **die schwedische/japanische ~bahn** the Swedish/Japanese National Railway; **~deutsch** *Adj.* within the German Reich *postpos.*; **~deutsche** *der/die* German citizen living within the German Reich; **~grenze** *die* frontier of the Empire; **~insignien** *Pl.* (hist.) imperial insignia *pl.*; **~kanzler** *der* **1** (1871-1918) Imperial Chancellor; **2** (Weimarer Republik) Chancellor of the Republic; **3** (Drittes Reich) Reich Chancellor; **~mark** *die; Pl.* **~~** (hist.) Reichsmark; **~präsident** *der* (hist.) President of Germany; **~regierung** *die* government of a/the nation (*under a monarch*); **~stadt** *die* (hist.) free city *or* town of the [Holy Roman] Empire; **~stände** *Pl.* (hist.) estates of the Empire; **~tag** *der* **1** (in Schweden) Riksdag; [Swedish] Diet; (in Finnland) Parliament; (in Japan) [Imperial *or* Japanese] Diet; **2** (hist.: bis 1806) Imperial Diet; Diet of the Holy Roman Empire; **3** (1871-1945 in Deutschland; Reichstagsgebäude) Reichstag; **~tags·brand** *der* (hist.) Reichstag Fire; **~unmittel·bar** *Adj.* (hist.) subordinate directly to the Kaiser *or* Emperor *postpos.*; **~verweser** *der;* **~~s, ~~** (hist.) Regent of the Empire; **~wehr** *die* (hist.) German *or* Imperial Army (*1919-35*); Reichswehr

> **Reichstag**
>
> This historic building in the centre of Berlin became the seat of the **Bundestag** in 1999. The refurbishment of the *Reichstag* included the addition of a glass cupola, with a walkway open to visitors, which provides a spectacular viewing platform and addition to the Berlin skyline.

Reichtum *der;* **~s, Reichtümer** /'raiçty:mɐ/ **1** (Vermögen, Besitz) wealth (**an** + *Dat.* of); **sein seelischer/innerer ~** (fig.) the richness of his spirit/inner life **2** *Pl.* (Vermögenswerte) riches; **die Reichtümer der Erde** the riches of the earth; **damit kann man keine Reichtümer erwerben** one cannot get rich that way **3** (Reichhaltigkeit) wealth (**an** + *Dat.* of); **der ~ an Singvögeln** the abundance of songbirds; **der ~ seiner Kompositionen** the richness of his compositions

reich·verziert ▸**reich B**

Reich·weite *die* **1** reach; (eines Geschützes, Senders, Flugzeugs) range ; **sich außer ~ halten** keep out of reach/range; **in ~ sein/kommen** be/come within reach/range; **Geschütze mit großer ~:** long-range guns **2** (Physik: Strahlungsweite) range

reif /raif/ *Adj.* **1** (voll entwickelt) ripe ‹*fruit, grain, cheese*›; mature ‹*brandy, cheese*›; **das Geschwür ist ~:** the boil has come to a head; **~ für etw. sein** (ugs.) be ready for sth.; **er ist ~ fürs Irrenhaus** (ugs.) he belongs in the loony bin (sl.); **er brauchte nur die ~e Frucht zu pflücken** (fig.) it just fell into his lap **2** (erwachsen, erfahren) mature; **in [den] ~eren Jahren, im ~eren Alter** in one's mature years; **die ~eren Jahrgänge** those of mature age **3** (ausgewogen, durchdacht) mature; **eine ~e Leistung** (ugs.) a solid achievement; **~ für die** *od.* **zur Veröffentlichung sein** be ready for publication; **die Zeit ist noch nicht ~:** the time is not yet ripe

-reif ready for …; **kino-/test-/olympia~:** ready for the cinema/for testing/for the Olympics; **aufführungs~:** ready to be performed

Reif[1] *der;* **~[e]s** hoar frost

Reif[2] *der;* **~[e]s, ~e** (geh.) (Fingerring) ring; (Arm~) bracelet; (Diadem) circlet

Reife *die;* **~** **1** (das Reifsein) ripeness; (das Reifen) ripening; **während der ~:** during ripening; **zur ~ kommen** ripen **2** (von Menschen) maturity; **Zeugnis der ~:** Abitur certificate **3** (von Gedanken, Produkten) maturity; **mittlere ~** (Schulw.) *school-leaving certificate usually taken after the fifth year of secondary school*

Reife·grad *der* degree of ripeness

reifen[1]
A *itr. V.* **1** *mit sein* (reif werden) ‹*fruit, cereal, cheese*› ripen; ‹*ovum, embryo, cheese*› mature **2** *mit sein*

(geh.: älter, reifer werden) mature (**zu** into); **diese Erfahrungen haben ihn [zum Manne] ~ lassen** (geh.) these experiences made a man of him; **ein gereifter Mann** (geh.) a mature man **3** *mit sein* ‹*idea, plan, decision*› mature; ‹*resistance*› develop, grow; **zur Gewissheit ~** (geh.) grow *or* harden into certainty
B *tr. V.* (geh.) ripen ‹*fruit, cereal*›; mature ‹*person*›

reifen² *itr. V.* **es hat gereift** there is/was a hoar frost

Reifen *der;* **~s, ~ 1** (Metallband, Sportgerät) hoop **2** (Gummi~) tyre **3** (Schmuckstück) (Fingerring) ring; (Arm~) bracelet; (Diadem) circlet

Reifen-: ~druck *der; Pl.* **~drücke** tyre pressure; **~panne** *die* flat tyre; puncture; **~profil** *das* [tyre] tread; **~schaden** *der* tyre defect; faulty tyre; **~wechsel** *der* tyre change

Reife-: ~prüfung *die: school-leaving examination for university entrance qualification;* **~zeugnis** *das* Abitur certificate

Reif·glätte *die* ice on the roads

reiflich
A *Adj.* [very] careful; **bei/nach ~er Überlegung** on mature consideration/after [very] careful consideration
B *adv.* [very] carefully; **über etw.** (*Akk.*) **~ nachdenken** give [very] careful thought *or* consideration to sth.; consider sth. [very] carefully

Reif·rock *der* (hist.) hooped skirt

Reifung *die;* **~** ▸ **reifen¹ A**: ripening; maturing; maturation

Reifungs·prozess, ***Reifungs·prozeß** *der* ▸ **reifen¹ A**: process of ripening *or* maturing; (eines Menschen) stage of becoming mature

Reigen /ˈraign/ *der;* **~s, ~ 1** round dance; **den ~ eröffnen/anführen** lead off [in the round dance] **2** (fig.) **den ~ eröffnen** start off; **den ~ der Gratulanten eröffnen** be the first to offer congratulations; **den ~ schließen** close; finish off; **ein bunter ~ von Melodien** a medley of tunes

Reihe /ˈraiə/ *die;* **~, ~n 1** row; **Geräte in ~ schalten** (Elektrot.) connect pieces of equipment in series; **in ~n** (*Dat.*) **antreten** line up; (Milit.) fall in; **sich in fünf ~n aufstellen** line up in five rows; form five lines; **die ~n der älteren Generation lichten sich** (fig.) the ranks of the older generation are thinning out; **in Reih und Glied** (Milit.) in rank and file; **aus der ~ tanzen** (fig. ugs.) be different; **nicht in der ~ sein** (fig. ugs.) be feeling below par; **etw. in die ~ bringen** (fig. ugs.) put sth. straight *or* in order; **[wieder] in die ~ kommen** (fig. ugs.) get [back] on one's feet **2** (Reihenfolge) series; **die ~ ist an ihm/ihr** *usw.*, **er/sie** *usw.* **ist an der ~**: it's his/her *etc.* turn; **wer ist an der ~?** (ugs.) whose turn is it?; **Punkt drei der Tagesordnung ist jetzt an der ~**: we now come to the third item on the agenda; **du kommst jetzt an die ~** (ugs.) it's your turn now; **der ~ nach, nach der ~**: in turn; one after the other **3** (größere Anzahl) number; **eine ganze ~ Frauen** a whole lot of women (coll.) **4** (Gruppe) ranks *pl.*; **die ~n schließen** close ranks; **aus den eigenen ~n** from one's/its own ranks **5** (bes. Fußball) **aus der zweiten ~ schießen** take a long shot/long shots [at goal] **6** (Math.) series **7** (Schach) rank **8** (Musik) series

reihen¹ (geh.)
A *tr. V.* (auf~) string; thread; **Perlen auf eine Schnur ~**: string pearls [on a thread]; **um etw. gereiht sein** be ranged around sth.; **Zahl an Zahl ~**: string numbers together
B *refl. V.* (sich an~, ein~) follow; **sich um jmdn. ~**: gather round sb.

reihen² *tr. V.* (heften) tack; baste

Reihen *der;* **~s, ~** (veralt.) ▸ **Reigen**

reihen-, Reihen-: ~dorf *das* ▸ **Straßendorf**; **~folge** *die* order; **die ~folge einhalten** keep in order *or* sequence; **in kurzer ~folge** in quick succession; **~haus** *das* terraced house; **~schaltung** *die* (Elektrot.) series connection; **~untersuchung** *die* (Med.) mass screening; **~weise** *Adv.* **1** (ugs.: in großer Zahl) by the dozen; **2** (in ~) in rows *or* lines

Reiher *der;* **~s, ~**: heron

Reiher·feder *die* heron feather

reihern *itr. V.* (salopp) puke (coarse)

Reih·garn *das* tacking *or* basting thread

reih·um *Adv.* **etw. ~ gehen lassen** pass sth. round; **die Flasche ging ~**: the bottle went *or* was passed round; **etw. ~ tun** do sth. in turn

Reihung *die;* **~, ~en** ▸ **reihen¹ A**: stringing; threading; ranging

Reim /raim/ *der;* **~[e]s, ~e** rhyme; **einen ~ auf ein Wort suchen** try to find something to rhyme with a word; **sich** (*Dat.*) **keinen ~ auf etw.** (*Akk.*) **machen [können]** (fig.) not [be able] to see rhyme or reason in sth.

reimen
A *itr. V.* make up rhymes
B *tr. V.* rhyme; **ein Wort auf ein anderes ~**: rhyme one word with another; **eine gereimte Fabel** a fable in rhyme
C *refl. V.* rhyme (**auf** + *Akk.* with); **das reimt sich nicht** (fig.) that makes no sense

Reimerei *die;* **~, ~en** (abwertend) **eine ~**: a piece of doggerel; **~en** doggerel *sing.*

Reime·schmied *der* (abwertend) rhymester

reim-, Reim-: ~lexikon *das* rhyming dictionary; **~los** *Adj.* unrhymed; rhymeless; **~paar** *das* (Verslehre) rhyming couplet

Reimport *der* (Wirtsch.) reimport

Reim-: ~wort *das; Pl.* **~wörter** rhyme word; **~wörter·buch** *das* rhyming dictionary

rein¹ /rain/ (ugs.) **~ mit dir!** in you go/come!

rein²
A *Adj.* **1** (unvermischt) pure; **~es Hochdeutsch sprechen** speak faultless *or* perfect German **2** (nichts anderes als) pure; sheer; **etw. aus ~em Trotz tun** do sth. out of sheer *or* pure contrariness; **~e Theorie/Mathematik** pure theory/mathematics; **die ~e Wahrheit sagen** tell the plain *or* unvarnished truth **3** (ohne Ausnahme) **es war ~e Männersache** it was exclusively a men's affair; **eine ~e Arbeitergegend** a purely *or* entirely working-class district **4** (ugs.: intensivierend) pure; sheer; **das ist der ~ste Quatsch** that's pure *or* sheer *or* absolute nonsense; **Sie sind der ~ste Dichter** you are a real poet; **dein Zimmer ist der ~ste Saustall** (derb) your room is a real pigsty **5** (meist geh.: frisch, sauber) clean; fresh ‹*clothes, sheet of paper, etc.*›; pure, clean ‹*water, air*›; clear, fresh ‹*complexion*›; (fig.) **ein ~es Gewissen haben** have a clear conscience; **sein Gewissen ~waschen** (ugs.) appease one's conscience; **jmdn./jmds. Namen/sich ~waschen** (ugs.) clear sb./sb.'s name/oneself; **~ klingen** make *or* have a pure sound; **etw. ins Reine schreiben** make a fair copy of sth.; **etw. ins Reine bringen** clear sth. up; put sth. straight; **mit jmdm./etw. ins Reine kommen** get things straightened out with sb./get sth. sorted *or* straightened out; **mit sich [selbst] ins Reine kommen** sort things out in one's own mind; **mit etw. im Reinen sein** have got sth. sorted out; **mit jmdm. im Reinen sein** have got things straightened out with sb.
B *Adv.* **1** (ausschließlich) purely **2** (vor allem, besonders) purely; **~ zufällig/unmöglich** purely *or* quite by chance/quite impossible; **~ zeitlich** purely from the point of view of time **3** (ugs.: intensivierend) **~ gar nichts** absolutely nothing

rein-: ~beißen *unr. itr. V.* (ugs.) take a bite; **in etw.** (*Akk.*) **~beißen** take a bite of sth.; **zum Reinbeißen sein** *od.* **aussehen** (ugs.) ‹*cake etc.*› look tempting; (fig.) ‹*girl*› look good enough to eat; **~blasen** (ugs.) **A** *tr. V.* blow in; **etw. in etw.** (*Akk.*) **~blasen** blow sth. into sth.; **B** *itr. V.* blow in; **in etw.** (*Akk.*) **~blasen** blow into sth.; **~bringen** *unr. tr. V.* (ugs.) ▸ **hereinbringen, hineinbringen**; **~dürfen** *unr. itr. V.* be allowed in

Reineclaude /rɛːnəˈkloːdə/ ▸ **Reneklode**

Reineke /ˈrainəkə/ *der;* **~s, ~s** Reynard *no art.*; **Meister ~, ~ Fuchs** Reynard the Fox

Reine·mache·frau *die* cleaning lady; cleaner

Reine·machen *das;* **~s** (bes. nordd.) cleaning session; **beim ~ sein** be doing the cleaning; **eine Frau kommt zum ~**: a woman comes to do the cleaning

rein-, Rein-: ~erbig *Adj.* (Biol.) homozygous; **~erlös** *der,* **~ertrag** *der* net profits *pl. or* proceeds *pl.*

Reinette /rɛˈnɛtə/ ▸ **Renette**

reine·weg *Adv.* (ugs.) really; (ganz u. gar) absolutely; **das ist ~ zum Verzweifeln** it's enough to drive you to despair

rein|fahren
A *unr. itr. V.; mit sein* (ugs.) ▸ **hineinfahren A**.
B *unr. tr. V.* (ugs.) ▸ **hineinfahren B**

Rein·fall *der* (ugs.) let-down; **das Stück war ein böser ~**: the play was a complete flop (coll.); **mit unserem letzten Auto haben wir einen großen ~ erlebt** our last car was a complete disaster

rein|fallen *unr. itr. V.; mit sein* (ugs.) ▸ **hereinfallen 1, hineinfallen**

rein|feiern *itr. V.* (ugs.) **ins neue Jahr** *usw.* **~**: go on celebrating into the New Year *etc.*

Reinfektion *die* (Med.) reinfection

rein|fließen *unr. itr. V.; mit sein* (ugs.); **in etw.** (*Akk.*) **~**: run *or* flow into sth.; (fig.) ‹*money*› pour into sth.; ‹*work, time*› be put into sth.

rein|gehen *unr. itr. V.; mit sein* (ugs.) ▸ **hineingehen**

Reingeschmeckte /-gəʃmɛktə/ *der/die; adj. Dekl.* (scherzh.) outsider

Rein-: ~gewicht *das* net weight; **~gewinn** *der* net profit

Rein·haltung *die:* **die ~ der Seen/der Luft** keeping the lakes/air clean *or* pure; **die ~ der Sprache** keeping the language pure

rein|hauen *unr. tr. V.* (salopp) **1** (schlagen) bash; **in die Tasten ~**: pound *or* thump the keys; **Kokain haut viel mehr rein** (fig.) cocaine gives you much more of a kick (coll.); **jmdm. eine ~**: thump sb. [one] (coll.) **2** (essen) tuck in (coll.)

Reinheit *die;* **~ 1** (Klarheit) purity **2** (Sauberkeit) cleanness; (des Wassers, der Luft) purity; (der Haut) clearness

Reinheits-: ~gebot *das* beer purity regulations *pl.*; **~grad** *der* degree of purity

reinigen /ˈrainɪgn̩/ *tr. V.* clean; clean, cleanse ‹*wound, skin*›; purify ‹*effluents, air, water, etc.*›; **Kleider [chemisch] ~ lassen** have clothes [dry-]cleaned; **das Gewitter hat die Luft gereinigt** the storm has cleared the air; **ein ~des Gewitter** (fig.) an argument that clears the air; **die Atmosphäre ~** (fig.) clear the air

Reinigung *die;* **~, ~en 1** ▸ **reinigen**: cleaning; cleansing; purification; dry-cleaning **2** (Betrieb) [dry-]cleaner's

Reinigungs-: ~creme *die* cleansing cream; **~milch** *die* cleansing milk; **~mittel** *das* cleaning agent; (für die Haut) cleanser; cleansing product

Reinkarnation *die;* **~, ~en** reincarnation

rein-, Rein-: ~|knien *refl. V.* (ugs.) ▸ **hineinknien**; **~|kommen** *unr. itr. V.; mit sein* (ugs.) ▸ **herein-, hineinkommen**; **~|können** *unr. itr. V.* be able to go/come in; **~|kriechen** *unr. itr. V.; mit sein* (ugs.) crawl in; **in etw.** (*Akk.*) **~kriechen** crawl into sth.; **jmdm. hinten ~kriechen** (derb) lick sb.'s arse (coarse); **~|kriegen** *tr. V.* (ugs.) ▸ **hereinbekommen; hineinbekommen**; **~kultur** *die* **1** (Landw.) monoculture; **2** (Biol.) pure culture; **Kitsch/Konservatismus in ~kultur** (fig.) pure *or* unadulterated kitsch/pure *or* sheer Conservatism; **~|legen** *tr. V.* (ugs.) ▸ **hereinlegen**; **~leinen** *Adj.* pure linen

reinlich
A *Adj.* **1** (~keitsliebend) cleanly **2** (sauber) clean; neat ‹*dress*› **3** (gründlich) clear[-cut] ‹*division, distinction, etc.*›
B *adv.* **1** (sauber) cleanly; neatly ‹*dressed, folded*› **2** (gründlich) clearly

Reinlichkeit *die;* **~** ▸ **reinlich**: cleanliness; neatness; clearness

rein-, Rein-: ~mache·frau *die* ▸ **Reinemachefrau**; **~|müssen** *unr. itr. V.* have to go/come in; **~|passen** *itr. V.* (ugs.) ▸ **hineinpassen**; **~|pusten** (ugs.) **A** *tr. V.* blow in;

etw. in etw. (*Akk.*) **~pusten** blow sth. into sth.; **B** *itr. V.* blow in; **in etw.** (*Akk*) **~pusten:** blow into sth.; **~rassig** *Adj.* pure-bred, thoroughbred ‹*animal*›; **~rassigkeit** *die* purity of breeding; **~|reden** *itr. V.* (ugs. abwertend) ▸**hineinreden 2**; **~|reißen** *unr. tr. V.* (ugs.) **jmdn. ~reißen** drag sb. in (fig.); **~|reiten** *unr. tr. V.* (ugs.) **jmdn. ~reiten** drag sb. in (fig.); **~|riechen** *unr. itr. V.* (ugs.) **in die Exportabteilung ~riechen** get a taste of work in the export department; **~|schauen** *itr. V.* (ugs.) look in; **~schiff** (*das*) (Seemannsspr.) *in* **~schiff machen** clean the decks [thoroughly]; **~|schlagen** *unr. tr. V.* **1** (ugs.) knock in; **etw. in etw.** (*Akk.*) **~schlagen** knock sth. into sth.; **2** **jmdm. eine ~schlagen** (salopp) thump sb. [one] (coll.); **~|schmuggeln** *tr. V.*: ▸**hineinschmuggeln**; **~schrift** *die* fair copy; **~schriftlich** *Adj.* **eine ~schriftliche Fassung** a fair copy; **~seiden** *Adj.* pure silk; **~|sollen** *itr. V.* be supposed to go/come in; **~|stecken** *itr. V.* put in; **~|steigern** *refl. V.* (ugs.) work oneself up; become worked up

Reintegration /reɪntegra'tsjo:n/ *die;* **~, ~en** reintegration

reintegrieren /reɪnte'gri:rən/ *tr. V.* reintegrate (**in** + *Akk.* into)

rein-: **~|treten** (ugs.) **A** *unr. itr. V.; mit sein* (hineintreten) **in etw.** (*Akk.*) **~treten** step in[to] sth.; **B** *unr. tr., itr. V.* **jmdm.** *od.* **jmdn. hinten ~treten** kick sb. up the backside; **~|waschen** *unr. tr. V.* clear ‹*person, sb.'s name*›; **~weg** *Adv.* ▸**reineweg**; **~wollen¹** *Adj.* pure wool; **~|wollen²** *unr. itr. V.* (ugs.) want to come/go in; **seltsam, dass so viele Leute ins Kino ~wollten** it's odd that so many people wanted to get into the cinema; **~|würgen** *tr. V.* **1** (ugs.) **sich** (*Dat.*) **~würgen** force ‹*food, medicine, etc.*› down; **etw. in sich** (*Akk.*) **~würgen** force sth. down; **2** **jmdm. eine** *od.* **eins ~würgen** come down on sb. like a ton of bricks (coll.); **er hat einen ~gewürgt gekriegt** he/she/they *etc.* came down on him like a ton of bricks (coll.) **~|ziehen** *tr. V.* **1** ▸**hineinziehen A**; **2** **sich** (*Dat.*) **etw. ~ziehen** (salopp) take ‹*drug*›; watch ‹*film, show, video*›

Reis¹ /rais/ *der;* **~es** rice

Reis² *das;* **~es, ~er** **1** (geh.: Zweig) twig; **~er** (**~ig**) brushwood *sing.* **2** (geh.: Spross) shoot **3** (Pfropfreis) scion

Reis-: **~auflauf** *der* (Kochk.) baked rice dish; (süß) *baked pudding of rice with layers of fruit etc.*; **~bauer** *der;* **~~n, ~~n, ~bäuerin** *die;* **~~, ~~nen** rice grower; **~brei** *der* rice pudding

-reise *die;* **~, ~n** ... journey/trip; **Schweiz~/Afrika~:** journey/trip to Switzerland/Africa; **Bus~:** bus trip *or* journey

Reise /'raizə/ *die;* **~, ~n** **1** journey; (kürzere Fahrt, Geschäfts~) trip; (Ausflug) outing; excursion; trip; (Schiffs~) voyage; (ins Weltall) voyage; flight; (im Flugzeug) flight; (Kreuzfahrt) cruise; (Überfahrt) crossing; **eine ~ mit dem Auto/der Eisenbahn** a journey by car/train; a car/train journey; **eine ~ zur See** a sea voyage; (Kreuzfahrt) a cruise; **eine dienstliche ~:** a business trip; **eine ~ um die Welt** a journey round the world; **auf meinen ~n** on my travels; **eine ~ machen** make a journey/go on a trip/an outing; **auf ~n sein** travel; (nicht zu Hause sein) be away; **viel auf ~n sein** *od.* **gehen** travel a lot; do a lot of travelling; **jeden Sommer gehen wir auf die ~** *od.* **auf ~n** we travel every summer; **auf der ~ gabs viel zu sehen** there was a lot to see during *or* on the journey/trip; **wohin soll diesmal die ~ gehen?** where will you/shall we go this time?; **glückliche** *od.* **gute ~!** have a good journey; **wenn einer eine ~ tut, dann kann er was erzählen** (Spr.) travelling is always eventful; **die** *od.* **seine letzte ~ antreten** (geh. verhüll.) go to meet one's Maker **2** (Drogenjargon) trip (coll.)

reise-, Reise-: **~andenken** *das* souvenir; **~apotheke** *die* [traveller's] first aid kit; **~bedarf** *der* travel requisites *pl.*; **~begleiter** *der,* **~begleiterin** *die* travelling companion; (~leiter[in]) courier; (für Kinder) chaperone; **~bekanntschaft** *die* acquaintance made on a/the journey; **ich habe eine interessante ~bekanntschaft gemacht** I met somebody interesting on the journey; **~bericht** *der* (privat) account of one's journey; (offiziell) report of one's journey; (Buch) travel book; (Film) travelogue; travel film; (Artikel) travel story; **~beschreibung** *die* account of a journey/one's travels; (Buch) travel book; **~büro** *das* travel agent's; travel agency; **~bus** *der* coach; **~decke** *die* travelling rug; **~fähig** *Adj.* **~fähig sein** be able to travel; **ein ~fähiger Patient** a patient able to travel; **~fertig** *Adj.* **~fertig sein** be ready to leave; **~fieber** *das* (ugs.) nervous excitement about the journey; **~fieber haben** be nervous and excited about the journey; **~führer** *der* **1** (~leiter) courier; **2** (Buch) guidebook; **~führerin** *die* courier; **~geld** *das* **1** (Geld für die ~) money for the journey; **2** ▸**~spesen**; **~gepäck** *das* luggage (Brit.); baggage (Amer.); (am Flughafen) baggage; **~gepäck·versicherung** *die* luggage/baggage insurance; **~geschwindigkeit** *die* average speed for a/the journey; **~gesellschaft** *die* **1** (~gruppe) party of tourists; **eine deutsche ~gesellschaft** a party of German tourists **2** (ugs.: ~veranstalter) travel firm; tour operator; **~gruppe** *die* ▸**~gesellschaft 1**; **~kasse** *die* holiday fund; **~koffer** *der* suitcase; **~kosten** *Pl.* travel expenses; **~kosten·abrechnung** *die* travel expenses claim; **~krankheit** *die* travel sickness *no pl.*; **~land** *das:* **ein beliebtes/teures ~land sein** be a popular country with/an expensive country for tourists; **Spanien ist ~land Nr. 1 für die Deutschen** Spain is the most popular holiday destination for the Germans; **~leiter** *der,* **~leiterin** *die* ▸**❶ S. 113** courier; **~leitung** *die* **1** (das Leiten) **er hat die ~leitung übernommen** he has taken on the job of courier; **~leitung durch erfahrene Mitarbeiter** only experienced couriers are used; **2** (Person) courier/couriers; **~lektüre** *die* reading matter for the journey; **etw. als ~lektüre kaufen** buy sth. to read on the journey; **~lustig** *Adj.* **~lustig sein** (häufig ~n unternehmend) be a keen traveller; (zum Reisen aufgelegt sein) be keen to travel

reisen *itr. V.; mit sein* **1** travel; **viel gereist sein** be well-travelled; **er reist für einige Tage nach Paris** he's going to Paris for a few days; **in Unterwäsche/Hundefutter** *usw.* **~** (ugs.) travel in underwear/dog food *etc.* **2** (ab~) leave; set off

Reisende *der/die; adj. Dekl.* **1** traveller; (Fahrgast) passenger **2** (Vertreter) [travelling] sales representative; [commercial] traveller

Reise-: **~necessaire** *das* sponge bag (Brit.); toiletries bag (Amer.); **~pass,** ***~paß** *der* passport; **~pläne** *Pl.* travel plans; **~prospekt** *der* travel brochure; **~rad** *das* touring bicycle; tourer; **~route** *die* route; **~ruf** *der* SOS message for travellers; **~scheck** *der* **1** ▸**❶ S. 299** traveller's cheque; **2** (DDR) *coupon of entitlement to a holiday at a specified place*; **~schreibmaschine** *die* portable typewriter; **~spesen** *Pl.* travelling expenses; **~tag** *der* **1** (Abreisetag) departure day; **2** **am dritten ~tag erreichten sie Athen** on the third day after setting out they reached Athens; **~tasche** *die* holdall; **~verkehr** *der* holiday traffic; **~wecker** *der* travel alarm; **~welle** *die* surge of holiday traffic; **~wetter** *das* weather for travelling; **das ist ideales/kein ~wetter** that's ideal/no weather for travelling; **~wetterbericht** *der* holiday weather forecast; **~zeit** *die* **1** (Zeit der An-, Abreise) travelling time; **2** (günstige Zeit) time to travel; **3** (Urlaubszeit) holiday time *or* season; **~ziel** *das* destination; **unser ~ziel für diesen Sommer ist Mallorca** we're going on holiday to Mallorca this summer; **Paris ist ein beliebtes ~ziel** Paris is a popular holiday destination; **~zug** *der* (Eisenb.) holiday train

Reis·feld *das* paddy field

Reisig *das;* **~s** brushwood

Reisig-: **~besen** *der* besom; **~bündel** *das* bundle of brushwood

Reis-: **~korn** *das* grain of rice; **~mehl** *das* rice flour; **~papier** *das* rice paper

reiß-, Reiß-: **~ahle** *die* scriber; **~aus** *der: in* **~aus nehmen** (ugs.) scram (coll.); scarper (Brit. coll.); **~brett** *das* drawing board; **~brett·stift** *der* ▸**~zwecke**

reißen /'raisn̩/

A *unr. tr. V.* **1** (zer~) tear; (in Stücke) tear up; **ein Loch in die Hose ~:** tear *or* rip a hole in one's trousers **2** (ab~, weg~) tear; **eine Pflanze aus dem Boden ~:** tear a plant out of the ground; **jmdm. etw. aus den Händen/Armen ~:** snatch *or* tear sth. from sb.'s hands/arms; **der Sturm riss die Ziegel von den Dächern** the gale ripped *or* tore the tiles off the roofs; **sich** (*Dat.*) **die Kleider vom Leibe ~:** tear one's clothes off; **jmdn. aus seinen Gedanken ~** (fig.) awaken sb. rudely from his/her thoughts; **etw. aus dem Zusammenhang ~:** take sth. out of context **3** (ziehen an) pull; (heftig) yank (coll.) **4** (werfen, ziehen) **eine Welle riss ihn zu Boden** a wave knocked him to the ground; **er riss den Wagen zur Seite** he wrenched the [steering] wheel over; **jmdn. in die Tiefe ~:** drag sb. down into the depths; **der Fluss hat die Brücke mit sich gerissen** the river swept *or* carried the bridge away; **das Boot wurde in den Strudel gerissen** the boat was sucked into the whirlpool; **er riss sie in seine Arme** he pulled her into his arms; **[innerlich] hin und her gerissen sein** *od.* **werden** (fig.) be torn [two ways]; **von Zweifeln hin und her gerissen werden** (fig.) be torn by doubt **5** (töten) ‹*wolf, lion, etc.*› kill, take ‹*prey*› **6** (sich einer Sache bemächtigen) **an sich ~:** seize ‹*object, power, control, advantage, etc.*›; **er will immer das Gespräch an sich ~:** he always wants to monopolize the conversation **7** (ugs.: machen) crack ‹*joke*›; make ‹*remark*› **8** (Leichtathletik) **die Latte/eine Hürde ~:** knock the bar down/knock a hurdle over **9** *unpers.* (schmerzen) **es reißt mich in den Waden** my calves are aching **10** (veralt.: zeichnen) draw **11** *in* **jmdm. eine ~** (österr. salopp) stick one on sb. (sl.)

B *unr. itr. V.* **1** *mit sein* ‹*paper, fabric*› tear, rip; ‹*rope, thread*› break, snap; ‹*film*› break; ‹*muscle*› tear; **wenn alle Stricke** *od.* **Stränge ~** (fig.) if all else fails **2** (ziehen) **an etw.** (*Dat.*) **~:** pull at sth.; **der Hund riss an der Leine** the dog strained at the leash **3** (Leichtathletik) bring the bar down/knock the hurdle over **4** (Schwerathletik) snatch

C *unr. refl. V.* **1** (sich los~) tear oneself/itself (**aus, von** from); **sich aus seinen Träumen ~:** jerk oneself out of one's reveries **2** (ugs.: sich bemühen um) **ich reiße mich nicht um diese Arbeit** I'm not all that keen on this work (coll.); **sie ~ sich um die Eintrittskarten** they are scrambling to *or* fighting each other to get tickets; **sie ~ sich alle darum, mitzuspielen** they are all after the chance to play **3** (sich verletzen) scratch oneself **4** (sich beibringen) **sich eine Wunde ~:** cut oneself

Reißen *das;* **~s** (ugs.) **ich habe ein ~ in allen Gliedern** all my limbs are aching; **das ~ haben** have got rheumatism

reißend *Adj.* rapacious ‹*animal*›; stabbing ‹*pain*›; **~en Absatz finden** sell like hot cakes; **ein ~er Fluss** a raging torrent

Reißer *der;* **~s, ~** **1** (ugs., oft abwertend) thriller **2** (ugs.: Verkaufserfolg) big seller

reißerisch (abwertend)

A *Adj.* sensational; lurid ‹*headline*›; garish, lurid ‹*colour*›

B *adv.* sensationally

reiß-, Reiß-: **~feder** *die* ruling pen; **~fest** *Adj.* unbreakable; non-tear ‹*fabric*›; **~festigkeit** *die* breaking strength; **~leine** *die* (Flugw.) ripcord; **~nadel** *die* scriber; **~nagel** *der* ▸**~zwecke**; **~schiene** *die* T-square; **~stift** *der* ▸**~zwecke**

Reis·stroh *das* rice grass

Reiß-: **~verschluss,** ***~verschluß** *der* zip [fastener]; **den ~verschluss an etw.** (*Dat.*) **aufmachen/zumachen** undo/do up the zip on sth.; unzip/zip up sth.; **jmdm. den ~verschluss aufmachen** undo sb.'s zip; **~wolf** *der* shredder; (Textilw.) devil; **~wolle** *die*

r

shoddy; ~**zahn** *der* (Zool.) carnassial [tooth]; ~**zeug** *das* drawing instruments *pl.*; ~**zwecke** *die* drawing pin (Brit.); thumbtack (Amer.)

Reis-: ~**tafel** *die* (Kochk.) rijsttafel; ~**wein** *der* rice wine

Reit·bahn *die* riding arena

reiten /ˈraitn̩/

[A] *unr. itr. V.; meist mit sein* ride; **auf etw.** (*Dat.*) ~: ride [on] sth.; **im Schritt/Trab/Galopp** ~: ride at a walk/trot/gallop

[B] *unr. tr. V.; auch mit sein* [1] ride; **Schritt/Trab/Galopp** ~: ride at a walk/trot/gallop; **ein Pferd müde** ~: ride a horse until it is tired; **ein Turnier/einen Wettbewerb** ~: ride in a tournament/competition; **ein scharfes Tempo** ~: ride at a furious pace; **ich habe mir die Knie steif geritten** I rode until my knees were stiff; **was reitet denn den?** (fig. ugs.) what's eating him? (coll.) [2] (begatten) ride; mount

[C] *unr. refl. V.* **im Regen reitet es sich schwerer** riding is more difficult in the rain

Reiten *das;* ~**s** riding *no art.*

Reiter *der;* ~**s,** ~ [1] rider; **ich bin kein guter** ~: I'm not a good rider *or* horseman; *s. auch* **apokalyptisch** [2] (Milit.: Absperrung) barrier; **spanischer** ~: barbed wire barricade [3] (österr.: Heu~) rickstand [4] (an der Waage) rider [5] (Kartei~) tab

Reiterei *die;* ~, ~**en** [1] (Kavallerie) cavalry [2] (ugs.: das Reiten) riding *no art.*

Reiterin *die;* ~, ~**nen** rider; **sie ist eine gute** ~: she is a good rider *or* horsewoman

Reiter·regiment *das* (Milit.) cavalry regiment

Reiters·mann *der; Pl.* ~**männer** *od.* ~**leute** (veralt.) horseman

Reiter-: ~**staffel** *die* mounted police unit; ~**standbild** *das* equestrian statue

Reit-: ~**gerte** *die* riding whip; ~**hose** *die* riding breeches *pl.*; ~**knecht** *der* (veralt.) groom; ~**kunst** *die* riding skills *pl.*; equestrian skills *pl.*; ~**peitsche** *die* riding whip; ~**pferd** *das* saddle horse; ~**schule** *die* riding school; ~**sitz** *der* [1] (auf Pferd) **im** ~**sitz auf etw.** (*Dat.*) **sitzen** sit astride sth.; [2] (Turnen) straddle seat; ~**sport** *der* [horse] riding; ~**stall** *der* riding stable; ~**stiefel** *der* riding boot; ~**stunde** *die* riding lesson; ~**tier** *das* mount; **das ist ein** ~**tier** this animal is used for riding; ~**turnier** *das* riding event; ~**unfall** *der* riding accident; ~**weg** *der* bridle path; bridleway

Reiz /raits/ *der;* ~**es,** ~**e** [1] (Physiol.) stimulus [2] (Anziehungskraft) attraction; appeal *no pl.*; (des Verbotenen, Fremdartigen, der Ferne usw.) lure; **etw. übt einen großen** ~ **auf jmdn. aus** sth. holds *or* has great attraction *or* appeal for sb.; **in dieser Aufgabe liegt für mich ein besonderer** ~: this task has a particular attraction *or* appeal for me; **ich kann dieser Sache** (*Dat.*) **keinen** ~ **abgewinnen** this has no appeal for me; **die neue Aufgabe hat gewiss ihre** ~**e** the new job certainly has its attractions; **an** ~ **verlieren** lose some of its attraction *or* appeal [3] (Zauber) charm; **weibliche** ~**e** female charms; **sie ließ alle ihre** ~**e spielen** she used all her charms

reizbar *Adj.* [1] (leicht zu verärgern) irritable; **leicht** ~ **sein** be very irritable [2] (empfindlich) sensitive

Reizbarkeit *die;* ~ [1] (Erregbarkeit) irritability [2] (Empfindlichkeit) sensitivity

reizen

[A] *tr. V.* [1] annoy; tease ‹*animal*›; (herausfordern, provozieren) provoke; (zum Zorn treiben) anger; **jmds. Zorn** ~, **jmdn. zum Zorn** ~: provoke sb. to anger; **jmdn. bis aufs Blut** ~: make sb.'s blood boil; *s. auch* **gereizt** [2] (anziehen) attract; **jmds. Verlangen** ~: rouse sb.'s desire [3] (Physiol.) irritate; **seine Nerven waren zu sehr gereizt** his nerves were too much on edge [4] (Interesse erregen bei) **jmdn.** ~: attract sb.; appeal to sb.; **jmds. Hass/Widerspruch** ~: arouse sb.'s hatred/make sb. want to contradict; **es würde mich sehr** ~, **das zu tun** I'd love to do that; **das Angebot reizt mich** I find the offer tempting [5] (Kartenspiele) bid

[B] *itr. V.* [1] (Physiol.) irritate; **der Qualm reizt zum Husten** the smoke makes you cough [2] (anregen) **das reizt zum Lachen** it makes people laugh; **eine solche Ansicht reizt zum Widerspruch** such an opinion invites contradiction [3] (Kartenspiele) bid; **hoch** ~ (fig.) play for high stakes

reizend

[A] *Adj.* charming; delightful, lovely ‹*child*›; **das ist ja** ~ (iron.) [that's] charming! (iron.)

[B] *adv.* charmingly; **wir haben uns** ~ **unterhalten** we had a delightful chat

Reiz-: ~**figur** *die* person who arouses strong feelings; (verhasst) hate figure; ~**gas** *das* irritant gas; ~**husten** *der* ▸ⓘ **S. 439** (Med.) dry cough

Reizker /ˈraitskɐ/ *der;* ~**s,** ~ (Bot.) Lactarius; **[Echter]** ~: saffron milk cap

reiz-, Reiz-: ~**klima** *das* (Med., Met.) bracing climate; ~**los** [A] *Adj.* unattractive ‹*person, face, task, etc.*›; ‹*landscape, scenery*› lacking in charm; bland ‹*food, diet*›; [B] *adv.* unattractively; ~**losigkeit** *die;* ~~: ▸~**los**: unattractiveness; lack of charm; blandness; ~**mittel** *das* (Med.) stimulant; ~**schwelle** *die* (Med., Psych.) stimulus threshold; absolute threshold; ~**stoff** *der* irritant; ~**thema** *das* emotive issue; ~**über·flutung** *die;* ~**en** (Psych.) overstimulation

Reizung *die;* ~, ~**en** [1] annoyance; (Herausforderung) provocation; (eines Tieres) teasing [2] ▸ⓘ **S. 439** (Physiol., Med.) irritation

reiz-, Reiz-: ~**voll** [A] *Adj.* [1] (hübsch) charming; delightful; [2] (interessant) attractive; **das ist wenig** ~**voll für ihn** it doesn't appeal to him much; **es wäre** ~**voll, mit ihm darüber zu sprechen** it would be interesting to talk to him about it; **die Aussicht ist nicht gerade** ~**voll** the prospect isn't exactly enticing. [B] *adv.* (hübsch) charmingly; delightfully; ~**wäsche** *die* (ugs.) sexy underwear; ~**wort** *das; Pl.* ~**wörter** [1] (Emotionen hervorrufend) emotive word; [2] (Psych.) stimulus word

Rekapitulation *die* (auch Biol.) recapitulation

rekapitulieren *tr. V.* recapitulate

rekeln /ˈreːkl̩n/ *refl. V.* (ugs.) stretch; **sich in der Sonne/im Liegestuhl** ~: stretch out in the sun/in the deckchair

Reklamation /reklamaˈtsi̯oːn/ *die;* ~, ~**en** complaint (**wegen** about); **spätere** ~**[en] ausgeschlossen!** money cannot be refunded after purchase

Reklame /reˈklaːmə/ *die;* ~, ~**n** [1] (Werbung) advertising *no indef. art.*; (Ergebnis) publicity *no indef. art.*; **schlechte** ~: poor advertising/publicity; ~ **für jmdn./etw. machen** promote sb./advertise *or* promote sth. [2] (ugs.: Werbemittel) advert (Brit. coll.); ad (coll.); advertisement; (im Fernsehen, Radio auch) commercial; **nichts als** ~: nothing but adverts/commercials; **die BBC bringt keine** ~: there are no adverts *etc.*/commercials on BBC

Reklame-: ~**rummel** *der* (ugs. abwertend) [publicity] ballyhoo, hype (coll.) (**um** surrounding); ~**sendung** *die* ▸**Werbesendung**; ~**schild** *das* advertising sign; ~**trommel** *die:* *in* **für jmdn./etw. die** ~**trommel rühren** (ugs.) promote sb./advertise *or* promote sth. in a big way; ~**zettel** *der* advertising leaflet

reklamieren

[A] *itr. V.* (sich beschweren) complain; make a complaint

[B] *tr. V.* [1] (beanstanden) complain about, make a complaint about (**bei** to, **wegen** on account of); **reklamierte Güter** goods about which there has been a complaint [2] (beanspruchen) claim; **jmdn. für sich** ~: monopolize sb.; **etw. für sich** ~: claim sth. for oneself

rekognoszieren /rekɔgnɔsˈtsiːrən/ *tr. V.* (österr., schweiz., Milit.) reconnoitre

Rekommandation /rekɔmandaˈtsi̯oːn/ *die;* ~, ~**en** [1] (österr.) recommendation [2] (österr. Postw.) registered letter

rekommandieren *tr. V.* (österr. Postw.) register

rekonstruierbar *Adj.* reconstructible; **leicht/schwer** ~ **sein** be easy/difficult to reconstruct

rekonstruieren *tr. V.* [1] reconstruct [2] (regional: modernisieren) modernize; renovate ‹*building*›

Rekonstruktion *die* [1] reconstruction [2] (regional: Modernisierung) modernization/renovation

Rekonvaleszent /rekɔnvalɛsˈtsɛnt/ *der;* ~**en,** ~**en, Rekonvaleszentin** *die;* ~, ~**nen** convalescent

Rekonvaleszenz /rekɔnvalɛsˈtsɛnts/ *die* ▸ⓘ **S. 439** (Med.) convalescence *no art.*

Rekord /reˈkɔrt/ *der;* ~**[e]s,** ~**e** record; **einen** ~ **aufstellen/innehaben** set up/hold a record

Rekord- record ‹*harvest, temperature, fee*›

Rekorder ▸**Recorder**

Rekord-: ~**halter** *der,* ~**halterin** *die,* ~**inhaber** *der,* ~**inhaberin** *die* record holder; ~**lauf** *der* record-breaking run; ~**leistung** *die* record

Rekordler /reˈkɔrtlɐ/ *der;* ~**s,** ~, **Rekordlerin** *die;* ~, ~**nen** record holder

rekord-, Rekord-: ~**marke** *die* record; ~**tief** *das* record low; all-time low; ~**umsatz** *der* record turnover; ~**verdächtig** (Jargon) [A] *Adj.* ‹*figure, growth, etc.*› which must be a record; [B] *adv.* ~**verdächtig lang/niedrig sein** be long/low enough to be a record; ~**versuch** *der* attempt at a/the record; ~**zeit** *die* record time

Rekrut /reˈkruːt/ *der;* ~**en,** ~**en** (Milit.) recruit

rekrutieren

[A] *refl. V.* **sich aus einem bestimmten Kreis** ~: be drawn from a particular sphere; **sich aus Beamten/Selbstständigen** ~: consist *or* be composed of civil servants/self-employed people

[B] *tr. V.* (Milit. veralt., auch fig.) recruit (**aus** from)

Rekrutierung *die;* ~, ~**en** recruitment; recruiting

Rekrutin *die;* ~, ~**nen** ▸**Rekrut**

Rekta ▸**Rektum**

rektal /rɛkˈtaːl/ (Med.)

[A] *Adj.* rectal

[B] *adv.* rectally

Rektion /rɛkˈtsi̯oːn/ *die;* ~, ~**en** (Grammatik) **die** ~ **einer Präposition** the case governed by a preposition; **nur bei einigen Präpositionen schwankt die** ~: only a few prepositions can take more than one case

Rektor /ˈrɛktɔr/ *der;* ~**s,** ~**en** /-ˈtoːrən/ [1] (Schulleiter) head[master] [2] (Universitäts~) Rector; ≈ Vice-Chancellor (Brit.); (einer Fachhochschule) principal

Rektorat /rɛktoˈraːt/ *das;* ~**[e]s,** ~**e** [1] (Amt, Amtszeit) headship; (an der Universität) Rectorship; ≈ Vice-Chancellorship (Brit.) [2] (Amtszimmer) head[master]'s room *or* office; (an der Universität) Rector's office; ≈ Vice-Chancellor's office (Brit.)

Rektorin *die;* ~, ~**nen** [1] (Schulleiterin) head[-mistress] [2] ▸**Rektor 2**

Rektoskop /rɛktoˈskoːp/ *das;* ~**s,** ~**e** (Med.) proctoscope; rectoscope

Rektoskopie /rɛktoskoˈpiː/ *die;* ~, ~**n** (Med.) proctoscopy

Rektum /ˈrɛktʊm/ *das;* ~**s, Rekta** /ˈrɛkta/ (Anat.) ▸ⓘ **S. 435** rectum

rekultivieren *tr. V.* (Landw.) recultivate

rekurrieren /rekuˈriːrən/ *itr. V.* [1] (geh.: Bezug nehmen) **auf etw.** (*Akk.*) ~: refer back to sth. [2] (österr. Rechtsspr.) **gegen etw.** ~: appeal against sth.

Rekurs *der* [1] (geh.: Bezug) reference (**auf** + *Akk.* to); **auf etw.** (*Akk.*) ~ **nehmen** refer back to sth. [2] (Rechtsspr.) appeal; ~ **einlegen** lodge an appeal

Relais /rəˈlɛː/ *das;* ~ /rəˈlɛː(s)/, ~ /rəˈlɛːs/ (Elektrot.) relay

Relais-: ~**schaltung** *die* (Elektrot.) relay circuit; ~**station** *die* (Elektrot.) relay station

Relation /relaˈtsi̯oːn/ *die;* ~, ~**en** (auch Math.) relation; **in einer/keiner** ~ **zu etw. stehen**

bear a/no relation to sth.

relativ /rela'ti:f/
A *Adj.* relative; *s. auch* **Mehrheit**; **Gehör**
B *adv.* [1] (ziemlich) relatively [2] (vergleichsweise) **~ zu** relative to

relativieren *tr. V.* relativize

Relativierung *die;* **~, ~en** relativization

Relativismus *der;* **~** (Philos.) relativism

relativistisch *Adj.* (auch Philos., Physik) relativistic

Relativität /relativi'tɛ:t/ *die;* **~, ~en** relativity

Relativitäts·theorie *die* (Physik) theory of relativity

Relativ-: ~pronomen *das* (Sprachw.) relative pronoun; **~satz** *der* (Sprachw.) relative clause

Relaxans /re'laksans/ *das;* **~, Relaxantien** (Med.) relaxant

relaxed /ri'lɛkst/ *Adj.* (salopp) laid-back (coll.)

Relegation /relega'tsi̯o:n/ *die;* **~, ~en** expulsion

relegieren /rele'gi:rən/ *tr. V.* expel

relevant /rele'vant/ *Adj.* relevant (**für** to)

Relevanz *die;* **~:** relevance (**für** to)

Relief /re'li̯ɛf/ *das;* **~s, ~s** *od.* **~e** (bild. Kunst; Geogr.) relief

relief-, Relief-: ~artig **A** *Adj.* raised in relief *postpos.*; **B** *adv.* **~artig erhoben** raised in relief *postpos.*; **~druck** *der; Pl.* **~~e** [1] (Verfahren) relief printing; [2] (Erzeugnis) relief print; **~karte** *die* relief map

Religion /reli'gi̯o:n/ *die;* **~, ~en** [1] (auch fig.) religion [2] (Unterrichtsfach) religious instruction *or* education; RI; RE

religions-, Religions-: ~ausübung *die* practice of religion; **freie ~ausübung** freedom to practise one's religion; **~bekenntnis** *das* religion; denomination; [religious] confession; **~freiheit** *die* religious freedom; **~friede** *der* religious peace; **~gemeinschaft** *die* denomination; **~geschichte** *die* history of religion; **~krieg** *der* religious war; **~lehre** *die* ▸ **Religion 2**; **~lehrer** *der,* **~lehrerin** *die* religious instruction *or* education teacher; RI *or* RE teacher; **~los** *Adj.* [1] ‹*person*› who has no religious beliefs; **ich bin ~los** I'm not religious; [2] (gottlos) irreligious; **~philosophie** *die* philosophy of religion; **~stifter** *der,* **~stifterin** *die* founder of a/the religion; **~streit** *der* religious dispute; **~stunde** *die* religious instruction *or* education lesson; RI *or* RE lesson; **~unterricht** *der* ▸ **Religion 2**; *s. auch* **Englischunterricht**; **~wissenschaft** *die* religious studies *pl., no art.*; **vergleichende ~wissenschaft** comparative religion; **~wissenschaftler** *der,* **~wissenschaftlerin** *die* religious scholar; **~zugehörigkeit** *die* religion; religious confession; **~zwang** *der: compulsion to belong to a particular denomination*

religiös /reli'gi̯ø:s/
A *Adj.* religious
B *adv.* in a religious manner; **~ erzogen werden** have *or* receive a religious upbringing; **~ leben** live a religious life

Religiosität /religi̯ozi'tɛ:t/ *die;* **~:** religiousness

Relikt /re'lɪkt/ *das;* **~[e], ~e** [1] (auch Sprachw.) relic [2] (Biol.) relict; relic

Reling /'re:lɪŋ/ *die;* **~, ~s** *od.* **~e** (Seew.) [deck] rail

Reliquie /re'li:kvi̯ə/ *die;* **~, ~n** (Rel., bes. kath. Kirche) relic

Reliquien·schrein *der* reliquary

Rembours·geschäft /rã'bu:ɐ̯-/ *das* (Finanzw.) documentary credit trading; **ein ~:** a documentary credit transaction

Remigrant /remi'grant/ *der;* **~en, ~en, Remigrantin** *die;* **~, ~nen** returning emigrant; (nach der Rückkehr) returned emigrant; **türkische ~en** returning/returned Turkish emigrants

remilitarisieren *tr. V.* remilitarize

Remilitarisierung *die* remilitarization

Reminiszenz /reminɪs'tsɛnts/ *die;* **~, ~en** (geh.) reminiscence (**an** + *Akk.* of)

remis /rə'mi:/ *indekl. Adj.* (bes. Schach) drawn; **~ enden/ausgehen** end in a draw; **sie trennten sich ~:** they held each other to a draw; **~ spielen** draw

Remis *das;* **~** /rə'mi:(s)/, **~** /rə'mi:s/ *od.* **~en** (bes. Schach) draw; **~ anbieten** offer a draw

Remise /re'mi:zə/ *die;* **~, ~n** [1] (veralt.) coach house; (Geräteschuppen) shed [2] (Schach) ▸ **Remis**

Remission *die* [1] (Buchw.) return [2] (Med.) remission

Remittende /remɪ'tɛndə/ *die;* **~, ~n** (Buchw.) return

Remittent /remɪ'tɛnt/ *der;* **~en, ~en, Remittentin** *die;* **~, ~nen** (Finanzw.) payee

remittieren /remɪ'ti:rən/
A *tr. V.* (Buchw.) return
B *itr. V.* (Med.) remit

Remmidemmi /rɛmi'dɛmi/ *das;* **~** (ugs.) row (coll.); racket; **~ machen** make a row (coll.) *or* racket

Remoulade /remu'la:də/ *die;* **~, ~n, Remouladen·soße** *die* remoulade

Rempelei *die;* **~, ~en** (ugs.) pushing and shoving; jostling; (Sport) pushing; **hören Sie doch mit der ~ auf!** stop pushing and shoving!

rempeln /'rɛmpl̩n/ (ugs.) push; shove; jostle; (Sport) push

REM-Phase /'rɛm-/ *die* (fachspr.) REM phase [of sleep]

Rempler *der;* **~s, ~** (ugs.) **jmdm. einen ~ geben** push against sb.

REM-Schlaf /'rɛm-/ *der* (fachspr.) REM sleep

Remuneration /remunera'tsi̯o:n/ *die;* **~, ~en** (österr., sonst veralt.) compensation

Ren /rɛn/ *das;* **~s, ~s** *od.* **~e** reindeer

Renaissance /rənɛ'sã:s/ *die;* **~, ~n** [1] Renaissance [2] (Wiederaufleben) revival; **eine ~ erleben** enjoy a renaissance

Renaissance·musik *die* Renaissance music

Rendezvous /rãde'vu:/ *das;* **~** /-'vu:(s)/, **~** /'rãde'vu:s/ rendezvous

Rendezvous·manöver *das* (Raumf.) rendezvous manoeuvre

Rendite /rɛn'di:tə/ *die;* **~, ~n** (Wirtsch.) [annual] yield *or* return

Rendite·objekt *das* investment property

rendite·trächtig
A *Adj.* profitable; ‹*share, stock*› with a good yield; **~/wenig ~ sein** give a good/poor return
B *adv.* profitably

Renegat /rene'ga:t/ *der;* **~en, ~en** (abwertend) renegade

Renegatentum *das;* **~s** (abwertend) apostasy; **jmdm. ~ vorwerfen** accuse sb. of being a renegade

Renegatin *die;* **~, ~nen** ▸ **Renegat**

Reneklode /re:nə'klo:də/ *die;* **~, ~n** greengage

Renette /re'nɛtə/ *die;* **~, ~n** rennet

renitent /reni'tɛnt/
A *Adj.* refractory
B *adv.* refractorily

Renitenz /reni'tɛnts/ *die;* **~:** refractoriness

Renn-: ~auto *das* racing car; **~bahn** *die* (Sport) racetrack; (für Pferde) racecourse; racetrack; **~boot** *das* (Motorboot) power boat; (Segelboot) racing yacht; (Ruderboot) racing shell

rennen /'rɛnən/
A *unr. itr. V.; mit sein* [1] run; **um die Wette ~:** have a race; race each other; **wütend aus dem Zimmer ~:** storm out of the room; **in sein Verderben/den Tod ~** (fig.) rush headlong to one's doom/hasten to one's death; **meine Uhr rennt wieder** (fig. ugs.) my watch is fast again [2] (ugs. abwertend: hingehen) run [off]; **dauernd ins Kino/zur Polizei ~:** be always going to the cinema/running to the police [3] (stoßen an) **an/gegen jmdn./etw. ~:** run *or* bang into sb./sth.; **mit dem Kopf an** *od.* **gegen etw.** (*Akk.*) **~:** bang one's head against *or* on sth.
B *unr. tr. V.* [1] (sich zuziehen) **sich** (*Dat.*) **an etw.** (*Dat.*) **ein Loch in den Kopf/ins Knie ~:** run *or* bang into sth. and hurt one's head/knee [2] (ugs.: stoßen) **jmdm. etw. in das Bein/die Rippen ~:** run sth. into sb.'s leg/ribs

Rennen *das;* **~s, ~:** running; (Pferde~, Auto~) racing; (einzelner Wettbewerb) race; **zum ~ gehen** (Pferde~) go to the races; (Auto~) go to the racing; **gut im ~ liegen** be well placed; (fig.) be one of the front runners; **das ~ ist gelaufen** the race is over *or* has been run; (fig.) it's all over; **ein totes ~** (Sport) a dead heat; **das ~ machen** (ugs.) win; **das ~ aufgeben** give up

Renner *der;* **~s, ~** [1] (ugs.: Verkaufserfolg) big seller [2] (Pferd) racer

Rennerei *die;* **~, ~en** (ugs.) running around; **du glaubst nicht, was das für eine ~ war** you wouldn't believe how much running *or* chasing around it involved; **die ~ mit den Weihnachtsgeschenken** running around getting the Christmas presents; **das Schlimmste ist die ewige ~ zum Klo** the worst thing is having to run to the loo (Brit. coll.) *or* (Amer. coll.) john all the time

Renn-: ~fahrer *der,* **~fahrerin** *die* ▸ **i S. 113** racing driver; (Radsport) racing cyclist; (Motorradsport) racing motorcyclist; **~jacht** *die* racing yacht; **~leitung** *die* [1] (das Leiten) race organization; [2] (Personen) race organizers *pl.*; **~lenker** *der* drop[ped] handlebars *pl.*; **~maschine** *die* (Jargon) racing bike; **~pferd** *das* racehorse; **~platz** *der* ▸ **~bahn**; **~rad** *das* racing cycle; **~rodel** *der* ▸ **~schlitten**; **~rodeln** *das* luge racing; **im ~rodeln** in the luge; **~schlitten** *der* luge; **~sport** *der* racing *no art.*; **~stall** *der* [1] racing stable; (die Pferde allein) string; [2] (Mannschaft) team; **~strecke** *die* (**~bahn**) racetrack; (Distanz) race distance; **~wagen** *der* racing car

Renommee /renɔ'me:/ *das;* **~s, ~s** (geh.) reputation

renommieren /renɔ'mi:rən/ *itr. V.* show off; **mit etw. ~:** brag about sth.; **mit seinem Titel/Wissen ~:** flaunt one's title/show off *or* flaunt one's knowledge

Renommier-: ~stück *das:* **das ~stück des Museums** the museum's showpiece [exhibit]; **ihr ~stück, das dreireihige Perlen hat** her finest piece of jewelry with its three rows of pearls; **~sucht** *die* (abwertend) urge to show off

renommiert *Adj.* renowned (**wegen** for)

renovieren /reno'vi:rən/ *tr. V.* renovate; redecorate ‹*room, flat*›

Renovierung *die;* **~, ~en** renovation; (eines Zimmers, einer Wohnung) redecoration

rentabel /rɛn'ta:bl̩/
A *Adj.* profitable; **~ sein** be profitable; ‹*equipment, machinery*› pay its way
B *adv.* profitably

Rentabilität /rɛntabili'tɛ:t/ *die;* **~** (bes. Wirtsch.) profitability; (von Geräten usw.) cost-effectiveness

Rentabilitäts·prüfung *die* (Wirtsch.) profitability analysis

Rente /'rɛntə/ *die;* **~, ~n** [1] pension; **auf** *od.* **in ~ gehen** (ugs.) retire; **auf** *od.* **in ~ sein** (ugs.) be retired; **jmdn. auf ~ setzen** (ugs.) pension sb. off [2] (Kapitalertrag) annuity

renten-, Renten-: ~alter *das* pensionable age *no art.*; **im ~alter sein** *od.* **stehen** be of pensionable age; **~anpassung** *die* index-linking of pensions (*to the average national wage*); **~anspruch** *der* pension entitlement; **~berechtigt** *Adj.* entitled to a pension *postpos.*; **~beitrag** *der* pension contribution; **~empfänger** *der,* **~empfängerin** *die* pensioner; **~erhöhung** *die* pension increase; **~fonds** *der* (Finanzw.) fixed income fund; **~kasse** *die* [state] pension fund; **~markt** *der* (Börsenw.) fixed securities market; **~papier** *das* (Finanzw.) fixed interest security; **~pflichtig** *Adj.* responsible for providing a pension *postpos.*; **~system** *die* pension system; **~versicherung** *die* [1] (Versicherung) pension scheme; **eine private**

r

~versicherung abschließen join a private pension scheme; **2** (Behörde) *state pension authority*

Rentenversicherung

This is the compulsory state pension insurance in Germany. All employees have to pay into it as part of their **Sozialabgaben**, with employers and the state also making a contribution. The amount of the German state pension depends on the contributions made by the individual, with allowances for years spent as a student or carer.

Ren·tier[1] *das* reindeer

Rentier[2] /rɛnˈtie:/ *der;* ~s, ~s **1** (veralt.: mit Vermögen) man with a private income **2** (selten: Rentner) pensioner

rentieren /rɛnˈti:rən/ *refl. V.* be profitable; ‹*equipment, machinery*› pay its way; ‹*effort, visit, etc.*› be worth while; **eine Geschirrspülmaschine rentiert sich für uns nicht** it's not worth our having *or* not worth our while to have a dishwasher

rentierlich
A *Adj.* profitable.
B *adv.* profitably

Rentner /ˈrɛntnɐ/ *der;* ~s, ~, **Rentnerin** *die;* ~, ~nen pensioner

Rentner-: **~dasein** *das* life of a pensioner; **~paradies** *das* pensioners' paradise

Reorganisation *die* reorganization

reorganisieren *tr. V.* reorganize

Reorganisierung *die* reorganization

reparabel /repaˈra:bl̩/ *Adj.* repairable; **nicht mehr ~ sein** be no longer repairable; be beyond repair; **die Ehe ist nicht mehr ~** (fig.) the marriage has failed irretrievably

Reparationen /reparaˈtsi̯o:nən/ *Pl.* (Politik) reparations; **~ leisten** *od.* **zahlen** make *or* pay reparations

Reparations·zahlung *die* reparation payment

Reparatur /reparaˈtu:ɐ̯/ *die;* ~, ~en repair (**an** + *Dat.* to); **in ~ sein** be being repaired; **etw. in ~ geben** take sth. in to have it repaired

reparatur-, Reparatur-: **~anfällig** *Adj.* prone to break down *postpos.*; **~arbeit** *die* repair work; **~en** repair work *sing.*; repairs; **~bedürftig** *Adj.* ‹*device, appliance, vehicle, etc.*› [which is] in need of repair; **~bedürftig sein** be in need of repair; need repairing; **~kosten** *Pl.* repair costs; **die ~kosten für das Auto** the cost of repairing the car; **~werkstatt** *die* repair [work]shop; (für Autos) garage

reparieren /repaˈri:rən/ *tr. V.* repair; mend; (bei komplexeren Geräten, größeren Schäden) repair; **einen Fehler ~** (fig.) put right an error

repatriieren /repatriˈi:rən/ *tr. V.* (Politik, Rechtsw.) **1** (wieder einbürgern) **jmdn. ~:** restore sb.'s citizenship **2** (wieder heimführen) repatriate

Repatriierung *die;* ~, ~en **1** (Wiedereinbürgerung) **jmds. ~:** the restoration of sb.'s citizenship **2** (Heimführung) repatriation

Repertoire /repɛrˈto̯a:ɐ̯/ *das;* ~s, ~s (auch fig.) repertoire

Repertoire·stück *das* stock play

Repertorium /repɛrˈto:ri̯ʊm/ *das;* ~s, **Repertorien** reference work

repetieren /repeˈti:rən/ *tr. V.* **1** (einüben) learn by repetition **2** (veralt.: wiederholen) repeat ‹*year*›

Repetier-: **~gewehr** *das* repeating rifle; repeater; **~uhr** *die* repeating watch; repeater

Repetitor /repeˈti:tɔr/ *der;* ~s, ~en /-tiˈto:rən/, **Repetitorin** *die;* ~, ~nen **1** (für Studenten) *private tutor who coaches (esp. law) students for examinations* **2** (Musik) répétiteur

Replik /reˈpli:k/ *die;* ~, ~en **1** (geh.: Erwiderung) reply; rejoinder **2** (Rechtsw.) reply; replication **3** (Kunst) replica

Replikat /repliˈka:t/ *das;* ~[e]s, ~e (bes. Kunstwiss.) replica

Report /reˈpɔrt/ *der;* ~[e]s, ~e **1** (Bericht) report **2** (Finanzw.) premium

Reportage /repɔrˈta:ʒə/ *die;* ~, ~n report

Reporter /reˈpɔrtɐ/ *der;* ~s, ~, **Reporterin** *die;* ~, ~nen ▸ **i** S. 113 reporter; *s. auch* **-in**

repräsentabel /reprɛzɛnˈta:bl̩/
A *Adj.* imposing
B *adv.* imposingly

Repräsentant /reprɛzɛnˈtant/ *der;* ~en, ~en representative

Repräsentanten·haus *das* House of Representatives

Repräsentantin *die;* ~, ~nen representative; *s. auch* **-in**

Repräsentanz /reprɛzɛnˈtants/ *die;* ~, ~en **1** (Interessenvertretung) representation **2** (Wirtsch.) branch

Repräsentation *die;* ~, ~en **1** (bes. Politik) representation **2** (das Typischsein) representativeness **3** (Vertretung in der Öffentlichkeit) **die Rolle des Präsidenten besteht vorwiegend in der ~:** the role of the President is primarily that of official figurehead; **die wichtigste Pflicht einer Diplomatenfrau ist die ~:** the most important duty of a diplomat's wife is attending official and social functions **4** (aufwendiger Lebensstil) **etw. dient nur der ~:** sth. is for prestige purposes only

repräsentativ /reprɛzɛntaˈti:f/
A *Adj.* **1** (auch Politik) representative; **für etw. ~ sein** be representative of sth. **2** (ansehnlich) imposing; (mit hohem Prestigewert) prestigious; **eine ~e Erscheinung** a man/woman of distinguished *or* imposing appearance
B *adv.* **1** (bes. Politik) representatively; **ein ~ strukturiertes politisches System** a political system with a representative structure **2** (luxuriös) imposingly

Repräsentativ·umfrage *die* (Statistik) representative survey

repräsentieren /reprɛzɛnˈti:rən/
A *tr. V.* represent
B *itr. V.* (Repräsentation betreiben) attend official and social functions

Repressalie /reprɛˈsa:li̯ə/ *die;* ~, ~n repressive measure; (Vergeltungsmaßnahme) reprisal; **~n anwenden** *od.* **ergreifen** resort to repressive measures/take reprisals

Repression /reprɛˈsi̯o:n/ *die;* ~, ~en repression

repressions·frei
A *Adj.* free of repression *postpos*
B *adv.* **~ erzogen werden** have an upbringing that is/was free of repression

repressiv /reprɛˈsi:f/
A *Adj.* repressive
B *adv.* repressively

Reprint /reˈprɪnt/ *der;* ~s, ~s (Buchw.) reprint

Reprise *die* **1** (Theater) revival; (Film) re-run **2** (einer Schallplatte) re-issue **3** (Musik) reprise **4** (Börsenw.) recovery

reprivatisieren *tr. V.* (Wirtsch., Politik) re-privatize

Reprivatisierung *die* (Wirtsch., Politik) re-privatization

Repro /ˈre:pro/ *die;* ~, ~s (Druckw.) repro

Reproduktion *die* reproduction

Reproduktions-: **~bedingungen** *Pl.* (polit. Ökonomie) conditions of reproduction; **~kamera** *die* (Druckw.) process camera; **~kosten** *Pl.* (Wirtsch.) reproduction costs; **~medizin** *die* reproductive medicine; **~mediziner** *der,* **~medizinerin** *die* specialist in reproductive medicine; **~prozess**, ***~prozeß** *der* (polit. Ökonomie) reproduction process; **~verfahren** *das* (Druckw.) reproduction process

reproduzierbar
A *Adj.* reproducible.
B *adv.* in a reproducible way

Reproduzierbarkeit *die;* ~, ~en reproducibility

reproduzieren *tr. V.* (auch Druckw., polit. Ökonomie) reproduce

Repro-: **~graphie** *die* (Druckw.) **1** (Verfahren) reprography *no art.*; **2** (Erzeugnis) reproduction; **~technik** /ˈ---/ *die* reproduction technology *no art.*

Reps /rɛps/ *Pl.* (ugs.) Republicans

Reptil /rɛpˈti:l/ *das;* ~s, ~ien /rɛpˈti:li̯ən/ reptile

Reptilien·fonds *der* (Politik) slush fund

Republik /repuˈbli:k/ *die;* ~, ~en republic

Republikaner /republiˈka:nɐ/ *der;* ~s, ~, **Republikanerin** *die;* ~, ~nen **1** republican **2** (Angehörige[r] der republikanischen Partei) Republican

Die Republikaner

This ultra-right-wing party was founded in 1983 and quickly became notorious for its xenophobic and nationalistic aims. After some success in the early 90s it now has very little support and is not represented in the Bundestag.

republikanisch
A *Adj.* **1** republican **2** (eine ~e Partei betreffend) Republican
B *adv.* **1** **ein ~ aufgebauter Staat** a state with a republican structure **2** **~ wählen** vote Republican

republik-, Republik-: **~flucht** *die* (DDR) illegal emigration; **~flüchtling** *der* (DDR) illegal emigrant; **~weit** **A** *Adj.* throughout the republic *postpos.*; (in ganz Deutschland) all over Germany; **B** *adv.* throughout the republic; (in ganz Deutschland) all over Germany

Repulsions·motor /repʊlˈzi̯o:ns-/ *der* (Technik) repulsion motor

repulsiv /repʊlˈzi:f/ *Adj.* (Physik) repulsive

Repunze /reˈpʊntsə/ *die;* ~, ~n hallmark

Reputation /reputaˈtsi̯o:n/ *die;* ~, ~en reputation; standing

reputierlich *Adj.* (veralt.) upright; decent

Requiem /ˈre:kvi̯ɛm/ *das;* ~s, ~s requiem

requirieren /rekviˈri:rən/ *tr. V.* (veralt.) requisition

Requisit /rekviˈzi:t/ *das;* ~[e]s, ~en **1** (Theater) prop (coll.); property **2** (fig.) requisite

Requisiten·kammer *die* (Theater) prop store *or* room (coll.); property store *or* room

Requisiteur /rekviziˈtø:ɐ̯/ *der;* ~s, ~e (Theater) prop man (coll.); property man

Requisiteurin *die;* ~, ~nen (Theater) prop woman (coll.); property woman

Requisition *die;* ~, en (veralt.) requisition

resch /rɛʃ/ *Adj.* (bayr., österr.) **1** (knusprig) crusty ‹*rolls, bread*›; crisp ‹*fried potatoes, batter*› **2** (ugs.: lebhaft) vivacious

Reseda /reˈze:da/ *die;* ~, ~s, **Resede** *die;* ~, ~n Reseda; (Garten~) mignonette

Reservat /rezɛrˈva:t/ *das;* ~[e]s, ~e **1** (Tier~) reserve **2** (für Volksstämme) reservation

Reserve /reˈzɛrvə/ *die;* ~, ~n **1** (Vorrat) reserve (**an** + *Dat.* of); **etw. in ~ haben** have sth. in reserve; **etw. in ~ halten** keep *or* hold sth. in reserve; *s. auch* **eisern A 4**; **still A 6** **2** (Milit.) reserves *pl.*; **Offizier der ~:** reserve officer **3** (Sport) reserves *pl.* **4** (Zurückhaltung) reserve; **jmdn. aus der ~ [heraus]locken** (ugs.) bring sb. out of his/her shell **5** (Bedenken) reservation

Reserve-: **~armee** *die* reserve army; (fig.) reserve force; **~bank** *die; Pl.* **~bänke** (Sport) substitutes' bench; **~fonds** *der* (Wirtsch.) reserve [fund]; **~frau** *die* ▸ **~mann**; **~kanister** *der* spare [petrol (Brit.) *or* (Amer.) gasoline] can; **~mann** *der; Pl.* **~männer** *od.* **~leute** replacement; (Sport) substitute; reserve; **~offizier** *der* reserve officer; **~rad** *das* spare wheel; **~reifen** *der* spare tyre; **~schlüssel** *der* spare key; **~spieler** *der,* **~spielerin** *die* (Sport) substitute; reserve; **~tank** *der* reserve [fuel] tank; **~truppe** *die* (Milit.) reserve troops *pl.*; **~übung** *die* (Milit.) reservists' exercise

reservieren *tr. V.* reserve

r

reserviert
A *Adj.* reserved
B *adv.* in a reserved way

Reserviertheit *die;* ~: reserve

Reservierung *die;* ~, ~**en** reservation

Reservist *der;* ~**en**, ~**en** (Milit.) reservist; (Sportjargon) substitute; reserve

Reservisten·übung *die* (Milit.) reservists' exercise

Reservoir /rezɛr'vo̯aːɐ̯/ *das;* ~**s**, ~**e** (auch fig.) reservoir (**an** + *Dat.* of)

Residenz /rezi'dɛnts/ *die;* ~, ~**en** 1 (Wohnsitz) residence 2 (Hauptstadt) [royal] capital

Residenz-: ~**pflicht** *die* 1 (von Beamten) obligation to live within a reasonable distance of one's place of work; 2 (ev. u. kath. Kirche) obligation [on a clergyman] to live in the accommodation provided with the post; ~**stadt** *die* ▸ **Residenz 2**

residieren /rezi'diːrən/ *itr. V.* reside

Resignation /rezɪgna'tsi̯oːn/ *die;* ~, ~**en** resignation; **in** ~ **versinken** become resigned

resignativ /rezɪgna'tiːf/ *Adj.* ‹*mood, atmosphere*› of resignation

resignieren /rezɪ'gniːrən/ *itr. V.* give up

resigniert
A *Adj.* resigned
B *adv.* resignedly

Resistance /rezis'tãːs/ *die;* ~ (hist.) Resistance

resistent /rezɪs'tɛnt/ *Adj.* (Biol., Med.) resistant (**gegen** to)

Resistenz /rezɪs'tɛnts/ *die;* ~, ~**en** (auch Biol., Med.) resistance (**gegen** to)

resolut /rezo'luːt/
A *Adj.* resolute
B *adv.* resolutely

Resolutheit *die;* ~: resoluteness

Resolution /rezolu'tsi̯oːn/ *die;* ~, ~**en** resolution

Resonanz /rezo'nants/ *die;* ~, ~**en** 1 (Physik, Musik) resonance 2 (Reaktion) response (**auf** + *Akk.* to); ~/**keine** ~ **finden**, **auf** ~/**auf keine** ~ **stoßen** meet with a/no response

Resonanz-: ~**boden** *der* (Musik) sounding board; soundboard; ~**körper** *der* (Musik) soundbox

Resopal Ⓦⓩ /rezo'paːl/ *das;* ~**s** ≈ melamine

resorbieren /rezɔr'biːrən/ *tr. V.* (Biol., Med.) absorb

Resorption /rezɔrp'tsi̯oːn/ *die;* ~, ~**en** (Biol., Med.) absorption

resozialisierbar *Adj.* (bes. Rechtsspr.) able to be reintegrated into society *postpos.*

resozialisieren *tr. V.* (bes. Rechtsspr.) reintegrate into society

Resozialisierung *die;* ~, ~**en** (bes. Rechtsspr.) reintegration into society

Respekt /re'spɛkt/ *der;* ~**[e]s** 1 (Achtung) respect; ~ **vor jmdm./etw. haben** have respect for sb./sth.; **jmdm.** ~ **einflößen** *od.* **abnötigen** command sb.'s respect; **bei allem** ~: with all due respect (**vor** + *Dat.* to); **allen** ~!, ~, ~! good for you!; well done! 2 (Furcht) **jmdm.** ~ **einflößen** intimidate sb.; **vor jmdm./etw. [größten]** ~ **haben** be [much] in awe of sb./sth.; **sich** (*Dat.*) **den nötigen** ~ **verschaffen** command proper respect 3 (Schrift- u. Buchw., Kunstwiss.) margin

respektabel /respɛk'taːbl̩/
A *Adj.* respectable
B *adv.* respectably

respekt·einflößend *Adj.* impressive; fearsome ‹*claws, teeth*›

respektieren *tr. V.* 1 respect 2 (Finanzw.) honour ‹*bill of exchange etc.*›

respektierlich *Adj.* (veralt.) respectable

respektive /rɛspɛk'tiːvə/ *Konj.* (geh.) 1 (oder) or 2 (oder vielmehr) or rather; (oder genauer gesagt) or more precisely 3 (und im anderen Fall) **grün** ~ **blau** green and blue respectively

respekt·los
A *Adj.* disrespectful
B *adv.* disrespectfully

Respektlosigkeit *die;* ~, ~**en** 1 (Haltung) disrespectfulness; lack of respect 2 (Äußerung) disrespectful remark; (Handlung) impertinence

Respekts·person *die* person who commands/commanded respect

respekt·voll
A *Adj.* respectful
B *adv.* respectfully

Respiration /respira'tsi̯oːn/ *die;* ~ (Med.) respiration

Respirator /rɛspi'raːtɔr/ *der;* ~**s**, ~**en** /-ra'toːrən/ (Med.) respirator

respirieren /rɛspi'riːrən/ *itr. V.* (Med.) respire

Ressentiment /rɛsãti'mãː/ *das;* ~**s**, ~**s** 1 (geh.: Abneigung) antipathy (**gegen** towards) 2 (Psych.) resentment

Ressort /rɛ'soːɐ̯/ *das;* ~**s**, ~**s** area of responsibility; (Abteilung) department; **in jmds.** ~ **fallen** come within sb.'s area of responsibility; **das Abwaschen ist mein** ~ (scherzh.) the washing-up is my department

Ressort-: ~**chef** *der*, ~**chefin** *die*, ~**leiter** *der*, ~**leiterin** *die* head of department; ~**minister** *der*, ~**ministerin** *die* departmental minister

Ressource /rɛ'sʊrsə/ *die;* ~, ~**n** 1 resource 2 *Pl.* (Ersparnisse) resources

Rest /rɛst/ *der;* ~**[e]s**, ~**e** 1 rest; (~betrag) rest; balance; ~**e** (historische ~e, Ruinen, Leiche) remains; (einer Kultur) relics; **jmdm./einer Sache den** ~ **geben** (ugs.) finish sb./sth. off; **das ist der** ~ **von meinem Vermögen** this is all that's left of my fortune; **ein** ~ **von Farbe/Leim/Käse/Wein ist noch da** there's still a little bit of paint/glue/cheese/a little bit *or* a drop of wine left; **bis auf einen** ~ **ist es alles verbraucht** it's all been used up apart from a little bit; **der letzte** ~: the last bit; **ein trauriger** ~ **von Käse/Kuchen** a few pathetic scraps *pl.* of cheese/cake; **morgen gibt es** ~**e** tomorrow we're having leftovers; ~ **machen** (nordd.) finish up what's left; **machen Sie doch** ~ **mit dem Fleisch** (nordd.) do finish up the meat; **das ist der** ~ **vom Schützenfest** (ugs.) that's all there is left; **hast du den letzten** ~ **von Verstand verloren?** have you lost all the sense you had left?; **der** ~ **ist Schweigen** (man schweigt besser darüber) the less said, the better; (das Weitere ist unbekannt) the rest is a mystery 2 (Endstück) remnant 3 (Math.) remainder; **20 durch 6 ist 3,** ~ **2** 20 divided by 6 is 3 with *or* and 2 left over

Rest-: ~**alkohol** *der* residual alcohol; ~**auflage** *die* remaindered stock

Restaurant /rɛsto'rãː/ *das;* ~**s**, ~**s** restaurant

Restaurant·besuch *der* visit to a/the restaurant

Restauration /restaura'tsi̯oːn/ *die;* ~, ~**en** 1 (auch Politik) restoration 2 (hist.) Restoration 3 (österr., sonst veralt.) restaurant

Restaurations-: ~**arbeit** *die* restoration work; ~**arbeiten** restoration work *sing.*; ~**betrieb** *der* restaurant; ~**zeit** *die* restoration; (hist.) Restoration

restaurativ /restaura'tiːf/
A *Adj.* 1 (Geschichte, Politik) ‹*efforts*› to restore the old order; ‹*phase, time*› in which the old order is/was restored; ‹*policies*› aimed at restoring the old order 2 (das Restaurieren betreffend) restorative; **eine** ~**e Meisterleistung** a masterpiece of restoration
B *adv.* (das Restaurieren betreffend) **etw.** ~ **aufarbeiten** restore sth.; **etw.** ~ **retten** save sth. by restoration

Restaurator /restau̯'raːtɔr/ *der;* ~**s**, ~**en** /-ra'toːrən/, **Restauratorin** *die;* ~, ~**nen** restorer

restaurieren /restau̯'riːrən/
A *tr. V.* restore
B *refl. V.* (ugs. scherzh.: sein Äußeres herrichten) make oneself presentable

Restaurierung *die;* ~, ~**en** restoration

Rest-: ~**bestand** *der* remaining stock; (an Büchern) remaindered stock; ~**betrag** *der* balance; amount *or* sum remaining

Reste-: ~**essen** *das* (fam.) leftovers *pl.*; ~**verkauf** *der* remnants sale; ~**verwertung** *die* making use of leftovers

restituieren /restitu'iːrən/ *tr. V.* (bes. Rechtsw.) 1 (aufheben) set aside ‹*judgement, decision*› 2 (erstatten) **etw.** ~: make restitution for sth.

Restitution /restitu'tsi̯oːn/ *die;* ~, ~**en** 1 (bes. Rechtsw.: Wiederherstellung) restitution 2 (Rechtsw.: Aufhebung) setting aside 3 (Biol.) regeneration

Restitutions·klage *die* (Rechtsw.) action for a retrial

restlich *Adj.* remaining; **die** ~**en** the rest

rest·los
A *Adj.* complete; total
B *adv.* completely; totally; ~ **verzweifelt sein** be in complete *or* total despair; **alles** ~ **aufessen** eat every last morsel; ~ **ausverkauft sein** be completely sold out

Rest-: ~**müll** *der* general waste; non-recyclable waste; ~**posten** *der* (Kaufmannsspr.) remaining stock *no indef. art.*

Restmüll
▸ Recycling

Restriktion /restrɪk'tsi̯oːn/ *die;* ~, ~**en** (auch Sprachw.) restriction

restriktiv /restrɪk'tiːf/
A *Adj.* (auch Sprachw.) restrictive
B *adv.* restrictively; **sich** ~ **auf etw.** (*Akk.*) **auswirken** have a restrictive effect on sth.

restringieren /restrɪŋ'giːrən/ *tr. V.* (Sprachw.) **restringierter Kode** restricted code

Rest-: ~**strafe** *die* remainder of a/the/one's sentence; ~**summe** *die* amount remaining; (von Geld) balance; ~**zahlung** *die* payment of the balance; **eine** ~**zahlung von 500 Euro leisten** pay off the balance of 500 euros

Resultante /rezʊl'tantə/ *die;* ~, ~**n** (Physik) resultant

Resultat /rezʊl'taːt/ *das;* ~**[e]s**, ~**e** result; **zum** ~ **kommen, dass ...** come to the conclusion that ...

resultieren /rezʊl'tiːrən/ *itr. V.* result (**aus** from); **daraus resultiert, dass ...** the result *or* upshot of this is that ...

Resultierende *die; adj. Dekl.* (Physik) resultant

Resümee /rezʏ'meː/ *das;* ~**s**, ~**s** résumé

resümieren /rezʏ'miːrən/
A *tr. V.* **etw.** ~: summarize sth.; give a résumé of sth.
B *itr. V.* sum up

retardieren /retar'diːrən/ *tr. V.* retard; ~**des Moment** (Literaturw.) retardation

retirieren /reti'riːrən/ *itr. V.* (Milit.) retreat; (geh.: sich zurückziehen) retire

Retorte /re'tɔrtə/ *die;* ~, ~**n** (Chemie) retort; **aus der** ~ (ugs., oft abwertend) artificial; **ein Baby aus der** ~: a test-tube baby (coll.)

Retorten·baby *das* (ugs.) test-tube baby (coll.)

retour /re'tuːɐ̯/ *Adv.* (bes. südd., österr., schweiz.) back; **1,50 Euro** ~: you get 1.50 euros back

Retour-: ~**fahr·karte** *die* (österr.) return ticket; ~**gang** *der* (österr.) reverse gear; ~**kutsche** *die* (ugs.) tit-for-tat response

retournieren /retʊr'niːrən/
A *tr. V.* return
B *itr. V.* (Sport, bes. Tennis) make a return; return the ball

retro /'reːtro/ *Adj.* retro

retrograd /retro'graːt/ *Adj.* (Med.) ~**e Amnesie** retroactive *or* retrograde amnesia

Retro·look *der* retro look; **im** ~: with the retro look; **Jacken im** ~: retro-look jackets

Retrospektive /retrospɛk'tiːvə/ *die;* ~, ~**n** 1 (Rückblick) retrospective view; **in der** ~: in retrospect 2 (Ausstellung) retrospective

retten /'rɛtn̩/
A *tr. V.* save; rescue; (vor Gefahr) save; rescue; (befreien) rescue; **jmdm. das Leben** ~: save sb.'s life; **jmdn. aus der Gefahr** ~: save sb. from danger; **jmdn. vor jmdm./etw.** ~: save sb. from sb./sth.; **jmdm. kommt die** ~**de Idee** sb. sees the perfect answer; **das** ~**de Ufer erreichen** reach the safety of the shore; **versuchen**

r

zu ~, was zu ~ ist try to save what can be saved; **ist er noch zu ~?** (ugs. fig.) has he gone [completely] round the bend? (coll.); **das alte Haus/der Patient ist nicht mehr zu ~:** the old house is past saving/the patient is beyond help; **nicht mehr zu ~ sein** (ugs.) be a hopeless case; **seine Habe über den Krieg ~:** manage to keep one's possessions through the war
[B] *refl. V.* (fliehen) escape (**aus** from); **sich vor etw.** (*Dat.*) **~:** escape [from] sth.; **sich ans Ufer ~:** manage to reach the bank; **der Pilot rettete sich mit dem Schleudersitz** the pilot saved himself by using the ejector seat; **rette sich, wer kann!** [it's] every man for himself!; **sich vor jmdm./etw. nicht [mehr]** *od.* **kaum [noch] ~ können** be besieged by sb./be swamped with sth.; **sich ins Ziel ~** (Sport) just hold on to cross the line first
[C] *itr. V.* (Ballspiele) save

Retter *der;* **~s, ~, Retterin** *die;* **~, ~nen** rescuer; (eines Landes, einer Bewegung o. Ä.) saviour; **der/ein ~ in der Not** the/a helper in my/our *etc.* hour of need; **Christ der ~:** Christ the Saviour

Rettich /ˈrɛtɪç/ *der;* **~s, ~e** radish

Rettung *die* [1] rescue; (Rel., eines Landes usw.) salvation; (vor Zerstörung) saving; **jmdm. ~ bringen** rescue *or* save sb.; **die ~ kam in der letzten Minute** rescue came at the last moment *or* the eleventh hour; **er verdankt dem Medikament seine ~:** he owes his life to the medicine; **er dachte nur an seine eigene ~:** he thought only of saving himself *or* saving his own skin; **auf ~ warten/hoffen** wait for rescue/hope to be rescued; **für jmdn/etw. gibt es keine ~:** sb. is beyond help/sth. is past saving; **es war jmds. ~, dass ...** sb. was saved by the fact that ...; **das war meine letzte ~:** that was my last hope [of salvation]; (es hat mich schließlich gerettet) that was my salvation [2] (österr.: ~sdienst) ambulance service [3] (österr.: ~swagen) ambulance

rettungs-, Rettungs-: ~aktion *die* rescue operation; **~anker** *der* sheet anchor; **~boje** *die* (Seew.) lifebuoy; **~boot** *das* lifeboat; **~dienst** *der* ambulance service; (Bergwacht, Seerettungsdienst, bei Katastrophen) rescue service; **~flugzeug** *das* rescue aircraft *or* plane; **~gürtel** *der* lifebelt; **~hubschrauber** *der* rescue helicopter; **~insel** *die* (Seew.) [inflatable] life raft; **~kommando** *das* rescue team; **~los** [A] *Adj.* hopeless; inevitable ‹*disaster*›; [B] *adv.* hopelessly; **~mannschaft** *die* rescue team; **~medaille** *die* life-saving medal; **~ring** *der* [1] lifebelt; [2] (ugs.: Fettwulst) spare tyre (coll.); **~schuss, *~schuß** *der: in* **finaler ~schuss** fatal shot fired to save lives; **~schwimmen** *das* life-saving *no art.*; **~schwimmer** *der,* **~schwimmerin** *die* lifesaver; (am Strand, im Schwimmbad) lifeguard; **~trupp** *der* rescue team; **~versuch** *der* rescue attempt; **~wagen** *der* ambulance; (der Bergwacht, bei Katastrophen) rescue vehicle; **~weste** *die* (Seew.) life jacket

Return·taste /riˈtœːn-/ *die* (DV) return key

Retusche /reˈtʊʃə/ *die;* **~, ~n** (bes. Fot., Druckw.) retouching; (Stelle) retouch; **eine ~/~n vornehmen** retouch

Retuscheur /retʊˈʃøːɐ̯/ *der;* **~s, ~e, Retuscheurin** *die;* **~, ~nen** (bes. Fot., Druckw.) retoucher

retuschieren *tr. V.* (bes. Fot., Druckw.) retouch; (fig.) gloss over ‹*statement, remark*›

Reue /ˈrɔy̯ə/ *die;* **~:** remorse (**über** + *Akk.* for); (Rel.) repentance; *s. auch* **tätig**

Reue·gefühl *das* (geh.) feeling of remorse; **~ überkam sie** she was overcome by [feelings of] remorse

reuen *tr. V.* (meist geh.) **etw. reut jmdn.** sb. regrets sth.; **das Geld reut mich** I regret having spent the money

reue·voll (geh.) ▸**reumütig**

Reu·geld *das* (Rechtsw., Wirtsch., Pferderennen) forfeit

reuig (geh.) ▸**reumütig**

reu·mütig
[A] *Adj.* remorseful; repentant, penitent ‹*sinner*›
[B] *adv.* remorsefully; **~ gestand er seine Sünden** repentantly *or* penitently he confessed his sins; **du wirst ~ zurückkehren** you'll be back, saying you're sorry

Reuse /ˈrɔy̯zə/ *die;* **~, ~n** fish trap

reüssieren /reʏˈsiːrən/ *itr. V.* be successful; succeed; achieve success

Revalvation /revalvaˈt͜si̯oːn/ *die;* **~, ~en** (Wirtsch.) revaluation

Revanche /reˈvãːʃ(ə)/ *die;* **~, ~n** revenge; (Sport: Rückkampf, ~spiel) return match/fight/game; **jmdm. ~ geben** give sb. his/her revenge; **~ nehmen** *od.* **üben** get one's revenge; **~ fordern** (Sport, Spiel) demand a return match/fight/game

Revanche-: ~kampf *der* (Sport) return fight; **~partie** *die* (bes. Schach) return match; **~politik** *die* revanchist policy

revanchieren *refl. V.* [1] get one's revenge, (coll.) get one's own back (**bei** on) [2] (ugs.: sich erkenntlich zeigen) **sich bei jmdm. für eine Einladung/seine Gastfreundschaft ~:** return sb.'s invitation/repay sb.'s hospitality; **ich werde mich für eure Hilfe beim Umzug ~:** I'll return your favour of helping me move

Revanchismus *der;* **~** (Politik) revanchism *usu. no art.*

Revanchist *der;* **~en, ~en, Revanchistin** *die;* **~, ~nen** (Politik) revanchist

revanchistisch *Adj.* (Politik) revanchist

Revenue /rəvəˈnyː/ *die;* **~, ~n** (Wirtsch.) revenue

Reverenz /reveˈrɛnt͜s/ *die;* **~, ~en** [1] (Hochachtung) esteem, respect (**vor** + *Dat.* for); **jmdm. seine ~ erweisen** pay sb. one's respects [2] (Verbeugung) bow; **seine ~ vor jmdm. machen** bow to sb.

Revers[1] /rəˈveːɐ̯/ *das od.* (österr.) *der;* **~** /rəˈveːɐ̯(s)/, **~** /rəˈveːɐ̯s/ lapel

Revers[2] /reˈvɛrs/ *der;* **~es, ~e** (Münzk.) reverse

Revers[3] /reˈvɛrs/ *der;* **~es, ~e** (Rechtsw.) [written] undertaking

reversibel /revɛrˈziːbl̩/ *Adj.* (Technik, Med.) reversible

reversieren *itr. V.* (österr.) reverse

Reversion /revɛrˈzi̯oːn/ *die;* **~, ~en** (Biol., Psych.) reversion

revidieren /reviˈdiːrən/ *tr. V.* [1] (abändern) revise; amend ‹*law, contract*› [2] (kontrollieren) check; (Buchf.) audit ‹*accounts, books*›

Revier /reˈviːɐ̯/ *das;* **~s, ~e** [1] (Aufgabenbereich) province; **der Weinkeller ist mein ~** (scherzh.) the wine cellar is my province *or* preserve [2] (Zool.) territory [3] (Polizei~) (Dienststelle) [police] station; (Bereich) district; (des einzelnen Polizisten) beat [4] (Forst~) district [5] (Jagd~) preserve; shoot [6] (Bergbau) coalfield; **das ~:** the Ruhr/Saar coalfields *pl.* [7] (Milit. veralt.: Unterkunft) barracks *sing. or pl.* [8] (Milit. veralt.: Kranken~) sickbay

Revier-: ~förster *der,* **~försterin** *die* forest warden; forester; **~stube** *die* (Milit. veralt.) sickbay; **~verhalten** *das* (Verhaltensf.) territorial behaviour; **~wache** *die* police station

Revirement /revirəˈmãː/ *das;* **~s, ~s** reshuffle

Revision /reviˈzi̯oːn/ *die;* **~, ~en** [1] (das Ändern) revision; (eines Gesetzes, Vertrags) amendment [2] (Rechtsw.) appeal [on a point/points of law]; **~ einlegen, in die ~ gehen** lodge an appeal [on a point/points of law] [3] (Kontrolle) inspection; (Buchf.) audit [4] (Druckw.) revision of the page proofs; **~ lesen** read the page proofs

Revisionismus *der;* **~** (Politik) revisionism *usu. no art.*

Revisionist *der;* **~en, ~en, Revisionistin** *die;* **~, ~nen** (Politik) revisionist

revisionistisch *Adj.* (Politik) revisionist

Revisions-: ~bogen *der* (Druckw.) final page proof; **~gericht** *das* (Rechtsw.) court of appeal [dealing with points of law]; **~verfahren** *das* (Rechtsw.) appeal proceedings *pl.* [on a point/points of law]; **~verhandlung** *die* (Rechtsw.) hearing of an/the appeal [on a point/points of law]

Revisor /reˈviːzɔr/ *der;* **~s, ~en** /reviˈzoːrən/, **Revisorin** *die;* **~, ~nen** [1] (Buchf.) auditor [2] (Druckw.) reader of the page proofs

Revolte /reˈvɔltə/ *die;* **~, ~n** revolt

revoltieren *itr. V.* revolt, rebel (**gegen** against); (fig.) ‹*stomach*› rebel

Revolution /revoluˈt͜si̯oːn/ *die;* **~, ~en** [1] (auch fig.) revolution [2] (Skat) revolution

revolutionär /revolut͜si̯oˈnɛːɐ̯/
[A] *Adj.* revolutionary
[B] *adv.* in a revolutionary way

Revolutionär *der;* **~s, ~e, Revolutionärin** *die;* **~, ~nen** revolutionary

revolutionieren *tr. V.* revolutionize; **eine ~de Entdeckung** a revolutionary discovery

Revolutions-: ~führer *der,* **~führerin** *die* revolutionary leader; **~held** *der,* **~heldin** *die* revolutionary hero; **~rat** *der* (Politik) revolutionary council; **~regierung** *die* revolutionary government; **~tribunal** *das* (hist.) Revolutionary Tribunal

Revoluzzer /revoˈlʊt͜sɐ/ *der;* **~s, ~, Revoluzzerin** *die;* **~, ~nen** (abwertend) phoney revolutionary

Revoluzzertum *das;* **~s** (abwertend) phoney revolutionary fervour

Revolver /reˈvɔlvɐ/ *der;* **~s, ~** [1] revolver [2] (Technik) turret

Revolver-: ~blatt *das* (abwertend) scandal rag; **~held** *der* (abwertend) gunslinger; **~kopf** *der* (Technik) turret; **~lauf** *der* revolver barrel; **~presse** *die* (abwertend) yellow press; scandal rags *pl.*; **~schnauze** *die* (ugs. abwertend) [1] (Mundwerk) big trap (sl.) *or* mouth; [2] (Mensch) loudmouth; **~tasche** *die* holster

Revue /reˈvyː/ *die;* **~, ~n** [1] (Theater) revue [2] (Truppe) revue company [3] (Zeitschrift) review [4] (Milit.) review; **etw. ~ passieren lassen** (fig.) review sth.; **er ließ seine Freunde ~ passieren** (fig.) he brought back to mind *or* he recalled his friends

Revue·theater *das* revue theatre

Rezensent /ret͜sɛnˈt͜sɛnt/ *der;* **~en, ~en, Rezensentin** *die;* **~, ~nen** reviewer

rezensieren /ret͜sɛnˈziːrən/
[A] *tr. V.* review
[B] *itr. V.* write reviews

Rezension /ret͜sɛnˈzi̯oːn/ *die;* **~, ~en** review

Rezensions·exemplar *das* review copy

rezent /reˈt͜sɛnt/ *Adj.* (Geol.) Recent

Rezept /reˈt͜sɛpt/ *das;* **~[e]s, ~e** [1] (Med.) prescription; (fig.) remedy (**gegen** for); **nur auf ~:** only on prescription [2] (Anleitung) recipe; (fig.) formula

Rezept·block *der; Pl.* **~s** *od.* **Rezept·blöcke** prescription pad

rezept·frei
[A] *Adj.* **~e Mittel** medicines obtainable without a prescription
[B] *adv.* **etw. ~ verkaufen/erhalten** sell/obtain sth. without a prescription *or* over the counter

rezeptieren *tr.* (*auch itr.*) *V.* prescribe

Rezeption /ret͜sɛpˈt͜si̯oːn/ *die;* **~, ~en** [1] (im Hotel) reception *no art.* [2] (Aufnahme) reception

rezeptiv /ret͜sɛpˈtiːf/ *Adj.* receptive (**für** to)

rezept·pflichtig *Adj.* ‹*medicine, drug, etc.*› obtainable only on prescription; **nicht ~ sein** be obtainable without a prescription *or* over the counter

Rezeptur /ret͜sɛpˈtuːɐ̯/ *die;* **~, ~en** [1] (das Rezeptieren) prescription [2] (für Nahrungsmittel) recipe (*Gen.* for); (für Arzneimittel, Farbe, Baustoff) formula

Rezession /ret͜sɛˈsi̯oːn/ *die;* **~, ~en** (Wirtsch.) recession

rezessiv /ret͜sɛˈsiːf/ (Biol.)
[A] *Adj.* recessive
[B] *adv.* recessively

rezipieren /ret͜siˈpiːrən/ *tr. V.* receive; (übernehmen) adapt

reziprok /ret͜siˈproːk/ *Adj.* (bes. Math., Sprachw.) reciprocal

Rezitation /retsita'tsio:n/ *die;* **~, ~en** recitation

Rezitations·abend *der* [evening] recitation; (mit Rezitation von Gedichten) [evening] poetry-reading; poetry evening

Rezitativ /retsita'ti:f/ *das;* **~s, ~e** (Musik) recitative

rezitieren /retsi'ti:rən/ *tr. (auch itr.) V.* recite; **er rezitierte aus seinem Roman** he gave a reading *or* he read from his novel; **er rezitiert gern** he enjoys giving recitations

RE-Zug *der* local express

R-Gespräch /'ɛr-/ *das* (Fernspr.) reverse-charge call (Brit.); collect call (Amer.)

RGW *Abk.* **= Rat für Gegenseitige Wirtschaftshilfe** COMECON

rh /ɛr'ha:/ *Abk.* (Med.) **= Rhesusfaktor negativ** Rh negative

Rh /ɛr'ha:/ *Abk.* (Med.) **= Rhesusfaktor positiv** Rh positive

Rhabarber[1] /ra'barbɐ/ *der;* **~s** rhubarb

Rhabarber[2] *das;* **~s** (ugs.) **sie murmelten „~, ~"** they mumbled 'rhubarb, rhubarb' (coll.)

Rhapsode /ra'pso:də/ *der;* **~n, ~n** (Musik, Literaturw.) rhapsodist; rhapsode; (fig.) rhapsodic composer

Rhapsodie /rapso'di:/ *die;* **~, ~n** (Musik, Literaturw.) rhapsody

rhapsodisch *Adj.* rhapsodic

Rhein /rain/ *der;* **~[e]s** ▸ⓘ **S. 267** Rhine

Rhein·fall *der* Rhine Falls *Pl.*

rheinisch *Adj.* Rhenish; **eine ~e Spezialität** a speciality of the Rhine region

Rheinland *das;* **~[e]s** Rhineland

Rheinländer *der;* **~s, ~, Rheinländerin** *die;* **~, ~nen** Rhinelander

Rheinland-Pfalz *(das);* **~'** the Rhineland-Palatinate; **in/aus ~:** in/from the Rhineland-Palatinate

rheinland-pfälzisch *Adj.* ‹*capital, citizen, etc.*› of the Rhineland-Palatinate

Rhein·wein *der* Rhine wine; Rhenish [wine]; (Weißwein auch) hock

Rhesus- /'re:zʊs/: **~affe** *der* rhesus monkey; **~faktor** *der* (Med.) rhesus factor; Rh factor

Rhetorik /re'to:rɪk/ *die;* **~, ~en** rhetoric

Rhetoriker *der;* **~s, ~, Rhetorikerin** *die;* **~, ~nen** rhetorician

rhetorisch

A *Adj.* rhetorical; **eine ~e Frage** a rhetorical question

B *adv.* rhetorically

Rheuma /'rɔyma/ *das;* **~s** ▸ⓘ **S. 439** (ugs.) rheumatism; rheumatics *pl.* (coll.)

Rheuma-: **~decke** *die* thermal blanket; **~mittel** *das* (ugs.) rheumatism pills *pl.*/cream *etc.*; **~wäsche** *die* thermal underwear

Rheumatiker /rɔy'ma:tikɐ/ *der;* **~s, ~, Rheumatikerin** *die;* **~, ~nen** (Med.) rheumatic; rheumatism sufferer

rheumatisch (Med.)

A *Adj.* rheumatic

B *adv.* rheumatically

Rheumatismus /rɔyma'tɪsmʊs/ *der;* **~, Rheumatismen** ▸ⓘ **S. 439** (Med.) rheumatism

Rhinozeros /ri'no:tserɔs/ *das;* **~[ses], ~se** **1▸** (Nashorn) rhinoceros; rhino (coll.) **2▸** (ugs.: Trottel) nitwit (coll.); fathead (coll.)

Rhizom /ri'tso:m/ *das;* **~s, ~e** (Bot.) rhizome

Rhododendron /rodo'dɛndrɔn/ *der od. das;* **~s, Rhododendren** rhododendron

Rhodos /'ro:dɔs/ *(das);* **~'** Rhodes

Rhomben ▸**Rhombus**

rhombisch *Adj.* (bes. Math.) rhombic

Rhomboid /rɔmbo'i:t/ *das;* **~[e]s, ~e** (Math.) rhomboid

Rhombus /'rɔmbʊs/ *der;* **~, Rhomben** /'rɔmbn̩/ rhombus

Rhythm and Blues /'rɪðm ɛnt 'blu:s/ *der;* **~:** rhythm and blues

Rhythmen ▸**Rhythmus**

Rhythmik /'rʏtmɪk/ *die;* **~** **1▸** (auch Musik) rhythm **2▸** (Päd.) rhythmics *sing., no art.*

Rhythmiker *der;* **~s, ~, Rhythmikerin** *die;* **~, ~nen** rhythmist

rhythmisch

A *Adj.* rhythmical; rhythmic; **~e Instrumente** rhythm instruments; **~e Gymnastik** rhythmic gymnastics *sing*

B *adv.* rhythmically

Rhythmus /'rʏtmʊs/ *der;* **~, Rhythmen** /'rʏtmən/ (auch fig.) rhythm; **aus dem ~ kommen** lose the rhythm

Rhythmus-: **~gitarre** *die* rhythm guitar; **~gruppe** *die* rhythm section; **~instrument** *das* rhythm instrument

RIAS, Rias /'ri:as/*der;* **~** *Abk.* (hist.) **= Rundfunk im amerikanischen Sektor [Berlin]** RIAS; Radio in the American Sector [of Berlin]

ribbeln /'rɪbl̩n/ *tr. V.* (landsch.) rub

Ribisel /'ri:bi:zl/ *die;* **~, ~[n]** (österr.) ▸**Johannisbeere**

Ribosom /ribo'zo:m/ *das;* **~s, ~en** (Biochem.) ribosome

Richt-: **~antenne** *die* directional aerial *or* (Amer.) antenna; **~baum** *der: tree used for topping-out ceremony;* **~beil** *das* (hist.) executioner's axe; **~blei** *das* (Bauw.) plumb [bob]; **~block** *der; Pl.* **~blöcke** [execution] block

richten /'rɪçtn/

A *tr. V.* **1▸** (lenken) direct ‹*gaze*› (**auf** + *Akk.* at, towards); turn ‹*eyes, gaze*› (**auf** + *Akk.* towards); point ‹*torch, telescope, gun*› (**auf** + *Akk.* at); aim, train ‹*gun, missile, telescope, searchlight*› (**auf** + *Akk.* on); (fig.) direct ‹*activity, attention*› (**auf** + *Akk.* towards); **etw. nach jmdm./etw. ~:** arrange sth. to suit sb./sth.; **die Augen gen Himmel ~:** look heavenwards; **die Waffe gegen sich selbst ~:** turn the weapon on oneself; **das Schiff/den Kurs eines Schiffes nach Norden ~:** steer the ship on/steer a northerly course **2▸** (zukommen lassen) address ‹*letter, remarks, words*› (**an** + *Akk.* to); direct, level ‹*criticism*› (**an** + *Akk.* at); send ‹*letter of thanks, message of greeting*› (**an** + *Akk.* to); **eine Bitte/Frage an jmdn. ~:** put a request/question to sb.; **ein Gesuch an jmdn. ~:** petition sb.; **eine Mahnung an jmdn. ~:** give sb. a warning; **das Wort an jmdn. ~** (geh.) address sb. **3▸** (gerade **~**) straighten; set ‹*fracture*› **4▸** (einstellen) aim ‹*cannon, missile*›; direct ‹*aerial*› **5▸** (aburteilen) judge; (verurteilen) condemn **6▸** (bes. südd., österr., schweiz.: instand setzen, in Ordnung bringen) fix; repair ‹*shoes*›; (einrichten) arrange; fix; **[sich** *(Dat.)*] **die Haare/den Schlips ~:** do one's hair/adjust *or* straighten one's tie; **es wird sich schon alles ~:** everything will sort itself out; **das lässt sich schon ~:** it can be arranged **7▸** (bes. südd., österr., schweiz.: vorbereiten) get ready; prepare; make ‹*bed, nest*›; get ‹*food, meal*›; **den Tisch/das Zimmer ~:** lay *or* set the table/get the room ready; **[jmdm.] ein Bad ~:** run a bath [for sb.] **8▸** (geh. veralt.: hin~) execute; **sich selbst ~:** die by one's own hand

B *refl. V.* **1▸** (sich hinwenden) **sich auf jmdn./etw. ~** (auch fig.) be directed towards sb./sth.; **ihre Augen richteten sich auf mich** her gaze was turned towards me **2▸** (sich wenden) **sich an jmdn./etw. ~** ‹*person*› turn on sb./sth.; ‹*appeal, explanation*› be directed at sb./sth. **3▸** (kritisieren, schädigen) **sich gegen jmdn./etw. ~** ‹*person*› criticize sb./sth.; ‹*criticism, accusations, etc.*› be aimed *or* levelled *or* directed at sb./sth.; **diese Lehre richtet sich gegen den Staat** this doctrine is directed against the state **4▸** (sich orientieren) **sich nach jmdm./jmds. Wünschen ~:** fit in with sb./sb.'s wishes; **sich nach jmds. Anweisungen ~:** comply with sb.'s instructions; **sich nach den Vorschriften ~:** keep to *or* follow the rules; **sich nach den Wünschen seiner Kunden ~:** be guided by one's customers' wishes **5▸** (abhängen) **sich nach jmdm./etw. ~:** depend on sb./sth. **6▸** (Milit.) **richt't euch!** right dress!

C *itr. V.* (urteilen) judge; pass judgement; **über jmdn. ~:** judge sb.; pass judgement on sb.; (zu Gericht sitzen) sit in judgement over sb.

Richter *der;* **~s, ~** ▸ⓘ **S. 113** judge; **die ~** (**~**schaft) the judiciary *sing.*; **sich zum ~ über jmdn./etw. aufwerfen** presume to pass judgement *or* sit in judgement on sb./sth.; **jmdn. vor den ~ bringen** take sb. to court; **der himmlische/höchste ~:** the Heavenly/Supreme Judge; **vor dem höchsten ~ stehen** stand before the Judgement Seat *or* the Throne of Judgement

Richter·amt *das* office of judge

Richterin *die;* **~, ~nen** ▸ⓘ **S. 113** judge

richterlich

A *Adj.* judicial

B *adv.* ‹*examined, approved, etc.*› by a judge

Richterschaft *die;* **~, ~en** judiciary

Richter-: **~skala** *die* Richter scale; **~spruch** *der* judge's verdict; (Verkündigung der Strafe) sentence; **~stuhl** *der* bench; **der ~stuhl Gottes** the Judgement Seat; the Throne of Judgement

Richt-: **~fest** *das* topping-out ceremony; **~funk** *der* (Funkw.) directional radio; **~geschwindigkeit** *die* (Verkehrsw.) recommended maximum speed

richtig

A *Adj.* **1▸** right; (zutreffend) right; correct; correct ‹*realization*›; accurate ‹*prophecy, premonition*›; **sehr ~!** quite right!; **bin ich hier ~ bei Schulzes?** is this the Schulzes' home?; **die ~e Haltung von Katzen** the right way to keep cats; **ich halte es für das Richtigste, wenn du mitkommst** I think the best thing would be for you to come [too]; **das ist genau das Richtige für mich** that's just right for me; **mit etw. ~ liegen** (ugs.) get it right with sth.; **ich habe ~ gelegen** (ugs.) I was right; **etw. ~ stellen** correct sth. **2▸** (ordentlich) proper; **ein ~er Mann/Fachmann** a real man/expert; **er ist ~** (ugs.) he's OK (coll.) *or* all right; **nicht ganz ~ [im Kopf** *od.* (ugs.) **im Oberstübchen] sein** be not quite right in the head (coll.) *or* not quite all there (coll.) **3▸** (wirklich, echt) real; (regelrecht) real; proper (coll.); **du bist ein ~er Esel** you're a right *or* proper idiot (coll.)

B *adv.* **1▸** right; correctly; **sehe ich das ~?** (fig.) am I right?; **habe ich ~ gehört?** (fig.) do my ears deceive me?; **~ sitzen** *od.* **passen** ‹*clothes*› fit properly; **meine Uhr geht ~:** my watch is right; **eine ~ gehende Uhr** an accurate clock/watch; **das Radio funktioniert nicht mehr ~:** the radio doesn't work properly anymore; **etw. ~ anpacken** tackle sth. the right way; **~ wählen** make the right choice; **du kommst [mir] gerade ~!** you've come at just the right moment; (ugs. iron.) nothing doing! **2▸** (ordentlich) properly; **~ ausschlafen/frühstücken** have a good sleep/breakfast **3▸** (**~**gehend) really **4▸** (in der Tat) yes; **ja ~!** yes, that's right!; **das habe ich doch ~ wieder versäumt** sure enough, I've missed it again

Richtige[1] *der/die; adj. Dekl.* right man/woman/person; **sie sucht noch den ~n** she's still looking for Mr Right; **an die ~/den ~n geraten** (iron.) choose the wrong person to try it on with (Brit. coll.); **du bist mir der ~!** (ugs.) you're a right one!

Richtige[2] *der; adj. Dekl.* **drei/sechs ~ im Lotto** three/six right in the lottery

Richtige[3] *das; adj. Dekl.* right thing; **das ~ sein** be right; **hast du was ~s gegessen?** have you eaten properly?; have you had a proper meal?; **nichts ~s gefunden haben** not have found anything suitable; **nichts ~s gelernt haben** have had no proper education

richtig·gehend

A *Adj.* real; proper (coll.)

B *adv.* really

Richtigkeit *die;* **~:** correctness; (einer Ahnung, Prophetie) accuracy; **die ~ einer Abschrift bescheinigen** certify a copy as [being] accurate; **etw. hat seine ~, mit etw. hat es seine ~:** sth. is right; **das wird schon seine ~ haben** I'm sure it's all right *or* (coll.) OK

richtig-, Richtig-: ***~|liegen** ▸**richtig A1**; ***~|stellen** ▸**richtig A1**; **~stellung** *die* correction

Richt-: **~kranz** *der: wreath used in the topping-out ceremony;* **~linie** *die* **1▸** guideline;

2 (Direktive) directive; **~mikrofon** *das* directional microphone; **~platz** *der* place of execution; **~preis** *der* recommended price; **unverbindlicher ~preis** manufacturer's recommended price; **~scheit** *das* (Bauw.) straight edge; **~schnur** *die; Pl.* **~en** **1** (fig.) guiding principle; **2** (Bauw.) line; **~schwert** *das* (hist.) executioner's sword; **~spruch** *der* **1** *(beim Richtfest) verse address at the topping-out ceremony;* **2** (veralt.: Urteilsspruch) judgement; (Verkündigung der Strafe) sentence; **~stätte** *die* (geh.) ►**Richtplatz**; **~strahler** *der* (Funkt.) directional aerial *or* (Amer.) antenna

Richtung *die;* **~, ~en** **1** ►❶ **S. 363** direction; **die ~ ändern** *od.* **wechseln** change direction; **in ~ Osten** in an easterly direction; eastwards; (auf der Autobahn) on the eastbound carriageway; **in ~ Ulm** in the direction of Ulm; **nach/aus allen ~en** in/from all directions; **der Zug/die Autobahn ~ Ulm** the train to Ulm/the motorway in the direction of Ulm; **eine ~ einschlagen** head in a direction; **eine andere ~ einschlagen** change direction; ‹*ship, aircraft*› change course; **~ auf den Wald nehmen, die ~ zum** *od.* **nach dem Wald einschlagen** head in the direction of the wood; **[in] ~** *(Akk.)* **Bad verschwinden** (ugs.) disappear in the direction of the bathroom (coll.); **aus welcher ~ kam der Schuss?** from what direction did the shot come?; **wir gehen in diese ~:** we're going this way *or* in this direction; **ihre Gedanken nahmen eine andere ~** (fig.) her thoughts took a different turn; **ein erster Schritt in ~ auf die Integration** (fig.) a first step towards *or* in the direction of integration; **der Pullover lag nicht so ganz in meiner ~** *od.* **war nicht so ganz meine ~** (fig.) the pullover wasn't quite [to] my taste; **er hat Angst, sich in irgendeine ~ festzulegen** (fig.) he's afraid to commit himself in any way; **der erste Versuch in dieser ~** (fig.) the first experiment of this kind; **die ~ stimmt** (fig. ugs.) it's/he's *etc.* on the right lines; **ich hätte jetzt Lust auf Fisch oder irgendetwas in dieser ~:** I could just fancy some fish or something in that line **2** (fig.: Tendenz) movement; trend; (die Vertreter einer ~) (in der Kunst, Literatur) movement; (in einer Partei) faction; (Denk~, Lehrmeinung) school of thought; **die ganze ~ seiner Äußerungen** the whole tendency *or* drift of his remarks

richtung·gebend ►**richtungsweisend**

richtungs-, Richtungs-: ~änderung *die* change in *or* of direction; (eines Schiffs, Flugzeugs) change of course; **die politische ~änderung XYs** (fig.) XY's change of political course; **~gewerkschaft** *die: trade union linked to one party, ideology, etc.*; **~kämpfe** *Pl.* factional struggles; **~los** **A** *Adj.* lacking [a sense of] direction *postpos.*; **~los sein** lack [a sense of] direction; **B** *adv.* aimlessly; **~losigkeit** *die;* **~~:** lack of [a sense of] direction

richtungs·weisend
A *Adj.* ‹*idea, resolution, paper, speech*› that points the way ahead; (in der Mode) trendsetting; **für jmdn./etw. ~ sein** point the way ahead for sb./sth.
B *adv.* **sie hat sich zu diesem Thema ~ geäußert** she set out ideas on this subject which point the way ahead; **Kunststoffe haben die heutige Technik ~ beeinflusst** plastics have had a determining influence on the direction in which today's technology has developed

Richt·waage *die* spirit level

Ricke /ˈrɪkə/ *die;* **~, ~n** (Jägerspr.) doe *(of roe-deer)*

rieb /riːp/ *1. u. 3. Pers. Sg. Prät. v.* **reiben**

riechen /ˈriːçn̩/
A *unr. tr. V.* **1** smell; **ich rieche Tabak gern** I like the smell of tobacco; **ich rieche Gas** I [can] smell gas; **jmdn./etw. nicht ~ können** (fig. salopp) not be able to stand sb./sth. **2** (wittern) ‹*dog etc.*› scent, pick up the scent of ‹*animal*›; **er roch die Gefahr sofort** (fig.) he scented *or* sensed danger immediately; **ich konnte ja nicht ~, dass ...** (fig.) [I'm not psychic,] I couldn't know that ...
B *unr. itr. V.* **1** (Gerüche wahrnehmen) smell; **Hunde können sehr gut ~:** dogs have a very good sense of smell; **an jmdm./etw. ~:** smell sb./sth.; **lass mich mal [daran] ~:** let me have a sniff **2** (einen Geruch haben) smell (**nach** of); **gut/schlecht ~:** smell good/bad; **diese Blumen ~ nicht** these flowers have no smell *or* scent; **hier riecht es verbrannt/nach Krankenhaus** there is a burnt/hospital smell *or* smell of burning/hospital here; **er roch aus dem Mund** he had bad breath; his breath smelt; **das riecht nach Betrug** (fig.) that smells *or* smacks of deceit

Riecher *der;* **~s, ~** (salopp) **1** (Nase) conk (coll.) **2** (fig.: Gespür) nose; **einen guten ~ für etw. haben** have a sixth sense for sth.

Riech-: ~fläschchen *das* smelling bottle; **~kolben** *der* (salopp scherzh.) conk (sl.); **~organ** *das* olfactory organ; **~salz** *das* smelling salts *pl.*; **~zentrum** *das* (Anat.) olfactory centre

Ried[1] /riːt/ *das;* **~[e]s, ~e** **1** (Schilf) reeds *pl.* **2** (Gebiet) reedy marsh

Ried[2] *die;* **~, ~en, Riede** *die;* **~e, ~en** (österr.) [patch of] vineyard

Ried·gras *das* (Bot.) sedge

rief /riːf/ *1. u. 3. Pers. Sg. Prät. v.* **rufen**

Riefe *die;* **~, ~n** groove

Riege /ˈriːgə/ *die;* **~, ~n** (Turnen) squad; (fig.) team

Riegel /ˈriːgl̩/ *der;* **~s, ~** **1** (an der Tür usw.) bolt; **einer Sache** *(Dat.)* **einen ~ vorschieben** (fig.) put a stop to sth.; (etw. verhindern) not let sth. happen **2** **ein ~ Schokolade** a bar of chocolate **3** (bes. Fußball: Abwehr) packed defence **4** (Milit.) [defensive] wall **5** (Schneiderei) (Lasche) loop; (an Jacke, Mantel usw.) half-belt

Riegel·haus *das* (schweiz.) half-timbered house

Riemchen *das;* **~s, ~:** [small] strap *or* belt

Riemchen·pumps *der* ankle strap pumps

Riemen /ˈriːmən/ *der;* **~s, ~** **1** (Gurt) strap; (Treib~, Gürtel) belt; **sich am ~ reißen** (ugs.) pull oneself together; get a grip on oneself; **den ~ enger schnallen** (fig. ugs.) tighten one's belt **2** (Schnürsenkel) leather shoelace **3** (derb: Penis) prick (coarse) **4** (Ruder) [long] oar; **sich [kräftig] in die ~ legen** (auch fig.) put one's back into it

Riemen-: ~antrieb *der* belt drive; **~scheibe** *die* belt pulley

Ries /riːs/ *das;* **~es, ~e** (veraltet) two reams; **vier ~ Papier** eight reams of paper

-riese *der;* **~n, ~n** giant; **Automobil~:** giant car manufacturer; **Chemie~:** giant chemical firm; **Branchen~:** giant of the industry

Riese /ˈriːzə/ *der;* **~n, ~n** **1** giant; **ein ~ von einem Menschen** a giant of a man/woman; *s. auch* **abgebrochen B 2** **2** (salopp: Geldschein) thousand-franc/dollar *etc.* note; **das kostet drei ~n** that costs three grand [in euros *etc.*] (coll.)

Riesel·feld *das* (Landw.) field irrigated with sewage

rieseln /ˈriːzl̩n/ *itr. V.; mit Richtungsangabe mit sein;* **1** (rinnen) trickle **2** (fallen) ‹*sand, lime*› trickle [down]; ‹*snow*› fall gently *or* lightly; **der Kalk rieselte von den Wänden** lime was crumbling off the walls

Riesen- giant ‹*building, tree, salamander, tortoise, etc.*›; enormous ‹*task, selection, profit, sum, portion*›; tremendous (coll.) ‹*effort, rejoicing, success, hit*›; (abwertend: schrecklich) terrific (coll.), terrible (coll.) ‹*stupidity, mess, scandal, fuss*›; **ich habe einen ~hunger** I am tremendously *or* terribly hungry (coll.); **ein ~rindvieh** (ugs.) an almighty idiot (coll.); **ein ~spaß** (ugs.) tremendous *or* terrific fun (coll.)

riesen-, Riesen-: ~auswahl *die* huge selection; **~baby** *das* (ugs.) **1** oversize baby (joc.); **2** (abwertend) ►**Elefantenküken**; **~bockwurst** *die* giant bockwurst; **~groß** *Adj.* enormous; huge; gigantic; terrific (coll.) ‹*surprise*›; **eine ~große Dummheit** something terribly stupid (coll.); **~haft** *Adj.* enormous; huge; gigantic; **~rad** *das* big wheel; Ferris wheel; **~rad fahren** go on the big wheel *or* Ferris wheel; **~saurier** *der* giant dinosaur; **~schlange** *die* boa; **~schritt** *der* giant stride; **~slalom** *der* (Skisport) giant slalom; **~stern** *der* (Astron.) giant [star]; **~welle** *die* giant wave; **~wuchs** *der* (Biol.) gigantism

riesig
A *Adj.* **1** (sehr groß) enormous; huge; gigantic; vast ‹*country*›; tremendous ‹*joy, enthusiasm, effort, progress, strength*›; terrific (coll.), terrible (coll.) ‹*hunger, thirst*›; **~e Ausmaße haben** be of enormous size; **ein ~er Spaß** terrific *or* tremendous fun (coll.) **2** (ugs.: großartig) fabulous (coll.), tremendous (coll.) ‹*party, film, etc.*›
B *adv.* (ugs.) tremendously (coll.); terribly (coll.)

Riesin *die;* **~, ~nen** giantess

Riesling /ˈriːslɪŋ/ *der;* **~s, ~e** Riesling

riet /riːt/ *1. u. 3. Pers. Sg. Prät. v.* **raten**

Riff[1] /rɪf/ *das;* **~[e]s, ~e** reef

Riff[2] *der;* **~s, ~s** (Jazz) riff

Riffel /ˈrɪfl̩/ *die;* **~, ~n** **1** corrugation; (Vertiefung) groove; (in einer Säule) flute; (Erhöhung) rib **2** (Textilw.) (Maschine) ripple [machine]; (Kamm) ripple

riffeln *tr. V.* **1** rib ‹*glass*›; ripple ‹*lake*›; *s. auch* **geriffelt** **2** (Textilw.) ripple ‹*flax*›

Rififi /ˈrɪfifi/ *das;* **~s** (ugs.) master crime

Rigg /rɪk/ *das;* **~s, ~s** (Seemannsspr.) rig

rigid /riˈgiːt/, **rigide**
A *Adj.* (geh., Med.) rigid
B *adv.* (geh.) rigidly

Rigidität /rigidiˈtɛːt/ *die;* **~** (geh., Med.) rigidity

Rigorismus /rigoˈrɪsmʊs/ *der;* **~** (geh.) rigorism

rigoros /rigoˈroːs/
A *Adj.* rigorous
B *adv.* rigorously; **etw. ~ ablehnen** reject sth. categorically

Rigorosität *die;* **~** (geh.) rigorousness

Rigorosum /rigoˈroːzʊm/ *das;* **~s, Rigorosa** *od. bes. österr.* **Rigorosen** (Hochschulw.) *oral part of the doctoral examination*

Rikscha /ˈrɪkʃa/ *die;* **~, ~s** rickshaw

Rille /ˈrɪlə/ *die;* **~, ~n** groove; (in einer Säule) flute

Rind /rɪnt/ *das;* **~[e]s, ~er** **1** cow; (Stier) bull; **~er** cattle *pl.*; **20 ~er** twenty head of cattle; **ein gemästetes ~:** a fattened ox; **Hackfleisch/ein Steak vom ~:** minced *or* (Amer.) ground beef/a beef steak **2** (ugs.: ~fleisch) beef **3** (Zool.) bovine

Rinde *die;* **~, ~n** **1** (Baum~) bark **2** (Brot~) crust; (Käse~) rind **3** (Hirn~) cortex

Rinder-: ~braten *der* (gebraten) roast beef *no indef. art.*; (roh) roasting beef *no indef. art.*; **ein ~braten** a joint of roast beef; (roh) a joint of [roasting] beef; **~bremse** *die* horsefly; **~brust** *die* brisket of beef; **~filet** *das* fillet of beef; **~herde** *die* herd of [beef] cattle; **~leber** *die* ox liver; **~lende** *die* loin of beef; **~pest** *die* rinderpest; cattle plague; **~roulade** *die* beef olive; **~seuche** *die* cattle disease; **~talg** *der* (zum Kochen) beef suet; (für Salbe usw.) beef tallow; **~wahnsinn** *der* ►❶ **S. 439** mad cow disease; **~zucht** *die* cattle breeding *or* -rearing *no art.*

Rind-: ~fleisch *das* beef; **~fleisch·brühe** *die* beef broth; **~fleisch·suppe** *die* beef soup

rinds-, Rinds-: ~braten *der* (bes. südd., österr.) ►**Rinderbraten**; **~fett** *das* (südd., österr.) clarified butter; **~leber** *die* (bes. südd., österr.) ►**Rinderleber**; **~leder** *das* cowhide; oxhide; **~ledern** *Adj.* cowhide; oxhide; **~lende** *die* (bes. südd., österr.) ►**Rinderlende**; **~roulade** *die* (bes. südd., österr.) ►**Rinderroulade**

Rind·vieh *das; Pl.* **Rindviecher** **1** cattle *pl.*; **20 Stück ~:** twenty head of cattle **2** (ugs. abwertend) ass; [stupid] fool; **ich ~!** what an idiot I am! (coll.)

Ring /rɪŋ/ *der;* **~[e]s, ~e** **1** ring; **die ~e tauschen** *od.* **wechseln** (geh.) exchange rings; **an den ~en turnen** perform *or* exercise on the rings; **10 ~e schießen** shoot *or* score a ten; **einen ~ bilden** ‹*spectators etc.*› form a ring *or* circle; ‹*stones, road*› form a ring **2)** (~straße) ring road; **den ~ fahren** take the ring road **3)** (Box~) ring; **~ frei zur zweiten Runde** seconds out for the second round **4)** (Vereinigung) **ein ~ für Theaterbesuche** a theatre-going circle; **ein ~ von Händlern** a ring of dealers **5)** (Wurf~) hoop

Ring-: ~bahn *die* circle line; **~buch** *das* ring binder

Ringel /ˈrɪŋl/ *der;* **~s, ~:** [small] ring; **die ~ ihrer Haare** the ringlets in her hair

Ringel·blume *die* marigold

ringelig *Adj.* curly; ‹*hair*› in ringlets

Ringel·locke *die* ringlet

ringeln

A *tr. V.* curl; coil ‹*tail*›; *s. auch* **geringelt**

B *refl. V.* curl

Ringel-: ~natter *die* ring snake; **~piez** /-piːt͜s/ *der;* **~~[es], ~~e** (ugs. scherzh.) **~piez [mit Anfassen]** hop (coll.); hoedown (Amer.); **~reigen** *der,* **~reihen** *der;* **~~s, ~~:** ring-a-ring-o'-roses; **~reigen tanzen** *od.* **spielen** play ring-a-ring-o'-roses; **~schwanz** *der* curly tail; **~söckchen** *das,* **~socke** *die* [horizontally] striped sock; **~spiel** *das* (österr.) merry-go-round; **~taube** *die* wood pigeon; ringdove; **~wurm** *der* (Zool.) annelid

ringen

A *unr. itr. V.* (Sport, fig.) wrestle; (fig.: kämpfen) struggle, fight (**um** for); **gegen jmdn.** *od.* **mit jmdm. ~** (Sport) wrestle with sb.; (fig.) **mit den Tränen ~:** fight back one's tears; **die Ärzte ~ um sein Leben** the doctors are struggling *or* fighting to save his life; **nach Atem** *od.* **Luft ~:** struggle for breath; **nach** *od.* **um Fassung ~:** fight to maintain one's composure; **er rang nach Worten** *od.* **um Worte** he struggled to find the right words; **ich habe lange mit mir gerungen, ob ...** I had a long struggle with my conscience to decide whether ...

B *unr. tr. V.* **1)** (bes. Sport) **den Gegner zu Boden ~:** bring one's opponent down **2)** (gewaltsam reißen) **jmdm. etw. aus den Händen/der Hand ~:** wrest sth. from sb.'s hands/hand **3)** *in* **die Hände ~:** wring one's hands

C *unr. refl. V.* (geh.) **ein Seufzer rang sich aus ihrer Brust** a sigh forced its way up from deep within her

Ringen *das;* **~s** (Sport) wrestling *no art.*

Ringer *der;* **~s, ~, Ringerin** *die;* **~, ~nen** wrestler

ring-, Ring-: ~fahndung *die* intensive manhunt [over a wide area]; **~finger** *der* ring finger; **~förmig A** *Adj.* in the shape of a ring *postpos.;* circular; annular ‹*eclipse*›; **~förmige Verbindungen** (Chem.) ring *or* cyclic compounds; **B** *adv.* ‹*arrange*› in a ring *or* circle; ‹*spread out*› in rings *or* circles; **die Straße verläuft ~förmig um die ganze Stadt** the road rings the whole town; **~impfung** *die* ring vaccination; **~kampf** *der* **1)** [stand-up] fight; **2)** (Sport) (Wettbewerb) wrestling bout; (Sportart) ▸ **Ringen**; **~kämpfer** *der,* **~kämpferin** *die* wrestler

Ringlein *das;* **~s, ~:** [little] ring

Ringlotte /rɪŋˈglɔtə/ *die;* **~, ~n** (bes. österr.) greengage

Ring-: ~mauer *die* ringwall; **~muskel** *der* ▸ⓘ **S. 435** (Anat.) sphincter; **~richter** *der,* **~richterin** *die* (Boxen) referee

rings /rɪŋs/ *Adv.* all around; **sich ~ im Kreise umsehen** look all around one; **~ von Bergen umgeben** completely surrounded by mountains

Ring·schlüssel *der* ring spanner

rings·herum *Adv.* all around [it/them *etc.*]; *s. auch* **rings**

Ring·straße *die* ring road; (um den Stadtkern) inner ring road

rings-: ~um, ~umher *Adv.* all around; *s. auch* **rings**

Ring-: ~tennis *das* deck tennis; **~wall** *der* (Archäol.) ringwall

Rinne /ˈrɪnə/ *die;* **~, ~n** channel; (Dach~, Rinnstein) gutter; (tiefer) gully; (Abfluss) drainpipe; (Rille) groove; (im Meeresboden) trench

rinnen *unr. itr. V.* **1)** *mit sein* run; **das Geld rinnt ihm durch die Finger** money just slips through his fingers **2)** (südd.: undicht sein) leak

Rinnsal /ˈrɪnzaːl/ *das;* **~[e]s, ~e** (geh.) rivulet; **ein ~ von Blut/Öl** a trickle of blood/oil

Rinn·stein *der* gutter; **jmdn. aus dem ~ auflesen** (fig.) pick sb. out of the gutter; **im ~ enden** *od.* **landen** (fig.) end up in the gutter

Riposte /riˈpɔstə/ *die;* **~, ~n** (Fechten) riposte

Rippchen *das;* **~s, ~** (Kochk. südd.) rib [of pork]

Rippe /ˈrɪpə/ *die;* **~, ~n 1)** ▸ⓘ **S. 435** (Anat., Bot., Technik, Textilw., Bautechnik, fig.) rib; (Technik: Kühl~) fin; **sie hat nichts auf den ~n** (ugs.) she is only skin and bone; **bei ihm kann man die ~n zählen** (ugs.) you can see his ribs sticking out; **dass er was auf die ~n kriegt** (ugs.) to put some flesh on his bones; **ich kann es mir nicht aus den ~n schneiden** (ugs.) I can't just produce it out of thin air **2)** (einer Zitrusfrucht) segment; (einer Tafel Schokolade) strip

Rippen-: ~bogen *der* ▸ⓘ **S. 435** (Anat.) costal arch; **~bruch** *der* ▸ⓘ **S. 439** (Med.) rib fracture; **~fell** *das* ▸ⓘ **S. 435** (Anat.) costal pleura; **~fell·entzündung** *die* ▸ⓘ **S. 439** (Med.) pleurisy *no indef. art.;* **~speer** *der od. das;* **~~[e]s: [Kasseler] ~speer** cured rib of pork; **~stoß** *der* dig in the ribs; (sanfter, auch fig.) nudge; **~stück** *das* (Kochk.) piece of rib

Ripp·samt *der* corduroy

Rips /rɪps/ *der;* **~es, ~e** (Textilw.) rep[p]

Risiko /ˈriːziko/ *das;* **~s, Risiken** *od.* **~s** *od. österr.* **Risken** risk; **das ~ eingehen, dass etw. geschieht** run the risk of sth. happening; **ein/kein ~ eingehen** take a risk/not take any risks; **die Sache ist mit einem gewissen ~ verbunden** there is a certain amount of risk involved [in it]; **auf eigenes/dein/mein ~:** at one's/your/my own risk

risiko-, Risiko-: ~arm A *Adj.* low-risk; **B** *adv.* with little risk; **möglichst ~arm** with the lowest possible risk; **~bereit A** *Adj.* ready to take risks *postpos.;* **B** *adv.* ready to take risks; (wagemutig) daringly; **~bereitschaft** *die* readiness to take risks; **~faktor** *der* risk factor; **der ~faktor Alkohol** the risk factor represented by alcohol; **~frei** ▸ **~los**; **~freudig A** *Adj.* risky ‹*driving*›; ‹*player, speculator*› who likes taking risks; **er ist sehr ~freudig** he likes playing with fire *or* taking [a lot of] risks; **B** *adv.* **er fährt/spielt sehr ~freudig** he likes to take [a lot of] risks when he drives/plays; **~geburt** *die* (Med.) difficult *or* complicated birth; **~gruppe** *die* risk group; **~los A** *Adj.* safe; without risk *postpos.;* **B** *adv.* safely; without taking risks; **~reich** *Adj.* very risky; **~schwangerschaft** *die* pregnancy involving some risk

riskant /rɪsˈkant/

A *Adj.* risky

B *adv.* riskily; **er fährt zu ~:** he takes too many risks [in his driving]

riskieren /rɪsˈkiːrən/ *tr. V.* risk; venture ‹*smile, remark*›; run the risk of ‹*accident, thrashing, etc.*›; (gefährden) put ‹*reputation, job*› at risk; risk ‹*life, reputation*›; **etwas/nichts ~:** take a risk/not take any risks; **einen verstohlenen Blick ~:** steal a furtive glance

Rispe /ˈrɪspə/ *die;* **~, ~n** (Bot.) panicle

riss, *riß /rɪs/ *1. u. 3. Pers. Sg. Prät. v.* **reißen**

Riss, *Riß /rɪs/ *der;* **Risses, Risse 1)** (im Stoff, Papier, Gewebe) tear; (im Tonband) break; **die Hose hat einen ~/du hast einen ~ in der Hose** the trousers/your trousers are torn *or* have a tear; **einen ~ bekommen** tear **2)** (Spalt, Sprung) crack; (fig.: Kluft) rift; split; **einen ~ bekommen** become cracked; (fig.) ‹*friendship*› begin to break up **3)** (Zeichnung) plan; (Entwurf) sketch

rissig *Adj.* cracked; chapped ‹*lips*›

Rist /rɪst/ *der;* **~es, ~e** (des Fußes) instep; (der Hand) back [of the hand]

Rist·griff *der* (Turnen) overgrasp

rite /ˈriːtə/ *Adv.* (Hochschulw.) **~ bestehen** get a pass (*in one's doctoral examination*); **mit „~" bewertet werden** be given a pass

Riten ▸ **Ritus**

ritsch *Interj.* rip; zip; **~, ratsch** rip, rip

ritt *1. u. 3. Pers. Sg. Prät. v.* **reiten**

Ritt *der;* **~[e]s, ~e** ride; **einen weiten/scharfen ~ machen** go for a long/hard ride; **auf einen** *od.* **in einem ~** (ugs.) in one go (coll.)

Rittberger /ˈrɪtbɛrgɐ/ *der;* **~s, ~** (Sport) loop jump; **einen ~ springen** do a loop jump

Ritter *der;* **~s, ~ 1)** knight; **jmdn. zum ~ schlagen** (hist.) knight sb.; dub sb. [a] knight; **fahrender ~** (hist.) knight errant; **~ ohne Furcht und Tadel** chevalier sans peur et sans reproche; (fig. geh., oft scherzh.) knight in shining armour **2)** (Adelstitel) (als Teil eines Namens) Ritter; (Ordens~) Knight **3)** *in* **arme ~** (Kochk.) French toast

Ritter-: ~burg *die* knight's castle; **~dichtung** *die* (Literaturwiss.) knightly poetry; **~gut** *das* (hist.) ≈ manor; feudal estate; **~kreuz** *das* (ns.) Knight's Cross

ritterlich

A *Adj.* **1)** chivalrous **2)** (zum Rittertum gehörend) knightly ‹*life, culture, virtues, ideals*›

B *adv.* chivalrously

Ritterlichkeit *die;* **~:** chivalrousness; chivalry

Ritter-: ~orden *der* order of knights; knightly order; **~roman** *der* romance of chivalry; knightly romance

Ritterschaft *die;* **~** (hist.) knighthood

Ritter-: ~schlag *der* (hist.) knightly accolade; **den ~schlag empfangen** be knighted; be dubbed [a] knight; **~sporn** *der;* **~~[e]s, ~~e** (Bot.) larkspur; (Gartenrittersporn) delphinium; **~stand** *der* (hist.) knighthood; **jmdn. in den ~stand aufnehmen** make sb. a knight

Rittertum *das;* **~s** (hist.) knighthood

Ritter·zeit *die* days *pl.* of the knights; (Zeit der Ritterlichkeit) Age of Chivalry

rittlings /ˈrɪtlɪŋs/ *Adv.* astride; **~ auf einem Stuhl sitzen** sit astride a chair

Ritt·meister *der* (Milit. hist.) cavalry captain

Ritual /riˈtu̯aːl/ *das;* **~s, ~e** *od.* **Ritualien** /-li̯ən/ (Rel., fig.) ritual

ritualisieren *tr. V.* (geh.) ritualize

Ritualisierung *die;* **~, ~en** ritualization

Ritual·mord *der* ritual murder

rituell /riˈtu̯ɛl/ (Rel., fig.)

A *Adj.* ritual

B *adv.* ritually

Ritus /ˈriːtʊs/ *der;* **~, Riten** (Rel., fig.) rite

Ritz /rɪt͜s/ *der;* **~es, ~e 1)** (Kratzer) scratch **2)** ▸ **Ritze**

Ritze *die;* **~, ~n** crack; [narrow] gap; **durch eine ~ spähen** peer through a crack *or* slit; **auf der ~ schlafen** (ugs. scherzh.) sleep on the join (*of a pair of* [*twin*] *beds*)

Ritzel /ˈrɪt͜sl/ *das;* **~s, ~** (Technik) pinion

ritzen *tr. V.* **1)** scratch; (tiefer) cut; **sich** (*Dat.*) **das Kinn ~:** scratch/cut one's chin **2)** (ein~) carve ‹*name etc.*› (**in** + *Akk.* in); (in eine Metallplatte) engrave ‹*drawing etc.*›

Rivale /riˈvaːlə/ *der;* **~n, ~n, Rivalin** *die;* **~, ~nen** rival

rivalisieren *itr. V.* **mit jmdm. um etw. ~:** compete with sb. for sth.; **~de Gruppen** rival groups

Rivalität /rivaliˈtɛːt/ *die;* **~, ~en** rivalry *no indef. art.*

Riviera /riˈvi̯eːra/ *die;* **~:** Riviera

Rizinus /ˈriːt͜sinʊs/ *der;* **~, ~** *od.* **~se 1)** (Pflanze) castor-oil plant **2)** (~öl) castor oil

RK *Abk.* (EU) **= Regierungskonferenz** IGC

Roaming /ˈroʊmɪŋ/ *das;* **~s** (Fernspr.) roaming

Roastbeef /ˈroːstbiːf/ *das;* **~s, ~s 1)** (roh) sirloin (Brit.) **2)** (gebraten) roast [sirloin (Brit.) of] beef

Robbe /ˈrɔbə/ *die;* **~, ~n** seal

robben *itr. V.; meist, mit Richtungsangabe nur, mit sein* crawl

Robben-: ~fang *der* sealing; seal-hunting; **~kolonie** *die* seal colony; **~schlag** *der* seal cull

Robe /ˈroːbə/ *die;* **~, ~n 1)** robe; (schwarz) gown **2)** (Abendkleid) evening gown

r

Robinie /ro'bi:ni̯ə/ *die;* **~, ~n** (Bot.) robinia; false acacia

Robinsonade /robɪnzo'na:də/ *die;* **~, ~n** (Roman/Abenteuer) Robinson-Crusoe style novel/adventure

roboten /'rɔbɔtn̩/ *itr. V.* (ugs.) slave [away]

Roboter /'rɔbɔtɐ/ *der;* **~s, ~:** robot

Robotik /ro'bɔtik/ *die;* **~:** robotics

robust /ro'bʊst/ *Adj.* robust

Robustheit *die;* **~:** robustness; (Gesundheit) robust constitution

roch /rɔx/ *1. u. 3. Pers. Sg. Prät. v.* **riechen**

Rochade /rɔ'xa:də/ *die;* **~, ~n** (Schach) castling; **kleine/große ~:** short/long castling; **die ~ ausführen** castle

röcheln /'rœçl̩n/ *itr. V.* breathe stertorously; ‹*dying person*› give the death rattle

Rochen /'rɔxn̩/ *der;* **~s, ~** (Zool.) ray

rochieren /rɔ'xi:rən/ *itr. V.* **1** (Schach) castle **2** *mit Richtungsangabe mit sein* (Sport) change over; switch positions

Rock¹ /rɔk/ *der;* **~[e]s, Röcke** /'rœkə/ **1** skirt; (Schotten~) kilt; **hinter jedem ~ her sein** *od.* **herlaufen** (ugs.) be after *or* chase every bit of skirt (sl.) **2** (landsch.: Jacke) jacket; **der grüne ~ [des Försters]** the [forester's] green coat; **den bunten ~ anziehen/ausziehen** (fig. veralt.) go for a soldier (arch.)/leave the army; **des Königs ~ tragen** (fig. veralt.) be a soldier of the King; **der letzte ~ hat keine Taschen** (fig.) you can't take it with you

Rock² *der;* **~[s]** (Musik) rock [music]

Rock and Roll /'rɔk ɛnt 'rɔl/ *der;* **~[s], ~[s]** rock and roll *no pl.*

Rock·aufschlag *der* [jacket] lapel; **am ~:** in one's lapel

Röckchen /'rœkçən/ *das;* **~s, ~:** little skirt; (kurz) short skirt

rocken *itr. V.* rock

Rocker *der;* **~s, ~:** rocker

Rockerin *die;* **~, ~nen** [female] rocker

Rock·idol *das* rock idol

rockig *Adj.* rock ‹*music*›; rock-like ‹*jazz etc.*›

Rock-: ~konzert *das* rock concert **~musik** *die* rock music; **~musiker** *der,* **~musikerin** *die* rock musician; **~oper** *die* rock opera; **~sänger** *der* **~sängerin** *die* rock singer; **~schoß** *der* coat-tail; *s. auch* **~zipfel**; **~star** *der* rock star; **~zipfel** *der: in* **an jmds.** *od.* **jmdm. am ~zipfel hängen** cling *or* hang on to sb.; (fig.: unselbstständig sein) lean on *or* be dependent on sb.; **jmdn. [gerade noch] am ~zipfel erwischen** just [manage to] catch sb.; *s. auch* **Rock¹ 1**

Rodel /'ro:dl̩/ *der;* **~s, ~** (südd.) ▸**Rodelschlitten**

Rodel·bahn *die* toboggan run; (bei sportlichen Veranstaltungen) luge run

rodeln /'ro:dl̩n/ *itr. V.; meist, mit Richtungsangabe nur, mit sein* sledge; toboggan; (als Sport) luge

rödeln *itr. V.* beaver away

Rodeln *das;* **~s** sledging *no art.;* tobogganing *no art.;* (Sport) luge

Rodel·schlitten *der* sledge; toboggan; (bei sportlichen Veranstaltungen) luge

roden /'ro:dn̩/
A *tr. V.* **1** clear ‹*wood, land*›; (ausgraben) grub up ‹*tree*› **2** (ernten) lift ‹*potatoes etc.*›
B *itr. V.* clear the land

Rodeo /ro'de:o/ *das od. der;* **~s, ~s** rodeo

Rodler /'ro:dlɐ/ *der;* **~s, ~, Rodlerin** *die;* **~, ~nen** tobogganer; (bei sportlichen Veranstaltungen) luger

Rodung *die;* **~, ~en 1** (das Roden) clearing; clearance; (das Ausgraben) grubbing up **2** (gerodete Fläche) clearance

Rogen /'ro:gn̩/ *der;* **~s, ~:** roe

roger /'rɔdʒɐ/ *Adv.* (Funkw.) roger; **alles ~** (ugs.) everything fine

Roggen /'rɔgn̩/ *der;* **~s** rye

Roggen-: ~brot *das* rye bread; **ein ~brot** a loaf of rye bread; **~brötchen** *das* rye-bread roll

Rogner /'ro:gnɐ/ *der;* **~s, ~:** spawner

roh /ro:/
A *Adj.* **1** raw ‹*food*›; unboiled ‹*milk*›; raw, uncooked ‹*ham*›; **jmdn./etw. wie ein ~es Ei behandeln** handle sb./sth. with kid gloves **2** (nicht bearbeitet) rough, unfinished ‹*wood*›; rough, uncut ‹*diamond*›; rough-hewn, undressed ‹*stone*›; crude ‹*ore, metal*›; unbleached ‹*cloth*›; untreated ‹*skin*›; raw ‹*silk, sugar*› **3** (ungenau) rough **4** (brutal) brutish ‹*person, treatment, etc.*›; (grausam) callous ‹*person, treatment*›; (grob) coarse, uncouth ‹*manners, words, joke*›; brute *attrib.* ‹*force*›
B *adv.* **1** (ungenau) roughly; **~ zusammengeschlagen** crudely knocked together **2** (brutal) brutishly; (grausam) callously; (grob) coarsely; in an uncouth manner

Roh-: ~bau *der; Pl.* **~~ten** shell [of a/the building]; **das Haus ist im ~bau fertig** the shell of the house is complete; **~daten** *die Pl.* (DV) raw data; **~diamant** *der* rough *or* uncut diamond; **~eisen** *das* pig iron

***Roheit** ▸**Rohheit**

Roh-: ~ertrag *der* (Wirtsch.) gross return; **~erz** *das* crude ore; **~erzeugnis** *das* ▸**~produkt**; **~fassung** *die* unfinished version

Rohheit /'ro:hai̯t/ *die;* **~, ~en 1** (Brutalität) brutishness; (Grausamkeit) callousness; (Grobheit) coarseness; uncouthness **2** (Handlung) brutish/callous deed; (Äußerung) callous remark

Roh·kost *die* raw fruit and vegetables *pl.*

Rohköstler /'ro:kœstlɐ/ *der;* **~s, ~, Rohköstlerin** *die;* **~, ~nen** *person who eats raw fruit and vegetables only*

Rohling /'ro:lɪŋ/ *der;* **~s, ~e 1** (abwertend: Mensch) brute; beast **2** (Technik) blank

Roh-: ~material *das* raw material; **~öl** *das* crude oil; **~produkt** *das* natural product [requiring further treatment]; (**~stoff**) raw material

Rohr /ro:ɐ̯/ *das;* **~[e]s, ~e 1** (Leitungs~) pipe; (als Bauteil) tube; (Geschütz~) barrel; **das Schiff feuerte aus allen ~en** the ship fired with all its guns **2** (Röhricht) reeds *pl.* **3** (Schilf usw. als Werkstoff) reed; (Bambus, Zucker~ usw.) cane; **ein aus ~ geflochtener Korb/Stuhl** a reed basket/chair; **ein Korb/Stuhl aus ~** (aus Peddigrohr) a cane basket/chair; **spanisches ~:** rattan cane **4** (Schilf-, Riedhalm) reed **5** (südd., österr.: Backofen) oven

Rohr-: ~ammer *die* (Zool.) reed bunting; **~blatt** *das* reed; **~bruch** *der* burst pipe

Röhrchen /'rø:ɐ̯çən/ *das;* **~s, ~:** small pipe; (Behälter) small tube; (Reagenzglas) test tube; **ins ~ blasen** take the breathalyser test

Rohrdommel /-dɔməl/ *die;* **~, ~n** (Zool.) bittern

Röhre /'rø:rə/ *die;* **~, ~n 1** (Rohr) tube; (Leitungs~) pipe; (Tunnel~) bore; (Jägerspr.: Gang eines Baus) gallery; *s. auch* **kommunizieren 1** **2** (Leuchtstoff~) [fluorescent] tube; (Elektronen~) valve (Brit.); tube (Amer.); (ugs.: Bild~) [picture] tube; **vor der ~ sitzen** sit in front of the box (coll.) **3** (Behälter) **eine ~ [mit] Tabletten** a tube of pills **4** (eines Ofens) oven; **in die ~ sehen** *od.* **gucken** (fig. ugs.) be left out [in the cold]

röhren *itr. V.* ‹*stag etc.*› bell; (fig.) roar

röhren-, Röhren-: ~förmig *Adj.* tubular; **~hose** *die* drainpipe trousers; **~knochen** *der* long bone; **~pilz** *der* boletus

Rohr-: ~flöte *die* reed pipe; (Panflöte) pan pipes *pl.*; **~geflecht** *das* woven cane

Röhricht /'rø:rɪçt/ *das;* **~s, ~e** reeds *pl.*

Rohr-: ~kolben *der* reed mace; cat's-tail; **~krepierer** *der;* **~~s, ~~:** barrel burst; **~leger** *der;* **~~s, ~~, ~legerin** *die;* **~~, ~~nen** pipelayer; **~leitung** *die* pipe; (über längere Entfernung) pipeline

Röhrling /'rø:ɐ̯lɪŋ/ *der;* **~s, ~e** boletus

Rohr-: ~post *die* pneumatic dispatch; **etw. mit ~post befördern** convey sth. by pneumatic tube; **~sänger** *der* (Zool.) reed warbler; **~spatz** *der: in* **schimpfen wie ein ~spatz** (ugs.) really create (coll.); **~stock** *der* cane [walking stick]; **~zange** *die* footprint; **~zucker** *der* cane sugar

Roh·seide *die* raw silk

roh·seiden *Adj.* raw-silk *attrib.*

Roh·stoff *der* raw material

Rohstoff-: ~mangel *der* lack of raw materials; **~preis** *der* raw material price; **~reserve** *die* reserve of raw materials

Roh-: ~übersetzung *die* rough translation; **~zucker** *der* raw *or* unrefined sugar; **~zustand** *der* raw state; **im ~zustand** in a raw state; (von Gütern) in an unfinished state; (von einem Schriftstück usw.) in a rough draft

Rokoko /'rɔkoko/ *das;* **~[s]** rococo; (Zeit) rococo period

Rokoko·möbel *das* piece of rococo furniture; **teure ~:** expensive rococo furniture *sing.*

***Rolladen** ▸**Rollladen**

Roll·bahn *die* (Flugw.) taxiway

Röllchen /'rœlçən/ *das;* **~s, ~ 1** (Spule) little reel *or* spool **2** (etwas Zusammengerolltes) little roll **3** (Walze) little roller **4** ▸**Rolle 4**

Rolle /'rɔlə/ *die;* **~, ~n 1** (Spule) reel; spool; **eine ~ Film** a spool of film; (Schmalfilm) a reel of film **2** (zylindrischer [Hohl]körper; Zusammengerolltes) roll; (zum Verschicken von Plakaten o. Ä.) [cardboard] tube; (von Papier zum Drucken) reel; (Schrift~) scroll; **eine ~ Bindfaden/Drops/Frankenstücke/Kekse** a reel of string/tube of fruit drops/roll of one-franc pieces/[round] packet of biscuits **3** (Walze) roller; (Teig~) rolling pin **4** (Rad) [small] wheel; (an Möbeln usw.) castor; (für Gardine, Schiebetür usw.) runner; (mit einer Rille für ein Seil o. Ä.) pulley **5** (Turnen, Kunstflug) roll; **eine ~ [vorwärts/rückwärts] machen** do a [forward/backward] roll **6** (Theater, Film usw., fig.) role; part; (Soziol.) role; **sich in die ~ eines anderen versetzen** put oneself in sb. else's position; **[bei jmdm./einer Sache] eine entscheidende/überragende ~ spielen** be of crucial/overriding importance [to sb./for sth.]; **es spielt keine ~:** it is of no importance; (es macht nichts aus) it doesn't matter; (es gehört nicht zur Sache) it is irrelevant; **Geld spielt [bei ihm] keine ~:** money is no object [for him]; **solche Erwägungen dürfen dabei keine ~ spielen** such considerations must not be allowed to enter into it *or* influence things; **aus der ~ fallen** forget oneself **7** (Radsport) roller (*on a pacing motorcycle*); (fig. ugs.) **von der ~ kommen** get left behind; lose ground

***Rolleine** ▸**Rollleine**

rollen
A *tr. V.* **1** roll; (im Rollstuhl) wheel; **die Augen ~:** roll one's eyes; **das R ~:** roll one's r's; **sich** (*Dat.*) **eine Zigarette ~:** roll oneself a cigarette **2** (auf~, zusammen~, ein~) roll up ‹*blanket, carpet, map, etc.*›; **jmdn./etw./sich in eine Decke ~:** roll sb./sth./oneself up in a blanket **3** (aus~) roll out ‹*dough*›
B *itr. V.* **1** *mit sein* ‹*ball, wheel, etc.*› roll; ‹*vehicle*› move; ‹*aircraft*› taxi; **mit den Augen ~:** roll one's eyes; **ins R~ kommen** start to move; get under way (lit. or fig.); (unbeabsichtigt) start to move; **es werden Köpfe ~** (fig.) heads will roll; **etw. ins R~ bringen** set sth. in motion; get sth. going (lit. or fig.); (unbeabsichtigt) set sth. moving **2** (Seemannsspr.: schlingern [und stampfen]) ‹*ship*› roll [and pitch] **3** (donnern) *mit Richtungsangabe mit sein* ‹*thunder, guns, echo*› rumble
C *refl. V.* **1** (sich ein~) ‹*paper, carpet*› curl [up] **2** (sich wälzen) roll; **er rollte sich in die Rückenlage** he rolled over on to his back

rollen-, Rollen-: ~fach *das* (Theater) type of role; **das ~fach der Naiven** the ingénue type of role; **~förmig** *Adj.* cylindrical; **~konflikt** *der* (Soziol.) role conflict; **~lager** *das* (Technik) roller bearing; **~spiel** *das* (Sozialpsych.) role playing *no pl., no art.;* role play *no pl., no art.;* **~tausch** *der* exchange of roles; (bei entgegengesetzten ~) role reversal; **~verhalten** *das* role[-specific] behaviour; **~verteilung** *die* (Sozialpsych.) allocation of roles

Roller *der;* **~s, ~ 1** scooter; **~ fahren** ride a/one's scooter **2** (Fußball) half-hit shot along the ground **3** (Deo~) roll-on [container]

Rollerblade (Wz) /'roʊləbleɪd/ *der;* **~s, ~s** Rollerblade ®

Roller·fahrer *der*, **Roller·fahrerin** *die* scooter rider

rollern *itr. V.; meist, mit Richtungsangabe nur, mit sein* ride a/one's scooter

Rollerskate /'roʊləskeɪt/ *der;* **~s, ~s** roller skate

Roll-: ~feld *das* [operational] airfield; landing field; **~film** *der* roll film; **~geld** *das* (Eisenb.) parcel freight [charge] (*for delivery to and collection from station or depot*); **~gut** *das* (Eisenb.) freight (*delivered to and collected from station or depot*); **~kommando** *das* party of bully boys; **~kragen** *der* polo neck; **~kragen·pullover** *der* polo neck[ed] sweater; **~kur** *die* (Med.) *treatment in which the patient takes medicine and then lies in different positions;* **~laden** *der; Pl.* **~läden,** *auch* **~~**: [roller] shutter; **~mops** *der* rollmops

Rolli /'rɔli/ *der;* **~s, ~s** 1▸ (ugs.: Rollkragenpullover) polo neck; 2▸ (Jargon) (Rollstuhlfahrer/-fahrerin) wheelchair user

rollig /'rɔlɪç/ (fachspr.)

A *Adj.* on heat *postpos.*; (fig.) randy (coll.); horny (coll.)

B *adv.* on heat

Roll·leine *die* retractable dog lead

Rollo /'rɔlo/ *das;* **~s, ~s** [roller] blind

Roll-out, *auch* **Rollout** /roʊl'|aʊt/ *der od. das;* **~s, ~s** (auch fig.) roll-out

Roll-: ~schinken *der* rolled smoked ham; **~schuh** *der* roller skate; **~schuh laufen** roller skate

Rollschuh-: ~bahn *die* roller skating rink; **~laufen** *das;* **~~s** roller skating *no art.*; **~läufer** *der*, **~läuferin** *die* roller skater

Roll-: ~splitt *der* loose chippings *pl.*; **~sprung** *der* (Leichtathletik) Western roll; **~stuhl** *der* wheelchair; **~stuhl·fahrer** *der*, **~stuhl·fahrerin** *die* wheelchair user; **~treppe** *die* escalator; **~wagen** *der* trolley

Rom¹ /ro:m/ *(das);* ▸❶ **S. 675 ~s** Rome; **viele Wege führen nach ~** (Spr.) there is more than one way to skin a cat (prov.); **Zustände wie im alten ~** (fig.) everything in chaos; **~ ist auch nicht an einem Tag erbaut worden** (Spr.) Rome wasn't built in a day (prov.)

Rom² /rɔm/ *der;* **~s, ~a** European gypsy

Roman /ro'ma:n/ *der;* **~s, ~e** novel; **einen ganzen/langen ~ erzählen** (fig.) tell a very long story *or* (derog.) a long rigmarole; **erzähl keine ~e** (fig.) don't tell stories; (fass dich kürzer) we don't want any long rigmaroles

Romancier /romã'sie:/ *der;* **~s, ~s** novelist

Romane /ro'ma:nə/ *der;* **~n, ~n** speaker of a Romance language; Latin

Roman-: ~figur *die* character from *or* in a novel; **eine ~figur bei Dickens** a character from *or* in a Dickens novel; **~form** *die* novel form; **in ~form** in the form of a novel; **~heft** *das* [paper-covered] novelette

Romani /'romani/ *das;* **~s** (Sprachw.) Romany

Romanik /ro'ma:nɪk/ *die;* **~:** Romanesque; (Zeit) Romanesque period

Romanin *die;* **~, ~nen** ▸**Romane**; *s. auch* **-in**

romanisch

A *Adj.* 1▸ ▸❶ **S. 670** Romance ‹*language, literature*›; Latin ‹*people, country, charm*›; ‹*Department*› of Romance Studies 2▸ (Kunstwiss.: der Romanik) Romanesque

B *adv.* ‹*build*› in a Romanesque style

romanisieren *tr. V.* 1▸ (romanisch machen) give ‹*town etc.*› a Latin character 2▸ (hist.: römisch machen) romanize ‹*country etc.*›

Romanist *der;* **~en, ~en** Romance scholar; Romanist; (Student) student of Romance languages and literature

Romanistik /roma'nɪstɪk/ *die;* **~:** Romance studies *pl., no art.*; (Sprache und Literatur) Romance languages and literature *no art.*

Romanistin *die;* **~, ~nen** ▸**Romanist**

romanistisch *Adj.* Romance ‹*studies*›; ‹*periodical*› for Romance studies

Romantik /ro'mantɪk/ *die;* **~** 1▸ (romantischer Charakter) romanticism; romantic nature; **die ~ des Zigeunerlebens/der Straße** the romance of gypsy life/of the road 2▸ (Literaturw., Musik usw.) (Bewegung) Romanticism *no art.*; Romantic movement; (Epoche) Romantic period; **die jüngere/ältere ~:** the younger/older Romantics *pl.*

Romantiker *der;* **~s, ~, Romantikerin** *die;* **~, ~nen** 1▸ (Kunstwiss.) Romantic 2▸ (romantischer Mensch) romantic

romantisch

A *Adj.* 1▸ romantic 2▸ (Literaturw., Musik usw.) Romantic

B *adv.* romantically; **~ veranlagt sein** have a romantic disposition

romantisieren *tr. V.* romanticize

Roman-: ~vorlage *die* source novel; **nach einer ~vorlage von X** based on a novel by X; **~werk** *das* 1▸ (Roman) novel; 2▸ (Romane eines Autors) novels *pl.*

Romanze /ro'mantsə/ *die;* **~, ~n** (Literaturw., Musik, fig.) romance

Römer /'rø:mɐ/ *der;* **~s, ~** 1▸ ▸❶ **S. 520,** ▸❶ **S. 675** (Person) Roman; **die [alten] ~:** the [ancient] Romans 2▸ (Weinglas) rummer

Römer·brief *der* Epistle to the Romans

Römerin *die;* **~, ~nen** ▸❶ **S. 520** Roman; *s. auch* **-in**

Römer·topf Ⓦⓩ *der: oval earthenware cooking pot;* ≈ cooking brick

römisch

A *Adj.* ▸❶ **S. 520,** ▸❶ **S. 675** Roman; **die R~en Verträge** the Treaty of Rome

B *adv.* **das ~ besetzte Gallien** the part of Gaul occupied by the Romans

römisch-katholisch

A *Adj.* Roman Catholic

B *adv.* **~ getauft** baptized into the Roman Catholic church

röm.-kath. *Abk.* = **römisch-katholisch** RC

Rommé /'rɔme/ *das;* **~s, ~s** (Kartenspiele) rummy *no art.*

Rondeau /rõ'do/ *das;* **~s, ~s** 1▸ (Literaturw.) rondeau 2▸ (österr.: Beet, Platz) ▸**Rondell 1, 2**

Rondell /rɔn'dɛl/ *das;* **~s, ~e** 1▸ (Beet) circular flower bed 2▸ (Platz) circus 3▸ (österr.: Weg) circular path 4▸ (Archit.: Turm) round tower

Rondo /'rɔndo/ *das;* **~s, ~s** 1▸ (Literaturw.) rondeau 2▸ (Musik) rondo

röntgen /'rœntgn̩/ *tr. V.* X-ray; **sich** *(Akk.)*/**sich** *(Dat.)* **den Magen ~ lassen** have an X-ray/have one's stomach X-rayed

Röntgen-: ~aufnahme *die* X-ray [image/photograph]; **~augen** *Pl.* (scherzh.) X-ray eyes; **~bild** *das* ▸**~aufnahme**; **~blick** *der* (scherzh.) X-ray vision *no art.*; **~gerät** *das* X-ray apparatus

röntgenisieren *tr. V.* (österr.) ▸**röntgen**

Röntgenologe /rœntgeno'lo:gə/ *der;* **~n, ~n** ▸❶ **S. 113** radiologist

Röntgenologie *die;* **~:** radiology *no art.*

Röntgenologin *die;* **~, ~nen** ▸❶ **S. 113** radiologist

Röntgen-: ~schirm *der* X-ray screen; **~strahlen** *Pl.* X-rays; **~therapie** *die* X-ray treatment *no indef. art.*; **eine ~therapie** a course of X-ray treatment; **~untersuchung** *die* X-ray examination

Roquefort /'rɔkfo:ɐ̯/ *der;* **~s, ~s** Roquefort

Ro-Ro-Schiff /ro'ro:-/ *das* ro-ro *or* roll-on roll-off ship

rosa /'ro:za/

A *indekl. Adj.* pink; *s. auch* **Brille**

B *adv.* pink

Rosa *das;* **~s, ~** *od.* **~s** pink

rosa-: ~farben, ~farbig *Adj.* pink; **~rot** *Adj.* [deep] pink; (fig.) rosy; *s. auch* **Brille**

rösch /rø:ʃ/ *Adj.* (südd.) crisp

Röschen /'rø:sçən/ *das;* **~s, ~** 1▸ (kleine Rose) [little] rose 2▸ (Blumenkohl~) [cauliflower] floweret; (Rosenkohl~) [Brussels] sprout

rosé /ro'ze:/

A *indekl. Adj.* pale pink

B *adv.* pale pink

Rose /'ro:zə/ *die;* **~, ~n** 1▸ rose; **sie sind nicht [gerade] auf ~n gebettet** their life is no bed of roses; **keine ~ ohne Dornen** (Spr.) no rose without a thorn 2▸ (Fenster~) rose window 3▸ (Jägerspr.) burr

Rosé¹ *das;* **~s, ~** *od.* **~s** pale pink

Rosé² *der;* **~s, ~s** rosé [wine]

rosen-, Rosen-: ~beet *das* rose bed; **~blatt** *das* rose petal; (Laubblatt) rose leaf; **~blüte** *die* 1▸ rose [bloom]; 2▸ (das Blühen) flowering period for roses; **die ~blüte hat begonnen** the roses have started to flower *or* bloom; **~duft** *der* scent of roses; **~garten** *der* rose garden; **~gewächs** *das* (Bot.) rose; rosaceous plant; **die ~gewächse** the Rosaceae; **~holz** *das* rosewood; **~kohl** *der* [Brussels] sprouts *pl.*; **~kranz** *der* (kath. Kirche) rosary; **einen ~kranz beten** say a rosary; **~krieg** *der* (hist.) War of the Roses; (fig.) feud; **~montag** *der* the day before Shrove Tuesday; **~montags·zug** *der: carnival procession on the day before Shrove Tuesday;* **~öl** *das* attar of roses; **~quarz** *der* rose quartz; **~rot** *Adj.* deep pink; **~stock** *der* rose tree; standard rose; **~strauß** *der; Pl.* **~sträuße** bunch *or* bouquet of roses; **~verkäufer** *der*, **~verkäuferin** *die* rose-seller; **~wasser** *das; Pl.* **~wässer** rose water; **~züchter** *der*, **~züchterin** *die* rose grower

Rosette /ro'zɛtə/ *die;* **~, ~n** 1▸ (Archit.) rose window 2▸ (Verzierung, Bot.) rosette

Rosé·wein *der* rosé wine

rosig

A *Adj.* 1▸ rosy ‹*face, complexion, etc.*›; pink ‹*piglet etc.*›; **~ und gesund aussehen** be glowing with health 2▸ (fig.) rosy; optimistic ‹*mood*›; **etw. in den ~sten Farben schildern** paint sth. in the most glowing colours

B *adv.* **ihm geht es nicht gerade ~:** things aren't too good with him

Rosine /ro'zi:nə/ *die;* **~, ~n** raisin; (Korinthe) currant; **[große] ~n im Kopf haben** (fig. ugs.) have big ideas; **sich** *(Dat.)* **die ~n herauspicken** *od.* **aus dem Kuchen picken** (fig. ugs.) take the pick of the bunch [for oneself]

Rosinen-: ~brot *das* currant bread; (Laib) currant loaf; **~kuchen** *der* currant cake

Rosmarin /'ro:smari:n/ *der;* **~s** rosemary

Ross, *Roß /rɔs/ *das;* **Rosses, Rosse** *od.* **Rösser** /'rœsɐ/ 1▸ (geh.; südd., österr., schweiz. noch Normalspr.) horse; steed (poet./joc.); **hoch zu ~:** on horseback; (scherzh.) on one's [trusty] steed (joc.); **auf dem** *od.* **seinem hohen ~ sitzen** be on one's high horse; **von seinem** *od.* **vom hohen ~ herunterkommen** *od.* **-steigen** get down off one's high horse; **~ und Reiter nennen** name names 2▸ *Pl.* **Rösser** (ugs.: Trottel) fool; idiot

Ross-, *Roß- *s. auch* **Pferde-**

Rössel /'rœsl̩/ *das;* **~s, ~** 1▸ (landsch.) small horse 2▸ (Schach) knight

Rössel·sprung *der: puzzle in which certain syllables make up a phrase or saying when taken in a sequence of knight's moves in a squared diagram*

Ross-, *Roß-: ~haar *das* horsehair; **~kastanie** *die* horse chestnut; **~kur** *die* (ugs.) drastic cure *or* remedy; **~täuscher** *der* (abwertend) confidence trickster; con artist (coll.); con man (coll.); **~täuscherei** *die;* **~~, ~~en** (abwertend) confidence *or* (coll.) con trick; **~täuscherin** *die* (abwertend) confidence trickster; con artist (coll.)

Rost¹ /rɔst/ *der;* **~[e]s, ~e** 1▸ (Gitter) grating; grid; (eines Ofens, einer Feuerstelle) grate; (Brat~) grill; (im Freien) barbecue; **vom ~** (Gastr.) fresh from the grill; **auf dem ~ gegrillte Steaks** grilled steaks; (im Freien) barbecued steaks 2▸ (Bett~) base; frame

Rost² *der;* **~[e]s** (auch Bot.) rust; **~ ansetzen** begin to rust; go rusty

rost-, Rost-: ~beständig *Adj.* rust-resistant; (absolut) rustproof; **~bildung** *die* rust formation; rusting; **~braten** *der* grilled steak; (österr.: Entrecote) entrecôte; rib steak; **~brat·wurst** *die* grilled sausage; **~braun** *Adj.* reddish-brown; russet; auburn ‹*hair*›

Röst·brot /'rœst-, 'rø:st-/ *das* toast

Röste /'rø:stə/ *die;* **~, ~n** (Hüttenw.) roasting furnace

rosten *itr. V.; auch mit sein* rust; (auch fig.) get rusty; **alte Liebe rostet nicht** (scherzh.) old habits die hard; **eine nicht ~de Klinge** a non-rusting blade; **nicht ~der Stahl** stainless steel

rösten /ˈrœstn̩, ˈrøːstn̩/ *tr. V.* 1 roast ‹*coffee, malt, chestnuts, etc.*›; toast ‹*bread*›; **sich [in der Sonne] ~ lassen** roast oneself in the sun 2 (bes. südd., österr., schweiz.: braten) roast ‹*meat*›; (auf dem Grill) grill ‹*meat*›; (in der Pfanne) fry ‹*meat, fish, egg, potatoes, etc.*›; (in der heißen Asche/Glut) bake ‹*potatoes*› 3 (Hüttenw.) roast, calcine ‹*ore*›

Röster *der;* **~s, ~** 1 (Toaster) toaster 2 (österr.) (Zwetschgenmus) plum purée; (Holunderbeerenmus) elderberry purée

Rösterei *die;* **~, ~en** [coffee *etc.*] roasting establishment

rost-, Rost-: ~farben, ~farbig *Adj.* rust-coloured; russet; **~fleck** *der* 1 rust stain; 2 (rostige Stelle) rust spot; (größer) patch of rust; **~fraß** *der* rusting process; rusting *no art.*; **~frei** *Adj.* 1 (nicht ~end) stainless ‹*steel*›; 2 (ohne ~) rust-free

Rösti /ˈrøːsti/ *die;* ~ (schweiz. Kochk.) thinly sliced fried potatoes *pl.*

rostig *Adj.* rusty

Röst-kartoffeln *Pl.* fried potatoes

rost-, Rost-: ~laube *die* (ugs.) picturesque old rust-heap; **~mühle** *die* (ugs. abwertend) (Auto) rusty heap; (Schiff) rust bucket (coll.); **~rot** *Adj.* rust-coloured; russet; **~schutz** *der* 1 protection *no art.* against rust; rust protection *no art.*; 2 (Mittel) rustproofing agent; **~schutz·farbe** *die* anti-rust paint; **~schutz·mittel** *das* ▸**~schutz 2**; **~stelle** *die* patch of rust; (kleiner) rust spot

rot /roːt/

A *Adj.* red; **ein Roter** (ugs.: Wein) a red [wine]; **ein Roter/eine Rote** (ugs.) (Mensch mit ~en Haaren) a redhead; (Sozialist) a red (coll.); a leftie (coll.); **der Rote Platz** Red Square; **die Rote Armee** (hist.) the Red Army; **das Rote Meer** the Red Sea; **das Rote Kreuz** the Red Cross; **der Rote Halbmond/Löwe/Davidstern/die Rote Sonne** the Red Crescent/Lion/Star of David/Sun; **~ werden** turn red; ‹*person*› go red; blush; ‹*traffic light*› change to red; **er bekam einen ~en Kopf** he went red in the face; he blushed; **heute ~, morgen tot** (Spr.) here today, gone tomorrow; **lieber ~ als tot** (ugs.) better red than dead; **~ geweinte Augen** eyes red from crying; *s. auch* **Faden 1**; **Zahl**

B *adv.* red; **~ gepunktet** with red dots *postpos., not pred.*; **etw. ~ schreiben/anstreichen** write/mark sth. in red; **[im Gesicht] ~ anlaufen** go red in the face; **~ glühend** red-hot

Rot *das;* **~s, ~** *od.* **~s** 1 red; (Schminke) rouge; **die Ampel zeigt ~:** the traffic lights are red; **bei ~ über die Kreuzung fahren** cross the junction on the red 2 (Spielkartenfarbe) hearts *pl.*; *s. auch* **Pik²**

Rotarier /roˈtaːri̯ɐ/ *der;* **~s, ~, Rotarierin** *die;* **~, ~nen** Rotarian

Rotarmist /ˈroːtarmɪst/ *der;* **~en, ~en** (hist.) Red Army soldier

Rotation /rotaˈt͜si̯oːn/ *die;* **~, ~en** rotation

Rotations-: ~achse *die* axis [of rotation]; **~druck** *der* rotary printing *no art.*; **~fläche** *die* (Math.) surface of revolution; **~körper** *der* (Math.) solid of revolution; **~maschine** *die* (Druckw.) rotary press

rot-, Rot-: ~auge *das* (Zool.) roach; **~backig, ~bäckig** *Adj.* rosy-cheeked ‹*child, girl*›; ruddy-cheeked ‹*old man, farmer, etc.*›; **~barsch** *der* rosefish; **~bart** *der* (ugs.) red-beard; red-bearded type (coll.); **~blond** *Adj.* sandy ‹*hair*›; sandy-haired ‹*person*›; **~braun** *Adj.* reddish-brown; russet; **~buche** *die* [European] beech; **~dorn** *der; Pl.* **~~e** [pink] hawthorn

Röte /ˈrøːtə/ *die;* **~, ~n** 1 red[ness]; **eine ~ stieg ihm ins Gesicht** his face reddened; he blushed 2 (Bot.) madder

Rötel /ˈrøːtl̩/ *der;* **~s, ~:** red chalk

Röteln /ˈrøːtl̩n/ *Pl.* **[die] ~** ▸ⓘ **S. 439** German measles *sing.*

röten

A *tr. V.* redden; make red; **Scham rötete ihr Gesicht** her face went red with embarrassment

B *refl. V.* go *or* turn red

rot-, Rot-: ~fuchs *der* 1 (Tier, Pelz) red fox; 2 (Pferd) chestnut; (heller) sorrel; 3 (ugs.: Rothaariger) redhead; **~gardist** *der,* **~gardistin ~~, ~~nen** *die* Red Guard; **~gesichtig** *Adj.* red-faced; (gesund, mit roten Backen) ruddy-cheeked; **~geweint** ▸**rot A**; **~glühend** ▸**rot B**; **~glut** *die* red heat; **~gold** *das* red gold; **~grün** *Adj.* (Politik) ‹*coalition*› of Greens and Socialists; red-green ‹*coalition*›; **~-Grün** *(das);* **~~s** (Politik) the coalition between the SPD and the Green Party; **~grün·blindheit** /-ˈ--/ *die* ▸ⓘ **S. 439** (Med.) [red-green] colour-blindness; daltonism; **~guss,** ***~guß** *der* red brass; **~haarig** *Adj.* red-haired; **eine ~haarige/ein ~haariger** a redhead; **~haut** *die* (ugs. scherzh.) redskin; **~hirsch** *der* red deer

rotieren /roˈtiːrən/ *itr. V.* 1 rotate; **~de Präsidentschaft** rotating presidency 2 (ugs.: hektisch sein) flap (coll.); get into a flap (coll.); **er ist am R~:** he is in a flap (coll.)

Rot-: ~käppchen *(das);* **~~s** Little Red Riding Hood; **~kehlchen** *das;* **~~s, ~~:** robin [redbreast]; **~kohl** *der,* (bes. südd., österr.) **~kraut** *das* red cabbage; **~kreuz·schwester** *die* Red Cross nurse; **~lauf** *der* (Tiermed.) swine erysipelas

rötlich /ˈrøːtlɪç/

A *Adj.* reddish

B *adv.* **~ braun** reddish-brown

***rötlich·braun** ▸**rötlich B**

rot-, Rot-: ~licht *das; Pl.* **~lichter** red light; **bei ~licht** under a red light; **~licht·bezirk** *der* red-light district; **~licht·milieu** *das* world of pimps and prostitutes; **~licht·viertel** *das* red-light district; **~liegende** *das; adj. Dekl.* (Geol.) Rothliegende; **~nasig** *Adj.* red-nosed

Rotor /ˈroːtɔr/ *der;* **~s, ~en** /roˈtoːrən/ (Technik) rotor

rot-, Rot-: ~schopf *der* (ugs.) shock of red hair; (Person) redhead; **~schwanz** *der,* **~schwänzchen** *das* redstart; **~|sehen** *unr. itr. V.* (ugs.) see red; **~stichig** /-ʃtɪçɪç/ *Adj.* (Fot.) with a red cast *postpos., not pred.*; **~stichig sein** have a red cast; **~stift** *der* red pencil; (Kugelschreiber) red ballpoint; **dem ~stift zum Opfer fallen** (aufgegeben werden) be scrapped; (gestrichen werden) be deleted; **den ~stift ansetzen** (fig.) make economies; **~tanne** *die* common *or* Norway spruce

Rotte /ˈrɔtə/ *die;* **~, ~n** 1 gang; mob 2 (Milit.) pair [operating together] 3 (Jägerspr.) (von Wildschweinen) herd; (von Wölfen) pack 4 (Eisenb.) gang

rotten *tr. V.* (Textilw.) ret ‹*flax, hemp*›

Rotten·führer *der* (Eisenb.) foreman

Rottweiler /ˈrɔtvai̯lɐ/ *der;* **~s, ~** (Hunderasse) Rottweiler

Rotunde /roˈtʊndə/ *die;* **~, ~n** (Archit.) rotunda

Rötung *die;* **~, ~en** reddening

rot·wangig /-vaŋɪç/ *Adj.* (geh.) ▸**rotbackig**

Rot·wein *der* red wine

Rotwein-: ~glas *das* glass for red wine; **~fleck** *der* red wine stain

Rotwelsch *das;* **~[s]** thieves' cant *or* argot

Rot-: ~wild *das* (Jägerspr.) red deer; **~wurst** *die* blood sausage

Rotz /rɔt͜s/ *der;* **~es** (salopp) 1 snot (sl.); **frech wie ~** (salopp) cheeky as anything; **~ und Wasser heulen** (salopp) cry one's eyes out; **der ganze ~** (salopp) the whole bloody (Brit. sl.) *or* (coll.) damn lot 2 (Tiermed.) glanders *pl.*

Rotz·bengel *der* (derb abwertend) snotty brat (sl.)

Rotze /ˈrɔt͜sə/ *die;* **~** (landsch. salopp) snot (sl.)

rotzen (derb)

A *itr. V.* 1 blow one's nose loudly 2 (Schleim in den Mund ziehen) sniff back one's snot (sl.) 3 (ausspucken) gob (sl.)

B *tr. V.* spit

Rotz·fahne *die* (derb) snot rag (sl.)

rotz·frech (salopp)

A *Adj.* insolent; snotty (sl.); **ein ~er Bengel** a snotty little brat (sl.)

B *adv.* insolently; snottily (sl.)

rotzig

A *Adj.* 1 (derb) snotty (sl.) ‹*nose, handkerchief, child*› 2 (salopp: frech) insolent; snotty (sl.)

B *adv.* (salopp abwertend) insolently; snottily (sl.)

Rotz·nase *die* 1 (derb) snotty nose (sl.) 2 (salopp abwertend: Bengel) snotty little brat (sl.)

rotznäsig /-nɛːzɪç/ (derb abwertend)

A *Adj.* 1 snotty-nosed (sl.) 2 (ungezogen) snotty (sl.)

B *adv.* snottily (sl.)

Rouge /ruːʒ/ *das;* **~s, ~s** rouge

Roulade /ruˈlaːdə/ *die;* **~, ~n** (Kochk.) [beef/veal/pork] olive

Rouleau /ruˈloː/ *das;* **~s, ~s** [roller] blind

Roulett /ruˈlɛt/ *das;* **~[e]s, ~e, Roulette** /ruˈlɛtə/ *das;* **~s, ~s** roulette

Roulette·tisch *der* roulette table

Route /ˈruːtə/ *die;* **~, ~n** route

Routen·planer *der* route planner

Router /ˈruːtɐ/ *der;* **~s, ~** (DV) router

Routine /ruˈtiːnə/ *die;* **~** 1 (Erfahrung) experience; (Übung) practice; (Fertigkeit) proficiency; expertise 2 (gewohnheitsmäßiger Ablauf) routine *no def. art.*; **in ~ erstarrt sein** have got into a rut

routine-, Routine-: ~angelegenheit *die* routine matter; **~mäßig** **A** *Adj.* routine; **B** *adv.* as a matter of routine; **~sache** *die* ▸**~angelegenheit**; **~untersuchung** *die* routine examination

Routinier /rutiˈni̯eː/ *der;* **~s, ~s** experienced man; (Experte) expert

routiniert /rutiˈniːɐ̯t/

A *Adj.* (gewandt) expert; skilled; (erfahren) experienced; **ihr Auftreten ist mir zu ~:** her manner is too slick for my taste

B *adv.* expertly; skilfully

Rowdy /ˈrau̯di/ *der;* **~s, ~s** (abwertend) hooligan

Rowdytum *das;* **~s** (abwertend) hooliganism

Royalist /ro̯ajaˈlɪst/ *der;* **~en, ~en, Royalistin** *die;* **~, ~nen** royalist

royalistisch

A *Adj.* royalist

B *adv.* along royalist lines; **~ eingestellt sein** have royalist ideas

> **RTL — Radio Télévision Luxembourg**
>
> Germany's largest privately-owned television channel is the market leader in commercial television. It broadcasts films, sport, news, and entertainment, and regularly achieves top viewing figures.

Ruanda /ˈru̯anda/ *(das);* **~s** Rwanda

rubbeln /ˈrʊbl̩n/ *tr., itr. V.* (bes. nordd.) rub [vigorously]

Rübe /ˈryːbə/ *die;* **~, ~n** 1 turnip; (Zucker~) [sugar] beet; **rote ~:** beetroot; **gelbe ~** (südd.) carrot 2 (salopp: Kopf) nut (coll.); **eins auf die ~ kriegen** get a bonk *or* bash on the nut (coll.); **~ runter** *od.* **ab!** off with his/her head!

Rubel /ˈruːbl̩/ *der;* **~s, ~** ▸ⓘ **S. 299** rouble; **der ~ rollt** (fig. ugs.) the money keeps rolling in

Rüben-: ~kraut *das* (westdt.) [sugar beet] syrup; **~zucker** *der* beet sugar

rüber /ˈryːbɐ/ *Adv.* (ugs.) over

rüber-: ~|dürfen *unr. itr. V.* be allowed over; **über etw.** (*Akk.*) **~dürfen** be allowed to cross sth.; **~|faxen** *tr. V.* fax over; **jmdm. etw. ~faxen** fax sth. over to sb.; **~|gehen** *unr. itr. V.; mit sein* go over; **bei Rot ~gehen** cross over when the lights are red; **~|kommen** *unr. itr. V.; mit sein* 1 come over; **komm doch einen Moment ~:** come over here a moment; 2 (~können) manage to get over/across; **über die Straße/die Mauer nicht ~kommen** be unable to cross the road/get over the wall; 3 (salopp: verstanden werden) come across; **~|können** *unr. itr. V.* be able to get over *or* across; **über etw.** (*Akk.*) **~können** be able to

r

cross sth.; **~|müssen** *unr. itr. V.* have to get over *or* across; **über etw.** *(Akk.)* **~müssen** have to cross sth.; **er muss wieder ~ nach Amerika** he has to go back to America; **~|schicken** *tr. V.* send over; **~|sollen** *itr. V.* be supposed to go over; **soll der Schrank auch ~?** is the cupboard to go over there too?; **~|steigen** *unr. itr. V.; mit sein* **[über etw.** *(Akk.)***] ~steigen** climb over [sth.]; **~|wollen** *unr. itr. V.* want to get over *or* across; **über etw.** *(Akk.)* **~wollen** want to cross sth.; **[in den Westen/Osten] ~wollen** want to cross over to the West/East

Rübezahl /'ry:bətsa:l/ *(der);* **~s** Rübezahl (spirit of the Sudeten Mountains)

Rubikon /'ru:bikɔn/ *der;* **~s** (hist.) *in:* **den ~ überschreiten** (geh.) cross the Rubicon

Rubin /ru'bi:n/ *der;* **~s, ~e** ruby

rubin·rot *Adj.* ruby[-red]

Rüb- /'ry:p-/: **~kohl** *der* (schweiz.) kohlrabi; **~öl** *das* rape oil

Rubrik /ru'bri:k/ *die;* **~, ~en** (Spalte) column; (Zeitungs~) column; section; (fig.: Kategorie) category; **unter der ~ ...** under the heading [of] ...; (in der Zeitung usw.) in the ... section

Rüb·samen *der* oilseed rape

Ruch /ru:x/ *der;* **~[e]s** [bad] reputation; **im ~ der Korruption stehen** have the reputation of being corrupt

ruch·bar *Adj.* *in* **~ werden** (geh.) become known

ruch·los (geh.)
A *Adj.* dastardly; heinous ‹*crime*›
B *adv.* in a dastardly fashion

Ruchlosigkeit *die;* **~:** dastardliness

ruck, zuck /rʊk 'tsʊk/ *Interj.* in no time; **~, ~ gehen** only take a moment *or* second

Ruck /rʊk/ *der;* **~[e]s, ~e** jerk; **ein ~ nach links** (Politik) a sudden swing to the left; **in einem ~** (fig. ugs.) in one go; **sich** *(Dat.)* **einen ~ geben** (fig.) pull oneself together

rück-, Rück-: ~ab|wickeln *tr. V.* (Wirtsch.) cancel ‹*contract, deal, loan*›; **~abwicklung** *die* cancellation; **~antwort** *die* reply; **um ~antwort wird gebeten** please reply

ruck·artig
A *Adj.* jerky
B *adv.* (mit einem Ruck) with a jerk

rück-, Rück-: ~besinnung *die* recollection (**auf** + *Akk.* of); **eine ~besinnung auf bewährte Tugenden** a return to traditional virtues; **~bezüglich** (Sprachw.) **A** *Adj.* reflexive; **B** *adv.* reflexively; **~bildung** *die* 1 (Biol.) atrophy; 2 (Med.) regression; 3 (Sprachw.) back-formation; **~blende** *die* flashback; **~blick** *der* look back (**auf** + *Akk.* at); retrospective view (**auf** + *Akk.* of); **im ~blick** in retrospect; **~blickend** **A** *Adj.* retrospective; **B** *adv.* retrospectively; in retrospect; **~datieren** *tr. V.; nur im Inf. u. 2. Part.* backdate

ruckeln /'rʊk]n/ *itr. V.* (bes. nordd., mitteld.) give a slight jolt

rucken
A *itr. V.* jerk; give a jerk; ‹*car*› jolt; give a jolt;
B *tr. V.* jerk

rücken /'rʏkn̩/
A *tr. V.* move; **den Tisch an die Wand ~:** move *or* push the table against the wall; **es ließ sich nicht von der Stelle ~:** it was impossible to shift it; **etw. in ein völlig neues Licht ~** (fig.) show sth. in a completely new light
B *itr. V.* 1 *mit sein* move; **der Zeiger rückte auf 12** the hand moved up to 12; **mit seinem Stuhl näher an den Tisch ~:** move one's chair closer to the table; **jmdm. auf den Balg** *od.* **Pelz** *od.* **die Pelle ~** (ugs.) squeeze right up to sb; **die Polizei ist mir auf die Pelle** *od.* **den Pelz gerückt** (fig.) the police are breathing down my neck; **kannst du ein bisschen ~?** could you move up/over a bit?; **mit dem König ein Feld nach vorn ~** (Schach) move the king forwards one square; **ins Feld/ins Manöver ~** (Milit.) move into the field/go on manoeuvres; **in weite Ferne ~** (fig.) recede into the distance; ‹*project*› become an increasingly remote possibility 2 **an etw.** *(Dat.)* **~** (ziehen) pull at sth.; (schieben) push at sth.; **an seiner Krawatte/Brille ~:** adjust one's tie/glasses; **hört auf, mit den Stühlen zu ~:** stop shifting your chairs

Rücken *der;* **~s, ~** 1 ▸❶ **S. 435** back; **ein Stück vom ~** (Rindfleisch) a piece of chine; (Hammel, Reh) a piece of saddle; **auf dem ~ liegen** lie on one's back; **legen Sie sich bitte auf den ~!** please lie [down] on your back; **jmdm. die Hände auf den ~ binden** tie sb.'s hands behind his/her back; **~ gegen** *od.* **an ~ stehen** stand back to back; **es lief mir [heiß und kalt] über den ~:** [hot and cold] shivers ran down my spine; **die Sonne/den Wind im ~ haben** have the sun/wind behind one; **verlängerter ~** (scherzh.) backside; posterior (joc.); **jmdm. den ~ zuwenden** turn one's back on sb.; **jmdm./einer Sache den ~ kehren** (fig.) turn one's back on sb./sth.; give sb./sth. up; **jmdm. den ~ stärken** *od.* **steifen** (fig.) give sb. moral support; **den ~ frei haben** (fig.) be free of any obligations; not be tied [down]; **sich** *(Dat.)* **den ~ freihalten** (fig.) not commit oneself; not enter into any obligations; **jmdm. den ~ freihalten** *od.* **decken** (fig.) ensure sb. is not troubled with other problems; **hinter jmds. ~** *(Dat.)* (fig.) behind sb.'s back; **im ~** (fig.) behind one; **er hat die Gewerkschaft im ~** (fig.) he has the backing of the union; **jmdm. in den ~ fallen** (fig.) stab sb. in the back; **mit dem ~ an der** *od.* **zur Wand** (fig.) with one's back to the wall; **mit dem ~ zur Wand stehen** (fig.) have one's back to the wall 2 (Rückseite) back; (Buch~) spine; (der Nase) bridge; (des Berges) ridge 3 ▸ **~schwimmen**

rücken-, Rücken-: ~aus·schnitt *der* back neckline; **mit tiefem ~ausschnitt** with a low[-cut] back; **~deckung** *die* 1 (bes. Mittel) rear cover; 2 (Unterstützung) backing; **jmdm. ~deckung geben** give sb. one's backing; **~flosse** *die* dorsal fin; **~frei** *Adj.* backless ‹*dress*›; **~lage** *die* supine position; **in [der] ~lage** on one's back; **~lehne** *die* [chair/seat] back; **~mark** *das* ▸❶ **S. 435** (Anat.) spinal marrow *or* cord

Rücken·mark[s]-: ~entzündung *die* ▸❶ **S. 439** (Med.) myelitis *no indef. art.*; **~erweichung** *die* ▸❶ **S. 439** (Med.) myelomalacia *no indef. art.*; **~punktion** *die* (Med.) spinal puncture

Rücken-: ~massage *die* back massage; **~muskulatur** *die* ▸❶ **S. 435** back *or* (Anat.) dorsal muscles *pl.*; **~schild** *das* (Bürow.) spine label; **~schmerzen** *Pl.* backache *sing.*; **~schule** *die* (Med.) *programme of back exercises [and advice on posture]*; **~schwimmen** *das* backstroke; **~stärkung** *die* [moral] support

Rück·entwicklung *die* ▸ **Rückbildung 1, 2**

Rücken-: ~wind *der* tail *or* following wind; **~wind haben** have a tail *or* following wind; (fig.) be making good progress; **mit ~wind spielen** play with the wind behind one; **~wirbel** *der* ▸❶ **S. 435** (Anat.) dorsal vertebra

rück-, Rück-: ~erinnerung *die* recollection; reminiscence; **~|erstatten** *tr. V.; nur im Inf. u. 2. Part.* repay; **jmdm. die Reisekosten ~erstatten** repay *or* reimburse sb. his/her travelling expenses; **~erstattung** *die* repayment; reimbursement; (von Steuern) rebate; **~fahr·karte** *die;* **~fahr·schein** *der* return [ticket]; **~fahr·scheinwerfer** *der* (Kfz-W.) reversing light; **~fahrt** *die* return journey; **auf der ~fahrt** on the return journey *or* way back; **~fall** *der* 1 (Med., auch fig.) relapse; **einen ~fall bekommen** *od.* **erleiden** have *or* suffer a relapse; **ein ~fall in alte Gewohnheiten/in die Barbarei** *usw.* (fig.) a relapse into *or* return to old habits/to barbarism *etc.*; 2 (Rechtsspr.) **Diebstahl/Einbruch im ~fall** subsequent *or* second offence of theft/burglary; **~fall·gefahr** *die* (Med.) danger of [a] relapse; (Rechtsw.) danger of reoffending; **~fällig** *Adj.* 1 (Med., auch fig.) relapsed ‹*patient, alcoholic, etc.*›; **[wieder] ~fällig werden** have a relapse; ‹*alcoholic etc.*› go back to one's old ways; 2 (Rechtsspr.); **~fällig werden** reoffend; commit a second offence; **~fall·quote** *die* (Med.) relapse rate; (Rechtsw.) reoffending rate; **~fall·täter** *der,* **~fall·täterin** *die* (Rechtsspr.) recidivist; subsequent *or* second offender; **~fettend** *Adj.* fat-replenishing *attrib.*; **~flug** *der* return flight; **~fluss,** **~fluß *der* reflux; return flow; **~frage** *die* query; **nach telefonischer ~frage** after checking up on the telephone; **~|fragen** *itr. V.; nur im Inf. u. 2. Part.* query it; **bei jmdm. ~fragen** raise a query with sb.; check with sb.; **~front** *die* back; rear; **~führung** *die* return; (in die Heimat) repatriation; **~gabe** *die* 1 return; **gegen ~gabe der Eintrittskarte** upon returning the [entrance] ticket; 2 (Ballspiele) back pass; **~gabe·recht** *das* right of return; **~gang** *der* drop, fall (+ *Gen.* in); (qualitätsmäßig) decline (+ *Gen.* in); **ein ~gang an Besuchern/Geburten** *usw.* a decrease in the number of visitors/births *etc.*

-rückgang *der* decrease in ...; **Preis-/Produktions~:** drop in price/fall in output

rück-, Rück-: ~gängig *Adj.* 1 **~gängig machen** cancel ‹*agreement, decision, etc.*›; break off ‹*engagement*›; **einen Kauf ~gängig machen** return what one has bought; **es lässt sich nicht mehr ~gängig machen** what's done cannot be undone; 2 (im ~gang begriffen) on the decline *postpos.*; **~gebildet** *Adj.* 1 (Biol.) atrophied; 2 (Sprachw.) produced by back-formation; **~gewinnung** *die* recovery (**aus** from); **die ~gewinnung von Rohstoffen aus Müll** the recovery *or* reclaiming of raw materials from waste products; **der Partei ist die ~gewinnung des Rathauses nicht gelungen** the party did not succeed in regaining control of the town council; **~grat** *das* ▸❶ **S. 435** spine; (bes. fig.) backbone; **~grat haben/kein ~grat haben** have guts (coll.)/be spineless; **~grat zeigen** show [real] guts (coll.) *or* fight; **jmdm. das ~grat brechen** (fig.) break sb.'s resistance; **~grat[s]·verkrümmung** *die* ▸❶ **S. 439** (Med.) spinal curvature; **~griff** *der* 1 recourse; **es bleibt immer noch der ~griff auf unsere Reserven** we can always have recourse to our reserves; 2 (das Wiederaufgreifen) return (**auf** + *Akk.* to); **~halt** *der* 1 support; backing; **er hat an seinen Freunden einen festen ~halt** he gets firm support *or* backing from his friends; 2 *in* **ohne ~halt** without reservation; unreservedly; **~halt·los** **A** *Adj.* unreserved, unqualified ‹*criticism, support*›; complete, absolute ‹*frankness*›; ‹*fight*› with no holds barred; **B** *adv.* unreservedly; without reservation; ‹*trust*› completely, absolutely; ‹*confess*› with complete frankness; ‹*fight*› with total commitment; **~hand** *die* (Sport, bes. Tennis) backhand; **einen Ball mit [der] ~hand schlagen/annehmen** hit/take the ball on one's backhand; **~kanal** *der* (Hörfunk, Ferns.) return channel; **~kauf** *der* repurchase; (einer Versicherung) surrender

Rückkehr /'rʏkke:ɐ̯/ *die;* **~:** return; **jmdn. zur ~ [nach Litauen] bewegen** persuade sb. to return [to Lithuania]

Rückkehrer *der;* **~s, ~:** homecomer; **~ aus dem Urlaub** people returning from holiday

Rückkehr·recht *das* right to return; (von Flüchtlingen) right of return

rückkoppeln *tr. V.; nur im Inf. u. 2. Part.* (Elektrot.) feed back; **A mit B ~** (fig.) [re]create links between A and B

Rück·kopp[e]lung *die* (Elektrot.) feedback; (fig.) [re]creation of links

Rückkunft /-kʊnft/ *die;* **~** (geh.) return

rück-, Rück-: ~lage *die* 1 (Spargeld) savings *pl.*; **eine kleine ~lage haben** have a small sum saved up; have a small nest egg; 2 (Wirtsch.: Reserve) reserves *pl.*; (Sozialw.) credit reserve; **~lauf** *der* 1 (~fluss) return flow; 2 (~transport) return; 3 (bei Maschinen) return travel; (beim Tonbandgerät) rewind; **~läufig** **A** *Adj.* 1 (sinkend) decreasing ‹*number*›; declining ‹*economic growth etc.*›; falling ‹*rate, production, etc.*›; **~e Entwicklung** downward trend; decline; 2 (~wärts verlaufend) reverse ‹*process, dictionary*›; reverse, retrograde ‹*motion*›; **~läufiges Wachstum** reversal of growth; **B** *adv.* in

r

reverse order; **~licht** *das; Pl.* **~~er** rear *or* tail light

rücklings *Adv.* 1 (auf dem Rücken) on one's back 2 (mit dem Rücken nach vorn) facing backwards

Rück-: ~marsch *der* march back; (~zug) retreat; **sich auf dem ~marsch befinden** ‹*troops, tanks*› be returning from the front/be retreating; **~nahme** /-na:mə/ *die;* **~~, ~~n** taking back; (einer Behauptung, einer Anordnung, einer Klage usw.) withdrawal; (eines Verbotes) cancellation; **die ~nahme von etw. verweigern** refuse to take sth. back; **~nahme·pflicht** *die:* **~nahme·pflicht von** *od.* **für ...** requirement to take back ...; **~pass,** ***~paß** *der* (Sport) back pass; **~porto** *das* return postage; **~prall** *der;* **~~[e]s, ~~e** rebound; (eines Geschosses) ricochet; **~reise** *die* return journey; **~ruf** *der* 1 (Fernspr.) return call; **ich erwarte deinen ~ruf** I shall wait for you to phone back; 2 (das Zurückbeordern) recall; **~ruf·aktion** *die* (Wirtsch.) [product] recall (**für** of)

Rụck·sack *der* rucksack; (Touren~) backpack

Rụcksack·tourist *der,* **Rụcksack·touristin** *die* backpacker

rụ̈ck-, Rụ̈ck-: ~schau *die* review (**auf** + *Akk.* of); **~schau halten** look back; **~schau auf etw.** (*Akk.*) **halten** pass sth. in review; review sth.; **~schlag** *der* 1 setback; **in seinem Leben gab es immer wieder ~schläge** throughout his life he suffered repeated setbacks; 2 (Tennis, Tischtennis usw.) return; **~schlag·ventil** *das* (Technik) non-return valve; check valve; **~|schließen** *unr. itr. V.* conclude (**aus** from); **aus** *od.* **von etw. auf etw.** (*Akk.*) **~schließen** draw conclusions about sth. from sth.; **~schluss,** ***~schluß** *der* conclusion (**auf** + *Akk.* about); **aus etw. ~schlüsse auf etw.** (*Akk.*) **ziehen** draw conclusions from sth. about sth.; **~schritt** *der* retrograde step; **das ist kein Fortschritt, sondern ein ~schritt** that's not a forward, but a backward step; **~schrittlich** A *Adj.* reactionary; retrograde ‹*development*›; B *adv.* **~schrittlich eingestellt sein** have reactionary ideas; **~schwung** *der* (Turnen) backward swing; **~seite** *die* back; (eines Gebäudes usw.) back; rear; (einer Münze usw.) reverse; (des Mondes) far side; **siehe ~seite** see over[leaf]; **auf der ~seite eines Tiefs** (Met.) in the rear of *or* behind a depression; **~seitig** A *Adj.* rear, back ‹*entrance*›; ‹*explanation etc.*› overleaf; B *adv.* **~seitig gelegen** situated at the back *or* rear; **~sendung** *die* return; **~sicht** *die* 1 consideration; **mit ~sicht auf etw.** (*Akk.*) taking sth. into consideration; in view of sth.; **~sicht auf jmdn. nehmen** show consideration for *or* towards sb.; (Verständnis haben) make allowances for sb.; **ohne ~sicht auf etw.** (*Akk.*) with no regard for *or* regardless of sth.; **ohne ~sicht auf Verluste** (ugs.) regardless; **keine ~sicht kennen** show no consideration; (unbarmherzig sein) be ruthless; 2 (Erwägung, Grund) **~en** considerations; **aus finanziellen ~sichten** for financial reasons; 3 (Sicht nach hinten) rear view; **~sicht·nahme** *die;* **~~:** consideration; **unter ~sichtnahme** (*Dat.*) **auf etw.** (*Akk.*) taking sth. into consideration/making allowances for sth.; **gegenseitige ~sichtnahme ist notwendig** it is essential that people show mutual consideration

rụ̈cksichts-, Rụ̈cksichts-: ~los A *Adj.* 1 inconsiderate; thoughtless; **ein ~loser Autofahrer** an inconsiderate driver; (verantwortungslos) a reckless driver; 2 (schonungslos) ruthless; **ein ~loser Kampf** a bitter struggle; a fight with no holds barred; B *adv.* 1 inconsiderately; thoughtlessly; (verantwortungslos) recklessly; **sich ~los durch die Menge schieben** shove one's way through the crowd regardless of anyone else; 2 (schonungslos) ruthlessly; **jmdm. ~los die Wahrheit sagen** tell sb. the truth regardless of his/her feelings; **~losigkeit** *die;* **~~, ~~en** 1 lack of consideration; thoughtlessness; (Verantwortungslosigkeit) recklessness; **so eine ~losigkeit!** how inconsiderate *or* thoughtless!; 2 (Schonungslosigkeit) ruthlessness; **~voll** A *Adj.* considerate; thoughtful; B *adv.* considerately; thoughtfully

rụ̈ck-, Rụ̈ck-: ~sitz *der* back seat; **auf dem ~sitz/den ~sitzen** in the back; in *or* on the back seat/seats; **~spiegel** *der* rear-view mirror; **~spiel** *das* (Sport) second *or* return leg; **~sprache** *die* consultation; **[mit jmdm.] ~sprache nehmen** *od.* **halten** (Papierdt.) consult [sb.]; **~stand** *der* 1 (Übriggebliebenes, Rest) residue; **radioaktive ~stände** traces of radioactivity; 2 (offener Rechnungsbetrag) **~stände/ein ~stand** arrears *pl.;* **~stände eintreiben** collect outstanding debts; **ein ~stand in der Miete** rent arrears *pl.;* 3 (Zurückbleiben hinter dem gesetzten Ziel, Soll usw.) backlog; (bes. Sport: hinter dem Gegner) deficit; **[mit den Zahlungen/mit der Arbeit** *usw.***] im ~stand sein/in ~stand** (*Akk.*) **geraten** be/get behind [with one's payments/work *etc.*]; **seinen/einen ~stand aufholen** (bei der Arbeit) make up *or* catch up one's/a backlog; (bei einem Spiel/Rennen/(fig.) *bei der Rüstung usw.*) make up the deficit; close the gap; **die Mannschaft lag mit 0:3 im ~stand** (Sport) the team was trailing by three to nil; **mit 38 hundertstel Sekunden ~stand auf den zweiten Platz kommen** (Sport) take second place .38 of a second behind; **~stand·frei** ▸**~standsfrei; ~stand·los** ▸**~standslos; ~ständig** *Adj.* 1 (unterentwickelt) underdeveloped; backward; 2 (überholt) outdated; antiquated; **~ständig sein** be behind the times; 3 (schon länger fällig) outstanding ‹*payment, amount*›; ‹*wages*› still owing; **~ständige Steuern** tax arrears; **~ständigkeit** *die;* **~~** 1 backwardness; 2 (Überholtheit) outdated nature; (Ansichten) old-fashioned *or* antiquated ideas *pl.;* **~stands·frei** A *Adj.* residue-free; B *adv.* without leaving a residue; **~stands·los** A *Adj.* residue-free; total, complete ‹*incineration, breakdown*›; B *adv.* without leaving a trace; **~stau** *der* (von Wasser) backing up; backwater; (von Fahrzeugen) tailback; **~stellung** *die* 1 (das Zurückstellen) postponement (**um** by); **eine ~stellung vom Wehrdienst** a temporary exemption from military service; 2 (Wirtsch.) reserve [fund]; **~stoß** *der* (Physik) reaction; (einer Feuerwaffe) recoil; **~strahler** *der* reflector; **~stufung** *die;* **~~, ~~en** downgrading; **~taste** *die* backspacer; backspace key; **~tausch** *der:* **beim ~tausch [von Devisen]** when changing currency back; **~tritt** *der* 1 (von einem Amt) resignation (**von** from); (von einer Kandidatur, von einem Vertrag usw.) withdrawal (**von** from); 2 ▸**~trittbremse; ~tritt·bremse** *die* back-pedal brake

Rụ̈cktritts-: ~drohung *die* threat to resign; **~erklärung** *die* announcement of one's intention to resign; **~forderung** *die* resignation demand; **eine ~forderung an X** a demand for X's resignation; **~gesuch** *das* offer of resignation; **sein ~gesuch einreichen** hand in *or* tender one's resignation; **~recht** *das* right to withdraw [from a contract]

rụ̈ck-, Rụ̈ck-: ~|übersetzen *tr. V.; nur im Inf. u. 2. Part.* translate back; **~übersetzung** *die* back-translation; **~übertragen** *unr. tr. V.* return, give back (**an** + *Akk.* to); **~umschlag** *der* return envelope; **frankierter [adressierter] ~umschlag** stamped addressed envelope; SAE; **~|vergüten** *tr. V.; nur im Inf. u. 2. Part.* refund; **~vergütung** *die* refund; **~verkaufs·recht** (Rechtsw.) right of repurchase; **~|versichern** *refl. V.; nur im Inf. u. 2. Part.* 1 cover oneself [two ways]; hedge one's bets; 2 (Versicherungsw.) reinsure; **~versicherung** *die* 1 [double] insurance; (Schutz) safeguard; protection; 2 (Versicherungsw.) reinsurance; **~wand** *die* back wall; (eines Regals usw.) back; **~wanderer** *der,* **~wanderin** *die* repatriate

rụ̈ckwärtig /-vɛrtɪç/

A *Adj.* 1 back; rear; **die ~e Seite** the back *or* rear; **auf den ~en Verkehr achten** keep an eye on the traffic behind [one] 2 (Milit.) rearward ‹*lines of communication*›

B *adv.* **die ~ gelegene Tür** the door at the back

rụ̈ckwärts /-vɛrts/ *Adv.* 1 backwards; **ein Blick [nach] ~:** a look back; a backward look; **ein Salto/eine Rolle ~:** a back somersault/backward roll; **~ fahren** reverse; **~ einparken** reverse *or* back into a parking space; **es ging ~** (fig.) it got worse; **mit dem Umsatz ist es immer mehr ~ gegangen** the turnover has gone down and down; **~ gewandt** turned backwards *postpos.* 2 (südd., österr.: hinten) behind; **[etwas] weiter ~:** [a little] further back; **~ einsteigen!** enter at the rear [of the vehicle]; **sich nach ~ fallen lassen/lehnen** fall/lean back

rụ̈ckwärts-, Rụ̈ckwärts-: ~bewegung *die* backward movement; **~drehung** *die* turn backwards; **durch ~drehung einer Sache** (*Gen.*) by turning sth. back; **~gang** *der* (Kfz-W.) reverse [gear]; **im ~gang** in reverse; **den ~gang einlegen** (auch fig.) go into reverse; ***~|gehen** ▸**rückwärts 1; ~gewandt** ▸**rückwärts 1**

Rụ̈ckweg *der* return journey; **auf dem ~:** on the way back; **den ~ antreten, sich auf den ~ machen** set off *or* start on one's way back; **jmdm. den ~ abschneiden** cut off sb.'s line of retreat

rụck·weise

A *Adv.* (mit einem Ruck) with a jerk; (mit mehreren) in a series of jerks

B *adj.* jerky

rụ̈ck-, Rụ̈ck-: ~wendung *die* reorientation; **~wirkend** A *Adj.* retrospective; backdated ‹*pay increase*›; B retrospectively; **~wirkend vom** *od.* **zum 1. April in Kraft treten** take effect [retrospectively] as from 1 April; **die Gehaltserhöhung erfolgt ~wirkend vom 1. Januar** the rise (Brit.) *or* (Amer.) raise is *or* has been backdated to 1 January; **~wirkung** *die* 1 (zeitlich) retrospective force; **mit ~wirkung vom ...** [retrospectively] as from ...; 2 (Auswirkung) repercussion (**auf** + *Akk.* on); **~zahlbar** *Adj.* repayable; **~zahlung** *die* repayment; **~zahlungs·bedingungen** *Pl.* repayment terms; **~zieher** *der* 1 (Fußball) overhead kick; 2 (fig. ugs.) (von Behauptungen, Forderungen usw.) climbdown; (von einem Vorhaben) backing out *no art.*; **einen ~zieher machen** climb down/back out; (salopp: Coitus interruptus) pull out (coll.)

Rụ̈ck·zug *der* retreat; **auf dem ~ sein** be retreating; **jmdn. zum ~ zwingen** force sb. to retreat

Rụ̈ckzugs-: ~gebiet *das* reserve (*for native inhabitants/wild animals*); **~gefecht** *das* (Milit., fig.) rearguard action

rüde /'ry:də/

A *Adj.* uncouth; coarse ‹*language*›

B *adv.* in an uncouth manner

Rü̱de *der;* **~n, ~n** 1 (Hund) [male] dog; (Fuchs/Wolf) [male] fox/wolf; **unser Hund ist ein ~:** our dog is a male 2 (Jägerspr.: Hetzhund) hound; hunting dog

Rudel /'ru:dl̩/ *das;* **~s, ~** (von Hirschen, Gämsen) herd; (von Wölfen, Hunden) pack; (fig.: von Menschen) horde

Ru̱del·führer *der,* **Ru̱del·führerin** *die* leader of the pack (also fig.)

Ruder /'ru:dɐ/ *das;* **~s, ~** 1 (Riemen) oar; **sich in die ~ legen** (kräftig rudern) row strongly *or* vigorously; (fig. ugs.: etw. in Angriff nehmen) put one's back into it 2 (Steuer~) rudder; (Steuerrad) helm; **am ~ sein/bleiben** (fig.) be/stay at the helm; **das ~ fest in der Hand haben** (fig.) be firmly in control; **das ~ herumwerfen** (fig.) change course *or* tack; **ans ~ kommen** (fig.) take the helm; party, leader come to power; **aus dem ~ laufen** (auch fig.) go off course 3 (eines Flugzeugs) (Höhen~) elevator; (Quer~) aileron; (Seiten~) rudder

Ru̱der-: ~bank *die; Pl.* **~bänke** thwart; (einer Galeere) oarsman's bench; **~blatt** *das* 1 (eines Steuerruders) rudder [blade]; 2 (eines Riemens) blade; **~boot** *das* rowboat; rowing boat (Brit.)

Ru̱derer *der;* **~s, ~:** oarsman; rower

Ru̱der-: ~gänger *der;* **~~s, ~~, ~gast** *der* (Seemannsspr.) helmsman; **~haus** *das* (Seemannsspr.) wheelhouse

-ruderig *Adj.* -oared

Ru̱derin *die;* **~, ~nen** oarswoman; rower

rudern
A *itr. V.* **1** *meist, mit Richtungsangabe nur, mit sein* row **2** (fig.) **mit den Armen ~:** swing one's arms [about] **3** *mit sein ‹waterfowl›* paddle
B *tr. V.* row ‹*boat, person, object*›

Ruder-: ~pinne *die* tiller; **~regatta** *die* rowing regatta; **~sport** *der* rowing *no art.*

Rudiment /rudiˈmɛnt/ *das;* **~[e]s, ~e** **1** (Biol., geh.) vestige **2** *Pl.* (veralt.: Grundbegriffe) rudiments

rudimentär /rudimɛnˈtɛːɐ̯/ (Biol., geh.)
A *Adj.* rudimentary
B *adv.* in a rudimentary form

Ruf /ruːf/ *der;* **~[e]s, ~e** **1** call; (Schrei) shout; cry; (Tierlaut) call **2** (fig.: Aufforderung, Forderung) call (**nach** for); **der ~ zu den Waffen** (geh.) the call to arms; **dem ~ des Herzens/Gewissens/der Natur folgen** *od.* **gehorchen** follow one's heart/listen to the voice of conscience/nature; **der ~ nach der Todesstrafe** the call for the death penalty **3** (Berufung) **sie bekam einen ~ an die Universität Bremen** *od.* **nach Bremen** she was offered a chair *or* professorship at Bremen University **4** (Papierdt.: Telefonnummer) telephone [number]; **~ 33700** tel. [no.] 33700 **5** (Leumund) reputation; **eine Firma von ~:** a firm of repute *or* with a good reputation; **ein Mann von gutem/schlechtem ~:** a man with a good/bad reputation; **jmdn./etw. in schlechten ~ bringen** give sb./sth. a bad name; **besser als sein ~ sein** be not as bad as one/it is made out to be; **ist der ~ erst ruiniert, lebt es sich ganz ungeniert** (Spr.) you needn't worry if you've no reputation to lose

Rufe /ˈruːfə/ *die;* **~, ~n, Rüfe** /ˈryːfə/ *die;* **~, ~n** (schweiz.) landslide

rufen
A *unr. itr. V.* **1** call (**nach** for); (schreien) shout (**nach** for); ‹*animal*› call; **hast du sein Rufen nicht gehört?** didn't you hear him calling?; **jmdm. ~** (südwestd., schweiz.) call to sb.; **Mutter/der Gong ruft zum Essen** mother is calling [out] that lunch/dinner is ready/the gong is sounding for lunch/dinner; **die Glocke ruft zum Gottesdienst/Gebet** the bell is calling to worship/prayer; **die Pflicht/die Arbeit ruft** (fig.) duty calls **2** (schweiz.: hervor~) **einer Sache** (*Dat.*) **~:** cause sth.; give rise to sth.
B *unr. tr. V.* **1** **etw. ~:** call sth.; (schreien) shout sth.; (unpers.) **aus dem Zimmer rief es: „Herein!"** from inside the room a voice called 'come in!' **2** (herbei-) **jmdn. ~:** call sb.; **jmdn. zu Hilfe ~:** call to sb. to help; **dringende Geschäfte riefen ihn nach München** (fig.) he was called to Munich on urgent business; **jmdm./sich** (*Dat.*) **etw. ins Gedächtnis** *od.* **in Erinnerung ~:** remind sb. of sth./recall sth.; **[jmdm.] wie ge~ kommen** (ugs.) come at just the right moment; **du kommst/der Wind kommt mir wie ge~:** you're just the person I wanted/the wind is just what I wanted **3** (telefonisch) call; **jmdn. [unter der Nummer 347106] ~:** call *or* ring sb. [on 347106]; **~ Sie 888666** ring 888666; (über Funk) **Teddybär ruft Zeppelin** Teddy Bear calling Zeppelin **4** (nennen) **jmdn./** (südwestd., schweiz.:) **jmdm. etw. ~:** call sb. sth. **5** (geh., veralt.: anreden) **jmdn. bei** *od.* **mit seinem Namen ~:** address sb. by name
C *refl. V.* **sich heiser ~:** call until one is hoarse; (schreien) shout oneself hoarse

Rufer *der;* **~s, ~, Ruferin** *die;* **~, ~nen** person calling; **ein Rufer in der Wüste** (fig. geh.) a voice [crying] in the wilderness

Rüffel /ˈrʏfl̩/ *der;* **~s, ~** (ugs.) ticking-off (coll.)

rüffeln *tr. V.* (ugs.) **jmdn. ~:** tick sb. off (coll.)

Ruf-: ~mord *der* character assassination; **~mord·kampagne** *die* smear campaign; **~name** *der* first name (*by which one is generally known*); **~nummer** *die* telephone number; **~säule** *die* emergency telephone (mounted in a pillar); **~umleitung** *die* call diversion; **~weite** *die:* **in/außer ~weite sein** be within/beyond hailing distance; **~zeichen** *das* **1** (Fernspr.) ringing tone; **2** (österr.: Ausrufezeichen) exclamation mark

Rugby /ˈrakbi/ *das;* **~[s]** rugby [football]

Rüge /ˈryːgə/ *die;* **~, ~n** reprimand; **jmdm. eine ~ wegen etw.** (*Gen.*) **erteilen** reprimand sb. for sth.; **eine ~ erhalten** be reprimanded

rügen *tr. V.* reprimand ‹*person*› (**wegen** for); (mit Nachdruck kritisieren) censure ‹*carelessness etc.*›; **Mängel ~:** complain about faults *or* defects

Ruhe /ˈruːə/ *die;* **~** **1** (Stille) silence; **im Saal herrschte absolute ~:** there was dead silence *or* a complete hush in the hall; **endlich war im Klassenzimmer ~ eingetreten** at last the classroom had become quiet; **die nächtliche ~ stören** disturb the nocturnal peace; **~ [bitte]!** quiet *or* silence [please]!; **[einen Moment] um ~ bitten** ask for [a moment's] silence; **jmdn. um ~ bitten** ask sb. to be quiet; **~ geben/halten** be/keep quiet; **jmdn. zur ~ ermahnen** tell sb. to be quiet **2** (Ungestörtheit) peace; **in ~ [und Frieden]** in peace [and quiet]; **vor jmdm. ~ haben** not be bothered by sb.; **ich möchte mal meine ~ haben** I should like [to have] some peace [and quiet]; **er braucht ~ bei seiner Arbeit** he needs peace and quiet *or* must not be disturbed while he is working; **die [öffentliche] ~ wiederherstellen** restore [law and] order; **für ~ und Ordnung sorgen** uphold *or* preserve law and order; **jmdn. in ~ lassen** leave sb. in peace; **lass mich in ~!** leave me alone!; **jmdn. mit etw. in ~ lassen** stop bothering sb. with sth.; **jmdn. nicht zur ~ kommen lassen** give sb. no peace; **keine ~ geben** not stop pestering; (nicht nachgeben) not give up; (weiter protestieren) go on protesting; **hier hast du fünf Euro, aber nun gib auch ~!** here's five euros, [but] now stop bothering me/us! **3** (Unbewegtheit) rest; **zur ~ kommen** come to rest; ‹*weel*› stop turning; **die ~ vor dem Sturm** the calm before the storm **4** (Erholung, das Sichausruhen) rest *no def. art.*; **der ~ pflegen** (geh.) take it *or* things easy; seek repose (literary); **angenehme ~** (geh.) sleep well; **sich zur ~ begeben** (geh.) retire [to bed]; **die ewige ~** (geh.) eternal rest; **jmdn. zur letzten ~ betten** (geh.) lay sb. to rest **5** (**~stand**) **sich zur ~ setzen** take one's retirement; retire (**in** + *Dat.* to) **6** (Gelassenheit) calm[ness]; composure; **er ist die ~ selbst** (ugs.) he is calmness itself; **[die] ~ bewahren/die ~ verlieren** keep calm/lose one's composure; keep/lose one's cool (coll.); **sich aus der ~ bringen lassen** let oneself get worked up; (ängstlich werden) let oneself get rattled (coll.); **in [aller] ~:** [really] calmly; **lesen Sie sich die Prüfungsaufgaben in [aller] ~ durch** read through the examination questions calmly and in your own time; **ich muss mir das in [aller] ~ überlegen** I must have a quiet think about it; **jmdn. keine ~ lassen** not give sb. any peace; **der Gedanke lässt ihm keine ~ mehr** he can't stop thinking about it; **die ~ weghaben** (ugs.) be completely unflappable (coll.); **~ ist die erste Bürgerpflicht** (veralt.) orderly behaviour is the first duty of the citizen; (scherzh.) the main thing is to keep calm; **immer mit der ~!** (nur keine Panik) don't panic!; (nichts überstürzen) one thing at a time; no need to rush

ruhe-, Ruhe-: ~bank *die; Pl.* **~bänke** bench; **~bedürfnis** *das* need of rest; **~bedürftig** *Adj.* in need of rest *postpos.*; **~gehalt** *das* [retirement] pension; **~geld** *das* [old-age] pension; **~genuss, *~genuß** *der* (österr. Amtsspr.) [retirement] pension; **~kissen** *das* cushion; (Kopfkissen) pillow; *s. auch* **Gewissen**; **~lage** *die* **1** (Körperlage) [fully] relaxed position; **2** (eines beweglichen Gegenstands) neutral position; (unbeweglich) immobile position; **~los** **A** *Adj.* restless; **B** *adv.* restlessly; **~losigkeit** *die;* **~~:** restlessness

ruhen *itr. V.* **1** (aus~) rest; **hier lässt es sich gut ~:** it's very restful here; **nach dem Essen sollst du ~ oder tausend Schritte tun** (Spr.) after a meal one should take either a rest or a good walk **2** (geh.: schlafen) sleep; **ich wünsche gut** *od.* **wohl zu ~:** I hope you sleep well **3** **im Grabe ~:** lie in one's grave; **in fremder Erde ~:** be buried in foreign soil; **„Ruhe sanft"** *od.* **„in Frieden!"** 'Rest in Peace'; **„Hier ruht in Gott ..."** 'Here lies ...' **4** (stillstehen) ‹*work, business*› have stopped; ‹*production, firm*› be at a standstill; ‹*field*› rest; ‹*employment, insurance*› be suspended; **der Verkehr ruht fast völlig** there is hardly any traffic; **die Waffen ~:** there is a ceasefire; **ihre Hände ~ nie** her hands are never still; **nicht ~ [und rasten]** *od.* **nicht ~ noch rasten** *od.* **weder ~ noch rasten, bis ...** not rest until ... **5** (liegen) rest; **der Braten muss zehn Minuten ~:** the roast must be left to stand for ten minutes; **in sich** (*Dat.*) **[selbst] ~:** be a well-balanced [and harmonious] person **6** **eine Angelegenheit ~ lassen** let a matter rest; (vorläufig) shelve a matter; **ein Problem ~ lassen** leave a problem [on one side]

ruhend *Adj.* (unbeweglich) stationary; (liegend) reclining ‹*Venus etc.*›; **~er Verkehr** parked vehicles *pl.*

***ruhen|lassen** ▸ **ruhen 6**

ruhe-, Ruhe-: ~pause *die* break; **eine ~pause einlegen** take a break; **~pol** *der* point of rest; (Ort) place of rest; **der ~pol in seinem Leben** the still point in his life; **~punkt** *der* resting point; (in einer Entwicklung) restful *or* quiet point; **~stand** *der* retirement; **in den ~stand gehen/versetzt werden** go into retirement/be retired; **er ist im ~stand/Lehrer im ~stand** he is retired/a retired teacher; **seine Versetzung in den ~stand** his retirement; **~ständler** *der;* **~~s, ~~, ~ständlerin** *die;* **~~, ~~nen** retired person; **~statt** *die;* **~~, ~stätten, ~stätte** *die* (fig. geh.) [last] resting place; **~störend** *Adj.* **~störender Lärm** disturbance of the peace; **~störung** *die* disturbance; (Rechtsw.) disturbance of the peace; **jmdn. wegen ~störung anzeigen** report sb. [to the police] for disturbing the peace; **~strom** *der* (Elektrot.) closed-circuit current; **~tag** *der* **1** (einer Gaststätte) closing day; **[wir haben] dienstags** *od.* **Dienstag ~tag** [we are] closed on Tuesdays; **2** (arbeitsfreier Tag) day of rest; **~zeit** *die* rest period; time of rest; (für Bäume usw.) dormant period *or* season; **~zustand** *der* state of inactivity; **im ~zustand** when at rest; when inactive

Ruhezeit

This is an accepted period of quiet, usually between one and three o'clock in the afternoon. *Ruhezeit* applies to loud music and noisy work on Sundays, when there should be no hammering or drilling. But most young Germans no longer adhere to the letter of the *Ruhezeit*, which seems to have fallen victim to a noisier modern lifestyle.

ruhig /ˈruːɪç/
A *Adj.* **1** (still, leise) quiet; **seid doch mal ~!** do be quiet!; **um diese Angelegenheit/diesen Politiker ist es sehr ~ geworden** one does not hear much about this matter/politician any more **2** (friedlich, ungestört) peaceful ‹*times, life, scene, valley, etc.*›; quiet ‹*talk, reflection, life*›; **wir suchten uns ein ~es Plätzchen** we looked for a quiet *or* peaceful spot; **überleg es dir mal in einer ~en Stunde** think about it when you have a quiet moment; **er hat keine ~e Minute** he doesn't have a moment's peace; **ein ~er Job** *od.* **Posten** (ugs.) a cushy job *or* number (coll.); **einen ~en Verlauf nehmen** go smoothly; be uneventful **3** (unbewegt) calm ‹*sea, weather*›; still ‹*air*›; (fig.) peaceful ‹*melody*›; quiet ‹*pattern*›; (gleichmäßig) steady ‹*breathing, hand, flame, steps*›; smooth ‹*flight, crossing*›; **eine Gliedmaße ~ stellen** immobilize a limb **4** (gelassen) calm ‹*voice etc.*›; quiet, calm ‹*person*›; **er gab sich Mühe, ~ zu bleiben** he made an effort to keep calm *or* (coll.) keep his cool; **~en Gewissens** with an easy *or* a clear conscience; **sei ganz ~:** you needn't worry; **[nur immer] ~ Blut!** (ugs.) keep your hair on! (coll.); **einen Patienten ~ stellen** (verhüll.) calm a patient
B *adv.* **1** (still, leise) quietly; **wir wohnen sehr ~:** we live in a very quiet area; **sich ~ verhalten** keep quiet **2** (friedlich, ohne Störungen) ‹*sleep*› peacefully; ‹*go off*› smoothly, peacefully; (ohne Zwischenfälle) uneventfully; ‹*work, think*› in peace; **hier geht es sehr ~ zu** it is very peaceful here; **ich kann nicht ~ schlafen** I can't sleep properly **3** (unbewegt) ‹*sit, lie, stand*› still; (gleichmäßig) ‹*burn, breathe*› steadily; ‹*run, fly*› smoothly **4** (gelassen) ‹*speak, watch, sit*› calmly; **sie sahen ~ zu, wie das Kind geschlagen**

wurde they watched unmoved as the child was beaten
C *Adv.* by all means; **du kannst ~ mitkommen** by all means come along; you're welcome to come along; **streichle ihn ~ mal** go ahead and stroke him; **man kann ihm das ~ ganz direkt sagen** there's no harm in telling him to his face; **du kannst es mir ~ glauben/sagen** it's OK, you can take my word for it/you can tell me; **du könntest dich ~ entschuldigen/ihm ~ etwas helfen** it wouldn't hurt you to apologize/to help him a bit; **lach mich ~ aus** all right *or* go ahead, laugh at me[, I don't care]; **soll er ~ meckern** (ugs.) let him moan[, I don't care]

***ruhig|stellen** ▸**ruhig A3, 4**

Ruhm /ru:m/ *der;* **~[e]s** fame; **diese Erfindung begründete seinen ~:** this invention made him famous *or* made his name; **sich mit ~ bedecken** (geh.) cover oneself with glory; **er hat sich nicht [gerade] mit ~ bekleckert** (ugs. iron.) he didn't exactly cover himself with glory *or* distinguish himself; **der zweifelhafte ~ dieser Erfindung** (fig.) the dubious reputation of this invention

rühmen /ˈry:mən/
A *tr. V.* praise
B *refl. V.* **sich einer Sache** (*Gen.*) **~:** boast about sth.; **wenige dürfen sich ~, ihn gesehen zu haben** only a few can claim to have seen him

rühmens·wert *Adj.* laudable; praiseworthy

Ruhmes·blatt *das:* **das war kein ~ für ihn/die Bundesrepublik** it did not reflect any credit on him/the Federal Republic; it did him/the Federal Republic no credit

rühmlich *Adj.* laudable, praiseworthy ‹*behaviour, action, etc.*›; notable ‹*exception*›; **er hat kein ~es Ende genommen** he came to a discreditable end

ruhm·los
A *Adj.* inglorious
B *adv.* ingloriously

ruhm·reich
A *Adj.* glorious ‹*victory, history*›; celebrated ‹*general, army, victory*›
B *adv.* **~ kämpfen** fight with great glory; **~ siegen** win a famous *or* glorious victory

Ruhr /ru:ɐ̯/ *die;* **~, ~en** ▸ⓘ **S. 439** dysentery *no art.*

Rühr·ei *das* scrambled egg[s *pl.*]

rühren /ˈry:rən/
A *tr. V.* [1] (um~) stir ‹*sauce, dough, etc.*›; (ein~) stir ‹*egg, powder, etc.*› **(an, in** + *Akk.* into) [2] (bewegen) move ‹*limb, fingers, etc.*›; **ich konnte die Glieder nicht mehr ~:** I could no longer move; *s. auch* **Finger 2** [3] (erweichen) move; touch; **jmdn. zu Tränen ~:** move sb. to tears; **es rührte ihn überhaupt nicht, dass ...** it didn't bother him at all that ...; *s. auch* **gerührt**; **rührend** [4] (geh. veralt.) **die Trommel/die Leier ~:** beat the drum/play the lyre
B *itr. V.* [1] (um~) stir; **im Kaffee** *od.* **in der Kaffeetasse ~:** stir one's coffee [2] (Milit.) stand at ease [3] (geh.: her~) **das rührt daher, dass ...** that stems from the fact that ... [4] (geh.: vorsichtig anfassen) **an etw.** (*Akk.*) **~:** touch sth.; (fig.: im Gespräch be~) touch on sth.; **wir wollen nicht [mehr] daran ~:** let's not go into that [any further]
C *refl. V.* [1] (sich bewegen) move; **er rührte sich nicht von der Stelle** he did not budge *or* stir; **niemand rührte sich** nobody moved *or* stirred; (fig.: unternahm etwas) nobody did anything; **kein Blatt/kein Lüftchen rührte sich** not a leaf stirred/there was not a breath of wind; **es rührte sich nichts** there was no sign of movement; (nichts geschah) nothing happened; **er hat sich seit zwei Monaten nicht gerührt** (ugs.: nicht geschrieben) he has given no sign of life for two months [2] (Milit.) **rührt euch!** at ease!

Rühren *das;* **~s** [1] stirring *no art.*; **beim ~ des Teigs** when stirring the dough [2] **ein menschliches ~ verspüren** (scherzh.) feel the call of nature

rührend
A *Adj.* touching; **er sorgt in ~er Weise für seine Eltern** it is touching how he looks after his parents; **das ist ~ von Ihnen** that is terribly sweet *or* kind of you (coll.); **das ist ja ~!** (auch iron.) that's really charming!
B *adv.* touchingly; **er sorgt ~ für sie** it is touching the way he looks after her/them

Ruhrgebiet *das;* **~[e]s** Ruhr [district]

rührig
A *Adj.* active; (mit Unternehmungsgeist) enterprising; go-ahead; (emsig) busy; industrious
B *adv.* actively; (mit Unternehmungsgeist) enterprisingly; (emsig) busily; industriously

Rührigkeit *die;* **~:** active nature; (Unternehmungsgeist) enterprise

rühr-, Rühr-: ~löffel *der* mixing spoon; **~mich·nicht·an** *das;* **~~, ~~** (Bot.) touch-me-not; *s. auch* **Kräutchen**

Ruhr·pott *der* (ugs.) **der ~:** the Ruhr

rühr, Rühr-: ~selig A *Adj.* [1] emotional ‹*person*›; [2] (allzu gefühlvoll) over-sentimental ‹*manner, mood, etc.*›; maudlin, (coll.) tear-jerking ‹*play, song, etc.*›; **B** *adv.* in an over-sentimental manner; **der Film endete ~selig** the film had a tear-jerking *or* weepy ending (coll.); **~seligkeit** *die* sentimentality; **~stück** *das* (Literaturw.) sentimental drama; melodrama; **~teig** *der* [cake] mixture

Rührung *die;* **~:** emotion; **von tiefer ~ ergriffen** deeply moved

Ruin /ruˈi:n/ *der;* **~s** ruin; **jmdn. an den Rand des ~s bringen** bring sb. to the brink of ruin; **du bist noch mein ~** (ugs.) you'll be the ruin *or* end of me

Ruine *die;* **~, ~n** ruin

Ruinen-: ~feld *das* [expanse *sing.* of] ruins *pl.*; **~stadt** *die* ruined town/city

ruinieren *tr. V.* ruin; **sich finanziell ~:** ruin oneself [financially]; **du ruinierst meine Nerven** you are turning me into a nervous wreck; *s. auch* **Ruf 5**

ruinös /ruiˈnø:s/ *Adj.* ruinous

Ruländer /ˈru:lɛndɐ/ *der;* **~s, ~:** Ruländer [grape/wine]

rülpsen /ˈrʏlpsn̩/ *itr. V.* (ugs.) belch

Rülpser *der;* **~s, ~** (ugs.) belch

rum /rʊm/ *Adv.* (ugs.) ▸**herum**

Rum /rʊm/ *der;* **~s, ~s** rum

rum|albern *itr. V.* (ugs.) ▸**herumalbern**

Rumäne /ruˈmɛ:nə/ *der;* **~n, ~n** ▸ⓘ **S. 520** Romanian

Rumänien *(das);* **~s** Romania

Rumänin *die;* **~, ~nen** ▸ⓘ **S. 520** Romanian

rumänisch ▸ⓘ **S. 520**, ▸ⓘ **S. 670**
A *Adj.* Romanian
B *adv.* Romanian; *s. auch* **deutsch**; **Deutsch**; **Deutsche²**

rum|ärgern *refl. V.* (ugs.) ▸**herumärgern**

Rumba /ˈrʊmba/ *die;* **~, ~s** *od. der;* **~s, ~s** rumba

rum-: ~|ballern *itr. V.* (ugs.) blast away; **~|brüllen** *itr. V.* (ugs.) ▸**herumbrüllen**; **~|diskutieren** *itr. V.* (ugs.) keep on and on discussing the problem/point *etc.*; **~|drucksen** *itr. V.* (ugs.) ▸**herumdrucksen**; **~|eiern** *itr. V.* (ugs.) beat about the bush; avoid the issue; **~|fliegen** (ugs.) **A** *unr. itr. V.; mit sein* [1] ▸**herumfliegen A 1**; [2] (herumliegen) lie about *or* around; **im Zimmer ~fliegen** litter the room; **B** *unr. tr. V.* ▸**herumfliegen B**; **~|fummeln** *itr. V.* (ugs.) ▸**herumfummeln**; **~|gammeln** *itr. V.* (ugs.) ▸**gammeln 2**; **~|gehen** *unr. itr. V.; mit sein* (ugs.) ▸**herumgehen**; **~|hampeln** *itr. V.* (ugs.) hop *or* jig about; **~|hängen** *unr. itr. V.* (ugs.) [1] (sich ziellos aufhalten/untätig od. arbeitslos sein) hang about *or* around; [2] ▸**herumhängen 1**; **~|hocken** *itr. V.* (ugs.) sit around [doing nothing]; **~|kriegen** *tr. V.* (ugs.) ▸**herumkriegen**; **~|knutschen** *itr. V.* (ugs.) **mit jmdm. ~knutschen** smooch around with sb.; **~|kommandieren A**; **B** *itr. V.* ▸**herumkommandieren B**; **~|kommen** (ugs.) **A** *unr. tr. V.; mit sein* **bei etw. ~kommen** come out of sth.; **dabei ist für mich nicht viel rumgekommen** I didn't get much out of it; **B** *unr. itr. V.; mit sein* ▸**herumkommen**; **~|labern** *itr. V.* (salopp abwertend) natter (Brit. coll.) *or* chatter away (coll.); rabbit on (Brit. coll.); **~|laufen** *unr. itr. V.; mit sein* (ugs.) ▸**herumlaufen**; **~|liegen** *unr. itr. V.* (ugs.) ▸**herumliegen**; **~|lungern** *itr. V.* (salopp) ▸**herumlungern**; **~|machen** *itr. V.* (salopp) [1] ▸**herummachen**; [2] ▸**herumfummeln 1**; [3] (sich [sexuell] einlassen) play around; (koitieren) do it (sl.); (schmusen) neck (coll.); **~|mäkeln** *itr. V.* (ugs.) ▸**herummäkeln**; **~|meckern** *itr. V.* (ugs. abwertend) keep on moaning (**an** + *Dat.* at)

Rummel /ˈrʊml̩/ *der;* **~s** (ugs.) [1] (laute Betriebsamkeit) commotion; (Aufhebens) fuss, to-do (**um** about); **der ganze ~:** the whole business [2] (bes. nordd.: Jahrmarkt) fair; **auf den ~ gehen** go to the fair

Rummel·platz *der* (bes. nordd.) fairground

rum|mosern *itr. V.* (ugs.) keep on bellyaching (coll.)

Rummy /ˈrœmi/ *das;* **~s, ~s** (österr.) ▸**Rommé**

rumoren /ruˈmo:rən/ *itr. V.* (ugs.) [1] (rumpeln) make a noise; (poltern) ‹*person*› bang about; **es rumorte in seinem Bauch** (fig.) his stomach rumbled [2] (aufbegehren) protest; stage a protest/protests

Rumpel·kammer *die* (ugs.) boxroom (Brit.); junk room

rumpeln /ˈrʊmpl̩n/ *itr. V.* (ugs.) [1] (poltern) bump and bang about; **es rumpelte** *unpers.* there was banging and bumping; (im Magen) there was a rumble *or* rumbling [2] *mit sein* (sich **~d** fortbewegen) rumble; bump and bang

Rumpelstilzchen /ˈrʊmpl̩ʃtɪltsçən/ *(das);* **~s** Rumpelstiltskin *no art.*

Rumpf /rʊmpf/ *der;* **~[e]s, Rümpfe** /ˈrʏmpfə/ [1] (bei Lebewesen) trunk [of the body]; **den ~ drehen/beugen** turn one's body/bend from the hips [2] (beim Schiff) hull [3] (beim Flugzeug) fuselage

Rumpf·beuge *die* (Gymnastik) trunk-bend; bend from the hips; **~ rückwärts** arch

rümpfen /ˈrʏmpfn̩/ *tr. V.* **die Nase [bei etw.] ~:** wrinkle one's nose at sth.; **über jmdn./etw. die Nase ~** (fig.) look down one's nose at sb./turn up one's nose at sth.

rum-: ~|pienzen *itr. V.* (ugs.) keep on moaning (coll.); **~|pöbeln** *itr. V.* (ugs.) be always effing and blinding (coll.)

Rumpsteak /ˈrʊmp-ste:k/ *das;* **~s, ~s** rump steak

rum-: ~|reißen *tr. V.* (ugs.) ▸**herumreißen**; **~|rennen** *unr. itr. V.; mit sein* (ugs.) ▸**herumrennen**

rums /rʊms/ *Interj.* (Geräusch) bump; (lauter, heller) bang; (beim Zusammenstoß) crash

rum-: ~|schleichen *unr. itr. V.; mit sein* (ugs.) ▸**herumschleichen**; **~|schnüffeln** *itr. V.* (ugs. abwertend) ▸**herumschnüffeln**; **~|schreien** *unr. itr. V.* (ugs. abwertend) (schimpfen) curse away (coll.); (sehr laut singen/sprechen) shout away (coll.)

rumsen *itr. V.* (ugs.) [1] *unpers.* **es rumst** there's a bump *or* bang; (wiederholt) there's bumping and banging; (laut, beim Zusammenstoß) there's a crash [2] *mit sein* (auftreffen) **gegen etw. ~:** bang into sth.

rum-: ~|sitzen *unr. itr. V.* (ugs.) ▸**herumsitzen**; **~|spinnen** *unr. itr. V.* (ugs.) let one's imagination run riot; **~spinnen, was/wie ...** come up with crazy ideas as to what/how ...; **~|spuken** *itr. V.* (ugs.) ▸**herumspuken**; **~|stänkern** *itr. V.* (ugs. abwertend) ▸**herumstänkern**; **~|stehen** *unr. itr. V.* (ugs.) ▸**herumstehen**; **~|stöbern** *itr. V.* (ugs.) ▸**herumstöbern**; **~|sülzen** *itr. V.* (salopp) waffle on (coll.); **hier wird rumgesülzt** there's a load of waffle here (coll.); **~|toben** *itr. V.* (ugs.) [1] *auch mit sein* ‹*child*› charge *or* romp [noisily] about; ‹*students etc.*› rag; [2] (wüten) rant and rave

Rum·topf *der: fruits preserved in rum and sugar*

rum|treiben *unr. refl. V.* (ugs.) ▸**herumtreiben**

Rum·verschnitt *der* rum blend (*with other spirits*)

rum-: ~|**wühlen** *itr. V.* (ugs.) ▸**herumwühlen**; ~|**zappen** *itr. V.* (ugs.) zap around (coll.); ~|**zicken** *itr. V.* (ugs.) (Unfug machen) cause trouble; (Theater machen) kick up a fuss; ~|**ziehen** *unr. tr., itr. V.* (ugs.) ▸**herumziehen**

Run /ran/ *der;* ~**s,** ~**s** [big] rush; **ein [starker]** ~ **auf etw.** (*Akk.*) a [big] run on sth.

rund /rʊnt/

A *Adj.* [1] (kreis~) round; ~**e Augen machen** (ugs.) ‹*child*› gaze wide-eyed; **ein Gespräch am** ~**en Tisch** (fig.) a round-table conference [2] (dicklich) plump ‹*arms etc.*›; chubby ‹*cheeks*›; fat ‹*stomach*›; **er ist dick und** ~ **geworden** he has become rather rotund *or* stout [3] (ugs.: ganz) round ‹*dozen, number, etc.*›; ~**e drei Jahre** three years or as near as makes no difference [4] (abgerundet) full, rounded ‹*tone, sound, flavour*›; **eine** ~**e Sache** a nice piece of work

B *adv.* ~ **laufen** (Kfz-W.) ‹*engine*› run smoothly; *s. auch* **rundgehen**

C *Adv.* [1] (ugs.: etwa) about; approximately [2] ~ **um jmdn./etw.** [all] around sb./sth.; **eine Sendung** ~ **um das Kind** a broadcast on all aspects of childhood; *s. auch* **Uhr**

Rund *das;* ~**[e]s,** ~**e** (geh.) [1] (runde Form) round; (Mond usw.) orb (literary) [2] (runde Fläche) circle

Rund-: ~**bau** *der; Pl.* ~~**ten** circular building; rotunda; ~**blick** *der* panorama; view in all directions; ~**bogen** *der* (Kunstwiss., Archit.) round arch; ~**brief** *der* circular [letter]; ~**bürste** *der* styling brush

Runde /ˈrʊndə/ *die;* ~, ~**n** [1] (Sport: runde Strecke) lap; **die schnellste** ~ **fahren** do the fastest lap; **seine** ~**n ziehen** *od.* **drehen** do one's laps [2] (Sport: Durchgang, Partie; Boxen: Abschnitt) round; **eine** ~ **Golf/Skat** a round of golf/skat; **über die** ~**n kommen** (fig. ugs.) get by; manage [3] (Personenkreis) circle; (Gesellschaft) company; **in fröhlicher** ~ **beisammensitzen** sit together in a happy circle *or* group [4] (Umkreis) **in der** ~: round about; **in die** ~ **blicken** look all around one [5] (Rundgang) round; (Spaziergang) walk; **eine** ~ **durch die Kneipen machen** go on a pub crawl (Brit. coll.); go barhopping (Amer.); **die** ~ **machen** (ugs.) ‹*drink, rumour*› go the rounds *pl.*; circulate [6] **eine** ~ **Bier schmeißen** (ugs.) buy *or* stand a round of beer; **die** ~ **geht auf mich/auf den Wirt** this round is on me/on the house

runden

A *tr. V.* [1] (rund machen) round [2] (fig.: ab~) round off, fill out ‹*picture, impression*›

B *refl. V.* become round

Runden·rekord *der* (Motorsport) lap record

rund-, Rund-: ~**erneuern** *tr. V.* (Kfz-W.) remould; retread; ~**erneuerte Reifen** remoulds; retreads; ~**erneuerung** *die* (Kfz-W.) remoulding; retreading; ~**fahrt** *die* (auch Sport) tour (**durch** of); **eine** ~**fahrt durch Amsterdam** a circular tour of *or* a trip round Amsterdam; **eine** ~**fahrt machen** go on a [circular] tour; ~**flug** *der* [short] circular flight; circuit; ~**frage** *die* survey (*using a questionnaire*); questionnaire

Rund·funk *der* [1] radio; (das Senden) radio broadcasting *no art.*; **im** ~: on the radio; ~ **hören** listen to the radio [2] (Einrichtung, Gebäude) radio station; **sie ist** *od.* **arbeitet beim** ~: she works in radio

Rundfunk-: ~**anstalt** *die* broadcasting corporation; (Sender) radio station; ~**empfang** *der* radio reception *no indef. art.*; ~**empfänger** *der* radio receiver; ~**gebühren** *Pl.* radio licence fees; ~**gerät** *das* radio set; ~**hörer** *der*, ~**hörerin** *die* [radio] listener; ~**programm** *das* [1] (Sendefolge) [schedule *sing.* of] radio programmes *pl.*; [2] (Programmheft) radio programme guide; ~**redakteur** *der*, ~**redakteurin** *die* radio producer; ~**reporter** *der*, ~**reporterin** *die* radio reporter; ~**sender** *der* radio station; (technische Anlage) radio transmitter; ~**sendung** *die* radio programme; ~**sprecher** *der*, ~**sprecherin** *die* radio announcer; ~**station** *die* radio station; ~**techniker** *der*, ~**technikerin** *die* radio engineer; ~**teilnehmer** *der*, ~**teilnehmerin** *die* radio licence holder; (Hörer) radio listener; ~**übertragung** *die* radio broadcast

rund-, Rund-: ~**gang** *der* [1] (des Wachmanns, Chefarztes usw.) round (**durch** of); **einen** ~**gang durch die Stadt machen** go for a walk round the town; [2] (Umgang) gallery; ~|**gehen** *unr. itr. V.; mit sein* [1] *unpers.* (ugs.) **es geht** ~ (es ist viel Betrieb) it's all go (coll.); (es geht flott zu) things are going with a swing; [2] (herumgereicht werden) be passed round; (fig.) ‹*story, rumours*› go *or* do the rounds; **er ließ die Flasche** ~**gehen** he passed the bottle round; ~**heraus** *Adv.* straight out; ‹*say, ask*› bluntly; ‹*refuse*› flatly; ~**herum** *Adv.* [1] (ringsum) all around; (darum herum) all round it; ~**herum an der Wand** all round the walls; [2] (völlig) completely; (fig.) entirely ‹*satisfied, practical*›; ~**kurs** *der* (bes. Motor-, Fahrradsport) circuit

rundlich *Adj.* [1] (fast rund) roundish [2] (mollig) plump; chubby

rund-, Rund-: ~**reise** *die* [circular] tour (**durch** of); **eine** ~**reise [mit dem Bus/Auto] durch den Schwarzwald machen** tour the Black Forest [by coach/car]; ~**schädel** *der* (Anthrop.) round *or* (as tech. term) brachycephalic skull; ~**schau** *die* [1] (geh.) ▸ ~**blick**; [2] (in Zeitungstiteln) review; ~**schlag** *der* (Boxen, Faustball, Eishockey) swing; (fig.) [general] broadside; ~**schreiben** *das* ▸ ~**brief**; ~**sicht** *die* ▸ ~**blick**; ~**spruch** *der* (schweiz.) ▸**Rundfunk**; ~**strecke** *die* circuit; ~**strick·nadel** *die* circular-knitting needle; ~**stück** *das* (nordd.) [oval] roll; ~**um** *Adv.* ▸ ~**herum**

Rundum-: ~**grün** *das* (Verkehrsw.) green [pedestrian] light at all crossing points; ~**sicht** *die* (Kfz.-W.) all-round vision; ~**versorgung** *die* comprehensive care; (für Kunden) comprehensive support *or* service

Rundung *die;* ~, ~**en** curve; (hervortretend) bulge

rund·weg *Adv.* ‹*refuse, deny*› flatly, point-blank

Rund·weg *der* circular path *or* walk

Rune /ˈruːnə/ *die;* ~, ~**n** rune

Runen-: ~**schrift** *die* runic alphabet; ~**stein** *der* rune stone; ~**zeichen** *das* runic character

Runge /ˈrʊŋə/ *die;* ~, ~**n** [load-retaining] stanchion

Runkel·rübe /ˈrʊŋkl̩ryːbə/ *die* mangel-wurzel

runter /ˈrʊntɐ/ *Adv.* (ugs.) ~ **[da, das ist mein Platz]!** get off [there, that's my seat]!; ~ **mit den Klamotten** off with your clothes; get those clothes off; ~ **mit den Füßen** take your feet [down] off the table; **Kopf** ~! head/heads down!; *s. auch* **herunter**; **hinunter**

runter-: ~|**beten** *tr. V.* (ugs. abwertend) ▸**herunterbeten**; ~|**beugen** *refl. V.* (ugs.) bend down; ~|**bringen** *unr. tr. V.* ▸**herunterbringen**; ~|**drehen** *tr. V.* (ugs.) turn down ‹*gas, heating, sound*›; wind down ‹*window*› ~|**dürfen** *unr. itr. V.* (ugs.) be allowed to come down; (hinausgehen dürfen) be allowed out; ~|**fahren** (ugs.) **A** *unr. itr. V.; mit sein* ▸**herunterfahren A**; **B** *unr. tr. V.*: ▸**herunterfahren B**; ~|**fallen** *unr. itr. V.; mit sein* (ugs.) fall down; (von der Leiter usw.) fall off; **die Leiter/von der Leiter** ~**fallen** fall off the ladder; **die Kreide fiel ihm** ~: he dropped the chalk; ~|**gehen** *unr. itr. V.; mit sein* (ugs.) [1] (nach unten gehen) go down; [2] (niedriger werden) ‹*price, temperature, pressure, etc.*› go down, drop; [3] (die Höhe senken) go down (**auf** + *Akk.* to); (langsamer fahren) slow down (**auf** + *Akk.* to); **wir müssen mit den Preisen** ~**gehen** we must reduce our prices; *s. auch* **heruntergehen 4, 5**; **hinuntergehen**; ~|**hängen** *unr. itr. V.* (ugs.) ▸**herunterhängen**; ~|**hauen** *unr. tr. V.* **jmdm. eine/ein paar** ~**hauen** (salopp) give sb. a clip/a couple of clips round the ear; ~|**holen** *tr. V.* (ugs.) [1] fetch down; *s. auch* **herunterholen 2**; [2] **sich/jmdm. einen** ~**holen** (vulg.) jerk off (coarse) *or* (Brit. coarse) wank/jerk (coarse) *or* (Brit. coarse) wank sb. off; ~|**kommen** *unr. itr. V.; mit sein* (ugs.) come down; *s. auch* **herunterkommen 2, 3**; ~|**können** *unr. itr. V.* (ugs.) ▸**herunterkönnen**; ~|**kriegen** *tr. V.* (ugs.) [1] get down; **etw.** ~**kriegen [können]** manage to get sth. down; [2] (wegbekommen) get off ‹*dirt, sth. sticky*›; ~|**kurbeln** *tr. V.* (ugs.) wind down; ~|**laden** *unr. tr. V.* (DV) ▸**herunterladen**; ~|**lassen** *unr. tr. V.* (ugs.) ▸**herunterlassen**; **hinunterlassen**; ~|**machen** *tr. V.* (salopp) ▸**heruntermachen**; ~|**müssen** *unr. itr. V.* (ugs.) have to go/come down; **ich muss von der Autobahn** ~ (fig.) I'll have to get off the motorway; ~|**reißen** *unr. tr. V.* (ugs.) ▸**herunterreißen**; ~|**rollen** (ugs.) **A** *itr. V.; mit sein* roll down; **B** *tr. V.* roll down ‹*sleeve, trouser leg, blind*›; ~|**rutschen** *itr. V.; mit sein* (ugs.) ▸**herunterrutschen**; *s. auch* **Buckel 1**; ~|**schrauben** *tr. V.* (ugs.) ▸**herunterschrauben**; ~|**scrollen** *tr., auch itr. V.* (DV) scroll down; ~|**spülen** *tr. V.* (ugs.) ▸**hinunterspülen**; ~|**tragen** *unr. tr. V.* (ugs.) ▸**heruntertragen**; ~|**werfen** *unr. tr. V.* (ugs.) ▸**herunterwerfen**; ~|**ziehen** **A** *unr. tr. V.*: ▸**herunterziehen A**; **B** *unr. itr. V.; mit sein* ▸**herunterziehen B**

Runzel /ˈrʊntsl̩/ *die;* ~, ~**n** wrinkle

runzelig *Adj.* wrinkled

runzeln

A *tr. V.* **die Stirn/die Brauen** ~: wrinkle one's brow/knit one's brows; (ärgerlich) frown; **mit gerunzelter Stirn** with wrinkled brow; (ärgerlich) frowning

B *refl. V.* wrinkle

runzlig *Adj.* ▸**runzelig**

Rüpel /ˈryːpl̩/ *der;* ~**s,** ~ (abwertend) lout

Rüpelei *die;* ~, ~**en** (abwertend) [1] (Benehmen) loutishness; loutish behaviour [2] (Handlung) piece of coarseness; **noch so eine** ~ **von dir, und wir gehen nach Hause** any more of that coarseness from you and we're going home; ~**en** coarseness *sing.*

rüpelhaft (abwertend)

A *Adj.* loutish

B *adv.* in a loutish manner

rupfen /ˈrʊpfn̩/ *tr. V.* [1] pluck ‹*goose, hen, etc.*›; *s. auch* **Hühnchen** [2] (abreißen) pull up ‹*weeds, grass*›; pull off ‹*leaves etc.*› [3] (ugs.: übervorteilen) fleece ‹*person*› [of his/her money]

Rupfen *der;* ~**s** hessian

Rupie /ˈruːpi̯ə/ *die;* ~, ~**n** ▸❶ **S. 299** rupee

ruppig /ˈrʊpɪç/

A *Adj.* (abwertend) gruff ‹*person, behaviour*›; sharp ‹*tone*›; **er war** ~ **zu ihr** he was short with her; he snapped at her

B *adv.* (abwertend) gruffly; ~ **spielen** play rough *or* a rough game

Ruppigkeit *die;* ~, ~**en** (abwertend) [1] (Benehmen) gruffness [2] (Handlung) piece of uncouthness; ~**en** rough *or* uncouth behaviour *sing.*

Ruprecht ▸**Knecht 2**

Rüsche /ˈryːʃə/ *die;* ~, ~**n** ruche; frill

Ruß /ruːs/ *der;* ~**es** soot

Russe /ˈrʊsə/ *der;* ~**n,** ~**n** ▸❶ **S. 520** Russian; **der** ~ (ugs.) Russians *pl.*; (die russische Regierung) the Russians *pl.*

Rüssel /ˈrʏsl̩/ *der;* ~**s,** ~ [1] (des Elefanten) trunk; (des Schweins) snout; (bei Insekten u. Ä.) proboscis [2] (salopp: Nase) conk (coll.)

Rüssel·tier *das* proboscidean

rußen

A *itr. V.* give off sooty smoke

B *tr. V.* (schwärzen) blacken with soot

Russen·bluse *die,* **Russen·kittel** *der* Russian blouse

Russen·mafia *die* Russian Mafia

Ruß·fleck *der* soot mark

ruß·geschwärzt *Adj.* blackened with soot *postpos.*

rußig *Adj.* sooty

Russin *die;* ~, ~**nen** ▸❶ **S. 520** Russian; *s. auch* **-in**

russisch ▸❶ **S. 520**, ▸❶ **S. 670**

A *Adj.* Russian; ~**es Roulett** Russian roulette; *s. auch* **Ei 1**

B *adv.* [1] ~ **verwaltet/besetzt** administered/occupied by Russia [2] (auf Russisch) in Russian; *s. auch* **deutsch**; **Deutsche**[2]

r

Russisch *das;* ~[s] ▸ⓘ S. 670 Russian; *s. auch* **Deutsch**

Russisch·brot, *Russisch Brot *das* alphabet biscuits *pl.* (Brit.) *or* (Amer.) cookies

Russisch·grün *das* Russian green

Russland, *Rußland *(das);* ~s Russia

Russland·deutsche *der/die* Russian German; *German national born in, and living in, Russia*

ruß, Ruß: ~schwaden *der* sooty cloud of smoke; **~verschmiert** *Adj.* covered in soot *postpos.*; soot-blackened ‹*face*›

rüsten /ˈrʏstn̩/

A *itr. V.* (sich bewaffnen) arm; **zum Krieg ~:** arm for war

B *itr., refl. V.* (geh.: sich bereit machen, auch fig.) get ready; prepare; **sich zur Reise ~:** get ready *or* prepare oneself for the journey

Rüster /ˈryːstɐ/ *die;* ~, ~n [1] ▸**Ulme** [2] ▸**Rüsternholz**

Rüstern·holz *das* elmwood

rüstig

A *Adj.* [1] (leistungsfähig) sprightly; active; **er ist noch ~:** he is still hale and hearty [2] (geh.: kraftvoll) strong

B *adv.* (geh.: kraftvoll) strongly; **~ ausschreiten** stride out vigorously

rustikal /rʊstiˈkaːl/

A *Adj.* country-style ‹*food, inn, clothes, etc.*›; farmhouse *attrib.* ‹*food*›; rustic ‹*pattern*›; rustic, farmhouse *attrib.* ‹*furniture*›; (als Nachahmung) rustic-style ‹*furniture etc.*›; **ein Schrank aus Eiche ~:** a rustic-style oak cupboard

B *adv.* in [a] country style; **~ essen** eat farmhouse *or* country-style food; ‹*furnish*› in a rustic *or* farmhouse style

Rustikalität *die;* rusticity; rustic nature

Rüst-: ~kammer *die* (hist.) armoury; **~tag** *der* (jüd. Rel.) day of preparation

Rüstung *die;* ~, ~en [1] (Bewaffnung) armament *no art.*; (Waffen) arms *pl.*; weapons *pl.* [2] (hist.: Schutzbekleidung) suit of armour; **in voller ~:** in full armour

Rüstungs-: ~auftrag *der* arms order; **~ausgaben** *Pl.* arms expenditure *sing.*; **~begrenzung** *die* arms limitation; **~betrieb** *der* armaments factory; **~export** *der* arms export; (das Exportieren) exporting of arms; arms exports *pl.*; **~fabrik** *die* ▸**~betrieb**; **~firma** *die* armaments company; **~geschäft** *das* arms deal; **~gut** *das* armaments *pl.*; **~haushalt** *der* armaments *or* arms budget; **~industrie** *die* armaments *or* arms industry; **~kontrolle** *die* arms control; **~konzern** *der* armaments concern; **~politik** *die* arms policy; **~produktion** *die* arms production *no art.*; **~schmiede** *die* armaments manufacturer; **~stopp** *der* arms freeze; **~wettlauf** *der* arms race

Rüst-: ~zeit *die* [1] (ev. Kirche) period of reflection; retreat; [2] (Arbeitswiss.) set-up time; **~zeug** *das* [1] (Wissen) requisite know-how; [2] (Ausrüstung) equipment [for the job *or* task]

Rute /ˈruːtə/ *die;* ~, ~n [1] (Stock) switch; (Birken~, Angel~, Wünschel~) rod; (zum Züchtigen) cane; (Bündel) birch [2] (veralt.: Längenmaß) rod; perch [3] (Jägerspr.: männliches Glied) penis; (derb: menschlicher Penis) prick (coarse) [4] (Jägerspr.: Schwanz) tail

Ruten-: ~bündel *das* [1] bundle of [birch] rods; [2] (altröm.: Faszes) fasces *pl.*; **~gänger** *der;* **~~s, ~~, ~gängerin** *die;* **~~, ~~nen** dowser; diviner

Ruthenium /ruˈteːni̯ʊm/ *das;* ~s (Chemie) ruthenium

Rutsch /rʊtʃ/ *der;* ~[e]s, ~e [1] (das ~en) slide; **in einem** *od.* **auf einen ~** (fig. ugs.) in one go [2] (Erdmasse) landslide [3] (ugs.: Ausflug) trip; jaunt; **guten ~ [ins neue Jahr]!** happy New Year!

Rutsch·bahn *die* slide; (auf dem Rummelplatz) helter-skelter

Rutsche *die;* ~, ~n chute

rutschen *itr. V.; mit sein* [1] slide; ‹*clutch, carpet*› slip; (aus~) ‹*person*› slip; ‹*car etc.*› skid; (nach unten) slip [down]; **rutsch mal zur Seite!** (ugs.) move up a bit! (coll.); **ins R~ kommen** ‹*person*› [start to] slip; ‹*car etc.*› go into a skid; **auf seinem Platz hin und her ~:** slide *or* shift about on one's seat; **von/aus etw. ~:** slip *or* slide off/out of sth.; **die Brille/der Rock rutscht** the glasses keep/skirt keeps slipping [down]; **das trockene Brot rutscht schlecht/will nicht ~** (ugs.) the dry bread doesn't go down easily/won't go down [2] (ugs.: kurz verreisen) slip off

rutsch·fest *Adj.* [1] (strapazierfähig) hard-wearing [2] (nicht rutschig) anti-skid ‹*tyre*›; skid-proof ‹*road surface*›; non-slip ‹*mat, material*›

Rutsch·gefahr *die* danger of skidding

rutschig *Adj.* slippery

Rutsch·partie *die* (ugs.) succession of slides; (im Auto) succession of skids

rütteln /ˈrʏtl̩n/

A *tr. V.* [1] shake; **jmdn. aus dem Schlaf ~:** shake sb. out of his/her sleep; **jmdn. am Arm/an der Schulter ~:** shake sb. by the arm/shoulder [2] (Bauw.) vibrate ‹*concrete etc.*›

B *itr. V.* [1] shake; **an der Tür/den Fenstern ~:** shake the door/windows; (sodass es klappert) rattle at the door/windows; ‹*wind*› make the door/windows rattle; **an den Fundamenten von etw. ~** (fig.) rock *or* shake the foundations of sth.; **daran ist nicht** *od.* **gibt es nichts zu ~** (fig.) there's nothing you can do about that [2] (sich ruckartig hin u. her bewegen) shake about; ‹*engine*› hunt; run unevenly

Rüttler /ˈrʏtlɐ/ *der;* ~s, ~ (Bauw.) vibrator

Ss

s, S /ɛs/ *das;* ~, ~: s/S; *s. auch* **a, A**

s *Abk.* = **Sekunde** sec.; s.

S *Abk.* ① = **Süden** ▸ⓘ **S. 363** S ② (österr.) = **Schilling** Sch.

s. *Abk.* = **siehe**

S. *Abk.* = **Seite** p.

s. a. *Abk.* = **siehe auch**

Sa. *Abk.* = **Samstag** Sat.

SA *Abk.* (ns.) = **Sturmabteilung** SA

Saal /za:l/ *der;* **~[e]s, Säle** /ˈzɛ:lə/ ① hall; (Ball~) ballroom; (für Konzerte) **der große/kleine ~:** the large/small auditorium ② (Publikum) audience

Saal-: ~ordner *der,* **~ordnerin** *die* steward; **~schlacht** *die* [violent] brawl, roughhouse (between rival political factions)

Saarland /ˈza:ɐ̯lant/ *das;* **~[e]s** Saarland; Saar (esp. Hist.); **das ~:** the Saarland; (Hist.) the Saar; **im/aus dem ~:** in/from the Saarland

Saarländer /-lɛndɐ/ *der;* **~s, ~, Saarländerin** *die;* **~, ~nen** Saarlander

saarländisch *Adj.* Saarland *attrib.* ‹*government, population, etc.*›; Saar *attrib.* ‹*industry, miners, etc.*›; ‹*history*› of the Saar

Saat /za:t/ *die;* **~, ~en** ① (Getreide usw.) [young] crops *pl.;* (fachspr.: Pflanzgut) seedlings *pl.;* young plants *pl.;* **die ~ des Bösen ist aufgegangen** (fig. geh.) the seeds of evil have borne fruit ② (das Säen) sowing; **mit der ~ beginnen** start sowing ③ (Samenkörner) seed[s *pl.*]

Saat-: ~gut *das* seed[s *pl.*]; **~kartoffel** *die* seed potato; **~korn** *das* ① (zum Aussäen) seedcorn; ② (Samenkorn) grain; **~krähe** *die* rook

Sabbat /ˈzabat/ *der;* **~s, ~e** sabbath; **es ist ~:** it is the sabbath

Sabbatical /səˈbɛtɪkl/ *das;* **~s, ~s** sabbatical

Sabbat·jahr *das* (jüd. Rel.) sabbatical year

Sabbel /ˈzabl̩/ *der;* **~s, ~** (nordd. abwertend) ① (Mund) gob (sl.); **halt den ~:** shut your trap (sl.) ② ▸ **Sabber**

sabbeln (nordd.)

A *itr. V.* ① (abwertend: sprechen) natter (Brit. coll.) *or* chatter [on]; rabbit on (Brit. coll.) ② ▸ **sabbern A 1**

B *tr. V.* (abwertend) jabber ‹*nonsense, rubbish*›

Sabber /ˈzabɐ/ *der;* **~s** (ugs.) slobber; (eines Kindes) dribble

sabbern

A *itr. V.* ① ‹*dog, person*› slaver, slobber; ‹*baby*› dribble ② (abwertend) ▸ **sabbeln A 1**

B *tr. V.* (abwertend) ▸ **sabbeln B**

Säbel /ˈzɛ:bl̩/ *der;* **~s, ~:** sabre; **mit dem ~ rasseln** (fig. abwertend) rattle the sabre

Säbel-: ~beine *Pl.* (ugs. scherzh.) bandy *or* bow legs; **~fechten** *das* (Fechten) sabre fencing *no art.;* **Weltmeister im ~fechten** world champion at sabre; world sabre champion; **~gerassel** *das* (abwertend) sabre-rattling

säbeln *tr. V.* (ugs.) hack, saw ‹*bread etc.*›

Säbel·rasseln *das;* **~s** (abwertend) sabre-rattling

säbel·rasselnd *Adj.* (abwertend) sabre-rattling

Sabotage /zaboˈta:ʒə/ *die;* **~, ~n** sabotage *no art.;* **Versuch der ~:** attempted sabotage

Sabotage·akt *der* act of sabotage

Saboteur /zaboˈtø:ɐ̯/ *der;* **~s, ~e, Saboteurin** *die;* **~, ~nen** saboteur

sabotieren *tr. V.* sabotage; disobey ‹*order*›

Saccharin /zaxaˈri:n/ *das;* **~s** saccharin

sach-, Sach-: ~bearbeiter *der,* **~bearbeiterin** *die* person responsible (**für** for); (Experte) specialist, expert (**für** on); **~bereich** *der* area; field; **der ~bereich Öffentlichkeitsarbeit** the field of public relations; all matters *pl.* concerning public relations; **~beschädigung** *die* (Rechtsw.) wilful damage to property; **~bezogen A** *Adj.* relevant; pertinent ‹*remark*›; **B** *adv.* to the point; **~bezüge** *Pl.* payment *sing.* in kind; **~buch** *das* [popular] non-fiction *or* informative book; **~bücher lesen** read non-fiction *sing.;* **~dienlich** *Adj.* (Papierdt.) useful; helpful

Sache /ˈzaxə/ *die;* **~, ~n** ① thing; **scharfe ~n trinken** drink the hard stuff (coll.); **bewegliche/unbewegliche ~n** (Rechtsspr., Wirtsch.) movable/fixed assets; (Rechtsw.: Eigentum) movables *or* chattels/immovables *or* real estate *sing.* ② (Angelegenheit) matter; business (esp. derog.); **das ist eine andere ~/eine ~ für sich** that's a different/a separate matter; **eine ernste/schlimme/heikle/faule ~:** a serious/a bad/an awkward/a shady business; **es ist beschlossene ~[, dass ...]** it's [all] arranged *or* settled [that ...]; **es ist die einfachste ~ [von] der Welt** it's the simplest thing in the world; **das ist meine/seine ~:** that's my business/his own affair; **das ist so eine ~:** it's a bit tricky; **das ist nicht jedermanns ~:** it's not everyone's cup of tea; **du hast dir die ~ sehr leicht gemacht** you made it *or* things *pl.* very easy for yourself; **so kommen wir der ~ näher** we are getting warmer *or* coming to the point; **~n gibts[, die gibts gar nicht]!** (ugs.) would you believe *or* credit it!; **mach ~n!** you don't say!; **was sind denn das für ~n!** (ugs.) what's all this then!; what's going on!; **von dir hört man ja nette ~n!** (iron.) I've heard some things about you!; **[mit jmdm.] gemeinsame ~ machen** join forces [with sb.]; **sagen/jmdm. sagen, was ~ ist** (ugs.) come out with it/come clean with sb. (coll.); (die Dinge beim Namen nennen) say/tell sb. what's what; (sagen, worum es geht) say/tell sb. what gives (coll.); (bestimmen) say/tell sb. what goes (coll.); **[sich (*Dat.*)] seiner ~ sicher** *od.* **gewiss sein** be sure one is right; **bei der ~ sein/bleiben** concentrate/keep one's mind on it; (im Gespräch usw.) stick to the point; **nicht bei der ~ sein** let one's mind wander; **zur ~ kommen** come to the point; **das tut nichts zur ~:** that's irrelevant; that's got nothing to do with it ③ (Rechts~) case; **die Verhandlung in ~n Maier gegen Schulze** the hearing in the case of Maier versus Schulze; **Fragen/Angaben zur ~:** questions/statements about the case ④ (Anliegen) cause; **es dient der großen ~:** it's in a good cause ⑤ *Pl.* (ugs.: Stundenkilometer) **100 ~n** 100 kilometres per hour; **wie viel ~n hat er draufgehabt?** how fast was he going?

Sach·einlage *die* (Wirtsch.) investment in kind

Sächelchen /ˈzɛçlçən/ *das;* **~s, ~:** [little] thing

Sachen·recht *das* (Rechtsw.) law of property

Sacher·torte /ˈzaxɐ-/ *die: rich iced chocolate cake;* Sachertorte

sach-, Sach-: ~frage *die* question about the matter/issue itself (as opposed to personalities, methods, etc.); **~gebiet** *das* subject [area]; field; **das ~gebiet Ornithologie** the field of ornithology; **~gemäß, ~gerecht A** *Adj.* proper; correct; **B** *adv.* properly; correctly; **~katalog** *der* (Buchw.) subject catalogue; **~kenner** *der,* **~kennerin** *die* expert; **~kenntnis** *die* expertise; knowledge of the subject; **von keiner ~kenntnis getrübt** (scherzh.) without having the faintest idea [what it's all about]; **~kompetenz** *die* ① expertise [in the subject]; ② (Kompetenzbereich) area of responsibility; **~kunde** *die* ① ▸ **~kenntnis;** ② ≈ general subjects *pl.;* **~kundig A** *Adj.* with a knowledge of the subject *postpos., not pred.;* **sich ~kundig machen** acquaint oneself with the subject; **B** *adv.* expertly; **~lage** *die* situation; **~leistung** *die* (Amtsspr., Versicherungsw.) benefit in kind

sachlich

A *Adj.* ① (objektiv) objective; (nüchtern) functional ‹*building, style, etc.*›; matter-of-fact, down-to-earth ‹*letter etc.*› ② (sachbezogen) factual ‹*error*›; actual, material ‹*difference*›; material ‹*consideration*›; **aus ~en Gründen** for practical reasons

B *adv.* ① (objektiv) objectively; ‹*state*› as a matter of fact; (nüchtern) ‹*furnished*› in a functional style; ‹*written*› in a matter-of-fact way ② (sachbezogen) factually ‹*wrong*›; actually ‹*justified*›

sächlich /ˈzɛçlɪç/ *Adj.* (Sprachw.) neuter

Sachlichkeit *die;* **~:** objectivity; (Nüchternheit) functionalism; **Neue ~** (Kunstwiss.) new objectivity

Sach-: ~mangel *der* (Rechtsw.) material defect; **~preis** *der* non-money prize; **~register** *das* [subject] index; **~schaden** *der* damage [to property] *no indef. art.;* **ein ~schaden von 30 000 Euro** damage amounting to 30,000 euros

Sachse /ˈzaksə/ *der;* **~n, ~n** Saxon

sächseln /ˈzɛksl̩n/ *itr. V.* **er sächselt** he speaks in Saxon dialect

Sachsen *(das);* **~s** Saxony

Sachsen-Anhalt *(das);* **~s** Saxony-Anhalt

Sachsen-Anhalter, *der;* **~s, ~, Sachsen-Anhalterin** *die;* **~, ~nen, Sachsen-Anhaltiner** *der;* **~s, ~, Sachsen-Anhaltinerin** *die;* **~, ~nen** native of Saxony-Anhalt; (Einwohner[in]) inhabitant of Saxony-Anhalt

sachsen-anhaltinisch, sachsen-anhaltisch *Adj.* Saxony-Anhalt *attrib.*

Sächsin /ˈzɛksɪn/ *die;* **~, ~nen** ▸ **Sachse**

sächsisch /ˈzɛksɪʃ/

A *Adj.* Saxon; ‹*capital, economy, etc.*› of Saxony

B *adv.* ‹*speak, write*› in Saxon dialect; *s. auch* **badisch**

Sach·spende *die* gift *or* contribution in kind

sacht /zaxt/

A *Adj.* ① (behutsam) gentle; (langsam) smooth ‹*take-off*›; gentle, gradual ‹*acceleration*› ② (leise) quiet

B *adv.* ① gently ② (leise) quietly

sachte

A ▸ **sacht**

B *adv.* (ugs.) ① (Beschwichtigung) **~[, ~]** take it

easy; (nicht so hastig) not so fast **2** **so [ganz] ~** (allmählich) gradually

sạch-, Sạch-: ~thema *das* topic; (Frage) issue; **~verhalt** *der;* **~~[e]s, ~~e** facts *pl.* [of the matter]; **~versicherung** *die* (Versicherungsw.) property insurance; **~verstand** *der* expertise; grasp of the subject; **~verständig** **A** *Adj.* expert ‹*opinion etc.*›; knowledgeable ‹*person*›; **B** *adv.* expertly; knowledgeably; **~verständige** *der/die; adj. Dekl.* expert; **~verständigenausschuss**, ***~verständigenausschuß** *der* committee of experts; **~verständigen·gutachten** *das* expert's report; (von mehreren) experts' report; **~walter** /-valtɐ/ *der;* **~~s, ~~, ~walterin** *die;* **~~, ~~nen** **1** (geh.: Fürsprecher) champion; **2** (Rechtsw.: Interessenvertreter der Gläubiger) trustee in bankruptcy; **~wert** *der* **1** intrinsic *or* real value; **2** (Wertobjekt) material asset; **~wissen** *das* specialist knowledge; **~wörterbuch** *das* specialist *or* subject dictionary; **ein ~wörterbuch der Literatur** a dictionary of literature; **~zwang** *der* [factual *or* material] constraint

Sack /zak/ *der;* **~[e]s, Säcke** /ˈzɛkə/ **1** (Behältnis) sack; (aus Papier, Kunststoff) bag; **ein ~ Zement** a bag of cement; **drei Säcke [voll] Kartoffeln** three sacks of potatoes; **einen ~ voll ...** (fig.) a [whole] load *or* mass of ... (coll.); **den ~ schlägt man, den Esel meint man** (Spr.) he/she is being used as a scapegoat; **jmdn. im ~ haben** (salopp) have got round sb.; **etw. im ~ haben** (salopp) have sth. in the bag (coll.); **jmdn. in den ~ stecken** (ugs.) put sb. in the shade; **mit ~ und Pack** with bag and baggage; *s. auch* **nass A 1**; **schlafen A 1** **2** (Hautfalte) **Säcke unter den Augen haben** have bags under one's eyes **3** (derb: Hoden~) balls *pl.* (coarse) **4** (derb abwertend: Mensch) sod (Brit. sl.) **5** (bes. südd., österr., schweiz.) (Hosentasche) [trouser] pocket; (Geldbeutel) purse

Sack·bahn·hof *der* ▸ **Kopfbahnhof**

Säckchen /ˈzɛkçən/ *das;* **~s, ~:** small sack; bag

Säckel /ˈzɛkl̩/ *der;* **~s, ~** (bes. südd., österr.) **1** (veralt.: Geldbeutel) money bag; purse **2** (Hosentasche) [trouser] pocket **3** ▸ **Sack 4**

sạcken *itr. V.; mit sein* ‹*person*› slump; ‹*ship etc.*› sink; ‹*plane*› drop rapidly, plummet; **er sackte in die Knie** his knees gave way

säcke·weise *Adv.* ▸ **sackweise 2**

sạck-, Sạck-: ~gasse *die* cul-de-sac; (fig.) impasse; **~hüpfen** *das;* **~~s** sack race; **beim ~hüpfen** in the sack race; **~kleid** *das* sack; **~leinen** *das,* **~leinwand** *die* sacking; **~pfeife** *die* bagpipes *pl.;* **~tuch** *das; Pl.* **~tücher** (südd., österr., schweiz.) handkerchief; **~weise** *Adv.* **1** (in Säcken) in sacks; **2** (massenhaft) loads *or* masses of (coll.)

Sadismus /zaˈdɪsmʊs/ *der;* **~, Sadịsmen** **1** (Veranlagung; abwertend: Quälerei) sadism *no art.* **2** (Handlung) act of sadism

Sadịst *der;* **~en, ~en, Sadịstin** *die;* **~, ~nen** sadist

sadịstisch
A *Adj.* sadistic
B *adv.* sadistically; **~ veranlagt sein** have sadistic tendencies

Sado·masochismus /zadomazɔˈxɪsmʊs/ *der* (Med.) sadomasochism *no art.*

sado·masochịstisch (Med.)
A *Adj.* sadomasochistic
B *adv.* sadomasochistically; **~ veranlagt sein** have sadomasochistic tendencies

säen /ˈzɛːən/ *tr.* (*auch itr.*) *V.* (auch fig.) sow; **dünn** *od.* **nicht gerade dicht gesät sein** (fig.) be thin on the ground

Safari /zaˈfaːri/ *die;* **~, ~s** safari

Safe /seɪf/ *der od. das;* **~s, ~s** **1** safe **2** (Schließfach) safe-deposit box

Saffian /ˈzafi̯an/ *der;* **~s, Saffian·leder** *das* morocco [leather]

Safran /ˈzafran/ *der;* **~s, ~e** saffron

Saft /zaft/ *der;* **~[e]s, Säfte** /ˈzɛftə/ **1** juice; **jmdn. im eigenen ~ schmoren lassen** (fig. ugs.) let sb. stew in his/her own juice **2** (in Pflanzen) sap; **Blut ist ein ganz besonderer ~:** blood is thicker than water (fig.); **ohne ~ und Kraft** (abwertend) weak and lifeless; (adv.) without any zest **3** (salopp: Elektrizität) juice (sl.) **4** (veralt.: Körperflüssigkeit) fluid **5** (österr.: Soße) gravy

sạft·grün *Adj.* lush green

Sạft·heini *der* (ugs.) right twit (Brit. coll.); jerk (coll.)

saftig
A *Adj.* **1** (voll Saft) juicy; sappy ‹*stem*›; lush ‹*meadow, green*›; (fig.: lebensvoll) lusty **2** (ugs.: stark, intensiv) hefty ‹*slap, blow*›; good ‹*thrashing*›; steep (coll.) ‹*prices, bill*›; terrific, big ‹*surprise, punch-up*›; crude, coarse ‹*joke, song, etc.*›; strong-ly-worded ‹*letter etc.*›; strong, juicy ‹*curse*›
B *adv.* **1** **eine ~ grüne Wiese** a lush green meadow **2** (ugs.: kräftig) ‹*curse, hit out*› well and truly, good and proper

Sạftigkeit *die;* **~, ~en** **1** juiciness; **die ~ der Wiesen** the lushness of the meadows **2** (Äußerung) crude remark

sạft-, Sạft-: ~kur *die* juice diet; **~laden** *der; Pl.* **~läden** (salopp abwertend) lousy outfit (coll.); **~los** *Adj.* **1** juiceless; **~los sein** have *or* contain no juice; **2** (fig.) feeble, anodyne ‹*language*›; **~- und kraftlos** feeble; wishy-washy; (adv.) without any zest; **~presse** *die* juice extractor; **~sack** *der* (derb abwertend) bastard (coll.); **~tag** *der* juice[-diet] day

Saga /ˈza(ː)ga/ *die;* **~, ~s** (Literaturw.) saga

Sage /ˈzaːgə/ *die;* **~, ~n** legend; (bes. nordische) saga; (fig.: Gerücht) rumour

Säge /ˈzɛːgə/ *die;* **~, ~n** **1** saw **2** (bayr., österr.: **~werk**) sawmill

Sä̲ge-: ~blatt *das* saw blade; **~bock** *der* sawhorse; **~fisch** *der* sawfish; **~mehl** *das* sawdust; **~mühle** *die* sawmill

sagen
A *tr. V.* **1** (äußern, behaupten) say; **so etwas sagt man nicht** it's not done to say things like that; **das kann man nicht [so ohne weiteres] ~:** you can't really say *or* tell; **das kann jeder ~:** anybody can claim that; it's easy to talk; **das ist nicht zu viel gesagt** that's not overstating the case *or* no exaggeration; **man sagt [von ihm** *od.* **über ihn], dass ...** it is said [of him] that ...; **das sagst du so einfach!** that's easy to say *or* easily said; **da soll noch einer ~** *od.* **da sage noch einer, dass ...** never let it be said that ...; **na, wer sagts denn!** (ugs.) there you are[, I knew it]!; **sag dạs nicht!** (ugs.) don't [just] assume that!; not necessarily!; **das ist nicht gesagt** it's not necessarily the case; it's by no means certain; **dann will ich nichts gesagt haben** in that case forget I said anything; **was ich noch ~ wollte** [oh] by the way; before I forget; **unter uns gesagt** between you and me; **das oben Gesagte** what has been said above; the above remarks *pl.;* (in einem Vortrag) the foregoing [remarks]; **das musste einmal gesagt werden** it had to be said; **wie gesagt** as I've said *or* mentioned; **das ist leichter gesagt als getan** that's easier said than done; **das kann man wohl ~, das kann man** *od.* **kannst du laut ~** (ugs.) you can say 'that again; **gesagt, getan** no sooner said than done; **das kostet Tausende, [ach,] was sage ich, Millionen!** it costs thousands, what am I talking about, millions!; **~ wir einmal** *od.* (ugs.) **mal** let's say; **wir treffen uns, ~ wir, um 10 vor 8** let's meet at, say, ten to eight; **sage und schreibe** (ugs.) believe it or not; would you believe; **um nicht zu ~:** not to say; **sag bloß, du hast es vergessen!** (ugs.) don't say you've forgotten it! **2** (meinen) say; **was ~ Sie dazu?** what do you think about that?; **was soll man dazu noch ~?** (ugs.) what 'can one say; **was sagst du nun?** (ugs.) now what do you say?; what do you say to that? **3** ▸ ℹ **S. 800** (mitteilen) **jmdm. etw. ~:** say sth. to sb.; (zur Information) tell sb. sth.; **[jmdm.] seinen Namen/seine Gründe ~:** give [sb.] one's name/reasons; **[jmdm.] die Wahrheit ~:** tell [sb.] the truth; **sag mal/~ Sie [mal], gibt es ...?** tell me, is there ...?; **ich habe mir ~ lassen, dass ...** I've been told that ...; **das sag ich dir** (ugs.) I'm telling *or* warning you; **ich habs [dir] ja gleich gesagt!** (ugs.) I told you so!; (habe dich gewarnt) I warned you!; **ich will dir mal was ~:** let me tell you something; **lass dir das gesagt sein** (ugs.) make a note of *or* remember what I'm saying; **das sag ich [deinen Eltern** *usw.***]** (Kinderspr.) I'll tell on you [to your parents *etc.*]; **wem ~ Sie das!** (ugs.) you don't need to tell me [that]!; **das brauchst du mir nicht zu ~** (ugs.) you don't need to tell me that; I know that only too well; **was Sie nicht ~!** (ugs., oft iron.) you don't say!; **das kann ich dir ~!** (ugs.) you can be sure of that *or* bank on that; **wenn ich es [dir] sage!** (ugs.) I promise [you]; **jmdm. Grobheiten ~:** speak rudely to sb.; **und dann muss ich mir von ihm auch noch ~ lassen, dass ...** and then I have to put up with him telling me that ...; **er lässt sich** (*Dat.*) **nichts ~:** he won't be told; you can't tell him anything; **das ist zu viel gesagt** that's going too far; that's an exaggeration **4** (nennen) **zu jmdm./etw. X ~:** call sb./sth. X; **du kannst du zu mir ~:** you can call me 'du' *or* say 'du' to me **5** (formulieren, ausdrücken) say; **das hast du gut gesagt** you put that well; that was well said; **so kann man es auch ~:** you could put it like that; **etw. in aller Deutlichkeit ~:** make sth. perfectly clear; **das sagt er nur so** he doesn't mean it; **es ist nicht zu ~, wie ...** no words can express *or* say *or* there is no expressing how ...; **du sagst es!** very true!; **willst du damit ~, dass ...?** are you trying to say *or* do you mean [to say] that ...?; **das wollte ich damit nicht ~:** I didn't mean that; **will ~:** or rather; that is to say **6** (bedeuten) mean; **damit ist viel/wenig/nichts gesagt** that's saying a lot/not saying much/that doesn't mean anything; **das will** *od.* **hat nichts zu ~:** that doesn't mean anything; that isn't important; **hat das etwas zu ~?** does that mean anything? **7** (anordnen, befehlen) tell; **du hast mir gar nichts zu ~:** you've no right to order me about; **von ihm lasse ich mir nichts ~:** I'm not taking any orders from him; **sich** (*Dat.*) **etw. nicht zweimal ~ lassen** (ugs.) not need to be told *or* asked twice; **das lass/ließ ich mir nicht zweimal ~:** I'd love to/I jumped at it; **etwas/nichts zu ~ haben** ‹*person*› have a/no say; (zuständig/nicht zuständig sein) be in authority/have no authority
B *refl. V.* **1** **sich** (*Dat.*) **etw. ~:** say sth. to oneself; **das hättest du dir damals schon ~ können** you should have realized [that] then **2** **das sagt sich so einfach** (ugs.) that's easy to say *or* easily said
C *itr. V.* **wie sagt man [da]?** what does one say?; what's the [right] word?; (Aufforderung an ein Kind) what do you say [now]?; **wenn ich so ~ darf** if I may put it this way; (bei einem etwas gewagten Ausdruck) if you will pardon the expression; **sag bloß!** (ugs.) you don't say!

sägen /ˈzɛːgn̩/
A *itr. V.* **1** saw; (fig.: auf einer Geige usw.) saw away; **an jmds. Stuhl ~** (fig.) try to undermine sb.'s position **2** (ugs. scherzh.: schnarchen) snore loudly
B *tr. V.* saw; (zersägen) saw up ‹*tree etc.*›

Sa̲gen-: ~buch *das* book of legends; **~gestalt** *die* legendary figure

sagenhaft
A *Adj.* **1** (ugs.) incredible (coll.) ‹*wealth, mess, memory, etc.*›; fabulous (coll.) ‹*party, wealth*› **2** (der Sage angehörend) legendary
B *adv.* incredibly (coll.)

sa̲gen·umwoben *Adj.* (geh.) ‹*castle, place*› steeped in legend; ‹*historical figure*› at the centre of many legends

Sa̲gen·welt *die* legendary world

Sä̲ge-: ~späne *Pl.* wood shavings; **~werk** *das* sawmill; **~zahn** *der* sawtooth

Sago /ˈzaːgo/ *der od. das;* **~s** sago

sah /zaː/ *1. u. 3. Pers. Sg. Prät. v.* **sehen**

Sahelzone /ˈzaːhɛl- *od.* zaˈheːl-/ *die;* **~:** Sahel

Sahne /ˈzaːnə/ *die;* **~:** cream

Sa̲hne-: ~bonbon *der od. das* cream toffee; **~eis** *das* cream ice; **~häubchen** *das;* **~~s, ~~:** layer of cream (*on drink*); (fig.) icing on the cake; **~quark** *der* creamy quark;

quark with a high fat content; **~torte** *die* cream cake *or* gateau

sahnig *Adj.* creamy

Saison /zɛ'zõ:/ *die;* **~, ~s** season; **während/außerhalb der ~:** during the season/out of season *or* in the off-season; **~ haben** have one's busy time *or* season; ‹*hotel*› be open for the season; (ugs.: sehr gefragt sein) ‹*goods*› be much in demand

saisonal /zɛzo'na:l/

A *Adj.* seasonal

B *adv.* ‹*fluctuate*› according to the season

saison-, Saison-: ~arbeit *die* seasonal work; **~arbeiter** *der,* **~arbeiterin** *die* seasonal worker; **~ausverkauf** *der* end-of-season sale; **~bedingt** **A** *Adj.* seasonal; **B** *adv.* due to seasonal influences; **~zuschlag** *der* seasonal supplement

Saite /'zaitə/ *die;* **~, ~n** (Musik, Sport) string; **das/sie brachte in mir eine verwandte ~ zum Klingen** (fig.) it/she struck a responsive chord in me; **andere** *od.* **strengere ~n aufziehen** (fig.) take stronger measures; get tough (coll.)

Saiten-: ~halter *der* (Musik) (an der Geige) tailpiece; (an der Laute, Gitarre) string holder; **~instrument** *das* stringed instrument; **~spiel** *das* (geh.) string playing; (Musik) string music

-saitig /-zaitɪç/ -string[ed]

Sakko /'zako/ *der od. das;* **~s, ~s** jacket

sakral /za'kra:l/ *Adj.* religious; **~e Gewänder** priest's vestments; **~e Gesänge** sacred songs *or* chants

Sakral·bau *der; Pl.* **~ten** (Archit., Kunstwiss.) religious building

Sakrament /zakra'mɛnt/ *das;* **~[e]s, ~e** **1** (christl., bes. kath. Kirche) sacrament **2** **~ [noch mal]!** for Heaven's sake

sakramental /zakramɛn'ta:l/ *Adj.* sacramental

Sakramentalien /zakramɛn'ta:liən/ *Pl.* (kath. Rel.) sacramentals

Sakrileg /zakri'le:k/ *das;* **~s, ~e** act of sacrilege; **ist es ein ~?** is it sacrilege?

Sakristan /zakrɪs'ta:n/ *der;* **~s, ~e, Sakristanin** *die;* **~, ~nen** sacristan

Sakristei /zakrɪs'tai/ *die;* **~, ~en** sacristy

sakrosankt /zakro'zaŋkt/ *Adj.* sacrosanct

säkular /zɛku'la:ɐ/ *Adj.* **1** (geh.: weltlich; auch Astron., Geol.) secular **2** (geh.: herausragend) outstanding

säkularisieren *tr. V.* secularize ‹*property, art, etc.*›; deconsecrate ‹*church*›

Salamander /zala'mandɐ/ *der;* **~s, ~:** salamander; **einen** *od.* **den ~ reiben** (Studentenspr.): *scrape one's glass three times on the table, empty it, and after brief drumming put it down with a bang (as a mark of honour)*

Salami /za'la:mi/ *die;* **~, ~[s]** salami

Salami·taktik *die* step-by-step policy

Salär /za'lɛ:ɐ/ *das;* **~s, ~e** (bes. schweiz., auch südd., österr., sonst veralt.) salary

Salat /za'la:t/ *der;* **~[e]s, ~e** **1** salad **2** **[grüner] ~:** lettuce; **ein Kopf ~:** a [head of] lettuce **3** (ugs.: Wirrwarr) muddle; mess; **jetzt haben wir den ~!** (ugs. iron.) now we're in a right mess!

Salat-: ~bar *die* salad bar; **~besteck** *das* salad servers *pl.;* **~blatt** *das* lettuce leaf; **~büfett** *das* salad buffet; **~gurke** *die* cucumber; **~kartoffel** *die: potato suitable for potato salad;* **~kopf** *der* lettuce; **~öl** *das* salad oil; **~schüssel** *die* salad bowl; **~soße** *die* salad dressing

salbadern /zal'ba:dɐn/ *itr. V.* (ugs. abwertend) waffle [pretentiously]

Salbe /'zalbə/ *die;* **~, ~n** ointment; (gegen Muskelkater usw.) embrocation

Salbei /'zalbai/ *der od. die;* **~:** sage

salben *tr. V.* **1** (einreiben) put ointment on ‹*part of body*› **2** (kath. Kirche) anoint ‹*sick or dying person, (Hist.) king, emperor, etc.*›; (hist.) **jmdn. zum Kaiser ~:** anoint sb. emperor

Salbung *die;* **~, ~en** (Weihung) anointing; (kath. Kirche) unction; **die letzte ~:** extreme unction

salbungs·voll (abwertend)

A *Adj.* unctuous

B *adv.* unctuously

saldieren /zal'di:rən/

A *tr. V.* **1** (Buchf., Finanzw.) balance ‹*credit and debit sides*›; **einen Gewinn ~:** produce a profit balance **2** (österr.: quittieren) confirm payment of; give a receipt for

B *itr. V.* **1** (Buchf., Finanzw.) balance the books **2** (österr.: quittieren) confirm payment

Saldo /'zaldo/ *der;* **~s, ~s** *od.* **Saldi** *od.* **Salden** (Buchf., Finanzw.) balance; **im ~ sein/bleiben** be/remain in debt

Saldo-: ~übertrag *der,* **~vortrag** *der* (Buchf.) balance brought forward

Säle ▸ **Saal**

Salicylsäure (chem. fachspr.) ▸ **Salizylsäure**

Salier /'za:liɐ/ *der;* **~s, ~, Salierin** *die;* **~, ~nen** (hist.) Salian

Saline /za'li:nə/ *die;* **~, ~n** salt works *sing. or pl.*

Salizyl·säure /zali'tsy:l-/ *die* (Chemie) salicylic acid

Salm /zalm/ *der;* **~[e]s, ~e** (bes. rhein.) salmon

Salmiak /zal'miak/ *der od. das;* **~:** sal ammoniac

Salmiak-: ~geist *der* [liquid] ammonia; ammonia water; **~pastille** *die* sal ammoniac pastille

Salmonelle /zalmo'nɛlə/ *die;* **~, ~n** salmonella

Salomon /'za:lomɔn/ *(der)* Solomon

Salomonen /zalo'mo:nən/ *Pl.* Solomon Islands

salomonisch (geh.)

A *Adj.* Solomon-like; **ein ~es Urteil** a judgment of Solomon

B *adv.* with the wisdom of Solomon

Salon /za'lõ:/ *der;* **~s, ~s** **1** (Raum) drawing room; salon **2** (Geschäft) [hair *etc.*] salon **3** (veralt.: Zirkel) [literary] salon **4** (Ausstellung) Salon

salon-, Salon-: ~fähig **A** *Adj.* socially acceptable; (nach einem Bad o. Ä.) **ich bin noch nicht ~fähig** I am not yet presentable; **B** *adv.* in a socially acceptable manner; properly ‹*dressed*›; **~kommunist** *der,* **~kommunistin** *die* (iron.) parlour communist; **~löwe** *der* (abwertend) society man; **~musik** *die* salon music; **~wagen** *der* Pullman car *or* coach

salopp /za'lɔp/

A *Adj.* casual ‹*clothes*›; free and easy, informal ‹*behaviour, household, etc.*›; very colloquial, slangy ‹*saying, expression, etc.*›

B *adv.* ‹*dress*› casually; informally; **~ reden** use slangy *or* [very] colloquial language

Salpeter /zal'pe:tɐ/ *der;* **~s** saltpetre

Salpeter·säure *die* nitric acid

salpetrig *Adj.* **~e Säure** nitrous acid

Salto /'zalto/ *der;* **~s, ~s** *od.* **Salti** **1** somersault; (beim Turnen auch) salto; **ein ~ vorwärts/rückwärts** a forward/backward somersault; **einen ~ springen** do *or* turn a somersault **2** (Fliegerspr.) ▸ **Looping**

Salto mortale /- mɔr'ta:lə/ *der;* **~ ~, ~ ~** *od.* **Salti mortali** salto mortale

Salut /za'lu:t/ *der;* **~[e]s, ~e** (Milit.) salute; **~ schießen** fire a salute; **21 Schuss ~ abgeben** fire a twenty-one-gun salute

salutieren *itr. V.* (bes. Milit.) salute; **vor jmdm. ~:** salute sb.

Salut·schuss, ***Salut·schuß** *der* (Milit.) gun salute; **sieben Salutschüsse** a seven-gun salute

Salvadorianer /zalvado'ria:nɐ/ *der;* **~s, ~, Salvadorianerin** *die;* **~, ~nen** Salvadoran

Salve /'zalvə/ *die;* **~, ~n** (Milit.) salvo; (aus Gewehren) volley; **eine ~ des Beifalls/von Gelächter** (fig.) a burst of applause/laughter

Salz /zalts/ *das;* **~es, ~e** salt; **das ~ der Ironie** (fig.) the spice of irony; **~ auf die** *od.* **in die Wunde streuen** (fig.) rub salt into the wound; **jmdm. nicht das ~ in der Suppe gönnen** (ugs.) begrudge sb. everything

salz-, Salz-: ~arm **A** *Adj.* low in salt *postpos.;* low-salt; **B** *adv.* **~arm kochen** use little salt in cooking; **~arm essen** eat food containing little salt; **~berg·werk** *das* salt mine; **~brezel** *die* [salted] pretzel

> **Salzburger Festspiele**
>
> Salzburg, the home of Wolfgang Amadeus Mozart (1756-91), hosts this annual festival as a tribute to the great composer. Every summer since 1920, Mozart-lovers have been enjoying his music at the *Salzburger Festspiele*.

salzen *tr. V.* salt; **die Suppe ist stark/zu wenig/kaum gesalzen** the soup has a lot of/too little/hardly any salt in it

salz-, Salz-: ~fässchen, ***~fäßchen** *das* **1** salt cellar; **2** (ugs. scherzh.: beim Menschen) hollow between the collarbones; **~fleisch** *das* ▸ **Pökelfleisch**; **~haltig** *Adj.* containing salt *postpos., not pred.;* salty; **sehr ~haltig sein** have a high salt content; **~hering** *der* salted herring

salzig *Adj.* salty

salz-, Salz-: ~kartoffel *die* boiled potato; **~korn** *das* grain of salt; **~lake** *die* brine; **~lecke** *die* (Jägerspr.) salt lick; **~los** **A** *Adj.* salt-free; (nicht gesalzen) unsalted; **B** *adv.* ‹*cook*› without any salt; **~los essen** eat unsalted food; **~lösung** *die* saline solution; **~mandel** *die* salted almond; **~napf** *der* salt cellar; **~säule** *die* pillar of salt; **zur ~säule erstarren** (fig.) be rooted to the spot *or* turned to stone; **~säure** *die* (Chemie) hydrochloric acid; **~see** *der* salt lake; (ausgetrocknet) salt flats *pl.;* **~sole** *die* brine; **~stange** *die* salt stick; **~streuer** *der;* **~~s, ~~:** salt sprinkler; salt shaker (Amer.); **~wasser** *das; Pl.* **~wässer** **1** (zum Kochen) salted water; **2** (Meerwasser) salt water; **3** (Lake) brine; **~werk** *das* salt works *sing. or pl.;* **~wüste** *die* salt desert

Sä·mann *der* (dichter.) sower

SA-Mann /ɛs'|a:-/ *der; Pl.* **SA-Männer** *od.* **SA-Leute** (ns.) SA man; stormtrooper

Samariter /zama'ri:tɐ/ *der;* **~s, ~** **1** **[barmherziger] ~:** good Samaritan; **bei jmdm. ~ spielen** play *or* act the good Samaritan to sb. **2** (schweiz.) ▸ **Sanitäter**

Samariter·dienst *der* selfless act [of kindness]

Samariterin *die;* **~, ~nen** **1** ▸ **Samariter 1** **2** (schweiz.) ▸ **Sanitäterin**

Sä·maschine *die* seeder, (esp.) seed drill

Samba /'zamba/ *der;* **~s, ~s** *od. die;* **~, ~s** samba

Sambesi /zam'be:zi/ *der;* **~[s]** ▸ **ⓘ S. 267** Zambezi

Sambia /'zambia/ *(das);* **~s** Zambia

Sambier /'zambiɐ/ *der;* **~s, ~, Sambierin** *die;* **~, ~nen** Zambian

Same[1] /'za:mə/ *der;* **~n, ~n** ▸ **Lappe**

Same[2] *der;* **~ns, ~n** (geh.) seed

Samen /'za:mən/ *der;* **~s, ~** **1** (**~korn**) seed **2** (**~körner**) seed[s. *pl.*] **3** (Sperma) sperm; semen

Samen-: ~anlage *die* (Bot.) ovule; **~bank** *die; Pl.* **~en** (Med., Tiermed.) sperm bank; **~erguss,** ***~erguß** *der* ejaculation; **~faden** *der* ▸ **Spermium**; **~flüssigkeit** *die* seminal fluid; **~handlung** *die* seed merchant's [shop *or* (Amer.) store]; **~kapsel** *die* seed capsule; **~korn** *das* seed; **~leiter** *der* ▸ **ⓘ S. 435** (Anat.) sperm[atic] duct; **~spender** *der* (Med.) sperm donor; **~strang** *der* ▸ **ⓘ S. 435** (Anat.) spermatic cord; **~zelle** *die* sperm cell

Sämereien /zɛːmə'raiən/ *Pl.* seeds

sämig /'zɛ:mɪç/ *Adj.* thick ‹*sauce, soup, etc.*›; viscous ‹*liquid*›

Samin *die;* **~, ~nen** ▸ **Same**[1]

Sämisch·leder *das* chamois leather

Sämling /'zɛ:mlɪŋ/ *der;* **~s, ~e** seedling

Sammel-: ~album *das* [collector's] album; **~auftrag** *der* (Postw.) multiple *or* combined transfer; **~band** *der* anthology (**über** + *Akk.*

S

of); **~becken** *das* collecting basin; reservoir; (fig.) gathering point *or* place; **~bestellung** *die* joint order; **~bezeichnung** *die* (Sprachw.) collective term; **~büchse** *die* collecting box; **~fahrschein** *der* group ticket; **~klage** *die* (Rechtsw.) class action (Amer.); **~konto** *das* (Buchf.) collation account; **~lager** *das* assembly *or* transit camp; **~mappe** *die* folder; file

sammeln /'zamln/
A *tr.* (*auch itr.*) *V.* ① collect; gather ‹*honey, firewood, fig.: material, experiences, impressions, etc.*›; gather, pick ‹*berries, herbs, mushrooms, etc.*›; **Kräfte ~:** summon up one's strength; **die gesammelten Werke Tolstois** Tolstoy's collected works ② (zusammenkommen lassen) gather ‹*people*› [together]; assemble ‹*people*›; cause ‹*light rays*› to converge
B *refl. V.* ① (sich versammeln) gather [together]; ‹*light rays*› converge; **sich um jmdn./etw. ~:** gather round sb./sth. ② (sich konzentrieren) collect oneself; gather oneself together

Sammel-: ~platz *der* (für Gegenstände) collection *or* collecting point; (für Menschen) assembly point; **~punkt** *der* ① (~platz) assembly point; ② (Brennpunkt) focal point; **~stelle** *die* ▸ **~platz**

Sammelsurium /zaml'zu:ri̯ʊm/ *das;* **~s, Sammelsurien** (abwertend) hotchpotch; **ein ~ von alten Gläsern und Flaschen** a jumble of old glasses and bottles

Sammel-: ~tasse *die* [collector's] ornamental cup and saucer; **~transport** *der* (von Menschen, Vieh) mass transport; (von Gütern) bulk shipment; **~visum** *das* collective *or* group visa; **~wut** *die* collecting mania

Sammet /'zamət/ *der;* **~s, ~e** (schweiz., sonst veralt.) ▸ **Samt**

Sammler /'zamlɐ/ *der;* **~s, ~** ① collector; (von Pilzen, Kräutern, Beeren usw.) gatherer; picker ② (Technik: Akkumulator) accumulator; storage battery

Sammler·fleiß *der* keenness *or* dedication to collecting; **mit ~:** with the dedication of a true collector

Sammlerin *die;* **~, ~nen** ▸ **Sammler 1**

Sammler-: ~objekt *das,* **~stück** *das* collector's item; **~wert** *der* value to collectors; **~wert haben** be of value to collectors

Sammlung *die;* **~, ~en** ① collection ② **[innere] ~:** composure

Sammlungs·bewegung *die* movement combining disparate elements; all-embracing movement

Samoa·inseln /za'mo:a-/ *Pl.* **die ~** (als Ganzes) Samoa *sing.;* (als einzelne Inseln) the Samoan Islands

Samoaner /zamo'a:nɐ/ *der;* **~s, ~, Samoanerin** *die;* **~, ~nen** Samoan

samoanisch *Adj.* Samoan

Samowar /zamo'va:ɐ̯/ *der;* **~s, ~e** samovar

sampeln *tr. V.* sample

Sampler *der;* **~s, ~s** sampler

Samstag /'zamsta:k/ *der;* **~[e]s, ~e** ▸ ❶ **S. 165,** ▸ ❶ **S. 816** Saturday; **langer ~:** Saturday on which the shops stay open late; *s. auch* **Dienstag; Dienstag-**

samstägig /'zamstɛ:gɪç/ *Adj.* on Saturday *postpos.*

samstäglich
A *Adj.* [regular] Saturday
B *adv.* on Saturdays

samstags *Adv.* ▸ ❶ **S. 816** on Saturdays

samt /zamt/
A *Präp. mit Dat.* together with
B *Adv.* **~ und sonders** one and all; without exception

Samt *der;* **~[e]s, ~e** velvet; **eine Haut wie ~:** a velvety skin; **in ~ und Seide** (veralt.) in all one's finery

samt·artig
A *Adj.* velvety
B *adv.* ‹*soft etc.*› as velvet

Samt·band *das; Pl.* **~bänder** velvet ribbon; (breit) velvet band

samten *Adj.* ① (aus Samt) velvet ② (wie Samt) velvety

Samt·handschuh *der* velvet glove; **jmdn. mit ~en anfassen** (fig.) handle sb. with kid gloves

samtig *Adj.* velvety

Samt·kleid *das* velvet dress

sämtlich /'zɛmtlɪç/ *Indefinitpron. u. unbest. Zahlwort* ① *attr.* all the; **die Kleidung ~er Gefangener** *od.* **Gefangenen** all the prisoners' clothes; **Goethes ~e Werke** the complete works of Goethe ② *allein stehend* all

Samt·pfötchen *das* velvety paw; **wie auf ~ gehen** tread softly

samt·weich *Adj.* velvety[-soft]; soft as velvet *postpos.*

Sanatorium /zana'to:ri̯ʊm/ *das;* **~s, Sanatorien** sanatorium

Sand /zant/ *der;* **~[e]s, ~e** *od.* **Sände** /'zɛndə/ ① sand; **... gibt es wie ~ am Meer** (ugs.) there are countless ...; ... are pretty thick on the ground (coll.); **da ist ~ im Getriebe** (fig. ugs.) there's something gumming up the works (coll.); **jmdm. ~ ins Getriebe streuen** (fig. ugs.) put a spanner in sb.'s works; **jmdm. ~ in die Augen streuen** (fig.) pull the wool over sb.'s eyes; **da habe ich auf ~ gebaut** (fig.) I was on shaky ground; **im ~[e] verlaufen** (fig. ugs.) come to nothing; **etw. [total] in den ~ setzen** (fig. ugs.) make a [complete] mess of sth. ② *Pl.* **~e** (bes. Geol.: ~art) [type of] sand ③ (Seemannsspr.) sands *pl.;* sandbank; **auf [einen] ~ geraten** *od.* **laufen** run aground on a sandbank

Sandale /zan'da:lə/ *die;* **~, ~n** sandal

Sandalette /zanda'lɛtə/ *die;* **~, ~n** [high-heeled] sandal

Sand-: ~bahn·rennen *das* (Motorradsport) speedway racing; **~bank** *die; Pl.* **~bänke** sandbank; **~boden** *der* sandy soil; **~burg** *die* sandcastle; **~dorn** *der; Pl.* **~~e** (Bot.) hippophaë; **[Echter] ~dorn** sea buckthorn

Sandel- /'zandl-/: **~holz** *das* sandalwood; **~öl** *das* sandalwood oil

sand-, Sand-: ~farben, ~farbig *Adj.* sand-coloured; **~förmchen** /-fœrmçən/ *das;* **~~s, ~~:** sand mould; **~haufen** *der* pile of sand; **~hose** *die* sand spout

sandig *Adj.* sandy

Sandinist /zandi'nɪst/ *der;* **~en, ~en, Sandinistin** *die;* **~, ~nen** Sandinista

sand-, Sand-: ~kasten *der* ① [child's] sandpit; sandbox (Amer.); ② (Milit.) sand table; **~kasten·spiel** *das* (Milit.) sand table exercise; **~korn** *das* grain of sand; **~kuchen** *der* Madeira cake; **~mann** *der,* **~männchen** *das* sandman; **~papier** *das* sandpaper; **~sack** *der* ① sandbag; ② (Boxen) punch bag; **~stein** *der* ① sandstone; ② (als Baustein) sandstone block; **~strahlen** *tr. V.* (Technik) sandblast; **~strahl·gebläse** *das* (Technik) sandblaster; **~strand** *der* sandy beach; **~sturm** *der* sandstorm

sandte /'zantə/ *1. u. 3. Pers. Sg. Prät. v.* **senden**

Sand·uhr *die* sandglass

Sandwich /'zɛntvɪtʃ/ *der od. das;* **~s, ~[e]s** sandwich

Sandwich·bauweise *die* sandwich construction

Sand·wüste *die* [sandy] desert

sanforisieren (Wz) /zanfori'zi:rən/ *tr. V.* Sanforize ®

sanft /zanft/
A *Adj.* gentle; (leise, nicht intensiv) soft ‹*music, colour, light*›; (friedlich) peaceful; **kommen Sie mir bloß nicht auf die ~e [Tour]** (ugs.) it's no use trying to soft-soap me; **es auf die ~e Tour versuchen** (ugs.) try the gentle *or* diplomatic approach; (bei Bitten) try wheedling *or* cajolery
B *adv.* gently; (leise) ‹*speak, play*› softly; (friedlich) peacefully; **ruhe ~** (auf Grabsteinen) rest in peace; **es regnete ~:** a gentle rain was falling

Sänfte /'zɛnftə/ *die;* **~, ~n** litter; (geschlossen) sedan chair

Sanftheit *die;* **~:** gentleness; (von Klängen, Licht, Farben) softness

Sanft·mut *die;* **~:** gentleness; **mit ~:** gently; (nachsichtig) leniently

sanftmütig /-my:tɪç/
A *Adj.* gentle; docile ‹*horse*›
B *adv.* gently

Sanftmütigkeit *die;* **~:** gentleness; (Fügsamkeit) docility

sang /zaŋ/ *1. u. 3. Pers. Sg. Prät. v.* **singen**

Sang *der;* **~[e]s** (veralt.) song; singing; **mit ~ und Klang** singing and playing [music]; **er ist mit ~ und Klang durchs Examen gefallen** (ugs. iron.) he failed the exam in style (iron.)

Sänger /'zɛŋɐ/ *der;* **~s, ~** ▸ ❶ **S. 113** ① (Singender) singer; (Vogel) songbird; **darüber schweigt des ~s Höflichkeit** let's draw a veil over that ② (veralt.: Dichter) bard; **ein fahrender** *od.* **wandernder ~** (hist.) a wandering minstrel

Sänger-: ~bund *der* choral union; **~fest** *das* choral *or* choir festival

Sängerin *die;* **~, ~nen** ▸ ❶ **S. 113** singer; *s. auch* **-in**

Sänger·knabe *der* ▸ **Wiener[2]**

Sanges·bruder *der* (geh., veralt.) fellow choir-member

sang·los *Adv. in* **sang- und klanglos** (ugs.) (ohne viel Aufhebens) simply; without any ado *or* fuss; (unbemerkt) unnoticed

Sanguiniker /zaŋ'gui:nikɐ/ *der;* **~s, ~, Sanguinikerin** *die;* **~, ~nen** sanguine person

sanguinisch
A *Adj.* sanguine
B *adv.* sanguinely; **~ veranlagt sein** have a sanguine disposition

sanieren /za'ni:rən/
A *tr. V.* ① (umgestalten) redevelop ‹*area*›; rehabilitate ‹*building*›; (renovieren) renovate [and improve] ‹*flat etc.*› ② (Wirtsch.) restore ‹*firm*› to profitability; (rehabilitieren) put ‹*firm*› back on its feet; rehabilitate ‹*agriculture, coal mining, etc.*› ③ (Med.: heilen) heal ‹*wound, ulcer, etc.*›; clear up the infection in, treat ‹*tooth etc.*›
B *refl. V.* ‹*company etc.*› restore itself to profitability, get back on its feet again; ‹*person*› get oneself out of the red

Sanierung *die;* **~, ~en** ① ▸ **sanieren 1:** redevelopment; rehabilitation; renovation ② (Wirtsch.) restoration to profitability ③ (Med.: Heilung) healing; (Behandlung) treatment

Sanierungs-: ~gebiet *das* redevelopment area; **~maßnahme** *die* ① (bei einem Stadtteil usw.) redevelopment measure; ② (Wirtsch.) [financial] rehabilitation measure

sanitär /zani'tɛ:ɐ̯/ *Adj.* sanitary; **~e Anlagen** sanitary installations

Sanitär-: ~bereich *der* [field of] sanitation; **~installation** *die* ① (das Einbauen) fitting of sanitation *no indef. art.;* ② (Anlage) sanitary installation

Sanität /zani'tɛ:t/ *die;* **~, ~en** (schweiz., österr.) ① (Milit.) medical service ② (ugs.: Sanitätswagen) ambulance

Sanitäter /zani'tɛ:tɐ/ *der;* **~s, ~** ① (Krankenpfleger) first-aid worker; first-aid man; (im Krankenwagen) ambulance man ② (Soldat) medical orderly

Sanitäterin *die;* **~, ~nen** ① (Krankenpflegerin) first-aid worker; (im Krankenwagen) ambulance worker ② (Soldatin) medical orderly

Sanitäts-: ~auto *das* (ugs.) ambulance; **~dienst** *der* ① first-aid duty; (im Krankenwagen) ambulance duty; ② (Milit.) medical service *or* corps; **~kasten** *der* (bes. Milit.) first-aid box *or* kit; **~offizier** *der* (Milit.) medical officer; **~truppe** *die* (Milit.) medical corps; **~wache** *die* first-aid post; **~wagen** *der* ambulance; **~wesen** *das* (bes. Milit.) medical service

sank /zaŋk/ *1. u. 3. Pers. Sg. Prät. v.* **sinken**

Sanktion /zaŋk'tsi̯o:n/ *die;* **~, ~en** ① (geh., Rechtsspr.: Billigung) approval; sanction ② (Völkerr., Soziol.) sanction; (geh.: Bestrafung) punitive measure *or* sanction ③ (Rechtsw.) (Gesetzesklausel) penalty [clause]; sanction

S

sanktionieren *tr. V.* sanction

Sanktionierung *die;* ~, **~en** sanctioning *no indef. art.*

Sankt-Lorenz-Strom /zaŋkt'lo:rɛntsʃtro:m/ *der;* **~[e]s** St Lawrence [river]

Sankt-Nimmerleins-Tag /zaŋkt 'nɪmɐlains-/ *der* ▸ **Nimmerleinstag**

sann /zan/ *1. u. 3. Pers. Sg. Prät. v.* **sinnen**

Sansibar /'zanziba:ɐ̯/ *(das);* **~s** Zanzibar

Sanskrit /'zanskrɪt/ *das;* **~s** ▸❶ **S. 670** Sanskrit

Saphir /'za:fɪr/ *der;* **~s, ~e** sapphire

sapperlot /zapɐ'lo:t/ *Interj.* (veralt.) upon my soul (dated)

sapphisch /'zapfɪʃ/
A *Adj.* 1 Sapphic; **~e Strophe** sapphic verse *or* stanza 2 (geh.: lesbisch) sapphic; lesbian
B *adv.* 1 (wie Sappho) in the style of Sappho 2 (geh.) **~ veranlagt** with sapphic *or* lesbian tendencies

Sarabande /zara'bandə/ *die;* ~, **~n** (Musik) saraband

Sarde /'zardə/ *der;* **~n, ~n** Sardinian

Sardelle /zar'dɛlə/ *die;* ~, **~n** anchovy

Sardellen·paste *die* anchovy paste

Sardin *die;* ~, **~nen** Sardinian

Sardine /zar'di:nə/ *die;* ~, **~n** sardine

Sardinen·büchse *die* tin of sardines; (leer) sardine tin; **das Schiff war eine schwimmende ~** (fig.) they were packed like sardines on the ship

Sardinien /zar'di:ni̯ən/ *(das);* **~s** Sardinia

sardisch *Adj.* ▸❶ **S. 670** Sardinian

sardonisch /zar'do:nɪʃ/ (geh.)
A *Adj.* sardonic
B *adv.* sardonically

Sarg /zark/ *der;* **~[e]s, Särge** /'zɛrgə/ coffin; *s. auch* **Nagel 2**

Sarg-: **~deckel** *der* coffin lid; **~nagel** *der* (Nagel, ugs. scherzh.: Zigarette) coffin nail (lit., or fig. sl.); **~träger** *der,* **~trägerin** *die* pallbearer

Sari /'za:ri/ *der;* **~[s], ~s** sari

Sarkasmus /zar'kasmʊs/ 1 (Spott) sarcasm 2 (Äußerung) sarcastic remark

sarkastisch
A *Adj.* sarcastic
B *adv.* sarcastically

Sarkophag /zarko'fa:k/ *der;* **~s, ~e** sarcophagus

SARS, Sars /zars/ *das;* **~:** SARS

saß /za:s/ *1. u. 3. Pers. Sg. Prät. v.* **sitzen**

> **SAT 1**
>
> Germany's second largest privately-owned television channel broadcasts films, news, sport, and entertainment. It was the first commercial channel in the country.

> **3sat**
>
> This satellite TV channel is run jointly by **ARD**, **ZDF**, and Swiss and Austrian TV. It offers programmes that are not broadcast by other TV stations, and almost half of *3sat*'s output is devoted to cultural reports.

Satan /'za:tan/ *der;* **~s, ~e** 1 (bibl.) Satan *no def. art.; s. auch* **Teufel** 2 (ugs. abwertend: Mensch) fiend

satanisch
A *Adj.* satanic; fiendish
B *adv.* satanically

Satanismus *der;* **~:** Satanism

Satanist *der;* **~en, ~en**, **Satanistin** *die;* ~, **~nen** satanist

satanistisch
A *Adj.* satanist
B *adv.* **~ orientiert** *od.* **ausgerichtet** with satanist orientation

Satans·braten *der* (ugs.) devil

Satellit /zatɛ'li:t/ *der;* **~en, ~en** (Raumf., Astron., auch fig.) satellite

Satelliten-: **~anlage** *die* (ugs.) satellite receiver; **~antenne** *die* satellite aerial; satellite antenna (Amer.); **~aufnahme** *die* satellite photograph; **~bild** *das* ▸**~foto**; **~empfänger** *der* satellite receiver; **~fernsehen** *das* satellite television; **~film** *der* (bes. Met.) satellite film; **~foto** *das* (bes. Met.) satellite picture; **~navigation** *die* satellite navigation; **~receiver** *der* satellite receiver; **~schüssel** *die* (ugs.) satellite dish; **~staat** *der* (abwertend) satellite [state]; **~technik** *die* satellite technology; **~telefon** *das* satellite telephone; **~übertragung** *die* (Ferns.) satellite transmission

Satin /za'tɛ̃:/ *der;* **~s, ~s** satin

Satire /za'ti:rə/ *die;* ~, **~n** satire

Satiriker *der;* **~s,** ~, **Satirikerin** *die;* ~, **~nen** 1 satirist 2 (Spötter) lampooner; mocker

satirisch
A *Adj.* 1 satirical 2 (spöttisch) mocking ‹*remarks*›
B *adv.* 1 satirically; with a satirical touch 2 (spöttisch) mockingly; in a satirical vein

Satisfaktion /zatɪsfak'tsi̯o:n/ *die;* ~, **~en** (geh. od. Studentenspr. veralt.) satisfaction

satisfaktions·fähig *Adj.* (veralt.) able to give/demand satisfaction [in a duel] *pred.*

satt /zat/
A *Adj.* 1 full [up] *pred.;* well-fed; **~ sein** be full [up]; have had enough [to eat]; **~ werden** have enough [to eat]; eat one's fill; **von so einem Salat werde ich nicht ~:** a salad like that is not enough for me *or* to fill me up; **sich ~ essen/trinken** eat/drink as much as one wants; eat/drink one's fill; **etw. macht ~:** sth. is filling; **ich kann mich an ihr/an der Akropolis nicht ~ sehen** (fig.) I can't take my eyes off her/I can gaze endlessly at the Acropolis 2 (selbstgefällig) smug, self-satisfied ‹*person, smile, expression, etc.*› 3 **jmdn./etw. ~ haben** (ugs.) be fed up with sb./sth. (coll.); **ich habe es ~, allein zu fahren** I'm fed up with travelling alone (coll.); **etw. ~ bekommen** *od.* **kriegen** (ugs.) get fed up with sth. 4 (intensiv) rich, deep ‹*colour*›; rich, pure ‹*sound*› 5 (ugs.: beeindruckend) tremendous (coll.) ‹*price*›; **ein ~er Schuss** a super shot (coll.); **~e 100000 Euro** a cool 100,000 euros (coll.); **~e 180 km/h** an impressive 180 k.p.h
B *adv.* 1 (selbstgefällig) smugly; complacently 2 (reichlich) **nicht ~ zu essen haben** not have enough to eat; **Hummer ~:** as much lobster as one can eat; **Tennis ~** (fig.) as much tennis as one could possibly want 3 (schweiz.: straff) tightly

satt·blau *Adj.* deep blue

Sattel /'zatl̩/ *der;* **~s, Sättel** /'zɛtl̩/ 1 saddle; **ohne ~ reiten** ride bareback; **jmdm. in den ~ helfen, jmdn. in den ~ heben** help sb. into the saddle; (fig.: fördern) give sb. a leg up; (fig.: an die Macht bringen) put sb. in the driving seat; **jmdn. aus dem ~ heben** unseat sb.; (fig.: jmdm. die Macht nehmen) depose sb.; remove sb. from office; **fest im ~ sitzen** (fig.) be firmly in the saddle; **in allen Sätteln gerecht sein** (fig.) be able to turn one's hand to anything 2 (Berg~) saddle; col 3 (Schneidern: Passe) yoke 4 (bei Saiteninstrumenten) nut 5 (Turnen: beim Seitpferd) saddle

sattel-, Sattel-: **~dach** *das* gable *or* saddle roof; **~decke** *die* saddlecloth; **~fest** *Adj.* experienced; **in etw.** *(Dat.)* **~fest sein** be au fait with sth.; be well up in sth.; **weniger ~feste Kandidaten** candidates less sure of their facts; **~gurt** *der* girth

satteln
A *tr. V.* saddle
B *itr. V.* saddle the/one's horse

Sattel-: **~nase** *die* saddle nose; **~punkt** *der* (Math.) saddle point; **~schlepper** *der* tractor [unit]; (mit Anhänger) articulated lorry (Brit.); semi[-trailer] (Amer.); **~stütze** *die* seatpost; seat pillar; **~tasche** *die* (am Pferd, Fahrrad) saddlebag; **~zeug** *das* saddle equipment; saddlery; **~zug** *der* articulated vehicle

Sattheit *die;* ~ 1 repleteness *no def. art.;* **die ~ der Konsumgesellschaft** the satiety of the consumer society 2 (Selbstgefälligkeit) smugness; complacency 3 (Intensität) richness; fullness

sättigen /'zɛtɪgn̩/
A *itr. V.* be filling
B *tr. V.* 1 (ausfüllen) saturate ‹*market, colour*› 2 (erfüllen) **gesättigt sein von etw.** be filled with *or* full of sth. 3 (geh.: satt machen) fill ‹*sb.*›; satisfy ‹*sb., fig.: curiosity, ambition, etc.*›
C *refl. V.* **sich mit** *od.* **an etw.** *(Dat.)* **~** (geh.) satisfy one's appetite with sth.

sättigend *Adj.* filling

Sättigung *die;* ~, **~en** 1 (bes. Chemie, Physik) saturation 2 (das Sattsein) repleteness *no def. art.;* (das Sättigen) satisfying; **die ~ der Hungernden** the feeding of the starving

Sättigungs-: **~beilage** *die* (Gastr. regional) filling side dish; **~grad** *der* (Wirtsch.) [degree of] saturation; **~punkt** *der* (Chemie) saturation point

Sattler /'zatlɐ/ *der;* **~s,** ~ ▸❶ **S. 113** saddler; (allgemein: Hersteller von Lederwaren) leather worker

Sattlerei *die;* ~, **~en** 1 (Handwerk) saddlery 2 (Werkstatt) saddler's workshop

Sattlerin *die;* ~, **~nen** ▸❶ **S. 113** ▸**Sattler**

sattsam *Adv.* ad nauseam; **~ bekannt** only too well known; notorious

saturiert /zatu'ri:ɐ̯t/ *Adj.* (geh.) 1 (zufrieden gestellt) satisfied 2 (abwertend: selbstgefällig) **~e Wohlstandsbürger** sated and self-satisfied members of the affluent society

Saturn[1] /za'tʊrn/ *der;* **~s** (Astron.), **Saturn**[2] *(der)* (Myth.) Saturn *no def. art.*

Satyr /'za:tʏr/ *der;* **~s** *od.* **~n, ~n** satyr

Satyr·spiel *das* satyric drama

Satz /zats/ *der;* **~es, Sätze** /'zɛtsə/ 1 (sprachliche Einheit) sentence; (Teil~) clause; **in** *od.* **mit einem ~:** in one sentence; briefly 2 (Teil eines Musikwerks) movement; (Periode) period 3 (Musik: Kompositionsweise) [method of] composition; **der vierstimmige/kontrapunktische ~:** four-part/contrapuntal writing 4 (Sport) (Tennis, Volleyball) set; (Tischtennis, Badminton) game 5 (Sprung) leap; jump; **einen ~ über etw.** *(Akk.)* **machen** *od.* **tun** jump *or* leap across sth.; **er war mit einem ~ an der Tür** in one bound he was at the door; **in** *od.* **mit wenigen Sätzen** in a few strides 6 (Amtsspr.: Tarif) rate 7 (Set) set; **ein ~ Reifen** a set of tyres 8 (Boden~) sediment; (von Kaffee) grounds *pl.* 9 (Druckw.: das Setzen) setting; (Gesetztes) type matter; **mit dem ~ beginnen** start setting; **das Manuskript ist in ~/geht in [den] ~:** the manuscript is being set/is being sent for setting 10 (DV) record

Satz-: **~anweisung** *die* (Druckw.) setting instructions *pl.;* **~aussage** *die* (Sprachw.) predicate; **~ball** *der* (Tennis, Volleyball) set point; (Tischtennis, Badminton) game point; **~bau** *der* sentence construction; **~bauplan** *der* (Sprachw.) sentence pattern

Sätzchen /'zɛtsçən/ *das;* **~s,** ~ 1 (Sprung) little jump 2 (Äußerung) little sentence

satz-, Satz-: **~ergänzung** *die* (Sprachw.) complement; **~fehler** *der* (Druckw.) literal; printer's error; **~fertig** *Adj.* (Druckw.) ready for setting *postpos.;* **~gefüge** *das* (Sprachw.) complex sentence; **~gegenstand** *der* (Sprachw.) subject [of a/the sentence]; **~glied** *das* (Sprachw.) component part [of a/the sentence]; **~konstruktion** *die* (Sprachw.) sentence construction; **~lehre** *die* 1 (Sprachw.) syntax *no art.;* 2 (Musik) composition theory *no art.;* **~rechner** *der* (Druckw.) composer; **~reif** *Adj.* (Druckw.) ready for setting *postpos.;* **~spiegel** *der* (Druckw.) type area; **~technisch** (Druckw.) A *Adj.* **aus ~technischen Gründen** for reasons of setting; B *adv.* **~technisch gesehen** from the typographic point of view; **~teil** *der* (Sprachw.) ▸**~glied**

Satzung /'zatsʊŋ/ *die;* ~, **~en** articles of association *pl.;* statutes *pl.*

satzungs-: **~gemäß** *Adj., adv.* in accordance with the articles of association *or* the statutes; **~widrig** *Adj., adv.* contrary to the articles of association *or* the statutes

satz-, Satz-: **~weise** *Adv.* sentence by sentence; **~wertig** *Adj.* (Sprachw.) forming a clause *postpos.*; **~wertiger Infinitiv/~wertiges Partizip** infinitive/participial clause; **~zeichen** *das* (Sprachw.) punctuation mark; **~zusammenhang** *der* (Sprachw.) sentence correlation *or* interrelation

sau-, Sau- (salopp) bloody ... (Brit. sl.); damn ... (coll.); (sehr schlecht) lousy ... (coll.); **~dreckig/~schwer** bloody (Brit. sl.) *or* (coll.) damn filthy/difficult

-sau *die* (derb) ... pig *or* swine; pig *or* swine of a/an ...

Sau /zau/ *die;* ~, **Säue** /ˈzɔyə/ 1 (weibliches Schwein) sow 2 (bes. südd.: Schwein) pig; **jmdn. zur ~ machen** (derb) tear a strip off sb. (sl.); **wie eine gesengte ~ fahren** (derb) drive like a madman; **unter aller ~** (derb abwertend) bloody awful (Brit. sl.); the pits (coll.); **keine ~** (derb) not a bloody (Brit. sl.) *or* (coll.) damn soul 3 (derb abwertend: schmutziger Mensch) (Mann) dirty pig; (Frau) dirty cow (sl.) 4 (derb abwertend: gemeiner Mensch) swine 5 **die ~ rauslassen** (fig. ugs.) let one's hair down

Sau-: **~arbeit** *die* (salopp) bloody awful job (Brit. sl.); hell of a job (coll.); **~bande** *die* (salopp) wretched swine (derog.) *pl.*; (mehr scherzh.) bunch of good-for-nothings (sl.)

sauber /ˈzaubɐ/

A *Adj.* 1 clean; **~e Flüsse/Wälder** unpolluted rivers/forests; **etw. ~ machen** clean sth.; **~ machen** (putzen) clean; do the cleaning; **bei jmdm. ~ machen** clean for sb.; **etw. ~ halten** keep sth. clean; **das Kind ist ~:** the child is toilet-trained; **ein Glas ~ ausspülen** rinse [out] a glass; **der ~e Bildschirm** (fig.) the unpolluted TV screen; **mein Tor bleibt ~** (fig. Fußball) I'll keep a clean sheet 2 (sorgfältig) neat ‹*handwriting, division, work, etc.*› 3 (fehlerlos) perfect, faultless ‹*accent, technique, etc.*› 4 (anständig) upstanding ‹*attitude, person*›; upright ‹*young man*›; unsullied ‹*character*›; **er ist ~** (ugs.) he is straight; (hat nichts Kriminelles gemacht) he has a clean record; **~ bleiben** keep one's hands clean (coll.); **nicht [ganz] ~ sein** (ugs.) be a bit shady *or* dodgy (coll.); **also dann alles Gute, und bleib ~!** (ugs. scherzh.) all the best, and be good! 5 (gerecht) fair ‹*solution, description*›; equitable ‹*solution, plan*› 6 (iron.: unanständig) nice, fine (iron.); *s. auch* **Früchtchen** 7 (ugs., bes. südd., österr., schweiz.: beachtlich) fantastic (coll.); **ein ~es Sümmchen** a tidy little sum (coll.) 8 (südd., österr., schweiz.: schmuck) smart ‹*girl etc.*›

B *adv.* 1 (sorgfältig) neatly ‹*written, dressed, mended, etc.*› 2 (fehlerlos) **[sehr] ~:** [quite] perfectly *or* faultlessly 3 (anständig) conscientiously 4 (gerecht) ‹*judge etc.*› fairly 5 (iron.: unanständig) nicely (iron.); **das hast du ~ hingekriegt** a nice *or* fine job you made of that

***sauber|halten** ▸ **sauber A 1**

Sauberkeit *die;* ~ 1 cleanness; (bes. der Person) cleanliness; **ihre Wohnung blitzt vor ~:** her flat (esp. Brit.) *or* (esp. Amer.) apartment is sparkling clean 2 (Sorgfältigkeit) neatness 3 (Anständigkeit) uprightness

Sauberkeits·fimmel *der* (ugs. abwertend) mania for cleanliness; **einen ~ haben** have a thing about cleanliness (coll.)

säuberlich /ˈzɔybɐlɪç/

A *Adj.* neat

B *adv.* neatly; **fein ~ geordnet/verpackt** *usw.* neatly arranged/packed *etc.*

***sauber|machen** ▸ **sauber A 1**

Sauber·mann *der* (iron.) decent and upright fellow; nice guy (coll.); (Moralapostel) upholder of moral standards

säubern /ˈzɔybɐn/ *tr. V.* 1 (sauber machen) clean; **die Schuhe vom Lehm ~:** clean the mud off the shoes; **eine Wunde ~:** cleanse a wound; **das Wasser von Schadstoffen ~:** cleanse the water of pollutants; purify the water 2 (befreien) clear, rid (**von** of); purge ‹*party, government, etc.*› (**von** of); **Bibliotheken von verbotenen Büchern ~:** rid libraries of banned books

Säuberung *die;* ~, **~en** 1 (das Saubermachen) cleaning 2 (Entfernung) purging; **einer ~ zum Opfer fallen** be the victim of a purge 3 (Politik: ~saktion) purge; **ethnische ~** (verhüll.) ethnic cleansing

Säuberungs·aktion *die* purge; clean-up operation

sau·blöd[e] (salopp abwertend)

A *Adj.* bloody silly *or* stupid (sl.)

B *adv.* in a bloody silly *or* stupid manner (sl.); **frag doch nicht so ~:** don't ask such bloody silly *or* stupid questions (sl.)

Sauce ▸ **Soße 1**

Saucier /zoˈsi̯eː/ *der;* ~**s**, ~**s** sauce chef

Sauciere /zoˈsi̯ɛːrə/ *die;* ~, ~**n** sauceboat

Saudi /ˈzaudi/ *der;* ~**s**, ~**s**, **Saudi-Araber** *der*, **Saudi-Araberin** *die* ▸ ℹ **S. 520** Saudi

Saudi-Arabien *(das);* ~**s** Saudi Arabia

saudi-arabisch, saudisch *Adj.* ▸ ℹ **S. 520** Saudi Arabian; Saudi

sau·dumm ▸ **saublöd**

sauer /ˈzauɐ/

A *Adj.* 1 sour; sour, tart ‹*fruit*›; sharp-tasting ‹*bread, coffee, etc.*›; pickled ‹*herring, gherkin, etc.*›; acid[ic] ‹*wine, vinegar*›; **saure Drops** acid drops (Brit.); **saure Nieren** (Kochk.) *dish of sliced kidneys with lemon-flavored sauce;* **saurer Regen** acid rain; *s. auch* **Apfel 1**; **Bier** 2 (ugs.: verärgert) cross, annoyed (**auf** + *Akk.* with); (verdrossen) sour 3 (bes. Landw.) acidic 4 (Chemie) acid[ic] 5 (mühselig) hard; difficult; **gib ihm Saures!** (ugs.) let him have it! (coll.)

B *adv.* 1 (in, mit Essig) in vinegar 2 (ugs.: verärgert) crossly; **~ [auf jmdn./etw.] reagieren** get annoyed *or* cross [with sb./sth.] 3 (Chemie) **~ reagieren** react acidically 4 (mühsam) with difficulty; **~ erspartes/verdientes Geld** hard-saved/hard-earned money; **jmdn. ~ ankommen** be hard for sb. to take *or* accept 5 **~ aufstoßen** belch (*with acid taste*); **das wird ihm noch einmal ~ aufstoßen** (fig. ugs.) he will live to regret that

Sauer-: **~ampfer** /-ampfɐ/ *der* sorrel; **~braten** *der: braised beef marinated in vinegar and herbs;* sauerbraten (Amer.); **~brunnen** *der* 1 (Quelle) mineral spring containing carbon dioxide; 2 (Wasser) mineral water containing carbon dioxide

Sauerei *die;* ~, **~en** (salopp abwertend) 1 (Unflätigkeit) obscenity; **~en erzählen** tell filthy stories 2 (Gemeinheit) bloody (Brit. sl.) *or* (coll.) damn scandal (sl.)

Sauer-: **~kirsche** *die* sour cherry; **~klee** *der* wood sorrel; **~kohl** *der* (bes. nordd.); **~kraut** *das* sauerkraut; pickled cabbage

säuerlich

A *Adj.* 1 **[leicht] ~:** slightly sour; slightly sharp ‹*sauce*›; slightly sour *or* tart ‹*fruit*›; **ein leicht ~er Riesling** a Riesling with a touch of acidity 2 (verdorben) sourish; slightly sour 3 (missvergnügt) sourish; slightly sour

B *adv.* (missvergnügt) somewhat sourly

Säuerling *der;* ~**s**, ~**e** 1 (Mineralwasser) ▸ **Sauerbrunnen 2** 2 (ugs.: Wein) acidy wine

Sauer·milch *die* sour milk

säuern /ˈzɔyɐn/

A *tr. V.* 1 (gären lassen) leaven ‹*bread, dough, etc.*›; pickle ‹*cabbage, cucumber, etc.*› 2 (Kochk.: würzen) give zest *or* piquancy to

B *itr. V.; auch mit sein* (gären) turn sour; **der Kohl säuert in Fässern** the cabbage is pickling in vats

Sauer-: **~rahm** *der* sour cream; **~rahm·butter** *die* butter made from sour cream

Sauer·stoff *der* oxygen

sauerstoff-, Sauerstoff-: **~apparat** *der* oxygen apparatus; **~arm** *Adj.* low in oxygen *postpos.*; **~flasche** *die* oxygen cylinder; **~gerät** *das* oxygen apparatus; **~haltig** *Adj.* containing oxygen *postpos., not pred.*; **~haltig sein** contain oxygen; **~mangel** *der* lack of oxygen; **~mangel im Blut/Zellgewebe** oxygen deficiency in the blood/cell tissue; **~maske** *die* oxygen mask; **~reich** *Adj.* oxygen-rich; **~zelt** *das* (Med.) oxygen tent; **~zufuhr** *die* oxygen supply

Sauer·teig *der* leaven

sauer·töpfisch /-tœpfɪʃ/ *Adj.* (ugs. abwertend) sour ‹*expression, look, etc.*›; sour-faced ‹*person*›

Säuerung *die;* ~, **~en** (von Brot, Teig) leavening; (von Kohl, Kraut usw.) pickling

Saufbold /-bɔlt/ *der;* **~[e]s**, **~e** (veralt. abwertend) drunkard; boozer (coll.)

Sauf·bruder *der* (salopp, oft abwertend) boozing companion (coll.)

saufen /ˈzaufn̩/

A *unr. itr. V.* 1 drink 2 (salopp) (trinken) drink; swig (coll.); (Alkohol trinken) drink; booze (coll.); **~ wie ein Loch** drink like a fish 3 (salopp: alkoholabhängig sein) drink

B *unr. tr. V.* 1 drink 2 (salopp: trinken) drink; **er hat so viel [Schnaps] gesoffen, dass ...** he knocked back so much booze that ... (coll.); **einen ~ gehen** go for a drink

C *unr. refl. V.* (salopp) **sich dumm/zu Tode ~:** drink oneself stupid/to death; **sich arm ~:** drink one's last penny away; **sich** (*Dat.*) **die Jacke** *od.* **Hucke voll ~:** get tanked up (sl.)

Säufer /ˈzɔyfɐ/ *der;* ~**s**, ~ (salopp, oft abwertend) boozer (coll.); piss artist (sl.)

Sauferei *die;* ~, **~en** (salopp) 1 (Gelage) booze-up (coll.) 2 (das Saufen) boozing *no def. art.* (coll.)

Säuferin *die;* ~, **~nen** (salopp, oft abwertend) boozer (coll.); drunkard

Säufer-: **~leber** *die* (ugs.) hobnail[ed] liver; **~nase** *die* (ugs.) drinker's nose; **~wahn** *der* ▸ ℹ **S. 439** (Med. veralt.) delirium tremens

Sauf-: **~gelage** *das* (salopp) booze-up (coll.); **~kumpan** *der* (salopp) boozing companion (coll.)

Sau·fraß *der* (salopp abwertend) pigswill (coll.); rubbish

säufst /zɔyfst/ *2. Pers. Sg. Präsens v.* **saufen**

säuft /zɔyft/ *3. Pers. Sg. Präsens v.* **saufen**

Sauf·tour *die* (salopp) pub crawl (Brit. coll.); **eine ~ machen, auf ~ gehen** go on a pub crawl (Brit. coll.); bar-hop (Amer. coll.)

saugen /ˈzaugn̩/

A *tr. V.* 1 *auch unr.* (aufnehmen) suck; *s. auch* **Finger 2** 2 *auch itr.* (mit dem Staubsauger) vacuum; hoover (coll.) 3 (entfernen) suck up

B *regelm. (auch unr.) itr. V.* **an etw.** (*Dat.*) **~:** suck [at] sth.; **an einer Pfeife/Zigarette ~:** draw on a pipe/cigarette

C *unr. (auch regelm.) refl. V.* 1 (eindringen) soak (**in** + *Akk.* into) 2 (aufnehmen) **sich voll etw. ~:** become soaked with sth.

säugen /ˈzɔygn̩/ *tr. V.* suckle

Sauger *der;* ~**s**, ~ 1 (auf Flaschen) teat 2 (Saugheber) siphon 3 ▸ **Schnuller**

Säuger /ˈzɔygɐ/ *der;* ~**s**, ~, **Säuge·tier** *das* (Zool.) mammal

saug-, Saug-: **~fähig** *Adj.* absorbent; **~fähigkeit** *die* absorbency; **~glocke** *die* (Med.) suction cup; (zur Geburtshilfe) vacuum extractor; venteuse; **~heber** *der* siphon; **~kraft** *die* suction [strength]

Säugling /ˈzɔyklɪŋ/ *der;* ~**s**, ~**e** baby; infant

Säuglings-: **~alter** *das* infancy; babyhood; **im ~alter** in *or* during infancy; **~heim** *das* home for babies; **~pflege** *die* baby care; **~schwester** *die* infant *or* baby nurse; **~station** *die* baby ward; **~sterblichkeit** *die* infant mortality

Saug-: **~napf** *der* (Zool.) sucker; **~organ** *das* (Biol.) suctorial organ; **~reflex** *der* sucking reflex; **~rüssel** *der* (Zool.) proboscis; **~wurm** *der* (Zool.) trematode

Sau-: **~hatz** *die* (Jägerspr.) [wild] boar hunt; **~haufen** *der* (salopp abwertend) bunch of layabouts (sl.); **~hund** *der* (derb abwertend) bastard (coll.); bloody (Brit. sl.) *or* (coll.) damn swine

säuisch /ˈzɔyɪʃ/ (salopp)

A *Adj.* 1 (abwertend: unanständig) obscene ‹*phone call*›; filthy, obscene ‹*book, joke, behaviour*› 2 (stark, groß) hellish (coll.)

B *adv.* (sehr) hellishly (coll.); **~ viel Glück haben** have a hell of a lot of luck (coll.)

sau-, Sau-: **~kalt** *Adj.* (salopp) bloody cold (Brit. sl.); damn cold (coll.); **~kälte** *die* (salopp) bloody cold (Brit. sl.) *or* (coll.) damn cold weather; **das ist eine ~kälte** it's bloody (Brit. sl.) *or* (coll.) damn cold *or* freezing; **~kerl** *der* (salopp abwertend) bastard (coll.); **~laden** *der; Pl.* **~läden** (salopp abwertend) dump (coll.)

S

Säule /ˈzɔyla/ *die;* **~, ~n** 1 column; (nur als Stütze, auch fig.) pillar 2 (Zapf~) [petrol (Brit.) *or* (Amer.) gasoline] pump

Säulen-: **~bau** *der; Pl.* **~ten** building with columns; **~fuß** *der* base [of a/the column/pillar]; **~gang** *der* colonnade; **~halle** *die* columned hall; **~heilige** *der* stylite; **er ist ja kein ~heiliger** (fig.) he's no plaster saint; **~kaktus** *der* cereus; **~ordnung** *die* (Archit.) order [of columns]; **die dorische ~ordnung** the Doric order; **~portal** *das* (Archit.) columned doorway

Saum /zaum/ *der;* **~[e]s, Säume** /ˈzɔyma/ hem; (fig. geh.) edge

Sau·magen *der* (Kochk.) stuffed pig's stomach

sau·mäßig (salopp)

A *Adj.* 1 (sehr groß) **das ist eine ~e Arbeit/Hitze** that's a hell of a job/temperature (coll.); **~es Glück haben** be damned lucky (coll.) 2 (abwertend: schlecht) lousy (coll.)

B *adv.* 1 (sehr) damned (coll.); **~ viel verdienen** earn a hell of a lot (coll.); **es tat ~ weh** it hurt like hell 2 (abwertend: sehr schlecht) lousily (coll.)

säumen[1] /ˈzɔyman/ *tr. V.* hem; (fig. geh.) line

säumen[2] *itr. V.* (geh.: zögern) tarry (literary)

säumig *Adj.* (geh.) tardy; dilatory

Säumigkeit *die;* **~** (geh.) tardiness; dilatoriness

Säumnis /ˈzɔymnɪs/ *die;* **~, ~se** *od. das;* **~ses, ~se** (geh.) 1 delay 2 (Unterlassung) omission; failing

saum-, Saum-: **~pfad** *der* mule track; **~selig** (geh.) **A** *Adj.* dilatory; slow; **B** *adv.* in a dilatory manner; slowly; **~seligkeit** *die* (geh.) dilatoriness; slowness

Saum·tier *das* pack animal

Sauna /ˈzauna/ *die;* **~, ~s** *od.* **Saunen** sauna

Sauna·bad *das* sauna

saunieren /zauˈniːran/ *itr. V.* have *or* take a sauna

Säure /ˈzɔyra/ *die;* **~, ~n** 1 (von Früchten) sourness; tartness; (von Wein, Essig) acidity; (von Soßen) sharpness 2 (Chemie) acid

säure-, Säure-: **~arm** *Adj.* low in acid *postpos.*; **~beständig** *Adj.* acid-resistant; **~fest** *Adj.* acid-proof; **~frei** *Adj.* acid-free; **~gehalt** *der* acid content

Saure·gurken·zeit, Saure-Gurken-Zeit *die* (ugs.) slack *or* dead season; (in den Medien) silly season (Brit.)

säure·haltig *Adj.* acid[ic]

Saurier /ˈzauri̯ɐ/ *der;* **~s, ~:** large prehistoric reptile

Saus /zaus/ *in* **in ~ und Braus leben** live the high life

Sause *die;* **~, ~n** (ugs. veralt.) 1 (Gelage) booze-up (coll.) 2 (Zug durch die Kneipen) pub crawl (Brit. coll.); **eine ~ machen** go on a pub crawl (Brit. coll.); go barhopping (Amer.)

säuseln /ˈzɔyzl̩n/

A *itr. V.* (rascheln) ‹*leaves, branches, etc.*› rustle; ‹*wind*› murmur

B *tr. V.* (iron.: sagen) whisper

sausen *itr. V.* 1 (Geräusch machen) ‹*wind*› whistle; ‹*storm*› roar; ‹*head, ears*› buzz; ‹*propeller, engine, etc.*› whirr. **das Blut sauste ihm in den Ohren** blood was pounding in his ears 2 *mit sein* (hinfahren, -gehen) ‹*person*› rush; ‹*vehicle*› roar; **er sauste mit dem Fahrrad um die Ecke** he sped round the corner on his bike; **durchs Examen ~** (fig.) fail one's exam 3 *mit sein* ‹*whip, bullet, etc.*› whistle 4 **einen ~ lassen** (salopp) blow off (sl.) 5 (salopp) **ein Konzert ~ lassen** give a concert a miss; **eine Einladung ~ lassen** not take up an invitation; **eine Stellung/ein Geschäft ~ lassen** let a job/a business deal go; **ein Vorhaben ~ lassen** not bother to follow up a plan 6 **jmdn. ~ lassen** (salopp) drop sb.

***sausen|lassen** ▸ **sausen 5, 6**

Sauser *der;* **~s, ~** (bes. südwestd., österr., schweiz.) new wine

Sause-: **~schritt** *der: in* **im ~schritt** (ugs.) at breakneck speed; **~wind** *der* 1 (Kinderspr.) wind; 2 (ugs.: Mensch) live wire

sau-, Sau-: **~stall** *der* 1 pigsty; 2 (fig. salopp abwertend) hole (coll.); dump (coll.); **~teuer** *Adj.* (salopp) hideously expensive; **~teuer sein** cost a bomb (coll.); **~wetter** *das* (salopp abwertend) lousy weather (coll.); **~wohl** *Adj.; in* **sich ~wohl fühlen** (salopp) feel bloody (Brit. sl.) *or* (coll.) damn good *or* great; **~wut** *die* (salopp) **eine ~wut [auf jmdn.] haben** be bloody (Brit. sl.) *or* (coll.) damn mad [with sb.]

Savanne /zaˈvana/ *die;* **~, ~n** savannah

Savoyen /zaˈvɔyan/ *(das);* **~s** Savoy

Sax *das;* **~es, ~e** (Musikerjargon) sax (coll.)

Saxer, *der;* **~s, ~, Saxerin** *die;* **~, ~nen** (Musikerjargon) sax player (coll.)

Saxophon /zaksoˈfoːn/ *das;* **~s, ~e** saxophone

Saxophonist *der;* **~en, ~en, Saxophonistin** *die;* **~, ~nen** ▸ⓘ **S. 113** saxophonist

S-Bahn /ˈɛs-/ *die* city and suburban railway; S-bahn

S-Bahn

▸ **U-Bahn**

S-Bahn-: **~hof** *der,* **~-Station** *die* S-bahn station; **~-Zug** *der* city and suburban train; S-bahn train

S-Bahn-Surfen *das;* **~s** train surfing

SBB *Abk.* = **Schweizerische Bundesbahn** Swiss Federal Railways

SB-/ɛsˈbeː-/: **~-Laden** *der; Pl.* **~-Läden** self-service shop; **~-Tank·stelle** *die* self-service petrol (Brit.) *or* (Amer.) gasoline station

SBZ /ɛsbeːˈtsɛt/*die;* **~** *Abk.* = **Sowjetische Besatzungszone** Soviet occupied zone

Scampi /ˈskampi/ *Pl.* scampi

Scanner /ˈskɛnɐ/ *der;* **~s, ~** (DV, Med., graf. Technik) scanner

scatten /ˈskɛtn̩/ *itr. V.* scat

Scene /siːn/ *die;* **~, ~s** (salopp) scene

sch /ʃ/ *Interj.* 1 (ruhig) sh[h]; hush 2 (weg da) shoo

Schabe /ˈʃaːba/ *die;* **~, ~n** 1 cockroach 2 (südd., schweiz.: Motte) moth

Schabe·fleisch *das* minced beef

Schab·eisen *das* scraper

schaben

A *tr. V.* 1 (schälen) scrape ‹*carrots, potatoes, etc.*›; (glätten) shave ‹*leather, hide, etc.*›; plane ‹*wood, surface, etc.*›; **sich** *(Dat.)* **den Bart ~** (ugs. scherzh.) have a shave; shave 2 (scheuern) rub 3 (entfernen) scrape

B *itr. V.* scrape; **an/auf etw.** *(Dat.)* **~:** scrape against sth./scrape sth.

Schaber *der;* **~s, ~:** scraper

Schabernack /ˈʃaːbɐnak/ *der;* **~[e]s, ~e** 1 (Streich) prank; **jmdm. einen ~ spielen, mit jmdm. seinen ~ treiben** play a prank on sb. 2 (Scherz, Spaß) **aus ~ etw. tun** do sth. for a joke 3 (scherzh.: Kind) monkey; rascal

schäbig /ˈʃɛːbɪç/

A *Adj.* 1 (abgenutzt) shabby 2 (jämmerlich, gering) pathetic; miserable; **~e Gehälter** paltry wages 3 (gemein) shabby; mean 4 (geizig) stingy

B *adv.* 1 (abgenutzt) shabbily 2 (jämmerlich) miserably; **~ bezahlen** pay poorly 3 (gemein) meanly

Schäbigkeit *die;* **~:** shabbiness; (des Gehalts) paltriness; (Geiz) stinginess

Schablone /ʃaˈbloːna/ *die;* **~, ~n** 1 pattern 2 (fig., meist abwertend) **in ~n denken/sprechen** *od.* **reden** think in stereotypes/speak in clichés; **nach ~ arbeiten** work according to a set pattern *or* routine

schablonen-, Schablonen-: **~denken** *das* stereotyped way of thinking; **~druck** *der* 1 (Vervielfältigungsverfahren) stencil printing; 2 (Siebdruck) screen printing; **~haft** **A** *Adj.* stereotyped ‹*thinking*›; clichéd ‹*remark, expression, etc.*›; **B** *adv.* ‹*speak*› in a clichéd manner; ‹*think, act, argue, etc.*› in a stereotyped manner

Schab·messer *das* 1 (Schabeisen) scraper; scraping knife 2 (zur Holzbearbeitung) spokeshave

Schabracke /ʃaˈbraka/ *die;* **~, ~n** 1 (Pferdedecke) caparison 2 (an Fenstern) pelmet

Schabsel /ˈʃaːpsl̩/ *das;* **~s, ~:** shavings *pl.*

Schab·technik *die* mezzotint technique

Schach /ʃax/ *das;* **~s, ~s** 1 (Spiel) chess 2 (Schachspiel: Stellung) check; **~ [dem König]!** check; **[dem gegnerischen König/dem Gegner] ~ bieten** check the opponent's king/the opponent; **der Turm/der Gegner bietet ~:** the rook/the opponent gives check; **ewiges ~:** perpetual check; **im ~:** in check; **jmdn./etw. in ~ halten** (ugs. fig.) keep sb./sth. in check; *s. auch* **matt A 6**

Schach-: **~aufgabe** *die* chess problem; **~brett** *das* chessboard; **~brett·muster** *das* chequerboard pattern; (auf Stoff) chequered pattern; **~ecke** *die* (ugs.) chess column

Schacher /ˈʃaxɐ/ *der;* **~s** (abwertend) haggling (**um** over); (bes. Politik) horse-trading (**um** about)

Schächer /ˈʃɛçɐ/ *der;* **~s, ~** (bibl.) thief

schachern *itr. V.* haggle (**um** over)

schach-, Schach-: **~figur** *die* chess piece; chessman; **~matt** *Adj.* 1 (Schachspiel) **~matt!** checkmate!; **~matt sein** be checkmated; **jmdn. ~matt setzen** (Schachspiel) checkmate sb.; (fig.: ausschalten) render sb. powerless; 2 (erschöpft) exhausted; **~partie** *die* game of chess; **~spiel** *das* 1 (Spiel) chess; 2 (das Spielen) chess-playing; 3 (Partie) game of chess; 4 (Brett und Figuren) chess set; **~spieler** *der,* **~spielerin** *die* chess player

Schacht /ʃaxt/ *der;* **~[e]s, Schächte** /ˈʃɛçta/ shaft

Schachtel /ˈʃaxtl̩/ *die;* **~, ~n** 1 box; **eine ~ Zigaretten** a packet *or* (Amer.) pack of cigarettes; **eine ~ Pralinen/Streichhölzer** a box of chocolates/matches 2 *in* **alte ~** (salopp abwertend) old bag (sl.)

Schächtelchen /ˈʃɛçtl̩çan/ *das;* **~s, ~:** [little] box

Schachtel-: **~halm** *der* (Bot.) horsetail; **~satz** *der* (Sprachw.) involved sentence

schächten /ˈʃɛçtn̩/ *tr., itr. V.* slaughter according to Jewish rites

Schach-: **~turnier** *das* chess tournament; **~zug** *der* 1 (Schachspiel) move [in chess]; 2 (fig.) move

schade /ˈʃaːda/ *Adj.* **[ach, wie] ~!** [what a] pity *or* shame; **es/das ist [sehr] ~!** it's/that's a [terrible] pity *or* shame; **[es ist zu] ~, dass ...** it's a [real] pity *or* shame that ...; **nur ~** *od.* **~ nur, dass ...** it's just a pity *or* shame that ...; **[es ist] ~ um jmdn./etw.** it's a pity *or* shame about sb./sth.; **~ drum!** what a pity *or* shame; **um die Vase ist es nicht weiter ~:** it doesn't matter about the vase; the vase is no great loss; **für jmdn./für** *od.* **zu etw. zu ~ sein** be too good for sb./sth.; **sich** *(Dat.)* **zu ~ für** *od.* **zu etw./für jmdn. sein** consider oneself too good for sth./sb.

Schade *in* **es soll dein ~ nicht sein** (veralt.) it will not be to your disadvantage

Schädel /ˈʃɛːdl̩/ *der;* **~s, ~** 1 ▸ⓘ **S. 435** head; (Skelett) skull; **jmdm. eins auf** *od.* **über den ~ geben** (ugs.) hit *or* knock sb. over the head; **mir brummt der ~** (ugs.) my head is throbbing; **einen dicken** *od.* **harten ~ haben** (fig.) be stubborn *or* pigheaded; **sich** *(Dat.)* **[an etw.** *(Dat.)***] den ~ einrennen** (fig.) beat *or* run one's head against a brick wall [with sth.] 2 (fig.: Verstand) **streng deinen ~ mal an!** tax your brains a bit!; **es geht** *od.* **will nicht in seinen ~ [hinein], dass ...** (ugs.) he can't get it into his head that ...

Schädel-: **~basis·bruch** *der* ▸ⓘ **S. 439** (Med.) basal skull fracture; **~bruch** *der* ▸ⓘ **S. 439** (Med.) skull fracture; **~decke** *die* ▸ⓘ **S. 435** (Anat.) skullcap; calvaria; **~lage** *die* (Med.) cephalic *or* head presentation; **~naht** *die* ▸ⓘ **S. 435** (Anat.) suture

schaden *itr. V.* **jmdm./einer Sache ~:** damage *or* harm sb./sth.; **Rauchen schadet Ihrer Gesundheit/Ihnen** smoking damages your health/is bad for you; **jmds. Ansehen [sehr] ~:** do [great] damage to sb.'s reputation; **das würde dir nichts ~** (ugs.) that wouldn't hurt you *or* do you any harm; **das**

S

schadet nichts (ugs.) (ist nicht schlimm) that doesn't matter; (ist ganz gut) that won't do any harm; es kann nichts ~, wenn ... (ugs.) it would do no harm if ...

Schaden der; ~s, Schäden /ˈʃɛːdn̩/ 1 (Beschädigung) damage *no pl., no indef. art.*; ein kleiner/großer ~: little/major damage; jmdm. [einen] ~ zufügen harm sb.; ~ leiden (geh.) suffer; wer den ~ hat, braucht für den Spott nicht zu sorgen (Spr.) the laugh is always on the loser; aus ~ wird man klug (Spr.) once bitten, twice shy (prov.); er hat an seiner Gesundheit ~ genommen (geh.) his health has suffered 2 (Nachteil) disadvantage; es ist dein eigener *od.* zu deinem eigenen ~: it is to your own disadvantage; es soll Ihr ~ nicht sein it will not be to your disadvantage; zu ~ kommen suffer; be adversely affected 3 (Defekt) damage *no pl., no indef. art.*; das Haus weist einige Schäden auf the house has some defects 4 (Verletzung) injury; zu ~ kommen be hurt *or* injured

schaden-, Schaden-: ~ersatz *der* (Rechtsw.) damages *pl.*; (Versicherungsw.) ~ersatz leisten pay damages/compensation; jmdn. auf ~ersatz verklagen sue sb. for damages/compensation; **~ersatz·anspruch** *der,* **~ersatz·forderung** *die* (Rechtsw.) claim for damages; (Versicherungsw.) claim for compensation; **~ersatz·klage** *die* (Rechtsw.) action for damages; **~ersatz·pflichtig** *Adj.* (Rechtsw.) liable for damages *pred.*; **~freude** *die* malicious pleasure; ..., sagte er voller ~freude ... he said gloatingly; **~froh** A *Adj.* gloating; ~froh sein gloat; B *adv.* with malicious pleasure

Schadens·fall *der* (Rechtsw., Versicherungsw.) case of damage; (Verlust) case of loss; im ~: in the event of damage/loss

schadhaft /ˈʃaːthaft/ *Adj.* defective

Schadhaftigkeit *die;* ~: defectiveness

schädigen /ˈʃɛːdɪgn̩/ *tr. V.* damage ‹*health, reputation, interests*›; harm, hurt ‹*person*›; cause losses to ‹*firm, industry, etc.*›; er hat den Betrieb um mehrere tausend Euro geschädigt he caused losses of several thousand euros to the firm; jmdn. gesundheitlich ~: damage sb.'s health

Schädigung *die;* ~, ~en damage *no pl., no indef. art.* (*Gen.* to); materielle/gesundheitliche ~en financial losses/damage to one's/your *etc.* health

schädlich /ˈʃɛːtlɪç/ *Adj.* harmful; ~ für die Gesundheit damaging *or* injurious to the health; ~e Folgen/Wirkungen/Einflüsse damaging or detrimental consequences/effects/influences

Schädlichkeit *die;* ~: harmfulness

Schädling /ˈʃɛːtlɪŋ/ *der;* ~s, ~e pest

Schädlings-: ~befall *der* infestation [by pests]; **~bekämpfer** *der;* ~~s, ~~, **~bekämpferin** *die;* ~~, ~~nen pest control expert; **~bekämpfung** *die* pest control; **~bekämpfungs·mittel** *das* pesticide

schad·los *Adj.* in sich an jmdm./etw. ~ halten take advantage of sb./sth.

Schad·stoff *der* harmful chemical

schadstoff·arm *Adj.* (bes. Kfz-W.) low in harmful substances *postpos.*; clean-exhaust ‹*vehicle*›; (mit Katalysator) ‹*vehicle*› with exhaust emission control

Schaf /ʃaːf/ *das;* ~[e]s, ~e 1 sheep; *s. auch* Bock 1; schwarz 2 2 (ugs.: Dummkopf) twit (Brit. coll.); idiot (coll.)

Schaf·bock *der* ram

Schäfchen /ˈʃɛːfçən/ *das;* ~s, ~ 1 [little] sheep; (Lamm) lamb; sein[e] ~ ins Trockene bringen (ugs.) take care of number one (coll.); sein[e] ~ im Trockenen haben (ugs.) have taken care of number one (coll.); ~ zählen (zum Einschlafen) count sheep 2 *Pl.* (ugs.: Schutzbefohlene) flock *sing. or pl.* 3 (fam.: einfältiger Mensch) silly thing

Schäfchen·wolke *die* fleecy cloud

Schäfer *der;* ~s, ~ ▸ℹ S. 113 shepherd

Schäfer·dichtung *die* (Literaturw.) pastoral *or* bucolic poetry

Schäferei *die;* ~, ~en 1 sheep farming; sheep rearing 2 (Betrieb) sheep farm

Schäfer·hund *der* 1 (Rasse) Alsatian (Brit.); German shepherd; ein deutscher ~: an Alsatian (Brit.); a German shepherd 2 (Hirtenhund) sheepdog

Schäferin *die;* ~, ~nen ▸ℹ S. 113 shepherdess

Schäfer-: ~spiel *das* (Literaturw.) pastoral [play]; **~stündchen** *das* lovers' tryst

Schaf·fell *das* sheepskin

schaffen /ˈʃafn̩/

A *unr. tr. V.* 1 (schöpferisch gestalten) create; der ~de Mensch creative man; für jmdn./etw. *od.* zu jmdm./etw. wie ge~ sein be made *or* perfect for sb./sth. 2 *auch regelm.* (herstellen) create ‹*conditions, jobs, situation, etc.*›; make ‹*room, space, fortune*›; klare Verhältnisse ~: clear things up; straighten things out; *s. auch* Abhilfe; Ordnung 1

B *tr. V.* 1 (bewältigen) etw. ~: manage to do sth.; viel ~: manage to do a great deal; eine Arbeit ~: get a job done; wenn wir uns beeilen, ~ wir es vielleicht noch we might still make it if we hurry; das schafft er nie he'll never manage it; das hätten wir geschafft, das wäre geschafft there, that's done; er hat die Prüfung nicht geschafft (ugs.) he didn't pass the exam 2 (ugs.: erschöpfen) wear out; die Hitze/Arbeit hat mich geschafft the heat/work took it out of me 3 (befördern) etw. aus etw./in etw. (*Akk.*) ~: get sth. out of/into sth.; die Kisten auf den Speicher/in den Keller ~: take the boxes to the attic/cellar

C *itr. V.* 1 (südd.: arbeiten) work 2 sich (*Dat.*) zu ~ machen (an etw. hantieren) busy oneself; (Tätigkeit vortäuschen) fiddle *or* tinker about; was machst du dir an meinem Schreibtisch zu ~? what are you doing at my desk?; mit ihm will ich nichts zu ~ haben I don't want to have anything to do with him; was habe ich mit dieser Angelegenheit zu ~? what does this matter have to do with me?; jmdm. zu ~ machen cause sb. trouble

Schaffen *das;* ~s work; im Zenit seines ~s at the peak of his creative work

Schaffens-: ~drang *der* energy; **~freude** *die* enthusiasm [for one's work]; (eines Künstlers) pleasure in creating things; **~kraft** *die* energy for work; (eines Künstlers) creativity; creative power

Schaffer *der;* ~s, ~ (bes. südd.) hard worker

Schafferei *die;* ~ (bes. südd.) hard work

Schafferin *die;* ~, ~nen ▸ Schaffer

Schaf·fleisch *das* mutton

Schaffner /ˈʃafnɐ/ *der;* ~s, ~ ▸ℹ S. 113 (im Bus) conductor; (im Zug) guard (Brit.); conductor (Amer.); (der Fahrausweise verkauft/kontrolliert) inspector

Schaffnerin *die;* ~, ~nen ▸ℹ S. 113 (im Bus) conductress (Brit.); (im Zug) guard (Brit.); conductress (Amer.); (die Fahrausweise verkauft/kontrolliert) inspector

schaffner·los *Adj.* (Verkehrsw.) ‹*bus, tram, etc.*› without a conductor; ‹*train*› without a guard (Brit.) *or* (Amer.) conductor/an inspector *postpos.*

Schaffung *die;* ~: creation

Schaf-: ~garbe *die* yarrow; **~herde** *die* flock of sheep; **~hirt** *der* shepherd; **~hirtin** *die* shepherdess; **~kälte** *die: spell of cold weather frequently occurring in mid-June;* **~kopf** ▸ Schafskopf

Schäflein /ˈʃɛːflain/ *das;* ~s, ~ ▸ Schäfchen 1, 2

Schafott /ʃaˈfɔt/ *das;* ~[e]s, ~e scaffold

Schaf·schur *die* sheep shearing

Schafs-: ~käse *der* sheep's milk cheese; **~kopf** *der* 1 (Kartenspiel) sheep's head; 2 (ugs.: Trottel) dope (coll.); idiot (coll.); **~pelz** *der* sheepskin

Schaf·stall *der* sheepfold

Schaft /ʃaft/ *der;* ~[e]s, Schäfte /ˈʃɛftə/ 1 (Griff; auch Archit.) shaft; (eines Messers, Beils, Meißels) handle; (eines Gewehrs usw.) stock 2 (eines Baumes, einer Feder) shaft 3 (am Schuh) upper 4 (am Stiefel) leg 5 (Bot.) stem; stalk

Schaft·stiefel *der* high boot

Schaf-: ~wolle *die* sheep's wool; **~zucht** *die* 1 (das Züchten) sheep breeding *no art.*; 2 (Betrieb) sheep farm

Schah /ʃaː/ *der;* ~s, ~s Shah

Schakal /ʃaˈkaːl/ *der;* ~s, ~e jackal

Schäker /ˈʃɛːkɐ/ *der;* ~s, ~ (veralt.) 1 (Witzbold) joker 2 (jmd., der flirtet) flirt

schäkern *itr. V.* (veralt.) 1 (spaßen) fool about 2 (flirten) flirt

schal /ʃaːl/ *Adj.* stale ‹*drink, taste, smell, joke*›; empty ‹*words, feeling*›

Schal *der;* ~s, ~s *od.* ~e 1 (Halstuch) scarf 2 (Vorhang~) curtain

Schälchen /ˈʃɛːlçən/ *das;* ~s, ~: small bowl *or* dish

Schale /ˈʃaːlə/ *die;* ~, ~n 1 (Obstschale) skin; (abgeschälte ~) peel *no pl.*; Kartoffeln in der ~ (Kochk.) jacket potatoes 2 (Nuss~, Eier~) shell 3 (tieferes Gefäß) bowl; (flacheres Gefäß) dish; (Waag~) pan; scale; (Sekt~) champagne glass 4 *in* [groß] in ~ sein (ugs.) be dressed up to the nines; sich in ~ werfen *od.* schmeißen (ugs.) get dressed [up] to the nines 5 (Zool.) shell 6 (bes. österr.: Tasse) [shallow] cup 7 (des BH) cup

schälen /ˈʃɛːlən/

A *tr. V.* peel ‹*fruit, vegetable*›; shell ‹*egg, nut, pea*›; skin ‹*tomato, almond*›; einen Baumstamm ~: remove the bark from a tree trunk; den Knochen aus einem Schinken ~: bone a ham; etw. aus der Verpackung ~ (fig.) get sth. out of its wrappings; sich aus den Kleidern ~ (fig.) get oneself out of one's clothes

B *refl. V.* 1 (sich ~ lassen) peel; Tomaten/Eier ~ sich leichter tomatoes/eggs can be skinned/shelled more easily 2 ‹*person, skin, nose, etc.*› peel; du schälst dich am Rücken/auf der Nase/im Gesicht your back/nose/face is peeling

Schalen-: ~obst *das* nuts *pl.*; **~sitz** *der* bucket seat; **~tier** *das* shell animal; **~wild** *das* (Jägerspr.) hoofed game

Schalheit *die;* ~ ▸ schal: staleness; emptiness

Schalk /ʃalk/ *der;* ~[e]s, ~e *od.* Schälke /ˈʃɛlkə/ rogue; prankster; jmdm. sitzt der ~/jmd. hat den ~ im Nacken (fig.) sb. is really roguish *or* mischievous; jmdm. schaut der ~ aus den Augen (fig.) sb. has a roguish *or* mischievous look in his eye

schalkhaft (geh.)

A *Adj.* roguish; mischievous

B *adv.* roguishly; mischievously

Schal·kragen *der* shawl collar

Schalks·narr *der* (veralt.) 1 (Hofnarr) jester; fool 2 (Schalk) rogue; prankster; wag

Schall /ʃal/ *der;* ~[e]s, ~e *od.* Schälle /ˈʃɛlə/ 1 (Klang) sound; mit lautem ~: loudly; leerer ~ sein be meaningless *or* irrelevant; ~ und Rauch sein not mean anything; Name ist ~ und Rauch names mean nothing 2 (Physik) sound *no art.*

schall-, Schall-: ~dämmend *Adj.* sound-deadening; sound-absorbing; **~dämmung** *die* sound insulation; **~dämpfer** *der* 1 (am Auto, für Feuerwaffen) silencer; 2 (Musik) mute; **~dicht** *Adj.* soundproof

***Schallehre** ▸ Schalllehre

schallen *regelm.* (*auch unr.*) *itr. V.* ring out; (nachhallen) resound; echo; eine ~de Ohrfeige a resounding slap; ~des Gelächter ringing laughter; ~d lachen roar with laughter

Schall-: ~geschwindigkeit *die* speed *or* velocity of sound; **~lehre** *die* acoustics *sing., no art.*; **~loch** *das* 1 (Musik) soundhole; 2 (an einem Turm usw.) belfry window; **~mauer** *die* sound *or* sonic barrier

***Schalloch** ▸ Schallloch

Schall·platte *die* record

Schallplatten-: ▸ Platten-

schall-, Schall-: ~quelle *die* sound source; **~schluckend** *Adj.* sound-absorbent; sound-deadening; **~trichter** *der* (am Grammophon) horn; (am Blasinstrument) bell;

S

~**welle** *die* (Physik) sound wave; ~**wort** *das Pl.* ~**wörter** (Sprachw.) onomatopoeic word

Schalmei /ʃal'mai/ *die;* ~, ~**en** shawm

Schalotte /ʃa'lɔtə/ *die;* ~, ~**n** shallot

schalt /ʃalt/ *1. u. 3. Pers. Sg. Prät. v.* **schelten**

Schalt·anlage *die* (Elektrot.) switchgear

Schalte /'ʃaltə/ *die;* ~, ~**n** (Ferns. Jargon) ▸**Schaltung 1**

schalten /'ʃaltn̩/

A *tr. V.* **1** switch; **ein Gerät auf „aus" ~:** turn an appliance to 'off' **2** (Elektrot.: verbinden) connect; **in Reihe/parallel ~:** connect in series/in parallel

B *itr. V.* **1** (Schalter betätigen) switch, turn (**auf** + *Akk.* to); **du musst zweimal ~:** you have to operate the switch twice; **er schaltet immer gleich auf stur** (fig. ugs.) he immediately digs his heels in (fig.) **2** ‹*machine*› switch (**auf** + *Akk.* to); ‹*traffic light*› change (**auf** + *Akk.* to) **3** (im Auto) change [gear]; **in den 4. Gang ~:** change into fourth gear **4** (geh.: verfahren) act; **er kann mit dem Geld frei ~:** he can do as he pleases with the money; he has a free hand with the money; **~ und walten** manage one's affairs; **sie kann ~ und walten, wie sie will** she can manage things as she pleases **5** (ugs.: begreifen) twig (coll.); catch on (coll.)

C *refl. V.* (sich ~ lassen) **das Gerät schaltet sich leicht/schwer** the switch on this device is easy/difficult to operate; **der Wagen schaltet sich schlecht** it's difficult to change gear in this car

Schalter /'ʃaltɐ/ *der;* ~**s,** ~ **1** (Strom~) switch **2** (Post~, Bank~, Fahrkarten~ usw.) counter; (mit Fenster auch) window **3** (am Fahrrad) gear lever

Schalter-: ~**beamte** *der,* ~**beamtin** *die* counter clerk; (im Bahnhof) ticket clerk; ~**halle** *die* hall; (im Bahnhof) booking hall (Brit.); ticket office; ~**raum** *der* counter room; (im Bahnhof) ticket office; ~**schluss,** *~**schluß** *der* closing time; ~**stunden** *Pl.* business hours; hours of business

Schalt-: ~**fläche** *die* (DV) button; ~**getriebe** *das* (Kfz-W.) [manual] gearbox; ~**hebel** *der* **1** (am Schalter) switch; **an den ~hebeln der Macht sitzen** (fig.) hold the reins of power; **2** (einer Gangschaltung) gear lever; gear shift (Amer.); ~**jahr** *das* leap year; **alle ~jahre [ein]mal** (ugs.) once in a blue moon; ~**knüppel** *der* [floor-mounted] gear lever; ~**kreis** *der* (Elektrot.) circuit; ~**pause** *die* (Rundfunk) pause [in transmission]; ~**plan** *der* (Elektrot.) wiring *or* circuit diagram; ~**pult** *das* control desk; (kleiner) control panel; ~**satz** *der* (Sprachw.) parenthetic clause; ~**stelle** *die* control centre; ~**tafel** *die* (Elektrot.) control panel; ~**tag** *der* leap day

Schaltung *die;* ~, ~**en** **1** (Rundfunk: Verbindung) link-up **2** (Gangschaltung) manual gear change **3** (Elektrot.) circuit; wiring system **4** ▸~**plan**

Schaltwerk *das* changer; derailleur

Schalt·zentrale *die* (Technik) control centre

Schaltzug *der* gear cable

Schaluppe /ʃa'lʊpə/ *die;* ~, ~**n** (Frachtschiff) sloop

Scham /ʃa:m/ *die;* ~ **1** shame; **ohne/ohne jede ~:** unashamedly/without the slightest shame; **ich hätte vor ~ in den Boden versinken können** I could have sunk through the floor with embarrassment *or* shame; **aus/vor ~ erröten** blush with shame; **nur keine falsche ~:** no need for any false modesty **2** (geh. verhüll.: ~gegend) private parts *pl.*

Schamane /ʃa'ma:nə/ *der;* ~**n,** ~**n, Schamanin** *die;* ~, ~**nen** (Völkerk.) shaman

Schamanismus *der;* ~ (Völkerk.) shamanism

schamanistisch (Völkerk.)

A *Adj.* shamanist[ic]

B *adv.* shamanistically

Scham·bein *das* ▸ℹ **S. 435** (Anat.) pubic bone

schämen /'ʃɛmən/ *refl. V.* be ashamed; **sich einer Sache** (*Gen.*) *od.* **für etw.** *od.* **wegen etw. ~:** be ashamed of sth.; **sich für jmdn. ~:** be ashamed for sb.; **du solltest dich [was** (ugs.)**] ~!** you [really] should be ashamed of yourself; **schäm dich** shame on you

Scham-: ~**gefühl** *das* sense of shame; ~**haar** *das* pubic hair

schamhaft

A *Adj.* bashful ‹*person, look, etc.*›; modest ‹*clothing*›

B *adv.* ‹*look, smile, etc.*› bashfully; ‹*dress, behave*› modestly

Schamhaftigkeit *die;* ~**:** modesty

scham-, Scham-: ~**lippe** *die* ▸ℹ **S. 435** (Anat.) labium; **innere/äußere ~lippen** labia minora/majora; ~**los** **A** *Adj.* **1** (skrupellos, dreist) shameless; barefaced, shameless ‹*lie, slander*›; **2** (unanständig) indecent ‹*gesture, remark, dress, etc.*›; shameless ‹*person*›; **B** *adv.* **1** (skrupellos, dreist) shamelessly; **2** (unanständig) indecently; ~**losigkeit** *die;* ~~, ~~**en** (Skrupellosigkeit, Dreistigkeit) shamelessness; (Unanständigkeit) indecency; shamelessness; **ich kann solche ~losigkeiten nicht dulden** I cannot tolerate such shameless behaviour *sing.*

Schamotte·stein /ʃa'mɔtə-/ *der* firebrick

Schampon /'ʃampɔn/ ▸**Shampoo**

schamponieren *tr. V.* shampoo

Schampus /'ʃampʊs/ *der;* ~ (ugs.) bubbly (coll.); champers *sing.* (Brit. coll.)

scham·rot *Adj.* red with shame *postpos.;* ~ **werden** blush with shame

Scham·röte *die:* **ihm stieg die ~ ins Gesicht** he blushed with shame

schandbar ▸**schändlich**

Schande /'ʃandə/ *die;* ~**:** disgrace; shame; **es ist eine [wahre] ~:** it is a[n absolute] disgrace; **es wäre doch eine ~, das wegzuwerfen** it would be a shame to throw it away; **zu meiner ~ muss ich sagen, dass ...** it must be said to my shame that ...; **~ über dich!** shame on you!; **jmdm./einer Sache [keine] ~ machen** [not] disgrace sb./sth.; bring [no] disgrace *or* shame on sb./sth.; **etw. gereicht jmdm. zur ~** (geh.) sth. is a disgrace to sb.; **zu ~n** ▸**zuschanden**

schänden /'ʃɛndn̩/ *tr. V.* **1** dishonour, discredit ‹*name, reputation, etc.*› **2** (beschädigen) defile ‹*memorial, work of art, etc.*›; desecrate, defile ‹*holy place, grave, relic*›; violate ‹*corpse*› **3** (veralt.: vergewaltigen) violate; *s. auch* **Arbeit 1**

Schand·fleck *der* blot; **ein ~ in der Landschaft sein** be a blot on the landscape; **er war schon immer der ~ [in] unserer Familie** he always 'was the disgrace of our family

schändlich

A *Adj.* **1** (verwerflich) shameful; disgraceful **2** (ugs.: scheußlich) disgraceful; dreadful (coll.), terrible (coll.) ‹*weather*›

B *adv.* **1** (verwerflich) shamefully; disgracefully **2** (ugs.: überaus) dreadfully (coll.), terribly (coll.)

Schändlichkeit *die;* ~, ~**en** **1** (Eigenschaft) shamefulness; disgracefulness **2** (Handlung) shameful action

Schand-: ~**mal** *das; Pl.* ~~**e,** *od.* ~**mäler** **1** mal (hist.) brand; **2** (geh.: Schandfleck) blemish; ~**tat** *die* disgraceful *or* abominable deed; **zu jeder ~tat** *od.* **zu allen ~taten bereit sein** (ugs. scherzh.) be game for anything

Schändung *die;* ~, ~**en** **1** ▸**schänden 1, 2:** dishonouring; discrediting; desecration; defilement **2** (veralt.: Vergewaltigung) violation

Schanker /'ʃaŋkɐ/ *der;* ~**s,** ~ ▸ℹ **S. 439** (Med.) chancre; **harter/weicher ~:** hard/soft chancre

Schank-: ~**erlaubnis** *die* licence [to sell alcohol]; ~**tisch** *der* bar; ~**wirtschaft** *die* public house (Brit.); bar (Amer.)

Schanze /'ʃantsə/ *die;* ~, ~**n** **1** (Milit. veralt.) entrenchment; fieldwork **2** (Sprung~) [ski] jump

Schanzen·rekord *der* (Skispringen) ski jump record

Schar /ʃa:ɐ̯/ *die;* ~, ~**en** crowd; horde; (von Vögeln) flock; **in [großen** *od.* **hellen] ~en** in swarms *or* droves

Scharade /ʃa'ra:də/ *die;* ~, ~**n** charade

Schäre /'ʃɛ:rə/ *die;* ~, ~**n** skerry

scharen

A *refl. V.* (sich zusammenfinden) gather

B *tr. V.* **die Kinder/Klasse um sich ~:** gather the children/class around one[self]

Schären·küste *die* skerry coast

scharen·weise *Adv.* in swarms *or* hordes

scharf /ʃarf/; **schärfer** /'ʃɛrfɐ/, **schärfst...** /'ʃɛrfst.../

A *Adj.* **1** sharp **2** (stark gewürzt, brennend, stechend) hot; strong ‹*drink, vinegar, etc.*›; caustic ‹*chemical*›; pungent, acrid ‹*smell*› **3** (durchdringend) shrill; (hell) harsh; (kalt) biting ‹*cold, wind, air, etc.*›; sharp ‹*frost*› **4** (deutlich wahrnehmend) keen; sharp **5** (stark) strong ‹*spectacles*›; powerful ‹*lens, microscope, telescope, etc.*› **6** (deutlich hervortretend) sharp ‹*contours, features, nose, photograph*› **7** (schonungslos) tough, fierce ‹*resistance, competition, etc.*›; sharp ‹*criticism, remark, words, etc.*›; strong, fierce ‹*opponent, protest, etc.*›; severe, harsh ‹*sentence, law, measure, etc.*›; strict, tough ‹*examiner, teacher*›; tough, rigorous ‹*inquiry, interrogation*›; bitter, fierce ‹*fighting, argument, etc.*›; fierce ‹*dog*›; **eine ~e Zunge haben** have a sharp tongue; **jmdn./etw. in ~er Form kritisieren** criticize sb./sth. in strong terms **8** (schnell) fast; hard ‹*ride, gallop, etc.*›; **ein ~es Tempo fahren** drive at quite a speed **9** (explosiv) live; (Ballspiele) powerful ‹*shot*›; **~e Schüsse abgeben** fire live bullets **10** (Sprachw.) pronounced; clear; **das ~e S** (bes. österr.) the German letter 'ß' **11** (ugs.: großartig) great (coll.) **12** (ugs. empörend) outrageous **13** (ugs.: geil) sexy ‹*girl, clothes, pictures, etc.*›; randy ‹*fellow, thoughts, etc.*› **14** *in* ~ **auf jmdn./etw. sein** (ugs.) really fancy sb. (coll.)/be really keen on sth.

B *adv.* **1** ~ **würzen/abschmecken** season/flavour highly; ~ **riechen** smell pungent *or* strong **2** (durchdringend) shrilly; (hell) harshly; (kalt) bitingly **3** (deutlich wahrnehmend) ‹*listen, watch, etc.*› closely, intently; ‹*think, consider, etc.*› hard; ~ **aufpassen** pay close attention **4** (deutlich hervortretend) sharply; **einen Sender ~ einstellen** tune in a radio station properly; **etw. ~ umreißen** (fig.) outline sth. clearly *or* precisely **5** (schonungslos) ‹*attack, criticize, etc.*› sharply, strongly; ‹*contradict, oppose, etc.*› strongly, fiercely; ‹*examine, investigate, etc.*› rigorously; ‹*watch, observe, etc.*› closely; ‹*fight, quarrel, etc.*› fiercely, bitterly; ~ **durchgreifen** take vigorous *or* strong action **6** (schnell) fast; ~ **bremsen** brake hard *or* sharply; **das Auto fuhr ~ rechts heran** the car pulled up well over to the right **7** **das Gewehr ist ~ geladen** the rifle is loaded with live ammunition; ~ **schießen** shoot with live ammunition; **den Ball ~ ins Netz schießen** hammer the ball into the net (coll.) **8** (akzentuiert) clearly **9** (ugs.: großartig) splendidly

Scharf·blick *der* perspicacity

Schärfe /'ʃɛrfə/ *die;* ~, ~**n** **1** (von Messer usw.) sharpness **2** (von Geschmack) hotness; (von Chemikalien) causticity; (von Geruch) pungency **3** (Intensität) shrillness; (von Licht, Farbe usw.) harshness; (des Windes) bitterness; (des Frostes) sharpness **4** (Empfindlichkeit, analytische Fähigkeit) sharpness; keenness **5** (Klarheit) clarity; sharpness **6** (Härte) ▸**scharf A 7:** toughness; ferocity; sharpness; strength; severity; harshness; strictness; rigour; bitterness **7** (Heftigkeit) harshness **8** (Ballspiele) power

schärfen

A *tr. V.* (auch fig.) sharpen

B *refl. V.* become sharper *or* keener

Schärfen·tiefe *die* (Fot.) depth of focus

schärfer ▸**scharf**

scharf-, Scharf-: ~**kantig** *Adj.* sharp-edged; ~|**machen** *tr. V.* (ugs.) stir up; **einen Hund ~machen** urge a dog on; ~**macher** *der* (ugs.) rabble-rouser; ~**macherei** /-maxə'rai/ *die;* ~~, ~~**en** (ugs.) rabble-rousing; ~**macherin** *die* ▸~**macher;** ~**richter** *der* hangman; executioner; ~**schütze** *der* (Milit.) marksman; (auch fig. Ballspiele) sharpshooter; ~**schützin** *die* (Milit.) markswoman; (auch fig. Ballspiele) sharpshooter; ~**sichtig** /-zɪçtɪç/ **A** *Adj.* sharp-sighted; perspicacious; **B** *adv.* with sharp-sightedness; ~**sinn** *der*

S

astuteness; acumen; **~sinnig** [A] *Adj.* astute; [B] *adv.* astutely

schärfst... ▸**scharf**

Schärfung *die;* ~, ~**en** sharpening

scharfzüngig /-tsʏŋɪç/
[A] *Adj.* sharp-tongued
[B] *adv.* sharply; in a sharp-tongued manner

Scharlach /ˈʃarlax/ *der;* ~**s** ▸❶ **S. 439** (Med.) scarlet fever

scharlach·rot *Adj.* scarlet

Scharlatan /ˈʃarlatan/ *der;* ~**s,** ~**e** (abwertend) charlatan

Scharlatanerie *die;* ~, ~**n** [1] charlatanism [2] (einzelne Handlung) charlatanry

Scharlatanin *die;* ~, ~**nen** (abwertend) charlatan

Scharmützel /ʃarˈmʏtsl̩/ *das;* ~**s,** ~ (Milit.) skirmish

Scharnier /ʃarˈniːɐ̯/ *das;* ~**s,** ~**e** hinge

Schärpe /ˈʃɛrpə/ *die;* ~, ~**n** sash

scharren /ˈʃarən/
[A] *itr. V.* [1] (schaben, schleifen) scrape; **die Pferde ~ ungeduldig** the horses are pawing at the ground impatiently; **der Hund scharrte an der Tür** the dog scratched *or* pawed at the door; **mit den Füßen ~:** scrape one's feet [2] (wühlen) scratch
[B] *tr. V.* [1] scrape ‹*fallen leaves, twigs, sand, dirt*› [2] (herstellen) scrape, scratch out ‹*hole, hollow, etc.*›

Scharte /ˈʃartə/ *die;* ~, ~**n** [1] nick; **eine ~ auswetzen** (fig.) make good a/the mistake [2] (Gebirgs~) wind gap [3] (Schieß~) crenel

Scharteke /ʃarˈteːkə/ *die;* ~, ~**n** (abwertend) [1] (Buch) trashy old tome [2] (Frau) [old] hag; [old] bag (sl.)

schartig *Adj.* nicked; jagged

Schaschlik /ˈʃaʃlɪk/ *der od. das;* ~**s,** ~**s** (Kochk.) shashlik

schassen /ˈʃasn̩/ *tr. V.* (ugs.) throw *or* (coll.) chuck out

Schatten /ˈʃatn̩/ *der;* ~**s,** ~ [1] shadow; **nur noch ein ~ seiner selbst sein** (fig.) be only a shadow of one's former self; **einen** *od.* **seinen ~ auf etw.** (*Akk.*) **werfen** (fig. geh.) cast a *or* its shadow over sth.; **das große Ereignis wirft schon seine ~ voraus** (fig.) the big event is already making itself felt; **jmd./man kann nicht über seinen [eigenen] ~ springen** a leopard cannot change its spots (prov.) [2] (schattige Stelle) shade; **40° im ~:** 40° in the shade; **das Tal lag im ~:** the valley lay in shadow; **in jmds. ~ stehen** (fig.) be in sb.'s shadow; **jmdn./etw. in den ~ stellen** (fig.) put sb./sth. in the shade [3] (dunkle Stelle, auch fig.) shadow; **nicht der ~ eines Verdachts** not a shadow of suspicion [4] (Gestalt) shadow [5] **das Reich der ~** (Myth.) the realm of shades [6] (Beobachter) shadow

Schatten-: ~**bild** *das* [1] (Schatten) shadow; [2] (Schattenriss) silhouette; ~**boxen** *das;* ~~**s** shadow boxing; ~**dasein** *das: in* **ein ~dasein fristen** lead a shadowy existence; **aus dem** *od.* **seinem ~dasein heraustreten** emerge from its/one's shadowy existence; ~**gestalt** *die* [1] (Spukgestalt) ghostly figure; [2] (fig.) shadowy figure

schattenhaft *Adj.* shadowy; **etw. ist nur ~ zu erkennen** sth. is only vaguely recognizable

schatten-, Schatten-: ~**kabinett** *das* (Politik) shadow cabinet; ~**los** *Adj.* shadeless; without shade *postpos.;* ~**morelle** /-morɛlə/ *die;* ~, ~**n** morello cherry; ~**reich** *das* (Myth.) realm of shades; ~**riss,** *~**riß** *der* silhouette; ~**seite** *die* [1] shady side; **die ~seiten des Lebens kennen lernen** (fig.) get to know the dark side of life; [2] (Kehrseite) disadvantage; negative aspect; ~**spender** *der* (geh.) source of shade; ~**spiel** *das* [1] (Theater) shadow theatre; [2] (Stück) shadow play; shadow show; [3] (Kinderspiel) ~**spiele machen** make shadow pictures; ~**wirtschaft** *die* ≈ black economy [and social security scrounging]

schattieren *tr. V.* shade

Schattierung *die;* ~, ~**en** [1] shading [2] (Variante, Nuance) shade; **aller ideologischen/religiösen ~en** of every ideological/religious shade *or* (Amer.) stripe

schattig *Adj.* shady

Schatt·seite *die* (österr., schweiz.) ▸**Schattenseite**

Schatulle /ʃaˈtʊlə/ *die;* ~, ~**n** casket

Schatz /ʃats/ *der;* ~**es, Schätze** /ˈʃɛtsə/ [1] treasure *no indef. art.;* **ein ~ von Erinnerungen/Erfahrungen** (fig.) a wealth of memories/experience [2] *Pl.* (Bodenschätze) natural resources [3] (ugs.: Anrede) love (coll.); darling [4] (ugs.: hilfsbereiter Mensch) treasure (coll.); **sei ein ~ und räum schnell auf** be a dear and clear up quickly

Schätzchen /ˈʃɛtsçən/ *das;* ~**s,** ~**:** darling

schätzen /ˈʃɛtsn̩/
[A] *tr. V.* [1] (ein~, bewerten) estimate; **wie alt schätzt du ihn?** how old do you think he is?; **sich glücklich ~:** deem oneself lucky; **grob geschätzt** at a rough estimate; **ein Haus/einen Gebrauchtwagen ~:** value a house/a second-hand car [2] (ugs.: annehmen) reckon; think [3] (würdigen, hoch achten) **jmdn. ~:** hold sb. in high regard *or* esteem; **hoch geschätzt** highly esteemed *or* respected; **ein geschätzter Künstler** a highly regarded artist; **etw. zu ~ wissen** appreciate sth.; **ich weiß es zu ~, dass ...** I appreciate the fact that ...; **jmdn./etw. ~ lernen** come to appreciate or value sb./sth.
[B] *itr. V.* guess; **schätz mal** guess; have a guess

***schätzenlernen** ▸**schätzen A 3**

Schatz-: ~**kammer** *die* (hist.) treasure chamber; ~**kanzler** *der,* ~**kanzlerin** *die* Chancellor of the Exchequer (Brit.); ~**meister** *der,* ~**meisterin** *die* treasurer

Schätzung *die;* ~, ~**en** estimate; (eines Gebäudes, Grundstückwerts usw.) valuation; **nach grober/vorsichtiger ~:** at a rough/cautious estimate; **nach meiner ~:** according to my reckoning

schätzungs·weise *Adv.* roughly; approximately

Schätz·wert *der* estimated value

Schau /ʃau̯/ *die;* ~, ~**en** [1] (Ausstellung) exhibition [2] (Vorführung) show; **es war eine reine ~:** it was all show; **die** *od.* **eine ~ sein** (Jugendspr.) be really something; be something else (coll.); **eine ~ machen** *od.* **abziehen** (ugs.) (sich in Szene setzen) put on a show; (sich aufspielen) show off; (sich lautstark ereifern) make a scene *or* fuss; **jmdm. die ~ stehlen** steal the show from sb. [3] *in* **zur ~ stellen** (ausstellen) exhibit; display; (offen zeigen) display; **seine Gefühle zur ~ tragen** make a show of one's emotions [4] (geh.: Betrachtung) vision [5] (geh.: Blickwinkel) perspective

Schau-: ~**bild** *das* [1] (Diagramm) chart; [2] (Nachbildung) diagram; ~**bude** *die* show booth; ~**bühne** *die* (veralt.) theatre

Schauder /ˈʃau̯dɐ/ *der;* ~**s,** ~ (vor Kälte, Angst) shiver; (vor Angst) shudder; **mir lief ein ~ den Rücken hinunter** a shiver/shudder ran down my spine

schauderbar (ugs. scherzh.) ▸**schauderhaft**

schauder·erregend *Adj.* terrifying; horrifying

schauderhaft
[A] *Adj.* [1] (fürchterlich) terrible; dreadful; awful [2] (schaudererregend) ghastly; terrible; horrifying
[B] *adv.* [1] (fürchterlich) terribly; dreadfully [2] (überaus) terribly (coll.); dreadfully (coll.)

schaudern *itr. V.* [1] (vor Kälte) shiver [2] (vor Angst) shudder [3] *unpers.* **es schauderte ihn [vor Kälte]** he shivered [with cold]; **bei dem Gedanken schauderte [es] ihn** he shuddered at the thought

schauen
[A] *itr. V.* (bes. südd., österr., schweiz.) [1] (sehen) look; **jmdm./einander [fest] in die Augen ~:** look [straight] into sb.'s/each other's eyes; **auf jmdn./etw. ~:** look at sb./sth.; (fig.) look to sb./sth.; **um sich ~:** look around [one]; **zu tief in den Becher** *od.* **ins Glas geschaut haben** have had a drop too much [to drink]; have had one too many [2] (dreinblicken) look; **der hat vielleicht geschaut, als er uns sah** his eyes opened wide when he saw us; **seine Augen schauten vergnügt/spöttisch** amusement/mockery showed in his eyes [3] **schau, schau!** well, well; what do you know; **da schau her!** (Verwunderung ausdrückend) well, well; how about that?; (Empörung ausdrückend) well, what about 'that?; **da schau her, was du ...** just look what you ...; **schau [mal], ich finde, du solltest ...** look, I think you should ... [4] (sich kümmern um) **nach jmdm./etw. ~:** take *or* have a look at sb./sth.; **die Nachbarn haben nach den Blumen geschaut** the neighbours looked after the flowers [5] (Acht geben) **auf etw.** (*Akk.*) **~:** set store by sth.; **er schaut darauf, dass alle pünktlich sind** he sets store by everybody being punctual [6] (ugs.: sich bemühen) **schau, dass du ...** see *or* mind that you ... [7] (nachsehen) have a look
[B] *tr. V.* [1] (sich ansehen) **Fernsehen ~:** watch television; **~ Sie, was ich gefunden habe** look what I've found [2] (geh.: erfassen) behold

Schauer *der;* ~**s,** ~ [1] (Met.) shower [2] (geh.) ▸**Schauder**

schauer·artig *Adj.* (Met.) ~**e Regenfälle** showers; ~**e Schneefälle** snow showers

Schauer·geschichte *die* horror story

schauerlich
[A] *Adj.* [1] (schauererregend) horrifying; ghastly [2] (ugs.: fürchterlich) terrible (coll.); dreadful (coll.)
[B] *adv.* [1] (ugs.: fürchterlich) dreadfully (coll.), terribly (coll.); **ein ~ gemusterter Teppich** a hideously patterned carpet [2] (überaus) terribly (coll.); dreadfully (coll.)

Schauer·roman *der* Gothic novel

Schaufel /ˈʃau̯fl̩/ *die;* ~, ~**n** [1] shovel; (für Mehl usw.) scoop; (Kehrschaufel) dustpan; (vom ~rad, Mühlrad) paddle; **zwei ~n Erde** two shovelfuls of soil [2] (Jägerspr.: vom Geweih) palm

schaufeln /ˈʃau̯fl̩n/ *tr. itr. V.* shovel; dig ‹*hole, grave, trench, etc.*›

Schaufel-: ~**rad** *das* paddle wheel; ~**rad·dampfer** *der* paddle steamer; ~**rad·bagger** *der* bucket excavator

Schau·fenster *das* shop window

Schaufenster-: ~**auslage** *die* window display; ~**bummel** *der* window shopping expedition; **einen ~bummel machen** go window shopping; ~**dekorateur** *der,* ~**dekorateurin** *die* ▸❶ **S. 113** window dresser; ~**puppe** *die* mannequin

Schau-: ~**flug** *der* air display; (von einem Flugzeug) aerobatics demonstration; ~**geschäft** *das* show business *no art.;* ~**kampf** *der* (Boxen) exhibition fight; ~**kasten** *der* display case; showcase

Schaukel /ˈʃau̯kl̩/ *die;* ~, ~**n** [1] swing [2] (bes. südd.: Wippe) see-saw

schaukeln
[A] *itr. V.* [1] swing; (im Schaukelstuhl) rock; **auf einem Stuhl ~:** rock one's chair backwards and forwards [2] (sich hin und her bewegen) sway [to and fro]; (sich auf und ab bewegen) ‹*ship, boat*› pitch and toss; ‹*vehicle*› bump [up and down] [3] (unpers.) **auf der Überfahrt/in dem klapprigen Bus hat es ganz schön geschaukelt** the boat pitched and tossed quite a bit during the crossing/it was a pretty bumpy ride in the rickety bus
[B] *tr. V.* [1] rock; **ein Kind auf den Knien ~:** dandle a child on one's knee [2] (ugs.: fahren) take; **jmdn. durch die Gegend ~:** drive sb. round the area [3] (ugs.: bewerkstelligen) manage; **wir werden die Sache schon ~:** we'll manage it somehow

Schaukel-: ~**pferd** *das* rocking horse; ~**stuhl** *der* rocking chair

schau-, Schau-: ~**laufen** *das;* ~~**s** (Eislauf) exhibition skating *no art.;* ~**lustig** *Adj.* curious; ~**lustige** *der/die; adj. Dekl.* curious onlooker

Schaum /ʃau̯m/ *der;* ~**s, Schäume** /ˈʃɔy̯mə/ [1] foam; (von Seife usw.) lather; (von Getränken, Suppen usw.) froth; **etw. zu ~ schlagen** (Kochk.) beat sth. until frothy; **den ~ von etw. abschöpfen** (Kochk.) skim sth.; **~ schlagen** (fig.

ugs.) talk big 2 (Geifer) foam; froth; ~ **vor dem Mund haben** (auch fig.) foam *or* froth at the mouth

Schaum·bad *das* 1 (Badezusatz) bubble bath 2 (Wannenbad) bubble *or* foam bath

schäumen /ˈʃɔymən/

A *itr. V.* 1 (Schaum bilden) foam; froth; ‹*soap etc.*› lather; ‹*beer, fizzy drink, etc.*› froth [up] 2 (mit Wasser) produce lather; **stark/schwach** ~: produce a large amount of/little lather; **eine stark ~de Zahnpasta** a very frothy toothpaste 3 (wütend sein) fume; **vor Wut** ~: fume with anger

B *tr. V.* (Technik) foam ‹*plastics, concrete, etc.*›; **geschäumter Kunststoff** foamed plastic

Schaum-: ~**gebäck** *das* meringues *pl.*; ~**gummi** *der* foam rubber

schaumig *Adj.* frothy ‹*drink, dessert, etc.*›; sudsy, lathery ‹*water*›; **Butter und Zucker ~ rühren** beat butter and sugar until fluffy

Schaum-: ~**krone** *die* 1 (auf Wellen) white crest; 2 (auf Bier) head [of froth]; ~**schläger** *der* 1 (abwertend) boaster; 2 ▸**Schneebesen**; ~**schlägerei** *die* (abwertend) boasting; ~**schlägerin** *die* ▸~**schläger 1**; ~**stoff** *der* [plastic] foam; ~**wein** *der* sparkling wine

Schau-: ~**platz** *der* scene; **direkt vom ~platz berichten** give an on-the-spot report; ~**prozess**, *~**prozeß** *der* show trial

schaurig /ˈʃaurɪç/

A *Adj.* 1 (furchtbar) dreadful; frightful; (unheimlich) eerie; **eine ~e Geschichte** a blood-curdling story 2 (ugs.: grässlich, geschmacklos) hideous; dreadful (coll.)

B *adv.* 1 (fürchterlich) dreadfully; (unheimlich) eerily 2 (ugs.: grässlich, geschmacklos) hideously; horribly (coll.) 3 (ugs.: überaus) dreadfully (coll.)

schau-, Schau-: ~**spiel** *das* 1 (Drama) drama *no art.*; 2 (ernstes Stück) play; 3 (geh.: Anblick) spectacle; ~**spieler** *der* ▸❶ **S. 113** (auch fig.) actor; ~**spielerei** *die* 1 (Beruf) acting *no art.*; 2 (fig. ugs.: das Sichverstellen) play-acting; ~**spielerin** *die* (auch fig.) ▸❶ **S. 113** actress; ~**spielerisch** A *Adj.*; acting ‹*career*›; **eine großartige ~spielerische Leistung** a great piece of acting; **eine ~spielerische Begabung** a gift of *or* talent for acting B *adv.* **etw. ~spielerisch darstellen** act sth.; **sie ist ~spielerisch begabt** she has acting talent

schauspielern *itr. V.* (ugs.) 1 (als Schauspieler) act 2 (fig.) play-act

Schauspiel-: ~**führer** *der* theatre goer's guide; ~**haus** *das* theatre; playhouse; ~**kunst** *die* dramatic art

Schausteller /-ʃtɛlɐ/ *der;* ~**s**, ~ ▸❶ **S. 113** showman

Schaustellerin *die;* ~, ~**nen** ▸❶ **S. 113** show-woman

Schau-: ~**tafel** *die* illustrated chart; ~**turnen** *das* gymnastic display

Scheck /ʃɛk/ *der;* ~**s**, ~**s** ▸❶ **S. 299** cheque

Scheck·buch *das* (veralt.) chequebook

Schecke[1] /ˈʃɛkə/ *der;* ~**n**, ~**n** (Pferd) piebald; (Rind) mottled bull

Schecke[2] *die;* ~, ~**n** (Pferd) piebald; (Rind) mottled cow

Scheckheft *das* chequebook

scheckig *Adj.* 1 ▸**gescheckt** 2 (voller Flecken) blotchy ‹*face, skin, etc.*›; **sich ~ lachen** (ugs.) laugh oneself silly

Scheck·karte *die* ▸❶ **S. 299** cheque card

scheel /ʃe:l/ (ugs.)

A *Adj.* disapproving; (misstrauisch) suspicious; (neidisch) envious; jealous

B *adv.* disapprovingly; (misstrauisch) suspiciously; (neidisch) enviously; jealously

Scheffel /ˈʃɛfl̩/ *der;* ~**s**, ~: bushel; *s. auch* **Licht**

scheffeln *tr. V.* (ugs.) rake in (coll.) ‹*money, profits, etc.*›; pile up, accumulate ‹*medals, awards, etc.*›

scheffel·weise *Adv.* (ugs.) by the sackful; in large quantities; ~ **Geld haben/verdienen** have/earn stacks of money (coll.)

Scheibchen /ˈʃaipçən/ *das;* ~**s**, ~ (von Fleisch, Brot usw.) [small] slice; (aus Kunststoff, Metall usw.) [small] disc

Scheibe /ˈʃaibə/ *die;* ~, ~**n** 1 (flacher, runder Gegenstand) disc; (Sportjargon: Puck) puck; (Schieß~) target; (Wähl~) dial 2 (abgeschnittene ~) slice; **etw. in ~n schneiden** slice sth. up; cut sth. [up] into slices; **sich** (*Dat.*) **von jmdm./etw. eine ~ abschneiden können** (fig.) be able to learn a thing or two from sb./sth.; **... in ~n** slices of *or* sliced ... 3 (Glas~) pane [of glass]; (Fenster~) [window] pane; (Windschutz~) windscreen (Brit.); windshield (Amer.); (Spiegel~) glass; **die ~n des Wagens herunterdrehen** wind down the car windows 4 (ugs.: Schallplatte) disc; record

Scheiben-: ~**bremse** *die* (Technik) disc brake; ~**gardine** *die* net curtain; ~**honig** *der* 1 comb honey; 2 ▸~**kleister**; ~**kleister** *der* (ugs. verhüll.) ~**kleister!** blast [it]! (coll.); damn it! (coll.); **so ein ~kleister!** what a blasted nuisance *or* mess!; ~**rad** *das* disc wheel; ~**schießen** *das;* ~~**s** (Milit., Sport) target-shooting; ~**waschanlage** *die* (Kfz-W.) windscreen washer system *or* unit; ~**wischer** *der* windscreen wiper

Scheich /ʃaiç/ *der;* ~**[e]s**, ~**s** *od.* ~**e** 1 sheikh 2 (ugs.: Freund) guy (coll.); bloke (Brit. sl.)

Scheichtum *das;* ~**s**, **Scheichtümer** /-ty:mɐ/ sheikhdom

Scheide /ˈʃaidə/ *die;* ~, ~**n** 1 (Waffen~) sheath; (des Schwerts, Säbels) scabbard; sheath 2 ▸❶ **S. 435** (Anat.) vagina

scheiden

A *unr. tr. V.* 1 dissolve ‹*marriage*›; divorce ‹*married couple*›; **eine geschiedene Frau** a divorced woman; a divorcee; **sich [von jmdm.] ~ lassen** get divorced *or* get a divorce [from sb.]; **sie lässt sich nicht [von ihm] ~:** she won't give him a divorce; **ich bin [schuldig/unschuldig] geschieden** I am divorced [and I was the guilty/innocent party] 2 (geh.: trennen) divide; separate; **von dem Moment an waren wir geschiedene Leute** from that moment on, we went our separate ways; **wir sind geschiedene Leute!** you and I must part 3 (geh.: unter~) distinguish 4 (bes. Chemie) separate; extract

B *unr. itr. V.; mit sein* (geh.) 1 (auseinander gehen) part 2 (sich entfernen) depart; leave; **von jmdm. ~:** part from sb.; **aus dem Dienst/Amt ~:** retire from service/one's post *or* office; **aus dem Leben ~:** depart this life

C *unr. refl. V.* (sich unter~) diverge; differ; *s. auch* **Geist 4**

Scheide·weg *der:* *in* **am** *od.* **an einem ~ stehen** face a crucial decision

Scheidung *die;* ~, ~**en** 1 (Ehe~) divorce; **die ~ einreichen** file [a petition] for divorce; **die ~ aussprechen** grant the divorce; **in ~ leben** be in the process of getting a divorce 2 (Unter~) distinction

Scheidungs-: ~**grund** *der* grounds *pl.* for divorce; **sie war der ~grund** they got divorced because of her; ~**kind** *das* (Jargon) child of a/the divorced couple; ~**klage** *die* petition for divorce; ~**rate** *die* divorce rate; ~**urkunde** *die* divorce certificate; ~**waise** *die* (Jargon) [neglected] child of a/the divorced couple

Schein /ʃain/ *der;* ~**[e]s**, ~**e** 1 (Licht~) light; **der ~ des brennenden Hauses/der sinkenden Sonne** the glow of the burning house/setting sun 2 (An~) appearances *pl.*, *no art.*; (Täuschung) pretence; **den ~ wahren** keep up appearances; **der ~ spricht gegen ihn** appearances are against him; **der ~ trügt** appearances are deceptive; **~ und Wirklichkeit** *od.* **Sein** appearances and reality; **etw. nur zum ~ tun** [only] pretend to do sth.; make a show of doing sth. 3 (Bescheinigung) receipt; (vom Arzt) doctor's certificate; (Hochschulw.) certificate 4 ▸❶ **S. 299** (Geld~) note

Schein·argument *das* spurious argument

scheinbar

A *Adj.* (nicht wirklich) apparent; seeming

B *adv.* 1 (nicht wirklich) seemingly 2 (ugs.) ▸**anscheinend**

Schein·blüte *die* 1 (Bot.) composite flower 2 (fig.) illusory boom

scheinen *unr. itr. V.* 1 (Helligkeit ausstrahlen) shine 2 (den Eindruck erwecken) seem; appear; **es scheint, dass .../als ob ...** it appears that .../as if ...; **mir scheint, [dass] ...** it seems *or* appears to me that ...; **wie es scheint ...** apparently; **er kommt scheints nicht mehr** (ugs.) it doesn't look as though he's coming now; **sie schienen es zufrieden zu sein** (veralt.) they seemed to be satisfied *or* happy with it

schein-, Schein-: ~**gefecht** *das* (auch fig.) mock fight *or* battle; ~**heilig** A *Adj.* (heuchlerisch) hypocritical; (Nichtwissen vortäuschend) innocent; B *adv.* (heuchlerisch) hypocritically; (Nichtwissen vortäuschend) innocently; ~**heiligkeit** *die* hypocrisy; ~**schwangerschaft** *die* (Med.) false pregnancy; ~**tod** *der* (Med.) apparent death; ~**tot** *Adj.* 1 (Med.) apparently *or* seemingly dead; 2 (salopp: alt) with one foot in the grave *postpos.*; ~**tot sein** have one foot in the grave; ~**welt** *die* illusory *or* unreal world; ~**werfer** *der* floodlight; (am Auto) headlight; (im Theater, Museum usw.) spotlight; (Suchscheinwerfer) searchlight; ~**werfer·licht** *das* floodlight; (des Autos) headlights *pl.*; (im Theater, Museum usw.) spotlight [beam]; (des Suchscheinwerfers) searchlight [beam]; **im ~werferlicht [der Öffentlichkeit] stehen** be in the [public] spotlight

scheiß-, Scheiß- (derb) bloody (Brit. sl.)

Scheiß /ʃais/ *der;* ~ (salopp) shit *no indef. art.* (coarse); crap *no indef. art.* (coarse); **so ein ~!** oh, shit! (coarse); ~ **machen** (Fehler machen) make a bloody mess (Brit. sl.); (unklug handeln) act in a bloody silly way (Brit. sl.)

Scheiß·dreck *der* (derb) 1 (Kot) shit (coarse); crap (coarse) 2 (Blödsinn, Minderwertiges) shit *no indef. art.* (coarse); crap *no indef. art.* (*coarse*); (Angelegenheiten) bloody (Brit.) *or* damned business (sl.); **red keinen ~!** don't talk crap! (coarse); **das geht dich einen ~ an** that's none of your bloody business (Brit. sl.); **einen ~ werde ich tun** like hell I will (coll.)

Scheiße /ˈʃaisə/ *die;* ~ (derb) (auch fig.) shit (coarse); crap (coarse); **[bis zum Hals] in der ~ sitzen** *od.* **stecken** (fig.) be in the shit (coarse); be up shit creek (coarse); **der Film ist große ~** (fig.) the film is a load of shit *or* crap (coarse); **verdammte/schöne ~!** shit (coarse); bloody hell (Brit. sl.)

scheiß·egal *Adj.:* *in* **~ sein** (derb) not matter a damn (sl.); **das ist mir ~:** I don't give a damn (sl.) *or* (coarse) shit; **das kann dir doch ~ sein** you needn't give a damn (sl.) *or* (coarse) shit about that

scheißen *unr. itr. V.* (derb) 1 (den Darm entleeren) [have *or* (Amer.) take a] shit (coarse); crap (coarse); have a crap (coarse); **in die Hose ~:** shit one's pants (coarse); **auf jmdn./etw. ~** (fig.) not give a shit (coarse) *or* (sl.) damn about sb./sth.; **wir ~ auf ihn/drauf** (fig.) to hell with him/with it/that (coll.) 2 **[einen] ~** (eine Blähung entweichen lassen) fart (coarse)

Scheißer *der;* ~**s**, ~ 1 (derb) bastard (coll.); shithead (coarse) 2 (salopp: unbedeutender Mensch) arsehole (Brit. coarse); asshole (Amer. coarse) 3 (fam.: Kosewort) monkey

scheiß-, Scheiß-: ~**freundlich** *Adj., adv.* (derb) as nice as pie; ~**haufen** *der* (derb) pile of shit (coarse); ~**haus** *das* (derb) bog (sl.); shithouse (coarse); ~**kerl** *der* (derb) bastard (coll.); ~**vornehm** *Adj.* (derb) bloody (Brit. sl.) *or* (coll.) damn posh

Scheit /ʃait/ *das;* ~**[e]s**, ~**e** *od.* ~**er** ▸**Holzscheit**

Scheitel /ˈʃaitl̩/ *der;* ~**s**, ~ 1 parting; (geh.: Haar) hair; **einen ~ ziehen** make a parting 2 (oberste Stelle) top of one's head; **vom ~ bis zur Sohle** from head to toe 3 (höchster Punkt) vertex 4 (Math.: bei Winkel) apex; vertex 5 (Math.: bei Kurve) vertex

scheiteln *tr. V.* part ‹*hair*›

Scheitel-: ~**punkt** *der* vertex; ~**winkel** *der* (Math.) vertically opposite angle

Scheiter·haufen *der:* **auf dem ~ sterben/verbrannt werden** die/be burned at the stake;

S

einen ~ für die Hexe errichten build a pile of wood on which the witch is to be burnt

scheitern /ˈʃaitɐn/ *itr. V.; mit sein* fail; ‹*talks, marriage*› break down; ‹*plan, project*› fail, fall through; **an jmdn./etw. ~:** fall through *or* fail because of sb./sth.; **die Partei scheiterte an der Fünfprozentklausel** the party was defeated by the five-per-cent clause; **jmds. Pläne zum Scheitern bringen** thwart *or* frustrate sb.'s plans; **zum Scheitern verurteilt sein** be doomed to failure; **eine gescheiterte Existenz sein** be a failure

Schekel /ˈʃeːkl̩/ *der;* **~s, ~** ▸ⓘ **S. 299** shekel

Schelde /ˈʃɛldə/ *die;* **~:** Schelde [tributary]

Schelf /ʃɛlf/ *der od. das;* **~s, ~e** (Geogr.) continental shelf

Schellack /ˈʃɛlak/ *der;* **~s, ~e** shellac

Schelle /ˈʃɛlə/ *die;* **~, ~n** 1 bell 2 *Pl.* (Spielkartenfarbe) bell; *s. auch* **Pik²**

schellen *itr. V.* (westd.) ring; **an der Tür dreimal ~:** ring the [door] bell three times; **nach jmdm. ~:** ring for sb.; **es schellt** the bell is ringing

Schellen-: ~baum *der* Turkish crescent; pavillon chinois; **~kranz** *der* tambourine (*without drumskin*); **~trommel** *die* tambourine

Schell·fisch *der* cod

Schell·kraut *das:* **[großes] ~:** [greater] celandine

Schelm /ʃɛlm/ *der;* **~[e]s, ~e** rascal; rogue

Schelmen-: ~roman *der* (Literaturw.) picaresque novel; **~streich** *der,* **~stück** *das* roguish prank

Schelmerei *die;* **~, ~en** 1 (Eigenschaft) roguishness; roguery 2 roguish prank

Schelmin *die;* **~, ~nen** rascal; rogue

schelmisch

A *Adj.* roguish; mischievous

B *adv.* roguishly; mischievously

Schelte /ˈʃɛltə/ *die;* **~, ~n** (geh.) scolding; **~ bekommen** be given *or* get a scolding; **sei pünktlich, sonst gibt es ~:** be punctual, otherwise you'll get a scolding

schelten (bes. südd., sonst geh.)

A *unr. itr. V.* **auf** *od.* **über jmdn./etw. ~:** moan about sb./sth.; **[mit jmdm.] ~:** scold [sb.]

B *unr. tr. V.* 1 (tadeln) scold 2 (geh.: nennen) call

Schelt·wort *das; Pl.* **~~e** (geh.) oath

Schema /ˈʃeːma/ *das;* **~s, ~s** *od.* **~ta** *od.* **Schemen** 1 (Muster) pattern; **sie lässt sich in kein ~ pressen** (fig.) she does not fit into any pattern *or* mould; *s. auch* **F** 2 (Skizze) diagram

schematisch

A *Adj.* 1 (einem Schema folgend) diagrammatic 2 (mechanisch) mechanical

B *adv.* 1 (als Schema) in diagram form 2 (mechanisch) mechanically

schematisieren *tr. V.* 1 schematize; **etw. schematisiert darstellen** describe sth. by means of a simple formula 2 (vereinfachen) simplify

Schematisierung *die;* **~, ~en** 1 schematization 2 (Vereinfachung) simplification

Schemel /ˈʃeːml̩/ *der;* **~s, ~** 1 (Hocker) stool 2 (südd.: Fußbank) footstool

Schemen¹ ▸ **Schema**

Schemen² /ˈʃeːmən/ *der od. das;* **~s, ~:** shadowy figure

schemenhaft

A *Adj.* shadowy

B *adv.* **etw. ~ erkennen/sehen** make out/see only the outline *or* silhouette of sth.

Schenke /ˈʃɛŋkə/ *die;* **~, ~n** pub (Brit.); bar (Amer.); (bes. auf dem Lande) inn

Schenkel /ˈʃɛŋkl̩/ *der;* **~s, ~** 1 ▸ⓘ **S. 435** (Ober~) thigh; **sich** (*Dat.*) **auf die ~ schlagen** slap one's thigh; **dem Pferd die ~ geben** press one's horse on 2 (Math.) side 3 (von einer Zange, Schere) shank; (vom Zirkel) leg

Schenkel-: ~bruch *der* ▸ⓘ **S. 439** (Med.) fracture of the femur; **~druck** *der; Pl.* **~drücke, ~hilfe** *die* (Reiten) knee pressure *no indef. art.*; **~klatschend** *Adj.* thigh-slapping

schenken

A *tr. V.* 1 (geben) give; **jmdm. etw. [zum Geburtstag] ~:** give sb. sth. *or* sth. to sb. [as a birthday present *or* for his/her birthday]; **etw. geschenkt bekommen** be given sth. [as a present]; **sich gegenseitig etw. ~:** give each other presents; exchange presents; **den Rest des Geldes schenke ich dir** you can keep the rest of the money; **ich möchte nichts geschenkt haben** I don't want any presents; (bevorzugt werden) I don't want to be given special *or* preferential treatment; **das möchte ich nicht geschenkt haben, das wäre mir geschenkt zu teuer** (ugs.) I wouldn't want that if it was given to me; **das ist ja geschenkt!** (ugs.) it's a gift!; **geschenkt ist geschenkt** a gift is a gift; **sie schenkte ihm fünf Kinder** (fig. geh.) she bore him five children; *s. auch* **Gaul** 2 (verleihen) give 3 (ugs.: erlassen) **jmdm./sich etw. ~:** spare sb./oneself sth.; **ihr ist im Leben nichts geschenkt worden** she has never had it easy in life 4 **jmdm./einer Sache Beachtung/Aufmerksamkeit ~:** give sb./sth. one's attention; **jmdm. das Leben ~:** spare sb.'s life; **einem Kind das Leben ~** (geh.) give birth to a child 5 (geh. veralt.: eingießen) pour

B *refl. V.* (ugs.: erlassen) **sich** (*Dat.*) **etw. ~:** give sth. a miss; **deine Ausreden kannst du dir ~:** you can save your excuses

C *itr. V.* give presents *or* gifts

Schenker *der;* **~s, ~, Schenkerin** *die;* **~, ~nen** 1 giver 2 (Rechtsspr.) donator

Schenkung *die;* **~, ~en** (Rechtsw.) gift

scheppern /ˈʃɛpɐn/ *itr. V.* (ugs.) clank; ‹*bell*› clang; **es hat gescheppert** there was a clatter *or* clanking; (beim Autounfall) there was a smash *or* crash; (es gab eine Ohrfeige) he/she got a box on the ears

Scherbe /ˈʃɛrbə/ *die;* **~, ~n** fragment; (archäologischer Fund) [pot]sherd; **die ~n zusammenkehren** sweep up the [broken] pieces; **die ~n des Tellers/Spiegels** the fragments *or* [broken] pieces of the plate/mirror; **beim Spülen hat es ~n gegeben** something got broken during the washing-up; **es gab ~n** (fig.) sparks flew; **in tausend ~n zerspringen** be smashed to smithereens; **die ~n ihrer Ehe** (fig.) the shattered remains of their marriage; **~n bringen Glück** (Spr.) break a thing, mend your luck

Scherben-: ~gericht *das* ostracism *no art.*; **ein ~gericht über jmdn. veranstalten** (fig.) judge sb. with unnecessary harshness; **~haufen** *der* pile of broken fragments *or* pieces; (fig.) shattered remains

Schere /ˈʃeːrə/ *die;* **~, ~n** 1 (Werkzeug) scissors *pl.*; **eine ~:** a pair of scissors 2 (Zool.) claw 3 (Turnen) scissors

scheren¹ *unr. tr. V.* 1 crop; (von Haar befreien) shear, clip ‹*sheep*›; clip ‹*dog, horse, etc.*›; **sich** (*Dat.*) **den Bart ~** (veralt.) trim one's beard; (abrasieren) shave one's beard 2 (Textilind.) shear 3 (kürzen) cut, mow ‹*lawn*›; clip, trim ‹*hedge, bush, etc.*›

scheren² *tr., refl. V.* **sich um jmdn./etw. nicht ~:** not care about sb./sth.; **es schert ihn [herzlich] wenig** *od.* **nicht im Geringsten** he could not care less *or* in the least

scheren³ *refl. V.* **scher dich in dein Zimmer** go *or* get [off] to your room; **~ Sie sich an die Arbeit/in Ihr Büro** get to work/[off] to your office; **sich ins Bett ~:** get [off] to bed; *s. auch* **Henker 2; Teufel**

Scheren-: ~gitter *das* [folding] grille; **~griff** *der* (Turnen) scissors hold; **~schlag** *der* (Fußball) scissors kick; **~schleifer** *der,* **~schleiferin** *die* knife grinder; **~schnitt** *der* silhouette

Schererei *die;* **~, ~en** (ugs.) trouble *no pl.*

Scherflein /ˈʃɛrflain/ *das;* **~s, ~** (geh.) mite; **[s]ein ~ [zu etw.] beitragen** *od.* **beisteuern** make one's/a little contribution [to sth.]

Scherge /ˈʃɛrgə/ *der;* **~n, ~n** (geh.) henchman

Scher-: ~messer *das* [cutting] blade; **~sprung** *der* (bes. Turnen) scissors jump

Scherung *die;* **~, ~en** 1 (Math.) shearing 2 (Mechanik) shear[ing]

Scherz /ʃɛrts/ *der;* **~es, ~e** joke; **seine ~e mit jmdm. treiben** play jokes on sb.; **er versteht keinen ~:** he can't take a joke; **mach keine ~e** you must be joking; **seine ~e über jmdn./etw. machen** make *or* crack jokes about sb./sth.; **etw. aus** *od.* **zum ~ sagen** say sth. as a joke *or* in jest; **... und solche** *od.* **ähnliche ~e** (ugs.) ... and what have you (coll.); **~ beiseite** joking aside *or* apart; **[ganz] ohne ~** (ugs.) no kidding (coll.)

Scherz·artikel *der* joke article

scherzen *itr. V.* joke; **mit etw.** *od.* **über etw.** (*Akk.*) **~:** joke about sth.; **Sie belieben zu ~** (geh., oft iron.) you jest; **ich scherze nicht** I'm not joking; **mit jmdm./etw. ist nicht zu ~:** sb./sth. is not to be trifled with

Scherz-: ~frage *die* riddle; **~gedicht** *das* humorous poem

scherzhaft

A *Adj.* jocular; joking *attrib*

B *adv.* jocularly; jokingly; **etw. ~ sagen/meinen** say/mean sth. as a joke *or* in fun

Scherzo /ˈskɛrtso/ *das;* **~s, ~s** *od.* **Scherzi** (Musik) scherzo

Scherz·wort *das; Pl.* **~~e** joke; witticism

schesen /ˈʃeːzn̩/ *itr. V.; mit sein* (bes. nordd.) rush

scheu /ʃɔy/

A *Adj.* (schüchtern) shy; timid ‹*animal*›; (ehrfürchtig) awed; **~ machen** frighten ‹*animal*›; *s. auch* **Pferd**

B *adv.* 1 (schüchtern) shyly 2 (von Tieren) timidly

Scheu *die;* **~** 1 (Schüchternheit) shyness; (Ehrfurcht) awe; **voller ~ sein** be very shy *or* timid/be full of awe; **ohne jede ~:** without any inhibitions 2 (von Tieren) timidity

Scheuche /ˈʃɔyçə/ *die;* **~, ~n** scarecrow

scheuchen *tr. V.* 1 (treiben) shoo; drive 2 (fig.) force; **jmdn. zum Arzt/an die Arbeit ~:** make sb. go *or* urge sb. to go to the doctor/to work

scheuen

A *tr. V.* (meiden) shrink from; shun ‹*people, light, company, etc.*›; **weder Kosten noch Mühe ~:** spare neither expense nor effort; **Arbeit scheue ich nicht** I'm not afraid of work

B *refl. V.* **sich vor etw.** (*Dat.*) **~:** be afraid of *or* shrink from sth.

C *itr. V.* ‹*horse*› shy (**vor** + *Dat.* at)

Scheuer *die;* **~, ~n** (bes. südd.) barn

Scheuer-: ~bürste *die* scrubbing brush; **~lappen** *der* cleaning cloth (*for wiping surfaces*); **~leiste** *die* 1 (Fußleiste) skirting [board] (Brit.); baseboard (Amer.); 2 (Seew.) rubbing strake; **~mittel** *das* scouring agent

scheuern

A *tr., itr. V.* 1 (reinigen) scour; scrub 2 (reiben) rub; chafe

B *tr. V.* 1 (reiben an) rub 2 *in* **jmdm. eine ~** (ugs.) give sb. a clout; clout sb.; **eine gescheuert kriegen** (ugs.) get a clout round the ears (coll.)

C *refl. V.* (reiben) **sich** (*Akk.*) **wund ~:** rub oneself raw; chafe oneself; **sich** (*Dat.*) **das Knie [wund] ~:** rub one's knee raw; chafe one's knee

Scheuer-: ~pulver *das* scouring powder; **~sand** *der* scouring sand; **~tuch** *das; Pl.* **~tücher** scouring cloth

Scheu·klappe *die* blinker; **~n haben** *od.* **tragen** wear blinkers; be blinkered (also fig.)

Scheune /ˈʃɔynə/ *die;* **~, ~n** barn

Scheunen-: ~drescher *der: in* **wie ein ~drescher essen** *od.* **fressen** (salopp) eat like a horse (coll.); **~tor** *das* barn door; *s. auch* **dastehen 1**

Scheusal /ˈʃɔyzal/ *das;* **~s, ~e** *od.* (ugs.) **Scheusäler** /ˈʃɔyzɛlɐ/ (abwertend) monster

scheußlich /ˈʃɔyslɪç/

A *Adj.* 1 dreadful 2 (ugs.: äußerst unangenehm) terrible (coll.); dreadful (coll.); dreadful (coll.), ghastly (coll.) ‹*weather, taste, smell*›

B *adv.* 1 dreadfully 2 (ugs.: sehr) terribly (coll.);

dreadfully (coll.); **sich ~ erkälten** catch a dreadful cold (coll.)

Scheußlichkeit *die; ~, ~en* 1 dreadfulness 2 (etw. Scheußliches) dreadful thing; (Grausamkeit) atrocity

Schi /ʃiː/ *usw.* ▸**Ski** *usw.*

Schicht /ʃɪçt/ *die; ~, ~en* 1 (Lage) layer; (Geol.) stratum; (von Farbe) coat; (sehr dünn) film 2 (Gesellschafts~) stratum; **breite ~en [der Bevölkerung]** broad sections of the population; **in allen ~en** at all levels of society; **die besitzenden ~en** the propertied classes 3 (Abschnitt eines Arbeitstages, Arbeitsgruppe) shift; **~ haben, auf ~ sein** be working one's shift; **er geht morgens zur ~:** he's on the morning shift; **~ arbeiten** work shifts; be on shift work

Schicht-: ~arbeit *die* shift work; **~arbeiter** *der,* **~arbeiterin** *die* shift worker

schichten *tr. V.* stack; **die Bretter zu einem Stapel ~:** stack the boards [up]

Schicht-: ~gestein *das* (Geol.) ▸**Sedimentgestein**; **~käse** *der: low-fat quark containing a layer of higher-fat quark;* **~stufe** *die* (Geol.) cuesta

Schichtung *die; ~, ~en* stacking; (Geol., Met., Soziol.) stratification

schicht-, Schicht-: ~unterricht *der* teaching *no art.* in shifts; **~wechsel** *der* change of shifts; **~wechsel ist um 6** we/they *etc.* change shifts at 6; **~weise** *Adv.* 1 in layers; layer by layer; (bei Farben) in coats; 2 (in Gruppen) in shifts

schick /ʃɪk/

A *Adj.* 1 stylish; stylish, chic ‹*clothes, fashions*›; (elegant) smart ‹*woman, girl, man*› 2 (ugs.: großartig, toll) great (coll.); fantastic (coll.)

B *adv.* 1 stylishly; stylishly, smartly ‹*furnished, decorated*›; **~ frisiert sein** have a fashionable hairstyle *or* (coll.) hairdo 2 (ugs.: großartig, toll) **abends sind wir ~ ausgegangen** we had a great evening out (coll.)

Schick *der; ~[e]s* 1 style; (von Frauenmode, Frau) chic; style 2 (oberd., niederd.) **nun hat** *od.* **kriegt alles wieder seinen ~!** now everything's as it should be

schicken

A *tr. V.* send; **jmdm. etw. ~, etw. an jmdn. ~:** send sth. to sb.; send sb. sth.; **jmdm. etw. ins Haus ~:** send sth. to sb.'s home; **jmdn. nach Hause/auf** *od.* **in die** *od.* **zur Schule/ins** *od.* **zu Bett/in den Krieg ~:** send sb. home/to school/to bed/to war; **jmdn. einkaufen** *od.* **zum Einkaufen ~:** send sb. to do the shopping

B *itr. V.* (rufen, holen lassen) **nach jmdm. ~:** send for sb.

C *refl. V.* 1 (unpers. veralt.: sich ziemen) be proper *or* fitting; **das schickt sich nicht für eine junge Dame** it does not befit *or* become a young lady; it is not proper for a young lady 2 (geduldig ertragen) **sich in etw.** (*Akk.*) **~:** resign *or* reconcile oneself to sth.

Schickeria /ʃɪkəˈriːa/ *die; ~* (ugs.) smart set

Schicki[micki] /ˈʃɪkɪ(ˈmɪkɪ)/ *der; ~s, ~s* (ugs.) 1 (Mensch) trendy (coll.) 2 (Modisches) trendy (coll.) goods *pl.*/clothes *pl.*/architecture *etc.*

schicklich (veralt.)

A *Adj.* proper; fitting; (dezent) seemly

B *adv.* fittingly; (dezent) in a seemly way

-schicksal *das:* **ein Emigranten~/Flüchtlings~/Behinderten~:** life *or* experiences as an emigré/a refugee/a handicapped person

Schicksal /ˈʃɪkzaːl/ *das; ~s, ~e* 1 (Geschick, Los) fate; destiny; (schweres Los) fate; **ich habe manche schwere ~e miterlebt** I've witnessed many a hard fate; **[das ist] ~** (ugs.) it's just fate; **er hat ein schweres ~ gehabt** fate has been unkind to him 2 (höhere Macht) fate *no art.*; destiny *no art.*; **das ~ hat es mit ihm gut gemeint** fortune smiled on him; **~ spielen** play the role of fate *or* destiny

schicksalhaft

A *Adj.* fateful

B *adv.* **~ bedingt/verbunden** determined/linked by fate; **sie sind ~ aufeinander angewiesen** their fates are inextricably linked

schicksals-, Schicksals-: ~drama *das* (Literaturw.) fate drama; **~frage** *die* crucial question; (Angelegenheit) fundamental issue; **~gefährte** *der,* **~gefährtin** *die* companion in misfortune; **die drei waren ~gefährten** the three shared the same fate; **~gemeinschaft** *die:* **sie bildeten** *od.* **waren eine ~gemeinschaft** they shared a common fate; **~genosse** *der,* **~genossin** *die* ▸**~gefährte**; **~glaube** *der* fatalism; **~göttin** *die* goddess of fate; **die ~göttinnen** the Fates; **~schlag** *der* stroke of fate; **~schwer** *Adj.* momentous ‹*day, decision*›; **~tragödie** *die* (Literaturw.) ▸**~drama**

Schickse /ˈʃɪksə/ *die; ~, ~n* (salopp abwertend) floozie (coll.)

Schickung *die; ~, ~en* (geh.) stroke of fate

Schiebe-: ~dach *das* sliding roof; sunroof; **~fenster** *das* sliding window

schieben /ˈʃiːbn̩/

A *unr. tr. V.* 1 push; push, wheel ‹*bicycle, pram, shopping trolley*›; (drängen) push; shove; **die Lokomotive schob die Waggons auf ein Nebengleis** the locomotive shunted the wagons into a siding 2 (stecken) put; (gleiten lassen) slip; **den Riegel vor die Tür ~:** slip the bolt across; **den Ball ins Tor ~** (Fußballjargon) slip the ball into the net; **etw. von einem Tag auf den anderen ~** (fig.) keep putting sth. off from one day to the next 3 **etw. auf jmdn./etw. ~:** blame sb./sth. for sth.; **die Schuld/die Verantwortung auf jmdn. ~:** put the blame on sb. *or* lay the blame at sb.'s door/lay the responsibility at sb.'s door 4 (salopp: handeln mit) traffic in; push ‹*drugs*›

B *unr. refl. V.* 1 (sich zwängen) **sich durch die Menge ~:** push one's way through the crowd 2 (sich bewegen) move; **ihr Rock schob sich nach oben** her skirt slid up; **sich an die Spitze ~** (Sportjargon) move up to the front

C *unr. itr. V.* 1 push; (heftig) push; shove 2 *mit sein* (salopp: gehen) mooch (coll.) 3 (ugs.: mit etw. handeln) **mit etw. ~:** traffic in sth. 4 (Skat) shove

Schieber *der; ~s, ~* 1 (an einer Tür) bolt; (am Ofen) damper; (an Rohrleitungen) sluice valve 2 (ugs.: Schwarzhändler) black marketeer; (Drogen~) pusher; (Waffen~) gun-runner 3 (ugs.: Tanz) one-step

Schiebe-: ~regler *der* 1 (Tech.) slide control; 2 (DV) scroll box; **~tür** *die* sliding door; **~wand** *die* sliding partition

Schieberin *die; ~, ~nen* ▸**Schieber 2**

Schieber·mütze *die* ▸**Schlägermütze**

Schieb-: ~lade *die* ▸**Schublade**; **~lehre** *die* (Technik) vernier [calliper] gauge

Schiebung *die; ~, ~en* (ugs.) 1 (betrügerisches Geschäft) shady deal 2 (Begünstigung) pulling strings; (bei einer Wahl, einem Wettbewerb) rigging; (bei einem Wettlauf, -rennen) fixing; **„[das ist ja] ~!", riefen die Zuschauer** the spectators shouted '[it's a] fix!'

schied /ʃiːt/ *1. u. 3. Pers. Sg. Prät. v.* **scheiden**

schiedlich-friedlich *Adv.* amicably

Schieds-: ~frau *die* arbitrator; **~gericht** *das* 1 (Rechtsw.) arbitration tribunal; 2 (Sport) panel of judges; (Fechten) jury; **~kommission** *die* (Rechtsw.) ▸**~gericht 1**; **~mann** *der; Pl.* **~leute** *od.* **~männer** arbitrator; **~richter** *der* ▸**i S. 113** 1 (Sport) referee; (Tennis, Tischtennis, Hockey, Kricket, Federball) umpire; (Eislauf, Ski, Schwimmen) judge; 2 (Rechtsw.) arbitrator; **~richter·ball** *der* (Fußball) drop ball; (Basketball) jump ball; (Wasserball) neutral throw; **~richterin** *die* ▸**i S. 113** ▸**~richter**; **~richterlich** *Adj.* 1 (Sport) ‹*decision, permission, etc.*› of the referee/umpire; 2 (Rechtsw.) **die ~richterliche Entscheidung** the decision of the arbitrator/arbitrators; **~richtern** *itr., tr. V.* (Sport) referee; (Tennis, Tischtennis, Hockey, Kricket, Federball) umpire; **~spruch** *der* (Rechtsw.) arbitration decision

schief /ʃiːf/

A *Adj.* 1 (schräg) leaning ‹*wall, fence, post*›; (nicht parallel) crooked; not straight *pred.*; crooked ‹*nose*›; sloping, inclined ‹*surface*›; worn[-down] ‹*heels*›; (fig.) wry ‹*smile, look*›; **eine ~e Schulter haben** have one shoulder higher than the other; **er hält den Kopf ~:** he holds his head to one side; **der Schiefe Turm von Pisa** the Leaning Tower of Pisa; **eine ~e Ebene** (Math., Phys.) an inclined plane; **sich die Absätze ~ laufen** *od.* **treten** wear down one's heels on one side; *s. auch* **Bahn 1**; **Gesicht 1** 2 (fig.: verzerrt) distorted ‹*picture, presentation, view, impression*›; false ‹*comparison*›

B *adv.* 1 (schräg) **der Baum ist ~ gewachsen** the tree has grown crooked *or* hasn't grown straight; **das Bild hängt/der Teppich liegt ~:** the picture/carpet is crooked; **der Tisch steht ~:** the table isn't level; **sich** (*Dat.*) **die Mütze ~ aufsetzen** put one's cap on at an angle; **jmdn. ~ ansehen** (ugs.) look at sb. askance; **~ gewickelt sein** (*ugs.*) be very much mistaken; **~ liegen** (*ugs.*) be on the wrong track; *s. auch* **Haussegen** 2 (fig.: verzerrt) **etw. ~ darstellen** give a distorted account of sth.

Schiefer /ˈʃiːfɐ/ *der; ~s* 1 (Gestein) slate 2 (südd., österr.: Splitter) splinter

schiefer-, Schiefer-: ~dach *das* slate roof; **~grau** *Adj.* slate-grey; **~tafel** *die* slate

schief-: *~|**gehen** ▸**gehen 9**; **~gewickelt** ▸**schief B 1**; ~|**lachen** *refl. V.* (ugs.) kill oneself laughing (coll.); laugh one's head off; *~|**laufen** ▸**schief A 1**, **laufen A 11**; *~|**liegen** ▸**schief B 1**; *~|**treten** ▸**schief A 1**

schielen /ˈʃiːlən/ *itr. V.* 1 squint; have a squint; **leicht/stark ~:** have a slight/pronounced squint; **auf dem rechten Auge ~:** have a squint in one's right eye 2 (ugs.: blicken) look out of the corner of one's eye; **nach etw. ~:** steal a glance at sth.; (fig.) have one's eye on sth. 3 (ugs.: spähen) peep; **nach rechts und links ~:** glance right and left

schien /ʃiːn/ *1. u. 3. Pers. Sg. Prät. v.* **scheinen**

Schien·bein *das* ▸**i S. 435** shinbone; **sich ans** *od.* **am ~ stoßen** bang one's shin; **jmdm.** *od.* **jmdn. vor das ~ treten** kick sb. on the shin

-schiene *die:* **Nord~/Süd~/Rhein~:** northern/southern/Rhine sector

Schiene /ˈʃiːnə/ *die; ~, ~n* 1 rail; **~n legen** lay track; **aus den ~n springen** come off the rails 2 (Gleit~) runner; **in einer ~ laufen** move on a runner 3 (Med.: Stütze) splint 4 (Reiß~) T-square 5 (schmale Leiste) right-angle moulding; (in Korbwaren) rib 6 (hist.: Teil der Rüstung) splint

schienen *tr. V.* **jmds. Arm/Bein ~:** put sb.'s arm/leg in a splint/splints; put a splint/splints on sb.'s arm/leg

Schienen-: ~bus *der* railbus; **~fahrzeug** *das* track vehicle; **~strang** *der* [railway] line *or* track; **~verkehr** *der* rail traffic

schier[1] /ʃiːɐ̯/ *Adv.* (veralt.: geradezu) well-nigh; almost

schier[2] *Adj.* (bes. nordd.) pure; (fig.) sheer ‹*malevolence, stupidity*›

Schierling /ˈʃiːɐ̯lɪŋ/ *der; ~s, ~e* hemlock

Schierlings·becher *der* cup of hemlock

Schieß-: ~befehl *der* order to shoot; **~bude** *die* shooting gallery; **~buden·figur** *die* target [in a shooting gallery]; **du siehst aus wie eine ~budenfigur** (ugs.) you look a real clown; **~eisen** *das* (ugs.) shooting iron (coll.)

schießen /ˈʃiːsn̩/

A *unr. itr. V.* 1 shoot; ‹*pistol, rifle*› shoot, fire; **auf jmdn./etw. ~:** shoot/fire at sb./sth.; **gut/schlecht ~** ‹*person*› be a good/bad shot; **es wurde aus dem Fenster geschossen** a shot/shots came from the window; **sie schoss ihm/sich ins Bein** she shot him/herself in the leg; **mit Schrot/einem Pfeil ~:** fire shot/shoot an arrow 2 (Fußball) shoot; **der Stürmer schoss hoch über das Tor** the forward's shot went high over the goal 3 *mit sein* (ugs.: schnellen) shoot; **er schoss vom Stuhl in die Höhe** he shot up out of his chair; **ein Gedanke schoss ihr durch den Kopf** (fig.) a thought flashed through her mind; **zum Schießen sein** (ugs.) be a scream (coll.); **jmdn. ~ lassen**

S

(salopp) drop sb.; **einen Plan ~ lassen** (salopp) ditch (coll.) or drop a plan **4** mit sein (fließen, heraus~) gush; (spritzen) spurt; **ich spürte, wie mir das Blut in den Kopf schoss** I felt the blood rush to my head; **aus dem Dachstuhl schossen Flammen** flames were shooting from the attic **5** mit sein (schnell wachsen) shoot up; (fig.) ‹building› spring up; **der Junge ist sehr in die Höhe geschossen** the boy has shot up a lot; **die Preise ~ in die Höhe** (fig.) prices are shooting up or rocketing **6** (Drogenjargon) fix

B unr. tr. V. **1** shoot; fire ‹bullet, missile, rocket›; **jmdn./etw. in den Weltraum ~:** launch sb./sth. into space; **an der Schießbude einen Preis ~:** win a prize at the shooting gallery; **jmdn. zum Krüppel ~:** shoot and maim sb. **2** (Fußball) score ‹goal›; **den Ball ins Netz ~:** put the ball in the net; **er schoss seine Mannschaft in Führung** he scored the goal that put his team ahead; **das 3:2 ~:** make it 3-2 **3** (ugs.: fotografieren) **einige Aufnahmen ~:** take a few snaps

***schießen|lassen** ▸ **schießen A 3**

Schießerei die; ~, ~en **1** shooting no indef. art., no pl. **2** (Schusswechsel) gun battle; **die ~ am Ende des Films** the shoot-out at the end of the film

Schieß-: **~gewehr** das (Kinderspr.) rifle; **~hund** der (Jägerspr., veralt.: Jagdhund) gun dog; **aufpassen wie ein ~hund** (ugs.) be on one's toes; **~platz** der firing range; **~pulver** das gunpowder; **er hat das ~pulver [auch] nicht erfunden** (ugs.) he's not exactly a genius; **~scharte** die crenel; **~scheibe** die target; **~sport** der shooting no art.; **~stand** der **1** shooting range; **2** ▸ **~bude**; **~übung** die target practice

Schiff /ʃɪf/ das; **~[e]s, ~e** **1** ship; **mit dem** od. **per** od. **zu ~:** by ship or sea; **~ voraus!** ship ahead!; **das ~ der Wüste** (fig.) the ship of the desert **2** (Archit.: Kirchen~) (Mittel~) nave; (Quer~) transept; (Seiten~) aisle **3** (Druckw.) galley

***Schiffahrt** usw. ▸ **Schifffahrt** usw.

schiffbar Adj. ▸ ❶ **S. 267** navigable

Schiffbarmachung die; **~: seit der ~ dieses Flusses** since this river was made navigable

schiff-, Schiff-: **~bau** der; shipbuilding no art.; **~bauer** der; ~~s, ~~, **~bauerin** die; ~~, ~~nen ▸ ❶ **S. 113** shipbuilder; **~bruch** der (veralt.) shipwreck; **~bruch erleiden** ‹ship› be wrecked; ‹person› be shipwrecked; **[mit etw.] ~bruch erleiden** (fig.) fail [in sth.]; **~brüchig** Adj. shipwrecked; **~brüchige** der/die; adj. Dekl. shipwrecked man/woman; **die ~brüchigen** those shipwrecked

Schiffchen das; ~s, ~ **1** (Spielzeug) [little] boat **2** (ugs.: Kopfbedeckung) forage cap **3** (Weberei, Handarbeit, Nähen) shuttle

schiffen itr. V. **1** mit sein (veralt.: mit dem Schiff fahren) ship; travel by ship **2** (derb: urinieren) piss (coarse) **3** (unpers. salopp: regnen) **es schifft** it's pissing down (sl.); it's chucking it down (sl.)

Schiffer der; ~s, ~, **Schifferin** die; ~, ~nen boatman/boatwoman; (eines Lastkahns) bargee; (Kapitän[in]) skipper

Schiffer-: **~klavier** das accordion; **~knoten** der seaman's knot; **~mütze** die [peaked] sailor's cap

Schiff·fahrt die **1** (Schiffsverkehr) shipping no indef. art.; **die ~ einstellen** suspend all shipping movements **2** (Schifffahrtskunde) navigation

Schifffahrts-: **~gesellschaft** die shipping company; **~linie** die shipping route; **~straße** die, **~weg** der [navigable] waterway

Schiffs-: **~arzt** der, **~ärztin** die ship's doctor; **~ausrüster** der; ~~s, ~~, **~ausrüsterin** die; ~~, ~~nen ship's chandler; **~bau** der; ▸ **Schiffbau**; **~bauch** der (ugs.) belly of a/the ship; **~brücke** die pontoon bridge

Schiff·schaukel die swingboat; **~ fahren** go on a/the swingboat

Schiffs-: **~eigner** der, **~eignerin** die shipowner; **~fahrt** die boat trip; (länger) cruise; **~führer** der, **~führerin** die ▸ **Schiffer**; **~glocke** die ship's bell; **~junge** der ▸ ❶ **S. 113** ship's boy; **~ladung** die [ship's] cargo; **eine ganze ~ladung** an entire shipload; **~laterne** die (Seemannsspr.) ship's lantern; **~makler** der, **~maklerin** die shipbroker; **~modell** das model ship; **~name** der ship's name; **~papiere** Pl. ship's papers; **~passage** die passage; **~reise** die voyage; (Vergnügungsreise) cruise; **~rumpf** der [ship's] hull; **~schraube** die ship's propeller or screw; **~sirene** die ship's siren; **~taufe** die naming of a/the ship; **~verkehr** der shipping traffic; **auf dem Fluss war lebhafter** od. **reger ~verkehr** the river was busy with traffic; **~zwieback** der hard tack; ship's biscuit

Schiit /ʃi'i:t/ der; **~en, ~en, Schiitin** die; **~, ~nen** Shiite

schiitisch Adj. Shiite

Schikane /ʃi'ka:nə/ die; ~, **~n** **1** (Bosheit) harassment no indef. art.; **das ist eine ~:** that amounts to or is harassment; **aus reiner ~:** purely in order to harass him/her etc.; **Beschimpfungen und ~n** abuse and harassment **2** in **mit allen ~n** (ugs.) ‹kitchen, house› with all mod cons (Brit. coll.); ‹car, bicycle, stereo› with all the extras **3** (Motorsport) chicane

schikanieren tr. V. **jmdn. ~:** harass sb.; mess sb. about (coll.); **Rekruten/seine Ehefrau ~:** bully recruits/one's wife

schikanös /ʃika'nø:s/

A Adj. harassing ‹action, measure›; bullying ‹husband, superior officer›; **~e Behandlung** harassment/bullying

B adv. **jmdn. ~ behandeln** harass sb.

Schild[1] /ʃɪlt/ der; **~[e]s, ~e** **1** shield; **jmdn. auf den ~ [er]heben** (geh.) (als Anführer) make sb. one's leader; (als Leitbild) make sb. one's figurehead; **etw./nichts im ~e führen** be up to something/not be up to anything; **etwas gegen jmdn./etw. im ~e führen** be plotting against sb./sth. **2** (Wappen~) shield; escutcheon **3** ▸ **Schirm 3**

Schild[2] das; **~[e]s, ~er** (Verkehrs~) sign; (Nummern~) number plate; (Namens~) nameplate; (Plakat) placard; (an einer Mütze) badge; (auf Denkmälern, Gebäuden, Gräbern) plaque; (Etikett) label

Schild-: **~bürger** der (abwertend) ≈ wise man of Gotham; Gothamite; fool; **~bürgerin** die (abwertend) Gothamite; fool; **~bürgerstreich** der (abwertend) act of monumental dim-wittedness; **~drüse** die ▸ ❶ **S. 435** (Med.) thyroid [gland]

Schilder-: **~brücke** die (Verkehrsw.) sign gantry; **~haus** das, **~häuschen** das sentry box

schildern /'ʃɪldɐn/ tr. V. describe; (in einer Erzählung) portray; describe; **die Gräuel dieses Krieges sind kaum zu ~:** the atrocities committed in this war beggar description; s. auch **Farbe 2**

Schilderung die; ~, **~en** description; (von Ereignissen) account; description; (in einer Erzählung) portrayal; description

Schilder·wald der (Verkehrsw. abwertend) maze of traffic signs

Schild-: **~knappe** der (hist.) squire; shield-bearer; **~kröte** die tortoise; (Seeschildkröte) turtle; **~kröten·suppe** die turtle soup; **~laus** die scale insect; **~patt** das tortoiseshell; **~wache** die (veralt.) sentry; **~wache stehen** stand sentry

Schilf /ʃɪlf/ das; **~[e]s, ~e** **1** (~rohr) reed **2** (Röhricht) reeds pl.

Schilf-: **~dach** das roof thatched with reeds; **~gras** das, **~rohr** das ▸ **Schilf 1**; **~rohrsänger** der sedge warbler

Schiller-: **~kragen** der large open-necked collar; **~locke** die **1** (Gebäck) cream horn; **2** (Räucherfisch) strip of smoked fish (esp. dogfish)

schillern /'ʃɪlɐn/ itr. V. shimmer; **in allen Regenbogenfarben ~:** shimmer with all the colours of the rainbow; **ein ~der Charakter** (fig.) an ambivalent character; **ein ~der Begriff** (fig.) a shifting concept

Schilling /'ʃɪlɪŋ/ der; **~s, ~e** ▸ ❶ **S. 299** schilling; **das kostet 30 ~:** that costs 30 schillings

Schillum /'ʃɪlʊm/ das; **~s, ~s** chillum

schilpen /'ʃɪlpn̩/ ▸ **tschilpen**

schilt /ʃɪlt/ 3. Pers. Sg. Präsens v. **schelten**

Schimäre /ʃi'mɛ:rə/ die; **~, ~n** chimera

schimärisch Adj. chimerical

Schimmel /'ʃɪml̩/ der; **~s, ~** **1** (Belag) mould; (auf Leder, Papier) mildew **2** (Pferd) white horse

schimmelig Adj. mouldy; mildewy ‹paper, leather›; **~ werden** go mouldy/get covered with mildew

schimmeln itr. V.; auch mit sein go mouldy; ‹leather, paper› get covered with mildew

Schimmel·pilz der mould

Schimmer /'ʃɪmɐ/ der; **~s** **1** (Schein) gleam; (von Perlmutt) lustre; shimmer; (von Seide) shimmer; sheen; (von Haar) sheen; (von Kerzen) [soft] glow **2** (Anflug, Hauch) glimmer; **noch einen ~ [von] Anstand haben** still have a scrap of decency; **keinen [blassen]** od. **nicht den leisesten ~ [von etw.] haben** (ugs.) not have the faintest or foggiest idea [about sth.] (coll.)

schimmern itr. V. **1** (matt glänzen) gleam; ‹water, sea› glisten, shimmer; ‹teeth› glisten; ‹metal› glint, gleam; ‹silk, mother-of-pearl› shimmer; **der Stoff/die Seide schimmert rötlich** the material has a reddish tinge/the silk has a reddish sheen **2** (durch~) show (**durch** through)

schimmlig ▸ **schimmelig**

Schimpanse /ʃɪm'panzə/ der; **~n, ~n** chimpanzee

Schimpf der; **~[e]s** (geh.) affront; **jmdm. einen ~ antun/zufügen** affront sb.; **mit ~ und Schande** in disgrace

Schimpfe die; ~ (ugs.) **~ bekommen** get an earful (coll.)

schimpfen

A itr. V. **1** carry on (coll.) (**auf, über** + Akk. about); (meckern) grumble, moan (**auf, über** + Akk. at) **2** (zurechtweisen) **mit jmdm. ~:** tell sb. off; scold sb.

B tr. V. **1** (bes. md.: aus~) **jmdn. ~:** tell sb. off; scold sb. **2** **jmdn. dumm/faul ~:** call sb. stupid/lazy

C refl. V. (spött.: vorgeben zu sein) **sich Professor/Dichter ~:** call oneself a professor/poet

Schimpferei die; **~, ~en** (abwertend) carrying on (coll.); (Meckerei) grumbling; moaning; (das Zurechtweisen) telling off, scolding (**mit** of)

schimpflich (geh.)

A Adj. shameful, disgraceful ‹behaviour, treatment›; dishonourable ‹occupation›; (entwürdigend) humiliating ‹defeat, terms, etc.›

B adv. shamefully; disgracefully; (entwürdigend) humiliatingly

Schimpf-: **~name** der [abusive] nickname; **jmdn. mit ~namen belegen** call sb. names; **~wort** das; Pl. **~wörter** (Beleidigung) insult; (derbes Wort) swear word

Schindel /'ʃɪndl̩/ die; **~, ~n** shingle

Schindel·dach das shingle roof

schinden /'ʃɪndn̩/

A unr. tr. V. **1** maltreat; ill-treat; (ausbeuten) slave-drive; **jmdn./ein Tier zu Tode ~:** work sb./an animal to death **2** (ugs.: herausschlagen) **Zeilen ~:** pad as much as possible; fill up space with as little as possible; **[bei jmdm.] Eindruck ~:** make an impression [on sb.]; **Applaus ~ wollen** fish for applause; **Zeit ~:** play for time

B unr. refl. V. (ugs.: sich abplagen) slave away; **sich mit einer Arbeit ~:** slave away at a job

Schinder der; **~s, ~** **1** slave driver **2** (veralt.: Abdecker) knacker (Brit.)

Schinderei die; **~, ~en** **1** ill-treatment no pl.; (Ausbeutung) slave-driving no pl. **2** (Strapaze, Qual) struggle; (Arbeit) toil

Schinderin die; **~, ~nen** ▸ **Schinder 1**

Schind-: **~luder** das: in **mit etw. ~luder treiben** (ugs.) (ausbeuten) take advantage of or

S

abuse sth.; (vergeuden) squander sth.; **wir dürfen nicht länger mit der Natur ~luder treiben** we must stop this appalling waste of natural resources; **~mähre** *die* (abwertend) nag

Schinken /ˈʃɪŋkn̩/ *der;* **~s, ~** **1** ham **2** (ugs.) (Buch) great tome; (Gemälde) enormous painting; (Film, Theaterstück) epic

Schinken-: ~brot *das* slice of bread and ham; (zugeklappt) ham sandwich; **~speck** *der* bacon

Schintoismus /ʃɪntoˈɪsmʊs/ *der;* **~:** Shintoism *no art.*

Schippe /ˈʃɪpə/ *die;* **~, ~n** **1** (nordd., md.: Schaufel) shovel; **~ und Eimer** bucket and spade; **~ und Handfeger** dustpan and brush; **jmdn. auf die ~ nehmen** (fam.) kid sb. (sl.); pull sb.'s leg; **dem Tod von der ~ springen** (ugs.) escape death by a hair's breadth **2** (Kartenspiel) ▸**Pik²** **3** (ugs.: Flunsch) **eine ~ ziehen** *od.* **machen** pout

schippen *tr. V.* (nordd., md.) **1** shovel **2** (ausheben) dig ‹*ditch, grave, etc.*›

Schipper *der;* **~s, ~** (nordd.) ▸**Schiffer**

schippern (ugs.)

A *itr. V.; mit sein* cruise

B *tr. V.* ship ‹*goods, materials*›; skipper ‹*ship*›

Schirm /ʃɪrm/ *der;* **~[e]s, ~e** **1** umbrella; brolly (Brit. coll.); (Sonnen~) sunshade; parasol **2** (Lampen~) shade **3** (Mützen~) peak **4** (gegen Licht) eyeshade; (Ofen~, Kamin~) guard; (Strahlen~) shield; (beim Schweißen o. Ä.) mask; visor **5** (Bild~) screen **6** (Schutz) shield

Schirm-: ~bild *das* (Med.) X-ray [picture]; **~bild·gerät** *das* (Med.) X-ray machine; **~herr** *der* patron; **~herrin** *die* patroness; **~herrschaft** *die* patronage; **die ~herrschaft über etw.** (*Akk.*) **übernehmen** become patron of sth.; **~mütze** *die* peaked cap; **~pilz** *der* parasol mushroom; **~ständer** *der* umbrella stand

Schirokko /ʃiˈrɔko/ *der;* **~s, ~s** sirocco

Schisma /ˈʃɪsma/ *das;* **~s, Schismen** *od.* **~ta** (Kirche, Politik) schism

schiss, *schiß /ʃɪs/ *1. u. 3. Pers. Sg. Prät. v.* **scheißen**

Schiss, *Schiß *der;* **Schisses** (salopp: Angst) **[vor etw.] ~ haben** be shit-scared [of sth.] (coarse); **~ kriegen** get the shits (coarse)

schizoid /ʃɪtsoˈiːt/ (Med.)

A *Adj.* schizoid

B *adv.* **~ veranlagt sein** have schizoid tendencies

schizophren /ʃɪtsoˈfreːn/ (Med., auch fig.)

A *Adj.* schizophrenic

B *adv.* schizophrenically

Schizophrenie *die;* **~, ~n** (Med., auch fig.) schizophrenia

schlabberig *Adj.* (ugs.) **1** (locker fallend) baggy ‹*clothes*›; loose, limp ‹*material*› **2** (abwertend: wässrig) watery

schlabbern /ˈʃlabɐn/

A *tr. V.* (ugs.) (schlürfen) ‹*person*› slurp; ‹*animal*› lap up

B *itr. V.* **1** (abwertend) slobber **2** (schlenkern) ‹*dress*› flap; ‹*trousers*› be baggy

schlabbrig *Adj.* ▸**schlabberig**

Schlacht /ʃlaxt/ *die;* **~, ~en** battle; **die ~ bei** *od.* **von/um X** the battle of/for X; **in die ~ ziehen** go into battle; **sich eine ~ liefern** do battle; **sich eine erbitterte ~ liefern** (fig.) fight fiercely; **jmdn. eine ~ liefern** do battle with sb.; **eine ~ schlagen** fight a battle

Schlacht·bank *die; Pl.* **Schlachtbänke** slaughtering block; **sich wie ein Lamm zur ~ führen lassen** (geh.) let oneself be led like a lamb to the slaughter

schlachten *tr.* (*auch itr.*) *V.* slaughter; kill ‹*rabbit, chicken, etc.*›; **sein Sparschwein ~** (scherzh.) raid one's piggy bank

Schlachtenbummler /-bʊmlɐ/ *der,* **Schlachtenbummlerin** *die* (Sportjargon) away supporter; **die englischen ~:** the visiting English supporters

Schlachter *der;* **~s, ~, Schlächter** *der;* **~s, ~** (nordd.) ▸**i S. 113** butcher

Schlachterei *die;* **~, ~en, Schlächterei** *die;* **~, ~en** **1** (nordd.: Fleischerei) butcher's [shop] **2** (abwertend: Gemetzel) slaughter; butchery *no indef. art.*

schlacht-, Schlacht-: ~feld *das* battlefield; **auf dem ~feld bleiben** (veralt. verhüll.) fall in battle; **das Zimmer sah wie ein ~feld aus** the room looked as if a bomb had hit it; **~fest** *das: feast at which the meat of freshly slaughtered animals, esp. pork, is eaten;* **~haus** *das* slaughterhouse; **~hof** *der* slaughterhouse; abattoir; **~opfer** *das* (Rel.) animal sacrifice; **~ordnung** *die* (Milit. hist.) battle order; **~plan** *der* (Milit.) plan of battle; battle plan; (fig.) plan of action; **~platte** *die: dish with assorted cooked meats, sausages, and sauerkraut;* **~reif** *Adj.* ready for slaughtering *postpos.;* **~ross, *~roß** *das* (veralt.) warhorse; charger; **ein altes ~ross** (fig. scherzh.) an old warhorse; **~schiff** *das* (Milit.) battleship; **~tier** *das* animal kept for meat; (kurz vor der Schlachtung) animal for slaughter

Schlachtung *die;* **~, ~en** slaughter[ing]

Schlacht·vieh *das* animals *pl.* kept for meat; (kurz vor der Schlachtung) animals *pl.* for slaughter

Schlacke /ˈʃlakə/ *die;* **~, ~n** **1** cinders *pl.;* (größere Stücke) clinker **2** *Pl.* (Physiol.: Ballaststoffe) roughage *sing.* **3** (Hochofen~) slag **4** (Geol.: Lava) slag; clinker

schlackern /ˈʃlakɐn/ *itr. V.* (nordd., westmd.) **1** (schlenkern) ‹*dress*› flap; ‹*bag*› dangle; ‹*trousers*› be baggy **2** (wackeln, zittern) shake; tremble; **mit den Armen ~:** flap one's arms about; *s. auch* **Ohr**

Schlack·wurst *die* ▸**Zervelatwurst**

Schlaf /ʃlaːf/ *der;* **~[e]s** sleep; **einen leichten/festen/gesunden ~ haben** be a light/heavy/good sleeper; **keinen ~ finden** (geh.) be unable to sleep; **jmdn. um den** *od.* **seinen ~ bringen** ‹*worry etc.*› give sb. sleepless nights/a sleepless night; ‹*noise*› stop sb. from sleeping; **jmdn. in den ~ singen/wiegen** sing/rock sb. to sleep; **jmdn. aus dem ~ reißen** wake sb. up with a start; **den ~ des Gerechten schlafen** (scherzh.) sleep the sleep of the just; **das kann** *od.* **mache ich im ~** (fig.) I can do that with my eyes closed *or* shut; **halb im ~:** half asleep

Schlaf-: ~anzug *der* pyjamas *pl.;* **ein ~anzug** a pair of pyjamas; **~bedürfnis** *das* need for sleep

Schläfchen /ˈʃlɛːfçən/ *das;* **~s, ~:** nap; snooze (coll.); **ein ~ halten** have a nap *or* (coll.) snooze

Schlaf-couch *die* bed settee; sofa-bed

Schläfe /ˈʃlɛːfə/ *die;* **~, ~n** ▸**i S. 435** temple; **er hat/bekommt graue ~n** his hair has gone/is going grey at the temples

schlafen

A *unr. itr. V.* **1** (auch fig.) sleep; **tief** *od.* **fest ~** (zurzeit) be sound asleep; (gewöhnlich) sleep soundly; be a sound sleeper; **lange ~:** sleep for a long time; (am Morgen) sleep in; **~ gehen** go to bed; **sich ~ legen** lie down to sleep; (ins Bett gehen) go to bed; **im Hotel/bei Bekannten ~:** stay in a hotel/with friends; **schlaf gut!** sleep well!; **hast du gut ge~?** did you sleep well?; **schläft sie immer noch?** is she still asleep?; **er schläft noch halb** he's still half asleep; **darüber muss ich noch ~:** I'd like to sleep on it; **~ wie ein Murmeltier** *od.* **Bär** *od.* **Sack** *od.* **Stein** (ugs.) sleep like a log *or* top; **bei jmdm. ~:** sleep at sb.'s house/in sb.'s room *etc.;* **mit jmdm. ~** (verhüll.) sleep with sb. (euphem.) **2** (ugs.: nicht aufpassen) be asleep

B *unr. refl. V.* (unpers.) **auf dem Sofa schläft es sich gut** the sofa's good to sleep on

Schläfen·bein *das* ▸**i S. 435** (Anat.) temporal bone

Schlafen·gehen *das;* **~s** going *no def. art.* to bed

Schlafens·zeit *die* bedtime

Schläfer /ˈʃlɛːfɐ/ *der;* **~s, ~, Schläferin** *die;* **~, ~nen** sleeper

schlaff /ʃlaf/

A *Adj.* **1** (nicht straff, nicht fest) slack ‹*cable, rope, sail*›; flaccid, limp ‹*penis*›; loose, slack ‹*skin*›; sagging ‹*breasts*›; flabby ‹*stomach, muscles*›; **die Fahne war ~:** the flag hung limply **2** (schlapp, matt) limp ‹*body, hand, handshake*›; shaky ‹*knees*›; feeble ‹*blow*› **3** (abwertend: träge) lethargic; **~e Nachfrage** (fig.) weak demand

B *adv.* **1** (locker, nicht straff) slackly; **das Segel hing ~:** the sail hung limply; **ihre Brüste hingen ~:** her breasts sagged **2** (schlapp, matt) limply; **er saß ~ herum** (ugs.) he sat around listlessly

Schlaffheit *die;* **~:** limpness; (der Haut) looseness, slackness; (des Bauches, der Muskeln) flabbiness

Schlaffi /ˈʃlafi/ *der;* **~s, ~s** (ugs. abwertend) wet (coll.)

schlaf-, Schlaf-: ~forscher *der,* **~forscherin** *die* sleep researcher; **~forschung** *die* sleep research; **~gast** *der* overnight guest; **~gelegenheit** *die* place to sleep; **~gewohnheiten** *Pl.* sleeping habits

Schlafittchen /ʃlaˈfɪtçən/ *das:* **in jmdn. am** *od.* **beim ~ kriegen** *od.* **fassen** (ugs.) collar *or* (coll.) nab sb.

Schlaf-: ~krankheit *die* sleeping sickness; **~labor** *das* sleep laboratory; **~lied** *das* lullaby; **~los** *Adj.* sleepless ‹*night*›; **~los liegen** lie awake, unable to sleep; **~losigkeit** *die;* **~~:** sleeplessness; insomnia; **an ~losigkeit leiden** be an insomniac; suffer from insomnia; **~mittel** *das* sleep-inducing drug; soporific [drug]; **dieser Roman ist das reinste ~mittel** (fig.) this novel sends you [right off] to sleep; **~mütze** *die* **1** (ugs.) sleepyhead; (jmd., der unaufmerksam ist) daydreamer; **2** (veralt.: Nachtmütze) nightcap; **~mützig** *Adj.* (ugs.) dozy (coll.); **~raum** *der* bedroom; (in Heim o. Ä.) dormitory

schläfrig /ˈʃlɛːfrɪç/

A *Adj.* sleepy; **~ sein/werden** ‹*person*› be/become sleepy *or* drowsy

B *adv.* sleepily

Schläfrigkeit *die;* **~:** sleepiness; drowsiness

Schlaf-: ~rock *der* (veralt.) nightgown; *s. auch* **Apfel 1**; **~saal** *der* dormitory; **~sack** sleeping bag

schläfst /ʃlɛːfst/ *2. Pers. Sg. Präsens v.* **schlafen**

Schlaf-: ~stadt *die* dormitory town; **~stelle** *die* place to sleep; (Bett) bed; **~störungen** *Pl.* ▸**i S. 439** (Med.) insomnia *sing.*

schläft /ʃlɛːft/ *3. Pers. Sg. Präsens v.* **schlafen**

schlaf-, Schlaf-: ~tablette *die* sleeping pill *or* -tablet; **~trunk** *der* nightcap; **~trunken** **A** *Adj.* (geh.) drowsy; **B** *adv.* drowsily; [still] half asleep; **~wagen** *der* sleeping car; sleeper; **~wandeln** *itr. V.; auch mit sein* sleepwalk; **~wandler** *der;* **~~s, ~~, ~wandlerin** *die;* **~~, ~~nen** sleepwalker; **~wandlerisch** *Adj.* somnambulistic; **mit ~wandlerischer Sicherheit** with the sureness of a sleepwalker; with instinctive sureness; **~zimmer** *das* bedroom; (Einrichtung) bedroom suite; **~zimmerblick** *der* (scherzh.) bedroom eyes *pl.;* seductive eyes *pl.*

Schlag /ʃlaːk/ *der;* **~[e]s, Schläge** /ˈʃlɛːɡə/ **1** blow; (Faust~) punch; blow; (Klaps) slap; (leichter) pat; (als Strafe für ein Kind) smack; (Peitschenhieb) lash; (Tennis~, Golf~) stroke; shot; **ein ~ auf den Kopf/ins Genick** a blow on the head/neck; **Schläge kriegen** (ugs.) get *or* be given a thrashing *or* beating; **~ auf ~** (fig.) in quick *or* rapid succession; **alles ging ~ auf ~:** everything went quickly; **die Fragen/Nachrichten kamen ~ auf ~:** the questions/news came thick and fast; **ein ~ ins Gesicht sein** (fig.) be a slap in the face; **das war ein ~ ins Kontor** (ugs.) that was a real blow (coll.); **ein ~ ins Wasser** a washout (coll.); **einen ~ [weg]haben** (salopp) be round the bend (coll.); be nuts (coll.); **keinen ~ tun** (ugs.) not do a stroke [of work]; **jmdm. einen ~ versetzen** deal sb. a blow; (fig.) be a blow to sb.; **einen vernichtenden ~ gegen jmdn. führen** (fig.) deal sb. a crushing blow; **auf einen ~** (ugs.) at one go; all at once; **mit einem ~[e]** (ugs.) suddenly; all at once; **mit einem ~ berühmt werden** become famous overnight; **zum entscheidenden ~ ausholen** (fig.) prepare to deal the decisive

S

blow; *s. auch* **Gürtellinie** **2** (Auf~, Aufprall) bang; (dumpf) thud; (Klopfen) knock **3** (des Herzens, Pulses, der Wellen) beating; (eines Pendels) swinging **4** (einzelne rhythmische Bewegung) (Herz~, Puls~, Takt~) beat; (eines Pendels) swing; (Ruder~, Kolben~) stroke **5** (*Töne*) (einer Uhr) striking; (einer Glocke) ringing; (einer Trommel) beating; (eines Gongs) clanging **6** (einzelner Ton) (Stunden~) stroke; (Glocken~) ring; (Trommel~) beat; (Gong~) clang; ~ *od.* (österr., schweiz.) **schlag acht Uhr** on the dot *or* stroke of eight **7** (Vogelgesang) song **8** (Blitz~) flash [of lightning] **9** (Stromstoß) shock **10** (ugs.: ~anfall) stroke; **jmdn. trifft** *od.* **rührt der ~** (ugs.) sb. is flabbergasted; **ich dachte, mich trifft** *od.* **rührt der ~** (ugs.) I was flabbergasted; you could have knocked me down with a feather; **wie vom ~ getroffen** *od.* **gerührt** (ugs.) as if thunderstruck **11** (Schicksals~) blow **12** (Tauben~) cote **13** (ugs.: Portion) helping; **[einen] ~ bei jmdm. haben** (fig. ugs.) be well in with sb. (coll.) **14** (österr.: ~sahne) whipped cream **15** (Wagen~, Kutschen~) door **16** (Menschen~) type; **ein Beamter vom alten ~:** a civil servant of the old school

schlag-, Schlag-: ~abtausch *der* exchange of blows; (fig.) clash; **~ader** *die* ▸ℹ **S. 435** artery; **~anfall** *der* stroke; **einen ~anfall bekommen [haben]** have [had] a stroke; **~artig** **A** *Adj.* very sudden; (innerhalb kürzester Zeit geschehend) instantaneous; **B** *adv.* quite suddenly; (innerhalb kürzester Zeit) instantly; **~ball** *der* **1** (Ballspiel) *ball game similar to rounders;* **2** (Ball) *ball used in Schlagball;* **~bass**, ***~baß** *der* (Musik) plucked bass; **~baum** *der* barrier; **~bohrer** *der*, **~bohrmaschine** *die* percussion drill; hammer drill

Schlägel /ˈʃlɛːɡl̩/ *der;* **~s, ~:** **1** (Werkzeug) mallet **2** (Trommelstock) stick

schlagen

A *unr. tr. V.* **1** hit; beat; strike; (mit der Faust) punch; hit; (mit der flachen Hand) slap; (mit der Peitsche) lash; **ein Kind ~:** smack a child; (aufs Hinterteil) spank a child; **jmdn. bewusstlos/zu Boden ~:** beat sb. senseless/to the ground; (mit einem Schlag) knock sb. senseless/to the ground; **jmdn. zum Krüppel ~:** cripple sb. with a beating; **ich schlage dich zum Krüppel!** (derb) I'll beat you to a pulp (coll.); **etw. in Stücke ~:** smash sth. to pieces; **die Hände vors Gesicht ~:** cover one's face with one's hands; **jmdm. einen Schirm auf den Kopf ~:** hit sb. over the head with an umbrella; **sie schlug ihm das Buch aus der Hand** she knocked the book out of his hand; **ein Loch ins Eis ~:** break *or* smash a hole in the ice; **er hat ihr ein Loch in den Kopf ge~:** he hit her and cut her head open; *s. auch* **grün 1**
2 (mit Richtungsangabe) hit ‹*ball*›; (mit dem Fuß) kick; **einen Nagel in etw.** (*Akk.*) **~:** knock a nail into sth.; **einen Pflock in den Boden ~:** knock a post into the ground; **die Eier in die Pfanne ~:** crack the eggs into the pan; **etw. durch ein Sieb ~:** press sth. through a sieve; **der Adler schlug die Fänge in seine Beute** the eagle sank its talons into its prey
3 (rühren) beat ‹*mixture*›; whip ‹*cream*›; (mit einem Schneebesen) whisk; **die Sahne steif ~:** beat the cream till stiff
4 (läuten) ‹*clock*› strike; ‹*bell*› ring; **die Uhr schlägt acht** the clock strikes eight; **eine geschlagene Stunde** (ugs.) a whole hour; **die Stunde der Rache/Wahrheit hat ge~** (fig.) the moment of revenge/truth has come; *s. auch* **dreizehn**; **Stunde 1**
5 (legen) throw; **die Decke zur Seite ~:** throw aside the blanket; **ein Bein über das andere ~:** lay *or* put one leg over the other; cross one's legs
6 (einwickeln) wrap (**in** + *Akk.* in)
7 (besiegen, übertreffen) beat; **jmdn. in etw.** (*Dat.*) **~:** beat sb. at sth.; **jmdn. um einige Meter ~:** beat sb. by a few metres; **eine Mannschaft [mit] 2 : 0 ~:** beat a team [by] 2-0; **sich ge~ geben** admit defeat
8 *auch itr.* (bes. Schach) take ‹*chessman*›
9 (fällen) fell ‹*tree*›
10 ▸**Alarm 1**; **Bogen 1**; **Falte 1**; **Haken 1**; **Krach 3**; **Kreis 1**; **Kreuz 3**; **Lärm**; **Rad[1] 3, 5**
11 (spielen) beat ‹*drum*›; (geh.) play ‹*lute, zither, harp*›; **einen Wirbel auf der Trommel ~:** play a roll on the drum; **den Takt/Rhythmus ~:** beat time
12 (hinzufügen) annex ‹*territory*›; **etw. in etw./auf etw.** (*Akk.*) **~:** add sth. to sth.
13 (befestigen) (mit Nägeln) nail; (mit Reißzwecken) pin; (mit Krampen) staple
14 (prägen) mint, strike ‹*coin*›; strike ‹*medal*›
15 (geh.) **ein geschlagener Mann** a broken man; **das Schicksal hat ihn schwer ge~:** fate has treated him cruelly; **Gott hat ihn mit Blindheit ge~:** God struck him blind

B *unr. itr. V.* **1** (hauen) **er schlug mit der Faust auf den Tisch/gegen die Tür** he beat the table/beat [on] the door with his fist; **jmdm. auf die Hand/ins Gesicht ~:** slap sb.'s hand/hit sb. in the face; **er hat nach mir ge~:** he hit *or* lashed out at me; **sie schlug wie wild um sich** she lashed *or* hit out wildly all round her
2 **mit den Flügeln ~** ‹*bird*› beat or flap its wings
3 *mit sein* (prallen) bang; **mit dem Kopf auf etw.** (*Akk.*)/**gegen etw. ~:** bang one's head on/against sth.; **auf den Boden ~:** land with a thud on the floor; **die Wellen schlugen über den Deich** the waves broke over the dyke
4 *mit sein* (schädigen) **jmdm. auf den Magen ~:** affect sb.'s stomach
5 (pulsieren) ‹*heart, pulse*› beat; (heftig) ‹*heart*› pound; ‹*pulse*› throb; **ihr schlug das Gewissen** (fig.) her conscience pricked her
6 (läuten) ‹*clock*› strike; ‹*bell*› ring; ‹*funeral bell*› toll
7 *auch mit sein* (auftreffen) **gegen/an etw.** (*Akk.*) **~** ‹*rain, waves*› beat against sth.; **das Segel schlug gegen den Mast** the sail flapped against the mast
8 *meist mit sein* (ein~) **in etw.** (*Akk.*) **~** ‹*lightning, bullet, etc.*› strike *or* hit sth.
9 *mit sein* (ähnlich werden) **nach dem Großvater/Onkel** *usw.* **~:** take after one's grandfather/uncle *etc.*
10 (sich hin und her bewegen) bang; ‹*sail, flag*› flap
11 *meist mit sein* (sich irgendwohin bewegen) ‹*flames*› shoot, leap; ‹*smoke*› billow
12 *mit sein* (irgendwohin dringen) **der Lärm schlug an mein Ohr** the noise reached my ears; **die Röte/das Blut schlug ihr ins Gesicht** the colour/blood rushed to her face
13 (singen) ‹*nightingale, thrush, etc.*› sing
14 *auch mit sein* (gehören) **in jmds. Fach/Gebiet/Branche ~:** be sb.'s line

C *unr. refl. V.* **1** (sich prügeln) fight; **sich mit jmdm. ~:** fight with sb.; **sich um etw. ~** (auch fig.) fight over sth.
2 (ugs.: sich behaupten) hold one's own; **sich gut** *od.* **wacker** *od.* **tapfer ~:** hold one's own well; put up a good showing
3 (sich schädlich auswirken) **sich/sich jmdm. auf das Gehirn/die Leber ~:** affect the/sb.'s brain/liver
4 (veralt.: sich duellieren) **sich mit jmdm. ~:** fight a duel with sb.; *s. auch* **Mensur 1**
5 (sich begeben) make one's way; **sich ins Gebüsch/Kornfeld ~:** slip away into the bushes/corn

schlagend

A *Adj.* cogent, compelling ‹*argument, reason*›; cogent ‹*comparison*›; conclusive ‹*proof, evidence*›; *s. auch* **Verbindung 10**; **Wetter[2] 3**
B *adv.* ‹*prove, disprove*› conclusively; ‹*formulate*› cogently

Schlager *der;* **~s, ~** **1** (Lied) pop song; (Hit) hit **2** (Erfolg) (Buch) best seller; (Ware) best-selling line; (Film, Stück) hit

Schläger /ˈʃlɛːɡɐ/ *der;* **~s, ~** **1** (abwertend: Raufbold) tough; thug **2** (Tennis~, Federball~, Squash~) racket; (Tischtennis~, Kricket~) bat; ([Eis]hockey~, Polo~) stick; (Golf~) club **3** (Baseball, Schlagball: Spieler) batter **4** (Fechten: Waffe) straight-edged sabre

Schlägerei *die;* **~, ~en** brawl; fight

Schlägerin *die;* **~, ~nen** ▸**Schläger 1, 3**

Schlager·musik *die* popular music; pop music

Schläger·mütze *die: large soft peaked cap*

Schlager-: ~sänger *der*, **~sängerin** *die* pop singer; **~spiel** *das* (Sportjargon) big match; **~text** *der* pop [song] lyric; **~texter** *der*, **~texterin** *die* pop [song] lyricist

Schläger·typ *der* (abwertend) tough; thug

schlag-, Schlag-: ~fertig **A** *Adj.* quick-witted ‹*reply*›; ‹*person*› who is quick at repartee; **er ist ~fertig** he is quick at repartee; **B** *adv.* **~fertig antworten/parieren** give a quick-witted reply/riposte; **~fertigkeit** *die* quickness at repartee; **~fluss**, ***~fluß** *der* (veralt.) ▸**~anfall**; **~frau** *die* (Rudern) stroke; **~hose** *die* flared trousers; flares; **~instrument** *das* percussion instrument; **~kraft** *die* **1** (Kraft zum ~en) weight of punch; **2** (Milit.: Kampfkraft) strike power; **3** (fig.: Wirkungskraft) effectiveness; (von Argumenten) compellingness; (von Beispielen) convincingness; **~kräftig** **A** *Adj.* **1** (Milit.: über große Kampfkraft verfügend) powerful; **2** (überzeugend) compelling ‹*argument*›; convincing ‹*example*›; **3** (effektiv) strong, effective ‹*support, back-up, team*›; **B** *adv.* (überzeugend) ‹*argue*› compellingly; **~licht** *das* *Pl.* **~~er** (Kunst, Fot.) shaft of light; **ein ~licht auf etw. werfen** highlight sth.; **~loch** *das* pothole; **~mann** *der* (Rudern) stroke; **~obers** /-oːbɐs/ *das;* **~~** (österr.), **~rahm** *der* (bes. südd., österr., schweiz.) ▸**~sahne**; **~ring** *der* knuckleduster; **~sahne** *die* whipping cream; (geschlagen) whipped cream; **~schatten** *der* [harsh] shadow; **~seite** *die* list; **[starke** *od.* **schwere] ~seite haben/bekommen** be listing [heavily] *or* have a [heavy] list/develop a [heavy] list; **~seite haben** (ugs. scherzh.) be rolling drunk; **~stock** *der* cudgel; (für Polizei) truncheon; **die Polizisten setzten ~stöcke ein** the police used their truncheons; **~werk** *das* striking mechanism; **~wetter** *Pl.* (Bergbau) firedamp *sing.*; **~wort** *das* **1** *Pl. meist* **~worte** (Parole) slogan; catchphrase; **2** *Pl. meist* **~worte** (abwertend: Redensart) cliché; **3** *Pl.* **~wörter** (Buchw.: Stichwort) headword; **nach ~wörtern und Verfassern katalogisieren** catalogue by subject and author; **~wort·katalog** *der* (Buchw.) subject catalogue; **~zeile** *die* (Zeitungsw.) headline; **~zeilen machen** (fig.) make headlines; **~zeug** *das* drums *pl.*; (~instrumente) percussion instruments *pl.*; **~zeuger** *der;* **~~s, ~~**, **~zeugerin** *die;* **~~, ~~nen** ▸ℹ **S. 113** drummer; (Perkussionist[in]) percussionist

schlaksig /ˈʃlaːksɪç/ (ugs.)
A *Adj.* gangling; lanky
B *adv.* lankily

Schlamassel /ʃlaˈmasl̩/ *der od. das;* **~s** (ugs.) mess; **da haben wir den ~!** a right *or* fine mess we're in now!

Schlamm /ʃlam/ *der;* **~[e]s, ~e** *od.* **Schlämme** /ˈʃlɛmə/ **1** (aufgeweichte Erde) mud **2** (Schlick) sludge; silt

Schlamm·bad *das* (Med.) mudbath

schlammig *Adj.* **1** muddy **2** (schlickig) sludgy; muddy

Schlämm·kreide /ˈʃlɛm-/ *die* whiting

Schlamm·schlacht *die* (fig.) mud-slinging *no indef. art.*

Schlampe *die;* **~, ~n** (ugs. abwertend) slut

schlampen *itr. V.* (ugs. abwertend) be sloppy; **bei etw. ~:** do sth. sloppily; **sie haben bei der Reparatur geschlampt** they made a sloppy job of the repair

Schlamperei *die;* **~, ~en** (ugs. abwertend) **1** (Unordentlichkeit) sloppiness; (Nachlässigkeit) slackness; **eine unerhörte ~!** an outrageous example of sloppiness/slackness **2** (Unordnung) mess

schlampert /ˈʃlampɐt/ (österr.), **schlampig** (ugs. abwertend)
A *Adj.* **1** (liederlich) slovenly **2** (nachlässig) sloppy, slipshod ‹*work*›
B *adv.* **1** (liederlich) in a slovenly way **2** (nachlässig) sloppily; in a sloppy *or* slipshod way

Schlampigkeit *die;* **~, ~en** (ugs. abwertend) **1** (Liederlichkeit) slovenliness **2** (Nachlässigkeit) sloppiness

schlang /ʃlaŋ/ *1. u. 3. Pers. Sg. Prät. v.* **schlingen**

schlänge /ˈʃlɛŋə/ *1. u. 3. Pers. Sg. Konjunktiv II v.* **schlingen**

Schlange *die;* ~, ~n [1] snake; *s. auch* **Busen 1** [2] (Menschen~) queue; line (Amer.); ~ **stehen** queue; stand in line (Amer.) [3] (Auto~) tailback (Brit.); backup (Amer.) [4] (abwertend: Frau) viper

schlängeln /ˈʃlɛŋl̩n/ *refl. V.* [1] ‹*snake*› wind [its way]; ‹*road*› wind, snake [its way]; **eine geschlängelte Linie** a wavy line [2] (sich irgendwo hindurch bewegen) wind one's way

Schlangen-: ~beschwörer *der;* ~~s, ~~, **~beschwörerin** *die;* ~~, ~~nen snake charmer; **~biss**, ***~biß** *der* snakebite; **~brut** *die* (geh. abwertend) brood of vipers; **~fraß** *der* (salopp abwertend) muck (coll.); **~gift** *das* snake venom *or* poison; **~haut** *die* snake's skin; **~leder** *das* snakeskin; **~linie** *die* wavy line; **er fuhr mit seinem Moped ~linien** he weaved along on his moped; **~mensch** *der* contortionist

schlank /ʃlaŋk/ *Adj.* slim ‹*person*›; slim, slender ‹*build, figure*›; slender ‹*column, tree, limbs*›; **~ werden** get slimmer; slim down; **dieser Rock macht [dich] ~**: this skirt makes you look slim; **Joghurt macht ~**: yoghurt helps you slim; **sich ~ machen** (fig.) breathe in; *s. auch* **Linie 1**

Schlankheit *die;* ~ ▸**schlank**: slimness; slenderness

Schlankheits-: ~kur *die* slimming diet; **eine ~ machen/beginnen** be/go on a slimming diet; (in einer Klinik usw.) have/start a course of slimming treatment; **~pille** *die* slimming pill; **~wahn** *der* obsession with slimness

schlank·weg *Adv.* (ugs.) ‹*refuse*› flatly, point-blank; ‹*accept*› straight away; **jmdn. ~ einen Lügner nennen** come right out and call sb. a liar; **das ist alles ~ erfunden** that's all pure invention

schlankwüchsig /-vyːksɪç/ *Adj.* ‹*person*› of slender *or* slim build; slender ‹*tree*›

schlapp /ʃlap/
[A] *Adj.* [1] worn out; tired out; (wegen Schwüle) listless; (wegen Krankheit) run-down; listless [2] (ugs.: ohne Schwung) wet (coll.); feeble [3] slack ‹*rope, cable*›; loose, slack ‹*skin*›; flabby ‹*stomach, muscles*›
[B] *adv.* (schlaff) slackly; **das Segel hing ~**: the sail hung limply

Schlappe *die;* ~, ~n setback; **eine [schwere] ~ einstecken [müssen]** *od.* **erleiden** suffer a [severe] setback

schlappen
[A] *itr. V.* [1] (zu weit sein) ‹*shoe*› be too wide [2] *mit sein* (schlurfend gehen) shuffle
[B] *tr. V.* (schlabbern) lap [up]

Schlappen *der;* ~s, ~ (ugs.) slipper

Schlappheit *die;* ~: weariness; (wegen Krankheit, Schwüle) listlessness; (ugs.: Schwunglosigkeit) feebleness

schlapp-, Schlapp-: ~hut *der* slouch hat; **~|machen** *itr. V.* (ugs.) flag; (zusammenbrechen) flake out (coll.); (aufgeben) give up; **~ohr** *das* lop ear; **~schwanz** *der* (salopp abwertend) weed; wet (coll.)

Schlaraffenland /ʃlaˈrafn̩-/ *das;* ~[e]s Cockaigne

schlau /ʃlau̯/
[A] *Adj.* [1] shrewd; astute; (gerissen) wily; crafty; cunning; **sich** (*Dat.*) **ein ~es Leben machen** (ugs.) make life cushy for oneself (coll.); **das war besonders ~ [von dir]** (iron.) that was very clever *or* bright [of you] (iron.) [2] (ugs.: gescheit) clever; bright; smart; **aus etw. nicht ~ werden** (ugs.) not be able to make head or tail of sth.; **aus jmdm. nicht ~ werden** (ugs.) not be able to make sb. out; *s. auch* **Buch 1**
[B] *adv.* shrewdly; astutely; (gerissen) craftily; cunningly

Schlauberger /ˈʃlau̯bɛrgɐ/ *der;* ~s, ~ (ugs. scherzh.) wily *or* crafty customer (coll.)

Schlaubergerin *die;* ~, ~nen (ugs. scherzh.) wily lady

Schlauch /ʃlaux/ *der;* ~[e]s, **Schläuche** /ˈʃlɔyçə/ [1] hose; **das war ein [ganz schöner] ~!** (fig. ugs.) it was a [real] slog [2] (Fahrrad~, Auto~) tube [3] (für Wein usw.) skin [4] (ugs.: schmaler Raum) tunnel

Schlauch·boot *das* rubber dinghy; inflatable [dinghy]

schlauchen *tr. V.* (ugs.) [1] *auch itr.* (anstrengen) **jmdn. ~**: take it out of sb.; **geschlaucht sein** be whacked (Brit. coll.); be worn out [2] (scharf herannehmen) **jmdn. ~**: put sb. through the mill

schlauch·los *Adj.* tubeless ‹*tyre*›

Schläue /ˈʃlɔyə/ *die;* ~: shrewdness; astuteness; (Gerissenheit) wiliness; craftiness; cunning

Schlaufe /ˈʃlau̯fə/ *die;* ~, ~n (zum Festhalten) strap; (Gürtel~, Verschluss) loop

Schlau-: ~kopf *der* (ugs.), **~meier** *der* (ugs. scherzh.) ▸**Schlauberger**

Schlawiner /ʃlaˈviːnɐ/ *der;* ~s, ~ (ugs.) trickster; (scherzh.: Schlingel) rogue; rascal

Schlawinerin *die;* ~, ~nen trickster; (Kind) rascal

schlecht /ʃlɛçt/
[A] *Adj.* [1] bad; poor, bad ‹*food, quality, style, harvest, health, circulation*›; poor ‹*salary, eater, appetite*›; poor-quality ‹*goods*›; bad, weak ‹*eyes*›; **nicht ~!** not bad!; **in Mathematik ~ sein** be bad at mathematics; **[ein] ~es Englisch sprechen** speak poor English; **~ für die Gesundheit sein** be bad for one's health; **das wäre nicht ~/das Schlechteste** that wouldn't be a bad idea/a bad idea at all; **mit jmdm.** *od.* **um jmdn./mit etw. steht es ~**: sb./sth. is in a bad way; (jmd./etw. hat ~e Aussichten) things look bad for sb./sth. [2] (böse) bad; wicked; **das Schlechte im Menschen/in der Welt** the evil in man/the world; **ich hatte nur Schlechtes über ihn gehört** I had heard only bad things about him; **sie ist nicht die Schlechteste** she's not too bad; **jmdn. ~ machen** run sb. down; disparage sb.; *s. auch* **Eltern** [3] (ungenießbar) off; **die Milch/das Fleisch ist ~ geworden** the milk/meat has gone off [4] (unwohl, elend) **jmdm. ist [es] ~**: sb. feels ill *or* unwell *or* poorly; **in ~er Verfassung sein** be in a bad way; **da kann einem ja ~ werden!** (fig. ugs.) it's enough to make you ill
[B] *adv.* [1] badly; **er verdient ziemlich ~**: he is badly *or* poorly paid; **die Vorstellung war ~ besucht** the performance was poorly attended; **sie vertragen sich ~**: they don't get on well; **sie spricht ~ Englisch** she speaks poor English; **die Farben vertragen sich ~**: the colours don't go well together; **er sieht/hört ~**: his sight is poor/he has poor hearing; **sie waren nicht ~ beeindruckt** (ugs.) they weren't half impressed (sl.); **die Geschäfte gehen im Moment ~**: business is bad at the moment; **über jmdn.** *od.* **von jmdm. ~ sprechen** speak ill of sb.; **~ beraten** badly-advised; **~ bezahlt** badly *or* poorly paid; **~ sitzend** ill-fitting [2] (schwer) **heute geht es ~**: today is difficult; **heute passt es mir ~**: it's not very convenient for me today; **das lässt sich ~ machen** that's difficult to manage; **das kann ich ~ sagen** I can't really say; **das wird sich ~ vermeiden lassen** it can hardly be avoided; **das kann er sich** (*Dat.*) **als Pfarrer ~ leisten** *od.* **erlauben** [in his position] as a vicar he really cannot afford to do that [3] *in* **~ und recht, mehr ~ als recht** after a fashion; **sie hat sich ~ und recht durchs Leben geschlagen** she got by in life as best she could

***schlechtberaten, schlechtbezahlt** ▸**schlecht B 1**

schlechter·dings *Adv.* simply

schlecht-: *~gehen ▸**gehen A 11**; **~gelaunt** ▸**gelaunt**; **~hin** *Adv.* [1] *einem Subst. nachgestellt* **er war der Romantiker ~hin** he was the quintessential Romantic *or* the epitome of the Romantic; **das Prinzip des Privateigentums ~hin anfechten** attack the very principle of private property; [2] (geradezu, ganz einfach) quite simply

Schlechtigkeit *die;* ~, ~en [1] badness; wickedness [2] (böse Tat) bad *or* wicked deed

schlecht-, Schlecht-: *~|machen ▸**schlecht A 2**; ***~sitzend** ▸**schlecht B 1**; **~weg** *Adv.:* ▸**~hin 2**; **~wetter·geld** /-ˈ---/ *das* bad weather allowance (*paid to building workers to make up for work lost due to bad weather*); **~wetter·periode** /-ˈ-----/ *die* (Met.) period of bad weather

schlecken /ˈʃlɛkn̩/ (bes. südd., österr.)
[A] *tr. V.* lap up
[B] *itr. V.* [1] **an etw.** (*Dat.*) **~**: lick sth. [2] ▸**naschen A 1**

Schleckerei *die;* ~, ~en (bes. südd., österr.) [1] (das Naschen) ▸**Nascherei** [2] (Süßigkeit) sweet

Schlegel /ˈʃleːgl̩/ *der;* ~s, ~ [1] (Werkzeug) mallet [2] (für Schlaginstrumente) stick [3] (südd., österr.) ▸**Keule 3**

Schleh·dorn *der; Pl.* ~e blackthorn; sloe

Schlehe /ˈʃleːə/ *die;* ~, ~n sloe

Schleiche *die;* ~, ~n (Zool.) one of the Anguidae; **die ~n** the Anguidae

schleichen /ˈʃlai̯çn̩/
[A] *unr. itr. V.; mit sein* creep; (heimlich) creep; steal; sneak; ‹*cat*› slink, creep; (langsam fahren) crawl along; **die Zeit schlich** time crept by
[B] *unr. refl. V.* creep; steal; sneak; ‹*cat*› slink, creep; **Misstrauen schlich sich in ihr Herz** (geh.) distrust crept into her heart; **schleich dich!** (ugs., bes. österr.) get lost! (coll.); buzz off! (sl.)

schleichend *Adj.* insidious ‹*disease*›; slow[-acting], insidious ‹*poison*›; creeping ‹*inflation*›; gradual ‹*crisis*›

Schleicher *der;* ~s, ~, **Schleicherin** *die;* ~, ~nen (abwertend) toadying hypocrite

Schleich-: ~handel *der* black marketeering (**mit** in); **im ~handel** on the black market; **~katze** *die* viverrid (Zool.); **~weg** *der* secret path; **auf ~wegen, auf dem ~weg** (fig.) clandestinely; (unrechtmäßig) illicitly; by illicit means; **~werbung** *die* surreptitious advertising

Schleie /ˈʃlai̯ə/ *die;* ~, ~n (Zool.) tench

Schleier /ˈʃlai̯ɐ/ *der;* ~s, ~ [1] (durchsichtiges Gewebe) veil; **den ~ nehmen** (fig. geh.) take the veil; **den ~ [des Geheimnisses] lüften** (fig. geh.) lift the veil of secrecy; **den ~ der Vergessenheit** *od.* **des Vergessens über etw.** (*Akk.*) **breiten** (fig. geh.) draw a veil over sth. [2] (Nebel~, Dunst~) veil of mist/smoke [3] (Fot.: Farb~) fog; **einen ~ haben** be fogged

schleier-, Schleier-: ~eule *die* barn owl; **~haft** *Adj.* **jmdm. [völlig** *od.* **vollkommen] ~haft sein/bleiben** be/remain a [total *or* complete] mystery to sb.; **~kraut** *das* (Bot.) baby's breath; **~schwanz** *der* (Zool.) fantail; **~tanz** *der* dance of the veils

Schleife /ˈʃlai̯fə/ *die;* ~, ~n [1] bow; (Fliege) bow tie [2] (starke Biegung) loop; (eines Flusses) loop; horseshoe bend [3] (Kranz~) [inscribed] ribbon (*attached to a wreath*)

schleifen[1] *unr. tr. V.* [1] (schärfen) sharpen; grind, sharpen ‹*axe*› [2] (glätten) grind; cut ‹*diamond, glass*›; (mit Sand-/Schmirgelpapier) sand; *s. auch* **geschliffen** [3] (bes. Soldatenspr.: drillen) **jmdn. ~**: drill sb. hard

schleifen[2]
[A] *tr. V.* [1] (auch fig.) drag; **jmdn. ins Kino ~** (fig.) drag sb. along to the cinema (Brit.) *or* (Amer.) movie [2] (niederreißen) **etw. ~**: raze sth. [to the ground]
[B] *itr. V.; auch mit sein* drag; **die Kette schleift am Schutzblech** the chain scrapes the guard; **die Kupplung ~ lassen** (Kfz-W.) slip the clutch; **etw. ~ lassen** (fig.) let sth. slide; *s. auch* **Zügel**

Schleifer *der;* ~s, ~ [1] grinder; (Diamanten~) cutter [2] (Soldatenspr.) slave driver [3] (Musik) slur

Schleiferei *die;* ~, ~en [1] ▸**schleifen**[1] **1, 2**: sharpening; grinding; cutting; sanding [2] (bes. Soldatenspr.: das Drillen) hard drilling [3] (Betrieb) grinding shop

Schleiferin *die;* ~, ~nen ▸**Schleifer 1**

Schleif-: ~lack·möbel *das* piece of matt-lacquered furniture; **weiße ~~**: white matt-lacquered furniture *sing.*; **~spur** *die* drag mark; **~stein** *der* grindstone; **dasitzen wie ein Affe auf dem ~stein** (ugs. scherzh.) sit crouched there looking a proper charlie (coll.)

S

Schleifung *die;* ~, ~**en** razing [to the ground]

Schleim /ʃlaim/ *der;* ~**[e]s,** ~**e** **1** mucus; (im Hals) phlegm; (von Schnecken, Aalen) slime; (Bot.) mucilage **2** (sämiger Brei) gruel

Schleim-: ~**beutel** *der* ▸**i** **S. 435** (Anat.) synovial bursa; mucous bursa; ~**haut** *die* ▸**i** **S. 435** mucous membrane

schleimig

A *Adj.* **1** slimy; (Physiol., Zool.) mucous **2** (abwertend: heuchlerisch) slimy

B *adv.* (abwertend) slimily

schleim-, Schleim-: ~**lösend** *Adj.* expectorant; ~**pilz** *der* slime mould *or* fungus; ~**suppe** *die* (Kochk.) gruel

schleißen /ˈʃlaisn̩/ *regelm. (auch unr.) tr. V.* **1** strip ‹*feathers*› **2** (bes. südd.: spalten) split ‹*wood*›

Schlemihl /ʃleˈmiːl/ *der;* ~**s,** ~**e** **1** (Pechvogel) unlucky devil **2** (ugs.: Schlitzohr) crafty devil

schlemmen /ˈʃlɛmən/

A *itr. V.* (prassen) have a feast

B *tr. V.* (verzehren) feast on

Schlemmer *der;* ~**s,** ~: gourmet

Schlemmerei *die;* ~, ~**en** (oft abwertend) **1** (das Schlemmen) feasting; gormandizing (derog.) **2** ▸**Schlemmermahl**

Schlemmerin *die;* ~, ~**nen** ▸**Schlemmer**

Schlemmer-: ~**lokal** *das* gourmet restaurant; ~**mahl** *das* gourmet meal

schlendern /ˈʃlɛndɐn/ *itr. V.; mit sein* stroll

Schlendrian /ˈʃlɛndriaːn/ *der;* ~**[e]s** (ugs. abwertend) slackness

Schlenker /ˈʃlɛŋkɐ/ *der;* ~**s,** ~ (ugs.) **1** (Bogen) swerve; **einen** ~ **machen** swerve; (fig.) dodge **2** (Umweg) detour

schlenkern

A *itr. V.* **1** swing; dangle; **mit den Armen/mit den Beinen** ~: swing *or* dangle one's arms/legs **2** ‹*curtain, dress*› flap; ‹*car*› swerve

B *tr. V.* swing, dangle ‹*arms, legs*›

schlenzen /ˈʃlɛntsn̩/ *tr. V.* flick ‹*ball, puck*›

Schlepp /ʃlɛp/ *der:* **in** **ein Fahrzeug in** ~ **nehmen** take a vehicle in tow

Schlepp-: ~**bügel** *der* (Skisport) T-bar; ~**dampfer** *der* (Seew.) [steam-driven] tug

Schleppe *die;* ~, ~**n** **1** train **2** (Pferdesport, Jagdw.: künstliche Fährte) drag

schleppen

A *tr. V.* **1** (hinter sich herziehen) tow ‹*vehicle, ship*› **2** (tragen) carry; lug **3** (ugs.: mitnehmen) drag; **jmdn. vor den Richter** ~: haul sb. up before the judge

B *refl. V.* **1** drag *or* haul oneself **2** (sich hinziehen) ‹*trial, negotiations, etc.*› drag on **3** (bes. nordostd.: sich abmühen) **ich musste mich allein mit dem Kasten** ~: I had to lug the box around by myself

C *itr. V.* (schleifen) drag

schleppend

A *Adj.* **1** (schwerfällig) shuffling, dragging ‹*walk, steps*› **2** (gedehnt) dragging ‹*speech*›; slow ‹*song, melody*› **3** (nicht zügig) slow ‹*service*›; **er beklagte sich über die** ~**e Bearbeitung seines Antrags** he complained about the delays in processing his application; **die Unterhaltung wurde immer** ~**er** the conversation dragged more and more

B *adv.* **1** (schwerfällig) ~ **gehen** shuffle along **2** (gedehnt) ‹*speak*› in a dragging voice; ‹*sing, play*› slowly **3** (nicht zügig) **die Unterhaltung kam nur** ~ **in Gang** conversation was slow to get going; **die Arbeiten gehen nur** ~ **voran** the work is progressing slowly

Schlepper *der;* ~**s,** ~ **1** (Schiff) tug **2** (Traktor) tractor; (Sattel~) tractor [unit] **3** (ugs.: jmd., der Kunden zuführt) tout **4** (ugs.: Fluchthelfer) *person who aids the entry of illegal immigrants or escape of illegal emigrants*

Schlepperei *die;* ~, ~**en** (ugs. abwertend) lugging around

Schlepperin *die;* ~, ~**nen** ▸**Schlepper 3, 4**

Schlepp-: ~**kahn** *der* dumb barge; ~**lift** *der* T-bar [lift]; ~**netz** *das* trawl [net]; ~**seil** *das* ▸~**tau**; ~**start** *der* (Segelfliegen) aerotow; ~**tau** *das* towline; tow rope; (aus Draht) towline; tow cable; **etw. ins** ~**tau nehmen** take sth. in tow; **in jmds.** ~**tau** (fig.) in sb.'s wake; ~**zug** *der* (Schifffahrt) train of barges

Schlesien /ˈʃleːzi̯ən/ *(das);* ~**s** Silesia

Schlesier /ˈʃleːzi̯ɐ/ *der;* ~**s,** ~, **Schlesierin** *die;* ~, ~**nen** Silesian

schlesisch *Adj.* Silesian

Schleswig-Holstein *(das);* ~**s** Schleswig-Holstein

Schleswig-Holsteiner

A *indekl. Adj.* Schleswig-Holstein

B *der;* ~**s,** ~: native of Schleswig-Holstein; (Einwohner) inhabitant of Schleswig-Holstein

schleswig-holsteinisch *Adj.* Schleswig-Holstein *attrib.*

Schleuder /ˈʃlɔydɐ/ *die;* ~, ~**n** **1** sling; (mit Gummiband) catapult (Brit.); slingshot (Amer.) **2** ▸**Wäscheschleuder** **3** ▸**Zentrifuge**

Schleuder-: ~**ball** *der* **1** *team game played with a 'Schleuderball' 2;* **2** (Ball) *leather ball with a strap attached for throwing;* ~**honig** *der* extracted honey

schleudern

A *tr. V.* **1** (werfen) hurl; fling; **der Wagen wurde aus der Kurve geschleudert** the car was sent skidding off the bend; **jmdm. Beleidigungen ins Gesicht** ~ (fig.) hurl insults at sb. **2** (rotieren lassen) centrifuge; spin ‹*washing*›

B *itr. V.* **1** *mit sein* (rutschen) skid; **ins Schleudern geraten** *od.* **kommen** go into a skid; (fig. ugs.) run into trouble; **dein Argument hat ihn ins Schleudern gebracht** (ugs.) your argument completely threw him (coll.) **2** (rotieren) spin

Schleuder-: ~**preis** *der* (ugs.) knock-down price; ~**sitz** *der* ejector seat; ~**ware** *die* (ugs.) cut-price item

schleunig /ˈʃlɔynɪç/

A *Adj.* **1** (unverzüglich) speedy; rapid **2** (eilig) hurried

B *adv.* **1** (unverzüglich) rapidly; speedily **2** (eilig) hurriedly

schleunigst *Adv.* **1** (auf der Stelle) at once; immediately; straight away **2** (eilends) hastily; with all haste

Schleuse /ˈʃlɔyzə/ *die;* ~, ~**n** **1** sluice [gate]; **die** ~**n des Himmels öffneten sich** (fig.) the heavens opened **2** (Schiffs~) lock **3** (Luft~) airlock

schleusen *tr. V.* **1** **ein Schiff** ~: pass a ship through a/the lock **2** (geleiten) shepherd **3** (schmuggeln) smuggle ‹*secrets*›; infiltrate ‹*spy, agent, etc.*› **(in** + *Akk.* into)

Schleusen-: ~**kammer** *die* lock chamber; ~**tor** *das* lock gate; ~**wärter** *der,* ~**wärterin** *die* lock-keeper

schlich /ʃlɪç/ *1. u. 3. Pers. Sg. Prät. v.* **schleichen**

Schlich *der;* ~**[e]s,** ~**e** trick; **alle** ~**e kennen** know all the tricks; **jmdm. auf die** ~**e** *od.* **hinter jmds.** ~**e kommen** get on to sb.

schlicht /ʃlɪçt/

A *Adj.* **1** simple; plain, simple ‹*pattern, furniture*›; (geh.: glatt) smooth ‹*hair*›; **in** ~**en Verhältnissen leben** live in modest circumstances **2** (unkompliziert) simple, unsophisticated ‹*person, view, etc.*› **3** (bloß, rein) simple; pure; **ein** ~**es Ja oder Nein** a simple yes or no

B *adv.* simply; simply, plainly ‹*dressed, furnished*›; **wir haben ihn** ~ **Karl genannt** we gave him the plain, straightforward name Karl; ~ **und einfach** (ugs.) quite *or* just simply; **er hat es** ~ **und ergreifend vergessen** (ugs. scherzh.) he just plain forgot

schlichten

A *tr. V.* **1** settle ‹*argument, difference of opinion*›; settle ‹*industrial dispute etc.*› by mediation **2** (fachspr.) smooth ‹*wood, metal*›; dress ‹*stone, leather*›; size ‹*warp threads*›

B *itr. V.* mediate **(in** + *Dat.* in, **zwischen** between); **in einem Konflikt** ~**d eingreifen** intervene as mediator in a dispute

Schlichter *der;* ~**s,** ~, **Schlichterin** *die;* ~, ~**nen** mediator; (durch Schiedsspruch) arbitrator

Schlichter·spruch *der* arbitrator's award

Schlichtheit *die;* ~ ▸**schlicht 1, 2**: simplicity; plainness; unsophisticatedness

Schlichtung *die;* ~, ~**en** settlement; (in einem Arbeitskampf usw.) mediation; (durch Schiedsspruch) arbitration

Schlichtungs-: ~**ausschuss,** *~**ausschuß** *der* arbitration committee; ~**verfahren** *das* arbitration process

schlicht·weg *Adv.* **er gab es** ~ **zu** he simply admitted it; **das ist** ~ **kriminell** that's just plain criminal

Schlick /ʃlɪk/ *der;* ~**[e]s,** ~**e** silt

schlief /ʃliːf/ *1. u. 3. Pers. Sg. Prät. v.* **schlafen**

Schliere /ˈʃliːrə/ *die;* ~, ~**n** (Technik, Optik, Geol.) schliere

Schließe /ˈʃliːsə/ *die;* ~, ~**n** clasp; (Schnalle) buckle

schließen

A *unr. tr. V.* **1** (zumachen) close; shut; put the top on ‹*bottle*›; turn off ‹*tap*›; fasten ‹*belt, bracelet*›; do up ‹*button, zip*›; close ‹*street, route, electrical circuit*›; close off ‹*pipe*›; (fig.) close ‹*border*›; fill, close ‹*gap*›; **mit geschlossenen Beinen** with one's legs together; **die Augen für immer geschlossen haben** (geh. verhüll.) have passed away **2** (unzugänglich machen) close, shut ‹*shop, factory*›; (außer Betrieb setzen) close [down] ‹*shop, school*›; close *or* shut [down] ‹*factory*› **3** (ein~) **etw./jmdn./sich in etw.** (*Akk.*) ~: lock sth./sb./oneself in sth. **4** (beenden) close ‹*meeting, proceedings, debate*›; end, conclude ‹*letter, speech, lecture*›; **die Rednerliste ist geschlossen** the list of speakers is closed **5** (befestigen) **etw. an etw.** (*Akk.*) ~: connect sth. to sth.; (mit Schloss) lock sth. to sth. **6** (eingehen, vereinbaren) conclude ‹*treaty, pact, ceasefire, agreement*›; reach ‹*settlement, compromise*›; enter into ‹*contract*›; **wann wurde Ihre Ehe geschlossen?** when did you get married?; **Freundschaft/Bekanntschaft mit jmdm.** ~: make friends with/get to know sb.; *s. auch* **Frieden** **7** (umfassen) **jmdn. in die Arme** ~: take sb. in one's arms; embrace sb.; **etw. in seine Hand** ~: clasp sth. in one's hand; **etw. in sich** ~ (fig.) contain sth. **8** (folgern) **etw. aus etw.** ~: infer *or* conclude sth. from sth.; **aus etw.** ~, **dass ...** infer *or* conclude from sth. that ...

B *unr. itr. V.* **1** close; shut; **der Schlüssel/das Schloss schließt schlecht** the key won't turn properly/the lock doesn't work properly **2** ‹*shop*› close, shut; ‹*stock exchange*› close; (den Betrieb einstellen) ‹*shop*› close [down]; ‹*factory*› close *or* shut [down] **3** (enden) end; conclude **4** (urteilen) **[aus etw.] auf etw.** (*Akk.*) ~: infer *or* conclude sth. [from sth.]; **die Symptome lassen auf Hepatitis** ~: the symptoms indicate hepatitis; **etw. lässt darauf** ~, **dass ...** sth. indicates *or* suggests that ...; **vom Besonderen auf das Allgemeine** ~: proceed from the particular to the general; **von sich auf andere** ~: judge others by one's own standards

C *unr. refl. V.* **1** ‹*door, window*› close, shut; ‹*wound, circle*› close; ‹*flower*› close [up]; **sich um etw.** ~: close around sth.; *s. auch* **geschlossen** **2** (sich an~) **an den Vortrag schloss sich eine Diskussion** the lecture was followed by a discussion

Schließer *der;* ~**s,** ~ **1** (Tür~) doorkeeper; (Vorrichtung) [door-]closer **2** (im Gefängnis) warder

Schließerin *die;* ~, ~**nen** **1** doorkeeper **2** (im Gefängnis) warder

Schließ-: ~**fach** *das* locker; (bei der Post) post office box; PO box; (bei der Bank) safe-deposit box; ~**frucht** *die* (Bot.) indehiscent fruit; ~**korb** *der* hamper

schließlich *Adv.* **1** finally; in the end; (bei Erwünschtem auch) at last; ~ **und endlich** (ugs.) in the end; finally **2** (bei einer Aufzählung) **..., und** ~ **...** ... and finally ... **3** (immerhin, doch) after all; **er ist** ~ **mein Freund** he is my friend, after all; **er hat** ~ **nur seine Pflicht getan** after all, he was only doing his duty

Schließ·muskel *der* ▸**i** **S. 435** (Anat.) sphincter

Schließung *die;* ~, ~**en** 1 (der Geschäfte, Büros usw.) closing; shutting; (Stilllegung, Einstellung) closure; closing; (fig.: einer Grenze) closing; **zur ~ seiner Haushaltslücke** to fill the gap in his budget 2 (Beendigung) **vor/nach ~ der Versammlung** before/after the meeting was closed; before/after the conclusion of the meeting; **die ~/einstweilige ~ der Debatte** the closure/adjournment of the debate 3 ▸**schließen A 6**: conclusion; reaching; **die ~ einer Ehe** the solemnization of a marriage

schliff /ʃlɪf/ *1. u. 3. Pers. Sg. Prät. v.* **schleifen**

Schliff *der;* ~**[e]s,** ~**e** 1 (das Schleifen) cutting; (von Messern, Sensen usw.) sharpening 2 (Art, wie etw. geschliffen wird) cut; (von Messern, Scheren, Schneiden) edge 3 (Lebensart) refinement; polish 4 (Vollkommenheit) **einem Brief/Text** *usw.* **den letzten ~ geben** put the finishing touches *pl.* to a letter/text *etc.*; **der Mannschaft den letzten ~ geben** put the finishing touches *pl.* to the team's training

schlimm /ʃlɪm/

A *Adj.* 1 (schwerwiegend) grave, serious ‹*error, mistake, accusation, offence*›; bad, serious ‹*error, mistake*›; **man hat ihm die ~sten Dinge nachgesagt** the most terrible things have been said about him; **das ist ~ für ihn** that's serious for him 2 (übel) bad; nasty, bad ‹*experience*›; **das war eine ~e Geschichte für ihn** that was a nasty business for him; **im ~sten Fall muss ich ...** if the worst comes to the worst I'll have to ...; **ist es ~, wenn wir erst morgen kommen?** does it matter if we don't come till tomorrow?; **[das ist alles] halb so ~:** it's not as bad as all that; **das Schlimmste ist, dass ...** the worst thing is *or* the worst of it is that ...; **es wurde immer ~er** it got worse and worse; **es ist nichts Schlimmes** it's nothing serious; **wenn es nichts Schlimmeres ist!** if it's nothing worse than that!; **ist nicht ~!** [it] doesn't matter; **es gibt Schlimmeres** there are worse things 3 (schlecht, böse) wicked; (ungezogen) naughty ‹*child*›; **er ist ein ganz Schlimmer** (scherzh.) he's really wicked 4 (fam.: schmerzend, entzündet) bad; sore; bad, nasty ‹*wound*›

B *adv.* (übel, arg) **~ d[a]ran sein** (körperlich, geistig) be in a bad way; (in einer ~en Situation) be in dire straits; **es steht ~ um jmdn.** things look bad *or* serious for sb.; **es hätte ~er ausgehen können** things could have turned out worse

schlimmsten·falls *Adv.* if the worst comes to the worst; **~ kriegt man eine Verwarnung** at worst you'll get a caution

Schlinge /ˈʃlɪŋə/ *die;* ~, ~**n** 1 (Schlaufe) loop; (für den gebrochenen Arm o. Ä.) sling; (zum Aufhängen) noose; **jmdm. die ~ um den Hals legen** put a noose round sb.'s neck; **die ~ zusammenziehen** (fig.) tighten the noose; *s. auch* **Kopf 1** 2 (Fanggerät) snare; **~n legen** lay *or* set snares; **sich in der eigenen ~ fangen** (fig.) be hoist with one's own petard; **in jmds. ~ geraten** (fig.) fall into sb.'s trap

Schlingel /ˈʃlɪŋl/ *der;* ~**s,** ~**:** rascal; rogue

schlingen

A *unr. tr. V.* 1 (winden) **etw. um etw. ~:** loop sth. round sth.; (und zusammenbinden) tie sth. round sth.; **sich** (*Dat.*) **einen Schal um den Hals ~:** wrap a scarf round one's neck; **die Arme um jmdn./etw. ~:** wrap one's arms round sb./sth. 2 (binden) tie ‹*knot*›; **etw. zu einem Knoten ~:** tie sth. up in a knot 3 (flechten) plait

B *unr. refl. V.* (sich winden) **sich um etw. ~** ‹*snake*› wind *or* coil itself round sth.; ‹*plant*› wind *or* twine itself round sth.

C *unr. itr. V.* bolt one's food; wolf one's food [down]; **schling nicht so hastig!** don't bolt your food like that!

Schlinger-: ~**bewegung** *die* (Seew.) rolling motion; **in ~bewegungen geraten** start to roll; ~**kurs** *der* (bes. Politik Jargon) wavering course; **einen ~kurs fahren** steer *or* follow a wavering course

schlingern /ˈʃlɪŋɐn/ *itr. V.; meist, mit Richtungsangabe nur, mit sein* ‹*ship, boat*› roll; ‹*train, vehicle*› lurch from side to side; **ins Schlingern kommen** (fig. ugs.) run into trouble

Schling·pflanze *die* creeper

Schlips /ʃlɪps/ *der;* ~**es,** ~**e** tie; **jmdm. auf den ~ treten** (fig. ugs.) tread on sb.'s toes; **sich auf den ~ getreten fühlen** (fig. ugs.) feel *or* be put out; **mit ~ und Kragen** (fig. ugs.) wearing a collar and tie; with a collar and tie on

Schlitten /ˈʃlɪtn/ *der;* ~**s,** ~ 1 sledge; sled; (Pferde~) sleigh; (Rodel~) toboggan; **~ fahren** go tobogganing; **die Kinder fuhren mit dem ~ den Hang hinunter** the children tobogganed down the slope; **mit jmdm. ~ fahren** (fig. ugs.) bawl sb. out (coll.); **ich werde mit ihm ~ fahren** (fig. ugs.) I'm going to give him hell (coll.) 2 (salopp: Auto) car; motor (Brit.); **ein alter ~:** an old banger (Brit. sl.); a jalopy 3 (Technik: Maschinenteil) carriage

Schlitten-: ~**fahrt** *die* sleigh ride; ~**hund** *der* sled dog

schlittern /ˈʃlɪtɐn/ *itr. V.* 1 *auch mit sein* (rutschen) slide 2 *mit sein* (ins Rutschen kommen) slip; slide; ‹*vehicle*› skid; ‹*wheel*› slip 3 *mit sein* (fig.) **in die Pleite ~:** slide into bankruptcy; **in ein Abenteuer ~:** stumble into an adventure

Schlitt-: ~**schuh** *der* [ice] skate; **~schuh laufen** *od.* **fahren** [ice-]skate; ~**schuh·laufen** *das;* ~~**s** [ice] skating *no art.*; ~**schuh·läufer** *der,* ~**schuh·läuferin** *die* [ice] skater

Schlitz /ʃlɪts/ *der;* ~**es,** ~**e** 1 slit; (Briefkasten~, Automaten~) slot; **seine Augen wurden zu ~en** (fig.) his eyes narrowed to slits 2 (Hosen~) flies *pl.*; fly; (Jacken~) vent

Schlitz·auge *das* slit eye

schlitzäugig /-ɔygɪç/ *Adj.* slit-eyed

schlitzen *tr. V.* slit; (auf~) slit open

Schlitz·ohr *das* (ugs.) wily *or* crafty devil

schlitzohrig (ugs.)

A *Adj.* wily; crafty

B *adv.* craftily

schloh·weiß /ˈʃloːˈvais/ *Adj.* snow-white ‹*hair, head*›; **er ist ~:** he has snow-white hair

schloss, *schloß /ʃlɔs/ *1. u. 3. Pers. Sg. Prät. v.* **schließen**

Schloss, *Schloß *das;* **Schlosses, Schlösser** /ˈʃlœsɐ/ 1 (Tür~, Gewehr~) lock; **die Tür fiel/fiel krachend ins ~:** the door clicked/slammed to *or* shut 2 (Vorhänge~) padlock; **hinter ~ und Riegel** (ugs.) behind bars 3 (Verschluss) clasp 4 (Wohngebäude) castle; (Palast) palace; (Herrschaftshaus) mansion; (in Frankreich) chateau

Schloss-, *Schloß-: ~**anlage** *die* 1 castle buildings *pl.*; 2 *Pl.*; ▸~**park**; ~**berg** *der* castle hill

Schlösschen, *Schlößchen /ˈʃlœsçən/ *das;* ~**s,** ~ ▸**Schloss 4**: small castle *etc.*

Schloße /ˈʃloːsə/ *die;* ~, ~**n;** (bes. md.) hailstone

Schlosser *der;* ~**s,** ~ ▸❶ **S. 113** metalworker; (Maschinen~) fitter; (für Schlösser) locksmith; (Auto~) mechanic

Schlosserei *die;* ~, ~**en** 1 (Werkstatt) metalworking shop; (für Schlösser) locksmith's workshop 2 ▸**Schlosserhandwerk**

Schlosser-: ~**handwerk** *das;* ▸**Schlosser**: metalworking; fitter's trade; locksmithery; mechanic's trade; **das ~handwerk lernen** train to be a metalworker/fitter/locksmith/mechanic

Schlosserin, *die;* ~, ~**nen** ▸**Schlosser**

Schlosser·werkstatt, *die* ▸**Schlosserei 1**

Schloss-, *Schloß-: ~**garten** *der* castle *etc.* gardens *pl.*; ~**herr** *der,* ~**herrin** *die* owner of a/the castle *etc.*; ~**hof** *der* castle *etc.* courtyard; ~**hund** *der:* *in* **heulen wie ein ~hund** (ugs.) cry one's eyes out; ~**kapelle** *die* castle *etc.* chapel; ~**park** *der* castle *etc.* grounds *pl.*; ~**ruine** *die* ruined castle *etc.*

Schlot /ʃloːt/ *der;* ~**[e]s,** ~**e** *od.* **Schlöte** /ˈʃløːtə/ 1 (bes. md.: Schornstein) chimney [stack]; (eines Schiffes) funnel; **rauchen** *od.* **qualmen wie ein ~** (ugs.) smoke like a chimney 2 (Geol.: Eruptionsschacht) chimney; vent 3 (ugs. abwertend: Nichtsnutz) good-for-nothing

Schlot·baron *der* (abwertend) industrial baron *or* tycoon

schlotterig ▸**schlottrig**

schlottern /ˈʃlɔtɐn/ *itr. V.* 1 shake; tremble; **jmdm. ~ die Knie** sb.'s knees are shaking *or* trembling; **am ganzen Leibe ~:** shake *or* tremble all over 2 ‹*clothes*› hang loose

schlottrig *Adj.* 1 trembling; shaking 2 baggy ‹*clothes*›

Schlucht /ʃlʊxt/ *die;* ~, ~**en** ravine; gorge

schluchzen /ˈʃlʊxtsn̩/ *itr. V.* sob; **unter Schluchzen** sobbing; **in heftiges Schluchzen ausbrechen** burst into heavy sobbing; **die ~den Klänge der Geigen** (fig.) the sobbing strains of the violins

Schluchzer *der;* ~**s,** ~**:** sob

Schluck /ʃlʊk/ *der;* ~**[e]s,** ~**e** *od.* **Schlücke** /ˈʃlʏkə/ 1 swallow; mouthful; (großer ~) gulp; (kleiner ~) sip; **einen tüchtigen ~ [Bier] trinken** take a good *or* long swig [of beer] (coll.); **sein Glas mit** *od.* **in einem** *od.* **in einem ~ leeren** empty one's glass in one go *or* (coll.) swig; **hast du einen ~ zu trinken für uns?** have you got a drop of something for us to drink? 2 (ugs.: Getränk) **ein guter ~:** a good drop [of stuff] (coll.); (Wein) a pleasant little number (coll.)

Schluck·auf *der;* ~**s** hiccups *pl.*; hiccoughs *pl.*; **[den** *od.* **einen] ~ haben/bekommen** have/get [the] hiccups *or* hiccoughs

Schlückchen /ˈʃlʏkçən/ *das;* ~**s,** ~**:** sip; **du nimmst doch noch ein ~?** you'll have another drop, won't you?; **ich geh zu Peter auf ein ~:** I'm off to Peter's for a drink

schlucken

A *tr. V.* 1 (auch fig. ugs.) swallow; **etw. hastig ~:** gulp sth. down 2 (ugs.: einatmen) swallow ‹*dust*›; breathe in ‹*gas*› 3 (ugs. abwertend: in seinen Besitz bringen) swallow [up] 4 (ugs.: verbrauchen) swallow up; guzzle ‹*petrol*›

B *itr. V.* (auch fig.) swallow; **Beschwerden beim S~ haben** have difficulty swallowing; **an etw.** (*Dat.*) **zu ~ haben** (fig. ugs.) find sth. hard to come to terms with

Schlucken *der;* ~**s** ▸**Schluckauf**

Schlucker *der;* ~**s,** ~**:** *in* **armer ~** (ugs.) poor devil *or* (Brit. coll.) blighter

Schluck·impfung *die* oral vaccination

schlucksen /ˈʃlʊksn̩/ *itr. V.* (ugs.) hiccup; hiccough

schluck·weise *Adv.* in sips

Schluderei *die;* ~, ~**en** (ugs. abwertend) 1 sloppiness; slipshod work 2 (Fall von Nachlässigkeit) slipshod piece of work; botched job; **~en** slipshod work *sing.*; botching *sing.*

schluderig ▸**schludrig**

schludern /ˈʃluːdɐn/ *itr. V.* (ugs. abwertend) work sloppily; **bei etw. ~:** make a botched job of sth.; (etw. oberflächlich bearbeiten) skimp sth.; **es wird zu viel geschludert** too much work is being botched

schludrig (ugs. abwertend)

A *Adj.* 1 (nachlässig) slipshod ‹*work, examination*›; botched ‹*job*›; slapdash ‹*person, work*›; **eine ~e Schrift** a messy scrawl 2 (schlampig [aussehend]) scruffy

B *adv.* 1 (nachlässig) in a slipshod *or* slapdash way 2 (schlampig [aussehend]) scruffily

Schludrigkeit *die;* ~, ~**en** (ugs. abwertend) 1 sloppiness; (eines Menschen) slapdash ways *pl.*; (der Kleidung) scruffiness 2 (Fall von Nachlässigkeit) sloppiness; **diese ~en im Detail** this sloppiness when it comes to detail; this slipshod treatment of detail

schlug /ʃluːk/ *1. u. 3. Pers. Sg. Prät. v.* **schlagen**

Schlummer /ˈʃlʊmɐ/ *der;* ~**s** (geh.) slumber (poet./rhet.); (Nickerchen) doze; **nach langem ~:** after a long slumber (poet./rhet.)

Schlummer·lied *das* (geh.) lullaby; cradle song

schlummern *itr. V.* 1 (geh.: schlafen) slumber (poet./rhet.); (dösen) doze; **tief ~d** in a deep slumber 2 (fig.: verborgen liegen) **[in jmdm.] ~:** lie dormant [in sb.]; **~des Talent/~de Energie** latent talent/energy

Schlummer·rolle *die* bolster

Schlumpf /ʃlʊmpf/ *der;* ~**s, Schlümpfe** /ˈʃlʏmpfə/ (Comicfigur) smurf

S

Schlund /ʃlʊnt/ *der;* ~[e]s, **Schlünde** /ˈʃlʏndə/ 1▸ ▸❶ S. 435 (Rachen) [back of the] throat; pharynx (Anat.); (eines Tieres) maw 2▸ (geh.: gähnende Öffnung) [gaping] mouth; (Abgrund) chasm; abyss

Schlunze /ˈʃlʊntsə/ *die;* ~, ~n (salopp abwertend, bes. nordd.) slut

schlüpfen /ˈʃlʏpfn̩/ *itr. V.; mit sein* slip; **in ein/aus einem Kleid** *usw.* **~:** slip into *or* slip on/slip out of *or* slip off a dress *etc.*; **[aus dem Ei] ~** ‹*chick*› hatch out; **keiner kann aus seiner Haut ~** (fig.) nobody can completely change his/her identity

Schlüpfer *der;* ~s, ~ (veralt.) (für Damen) knickers *pl.* (Brit.); panties *pl.*; (für Herren) [under]pants *pl. or* trunks *pl.*; **ein ~:** a pair of knickers/ underpants

Schlupf·loch /ˈʃlʊpf-/ *das* 1▸ (Schlupfwinkel) hiding place 2▸ (Durchschlupf) hole; (Lücke im Gesetz usw.) loophole

schlüpfrig /ˈʃlʏpfrɪç/ *Adj.* 1▸ (feucht u. glatt) slippery 2▸ (abwertend: anstößig) lewd

Schlüpfrigkeit *die;* ~, ~en 1▸ (feuchte Glätte) slipperiness 2▸ (Anstößigkeit) lewdness

Schlupf-: **~wespe** *die* ichneumon fly; **~winkel** *der* hiding place; (von Banditen, Flüchtlingen usw.) hideout

schlurfen /ˈʃlʊrfn̩/ *itr. V.; mit sein* shuffle; (ohne Richtungsangabe) shuffle along

schlürfen /ˈʃlʏrfn̩/

A *tr. V.* (geräuschvoll) slurp [up]; drink noisily; (genussvoll) savour; (in kleinen Schlucken) sip

B *itr. V.* slurp; drink noisily

Schluss, *Schluß /ʃlʊs/ *der;* **Schlusses, Schlüsse** /ˈʃlʏsə/ 1▸ (Endzeitpunkt) end; (eines Vortrags o. Ä.) conclusion; (Laden~) closing time; (Dienst~) knocking-off time; **nach/gegen ~ der Aufführung** after/towards the end of the performance; **mit etw. ist ~:** sth. is at an end *or* over; (ugs.: etw. ist ruiniert) sth. has had it (coll.); **mit ihm ist ~** (ugs.) it's all up with him; (das Verhältnis ist beendet) it's all over with him; (seine Karriere ist beendet) he's past it; **mit dem Rauchen/Trinken ist jetzt ~:** there's to be no more smoking/drinking; you must stop smoking/drinking; (auf sich bezogen) I've given up smoking/drinking; **jetzt ist aber ~ [damit]!** that's enough of that; **~ jetzt!, ~ damit!** stop it!; that'll do!; **~ für heute!** that's it *or* that'll do for today; **am** *od.* **zum ~:** at the end; (schließlich) in the end; finally; **am** *od.* **zum ~ des Jahres** at the end of the year; **zum ~ möchte ich noch darauf hinweisen, dass ...** finally *or* in conclusion I should like to mention that ...; **kurz vor ~:** just before closing time; (im Büro) just before knocking-off time; **~ machen** (ugs.) stop; (Feierabend machen) knock off; (seine Stellung aufgeben) pack in one's job (coll.); (eine Freundschaft usw. lösen) break it off; (sich das Leben nehmen) end it all (coll.); **ich mache ~ für heute** I'm calling it a day; **ich muss jetzt ~ machen** (am Telefon) I'll have to go now; (am Briefende) I must stop now; **mit etw. ~ machen** stop sth.; **mit jmdm. ~ machen** finish with sb.; break it off with sb. 2▸ (letzter Abschnitt) end; (eines Zuges) back; (eines Buchs, Schauspiels usw.) ending 3▸ (Folgerung) conclusion (**auf** + *Akk.* regarding); (Logik: Ableitung) deduction; **Schlüsse aus etw. ziehen** draw conclusions from sth.; **ich werde meine Schlüsse daraus ziehen** I shall draw my own conclusions 4▸ (Technik, Bauw.) **einen guten ~ haben** ‹*piston*› form a good seal; ‹*door, window*› be a good fit 5▸ (Reiten) **diese Reiterin hat einen guten ~:** this rider keeps a good leg position; **mit den Knien ~ nehmen** grip with one's knees 6▸ (Musik) cadence

Schluss-, *Schluß-: **~abstimmung** *die* (Parl.) final vote; **~akkord** *der* (Musik) final chord; (geh. fig.: Ausklang) conclusion; finale; **~akte** *die* (Dipl.) final communiqué; **~bemerkung** *die* concluding remark; **~bilanz** *die* (Kaufmannsspr.) annual balance sheet; (nach Abwicklung eines Unternehmens) final balance [sheet]; **~drittel** *das* (Eishockey) third *or* final period

Schlüssel /ˈʃlʏsl̩/ *der;* ~s, ~ 1▸ key; **der ~ zur Wohnung/Wohnungstür** the key to the flat (esp. Brit.) *or* (esp. Amer.) apartment/the front door key 2▸ (Schrauben~) spanner 3▸ (Lösungsweg, Lösungsheft) key; (Kode) code; cipher; **der ~ zum Erfolg** (fig.) the key to *or* secret of success 4▸ (Musik) clef 5▸ (Aufgliederungsschema) scheme *or* pattern [of distribution]

schlüssel-, Schlüssel-: **~bart** *der* bit [of a/the key]; **~anhänger** *der* key fob; **~begriff** key concept; (Wort) key word; **~bein** *das* ▸❶ S. 435 (Anat.) collarbone; clavicle (Anat.); **~blume** *die* cowslip; (Primel) primula; **~brett** *das* keyboard; **~bund** *der od. das* bunch of keys; **~erlebnis** *das* (Psych.) crucial experience; **~fertig** *Adj.* ready to move into *postpos.*; **~figur** *die* key figure; **~industrie** *die* (Wirtsch.) key industry; **~kind** *das* (ugs.) latchkey child; **~loch** *das* keyhole; **~position** *die* ▸ **~stellung**; **~qualifikation** *die* key qualification; **~ring** *der* key ring; **~roman** *der* (Literaturw.) roman à clef; **~stellung** *die* key position; **~technologie** *die* key technology; **~wort** *das; Pl.* **~wörter** keyword; (für ein Kombinationsschloss, fig.: verschlüsseltes Wort) code word

schluss-, Schluss-, *schluß-, *Schluß-: **~endlich** *Adv.* (bes. schweiz.) finally; (immerhin) after all; **~folgern** *tr. V.* conclude (**aus** from); **~folgerung** *die* conclusion, inference (**aus** from); **~formel** *die* conventional ending; **~frau** *die* (Ballspiele) goalie (coll.)

schlüssig /ˈʃlʏsɪç/

A *Adj.* 1▸ conclusive ‹*proof, evidence*›; convincing, logical ‹*argument, conclusion, statement*› 2▸ **sich** (*Dat.*) **[darüber] ~ sein** have made up one's mind; **sich** (*Dat.*) **[darüber] ~ werden** make up one's mind

B *adv.* conclusively

Schlüssigkeit *die;* ~: conclusiveness

Schluss-, *Schluß-: **~kapitel** *das* (auch fig.) final *or* closing chapter; **~leuchte** *die* ▸ **~licht 1**; **~licht** *das; Pl.* **~~er** 1▸ (an Fahrzeugen) tail *or* rear light; 2▸ (ugs.: Letzter einer Kolonne) **das ~licht machen** *od.* **bilden/sein** bring up the rear; 3▸ (ugs.: Letzter, Schlechtester) **das ~licht der Bundesliga/Klasse sein** be bottom of the [national] league table/class; **~mann** *der;* (Ballspiele) goalie (coll.); **~pfiff** *der* (Ballspiele) final whistle; **~phase** *die* final phase; final stages *pl.*; **~punkt** *der* 1▸ (Satzzeichen) full stop; 2▸ (Abschluss) conclusion; (einer Feier) finale; **einen ~punkt unter etw.** (*Akk.*) **setzen** put an end to sth. once and for all; (etw. beendet sein lassen) declare sth. to be over and done with; **~runde** *die* (Sport: eines Rennens) final *or* last lap; (Boxen, Ringen, fig.: des Wahlkampfes usw.) final *or* last round; **~satz** *der* 1▸ (abschließender Satz) last *or* concluding sentence; 2▸ (Musik) last movement; finale; 3▸ (bes. Philos.) conclusion; **~sprung** *der* (Turnen) jump with legs together; **~stein** *der* (Archit.) keystone; (im Rippengewölbe) boss; **~strich** *der* [bottom] line; **einen ~strich ziehen/unter etw.** (*Akk.*) **ziehen** (fig.) make a clean break/draw a line under sth.; **~verkauf** *der* [end-of-season] sale[s *pl.*]; **~wort** *das; Pl.* **~~e** final word[s]; **ein kurzes ~wort** a few closing remarks; **das ~wort haben** make the closing speech; (in einer Debatte) wind up

Schmach /ʃmaːx/ *die;* ~ (geh.) ignominy; shame; (Demütigung) humiliation; **etw. als ~ empfinden** consider sth. a disgrace; regard sth. as ignominious; **jmdm. [eine] ~ antun** *od.* **bereiten** bring shame/humiliation upon sb.; **[mit] ~ und Schande** [in] deep disgrace

schmachten /ˈʃmaxtn̩/ *itr. V.* (geh.) 1▸ (leiden) languish; **in der Hitze ~:** fade away in the heat; **jmdn./einen Liebhaber ~ lassen** leave sb. to suffer *or* (coll.) stew/let a lover pine away 2▸ (spött.: sich sehnen) **nach jmdm./etw. ~:** pine *or* yearn for sb./sth.

schmachtend (spött.)

A *Adj.* soulful (coll.) ‹*look, song*›; languishing ‹*tones*›; schmaltzy (coll.) ‹*song, music*›

B *adv.* soulfully (coll.)

Schmacht·fetzen *der* (salopp abwertend) tear jerker (coll.)

schmächtig *Adj.* slight; weedy (coll. derog.); **einen ~en Körper haben** be of slight build

Schmacht·locke *die* (ugs. spött.) kiss-curl

schmach·voll (geh.)

A *Adj.* ignominious; (erniedrigend) humiliating

B *adv.* ignominiously; (erniedrigend) humiliatingly; **~ untergehen** come to an ignominious end

schmackhaft /ˈʃmakhaft/

A *Adj.* tasty; **jmdm. etw. ~ machen** (fig. ugs.) make sth. palatable to sb.

B *adv.* in a tasty way; **etw. ~ zubereiten** make sth. tasty

Schmäh *der;* ~s, ~[s] (österr. ugs.) 1▸ [tall] story; (Trick) con (coll.); **einen ~ führen** entertain; tell jokes 2▸ (Sarkasmus) sarcasm; **Wiener ~:** Viennese snide humour (coll.)

schmähen /ˈʃmɛːən/ *tr. V.* (geh.) revile

schmählich

A *Adj.* shameful; (verächtlich) despicable

B *adv.* shamefully; (in verächtlicher Weise) despicably

Schmäh-: **~rede** *die* diatribe; **~schrift** *die* piece of invective; (Pamphlet) defamatory pamphlet

Schmähung *die;* ~, ~en diatribe; **~en** abuse *sing.*; invective *sing.*; **jmdn. mit ~en überschütten** heap invective *or* abuse on sb.

Schmäh·wort *das; Pl.* **~e** term of abuse; **~e** abuse *sing.*

schmal /ʃmaːl/; **schmaler** *od.* **schmäler** /ˈʃmɛːlɐ/, **schmalst...** *od.* **schmälst...**

A *Adj.* 1▸ narrow; slim, slender ‹*hips, hands, figure, etc.*›; thin ‹*lips, face, nose, etc.*›; **ein ~er Band, ein ~es Büchlein** a slim volume; **~er werden** ‹*person, face*› get thinner 2▸ (geh.: knapp, karg) meagre ‹*income, profit, etc.*›; meagre, scanty ‹*food, selection*›; **mit ~em Geldbeutel** of restricted means

B *adv.* 1▸ **eine ~ geschnittene Hose** slim-fit trousers 2▸ (geh.: knapp, karg) meagrely

schmalbrüstig /-brʏstɪç/ narrow-chested; (fig.) narrow ‹*cupboard, views, etc.*›

schmäler ▸ **schmal**

schmälern *tr. V.* diminish; reduce; restrict, curtail ‹*rights*›; (herabsetzen) belittle

Schmälerung *die;* ~, ~en reduction; (Herabsetzung) belittlement

Schmal-: **~film** *der* 8 mm/16 mm cine film; **~film·kamera** *die* 8 mm/16 mm cine camera; **~hans** *in* **bei ihnen ist ~hans Küchenmeister** (ugs. veralt.) they are on short commons; **~seite** *die* short side; (eines Korridors usw.) end; **~spur** *die* (Eisenb.) narrow gauge

Schmalspur- (ugs.) small-time (coll.) ‹*politician, academic*›; (dilettantisch) lightweight ‹*academic*›; amateur ‹*engineer*›

Schmalspur·bahn *die* narrow-gauge railway

schmälst... ▸ **schmal**

schmal·wüchsig *Adj.* slender ‹*person, tree, etc.*›; ‹*person*› of slender build

Schmalz[1] /ʃmalts/ *das;* ~es (Schweine~) lard

Schmalz[2] *der;* ~es (ugs. abwertend) 1▸ (Sentimentalität) schmaltz (coll.); **mit viel ~:** with plenty of slushy *or* soppy sentimentality (coll.) 2▸ (Lied o. Ä.) schmaltz *no indef. art.* (coll.)

Schmalz·brot *das* slice of bread and dripping

schmalzig (abwertend)

A *Adj.* schmaltzy (coll.); slushy[-sentimental]

B *adv.* with schmaltzy (coll.) *or* slushy sentimentality; **~ sprechen** talk in a slushy-sentimental way; ‹*lover*› talk in a lovey-dovey tone (coll.)

Schmalzler /ˈʃmaltslɐ/ *der;* ~s (bayr.) snuff (*containg a trace of animal fat*)

Schmalz·tolle *die* (ugs. scherzh.) greased-up quiff

Schmankerl /ˈʃmaŋkɐl/ *das;* ~s, ~n (bayr., österr.) delicacy; (fig.) treat

schmarotzen /ʃmaˈrɔtsn̩/ *itr. V.* 1▸ (abwertend) sponge; freeload (sl.); **bei jmdm. ~:** sponge on sb. 2▸ (Biol.) live as a parasite (**in/auf** + *Dat.* in/on); **~d** parasitic

Schmarotzer *der;* ~s, ~ 1▸ (abwertend) sponger; freeloader (coll.) 2▸ (Biol.) parasite

Schmarotzerin, *die;* ~, ~nen ▸**Schmarotzer 1**

Schmarotzer·pflanze *die* parasitic plant

Schmarotzertum *das;* ~s **1** (Biol.) parasitism **2** (abwertend) sponging; freeloading (sl.)

Schmarren /ˈʃmarən/ *der;* ~s, ~ **1** (österr., auch südd.) *pancake broken up with a fork after frying* **2** (ugs. abwertend: Unsinn) trash; rubbish; **das ist ein ~:** it's a load (coll.) of trash *or* rubbish **3** **einen ~** (salopp: nichts) not a thing; damn all (Brit. coll.); (adverbiell) not at all; no way; **das geht dich einen ~ an** it's none of your damn business (coll.)

Schmatz /ʃmats/ *der;* ~es, ~e *od.* **Schmätze** /ˈʃmɛtsə/ (ugs.) loud kiss; smacker (coll.)

schmatzen *itr. V.* smack one's lips; (geräuschvoll essen) eat/drink noisily; (fig.) ‹*mud, wet ground*› squelch; **sie küssten sich, dass es schmatzte** they gave one another a resounding kiss *or* a (coll.) real smacker

schmauchen /ˈʃmauxn̩/

A *tr. V.* puff away at ‹*pipe, cigar, etc.*›

B *itr. V.* puff away

Schmaus /ˈʃmaus/ *der;* ~es, **Schmäuse** /ˈʃmɔyzə/ (veralt., noch scherzh.) [good] spread (coll.); (reichhaltig) feast; **ein köstlicher ~:** a delicious repast (formal/joc.) *or* (coll.) spread

schmausen (veralt.)

A *itr. V.* eat with relish; **vergnügt ~:** tuck in contentedly (coll.)

B *tr. V.* eat ‹*food*› with relish

schmecken /ˈʃmɛkn̩/

A *itr. V.* taste (**nach** of); **[gut] ~:** taste good; **das hat geschmeckt** that was good; (war köstlich) that was delicious; **nach nichts ~:** not taste of anything; be tasteless; **das schmeckt nach mehr** (ugs.) it tastes *or* it's moreish (coll.); **schmeckt es [dir]?** are you enjoying it *or* your meal?; [how] do you like it?; **wenn man krank ist, schmeckt es einem oft nicht [richtig]** when you're ill you're often off your food; **bei dir schmeckt es mir immer ausgezeichnet** your meals are always delicious; **lasst es euch ~!** enjoy your food!; tuck in (coll.)!; **wie schmeckt dir die Ehe?** (fig.) how do you like married life?; **diese Kritik schmeckte ihm gar nicht** (fig.) this criticism was not at all to his liking

B *tr. V.* taste; (kosten) sample; **die Rute zu ~ bekommen** (fig.) get a taste of the rod

Schmeichelei *die;* ~, ~en flattering remark; blandishment; **die ~en, die er ihr sagte** the flattering things he said to her

schmeichelhaft

A *Adj.* flattering; complimentary ‹*words, speech*›; **wenig ~:** not very flattering

B *adv.* flatteringly

schmeicheln /ˈʃmaiçl̩n/ *itr. V.* **1** **jmdm. ~:** flatter sb.; **er schmeichelte ihr, sie sei ...** *od.* **dass sie ... sei** he flattered her by saying she was ...; **etw. in ~dem Ton sagen** say sth. in honeyed tones; **es schmeichelt ihm, dass ...** he finds it flattering that ...; **„Zwerg" ist noch geschmeichelt** 'dwarf' is putting it mildly **2** (liebkosen) be affectionate; **die Katze strich ~d um ihre Füße** the cat rubbed affectionately against her feet

Schmeichel·wort *das; Pl.* ~e; blandishment; ~e honeyed words; flattery *sing.*

Schmeichler /ˈʃmaiçlɐ/ *der;* ~s, ~, **Schmeichlerin** *die;* ~, ~nen flatterer

schmeichlerisch

A *Adj.* flattering; honeyed ‹*words, tone*›; (sich anbiedernd) cajoling ‹*words, tone, glance*›

B *adv.* cajolingly; (im ~en Ton) in honeyed tones

schmeißen /ˈʃmaisn̩/ (ugs.)

A *unr. tr. V.* **1** (werfen) chuck (coll.); sling (coll.); (schleudern) fling; hurl; **etw. nach jmdm. ~:** throw *or* (coll.) chuck sth. at sb.; **die Tür [ins Schloss] ~:** slam the door; **jmdn. aus dem Zimmer/der Schule ~:** chuck sb. out of the room/school (coll.) **2** (abbrechen, aufgeben) chuck in (coll.) ‹*job, studies, etc.*› **3** (spendieren) stand ‹*drink*›; **eine Lage** *od.* **Runde [Bier] ~:** get *or* stand a round [of beer]; **[für jmdn.] eine Party ~:** throw a party [for sb.] **4** (bewältigen) handle; deal with; **wir werden den Laden schon ~:** we'll manage OK (coll.) **5** (Theater-, Fernsehjargon: misslingen lassen) fluff (coll.) ‹*scene, number*›; make a mess of ‹*performance*›

B *unr. refl. V.* **1** (sich werfen) throw oneself; (mit Wucht) hurl oneself; **sich jmdm. an den Hals ~** ‹*woman*› throw oneself at sb.; *s. auch* **Schale 4** **2** **sich in seinen Smoking/in ein festliches Kleid** *usw.* **~:** get togged up (coll.) in one's dinner jacket/a party dress *etc*

C *unr. itr. V.* **mit Steinen/Tomaten** *usw.* **[nach jmdm.] ~:** chuck stones/tomatoes *etc.* [at sb.] (coll.); **mit Geld um sich ~** (fig.) throw one's money around; lash out (coll.); **mit Geschenken um sich ~** (fig.) lash out (coll.) on masses of presents

Schmeiß·fliege *die* blowfly; (blaue ~) bluebottle

Schmelz *der;* ~es, ~e **1** (Glasur) glaze; (Email, Zahn~) enamel **2** (geh.: Lieblichkeit) (der Jugend) bloom; (von Farben) lustre; soft gleam; (Wohlklang) mellifluousness

Schmelze *die;* ~, ~n **1** (das [Zer]schmelzen) [process of] melting **2** (Technik: verflüssigtes Material) melt

schmelzen /ˈʃmɛltsn̩/

A *unr. itr. V.; mit sein* **1** melt; (fig.) ‹*doubts, apprehension, etc.*› dissolve, fade away; **sein Vermögen war geschmolzen** (fig.) his fortune had melted away **2** (fig.: weich werden) soften; **ihm schmolz das Herz** his heart melted

B *unr. tr. V.* melt; smelt ‹*ore*›; render ‹*fat*›

schmelzend

A *Adj.* melting ‹*glance, tones*›; mellifluous, mellow ‹*voice, tones, etc.*›

B *adv.* **~ singen** sing in melting tones

Schmelz-: **~hütte** *die* smelting works *sing. or pl.*; **~käse** *der* processed cheese; **~ofen** *der* (Technik) smelting furnace; **~punkt** *der* melting point; **~tiegel** *der* crucible; melting pot (esp. fig.); **~wasser** *das; Pl.* ~: melted snow and ice; meltwater (Geol.)

Schmerbauch /ˈʃmeːɐ̯-/ *der* (ugs.) **1** (dicker Bauch) potbelly; paunch **2** (dickbäuchiger Mensch) potbelly

Schmerle /ˈʃmɛrlə/ *die;* ~, ~n (Zool.) loach

Schmerz /ʃmɛrts/ *der;* ~es, ~en **1** ▸ⓘ **S. 439** (physisch) pain; (dumpf u. anhaltend) ache; **wo haben Sie ~en?** where does it hurt?; **~en im Rücken/Arm** pain in one's back/arm; (an verschiedenen Stellen) pains in one's back/arm; **~en haben** be in pain; **etw. mit** *od.* **unter ~en tun** do sth. in pain *or* agony; **vor ~[en] weinen/sich vor ~en winden** cry with/writhe in pain *or* agony; **~, lass nach!** (ugs. scherzh.) oh no! it can't be!; that's the last straw! **2** ▸ⓘ **S. 439** (psychisch) pain; (Kummer) grief; **ein seelischer ~:** mental anguish *or* suffering; **jmdm. ~en bereiten** cause sb. pain/grief; **der ~ um jmdn.** grief for sb.; **tiefen ~ über etw.** (*Akk.*) **empfinden** be deeply grieved by sth.; **etw. mit ~en erkennen** realize sth. with a sense of grief; **jmdn./etw. mit ~en erwarten** wait for sb./sth. in an agony of impatience; **hast du sonst noch ~en?** (ugs. spött.) is there anything else you want?

schmerz-, Schmerz-: **~ambulanz** *die* outpatient pain clinic; **~empfindlich** *Adj.* sensitive to pain *pred.*; **~ sein** have a low pain threshold; **~empfindlichkeit** *die;* ~: sensitivity to pain

schmerzen ▸ⓘ **S. 439**

A *tr. V.* **jmdn. ~:** hurt sb.; (Kummer bereiten) grieve sb.; cause sb. sorrow; **es schmerzt mich, dass ...** it grieves *or* pains me that ...

B *itr. V.* hurt; **seine Wunde schmerzt** his wound is hurting *or* painful; **heftig ~:** be intensely painful

Schmerzens-: **~geld** *das* (Rechtsspr.) compensation (*for pain and suffering caused*); exemplary damages (Law); **~laut** *der* cry of pain; (stöhnend) moan; **~mann** *der* (Kunstwiss.) Ecce Homo; **~mutter** *die; Pl.* **~mütter** (Kunstwiss.) Mater Dolorosa; **~schrei** *der* cry of pain; (laut) scream [of pain]

schmerz·frei *Adj.* free of pain *pred.*; painless ‹*operation*›

Schmerz·grenze *die* (fig.) **jetzt/dann ist die ~ erreicht** this/that is the absolute limit

schmerzhaft *Adj.* painful; (wund) sore

schmerzlich

A *Adj.* painful; distressing; **die ~e Gewissheit haben, dass ...** be painfully aware that ...; **es ist mir eine ~e Pflicht, Ihnen mitteilen zu müssen, dass ...** it is my painful duty to inform you that ...

B *adv.* painfully

schmerz-, Schmerz-: **~lindernd** **A** *Adj.* pain-relieving; **~linderndes Mittel** pain-relieving drug; palliative; **B** *adv.* **~lindernd wirken** relieve pain; **~los** **A** *Adj.* painless; **B** *adv.* painlessly; *s. auch* **kurz B 3**; **~schwelle** *die* (Physiol.) pain threshold; **~stillend** **A** *Adj.* pain-killing; analgesic (Med.); **~stillendes Mittel** painkiller; analgesic; **B** *adv.* **~stillend wirken** have a painkilling *or* analgesic effect; **~tablette** *die* pain-killing *or* (Med.) analgesic tablet; **~therapie** *die* pain therapy; **~unempfindlich** *Adj.* insensitive to pain *pred.*; **~verzerrt** *Adj.* ‹*face, smile*› distorted *or* twisted with pain; **~voll** **A** *Adj.* **1** (physisch) [very] painful; **2** (psychisch) painful; distressing; **B** *adv.* painfully

Schmetter·ball *der* (Tennis usw.) smash

Schmetterling *der;* ~s, ~e **1** butterfly; (Nachtfalter) moth; **~e Europas** butterflies and moths of Europe **2** (Schwimmen) butterfly

Schmetterlingsblütler /-blyːtlɐ/ *der;* ~s, ~: papilionaceous plant

Schmetterlings·stil *der* (Schwimmen) butterfly [stroke]

schmettern /ˈʃmɛtɐn/

A *tr. V.* **1** (schleudern) hurl (**an** + *Akk.* at, **gegen** against); **jmdn./etw. zu Boden ~:** send sb./sth. crashing to the ground; **die Tür ins Schloss ~:** slam the door hard **2** (laut spielen, singen usw.) blare out ‹*march, music*›; ‹*person*› sing lustily ‹*song*›; bellow ‹*order*›; **einen Tusch ~:** unleash a loud flourish **3** (Tennis usw.) smash ‹*ball*›

B *itr. V.* **1** *mit sein* (aufprallen) crash; smash **2** (schallen) ‹*trumpet, music, etc.*› blare out; **ein ~der Klang** a blare

Schmetter·schlag *der* (bes. Faustball, Volleyball) smash

Schmied /ʃmiːt/ *der;* ~[e]s, ~e ▸ⓘ **S. 113** blacksmith; *s. auch* **Glück 2**

schmiedbar *Adj.* malleable

Schmiede *die;* ~, ~en smithy; forge

schmiede-, Schmiede-: **~arbeit** *die* piece of wrought-iron work; **~arbeiten** [pieces *pl.* of] wrought-iron work *sing.*; **~eisen** *das* wrought iron; (schmiedbares Eisen) forgeable iron; **~eisern** *Adj.* wrought-iron; **~hammer** *der* drop hammer; **~kunst** *die* blacksmith's craft

schmieden *tr. V.* (auch fig.) forge (**zu** into, **aus** from, out of); **Pläne/ein Komplott ~** (fig.) hatch plans/a plot; **Verse** *od.* **Reime ~** (spött.) concoct verses; **an eine Mauer** *usw.* **geschmiedet werden** ‹*prisoner*› be fettered to a wall *etc.*

Schmiedin *die;* ~, ~nen ▸ⓘ **S. 113** blacksmith

schmiegen /ˈʃmiːgn̩/

A *refl. V.* snuggle, nestle (**in** + *Akk.* in); **sich an jmdn. ~:** snuggle [close] up to sb.; **sie schmiegte sich eng an seine Seite** she pressed *or* nestled close to his side; **sich an etw.** (*Akk.*) **~** (fig.) ‹*road*› hug sth.; ‹*village*› cling to sth.; **sich an jmds. Körper ~** (fig.) ‹*dress*› hug sb.'s figure

B *tr. V.* press (**an** + *Akk.* against)

schmiegsam *Adj.* supple ‹*leather, material*›

Schmierage /ʃmiˈraːʒə/ *die;* ~ (ugs. scherzh.) ▸**Schmiererei 1**

Schmiere[1] *die;* ~, ~n **1** (Schmierfett) grease **2** (schwieriger Schmutz) greasy *or* slimy mess **3** (ugs. abwertend: Provinztheater) fleapit (coll.) of a provincial theatre; (veralt.: Wanderbühne) troop of second-rate barnstormers

Schmiere[2] *die;* ~: *in* **[bei etw.] ~ stehen** (ugs.) act as lookout [while sth. takes place]; (in der Schule) keep cave (Sch. sl.) [while sth. is going on]

schmieren /ˈʃmiːrən/

A *tr. V.* **1** (mit Schmiermitteln) lubricate; (mit Schmierfett) grease; **[gehen** *od.* **laufen] wie geschmiert**

S

(ugs.) [go] like clockwork *or* without a hitch **2** (streichen, auftragen) spread ‹*butter, jam, etc.*› (**auf** + *Akk.* on); **Salbe auf eine Wunde ~:** apply ointment to a wound; **sich** (*Dat.*) **Creme ins Gesicht/Pomade ins Haar ~:** rub cream into one's face/hair cream into one's hair **3** (mit Aufstrich) **Brote/Schmalzbrote ~:** spread slices of bread/bread and dripping **4** (abwertend: unsauber schreiben) scrawl ‹*essay, school work*›; (schnell und nachlässig schreiben) scribble, dash off ‹*article, play, etc.*›; **Parolen an Wände** *usw.* **~:** scrawl *or* daub slogans on walls *etc.* **5** (salopp: bestechen) **jmdn. ~:** grease sb.'s palm **6** **jmdm. eine ~** (salopp) give sb. a clout (coll.); **eine geschmiert kriegen** (salopp) get a clout (coll.) **7** (Kartenspiel, bes. Skatjargon) play ‹*high-counting card*› to a trick won by one's partner
B *itr. V.* **1** ‹*oil, grease*› lubricate **2** (ugs. unsauber schreiben) ‹*person*› scrawl, scribble; ‹*pen, ink*› smudge, make smudges

Schmieren-: ~komödiant *der,* **~komödiantin** *die* (abwertend) cheapjack play-actor; **~komödie** *die,* **~theater** *das* (abwertend) shoddy farce

Schmiererei *die;* **~, ~en** (ugs. abwertend) **1** (unsauberes Schreiben) scrawling; scribbling; **eine einzige ~:** one long scrawl; (Kleckserei) nothing but a smudgy mess **2** (unsauber Geschriebenes) scrawl; scribble

Schmier-: ~fett *das* grease; **~film** *der* **1** (auf der Straße usw.) greasy surface; **2** (Technik) film of lubricant; **~fink** *der* (ugs. abwertend) **1** (im Schreiben) messy writer; (jmd., der Wände beschmiert) graffiti writer; (jmd., der Diffamierendes schreibt) muckraker; **2** (Kind, das sich/etw. schmutzig macht) mucky pup (coll.); **~geld** *das* (ugs. abwertend) slush money; **~heft** *das* rough book

schmierig *Adj.* **1** (feucht-klebrig) greasy ‹*surface, clothes, hands, step, etc.*›; slimy ‹*earth, surface*› **2** (schmutzig) mucky; (dreckig) filthy **3** (abwertend: widerlich freundlich) slimy, (coll.) smarmy ‹*person*› **4** (abwertend: zweideutig) dirty, smutty ‹*joke etc.*›

Schmier-: ~käse *der* (bes. nordd.) ▸**Streichkäse**; **~mittel** *das* lubricant; **~öl** *das* lubricating oil; **~papier** *das* scrap paper; **~seife** *die* soft soap

schmilzt /ʃmɪltst/ *2. u. 3. Pers. Sg. Präsens v.* **schmelzen**

Schminke /ˈʃmɪŋkə/ *die;* **~, ~n** make-up

schminken
A *tr. V.* make up ‹*face, eyes*›; **die Lippen ~:** put lipstick on; **der Bericht ist stark geschminkt** (fig.) the report has been given a very favourable slant
B *refl. V.* make oneself up; put on make-up; **sich leicht/stark** *od.* **kräftig ~:** put on a little/a lot of make-up

Schmink-: ~stift *der* stick of make-up *or* greasepaint; **~tisch** *der* make-up table; **~topf** *der* make-up jar

Schmirgel /ˈʃmɪrgl̩/ *der;* **~s** emery

schmirgeln /ˈʃmɪrgl̩n/ *tr. V.* **1** (schleifen) rub down; (bes. mit Sandpapier) sand **2** (durch Schmirgeln entfernen) remove ‹*paint, rust*› with emery paper/sandpaper

Schmirgel·papier *das* emery paper; (Sandpapier) sandpaper

schmiss, *schmiß /ʃmɪs/ *1. u. 3. Pers. Sg. Prät. v.* **schmeißen**

Schmiss, *Schmiß *der;* **Schmisses, Schmisse** **1** (Fechtwunde) [sabre] cut; (Narbe) duelling scar **2** (veralt.: Schwung, Elan) punch; zip

schmissig (veralt.)
A *Adj.* rousing ‹*march, song*›; zippy ‹*couplets etc.*›
B *adv.* rousingly; with a swing

Schmock /ʃmɔk/ *der;* **~[e]s, Schmöcke** /ˈʃmœkə/ (abwertend: Schreiberling) hack writer

Schmöker /ˈʃmøːkɐ/ *der;* **~s, ~** (ugs.) lightweight adventure story/romance; **ein dicker ~:** a thick tome of light reading

schmökern (ugs.)
A *itr. V.* bury oneself in a book
B *tr. V.* bury oneself in ‹*book*›

schmollen /ˈʃmɔlən/ *itr. V.* sulk; ‹*lips, mouth*› pout; **mit jmdm. ~:** be in a huff and refuse to speak to sb.

Schmoll-: ~mund *der* pouting mouth; **einen ~mund machen** *od.* **ziehen** pout; **~winkel** *der:* *in* **sich in den ~winkel zurückziehen** (ugs.) go off into a corner to sulk; get a fit of the sulks; **im ~winkel sitzen** (ugs.) have [a fit of] the sulks

schmolz /ʃmɔlts/ *1. u. 3. Pers. Sg. Prät. v.* **schmelzen**

Schmonzes /ˈʃmɔntsəs/ *der;* **~** (ugs. abwertend) idle chatter; silly talk

Schmonzette /ʃmɔnˈtsɛtə/ *die;* **~, ~n** (ugs. abwertend) trashy play; (Film) trashy film

Schmor·braten *der* pot roast; braised beef

schmoren /ˈʃmoːrən/
A *tr. V.* braise; **jmdn. [im eigenen Saft] ~ lassen** (ugs.) leave sb. to stew in his/her own juice
B *itr. V.* **1** (garen) braise **2** (ugs.: schwitzen) swelter; **in der Sonne ~:** roast in the sun

Schmor·fleisch *das* braising steak

Schmu /ʃmuː/ *der;* **~s** (ugs.) little game; **erzähl mir keinen ~!** don't tell me any stories (coll.); **~ machen** cheat; work a fiddle (coll.)

schmuck /ʃmʊk/ (veralt.)
A *Adj.* attractive; pretty; (schick) smart ‹*clothes, house, ship, etc.*›
B *adv.* attractively; smartly

Schmuck *der;* **~[e]s** **1** (**~stücke**) jewelry; jewellery (esp. Brit.) **2** (**~stück**) piece of jewelry/jewellery **3** (Zierde) decoration; **ornamentaler ~:** ornamentation; **die Stadt zeigte sich im ~ der Fahnen** (geh.) the town was decked with flags

schmücken /ˈʃmʏkn̩/ *tr. V.* decorate; embellish ‹*writings, speech*›; **sie schmückten sich mit Blumenkränzen** they adorned themselves with garlands; **~de Beiwörter/Zusätze** embellishments

schmuck-, Schmuck-: ~kästchen *das,* **~kasten** *der* jewelry *or* (esp. Brit.) jewellery box; **ihr Haus ist das reinste ~kästchen** her house is an absolute picture; **~los** *Adj.* plain; bare ‹*room*›; **ein ~loses Grab** an undecorated grave

Schmucklosigkeit *die;* **~:** plainness; (eines Zimmers) bareness

Schmuck-: ~sachen *Pl.* jewelry *sing.*; jewellery *sing.* (esp. Brit.); **~stein** *der* attractive stone (*used in jewelry*); gemstone; **~stück** *das* piece of jewelry *or* (esp. Brit.) jewellery; **ein ~stück/das ~stück seiner Sammlung** (fig.) one of the jewels/the jewel of his collection; **~waren** *Pl.* jewelry *sing.*; jewellery *sing.* (esp. Brit.)

Schmuddel *der;* **~s** (ugs. abwertend) muck (coll.); grime

schmuddelig *Adj.* (ugs. abwertend) grubby; mucky (coll.); (schmutzig u. unordentlich) messy; grotty (Brit. coll.)

Schmuddel-: ~kind *das* (ugs. abwertend) grubby kid (coll.); (Straßenkind) [street] urchin; **~kinder** (fig.: Gesindel) lowlife; **~wetter** *das* (ugs.) dirty weather

Schmuggel /ˈʃmʊgl̩/ *der;* **~s** smuggling *no art.*; **~ treiben** smuggle

schmuggeln *tr.* (*auch itr.*) *V.* smuggle (**in** + *Akk.* into; **aus** out of); **jmdm. einen Zettel in die Handtasche ~** (fig.) smuggle a note into sb.'s handbag

Schmuggel·ware *die* smuggled goods *pl.*; contraband *no pl.*

Schmuggler *der;* **~s, ~, Schmugglerin** *die;* **~, ~nen** smuggler

schmunzeln /ˈʃmʊntsl̩n/ *itr. V.* **[vor sich** (*Akk.*) **hin] ~:** smile [quietly] to oneself; **ein Schmunzeln unterdrücken** suppress a smile

Schmus /ʃmuːs/ *der;* **~es** (ugs.) (Angeberei) big talk; (Geschwafel) waffle; (Schmeicheleien) soft soap; **so ein ~!** what a load of waffle/soft soap

Schmuse·katze *die* (fam.) cuddly sort (coll.); (kleines Mädchen) cuddly little thing (coll.); **eine ~ sein** be the cuddly sort (coll.)

schmusen /ˈʃmuːzn̩/ *itr. V.* (ugs.) **1** (zärtlich sein) cuddle; ‹*couple*› kiss and cuddle; (knutschen) neck (coll.); **mit jmdm. ~:** cuddle sb.; ‹*lover*› kiss and cuddle *or* (coll.) neck with sb.; **miteinander ~:** have a cuddle; ‹*couple*› have a kiss and a cuddle; **~de Pärchen** snogging (Brit. coll.) *or* (coll.) necking couples **2** (abwertend: schmeicheln) softsoap

Schmuser *der;* **~s, ~** (ugs.) affectionate type; cuddly sort (coll.); **er ist ein kleiner ~:** he's a cuddly little thing

Schmuserin, *die;* **~, ~nen** (ugs.) affectionate type; cuddly sort (coll.); **sie ist eine kleine ~:** she's a cuddly little thing

Schmutz /ʃmʊts/ *der;* **~es** **1** dirt; (Schlamm) mud; **der ~ von den Malern** the mess left by the painters; **etw. macht viel/keinen ~:** sth. makes a great deal of/leaves no mess; **durch den dicksten ~ laufen** walk through the worst bit of mud; **jmdn./etw. durch den ~ ziehen** *od.* **in den ~ treten** (fig.) drag sb./sth. through the mud (fig.) **2** (abwertend: minderwertige, geschmacklose Literatur, Filme usw.) filth; **~ und Schund** trash and filth; *s. auch* **bewerfen 1**

schmutz·abweisend *Adj.* dirt-resistant

schmutzen *itr. V.* get dirty

Schmutz-: ~fänger *der* **1** (etw., das ~ anzieht) dirt trap; **2** (bei Fahrzeugen) mudflap; **~fink** *der;* **~en** *od.* **~s, ~en** (ugs.) **1** (unsauberer Mensch) [dirty] pig (coll.); (Kind) dirty brat; **2** (unmoralischer Mensch) depraved type (coll.); **alter ~fink** dirty old man; **~fleck** *der* dirty mark (**in** + *Dat.* on); (in der Landschaft usw.) blot

schmutzig
A *Adj.* **1** (unsauber) dirty; (ungepflegt) dirty, slovenly ‹*person, restaurant, etc.*›; **sich/sich** (*Dat.*) **die Finger ~ machen** get [oneself] dirty/get one's fingers dirty *or* grubby; *s. auch* **Finger 1** **2** (abwertend: unverschämt) cocky ‹*remarks*›; **ein ~es Lächeln** a smirk **3** (abwertend: obszön) smutty ‹*joke, song, story*›; dirty ‹*thoughts*› **4** (abwertend: unlauter) dirty ‹*business, war*›; crooked, shady ‹*practices, deal*›; **eine ~e Gesinnung** a devious cast of mind
B *adv.* (abwertend) **~ grinsen** smirk

Schmutzigkeit *die;* **~:** dirtiness

Schmutz-: ~titel *der* (Druckw.) half-title; **~wäsche** *die* dirty washing; **~wasser** *das;* *Pl.* **~wässer** dirty water; (Abwasser) sewage

Schnabel /ˈʃnaːbl̩/ *der;* **~s, Schnäbel** /ˈʃnɛːbl̩/ **1** beak **2** (ugs.: Mund) gob (sl.); **reden, wie einem der ~ gewachsen ist** say just what one thinks **3** (an einer Kanne) spout; (an einem Krug) lip **4** (hist.: an Schiffen) prow **5** (Musik: Mundstück) mouthpiece

Schnabel·hieb *der* peck

schnäbeln /ˈʃnɛːbl̩n/ *itr. V.* **1** ‹*birds*› bill **2** (ugs. scherzh.: sich küssen) bill and coo

Schnabel-: ~schuh *der* (hist.) pointed shoe (*often with turned-up toe*); **~tier** *das* duck-billed platypus

schnabulieren /ʃnabuˈliːrən/ *tr., itr. V.* (fam.) eat with great enjoyment

Schnack /ʃnak/ *der;* **~[e]s, ~s** *od.* **Schnäcke** /ˈʃnɛkə/ (nordd.) **1** (Unterhaltung) chat **2** (abwertend: Gerede) [idle] chatter; gossip **3** (witziger Spruch) witty saying; bon mot

schnackeln *itr. V.* (ugs.) **1** (bes. bayr.: schnalzen) **mit der Zunge/den Fingern ~:** click one's tongue/snap one's fingers **2** (unpers.) **es hat geschnackelt** (bes. südd.) (es ist geglückt) it's come off; success [at last]!; (jmd. hat begriffen) it's clicked (sl.); **bei den beiden hats geschnackelt** those two have fallen for one another (coll.)

schnacken *itr. V.* (nordd.) chat; **platt ~:** talk in Low German dialect

Schnake /ˈʃnaːkə/ *die;* **~, ~n** **1** daddy-long-legs; crane fly **2** (bes. südd.: Stechmücke) mosquito

Schnaken·stich *der* (bes. südd.) mosquito bite

Schnalle /ˈʃnalə/ *die;* **~, ~n** **1** (Gürtelschnalle) buckle **2** (österr.: Türklinke) door handle **3** (salopp: weibliche Person) cow (sl. derog.); (Prostituierte) tart (sl.)

schnallen *tr. V.* **1** (mit einer Schnalle festziehen) buckle ‹*shoe, belt*›; fasten ‹*strap*›; **den Gürtel/**

Riemen enger/weiter ~: tighten/loosen one's belt/the strap **2** (mit Riemen/Gurten befestigen) strap (**auf** + *Akk.* on to) **3** (los~) **etw. von etw. ~:** unstrap sth. from sth. **4** (salopp: begreifen) twig (coll.)

Schnallen·schuh *der* buckle shoe

schnalzen *itr. V.* **[mit der Zunge/den Fingern] ~:** click one's tongue/snap one's fingers; **mit der Peitsche ~:** crack the whip

schnapp *Interj.* click; (beim Zufallen eines Deckels o. Ä.) bang; (beim Schneiden) snip; **~ machen** go click/bang/snip

Schnäppchen /ˈʃnɛpçən/ *das;* **~s, ~** (ugs.) snip (Brit. coll.); [real] bargain; **ein ~ machen** get a [real] bargain

Schnäppchen-: ~jäger *der,* **~jägerin** *die* (ugs.) bargain hunter; **~preis** *der* bargain price; giveaway price

schnappen /ˈʃnapn̩/

A *itr. V.* **1** **nach jmdm./etw. ~** ‹*animal*› snap *or* take a snap at sb./sth.; **nach Luft ~** (fig.) gasp for breath *or* air **2** *mit sein* (schnellen) **[in die Höhe] ~:** spring up [with a snap]; **ins Schloss ~** ‹*door*› click shut; ‹*bolt*› snap home **3** (leise knallen) snap; ‹*scissors*› snip

B *tr. V.* **1** ‹*dog, bird, etc.*› snatch; **[sich** *(Dat.)***] jmdn./etw. ~** (ugs.) ‹*person*› grab sb./sth.; (mit raschem Zugriff) snatch sb./sth.; *s. auch* **Luft 1** **2** (ugs.: festnehmen) catch, (coll.) nab ‹*thief etc.*›

Schnapper *der;* **~s, ~** (Türfalle) latch

Schnapp-: ~messer *das* **1** clasp knife; **2** (Stichwaffe) flick knife; **~schloss,** ***~schloß** *das* spring lock; **~schuss,** ***~schuß** *der* snapshot

Schnaps /ʃnaps/ *der;* **~es, Schnäpse** /ˈʃnɛpsə/ **1** spirit; (Klarer) schnapps; **zwei Schnäpse** two glasses of spirit/schnapps **2** (Spirituosen) spirits *pl.*

Schnaps·brennerei *die* distillery

Schnaps·bruder *der* (ugs. abwertend) boozer (coll.)

Schnäpschen /ˈʃnɛpsçən/ *das;* **~s, ~** (fam.) small schnapps

Schnaps·drossel *die* (scherzh.) boozer (coll.)

schnäpseln /ˈʃnɛpsl̩n/ *itr. V.* (ugs. scherzh.) booze [the hard stuff] (coll.)

Schnaps-: ~flasche *die* spirits/schnapps bottle; **~glas** *das* schnapps glass; **~idee** *die* (ugs.) hare-brained idea; **~zahl** *die:* (scherzh.) *number in which all the digits are the same*

schnarchen /ˈʃnarçn̩/ *itr. V.* snore

Schnarcher *der;* **~s, ~** (ugs.) **1** (Mensch) snorer **2** (Geräusch) snore

Schnarcherin, *die;* **~, ~nen** ▸ **Schnarcher 1**

schnarchnasig (ugs. abwertend)

A *Adj.* dozy (coll.); half asleep *pred.*; soporific ‹*film, book*›

B *adv.* dozily (coll.)

schnarren /ˈʃnarən/ *itr. V.* ‹*alarm clock, telephone, doorbell*› buzz [shrilly]; **mit ~der Stimme** in a rasping voice

schnattern /ˈʃnatɐn/ *itr. V.* **1** ‹*goose etc.*› cackle, gaggle **2** (ugs.: eifrig schwatzen) jabber [away]; chatter **3** (bes. nordd.: zittern) **er schnatterte vor Kälte** his teeth were chattering with the cold

schnauben /ˈʃnaubn̩/ *regelm.* (*auch unr.*) *itr. V.* **1** ‹*person, horse*› snort (**vor** with); (fig.) ‹*steam locomotive*› puff, chuff; **heftig ~:** pant heavily; **wütend ~:** snort with fury **2** (bes. südd.: atmen) breathe

schnaufen /ˈʃnaufn̩/ *itr. V.* puff, pant (**vor** with); (fig.) ‹*steam locomotive*› puff, chuff

Schnaufer *der;* **~s, ~** (ugs.) breath; **einen ~ lang** for a second; **den letzten ~ tun** (verhüll.) breathe one's last

Schnauferl *das;* **~s, ~,** (österr.:) **~n** (ugs. scherzh.) venerable old vehicle; oldie (coll.)

Schnauz /ʃnauts/ *der;* **~es, Schnäuze** /ˈʃnɔytsə/ (bes. schweiz.) ▸ **Schnauzbart 1**

Schnauz·bart *der* **1** (Bartform) large moustache; mustachio (arch.); (an den Seiten herabhängend) walrus moustache **2** (ugs.: Bartträger) heavily mustachioed fellow (dated/literary)

schnauz·bärtig *adj.* mustachioed (dated/literary)

Schnäuzchen /ˈʃnɔytsçən/ *das* **1** (von Tieren) little nose; (der Maus usw.) little snout **2** (von Menschen) little mouth

Schnauze *die;* **~, ~n** **1** (von Tieren) muzzle; (der Maus usw.) snout; (Maul) mouth; **eine kalte ~:** a cold nose **2** (derb: Mund, Mundwerk) gob (sl.); **jmdm. in die ~ hauen** smack sb. in the gob (sl.); **die ~ voll haben** (salopp) be fed up to the back teeth (coll.); **eine große ~ haben** shoot one's mouth off (sl.); **eine freche/lose ~ haben** be a cheeky so-and-so (coll.)/have a loose tongue; **die ~ halten** keep one's trap shut (sl.); **[halt die] ~!** shut your trap! (sl.); **frei [nach] ~, nach ~** (salopp) as one thinks fit; as the mood takes one; *s. auch* **verbrennen B 2** **3** (ugs.) ▸ **Schnabel 3** **4** (ugs.: Vorderteil) (eines Flugzeugs) nose; (eines Fahrzeugs) front

schnauzen *tr., itr. V.* (ugs.) bark; (ärgerlich) snap; snarl

schnäuzen

A *tr. V.* **einem Kind die Nase ~:** blow a child's nose; **sich** *(Dat.)* **die Nase ~:** blow one's nose

B *refl. V.* (geh.) blow one's nose

Schnauzer *der;* **~s, ~** **1** (Hund) schnauzer **2** (ugs.) ▸ **Schnauzbart 1**

Schnecke /ˈʃnɛkə/ *die* **1** (Tier) snail; (Nackt~) slug; **jmdn. [so] zur ~ machen** (ugs.) give sb. [such] a good carpeting (coll.) **2** (ugs.: Gebäck) Belgian bun **3** (Frisur) coiled plait (*over the ear*); earphone **4** (Anat.: im Ohr) cochlea **5** (bei Streichinstrumenten) scroll **6** (Kunstwiss.) ▸ **Volute**

Schnecken-: ~frisur *die* earphones *pl.*; **~gewinde** *das* (Technik) worm; **~haus** *das* snail shell; **~nudel** *die* (bes. südd.) ▸ **Schnecke 2**; **~post** *die* (ugs.) snail mail (coll.); **etw. mit der/per ~post schicken** send sth. by snail mail; **~tempo** *das* (ugs.) snail's pace; **im ~tempo** at a snail's pace

Schnee /ʃneː/ *der;* **~s** **1** snow; **in tiefem ~ liegen** lie under deep snow; **~ von gestern** (ugs.) things *pl.*/a thing of the past; ancient history (fig.); **anno ~, im Jahre ~** (österr.) in the year dot (coll.) **2** (Eier~) beaten egg white; **das Eiweiß zu ~ schlagen** beat the egg white until stiff **3** (Jargon: Kokain) snow (sl.)

Schnee·ball *der* **1** snowball **2** (Strauch) snowball tree; guelder rose

Schneeball-: ~prinzip *das* snowball principle; **~schlacht** *die* snowball fight; **eine ~schlacht machen** have a snowball fight; **~system** *das* **1** (Form des Warenabsatzes) pyramid selling *no art.*; **2** (Verbreitungsart) cumulative [distribution] process; snowball; (Fernspr.) cascade system; (von Briefen) chain-letter system

schnee-, Schnee-: ~bedeckt *Adj.* snow-covered; **~besen** *der* whisk; **~blind** *Adj.* snowblind; **~blindheit** *die* snow blindness; **~brett** *das* [stretch of] windslab; **~brille** *die* snow goggles *pl.*; **~decke** *die* blanket *or* covering of snow; **~fall** *der* snowfall; fall of snow; **dichter ~fall setzte ein** thick snow began to fall; **~flocke** *die* snowflake; **~fräse** *die* rotary [snow]plough; **~frau** *die* snow-woman; **~frei** *Adj.* free of snow *postpos.*; **~gestöber** *das* snow flurry; **~glatt** *Adj.* slippery with [packed] snow *postpos.*; **~glätte** *die* [slippery surface due to] packed snow; **bei ~glätte** when the roads are slippery because of packed snow; **~glöckchen** *das* snowdrop; **~grenze** *die* ▸ **❶ S. 374** snowline; (beweglich) snow limit; **~hase** *der* snow hare; **~huhn** *das* snow grouse; ptarmigan

schneeig *Adj.* snowy

schnee-, Schnee-: ~kette *die* snow chain; **~könig** *der:* *in* **sich freuen wie ein ~könig** (ugs.) be as pleased as Punch; **~landschaft** *die* snowy *or* snow-covered landscape; **~mann** *der* snowman; **~matsch** *der* slush; **~mobil** *das* snowmobile; **~pflug** *der* (auch Ski) snowplough; **~raupe** *die* snowmobile (*for preparing ski runs*); **~regen** *der* sleet; **~schauer** *der* snow shower; **~schmelze** *die* melting of the snow; thaw; **~schuh** *der* **1** (veralt.) ski; **2** (Lauffläche) snowshoe; **~sturm** *der* snowstorm; **~treiben** *das* driving snow; **~verhältnisse** *Pl.* snow conditions; **~verwehung** *die:* **~verwehung[en]** snowdrifts *pl.*; **eine ~verwehung** a mass of snowdrifts; ***~wächte, ~wechte** *die* cornice; **~wehe** *die* snowdrift; **~weiß** *Adj.* snow-white; as white as snow *postpos.*

Schneewittchen /-ˈvɪtçən/ *(das);* **~s** Snow White

Schneid *der;* **~[e]s,** *südd., österr.: die;* **~** (ugs.) guts *pl.* (coll.); **ihm fehlt der ~:** he hasn't got the guts [to do it]; **dazu gehört ~:** that takes some nerve; **jmdm. den** *od.* **die ~ abkaufen** take the fight out of sb.

Schneid·brenner *der* (Technik) cutting torch; oxyacetylene cutter

Schneide /ˈʃnaidə/ *die;* **~, ~n** [cutting] edge; (Klinge) blade; **eine doppelte ~ haben** be two-edged

schneiden

A *unr. itr. V.* **1** cut (**in** + *Akk.* into) **2** (Medizinerjargon: operieren) operate **3** (beim Fahren) **bei Überholmanövern ~:** cut in after overtaking **4** (Schmerz verursachen) ‹*wind, cold*› be biting; **~d** biting ‹*wind, cold, voice, sarcasm*›; **es schnitt ihm ins Herz** (fig.) it cut him to the quick

B *unr. tr. V.* **1** cut; cut, reap ‹*corn etc.*›; cut, mow ‹*grass*›; (in Scheiben) slice ‹*bread, sausage, etc.*›; (klein ~) cut up, chop ‹*wood, vegetables*›; (zu~) cut out ‹*dress*›; (stutzen) prune ‹*tree, bush*›; trim ‹*beard*›; **Kräuter in die Suppe/Wurst unter die Kartoffeln ~:** cut up herbs/sausage and add them/it to the soup/potatoes; **sich** *(Dat.)* **von jmdm. die Haare ~ lassen** have one's hair cut by sb.; **hier ist eine Luft zum Schneiden** (fig.) there's a terrible fug in here (coll.); **ein eng/weit/gut geschnittenes Kleid** a tight-fitting/loose-fitting/well-cut dress; **ein regelmäßig geschnittenes Gesicht** (fig.) a face with regular features **2** (Medizinerjargon: auf~) operate on ‹*patient*›; cut [open] ‹*tumour, ulcer, etc.*›; lance ‹*boil, abscess*› **3** (Film, Rundf., Ferns.: cutten) cut, edit ‹*film, tape*› **4** (beim Fahren) **eine Kurve ~:** cut a corner; **jmdn./einen anderen Wagen ~:** cut in on sb./another car **5** (kreuzen) ‹*line, railway, etc.*› intersect, cross; **die Linien/Straßen ~ sich** the lines/roads intersect **6** (Tennis usw.) slice, put spin on ‹*ball*›; (Fußball) curve ‹*ball, free kick*›; (Billard) put side on ‹*ball*› **7** **eine Grimasse ~:** grimace **8** (ignorieren) **jmdn. ~:** cut sb. dead; send sb. to Coventry (Brit.)

C *refl. V.* **ich habe mir** *od.* **mich in den Finger geschnitten** I've cut my finger; **wenn du das meinst, hast du dich geschnitten** (fig.) it you think that, you've made a big mistake

Schneider *der;* **~s, ~** **1** ▸ **❶ S. 113** tailor; (Damen~) dressmaker; **frieren wie ein ~** (ugs.) be frozen stiff **2** (ugs.: Schneidegerät) cutter; (für Scheiben) slicer **3** (Skat: 30 Punkte) schneider; **[im] ~ sein** have less than 30 points; be schneidered; **~ ansagen** declare schneider; **aus dem ~ sein** have made schneider; (fig. ugs.: eine schwierige Situation überwunden haben) be in the clear; be clear of trouble **4** (Tischtennis: unter 11 Punkte) [score of] less than 11 points

Schneide·raum *der* (Film, Rundf. Ferns.) cutting room

Schneiderei *die;* **~, ~en** **1** tailor's shop; (Damen~) dressmaker's shop **2** (das Schneidern) tailoring; (von Damenkleidern) dressmaking

Schneiderin *die;* **~, ~nen** ▸ **❶ S. 113** tailor; (Damen~) dressmaker

Schneider-: ~kostüm *das* tailor-made *or* tailored suit; **~kreide** *die* tailor's chalk; French chalk; **~meister** *der,* **~meisterin** *die* master tailor; (für Damenkleider) master dressmaker

schneidern

A *tr. V.* make ‹*dress, clothes*›; make, tailor ‹*suit*›; **sie schneidert ihre Sachen selbst** she makes her own clothes

B *itr. V.* make clothes/dresses; (beruflich) work as a tailor; (als Schneiderin) work as a dressmaker

Schneider-: **~puppe** *die* tailor's dummy; (eines Damenschneiders) dressmaker's dummy; **~sitz** *der* cross-legged position; **im ~sitz** cross-legged

Schneide-: **~tisch** *der* (Film, Ferns.) editing *or* cutting table; **~zahn** *der* ▸ℹ S. 435 incisor

schneidig

A *Adj.* **1** (forsch, zackig) dashing; (waghalsig) daring; bold; rousing, brisk ‹*music*› **2** (flott, sportlich) dashing ‹*appearance, fellow*›; trim ‹*figure*›

B *adv.* briskly; **~ spielen** play in a rousing/lively manner

schneien /ˈʃnaiən/

A *itr., tr. V.* (unpers.) **es schneit** it is snowing; **es schneit/schneite jeden Tag** it snows/snowed every day; **es schneit dicke Flocken** *od.* **in dicken Flocken** big flakes of snow are falling; **es schneit auf dem Bildschirm** (fig.) there's a snowstorm on the screen

B *itr. V.*; *mit sein* (fig.) ‹*blossom, confetti, etc.*› rain down, fall like snow

Schneise /ˈʃnaizə/ *die*; **~, ~n** **1** (Wald~) aisle; (als Feuerschutz) firebreak **2** (Flug~) [air] corridor

schnell /ʃnɛl/ ▸ℹ S. 310

A *Adj.* quick ‹*journey, decision, service, etc.*›; fast ‹*car, skis, road, track, etc.*›; quick, rapid, swift ‹*progress*›; quick, swift ‹*movement, blow, action*›; **ein ~es Tempo** a high speed; a fast pace; **um ~e Erledigung der Angelegenheit bitten** request that the matter be handled speedily; **sie ist sehr ~ bei der Arbeit** she is a very quick worker; **~es Geld** (ugs.) money for jam (coll.); **dem** *od.* **einen ~en Euro machen** (salopp) make a fast buck (sl.); **auf die Schnelle** (ugs.) in a trice; (übereilt) in [too much of] a hurry; in a rush; (kurzfristig) at short notice; quickly; **auf die Schnelle ein Bier/eins auf die Schnelle trinken** have a quick beer/a quick one

B *adv.* quickly; ‹*drive, move, etc.*› fast, quickly; ‹*spread*› quickly, rapidly; (bald) soon ‹*sold, past, etc.*›; **nicht so ~!** not so fast!; **mach ~!** (ugs.) move it! (coll.); **so ~ macht ihm das keiner nach** nobody is going to equal that in a hurry; **wie heißt er noch ~?** (ugs.) what's his name again?; **es ging ~er, als man dachte** it went quicker than expected; **das geht mir zu ~:** that's too quick for me

Schnell-: **~bahn** *die* (Verkehrsw.) municipal railway; **~boot** *das* high-speed patrol boat; (Torpedoschnellboot) motor torpedo boat; PT boat (Amer.); **~dienst** *der* express service; **~durchlauf** *der* fast forward; **im ~durchlauf** in fast forward *or* fast frame

Schnelle *die*; **~, ~n** **1** (Schnelligkeit) rapidity; (Tempo) speed **2** (Geog.: Strom~) rapids *pl.*

***schnellebig** ▸**schnelllebig**

schnellen

A *itr. V.*; *mit sein* shoot (**aus** + *Dat.* out of; **in** + *Akk.* into); **in die Höhe ~** ‹*person*› leap to one's feet *or* up; ‹*rocket, fig.: prices etc.*› shoot up

B *tr. V.* send ‹*ball, stone, etc.*› flying; hurl ‹*ball, stone, etc.*›; whip ‹*fishingline*›; **sich mit dem Trampolin in die Höhe ~:** leap high into the air on a/the trampoline

Schnell-: **~feuer** *das* (Milit.) rapid fire; **~feuer·gewehr** *das* semi-automatic rifle; **~gaststätte** *die* fast-food restaurant; (~imbiss) snackbar; **~gericht** *das* convenience food; (in Lokalen) quick snack; **~hefter** *der* loose-leaf binder; quick-release file

Schnelligkeit *die*; **~, ~en** **1** (Tempo) speed; **die ~, mit der sie arbeitet** the speed at which she works **2** (das Schnellsein) rapidity; speed

schnell-, Schnell-: **~imbiss**, ***~imbiß** *der* snackbar; **~kochplatte** *die* high-speed ring; **~kochtopf** *der* pressure cooker; **~kraft** *die* springiness; **~kurs** *der* crash course; **~lebig** /-le:bɪç/ *Adj.* **1** (Biol.: kurzlebig) short-lived ‹*animal, insect*›; **2** (hektisch, betriebsam) fast-moving ‹*age*›; **~paket** *das* (Postw.) express parcel; **~reinigung** *die* express cleaner's; **~spanner** *der* quick-release; **~spann·nabe** *die* quick-release hub

> **Schnellimbiss**
>
> This is a place where you can eat or take away a cheap, quick snack. Usually a *Schnellimbiss* is just a stand that sells different kinds of Würstchen (sausages), rissoles, *Döner* (doner kebab) or *Leberkäse*, depending on which region you are in. *Currywurst* is a favourite *Schnellimbiss* meal. Sausages are served on a long paper plate with a dab of mustard. Wherever you are, you won't have to go far to find a *Schnellimbiss*.

schnellstens *Adv.* as quickly as possible; (möglichst bald) as soon as possible

schnellst·möglich

A *Adj.* quickest possible; **auf ~e Erledigung der Arbeit drängen** press for the earliest possible completion of the work

B *adv.* ▸**schnellstens**

Schnell-: **~straße** *die* expressway (*on which slow-moving vehicles are prohibited*); **~test** *der* high-speed test; **~verfahren** *das* **1** (bes. Technik) high-speed process; **im ~verfahren** (fig.) at high speed; in a crash programme; **2** (Rechtsw.) summary trial; summary proceedings *pl.*; **im ~verfahren** in summary proceedings; **~verkehr** *der* (Kfz-W.) fast-moving traffic; (~verkehrsnetz) express services *pl.*; **~zug** *der* express [train]; **~zug·zuschlag** *der* express train supplement

Schnepfe /ˈʃnɛpfə/ *die*; **~, ~n** **1** (Vogel) snipe; (Wald~) woodcock **2** (salopp abwertend: weibliche Person) **[blöde] ~:** [silly] cow (sl. derog.) **3** (salopp abwertend: Prostituierte) tart (sl.)

schnetzeln /ˈʃnɛtsl̩n/ (bes. südd.) cut ‹*meat*› into thin strips

***schneuzen** ▸**schnäuzen**

Schnick·schnack *der* (ugs.; meist abwertend) **1** (wertloses Zeug) trinkets *pl.*; (Zierrat) frills *pl.* (fig.); **überflüssiger ~:** superfluous paraphernalia *sing.* **2** (Geschwätz) waffle; (Unsinn) drivel; **~!** rubbish!

schniefen /ˈʃni:fn̩/ *itr. V.* sniffle; (bes. beim Weinen) snivel

schniegeln /ˈʃni:gl̩n/ *refl. V.* spruce oneself up; *s. auch* **geschniegelt**

schnieke /ˈʃni:kə/

A *Adj.* (berlin.) **1** (schick, elegant) snazzy (coll.) ‹*clothes, fashion, etc.*› **2** (großartig) super (Brit. coll.)

B *adv.* snazzily (coll.)

schnipp *Interj.* snip; **~, schnapp!** snip, snip

Schnippchen *das*; **~s** trick; **jmdm. ein ~ schlagen** (ugs.) outsmart sb. (coll.); put one over on sb. (sl.); **dem Tod/Schicksal ein ~ schlagen** (ugs.) cheat death/fate

Schnippel *der od. das*; **~s, ~** (ugs.) scrap; (Papier~, Stoff~) snippet; shred

Schnippelchen *das*; **~s, ~:** tiny scrap; (Papier~, Stoff~) tiny snippet *or* shred

schnippeln (ugs.)

A *itr. V.* (mit der Schere) snip [away] (**an** + *Dat.* at); **an der Wurst ~** (mit dem Messer) cut little snippets of sausage

B *tr. V.* **1** (ausschneiden) snip [out] **2** (zerkleinern) shred ‹*vegetables*›; chop ‹*beans etc.*› [finely]

schnippen /ˈʃnɪpn̩/

A *itr. V.* **1** (mit der Schere) snip **2** (mit den Fingern) snap one's fingers (**nach** at); **mit Daumen und Mittelfinger ~:** snap one's thumb and middle finger together

B *tr. V.* **1** (wegschleudern) flick (**von** off, from); **die Asche von der Zigarette ~:** flick the ash off one's cigarette **2** (herausschleudern) tap ‹*cigarette, card, etc.*› (**aus** out of)

schnippisch (abwertend)

A *Adj.* pert ‹*reply, tone, etc.*›; (anmaßend) cocky ‹*girl, tone, expression*›

B *adv.* pertly; (anmaßend) cockily

Schnipsel /ˈʃnɪpsl̩/ *der od. das*; **~s, ~:** scrap; (Papier~, Stoff~) snippet; shred

schnipseln ▸**schnippeln**

schnitt /ʃnɪt/ *1. u. 3. Pers. Sg. Prät. v.* **schneiden**

Schnitt *der*; **~[e]s, ~e** **1** cut; (Operationsschnitt) incision; cut; **etw. mit einem [schnellen] ~ durchtrennen** divide sth. by cutting it [quickly]; **sich** (*Dat.*) **einen ~ beibringen** cut oneself **2** (das Mähen) (von Gras) mowing; cut; (von Getreide) harvest; **das Korn ist reif für den ~:** the corn is ready for reaping *or* harvesting; **einen** *od.* **seinen ~ [bei etw.] machen** (fig. ugs.) make a profit [from sth.] **3** (Form von Kleidung, Haar, Edelsteinen usw.) cut; **eine Wohnung mit gutem ~** (fig.) a well-planned flat (esp. Brit.) *or* (esp. Amer.) apartment; **ihr Profil hat einen klassischen ~** (fig.) she has a classical profile **4** (Film, Ferns.) editing; cutting; **ein harter/weicher ~:** editing with straight *or* sudden/gradual cuts; **~: Gisela Meyer** edited by *or* editor Gisela Meyer **5** (Schnittmuster) [dressmaking] pattern **6** (Längs-, Quer-, Schrägschnitt) section; **etw. im ~ darstellen** show sth. in section **7** (ugs.: Durch~) average; **er fährt einen ~ von 200 km/h** he is driving at *or* doing an average [speed] of 125 mph; **im ~:** on average **8** (Math.) ▸**golden A 3** **9** (Geom.: Schnittfläche) intersection **10** (Ballspiele: Drall) spin; **den Ball mit ~ spielen** *od.* **schlagen** put spin on the ball

Schnitt-: **~blume** *die* cut flower; **~bohne** *die* French bean; **~brot** *das* cut *or* sliced bread

Schnittchen *das*; **~s, ~:** canapé; [small] open sandwich

Schnitte *die*; **~, ~n** **1** (bes. nordd.: Scheibe) slice; **eine ~ [Brot]** a slice of bread; **eine [belegte] ~:** an open sandwich **2** (österr.: Waffel) wafer

Schnitter *der*; **~s, ~**, **Schnitterin** *die*; **~, ~nen** (veralt.) reaper

schnitt-, Schnitt-: **~fest** *Adj.* firm ‹*tomato, sausage, etc.*›; **~fläche** *die* cut surface; **die ~fläche des Käses** the cut end of the cheese; **~holz** *das* cut timber

schnittig

A *Adj.* stylish, smart ‹*suit, appearance, etc.*›; (sportlich) racy ‹*car, yacht, etc.*›; (stromlinienförmig) streamlined ‹*car, bow, etc.*›

B *adv.* stylishly; (sportlich) racily

schnitt-, Schnitt-: **~käse** *der* cheese suitable for slicing; hard cheese; (in Scheiben) cheese slices *pl.*; **~lauch** *der* chives *pl.*; **~linie** *die* line of intersection; (Linie, die eine andere kreuzt) intersecting line; **~menge** *die* (Math.) **die ~menge A ∩ B** the intersection of the sets A and B; **~muster** *das* **1** [dressmaking] pattern; **2** (ugs.) ▸**~musterbogen**; **~muster·bogen** *der* pattern chart; **~punkt** *der* intersection; (Geom.) point of intersection; **~reif** *Adj.* ‹*corn etc.*› ready for reaping *or* harvesting; **~stelle** *die* (DV) interface; **~wunde** *die* cut; (lang u. tief) gash

Schnitz·arbeit *die* carving

Schnitzel /ˈʃnɪtsl̩/ *das*; **~s, ~** **1** (Fleisch) [veal/pork] escalope **2** (Stückchen) (von Papier) scrap; snippet; (von Holz) shaving; (von Früchten usw.) sliver

Schnitzel·jagd *die* paperchase

schnitzeln *tr. V.* chop up ‹*vegetables etc.*› [into small pieces]; shred ‹*cabbage*›

schnitzen

A *itr. V.* carve; **an etw.** (*Dat.*) **~:** carve away at sth.

B *tr. V.* carve

Schnitzer *der*; **~s, ~** **1** (Handwerker) carver **2** (ugs.: Fehler) boob (Brit. coll.); goof (coll.); **sich** (*Dat.*) **einen groben ~ leisten** make an awful boob (Brit. coll.) *or* (coll.) goof; (mit einer Bemerkung) drop an awful clanger (coll.)

Schnitzerei *die*; **~, ~en** **1** (Geschnitztes) carving (*Gen.* by) **2** (das Schnitzen) carving *no art.*

Schnitzerin, *die*; **~, ~nen** ▸**Schnitzer 1**

Schnitz-: **~messer** *das* wood carving knife; **~werk** *das* carving; (mehrere Stücke) carvings *pl.*

schnob /ʃno:p/ *1. u. 3. Pers. Sg. Prät. v.* **schnauben**

schnöd /ʃnø:t/ *Adj.* (bes. südd., österr.) ▸**schnöde**

schnodderig /ˈʃnɔdərɪç/ (ugs. abwertend)

A *Adj.* brash; **ein ~es Mundwerk haben** have a big mouth

B *adv.* brashly

S

Schnodderigkeit *die;* ~, ~**en** (ugs.) 1 (Art, Wesen) brashness 2 (Äußerung/Handlung) brash remark/action

schnoddrig ▸**schnodderig**

schnöde (geh. abwertend)
A *Adj.* 1 (verachtenswert) despicable; contemptible; base ‹*cowardice*›; *s. auch* **Mammon** 2 (gemein) contemptuous, scornful ‹*glance, reply, etc.*›; harsh ‹*reprimand*›; ~**r Undank** blatant ingratitude
B *adv.* (gemein) contemptuously; ‹*reprimand*› harshly; ‹*exploit, misuse*› flagrantly, blatantly

Schnorchel /ˈʃnɔrçl̩/ *der;* ~**s,** ~: snorkel

Schnörkel /ˈʃnœrkl̩/ *der;* ~**s,** ~: scroll; curlicue; (der Handschrift, in der Rede) flourish

schnorren /ˈʃnɔrən/ *tr., itr. V.* (ugs.) scrounge (coll.); **etw. bei** *od.* **von jmdm.** ~: scrounge (coll.) *or* cadge sth. off sb.

Schnorrer *der;* ~**s,** ~, **Schnorrerin** *die;* ~, ~**nen** (ugs.) scrounger (coll.); sponger

Schnösel /ˈʃnøːzl̩/ *der;* ~**s,** ~ (ugs. abwertend) young whippersnapper

schnöselig (ugs. abwertend)
A *Adj.* cheeky; insolent
B *adv.* cheekily; insolently

Schnuckelchen /ˈʃnʊkl̩çən/ *das;* ~**s,** ~ (fam.) sweetie[-pie] (coll.); **mein kleines** ~: my little darling *or* pet

schnuckelig *Adj.* (ugs.) sweet; cute (Amer. coll.)

Schnüffelei *die;* ~, ~**en** (ugs. abwertend) 1 (dauerndes Schnüffeln) [constant] snooping (coll.) 2 (Vorfall von ~) case of snooping (coll.)

schnüffeln /ˈʃnʏfl̩n/
A *itr. V.* 1 (riechen) sniff; **an etw.** (*Dat.*) ~: sniff sth. 2 (ugs. abwertend: heimlich suchen; spionieren) snoop [about] (coll.); **in etw.** (*Akk.*) ~: pry into sth.; stick one's nose into sth. (coll.); **in jmds. Papieren** ~: nose about in sb.'s papers 3 (Drogenjargon: Dämpfe ~) sniff [glue/paint *etc.*] 4 (ugs.: die Nase hochziehen) sniff
B *tr. V.* (Drogenjargon: zum S~ benutzen) sniff ‹*glue etc.*›

Schnüffler *der;* ~**s,** ~, **Schnüfflerin** *die;* ~, ~**nen** 1 (ugs. abwertend) Nosey Parker; (Spion) snooper (coll.) 2 (Drogenjargon) [glue-, paint-, *etc.*]sniffer

Schnuller /ˈʃnʊlɐ/ *der;* ~**s,** ~: dummy (Brit.); pacifier (Amer.)

Schnulze /ˈʃnʊltsə/ *die;* ~, ~**n** (ugs. abwertend) (Lied/Melodie) slushy song/tune; (Theaterstück, Film, Fernsehspiel) tear jerker (coll.); slushy play; **etw. als** ~ **singen** sing sth. in a slushy version

schnupfen /ˈʃnʊpfn̩/
A *itr. V.* 1 (Tabak ~) take snuff 2 (bei Tränen, Nasenschleim) sniff
B *tr. V.* take a sniff of ‹*cocaine etc.*›; (gewohnheitsmäßig) sniff ‹*cocaine etc.*›; **Tabak** ~: take snuff

Schnupfen *der;* ~**s,** ~: [head] cold; **[den** *od.* **einen]** ~ **haben** have a [head] cold; **sich** (*Dat.*) **den** ~ **holen** catch a [head] cold

Schnupfer *der;* ~**s,** ~, **Schnupferin** *die;* ~, ~**nen** snuff-taker

Schnupf-: ~**tabak** *der* snuff; ~**tabak[s]·dose** *die* snuff box

schnuppe /ˈʃnʊpə/ *in* ~ **sein** (ugs.) be neither here nor there; **das/er ist mir** ~/**mir völlig** ~ (ugs.) I don't care/I couldn't care less about it/him (coll.)

schnuppern /ˈʃnʊpɐn/
A *itr. V.* sniff; **an etw.** (*Dat.*) ~: sniff sth.
B *tr. V.* sniff; **Seeluft** ~ (fig.) get some sea air

Schnur /ʃnuːɐ̯/ *die;* ~, **Schnüre** /ˈʃnyːrə/ *od.* **Schnuren** 1 (Bindfaden) piece of string; (Kordel) piece of cord; (Zelt~) guy [rope]; (für Marionette, Drachen usw.) string; **eine** ~ **um ein Paket binden** tie string round a parcel; **Perlen auf eine** ~ **aufziehen** string pearls 2 (Zierkordel) piece of braid; **mit vielen Schnüren** with much braid[ing] *sing.* 3 (ugs.: Kabel) flex (Brit.); lead; cord (Amer.)

Schnür·boden *der* 1 (Theater) flies *pl.* 2 (Schiffbau) mould loft

Schnürchen *das;* ~**s,** ~ *in* **wie am** ~ **[gehen** *od.* **klappen]** (ugs.) [go] like clockwork *or* without a hitch; **ein Gedicht wie am** ~ **aufsagen** (ugs.) say a poem off pat

schnüren /ˈʃnyːrən/
A *tr. V.* 1 tie ‹*bundle, string, sb.'s hands, etc.*›; tie [up] ‹*parcel, person*›; tie, lace up ‹*shoe, corset, etc.*›; **etw. zu Bündeln/Paketen** ~: tie sth. up in bundles/parcels; **etw. um/auf etw.** (*Akk.*) ~: tie sth. round/[on] to sth. 2 **Angst schnürte ihm die Kehle/den Atem** (fig.) fear constricted his throat/almost stopped him from breathing
B *refl. V.* (sich hineindrücken) **sich in das Fleisch** *usw.* ~: cut into the flesh *etc*
C *itr. V.* 1 (zu eng sein) be too tight; pinch 2 *mit sein* (Jägerspr.) ‹*fox, lynx, wolf*› trot in a straight line; ‹*fig.: person*› trot

schnur·gerade, schnur·grade (ugs.)
A *Adj.* dead straight
B *adv.* dead straight; ~ **auf sein Ziel losgehen** (fig.) make straight for one's goal

Schnur·keramik *die* (Archäol.) corded ware

schnurlos *Adj.* cordless

Schnurlos·telefon *das* cordless phone

Schnürl- /ˈʃnyːɐ̯l-/: ~**regen** *der* (österr.) persistent rain; ~**samt** *der* (österr.) corduroy

Schnurr·bart *der* moustache

schnurr·bärtig *Adj.* with a moustache *postpos.;* ~ **sein** have a moustache

Schnurre *die;* ~, ~**n** (veralt.) anecdote

schnurren /ˈʃnʊrən/ *itr. V.* ‹*cat*› purr; ‹*machine*› hum; ‹*camera, spinning wheel, etc.*› whirr

Schnurr·haar *das* (Zool.) whiskers *pl.*

Schnür·riemen *der* 1 strap 2 ▸**Schnürsenkel**

schnurrig *Adj.* (veralt.) droll; comic; funny; comic ‹*old man etc.*›

Schnür-: ~**schuh** *der* lace-up shoe; ~**senkel** *der* (bes. nordd.) [shoe]lace; (für Stiefel) bootlace; **sich** (*Dat.*) **die** ~**senkel binden** tie one's shoelaces

schnur·springen *unr. itr. V.; nur im Inf. und 2. Partizip; mit sein* (österr.) skip

Schnür·stiefel *der* lace-up boot

schnur·stracks *Adv.* (ugs.) straight; **der Weg geht** ~ **geradeaus** the way goes straight ahead; ~ **auf jmdn./etw. zugehen** make a beeline for sb./sth.

Schnürung *die;* ~, ~**en** lacing; (Schnürsenkel) laces *pl.*

schnurz /ʃnʊrts/ *Adj.* (ugs.) *in* **es ist [jmdm.]** ~ (salopp) it doesn't matter a hoot [to sb.] (sl.); **ihm ist jmd./etw./alles** ~ **[und piepe]** he doesn't give a damn *or* couldn't care less about sb./sth./anything (coll.)

Schnute /ˈʃnuːtə/ *die;* ~, ~**n** (fam., bes. nordd.: Mund) mouth; gob (sl.); **eine** ~ **ziehen** *od.* **machen** make *or* pull a [sulky] face

schob /ʃoːp/ *1. u. 3. Pers. Prät. v.* **schieben**

Schober /ˈʃoːbɐ/ *der;* ~**s,** ~ 1 open-sided barn 2 (Heuhaufen) [hay]stack; [hay]rick

Schock[1] /ʃɔk/ *das;* ~**[e]s,** ~**e** 1 (veralt.: 60 Stück) **ein** ~: three score; five dozen; **7 bis 8** ~ **Eier** 35-40 dozen eggs 2 (ugs.: Menge) [whole] load of (coll.)

Schock[2] *der;* ~**[e]s,** ~**s** ▸ⓘ **S. 439** (auch Med.) shock; **jmdm. einen [schweren/leichten]** ~ **versetzen** *od.* **geben** give sb. a [nasty/slight] shock *or* a [nasty/bit of a] fright; **unter** ~ **stehen** be in [a state of] shock; be suffering from shock

Schock·behandlung *die* shock treatment

schocken *tr. V.* (ugs.: schockieren) shock

Schocker *der;* ~**s,** ~ (ugs.) (Roman/Film) sensational book/film; shocker (coll.); (Mensch) sensationalist

Schock·farbe *die* (ugs.) violent colour

schockieren *tr. V.* shock; **über etw.** (*Akk.*) **schockiert sein** be shocked at sth.

schock-, Schock-: ~**therapie** *die* (auch fig.) shock therapy *or* treatment; ~**weise** *Adv.* 1 (in Schocks) by the three score; five dozen at a time; 2 (ugs.: scharenweise) in droves; ~**wirkung** *die* shock effect; **unter** ~**wirkung stehen** be in a state of shock; be suffering from shock

schofel /ˈʃoːfl̩/, **schofelig** (ugs. abwertend)
A *Adj.* horrid (coll.); beastly (coll.); (schändlich) disgusting
B *adv.* horridly

Schöffe /ˈʃœfə/ *der;* ~**n,** ~**n** lay judge (*acting together with another lay judge and a professional judge*)

Schöffen·gericht *das: court presided over by a professional judge and two lay judges*

Schöffin *die;* ~, ~**nen** ▸**Schöffe**

Schoko /ˈʃoːko/ *die;* ~, ~**[s]** (ugs.) choccy (coll.)

Schokolade /ʃokoˈlaːdə/ *die;* ~, ~**n** 1 (Süßigkeit) chocolate 2 (Getränk) [drinking] chocolate

schokolade[n]-, Schokolade[n]-: ~**braun** *Adj.* chocolate[-brown]; ~**eis** *das* chocolate ice cream; ~**farben** *Adj.* chocolate-coloured; chocolate ‹*brown*›; ~**guss,** *~**guß** *der* chocolate icing

Schokoladen-: ~**pudding** *der* chocolate blancmange; ~**raspel** *Pl.* chocolate flakes; grated chocolate *sing.;* ~**seite** *die* (ugs.) best side; ~**torte** *die* chocolate cake *or* gateau

schokoladig
A *Adj.* chocolatey
B *adv.* ‹*taste*› chocolatey

Scholar /ʃoˈlaːɐ̯/ *der;* ~**en,** ~**en** (hist.) [itinerant] scholar

Scholastik /ʃoˈlastɪk/ *die;* ~ (Philosophie) scholasticism

Scholastiker *der;* ~**s,** ~, **Scholastikerin** *die;* ~, ~**nen** scholastic

scholastisch *Adj.* scholastic

scholl /ʃɔl/ *1. u. 3. Pers. Sg. Prät. v.* **schallen**

Scholle /ˈʃɔlə/ *die;* ~, ~**n** 1 (Erd~) clod [of earth] 2 (Eis~) [ice] floe 3 (Fisch) (Goldbutt) flounder, *esp.* plaice; **die** ~**n** the plaice; (als Familie) the Pleuronectidae 4 (Erdboden, Acker) soil; **die heimatliche** ~ (fig.) one's native soil; **auf eigener** ~ **sitzen** have a farm of one's own 5 (Geol.) massif

Scholli /ˈʃɔli/ *in* **mein lieber** ~**!** (ugs.) my goodness!; good heavens!

Schöll·kraut /ˈʃœl-/ *das* (Bot.) celandine

schon /ʃoːn/
A *Adv.* 1 (bereits) (oft nicht übersetzt) already; (in Fragen) yet; **er hat das** ~ **vergessen** he has already forgotten that; **hat Walter** ~ **angerufen?** has Walter telephoned yet?; **wollt ihr wirklich** ~ **gehen?** do you really mean to go already *or* so soon?; **er kommt** ~ **heute/ist** ~ **gestern gekommen** he's coming today/he came yesterday; **er ist** ~ **da/[an]gekommen** he is already here/has already arrived; ~ **die Römer hatten gute Heizungen** even the Romans *or* the Romans already had good heating systems; **er ist** ~ **gestern angekommen** he arrived as early as yesterday; **ich bin** ~ **seit Mai/**~ **ein Jahr in Bremen** I've been here in Bremen since May/for a year; **wie lange bist du** ~ **hier?** how long have you been here?; ~ **damals/jetzt** even at that time *or* in those days/even now; ~ **[im Jahre] 1926** as early as 1926; back in 1926; **er war** ~ **immer faul** he always was lazy; **wie** ~ **gesagt** ... as I have already said, ...; as I said before, ...; **gestern kam er, wie** ~ **so oft, zu spät zur Arbeit** yesterday he was late for work, as so often before *or* as has so often been the case
2 (fast gleichzeitig) there and then; **er schwang sich auf das Fahrrad, und** ~ **war er weg** he jumped on the bicycle and was away [in a flash]; **kaum hatte er sich umgedreht,** ~ **ging der Krach los** he had scarcely turned his back when the row broke out; **in demselben Augenblick** ~: at that very *or* at the selfsame moment; *s. auch* **kaum 5**
3 (jetzt) ~ **[mal]** now; (inzwischen) meanwhile; **wir treffen uns dann gleich, ihr könnt ja** ~ **mal vorgehen** we'll meet up in a minute, you can be going on ahead [meanwhile]
4 (selbst, sogar) even; (nur) only; ~ **ein Tropfen von dem Gift kann tödlich sein** even a small amount *or* a mere drop of this poison can be fatal; **das weiß normalerweise** ~ **ein Zwölfjähriger** even a child of twelve would usually know that; ~ **zwei Bier reichen aus, um ihn**

völlig betrunken zu machen it only takes two beers to get him completely drunk; **das bekommt man ~ für 150 Euro** you can get it for as little as 150 euros; **für so ein Essen muss man ~ 30 Euro hinlegen** you have to pay as much as 30 euros for a meal like that
5 (ohne Ergänzung, ohne weiteren Zusatz) on its own; **das ist auch so ~ genug** that's [already] enough as it is; **[allein] ~ der Gedanke daran ist schrecklich** the mere thought *or* just the thought of it is dreadful; **~ der Name ist bezeichnend** the very name is significant; **~ darum** *od.* **aus diesem Grund** for this reason alone

B *Partikel* 1 (verstärkend) really; (gewiss) certainly; **du wirst ~ sehen!** you'll see!; **ich kann mir ~ denken, was du willst** I can well imagine what you want; **wenn wir ~ eine neue Maschine kaufen müssen, dann aber eine ordentliche** if we have to get a new machine, let's get a decent one; **wenn du ~ so früh gehen musst** if you really have to go so early
2 (ugs. ungeduldig: endlich) **nun sagen Sie [doch] ~!** come on, out with it; **nun komm ~!** come on!; hurry up!; **du hast meine Zigaretten geklaut, nun gibs ~ zu!** you've pinched my cigarettes, go on, admit it (coll.); **und wenn ~!** so what; what if he/she/it does/did/was *etc.*
3 (beruhigend: wahrscheinlich) all right; **es wird ~ gehen** *od.* **werden** it'll work out all right [in the end]; **er wird sich ~ wieder erholen** he'll recover all right; he's sure to recover; **doch, doch, das wird ~ stimmen** yes, yes, that must be right
4 (zustimmend, aber etwas einschränkend) **~ gut** OK (coll.); **ich glaube dir ~:** I believe you all right; fair enough, I believe you; **Lust hätte ich ~, nur keine Zeit** I'd certainly like to, but I've no time; **das ist ~ möglich, nur ...** that is quite possible, only ...; **er hat ~ recht, aber ...** he's right enough, but ...
5 (andererseits) **er ist nicht besonders intelligent, aber sein Bruder ~:** he's not particularly intelligent, but his brother is; **ob Willy kommt, weiß ich nicht, aber ich [komme] ~:** I don't know whether Willy's coming, but 'I'm coming *or* 'I am
6 (einschränkend, abwertend) **was weiß der ~!** what does 'he know [about it]!; **was ist** *od.* **bedeutet ~ Geld!** what does money matter?; what's the good of money [anyway]?; **wem nützt das ~?** what's the use of that [to anybody]?; **Ist was? — Nee, was soll ~ sein?** (ugs.) Is anything the matter? — No, should anything be [wrong]?; **was soll das ~ heißen?** what's 'that supposed to mean?

schön /ʃøːn/

A *Adj.* 1 (anziehend, reizvoll) beautiful; handsome ‹*youth, man*›; **das ~e Geschlecht** the fair sex; **die ~en Künste** the fine arts; **sie ist ~ von Gestalt** (geh.) she has a lovely figure; **das Schöne** beauty; (~e Dinge) beautiful things *pl.*; **~e Literatur** belles-lettres *pl.*; **~e Frau, was wünschen Sie?** (scherzh.) what is your wish, my pretty one?; **ich finde das Buch ~:** the book appeals to me; **bring mir etwas Schönes mit** bring me back something nice
2 (angenehm, erfreulich) pleasant, nice ‹*day, holiday, dream, relaxation, etc.*›; fine ‹*weather*›; (nett) nice; **das war eine ~e Zeit** those were wonderful days; **einen ~en Tod haben** die peacefully; **das war alles nicht ~ für sie** it was all rather unpleasant for her; **mach dir ein paar ~e Stunden** enjoy yourself for a few hours; **das ist ~ von dir** it's nice of you; **das ist ein ~er Zug an ihm** that is one of the good *or* nice things about him; **das Schöne daran/an ihm** the nice thing about it/him; **das ist zu ~, um wahr zu sein** that is too good to be true; **alles war in ~ster Ordnung** everything was in perfect order; **was hier vor sich geht, das ist nicht mehr ~** (ugs.) the goings-on here are beyond a joke
3 (gut) good ‹*wine, beer, piece of work, etc.*›; **~ schmecken/riechen** (nordd. ugs.) taste/smell really good *or* (esp. Amer. coll.) real good
4 (in Höflichkeitsformeln) **~e Grüße** best wishes; **[ich soll Ihnen einen] ~en Gruß von meiner Mutter [bestellen]** my mother sends you her kind regards; **recht ~en Dank für ...** thank you very much for ...; many thanks for ...
5 (ugs.: einverstanden) OK (coll.); all right; **also ~:** right then; **~ und gut** (ugs.) all well and good; **das ist alles ~ und gut, aber ...** (ugs.) that's all very well but ...
6 (iron.: leer) **eine ~e Floskel** a splendid platitude; **~e Worte** fine[-sounding] words; (schmeichlerisch) honeyed words
7 (ugs.: beträchtlich) handsome, (coll.) tidy ‹*sum, fortune, profit*›; considerable ‹*quantity, distance*›; pretty good ‹*pension*›; **das hat ein ganz ~es Gewicht** it's quite a weight; **ein ~es Alter erreichen** reach a fine old age; **einen ~en Schrecken davontragen** get a real *or* quite a fright; **eine ~e Leistung** no mean *or* quite an achievement
8 (iron.: unerfreulich) nice (coll. iron.); **das sind ja ~e Aussichten!** this is a fine lookout *sing.* (iron.); what a delightful prospect! *sing.* (iron.); **eine ~e Bescherung** a nice *or* fine mess (coll. iron.); **ein ~er Reinfall** a real disaster; **du machst [mir] ja ~e Geschichten!** you do get up to some fine tricks (iron.)

B *adv.* 1 (anziehend, reizvoll) beautifully; **der Wein ist ~ klar** the wine is beautifully clear; **sie ist ~ eingerichtet** she has a lovely home; **sich ~ zurechtmachen** make oneself look nice
2 (angenehm, erfreulich) nicely; **~ warm/weich/langsam** nice and warm/soft/slow; **wir haben es ~ hier** we're very well off here
3 (gut, ausgezeichnet) well; **das habt ihr ~ gemacht** you did that well *or* nicely; you made a good job of that
4 (in Höflichkeitsformeln) **bitte ~, können Sie mir sagen, ...** excuse me, could you tell me ...; **grüß deine Mutter ~ von mir** give your mother my kind regards
5 (iron.) **wie es so ~ heißt, wie man so ~ sagt** as they say
6 (ugs.: beträchtlich) really; (vor einem Adjektiv) pretty; **ganz ~ arbeiten müssen** have to work jolly hard (Brit. coll.); **[ganz] ~ dämlich** damned stupid; **er sitzt [ganz] ~ in der Tinte** he's well and truly in the soup (coll.); **ganz ~ trinken/lügen** drink like a fish (coll.)/lie like anything (coll.)

C *Partikel* (ugs. verstärkend) **~ der Reihe nach!** one after the other in a nice orderly line; **~ ruhig bleiben/~ langsam fahren** be nice and quiet/drive nice and slowly; **bleib ~ liegen!** lie there and be good; **passt ~ auf!** pay careful attention; **jetzt gehst du ~ nach Hause** now go home like a good boy/girl; **sei ~ brav** be a good boy/girl

Schöne *die; adj. Dekl.* beauty; (iron.: Frau) member of the fair sex; **die ~n der Nacht** (geh.) the ladies of the night

schonen

A *tr. V.* treat ‹*clothes, books, furniture, etc.*› with care; (schützen) protect ‹*hands, furniture*›; (nicht strapazieren) spare ‹*voice, eyes, etc.*›; conserve ‹*strength*›; (nachsichtig behandeln) go easy on, spare ‹*person*›; **jmdm. eine Nachricht ~d beibringen** break news gently to sb.; **eine ~de Behandlung** gentle treatment

B *refl. V.* take care of oneself; (sich nicht überanstrengen) take things easy; **sich mehr ~:** take things easier; **er schont sich nicht, wenn es um seine Patienten geht** he doesn't spare himself when it comes to his patients

schönen *tr. V.* brighten ‹*colour*›; clarify ‹*wine*›; (mit Gelatine) fine ‹*wine*›; touch up ‹*picture*›; enhance ‹*picture, figure*›; **[idealistisch] geschönt** (fig.) idealized; flattering

Schoner *der;* **~s, ~** (Seemannsspr.) schooner

Schön·färberei *die;* **~, ~en** embellishment; **frei von jeder** *od.* **ohne jede ~:** without any whitewashing

Schon-: **~frist** *die* period of grace; (nach einer Operation) period of convalescence; **~gang** *der* 1 (Kfz-W.) high gear; (Overdrive) overdrive; 2 (bei Waschmaschinen) programme for delicate fabrics

Schön·geist *der* aesthete

schön·geistig *Adj.* aesthetic; **die ~e Literatur** belletristic literature

Schönheit *die;* **~, ~en** beauty; **die ~en der Umgebung** the attractions of the area

Schönheits-: **~chirurgie** *die* cosmetic surgery *no art.*; **~farm** *die* health farm; **~fehler** *der* blemish; (fig.) minor defect; (Nachteil) slight drawback; **~ideal** *das* ideal of beauty; **~königin** *die* beauty queen; **~konkurrenz** *die* beauty contest; **~pflästerchen** /-pflɛstɐçən/ *das;* **~~s, ~~** (Kosmetik) beauty spot; **~pflege** *die* beauty care *no art.*; **~reparatur** *die* cosmetic repair; (in einem Haus/einer Wohnung) redecorating *no pl.*; **~sinn** *der* sense of beauty; aesthetic sense; **~wettbewerb** *der* beauty contest

Schon-: **~klima** *das* benign climate; **~kost** *die* light food; **auf ~kost gesetzt werden** be put on a light diet

schön|machen (ugs.)

A *tr. V.* smarten ‹*person, thing*› up; make ‹*person, thing*› look nice; do up ‹*building*›

B *refl. V.* smarten oneself up; make oneself look smart

C *itr. V.* ‹*dog*› [sit up and] beg

Schon·platz *der* (DDR): *job given to someone temporarily incapacitated;* light job

schön-, Schön-: **~|reden** *itr. V.* (abwertend) turn on the smooth talk; sweet-talk (Amer.); **das ~reden** smooth talking; sweet talk (Amer.); **~redner** *der* (abwertend) smooth *or* (Amer.) sweet talker; **~rednerei** *die;* **~~, ~~en** (abwertend) smooth *or* (Amer.) sweet talk *no pl.*; **~en** blandishments; **~rednerin** *die* ▸ **~redner**; **~|schreiben** *unr. itr.* (*auch tr.*) *V.* write neatly; (~schrift schreiben) do calligraphy; **~schreiben** (als Unterrichtsfach) handwriting *no art.*; **~schreibheft** *das* writing book; (mit vorgedruckten Buchstaben) copybook; **~schrift** *die* 1 (Zierschrift) calligraphy; (sorgfältige Schrift) neat handwriting; **etw. in ~schrift abschreiben** copy sth. out neatly *or* in one's best handwriting; 2 (ugs.: Reinschrift) neat *or* clean copy; **~|tun** *unr. itr. V.* (ugs.) **jmdm. ~tun** soft-soap sb.; butter sb. up

-schonung *die* ‹*fir, spruce, etc.*› plantation

Schonung *die;* **~, ~en** 1 (Nachsicht) consideration; (nachsichtige Behandlung) considerate treatment; (nach Krankheit/Operation) [period of] rest; (von Gegenständen) careful treatment; **sein Zustand/Magen verlangt ~:** his condition/his stomach needs careful treatment; **sie braucht noch ~:** she still needs to be treated considerately; (muss sich selbst schonen) she must still take things easy; **er kannte ihr gegenüber keine ~:** he knew no mercy towards her; he did not spare her 2 (Jungwald) [young] plantation

schonungs-: **~bedürftig** *Adj.* in need of rest *postpos.*; **~bedürftig sein** need to take things carefully *or* easy; **~los** **A** *Adj.* unsparing, ruthless ‹*criticism etc.*›; blunt ‹*frankness*›; **eine ~lose Aufklärung der Affäre** a rigorous elucidation of the affair; **B** *adv.* unsparingly; ‹*say*› without mincing one's words

Schonungslosigkeit *die;* **~:** ruthlessness; (Strenge) rigour

Schön·wetter·periode *die* spell of fine weather; fine spell

Schon·zeit *die* 1 (Jagdw.) close season 2 (Schonung) period of rest; (Erholungszeit) period of convalescence; recovery period; (fig.: Anfangszeit, in der man nachsichtig behandelt wird) honeymoon period

Schopf /ʃɔpf/ *der;* **~[e]s, Schöpfe** /ˈʃœpfə/ 1 (Haar~) shock of hair; **die Gelegenheit beim ~[e] fassen** *od.* **nehmen** *od.* **packen** *od.* **ergreifen** (ugs.) seize *or* grasp the opportunity with both hands 2 (Jägerspr.: Kopffedern) crest

schöpfen[1] /ˈʃœpfn̩/

A *tr. V.* 1 scoop [up] ‹*water, liquid*›; (mit einer Kelle) ladle ‹*soup*›; **Wasser aus einem Brunnen ~:** draw water from a well; **Wasser aus dem Boot ~:** bale water out of the boat 2 (geh.: einatmen) draw, take ‹*breath*›; **frische Luft ~:** take a breath of fresh air 3 (geh.: für sich gewinnen) draw ‹*wisdom, strength, knowledge*› (**aus** from); **neuen Mut/neue Hoffnung ~:** take fresh heart/find fresh hope; **Argwohn** *od.* **Verdacht ~:** become suspicious

B *itr. V.* **aus der Fantasie/jahrelanger Erfahrung** *usw.* **~:** draw on one's imagination/on years of experience *etc.*

S

schọ̈pfen² *tr. V.* (veralt.: schaffen) create; coin ‹*word*›

Schọ̈pfer¹ *der;* **~s, ~:** creator; (Gott) Creator

Schọ̈pfer² *der;* **~s, ~** (Kelle) ladle

Schọ̈pferin *die;* **~, ~nen** creator

schọ̈pferisch

A *Adj.* creative; constructive ‹*criticism*›; **der ~e Augenblick** the moment of inspiration; **eine ~e Pause** a pause for inspiration

B *adv.* creatively; **~ tätig sein** be creative

Schọ̈pferkraft *die* creative powers *pl.*; creativity

Schọ̈pf-: ~kelle *die,* **~löffel** *der* ladle

Schọ̈pfung *die;* **~, ~en** **1** (geh.: Erschaffung) creation; (Erfindung) invention **2** (geh.: **~ der Welt**) **die ~:** the Creation; (von Gott Erschaffenes) Creation **3** (geh.: Kunstwerk, **~ der Mode** usw.) creation; (Werk) work

Schọ̈pfungs-: ~geschichte *die* Creation story; **~tag** *der* day of the Creation

Schọ̈ppchen /ˈʃœpçən/ *das;* **~s, ~:** small glass of wine/beer

Schọppen /ˈʃɔpn̩/ *der;* **~s, ~** **1** [quarter-litre/half-litre] glass of wine/beer **2** (veralt.: Hohlmaß) **ein ~:** ≈ half a litre

Schọppen·wein *der* wine by the glass

Schöps /ʃœps/ *der;* **~es, ~e** (österr.) ▸ **Hammel 1, 2**

Schöpserne /ˈʃœpsɐnə/ *das; adj. Dekl.* (österr.) mutton

schor /ʃoːɐ̯/ *1. u. 3. Pers. Sg. Prät. v.* **scheren**

Schorf /ʃɔrf/ *der;* **~[e]s, ~e** **1** ▸ⓘ **S. 439** (Wund~) scab **2** (Pflanzenkrankheit) scab *no art.*

schọrfig *Adj.* scabby ‹*wound*›

Schorle /ˈʃɔrlə/ *die;* **~, ~n** wine with mineral water; ≈ spritzer; (mit Apfelsaft) apple juice with mineral water

Schorn·stein /ˈʃɔrn-/ *der* chimney; (Schiffs~, Lokomotiv~) funnel; **der ~ raucht** (fig.) things are ticking over nicely; business is good; **Geld in den ~ schreiben** (fig. ugs.) write off money

Schọrnstein·feger *der;* **~s, ~, Schọrnstein·fegerin** *die;* **~, ~nen** ▸ⓘ **S. 113** chimney sweep

schoss, *schoß /ʃɔs/ *1. u. 3. Pers. Sg. Prät. v.* **schießen**

Schoß¹ /ʃoːs/ *der;* **~es, Schöße** /ˈʃøːsə/ **1** lap; **ein Kind auf den ~ nehmen** take *or* sit a child on one's lap; **seine Frau saß bei ihm auf dem ~:** his wife sat on his knee; **die Hände in den ~ legen** (fig.) sit back and do nothing; **jmdm. in den ~ fallen** (fig.) just fall into sb.'s lap; **im ~ der Familie/der Kirche** (fig.) in the bosom of the family/of Mother Church; *s. auch* **Abraham 2; Hand 6** **2** (geh.: Mutterleib) womb; **im ~ der Erde** (fig.) in the bowels of the earth **3** (geh.: Vulva) pudenda *pl.* **4** (Rock~) [coat-]tail

***Schọß², Schọss** *der;* **Schọsses, Schọsse** ▸ **Schössling**

Schọß·hund *der,* **Schọß·hündchen** *das* lapdog

Schössling, *Schößling /ˈʃœslɪŋ/ *der;* **~s, ~e** **1** (Trieb) shoot **2** (Ableger zum Pflanzen) cutting

Schot /ʃoːt/ *die;* **~, ~en** (Seew.) sheet

Schote /ˈʃoːtə/ *die;* **~, ~n** **1** pod; siliqua (as tech. term); **fünf ~n Paprika** five peppers **2** (landsch.: Erbse) **~n** peas

Schott /ʃɔt/ *das;* **~[e]s, ~en** (Seemannsspr.) bulkhead; **die ~en dicht machen** (fig. ugs.) shut all the doors and windows

Schotte /ˈʃɔtə/ *der;* **~n, ~n** ▸ⓘ **S. 520** Scot; Scotsman; **er ist ~:** he's a Scot; he's Scottish; **die ~n** the Scots; the Scottish

Schọtten *der;* **~s, ~** (Textilw.) tartan [material]

Schọtten-: ~muster *das* tartan pattern; **~rock** *der* tartan skirt; (Kilt) kilt; **~witz** *der* Scottish joke (*concerning thriftiness*)

Schọtter /ˈʃɔtɐ/ *der;* **~s, ~** **1** (für Straßen) [road] metal; gravel; (für Schienen) ballast **2** (Geol.) gravel **3** (salopp: Geld) dough (coll.); lolly (Brit. sl.)

Schọtter-: ~decke *die* [loose] gravel surface; **~piste** *die* **1** gravel track; **2** (Flugw.) gravel runway; **~straße** *die* road with [loose] gravel surface

Schọttin *die;* **~, ~nen** ▸ⓘ **S. 520** Scot; Scotswoman

schọttisch ▸ⓘ **S. 520**, ▸ⓘ **S. 670**

A *Adj.* Scottish; Scots, Scottish ‹*dialect, accent, voice, etc.*›; **~er Whisky** Scotch whisky

B *adv.* ‹*speak*› with a Scots *or* Scottish accent

Schọttland (*das*); **~s** Scotland

schraffieren /ʃraˈfiːrən/ *tr. V.* hatch; (feiner) shade ‹*drawing*›

Schraffierung *die;* **~, ~en, Schraffur** /ʃraˈfuːɐ̯/ *die;* **~, ~en** hatching *no indef. art.*; (feiner) shading *no indef. art.*

schräg /ʃrɛːk/

A *Adj.* **1** diagonal ‹*line, beam, cut, etc.*›; sloping ‹*surface, roof, wall, side, etc.*›; slanting, slanted ‹*writing, eyes, etc.*›; tilted ‹*position of the head etc., axis*›; (nicht genau diagonal) oblique ‹*line etc.*›; **ein ~er Blick** (fig. ugs.) a sideways *or* sidelong glance **2** (ugs.: unseriös) offbeat; weird ‹*ideas*›; (wild) hot ‹*music*› **3** (ugs.: zweifelhaft) shady, (coll.) dodgy ‹*type, firm, etc.*›

B *adv.* at an angle; (diagonal) diagonally; (nicht genau diagonal) obliquely; **den Kopf ~ halten** hold one's head to one side; tilt one's head; **~ stehende Augen** slanting eyes; **~ gegenüber** diagonally opposite; **~ links fahren/abbiegen** bear left; **die Sonnenstrahlen fallen ~ ein** the sun is slanting in; **er saß ~ vor/hinter mir** he was sitting in front of/behind me and to one side; **das Boot liegt ~:** the boat is listing *or* down at one side; **~ gedruckt** [printed] in italics *postpos.*; **jmdn. ~ angucken** (fig. ugs.) look askance at sb.

Schräge *die;* **~, ~n** **1** (schräge Fläche) sloping surface; (Hang) slope; **das Zimmer hat eine ~:** the room has a sloping wall **2** (Neigung) slope; (Dach~) pitch; slope; **eine ~ von 10°** a 10° slope *or* incline

Schräg-: ~heck *das* (Kfz-W.) ▸ **Fließheck**; **~lage** *die* angle; (eines Schiffes) list; (eines Kindes bei der Geburt) oblique position *or* presentation; (eines Flugzeugs) bank; **etw. in ~lage bringen** tilt *or* slant sth.; **das Schiff hat ~lage** the ship is listing *or* is at an angle; **~streifen** *der* diagonal stripe; **~strich** *der* oblique stroke

schrak /ʃraːk/ *1. u. 3. Pers. Sg. Prät. v.* **schrecken**

Schramme /ˈʃramə/ *die;* **~, ~n** scratch

Schrammel·musik /ˈʃraml̩-/ *die: Viennese popular music played on violins, guitar, and accordion;* Schrammeln ensemble music

Schrạmmeln *Pl. quartet playing violins, guitar, and accordion;* Schrammeln ensemble *sing.*

schrạmmen *tr. V.* scratch (**an** + *Dat.* on)

Schrank /ʃraŋk/ *der;* **~[e]s, Schränke** /ˈʃrɛŋkə/ **1** cupboard; closet (Amer.); (Glas~; kleiner Wand~) cabinet; (Kleider~) wardrobe; (Bücher~) bookcase; (im Schwimmbad, am Arbeitsplatz usw.) locker **2** (ugs.: großer Mann) **ein [ganz schöner] ~:** a hulking great fellow (coll.)

Schrạnk·bett *das* foldaway bed

Schränkchen /ˈʃrɛŋkçən/ *das;* **~s, ~:** cabinet

Schranke /ˈʃraŋkə/ *die;* **~, ~n** **1** (auch fig.) barrier; **jmdn. in die ~ fordern** (geh.) throw down the gauntlet to sb.; **vor den ~n des Gerichts** before a/the court **2** (fig.: Grenze) limit; **er kennt keine ~n** he knows no limits *or* bounds; **die ~n der Konvention durchbrechen** break the bounds of convention; **jmdn. in die** *od.* **seine ~n [ver]weisen** (geh.) put sb. in his/her place

Schrạnken *der;* **~s, ~** (österr.) barrier

schrạnkenlos

A *Adj.* boundless, unbounded ‹*admiration, confidence, loyalty, etc.*›; unlimited, limitless ‹*power, freedom, etc.*›; unbridled, untrammelled ‹*individualism, despotism*›; unrestrained, unrestricted ‹*exploitation*›; unrestrained ‹*brutality*›; **sein Egoismus/seine Habgier war ~:** his egoism/greed knew no bounds

B *adv.* boundlessly; ‹*exploit*› without restraint

Schrạnken·wärter *der,* **Schrạnken·wärterin** *die* level-crossing (Brit.) *or* (Amer.) grade-crossing attendant; crossing keeper

Schrạ̈nker *der;* **~s, ~, Schrạ̈nkerin** *die;* **~, ~nen** (ugs.) ▸ **Geldschrankknacker**

schrạnk-, Schrạnk-: ~fach *das* [cupboard *or* (Amer.) closet] shelf; **~fertig** *Adj.* laundered; washed and ironed ‹*laundry*›; **~koffer** *der* wardrobe trunk; **~tür** *die* cupboard door; (eines Kleiderschranks) wardrobe door; **~wand** *die* shelf *or* wall unit

Schranze /ˈʃrant͜sə/ *die;* **~, ~n** (abwertend) sycophantic courtier; (fig.) lackey

Schrapnell /ʃrapˈnɛl/ *das;* **~s, ~e** *od.* **~s** (Milit.) shrapnel [shell]

Schrat /ʃraːt/ *der;* **~[e]s, ~e** forest goblin

Schrat-segel *das* (Seew.) fore-and-aft sail

Schratt /ʃrat/ *der;* **Schratt[e]s, Schratte** ▸ **Schrat**

Schraub·deckel *der* screw top

Schraube /ˈʃraubə/ *die;* **~, ~n** **1** (Schlitz~) screw; (Sechskant~/Vierkant~) bolt; **eine ~ ohne Ende** (fig.) a vicious *or* never-ending spiral; **bei ihm ist eine ~ locker** *od.* **los** (fig. salopp) he has [got] a screw loose (coll.) **2** (Schiffs~) propeller; screw **3** (Turnen) twist; (Kunstspringen) twist dive **4** (Kunstflug) vertical spin

schrauben

A *tr. V.* **1** (befestigen) screw (**an, auf** + *Akk.* on to); (mit Sechskant-/Vierkant~) bolt (**an, auf** + *Akk.* [on] to); (entfernen) unscrew/unbolt (**von** from) **2** (drehen) screw ‹*nut, hook, lightbulb, etc.*› (**auf** + *Akk.* on to; **in** + *Akk.* into); (lösen) unscrew ‹*cap etc.*› (**von** from); **den Deckel vom Marmeladenglas ~:** twist the top off the jam jar **3** **etw. höher/niedriger ~:** screw sth. up/down; **die Preise/Erwartungen in die Höhe ~:** push prices up *or* make prices spiral/raise expectations

B *refl. V.* **sich [in die Höhe] ~:** spiral upwards; *s. auch* **geschraubt**

Schrauben-: ~dreher *der* (Technik) screwdriver; **~mutter** *die; Pl.* **~~n** nut; **~schlüssel** *der* spanner; **~zieher** *der* screwdriver

Schrauber *der* (ugs.) **1** [power] screwdriver **2** (salopp scherzh.) mechanic

Schraub-: ~glas *das* screw top jar; **~stock** *der* vice; **~verschluss, *~verschluß** *der* screw top; **~zwinge** *die* screw clamp

Schreber- /ˈʃreːbɐ-/: **~garten** *der* ≈ allotment (*cultivated primarily as a garden*); **~gärtner** *der,* **~gärtnerin** *die* ≈ allotment holder

> **Schrebergarten**
>
> A *Schrebergarten* is an enclosed mini-garden (similar to an allotment) in a large common garden, usually just outside an urban area. As most German city-dwellers live in blocks of flats, many rent a *Schrebergarten* to provide them with a place where they can grow fruit and flowers and go to relax. The gardens are named after the Leipzig physician D. G. M. Schreber (1808-61), who had the idea of creating playgrounds for children and small gardens for adult part-time gardeners set within a common plot. By law the size of each mini-garden is limited to no more than 400 square metres. Most *Schrebergärten* have a shed or summer house at one end that often looks like a fairy-tale cottage, and tidy flower beds. The gardeners are members of an association (*Schrebergartenverein*) which represents their interests.

Schreck /ʃrɛk/ *der;* **~[e]s, ~e** fright; scare; (Schock) shock; **jmdm. einen ~ einjagen** give sb. a fright *or* scare/shock; **vor ~:** with fright; ‹*run away*› in one's fright; **ein freudiger ~:** a thrill of joy; **ein heftiger ~ packte ihn** he was seized by a sudden terror; **auf den ~ [hin] muss ich einen trinken** (ugs. scherzh.) I must have a drink to get over the shock; **der ~ fuhr ihm in die Knochen** *od.* **Glieder** the fright/shock went right through him; **der ~ saß ihm noch in den Knochen** *od.* **Gliedern** he still

S

hadn't recovered from the fright/shock; **krieg keinen ~!** (ugs.) don't be [too] shocked; **ach du ~!** (ugs.) oh my God!; **[oh] ~, lass nach!** (scherzh.) God help us!; oh no, not that!

Schreck·bild *das* terrible *or* frightening sight; (Vorstellung) terrible vision

schrecken
A *tr. V.* [1] (geh.) frighten; scare [2] (auf~) startle (**aus** out of); make ‹*person*› jump; **du hast mich aus meinen Gedanken geschreckt** you startled me — I was thinking
B *regelm.* (*auch unr.*) *itr. V.* start [up]; **aus dem Schlaf ~:** awake with a start; start from one's sleep

Schrecken *der;* **~s, ~** [1] (Schreck) fright; scare; (Entsetzen) horror; (große Angst) terror; **jmdm. einen ~ einjagen** give sb. a fright *or* scare; **ein jäher ~ durchfuhr ihn** (geh.) he was seized by a sudden terror; **jmdn. voll[er] ~ ansehen** look at sb. with fear *or* terror in one's eyes; **Angst und ~ verbreiten** spread fear and terror; **jmdn. in Angst und ~ versetzen** terrify sb.; **zu meinem [großen] ~:** to my [great] horror; **mit dem [bloßen] ~ davonkommen** escape with no more than a scare *or* fright; **lieber ein Ende mit ~ als ein ~ ohne Ende** it's better to make a painful break than draw out the agony [2] (Schrecklichkeit, Schrecknis) horror; **ein Bild des ~s** a terrible *or* terrifying picture [3] (fig.: gefürchtete Sache, Person) **der ~ des Volkes**/ (scherzh.) **der Schule** *usw.* the terror of the nation/(joc.) the school *etc.*

schrecken·erregend
A *Adj.* terrifying
B *adv.* terrifyingly

schreckens-, Schreckens-: ~bleich *Adj.* (geh.) pale with terror *postpos.*; as white as a sheet *postpos.*; **~herrschaft** *die* reign of terror; **~nachricht** *die* terrible piece of news; **die ~nachricht vom ...** the terrible news of ...; **~tat** *die* terrible deed *or* act; atrocity

Schreck·gespenst *das* [1] spectre; (gegenwärtig) nightmare; **das ~ Aids** the spectre of Aids [2] (ugs. abwertend: hässlicher Mensch) (Frau) hideous hag; (Mann) ugly brute

schreckhaft
A *Adj.* [1] (leicht zu erschrecken) easily scared [2] (erschrocken) frightened, scared ‹*movement, reaction*›
B *adv.* ‹*react*› in a frightened *or* scared way; ‹*start, gaze*› in fright

Schreckhaftigkeit *die;* **~:** easily scared nature; tendency to take fright

schrecklich
A *Adj.* [1] terrible; **er war ~ in seinem Zorn** (geh.) he was terrible in his wrath [2] (ugs.: unerträglich) terrible (coll.); **es war mir ~, es zu tun** I felt terrible about doing it [3] (ugs.: sehr groß) **es hat ihm ~en Spaß gemacht** he found it terrific fun (coll.)
B *adv.* [1] terribly; horribly [2] (ugs. abwertend: unerträglich) terribly (coll.); dreadfully (coll.) [3] (ugs.: sehr, äußerst) terribly (coll.); **ich habe es ~ eilig** I'm in a terrible *or* terrific hurry (coll.)

Schrecknis *das;* **~ses, ~se** (geh.) horror

Schreck-: ~schraube *die* (ugs. abwertend) battleaxe; **~schuss**, ***~schuß** *der* (auch fig.) warning shot; **~schuss·pistole**, ***~schuß·pistole** *die* blank [cartridge] gun *or* pistol; **~sekunde** *die* moment of terror/shock; (Reaktionszeit) reaction time; **eine ~sekunde lang** for one horrifying moment

Schredder *der;* **~s, ~:** shredder

Schredder-: ~anlage *die* shredding plant; shredder; **~müll** *der* shredded waste

schreddern *tr. V.* shred

Schrei /ʃrai/ *der;* **~[e]s, ~e** cry; (lauter Ruf) shout; (durchdringend) yell; (gellend) scream; (kreischend) shriek; (des Hahns) crow; **der ~ nach Gerechtigkeit** (fig. geh.) the cry for justice; **der letzte ~** (fig. ugs.) the latest thing; **nach dem letzten ~ gekleidet** (fig. ugs.) dressed in the latest style

Schreib-: ~arbeit *die:* **an einer ~arbeit sitzen** sit doing some writing; **~arbeiten** clerical work *sing.*; **~automat** *der* word processor; **~bedarf** *der* stationery; **~block** *der; Pl.* **~~s** *od.* **~blöcke** writing pad

Schreibe *die;* **~** (ugs.: Schreibstil) style [of writing]

schreiben /ˈʃraibn̩/
A *unr. itr. V.* write; ‹*typewriter*› type; **orthographisch richtig ~:** spell correctly; **auf** *od.* **mit der Maschine ~:** type; **mit der Hand/mit dem Bleistift/mit Tinte ~:** write in longhand/ in pencil/in ink; **hast du mal was zum Schreiben?** have you got anything to write with?; **der Bleistift schreibt weich/hart** the pencil is soft/hard *or* has a soft/hard lead; **die Feder schreibt zu breit** the nib is too broad; **er hat großes Talent zum Schreiben:** he has great talent as a writer; **an einem Roman** *usw.* **~:** be writing a novel *etc.*; **jmdm.** *od.* **an jmdn. ~:** write to sb.
B *unr. tr. V.* [1] write; **etw. mit der Hand/Maschine ~:** write sth. by hand *or* in longhand/type sth.; **wie schreibt man dieses Wort?** how is this word spelt?; **das Wort ist falsch/richtig/ mit f geschrieben** the word is spelt wrongly *or* misspelt/spelt correctly/written *or* spelt with an f; **den Titel schreibt man groß** the title is written with capitals [at the beginning of each word]; **Noten ~:** write [out] music; **200 Anschläge pro Minute ~:** have a typing speed of 200 strokes *or* 40 words a minute; **wo steht das denn geschrieben?** (fig.) there's no law that says that, is there?; who says? (coll.); **die geschriebene Sprache/das geschriebene Wort** the written language/word; **er schreibt einen guten Stil** he has a good style [of writing]; **eine Klausur/Klassenarbeit ~:** do an exam/a class test; **die Zeitungen ~ viel Unsinn** the newspapers print a lot of nonsense; **was schreibt denn die NZZ darüber?** what does the NZZ have to say about it?; **Karl hat geschrieben. — So, was schreibt er denn?** I've had a letter from Karl. — Oh, what does he say?; **ich werde es ihm sofort ~/ihm ~, dass ...** I'll write and tell him at once/ write and tell him that ...; **bitte ~ Sie mir den Betrag auf die Rechnung** please put the amount on my bill [2] (veralt.) **wir ~ heute den 21. September** today is 21 September; **man schreibt das Jahr 1925** the year is 1925; **den Wievielten ~ wir heute?** what is the date today *or* today's date? [3] (erklären für) **er wollte sich vom Arzt arbeitsunfähig ~ lassen** he wanted the doctor to give him a certificate
C *unr. refl. V.* [1] (richtig geschrieben werden) be spelt; **schreibst du dich mit ei oder mit ey?** is your name spelt with ei or ey? [2] **sich mit jmdm. ~** (ugs.) correspond with sb. [3] **sich** (*Dat.*) **die Finger wund ~:** write until one's fingers are weary

Schreiben *das;* **~s, ~** [1] writing *no def. art.* [2] (Brief) letter; **mit ~ vom ...** in a letter dated ...; **auf Ihr ~ vom ... teilen wir Ihnen mit, ...** in reply to your letter of the ... we inform you ...

Schreiber *der;* **~s, ~** [1] writer; (Verfasser) author; **er ist ein armseliger ~** (abwertend) he is a miserable hack [writer] [2] (veralt.: Sekretär, Schriftführer) secretary; clerk [3] (ugs.: Schreibgerät) **ich habe keinen ~ bei mir** I've got nothing to write with

Schreiberin *die;* **~, ~en** writer; (Verfasserin) authoress

Schreiberling /ˈʃraibɐlɪŋ/ *der;* **~s, ~e** (abwertend) hack [writer]; scribbler

schreib-, Schreib-: ~faul *Adj.* lazy about [letter-]writing *postpos.*; **ich bin [sehr] ~faul** I'm a poor correspondent *or* not much of a letter writer; **~faulheit** *die* laziness about [letter-]writing; **~fehler** *der* spelling mistake; (Versehen) slip [of the pen]; **~gerät** *das* writing implement; **~heft** *das* (*usu. lined*) exercise book; (im Gegensatz zum Rechenheft) writing book; **~kraft** *die* ▸❶ **S. 113** clerical assistant; ([Steno]typistin) [shorthand] typist; **~krampf** *der* writer's cramp; **einen ~krampf haben/bekommen** have/get writer's cramp; **~kundig** *Adj.* able to write *postpos.*; **~mappe** *die* writing case; **~maschine** *die* typewriter; **etw. mit [der]** *od.* **auf der ~maschine schreiben** type sth.; **mit [der] ~maschine geschrieben** typewritten; typed; **sie kann gut ~maschine schreiben** she is a good typist; **~maschinen·papier** *das* typing paper; **~papier** *das* writing paper; **~programm** *das* (DV) word processing program; **~pult** *das* [writing] desk; **~schrift** *die* cursive writing; (gedruckt) [cursive] script; **~schutz** *der* (DV) write protection; **~stift** *der* pen; **~stil** *der* written style; **~stube** *die* [1] (veralt.) office (*for clerical staff*); (hist.) scriptorium; [2] (Milit.) orderly room; **~tafel** *die* [1] (hist.) [writing] tablet; [2] (für die Schule) slate; **~tisch** *der* desk; **~tisch·täter** *der* mastermind behind the scenes; (Beamter) deskbound director of operations; **~übung** *die* writing exercise

Schreibung *die;* **~, ~en** spelling; **eine falsche ~:** a misspelling; an incorrect spelling

Schreib-: ~unter·lage *die* desk pad; **~verbot** *das* writing ban; **ihm wurde ~verbot erteilt** he was banned from writing; **~waren** *Pl.* stationery *sing.*; writing materials; **~waren·geschäft** *das* stationer's; stationery shop *or* (Amer.) store; **~weise** *die* spelling; **~zeug** *das* writing things *pl.*

schreien
A *unr. itr. V.* ‹*person*› cry [out]; (laut rufen/sprechen) shout; (durchdringend) yell; (gellend) scream; ‹*baby*› yell, bawl; ‹*animal*› scream; ‹*owl, gull, etc.*› screech; ‹*cock*› crow; ‹*donkey*› bray; ‹*crow*› caw; ‹*cat*› howl; ‹*monkey*› shriek; **vor Lachen ~:** scream with laughter; **zum S~ sein** (ugs.) be a scream (coll.); **nach etw. ~:** yell for sth.; (fig.) cry out for sth.; (fordern) demand sth.; **die Kinder schrien nach der Mutter** the children were yelling *or* bawling for their mother
B *unr. tr. V.* shout; **Hilfe ~:** shout for help
C *unr. refl. V.* **sich heiser/müde ~:** shout *or* yell oneself hoarse/tire onself out with shouting *or* yelling

schreiend (fig.)
A *Adj.* [1] (grell) garish ‹*colour, poster, etc.*›; loud ‹*pattern*› [2] (empörend) glaring, flagrant ‹*injustice, anomaly*›; blatant ‹*wrong*›
B *adv.* [1] (grell) garishly; **~ bunt** garishly coloured [2] (empörend) flagrantly; blatantly

Schreier *der;* **~s, ~, Schreierin** *die;* **~, ~nen** noisy person; bawler; **die größten Schreier** the noisiest people; those who make/made the most noise

Schrei-: ~hals *der* (ugs.) [1] (Kind) bawler; [2] (abwertend: Randalierer) rowdy; **~krampf** *der* screaming fit

Schrein /ʃrain/ *der;* **~[e]s, ~e** (geh.) shrine

Schreiner *der;* **~s, ~** ▸❶ **S. 113** (bes. südd.) ▸**Tischler**

Schreinerei *die;* **~, ~en** (bes. südd.) ▸**Tischlerei**

Schreinerin *die;* **~, ~nen** ▸❶ **S. 113** ▸**Schreiner**

schreinern (bes. südd.)
A *itr. V.* do joinery; **er kann gut ~:** he is good at joinery *or* woodworking
B *tr. V.* make ‹*furniture etc.*›

schreiten /ˈʃraitn̩/ *unr. itr. V.; mit sein* (geh.) [1] walk; (mit großen Schritten) stride; (marschieren) march; **auf und ab ~:** pace up and down; **von Sieg zu Sieg ~** (fig.) march on from one victory to another [2] **zu etw. ~** (fig.) proceed to sth.; **zur Tat** *od.* **zum Werk ~:** go into action/ get down to work

schrickt /ʃrɪkt/ *3. Pers. Sg. Präsens v.* **schrecken**

schrie /ʃriː/ *1. u. 3. Pers. Sg. Prät. v.* **schreien**

schrieb /ʃriːp/ *1. u. 3. Pers. Sg. Prät. v.* **schreiben**

Schrieb *der;* **~[e]s, ~e** (ugs.) missive (coll.)

Schrift /ʃrɪft/ *die;* **~, ~en** [1] (System) script; (Alphabet) alphabet; **in kyrillischer/phonetischer ~:** in Cyrillic/phonetic script; in the Cyrillic/phonetic alphabet [2] (Hand~) [hand-]writing; **er hat eine gute/unleserliche ~:** he has good/illegible handwriting; his writing is good/illegible [3] (Druckw.: ~art) [type]face [4] (Text) text; (wissenschaftliche Abhandlung) paper; (Werk) work; (Bitt~) petition; **Karl Hubers [frühe/gesammelte] ~en** Karl Hubers [early/

S

collected] writings; **die [Heilige] ~:** the Scriptures *pl.* [5] *Pl.* (schweiz.: Ausweispapiere) [identity] papers

schrift-, Schrift-: ~art *die* (Druckw.) [type-]face; **~bild** *das* (bei Druck~) [appearance of the] type; (bei Hand~) [appearance of one's] writing; **~deutsch** *Adj.* [1] written German; [2] ▸**hochdeutsch**; **~deutsch** *das* [1] written German; **das schweizerische ~deutsch** written Swiss German; [2] ▸**Hochdeutsch**

Schriften·verzeichnis *das* bibliography

Schrift-: ~erkennung *die* (DV) handwriting recognition; (Programm) handwriting recognition program; **~form** *die* (Rechtsspr.) written form; **... bedarf der ~form** ... must be drawn up in writing [and signed] by the party in question; **~führer** *der,* **~führerin** *die* secretary; **~gelehrte** *der* scribe (Bibl.); (Islam) mullah; **~grad** *der,* **~größe** *die* (Druckw.) type size; **~leiter** *der,* **~leiterin** *die* (veralt.) editor; **~leitung** *die* (veralt.) [1] (Funktion) editorship; [2] (Abteilung) editorial department

schriftlich

A *Adj.* written; **das Schriftliche** written work; (ugs.: die ~e Prüfung) the written exam; **ich habe [darüber] leider nichts Schriftliches** I'm afraid I haven't got anything in writing

B *adv.* in writing; **soll ich es ~ machen?** should I put it in writing?; **jmdn. ~ einladen** send sb. a written invitation; **das lasse ich mir ~ geben** I'll get that in writing; **das kann ich dir ~ geben** (fig. ugs.) you can take that from me

schrift-, Schrift-: ~probe *die* [1] (einer Hand~) sample *or* specimen of [one's] handwriting; [2] (Druckw.) type specimen; **~rolle** *die* scroll; **~satz** *der* [1] (Druckw.) type matter; [2] (Rechtsw.: Erklärung) written statement; **~setzer** *der,* **~setzerin** *die* ▸❶ **S. 113** typesetter; **~sprache** *die* written language; **die deutsche ~sprache** written German; **~sprachlich** A *Adj.* used in the written language *postpos.*; B *adv.* in the written language; **sich ~sprachlich ausdrücken** express oneself in language appropriate to a written style; **~steller** *der;* **~~s, ~~:** ▸❶ **S. 113** writer; **die antiken ~steller** the authors of classical antiquity; **~stellerei** *die;* **~~:** writing *no def. art.*; **~stellerin** *die;* **~~, ~~nen** ▸❶ **S. 113** writer; **~stellerisch** A *Adj.* literary ‹*work, activity*›; ‹*talent*› as a writer; **die ~stellerische Tätigkeit** working as a writer; B *adv.* **~stellerisch begabt/tätig sein** be talented as a writer/work as a writer; **~stellern** *itr. V.* work as a writer; do literary work; **~stück** *das* [official] document

Schrifttum *das;* **~s** literature; **das ~ zu diesem Thema** the literature on this subject

Schrift-: ~verkehr *der* correspondence; **mit jmdm. in regem ~verkehr stehen** have an active correspondence with sb.; **~wechsel** *der* correspondence; **~zeichen** *das* character; **~zug** *der* [1] *Pl.* lettering *sing.*; (Handschrift) handwriting *sing.*; [2] (Namenszug) lettering; (als Firmenzeichen) logo

schrill /ʃrɪl/

A *Adj.* [1] shrill; (fig.) strident ‹*propaganda, colours, etc.*› [2] (Jugendspr.) fab (sl.)

B *adv.* shrilly

schrillen *itr. V.* shrill; sound shrilly

Schrippe /ˈʃrɪpə/ *die;* **~, ~n** (bes. berlin.) long [bread] roll

schritt /ʃrɪt/ *1. u. 3. Pers. Sg. Prät. v.* **schreiten**

Schritt *der;* **~[e]s, ~e** [1] step; **mit großen/gemessenen ~en** with big/measured strides; **die ersten ~e machen** (auch fig.) take one's first steps; **er verlangsamte/beschleunigte seine ~e** he slowed/quickened his pace; **die Freude beflügelte meine ~e** (geh.) joy gave me wings; **einen ~ zur Seite/nach vorn machen** *od.* **tun** take a step sideways/forwards; **der Schnee knirschte unter unseren ~en** the snow crunched under our footsteps; **~ für ~, ~ um ~** (auch fig.) step by step; **den ersten ~ machen** *od.* **tun** (fig.) (den Anfang machen) take the first step; (als Erster handeln) make the first move; **in einem zweiten ~** (fig.) as a second stage; **den zweiten ~ vor dem ersten machen** *od.* **tun** (fig.) put the cart before the horse; **der erste ~ zur Diktatur** *usw.* the first step on the road to dictatorship *etc.*; **auf ~ und Tritt** wherever one goes; at every step; **er folgte ihr auf ~ und Tritt** he followed her wherever she went [2] *Pl.* (Geräusch) footsteps [3] (als Längenmaß) pace; **nur ein paar ~e von uns entfernt** only a few yards away from us; **in etwa 100 ~[en] Entfernung** at [a distance of] about 100 paces; **ein paar ~e gehen** take a little walk; **einen ~ weiter gehen** (fig.) go a step *or* stage further; **einen ~ zu weit gehen** (fig.) go too far; overstep the mark; **jmdn. einen großen** *od.* **guten ~ weiterbringen** (fig.) take sb. a lot further; **er ist der Konkurrenz immer ein paar ~e voraus** (fig.) he is always a few steps ahead of the competition; **sich** (*Dat.*) **jmdn. drei ~e vom Leibe halten** (fig. ugs.) keep sb. at arm's length [4] (Gleich~) **aus dem ~ kommen** *od.* **geraten** get out of step; **im ~ gehen** walk in step [5] (des Pferdes) walk; **im ~:** at a walk [6] (Gangart) walk; **jmdn. am ~ erkennen** recognize sb. by his/her walk *or* gait; **seinen ~ verlangsamen/beschleunigen** slow/quicken one's pace; **[mit jmdm./etw.] ~ halten** (auch fig.) keep up *or* keep pace [with sb./sth.] [7] (~geschwindigkeit) walking pace; **[im] ~ fahren** go at walking pace *or* a crawl; **„~ fahren"** 'dead slow' [8] (fig.: Maßnahme) step; measure; **~e unternehmen** *od.* **veranlassen** take steps [9] (Teil der Hose, Genitalbereich) crotch

***Schrittempo** ▸**Schritttempo**

schritt-, Schritt-: ~geschwindigkeit *die* walking pace; **[mit] ~geschwindigkeit fahren** go at walking pace *or* a crawl; **~macher** *der,* **~macherin** *die* pacemaker; **~tempo** *das* walking pace; **im ~tempo fahren** go at a walking pace *or* at a crawl; **~weise** A *Adv.* step by step; gradually; B *adj.* step by step; gradual

schroff /ʃrɔf/

A *Adj.* [1] precipitous, sheer ‹*rock etc.*› [2] (plötzlich) sudden, abrupt ‹*transition, change*›; (krass) stark ‹*contrast*›; **im ~en Widerspruch zu etw. stehen** be totally incompatible with sth. [3] (barsch) abrupt, curt ‹*refusal, manner*›; brusque ‹*manner, behaviour, tone*›

B *adv.* [1] ‹*rise, drop*› sheer; ‹*fall away*› precipitously [2] (plötzlich, unvermittelt) suddenly; abruptly [3] (barsch) curtly; ‹*interrupt*› abruptly; ‹*treat*› brusquely

Schroffheit *die;* **~, ~en** [1] precipitousness [2] (Plötzlichkeit) suddenness; abruptness; (Krassheit) starkness [3] (Barschheit) curtness; abruptness; brusqueness; **mit ~:** curtly [4] **seine ~en** his curt *or* brusque behaviour *sing.*; (Bemerkungen) his curt remarks

schröpfen /ˈʃrœpfn̩/ *tr. V.* [1] (ugs.) fleece [2] (Med.) cup

Schrot /ʃroːt/ *der od. das;* **~[e]s, ~e** [1] coarse meal; (aus Getreide) whole meal (Brit.); whole grain; (aus Malz) grist; crushed malt [2] (aus Blei) shot; **einem Hasen eine Ladung ~ aufbrennen** pepper a hare with shot [3] *in* **ein Mann von echtem/bestem ~ und Korn** a man of sterling qualities; **ein Offizier/Kavalier** *usw.* **von altem ~ und Korn** an officer/a gentleman *etc.* of the old school

schroten *tr. V.* grind ‹*grain etc.*› [coarsely]; crush ‹*malt*› [coarsely]

Schrot-: ~flinte *die* shotgun; **~kugel** *die* pellet; **~ladung** *die* round of shot; small-shot charge

Schrott /ʃrɔt/ *der;* **~[e]s, ~e** [1] scrap [metal]; **das gehört auf den ~:** it belongs on the scrap heap; **ein Auto zu ~ fahren** (ugs.) write a car off [2] (salopp abwertend: minderwertiges Zeug) rubbish; junk

schrott-, Schrott-: ~händler *der* ▸❶ **S. 113** scrap dealer; scrap merchant; **~haufen** *der* scrap heap; (ugs. fig.) rusty heap; (Unfallwagen) heap of scrap; **~kiste** *die* (ugs. abwertend: Auto) heap [of scrap]; **~platz** *der* scrapyard; **~reif** *Adj.* ready for the scrap heap *postpos.*; fit for scrap *postpos.*; **ein Auto ~reif fahren** write a car off; **~wert** *der* scrap value

schrubben /ˈʃrʊbn̩/ *tr.* (*auch itr.*) *V.* scrub

Schrubber *der;* **~s, ~:** [long-handled] scrubbing brush

Schrulle /ˈʃrʊlə/ *die;* **~, ~n** [1] (seltsame Idee) cranky idea; (Marotte) quirk [2] (ugs. abwertend: Frau) **[alte] ~:** old crone

schrullen·haft, schrullig *Adj.* cranky ‹*person, idea*›; zany (coll.) ‹*story etc.*›

Schrulligkeit *die;* **~:** crankiness; zaniness

schrumpelig *Adj.* (ugs.) wrinkly; wrinkled

schrumpeln /ˈʃrʊmpl̩n/ *itr. V.; mit sein* (ugs.) ‹*skin*› go wrinkled; ‹*apple etc.*› shrivel

schrumpfen /ˈʃrʊmpfn̩/ *itr. V.; mit sein* shrink; ‹*metal, rock*› contract; ‹*apple etc.*› shrivel; ‹*skin*› go wrinkled; (abnehmen) decrease; ‹*supplies, capital, hopes*› dwindle

Schrumpf-: ~kopf *der* (Völkerk.) shrunken head; **~leber** *die* cirrhotic liver; **eine ~leber haben/kriegen** have/get cirrhosis of the liver; **~niere** *die* cirrhotic kidney; **eine ~niere haben** have cirrhosis of the kidney

schrumplig ▸**schrumpelig**

Schrunde /ˈʃrʊndə/ *die;* **~, ~n** crack; (von Kälte) chap

schrundig *Adj.* cracked, chapped ‹*skin, hands, etc.*›

Schub /ʃuːp/ *der;* **~[e]s, Schübe** /ˈʃyːbə/ [1] (Physik: ~kraft) thrust; (eines Kolbenmotors) pulling power [2] ▸❶ **S. 439** (Med.: Phase) phase; stage [3] (Gruppe, Anzahl) batch; **~ auf** *od.* **um ~:** [in] one batch after another [4] (bes. ostmd.: ~lade) drawer

Schuber /ˈʃuːbɐ/ *der;* **~s, ~** [1] slip case [2] (österr.: Riegel) bolt

Schub·fach *das* ▸**Schublade**

Schub-: ~karre *die,* **~karren** *der* wheelbarrow; **~kasten** *der* drawer; **~kraft** *die* thrust; **~lade** *die* drawer; (fig.: Kategorie) pigeon-hole; **in der ~lade liegen** (fig.) be ready for use

schubladisieren *tr. V.* (schweiz.) pigeon-hole

Schubs /ʃʊps/ *der;* **~es, ~e** (ugs.) shove; (fig.: Ermunterung) prod

Schub·schiff *das* push boat; pusher

schubsen *tr.* (*auch itr.*) *V.* (ugs.) push; shove

schub·weise

A *Adv.* [1] in batches [2] (Med.) in phases *or* stages

B *adj.* [1] in batches *postpos.* [2] (Med.) phased

schüchtern /ˈʃʏçtɐn/

A *Adj.* [1] shy ‹*person, smile, etc.*›; shy, timid ‹*voice, knock, etc.*› [2] (fig.: zaghaft) tentative, cautious ‹*attempt, beginnings, etc.*›; cautious ‹*hope*›

B *adv.* [1] shyly; ‹*knock, ask, etc.*› timidly; **er schwieg ~:** he was too shy to say anything [2] (fig.: zaghaft) tentatively; cautiously

Schüchternheit *die;* **~:** shyness

Schuft /ʃʊft/ *der;* **~[e]s, ~e** (abwertend) scoundrel; swine

schuften (ugs.)

A *itr. V.* slave *or* slog away; **er schuftet für zwei** he does the work of two [people]

B *refl. V.* **sich müde/krank** *usw.* **~:** tire oneself out/make oneself ill *etc.* with [over]work; **sich zu Tode ~:** work oneself to death

Schufterei *die;* **~** (ugs.) slaving away *no indef. art.*; slog

schuftig

A *Adj.* mean; despicable

B *adv.* meanly; despicably

Schuftigkeit *die;* **~, ~en** [1] meanness [2] (schuftige Handlung) mean *or* despicable thing

Schuh /ʃuː/ *der;* **~[e]s, ~e** shoe; (hoher ~, Stiefel) boot; **umgekehrt wird ein ~ draus** (fig. ugs.) the reverse *or* opposite is true; **wo drückt der ~?** (fig. ugs.) what's on your mind?; what's bugging you? (sl.); **wissen, wo jmdn. der ~ drückt** (fig. ugs.) know where sb.'s problems lie; **jmdm. etw. in die ~e schieben** (fig. ugs.) pin the blame for sth. on sb.

Schuh-: ~anzieher *der;* **~~s, ~~:** shoehorn; **~band** *das; Pl.* **~bänder** (bes. südd.) shoelace; **~bürste** *die* shoe brush

Schuhchen, Schühchen /ˈʃyːçən/ *das;* **~s, ~:** [little] shoe; (Stiefelchen) bootee

Schuh-: ~**creme** *die* shoe polish; ~**größe** *die* shoe size; **welche ~größe hast du?** what size shoe[s] do you take?; ~**löffel** *der* shoehorn; ~**macher** *der* ▸❶ S. 113 shoemaker; *s. auch* **Bäcker**; ~**macherei** *die;* ~~, ~~**en** **1** shoemaker's; **2** (Handwerk) shoemaking *no art.;* ~**macherin** *die* ▸~**macher**; ~**nummer** *die* shoe size; ~**plattler** /-platlɐ/ *der;* ~~**s**, ~~: *folk dance in Tirol, Bavaria and Carinthia, involving the slapping of the thighs, knees, and shoe soles;* ~**putzer** *der;* ~~**s**, ~~ **1** shoeblack; shoe cleaner; **2** (Gerät) shoe-cleaning machine; ~**putzerin** *die;* ~~, ~~**nen** ▸~**putzer 1**; ~**riemen** *der* **1** sandal strap; **2** (bes. westmd.: Schnürsenkel) shoelace; ~**sohle** *die* sole [of a/one's shoe]; **sich** (*Dat.*) **etw. an den ~sohlen abgelaufen haben** (fig. ugs.) have found sth. out ages ago; ~**spanner** *der* shoe tree; ~**werk** *das* footwear; shoes *pl.;* ~**wichse** *die* (veralt.) shoe polish

Schuko·stecker Ⓦⓩ /'ʃu:ko-/ *der* two-pin earthed (Brit.) *or* (Amer.) grounded plug

Schul-: ~**abgänger** *der;* ~~**s**, ~~, ~**abgängerin** *die;* ~~, ~~**nen** school leaver; ~**abschluss**, *~**abschluß** *der* school-leaving qualification; ~**alter** *das* school age; **Kinder im ~alter** children of school age; **er kommt bald ins ~alter** he will soon be of school age; ~**amt** *das* education authority; ~**an·fang** *der* **1** (Anfang des ~besuches) first day at school; **etw. zum ~anfang bekommen** get sth. for starting school; **2** (Anfang des ~tages) **um 8 Uhr ist ~anfang** school starts at 8 o'clock; ~**anfänger** *der,* ~**anfängerin** *die* child [just] starting school; ~**arbeit** *die* **1** ▸~**aufgabe**; **2** (österr.: Klassenarbeit) [written] class test; **3** (Praxis des Unterrichts) schoolwork *no art.;* ~**atlas** *der* school atlas; ~**aufgabe** *die* item of homework; ~**aufgaben** homework *sing.;* ~**aufsatz** *der* school essay; ~**ausflug** *der* school outing; ~**bank** *die; Pl.* ~**bänke** [school] desk; **die ~bank drücken** (ugs.) go to *or* be at school; ~**beginn** *der* ▸~**anfang**; ~**beispiel** *das* textbook example (**für** of); ~**besuch** *der* school attendance; ~**bildung** *die* [school] education; schooling; ~**brot** *das* sandwich (*eaten during break*); ~**buch** *das* school book; ~**bus** *der* school bus

schuld /ʃʊlt/ *Adj.: in* **[an etw.** (Dat.)**] ~ sein** be to blame [for sth.]; **er ist nicht ~ daran** it is not his fault; he is not to blame [for this]; **sie ist an allem ~:** it's all her fault

Schuld *die;* ~, ~**en** **1** (das Schuldigsein) guilt; **die Schwere einer ~:** the seriousness *or* degree of guilt; **er ist ohne [jede] ~:** he is [entirely] guiltless *or* blameless; **er ist sich** (*Dat.*) **keiner ~ bewusst** he is not conscious of having done any wrong; **~ und Sühne** crime and punishment; **... und vergib uns unsere ~** (bibl.) ... and forgive us our sins *or* trespasses **2** (Verantwortlichkeit) blame; **es ist [nicht] seine ~:** it is [not] his fault; **ihn trifft keine ~:** no blame attaches to him; **er sucht die ~ immer zuerst bei anderen** he always tries to blame others first; **der Unfallgegner hat seine ~ anerkannt** the other party admitted liability for the accident; **er ist durch eigene ~ in diese Lage geraten** it was his own fault that he got into this situation; **jetzt hat er durch deine ~ seinen Zug verpasst** now he has missed his train because of you; **[an etw.** (*Dat.*)**] ~ haben** be to blame [for sth.]; **zu ~en** ▸**zuschulden** **3** (Verpflichtung zur Rückzahlung) debt; (Hypothek) mortgage; **ich habe [bei der Bank] 5 000 Euro ~en** I have debts of 5,000 euros [with the bank]; I owe [the bank] 5,000 euros; **das Haus ist frei von ~en** the house is unmortgaged *or* free of mortgage; **in ~en geraten/sich in ~en stürzen** get into debt/into serious debt; **ich mache ungern ~en** I don't like getting into debt *or* running up debts; **er hat mehr ~en als Haare auf dem Kopf** (ugs.) he is up to his eyes *or* ears in debt **4** *in* **[tief] in jmds. ~ stehen** *od.* **sein** (geh.) be [deeply] indebted to sb.

Schuld·bekenntnis *das* **1** confession [of guilt] **2** (Rechtsw.) acknowledgement of indebtedness

schuld·bewusst, ***schuld·bewußt**
A *Adj.* guilty ‹*look, face, etc.*›
B *adv.* guiltily; **jmdn. ~ ansehen** give sb. a guilty look

schulden *tr. V.* owe ‹*money, respect, explanation*›; **was schulde ich Ihnen?** how much do I owe you?

schulden-, Schulden-: ~**berg** *der* (ugs.) pile of debts; ~**frei** *Adj.* debt-free ‹*person etc.*›; unmortgaged ‹*house etc.*›; **ich bin/das Haus ist ~frei** I am free of debt/the house is free of mortgage; ~**macher** *der,* ~**macherin** *die* (ugs. abwertend) [habitual] debtor

schuld-, Schuld-: ~**frage** *die* question of guilt; ~**gefühl** *das* feeling of guilt; guilty feeling; **~gefühle haben/bekommen** feel/start to feel guilty; ~**haft** **A** *Adj.* culpable; **B** *adv.* culpably

Schul·dienst *der* [school]teaching *no art.;* **in den ~ gehen** go into teaching; **im ~ tätig sein** be in the teaching profession

schuldig *Adj.* **1** (Schuld tragend) guilty; **jmdn. ~ sprechen** *od.* **für ~ erklären** find sb. guilty; **er hat sich des Diebstahls ~ gemacht** he has been guilty of *or* committed theft; **er bekennt sich ~:** he admits his guilt; **er wurde/ist ~ geschieden** (veralt.) he was the guilty party in the divorce; **auf ~ plädieren** ‹*public prosecutor*› ask for a verdict of guilty; **das Gericht erkannte auf ~:** the court returned a verdict of guilty **2** (verantwortlich) **der [an dem Unfall] ~e Autofahrer** the driver to blame *or* responsible [for the accident] **3** **jmdm. etw. ~ sein/bleiben** owe sb. sth.; **was bin ich Ihnen ~?** what *or* how much do I owe you?; **jmdm. eine Erklärung/Dank** *usw.* **~ sein** owe sb. an explanation/a debt of gratitude *etc.;* **dafür bin ich dir keine Rechenschaft ~:** I don't have to account to you for that; **den Beweis bist du mir immer noch ~:** you have still not given *or* shown me any proof; **das bin ich ihm/der Partei ~:** I owe it to him/the party; **das ist er seiner gesellschaftlichen Stellung ~:** his social position requires it of him; **jmdm. die Antwort/Erklärung ~ bleiben** [still] owe sb. an answer/explanation; **er blieb ihnen die Antwort nicht ~:** he did not fail to give them an answer *or* leave them without an answer **4** (gebührend) due; proper; **jmdm. den ~en Respekt erweisen** show sb. due respect *or* the respect due to him/her

Schuldige *der/die; adj. Dekl.* guilty person; (im Strafprozess) guilty party; **der an dem Unfall ~:** the person responsible for *or* to blame for the accident; **einer muss ja der ~ sein** 'someone must have done it'

Schuldiger *der;* ~**s**, ~ (bibl.) **wie wir vergeben unsern ~n** as we forgive those who sin *or* trespass against us

Schuldigkeit *die;* ~, ~**en** duty; **meine [verdammte] Pflicht und ~:** my bounden duty; **seine ~ getan haben** (fig.) have served its/his purpose

Schuld·komplex *der* guilt complex

schuld·los *Adj.* innocent (**an** + *Dat.* of); **er wurde/ist ~ geschieden** he was the innocent party in the divorce

Schuldner *der;* ~**s**, ~, **Schuldnerin** *die;* ~, ~**nen** debtor

Schuld-: ~**schein** *der* IOU; promissory note (Commerc.); (formell) bond; ~**spruch** *der* verdict of guilty; ~**turm** *der* (hist.) debtors' prison; ~**verschreibung** *die* (Wirtsch.) debenture bond; ~**zuweisung** *die* recrimination

Schule /'ʃu:lə/ *die;* ~, ~**n** **1** school; **die ~ wechseln** change schools; **zur** *od.* **in die ~ gehen, die ~ besuchen** go to school; **zur** *od.* **in die ~ kommen** come to school; (als Schulanfänger) start school; **von der ~ abgehen** leave school; **auf** *od.* **in der ~:** at school; **er ist an der ~:** he is a [school]teacher; he teaches school (Amer.); **er ist durch eine harte ~ gegangen** (fig.) he has been through a hard school; **aus der ~ plaudern** (fig.) reveal [confidential] information; spill the beans (coll.); **~ machen** (fig.) become the accepted thing; form a precedent; **ein Diplomat** *usw.* **alter** *od.* **der alten ~:** a diplomat *etc.* of the old school **2** (Ausbildung) training; **[keine] ~ haben** ‹*dog, singer, etc.*› [not] be trained; **hohe ~** (Reiten) haute école **3** (Lehr-, Übungsbuch) manual; handbook; **eine ~ des Klavierspiels** a piano tutor; **eine ~ der Liebe** a handbook of *or* guide to love

> **Schule**
>
> German children have to attend school from the ages of 6 to 18. Full-time schooling is compulsory for nine or ten years, until pupils are at least 15. All children go to a **Grundschule** for four years (six in Berlin) and move on to a **Hauptschule, Realschule, Gymnasium,** or **Gesamtschule,** depending on their ability. From the age of 15 some pupils attend a **Berufsschule,** a part-time vocational school. Some students stay at school until they are over 20 due to the system of **sitzen bleiben.**

schulen *tr. V.* train; **jmdn. politisch ~:** give sb. a political schooling; **er hat sich/seinen Stil an Adorno geschult** he modelled himself/his style on Adorno; **ein geschultes Auge** a practised *or* expert eye

Schul-: ~**englisch** *das* school English; ~**entlassene** *der/die; adj. Dekl.* school leaver (Brit.); school graduate (Amer.)

Schüler /'ʃy:lɐ/ *der;* ~**s**, ~ **1** pupil; (Schuljunge) schoolboy; **~ und Studenten** schoolchildren and students; **die ~ der Grundschule** the primary school children *or* pupils; **ein ehemaliger ~ [der Schule]** a former pupil *or* an old boy [of the school]; **er ist noch ~:** he is still at school; **als ~ bekomme ich ...** as I am [still] at school, I receive ... **2** (fig.: eines Meisters) pupil; (Jünger) disciple

schüler-, Schüler-: ~**austausch** *der* school exchange; ~**ausweis** *der* schoolchild's pass; ~**brigade** *die* (DDR) work team of schoolchildren (*usu. working on a farm*); ~**haft** **A** *Adj.* (wie ein Schuljunge) schoolboyish; (wie ein Schulmädchen) schoolgirlish; **B** *adv.* like a schoolboy/schoolgirl

Schülerin *die;* ~, ~**nen** pupil; schoolgirl; **eine ehemalige ~ [der Schule]** a former pupil *or* an old girl [of the school]

Schüler-: ~**karte** *die* schoolchild's season ticket; ~**lotse** *der,* ~**lotsin** *die: pupil trained to help other schoolchildren to cross the road;* ~**mit·verwaltung** *die* pupil participation *no art.* in school administration

Schülerschaft *die;* ~, ~**en** pupils *pl.*

Schüler-: ~**sprache** *die* school slang; ~**zeitung** *die* school magazine

schul-, Schul-: ~**fach** *das* school subject; **... ist ~fach** ... is taught in schools *or* is a school subject; ~**ferien** *Pl.* school holidays *or* (Amer.) vacation *sing.;* **es sind noch ~ferien** the schools are still on holiday *or* (Amer.) vacation; ~**fest** *das* school open day; ~**frei** *Adj.* ‹*day*› off school; **morgen ist/haben wir ~frei** there is/we have no school tomorrow; **~frei bekommen** be let off school; ~**freund** *der,* ~**freundin** *die* school friend; ~**funk** *der* schools broadcasting *no art.;* (Sendungen) [radio] programmes *pl.* for schools; ~**gebäude** *das* school [building]; ~**gebrauch** *der:* **für den ~gebrauch** for school use; for use in schools; ~**gegenstand** *der* (österr.) ▸~**fach**; ~**gelände** *das* school grounds *pl. or* premises *pl.;* ~**geld** *das* school fees *pl.;* **lass dir dein ~geld wiedergeben!** (ugs.) they can't have taught you a thing at school; ~**grammatik** *die* grammar [book] for schools; ~**haus** *das* schoolhouse; ~**heft** *das* exercise book; ~**hof** *der* school yard

schulisch
A *Adj.* ‹*conflicts, problems, etc.*› at school; school ‹*work etc.*›; scholastic ‹*questions etc.*›; **seine ~en Leistungen** [the standard of] his school work *sing.*
B *adv.* at school

S

schul-, Schul-: ~**jahr** *das* 1 school year; 2 (Klasse) year; **ein zehntes ~jahr** a tenth-year class; ~**jugend** *die* schoolchildren *pl.*; ~**junge** *der* schoolboy; ~**kamerad** *der*, ~**kameradin** *die* (veralt.) schoolmate; ~**kind** *das* schoolchild; ~**klasse** *die* [school] class; ~**landheim** *das* [school's] country hostel (*visited by school classes*); ~**lehrer** *der*, ~**lehrerin** *die* schoolteacher; ~**leiter** *der* ▸ⓘ **S. 113** headmaster; head teacher; ~**leiterin** *die* ▸ⓘ **S. 113** headmistress; head teacher; ~**leitung** *die* 1 [school] headship; 2 (Person) head teacher; (Personen) school management; ~**lektüre** *die* school reading [material]; (einzelner Text) school text; ~**mädchen** *das* schoolgirl; ~**mann** *der* (veralt.) schoolteacher; ~**mappe** *die* schoolbag; ~**medizin** *die* orthodox *or* traditional medicine *no art.*; ~**meister** *der* 1 (veralt., scherzh.) schoolmaster; 2 (abwertend: Krittler) schoolmasterly type; pedagogue; ~**meisterin** *die* 1 (veralt., scherzh.) schoolmistress; 2 schoolmistress type; pedagogue; ~**meistern** *tr.* (*auch itr.*) *V.* (abwertend) lecture; **er ~meistert gern** he likes lecturing people; ~**musik** *die* music *no art.* in schools; ~**orchester** *das* school orchestra; ~**ordnung** *die* school rules *pl.*; ~**pflicht** *die* obligation to attend school; **die Einführung der [allgemeinen] ~pflicht** the introduction of compulsory school attendance [for all children]; ~**pflichtig** *Adj.* required to attend school *postpos.*; **~pflichtig sein** have to attend school; **im ~pflichtigen Alter** of school age; ~**praktikum** *das* teaching practice; ~**ranzen** *der* [school] satchel; ~**rat** *der*, ~**rätin** *die* schools inspector; ~**reif** *Adj.* ready for school *postpos.*; ~**reife** *die* readiness for school; ~**schiff** *das* training ship; ~**schluss**, *~**schluß** *der* end of school; **nach ~schluss** after school; ~**schwänzer** *der*, ~**schwänzerin** *die* (ugs.) truant; ~**speisung** *die* school meals *pl.*; ~**sport** *der* sport *no art.* in schools; ~**sprecher** *der* pupils' representative; ≈ head boy; ~**sprecherin** *die* pupils' representative; ≈ head girl; ~**stunde** *die* [school] period; lesson; ~**system** *das* school system; ~**tag** *der* school day; **der erste/letzte ~tag** the first/last day of school; ~**tasche** *die* schoolbag; (Ranzen) [school] satchel

> **Schultag - 1. Schultag**
>
> The first day at school is a big event for a German child, involving a ceremony at school and sometimes at church. The child is given a *Schultüte*, a large cardboard cone containing pens, small gifts, and sweets, to mark this special occasion.

Schulter /ˈʃʊltɐ/ *die;* ~, ~**n** ▸ⓘ **S. 435** shoulder; **hängende ~n** drooping shoulders; (als Merkmal) round shoulders; **seine Frau reicht ihm gerade bis an die ~:** his wife only comes up to his shoulder; **er nahm das Kind auf die ~[n]** he lifted the child on to his shoulder[s]; **der Ringer zwang seinen Gegner auf die ~n** the wrestler forced his opponent on to his back; **~ an ~** (auch fig.) shoulder to shoulder; **mit den ~n** *od.* **die ~n zucken** shrug one's shoulders; **jmdn. über die ~ ansehen** (fig.) look down on sb.; look down one's nose at sb.; **jmdm. auf die ~ klopfen** pat sb. on the shoulder *or* (fig.) back; **sich** (*Dat.*) **selbst auf die ~ klopfen** (fig.) pat oneself on the back; **auf beiden ~n Wasser tragen** (fig.) have a foot in both camps; *s. auch* **kalt A**; **leicht 1**

schulter-, Schulter-: ~**blatt** *das* ▸ⓘ **S. 435** (Anat.) shoulder blade; ~**frei** *Adj.* off-the-shoulder ‹*dress*›; ~**halfter** *der* shoulder holster; ~**höhe** *die* shoulder height; ~**klappe** *die* shoulder strap; epaulette; ~**lang** *Adj.* shoulder-length

schultern *tr. V.* shoulder; **das Gewehr ~:** shoulder arms; **etw. geschultert tragen** carry sth. on one's shoulder

Schulter-: ~**riemen** *der* shoulder strap; (Milit.) shoulder belt; ~**schluss** *der*, *~**schluß** (Solidarität) solidarity; (Zusammenarbeit) collaboration; ~**stand** *der* (Turnen, Kunstfahren) shoulder stand; ~**stück** *das* 1 (~klappe) shoulder strap; epaulette; 2 (Stück Fleisch) piece of shoulder

Schultheiß /ˈʃʊltai̯s/ *der;* ~**en**, ~**en** (hist.) sheriff; (im Dorf) mayor

Schul·tüte *die:* *cardboard cone of sweets given to a child on its first day at school*

> **Schultüte**
>
> ▸ Schultag

Schulung *die;* ~, ~**en** training; (Veranstaltung) training course; **politische ~:** political schooling

Schulungs·kurs *der* training course

Schul-: ~**uniform** *die* school uniform; ~**unterricht** *der* school lessons *pl.*, *no art.*; ~**weg** *der* way to school; **er hat einen ~weg von 10 km/Minuten** he lives 10 kilometres/minutes from his school; ~**weisheit** *die* (abwertend) book learning; ~**wesen** *das* school system

Schulze /ˈʃʊltsə/ *der;* ~**n**, ~**n** (hist.) ▸ **Schultheiß**

Schul-: ~**zeit** *die* schooldays *pl.*; ~**zentrum** *das* school complex; ~**zeugnis** *das* school report; ~**zimmer** *das* schoolroom

Schummel /ˈʃʊml̩/ *der;* ~**s** (ugs.) cheating *no indef. art.*

Schummelei *die;* ~, ~**en** (ugs.) ▸ **Mogelei**

schummeln *itr.*, *tr.*, *refl. V.* (ugs.) ▸ **mogeln**

schummerig /ˈʃʊmərɪç/

A *Adj.* dim ‹*light etc.*›; dimly lit ‹*room etc.*›

B *adv.* dimly

Schummler *der;* ~**s**, ~, **Schummlerin** *die;* ~, ~**nen** (ugs.) cheat

schummrig ▸ **schummerig**

Schund *der;* ~**[e]s** (abwertend) trash

Schund-: ~**literatur** *die* (abwertend) pulp literature; trashy literature; ~**roman** *der* (abwertend) pulp novel; trashy novel

schunkeln /ˈʃʊŋkl̩n/ *itr. V.* rock to and fro together (in time to music, with linked arms)

schupfen /ˈʃʊpfn̩/ *tr. V.* (österr., schweiz., südd.) 1 (stoßen) give sb. a shove *or* push 2 (werfen) throw; chuck (coll.)

Schupfen *der;* ~**s**, ~ (österr., südd.) shed; (Wetterdach) [wooden] shelter

Schupo[1] /ˈʃuːpo/ *die;* ~ *Abk.* = **Schutzpolizei**

Schupo[2] *der;* ~**s**, ~**s** (veralt. ugs.) cop (coll.)

Schuppe /ˈʃʊpə/ *die;* ~, ~**n** 1 scale; **es fiel ihm wie ~n von den Augen** he had a sudden, blinding realization; the scales fell from his eyes 2 *Pl.* (auf dem Kopf) dandruff *sing.*; (auf der Haut) flaking skin *sing.*

schuppen

A *tr. V.* scale ‹*fish*›

B *refl. V.* ‹*skin*› flake; ‹*person*› have flaking skin

Schuppen *der;* ~**s**, ~ 1 shed 2 (ugs. abwertend) (hässliches Gebäude) dump (coll.); (kastenförmiger Bau) box 3 (ugs.: Lokal) joint (coll.)

schuppen·artig

A *Adj.* scale-like

B *adv.* like scales

Schuppen·flechte *die* ▸ⓘ **S. 439** (Med.) psoriasis

schuppig *Adj.* 1 scaly 2 (mit Haut-, Kopfschuppen bedeckt) flaky ‹*skin*›; dandruffy ‹*hair*›

Schur /ʃuːɐ̯/ *die;* ~, ~**en** 1 (das Scheren) shearing 2 (Landw.: das Mähen, Schneiden) cut

Schür·eisen *das* poker

schüren /ˈʃyːrən/ *tr. V.* 1 poke ‹*fire*›; (gründlich) rake ‹*fire, stove, etc.*› 2 (fig.) stir up ‹*hatred, envy, etc.*›; fan the flames of ‹*passion*›; **jmds. Hoffnung ~:** raise sb.'s hopes

schürfen /ˈʃʏrfn̩/

A *itr. V.* 1 scrape 2 (Bergbau) dig [experimentally] (**nach** for); **nach Gold** *usw.* **~:** prospect for gold *etc.*; **tiefer ~** (fig.) dig deeper

B *tr. V.* 1 **sich** (*Dat.*) **das Knie** *usw.* **[wund/blutig] ~:** graze one's knee *etc.* [and make it sore/bleed] 2 (Bergbau) mine ‹*ore etc.*› opencast *or* (Amer.) opencut

C *refl. V.* graze oneself

Schürf·wunde *die* graze; abrasion

Schür·haken *der* poker (*with hooked end;*) (*für den Ofen*) rake

schurigeln /ˈʃuːriːgl̩n/ *tr. V.* (ugs. abwertend) **jmdn. ~:** make life unpleasant for sb.; (schikanieren) bully sb.

Schurke /ˈʃʊrkə/ *der;* ~**n**, ~**n**, **Schurkin** *die;* ~, ~**nen** (abwertend) rogue; villain; **die Rolle des Schurken** the part of the villain *or* (coll.) baddy

Schurken·staat *der* (abwertend) rogue state

Schurkerei *die;* ~, ~**en** (veralt. abwertend) villainous deed

schurkisch (veralt. abwertend)

A *Adj.* villainous

B *adv.* villainously

Schur·wolle *die:* **[reine] ~:** pure new wool

Schurz /ʃʊrts/ *der;* ~**es**, ~**e** 1 apron 2 (Lenden~) loincloth

Schürze /ˈʃʏrtsə/ *die;* ~, ~**n** apron; (Frauen~, Latz~) pinafore; **jmdm. an der ~ hängen** (fig.) be tied to sb.'s apron strings; **hinter jeder ~ her sein** *od.* **herlaufen** (ugs.) run *or* chase after anything in a skirt

schürzen *tr. V.* 1 gather up 2 (aufwerfen) purse ‹*lips, mouth*› 3 (geh.: binden) tie ‹*knot*›; knot ‹*thread etc.*›

Schürzen-: ~**band** *das; Pl.* ~**bänder** ▸ **Schürzenzipfel**; ~**jäger** *der* (ugs. abwertend) skirt-chaser (sl.); ~**zipfel** *der* apron string; **jmdm. am ~zipfel hängen** (fig. ugs.) be tied to sb.'s apron strings

Schuss, ***Schuß** /ʃʊs/ *der;* **Schusses**, **Schüsse** /ˈʃʏsə/ 1 shot (**auf** + *Akk.* at); **21 ~ Salut** a 21-gun salute; **zum ~ kommen** get a chance of a shot; get a shot in; **weit** *od.* **weitab vom ~** (fig. ugs.) (in sicherer Entfernung) well away from the action; at a safe distance; (abseits) far off the beaten track; **der ~ kann nach hinten losgehen** (fig. ugs.) it could backfire *or* turn out to be an own goal; **ein ~ ins Schwarze** (fig.) a bull's eye; **ein ~ in den Ofen** (fig.) a complete waste of effort; **jmdm. einen ~ vor den Bug setzen** *od.* **geben** (fig.) fire a shot across sb.'s bows; **einen ~ haben** (salopp) be off one's rocker (coll.) 2 (Menge Munition/Schießpulver) round; **drei ~ Munition** three rounds of ammunition; **keinen ~ Pulver wert sein** (fig. ugs.) be worthless *or* not worth a thing 3 (~wunde) gunshot wound 4 (mit einem Ball, Puck usw.) shot (**auf** + *Akk.* at); **er ließ ihn nicht zum ~ kommen** he didn't let him get a shot in 5 (kleine Menge) dash; **ein ~ Whisky** a dash *or* shot of whisky; **Cola** *usw.* **mit ~:** Coke ® *etc.* with something strong; brandy/rum *etc.* and Coke ® *etc.*; **eine Weiße mit ~** *a light top-fermented beer with a dash of fruit syrup, esp. raspberry-flavoured* 6 (Drogenjargon) shot; fix (sl.); **jmdm./sich einen ~ setzen** give sb./oneself a fix; **der goldene ~:** the fatal shot 7 (Skisport) schuss; **~ fahren** schuss; **im ~ abfahren** schuss down; **in ~ kommen** (fig.) get speed up 8 (ugs.) **in ~ sein/kommen** be in/get into [good] shape; **etw. in ~ bringen** *od.* **kriegen/halten/haben** get sth. into/keep sth. in/have got sth. in [good] shape 9 (Weberei) weft

schuss·bereit, ***schuß·bereit** *Adj.* ready to shoot *postpos.*

Schussel /ˈʃʊsl̩/ *der;* ~**s**, ~ (ugs.) scatterbrain; wool-gatherer

Schüssel /ˈʃʏsl̩/ *die;* ~, ~**n** bowl; (flacher) dish; **vor leeren ~n sitzen** (fig.) go hungry; have nothing to eat

schusselig (ugs.)

A *Adj.* scatterbrained; (fahrig) dithery

B *adv.* in a scatterbrained way

Schusseligkeit *die;* ~ (ugs.) wool-gathering; muddle-headedness; (schusselige Art) scatterbrained way

schusseln *itr. V.* (ugs.) be scatterbrained; (bei der Arbeit) be careless; make careless *or* silly mistakes; **er hat mal wieder geschusselt** he's been wool-gathering again

Schusser *der;* ~**s**, ~ (bes. südd.) ▸ **Murmel**

schuss-, ***schuß-**, **Schuss-**, ***Schuß-:** ~**faden** *der* (Weberei) weft thread; ~**fahrt**

die [1] (Ski) schuss; [2] (fig.) wild career; headlong rush; **~feld** *das* field of fire; **er hatte freies ~feld** he had a clear view of the target; (Fußball usw.) he had a clear shot [at goal]; **ins ~feld geraten** (fig.) come under fire; **~fest** *Adj.* bulletproof

schusslig, *schußlig /ˈʃʊslɪç/ ▸**schusselig**

Schuss-, schuss-, *schuß-, Schuß-: ~linie *die* line of fire; **in die/jmds. ~linie geraten** *od.* **kommen** (auch fig.) come under fire/come under fire from sb.; **~sicher** *Adj.* bulletproof; **~verletzung** *die* gunshot wound; **~waffe** *die* weapon (*firing a projectile*); (Gewehr usw.) firearm; **~waffen·gebrauch** *der* use of firearms; **~wech·sel** *der* exchange of shots; **~wunde** *die* gunshot wound

Schuster /ˈʃuːstɐ/ *der;* **~s, ~** ▸❶ **S. 113** (ugs.) shoemaker; (Flick~) shoe repairer; cobbler (dated); **auf ~s Rappen** (scherzh.) on Shanks's pony; **~, bleib bei deinem Leisten!** (Spr.) the cobbler should stick to his last (prov.); don't meddle with things you don't understand; *s. auch* **Bäcker**

Schuster-: ~ahle *die* [shoemaker's] awl; **~draht** *der* waxed end; **~handwerk** *das* shoemaking *no art.*

Schusterin *die;* **~, ~nen** ▸❶ **S. 113** ▸**Schuster**

schustern *tr., itr. V.* (veralt.) cobble (dated)

Schuster-: ~palme *die* (volkst.) aspidistra; **~werkstatt** *die* shoemaker's workshop; (für Schuhreparaturen) shoe repairer's workshop

Schute /ˈʃuːtə/ *die;* **~, ~n** [1] (Wasserfahrzeug) barge; lighter [2] (Hut) poke bonnet

Schutt /ʃʊt/ *der;* **~[e]s** [1] rubble; **„~ abladen verboten"** 'no tipping'; 'no dumping'; **in ~ und Asche liegen/sinken** (geh.) lie in ruins/be reduced to rubble [2] (Geol.) debris; detritus

Schutt·ablade·platz *der* rubbish dump *or* (Brit.) tip; garbage dump (Amer.)

Schütte /ˈʃʏtə/ *die;* **~, ~n** [1] (Behälter) [kitchen] drawer-container (*for flour etc.*) [2] (Rutsche) chute [3] (landsch.: Bündel) sheaf

Schüttel·frost *der* ▸❶ **S. 439** [violent] shivering fit; **~ haben** have violent shivers

schütteln /ˈʃʏtl̩n/

A *tr.* (*auch itr.*) *V.* [1] shake; **den Kopf [über etw.** (*Akk.*)**]/die Faust [gegen jmdn.] ~:** shake one's head [over sth.]/one's fist [at sb.]; **jmdm. die Hand ~:** shake sb.'s hand; shake sb. by the hand; **das Fieber/die Angst/das Grauen schüttelte ihn** he was shivering *or* shaking with fever/fear/gripped with horror; **von Angst/Ekel geschüttelt sein/werden** be gripped with fear/filled with revulsion; **das von Katastrophen und Krieg geschüttelte Land** the country [that was] torn by catastrophe and war [2] (unpers.) **es schüttelte ihn [vor Kälte]** he was shaking [with *or* from cold]

B *refl. V.* shake oneself/itself; **sich im Fieber/vor Lachen ~:** be racked with fever/shake with laughter; **ich könnte mich [vor Ekel] ~:** I feel utterly revolted

C *itr. V.* **mit dem Kopf ~:** shake one's head

Schüttel·reim *der: humorous rhyming couplet with two pairs of rhyming words having interchanging initial consonants*

schütten /ˈʃʏtn̩/

A *tr. V.* [1] pour ‹*liquid, flour, grain, etc.*›; (unabsichtlich) spill ‹*liquid, flour, etc.*›; tip ‹*rubbish, coal, etc.*›; **jmdm./sich Wein über den Anzug ~:** spill wine on sb.'s/one's suit [2] **einen Eimer** *usw.* **voll Wasser** *usw.* (*Akk.*) **~** (ugs.) fill a bucket *etc.* with water *etc*

B *itr. V.* (unpers.) (ugs.: regnen) pour [down]

schütter /ˈʃʏtɐ/ *Adj.* sparse; thin

Schütter *der;* **~s, ~:** [coal] hod

Schütt·gut *das* bulk goods *pl.*

Schutt-: ~halde *die* pile *or* heap of rubble; **~haufen** *der* pile of rubble; (Abfallhaufen) rubbish heap; **~platz** *der* [rubbish] dump *or* (Brit.) tip; garbage dump (Amer.)

Schutz /ʃʊts/ *der;* **~es, ~e** [1] protection (**vor** + *Dat.*, **gegen** against); (Feuer~) cover; (Zuflucht) refuge; **im ~ der Dunkelheit/Nacht** under cover of darkness/night; **unter einem Baum ~ [vor dem Regen** *usw.***] suchen/finden** seek/find shelter *or* take refuge [from the rain *etc.*] under a tree; **jmdm. ~ gewähren** give *or* afford sb. protection; **jmdn. [vor jmdm.** *od.* **gegen jmdn./gegen etw.] in ~ nehmen** defend sb. *or* take sb.'s side [against sb./sth.]; *s. auch* **Trutz** [2] (Vorrichtung) guard

schutz-, Schutz-: ~anstrich *der* protective coating; **~bedürftig** *Adj.* in need of protection *postpos.;* **~befohlene** *der/die; adj. Dekl.* (veralt.) charge; **~behauptung** *die* (bes. Rechtsw.) attempt to justify one's behaviour; **~blech** *das* mudguard; **~brief** *der* (Kfz-W.) travel insurance; (Dokument) travel insurance certificate; **~brille** *die* [protective] goggles *pl.;* **~dach** *das* shelter; (über der Haustür usw.) canopy

Schütze /ˈʃʏtsə/ *der;* **~n, ~n** [1] marksman; **ein guter/schlechter ~:** a good/poor shot *or* marksman; **der ~ konnte ermittelt werden** it was possible to establish who fired the shot/shots [2] (Fußball usw.: Torschütze) scorer [3] (Mitglied eines ~nvereins) **er ist ~** *od.* **bei den ~n** he is a member of a/the shooting *or* rifle club [4] (Milit.: einfacher Soldat) private; **~ Arsch [im letzten** *od.* **dritten Glied]** (derb) the lowest of the low [5] (DDR Milit.) soldier in the motorized arm [6] (Astrol., Astron.) Sagittarius; **er/sie ist [ein] ~:** he/she is a Sagittarian

schützen

A *tr. V.* protect (**vor** + *Dat.* from, **gegen** against); (vor Regen, Wind usw.) ‹*roof, wall*› shelter (**vor** + *Dat.* from); ‹*coat*› protect (**gegen** against); (absichern) protect (**vor** + *Dat.* from); safeguard ‹*interest, property, etc.*› (**vor** + *Dat.* from); **sich ~d vor jmdn./etw. stellen** stand protectively in front of sb./sth.; **ein geschützter Platz** a sheltered spot; **geschützte Arten/Tiere/Pflanzen** protected species/animals/plants; **etw. patentrechtlich/urheberrechtlich/als Warenzeichen ~ lassen** patent sth./copyright sth./register sth. as a trade mark; **gesetzlich geschützt** registered [as a trade mark]; **„vor Wärme/Kälte/Licht ~"** 'keep away from heat/cold/light'; **„vor Nässe ~"** 'keep dry'

B *itr. V.* provide *or* give protection (**vor** + *Dat.* from, **gegen** against); (vor Wind, Regen) provide *or* give shelter (**vor** + *Dat.* from)

Schützen-: ~bruder *der* fellow member of a/the shooting *or* rifle club; **~fest** *das: shooting competition with fair*

> **Schützenfest**
>
> An annual festival celebrated in most towns, involving a shooting competition, parade, and fair. The winners of the shooting competition are crowned *Schützenkönig* and *Schützenkönigin* for the year.

Schutz·engel *der* guardian angel

Schützen-: ~graben *der* (Milit.) trench; **~haus** *das* [shooting *or* rifle club] clubhouse; **~hilfe** *die* (ugs.) support; **~könig** *der* shooting champion; champion marksman; **~königin** *die* shooting champion; champion markswoman; **~panzer** *der* armoured personnel carrier; **~platz** *der: fairground where the Schützenfest takes place*

schützens·wert *Adj.* worthy of protection *postpos.*

Schützen-: ~stand *der* (Milit.) firing point (*in a foxhole*); **~verein** *der* shooting *or* rifle club

Schutz-: ~film *der* protective film; **~gebiet** *das* [1] [nature] reserve; [2] (hist.: Kolonie) protectorate; **~gebühr** *die* [1] token *or* nominal charge; [2] (verhüll.: erpresste Zahlung) protection money *no pl., no indef. art.;* **~geld** *das* protection money; **~geld·erpressung** *die* extortion of protection money; protection racket/rackets; **~gitter** *das* protective grid; **~gott** *der* tutelary *or* protective god; **~göttin** *die* tutelary *or* protective goddess; **~hafen** *der* port of refuge; **~haft** *die* preventive detention; **~heilige** *der/die* (kath. Rel.) patron saint; **~helm** *der* helmet; (bei Renn-, Motorradfahrern) crash helmet; (bei Bauarbeitern usw.) safety helmet; **~herrschaft** *die* (Völkerr.) protectorate; **~hülle** *die* [protective] cover; (für Dokumente usw.) folder; (~umschlag) dust jacket; **~hund** *der* guard dog; **~hütte** *die* [1] (Unterstand) shelter; [2] (Berghütte) mountain hut; **~impfung** *die* vaccination; inoculation

Schützin *die* **~, ~nen** [1] markswoman; *s. auch* **Schütze 1** [2] (Fußball usw.: Tor~) scorer

Schutz-: ~kleidung *die* protective clothing; **~kontakt** *der* (Elektrot.) earth contact; **~leute** ▸**~mann**

Schützling /ˈʃʏtslɪŋ/ *der;* **~s, ~e** protégé; (Anvertrauter) charge

schutz-, Schutz-: ~los *Adj.* defenceless; unprotected; **dem Gegner/Wind ~los ausgeliefert sein** be completely at the mercy of the enemy/the wind; **~mann** *der; Pl.* **~männer** *od.* **~leute** (ugs. veralt.) [police] constable; copper (Brit. coll.); **~marke** *die:* **[eingetragene] ~marke** registered trade mark; **~maßnahme** *die* protective measure; **~patron** *der,* **~patronin** *die* patron saint; **~polizei** *die* constabulary; police [force]; **~polizist** *der* (veralt.) police constable; **~raum** *der* shelter; **~schicht** *die* protective layer (**aus** of); (flüssig aufgetragen) protective coating; **~schild** *der* shield; (der Polizei) riot shield; **menschlicher ~schild** human shield; **~suchend** *Adj.* seeking protection *postpos.;* **~truppe** *die* [1] peacekeeping force; [2] (hist.: Kolonialtruppe) colonial force *or* army; **~um·schlag** *der* dust jacket; (für Papiere) cover; **~verband** *der* protective bandage *or* dressing; **~vorrichtung** *die* safety device; (Geländer, Gitter usw.) safety measure; **~wall** *der* protective wall; (fig.) [protective] barrier; **der antifaschistische ~wall** (DDR Amtsspr.) the Berlin Wall; **~weg** *der* (österr.) pedestrian crossing; **~würdig** *Adj.* worthy of protection *postpos.;* **~zoll** *der* protective tariff; **~zone** *die* safe area

> **Schutzpolizei (Schupo)**
>
> Colloquially referred to as the *Schupo*, the *Schutzpolizei* is the general police force ensuring public security and order, dealing with traffic offences and minor disturbances. Most people know the *Schupo* only as traffic police.

Schwa /ʃvaː/ *das;* **~[s], ~[s]** (Sprachw.) schwa

schwabbelig /ˈʃvabəlɪç/ *Adj.* flabby ‹*stomach, person, etc.*›; wobbly ‹*jelly etc.*›

schwabbeln *itr. V.* (ugs.) wobble

schwabblig ▸**schwabbelig**

Schwabe /ˈʃvaːbə/ *der;* **~n, ~n** Swabian

schwäbeln /ˈʃvɛːbl̩n/ *itr. V.* **er schwäbelt** he speaks in Swabian dialect

Schwaben (*das*)*;* **~s** Swabia

Schwaben·streich *der* (scherzh.) piece of folly

Schwäbin /ˈʃvɛːbɪn/ *die;* **~, ~nen** Swabian

schwäbisch

A *Adj.* Swabian; **die Schwäbische Alb** the Swabian Mountains *pl.*

B *adv.* in Swabian dialect; (mit ~em Akzent) with a Swabian accent; *s. auch* **badisch**; **deutsch**; **Deutsch**

schwach /ʃvax/; **schwächer** /ˈʃvɛçɐ/, **schwächst...** /ˈʃvɛçst.../

A *Adj.* [1] (kraftlos) weak; weak, delicate ‹*child, woman*›; frail ‹*invalid, old person*›; low-powered ‹*engine, car, bulb, amplifier, etc.*›; weak, poor ‹*eyesight, memory, etc.*›; poor ‹*hearing*›; delicate ‹*health, constitution*›; **die Birne/die Brille ist ziemlich ~:** the lightbulb is of rather a low wattage/the glasses are not very strong; **auf ~en Beinen stehen** (fig.) ‹*theory, evidence, argument, etc.*› be shaky; **~ werden** grow weak; (fig.: schwanken) weaken; waver; (nachgeben) give in; **mir wird [ganz] ~:** I feel [quite] faint; **in einem ~en Moment, in einer ~en Stunde** in a weak moment; **er hat einen ~en Willen/Charakter** he is weak-willed/lacks strength of character [2] (nicht gut) poor ‹*pupil, player, runner, performance, result, effort, etc.*›; weak ‹*candidate, argument, opponent, play, film, etc.*›; **sein**

schwächstes Buch/der schwächste Schüler his worst book/the worst pupil; **er ist in Latein sehr ~:** he is very bad at Latin; **das ist aber ein ~es Bild!** (fig. ugs.) that's a poor show (coll.); **die Party war ~** (ugs.) the party wasn't up to much (coll.) [3] (gering, niedrig, klein) poor, low ‹*attendance etc.*›; sparse ‹*population*›; slight ‹*effect, resistance, gradient, etc.*›; light ‹*wind, rain, current*›; faint ‹*groan, voice, pressure, hope, smile, smell*›; weak, faint ‹*pulse*›; lukewarm ‹*applause, praise*›; faint, dim ‹*light*›; pale ‹*colour*›; low ‹*fire, heat*›; **die zahlenmäßig schwächere Gruppe** the group which is/was smaller in number; **die Nachfrage/das Geschäft ist zur Zeit ~:** demand/business is slack at the moment; **das ist nur ein ~er Trost** that is only a slight consolation; (ugs.: hilft nur wenig) that is little consolation *or* cold comfort; **das Licht wird schwächer** the light is fading [4] (wenig konzentriert) weak ‹*solution, acid, tea, coffee, beer, poison, etc.*›; **Sherry ist schwächer als Whisky** sherry is not as strong as whisky [5] (Sprachw.) weak ‹*conjugation, verb, noun, etc.*›

B *adv.* [1] (kraftlos) weakly [2] (nicht gut) poorly; **sehr ~ argumentieren** offer very weak arguments [3] (in geringem Maße) poorly ‹*attended, developed*›; sparsely ‹*populated*›; slightly ‹*poisonous, acid, alcoholic, sweetened, salted, inclined, etc.*›; ‹*rain*› slightly; ‹*remember, glow, smile, groan*› faintly; lightly ‹*accented*›; ‹*beat*› weakly; **der Saal war nur ~ besetzt** there was only a small audience in the hall; **es war ~ windig** there was a light wind; **er wehrte sich nur ~:** he offered only faint resistance [4] (Sprachw.) **~ gebeugt/konjugiert** weak

schwachbesiedelt, schwachbevölkert ▸ **schwach B 2**

Schwäche /ˈʃvɛçə/ *die;* ~, ~**n** [1] (Kraftlosigkeit) weakness; (plötzlich auftretend) [feeling of] faintness; **allgemeine ~:** general debility (Med.) [2] (Mangel an Können) weakness; **seine ~ in Mathematik** *usw.* his lack of ability in mathematics *etc.* [3] (Mangel) weakness; failing [4] (Vorliebe) weakness; **eine ~ für jmdn./etw. haben** have a soft spot for sb./a weakness for sth.

Schwäche-: ~anfall *der* sudden feeling of faintness; **~gefühl** *das* feeling of faintness

schwächen *tr. V.* weaken

schwächer ▸ **schwach**

Schwäche·zustand *der* [state of] weakness; weak condition

Schwachheit *die;* ~, ~**en** [1] weakness; **die ~ des Greises/des Alters** the frailty of the old man/of old age [2] (Mangel, Fehler) weakness; failing; **bilde dir nur keine ~en ein!** (fig. ugs.) don't kid yourself! (sl.)

Schwach·kopf *der* (salopp abwertend) bonehead (coll.); dimwit (coll.)

schwächlich *Adj.* weakly, delicate ‹*person*›; frail ‹*old person, constitution*›; delicate ‹*nerves, stomach, constitution*›

Schwächlichkeit *die;* ~, ~**en** weakness; (der Nerven, der Konstitution) delicateness

Schwächling /ˈʃvɛçlɪŋ/ *der;* ~**s,** ~**e** weakling

schwach-, Schwach-: ~punkt *der* weak point; **~sichtig** *Adj.* (Med.) weak-sighted; **~sichtigkeit** *die;* ~~: dimness of sight; amblyopia; **~sinn** *der* [1] ▸ ❶ **S. 439** (Med.) mental deficiency; [2] (ugs. abwertend: Unsinn) [idiotic (coll.)] rubbish *or* nonsense; **~sinnig** **A** *Adj.* [1] (Med.) mentally deficient; [2] (ugs. abwertend: unsinnig) idiotic (coll.), nonsensical ‹*measure, policy, etc.*›; rubbishy ‹*film etc.*›; **B** *adv.* (ugs. abwertend) idiotically (coll.); stupidly

schwächst... ▸ **schwach**

Schwach-: ~stelle *die* weak spot *or* point; **~strom** *der* (Elektrot.) current of low amperage; (mit niedriger Spannung) low-voltage current

Schwächung *die;* ~, ~**en** weakening

Schwaden /ˈʃvaːdn̩/ *der;* ~**s,** ~: [thick] cloud

Schwadron /ʃvaˈdroːn/ *die;* ~, ~**en** (Milit. hist.) squadron

Schwadroneur /ʃvadroˈnøːɐ̯/ *der;* ~**s,** ~**e** (geh. abwertend) windbag

schwadronieren *itr. V.* (abwertend) bluster; **von etw. ~:** sound off about sth. (coll.)

Schwafelei *die;* ~, ~**en** (ugs. abwertend) [1] rabbiting on (Brit. coll.) [2] (Bemerkung) rubbishy remark; **~en** blether *sing.*

schwafeln /ˈʃvaːfl̩n/ (ugs. abwertend)

A *itr. V.* rabbit on (Brit. coll.), waffle (**von** about)

B *tr. V.* blether ‹*nonsense*›

Schwager /ˈʃvaːgɐ/ *der;* ~**s, Schwäger** /ˈʃvɛːgɐ/ [1] brother-in-law [2] (veralt.: Postkutscher) mail coach driver

Schwägerin /ˈʃvɛːgərɪn/ *die;* ~, ~**nen** sister-in-law

Schwalbe /ˈʃvalbə/ *die;* ~, ~**n** [1] swallow; **eine ~ macht noch keinen Sommer** (Spr.) one swallow does not make a summer (prov.) [2] (ugs.: Papierflieger) paper aeroplane

Schwalben-: ~nest *das* [1] swallow's nest; [2] (Seemannsspr.) cockpit locker; **~schwanz** *der* [1] swallow's tail; [2] (Schmetterling) swallowtail; [3] (scherzh. veralt.: Frack) [swallow]tails *pl.;* [4] (Tischlerei) dovetail [joint]

Schwall /ʃval/ *der;* ~**[e]s,** ~**e** torrent; flood; **ein ~ Wasser/** (fig.) **von Lauten/Worten** a torrent of water/(fig.) sounds/words

schwallen *tr., itr. V.* (salopp) ▸ **schwafeln**

schwamm /ʃvam/ *1. u. 3. Pers. Sg. Prät. v.* **schwimmen**

Schwamm *der;* ~**[e]s, Schwämme** /ˈʃvɛmə/ [1] sponge; **~ drüber!** (ugs.) [let's] forget it [2] (südd., österr.: Pilz) mushroom; **giftige Schwämme** poisonous fungi [3] (Pilzbefall) dry rot *no art.*

Schwammerl /ˈʃvaməl/ *das;* ~**s,** ~**[n]** (bayr., österr.) mushroom; *s. auch* **Pilz 1**

schwammig

A *Adj.* [1] spongy [2] (abwertend: aufgedunsen) flabby, bloated ‹*face, body, etc.*› [3] (abwertend: unpräzise) woolly ‹*concept, manner of expression, etc.*›

B *adv.* (abwertend: unpräzise) vaguely

Schwammigkeit *die;* ~ [1] sponginess [2] (abwertend: Aufgedunsenheit) flabbiness; bloated appearance [3] (abwertend: Vagheit) woolliness

Schwan /ʃvaːn/ *der;* ~**[e]s, Schwäne** /ˈʃvɛːnə/ [1] swan; **mein lieber ~!** (ugs.) (staunend) my goodness!; good heavens!; (warnend) for heaven's sake! [2] (Sternbild) **der ~:** Cygnus

schwand /ʃvant/ *1. u. 3. Pers. Sg. Prät. v.* **schwinden**

schwanen *itr. V.* (ugs.) **jmdm. schwant etw.** sb. senses sth.; **ihm schwante nichts Gutes** he had a sense of foreboding

Schwanen-: ~gesang *der* (geh.) swansong; **~hals** *der* [1] swan's neck; [2] (oft scherzh.: langer Hals) swanlike neck; [3] (Technik) swan neck

schwang /ʃvaŋ/ *1. u. 3. Pers. Sg. Prät. v.* **schwingen**

Schwang *der: in* **im ~[e] sein** be in vogue; ‹*rumour*› be going the rounds; **in ~ kommen** come into vogue; ‹*rumour*› come into circulation

schwanger /ˈʃvaŋɐ/ *Adj.* pregnant (**von** by); **sie ist im vierten Monat ~:** she is in her fourth month [of pregnancy]; **mit etw. ~ gehen** (fig.) be big with sth. (literary); (mit etw. erfüllt sein) be full of sth.; (scherzh.) be mulling over sth.

Schwangere *die; adj. Dekl.* expectant mother; pregnant woman

schwängern /ˈʃvɛŋɐn/ *tr. V.* make ‹*woman*› pregnant; **sich von jmdm. ~ lassen** get [oneself] pregnant by sb.; **von Duft geschwängert sein** (fig. geh.) ‹*air*› be heavy with scent

Schwangerschaft *die;* ~, ~**en** pregnancy

Schwangerschafts-: ~abbruch *der* termination of pregnancy; abortion; **~streifen** *der* stretch mark

schwank *Adj. in* **wie ein ~es Rohr im Wind** (geh.) like a swaying reed

Schwank /ʃvaŋk/ *der;* ~**[e]s, Schwänke** /ˈʃvɛŋkə/ [1] (Literaturw.: Erzählung) comic tale; (auf der Bühne) farce [2] (komische Episode) comic event; **einen ~ aus seinem Leben erzählen** (scherzh.) tell the story of something funny that happened to one

schwanken *itr. V.* (mit Richtungsangabe mit sein) [1] sway; ‹*boat*› rock; (heftiger) roll; ‹*compass-needle etc.*› swing [to and fro]; ‹*ground, floor*› shake; **mit ~den Schritten** with wavering steps [2] (fig.: unbeständig sein) ‹*prices, temperature, etc.*› fluctuate; ‹*number, usage, etc.*› vary [3] (fig.: unentschieden sein) waver; (zögern) hesitate; **zwischen zwei Möglichkeiten ~:** be unable to decide between two possibilities; **er schwankt noch, ob ...** he is still undecided [as to] whether ...; **~d werden, ins Schwanken kommen** *od.* **geraten** begin to waver *or* hesitate; become undecided; **jmdn. ~[d] machen** make sb. waver *or* uncertain

Schwankung *die;* ~, ~**en** variation; (der Kurse usw.) fluctuation

Schwanz /ʃvants/ *der;* ~**es, Schwänze** /ˈʃvɛntsə/ [1] tail; **ein Tier am** *od.* **beim ~ fassen** catch an animal by the tail; **den ~ des Festzugs bilden** (fig.) bring up the rear of the procession; **kein ~** (fig. salopp) not a bloody (Brit. sl.) *or* (coll.) damn soul; **den ~ einziehen** *od.* **einklemmen** *od.* **einkneifen** (fig. salopp) draw in one's horns; **jmdm. auf den ~ treten** (fig. salopp) tread *or* step on sb.'s toes; **da beißt sich die Katze in den ~** (fig.) that is a circular argument [2] (salopp: Penis) prick (coarse); cock (coarse)

Schwänzchen *das;* ~**s,** ~ [1] [little] tail [2] (fam.: Penis) willy (coll.)

schwänzeln /ˈʃvɛntsl̩n/ *itr. V.* [1] wag its tail/their tails [2] *mit sein* (~d laufen) ‹*dog etc.*› run wagging its tail [3] *mit Richtungsangabe mit sein* (ugs. iron.: tänzeln) mince; trip; (ugs. abwertend: herumscharwenzeln) **vor jmdm. ~:** crawl to sb.

schwänzen /ˈʃvɛntsn̩/ *tr., itr. V.* (ugs.) skip, cut ‹*lesson etc.*›; **[die Schule] ~:** play truant *or* (Amer. coll.) hookey; **den Dienst ~:** skive [off] (Brit. coll.)

schwanz-, Schwanz-: ~feder *die* tail feather; **~flosse** *die* (Zool., Flugw.) tail fin; (des Wals) tail flukes *pl.;* **~lastig** *Adj.* tail-heavy; **~lurch** *der* (Zool.) caudate; **~wedelnd** *Adj.* tail-wagging *attrib.*; wagging its tail/their tails *postpos.;* **~wirbel** *der* ▸ ❶ **S. 435** (Anat., Zool.) caudal vertebra

schwappen /ˈʃvapn̩/

A *itr. V.* [1] **[hin und her] ~:** slosh [around]; **an die Bordwand ~:** splash *or* slap against the side of the boat [2] *mit Richtungsangabe mit sein* splash, slosh (**über** + *Akk.* over, **aus** out of)

B *tr. V.* slosh ‹*water, beer, etc.*› (**auf** + *Akk.* on)

Schwäre /ˈʃvɛːrə/ *die;* ~, ~**n** (geh.) [festering] ulcer

schwären *itr. V.* (geh.) fester; **eine ~de Wunde** (auch fig.) a festering wound *or* (esp. fig.) sore

Schwarm /ʃvarm/ *der;* ~**[e]s, Schwärme** /ˈʃvɛrmə/ [1] swarm; **ein ~ Krähen/Heringe** a flock of crows/shoal of herrings [2] (fam.: Angebetete[r]) idol; heart-throb; **sie hat einen neuen ~:** she's got a new flame [3] (Vorliebe) **mein/sein** *usw.* ~ (Tätigkeit) my/his *etc.* passion; (Gegenstand) the apple of my/his *etc.* eye

schwärmen /ˈʃvɛrmən/ *itr. V.* [1] *mit Richtungsangabe mit sein* swarm [2] (begeistert sein) **für jmdn./etw. ~:** be mad about *or* really keen on sb./sth.; **sie schwärmt für ihren Skilehrer** she has a crush on her skiing instructor (coll.); **von etw. ~:** go into raptures about sth.; **ins Schwärmen geraten** go into raptures

Schwärmer *der;* ~**s,** ~ [1] (Fantast) dreamer; (Begeisterter) [passionate] enthusiast [2] (Zool.: Schmetterling) hawkmoth [3] (Feuerwerkskörper) *firework emitting sparks and hopping short distances;* ≈ *jumping jack*

Schwärmerei *die;* ~, ~**en** [1] (Begeisterung) [passionate *or* rapturous] enthusiasm; **eine ~ für jmdn./etw.** a passion for sb./sth.; **romantische ~:** romantic rapture *or* ecstasy [2] (schwärmerische Worte) **[überschwängliche] ~[en]** rapturous hyperbole; (Beschreibung) rapturous description (**von** of) [3] (Fantasterei) fantasy

S

Schwärmerin *die;* ~, ~nen ▸**Schwärmer 1**

schwärmerisch

A *Adj.* rapturous ‹*enthusiasm, admiration, letter, etc.*›; effusive ‹*person, language*›; (begeistert) wildly enthusiastic

B *adv.* rapturously; ‹*speak*› effusively

Schwarm·geist *der* **1** woolly-headed enthusiast **2** (hist.) adventist

Schwarte /ˈʃvartə/ *die;* ~, ~n **1** (Speck~) rind; (Haut~) skin **2** (ugs. abwertend: dickes Buch) **[dicke] ~:** thick *or* weighty tome **3** (salopp: menschliche Haut) skin; hide (joc.); **arbeiten, dass die ~ kracht** (salopp) work one's fingers to the bone; work until one drops **4** (Jägerspr.: Tierhaut) skin; hide **5** (Brett mit Rinde) slab

Schwarten·magen *der* (Kochk.) brawn

schwarz /ʃvarts/; **schwärzer** /ˈʃvɛrtsɐ/, **schwärzest...** /ˈʃvɛrtsəst.../

A *Adj.* **1** black; Black ‹*person*›; filthy[-black] ‹*hands, fingernails, etc.*›; **~ wie die Nacht/wie Ebenholz** as black as pitch/jet-black; **mir wurde ~ vor den Augen** everything went black; **der Kaffee/Tee ist mir zu ~:** the coffee/tea is too strong for me; **der Kuchen ist schon ganz ~:** the cake is quite burnt **2** (fig.) **der ~e Erdteil** *od.* **Kontinent** the Dark Continent; **die ~e Rasse** the Blacks *pl.*; **~e Blattern** *od.* **Pocken** smallpox *sing.*; **das ~e Schaf sein** be the black sheep; **~e Liste** blacklist; **~e Messe** Black Mass; **~e Gedanken** black *or* dismal thoughts; **das habe ich ~ auf weiß** I've got it in black and white *or* in writing; **das kann ich dir ~ auf weiß geben** you can take that from me; **er kann warten, bis er ~ wird** (ugs.) he can wait till the cows come home (coll.); **~ werden** (Skat ugs.) lose every trick; get whitewashed (coll.); **~ von Menschen** packed with people; **die ~e Kunst** [the art of] printing; (Magie) the black art; (Kartenspiel) **~er Peter** ≈ old maid (*with a black cat card instead of an old maid*); **etw. ~ malen** paint a black *or* gloomy picture of sth.; **vielleicht male ich zu ~:** perhaps I'm painting too black a picture; **~ sehen** look on the black side; be pessimistic; **für jmdn./etw. ~ sehen** be pessimistic about sb./sth.; **er sieht/malt alles ~ in ~:** he is deeply pessimistic about everything/paints a black picture of everything; **der ~e Tod** (geh.) the Black Death; **das Schwarze Meer** the Black Sea; *s. auch* **Mann 1**; **Schwarz**; **schwarzsehen 3** (illegal) illicit, shady ‹*deal, exchange, etc.*›; **eine ~e Kasse führen** run a separate account for underhand purposes; **der ~e Markt** the black market **4** (ugs.: katholisch) Catholic **5** (ugs.: christdemokratisch) Christian Democrat

B *adv.* **1** ‹*write, underline, etc.*› in black; **~ gestreift/gemustert** with black stripes/a black pattern; **~ gerändert** black-edged; edged in black *postpos.*; dark-rimmed ‹*eyes*› **2** (illegal) illegally; illicitly; **etw. ~ kaufen/verkaufen** buy/sell sth. illegally *or* on the black market; **~ Straßenbahn fahren** go on the tram (Brit.) *or* (Amer.) streetcar without paying; **die Arbeiten lassen wir ~ machen** we're going to get the work done by a moonlighter (coll.) **3** (ugs.: christdemokratisch) ‹*vote*› Christian Democrat; ‹*ruled*› by the Christian Democrats

Schwarz *das;* ~[es], ~: black; **in ~ gehen, ~ tragen** wear black; **aus ~ Weiß machen [wollen]** (ugs.) [try to] argue that black is white

schwarz-, Schwarz-: ~afrika (*das*) Black Africa; **~arbeit** *die* work done on the side (*and not declared for tax*); (abends) moonlighting (coll.); **~|arbeiten** *itr. V.* do work on the side (*not declared for tax*); (abends) moonlight (coll.); **~arbeiter** *der,* **~arbeiterin** *die* person who does work on the side; (abends) moonlighter (coll.); **~äugig** *Adj.* black-eyed; **~bär** *der* black bear; **~beere** *die* (südd., österr.) bilberry; **~braun** *Adj.* blackish-brown; **~brenner** *der,* **~brennerin** *die* illicit distiller; moonshiner (Amer.); **~brot** *das* black bread; **ein [Laib] ~brot** a loaf of black bread; **~bunt** *Adj.* (Landw.) black pied, Frisian ‹*cattle*›; **~drossel** *die* blackbird

Schwarze[1] *der; adj. Dekl.* **1** (Neger) Black; (Dunkelhaariger) dark-haired man/boy **2** (österr.: Kaffee) black coffee **3** (ugs.: Konservativer) Conservative

Schwarze[2] *die; adj. Dekl.* **1** (Negerin) Black [woman/girl]; (Dunkelhaarige) dark haired woman/girl **2** (ugs.: Konservative) Conservative

Schwarze[3] *das; adj. Dekl.* **1** (der Zielscheibe) bull's eye; **ins ~ treffen** hit the bull's eye; (fig.) hit the nail on the head **2** **er gönnt ihr nicht das ~ unter den Nägeln** (ugs.) he begrudges her everything **3** **ihr kleines ~s** her plain black dress; her little black number (coll.)

Schwärze /ˈʃvɛrtsə/ *die;* ~, ~n **1** (Dunkelheit) blackness **2** (Farbstoff) black [dye]

schwärzen *tr. V.* blacken; black out ‹*words*›

schwarz-, Schwarz-: ~|fahren *unr. itr. V.; mit sein* travel without a ticket *or* without paying; dodge paying the fare; **~fahrer** *der,* **~fahrerin** *die* fare dodger; **er ist ~fahrer** he's a fare dodger; **~gerändert** ▸**schwarz B 1**; **~haarig** *Adj.* black-haired; **~handel** *der* black market (**mit** in); (Tätigkeit) black marketeering (**mit** in); **~händler** *der,* **~händlerin** *die* black marketeer; (mit Eintrittskarten) tout; **~|hören** *itr. V.* (Radio) use a radio without [having] a licence; dodge paying one's radio licence fee; **~hörer** *der,* **~hörerin** *die* (Radio) radio user without a licence; radio licence dodger; **~kittel** *der* **1** (scherzh.: Wildschwein) wild boar; **2** (abwertend: Geistlicher) [Catholic] priest

schwärzlich *Adj.* blackish

schwarz-, Schwarz-: *~|malen ▸**schwarz A 2**; **~malerei** *die* pessimism; gloominess; **hör auf mit dieser ewigen ~malerei!** stop always painting things so black!; **~markt** *der* black market; **~markt·preis** *der* black-market price; **~pulver** *das* black powder; **~rot·golden, ~-rot-golden** *Adj.* black, red, and gold; **~|schlachten** **A** *itr. V.* slaughter animals illegally; **B** *tr. V.* slaughter ‹*animal*› illegally; **~|sehen** *unr. itr. V.* (Ferns.) watch television without a licence; *s. auch* **schwarz A 2**; **~seher** *der,* **~seherin** *die* **1** (ugs.) pessimist; **2** (Ferns.) [television] licence dodger; **~sender** *der* pirate [radio] station; (beim Amateurfunk) pirate [radio] transmitter; **~specht** *der* black woodpecker; **~storch** *der* black stork

Schwärzung *die;* ~, ~en blackening

Schwarz·wald *der;* ~[e]s Black Forest

> **Schwarzwald**
>
> The Black Forest, a mountainous area in **Baden-Württemberg** in south-western Germany, is a popular holiday destination for Germans and foreign tourists alike. The name refers to the large coniferous forests in the region.

Schwarzwälder /-ˈvɛldɐ/ *die;* ~, ~ (Torte) Black Forest gateau

schwarz-weiß, schwarz-weiß *Adj.* black and white; **~ malen** (fig.) paint *or* put things in [crude] black-and-white terms

schwarzweiß-, Schwarzweiß-: ~aufnahme *die* black and white photograph; **~fernseher** *der,* **~fernsehgerät** *das* black and white television [set]; **~film** *der* black and white film; **~foto** *das* black and white photo; ***~|malen** ▸**schwarzweiß, schwarz-weiß**; **~malerei** *die:* **der Bericht ist eine einzige ~malerei** the report paints *or* puts things in [crude] black-and-white terms; **~rot** *Adj.* black, white, and red; **~zeichnung** *die* black-and-white drawing

Schwarz-: ~wild *das* (Jägerspr.) wild boars *pl.*; **~wurzel** *die* black salsify

Schwatz /ʃvats/ *der;* ~es, ~e (fam.) chat; natter (coll.); **einen ~ halten** have a chat *or* (coll.) natter

Schwätzchen /ˈʃvɛtsçən/ *das;* ~s, ~ (fam.) [little] chat; [little] natter (coll.); *s. auch* **Schwatz**

schwatzen, (bes. südd.) **schwätzen** /ˈʃvɛtsn̩/

A *itr. V.* **1** (sich unterhalten) chat; **schwatzt nicht über Politik** don't talk about politics **2** (sich über belanglose Dinge auslassen) chatter; natter (coll.) **3** (etw. ausplaudern) talk; blab **4** (in der Schule) talk

B *tr. V.* say; talk ‹*nonsense, rubbish*›

Schwätzer *der;* ~s, ~, **Schwätzerin** *die;* ~, ~nen (abwertend) chatterbox; (geistloser Redner) windbag; (klatschhafter Mensch) gossip

schwatzhaft *Adj.* (abwertend) talkative; garrulous; (klatschhaft) gossipy

Schwatzhaftigkeit *die;* ~ (abwertend) talkativeness; garrulousness; (Klatschsucht) gossipiness

Schwebe /ˈʃveːbə/ *die:* **in der ~ bleiben, sich in der ~ halten** keep one's balance; ‹*balloon*› float in the air, hover; **in der ~ sein/bleiben** (fig.) be/remain in the balance; **eine Frage in der ~ lassen** (fig.) leave a question open *or* undecided

Schwebe-: ~bahn *die* (Seilbahn) cableway; (Hängebahn) [overhead] monorail; (Magnetschwebebahn) levitation railway; **~balken** *der* (Turnen) [balance] beam

schweben *itr. V.* **1** ‹*bird, balloon, etc.*› hover; ‹*cloud, balloon, mist*› hang; (im Wasser) float; **ihr war, als ob sie schwebte** she felt as if she were standing on air; **in Gefahr ~** (fig.) be in danger; **zwischen Leben und Tod ~** (fig.) hover between life and death; **was mir vor Augen schwebt, ist ...** (fig.) what I have in mind is ... **2** *mit sein* (durch die Luft) float; (herab~) float [down]; (mit dem Fahrstuhl) glide; (wie schwerelos gehen) ‹*dancer etc.*› glide; **sich ~d fortbewegen** glide along **3** (unentschieden sein) be in the balance; **das Verfahren schwebt noch** the trial is still pending; **alle ~den Fragen/Probleme** all outstanding questions/problems

Schwebe·zustand *der* state of uncertainty

Schweb·stoff *der* matter in suspension; suspended matter

Schwede /ˈʃveːdə/ *der;* ~n, ~n **1** ▸ⓘ **S. 520** Swede; **er ist ~:** he's a Swede; he's Swedish **2** *in* **[du] alter ~!** (ugs.) old mate (coll.)

Schweden /ˈʃveːdn̩/ *(das);* ~s Sweden

Schweden-: ~bombe *die* (Wz) (österr.) ▸**Mohrenkopf 1**; **~platte** *die* (Gastr.) smorgasbord; **~punsch** *der* Swedish punch; arrack punch; **~stahl** *der* Swedish steel

Schwedin *die;* ~, ~nen ▸ⓘ **S. 520** Swede; *s. auch* **-in**; **Schwede 1**

schwedisch /ˈʃveːdɪʃ/ *Adj.* **1** ▸ⓘ **S. 520**, ▸ⓘ **S. 670** Swedish; *s. auch* **deutsch**; **Deutsch**; **Deutsche**[2] **2** *in* **hinter ~en Gardinen** (ugs.) behind bars (coll.)

Schwefel /ˈʃveːfl̩/ *der;* ~s sulphur

schwefel-, Schwefel-: ~blume, ~blüte *die* (Chemie) flowers of sulphur *pl.*; **~dioxid, ~dioxyd** /-ˈ---/ *das* (Chemie) sulphur dioxide; **~gelb** *Adj.* sulphur-yellow; **~haltig** *Adj.* containing sulphur *postpos., not pred.*; sulphurous ‹*Quelle, Boden*›; **schwach ~haltig sein** have a low sulphur content; **~holz** *das* (veralt.) lucifer (arch.); match

schwefelig ▸**schweflig**

schwefeln *tr. V.* sulphurize

Schwefel-: ~säure *die* (Chemie) sulphuric acid; **~wasser·stoff** *der* (Chemie) hydrogen sulphide

schweflig *Adj.* sulphurous ‹*acid*›

Schweif /ʃvaif/ *der;* ~[e]s, ~e (auch fig.: eines Kometen) tail; (eines Fuchses) brush; (fig.: von Anhängern, Fans o. Ä.) retinue

schweifen

A *itr. V.; mit sein* (geh.: umher~; auch fig.) wander; roam

B *tr. V.* (formen) curve

Schweif·säge *die* turning saw

Schweige-: ~gebot *das* duty of silence; **~geld** *das* hush money; **er deckte die Geschäfte des Chefs und bekam dafür ~geld** he covered up his boss's deals and received a bribe to keep quiet; **~gelübde** *das* (Rel., fig.) vow of silence; **~marsch** *der* silent [protest-]march; **~minute** *die* minute's silence

schweigen *unr. itr. V.* 1 (nicht sprechen) remain *or* stay *or* keep silent; say nothing; **kannst du ~?** can you keep a secret?; **~ Sie!** be silent *or* quiet! hold your tongue!; **auf etw.** *(Akk.) od.* **zu etw. ~:** say nothing in reply to sth.; **ganz zu ~ von ...** not to mention ...; let alone ...; **in ~der Andacht/Zustimmung** in silent worship/agreement; **die ~de Mehrheit** the silent majority 2 (aufhören zu tönen usw.) ‹*music, noise, etc.*› stop; **der Sender schwieg ab ein Uhr nachts** the radio station stopped broadcasting at 1 a.m.; **die Geschütze ~** (geh.) the guns are silent

Schweigen *das;* **~s** silence; **das/sein ~ brechen** break the/one's silence; **..., da herrschte ~ im Lande** *od.* **Walde** ... [then] nobody said a word; **sich in ~ hüllen** maintain one's silence; **jmdn. zum ~ bringen** (auch verhüll.) silence sb.

Schweige·pflicht *die* (eines Priesters) obligation of secrecy; (eines Arztes, Anwalts) duty to maintain confidentiality

schweigsam *Adj.* silent; quiet; (verschlossen) taciturn; (verschwiegen) discreet

Schweigsamkeit *die;* **~:** silence; quietness; (Verschlossenheit) taciturnity; (Verschwiegenheit) discretion

-schwein *das;* **~[e]s, ~e** (derb abwertend) pig; **Kapitalisten~/Kommunisten~:** capitalist pig/communist swine

Schwein /ʃvain/ *das;* **~[e]s, ~e** 1 pig; **Hackfleisch vom ~:** pork mince; **besoffen wie ein ~** (derb) pissed as a newt (sl.); **wie ein ~ bluten** (derb) bleed like a stuck pig; **sich benehmen wie ein ~/die ~e** (derb) behave like a pig/like pigs; **haben wir mal zusammen ~e gehütet?** (spött.) since when have we been on such familiar terms? 2 (Fleisch) pork 3 (salopp abwertend) (gemeiner Mensch) swine; (Schmutzfink) dirty *or* mucky devil (coll.); mucky pig (coll.) 4 (salopp: Mensch) **ein armes ~:** a poor devil; **kein ~ war da** there wasn't a bloody (Brit. sl.) *or* (coll.) damn soul there; **es macht kein ~ auf** nobody's opening the door 5 (ugs.: Glück) **[großes] ~ haben** have a [big] stroke of luck; (davonkommen) get away with it; **hast du ein ~!** you're a lucky beggar!; **ich habe ~ gehabt** I was in luck

Schweinchen *das;* **~s, ~:** piggy

Schweine- (salopp) **eine ~arbeit** a hell (coll.) *or* (Brit. sl.) sod of a job; **ein ~glück haben** be incredibly jammy (Brit. coll.) *or* (coll.) lucky; **heute ist wieder eine ~kälte** it's bloody (Brit. sl.) *or* (coll.) damn cold again today

Schweine-: ~bande *die* (derb) pack of so-and-sos (coll.); (stärker) pack of bastards (sl.); **~bauch** *der* (Kochk.) belly pork; **~braten** *der* (Kochk.) roast pork *no indef. art.*; **ein ~braten** a joint of pork; **~doping** *das* drugging of pigs; **~filet** *das* (Kochk.) fillet of pork; **~fleisch** *das* pork; **~fraß** *der* (derb abwertend) pigswill (coll.); **~geld** *das* (salopp) **ein ~geld kosten/verdienen** cost/earn a packet (coll.) *or* a fortune; **~hund** *der* (derb abwertend) bastard (sl.); swine; **der innere ~hund** lack of will power; **~koben** *der* (Stall) pigsty; pigpen (Amer.); (Verschlag) pen (*in a sty*); **~kotelett** *das* (Kochk.) pork chop; (vom Nacken) pork cutlet; **~lende** *die* (Kochk.) loin of pork; **~mast** *die* fattening of pigs; pig-fattening; **~pest** *die* swine fever

Schweinerei *die;* **~, ~en** (ugs. abwertend) 1 (Schmutz) mess; **so eine ~!** what a mess! 2 (Gemeinheit) mean *or* dirty trick; **es ist eine ~, dass das nicht erlaubt ist** it's disgusting that that's not allowed; **Er verdient mehr Geld als du? So eine ~!** He earns more money than you? Disgraceful! 3 (Zote) dirty *or* smutty joke; (Handlung) obscene act

schweinern *Adj.* (südd., österr.) pork

Schweinerne *das; adj. Dekl.* (südd., österr.) pork

schweine-, Schweine-: ~schmalz *das* lard; (zum Streichen) dripping; **~schnitzel** *das* (Kochk.) escalope of pork; **~stall** *der* (auch fig.) pigsty; pigpen (Amer.); **ich halte es nicht länger aus in diesem ~stall** (fig.) I can't stand it any longer in this lousy joint (coll.); **~steak** *das* pork steak; **~system** *das* (salopp abwertend) corrupt capitalist system; **~teuer** *Adj.* (salopp) hideously expensive; **~zucht** *die* pig breeding *no art.*; **~zucht betreiben** breed pigs; **~zyklus** *der* (Jargon) cycle of employment and unemployment; employment/unemployment cycle

Schwein-igel *der* (ugs. abwertend) 1 (Schmutzfink) dirty *or* mucky devil (coll.); mucky pig (coll.) 2 (unanständiger Mensch) dirty so-and-so (coll.)

Schweinigelei *die;* **~, ~en** (ugs. abwertend) 1 making *no art.* a [filthy] mess; (Schmutz) [filthy] mess 2 (Zote) dirty *or* smutty story

schweinigeln *itr. V.* (ugs. abwertend) 1 (Schmutz machen) make a [filthy] mess 2 (Zoten reißen) tell dirty *or* smutty stories

schweinisch (ugs. abwertend)
A *Adj.* 1 (schmutzig) filthy 2 (unanständig) dirty; smutty
B *adv.* (unanständig) ‹*behave*› obscenely, disgustingly

Schwein-kram *der* (salopp abwertend) filth

schweins-, Schweins-: ~äuglein *das* piggy eye; **~braten** *der* (Kochk., bes. südd., österr., schweiz.) ▸ **Schweinebraten**; **~galopp** *die* **im ~galopp** (scherzh.) at a gallop; **im ~galopp angerannt kommen** come charging up [at a gallop]; **~hachse** *die,* (bes. südd.) **~haxe** *die* (Kochk.) knuckle of pork; **~kopf** *der* (Kochk.) pig's head; **~leder** *das* pigskin; **~ledern** *Adj.* pigskin; **~stelze** *die* (österr.) ▸ **~hachse**

Schweiß /ʃvais/ *der;* **~es** 1 sweat; (höflicher: Transpiration) perspiration; **in ~ kommen** *od.* **geraten** start to sweat; **mir brach der ~ aus** I broke out in a sweat; **ihm brach der kalte ~ aus** he came out in a cold sweat; **in ~ gebadet sein** be bathed in sweat; **etw. im ~e seines Angesichts tun** (geh.) do sth. in *or* by the sweat of one's brow; **das hat viel ~ gekostet** that was a real sweat (coll.) 2 (Jägerspr.: Blut) blood

schweiß-, Schweiß-: ~ausbruch *der* sweat; **einen ~ausbruch bekommen** start to sweat; **~band** *das; Pl.* **~bänder** sweatband; **~bedeckt** *Adj.* covered in *or* with sweat *postpos.*; **~brenner** *der* (Technik) welding torch; **~draht** *der* (Technik) filler wire; welding wire; **~drüse** *die* ▸ **ⓘ S. 435** (Anat.) sweat gland

schweißen *tr., itr. V.* weld

Schweißer *der;* **~s, ~, Schweißerin** *die;* **~, ~nen** ▸ **ⓘ S. 113** welder

schweiß-, Schweiß-: ~fleck *der* sweat stain; **~fuß** *der* sweaty foot; **~gebadet** *Adj.* bathed in sweat *postpos.*; **~geruch** *der* smell of sweat

schweißig *Adj.* sweaty

schweiß-, Schweiß-: ~naht *die* (Technik) weld; **~nass, *~naß** *Adj.* sweaty; damp with sweat *pred.*; **~perle** *die* bead of sweat; **~treibend** *Adj.* sudorific; diaphoretic; **Holzhacken ist eine ~treibende Arbeit** chopping wood makes you work up a sweat; **~tropfen** *der* drop of sweat; **~tuch** *das; Pl.* **~tücher** (veralt.) sudarium; **das ~tuch der Veronika** (Bibl.) the sudarium; the Veronica; Veronica's veil

Schweiz /ʃvaits/ *die;* **~:** Switzerland *no art.*; **in die ~ reisen** travel to Switzerland; **aus der ~ stammen** come from Switzerland

Schweizer
A *indekl. Adj.* ▸ **ⓘ S. 520** Swiss
B *der;* **~s, ~:** 1 (Einwohner) Swiss 2 (Landw.: Melker) dairyman 3 (in der ~garde) Swiss Guard 4 (~ Käse) Swiss cheese

schweizer-, Schweizer-: ~bürger *der,* **~bürgerin** *die* Swiss citizen; **~deutsch** *Adj.* Swiss German; *s. auch* **deutsch; Deutsch; Deutsche²**; **~garde** *die* Swiss Guard

Schweizerin *die;* **~, ~nen** ▸ **ⓘ S. 520** Swiss; *s. auch* **-in**

schweizerisch *Adj.* ▸ **ⓘ S. 520** Swiss

Schweizerische Eidgenossenschaft

The Swiss Confederation is the official name for Switzerland. The confederation was established in 1291 when farmers from the mountain cantons of Uri, Schwyz, and Unterwalden swore that they would jointly defend their traditional rights against the House of Habsburg. The unified federal state as it is known today, with 26 self-governing cantons, was formed in 1848.

Schweizerland *das;* **~[e]s** (schweiz.) ▸ **Schweiz**

Schweizer-: ~psalm *der* Swiss national anthem; **~volk** *das:* **das ~volk** the Swiss people

Schwel·brand *der* smouldering fire

schwelen /ˈʃveːlən/
A *itr. V.* (auch fig.) smoulder
B *tr. V.* (Technik) carbonize ‹*coal, peat, etc.*› at low temperature

schwelgen /ˈʃvɛlgn̩/ *itr. V.* 1 (essen u. trinken) feast; **in etw.** *(Dat.)* **~:** feast on sth. 2 **in Erinnerungen/Gefühlen** *usw.* **~:** wallow in memories/emotions *etc.*; **in Farben ~** (geh.) revel in colours

schwelgerisch
A *Adj.* epicurean ‹*person*›; sumptuous, opulent ‹*meal, grandeur*›; rapturous ‹*look, expression*›; luxuriant ‹*blossom*›
B *adv.* rapturously; with rapturous pleasure

Schwelle /ˈʃvɛlə/ *die;* **~, ~n** 1 (auch Physiol., Psych., fig.) threshold; **ich werde keinen Fuß mehr über seine ~ setzen** (fig. geh.) I shall not set foot in his house/flat *etc.* again; **jmdn. von der ~ weisen** (fig. geh.) turn sb. from one's door; **sich an der ~ des Todes befinden** (fig. geh.) be at death's door 2 (Eisenbahn~) sleeper (Brit.); [cross] tie (Amer.) 3 (Geogr.) swell 4 (Bauw.) sill; sole plate; abutment piece (Amer.)

schwellen¹ *unr. itr. V.; mit sein* swell; ‹*limb, face, cheek, etc.*› swell [up], become swollen; ‹*river*› become swollen, rise; **~d** full ‹*lips*›; ample ‹*bosom*›; thick ‹*cushion, carpet*›; bulging ‹*wallet*›; **der Sturm schwoll zum Orkan** the storm rose to a hurricane force; *s. auch* **Kamm**

schwellen² *tr. V.* (geh.) belly, fill ‹*sail, curtain*›; **der Stolz schwellte ihm die Brust** (fig.) his breast swelled with pride

Schwellen-: ~angst *die* fear of entering a place; **~land** *das: country at the stage of economic take-off*

Schweller *der;* **~s, ~** (Musik) swell

Schwell·körper (Physiol.) *der* corpus cavernosum

Schwellung *die;* **~, ~en** (Med.) swelling

-schwemme *die;* **~, ~n** glut; **Tomaten~/Milch~:** tomato/milk glut; **Lehrer~/Juristen~:** glut of teachers/lawyers

Schwemme /ˈʃvɛmə/ *die;* **~, ~n** 1 (Wirtsch.) glut (**an** + *Dat.* of) 2 (Kneipe) bar; [basic] pub (Brit.) 3 (für Tiere) watering place 4 (österr.: im Warenhaus) bargain basement

schwemmen *tr. V.* 1 (treiben) wash; **an Land geschwemmt werden** be washed ashore 2 (bes. österr.: spülen) rinse

Schwemm-: ~land *das;* alluvial land; **~sand** *der* alluvial sand

Schwengel /ˈʃvɛŋl/ *der;* **~s, ~** 1 (Glocken~) clapper 2 (Pumpen~) handle 3 (salopp: Penis) tool (sl.)

Schwenk /ʃvɛŋk/ *der;* **~s, ~s** 1 (Drehung) swing; **die Kolonne machte einen ~ nach rechts** the column swung *or* wheeled to the right; **die Partei macht einen ~ nach links** (fig.) the party is swinging *or* shifting to the left 2 (Film, Ferns.) pan; **die Kamera machte einen ~ auf den Helden** the camera panned to the hero

Schwenk·arm *der* swivel arm; swivelling arm

schwenkbar *Adj.* swivelling; **das Periskop ist ~:** the periscope can be swivelled round

Schwenk·bereich *der* working range; jib range

S

schwenken

A *tr. V.* 1 (schwingen) swing; wave ‹*flag, handkerchief*› 2 (spülen) rinse 3 (drehen) swing round; swivel; pan ‹*camera*›; swing, traverse ‹*gun*› 4 (Kochk.) toss

B *itr. V.; mit sein* ‹*marching column*› swing, wheel; ‹*camera*› pan; ‹*path, road, car*› swing; **er schwenkte in den Hof** he turned into the courtyard; **rechts schwenkt!** (Milit.) right wheel!

Schwenker *der;* ~s, ~: balloon glass

Schwenk·kran *der* swing-jib crane

Schwenkung *die;* ~, ~en ▸ **Schwenk**

schwer /ʃveːɐ̯/

A *Adj.* 1 heavy; heavy[weight] ‹*fabric*›; (massiv) solid ‹*gold*›; **die Äste sind ~ von Früchten** the branches are heavy with fruit; **~es Geld kosten** (fig. ugs.) cost a packet (coll.) *or* a fortune; **mir wurden die Beine ~:** my legs grew heavy; **ihm wurde ~ ums Herz** (geh.) his heart grew heavy

2 ▸ ❶ **S. 315** (bestimmtes Gewicht habend) **2 Kilo ~ sein** weigh two kilos; **ein zwei Zentner ~er Sack** a two-centner sack; a sack weighing two centners; **wie ~ bist du?** how much do you weigh?; **eine mehrere Millionen ~e Frau** (fig. ugs.) a woman who's worth a few millions

3 (anstrengend, mühevoll) heavy ‹*work*›; hard, tough ‹*job*›; hard ‹*day*›; difficult ‹*birth*›; troubled ‹*dream*›

4 (schwierig) difficult; hard; **jmdm. fällt etw. ~:** sb. finds sth. difficult; **auch wenns ~ fällt** whether you like it or not; **es wird ~ halten, das zu tun** it will be difficult to do it *or* that; **es ~/nicht ~ haben** have it hard/easy; **sie hat es ~ mit ihrem Mann gehabt** she's had a hard time with her husband; **jmdm./sich etw. ~ machen** make sth. difficult for sb./oneself; **sich** (*Dat.*) **die Entscheidung ~ machen** find it hard to make a decision; find the decision a hard one; **etw. ~ nehmen** take sth. seriously; **sich** (*Akk. od. Dat.*) **mit** *od.* **bei etw. ~ tun** (ugs.) have trouble with sth; **sich** (*Akk. od. Dat.*) **mit jmdm. ~ tun** (ugs.) not get along with sb.; **Schweres durchmachen** go through hard times; **wir haben das Schwerste überstanden** we're over the worst

5 (schlimm) severe ‹*shock, disappointment, strain, storm*›; serious, grave ‹*wrong, injustice, error, illness, blow, reservation*›; serious ‹*accident, injury*›; heavy ‹*punishment, strain, loss, blow*›; grave ‹*suspicion*›; **ein ~er Junge** (ugs.) a crook with a record (coll.)

6 (~ verträglich) heavy ‹*food, wine*›

7 (intensiv) heavy ‹*fragrance, perfume, etc.*›

8 (anspruchsvoll) heavy ‹*book, music, etc.*›

9 (Seemannsspr.) heavy ‹*sea, weather*›

10 (schwül) heavy; oppressive ‹*air, atmosphere*›

B *adv.* 1 ▸ ❶ **S. 315** heavily ‹*built, armed*›; **~ beladen** heavily laden *or* loaded ‹*vehicle*›; heavily laden ‹*person, animal*›; **~ wiegen** be heavy; (fig.) carry weight; **~ tragen** be carrying sth. heavy [with difficulty]; **~ heben** lift heavy weights; **~ zu tragen haben** have a heavy load to carry; **daran hat er ~ zu tragen** (fig.) it is a hard cross for him to bear; **~ auf jmdm./etw. liegen** *od.* **lasten** (auch fig.) weigh heavily on sb./sth.; **das Essen lag mir ~ im Magen** (fig.) the food lay heavily on my stomach

2 (anstrengend, mühevoll) ‹*work*› hard; ‹*breathe*› heavily; **~ erkämpft sein** be hard won; **das habe ich mir ~ erkämpft** I gained it at great cost; **~ erkauft** dearly bought; bought at great cost *postpos.*; **er lernt nur ~:** he is a slow learner; **~ hören** be hard of hearing; **~ erziehbare Kinder** difficult children; **~ verdaulich sein** (auch fig.) be hard to digest; **~ verständlich** scarcely comprehensible

3 (schwierig) with difficulty; **ein ~ zu lesender Text** a text that is hard *or* difficult to read

4 (sehr) seriously ‹*injured, wounded*›; greatly, deeply ‹*disappointed*›; ‹*punish*› severely, heavily; **~ behindert** severely handicapped; (körperlich auch) severely disabled; **~ beschädigt** badly damaged; (veralt.: ~ behindert) severely disabled; **~ krank** seriously ill; **etw. ~ büßen** pay dearly for sth.; **~ aufpassen** (ugs.) take great care; **~ stürzen** fall heavily; have a heavy fall; **~ verunglücken** have a serious accident; **~ im Irrtum sein** (ugs.) be very much mistaken; **~ in Fahrt sein** (ugs.) be really worked up; **~ betroffen sein** be deeply affected; **~ beleidigt/betrunken sein** (ugs.) be deeply *or* very insulted/blind drunk; **sich ~ ärgern** (ugs.) get very annoyed; **sich ~ blamieren** (ugs.) make a proper fool of oneself; **das will ich ~ hoffen** (ugs.) I should jolly well think so (Brit. coll.); **er ist ~ in Ordnung** (ugs.) he's a good bloke (Brit. coll.) *or* (coll.) guy; **wir haben ~ einen draufgemacht** (ugs.) we really painted the town red (coll.)

5 (unverträglich) **~ essen** eat heavy food; **sie kocht zu ~:** the food she cooks is too heavy

schwer-, Schwer-: **~arbeit** *die;* heavy work; **~arbeiter** *der,* **~arbeiterin** *die* worker engaged in heavy physical work; **~athlet** *der* weightlifter/wrestler/boxer/judoka/shot-putter/discus-thrower; **~athletik** *die* weightlifting *no art.*/combat sports *no art.*/shot-putting *no art.*/discus-throwing *no art.*; **~behindert** ▸ **schwer B 4**; **~behinderte** *der/die* severely handicapped person; (körperlich auch) severely disabled person; **die ~behinderten** the severely handicapped/disabled; **~behinderten·ausweis** *der* disabled person's pass; **~beladen** ▸ **schwer B 1**; **~beschädigt** ▸ **schwer B 4**; **~beschädigte** *der/die; adj. Dekl.* severely disabled person; **die ~beschädigten** the severely disabled; **~bewaffnet** ▸ **schwer B 1**; **~blütig** *Adj.* stolid; phlegmatic

Schwere *die;* ~ 1 weight; **eine ~ in den Gliedern** a heaviness in one's limbs 2 (Physik: Schwerkraft) gravity 3 ▸ **schwer A 5**: severity; seriousness; gravity; heaviness 4 (Schwierigkeitsgrad) difficulty 5 (von Speisen, Parfums usw.) heaviness

Schwere·feld *das* (Geophysik) gravitational field; field of gravity

schwere·los

A *Adj.* weightless

B *adv.* weightlessly

Schwerelosigkeit *die;* ~: weightlessness

Schwerenöter /ˈʃveːrənøːtɐ/ *der;* ~s, ~ (ugs. scherzh.) ladykiller (coll.)

schwer-, Schwer-: *~**erziehbar** ▸ **schwer B 2**; *~|**fallen** ▸ **schwer A 4**; **~fällig** A *Adj.* ponderous, slow-moving ‹*animal*›; ponderous, heavy ‹*movement, steps*›; (auch geistig) ponderous ‹*person*›; (fig.) cumbersome ‹*bureaucracy, procedure*›; ponderous ‹*style, thinking*›; B *adv.* ponderously; **~fällig denken/antworten** think/answer slowly and ponderously; **~fälligkeit** *die* ▸ **~fällig**: ponderousness; heaviness; (fig.) cumbersomeness; ponderousness; **~gewicht** *das* 1 heavyweight; **die Meisterschaften im ~gewicht** the heavyweight championships; 2 (Sportler) heavyweight; 3 (Schwerpunkt) main focus; emphasis; **sie studiert Russisch mit ~gewicht Sprachwissenschaft** she's studying Russian, specializing in linguistics; 4 (ugs. scherzh.: dicker Mensch) heavyweight; **~gewichtig** *Adj.* heavyweight *attrib.*; **~gewichtler** /ˈɡəvɪçtlɐ/ *der;* ~s, ~ (~athletik) heavyweight; *~|**halten** ▸ **schwer A 4**; **~hörig** *Adj.* hard of hearing *pred.*; **auf dem Ohr ist er ~hörig** (fig.) when it comes to that sort of thing, he doesn't want to know; **~hörige** *der/die; adj. Dekl.* person who is hard of hearing; **die ~n** the hard of hearing; **~hörigkeit** *die* hardness of hearing; **~industrie** *die* heavy industry; **~kraft** *die* (Physik, Astron.) gravity; *~**krank** ▸ **schwer B 4**; **~kranke** *der/die* seriously ill person; **die ~kranken** the seriously ill; **~kriegsbeschädigte** *der/die* severely war disabled person; **die ~kriegsbeschädigten** the severely war disabled; **~laster** *der* (ugs.) heavy truck and trailer; heavy lorry (Brit.)

schwerlich *Adv.* hardly; **das wird dir ~ jemand glauben** it's hardly likely that anyone will believe you

schwer-, Schwer-: *~|**machen** ▸ **schwer A 4**; **~metall** *das* heavy metal; **~mut** *die* melancholy; **~mütig** A *Adj.* melancholic; B *adv.* melancholically; **er starrte ~mütig vor sich hin** he stared ahead full of melancholy; *~|**nehmen** ▸ **schwer A 4**; **~öl** *das* heavy oil; **~punkt** *der* (Physik) centre of gravity; (fig.) main focus; (Hauptgewicht) main stress; **der ~punkt seiner Tätigkeit liegt in** *od.* **auf der Forschung** his activity centres on research; **den ~punkt auf etw.** (*Akk.*) **legen** (fig.) put the main stress on sth.; focus mainly on sth.; **~punkt·mäßig** A *Adj.* selective ‹*strike, action*›; B *adv.* **im Lager und in der Packerei soll ~punktmäßig gestreikt werden** there are to be selective strikes in the warehouse and the packing department; **~punkt·programm** *das* programme of selective measures; **~reich** *Adj.* (ugs.) immensely rich (coll.)

Schwerst-: **~arbeiter** *der,* **~arbeiterin** *die* worker engaged in very heavy work; **~behinderte** *der/die; adj. Dekl.* severely disabled person (*with a disablement of over 80%*); *s. auch* **Schwerbehinderte**

Schwert /ʃveːɐ̯t/ *das;* ~[e]s, ~er 1 sword; **das ~ ziehen** *od.* **zücken** draw one's sword; **~er zu Pflugscharen** swords to ploughshares; *s. auch* **zweischneidig** 2 (Schiffbau) centreboard

Schwert-: **~fisch** *der* swordfish; **~leite** /ˈlaitə/ *die;* ~~, ~~n (hist.) accolade; dubbing ceremony; **~lilie** *die* iris; **~schlucker** *der,* **~schluckerin** *die;* ~~, ~~nen swordswallower

schwer, Schwer: *~**tun** ▸ **schwer A 4**; **~transport** *der* (Verkehrsw.) heavy goods transport; **~transporter** *der* heavy goods vehicle; (Flugw.) heavy transport aircraft

Schwert·wal *die* **[großer] ~:** killer whale; **[kleiner] ~:** false killer whale

schwer-, Schwer-: **~verbrecher** *der,* **~verbrecherin** *die* serious offender; **ich lasse mich nicht wie ein ~verbrecher behandeln** I won't be treated like a common criminal; *~**verdaulich** ▸ **schwer B 2**; **~verletzt** ▸ **schwer B 4**; **~verletzte** *der/die* seriously injured person; serious casualty; **die ~verletzten** the seriously injured; *~**verständlich** ▸ **schwer B 2**; **~verwundet** ▸ **schwer B 4**; **~verwundete** *der/die* seriously wounded person; **die ~verwundeten** the seriously wounded; **~wiegend** *Adj.* serious, grave ‹*reservation, consequence, objection, accusation, etc.*›; momentous ‹*decision*›; serious ‹*case, problem*›

Schwester /ˈʃvɛstɐ/ *die;* ~, ~n 1 sister 2 (Nonne) nun; (als Anrede) Sister; **~ Petra** Sister Petra 3 (Kranken~) nurse; (als Anrede) Nurse; (zur Ober~) Sister 4 (ugs.: ~firma) associate firm

Schwesterchen *das;* ~s, ~: little sister; **ein kleines ~:** a little sister

Schwester-: **~firma** *die* associate firm *or* company; **~herz** *das* (veralt., noch scherzh.) dear sister; **hör mal, ~herz** listen, sister dear

schwesterlich

A *Adj.* sisterly

B *adv.* **~ handeln** act in a sisterly way

Schwester-: **~liebe** *die* sisterly love; **~mord** *der* sororicide; **~mörder** *der,* **~mörderin** *die* sororicide

Schwestern·helferin *die* ▸ ❶ **S. 113** nursing auxiliary; auxiliary nurse

Schwesternschaft *die;* ~: nurses *pl.*; nursing staff

Schwestern-: **~schülerin** *die* probationer; **~wohn·heim** *das* nurses' home *or* hostel

Schwester-: **~partei** *die* sister party; **~schiff** *das* sister ship

Schwib·bogen /ˈʃvɪp-/ *der* (Archit.) flying buttress

schwieg /ʃviːk/ *1. u. 3. Pers. Prät. v.* **schweigen**

Schwieger- /ˈʃviːɡɐ-/: **~eltern** *Pl.* parents-in-law; **~mutter** *die; Pl.* **~mütter** mother-in-law; **~sohn** *der* son-in-law; **~tochter** *die* daughter-in-law; **~vater** *der* father-in-law

Schwiele /ˈʃviːlə/ *die;* ~, ~n callus; **~n an den Händen** horny hands

S

schwielig *Adj.* callused; **~e Hände** horny hands

schwierig /ˈʃviːrɪç/ *Adj.* difficult

Schwierigkeit *die;* **~, ~en** difficulty; **in ~en** *(Akk.)* **geraten** get into difficulties; **jmdm. ~en machen** make difficulties for sb.; **Latein macht ihm ~en** he has difficulty *or* trouble with Latin; **mach keine ~en!** don't make difficulties!; don't be difficult *or* awkward!; **~en bekommen** have problems *or* trouble; **jmdn./sich in ~en** *(Akk.)* **bringen** get sb./oneself into trouble; **ohne ~en** without difficulty

Schwierigkeits·grad *der* degree of difficulty; (von Lehrmaterial usw.) level of difficulty

Schwimm-: ~anzug *der* swimsuit; (für Taucher) wet suit; **~bad** *das* swimming baths *pl.* (Brit.); swimming pool; **~bagger** *der* dredger; **~becken** *das* swimming pool; **~blase** *die* swim bladder; air bladder; **~dock** *das* floating dock

***Schwimmeister** *usw.* ▸ **Schwimm-meister**

schwimmen

A *unr. itr. V.* **1** *meist mit sein* swim; **~ gehen** go swimming **2** *meist mit sein* (treiben, nicht untergehen) float; **die Kinder ließen ihre Schiffchen ~:** the children sailed their boats; **koreanische Schiffe ~ auf allen Meeren** Korean ships sail on all the seas of the world **3** (ugs.: unsicher sein) be all at sea; **ins Schwimmen geraten** *od.* **kommen** start to flounder **4** (überschwemmt sein) be awash **5** *mit sein* (triefen von) **in etw.** *(Dat.)* **~:** be swimming in sth.; **im [eigenen] Blut ~:** be bathed in [one's own] blood; **in** *od.* **im Geld ~** (fig.) be rolling in money *or* in it (coll.) **6** *mit sein* (ver~) swim; **mir schwimmt es vor den Augen** everything is swimming in front of my eyes **7** *in* **~des Fett** (Kochk.) deep fat; **etw. in ~dem Fett braten** deep-fry sth.; fry sth. in deep fat

B *unr. tr. V.; auch mit sein* swim; **einen neuen Rekord ~:** swim a new record time

Schwimmen *das;* **~s** swimming *no art.*

Schwimmer *der;* **~s, ~ 1** swimmer **2** (der Angel, Technik) float

Schwimmer·becken *das* swimmers' pool

Schwimmerin *die;* **~, ~nen** swimmer

schwimm-, Schwimm-: ~fähig *Adj.* buoyant ‹*material*›; amphibious ‹*vehicle*›; **~flosse** *die* flipper; **~fuß** *der* webbed foot; **~gürtel** *der* swimming belt; **~halle** *die* indoor swimming pool; **bevor man in die ~halle kommt, muss man durch den Duschraum gehen** before entering the pool area, you have to go through the showers; **~haut** *die* web (*of bird's webbed foot*); **~kran** *der* floating crane; **~lehrer** *der,* **~lehrerin** *die* swimming instructor; **~meister** *der,* **~meisterin** *die* swimming supervisor [and instructor]; **~sport** *der* [competitive] swimming *no art.*; **~stadion** *das* swimming stadium; **~stil** *der* stroke; **~vogel** *der* web-footed bird; **~weste** *die* life jacket

Schwindel /ˈʃvɪndl̩/ *der;* **~s 1** (Gleichgewichtsstörung) dizziness; giddiness; vertigo **2** (Anfall) dizzy *or* giddy spell; attack of dizziness *or* giddiness *or* vertigo **3** (abwertend) (Betrug) swindle; fraud; (Lüge) lie; **das ist alles ~, was er sagt** what he says is all lies; **den ~ kenne ich** (ugs.) that's an old trick; I know that trick; **er fällt auf jeden ~ rein** he'll fall for any trick **4** *in* **der ganze ~** (ugs. abwertend) the whole lot (coll.) *or* (sl.) shoot

Schwindel·anfall *der* ▸ **Schwindel 2**

Schwindelei *die;* **~, ~en** (ugs.) **1** fibbing **2** (Lüge) fib

schwindel-, Schwindel-: ~erregend *Adj.* vertiginous ‹*height, speed, depths*›; (fig.) meteoric ‹*career, success*›; **in ~erregender Höhe** at a dizzy height; **die Preise kletterten in ~erregende Höhe** (fig.) the prices rose sky high; **~frei** *Adj.* **~frei sein** have a head for heights; not suffer from vertigo; **~gefühl** *das* feeling of dizziness *or* giddiness *or* vertigo

schwindelig ▸ **schwindlig**

schwindeln

A *itr. V.* **1** (sich drehen) **mich** *od.* **mir schwindelt** I feel dizzy *or* giddy; **in ~der Höhe** at a dizzy height; **ein ~der Abgrund** a vertiginous drop **2** (lügen) tell fibs

B *tr. V.* (lügen) **„...", schwindelte sie** '...,' she said, lying; **das ist alles geschwindelt** that's all lies

C *refl. V.* **sich ins Kino/durch den Zoll ~:** trick *or* (coll.) wangle one's way in to the cinema/through the customs; **sich durchs Examen ~:** wangle one's way through the exam (coll.)

schwinden /ˈʃvɪndn̩/ *unr. itr. V.; mit sein* **1** (geh.: abnehmen) fade; ‹*sound*› die away, fade; ‹*supplies, money*› run out, dwindle; ‹*effect*› wear off; ‹*interest*› fade, wane, fall off; ‹*fear, mistrust*› lessen, diminish; ‹*powers, influence*› wane, decline; ‹*courage, strength*› fail; ‹*years, time*› pass by; ‹*snow, illusion*› disappear; **ihm schwand der Mut** his courage failed him; **im Schwinden [begriffen] sein** ‹*effect*› be wearing off; ‹*interest, powers, influence*› be on the wane **2** (fachspr.: Volumen verlieren) shrink; ‹*metal*› contract, shrink

Schwindler *der;* **~s, ~** (Lügner) liar; (Betrüger) swindler; (Hochstapler) confidence trickster; con man (coll.); con artist (coll.)

Schwindlerin *die;* **~, ~nen** (Lügnerin) liar; (Betrügerin) swindler; (Hochstaplerin) confidence trickster; con artist (coll.)

schwindlig *Adj.* dizzy; giddy; **jmdm. wird es ~:** sb. gets dizzy *or* giddy; **da wird einem ja ~!** (fig.) it fairly makes your head spin

Schwind·sucht *die* (veralt.) consumption; tuberculosis; *s. auch* **galoppieren**

schwind·süchtig *Adj.* (veralt.) consumptive; tubercular

Schwinge /ˈʃvɪŋə/ *die;* **~, ~n 1** (geh.; auch fig.) wing **2** (bes. österr.: Korb) shallow oval basket

schwingen

A *unr. itr. V.* **1** *mit sein* (sich hin- u. herbewegen) swing **2** (vibrieren) vibrate; **etw. zum Schwingen bringen** cause sth. to vibrate **3** (Physik) ‹*wave*› oscillate **4** (geh.: anklingen) **in ihren Worten schwang Kritik** her words had a tone of criticism **5** (nachklingen) linger **6** *mit sein* (Skilaufen) swing **7** (schweiz.: ringen) wrestle Swiss style (*with one's right hand on the belt of one's opponent's wrestling-suit and the left hand on his rolled-up right trouser leg*)

B *unr. tr. V.* **1** (hin- u. herbewegen) swing; wave ‹*flag, wand*›; (fuchteln mit) brandish ‹*sword, axe, etc.*›; **eine Rede ~** (ugs.) hold forth; **große Reden ~** (ugs.) talk big; *s. auch* **geschwungen B**; **Tanzbein 2** (Landw.) swingle ‹*flax, hemp*›

C *unr. refl. V.* **1** (sich schnell bewegen) **sich über die Mauer ~:** swing oneself *or* vault over the wall; **sich aufs Pferd/Fahrrad ~:** swing oneself *or* leap on to one's horse/bicycle; **sich ins Auto/hinters Steuer ~** (ugs.) jump into one's car/get behind the wheel; **der Vogel schwang sich in die Luft** (fig.) the bird soared [up] into the air **2** (geh.: in einem Bogen verlaufen) arch

Schwinger *der;* **~s, ~ 1** (Boxen) swing **2** (schweiz.: Ringer) [Swiss-style] wrestler; *see also* **schwingen A 7**

Schwing-: ~kreis *der* (Elektrot.) oscillatory circuit; **~tür** *die* swing door

Schwingung *die;* **~, ~en 1** swinging; (Vibration) vibration; **etw. in ~ versetzen** set sth. swinging/vibrating **2** (Physik) oscillation

Schwingungs·zahl *die* (Physik) frequency of oscillation

Schwipp- /ʃvɪp-/: **~schwager** *der* (ugs.) husband's/wife's/brother's/sister's brother-in-law; **~schwägerin** *die* (ugs.) husband's/wife's/brother's/sister's sister-in-law

Schwips /ʃvɪps/ *der;* **~es, ~e** (ugs.) **einen [kleinen] ~ haben** be [a bit] tipsy *or* (coll.) merry

schwirren /ˈʃvɪrən/ *itr. V.* **1** (tönen) ‹*insect*› buzz; ‹*bowstring*› twang **2** *mit sein* ‹*arrow, bullet, etc.*› whiz; ‹*bird*› whirr; ‹*insect*› buzz; **allerlei schwirrte mir durch den Kopf** (fig.) all sorts of things buzzed through my head; **von den vielen Zahlen schwirrte mir der Kopf** (fig.) my head was buzzing *or* spinning from all the figures **3** (erfüllt sein von) **die Stadt schwirrt von Gerüchten** the town is buzzing with rumours

Schwitz·bad *das* sweat bath

Schwitze *die;* **~, ~n** (Kochk.) roux

schwitzen

A *itr. V.* **1** (auch fig.) sweat; **ins S~ kommen** (auch fig.) start to sweat **2** (beschlagen) steam up **3** (Harz absondern) sweat

B *refl. V.* **sich bei der Arbeit klatschnass ~:** get soaked with sweat from working; **sich halb tot ~** (ugs.) sweat like anything (coll.)

C *tr. V.* (Kochk.: in heißem Fett) sweat

schwitzig *Adj.* (ugs.) sweaty

Schwitz-: ~kasten *der* (Ringen) headlock; **jmdn. in den ~kasten nehmen** get sb. in a headlock; **~kur** *die* sweat cure

schwofen /ˈʃvoːfn̩/ *itr. V.* (ugs.) shake a leg (coll.); **~ gehen** go and shake a leg

schwor /ʃvoːɐ̯/ *1. u. 3. Pers. Sg. Prät. v.* **schwören**

schwören /ˈʃvøːrən/

A *unr. tr., itr. V.* swear ‹*fidelity, allegiance, friendship*›; swear, take ‹*oath*›; **ich schwöre es[, so wahr mir Gott helfe]** I swear it[, so help me God]; **jmdm./sich etw. ~:** swear sth. to sb./oneself

B *unr. itr. V.* swear an/the oath; **auf die Bibel/die Verfassung ~:** swear on the Bible/the Constitution; **ich könnte darauf ~** (ugs.) I could swear to it; **sie schwört auf ihren Kräutertee** she swears by her herbal tea

Schwuchtel /ˈʃvʊxtl̩/ *die;* **~, ~n** (salopp) queen (sl.)

schwul /ʃvuːl/ *Adj.* (ugs.) gay (coll.)

schwül /ʃvyːl/ *Adj.* **1** (feuchtwarm) sultry; close **2** (beklemmend) oppressive **3** (sinnlich) sensuous ‹*perfume, fantasy, etc.*›; steamy ‹*eroticism*›; sultry ‹*look*›; seductive ‹*lighting, music*›

Schwule *der; adj. Dekl.* (ugs.) gay (coll.); (abwertend) queer (sl.)

Schwüle *die;* **~:** sultriness

Schwulen-: ~bar *die* (ugs.) gay bar; **~bewegung** *die* (ugs.) gay rights movement; **~lokal** *das* (ugs.) gay bar (coll.)

schwül·heiß *Adj.* hot and sultry

Schwulität /ʃvuliˈtɛːt/ *die;* **~, ~en** (ugs.) **in ~en kommen** *od.* **geraten** get into a fix *or* jam (coll.); **jmdn./sich in ~en bringen** get sb./oneself into a fix *or* jam (coll.)

Schwulst /ʃvʊlst/ *der;* **~[e]s** (abwertend) bombast; pompousness; (im Baustil) over-ornateness; **dieser Film ist sentimentaler ~:** this film is full of sentimental affectation

schwülstig /ˈʃvʏlstɪç/

A *Adj.* bombastic, pompous ‹*writing*›; bombastic, pompous, grandiloquent ‹*speech*›; over-ornate ‹*art, architecture*›

B *adv.* bombastically; pompously; ‹*speak*› bombastically, pompously, grandiloquently

schwül·warm *Adj.* [warm and] sultry

schwumm[e]rig /ˈʃvʊmərɪç/ *Adj.* (ugs.) **1** (unwohl) queasy; funny (coll.); **ihr wurde ~:** she started to feel queasy *or* (coll.) funny **2** (bang) jittery (coll.); nervous; apprehensive; **mir wird schon ~:** I'm already starting to get the jitters (coll.); I'm already getting butterflies [in my stomach]

Schwund /ʃvʊnt/ *der;* **~[e]s 1** decrease, drop (*Gen.* in); (an Interesse) waning; falling off; **einen ~ an Wählerstimmen befürchten** ‹*party*› fear a decline in its share of the vote **2** (Kaufmannsspr.) shrinkage **3** (Technik: Ausschuss) wastage **4** (Med.) atrophy **5** (Rundfunkt., Funkt.) fading

Schwung /ʃvʊŋ/ *der;* **~[e]s, Schwünge** /ˈʃvʏŋə/ **1** (Bewegung) swing **2** (Linie) sweep; **der elegante ~ ihrer Brauen/ihrer Nase** the elegant arch of her eyebrows/curve of her nose; **mit kühnem ~ überspannt die Brücke das Tal** the bridge crosses the valley in a bold arc **3** (Geschwindigkeit) momentum; **~ holen** build *or* get up momentum; (auf einer Schaukel usw.) work up a swing; **~ in etw.** *(Akk.)* **bringen, etw. in ~ bringen** (fig. ugs.) get sth. going; **jmdn. in ~ bringen, jmdm. ~ geben** (fig. ugs.)

S

put some life into sb.; get sb. going; **in ~ sein** (fig. ugs.) (in guter Stimmung) have livened up; (wütend) be worked up; (gut laufen) ‹*business, practice*› do a lively trade; (gut vorankommen) be getting on well; be right in the swing [of it]; **in ~ kommen** (fig. ugs.) (in gute Stimmung kommen) get going; liven up; (wütend werden) get worked up; (gut vorankommen) get right in the swing [of it]; ‹*business*› pick up; **jmdn./einen Betrieb in ~ haben** *od.* **halten** (ugs.) keep sb. on his/her toes/keep a firm doing a flourishing *or* good trade; **in die Sache kommt ~** (ugs.) things are picking up 4 (Antrieb) drive; energy 5 (mitreißende Wirkung) sparkle; vitality 6 (ugs.: größere Menge) stack (coll.); (von Menschen) crowd; bunch (sl.)

schwung·haft
A *Adj.* thriving; brisk, flourishing ‹*trade, business*›
B *adv.* **die Aktien werden ~ gehandelt** there's a brisk *or* flourishing trade in the shares; **das Geschäft entwickelt sich ~:** business is booming

schwung-, Schwung-: ~kraft *die* (Physik) centrifugal force; **~los** A *Adj.* 1 (antriebsschwach) lacking in energy *or* drive *postpos.*; listless; 2 (langweilig) lacklustre ‹*speech, performance, etc.*›; B *adv.* ‹*sing, dance, etc.*› in a lacklustre way; **~rad** *das* (Technik) flywheel; (an einer Nähmaschine) band wheel; **~voll** A *Adj.* 1 (mitreißend) lively; spirited; spirited ‹*words*›; lively, (coll.) snappy ‹*tune*›; 2 (kraftvoll) vigorous; **ein ~er Handel** a roaring trade; 3 (elegant) sweeping ‹*movement, gesture*›; bold ‹*handwriting, line, stroke*›; B *adv.* 1 (mitreißend) spiritedly; with verve; ‹*speak*› spiritedly; 2 (kraftvoll) with great vigour

Schwur /ʃvuːɐ̯/ *der;* **~[e]s, Schwüre** /ˈʃvyːrə/ 1 (Gelöbnis) vow 2 (Eid) oath; **die Hand zum ~ erheben** raise one's hand to take the oath

Schwur·gericht *das: court with a jury;* **vor das ~ kommen** be tried by a jury

Schwyzerdütsch /ˈʃviːt͜sɐdyːt͜ʃ/, **Schwyzertütsch** /ˈʃviːt͜sɐtyːt͜ʃ/ *das;* **~[s]** (schweiz.) Swiss German

Sciencefiction, ***Science-fiction** /ˈsaɪənsˈfɪkʃən/ *die;* **~:** science fiction

Scientologe /sai̯əntoˈloːgə/ *der;* **~n, ~n, Scientologin** *die;* **~, ~nen** scientologist

Scientology /sai̯ənˈtɔlədʒi/ *die;* **~:** scientology

Scorer /ˈskɔːrɐ/ *der;* **~s, ~, Scorerin** *die;* **~, ~nen** (Sport) 1 (Spieler[in]) (Fußball) [goal] scorer; (Basketball etc.) [points] scorer 2 (Funktionär) scorer

Scotch·terrier /ˈskɔtʃ-/ *der* Scotch terrier

scrollen /ˈskrolən/ *itr., tr. V.* (DV) scroll

Scylla /ˈstsyla/ ▸ **Szylla**

SDS *Abk.* = **Sozialistischer Deutscher Studentenbund** Socialist German Students' Federation

Séance /zeˈãːs(ə)/ *die;* **~, ~n** seance

Seborrhö, Seborrhöe /zebɔˈrøː/ *die;* **~, Seborrhöen** ▸ⓘ **S. 439** (Med.) seborrhoea

sechs /zɛks/ *Kardinalz.* ▸ⓘ **S. 29,** ▸ⓘ **S. 729,** ▸ⓘ **S. 826** six; *s. auch* **acht**

Sechs *die;* **~, ~en** six; **eine ~ schreiben/bekommen** (Schulw.) get a 'fail' mark; *s. auch* **Acht**[1] **1, 2, 4, 5, 7; Zwei 2**

sechs-, Sechs-: ~achtel·takt *der* six-eight time; **im ~achteltakt** in six-eight time; **~eck** *das* hexagon; **~eckig** *Adj.* hexagonal; *s. auch* **achteckig**

Sechser *der;* **~s, ~** (ugs.) (Ziffer, beim Würfeln) six; (Bahn, Bus) [number] six; (im Lotto) six winning numbers

sechserlei *Gattungsz.; indekl.* 1 *attr.* six kinds *or* sorts of; six different ‹*sorts, kinds, sizes, possibilities*› 2 *subst.* six [different] things

Sechser·pack *der,* **Sechser·packung** *die* pack of six; (bes. von Bier) six-pack

sechs-, Sechs-: ~fach *Vervielfältigungsz.* sixfold; *s. auch* **achtfach**; **~fache** *das; adj. Dekl.* **etw. um ein ~faches/um das ~fache erhöhen** increase sth. by a factor of six; *s. auch* **Achtfache**; **~flach** *das;* **~~[e]s, ~~e, ~flächner** /-flɛçnɐ/ *der;* **~~s, ~~:** hexahedron; **~hundert** *Kardinalz.* ▸ⓘ **S. 826** six hundred; **~jährig** *Adj.* (6 Jahre alt) six-year-old *attrib.*; six years old *postpos.*; (6 Jahre dauernd) six-year *attrib.*; *s. auch* **achtjährig**; **~kant·mutter** *die; Pl.* **~~n** hexagon nut; **~köpfig** *Adj.* six-headed ‹*monster*›; ‹*family, committee*› of six

Sechsling /ˈzɛkslɪŋ/ *der;* **~s, ~e** sextuplet

sechs-: ~mal *Adv.* six times; *s. auch* **achtmal**; **~malig** *Adj.* **nach ~maliger Wiederholung konnte er es auswendig** after repeating it six times, he knew it by heart; *s. auch* **achtmalig**; **~seitig** *Adj.* six-sided; six-page *attrib.* ‹*letter, article*›; **~stellig** *Adj.* six-figure; *s. auch* **achtstellig**; **~stöckig** *Adj.* six-storey *attrib.*; *s. auch* **achtstöckig**

sechst /zɛkst/ *in* **wir waren zu ~:** there were six of us; *s. auch* **acht**[2]

sechst... *Ordinalz.* ▸ⓘ **S. 165,** ▸ⓘ **S. 826** sixth; *s. auch* **acht...**

sechs-, Sechs-: ~tage·rennen *das* (Radsport) six-day race; **~tage·woche** *die* six-day week; **~tägig** *Adj.* (6 Tage alt) six-day-old *attrib.*; (6 Tage dauernd) six-day[-long] *attrib.*; *s. auch* **achttägig**; **~tausend** *Kardinalz.* ▸ⓘ **S. 826** six thousand

Sechste *der/die; adj. Dekl.* sixth; *s. auch* **Achte**

sechs·teilig *Adj.* six-piece ‹*tool set etc.*›; six-part ‹*serial*›; *s. auch* **achtteilig**

sechstel *Bruchz.* ▸ⓘ **S. 826** sixth

Sechstel *das, schweiz. meist der;* **~s, ~** ▸ⓘ **S. 826** sixth; *s. auch* **Achtel**

***sechste·mal, * sechsten·mal** ▸ **Mal**[1]

sechstens *Adv.* sixthly

Sechs-: ~tonner *der;* **~~s, ~~:** six-tonner; **~und·sechzig** *das;* **~:** sixty-six; **~zylinder·motor** *der* six-cylinder engine

sechzehn /ˈzɛçt͜seːn/ *Kardinalz.* ▸ⓘ **S. 29,** ▸ⓘ **S. 729,** ▸ⓘ **S. 826** sixteen; *s. auch* **achtzehn**

sechzehn-, Sechzehn-: ~jährig *Adj.* (16 Jahre alt) sixteen-year-old *attrib.*; sixteen years old *pred.*; (16 Jahre dauernd) sixteen-year *attrib.*; *s. auch* **achtjährig**; **~meter·raum** *der* (Fußball) penalty area; **~millimeter·film** *der* sixteen-millimetre film; 16-mm film

sechzehnt... *Ordinalz.* ▸ⓘ **S. 165** sixteenth

Sechzehntel *das;* **~s, ~:** sixteenth

Sechzehntel·note *die* sixteenth note

sechzig /ˈzɛçt͜sɪç/ *Kardinalz.* ▸ⓘ **S. 29,** ▸ⓘ **S. 826** sixty; *s. auch* **achtzig**

sechziger *indekl. Adj.* **die ~ Jahre** the sixties; **zwei ~ Briefmarken** two sixty-cent stamps; **eine ~ Glühbirne** a 60-watt bulb

Sechziger[1] *der;* **~s, ~** 1 (60-Jähriger) sixty-year-old; sexagenarian 2 (Bus, Bahn) number sixty 3 (Wein von 1960) **der ~:** the '60 vintage

Sechziger[2] *die;* **~, ~** 1 (Briefmarke) sixty-cent/centime *etc.* stamp 2 60-watt bulb

Sechziger[3] *Pl.* sixties; **in den ~n sein** be in one's sixties

Sechziger·jahre *Pl.* ▸ⓘ **S. 29,** ▸ⓘ **S. 165** sixties *pl.*

sechzig·jährig *Adj.* (60 Jahre alt) sixty-year-old *attrib.*; sixty years old *postpos.*; (60 Jahre dauernd) sixty-year *attrib.*

Sechzig·jährige *der/die; adj. Dekl.* sixty-year-old

sechzigst... /ˈzɛçt͜sɪçst/ *Ordinalz.* ▸ⓘ **S. 826** sixtieth; *s. auch* **achtzigst...**

SED *Abk.* = **Sozialistische Einheitspartei Deutschlands** Socialist Unity Party of Germany (*state party of the former GDR*)

Sedativum /zedaˈtiːvʊm/ *das;* **~s, Sedativa** (Med.) sedative

Sediment /zediˈmɛnt/ *das;* **~[e]s, ~e** (Geol., Chemie, Med.) sediment

Sediment·gestein *das* (Geol.) sedimentary rock

See[1] /zeː/ *der;* **~s, ~n** lake; **der Genfer ~:** Lake Geneva; **der Obere ~:** Lake Superior

See[2] *die;* **~, ~n** 1 (Meer) sea; **an die ~ fahren** go to the seaside; **an der ~:** by the sea[side]; **auf ~:** at sea; **er ist auf ~:** he is away at sea; **auf ~ bleiben** (geh. verhüll.) be lost at sea; **auf hoher ~:** on the high seas; **in ~ gehen** *od.* **stechen** put to sea; **Leutnant/Kapitän zur ~** (Marine) sub lieutenant/[naval] captain; **zur ~ fahren** be a seaman; **zur ~ gehen** (ugs.) go to sea 2 (~mannsspr.: ~gang) **ruhige/raue** *od.* **grobe** *od.* **schwere ~:** calm/rough or heavy sea 3 (~mannsspr.: Woge) sea

see-, See-: ~aal *der* flake; **~adler** *der* sea eagle; white-tailed [sea] eagle; **~anemone** *die* sea anemone; **~bad** *das* seaside health resort; **~bär** *der* 1 (Zool.) fur seal; 2 (fam.: ~mann) sea dog (coll.); **~beben** *das* seaquake; **~bestattung** *die* burial at sea; **~blockade** *die* naval blockade; **~bühne** *die* lake stage; **~elefant, ~-Elefant** *der* elephant seal; **~fahrend** *Adj.* seafaring; **~fahrer** *der* (veralt.) seafarer; **Sindbad der ~fahrer** Sinbad the Sailor; **~fahrer·volk** *das* seafaring people; **~fahrt** *die* 1 seafaring *no art.*; sea travel *no art.*; (~fahrtskunde) navigation; *s. auch* **christlich**; 2 (~reise) voyage; (Kreuzfahrt) cruise; **~fahrt[s]·buch** *das* (~w.) seaman's discharge book; **~fahrt[s]·schule** *die* merchant navy college; **~fest** *Adj.* 1 ▸ **~tüchtig**; 2 (nicht leicht ~krank) **~fest sein** not suffer from seasickness; not get seasick; 3 (gesichert, fest angebracht) secured [for sea]; **~fisch** *der* sea fish; saltwater fish; **~fracht** *die* sea freight; **~funk** *der* maritime radio; **~gang** *der:* **leichter/starker** *od.* **hoher** *od.* **schwerer ~gang** light/heavy *or* rough sea; **bei leichtem/schwerem ~gang** with a calm/heavy sea; **~gefecht** *das* naval engagement; sea battle; naval battle; **~gestützt** *Adj.* (Milit.) sea-based; **~gras** *das* eel grass; (als Polstermaterial) sea grass; **~hafen** *der* 1 (Hafenanlagen) harbour; 2 (Stadt) seaport; **~handel** *der* maritime trade; **~hase** *der* (Zool.) lumpsucker; **~herrschaft** *die* maritime supremacy; **~hund** *der* 1 common seal; 2 (Pelz) seal[skin]; **~igel** *der* sea urchin; **~jung·frau** *die* (Myth.) mermaid; **~karte** *die* sea chart; **~klar** *Adj.* (Seemannsspr.) ready to sail *pred.*; **~klima** *das* (Geogr.) maritime climate; **~krank** *Adj.* seasick; **~krankheit** *die* seasickness; **~krieg** *der* naval war; (Kriegsführung) naval warfare; **~lachs** *der* pollack

Seelchen /ˈzeˈlçən/ *das;* **~s, ~** (spött.) tender soul

Seele /ˈzelə/ *die;* **~, ~n** 1 (auch Rel., fig.) soul; (Psyche) mind; **nun hat die liebe ~ Ruh** (ugs.) now he's *etc.* satisfied at last; **zwei ~n, ein Gedanke** two minds with but a single thought; **sich** (*Dat.*) **die ~ aus dem Leib schreien** (ugs.) shout/scream one's head off (coll.); **jmdm. auf der ~ lasten** *od.* **liegen** (geh.) weigh on sb.['s mind]; **jmdm. aus der ~ sprechen** *od.* **reden** (ugs.) take the words out of sb.'s mouth; **aus tiefster** *od.* **ganzer ~:** with all one's heart; ‹*thank*› from the bottom of one's heart; ‹*sing*› with all one's heart and soul; **jmdn. in tiefster ~ kränken/enttäuschen** cut sb. to the quick/profoundly *or* deeply disappoint sb.; **das tut mir in der ~ weh** it hurts me deeply; **mit ganzer ~:** heart and soul; **sich** (*Dat.*) **etw. von der ~ reden** unburden oneself about sth.; **die ~ einer Sache** *od.* **von etw. sein** be the heart of sth.; **eine arme ~:** a poor soul; *s. auch* **aushauchen**; **Herz 2**; **Leib 1**; **Teufel** 2 (Mensch) soul; **eine ~ von Mensch** *od.* **von einem Menschen sein** be a good[-hearted] soul 3 (Waffent.) bore 4 (Technik: eines Kabels usw.) core

seelen-, Seelen-: ~amt *das* (kath. Kirche) requiem mass; **~arzt** *der,* **~ärztin** *die* psychoanalyst; **~friede[n]** *der* peace of mind; **~heil** *das* (christl. Rel.) salvation of one's/sb.'s soul; **ich mache das, wenn dein ~heil davon abhängt** (iron.) I'll do it, if it's a matter of life and death (joc.); **~klempner** *der,* **~klempnerin** *die* (scherzh.) psychotherapist; trick cyclist (Brit. joc.); **~leben** *das* (geh.) inner life; **~los** A *Adj.* soulless; B *adv.* soullessly; **~qual** *die* (geh.) mental anguish *or* torment *no pl.*; **~ruhe** *die* calmness; **in aller ~ruhe** calmly; **~ruhig** A *Adj.* calm; unruffled; B *adv.* calmly; **~striptease** *der od. das* revelation of one's innermost secrets; baring of one's soul; **~vergnügt** **A** *Adj.* cheerful; contented; **B** *adv.* cheerfully; contentedly; **~verkäufer** *der* (Seemannsspr. abwertend) coffin ship; **~verwandtschaft** *die* **unsere/ihre ~verwandtschaft** the fact that we/they are kindred spirits; **~voll** **A** *Adj.* soulful; **B** *adv.* soulfully; **~wanderung** *die* (bes. ind. Religionen) transmigration of souls; **~zustand** *der* mental state; state of mind

seelisch
A *Adj.* psychological ‹*cause, damage, tension*›; mental ‹*equilibrium, breakdown, illness, health*›; mental [and emotional] ‹*state, strain, low [point]*›
B *adv.* **~ bedingt sein** have psychological causes; **~ krank** mentally ill

See·löwe *der* sea lion

Seel·sorge *die* pastoral care

Seelsorger *der;* **~s, ~, Seelsorgerin** *die;* **~, ~nen** pastoral worker; (Geistliche[r]) pastor

seelsorgerisch, seelsorg[er]lich
A *Adj.* pastoral
B *adv.* **eine Gemeinde ~ betreuen** provide pastoral care for a parish

See-: ~luft *die* sea air; **~macht** *die* maritime *or* naval power; sea power; **~mann** *der; Pl.* **~leute** ▸ⓘ **S. 113** seaman; sailor

seemännisch /ˈzeːmɛnɪʃ/ *Adj.* nautical

Seemanns-: ~braut *die* sailor's lass; **~garn** *das* seaman's yarn; **~garn spinnen** spin yarns; **~grab** *das:* **ein ~grab finden** (geh.) go to a watery grave; **~heim** *das* sailors' home; **~knoten** *der* seaman's knot; **~lied** *das* sailors' song; **~sprache** *die* seaman's language; nautical language; **~tod** *der:* **den ~tod finden** *od.* **sterben** be drowned [at sea]

See-: ~meile *die* nautical mile; **~mine** *die* naval mine

Seen-: ~gebiet *das* lakeland [region]; **~kunde** *die* limnology *no art.*

See·not *die* distress [at sea]; **jmdn. aus ~ retten** rescue sb. in distress; **in ~ geraten** get into difficulties *pl.*

Seen·platte /ˈzeːən-/ *die* (Geogr.) lakeland area (*of glacial origin*)

see-, See-: ~pferd[chen] *das* sea horse; **~räuber** *der* pirate; **~räuberei** *die;* **~~:** piracy; **~recht** *das* maritime law; **~reise** *die* voyage; (Kreuzfahrt) cruise; **~rose** *die* **1** (Pflanze) waterlily; **2** (Seeanemone) sea anemone; **~sack** *der* kitbag; **~sand** *der* sea sand; **~schiff** *das* sea-going ship; ***~schiffahrt**, **~schifffahrt** *die* maritime shipping *no art.;* sea shipping *no art.;* **~schlacht** *die* sea battle; naval battle; **~schwalbe** *die* tern; **~stern** *der* starfish; **~streitkräfte** *Pl.* naval forces; **~stück** *das* (Kunstwiss.) seascape; (mit Schiffen usw.) marine; **~tang** *der* seaweed; **~tüchtig** *Adj.* seaworthy; **~ufer** *das* lake shore; shore of a/the lake; **~vogel** *der* seabird; **~wärts** *Adv.* seawards; **~weg** *der* sea route; **auf dem ~weg** by sea; **~wind** *der* onshore wind; **~zeichen** *das* seamark; navigation mark; **~zunge** *die* sole

Segel /ˈzeːgl̩/ *das;* **~s, ~:** sail; **mit vollen ~n** under full sail; (fig.) full speed ahead; **unter ~** (Seemannsspr.) under sail; **die ~ streichen** strike sail; (fig.) throw in the towel (**vor** + *Dat.* in the face of)

segel-, Segel-: ~boot *das* sailing boat; **~fahrt** *die* sailing trip; sail; (länger) sailing voyage; **~fliegen** *itr. V.; nur im Inf.* **~fliegen lernen** learn to fly a glider *or* to be a glider pilot; **man kann heute nicht ~fliegen** one can't go gliding today; **~fliegen** *das;* **~~s** gliding *no art.;* **~flieger** *der,* **~fliegerin** *die* glider pilot; **~flugzeug** *das* glider; **~jacht** *die* sailing yacht; **~macher** *der,* **~macherin** *die* ▸ⓘ **S. 113** sailmaker

segeln
A *itr. V.* **1** *mit sein, ohne Richtungsangabe auch mit haben* sail; **~ gehen** go sailing; go for a sail **2** *mit sein* (ugs.: fallen) fall; go flying; **durch die Prüfung ~** (fig.) fail *or* (Amer. coll.) flunk the examination **3** *mit sein* (schweben) ‹*cloud, bird, leaf*› sail
B *tr. V.; auch mit sein* sail in ‹*regatta*›; **die Strecke in drei Stunden ~:** sail the course in three hours

Segel-: ~regatta *die* sailing regatta; **~schiff** *das* sailing ship; **~sport** *der* sailing *no art.;* **~törn** *der* (Seemannsspr.) sailing trip; **~tuch** *das; Pl.* **~~e** sailcloth

Segen /ˈzeːgn̩/ *der;* **~s, ~** **1** blessing; (Gebet in der Messe) benediction; **jmdm. den ~ erteilen** *od.* **spenden** ‹*priest*› pronounce the blessing on sb.; **über jmdn./etw. den ~ sprechen** bless sb./sth.; **[jmdm.] seinen ~ [zu etw.] geben** (ugs.) give [sb.] one's blessing [on sth.]; **meinen ~ hat er!** (ugs.) I have no objection [to his doing that]; (iron.) the best of luck to him! **2** (Glück, Wohltat) blessing; **ein wahrer ~:** a real blessing *or* boon; **darauf ruht kein ~** (geh.) no good will come of it; **etw. zum ~ der Menschheit nutzen** exploit sth. to the benefit of mankind **3** (geh.: Ertrag) yield; **der ganze ~** (ugs.) the whole lot (coll.); **reichen ~ tragen** (fig. geh.) have rich rewards

segen·bringend
A *Adj.* beneficent
B *adv.* **sich auf etw.** (*Akk.*) **~ auswirken** have a beneficent effect on sth.

segens·reich *Adj.* **1** prosperous ‹*life, future*› **2** ▸ **segenbringend A**

Segens·wunsch *der* **1** (Bitte) blessing **2** *Pl.* (geh.: Glückwünsche) good wishes

Segler *der;* **~s, ~** **1** (Schiff) sailing ship *or* -vessel **2** (Sportler) yachtsman **3** (Zool.) swift

Seglerin *die;* **~, ~nen** yachtswoman

Segment /zɛˈgmɛnt/ *das;* **~[e]s, ~e** segment

segmentieren *tr. V.* segment

segnen /ˈzeːgnən/ *tr. V.* **1** bless; **er hob ~d die Hände** he raised his hands in blessing **2** (ausstatten mit) **mit jmdm./etw. gesegnet sein** (auch iron.) be blessed with sb./sth.; **im gesegneten Alter von 88 Jahren** at the venerable age of 88 years; **gesegneten Leibes sein** (geh. veralt.) be with child; **einen gesegneten Appetit/Schlaf haben** (fam.) have a healthy appetite/sleep like a log

Segnung *die;* **~, ~en** **1** (Wirkung) blessing; (iron.) dubious blessing **2** (das Segnen) blessing

seh·behindert *Adj.* partially sighted; visually handicapped; **stark ~ sein** have severely impaired vision

sehen /ˈzeːən/
A *unr. itr. V.* **1** see; **schlecht/gut ~:** have bad *or* poor/good eyesight; **sehe ich recht?** am I seeing things?; **hast du ge~?** did you see?; **mal ~, wir wollen** *od.* **werden ~** (ugs.) we'll see; **siehste!** (ugs.), **siehst du wohl!** there, you see!; **lass mal ~:** let me *or* let's see; let me *or* let's have a look; **siehe oben/unten/Seite 80** see above/below/page 80; **wie ich sehe, haben Sie zu tun** I see you're busy; **da kann man** *od.* (ugs.) **kannste mal ~, …** that just goes to show …
2 (hin~) look; **auf etw.** (*Akk.*) **~:** look at sth.; **nach der Uhr ~:** look at one's watch; **jmdm. über die Schulter ~:** look over sb.'s shoulder; **sieh mal** *od.* **doch!** look!; **siehe da!** lo and behold!; **sieh einmal!** just look!; **alle Welt sieht auf Washington** (fig.) all eyes are turned on Washington; **in die Zukunft ~** (fig.) look into the future
3 (zeigen, liegen) **nach Süden/Norden ~:** face south/north
4 (nach~) have a look; see; **kannst du mal ~?** can you just have a look?; **nach der Post ~:** see whether there is any post
5 **nach jmdm. ~** (betreuen) keep an eye on sb.; (besuchen) drop by to see sb.; (nach~) look in on sb.; **nach etw. ~** (betreuen) keep an eye on sth.; (nach~) take a look at sth.
6 (suchen) **nach jmdm./etw. ~:** look for sb./sth.
7 (achten) **auf Sauberkeit/Ordnung ~:** be particular about cleanliness/tidiness; **er sieht nur auf seinen Vorteil/aufs Geld** he's only out for himself/he's only concerned about the money; **darauf ~, dass die Bestimmungen eingehalten werden** make sure that the regulations are adhered to
8 (zu~, sich bemühen) see; **wir müssen ~, dass wir pünktlich sind** we must see [to it] that we're on time; **man muss ~, wo man bleibt** (ugs.) you've got to take what chances you get
9 (hervorragen) show; **das Boot sah nur ein Stück aus dem Wasser** only a part of the boat showed above the water
B *unr. tr. V.* **1** (erblicken) see; **jmdn./etw. [nicht] zu ~ bekommen** [not] get to see sb./sth.; **sich am Fenster ~ lassen** show oneself at the window; **siehst du meine Brille?** can you see my glasses?; **von ihm/davon ist nichts zu ~:** he/it is nowhere to be seen; **hier gibt es nichts/etwas zu ~:** there's nothing/something to see here; **ich habe ihn kommen [ge]~:** I saw him coming; **das sieht man** you can see that; **sieht man das?** does it show?; **den möchte ich ~, der das gern tut** I'd like to meet the person who 'does enjoy doing it; **wenn ich das schon sehe, wird mir übel** just looking at it makes me feel sick; I feel sick just looking at it; **hat man so was schon ge~!** did you ever see anything like it!; **er hat schon bessere Zeiten ge~:** he has seen better days; **ich habe ihn selten so fröhlich ge~:** I've rarely seen him so happy; **[überall] gern ge~ sein** be welcome [everywhere]; **jmdn. vom Sehen kennen** know sb. by sight; **etw. gern ~:** approve of sth.; **er sieht es nicht gern, wenn seine Frau raucht** he doesn't like his wife to smoke; **jmdn./etw. nicht mehr ~ können** (fig. ugs.) not be able to stand the sight of sb./sth. any more; **kein Blut ~ können** (ugs.) not be able to stand the sight of blood; **er kann sich in dieser Gegend nicht mehr ~ lassen** he can't show his face around here any more; **mit ihm kann sie sich ~ lassen** she needn't be ashamed to be seen with him; **mit dieser Frisur kann ich mich nicht ~ lassen** I can't let people see me with my hair like this; **eine Leistung, die sich ~ lässt** an impressive *or* a considerable achievement; **du lässt dich ja überhaupt nicht mehr ~:** we never see anything of you any more
2 (an~, betrachten) watch ‹*television, performance*›; look at ‹*photograph, object*›; **hast du ihn gestern im Fernsehen ge~?** did you see him yesterday on television?
3 (treffen) see; **wann ~ wir uns?** when shall we see each other next?; **wir ~ uns morgen!** see you tomorrow!; **in letzter Zeit ~ wir Schulzes häufiger** we've seen more of the Schulzes [just] recently
4 (sich vorstellen) see; **er sah sich schon als neuen Chef** he already saw himself as the new boss (coll.)
5 (feststellen, erkennen) see; **ich möchte doch einmal ~, ob er es wagt** I'd just like to see whether he dares [to]; **das sieht man an der Farbe** you can tell by the colour; **er sieht nur seinen Vorteil** he's only out for himself; **ich sehe schon, ich komme zu spät** I see I've come too late; **wir sahen, dass wir nicht mehr helfen konnten** we saw that we could not help any more; **etw. in jmdm. ~:** see sth. in sb.; **das wollen wir [doch] erst mal ~!** we'll 'see about that; **man wird ~ [müssen]** we'll [just have to] see; **das sehe ich noch nicht** (ugs.) I can't see that happening; **da sieht man es [mal] wieder** it's the same old story
6 (beurteilen) see; **das sehe ich anders** I see it differently; **so sehe ich das nicht** that's not how I see it; **so darf man das nicht ~:** you mustn't look at it that way *or* like that; **das darfst du nicht so eng ~:** you mustn't take such a narrow view; **so ge~:** looked at that way *or* in that light; **dienstlich/menschlich/rechtlich ge~:** seen from a professional/human/legal point of view; **…, oder wie sehe ich das?** (ugs.) …, am I right?; **ich werde ~, was ich für Sie tun kann** I'll see what I can do for you
C *unr. refl. V.* **1** **er kann sich nicht satt ~:** he can't see enough (**an** + *Dat.* of); **ich habe mich müde ge~:** I've seen more than enough
2 (sich betrachten als) **ich sehe mich getäuscht** I feel cheated; **sich genötigt/veranlasst ~, …**

S

zu ... feel compelled to ...; **sich in der Lage ~, ... zu ...** feel able to ...; think one is able to ...; **ich sehe mich außerstande, Ihnen zu helfen** I do not feel able to help you

sehens-, Sehens-: ~wert, ~würdig *Adj.* worth seeing *postpos.*; **~würdigkeit** *die* sight; **die ~würdigkeiten [der Stadt] besichtigen** go sightseeing [in the town]; see the sights [of the town]

Seher *der;* **~s, ~:** seer; prophet

Seher·blick *der* prophetic *or* visionary powers *pl.*

Seherin *die;* **~, ~nen** seer; prophetess

Seh-: ~fehler *der* sight defect; defect of vision; **~kraft** *die* sight

Sehne /ˈzeːnə/ *die;* **~, ~n** 1 ▸❶ **S. 435** (Anat.) tendon; sinew 2 (Bogen~) string 3 (Geom.) chord

sehnen *refl. V.* **sich nach jmdm./etw. ~:** long *or* yearn for sb./sth.; **sich [danach] ~, etw. zu tun** long *or* yearn to do sth.; **er sehnt sich nach Hause** he longs to go home; **~des Verlangen** (geh.) longing; yearning

Sehnen *das;* **~s** (geh.) longing; yearning

Sehnen·scheiden·entzündung *die* ▸❶ **S. 439** (Med.) tendosynovitis *no indef. art.*

Seh·nerv *der* ▸❶ **S. 435** (Anat.) optic nerve

sehnig *Adj.* 1 stringy ‹*meat*› 2 (kräftig) sinewy ‹*figure, legs, arms, etc.*›

sehnlich
A *Adj.* **das ist mein ~stes Verlangen/mein ~ster Wunsch** that's what I long for most/ that's my dearest wish
B *adv.* **etw. ~[st] herbeiwünschen** look forward longingly to sth.; **sich** (*Dat.*) **etw. ~st wünschen** long *or* yearn for sth.; **jmdn. ~st erwarten** look forward eagerly to sb. coming

Sehn·sucht *die* longing; yearning; **~ nach jmdm. haben** long *or* yearn to see sb.; **die ~ nach der Ferne** the longing for faraway parts

sehn·süchtig
A *Adj.* longing *attrib.*, yearning *attrib.* ‹*desire, look, gaze, etc.*›; ‹*letter*› full of longing *or* yearning; (wehmütig verlangend) wistful ‹*gaze, sigh, etc.*›; **~es Verlangen** longing; yearning
B *adv.* longingly; (wehmütig verlangend) wistfully; **jmdn./etw. ~ erwarten** look forward longingly to seeing sb./to sth.; long for sb. to come/for sth.

sehnsuchts·voll (geh.)
A *Adj.* longing *attrib.*, yearning *attrib.* ‹*desire, look, gaze, etc.*›; ‹*letter, lines, song*› full of longing *or* yearning; (wehmütig) wistful ‹*gaze, sigh, tremolo, etc.*›
B *adv.* longingly; yearningly; (wehmütig) wistfully

sehr /zeːɐ̯/ *Adv.* 1 *mit Adj. u. Adv.* very; **~ viel** a great deal; **ich bin ~ dafür/dagegen** I'm very much in favour/against [it]; **~ zu meiner Überraschung** [very] much to my surprise; **ich bin Ihnen ~ dankbar** I'm most grateful to you; **ich bin Ihnen ~ verbunden** I'm [very] much obliged to you; **jmdn. ~ gern haben** like sb. a lot (coll.) *or* a great deal; **er wäre ~ wohl imstande gewesen, es zu tun** he would perfectly well have been able to do it 2 *mit Verben* very much; greatly; **er hat ~ geweint** he cried a great deal *or* (coll.) a lot; **er hat sich darüber ~ geärgert** he was greatly *or* very annoyed about it; **das muss ich mir ~ überlegen** I'll have to give that a great deal of thought; I'll have to consider that very carefully; **du musst dich ~ vorsehen** you must be very careful; **es regnet ~:** it's raining hard; **danke ~!** thank you *or* thanks [very much]; **bitte ~, Ihr Schnitzel!** here's your steak, sir/ madam; **Danke ~! — Bitte ~!** Thank you — You're welcome; **er hat sich so ~ geärgert/ gefreut, dass ...** he was so annoyed/delighted that ...; **du glaubst nicht, wie ~ er sich gefreut hat** you wouldn't believe how delighted he was; **ja, ~!** yes, very much!; **nein, nicht ~!** no, not much!; **Langweilst du dich? — Sehr sogar!** Are you bored? — Yes, very!; **zu ~:** too much; **Hat es ihr gefallen? — Nicht so ~!** Did she like it? — Not all that much!

Seh-: ~rohr *das* periscope; **~schärfe** *die* visual acuity; **~schlitz** *der* observation slit; **~schwäche** *die* weak vision *or* sight *no indef. art.*; **~störung** *die* sight defect; visual defect; **~störungen** impaired vision *sing.*; **~test** *der* eye test; **~vermögen** *das* sight; **~zentrum** *das* (Anat.) centre of vision

sei /zai/ *1. u. 3. Pers. Sg. Präsens Konjunktiv u. Imperativ Sg. v.* **sein**

seibern /ˈzaibɐn/ *itr. V.* dribble

seichen /ˈzaiçn̩/ *itr. V.* (bes. schwäb. salopp) 1 pee (coll.); **ins Bett ~:** wet the bed 2 (dummes Zeug reden) talk drivel

seicht /zaiçt/
A *Adj.* ▸❶ **S. 267**, ▸❶ **S. 374** shallow; (fig.) shallow; superficial
B *adv.* (fig.) shallowly; superficially

Seichtheit *die;* **~** (auch fig.) shallowness

seid /zait/ *2. Pers. Pl. Präsens u. Imperativ Pl. v.* **sein**

Seide /ˈzaidə/ *die;* **~, ~n** silk

Seidel /ˈzaidl̩/ *das;* **~s, ~** (half-litre) beer mug

Seidel·bast *der* daphne

seiden
A *Adj.* 1 (aus Seide) silk 2 (wie Seide) silky
B *adv.* silkily

seiden-, Seiden-: ~atlas *der* silk satin; **~bau** *der* sericulture *no art.*; **~kleid** *das* silk dress; **~papier** *das* tissue paper; **~raupe** *die* silkworm; **~raupen·zucht** *die* sericulture *no art.*; **~spinner** *der* (Zool.) silk[worm] moth; **~straße** *die* (hist.) silk road; **~strumpf** *der* silk stocking; **~weich** *Adj.* silky-soft

seidig
A *Adj.* silky
B *adv.* silkily

Seiende /ˈzaiəndə/ *das; adj. Dekl.* (Philos.) **das ~:** that which exists

Seife /ˈzaifə/ *die;* **~, ~n** 1 soap 2 (Geol.) alluvial deposit; placer

Seifen-: ~blase *die* soap bubble; (fig.) bubble; **~blasen machen** blow bubbles; **~kisten·rennen** *das* soapbox race; **~lauge** *die* [soap]suds *pl.*; **~oper** *die* (ugs.) soap opera; **~pulver** *das* soap powder; **~schale** *die* soap dish; **~schaum** *der* lather; **~spender** *der* soap dispenser

seifig *Adj.* soapy

seihen /ˈzaiən/ *tr. V.* strain

Seil /zail/ *das;* **~s, ~e** rope; (Draht~) cable; **auf dem ~ tanzen** dance on the high wire; **in den ~en hängen** (Boxen) be on the ropes; (fig. ugs.: müde sein) be knackered (Brit. coll.) *or* shattered (Brit. coll.) *or* (Amer. coll.) tuckered

Seil·bahn *die* cableway

Seiler *der;* **~s, ~** ▸❶ **S. 113** rope maker

Seilerei *die;* **~, ~en** 1 (Herstellung) rope making *no art.* 2 (Betrieb) rope maker's

Seilerin *die;* **~, ~nen** ▸❶ **S. 113** ▸**Seiler**

seil·hüpfen *itr. V.; nur im Inf. u. im 2. Part.; mit sein* ▸**seilspringen**

Seilschaft *die;* **~, ~en** (Bergsteigen) rope; (fig.) followers *pl.*

seil-, Seil-: ~springen *unr. itr. V.; nur im Inf. u. im 2. Part.; mit sein* skip; **~tanz** *der* tightrope *or* high-wire act; **~tanzen** *itr. V.; nur im Inf. u. im 2. Part.* walk the tightrope *or* high wire; **~tänzer** *der,* **~tänzerin** *die* tightrope walker; **~winde** *die* cable winch

Seim /zaim/ *der;* **~[e]s, ~e** (geh.) glutinous *or* viscid mass; (Honig~) honey

seimig *Adj.* glutinous; viscid

sein[1] /zain/
A *unr. itr. V.* 1 be; **wie ist der Wein?** how is the wine?; **wie ist das Wetter?** what is the weather like?; **wie wäre es mit einem Schnaps?** how about a schnaps?; **wie war das noch mit dem Scheck?** what was that again about a cheque?; **nun, wie ist es, gehst du mit oder nicht?** well, what about it? are you going too, or not?; **wie ist es mit dir, möchtest du ein Glas Glühwein?** how about you, would you like a glass of mulled wine?; **ist das kalt heute!** it's so cold today; **wie dem auch sei, sei es, wie es wolle** (geh.) be that as it may; **seien Sie bitte so freundlich und geben Sie mir ...** [would you] be so kind as to give me ...; **das Buch ist meins** *od.* (ugs.) **mir** the book is mine; **die Sache ist die: ...** it's like this: ...; **wenn ich du wäre ...** if I were you ...; **das wären neun Euro** that will be nine euros; **hier wären wir** here we are; **das wärs** that's that; (beim Einkaufen) that's all; that's it (coll.); **und das wäre?** and what might *or* would that be?; **er ist Schwede/Lehrer** he is Swedish *or* a Swede/a teacher; **was ist er [von Beruf]?** what does he do [for a living]?; **bist du es?** is that you?; **Karl wars** (ist verantwortlich) it was Karl [who did/said *etc.* it]; **keiner will es gewesen ~:** no one will admit it was him; **wer** (ugs.) *od.* **jemand ~:** be somebody; **nichts ~** (ugs.) be a nothing *or* a nonentity; **Everton ist Fußballmeister** Everton are football champions; **x sei 4** let x be 4
2 (unpers.) **mir ist kalt/besser** I am *or* feel cold/better; **mir ist schlecht** I feel sick; **ist dir etwas?** are you all right?; is something the matter?; **jmdm. ist, als [ob] ...** sb. feels as if ...; (jmd. hat den Eindruck [als]) sb. has a feeling that ...; **jmdm. ist nach etw.** (ugs.) sb. feels like *or* fancies sth.; **mir ist nicht nach Scherzen** (ugs.) I'm not in a mood for joking
3 (ergeben) be; make; **drei und vier ist** *od.* (ugs.) **sind sieben** three and four is *or* makes seven
4 (unpers.) (bei Zeitangabe) be; **es ist drei Uhr/ Mai/Winter** it is three o'clock/May/winter
5 (sich befinden) be; **ist noch Bier im Haus?** is there any more beer in the house?; **morgen bin ich zu Hause** I shall be [at] home tomorrow; **wo warst du so lange?** where have you been all this time?; **bist du schon mal bei Eva gewesen?** have you ever been to Eva's?
6 (stammen) be; come; **er ist aus Berlin** he is *or* comes from Berlin
7 (stattfinden) be; (sich ereignen) be; happen; **es war an einem Sonntag im April** it was on a Sunday in April; **muss das ~?** is that really necessary?; **es hat nicht sollen ~** (veralt., geh.) it was not meant to be; **was darf es ~?** (im Geschäft) what can I get you?; **das kann schon ~:** that may well be; **das kann doch nicht ~!** that's just not possible!; **wenn etwas ist, ruf mich an** (ugs.) if anything comes up, give me a ring; **war etwas während meiner Abwesenheit?** did anything happen during my absence?; **es sei!** so be it; **was ~ muss, muss ~:** what must be, must be; **seis drum!** all right!; **sei es ..., sei es ...** (geh.) whether ... or ...
8 (existieren) be; exist; **er ist nicht mehr** (verhüll.) he is no longer with us; **ist was?** (ugs.) is anything wrong *or* the matter?; **sie taten, als ob nichts wäre** they acted as if nothing had happened; **das war einmal** that's all past now; **es war einmal ein Prinz** once upon a time there was a prince; **es ist keine Hoffnung mehr** there is no hope [left]; **was nicht ist, kann noch werden** things can always change; **wenn du nicht gewesen wärest** if it hadn't been for you
9 (ugs.) **etw. ~ lassen** stop sth.; **lassen wir die Idee/das Ganze lieber ~!** let's drop the idea/the whole thing; **jmdn./etw. ~ lassen** (ugs.: in Ruhe lassen) leave sb. alone *or* (coll.) be/leave sth. alone
B *Hilfsverb* 1 (... werden können) **es ist niemand zu sehen** there's no one to be seen; **das war zu erwarten** that was to be expected; **die Schmerzen sind kaum zu ertragen** the pain is hardly bearable; **mit ihm ist zu reden** he's quite approachable; **es ist zu verkaufen** it is for sale
2 (... werden müssen) **das Bemalen der Wände ist zu unterlassen** painting on the walls is prohibited; **die Richtlinien sind strengstens zu beachten** the guidelines are to be strictly followed
3 (zur Perfektumschreibung) have; **er ist gestorben** he has died; **sie sind gerade mit dem Wagen in die Stadt** (ugs.) they've just driven off into town; **gestern bin ich gleich von der Arbeit nach Hause** (ugs.) I went straight home from work yesterday; **die Kinder sind spielen** (ugs.) the children have gone off to play
4 (zur Bildung des Zustandspassivs) be; **wir waren gerettet** we were saved

S

ℹ seit

1. Als Präposition

Mit einem Zeitpunkt = since

Wir wohnen seit 1995 hier
= We have been living here since 1995

Seit damals leidet er an Depressionen
= Since then he has suffered from fits of depression

Mit einer Zeitspanne = for

Wir wohnen seit zwei Jahren hier
= We have been living here for two years

Er ist seit 20 Jahren bei der Firma
= He has been with the firm for 20 years

Ich kenne ihn schon seit einiger Zeit
= I have known him for some time

Die Übersetzungen von *seit* sind also nicht problematisch, aber die Zeiten des Verbs sind in den beiden Sprachen meist unterschiedlich: im Deutschen steht durchweg das Präsens, während man im Englischen das Perfekt oder – bei einem ununterbrochenen Vorgang – vor allem seine Verlaufsform, das Perfect Continuous, verwendet (mit **know** und **love** z.B. kann man aber das Perfect Continuous nicht verwenden). Ähnlich wird ein Verb im Imperfekt durch ein Verb im Plusquamperfekt übersetzt:

Ich wartete seit 8 Uhr/zwei Stunden
= I had been waiting since 8 o'clock/for two hours

Negative und andere Beispiele, bei denen kein ununterbrochener Vorgang vorliegt, weisen aber in beiden Sprachen die gleichen Zeiten auf:

Wir haben sie seit der Hochzeit nicht gesehen/nur einmal gesehen
= We haven't seen her/have only seen her once since the wedding

Ich war seit 1980 nicht dort gewesen
= I hadn't been there since 1980

2. Als Konjunktion

Auch hier wird das englische Perfect Continuous bzw. das Perfekt bei einem ununterbrochenen Vorgang verwendet, wo im Deutschen das Präsens steht:

Seit sie in Deutschland lebt, haben wir keinen Kontakt mehr
= Since she has been living in Germany we are no longer in touch

Seit er dieses Mittel nimmt, hat er keine Schmerzen mehr
= Since he has been taking this medication, he no longer has any pain

Seit ich sie kenne, hat sie nie gelacht
= Since I have known her, she has never laughed

Und in der Vergangenheit (etwa in der Erzählform):

Seit sie in Deutschland lebte, hatten wir keinen Kontakt mehr
= Since she had been living in Germany, we were no longer in touch

Seit ich sie kannte, hatte sie nie gelacht
= Since I had known her, she had never laughed

Aber bei einem Geschehen, das nicht andauert, wird das deutsche Perfekt mit dem englischen Simple Past übersetzt:

Seit er das gehört hat, ist er wie verwandelt
= Since he heard that, he's a changed man

sein² *Possessivpron.* (bei Männern) his; (bei Mädchen) her; (bei Dingen, Abstrakta) its; (bei Tieren) its; (bei Männchen auch) his; (bei Weibchen auch) her; (bei Ländern) its; her; (bei Städten) its; (bei Schiffen) her; its; (nach man) one's; his (Amer.); **jeder hat ~e Sorgen** everyone has his *or* (coll.) their troubles; **er trinkt am Tag ~e acht Tassen Kaffee** (ugs.) he regularly drinks eight cups of coffee a day; **das hat ~e zwei Millionen gekostet** (ugs.) it cost a good two million; **wenn man sich** (*Dat.*) **~er eigenen Unzulänglichkeit bewusst ist** when you're aware of your own inadequacy; when one is aware of one's own inadequacy; **dem Willi ~ Hund** (salopp) Willi's dog; his; **endlich war sie Sein** (geh. veralt.) at last she was his; **der/die/das ~e** (geh.) his; **die ~e** *od.* **Seine** (veralt.) his wife; **die ~en** *od.* **Seinen** (geh.) his family; **das ~e** *od.* **Seine** (Eigentum) what is his; **er hat das ~e** *od.* **Seine getan** (was er konnte) he has done what *or* all he could; (~ Teil) he has done his part *or* (coll.) bit; **jedem das ~e** *od.* **Seine** to each his own; (jeder nach ~em Geschmack) each to his own; **den ~en** *od.* **Seinen gibts der Herr im Schlaf** some people have all the luck

sein³ *Gen. der Personalpronomen* **er, es** (dichter. veralt.) ▸ **seiner**

Sein *das;* **~s** (Philos.) being; (Dasein) existence; **~ und Schein** appearance and reality

seiner (geh.)
A *Gen. des Personalpronomens* **er: sich ~ erbarmen** have pity on him; **~ gedenken** remember him
B *Gen. des Personalpronomens* **es: das Tier lag dort, bis sich jemand ~ annahm** the animal lay there until somebody came and looked after it

seiner-: ~seits *Adv.* for his part; (von ihm) on his part; **er ~seits wollte nichts davon wissen** he for his part wanted nothing to do with it; **er unternimmt auch ~seits nichts** he doesn't do anything himself either; **~zeit** *Adv.* **1** (damals) at that time; in those days; **2** (österr. veralt.: später) later; **~zeitig** *Adj.* **der ~zeitige Präsident** the President at that time; the then President; **die ~zeitigen Verhältnisse** the conditions prevailing then *or* at that time

seines·gleichen *indekl. Pron.* **1** (nach er) his own kind; people *pl.* like himself; **er verkehrt am liebsten mit ~:** he prefers to associate with his own kind; **der König hat mich wie ~ behandelt** the King treated me as an equal **2** (nach man) one's own kind **3** (nach es) **das Kind soll mit ~ spielen** the child should play with others its own age; **das sucht** *od.* **hat nicht ~:** it is without equal *or* is unequalled

seinet-: ~halben (veralt.), **~wegen** *Adv.* **1** (wegen seiner) because of him; on his account; **das Kind ist schon lange weg: die Mutter macht sich ~wegen Sorgen** the child's been gone for a long time: the mother is worried for him/her; **2** (ihm zuliebe, für ihn) for his sake; for him; **3** (von ihm aus) **er sagte, ~wegen sollten wir ruhig gehen** he said as far as he was concerned we could go; **~willen** *Adv. in* **um ~willen** for his sake; for him

seinige /ˈzainɪgə/ *Possessivpron.* (geh. veralt.) **der/die/das ~:** his; **er hat das ~** *od.* **Seinige getan** (was er konnte) he had done what *or* all he could; (sein Teil) he has done his part; **die ~** *od.* **Seinige** his wife; **die ~n** *od.* **Seinigen** his family

***sein|lassen** ▸ **sein¹ A 9**

seismisch
A *Adj.* seismological; (Erdbeben betreffend) seismic
B *adv.* seismologically

seismo-, Seismo- /zaismo-/: **~gramm** *das* seismogram; **~graph** *der* seismograph; **~graphisch A** *Adj.* seismographic; **B** *adv.* seismographically (also fig.); **~loge** *der;* **~~n, ~~n** ▸ℹ **S. 113** seismologist; **~logie** *die;* **~~:** seismology *no art.;* **~login** *die;* **~~, ~~nen** ▸ℹ **S. 113** seismologist

seit /zait/ ▸ℹ **S. 649**
A *Präp. mit Dat.* (Zeitpunkt) since; (Zeitspanne) for; **~ dem Zweiten Weltkrieg/1955/dem Unfall** since the Second World War/1955/the accident; **~ Wochen/Jahren/einiger Zeit** for weeks/years/some time [past]; **ich bin ~ zwei Wochen hier** I've been here [for] two weeks; **er geht ~ vier Wochen zur Schule** he has been going to school for four weeks; **~ damals, ~ der Zeit** since then; **~ wann hast du ihn nicht mehr gesehen?** when was the last time you saw him?
B *Konj.* since; **~ du hier wohnst** since you have been living here; **~ er das gehört hat** since he heard that

seit·dem
A *Adv.* since then; **das Haus steht ~ leer** since then the house has stood empty
B *Konj.* ▸ **seit B**

Seite /ˈzaitə/ *die;* **~, ~n 1** side; **auf** *od.* **zu beiden ~n der Straße/des Tores** on both sides of the road/gate; **die hintere/vordere ~:** the back/front; **mit der ~ nach vorne** sideways [on]; **zur** *od.* **auf die ~ gehen** *od.* **treten** move aside *or* to one side; move out of the way; **zur ~!** make way!; **die ~n wechseln** (Fußball) change ends; **ein Auto auf die ~ winken** wave a car [over] to the side [of the road]; **jmdn. zur ~ nehmen** take sb. aside; **etw. zur ~ legen** *od.* **räumen** move *or* put sth. to one side *or* aside; **etw. auf die ~ schaffen** (ugs.) help oneself to sth.; **etw. auf die ~ legen** (ugs.: sparen) put sth. away *or* aside; **zur ~** (Theater) aside; **die eine/die andere ~ der Medaille** (fig.) the one/the other side of the coin; **alles** *od.* **jedes Ding hat seine zwei ~n** (fig.) there are two sides to everything; **ich schlafe auf der ~:** I sleep on my side; **er ist auf einer ~ gelähmt** he's paralysed down one side; **ich wünsche dir, dass du an seiner ~ glücklich wirst** (geh.) I hope you'll be happy with him; **halte dich an meiner ~:** stay beside me *or* by my side; **~ an ~:** side by side; **~ an ~ kämpfen** (fig.) stand shoulder to shoulder and fight; **jmdm. zur ~ stehen** stand by sb.; **jmdm. nicht von der ~ gehen** *od.* **weichen** not move from *or* leave sb.'s side; **setz dich an meine grüne ~!** (scherzh.) come and sit by me *or* by my side; **jmdn. von der ~ ansehen** look at sb. from the side; (fig.) look at sb. askance; **eine ~ Speck** a side of bacon **2** (Richtung) side; **von allen ~n** (auch fig.) from all sides; **nach allen ~n** in all directions; (fig.) on all sides **3** (Buch~, Zeitungs~) page; **die erste/letzte ~** (eines Buchs) the first/last page; (einer Zeitung) the front/back page; **~ wie viel?** (ugs.) what page? **4** (Eigenschaft, Aspekt) side; **auf der einen ~, ... auf der anderen ~ ...** on the one hand ... on the other hand ...; **von der ~ kenne ich ihn noch nicht** I haven't seen that side of him yet; **etw. ist jmds. schwache ~** (ugs.) sth. is not exactly sb.'s forte; (ist jmds. Schwäche) sb. has a weakness for sth.; **jmds. starke ~ sein** (ugs.) be sb.'s forte *or* strong point; **sich von der besten ~ zeigen** show one's best side **5** (Partei) side; **sich auf jmds. ~** (*Akk.*) **schlagen** take sb.'s side; **die ~n wechseln** (fig.) change sides; **auf jmds. ~ stehen** *od.* **sein** be on sb.'s side; **jmdn. auf seine ~ bringen** *od.* **ziehen** win sb. over; **auf/von ~n der Direktion** on/from the management side; **von anderer/offizieller ~ verlautete, dass ...** it was learned from other/official sources that ...; **ich werde von meiner ~ aus nichts unternehmen** I for my part will not do anything **6** (Familie) side; **auf der väterlichen ~**

stammt sie von ... on her father's side she descends from ...

***seiten** *in* **auf/von ~ ▸Seite 5; aufseiten, vonseiten**

seiten-, Seiten-: ~airbag *der* (Kfz.-W.) side airbag; **~altar** *der* side altar; **~ansicht** *die* side view; (Aufriss) side elevation; **~arm** *der* arm; branch; **~ausgang** *der* side exit; **~blick** *der* sidelong look; (kurzer Blick) sidelong glance; **~eingang** *der* side entrance; **~flügel** *der* 1 (eines Gebäudes) wing; 2 (eines Flügelaltars) side panel; **~gebäude** *das* annex; (eines Bauernhofs o. Ä.) outbuilding; **~gewehr** *das* (Milit.) bayonet; **~halbierende** *die; adj. Dekl.* (Math.) median; **~hieb** *der* 1 (fig.) sideswipe (**auf** + *Akk.* at); 2 (Fechten) flank cut; **~lage** *die:* **in ~lage schlafen/schwimmen** sleep/swim on one's side; **den Verletzten in ~lage bringen** put the injured man on his side; **stabile ~lage** recovery position; **~lang** A *Adj.* ‹letter› that goes on for pages; B *adv.* **so geht es ~lang weiter!** it goes on like that for pages; **~leitwerk** *das* (Flugw.) vertical tail; **~linie** *die* 1 (Geneal.) offset; offshoot; 2 (Fußball, Rugby) touchline; (Tennis, Hockey, Federball) sideline; **~ruder** *das* (Flugw.) rudder

seitens *Präp. mit Gen.* (Papierdt.) on the part of; **~ der Arbeitgeber wird noch beraten** the employers are still discussing the matter

seiten-, Seiten-: ~schiff *das* [side] aisle; **~sprung** *der* infidelity; **einen ~sprung machen** have an affair; **~stechen** *das:* **~stechen haben/bekommen** have/get a stitch; **~straße** *die* side street; **eine ~straße der Schillerstraße** a side street off the Schillerstrasse; **~streifen** *der* verge; (einer Autobahn) hard shoulder; **„~streifen nicht befahrbar"** 'Soft Verges'; **~tal** *das* side valley; **~tasche** *die* side pocket; **~verkehrt** *Adj.* reversed; **~wand** *die* side wall; **~wechsel** *der* (Ballspiele) change of ends; **~wind** *der* side wind; crosswind; **~zahl** *die* 1 page number; 2 (Anzahl der Seiten) number of pages

seit·her *Adv.* since then; **~ habe ich ihn nicht gesprochen** I haven't spoken to him since [then]

seitherig *Adj.* **seine ~e Abwesenheit/Arbeit** his absence/work since then

-seitig *adj.* -page; **tausend~:** thousand-page *attrib.*; **ein mehrseitiger Brief/Bericht** a letter/report several pages long

seitlich

A *Adj.* **der Eingang ist ~:** the entrance is at the side; **ein ~er Wind** a side wind; a crosswind

B *adv.* (an der Seite) at the side; (von der Seite) from the side; (nach der Seite) to the side; **~ von jmdm. stehen** stand to the side of sb.; **~ gegen etw. prallen** crash sideways into sth.

C *Präp. mit Gen.* beside; to the side of

seitlings /'zaitlɪŋs/ *Adv.* (veralt.) **~ reiten** ride side-saddle; **~ schlafen/liegen/fallen** sleep/lie/fall on one's side

Seit·pferd *das* (Turnen) side horse; pommel horse

-seits *adv.* **französischer~:** from the French side; **ärztlicher~:** from the medical angle

seit·wärts

A *Adv.* 1 (zur Seite) sideways 2 (an, auf der Seite) to one side; **~ von etw.** to the side of sth.

B *Präp. mit Gen.* beside; to the side of

sek., Sek. *Abk.* = **Sekunde** sec.

Sekante /ze'kantə/ *die;* **~, ~n** (Math.) secant

sekkant /zɛ'kant/ (österr., sonst veralt.)

A *Adj.* tiresome

B *adv.* tiresomely

sekkieren *tr. V.* (österr., sonst veralt.) annoy; (bedrängen) pester

Sekret /ze'kre:t/ *das;* **~[e]s, ~e** (Med., Biol.) secretion

Sekretär /zekre'tɛ:ɐ̯/ *der;* **~s, ~e** 1 ▸❶ S. 113 secretary 2 ▸❶ S. 113 (Beamter) middle-ranking civil servant 3 (Schreibschrank) secretaire; secretary; bureau (Brit.) 4 (Zool.) secretary bird

Sekretariat /zekreta'ria:t/ *das;* **~[e]s, ~e** [secretary's/secretaries'] office

Sekretärin *die;* **~, ~nen** ▸❶ S. 113 secretary

Sekretion /zekre'tsi̯o:n/ *die;* **~, ~en** (Med., Biol.) secretion

Sekt /zɛkt/ *der;* **~[e]s, ~e** high-quality sparkling wine; ≈ champagne

Sekte /'zɛktə/ *die;* **~, ~n** sect

Sekten-: ~anhänger *der,* **~anhängerin** *die* member of a/the sect; **~führer** *der,* **~führerin** *die* leader of a/the sect; **~mitglied** *das* member of a/the sect

Sekt·flasche *die* champagne bottle

Sektierer *der;* **~s, ~, Sektiererin** *die;* **~, ~nen** sectarian; (Politik: Abweichler) deviationist

sektiererisch

A *Adj.* sectarian; (Politik) deviationist

B *adv.* in a sectarian way; (Politik) in a deviationist way

Sektierertum *das;* **~s** sectarianism; (Politik) deviationism

Sektion /zɛk'tsi̯o:n/ *die;* **~, ~en** 1 (Abteilung) section; (im Ministerium) department 2 (DDR: an Hochschulen) department 3 (Med.) autopsy; postmortem [examination] (+ *Gen.* on)

Sektions·chef *der,* **Sektions·chefin** *die* (österr.) *head of a ministry department*

Sekt-: ~kellerei *die* champagne producer's; (Gebäude) champagne cellars *pl.*; **~kühler** *der* champagne cooler; **~laune** *die* (scherzh.) champagne mood; (verrückte Laune) crazy mood

Sektor /'zɛktɔr/ *der;* **~s, ~en** /-'to:rən/ 1 (Fachgebiet) field; sphere; **industrieller/wirtschaftlicher ~:** industrial/economic sector 2 (Geom.; Besatzungszone) sector

Sektoren·grenze *die* sector boundary

Sekunda /ze'kʊnda/ *die;* **~, Sekunden** (Schulw.) 1 (veralt.) sixth and seventh years (*of a Gymnasium*) 2 (österr.) second year (*of a Gymnasium*)

Sekundaner *der;* **~s, ~, Sekundanerin** *die;* **~, ~nen** (Schulw.) 1 (veralt.) (Ober~) pupil in the seventh year (*of a Gymnasium*); (Unter~) pupil in the sixth year (*of a Gymnasium*) 2 (österr.) pupil in the second year (*of a Gymnasium*)

Sekundant /zekʊn'dant/ *der;* **~en, ~en, Sekundantin** *die;* **~, ~nen** second (*in a duel or match*)

sekundär /zekʊn'dɛ:ɐ̯/

A *Adj.* secondary

B *adv.* secondarily

Sekundar·lehrer *der,* **Sekundar·lehrerin** *die* (schweiz.) secondary-school teacher

Sekundär·literatur *die* secondary literature

Sekundar-: ~schule *die* (schweiz.) secondary school; **~stufe** *die* secondary stage (*of education*)

Sekunde /ze'kʊndə/ *die;* **~, ~n** 1 ▸❶ S. 729 (auch Math., Musik) second; **es ist auf die ~ 12 Uhr** it is twelve o'clock precisely; **meine Uhr geht auf die ~ genau** my watch keeps perfect time 2 (ugs.: Augenblick) second; moment

sekundenlang

A *Adj.* momentary

B *adv.* for a moment; momentarily

Sekunden-: ~schlaf *der* microsleep; **~schnelle** *die:* **in ~schnelle** in a matter of seconds; (blitzschnell) in a flash; **~zeiger** *der* second hand

sekundieren *itr. V.* (geh.) **jmdm. [bei etw.] ~:** support sb., back sb. up [in sth.]; **jmdm. [bei einem Duell] ~:** act as sb.'s second [in a duel]

Sekurit Ⓦⓩ /zeku'ri:t/ *das;* **~s** [toughened] safety glass

selb... /zɛlp.../ ▸**derselbe**

selber /'zɛlbɐ/ *indekl. Demonstrativpron.* ▸**selbst A**

Selber·machen *das;* **~s** (ugs.) do-it-yourself *no art.*; **Möbel zum ~:** furniture to make oneself *or* for the do-it-yourselfer

selbig *Demonstrativpron.* (veralt.) [the] same; **am ~en Tag** that same *or* very day

selbst /zɛlpst/

A *indekl. Demonstrativpron.* **ich/du/er ~:** I myself/you yourself/he himself; **wir/ihr ~:** we ourselves/you yourselves; **sie ~:** she herself; (*Pl.*) they themselves; **Sie ~:** you yourself; (*Pl.*) you yourselves; **das Haus/der König ~:** the house itself/the king himself; **du hast es ~ gesagt** you said so yourself; (stärker betont) you yourself said so; **ich habe nicht ~ mit ihm gesprochen** I didn't speak to him myself; **sie backt/kocht ~:** she does the baking/cooking herself; **~ gebacken** home-made; home-baked; **~ gebraut** home-brewed; **~ gemacht** home-made ‹*jam, liqueur, sausages, basket, etc.*›; self-made ‹*dress, pullover, etc.*;› ‹*dress, pullover, etc.*› one has made oneself; **~ gestrickt** home-made, hand-knitted; (fig. ugs.) homespun ‹*ideology etc.*›; **~ gedrehte Zigaretten** [one's own] rolled cigarettes; **mein erstes ~ verdientes Geld** the first money I earned myself; **~ verfasste Gedichte/Lieder** poems/songs of one's own composition; **er denkt nur an sich ~:** he only thinks of himself; **Wie geht's dir? — Gut! Und ~?** (ugs.) How are you? — Fine! And how about you?; **von ~:** automatically; **etw. läuft ganz von ~:** sth. runs itself *or* requires no attention; **es versteht sich von ~:** it goes without saying; **die Ruhe/Bescheidenheit ~ sein** (ugs.) be calmness/modesty itself; **~ ist der Mann** you have to get on and do things for yourself

B *adv.* even; **~ wenn er wollte** even if he wanted [to]

Selbst *das;* **~** (geh.) self; **das eigene ~:** one's own self

Selbst-: ~abholer *der,* **~abholerin** *die* 1 (Kaufmannsspr.) *buyer who collects the goods himself/herself*; **ein Möbelmarkt für ~abholer** a cash-and-carry furniture store; 2 (Postw.) *person who collects his post himself*; **~abholer sein** collect the post oneself; **~achtung** *die* self-respect; self-esteem

selb·ständig

A *Adj.* ▸❶ S. 113 independent; **an ~es Arbeiten gewöhnt sein** be used to working on one's own *or* independently; **ein ~er Unternehmer** a self-employed business man; **sich ~ machen** set up on one's own; (fig. scherzh.) ‹*pram, child, etc.*› take off [on its/his/her own]

B *adv.* independently; **~ arbeiten** work on one's own *or* independently; **~ denken** think for oneself

Selbständige *der/die; adj. Dekl.* ▸❶ S. 113 self-employed [business] person

Selbständigkeit *die;* **~:** independence

selbst-, Selbst-: ~anzeige *die* (Rechtsw.) self-denunciation; **~aufgabe** *die* sacrifice of one's identity; **~aufopferung** *die* self-sacrifice *no art.*; **unter großer ~aufopferung** at the cost of considerable self-sacrifice; **~ausbeutung** *die* self-exploitation; **~auslöser** *der* (Fot.) delayed-action shutter release; **~bedienung** *die* self-service *no art.*; **hier ist ~bedienung** it's self-service here; **~bedienungs·laden** *der; Pl.* **~bedienungsläden** self-service shop; **~befriedigung** *die* 1 masturbation *no art.*; 2 (fig.) **er tut das aus reiner ~befriedigung** he only does it for self-gratification; **~behauptung** *die* self-assertion *no art.*; **~beherrschung** *die* self-control *no art.*; **die ~beherrschung bewahren/verlieren** keep/lose one's self-control; **~beobachtung** *die* self-observation *no art.*; **~beschränkung** *die* self-restraint *no art.*; **in kluger ~beschränkung** wisely exercising self-restraint; **~besinnung** *die* (geh.) [inward] contemplation *no art.*; **~bestätigung** *die* (Psych.) self-affirmation *no art.*; **eine ~bestätigung** a boost to the ego; **~bestimmung** *die* self-determination *no art.*; **~bestimmungs·recht** *das* right of self-determination; **~beteiligung** *die* (Versicherungsw.) [personal] excess; **~betrug** *der* self-deception *no art.*; **~beweih·räucherung** *die* (ugs.) self-adulation *no art.*; **~bewusst, *~bewußt**

A *Adj.* 1 self-confident; self-possessed; 2 (Philos.) self-aware; B *adv.* self-confidently; **~bewusst·sein, *~bewußt·sein** *das* 1 self-confidence *no art.*; (einer sozialen Schicht o.

S

Ä.) self-assurance; **nationales ~bewusstsein** sense of national identity; **2** (Philos.) self-awareness *no art.*; **~bezogen** *Adj., adv.* ▸**ichbezogen**; **~bild** *das* ([Sozial]psych.) self-image; **~bildnis** *das* self-portrait; **~darstellung** *die* self-presentation; **~disziplin** *die* self-discipline *no art.*; **~einschätzung** *die* self-assessment *no art.*; self-appraisal *no art.*; **~entfaltung** *die* blossoming of one's personality; **sie hatte keine Möglichkeit zur ~entfaltung** there was no opportunity for her to develop as an individual; **~entfremdung** *die* (Soziol., Philos.) self-alienation *no art.*; **~erfahrungs·gruppe** *die* (Psych.) sensitivity group; **~erhaltung** *die* self-preservation *no art.*; **~erhaltungs·trieb** *der* instinct for self-preservation; survival instinct; **~erkenntnis** *die* self-knowledge *no art.*; **~erkenntnis ist der erste Schritt zur Besserung** knowing your faults is the first step towards curing them; **~fahrer** *der* **1** *person who drives a car himself/herself*; **Autovermietung an ~fahrer** self-drive car hire; **2** (Krankenfahrstuhl) self-propelled wheelchair; **~fahrerin** *die* ▸**~fahrer 1**; **~findung** *die; ~~:* self-discovery *no art.*; **~gebacken** ▸**selbst A**; **~gebrannte¹** *der; adj. Dekl.* home-made spirit; ≈ moonshine; **~gebrannte²** *die* home-made copy (*of a CD etc.*); **~gebraut** ▸**selbst A**; **~gedreht** ▸**selbst A**; **~gefällig** (abwertend) **A** *Adj.* self-satisfied; smug; **B** *adv.* smugly; in a self-satisfied way; **~gefälligkeit** *die* self-satisfaction; smugness; **~gemacht** ▸**selbst A**; **~genügsam** **A** *Adj.* modest [in one's demands]; **B** *adv.* modestly; **~gerecht** (abwertend) **A** *Adj.* self-righteous; **B** *adv.* self-righteously; **~gespräch** *das* conversation with oneself; **~gespräche führen** talk to oneself; **~gestrickt** ▸**selbst A**; **~hass**, ***~haß** *der* self-hatred; **~heilung** *die* self-healing; **~heilungs·kraft** *die* self-healing power; **~herrlich** **A** *Adj.* high-handed; autocratic ‹ruler, decision›; **B** *adv.* high-handedly; in a high-handed manner; ‹decide, rule› autocratically; **~hilfe** *die* self-help *no art.*; **Hilfe zur ~hilfe leisten** help people to help themselves; **~hilfe·gruppe** *die* self-help group; **~inszenierung** *die* self-promotion; **~ironie** *die* self-mockery; **~justiz** *die* self-administered justice; **~justiz üben** take the law into one's own hands; **~kasteiung** *die* self-chastisement; **~klebe·folie** *die* self-adhesive plastic sheeting; **~klebend** *Adj.* self-adhesive; **~kontrolle** *die* self-restraint; (in den Medien) self-regulation; **~korrektur** *die* self-correction; **~kosten** *Pl.* (Wirtsch.) prime costs; **~kosten·preis** *der* (Wirtsch.) cost price; **zum [reinen] ~kostenpreis** at [no more than] cost; **etw. unter dem ~kostenpreis abgeben** sell sth. below cost *or* at less than cost; **~kritik** *die* self-criticism; **~kritisch** **A** *Adj.* self-critical; **B** *adv.* self-critically; **~laut** *der* vowel; **~los** **A** *Adj.* selfless; **B** *adv.* selflessly; unselfishly; **~mitleid** *das* self-pity; **~montage** *die* self-assembly; **~mord** *der* suicide *no art.*; **~mord begehen** *od.* **verüben** commit suicide; **mit ~mord drohen** threaten [to commit] suicide; **~mord mit Messer und Gabel** (ugs. scherzh.) suicide by unhealthy eating; eating one's way to an early grave; **~mord·anschlag** *der,* **~mord·attentat** *das* suicide attack; **~mord·attentäter** *der,* **~mord·attentäterin** *die* suicide attacker; **~mörder** *der,* **~mörderin** *die* suicide; **~mörderisch** *Adj.* suicidal

selbstmord-, Selbstmord-: **~gedanken** *Pl.* thoughts of suicide; **sich mit ~gedanken tragen** contemplate suicide; **~gefährdet** *Adj.* potentially suicidal; **~kandidat** *der,* **~kandidatin** *die* potential suicide; **~kommando** *das* suicide squad; **~versuch** *der* suicide attempt; **einen ~versuch unternehmen** attempt suicide

selbst-, Selbst-: **~porträt** *das* self-portrait; **~redend** *Adv.* naturally; of course; ***~schuß**, **~schuss** *der* automatic firing device; **~schutz** *der* self-protection *no art.*; **~sicher** **A** *Adj.* self-confident; **B** *adv.* in a self-confident manner; full of self-confidence; **~sicherheit** *die* self-confidence; **~ständig** *usw.* ▸**selbständig** *usw.*; **~studium** *das* self-study; private study; **im ~studium** through self-study; by studying on one's own; **~sucht** *die* selfishness; self-interest; **~süchtig** **A** *Adj.* selfish; **B** *adv.* selfishly; **~tätig** **A** *Adj.* automatic; **B** *adv.* automatically; **~täuschung** *die* self-deception; delusion; **~tötung** *die* (Amtsspr.) suicide; **~überschätzung** *die* overestimation of one's abilities; **er leidet an ~überschätzung** (ugs.) he has an exaggerated opinion of himself; **~überwindung** *die* will power *no indef. art.*; **das kostete mich viel ~überwindung** I really had to force myself to do it; **~verachtung** *die* self-contempt; **~verbrennung** *die* self-immolation *no art.* [by burning]; **~verdient** ▸**selbst A**; **~verfaßt** ▸**selbst A**; **~vergessen** (ugs.) **A** *Adj.* oblivious of all around one *postpos.*; lost to the world *postpos.*; **B** *adv.* obliviously; **~verlag** *der* private publishing venture; **~verleugnung** *die* self-denial; **~vernichtung** *die* self-destruction; **~verschulden** *das* (Amtsspr.) **das war ~verschulden** it was his/their *etc.* own fault; **~verschuldet** *Adj.* **~verschuldete Unfälle** accidents for which people are themselves to blame; **deine Notlage ist ~verschuldet** you have brought your predicament on yourself; **~versorger** *der,* **~versorgerin** *die* self-sufficient person; (im Urlaub) self-caterer; **~verständlich** **A** *Adj.* natural; **es war für ihn ~verständlich** it was completely natural *or* a matter of course for him; **etw. für ~verständlich halten, etw. als ~verständlich betrachten** regard sth. as a matter of course; (für gegeben hinnehmen) take sth. for granted; **das ist doch ~verständlich** that goes without saying; **B** *adv.* naturally; of course; **~verständlich nicht!** of course not!; **~verständlichkeit** *die* matter of course; **ein Badezimmer ist heute eine ~verständlichkeit** a bathroom is no longer considered a luxury; **etw. mit der größten ~verständlichkeit tun** do sth. as if it were the most natural thing in the world; **~verständnis** *das* conception of oneself; **~verstümmelung** *die* self-mutilation; self-inflicted injury; **~verteidigung** *die* self-defence *no art.*; **~vertrauen** *das* self-confidence; **~verwaltung** *die* self-government *no art.*; **~verwirklichung** *die* self-realization *no art.*; **~wähl·fern·dienst** *der* (Postw.) direct dialling; STD; **~wahrnehmung** *die* self-perception; **~wert·gefühl** *das* (Psych.) [sense of] self-esteem; **~zerstörerisch** *Adj.* self-destructive; **~zerstörung** *die* self-destruction; **~zufrieden** (oft abwertend) **A** *Adj.* self-satisfied; **B** *adv.* in a self-satisfied manner; smugly; **~zweck** *der* end in itself; **~zweck sein/zum ~zweck werden** be/become an end in itself

selchen /ˈzɛlçn̩/ *tr. V.* (bayr., österr.) smoke ‹meat, ham, etc.›

selektieren /zelɛkˈtiːrən/
A *tr. V.* select; pick out
B *itr. V.* make a choice; **~de Methoden** selective methods

Selektion *die; ~, ~en* selection

selektiv
A *Adj.* selective
B *adv.* selectively; on a selective basis

Selen /zeˈleːn/ *das; ~s* (Chemie) selenium

Selfmademan /ˈzɛlfmeːtmɛn/ *der; ~s,* **Selfmademen** self-made man

selig /ˈzeːlɪç/
A *Adj.* **1** (Rel.) blessed; **jmdn. ~ preisen** declare sb. blessed; **bis an sein ~es Ende** until his dying day; **Gott hab ihn ~:** God rest his soul; *s. auch* **Angedenken**; **geben 1**; **glauben 2** **2** (tot) late [lamented]; **Schwester Modesta ~** (veralt.) Sister Modesta of blessed memory **3** (kath. Kirche) **die ~e Dorothea** the blessed Dorothy; **jmdn. ~ sprechen** beatify sb. **4** (glücklich) blissful ‹idleness, slumber, etc.›; blissfully happy ‹person›; **~ [über etw.** (*Akk.*)**] sein** be overjoyed *or* (coll.) over the moon [about sth.]; **werde ~ mit deinem Geld!** (ugs.) you can keep *or* (sl.) stuff your money; **jmdn./sich ~ preisen** (geh.) consider s.b./onself remarkably fortunate
B *adv.* blissfully

Selige *der/die; adj. Dekl.* **1** (veralt., noch scherzh.) **mein ~r/meine ~:** my late lamented *or* dear departed husband/wife **2** *Pl.* **die ~n** (die Toten) the blessed spirits [of the departed]; **die Gefilde der ~n** the Elysian fields **3** (kath. Kirche: Seliggesprochene[r]) beatified person

Seligkeit *die; ~, ~en* **1** (Rel.) [state of] blessedness; beatitude; **die ewige ~:** eternal bliss; **von dieser Reise hängt doch nicht seine ~ ab** (fig.) he won't be heartbroken if he doesn't go on this trip **2** (Glücksgefühl) bliss *no pl.*; [blissful] happiness *no pl.*

selig-, Selig-: ***~|preisen** ▸**selig A1, 4**; **~preisung** *die; ~~, ~~en:* **die ~preisungen** (bibl.) the Beatitudes; **~|sprechen** ▸**selig A 3**; **~sprechung** *die; ~, ~en* (kath. Kirche) beatification

Sellerie /ˈzɛləri/ *der; ~s, ~[s] od. die; ~, ~* (Stauden~) celeriac; (Stangen~) celery

selten /ˈzɛltn̩/
A *Adj.* rare; infrequent ‹visit, visitor›; **in den ~sten Fällen** very rarely; **seine Besuche sind ~ geworden** his visits have become few and far between; **ein ~er Vogel** (fig. ugs.) an odd character; a queer fish (coll.)
B *adv.* **1** rarely; **wir sehen uns nur noch ~:** we seldom *or* hardly ever see each other now; **ein Sommer wie ~ einer** a summer such as is only too rare; **~ so gelacht!** that was a good laugh!; (iron.: gar nicht komisch) very funny[, I don't think] **2** (sehr) exceptionally; uncommonly

Seltenheit *die; ~, ~en* rarity; **es ist eine ~, dass ...** it is rare that ...

Seltenheits·wert *der; ~[es]* rarity value

Selters·wasser /ˈzɛltɐs-/ *das; Pl.* **Selters·wässer** seltzer [water]

seltsam
A *Adj.* strange; peculiar; odd; **alt und ~ werden** become rather odd in one's old age
B *adv.* strangely; peculiarly

seltsamerweise *Adv.* strangely enough

Seltsamkeit *die; ~, ~en* **1** (Art) strangeness; oddness **2** (Ereignis, Merkmal) peculiarity; oddity

Semantik /zeˈmantɪk/ *die; ~* (Sprachw.) semantics *sing., no art.*

semantisch (Sprachw.)
A *Adj.* semantic
B *adv.* semantically

Semasiologie /zemaziolo'giː/ *die; ~* (Sprachw.) semasiology *no art.*

Semester /zeˈmɛstɐ/ *das; ~s, ~* **1** semester; **er hat 14 ~ Jura studiert** he studied law for seven years; **Studenten des dritten ~s** students in their third semester; ≈ second-year students **2** (ugs.: Student) **ein höheres ~:** a senior student; **die ersten ~:** the first-year students; **ein älteres ~** (fig. scherzh.) a member of the older generation

Semesterferien *Pl.* [university] vacation *sing.*

semi-, Semi- /zemi-/ semi-

Semi·finale *das* (Sport) semi-final

Semikolon /zemiˈkoːlɔn/ *das; ~s, ~s od.* **Semikola** semicolon

Seminar /zemiˈnaːɐ̯/ *das; ~s, ~e, österr., schweiz. auch* **~ien** /...i̯ən/ **1** (Lehrveranstaltung) seminar (**über** + *Akk.* on) **2** (Institut) department; **das juristische ~/~ für Alte Geschichte** the Law Department/Department of Ancient History **3** (Priester~) seminary **4** (für Referendare) *course for student teachers prior to their second state examination*

Seminar·arbeit *die* seminar paper

Seminarist *der; ~en, ~en,* **Seminaristin** *die; ~, ~nen* seminarist

Seminar-: **~leiter** *der,* **~leiterin** *die* seminar leader; **~schein** *der* certificate of attendance [at a seminar]; **~teilnehmer**

der, **~teilnehmerin** *die* seminar participant *or* member

Semiotik /ze'mi̯o:tɪk/ *die;* ~ (Philos., Sprachw.) semiotics *sing., no art.*

semi·professionell
A *Adj.* semi-professional
B *adv.* semi-professionally

Semit /ze'mi:t/ *der;* **~en, ~en, Semitin** *die;* **~, ~nen** Semite

semitisch *Adj.* Semitic

Semmel /'zɛml̩/ *die;* **~, ~n** (bes. österr., bayr., ostmd.) [bread] roll; **weggehen wie warme ~n** (ugs.) sell like hot cakes

semmel-, Semmel-: ~blond *Adj.* flaxen ‹*hair*›; flaxen-haired ‹*person*›; **~brösel** *der od. österr.: das* breadcrumb; **~knödel** *der* (bayr., österr.) bread dumpling

sen. *Abk.* **= senior** sen.

Senat /ze'na:t/ *der;* **~[e]s, ~e** [1] (Hist., Politik, Hochschulw.) senate; **der US-~:** the US Senate [2] (an Gerichten) panel of judges

Senator *der;* **~s, ~en, Senatorin** *die;* **~, ~nen** senator; **Herr Senator X** Senator X

Senats·ausschuss, *Senats·ausschuß *der* senate committee

Send·bote *der,* **Send·botin** *die* (veralt.) envoy; (fig.) ambassador

Sende- /'zɛndə-/: **~anlage** *die* (Elektrot.) transmitter; **~bereich** *der* (Rundf., Ferns.) transmitting area; **~folge** *die* (Rundf., Ferns.) [1] (Reihenfolge) sequence [of programmes]; [2] (einer Geschichte) episode; **~format** *das* (Rundf., Ferns.) programme format; **~gebiet** *das* (Rundf., Ferns.) ▸ **~bereich; ~mast** *der* transmitter mast

senden[1] *unr. (auch regelm.) tr. V.* (geh.) send; **jmdm. etw. ~:** send sb. sth.; **etw. an jmdn. ~:** send sth. to sb.; **wir ~ Ihnen die Waren ins Haus** we will despatch the goods to you at your home address

senden[2] *regelm. (schweiz. unr.) tr., itr. V.* broadcast ‹*programme, play, etc.*›; transmit ‹*concert, signals, Morse, etc.*›; **Hilferufe ~:** send out distress signals

Sende-: ~pause *die* (Rundf., Ferns.) intermission; **~platz** *der* (Rundf., Ferns.) spot on the schedule

Sender *der;* **~s, ~:** [broadcasting] station; (Anlage) transmitter

Sende-: ~raum *der* (Rundf., Ferns.) [broadcasting] studio; **~reihe** *die* (Rundf., Ferns.) series [of programmes]

Sender·such·lauf *der* (Rundf., Ferns.) [automatic] station search

Sende-: ~saal *der* (Rundf., Ferns.) [broadcasting] studio; **~schluss, *~schluß** *der* (Rundf., Ferns.) close-down; end of broadcasting; **zum ~schluss noch ein Krimi** now as our last programme, a thriller; **~station** *die* (Funk, Rundf., Ferns.) broadcasting station; (Anlage) transmitter; **~termin** *der* (Rundf., Ferns.) time of transmission; **~termin 15. April** to be broadcast on April 15th; **~zeit** *die* (Rundf., Ferns.) broadcasting time; **die ~zeit um zehn Minuten überschreiten** overrun by ten minutes; **~zentrale** *die* (Rundf., Ferns.) main studio; **wir geben zurück in die ~zentrale** we return you to the studio

Sendschreiben *das* (veralt.) circular letter; (des Papstes) encyclical

Sendung *die;* **~, ~en** [1] consignment [2] (geh.: Aufgabe) mission [3] (Rundf., Ferns.: Darbietung) programme; broadcast [4] (Rundfunkt., Ferns.: Ausstrahlung) transmission; broadcast[ing]; **auf ~ sein** be on the air

Sendungs·bewusstsein, *Sendungs·bewußtsein *das* sense of mission

Senegal /'ze:negal/ *(das);* **~s** *od. der;* **~[s] [der] ~:** Senegal

Senegalese /zenega'le:zə/ *der;* **~n, ~n, Senegalesin** *die;* **~, ~nen** Senegalese

Seneschall /'ze:nəʃal/ *der;* **~s, ~e** (hist.) seneschal

Senf /zɛnf/ *der;* **~[e]s, ~e** mustard; **seinen ~ dazugeben** (fig. ugs.) get one's word in *or* have one's say

Senf-: ~gas *das* mustard gas; **~gurke** *die: gherkin pickled with mustard seeds;* **~korn** *das* mustard seed; **~soße** *die* mustard sauce; **~topf** *der* mustard pot

Senge /'zɛŋə/ *Pl.* (ostmd. ugs.) ▸ **Prügel 2**

sengen
A *tr. V.* singe
B *itr. V.* [1] (brennen) singe [2] (heiß sein) be scorching; **eine ~de Hitze** a scorching heat [3] **~ und brennen** (veralt.) burn and pillage

senil /ze'ni:l/
A *Adj.* (Med., auch abwertend) senile
B *adv.* in a senile manner

Senilität *die;* ~ (Med., auch abwertend) senility

senior /'ze:ni̯ɔr/ *indekl. Adj.; nach Personennamen* senior

Senior *der;* **~s, ~en** /ze'ni̯o:rən/ [1] (Kaufmannsspr.) senior partner [2] (Sport) senior [player] [3] (Rentner) senior citizen [4] (Ältester) oldest member [5] (scherzh.: Vater) old man (coll.) [6] (Werbesprache: älterer Mensch) older person

Senior·chef *der,* **Senior·chefin** *die* (Kaufmannsspr.) boss (coll.) (*in a family firm*)

Senioren-: ~heim *das* home for the elderly; **~mannschaft** *die* senior team; **~meister** *der* [1] senior champion; [2] (Mannschaft) senior champions *pl.;* **~meisterin** *die* ▸ **~meister 1**

Seniorin /ze'ni̯o:rɪn/ *die;* **~, ~nen** ▸ **Senior 1, 2, 4**

Senk·blei *das* (Bauw.) plumb [bob]

Senke /'zɛŋkə/ *die;* **~, ~n** hollow

Senkel /'zɛŋkl̩/ *der;* **~s, ~** [1] (Schnür~) shoelace [2] **jmdn. in den ~ stellen** (ugs.) put sb. in his/her place

senken
A *tr. V.* [1] lower; (Bergbau) sink ‹*shaft*›; lower ‹*flag*›; drop ‹*starting flag*›; **den Kopf ~:** bow one's head; **die Augen** *od.* **den Blick/die Stimme ~:** lower one's eyes *or* glance/voice; **mit gesenktem Blick** with [one's] eyes cast down [2] (herabsetzen) reduce ‹*fever, pressure, prices, etc.*› [3] (Technik) countersink ‹*hole*›
B *refl. V.* ‹*curtain, barrier, etc.*› fall, come down; ‹*ground, building, road*› subside, sink; ‹*water level*› fall, sink; ‹*lift cage*› go down, descend; **sein Brustkorb hob und senkte sich** his chest rose and fell

senk-, Senk-: ~fuß *der* (Anat.) flat foot; **~grube** *die* (Bauw.) cesspit; **~kasten** *der* (Technik) caisson; **~lot** *das* (Technik) plumb [bob]; **~recht A** *Adj.* vertical; **~rechte Linie** (Geom.) perpendicular line; perpendicular; **in ~rechter Stellung** in an upright position; **bleib** *od.* **halt dich ~recht!** (ugs.) stay upright *or* (coll.) on your two pins; **das ist das einzig Senkrechte** (ugs.) that's the only thing worth doing/eating/reading *etc.;* **B** *adv.* vertically; **~recht aufeinander stehen** (Geom.) be perpendicular *or* at right angles to each other; **~recht von oben** from vertically above; **~rechte** *die; adj. Dekl.* [1] (Geom.) perpendicular; [2] vertical line; vertical; upright; **~recht·starter** *der* [1] (Flugzeug) vertical take-off aircraft; [2] (ugs.) (Aufsteiger) whizz-kid (coll.); (Sache) instant success; **~recht·starterin** *die;* **~~, ~~nen** (ugs.) whizz-kid (coll.)

Senkung *die;* **~, ~en** [1] lowering [2] (Reduzierung) reduction; lowering; **eine ~ des Preises um 5%** a reduction of the price by 5% [3] (Geol.) [case of] subsidence [4] (Verslehre) unstressed syllable

Senk·waage *die* hydrometer

Senne /'zɛnə/ *die;* **~, ~n** (bayr., österr.) Alpine pasture

Senner *der;* **~s, ~** (bayr., österr.) *Alpine herdsman and dairyman*

Sennerin *die;* **~, ~nen** (bayr., österr.) *Alpine herdswoman and dairywoman*

Sennes·blätter /'zɛnəs-/ *Pl.* senna leaves

Senn·hütte *die* (bayr., österr.) Alpine hut

Sensation /zɛnza'tsi̯o:n/ *die;* **~, ~en** sensation; (Darbietung) sensational performance; **~en sehen wollen** want to see something sensational *or* spectacular

sensationell
A *Adj.* sensational
B *adv.* in a sensational manner; sensationally; **eine ~ aufgemachte Story** a sensationalized story

Sensations-: ~gier *die* (abwertend) craving for sensation; **~meldung** *die* sensational report *or* piece of news; **~prozess, *~prozeß** *der* sensational trial

Sense /'zɛnzə/ *die;* **~, ~n** [1] scythe [2] (salopp) **jetzt ist ~:** this really is [the end of] it (coll.)

Sensen·mann *der* (verhüll.) Great Reaper

sensibel /zɛn'zi:bl̩/
A *Adj.* sensitive
B *adv.* sensitively

Sensibelchen *das;* **~s, ~** (ugs.) sensitive soul

sensibilisieren *tr. V.* [1] (geh.) make ‹*person*› more sensitive (**für** to) [2] (Physiol.) sensitize

Sensibilität *die;* **~:** sensitivity

sensitiv /zɛnzi'ti:f/ *Adj.* sensitive

Sensor /'zɛnzɔr/ *der;* **~s, ~en** /-'zo:rən/ (Technik) [1] sensor [2] ▸ **~taste**

Sensorik *die;* **~** [1] (Sensoren) system of sensors; (bei Lebewesen) sense organs [2] (Disziplin) sensor technology

sensorisch *Adj.* (Physiol.) sensory

Sensorium /zɛn'zo:ri̯ʊm/ *das;* **~s, Sensorien** /...ri̯ən/ (Physiol.) sensorium

Sensor·taste *die* (Technik) touch panel; touch pad (Computing)

Sensualismus *der;* **~** (Philos.) sensationalism

Sentenz /zɛn'tɛnts/ *die;* **~, ~en** aphorism; maxim

sentimental /zɛntimɛn'ta:l/
A *Adj.* sentimental
B *adv.* sentimentally

Sentimentalität *die;* **~, ~en** sentimentality; **das sind bloße/überflüssige ~en** that is mere/unnecessary sentimentality

separat /zepa'ra:t/
A *Adj.* separate; **~e Wohnung** self-contained flat (esp. Brit.) *or* (esp. Amer.) apartment
B *adv.* separately; **er wohnt ~:** he has self-contained accommodation

Separat·friede[n] *der* separate peace [treaty]

Separatismus *der;* **~:** separatism *no art.*

Separatist *der;* **~en, ~en, Separatistin** *die;* **~, ~nen** separatist

separatistisch *Adj.* separatist

Separee, Séparée/zepa're:/ *das;* **~s, ~s** private room

separieren *tr. V.* separate

Sepia /'ze:pi̯a/ *die;* **~, Sepien** [1] (Tier) cuttlefish [2] (Farbstoff) sepia

Sepia·zeichnung *die* sepia drawing

Sepp[e]l·hose /'zɛpl̩-/ *die* (scherzh.) lederhosen *pl.*

Sepsis /'zɛpsɪs/ *die;* **~, Sepsen** ▸ ❶ **S. 439** (Med.) sepsis

Sept. *Abk.* **= September** Sept.

September /zɛp'tɛmbɐ/ *der;* **~[s], ~** ▸ ❶ **S. 165** September; *s. auch* **April**

Septett /zɛp'tɛt/ *das;* **~[e]s, ~e** (Musik) septet

Septime /zɛp'ti:mə/ *die;* **~, ~n** (Musik) seventh

septisch *Adj.* (Med.) septic

Septuaginta /zɛptu̯a'gɪnta/ *die;* **~:** Septuagint

Sequenz /ze'kvɛnts/ *die;* **~, ~en** sequence

sequestrieren /zekvɛs'tri:rən/ *tr. V.* (Rechtsw.) sequestrate; sequester

Serail /ze'ra:j/ *das;* **~s, ~s** seraglio

Seraph /'ze:raf/ *der;* **~s, ~e** *od.* **~im** (Rel.) seraph

Serbe /'zɛrbə/ *der;* **~n, ~n** Serb; Serbian; **~ sein** be a Serb *or* Serbian

Serbien /'zɛrbi̯ən/ *(das);* **~s** Serbia

Serbien und Montenegro /... mɔntə'ne:gro/ *(das);* **~s** Serbia and Montenegro

S

Serbin *die;* ~, ~nen ▸Serbe

serbisch *Adj.* ▸❶ **S. 670** Serbian; *s. auch* **deutsch**; **Deutsch**; **Deutsche²**

serbo·kroatisch /zɛrbokro'a:tɪʃ/ *Adj.* ▸❶ **S. 670** Serbo-Croat; *s. auch* **deutsch**; **Deutsch**; **Deutsche²**

Serenade /zere'na:də/ *die;* ~, ~n (Musik) serenade

Sergeant /zɛr'ʒant/ *der;* ~en, ~en *od.* (bei engl. Ausspr.:) /'sa:dʒənt/ ~s, ~s (Milit.) sergeant

Serie /'ze:ri̯ə/ *die;* ~, ~n 1 series; **eine ~ Briefmarken** a set of stamps; **etw. in ~ herstellen** *od.* **fertigen** produce *or* manufacture sth. in series; **in ~ gehen** go into [series *or* full-scale] production 2 ▸**Fernsehserie**

seriell *Adj.* (Musik) serial

serien-, Serien-: ~**fertigung** *die* series production; ~**held** *der,* ~**heldin** *die* leading character in a/the serial; (einer Seifenoper) soap hero/heroine; ~**mäßig** A *Adj.* standard ‹*product, model, etc.*›; (immer eingebaut) ‹*feature, accessory*› fitted as standard; B *adv.* 1 ~**mäßig gefertigt** *od.* **gebaut** produced in series; 2 (nicht als Sonderausstattung) ‹*fitted, supplied, etc.*› as standard; ~**mäßig mit etw. ausgerüstet sein** have sth. as a standard fitting; ~**mörder** *der,* ~**mörderin** *die* serial killer; ~**produktion** *die* series production; ~**reif** *Adj.* ready for [series] production *postpos.*; production ‹*version, model*›; ~**weise** *Adv.* 1 ~**weise gebaut** *od.* **hergestellt werden** be in series production; 2 (ugs.: in großer Zahl) en masse; wholesale

Serigraphie /zerigra'fi:/ *die;* ~, ~n serigraphy *no art.*

seriös /ze'ri̯ø:s/
A *Adj.* 1 (solide) respectable ‹*person, hotel, etc.*›; (vertrauenswürdig) reliable, trustworthy ‹*firm, partner, etc.*› 2 (ernst gemeint) serious ‹*offer, applicant, artist, etc.*›
B *adv.* 1 (solide) respectably; (vertrauenswürdig) in a trustworthy manner 2 (ernst gemeint) seriously

Seriosität /zeri̯ozi'tɛ:t/ *die;* ~ (geh.) 1 (Solidität) respectability; (Vertrauenswürdigkeit) reliability; trustworthiness; (eines Geschäftsmanns, einer Firma) probity 2 (Ernsthaftigkeit) seriousness

Sermon /zɛr'mo:n/ *der;* ~s, ~e 1 (veralt.: Predigt) sermon 2 (abwertend: langatmige Rede) [long] lecture

serologisch *Adj.* serological

Serotonin /zeroto'ni:n/ *das;* ~s, ~e (Biol.) serotonin

Serpentine /zɛrpɛn'ti:nə/ *die;* ~, ~n 1 (Weg) zigzag mountain road (*with numerous hairpin bends*) 2 (Kehre) hairpin bend

Serum /'ze:rʊm/ *das;* ~s, **Seren** *od.* **Sera** (Med., Physiol.) serum

Server /'sə:vɐ/ *der;* ~s, ~ (DV) server

Service¹ /zɛr'vi:s/ *das;* ~, ~: [dinner *etc.*] service

Service² /'zø:ɐ̯vɪs/ *der od. das;* ~, ~s /'zø:ɐ̯vɪsɪs/ 1 (Bedienung, Kundendienst) service; (Kundendienstabteilung) service department 2 (Tennis: Aufschlag) serve; service; **beim ~:** when serving

Service-: ~**center** *das* service centre; ~**leistung** *die* service

servieren /zɛr'vi:rən/
A *tr. V.* 1 (auftragen) serve ‹*food, drink*›; (fig.) serve up ‹*information*›; deliver ‹*line, punchline, etc.*›; **jmdm. etw. ~:** serve sb. sth. 2 (Ballspiele) **jmdm. den Ball ~:** feed/(Tennis) serve the ball to sb.
B *itr. V.* 1 serve [at table]; **gleich wird serviert** dinner/lunch *etc.* is [about to be] served 2 (Fußball) pass; make a pass; (Tennis) serve

Serviererin *die;* ~, ~nen ▸❶ **S. 113** waitress

Servier-: ~**tochter** *die* (schweiz.) waitress; ~**wagen** *der* [serving] trolley

Serviette /zɛr'vi̯ɛtə/ *die;* ~, ~n napkin; serviette (Brit.)

Servietten·ring *der* napkin *or* (Brit.) serviette ring

servil /zɛr'vi:l/ (geh. abwertend)
A *Adj.* obsequious; servile
B *adv.* obsequiously; in a servile manner

Servilität *die;* ~ (geh. abwertend) servility; obsequiousness

Servo- /'zɛrvo-/: ~**bremse** *die* servo[-assisted] brake; ~**lenkung** *die* power[-assisted] steering *no indef. art.*

servus /'zɛrvʊs/ *Interj.* (bes. südd., österr.) (beim Abschied) goodbye; so long (coll.); (zur Begrüßung) hello

Sesam /'ze:zam/ *der;* ~s, ~s 1 (Pflanze) sesame; (Samen) sesame seeds *pl.* 2 **~, öffne dich!** open sesame!

Sesam·brötchen *das* sesame-seed roll

Sessel /'zɛsl̩/ *der;* ~s, ~ 1 easy chair; (mit Armlehne) armchair 2 (österr.: Stuhl) chair

Sessel-: ~**lehne** *die* chair back; ~**lift** *der* chairlift

sesshaft, *seßhaft /'zɛshaft/ *Adj.* settled ‹*tribe, way of life*›; ~ **werden** settle [down]

Sesshaftigkeit, *Seßhaftigkeit *die;* ~: settled way of life

Session /zɛ'si̯o:n/ *die;* ~, ~en (bes. Parl.) [parliamentary *etc.*] session

Set /zɛt/ *das od. der;* ~[s], ~s 1 (Satz) set, combination (**aus** of) 2 (Deckchen) table mat; place mat 3 (Sozialpsych.) set

Setter *der;* ~s, ~: setter

Setup /'sɛtlap/ *das;* ~s, ~s 1 (DV) setup 2 (Anordnung) set-up

Setz·ei *das* (bes. nordostd.) ▸**Spiegelei**

setzen /'zɛtsn̩/
A *refl. V.* 1 (hin~) sit [down]; **setz dich/setzt euch/~ Sie sich** sit down; take a seat; **sich aufs Sofa/in den Sessel/in den Schatten** *usw.* **~:** sit on the sofa/in the chair/in the shade *etc.*; **sich zu jmdm. ~:** [go and] sit with sb.; join sb.; **setz dich zu uns** come and sit with us; **der Vogel setzte sich auf seine Schulter** the bird landed *or* alighted on his shoulder; **sich an den Tisch** *od.* **zu Tisch ~:** sit [down] at the table 2 (sinken) ‹*coffee, solution, froth, etc.*› settle; ‹*sediment*› sink to the bottom; **das Erdreich setzt sich** there is some settlement *or* subsidence 3 (in präp. Verbindungen) **sich mit jmdm. ins Einvernehmen ~:** come to an agreement with sb.; *s. auch* **Spitze 4, 5**; **Unrecht 2**; **Verbindung 8**; **Wehr** 4 (dringen) **der Staub/Geruch/Rauch setzt sich in die Kleider** the dust/smell/smoke gets into one's clothes
B *tr. V.* 1 (platzieren) put; **ein Kind jmdm. auf den Schoß ~:** put *or* sit a child on sb.'s lap; **ein Schiff auf Grund ~:** run a ship aground; **eine Figur/einen Stein ~:** move a piece/man; *s. auch* **Fuß 1** 2 (einpflanzen) plant ‹*tomatoes, potatoes, etc.*› 3 (aufziehen) hoist ‹*flag etc.*›; set ‹*sails, navigation lights*› 4 (Druckw.) set ‹*manuscript etc.*› 5 (schreiben) put ‹*name, address, comma, etc.*›; **seinen Namen unter etw.** (*Akk.*) **~:** put one's signature to sth.; sign sth.; **einen Punkt/ein Komma [falsch] ~:** put a full stop/comma [in the wrong place] 6 (in präp. Verbindungen) **jmdn. auf schmale Kost ~:** put sb. on short rations; **in/außer Betrieb ~:** start up/stop ‹*machine etc.*›; put ‹*lift etc.*› into operation/take ‹*lift etc.*› out of service; (ein-/ausschalten) switch on/off; **jmdn. in Erstaunen ~** (geh.) astonish sb.; *s. auch* **Fuß 2**; **Musik 1**; **Stelle 1**; **Szene 1**; **Trab**; **Umlauf 2**; **Werk 1**; **Wort 2**; **Zeitung** 7 (aufstellen) put up, build ‹*stove*›; stack ‹*logs, bricks*›; *s. auch* **Denkmal** 8 **sein Geld auf etw.** (*Akk.*) **~:** put one's money on sth.; **seine Hoffnungen auf jmdn. ~:** place one's hopes in sb.; *s. auch* **Vertrauen** 9 (festlegen) set ‹*limit, deadline*›; **einer Sache** (*Dat.*) **Grenzen** *od.* **Schranken ~:** keep sth. within limits; **sich** (*Dat.*) **ein Ziel ~:** set oneself a goal; *s. auch* **Akzente**; **Ende**; **Priorität**; **Zeichen 2** 10 (ugs.) **es setzt was** *od.* **Prügel** *od.* **Hiebe** he/she *etc.* gets a hiding (coll.) *or* thrashing 11 (Jägerspr.: zur Welt bringen) give birth to
C *itr. V.* 1 *meist mit sein* (im Sprung) leap, jump (**über** + *Akk.* over); **über einen Fluss ~** (mit einer Fähre o. Ä.) cross a river 2 (beim Wetten) bet; **auf ein Pferd/auf Rot ~:** back a horse/put one's money on red 3 (Jägerspr.: Junges, Junge zur Welt bringen) give birth

Setzer *der;* ~s, ~ (Druckw.) [type]setter

Setzerei *die;* ~, ~en (Druckw.) composing room

Setzerin *die;* ~, ~nen ▸**Setzer**

Setz-: ~**fehler** *der* (Druckw.) setting error; misprint; ~**holz** *das* dibber; dibble; ~**kasten** *der* 1 (Gartenbau) seedling box; 2 (Druckw.) [type] case

Setzling /'zɛtslɪŋ/ *der;* ~s, ~e 1 (Pflanze) seedling 2 (Fisch) young fish; ~**e** fry *pl.*

Setz·maschine *die* (Druckw.) composing *or* typesetting machine

Seuche /'zɔy̯çə/ *die;* ~, ~n epidemic; (fig.) scourge

seuchen-, Seuchen-: ~**artig** A *Adj.* epidemic-like; B *adv.* ‹*spread*› like an epidemic; ~**bekämpfung** *die* epidemic control *no art.*; ~**erreger** *der* epidemic virus; ~**gefahr** *die* danger of an epidemic; ~**herd** *der* source of the epidemic

seufzen /'zɔy̯ftsn̩/ *itr., tr. V.* sigh; **schwer/erleichtert ~:** give *or* heave a deep sigh/a sigh of relief

Seufzer *der;* ~s, ~: sigh; **seinen letzten ~ tun** (verhüll.) breathe one's last

Seufzer·brücke *die* Bridge of Sighs

Sevilla /ze'vɪlja/ (*das*); ~s ▸❶ **S. 675** Seville

Sex /zɛks/ *der;* ~[es] sex *no art.*; (Anziehungskraft) sex appeal; sexiness

sex-, Sex-: ~**appeal**, ~**-Appeal** /-ə'pi:l/ *der;* ~s sex appeal; ~**besessen** *Adj.* sex-obsessed; ~**bombe** *die* (salopp) sex bomb (coll.); sexpot (coll.); ~**boutique** *die* sex shop; ~**droge** *die* sex drug; ~**film** *der* sex film; ~**gier** *die* sexual lust; ~**hungrig** *Adj.* sex-hungry

Sexismus *der;* ~: sexism *no art.*

sexistisch
A *Adj.* sexist
B *adv.* ‹*behave, think, etc.*› in a sexist manner

Sex-: ~**leben** *das* sex life; ~**muffel** *der* (scherzh.) *person not interested in sex;* sexless wonder (joc.)

Sexologie *die;* ~: sexology *no art.*

sex-, Sex-: ~**protz** *der* (ugs.) sexual athlete; ~**shop** *der* sex shop; ~**süchtig** *Adj.* addicted to sex *pred.*; sex-addicted *attrib.*; ~**symbol** *das* sex symbol

Sexta /'zɛksta/ *die;* ~, **Sexten** (Schulw.) 1 (veralt.) first year (*of a Gymnasium*) 2 (österr.) sixth year (*of a Gymnasium*)

Sextaner *der;* ~s, ~ (Schulw.) 1 (veralt.) pupil in the first year (*of a Gymnasium*) 2 (österr.) pupil in the sixth year (*of a Gymnasium*)

Sextaner·blase *die* (ugs. scherzh.) bladder of a five-year-old

Sextanerin *die;* ~, ~nen ▸**Sextaner**

Sextant /zɛks'tant/ *der;* ~en, ~en sextant

Sexte *die;* ~, ~n (Musik) sixth

Sextett /zɛks'tɛt/ *das;* ~[e]s, ~e (Musik) sextet

Sex-: ~**tourismus** *der* sex tourism; ~**tourist** *der,* ~**touristin** *die* sex tourist

Sexual- /zɛ'ksu̯a:l-/: ~**erziehung** *die* sex education; ~**ethik** *die* sexual ethics *pl.*; ~**hormon** *das* sex hormone

Sexualität /zɛksu̯ali'tɛ:t/ *die;* ~: sexuality *no art.*

Sexual-: ~**kunde** *die* (Schulw.) sex education *no art.*; ~**leben** *das* sex life; ~**lockstoff** *der* (Biol.) sexual attractant [scent]; ~**mord** *der* sex murder; ~**mörder** *der* sex killer; ~**objekt** *das* sex object; ~**partner**, *der,* ~**partnerin** *die* sexual partner; ~**praktik** *die* sexual practice; ~**trieb** *der* sex[ual] drive *or* urge; ~**verbrechen** *das* sex crime; ~**verbrecher** *der* sex offender; ~**wissenschaft** *die* sexology *no art.*

sexuell
A *Adj.* sexual
B *adv.* sexually; **sich ~ befriedigen** get sexual satisfaction; (masturbieren) masturbate

Sexus /'zɛksu:s/ *der;* ~, ~ (geh.) sexuality *no art.*

sexy /'zɛksi/ (ugs.)
A *indekl. Adj.* sexy

S

B *adv.* sexily

Seychellen /ze'ʃɛlən/ *Pl.* Seychelles

Sezession /zetse'sio:n/ *die;* ~, ~**en** secession

Sezessionist *der;* ~**en**, ~**en**, **Sezessionistin** *die;* ~, ~**nen** secessionist

sezessionistisch *Adj.* secessionist

Sezessions·krieg *der* [American] Civil War

sezieren /ze'tsi:rən/

A *tr. V.* dissect ‹*corpse*›; (fig.) analyse ‹*policy etc.*›; dissect ‹*language etc.*›

B *itr. V.* perform dissections/a dissection

Sezier·messer *das* dissecting knife

SFB *Abk.* = **Sender Freies Berlin** Radio Free Berlin

s-förmig, S-förmig /'ɛs-/ *Adj.* S-shaped

sfr., (schweiz. nur:) **sFr.** *Abk.* = **Schweizer Franken**

Sg. *Abk.* = **Singular** sing.

SGB *Abk.* = **Schweizerischer Gewerkschaftsbund** Swiss Trades Union Federation

SGML *die;* ~: SGML

Shampoo /ʃam'pu:/ *das;* ~**s**, ~**s**, **Shampoon** /ʃam'po:n/ *das;* ~**ns**, ~**ns** shampoo

shampoonieren /ʃampo'ni:rən/ shampoo

Shareholder /'ʃɛ:ɐ̯hoʊldɐ/ *der;* ~**s**, ~ (Wirtsch.) shareholder

Shareholdervalue, Shareholder-Value /'ʃɛ:ɐ̯hoʊldɐvɛlju/ *der;* ~**s**, ~**s** (Wirtsch.) shareholder value

Sheriff /'ʃɛrɪʃ/ *der;* ~**s**, ~**s** sheriff

Sheriff·stern *der* sheriff's star

Sherry /'ʃɛri/ *der;* ~**s**, ~**s** sherry; *s. auch* **Bier**

Shetland- /'ʃɛtlənd-/: ~**inseln** *Pl.* Shetland Islands; Shetlands; ~**pony** *das* Shetland pony; ~**wolle** *die* Shetland wool

Shiatsu /ʃi'atsu/ *das;* ~**[s]** shiatsu

Shooting·star /'ʃu:tɪŋsta:/ *der;* ~**s**, ~**s** whizz-kid (coll.)

Shop /ʃɔp/ *der;* ~**s**, ~**s** shop

Shopaholic /ʃɔpə'hɔlɪk/ *der;* ~**s**, ~**s** shopaholic (coll.)

Shoppingmall, Shopping-Mall /'ʃɔpɪŋmɔ:l/ *die* shopping mall

Shorts /ʃɔrts/ *Pl.* shorts

Show /ʃoʊ/ *die;* ~, ~**s** show; *s. auch* **Schau**

Show-: ~**branche** *die* show business *no def. art.*; ~**master** /'-ma:stɐ/ *der,* ~**masterin** *die* compère; ~**room** /-ru:m/ *der* ~**s**, ~**s** showroom

Shuttle·bus /'ʃatl-/ *der* shuttle bus

Siam /zi:am/ *(das);* ~**s** (hist.) Siam

Siamese /zia'me:zə/ *der;* ~**n**, ~**n**, **Siamesin** *die;* ~, ~**nen** Siamese

siamesisch *Adj.* Siamese

Siam·katze *die* Siamese cat

Sibirien /zi'bi:ri̯ən/ *(das);* ~**s** Siberia

sibirisch *Adj.* Siberian; ~**e Kälte** Arctic temperatures *pl.*

Sibylle /zi'bʏlə/ *die;* ~, ~**n** sibyl; fortune teller

sibyllinisch (geh.)

A *Adj.* sibylline, mysterious ‹*words, expression*›

B *adv.* in a sibylline manner; mysteriously

sich /zɪç/ *Reflexivpron. der 3. Pers. Sg. und Pl. Akk. und Dat.*

A *Akk.* **1** (*nach* **man** *od. Inf.*) oneself; (3. Pers. Sg.) himself/herself/itself; (3. Pers. Pl.) themselves; (Höflichkeitsform Sg./Pl.) yourself/yourselves; **er/sie hat** ~ **umgebracht** he killed himself/she killed herself; **sie versteckten** ~: they hid [themselves] **2** (bei reflexiven Verben) ~ **freuen/wundern/schämen/täuschen** be pleased/surprised/ashamed/mistaken

B *Dat.* **1** (*nach* **man** *od. Inf.*) oneself; (3. Pers. Sg.) himself/herself/itself; (3. Pers. Pl.) themselves; (Höflichkeitsform Sg./Pl.) yourself/yourselves **2** (bei reflexiven Verben) ~ **etw. einbilden** imagine sth.; ~ **etw. erhoffen** hope for sth. [for oneself]; **sie hat** ~ **den Fuß verstaucht/verrenkt** she sprained/twisted her ankle

C *nach Präp.* (*nach* **man** *od. Inf.*) oneself; (3. Pers. Sg.) himself/herself/itself; (3. Pers. Pl.) themselves; (Höflichkeitsform Sg./Pl.) yourself/yourselves; **die Schuld auf** ~ **nehmen** take the blame upon oneself; **das ist eine Sache für** ~: that is a separate question; **das hat nichts auf** ~: that is of no consequence; **das hat etwas/viel für** ~: there is something/a great deal in that; **das Ding an** ~ (Philos.) the thing in itself; **von** ~ **aus** on one's own initiative; without being told to; *s. auch* **an B 2**; **für A 1**; **kommen 17**

D (*in unpers. Ausdrucksweisen für* **man** *od. passivisch*) **auf dieser Straße fährt es** ~ **gut** this is a good road to drive on; **es lässt** ~ **nicht schneiden/öffnen** it cannot be cut/opened; it is impossible to cut/open it

E (einander) one another; each other; **sie küssten** ~: they kissed [one another]; **sie sind** ~ **spinnefeind** they are at daggers drawn [with one another]; **sie sehen** ~ **ähnlich** they look alike

Sichel /'zɪçl̩/ *die;* ~, ~**n** sickle

sichel·förmig

A *Adj.* crescent- *or* sickle-shaped

B *adv.* in [the shape of] a crescent *postpos.*

sicher /'zɪçɐ/

A *Adj.* **1** (ungefährdet) safe ‹*road, procedure, etc.*›; secure ‹*job, investment, etc.*›; **in** ~**em Abstand** at a safe distance; **vor jmdm./etw.** ~ **sein** be safe from sb./sth.; ~ **ist** ~: it's better to be on the safe side; better safe than sorry; *s. auch* **Nummer 1** **2** (zuverlässig) reliable ‹*evidence, source*›; secure ‹*income*›; certain, undeniable ‹*proof*›; (vertrauenswürdig) reliable, sure ‹*judgment, taste, etc.*›; **eine** ~**e Hand** a sure *or* steady hand **3** (selbstbewusst) [self-]assured, [self-]confident ‹*person, manner*› **4** (gewiss) certain; sure; **der** ~**e Sieg/Tod** certain victory/death; **er war sich** (*Dat.*) **seines Erfolges** ~: he was confident of success; **eine Strafe ist ihm** ~: he is certain *or* sure to be punished; **seiner** (*Gen.*) **selbst sehr** ~ **sein** be very sure of oneself

B *adv.* **1** (ungefährdet) safely; ~ **die Straße überqueren** cross the street in safety; **Geld** ~ **aufbewahren** keep money in a safe place; **um ganz** ~ **zu gehen** to be quite sure **2** (zuverlässig, vertrauenswürdig) reliably; ~ **[Auto] fahren** be a safe driver; **[nicht mehr]** ~ **auf den Beinen stehen** be [un]steady on one's legs **3** (selbstbewusst) [self-]confidently; ~ **auftreten** behave in a self-assured *or* self-confident manner

C *Adv.* certainly; (plädierend) surely; **Kommst du? — Aber** ~: Are you coming? — Certainly; Of course; **du hast** ~ **schon gehört, dass ...** you are bound to *or* must have heard that ...; ~ **kommt er bald** he is sure to come soon

sicher|gehen *unr. itr. V.; mit sein* play safe; **um sicherzugehen** to be on the safe side

Sicherheit *die;* ~, ~**en** **1** safety; (der Öffentlichkeit) security; **die** ~ **der Arbeitsplätze** job security; **ein Gefühl der** ~: a sense of security; **in** ~ **sein** be safe; **jmdn./etw. in** ~ **[vor etw.** (*Dat.*)**] bringen** save *or* rescue sb./sth. [from sth.]; **sich vor etw.** (*Dat.*) **in** ~ **bringen** escape from sth.; **zur** ~: to be on the safe side; for safety's sake; **jmdn./sich in** ~ **wiegen** lull sb./[allow oneself to] be lulled into a [false] sense of security; *s. auch* **öffentlich A** **2** (Gewissheit) certainty; **mit an** ~ (*Akk.*) **grenzender Wahrscheinlichkeit** with almost complete certainty; almost certainly; **mit** ~! (als Antwort) certainly!; of course! **3** (Wirtsch.: Bürgschaft) security **4** (Zuverlässigkeit, Vertrauenswürdigkeit) reliability; soundness **5** (Selbstbewusstsein) [self-] confidence; [self-]assurance; ~ **im Auftreten/Benehmen** [self-]confidence of manner

sicherheits-, Sicherheits-: ~**abstand** *der* (Verkehrsw.) safe distance between vehicles; **einen zu geringen** ~**abstand einhalten** drive too close to the vehicle in front; ~**beauftragte** *der/die* security officer; ~**bindung** *die* (Ski) safety binding; ~**glas** *das* safety glass; ~**gurt** *der* **1** (im Auto, Flugzeug) seat belt; **2** (für Bauarbeiter, Segler) safety harness; ~**halber** *Adv.* to be on the safe side; for safety's sake; ~**kette** *die* safety *or* door chain; ~**kraft** *die* security guard; ~**kräfte** security forces; **79** ~**kräfte** 79 members of the security forces; ~**maßnahme** *die* safety measure; precaution; ~**nadel** *die* safety pin; ~**organe** *Pl.* security service *sing. or* services *pl.*; ~**rat** *der* Security Council; ~**risiko** *das* security risk; ~**schloss**, *~**schloß** *das* safety lock; ~**ventil** *das* (Technik) safety valve; ~**verschluss**, *~**verschluß** *der* safety catch; ~**vorkehrung** *die* [safety] precaution; safety measure; ~**vorschrift** *die* safety regulation

sicherlich *Adv.* certainly; **er wird es** ~ **tun** he is certain *or* sure to do it

sichern

A *tr. V.* **1** make ‹*door etc.*› secure; (garantieren) safeguard ‹*rights, peace*›; (schützen) protect ‹*rights etc.*›; **etw./sich gegen etw.** *od.* **vor etw.** (*Dat.*) ~: protect sth./oneself against sth.; **ein gesichertes Einkommen** a secure *or* guaranteed income; **eine Schusswaffe** ~: put the safety catch on a firearm **2** (verschaffen; polizeilich ermitteln) secure ‹*ticket, clue, etc.*›; **[sich** (*Dat.*)**] etw.** ~: secure sth.

B *itr. V.* (Jägerspr.) scent; test the wind

sicher|stellen *tr. V.* **1** (beschlagnahmen) impound ‹*goods, vehicle*›; seize ‹*stolen goods*›; confiscate ‹*licence etc.*› **2** (gewährleisten) guarantee ‹*supply, freedom, etc.*› **3** (beweisen) establish [beyond doubt]

Sicher·stellung *die* **1** ▸ **sicherstellen 1**: impounding; seizure; confiscation **2** (Gewährleistung) guarantee

Sicherung *die;* ~, ~**en** **1** (das Sichern) safeguarding (**vor** + *Dat.*, **gegen** from, against); (das Schützen) protection (**vor** + *Dat.*, **gegen** from, against) **2** (Elektrot.) fuse; *s. auch* **durchbrennen 1** **3** (tech. Vorrichtung) safety catch **4** (Schutz) safeguard (**gegen** against)

Sicherungs-: ~**kasten** *der* fuse box; ~**kopie** *die* (DV) back-up [copy]; ~**verwahrung** *die* (Rechtsw.) preventive detention

Sicht /zɪçt/ *die;* ~, ~**en** **1** (~weite) visibility *no art.*; (Ausblick) view (**auf** + *Akk.*, **in** + *Akk.* of); **gute** *od.* **klare/schlechte** ~: good/poor visibility; **die** ~ **beträgt nur fünfzig Meter** visibility is down to fifty metres; **in** ~ **kommen** come into sight; **außer** ~ **sein** be out of sight; **Land in** ~! land ahoy!; **auf** ~ **fliegen** fly by VFR **2** (Kaufmannsspr.) **Wechsel auf** ~: bill payable on demand *or* at sight **3** **auf lange/kurze** ~: in the long/short term; **auf lange** *od.* **weite** ~ **planen** plan on a long-term basis **4** (Betrachtungsweise) point of view; **aus meiner** ~/**in der** ~ **des Historikers** as I see it/as the historian sees it; in my/the historian's view

sichtbar

A *Adj.* visible; (fig.) apparent ‹*reason*›; **für jedermann** ~ **sein** be obvious *or* evident to everyone; **sich** (*Dat.*) ~**e Mühe geben** go to obvious *or* appreciable trouble; **etw.** ~ **machen** clarify sth.

B *adv.* visibly; **immer** ~**er zutage treten** (fig.) become increasingly obvious *or* apparent

Sicht·blende *die* screen; (Jalousie) blind

sichten *tr. V.* **1** (erspähen) sight **2** (durchsehen) sift [through]; (prüfen) examine

Sicht-: ~**flug** *der* contact *or* VFR flying; ~**gerät** *das* VDU; ~**grenze** *die:* **die** ~**grenze liegt bei 30 Metern** [maximum] visibility is 30 metres; ~**karte** *die* pass

sichtlich

A *Adj.* obvious; evident

B *adv.* obviously; evidently; visibly ‹*impressed*›

Sicht-: ~**linie** *die* (bes. Astron.) line of sight; ~**schutz** *der* [concealing] screen; ~**schutz·zaun** *der* concealing fence; (um seinen privaten Bereich abzuschirmen) privacy fence

Sichtung *die;* ~, ~**en** **1** sighting **2** (das Durchsehen) sifting; (das Prüfen) examination; inspection

Sicht-: ~**verhältnisse** *Pl.* visibility *sing.*; ~**vermerk** *der* visa; ~**weite** *die* visibility *no art.*; **außer/in** ~**weite sein** be out of/in sight; **in** ~**weite kommen** come into sight

sickern /'zɪkɐn/ *itr. V.; mit sein* seep; (spärlich fließen) trickle; (fig.) ‹*money*› leak away

Sicker·wasser *das* **1** (im Boden) gravitational *or* drainage water **2** (aus einem Damm o. Ä.) seepage (*from a dam etc.*)

S

sie /ziː/

A *Personalpron.; 3. Pers. Sg. Nom. Fem.* (bei weiblichen Personen und Tieren) she; (bei Dingen, Tieren) it; (bei Behörden) they *pl.*; **Wer hat es gemacht? — Sie war es/Sie:** Who did it? — It was her/She did; **ich weiß mehr als ~:** I know more than she does; I know more than her (coll.); *s. auch* **ihr**[1]; **ihrer 1**

B *Personalpron.; 3. Pers. Pl. Nom.* **1** they; **Wer hat es gemacht? — Sie waren es/Sie:** Who did it? — It was them/They did; **ich weiß mehr als ~:** I know more than they do; I know more than them (coll.); *s. auch* **ihnen**; **ihrer 2** **2** (ugs.: man) **mir haben ~ mein Rad gestohlen** somebody's stolen my bike; **hier wollen ~ das neue Rathaus bauen** here's where they are going to build the new town hall; **den haben ~ verhaftet** he's been arrested

C *Akk. des Personalpron.* **sie A** (bei weiblichen Personen und Tieren) her; (bei Dingen und Tieren) it; (bei Behörden) them *pl.*

D *Akk. des Personalpron.* **sie B 1** them

Sie[1] *Personalpron.* **1** *Anrede an eine od. mehrere Personen* you; **jmdn. mit ~ anreden** address sb. as 'Sie'; use the polite form of address to sb.; **kommen ~ her!** come here! **2** (veralt.: Anrede an eine Untergebene) you

Sie[2] *die;* **~, ~s** (ugs.) she

Sieb /ziːp/ *das;* **~[e]s, ~e** **1** sieve; (Kaffee~, Tee~) strainer; (für Sand, Kies usw.) riddle; (Technik: Filter) filter; **er hat ein Gedächtnis wie ein ~:** he's got a memory like a sieve **2** (Druckw.) screen

Sieb·druck *der; Pl.* **~e** **1** (Verfahren) [silk-]screen printing *no art.* **2** (Erzeugnis) [silk-]screen print

sieben[1]

A *tr. V.* **1** (durch~) sieve ‹*flour etc.*›; riddle ‹*sand, gravel, etc.*› **2** (auswählen) screen ‹*candidates, visitors, etc.*›

B *itr. V.* **1** use a sieve/strainer/riddle **2** (auswählen) pick and choose; **bei der Prüfung haben sie [schwer] gesiebt** (ugs.) they weeded out [a lot of] people in the examination

sieben[2] *Kardinalz.* ▸**i** **S. 29**, ▸**i** **S. 729**, ▸**i** **S. 826** seven; **die ~ fetten/mageren Jahre** the seven years of plenty/lean years; **die ~ Freien Künste** the liberal arts; *s. auch* **acht**

Sieben *die;* **~, ~en** **1** (Ziffer) seven **2** (Spielkarte) seven **3** (ugs.: Bus-, Bahnlinie) number seven; *s. auch* **Acht 1, 7; böse A 2**

sieben·armig *Adj.* seven-armed; **~er Leuchter** (jüd. Rel.) seven-branched candelabrum; menorah

Sieben·bürgen *(das);* **~s** Transylvania

Sieben·eck *das* heptagon

sieben·eckig *Adj.* heptagonal

Siebener *der;* **~s, ~** (ugs.) **1** (im Lotto usw.) seven winning numbers *pl.* **2** ▸**Sieben 1, 2, 3**

siebenerlei *Gattungsz.; indekl.* **1** *attr.* seven kinds *or* sorts of; seven different ‹*sorts, kinds, sizes, possibilities*› **2** *subst.* seven [different] things

sieben-, Sieben-: **~fach** *Vervielfältigungsz.* sevenfold; *s. auch* **achtfach**; **~fache** *das; adj. Dekl.* **das ~fache** seven times as much; *s. auch* **Achtfache**; **~gestirn** *das;* **~~s** Pleiades *pl.*; **~hundert** *Kardinalz.* ▸**i** **S. 826** seven hundred; **~jährig** *Adj.* **1** (7 Jahre alt) seven-year-old *attrib.*; seven years old *pred.*; **2** (7 Jahre dauernd) seven-year *attrib.*; **der ~jährige Krieg** the Seven Years War; *s. auch* **achtjährig**; **~köpfig** *Adj.* seven-headed ‹*monster*›; ‹*family, committee*› of seven; **~mal** *Adj.* seven times; *s. auch* **achtmal**; **~malig** *Adj.* **nach ~maligem Versuch** after the seventh attempt; *s. auch* **achtmalig**; **~meilen·stiefel** *Pl.* (scherzh.) seven-league boots; **~meilenstiefel anhaben** (ugs. scherzh.) have got one's seven-league boots on; **mit ~meilenstiefeln** (ugs. scherzh.) with giant strides; **~meter** *der* (Hockey) penalty [shot]; (Hallenhandball) penalty [throw]; **~monats·kind** *das* child born two months prematurely; **~sachen** *Pl.* (ugs.) **meine/deine** *usw.* **~sachen** my/your *etc.* belongings *or* (coll.) bits and pieces; **~schläfer** *der* **1** (Tier) dormouse; **2** (volkst.: Tag) 27 June (*rain on which is supposed to foretell rain for seven weeks*); ≈ St. Swithin's Day; **~seitig** *Adj.* seven-sided ‹*figure*›; seven-page ‹*letter, article, etc.*›; **~stöckig** *Adj.* seven-storey ‹*building*›; *s. auch* **achtstöckig**

siebent ▸**siebt**

siebent... *Ordinalz.* ▸**i** **S. 826** ▸**siebt...**

sieben·tausend *Kardinalz.* ▸**i** **S. 826** seven thousand

Siebente *der/die; adj. Dekl.* ▸**Siebte**

sieben·teilig *Adj.* seven-piece ‹*tool set etc.*›; seven-part ‹*serial*›; *s. auch* **achtteilig**

siebentel /ˈziːbn̩tl̩/ ▸**i** **S. 826** ▸**siebtel**

Siebentel *das;* **~s, ~** ▸**i** **S. 826** ▸**Siebtel**

siebentens *Adv.* ▸**siebtens**

sieben·zehn (veralt., zur Verdeutlichung) ▸**siebzehn**

siebt /ziːpt/ *in* **wir waren zu ~:** there were seven of us; *s. auch* **acht**[2]

siebt... /ziːpt.../ *Ordinalz.* ▸**i** **S. 165**, ▸**i** **S. 826** seventh; *s. auch* **acht...**

Siebte *der/die; adj. Dekl.* seventh; *s. auch* **Achte**

siebtel /ˈziːptl̩/ *Bruchz.* ▸**i** **S. 826** seventh

Siebtel *das* (schweiz. meist *der*); **~s, ~:** ▸**i** **S. 826** seventh

***siebte·mal, *siebten·mal** ▸**Mal**[1]

siebtens *Adv.* seventhly

sieb-, Sieb-: **~zehn** *Kardinalz.* ▸**i** **S. 29**, ▸**i** **S. 729**, ▸**i** **S. 826** seventeen; **~zehn·jährig** *Adj.* (17 Jahre alt) seventeen-year-old *attrib.*; seventeen years old *postpos.*; (17 Jahre dauernd) seventeen-year *attrib.*; *s. auch* **achtjährig**; **~zehnt...** *Ordinalz.* ▸**i** **S. 165** seventeenth; **~zehntel** *das* seventeenth; **~zehn·und·vier** *das;* **~~:** vingt-et-un

siebzig /ˈziːptsɪç/ *Kardinalz.* ▸**i** **S. 29**, ▸**i** **S. 826** seventy; *s. auch* **achtzig**

Siebziger[1] *der;* **~s, ~** **1** (70-Jähriger) seventy-year-old **2** (ugs.: Autobus usw.) number seventy **3** (Wein) '70 vintage

Siebziger[2] *die;* **~, ~** (ugs. Briefmarke): seventy-cent/centime *etc.* stamp

Siebziger·jahre *Pl.* ▸**i** **S. 29**, ▸**i** **S. 165** seventies *pl.*

siebzig·jährig *Adj.* (70 Jahre alt) seventy-year-old *attrib.*; seventy years old *pred.*; (70 Jahre dauernd) seventy-year *attrib.*; *s. auch* **achtjährig**

siebzigst... *Ordinalz.* ▸**i** **S. 826** seventieth

siech /ziːç/ *Adj.* (geh.) infirm; ailing

Siechtum *das;* **~s** (geh.) [long] infirmity

siedeln /ˈziːdl̩n/ *itr. V.* settle

sieden /ˈziːdn̩/

A *unr. od.* (fachspr. nur) *regelm. itr. V.* (bes. südd.) boil; **~d heiß** boiling hot

B *tr. V.* **1** *unr., auch regelm.* (bes. südd.) boil **2** *unr. od. regelm.* (veralt.) obtain ‹*salt, soap, etc.*› by boiling

***siedend·heiß** ▸**sieden A**

Siede-: **~punkt** *der* ▸**i** **S. 703** (Physik; auch fig.) boiling point; **auf den ~punkt steigen** (fig.) reach boiling point; **~wasser·reaktor** *der* (Kerntechnik) boiling-water reactor

Siedler *der;* **~s, ~, Siedlerin** *die;* **~, ~nen** settler

Siedlung *die;* **~, ~en** **1** (Wohngebiet) [housing] estate **2** (Niederlassung) settlement

Siedlungs·haus *das* house on an estate; estate house

Sieg /ziːk/ *der;* **~[e]s, ~e** victory, (bes. Sport) win (**über** + *Akk.* over); **auf ~ spielen** go for a win; **den ~ davontragen** *od.* **erringen** (geh.) be victorious; (Sport) be the winner/winners; **ein ~ der Vernunft** (fig.) a victory for common sense

Siegel /ˈziːgl̩/ *das;* **~s, ~:** seal; (von Behörden) stamp; (des Gerichtsvollziehers) bailiff's seal; **unter dem ~ der Verschwiegenheit** (fig.) under the seal of secrecy

Siegel·lack *der* sealing wax

siegeln *tr. V.* seal

Siegel·ring *der* signet ring

siegen *itr. V.* win; **über jmdn. ~:** gain *or* win a victory over sb.; (bes. Sport) win against sb.; beat sb.; **mit 2 : 0 ~** (Sport) win 2-0 *or* by two goals to nil

Sieger *der;* **~s, ~:** winner; (Mannschaft) winners *pl.*; (einer Schlacht) victor; **als ~ hervorgehen** emerge victorious (**aus** from); **zweiter ~ sein** (Sportjargon) be runner-up/runners-up

Sieger·ehrung *die* presentation ceremony; awards ceremony

Siegerin *die;* **~, ~nen** ▸**Sieger**

Sieger-: **~macht** *die* victorious power; **~podest** *das* winners' rostrum; **~straße** *die* (bes. Sport Jargon) **auf der ~straße sein/fahren/marschieren** be on the road to victory/(fig.) success; **auf die ~straße kommen** get into winning ways; **~urkunde** *die* winner's certificate

sieges-, Sieges-: **~bewusst**, ***~bewußt** **A** *Adj.* confident of victory *postpos.*; (erfolgssicher) confident of success *postpos.*; **B** *adv.* confident of victory; confidently; **~gewiss**, ***~gewiß** (geh.) ▸**~sicher**; **~göttin** *die* (Myth.) goddess of victory; **~palme** *die* palm [of victory]; **die ~palme davontragen** (fig.) carry off the palm; **~säule** *die* victory column; **~sicher** **A** *Adj.* certain *or* confident of victory *pred.*; (erfolgssicher) certain *or* confident of success *pred.*; **B** *adv.* confident of victory; ‹*say, smile*› confidently; **~trunken** (geh.) **A** *Adj.* intoxicated *or* drunk with victory *pred.*; **B** *adv.* intoxicated *or* drunk with victory; **~zug** *der* (auch fig.) triumphant progress

sieg-, Sieg-: **~gewohnt** *Adj.* ‹*army*› accustomed to victory; ‹*team*› used to winning; **~los** *Adj.* without a victory *postpos.*; (Sport) without a win *postpos.*; **~reich** *Adj.* victorious; winning ‹*team*›; successful ‹*campaign*›; **nach einer ~reichen Schlacht** after winning a battle; **~treffer** *der* (bes. Fußball) winning goal

sieh /ziː/, **siehe** *Imperativ Sg. v.* **sehen**

siehst /ziːst/ *2. Pers. Sg. Präsens v.* **sehen**

sieht /ziːt/ *3. Pers. Sg. Präsens v.* **sehen**

Siel /ziːl/ *der od. das;* **~[e]s, ~e** (nordd.) **1** (Deichschleuse) dyke sluice *or* floodgate **2** (Abwasserkanal) sewer

Siele *die;* **~, ~n** (veralt.) breast harness; **in den ~n sterben** (fig.) die in harness

siena /ˈzi̯eːna/ *indekl. Adj.* sienna

siezen /ˈziːtsn̩/ *tr. V.* call 'Sie' (*the polite form of address*); **sich ~:** call each other 'Sie'; **sich mit jmdm. ~:** call sb. 'Sie'

siezen/duzen

German has two forms for 'you', the formal *Sie* and the familiar *du*. *Du* is used when speaking to a friend, a child, or a family member. Young people always address each other as *du*. If someone says, *wir duzen uns* (we call each other *du*), it means that they are friends. When speaking to a person or group of people you do not know very well, the polite form *Sie* is used. Even though there has been a tendency for less formality in recent years, it is still best to say *Sie*, especially in work situations and when you would normally address someone in English with Mrs or Mr.

Siff *der;* **~s** (ugs.) filth; muck

siffig *Adj.* (ugs.) filthy

Sigel /ˈziːgl̩/ *das;* **~s, ~** (Zeichen) logogram; (in der Stenografie) grammalogue; (Kürzel) abbreviation

Signal /zɪˈgnaːl/ *das;* **~s, ~e** signal; **das ~ zum Angriff geben** give the signal to attack; **~e setzen** (fig.) set a new direction; **das ~ steht auf „Halt"** the signal is at 'stop'

Signal-: **~anlage** *die* (Verkehrsw.) signals *pl.*; **~brücke** *die* (Eisenb.) [signal] gantry

Signalement /zɪgnaləˈmɛnt/ *das;* **~s, ~e** (schweiz.) personal description *or* details *pl.*

Signal-: **~flagge** *die* (Seew.) signal flag; **~horn** *das* horn; hooter (Brit.)

signalisieren *tr. V.* indicate ‹*danger, change, etc.*›; (fig.: übermitteln) signal ‹*message, warning, order*› (+ *Dat.* to)

Signal-: **~lampe** *die* indicator light; **~mast** *der* [1] (Seew.) signalling mast; [2] (Eisenb.) signal post *or* mast; **~wirkung** *die* knock-on effect

Signatar·macht /zɪgna'ta:ɐ̯-/ *die* (Politik) signatory power

Signatar·staat *der* (Politik) signatory state

Signatur /zɪgna'tu:ɐ̯/ *die;* ~, ~en [1] (Namenszeichen) initials *pl.*; (Kürzel) abbreviated signature; (des Künstlers) autograph [2] (veralt.: Unterschrift) signature [3] (in einer Bibliothek) shelf mark [4] (auf Landkarten) [map] symbol

Signet /zɪn'je/ *das;* ~s, ~s (Buchw.) [publisher's] imprint

signieren
[A] *tr. V.* sign; autograph ‹*one's own work*›
[B] *itr. V.* sign *or* autograph one's work

signifikant /zɪgnifi'kant/ (geh.)
[A] *Adj.* [1] (wesentlich) significant [2] (typisch) characteristic, typical (**für** of)
[B] *adv.* significantly

Signifikanz *die;* ~ (geh.) significance

Sigrist /'zi:grɪst/ *der;* ~en, ~en (schweiz.) sexton

Silbe /'zɪlbə/ *die;* ~, ~n syllable; **etw. mit keiner ~ erwähnen** not say a word about sth.

Silben-: **~rätsel** *das: puzzle in which syllables must be combined to form words;* **~trennung** *die* word division (*by syllables*)

Silber /'zɪlbɐ/ *das;* ~s [1] (Edelmetall, Farbe) silver [2] (silbernes Gerät) silver[ware] [3] (Sport: ~medaille) silver [medal]; **sie hat schon zweimal olympisches ~ geholt** she has already won two Olympic silver medals

silber-, Silber-: **~ader** *die* vein of silver; **~arbeit** *die* silverwork; (Gegenstand) piece of silverwork; **~auf·lage** *die* silver plating *no indef. art.*; **~barren** *der* silver bar *or* ingot; **~blech** *das* rolled silver; **~besteck** *das* silver cutlery; **~blick** *der* (ugs. scherzh.) [slight] squint; **~blond** *Adj.* silver-blond; **~distel** *die* carline thistle; **~farben**, **~farbig** *Adj.* silver; **~fischchen** *das;* ~~s, ~~: silverfish; **~fuchs** *der* silver fox; **~führend** *Adj.* ▸ **~haltig**; **~gehalt** *der* silver content; **~geld** *das* silver; **~geschirr** *das* silver plate; silverware; **~grau** *Adj.* silver-grey; **~haar** *das* (geh.) silvery hair; **~haltig** *Adj.* silver-bearing; argentiferous; **~hoch·zeit** *die* silver wedding; **~kette** *die* silver necklace; **~legierung** *die* silver alloy

Silberling *der;* ~s, ~e (veralt.) piece of silver

Silber-: **~medaille** *die* silver medal; **~mine** *die* silver mine; **~möwe** *die* herring gull; **~münze** *die* silver coin

silbern
[A] *Adj.* [1] (aus Silber) silver [2] (silberfarben) silver; silvery ‹*moonlight, shade, gleam, etc.*›
[B] *adv.* [1] (mit Silber) ‹*ornament, coat, etc.*› with silver [2] ‹*shine, shimmer, etc.*› with a silvery lustre [3] (wohltönend) ‹*chime etc.*› with a silvery sound

silber-, Silber-: **~papier** *das* silver paper; **~pappel** *die* white poplar; **~scheibe** *die* (Jargon) compact disc; **~schmied** *der*, **~schmiedin** *die* ▸ⓘ S. 113 silversmith; **~streif** *der*, **~streifen** *der* silver line *or* strip; **ein ~streifen am Horizont** (fig.) a ray of hope on the horizon; **~weiß** *Adj.* silvery-white; **~zwiebel** *die* ▸ **Perlzwiebel**

-silbig *Adj.* -syllable

silbrig *Adj.* (geh.) silvery

Silhouette /zi'lu̯ɛtə/ *die;* ~, ~n [1] silhouette [2] (Mode) line; **mit** *od.* **in modischer ~:** with a fashionable line *or* shape

Silicat (fachspr.) ▸ **Silikat**

Silicium /zi'li:tsi̯ʊm/ *das;* ~s silicon

Silicon (fachspr.) ▸ **Silikon**

Silikat /zili'ka:t/ *das;* ~[e]s, ~e (Chemie) silicate

Silikon /zili'ko:n/ *das;* ~s, ~e (Chemie) silicone

Silikon-: **~busen** *der* silicon breasts *pl.*; **~implantat** *das* silicon [breast] implant

Silikose /zili'ko:zə/ *die;* ~, ~n (Med.) silicosis

Silizium ▸ **Silicium**

Silo /'zi:lo/ *der od. das;* ~s, ~s silo

Silur /zi'lu:ɐ̯/ *das;* ~s (Geol.) Siluran

Silvaner /zɪl'va:nɐ/ *der;* ~s, ~: silvaner [wine]

Silvester /zɪl'vɛstɐ/ *der od. das;* ~s, ~: New Year's Eve; **~ feiern** see the New Year in

Silvester·nacht *die* night of New Year's Eve

Simbabwe /zɪm'ba:bvə/ *(das);* ~s Zimbabwe

Simili·stein /'zi:mili-/ *der* (bes. Mineralogie) imitation stone

Sim-Karte, SIM-Karte /'zɪm-/ *die* SIM card

Simmer·ring Ⓦz /'zɪmɐ-/ *der* (Technik) ring type oil seal

Simonie /zimo'ni:/ *die;* ~, ~n (kath. Kirche) simony

simpel /'zɪmpl̩/
[A] *Adj.* [1] (einfach) simple ‹*question, task*› [2] (abwertend: beschränkt) simple-minded ‹*person*›; simple ‹*mind*› [3] (oft abwertend: schlicht) basic ‹*toy, dress, etc.*›
[B] *adv.* [1] (einfach) simply [2] (abwertend: beschränkt) in a simple-minded manner [3] (oft abwertend: schlicht) simply; basically

Simpel *der;* ~s, ~ (bes. südd. ugs.) simpleton; fool; **ich ~:** fool that I am/was

Simplex /'zɪmplɛks/ *das;* ~, ~e *od.* **Simplizia** /zɪm'pli:tsi̯a/ (Sprachw.) simplex

simplifizieren *tr., itr. V.* oversimplify

Simplizität *die;* ~: simplicity

Sims /zɪms/ *der od. das;* ~es, ~e ledge; sill; (Kamin~) mantelpiece

Simse /'zɪmzə/ *die;* ~, ~n (Bot.) bulrush

simsen /'zɪmzn̩/ *itr. V.* (ugs.) send a text message/text messages

Simson /'zɪmzɔn/ *(der);* ~s Samson

Simulant /zimu'lant/ *der;* ~en, ~en, **Simulantin** *die;* ~, ~nen malingerer

Simulation *die;* ~, ~en simulation

Simulator /zimu'la:tɔr/ *der;* ~s, ~en /-'to:rən/ (Technik) simulator

simulieren
[A] *tr. V.* feign, sham ‹*illness, emotion, etc.*›; simulate ‹*situation, condition, etc.*›
[B] *itr. V.* (Krankheit vortäuschen) feign illness; pretend to be ill; **er simuliert nur** he's just putting it on

simultan /zimʊl'ta:n/
[A] *Adj.* simultaneous
[B] *adv.* simultaneously

Simultan-: **~dolmetschen** *das;* ~~s simultaneous interpreting *no art.*; **~dolmetscher** *der*, **~dolmetscherin** *die* simultaneous interpreter

Sinai·halb·insel /'zi:nai-/ *die* Sinai Peninsula

sind /zɪnt/ *1. u. 3. Pers. Pl. Präsens v.* **sein**

sine tempore /'zi:nə 'tɛmporə/ (Hochschulw.) at the time stated

Sinfonie /zɪnfo'ni:/ *die;* ~, ~n (auch fig.) symphony

Sinfonie-: **~konzert** *das* symphony concert; **~orchester** *das* symphony orchestra

Sinfoniker *Pl.* (Orchester) symphony orchestra *sing.*

sinfonisch (Musik)
[A] *Adj.* symphonic
[B] *adv.* symphonically

Singapur /'zɪŋgapu:ɐ̯/ *(das);* ~s ▸ⓘ S. 675 Singapore

Sing·drossel *die* song thrush

singen /'zɪŋən/
[A] *unr. itr. V.* [1] sing; **einen ~den Tonfall haben** have a lilting cadence [2] (salopp: vor der Polizei aussagen) squeal (sl.); **jmdn. zum S~ bringen** make sb. talk [3] (dichter. veralt.) **von etw. ~** ‹*poet, poem*› sing of sth.
[B] *unr. tr. V.* [1] sing ‹*song, aria, contralto, tenor, etc.*›; **jmds. Lob/Ruhm ~** (fig. geh.) sing sb.'s praises; **das kannst du ~** (fig. ugs.) you can bet your life on that [2] **sich heiser/müde ~:** sing until one is hoarse/tired; **jmdn. in den Schlaf ~:** sing sb. to sleep

Single[1] /'zɪŋl̩/ *die;* ~, ~s (Schallplatte) single

Single[2] *der;* ~[s], ~s single person; **~s** single people *no art.*

Single[3] *das;* ~[s], ~[s] (Badminton, Tennis) singles *sing. or pl.*

Sing-: **~sang** *der* [1] (das Singen) singsong; [2] (Melodie) simple tune; **~spiel** *das* (Musik) Singspiel; **~stimme** *die* voice

singulär (geh.)
[A] *Adj.* [1] rare [2] (einzigartig) unique; singular
[B] *adv.* rarely

Singular /'zɪŋgula:ɐ̯/ *der;* ~s, ~e [1] singular; **Sinto ist der ~ von** *od.* **zu Sinti** 'Sinto' is the singular of 'Sinti' [2] (Wort) word in the singular; singular form; **im ~ stehen** be [in the] singular

Singularetantum /zɪŋgula:rə'tantʊm/ *das;* ~s, **Singulariatantum** singular-only noun

singularisch (Sprachw.)
[A] *Adj.* singular ‹*form, ending*›
[B] *adv.* in the singular

Sing·vogel *der* songbird

sinken /'zɪŋkn̩/ *unr. itr. V.; mit sein* [1] ‹*ship, sun*› sink, go down; ‹*plane, balloon*› descend, go down; (geh.) ‹*leaves, snowflakes*› fall; **die ~de Sonne** the setting sun; **er ist tief gesunken** (fig.) he has sunk low; **er wäre am liebsten in den Boden gesunken** he wished the earth would [open and] swallow him up; **ins Bett/in einen Sessel ~** (fig.) fall into bed/sink into a chair; **in Ohnmacht ~** (geh.) swoon; fall into a faint; **in Schlaf ~** (geh.) sink into a sleep [2] (nieder~) fall; **jmdm. an die Brust ~:** fall upon sb.'s breast; **den Kopf ~ lassen** let one's head drop; **der Kopf sank ihm auf die Brust** his head dropped to his chest; **auf** *od.* (geh.) **in die Knie ~:** sink *or* fall to one's knees; **die Hände in den Schoß ~ lassen** let one's hands drop to one's lap [3] (niedriger werden) ‹*temperature, level*› fall, drop; **das Thermometer/Barometer sinkt** the temperature is falling/the barometer is going back [4] (an Wert verlieren) ‹*price, value*› fall, go down; **in jmds. Gunst/Achtung ~:** go down in sb.'s favour/estimation [5] (nachlassen, abnehmen) fall; go down; ‹*excitement, interest*› diminish, decline; **jmds. Mut/Vertrauen sinkt** sb. loses courage/confidence; **ihre gute Laune sank** her good mood gradually disappeared

Sinn /zɪn/ *der;* ~[e]s, ~e [1] sense; **den** *od.* **einen sechsten ~ [für etw.] haben** have a sixth sense [for sth.]; **seine fünf ~e nicht beisammenhaben** (ugs.) be not quite right in the head [2] *Pl.* (geh.: Bewusstsein) senses; mind *sing.*; **ihm schwanden die ~e** he lost consciousness; **nicht bei ~en sein** be out of one's senses *or* mind; **bist du noch bei ~en?** have you gone out of your mind?; have you taken leave of your senses?; **wie von ~en** as if he/she had gone out of his/her mind [3] (Gefühl, Verständnis) feeling; **einen ~ für Schönheit/Stil/Gerechtigkeit/Humor** *usw.* **haben** have a sense of beauty/style/justice/humour *etc.*; **er hatte wenig ~ für Familienfeste** he didn't care much for family parties [4] (geh.: Gedanken, Denken) mind; **er hat ganz in meinem ~ gehandelt** he acted correctly to my mind *or* my way of thinking; **das ist nach meinem ~:** I like that; I agree with that; **mir steht der ~ [nicht] danach/nach etw.** I [don't] feel like it/sth.; **sich** (*Dat.*) **etw. aus dem ~ schlagen** put [all thoughts of] sth. out of one's mind; **etw. im ~ haben** have sth. in mind; **jmdm. in den ~ kommen** come to sb.'s mind; **das will mir nicht in den ~** (veralt.) I simply can't understand it [5] (geh.: Denkungsart) mind; way of thinking [6] (~gehalt, Bedeutung) meaning; **im strengen/wörtlichen ~:** in the strict/literal sense; **jmds. Rede dem ~e nach wiedergeben** convey the gist of sb.'s speech [7] (Ziel u. Zweck) point; **der ~ des Lebens** the meaning of life; **ohne ~ sein** be pointless *or* meaningless; **ohne ~ und Verstand** without thinking [about it/them] [8] *Pl.* (sexuelles Verlangen) desire *sing.*; desires

S

Sinn·bild *das* symbol

sinn·bildlich
A *Adj.* symbolic
B *adv.* symbolically

sinnen *unr. itr. V.* (geh.) 1 (nachdenken) think; ponder; **sie schaute ~d aus dem Fenster** she looked thoughtfully out of the window 2 (planen) **auf etw.** (*Akk.*) **~:** plan *or* plot sth.; **auf Rache ~:** be out for revenge

sinnen-, Sinnen-: ~freude *die* (geh.) joie de vivre; zest for life; **~froh** *Adj.* (geh.) sensuous; **~lust** *die* sensuality; **~rausch** *der* (geh.) [sensual] passion

sinn·entstellend
A *Adj.* which distorts/distorted the meaning *post-pos., not pred.*
B *adv.* ‹*translate, shorten*› so that the *or* its meaning is distorted

Sinnes-: ~art *die* disposition; **~eindruck** *der* sense impression; sensation; **~organ** *das* sense organ; sensory organ; **~täuschung** *die* trick of the senses; **~wandel** *der* change of mind *or* heart

sinn-, Sinn-: ~fällig A *Adj.* obvious; visible ‹*expression*›; B *adv.* **etw. ~fällig zum Ausdruck bringen** express sth. intelligibly *or* in an easily understood way; **~frei** A *Adj.* 1 (ohne Bedeutung) meaningless; 2 (sinnlos) senseless; B *adv.* 1 meaninglessly; 2 (sinnlos) senselessly; **~gebung** /-ge:bʊŋ/ *die;* **~~, ~~en** (geh.) meaning; **~gedicht** *das* (Literaturw.) epigram; **~gehalt** *der* ▸ **Sinn 6**; **~gemäß** A *Adj.* 1 **eine ~gemäße Übersetzung** a translation which conveys the general sense; 2 (folgerichtig) logical; B *adv.* 1 (inhaltlich) **etw. ~gemäß übersetzen/wiedergeben** translate the general sense of sth./give the gist of sth.; 2 (folgerichtig) logically; **~haft** A *Adj.* meaningful; B *adv.* meaningfully; **~haftigkeit** *die;* **~~:** meaningfulness

sinnieren *itr. V.* ponder (**über** + *Akk.* over); muse (**über** + *Akk.* [up]on)

sinnig *Adj.* (meist spött. od. iron.) clever; sensible (iron.)

Sinn·krise *die* crisis of belief in the meaning of life

sinnlich
A *Adj.* 1 sensory ‹*impression, perception, stimulus*› 2 (sexuell) sensual ‹*love, mouth*›; **~es Verlangen** sexual desire 3 (sinnenfroh) sensuous ‹*pleasure, passion*›
B *adv.* 1 ‹*perceive, understand*› through the senses; **die ~ wahrnehmbare Welt** the world perceived by the senses 2 (sexuell) sensually; **jmdn. ~ erregen** arouse sb. sexually

Sinnlichkeit *die;* **~** 1 sensuality 2 (sinnliche Wahrnehmbarkeit) sensuousness

sinn·los
A *Adj.* 1 (unsinnig) senseless 2 (zwecklos) pointless 3 (abwertend: übermäßig) mad; wild
B *adv.* 1 (unsinnig) senselessly 2 (zwecklos) pointlessly 3 (abwertend: übermäßig) like mad (coll.); **~ betrunken** blind drunk; **sich ~ besaufen** (salopp) get completely plastered (sl.)

Sinnlosigkeit *die* 1 (Wesen, Art) senselessness 2 (Zwecklosigkeit) pointlessness

sinn-, Sinn-: ~reich *Adj.* 1 (zweckmäßig) useful; 2 (tiefsinnig) profound; **~spruch** *der* saying; **~stiftend** *Adj.* ‹*activity, event*› giving a sense of meaning and purpose; **~stiftung** *die:* **~stiftung durch Kunst** the endowment of life with meaning through art; **~suche** *die* search for meaning; **~verwandt** *Adj.* (Sprachw.) synonymous ‹*words*›; **~verwandte Wörter** synonyms; **~voll** A *Adj.* 1 (vernünftig) sensible; 2 (mit ~ erfüllt, einen ~ ergebend) meaningful; **dieser Satz ist nur ~voll, wenn …** this sentence only makes sense if …; B *adv.* 1 (vernünftig) sensibly; 2 (mit ~ erfüllt, einen ~ ergebend) meaningfully; **~widrig** *Adj.* (geh.) nonsensical; **~zusammenhang** *der* context

Sinologe /zino'lo:gə/ *der;* **~n, ~n** sinologist; sinologue

Sinologie *die;* **~:** sinology *no art.*

Sinologin *die;* **~, ~nen** ▸ **Sinologe**

sinte·mal /'zɪntə'ma:l/ *Konj.* (veralt., noch scherzh.) because; since

Sinter /'zɪntɐ/ *der;* **~s, ~:** sinter

sintern *tr., itr. V.* (Technik) sinter

Sint·flut /'zɪnt-/ *die* Flood; Deluge; **nach mir/uns die ~:** I/we don't care what happens after I've/we've gone

sintflut·artig
A *Adj.* torrential
B *adv.* in torrents

Sinto /'zɪnto/ *der;* **~, Sinti** Sinte

Sinus /'zi:nʊs/ *der;* **~, ~** *od.* **~se** 1 (Math.) sine 2 ▸ **❶ S. 435** (Anat.) sinus

Sinus·kurve *die* sine curve

Siphon /'zi:fõ/ *der;* **~s, ~s** 1 siphon 2 (Geruchsverschluss) [anti-siphon] trap 3 (österr.: Sodawasser) soda [water]

Sippe /'zɪpə/ *die;* **~, ~n** 1 (Völkerk.) sib 2 (meist scherzh. od. abwertend: Verwandtschaft) clan 3 (Biol.) species

Sippen·haft *die: punishment of other members of a family or group for the crimes of one member*

Sippschaft *die;* **~, ~en** 1 (meist abwertend: Sippe) clan 2 (abwertend: Gesindel) bunch (coll.); crowd (coll.)

Sirene /zi're:nə/ *die;* **~, ~n** 1 siren 2 (Zool.) sirenian

Sirenen·geheul *das* wail of a/the siren/of sirens

sirren /'zɪrən/ *itr. V.* buzz

Sirtaki /zɪr'ta:ki/ *der;* **~, ~s** syrtos

Sirup /'zi:rʊp/ *der;* **~s, ~e** syrup; (streichfähig auch) treacle (Brit.); molasses *sing.* (Amer.)

Sisal /'zi:zal/ *der;* **~s** sisal

sistieren /zɪs'ti:rən/ *tr. V.* (Rechtsw.) detain

Sistierung *die;* **~, ~en** (Rechtsw.) detention

Sisyphus·arbeit /'zi:zyfʊs-/ *die* Sisyphean task; never-ending task

Sitemap /'saitmɛp/ *die;* **~, ~s** (DV) site map

Sitte /'zɪtə/ *die;* **~, ~n** 1 (Brauch) custom; tradition; **es ist in England [nicht] ~ …** it is [not] the custom in England …; **die ~n und Gebräuche eines Volkes** the customs and traditions of a people; **nach alter ~:** in the traditional way *or* manner 2 (moralische Norm) common decency; **gegen die guten ~n verstoßen** offend [against] common decency 3 *Pl.* (Benehmen) manners; **das sind ja feine ~n!** (iron.) that's a nice way to behave! (iron.) 4 (ugs.: Sittenpolizei) vice squad

sitten-, Sitten-: ~dezernat *das* vice squad; **~geschichte** *die* history of life and customs; **~lehre** *die* ethics *sing.;* moral philosophy; **~los** A *Adj.* immoral; B *adv.* immorally; **~polizei** *die* (volkst.) vice squad; **~richter** *der,* **~richterin** *die* (oft abwertend) moralist; moralizer; **sich zum ~richter erheben** sit in moral judgement [over sb.]; **~streng** *Adj.* (veralt.) morally strict; puritanical; **~strolch** *der* (Pressejargon) [sexual] molester; **~verfall** *der* moral decline; decline in moral standards; **~widrig** A *Adj.* 1 (Rechtsw.) illegal ‹*methods, advertising, etc.*›; 2 (unmoralisch) immoral ‹*behaviour*›; B *adv.* ▸ **A:** illegally; immorally

Sittich /'zɪtɪç/ *der;* **~s, ~e** parakeet

sittlich
A *Adj.* moral; **ihm fehlt die ~e Reife** he is morally immature
B *adv.* morally

Sittlichkeit *die* morality; morals *pl.*

Sittlichkeits-: ~verbrechen *das* sexual crime; **~verbrecher** *der* sex offender

sittsam (veralt.)
A *Adj.* 1 well-behaved ‹*child etc.*›; decorous ‹*behaviour*› 2 (keusch) demure
B *adv.* 1 in a well-behaved way 2 (keusch) demurely

Situation /zitu̯a'tsi̯o:n/ *die;* **~, ~en** situation

Situations·komik *die* comedy deriving from a/the situation

situiert *Adj.* **gut/schlechter ~ [sein]** [be] well off/worse off

Sitz /zɪts/ *der;* **~es, ~e** 1 seat; **er hat sich einen Stein als ~ ausgesucht** he picked a rock to sit on 2 (mit Stimmrecht) seat; **~ und Stimme haben** have a seat and a vote 3 (Regierungs~) seat; (Verwaltungs~) headquarters *sing. or pl.*; (einer Firma) head office; headquarters *sing. or pl.* 4 (sitzende Haltung) sitting position; (beim Reiten) seat 5 (von Kleidungsstücken) fit 6 **auf einen ~** (ugs.) in *or* at one go

Sitz-: ~bad *das* sitz-bath; hip bath; **~badewanne** *die* sitz-bath; hip bath; **~bank** *die; Pl.* **~bänke** bench; **~blockade** *die* sit-down blockade; **~ecke** *die* sitting area; (Möbelstück) corner seating unit

sitzen *unr. itr. V.; südd., österr., schweiz. mit sein* 1 sit; **eine ~de Lebensweise** a sedentary life; **bleiben Sie bitte ~:** please don't get up; please remain seated; **er saß den ganzen Tag an der Schreibmaschine/in der Kneipe** he spent the whole day at the typewriter/in the pub (Brit.); **auf der Anklagebank ~:** be in the dock; **er sitzt noch bei Tisch** *od.* **beim Essen** he is still eating *or* having his meal; **ich habe stundenlang beim Friseur ~ müssen** I had to spend hours at the hairdresser's; **im Sattel ~:** be in the saddle; **er sitzt viel über den Büchern** he spends a lot of time sitting over his books; **auf etw.** (*Dat.*) **~** (salopp: etw. nicht hergeben) hang on to sth.; not let go of sth.; **jmdm. auf der Pelle** *od.* **dem Pelz ~** (salopp) keep bothering sb.; keep on at sb. (coll.) 2 (sein) be; **die Firma sitzt in Berlin** the firm is based in Berlin; **die Tür sitzt schief in den Angeln** the door is not hanging straight; **der Schreck sitzt ihr noch in den Gliedern** she is still suffering from the shock; **einen ~ haben** (salopp) have had one too many; **etw. nicht auf sich** (*Dat.*) **~ lassen** not take sth.; not stand for sth. 3 ([gut] passen) fit; **die Krawatte sitzt nicht** the tie isn't straight 4 (ugs.: gut eingeübt sein) **Lektionen so oft wiederholen, bis sie ~:** keep on repeating lessons till they stick (coll.); **wir hatten so lange geübt, bis jede Schrittkombination wie im Schlafe saß** we had practised till we could do every step in our sleep 5 (ugs.: wirksam treffen) hit home 6 (Mitglied sein) be, sit (**in** + *Dat.* on) 7 (ugs.: eingesperrt sein) be in prison *or* (sl.) inside 8 (ugs.) **~ bleiben** (nicht versetzt werden) stay down [a year]; have to repeat a year; (abwertend: als Frau unverheiratet bleiben) be left on the shelf; **auf etw.** (*Dat.*) **~ bleiben** (etw. nicht verkaufen können) be left *or* (coll.) stuck with sth.; **jmdn. ~ lassen** (vergeblich warten lassen) stand sb. up (coll.); (im Stich lassen) leave sb. in the lurch; (nicht heiraten) jilt sb.; **er hat Frau und Kinder ~ lassen** he left his wife and children

°sitzen|bleiben ▸ **sitzen 8**

sitzen bleiben

If German pupils fail more than one subject in their end-of-year school report, they have to repeat the year. This is colloquially referred to as *sitzen bleiben*, and it means that some pupils do not manage to sit their **Abitur** until they are 20.

Sitzenbleiber *der;* **~s, ~, Sitzenbleiberin** *die;* **~, ~nen** (ugs. abwertend) pupil repeating a year; pupil who has to repeat a year

°sitzen|lassen ▸ **sitzen 2, 8**

Sitz-: ~erhöhung *die* booster cushion; booster seat; **~fleisch** *das* (ugs. scherzh.) **kein ~fleisch haben** not have the staying power; not be able to stick at it; (nicht stillsitzen können) not be able to sit still; **~gelegenheit** *die* seat; **~gruppe** *die* group of seats; **~kissen** *das* (im Sessel, Sofa) [seat] cushion; (auf dem Fußboden) [floor] cushion; **~ordnung** *die* seating plan *or* arrangement; **~platz** *der* seat; **~riese** *der* (ugs. scherzh.): *person who looks tall when sitting down;* **~rohr** *das* seat tube; saddle tube; **~stange** *die* perch; **~streik** *der* sit-down strike

Sitzung *die;* **~, ~en** 1 meeting; (Parlaments~) sitting; session 2 (beim Zahnarzt) visit; (beim Psychotherapeuten) session; (ugs. scherzh.: Toilettenbesuch) session 3 (das Porträtsitzen) sitting

Sitzungs-: ~bericht *der* minutes *pl.;* **~periode** *die* session; **~saal** *der* conference hall; (eines Gerichts) courtroom; **~zimmer** *das* conference room

sixtinisch /zɪks'ti:nɪʃ/ *Adj.* Sistine

S

Sizilianer /zitsi'li̯a:nɐ/ *der;* **∼s, ∼, Sizilianerin** *die;* **∼, ∼nen** Sicilian; *s. auch* **-in**
sizilianisch /zitsi'li̯a:nɪʃ/ *Adj.* Sicilian
Sizilien /zi'tsi:li̯ən/ *(das);* **∼s** Sicily
Skagerrak·schlacht /'ska:gərak-/ *die* (hist.) Battle of Jutland
Skala /'ska:la/ *die;* **∼, Skalen** 1) (Maßeinteilung, Musik) scale 2) (Reihe) range
Skalar *der;* **∼s, ∼s** (Math., Physik) scalar
Skalde /'skaldə/ *der;* **∼n, ∼n** skald
Skalden·dichtung *die* skaldic poetry
skalierbar *Adj.* (DV) scalable
skalieren *tr. V.* (DV) scale
Skalp /skalp/ *der;* **∼s, ∼e** scalp
Skalpell /skal'pɛl/ *das;* **∼s, ∼e** scalpel
skalpieren *tr. V.* scalp
Skandal /skan'da:l/ *der;* **∼s, ∼e** 1) scandal 2) (bes. nordd.: Lärm) row (coll.)
Skandal-: ∼geschichte *die* [piece of] scandal; **∼nudel** *die* (ugs.) **sie ist eine ∼nudel** she is always involved in some scandal or other
skandalös *Adj.* scandalous
skandieren /skan'di:rən/ *tr. V.* 1) chant 2) (Verslehre) scan
Skandinavien /skandi'na:vi̯ən/ *(das);* **∼s** Scandinavia
Skandinavier /skandi'na:vi̯ɐ/ *der;* **∼s, ∼, Skandinavierin** *die;* **∼, ∼nen** Scandinavian; *s. auch* **-in**
skandinavisch *Adj.* Scandinavian
Skarabäus /skara'bɛ:ʊs/ *der;* **∼, Skarabäen** scarab
Skat /ska:t/ *der;* **∼[e]s, ∼e** *od.* **∼s** skat; **∼ dreschen** *od.* **klopfen** (salopp) play skat

> **Skat**
> A popular card game for three players playing with 32 German cards. Keen players meet regularly for a game or even join a *Skat* club.

Skat·blatt *das* skat pack (Brit.) *or* (Amer.) deck
Skateboard /'skeɪtbɔ:d/ *das;* **∼s, ∼s** skateboard
skateboarden /'skeɪtbɔ:dn̩/ *itr. V.; mit sein* skateboard
Skateboarder /'skeɪtbɔ:dɐ/ *der;* **∼s, ∼:** skateboarder
skaten *itr. V.* 1) (ugs.) play skat 2) *mit sein* skate
Skater /'skeɪtɐ/ *der;* **∼s, ∼:** skater
Skat·spieler *der,* **Skat·spielerin** *die* skat player
Skeet·schießen /'ski:t-/ *das;* **∼s** (Sport) skeet [shooting] *no art.*
Skelett /ske'lɛt/ *das;* **∼[e]s, ∼e** skeleton; **er ist nur noch ein ∼** *od.* **das reinste ∼:** he is little more than a skeleton
Skelett·bauweise *die* (Bauw.) skeleton construction
Skepsis /'skɛpsɪs/ *die;* **∼:** scepticism
Skeptiker *der;* **∼s, ∼, Skeptikerin** *die;* **∼, ∼nen** sceptic
skeptisch
A *Adj.* sceptical
B *adv.* sceptically
Skeptizismus *der;* **∼:** scepticism
Sketch /skɛtʃ/ *der;* **∼[es], ∼e[s]** *od.* **∼s** sketch
Ski /ʃi:/ *der;* **∼s, ∼er** *od.* **∼:** ski; **∼ laufen** *od.* **fahren** ski; **er läuft** *od.* **fährt gut ∼:** he is a good skier; **∼ Heil!** ski heil!; good skiing!
Ski-: ∼bindung *die* ski binding; **∼bob** *der* ski-bob; **∼fliegen** *das;* **∼∼s, ∼flug** *der* ski flying *no art.*; **∼haserl** *das;* **∼∼s, ∼∼n** (südd., österr. scherzh.) [girl] skier; **∼lauf** *der,* **∼laufen** *das;* **∼∼s** skiing *no art.*; **∼läufer** *der,* **∼läuferin** *die* skier; **∼lehrer** *der,* **∼lehrerin** *die* ski instructor; **∼lift** *der* ski lift
Skinhead /'skɪnhɛd/ *der;* **∼s, ∼s** skinhead
Ski-: ∼springen *das;* **∼∼s** ski jumping *no art.*; **∼springer** *der,* **∼springerin** *die* ski jumper; **∼stiefel** *der* ski boot; **∼stock** *der* ski stick; ski pole; **∼zirkus** *der* (Sportjargon) ski circus
Skizze /'skɪtsə/ *die;* **∼, ∼n** 1) (Zeichnung) sketch 2) (Konzept) outline 3) (kurze Aufzeichnung) [brief] account
Skizzen·block *der; Pl.* **∼s** *od.* **Skizzenblöcke** sketch pad; sketch block
skizzen·haft
A *Adj.* rough ‹*drawing, outline*›
B *adv.* roughly
skizzieren *tr. V.* 1) (zeichnen) sketch 2) (aufzeichnen) outline 3) (entwerfen) draft
Sklave /'skla:və/ *der;* **∼n, ∼n** slave; **jmdn. zum ∼n machen** make a slave of sb.; **er ist der ∼ seiner Gewohnheiten** (fig. abwertend) he is a slave to habit
Sklaven-: ∼arbeit *die* 1) slavery *no art.*; work as slaves *no art.*; 2) (abwertend: schwere Arbeit) drudgery *no art.*; **∼halter** *der,* **∼halterin** *die* slave owner; **∼haltergesellschaft** *die* (bes. marx.) slave-owning society; **∼händler** *der,* **∼händlerin** *die* (auch fig. abwertend) slave trader
Sklaverei *die;* **∼** 1) (auch fig. abwertend) slavery *no art.* 2) (oft abwertend: harte Arbeit) drudgery *no art.*
Sklavin *die;* **∼, ∼nen ▸Sklave**; *s. auch* **-in**
sklavisch /'skla:vɪʃ/ (abwertend)
A *Adj.* slavish
B *adv.* slavishly
Sklerose /skle'ro:zə/ *die;* **∼, ∼n ▸ⓘ S. 439** (Med.) sclerosis *no art.*
skontieren /skɔn'ti:rən/ *tr. V.* (Kaufmannsspr.) **eine Rechnung ∼:** allow a [cash] discount on a bill
Skonto /'skɔnto/ *der od. das;* **∼s, ∼s** (Kaufmannsspr.) [cash] discount; **bei Barzahlung binnen 10 Tagen gewähren wir 3% ∼ auf den Rechnungsbetrag** we allow a 3% discount if payment is made in cash within ten days
Skooter /'sku:tɐ/ *der;* **∼s, ∼:** dodgem; bumper car
Skorbut /skɔr'bu:t/ *der;* **∼[e]s ▸ⓘ S. 439** (Med.) scurvy *no art.*
Skorpion /skɔr'pi̯o:n/ *der;* **∼s, ∼e** 1) (Tier) scorpion 2) (Astrol.) Scorpio; *s. auch* **Fisch**
Skribent /skri'bɛnt/ *der;* **∼en, ∼en, Skribentin** *die;* **∼, ∼nen** (veralt. abwertend) scribbler
Skript /skrɪpt/ *das;* **∼[e]s, ∼en** *od.* **∼s** script; (Manuskript) manuscript
Skript·girl *das* **▸ⓘ S. 113** (Film) script girl
Skriptum /'skrɪptʊm/ *das;* **∼s, Skripten** *od.* **Skripta** (österr., sonst veralt.) manuscript
Skrotum /'skro:tʊm/ *das;* **∼s, Skrota ▸ⓘ S. 435** (Anat.) scrotum
Skrupel /'skru:pl̩/ *der;* **∼s, ∼:** scruple; **∼ haben** *od.* **kennen** have scruples
skrupel·los (abwertend)
A *Adj.* unscrupulous
B *adv.* unscrupulously
Skrupellosigkeit *die;* **∼** (abwertend) unscrupulousness
skrupulös /skrupu'lø:s/ *Adj.* (veralt.) scrupulous
Skull /skʊl/ *das;* **∼s, ∼s** (Seemannsspr., Rudersport) scull
skullen *itr. V.; auch mit sein* (Seemannsspr., Rudersport) scull
Skulptur /skʊlp'tu:ɐ̯/ *die;* **∼, ∼en** sculpture
skurril /skʊ'ri:l/
A *Adj.* absurd; droll ‹*person*›
B *adv.* absurdly
Skurrilität *die;* **∼, ∼en** absurdity
S-Kurve /'ɛs-/ *die* S-bend; double bend
Sky·beamer /'skai̯-/ *der;* **∼s, ∼:** laser projector
Slalom /'sla:lɔm/ *der;* **∼s, ∼s** (Ski-, Kanusport) slalom; **im ∼ fahren** (fig.) zigzag
Slang /slɛŋ/ *der;* **∼s** 1) (oft abwertend: Umgangssprache) slang 2) (Jargon) jargon
Slash /slɛʃ/ *der;* **∼s, ∼s** [forward] slash
s-Laut, *S-Laut /'ɛs-/ *der* (stimmlos) s-sound; (stimmhaft) z-sound
Slawe /'sla:və/ *der;* **∼n, ∼n, Slawin** *die;* **∼, ∼nen** Slav; *s. auch* **-in**
slawisch *Adj.* **▸ⓘ S. 670** Slav[ic]; Slavonic
Slawist *der;* **∼en, ∼en** Slavicist; Slavist
Slawistik *die;* **∼:** Slavonic studies *pl., no art.*
Slawistin *die;* **∼, ∼nen ▸Slawist**
Slibowitz /'sli:bovɪts/ *der;* **∼[es], ∼e** slivovitz
Slip /slɪp/ *der;* **∼s, ∼s** briefs *pl.*
Slipper *der;* **∼s, ∼[s]** slip-on [shoe]
Slogan /'slo:gn̩/ *der;* **∼s, ∼s** slogan
Slot /slɔt/ *der;* **∼[s], ∼** 1) (DV) slot 2) (Flugw.) slot
Slowake /slo'va:kə/ *der;* **∼n, ∼n ▸ⓘ S. 520** Slovak
Slowakei *die;* **∼:** Slovakia *no art.*
Slowakin *die;* **∼, ∼nen ▸ⓘ S. 520** Slovak
slowakisch *Adj.* **▸ⓘ S. 520, ▸ⓘ S. 670** Slovak; Slovakian
Slowene /slo've:nə/ *der;* **∼n, ∼n** Slovene; Slovenian
Slowenien *(das);* **∼s** Slovenia
Slowenin *die;* **∼, ∼nen** Slovene; Slovenian
Slowenisch *das;* **∼en ▸ⓘ S. 670** Slovene; Slovenian; *s. auch* **Deutsch**
Slow·fox /'slo:fɔks/ *der* slow foxtrot
Slum /slam/ *der;* **∼s, ∼s** slum
Smaragd /sma'rakt/ *der;* **∼[e]s, ∼e** emerald
Smaragd·eidechse *die* green lizard
smaragden *Adj.* emerald
smaragd·grün *Adj.* emerald green
smart /sma:ɐ̯t/ *Adj.* smart
Smartie /'sma:ti/ *der;* **∼s, ∼s** (ugs.) smart guy (coll.)
Smartphone /'sma:tfoʊn/ *das;* **∼s, ∼s** smartphone
Smog /smɔk/ *der;* **∼[s], ∼s** smog
Smog·alarm *der* smog warning; **bei ∼:** if there is a smog warning
Smoking /'smo:kɪŋ/ *der;* **∼s, ∼s** dinner jacket *or* (Amer.) tuxedo and dark trousers
SMS *die;* **∼, ∼** SMS (message)
Smutje /'smʊtjə/ *der;* **∼s, ∼s** (Seemannsspr.) ship's cook
Snaredrum /'snɛ:ɐdram/ *die;* **∼, ∼s** (Musik) snare drum
Sneaker /'sni:kɐ/ *der;* **∼s, ∼s** sneaker
Sneakpreview /'sni:kpri:vju:/ *die;* **∼, ∼s** (Film) sneak preview
Snob /snɔp/ *der;* **∼s, ∼s** (abwertend) snob
Snobismus *der;* **∼** (abwertend) snobbery; snobbishness
snobistisch *Adj.* (abwertend) snobbish
Snowboard /'snoʊbɔ:d/ *das;* **∼s, ∼s** snowboard
snowboarden /'snoʊbɔ:dn̩/ *itr. V.; mit sein* snowboard
Snowboarder /'snoʊbɔ:dɐ/ *der;* **∼s, ∼:** snowboarder
so /zo:/
A *Adv.* 1) (auf diese Weise; in, von dieser Art) like this/that; this/that way; **schreibe den Brief so, wie ich es dir gesagt habe** write the letter as I told you; **er hat sich nicht so verhalten, wie allgemein erwartet wurde** he did not behave in the way that was generally expected; **ihr sollt alles so lassen, wie es ist** you are to leave everything the way it is; **wenn du es so nennen willst** if you want to call it that; **die so genannte Rechtschreibreform** the so-called spelling reform; **so ist sie nun einmal** that's the way she is; **ist das [wirklich] so?** is that [really] true?; **so?** really?; **wenn dem so ist** if that's the case; **sei doch nicht so** don't be like that; **ich will [mal] nicht so sein** I don't want to be awkward; **so ist das!** (resigniert) that's the way it goes!; that's how it goes!; **so ist es!** (zustimmend) that's correct *or* right!; **ach, so ist das!** (begreifend) oh, I 'see!; **so, so** (meist iron.) oh, I 'see! **recht so!, gut so!** right!; that's fine!; **mir ist so, als ob ...** I have a feeling that ...; **so kann es einem gehen, wenn ...** that's what can happen if ...;

und das kam so and this is what happened; and it happened like this; **du musst dich entscheiden, so oder so** you must make up your mind one way or the other; **so oder so gerät der Minister unter Druck** either way the minister will come under pressure; **weiter so!** carry on in the same way!; **die Religion, so** (so sagt/schreibt) **Marx, ist ...** religion, according to Marx is ...; **„die Ausgaben", so** (so sagte) **der Minister, „..."** 'the expenditure', said the minister *or* the minister said, '...'
2▸ (in dem Maße, Grade; überaus) so; **eine so große Frau** such a big woman; **er ist nicht so dumm, das zu tun** he is not so stupid as to do that; **er ist [nicht] so groß wie du** he is [not] as tall as you [are]; **so weiß wie Schnee** as white as snow; **so viel wie** *od.* **als** as much as; **das war so viel wie eine Zusage** that was tantamount to a commitment; **das ist so viel wie gar nichts** this is almost nothing; **nimm, so viel [wie] du willst** take as much as you like; **noch einmal so viel** the same again; **halb/doppelt so viel** half/twice as much; **so viel für heute** (ugs.) that's all *or* enough for today; **wo wenig wie** *od.* **als möglich** as little as possible; **ich kann es so wenig wie du** I can't do it any more than you can; **so weit** (im großen Ganzen) by and large; on the whole; (bis jetzt) up to now; **so weit wie** *od.* **als möglich** as far as possible; **so weit sein** (ugs.) be ready; **es ist so weit** the time has come; **so gut es geht** as best I/he *etc.* can; **so gut ich konnte** as best I could; **sei doch nicht so laut!** don't make such a noise!; **reg dich doch nicht so auf!** don't get so worked up!; **was schreist du so?** why are you yelling like that?; **so... [wie...]** as... [as...]; **so bald wie möglich** as soon as possible; **fast so groß wie...** almost as tall as...; **du weißt so gut wie ich, dass...** you know as well as I do that...; **er ist ja so nett!** he's so nice!
3▸ (ugs.: solch...) such; **so ein Mann/so eine Frau/so ein Kind** such a man/woman/child; **ein so schönes Fest** such a lovely party; **so ein Pech/eine Frechheit!** what bad luck/a cheek!; **so ein Idiot!** what an idiot!; **hast du so etwas schon mal gesehen?** have you ever seen such a thing *or* anything like it?; **so etwas kann passieren** such things *pl.* can happen; **so etwas ist mir noch nie passiert** a thing like that has never *or* nothing like that has ever happened to me before; **so was von fett habe ich noch nie gesehen** I've never seen anyone so fat; **die Suppe war so was von ekelhaft** the soup was absolutely disgusting; **er ist so was von dämlich** he is so stupid; **so was von dämlich!** talk about stupidity! (coll.); **ist sie nicht Kontoristin oder so was?** isn't she a clerk or something?; **[na** *od.* **nein** *od.* **also] so was!** (überrascht/empört) well, I never!; **so etwas Schönes** something as beautiful as that; such a beautiful thing; **und so was nennt** *od.* **schimpft sich Wissenschaft/Mutter** and they call that science/she calls herself a mother; **so einer/eine/eins** one like that; one of those; **mit so einer würde ich mich nicht einlassen** I wouldn't get mixed up with that sort of woman *or* a woman of that sort; **so einer** *od.* **jemand wie Schmidt** somebody like Schmidt; **Ein Grahambrötchen? — Nein, so eins** A granary roll? — No, one of those *or* one like that; **das ist so ein** *od.* **so'n kleiner Dicker** (ugs.) he's a little fat man; **so nennt man das also** so 'that's what it's called; **so einer bist du also!** so 'that's the sort of person you are!; **Banker und so** bankers and people like that; **heißt sie nicht Karobowski oder so [ähnlich]?** isn't her name Karobowski or something like that?; **ich spiele ein bisschen Tischtennis, Billard und so** I play a bit of table tennis, billiards and that sort of thing
4▸ (ugs.: ungefähr) about; **so [um die** *od.* **an die** *od.* **etwa** *od.* **ungefähr] 50 Euro** about 50 euros
5▸ (ugs.: ohne etw. Bestimmtes) **ich brauche keine Leiter, da komme ich auch so ran** I don't need a ladder, I can reach it [without one]; **geht es so, oder soll ich Ihnen eine Tüte geben?** can you manage, or shall I give you a bag?; **Nimmst du Zucker zum Kaffee? — Nein, ich trinke ihn so** do you take sugar in coffee? — no, without; **du kannst sie kochen oder einfach so essen** you can cook it or eat it raw *or* just as it is; **die können Sie so** (ohne sie zu bezahlen) **mitnehmen** you can take these — they're free; **kosten die was oder kriegt man die so?** do you have to pay for them, or are they free?; **Warum fragst du? — Ach nur so** (ohne einen bestimmten Grund) Why do you ask? — Oh, no particular reason
B *Konj.* **1▸ so dass ▸sodass**
2▸ (konzessiv) however; **so sehr ich ihn auch immer unterstützt habe, dieses Mal kann ich ihm nicht helfen** however much I have always supported him, this time I can't help him ; **so Leid es mir tut, ich muss absagen** much as I regret it, I'll have to cry off
3▸ (geh.: wenn, falls) **so Gott will** God willing
C *Partikel* **1▸ wie ich so ging, da sah ich ...** I was just walking along, when I saw ...; **ich weiß nicht so recht, ob ich gehen soll** I'm not really sure if I should go; **ach, das hab ich nur so gesagt** oh, I didn't mean anything by that; **das ist mir nur so rausgerutscht** (ugs.) it just slipped out; **wie ist der neue Chef denn so?** (ugs.) what's the new boss like, then? (coll.); **er schlug die Tür zu, dass es nur so knallte** he slammed the door shut
2▸ (eine Zäsur ausdrückend) right; OK; **so, und nun?** right, [and] now what?
3▸ (in Aufforderungen verstärkend) **so halt doch endlich deinen Mund!** just hold your tongue, will you!; **so komm doch** come on now; **so glaub mir doch** you must believe me

s. o. *Abk.* **= siehe oben**

So. *Abk.* **= Sonntag** Sun.

SO *Abk.* **= Südost[en] ▸❶ S. 363** SE

Soap /soʊp/ *die;* ~, ~**s** (TV) soap

sobald *Konj.* as soon as

Söckchen /ˈzœkçən/ *das;* ~**s**, ~ **1▸** [little] sock **2▸** (Damen-, Kinderstrumpf) [short] sock; ankle sock

Socke /ˈzɔkə/ *die;* ~, ~**n** sock; **sich auf die ~n machen** (ugs.) get going; **von den ~n sein** (ugs.) be flabbergasted

Sockel /ˈzɔkl̩/ *der;* ~**s**, ~ **1▸** (einer Säule, Statue) plinth **2▸** (unterer Teil eines Hauses, Schrankes) base **3▸** (Elektrot.) base

Sockel·betrag *der* (Wirtsch.) basic sum

Socken *der;* ~**s**, ~ (südd., österr., schweiz.) **▸ Socke**

Socken·halter *der* [sock] suspender

Soda /ˈzoːda/ *die;* ~ *od. das;* ~**s** soda

so·dann *Adv.* **1▸** (danach) then; thereupon **2▸** (außerdem) and furthermore

so·dass, *so daß *Konj.* so that; **er war krank, ~ er die Reise verschieben musste** he was sick, [and] so he had to postpone the trip

Soda·wasser *das; Pl.* **Sodawässer** soda; soda water

Sod·brennen *das;* ~**s** heartburn; pyrosis

Sodom /ˈzoːdɔm/ *das;* ~**: Sodom; ~ und Gomorrha** Sodom and Gomorrah

Sodomie *die;* ~**:** sodomy *no art.*

sodomitisch *Adj.* sodomitic[al]

so·eben *Adv.* just; **die Nachricht kam ~:** the news came just now

Sofa /ˈzoːfa/ *das;* ~**s**, ~**s** sofa; settee

Sofa·kissen *das* [sofa] cushion; scatter cushion

so·fern *Konj.* provided [that]

soff /zɔf/ *1. u. 3. Pers. Sg. Prät. v.* **saufen**

so·fort *Adv.* immediately; at once; **er war ~ tot** he died instantly; **komm ~ her!** come here this instant *or* at once!; **diese Regelung gilt ab ~:** this ruling has immediate effect *or* takes effect immediately; **Ingenieure ab ~ gesucht** engineers required, should be ready to start immediately; **ich bin ~ fertig** I'll be ready in a moment; (mit einer Arbeit) I'll be finished in a moment; **[ich] komme ~:** [I'm] just coming; (Bedienung) I'll be right with you

Sofort·bild·kamera *die* (Fot.) instant-picture camera

Sofort·hilfe *die* emergency relief *or* aid

sofortig *Adj.* (unmittelbar) immediate

Sofort·maß·nahme *die* immediate measure

Soft·eis, *Soft-Eis /ˈzɔft|ais/ *das* soft ice cream

Softie /ˈzɔfti/ *der;* ~**s**, ~**s** (ugs.) softy

Software /ˈzɔftvɛːɐ̯/ *die;* ~, ~**s** (DV) software

sog /zoːk/ *1. u. 3. Pers. Sg. Prät. v.* **saugen**

sog. *Abk.* **= so genannt**

Sog *der;* ~**[e]s**, ~**e 1▸** (saugende Strömung) suction; (bei Schiffen) wake; (bei Fahr-, Flugzeugen) slipstream; (von Wasser, auch fig.) current **2▸** (Meeresk.) undertow

so·gar *Adv.* even; **sie ist krank, ~ schwer krank** she is ill, in fact *or* indeed seriously ill

***so·genannt ▸ so A 1**

so·gleich *Adv.* immediately; at once

Sohle /ˈzoːlə/ *die;* ~, ~**n 1▸** (Schuh~) sole; **eine kesse** *od.* **heiße ~ aufs Parkett legen** (ugs.) put up a good show on the dance floor; **auf leisen ~n** softly; noiselessly **2▸** (Fuß~) sole [of the foot]; **auf** *od.* **mit nackten ~n** barefoot; with bare feet **3▸** (Tal~) bottom; (eines Flusses) bottom; bed **4▸** (Bergmannsspr.) level; (Gruben~) floor **5▸** (Einlege~) insole

sohlen *tr. V.* sole

Sohn /zoːn/ *der;* ~**es**, **Söhne** /ˈzøːnə/ **1▸** (männlicher Nachkomme) son; **der ~ Gottes** the Son of God; **der verlorene ~:** the prodigal son **2▸** (fam.: Anrede an einen Jüngeren) son; boy

Söhnchen /ˈzøːnçən/ *das;* ~**s**, ~**:** little son; little boy

Sohne·mann *der* (fam.) son

soigniert /zoanˈjiːɐ̯t/ *Adj.* (geh.) soigné ‹*man, appearance*›; soignée ‹*woman*›

Soiree /zoaˈreː/ *die;* ~, ~**n** (geh.) soirée

Soja- /ˈzoːja-/: **~bohne** *die* soy[a] bean; **~soße** *die* soy[a] sauce

Sokrates /ˈzoːkratɛs/ *(der);* **Sokrates'** Socrates

Sokratiker /zoˈkraːtikɐ/ *der;* ~**s**, ~, **Sokratikerin** *die;* ~, ~**nen** Socratic

sokratisch *Adj.* Socratic

Sol *das;* ~**s**, ~**e** (Chemie) sol

so·lang[e] *Konj.* so *or* as long as; **~ du nicht alles aufgegessen hast** unless *or* until you have eaten everything up

solar /zoˈlaːɐ̯/ *Adj.* solar

solar-, Solar-: ~anlage *die* solar power plant; **~batterie** *die* (Elektrot.) solar battery; **~betrieben** *Adj.* solar-powered; ‹*housing development*› relying on solar energy; **~energie** *die* (Physik) solar energy

Solarium /zoˈlaːri̯ʊm/ *das;* ~**s**, **Solarien** /...i̯ən/ solarium

Solar-: ~kraftwerk *das* **▸ Sonnenkraftwerk**; **~mobil** *das;* ~~**s**, ~~**e** solar-powered vehicle; **~panel** /-pɛnl̩/ *das;* ~~**s**, ~~**s** solar panel; **~plexus** /-plɛksʊs/ *der;* ~~, ~~ /-plɛksuːs/ **▸❶ S. 435** (Anat.) solar plexus; **~technik** *die* (Energietechnik) solar technology *no art.*; **~zelle** *die* (Physik, Elektrot.) solar cell

Sol·bad *das* **1▸** (Kurort) saltwater spa **2▸** (Bad) saltwater bath; brine bath

solch /zɔlç/ *Demonstrativpron.* **1▸** *attr.* such; **~e Leute** such people; people like that; **[ein] ~er Glaube** such a belief; **ich habe ~en Hunger** I am so hungry; **ich habe ~e Kopfschmerzen** I've got such a headache; **das macht ~en Spaß!** it's so much fun! **2▸** *selbstständig* **~e wie die** people like that; **sie ist keine ~e** she is not like that; **die Sache als ~e** the thing as such; **es gibt ~e und ~e** (ugs.) it takes all sorts *or* kinds [to make a world]; **Ärzte gibt es ~e und ~e** there are doctors and doctors **3▸** *ungebeugt* (geh.: so [ein]) such; **bei ~ einem herrlichen Wetter** when the weather is so beautiful

solcher-: ~art A *indekl. Demonstrativpron.* such; **B** *Adv.* thus; **~gestalt** *Adv.* thus; in such a way

solcherlei *indekl. Adj.;* **▸ derlei**

solcher·maßen *Adv.* in such a way; in this way; (in solchem Grade) to such an extent

S

ℹ sollen

1. Verpflichtung

Im Präsens:

soll, sollst,sollt, sollen
= am/is/are to; (*vor allem bei Nichterfüllung*)
= am/is/are supposed to

Er soll morgen zum Arzt
= He is to go to the doctor tomorrow

Er soll morgen zum Arzt, aber er hat keine Möglichkeit hinzukommen
= He's supposed to go to the doctor tomorrow, but he has no way of getting there

Bei Dingen wird ausgesagt, wie etwas gewünscht wird:

Die beiden Flächen sollen fluchten
= The two surfaces are meant to be *od.* should be in alignment

Besonders in der 2. Person wirkt es oft als Befehl:

Du sollst sofort damit aufhören!
= You're to stop that at once!

Sie sollen die Pillen jeden Tag einnehmen
= You're to *od.* You must take the pills every day; (*wenn man es nicht tut*) You're supposed to take the pills every day

Er soll hereinkommen
= He is to come in; (*sagen Sie es ihm*) Tell him to come in

Und in der Vergangenheit:

Er sollte gestern zum Arzt
= He was [supposed] to go to the doctor yesterday

Sie sollte die Hauptrolle spielen
= She was [meant] to play the lead

Du solltest ihn anrufen* od. *hättest ihn anrufen sollen
= You were meant to phone him *od.* should have phoned him

Im Konjunktiv:

sollte, solltest, solltet, sollten
= should, ought to

Wir sollten früher aufstehen
= We ought to *od.* should get up earlier

Du solltest dich schämen!
= You ought to be ashamed!

In der Vergangenheit:

hätte/hättest/hätten ... sollen
= should have

Das hätte er nicht tun/sagen sollen
= He shouldn't have done/said that

Du hättest dort hingehen sollen
= You should have gone there

2. Zukunft

soll, sollst, sollt, sollen
= am/is/are to;

sollte, solltest, solltet, sollten
= was/were to

Hier wird vor allem das Geplante ausgedrückt:

Ich soll die Abteilung übernehmen
= I am to take over the department

Er sagte mir, ich sollte die Abteilung übernehmen
= He told me I was to take over the department

Hier soll ein Bürogebäude gebaut werden
= An office block is to be built here

Du sollst dein Geld zurückbekommen
= You shall get your money back

Es soll nicht wieder vorkommen
= It won't happen again

Vor allem in Fragen kommt Ratlosigkeit zum Ausdruck:

Was soll man da machen?
= What is one to do?, What shall I/we do?

Ich weiß nicht, was ich machen soll
= I don't know what I should do *od.* what to do

Die Vergangenheit *sollte, solltest, solltet, sollten* kann auch von einem Zeitpunkt in der Vergangenheit auf damals noch zukünftige Ereignisse bezogen sein:

Sie sollten ihr Reiseziel nie erreichen
= They were never to reach their destination

Es sollte ganz anders kommen
= Things were to turn out quite differently

3. Allgemein verbreitete Meinung, Bericht

***soll/sollte* usw.**
= is/was supposed to

***Er soll sehr reich sein* (= Es heißt, dass er sehr reich ist)**
= He is supposed *od.* is said to be very rich

Sie soll geheiratet haben
= They say *od.* I gather she has got married

Seine Worte sollten als Warnung aufgefasst werden
= His words were meant *od.* supposed to be taken as a warning

Was soll dieses Bild darstellen?
= What is this picture supposed *od.* meant to represent?

Was soll das heißen?
= What is that supposed to mean?

Die drei letzten Beispiele beziehen sich auf die Absicht des Sprechenden bzw. des Urhebers.

4. Konditional

***sollte* usw. in Bedingungssätzen**
= should

Sollte er anrufen* od. *Falls er anrufen sollte, ...
= Should he *od.* If he should telephone, ...

Sold /zɔlt/ *der;* **~[e]s, ~e** 1 (veralt.) pay; **in jmds. ~ stehen** be in the pay of sb. *or* sb.'s pay; **im ~e des Kaisers stehen** be in the service of the emperor 2 ▸**Wehrsold**

Soldat /zɔlˈdaːt/ *der;* **~en, ~en** ▸ℹ **S. 113** soldier; **~ auf Zeit** soldier serving for a fixed period

Soldaten-: ~fried·hof *der* military *or* war cemetery; **~sprache** *die* army *or* soldiers' slang

Soldatin *die;* **~, ~nen** ▸ℹ **S. 113** [female *or* woman] soldier; **sie ist ~:** she is a soldier

soldatisch
A *Adj.* military ‹*discipline, expression, etc.*›; soldierly ‹*figure, virtue*›
B *adv.* in a military *or* soldierly manner

Sold·buch *das* (hist.) [military] pay-book

Söldner /ˈzœldnɐ/ *der;* **~s, ~:** mercenary

Söldner·heer *das* mercenary army; army of mercenaries

Söldnerin *die;* **~, ~nen** mercenary

Söldner·truppe *die* mercenary force; force of mercenaries

Sole /ˈzoːlə/ *die;* **~, ~n** salt water; brine

Sol·ei *das* pickled egg

solid /zoˈliːt/ ▸**solide**

Solidar·gemeinschaft *die* mutually supportive group; (die Gesellschaft) caring society

solidarisch
A *Adj.* **~es Verhalten zeigen** show one's solidarity; **sich mit jmdm. ~ erklären** declare one's solidarity with sb.
B *adv.* **~ handeln/sich ~ verhalten** act in/show solidarity

solidarisieren *refl. V.* show [one's] solidarity

Solidarität *die;* **~:** solidarity

Solidaritäts-: ~adresse *die* expression of solidarity; **~streik** *der* solidarity strike

> **Solidaritätszuschlag**
> A tax surcharge introduced to help pay for the enormous cost of German reunification and rebuilding the economy in the East. It is payable by every German taxpayer and firm.

Solidar·prinzip *das* principle of mutual support

solide
A *Adj.* 1 (massiv, gediegen) solid ‹*rock, wood, house*›; sturdy ‹*shoes, shed, material, fabric*›; solid, sturdy ‹*furniture*›; [good-]quality ‹*goods*› 2 (gut fundiert) sound ‹*work, workmanship, education, knowledge*›; solid ‹*firm, business*› 3 (anständig) respectable ‹*person, life, occupation, profession*›
B *adv.* 1 (gediegen) solidly ‹*built*›; sturdily ‹*made*› 2 (gut fundiert) soundly ‹*educated, constructed*› 3 (anständig) ‹*live*› respectably, steadily

Solidität *die;* **~** ▸**solide A 1-3**: solidness; sturdiness; soundness; respectability

Solipsismus /zoliˈpsɪsmʊs/ *der;* **~** (Philos.) solipsism *no art.*

Solist /zoˈlɪst/ *der;* **~en, ~en**, **Solistin** *die;* **~, ~nen** soloist

solistisch *Adj.* solo

Solitär /zoliˈtɛːɐ̯/ *der;* **~s, ~e** solitaire

soll *1. u. 3. Pers. Sg. Präsens v.* **sollen**

Soll /zɔl/ *das;* **~[s], ~[s]** 1 (Kaufmannsspr., Bankw.: Schulden) debit; **~ und Haben** debit and credit; **im ~:** in debit 2 (Kaufmannsspr.: linke Buchführungsseite) debit side; **etw. im ~ verbuchen** enter sth. on the debit side 3 (Wirtsch.: Arbeits~) quota; **sein ~ erfüllen** *od.* **erreichen** achieve *or* meet one's target 4 (Wirtsch.: Plan~) quota; target

Soll·bruch·stelle, *Soll-Bruch·stelle *die* (Technik) predetermined breaking point

sollen
A *unr. Modalverb; 2. Part.* **~** 1 (bei Aufforderung, Anweisung, Auftrag) **er soll sofort kommen** he is to come immediately; **solltest du nicht bei ihm anrufen?** were you not supposed to ring him?; **was soll ich als nächstes tun?** what shall I do next?; what do you want me to do next?; **du sollst Vater und Mutter ehren** (bibl.) honour thy father and thy mother; **du sollst das lassen!** stop that *or* it!; **soll ich dir mal erzählen, was mir gestern passiert ist?** shall I tell you what happened to me yesterday?; **du weißt, dass du das nicht tun sollst** you know that you shouldn't *or* are not supposed to do that; **sie sagte, dass das nicht mehr vorkommen soll** she said it wouldn't happen again; **[sagen Sie ihm,] er soll hereinkommen** tell him to come in; **der soll mir nur mal kommen, dem werde ichs schon zeigen!** (ugs.) just let him come and I'll show him what for! (sl.); **und da soll man nicht böse werden/nicht lachen** and I'm not supposed to get angry/laugh; **ich soll dir schöne Grüße von Herrn Meier bestellen** Herr Meier asked me to give you *or* sends his best wishes 2 (bei Wunsch, Absicht, Vorhaben) **es soll ihm nützen** may it be of use to him; **du sollst dich hier wie zu Hause fühlen** I/we should like you to feel at home here; **niemand soll sagen, dass ich meine Pflicht vernachlässigt hätte** let no one say *or* no one shall say [that] I neglected my duty; **das soll dich doch nicht stören** don't let it bother you; **~ wir heute ein wenig früher gehen?** should we leave a little earlier today?; **du sollst alles haben, was du brauchst** you shall have everything you require; **der Schal soll zum Mantel**

passen the scarf is to *or* should match the coat; **er hat alles für sich behalten; soll er doch!** (ugs. abwertend) he has kept everything to himself; well, let him, if he wants to!; **das sollte ein Witz sein** that was meant to be a joke; **was soll denn das heißen?** what is that supposed to mean?; **wozu soll denn das gut sein?** what's the good of that?

[3]▸ (bei Ratlosigkeit) **was soll ich nur machen?** what am I to do?; **was soll nur aus ihm werden?** what is to become of him?; **er wusste nicht, wie er aus der Situation herauskommen sollte** he didn't know how to get out of the situation

[4]▸ (Notwendigkeit ausdrückend) **man soll so etwas nicht unterschätzen** it's not to be taken *or* it shouldn't be taken so lightly

[5]▸ *häufig im Konjunktiv II* (Erwartung, Wünschenswertes ausdrückend) **du solltest dich schämen** you ought to be ashamed of yourself; **das hättest du besser nicht tun ~:** it would have been better if you hadn't done that; **mit deiner Erkältung solltest du besser zu Hause bleiben** with your cold you had better stay at home; **wie sollte ich das wissen?** how was I to know that?

[6]▸ (jmdm. beschieden sein) **er sollte seine Heimat nicht wiedersehen** he was never to see his homeland again; **es hat nicht sein ~** *od.* **nicht ~ sein** it was not to be; **es sollte ganz anders kommen, als man erwartet hatte** things were to turn out quite differently than expected

[7]▸ *im Konjunktiv II* (eine Möglichkeit ausdrückend) **sollte es regnen, [dann] bleiben wir zu Hause** if it should rain, we will stay at home; **sollte ich mich geirrt haben, tut es mir Leid** if I have made *or* should I have made a mistake, I'm sorry; **wenn du ihn sehen solltest, sage ihm bitte ...** if you should see him, please tell him ...; **ich versuche es, und sollte ich auch verlieren** (geh.) I'll try, even though I may lose

[8]▸ *im Präsens* (sich für die Wahrheit nicht verbürgend) **das Restaurant soll sehr teuer sein** the restaurant is supposed *or* said to be very expensive; **wir ~ eine Gehaltserhöhung bekommen** we are supposed to be getting a pay rise; **das soll vorkommen** things like that can happen

[9]▸ *im Konjunktiv II* (Zweifel ausdrückend) **sollte das sein Ernst sein?** is he really being serious?; **sollte das wirklich wahr sein?** is that really true?

[10]▸ (können) **mir soll es gleich sein** it's all the same to me; it doesn't matter to me; **man sollte glauben, dass ...** you would think that ...; **so etwas soll es geben** it's not unheard of

[B] *tr., itr. V.* **was soll das?** what's the idea?; **Was solls? Ich kann ja doch nichts ändern** So what? I can't change anything anyway; **Soll ich? — Ja, du sollst!** Should I? — Yes, you should!; **was soll ich dort?** what would I do there?; **was soll der Unsinn?** what's all this nonsense about?; **warum soll ich das?** why am I to do that?; why should I do that?; **was man nicht alles soll/sollte!** the things one has to do!/is supposed to do!

Söller /ˈzœlɐ/ *der;* **~s, ~** (Archit.) balcony

Soll-: ~seite *die* (Kaufmannsspr., Bankw.) debit side; **~zinsen** *Pl.* interest *sing.* on [one's] debit balance; **~zustand** *der* desired state

Solmisation /zɔlmizaˈtsi̯oːn/ *die;* **~** (Musik) solmization

solo /ˈzoːlo/ *indekl. Adj.* [1]▸ (bes. Musik: als Solist) solo [2]▸ (ugs., oft scherzh.: ohne Begleitung) on one's own *postpos.*

Solo /ˈzoːlo/ *das;* **~s, ~s** *od.* **Soli** /ˈzoːli/ [1]▸ (bes. Musik) solo [2]▸ (bes. Fußballjargon) solo run

Solo-: ~album *das* solo album; **~-CD** *die* solo CD; **~gesang** *der* solo; **~platte** *die* solo disc; **~tänzer** *der,* **~tänzerin** *die* soloist

Sol·quelle *die* salt water *or* brine spring

solvent /zɔlˈvɛnt/ *Adj.* (bes. Wirtsch.) solvent

Solvenz /zɔlˈvɛnts/ *die;* **~, ~en** (bes. Wirtsch.) solvency

Somalia /zoˈmaːli̯a/ *(das);* **~s** Somalia

Somalier *der;* **~s, ~, Somalierin** *die;* **~, ~nen** Somali

somatisch /zoˈmaːtɪʃ/ *Adj.* (Physiol.) somatic

Sombrero /zɔmˈbreːro/ *der;* **~s, ~s** sombrero

so·mit /*auch:* ˈ--/ *Adv.* consequently; therefore; **... und somit kommen wir zu Punkt 3** ... and so *or* thus we come to number 3

Sommer /ˈzɔmɐ/ *der;* **~s, ~** ▸➊ **S. 395** summer; *s. auch* **Frühling**

Sommer-: ~abend *der* summer['s] evening; **~anfang** *der* beginning of summer; **~anzug** *der* summer suit; **~fahrplan** *der* summer timetable; **~fell** *das* summer coat; **~ferien** *Pl.* summer holidays; **~frische** *die* (veralt.) [1]▸ (Aufenthalt) summer holiday; **~frische machen** be on one's summer holiday; [2]▸ (Ort) summer [holiday] resort; **~frischler** *der;* **~~s, ~~, ~frischlerin** *die;* **~~, ~~nen** (veralt.) summer holidaymaker; **~gast** *der* summer visitor *or* holidaymaker; **~getreide** *das* (Landw.) summer cereal *or* corn; **~halbjahr** *das* summer season; **~haus** *das* [summer] holiday house; **~hit** *der* summer hit; **~kleid** *das* summer dress; **~kleidung** *die* summer clothes *pl. or* clothing

sommerlich ▸➊ **S. 395**
[A] *Adj.* summer; summery ‹*warmth, weather*›; summer's *attrib.* ‹*day, evening*›; **draußen ist es schon ganz ~:** it is already quite summery outside
[B] *adv.* **es war oft schon ~ warm** it was often as warm as summer; **sich ~ kleiden** wear summer clothes

Sommer-: ~loch *das* (ugs.) summer recess; **~mantel** *der* summer coat; **~mode** *die* summer fashions *pl.;* (eines Modehauses) summer collection; **~monat** *der* summer month; **~nacht** *die* summer['s] night; **~olympiade** *die* Summer Olympics *pl.;* **~pause** *die* summer break; (im Parlament) summer recess; **das Theater hat ~pause** the theatre is closed for the summer; **~reifen** *der* standard tyre; **~residenz** *die* summer residence; **~rodelbahn** *die* summer toboggan run; (Sport) summer luge run

sommers *Adv.* in summer

sommer-, Sommer-: ~saison *die* summer season; **~schlussverkauf,** ***~schlußverkauf** *der* summer sale/sales; **wann ist ~schlussverkauf?** when are the summer sales?; **~semester** *das* summer semester; **~sitz** *der* summer seat; **~smog** *der* summer smog; **~sonnenwende** *die* summer solstice; **~spiele** *Pl.* [1]▸ (Theater) summer festival *sing.;* [2]▸ (Olympische ~spiele) Summer Olympics; **~sprosse** *die* freckle; **~sprossig** *Adj.* freckled; **~tag** *der* summer['s] day; **~wetter** *das* summer weather; **~zeit** *die* [1]▸ (Jahreszeit) summertime; **zur ~zeit** in summertime; [2]▸ (Uhrzeit) summer time

Somnambulismus *der;* **~** ▸➊ **S. 439** (Med.) somnambulism *no art.*

son /zoːn/ *Demonstrativpron.* (salopp) **~e nette Person/~ altes Haus** such a nice person/an old house; **~ Idiot!** what an idiot!

so·nach *Adv.* (veralt.) therefore; consequently

Sonate /zoˈnaːtə/ *die;* **~, ~n** (Musik) sonata

Sonatine *die;* **~, ~n** (Musik) sonatina

Sonde /ˈzɔndə/ *die;* **~, ~n** [1]▸ (Med.) (zur Untersuchung) probe; (zur Ernährung) tube [2]▸ (Raum~) [space] probe

sonder /ˈzɔndɐ/ *Präp. mit Akk.* (veralt.) without; **~ Zahl** innumerable

Sonder-: ~abschreibung *die* (Wirtsch., Steuerw.) (das Abschreiben) special amortization; (Betrag) special depreciation provision; **~anfertigung** *die* special design; **das Auto ist eine ~anfertigung** the car has been custom-built *or* specially made; **~angebot** *das* special offer; **etw. im ~angebot anbieten** have a special offer on sth.; **~ausgabe** *die* [1]▸ special edition; [2]▸ (Steuerw.: private Aufwendungen) tax-deductible expenditure (*e.g. pensions, insurance contributions, interest payment*); [3]▸ (Extraausgabe) extra expense

sonderbar
[A] *Adj.* strange; odd
[B] *adv.* strangely; oddly

sonderbarer·weise *Adv.* strangely *or* oddly enough

Sonderbarkeit *die;* **~:** strangeness; oddness

Sonder-: ~behandlung *die* [1]▸ special treatment; [2]▸ (ns. verhüll.: Liquidierung) liquidation; **~botschafter** *der,* **~botschafterin** *die* ambassador extraordinary; **~druck** *der; Pl.* **~~e** offprint; **~fahrt** *die* special excursion; **~fall** *der* special case; exception; **~genehmigung** *die* special permit

sonder·gleichen *Adv., nachgestellt* **eine Frechheit/Unverschämtheit ~:** the height of cheek/impudence; **mit einer Hartnäckigkeit ~:** with unparalleled obstinacy

Sonderheit *in* **in ~** (geh.) particularly; in particular

Sonder-: ~kommando *das* special unit; **~konto** *das* special account

sonderlich
[A] *Adj.* [1]▸ (besonders groß, stark) particular; [e]special [2]▸ (sonderbar) strange; peculiar; odd
[B] *adv.* [1]▸ (besonders, sehr) particularly; especially; **ihm geht es nicht ~:** he is not particularly *or* (coll.) all that well [2]▸ (sonderbar) strangely

Sonderling *der;* **~s, ~e** strange *or* odd person

Sonder-: ~marke *die* special issue [stamp]; **~maschine** *die* special plane *or* aircraft; **~meldung** *die* (Rundf., Ferns.) news flash; **~müll** *der* hazardous waste

sondern[1] *tr. V.* (geh.) separate (**von** from)

sondern[2] *Konj.* but; **nicht er hat es getan, ~ sie** 'he didn't do it, 'she did; **nicht nur ..., ~ [auch] ...** not only ... but also ...; **Er ist kein Linguist. — Sondern?** He is not a linguist. — What is he then?; **es ist kein Original, ~ nur eine Reproduktion** it is not an original, but only a reproduction

Sonder-: ~nummer *die* special edition *or* issue; **~parteitag** *der* special party conference; **~posten** *der* (Wirtsch.) exceptional item; **~preis** *der* special *or* reduced price; **~reg[e]lung** *die* special ruling; **~rolle** *die* special role

sonders ▸**samt B**

Sonder-: ~schule *die* special school; **~sendung** *die* (Ferns., Rundf.) special programme; **~stempel** *der* special postmark; **~urlaub** *der* [1]▸ (Milit.) special leave; [2]▸ (zusätzlicher Urlaub) special *or* extra holiday; **~wunsch** *der* special request *or* wish; **~ziehungs·rechte** *Pl.* (Wirtsch.) special drawing rights; **~zug** *der* special train

sondieren /zɔnˈdiːrən/ *tr. V.* [1]▸ sound out; **das Terrain ~:** see *or* find out how the land lies [2]▸ (Med.) probe

Sondierungs·gespräch *das* exploratory talks *pl.*

sone ▸**son**

Sonett /zoˈnɛt/ *das;* **~[e]s, ~e** sonnet

Song /sɔŋ/ *der;* **~s, ~s** song

Songwriter /ˈsɔŋrai̯tɐ/ *der;* **~s, ~, Songwriterin** *die;* **~, ~nen** songwriter

Sonn·abend /ˈzɔn|aːbn̩t/ *der* ▸➊ **S. 165,** ▸➊ **S. 816** (bes. nordd.) Saturday; **an ~en und Sonntagen** on Saturdays and Sundays; **der verkaufsoffene** *od.* **lange ~:** Saturday on which the shops are open all day; *s. auch* **Dienstag; Dienstag-**

sonn·abends *Adv.* ▸➊ **S. 816** on Saturday[s]; *s. auch* **dienstags**

Sonne *die;* **~, ~n** sun; (Licht der ~) sun[light]; **das Zimmer hat den ganzen Tag über ~:** the room gets sun[light] all day long

sonnen *refl. V.* sun oneself; **sich in etw.** (*Dat.*) **~** (fig.) bask in sth.

sonnen-, Sonnen-: ~anbeter *der;* **~~s, ~~, ~anbeterin** *die;* **~~, ~~nen** (scherzh.) sun worshipper; **~aufgang** *der* sunrise; **~bad** *das* sunbathing *no pl., no indef.*

S

art.; ein ~bad nehmen sunbathe; ~baden itr. V. sunbathe; das ~baden sunbathing no art.; ~bahn die (Astron.) path of the sun; sun's path; ~bank die; Pl. ~bänke sunbed; ~beschienen Adj. (geh.) sunny; ~bestrahlung die: bestimmte Pflanzen dürfen keiner direkten ~bestrahlung ausgesetzt werden certain plants are not supposed to be put in direct sunlight; ~blende die 1 (Fot.) lens hood; 2 (im Auto) sun visor; ~blume die sunflower; ~blumen·kern der sunflower seed; ~brand der ▸ⓘ S. 439 sunburn no indef. art.; ~bräune die suntan; ~brille die sunglasses pl.; ~creme die sun cream; ~dach das sun canopy; ~deck das sun deck; ~durchflutet Adj. (geh.) sunny; ~einstrahlung die (Met.) insolation; ~energie die (Physik) solar energy; ~finsternis die (Astron.) solar eclipse; eclipse of the sun; ~fleck der (Astron.) sunspot; ~gebräunt Adj. suntanned; ~geflecht das ▸ⓘ S. 435 (Anat.) solar plexus; ~gott der (Rel.) sun god; ~göttin die (Rel.) sun goddess; ~hut der sunhat; ~klar Adj. (ugs.) crystal clear; die Sache ist ~klar, er ist der Dieb he is the thief — it's as clear as daylight; ~kollektor der (Energietechnik) solar collector; ~kraftwerk das solar power station; ~licht das sunlight; ~öl das suntan oil; sun oil; ~schein der 1 sunshine; bei ~schein in sunshine; bei ~schein steigen die Temperaturen bis auf 24 °C where the sun shines temperatures will rise to 24 °C; 2 (fam.: geliebtes Kind) [little] ray of sunshine; ~schirm der sunshade; (zum Tragen) parasol; sunshade; ~schutz·creme die suntan lotion; ~segel das 1 (Schutzdach) awning; 2 (bei Raumflugkörpern) solar sail; ~seite die sunny side; die ~seite des Lebens (fig.) the bright side of life; ~stich der ▸ⓘ S. 439 (Med.) sunstroke no indef. art.; du hast wohl einen ~stich (fig. salopp) you must be mad; ~strahl der ray of sun[shine]; ~system das (Astron.) solar system; ~tag der 1 sunny day; day of sunshine; 2 (Astron.) solar day; ~tau der (Bot.) sundew; ~uhr die sundial; ~untergang der sunset; ~wende die solstice; ~wind der (Astron.) solar wind; ~zelle die (Physik, Elektrot.) solar cell

sonnig Adj. 1 sunny; (fig.) happy ‹youth, childhood, time›; cheerful ‹sense of humour, ways› 2 (iron.: naiv) naive

Sonn·tag der ▸ⓘ S. 165, ▸ⓘ S. 816 Sunday; s. auch Dienstag; Dienstag-

sonn·täglich ▸ⓘ S. 816

A Adj. Sunday attrib.

B adv. ~ gekleidet sein be dressed in one's Sunday best

sonntags Adv. ▸ⓘ S. 816 on Sunday[s]; s. auch dienstags

Sonntags-: ~arbeit die Sunday working no art.; ~ausflug der Sunday outing; ~ausgabe die Sunday issue or edition; ~beilage die Sunday supplement; ~braten der Sunday roast; ~dienst der Sunday duty; ~fahrer der, ~fahrerin die (abwertend) Sunday driver; ~kind das 1 Sunday's child; 2 (Glückskind) lucky person; er ist ein ~kind he was born lucky or under a lucky star; ~predigt die Sunday sermon; ~reden Pl. (abwertend) soapbox oratory no pl., no art.; ~schule die Sunday school; ~staat der (scherzh.) Sunday best; im ~staat in one's Sunday best; ~zeitung die Sunday [news-]paper

Sonnwend·feier die midsummer/midwinter festival or celebrations pl.

Sonny·boy /'sanɪ-/ der; ~s, ~s golden boy

sonor /zo'no:ɐ̯/ Adj. sonorous

sonst /zɔnst/ Adv. 1 der ~ so freundliche Mann ... the man, who is/was usually so friendly, ...; er hat es wie ~ gemacht/besser als ~ gemacht he did it as usual/better than usual; alles war wie ~: everything was [the same] as usual; war das auch ~ so? has it always been like that? 2 (außerdem, im Übrigen) otherwise; ~ war alles unverändert otherwise nothing had changed; wie gehts ~? how are things otherwise?; haben Sie ~ noch Fragen? have you any other questions?; kommt ~ noch jemand od. wer? is anybody else coming?; es wusste ~ niemand nobody or no one else knew; hat er ~ nichts erzählt? [apart from that,] he didn't say anything else?; er war ganz gut in Mathematik, aber ~? he was quite good in mathematics, but apart from that?; ~ noch was? (ugs., auch iron.) anything else?; ~ nichts, nichts ~: nothing else; und wer weiß wer ~ noch and goodness knows who else; [aber] ~ gehts dir gut od. ~ tut dir nichts weh? (salopp iron.) anything else [you'd want]? (iron.); wer/was/wie/wo [denn] ~? who/what/how/where else?; ~ jemand od. wer (ugs.) somebody else; (fragend, verneint) anybody else; da könnte ja ~ jemand kommen (ugs.) anybody could or might come; er meint, er ist ~ wer (ugs.) he thinks he's really something or he's the bee's knees (coll.); ~ was (ugs.) anything else; er hat ~ was unternommen (ugs.) he has tried all sorts of things; man hätte annehmen können, die Kinder hätten ~ was angestellt you would have thought the children had done something terrible; ~ wie (ugs.) in some other way; (fragend, verneint) in any other way; ~ wo/wohin (ugs.) somewhere else; (fragend, verneint) anywhere else; ~ woher (ugs.) [from] somewhere else; (fragend, verneint) [from] anywhere else 3 (andernfalls) otherwise; or

sonstig... Adj. other; further; sein ~es Verhalten war gut his behaviour was otherwise good; „Sonstiges" 'miscellaneous'

***sonst-:** ~jemand, ~was usw. ▸ sonst 2

so·oft Konj. whenever; ich komme, ~ du es wünschst I'll come as often as you wish

Soor /zo:ɐ̯/ der; ~[e]s, ~e ▸ⓘ S. 439 (Med.) thrush no art.

Sophismus /zo'fɪsmʊs/ der; ~, Sophismen (Philos.) sophism

Sophisterei die; ~, ~en (abwertend) sophistry

Sophistik die; ~ (Philos.) sophistry

sophistisch

A Adj. sophistic[al]

B adv. sophistically

Sophokles /'zo:foklɛs/ (der); Sophokles' Sophocles

Sopran /zo'pra:n/ der; ~s, ~e (Musik) 1 (Stimmlage) soprano [voice] 2 (im Chor) sopranos pl. 3 (Sängerin) soprano

Sopranist der; ~en, ~en sopranist

Sopranistin die; ~, ~nen soprano

Sorbe /'zɔrbə/ der; ~n, ~n Sorb

Sorbet /'zɔrbɛt/ der od. das; ~s, ~s (Gastr.) sorbet

Sorbin die; ~, ~nen ▸ Sorbe

Sore /'zo:rə/ die; ~, ~n (Gaunerspr.) loot

Sorge /'zɔrgə/ die; ~, ~n 1 (Unruhe, Angst) worry; keine ~: don't [you] worry; [keine] ~ haben, dass ... [not] be worried that ...; in ~ um jmdn./etw. sein be worried about sb./sth.; etw. erfüllt jmdn. mit ~: sth. worries sb. 2 (sorgenvoller Gedanke) worry; ich mache mir ~n um dich/um deine Gesundheit I am worried about you/about your health; mach dir darum od. darüber od. deswegen keine ~: don't worry about that; der hat ~n! (ugs. iron.) and he thinks 'he's got problems (coll. iron.); lassen Sie das meine ~ sein let 'me worry about that; er ertränkte seine ~n im Alkohol he drowned his sorrows in alcohol 3 (Mühe, Fürsorge) care; die ~ für die Familie caring for the family; die ~ um das tägliche Brot the worry of providing one's daily bread; für etw./(schweiz. auch:) einer Sache (Dat.) ~ tragen (geh.) take care of sth.; ich werde dafür ~ tragen, dass ... I will see to it or make sure that ...; das lass nur meine ~ sein let that be 'my concern or responsibility

sorgen

A refl. V. worry, be worried (um about); sie sorgt sich wegen jeder Kleinigkeit she worries about every little detail

B itr. V. 1 für jmdn./etw. ~: take care of or look after sb./sth.; für das Essen/Ruhe und Ordnung/gute Laune ~: look after the food/make sure that law and order prevail/make sure that people are in a good mood; für die Zukunft der Kinder ist gesorgt the children's future is provided for 2 (verblasst: bewirken) für etw. ~: cause sth.

sorgen-, Sorgen-: ~frei A Adj. carefree ‹person, future, existence, etc.›; B adv. ~frei leben live in a carefree manner; ~kind das (auch fig.) problem child; ~voll A Adj. worried; anxious; B adv. worriedly; anxiously

Sorge-: ~pflicht die: eine ~pflicht gegenüber seinen Kindern haben have a duty to provide for one's children; ~recht das (Rechtsw.) custody (für of)

Sorg·falt /'zɔrkfalt/ die; ~: care; große ~ auf etw. (Akk.) verwenden od. legen take great or a great deal of care over sth.

sorg·fältig

A Adj. careful; eine ~e Arbeit a job/piece of work done with care

B adv. carefully

Sorgfältigkeit die; ~: carefulness

Sorgfalts·pflicht die duty of care

sorg·los

A Adj. 1 (ohne Sorgfalt) careless 2 (unbekümmert) carefree

B adv. ~ mit etw. umgehen treat sth. carelessly

Sorglosigkeit die; ~ 1 (Mangel an Sorgfalt) carelessness 2 (Unbekümmertheit) carefreeness

sorgsam

A Adj. careful

B adv. carefully

sorry /'sɔri/ Interj. sorry

Sorte /'zɔrtə/ die; ~, ~n 1 sort; type; kind; (Marke) brand; bitte ein Pfund von der besten ~: a pound of the best quality, please 2 Pl. (Devisen) foreign currency sing.

Sorten·kurs der (Bankw.) exchange rate

sortieren tr. V. sort [out] ‹pictures, letters, washing, etc.›; grade ‹goods etc.›; (fig.) arrange ‹thoughts›; die Stücke werden nach der Größe sortiert the pieces are sorted according to size

Sortier·maschine die sorter; sorting machine

sortiert Adj. 1 ein gut/schlecht ~es Lager a well-stocked/badly stocked warehouse; dieses Geschäft ist sehr gut in französischen Rotweinen ~: this shop has a good range of French red wines 2 (erlesen) selected

Sortiment /zɔrti'mɛnt/ das; ~[e]s, ~e 1 range (an + Dat. of) 2 (Buchhandel) retail book trade

Sortimenter der; ~s, ~, Sortimenterin die; ~, ~nen retail bookseller; book retailer

Sortiments-: ~buchhandel der retail book trade; ~buchhandlung die retail bookshop

SOS /ɛs|o:'|ɛs/ das; ~: SOS; ~ funken send or put out an SOS

so·sehr Konj. however much

so·so

A Interj. 1 (ironisch, zweifelnd) I see 2 (gleichgültig) oh yes?; really?

B Adv. (ugs.) so-so

SOS-Ruf /ɛs|o:'|ɛs-/ der SOS [call]

Soße /'zo:sə/ die; ~, ~n 1 sauce; (Braten~) gravy; sauce; (Salat~) dressing 2 (salopp abwertend: schmutzige Flüssigkeit) muck (coll.)

Soßen-: ~löffel der gravy or sauce ladle; ~schüssel die gravy or sauce boat

sott /zɔt/ 1. u. 3. Pers. Sg. Prät. v. sieden

Soubrette /zu'brɛtə/ die; ~, ~n (Musik, Theater) soubrette

Soufflé /zu'fle:/ das; ~s, ~s (Gastr.) soufflé

Souffleur /zu'flø:ɐ̯/ der; ~s, ~e ▸ⓘ S. 113 (Theater) prompter

Souffleur·kasten der prompt box

Souffleuse /zu'flø:zə/ die; ~, ~n ▸ⓘ S. 113 prompter

soufflieren /zu'fli:rən/ tr. V. prompt; jmdm. etw. ~: prompt sb. by whispering sth.

soulig /'soʊlɪç/

A Adj. soul-influenced

B adv. with a soul feel; ‹sound› like soul

S

Soul·musik /'soul-/ *die* soul music
Sound-: ~check /-tʃɛk/ *der;* **~~s, ~~s** sound check; **~karte** *die* (DV) sound card
so·und·so
A *Adv.; vorangestellt* **~ groß/breit/lang** [of] such-and-such a size/width/length; **~ viel kosten** cost such-and-such; cost so-and-so much
B *Adj.; nachgestellt* **Paragraph ~:** paragraph such-and-such *or* so-and-so; **Fanny ~:** Fanny something-or-other; **die Soundso** what's-her-name
Soundtrack /'-træk/ *der;* **~s, ~s** soundtrack
Souper /zu'pe:/ *das;* **~s, ~s** (geh.) dinner [party]
soupieren *itr. V.* (geh.) dine
Soutane /zu'ta:nə/ *die;* **~, ~n** soutane
Souterrain /'zu:tɛrɛ̃/ *das;* **~s, ~s** basement
Souvenir /zuvə'ni:ɐ̯/ *das;* **~s, ~s** souvenir
souverän /zuvə'rɛ:n/
A *Adj.* **1** (unabhängig) sovereign **2** (geh.: überlegen) superior
B *adv.* **die Lage ~ meistern** be in total command of the situation; **er siegte ganz ~:** he won in a very impressive way
Souverän *der;* **~s, ~e** **1** (Herrscher, Fürst) sovereign **2** (schweiz.: die Stimmbürger) electorate
Souveränität *die;* **~:** sovereignty
so·viel *Konj.* **1** (nach dem, was) as *or* so far as; **~ mir bekannt ist** so far as I know; **~ ich sehe** as far as I can see **2** (in wie großem Maße auch immer) however much; *s. auch* **so A 2**
Sowchose /'zɔfço:zə/ *die;* **~, ~n** sovkhoz
so·weit *Konj.* **1** (nach dem, was) as *or* so far as; **~ mir bekannt ist** so far as I know; **~ ich sehe** as far as I can see **2** (in dem Maße, wie) [in] so far as; **~ ich dazu in der Lage bin, will ich gerne helfen** [in] so far as I am in a position to do so *or* am able to, I should like to help; *s. auch* **so A 2**
so·wenig *Konj.* however little; *s. auch* **so A 2**
so·wie *Konj.* **1** (und auch) as well as **2** (sobald) as soon as
so·wie·so *Adv.* anyway; **das ~!** (ugs.) that goes without saying!; of course!; **Herr S~:** Mr What's-his-name
Sowjet /zɔ'vjɛt/ *der;* **~s, ~s** **1** (Behörde) soviet; **der Oberste ~:** the Supreme Soviet **2** *Pl.* (Führung) Soviets; Russians
Sowjet-: ~armee *die* Soviet army; **~bürger** *der,* **~bürgerin** *die* Soviet citizen
sowjetisch *Adj.* Soviet
sowjetisieren *tr. V.* sovietize
Sowjet·mensch *der* Soviet citizen
Sowjetologie *die;* **~:** sovietology *no art.*
Sowjet-: ~republik *die* **1** (Gliedstaat) Soviet republic; **Union der Sozialistischen ~republiken** Union of Soviet Socialist Republics; **2** (hist.) soviet republic; **~russe** *der,* **~russin** *die* Soviet Russian; **~stern** *der* Soviet star; star of the Soviets; **~union** *die* Soviet Union; **~zone** *die* (hist.) Soviet zone
so·wohl *Konj.* **~ ... als** *od.* **wie [auch] ...** both ... and ...; ... as well as ...
Sozi /'zo:tsi/ *der;* **~s, ~s** (ugs., auch abwertend) socialist
sozial /zo'tsia:l/
A *Adj.* social; **die ~e Frage** (hist.) the social question; **~e Einrichtungen** public amenities; **ich habe heute meinen ~en Tag** (ugs.) I'm feeling charitable *or* generous today; **dieses Verhalten ist nicht sehr ~:** this behaviour is not very public-spirited; **~e Marktwirtschaft** social market economy
B *adv.* socially; **~ denken** be socially minded; **~ handeln** act in a socially conscious *or* public-spirited way
sozial-, Sozial-: ~abbau *der* dismantling of the welfare state; **~abgaben** *Pl.* social welfare contributions; **~amt** *das* social welfare office; **~arbeit** *die* social work; **~arbeiter** *der,* **~arbeiterin** *die* ▸ℹ S. 113 social worker; **~beruf** *der* social services profession; **in ~berufen arbeiten** work for *or* in the social services; **~charta** *die* (EU) Social Charter; **~demokrat** *der* Social Democrat; **~demokratie** *die* social democracy *no art.;* **~demokratin** *die* ▸**~demokrat;** **~demokratisch** *Adj.* social democratic; **Sozialdemokratische Partei [Deutschlands]** [German] Social Democratic Party; **~ethik** *die* social ethics *sing.;* **~fall** *der* hardship case; **~fonds** *der* (EU) Social Fund; **~gericht** *das* social welfare court; **~geschichte** *die* social history; **~gesetzgebung** *die* social welfare legislation; **~hilfe** *die* social welfare; **~hygiene** *die* community medicine; **~imperialismus** *der* social imperialism

> **Sozialabgaben**
>
> This term refers to the contributions every German taxpayer has to make towards the four main state insurance schemes: pension, health, nursing care, and unemployment. Altogether this amounts to over 40% of gross income, with employee and employer paying half each.

Sozialisation *die;* **~** (Soziol., Psych.) socialization
sozialisieren *tr. V.* **1** (Wirtsch.: vergesellschaften) nationalize **2** (Soziol., Psych.: zum Gemeinschaftsleben befähigen) socialize
Sozialismus *der;* **~:** socialism *no art.*
Sozialist *der;* **~en, ~en, Sozialistin** *die;* **~, ~nen** socialist
sozialistisch
A *Adj.* socialist
B *adv.* **~ regierte Länder** countries with socialist governments
sozial-, Sozial-: ~kapitel *das* (EU) Social Chapter; **~kontakt** *der* social contact; **~kritisch** *Adj.* socially critical; critical of society *postpos.;* **~kunde** *die* social studies *sing., no art.;* **~kürzung** *die* cut in social welfare [benefits]; **~leistungen** *Pl.* social welfare benefits; **~liberal** *Adj.* **1** (sozial und liberal) liberal socialist ‹*politician etc.*›; **2** (aus SPD und FDP) liberal-social democrat ‹*coalition etc.*›; **~pädagogik** *die* social education *no art.;* **~partner** *der:* **die ~partner** employers and employees *or* trade unions; **~plan** *der: written agreement between employer and works council which seeks to protect employees;* **~politik** *die* social policy; **~prestige** *das* social status; **~produkt** *das* (Wirtsch.) national product; **~psychologie** *die* social psychology *no art.;* **~rente** *die* state pension; **~rentner** *der,* **~rentnerin** *die* old-age pensioner; **~staat** *der* welfare state; **~struktur** *die* social structure; **~union** *die* unified social welfare system; *s. auch* **Währungsunion;** **~versichert** *Adj.* covered by social security *postpos.;* **~versicherung** *die* social security; **~wissenschaft** *die* social science *no art.;* **die ~wissenschaften** the social sciences; **~wohnung** *die* ≈ council flat (esp. Brit.); municipal housing unit (esp. Amer.)
Sozietät /zotsie'tɛ:t/ *die;* **~, ~en** **1** (Soziol.) society *no art.* **2** (Verhaltensf.) society; social unit **3** (gemeinsame Praxis) joint practice
Sozio·gramm *das* (Soziol.) sociogram

> **Soziokultur**
>
> The sociocultural movement has its origins in the alternative cultural scene which developed in the 1970s in Germany to counteract the established cultural facilities. Independent groups of artists and performers developed new centres for artistic and cultural activities, such as independent theatres, art schools, and women's cultural groups.

sozio·kulturell *Adj.* sociocultural
Soziolekt /zotsio'lɛkt/ *der;* **~[e]s, ~e** (Sprachw.) sociolect; social dialect
Sozio·linguistik *die* sociolinguistics *sing.*
Soziologe /zotsio'lo:gə/ *der;* **~n, ~n** ▸ℹ S. 113 sociologist
Soziologie *die;* **~:** sociology; **die ~ lehrt uns, dass ...** sociology teaches us that ...
Soziologin *die;* **~, ~nen** ▸ℹ S. 113 sociologist
soziologisch
A *Adj.* sociological
B *adv.* sociologically
sozio·ökonomisch *Adj.* socio-economic
Sozius /'zo:tsiʊs/ *der;* **~, ~se** **1** *Pl. auch:* **Sozii** /'zo:tsii/ (Wirtsch.: Teilhaber) partner **2** (beim Motorrad) pillion
Sozius·sitz *der* pillion
so·zu·sagen *Adv.* so to speak; as it were; **es geschah ~ offiziell** it took place officially, so to speak *or* as it were
Spachtel /'ʃpaxtl/ *der;* **~s, ~** *od. die;* **~, ~n** **1** (für Kitt) putty knife; (zum Abkratzen von Farbe) paint scraper; (zum Malen) palette knife; spatula **2** (**~**masse) filler
Spachtel·masse *die* filler
spachteln *tr. V.* **1** stop, fill ‹*hole, crack, etc.*›; smooth over ‹*wall, panel, surface, etc.*›; smooth ‹*filler, putty*› (**in** + *Akk.* into); apply ‹*paints*› with a palette knife **2** (ugs.: essen) put away (coll.) ‹*food, meal*›
spacig /'speisɪç/
A *Adj.* **1** space-age ‹*design, aesthetics, material, costume, hair style*› **2** (wie aus dem Weltraum kommend) ‹*sound, music*› from outer space; ethereal ‹*sound*›; **~e Traumwelt** dream world of outer space
B *adv.* in space-age style
Spagat[1] /ʃpa'ga:t/ *der od. das;* **~[e]s, ~e** **1** splits *pl.;* **[einen] ~ machen** do the splits **2** (fig.) **der ~ zwischen ... und ...:** the balancing act between ... and ...; **den ~ zwischen ... und ... schaffen/beherrschen** achieve the balancing act between ... and ...; succeed in bridging the gap between ... and ...
Spagat[2] *der;* **~[e]s, ~e** (südd., österr.) string
Spaghetti[1] /ʃpa'gɛti/ *Pl.* spaghetti *sing.*
Spaghetti[2] *der;* **~[s], ~s** (salopp abwertend) ▸**Spaghettifresser**
Spaghetti-: ~fresser *der,* **~fresserin** *die* (salopp abwertend) Eyetie (sl. derog.); wop (sl. derog.); **~träger** *der* (Mode) spaghetti strap
spähen /'ʃpɛ:ən/ *itr. V.* peer; (durch ein Loch, eine Ritze usw.) peep
Späher *der;* **~s, ~, Späherin** *die;* **~, ~nen** (Milit.) scout; (Posten) lookout; (Spitzel) informer
Späh·trupp *der* (Milit.) reconnaissance *or* scouting patrol *or* party
Spalett /ʃpa:lɛt/ *das;* **~[e]s, ~e** (österr.) [wooden] shutter
Spalier /ʃpa'li:ɐ̯/ *das;* **~s, ~e** **1** trellis; (für Obstbäume) espalier **2** (aus Menschen) double line; (Ehren**~**) guard of honour; **~ stehen** line the route; ‹*soldiers*› form a guard of honour
Spalier·obst *das* **1** (Früchte) espalier fruit **2** (Pflanzen) espalier
Spalt /ʃpalt/ *der;* **~[e]s, ~e** opening; (im Fels) fissure; crevice; (zwischen Vorhängen) chink; gap; (langer Riß) crack; **die Tür einen ~ [weit] öffnen** open the door a crack *or* slightly; **einen ~ [weit] offen sein** ‹*door*› be open a crack, be *or* stand slightly ajar
spalt-, Spalt-: ~bar *Adj.* (Physik) fissionable ‹*material, element, etc.*›; **~breit** *Adj.* narrow ‹*opening*›; **~breit** *der;* **~~s, ~~:** crack
Spalte *die;* **~, ~n** **1** crack; (Fels**~**) crevice; cleft; (Gletscher**~**) crevasse; crack **2** (Druckw.: Druck**~**) column **3** (derb: Scham-, Gesäß**~**) crack (coarse) **4** (österr.: Scheibe) slice
spalten
A *unr. (auch regelm.) tr. V.* **1** (auch Physik, fig.) split; **Holz ~:** chop wood **2** (Chemie) split; break down
B *unr. (auch regelm.) refl. V.* **1** (auch Physik, fig.) split **2** (Chemie) split; break down
-spaltig *adj.* (Druckw.) -column
Spalt-: ~pilz *der* **1** (Biol.) bacterium; **2** (fig.) divisive tendency; **~produkt** *das* (Physik) fission product
Spaltung *die;* **~, ~en** **1** (auch fig.) splitting; (fig.: durch eine Grenze) division **2** (fig.: das Gespaltensein) split (*Gen.* in; **zwischen** + *Dat.* between); (durch eine Grenze) division **3** (Physik) fission; splitting **4** (Chemie) splitting; breaking down

S

Spam /spɛm/ *das;* **~s, ~s** (DV) spam

Spam·filter *der* (DV) spam filter

Spammer /ˈspɛmɐ/ *der;* **~s, ~, Spammerin** *die;* **~, ~nen** spammer

Span /ʃpaːn/ *der;* **~[e]s, Späne** /ˈʃpɛːnə/ (Hobel~) shaving; (Feil~) filing *usu. in pl.;* (beim Bohren) boring *usu. in pl.;* (beim Drehen) turning *usu. in pl.;* (zum Feueranzünden) splint; **feine [Metall]späne** swarf *sing.;* **wo gehobelt wird, [da] fallen Späne** (Spr.) you cannot make an omelette without breaking eggs (prov.)

spänen /ˈʃpɛːnən/ *tr. V.* (Technik) scour with steel wool

Span·ferkel *das* suckling pig

Spange /ˈʃpaŋə/ *die;* **~, ~n** clasp; (Haar~) hairslide (Brit.); barrette (Amer.); (Arm~) bracelet; bangle

Spangen·schuh *der* strap shoe

Spaniel /ˈʃpaːnjəl/ *der;* **~s, ~s** spaniel

Spanien /ˈʃpaːnjən/ *(das);* **~s** Spain

Spanier /ˈʃpaːnjɐ/ *der;* **~s, ~** ▸❶ **S. 520** Spaniard; **die ~:** the Spanish *or* Spaniards; **seid ihr ~?** are you Spanish?; **stolz wie ein ~** (scherzh.) as proud as a peacock

Spanierin *die;* **~, ~nen** ▸❶ **S. 520** ▸**Spanier**

spanisch ▸❶ **S. 520,** ▸❶ **S. 670**
A *Adj.* Spanish; **das kommt mir/dir** *usw.* **~ vor** (ugs.) that strikes me/you *etc.* as odd
B *adv.* **sich ~ unterhalten** talk Spanish; *s. auch* **deutsch; Deutsch; Reiter 1; Rohr 3; Wand 2**

Span·korb *der* chip basket; chip

spann /ʃpan/ *1. u. 3. Pers. Sg. Prät. v.* **spinnen**

Spann *der;* **~[e]s, ~e** instep

Spann·beton *der* (Bauw.) pre-stressed concrete

Spanne *die;* **~, ~n** [1] (Zeit~) span of time; **eine ~ von 12 Tagen/fünfzig Jahren** a period of twelve days/span *or* period of fifty years [2] (veralt.: Längenmaß) span [3] (Handels~) margin

spannen
A *tr. V.* [1] tighten, tauten ‹*violin string, violin bow, etc.*›; draw ‹*bow*›; tension ‹*spring, tennis net, drumhead, saw-blade*›; stretch ‹*fabric, shoe, etc.*›; draw *or* pull ‹*line*› tight *or* taut; tense, flex ‹*muscle*›; cock ‹*gun, camera shutter*›; **eine Kamera ~:** cock the shutter on a camera; **seine Nerven waren zum Zerreißen gespannt** (fig.) his nerves were stretched to breaking point [2] (befestigen) put up ‹*washing line*›; stretch ‹*net, wire, tarpaulin, etc.*› (**über** + *Akk.* over); **einen Bogen Papier in die Schreibmaschine ~:** insert *or* put a sheet of paper in the typewriter; **etw. in einen Schraubstock ~:** clamp sth. in a vice [3] (schirren) hitch up, harness (**vor, an** + *Akk.* to) [4] (bes. südd., österr.: merken) notice; *s. auch* **Lage 3**
B *refl. V.* [1] become *or* go taut; ‹*muscles*› tense [2] (geh.: sich wölben) **sich über etw.** *(Akk.)* **~** ‹*bridge, rainbow*› span sth.
C *itr. V.* [1] (zu eng sein) ‹*clothing*› be [too] tight; ‹*skin*› be taut [2] **auf jmdn./etw. ~** (ugs.) (warten) wait [impatiently] for sb./sth.; (lauern) lie in wait for sb./sth.

spannend
A *Adj.* exciting; (stärker) thrilling; **machs nicht so ~!** (ugs.) don't keep me/us in suspense
B *adv.* excitingly; (stärker) thrillingly

spannen·lang *Adj.* (veralt.) a span tall/in length *postpos.*

Spanner *der;* **~s, ~** [1] (Schuh~) shoe tree; (Stiefel~) boot tree; (Hosen~) [trouser] hanger; (Gardinen~) curtain-stretcher; (für Tennisschläger) [racket] press [2] (Zool.) geometer [3] (ugs.: Voyeur) peeping Tom

Spann·kraft *die* vigour

Spannung *die;* **~, ~en** [1] excitement; (Neugier) suspense; tension; **jmdn. mit** *od.* **voll ~ erwarten** await sb. eagerly [2] (eines Romans, Films usw.) suspense [3] (Zwistigkeit, Nervosität) tension [4] (das Straffsein) tension; tautness [5] (elektrische ~) tension; (Voltzahl) voltage; **unter ~ stehen** be live [6] (Mechanik) stress

spannungs-, Spannungs-: ~gebiet *das* (Politik) area of tension; **~geladen** *Adj.* [1] (gespannt) ‹*atmosphere etc.*› charged with tension; [2] (spannend) ‹*novel, film, etc.*› full of suspense; **~messer** *der;* **~~s, ~~** (Elektrot.) voltmeter; **~verhältnis** *das* relationship of tension; **~zustand** *der* [1] (Psych.) state of tension; [2] (Mechanik) condition of stress

Spann·weite *die* [1] (Zool.: Flügel~) [wing]span; wingspread; (eines Flugzeugs) [wing]span [2] (Bauw.) span

Span-: ~platte *die* chipboard; **~schachtel** *die* small box made of thin strips of wood (*for storing jewellery, letters, etc.*)

Spant /ʃpant/ *das od. der;* **~[e]s, ~en** (eines Schiffs) rib; (eines Flugzeugs) frame; former

Spar-: ~brief *der* (Bankw.) savings certificate; **~buch** *das* (Bankw.) savings book; passbook; (bei der Bank auch) bank book; **~büchse** *die* money box; **~einlage** *die* (Bankw.) savings deposit

sparen /ˈʃpaːrən/
A *tr. V.* save; (zurücklegen) save, put away ‹*money*›; **die Mühe/den Ärger hätten wir uns ~ können** we could have saved *or* spared ourselves the effort/trouble; **du kannst dir jedes Wort ~:** you can save your breath; **deine Ratschläge kannst du dir ~:** you can keep your advice
B *itr. V.* [1] (Geld zurücklegen) save; **für** *od.* **auf etw.** *(Akk.)* **~:** save up for sth.; **spare in der Zeit, so hast du in der Not** (Spr.) waste not, want not (prov.) [2] (sparsam wirtschaften) economize (**mit** on); **er sparte nicht mit Lob** (fig.) he was unstinting *or* generous in his praise; **an etw.** *(Dat.)* **~** (weniger nehmen) be sparing with sth.; (Billigeres nehmen) economize on sth.; **am falschen Ort** *od.* **Ende ~:** make a false economy/false economies

Sparer *der;* **~s, ~, Sparerin** *die;* **~, ~nen** saver

Spar·flamme *die* low flame *or* heat; **auf ~:** on a low flame *or* heat

Spargel /ˈʃpargl̩/ *der;* **~s, ~,** *schweiz. auch die;* **~, ~n** asparagus *no pl., no indef. art.;* **ein ~:** an asparagus stalk

Spargel-: ~creme·suppe *die* cream of asparagus soup; **~kraut** *das* asparagus fern; **~spitze** *die* asparagus tip

Spar-: ~groschen *der* (ugs.) nest egg; savings *pl.;* **~guthaben** *das* credit balance (*in a savings account*); **ein ~guthaben von 500 Euro haben** have 500 euros in one's savings *or* deposit account; **~kasse** *die* savings bank; **~kassen·buch** *das* savings book; passbook; **~konto** *das* savings *or* deposit account; **~kurs** *der* economy programme

spärlich /ˈʃpɛːɐ̯lɪç/
A *Adj.* sparse ‹*vegetation, beard, growth*›; thin ‹*hair, applause*›; scanty ‹*leftovers, knowledge, news, evidence*›; scanty, skimpy ‹*clothing*›; slack ‹*demand*›; scattered ‹*remains, remnants*›; poor ‹*lighting, harvest, result, source*›; meagre ‹*income, salary*›; meagre, frugal ‹*food, meal*›
B *adv.* sparsely, thinly ‹*populated, covered*›; poorly ‹*lit, attended*›; scantily, skimpily ‹*dressed*›; **die Nachrichten kamen/die Geldmittel flossen nur ~:** news/money was only coming in in dribbs and drabs

Spar-: ~maßnahme *die* economy measure; **~paket** *das* austerity package; **~prämie** *die* savings premium; **~programm** *das* [1] (bes. Politik) programme of economy measures; [2] (Technik) economy programme

Sparren /ˈʃparən/ *der;* **~s, ~** [1] (Dach~) rafter [2] (Her.) chevron [3] (ugs.: Spleen) daft idea; **er hat einen ~ [zu viel** *od.* **zu wenig im Kopf]** (ugs.) he has a screw loose (coll.)

Sparring /ˈʃparɪŋ/ *das;* **~s** (Boxen) sparring *no art.*

Sparrings·partner *der,* **Sparrings·partnerin** *die* (Boxen) sparring partner

sparsam
A *Adj.* [1] thrifty ‹*person*›; (wirtschaftlich) economical; **durch ~en Umgang mit dem Material** by being economical *or* sparing with the material; **durch ~es Wirtschaften** by economizing; **mit etw. ~ sein** be economical with sth.; **er ist mit Worten/Lob immer sehr ~** (fig.) he is a man of few words/he is very sparing in his praise [2] (im Verbrauch) economical [3] (fig.: gering, wenig, klein) sparse ‹*detail, decoration, interior, etc.*›; economical ‹*movement, manner of expression, etc.*›; **er machte von dieser Möglichkeit nur ~en Gebrauch** he made little use of this opportunity; **die Wirkung ist schon bei ~ster Dosierung groß** even the most sparing dose has a strong effect
B *adv.* [1] **~ mit der Butter/dem Papier umgehen** use butter/paper sparingly; economize on butter/paper; **~ leben** live frugally; **~ mit seinen Kräften umgehen** conserve one's energy; **~ wirtschaften** economize; budget carefully [2] (wirtschaftlich) economically [3] (fig.: in geringem Maße) ‹*use*› sparingly; sparsely ‹*decorated, furnished*›; **etw. ~ dosieren** use sth. in small doses

Sparsamkeit *die;* **~** [1] thrift[iness]; **das ist ~ am falschen Platze** that's a false economy; **aus ~:** for the sake of economizing [2] (Wirtschaftlichkeit) economicalness [3] (fig.: geringes Maß) economy

Spar-: ~schwein *das* piggy bank; **~strumpf** *der* stocking for keeping one's savings in

Spartakiade /ʃpartaˈki̯aːdə/ *die;* **~, ~n** Spartakiad

Spartakist /ʃpartaˈkɪst/ *der;* **~en, ~en, Spartakistin** *die;* **~, ~nen** Spartacist; Spartakist

Spartaner /ʃparˈtaːnɐ/ *der;* **~s, ~, Spartanerin** *die;* **~, ~nen** (hist.) Spartan

spartanisch
A *Adj.* (auch fig.). Spartan
B *adv.* **~ leben** lead a Spartan life

Sparte /ˈʃpartə/ *die;* **~, ~n** [1] (Teilbereich) area; branch; (eines Geschäfts) line [of business]; (des Wissens) branch; field; speciality; (des Sports, der Kunst) discipline [2] (Rubrik) section; (Spalte) column

Sparten-: ~kanal *der* special-interest channel; **~sender** *der* special-interest station

Spar-: ~version *die* economy version; **~vertrag** *der* savings agreement; **~zins** *der; Pl.* **~~en,** interest *no pl.* on a savings account

spasmisch /ˈʃpasmɪʃ/ (Med.)
A *Adj.* spasmodic
B *adv.* spasmodically

Spasmus /ˈʃpasmʊs/ *der;* **~, Spasmen** ▸❶ **S. 439** (Med.) spasm

Spaß /ʃpaːs/ *der;* **~es, Späße** /ˈʃpɛːsə/ [1] (Vergnügen) fun; **wir hatten alle viel ~:** we all had a lot of fun *or* a really good time; we all really enjoyed ourselves; **~ an etw.** *(Dat.)* **haben** enjoy sth.; **verdirb ihm doch nicht seinen ~:** don't spoil his fun; **lass ihn doch, wenn er ~ dran hat!** let him, if it makes him happy; **meinetwegen, wenn du ~ daran hast** all right, if you want to; **~ an etw.** *(Dat.)* **finden** find sth. fun; **[jmdm.] ~/keinen ~ machen** be fun/no fun [for sb.]; **die Schule macht ihm großen/keinen/nicht viel ~:** he likes *or* enjoys school a great deal/doesn't like school/doesn't like school very much; **du machst mir [vielleicht] ~!** (iron.) you must be joking *or* (sl.) kidding; **sich** *(Dat.)* **einen ~ daraus machen, etw. zu tun** take great delight in doing sth.; **ein teurer ~** (ugs.) an expensive business; **was kostet der ~?** (ugs.) how much will that little lot cost? (coll.); **viel ~!** have a good time!; (iron.) have fun!; **das ist kein ~!** it's no fun [2] (Scherz) joke; (Streich) prank; antic; **er macht nur ~:** he's only joking *or* (sl.) kidding; **~ beiseite!** joking aside *or* apart; **~ muss sein!** there's no harm in a joke; **da hört [für mich] der ~ auf** that's getting beyond a joke; **~/keinen ~ verstehen** be able/not be able to take a joke; have a/have no sense of humour; **in Gelddingen versteht er keinen ~:** he won't stand for any nonsense where money is concerned; **lass diese albernen Späße!** stop fooling around!; **er ist immer zu Späßen aufgelegt** he's always ready for a laugh; **im** *od.* **zum** *od.* **aus ~:** as a joke; for fun; **aus ~ an der Freude** (scherzh.) for the [sheer] fun of it; **sich** *(Dat.)* **einen ~ mit jmdm. machen** *od.* **erlauben** play

S

a joke on sb.; **macht keine Späße!** surely you don't mean it; **aus [lauter] ~ und Tollerei** (ugs.) [just] for a laugh; just for the hell of it (coll.); **das ist kein ~ mehr!** that's gone beyond a joke; **seine Späße mit jmdm. treiben** get a laugh at sb.'s expense

Späßchen /ˈʃpɛːsçən/ *das;* **~s, ~:** little joke

spaßen /ˈʃpaːsn̩/ *itr. V.* 1 (Spaß machen) joke; kid (coll.); **Sie ~ wohl!** you must be joking *or* (coll.) kidding 2 **er lässt nicht mit sich ~:** he won't stand for any nonsense; **mit ihm/damit ist nicht zu ~:** he/it is not to be trifled with; **mit so einer Entzündung ist nicht zu ~:** an inflammation like that shouldn't be shrugged off lightly

spaßes·halber *Adv.* for the fun of it; for fun

Spaß·gesellschaft *die* hedonistic society

spaßhaft *Adj.* amusing; comical; funny

spaßig
A *Adj.* funny; comical; amusing
B *adv.* in an amusing way

Spaß-: ~macher *der,* **~macherin** *die* joker; **~verderber** *der;* **~~s, ~~, ~verderberin** *die;* **~~, ~~nen** spoilsport; killjoy; wet blanket; **~vogel** *der* joker; **du bist vielleicht ein ~vogel!** you must be joking *or* (coll.) kidding

spastisch (Med.)
A *Adj.* spastic
B *adv.* **~ gelähmt sein** suffer from spastic paralysis; **ein ~ Gelähmter** a spastic

spät /ʃpɛːt/
A *Adj.* ▸ⓘ **S. 729** late; belated ‹*fame, repentance*›; **am ~en Abend** in the late evening; **bis in die ~e Nacht** until late into the night; **die Werke des ~en Goethe** Goethe's late works; **wie ~ ist es?** what time is it?; **bei der Party ist es ziemlich ~ geworden** the party went on until quite late; **er kam zu ~er Stunde** (geh.) he came at a late hour; **ein ~es Mädchen** (scherzh.) an old maid; **ein ~es Glück** happiness late in life
B *adv.* late; **~ am Abend** late in the evening; **du kommst aber ~!** you're very late; **wenn ich jetzt nicht losfahre, komme ich zu ~:** if I don't leave now I'll be late; **wir sind eine Station zu ~ ausgestiegen** we got out one station too far down the line; **wir sind [schon ziemlich] ~ dran** (ugs.) we're late [enough already]; **so ~ am Tage** so late in the day; **er hat erst ~ angefangen zu studieren** he began studying late in life; *s. auch* **früh B**

Spat /ʃpaːt/ *der;* **~[e]s, ~e** *od.* **Späte** /ˈʃpɛːtə/ (Mineral) spar

spät-, Spät-: ~abends *Adv.* /-ˈ--/ late in the evening; in the late evening; **~aussiedler** *der,* **~aussiedlerin** *die: person of German origin who emigrated from countries East of the Oder-Neisse border relatively late after 1945;* **~barock** *das od. der* (Kunstwiss.) late Baroque; **~dienst** *der* late duty; (im Betrieb) late shift; **~dienst haben** be on late shift

Spatel /ˈʃpaːtl̩/ *der;* **~s, ~** 1 spatula 2 ▸ **Spachtel 1**

Spaten /ˈʃpaːtn̩/ *der;* **~s, ~:** spade

Spaten·stich *der* cut of the spade; **das Foto zeigt den Oberbürgermeister beim ersten ~:** the photo shows the mayor digging the first turf

Spät·entwickler *der,* **Spät·entwicklerin** *die;* **~, ~nen** late developer

später
A *Adj.* 1 (nachfolgend, kommend) later ‹*years, generations, etc.*› 2 (zukünftig) future ‹*owner, wife, etc.*›
B *Adv.* later; **er soll ~ [einmal] die Leitung der Firma übernehmen** he is to take over management of the firm at some future date; **was willst du denn ~ [einmal] werden?** what do you want to do when you grow up?; **jmdn. auf ~ vertrösten** put sb. off until later; **ich hebe es mir für ~ auf** I'll save it for later [on]; **[also dann] bis ~!** see you later!

später·hin *Adv.* (geh.) later [on]

spätestens *Adv.* at the latest; **~ gestern/[am] Freitag** yesterday/[on] Friday at the latest

Spät-: ~folge *die* long-term consequence; (Med.) late sequela; **~geburt** *die* post-term birth; **~gotik** *die* (Kunstwiss.) late Gothic; **~heimkehrer** *der,* **~heimkehrerin** *die* late returnee (*from a prisoner-of-war camp*); **~herbst** *der* late autumn *or* (Amer.) fall; **~lese** *die* late vintage; **~nachmittag** *der* late afternoon; **~schaden** *der* long-term damage *no pl., no indef. art.;* **~schalter** *der: counter that is open late;* **~schicht** *die* late shift; **~sommer** *der* late summer; **~vorstellung** *die* (Film) late showing; (Theater) late performance; **~werk** *das* late work

Spatz /ʃpats/ *der;* **~en, ~en** 1 sparrow; **er isst wie ein ~:** he eats like a bird; **besser ein ~ in der Hand als eine Taube auf dem Dach** (Spr.) a bird in the hand is worth two in the bush (prov.); **die ~en pfeifen es von den** *od.* **allen Dächern** it's common knowledge 2 (fam.: Liebling) pet 3 (fam.: kleines Kind) mite; tot (coll.)

Spätzchen /ˈʃpɛtsçən/ *das;* **~s, ~** 1 little sparrow 2 ▸ **Spatz 2, 3**

Spätzeit *die* end; **in der ~ der Renaissance** in the late Renaissance; **Dürers Bildnisse der ~:** Dürer's late portraits

Spatzen·[ge]hirn *das* (salopp abwertend) birdbrain (coll.); **sie hat ein ~:** she's birdbrained (coll.); she's a birdbrain (coll.)

Spätzle /ˈʃpɛtslə/ *Pl.* spaetzle; spätzle; *kind of noodles*

Spät-: ~zug *der* late train; **~zünder** *der* (ugs. scherzh.) **ein ~zünder sein** be slow on the uptake; **~zündung** *die* (Technik) retarded ignition

spazieren /ʃpaˈtsiːrən/ *itr. V.; mit sein* 1 stroll; **~ fahren** (im Auto) go for a drive *or* ride *or* spin; (im Bus usw., mit dem Fahrrad od. Motorrad) go for a ride; (mit einem Schiff) go for a [boat] trip; (mit einem Ruderboot) go for a row; (mit einem Segelboot) go for a sail; **jmdn. ~ fahren** (im Auto) take sb. for a drive *or* ride *or* spin; **ein Kind [im Kinderwagen] ~ fahren** take a baby for a walk [in a pram]; **die Kinder mit dem Schlitten/im Boot ~ fahren** take the children out on the sledge/on a boat trip; **~ gehen** go for a walk *or* stroll; **ein Stück ~ gehen** go for a little walk *or* stroll; **hier kann man schön ~ gehen** you can go for pleasant walks here; **eine schöne Gegend zum Spazierengehen** a pleasant area for walks 2 (veralt.: spazieren gehen) go for a walk *or* stroll; **wir sind ~ gewesen** we went for a walk *or* stroll

***spazieren|fahren, *spazieren|gehen** ▸ **spazieren 1**

Spazier-: ~fahrt *die* (mit dem Auto) drive; ride; spin; (mit dem Bus usw., mit dem Fahrrad od. Motorrad) ride; (mit einem Schiff) [boat] trip; (mit einem Ruderboot) row; (mit einem Segelboot) sail; **~gang** *der* walk; stroll; **~gänger** *der;* **~~s, ~~, ~gängerin** *die;* **~~, ~~nen** person out for a walk *or* stroll; **~ritt** *der* ride; **~stock** *der; Pl.* **~stöcke** walking stick; **~weg** *der* footpath

SPD *Abk.* **= Sozialdemokratische Partei Deutschlands** SPD

> **SPD – Sozialdemokratische Partei Deutschlands**
>
> One of the main German political parties and the party with the biggest membership. Re-formed after the war in 1945, it is a workers' party supporting social democratic values.

Specht /ʃpɛçt/ *der;* **~[e]s, ~e** woodpecker

spechten *itr. V.* (bes. bayr., ugs.) peer; **auf etw./jmdn. ~:** have one's eye on sth./sb.; **darauf ~, etw. zu tun** be out to do sth.

Special /ˈspɛʃl̩/ *das;* **~s, ~s** special [programme/feature/edition]

Speck /ʃpɛk/ *der;* **~[e]s, ~e** 1 bacon fat; (Schinken~) bacon; **durchwachsener ~:** streaky bacon; **fetter ~:** bacon fat; **ran an den ~!** (ugs.) get stuck in! (coll.); get to it! (coll.); **mit ~ fängt man Mäuse** (Spr.) if the bait is tempting enough, the fish will bite 2 (von Walen, Robben) blubber 3 (ugs. scherzh.: Fettpolster) fat; flab (sl.); **er hat ganz schön ~ auf den Rippen** he's well padded

Speck-: ~bauch *der* (ugs.) potbelly; paunch; **~gürtel** *der* (Jargon) ring of new development (*surrounding a big city and offering lower living costs and tax advantages to firms*)

speckig *Adj.* greasy

Speck-: ~nacken *der* (ugs.) fat neck; **~scheibe** *die* rasher *or* slice of bacon; **~schwarte** *die* bacon rind; **~seite** *die* side of bacon; **~stein** *der* (Mineral) lard stone; soapstone; steatite

Spediteur /ʃpediˈtøːɐ̯/ *der;* **~s, ~e, Spediteurin** *die;* **~, ~nen** 1 (Vermittler[in]) forwarding agent; (per Schiff) shipping agent; (per Flugzeug) air freight agent 2 (Beförderer/Beförderin) carrier; haulier; haulage contractor; (per Schiff) carrier; (Möbelspediteur[in]) furniture remover

Spedition /ʃpediˈtsioːn/ *die;* **~, ~en** 1 (Beförderung) carriage; transport 2 ▸ **Speditionsfirma**

Speditions-: ~firma *die* forwarding agency; (per Schiff) shipping agency; (Transportunternehmen) haulage firm; firm of hauliers; (per Schiff) firm of carriers; (Möbelspedition) removal firm; **~kauffrau** *die,* **~kaufmann** *der* forwarding agent; shipping agent; (für Möbelspedition) furniture remover

Speedmetal /ˈspiːtmɛtl̩/ *der;* **~[s]** (Musik) speed metal

Speedway·rennen /ˈspiːdweɪ-/ *das* (Motorsport) speedway racing; (Veranstaltung) speedway race

Speer /ʃpeːɐ̯/ *der;* **~[e]s, ~e** 1 spear 2 (Sportgerät) javelin

Speer-: ~spitze *die* 1 (auch fig.) spearhead; 2 (des Sportgeräts) tip of a/the javelin; **~werfen** *das;* **~~s** ▸ **~wurf 1; ~werfer** *der,* **~werferin** *die* (Sport) javelin-thrower; **~wurf** *der* 1 (Disziplin) javelin-throwing; 2 (Wurf) javelin-throw

Speiche /ˈʃpaiçə/ *die;* **~, ~n** 1 spoke 2 ▸ⓘ **S. 435** (Anat.) radius

Speichel /ˈʃpaiçl̩/ *der;* **~s** saliva; spittle

Speichel-: ~drüse *die* salivary gland; **~fluss, *~fluß** *der* 1 salivation *no art.;* 2 (Med.: übermäßige Sekretion) salivation *no art.;* ptyalism *no art.*

speicheln *itr. V.* salivate

Speichen-: ~dynamo *der* spoke dynamo; **~rad** *das* spoked wheel

Speichen·reflektor *der* wheel reflector

Speicher /ˈʃpaiçɐ/ *der;* **~s, ~** 1 storehouse; (Lagerhaus) warehouse; (~becken) reservoir; (fig.) store 2 (südd.: Dachboden) loft; attic; **auf dem ~:** in the loft *or* attic 3 (Elektronik) memory; store

Speicher·kapazität *die* storage capacity; (DV) memory *or* storage capacity

speichern *tr. V.* store

Speicherung *die;* **~, ~en** storing; storage

speien /ˈʃpaiən/ *unr. tr., itr. V.*(geh.) 1 (spucken) spit; spew [forth] ‹*lava, fire, etc.*›; belch ‹*smoke*›; spout ‹*water*›; **der Drache spie Feuer** the dragon breathed fire 2 (erbrechen) vomit

Speise /ˈʃpaizə/ *die;* **~, ~n** 1 (Gericht) dish; **~n und Getränke** food and drink; **„kalte/warme ~n"** 'cold/hot dishes' 2 (geh.: Nahrung) food 3 (nordd.: süße Nachspeise) dessert; sweet (Brit.)

Speise-: ~eis *das* ice cream; **~fett** *das* edible fat; **~fisch** *der* food fish; **~gaststätte** *die* restaurant; **~kammer** *die* larder; pantry; **~karte** *die* menu; **~lokal** *das* restaurant

speisen
A *itr. V.* (geh.) eat; (dinieren) dine; **haben Sie schon gespeist?** have you eaten yet?; **zu Mittag/Abend ~:** lunch *or* have lunch/dine *or* have dinner
B *tr. V.* 1 (geh.: verzehren) eat; (dinieren) dine on; **was wünschen Sie zu ~?** what do you wish to eat? 2 (geh.) (ernähren, auch fig.) feed; (bewirten) dine 3 (Technik) **etw. mit Strom/Wasser ~:**

supply sth. with electricity/water; **ein von Batterien gespeister Elektromotor** an electric motor powered by batteries; **Strom in das öffentliche Netz ~:** feed electricity [in]to the national grid

C *refl. V.* be fed (**aus, von** by)

Speisen-: ~aufzug *der* dumb waiter; **~folge** *die* (geh.) menu

Speise-: ~öl *das* edible oil; **~plan** *der* menu (*for the week etc.*); **~reste** *Pl.* leftovers; (zwischen den Zähnen) food particles; **~röhre** *die* ▸ℹ **S. 435** (Anat.) gullet; oesophagus (Anat.); **~saal** *der* dining hall; (im Hotel, in einer Villa usw.) dining room; (auf Schiffen) dining saloon; dining room; **~schrank** *der* food cupboard; **~wagen** *der* dining car; restaurant car (Brit.); **~würze** *die* seasoning additive; **~zettel** *der* menu; **auf dem ~zettel des Eichhörnchens stehen auch Vogeleier** (fig.) the squirrel's diet also includes birds' eggs; **~zimmer** *das* dining room

Speisung *die;* **~, ~en** **1** (geh.) feeding **2** (Technik) supplying

spei·übel *Adj.* **mir ist ~:** I think I'm going to be violently sick

Spektabilität /ʃpɛktabiliˈtɛːt/ *die;* **~, ~en** (Hochschulw.) *title of the dean of a university;* **an seine ~ den Dekan der ... Fakultät** to the Dean of the Faculty of ...

Spektakel[1] /ʃpɛkˈtaːkl̩/ *der;* **~s, ~** (ugs.) **1** (Lärm) row (coll.); rumpus (coll.); racket **2** (laute Auseinandersetzung, Theater) fuss; **einen ~ machen** kick up *or* make a fuss

Spektakel[2] *das;* **~s, ~** **1** (veralt.) spectacle; show **2** (fig.) spectacle

spektakulär /ʃpɛktakuˈlɛːɐ̯/

A *Adj.* spectacular; (sensationell) sensational

B *adv.* spectacularly; (sensationell) sensationally

Spektral-: ~analyse *die* (Technik) spectral analysis; **~farbe** *die* colour of the spectrum

Spektren ▸ **Spektrum**

Spektroskop /ʃpɛktroˈskoːp/ *das;* **~s, ~e** (Technik) spectroscope

Spektrum /ˈʃpɛktrʊm/ *das;* **~s, Spektren** (auch fig.) spectrum

Spekula ▸ **Spekulum**

Spekulant /ʃpekuˈlant/ *der;* **~en, ~en, Spekulantin** *die;* **~, ~nen** speculator

Spekulation /ʃpekulaˈtsi̯oːn/ *die;* **~, ~en** **1** (Mutmaßung, Erwartung; auch Philos.) speculation; **das sind alles nur ~en** that is all merely speculation *sing. or* conjecture *sing.* **2** (Wirtsch.) speculation (**mit** in); **die ~ mit Grundstücken** property speculation

Spekulations-: ~geschäft *das* (Wirtsch.) speculative deal; **~objekt** *das* object of speculative investment

Spekulatius /ʃpekuˈlaːtsi̯ʊs/ *der;* **~, ~:** *spiced biscuit in the shape of a human or other figure, eaten at Christmas*

spekulativ /ʃpekulaˈtiːf/

A *Adj.* speculative

B *adv.* speculatively

spekulieren /ʃpekuˈliːrən/ *itr. V.* **1** (ugs.) **darauf ~, etw. tun zu können** count on being able to do sth.; **er spekuliert auf den Laden** he's counting on getting the shop **2** (mutmaßen) speculate **3** (Wirtsch.) speculate (**mit** in); *s. auch* **Baisse**; **Hausse**

Spekulum /ˈʃpeːkulʊm/ *das;* **~s, Spekula** (Med.) speculum

Spelunke /ʃpeˈlʊŋkə/ *die;* **~, ~n** (ugs. abwertend) dive (coll.)

Spelze /ˈʃpɛltsə/ *die;* **~, ~n** (des Getreidekorns) husk; (der Grasblüte) glume

spelzig *Adj.* full of husks *postpos.*

spendabel /ʃpɛnˈdaːbl̩/ *Adj.* generous; openhanded

Spende /ˈʃpɛndə/ *die;* **~, ~n** donation; contribution; **eine kleine ~ bitte!** would you like to make a small donation?

spenden *tr., itr. V.* **1** donate; give; contribute; **[etw.] fürs Rote Kreuz ~:** contribute [sth.] to *or* for the Red Cross; **Blut/eine Niere ~:** give blood/donate a kidney **2** (fig. geh.) give ‹*light*›; afford, give ‹*shade*›; give off ‹*heat*›; provide ‹*water*›; administer ‹*communion, baptism*›; give, bestow ‹*blessing*›; confer ‹*holy orders*›; **jmdm. Beifall/Trost ~:** give sb. applause/comfort; applaud/comfort sb.; **Leben ~d** life-giving

Spenden-: ~aktion *die* campaign for donations; **~aufruf** *der* appeal for donations; **~gelder** *Pl.* money from donations; **~konto** *das* donations account

Spender *der;* **~s, ~** **1** donor; donator; contributor; (Organ~, Blut~) donor; **wer war der edle ~?** to whom am I indebted? **2** (Behälter) dispenser

Spenderherz *das* donor heart

Spenderin *die;* **~, ~nen** ▸ **Spender 1**

Spender-: ~niere *die* donor kidney; **~organ** *das* donor organ

spendieren *tr. V.* (ugs.) get, buy ‹*drink, meal, etc.*›; stand ‹*round*›; **jmdm. ein Bier/eine Tafel Schokolade ~:** stand *or* get sb. a beer/buy *or* get sb. a bar of chocolate

Spendier·hosen *Pl.* in **die/seine ~ anhaben** be in a generous mood; be feeling generous

Spengler /ˈʃpɛŋlɐ/ *der;* **~s, ~, Spenglerin** *die;* **~, ~nen** (südd., österr., schweiz.) ▸ **Klempner**

Spenzer /ˈʃpɛntsɐ/ *der;* **~s, ~** **1** (Jacke) spencer **2** (Unterhemd) tight-fitting short-sleeved vest

Sperber /ˈʃpɛrbɐ/ *der;* **~s, ~:** sparrowhawk

Sperenzchen /ʃpeˈrɛntsçən/ *Pl.* (ugs.) **~ machen** give trouble; **mach keine ~!** don't be difficult!

Sperling /ˈʃpɛrlɪŋ/ *der;* **~s, ~e** sparrow; **besser ein ~ in der Hand als eine Taube auf dem Dach** (Spr.) a bird in the hand is worth two in the bush (prov.)

Sperma /ˈʃpɛrma/ *das;* **~s, Spermen** *od.* **Spermata** sperm; semen

Spermium /ˈʃpɛrmi̯ʊm/ *das;* **~s, Spermien** (Biol.) spermatozoon; sperm

sperr·angel·weit *Adv.* (ugs.) **~ offen** *od.* **geöffnet** wide open

Sperr·bezirk *der* **1** restricted *or* prohibited area **2** (für Prostituierte) *area in which prostitution is prohibited* **3** (Gesundheitswesen) infected area

Sperre *die;* **~, ~n** **1** (Barriere) barrier; (Straßen~) roadblock **2** (Milit.) obstacle; (Draht~) entanglement **3** (Eisenb.) barrier **4** (fig.: Verbot, auch Sport) ban; (Handels~) embargo; (Import~, Export~) blockade; (Nachrichten~) [news] blackout **5** (Psych.: Blockierung, Hemmung) block **6** (Technik) locking device

sperren

A *tr. V.* **1** close ‹*road, tunnel, bridge, entrance, border, etc.*›; close off ‹*area*›; **etw. für jmdn./etw. ~:** close sth. to sb./sth. **2** (blockieren) block ‹*entrance, access, etc.*› **3** (Technik) lock ‹*mechanism etc.*› **4** **jmdm. das Gehalt/den Urlaub ~:** stop sb.'s salary/leave; **einem Soldaten den Ausgang ~:** confine a soldier to barracks **5** cut off, disconnect ‹*water, gas, electricity, etc.*›; **jmdm. den Strom/das Telefon ~:** cut off *or* disconnect sb.'s electricity/telephone **6** (Bankw.) stop ‹*cheque, overdraft facility*›; freeze ‹*bank account*›; **jmdm. das Konto ~:** freeze sb.'s account **7** (ein~) **ein Tier/jmdn. in etw.** (*Akk.*) **~:** shut *or* lock an animal/sb. in sth.; **jmdn. ins Gefängnis ~:** put sb. in prison; lock sb. up [in prison] **8** (Sport: behindern) obstruct **9** (Sport: von der Teilnahme ausschließen) ban **10** (Druckw.: spationieren) print ‹*word, text*› with the letters spaced

B *refl. V.* **sich [gegen etw.] ~:** balk *or* jib [at sth.]

C *itr. V.* (Sport) obstruct; **Sperren ohne Ball** obstruction off the ball

Sperr-: ~feuer *das* (Milit.) barrage; **~frist** *die* (auch Rechtsspr.) waiting period; **~gebiet** ▸ **~bezirk**; **~gürtel** *der* cordon; **~holz** *das* plywood

sperrig *Adj.* unwieldy

Sperr-: ~konto *das* (Bankw.) blocked account; **~minorität** *die* (Wirtsch., Politik) blocking minority; **~müll** *der* bulky refuse (*for which there is a separate collection service*); **morgen ist ~müll** (ugs.) they're collecting bulky refuse tomorrow; **~sitz** *der* (im Kino) seat in the back stalls; (im Zirkus) front seat; (im Theater) seat in the front stalls; **wir saßen ~sitz** we sat in the back stalls/front seats/front stalls; **~stunde** *die* closing time

Sperrung *die;* **~, ~en** ▸ **sperren A 1-6, 9**: closing; closing off; blocking; locking; stopping; cutting off; disconnection; freezing; banning

Sperr·vermerk *der* restriction note (*regarding sale of property, withdrawal of investment, disclosure of information, etc.*)

Spesen /ˈʃpeːzn̩/ *Pl.* expenses; **auf ~:** on expenses; **~ machen** incur expenses; **außer ~ nichts gewesen** (scherzh.) [it was] a waste of time and effort

Spezerei /ʃpeːtsəˈrai̯/ *die;* **~, ~en** (veralt.) spice

Spezi /ˈʃpeːtsi/ *der;* **~s, ~[s]** **1** (südd., österr., schweiz. ugs.) [bosom] pal (coll.); chum (coll.) **2** (Wz) (ugs.: Getränk) lemonade and cola

Spezial *das;* **~s, ~e** ▸ **Special**

Spezial-: ~einheit *die* special unit; **~gebiet** *das* special *or* specialist field; **~geschäft** *das* specialist shop

spezialisieren *refl. V.* specialize (**auf** + *Akk.* in)

Spezialist *der;* **~en, ~en, Spezialistin** *die;* **~, ~nen** specialist

Spezialität /ʃpetsi̯aliˈtɛːt/ *die;* **~, ~en** speciality; specialty

Spezialitäten·restaurant *das* speciality restaurant

Spezial·slalom *der* (Ski) special slalom

speziell /ʃpeˈtsi̯ɛl/

A *Adj.* special; specific ‹*question, problem, etc.*›; specialized ‹*book, knowledge, etc.*›; **er ist mein ~er Freund** he's a special friend of mine; (iron.) we're the best of enemies (joc.); **auf dein Spezielles!** your very good health!

B *adv.* (besonders, gerade) especially; (eigens) specially; **~ du** you especially; you of all people

Spezies /ˈʃpeːtsi̯ɛs/ *die;* **~, ~:** species; **eine besondere ~ [von] Mensch** a special type of person

Spezifikation /ʃpetsifikaˈtsi̯oːn/ *die;* **~, ~en** specification

Spezifikum /ʃpeˈtsiːfikʊm/ *das;* **~s, Spezifika** **1** (Besonderheit) specific characteristic **2** (Pharm.) specific

spezifisch

A *Adj.* specific; characteristic ‹*smell, style*›; **~es Gewicht/~e Wärme** (Phys.) specific gravity/heat

B *adv.* specifically

spezifizieren *tr. V.* specify; (einzeln aufführen) itemize ‹*bill, expenses, etc.*›

Spezifizierung *die;* **~, ~en** specification; (einer Rechnung, von Kosten) itemization

Sphäre /ˈsfɛːrə/ *die;* **~, ~n** (auch fig.) sphere; **in höheren ~n schweben** (scherzh.) have one's head in the clouds

Sphären·harmonie *die* (Philos.) harmony of the spheres

sphärisch *Adj.* **1** spherical **2** (fig.: himmlisch) heavenly

Sphäroid /sfɛroˈiːt/ *das;* **~[e]s, ~e** (Geom.) spheroid

Sphinx[1] /sfɪŋks/ *die od. der;* **~, ~e** *od.* **Sphingen** /ˈsfɪŋən/ (Ägyptologie, Kunstwiss.) sphinx; **die ~ von Gise** the Sphinx at Giza

Sphinx[2] *die;* **~, ~e** *od.* **Sphingen** (griech. Myth., Kunstwiss.) Sphinx

Spick·aal *der* (bes. nordd.) smoked eel

spicken /ˈʃpɪkn̩/

A *tr. V.* **1** (Kochk.) lard; **jmdn. ~** (fig. ugs.) grease sb.'s palm **2** (fig. ugs.: reichlich versehen) **eine Rede mit Zitaten ~:** lard a speech with quotations; **das Diktat war mit Fehlern gespickt** the dictation was full of mistakes

B *itr. V.* (bes. südd. ugs.) crib (coll.)

Spick-: ~nadel *die* larding needle; **~zettel** *der* (bes. südd. ugs.) crib (coll.); (fig.: eines Redners) notes *pl.*

spie /ʃpiː/ *1. u. 3. Pers. Sg. Prät. v.* **speien**

S

Spiegel /ˈʃpi:gl̩/ *der;* ~s, ~ **1** mirror; **in den ~ sehen** *od.* **schauen** look in the mirror; **im ~ der Presse** (fig.) as mirrored *or* reflected in the press; **dieser Roman ist ein ~ unserer Zeit** (fig.) this novel is a reflection of our time; **jmdm. den ~ vorhalten** (fig.) hold the mirror up to sb.; **das kannst du dir hinter den ~ stecken!** (fig. ugs.) you'll do well to remember that! **2** (Wasserstand, Blutzucker~, Alkohol~ usw.) level; (Wasseroberfläche) surface **3** (am Frack, Smoking) [silk] lapel **4** (am Kragen) tab **5** (Jägerspr., Zool.) (bei Rehen, Hirschen usw.) [white] rump patch; (bei Vögeln) speculum **6** (fig.: Übersicht) breakdown

Der Spiegel

One of Germany's best-selling weekly news and current affairs magazines, *Der Spiegel* was founded in 1947 and is published in Hamburg. It has a liberal outlook and has become synonymous with investigative journalism in Germany, as it has brought to light a number of major scandals in German business and politics over the years.

spiegel-, Spiegel-: **~bild** *das* (auch fig., Math.) reflection; **~bildlich** **A** *Adj.* **eine ~bildliche Abbildung** a mirror image; **B** *adv.* **~bildlich abgebildet** reproduced as a *or* in mirror image; **~blank** *Adj.* shining; **den Fußboden ~blank bohnern** polish the floor until it shines [like a mirror]; **~ei** *das* fried egg; **~fechterei** *die;* ~~, ~~en: **das ist ~fechterei/sind ~fechtereien** that's all a sham; **~glas** *das* mirror glass; **~glatt** *Adj.* like glass *postpos.;* as smooth as glass *postpos.;* **die Straße war ~glatt gefroren** the road was like a sheet of glass; **~karpfen** *der* mirror carp

spiegeln

A *itr. V.* **1** (glänzen) shine; gleam **2** (als Spiegel wirken) reflect the light; **nicht ~des Glas** non-reflective glass

B *tr. V.* **1** (reflektieren) reflect; mirror **2** (Med.) examine ‹*body cavity*› with a speculum

C *refl. V.* (auch fig.) be mirrored *or* reflected; **in ihrem Gesicht spiegelte sich Freude** (fig.) her face shone with delight

Spiegel-: **~reflex·kamera** *die* reflex camera; **~saal** *der* hall of mirrors; **~schrank** *der* wardrobe/cupboard/cabinet with mirror doors; **~schrift** *die* mirror writing; **~teleskop** *das* reflecting telescope; reflector

Spiegelung *die;* ~, ~en **1** (auch fig., Math.) reflection **2** (Med.) speculum examination

spiegel·verkehrt

A *Adj.* back-to-front ‹*lettering*›; **eine ~e Abbildung** a mirror image

B *adv.* **etw. ~ abbilden** reproduce sth. as a *or* in mirror image

Spiel /ʃpi:l/ *das;* ~[e]s, ~e **1** (das ~en, ~erei) play; **er treibt ein ~ mit ihr** he's playing games *pl.* with her; **für ihn ist alles nur ein ~:** everything's just a game to him; **pass auf, dass du das ~ nicht zu weit treibst** be careful that you don't push your luck too far; **das ist doch ein ~ mit dem Leben** that's risking your/his *etc.* life; **wie im ~:** as if it were child's play; **ein ~ mit dem Feuer** (fig.) playing with fire; **ein [merkwürdiges] ~ des Zufalls/Schicksals** a whim of chance/fate; **ein seltsames ~ der Natur** a freak of nature; **freies ~ haben** be able to do what one wants *or* as one pleases; **genug des grausamen ~s!** (scherzh.) enough is enough! **2** (Glücks~; Gesellschafts~) game; (Wett~) game; match; **ein ~ spielen/gewinnen** play/win a game; **einen ~er aus dem ~ nehmen/ins ~ schicken** take a player off/send a player on; **dem ~ verfallen sein** be addicted to gambling *or* gaming; **sein Geld beim ~ verlieren** gamble one's money away; **machen Sie Ihr ~!** (Roulette) place your bets; faites vos jeux; **das ~ ist aus** the game is up; **gewonnenes ~ haben** be home and dry; **leichtes ~ [mit jmdm.] haben** have an easy job [with sb.]; **mit Frauen ihres Typs hat ein Casanova wie er leichtes ~:** women like her are easy game for a Casanova like him; **das ~ verloren geben** give the game up for lost; (fig.) throw in the towel *or* one's hand; **auf dem ~ stehen** be at stake; **etw. aufs ~ setzen** put sth. at stake; risk sth.; **ein falsches/doppeltes/unfaires ~ spielen** *od.* **treiben** play sb. false/double-cross sb./treat sb. unfairly; **jmdn./etw. aus dem ~ lassen** (fig.) leave sb./sth. out of it; **aus dem ~ bleiben** (fig.) ‹*person*› stay out of it; **jmdn./etw. ins ~ bringen** (fig.) bring sb./sth. into it; **ins ~ kommen** (fig.) ‹*factor*› come into play; ‹*person, authorities, etc.*› become involved; ‹*matter, subject, etc.*› come into it; **im ~ sein** (fig.) be involved; *s. auch* **Hand 6** **3** (Utensilien) game; **ein ~ Karten** a pack of cards; **das ~ ist nicht mehr vollständig** there's something missing from the set; **ein ~ Stricknadeln/Saiten** (fig.) a set of knitting needles/strings **4** (eines Schauspielers) performance **5** (eines Musikers) performance; playing; *s. auch* **klingend B** **6** (Sport: ~weise) game **7** (Schau~) play **8** (Technik: Bewegungsfreiheit) [free] play **9** (fig.: Bewegung) play

Spiel-: **~alter** *das* playing stage; **~anzug** *der* playsuit; rompers *pl.;* **~art** *die* variety; **~automat** *der* gaming machine; (Geschicklichkeitsspiel) amusement machine; **~ball** *der* **1** (Sport) (Tennis) game point; (Volleyball) match ball; **2** (Billard) red [ball]; **3** (fig.) plaything; **das Boot war ein ~ball der Wellen** the boat was at the mercy of *or* was tossed about by the waves; **sie ist der ~ball ihrer Leidenschaften** she allows herself to be torn hither and thither by her passions; **4** (Ball, mit dem gespielt wird) match ball; **~bank** *die; Pl.* ~~en casino; **~bein** *das* (Sport) free leg; (Fußball) striking leg; **~dose** *die* musical box (Brit.); music box (Amer.)

spielen

A *itr. V.* **1** play; **~ gehen** go off to play; **der Wind spielte mit ihrem Haar** (fig.) the wind played in her hair; **um die Meisterschaft ~:** play for the championship; **sie haben 1:0/unentschieden gespielt** the match ended 1-0/in a draw; **er spielt in der Abwehr/als Libero** he plays in defence/as sweeper; **auf der Gitarre ~:** play the guitar; **er kann vom Blatt/nach Noten ~:** he can sight-read/play from music; **vierhändig ~:** play a [piano] duet/[piano] duets; **sie spielt nur mit ihm/seinen Gefühlen** she's only playing a game with him/playing with his feelings; **du darfst nicht mit deinem Leben ~:** you mustn't gamble with *or* risk your life

2 (um Geld) play; **er begann zu trinken und zu ~:** he began to drink and to gamble; **um Geld ~:** play for money; **mit hohem Einsatz ~:** play for high stakes; **an einem Spielautomaten ~:** play a fruit machine/ (Geschicklichkeitsspiel) an amusement machine; *s. auch* **Lotto**

3 (als Schauspieler) act; perform

4 (sich ab~) **der Roman/Film spielt im 17. Jahrhundert/in Berlin** the novel/film is set in the 17th century/in Berlin

5 (fig.: sich bewegen) ‹*wind, water, etc.*› play; **ein Lächeln spielte um ihre Lippen** (fig.) a smile played on her lips; **seine Muskeln ~ lassen** flex one's muscles; **seinen Charme/seine Beziehungen ~ lassen** (fig.) bring one's charm/connections to bear; **seine Fantasie ~ lassen** use one's imagination

6 (fig.: übergehen) **das Blau spielt ins Violette** the blue is tinged with purple; **ein ins Bräunliche ~des Rot** a red with a brownish tinge

B *tr. V.* **1** play; **Räuber und Gendarm ~:** play cops and robbers; **Cowboy ~:** play at being a cowboy; **er spielt hervorragend Schach/Tennis** he's an excellent chess/tennis player; **Geige/Akkordeon/Gitarre** *usw.* **~:** play the violin/accordion/guitar *etc.;* **er spielt hervorragend Gitarre** he's an outstanding guitarist; **Trumpf/Pik/ein As ~:** play a trump/spades/an ace

2 (aufführen, vorführen) put on ‹*play*›; show ‹*film*›; perform ‹*piece of music*›; play ‹*record*›; **spiel doch mal die Beatles** put the Beatles on; **das Radio spielte Jazz** there was jazz on the radio; **was wird hier gespielt?** (fig. ugs.) what's going on here?

3 (schauspielerisch darstellen) play ‹*role*›; **den Beleidigten/Unschuldigen ~** (fig.) act offended/play the innocent; **sie spielt gern die große Dame** (fig.) she likes playing *or* acting the grand lady; **[für jmdn.] den Chauffeur ~:** act as chauffeur for sb.; **[bei jmdm.] Babysitter ~** (fig.) be babysitter *or* do the babysitting [for sb.]; **sie reagierte mit gespielter Gleichgültigkeit** she reacted with feigned indifference; **sein Interesse war [nur] gespielt** he [only] pretended to be interested; his interest was [merely] feigned; **in gespieltem Ernst** with mock seriousness

4 (Sport: werfen, treten, schlagen) play; **einen Ball mit Rückhand/mit dem linken Fuß ~:** play a ball backhand/with the left foot; **den Ball ins Aus/vors Tor ~:** put the ball out/play the ball in towards the goal; **einen Ball mit dem Kopf ~:** head a ball

C *refl. V.* **sich warm ~:** warm up; **sich hungrig/müde ~:** work up an appetite/tire oneself out playing

spielend

A *Adj.* **mit ~er Leichtigkeit** with consummate *or* effortless ease

B *adv.* easily; **etw. ~ beherrschen** master sth. effortlessly; **~ leicht** without the slightest effort

Spieler *der;* ~s, ~ **1** (auch Sport, Musik) player **2** (Glücks~) gambler **3** (Schau~) actor

Spielerei *die;* ~, ~en **1** playing *no art.;* (im Glücksspiel) gambling *no art.;* (das Herumspielen) playing *or* fiddling about *or* around (**an** + *Dat.* with) **2** (müßiges Tun, Spiel) **eine ~ mit Worten/Zahlen** playing [around] with words/numbers; **eine mathematische ~:** a mathematical game; **für ihn ist das nur eine ~:** he's just playing about **3** (Kinderspiel, Leichtigkeit) child's play *no art.;* **das ist keine ~:** it has to be taken seriously **4** (Tand) gadget; **technische ~en** technical gadgetry *sing.*

Spielerin *die;* ~, ~nen **1** ▸**Spieler 1, 2** **2** (Schau~) actress

spielerisch

A *Adj.* **1** playful; **mit ~er Leichtigkeit** with consummate *or* effortless ease **2** (Sport) **sein ~es Können** his skill as a player; **~e Elemente** playing skills; **eine ausgezeichnete ~e Leistung** an outstanding [playing] performance **3** (Musik) **~es Können** playing ability

B *adv.* **1** playfully; **seine Hände glitten ~ über die Tasten** his hands glided lightly and easily over the keys **2** (Sport) in playing terms **3** (Musik) in terms of performance

spiel-, Spiel-: **~feld** *das* (Fußball, Hockey, Rugby usw.) field; pitch (Brit.); (Tennis, Squash, Federball, Volleyball usw.) court; **~figur** *die* piece; **~film** *der* feature film; **~frei** *Adj.* **ein ~freier Tag** (Theater) a day when there is no performance/are no performances; (Sport) a day without a match; **~führer** *der,* **~führerin** *die* (Sport) [team] captain; **~gefährte** *der,* **~gefährtin** *die* (geh.) playmate; playfellow; **~geld** *das* play *or* toy money; **~hölle** *die* (ugs. abwertend) gambling den

Spieliothek /ʃpi:lioˈte:k/ *die;* ~, ~en games library

Spiel-: **~kamerad** *der,* **~kameradin** *die* playmate; playfellow; **~karte** *die* playing card; **~kasino** *das* casino; **~konsole** *die* games console; **~leidenschaft** *die* passion for gambling; **~leiter** *der* **1** (im Fernsehen) quizmaster; (im Roulett) tourneur; **2** ▸**Regisseur**; **~leiterin** *die* **1** (im Fernsehen) quizmaster; (im Roulett) tourneuse; **2** ▸**Regisseurin**; **~macher** *der,* **~macherin** *die* (Sportjargon) key player; **~mann** *der; Pl.* **~leute** **1** (hist.: fahrender Sänger) minstrel; **2** (Mitglied eines ~mannszuges) bandsman; **~manns·zug** *der* marching band; **~marke** *die* chip; jetton; **~minute** *die* (Sport) minute [of play]

Spielothek /ʃpi:loˈte:k/ *die;* ~, ~en games library

Spiel-: **~phase** *die* stage of the game; **~plan** *der* **1** (Theater) programme; **das Stück steht noch bis nächsten Monat auf dem ~plan** the play will continue running until next month; **2** (eines Brettspiels) board; **~platz** *der* playground; **~raum** *der*

S

1 room to move (fig.); scope; latitude; (bei Ausgaben, Budget) leeway; 2 (Technik) clearance; **~regel** *die* (auch fig.) rule of the game; **gegen die ~regeln verstoßen** (auch fig.) break the rules; **~runde** *die* round [of the game]; **~saal** *der* gambling room; **~sachen** *Pl.* toys; **~salon** *der* gaming room; **~schuld** *die* gambling debt; **~stand** *der*: **beim ~stand 1:1** with the score at 1-1; **bei diesem ~stand muss Schwarz gewinnen** as the game stands, Black must win; **~stärke** *die*: **der FC Sachsenfurt demonstrierte seine ~stärke** FC Sachsenfurt demonstrated the strength of its play; **~stein** *der* piece; (beim Damespiel, Schach) piece; man; **~straße** *die* play street; **~tag** *der* day of play; **~teufel** *der*: **dem ~teufel verfallen** *od.* **vom ~teufel besessen sein** have been bitten by the gambling bug (coll.); **~tisch** *der* 1 games table; (für Glücksspiele) gaming table; (für Kartenspiele) card table; 2 (der Orgel) console; **~trieb** *der* play instinct; **~uhr** *die* 1 musical clock; 2 musical box (Brit.); music box (Amer.); **~verderber** *der*; **~~s, ~~, ~verderberin** *die*; **~~, ~~nen** spoilsport; **~verlauf** *der* (Sport) **der weitere ~verlauf** the rest of the game; **~waren** *Pl.* toys; **~warengeschäft** *das* toyshop; **~wiese** *die* grass play area; (fig.) playground; **~zeit** *die* 1 (Theater: Saison) season; 2 (Aufführungsdauer) run; 3 (Sport) playing time; **die normale ~zeit** normal time; **~zeug** *das* 1 toy; (fig.) toy; plaything; 2 (~sachen, ~waren) toys *pl.*; **~zeug·eisenbahn** *die* [toy] train set; **~zimmer** *das* playroom; **~zug** *der* (Sport, in einem Brettspiel) move

Spieß /ʃpiːs/ *der*; **~es, ~e** 1 (Waffe) spear; **den ~ umdrehen** *od.* **umkehren** (ugs.) turn the tables; **wie am ~ schreien** *od.* **brüllen** (ugs.) scream one's head off; scream blue murder (coll.) 2 (Brat~) spit; (Schaschlik~) skewer; (Cocktail~) cocktail stick; **ein am ~ gebratener Ochse** an ox roasted on the spit; a spit-roasted ox 3 (Fleisch~) kebab 4 (Soldatenspr.: Kompaniefeldwebel) [company] sergeant major 5 (Jägerspr.) spike; pricket

spieß-, Spieß-: ~bürger *der*, **~bürgerin** *die* (abwertend) [petit] bourgeois; **~bürgerlich** ▸ **spießig**; **~bürgertum** *das* (abwertend) 1 [petit] bourgeois existence; (spießiges Wesen) [petit] bourgeois conformism; 2 (die ~bürger) [petite] bourgeoisie

Spießchen *das*; **~s, ~** 1 (Cocktailspieß) cocktail stick 2 (Schaschlikspieß) skewer 3 (Fleischspieß) kebab

spießen *tr. V.* **die Fleischstücke werden auf einen Schaschlikspieß gespießt** the pieces of meat are pushed on to a skewer; **ein Stück Käse/eine Olive auf einen Cocktailspieß ~**: spear a piece of cheese/an olive with a cocktail stick; **etw. in etw.** (Akk.) **~**: stick sth. in sth.

Spießer *der*; **~s, ~** (abwertend) [petit] bourgeois

spießerhaft ▸ **spießig**

Spießerin *die*; **~, ~nen** ▸ **Spießer**

Spießertum *das*; **~s** (abwertend) ▸ **Spießbürgertum**

Spieß·geselle *der*, **Spieß·gesellin** *die* 1 (abwertend: Komplize) accomplice 2 (veralt.: Kumpan) companion

spießig (abwertend)
A *Adj.* [petit] bourgeois; **~e Kleinbürgerlichkeit** petit bourgeois narrow-mindedness
B *adv.* ‹think, behave, etc.› in a [petit] bourgeois way; **eine ~ eingerichtete Wohnung** a flat (esp. Brit.) *or* (esp. Amer.) apartment furnished in a typically petit bourgeois style

Spießigkeit *die*; **~** (abwertend) [petit] bourgeois narrow-mindedness; (einer Wohnungseinrichtung) [petit] bourgeois style

Spieß·rute *die*: **in ~n laufen** (auch fig.) run the gauntlet

Spike /ʃpaik/ *der*; **~s, ~s** 1 spike 2 *Pl.* (Schuhe) spikes 3 (eines Reifens) stud 4 *Pl.* (Reifen) studded tyres

Spike[s]·reifen *der* studded tyre

spillerig /ˈʃpɪlərɪç/ *Adj.* (bes. nordd.) spindly, skinny ‹limbs›; skinny ‹person›

spinal /ʃpiˈnaːl/ (Anat.)
A *Adj.* spinal; **~e Kinderlähmung** infantile paralysis; polio [myelitis]
B *adv.* **~ gelähmt sein** suffer from spinal paralysis

Spinat /ʃpiˈnaːt/ *der*; **~[e]s, ~e** spinach

Spinat·wachtel *die* (ugs. abwertend) skinny old bag (sl.)

Spind /ʃpɪnt/ *der od. das*; **~[e]s, ~e** locker

Spindel /ˈʃpɪndl̩/ *die*; **~, ~n** 1 spindle 2 (einer Treppe) newel

spindel·dürr *Adj.* skinny ‹person›; spindly, skinny ‹limbs, finger›; **sie ist ~**: she's as thin as a rake

Spinett /ʃpiˈnɛt/ *das*; **~[e]s, ~e** spinet

Spinnaker /ˈʃpɪnakɐ/ *der*; **~s, ~** (Seemannsspr.) spinnaker

Spinne /ˈʃpɪnə/ *die*; **~, ~n** spider

spinne·feind (ugs.) *in* **jmdm. ~ sein** hate sb.'s guts (coll.)

spinnen /ˈʃpɪnən/
A *unr. tr. V.* 1 spin (fig.); plot ‹intrigue›; think up ‹idea›; hatch ‹plot›; **ein Lügengewebe/Netz von Intrigen ~**: weave a tissue of lies/a web of intrigue 2 (ugs.: lügen) make up; **das spinnst du!** you're making it up!
B *unr. itr. V.* 1 spin; **an einer Intrige ~**: plot an intrigue 2 (ugs.: verrückt sein) be crazy *or* (coll.) nuts *or* (sl.) crackers; **Ich soll bezahlen? Du spinnst wohl!** [What,] me pay? You must be joking *or* (sl.) kidding; **ich glaube, ich spinne!** I don't believe it!; **du spinnst wohl [, das zu tun]** you must be crazy [to do it] 3 (ugs.: Unsinn reden) talk rubbish 4 (ugs.: lügen) make it up

Spinnen-: ~gewebe *das* ▸ **Spinngewebe**; **~netz** *das* spider's web

Spinner *der*; **~s, ~** 1 ▸ **i** S. 113 (Beruf) spinner 2 (ugs. abwertend) nutcase (coll.); idiot 3 (Zool. veralt.) silk moth 4 (Angeln) spinner

Spinnerei *die*; **~, ~en** 1 spinning *no art.* 2 (Werkstatt) spinning mill 3 (ugs. abwertend) crazy idea

Spinnerin *die*; **~, ~nen** 1 ▸ **i** S. 113 (Beruf) spinner 2 (ugs. abwertend) nutcase (coll.); idiot

spinnert /ˈʃpɪnɐt/ *Adj.* (ugs., bes. südd.) slightly potty (coll.)

Spinn·gewebe *das* cobweb

spinnig *Adj.* (ugs.) slightly potty (coll.)

Spinn-: ~rad *das* spinning wheel; **~rocken** *der* distaff; **~webe** *die*; **~~, ~~n** cobweb; **~wirtel** *der* whorl; wharve

Spin-off /spɪnˈɔf/ *das od. der*; **~[s], ~s** spin-off

spintisieren /ʃpɪntiˈziːrən/ *itr. V.* (ugs.) get weird *or* crazy ideas (coll.)

Spintisiererei *die*; **~, ~en** (ugs.) crazy fantasizing *no indef. art.*

Spion /ʃpiˈoːn/ *der*; **~s, ~e** 1 spy 2 (Guckloch) spyhole 3 (Spiegel am Fenster) telltale mirror

Spionage /ʃpioˈnaːʒə/ *die*; **~**: spying; espionage; **~ treiben** spy; carry out espionage

Spionage-: ~abwehr *die* 1 (Tätigkeit) counter-espionage; counter-intelligence; 2 (Dienst) counter-espionage *or* counter-intelligence service; **er arbeitet in der ~abwehr** he works in counter-espionage *or* counter-intelligence; **~fall** *der* spy *or* espionage case; **~netz** *das* spy *or* espionage network; **~ring** *der* spy ring

spionieren *itr. V.* 1 spy (**gegen** against) 2 (fig. abwertend) spy; snoop [about] (coll.)

Spioniererei *die*; **~, ~en** (fig. abwertend) snooping [about] *no pl.* (coll.)

Spionin *die*; **~, ~nen** spy

Spiral·bohrer *der* twist drill *or* bit

Spirale /ʃpiˈraːlə/ *die*; **~, ~n** 1 (auch Geom., fig.) spiral; (Heiz~) coil 2 (zur Empfängnisverhütung) coil

Spiral·feder *die* coil spring

spiral·förmig
A *Adj.* spiral[-shaped]
B *adv.* spirally

spiralig
A *Adj.* spiral
B *adv.* spirally

Spiral·nebel *der* (Astron.) spiral nebula

Spirant /spiˈrant/ *der*; **~en, ~en** (Sprachw.) spirant

Spiritismus /ʃpiriˈtɪsmʊs/ *der*; **~**: spiritualism; spiritism

Spiritist *der*; **~en, ~en**, **Spiritistin** *die*; **~, ~nen** spiritualist; spiritist

spiritistisch
A *Adj.* spiritualist[ic]; spiritistic
B *adv.* spiritualistically; spiritistically

Spiritual /ˈspɪrɪtjʊəl/ *das od. der*; **~s, ~s** [negro] spiritual

spiritualisieren *tr. V.* spiritualize

Spiritualismus /spiritu̯aˈlɪsmʊs/ *der*; **~** (Philos.) spiritualism

spiritualistisch
A *Adj.* spiritualist[ic]
B *adv.* spiritualistically

Spiritualität /spiritu̯aliˈtɛːt/ *die*; **~**: spirituality

Spirituose /spiriˈtu̯oːzə/ *die*; **~, ~n** spirit *usu. in pl.*

Spiritus /ˈʃpiːritʊs/ *der*; **~, ~se** spirit; ethyl alcohol; **ein Organ in ~ konservieren** preserve an organ in alcohol; **mit ~ kochen** cook on a spirit stove

Spiritus·kocher *der* spirit stove

Spital /ʃpiˈtaːl/ *das*; **~s, Spitäler** /ʃpiˈtɛːlɐ/ (bes. österr., schweiz.) hospital; (veralt.: Altersheim) old people's home; (veralt.: Armenhaus) almshouse

Spittel /ˈʃpɪtl̩/ *das*, (schweiz.:) *der*; **~s, ~** (bes. schweiz. ugs.) hospital

spitz /ʃpɪts/
A *Adj.* 1 (nicht stumpf) pointed ‹tower, arch, shoes, nose, beard, etc.›; sharp ‹pencil, needle, stone, etc.›; fine ‹pen nib›; (Geom.) acute ‹angle› 2 (schrill) shrill ‹cry etc.› 3 (ugs.: abgezehrt) haggard; haggard, pinched ‹face› 4 (boshaft) cutting ‹remark, etc.›; **~ werden** get spiteful 5 (ugs.: geil) randy; horny (sl.); **~ auf jmdn. sein** really fancy sb.
B *adv.* 1 **~ zulaufen** taper to a point; **~ zulaufend** pointed 2 (boshaft) cuttingly

Spitz *der*; **~es, ~e** (Hund) spitz

spitz-, Spitz-: ~ahorn *der* Norway maple; **~bart** *der* 1 goatee; pointed beard; 2 (Mann) man with a/the goatee or pointed beard; **~bauch** *der* potbelly; **~|bekommen** *unr. tr. V.* (ugs.) ▸ **~kriegen**; **~bogen** *der* pointed arch; **~bogen·fenster** *das* lancet window; **~bube** *der* 1 (veralt. abwertend: Gauner) rogue; scoundrel; 2 (scherzh.: Schlingel) rascal; scallywag; scamp; 3 (österr.: Plätzchen) *sandwich of two or three biscuits stuck together with jam*; **~büberei** /-byːbəˈrai/ *die*; **~~, ~~en** 1 piece of roguery; 2 roguery; **~bübin** *die*; **~~, ~~nen** ▸ **~bube 1, 2**; **~bübisch** **A** *Adj.* 1 (verschmitzt) roguish; mischievous; 2 (veralt. abwertend: schurkisch) villainous; **B** *adv.* 1 (verschmitzt) roguishly; mischievously; 2 (veralt. abwertend: schurkisch) villainously

spitze *indekl. Adj.* (ugs.) ▸ **klasse**

Spitze *die*; **~, ~n** 1 (Nadel~, Bleistift~ usw.) point; (Pfeil~, Horn~ usw.) tip; **einer Sache** (Dat.) **die ~ nehmen** *od.* **abbrechen** (fig.) take the sting out of sth. (fig.) 2 (Turm~, Baum~, Mast~ usw.) top; (eines Dreiecks, Kegels, einer Pyramide) top; apex; vertex (Math.); (eines Berges) summit; top; **ein auf der ~ stehendes Dreieck** an inverted triangle 3 (Zigarren~, Haar~, Zweig~) end; (Schuh~) toe; (Finger~, Nasen~, Schwanz~, Flügel~, Spargel~) tip; (Lungen~) apex; **die südliche ~ der Insel** the southern tip of the island 4 (vorderes Ende) front; **an der ~ des Zuges/der Kolonne marschieren** march at the head of the procession/column; **an der ~ liegen** (Sport) be in the lead *or* in front; **sich an die ~ [des Feldes] setzen** (Sport) go into *or* take the lead 5 (führende Position) top; **an der ~ [der Tabelle] stehen** *od.* **liegen** (Sport) be [at the] top [of the table]; **sich an die ~ [einer Bewegung] setzen** put oneself at the head [of a movement]; **die ~ halten/übernehmen** stay top/go to the top

S

[6] (einer Firma, Organisation usw.) head; (einer Hierarchie) top; (leitende Gruppe) management; **an der ~ des Unternehmens/der Partei stehen** be at the head of the company/party; **die ~n der Gesellschaft/der Partei** the leading figures of society/in the party [7] ▸❶ **S. 310** (Höchstwert) maximum; peak; (ugs.: **~nzeit**) peak period; **das Auto fährt 160 km ~:** the car has *or* does a top speed of 160 km. per hour; **wir wollen die Sache doch nicht auf die ~ treiben** we don't want to carry things too far [8] **[absolute/einsame] ~ sein** (ugs.) be [absolutely] great (coll.) [9] (fig.: Angriff) dig (**gegen** at); **~n austeilen** make pointed remarks [10] (Textilwesen) lace [11] (Sport: Sturm~) striker [12] (Zigaretten~, Zigarrenhalter) [cigarette/cigar] holder [13] (Wirtsch.: Überschuss) surplus

Spitzel *der;* **~s, ~** (abwertend) informer; **ein ~ der Polizei** a police informer; a copper's nark (Brit. coll.)

Spitzel·dienste *Pl.* (abwertend) **für jmdn. ~ leisten** act as an informer for sb.; **für ~ bin ich mir zu schade** I couldn't stoop to acting as *or* being an informer

spitzeln *itr. V.* (abwertend) act as an informer

spitzen
A *tr. V.* sharpen ‹*pencil*›; purse ‹*lips, mouth*›; **die Ohren ~** ‹*dog*› prick up its ears; (fig.) ‹*person*› prick up one's ears
B *refl. V.* **sich auf etw.** (*Akk.*) **~** (ugs.) look forward [expectantly] to sth.; (dringlich erhoffen) have one's heart set on sth.
C (landsch.: aufmerken) prick up one's ears

Spitzen-: ~bluse *die* lace blouse; **~deckchen** *das* lace mat; **~erzeugnis** *das* top-quality product; **~funktionär** *der,* **~funktionärin** *die* top official; **~gehalt** *das* top-level salary; **~geschwindigkeit** *die* ▸❶ **S. 310** top speed; **~kandidat** *der,* **~kandidatin** *die* leading *or* top candidate; **~klasse** *die* [1] top class; **ein Hotel der ~klasse** a top-class hotel; **zur ~klasse gehören** be top-class; [2] **~klasse sein** (ugs.) be really great (coll.); **~könner** *der,* **~könnerin** *die* top-class talent; **~kraft** *die* top-class *or* top-flight professional; **~kragen** *der* lace collar; **~leistung** *die* top-class performance; **eine ~leistung der Ingenieurskunst** a supreme achievement of engineering; **~politiker** *der,* **~politikerin** *die* top *or* leading politician; **~position** *die* [1] (Sport) leading position; [2] (leitende Position) top position; **~qualität** *die* top quality; **Erzeugnisse in ~qualität** top-quality products; **~reiter** *der* [1] top rider; (fig.) leader; [2] (Mannschaft) top team; [3] (Ware) top *or* best seller; **~reiterin** *die* ▸ **~reiter 1**; **~spiel** *das* (Sport) top match *or* game; **~spieler** *der,* **~spielerin** *die* top[-class] player; **~sportler** *der* top sportsman; **~sportlerin** *die* top sportswoman; **~steuersatz** *der* highest tax rate; **~stellung** *die* top position; **~tanz** *der* dancing *no art.* on points *or* on [full] point; **~technologie** *die* state-of-the-art technology; **~wein** *der* top[-quality] wine; **~wert** *der* peak; maximum [value]; **~zeit** *die* [1] peak time *or* period; [2] (Sport) (beste Zeit) best time; (sehr gute Zeit) outstanding *or* excellent time

Spitzer *der;* **~s, ~:** [pencil] sharpener

spitz-, Spitz-: ~findig A *Adj.;* hair-splitting, oversubtle; quibbling ‹*distinction*›; pettifogging ‹*quibble*›; **jetzt wirst du [zu] ~findig** now you're splitting hairs *or* being too subtle; B *adv.* in an oversubtle way; **[zu] ~findig argumentieren** be oversubtle in one's arguments; split hairs; **~findigkeit** *die;* **~~, ~~en** [1] over subtlety; (Haarspalterei) hair-splitting; [2] (etwas ~findiges) nicety; (Äußerung) hair-splitting remark; **~hacke** *die* pick; pickaxe

spitzig *Adj.* (veralt.) ▸ **spitz A 1-4, B**

spitz-, Spitz-: ~kehre *die* [1] (Haarnadelkurve) hairpin bend; [2] (Ski) kick turn; **~|kriegen** *tr. V.* (ugs.) tumble to (coll.); get wise to (sl.); **[es] ~kriegen, dass ...** tumble to *or* get wise to the fact that ...; **~maus** *die* [1] shrew; [2] (ugs. abwertend) weasel-faced female (derog.); **~name** *der* nickname; **~wegerich** *der* (Bot.) ribwort; **~winklig** A *Adj.* acute-angled ‹*triangle*›; B *adv.* at an acute angle; **~züngig** A *Adj.* sharp-tongued; B *adv.* ‹*reply*› sharply

Spleen /ʃpliːn/ *der;* **~s, ~e** *od.* **~s** strange *or* peculiar habit; eccentricity; **du hast ja einen ~!** there must be something the matter with you!; you must be dotty (coll.); **die Lexikographen haben doch alle einen kleinen ~:** lexicographers are all a bit cracked (coll.)

spleenig *Adj.* eccentric; dotty (coll.)

spleißen /ˈʃplaisn̩/ (Seemannsspr.)
A *unr. od. regelm. tr. V.* splice ‹*rope*›
B *unr. od. regelm. itr. V.* make a splice/splices

splendid /ʃplɛnˈdiːt/ (veralt.)
A *Adj.* [1] generous [2] (kostbar) sumptuous; magnificent
B *adv.* [1] generously [2] (kostbar) sumptuously; magnificently

Splint /ʃplɪnt/ *der;* **~[e]s, ~e** (Technik) split pin

Splint·holz *das* sapwood; alburnum

spliss, *spliß /ʃplɪs/ *1. u. 3. Pers. Sg. Prät. v.* **spleißen**

Splitt /ʃplɪt/ *der;* **~[e]s, ~e** [stone] chippings *pl.;* (zum Streuen) grit; (in Beton) aggregate

splitten *tr. V.* (Wirtsch.) [1] split ‹*shares*› [2] (Politik) **die Stimmen ~:** *give one's first vote to a particular candidate and one's second to a party other than that of the chosen candidate*

Splitter[1] /ˈʃplɪtɐ/*der;* **~s, ~:** splinter; (Granat~, Bomben~) splinter; fragment; **du siehst den ~ im fremden Auge, aber nicht den Balken im eigenen** (geh.) you can see a mote in another's eye but not the beam that is in your own

Splitter[2] /ˈsplɪtɐ/ *der;* **~s, ~s,** (DV) splitter

splitter-, Splitter-: ~bombe *die* fragmentation bomb; **~bruch** *der* ▸❶ **S. 439** (Med.) comminuted fracture; **~faser·nackt** *Adj.* (ugs.) absolutely stark naked; completely starkers *pred.* (Brit. coll.); **~frei** *Adj.* shatterproof; **~gruppe** *die* splinter group

splitterig *Adj.* [1] (leicht splitternd) ‹*wood, plastic, etc.*› that splinters easily; **~ sein** splinter easily [2] (voller Splitter) splintery

splittern *itr. V.* [1] (Splitter bilden) splinter [2] *mit sein* (in Splitter zerbrechen) ‹*glass, windscreen, etc.*› shatter

splitter·nackt *Adj.* (ugs.) stark naked; starkers *pred.* (Brit. coll.)

Splitter·partei *die* splinter party

Splitting /ˈʃplɪtɪŋ/ *das;* **~s, ~s** [1] (Steuerw.) *taxation of husband and wife whereby each is taxed on half the total of their combined incomes* [2] (Wirtsch.) splitting [3] (Politik) *division of one's first and second votes between a particular candidate and a party other than that of the chosen candidate*

Splitting·system *das* (Steuerw.) *tax system in which husband and wife each pay income tax on half the total of their combined incomes*

splittrig ▸ **splitterig**

SPÖ *Abk.* **= Sozialistische Partei Österreichs** Austrian Socialist Party

> **SPÖ – Sozialistische Partei Österreichs**
>
> The Austrian Social Democratic Party was founded in 1888 as the *Sozialdemokratische Arbeiterpartei Österreichs* (Social Democratic Workers' Party of Austria). It was re-formed in 1945 and is the largest political party in Austria.

Spoiler /ˈʃpɔylɐ/ *der;* **~s, ~** (Kfz-W.) spoiler

Spökenkieker /ˈʃpøːkn̩kiːkɐ/ *der;* **~s, ~** [1] (nordd.: Hellseher) clairvoyant; person who has second sight [2] (ugs.: spintisierender Mensch) crazy fantasist

Spökenkiekerei *die;* **~, ~en** (ugs.) crazy fantasizing *no indef. art.*

Spökenkiekerin *die;* **~, ~nen** ▸ **Spökenkieker**

Spondeus /ʃpɔnˈdeːʊs/ *der;* **~, Spondeen** (Verslehre) spondee

sponsern /ˈʃpɔnzɐn/ *tr. V.* sponsor

Sponsor /ˈʃpɔnzɐ/ *der;* **~s, ~en** /-ˈzoːrən/, **Sponsorin** *die;* **~, ~nen** sponsor

spontan /ʃpɔnˈtaːn/
A *Adj.* spontaneous
B *adv.* spontaneously

Spontaneität /ʃpɔntaneiˈtɛːt/ *die;* **~** (auch Psych., Med.) spontaneity

Sponti /ˈʃpɔnti/ *der;* **~s, ~s** (ugs.) *member of an undogmatic leftist group*

sporadisch /ʃpoˈraːdɪʃ/
A *Adj.* sporadic
B *adv.* sporadically

Spore /ˈʃpoːrə/ *die;* **~, ~n** (Biol.) spore

Sporen ▸ **Spore, Sporn**

sporen-, Sporen-: ~klirrend *Adv.* with a clatter of spurs; **~pflanze** *die* (Bot.) cryptogam; **~tierchen** *das* (Zool.) sporozoan

Sporn /ʃpɔrn/ *der;* **~[e]s, ~e** *od.* **Sporen** /ˈʃpoːrən/ [1] *Pl.* **Sporen** *od.* (Zool.) **~e** spur; **einem Pferd die Sporen geben** spur a horse; **sich die [ersten] Sporen verdienen** (fig.) win one's spurs [2] *Pl.* **~e** (hist.: am Schiff) ram [3] *Pl.* **~e** (eines Flugzeugs) tail skid

spornen *tr. V.* spur ‹*horse*›

sporn·streichs *Adv.* (veralt.) straight away

Sport /ʃpɔrt/ *der;* **~[e]s** [1] sport; (als Unterrichtsfach) sport; physical education; PE; **~ treiben** do sport; **beim ~:** while doing sport; **und hier noch eine Meldung vom ~:** and finally an item of sports news [2] (**~art**) sport [3] (Hobby, Zeitvertreib) hobby; pastime; **sich** (*Dat.*) **einen ~ aus etw. machen** get a kick (coll.) out of sth.

Sport-: ~abzeichen *das* sports badge; **~angler** *der,* **~anglerin** *die* club angler; **~anlage** *die* sports complex; **~art** *die* [form of] sport; **~artikel** *der* piece of sports equipment; **~artikel** *Pl.* sports equipment *sing.;* **~arzt** *der,* **~ärztin** *die* sports doctor; **~bericht** *der* sports report; **~berichterstattung** *die* sports reporting; **~boot** *das* sports boat; **~coupé** *das* sports coupé; **~dress,** ***~dreß** *der* ▸ **Dress 1**; **~feld** *das* sports ground; (Stadion) sports stadium; **~fest** *das* sports festival; (einer Schule) sports day; **~fischen** *das;* **~~s** club fishing *no art. or* angling *no art.;* **~flieger** *der,* **~fliegerin** *die* sports pilot; **~flugzeug** *das* sports plane; **~freund** *der,* **~freundin** *die* [1] sports fan; [2] (Kamerad[in]) sporting friend; **~funktionär** *der,* **~funktionärin** *die* sports official; **~geist** *der* sportsmanship; sporting spirit; **~gerät** *das* piece of sports apparatus; **~geräte** (als Gesamtheit) sports apparatus *sing.;* **~hemd** *das* sports shirt; **~hochschule** *die* college of physical education

sportiv /spɔrˈtiːf/
A *Adj.* sporty
B *adv.* sportily

Sport-: ~journalist *der,* **~journalistin** *die* sports journalist; **~kamerad** *der,* **~kameradin** *die* sporting friend; **~kleidung** *die* sportswear; sports clothes *pl.;* **~lehrer** *der,* **~lehrerin** *die* sports instructor; (in einer Schule) PE *or* physical education teacher; games teacher

Sportler /ˈʃpɔrtlɐ/ *der;* **~s, ~:** sportsman

Sportler·herz *das* athletic heart

Sportlerin *die;* **~, ~nen** sportswoman

sportlich
A *Adj.* [1] sporting *attrib.* ‹*success, performance, interests, etc.*›; **~e Veranstaltungen** sports events; sporting events; **auf ~em Gebiet** in the field of sport [2] (fair) sportsmanlike; sporting [3] (fig.: flott, rasant) sporty ‹*car, driving, etc.*› [4] (zu **~er** Leistung fähig) sporty, athletic ‹*person*› [5] (jugendlich wirkend) sporty, smart but casual ‹*clothes*›; smart but practical ‹*hairstyle*›
B *adv.* [1] as far as sport is concerned; **~ aktiv sein** be an active sportsman/sportswoman [2] (fair) sportingly [3] (fig.: flott, rasant) in a sporty manner

sportlich-elegant
A *Adj.* casually elegant
B *adv.* casually but elegantly ‹*dressed*›

sport-, Sport-: ~maschine *die* sports plane; **~medizin** *die* sports medicine *no art.;* **~medizinisch** *Adj.* **~medizinische**

S

ℹ Sprachen

Wie die Nationalitätsbezeichnungen, werden die englischen Bezeichnungen der Sprachen (auch die Adjektive) groß geschrieben:

französische Verben
= French verbs

Das Buch ist deutsch geschrieben
= The book is written in German

In Finnland spricht man Finnisch
= In Finland they speak Finnish

Die Belgier sprechen meist entweder Flämisch oder Französisch
= The Belgians mostly speak either Flemish or French

Hindi, die Amtssprache Indiens, wird von den Hindus gesprochen
= Hindi, India's official language, is spoken by the Hindus

auf/in/zu Deutsch usw.

Die verschiedenen Kombinationen von Präposition und Sprache, sowie in den meisten Fällen das deutsche Adverb, werden durch **in** + Sprachbezeichnung übersetzt:

Die Rede wurde auf Englisch gehalten* od. *englisch gehalten
= The speech was given in English

Sagen Sie es auf Deutsch
= Say it in German

Der Brief ist in Suaheli geschrieben
= The letter is written in Swahili

„Aquaplaning", zu Deutsch das Gleiten eines Kfzs auf einer Wasserschicht
= 'Aquaplaning', in plain English the skidding of a vehicle on a film of water

Dort war ein Engländer, der italienisch sprach
= There was an Englishman there who was speaking [in] Italian

Das substantivierte Adjektiv

Das Englische, das Deutsche usw. = **English, German** usw., also ohne Artikel. Vergleichen Sie:

Das Englische hat* od. *Im Englischen gibt es eine Verlaufsform
= English has *od.* In English there is a continuous form

Es wurde aus dem* od. *vom Italienischen ins Deutsche übersetzt
= It was translated from Italian into German

Das Substantiv

Das englische Substantiv zur Bezeichnung einer Sprache wird selten mit einem bestimmten Artikel verwendet, und zwar nur dann (wie im Deutschen), wenn es sich um eine näher bezeichnete Form der Sprache handelt:

das Latein der Mönche des Mittelalters
= the Latin of the medieval monks

Der unbestimmte Artikel **a, an** wird meist vermieden.

Sie schreibt ein fehlerfreies/gepflegtes Englisch
= She writes [a] faultless/cultivated English

Er spricht ein fließendes, akzentfreies Spanisch
= He speaks fluent Spanish without an accent

Die Quäker sprachen ein altmodisches Englisch
= The Quakers spoke an old-fashioned form of English

Das Adjektiv

Das englische Adjektiv übersetzt auch den ersten Teil von Zusammensetzungen wie

Deutschstunde, Französischunterricht, Englischlehrer
= German lesson, French teaching, English teacher

Letzteres kann natürlich auch "englischer Lehrer" heißen, diese Bedeutung wird aber in der gesprochenen Sprache durch stärkere Betonung des Substantivs gekennzeichnet (English 'teacher), wohingegen, wenn ein Englischlehrer gemeint ist, das Adjektiv betont wird ('English teacher). Um Verwechslungen in der Schriftsprache zu vermeiden, kann man im letzteren Fall 'teacher of English' schreiben.

Die Adjektive, die mit **-sprachig** enden, haben zweierlei Bedeutungen (eine bestimmte Sprache sprechend oder in dieser Sprache verfasst bzw. gehalten) und Übersetzungen:

Die deutschsprachige Bevölkerung
= the German-speaking population

Aber:

eine englischsprachige Zeitung
= an English-language newspaper

französischsprachiger Unterricht
= teaching in French

Betreuung/Forschung medical care of sportsmen/research into sports medicine; **~nachrichten** *Pl.* sports news *sing.*; **~platz** *der* sports field; (einer Schule) playing field/fields *pl.*; **~presse** *die* sports press; **~rad** *das* sports bike; **~schuh** *der* 1▸ sports shoe; 2▸ (sportlicher Schuh) casual shoe; **~sendung** *die* sports programme

Sports-: ~freund *der*, **~freundin** *die* sports enthusiast; **Hallo, ~freund! Wie gehts?** (ugs.) hello, mate (coll.), how are you?; **~kanone** *die* (ugs.) sporting ace; **~mann** *der*; *Pl.* **~männer** *od.* **~leute** sportsman

Sport-: ~stadion *das* [sports] stadium; **~student** *der*, **~studentin** *die* sports student; **~taucher** *der*, **~taucherin** *die* skin-diver; **~unfall** *der* sporting *or* sports accident; **~verband** *der* sports association; **~verein** *der* sports club; **~verletzung** *die* sports injury; **~wagen** *der* 1▸ (Auto) sports car; 2▸ (Kinderwagen) pushchair (Brit.); stroller (Amer.); **~wissenschaft** *die* sports science *no art.*

Spot /spɔt/ *der*; **~s, ~s** 1▸ (Werbe~) commercial; advertisement; ad (coll.) 2▸ (Leuchte) spotlight; spotlamp 3▸ (Theat., Film, Fernsehen) spot[light]

Spot·markt *der* (Wirtsch.) spot market

Spott /ʃpɔt/ *der*; **~[e]s** mockery; (höhnischer) ridicule; derision; **~ und Hohn** scorn and derision; **jmdn./etw. dem ~ preisgeben** hold sb./sth. up to ridicule; **seinen ~ mit jmdm./etw. treiben** make fun of sb./sth.

spott-, Spott-: ~bild *das* travesty; mockery; (eines Menschen) caricature; **~billig** (ugs.) **A** *Adj.* dirt cheap; **B** *adv.* **da kann man ~billig einkaufen** you can get *or* buy things dirt cheap there; **~drossel** *die* 1▸ mocking thrush; **[Eigentliche] ~drossel** mockingbird; 2▸ (fig.) ▸ **Spötter**

Spöttelei *die*; **~, ~en** 1▸ [gentle] mocking; [gentle] mockery 2▸ (spöttelnde Äußerung) mocking remark

spötteln /ˈʃpœtl̩n/ *itr. V.* mock [gently]; poke *or* make [gentle] fun; **über jmdn./etw. ~:** mock sb./sth. gently; poke gentle fun at *or* make [gentle] fun of sb./sth.

spotten /ˈʃpɔtn̩/ *itr. V.* 1▸ mock; poke *or* make fun; (höhnischer) ridicule; be derisive; **über jmdn./etw. ~:** mock sb./sth.; make fun of sb./sth.; (höhnischer) ridicule sb./sth.; be derisive about sb./sth.; **du hast gut/leicht ~:** it's easy *or* all very well for you to mock *or* laugh; **jmds./einer Sache ~** (geh.) mock sb./sth. 2▸ (fig.) be contemptuous of; scorn; **er spottete der Gefahr** (*Gen.*) (geh.) he was contemptuous of *or* scorned the danger; **das spottet jeder Beschreibung** (ugs.) it defies *or* beggars description

Spötter /ˈʃpœtɐ/ *der*; **~s, ~:** mocker

Spötterei *die*; **~, ~en** 1▸ mockery; mocking; making fun 2▸ (spottende Äußerung) mocking remark

Spötterin *die*; **~, ~nen** ▸ **Spötter**

Spott-: ~geburt *die* (geh. abwertend) monstrosity; **~gedicht** *das* satirical poem, verse satire (**auf** + *Akk.* about); **~geld** *das* (ugs.) **etw. für** *od.* (veralt.) **um ein ~geld bekommen** get sth. dirt cheap

spöttisch /ˈʃpœtɪʃ/

A *Adj.* mocking ‹*smile, remark, speech, etc.*›; (höhnischer) derisive, ridiculing ‹*remark, speech, etc.*›; **ein ~er Mensch** a person who likes poking fun

B *adv.* mockingly; **~ lächeln** give a mocking smile

Spott-: ~lust *die* love of *or* delight in mockery *or* poking fun; **~name** *der* [derisive] nickname; **~preis** *der* (ugs.) ridiculously low price; **etw. für einen** *od.* **zu einem ~preis bekommen** get sth. dirt cheap *or* for a song

sprach /ʃpraːx/ *1. u. 3. Pers. Sg. Prät. v.* **sprechen**

Sprach-: ~barriere *die* (Soziol.) language barrier; (zwischen Gesellschaftsklassen) linguistic barrier; **~bau** *der* (Sprachw.) linguistic structure; **~begabung** *die* talent *or* gift for languages; **~computer** *der* speech-synthesizing computer; **~denkmal** *das* linguistic monument

spräche /ˈʃprɛːçə/ *1. u. 3. Pers. Sg. Konjunktiv II v.* **sprechen**

Sprache /ˈʃpraːxə/ *die*; **~, ~n** 1▸ ▸ ℹ **S. 670** language; **in englischer ~:** in English; **die ~ der Jäger/Mediziner** the language of the hunt/of medicine; hunting/medical language; **ihm blieb die ~ weg** (ugs.) he was speechless; he was at a loss for words; **es verschlug** *od.* **raubte mir die ~:** it took my breath away; **hast du die ~ verloren?** (ugs.) haven't you got a tongue in your head? 2▸ (Sprechweise) way of speaking; speech; (Stil) style; **eine deutliche/unmissverständliche ~ [mit jmdm.] sprechen** speak bluntly [to sb.] 3▸ (Rede) **die ~ auf jmdn./etw. bringen** bring the conversation round to sb./sth.; **etw. zur ~ bringen** bring sth. up; raise sth.; **zur ~ kommen** be brought up *or* raised; come up; **mit der ~ herausrücken/herauswollen** come out/want to come out with it; **heraus mit der ~!** come on, out with it!

Sprachen-: ~schule *die* language school; **~studium** *das* language studies *pl.*, *no art.*

sprach-, Sprach-: ~entwicklung *die* development of a/the language; **~erkennung** *die* voice recognition; **~erwerb** *der* (Sprachw.) language acquisition; **~familie** *die* language family; family of languages; **~fehler** *der* speech impediment *or* defect; **~forscher** *der*, **~forscherin** *die* linguistic researcher; **~führer** *der* phrase book; **~gebrauch** *der* [linguistic] usage; **im ~gebrauch der Nazis** in Nazi usage *or* language; in the language of the Nazis; **~gefühl** *das* feeling for language; **~genie** *das* linguistic genius; **~geographie** *die* linguistic geography *no art.*; **~geschichte** *die* 1▸ history of a/the language; (Teilgebiet der ~Sprachwissenschaft) historical linguistics *sing.*, *no art.*; 2▸ (Buch) history of a/the language;

S

~geschichtlich **A** *Adj.* historical-linguistic ‹*studies, dissertation, etc.*›; **B** *adv.* from the point of view of historical linguistics; **~gewaltig** *Adj.* powerfully eloquent; **~grenze** *die* language boundary; **~insel** *die* linguistic enclave *or* island; **~kenntnisse** *Pl.* knowledge *sing.* of a language/languages; **seine französischen ~kenntnisse** his knowledge of French; **~kompetenz** *die* linguistic competence; **~kritik** *die* critique of language; **~kultur** *die* level of compliance with linguistic norms; **~kundig** *Adj.* proficient in *or* conversant with the language *postpos.*; **~kurs** *der* language course; **~labor** *das* language laboratory *or* (coll.) lab; **~lehre** *die* **1** grammar; **2** (Buch) grammar [book]

sprachlich
A *Adj.* linguistic; **~e Feinheiten** subtleties of language
B *adv.* linguistically; **ein ~ hervorragender Aufsatz** an excellently written essay

sprach-, Sprach-: ~los *Adj.* speechless; dumbfounded; **~losigkeit** *die;* **~~:** speechlessness; dumbfoundedness; **~mittler** *der,* **~mittlerin** *die* mediator between languages; **~norm** *die* linguistic norm; **~pflege** *die* language cultivation; **~philosophie** *die* philosophy of language; **~raum** *der* language area; **~regelung** *die* instructions *pl.* as to the wording to be used; **nach der offiziellen ~regelung ist er „aus gesundheitlichen Gründen" zurückgetreten** according to the official version *or* as the official version has it, he resigned 'for reasons of health'; **~rohr** *das* (Repräsentant) spokesman; (Propagandist) mouthpiece; **~schöpfer** *der,* **~schöpferin** *die* linguistic innovator; **~schöpferisch** *Adj.* linguistically innovative *or* creative; **~silbe** *die* word element; element of word formation; **~spiel** *das* (Sprachw.) language game; **~spielerei** *die* game with words; **~störung** *die* (Med., Psych.) language disorder; (Sprechstörung) speech disorder; **~studium** *das* **▸Sprachenstudium**; **~übung** *die* language exercise; linguistic exercise; **~unterricht** *der* language teaching *or* instruction; **~verwirrung** *die* linguistic confusion; **~wissenschaft** *die* linguistics *sing., no art.*; **~wissenschaftler** *der,* **~wissenschaftlerin** *die* linguist; **~wissenschaftlich** **A** *Adj.* linguistic; **eine ~wissenschaftliche Abhandlung** a linguistics dissertation; **B** *adv.* linguistically; **~wissenschaftlich interessierte Laien** laymen interested in linguistics; **~witz** *der* linguistic wit; (Wortspiel) wordplay

sprang /ʃpraŋ/ *1. u. 3. Pers. Sg. Prät. v.* **springen**

spränge /ˈʃprɛŋə/ *1. u. 3. Pers. Sg. Konjunktiv II v.* **springen**

Spray /ʃpreː/ *das od. der;* **~s, ~s** spray

Spray·dose *die* aerosol [can]

sprayen *tr., itr. V.* spray

Sprayer /ˈspreːɐ/ *der;* **~s, ~:** graffiti artist

Sprech-: ~anlage *die* intercom (coll.); **~blase** *die* balloon (coll.); **~bühne** *die* theatre staging plays only; **~chor** *der* chorus; **im ~chor rufen** shout in chorus; chant ‹*slogan*›

sprechen /ˈʃprɛçn̩/
A *unr. itr. V.* speak (**über** + *Akk.* about; **von** about, of); (sich unterhalten, sich be~ auch) talk (**über** + *Akk.*, **von** about); ‹*parrot etc.*› talk; **deutsch/flüsternd ~:** speak German/in a whisper *or* whispers; **er spricht wenig** he doesn't say *or* talk much; **Das war das Hörspiel „...". Es sprachen: ...** That was the play for radio '...'. Taking part were: ...; **es spricht Pfarrer N.** the speaker is the Revd. N.; **für/gegen etw. ~:** speak in favour of/against sth.; **das Sprechen fiel ihr noch schwer** she still found it difficult to speak; **mit jmdm. ~:** speak *or* talk with *or* to sb.; **seit dem Streit ~ sie nicht mehr miteinander** since the quarrel they are no longer on speaking terms *or* haven't been speaking to each other; **ich muss mit dir ~:** I must talk *or* speak with you; **er spricht mit sich selbst** he talks to himself; **wie sprichst du mit mir?** who do you think you're talking to?; **so spricht man nicht mit seiner Mutter** that's no way to talk *or* speak to one's mother; **sie spricht nicht mit jedem** she doesn't speak *or* talk to just anybody; **mit wem spreche ich?** who is speaking please?; who am I speaking to, please?; **~ Sie noch?** (am Telefon) are you still there?; **er spricht gerade** (telefoniert) he's on the phone; **worüber habt ihr gesprochen?** what were you talking about?; **es wurde über alles Mögliche gesprochen** we/they *etc.* talked about all sorts of things; **darüber spricht er nicht gern** he doesn't like talking about that; **gut/schlecht von jmdm.** *od.* **über jmdn. ~:** speak well/ill of sb.; **für jmdn. ~:** speak for sb.; speak on *or* (Amer.) in behalf of sb.; **ich kann nur für mich ~:** I can only speak for myself; **vor einer Hörerschaft/der Betriebsversammlung ~:** speak in front of an audience/speak to *or* address a meeting of the workforce; **zu einem** *od.* **über ein Thema ~:** speak on *or* about a subject; **frei ~:** extemporize; speak without notes; **~ Sie!/bitte ~!** (am Telefon) you're through [now]; go ahead, please; **sprich!** (geh.) speak! (literary); **also sprach der Herr/Buddha/Zarathustra** (dichter.) thus spake the Lord/Buddha/Zarathustra (Bibl./literary); **lass Blumen ~!** say it with flowers!; **sein Herz ~ lassen** follow the dictates of one's heart; **aus seinen Worten/seinem Blick sprach Hass/Neid/Angst** *usw.* his words/the look in his eyes expressed hatred/envy/fear *etc.*; **auf jmdn./etw. zu ~ kommen** get to talking about sb./sth.; **auf jmdn. schlecht/nicht gut zu ~ sein** be ill-disposed towards sb.; **für/gegen jmdn./etw. ~** (in günstigem/ungünstigem Licht erscheinen lassen) be a point in sb.'s/sth.'s favour/against sb./sth.; **es scheint alles dafür/dagegen zu ~, dass die Regierung im Amt bleiben wird** it seems there is every reason to believe that the government will/won't stay in power; **was spricht denn dafür/dagegen?** what is there to be said for/against it?; **für sich [selbst] ~** (fig.) speak for itself/themselves
B *unr. tr. V.* **1** **▸❶ S. 670** speak ‹*language, dialect*›; say ‹*word, sentence*›; **~ Sie Französisch?** do you speak French?; **„Hier spricht man Deutsch"** 'German spoken'; 'we speak German'
2 (rezitieren) say, recite ‹*poem, text*›; say ‹*prayer*›; recite ‹*spell*›; pronounce ‹*blessing, oath*›; **ein Schlusswort ~:** give *or* make a concluding speech; *s. auch* **Recht 1; Urteil**
3 **jmdn. ~:** speak to sb.; **Sie haben mich ~ wollen?** you wanted to see me *or* speak to me?; **ich bin heute für niemanden mehr zu ~:** I can't see anyone else today; **kann ich Sie mal einen Moment ~?** can I see you for a moment?; can I have a quick word?; **wir [beide] ~ uns noch!** you haven't heard the last of this
4 (aus~) pronounce ‹*name, word, etc.*›; **sprich ...** (auszu~) pronounced ...; (das heißt) that is to say ...
5 (sagen) say; **und Gott sprach: „Es werde Licht!"** and God said, 'Let there be light'; **die Wahrheit ~:** speak the truth; **was spricht denn die Uhr?** (fig. scherzh.) what's the time?

sprechend *Adj.* convincing ‹*example, evidence*›; expressive ‹*face, eyes*›; eloquent ‹*facial expression, glance, portrayal*›; descriptive ‹*name*›

Sprecher *der;* **~s, ~ 1** spokesman **2** (Ansager) announcer; (Nachrichten~) newscaster; newsreader **3** (Kommentator, Erzähler) narrator **4** (Sprachw.: Sprachteilhaber, Sprechender) speaker

Sprecherin *die;* **~, ~nen 1** spokeswoman **2** **▸Sprecher 2, 3, 4**

sprech-, Sprech-: ~erziehung *die* speech training; elocution; **~faul** *Adj.* uncommunicative; reluctant to talk *pred.*; **~funk** *der* radio-telephone system; **~funkgerät** *das* radio-telephone; (Walkie-Talkie) walkie-talkie; **~gesang** *der* sprechgesang; **sein Vortrag war eine Art ~gesang** he delivered his speech in a kind of singsong; **~muschel** *die* mouthpiece; **~platte** *die* spoken-word record; **~rolle** *die* speaking part; **~silbe** *die* [phonological] syllable; **~stimme** *die* speaking voice; (Mus.) sprechstimme; **~stunde** *die* consultation hours *pl.*; (eines Arztes) surgery; consulting hours *pl.*; (eines Rechtsanwalts usw.) office hours *pl.*; **wann haben Sie ~stunde?** when are your consultation hours/when is your surgery *or* what are your surgery hours?; **zum Zahnarzt/zu einem Abgeordneten in die ~stunde gehen** go to the dentist's/MP's surgery; **~stunden·hilfe** *die* (eines Arztes) receptionist; (eines Zahnarztes) assistant; **~tag** *der: day on which authorities' offices are open to the public;* **heute ist kein ~tag** we/they are not open today; **~übung** *die* elocution *or* speech exercise; (zu therapeutischen Zwecken) speech exercise; **~weise** *die* manner of speaking; **~werkzeuge** *Pl.* speech organs; organs of speech; **~zeit** *die* visiting time; **~zelle** *die* telephone booth; **~zimmer** *das* consulting room

Spree-Athen (*das*) (scherzh.) Berlin

Spreißel /ˈʃpraisl̩/ *der,* (österr.) *das;* **~s, ~ 1** (bes. südd.: Splitter) splinter **2** (bes. österr.: Span) splint

Spreiz·dübel *der* expanding anchor

Spreize /ˈʃpraitsə/ *die;* **~, ~n 1** (Bauw.) horizontal stay *or* brace **2** (Turnen) **in der ~ stehen** stand with one leg extended behind/forward/to the side

spreizen
A *tr. V.* spread ‹*fingers, toes, etc.*›; **die Flügel/den Schwanz ~** ‹*bird*› spread its wings/tail; **die Beine ~:** spread one's legs apart; open one's legs; **mit gespreizten Beinen stehen/sitzen** stand/sit with one's legs apart; **das rechte Bein vorwärts/seitwärts ~:** extend one's right leg in front/to the side
B *refl. V.* (geh.) **1** (sich zieren) **sie spreizte sich erst dagegen, dann stimmte sie zu** she made a fuss at first, [but] then agreed **2** (sich aufspielen) give oneself airs; put on airs; **sie spreizte sich vor ihren Bewunderern** she strutted about in front of her admirers

Spreiz-: ~fuß *der* **▸❶ S. 439** (Med.) spread foot; **~hose** *die* ≈ Frejka pillow (kind of romper incorporating a padded steel splint for keeping an infant's legs in the frog position)

Spreng·bombe *die* high-explosive bomb

Sprengel /ˈʃprɛŋl̩/ *der;* **~s, ~ 1** (Kirchen~) parish; (Diözese) diocese **2** (österr.) administrative district

sprengen /ˈʃprɛŋn̩/
A *tr. V.* **1** blow up; blast ‹*rock*›; **etw. in die Luft ~:** blow sth. up **2** (gewaltsam öffnen, aufbrechen) force [open] ‹*door*›; force ‹*lock*›; break open ‹*burial chamber etc.*›; burst, break ‹*bonds, chains*›; (fig.) break up ‹*meeting, demonstration*›; **Eis sprengt den Felsen** ice is breaking up the rock; **die Freude sprengte ihm fast die Brust** (fig.) his heart was bursting with joy; *s. auch* **Bank² 2; Rahmen 2** **3** (be~) water ‹*flower bed, lawn*›; sprinkle ‹*street, washing*› with water; (verspritzen) sprinkle; (mit dem Schlauch) spray
B *itr. V.* **1** **im Steinbruch wird wieder gesprengt** they're blasting again in the quarry **2** *mit sein* (geh.) ‹*rider*› thunder

Spreng-: ~kammer *die* blast *or* charge chamber; **~kapsel** *die* blasting cap; **~kommando** *das* demolition squad; **~kopf** *der* warhead; **~kraft** *die* explosive power; **~ladung** *die* explosive charge; **~meister** *der,* **~meisterin** *die* (im Steinbruch) blaster; shot firer; (bei Abbrucharbeiten) demolition expert; **~satz** *der* explosive charge

Sprengsel /ˈʃprɛŋzl̩/ *der od. das;* **~s, ~** (ugs.) **▸Sprenkel**

Spreng-: ~stoff *der* explosive; **~stoff·anschlag** *der* bomb attack

Sprengung *die;* **~, ~en 1** blowing-up; (im Steinbruch) blasting; **er drohte mit der ~ des Gebäudes** he threatened to blow up the building **2** **▸sprengen A2**: forcing [open]; forcing; breaking open; bursting; breaking; (fig.) breaking up **3** (das Besprengen) sprinkling; (mit dem Schlauch) spraying

Spreng·wagen *der* watering cart; [street] sprinkler

Sprenkel /ˈʃprɛŋkl̩/ *der;* **~s, ~:** spot; dot; speckle

sprenkeln *tr. V.* [1] (mit Flecken versehen) sprinkle spots of ‹*colour*› [2] (spritzen) sprinkle ‹*water*›

Spreu /ʃprɔy/ *die;* ~: chaff; **die ~ vom Weizen trennen** *od.* (geh.) **sondern** (fig.) separate the wheat from the chaff

sprich /ʃprɪç/ *Imperativ Sg. v.* **sprechen**

sprichst /ʃprɪçst/ *2. Pers. Sg. Präsens v.* **sprechen**

spricht /ʃprɪçt/ *3. Pers. Sg. Präsens v.* **sprechen**

Sprich·wort *das; Pl.* **Sprichwörter** proverb

sprich·wörtlich
[A] *Adj.* [1] proverbial [2] (fig.: notorisch) proverbial
[B] *adv.* [1] **..., so heißt es ~:** ..., as the proverb has it [2] (fig.: notorisch) proverbially

sprießen /ˈʃpriːsn̩/ *unr. itr. V.; mit sein* ‹*leaf, bud*› shoot, sprout; ‹*seedlings*› come *or* spring up; ‹*beard*› sprout; (fig.) ‹*mistrust, envy, etc.*› well up; ‹*club, organization, etc.*› spring up

Spriet /ʃpriːt/ *das;* **~[e]s, ~e** (Seemannsspr.) sprit

Spriet·segel *das* (Seemannsspr.) spritsail

Spring·brunnen *der* fountain

springen /ˈʃprɪŋən/
[A] *unr. itr. V.* [1] *mit sein* jump; (mit Schwung) leap; spring; jump; ‹*frog, flea*› hop, jump; **vom Fünfmeterbrett ~:** dive from the five-metre board; **mit Anlauf/aus dem Stand ~:** take a running/standing jump; **jmdm. an die Kehle ~:** leap at sb.'s throat; **auf die Beine** *od.* **Füße ~:** jump to one's feet [2] *meist mit sein* (Sport) jump; (beim Stabhochsprung, beim Kasten, Pferd) vault; (beim Turm~, Kunst~) dive [3] *mit sein* (sich in Sprüngen fortbewegen) bound; **wenn sie einen Wunsch hat, springt die ganze Familie** when she wants something the whole family jumps to it [4] (ugs.) *in* **eine Runde Bier ~ lassen** stand a round of beer; **er könnte ruhig mal was ~ lassen** he could easily fork out something just once in a while (sl.) [5] *mit sein* (fig.: schnellen, hüpfen, fliegen) ‹*pointer, milometer, etc.*› jump (**auf** + *Akk.* to); ‹*traffic lights*› change (**auf** + *Akk.* to); ‹*spark*› leap; ‹*ball*› bounce; ‹*cork*› pop out (**aus** + *Dat.* of); ‹*spring*› jump out; **[von etw.] ~** ‹*fan belt, bicycle-chain, button, tyre, etc.*› come off [sth.]; **die Lokomotive ist aus dem Gleis gesprungen** the locomotive jumped the rails [6] *mit sein* (zer~, zerbrechen, zerreißen) ‹*string, glass, porcelain, etc.*› break [7] *mit sein* (aufplatzen, bersten) ‹*seed-pod*› burst [open]; **gesprungene Lippen** cracked *or* chapped lips [8] *mit sein* (Risse, Sprünge bekommen) crack [9] *mit sein* (fig. geh.: spritzen, sprudeln) ‹*fountain, jet of water, blood, etc.*› spurt [10] *mit sein* (südd.: laufen) run; (eilen) hurry
[B] *unr. tr. V.; auch mit sein* (Sport) perform ‹*somersault, twist dive, etc.*›; **5,20m/einen neuen Rekord ~:** jump 5.20m/make a record jump

Springen *das;* **~s, ~** (Pferdesport) jumping event

Springer *der;* **~s, ~** [1] (Weit~, Hoch~, Ski~) jumper; (Stabhoch~) [pole] vaulter; (Kunst~, Turm~) diver; (Fallschirm~) parachutist [2] (Schachfigur) knight [3] **junger ~** (ugs.) greenhorn [4] (Arbeiter) worker who is moved from job to job as required

Springerin *die;* **~, ~nen** ▸ **Springer 1, 4**

spring-, Spring-: ~flut *die* spring tide; **~form** *die* spring form; **~ins·feld** *der;* **~~[e]s, ~~e** (scherzh.) (leichtsinniger junger Mensch) [young] madcap; (lebhaftes Kind) lively little nipper (Brit. sl.); **~kraut** *das* impatience; **~lebendig** *Adj.* extremely lively; full of beans *pred.* (coll.); **er ist trotz seines hohen Alters noch ~lebendig** he is still extremely sprightly despite his age; **~maus** *die* jerboa; **~messer** *das* flick knife; **~pferd** *das* jumper; **~quell** *der* (dichter.) fountain; **~reiten** *das* showjumping *no art.*; **~rollo** *das* roller blind; **~seil** *das* skipping rope (Brit.); jump rope (Amer.); **~turnier** *das* (Reiten) showjumping competition

Sprinkler /ˈʃprɪŋklɐ/ *der;* **~s, ~:** sprinkler

Sprint /ʃprɪnt/ *der;* **~s, ~s** (auch Sport) sprint; **die letzten 100 Meter im ~ zurücklegen** sprint the last 100 metres

sprinten *itr.* (*auch tr.*) *V.; meist, mit Richtungsangaben nur, mit sein* (Sport; ugs.: schnell laufen) sprint

Sprinter *der;* **~s, ~, Sprinterin** *die;* **~, ~nen** (Sport) sprinter

Sprint·strecke *die* sprint distance

Sprit /ʃprɪt/ *der;* **~[e]s, ~e** [1] (ugs.: Treibstoff) gas (Amer. coll.); juice (sl.); petrol (Brit.) [2] (ugs.: Schnaps) shorts *pl.* [3] (Äthylalkohol) ethanol; ethyl alcohol

Sprit-: ~kosten *Pl.* (ugs.) fuel costs; **~preis** *der* (ugs.) price of fuel; (bei Benzin) petrol price; gas price (Amer.); **~verbrauch** *der* (ugs.) fuel consumption

Spritze /ˈʃprɪtsə/ *die;* **~, ~n** [1] (zum Vernichten von Ungeziefer) spray; (Teig~, Torten~, Injektions~) syringe [2] (Injektion) injection; jab (coll.); **eine ~ bekommen** have an injection *or* (coll.) jab; **an der ~ hängen** (salopp) be on the needle (sl.) [3] (Feuer~) hose; (Löschfahrzeug) fire engine

spritzen /ˈʃprɪtsn̩/
[A] *tr. V.* [1] (versprühen) spray; (ver~) splash ‹*water, ink, etc.*›; spatter ‹*ink etc.*›; (in Form eines Strahls) spray, squirt ‹*water, foam, etc.*›; pipe ‹*cream etc.*› [2] (be~, besprühen) water ‹*lawn, tennis court*›; water, spray ‹*street, yard*›; spray ‹*plants, crops, etc.*›; pump ‹*concrete*›; (mit Lack) spray ‹*car etc.*›; **jmdn. nass ~:** splash sb.; (mit Wasserpistole, Schlauch) spray sb.; **den Fußboden/die Wände nass ~:** splash/spray water over the floor/walls; **jmdn. ~** (ugs.: nass~) squirt sb. [3] (injizieren) inject ‹*drug etc.*› [4] (~d herstellen) create ‹*ice rink*› by spraying; pipe ‹*cake decoration etc.*›; produce ‹*plastic article*› by injection moulding [5] (ugs.: einer Injektion unterziehen) **jmdn./sich ~:** give sb. an injection/inject oneself; **er hat sich mit einer Überdosis Heroin zu Tode gespritzt** he gave himself a fatal shot of heroin; **jmdm. ein Schmerzmittel ~:** give sb. a pain-killing injection [6] (verdünnen) dilute ‹*wine etc.*› with soda water/lemonade *etc*
[B] *itr. V.* [1] **die Kinder planschten und spritzten** the children splashed and threw water about; **in meinem Garten wird nicht gespritzt** chemical sprays aren't used in my garden [2] *mit Richtungsangabe mit sein* ‹*hot fat*› spit; ‹*mud etc.*› spatter, splash; ‹*blood, water*› spurt; **das Wasser spritzte ihm ins Gesicht** the water splashed up into his face [3] *mit sein* (ugs.: rennen) dash; (diensteifrig) dash *or* chase about [4] (ugs.: sich Rauschgift injizieren) shoot (sl.) [5] (derb: ejakulieren) come [off] (coll.)

Spritzen·haus *das* (veralt.) fire station

Spritzer *der;* **~s, ~** (kleiner Tropfen) splash; (von Farbe) splash; spot; (Schuss) dash; splash; **ein paar ~ Spülmittel** a few squirts of washing-up liquid

Spritz-: ~flasche *die* [1] spray bottle; [2] (Chemie) wash bottle; **~gebäck** *das: biscuit[s]/small cake[s] made by squeezing the dough through a piping bag;* **~guss, *~guß** *der* injection moulding *no art.*

spritzig
[A] *Adj.* [1] sparkling ‹*wine*›; tangy ‹*fragrance, perfume*› [2] (lebendig) lively ‹*show, music, article*›; sparkling ‹*production, performance*›; racy ‹*style*› [3] (temperamentvoll) nippy (coll.); zippy ‹*car, engine*› [4] (flink) agile, nimble ‹*person*›
[B] *adv.* sparklingly ‹*produced, performed, etc.*›; racily ‹*written*›; **die Mannschaft spielte sehr ~:** the team played with great speed and agility

Spritz-: ~lack *der* spray paint; **~pistole** *die* spray gun; **~tour** *die* (ugs.) spin

spröd, spröde /ʃprøːt/ *Adj.* [1] brittle ‹*glass, plastic, etc.*›; dry ‹*hair, lips, etc.*›; (rissig) chapped ‹*lips, skin*›; (rau) rough ‹*skin*› [2] (fig.: rau klingend) harsh, rough ‹*voice*› [3] (fig.: schwer handhabbar) unwieldy ‹*subject, problem*›; refractory ‹*material*› [4] (fig.: abweisend) aloof ‹*person, manner, nature*›; **eine Landschaft von spröder Schönheit** a landscape of forbidding beauty

Sprödheit, Sprödigkeit *die;* **~** [1] ▸ **spröde 1**: brittleness; dryness; roughness [2] (fig.: rauer Klang) harshness; roughness [3] ▸ **spröde 3**: unwieldiness; refractoriness [4] (fig.: abweisendes Wesen) aloofness

spross, *sproß /ʃprɔs/ *1. u. 3. Pers. Sg. Prät. v.* **sprießen**

Spross, *Sproß *der;* **Sprosses, Sprosse** *od.* **Sprossen** [1] *Pl.* **Sprosse** (Bot.) shoot [2] *Pl.* **Sprosse** (geh.: Nachkomme) scion [3] *Pl.* **Sprossen** (Jägerspr.) ▸ **Sprosse 3**

Sprosse *die;* **~, ~n** [1] (auch fig.) rung [2] (eines Fensters) glazing bar; sash bar [3] (Jägerspr.) point; tine

sprossen *itr. V.* ‹*plant*› shoot, put forth shoots

Sprossen-: ~fenster *das* window with glazing bars; **~kohl** *der* (österr.) ▸ **Rosenkohl**; **~wand** *die* wall bars *pl.*

Sprössling, *Sprößling /ˈʃprœslɪŋ/ *der;* **~s, ~e** (ugs. scherzh.) offspring; **seine ~e** his offspring *pl.*

Spross·vokal, *Sproß·vokal *der* (Sprachw.) svarabhakti

Sprotte /ˈʃprɔtə/ *die;* **~, ~n** sprat; **Kieler ~n** smoked [Kiel] sprats

Spruch /ʃprʊx/ *der;* **~[e]s, Sprüche** /ˈʃprʏçə/ [1] (Wahl~) motto; (Sinn~) maxim; adage; (Aus~) saying; aphorism; (Zitat) quotation; quote; (Parole) slogan; (Bibel~) quotation; saying [2] *Pl.* (ugs. abwertend: Phrase) **das sind doch alles nur Sprüche** that's just talk *or* empty words *pl.*; **Sprüche machen** *od.* **klopfen** talk big (coll.) [3] (Gedicht, Lied) medieval lyric poem; **das Buch der Sprüche** *od.* **die Sprüche Salomos** (bibl.) [the Book of] Proverbs [4] (Richter~) judgement; (Schieds~) ruling; (Orakel~) oracle

Spruch-: ~band *das; Pl.* **~bänder** [1] banner; [2] (auf einem Bild) banderol[e]; **~dichtung** *die* [medieval] didactic poetry

Sprüche·klopfer *der;* **~s, ~, Sprüche·klopferin** *die;* **~, ~nen** (ugs. abwertend) big mouth (coll.)

Spruch·kammer *die* (Rechtsw. hist.) denazification court

Sprüchlein /ˈʃprʏçlain/ *das;* **~s, ~** [1] (kleiner Spruch) short maxim [2] (vorgefertigter Text) little piece

spruch·reif *Adj.* **das ist noch nicht ~:** that's not definite, so people mustn't start talking about it yet; **die Angelegenheit ist jetzt ~:** the matter can now be discussed/decided

Spruch·weisheit *die* wise saying

Sprudel /ˈʃpruːdl̩/ *der;* **~s, ~** [1] (Selterwasser) sparkling mineral water [2] (österr.: Erfrischungsgetränk) fizzy drink

sprudeln
[A] *itr. V.* [1] *mit sein* ‹*spring, champagne, etc.*› bubble (**aus** out of) [2] (beim Kochen) bubble [3] (beim Entweichen von Gas) ‹*lemonade, champagne, etc.*› fizz, effervesce; **ein ~des Getränk** a fizzy drink [4] (fig.: überschäumen) ‹*person*› bubble [over] (**vor** + *Dat.* with); **ein ~des Temperament** a bubbly *or* an effervescent temperament
[B] *tr. V.* (österr.: quirlen) whisk

Sprudel·wasser *das; Pl.* **Sprudelwässer** sparkling mineral water

Sprudler *der;* **~s, ~** (österr.) whisk

Sprüh·dose *die* aerosol [can]

sprühen /ˈʃpryːən/
[A] *tr. V.* spray; **Wasser auf die Blätter ~:** spray the leaves with water; **ich sprühte mir etwas Spray aufs Haar** I put some spray on my hair; **seine Augen sprühten Feuer** *od.* **Funken/Hass** (fig.) his eyes flashed fire/hatred
[B] *itr. V.* [1] *mit Richtungsangabe mit sein* ‹*sparks, spray*› fly; ‹*flames*› spit; ‹*waterfall*› send out a fine spray; (fig.) ‹*eyes*› sparkle (**vor** + *Dat.* with); ‹*intellect, wit*› sparkle; **ein feiner Regen sprühte gegen die Scheibe** a fine rain drifted against the window pane; **aus seinen Augen sprühte Feuer/Zorn** (fig.) fire/anger flashed in his eyes; **~der Witz** sparkling wit; **ein ~des Temperament** a bubbly *or* effervescent temperament; **von Ideen/vor Witz** (*Dat.*) **~** (fig.) bubble [over] with ideas/sparkle with wit [2] *unpers.* (regnen) **es sprüht** it is drizzling

Sprüh-: ~flasche *die* spray bottle; **~pflaster** *das* spray dressing; **~regen** *der* drizzle; fine rain

S

Sprung /ʃprʊŋ/ *der;* **~[e]s, Sprünge** /'ʃprʏŋə/ [1] (auch Sport) jump; (schwungvoll) leap; (Satz) bound; (~ über das Pferd) vault; (Wassersport) dive; (fig.) leap; **zum ~ ansetzen** ‹*tiger etc.*› get ready to pounce; **sein Herz machte vor Freude einen ~** (fig.) his heart leapt for joy; **ein [großer] ~ nach vorn** (fig.) a [great] leap forward; **sie hat den ~ zum Film nicht geschafft** (fig.) she didn't manage to move into films; **ein qualitativer ~** (Philos.) a qualitative leap; **~ auf, marsch, marsch!** (Milit.) on your feet, quick march!; **ein ~ ins kalte Wasser** (fig.) jumping in at the deep end; **keine großen Sprünge machen können** (fig. ugs.) not be able to afford many luxuries; **auf einen ~** (fig. ugs.) for a few minutes; **auf dem ~[e] sein** (fig. ugs.) be in a rush [2] (ugs.: kurze Entfernung) stone's throw; (mit dem Auto) short drive [3] (Riß) crack; **einen ~ haben/bekommen** be cracked/crack; **einen ~ in der Schüssel haben** (salopp) be cracked (coll.) [4] *in* **jmdm. auf die Sprünge helfen** (ugs.) help sb. on his/her way; **jmds. Gedächtnis auf die Sprünge helfen** jog sb.'s memory; **jmdm. auf** *od.* **hinter die Sprünge kommen** (fig. ugs.) get on to sb. [5] (Jägerspr.: Gruppe von Rehen) herd [6] (Geol.) fault

sprung-, Sprung-: ~bein *das* [1] take-off leg; [2] ▸❶ **S. 435** (Anat.) ankle bone; **~bereit** *Adj.* ready to jump *pred.;* ‹*cat*› ready to pounce *pred.;* **~brett** *das* (auch fig.) springboard; **~deckel** *der* spring lid; **~feder** *die* [spiral] spring; **~gelenk** *das* ▸❶ **S. 435** (Anat.) ankle joint

sprunghaft

A *Adj.* [1] (unstet) erratic ‹*person, character, manner*› [2] (unzusammenhängend) disjointed ‹*conversation, thoughts*› [3] (unvermittelt) sudden; abrupt [4] (ruckartig) rapid ‹*change*›; sharp ‹*increase*›

B *adv.;* ▸ **A 2-4:** disjointedly; suddenly; abruptly; rapidly; sharply

Sprunghaftigkeit *die;* ~ ▸ **sprunghaft A 1, 2:** erraticness; disjointedness

Sprung-: ~höhe *die* height; **~lauf** *der* (Ski) ski jumping *no art.*; **~rahmen** *der* spring bedframe; **~schanze** *die* (Ski) ski jumping hill; **~seil** *das* skipping rope (Brit.); jump rope (Amer.); **~tuch** *das; Pl.* **~tücher** safety blanket; **~turm** *der* (Sport) diving platform

Spucke *die;* **~:** spit; **mir blieb die ~ weg** (ugs.) it took my breath away; I was speechless; *s. auch* **Geduld**

spucken /'ʃpʊkn̩/

A *itr. V.* [1] spit; **in die Hände ~** (fig.: an die Arbeit gehen) go to work with a will [2] (ugs.: erbrechen) throw up (coll.); be sick (Brit.) [3] **auf etw.** (*Akk.*) **~** (salopp) not give a damn about sth.

B *tr. V.* spit; spit [up], cough up ‹*blood, phlegm*›; spew out ‹*lava*›; **Feuer ~:** breathe fire; ‹*volcano*› belch fire; *s. auch* **Ton² 4**

Spuck-napf *der* spittoon

Spuk /ʃpu:k/ *der;* **~[e]s, ~e** [1] [ghostly *or* supernatural] manifestation [2] (abwertend: schreckliches Geschehen) horrific episode

spuken *itr. V.* [1] *auch unpers.* **in dem Haus spukt ein Geist** this house is haunted by a ghost; **hier/in dem Haus spukt es** this place/the house is haunted; **gestern hat es wieder gespukt** there was another manifestation *or* haunting yesterday; **dieser Aberglaube spukt noch immer in den Köpfen vieler Menschen** (fig.) this superstition still lurks in many people's minds [2] *mit sein* **durch die Gänge ~:** walk *or* haunt the corridors

Spuk-: ~gestalt *die* ghostly figure; **~schloss, *~schloß** *das* haunted castle

Spül-: ~becken *das* [1] sink; [2] (beim Zahnarzt usw.) basin; **~bürste** *die* washing-up brush

Spule /'ʃpu:lə/ *die;* **~, ~n** [1] spool; bobbin; (für Tonband, Film) spool; reel [2] (Elektrot.) coil

Spüle *die;* **~, ~n** sink unit; (Becken) sink

spulen *tr., itr. V.* spool; (am Tonbandgerät) wind; **etw. auf etw.** (*Akk.*) **~:** wind sth. on to sth.

spülen /'ʃpy:lən/

A *tr. V.* [1] rinse; bathe ‹*wound*› [2] (landsch.: abwaschen) wash up ‹*dishes, glasses, etc.*›; **Geschirr ~:** wash up [3] (schwemmen) wash

B *itr. V.* [1] (beim WC) flush [the toilet] [2] (den Mund aus~) rinse out [one's mouth] [3] (landsch.) ▸ **abwaschen B**

Spül-: ~kasten *der* cistern; **~maschine** *die* dishwasher; **~mittel** *das* washing-up liquid; **~schwamm** *der* washing-up sponge; **~tuch** *das; Pl.* **~tücher** dish cloth

Spülung *die;* **~, ~en** [1] (Med.) irrigation; (der Vagina) douche [2] (beim WC) flush

Spül-wasser *das; Pl.* **Spülwässer** [1] rinse water [2] (Abwaschwasser) dishwater

Spul-wurm *der* ascarid

Spund /ʃpʊnt/ *der;* **~[e]s, ~e/Spünde** /'ʃpyndə/ [1] *Pl.* **Spünde** (Zapfen) bung [2] *Pl.* **~e** (ugs.) **[junger** *od.* **grüner] ~:** young greenhorn *or* tyro

Spund-: ~loch *das* bunghole; **~wand** (Bauw.) sheet-pile wall

Spur /ʃpu:ɐ/ *die;* **~, ~en** [1] (Abdruck im Boden) track; (Folge von Abdrücken) tracks *pl.;* (Blut~, Schleim~ usw.) trail; **von dem Vermissten fehlt jede ~:** there is no trace of the missing person; **eine heiße ~** (fig.) a hot trail; **eine heiße ~ haben** (fig.) have a really good lead; **jmdm./einer Sache auf die ~ kommen** get on to the track of sb./sth.; **jmdm./einer Sache auf der ~ sein** be on the track *or* trail of sb./sth. [2] (Anzeichen) trace; (eines Verbrechens) clue (*Gen.* to); **die ~en des Krieges/häufigen Gebrauchs** the marks of war/frequent use [3] (sehr kleine Menge; auch fig.) trace; **da fehlt noch eine ~ Paprika** it needs just a touch of paprika; **er hat keine ~ [von] Ehrgefühl** he has not the slightest sense of honour; **von Reue/Mitgefühl keine ~/nicht die leiseste ~:** not a trace *or* sign/not the slightest trace *or* sign of penitence/sympathy; **keine** *od.* **nicht die ~** (ugs.: als Antwort) not in the slightest [4] (Verkehrsw.: Fahr~) lane; **die ~ wechseln** change lanes; **in** *od.* **auf der rechten/linken ~ fahren** drive in the right-hand/left-hand lane [5] (Fahrlinie) **[die] ~ halten** stay on its line; **aus der ~ kommen** be thrown off its line [6] (Technik) ▸ **~weite** [7] (Elektrot., DV) track

spürbar

A *Adj.* noticeable; perceptible; distinct, perceptible ‹*improvement*›; evident ‹*relief, embarrassment*›

B *adv.* noticeably; perceptibly; (sichtlich) clearly ‹*relieved, on edge*›; **die Temperatur ist ~ gesunken/gestiegen** there has been a noticeable drop/rise in temperature; **~ besser/schlechter werden** distinctly improve/deteriorate

Spur-breite *die* ▸ **~weite**

spuren

A *itr. V.* (ugs.) toe the line (coll.); do as one's told

B *tr. V.* (Ski) prepare ‹*cross-country course*›

spüren /ʃpy:rən/

A *tr. V.* feel; (instinktiv) sense; (merken) notice; **nach der Anstrengung spürte ich alle Knochen** I could feel every bone in my body after the exertion; **ich spüre mein Kreuz/meinen Magen** I have a pain in my back/my stomach; **die Peitsche zu ~ bekommen** get a taste of the whip; **jmds. Hass zu ~ bekommen** suffer sb.'s hatred; **von Kameradschaft war nichts zu ~:** there wasn't a sign *or* trace of comradeship; **er ließ uns seine Verärgerung nicht ~:** he gave [us] no sign of his annoyance; **sie ließ ihn ~, dass sie ihn nicht mochte** she made it plain [to him] *or* let him see that she didn't like him

B *itr. V.* (Jägerspr.) **[nach einem Tier] ~:** track [an animal]

Spuren-: ~element *das* (Biochemie) trace element; **~sicherung** *die* (Polizeiw.) [1] (Vorgang) collection of evidence; [2] (Abteilung) scene-of-crime *or* forensic unit

Spür-hund *der* tracker dog; (fig.: Spitzel) bloodhound; snooper (coll.)

spur-los

A *Adj.* total, complete ‹*disappearance*›

B *adv.* ‹*disappear*› completely *or* without trace; **an jmdm. ~ vorübergehen** leave sb. untouched; have no effect on sb.; **es ist nicht ~ an ihm vorübergegangen** it has not failed to leave its mark on him

Spür-: ~nase *die* (ugs.) [1] (Geruchssinn, fig.) nose; [2] (Person) bloodhound; snooper (coll.); **~panzer** *der* NBC reconnaissance armoured vehicle; [NBC] weapons-detecting tank; **~sinn** *der* (feiner Instinkt) intuition

Spurt /ʃpʊrt/ *der;* **~[e]s, ~s** *od.* **~e** [1] spurt [2] (Sport.: ~vermögen) turn of speed

spurten *itr. V.* [1] *mit Richtungsangabe mit sein* spurt [2] *mit sein* (ugs.: schnell laufen) sprint

spurt-stark *Adj.* (bes. Sport) capable of putting on a strong spurt *or* of sprinting strongly *postpos.*; nippy (coll.) ‹*car*›

Spur-: ~wechsel *der* change of lane; **~weite** *die* (Kfz-W.) track; (Eisenb.) gauge

sputen /'ʃpu:tn̩/ *refl. V.* (veralt.) make haste

Sputnik /'ʃpʊtnɪk/ *der;* **~s, ~s** sputnik

Squash /skvɔʃ/ *das;* ~ (Sport) squash *no art.*

Squaw /skwɔ:/ *die;* **~, ~s** squaw

SR *Abk.* **= Saarländischer Rundfunk** Saarland Radio

SRG *Abk.* **= Schweizerische Radio- und Rundfunkgesellschaft** Swiss Broadcasting Company

Sri Lanka /'sri: 'laŋka/ *(das);* **~s** Sri Lanka

***Srilanker, Sri-Lanker** *der;* **~s, ~, *Srilankerin, Sri-Lankerin** *die;* **~, ~nen** Sri Lankan

***srilankisch, sri-lankisch** *Adj.* Sri Lankan

SS¹ *Abk.* (ns.) **= Schutzstaffel** SS

SS² *Abk.* **= Sommersemester**

SSD (DDR) *Abk.* **= Staatssicherheitsdienst**

SS-Mann *der; Pl.* **SS-Männer** *od.* **SS-Leute** SS man

SSO *Abk.* **= Südsüdost[en]** ▸❶ **S. 363** SSE

SSV *Abk.* **= Sommerschlussverkauf**

SSW *Abk.* **= Südsüdwest[en]** ▸❶ **S. 363** SSW

s. t. *Abk.* **= sine tempore**

St. *Abk.* [1] **= Sankt** St. [2] **= Stück**

Staat /'ʃta:t/ *der;* **~[e]s, ~en** [1] state; **die ~en** (die USA) the States; **von ~s wegen** on the part of the [state] authorities; **beim ~ [angestellt] sein** be a civil servant *or* in the civil service; **der schlanke ~:** the slimmed-down state; *s. auch* **Vater 1** [2] (ugs.: Festkleidung, Pracht) finery; **in vollem ~:** in all one's finery; **damit ist kein ~ zu machen** (fig.) it's not up to much (coll.); **mit diesem Mantel ist kein ~ mehr zu machen** (fig. ugs.) this coat is past it (coll.) [3] (Zool.: Insekten~) colony; **~en bildend** social ‹*insect*›

staaten-, Staaten-: ~bildend ▸ **Staat 3;** **~bund** *der* confederation; **~los** *Adj.* stateless; **~lose** *der/die; adj. Dekl.* stateless person *or* subject; **~system** *das* (Politik) system of nation states

staatlich

A *Adj.* state *attrib.* ‹*sovereignty, institutions, authorities, control, etc.*›; ‹*power, unity, etc.*› of the state; state-owned ‹*factory etc.*›; **~e Mittel** government *or* public money *sing*

B *adv.* by the state; **~ anerkannt/geprüft/gelenkt/finanziert** state-approved/-certified/-managed/-financed; **~ subventioniert werden** receive a state subsidy

staats-, Staats-: ~affäre *die:* **eine ~affäre aus etw. machen** (ugs.) make a song and dance about sth. (coll.); **~akt** *der* [1] (Festakt) state ceremony; [2] (Rechtsvorgang) act of state; **~aktion** *die:* **eine ~aktion aus etw. machen** (ugs.) make a song and dance about sth. (coll.); **~amateur** *der,* **~amateurin** *die* (Sport): *state-sponsored, nominally amateur, sportsman/sportswoman;* **~amt** *das* public office; **~angehörige** *der/die* national; **~angehörigkeit** *die;* **~~, ~~en** nationality; **~anleihe** *die* government bond; **~anwalt** *der,* **~anwältin** *die* ▸❶ **S. 44,** ▸❶ **S. 113** public prosecutor; **~anwaltschaft** *die* public prosecutor's office; **~apparat** *der* state machine; **~ausgaben** *Pl.* public expenditure *sing.;* **~bank** *die; Pl.* **~~en** national bank; **~beamte** *der,* **~beamtin** *die* ▸❶ **S. 113** civil servant; **~begräbnis** *das* state funeral; **~besuch** *der* state visit; **~bürger** *der,* **~bürgerin**

S

die ▸ⓘ **S. 520** citizen; **er ist deutscher ~bürger** he is a German citizen *or* national; *s. auch* **Uniform**; **~bürger·kunde** *die* (DDR): *school subject involving ideological education of socialist citizens;* ≈ civics *sing. no art.*; **~bürgerlich** *Adj.* civil ‹*rights*›; civic ‹*duties, loyalty*›; ‹*education, attitude*› as a citizen; **~bürgerschaft** *die* ▸**~angehörigkeit**; **~chef** *der*, **~chefin** *die* head of state; **~diener** *der*, **~dienerin** *die* (meist scherzh.) public servant; **~dienst** *der* civil service; **~eigen** *Adj.* state-owned; **~eigentum** *das* state property; **~examen** *das: final university examination;* **~examen machen** ≈ take one's finals; **~feind** *der*, **~feindin** *die* enemy of the state; **~feindlich** *Adj.* anti-state; ‹*organization, attitude*› hostile to the state; **~finanzen** *Pl.* public finances; **~flagge** *die* state flag; (Nationalflagge) national flag; **~form** *die* type of state; state system; **~gebiet** *das* territory [of a/the state]; **~gefährdend** *Adj.* subversive; anti-state; **~gefährdung** *die* subversion [of the state]; **~geheimnis** *das* (auch fig.) state secret; **~geschäft** *das* affair of state; **~gewalt** *die* authority of the state; (Exekutive) executive power; **~grenze** *die* state frontier *or* border; **~haushalt** *der* national budget; **~hoheit** *die* sovereignty; **~hymne** *die* (bes. DDR) national anthem; **~kanzlei** *die* Minister-President's Office; (Schweiz) Cantonal Chancellery; **~karosse** *die* state coach; (fig. scherzh.) prestige limo (Amer. coll.) *or* limousine; **~kasse** *die* [1] public purse; [2] (Fiskus) treasury; **~kirche** *die* state *or* established church; **~kosten** *Pl.* **auf ~kosten** at public expense; **~kunst** *die* (geh.) statemanship; statecraft; **~macht** *die* power [of government]; **~mann** *der* statesman; **~männin** *die* stateswoman; **~männisch** /-mɛnɪʃ/ [A] *Adj.* statesmanlike ‹*wisdom, farsightedness, etc.*›; ‹*abilities, skill*› of a statesman; [B] *adv.* in a statesmanlike manner; **~minister** *der*, **~ministerin** *die* minister of state; (Minister[in] ohne Ressort) minister without portfolio; (Staatssekretär[in]) secretary of state; **~oberhaupt** *das* head of state; **~oper** *die* State Opera; **~organ** *das* organ *or* instrument of state; **~partei** *die* [totalitarian] government party; **~politisch** [A] *Adj.* ‹*aims, tasks, etc.*› of national policy; [B] *adv.* from the point of view of national policy; **~polizei** *die* state police; **~präsident** *der*, **~präsidentin** *die* [state] president; **~prüfung** *die* state examination; **~quote** *die* (Wirtsch.) state share (*in domestic product*); **~raison** *die*, **~räson** *die* reasons *pl.* of State *no def. art.*; **aus [Gründen der] ~raison** for reasons of state; **~recht** *das* constitutional law; **~rechtler** /-rɛçtlɐ/ *der;* **~~s, ~~, ~rechtlerin** *die;* **~~, ~~nen** expert in constitutional law; **~regierung** *die* national government; **~religion** *die* state religion; **~säckel** *der* (scherzh.) state coffers *pl.*; **~schatz** *der* national *or* state reserves *pl.*; **~schiff** *das* (geh.) ship of state; **~schuld** *die* national debt; **~sekretär** *der*, **~sekretärin** *die* ▸ⓘ **S. 113** permanent secretary; **~sicherheit** *die* [1] state security; [2] (DDR ugs.) ▸**~sicherheitsdienst**; **~sicherheits·dienst** *der* (DDR) State Security Service; **~streich** *der* coup d'état; **~theater** *das* state theatre; **~tragend** [A] *Adj.* ‹*programme, party*› supportive of the state; ‹*democracy*› embodying state principles; ‹*speech*› in support of [the role of] the state; [B] *adv.* in a way that supports the state; **~trauer** *die* national mourning *no indef. art.*; **~verbrechen** *das* crime against the state; **~verschuldung** *die* national debt; **~vertrag** *der* international treaty; (zwischen Gliedstaaten) interstate treaty *or* agreement; **der Österreichische ~vertrag** the Austrian State Treaty; **~wesen** *das* state [system]; **~wohl** *das* welfare *or* good of the state

Stab /ʃta:p/ *der;* **~[e]s, Stäbe** /ˈʃtɛ:bə/ [1] rod; (länger, für Stabhochsprung o. Ä.) pole; (eines Käfigs, Gitters, Geländers) bar; (Staffel~; geh.: Taktstock) baton; (Bischofs~) crosier; (Hirten~) crook; **den ~ über jmdn./etw. brechen** (geh.) condemn sb./sth. out of hand [2] (Milit.) staff [3] (Team) team

Stäbchen /ˈʃtɛ:pçən/ *das;* **~s, ~** [1] (kleiner Stab) little rod; [small] stick [2] (Ess~) chopstick

Stabelle /ʃtaˈbɛlə/ *die;* **~, ~n** (schweiz.) stool

Stab-: **~hochspringen** *das;* **~~s** pole-vaulting *no art.*; **~hochspringer** *der*, **~hochspringerin** *die* pole vaulter; **~hochsprung** *der* [1] (Disziplin) pole-vaulting *no art.*; **im ~hochsprung** in the pole vault; [2] (Sprung) pole vault

stabil /ʃtaˈbi:l/
[A] *Adj.* [1] (solide, kräftig) sturdy ‹*chair, cupboard*›; solid, sturdy ‹*construction*›; robust, sound ‹*health, constitution*› [2] (beständig, dauerhaft) stable ‹*prices, government, economy, Chem.: solution, etc.*›
[B] *adv.* **~ gebaut** solidly built

Stabilisator /ʃtabiliˈza:tɔr/ *der;* **~s, ~en** /-ˈto:rən/ (Technik, Chemie) stabilizer; (Kfz-W.) anti-roll bar

stabilisieren
[A] *tr. V.* stabilize
[B] *refl. V.* [1] stabilize; become more stable [2] ‹*health, circulation, etc.*› become stronger

Stabilisierung *die;* **~, ~en** [1] stabilization [2] (Kräftigung) strengthening

Stabilität /ʃtabiliˈtɛ:t/ *die;* **~** [1] (einer Konstruktion) sturdiness; (von Gesundheit, Konstitution usw.) robustness; soundness [2] (das Beständigsein) stability

Stabilitäts-: **~pakt** *der* (EU) Stability Pact; **~- und Wachstumsspakt** *der* (EU) Stability and Growth Pact

Stab-: **~lampe** *die* torch (Brit.); flashlight (Amer.); **~magnet** *der* bar magnet; **~reim** *der* (Verslehre) stave rhyme; head rhyme

Stabs-: **~abteilung** *die* specialist department *or* team; (Milit.) staff department; **~arzt** *der*, **~ärztin** *die* (Milit.) medical officer, MO (*with the rank of captain*); **~chef** *der*, **~chefin** *die* (Milit.) Chief of Staff; (Politik, Wirtsch.) chief of staff; **~feldwebel** *der* (Milit.) warrant officer 2nd class; **~offizier** *der*, **~offizierin** *die* (Milit.) staff officer; **~stelle** *die* [specialist] department; **~stelle Öffentlichkeitsarbeit** department for public relations; public relations department; **~unteroffizier** *der*, **~unteroffizierin** *die* (Milit.) ≈ staff sergeant

Staccato /staˈka:to/ ▸**Stakkato**

stach /ʃta:x/ *1. u. 3. Pers. Sg. Prät. v.* **stechen**

Stachel /ˈʃtaxl̩/ *der;* **~s, ~n** [1] spine; (Dorn) thorn [2] (Gift~) sting [3] (spitzes Metallstück) spike; (von ~draht) barb; *s. auch* **löcken** [4] (geh.: etw. Quälendes) barb; **der ~ der Eifersucht** the torment of jealousy; **einer Sache** (*Dat.*) **den ~ nehmen** take the sting out of sth.; **ein ~ im Fleisch** a thorn in the flesh [5] (etw. Stimulierendes) **der ~ des Ehrgeizes** the spur of ambition

Stachel-: **~beere** *die* gooseberry; **~draht** *der* barbed wire; **~häuter** /-hɔytɐ/ *der;* **~~s, ~~** (Zool.) echinoderm

stachelig *Adj.* prickly

stacheln *itr. V.* prick; ‹*beard*› prickle

Stachel·schwein *das* porcupine

stachlig ▸**stachelig**

Stadel /ʃta:dl̩/ *der;* **~s, ~** *od.* (schweiz.) **Städel** *od.* (österr.) **~n** (südd., österr., schweiz.) barn

Stadion /ˈʃta:di̯ɔn/ *das;* **~s, Stadien** stadium

Stadium /ˈʃta:di̯ʊm/ *das;* **~s, Stadien** stage

Stadt /ʃtat/ *die;* **~, Städte** /ˈʃtɛ(:)tə/ [1] town; (Groß~) city; **die ~ Basel** the city of Basel; **in die ~ gehen** go into town; go downtown (Amer.); **~ und Land** town and country; **in ~ und Land** throughout the country [2] (Verwaltung) town council; (in der Großstadt) city council; city hall *no art.* (Amer.); **bei der ~ [angestellt] sein/arbeiten** work for the council *or* (Amer.) for city hall

stadt-, Stadt-: **~auswärts** *Adv.* out of town; **~autobahn** *die* urban motorway (Brit.) *or* (Amer.) freeway; **~bahn** *die* urban railway; **~bekannt** *Adj.* well known in the town/city *postpos.*; known all over the town/city *postpos.*; (berüchtigt) notorious throughout the town/city *postpos.*; **~bevölkerung** *die* urban population; (einer bestimmten Stadt) townspeople *pl.*; **~bewohner** *der*, **~bewohnerin** *die* town-/city-dweller; **~bibliothek** *die* municipal library; **~bild** *das* townscape; (einer Großstadt) cityscape; **~bücherei** *die* municipal [lending] library; **~bummel** *der* (ugs.) **einen ~bummel machen** take a stroll through the town/city centre

Städtchen /ˈʃtɛ(:)tçən/ *das;* **~s, ~:** little town; **andere ~, andere Mädchen** move to a new town and you find a new girl

Stadt·chronik *die* history of the town/city

Städte·bau *der* urban building *or* development *no art.*; (Planung) town planning *no art.*

städte·baulich
[A] *Adj.* ‹*development*› of urban building/town planning; town-planning ‹*measure*›
[B] *adv.* from the point of view of town planning

stadt·einwärts *Adv.* into town; downtown (Amer.)

Städte·partnerschaft *die* twinning (Brit.) *or* (Amer.) sister-city arrangement (between towns/cities)

Städter *der;* **~s, ~, Städterin** *die;* **~, ~nen** [1] town-dweller; (Großstädter, -städterin) city-dweller [2] (Stadtmensch) townie (coll.)

Stadt-: **~flucht** *die* migration from the city; **~führer** *der* town/city guidebook; **~gas** *das* town gas; **~gespräch** *das* [1] (Telefongespräch) local call; [2] *in* **~gespräch sein** be the talk of the town; **~guerilla**[1] *die* urban guerilla group; **~guerilla**[2] *der* urban guerrilla; **~halle** *die* civic *or* municipal hall; **~haus** *das* [1] (Verwaltungsgebäude) council office building; [2] (Wohnhaus) town house

städtisch
[A] *Adj.* [1] (kommunal) municipal; **das Altersheim ist ~:** the old people's home is owned by the town/city [2] (urban) urban ‹*life, way of life, etc.*›; town ‹*clothes*›; ‹*manners, clothes*› of a town-dweller
[B] *adv.* [1] (kommunal) municipally; **~ verwaltet** run by the town/city council [2] (urban) **~/ausgesprochen ~ gekleidet** wearing town clothes/wearing clothes with a decidedly town style

Stadt-: **~kämmerer** *der*, **~kämmerin** *die* town/city treasurer; **~kasse** *die* [1] (Geldmittel) municipal funds *pl., no art.*; [2] (Stelle) town/city treasurer's office; **~kern** *der* ▸**~mitte**; **~kind** *das* [1] town/city child; [2] (~mensch) townie (coll.); **~kreis** *der* urban district; **~landschaft** *die* townscape; urban landscape; **~mauer** *die* town/city wall; **~mensch** *der* townie (coll.); **~mission** *die* town/city mission; **~mitte** *die* town centre; (einer Großstadt) city centre; downtown area (Amer.); **~park** *der* municipal park; **~parlament** *das* city council; **~plan** *der* [town/city] street plan *or* map; **~planer** *der*, **~planerin** *die* ▸ⓘ **S. 113** town planner; **~planung** *die* town planning *no art.*; **~rand** *der* outskirts *pl.* of the town/city; **am ~rand** on the outskirts of the town/city; **~rat** *der* [1] town/city council; [2] (Mitglied) town/city councillor; **~rätin** *die* ▸**~rat 2**; **~recht** *das* town ordinances and privileges *pl.*; **~recht erhalten** receive its town charter; **~rundfahrt** *die* sightseeing tour round a/the town/city; **~sanierung** *die* town/city redevelopment; **~schreiber** *der*, **~schreiberin** *die* [1] (hist.) town clerk; [2] (Schriftsteller) writer-in-residence (*living in a town/city and writing about it*); **~staat** *der* city state; **~streicher** *der*, **~streicherin** *die* town/city tramp; **~teil** *der* district; part [of a/the town]; **~theater** *das* municipal theatre; **~tor** *das* town/city gate; **~väter** *Pl.* (ugs. scherzh.) city fathers; **~verkehr** *der* town/city traffic; **~verordnete** *der/die; adj. Dekl.* town/city councillor; **~verwaltung** *die* municipal authority; town/city council; **~viertel** *das* district; **~wappen** *das*

ℹ Städte

Nur für wenige deutsche Städte gibt es besondere englische Namensformen: Am bekanntesten sind *Köln* = Cologne, *München* = Munich und *Hannover* = Hanover. In Österreich *Wien* = Vienna, in der Schweiz *Genf* = Geneva, *Basel* = Basle und *Luzern* = Lucerne. Unter den europäischen Hauptstädten fallen auf: *Brüssel* = Brussels, *Den Haag* = The Hague, *Rom* = Rome, *Athen* = Athens, *Prag* = Prague, *Warschau* = Warsaw und *Moskau* = Moscow. Überhaupt gibt es viele Unterschiede in der Transliteration von slawischen, griechischen, indischen und anderen fremdländischen Ortsnamen. Am besten schlägt man im Hauptteil dieses Wörterbuchs nach, der alle wichtigen geographischen Namen aufführt, oder auf einer englischsprachigen Landkarte.

Einwohnerbezeichnungen und Adjektive

Die von den Städtenamen abgeleiteten Einwohnerbezeichnungen und Adjektive haben im Englischen verschiedene Formen, aber es gibt sie nur für bestimmte größere Städte. Einige Substantive haben die gleiche Form wie die deutschen, die auf **-er** enden (Londoner, New Yorker usw.).

Für britische Städte gibt es einige ganz ausgefallene Ableitungen:

Glasgow→Glaswegian Aberdeen→Aberdonian
Bath→Bathonian Liverpool→Liverpudlian
Manchester→Mancunian Oxford→Oxonian

Die Endung **-ian** kommt recht häufig vor (z.B. Bristol →Bristolian, Lancaster→Lancastrian), aber für die meisten britischen Städte gibt es keine Einwohnerbezeichnungen. Die hier angegebenen werden sowohl als Adjektive wie auch als Substantive verwendet; die Adjektive beziehen sich meist auf Charaktereigenschaften (*Liverpooler Humor* = Liverpudlian humour).

Weitere Beispiele im europäischen Ausland:

Paris→Parisian Rome→Roman
Vienna→Viennese Milan→Milanese
Venice→Venetian Athens→Athenian
Florence→Florentine Moscow→Muscovite

In Deutschland gibt es lediglich *Hannoveraner* = Hanoverian (das sich hauptsächlich auf das englische Königshaus und die Pferderasse bezieht). Man kann aber in vielen Fällen die deutsche Form mit der Endung auf **-er** verwenden (Berliner, Frankfurter usw.), die sich aber nur als Einwohnerbezeichnung eignet. Sonst muss man auf die Formel 'inhabitant of ...' bzw. bei einer Großstadt, die als city gilt, 'citizen of ...' zurückgreifen:

ein Dinkelsbühler/eine Dinkelsbühlerin
= an inhabitant of Dinkelsbühl, a Dinkelsbühler

die Münchener
= the citizens *od.* people of Munich

Das gleiche gilt natürlich für Städte in anderen Ländern. Wenn man das Geschlecht hervorheben will, kann man 'a man/woman from ...' oder sogar den landessprachlichen Ausdruck verwenden:

ein alter Bremer
= an old man from Bremen, an old Bremen man

eine schöne Madriderin
= a beautiful woman/girl from Madrid, a beautiful madrileña

eine junge Römerin
= a young Roman girl

viele Wiener/Wienerinnen
= many Viennese men/women

An Stelle eines fehlenden abgeleiteten Adjektivs verwendet man einfach den Namen attributiv vor dem Substantiv (ohne Artikel bei Gebäuden und Einrichtungen), oder nachgestellt mit **of** bzw. **in**:

der Aachener Dom
= Aachen Cathedral

der Ravensburger Stadtrat
= Ravensburg Town Council, the Town Council of Ravensburg

der Berliner Dialekt
= Berlin dialect

die New Yorker Gegend
= the New York area

die Pariser Straßen
= the streets of Paris

der Londoner Verkehr
= the London traffic, the traffic in London

Der attributive Gebrauch von Städtenamen erstreckt sich auch auf Straßen:

die Straße nach Portsmouth
= the road to Portsmouth, the Portsmouth road

Die Adjektive, die auf **-isch** enden, werden auf ähnliche Weise übersetzt.

hamburgischer Humor
= Hamburg humour

hannoverischer Gleichmut
= Hanoverian equanimity

Die Dialekte, die auf **-erisch** enden, kann man nur als '... dialect' wiedergeben:

Wienerisch
= Viennese [dialect]

Berlinerisch
= Berlin dialect

town/city coat-of-arms; **~werke** *Pl.* municipal *or* council services; **~wohnung** *die* town/city flat (esp. Brit.) *or* (esp. Amer.) apartment; **~zentrum** *das* town/city centre; downtown area (Amer.)

Stafette /ʃtaˈfɛtə/ *die;* **~, ~n** [1] (hist.: reitender Bote) courier (*as one of a relay*) [2] (Gruppe von Kurieren) relay [3] (Formation als Begleitung) formation of outriders

Staffage /ʃtaˈfaːʒə/ *die;* **~, ~n,** [1] (Beiwerk) accessories *pl.;* (Dekoration) decoration [2] (bild. Kunst) staffage

Staffel /ˈʃtafl̩/ *die;* **~, ~n** [1] (Sport: Mannschaft) team; (für den **~lauf**) relay team [2] (Sport: **~lauf**) relay race [3] (Luftwaffe: Einheit) flight [4] (Formation von Schiffen, begleitenden Polizisten usw.) escort formation

Staffelei *die;* **~, ~en** easel

Staffel-: ~lauf *der* (Sport) relay race; **~läufer** *der,* **~läuferin** *die* (Sport) relay runner/skier

staffeln *tr. V.* [1] (aufstellen, formieren) arrange in a stagger *or* in an echelon; **gestaffelte Abwehr** (Fußball) staggered defence [line-up] [2] (einteilen, abstufen) grade ‹*salaries, fees, prices*›; stagger ‹*times, arrivals, starting places*›

Staffelung *die;* **~, ~en** [1] (Anordnung) staggered arrangement [2] (Einteilung, Abstufung) (von Gebühren, Gehältern, Preisen) grad[u]ation; (von Vorgängen) staggering

Stag /ʃtaːk/ *das;* **~[e]s, ~e[n]** (Seew.) stay

Stagflation /ʃtakflaˈtsi̯oːn/ *die;* **~, ~en** (Wirtsch.) stagflation

Stagnation /ʃtagnaˈtsi̯oːn/ *die;* **~, ~en** stagnation

stagnieren *itr. V.* stagnate

Stag·segel *das* (Seew.) staysail

stahl /ʃtaːl/ *1. u. 3. Pers. Sg. Prät. v.* **stehlen**

Stahl *der;* **~[e]s, Stähle** /ˈʃtɛːlə/ *od.* **~e** [1] steel; **die ~ verarbeitende Industrie** the steel-processing *or* steel industry; **Nerven wie** *od.* **aus ~ haben** have nerves of steel [2] (dichter.: Dolch, Schwert) blade

stahl-, Stahl-: ~arbeiter *der* ▸ℹ S. 113 steelworker; **~bau** *der; Pl.* **~~ten** [1] (Bautechnik) steel construction *no art.;* [2] (Gebäude) steel-frame building; **~besen** *der* (Musik) wire brush; **~beton** *der* (Bauw.) reinforced concrete; ferroconcrete; **~beton·bau** *der* reinforced concrete construction; **~blau** *Adj.* steel-blue; **~blech** *das* sheet steel

stählen *tr. V.* (geh.) toughen; harden

stählern *Adj.* [1] (aus Stahl) steel [2] (fig. geh.) ‹*muscles, nerves*› of steel; ‹*will*› of iron

stahl-, Stahl-: ~grau *Adj.* steel-grey; **~hart** *Adj.* as hard as steel *postpos.;* **~helm** *der* (Milit.) steel helmet; **~kammer** *die* strongroom; **~kocher** *der,* **~kocherin** *die;* **~~, ~~nen** (ugs.) steelworker; **~mantel·geschoss,** ***~mantel·geschoß** *das* (Milit.) steel-jacketed bullet; **~rohr** *das* steel tube; **~rohr·möbel** *das* piece of tubular steel furniture; **moderne ~rohrmöbel** modern tubular steel furniture *sing.;* **~ross,** ***~roß** *das* (ugs. scherzh.) bike (coll.); trusty steed (coll. joc.); **~stich** *der* (Grafik) steel engraving; **~verarbeitend** ▸**Stahl 1;** **~waren** *Pl.* steelware *sing.;* **~wolle** *die* steel wool

stak /ʃtaːk/ *1. u. 3. Pers. Sg. Prät. v.* **stecken**

Stake *die;* **~, ~n, Staken** *der;* **~s, ~** (nordd.) pole

staken
[A] *tr. V.* punt ‹*boat*›
[B] *itr. V.; mit sein* punt

Staket /ʃtaˈkeːt/ *das;* **~[e]s, ~e** [1] (Lattenzaun) paling [fence] [2] (Latte) pale

Stakete *die;* **~, ~n** (bes. österr.) ▸**Staket 2**

Staketen·zaun *der* paling fence

Stakkato /ʃtaˈkaːto/ *das;* **~s, ~s** *od.* **Stakkati** (Musik; auch fig.) staccato

staksen /ˈʃtaːksn̩/ *itr. V.; mit sein* (ugs.) stalk; (taumelnd) teeter

staksig (ugs.)
[A] *Adj.* spindly, shaky-legged ‹*foal etc.*›; teetering ‹*steps*›; **einen ~en Gang haben** walk as though on stilts
[B] *adv.* **~ gehen** walk as though on stilts; (unsicher) walk with teetering steps

Stalagmit /ʃtalakˈmiːt/ *der;* **~s** *od.* **~en, ~e[n]** (Geol.) stalagmite

Stalaktit /ʃtalakˈtiːt/ *der;* **~s** *od.* **~en, ~e[n]** (Geol.) stalactite

Stalinismus /stalɪˈnɪsmʊs/ *der;* **~:** Stalinism *no art.*

Stalinist *der;* **~en, ~en** Stalinist

stalinistisch
[A] *Adj.* Stalinist
[B] *adv.* in a Stalinist way; along Stalinist lines

Stalin·orgel *die* (Soldatenspr.) multiple rocket launcher

Stall /ʃtal/ *der;* **~[e]s, Ställe** /ˈʃtɛlə/ [1] (Pferde~, Renn~) stable; (Kuh~) cowshed; (Hühner~) [chicken] coop; (Schweine~) [pig]sty; (für Kaninchen, Kleintiere) hutch; (für Schafe) pen; **aus einem guten/demselben ~ kommen** (fig. ugs. scherzh.) have a good/the same background; **ein ganzer ~ voll Kinder** (ugs.) a whole horde of kids (coll.); *s. auch* **Pferd 1** [2] (Sportjargon: Rennfahrermannschaft) [racing] team

***Stallaterne** *die* ▸**Stalllaterne**

Stall·bursche *der* ▸ℹ **S. 113** stable lad

Ställchen /ˈʃtɛlçən/ *das;* **~s, ~** ▸**Stall 1:** little stable/cowshed/coop/sty/hutch/pen

Stall-: ~dung *der* (von Kühen/Schweinen/Schafen) cow/pig/sheep dung; (von Pferden) horse manure; **~hase** *der* (ugs.) domestic rabbit; **~knecht** *der* ▸ℹ **S. 113** (veralt.) stable lad;

S

(für Kühe) cowhand; **∼laterne** *die* stable lamp; **∼meister** *der*, **∼meisterin** *die* ▸❶ **S. 113** head groom; **∼mist** *der* ▸ **∼dung**

Stallung *die;* **∼, ∼en** (Pferdestall) stable; (Kuhstall) cowshed; (Schweinestall) [pig]sty; **die ∼en** the stables and other animal buildings

Stallwache *die* (fig.) caretakers *pl.;* **∼ halten** keep an eye on things; hold the fort

Stamm /ʃtam/ *der;* **∼[e]s, Stämme** 1 (Baum∼) trunk; **eine Hütte aus rohen Stämmen** a hut of rough-hewn boles; *s. auch* **Apfel 1** 2 (Volks∼, Geschlecht) tribe; **der ∼ Davids** the house of David; **vom ∼e Nimm sein** (ugs. scherzh.) be out for what one can get (coll.) 3 (fester Bestand) core; (von Fachkräften, Personal) permanent staff; **zum ∼ gehören** be one of the regulars (coll.); (der Belegschaft einer Firma) be a permanent member of staff; **ein [fester] ∼ von Kunden/Gästen** a number of regular customers/patrons 4 (Sprachw.) stem 5 (Biol.: Kategorie) phylum; (Mikrobiol.: Bakterien∼; Tierzucht) strain

Stamm-: ∼aktie *die* (Wirtsch.) ordinary share; **∼baum** *der* family tree; (eines Tieres) pedigree; (Biol.) phylogenetic tree; **∼buch** *das* 1 **jmdm. etw. ins ∼buch schreiben** (fig.) make sb. take sth. to heart; 2 (Familien∼buch) family album (recording births, marriages, deaths, etc.)

stammeln /ˈʃtamln̩/ *tr., itr. V.* stammer

Stamm-eltern *Pl.* progenitors

stammen *itr. V.* ▸❶ **S. 520** come (**aus, von** from); (datieren) date (**aus, von** from); **aus einem alten Geschlecht ∼:** be descended from an ancient lineage; **der Schmuck stammt von meiner Mutter** the jewellery used to belong to my mother; **der Satz/die Idee stammt nicht von ihm** the saying/idea isn't his

stammes-, Stammes-: ∼fürst, *der,* **∼fürstin** *die* tribal chieftain; **∼geschichte** *die* (Biol.) phylogenesis *no art.;* **∼geschichtlich** **A** *Adj.* phylogenetic; **B** *adv.* phylogenetically; **∼häuptling** *der* tribal chief

Stamm-: ∼essen *das* set meal; **∼form** *die* (Sprachw.) principal part; **∼gast** *der* (im Lokal/Hotel) regular customer/visitor; regular (coll.); **∼gericht** *das* set dish; **∼halter** *der* (oft scherzh.) son and heir (esp. joc.); **∼haus** *das* original building; **∼hirn** *das* (Anat.) ▸ **Hirnstamm;** **∼holz** *das* (Forstw.) round timber

stämmig /ˈʃtɛmɪç/ *Adj.* burly; sturdy ‹*arms, legs*›

Stamm-: ∼kapital *das* (Wirtsch.) authorized *or* registered capital; **∼kneipe** *die* (ugs.) favourite *or* usual pub (Brit.) *or* (Amer.) bar; **∼kunde** *der* regular customer; **∼land** *das; Pl. geh. auch* **∼e** ancestral homeland; (fig.) home territory; **∼lokal** *das* favourite *or* usual restaurant/pub (Brit.) *or* bar (Amer.)/café; **dieses Café ist sein ∼lokal** this café is his favourite haunt; **∼mutter** *die; Pl.* **∼mütter** progenitrix; **∼personal** *das* permanent staff; **∼platz** *der* (auch fig.) regular place; (Sitz) regular *or* usual seat; (für Wohnwagen, Zelt usw.) regular site; **∼schloss,** ***∼schloß** *das* ancestral castle; **∼silbe** *die* (Sprachw.) stem syllable; **∼sitz** *der* 1 (eines Adelsgeschlechts) family seat; 2 **der ∼sitz der Firma ist [in] X** the firm's head office is in X; **∼tafel** *die* genealogical table; **∼tisch** *der* 1 (Tisch) regulars' table (coll.); 2 (∼tischrunde) group of regulars (coll.); 3 (Treffen) get-together with the regulars (coll.); **∼tisch-politik** *die* (abwertend) bar-room politics *pl.;* **∼tisch-runde** *die* group of regulars (coll.)

> **Stammtisch**
>
> A large table reserved for regulars in most German pubs. The word is also used to refer to the group of people who meet around this table for a drink and lively discussion.

***Stammutter** ▸ **Stammmutter**

Stamm-: ∼vater *der* progenitor; **∼vokal** *der* (Sprachw.) stem vowel; **∼wähler** *der,* **∼wählerin** *die* committed *or* loyal voter; **∼würze** *die* (Brauerei) original wort; (Gehalt) original gravity; **∼zelle** *die* (Biol.) stem cell; **∼zellen-forschung** *die* stem cell research

Stamperl /ˈʃtampɐl/ *das;* **∼s, ∼n** (südd., österr. ugs.) [small] schnaps glas; **trinken wir ein ∼:** let's have a snifter (coll.)

stampfen /ˈʃtampfn̩/
A *itr. V.* 1 (laut auftreten) stamp; **mit den Füßen/dem Fuß/den Hufen ∼:** stamp one's feet/foot/its hoofs 2 *mit sein* (sich fortbewegen) tramp; (mit schweren Schritten) trudge 3 (mit wuchtigen Stößen sich bewegen) ‹*machine, engine, etc.*› pound 4 (Seemannsspr.) ‹*ship*› pitch
B *tr. V.* 1 **mit den Füßen den Rhythmus ∼:** tap the rhythm with one's feet; **etw. aus dem Boden** *od.* **der Erde ∼** (fig.) produce sth. out of thin air 2 (fest∼) compress; (rammen) drive ‹*pile*› (**in** + *Akk.* into) 3 (zerkleinern) mash ‹*potatoes*›; pulp ‹*fruit*›; crush ‹*sugar*›; pound ‹*millet, flour*›

Stampfer *der;* **∼s, ∼** 1 (für Erde usw.) tamper; (Stößel) pestle 2 (Küchengerät) masher

Stampf-kartoffeln *Pl.* (nordd.) mashed potatoes

stand /ʃtant/ *1. u. 3. Pers. Sg. Prät. v.* **stehen**

Stand *der;* **∼[e]s, Stände** /ˈʃtɛndə/ 1 (das Stehen) standing position; **keinen guten/sicheren ∼ haben** not have a good/secure footing; **aus dem ∼** (Sport) from a standing position; **ein Sprung/Start aus dem ∼:** a standing jump/start; **[bei jmdm.** *od.* **gegen jmdn.] einen schweren/keinen leichten ∼ haben** (fig.) have a tough/not have an easy time [of it] [with sb.]; **etw. aus dem ∼ [heraus] beantworten** (ugs.) answer sth. off the top of one's head (coll.); **die neue Partei schaffte aus dem ∼ [heraus] fast 7%** starting from scratch, the new party managed to get almost 7% [of the vote] 2 (∼ort) position 3 (Verkaufs∼; Box für ein Pferd) stall; (Messe∼, Informations∼) stand; (Zeitungs∼) [newspaper] kiosk; (Taxi∼) rank (Brit.); stand 4 (erreichte Stufe; Zustand) state; **jmdn. in den ∼ setzen, etw. zu tun** put sb. in a position *or* enable sb. to do sth.; **der heutige ∼ der Technik** the state of technological development today; **etw. auf den neu[e]sten ∼ [der Wissenschaft] bringen** bring sth. up to date *or* update sth. [in line with the latest scientific research]; **ich werde Sie über den ∼ der Dinge informieren** I'll keep you informed about how things stand; **bei dem jetzigen ∼ der Dinge** as things stand *or* are now; **außer ∼,** **außer ∼e** ▸ **außerstand, außerstande; im ∼e** ▸ **imstande; in ∼** ▸ **instand; zu ∼e** ▸ **zustande** 5 (des Wassers, Flusses) level; (des Thermometers, Zählers, Barometers) reading; (der Kasse, Finanzen) state; (eines Himmelskörpers) position; **den ∼ des Thermometers ablesen** take the thermometer reading 6 (Familien∼) status; **in den [heiligen] ∼ der Ehe treten** (geh., auch scherzh.) enter the state of [holy] matrimony 7 (Gesellschaftsschicht) class; (Berufs∼) trade; (Ärzte, Rechtsanwälte) [professional] group; **der geistliche ∼:** the clergy; **Leute von ∼:** persons of rank; **der dritte ∼** (hist.) the third estate; **die Stände** (hist.) the estates 8 (schweiz.: Kanton) canton

Standard /ˈʃtandart/ *der;* **∼s, ∼s** standard

Standard-: standard ‹*equipment, example, letter, form, solution, model, work, language*›

> **Der Standard**
>
> An Austrian daily printed on pink paper and considered to be liberal in its views.

standardisieren *tr. V.* standardize

Standardisierung *die;* **∼, ∼en** standardization

Standard-: ∼situation *die* (Sport) set piece; **∼software** *die* (DV) standard software

Standarte /ʃtanˈdartə/ *die;* **∼, ∼n** 1 (Feldzeichen, Fahne) standard 2 (ns.: Verband) [SA/SS] unit 3 ▸ **Lunte 2**

Stand-: ∼bein *das* (bes. Sport) support leg; (Fechten) rear leg; (Basketball) pivot leg; (Eislauf) tracing leg; **∼bild** *das* 1 statue; 2 (Film, Elektronik) freeze-frame

Ständchen /ˈʃtɛntçən/ *das;* **∼s, ∼:** serenade; **jmdm. ein ∼ bringen** serenade sb.

Stände-ordnung *die* (hist.) system of estates

Stander /ˈʃtandɐ/ *der;* **∼s, ∼:** pennant

Ständer /ˈʃtɛndɐ/ *der;* **∼s, ∼** 1 (Gestell, Vorrichtung) stand; (Kleider∼) coat stand; (Wäsche∼) clothes horse; (Kerzen∼) candle holder; (Pfeifen∼, Platten∼, Geschirr∼) rack 2 (Elektrot.) stator 3 (salopp: erigierter Penis) hard-on (sl.)

Stände-rat *der* (schweiz.) 1 (Vertretung) upper chamber 2 (Mitglied) member of the upper chamber

> **Ständerat**
>
> The *Ständerat* (Council of States) is the upper chamber in Switzerland. It is composed of 46 representatives from the various cantons.

Stände-rätin *die* ▸ **Ständerat 2**

Ständer-pilz *der* basidiomycete

standes-, Standes-: ∼amt *das* registry office; **∼amtlich** **A** *Adj.* registry office ‹*wedding, document*›; **B** *adv.* **sich ∼amtlich trauen lassen, ∼amtlich heiraten** get married in a registry office; **∼beamte** *der,* **∼beamtin** *die* registrar; **∼bewusst,** ***∼bewußt** *Adj.* conscious of one's social standing *or* rank *postpos.;* **∼bewusstsein,** ***∼bewußtsein** *das* consciousness of one's social standing *or* rank; **∼dünkel** *der* (abwertend) snobbery; **∼gemäß** **A** *Adj.* befitting sb.'s station *or* social standing *postpos.;* **∼gemäß sein** befit sb.'s station *or* social standing; **B** *adv.* as befits one's station *or* social standing; **∼organisation** *die* professional association; **∼person** *die* (veralt.) person of rank; **∼schranke** *die; meist Pl.* class barrier

Stände-staat *der* (hist.) corporative state

Standes-unterschied *der* difference of rank; class difference

Stände-wesen *das* corporative system

stand-, Stand-: ∼fest *Adj.* 1 (fest stehend) steady; stable; strong ‹*stalk, stem*›; **nicht mehr ganz ∼fest sein** (ugs. scherzh.) be a bit wonky (Brit. coll.) *or* shaky on one's feet; 2 (∼haft) steadfast; **∼festigkeit** *die* 1 stability; (eines Gebäudes) structural strength; 2 (∼haftigkeit) steadfastness; **∼foto** *das* (Film) still; **∼gas** *das* (Kfz-W.) idling speed; **∼gebühr** *die* (für Marktstand) stall fee; (Miete) stall rental; (bei Messen, für Taxis) stand fee; **∼geld** *das* stall fee; **∼gericht** *das* drumhead court martial; **∼haft** **A** *Adj.* steadfast; **B** *adv.* steadfastly; **∼haftigkeit** *die;* **∼∼:** steadfastness; **∼|halten** *unr. itr. V.* stand firm; **einer Sache** (*Dat.*) **∼halten** withstand *or* stand up to sth.; **der Kritik ∼halten** stand [up to] criticism; **einer näheren Überprüfung nicht ∼halten** not stand [up to] *or* bear closer scrutiny

ständig
A *Adj.* 1 (andauernd) constant ‹*noise, worry, pressure, etc.*›; **mit jmdm. in ∼er Feindschaft leben** live in a permanent state of enmity with sb. 2 (fest) permanent ‹*residence, correspondent, staff, member, etc.*›; standing ‹*committee*›; regular ‹*income*›
B *adv.* constantly; **musst du sie ∼ unterbrechen?** do you have to keep [on] interrupting her?; **sie kommt ∼ zu spät/ist ∼ krank** she's forever coming late/[being] ill; **Macht er das oft? — Ständig** Does he do that often? — All the time

ständisch
A *Adj.* corporative; **eine ∼e Gesellschaftsordnung** a social order based on privilege
B *adv.* corporatively

stand-, Stand-: ∼licht *das; Pl.* **∼∼er** (Kfz-W.) (Beleuchtung) sidelights *pl.;* (Leuchte, Lampe) sidelight; **mit ∼licht fahren** drive on sidelights; **∼miete** *die* stall rental; **∼ort** *der* 1 position; (einer Firma, Fabrik usw.) location; site; **von seinem ∼ort aus konnte er nichts sehen** he couldn't see anything from where he was standing; **jmds. politischer ∼ort** (fig.) sb.'s political stance *or* position; 2 (Milit.: Garnison) garrison; base; 3 (Wirtsch.) industrial location; **der ∼ort Deutschland** Germany as an industrial location *or* as a place for industrial investment; ~**ort·katalog** *der* shelf catalogue; ~**ort·kommandant** *der* (Milit.) garrison commander; ~**ort·vorteil** *der* (Wirtsch.) locational advantage; ~**pauke** *die* (ugs.) dressing down; **jmdm. eine [gehörige] ~pauke halten** give sb. a [good] dressing down; ~**punkt** *der* (fig.) point of view; viewpoint; **den ~punkt vertreten/auf dem ~punkt stehen/sich auf den ~punkt stellen, dass ...** take the view that ...; **das ist doch kein ~punkt!** (ugs.) that's no attitude to take!; ~**quartier** *das* base; ~**rechtlich** **A** *Adj.* summary ‹*execution, shooting*›; **B** *adv.* **jmdn. ~rechtlich erschießen** shoot sb. summarily; ~**spur** *die* (Verkehrsw.) hard shoulder; ~**streifen** *der* (Verkehrsw.) hard shoulder; ~**uhr** *die* grandfather clock; ~**vogel** *der* (Zool.) sedentary bird

Stange /ˈʃtaŋə/ *die;* ~, ~**n** **1** (aus Holz) pole; (aus Metall) bar; (dünner) rod; (Kleider~) rail; (Vogel~) perch; **Kleider/Anzüge von der ~** (ugs.) off-the-peg dresses/suits; **von der ~ kaufen** (ugs.) buy off-the-peg clothes; **jmdm. die ~ halten** (ugs.) stick up for sb. (coll.); **jmdn. bei der ~ halten** (ugs.) keep sb. at it (coll.); **bei der ~ bleiben** (ugs.) keep at it (coll.) ; **eine ~ Zimt/Vanille/Lakritze** *usw.* a stick of cinnamon/vanilla/liquorice *etc.*; **eine ~ Zigaretten** *a carton containing ten packets of cigarettes*; **eine [schöne] ~ Geld** (ugs.) a small fortune (coll.) **2** (bes. md.: zylindrisches Glas) [straight] glass **3** (Jägerspr.: Teil des Geweihs) beam

Stängel /ʃtɛŋl/ *der;* ~**s**, ~: stem; stalk

Stangen-: ~**bohne** *die* runner bean; ~**brot** *das* French bread; **ein französisches ~brot** a baguette; ~**spargel** *der* asparagus spears *pl. or* stalks *pl.*

stank /ʃtaŋk/ *1. u. 3. Pers. Sg. Prät. v.* **stinken**

Stänkerer *der;* ~**s**, ~, **Stänkerin** *die;* ~, ~**nen** (ugs. abwertend) grouser (coll.); stirrer

stänkern /ˈʃtɛŋkɐn/ *itr. V.* (ugs. abwertend) stir (coll.); **gegen jmdn./etw. ~:** go on about sb./sth.

Stanniol /ʃtaˈnio:l/ *das;* ~**s**, ~**e** tin foil; (Silberpapier) silver paper

Stanniol-papier *das* silver paper

stante pede /ˈstantə ˈpe:də/ *Adv.* (ugs. scherzh.) post-haste; lickety-split (coll.)

Stanze[1] /ˈʃtantsə/ *die;* ~, ~**n** (Verslehre) ottava rima (*with eleven-syllable lines*)

Stanze[2] *die;* ~, ~**n** press; (Prägestempel) die; (zum Lochen) punch

stanzen *tr. V.* press; (prägen) stamp; (aus~) punch ‹*holes, numbers, punchcards, discs, etc.*›

Stapel /ˈʃta:pl/ *der;* ~**s**, ~ **1** pile; **ein ~ Holz** a pile *or* stack of wood **2** (Schiffbau) stocks *pl.*; **vom ~ laufen** be launched; **vom ~ lassen** launch ‹*ship*›; (ugs. abwertend: von sich geben) trot out (coll. derog.) ‹*sayings, jokes, slogans, etc.*›

Stapel·lauf *der* launch[ing]

stapeln
A *tr. V.* (schichten) pile up; stack; (fig.: ansammeln) accumulate
B *refl. V.* pile up; (gestapelt sein) be piled up

stapel·weise *Adv.* ~ **Briefe** piles *or* stacks of letters; **ich habe sie ~:** I have piles of them

Stapfe /ˈʃtapfə/ *die;* ~, ~**n**, **Stapfen** *der;* ~**s**, ~ footprint

stapfen *itr. V.; mit sein* tramp; **in jede Pfütze ~:** stamp in every puddle

Stapler /ˈʃta:plɐ/ *der;* ~**s**, ~: ▸**Gabelstapler**

Star[1] /ʃta:ɐ/ *der;* ~**[e]s**, ~**e** *od.* (schweiz.) ~**en** (Vogel) starling

Star[2] *der;* ~**s**, ~**s** (berühmte Persönlichkeit) star

Star[3] *der;* ~**[e]s**, ~**e** ▸ⓘ **S. 439 der graue ~:** cataract; **der grüne ~:** glaucoma; **er ist am ~ operiert worden** he has been operated on for cataract/glaucoma

Star-: star ‹*conductor, guest singer, etc.*›; top ‹*lawyer, model, agent*›

Star·allüren *Pl.* prima donna behaviour *sing.*; ~ **zeigen/haben** put on the airs of a star

starb /ʃtarp/ *1. u. 3. Pers. Sg. Prät. v.* **sterben**

Star·besetzung *die* all-star cast

Staren·kasten *der* starlings' nest box

stark /ʃtark/; **stärker** /ˈʃtɛrkɐ/, **stärkst...** /ˈʃtɛrkst.../
A *Adj.* **1** strong ‹*man, current, structure, team, drink, verb, pressure, wind, etc.*›; potent ‹*drink, medicine, etc.*›; powerful ‹*engine, lens, voice, etc.*›; (ausgezeichnet) excellent ‹*runner, player, performance*›; **den ~en Mann markieren** *od.* **mimen** (ugs.) put on a strongman act (coll.); **sein stärkstes Werk/Theaterstück** his best work/play; **jetzt heißt es ~ bleiben** we must not yield now; **sich für jmdn./etw. ~ machen** (ugs.) throw one's weight behind sb./sth.; *s. auch* **Seite 4**; **Stück 3**; **Tobak** **2** (dick) thick; stout ‹*rope, string*›; (verhüll.: korpulent) well-built (euphem.); **Kleidung für stärkere Damen** clothes for the fuller figure; **eine 20 cm ~e Wand** a wall 20 cm thick **3** (zahlenmäßig groß, umfangreich) sizeable, large ‹*army, police, presence, entourage*›; big ‹*demand*›; **wir hoffen auf ~e Beteiligung** we hope a large number of people will take part; **eine 100 Mann ~e Truppe** a 100-strong unit; **das Kontingent ist 1 400 Mann ~:** the contingent is 1,400 strong **4** (heftig, intensiv) heavy ‹*rain, snow, traffic, smoke, heat, cold, drinker, smoker, demand, pressure*›; severe ‹*heat, cold, frost, pain*›; strong ‹*impression, influence, current, resistance, sign, dislike*›; grave ‹*doubt, reservations*›; great ‹*heat, hunger, thirst, exaggeration, interest*›; hearty ‹*eater, appetite*›; loud ‹*applause*›; ~**es Fieber** high temperature; **unter ~er Anteilnahme der Bevölkerung** with large numbers of the population attending; ~**er Widerhall** (fig.) a considerable response; **das ist [wirklich] ~** (ugs.) that [really] is a bit much! (coll.) **5** (Jugendspr.: großartig) great (coll.); fantastic (coll.)
B *adv.* **1** (sehr, überaus, intensiv) (mit Adj.) very; heavily ‹*indebted, stressed*›; greatly ‹*increased, reduced, enlarged*›; strongly ‹*emphasized, characterized*›; badly ‹*damaged, worn, affected*›; thickly, densely ‹*populated*›; (mit Verb) ‹*rain, snow, drink, smoke, bleed*› heavily; ‹*exaggerate, impress*› greatly; ‹*enlarge, reduce, increase*› considerably; ‹*support, oppose, suspect*› strongly; ‹*remind*› very much; ~ **wirkend** with a powerful effect *postpos.*; **es erinnert ~ an ...** it is very reminiscent of ...; ~ **riechen/duften** have a strong smell/scent; ~ **gewürzt** strongly seasoned; **es ist ~/zu ~ gesalzen** it is very/too salty; ~ **erkältet sein** have a heavy *or* bad cold; **er geht ~ auf die Sechzig zu** (ugs.) he's pushing sixty (coll.) **2** (Jugendspr.: großartig) fantastically (coll.) **3** (Sprachw.) ~ **flektieren** *od.* **flektiert werden** be a strong noun/verb

Stark·bier *das* strong beer

Stärke /ˈʃtɛrkə/ *die;* ~, ~**n** **1** strength; (eines Motors) power; (einer Glühbirne) wattage; **eine Politik der ~:** power politics *sing.* **2** (Dicke) thickness; (Technik) gauge **3** (zahlenmäßige Größe) strength; size; **eine Truppe von 300 Mann ~:** a 300-strong unit **4** (besondere Fähigkeit, Vorteil) strength; **jmds. ~/nicht jmds. ~ sein** be sb.'s forte/not be sb.'s strong point **5** (von Wind, Strömung, Eindruck, Einfluss, Nachfrage, Empfindung, Widerstand usw.) strength; (von Hitze, Kälte, Licht, Druck, Regenfall, Sturm, Schmerzen, Abneigung) intensity; (von Frost) severity; (von Lärm, Verkehr) volume; (von Appetit) heartiness **6** (organischer Stoff) starch

stärke·haltig *Adj.* starchy

Stärke·mehl *das* cornflour (Brit.); cornstarch (Amer.)

stärken
A *tr. V.* **1** (kräftigen, festigen; auch fig.) strengthen; boost ‹*power, prestige*›; ‹*drink, food, etc.*› fortify ‹*person*›; **die** *od.* **jmds. Gesundheit ~:** fortify *or* strengthen sb.'s constitution; **jmds. Selbstbewusstsein ~** (fig.) give sb.'s self-confidence a boost; **jmdn. in seinem Glauben ~:** reinforce sb.'s faith; *s. auch* **Rücken 1** **2** (steif machen) starch ‹*washing etc.*›
B *refl. V.* (sich erfrischen) fortify *or* refresh oneself; **nun stärkt euch erst mal** have something to give you strength
C *itr. V.* **ein ~des Mittel** a tonic

stärker ▸**stark**

Stärke·zucker *der* glucose

stärkst... ▸**stark**

Stark-: ~**strom** *der* (Elektrot.) heavy current; (mit hoher Spannung) high-voltage current; ~**strom·leitung** *die* (Elektrot.) power line; ~**ton** *der; Pl.* ~**töne** (Sprachw.) stress

Star·kult *der* (abwertend) star worship (**um** of)

Stärkung *die;* ~, ~**en** **1** strengthening; **zur ~ trank er erst mal einen Whisky** he drank a whisky to fortify himself; **die ~ des Parlaments** the increase in the power *or* influence vested in parliament **2** (Erfrischung) refreshment

Stärkungs·mittel *das* tonic

Starlet[t] /ˈʃta:lɛt/ *das;* ~**s**, ~**s** (spött. abwertend) starlet

starr /ʃtar/
A *Adj.* **1** rigid; (steif) stiff (**vor** + *Dat.* with); fixed ‹*expression, smile, stare*›; ~ **vor Schreck** paralysed with terror **2** (nicht abwandelbar) inflexible, rigid ‹*law, rule, principle*› **3** (unnachgiebig) inflexible, obdurate ‹*person, attitude, etc.*›
B *adv.* **1** rigidly; (steif) stiffly; **jmdn. ~ ansehen/~ geradeaus schauen** look at sb./look straight in front of one with a fixed stare **2** (unnachgiebig) ~ **bleibt er bei seiner Meinung** he sticks obdurately to his opinion

Starre *die;* ~ ▸**Starrheit**

starren *itr. V.* **1** (starr blicken) stare (**in** + *Akk.* into, **auf, an, gegen** + *Akk.* at); **jmdm. ins Gesicht ~:** stare sb. in the face **2** (ganz bedeckt sein mit) **vor/von Schmutz** *od.* **Dreck ~:** be filthy; be covered in filth; **vor Perlen und Diamanten/Gold und Geschmeiden ~:** be covered in *or* laden with pearls and diamonds/gold and precious stones; **vor Waffen ~:** be bristling with weapons

Starrheit *die;* ~ ▸**starr A**: **1** rigidity; stiffness; fixity **2** inflexibility; rigidity **3** inflexibility; obduracy

starr-, Starr-: ~**kopf** *der* (abwertend) pigheaded person; **ein ~kopf sein** be pigheaded; ~**köpfig** *Adj.* (abwertend) pigheaded; ~**krampf** *der* ▸**Wundstarrkrampf**; ~**sinn** *der* pigheadedness; ~**sinnig** *Adj.* (abwertend) pigheaded

Start /ʃtart/ *der;* ~**[e]s**, ~**s** **1** (Sport; auch fig.) start; **einen guten/schlechten/langsamen ~ haben** get off to *or* make a good/bad/slow start; **den ~ freigeben** give clearance to start; **das Zeichen zum ~ geben** give the starting signal **2** (Sport: ~platz) start; **an den ~ gehen/am ~ sein** (fig.: teilnehmen) start **3** (Sport: Teilnahme) participation; **sein ~ ist infrage gestellt** it is uncertain whether he will start **4** (eines Flugzeugs) take-off; (einer Rakete) launch; **den ~ der Maschine freigeben** give the aircraft clearance for take-off; **zum** *od.* **an den ~ rollen** taxi to the runway for take-off

start-, Start-: ~**automatik** *die* (Kfz-W.) automatic choke; ~**bahn** *die* [take-off] runway; ~**bereit** *Adj.* ready to start *postpos.*; ‹*aircraft*› ready for take-off; (zum Aufbruch bereit) ready to set off *postpos.*; ~**block** *der; Pl.* ~**blöcke** (Leichtathletik, Schwimmen) starting block

starten
A *itr. V.; mit sein* **1** start; ‹*aircraft*› take off; ‹*rocket*› blast off, be launched; **zu früh ~** (Sport) jump the start; **gut/schnell ~** (Sport) make a good/quick start; get away well/quickly **2** (an einem Wettkampf teilnehmen) compete; (bei einem Rennen) start (**bei, in** + *Dat.* in) **3** (den Motor anlassen) start the engine **4** (aufbrechen) set off; set out; **in den Urlaub ~:** set off on holiday **5** (beginnen) start; begin
B *tr. V.* start ‹*race, campaign, tour, production, etc.*›; launch ‹*missile, rocket, satellite, attack*›; start [up] ‹*engine, machine, car*›

Starter *der;* ~**s**, ~ (Sport, Kfz-W.) starter

Starterin *die;* ~, ~**nen** (Sport) starter

Starter-: ~**kit** *das;* ~~**s**, ~~**s** starter kit; ~**klappe** *die* (Kfz-W.) choke flap

start-, Start-: ~**erlaubnis** *die* **1** (Sport) authorization to compete; **2** (Flugw.) clearance [for take-off]; ~**geld** *das* (Sport) **1** (vom Teilnehmer bezahlt) entry fee; **2** (vom Veranstalter bezahlt) starting money; ~**guthaben** *das* starting credit; ~**hilfe** *die* **1** (Unterstützung) financial help, backing (*to get a project off the ground*); **jmdm. [finanzielle] ~hilfe geben** help sb. [financially] to get started; **2 ich brauche ~hilfe** I need help to get my car started; **~hilfe·kabel** *das* jump leads *pl.*; **~kapital** *das* starting capital; **~klar** *Adj.* ready to start *postpos.*; ‹*aircraft*› clear *or* ready for take-off; **~kommando** *das* (Sport) starter's order[s]; **~linie** *die* (Sport) starting line; **~loch** *das* (Leichtathletik) **in die ~löcher gehen** get on one's marks; **in den ~löchern kauern/hocken** (fig.) be waiting in the wings; **~nummer** *die* (Sport) [start] number; **~platz** *der* (Sport) starting position; **~rampe** *die* (Raumflug; auch fig.) launching pad; **~schuss**, ***~schuß** *der* (Sport) **der ~schuss fiel** the starter's gun went off; **den ~schuss zum 100-m-Lauf geben** fire the gun for the start of the 100 metres; **vor dem ~schuss loslaufen** jump the gun; **den ~schuss zu** *od.* **für etw. geben** (fig.) give sth. the go-ahead *or* the green light

Start-up /ˈstaːtlap/ *das;* **~s, ~s, Start-up-Unternehmen** *das* start-up [company]

Startverbot *das* **1** (Flugw.) grounding; **~ bekommen** be grounded; **2** (Sport) ban

Stasi[1] /ˈʃtaːzi/ *die;* **~** *od. der;* **~s** *Abk.* (DDR ugs.) **= Staatssicherheit[sdienst]**

Stasi[2] *der;* **~s, ~s** (DDR ugs.) state security man

> **Stasi, Staatssicherheitsdienst**
>
> *Stasi* is the shortened nickname of the State Security Service, the much despised secret police and their agents in the former GDR. With the help of an extensive network of informers, the *Stasi* built up personal files on a third of the East German population. It was disbanded a year before the **Wiedervereinigung**. Since then there have been many charges concerning political crimes committed by *Stasi* agents, as well as enquiries into the number of former GDR citizens who co-operated with the *Stasi*. See also **IM**.

Statement /ˈsteɪtmənt/ *das;* **~s, ~s** statement

Statik /ˈʃtaːtɪk/ *die;* **~ 1** (Physik) statics *sing.*, *no art.* **2** (Bauw.) static equilibrium **3** (geh.: statischer Zustand) stasis

Statiker *der;* **~s, ~, Statikerin** *die* structural engineer [concerned with statics]

Station /ʃtaˈtsi̯oːn/ *die;* **~, ~en 1** (Haltestelle) stop **2** (Bahnhof, Sender, Forschungs~, Raum~) station **3** (Zwischen~, Aufenthalt) stopover; **die ~en seiner Reise waren ...** the places where he stopped [off] on his journey were ...; **~ machen** stop over *or* off; make a stopover **4** (Kranken~) ward; **auf ~ sein** ‹*doctor*› be on ward duty **5** (einer Entwicklung, Karriere usw.) stage

stationär /ʃtatsi̯oˈnɛːɐ̯/

A *Adj.* **1** (Med.) ‹*admission, examination, treatment*› in hospital, as an inpatient; **ein ~er Patient** an inpatient **2** (ortsfest) permanently stationed ‹*troops, units*› **3** (Raumf.) fixed ‹*orbit*›; **ein ~er Satellit** a satellite in a fixed orbit

B *adv.* **1** (Med.) in hospital; **jmdn. ~ behandeln/aufnehmen** treat/admit sb. as an inpatient **2** (ortsfest) in one place

stationieren *tr. V.* station ‹*troops*›; deploy ‹*weapons, bombers, etc.*›

Stationierung *die;* **~, ~en** stationing; (von Waffen, Raketen usw.) deployment

Stations-: ~arzt *der*, **~ärztin** *die* ward doctor; **~schwester** *die* ward sister; **~taste** *die* (Rundf.) preset [tuning] button; preset; **~vorsteher** *der*, **~vorsteherin** *die* (Eisenb.) station master

statisch /ˈʃtaːtɪʃ/

A *Adj.* static; ‹*laws*› of statics; **~er Auftrieb** (Physik) static lift; **~e Berechnungen** (Bauw.) calculations relating to static equilibrium

B *adv.* (Bauw.) with regard to static equilibrium

Statist /ʃtaˈtɪst/ *der;* **~en, ~en** (Theater, Film) extra; (fig.) bystander; supernumerary; **zum ~en degradiert werden** (fig.) be demoted to the role of a mere accessory

Statisten·rolle *die* (Theater, Film) walk-on part

Statistik /ʃtaˈtɪstɪk/ *die;* **~, ~en 1** (Wissenschaft) statistics *sing.*, *no art.* **2** (Zusammenstellung) statistics *pl.*; **eine ~:** a set of statistics; **eine ~ über etw.** (*Akk.*) **erstellen** make a statistical study of sth.

Statistiker *der;* **~s, ~, Statistikerin** *die;* **~, ~nen ▸ⓘ S. 113** statistician

Statistin *die;* **~, ~nen ▸ Statist**

statistisch

A *Adj.* statistical; **~es Amt/~e Behörde** office of statistics

B *adv.* statistically

Stativ /ʃtaˈtiːf/ *das;* **~s, ~e** tripod

statt /ʃtat/

A *Konj.* **▸ anstatt A**

B *Präp. mit Gen.* instead of; **~ dessen** instead of this; (relativisch) instead of which

Statt *die;* **~, Stätten** (veralt., geh.) abode (arch.); **an jmds./einer Sache ~:** in sb.'s place/in place of sth.; instead of sb./sth.; *s. auch* **Eid; Kind 1**

statt·dessen *Adv.* instead; *s. auch* **statt B**

Stätte /ˈʃtɛtə/ *die;* **~, ~n** (geh.) place; **eine heilige/historische ~:** a holy/historic site; **die ~ des Sieges/der Niederlage** the scene of the victory/defeat

statt-, Statt-: ~|finden *unr. itr. V.* take place; ‹*process, development*› occur; **~|geben** *unr. itr. V.* (Amtsspr.) **einer Sache** (*Dat.*) **~geben** accede to sth.; **einer Klage ~geben** uphold a complaint; **~|haben** *unr. itr. V.* (veralt.) **▸ ~finden**; **~haft** *Adj.* permissible; **~halter** *der* (hist.) governor; **~halterschaft** *die;* **~~, ~~en** (hist.) governorship

stattlich

A *Adj.* **1** well-built; strapping ‹*lad*›; (beeindruckend) imposing ‹*figure, stature, building, etc.*›; fine ‹*farm, estate*›; impressive ‹*trousseau, collection*›; **ein ~er Mann/eine ~e Frau** a fine figure of a man/woman **2** (beträchtlich) considerable; sizeable ‹*part*›; considerable, appreciable ‹*sum, number*›; **~e 8 000 Euro** an impressive 8,000 euros; all of 8,000 euros (coll.)

B *adv.* impressively; splendidly

Stattlichkeit *die;* **~:** imposing nature; (von Statur) fine build *or* figure; **seine ~/die ~ seiner Erscheinung** his fine build *or* imposing stature

Statue /ˈʃtaːtu̯ə/ *die;* **~, ~n** statue

statuenhaft

A *Adj.* statuesque

B *adv.* like a statue; statuesquely

Statuette /ʃtaˈtu̯ɛtə/ *die;* **~, ~n** statuette

statuieren *tr. V.* (geh.) establish ‹*principle, purpose*›; lay down ‹*right, principle*›; *s. auch* **Exempel**

Statur /ʃtaˈtuːɐ̯/ *die;* **~, ~en** build; **kräftig von ~** *od.* **von kräftiger ~ sein** have a powerful build; **seine große/kleine/imponierende ~:** his tall/small/imposing stature

Status /ˈʃtaːtʊs/ *der;* **~, ~** /ˈʃtaːtuːs/ **1** (geh.: Stand, Zustand) state **2** ([rechtliche] Stellung) status

Status·leiste *die*, **Status·zeile** *die* (DV) status bar

Status quo /ˈstaːtʊs kvoː/ *der;* **~** (geh.) status quo

Status·symbol *das* status symbol

Statut /ʃtaˈtuːt/ *das;* **~[e]s, ~en** statute

Stau *der;* **~[e]s, ~s** *od.* **~e 1** (von Wasser, Blut usw.) build-up **2** (von Fahrzeugen) tailback (Brit.); backup (Amer.); **3 km ~:** a tailback (Brit.) *or* backup (Amer.) *or* jam stretching for three kilometres; **im ~ stehen** sit *or* be stuck in a jam

Staub /ʃtau̯p/ *der;* **~[e]s** dust; **[im ganzen Haus] ~ wischen** dust [the whole house]; **[im Wohnzimmer] ~ saugen** vacuum *or* (Brit. coll.) hoover [the sitting room]; **[viel] ~ aufwirbeln** (fig. ugs.) stir things up [quite a bit] (coll.); cause [a lot of] aggro (Brit. sl.); **sich aus dem ~[e] machen** (fig. ugs.) make oneself scarce (coll.)

Staub-: ~allergie *die* dust allergy; **~beutel** *der* **1** (Bot.) anther; **2** (eines ~saugers) dust bag; **~blatt** *das* (Bot.) stamen

Stäubchen /ˈʃtɔy̯pçən/ *das;* **~s, ~:** speck of dust

Stau·becken *das* reservoir

stauben *itr. V.* cause dust; ‹*person*› cause *or* raise dust; **es staubt sehr/mehr** there is a lot of dust/more dust; **er galoppierte davon, dass es nur so staubte** he galloped off raising clouds of dust

stäuben /ˈʃtɔy̯bn̩/

A *tr. V.* **etw. auf/über etw.** (*Akk.*) **~:** sprinkle sth. on/over sth.; **dem Baby Puder auf die Haut ~:** dust the baby's skin with powder

B *itr. V.* **1** (zerstieben) scatter; ‹*water*› form spray, spray out; ‹*sparks*› fly **2 ▸ stauben**

Staub-: ~faden *der* (Bot.) filament; **~fänger** *der* (abwertend) dust trap; **ein ~fänger sein** catch the dust; **~gefäß** *das* (Bot.) stamen

staubig *Adj.* dusty

staub-, Staub-: ~korn *das* speck *or* particle of dust; **~lappen** *der* duster; **~lunge** *die:* **▸ⓘ S. 439 eine ~lunge haben** have pneumoconiosis (Med.); **~saugen A** *tr. V.* vacuum, (Brit. coll.) hoover ‹*room, carpet, etc.*›; **B** *itr. V.* hoover (Brit. coll.); **~sauger** *der* vacuum cleaner; Hoover (*Brit.* ®); **~tuch** *das; Pl.* **~tücher** duster; **~wedel** *der* feather duster; **~wolke** *die* cloud of dust; **~zucker** *der* (veralt., südd., österr.) **▸ Puderzucker**

stauchen /ˈʃtau̯xn̩/ *tr. V.* **1** compress; (Technik) upset ‹*metal*› **2** (stoßen) thrust; jab ‹*stick, arms, etc.*›

Stau·damm *der* dam

Staude /ˈʃtau̯də/ *die;* **~, ~n 1** (Bot.) herbaceous perennial **2** (bes. südd.: Strauch) bush

Stauden·gewächs *das* (Bot.) herbaceous perennial

stauen /ˈʃtau̯ən/

A *tr. V.* **1** dam [up] ‹*stream, river*›; staunch *or* stem flow of ‹*blood*› **2** (Seemannsspr.: verladen) stow

B *refl. V.* ‹*water, blood, etc.*› accumulate, build up; ‹*people*› form a crowd; ‹*traffic*› form a tailback/tailbacks (Brit.) *or* (Amer.) backup/backups; (fig.) ‹*anger*› build up

Stauer *der;* **~s, ~, Stauerin** *die* stevedore

Staufer /ˈʃtau̯fɐ/ *der;* **~s, ~, Stauferin** *die;* **~, ~nen** (hist.) Hohenstaufen; **die Staufer** the Hohenstaufen dynasty *sing.*

Stau·mauer *die* dam [wall]

staunen /ˈʃtau̯nən/ *itr. V.* be amazed *or* astonished (**über** + *Akk.* at); (beeindruckt sein) marvel (**über** + *Akk.* at); **er staunte nicht schlecht, als er das hörte/sah** (ugs.) he was flabbergasted when he heard it/saw it; **da staunst du, was?** (ugs.) quite a shock, isn't it?; shattered, eh? (coll.); **da kann man nur [noch] ~:** one can only marvel *or* wonder at it; **~d** with *or* in amazement; **sie betrachtete ihn mit ~den Augen** she gazed at him wide-eyed with amazement; *s. auch* **Bauklotz; hören B 3**

Staunen *das;* **~s** amazement, astonishment (**über** + *Akk.* at); (staunende Bewunderung) wonderment; **jmdn. in ~ [ver]setzen** astonish *or* amaze sb.; **er kam aus dem ~ nicht mehr heraus** he couldn't get over it

Staupe /ˈʃtau̯pə/ *die;* **~, ~n** distemper *no art.*

Stau-: ~see *der* reservoir; **~stufe** *die* barrage

Stauung *die;* **~, ~en 1** (eines Bachs, Flusses) damming; (des Blutes, Wassers) stemming the flow; (das Sichstauen) build-up **2** (Verkehrsstau) tailback (Brit.); backup (Amer.); jam

Stau·werk *das* barrage

Std. *Abk.* **= Stunde** hr.

Steak /steːk/ *das;* **~s, ~s** steak

Stearin /ʃteaˈriːn/ *das;* **~s, ~e** stearin

Stech·apfel *der* (Bot.) thorn apple; **[Gemeiner] ~:** jimson weed

stechen /ˈʃtɛçn̩/

A *unr. itr. V.* **1** ‹*thorn, thistle, spine, needle*› prick; ‹*wasp, bee*› sting; ‹*mosquito*› bite; ‹*fig.: sun*› be scorching; **das Insekt hat ihm ins Bein gestochen** the insect bit him in the leg; **sich** (*Dat.*) **in den Finger ~:** prick one's finger

S

2 (hinein~) **mit etw. in etw.** (*Akk.*) **~:** stick *or* jab sth. into sth.; **jmdm. mit einer Nadel in den Hintern ~:** jab a needle into sb.'s behind; **nach jmdm. ~:** stab at sb.; try to stab sb. **3** (die Stechuhr betätigen) (bei Arbeitsbeginn) clock on; (bei Arbeitsende) clock off **4** (Kartenspiel) ‹*suit*› be trumps **5** (Sport) jump-off **6** ▸ **See² 1**

B *unr. tr. V.* **1** (mit dem Messer, Schwert) stab; (mit der Nadel, mit einem Dorn usw.) prick; ‹*bee, wasp*› sting; ‹*mosquito*› bite; (Fischereiw.: fangen) spear ‹*eel, pike*›; (ab~) stick ‹*pig, calf*›; **sich an etw.** (*Dat.*) **~:** prick oneself on sth.; **sich in den Finger ~:** prick one's finger **2** (hervorbringen) make ‹*hole, pattern*›; **jmdm. Löcher in die Ohren ~:** pierce sb.'s ears **3** (unpers.) **es sticht mich in der Seite** I've got a stabbing pain in my side **4** (herauslösen) cut ‹*peat, turf, asparagus, etc.*›; pick ‹*lettuce, mushrooms*› **5** (gravieren) engrave ‹*design etc.*› **6** (Kartenspiel) take ‹*card*›

Stechen *das;* **~s, ~** (Sport) jump-off

stechend *Adj.* penetrating, pungent ‹*smell*›; penetrating ‹*glance, eyes*›

Stech-: ~fliege *die* stomoxyine fly; (Wadenstecher) stable fly; **~ginster** *der* (Bot.) gorse; **~kahn** *der* punt; **~karte** *die* clocking-on card; **~mücke** *die* mosquito; gnat; **~palme** *die* holly; **~schritt** *der* (Milit.) goose step; **im ~schritt marschieren** goose-step; **~uhr** *die* time clock; **~zirkel** *der* dividers *pl.*

steck-, Steck-: ~brief *der* description [of a/the wanted person]; (Plakat) 'wanted' poster; (fig.: eines Menschen) personal details *pl.*; (fig.: eines Geräts) [brief] specification; **~brieflich** *Adv.* **der ~brieflich Gesuchte** the wanted man; **der Mörder wird ~brieflich gesucht** descriptions/'wanted' posters of the murderer have been circulated; **~dose** *die* socket; power point

stecken /ˈʃtɛkn̩/

A *tr. V.* **1** put; **etw. in die Tasche ~:** put *or* (coll.) stick sth. in one's pocket; **steck dein Hemd in die Hose** tuck your shirt in[to your trousers]; **ein Kind ins Bett ~:** put a child to bed; **sein ganzes Vermögen in etw.** (*Akk.*) **~:** put *or* invest all one's money in sth.; **sich hinter etw. ~** (ugs.) set to work on sth. with a will **2** (mit Nadeln) pin ‹*hem, lining, etc.*›; pin [on] ‹*badge*›; pin up ‹*hair*› **3** (pflanzen) put in, plant ‹*potatoes, onions, beans*› **4** (ugs.: mitteilen) **etw. der Polizei** *usw.* **~:** tip the police *etc.* off about sth.; **es jmdm. ~** (ugs.) give sb. a piece of one's mind (coll.)

B *regelm.* (*geh. auch unr.*) *itr. V.* be; **der Schlüssel steckt [im Schloss]** the key is in the lock; **voller Ideen ~:** be full of ideas; **wo hast du denn so lange gesteckt?** (ugs.) where did you get to *or* have you been all this time?; **wo steckt meine Brille?** (ugs.) where have my glasses got to *or* gone?; **er steckt in Schwierigkeiten** (ugs.) he's having problems; **in den Anfängen ~:** be in the early stages; **ein Abzeichen steckte an seinem Revers** a badge was pinned to his lapel; **hinter etw.** (*Dat.*) **~** (fig. ugs.) be behind sth.; **~ bleiben** get stuck; (fig.) ‹*negotiations etc.*› get bogged down; **die Kugel ist in der Lunge ~ geblieben** the bullet lodged in the lung; **es blieb in den Anfängen ~** (fig.) it never got beyond the early stages; **das Wort blieb ihm vor Angst im Halse** *od.* **in der Kehle ~:** he was speechless with fear; **den Schlüssel [im Schloss] ~ lassen** leave the key in the lock; **lassen Sie ~!** (ugs.: lassen Sie mich bezahlen) put your money away!

Stecken *der;* **~s, ~** (bes. südd.) stick

Stecken·pferd *das* **1** (Spielzeug) hobby horse **2** (Liebhaberei) hobby; **sein ~ reiten** go on about one's hobby horse; (sich seinem Hobby widmen) pursue one's [favourite] hobby

Stecker *der;* **~s, ~:** plug

Steck·kissen *das* papoose carrier; carry-nest

Steckling /ˈʃtɛklɪŋ/ *der;* **~s, ~e** cutting

Steck-: ~modul *das* (DV) plug-in module; **~nadel** *die* pin; **es ist so still, man könnte eine ~nadel fallen hören** it's so quiet you could hear a pin drop; **jmdn./etw. suchen wie eine ~nadel** (ugs.) search high and low for sb./sth.; **eine ~nadel im Heuhaufen suchen** (ugs.) look for a needle in a haystack; **~nadel·kopf** *der* pinhead; **~platz** *der* (DV) slot; **~rübe** *die* (bes. nordd.) swede; **~schloss, *~schloß** *das* safety lock (inserted in main lock); **~schlüssel** *der* socket spanner; **~schuss, *~schuß** *der: internal gunshot wound with bullet;* **er hat einen ~schuss in der Lunge** he has a bullet/pellet lodged in his lung; **~tuch** *das;* **~tücher** dress handkerchief

Steg /ʃteːk/ *der;* **~[e]s, ~e** **1** (schmale Brücke) [narrow] bridge; (Fußgänger~) footbridge; (Laufbrett) gangplank; (Boots~) landing stage **2** (veralt.: Pfad) path **3** (bei Saiteninstrumenten, Brillen) bridge

Steg·reif *der:* **aus dem ~:** impromptu; **er hielt aus dem ~ eine kleine Rede** he gave a short speech extempore *or* off the cuff; **etw. aus dem ~ beantworten** answer sth. off the top of one's head (coll.); **aus dem ~ spielen** improvise; ad lib

Stegreif·rede *die* impromptu *or* extempore speech

Steh-: ~auf·männchen *das* tumbling figure; tumbler; **er/sie ist ein [richtiges] ~aufmännchen** (fig. ugs.) nothing gets him/her down; **~bier·halle** *die* stand-up beer hall; **~café** *das* stand-up café; **~empfang** *der* stand-up reception

stehen /ˈʃteːən/

A *unr. itr. V.; südd., österr., schweiz. mit sein*

1 stand; **den ganzen Tag am Herd ~:** stand over the cooker all day; **er arbeitet ~d** *od.* **im Stehen** he works standing up; **jmdn. ~ lassen** walk off and leave sb. standing there; **sie steht zwischen ihnen** (fig.) she comes between them; **mit jmdm./etw. ~ und fallen** (fig.) stand or fall with sb./sth.; **das Haus steht noch/ist stehen geblieben** the house is still standing/was left standing; **er steht ihm** (salopp) he's got a hard-on (sl.)

2 (sich befinden) be; ‹*upright object, building*› stand; **~ bleiben** (unverändert gelassen werden) stay; be left; (zurückgelassen werden) be left behind; **etw. ~ lassen** leave sth.; (vergessen) leave sth. [behind]; **du kannst es nicht so ~ lassen** you can't leave it as it is; **lass die Vase ~!** leave the vase where it is; **den Teig eine Stunde ~ lassen** leave the dough to stand for an hour; **alles ~ und liegen lassen** drop everything; **sich** (*Dat.*) **einen Bart ~ lassen** grow a beard; **das Verb steht am Satzende** the verb comes at the end of the sentence; **wo steht dein Auto?** where is your car [parked]?; **sie haben dort einen Schrank ~:** they have a cupboard *or* (Amer.) closet [standing] there; **Schweißperlen standen auf seiner Stirn** beads of sweat stood out on his brow; **ich tue alles, was in meinen Kräften** *od.* **meiner Macht steht** I'll do everything in my power; **im Rentenalter ~:** be of pensionable age; **vor einer Entscheidung/dem Bankrott ~:** be faced with a decision/with bankruptcy

3 (einen bestimmten Stand haben) **auf etw.** (*Dat.*) **~** ‹*needle, hand*› point to sth.; **das Barometer steht hoch/tief/auf Regen** the barometer is reading high/low/indicating rain; **die Uhr steht auf 12** the clock shows 12; **die Ampel steht auf Rot** the traffic lights are [on] red; **es steht mir bis zum Hals[e]** *od.* **bis oben** *od.* **bis hier[hin]** I'm fed up to the back teeth with it (coll.); I'm sick to death of it (coll.); **der Wind steht günstig/nach Norden** (Seemannsspr.) the wind stands fair/is from the north; **das Spiel/es steht 1 : 1** (Sport) the score is one all; **wie steht es/ das Spiel?** (Sport) what's the score?; **die Chancen ~ fifty-fifty** the chances are fifty-fifty; **die Sache steht gut/schlecht** things are going well/badly; **[wie gehts,] wie stehts?** how are things?; **wie steht es mit deinen Finanzen/mit deiner Gesundheit?** how are your finances/how is your health?; **wie steht es mit deinen Ferien?** what is happening about your holidays?; **der Weizen steht gut** the wheat is growing well; **in Blüte ~:** be in bloom

4 (einen bestimmten Kurs, Wert haben) ‹*currency*› stand (**bei** at); **wie steht das Pfund?** what is the rate for the pound?; how is the pound doing? (coll.); **der Schweizer Franken steht am besten** the Swiss franc is currently strongest; **die Aktie steht gut/schlecht** the share price is high/low

5 (nicht in Bewegung sein) be stationary; ‹*machine etc.*› be at a standstill; **meine Uhr steht** my watch has stopped; **~ bleiben** (anhalten) stop; ‹*time*› stand still; **~ bleiben!** (Milit.) halt!; **wo sind wir ~ geblieben?** (fig.) where had we got to?; where were we?; **das Kind ist in der Entwicklung ~ geblieben** the child is a case of arrested development; **ein ~der Zug** a stationary train; **etw./den Verkehr zum Stehen bringen** stop sth./bring traffic to a standstill; **zum Stehen kommen** come to a standstill

6 (geschrieben, gedruckt sein) be; **auf einer Liste ~:** be *or* appear on a list; **was steht in dem Brief?** what does it say in the letter?; **in der Zeitung steht, dass …** it says in the paper that …; **das Zitat steht bei Schiller** the quotation is from Schiller

7 (Sprachw.: gebraucht werden) ‹*subjunctive etc.*› occur; be found; **mit dem Dativ ~:** be followed by *or* take the dative

8 **zu jmdm./etw. ~:** stand by sb./sth.; **wie stehst du dazu?** what's your view on this?; **hinter jmdm./etw. ~** (jmdn. unterstützen) be [right] behind sb./sth.; support sb./sth.

9 **jmdm. [gut] ~** ‹*dress etc.*› suit sb. [well]; **Lächeln steht dir gut** (fig.) it suits you *or* you look nice when you smile

10 (sich verstehen) **mit jmdm. gut/schlecht ~:** be on good/bad terms *or* get on well/badly with sb.

11 **das** *od.* **die Entscheidung steht [ganz] bei Ihnen** that's [entirely] up to you; it's for you to decide

12 **auf etw.** (*Akk.*) **steht Gefängnis** sth. is punishable by imprisonment

13 (ugs.: fertig-, zusammengestellt sein) ‹*plan, speech, team, programme, etc.*› be finalized

14 **für etw. ~** (Gewähr bieten) be a guarantee of sth.; (stellvertretend) stand for sth.

15 **auf etw.** (*Akk.*) **~** (ugs., bes. Jugendspr.: mögen) be into sth. (coll.); **sie steht total auf ihn** she's nuts about him (coll.); *s. auch* **Modell**; **Pate 1**; **Posten 2**; **Spalier 2**; **Wache 1**

B *unr. refl. V.; südd., österr., schweiz. mit sein* (ugs.)

1 (in bestimmten Verhältnissen leben) **sich gut/schlecht/auf 3 000 Euro monatlich ~:** be comfortably/badly off/on 3,000 euros a month

2 (sich verstehen) **sich gut/schlecht mit jmdm. ~:** be on good/bad terms *or* get on well/badly with sb.

C *tr. V.* (Skisport, Eislauf) **einen Sprung ~:** perform a jump without falling

***stehen|bleiben, *~|lassen** ▸ **stehen A 1, 2, 5**

Steher *der;* **~s, ~, Steherin** *die;* **~, ~nen** **1** (Pferdesport) stayer **2** (Radsport) motor-paced racer

Steher·rennen *das* (Radsport) motor-paced race

Steh-: ~geiger *der,* **~geigerin** *die* café violinist; **~kneipe** *die* stand-up bar; **~konvent** *der* (scherzh. fig.) [stand-up] chat; **einen ~konvent halten** *od.* **machen** stand around chatting *or* (Brit. coll.) having a good natter; **~kragen** *der* stand-up collar; (für Herrenhemden) choker; (mit Ecken) wing collar; **~lampe** *die* standard lamp (Brit.); floor lamp (Amer.); **~leiter** *die* stepladder

stehlen /ˈʃteːlən/

A *unr. tr., itr. V.* steal; **jmdm. etw. ~:** steal sth. from sb.; **jmdm. das Portemonnaie ~:** steal sb.'s purse; **jmdm. die Zeit ~** (fig.) take up *or* waste sb.'s time; *s. auch* **gestohlen B**; **nehmen 1**

B *unr. refl. V.* steal; creep

Steh-: ~platz *der* (im Theater/Stadion) standing place; (im Bus) space to stand; **40 ~plätze** standing room for 40; **es gab nur noch ~plätze** there was standing room only; **~pult** *das* high desk; **~vermögen** *das* stamina; staying power

Steiermark /ˈʃtaiɐmark/ *die;* **~:** Styria *no art.*

steif /ʃtaif/

A *Adj.* [1] stiff; (ugs.: erigiert) erect ‹*penis*›; **~ vor Kälte** stiff with cold; **~ gefroren** frozen stiff; **die Sahne ~ schlagen** beat the cream until stiff; **der Pudding ist noch nicht ~:** the blancmange has not set yet; **~ wie ein Stock** as stiff as a ramrod; **er kam uns mit ~en Schritten entgegen** he walked towards us stiffly; **einen Steifen haben** (salopp) have a hard-on (sl.); [2] (förmlich) stiff, formal ‹*person, greeting, style*›; formal ‹*reception*› [3] (Seemannsspr.: stark) stiff ‹*wind, breeze*› [4] (ugs.: stark) strong ‹*coffee*›; stiff, strong ‹*alcoholic drink*›

B *adv.* [1] stiffly; **bei ihnen geht es sehr ~ zu** things are very formal at their house [2] (Seemannsspr.: stark) **der Wind steht** *od.* **weht ~ aus Südost** there's a stiff wind blowing from the south-east [3] **~ und fest behaupten/glauben, dass ...** (ugs.) swear blind/be completely convinced that ...

***steif|halten** ▸ **Nacken**; **Ohr 2**

Steifheit *die;* **~:** stiffness; (Förmlichkeit) formality; stiffness

Steif·leinen *das* buckram

Steig *der;* **~[e]s, ~e** [mountain] path

Steig-: ~bügel *der* ▸ⓘ **S. 435** (auch Anat.) stirrup; **~bügel·halter** *der,* **~bügel·halterin** *die* (abwertend) backer; **die ~bügelhalter für Xs Karriere** those who advance/advanced X's career

Steige *die;* **~, ~n** [1] (bes. südd., österr.: Steig) [mountain] path [2] (bes. nordd.: Treppe) steps *pl.*; (Leiter) ladder [3] (bes. südd., österr.: Lattenkiste) open crate

Steig·eisen *das* (in Schächten usw.) step-iron; (am Schuh anschnallbar) climbing iron; (Bergsteigen) crampon

steigen /ˈʃtaign̩/

A *unr. itr. V.; mit sein* [1] ‹*person, animal, aircraft, etc.*› climb; ‹*mist, smoke, sun, object*› rise; ‹*balloon*› climb, rise; **Drachen ~ lassen** fly kites; **ins Tal/in den Keller ~:** climb *or* go down into the valley/go down into the cellar; **auf einen Turm/eine Leiter ~:** climb a tower/ladder; **auf die Leiter ~:** get on to the ladder; **aus dem Wasser/Auto/Bett/aus der Wanne ~:** get out of the water/out of the car/out of bed/out of the bath; **ins Wasser/ins Auto/in die Wanne/ins Bett ~:** get into the water/car/bath/into bed; **in den/aus dem Bus/Zug ~:** board *or* get on/get off *or* out of the bus/train; **ins/aus dem Flugzeug ~:** board/leave the aircraft; **aufs/vom Fahrrad ~:** get on [to]/off one's bicycle; **aufs Pferd/aus dem Sattel** *od.* **vom Pferd ~:** mount *or* get on [to]/get off one's horse; **auf die Bremse/aufs Gas ~** (ugs.) step on the brakes/the gas (coll.); **in die Kleider ~** (ugs.) slip into one's clothes; **das Blut/eine Röte stieg ihm ins Gesicht** the blood rose into *or* rushed to his face/he blushed; **der Duft steigt mir in die Nase** the scent gets up my nose; *s. auch* **Kopf 1** [2] (an~, zunehmen) rise (**auf** + *Akk.* to, **um** by) ‹*price, cost, salary, output*› increase, rise; ‹*debts, tension*› increase, mount; ‹*chances*› improve; **~de Preise** rising prices; **~de Ansprüche** growing *or* increasing demands; **in jmds. Achtung ~** (fig.) go up *or* rise in sb.'s estimation [3] (ugs.: stattfinden) be on; **morgen soll ein Fest ~:** there's to be a party tomorrow [4] (Reitsport: sich aufbäumen) ‹*horse*› rear

B *unr. tr. V.; mit sein* climb ‹*stairs, steps*›

Steiger *der;* **~s, ~** ▸ⓘ **S. 113** (Bergbau) overman

steigern

A *tr. V.* [1] increase ‹*speed, value, sales, consumption, etc.*› (**auf** + *Akk.* to); step up ‹*demands, production, etc.*›; raise ‹*standards, requirements*›; (verstärken) intensify ‹*fear, tension*›; heighten, intensify ‹*effect*›; exacerbate ‹*anger*›; **das Tempo ~:** step up the pace; **seine Leistung ~:** improve one's performance [2] (Sprachw.) compare ‹*adjective*›

B *refl. V.* [1] ‹*confusion, speed, profit, etc.*› increase; ‹*pain, excitement, tension*› become more intense; ‹*excitement, tension*› mount; ‹*hate, anger*› grow, become more intense; ‹*costs*› escalate; ‹*effect*› be heightened *or* intensified; **der Sturm steigerte sich zum Orkan** the gale increased to hurricane strength; **sich** *od.* **seine Leistung[en] ~:** improve one's performance [2] (hinein~) **sich [mehr und mehr] in Wut/Zorn/einen Erregungszustand ~:** work oneself up into [more and more of] a fury/rage/state [of excitement]

Steigerung *die;* **~, ~en** [1] increase (+ *Gen.* in); (Verstärkung) intensification; (einer Wirkung) heightening; (des Zorns) exacerbation; (Verbesserung) improvement (+ *Gen.* in); (bes. Sport: Leistungs~) improvement [in performance]; **~ der Produktion/des Absatzes** increase in production/in sales [2] (Sprachw.) comparison

Steigerungs-: ~form *die* (Sprachw.) comparative [form]; **~stufe** *die* (Sprachw.) degree of comparison

Steigung *die;* **~, ~en** gradient; (ansteigende Strecke) gradient; climb; **in sanfter ~:** climbing gently

Steigungs·winkel *der* [angle of] gradient

steil /ʃtail/

A *Adj.* [1] steep; upright, straight ‹*handwriting, flame*›; meteoric ‹*career*›; rapid ‹*rise*› [2] (Jugendspr. veralt.: beeindruckend) fabulous (coll.); super (coll.) [3] (Ballspiele) deep ‹*pass, ball*›

B *adv.* [1] steeply; **sie saß ~ aufgerichtet** she sat bolt upright [2] (Ballspiele) **jmdn. ~ anspielen** play a deep ball to sb.; **er spielt [immer wieder] zu ~:** he's playing too many deep balls

Steil·hang *der* steep escarpment

Steilheit *die;* **~:** steepness

Steil-: ~küste *die* (Geogr.) cliffs *pl.*; **~pass**, ***~paß** *der* (Fußball) deep [forward] pass; **~ufer** *das* steep bank; **~wand** *die* rock wall; **~wand·fahrer** *der,* **~wand·fahrerin** *die* wall-of-death rider; **~wand·zelt** *das* frame tent

Stein /ʃtain/ *der;* **~[e]s, ~e** [1] stone; (Fels) rock; **ihr Gesicht war zu ~ geworden** (fig.) her face had hardened [2] (losgelöstes Stück, Kern, Med., Edel~, Schmuck~) stone; (Kiesel~) pebble; **der ~ der Weisen** (geh.) the philosophers' stone; **ein ~ des Anstoßes** (geh.) a bone of contention; **mir fällt ein ~ vom Herzen** that's a weight off my mind; **es friert ~ und Bein** (ugs.) it's freezing hard; **~ und Bein schwören** (ugs.) swear blind; **den ~ ins Rollen bringen** (fig.) set the ball rolling; **jmdm. [die** *od.* **alle] ~e aus dem Weg räumen** (fig.) smooth sb.'s path; make things easy for sb.; **jmdm. ~e in den Weg legen** (fig.) create obstacles *or* make things difficult for sb.; **eine Uhr mit 12 ~en** a 12-jewel watch; *s. auch* **Krone 1** [3] (Bau~) [stone] block; (Ziegel~) brick; **keinen ~ auf dem anderen lassen** not leave one stone upon another [4] (Spiel~) piece; (rund, flach) counter; **bei jmdm. einen ~ im Brett haben** (fig.) be in sb.'s good books [5] (Grab~) gravestone

stein-, Stein-: ~adler *der* golden eagle; **~alt** *Adj.* aged; ancient; **~alt werden** live to a great age; **~axt** *die* (hist.) stone axe; **~bau** *der; Pl.* **~~ten** stone building; **~block** *der; Pl.* **~blöcke** block of stone; **~bock** *der* [1] (Tier) ibex; [2] (Astrol.) Capricorn; the Goat; *s. auch* **Fisch 3**; **~boden** *der* stone floor; **~brech** /-brɛç/ *der;* **~~[e]s, ~~e** (Bot.) saxifrage; **~bruch** *der* quarry; **~butt** *der* turbot

Steinchen *das;* **~s, ~:** little stone; (Kiesel~) pebble

Stein·druck *der; Pl.* **~e** [1] (Verfahren) lithography *no art.* [2] (Grafik) lithograph

Stein·druck·eiche *die* holm oak

steinern *Adj.* [1] stone ‹*floor, bench, etc.*› [2] (wie versteinert) stony ‹*face, features*›; **ein ~es Herz** a heart of stone

stein-, Stein-: ~erweichen *in* **zum ~erweichen** so as to make your heart bleed; heart-rendingly; **~frucht** *die* (Bot.) stone fruit; **~fuß·boden** *der* ▸ **~boden**; **~garten** *der* rockery; rock garden; **~gut** *das* earthenware; **~hart** *Adj.* rock-hard

steinig *Adj.* stony

steinigen *tr. V.* stone ‹*person*›

stein-, Stein-: ~kauz *der* little owl; **~kohle** *die* [hard] coal; **~krug** *der* earthenware jug; **~marder** *der* stone marten; **~metz** /-mɛts/ *der;* **~~en, ~~en, ~metzin** *die;* **~~, ~~nen** ▸ⓘ **S. 113** stonemason; **~obst** *das* stone fruit; **~pilz** *der* cep; **~reich** *Adj.* (ugs.) filthy rich; **~reich sein** be rolling [in money] (coll.); **~reich werden** make pots of money (coll.); **~salz** *das* rock salt; **~schlag** *der* (Fachspr.) rock fall; **„Achtung ~schlag"** 'beware falling rocks'; **~schleuder** *die* catapult (Brit.); slingshot (Amer.); **~topf** *der* earthenware pot; **~wurf** *der:* **jmdn. mit ~würfen wegjagen** chase sb. away by throwing stones [at him/her]; **[nur] einen ~wurf weit [entfernt]** (fig.) [only] a stone's throw away; **~wüste** *die* rocky desert; (fig.: leere Stadt) waste land of stone and concrete; **~zeit** *die* Stone Age (also fig.); **~zeitlich** *Adj.* Stone-Age *attrib.*; (fig.: völlig veraltet) antediluvian (coll.); **~zeug** *das* stoneware

Steirer /ˈʃtairɐ/ *der;* **~s, ~, Steierin** *die;* **Steierin, Steierinnen** Styrian

steirisch /ˈʃtairɪʃ/ *Adj.* Styrian

Steiß /ʃtais/ *der;* **~es, ~e** [1] (~bein) coccyx [2] (ugs.: Gesäß) backside; behind (coll.)

Steiß-: ~bein *das* ▸ⓘ **S. 435** (Anat.) coccyx; **~lage** *die* (Med.) breech presentation

Stellage /ʃtɛˈlaːʒə/ *die;* **~, ~n** rack

Stell·dich·ein *das;* **~[s], ~[s]** (veralt.) rendezvous; tryst (arch./literary); **sich** (*Dat.*) **ein ~ geben** (fig.) gather; assemble

Stelle /ˈʃtɛlə/ *die;* **~, ~n** [1] place; **eine schöne ~ zum Campen** a nice spot for camping; **an dieser ~ ereignete sich der Unfall** this is the spot where the accident happened; **die Truhe ließ sich nicht von der ~ rücken** the chest could not be shifted *or* would not budge; **sich nicht von der ~ rühren** not budge *or* move; **an jmds. ~ treten** take sb.'s place; **ich an deiner ~ würde das nicht machen** I wouldn't do it if I were you; **ich möchte nicht an deiner ~ sein** I shouldn't like to be in your place; **A an die ~ von B setzen** replace B with A; **an ~ +** *Gen.* instead of; **auf der ~:** immediately; **er war auf der ~ tot** he died instantly; **ich könnte auf der ~ einschlafen** I could go to sleep here and now; **auf der ~ treten** (ugs.), **nicht von der ~ kommen** (fig.) make no headway; not get anywhere; **zur ~ sein** be there *or* on the spot; **pünktlich zu ~ sein** arrive punctually; **Gefreiter Schulz meldet sich zur ~!** (Milit.) Lance Corporal Schulz reporting [2] (begrenzter Bereich) patch; (am Körper) spot; **eine kahle ~:** a bare patch; (am Kopf) a bald patch; **seine empfindliche ~** (fig.) his sensitive *or* sore spot; **eine schwache ~ in der Argumentation** (fig.) a weak point in the argument [3] (Passage) passage; **an anderer ~:** elsewhere; in another passage [4] (Punkt im Ablauf einer Rede usw.) point; **an dieser/früherer ~:** at this point *or* here/earlier [5] (Platz in einer Rangordnung, Reihenfolge) place; **an achter ~ liegen** be in eighth place; **er steht an führender ~:** he has a leading position; **etw. kommt an vorderster** *od.* **oberster ~:** sth. has top priority; **an erster ~ geht es hier um ...** here it is primarily a question of ... [6] (Math.) figure; **die erste ~ hinter** *od.* **nach dem Komma** the first decimal place; **etw. bis auf zwei ~n hinter dem Komma ausrechnen** calculate sth. to two decimal places [7] (Arbeits~) job; (formeller) position; (bes. als Beamter) post; **eine halbe/ganze ~:** a half-time/full-time job; **ohne ~ sein** be unemployed; **eine freie ~:** a vacancy [8] (Dienst~) office; (Behörde) authority; **die zuständige ~:** the competent authority

stellen

A *tr. V.* [1] put; (mit Sorgfalt, ordentlich) place; (aufrecht hin~) stand; **die Stühle um den Tisch ~:** place *or* put the chairs round the table; **wie sollen wir die Möbel ~?** how should we position the furniture?; **man soll die Flaschen ~, nicht legen** one should stand the bottles [up], not lay them down; **jmdn. wieder auf die Füße ~** (fig.) put sb. back on his/her feet; **jmdn. vor eine Entscheidung ~** (fig.) confront sb. with a decision; **auf sich [selbst] gestellt**

sein (fig.) be thrown back on one's own resources; **etw. in den Mittelpunkt der Diskussion ~** (fig.) make sth. the focus of discussion

2 (ein~, regulieren) set ‹*points, clock, scales*›; set ‹*clock*› to the right time; **den Wecker auf 6 Uhr ~:** set the alarm for 6 o'clock; **den Schalter auf null ~:** turn the switch to zero; set the switch at zero; **das Radio lauter/leiser ~:** turn the radio up/down; **die Heizung höher/niedriger ~:** turn the heating up/down

3 (bereit~) provide; produce ‹*witness*›; **jmdm. etw. ~:** provide sb. with sth.; *s. auch* **Verfügung 2**

4 **jmdn. besser ~** ‹*firm*› improve sb.'s pay; **gut/schlecht/besser gestellt** comfortably/badly/better off

5 (auf~) set ‹*trap*›; lay ‹*net*›

6 **kalt ~:** put ‹*food, drink*› in a cold place; leave ‹*champagne etc.*› to chill; **warm ~:** put ‹*plant*› in a warm place; keep ‹*food*› warm *or* hot

7 (fassen, festhalten) catch ‹*game*›; apprehend ‹*criminal*›

8 (aufrichten) ‹*dog, horse, etc.*› prick up ‹*ears*›; stick up ‹*tail*›

9 (er~) prepare ‹*horoscope, bill*›; make ‹*diagnosis, prognosis*›

10 *verblasst* put ‹*question*›; set ‹*task, essay, topic, condition*›; make ‹*application, demand, request*›; **jmdm. eine Frage/Aufgabe ~:** ask sb. a question/set sb. a task; **jmdn. unter Aufsicht/etw. unter Denkmalschutz ~:** place sb. under supervision/sth. under a conservation order; **jmdn. vor Gericht/unter Anklage ~:** take sb. to court/charge sb.

11 (bes. Theater, Film: arrangieren) block in the moves for ‹*scene*›; **das Foto wirkt gestellt** the photo looks posed

B *refl. V.* **1** place oneself; **sie stellte sich auf eine Leiter** she got on a ladder; **stell dich neben mich/ans Ende der Schlange/in die Reihe** come and stand by me/go to the back of the queue (Brit.) *or* (Amer.) line/get into line; **sich auf die Zehenspitzen ~:** stand on tiptoe; **ich stelle mich lieber** (ugs.) I'd rather stand; **sich gegen jmdn./etw. ~** (fig.) oppose sb./sth.; **sich hinter jmdn./etw. ~** (fig.) give sb./sth. one's backing; **sich vor jmdn. ~** (fig.) take sb.'s part; (verteidigen) defend sb.; *s. auch* **Standpunkt**

2 **sich schlafend/taub/tot** *usw.* **~:** feign sleep/deafness/death *etc.*; pretend to be asleep/deaf/dead *etc.*; *s. auch* **dumm A 1**

3 (sich ausliefern) **sich [der Polizei] ~:** give oneself up [to the police]

4 (nicht ausweichen) **sich einem Herausforderer/der Presse ~:** face a challenger/the press; **sich einer Diskussion ~:** consent to take part in a discussion; **er stellte sich der Kamera** he made himself available for photographs

5 (Stellung beziehen) **sich positiv/negativ zu jmdm./etw. ~:** take a positive/negative view of sb./sth.; **sich mit jmdm. gut ~:** try to get on good terms with sb.

stellen-, Stellen-: **~angebot** *das* offer of a job; (Inserat) job advertisement; **„~angebote"** 'situations vacant'; **~anzeige** *die* job advertisement; **~gesuch** *das* 'situation wanted' advertisement; **„~gesuche"** 'situations wanted'; **~markt** *der* job market; **~suche** *die* job-hunting *no art.*; search for a job; **auf ~suche sein** be looking for a job; be job-hunting; **~vermittlung** *die* employment agency; **~weise** *Adv.* in places; **~weise Nebel/Schauer** fog patches/scattered showers; **~wert** *der* **1** (Math.) place value; **2** (fig.: Bedeutung) standing; status

-stellig -figure ‹*number, salary*›; -place ‹*decimal*›

Stell-: **~macher** *der*, **~macherin** *die* cartwright; **~platz** *der* space; (auf einem Campingplatz) pitch; site; **~probe** *die* (Theater) blocking rehearsal; **~schraube** *die* adjusting screw

Stellung *die*; **~, ~en** **1** position; **in gebückter/kniender ~:** in a bent/kneeling posture; **die ~ der Frau in der Gesellschaft** the position *or* standing of women in society; **in ~ gehen** (Milit.) take up [one's] position; **geh nur, ich halte in der Zwischenzeit die ~** (fig.) you can go while I hold the fort; **[zu/gegen etw.] ~ beziehen** (fig.) take a stand [on/against sth.] **2** (Posten) job; (formeller) position; (bes. als Beamter) post **3** (Einstellung) attitude (**zu** to, towards); **zu etw. ~ nehmen** express one's opinion *or* state one's view on sth.; **er hat zu dem Vorschlag offiziell ~ genommen** he made an official statement on the proposal

Stellungnahme *die*; **~, ~n** opinion; (kurze Äußerung) statement; **eine ~ zu etw. abgeben** give one's opinion *or* views on sth.; (sich kurz zu etw. äußern) make a statement on sth.

stellungs-, Stellungs-: **~befehl** *der* (Milit.) call-up papers *pl.*; draft card (Amer.); **~krieg** *der* positional warfare *no pl., no indef. art.*; **~los** *Adj.* unemployed; jobless; **~spiel** *das* (Fußball) positioning; **~suche** *die* ▸ **Stellensuche**; **~suchende** *der/die*; *adj. Dekl.* job-hunter; **~wechsel** *der* change of position; (Wechsel der Arbeitsstelle) change of job

stell-, Stell-: **~vertretend** **A** *Adj.* acting; (von Amts wegen) deputy ‹*minister, director, etc.*›; **B** *adv.* as a deputy; **~vertretend für jmdn.** deputizing for sb.; on sb.'s behalf; **~vertreter** *der*, **~vertreterin** *die* deputy; **jmdn. als seinen ~vertreter schicken** send sb. as one's representative; **der ~vertreter Christi** (kath. Rel.) the Vicar of Christ; **~vertreterkrieg** *der* proxy war; **~vertretung** *die* deputizing *no art.*; acting as deputy *no art.*; **die ~vertretung für jmdn.** *od.* **jmds. ~vertretung übernehmen** stand in *or* deputize for sb.; **~wand** *die* partition; **~werk** *das* (Eisenb.) signal box (Brit.); switch tower (Amer.); (Anlage) control gear for signals and points (Brit.) *or* (Amer.) switches

Stelze *die*; **~, ~n** **1** stilt **2** (ugs.: Bein) leg; **der hat vielleicht ~n!** what long skinny legs *or* spindle-shanks he's got!

stelzen *itr. V.*; *mit sein* strut; stalk

Stemm-: **~bogen** *der* (Skisport) stem [turn]; **~eisen** *das* chisel

stemmen /ˈʃtɛmən/

A *tr. V.* **1** (hoch~) lift [above one's head]; (Gewichtheben) lift ‹*weight*› **2** (drücken) brace ‹*feet, knees*› (**gegen** against); **die Arme in die Hüften/Seiten ~:** place one's arms akimbo; put one's hands on one's hips; **die Arme in die Hüften gestemmt** with arms akimbo **3** (meißeln) chisel ‹*hole etc.*›

B *refl. V.* **sich gegen etw. ~:** brace oneself against sth.; (fig.: sich auflehnen) resist sth.; **sich in die Höhe ~:** haul oneself to one's feet

C *itr. V.* (Skisport) stem

Stempel /ˈʃtɛmpl̩/ *der*; **~s, ~** **1** stamp; (Post~) postmark; **jmdm./einer Sache seinen** *od.* **den ~ aufdrücken** (fig.) leave one's mark on sb./sth.; **den ~ einer Person/Sache tragen** (fig.) bear the stamp *or* imprint of sb./sth. **2** (Punze) hallmark **3** (Bot.: Teil der Blüte) pistil **4** (Technik) (zum Stanzen) punch; (zum Formen) die **5** (Bauw., Bergbau: Stütze) prop **6** (salopp: dicke Beine) **[richtige] ~ haben** have legs like tree trunks

Stempel-: **~farbe** *die* stamp pad ink; **~geld** *das* (ugs. veralt.) dole [money] (coll.); **~kissen** *das* stamp pad; ink pad

stempeln

A *tr. V.* **1** stamp ‹*passport, form*›; postmark ‹*letter*›; cancel ‹*postage stamp*›; **das Eingangsdatum auf die Briefe ~:** stamp the letters with the date of receipt **2** hallmark ‹*gold, silver, ring, brooch, etc.*› **3** (brandmarken) **jmdn. zum Verbrecher ~:** brand sb. [as] a criminal

B *itr. V.* (ugs. veralt.) be on the dole (coll.); **~ gehen** be on the dole (coll.); **er muss ~ gehen** he has to go on the dole

stempelpflichtig /-pflɪçtɪç/ *Adj.* (österr.) ▸ **gebührenpflichtig**

***Stengel** ▸ **Stängel**

Steno[1] /ˈʃteːno/ *die*; **~** (ugs.) shorthand; **kannst du ~?** do you know shorthand?

Steno[2] *das*; **~s, ~s** (ugs.) ▸ **Stenogramm**

steno-, Steno-: **~block** /ˈ---/ *der*; *Pl.* **~~s** *od.* **~blöcke** ▸ **~grammblock**; **~gramm** *das* shorthand text; **ein ~gramm aufnehmen** take a dictation in shorthand; **~grammblock** *der*; *Pl.* **~blöcke** *od.* **~~s** shorthand pad; **~graf** *usw.* ▸ **~graph** *usw.*; **~graph** *der* ▸ **i S. 113** stenographer; **~graphie** *die* stenography *no art.*; shorthand *no art.*; **~graphie lernen/können** learn shorthand/be able to do shorthand; **~graphieren** **A** *itr. V.* do shorthand; **sie kann gut ~graphieren** her shorthand is good; **B** *tr. V.* **etw. ~graphieren** take sth. down in shorthand; **~graphin** *die*; **~~, ~~nen** ▸ **i S. 113** ▸ **~graph**; **~graphisch** **A** *Adj.* shorthand *attrib.*; stenographic ‹*symbols*›; **B** *adv.* **~grafisch abgefasste Notizen** shorthand notes; **~stift** /ˈ--/ *der* shorthand pencil; **~typistin** *die*; **~~, ~~nen** shorthand typist

Stentor·stimme /ˈʃtɛntɔr-/ *die* stentorian voice; **mit ~:** in a stentorian voice

Stenz /ʃtɛnt͡s/ *der*; **~es, ~e** (ugs. abwertend) dandy; fop

***Step, Stepp** /ʃtɛp/ *der*; **~s, ~s** tap dance

Stepp·decke *die* quilt

Steppe /ˈʃtɛpə/ *die*; **~, ~n** steppe

steppen[1] *tr.* (*auch itr.*) *V.* (nähen) backstitch; **eine gesteppte Jacke** a quilted jacket

steppen[2] *itr. V.* (tanzen) tap dance

Steppen-: **~fuchs** *der* corsac; **~wolf** *der* ▸ **Präriewolf**

Stepperei *die*; **~, ~en** backstitching *no pl.*

Stepp-: **~futter** *das* quilted lining; **~jacke** *die* quilted jacket

Steppke /ˈʃtɛpkə/ *der*; **~[s], ~s** (ugs., bes. berlin.) lad; nipper (coll.)

Stepp-: **~naht** *die* backstitched seam; **~stich** *der* backstitch

Stepp-, *Step-: **~tanz** *der* tap dance; **~tänzer** *der*, **~tänzerin** *die* tap dancer

Sterbe-: **~bett** *das* deathbed; **auf dem ~bett liegen** be on one's deathbed; **~datum** *das* date of death; **~fall** *der* ▸ **Todesfall**; **~geläut** *das* death knell; **~glocke** *die* funeral bell; **~hilfe** *die* ▸ **Euthanasie**

sterben /ˈʃtɛrbn̩/

A *unr. itr. V.*; *mit sein* die; **eines sanften Todes ~** (geh.) die peacefully; **er starb als Christ** he died a Christian; **im Sterben liegen** lie dying; **und wenn sie nicht gestorben sind, dann leben sie noch heute** and they lived happily ever after; **davon stirbt man/stirbst du nicht gleich** (ugs.) it/they won't kill you; **zum Sterben langweilig/müde** deadly boring/dead tired; **er ist für mich gestorben** (fig.) he's finished *or* he doesn't exist as far as I'm concerned; **gestorben!** (Film-, Fernsehjargon) (abgeschlossen) [OK,] in the can!; (abgebrochen) cut!; **vor Angst/Scham/Neugier ~** (ugs.) die of fright/shame/be dying of curiosity

B *unr. tr. V.*; *mit sein* **den Hungertod ~:** die of starvation; starve to death; **den Heldentod ~:** die a hero's death

sterbens-, Sterbens-: **~angst** *die* terrible fear; **eine ~angst haben** be scared to death; be terribly afraid; be terrified; **~elend** *Adj.* wretched; **~krank** *Adj.* **1** ▸ **~elend**; **2** (sehr krank) mortally ill; **~langweilig** *Adj.* deadly boring; **~wort**, **~wörtchen** *das*: **in kein** *od.* **nicht ein ~wort** *od.* **~wörtchen** not a [single] word; **darüber haben wir kein ~wort** *od.* **~wörtchen gesagt** we didn't breathe a word [of it]

Sterbe-: **~sakramente** *Pl.* (kath. Kirche) last rites; **~stunde** *die* ▸ **Todesstunde**; **~tafel** *die* (Versicherungsw.) life expectancy table; **~urkunde** *die* death certificate; **~zimmer** *das*: **sein ~zimmer** the room in which he died

sterblich *Adj.* mortal; *s. auch* **Hülle 1**; **Überrest**

Sterbliche *der/die*; *adj. Dekl.* **1** (dichter.) mortal **2** **ein gewöhnlicher ~r** an ordinary mortal *or* person

Sterblichkeit *die*; **~:** mortality

stereo /ˈʃteːreo/ *Adv.* (Akustik) in stereo

stereo-, Stereo- stereo-

Stereo *das*; **~s** (Akustik) stereo

stereo-, Stereo-: **~anlage** *die* stereo [system]; **~aufnahme** *die* stereo recording;

S

~empfang *der* stereo reception; **~kamera** *die* stereocamera; stereoscopic camera; **~metrie** /-me'tri:/ *die;* **~~** (Math.) stereometry *no art.;* **~phon** /-'fo:n/ (Akustik) **A** *Adj.* stereophonic; **B** *adv.* stereophonically; **~phonie** /-fo'ni:/ *die;* **~~** (Akustik) stereophony *no art.;* **~skop** /-'sko:p/ *das;* **~~s, ~~e** stereoscope; **~skopie** /-sko'pi:/ *die;* **~~:** stereoscopy *no art.;* **~skopisch** *Adj.* stereoscopic; **~ton** *der; Pl.* **~töne** stereo sound; **~typ** /---'-/ **A** *Adj.* **1)** stereotyped ‹*discussion, pattern, etc.*›; stereotyped, stock ‹*question, reply, phrase, utterance*›; mechanical ‹*smile*›; **2)** (Druckw.) stereotype; **B** *adv.* **1)** in a stereotyped way; **2)** (Druckw.) in stereotype; **~typie** /-ty'pi:/ *die;* **~~** **1)** (Druckw.) stereotyping *no art.;* **2)** (Psychiatrie, Med.) stereotypy

steril /ʃte'ri:l/
A *Adj.* (auch fig. abwertend) sterile; **etw. ~ machen** sterilize sth.
B *adv.* **1)** (keimfrei) **~ verpackt sein** be in a sterile pack/sterile packs; **etw. ~ auskochen** sterilize sth. by boiling **2)** (fig. abwertend: unschöpferisch, nüchtern) sterilely

Sterilisation /ʃteriliza'tsi̯o:n/ *die;* **~, ~en** sterilization

sterilisieren *tr. V.* sterilize

Sterilität /ʃterili'tɛ:t/ *die;* **~** (auch fig. abwertend) sterility

Sterling /'stɛ:lɪŋ/ ▸ⓘ **S. 299** *in* **1 Pfund ~:** £1 sterling; **einen Betrag in Pfund ~ tauschen** change a sum into sterling; **in ~ bezahlen** pay in sterling

Sterling·silber *das* sterling silver

Stern /ʃtɛrn/ *der;* **~[e]s, ~e** **1)** star; **~e sehen** (ugs.) see stars; **unter fremden ~en** (geh.) in foreign parts; **nach den ~en greifen** (geh.) reach for the moon; **in den ~en stehen** (fig.) be in the lap of the gods; **unter einem guten** *od.* **günstigen/ungünstigen ~ stehen** (geh.) have an auspicious start/be ill-starred **2)** (Orden, Auszeichnung) star; **ein Hotel mit fünf ~en** a five-star hotel **3)** (bei Pferden, Rindern) blaze **4)** (Jägerspr.) iris

Stern·bild *das* constellation

Sternchen *das;* **~s, ~** **1)** [little] star **2)** (als Verweis) asterisk **3)** ▸ **Starlet[t]**

Stern-: ~deuter /-dɔytɐ/ *der,* **~deuterin** *die* astrologer; **~deutung** *die* astrology *no art.*

sternen-, Sternen-: ~banner *das* Star-spangled Banner, Stars and Stripes *pl.;* **~himmel** *der* (geh.) starry sky; **~klar** *Adj.* starlit, starry ‹*sky, night*›; **~licht** *das* (geh.) starlight; **~zelt** *das* (dichter.) starry canopy

stern-, Stern-: ~fahrt *die* rally (in which the participants converge from various starting points); **eine ~fahrt nach X** a rally converging on X; **~förmig** *Adj.* star-shaped; stellate ‹*leaf*› (Bot.); **~globus** *der* (Astron.) celestial globe; **~gucker** *der;* **~~s, ~~,** **~guckerin** *die;* **~~, ~~nen** (ugs. scherzh.: Astronom) stargazer; **~hagel·voll** *Adj.* (salopp) paralytic (Brit. coll.); blotto (coll.); **~haufen** *der* (Astron.) star cluster; **~hell** *Adj.* (geh.) starlit; starry; **~himmel** *der* starry sky; **~jahr** *das* sidereal year; **~karte** *die* ▸ **Himmelskarte;** **~klar** *Adj.* starlit, starry ‹*sky, night*›; **~kunde** *die* astronomy *no art.;* **~kundig** *Adj.* **~kundig sein** have a knowledge of astronomy; **~los** *Adj.* starless; **~marsch** *der* [protest] march (*with marchers converging from various starting points*); **~miere** /-mi:rə/ *die;* **~~, ~~n** (Bot.) starwort; **~schnuppe** *die;* **~~, ~~n** shooting star; **~stunde** *die* (geh.) great moment; **seine ~stunde haben** have one's moment *or* hour of glory; **~tag** *der* (Astron.) sidereal day; **~warte** *die* observatory; **~zeichen** *das* ▸ **Tierkreiszeichen;** **~zeit** *die* sidereal time

Steroid /stero'i:t/ *das;* **~[e]s, ~e** (Biochem.) steroid

Sterz[1] /ʃtɛrts/ *der;* **~es, ~e** (südd., österr.: Speise) (boiled or fried) dumpling pieces *pl.*

Sterz[2] *der;* **~es, ~e** (Bürzel) rump

stet /ʃte:t/ *Adj.* (geh.) **1)** constant ‹*goodwill, devotion, companion*›; steady ‹*rhythm*› **2)** (ständig) constant; continous

Stethoskop /ʃteto'sko:p/ *das;* **~s, ~e** (Med.) stethoscope

stetig /'ʃte:tɪç/
A *Adj.* steady ‹*growth, increase, decline*›; constant, continuous ‹*movement, vibration*›
B *adv.* ‹*grow, increase, drop*› steadily; ‹*move, vibrate*› constantly, continuously

Stetigkeit *die;* **~** ▸ **stetig:** steadiness; constancy; continuousness

stets /ʃte:ts/ *Adv.* always

Steuer[1] /'ʃtɔyɐ/ *das;* **~s, ~** (von Fahrzeugen) [steering] wheel; (von Schiffen) helm; **ins ~ greifen** grab the [steering] wheel; **sich ans** *od.* **hinters ~ setzen** get behind the wheel; **das ~ herumreißen** pull the [steering] wheel over hard; **das ~ übernehmen** take over the wheel *or* the driving; (bei Schiffen, fig.) take over the helm; **Trunkenheit am ~:** drunken driving; being drunk at the wheel; **das ~ fest in der Hand haben** (fig.) have one's hand firmly on the helm

Steuer[2] *die;* **~, ~n** **1)** tax; **~n zahlen** (Lohn-/Einkommensteuer) pay tax; **etw. von der ~ absetzen** set sth. off against tax; **etw. mit einer ~ belegen** impose a tax on sth. **2)** (ugs.: Behörde) tax authorities *pl.*

steuer-, Steuer-: ~aufkommen *das* (Steuerw.) tax revenue; **~bar** *Adj.* controllable; **~behörde** *die* tax authorities *pl.;* **~berater** *der,* **~beraterin** *die* ▸ⓘ **S. 113** (Steuerw.) tax consultant *or* adviser; **~bescheid** *der* (Steuerw.) tax assessment; **~bevollmächtigte** *der/die; adj. Dekl.* (Steuerw.) tax consultant *or* adviser; **~bord** *das od.* (*österr.*) *der* (Seew., Flugw.) starboard; **nach ~bord gehen** turn to starboard; **~bord[s]** *Adv.* (Seew., Flugw.) to starboard; **~erhöhung** *die* (Steuerw.) tax increase; **~erklärung** *die* (Steuerw.) tax return; **~ermäßigung** *die* (Steuerw.) tax relief; **~erstattung** *die* (Steuerw.) tax refund; **~experte** *der,* **~expertin** *die* tax expert; **~fahnder** *der;* **~~s, ~~,** **~fahnderin** *die;* **~~, ~~nen** tax investigator; **~fahndung** *die* (Steuerw.) tax investigation; **~finanziert** *Adj.* funded from taxation *postpos.;* **~flucht** *die* (Steuerw.) tax evasion (*by transferring capital out of the country or living abroad*); **~frau** *die* (Rudern) cox; **~frei** *Adj.* (Steuerw.) tax-free; free of tax *pred.;* **~freibetrag** *der* (Steuerw.) tax allowance; **~gelder** *Pl.* (Steuerw.) taxes; **~gerät** *das* **1)** (Rundfunkt.) receiver; **2)** (Elektrot.) control device *or* unit; **~gesetz** *das* (Steuerw.) tax law; **~hinterziehung** *die* (Steuerw.) tax evasion; **~klasse** *die* (Steuerw.) tax category (dependent on marital status [and number of children]); **~knüppel** *der* control column; joystick (coll.)

steuerlich
A *Adj.* tax ‹*advantages, benefits, etc.*›
B *adv.* **~ absetzbar** tax-deductible

steuer-, Steuer-: ~los *Adj.* out of control; **~mann** *der; Pl.* **~leute** *od.* **~männer** **1)** (Seew. veralt.) helmsman; steersman; **2)** (Seew.) ▸ **Bootsmann 2; 3)** (Rudern) cox; **Vierer mit/ohne ~mann** coxed/coxless fours; **Einer mit ~mann** coxed single; **4)** (Elektrot.) controller; **~marke** *die* revenue stamp; (für Hunde) licence disc; **~moral** *die* tax-payer honesty; attitude to paying tax

steuern
A *tr. V.* **1)** (fahren) steer; (fliegen) pilot, fly ‹*aircraft*›; fly ‹*course*› **2)** (Technik) control **3)** (beeinflussen) control, regulate ‹*process, activity, price, etc.*›; steer ‹*discussion etc.*›; influence ‹*opinion etc.*›
B *itr. V.* **1)** (im Fahrzeug) be at the wheel; (auf dem Schiff) be at the helm **2)** *mit sein* (Kurs nehmen, ugs.: sich hinbewegen; auch fig.) head **3)** (geh.: entgegenwirken) **jmdm./einer Sache ~:** curb sb./remedy sth.

steuer-, Steuer-: ~oase *die* (ugs.) tax haven; **~pflicht** *die* (Steuerw.) liability to [pay] tax; **~pflichtig** *Adj.* (Steuerw.) ‹*person*› liable to [pay] tax; taxable ‹*goods, assets, income, profits, etc.*›; **~pflichtige** *der/die; adj. Dekl.* (Steuerw.) person liable to [pay] tax; **~progression** *die* progressive taxation; **~prüfer** *der,* **~prüferin** *die* ▸ **Wirtschaftsprüfer;** **~pult** *das* (Elektrot.) ▸ **Schaltpult;** **~rad** *das* **1)** ▸ **Lenkrad;** **2)** (Seew.) [ship's] wheel; helm; **~recht** *das* tax law; **~rechtlich** *Adj.* (Steuerw.) under the tax laws *postpos.;* **~ruder** *das* (Seew.) rudder; **~satz** *der* (Steuerw.) tax rate; rate of tax; **~schätzung** *die* estimate of tax revenue[s]; **~schraube** *die:* **in die ~schraube anziehen/überdrehen** (ugs.) squeeze the taxpayer/squeeze the taxpayer too hard (coll.); **~schuld** *die* (Steuerw.) tax[es] owing *no indef. art.;* (Verpflichtung) tax liability; **~senkung** *die* (Steuerw.) tax cut; reduction in taxation; **~system** *das* (Technik) ▸ **Steuerung 1;** **~tabelle** *die* (Steuerw.) ≈ tax table

Steuerung *die;* **~, ~en** **1)** (System) controls *pl.;* **die automatische ~** (Flugw.) the automatic pilot; the autopilot **2)** ▸ **steuern A 1, 3, 4:** steering; piloting; flying; control; regulation; steering; influencing; **die ~ übernehmen** (Flugw.) take over the controls **3)** ▸ **Steuergerät 2**

Steuer-: ~verkürzung *die* (Steuerw.) tax evasion; **~vorteil** *der* (Steuerw.) tax advantage; **~zahler** *der;* **~~s, ~~,** **~zahlerin** *die;* **~~, ~~nen** taxpayer

Steven /'ʃte:vn̩/ *der;* **~s, ~** (Vorder~) stem; (Achter~) sternpost

Steward /'stju:ɐt/ *der;* **~s, ~s** ▸ⓘ **S. 113** steward

Stewardess, *Stewardeß /'stju:ɐdɛs/ *die;* **~, Stewardessen** ▸ⓘ **S. 113** stewardess

StGB *Abk.* **= Strafgesetzbuch**

stibitzen /ʃti'bɪtsn̩/ *tr. V.* (fam.) pinch (coll.); swipe (coll.)

stich /ʃtɪç/ *Imperativ Sg. v.* **stechen**

Stich *der;* **~[e]s, ~e** **1)** (mit einer Waffe) stab; (fig.: böse Bemerkung) dig; gibe **2)** (Dornen~, Nadel~) prick; (von Wespe, Biene, Skorpion usw.) sting; (Mücken~ usw.) bite **3)** (~wunde) stab wound **4)** (beim Nähen) stitch **5)** (Schmerz) stabbing *or* shooting *or* sharp pain; **es gab mir einen ~ [ins Herz]** (fig.) I was cut to the quick **6)** (Kartenspiel) trick **7)** **jmdn. im ~ lassen** leave sb. in the lurch; **mein Gedächtnis hat mich im ~ gelassen** my memory has failed me; **etw. im ~ lassen** abandon sth.; **~ halten** ‹*argument, alibi, etc.*› hold water **8)** (Fechten) hit **9)** (bild. Kunst) engraving **10)** (Farbschimmer) tinge; **ein ~ ins Blaue** a tinge of blue; **sie hat einen ~ ins Ordinäre** (fig.) she is a touch vulgar **11)** **einen [leichten] ~ haben** (ugs.) ‹*food, drink*› be off, have gone off; (salopp) ‹*person*› be nuts (coll.); be round the bend (coll.) **12)** (Kochk. landsch.) **ein ~ Butter** a knob of butter

Stichel *der;* **~s, ~:** graver; burin

Stichelei *die;* **~, ~en** (ugs. abwertend) **1)** (Bemerkung) dig; gibe **2)** **hör auf mit deiner ~:** stop getting at me/his *etc.* (coll.)

sticheln *itr. V.* **1)** (Anspielungen machen) make snide remarks (coll.) **(gegen** about) **2)** (nähen) sew; (sticken) embroider

stich-, Stich-: ~fest ▸ **hiebfest;** **~flamme** *die* tongue *or* jet of flame; **~|halten** (österr.) ▸ ~ **7;** **~haltig,** (österr.) **~hältig** **A** *Adj.* sound, valid ‹*argument, reason*›; valid ‹*assertion, reply*›; conclusive ‹*evidence*›; **dieses Argument ist nicht ~haltig** this argument doesn't hold water; **B** *adv.* **etw. ~haltig begründen** back sth. with sound *or* valid reasons; **~haltigkeit** *die;* **~~,** (österr.) **~hältigkeit** *die;* **~~:** ▸ **~haltig:** soundness; validity; conclusiveness; **~kampf** *der* (Sport) play-off **(um** for)

Stichling /'ʃtɪçlɪŋ/ *der;* **~s, ~e** stickleback

Stich-: ~probe *die* [random] sample; (bei Kontrollen) spot check; **~säge** *die* compass saw

stichst /ʃtɪçst/ *2. Pers. Sg. Präsens v.* **stechen**

Stich·straße *die* cul-de-sac

sticht /ʃtɪçt/ *3. Pers. Sg. Präsens v.* **stechen**

Stich-: ~tag *der* set date; (letzter Termin) deadline; **~waffe** *die* stabbing weapon; **~wahl** *die* final *or* deciding ballot; run-off; **~wort** *das* **1)** *Pl.* **~wörter** headword; (in Registern) entry; **2)** *Pl.* **~~e** (Theater) cue; **3)** *Pl.* **~~e** (Äußerung) cue **(zu** for); **4)** *Pl.* **~~e** (Gedächtnisstütze) keyword; (Notiz) note; **~wort-**

verzeichnis *das* [subject] index; **~wunde** *die* stab wound

Stick·arbeit *die* (Handarb.) piece of embroidery

sticken /ˈʃtɪkn̩/
A *itr. V.* do embroidery
B *tr. V.* embroider

Sticker[1] *der*; **~s, ~:** embroiderer

Sticker[2] /ˈstɪkɐ/ *der*; **~s, ~** (Aufkleber) sticker

Stickerei *die*; **~, ~en** (Handarb.) 1 (Verzierung) embroidery *no pl.*; embroidered pattern; **~en** embroidery *sing.* 2 (gestickte Arbeit) piece of embroidery

Stickerin *die*; **~, ~nen** embroiderer; embroideress

Stick·garn *das* embroidery thread

stickig *Adj.* stuffy; stale ‹air›

stick-, Stick-: ~luft *die* stale air; **~muster** *das* (Handarb.) embroidery pattern; **~oxid**, **~oxyd** *das* (Chemie) nitrogen oxide; **~rahmen** *der* embroidery frame; **~stoff** *der* nitrogen; **~stoff·haltig** *Adj.* nitrogenous; containing nitrogen *postpos.*; **~stoff·oxid**, **~stoff·oxyd** *das* (Chemie) nitrogen oxide

stieben /ˈʃtiːbn̩/ *unr.* (*auch regelm.*) *itr. V.* (geh., veralt.) 1 *auch mit sein* (auseinander wirbeln) ‹*dust, snow*› be thrown up in a cloud; ‹*sparks*› fly; ‹*water*› spray; **sie rannten davon, dass es nur so stiebte** you couldn't see them for dust 2 *mit sein* **Schnee stiebt durch die Ritzen** snow blows through the cracks 3 *mit sein* (davoneilen) dash; **nach allen Seiten ~:** scatter in all directions

Stief·bruder /ˈʃtiːf-/ *der* stepbrother; (ugs.: Halbbruder) half-brother

Stiefel /ˈʃtiːfl̩/ *der*; **~s, ~** 1 boot; **das sind zwei Paar ~** (fig.) they are totally different things; **er kann einen [tüchtigen** *od.* **gehörigen] ~ vertragen** (ugs.) he can really put away the beer (coll.) 2 **einen ~ zusammenreden/-schreiben** (ugs. abwertend) talk/write a lot of nonsense *or* a load of rubbish; **seinen** *od.* **den [alten] ~ weitermachen** (ugs.) carry on in the same old way

Stiefelette /ʃtiːfəˈlɛtə/ *die*; **~, ~n** ankle boot

Stiefel·knecht *der* bootjack

stiefeln *itr. V.*; *mit sein* (ugs.) stride

Stiefel·schaft *der* boot leg; leg of a/the boot

stief-, Stief-: ~eltern *Pl.* step-parents; **~geschwister** *Pl.* 1 stepbrother[s] and [step]sister[s]; (ugs.: Halbgeschwister) half-brother[s] and -sister[s]; **~kind** *das* stepchild; (fig.) poor relation (fig.); **sie ist ein ~kind des Glücks** (geh.) she's always having bad luck; **~mutter** *die*; *Pl.* **~mütter** stepmother; **~mütterchen** *das* (Bot.) pansy; **~mütterlich** A *Adj.* poor, shabby ‹*treatment*›; B *adv.* **~mütterlich behandeln** treat ‹*person*› poorly *or* shabbily; neglect ‹*pet, flowers, doll, problem*›; **~schwester** die stepsister; (ugs.: Halbschwester) half-sister; **~sohn** *der* stepson; **~tochter** *die* stepdaughter; **~vater** *der* stepfather

stieg /ʃtiːk/ *1. u. 3. Pers. Sg. Prät. v.* **steigen**

Stiege[1] *die*; **~, ~n** 1 (Holztreppe) [wooden] staircase; [wooden] stairs *pl.* 2 (südd., österr.: Treppe) stairs *pl.*; steps *pl.* 3 (Kiste für Gemüse, Obst) [wooden] box; (größer) [wooden] crate

Stiege[2] *die*; **~, ~n** (nordd. veralt.) score

Stiegen·haus *das* (südd., österr.) ▸ **Treppenhaus**

Stieglitz /ˈʃtiːglɪts/ *der*; **~es, ~e** goldfinch

stiehl /ʃtiːl/ *Imperativ Sg. v.* **stehlen**

stiehlst *2. Pers. Sg. Präsens v.* **stehlen**

stiehlt *3. Pers. Sg. Präsens v.* **stehlen**

stiekum /ˈʃtiːkʊm/ *Adv.* (ugs.) secretly; on the quiet

Stiel /ʃtiːl/ *der*; **~[e]s, ~e** 1 (Griff) handle; (Besen~) [broom]stick; (für Süßigkeiten) stick; **ein Eis am ~:** an ice lolly (Brit.); a Popsicle (*Amer.* ®) 2 (bei Gläsern) stem 3 (bei Blumen) stem; stalk; (an Obst, Obstblüten usw.) stalk

Stiel-: ~auge *das* stalked eye; **er machte** *od.* **bekam ~augen** (ugs. scherzh.) (erstaunt) his eyes nearly popped out of his head; he stared goggle-eyed; (begehrlich) his eyes stood out on stalks; **~kamm** *der* tail comb; **~stich** *der* (Handarb.) stem stitch

stier
A *Adj.* vacant
B *adv.* vacantly

Stier /ʃtiːɐ̯/ *der*; **~[e]s, ~e** 1 bull; **brüllen wie ein ~:** bellow like a bull; **den ~ bei den Hörnern fassen** *od.* **packen** take the bull by the horns 2 (Astrol.) Taurus; the Bull; **er/sie ist [ein] ~:** he/she is a Taurus *or* Taurean

stieren *itr. V.* stare [vacantly] (**auf** + *Akk.* at); **in die Luft** *od.* **vor sich hin ~:** stare [vacantly] into space

Stier-: ~kampf *der* bullfight; **~kämpfer** *der* bullfighter; **~nacken** *der* (fig.) bull neck

Stiesel /ˈʃtiːzl̩/ *der*; **~s, ~** (ugs.: abwertend) boor; churl

stieß /ʃtiːs/ *1. u. 3. Pers. Sg. Prät. v.* **stoßen**

Stift[1] /ʃtɪft/ *der*; **~[e]s, ~e** 1 (aus Metall) pin; (aus Holz) peg 2 (Blei~, Bunt~, Zeichen~) pencil; (Mal~) crayon; (Schreib~) pen 3 (ugs.: Lehrling) apprentice

Stift[2] *das*; **~[e]s, ~e** 1 (christl. Kirche: Institution) foundation 2 (österr.: Kloster) monastery 3 (Schule) seminary; (für Mädchen) convent [school] 4 (Altenheim) home for elderly gentlewomen

stiften
A *tr. V.* 1 found, establish ‹*monastery, hospital, prize, etc.*›; endow ‹*prize, professorship, scholarship*›; (als Spende) donate, give (**für** to) 2 (herbeiführen) cause, create ‹*unrest, confusion, strife, etc.*›; bring about ‹*peace, order, etc.*›; arrange ‹*marriage*›
B *in* **~ gehen** (ugs.) disappear; hop it (coll.); do a bunk (coll.)

***stiften|gehen** ▸ **stiften B**

Stifter *der*; **~s, ~:** founder; (Spender) donor

Stifter·figur *die* (bild. Kunst) likeness of the founder/donor

Stifterin *die*; **~, ~nen** ▸ **Stifter**

Stifts-: ~hütte *die* (jüd. Rel.) tabernacle; **~kirche** *die* collegiate church

Stiftung *die*; **~, ~en** 1 (Rechtsspr.) foundation; endowment 2 (Anstalt) foundation 3 (Spende) donation (*Gen.* by) 4 (das Spenden) donation (*Gen.*, **von** of)

Stift·zahn *der* (Zahnmed.) post crown

Stigma /ˈstɪgma/ *das*; **~s, Stigmen** *od.* **~ta** (auch fig., kath. Kirche) stigma

Stigmatisation /stɪgmatizaˈtsi̯oːn/ *die*; **~, ~en** stigmatization

stigmatisieren *tr. V.* stigmatize

Stigmen ▸ **Stigma**

-stil *der* style of …; **Schreib~:** style of writing

Stil /ʃtiːl/ *der*; **~[e]s, ~e** 1 style; **einen flüssigen ~ schreiben** write in a flowing style; **das ist schlechter politischer ~:** that is bad form politically; **in dem ~ ging es weiter** (ugs.) it went on in that vein; **im großen** *od.* **in großem ~:** on a grand scale 2 **alten/neuen ~s** according to the old *or* Julian calendar/new *or* Gregorian calendar

stil-, Stil-: ~bildend *Adj.* that influences *or* shapes style *postpos., not pred.*; **~bildend wirken** influence *or* shape style; **~blüte** *die* howler (coll.); **~bruch** *der* inconsistency of style; **~ebene** *die* style level; **~echt** A *Adj.* period *attrib.* ‹*furniture*›; B *adv.* true to style; **~element** *das* stylistic element

Stilett /ʃtiˈlɛt/ *das*; **~s, ~e** stiletto

Stil·gefühl *das* sense of *or* feeling for style

stilisieren *tr. V.* stylize

Stilisierung *die*; **~, ~en** stylization

Stilist *der*; **~en, ~en** stylist

Stilistik *die*; **~, ~en** 1 (Lehre) stylistics *sing., no art.* 2 (Buch) book on stylistics

Stilistin *die*; **~, ~nen** stylist

stilistisch
A *Adj.* stylistic
B *adv.* stylistically

Stil·kunde *die* ▸ **Stilistik 1, 2**

still /ʃtɪl/
A *Adj.* 1 (ruhig, leise) quiet; (ganz ohne Geräusche) silent; still; quiet, peaceful ‹*valley, area, etc.*›; **sei ~!** be quiet!; **im Saal wurde es ~:** the hall went quiet; **um ihn ist es ~ geworden** (fig.) you don't hear much about him any more; **in ~em Gedenken** in loving memory 2 (reglos) still; **~es [Mineral-/Tafel-]wasser** still [mineral/table] water 3 (ohne Aufregung, Hektik) quiet ‹*day, life*›; quiet, calm ‹*manner*›; **in einer ~en Stunde** in a quiet moment 4 (nicht gesprächig) quiet; *s. auch* **Wasser 2** 5 (wortlos) silent ‹*reproach, grief, etc.*› 6 (heimlich) secret; **im Stillen** in secret; **~e Reserven** (Wirtsch.) secret *or* hidden reserves; (ugs.) [secret] savings 7 **der Stille Ozean** the Pacific [Ocean]
B *adv.* 1 (ruhig, leise) quietly; (geräuschlos) silently 2 (zurückhaltend) quietly 3 (wortlos) in silence

Still /stɪl/ *das*; **~s, ~s** (DV) still

Still-BH *der* nursing bra

Stille *die*; **~** 1 (Ruhe) quiet; (Geräuschlosigkeit) silence; stillness; **in der ~ der Nacht** in the still of the night; **tiefe ~:** deep silence; **gefräßige ~** (scherzh.) silence of people too busy eating to talk 2 (Regungslosigkeit) (des Meeres) calm[ness]; (der Luft) stillness 3 **in aller ~ heiraten** have a quiet wedding; **die Beerdigung fand in aller ~ statt** it was a quiet funeral

***Stilleben** ▸ **Stillleben**

***stillegen** ▸ **stilllegen**

***Stillegung** ▸ **Stilllegung**

stillen
A *tr. V.* 1 **ein Kind ~:** breastfeed a baby; **ich muss das Baby jetzt ~:** I must feed the baby *or* give the baby a feed now 2 (befriedigen) satisfy ‹*hunger, desire, curiosity*›; quench ‹*thirst*›; still (literary) ‹*hunger, thirst, desire*› 3 (eindämmen) stop ‹*bleeding, tears, pain*›; staunch ‹*blood*›
B *itr. V.* breastfeed; **~de Mütter** nursing mothers

Still·halte·abkommen *das* (Polit., Finanzw.) moratorium; standstill agreement

still|halten *unr. itr. V.* 1 (sich nicht bewegen) keep *or* stay still 2 (nicht reagieren) keep quiet

still-, Still-: ~leben *das* (bild. Kunst) still life; **~|legen** *tr. V.* close *or* shut down; close ‹*railway line*›; lay up ‹*ship, vehicle, fleet*› **eine ~gelegte Bahn** a disused railway; **~legung** *die*; **~~, ~~en** closure; shut-down; (von Schiff, Fahrzeug, Flotte) laying up; (einer Eisenbahnstrecke) closure

stil·los
A *Adj.* 1 (ohne Stil) lacking *or* without any definite *or* recognizable style *postpos.* 2 (gegen den Stil) in bad *or* poor style *postpos.*; lacking in style *postpos.*; styleless; **Wein aus Biergläsern zu trinken ist ~:** drinking wine out of beer glasses shows a lack of style
B *adv.* 1 (ohne Stil) without any definite *or* recognizable style 2 (gegen den Stil) in bad *or* poor style; stylelessly

Stillosigkeit *die*; **~, ~en** 1 lack of any definite *or* recognizable style 2 ▸ **stillos 2**: bad *or* poor style; lack of style; stylelessness 3 (stilloses Verhalten) [piece of] styleless behaviour

still-, Still-: ~schweigen *das* 1 (Schweigen) silence; **mit ~schweigen** in silence; 2 (Diskretion) **~schweigen bewahren** maintain silence; keep silent; **~schweigend** A *Adj.* 1 (wortlos) silent; 2 (ohne Abmachung) tacit ‹*assumption, agreement*›; B *adv.* 1 (wortlos) in silence; 2 (ohne Abmachung) tacitly; **das Projekt wurde ~schweigend eingestellt** the project was quietly shelved; **~|sitzen** *unr. itr. V.* sit still; **~stand** *der* standstill; **den Motor/die Entzündung/den Zug/den Verkehr zum ~stand bringen** stop the engine/inflammation/train/bring the traffic to a standstill; **die Blutung ist zum ~stand gekommen** the bleeding has stopped; **~|stehen** *unr. itr. V.* 1 ‹*factory, machine*› be *or* stand idle; ‹*traffic*› be at a standstill; ‹*heart etc.*› stop; **ihr Mundwerk steht nie ~** (ugs.) she never stops talking; **die Zeit schien ~zustehen** time seemed to stand still; 2 (Milit.) stand at *or* to attention;

S

~gestanden! attention!

Stillung *die;* ~ ▸**stillen A 2, 3**: satisfying; quenching; stilling (literary); stopping; staunching; relieving

still·vergnügt
A *Adj.* inwardly contented
B *adv.* ‹*listen, smile, etc.*› with inner contentment

Still·zeit *die* lactation period

stil-, Stil-: ~mittel *das* stylistic device; **~mix** *der* mixture of styles; **~möbel** *das* piece of period furniture; **französische ~möbel** French period furniture *sing.*; **~richtung** *die* style; **~voll A** *Adj.* stylish; **B** *adv.* stylishly

stimm-, Stimm-: ~abgabe *die* voting *no art.*; **zur ~abgabe erscheinen** come to vote *or* to cast one's vote; **~band** *das; Pl.* **~bänder** vocal cord; **~berechtigt** *Adj.* entitled to vote *postpos.*; **~bruch** *der:* **er ist im ~bruch** his voice is breaking; **~bürger** *der* (schweiz.) voter; elector

Stimmchen *das;* **~s, ~:** little *or* small voice

Stimme /ˈʃtɪmə/ *die;* **~, ~n 1** voice; **die ~ des Blutes** (fig.) the call of the blood; **der ~ der Vernunft folgen** (fig.) listen to the voice of reason; **der ~ des Herzens/Gewissens folgen** (fig. geh.) follow [the dictates of] one's heart/conscience; **mit stockender ~:** in a faltering voice; **mit halber ~ singen** sing at half-power; **gut/nicht bei ~ sein** be in good/bad voice **2** (Meinung) voice; **die ~n in der Presse waren kritisch** press opinion was critical **3** (bei Wahlen, auch Stimmrecht) vote

stimmen
A *itr. V.* **1** (zutreffen) be right *or* correct; **stimmt es, dass ...?** is it true that ...?; **das kann unmöglich ~:** that can't possibly be right; **stimmts, oder hab ich Recht?** (ugs. scherzh.) am I not right? **2** (in Ordnung sein) ‹*bill, invoice, etc.*› be right *or* correct; **stimmt so** that's all right; keep the change; **hier stimmt etwas nicht** there's something wrong here; **bei ihm stimmt es** *od.* **etwas nicht** (salopp) there must be something wrong with him **3** (seine Stimme geben) vote; **mit Ja ~:** vote yes *or* in favour
B *tr. V.* **1** (in eine Stimmung versetzen) make; **das stimmt mich traurig** that makes me [feel] sad; **sentimental gestimmt sein** be feeling sentimental **2** (Musik) tune ‹*instrument*›; **eine Gitarre höher/tiefer ~:** raise/lower the pitch of a guitar

Stimmen-: ~fang *der* vote-catching *no art.*; **er ist auf ~fang** he is out to catch votes; **~gewinn** *der* gain in votes; **~gewirr** *das* babble of voices; **~gleichheit** *die* tied vote; tie; **bei ~gleichheit** in the event of a tied vote *or* a tie; **~kauf** *der* vote-buying *no art.*; buying votes *no art.*; **~mehrheit** *die* majority [of votes]

Stimm·enthaltung *die* abstention; **~ üben** abstain; **bei vier ~en angenommen** accepted with four abstentions

Stimmen·verlust *der* loss of votes; **~e erleiden** lose votes

Stimm·gabel *die* (Musik) tuning fork

stimm·gewaltig
A *Adj.* ‹*singer etc.*› with a strong *or* powerful voice; strong, powerful ‹*bass, contralto, etc.*›
B *adv.* ‹*sing, speak*› with *or* in a strong *or* powerful voice

stimmhaft (Sprachw.)
A *Adj.* voiced
B *adv.* **~ gesprochen werden** be voiced

stimmig *Adj.* harmonious; **die Argumentation ist [in sich** *(Dat.)***] ~:** the argument is consistent

Stimm·lage *die* **1** voice **2** (Musik) voice; register

stimmlich
A *Adj.* vocal
B *adv.* vocally

stimm-, Stimm-: ~los (Sprachw.) **A** *Adj.* voiceless; unvoiced; **B** *adv.* **~los ausgesprochen werden** not be voiced; **~recht** *das* right to vote; **~um·fang** *der* vocal range

Stimmung *die;* **~, ~en 1** mood; **er ist in gereizter ~:** he is in a very touchy mood; **in ~ sein** be in a good mood; **in ~ kommen** get in the mood; liven up; **jmdn. in ~ bringen** liven sb. up; **jmdm. die ~ verderben** spoil sb.'s [good] mood; **nicht in der [rechten] ~ sein, etw. zu tun** not be in the [right] mood to do sth.; **~en unterworfen sein** be moody; **für gute ~ sorgen** ensure a good atmosphere **2** (Atmosphäre) atmosphere **3** (öffentliche Meinung) opinion; **~ für/gegen jmdn./etw. machen** stir up [public] opinion in favour of/against sb./sth. **4** (Musik) pitch

stimmungs-, Stimmungs-: ~barometer *das:* **in das ~barometer steht auf null** (ugs.) the mood is bleak; **~bild** *das:* **ein ~bild von dem Ball geben** report on the atmosphere at the ball; **~kanone** *die* (ugs. scherzh.) entertainer who is always the life and soul of the party; **~umschwung** *der* change of mood; **~voll A** *Adj.* atmospheric; **B** *adv.* ‹*describe, light*› atmospherically; ‹*sing, recite*› with great feeling; **~wandel** *der* change of mood; (Meinungswandel) change of opinion

Stimm-: ~vieh *das* (abwertend) **für ihn sind die Wähler doch nur ~vieh** he sees voters as nothing more than a means of getting to power; **~zettel** *der* ballot paper

Stimulans /ˈstiːmulans/ *das;* **~, Stimulanzien** *od.* **Stimulantia** /stimuˈlantsi̯a/ (auch fig.) stimulant

Stimuli ▸**Stimulus**

stimulieren *tr. V.* stimulate

Stimulus /ˈstiːmulʊs/ *der;* **~, Stimuli** (Psych., fig.) stimulus (**für** to)

stink-, Stink- (salopp) stinking (sl.) ‹*drunk, mood*›; terribly (coll.) ‹*bourgeois, posh*›

Stink·bombe *die* stink bomb

Stinke·finger *der* (ugs.) *middle finger pointing up as a gesture of abuse, contempt, etc.*; **jmdm. den ~ zeigen** give sb. a one-finger salute (coll.)

stinken /ˈʃtɪŋkn̩/ *unr. itr. V.* **1** (abwertend) stink; pong (coll.); **nach etw. ~:** stink *or* reek of sth.; **es stinkt nach Chemikalien/faulen Eiern** there's a stink *or* reek *or* stench of chemicals/bad eggs; **nach Geld ~** (fig. ugs.) be stinking rich (coll.); **vor Faulheit/Selbstgerechtigkeit ~** (fig. ugs.) be bone idle (coll.)/appallingly self-righteous **2** (ugs.: Schlechtes vermuten lassen) **die Sache/es stinkt** it smells; it's fishy (coll.) **3** (salopp: missfallen) **die Hausarbeit stinkt mir** I'm fed up to the back teeth with housework (coll.); **mir stinkts** I'm fed up to the back teeth (sl.)

stink·faul *Adj.* (salopp abwertend) bone idle (coll.)

stinkig *Adj.* (salopp abwertend) **1** (stinkend) stinking; smelly **2** (widerwärtig) vile (coll.), stinking (coll.) ‹*mood*›; **du bist heute so ~** (fig.) you're in such a vile *or* stinking mood today

stink-, Stink-: ~langweilig (ugs.) **A** *Adj.* deadly boring; **B** *adv.* in a deadly boring way; **~morchel** *die* (Bot.) stinkhorn; **~normal** (salopp) **A** *Adj.* dead (coll.) *or* boringly ordinary; **B** *adv.* in a dead ordinary way (coll.); **~reich** *Adj.* (salopp) stinking rich (coll.); **~tier** *das* skunk; **~vornehm** *Adj.* (salopp) terribly posh (coll.); **~wut** *die* (salopp) towering rage; **eine ~wut [auf jmdn.] haben** be livid (Brit. coll.) *or* furious [with sb.]

Stint /ʃtɪnt/ *der;* **~[e]s, ~e 1** (Fisch) smelt **2** (nordd.: Junge) boy; lad

Stipendiat /ʃtipɛnˈdi̯aːt/ *der;* **~en, ~en, Stipendiatin** *die;* **~, ~nen** person receiving a scholarship/grant

Stipendium /ʃtiˈpɛndi̯ʊm/ *das;* **~s, Stipendien** (als Auszeichnung) scholarship; (als finanzielle Unterstützung) grant

Stippe *die;* **~, ~n** (bes. nordd.) [thick] gravy

stippen /ˈʃtɪpn̩/ *tr. V.* (bes. nordd.) dunk

Stipp·visite *die* (ugs.) flying visit

stipulieren /stipuˈliːrən/ *tr. V.* establish; lay down; (als Bedingung) stipulate

stirb /ʃtɪrp/ *Imperativ Sg. v.* **sterben**

stirbst *2. Pers. Sg. Präsens v.* **sterben**

stirbt *3. Pers. Sg. Präsens v.* **sterben**

Stirn /ʃtɪrn/ *die;* **~, ~en** ▸**❶ S. 435** forehead; brow; **sich** *(Dat.)* **die Haare aus der ~ kämmen** comb one's hair from one's forehead; **jmdm./einer Sache die ~ bieten** (fig.) stand *or* face up to sb./sth.; **die ~ haben, etw. zu tun** (fig.) have the nerve *or* gall to do sth.; **jmdm. an** *od.* **auf der ~ geschrieben stehen** (geh.) be written in *or* all over sb.'s face

Stirn-: ~band *das; Pl.* **~bänder** headband; **~bein** *das* ▸**❶ S. 435** (Anat.) frontal bone

Stirne *die;* **~, ~n** ▸**Stirn**

Stirn-: ~falte *die* wrinkle [on one's forehead]; **~höhle** *die* ▸**❶ S. 435** (Anat.) frontal sinus; **~höhlen·vereiterung** *die* suppurative *or* purulent frontal sinusitis; **~locke** *die* quiff (Brit.); cowlick; **~rad** *das* (Technik) spur wheel; spur gear; **~runzeln** *das;* **~~s** frown; **mit ~runzeln** with a frown; **~seite** *die* front [side]

stob /ʃtoːp/ *1. u. 3. Pers. Sg. Prät. v.* **stieben**

stöbern /ˈʃtøːbɐn/ *itr. V.* (ugs.) rummage

Stochastik *die* stochastic theory

stochastisch *Adj.* stochastic

stochern /ˈʃtɔxɐn/ *itr. V.* poke; **sich** *(Dat.)* **in den Zähnen ~:** pick one's teeth; **mit dem Feuerhaken im Feuer ~:** poke the fire; **im Essen ~:** pick at one's food

Stock[1] /ʃtɔk/ *der;* **~[e]s, Stöcke** /ˈʃtœkə/ **1** (Ast, Spazier~) stick; (Zeige~) pointer; stick; (Takt~) baton; **steif wie ein ~:** as stiff as a poker; **den ~ gebrauchen/zu spüren bekommen** use/get the stick *or* cane; **am ~ gehen** walk with a stick; (ugs.: erschöpft sein) be whacked (Brit. coll.) *or* dead beat; (ugs.: finanzielle Schwierigkeiten haben) be [completely] broke (coll.) **2** (Ski~) pole; stick **3** (Pflanze) (Rosen~) [rose] bush; (Reb~) vine **4** (Eishockey, Hockey, Rollhockey) stick **5** (veralt.: Baumstumpf) stump [and roots]; **über ~ und Stein** over hedge and ditch

Stock[2] *der;* **~[e]s, ~** (Etage) floor; storey; **das Haus hat vier ~:** the house is four storeys high; **in welchem ~?** on which floor?; **im fünften ~:** on the fifth (Brit.) *or* (Amer.) sixth floor

stock-: ~besoffen *Adj.* (derb) pissed as a newt/as newts *pred.* (sl.); blind drunk; **~blind** *Adj.* (ugs.) as blind as a bat *pred.* (coll.); totally blind

Stöckchen /ˈʃtœkçən/ *das;* **~s, ~:** little stick

stock·dunkel *Adj.* (ugs.) pitch-dark

Stöckel·absatz *der* high *or* stiletto heel

stöckeln /ˈʃtœkl̩n/ *itr. V.; mit sein* (ugs.) totter [on high heels]

Stöckel·schuh *der* high- *or* stiletto-heeled shoe; **~e** high heels; high- *or* stiletto-heeled shoes

stocken *itr. V.* **1** (aussetzen, stillstehen) **ihm stockte das Herz/der Puls** his heart/pulse missed *or* skipped a beat; **ihm stockte der Atem** he caught his breath; **das Blut stockte ihm in den Adern** (fig.) the blood froze in his veins **2** (unterbrochen sein) ‹*traffic*› be held up, come to a halt; ‹*conversation, production*› stop; ‹*business*› slacken *or* drop off; ‹*journey*› be interrupted; **die Antwort kam ~d** he/she gave a hesitant reply; **ins Stocken geraten** ‹*traffic*› be held up, come to a halt; ‹*conversation, production*› stop; ‹*talks, negotiations, etc.*› grind to a halt **3** (innehalten) falter; **er sprach ein wenig ~d** he faltered a little **4** *auch mit sein* (bes. südd., österr., schweiz.: gerinnen) ‹*milk*› curdle

stock-, Stock-: ~ente *die* mallard; **~finster** *Adj.* (ugs.) pitch-dark; **~fisch** *der* **1** stockfish; **2** (ugs. abwertend: Mensch) boring *or* dull old stick; **~fleck** *der* mildew *or* mould spot; **~fleckig** *Adj.* mildewed; mouldy

stockig *Adj.* **1** (muffig) musty ‹*clothes, smell, etc.*› **2** (stockfleckig) mildewed; mouldy

-stöckig /ʃtœkɪç/ -storey *attr.*; -storeyed

stock-, Stock-: ~konservativ *Adj.* (ugs.) arch-conservative; **~nüchtern** *Adj.* (ugs.) stone-cold sober; **~sauer** *Adj.* (salopp) pissed off (Brit. sl.) (**auf** + *Akk.* with); **~schirm** *der* walking-length umbrella; **~schnupfen** *der* heavy cold; **~steif** (ugs.) **A** *Adj.* extremely

S

stiff ‹*gait*›; B *adv.* extremely stiffly; as stiff as a poker; **~taub** *Adj.* (ugs.) stone deaf; as deaf as a post

Stockung *die;* ~, ~en 1 (Unterbrechung) hold-up (+ *Gen.* in) 2 (des Pulses, der Atmung) stoppage

Stockwerk *das* floor; storey; **im dritten ~:** on the third (Brit.) *or* (Amer.) fourth floor; **ein Haus mit fünf ~en** a five-storey[ed] house

Stoff /ʃtɔf/ *der;* **~[e]s, ~e** 1 (für Textilien) material; fabric 2 (Materie) substance 3 (Philos.) matter 4 (Thema) subject [matter]; **~ für einen Roman sammeln** collect material for a novel; **einen ~ in der Schule durchnehmen** do a subject at school 5 (Gesprächsthema) topic; **viel ~ zum Nachdenken** much food for thought 6 (salopp: Alkohol) booze (coll.) 7 (salopp: Rauschgift) stuff (sl.); dope (sl.)

Stoff·druck *der* textile printing

Stoffel /ˈʃtɔfl̩/ *der;* **~s, ~** (ugs. abwertend) boor; churl

stoffelig *Adj.* (ugs. abwertend) boorish; churlish

stofflich *Adj.* 1 (materiell) material 2 (thematisch) thematic ‹*effect etc.*›; **die ~e Fülle des Buches** the richness *or* breadth of the book's subject matter

Stofflichkeit *die;* **~:** materiality

Stoff-: **~muster** *das* 1 (Zeichnung) pattern; 2 (kleines Stück) swatch; sample of material; **~puppe** *die* rag doll; **~rest** *der* remnant; **~wechsel** *der* metabolism; **~wechsel·krankheit** *die* ▸❶ S. 439 metabolic disease; **~wechsel·produkt** *das* product of metabolism

stöhnen /ˈʃtøːnən/ *itr. V.* moan; (vor Schmerz) groan

Stoiker /ˈʃtoːikɐ/ *der;* **~s, ~, Stoikerin** *die;* **~, ~nen** (Philos.) Stoic; (fig.) stoic

stoisch

A *Adj.* (Philos.) Stoic; (fig.) stoic

B *adv.* stoically

Stoizismus *der;* ~ (Philos.) Stoicism *no art.;* (fig.) stoicism

Stola /ˈʃtoːla/ *die;* **~, Stolen** 1 shawl; (Pelz~) stole 2 (bes. kath. Kirche) stole

Stolle *die;* **~, ~n** (bes. nordd.) stollen

Stollen /ˈʃtɔlən/ *der;* **~s, ~** 1 (Kuchen) Stollen 2 (unterirdischer Gang) gallery; tunnel 3 (Bergbau) gallery 4 (bei Sportschuhen) stud 5 (beim Hufeisen) caulk 6 (Verslehre) stollen (in Meistergesang)

stolpern /ˈʃtɔlpɐn/ *itr. V.; mit sein* 1 stumble; trip; **ins Stolpern kommen** stumble; trip; (fig.) lose one's thread; **über jmdn. ~** (fig. ugs.) bump *or* run into sb.; **ich bin über dieses Wort/diesen Satz gestolpert** (fig.) I was puzzled by that word/sentence 2 (fig.: straucheln) come to grief, (coll.) come unstuck (**über** + *Akk.* over)

Stolper·stein *der* stumbling block; **jmdm. ~e in den Weg legen** put obstacles in sb.'s way

stolz /ʃtɔlts/

A *Adj.* 1 proud (**auf** + *Akk.* of) 2 (überheblich) proud[-hearted]; **warum so ~?** don't you know me any more? 3 (imposant) proud ‹*building, castle, ship, etc.*› 4 (ugs.: beträchtlich) steep (coll.), hefty (coll.) ‹*price*›; tidy (coll.) ‹*sum*›; **~ wie ein Spanier** as proud as can be; **~ wie ein Pfau** as proud as a peacock

B *adv.* proudly

Stolz *der;* **~es** 1 pride; **sie setzte ihren ganzen ~ daran** she made it a point of pride 2 (Freude über etw.) pride (**auf** + *Akk.* in); **die Rosen sind sein ganzer ~:** his roses are his pride and joy

stolzgeschwellt /-gəʃvɛlt/ *Adj.* **mit ~er Brust** his/her breast swelling with pride

stolzieren *itr. V.; mit sein* strut

stop /stɔp/ *Interj.* stop; (Verkehrsw.) halt

***Stop** ▸**Stopp**

Stopf·ei *das* darning egg

stopfen /ˈʃtɔpfn̩/

A *tr. V.* 1 darn ‹*socks, coat, etc., hole*› 2 (hineintun) stuff; **jmdm./sich etwas in den Mund ~:** stuff sth. into sb.'s/one's mouth; **die ganze Familie ins Auto ~** (ugs.) cram the whole family into the car 3 (füllen) stuff ‹*cushion, quilt, etc.*›; fill ‹*pipe*›; **der Saal war gestopft voll** (fig. südd.) the hall was cram-full 4 (ausfüllen, verschließen) plug, stop [up] ‹*hole, leak*›; **jmdm. das Maul ~** (salopp) shut sb. up; **er hat fünf hungrige Mäuler zu ~** (fig. ugs.) he has five hungry mouths to feed 5 (mästen) stuff, cram ‹*poultry*›

B *itr. V.* 1 (den Stuhlgang hemmen) cause constipation 2 (ugs.: sehr sättigen) be very filling

Stopfen *der;* **~s, ~** (bes. westmd.) stopper; (Korken) cork

Stopf-: **~garn** *das* darning cotton *or* thread; **~nadel** *die* darning needle

Stopover /ˈstɔplouvɐ/ *der;* **~s, ~s** stopover

Stopp *der;* **~s, ~s** 1 (das Anhalten) stop; **ohne ~:** without stopping; **die Fahrer mussten zum ~ an die Boxen** the drivers had to make a pit stop 2 (Einstellung) freeze (*Gen.* on) 3 ▸**Stopp·ball**

Stopp·ball *der* (Badminton, [Tisch]tennis) drop shot

Stoppel[1] /ˈʃtɔpl̩/ *die;* **~, ~n** (auch Bart~) piece of stubble; **~n** *Pl.* stubble *sing.*

Stoppel[2] *der;* **~s, ~[n]** (österr.) stopper; (Korken) cork

Stoppel-: **~bart** *der* (ugs.) stubble; **~feld** *das* stubble field

stoppelig *Adj.* stubbly

stoppen

A *tr. V.* 1 stop; **den Ball ~** (Fußball) trap *or* stop the ball; **er war nicht mehr zu ~** (fig.) there was no stopping him 2 time ‹*athlete, run*›; **ich habe 11 Sekunden/103 km/h gestoppt** I made the time 11 seconds/the speed 103 k.p.h

B *itr. V.* stop; **der Angriff stoppte** (fig.) the attack got no further *or* fizzled out

Stopper *der;* **~s, ~, Stopperin** *die;* **~, ~nen** (Fußball) centre half; stopper

Stopp·licht *das; Pl.* **~er** stop light

stopplig *Adj.* ▸**stoppelig**

Stopp-: **~schild** *das* stop sign; **~signal** *das* stop signal; signal to stop; **~straße** *die* side road; road with a stop sign/stop signs; **~uhr** *die* stopwatch

Stöpsel /ˈʃtœpsl̩/ *der;* **~s, ~** 1 plug; (einer Karaffe usw.) stopper 2 (Elektrot.) [jack] plug

stöpseln (Fernspr.)

A *tr. V.* **jmdm. eine Verbindung ~:** put sb. through (**nach** to)

B *itr. V.* operate the plugs

Stör /ʃtøːɐ̯/ *der;* **~s, ~e** sturgeon

stör·anfällig *Adj.* susceptible to faults *postpos.*; liable to break down *postpos.*; (fig.) liable to break down *postpos.*

Storch /ʃtɔrç/ *der;* **~[e]s, Störche** /ˈʃtœrçə/ stork; **wie ein ~ im Salat gehen** walk clumsily and stiff-leggedly; **da brat mir einer einen ~** (ugs.) well, I'll be damned (coll.)

Storchen·nest *das* stork's nest

Storch·schnabel *der* 1 (Pflanze) cranesbill 2 (Zeichenhilfe) pantograph

Store /ʃtoːɐ̯/ *der;* **~s, ~s** net curtain

stören

A *tr. V.* 1 (behindern) disturb; disrupt ‹*court proceedings, lecture, church service, etc.*›; **bitte lassen Sie sich nicht ~:** please don't let me disturb you; **jmdn. in seiner Ordnung ~:** upset sb.'s routine 2 (stark beeinträchtigen) disturb ‹*relation, security, law and order, peaceful atmosphere, etc.*›; interfere with ‹*transmitter, reception*›; (absichtlich) jam ‹*transmitter*›; **ein gutes Verhältnis ~:** spoil a good relationship; **hier ist der Empfang oft gestört** there is often interference [with reception] here 3 (missfallen) bother; **das stört mich nicht** I don't mind; that doesn't bother me; **das stört mich an ihr** that's what I don't like about her; **stört es Sie, wenn ich das Fenster aufmache?** do you mind *or* will it bother you if I open the window?

B *itr. V.* 1 **darf ich reinkommen, oder störe ich?** may I come in, or am I disturbing you?; **entschuldigen Sie bitte, dass** *od.* **wenn ich störe** I'm sorry to bother you; **bitte nicht ~!** [please] do not disturb; **wenn ich störe, müsst ihr es mir sagen!** if I'm in the way, you must tell me; **sein Verhalten/seine Anwesenheit empfinde ich als ~d** I find his behaviour/presence irritating *or* annoying; **der Lärm machte sich sehr ~d bemerkbar** the noise was very intrusive 2 (als Mangel empfunden werden) spoil the effect 3 (Unruhe stiften) make *or* cause trouble

C *refl. V.* **sich an jmdm./etw. ~:** take exception to sb./sth.

Störenfried /ˈʃtøːrənfriːt/ *der;* **~[e]s, ~e** (abwertend) troublemaker

Störer *der;* **~s, ~, Störerin** *die;* **~, ~nen** troublemaker

Stör-: **~faktor** *der* disruptive factor *or* influence; **~fall** *der* (Technik) fault

stornieren *tr. V.* 1 (Finanzw., Kaufmannsspr.) reverse ‹*wrong entry*› 2 (Kaufmannsspr.) cancel ‹*order, contract*›

Storno /ˈʃtɔrno/ *der od. das;* **~s, Storni** (Finanzw., Kaufmannsspr.) reversal

störrisch /ˈʃtœrɪʃ/

A *Adj.* stubborn; obstinate; refractory ‹*child, horse*›; unmanageable ‹*hair*›; **~ wie ein Esel** as stubborn as a mule

B *adv.* stubbornly; obstinately

Stör·sender *der* jammer

Störung *die;* **~, ~en** 1 disturbance; (einer Gerichtsverhandlung, Vorlesung, eines Gottesdienstes) disruption; **bitte entschuldigen Sie die ~, aber ...** I'm sorry to bother you, but ... 2 (Beeinträchtigung) disturbance; disruption; **eine technische ~:** a technical fault; **eine nervöse ~:** a nervous disorder; **atmosphärische ~** (Met.) atmospheric disturbance; (Rundf.) atmospherics *pl.*

Story /ˈstɔrɪ/ *die;* **~, ~s** story

Stoß /ʃtoːs/ *der;* **~es, Stöße** /ˈʃtøːsə/ 1 (mit der Faust) punch; (mit dem Fuß) kick; (mit dem Kopf, den Hörnern) butt; (mit dem Ellbogen) dig; **jmdm. einen kleinen ~ mit dem Ellenbogen geben** nudge sb.; give sb. a nudge; **die Fahrgäste spürten einen leichten ~:** the passengers felt a slight bump; **jmdm. einen ~ versetzen** (fig.) give sb. a jolt 2 (mit einer Waffe) (Stich) thrust; (Schlag) blow 3 (beim Schwimmen, Rudern) stroke 4 (Stapel) pile; stack 5 (beim Kugel~en) put; throw 6 (stoßartige Bewegung) thrust; (Atem~) gasp 7 (Erd~) tremor 8 (Technik) joint 9 (Jägerspr.) tail [feathers]

Stoß-: **~band** *das; Pl.* **~bänder** edging tape; **~dämpfer** *der* (Kfz-W.) shock absorber

Stößel /ˈʃtøːsl̩/ *der;* **~s, ~:** pestle

stoß·empfindlich *Adj.* sensitive to shock *postpos.*; **meine Uhr ist nicht ~:** my watch is shockproof

stoßen

A *unr. tr. V.* 1 *auch itr.* (mit der Faust) punch; (mit dem Fuß) kick; (mit dem Kopf, den Hörnern) butt; (mit dem Ellbogen) dig; **jmdn.** *od.* **jmdm. in die Seite ~:** dig sb. in the ribs; (leicht) nudge sb. in the ribs 2 (hineintreiben) plunge, thrust ‹*dagger, knife*›; push ‹*stick, pole*›; **jmdm. ein Messer in die Rippen ~:** plunge *or* thrust a knife into sb.'s ribs 3 (~d hervorbringen) knock, bang ‹*hole*› 4 (schleudern) push; **den Ball mit dem Kopf ~:** head the ball; **die Kugel ~** (beim Kugel~) put the shot; (beim Billard) strike the ball; **jmdn. von der Leiter/aus dem Zug ~:** push sb. off the ladder/out of the train; **man muss ihn immer erst darauf ~** (fig.) he always has to have things pointed out to him 5 (zer~) pound ‹*sugar, cinnamon, pepper*› 6 (ugs.: hinweisen) **jmdm. etw. ~:** hammer sth. home to sb.; hammer sth. into sb.'s head

B *unr. itr. V.* 1 *mit sein* (auftreffen) bump (**gegen** into); **mit dem Kopf gegen etw. ~:** bump one's head on sth. 2 *mit sein* (begegnen) **auf jmdn. ~:** bump *or* run into sb. 3 *mit sein* (entdecken) **auf etw.** (*Akk.*) **~:** come upon *or* across sth.; **auf Erdöl ~:** strike oil; **auf Ablehnung ~** (fig.) meet with disapproval 4 *mit sein* **zu jmdm. ~** (jmdn. treffen) meet up with sb.; (sich jmdm. anschließen) join sb. 5 *mit sein* (zuführen) **auf etw.** (*Akk.*) **~** ‹*path, road*› lead [in]to sth. 6 (grenzen) **an etw.** (*Akk.*) **~** ‹*room, property, etc.*› be [right] next to sth. 7 *mit sein* (Jägerspr.) **auf etw.** (*Akk.*) **~** ‹*bird*› swoop down on sth. 8 (veralt.: blasen) **in die Trompete/ins Horn**

usw. ~: blow *or* sound the trumpet/horn *etc.*
C *unr. refl. V.* bump *or* knock oneself; **ich habe mich am Kopf ge~:** I bumped *or* banged my head; **sich** (*Dat.*) **den Kopf blutig ~:** bang one's head and cut it; **sich an etw.** (*Dat.*) **~** (fig.) object to *or* take exception to sth.

stoß-, Stoß-: ~fest *Adj.* shockproof ‹*watch, container, etc.*›; hard-wearing ‹*fabric, wallpaper, etc.*›; **~gebet** *das* quick prayer; **~kraft** *die* **1** force of the impact; **2** (vorwärts drängende Kraft) force and momentum; (Milit.) strike power; (Sport) striking power; **~seufzer** *der* heartfelt groan; **~stange** *die* bumper

stößt /ʃtø:st/ *3. Pers. Sg. Präsens v.* **stoßen**

stoß-, Stoß-: ~trupp *der* (Milit.) unit of shock troops; **~verkehr** *der* rush hour traffic; **~waffe** *die* thrust weapon; **~weise** *Adv.* **1** (ruckartig) spasmodically; ‹*breathe*› spasmodically, jerkily; **2** (in Stapeln) by the pile; in piles; **~zahn** *der* tusk; **~zeit** *die* rush hour

Stotterer *der;* **~s, ~, Stotterin** *die;* **~, ~nen** stutterer; stammerer

stottern /ˈʃtɔtɐn/
A *itr. V.* stutter; stammer; **sie stottert stark** she has a strong *or* bad stutter *or* stammer; **ins Stottern kommen** *od.* **geraten** start stuttering *or* stammering; **der Motor stottert** (fig.) the engine is spluttering; **etw. auf Stottern kaufen** (ugs.) buy sth. on the never-never (Brit coll.) *or* (Amer.) on installments
B *tr. V.* stutter [out]; stammer [out]

Stövchen /ˈʃtø:fçən/ *das;* **~s, ~:** [teapot *etc.*] warmer

StPo *Abk.* = **Strafprozessordnung**

Str. *Abk.* = **Straße** St./Rd.

StR. *Abk.* = **Studienrat**

stracks /ʃtraks/ *Adv.* **1** (direkt) straight **2** (sofort) straight away

Stradivari /stradiˈva:ri/ *die;* **~, ~[s]** Stradivarius

straf-, Straf-: ~androhung *die* threat of punishment; **~anstalt** *die* penal institution; prison; **~antrag** *der* **1** (des Klägers) action; legal proceedings *pl.;* **~antrag stellen** bring an action; institute legal proceedings; **2** (des Staatsanwalts) petition for a penalty *or* sentence; **~anzeige** *die* reporting of an offence; **[eine] ~anzeige erstatten** report an offence; **~arbeit** *die* imposition (Brit.); **~aufschub** *der* (Rechtsw.) **[bedingter] ~aufschub** [conditional] deferral of sentence; **~aussetzung** *die* suspension of sentence; **~bank** *die; Pl.* **~bänke** (Eishockey, Handball) penalty bench; **~bar** *Adj.* punishable; **das ist ~bar** that is a punishable offence; **sich ~bar machen** make oneself liable to prosecution

Strafe /ˈʃtra:fə/ *die;* **~, ~n** punishment; (Rechtsspr.) penalty; (Freiheits~) sentence; (Geld~) fine; **auf dieses Delikt steht eine hohe ~:** this offence carries a heavy penalty; **sie empfand die Arbeit als ~:** she found the work a real drag *or* (coll.) bind; **das ist bei ~ verboten/steht unter ~:** it is a punishable offence; **etw. unter ~ stellen** make sth. punishable; **die ~ folgt auf dem Fuße** punishment is swift to follow; **~ muss sein!** discipline is necessary; you'll/he'll *etc.* have to be punished; **das ist die ~ [dafür]** that's what you get; **das ist ja eine ~ Gottes!** it's a real pain [in the neck]; **es ist eine ~, mit ihm arbeiten zu müssen** it's a pain having to work with him; **zur ~:** as a punishment

strafen *tr. V.* punish; **ein ~der Blick** a reproachful look; **jmdn. ~d ansehen** give sb. a reproachful look; **jmdn. mit Verachtung ~:** treat sb. with contempt as a punishment; **er ist gestraft genug** (fig.) he has been punished enough; **Gott strafe mich, wenn ich lüge!** (veralt.) may God strike me down if I am lying; **mit ihm/dieser Arbeit sind wir gestraft** he/this work is a real pain; **das Schicksal hat ihn schwer gestraft** fate has been hard on him; *s. auch* **Lüge**

Straf-: ~entlassene *der/die; adj. Dekl.* ex-convict; ex-prisoner; **~erlass, *~erlaß** *der* (Rechtsw.) remission [of a/the sentence]; **bedingter ~erlass** conditional remission; **~expedition** *die* punitive expedition

straff /ʃtraf/
A *Adj.* **1** (fest, gespannt) tight, taut ‹*rope, lines, etc.*›; firm ‹*breasts, skin*›; erect ‹*posture, figure*›; tight ‹*rein[s]*› **2** (energisch) tight ‹*organization, planning, etc.*›; strict ‹*discipline, leadership, etc.*›
B *adv.* **1** (fest, gespannt) **die Saiten sind ~ gespannt** the strings are tight; **[zu] ~ sitzen** ‹*clothes*› be [too] tight; **die Jacke ~ über die Schultern ziehen** pull one's jacket tightly round one's shoulders; **er zog die Zügel ~ an** he pulled the reins tight; **~ zurückgekämmtes Haar** hair combed back tightly **2** (energisch) tightly, strictly ‹*organized, planned, etc.*›

straf-fällig *Adj.* **~ werden** commit a criminal offence; **die Zahl der Straffälligen** the number of offenders; **~e Jugendliche** young offenders

straffen
A *tr. V.* **1** (spannen) tighten; **diese Creme strafft die Haut** this cream firms the skin; **sich** (*Dat.*) **das Gesicht ~ lassen** have a facelift; **den Körper ~:** straighten oneself; draw oneself up **2** (raffen) tighten up ‹*text, procedure, organization, etc.*›
B *refl. V.* ‹*person*› straighten oneself, draw oneself up; ‹*rope etc.*› tighten; ‹*body, back*› stiffen; ‹*posture, bearing*› straighten

straf-, Straf-: ~frei *Adj.* **jmdn. für ~frei erklären** declare sb. exempt from punishment; **~frei ausgehen** go unpunished; get off [scot-]free (coll.); **~freiheit** *die* exemption from punishment; **~gefangene** *der/die* prisoner; **~gericht** *das* (fig.) judgement; **ein ~gericht des Himmels** divine judgement; **ein grausames ~gericht abhalten** mete out cruel judgement; **~gesetz** *das* criminal *or* penal law; **~gesetz·buch** *das* criminal *or* penal code; **~justiz** *die* criminal *or* penal justice; **~kammer** *die* (Rechtsw.) criminal division (*of a district court*); **~kolonie** *die* penal colony; **~kompanie** *die* punishment battalion; **~lager** *das* penal camp

sträflich /ˈʃtrɛ:flɪç/
A *Adj.* criminal
B *adv.* criminally

Sträfling /ˈʃtrɛ:flɪŋ/ *der;* **~s, ~e** prisoner

Sträflings·kleidung *die* prison clothing; prison clothes *pl.*

straf-, Straf-: ~los *Adj.* unpunished; **~mandat** *das* [parking, speeding, *etc.*] ticket; **~maß** *das* sentence; **~minute** *die* **1** (bes. Eishockey, Handball) minute of penalty time; **die drei ~minuten** the three-minute penalty *sing.;* **2** (Rennsport, Springreiten, Biathlon, usw.) penalty minute; **~mündig** *Adj.* (Rechtsw.) of the age of criminal responsibility *postpos.;* **er ist noch nicht ~mündig** he is under the age of criminal responsibility; **~porto** *das* surcharge; **~predigt** *die* (ugs.) lecture; **jmdm. eine ~predigt halten** lecture sb.; **~prozess, *~prozeß** *der* criminal proceedings *pl.;* **~prozess·ordnung, *~prozeß·ordnung** *die* (Rechtsw.) code of criminal procedure; **~punkt** *der* (Sport) penalty point; **~raum** *der* (bes. Fußball) penalty area; **~recht** *das* criminal law; **~rechtlich** **A** *Adj.* criminal *attrib.* ‹*case, investigation, responsibility*›; **~rechtliche Fragen/Probleme** questions/problems of criminal law; **im ~rechtlichen Sinne** according to criminal law; **B** *adv.* under criminal law; **etw. ~rechtlich verfolgen** prosecute sth.; **~register** *das* criminal records *pl.;* **~richter** *der,* **~richterin** *die* (Rechtsw.) criminal judge; **~sache** *die* criminal case; **~stoß** *der* (Fußball) ▸ **Elfmeter**; **~tat** *die* criminal offence; **~täter** *der,* **~täterin** *die* offender; **~verbüßung** *die* serving [of] one's sentence; **~verfahren** *das* criminal proceedings *pl.;* **~verfolgung** *die* (Rechtsw.) [criminal] prosecution; **~|versetzen** *tr. V. nur im Inf. u. Part. gebr.* transfer for disciplinary reasons; **~versetzung** *die* disciplinary transfer; **~verteidiger** *der,* **~verteidigerin** *die* defence lawyer *or* counsel; **~vollzug** *der* penal system; **~würdig** *Adj.* (Rechtsw.) punishable; **~zettel** *der* (ugs.) [parking, speeding, *etc.*] ticket

Strahl /ʃtra:l/ *der;* **~[e]s, ~en** **1** (Licht, fig.) ray; (von Scheinwerfern, Taschenlampen) beam; **ein ~ fiel durch den Türspalt** a shaft of light came through the crack of the door **2** (Flüssigkeit) jet; **ein dünner ~ Wasser** a thin trickle of water **3** (Math., Phys.) ray

Strahl·an·trieb *der* (Technik) jet propulsion

Strahle·mann *der* (ugs.) man/boy with the smiling face

strahlen *itr. V.* **1** shine; **ein ~d heller Morgen** a gloriously bright morning; **bei ~dem Wetter/Sonnenschein** in glorious sunny weather/in glorious sunshine; **eine ~de Schönheit/Stimme** (fig.) a radiant beauty/marvellously pure voice; **~d weiß** sparkling white **2** (glänzen) sparkle **3** (lächeln) beam (**vor** + *Dat.* with); **er strahlte über das ganze Gesicht** *od.* (ugs.) **über beide Backen** he was beaming all over his face **4** (Physik) radiate; emit rays

strahlen-, Strahlen-: ~behandlung *die* (Med.) radiotherapy *no art.;* **~belastung** *die* radioactive contamination; **~biologie** *die* radiobiology *no art.;* **~bündel** *das* (Optik, Math.) pencil of rays; **~förmig** **A** *Adj.* radial; **B** *adv.* radially; **~pilz** *der* (Biol.) ray fungus; **~schutz** *der* radiation protection; **~therapie** *die* (Med.) radiotherapy *no art.;* **~tierchen** *das* radiolarian; **~unfall** *der* radiation accident

Strahler *der;* **~s, ~** **1** radiator **2** (Heiz~) radiant heater

strahlig
A *Adj.* radial
B *adv.* radially

Strahl·triebwerk *das* jet engine

Strahlung *die;* **~, ~en** radiation

Strahlungs-: ~energie *die* (Physik) radiant energy; **~gürtel** *der* (Physik) radiation belt; **~intensität** *die* (Physik) intensity of radiation

Strähne /ˈʃtrɛ:nə/ *die;* **~, ~n** **1** (Haare) strand; **eine graue ~:** a grey streak **2** (fig.: Zeitspanne) streak

strähnig
A *Adj.* straggly ‹*hair*›
B *adv.* in strands

stramm /ʃtram/
A *Adj.* **1** (straff) tight, taut ‹*rope, line, etc.*›; tight ‹*clothes*› **2** (kräftig) strapping ‹*girl, boy*›; sturdy ‹*legs, body*›; *s. auch* **Max** **3** (gerade) upright, erect ‹*posture, etc.*›; **eine ~e Haltung einnehmen** stand to attention **4** (energisch) strict ‹*discipline*›; strict, staunch ‹*Marxist, Catholic, etc.*›; brisk ‹*step*›
B *adv.* **1** (straff) tightly; **die Hose saß ziemlich ~:** the trousers were rather tight; **der Gurt soll ~ am Körper anliegen** the belt is supposed to be tight **2** (kräftig) sturdily ‹*built*› **3** (energisch) ‹*bring up*› strictly; strictly, staunchly ‹*Marxist, Catholic, etc.*›; ‹*hold out*› resolutely **4** (ugs.: zügig) ‹*work*› hard; ‹*walk, march*› briskly; ‹*drive*› fast, hard

stramm|stehen *unr. itr. V.* stand to *or* at attention

Strampel·höschen *das,* **Strampel·hose** *die* rompers *pl.;* romper suit; playsuit

strampeln /ˈʃtrampl̩n/ *itr. V.* **1** ‹*baby*› kick [his/her feet] [and wave his/her arms about] **2** *mit sein* (ugs.: mit dem Rad) pedal **3** (ugs.: sich sehr anstrengen) sweat; struggle

Strampler *der;* **~s, ~** ▸ **Strampelhöschen**

Strand /ʃtrant/ *der;* **~[e]s, Strände** /ˈʃtrɛndə/ beach; (geh. veralt.: Flussufer) bank; strand; (geh. veralt.: Seeufer) shore; strand; **am ~:** on the beach; **an den ~ gehen** go to the beach; **auf ~ laufen** ‹*ship*› run aground; **ein Schiff auf ~ setzen** beach a ship

Strand-: ~bad *das* bathing beach (*on river, lake*); **~burg** *die* sand den (built as a windbreak); **~café** *das* beach café; **~distel** *die* sea holly

stranden *itr. V.; mit sein* **1** (festsitzen) ‹*ship*› run aground; (fig.) be stranded **2** (geh.: scheitern) fail

Strand-: **~gut** *das* flotsam and jetsam; **~haubitze** *die:* *in* **voll** *od.* **blau wie eine ~haubitze sein** (ugs.) be dead drunk; **~hotel** *das* beach hotel; **~kleid** *das* beach dress; **~korb** *der* basket chair; **~leben** *das* beach life; **~promenade** *die* promenade; **~räuber** *der,* **~räuberin** *die* wrecker; **~segeln** *das* (Sport) sand-yachting

Strang /ʃtraŋ/ *der;* **~[e]s, Stränge** /ˈʃtrɛŋə/ [1] (Seil) rope; **jmdn. zum Tod durch den ~ verurteilen** (geh.) sentence sb. to be hanged [2] (von Wolle, Garn usw.) hank; skein [3] (Nerven~, Muskel~, Sehnen~) cord; (der DNS) strand [4] (Leine) trace; **über die Stränge schlagen** (ugs.) kick over the traces; *s. auch* **reißen B 1**; **ziehen B 1**

strangulieren /ʃtraŋguˈliːrən/ *tr. V.* strangle

Strapaze /ʃtraˈpaːt͜sə/ *die;* **~, ~n** strain *no pl.*; **sich von den ~n erholen** recover from the strain *sing.*

strapaz̲-fähig *Adj.* (österr.) ▸ **strapazierfähig**

strapaz̲ieren

A *tr. V.* be a strain on ‹*person, nerves*›; **die tägliche Rasur strapaziert die Haut** shaving daily is hard on the skin; **die Reise würde ihn zu sehr ~:** the journey would be too much [of a strain] for him; **jmds. Geduld ~** (fig.) tax sb.'s patience; **wir haben unsere Wanderschuhe/Wintermäntel stark strapaziert** we gave our walking shoes/winter coats a great deal of hard wear; **diese Ausrede ist schon zu oft strapaziert worden** (fig.) this excuse has been flogged to death

B *refl. V.* strain *or* tax oneself

strapaz̲ier-fähig *Adj.* hard-wearing ‹*clothes, shoes*›; hard-wearing, durable ‹*material*›; sturdy ‹*book*›

Strapaz̲ier-fähigkeit *die* ▸ **strapazierfähig**: hard-wearingness; durability; sturdiness

strapaziös /ʃtrapaˈt͜si̯øːs/ *Adj.* wearing

Straps /ʃtraps/ *der;* **~es, ~e** suspender

Strass, °**Straß** /ʃtras/ *der;* **~** *od.* **Strasses, Str̲asse** [1] (Glasfluss) paste [2] (Nachbildung aus ~) paste gem

Straßburg /ˈʃtraːsbʊrk/ *(das);* **~s** ▸ⓘ **S. 675** Strasbourg

Sträßchen /ˈʃtrɛːsçən/ *das;* **~s, ~:** little *or* narrow street

Straße /ˈʃtraːsə/ *die;* **~, ~n** [1] ▸ⓘ **S. 800** (in Ortschaften) street; road; (außerhalb) road; (fig. abwertend: Pöbel) mob; rabble; **auf offener ~:** in [the middle of] the street; **man traut sich abends kaum noch auf die ~:** you hardly dare go out in the evenings any more; **Verkauf über die ~:** take away sales *pl.*; (von alkoholischen Getränken) off-licence sales *pl.*; **Jugendliche von der ~ holen** get young people off the streets; **der Mann auf der ~** (fig.) the man in the street; **mit jugendlichen Arbeitslosen/Prostituierten kann man hier die ~n pflastern** (ugs.) the place is full of young unemployed people/prostitutes (coll.); **jmdn. auf die ~ setzen** *od.* **werfen** (ugs.) (aus einer Stellung) sack sb. (coll.); give sb. the sack (coll.); (aus einer Wohnung) turn sb. out on to the street; **auf der ~ liegen** *od.* **sitzen** *od.* **stehen** (ugs.) (arbeitslos sein) be out of work; (ohne Wohnung sein) be on the streets; **auf die ~ gehen** (ugs.) (demonstrieren) take to the streets; (der Prostitution nachgehen) go on *or* walk the streets; **jmdn. auf die ~ schicken** (ugs.) send sb. out on the streets; **sich [nicht] dem Druck der ~ beugen** [not] bow to mob rule [2] (Meerenge) strait[s *pl.*]; **die ~ von Gibraltar/Hormus** the Straits of Gibraltar/Strait of Hormuz

Str̲aßen-: **~anzug** *der* lounge suit (Brit.); business suit (Amer.); **~bahn** *die* tram (Brit.); streetcar (Amer.); **~bahner** *der;* **~~s, ~~, ~bahnerin** *die;* **~~, ~~nen** (ugs.) tramway employee (Brit.)

Str̲aßen·bahn-: **~fahrer** *der,* **~fahrerin** *die* [1] (Führer[in]) tram driver (Brit.); [2] (Benutzer[in]) tram passenger (Brit.); **~halte·stelle** *die* tram stop (Brit.); **~linie** *die* tram route (Brit.); **die ~linie 24** the number 24 tram (Brit.); **~schaffner** *der,* **~schaffnerin** *die* tram conductor (Brit.); **~schiene** *die* tramline (Brit.); **~wagen** *der* tram[car] (Brit.)

Str̲aßen-: **~bau** *der* road building *no art.*; road construction *no art.*; **~bekanntschaft** *die:* **sie ist nur eine ~bekanntschaft** she is just someone I talk to when I meet her in the street; **~beleuchtung** *die* street lighting; **~benutzungs·gebühr** *die* ▸ **Maut**; **~bild** *das* street scene; **mehr und mehr gehörten Uniformen wieder zum ~bild** uniforms were increasingly seen in the streets again; **~café** *das* pavement café; street café; **~decke** *die* road surface; **~dorf** *das* street village; **~ecke** *die* street corner; **~fahrer** *der,* **~fahrerin** *die* (Rennsport) road racer; **~feger** *der* [1] ▸ⓘ **S. 113** (bes. nordd.) road sweeper; [2] (ugs. scherzh.: spannende Fernsehsendung) programme/series which pulls a huge audience; **~fegerin** *die;* **~~, ~~nen** ▸ⓘ **S. 113** ▸ **~feger 1**; **~fest** *das* street party; **~glätte** *die* slippery road surface; **~graben** *der* ditch [at the side of the road]; **~händler** *der,* **~händlerin** *die* street trader; **~junge** *der* (abwertend) street urchin; **~kampf** *der* [1] street fight; street battle; [2] (Taktik, Strategie) streetfighting; **~kämpfer** *der,* **~kämpferin** *die* streetfighter; **~karte** *die* road map; **~kehrer** *der;* **~~s, ~~, ~kehrerin** *die;* **~~, ~~nen** ▸ⓘ **S. 113** (bes. südd.) ▸ **~feger 1**; **~kreuzer** *der* (ugs. veralt.) limousine; **~kreuzung** *die* crossroads *sing.*; **~lage** *die* roadholding *no indef. art.*; **eine gute ~lage haben** have good roadholding; hold the road well; **~lärm** *der* street noise; **~laterne** *die* street lamp; **~mädchen** *das* (abwertend) streetwalker; **~musikant** *der,* **~musikantin** *die* street musician; busker; **~name** *der* street name; name of a/the street; **~netz** *das* road network; **~rand** *der* roadside; side of the road; **~raub** *der* street robbery; (gewalttätig) mugging; **~räuber** *der,* **~räuberin** *die* street robber; (gewalttätig) mugger; **~reinigung** *die* street cleaning; **~rennen** *das* (Rennsport) road race; **~sammlung** *die* street collection; **~schild** *das* street name sign; **~schlacht** *die* street battle; **~schmutz** *der* (auf der Straße) dirt in the street/streets; (von der Straße) dirt from the street/streets; **~schuh** *der* walking shoe; **~seite** *die* side of the street/road; (eines Gebäudes) street side; **das Fenster ging zur ~seite** the window looked out on [to] the street/road; **~sperre** *die* roadblock; **~sperrung** *die* closing [off] of a/the street/road; **~staub** *der* dust of the street/road; **~theater** *das* [1] street theatre; [2] (Ensemble) street theatre group; **~tunnel** *der* road tunnel; **~überführung** *die* (für Fußgänger) footbridge; (für Fahrzeuge) road bridge; **~unterführung** *die* (für Fußgänger) subway; (für Fahrzeuge) underpass; **~verhältnisse** *Pl.* road conditions; **~verkauf** *der* [1] (auf der Straße) street trading; [2] (über die Straße) take away sales *pl.*; (von alkoholischen Getränken) off-licence sales *pl.*; **~verkäufer** *der,* **~verkäuferin** *die* street vendor; **~verkehr** *der* traffic; **im ~verkehr** in traffic; **~verkehrs·ordnung** *die* road traffic act; **~zoll** *der* ▸ **Maut**; **~zug** *der* street; **~zustand** *der* road conditions *pl.*

Stratege /ʃtraˈteːgə/ *der;* **~n, ~n** strategist

Strategie /ʃtrateˈgiː/ *die;* **~, ~n** strategy

Strategi̲e·papier *das* strategy paper

Strate̲gin *die;* **~, ~nen** strategist

strate̲gisch

A *Adj.* strategic

B *adv.* strategically

Strato·sphä̲re /ʃtrato-/ *die* stratosphere

Stratus /ˈʃtraːtʊs/ *der;* **~, Stra̲ti** (Met.) stratus

Stra̲tus·wolke *die* stratus cloud

sträuben /ˈʃtrɔ̯ybn̩/

A *tr. V.* ruffle [up] ‹*feathers*›; bristle ‹*fur, hair*›

B *refl. V.* [1] ‹*hair, fur*› bristle, stand on end; ‹*feathers*› become ruffled; **bei dieser Nachricht sträubten sich mir die Haare** the news made my hair stand on end [2] (sich widersetzen) resist; **sich ~, etw. zu tun** resist doing sth.; **sie hat sich mit Händen und Füßen gegen die Versetzung gesträubt** she resisted the transfer with all her might; **die Feder sträubt sich, das zu schildern** (fig. geh.) one hesitates *or* is reluctant to put it on paper

Strauch /ʃtra̲ux/ *der;* **~[e]s, Sträucher** /ˈʃtrɔ̯yçɐ/ shrub

Stra̲uch·dieb *der* (veralt. abwertend) footpad (hist.); **wie ein ~ aussehen** (ugs.) look like a tramp

straucheln /ˈʃtra̲uxl̩n/ *itr. V.;* *mit sein* (geh.) [1] (stolpern) stumble; **sein Fuß strauchelte** (geh.) he stumbled [2] (scheitern) fail [3] (straffällig werden) go astray

Stra̲uch·werk *das* shrubbery; bushes *pl.*

Strauß[1] /ʃtra̲us/ *der;* **~es, Sträuße** /ˈʃtrɔ̯ysə/ bunch of flowers; (bes. als Geschenk, zu offiziellem Anlass) bouquet [of flowers]; (von kleinen Blumen) posy

Stra̲uß[2] *der;* **~es, ~e** (Vogel) ostrich; **wie der Vogel ~:** like an ostrich

Stra̲uß[3] *der;* **~es, Strä̲uße** (veralt.) [1] (Kampf) battle [2] (Streit) quarrel; **ich habe einen ~ mit dir auszufechten** I have a bone to pick with you

Str̲äußchen /ˈʃtrɔ̯ysçən/ *das;* **~s, ~:** posy

Stra̲ußen-: **~ei** *das* ostrich egg; **~feder** *die* ostrich feather *or* plume

Stra̲uß·wirtschaft *die:* (bes. südd.) [*temporarily opened*] *bar selling new wine when a bundle of twigs is displayed*

Straußwirtschaft

An inn set up temporarily by a local winegrower for a few weeks after the new wine has been made. A bunch of flowers and vine leaves above the door shows that the new vintage is ready for tasting. See also **Besenwirtschaft.**

Streaming /ˈstriːmɪŋ/ *das;* **~[s]** (DV) streaming

Strebe /ˈʃtreːbə/ *die;* **~, ~n** brace; strut

Stre̲be-: **~balken** *der* shore; prop; **~bogen** *der* (Archit.) flying buttress

stre̲ben *itr. V.* [1] *mit sein* (hinwollen) make one's way briskly; **er strebte zur Tür** he made briskly for the door; **die Pflanzen ~ zum Licht** the plants reach up towards the light; **die Partei strebt an die Macht** the party is reaching out for power [2] (trachten) strive (**nach** for); **danach ~, etw. zu tun** strive to do sth.; **das Streben nach Vollkommenheit** [the] striving for perfection [3] (abwertend) ‹*pupil*› swot (Brit. sl.); cram

Stre̲ben *das;* **~s** striving (**nach** for); **sein ~ ist darauf gerichtet, die Zustände zu verbessern** his efforts are directed towards improving conditions

Stre̲be·pfeiler *der* (Archit.) buttress

Stre̲ber *der;* **~s, ~** (abwertend) overambitious *or* pushing *or* (coll.) pushy person; (in der Schule) swot (Brit. sl.); cram

stre̲berhaft, stre̲berisch *Adj.* (abwertend) overambitious; pushing; pushy (coll.); **ein ~er Schüler** a swot (Brit. sl.); grind (Amer. sl.)

Stre̲berin *die;* **~, ~nen** ▸ **Streber**

Stre̲be·werk *das* (Archit.) [system *sing.* of] buttresses *pl.*

strebsam *Adj.* ambitious and industrious

Stre̲bsamkeit *die;* **~:** ambition and industriousness

Stre̲ck·bett *das* (Med.) orthopaedic bed

Strecke /ˈʃtrɛkə/ *die;* **~, ~n** [1] (Weg~) distance; **über weite ~n sah man kein einziges Dorf** for long distances there was not a single village to be seen; **das Land war über weite ~n überschwemmt** large parts of the countryside were flooded; **auf der ~ bleiben** (ugs.) fall by the wayside [2] (Abschnitt, Route) route; (Eisenbahn~) line; **er fliegt diese ~ oft** he often flies this route; **der Zug hielt auf freier** *od.* **offener ~:** the train stopped between stations [3] (Sport) distance; **viele Zuschauer waren an der ~:** there were a lot of spectators lining the route/track; **die Läufer gehen auf die ~:** the runners are setting off [4] (Geom.) line segment [5] (Bergbau) gallery

S

6▸ (Jägerspr.) bag; kill; **ein Tier zur ~ bringen** bag *or* kill an animal; **jmdn. zur ~ bringen** (fig.) hunt sb. down

strẹcken

A *tr. V.* 1▸ (gerade machen) stretch ‹*arms, legs*›; **ein gebrochenes Bein ~:** straighten a broken leg 2▸ (dehnen) stretch [out] ‹*arms, legs, etc.*›; **den Hals ~:** crane one's neck 3▸ (lehnen) stick (coll.); **den Kopf aus dem Fenster ~:** stick one's head out of the window (coll.) 4▸ (größer, länger, breiter machen) stretch; hammer/roll out ‹*metal*› 5▸ (verdünnen) thin down 6▸ (rationieren) eke out ‹*provisions, fuel, etc.*›

B *refl. V.* stretch out

strẹcken-, Strẹcken-: ~abschnitt *der* section; **~arbeiter** *der,* **~arbeiterin** *die* platelayer; track worker; **~begehung** *die* track inspection; **~führung** *die* routing; (Strecke) route; **~netz** *das* route network; (Eisenbahnw.) rail network; **~wärter** *der,* **~wärterin** *die* track inspector; **~weise** *Adv.* in places; (fig.: zeitweise) at times; **das Buch war ~weise langweilig** the book was boring in parts

Strẹcker *der;* **~s, ~** ▸❶ **S. 435** (Anat.) extensor

Strẹck-: ~muskel *der* ▸❶ **S. 435** (Anat.) extensor [muscle]; **~verband** *der* (Med.) extension *or* traction bandage

Streetball /'stri:tbɔ:l/ *der;* **~s** streetball

Streich /ʃtraiç/ *der;* **~[e]s, ~e** 1▸ (geh.: Hieb) blow; **jmdm. einen ~ versetzen** strike sb.; **auf einen ~** (veralt.) at one blow; (fig.) at one fell swoop; at one go 2▸ (Schabernack) trick; prank; **jmdm. einen ~ spielen** play a trick on sb.; **mein Gedächtnis hat mir wieder einen ~ gespielt** my memory has been playing tricks on me again

Strei̲chel·einheiten *Pl.* (ugs.) share *sing.* of kindness and affection; (bei Mitarbeitern) share *sing.* of encouragement and appreciation

streicheln /'ʃtraiçl̩n/ *tr.* (*auch itr.*) *V.* stroke; (liebkosen) stroke; caress; **einem Hund über den Rücken ~:** stroke a dog's back; **er streichelte ihr übers Haar** he stroked her hair

strei̲chen

A *unr. tr. V.* 1▸ stroke; **die Geige ~** (geh.) play the violin; *s. auch* **gestrichen B, C** 2▸ (an~) paint; **eine Wand grün/beige** *usw.* **~:** paint a wall green/beige *etc.*; **„frisch gestrichen"** 'wet paint' 3▸ (wegstreifen) sweep ‹*crumbs etc.*›; **sich** (*Dat.*) **das Haar aus der Stirn ~:** push *or* smooth the hair back from one's forehead 4▸ (drücken) **Kitt in die Fugen ~:** press putty into the joints; **Tomaten durch ein Sieb ~:** rub *or* press tomatoes through a sieve 5▸ (auftragen) spread ‹*butter, jam, ointment, etc.*› 6▸ (be~) **ein Brötchen [mit Butter]/mit Honig ~:** butter a roll/spread honey on a roll 7▸ (aus~, tilgen) delete; cross out; cancel ‹*train, flight*›; **jmdn. von der Liste ~:** cross sb. off the list; **Nichtzutreffendes bitte ~!** please delete as appropriate *or* applicable; **etw. aus seinem Gedächtnis** *od.* **seiner Erinnerung ~:** erase sth. from one's memory *or* mind; **einen Auftrag/Zuschuss ~:** cancel an order/a subsidy 8▸ (Rudern) **die Riemen ~:** back water 9▸ (Seemannsspr. veralt.) strike ‹*sail*›; *s. auch* **Flagge; Segel**

B *unr. itr. V.* 1▸ stroke; **jmdm. durch die Haare/über den Kopf ~:** run one's fingers through sb.'s hair/stroke sb.'s head; **er strich sich** (*Dat.*) **nachdenklich über den Bart** he stroked his beard thoughtfully; **mit der Hand über die Tischdecke ~:** smooth the tablecloth with one's hand 2▸ (an~) paint 3▸ *mit sein* (umhergehen) wander 4▸ (Geol.) ‹*stratum*› strike; (Geogr.) ‹*mountain range*› stretch 5▸ *mit sein* (bes. Jägerspr.) ‹*bird*› wing

Strei̲cher *der;* **~s, ~, Strei̲cherin** *die;* **~, ~nen** (Musik) string player; **die Streicher** the strings

strei̲ch·fähig *Adj.* easy to spread *pred.*

Strei̲ch·holz *das* match; (als Spielzeug) matchstick; **eine Schachtel Streichhölzer** a box of matches

Strei̲chholz-: ~briefchen *das* book of matches; **~spiel** *das* game with matchsticks

Strei̲ch-: ~instrument *das* string[ed] instrument; **~käse** *der* cheese spread; **~orchester** *das* string orchestra; **~quartett** *das* string quartet; **~trio** *das* string trio

Strei̲chung *die;* **~, ~en** 1▸ (Tilgung) deletion; (Kürzung) cutting *no indef. art.*; **~en vornehmen** make deletions/cuts 2▸ (gestrichene Stelle) deletion; (Kürzung) cut

Strei̲ch·wurst *die* [soft] sausage for spreading; ≈ meat spread

Streif /ʃtraif/ *der;* **~[e]s, ~e** (geh.) strip; (Licht~) shaft

Strei̲f·band *das; Pl.* **Strei̲fbänder** wrapper

Streife *die;* **~, ~n** 1▸ (Personen) patrol 2▸ (Streifengang) patrol; **auf ~ gehen/sein** go/be on patrol

strei̲fen

A *tr. V.* 1▸ (leicht berühren) touch; brush [against]; ‹*shot*› graze; **jmdn. am Arm/an der Schulter ~:** touch sb. on the arm *or* brush against sb.'s arm/touch sb. on the shoulder; **mit dem Wagen das Garagentor ~:** scrape the garage door with the car; **ein Windhauch streifte ihre Wangen** (geh.) she felt a breath of wind on her cheeks; **jmdn. mit einem Blick ~** (fig.) glance fleetingly at sb. 2▸ (kurz behandeln) touch [up]on ‹*problem, subject, etc.*› 3▸ **den Ring auf den/vom Finger ~:** slip the ring on/off one's finger; **die Ärmel nach oben ~:** pull/push up one's sleeves; **die Butter vom Messer ~:** wipe the butter off the knife; **sich** (*Dat.*) **die Kapuze/den Pullover über den Kopf ~:** pull the hood/slip the pullover over one's head; **sich die Strümpfe von den Beinen ~:** slip one's stockings off; **die Blätter von den Zweigen ~:** strip the leaves from the twigs; strip the twigs of leaves

B *itr. V. mit sein* roam; **durch die Wälder ~:** roam the forests

Strei̲fen *der;* **~s, ~** 1▸ (Linie) stripe; (auf der Fahrbahn) line; **ein heller ~ am Horizont** a streak of light on the horizon; **graue ~ im Haar haben** have grey streaks in one's hair 2▸ (Stück, Abschnitt) strip; (Speck~) rasher; (Tresse) braid 3▸ (ugs.: Film) film

Strei̲fen-: ~beamte *der* policeman on patrol duty; **~beamtin** *die* policewoman on patrol duty; **~dienst** *der* patrol duty; **~gang** *der* patrol; **~muster** *das* striped pattern; **ein Hemd mit ~muster** a striped shirt; **~wagen** *der* patrol car

strei̲fig *Adj.* streaky

Strei̲f-: ~licht *das; Pl.* **~~er** streak of light; **ein ~licht auf etw.** (*Akk.*) **werfen** (fig.) highlight sth.; **~schuss, *~schuß** *der* grazing shot; (Wunde) graze; **~zug** *der* expedition; (fig.) expedition; journey; (eines Tieres) prowl

Streik /ʃtraik/ *der;* **~[e]s, ~s** strike; **in den ~ treten** come out *or* go on strike; **den ~ ausrufen** call a strike; **jmdn. zum ~ aufrufen** call sb. out on strike; **mit ~ drohen** threaten to strike; threaten strike action; *s. auch* **wild A 2**

Strei̲k-: ~aufruf *der* strike call; **~brecher** *der,* **~brecherin** *die* strike-breaker; blackleg (derog.); scab (derog.); **~drohung** *die* strike threat; threat of strike action

strei̲ken *itr. V.* 1▸ strike; be on strike; (in den Streik treten) come out *or* go on strike; strike 2▸ (ugs.: nicht mitmachen) go on strike 3▸ (ugs.: nicht funktionieren) pack up (coll.); **der Kühlschrank streikt** the fridge has packed up (coll.)

Strei̲kende *der/die; adj. Dekl.* striker

Strei̲k-: ~front *die* strike; **an der ~front** in the strike/strikes; **~geld** *das* strike pay; **~kasse** *die* strike fund; **~leitung** *die* strike leadership; strike leaders *pl.*; **~posten** *der* picket; **~posten beziehen** picket; stand on the picket line; **vor einer Fabrik ~posten stehen** picket a factory; **~recht** *das* right to strike

Streit /ʃtrait/ *der;* **~[e]s** 1▸ quarrel; argument; (Zank) squabble; quarrel; (Auseinandersetzung) dispute; argument; **~ anfangen** start a quarrel *or* an argument; **sie sind im ~ auseinander gegangen** they parted in disharmony; **er sucht immer ~:** he is always looking for an argument *or* a quarrel; **die beiden haben oft ~:** those two are always arguing *or* quarrelling *or* fighting; **ein ~ der Meinungen** a clash of opinions; **mit jmdm. ~ bekommen** get into an argument *or* a quarrel with sb.; **er hat ihn im ~ erschlagen** he beat him to death during a quarrel; **miteinander in ~ leben** be always at loggerheads with each other; **ein ~ um des Kaisers Bart** an argument over nothing 2▸ (veralt.: Kampf) battle

Strei̲t·axt *die* battleaxe

strei̲t·bar *Adj.* (geh.) 1▸ pugnacious 2▸ (veralt.: tapfer) brave; valiant

strei̲ten

A *unr. itr., refl. V.* quarrel; argue; (sich zanken) squabble; quarrel; (sich auseinander setzen) argue; have an argument; **die Erben stritten [sich] um den Nachlass** the heirs argued *or* fought over *or* disputed the estate; **darüber lässt sich ~:** one can argue about that; that's a debatable point; **die ~den Parteien in einem Prozess** the litigants in a lawsuit; **die Streitenden** the quarrellers

B *unr. itr. V.* (geh.: kämpfen) fight

Strei̲ter *der;* **~s, ~** (geh.: Kämpfer) fighter (**für** for, **gegen** against); champion (**für** of)

Streiterei̲ *die;* **~, ~en** arguing *no pl., no indef. art.*; (Gezänk) quarrelling *no pl.*; **bei ihnen gibt es immer ~en** they are always quarrelling

Strei̲terin *die;* **~, ~nen** ▸ **Streiter**

Strei̲t-: ~fall *der* (Rechtsw.) case; (Kontroverse) dispute; conflict; **das ist ein ~fall** that is a disputed point; **im ~fall** in [the] case of dispute *or* conflict; **~frage** *die* disputed question *or* issue; **~gespräch** *das* debate; disputation; **~hahn** *der; Pl.* **~hähne** (ugs., oft scherzh.) quarreller; squabbler; (fig.: Kampfhahn) fighter; brawler; **~hammel** *der* (fam.) quarreller

strei̲tig *Adj.* 1▸ disputed ‹*question, issue*›; **jmdm. jmdn./etw. ~ machen** dispute sb.'s right to sb./sth. 2▸ (Rechtsw.) disputed

Strei̲tigkeit *die;* **~, ~en** 1▸ quarrel; argument 2▸ (Streitfall) dispute

strei̲t-, Strei̲t-: ~kräfte *Pl.* armed forces; **~kultur** *die* culture of [lively] debate; **~macht** *die* (veralt.) forces *pl.*; **~punkt** *der* contentious issue; **~roß** *das* (veralt.) ▸ **Schlachtross**; **~sache** *die* 1▸ dispute; 2▸ (Rechtsw.) ▸ **Rechtsstreit**; **~schrift** *die* polemical treatise; **~sucht** *die* quarrelsomeness; **~süchtig** *Adj.* quarrelsome; **~wagen** *der* chariot; **~wert** *der* amount in dispute

streng /ʃtrɛŋ/

A *Adj.* 1▸ (hart) strict ‹*teacher, parents, upbringing, principle*›; severe ‹*punishment*›; stringent, strict ‹*rule, regulation, etc.*›; stringent ‹*measure*›; rigorous ‹*examination, check, test, etc.*›; stern ‹*reprimand, look*› 2▸ (strikt) strict ‹*order, punctuality, diet, instruction, Catholic*›; absolute ‹*discretion*›; complete ‹*rest*›; **~ gegen sich selbst sein** be strict with oneself; **im ~en Sinne** in the strict sense 3▸ (schnörkellos) austere, severe ‹*cut, collar, style, etc.*›; severe ‹*hairstyle*›; **der ~e Aufbau eines Romans** the tight structure of a novel 4▸ (herb) severe ‹*face, features, etc.*› 5▸ (durchdringend) pungent, sharp ‹*taste, smell*›; **er riecht etwas ~:** he smells a bit strong 6▸ (rau) severe ‹*winter*›; sharp, severe ‹*frost*›

B *adv.* 1▸ (hart) ‹*mark, judge, etc.*› strictly, severely; ‹*punish*› severely; ‹*look, reprimand*› sternly; **~ durchgreifen** take rigorous action 2▸ (strikt) strictly; **~ verboten** strictly prohibited; **~ genommen** strictly speaking 3▸ (schnörkellos) **sie trug ein ~ geschnittenes Kostüm** she wore a severe suit 4▸ (durchdringend) ‹*smell*› strongly

Strẹnge *die;* **~** 1▸ ▸ **streng 1**: strictness; severity; stringency; rigour; sternness; **jmdn. mit äußerster ~ bestrafen** punish sb. extremely severely 2▸ (Striktheit) strictness 3▸ (von [Gesichts]zügen) severity 4▸ (von Geruch, Geschmack) pungency; sharpness; **ein Geruch von beißender ~** a bitingly pungent smell 5▸ ▸ **streng 6**: severity; sharpness 6▸ (Schnörkellosigkeit) austerity; severity

strẹng-, Strẹng-: ~genommen ▸ **streng B2**; **~gläubig** *Adj.* strict; **~gläubigkeit** *die* strict beliefs *pl.*

strengstens /ˈʃtrɛŋstn̩s/ *Adv.* [most] strictly

Streptokokkus /ʃtrɛptoˈkɔkʊs/ *der;* ~, **Streptokokken** streptococcus

Strese·mann *der: formal suit with dark jacket, grey waistcoat, and striped trousers*

Stress, ***Streß** /ʃtrɛs/ *der;* **Stresses, Stresse** stress; **im ~ sein** be under stress

Stress·abbau *der* reduction of stress

stressen (ugs.)
A *tr. V.* **jmdn. ~:** put sb. under stress; *s. auch* **gestresst**
B *itr. V.* be stressful

Stress·hormon *das* stress hormone

stressig *Adj.* (ugs.) stressful

Stress·situation, ***Streß·situation** *die* stress situation

Stretch /ʃtrɛtʃ/ *der;* **~[e]s, ~es** stretch fabric *or* material

Streu /ʃtrɔy/ *die;* **~, ~en** straw

Streu·büchse *die* shaker; (für Zucker) shaker; castor; (für Mehl) dredger

streuen
A *tr. V.* 1 spread ‹*manure, sand, grit*›; sprinkle ‹*salt, herbs, etc.*›; strew, scatter ‹*flowers*›; (fig.) spread ‹*rumour*›; **den Vögeln Futter ~:** scatter food for the birds; **weit gestreut** (fig.) scattered *or* spread over a wide area 2 (auch itr.) (mit Streugut) **die Straßen [mit Sand/Salz] ~:** grit/salt the roads; put grit/salt down on the roads; **[den Weg] ~:** put grit/salt *etc.* down [on the path]
B *itr. V.* 1 (beim Schießen) scatter 2 (bes. Physik) ‹*particles, ions, etc.*› scatter 3 (Med.) spread

Streu-: ~fahrzeug *das* gritter; gritting lorry; **~gut** *das* grit/salt (for icy roads etc.); **~licht** *das* (Optik) scattered light

streunen *itr. V.; meist mit sein* (oft abwertend) wander *or* roam about *or* around; **~de Katzen/Hunde** stray cats/dogs; **durch die Straßen/Felder ~:** roam *or* wander the streets/across the fields

Streuner *der;* **~s, ~, Streunerin** *die;* **~, ~nen** (abwertend) tramp

Streu-: ~salz *das* salt (for icy roads etc.); **~sand** *der* 1 grit (for icy roads etc.); 2 (veralt.: zum Trocknen) sand

Streusel *der od. das;* **~s, ~** *crumble* [*topping*] *made of butter, sugar, flour;* streusel

Streusel·kuchen *der* streusel cake

Streuung *die;* **~, ~en** 1 (Verbreitung) dissemination 2 (Ballistik) scattering 3 (Med.) generalization; metastasis (Med.)

Streu·zucker *der* granulated sugar

strich /ʃtrɪç/ *1. u. 3. Pers. Sg. Prät. v.* **streichen**

Strich *der;* **~[e]s, ~e** 1 (Linie) line; (in einer Zeichnung) stroke; line; (Gedanken~) dash; (Schräg~) diagonal; slash; (Binde~, Trennungs~) hyphen; (Markierung) mark; **beim Lesen ~e an den Rand machen** sideline passages when reading; **etw. mit groben** *od.* **in großen ~en zeichnen** *od.* (fig.) **umreißen** sketch sth. in broad strokes (lit. or fig.); **er ist nur noch ein ~ [in der Landschaft]** (ugs.) he's as thin as a rake; **keinen ~ tun** *od.* **machen** *od.* **arbeiten** not do a stroke *or* a thing; **jmdm. einen ~ durch die Rechnung/durch etw.** (*Akk.*) **machen** (ugs.) mess up *or* wreck sb.'s plans/ mess up sb.'s plans for sth.; **dem werden wir einen ~ durch die Rechnung machen!** we'll put a stop to his little game; **einen ~ unter etw.** (*Akk.*) **machen** *od.* **ziehen** put sth. behind one; make a [clean] break with sth.; **unter dem ~:** at the end of the day; all things considered; **unter dem ~ sein** (ugs.) not be up to scratch; be below par 2 (Winkeleinheit) point 3 **der ~** (salopp) (Prostitution) [street] prostitution; streetwalking; (Gegend) the streetwalkers' patch; the red-light district; **auf den ~ gehen** walk the streets 4 (streichende Bewegung) stroke 5 (Pinselführung) strokes *pl.*; **van Goghs kräftiger ~:** van Gogh's powerful brush strokes *pl. or* brush 6 (Streichung) deletion 7 (Bogen~) bowing *no indef. art.* 8 (Haar~, Fell~) lie; (eines Teppichs) pile; (von Samt o. Ä.) nap; **gegen den/mit dem ~ bürsten** brush ‹*hair, fur*› the wrong/right way; brush ‹*carpet*› against/with the pile; brush ‹*velvet*› against/with the nap; **jmdm. gegen den ~ gehen** (ugs.) go against the grain [with sb.]; **nach ~ und Faden** (ugs.) good and proper (coll.); well and truly; **jmdn. nach ~ und Faden belügen** (ugs.) lie through one's teeth to sb. 9 (bes. Jägerspr.) (Flug) flight; (Schwarm) flock

Strich·ätzung *die* (Druckw.) line block *or* plate

Strichelchen *das;* **~s, ~:** little line; (dünn) fine line

stricheln /ˈʃtrɪçl̩n/ *tr. V.* 1 (zeichnen) sketch in [with short lines]; **eine gestrichelte Linie** a broken line 2 (schraffieren) hatch

Strich-: ~junge *der* (salopp) [young] male prostitute; **~kode** *der* bar code

strichlieren (österr.) ▸ **stricheln**

strich-, Strich-: ~mädchen *das* (salopp) streetwalker; hooker (Amer. sl.); **~männchen** *das* matchstick man; **~punkt** *der* semicolon; **~vogel** *der* (Zool.) flocking bird; **~weise** (bes. Met.) **A** *Adv.* ‹*rain etc.*› in places; **B** *adj.* in places *postpos.*; local; **~zeichnung** *die* line drawing

Strick[1] /ʃtrɪk/ *der;* **~[e]s, ~e** 1 cord; (Seil) rope; **jmdm. aus etw. einen ~ drehen** (fig.) use sth. against sb.; **da kann ich mir ja gleich einen ~ nehmen** *od.* **kaufen!** I might as well end it all now; *s. auch* **reißen B 1; ziehen B 1** 2 (fam.: Schlingel) rascal

Strick[2] *das;* **~[e]s** (bes. Mode) knitted material; **in lässigem ~:** knitted in casual style

Strick-: ~arbeit *die* [piece of] knitting; **~bündchen** *das* knitted welt

stricken *tr., itr. V.* knit; **an etw.** (*Dat.*) **~:** be knitting sth.; **eine sauber gestrickte Story** (fig.) a neatly constructed story

Strickerei *die;* **~, ~en** 1 (Tätigkeit) knitting 2 (Produkt) piece of knitting

Strickerin *die;* **~, ~nen** knitter

Strick-: ~jacke *die* cardigan; **~kleid** *das* knitted dress; **~leiter** *die* rope ladder; **~maschine** *die* knitting machine; **~mode** *die* knitwear fashion; **~muster** *das* knitting pattern; (fig.) formula; **~nadel** *die* knitting needle; **~waren** *Pl.* knitwear *sing.*; **~zeug** *das* knitting

Striegel /ˈʃtriːgl̩/ *der;* **~s, ~:** curry-comb

striegeln *tr. V.* groom ‹*horse*›; **gestriegelt und gebügelt** (fig.) all spruced up

Strieme /ˈʃtriːmə/ *die;* **~, ~n, Striemen** *der;* **~ns, ~n** weal

Striezel /ˈʃtriːtsl̩/ *der;* **~s, ~** (bes. ostd.) long plaited bun

strikt /ʃtrɪkt/
A *Adj.* strict; exact ‹*opposite*›
B *adv.* strictly; **ich bin ~ dagegen** I am totally opposed to it

String /strɪŋ/ *der;* **~s, ~s** 1 (DV) string; 2 (Mode) string tanga

stringent /ʃtrɪŋˈgɛnt/ (geh.)
A *Adj.* compelling ‹*conclusion, reasoning, proof, argument*›
B *adv.* ‹*prove, deduce*› by compelling logic; ‹*prove, argue*› compellingly

Stringenz /ʃtrɪŋˈgɛnts/ *die;* **~** (geh.) compelling nature

String·tanga *der* string tanga

Strip /ʃtrɪp/ *der;* **~s, ~s** 1 (~tease) striptease 2 (Pflaster) strip [of sticking plaster]

Strippe /ˈʃtrɪpə/ *die;* **~, ~n** (ugs.) string; **an der ~ hängen** (fig.) be on the phone; (dauernd) hog the phone (coll.); **jmdn. an der ~ haben** (fig.) have sb. on the phone *or* line; **jmdn. an die ~ kriegen** (fig.) get sb. on the phone; **sich an die ~ hängen** (fig.) get on the phone

strippen *itr. V.* (ugs.) do striptease; strip

Stripper *der;* **~s, ~, Stripperin** *die;* **~, ~nen** ▸ⓘ S. 113 (ugs.) stripper

Striptease /ˈʃtrɪptiːs/ *der od. das;* **~:** striptease

Striptease·tänzerin *die* ▸ⓘ S. 113 striptease dancer

stritt /ʃtrɪt/ *1. u. 3. Pers. Sg. Prät. v.* **streiten**

strittig *Adj.* contentious ‹*point, problem*›; disputed ‹*territory*›; ‹*question*› in dispute, at issue; **~ ist nur, ob …** the only point at issue is whether …

Strizzi /ˈʃtrɪtsi/ *der;* **~s, ~s** (bes. südd., österr.) 1 (Zuhälter) pimp 2 (Strolch) rascal

Stroh /ʃtroː/ *das;* **~[e]s** straw; **mit ~ gedeckt** ‹*roof, cottage*› thatched with straw; **es brannte wie ~:** it went up like dry tinder; **~ im Kopf haben** (ugs.) have sawdust between one's ears (coll.)

stroh-, Stroh-: ~ballen *der* bale of straw; straw bale; **~blond** *Adj.* flaxen-haired ‹*person*›; straw-coloured, flaxen ‹*hair*›; **~blume** *die* 1 (Immortelle) immortelle; everlasting [flower]; 2 (Korbblütler) strawflower; **~dach** *das* roof thatched with straw; **~dumm** *Adj.* (ugs.) witless (coll.); thickheaded; **~feuer** *das:* **wie ein ~feuer aufflammen** flare up briefly; **das war nur ein ~feuer** (fig.) it was just a flash in the pan; **~frau** *die* (fig.) front woman; **~gedeckt** *Adj.* ‹*roof, house*› thatched with straw; **~gelb** *Adj.* straw-coloured; flaxen ‹*hair*›; **~halm** *der* straw; **sich [wie ein Ertrinkender] an einen ~halm klammern** (fig.) grasp at a straw [like a drowning man]; **der letzte ~halm** (fig.) the last ray of hope; **nach einem/jedem ~halm greifen** (fig.) clutch at a/any straw; **~hut** *der* straw hat

strohig *Adj.* strawy; **eine ~e Apfelsine** a dried-up orange; **~ sein/werden/schmecken** be/become/taste like straw

Stroh-: ~kopf *der* (ugs. abwertend) thickhead; **~mann** *der* (fig.) front man; **~puppe** *die* straw doll; **~sack** *der* palliasse; **[ach du] heiliger ~sack!** (ugs.) jeepers creepers! (coll.); goodness gracious [me]!; **~witwe** *die* (ugs. scherzh.) grass widow; **~witwer** *der* (ugs. scherzh.) grass widower

Strolch /ʃtrɔlç/ *der;* **~[e]s, ~e** 1 (veralt.) ruffian 2 (fam. scherzh.: Junge) rascal

strolchen *itr. V.; mit sein* roam *or* wander [aimlessly] about; **durch die Straßen ~:** roam the streets

Strom /ʃtroːm/ *der;* **~[e]s, Ströme** /ˈʃtrøːmə/ 1 ▸ⓘ S. 267 river; (von Blut, Schweiß, Wasser, fig.: Erinnerungen, Menschen, Autos usw.) stream; (große Menge) torrent; (fig.: von Tränen) flood; **ein reißender ~:** a raging torrent; **in Strömen regnen** *od.* (ugs.) **gießen** pour with rain; **in Strömen fließen** (fig.) flow freely; **das Blut floss in Strömen** (fig.) there was heavy bloodshed 2 (Strömung) current; **mit dem/gegen den ~ schwimmen** (fig.) swim with/against the tide (fig.) 3 (Elektrizität) current; (~versorgung) electricity; **das Kabel führt** *od.* **steht unter ~:** the cable is live; **ein ~ führendes Kabel** a live cable; **jmdm. den ~ sperren** *od.* **abstellen** cut off sb.'s electricity supply; **mit ~ betrieben sein** run on electricity; be electric; **der ~ ist ausgefallen** there has been a power failure

strom-, Strom-: ~ab *Adv.* downstream; **~abnehmer** /ˈ---/ *der* (Technik) current collector; **~abwärts** *Adv.* downstream; **~auf[wärts]** *Adv.* upstream; **~ausfall** /ˈ---/ *der* power failure

strömen /ˈʃtrøːmən/ *itr. V.; mit sein* stream; (intensiv) pour; (fließen) flow; **~der Regen** pouring rain

Stromer *der;* **~s, ~, Stromerin** *die;* **~, ~nen** (ugs.) vagabond; roamer

stromern *itr. V.; mit Richtungsangabe mit sein* (ugs.) roam *or* wander around; **durch die Gegend/Stadt ~:** roam *or* wander around the place/through the town

strom-, Strom-: ~führend ▸ **Strom 3**; **~kreis** *der* [electric] circuit; **~leitung** *die* power line *or* cable; **~linien·form** *die* streamlined shape; streamlining *no indef. art.*; **~linien·förmig** *Adj.* streamlined; **~netz** *das* electricity supply; mains [network]; **~rechnung** *die* electricity bill; **~schlag** *der* electric shock; **~schnelle** *die* rapids *pl.*; **~sparend A** *Adj.* power-saving; **~sparend sein** save electricity; **B** *adv.* in such a way that saves one electricity; **~stärke** *die* current strength; **~stoß** *der* electric shock

Strömung *die;* **~, ~en** 1 ▸ⓘ S. 267 current; (Met.) airstream 2 (fig.) (Bewegung) movement; (Tendenz) trend

Strom-: **~verbrauch** *der* electricity consumption; **~verbraucher** *der* (Technik) current-consuming device; **~versorgung** *die* electricity *or* power supply; **~zähler** *der* electricity meter

Strontium /ˈʃtrɔntsi̯ʊm/ *das;* **~s** strontium

Strophe /ˈʃtroːfə/ *die;* **~, ~n** verse; (einer Ode) strophe

Strophen·form *die* **1** verse form **2** (strophische Form) strophic form

-strophig *adj.* **drei~ sein** have three verses; **ein mehr~es/drei~es Lied** a song with several verses/a three-verse song

strophisch
A *Adj.* strophic
B *adv.* **~ gestaltet/gebaut** in strophic form

strotzen /ˈʃtrɔtsn̩/ *itr. V.* **von** *od.* **vor etw.** (*Dat.*) **~:** be full of sth.; **von** *od.* **vor Kraft/Gesundheit ~:** be bursting with strength/health

strubbelig /ˈʃtrʊb(ə)lɪç/ *Adj.* tousled; **du bist ja so ~!** your hair is in such a mess

Strubbel·kopf *der* (ugs.) **1** mop *or* shock of [tousled] hair **2** (Mensch) tousle-head

strubblig ▸ **strubbelig**

Strudel /ˈʃtruːdl̩/ *der;* **~s, ~** **1** whirlpool; (kleiner) eddy; **der ~ der Ereignisse** (fig.) the whirl of events **2** (bes. südd., österr.: Gebäck) strudel

strudeln *itr. V.* ‹*water*› eddy, swirl

Struktur /ʃtrʊkˈtuːɐ̯/ *die;* **~, ~en** **1** structure **2** (von Stoffen usw.) texture

Strukturalismus /ʃtrʊkturaˈlɪsmʊs/ *der;* **~:** structuralism *no art.*

strukturalistisch
A *Adj.* structuralist
B *adv.* structuralistically

Struktur·analyse *die* structural analysis

strukturell /ʃtrʊktuˈrɛl/
A *Adj.* structural
B *adv.* structurally

Struktur·fonds *der* (EU) Structural Fund

Struktur·formel *die* (Chemie) structural formula

strukturieren *tr. V.* structure; **neu ~:** restructure

Strukturierung *die;* **~, ~en** **1** structuring; organization **2** (Struktur) structure

struktur-, Struktur-: **~politik** *die* economic development policy; structural policy; **~schwach** *Adj.* (Wirtsch.) economically underdeveloped; **~wandel** *der* structural change

Strumpf /ʃtrʊmpf/ *der;* **~[e]s, Strümpfe** /ˈʃtrʏmpfə/ stocking; (Socke, Knie~) sock; **lange Strümpfe** stockings; **auf Strümpfen** in stockinged feet/in one's socks

Strumpf·band *das; Pl.* **Strumpfbänder** garter; (Straps) suspender (Brit.); garter (Amer.)

Strümpfchen /ˈʃtrʏmpfçən/ *das;* **~s, ~:** little stocking; (Socke, Kniestrumpf) little sock

Strumpf-: **~halter** *der* suspender (Brit.); garter (Amer.); **~hose** *die* tights *pl.* (Brit.); pantyhose (esp. Amer.); **eine ~hose** a pair of tights (Brit.); **~maske** *die* stocking mask

Strunk /ʃtrʊŋk/ *der;* **~[e]s, Strünke** /ˈʃtrʏŋkə/ stem; stalk; (Baum~) stump

struppig /ˈʃtrʊpɪç/ *Adj.* shaggy ‹*coat, dog, beard*›; tangled, tousled ‹*hair*›

Struwwel·peter /ˈʃtrʊvl̩-/ *der* tousle-head

Strychnin /ʃtrʏçˈniːn/ *das;* **~s** strychnine

Stübchen /ˈʃtyːpçən/ *das;* **~s, ~:** [little] room

Stube /ˈʃtuːbə/ *die;* **~, ~n** **1** (veralt.: Wohnraum) [living] room; parlour (dated); **in der ~ hocken** (ugs.) sit around indoors; **die gute ~:** the front room *or* (dated) parlour; **immer rein in die gute ~!** (ugs.) come on in! **2** (Milit.) [barrack] room

stuben-, Stuben-: **~älteste** *der/die; adj. Dekl.* (Milit.) senior man/woman in a/the barrack room; **~arrest** *der* (ugs.) detention (*in one's room*); **[zwei Tage] ~arrest bekommen** be kept in [for two days]; **~fliege** *die* [common] housefly; **~hocker** *der* (ugs. abwertend) stay-at-home; **~hockerei** *die;* **~~** (ugs. abwertend) sticking (coll.) *or* sitting around indoors *no art.;* **~hockerin** *die;* **~~, ~~nen** ▸ **~hocker**; **~kamerad** *der,* **~kameradin** *die* room-mate; **~rein** *Adj.* **1** house-trained; **2** (scherzh.: nicht zotig) clean ‹*joke etc.*›; **~wagen** *der* bassinet; wicker cot

Stuck /ʃtʊk/ *der;* **~[e]s** stucco

Stück /ʃtʏk/ *das;* **~[e]s, ~e** **1** piece; (kleines) bit; (Teil, Abschnitt) part; **ein ~ Kuchen** a piece *or* slice of cake; **ein ~ Zucker/Seife** a piece *or* lump of sugar/ a piece *or* bar of soap; **ein ~ [Weg** *od.* (geh.) **Weges]** a little [way]; a short distance; **ein ~ spazieren gehen** go for a little walk; **ein [gutes] ~ weiterkommen** get a [good] bit further; **ein ~ Autobahn** a section *or* stretch of motorway (Brit.) *or* (Amer.) freeway; **jmdn. wie ein ~ Dreck/Mist behandeln** (ugs. abwertend) treat sb. like dirt; **ein ~ Heimat** a bit of home; **ein gewaltiges/hartes ~ Arbeit** a really big/tough job; **ein ~ Hoffnung/Wahrheit** a ray of hope/a grain of truth; **alles in ~e schlagen** smash everything [to pieces]; **es ist nur ein ~ Papier** it's only a scrap of paper; **sich für jmdn. in ~e reißen lassen** (ugs.) do anything for sb.; **im** *od.* **am ~:** unsliced ‹*sausage, cheese, etc.*›; **aus einem ~ gemeißelt** carved from the solid; **in einem ~** (ugs.) ‹*talk, rain*› non-stop **2** (Einzel~) item; article; (Exemplar) specimen; (Möbel~) piece [of furniture]; **zwanzig ~ Vieh** twenty head of cattle; **ich nehme 5 ~/5 ~ von den Rosen** I'll take five [of them]/five of the roses; **30 Cent das ~, das ~ 30 Cent** thirty cents each; **~ für ~:** piece by piece; (eins nach dem andern) one by one; **das gute ~** (oft iron.) the precious thing; **große ~e auf jmdn. halten** (ugs.) think the world of sb.; **Vater, unser bestes ~** (scherzh.) father, our pride and joy; *s. auch* **frei A 17** **3** **das ist [ja] ein starkes** *od.* **tolles ~** (ugs.) that's a bit much *or* a bit thick (coll.); **da hast du dir aber ein [tolles] ~ geleistet** you've [really] gone too far there; **das ist ja ein ~ aus dem Tollhaus!** that's [a piece of] pure lunacy **4** (salopp abwertend: Person) **ein faules/freches ~:** a lazy/cheeky thing *or* devil; **ein dummes** *od.* **blödes ~:** a stupid thing **5** (Bühnen~) play **6** (Musik~) piece

Stuckateur /ʃtʊkaˈtøːɐ̯/ *der;* **~s, ~e, Stuckateurin** *die;* **~, ~nen** [stucco] plasterer

Stückchen *das;* **~s, ~:** [little] piece; bit; **es ist bloß noch ein kleines ~:** it's only another few yards

Stuck·decke *die* stucco[ed] ceiling

stückeln
A *tr. V.* put together ‹*sleeve, curtain*› with patches
B *itr. V.* sew on patches

Stücke·schreiber *der,* **Stücke·schreiberin** *die* playwright

stück-, Stück-: **~gut** *das* [individually] packaged goods *pl.;* **~lohn** *der* (Wirtsch.) piecework pay; (Akkordsatz) piece rate; **~preis** *der* unit price; **~weise** *Adv.* piece by piece; (einzeln) ‹*sell*› separately; **~werk** *das:* **~werk sein/bleiben** be/remain incomplete; ‹*book, work of art*› remain a torso; **unsere Korrekturen sind nur ~werk, wir müssen das ganze Buch neu bearbeiten** our corrections are only half measures, we must revise the whole book; **~zahl** *die* (Wirtsch.) number of units; **in hohen ~zahlen produzieren** manufacture in large numbers; **eine ~zahl von 300** an output of 300 units

Student /ʃtuˈdɛnt/ *der;* **~en, ~en** **1** student **2** (österr.: Schüler) [secondary-school] pupil

Studenten-: **~ausweis** *der* student card; **~bewegung** *die* student movement; **~bude** *die* (ugs.) student's room; **~heim** *das* student hostel; students' [hall of] residence; **~lokal** *das* students' [favourite] haunt; **~parlament** *das:* students' assembly

Studentenschaft *die;* **~, ~en** student body; **die verfasste ~** (Hochschulw.) the students' assembly

Studenten·verbindung *die* society; (für Männer) fraternity (Amer.); (für Frauen) sorority (Amer.)

> **Studentenwerk**
>
> The *Studentenwerke* (student welfare services) are responsible for the economic, social, cultural and health care of students at higher educational institutions. Sixty-five of these organizations are statutory bodies of the federal states and deal with **BAföG** payments. The local student welfare services have formed the national *Deutsches Studentenwerk* (*DSW*).

Studentin *die;* **~, ~nen** ▸ **Student**; *s. auch* **-in**

studentisch *Adj.* student

Studi[1] *der;* **~s, ~s** (Jargon) student

Studi[2] *die;* **~, ~s** (Jargon) student

Studie /ˈʃtuːdi̯ə/ *die;* **~, ~n** study

studien-, Studien-: **~assessor** *der,* **~assessorin** *die: graduate teacher who has recently passed the second State Examination;* ≈ probationary teacher; **~aufenthalt** *der* study visit (**in** + *Dat.* to); **~bewerber** *der,* **~bewerberin** *die: applicant for a place in higher education;* **~direktor** *der,* **~direktorin** *die* **1** deputy headteacher; **2** (DDR) *honorary title conferred on a secondary-school teacher;* **~fach** *das* subject [of study]; **~freund** *der,* **~freundin** *die* university/college friend; **~gang** *der* course of study; **~gebühr** *die* tuition fee; **~halber** *Adv.* for study purposes; **~kolleg** *das* (Hochschulw.) preparatory course (*esp. for foreign students*); **~kollege** *der,* **~kollegin** *die* fellow student; **~platz** *der* university/college place; **~rat** *der,* **~rätin** *die* ▸ℹ **S. 44** **1** *established graduate secondary-school teacher* (Brit.); *graduate high-school teacher with tenure* (Amer.); **2** (DDR) *honorary title conferred on a teacher;* **~referendar** *der,* **~referendarin** *die* probationary graduate teacher; **~reise** *die* study trip; **~zeit** *die* **1** (Zeit als Student) time as a student; student days *pl.;* **2** (Dauer) period of study

studieren /ʃtuˈdiːrən/
A *itr. V.* study; **er studiert in Berlin** he is studying *or* at university in Berlin; **er studiert noch** he is still a student
B *tr. V.* study

Studierende *der/die; adj. Dekl.* student

Studier·stube *die* (veralt., scherzh.) study

studiert *Adj.* (ugs.) ‹*person*› who has been to university; ‹*painter etc.*› with an academic training

Studierte *der/die; adj. Dekl.* (ugs.) person with a university education

Studio /ˈʃtuːdi̯o/ *das;* **~s, ~s** **1** studio **2** (Einzimmerwohnung) [one-room] flatlet (esp. Brit.); studio flat (esp. Brit.); studio apartment (esp. Amer.)

Studio·bühne *die* studio theatre

Studiosus /ʃtuˈdi̯oːzʊs/ *der;* **~, Studiosi** (veralt., scherzh.) student

Studium /ˈʃtuːdi̯ʊm/ *das;* **~s, Studien** **1** study; (Studiengang) course of study; **zum ~ der Medizin zugelassen werden** get a place to study medicine; **das ~ mit dem Staatsexamen abschließen** complete one's studies *or* course [of study] with the State Examination; **neben dem ~ arbeitet sie als Kellnerin** she works as a waitress while she is studying; **während seines ~s** (als er Student war) in his student days **2** (Erforschung) study; **Studien über etw.** (*Akk.*) **betreiben** carry out studies into sth. **3** (genaues Lesen) study; **beim ~ der Akten** while studying the files

Studium generale *das;* **~:** general studies course

Stufe /ˈʃtuːfə/ *die;* **~, ~n** **1** step; (einer Treppe) stair; (Gelände~) terrace; **„Achtung** *od.* **Vorsicht, ~!"** 'mind the step' **2** (Raketen~, Geol., fig.: Stadium) stage; (Niveau) level; (Steigerungs~, Grad) degree; (Rang) grade; **eine ~ der Entwicklung** a stage of development; **auf einer hohen ~ stehen** be of a high standard; **auf der gleichen ~ stehen [wie ...]** be of the same standard [as ...]; have the same status [as ...]; (gleichwertig sein) be equivalent [to ...]; **jmdn./etw. mit jmdm./etw. auf eine** *od.* **auf die gleiche ~ stellen** equate sb./sth. with sb./sth.; **zwei Dinge auf die gleiche ~ stellen** equate two things; **sich mit jmdm./etw. auf eine** *od.* **auf die gleiche ~ stellen** put oneself on a level with sb./sth. [3] (Technik) (Funktions~) mark; position; (Geschwindigkeits~) speed; (Heiz~) heat setting; **Gas: ~ III** gas mark III [4] (Musik) degree; **die erste ~ der Tonleiter** the first step on the scale

stufen *tr. V.* [1] step; terrace ‹*slope*› [2] (ab~) grade ‹*salaries*›; graduate ‹*prices*›

stufen-, Stufen-: ~barren *der* (Turnen) asymmetric bars *pl.*; **~heck** *das* (Kfz-W.) notchback; **~leiter** *die* (fig.) hierarchy; ladder (fig.); **~los** **A** *Adj.* continuously variable; **B** *adv.* **~los verstellbar** continuously adjustable; **~plan** *der* phased plan; **~pyramide** *die* (Kunstwiss.) step pyramid; **~weise** **A** *Adv.* in stages *or* phases; **B** *adj.* phased

stufig
A *Adj.* layered ‹*hair [style]*›; terraced ‹*terrain*›
B *adv.* **~ geschnittenes Haar** layered hair; hair cut in layers; **~ gegliedertes Gelände** terraced terrain

-stufig *adj.* -step; (fig.) -stage ‹*development, rocket, filter, etc*›; -phase ‹*plan*›

Stuhl /ʃtu:l/ *der;* **~[e]s, Stühle** /ˈʃty:lə/ [1] chair [2] (fig.) **sein ~ wackelt** his position is threatened *or* no longer secure; **der Minister klebt an seinem ~** (ugs.) the minister is not to be shifted [from office]; **jmdm. den ~ vor die Tür setzen** kick sb. out; show sb. the door; **[fast] vom ~ fallen** (ugs.) [nearly] have a fit (coll.); **jmdn. vom ~ reißen** *od.* **jagen/hauen** (ugs.) get sb. excited/take sb.'s breath away; **das hat mich fast** *od.* **bald vom ~ gehauen** (ugs.) you could have knocked me down with a feather; **sich zwischen zwei Stühle setzen/zwischen zwei Stühlen sitzen** fall/have fallen between two stools; *s. auch* **elektrisch A** [3] (kath. Kirche) see; **der ~ Petri** the Holy See *or* See of Rome; *s. auch* **apostolisch 2; heilig 1** [4] (Med.) stool [5] ▸ **Stuhlgang 1**

Stuhl·bein *das* chair leg

Stühlchen /ˈʃty:lçən/ *das;* **~s, ~:** little chair

Stuhl-: ~gang *der* [1] bowel movement[s]; [2] (Kot) stool; **~lehne** *die* [1] (Rückenlehne) chair back; [2] (Armlehne) chair arm; **~verstopfung** *die* constipation

Stuka /ˈʃtu:ka/ *der;* **~s, ~s** (Milit.) dive-bomber; (Ju 87) stuka

***Stukkateur, *Stukkateurin** ▸ **Stuckateur, Stuckateurin**

Stulle /ˈʃtʊlə/ *die;* **~, ~n** (nordostd.) slice of bread; (Butter~) piece of bread and butter; (belegt) sandwich

Stulpe /ˈʃtʊlpə/ *die;* **~, ~n** (am Ärmel) turned-up cuff; (am Stiefel) bucket-top

stülpen /ˈʃtʏlpn̩/ *tr. V.* **etw. auf** *od.* **über etw.** (*Akk.*) **~:** pull/put sth. on to *or* over sth.; **die Taschen nach außen ~:** turn the/one's pockets inside out

Stulpen·stiefel *der* bucket-top boot

stumm /ʃtʊm/ *Adj.* dumb ‹*person*›; (schweigsam) silent ‹*person, reproach, greeting, prayer, etc.*›; (wortlos) wordless ‹*greeting, complaint, prayer, gesture, dialogue*›; mute ‹*glance, gesture*›; (Theater) non-speaking ‹*part, character*›; **~ vor Schreck** speechless with fear; **sie sahen sich ~ an** they looked at one another without speaking *or* in silence; **ein ~er Konsonant/Vokal** (Sprachw.) a silent *or* mute consonant/vowel; **das ~e h** the silent h; the h mute; **~er Diener** (Kleiderständer) valet; (Serviertisch) dumb waiter

Stumme *der/die; adj. Dekl.* mute; **die ~n** the dumb

Stummel /ˈʃtʊml̩/ *der;* **~s, ~:** stump; (Bleistift~) stub; (Zigaretten~/Zigarren~) [cigarette/cigar] butt

Stummel·schwanz *der* stumpy tail

Stumm·film *der* silent film

Stummheit *die* dumbness; (Schweigsamkeit) silence

Stumpen /ˈʃtʊmpn̩/ *der;* **~s, ~:** stumpy cigar

Stümper /ˈʃtʏmpɐ/ *der;* **~s, ~** (abwertend) botcher; bungler

Stümperei *die;* **~, ~en** (abwertend) [1] botching; incompetence [2] (Ergebnis) botched job; piece of incompetence

stümperhaft (abwertend)
A *Adj.* incompetent; botched ‹*job*›; (laienhaft) amateurish ‹*attempt, drawing*›
B *adv.* incompetently; (laienhaft) amateurishly

Stümperin *die* ▸ **Stümper**

stümpern *itr. V.* (abwertend) work incompetently; (pfuschen) bungle

stumpf /ʃtʊmpf/
A *Adj.* [1] blunt ‹*pin, needle, knife, etc.*›; snub ‹*nose*›; flat-topped ‹*tower*›; (Math.) truncated ‹*cone, pyramid*›; obtuse ‹*angle*› [2] (glanzlos, matt) dull ‹*paint, hair, metal, colour, etc.*›; (rau) rough ‹*stone, wood*› [3] (Verslehre) masculine ‹*rhyme*› [4] (abgestumpft, teilnahmslos) impassive, lifeless ‹*person, glance*›; impassive, apathetic ‹*indifference, resignation*›; dulled ‹*senses*›; blank ‹*look, despair*› [5] (Med.) contused ‹*wound*›
B *adv.* (abgestumpft) ‹*sit, stare*› impassively

Stumpf *der;* **~[e]s, Stümpfe** /ˈʃtʏmpfə/ stump; **etw. mit ~ und Stiel ausrotten/vernichten** eradicate/destroy sth. root and branch

Stümpfchen /ˈʃtʏmpfçən/ *das;* **~s, ~:** [little] stump

Stumpfheit *die;* **~** [1] bluntness [2] (Abgestumpftheit) impassiveness; apathy; (des Blickes) lifelessness; blankness; (der Sinne) dullness

stumpf-, Stumpf-: ~sinn *der* [1] apathy; [2] (Monotonie) monotony; tedium; **~sinnig** **A** *Adj.* [1] apathetic; vacant ‹*look*›; [2] (monoton) tedious; dreary; soul-destroying ‹*job, work*›. **B** *adv.* [1] apathetically; ‹*stare*› vacantly; [2] (monoton) tediously; monotonously; **~winklig** *Adj.* obtuse-angled ‹*triangle, intersection*›

Stund /ʃtʊnt/ ▸ **Stunde 2**

Stündchen /ˈʃtʏntçən/ *das;* **~s, ~** (fam.) **[für** *od.* **auf] ein ~:** for an hour or so; **jmds. letztes ~ ist gekommen** *od.* **hat geschlagen** sb.'s last hour has come

stünde /ˈʃtʏndə/ *1. u. 3. Pers. Sg. Konjunktiv II v.* **stehen**

Stunde /ˈʃtʊndə/ *die;* **~, ~n** [1] ▸ⓘ **S. 224,** ▸ⓘ **S. 729** hour; **eine ~ Aufenthalt/Pause** an hour's stop/break; a stop/break of an hour; **drei ~n zu Fuß/mit dem Auto** three hours' walk/drive; **120 km in der ~ fahren** do 120 kilometres per hour; **20 Euro [für] die** *od.* **in der** *od.* **pro ~ bekommen** get 20 euros an hour *or* per hour; **jede ~:** once an hour; **nach ~n bezahlt werden** be paid by the hour; **zur vollen ~:** on the hour; **alle halbe ~:** every half hour; **~ um ~, ~n und ~n** [for] hours; [for] hour after hour; **jmds. letzte ~ hat geschlagen** *od.* **ist gekommen** sb.'s last hour has come; **wissen, was die ~ geschlagen hat** (fig.) know how things [really] stand; (wissen, was einem bevorsteht) know what's in store *or* what one is in for; **die Männer und Frauen der ersten ~** (einer Partei o. ä.) the founder members [2] (geh.) (Zeitpunkt) hour; (Zeit) time; (Augenblick) moment; **in ~n der Not/Gefahr** in times of need/danger; **in einer stillen ~:** in a quiet moment; **zu früher/vorgerückter** *od.* **später ~:** at an early/a late hour; **zur ~:** at the present time; **die Gunst der ~ nutzen** make hay while the sun shines (fig.); strike while the iron is hot (fig.); **seine [große] ~ war gekommen** his big moment had come; **die ~ der Wahrheit** the moment of truth; **die ~ null** [the time of] the new beginning (*esp. in Germany after World War II*); **von Stund an** (geh. veralt.) thenceforth (arch.); *s. auch* **blau; Gebot 5** [3] (Unterrichtsstunde) lesson; **in der dritten ~:** in the third period; **eine freie ~:** a free period

stunden *tr. V.* **jmdm. einen Betrag/eine Rate** *usw.* **~:** give sb. [extra] time to pay *or* allow sb. to defer payment of a sum/an instalment *etc.*; **können Sie mir den Rest bis morgen ~?** will you give me until tomorrow to pay you the rest?

stunden-, Stunden-: ~buch *das* (Hist., Kunstwiss.) book of hours; **~gebet** *das* (kath. Kirche) *prayer said at the canonical hours;* **~geschwindigkeit** *die:* ▸ⓘ **S. 310 bei/mit einer ~geschwindigkeit von 60 km** at a speed of 60 k.p.h.; **~glas** *das* (veralt.) hourglass; **~hotel** *das* sleazy hotel (*which lets rooms by the hour*); **~kilometer** *der* ▸ⓘ **S. 310** (ugs.) kilometre per hour; k.p.h.; **er fuhr 120 ~kilometer** he was driving at *or* doing 120 k.p.h.; **~lang** **A** *Adj.* lasting hours *postpos.*; **das ~lange Warten/Stehen** the hours of waiting/standing; **B** *adv.* for hours; **~lohn** *der* hourly wage; **sie bekommt 12 Euro ~lohn** she gets paid 12 euros an hour *or* per hour; **~plan** *der* timetable; **~schlag** *der* stroke [of the clock]; **mit dem ~schlag** on the stroke of the hour; **~weise** **A** *Adv.* for an hour or two [at a time]; **er wird ~weise bezahlt** he is paid by the hour; **B** *adj.* ‹*hiring, payment*› by the hour; **~zahl** *die* number of hours; (von Unterrichts~) number of lessons; **~zeiger** *der* hour hand

-stündig *adj.* -hour

Stündlein *das;* **~s, ~** ▸ **Stündchen**

stündlich ▸ⓘ **S. 729**
A *Adj.* hourly
B *adv.* [1] hourly; once an hour; **sich ~ verändern** change from hour to hour *or* from one hour to the next [2] (jeden Augenblick) at any moment; **etw. ~ erwarten** expect sth. hourly

-stündlich *adj.* -hourly; **zwei~/halb~:** two-hourly/half-hourly; *adv.* every two hours/half an hour

Stundung *die;* **~, ~en** deferment of payment

Stunk /ʃtʊnk/ *der;* **~s** (ugs.) trouble; **~ machen/anfangen** cause/start trouble

Stunt /stant/ *der;* **~s, ~:** stunt

Stunt-frau *die* stuntwoman

Stuntman /ˈstantmən/ *der;* **~s, Stuntmen** /ˈstantmən/ stuntman

stupid[e] /ʃtuˈpi:də/ (abwertend)
A *Adj.* [1] moronic, empty-headed ‹*person*›; moronic, vacuous ‹*expression*› [2] (monoton) soul-destroying
B *adv.* moronically

Stupidität /ʃtupidiˈtɛ:t/ *die;* **~** (abwertend) [1] moronic stupidity *or* vacuity [2] (Monotonie) deadly monotony *or* tedium

Stups /ʃtʊps/ *der;* **~es, ~e** (ugs.) push; shove; (leicht) nudge

stupsen *tr. V.* (ugs.) push; shove; (leicht) nudge

Stups·nase *die* snub nose

stur (ugs.)
A *Adj.* [1] (abwertend) (eigensinnig, unnachgiebig) obstinate; pigheaded; obstinate, dogged ‹*insistence*›; (phlegmatisch) stolid; dour; **ein ~er Bock** a pigheaded so-and-so (coll.); **du ~er Bock!** you're as obstinate as a mule!; **~ wie ein Panzer** stubborn as a mule; **auf ~ schalten** dig one's heels in; **sich ~ stellen, ~ bleiben** not give in [2] (unbeirrbar) dogged; persistent; **~es Geradeausgehen** just keeping straight on [3] (abwertend: stumpfsinnig) tedious; **~es Auswendiglernen** soul-destroying *or* mechanical learning by rote
B *adv.* [1] (abwertend: eigensinnig, unnachgiebig) obstinately [2] (unbeirrbar) doggedly; **sie las/redete ~ weiter** she carried on reading/kept on talking regardless [3] (abwertend: stumpfsinnig) tediously; ‹*learn, copy*› mechanically

stürbe /ˈʃtʏrbə/ *1. u. 3. Pers. Sg. Konjunktiv II v.* **sterben**

Sturheit *die;* **~** (ugs. abwertend) [1] (Eigensinnigkeit, Unnachgiebigkeit) obstinacy; pigheadedness; (phlegmatisches Wesen) stolidity; dourness [2] (Stumpfsinnigkeit) deadly monotony

Sturm /ʃtʊrm/ *der;* **~[e]s, Stürme** /ˈʃtʏrmə/ [1] storm; (heftiger Wind) gale; **bei** *od.* **in ~ und Regen** in the wind and rain; **ein ~ im Wasserglas** a storm in a teacup; **das Barometer steht auf ~** (fig.) there's a storm brewing; **ein ~ der Begeisterung/des Protests** tumultuous *or* tempestuous applause/a storm of protest; **~ und Drang** (Literaturw.) Storm and Stress; *s. auch* **Ruhe 3** [2] (Milit.: Angriff) assault (**auf +** *Akk.* on); **der ~ auf die Bastille** (hist.) the storming of the Bastille; **etw. im ~ erobern** *od.* **nehmen** (auch fig.) take sth. by storm; **gegen etw. ~ laufen** (fig.) be up in arms against sth.;

S

~ klingeln ring the [door]bell like mad (coll.); lean on the [door]bell (coll.) 3) (Sport: die Stürmer) forward line; **im ~ spielen** play up front 4) (österr.: Most) ▸**Federweiße**

Sturm-: ~abteilung *die* (ns.) *armed and uniformed branch of the NSDAP;* SA; **~angriff** *der* (Milit.) assault (**auf** + *Akk.* on); **~bock** *der* (hist.) battering ram

stürmen /ˈʃtʏrmən/

A *itr. V.* 1) *unpers.* **es stürmt [heftig]** it's blowing a gale 2) *mit sein* (rennen) rush; (verärgert) storm; **zum Ausgang ~:** make a rush for the exit 3) (Sport: als Stürmer spielen) play up front *or* as a striker 4) (Sport, Milit.: angreifen) attack

B *tr. V.* (Milit.) storm ‹*town, position, etc.*›; (fig.) besiege ‹*booking-office, shop, etc.*›; **den Saal ~:** force one's way into the hall

Stürmer /ˈʃtʏrmɐ/ *der:* **~s, ~** 1) (Sport) striker; forward 2) **~ und Dränger** (Literaturw.) Storm and Stress writer; **die ~ und Dränger in der Partei** (fig.) the radical faction in the party

Stürmerin *die;* **~, ~nen** ▸**Stürmer 1**

sturm-, Sturm-: ~feuerzeug *das* storm lighter; **~flut** *die* storm tide; **~frei** *Adj.* (scherzh.) **eine ~freie Bude haben** have a place where one can do as one likes [without interference/objections]; **~gepäck** *das* (Milit.) combat pack; **~gepeitscht** *Adj.* (geh.) ‹*forest, trees*› bending before the storm; storm-tossed ‹*sea*›

stürmisch /ˈʃtʏrmɪʃ/

A *Adj.* 1) stormy; (fig.) tempestuous, turbulent ‹*days, life, times, years*› 2) (ungestüm) tempestuous ‹*nature, outburst, welcome*›; tumultuous ‹*applause, welcome, reception*›; wild ‹*enthusiasm*›; passionate ‹*lover, embrace, temperament*›; vehement ‹*protest*›; **~es Gelächter** gales of laughter; **er näherte sich mit ~en Schritten** he approached with impetuous steps; **nicht so ~!** calm down!; take it easy! 3) (rasant) meteoric ‹*development, growth*›; lightning, breakneck ‹*speed*›

B *adv.* 1) ‹*protest*› vehemently; ‹*embrace*› impetuously, passionately; ‹*demand*› clamorously; ‹*applaud*› wildly; **jmdn. ~ begrüßen/empfangen** give sb. a tumultuous welcome/reception 2) (rasant) at a tremendous rate *or* speed; at lightning speed

sturm-, Sturm-: ~laterne *die* storm lantern (Brit.); hurricane lamp; **~lauf** *der:* **im ~lauf** at the double; **~leiter** *die* (Milit. hist.) scaling ladder; **~möwe** *die* seamew; common gull; **~reif** *Adj.* (Milit. hist.) ready to be stormed *postpos.*; **die Stadt ~reif schießen** soften the town up with a bombardment [preparatory to the assault]; **~schaden** *der* gale *or* storm damage *no pl., no indef. art.*; **~schritt** *der:* **im ~schritt** at the double; **~segel** *das* storm sail; **~tief** *das* (Met.) deep low

Sturm-und-Drang-Zeit *die* (Literaturw.) Storm and Stress period; **in meiner ~** (fig. scherzh.) [in the days] when I was sowing my wild oats

Sturm-: ~vogel *der* (Zool.) petrel; **~warnung** *die* (Seew.) gale warning; **~wind** *der* (dichter., geh.) tempest (literary)

Sturz /ʃtʊrts/ *der;* **~es, Stürze** /ˈʃtʏrtsə/ 1) fall (**aus, von** from); (Unfall) accident; **ein ~ in die Tiefe** a plunge into the depths; **bei einem ~ vom Pferd** falling off a horse 2) (fig.: von Preis, Temperatur usw.) [sharp] fall, drop (*Gen.* in) 3) (Verlust des Amtes, der Macht) fall; (Absetzung) overthrow; (Amtsenthebung) removal from office 4) (Kfz-W.) camber 5) *Pl. auch* **~e** (Fenster~, Tür~) lintel

Sturz·bach *der* [mountain] torrent; (fig.: von Fragen usw.) torrent

stürzen /ˈʃtʏrtsn̩/

A *itr. V.; mit sein* 1) fall (**aus, von** from); (in die Tiefe) plunge; plummet; (fig.) ‹*temperature, exchange rate, etc.*› drop [sharply]; ‹*prices*› tumble; ‹*government*› fall, collapse; **beim Rollschuhlaufen/auf dem Eis ~:** have a fall while roller skating/on the ice; **mit dem Pferd/Fahrrad ~:** come off one's horse/bicycle 2) (laufen) rush; dash; **er stürzte ins Zimmer** he burst into the room; **jmdm. in die Arme ~:** hurl *or* fling oneself into sb.'s arms 3) (fließen) stream; pour 4) (geh.: steil abfallen) plunge

B *refl. V.* **sich auf jmdn./etw. ~** (auch fig.) pounce on sb./sth.; **sich in etw.** (*Akk.*) **~:** throw oneself *or* plunge into sth.; **sich in die Arbeit ~:** throw oneself into one's work; **sich ins Vergnügen ~:** abandon oneself to pleasure

C *tr. V.* 1) throw; (mit Wucht) hurl; **sich aus dem Fenster/von der Brücke ~:** hurl oneself *or* leap out of the window/off the bridge; **sich in die Tiefe ~:** plunge into the depths; **jmdn. ins Verderben/Unglück ~:** plunge sb. into ruin/misfortune 2) (umdrehen) upturn, turn upside-down ‹*mould, pot, box, glass, cup*›; turn out ‹*pudding, cake, etc.*›; **„[bitte] nicht ~"** 'this way up' 3) (des Amtes entheben) oust ‹*person*› [from office]; (gewaltsam) overthrow, topple ‹*leader, government*›

Sturz-: ~flug *der* (Flugw.) [nose]dive; **im ~flug** in a [nose]dive; **~geburt** *die* (Med.) precipitate delivery; **~helm** *der* crash helmet; **~kampf·flugzeug** *das* dive-bomber; **~regen** *der* torrential downpour; **~see** *die,* **~welle** *die* breaking wave; [heavy] sea; (am Strand usw.) breaker

Stuss, *Stuß /ʃtʊs/ *der;* **Stusses** (ugs. abwertend) rubbish; twaddle (coll.)

Stute /ˈʃtu:tə/ *die;* **~, ~n** mare; (Esel~) she-ass

Stuten *der;* **~s, ~** (nordd.) currant bread; fruit loaf

Stut[en]-: ~fohlen *das,* **~füllen** *das* filly

Stütz *der;* **~es, ~e** (Geräteturnen) support

Stütze /ˈʃtʏtsə/ *die;* **~, ~n** 1) (auch fig.) support; (für die Wäscheleine) prop; **~n für Kopf, Arme und Füße** head, arm, and footrests; **an jmdm. eine ~ haben** (fig.) get support *or* help from sb.; **er ist die ~ der Familie** (fig.) he is the mainstay of the family; **die ~n der Gesellschaft** (fig.) the pillars of society 2) (salopp: Arbeitslosengeld) dole (coll.); **von der ~ leben** live on the dole (Brit. coll.)

stutzen[1] /ˈʃtʊtsn̩/ *itr. V.* stop short

stutzen[2] *tr. V.* trim; dock ‹*tail*›; clip ‹*ear, hedge, wing*›; prune ‹*tree, bush*›

stützen /ˈʃtʏtsn̩/

A *tr. V.* 1) support; (mit Pfosten o. Ä.) prop up; (auf~) rest ‹*head, hands, arms, etc.*› (**auf** + *Akk.* on); **die Hände in die Seiten/den Kopf in die Hände gestützt** hands on hips/head in hands; **wo sind die Beweise, auf die Sie Ihre Anschuldigungen ~?** where is the evidence to support your accusations *or* on which your accusations are based? 2) (Wirtsch.) support ‹*currency, exchange rate, price*›; (niedrig halten) peg ‹*prices*›

B *refl. V.* **sich auf jmdn./etw. ~:** lean *or* support oneself on sb./sth.; **sich auf Fakten** (*Akk.*) **~** (fig.) ‹*theory, statement etc.*› be based on facts; **er kann sich auf keinerlei Fakten ~:** he has no facts to support his case

Stutzen *der;* **~s, ~** 1) (Gewehr) carbine 2) (Technik: Rohrstück) pipe end; spout; (zum Einfüllen) filler pipe 3) (Kniestrumpf) [knee] sock (*without a foot*); (Fußball) [football] sock

Stutzer *der;* **~s, ~** (veralt. abwertend) dandy; fop

stutzerhaft

A *Adj.* dandyish

B *adv.* like a dandy

Stutz·flügel *der* (Musik) baby grand [piano]

Stütz·gewebe *das* ▸ **S. 435** (Anat., Biol.) stroma

stutzig *Adj.* **~ werden** begin to wonder; get suspicious; **jmdn. ~ machen** make sb. wonder; make sb. suspicious

Stütz-: ~korsett *das* [support] corset; **~mauer** *die* supporting wall; **~pfeiler** *der* [supporting] pillar; **~punkt** *der* (bes. Milit.) base; **~rad** *das* stabilizer (*for bicycle*); **~strumpf** *der* support stocking

Stützung *die;* **~, ~en** 1) support; **zur ~ seiner Behauptung sagte er ...** in support of his statement, he said ... 2) (Wirtsch.) (von Währung, Kursen) support; (von Preisen) pegging

Stützungs·kauf *der* (Wirtsch.) support purchase

Stütz·verband *der* (Med.) support bandage

StVO *Abk.* = **Straßenverkehrsordnung**

stylen /ˈstailən/ *tr. V.* (ugs.) style ‹*car etc.*›; do up ‹*person*›; **ein hervorragend gestyltes Modell** a model with outstanding lines

Styling /ˈstailɪŋ/ *das;* **~s, ~s** styling

Styropor Ⓦ /ʃtyroˈpo:ɐ̯/ *das;* **~s** polystyrene [foam]

Styx /ʃtʏks/ *der;* **~** (griech. Myth.) Styx

s.u. *Abk.* = **siehe unten** see below

SU *Abk.* = **Sowjetunion**

Suada /ˈzu̯a:da/ *die;* **~, Suaden** (geh. abwertend) harangue; diatribe

Suaheli /zu̯aˈhe:li/ *das;* **~[s]** ▸ **S. 670** Swahili; *s. auch* **Deutsch**

subaltern /zʊp|alˈtɛrn/ (geh.)

A *Adj.* 1) (untergeordnet) subordinate 2) (abwertend) (unselbstständig) unoriginal ‹*mind, literature*›; (unterwürfig) servile

B *adv.* (abwertend: unterwürfig) in a servile manner

Subbotnik /zʊˈbɔtnɪk/ *der;* **~[s], ~s** (DDR) *voluntary work (usually on a Saturday) done without payment*

Sub·dominante /ˈzʊp-/ *die* (Musik) subdominant; (Dreiklang) subdominant chord

Subjekt /zʊpˈjɛkt/ *das;* **~[e]s, ~e** 1) subject 2) (abwertend: Mensch) creature; type (coll.)

subjektiv /zʊpjɛkˈti:f/

A *Adj.* subjective

B *adv.* subjectively

subjektivieren *tr. V.* (geh.) subjectivize

Subjektivismus *der;* **~:** subjectivism

Subjektivität /zʊpjɛktiviˈtɛ:t/ *die;* **~:** subjectivity

Subjekt·satz *der* (Sprachw.) subject clause

Sub-: ~kontinent *der* (Geogr.) subcontinent; **~kultur** *die* (Soziol.) subculture

subkutan /zʊpkuˈta:n/ (Anat., Med.)

A *Adj.* subcutaneous

B *adv.* subcutaneously

sublim /zuˈbli:m/ (geh.)

A *Adj.* subtle; (erhaben) sublime

B *adv.* subtly

Sublimation /zublimaˈtsi̯o:n/ *die;* **~, ~en** (Chemie) sublimation

sublimieren *tr., itr. V.* sublimate

Sublimierung *die;* **~, ~en** sublimation

Sublimität /zublimiˈtɛ:t/ *die;* **~** (geh.) subtlety

submarin *Adj.* submarine

Subordination *die* (bes. Logik) subordination (**unter** + *Akk.* to)

subsidiär /zʊpziˈdi̯ɛ:ɐ̯/ (bes. Rechtsw.)

A *Adj.* 1) (unterstützend) supplementary ‹*measures*› 2) (als Behelf dienend) provisional ‹*law etc.*›

B *adv.* 1) **~ tätig werden** play a supporting role 2) (behelfsmäßig) on a provisional basis

Subsidiarität /zʊpzidi̯ariˈtɛ:t/ *die;* **~** (Politik, Soziol.) subsidiarity *no art.*

Subskribent /zʊpskriˈbɛnt/ *der,* **Subskribentin** *die;* **~, ~nen** (Buchw.) subscriber

subskribieren /zʊpskriˈbi:rən/ (Buchw.)

A *tr. V.* subscribe to

B *itr. V.* take out a subscription

Subskription /zʊpskrɪpˈtsi̯o:/ *die;* **~, ~en** (Buchw.) subscription

Subskriptions·preis *der* (Buchw.) subscription price

substantiell ▸**substanziell**

Substantiv /ˈzʊpstanti:f/ *das;* **~s, ~e** (Sprachw.) noun

substantivieren *tr. V.* (Sprachw.) nominalize

substantivisch (Sprachw.)

A *Adj.* nominal

B *adv.* **~ gebraucht** used as nouns/a noun; nominalized

Substanz /zʊpˈstants/ *die;* **~, ~en** 1) (auch fig.) substance 2) (Grundbestand) **die ~:** the reserves *pl.*; **etw. geht an die ~** (fig. ugs.) (seelisch, nervlich) sth. gets you down; (körperlich) sth. takes it out of you; **von der ~ zehren** live off one's reserves *or* capital

substanziell /zʊpstanˈtsi̯ɛl/ (geh.)

A *Adj.* substantial

B *adv.* substantially

substituieren /zʊpstituˈi:rən/ *tr. V.* (geh., fachspr.) replace

S

Substitut /zʊpsti'tu:t/ *der;* **~en, ~en**, **Substitutin** *die;* **~, ~nen** assistant manager

Substitution /zʊpstitu'tsi̯o:n/ *die;* **~, ~en** (geh., fachspr.) replacement

Substrat /zʊp'stra:t/ *das;* **~[e]s, ~e** (geh., fachspr.) substratum

subsumieren /zʊpzu'mi:rən/ *tr. V.* (geh.) subsume (**unter** + *Dat. od. Akk.* under)

subtil /zʊp'ti:l/ (geh.)
A *Adj.* subtle
B *adv.* subtly

Subtilität /zʊptili'tɛ:t/ *die;* **~, ~en** (geh.) subtlety

Subtrahend /zʊptra'hɛnt/ *der;* **~en, ~en** (Math.) subtrahend

subtrahieren *tr., itr. V.* (Math.) subtract

Subtraktion /zʊptrak'tsi̯o:n/ *die;* **~, ~en** (Math.) subtraction

Sub·tropen *Pl.* (Geogr.) subtropics

sub·tropisch *Adj.* subtropical

Subvention /zʊpvɛn'tsi̯o:n/ *die;* **~, ~en** (Wirtsch.) subsidy

subventionieren *tr. V.* (Wirtsch.) subsidize

Sub·version *die* (Politik) subversion

subversiv /zʊpvɛr'zi:f/ (Politik)
A *Adj.* subversive
B *adv.* subversively

Such-: **~aktion** *die* search [operation]; **~anzeige** *die* 1 missing-person report; 2 (in der Zeitung) 'lost' advertisement; **~bild** *das* ▸ **Vexierbild**

Suche /'zu:xə/ *die;* **~, ~n** search (**nach** for); **auf der ~ [nach jmdm./etw.] sein** be looking/(intensiver) searching [for sb./sth.]; **sich [nach jmdm./etw.] auf die ~ machen, [nach jmdm/etw.] auf die ~ gehen** start searching *or* start a search [for sb./sth.]

suchen
A *tr. V.* 1 look for; (intensiver) search for; **gesucht wird der 54-jährige XY** a search is going on for the 54-year-old XY; **„Kellner/Leerzimmer gesucht"** 'waiter/unfurnished room wanted'; **„Gesucht: Jesse James"** 'Wanted: Jesse James'; **die beiden haben sich gesucht und gefunden** (ugs.) those two were made for each other; **solche Menschen/jemanden wie ihn kann man ~** (ugs.) you don't come across people like that/someone like him every day; **seinesgleichen ~:** be without equal *or* unequalled 2 (bedacht sein auf, sich wünschen) seek ‹*protection, advice, company, warmth, etc.*›; look for ‹*adventure*›; **Kontakt** *od.* **Anschluss ~:** try to get to know people; **Streit ~:** seek a quarrel; **was sucht er denn hier?** what does he want here?; **er hat hier nichts zu ~** (ugs.) he has no business [to be] here; **an meinem Schreibtisch hat sie nichts zu ~** (ugs.) she's got no right *or* business to be at my desk 3 (geh.: trachten) **~, etw. zu tun** seek *or* endeavour to do sth.
B *itr. V.* search; **ich habe überall gesucht** I've looked everywhere; **nach jmdm./etw. ~:** look/search for sb./sth.; **da kannst du lange ~!** (ugs.) you're wasting your time looking for that; **sich ~d umsehen** look around; **such, such!** (an einen Hund) seek, seek!; **wer sucht, der findet** he who seeks shall find; seek, and ye shall find (Bibl.); **Suchen spielen** (landsch.) play hide-and-seek

Sucher *der;* **~s, ~** (Fot.) viewfinder

Sucherei *die;* **~, ~en** (ugs., oft abwertend) [endless] searching *no pl.*

Such-: **~funktion** *die* (DV) search function; **~hund** *der* tracker dog; **~maschine** *die* (DV) search engine; **~meldung** *die* announcement about a missing or wanted person; **~roboter** *der* (DV) ▸ **Suchmaschine**; **~scheinwerfer** *der* searchlight

Sucht /zʊxt/ *die;* **~, Süchte** /zʏçtə/ *od.* **~en** 1 addiction (**nach** to); **[bei jmdm.] zur ~ werden** (auch fig.) become addictive [in sb.'s case] 2 *Pl.* **Süchte** (übermäßiges Verlangen) craving, obsessive desire (**nach** for); **ihre krankhafte ~, immer alles besser zu wissen** her pathological obsession with knowing better all the time

süchtig /'zʏçtɪç/ *Adj.* 1 addicted; **~ machen** (auch fig.) be addictive; **~ [nach etw.] sein** (auch fig.) be an addict *or* addicted [to sth.] 2 (versessen, begierig) obsessive; **nach etw. ~ sein** be obsessed with sth.

-süchtig 1 ‹*drug-, heroin-, morphine-, etc.*› addicted; **alkohol~ sein** be an alcoholic 2 (fig.) addicted to ‹*television*›; obsessed with ‹*death*›; craving for ‹*liberation, love, home, sex*›

Süchtige *der/die; adj. Dekl.*, **Sucht·kranke** *der/die* addict

Sud /zu:t/ *der;* **~[e]s, ~e** 1 stock 2 (Extrakt) decoction

Süd¹ /zy:t/ ▸ ❶ **S. 363** 1 (Seemannsspr., Met.: Richtung) **nach ~:** southwards; to the south; **aus** *od.* **von ~:** from the south 2 (südliches Gebiet, Politik) South; *s. auch* **Nord¹ 2** 3 *einem Subst. nachgestellt* **Autobahnausfahrt Frankfurt ~:** Frankfurt South motorway (Brit.) *or* (Amer.) freeway exit; **Europa ~** (Milit.) Southern Europe

Süd² *der;* **~[e]s, ~e** (Seemannsspr., dichter.) southerly

süd-, Süd-: **~afrika** *(das)* South Africa; **~afrikanisch** *Adj.* South African; **~amerika** *(das)* South America; **~amerikanisch** *Adj.* South American

Sudan /zu'da:n/ *(das);* **~s** *od. der;* **~s** Sudan

Sudanese *der;* **~n, ~n**, **Sudanesin** *die;* **~, ~nen** Sudanese

süd·deutsch *Adj.* South German; *s. auch* **norddeutsch**

> **Süddeutsche Zeitung**
>
> This respected daily national newspaper was founded in 1945 and is published in Munich. It has a liberal outlook and is read mainly in southern Germany.

Süd·deutschland *(das)* South Germany

Sudelei *die;* **~, ~en** (ugs. abwertend) 1 (das Sudeln) making *no art.* a [disgusting] mess 2 (gesudelte Arbeit) **[eine] ~ sein** be a [disgusting] mess

sudeln /'zu:dl̩n/ *itr. V.* (ugs. abwertend) make a [disgusting] mess; (pfuschen) make a mess of it; botch it

Süden *der;* **~s** ▸ ❶ **S. 363** 1 (Richtung) south; *s. auch* **Norden 1** 2 (Gegend) southern part; **aus dem ~:** from the south 3 (Geogr.) South; **der tiefe/tiefste ~:** the far South

Süd·england *(das)* Southern England; the South of England

Sudeten /zu'de:tn̩/ *Pl.* **die ~:** the Sudeten [Mountains]

Sudeten·deutsche *der/die* Sudeten German

Sudetenland *das;* **~[e]s** Sudetenland

süd-, Süd-: **~europa** *(das)* Southern Europe; **~europäisch** *Adj.* Southern European; **~flanke** *die* (Met., Milit.) southern flank; (Geogr.: eines Gebirges) southern escarpment; **~frucht** *die* tropical [or subtropical] fruit; **~hang** *der* southern slope

Sud·haus *das* mashhouse

Süd-: **~insel** *die* South Island; **~korea** *(das)* South Korea; **~küste** *die* south coast

Südländer /'zy:tlɛndɐ/ *der;* **~s, ~**, **Südländerin** *die;* **~, ~nen** Southern European; Mediterranean type

südländisch *Adj.* Southern [European]; Mediterranean; Latin ‹*temperament*›; **~ aussehen** have Latin looks; look like a Southern European

südlich ▸ ❶ **S. 363**
A *Adj.* 1 (im Süden gelegen) southern; *s. auch* **Eismeer**; **nördlich A 1**; **Polarkreis**; **Wendekreis 1** 2 (nach Süden gerichtet, von Süden kommend) southerly 3 (aus dem Süden kommend, für den Süden typisch) Southern
B *adv.* southwards; *s. auch* **nördlich B**
C *Präp. mit Gen.* [to the] south of

süd-, Süd-: **~licht** /'--/ *das; Pl.* **~~er** 1 (Polarlicht) southern lights *pl.*; (einzelne Erscheinung) display of the southern lights; 2 (iron.: Mensch aus Süddeutschland) South German type; **~ost¹** (Seemannsspr., Met.) south-east; *s. auch* **Nord¹ 1**; **Nordost¹**; **~ost²** *der* (Seemannsspr.) southeaster[ly]; south-easter[ly] [wind]; **~osten** *der* ▸ ❶ **S. 363** south-east; **der ~osten [Englands]** the South-East [of England]; *s. auch* **Norden**; **~östlich** ▸ ❶ **S. 363** A *Adj.* south-eastern; south-easterly ‹*direction, wind, course*›; B *adv.* **~östlich [von X] liegen** be to the south-east [of X]; C *Präp. mit Gen.* [to the] south-east of; **~ost·wind** *der* south-east[erly] wind; **~pol** /'--/ *der* 1 South Pole; 2 (eines Magneten) south pole

Süd·polar-: **~gebiet** *das* Antarctic [Region]; **~meer** *das;* **~[e]s** Antarctic Ocean

süd-, Süd-: **~pol·expedition** /'-------/ *die* expedition to the South Pole; **~rand** /'--/ *der* southern edge; **~see** /'--/ *die;* **~: die ~see** the South Seas *pl.*; **~see·insel** /'----/ *die* South Sea island; **~seite** /'---/ *die* south side; **~staaten** /'---/ *Pl.* southern States; **~süd·ost¹** (Seemannsspr., Met.) south-south-east; *s. auch* **Nord¹ 1**; **~süd·ost²** *der* (Seemannsspr.) south-south-easterly; **~süd·osten** *der* south-south-east; *s. auch* **Norden 1**; **~süd·west¹** (Seemannsspr., Met.) south-south-west[erly]; *s. auch* **Nord¹ 1**; **~süd·west²** *der* (Seemannsspr.) south-south-westerly; **~südwesten** *der* south-south-west; *s. auch* **Norden 1**; **~tirol** /'---/ *(das)* South Tyrol; **~wand** /'--/ *die* south face; **~wärts** /'--/ *Adv.* southwards; **~wein** /'--/ *der* dessert wine; **~west¹** (Seemannsspr., Met.) south-west; *s. auch* **Nord¹ 1**; **Nordwest¹**; **~west²** *der* (Seemannsspr.) southwester[ly]; (dichter.) south-west[erly] wind; **~westafrika** *(das)* South-West Africa; **~westen** *der* ▸ ❶ **S. 363** south-west; **der ~westen [Deutschlands]** the South-West [of Germany]; *s. auch* **Norden 1**; **~wester** *der;* **~~s, ~~:** sou'wester; **~west·funk** *der* South West German Radio; **~westlich** ▸ ❶ **S. 363** A *Adj.* south-western; south-westerly ‹*direction, course, wind*›; B *adv.* **~westlich [von X] liegen** be to the south-west [of X]; C *Präp. mit Gen.* [to the] south-west of; **~west·rundfunk** *der* South West German Radio; **~west·wind** *der* south-west[erly] wind; **~wind** /'--/ *der* south *or* southerly wind

Sues·kanal /'zu:ɛs-/ *der;* **~s** Suez Canal

Suff /zʊf/ *der;* **~[e]s** (salopp) 1 **im ~:** while under the influence (coll.) 2 (Trunksucht) boozing (coll.); **dem ~ verfallen sein/sich dem ~ ergeben** be/become a victim of the demon drink; be on/take to the bottle (coll.)

süffeln /'zʏfl̩n/ *tr., itr. V.* (ugs.) tipple (coll.)

süffig *Adj.* (ugs.) [very] drinkable; **dieser Wein ist sehr ~:** this wine goes down very well

Süffisance /zʏfi'zã:s/ *die;* **~** ▸ **Süffisanz**

süffisant /zʏfi'zant/ (geh. abwertend)
A *Adj.* smug
B *adv.* smugly

Süffisanz /sʏfi'zants/ *die;* **~** (geh. abwertend) smugness

Suffix /zʊ'fɪks/ *das;* **~es, ~e** (Sprachw.) suffix

Suffragette /zʊfra'gɛtə/ *die;* **~, ~n** (hist.) suffragette; (veralt. abwertend: Frauenrechtlerin) campaigner for women's rights

suggerieren /zʊge'ri:rən/ *tr. V.* 1 (geh., Psych.) suggest; **jmdm. etw. ~:** suggest sth. to sb.; put sth. into sb.'s mind 2 (geh.: den Eindruck erwecken) suggest; give the *or* an impression of; **das musste ~, dass ...** this was bound to give the impression that ...

Suggestion /zʊgɛs'ti̯o:n/ *die;* **~, ~en** 1 (geh., Psych.) suggestion 2 (geh.: suggestive Wirkung) suggestive effect *or* power

suggestiv /zʊgɛs'ti:f/ (geh., Psych.)
A *Adj.* suggestive
B *adv.* suggestively

Suggestiv·frage *die* leading question

Suhle /'zu:lə/ *die;* **~, ~n** muddy pool

suhlen *refl. V.* wallow (**in** + *Dat.* in)

Sühne /'zy:nə/ *die;* **~, ~n** (geh.) atonement; expiation; **~ [für etw.] leisten** make atonement *or* atone [for sth.]

sühnen
A *tr., itr. V.* (abbüßen) **[für] etw. ~:** atone for *or* pay the penalty for sth.
B *tr. V.* (bestrafen) punish ‹*wrongdoing*›

Sühne-: **~opfer** *das* (Rel.) expiatory sacrifice; **~termin** *der* (Rechtsw.) conciliation hearing

S

Sühn·opfer *das* ▸ **Sühneopfer**
Suite /ˈsviːt(ə)/ *die;* ~, ~**n** suite
Suizid /zuiˈtsiːt/ *der od. das;* ~**[e]s,** ~**e** (bes. Med., Psych.) suicide
Sujet /zyˈʒeː/ *das;* ~**s,** ~**s** subject
Sukkade /zʊˈkaːdə/ *die;* ~, ~**n** candied peel
Sukkulente /zʊkuˈlɛntə/ *die;* ~, ~**n** (Bot.) succulent
sukzessiv /zʊktsɛˈsiːf/
A *Adj.* gradual
B *adv.* gradually
sukzessive *Adv.* gradually
Sulfat /zʊlˈfaːt/ *das;* ~**[e]s,** ~**e** (Chemie) sulphate
Sulfid /zʊlˈfiːt/ *das;* ~**[e]s,** ~**e** (Chemie) sulphide
Sulfit /zʊlˈfiːt/ *das;* ~**s,** ~**e** (Chemie) sulphite
Sulfonamid /zʊlfonaˈmiːt/ *das;* ~**[e]s,** ~**e** (Pharm.) sulphonamide
Sulky /ˈzʊlki/ *das;* ~**s,** ~**s** (Pferdesport) sulky
Sultan /ˈzʊltaːn/ *der;* ~**s,** ~**e** sultan
Sultanat /zʊltaˈnaːt/ *das;* ~**[e]s,** ~**e** sultanate
Sultanin *die;* ~, ~**nen** sultana
Sultanine /zʊltaˈniːnə/ *die;* ~, ~**n** sultana
Sülze /ˈzʏltsə/ *die;* ~, ~**n** **1** diced meat/fish in aspic; (vom Schweinskopf) brawn **2** (Aspik) aspic
sülzen /ˈzʏltsn̩/ *tr., itr. V.* (salopp) ▸ **quatschen A 1, B**
Sülz·kotelett *das* boned pork chop in aspic
Sumerer /zuˈmeːrɐ/ *der;* ~**s,** ~, **Sumererin** *die;* ~, ~**nen** Sumerian
summ /zʊm/ *Interj.* buzz
summa cum laude /ˈzʊma kʊm ˈlaudə/ *Adv.* (Hochschulw.) with the utmost distinction; *highest of four grades of successful doctoral examination*
Summand /zʊˈmant/ *der;* ~**en,** ~**en** (Math.) summand
summarisch /zʊˈmaːrɪʃ/ (geh.)
A *Adj.* summary; brief *(summary)*; **ein** ~**es Verfahren** (Rechtsw.) summary proceedings *pl*
B *adv.* summarily; briefly
summa summarum /ˈzʊma zʊˈmaːrʊm/ *Adv.* in all; altogether
Sümmchen /ˈzʏmçən/ *das;* ~**s,** ~ (ugs.) **ein hübsches** *od.* **nettes** ~: a tidy little sum (coll.)
Summe /ˈzʊmə/ *die;* ~, ~**n** sum
summen
A *itr. V.* hum; (lauter, heller) buzz; **es summt** there's a hum/buzzing
B *tr., auch itr. V.* hum *(tune, song, etc.)*
Summer *der;* ~**s,** ~: buzzer
summieren *refl. V.* add up (**auf** + *Akk.* to); (anwachsen) *(number)* grow, increase (**auf** + *Akk.* to)
Summ·ton *der; Pl.* **Summtöne** buzzing [tone]; (leiser) hum
Sumpf /zʊmpf/ *der;* ~**[e]s, Sümpfe** /ˈzʏmpfə/ marsh; (bes. in den Tropen) swamp; (fig.) morass; quagmire; **im** ~ **stecken bleiben** be stuck in the mire
Sumpf·dotter·blume *die* marsh marigold
sumpfen *itr. V.* (salopp) make whoopee (coll.) *or* live it up into the small hours
Sumpf-: ~**fieber** *das* malaria; ~**gas** *das* marsh gas; ~**gebiet** *das* marsh[land]; (bes. in den Tropen) swamp[land]; ~**huhn** *das* crake
sumpfig *Adj.* marshy
Sumpf·pflanze *die* marsh plant
Sums /zʊms/ *der;* ~**es** (ugs.) **viel** ~ **um etw. machen** make a lot of fuss about sth.
Sund /zʊnt/ *der;* ~**[e]s,** ~**e** (Geogr.) sound
Sünde /ˈzʏndə/ *die;* ~, ~**n** sin; (fig.) misdeed; transgression; **in** ~ **leben** (veralt.) live in sin; **faul wie die** ~: bone idle; **eine** ~ **wert sein** (scherzh.) be worth a little transgression; *(food)* be naughty but nice; **es ist eine** ~ **[und Schande]** it's a crying shame
Sünden-: ~**babel** *das* sink of iniquity; ~**bekenntnis** *das* confession of one's sins; ~**bock** *der* (ugs.) scapegoat; ~**fall** *der* (christl. Rel.) Fall of Man; (fig.) fall from grace; ~**geld** *das:* **ein** ~**geld** (ugs.) a small fortune; ~**pfuhl** *der* (abwertend) sink of iniquity; ~**register** *das* (ugs. scherzh.) catalogue of misdeeds
Sünder *der;* ~**s,** ~, **Sünderin** *die;* ~, ~**nen** sinner; **armer Sünder** (veralt.) condemned man; **sie saß da wie eine arme Sünderin** (ugs.) she sat there looking a picture of misery and remorse
Sünd·flut *die* ▸ **Sintflut**
sündhaft
A *Adj.* **1** sinful **2** (ugs.) **ein** ~**er Preis/**~**es Geld** an outrageous price/amount of money
B *adv.* **1** sinfully **2** (ugs.: sehr) outrageously *(expensive)*; stunningly *(beautiful)*; ~ **faul** bone idle
Sündhaftigkeit *die;* ~: sinfulness
sündig
A *Adj.* sinful; (lasterhaft) wicked
B *adv.* sinfully
sündigen *itr. V.* sin; (scherzh.: viel essen) indulge oneself [sinfully]; **gegen die Natur** ~ (fig.) offend against nature
Sunnit /zʊˈniːt/ *der;* ~**en,** ~**en, Sunnitin** *die;* ~, ~**nen** Sunnite
sunnitisch *Adj.* Sunnite
super (ugs.)
A *indekl. Adj.* super (coll.); fantastic (coll.); ~ **aussehen/ sich** ~ **fühlen** look/feel great (coll.)
B *adv.* fantastically (coll.)
super- ultra-*(long, high, fast, modern, masculine, etc.)*; ~**geheim** top secret; ~**günstig** extra cheap
Super /ˈzuːpɐ/ *das;* ~**s,** ~: four star (Brit.); premium (Amer.); *s. auch* **Normal**
Super- super-*(hero, figure, car, group, etc.)*; terrific (coll.), tremendous (coll.) *(success, offer, chance, idea, etc.)*
Super-8-Film *der* super 8 film
superb /zuˈpɛrp/, **süperb** /zyˈpɛrp/ (geh.)
A *Adj.* superb
B *adv.* superbly
Super·benzin *das* four-star petrol (Brit.); premium (Amer.)
Super-: ~**ding** *das; Pl.* ~~**er** (salopp) terrific thing (coll.); ~**frau** *die* (ugs.) superwoman
Superintendent /zupeˌlɪntɛnˈdɛnt/ *der;* ~**en,** ~**en** (ev. Kirche) dean
Superiorität /zuperi̯oriˈtɛːt/ *die;* ~ (geh.) **1** superiority (**über** + *Akk.* in relation to) **2** (Vormachtstellung) supremacy (**über** + *Akk.* over)
super·klug (iron.)
A *Adj.* extra clever; smart-aleck (coll. derog.)
B *adv.* in a smart-aleck way (coll. derog.)
Superlativ /ˈzuːpɐlatiːf/ *der;* ~**s,** ~**e** (Sprachw.) superlative
superlativisch *Adj.* (Sprachw.) superlative
super-, Super-: ~**mann** *der* (ugs.) superman; ~**markt** *der* supermarket; ~**modern** **A** *Adj.* ultra-modern; **B** *adv.* *(furnished, dressed)* in ultra-modern style; ~**schlau** *Adj.* (iron.) ▸ ~**klug**
Supernova /zupɐˈnoːva/ *die;* ~, **...vae** /-vɛ/ *auch* **...vä**/-vɛ/ (Astron.) supernova
super-, Super-: ~**schnell** (ugs.) **A** *Adj.* ultra-fast; **B** *adv.* at tremendous speed; ~**star** *der* superstar
supi *indekl. Adj.* ▸ **super**
Süppchen /ˈzʏpçən/ *das;* ~**s,** ~: soup; **sein** ~ **am Feuer anderer kochen** (ugs.) use others for one's own ends
Suppe /ˈzʊpə/ *die;* ~, ~**n** soup; **jmdm. die** ~ **versalzen** (ugs.) put a spoke in sb.'s wheel; put a spanner in sb.'s works; **jmdm. in die** ~ **spucken** (salopp) mess things up for sb.; *s. auch* **auslöffeln 1; einbrocken**
Suppen-: ~**einlage** *die: rice, noodles, dumplings, etc. put into a clear soup;* ~**fleisch** *das* beef for making soup; ~**grün** *das* green vegetables for making soup *(comprising parsley, carrots, celery, and leeks)*; ~**huhn** *das* boiling fowl; ~**kasper** *der* (ugs.) poor *or* finicky eater; ~**kelle** *die* soup ladle; ~**knochen** *der* soup bone; ~**löffel** *der* soup spoon; ~**nudel** *die* noodle *(for use in soup)*; ~**schüssel** *die* soup tureen; ~**tasse** *die* soup bowl *(with handles)*; ~**teller** *der* soup plate; ~**terrine** *die* soup tureen; ~**würfel** *der* stock cube
suppig *Adj.* watery; thin
Supplement /zʊpleˈmɛnt/ *das;* ~**[e]s,** ~**e** supplement
Suppositorium /zʊpoziˈtoːri̯ʊm/ *das;* ~**s, Suppositorien** (Pharm.) suppository
supraleitend *Adj.* (Physik) superconducting
Supra·leiter *der* (Physik) superconductor
Supra·leitung *die* (Physik) superconductivity; superconduction
supranational *Adj.* supranational
Supremat /zupreˈmaːt/ *der od. das;* ~**[e]s,** ~**e** supreme authority
Sure /ˈzuːrə/ *die;* ~, ~**n** sura
Surf·brett /ˈsəːf-/ *das* surfboard
surfen /ˈsəːfn̩/ *itr. V.* surf
Surfer /ˈsəːfɐ/ *der;* ~**s,** ~, **Surferin** *die;* ~, ~**nen** surfer
Sur·realismus /zʊreaˈlɪsmʊs/ *der;* ~: surrealism *no art.*
Sur·realist *der,* **Sur·realistin** *die* surrealist
surrealistisch
A *Adj.* surrealist *(movement, painting, literature)*; surrealistic *(image, story, scene)*
B *adv.* surrealistically; *(paint)* in a surrealistic style; *(influenced)* by surrealism
surren /ˈzʊrən/ *itr. V.* **1** (summen) hum; *(camera, fan)* whirr; **es surrt** there's a hum/whirr **2** *mit sein* (schwirren) whirr
Surrogat /zʊroˈgaːt/ *das;* ~**[e]s,** ~**e** (geh.) surrogate
suspekt /zʊsˈpɛkt/
A *Adj.* suspicious; **jmdm.** ~ **sein** seem suspicious to sb.; arouse sb.'s suspicions
B *adv.* suspiciously
suspendieren /zʊspɛnˈdiːrən/ *tr. V.* suspend; (entlassen) dismiss; **jmdn. vom Dienst/von seinem Amt** ~: suspend/dismiss sb. from his/her post
Suspendierung, Suspension /zʊspɛnˈtsi̯oːn/ *die;* ~, ~**en** suspension; (Entlassung) dismissal
Suspensorium /zʊspɛnˈzoːri̯ʊm/ *das;* ~**s, Suspensorien** (Med.) suspensory [bandage]
süß /zyːs/
A *Adj.* sweet; (geh.: lieblich klingend) melodious; sweet; (fig.: übertrieben freundlich) sweet, sugary *(smile, words)*; **er isst gern Süßes** he likes sweet things; he has a sweet tooth; **na, mein Süßer/meine Süße?** well, sweetheart?
B *adv.* sweetly; ~ **duften** give off a sweet scent; **den Salat** ~ **anmachen** sweeten the salad dressing; **träum** ~**!** sweet dreams!; **das hast du** ~ **gemalt** (fam.) you've painted this enchantingly
Süße *die;* ~: sweetness
süßen
A *tr. V.* sweeten
B *itr. V.* sweeten things; **mit Saccharin** ~: use saccharine as a sweetener
Süß·holz *das* liquorice [plant]; ~ **raspeln** (fig. ugs.) ooze charm
Süßholz·raspler *der;* ~**s,** ~, **Süßholz·rasplerin** *die;* ~, ~**nen** (ugs.) smoothie (coll.)
Süßigkeit *die;* ~, ~**en** **1** (Bonbon usw.) sweet (Brit.); candy (Amer.); ~**en** sweets (Brit.); candy *sing. (Amer.)*; (als Ware) confectionery *sing.* **2** (fig. geh.: Süße) sweetness
Süß·kirsche *die* sweet cherry
süßlich
A *Adj.* **1** [slightly] sweet; on the sweet side *pred.*; **ein widerlich** ~**er Geruch/Geschmack** an unpleasantly sickly *or* cloying smell/taste **2** (abwertend) (sentimental) sickly mawkish *(film)*; (heuchlerisch freundlich) sugary *(smile etc.)*; smarmy (coll.) *(expression, manners)*; honeyed *(words)*
B *adv.* (abwertend) *(write, paint)* mawkishly *or* in a sickly-sentimental style; *(smile)* smarmily (coll.)
süß-, Süß-: ~**most** *der* unfermented fruit juice; ~**rahm·butter** *die* sweet cream

butter; **~sauer** A *Adj.* sweet-and-sour; (fig.) wry ‹*smile, face*›; **etw. gern ~sauer essen** like eating sth. with a sweet-and-sour sauce; B *adv.* 1 **etw. ~sauer zubereiten** give sth. a sweet-and-sour flavour; 2 (fig.) ‹*smile*› wryly; **~speise** *die* sweet; dessert; **~stoff** *der* sweetener; **~waren** *Pl.* confectionery *sing.*; candy *sing.* (Amer.); **~wasser** *das; Pl.* **~:** fresh water; **~wasser·fisch** *der* freshwater fish; **~wein** *der* sweet wine

Sutane ▸ **Soutane**

Sütterlin·schrift /ˈzʏtɐliːn-/ *die* Sütterlin script

SV *Abk.* = **Sportverein** SC

SVP *Abk.* = **Schweizer Volkspartei**

svw. *Abk.* = **soviel wie**

SW *Abk.* = **Südwest[en]** ▸ⓘ **S. 363** SW

Swahili /svaˈhiːli/ ▸ **Suaheli**

Swastika /ˈsvastika/ *die;* **~, Swạstiken** swastika

Sweatshirt /ˈswɛt-ʃəːt/ *das;* **~s, ~s** sweat-shirt

Swimmingpool, Swimming-pool /ˈsvɪmɪŋpuːl/ *der;* **~s, ~s** [swimming] pool

Swing /svɪŋ/ *der;* **~[s]** 1 (Musik) swing *no art.* 2 (Wirtsch.) swing

swingen *itr. V.* 1 (Musik) ‹*player*› swing [it]; ‹*music*› have a swing [to it] 2 (tanzen) swing

SWR *Abk.* = **Südwestrundfunk**

Syllogismus /zʏloˈgɪsmʊs/ *der;* **~s, Syllogịsmen** (Philos.) syllogism

Sylphe /ˈzʏlfə/ *der;* **~n, ~n** sylph

Symbiose /zʏmˈbi̯oːzə/ *die;* **~, ~n** (Biol., fig.) symbiosis (**zwischen** + *Dat.* of); **eine ~ eingehen** (fig.) form a symbiotic relationship

symbiotisch *Adj.* (Biol., fig.) symbiotic

Symbol /zʏmˈboːl/ *das;* **~s, ~e** symbol

symbolhaft
A *Adj.* symbolic (**für** of)
B *adv.* symbolically

Symbolik /zʏmˈboːlɪk/ *die;* **~:** symbolism

symbolisch
A *Adj.* symbolic
B *adv.* symbolically

symbolisieren
A *tr. V.* symbolize
B *refl. V.* be symbolized (**in** + *Dat.* by)

Symbolismus *der;* **~:** symbolism; (Kunstrichtung) Symbolism *no art.*

Symbolist *der;* **~en, ~en, Symbolistin** *die;* **~, ~nen** Symbolist

symbolistisch *Adj.* Symbolist

Symbol·sprache *die* (DV) assembly language

Symmetrie /zymeˈtriː/ *die;* **~, ~n** symmetry

Symmetrie·achse *die* axis of symmetry

symmetrisch
A *Adj.* symmetrical
B *adv.* symmetrically

Sympathie /zʏmpaˈtiː/ *die;* **~, ~n** sympathy; **~ für jmdn. haben** sympathize with *or* have sympathy with sb.; **sich** (*Dat.*) **jmds./alle ~n verscherzen** forfeit sb.'s/everybody's sympathy; **bei aller ~:** with the best will in the world

Sympathie·streik *der* sympathy strike; **in ~ [mit jmdm.] treten** strike in sympathy [with sb.]

Sympathikus *der;* **~** ▸ⓘ **S. 435** (Anat., Physiol.) sympathetic nervous system

Sympathisant /zʏmpatiˈzant/ *der;* **~en, ~en, Sympathisantin** *die;* **~, ~nen** sympathizer (*Gen.* with)

sympathisch
A *Adj.* 1 congenial, likeable ‹*person, manner*›; appealing, agreeable ‹*voice, appearance, material*›; **jmdm. ~ sein** appeal to sb.; **er war mir gleich ~:** I took to him at once; I took an immediate liking to him 2 (Anat., Physiol.) sympathetic ‹*nerve, nervous system, etc.*›
B *adv.* in a likeable *or* appealing way; (angenehm) agreeably

sympathisieren *itr. V.* sympathize (**mit** with); **mit einer Partei ~:** be sympathetic towards a party

Symphonie /zʏmfoˈniː/ *usw.* ▸ **Sinfonie** *usw.*

Symposion /zʏmˈpoːzi̯ɔn/ *das;* **~s, Symposien, Symposium** /zʏmˈpoːzi̯ʊm/ *das;* **Symposiums, Symposien** symposium (**über** + Akk., **zu** on)

Symptom /zʏmpˈtoːm/ *das;* **~s, ~e** ▸ⓘ **S. 439** (Med., geh.) symptom (*Gen.*, **für, von** of)

Symptomatik /zʏmptoˈmaːtɪk/ *die;* **~** (Med., geh.) symptoms *pl.*; symptom complex

symptomatisch (Med., geh.)
A *Adj.* symptomatic (**für** of)
B *adv.* symptomatically

Synagoge /zynaˈgoːgə/ *die;* **~, ~n** synagogue

Synapse /zʏˈnapsə/ *die;* **~, ~n** synapse

Synästhesie /zynɛsteˈziː/ *die;* **~, ~n** (Med., Literaturw.) synaesthesia

synchron /zʏnˈkroːn/
A *Adj.* 1 synchronous 2 (Sprachw.) synchronic
B *adv.* 1 synchronously 2 (Sprachw.) synchronically

Synchronisation /zʏnkronizaˈtsi̯oːn/ *die;* **~, ~en** ▸ **Synchronisierung**

synchronisch *Adj.* (Sprachw.) synchronic

synchronisieren *tr. V.* 1 (Film) dub ‹*film*› 2 (Technik, fig.) synchronize ‹*watches, operations, etc.*›; fit synchromesh to ‹*gearbox*›; **alle Gänge sind synchronisiert** (Kfz-W.) there is synchromesh on all gears; **synchronisiertes Getriebe** synchromesh gearbox

Synchronisierung *die;* **~, ~en** 1 (Film) dubbing 2 (Technik, fig.) synchronization; (Kfz-W.) fitting of synchromesh (*Gen.* to)

Synchron-: ~schwimmen *das* (Sport) synchronized swimming; **~sprecher** *der*, **~sprecherin** *die* dubbing actor

Synchrotron /ˈzʏnkrotroːn/ *das;* **~s, ~e** *od.* **~s** (Kernphysik) synchrotron

Syndikalismus /zʏndikaˈlɪsmʊs/ *der;* **~:** syndicalism *no art.*

syndikalistisch *Adj.* syndicalist

Syndikat /zʏndiˈkaːt/ *das;* **~[e]s, ~e** (bes. Wirtsch.) syndicate

Syndikus /ˈzʏndikʊs/ *der;* **~, ~se** *od.* **Syndizi** /ˈzʏnditsi/ (Rechtsspr.) legal adviser; (Rechtsanwalt einer Firma) company lawyer *or* (Amer.) attorney

Syndrom /zʏnˈdroːm/ *das;* **~s, ~e** ▸ⓘ **S. 439** (Med.) syndrome

Synkope *die;* **~, ~n** 1 /zʏnˈkoːpə/ (Musik) syncopation 2 /ˈzʏnkope/ (Sprachw.) syncope

synkopieren /zʏnkoˈpiːrən/ *tr. V.* (Musik, Sprachw.) syncopate

synkopisch *Adj.* (Musik) syncopated

Synodale /zynoˈdaːlə/ *der/die; adj. Dekl.* synod member

Synode /zyˈnoːdə/ *die;* **~, ~n** (ev., kath. Kirche) synod

Synonomie /zynonyˈmiː/ *die;* **~, ~n** (Sprachw.) synonymity

synonym /zynoˈnyːm/ (Sprachw.)
A *Adj.* synonymous
B *adv.* synonymously

Synonym /zynoˈnyːm/ *das;* **~s, ~e** (Sprachw.) synonym

Synonym·wörterbuch *das* dictionary of synonyms

Synopse /zyˈnɔpsə/ *die;* **~, ~n, Synopsis** /ˈzyːnɔpsɪs/ *die;* **Synopsis, ~n** 1 textual comparison 2 (bibl.) comparative parallel text of the Synoptic Gospels 3 (geh.: Zusammenschau) overall view; survey

Synoptiker *der;* **~s, ~:** synoptist

syntaktisch /zʏnˈtaktɪʃ/ (Sprachw.)
A *Adj.* syntactic
B *adv.* syntactically

Syntax /ˈzʏntaks/ *die;* **~, ~en** (Sprachw.) syntax

Synthese /zʏnˈteːzə/ *die;* **~, ~n** synthesis (*Gen.*, **von, aus** of)

Synthesizer /ˈsɪntəsaɪzɐ/ *der;* **~s, ~** (Musik) synthesizer

Synthetik /zʏnˈteːtɪk/ *das;* **~s** (ugs.) synthetic material

synthetisch
A *Adj.* synthetic
B *adv.* synthetically

Syphilis /ˈzyːfilɪs/ *die;* **~** ▸ⓘ **S. 439** (Med.) syphilis

Syrakus /zyraˈkuːs/ (*das*); **~'** Syracuse

Syrer /ˈzyːrɐ/ *der;* **~s, ~, Syrerin** *die;* **~, ~nen** ▸ⓘ **S. 520** Syrian

Syrien /ˈzyːri̯ən/ (*das*); **~s** Syria

syrisch /ˈzyːrɪʃ/ *Adj.* ▸ⓘ **S. 520** Syrian

System /zʏsˈteːm/ *das;* **~s, ~e** system; **~ in etw.** (*Akk.*) **bringen** introduce some system into sth.; get sth. into some sort of order; **~ haben** be methodical; have system; **hinter etw.** (*Dat.*) **steckt ~:** there's method in sth.

System-: ~absturz *der* (DV) system crash; **~administrator** *der*, **~administratorin** *die* system administrator; **~analyse** *die* systems analysis; **~analytiker** *der*, **~analytikerin** *die* ▸ⓘ **S. 113** systems analyst

Systematik /zʏsteˈmaːtɪk/ *die;* **~, ~en** 1 systematics *sing.* 2 (Biol.) taxonomy

systematisch /zʏsteˈmaːtɪʃ/
A *Adj.* systematic
B *adv.* systematically

systematisieren *tr. V.* systematize

system-, System-: ~fehler *der* system error; **~immanent** A *Adj.* part of the system *pred.*; **~immanente Faktoren** factors inherent in the system; B *adv.* in a manner inherent in the system; **~kritiker** *der*, **~kritikerin** *die* critic of the system; **~los** A *Adj.* unsystematic; B *adv.* unsystematically; **~veränderung** *die* change in the system; **~wette** *die: betting based on an agreed system of permutations*; **~zwang** *der* pressure imposed by the system

Systole /ˈzʏstole/ *die;* **~, ~n** (Med.) systole

Szenario /stseˈnaːri̯o/ *das;* **~s, ~s, Szenarium** /stseˈnaːri̯ʊm/ *das;* **~s, Szenarien** (Theater, Film) scenario

-szene *die;* **~, ~n** (ugs.) scene (coll.); **die Terror[isten]~/Literatur~:** the terrorist/literary scene

Szene /ˈstseːnə/ *die;* **~, ~n** 1 scene; **hinter der ~:** backstage; behind the scenes; **er erhielt Beifall auf offener ~:** he was applauded during the scene; **die ~ beherrschen** (fig.) dominate the scene; **ein Theaterstück in ~ setzen** stage a play; **sich in ~ setzen** (fig.) put oneself in the limelight 2 (Auseinandersetzung) scene; **[jmdm.] eine ~ machen** make a scene [in front of sb.] 3 (ugs.: bestimmtes Milieu) scene (coll.)

Szene-: ~blatt *das* (ugs.) scene mag (coll.); **~kneipe** *die* (ugs.) scene pub (Brit. coll.); scene bar (Amer.)

Szenen-: ~applaus *der* applause during the scene; spontaneous burst of applause; **~folge** *die* sequence of scenes; **~wechsel** *der* (Theater) scene change

Szenerie /stsenəˈriː/ *die;* **~, ~n** 1 (Bühnendekoration) set (*Gen.* for) 2 (Schauplatz) scene; (eines Romans) setting

Szene·treff *der* (ugs.) 1 (Treffen) rendezvous for members of the/a scene; **~ der IT-Branche** rendezvous for the IT industry scene; 2 (Ort) [fashionable] meeting place for members of a/the scene; **~ der Rechtsextremisten** meeting place for the right-wing extremist scene

szenig *Adj.* ‹*person*› who is part of the scene; ‹*place, pub, bar*› that is part of the scene

szenisch *Adj.* dramatic; **~e Gestaltung/Effekte** staging/stage effects

Szepter /ˈstsɛptɐ/ *das;* **~s, ~** ▸ **Zepter**

Szientismus /stsi̯ɛnˈtɪsmʊs/ *der;* **~** (Fachspr.) scientism *no art.*

Szilla /ˈstsɪla/ *die;* **~, Szillen** (Bot.) scilla

Szylla /ˈstsʏla/ *in* **zwischen ~ und Charybdis** (geh.) between Scylla and Charybdis

t, T /teː/ *das;* ~, ~, (ugs.) ~**s**, ~**s** t/T; *s. auch* **a, A**
t *Abk.* **= Tonne** ▸ⓘ **S. 315**
Tab. *Abk.* **= Tabelle**
Tabak /ˈta(ː)bak/ *der;* ~**s**, ~**e** tobacco
Tabak-: ~**monopol** *das* (Wirtsch.) tobacco monopoly; ~**rauch** *der* tobacco smoke
Tabaks-: ~**beutel** *der* tobacco pouch; ~**dose** *die* tobacco tin; ~**pfeife** *die* [tobacco] pipe
Tabak-: ~**steuer** *die* duty *or* tax on tobacco; ~**trafik** /-ˈ---/ *die* (österr.) tobacconist['s] [shop]; ~**waren** *Pl.* tobacco *sing.*; ~**werbung** *die* tobacco advertising
Tabatiere /tabaˈtjeːrə/ *die;* ~, ~**n** **1** (veralt.) snuff box **2** (österr.) ▸**Tabaksdose** **3** (österr.) ▸**Zigarettenetui**
tabellarisch /tabɛˈlaːrɪʃ/
A *Adj.* tabular; **ein** ~**er Lebenslauf** a curriculum vitae in tabular form
B *adv.* in tabular form
Tabelle /taˈbɛlə/ *die;* ~, ~**n** **1** (Übersicht) table **2** (Sport) [league/championship] table; **die** ~ **anführen** be at the top of the [league/championship] table
Tabellen-: ~**führer** *der* (Sport) player in the [league/championship] table; ~**führer sein** be top of the table; ~**führerin** *die* top player in the [league/championship] table; ~**führerin sein** be top of the table; ~**kalkulation** *die* (DV) spreadsheet calculation; (Programm) spreadsheet program; (Software) spreadsheet software; ~**platz** *der* (Sport) position *or* place in the [league/championship] table; ~**stand** *der* (Sport) state of the [league/championship] table
tabellieren *tr. V.* (Fachspr.) tabulate
Tabernakel /tabɛrˈnaːkl̩/ *das od. der;* ~**s**, ~ (kath. Kirche, Archit.) tabernacle
Tableau /taˈbloː/ *das;* ~**s**, ~**s** (bes. Literaturw.) tableau
Tablet-PC /ˈtɛblɪt-/ *der* (DV) tablet PC
Tablett /taˈblɛt/ *das;* ~**[e]s**, ~**s** *od.* ~**e** tray; **jmdm. etw. auf einem silbernen** ~ **servieren** (fig.) hand sth. to sb. on a silver platter
Tablette *die;* ~, ~**n** tablet
tabletten-, Tabletten-: ~**form** *die* tablet form; ~**missbrauch**, *~**mißbrauch** *der* pill abuse; ~**röhrchen** *das* tablet tube; ~**süchtig** *Adj.* addicted to pills *postpos.*
tabu /taˈbuː/ *Adj.* taboo
Tabu *das;* ~**s**, ~**s** taboo
Tabu·bruch *der* breach *or* infringement of a/the taboo
tabuieren, tabuisieren *tr. V.* (geh.) **etw.** ~: taboo sth.; make sth. taboo
Tabula rasa /ˈtaːbula ˈraːza/ *in* ~ ~ **machen** make a clean sweep
Tabulator·taste *die* tab key
Tabulatur /tabulaˈtuːɐ̯/ *die;* ~, ~**en** (Musik) tablature
tabu·los
A *Adj.* free from taboos *postpos.*; (ungehemmt) uninhibited
B *adv.* without [any] taboos; (ungehemmt) uninhibitedly
Taburett /tabuˈrɛt/ *das;* ~**[e]s**, ~**e** (schweiz., sonst veralt.) tabouret
Tabu·wort *das; Pl.* **Tabuwörter** (Sprachw., Psych.) taboo word
Tacheles /ˈtaxələs/ *in* **[mit jmdm.]** ~ **reden** (ugs.) do some straight talking [to sb.]
tachinieren /taxiˈniːrən/ *itr. V.* (österr. ugs.) loaf [about]
Tachinierer *der;* ~**s**, ~, **Tachiniererin** *die* (österr. ugs.) slacker (coll.); loafer
Tachismus /taˈʃɪsmʊs/ *der;* ~ (Kunstwiss.) tachism *no art.*
Tacho /ˈtaxo/ *der;* ~**s**, ~**s** (ugs.) speedo (coll.)
Tacho·meter *der od. das* speedometer
Tacho·nadel *die* speedometer needle
Tacho·stand *der* (ugs.: Kilometerstand) milometer *or* odometer reading
Tacker /ˈtakɐ/ *der;* ~**s**, ~: stapler
tackern
A *tr. V.* staple (**an** + *Akk.* to)
B *itr. V.* go rat-tat-tat; ‹*Schreibmaschine, Faxgerät:*› clatter
Tadel /ˈtaːdl̩/ *der;* ~**s**, ~ **1** censure; **jmdm. einen** ~ **erteilen** give sb. a rebuke; rebuke sb.; **ihn trifft kein** ~: he is not to blame; **öffentlicher** ~ (DDR Rechtsw.) public censure **2** (im Klassenbuch) black mark **3** (geh.: Mangel, Makel) blemish; flaw; **ohne** ~: perfect, flawless ‹*figure, copy, etc.*›; impeccable ‹*dress, appearance, etc.*›; irreproachable ‹*life, character, person, etc.*›
tadel·los
A *Adj.* **1** (makellos) impeccable; immaculate ‹*hair, clothing, suit, etc.*›; perfect ‹*condition, teeth, pronunciation, German, etc.*› **2** (ugs.: sehr gut) excellent **3** /ˈ--ˈ-/ (ugs.: als Ausruf der Zustimmung) splendid (coll.)
B *adv.* **1** (makellos) ‹*dress*› impeccably, immaculately; ‹*fit, speak, etc.*› perfectly; ‹*live, behave, etc.*› irreproachably **2** (ugs.: sehr gut) **hier wird man** ~ **bedient** the service is excellent here
tadeln *tr. V.* **jmdn. [für sein Verhalten** *od.* **wegen seines Verhaltens]** ~: rebuke sb. [for his/her behaviour]; **jmds. Arbeit** ~: criticize sb.'s work; **er hatte an ihr/ihrer Handlungsweise etw. zu** ~: he found some fault with her/the way she behaved; ~**de Worte**/~**der Blick** reproachful words/look
tadelns·wert *Adj.* reprehensible
Tadels·antrag *der* (Parl.) censure motion
Tafel /ˈtaːfl̩/ *die;* ~, ~**n** **1** (Schiefer~) slate; (Wand~) blackboard **2** (plattenförmiges Stück) slab; **eine** ~ **Schokolade** a bar of chocolate **3** (Gedenk~) plaque **4** (geh.: festlicher Tisch) table; **die** ~ **aufheben** (fig.) rise from the table **5** (Druckw.) plate
Tafel-: ~**anschrieb** *der* (Schulw.) writing on the board *no art*; ~**apfel** *der* (Kaufmannsspr.) dessert apple; ~**aufsatz** *der* centrepiece; ~**berg** *der* (Geol.) mesa; ~**besteck** *das* cutlery *or* (Amer.) flatware service; ~**bild** *das* (bild. Kunst) panel painting
Täfelchen /ˈtɛːflçən/ *das;* ~**s**, ~ ▸**Tafel 2**: [small] slab; [small] bar
tafel-, Tafel-: ~**fertig** *Adj.* (Kochk.) ready to serve *postpos.*; (noch zu erwärmen) ready to heat and serve *postpos.*; ~**fertige Gerichte** ready-to-serve/ready-to-heat-and-serve dishes; ~**freuden** *Pl.* (geh.) culinary delights; ~**lappen** *der* blackboard cloth; ~**musik** *die* musical entertainment (provided at a banquet, festive dinner, etc.)
tafeln *itr. V.* (geh.) feast
täfeln /ˈtɛːfl̩n/ *tr. V.* panel
Tafel-: ~**obst** *das* [dessert] fruit; ~**runde** *die* (geh.) gathering [round a table]; **die** ~**runde des Königs Artus** King Arthur's Round Table; ~**salz** *das* table salt; ~**silber** *das* silver cutlery; (fig.) most valuable possessions; **das** ~**silber verkaufen** sell the family silver (fig.); ~**spitz** *der* (österr.) boiled fillet of beef
Täfelung *die;* ~, ~**en** **1** (das Täfeln) panelling **2** (Paneel) [wooden] panelling
Tafel-: ~**wasser** *das; Pl.* ~**wässer** [bottled] mineral water; ~**wein** *der* table wine
Taft /taft/ *der;* ~**[e]s**, ~**e** taffeta
Tag /taːk/ *der;* ~**[e]s**, ~**e** **1** ▸ⓘ **S. 331** day; **es wird/ist** ~: it's getting/it is light; **solange es noch** ~ **ist** while it's still light; **der** ~ **bricht an** *od.* **graut** *od.* **erwacht/neigt sich** (geh.) the day breaks/draws to an end *or* a close; **die** ~**e nehmen ab/zu** the days are getting shorter/longer; **am** ~**[e]** during the day[time]; **am helllichten** ~: in broad daylight; **bei** ~**[e] reisen/ankommen** travel during the day/arrive while it's light; **[drei Stunden] vor** ~ (geh.) [three hours] before daylight; **er redet viel, wenn der** ~ **lang ist** (ugs.) you can't put any trust in what he says; **sie sind wie** ~ **und Nacht** they are as different as chalk and cheese; **man soll den** ~ **nicht vor dem Abend loben** (Spr.) don't count your chickens before they're hatched (prov.); **es ist noch nicht aller** ~**e Abend** we haven't yet seen the end of the matter; **guten** ~**!** hello; (bei Vorstellung) how do you do?; (nachmittags auch) good afternoon; **jmdm. einen guten** ~ **wünschen** wish sb. good day; ~**!** (ugs.) hello; hi (Amer. coll.); (nachmittags auch) afternoon; **bei jmdm. Guten** ~ **sagen** (ugs.) pop in to sb. to say 'hello' (coll.); **etw. an den** ~ **legen** display sth.; **etw. an den** ~ **bringen** *od.* (geh.) **ziehen** bring sth. to light; reveal sth.; **an den** ~ **kommen** come to light; **unter** ~**s** (landsch.) during the day [time]; **über/unter** ~**[e]** (Bergmannsspr.) above ground/underground; **zu** ~**e** ▸**zutage**
2 ▸ⓘ **S. 816** (Zeitraum von 24 Stunden) day; ~ **und Stunde des Treffens stehen fest** the date and time of the meeting are fixed; **welchen** ~ **haben wir heute?** (Wochentag) what day is it today? what's today?; (Datum) what date is it today?; **heute in/vor drei** ~**en** three days from today/three days ago today; **den** ~ **über** during the day; **einen** ~ **um den anderen** every other day; **jmdm. den** ~ **stehlen** waste sb.'s time; **an diesem** ~: on this day; **dreimal am** ~: three times a day; **früh/spät am** ~**[e]** early/late in the day; **am** ~**e vorher** on the previous day; the day before; **auf den** ~ **[genau]** on the [very] day; ~ **für** ~: every [single] day; **von** ~ **zu** ~: day by day; **in den nächsten** ~**en** in the next few days; **der** ~ **X** the great day; **am folgenden** ~: the next day; **heute ist sein [großer]** ~: it's his big day today; **er hatte heute einen schlechten** ~: today was one of his bad days; **sich** (*Dat.*) **einen schönen/faulen** ~ **machen** (ugs.) have a nice/lazy day; **den lieben langen** ~: all day long; **der** ~ **des Herrn** (christl. Rel.) the Lord's Day; ~ **der offenen Tür** open day; **der Brief muss/kann jeden** ~ **ankommen** the letter will surely/can arrive any day now; **eines** ~**es** one day; some day; **eines schönen** ~**es** one of these days; **dieser** ~**e werde ich ...** in the next few days, I will ...; **dieser** ~**e kam ein**

Mann ... the other day *or* recently, a man came ...; **von einem ~ auf den anderen** from one day to the next; overnight; **jmdn. von einem ~ auf den anderen vertrösten** put sb. off from day to day; **in den ~ hinein leben** live from day to day; **den ~ über** during the day
[3] (Ehren~, Gedenk~) **~ der deutschen Einheit** (Bundesrepublik Deutschland) Day of German Unity; **~ der Republik** (DDR) Republic Day
[4] *Pl.* ([Lebens]zeit) days; **sie hat schon bessere ~e gesehen** she has seen better days; **seine ~e sind gezählt** his days are numbered; **bis in unsere ~e** until our day; **auf meine/deine** *usw.* **alten ~e** in my/your *etc.* old age
[5] *Pl.* (ugs. verhüll.: Menstruation) period *sing.*; **wenn sie ihre ~e hat** when it's her time of the month

tag-, Tag-: ~aktiv *Adj.* (Zool.) diurnal; **~aus** *Adv.* **~aus, tagein** day in, day out; day after day; **~dienst** *der* day duty; **~dienst haben** be on day duty

Tage-: ~bau *der*; *Pl.* **~~e** (Bergbau) [1] (Bergbau über Tage) opencast mining *no art.*; [2] (Anlage) opencast mine; **~blatt** *das* [1] (veralt.: Tageszeitung) daily [news]paper; [2] (in Namen) **das Offenburger ~blatt** the Offenburg Daily News; **~buch** *das* diary; **[über etw.** (*Akk.*)**] ~buch führen** keep a diary [about sth.]; **~buch·aufzeichnung** *die* diary entry; **~dieb** *der*, **~diebin** *die* (abwertend) idler; lazybones *sing.*; **~geld** *das* [1] (Verpflegungsbetrag) daily [expense] allowance; [2] *Pl.* (Diäten) daily [parliamentary] allowance *sing.*; [3] (Tagesvergütung) daily compensation

tag·ein *Adv.* ▸ **tagaus**

tage-, Tage-: ~lang [A] *Adj.*; lasting for days *postpos.*; **das ~lange Warten** the days of waiting; **nach ~langem Regen** after days of rain; [B] *adv.* for days [on end]; **~lohn** *der* daily *or* day's wage[s]; **im ~lohn arbeiten** be paid by the day; **~löhner** /-lø:nɐ/ *der*; **~~s, ~~**, **~löhnerin** *die*; **~~, ~~nen** day labourer

tagen *itr. V.* [1] (konferieren) meet; **das Gericht/Parlament tagt** the court/parliament is in session; **über etw.** (*Akk.*) **~:** confer about *or* meet to discuss sth.; **bis in den frühen Morgen hinein ~** (fig.) celebrate until the early hours [2] (geh.: dämmern) **es tagt** day is breaking *or* dawning

Tage·reise *die* day's journey; **nach Passau sind es zehn ~n** it's a ten-day journey to Passau

tages-, Tages-: ~ablauf *der* day; daily routine; **~aktuell** *Adj.* up-to-the-minute; **~anbruch** *der* daybreak; dawn; **~arbeit** *die* day's work; **~ausflug** *der* day's outing; **~auszug** *der* (Bankw.) daily statement of account transactions; **~bedarf** *der* daily requirement; **~befehl** *der* (Milit.) order of the day; **~creme** *die* (Kosmetik) day cream; **~decke** *die* bedspread; **~dessert** *das* dessert *or* (Brit.) sweet of the day; **~einnahme** *die* day's takings *pl.*; **~einrichtung** *die* day-care centre; **~ereignis** *das* event of the day; **~fahrt** *die* day trip; day excursion; **~gast** *der* (im Hotel, Restaurant) daytime guest; (im Schwimmbad) daytime user; **~geschäft** *das* day-to-day business; **~gespräch** *das* topic of the day; **~karte** *die* [1] (Gastron.) menu of the day; [2] (Fahr-, Eintrittskarte) day ticket; **~kasse** *die* [1] box office (*open during the day*); [2] (**~einnahme**) day's takings *pl.*; **~kilometerzähler** *der* trip mileage recorder; **~kurs** *der* (Börsenw.) current rate of exchange; **~lauf** *der* daily routine; **~licht** *das* daylight; **bei ~licht** in [the] daylight; **das ~licht scheuen** (fig.) shun the light of day; **etw. ans ~licht bringen** *od.* **ziehen** (fig.) bring sth. to light; **ans ~licht kommen** (fig.) come to light; **~licht·projektor** *der* overhead projector; **~losung** *die* day's password; **~marsch** *der* [1] (Fußmarsch) day's hike; [2] (Strecke eines **~marsches**) day's march; **drei ~märsche entfernt** three days' march away; **~menü** *das* set menu of the day; **~mutter** *die*; *Pl.* **~mütter** childminder; **~ordnung** *die* agenda; **einen Punkt auf die ~ordnung setzen/von der ~ordnung absetzen** place an item on the agenda/delete an item from the agenda; **an der ~ordnung sein** (fig.) be the order of the day; **zur ~ordnung übergehen** (fig.) proceed as if nothing had happened; **~ordnungs·punkt** *der* item on the agenda; **~politik** *die* day-to-day politics *sing.*; **~preis** *der* (Wirtsch.) current price; **~presse** *die* daily press; **~ration** *die* daily ration; **~raum** *der* day room; **~satz** *der* [1] (Rechtsw.: Geldstrafe) *unit, based on net daily income etc., used to calculate a fine*; [2] (Unterbringungskosten) daily rate; **~suppe** *die* soup of the day; **~tour** *die* ▸ **~fahrt**; **~wanderung** *die* day's hike; **~wanderungen** one-day hikes; **~zeit** *die* time of day; **um diese ~zeit** at this time; **jmdm. die ~zeit [ent]bieten** (veralt.) give sb. the time of day; **zu jeder ~- und Nachtzeit** at any time of the day or night; **~zeitung** *die* daily newspaper; daily

Tagetes /ta'ge:tεs/ *die*; **~, ~:** tagetes

tage·weise *Adv.* on some days

Tage·werk *das* (veralt. geh.) day's labour

Tag·falter *der* (Zool.) butterfly

tag·hell
[A] *Adj.* [1] (durch Tageslicht) [day]light [2] (wie am Tag) bright as daylight *postpos*
[B] *adv.* **etw. ist ~ erleuchtet** sth. is very brightly lit [up]

-tägig /-tε:gɪç/ [1] (... Tage alt) **ein sechstägiges Küken** a six-day-old chick [2] (... Tage dauernd) **nach dreitägiger Vorbereitung** after three days' preparation; **mit dreitägiger Verspätung** three days late

täglich /'tε:klɪç/
[A] *Adj.* daily
[B] *adv.* every day; **zweimal ~:** twice a day; **~ zwei Stunden** for two hours a day; **~ drei Tabletten einnehmen** take three tablets daily

Tag·pfauen·auge *das* (Zool.) peacock butterfly

tags *Adv.* [1] by day; in the daytime [2] **~ zuvor/davor** the day before; **~ darauf** the next *or* following day; the day after

Tag·schicht *die* day shift; **~ haben** be on [the] day shift; **in ~ arbeiten** work a day shift

tags·über *Adv.* during the day

tag·täglich (intensivierend)
[A] *Adj.* day-to-day; daily
[B] *adv.* every single day

tag-, Tag-: ~träumen *itr. V.* daydream (**von** about); **~träumer** *der*, **~träumerin** *die* daydreamer; **~träumerei** *die* daydreaming (**von** about); **~und·nacht·gleiche** *die*; **~~, ~~n** equinox

Tagung *die*; **~, ~en** conference

Tagungs-: ~ort *der* venue [for a/the conference]; **~teilnehmer** *der*, **~teilnehmerin** *die* participant in a/the conference

Taifun /tai'fu:n/ *der*; **~s, ~e** typhoon

Taiga *die*; **~:** taiga

Taille /'taljə/ *die*; **~, ~n** waist; **in der ~:** at the waist

Taillen·weite *die* waist measurement

Tailleur /ta'jø:ɐ/ *das*; **~s, ~s** (schweiz.) tailored suit/coat (fitted at the waist)

taillieren /ta'ji:rən/ *tr. V.* fit [at the waist]; **ein tailliertes Kostüm** a suit with the jacket fitted at the waist

Taillierung *die*; **~, ~en** (Schneiderei) fitting at the waist; **mit leichter ~:** taken in slightly at the waist

Taiwan /'taivan/ (*das*); **~s** Taiwan

Taiwaner *der*; **~s, ~, Taiwanerin** *die*; **~, ~nen** Taiwanese

Takelage /takə'la:ʒə/ *die*; **~, ~n** (Seew.) masts and rigging

takeln /'ta:kl̩n/ *tr. V.* (Seemannsspr.) rig

Takelung *die*; **~, ~en** (Seemannsspr.) rig

Takt /takt/ *der*; **~[e]s, ~e** [1] (Musik) time; (Einheit) bar; measure (Amer.); **im ~ bleiben** stay in time; **den ~ [ein]halten** keep in time; **den ~ angeben/schlagen/wechseln** give the beat/beat time/change the time *or* beat; **aus dem ~ kommen** lose the beat; **sich nicht aus dem ~ bringen lassen** not lose the beat; **mit ihm muss ich mal ein paar ~e reden** (fig. ugs.) I need to have a serious talk with him [2] (rhythmischer Bewegungsablauf) rhythm; **im/gegen den ~:** in/out of rhythm; **im ~ bleiben** keep the rhythm; **aus dem ~ kommen** lose the rhythm [3] (Feingefühl) tact; **etw. aus ~ tun** do sth. out of tact[fulness] [4] (Verslehre) foot

takt·fest (Musik)
[A] *Adj.* **ein nicht ganz ~er Pianist** a pianist who has some difficulty keeping time; **~ sein** keep good time
[B] *adv.* in time

Takt·gefühl *das* sense of tact; **etw. mit großem ~ tun** do sth. with great delicacy

taktieren *itr. V.* proceed tactically; **vorsichtig/klug ~:** use caution/clever tactics

Taktik /'taktɪk/ *die*; **~, ~en [eine] ~:** tactics *pl.*; **die ~ der verbrannten Erde** (Milit.) scorched-earth tactics

Taktiker *der*; **~s, ~:** tactician

taktil
[A] *Adj.* tactile
[B] *adv.* by tactile means; by [one's] sense of touch

taktisch
[A] *Adj.* tactical
[B] *adv.* tactically; **~ klug vorgehen** use clever *or* good tactics

takt·los
[A] *Adj.* tactless
[B] *adv.* tactlessly

Taktlosigkeit *die*; **~, ~en** [1] (taktlose Art) tactlessness [2] (taktlose Handlung) piece of tactlessness; **derartige ~en** such tactlessness *sing.*

Takt-: ~stock *der* baton; **den ~stock schwingen** (scherzh.) wield the baton; **~strich** *der* (Musik) bar [line]; **~verkehr** *der* regular service; **im ~verkehr** at regular intervals

takt·voll
[A] *Adj.* tactful
[B] *adv.* tactfully

Takt·wechsel *der* (Musik) change of time

Tal /ta:l/ *das*; **~[e]s, Täler** /'tε:lɐ/ valley; **das Vieh zu ~ treiben** drive the cattle down into the valley

tal·abwärts *Adv.* down the valley

Talar /ta'la:ɐ/ *der*; **~s, ~e** robe

tal·aufwärts *Adv.* up the valley

Tal·brücke *die* bridge across a/the valley

Tälchen /'tε:lçən/ *das*; **~s, ~:** [little] valley

Talent /ta'lεnt/ *das*; **~[e]s, ~e** [1] (Befähigung) talent (**zu, für** for); **~ für Sprachen haben** have a gift for languages; **sie hat das ~, immer das richtige Wort zu finden** she has a gift for always finding the right word [2] (Mensch) talented person; **junge ~e fördern** promote young talent

talentiert /talεn'ti:ɐt/ *Adj.* talented

Talent-: ~scout /-skaut/ *der*; **~~[s], ~~s** (Jargon) talent scout; **~suche** *die* search for talent; **zur ~suche in die Provinz kommen** come in search of talent in the provinces

Taler /'ta:lɐ/ *der*; **~s, ~** (hist.) thaler

Tal·fahrt *die* [1] (Schifffahrt) passage downstream [2] (Fahrt abwärts) drive down into the valley; (mit dem Lift) descent into the valley; (mit Skiern) skiing down into the valley; (fig.) fall; plunge; **die Wirtschaft befindet sich auf einer ~** (fig.) the economy is on the decline

Talg /talk/ *der*; **~[e]s, ~e** [1] (Speisefett) suet; (zur Herstellung von Seife, Kerzen usw.) tallow [2] (Haut~) sebum

Talg-: ~drüse *die* sebaceous gland; **~licht** *das*; *Pl.* **~~er** tallow candle

Talisman /'ta:lɪsman/ *der*; **~s, ~e** talisman

Talk /talk/ *der*; **~[e]s** talc

talken /'tɔ:kn̩/ *itr. V.* appear on a talk show; **über etw. ~:** talk about sth.

Talker /'tɔ:kɐ/ *der*; **~s, ~** (Jargon: Talkmaster) talk show host; chat show host

Talk-: /'tɔ:k-/ **~gast** *der* talk-show guest; chat-show guest; **~master** *der* talk show host; chat show host; **~runde** *die* talk show;

t

~show /'tɔ:kʃoʊ/ *die* (Ferns.) talk show; chat show

Talmi /'talmi/ *das;* **~s** 1) (wertloser Schmuck) imitation *or* cheap jewellery; (fig.) tinsel 2) (vergoldete Legierung) pinchbeck

Talmi·glanz *der* glitter

Talmud /'talmu:t/ *der;* **~[e]s, ~e** Talmud

Talschaft *die;* **~, ~en** (schweiz., westösterr.) valley people *pl. or* inhabitants *pl.*

Tal-: ~sohle *die* valley floor *or* bottom; (fig.) depression; **die Wirtschaft befindet sich auf** *od.* **in einer ~sohle** the economy is going through a depression; **~sperre** *die* dam (*with associated reservoir and power station*); **~station** *die* valley station

Tamarinde /tama'rɪndə/ *die;* **~, ~n** tamarind

Tamariske /tama'rɪskə/ *die;* **~, ~n** tamarisk

Tambour /'tambu:ɐ̯/ *der;* **~s, ~e** *od.* (schweiz.) **~en** (veralt.) drummer

Tambour·major *der* drum major

Tamburin /tambu'ri:n/ *das;* **~s, ~e** tambourine

Tampon /'tampɔn/ *der;* **~s, ~s** 1) (Med.: Wattebausch) tampon; plug 2) (Menstruations~) tampon

tamponieren *tr. V.* (Med.) plug

Tamtam /tam'tam/ *das;* **~s, ~s** 1) (Musikinstrument) tam-tam 2) (ugs. abwertend: großer Aufwand) **[großes] ~:** [a big] fuss; **~ machen** make a fuss

TAN /tan/ *die;* **~, ~s** (DV) TAN

Tand /tant/ *der;* **~[e]s** trumpery

Tändelei *die;* **~, ~en** 1) (Spielerei) dalliance 2) (Liebelei) flirtation

tändeln /'tɛndl̩n/ *itr. V.* 1) (spielen) dally 2) (schäkern) flirt

Tandem /'tandɛm/ *das;* **~s, ~s** tandem; (fig.) pair; **als ~ arbeiten** work in tandem

Tang /taŋ/ *der;* **~[e]s, ~e** seaweed

Tanga /'taŋga/ *der;* **~s, ~s** tanga

Tangens /'taŋgɛns/ *der;* **~, ~** (Math.) tangent

Tangente /taŋ'gɛntə/ *die;* **~, ~n** 1) (Math.) tangent 2) (Straße) ring road; bypass

tangential /taŋgɛn'tsia:l/ (Math.)

A *Adj.* tangential

B *adv.* tangentially

Tanger /'taŋɐ/ *(das);* **~s** ▸ℹ **S. 675** Tangier

tangieren /taŋ'gi:rən/ *tr. V.* 1) affect 2) (Math.) be tangent to

Tango /'taŋgo/ *der;* **~s, ~s** tango

Tank /taŋk/ *der;* **~s, ~s,** (seltener) **~e** tank

Tanke *die;* **~, ~n** (salopp) filling station

tanken *tr., itr. V.* fill up; **Benzin/Öl ~:** fill up with petrol (Brit.) *or* (Amer.) gasoline/oil; **er tankte dreißig Liter [Super]** he put in thirty litres [of four-star]; **hast du schon getankt?** have you already put petrol (Brit.) *or* (Amer.) gasoline in?; **frische Luft/Sonne ~** (fig.) get one's fill of fresh air/sun; **er hat aber reichlich getankt** (fig. salopp) he really got tanked up (sl.)

Tanker *der;* **~s, ~:** tanker

Tanker·flotte *die* fleet of tankers

Tank-: ~fahr·zeug *das* tanker; **~füllung** *die* 1) (das Füllen) filling of the tank; 2) **eine ~füllung reicht für ...** one full tank is enough for ...; **~lager** *das* tank farm; **~laster** *der* (ugs.), **~lastwagen** *der* tanker; **~säule** *die* petrol pump (Brit.); gasoline pump (Amer.); **~stelle** *die* petrol station (Brit.); gas station (Amer.); **freie ~stelle** unbranded petrol/gas station; **~stopp** *der* (ugs.) stop for fuel; (Flugw.) refuelling stop; **~uhr** *die* fuel gauge; **~wagen** *der* tanker; **~wart** /-vart/ *der;* **~~s, ~~e, ~wartin** *die;* **~~, ~~nen** ▸ℹ **S. 113** petrol pump attendant (Brit.)

Tann /tan/ *der;* **~[e]s, ~e** (dichter.) [pine] forest

Tanne /'tanə/ *die;* **~, ~n** 1) fir [tree]; **schlank wie eine ~:** slender as a reed 2) (Holz) fir

Tannen-: ~baum *der* 1) (ugs.: Tanne a) fir tree; 2) (Weihnachtsbaum) Christmas tree; **~grün** *das* fir sprigs *pl.;* **~holz** *das* fir; **~nadel** *die* fir needle; **~wald** *der* fir forest; **~zapfen** *der* fir cone; **~zweig** *der* fir branch

Tansania /tan'za:nia/ *(das);* **~s** Tanzania

Tansanier /tan'za:niɐ/ *der;* **~s, ~, Tansanierin** *die;* **~, ~nen** Tanzanian

Tantalus·qualen /'tantalʊs-/ *Pl.* **~ leiden** suffer agonizing frustration *sing.*

Tantchen *das;* **~s, ~:** auntie (coll.)

Tante /'tantə/ *die;* **~, ~n** 1) aunt 2) (Kinderspr.: Frau) lady 3) (ugs.: Frau) woman

Tante-Emma-Laden *der; Pl.* **Tante-Emma-Läden** [small] corner shop

tantenhaft

A *Adj.* old-maidish; (belehrend) nannyish

B *adv.* like an old maid; (belehrend) nannyishly

Tantieme /tã'tie:mə/ *die;* **~, ~n** 1) (Gewinnbeteiligung) percentage of the profits 2) (von Künstlern) royalty

Tanz /tants/ *der;* **~es, Tänze** /'tɛntsə/ 1) dance; **jmdn. zum ~ auffordern** ask sb. to dance *or* for a dance; **ein ~ auf dem Vulkan** (fig.) sitting on a powder keg; **der ~ ums Goldene Kalb** (fig.) worship of the golden calf 2) (~veranstaltung) dance; **heute Abend ist ~:** there is dancing this evening; **zum ~ gehen** go dancing; **ein ~ in den Mai/Frühling** a dance to mark the beginning of May/Spring 3) (Zank, Auftritt) song and dance (fig. coll.)

tanz-, Tanz-: ~abend *der* evening dance; **~bar** *Adj.* that you can dance to *postpos., not pred.;* **~bar** *die* night spot (coll.) with dancing; **~bär** *der* dancing bear; **~bein** *das: in* **das ~bein schwingen** (ugs. scherzh.) shake a leg (coll.); **~boden** *der* dance floor; **~café** *das* coffee house with dancing

Tänzchen /'tɛntsçən/ *das;* **~s, ~:** [little] dance; **ein ~ wagen** take a turn around the floor

Tanz·diele *die* (veralt.) dance hall

tänzeln /'tɛntsl̩n/ *itr. V.* 1) prance; **jmdm. mit ~den Schritten entgegenkommen** skip towards sb. 2) *mit sein* **sie tänzelte ins Zimmer** she skipped into the room

tanzen

A *itr. V.* 1) dance; **~ gehen** go dancing; **auf dem Seil ~:** walk the tightrope; **das Schiff tanzt auf den Wellen** the ship is bobbing up and down on the waves; **sich heiß/müde ~:** dance until one is hot/tired 2) *mit sein* (sich ~d fortbewegen) dance; skip

B *tr. V.* **Walzer/Tango ~:** dance a waltz/tango; waltz/tango

Tänzer /'tɛntsɐ/ *der;* **~s, ~** ▸ℹ **S. 113** 1) dancer 2) (Tanzpartner) dancing partner 3) (Balletttänzer) ballet dancer

Tanzerei *die;* **~, ~en** 1) (ugs.) [small] dancing party 2) (oft abwertend: dauerndes Tanzen) [continual] dancing *no pl.*

Tänzerin *die;* **~, ~nen** ▸ **Tänzer**

tänzerisch

A *Adj.* dance-like ‹*movement, rhythm, step*›; **~e Begabung** talent for dancing

B *adv.* **~ begabt sein** have a talent for dancing; **~ ausgebildet sein** be trained as a dancer; **eine ~ hervorragende Leistung** an outstanding achievement in dance

Tanz-: ~fläche *die* dance floor; **~gruppe** *die* dance group; **~kapelle** *die* dance band; **~kurs** *der* dancing class; **~lehrer** *der,* **~lehrerin** *die* dancing teacher; **~lokal** *das* café/restaurant with dancing; **~musik** *die* dance music; **~orchester** *das* dance band; **~partner** *der,* **~partnerin** *die* dancing partner; **~platte** *die* record of dance music; **~platz** *der* [open-air] dance floor; **~saal** *der* dance hall; (in hotel, castle, etc.) ballroom; **~schritt** *der* dance step; **~schuh** *der* dance *or* dancing shoe; **~schule** *die* dancing school; school of dancing; **~sport** *der* ballroom *or* competition dancing *no art.;* **~stunde** *die* 1) (~kurs) dancing class; **~stunde nehmen, in die ~stunde gehen** take dancing lessons; go to dancing class; 2) (einzelne Stunde) dancing lesson; **~tee** *der* tea dance; thé dansant; **~turnier** *das* dancing competition; **~veranstaltung** *die* dance; **~vergnügen** *das* dance

Taoismus /tao'ɪsmʊs/ *der;* **~:** Taoism *no art.*

Tapet *das: in* **aufs ~ kommen** (ugs.) be brought up; come up [for discussion]; **etw. aufs ~ bringen** (ugs.) bring sth. up; broach sth.

Tapete /ta'pe:tə/ *die;* **~, ~n** wallpaper; **die ~n wechseln** (ugs.) have a change of scene

Tapeten-: ~rolle *die* roll of wallpaper; **~tür** *die* concealed door; **~wechsel** *der* (ugs.) change of scene

Tape·verband /'teɪp-/ *der* tape bandage

tapezieren /tape'tsi:rən/ *tr. V.* [wall]paper

Tapezierer *der;* **~s, ~, Tapeziererin** *die;* **~, ~nen** ▸ℹ **S. 113** paperhanger

Tapezier-: ~nagel *der* tack; **~tisch** *der* pasteboard; paperhanger's bench

tapfer /'tapfɐ/

A *Adj.* brave; courageous; brave ‹*child*›; **~en Widerstand leisten** resist bravely

B *adv.* 1) bravely; courageously; (von Kindern) bravely; **sich ~ halten** be brave 2) (kräftig) ‹*eat, drink*› heartily; **~ zulangen** have *or* take a big helping

Tapferkeit *die;* **~:** courage; bravery

Tapioka /ta'pio:ka/ *die;* **~:** tapioca

Tapir /'ta:pi:ɐ̯/ *der;* **~s, ~e** (Zool.) tapir

Tapisserie /tapɪsə'ri:/ *die;* **~, ~n** tapestry

tapp /tap/ *Interj.* patter; **~, ~!** pitter patter!

tappen *itr. V.* 1) *mit sein* patter; **in eine Falle ~** (fig.) stumble into a trap 2) (tastend greifen) grope (**nach** for)

täppisch /'tɛpɪʃ/

A *Adj.* awkward; clumsy

B *adv.* awkwardly; clumsily

Taps /taps/ *der;* **~es, ~e** (ugs. abwertend) clumsy oaf

tapsig (ugs.)

A *Adj.* awkward; clumsy

B *adv.* awkwardly; clumsily

Tarantel /ta'rantl̩/ *die;* **~, ~n** (Zool.) tarantula; **er sprang wie von der ~ gestochen auf** he jumped up as if something had bitten him

Tarantella /taran'tɛla/ *die;* **~, ~s** *od.* **Tarantellen** (Musik) tarantella

Tarif /ta'ri:f/ *der;* **~s, ~e** 1) (Preis, Gebühr) charge; (Post~, Wasser~) rate; (Verkehrs~) fares *pl.;* (Zoll~) tariff 2) (~verzeichnis) list of charges/rates/fares; tariff; **der Fahrpreis beträgt laut ~ 1,20 Euro** the fare is fixed at 1.20 euros 3) (Lohn~) [wage] rate; (Gehalts~) [salary] scale; **weit über/unter ~ verdienen** earn well above/far below the agreed rate

Tarif-: ~auseinandersetzung *die* pay negotiations *pl;* **~autonomie** *die* [right to] free collective bargaining *no art.* (*without state intervention*); **~gruppe** *die* (Lohngruppe) wage group; (Gehaltsgruppe) salary group; **~kommission** *die* wages commission

tariflich

A *Adj.* wage ‹*demand, dispute, etc.*›

B *adv.* **Löhne und Gehälter sind ~ festgelegt** there are fixed rates for wages and salaries; **die Arbeitszeit ist ~ geregelt** the number of working hours is fixed [by collective agreement]

tarif-, Tarif-: ~lohn *der* wage under the collective agreement; **~los** *Adj.* **es herrscht ein ~loser Zustand** no wage agreement is in force; **~partei** *die* side [in the pay negotiations]; (nach abgeschlossenem Vertrag) party to the pay agreement; **~partner** *der:* **die ~partner** union and management; employers and employees; **wegen der Unnachgiebigkeit des ~partners** because of the inflexibility of management/the union; **~recht** *das* law governing [collective] pay agreements *or* settlements; **~rechtlich** A *Adj.* ‹*regulations, reforms*› relating to pay settlement law; **ohne ~rechtliche Absicherung** not covered by pay settlement law; B *adv.* from the point of view of pay settlement law; ‹*protected, covered*› by pay settlement law; **~streit** *der* pay dispute; **~verhandlung** *die* pay negotiations *pl.;* **~vertrag** *der* pay agreement

tarnen /'tarnən/

A *tr., itr. V.* camouflage; **seine Aufregung ~** (fig.)

disguise one's excitement
B *refl. V.* camouflage oneself; (fig.) disguise oneself
Tarn-: ~farbe *die* camouflage [colour]; **etw. mit ~farbe bemalen** paint sth. with camouflage paint; **~kappe** *die* (Myth.) magic hat (making the wearer invisible)
Tarnung *die;* **~, ~en** (auch fig.) camouflage; **zur ~ dienen** serve as camouflage
Tarock /ta'rɔk/ *das* (österr. nur so) *od. der* taroc
Tarot /ta'ro:/ *das od. der;* **~s, ~s** tarot
Tarot·karte *die* tarot card
Tartan·bahn /'tartan-/ *die* Tartan track ®
Täschchen /'tɛʃçən/ *das;* **~s, ~** ▸**Tasche**: [little] bag/pocket
Tasche /'taʃə/ *die;* **~, ~n** **1** bag **2** (in Kleidung, Koffer, Rucksack usw.) pocket **3** (fig.) **jmdm. die ~n leeren** (ugs.) fleece sb.; **sich** (*Dat.*) **die eigenen ~n füllen** (ugs.) line one's own pockets *or* purse; **jmdm. auf der ~ liegen** (ugs.) live off sb.; **etw. aus eigener** *od.* **der eigenen ~ bezahlen** pay for sth. out of one's own pocket; **jmdm. etw. aus der ~ ziehen** (ugs.) wangle money out of sb. (coll.); **[für etw.] tief in die ~ greifen [müssen]** (ugs.) [have to] dig deep in *or* into one's pocket [for sth.]; **etw. in die eigene ~ stecken** (ugs.) pocket sth.; put sth. in one's own pocket; **in die eigene ~ arbeiten** *od.* **wirtschaften** (ugs.) line one's own pocket[s]; **jmdn. in die ~ stecken** (ugs.) put sb. in the shade; **sich** (*Dat.*) **in die eigene ~ lügen** (ugs.) fool oneself; **etw. in der ~ haben** (ugs.) have sth. in one's pocket
Taschen-: ~buch *das* paperback; **~buchausgabe** *die* paperback edition; **~dieb** *der,* **~diebin** *die* pickpocket; **~fahrplan** *der* pocket timetable; **~format** *das* pocket size; **ein Wörterbuch im ~format** a pocket-size dictionary; **~geld** *das* pocket money; **~kalender** *der* pocket calendar; **~krebs** *der* edible crab; **~lampe** *die* [pocket] torch (Brit.) *or* (Amer.) flashlight; **~messer** *das* pocket knife; penknife; **~rechner** *der* pocket calculator; **~schirm** *der* telescopic umbrella; **~spiegel** *der* pocket mirror; **~spieler** *der,* **~spielerin** *die* (veralt.) conjuror; **~spieler·trick** *der* (abwertend) trick; **~träger** *der,* **~trägerin** *die* (Golf) caddie; (fig.) bag carrier; **~tuch** *das; Pl.* **~tücher** handkerchief; **~uhr** *die* pocket watch; **~wörterbuch** *das* pocket dictionary
Task·leiste /'ta:sk-/ *die* (DV) taskbar
Tässchen, °Täßchen /'tɛsçən/ *das;* **~s, ~**: [small] cup
Tasse /'tasə/ *die;* **~, ~n** **1** cup; **eine ~ Tee** a cup of tea; **trübe ~** (ugs. abwertend) drip (coll.); **komm, du trübe ~!** come on, don't be such a drip (coll.) **2** (~ mit Untertasse) cup and saucer; **nicht alle ~n im Schrank haben** (ugs.) not be right in the head (coll.)
Tastatur /tasta'tu:ɐ̯/ *die;* **~, ~en** keyboard
Taste /'tastə/ *die;* **~, ~n** **1** (eines Musikinstruments, einer Schreibmaschine) key; **[mächtig] in die ~n greifen** start to play with great gusto **2** (Fuß~) pedal [key] **3** (am Telefon, Radio, Fernsehgerät, Taschenrechner usw.) button
Tast·empfindung *die* sense of touch
tasten
A *itr. V.* (fühlend suchen) grope, feel (**nach** for); **~de Versuche/Fragen** (fig.) tentative attempts/ questions
B *refl. V.* (sich tastend bewegen) grope *or* feel one's way
C *tr. V.* **1** (über eine Tastatur eingeben) key in **2** (tastend feststellen) feel
Tasten-: ~druck *der; Pl.* **~drücke** touch of a/the button; **auf ~druck** at the touch of a/the button; **~feld** *das* (Elektrot.) keypad; **~instrument** *das* keyboard instrument; **~kombination** *die* (DV) key combination; **~telefon** *das* push-button telephone
Taster *der;* **~s, ~** **1** (Technik: Maschine) keyboard **2** ▸**ⓘ S. 113** (Fachspr.: Mensch) keyboard operator; keyboarder **3** (Taste~) button
Tasterin *die;* **~, ~nen** ▸**Taster 2**
Tast·sinn *der* sense of touch
tat /ta:t/ *1. u. 3. Pers. Sg. Prät. v.* **tun**

Tat *die;* **~, ~en** **1** (Handlung) act; (das Tun) action; **ein Mann der ~**: a man of action; **jmdm. mit Wort und ~ beistehen** stand by sb. in word and deed; **etw. durch ~en beweisen** prove sth. by one's actions; **zur ~ schreiten** proceed to action; **die gute Absicht/den guten Willen für die ~ nehmen** take the will for the deed; **jmdn. auf frischer ~ ertappen** catch sb. red-handed *or* in the act; **etw. in die ~ umsetzen** put sth. into action *or* effect; **das ist die ~ eines Wahnsinnigen** that is the action of a madman; **eine verbrecherische ~**: a crime; a criminal act; **eine gute ~ vollbringen** do a good deed; **ein Buch über Leben und ~en des ...** a book on the life and exploits of ...; **zu seiner ~ stehen** stand by one's action **2** **in der ~** (verstärkend) actually; (zustimmend) indeed
Tatar[1] /ta'ta:ɐ̯/ *der;* **~en, ~en** Tartar
Tatar[2] *das;* **~[s], Tatar-beefsteak** *das* steak tartare
Tataren·meldung *die* alarmist report
Tatarin *die;* **~, ~nen** ▸**Tatar**[1]
tatarisch *Adj.* Tartar
tatauieren /tatau'i:rən/ (Völkerk.) ▸**tätowieren**
Tat-: ~bestand *der* **1** facts *pl.* [of the matter *or* case]; **einen ~bestand feststellen** establish the facts [of a matter *or* case]; **2** (Rechtsw.) elements *pl.* of an offence; **der ~bestand der vorsätzlichen Tötung** the offence of premeditated murder; **~einheit** *die* (Rechtsw.) concomitance of offences; **Mord in ~einheit mit Raub** murder [in concomitance] with robbery
taten-, Taten-: ~drang *der* desire *or* thirst for action; **trotz seines hohen Alters war er noch voller ~drang** in spite of his old age he was still full of energy; **~durst** *der* (geh.) thirst for action; **er brennt vor ~durst** he is thirsting for action; **~durstig** *Adj.* (geh.) thirsty *or* eager for action *postpos.*; **~los** **A** *Adj.* idle; **B** *adv.* idly; **einer Sache** (*Dat.*) **~los zusehen** watch sth. without taking any action
Täter /'tɛ:tɐ/ *der;* **~s, ~**: culprit; **wer ist der ~?** who did it?; **der ~ hat sich der Polizei gestellt** the person who committed the crime gave himself/herself up to the police; **nach dem ~ fahnden** search *or* look for the person responsible [for the crime]; **die Polizei hat die ~ noch nicht gefunden** the police have not yet found those responsible [for the crime]
Täter·gruppe *die* group of criminals
Täterin *die;* **~, ~nen** ▸**Täter**
Täter·kreis *der* group of people involved in a/the crime; (bei mehreren Verbrechen) group of offenders
Täterschaft *die;* **~** **1** **seine ~ ist erwiesen** his responsibility for the crime has been proved **2** (schweiz.: Täter) culprit/culprits
Tat-: ~form *die* (Sprachw.) ▸**Aktiv**[1]; **~hergang** *der* [course *sing.* of] events *pl.*
tätig /'tɛ:tɪç/ *Adj.* **1** **~ sein** work; **der in unserer Firma ~e Ingenieur** the engineer who works for our firm; **~ werden** (bes. Amtsspr.) take action; **~e Reue** (Rechtsw.) *remorse for one's crime, accompanied by action to avert its effects* **2** (rührig, aktiv) active; **~e Nächstenliebe** charity [to one's neighbour]; brotherly love; **ein ~er Vulkan** an active volcano
tätigen /'tɛ:tɪgn̩/ *tr. V.* (Kaufmannsspr., Papierdt.) transact ‹*business, deal, etc.*›; **Einkäufe ~**: effect purchases; **Anrufe ~**: make [telephone] calls
Tätigkeit *die;* **~, ~en** **1** activity; (Arbeit) job; **eine fieberhafte ~**: a frenzy of activity; **das gehört zu den ~en einer Hausfrau** that is part of a housewife's work *sing.*; **eine ~ ausüben** do work; do a job; **seine ~ aufnehmen** start work; **nach zweijähriger ~**: after two years' work **2** (das In-Betrieb-Sein) operation; **in ~ treten** come into operation
Tätigkeits-: ~bereich *der* sphere *or* field of activity; **~bericht** *der* progress report; **~form** *die* (Sprachw.) ▸**Aktiv**[1]; **~merkmal** *das* key activity; **~wort** *das; Pl.* **~wörter** (Sprachw.) ▸**Verb**
Tat·kraft *die* energy; drive

tat·kräftig
A *Adj.* energetic, active ‹*person*›; active ‹*help, support*›
B *adv.* energetically; actively
tätlich /'tɛ:tlɪç/
A *Adj.* physical ‹*clash, attack, resistance, etc.*›; **gegen jmdn. ~ werden** become violent towards sb.
B *adv.* physically; **jmdn. ~ angreifen** attack sb. physically; assault sb.
Tätlichkeit *die;* **~, ~en** act of violence; **es kam zu ~en** violence occurred
Tat-: ~mensch *der* man/woman of action; **~motiv** *das* motive [for a/the crime]; **~ort** *der* scene of a/the crime
tätowieren /tɛto'vi:rən/ *tr. V.* tattoo; **sich** (*Dat.*) **etw. ~ lassen** have oneself tattooed with sth.
Tätowierer *der;* **~s, ~, Tätowiererin** *die;* **~, ~nen** ▸**ⓘ S. 113** tattooist; tattooer
Tätowierung *die;* **~, ~en** **1** tattoo **2** (das Tätowieren) tattooing
Tat·sache *die* fact; **es ist [eine] ~, dass ...** it's a fact that ...; **~!** (ugs.) it's true; it's a fact; **~?** (ugs.) really?; is that true?; **den ~n entsprechen** be true; **nackte ~n** hard facts; (scherzh.) naked bodies; **den ~n ins Auge sehen** face facts; **vollendete ~n schaffen** create a fait accompli; **jmdn. vor die vollendete ~** *od.* **vollendete ~n stellen** present sb. with a fait accompli; *s. auch* **Vorspiegelung**
Tatsachen-: ~bericht *der* factual report; **~material** *das* facts *pl.*
tatsächlich /'ta:tzɛçlɪç/
A *Adj.* actual; real; **der ~e Grund** the real reason
B *adv.* actually; really; **ist das ~ wahr?** is that really true?; **~?** really?; **ich habe mich ~ geirrt** I was indeed mistaken; **Er hat es geschafft. — Tatsächlich!** He made it. — So he did!
tätscheln /'tɛtʃl̩n/ *tr. V.* pat
tatschen /'tatʃn̩/ *itr. V.* (ugs. abwertend) **an/auf etw.** (*Akk.*) **~**: paw sth.
Tatter·greis /'tatɐ-/ *der* (ugs. abwertend) doddery old man
Tatter·greisin *die* (ugs. abwertend) doddery old woman
Tatterich /'tatərɪç/ *der;* **~s** (ugs.) **einen ~ kriegen** get shaking hands; **er hat einen ~**: his hands are shaking
tatterig, tattrig *Adj.* (ugs.) shaky ‹*hands, movements, etc.*›; doddery ‹*person*›
tatütata /ta'ty:ta'ta:/ *Interj.* pah-paw-pah-paw; **mit „Tatütata" und Blaulicht** with siren wailing and blue light flashing
tat·verdächtig *Adj.* suspected; **[dringend] ~ sein** be under [strong] suspicion
Tat·waffe *die* weapon [used in the crime]
Tatze /'tatsə/ *die;* **~, ~n** (auch fig. ugs.) paw
Tat·zeit *die:* **[zur] ~**: [at the] time of the crime
Tau[1] /tau/ *der;* **~[e]s** dew; **vor ~ und Tag** (dichter.) before dawn of day
Tau[2] *das;* **~[e]s, ~e** (Seil) rope
taub /taup/ *Adj.* **1** deaf; **~ werden** go deaf; **er war ~ gegen** *od.* **für alle Bitten** (fig.) he was deaf to all requests; **auf diesem Ohr ist er ~** (ugs. scherzh.) he's deaf to that sort of thing **2** (wie abgestorben) numb **3** (leer, unbefruchtet usw.) empty ‹*nut*›; unfruitful ‹*ear of corn*›; unfertilized ‹*bird's egg*›; dead ‹*rock*›
taub·blind *Adj.* deaf and blind
Täubchen /'tɔypçən/ *das;* **~s, ~**: [little] pigeon; (Turtel~) [little] dove; **mein ~** (fig.) my little dove
Taube[1] *die;* **~, ~n** pigeon; (Turtel~; auch Politik fig.) dove
Taube[2] *der/die; adj. Dekl.* deaf person; deaf man/woman; **die ~n** the deaf
tauben·blau *Adj.* greyish-blue
Tauben·ei *das* pigeon['s] egg
taubenei·groß *Adj.* as big as *or* the size of a golf ball *postpos.*; **~e Stücke** pieces as big as *or* the size of golf balls

t

Tauben-: ~plage *die* plague of pigeons; **~schlag** *der* pigeon loft; (für Turteltauben) dovecot; **hier geht es zu wie in einem** *od.* **im ~schlag** (ugs.) it's like Piccadilly Circus here (Brit. coll.); it's like being in the middle of Times Square (Amer.)

Tauber *der;* **~s, ~, Täuberich** /ˈtɔybərɪç/ *der;* **~s, ~e** cock pigeon

Taubheit *die;* **~:** deafness

taub-, Taub-: ~nessel *die* dead-nettle; **~stumm** *Adj.* deaf and dumb; **~stumme** *der/die; adj. Dekl.* deaf mute; **~stummen·sprache** *die* deaf-and-dumb language

tauchen
A *itr. V.* **1** *auch mit sein* dive (**nach** for); **früher habe ich viel getaucht** I used to do a lot of skin diving *or* underwater swimming; **er kann zwei Minuten [lang] ~:** he can stay under water for two minutes; **er ist 3 Meter tief getaucht** he dived down three metres; **die Sonne tauchte unter den Horizont** (fig.) the sun disappeared *or* sank below the horizon **2** *mit sein* (ein~) dive; (auf~) rise; emerge; **er tauchte ins Dunkel des Gartens** (fig.) he plunged into the darkness of the garden
B *tr. V.* **1** (ein~) dip; **der Raum war in Licht getaucht** (geh.) the room was bathed in light; **die Landschaft war in Dunkelheit getaucht** (geh.) the countryside was shrouded in darkness **2** (unter~) duck

Tauch·ente *die* scaup [duck]

Taucher *der;* **~s, ~** ▸❶ **S. 113** diver; (mit Flossen und Atemgerät) skin-diver

Taucher-: ~anzug *der* diving suit; **~ausrüstung** *die* diving equipment; **~brille** *die* diving goggles *pl.*; **~glocke** *die* diving bell

Taucherin *die;* **~, ~nen** ▸❶ **S. 113** ▸**Taucher**

Tauch-: ~gang *der* dive; **~gerät** *das* diving equipment *no pl., no indef. art.*; **~maske** *die* diving mask; **~sieder** *der;* **~~s, ~~:** portable immersion heater; **~sport** *der* skin diving *no art.*; **~station** *die:* **auf ~station gehen** (auf dem U-Boot) go to one's diving station; (fig. ugs.) go to ground; **~tiefe** *die* diving depth

tauen
A *itr. V.* **1** (unpers.) **es taut** it's thawing **2** *mit sein* (schmelzen) melt
B *tr. V.* melt; thaw

Tauf·becken *das* font

Taufe *die;* **~, ~n** **1** (christl. Rel.: Sakrament) baptism **2** (christl. Rel.: Zeremonie) christening; baptism; **jmdn. über die ~ halten** *od.* (veralt.) **aus der ~ heben** be [a] godparent to sb.; **etw. aus der ~ heben** (fig. ugs.) launch sth.

taufen *tr. V.* **1** (die Taufe vollziehen an) baptize; **katholisch getauft sein** be baptized a Catholic **2** (einen Namen geben) christen ‹*child, ship, animal, etc.*›; **ein Kind auf den Namen Peter ~:** christen a child Peter; **er wurde nach seinem Großvater [Hermann] getauft** he was named [Hermann] after *or* (Amer.) for his grandfather

Tauf-: ~kapelle *die* baptistery; **~kleid** *das* christening robe *or* gown

Täufling /ˈtɔyflɪŋ/ *der;* **~s, ~e** child to be baptized; (Erwachsener) person to be baptized

Tauf-: ~name *der* Christian name; **~pate** *der* godparent; (männlicher ~pate) godfather; **~patin** *die* godmother; **~register** *das* register of baptisms; baptismal register

tau·frisch **1** (feucht vom Tau) dew-covered; dewy **2** (ganz frisch) fresh; **sie ist auch nicht mehr ganz ~** (fig.) she's not exactly a spring chicken any more

Tauf-: ~schein *der* certificate of baptism; baptismal certificate; **~stein** *der* font

taugen /ˈtaugn̩/ *itr. V.* **nichts/wenig** *od.* **nicht viel/etwas ~:** be no/not much/some good *or* use; **zu** *od.* **für etw. ~** ‹*person*› be suited to sth.; ‹*thing*› be suitable for sth.; **zu einem** *od.* **zum Lehrer ~** ‹*person*› make a good teacher; **dazu ~, etw. zu tun** be good at doing sth.; **nicht wissen, was etw. wirklich taugt** not know how useful sth. really is

Taugenichts *der;* **~[es], ~e** (veralt. abwertend) good-for-nothing

tauglich *Adj.* **1** (geeignet, brauchbar) **[nicht] ~:** [un]suitable; **der Arzt hat ihn für ~ erklärt, ein Auto zu führen** the doctor has pronounced him fit to drive a car **2** (für Militärdienst) fit [for service]

Taumel *der;* **~s** **1** (Schwindel, Benommenheit) [feeling of] dizziness *or* giddiness; **ein ~ überkam ihn** he was overcome by a feeling of dizziness *or* giddiness **2** (Begeisterung, Rausch) frenzy; fever; **ein ~ der Begeisterung/Leidenschaft** a fever of excitement/passion; **ein ~ des Entzückens/Glücks** a transport of delight/happiness

taumelig
A *Adj.* dizzy; giddy; **ihm war/wurde ~ vor Glück** he was transported with happiness/went into transports of happiness
B *adv.* **~ gehen** reel *or* stagger

taumeln /ˈtaumḷn/ *itr. V.* **1** *auch mit sein* (wanken) reel, sway (**vor** + *Dat.* with); **das Flugzeug begann zu ~:** the aircraft began to roll **2** *mit sein* (sich ~d bewegen) stagger; **in den Abgrund/ins Unglück ~:** tumble into the abyss/plunge into disaster

tau·nass, *tau·naß *Adj.* wet with dew *postpos.*

Tau·punkt *der* (Physik) dew point

Tausch *der;* **~[e]s, ~e** exchange; **ein guter/schlechter ~:** a good/bad deal; **im ~ gegen** *od.* **für etw.** in exchange for sth.; **etw. durch ~ erwerben** acquire sth. through an exchange; **etw. zum ~ anbieten** offer to exchange sth. for sth.; **etw. im ~ erhalten** receive sth. in exchange

Tausch-: ~aktion *die* exchange; (Börsenw.) exchange operation; **~börse** *die* swapping service; (im Internet) file-sharing service; file-swapping service; (Veranstaltung) swapmeet

tauschen
A *tr. V.* exchange (**gegen** for); **Briefmarken/Münzen ~:** exchange *or* swap stamps/coins; **sie tauschten die Partner/Pferde/Plätze** they changed *or* swapped partners/horses/places; **wollen wir ~:** shall we swap (coll.); **Küsse ~** (geh.) kiss; **einen Händedruck ~:** shake hands
B *itr. V.* **mit den Rollen/Plätzen/Partnern ~:** change *or* swap roles/places/partners; **mit jmdm. ~** (fig.) change *or* swap places with sb.

täuschen /ˈtɔyʃn̩/
A *tr. V.* deceive; **ich sah mich in meinen Erwartungen getäuscht** I was disappointed in my expectations; **der Schüler versuchte zu ~:** the pupil tried to cheat; **der Schein täuscht uns oft** appearances are often deceiving; **wenn mich nicht alles täuscht** unless I'm completely mistaken
B *itr. V.* **1** (irreführen) be deceptive **2** (bes. Sport: ablenken) make a feint
C *refl. V.* be wrong *or* mistaken (**in** + *Dat.* about); **ich habe mich in ihm getäuscht** I was wrong about him; he disappointed me; **da täuschst du dich aber [gewaltig]** but that's where you're [very much] mistaken

täuschend
A *Adj.* remarkable, striking ‹*similarity, imitation*›
B *adv.* remarkably; **jmdm. ~ ähnlich sehen** look remarkably like sb.

Täuscher *der;* **~s, ~, Täuscherin** *die;* **~, ~nen** swindler

Tausch-: ~geschäft *das* exchange [deal]; **ein gutes ~geschäft machen** make a good deal in an/the exchange; **~gesellschaft** *die* (Soziol.) barter society; **~handel** *der* **1** bartering; **~handel treiben** barter; **2** (Wirtsch.) trade by barter; **~objekt** *das* object of barter[ing]

Täuschung *die;* **~, ~en** **1** (das Täuschen) deception; **auf eine ~ hereinfallen** be deceived **2** (Selbst~) delusion; illusion; **einer ~ unterliegen** be under an illusion; **er gibt sich der ~ hin, dass ...** he mistakenly believes that ...; **optische ~:** optical illusion

Täuschungs-: ~absicht *die* intent to deceive; **~manöver** *das* ploy

tausend /ˈtauzn̩t/ *Kardinalz.* **1** ▸❶ **S. 826** a *or* one thousand; **einige/mehrere Tausend Zuschauer** a few/several thousand spectators; **Tausend und Abertausend Ameisen** thousands and thousands of ants; *s. auch* **acht** **2** (ugs.: sehr viele) thousands of; **noch ~ Sachen zu erledigen haben** still have thousands of *or* a thousand things to do; **~ Dank/Küsse** a thousand thanks/kisses

Tausend[1] *das;* **~s, ~e** *od.* **~** (nach unbest. Zahlwörtern) **1** thousand; **ein volles/halbes ~:** a full/half a thousand; a thousand/five hundred; **vom ~:** per thousand **2** *Pl.* (große Anzahl) thousands; **~e Zuschauer** thousands of spectators; **die Kosten gehen in die ~e** (ugs.) the costs run into thousands; **die Tiere starben zu ~en** the animals died in [their] thousands

Tausend[2] *die;* **~, ~en** thousand

tausend·ein[s] *Kardinalz.* ▸❶ **S. 826** a *or* one thousand and one

Tausender *der;* **~s, ~** **1** (ugs.) (Tausendfrankenschein usw.) thousand-franc/-dollar *etc.* note; (Betrag) thousand francs/dollars *etc.* **2** (Math.) thousand

tausenderlei *Gattungsz.; indekl.* (ugs.) **1** (von verschiedener Art) a thousand and one different ‹*answers, kinds, etc.*› **2** (viele) a thousand and one; *s. auch* **hunderterlei**

tausendfach *Vervielfältigungsz.* thousandfold; (ugs.: sehr häufig) a thousand and one times; **die ~e Menge** a thousand times the amount; **~en Dank** a thousand thanks; *s. auch* **achtfach**

Tausendfüßer /ˈtauzn̩tfyːsɐ/ *der;* **~s, ~, Tausendfüßler** *der;* **Tausendfüßlers, Tausendfüßler** millipede

Tausend·gülden·kraut *das* (Bot.) centaury

Tausend·jahr·feier *die* millenary; millennial; (Festlichkeit auch) millenary *or* millennial celebrations *pl.*; *s. auch* **Hundertjahrfeier**

tausend·jährig *Adj.* **1** (tausend Jahre alt) [one-]thousand-year-old **2** (tausend Jahre dauernd) thousand-year[-long]; **~es Reich** (ns.) thousand-year Reich; **Tausendjähriges Reich** (Theol.) millennium

tausend·köpfig *Adj.* thousand-strong; (fig.) thousands strong *postpos.*

Tausend·künstler *der,* **Tausend·künstlerin** *die* (ugs. scherzh.) jack of all trades

tausend·mal *Adv.* a thousand times; **ich bitte [dich] ~ um Entschuldigung** (ugs.) a thousand pardons *or* apologies; *s. auch* **achtmal**

Tausendsas[s]a /ˈtauzn̩tsasa/ *der;* **~s, ~[s]** jack of all trades

Tausendschönchen /-ʃøːnçən/ *das;* **~s, ~:** daisy

tausendst... *Ordinalz.* ▸❶ **S. 826** thousandth; *s. auch* **acht...**

tausendstel /ˈtauzn̩tstl̩/ *Bruchz.* ▸❶ **S. 826** thousandth; *s. auch* **achtel**

Tausendstel *das* (*schweiz. meist der*); **~s, ~:** thousandth

Tausendstel·sekunde *die;* **~, ~n** thousandth of a second

tausend·und·ein[s] *Kardinalz.* ▸**tausend·ein[s]**

Tautologie /tautoloˈgiː/ *die;* **~, ~n** (Rhet., Stilk.) tautology

tautologisch *Adj.* (Rhet., Stilk.) tautological; tautologous

Tau-: ~tropfen *der* dewdrop; **~wasser** *das; Pl.* **~~:** meltwater; **~werk** *das* **1** (Material) rope; **2** (auf einem Schiff) rigging; **~wetter** *das* (auch fig.) thaw; **gestern war bei uns ~wetter** yesterday we had a thaw; **~ziehen** *das;* **~~s** (auch fig.) tug-of-war

Taverne /taˈvɛrnə/ *die;* **~, ~n** taverna

Taxa·meter /taxa-/ *der* [taxi]meter

Taxator /taˈksaːtɔr/ *der;* **~s, ~en** /taksaˈtoːrən/, **Taxatorin** *die;* **~, ~nen** (Wirtsch.) valuer

Taxe /ˈtaksə/ *die;* **~, ~n** **1** taxi **2** (Gebühr) charge **3** (taxierter Preis) valuation

t

Taxi /'taksi/ *das;* ~s, ~s taxi; **mit dem ~:** by taxi *or* in a taxi; **~ fahren** drive a taxi; (als Fahrgast) go by taxi

taxieren *tr. V.* 1) (ugs.: schätzen) estimate (**auf** + *Akk.* at); **er hat falsch taxiert** his estimate is wrong; **etw. zu hoch/niedrig ~:** overestimate/underestimate sth. 2) (den Wert ermitteln von) value (**auf** + *Akk.* at); **etw. zu hoch/niedrig ~:** overvalue/undervalue sth. 3) (ugs.: mustern, prüfen) size up (coll.) 4) (einschätzen) assess

Taxi-: **~fahrer** *der;* **~fahrerin** *die* ▸❶ **S. 113** taxi driver; **~fahrt** *die* taxi ride; **~stand** *der* taxi rank (Brit.); taxi stand

Taxus /'taksʊs/ *der;* ~, ~: yew [tree]

Tb, Tbc /te:'be:, te:be:'tse:/ *die;* ~ *Abk.* = **Tuberkulose** TB

Tb-krank /te:'be:-/ *Adj.* suffering from TB *postpos.;* **~e Patienten** patients with TB

Tb-Kranke /te:'be:-/ *der/die; adj. Dekl.* TB patient; patient with TB

Teak /ti:k/ *das;* ~s, **Teak·holz** *das* teak

Team /ti:m/ *das;* ~s, ~s team

Team·arbeit *die* teamwork

team-, Team-: **~chef** *der;* **~chefin** *die* (Sport) team manager; **~fähig** *Adj.* able to work as part of a team *postpos.;* **~fähig sein** be a [good] team player; **~fähigkeit** *die* ability to work as part of a team; (von einer Gruppe) ability to work [together] as a team; **~manager** *der,* **~managerin** *die* (Sport) team manager; **~player** /-pleɪə/ *der;* ~~s, ~~, **~playerin** *die;* ~~, ~~nen team player; **~unfähig** *Adj.* unable to work as part of a team; (von einer Gruppe) unable to work [together] as a team

Teamwork /'ti:mwə:k/ *das;* ~s teamwork

Tearoom /'ti:ru:m/ *der;* ~s, ~s (schweiz.) tearoom (*without alcoholic drinks*)

Technicolor Ⓦⓩ /teçniko'lo:ɐ̯/ *das;* ~s Technicolor ®

Technik /'teçnɪk/ *die;* ~, ~en 1) technology; (Studienfach) engineering *no art.;* **auf dem neuesten Stand der ~:** incorporating the latest technical advances; **im Zeitalter der ~ leben** live in the technological age *or* age of technology 2) (technische Ausrüstung) equipment; machinery 3) (Arbeitsweise, Verfahren) technique 4) (eines Gerätes) workings *pl.*

Techniker *der;* ~s, ~, **Technikerin** *die;* ~, ~nen ▸❶ **S. 113** 1) technical expert 2) (im Sport, in der Kunst) technician

technik-, Technik-: **~freak** *der* technology freak (coll.); **~gläubig** A *Adj.* ⟨*person, society*⟩ with a belief in technology; **~gläubig sein** believe in technology; B *adv.* with a belief in technology; **~gläubigkeit** *die* belief *or* faith in technology

Technikum /'teçnikʊm/ *das;* ~s, **Technika** *od.* **Techniken** technical college

technikverliebt *Adj.* technology-loving; **~ sein** be in love with technology; be a great technophile

technisch /'teçnɪʃ/
A *Adj.* technical; technological ⟨*progress, age*⟩; **ein ~er Fehler** a technical fault
B *adv.* technically; ⟨*interested*⟩ in technology; technologically ⟨*advanced*⟩; **~ begabt sein** have a technical flair

technisieren /teçni'zi:rən/ *tr. V.* mechanize

Technisierung *die;* ~, ~en mechanization

technizistisch *Adj.* technicist

Techno[1] /'tekno/ *das od. der;* ~s techno

Techno[2] /'tekno/ *der;* ~s, ~s techno fan

Technokrat /teçno'kra:t/ *der;* ~en, ~en technocrat

Technokratie /teçnokra'ti:/ *die;* ~: technocracy

Technokratin *die;* ~, ~nen technocrat

technokratisch *Adj.* technocratic

Technologie /teçnolo'gi:/ *die;* ~, ~n technology

Technologie-: **~park** *der* technology park; science park; **~unternehmen** *das* technology firm *or* company; **~wert** *der* (Wirtsch.) technology equity

technologisch
A *Adj.* technological
B *adv.* technologically

Techno-: **~musik** *die* techno [music]; **~party** *die* techno party

Techtelmechtel /teçtl̩'meçtl̩/ *das;* ~s, ~: affair

Teckel /'tekl̩/ *der;* ~s, ~: dachshund

Teddy·bär /'tedi-/ *der* teddy bear

Tedeum /te'de:ʊm/ *das;* ~s, ~s Te Deum

Tee[1] /te:/ *der;* ~s, ~s tea; **der ~ muss noch ziehen** the tea must stand *or* brew a while; **~ machen** make some tea; **einen ~ geben** (geh.) give a tea party; **einen im ~ haben** (fig. ugs.) be tipsy; have had one over the eight (coll.); **abwarten und ~ trinken** (fig. ugs.) just wait and see

Tee[2] /ti:/ *das;* ~s, ~s (Golf) tee

TEE *Abk.* = **Trans-Europ-Express** TEE

Tee-: **~beutel** *der* tea bag; **~butter** *die* (österr.) ▸**Markenbutter**; **~ei, ~-Ei** *das* tea ball; tea egg; **~gebäck** *das* [tea] biscuits *pl.* (Brit.) *or* (Amer.) cookies *pl.;* **~glas** *das; Pl.* **~gläser** tea glass; **~kanne** *die* teapot; **~kessel** *der* 1) tea kettle; 2) (Spiel) *game in which homonymous words must be guessed;* **~kesselchen** *das;* ~~s, ~~ ▸**~kessel 2**; **~küche** *die* [small] kitchen; **~licht** *das; Pl.* **~~er** *od.* **~e** tea warmer; **~löffel** *der* teaspoon

Teen /ti:n/ *der;* ~s, ~s, **Teenager** /'ti:neɪdʒə/ *der;* **~agers, ~ager** ▸❶ **S. 29** teenager

Teenie /'ti:ni/ *der;* ~s, ~s (ugs.) young teenager

Tee-: **~pause** *die* tea break; **~pflücker** *der,* **~pflückerin** *die* tea picker

Teer /te:ɐ̯/ *der;* ~[e]s, (Arten:) ~e tar

Teer·decke *die* tar surface

teeren *tr. V.* tar; **jmdn. ~ und federn** tar and feather sb.

teer-, Teer-: **~farbstoff** *der* aniline dye; **~fass, *~faß** *das* tar barrel; **~haltig** *Adj.* containing tar *postpos., not pred.*

Tee·rose *die* tea rose

Teer·pappe *die* bituminous roofing felt

Tee-: **~service** *das* tea service; teaset; **~sieb** *das* tea strainer; **~strauch** *der* tea plant; **~stube** *die* tearoom; **~tasse** *die* teacup; **~trinker** *der;* **~trinkerin** *die* tea drinker; **~wagen** *der* tea trolley; **~wasser** *das* water for the tea; *s. auch* **Kaffeewasser**; **~wurst** *die: soft German smoked sausage for spreading;* ≈ meat spread

Teich /taiç/ *der;* ~[e]s, ~e pond; **der große ~** (ugs. scherzh.: das Meer) the [herring] pond (joc.)

Teig /taik/ *der;* ~[e]s, ~e dough; (Kuchen~, Biskuit~) pastry; (Pfannkuchen~, Waffel~) batter; (in Rezepten auch) mixture; **~ für Fleischklößchen** meatball mixture; **den ~ gehen lassen** let the dough rise

teigig *Adj.* 1) (wie Teig) doughy 2) (blass u. schwammig) pasty ⟨*face, skin, complexion*⟩

Teig-: **~rolle** *die* 1) (Rolle aus Teig) roll of dough; 2) (Nudelholz) rolling pin; **~waren** *Pl.* pasta *sing.*

Teil /tail/ 1) *der;* ~[e]s, ~e (etw. von einem Ganzen) part; **weite ~e des Landes** wide areas of the country; **ein [großer** *od.* **guter] ~ der Presse/Bevölkerung** a [large] section of the press/population; **ich habe das Buch zum größten ~ gelesen** I have read most of the book; **zum ~:** partly; **es waren zum ~ schöne Exemplare** some of them were beautiful specimens; **fünfter ~:** fifth; **den größten ~ des Weges hat er zu Fuß zurückgelegt** he walked most of the way; **ein gut ~ Glück/Mut** a lot of *or* a good bit of luck/courage (coll.) 2) *der od. das;* ~[e]s, ~e (An~) share; **sein[en] ~ [schon noch] bekommen** *od.* **kriegen** get one's comeuppance (coll.); **sein[en] ~ weghaben** (ugs.) have [already] had one's due; (die verdiente Strafe bekommen haben) have got what was coming to one; **sich** (*Dat.*) **sein ~ denken** have one's own thoughts on the matter; **ich für mein ~ ...** for my part, I ... 3) *der od. das;* ~[e]s, ~e (Beitrag) share; **ich will gerne mein[en] ~ dazu beisteuern** I should like to do my share *or* bit; **sein[en] ~ geben** *od.* **[zu etw.] tun** do one's share *or* bit [towards sth.] 4) *der;* ~[e]s, ~e (beteiligte Person[en]; Rechtsw.: Partei) party 5) *das;* ~[e]s, ~e (Einzel~) part; **~e des Motors** [component] parts of the engine; **etw. in seine ~e zerlegen** take sth. apart *or* to pieces

Teil-: **~ansicht** *die* partial view; **~aspekt** *der:* **nur ein ~aspekt des Problems** only one aspect of the problem

teil·bar *Adj.* divisible (**durch** by)

Teilbarkeit *die;* ~: divisibility

Teil-: **~bereich** *der* (eines Fachs) branch; (einer Organisation) section; **~betrag** *der* instalment; (einer Rechnung) item

Teilchen *das;* ~s, ~ 1) (kleines Stück) [small] part 2) (Partikel) particle 3) (bes. nordd.: Gebäckstück) tart

Teilchen·beschleuniger *der;* ~s, ~ (Kerntechnik) particle accelerator

teilen
A *tr. V.* 1) (zerlegen, trennen) divide [up] 2) (dividieren) divide (**durch** by) 3) (auf~) share (**unter** + *Dat.* among) 4) (teilweise überlassen, gemeinsam nutzen, teilhaben an) share 5) (in zwei Teile ~) divide; **das Schiff teilt die Wellen** (geh.) the ship cuts through the waves; *s. auch* **Leid 1**
B *refl. V.* 1) **sich** (*Dat.*) **etw. [mit jmdm.] ~:** share sth. [with sb.]; **sich** (*Dat.*) **[mit jmdm.] in etw.** (*Akk.*) **~** (geh.) share sth. [with sb.] 2) (auseinander gehen) **der Vorhang teilt sich** the curtain opens; **der Weg teilt sich** the road forks; **geteilter Meinung sein** have different views *or* opinions
C *itr. V.* share

Teiler *der;* ~s, ~ (Math.) factor

Teil-: **~erfolg** *der* partial success; **~gebiet** *das* branch; **~habe** *die* participation (**an** + *Dat.* in)

teil|haben *unr. itr. V.* share (**an** + *Dat.* in)

Teilhaber *der;* ~s, ~, **Teilhaberin** *die;* ~, ~nen partner; **stiller Teilhaber** sleeping partner

Teilhaberschaft *die;* ~, ~en participation, (Anteil) share (**an** + *Dat.* in)

teilhaftig /-'haftɪç/ *Adj.* in **einer Sache** (*Gen.*) **~ werden/sein** (geh. veralt.) be blessed with sth.; **eines Anblicks ~ werden** be privy to a sight

Teil·kasko·versicherung *die: insurance giving limited cover*

teil·möbliert
A *Adj.* partially furnished
B *adv.* **~ wohnen** live in partly furnished accommodation

Teilnahme /'tailna:mə/ *die;* ~, ~n 1) (das Mitmachen) participation (**an** + *Dat.* in); **~ an einem Kurs** attendance at a course 2) (Interesse) interest (**an** + *Dat.* in) 3) (geh.: Mitgefühl) sympathy

teilnahme·berechtigt *Adj.* eligible (**bei** for)

Teilnahme·berechtigung *die* eligibility

Teilnahme·gebühr *die* (für Wettbewerb) entry fee; (für Kurs usw.) attendance fee

teilnahms·los *Adj.* (gleichgültig) indifferent; (apathisch) apathetic

Teilnahmslosigkeit *die* (Gleichgültigkeit) indifference; (Apathie) apathy

teilnahms·voll
A *Adj.* compassionate
B *adv.* compassionately; **jmdn. ~ ansehen** look at sb. with compassion

teil|nehmen /'tailne:mən/ *unr. itr. V.* 1) (dabei sein bei) **[an etw.** (*Dat.*)**] ~:** attend [sth.] 2) (beteiligt sein) **[an etw.** (*Dat.*)**] ~:** take part [in sth.]; **am Krieg ~:** fight in the war; **an einem Wettkampf ~:** take part in *or* enter a competition 3) (als Lernender) **[an einem Lehrgang] ~:** attend [a course]; **am Unterricht ~:** attend lessons 4) (Teilnahme zeigen) **an jmds. Schmerz/Glück ~:** share sb.'s pain/happiness

teilnehmend ▸**teilnahmsvoll**

t

Teilnehmer *der;* **~s, ~** [1] participant (*Gen.*, **an** + *Dat.* in); (bei Wettbewerb auch) competitor, contestant (**an** + *Dat.* in) [2] (Fernspr.) subscriber; **der ~ meldet sich nicht** there is no reply

Teilnehmerin *die;* **~, ~nen** ▸ **Teilnehmer**

Teilnehmer·zahl *die* number of participants; (Sport) number of competitors

teils /tails/ *Adv.* partly; **~ ... ~ ...** partly ... partly ...; **Kostüme, ~ mit Seitenschlitzen** costumes, some with side slits; **Wie hat es dir gestern gefallen? — T~, ~** (ugs.) How did you like it yesterday? — So so

Teil-: ~strecke *die* (einer Straße) stretch; (einer Buslinie usw.) stage; (Rennsport) stage; **~strich** *der* graduation line; **~stück** *das* piece; part

Teilung *die;* **~, ~en** division

teil-, Teil-: ~weise **A** *Adv.* partly; **~weise gut** good in parts. **B** *adj.* partial; **~zahlung** *die* instalment; **etw. auf ~zahlung kaufen** buy sth. on hire purchase (Brit.) *or* (Amer.) on installment plan; **~zeit** *die;* **~~:** part-time [working]; **~zeit arbeiten** work part-time

teilzeit-, Teilzeit-: ~arbeit *die* part-time work *no indef. art.*; (Stelle) part-time job; **~arbeitsplatz** *der* part-time job; **~beschäftigt** *Adj.* ‹*person*› in part-time work, working part-time; **~beschäftigt sein** work part-time; **~beschäftigte** *der/die; adj. Dekl.* part-time employee; **~beschäftigung** *die* part-time employment *or* work *no indef. art.*; (Stelle) part-time job; **~job** *der* part-time job; **~kraft** *die* part-time employee; **als ~kraft angestellt** working *or* employed part-time; **~stelle** *die* part-time job

Teint /tɛ̃:/ *der;* **~s, ~s** complexion

Tektonik /tɛk'to:nɪk/ *die;* **~** (Geol.) tectonics *sing., no art.*

tektonisch *Adj.* tectonic

tele-, Tele- /'te:le-/ tele-

Tele-: ~arbeit *die* teleworking; telecommuting; **~arbeiter** *der* teleworker; telecommuter

Tele·brief *der* fax message

Tele·fax *das* fax

Telefon /'te:lefo:n, *auch* tele'fo:n/ *das;* **~s, ~e** telephone; phone; **ans ~ gehen** answer the [tele]phone; **jmdn. ans ~ rufen** call sb. to the [tele]phone; **am ~ verlangt werden** be wanted on the [tele]phone; **am ~ hängen** (ugs.) be on the [tele]phone; **sich ans ~ hängen** (ugs.) get on the phone

Telefon-: ~anruf *der* [tele]phone call; **~anschluss, *~anschluß** *der* telephone; line; **~apparat** *der* telephone

Telefonat /telefo'na:t/ *das;* **~[e]s, ~e** telephone call

Telefon-: ~beratung *die* telephone advisory service; **~buch** *das* [tele]phone book *or* directory; **~gebühr** *die* telephone charge; **~gesellschaft** *die* telephone company; **~gespräch** *das* telephone conversation; **~häuschen** *das* ▸ **~zelle**; **~hörer** *der* telephone receiver

Telefonie *die;* **~:** telephony

telefonieren /telefo'ni:rən/ *itr. V.* make a [tele]phone call; **mit jmdm. ~:** talk to sb. [on the telephone]; **nach einem Taxi ~:** [tele-]phone a taxi; **du telefonierst zu viel** you're on the phone too much; you're making too many [tele]phone calls; **nach Hause ~:** phone home; **nach England ~:** make a [tele]phone call to England; **lange [mit jmdm.] ~:** be on the telephone [to sb.] for a long time; **er telefoniert gerade** he is on the phone at the moment; **bei jmdm. ~:** use sb.'s [tele]phone

telefonisch
A *Adj.* telephone; **die ~e Zeitansage** the speaking clock (Brit. coll.); the telephone time service; **~e Bestellung** telephone order; order by telephone
B *adv.* by telephone; **jmdm. etw. ~ mitteilen** inform sb. of sth. over the *or* by telephone; **ich bin ~ zu erreichen** *od.* **erreichbar** I can be contacted by telephone; **er hat sich ~ entschuldigt** he telephoned to apologize

Telefonist /telefo'nɪst/ *der;* **~en, ~en, Telefonistin** *die;* **~, ~nen** ▸ⓘ **S. 113** telephonist; (in einer Firma) switchboard operator

Telefon-: ~karte *die* phonecard; **~konferenz** *die* conference call; **~konzern** *der* telephone concern; **~leitung** *die* telephone line; **~marketing** *das* (Wirtsch) telephone marketing; **~nummer** *die* [tele]phone number; **~rechnung** *die* [tele]phone bill; **~seelsorge** *die* pastoral advice service; **die ~seelsorge** ≈ the Samaritans (Brit.); **~terror** *der* menacing *or* threatening calls *pl.*; **~überwachung** *die* telephone surveillance; **~umfrage** *die* telephone poll; **~verbindung** *die* telephone line; **~verkehr** *der* telephone traffic; **~verzeichnis** *das* telephone list; **~zelle** *die* [tele]phone booth *or* (Brit.) box; call box (Brit.); **~zentrale** *die* telephone exchange

tele·gen /tele'ge:n/ *Adj.* telegenic

Telegraf /tele'gra:f/ *der;* **~en, ~en** telegraph

Telegrafen-: ~amt *das* telegraph office; **~mast** *der* telegraph pole

Telegrafie *die;* **~:** telegraphy *no art.*

telegrafieren /telegra'fi:rən/ *itr., tr. V.* telegraph; **jmdm. ~:** send a telegram to sb.; **nach Berlin ~:** send a telegram to Berlin

telegrafisch
A *Adj.* telegraphic; **eine ~e Mitteilung** a message by telegraph *or* telegram
B *adv.* by telegraph *or* telegram; **~ überwiesenes Geld** money sent by telegram *or* cable

Telegramm *das* telegram

Telegrammstil *der* telegram style; telegraphese [style]; **im ~:** in telegraphese

Telegraph, Telegraphie *usw.* ▸ **Telegraf, Telegrafie** *usw.*

Telekinese /teleki'ne:zə/ *die;* **~** (Parapsych.) telekinesis *no art.*

Tele·kolleg *das* ≈ Open University (Brit.)

Telematik *die;* **~:** telematics *sing., no art.*

Tele·objektiv *das* (Fot.) telephoto lens

Teleologie /teleolo'gi:/ *die;* **~** (Philos.) teleology *no art.*

teleo·logisch /teleo'lo:gɪʃ/
A *Adj.* teleological
B *adv.* teleologically

Telepathie /telepa'ti:/ *die;* **~:** telepathy *no art.*

telepathisch
A *Adj.* telepathic; **auf ~em Weg** by telepathic means
B *adv.* telepathically

***Telephon, *telephonieren** *usw.:* ▸ **Telefon, telefonieren** *usw.*

Tele·prompter Ⓦⓩ *der;* **~s, ~** (Jargon) Autocue ® (Brit.); teleprompter ® (Amer.)

tele·scheu *Adj.* camera-shy

Tele·shopping *das* teleshopping

Tele·skop /tele'sko:p/ *das;* **~s, ~e** telescope

Teleskop·antenne *die* telescopic aerial *or* (Amer.) antenna

Tele·spiel *das* video game

Tele·vision /televi'zi̯o:n/ *die;* **~:** television *no art.*

Telex /'te:lɛks/ *das;* **~, ~[e]** telex

telexen *itr. V.* telex

Teller /'tɛlɐ/ *der;* **~s, ~** [1] plate; **ein ~ Suppe** a plate of soup [2] (beim Skistock) basket

Teller-: ~eisen *das* (Jagdw.) steel jaw trap; **~fleisch** *das* (bes. österr.): *pieces of boiled beef or pork served in soup;* **~gericht** *das* (Gastr.) one-course meal; **~mine** *die* Teller mine; anti-tank mine; **~rand** *der* rim; edge of a/the plate; **über den eigenen ~rand** (fig.) beyond one's own nose; **~wäscher** *der;* **~~s, ~~, ~wäscherin** *die* dishwasher; **vom ~wäscher zum Millionär werden** go from rags to riches

Tellur /tɛ'lu:ɐ/ *das;* **~s** (Chemie) tellurium

Tempel /'tɛmpl̩/ *der;* **~s, ~:** temple

Tempel-: ~herr *der* (hist.) Templar; **~orden** *der* (hist.) Order of the Knights Templars; **~ritter** *der* (hist.) Templar; **~schändung** *die* desecration of a/the temple

Tempera- /'tɛmpəra-/: **~farbe** *die* tempera colour; distemper; **~malerei** *die* [1] (Maltechnik) tempera painting *no art.*; painting *no art.* in distemper; [2] (Bild) tempera painting

Temperament /tɛmpəra'mɛnt/ *das;* **~[e]s, ~e** [1] (Wesensart) temperament; **die vier ~e** the four humours; **eine Sache des ~s** a matter *or* question of temperament [2] (Schwung, Lebhaftigkeit) **eine Frau mit ~:** a lively *or* vivacious woman; a woman with spirit; **[viel] ~ haben** be [very] lively; have [plenty of] spirit; **sie hat kein/wenig ~:** she is not a lively/not a very lively person; **sein ~ reißt alle mit** his vivacity infects everyone [3] (Erregbarkeit) **das ~ geht oft mit mir durch** I often lose my temper; **sein ~ zügeln** control one's temper

temperament·los *Adj.* spiritless; lifeless

Temperaments-: ~ausbruch *der* temperamental outburst; **~bolzen** *der* (ugs.) fireball; ball of fire; **~sache** *die: in* **etw./das ist ~sache** sth./that is a matter *or* question of temperament

temperament·voll *Adj.* spirited ‹*person, speech, dance, etc.*›; lively ‹*start etc.*›; nippy (coll.) ‹*car*›

Temperatur /tɛmpəra'tu:ɐ/ *die;* **~, ~en** ▸ⓘ **S. 703** [1] (Wärmezustand) temperature; **die richtige ~ haben** be [at] the right temperature [2] (Körper~) temperature; **[erhöhte] ~ haben** have *or* be running a temperature; **jmds. ~ messen** take sb.'s temperature

Temperatur-: ~anstieg *der* rise in temperature; **~gefälle** *das* temperature difference; difference in temperature; **~regler** *der* thermostat; **~rückgang** *der* drop *or* fall in temperature; **~schwankung** *die* fluctuation in temperature; **~sturz** *der* [sudden] fall *or* drop in temperature; **~unterschied** *der* difference in temperature

temperieren /tɛmpə'ri:rən/ *tr. V.* bring to the right temperature; **das Zimmer angenehm/richtig ~:** bring the room to a pleasant/the right temperature; **das Wasser ist gut temperiert** the water is [at] the right temperature; **ein schlecht temperierter Wein** a wine at the wrong temperature

Templer /'tɛmplɐ/ *der;* **~s, ~** (hist.) Templar

Tempo[1] /'tɛmpo/ *das;* **~s, ~s** *od.* **Tempi** [1] *Pl.* **~s** speed; **das ~ erhöhen** speed up; accelerate; **in** *od.* **mit hohem ~:** at high speed; **hier gilt ~ 100** there is a 100 k.p.h. speed limit here; **der hat ein ~ drauf!** (ugs.) he's going at quite a *or* (Brit. coll.) at a fair old speed!; **~ [~]!** (ugs.), **macht mal ein bisschen ~** (ugs.) get a move on [2] (Musik) tempo; time [3] (Fechten) period; (Hieb) stop cut; (Stoß) stop thrust *or* point

Tempo[2] Ⓦⓩ *das;* **~s, ~s** (ugs.) tissue

Tempo·limit *das* ▸ⓘ **S. 310** (Verkehrsw.) speed limit

> **Tempolimit**
>
> Speed limits are either compulsory - 50 km/h in towns, 100 km/h on other roads - or recommended when driving in bad weather conditions, on dangerous stretches, and in urban areas. On the *Autobahn* the *Richtgeschwindigkeit* (recommended maximum speed) is 130 km/h. In residential areas the limit can be as low as 30 km/h; the *30-Zone* was introduced to protect children and pedestrians.

Tempomat *der;* **~[e]s, ~e** *auch:* **~en, ~en** (Kfz-T.) cruise control

Tempora ▸ **Tempus**

temporal /tɛmpo'ra:l/ (Sprachw.) temporal

Temporal·satz *der* (Sprachw.) temporal clause

temporär /tɛmpo'rɛ:ɐ/ (geh.)
A *Adj.* temporary
B *adv.* temporarily

Tempo·taschentuch *das* (ugs.) paper tissue *or* handkerchief

Tempus /'tɛmpʊs/ *das;* **~, Tempora** /'tɛmpora/ (Sprachw.) ▸ **Zeitform**

ℹ Temperaturen

Temperaturen werden in Großbritannien zum Teil noch in Fahrenheit angegeben, obwohl alle Wetterberichte, Schulprüfungen und andere amtliche Quellen die Celsiusskala gebrauchen. In den USA dagegen sind Temperaturen in Fahrenheit noch gang und gäbe.

Um Celsius in Fahrenheit umzurechnen, benutzt man die folgende Formel: Grad in Celsius mal 9 dividiert durch 5 plus 32 (°C × 9 ÷ 5 + 32 = °F).

	Celsius (°C)	Fahrenheit (°F)	
Siedepunkt	100	212	Boiling point
	90	194	
	80	176	
	70	158	
	60	140	
	50	122	
	40	104	
Körpertemperatur	37	98.4	Body temperature
	30	86	
	20	68	
	10	50	
Gefrierpunkt	0	32	Freezing point
	– 10	14	
	– 17,8	0	
absoluter Nullpunkt	– 273,15	– 459.67	Absolute zero

Das Wetter

Wie viel Grad sind es?
= What's the temperature?
Die Außentemperatur beträgt 20 Grad [Celsius]
= The outside temperature is 20 degrees [centigrade *od.* Celsius] *od.* (*bes. amerik.*) 68 degrees Fahrenheit
Höchsttemperaturen um 27 Grad
= Maximum temperatures around 27 degrees, (*bes. amerik.*) Highs around 80 degrees
Tiefsttemperaturen um 10 Grad
= Temperatures falling to 10 degrees, (*bes. amerik.*) Lows around 50 degrees
Temperaturen um den Gefrierpunkt
= temperatures around freezing
zehn Grad unter Null
= ten degrees below freezing
– 15°C (minus fünfzehn Grad Celsius)
= – 15°C (minus fifteen degrees centigrade *od.* Celsius)
Die Temperatur liegt über/unter dem Gefrierpunkt
= The temperature is above/below freezing
In Berlin herrscht die gleiche Temperatur
= It's the same temperature *od.* The temperature is the same in Berlin

Bei Personen

Sie hat erhöhte Temperatur
= She has a [slight] temperature, Her temperature is above normal
Er hat [hohes] Fieber/40 Grad Fieber
= He has a high temperature/a temperature of 40 [centigrade] *od.* 104 [Fahrenheit]
Wie hoch ist od. Was ist Ihre Temperatur?
= What is your temperature?
Ich habe kein Fieber
= I haven't got a temperature, My temperature is normal
Sie hat bei ihm Fieber gemessen
= She took his temperature

Bei Dingen

Bei welcher Temperatur kocht Wasser?
= What temperature does water boil at?
Wasser kocht bei 100°C
= Water boils at 100°C *od.* 212°F
Welche Temperatur hat der Wein?
= What is the temperature of the wine?
Der Wein muss die richtige Temperatur haben
= The wine must be the right temperature
A hat die gleiche Temperatur wie B
= A is the same temperature as B

Tendenz /tɛn'dɛnts/ *die;* ~, ~**en** [1] trend; **es herrscht die ~/die ~ geht dahin, ... zu ...** there is a tendency to ...; the trend is to ...; **die Preise haben eine steigende/fallende ~:** prices are rising/falling; **..., ~ steigend ....** and rising [2] (Hang, Neigung) tendency; **die ~ haben, etw. zu tun** have a tendency to do sth.; **seine Ansichten haben eine ~ zum Dogmatismus** his attitudes tend towards dogmatism [3] (oft abwertend: Darstellungsweise) slant; bias

tendenziell /tɛndɛn'tsi̯ɛl/
A *Adj.* **der ~e Fall der Profitrate** the [general] trend towards a drop in profit margins
B *adv.* **~ scheint sich eine Verschärfung dieser Krise abzuzeichnen** the trend seems to indicate a deepening of the crisis; **eine ~ faschistische Haltung** an attitude tending towards fascism

tendenziös /...'tsi̯ø:s/ *Adj.* tendentious

Tendenz·wende *die* change in a/the trend *or* in direction

Tender /'tɛndɐ/ *der;* ~**s,** ~ (Eisenb., Seew.) tender

tendieren /tɛn'di:rən/ *itr. V.* tend (**zu** towards); **er tendiert zu solchen Auffassungen** he tends to [hold] such opinions; **nach links/rechts ~:** tend to[wards] the left/right; **der nach links ~de Flügel dieser Partei** the branch of the party with left-wing leanings

Teneriffa /tene'rɪfa/ *(das);* ~**s** Tenerife

Tenne /'tɛnə/ *die;* ~, ~**n** threshing floor (in barn)

Tennis /'tɛnɪs/ *das;* ~: tennis *no art.*

Tennis-: ~**arm** *der* ▸ℹ **S. 439** (Med.) tennis elbow; ~**ball** *der* tennis ball; ~**platz** *der* tennis court; ~**schläger** *der* tennis racket; ~**schuh** *der* tennis shoe; ~**spiel** *das* [1] (Tennis) tennis *no art.;* [2] (Einzelspiel) game of tennis; ~**spielen** *das;* ~~**s** tennis *no art.;* ~**spieler** *der,* ~**spielerin** *die* tennis player

Tenor[1] /te'no:ɐ̯/ *der;* ~**s, Tenöre** /te'nø:rə/, (österr. auch:) ~**e** (Musik) [1] (Stimmlage, Sänger) tenor; **den ~ singen** sing tenor *or* the tenor part [2] (im Chor) tenors *pl.;* tenor voices *pl.*

Tenor[2] /'te:nɔr/ *der;* ~**s** tenor

Tenor-: ~**saxophon** *das* tenor saxophone; ~**saxophonist** *der,* ~**saxophonistin** *die* tenor saxophonist; tenor saxophone player; ~**schlüssel** *der* (Musik) tenor clef

Tentakel /tɛn'ta:kl̩/ *der od. das;* ~**s,** ~ (Zool., Bot.) tentacle

Tenü, Tenue /tə'ny/ *das;* ~**s,** ~**s** (schweiz.) style of dress

Teppich /'tɛpɪç/ *der;* ~**s,** ~**e** carpet; (kleiner) rug; **auf dem ~ bleiben** (fig. ugs.) keep one's feet on the ground; **etw. unter den ~ kehren** (fig. ugs.) sweep sth. under the carpet

Teppich-: ~**boden** *der* fitted carpet; ~**fliese** *die* carpet tile; ~**kehrer** *der;* ~~**s,** ~~: carpet sweeper; ~**klopfer** *der* carpet beater; ~**stange** *die: frame for beating carpets*

Tera·bit /'te:ra-/ *das* (DV) terabit

Tera·byte /'te:ra-/ *das* (DV) terabyte

Term /tɛrm/ *der;* ~**s,** ~**e** (Math., Logik, Physik) term

Termin /tɛr'mi:n/ *der;* ~**s,** ~**e** [1] (festgelegter Zeitpunkt) date; (Anmeldung) appointment; (Verabredung) engagement; **der letzte** *od.* **äußerste ~ für die Zahlung** the deadline *or* final date for payment; **sich** *(Dat.)* **einen ~ geben lassen** make an appointment [2] (Rechtsw.) hearing; **heute ist ~ in Sachen ...** the ... case comes on today

Terminal /'tø:ɐ̯minəl/ *das;* ~**s,** ~**s** terminal

termin-, Termin-: ~**gebunden** *Adj.* scheduled; **~gebunden sein** have a deadline; ~**gemäß** A *Adj.* on time *postpos.;* **~gemäße Fertigstellung** completion on time *or* schedule; B *adv.* on time; on schedule; **~gemäß beginnen** start punctually; ~**geschäft** *das* (Börsenw.) forward transaction *or* operation

Termini ▸ **Terminus**

terminieren /tɛrmi'ni:rən/ *tr. V.* [1] (befristen) limit the duration of (**auf** + *Akk.* to) [2] (zeitlich festlegen) **eine Veranstaltung** *usw.* **~:** set *or* fix a date for an event *etc.*

Terminierung *die;* ~, ~**en** scheduling

Termini technici ▸ **Terminus technicus**

Termin·kalender *der* appointments book; (für gesellschaftliche Termine) engagements diary; **den ~ einhalten** (fig.) keep to the schedule

terminlich
A *Adj.* **~e Schwierigkeiten/Grenzen** difficulties/limits with regard to schedule; **~e Gründe** reasons of schedule
B *adv.* **es lässt sich ~ vereinbaren** it fits in with the/our/their *etc.* schedule

Terminologie /tɛrminolo'gi:/ *die;* ~, ~**n** terminology

terminologisch /tɛrmino'lo:gɪʃ/ *Adj.* terminological

Terminus /'tɛrminʊs/ *der;* ~, **Termini** term

Terminus technicus /- 'tɛçnikʊs/ *der;* ~, **Termini technici** /...nitsi/ technical term

Termite /tɛr'mi:tə/ *die;* ~, ~**n** termite

Termiten·hügel *der* termite hill

t

Terpentin /tɛrpɛn'ti:n/ *das,* (österr. meist:) *der;* **~s** [1] (Harz) turpentine [2] (ugs.: ~öl) turps *sing.* (coll.)

Terpentin·öl *das* oil of turpentine

Terrain /tɛ'rɛ̃:/ *das;* **~s, ~s** [1] (Gelände) terrain; **~ verlieren** lose ground; **es ist für ihn ein unbekanntes ~** (fig.) it is unknown territory to him; **das ~ sondieren** (fig. geh.) sound out the situation [2] (Baugelände) building land

Terrakotta /tɛra'kɔta/ *die;* **~, Terrakotten, Terrakotte** *die;* **~, ~n** terracotta

Terrarium /tɛ'ra:ri̯ʊm/ *das;* **~s, Terrarien** terrarium

Terrasse /tɛ'rasə/ *die;* **~, ~n** terrace

terrassen·förmig

A *Adj.* terraced

B *adv.* in terraces

Terrassen-: ~haus *das* block of flats (esp. Brit.) *or* (esp. Amer.) apartments/house built in terraces on a slope; **~tür** *die* patio door

Terrazzo /tɛ'ratso/ *der;* **~[s], Terrazzi** terrazzo

terrestrisch /tɛ'rɛstrɪʃ/

A *Adj.* terrestrial

B *adv.* terrestrially

Terrier /'tɛri̯ɐ/ *der;* **~s, ~:** terrier

Terrine /tɛ'ri:nə/ *die;* **~, ~n** tureen

territorial /tɛrito'ri̯a:l/ *Adj.* territorial

Territorial-: ~hoheit *die* territorial sovereignty; **~staat** *der* (hist.) territorial state

Territorium /tɛri'to:ri̯ʊm/ *das;* **~s, Territorien** [1] (Gebiet, Land) land; territory; **ein unbesiedeltes ~:** uninhabited land *or* territory; **ein riesiges ~:** a huge area *or* region [2] (Hoheitsgebiet) territory

Terror /'tɛrɔr/ *der;* **~s** [1] terrorism *no art.;* **blutiger ~:** terror and bloodshed; **~ ausüben** use terror tactics [2] (ugs.: Zank u. Streit) trouble [3] (ugs.: großes Aufheben) big row (coll.) *or* fuss; **~ machen** raise hell (coll.)

Terror-: ~akt *der* act of terrorism; **~angriff** *der* terrorist attack; **~anschlag** *der* terrorist attack; **~attacke** *die* terrorist attack; **~bekämpfung** *die* fight against terrorism; **~gruppe** *die* terrorist group

terrorisieren *tr. V.* [1] (durch Terror unterdrücken) terrorize [2] (ugs.: belästigen) pester

Terrorismus *der;* **~:** terrorism *no art.*

Terrorismus·bekämpfung *die* counterterrorism; **die ~:** the fight against terrorism

Terrorist *der;* **~en, ~en, Terroristin** *die;* **~, ~nen** terrorist

Terroristen-: ~führer *der,* **~führerin** *die* terrorist leader; **~gruppe** *die* terrorist group

terroristisch *Adj.* terrorist

Terror-: ~kommando *das* terrorist commando group; **~netz** *das,* **~netzwerk** *das* terrorist network; **~opfer** *das* terrorist victim; **~organisation** *die* terrorist organization; **~regime** *das* regime of terror; **~truppe** *die* terrorist unit; **~verdächtige** *der/die* terrorist suspect; **~warnung** *die* warning of a terrorist attack; **~welle** *die* wave of terror; **~zelle** *die* terrorist cell

Tertia /'tɛrtsi̯a/ *die;* **~, Tertien** (Schulw.) [1] (veralt.) fourth and fifth year (*of a Gymnasium*) [2] (österr.) third year (*of a Gymnasium*)

Tertianer /tɛr'tsi̯a:nɐ/ *der;* **~s, ~, Tertianerin** *die;* **~, ~nen** (Schulw.) [1] (veralt.) (Ober~) pupil in the fifth year (*of a Gymnasium*) (Unter~) pupil in the forth year (*of a Gymnasium*) [2] (österr.) pupil in the third year (*of a Gymnasium*)

tertiär /tɛr'tsi̯ɛ:ɐ̯/ *Adj.* (Geol.) Tertiary

Tertiär *das;* **~s** (Geol.) Tertiary [Period]

Tertium Comparationis /'tɛrtsi̯ʊm kɔmpara'tsi̯o:nɪs/ *das;* **~, Tertia Comparationis** (geh.) common element (*as a basis for comparison*)

Terz /tɛrts/ *die;* **~, ~en** [1] (Musik) third [2] (Fechten) tierce

Terzett /tɛr'tsɛt/ *das;* **~[e]s, ~e** [1] (Musik) trio; **[im] ~ singen** sing a trio [2] (Verslehre) triplet

Terzine /tɛr'tsi:nə/ *die;* **~, ~n** (Verslehre) terza rima

Tesa·film Ⓦⓩ /'te:za-/ *der;* **~[e]s** Sellotape (Brit.) ®; Scotch tape (Amer.) ®

Test /tɛst/ *der;* **~[e]s, ~s** *od.* **~e** test

Testament /tɛsta'mɛnt/ *das;* **~[e]s, ~e** [1] (letzte Verfügung eines Erblassers) will; **das ~ eröffnen** read the will; **ohne Hinterlassung eines ~s sterben** die intestate; **das politische ~** (fig.) the political legacy; **er kann sein ~ machen** (fig. ugs.) he is [in] for it (coll.) [2] (christl. Rel.) Testament; **das Alte/Neue ~:** the Old/New Testament

testamentarisch /tɛstamɛn'ta:rɪʃ/

A *Adj.* testamentary

B *adv.* **etw. ~ bestimmen** *od.* **festlegen** *od.* **verfügen** write sth. in one's will

Testaments-: ~eröffnung *die* reading of a/the will; **~vollstrecker** *der,* **~vollstreckerin** *die* executor

Testat /tɛs'ta:t/ *das;* **~[e]s, ~e** [1] certification [2] (Hochschulw. veralt.: Vorlesungsnachweis) certificate of attendance

Test·bild *das* (Ferns.) test card

testen *tr. V.* test (**auf** + *Akk.* for)

Test-: ~fall *der* test case; **~frage** *die* test question

testieren *tr. V.* (Hochschulw. veralt.) certify

Testosteron /tɛstoste'ro:n/ *das;* **~s** (Physiol.) testosterone

Test-: ~phase *die* test phase; **~pilot** *der,* **~pilotin** *die* test pilot; **~sieger** *der* winner in a/the test; **~sieger wurde X** X came out top in the test; **~verfahren** *das* test[ing] procedure; **~wagen** *der* test car; **~zweck** *der* purpose of the test

Tetanus /'te:tanʊs/ *der;* **~** ▸ⓘ **S. 439** (Med.) tetanus *no art.*

Tetanus·schutz·impfung *die* tetanus vaccination

Tete-a-Tete, Tête-à-tête /tɛta'tɛ:t/ *das;* **~s, ~s** (veralt., scherzh.) tête-à-tête

Tetraeder /tetra'|e:dɐ/ *das;* **~s, ~** (Geom.) tetrahedron

Tetralogie /tetralo'gi:/ *die;* **~, ~n** tetralogy

teuer /'tɔy̯ɐ/

A *Adj.* [1] expensive; dear *usu. pred.;* **wie ~ war das?** how much did that cost?; **das ist mir zu ~:** that's too expensive *or* too much [for me]; **Kaffee soll wieder teurer werden** coffee is supposed to be going up again; **zu teuren Preisen** at high prices; **teures Geld** (fig.) good money; **das ist ihn ~ zu stehen gekommen** (fig.) that cost him dear; *s. auch* **Rat 1** [2] (veralt.: geschätzt) dear; **teurer Freund!** [my] dear friend!; **[mein] Teuerster!** [my] dearest; (von Mann zu Mann) [my] dearest friend; *s. auch* **lieb A 4**

B *adv.* expensively; dearly; **etw. ~ kaufen/verkaufen** pay a great deal for sth./sell sth. at a high price; **~ essen gehen** eat in an expensive restaurant/expensive restaurants; **sie haben ihren Sieg ~ erkauft** they paid a high price for their victory; **ein ~ erkaufter Sieg** a victory won at a high price; **diese Gemeinheit wird er [mir] ~ bezahlen!** I'll make him pay for that dirty trick!

Teuerung *die;* **~, ~en** rise in prices

Teuerungs-: ~rate *die* rate of price increases; **~zuschlag** *der* cost-of-living supplement

Teufel /'tɔy̯fl̩/ *der;* **~s, ~:** devil; **der ~:** the Devil; **wie der ~ fahren/reiten** drive/ride in daredevil fashion; **armer ~:** poor devil; **der ~ steckt im Detail** it's [always] the little things that cause all the problems; **der ~ ist los** all hell's let loose (coll.); **dich reitet wohl der ~!** what's got into you?; **ich weiß auch nicht, was für ein ~ mich da geritten hat** I don't know what got into me; **hol dich/ihn** *usw.* **der ~!** (salopp) sod (Brit. sl.) *or* (coll.) damn you/him *etc.;* **hol's der ~!** (salopp) sod (Brit. sl.) *or* (coll.) damn it!; **der ~ soll dich/ihn/es** *usw.* **holen!** (salopp) sod (Brit. sl.) *or* (coll.) damn you/him/it *etc.;* **in ihn/dich** *usw.* **ist wohl der ~ gefahren** (salopp) (er ist/du bist usw. frech) what does he think he's/do you think you're *etc.* doing?; (er ist/du bist usw. leichtsinnig) he/you *etc.* must be mad; **~ auch!** (salopp) damn [it all]! (coll.); **das weiß der ~!** (salopp) God [only] knows; **weiß der ~, was/wie/wo ...** (salopp) God knows what/how/where ...; **hinter etw. her sein wie der ~ hinter der armen Seele** (ugs.) be greedy for sth.; **etw. fürchten/scheuen wie der ~ das Weihwasser** (ugs.) fear nothing more than sth./avoid sth. like the plague; **den ~ werde ich [tun]!** (salopp) like hell [I will]! (coll.); **mal bloß nicht den ~ an die Wand!** (ugs.) don't invite trouble/(stärker) disaster by talking like that!; **des ~s sein** (ugs.) be mad; have taken leave of one's senses; **des ~s Gebetbuch** *od.* **Gesangbuch** (scherzh.) a pack *or* (Amer.) deck of cards; **in ~s Küche kommen** (ugs.) get into a hell of a mess (coll.); **jmdn. in ~s Küche bringen** (ugs.) put sb. in a hell of a mess (coll.); **warum musst du den jetzt auf ~ komm raus überholen?** (ugs.) why are you so hell-bent on overtaking him now? (coll.); **vom ~ besessen sein** (fig.) (verrückt, wahnsinnig) be mad; (wild, ungestüm) be wild; **zum ~ gehen** (ugs.: kaputtgehen) be ruined; **scher dich** *od.* **geh zum ~!** (salopp) go to hell! (coll.); **er soll sich zum ~ scheren!** (salopp) he can go to hell (coll.) *or* blazes (coll.); **zum** *od.* **beim ~ sein** (ugs.: kaputt sein) have had it (coll.); be ruined; **jmdn./etw. zum ~ wünschen** (salopp) wish sb. in hell/curse sth.; **jmdn. zum ~ jagen** *od.* **schicken** (salopp) send sb. packing; **zum ~!** (salopp) damn it! (coll.); **zum ~ mit dir/damit!** (salopp) to hell with you/it! (coll.); **wer/wo** *usw.* **zum ~ ...** (salopp) who/where *etc.* the hell ... (coll.); **wenn man vom ~ spricht[, dann ist er nicht weit]** (scherzh.) speak *or* talk of the devil [and he will appear]

Teufelei *die;* **~, ~en** [1] devilry [2] (Handlung) piece of devilry; **diese ~en** this devilry *sing.*

Teufelin *die;* **~, ~nen** (abwertend) she-devil

Teufels-: ~austreibung *die* (Rel.) casting-out of devils; exorcism; **~braten** *der* (ugs.) devil; **~kerl** *der* (ugs.) amazing fellow; **~kreis** *der* vicious circle; **~messe** *die* Black Mass; **~rochen** *der* (Zool.) devil ray; **~weib** *das* (ugs.) [1] (bewundernd) **sie ist ein ~weib** she's some woman (coll.); [2] (abwertend) she-devil; **~werk** *das* devil's work *no indef. art.;* **~zeug** *das* (ugs.) terrible stuff (coll.)

teuflisch

A *Adj.* [1] devilish, fiendish ‹*plan, trick, etc.*›; fiendish, diabolical ‹*laughter, pleasure, etc.*›; **das Teuflische an dieser Krankheit** the devilish *or* diabolical thing about this illness [2] (ugs.: groß, intensiv) terrible (coll.); dreadful (coll.)

B *adv.* [1] fiendishly; diabolically [2] (ugs.) terribly (coll.); dreadfully (coll.)

Teutone /tɔy̯'to:nə/ *der;* **~n, ~n, Teutonin** *die;* **~, ~nen** Teuton

teutonisch (auch fig.)

A *Adj.* Teutonic

B *adv.* Teutonically; in a Teutonic way

Text /tɛkst/ *der;* **~[e]s, ~e** [1] text; (eines Gesetzes, auf einem Plakat) wording; (eines Theaterstücks) script; (einer Oper) libretto; **ein Telegramm mit folgendem ~: ...** a telegram which reads/read ...; **weiter im ~!** (ugs.) [let's] carry on! [2] (eines Liedes, Chansons usw.) words *pl.;* (eines Schlagers) words *pl.;* lyrics *pl.* [3] (zu einer Abbildung) caption

Text-: ~analyse *die* (Sprachw.) text analysis; (Literaturw.) textual analysis; **~aufgabe** *die* (Schule) problem; **~baustein** *der* textual unit; **~buch** *das* libretto; **~datei** *die* (DV) text file; **~dichter** *der,* **~dichterin** *die* librettist

texten

A *tr. V.* write ‹*song, advertisement, etc*›

B *itr. V.* ‹*composer*› write one's own words

Texter *der;* **~s, ~** ▸ⓘ **S. 113** writer; (in der Werbung) copywriter

Text·erfassung *die* text capture

Texterin *die;* **~, ~nen** ▸**Texter**

textil *Adj.* textile

textil-, Textil-: **~frei** *Adj.* (ugs. scherzh.) nude; **~gewerbe** *das* textile trade *or* industry; **~handwerk** *das* textile trade

Textilien *Pl.* 1 textiles 2 (Fertigwaren) textile goods

Textil-: **~industrie** *die* textile industry; **~ingenieur** *der* textile engineer; **~strand** *der* (ugs. scherzh.) beach where there is no nude bathing; **~waren** *Pl.* textile goods

text-, Text-: **~kritik** *die* textual criticism; **~kritisch** *Adj.* textual ‹*study, commentary*›; critical ‹*edition*›; **~linguistik** *die* text linguistics *sing., no art.*; **~passage** *die* passage [of text]; **~sorte** *die* (Sprachw.) type of text; **~stelle** *die* passage [in a/the text]

Textur /tɛksˈtuːɐ̯/ *die;* ~, ~en (geh., Geol.) texture

Text-: **~verarbeitung** *die* word processing; text processing; **~verarbeitungs·system** *das* (DV) word processor; word processing system

Thai[1] /tai/ *der;* ~[s], ~[s] Thai

Thai[2] *das;* ~s ▸ⓘ S. 670 (Sprache) Thai

Thailand *(das);* ~s Thailand

Thailänder *der;* ~s, ~, **Thailänderin** *die;* ~, ~nen Thai

thailändisch *Adj.* Thai

Thalamus /ˈtaːlamʊs/ *der;* ~, **Thalami** ▸ⓘ S. 435 (Anat.) thalamus

Thälmann·pionier /ˈtɛːl-/ *der* (DDR) Thälmann Pioneer

Theater /teˈaːtɐ/ *das;* ~s, ~ 1 theatre; **ins ~ gehen** got to the theatre; **im ~:** at the theatre; **zum ~ gehen** (ugs.) go into the theatre; tread the boards; **beim** *od.* **am ~ sein** be *or* work in the theatre; **das englische ~:** English theatre; **~ spielen** act; (fig.) play-act; pretend; put on an act 2 (fig. ugs.) fuss; **mach [mir] kein ~!** don't make a fuss; **das ist doch alles nur ~:** that's all just play-acting; **dieses ~ mache ich nicht mehr mit** I'm not having any more to do with this farce; **das war vielleicht ein ~[, bis ich mein Visum hatte]** what a performance *or* (coll.) palaver [it was, getting my visa]; **jetzt geht das ~ wieder los!** now we have to go through all 'that performance again

Theater-: **~abonnement** *das* theatre subscription [ticket]; **~besuch** *der* visit to the theatre; **~besucher** *der,* **~besucherin** *die* theatre goer; **~donner** *der* (spött.) sound and fury; **~ferien** *Pl.* theatre holidays; **~karte** *die* theatre ticket; **~kasse** *die* theatre box office; **~kritiker** *der,* **~kritikerin** *die* theatre *or* drama critic; **~macher** *der,* **~macherin** *die* (Jargon) [theatre] director; **~stück** *das* [stage] play; **~werkstatt** *die* theatre workshop; **~wissenschaft** *die* theatre studies *pl., no art.;* study of theatre arts

theatralisch /teaˈtraːlɪʃ/ (auch fig.)
A *Adj.* theatrical
B *adv.* theatrically

Theismus /teˈɪsmʊs/ *der;* ~ (Philos., Rel.) theism *no art.*

Theist /teˈɪst/ *der;* ~en, ~en, **Theistin** *die;* ~, ~nen (Philos., Rel.) theist

theistisch (Philos., Rel.)
A *Adj.* theistic
B *adv.* theistically

Theke /ˈteːkə/ *die;* ~, ~n 1 (Schanktisch) bar 2 (Ladentisch) counter; **unter der ~** (fig.) under the counter

Thema /ˈteːma/ *das;* ~s, **Themen** *od.* ~ta 1 subject; topic; (einer Abhandlung) subject; theme; (Leitgedanke) theme; **das ist für uns kein ~:** that's not a matter for discussion [as far as we are concerned]; **das ~ wechseln** change the subject; **vom ~ abkommen** *od.* **abschweifen** wander off the subject *or* point; **beim ~ bleiben** stick to the subject *or* point; **das ~ verfehlen** go completely off the subject; **damit ist das ~ [für mich] erledigt** [as far as I'm concerned] that's the end of the matter; **lassen wir das ~!** let's drop the subject; *s. auch* **Nummer 1** 2 (Musik) theme

Thematik /teˈmaːtɪk/ *die;* ~, ~en theme; (Themenkreis) themes *pl.;* (Themenkomplex) complex of themes

thematisch
A *Adj.* (auch Musik) thematic; **etw. nach ~en Gesichtspunkten ordnen** arrange sth. according to subject
B *adv.* (auch Musik) thematically; (was das Thema betrifft) as regards subject matter

thematisieren *tr. V.* take as a *or* one's/its theme

Thema·wechsel *der* change of subject

Themen ▸ **Thema**

Themen-: **~abend** *der* (Rundf., Ferns.) theme[d] evening; **~kreis** *der* group of themes; **~park** *der* theme park; **~stellung** *die* presentation of a/the subject; (Thema) subject; **~wahl** *die* choice of subject

Themse /ˈtɛmzə/ *die;* ~ ▸ⓘ S. 267 Thames

Theologe /teoˈloːɡə/ *der;* ~n, ~n theologian

Theologie /teoloˈɡiː/ *die;* ~, ~n theology *no art.*

Theologin *die;* ~, ~nen theologian

theologisch
A *Adj.* theological
B *adv.* theologically

Theorem /teoˈreːm/ *das;* ~s, ~e theorem

Theoretiker /teoˈreːtikɐ/ *der;* ~s, ~, **Theoretikerin** *die;* ~, ~nen theoretician; theorist

theoretisch /teoˈreːtɪʃ/
A *Adj.* theoretical
B *adv.* theoretically

theoretisieren *itr. V.* (geh.) theorize

Theorie /teoˈriː/ *die;* ~, ~n theory; **das ist graue ~:** that's just pure theory

Theosophie /teozoˈfiː/ *die;* ~, ~n theosophy *no art.*

theosophisch
A *Adj.* theosophical
B *adv.* theosophically

Therapeut /teraˈpɔy̯t/ *der;* ~en, ~en therapist; therapeutist

Therapeutik /teraˈpɔy̯tɪk/ *die;* ~ (Med.) therapeutics *no art.*

Therapeutikum *das;* ~s, **Therapeutika** (Med.) therapeutic agent

Therapeutin *die;* ~, ~nen therapist; therapeutist

therapeutisch
A *Adj.* therapeutic
B *adv.* therapeutically

Therapie /teraˈpiː/ *die;* ~, ~n therapy (**gegen** for); (fig.) remedy (**gegen** for); **eine ~ machen** (ugs.) undergo *or* have therapy *or* treatment

Therapie-: **~angebot** *das* range of therapies; **~einrichtung** *die* therapy unit; **~erfolg** *der* success of the therapy; **~platz** *der* therapy place

therapieren *tr. V.* treat

Therapierung *die;* ~, ~en treatment [with a therapy]

Therapie·zentrum *das* therapy centre

Thermal-: **~bad** *das* 1 (Ort) thermal spa; 2 (Bad) thermal bath; **~quelle** *die* thermal spring; **~wasser** *das; Pl.* **~wässer** thermal water

Therme /ˈtɛrmə/ *die;* ~, ~n 1 (Quelle) thermal spring 2 *Pl.* (Bäder) baths; thermae

Thermik /ˈtɛrmɪk/ *die;* ~ (Met.) thermal

thermisch
A *Adj.* thermal
B *adv.* thermally

thermo-, Thermo- /tɛrmo-/: **~dynamik** *die* thermodynamics *sing., no art.;* **~dynamisch** A *Adj.* thermodynamic; B *adv.* thermodynamically; **~meter** *das* (österr. u. schweiz. der od. das) thermometer

Thermos·flasche Ⓦⓩ /ˈtɛrmɔs-/ *die* Thermos flask ®; vacuum flask

Thermostat /tɛrmoˈstaːt/ *der;* ~[e]s *od.* ~en, ~e *od.* ~en thermostat

Thesaurus /teˈzau̯rʊs/ *der;* ~, **Thesauren** *od.* **Thesauri** thesaurus

These /ˈteːzə/ *die;* ~, ~n thesis

Thing /tɪŋ/ *das;* ~[e]s, ~e (hist.) thing

Thing·platz *der* (hist.) thingstead

Thinktank /ˈθɪŋktɛŋk/ *der;* ~s, ~s think tank

Thomas /ˈtoːmas/ *der;* ~, ~se *in* **ungläubiger ~:** doubting Thomas

Thora /toˈraː/ *die;* ~ (jüd. Rel.) Torah

Thora·rolle *die* (jüd. Rel.) Torah [scroll]

Thriller /ˈθrɪlɐ/ *der;* ~s, ~: thriller

Thrombose /trɔmˈboːzə/ *die;* ~, ~n thrombosis

Thron /troːn/ *der;* ~[e]s, ~e 1 throne; **sein ~ wackelt** (fig.) his position is becoming very shaky 2 (ugs. scherzh.: Nachttopf) pot (coll.)

Thron-: **~anwärter** *der,* **~anwärterin** *die* heir apparent; **~besteigung** *die* accession [to the throne]

thronen *itr. V.* sit enthroned; (fig.: erhöht liegen) tower

Thron-: **~folge** *die* succession [to the throne]; **die ~folge antreten** succeed [to the throne]; **~folger** *der;* ~~s, ~~, **~folgerin** *die;* ~~, ~~nen heir to the throne; **~jubiläum** *das:* **das silberne/goldene ~jubiläum von X** the silver/golden jubilee of X's accession to the throne; **~rede** *die* King's/Queen's speech; **~saal** *der* throne room

Thuja /ˈtuːja/ *die;* ~, **Thujen,** *österr. auch:* **Thuje** /ˈtuːjə/ *die;* **Thuje, Thujen** (Bot.) thuja

Thun·fisch /ˈtuːn-/ *der* tuna

Thüringen /ˈtyːrɪŋən/ *(das);* ~s Thuringia

Thüringer
A *der;* ~s, ~: Thuringian
B *indekl. Adj.* Thuringian.

Thüringerin *die;* ~, ~nen ▸ **Thüringer A**

Thüringer Wald *der* Thuringian Forest

thüringisch *Adj.* Thuringian; *s. auch* **badisch**

Thusnelda /tʊsˈnɛlda/ *die;* ~ (salopp abwertend) bird (sl.)

Thymian /ˈtyːmi̯aːn/ *der;* ~s, ~e thyme

Thymus·drüse /ˈtyːmʊs-/ *die* ▸ⓘ S. 435 (Anat.) thymus [gland]

Tiara /tiˈaːra/ *die;* ~, **Tiaren** tiara

Tibet /ˈtiːbɛt/ *(das);* ~s Tibet

tibetanisch *Adj.* ▸ **tibetisch**

Tibeter /tiˈbeːtɐ/ *der;* ~s, ~, **Tibeterin** *die;* ~, ~nen ▸ⓘ S. 520 Tibetan

tibetisch *Adj.* ▸ⓘ S. 520, ▸ⓘ S. 670 Tibetan; *s. auch* **deutsch; Deutsch; Deutsche**[2]

Tic /tɪk/ *der;* ~s, ~s ▸ⓘ S. 439 (Med.) tic

Tick *der;* ~[e]s, ~s 1 (ugs.: Schrulle) quirk; thing (coll.); **du hast wohl einen kleinen ~:** you must be round the bend (coll.) 2 ▸ⓘ S. 439 (Med.) tic 3 (ugs.: Nuance) tiny bit; shade

ticken
A *itr. V.* tick; **du tickst wohl nicht richtig** (salopp) you must be off your rocker (coll.)
B *tr. V.* (salopp: erkennen, merken) catch on to (coll.)

Ticker *der;* ~s, ~ (bes. Pressejargon) teleprinter; telex

Ticket /ˈtɪkət/ *das;* ~s, ~s ticket

ticktack /ˈtɪk ˈtak/ *Interj.* tick-tock

Tide /ˈtiːdə/ *die;* ~, ~n (nordd., bes. Seemannsspr.) tide

Tiden·hub *der* tidal range

tief /tiːf/
A *Adj.* 1 ▸ⓘ S. 267, ▸ⓘ S. 374 (auch fig.) deep; low ‹*neckline, bow*›; long ‹*fall*›; **eine fünf Meter ~e Grube** a pit five metres deep; **~es Einatmen** breathing in deeply 2 (niedrig) low ‹*table, chair, temperature, tide, level, cloud*›; **den Sattel/die Heizung etwas ~er stellen** lower the saddle/turn the heating down a bit 3 (intensiv, stark) deep; intense ‹*pain, suffering*›; utter ‹*misery*›; great ‹*need, want*› 4 (weit im Innern gelegen) **im ~en/~sten Afrika** in the depths of/in darkest Africa; **es freut mich aus ~stem Herzen/~ster Seele** I really am delighted; **in ~er/~ster Nacht** in the *or* at dead of night;

t

im ~en/~sten Winter in the depths of winter; im ~sten Mittelalter in the depths of the Middle Ages
B *adv.* 1 (weit unten) deep; 100 m ~ in/unter der Erde 100 metres [down] under the earth; ~ verschneit covered in deep snow *postpos.*; deep in snow *postpos.*; er war ~ in Gedanken he was deep in thought; die Mütze saß ihm ~ in der Stirn the cap was low over his forehead; ~ liegend low-lying ‹*area;*› deep-set ‹*eyes;*› die ~ stehende Sonne the sun low down on the horizon; ein moralisch ~ stehender Mensch a person of little moral principle 2 (weit nach unten) ‹*dig, drill*› deep; ‹*fall, sink*› a long way; ‹*stoop, bow*› low; ~er graben/bohren dig/drill deeper *or* more deeply; ein ~ ausgeschnittenes Kleid a low-cut dress; *s. auch* Glas[1] 2 3 (in nur geringer Höhe) ‹*fly, hover, etc.*› low; ~ liegen be at a lower level; er wohnt einen Stock ~er he lives one floor down 4 (nach unten) ‹*hang etc.*› low; ~er gehen ‹*pilot*› go lower ; einen Stock ~er gehen go one floor down; ~ herabhängende Äste low-hanging branches 5 (weit innen) deep; ~ in Afrika/im Dschungel deep in Africa/in the jungle 6 (weit nach innen) deep; ‹*breathe, inhale*› deeply; er sah ihr ~ in die Augen he looked deep into her eyes; ~er ins All vorstoßen push deeper into space; bis ~ in die Nacht/in den Winter (fig.) until deep *or* late into the night/well into winter; das geht bei ihm nicht sehr ~ (ugs.) it doesn't go very deep with him 7 er sprach ganz ~: he spoke in a deep voice; zu ~ gestimmt tuned too low; zu ~ singen sing flat; er spielt das Lied ~er/eine Terz ~er he plays the song in a lower key *or* lower/a third lower 8 (intensiv, stark) ‹*feel etc.*› deeply; ‹*sleep*› deeply, soundly; ~ betrübt/bewegt deeply distressed or saddened/moved; ~ empfunden deep[ly]-felt; heartfelt ‹*thanks, sympathy*› 9 ~ gehend, ~ greifend ▸tiefgehend, tiefgreifend; ~ schürfend ▸tiefschürfend

Tief *das;* ~s, ~s (Met.) low; depression; (fig.) low

tief-, Tief-: ~ausläufer *der* (Met.) trough [of low pressure]; ~bau *der* civil engineering *no art.* (*at or below ground level*); ~betrübt ▸tief B 8; ~bewegt ▸tief Bh; ~blau *Adj.* deep blue; ~druck[1] *der; Pl.* ~drücke (Met.) low pressure; ~druck[2] *der; Pl.* ~~e 1 intaglio *or* gravure [printing]; 2 (Erzeugnis) intaglio *or* gravure [print]; ~druck·gebiet *das* (Met.) area of low pressure; depression

Tiefe *die;* ~, ~n 1 ▸ⓘ S. 374 (Ausdehnung, Entfernung nach unten) depth; eine ~ von 300 m a depth of 300 metres; in großen ~n at great depths 2 (weit unten, im Innern gelegener Bereich; auch fig.) depths *pl.;* in die ~ stürzen plunge into the depths; in der ~ ihres Herzens (fig.) deep down in her heart; *s. auch* Höhe 8 3 (Ausdehnung nach hinten) depth; der Schrank hat eine ~ von 60 cm the cupboard is 60 cm deep 4 ▸tief A 3: depth; intensity; greatness 5 (von Tönen, Klängen, Stimmen) deepness 6 (fig.: Tiefgründigkeit) depth; profundity 7 *Pl.* (Akustik) bass *sing.* 8 (Geogr.: Meeres~) deep

Tief·ebene *die* (Georgr.) lowland plain

tief·empfunden ▸tief B 8

Tiefen-: ~gestein *das* (Geol.) plutonic rock; ~psychologie *die* depth psychology *no art.;* ~psychologisch A *Adj.* depth psychology ‹*analysis, methods etc.*›; B *adv.* by means of depth psychology; ~schärfe *die* (Fot.) ▸Schärfentiefe; ~wirkung *die* 1 deep action; 2 (optisch) effect of depth

tief-, Tief-: ~ernst A *Adj.* deadly serious; B *adv.* deadly seriously; ~flieger *der* low-flying aircraft; ~flug *der* low-altitude flight *no art.;* flying *no art.* at low altitude; im ~flug at low altitude; ~gang *der* (Schiffbau) draught; (fig.) depth; ~garage *die* underground car park; ~gefrieren *unr. tr. V.* [deep-]freeze; ~gehend, ~greifend A *Adj.* profound; far-reaching; profound, deep ‹*crisis*›; far-reaching ‹*improvement*›; B *adv.* profoundly; ~gründig /-grʏndɪç/ A *Adj.* profound; B *adv.* ‹*discuss, examine*› in depth; ~gründigkeit *die;* ~~: profundity; ~kühlen *tr. V.* [deep-]freeze

Tief·kühl-: ~fach *das* freezer [compartment]; ~kost *die* frozen food; ~truhe *die* [chest] freezer *or* deep-freeze

tief-, Tief-: ~lader *der;* ~~s, ~~: low-loader; ~land *das* lowlands *pl.;* *~liegend ▸tief B 1; ~punkt *der* 1 (fig.) low [point]; 2 (Math.: Minimum) minimum; ~religiös *Adj.* deeply religious; ~rot A *Adj.* deep red; (Politik) very left-wing; B *adv* ‹*coloured, painted*› deep red; ~schlaf *der* deep sleep; ~schlag *der* (Boxen) low punch; punch below the belt (lit. or fig.); ~schürfend A *Adj.* profound; B *adv.* profoundly; ~schwarz *Adj.* jet-black; ~see *die* (Geogr.) deep sea; ~see·graben *der* deep-sea trench; ~sinn *der* profundity; ~sinnig A *Adj.* profound; B *adv.* profoundly; ~stand *der* (auch fig.) (tiefer Stand) low level; (tiefster Stand) lowest level; ~stapelei /-ʃta:pəˈlai/ *die;* ~~: understatement; (aus Bescheidenheit) modesty; ~|stapeln *itr. V.* understate the case; (aus Bescheidenheit) be modest; ~stehend ▸tief B 1; ~strahler *der* floodlight

Tiefst-: ~temperatur *die* minimum *or* lowest temperature; ~wert *der* minimum *or* lowest value

tief-: ~traurig *Adj.* very *or* deeply sad; ~verschneit ▸tief B 1

Tiegel /ˈtiːgl̩/ *der;* ~s, ~ (zum Kochen) pan; (Schmelz~) crucible; (Behälter) pot

Tier /tiːɐ̯/ *das;* ~[e]s, ~e animal; (in der Wohnung gehaltenes) pet; niedere/höhere ~e lower/higher animals; er ist ein ~ (fig.) he is an animal; das ist das ~ im Menschen that's the beast in man; ein hohes *od.* großes ~ (ugs.) a big noise (coll.) *or* shot (sl.)

tier-, Tier-: ~art *die* animal species; species of animal; ~arzt *der,* ~ärztin *die* ▸ⓘ S. 113 veterinary surgeon; vet; ~ärztlich A *Adj.* veterinary; B *adv.* by a veterinary surgeon/veterinary surgeons; ~asyl *das* animal home

Tierchen *das;* ~s, ~: [little] animal; was für ein possierliches ~! what a funny little creature!; jedem ~ sein Pläsierchen (ugs.) each to his own; if that's what he/she wants

tier-, Tier-: ~fabel *die* animal fable; ~fänger *der,* ~fängerin *die* animal collector; ~freund *der,* ~freundin *die* animal-lover; ~futter *das* 1 (Landw.) animal feed; 2 (für Haustiere) pet food; ~garten *der* zoo; zoological garden; ~gerecht A *Adj.* animal-friendly; B *adv.* ‹*transport, keep*› in conditions fit for animals; ~geschichte *die* animal story

tierhaft *Adj.* animal *attrib.* ‹*behaviour, warmth, etc.*›

Tier-: ~halter *der,* ~halterin *die* animal owner; ~halter sein keep an animal/animals; ~haltung *die* keeping of animals; ~handlung *die* pet shop; ~heilkunde *die* ▸~medizin; ~heim *das* animal home

tierisch
A *Adj.* 1 animal *attrib.;* bestial, savage ‹*cruelty, crime*› 2 (ugs.: unerträglich groß) terrible (coll.); ~er Ernst deadly seriousness 3 (Jugendspr.: sehr gut, sehr schön) great (coll.)
B *adv.* 1 ‹*roar*› like an animal; savagely ‹*cruel*› 2 (ugs.: unerträglich) terribly (coll.); deadly ‹*monotonous, serious*›; baking ‹*hot*›; perishing (coll.) ‹*cold*› 3 (Jugendspr.: sehr) really; es hat ~ Spaß gemacht it was great fun

tier-, Tier-: ~kind *das* baby animal; ~kreis *der* (Astron., Astrol.) zodiac; ~kreis·zeichen *das* (Astron., Astrol.) sign of the zodiac; er ist im ~kreiszeichen der Jungfrau geboren he was born under [the sign of] Virgo; ~kunde *die* zoology *no art.;* ~lieb *Adj.* animal-loving *attrib.;* fond of animals *postpos.;* ~liebe *die* love of animals; ~liebend *Adj.* ▸~lieb; ~medizin *die* veterinary medicine; ~mehl *das* animal meal; ~park *der* zoo; ~pfleger *der,* ~pflegerin *die* ▸ⓘ S. 113 animal keeper; ~quäler *der;* ~~s, ~~, ~quälerin *die;* ~~, ~~nen person who is cruel to animals; ein ~quäler sein be cruel to animals; ~quälerei /---ˈ-/ *die* cruelty to animals; das ist ~quälerei (fig. ugs. scherzh.) that's cruelty to dumb animals (joc.); ~recht *das* animal rights *pl.*; ~rechtler *der* ~~s, ~~, ~rechtlerin *die;* ~~, ~~nen animal rights campaigner; ~reich *das* animal kingdom; ~schau *die* menagerie; ~schutz *der* animal protection; ~schützer *der;* ~~s, ~~, ~schützerin *die;* ~~, ~~nen animal protectionist; ~schutz·verein *der* society for the prevention of cruelty to animals; animal protection society; ~seuche *die* animal epidemic; ~versuch *der* animal experiment; ~welt *die* fauna; ~zucht *die* [animal] breeding *no art.*

Tiger /ˈtiːgɐ/ *der;* ~s, ~: tiger

Tiger-: ~auge *das* tiger['s] eye; ~hai *der* tiger shark

Tigerin *die;* ~, ~nen tigress

Tiger·katze *die* tiger cat; margay

tigern *itr. V.; mit sein* (ugs.) walk; go

Tiger·staat *der* tiger [economy]

Tilde /ˈtɪldə/ *die;* ~, ~n tilde

tilgen /ˈtɪlgn̩/ *tr. V.* 1 (geh.) delete ‹*word, letter, error*›; erase ‹*record, endorsement*›; (fig.) wipe out ‹*shame, guilt, traces*› 2 (Wirtsch., Bankw.) repay; pay off

Tilgung *die;* ~, ~en 1 (geh.) ▸tilgen 1: deletion; erasure; wiping out 2 (Wirtsch., Bankw.) repayment

Till /tɪl/ (der) *in* ~ Eulenspiegel Till Eulenspiegel; (fig.) practical joker

Tilsiter /ˈtɪlzɪtɐ/ *der;* ~s, ~: Tilsit [cheese]

Timbre /ˈtɛ̃:br(ə)/ *das;* ~s, ~s timbre

timen /ˈtaimən/ *tr. V.* time

Timing /ˈtaimɪŋ/ *das;* ~s, ~s timing

tingeln /ˈtɪŋl̩n/ *itr. V.* 1 play the [small] clubs/theatres/pubs *etc.* 2 *mit sein* er tingelte durch die Hamburger Clubs he played the Hamburg clubs

Tingeltangel /ˈtɪŋl̩taŋl̩/ *das od. der;* ~s, ~ (veralt. abwertend) 1 (Lokal) cheap nightclub/dance hall; honky-tonk (coll.) 2 (Unterhaltung) cheap nightclub entertainment

Tinktur /tɪŋkˈtuːɐ̯/ *die;* ~, ~en tincture

Tinnef /ˈtɪnɛf/ *der;* ~s (ugs. abwertend) 1 (wertloses Zeug) rubbish; junk 2 (Unsinn) rubbish; nonsense

Tinte /ˈtɪntə/ *die;* ~, ~n ink; das ist klar wie dicke ~ (ugs.) that's as clear as daylight; that's crystal clear; in der ~ sitzen (ugs.) be in the soup (coll.)

tinten-, Tinten-: ~blau *Adj.* deep blue; ~fass, *~faß *das* inkpot; (eingelassen) inkwell; ~fisch *der* cuttlefish; (Kalmar) squid; (Krake) octopus; ~fleck *der* ink stain; ~klecks *der* ink blot; ~kleckser *der* (ugs. abwertend) scribbler; ~stift *der* ▸Kopierstift; ~strahl·drucker *der* (DV) ink-jet printer

***Tip, Tipp** /tɪp/ *der;* ~s, ~s 1 (ugs.: Fingerzeig) tip; (an die Polizei) tip-off 2 (bei Toto, Lotto usw.) [row of] numbers

tipp, tapp *Interj.* pitter-patter; pit-a-pat

Tippel·bruder /ˈtɪpl̩-/ *der* (fam.) tramp

tippeln *itr. V.; mit sein* (ugs.) walk; wir mussten nach Hause ~: we had to foot it home

tippen /ˈtɪpn̩/
A *itr. V.* 1 an/gegen etw. (*Akk.*) ~: tap sth.; an seine Mütze ~: touch one's cap; sich (*Dat.*) an die Stirn ~: tap one's forehead; aufs Gaspedal ~: touch the accelerator; daran ist nicht zu ~ (ugs.) there's no question about that 2 (ugs.: Maschine schreiben) type 3 (ugs.: vermuten) reckon; auf jmds. Sieg ~: tip sb. to win; darauf hätte ich nicht getippt I hadn't reckoned with that; du hast gut/richtig getippt you were right 4 (wetten) do the pools/lottery *etc.;* im Lotto ~: do the lottery
B *tr. V.* 1 tap; jmdn. auf die Schulter ~: tap sb. on the shoulder 2 (ugs.: mit der Maschine schreiben) type 3 (bei der Registrierkasse) ring up 4 (setzen auf) choose; sechs Richtige ~: make six correct selections

t

Tipper *der;* ~s, ~, **Tipperin** *die;* ~, ~nen person who does the pools/lottery *etc.*

Tipp-: ~**fehler** *der* typing error *or* mistake; ~**gemeinschaft** *die* pools/lottery *etc.* syndicate; ~**schein** *der* [pools/lottery *etc.*]coupon

Tippse /ˈtɪpsə/ *die;* ~, ~n (ugs. abwertend) typist

tipp·topp (ugs.)
A *Adj.* (tadellos) immaculate; (erstklassig) tip-top
B *adv.* immaculately; ~ **in Ordnung** in immaculate *or* tip-top order

Tipp·zettel *der* (ugs.) ▸ **Tippschein**

Tirade /tiˈraːdə/ *die;* ~, ~n (geh. abwertend) interminable speech; **sich in langen ~n ergehen** talk interminably

tirilieren /tiriˈliːrən/ *itr. V.* trill; warble

Tirol /tiˈroːl/ *(das);* ~s [the] Tyrol

Tiroler *der;* ~s, ~, **Tirolerin** *die;* ~, ~nen Tyrolese; Tyrolean

Tisch /tɪʃ/ *der;* ~[e]s, ~e **1** table; (Schreib~) desk; **er zahlte bar auf den ~:** he paid cash down; **vor/nach ~:** before/after lunch/dinner/the meal *etc.*; **bei ~ sein** *od.* **sitzen** be at table; **zu ~ sein** be having one's lunch/dinner *etc.*; **zu ~ gehen** go to lunch/dinner *etc.*; **vom ~ aufstehen** get up from the table; ‹*child*› get down [from the table]; **bitte zu ~:** please take your places for lunch/dinner; **es wird gegessen, was auf den ~ kommt!** [you'll] eat what's put on the table!; **ein Gespräch am runden ~:** round-table talks *pl.* **2** (fig.) **am grünen ~, vom grünen ~ aus** merely academically; **reinen ~ machen** (ugs.) clear things up; sort things out; **reinen ~ mit etw. machen** (ugs.) clear sth. up; sort sth. out; **sich [mit jmdm.] an einen ~ setzen** get round the table [with sb.]; **auf den ~ hauen** (ugs.) take a hard line; **etw. auf den ~ legen** (Angebot machen) put sth. on the table; (bezahlen) lay sth. out; **jmdn. über den ~ ziehen** (ugs.) outmanoeuvre sb.; **unter den ~ fallen** (ugs.) go by the board; **jmdn. unter den ~ trinken** (ugs.) drink sb. under the table; **die Füße** *od.* **Beine unter jmds. ~** (Akk.) **strecken** (ugs.) live under sb.'s roof and eat at sb.'s table; **vom ~ sein** (ugs.) be out of the way; ‹*subject, topic*› be closed; *s. auch* **fegen A 2**

Tisch·bein *das* table leg; leg of the table

Tischchen *das;* ~s, ~: [little] table

Tisch-: ~**dame** *die* dinner partner; ~**decke** *die* tablecloth; ~**feuerzeug** *das* table lighter; ~**fußball** *der* table football; ~**gebet** *das* grace; **ein/das ~gebet sprechen** say grace; ~**gespräch** *das* breakfast/lunch/dinner conversation; ~**herr** *der* dinner partner; ~**karte** *die* place card; ~**lampe** *die* table lamp

Tischlein·deck·dich *das;* ~: easy life; **was er sucht, ist so eine Art ~:** he's looking to get on the gravy train (coll.)

Tischler *der;* ~s, ~ ▸❶ **S. 113** joiner; (bes. Kunst~) cabinetmaker

Tischlerei *die;* ~, ~en **1** (Werkstatt) joiner's/cabinetmaker's [workshop] **2** (Handwerk) joinery/cabinetmaking

Tischlerin *die;* ~, ~nen ▸ **Tischler**

tischlern
A *itr. V.* do woodwork
B *tr. V.* make ‹*shelves, cupboard, etc.*›

Tisch-: ~**manieren** *Pl.* table manners; ~**nachbar** *der,* ~**nachbarin** *die* person next to one [at table]; **wer ist dein ~nachbar?** who is sitting next to you?; ~**platte** *die* table top; ~**rede** *die* after-dinner speech; ~**rücken** *das;* ~~s table-turning *no art. or* -lifting *no art.*; ~**sitte** *die* table manners *pl.*; ~**tennis** *das* table tennis

Tisch·tennis-: ~**platte** *die* table-tennis table; ~**schläger** *der* table-tennis bat

Tisch-: ~**tuch** *das; Pl.* ~**tücher** tablecloth; ~**vorlage** *die* handout; ~**wäsche** *die* table linen; ~**wein** *der* table wine; ~**zeit** *die* lunchtime; **wir haben eine halbe Stunde ~zeit** we have half an hour for lunch

Titan[1] /tiˈtaːn/ *der;* ~en, ~en (Myth., fig.) Titan

Titan[2] *das;* ~s (Chemie) titanium

titanenhaft *Adj.* titanic

titanisch *Adj.* (Myth., fig.) titanic

Titel /ˈtiːtl̩/ *der;* ~s, ~ **1** ▸❶ **S. 44,** ▸❶ **S. 143** title; **unter dem ~ „…"** under the title '…' **2** (ugs.: Musikstück, Song usw.) number

Titel-: ~**anwärter** *der,* ~**anwärterin** *die* (Sport) title contender; contender for the title; ~**bild** *das* **1** cover picture; **2** (Frontispiz) frontispiece; ~**blatt** *das* title page

Titelei *die;* ~, ~en (Buchw.) prelims *pl.*

Titel-: ~**geschichte** *die* cover story *or* article; ~**held** *der,* eponymous hero; ~**heldin** *die* eponymous heroine; ~**kampf** *der* (Sport) final; (Boxen) title fight; ~**rolle** *die* title role; ~**schutz** *der* (Rechtsw.) copyright (*in a title*); ~**seite** *die* **1** (einer Zeitung, Zeitschrift) [front] cover; **2** (eines Buchs) title page; ~**story** *die* front page story; ~**sucht** *die* mania for titles; ~**träger** *der,* ~**trägerin** *die* **1** titled person; person with a title; **2** (Sport) title-holder; ~**verteidiger** *der,* ~**verteidigerin** *die* (Sport) title-holder; (Mannschaft) title-holders *pl.*

Titte /ˈtɪtə/ *die;* ~, ~n (derb) tit (coarse)

titulieren /tituˈliːrən/ *tr. V.* **1** (bezeichnen) call; **jmdn. als** *od.* **mit „Flasche" ~:** call sb. a dead loss (coll.) **2** (veralt.: mit dem Titel anreden) address; **jmdn. [als** *od.* **mit] Herr Doktor ~:** address sb. as Doctor

Titulierung *die;* ~, ~en **1** (Bezeichnung) name; **gegen seine ~ als … hatte er nichts einzuwenden** he had no objection to being called … **2** (veralt.: Anrede mit dem Titel, Nennung des Titels) title

Tizian /ˈtiːtsi̯aːn/ *(der);* ~s Titian

tizianrot *Adj.* Titian [red]

tja /tja(ː)/ *Interj.* [yes] well; (Resignation ausdrückend) oh, well

Toast /toːst/ *der;* ~[e]s, ~e *od.* ~s **1** (getoastetes Brot) toast; (Scheibe ~) piece of toast **2** (Trinkspruch) toast

Toast·brot *das* [sliced white] bread for toasting

toasten *tr. V.* toast

Toaster *der;* ~s, ~: toaster

Tobak /ˈtoːbak/ *der;* ~s *in* **starker ~ sein** (ugs.) be a bit thick (Brit. coll.) *or* (coll.) much; *s. auch* **Anno**

Tobel /ˈtoːbl̩/ *der od. das* (österr. *das*); ~s, ~ (Geogr., österr., schweiz., südd.) ravine

toben /ˈtoːbn̩/ *itr. V.* **1** go wild (**vor** + *Dat.* with); (fig.) ‹*storm, sea, battle*› rage; **wie ein Wilder** *od.* **Berserker ~:** go wild *or* berserk **2** (tollen) romp *or* charge about **3** *mit sein* (laufen) charge

Toberei *die;* ~: romping *or* charging about

tob-, Tob-: ~**sucht** *die* frenzied *or* mad rage; [mad] frenzy; ~**süchtig** *Adj.* frenzied; raving mad; ~**suchts·anfall** *der* fit of frenzied *or* mad rage; **einen ~suchtsanfall bekommen** *od.* **erleiden** fly into a fit of frenzied rage *or* into a frenzy

Toccata /toˈkaːta/ ▸ **Tokkata**

Tochter /ˈtɔxtɐ/ *die;* ~, **Töchter** /ˈtœçtɐ/ **1** daughter; **die ~ des Hauses** the daughter *or* young lady of the house; **Ihre Frau/Ihr Fräulein ~:** your daughter; **höhere ~:** young lady **2** (schweiz.: Mädchen, Bedienstete) girl **3** (Wirtschaftsjargon) subsidiary

Töchterchen /ˈtœçtɐçən/ *das;* ~s, ~: little daughter; (Kleinkind) baby daughter

Tochter-: ~**geschwulst** *die* ▸❶ **S. 439** (Med.) secondary tumour; ~**gesellschaft** *die* (Wirtsch.) subsidiary [company]

Tod /toːt/ *der;* ~[e]s, ~e (auch fig.) death; **es wäre unser aller sicherer ~:** it would mean certain death for us all; **diese Krankheit führt zum ~:** this illness is fatal; **eines natürlichen/gewaltsamen ~es sterben** die a natural/violent death; **jmdn. zum ~e/zum ~ durch den Strang/zum ~ durch Erschießen verurteilen** sentence sb. to death/to death by hanging/to death by firing squad; **~ durch Ersticken/Erfrieren** death by suffocation/freezing to death; **jmdm. den ~ wünschen** wish sb. dead; **bis in den ~:** till death; **das ist kein schöner ~:** that's not a pleasant way to die; **in den ~ gehen** go to one's death; **für jmdn./etw. in den ~ gehen** die for sb./sth.; **jmdn. vom ~[e] erretten** save sb.'s life; **sich zu ~e stürzen/trinken** fall to one's death/drink oneself to death; **zu ~e kommen, den ~ finden** die; lose one's life; **des ~es sein** (veralt.) be doomed; **jmdn./etw. auf den ~ nicht leiden/ausstehen können** (ugs.) not be able to stand or abide sb./sth.; **er hasste ihn auf den ~:** he utterly detested him; **sich zu ~e schämen/langweilen** be utterly ashamed/bored to death; **zu ~e betrübt** extremely distressed; **etw. zu ~e reiten** (fig. ugs.) flog sth. to death (coll.); **tausend ~e sterben** (ugs.) die a thousand deaths; **sich** (Dat.) **den ~ holen** (ugs.) catch one's death [of cold]; **der schwarze ~:** the Black Death; **der weiße ~:** death in the snow; **~ und Teufel!** (veralt.) by the devil!; **weder ~ noch Teufel fürchten** fear nothing

tod-: ~**bringend** *Adj.* fatal ‹*illness, disease, etc.*›; deadly, lethal ‹*poison etc.*›; ~**elend** *Adj.* utterly miserable; ~**ernst** **A** *Adj.* deadly serious; **B** *adv.* deadly seriously; **etw. ~ernst sagen** say sth. in deadly seriousness

todes-, Todes-: ~**ahnung** *die* presentiment *or* premonition of death; ~**angst** *die* **1** fear of death; **2** (große Angst) extreme fear; **~ängste ausstehen** be scared to death; ~**anzeige** *die* **1** (in einer Zeitung) death notice; **„~anzeigen"** 'Deaths'; **2** (Karte) *card announcing a person's death;* ~**art** *die:* **eine schreckliche ~art** a terrible way to die; ~**engel** *der* angel of death; ~**erklärung** *die* (Rechtsw.) declaration of death (*of missing person*); ~**fall** *der* **1** death; (in der Familie) bereavement; **2** (Versicherungsw.) **im ~fall** in [the] case *or* in the event of death; ~**folge** *die* (Rechtsw.) **Körperverletzung mit ~folge** bodily harm resulting in death; ~**furcht** *die* (geh.) fear of death; ~**gefahr** *die* mortal danger; ~**jahr** *das* year of death; **in seinem ~jahr** in the year of his death; ~**kampf** *der* death throes *pl.*; ~**kandidat** *der,* ~**kandidatin** *die* (Verurteilte[r]) condemned man/woman; (Schwerkranke[r]) terminal case; ~**mutig** **A** *Adj.* utterly fearless; **B** *adv.* utterly fearlessly; ~**nachricht** *die* news of his/her/their *etc.* death; ~**not** *die* (geh.) mortal danger; **in ~not** *od.* **~nöten** in mortal danger; ~**opfer** *das* death; fatality; **der Unfall forderte drei ~opfer** the accident claimed three lives; ~**qual** *die* (geh.) [terrible] agony; ~**schrei** *der* death cry; ~**schuss,** *~**schuß** *der* fatal shot; **war die Abgabe eines ~schusses zulässig?** was it permissible to shoot to kill?; ~**schütze** *der,* ~**schützin** *die* person who fired the fatal shot; (Attentäter[in]) assassin; killer; ~**schwadron** *die* death squad; ~**sehnsucht** *die* longing to die; ~**spirale** *die* (Eis-, Rollkunstlauf) death spiral; ~**stoß** *der* death blow; **jmdm./(fig.) einer Sache den ~stoß geben** deal sb. the death blow/the death blow to sth.; ~**strafe** *die* death penalty; ~**streifen** *der* death strip; ~**stunde** *die* hour of death; ~**ursache** *die* cause of death; ~**urteil** *das* death sentence; ~**verachtung** *die* [utter] fearlessness in the face of death; **etw. mit ~verachtung essen/trinken** (ugs.) force sth. down [without showing one's distaste]; ~**zelle** *die* death cell; ~**zone** *die* death zone

Tod·feind[1], ***tod·feind** *in* **jmdm. ~ sein** be sb's deadly enemy

Tod·feind[2] *der,* **Tod·feindin** *die* deadly enemy

tod-: ~**geweiht** *Adj.* (geh.) doomed [to die]; ~**krank** *Adj.* critically ill

tödlich /ˈtøːtlɪç/
A *Adj.* **1** fatal ‹*accident, illness, outcome, etc.*›; lethal, deadly ‹*poison, bite, shot, trap, etc.*›; lethal ‹*dose*›; deadly, mortal ‹*danger*› **2** (sehr groß, ausgeprägt) deadly
B *adv.* **1** fatally; **er ist ~ verunglückt/abgestürzt** he was killed in an accident/he fell to his death; **die Krankheit verläuft in der Regel ~:** the illness is usually fatal **2** (sehr) terribly (coll.); **sich ~ langweilen** be bored stiff *or* to death (coll.)

t

tod-, Tod-: **~müde** *Adj.* dead tired; **~schick** (ugs.) **A** *Adj.* dead smart (coll.); **B** *adv.* dead smartly (coll.); **~sicher** (ugs.) **A** *Adj.* sure-fire (coll.) ‹*system, method, tip, etc.*›; **eine ~sichere Sache** a dead certainty *or* (coll.) cert; **B** *adv.* for certain *or* sure; **~sterbenskrank** *Adj.* (ugs.) critically ill; **~sünde** *die* (auch fig.) deadly *or* mortal sin; **~traurig** **A** *Adj.* extremely sad; **B** *adv.* extremely sadly; with extreme sadness; **~unglücklich** *Adj.* (ugs.) extremely *or* desperately unhappy

Toffee /ˈtɔfi/ *das;* **~s, ~s** toffee

Toga /ˈtoːga/ *die;* **~, Togen** toga

Togo /ˈtoːgo/ *(das);* **~s** Togo

Togoer *der;* **~s, ~, Togoerin** *die;* **~, ~nen** Togolese

togoisch *Adj.* Togolese

Tohuwabohu /ˈtoːhuvaˈboːhu/ *das;* **~s, ~s** chaos; **im ganzen Haus war ein großes ~:** the whole house was in total *or* utter chaos

toi, toi, toi /ˈtɔy ˈtɔy ˈtɔy/ *Interj.* [1] (gutes Gelingen!) good luck!; **~ für deine Prüfung!** good luck in your exam! (coll.) [2] (unberufen!) touch wood!

Toilette /tọaˈlɛtə/ *die;* **~, ~n** [1] toilet; lavatory; **auf die** *od.* **zur ~ gehen** go to the toilet *or* lavatory; **eine öffentliche ~:** a public lavatory *or* convenience [2] (geh.: das Sichzurechtmachen) toilet; **~ machen** make one's toilet [3] (geh.: Aufzug) dress; toilet (arch.); **in großer ~:** in full dress

Toilette- (österr.), **Toiletten-:** **~artikel** *der* toiletry; **~becken** *das* lavatory *or* toilet bowl *or* pan; **~bürste** *die* toilet brush; **~frau** *die,* **~mann** *der* lavatory attendant; **~papier** *das* toilet paper; **~seife** *die* toilet soap; **~sitz** *der* lavatory *or* toilet seat

Tokaier /toˈkaịɐ/ *der;* **~s, ~:** Tokay

Tokio /ˈtoːkịo/ *(das);* **~s** ▸ⓘ **S. 675** Tokyo

Tokioter /toˈkịoːtɐ/ ▸ⓘ **S. 675**
A *der;* **~s, ~:** Tokyoite
B *indekl. Adj.* Tokyo *attrib.*; *s. auch* **Kölner**

Tokioterin *die;* **~, ~nen** ▸**Tokioter A**

Tokkata /tɔˈkaːta/ *die;* **~, Tokkaten** (Musik) toccata

tolerant /toleˈrant/
A *Adj.* tolerant (**gegen** of)
B *adv.* tolerantly

Toleranz *die;* **~, ~en** [1] (auch Med.) tolerance [2] (Technik) tolerance

Toleranz·grenze *die* [1] limit of tolerance [2] (Med.) tolerance level [3] (Technik) tolerance limit

tolerierbar *Adj.* tolerable

tolerieren /toleˈriːrən/ *tr. V.* tolerate

toll /tɔl/
A *Adj.* [1] (ugs.) (großartig) great (coll.); fantastic (coll.); (erstaunlich) amazing; (heftig, groß) enormous ‹*respect*›; terrific (coll.) ‹*noise, storm*› [2] (wild, ausgelassen, übermütig) wild; wild, mad ‹*tricks, antics*›; **die [drei] ~en Tage** the [last three] days of Fasching [3] (ugs.: schlimm, übel) terrible (coll.) [4] (veralt.) ▸**verrückt A 1** [5] (veralt.: ~wütig) rabid
B *adv.* [1] (ugs.: großartig) terrifically well (coll.); **~ hast du das gemacht** you've made a great job of that (coll.) [2] (ugs.: heftig, sehr) ‹*rain, snow*› like billy-o (coll.); **es regnet immer ~er** it's chucking it down harder and harder (coll.) [3] (wild, ausgelassen, übermütig) **bei dem Fest ging es ~ zu** it was a wild party [4] (ugs.: schlimm, übel) **treibt es nicht zu ~:** don't go too mad; **aber es kommt noch ~er** but that's not all

Tolle *die;* **~, ~n** quiff

tollen *itr. V.* [1] romp about [2] *mit sein* romp

Tollerei *die;* **~, ~en** (ugs.) romping about

Toll·haus *das* (veralt.) lunatic asylum (Hist.); **hier geht es ja zu wie in einem ~:** it's like a madhouse here

Tollheit *die;* **~, ~en** (veralt.) ▸**Verrücktheit**

toll-, Toll-: **~kirsche** *die* Atropa; **Schwarze ~kirsche** deadly nightshade; belladonna; **~kühn** **A** *Adj.* daredevil *attrib.*; daring; **B** *adv.* daringly; **~kühnheit** *die* [1] daring; [2] (~kühne Handlung) daredevil *or* daring exploit

Tollpatsch /ˈtɔlpatʃ/ *der;* **~[e]s, ~e** (ugs.) clumsy *or* awkward creature

tollpatschig (ugs.)
A *Adj.* clumsy; awkward
B *adv.* clumsily; awkwardly

toll-, Toll-: **~wut** *die* ▸ⓘ **S. 439** rabies *sing.*; **~wütig** *Adj.* rabid

***Tolpatsch** ▸**Tollpatsch**

***tolpatschig** ▸**tollpatschig**

Tölpel /ˈtœlpḷ/ *der;* **~s, ~** [1] (abwertend; einfältiger Mensch) fool [2] (Zool.) (Gattung Sula) booby; (Gattung Morus) gannet

tölpelhaft (abwertend)
A *Adj.* foolish
B *adv.* foolishly

Tomahawk /ˈtɔmahaːk/ *der;* **~s, ~s** tomahawk

Tomate /toˈmaːtə/ *die;* **~, ~n** tomato; **du hast wohl ~n auf den Augen!** (salopp) you must be blind!; **er wurde rot wie eine ~** (ugs. scherzh.) he turned *or* went as red as a beetroot; **du [bist vielleicht eine] treulose ~** (ugs. scherzh.) a fine friend you are

Tomaten- tomato ‹*juice, salad, sauce, soup, etc.*›

Tomaten·mark *das* tomato purée

tomaten·rot *Adj.* brilliant red

Tombola /ˈtɔmbola/ *die;* **~, ~s** *od.* **Tombolen** raffle

Tommy /ˈtɔmi/ *der;* **~s, ~s** (ugs.: Engländer) Tommy

Tomographie /tomograˈfiː/ *die;* **~** (Med.) tomography *no art.*

Ton¹ /toːn/ *der;* **~[e]s, ~e** clay

Ton² *der;* **~[e]s, Töne** /ˈtøːnə/ [1] (auch Physik, Musik; beim Telefon) tone; (Klang) note; **der ~ macht die Musik** (fig. ugs.) it's not what you say but the way that you say it; **den ~ angeben** (Musik) give the note; (fig.) (in der Mode, Kunst usw.) set the tone; (in einer Gruppe o. Ä.) have the most *or* greatest say; **jmdn./etw. in den höchsten Tönen loben** praise sb./sth. to the skies [2] (Film, Ferns. usw., ~wiedergabe) sound; **~ ab!** turn over sound!; **~ läuft** sound running [3] (Sprechweise, Umgangs~) tone; **den richtigen ~ finden** strike the right note; **ich verbitte mir diesen ~!** I will not be spoken to like that!; **sich im ~ vergreifen** adopt the wrong tone; strike the wrong note; **einen unverschämten/frechen** *usw.* **~ anschlagen** adopt an impudent/a cheeky tone; **der gute ~:** good form; **das gehört zum guten ~:** it is considered good form; **hier gehört es zum guten ~, ... zu ...** (iron.) here it's the done thing to ... (coll.) [4] (ugs.: Äußerung) word; **ich möchte keinen ~ mehr hören** I don't want to hear another word; **er konnte keinen ~ herausbringen** he couldn't say a word; **hast du/hat der Mensch [da noch] Töne?** that's just unbelievable; **große Töne reden** *od.* **spucken** (ugs.) talk big [5] (Farb~) shade; tone; **~ in ~ gehalten** colour coordinated [6] (Akzent) stress [7] (Sprachw.: ~höhe) tone

Ton·abnehmer *der;* **~s, ~:** pick-up

tonal /toˈnaːl/ *Adj.* (Musik) tonal

Tonalität /tonaliˈtɛːt/ *die;* **~** (Musik) tonality

ton-, Ton-: **~angebend** *Adj.* predominant; **~angebend sein** (in der Mode, Kunst usw.) set the tone; (in einer Gruppe o. Ä.) have the most *or* greatest say; **~arm** *der* pick-up arm; **~art** *die* [1] (Musik) key; [2] (fig.) tone; **eine andere/schärfere** *usw.* **~art anschlagen** take a stronger *or* tougher line; **~aufnahme** *die* [sound] recording

Tonband *das; Pl.* **~bänder** [1] tape [2] (ugs.: Gerät) tape recorder

Ton·band-: **~aufnahme** *die* tape recording; **~gerät** *das* tape recorder; **~protokoll** *das* tape transcript

Ton-: **~blende** *die* (Rundf., Ferns.) tone control; **~dichtung** *die* tone poem

tonen *tr. V.* (Fot.) tone

tönen /ˈtøːnən/
A *itr. V.* [1] (geh.) sound; ‹*bell*› sound, ring; (schallen, widerhallen) resound; **mit ~der Stimme** in a resounding voice; **~de Worte/Phrasen** empty words/phrases [2] (ugs. abwertend) boast
B *tr. V.* (färben) tint

Ton·erde *die* ▸**essigsauer**

tönern /ˈtøːnɐn/ *Adj.* clay; *s. auch* **Fuß 3**

Ton-: **~fall** *der* tone; (Intonation) intonation; **~film** *der* sound film; talkie (coll.); **~folge** *die* sequence of notes; **~frequenz** *die* (Akustik) sound frequency; audio frequency; **~gefäß** *das* earthen[ware] vessel; **~geschlecht** *das* (Musik) scale; **~höhe** *die* pitch

Toni ▸**Tonus**

Tonic /ˈtɔnɪk/ *das;* **~[s], ~s** tonic [water]

Tonika¹ ▸**Tonikum**

Tonika² /ˈtoːnika/ *die;* **~, Toniken** (Musik) tonic

Tonika-Do *das;* **~** (Musik) Tonika-Doh [method]

Tonikum /ˈtoːnikʊm/ *das;* **~s, Tonika** tonic

Ton·ingenieur *der,* **Ton·ingenieurin** *die* sound engineer

tonisch *Adj.* (Physiol.) tonic

ton-, Ton-: **~kopf** *der* head; **~krug** *der* earthenware jug; (für Blumen) earthenware pot; **~kunst** *die* (geh.) music; **~künstler** *der,* **~künstlerin** *die* (geh.) composer; **~lage** *die* (Musik) pitch; **~leiter** *die* (Musik) scale; **~los** **A** *Adj.* toneless; **B** *adv.* tonelessly; **~meister** *der,* **~meisterin** *die* sound engineer, recording engineer

Tonnage /tɔˈnaːʒə/ *die;* **~, ~n** (Seew.) tonnage

Tönnchen /ˈtœnçən/ *das;* **~s, ~** (ugs.: dicker Mensch) dumpling (coll.)

Tonne /ˈtɔnə/ *die;* **~, ~n** [1] (Behälter) drum; (Müll~) bin; (Regen~) water butt [2] ▸ⓘ **S. 315** (Gewicht) tonne; metric ton [3] (ugs.: dicker Mensch) fatty (coll.) [4] (Seew.) buoy

Tonnen·gewölbe *das* (Archit.) barrel *or* tunnel vault

tonnen·schwer
A *Adj.* weighing tons *postpos.*; (kolossal schwer) enormously heavy; **~ sein** weigh tons; be enormously heavy.
B *adv.* **~ lasten auf** (+ *Dat.*) be an enormous weight on

tonnen·weise
A *Adv.* by the tonne *or* metric ton; (in großer Menge) by the ton; **ich habe das Zeug ~:** I've got tons of the stuff (coll.)
B *adj.* by the ton *postpos.*

Ton-: **~pfeife** *die* clay pipe; **~scherbe** *die* potsherd; **~setzer** *der,* **~setzerin** *die* (veralt.) composer; **~spur** *die* soundtrack; **~störung** *die* (Rundf., Film, Ferns.) sound interference; (durch Geräteschaden usw.) fault on sound; **~studio** *das* recording studio; (Film, Ferns.) sound studio; **~stufe** *die* (Musik) note

Tonsur /tɔnˈzuːɐ̯/ *die;* **~, ~en** tonsure

Ton-: **~system** *das* (Musik) tone *or* tonic system; **~tafel** *die* clay tablet; **~taubenschießen** *das;* **~~s** clay-pigeon shooting *no art.*; **~techniker** *der,* **~technikerin** *die* (Rundf., Ferns., Film) sound technician; **~träger** *der* sound[-recording and] storage medium; **~umfang** *der* (Musik) register; range

Tönung *die;* **~, ~en** [1] (das Tönen) tinting [2] (Farbton) tint; shade

Tonus /ˈtoːnʊs/ *der;* **~, Toni** (Physiol.) tone

Ton·wahl *das* tone dialling

Ton·waren *Pl.* earthenware *sing.*

Tool /tuːl/ *das;* **~s, ~s** (DV) tool

top- ultra ‹*modern, topical*›

Top /tɔp/ *das;* **~s, ~s** (Mode) top

Top- top; outstanding ‹*location, performance, time*›

top-, Top-: **~adresse** *die* top address; **~aktuell** **A** *Adj.* [1] up-to-the-minute ‹*news, information etc.*›; ultra-topical ‹*subject*›; [2] (sehr modisch) latest *attrib.*; hot (coll.). **B** *adv.* [1] in up-to-the-minute form; **jmdn. ~ informieren** keep sb. right up-to-date; [2] (sehr modisch) in the latest fashion

Topas /toˈpaːs/ *der;* **~es, ~e** topaz

Top-: **~athlet** *der,* **~athletin** *die* top athlete; **~ereignis** *das* top event; **ein internationales/gesellschaftliches ~ereignis** a top international/social event

Topf /tɔpf/ *der;* **~es, Töpfe** /'tœpfə/ 1 pot; (Braten~, Schmor~) casserole; (Stielkasserolle) saucepan; **alles in einen ~ werfen** (fig. ugs.) lump everything together 2 (zur Aufbewahrung) pot; jar 3 (Krug) jug 4 (Nacht~) chamber pot; po (coll.); (für Kinder) potty (Brit. coll.) 5 (Blumen~) [flower]pot 6 (salopp: Toilette) loo (Brit. coll.); john (Amer. coll.)

Top·favorit *der,* **Top·favoritin** *die* (Sport) hot favourite

Topf·blume *die* [flowering] pot plant

Töpfchen /'tœpfçən/ *das;* **~s, ~** ▸**Topf 1-4**: [small] pot/saucepan/jug *etc.;* (Nachttopf) po (coll.); (für Kinder) potty (Brit. coll.)

Topfen *der;* **~s** (bayr., österr.) ▸**Quark**[1] **1**

Töpfer /'tœpfɐ/ *der;* **~s, ~** ▸❶ **S. 113** potter

Töpferei *die;* **~, ~en** 1 (Handwerk) pottery *no art.* 2 (Werkstatt) pottery; potter's workshop 3 (Erzeugnis) piece of pottery; **~en** pottery *sing.*

Töpferin *die;* **~, ~nen** ▸❶ **S. 113** potter

töpfern

A *itr. V.* do pottery

B *tr. V.* make ‹*vase, jug, etc.*›; **getöpferte Teller** handmade pottery plates

Töpfer-: **~scheibe** *die* potter's wheel; **~ware** *die* pottery *no pl.;* **~waren** pottery *sing.*

Topf·gucker *der;* **~s, ~, Topf·guckerin** *die;* **~, ~nen** (scherzh.) *Nosy Parker who looks into all the pots and saucepans to see what's cooking*

top·fit *Adj.* in *or* on top form *postpos.* (gesundheitlich) in fine fettle; as fit as a fiddle; **jetzt ist der Wagen wieder ~:** the car is in perfect order again now

Topf-: **~kuchen** *der* ▸**Napfkuchen**; **~lappen** *der* oven cloth

Top·form *die* (bes. Sport) top form; **in ~:** in *or* on top form

Topf-: **~pflanze** *die* pot plant; **~reiniger** *der* [pot] scourer; scouring pad

Top-: **~frau** *die* top woman; **~hit** *der* (ugs.) smash hit (coll.)

Topinambur /topinam'bu:ɐ/ *der;* **~s, ~s** *od.* **~e** *od. die;* **~, ~en** Jerusalem artichoke

top-, Top-: **~job** *der* top job; **~klub** *der* (Sport) top club; **~lage** *die* top location; **~leistung** *die* (Sport) outstanding performance; **~leute** *Pl.* top people; **~-Level-Domain** /-lɛvl̩domeɪn/ *die;* **~~, ~~s** *od. das;* **~~s, ~~s** (DV) top-level domain; **~management** *das* top management; **~manager** *der,* **~managerin** *die* top manager; **~mann** *der* top man; **~model** *das* top model; **~modern** A *Adj.* ultramodern; state-of-the-art ‹*PC etc.*›; (sehr modisch) really hip (coll.); B *adv.* ‹*furnished*› in ultramodern style; (sehr modisch) according to the latest fashion; ‹*equipped*› with all the latest gadgetry; ‹*produced*› by cutting-edge *or* state-of-the-art technology

Topographie /topogra'fi:/ *die;* **~, ~n** (Geogr.) topography *no art.*

topographisch (Geogr.)

A *Adj.* topographic[al]

B *adv.* topographically

Topologie /topolo'gi:/ *die;* **~** (Math.) topology *no art.*

topologisch (Math.) *Adj.* topological

Topos /'tɔpɔs/ *der;* **~, Topoi** /'tɔpɔy/ 1 (Literaturw.) topos 2 (geh.: Gemeinplatz) commonplace

topp /tɔp/ *Interj.* (veralt.) done! agreed!

Topp *der;* **~s, ~e[n]** *od.* **~s** (Seemannsspr.) masthead; **das Schiff war über die ~en geflaggt** the ship was dressed overall

Top·position *die* top position

Topp·segel *das* (Seew.) topsail

Top·qualität *die* top quality; **Lederbekleidung in ~:** top-quality leather clothing

Top-: **~scorer** *der,* **~scorerin** *die* (Sport) top scorer; **~spiel** *das* (Sport) top game; **~spieler** *der,* **~spielerin** *die* (Sport) top player; **~spin** /'tɔpspɪn/ *der;* **~~s, ~~s** (bes. Golf, Tennis, Tischtennis) top spin; **~star** *der* top star; **~ten** /-'tɛn/ *die;* **~~, ~~s** top ten; **~terrorist** *der,* **~terroristin** *die* top terrorist; **~verdiener** *der,* **~verdienerin** *die* top earner; highest earner; **~zustand** *der* top condition

Tor[1] /to:ɐ/ *das;* **~[e]s, ~e** 1 gate; (einer Garage, Scheune) door; (fig.) gateway; **vor den ~en der Stadt** just outside the town; *s. auch* **dastehen** 2 (Ballspiele) goal; **mit 3:2 ~en gewinnen** *od.* **siegen** win 3-2 *or* by three goals to two; **im ~ stehen** be in goal 3 (Ski) gate

Tor[2] *der;* **~en, ~en** (geh.: Narr) fool

Tor-: **~aus** *das* (Ballspiele) **der Ball ging ins ~aus** the ball went over the byline *or* went behind; **~bogen** *der* arch[way]

Torero /to're:ro/ *der;* **~[s], ~s** torero

Tores·schluss, *Tores·schluß *der:* in **kurz vor ~** (ugs.) at the last minute *or* the eleventh hour

Torf /tɔrf/ *der;* **~[e]s, ~e** peat

Torf-: **~ballen** *der* bale of peat; **~moor** *das* peat bog; **~mull** *der* [loose] garden peat

Tor·frau *die* (Ballspiele) goalkeeper

Torheit *die;* **~, ~en** (geh.) 1 foolishness 2 (Handlung) foolish act; **eine [große] ~ begehen** do something [extremely] foolish

Tor·hüter *der,* **Tor·hüterin** *die* (Ballspiele) goalkeeper

töricht /'tø:rɪçt/ (geh.)

A *Adj.* foolish ‹*behaviour, action, hope*›; stupid ‹*person, question, smile, face*›

B *adv.* ‹*behave, act*› foolishly; ‹*smile, ask*› stupidly

törichterweise *Adv.* (geh.) foolishly

Törin /'tø:rɪn/ *die;* **~, ~nen** fool

Tor·jäger *der,* **Tor·jägerin** *die* (Ballspiele) goal scorer

torkeln /'tɔrkl̩n/ *itr. V.; mit sein* stagger; reel

tor-, Tor-: **~linie** *die* (Ballspiele) [goal-]line; **~los** *Adj.* (Ballspiele) goalless; **~mann** *der; Pl.* **~männer** *od.* **~leute** (Ballspiele) goalkeeper

Törn /tœrn/ *der;* **~s, ~s** (Seemannsspr.) trip

Tornado /tɔr'na:do/ *der;* **~s, ~s** tornado

Tornister /tɔr'nɪstɐ/ *der;* **~s, ~** 1 knapsack 2 (Schulranzen) satchel

torpedieren /tɔrpe'di:rən/ *tr. V.* (Milit., fig.) torpedo

Torpedierung *die;* **~, ~en** (Milit., fig.) torpedoing

Torpedo /tɔr'pe:do/ *der;* **~s, ~s** torpedo

Torpedo·boot *das* torpedo boat

Tor-: **~pfosten** *der* (Ballspiele) [goal]post; **~raum** *der* (Ballspiele) goal area; ***~schluß, ~schluss** *der* ▸**Toresschluss**; **~schluss·panik, *~schluß·panik** *die* last-minute panic; (Furcht, keinen Partner mehr zu finden) fear of being left on the shelf; **~schlusspanik haben** *od.* **bekommen** *od.* **kriegen** panic at the last minute/be frightened of being left on the shelf; **~schuss, *~schuß** *der* (Ballspiele) shot [at goal]; **~schütze** *der,* **~schützin** *die* (Ballspiele) [goal] scorer

Torsi ▸**Torso**

Torsion /tɔr'zi̯o:n/ *die;* **~, ~en** (Physik, Technik, Math.) torsion

Torso /'tɔrzo/ *der;* **~s, ~s** *od.* **Torsi** (Kunstwiss., auch fig. geh.) torso

Tort /tɔrt/ *der;* **~[e]s** (ugs. veralt.) wrong; injury; **jmdm. einen ~ antun** do sb. wrong; **jmdm. etw. zum ~ tun** do sth. to spite sb.

Törtchen /'tœrtçən/ *das;* **~s, ~:** tartlet

Torte /'tɔrtə/ *die;* **~, ~n** (Creme~, Sahne~) gateau; (Obst~) [fruit] flan

Tortelett /tɔrtə'lɛt/ *das;* **~s, ~s, Tortelette** *die;* **~e, ~en** tartlet

Torten-: **~boden** *der* flan case; (ohne Rand) flan base; * **~guß, ~guss** *der* glaze; **~heber** *der* cake slice; **~platte** *die* cake plate; **~schaufel** *die* ▸**~heber**

Tortur /tɔr'tu:ɐ/ *die;* **~, ~en** 1 ordeal 2 (veralt.: Folter) torture

Tor-: **~verhältnis** *das* (Ballspiele) goal average; **~wächter** *der,* **~wächterin** *die* 1 gatekeeper; 2 (Ballspiele) goalkeeper; **~wart** *der;* **~~s, ~~e, ~wartin** *die;* **~~, ~~nen** (Ballspiele) goalkeeper; **~weg** *der* gateway

tosen /'to:zn̩/ *itr. V.; mit Richtungsangabe mit sein* ‹*sea, surf*› roar, rage; ‹*storm*› rage; ‹*torrent, waterfall*› roar, thunder; ‹*wind*› roar; **~der Lärm/Beifall** (fig.) thunderous noise/applause

Toskana /tɔs'ka:na/ *die;* **~:** Tuscany

tot /to:t/ *Adj.* 1 dead; **das Kind wurde ~ geboren** the baby was stillborn; **ein ~ geborenes Kind** a stillborn child; **das Projekt war ein ~ geborenes Kind** (fig.) the project was stillborn *or* did not get off the ground; **er war auf der Stelle ~:** he died instantly; **~ zusammenbrechen** collapse and die; **~ umfallen** drop dead; **ich will auf der Stelle ~ umfallen, wenn das nicht wahr ist** may I be struck down if it isn't true; **sich ~ stellen** pretend to be dead; play dead; **er ist [politisch] ein ~er Mann** (fig.) he is finished [as a politician]; **er ist ein ~er Mann** he is a dead man *or* (coll.) a goner; **halb ~ vor Angst/Schrecken** *usw.* (ugs.) paralysed with fear/shock; **den ~en Mann machen** (ugs.) float on one's back 2 (abgestorben) dead ‹*tree, branch, leaves, etc.*› 3 (fig.) dull ‹*colour*›; bleak ‹*region etc.*›; dead ‹*town, telephone line, socket, language*›; disused ‹*railway line*›; extinct ‹*volcano*›; dead, quiet ‹*time, period*›; useless ‹*knowledge*›; **ein ~er Flussarm** a backwater; (Schleife) an oxbow lake; **das Tote Meer** the Dead Sea; *s. auch* **Briefkasten 2; Hose 2; Punkt 4; Winkel 1**

total /to'ta:l/

A *Adj.* total

B *adv.* totally

Total·ausverkauf *der* clearance sale

Totale *die;* **~, ~n** *od. adj. Dekl.* complete view; (Film) long shot

Totalisator /totali'za:tɔr/ *der;* **~s, ~en** /-za'to:rən/ totalizator; tote (coll.)

totalitär /totali'tɛ:ɐ/ (Politik)

A *Adj.* totalitarian

B *adv.* in a totalitarian way; ‹*organized, run*› along totalitarian lines

Totalitarismus /totalita'rɪsmʊs/ *der;* **~** (Politik) totalitarianism *no art.*

totalitaristisch ▸**totalitär**

Totalität /totali'tɛ:t/ *die;* **~, ~en** (geh.) totality

Total-: **~operation** *die* (Med.) extirpation; (Gynäkologie) hysterectomy; **~schaden** *der* (Versicherungsw.) **an beiden Fahrzeugen entstand ~schaden** both vehicles were a write-off; **~verlust** *der* total loss

tot-: **~|arbeiten** *refl. V.* (ugs.) work oneself to death; **~|ärgern** *refl. V.* (ugs.) get livid (coll.); **ich könnte mich ~ärgern** I'm livid (coll.) *or* really furious

Tote /'to:tə/ *der/die; adj. Dekl.* dead person; dead man/woman; **die ~n** the dead; **es gab zwei ~:** two people died *or* were killed; there were two fatalities; **wie ein ~r schlafen** sleep like a log; **na, bist du von den ~n auferstanden?** (ugs. scherzh.) oh, you're back in the land of the living, are you?; **die ~n soll man ruhen lassen** (ugs.) let the dead rest in peace

Totem /'to:tɛm/ *das;* **~s, ~s** (Völkerk.) totem

Totem·pfahl *der* totem pole

töten /'tø:tn̩/ *tr., itr. V.* kill; deaden ‹*nerve etc.*›; **einen kranken Hund ~ lassen** have a sick dog put down; *s. auch* **Blick 1; Nerv 1**

toten-, Toten-: **~acker** *der* (veralt.) graveyard; **~ähnlich** *Adj.* deathlike ‹*sleep*›; **~amt** *das* (kath. Kirche) ▸**~messe**; **~bahre** *die* bier; **~bett** *das* deathbed; **~blass, *~blaß, ~bleich** *Adj.* deathly pale; pale as death *postpos.;* **~feier** *die* memorial service; **~glocke** *die* death knell; **~gräber** *der;* **~~s, ~~** ▸❶ **S. 113** 1 gravedigger; 2 (Zool.) burying beetle; sexton beetle; **~hemd** *das* shroud; **~klage** *die* 1 lamentation *or* bewailing of the dead; 2 (Literaturw.) lament; dirge; **~kopf** *der* 1 skull; 2 (als Symbol) death's head; (mit gekreuzten Knochen) skull and crossbones; **~kult** *der* (Völkerk.) cult

t

of the dead; **~maske** *die* death mask; **~messe** *die* (kath. Kirche) requiem [mass]; **~reich** *das* kingdom of the dead; **~schädel** *der* skull; **~schein** *der* death certificate; **~sonntag** *der:* (ev. Kirche) *Sunday before Advent on which the dead are commemorated;* **~starre** *die* rigor mortis; **~still** *Adj.* deathly quiet *or* silent; **~stille** *die* deathly quiet *or* silence; **~tanz** *der* (bild. Kunst) Dance of Death; **~wache** *die* vigil by the body; **die ~wache halten** keep vigil by the body

tot-, Tot-: **~|fahren** **A** *unr. tr. V.* [run over and] kill; **B** *unr. refl. V.* kill oneself; **~geboren** ▸**tot 1**; **~geburt** *die* [1] still birth; [2] (Kind) still birth; stillborn baby; **ihr erstes Kind war eine ~geburt** her first child was stillborn; **~geglaubte** *der/die; adj. Dekl.* person believed dead; **~gesagte** *der/die; adj. Dekl.* person declared dead; **~holz** *das* dead wood (also fig.); (Bäume) dead timber; **~|kriegen** *tr. V.* (ugs.) kill; kill, get rid of ‹*insect pests, weeds, etc.*›; **er/dieser Mantel ist nicht ~zukriegen** (fig.) he's irrepressible/this coat just never wears out; **~|lachen** *refl. V.* (ugs.) kill oneself laughing; **zum ~lachen sein** be killing (coll.); be killingly funny (coll.); **~|laufen** *unr. refl. V.* (ugs.) ‹*movement, trend, fashion*› peter *or* die out; ‹*talks, discussions*› peter out; **~|machen** *tr. V.* (ugs.) kill

Toto /'to:to:/ *das od. der;* **~s, ~s** [1] (Pferde~) tote (coll.); **im ~:** on the tote [2] (Fußball~) [football] pools *pl.;* **[im] ~ spielen** do the pools

Toto-: **~gewinn** *der* win on the pools/(coll.) tote; **~schein** *der* pools coupon/(coll.) tote ticket

tot-, Tot-: **~|reden** *tr. V.* (ugs.) [1] (beseitigen) talk down [and destroy]; [2] (mundtot machen) **jmdn. ~reden** talk sb. into the ground; silence sb. with a torrent of words; **~|sagen** *tr. V.* declare ‹*person*› dead; **eine Partei** *usw.* **~sagen** (fig.) say a party *etc.* is dead *or* finished; **~|schießen** *unr. tr. V.* (ugs.) **jmdn. ~schießen** shoot sb. dead; **~schlag** *der* (Rechtsw.) manslaughter *no indef. art.;* **~schlag·argument** *das* (ugs. abwertend) killer argument; **~|schlagen** *unr. tr. V.* beat to death; **und wenn du mich ~schlägst** for the life of me; **eher/lieber lasse ich mich ~schlagen** (ugs.) I'd rather die *or* be dead; **die Zeit ~schlagen** kill time; **~schläger** *der* [1] (Mensch) manslaughterer; [2] (Waffe) cosh (Brit. coll.); blackjack (Amer.); **~schlägerin** *die* ▸**schläger 1**; **~|schweigen** *unr. tr. V.* hush up; **jmdn. ~schweigen** keep quiet about sb.; ***~|stellen** ▸**tot 1**; **~|treten** *unr. tr. V.* trample ‹*person*› to death; step on and kill ‹*insect*›

Tötung *die;* **~, ~en** killing; **fahrlässige ~** (Rechtsspr.) manslaughter by culpable negligence

Tötungs-: **~absicht** *die* (Rechtsw.) intent *or* intention to kill; **~versuch** *der* (Rechtsw.) attempted murder

Touch /tatʃ/ *der;* **~s, ~s** (ugs.) touch

Toupet /tu'pe:/ *das;* **~s, ~s** toupee

toupieren /tu'pi:rən/ *tr. V.* backcomb

Tour /tu:ɐ̯/ *die;* **~, ~en** [1] tour (**durch** of); (Kletter~) [climbing] trip; (kürzere Fahrt, Ausflug) trip; (mit dem Auto) drive; (mit dem Fahrrad) ride; (Zech~) pub crawl (Brit. coll.); **eine ~ machen** go on a tour/trip *or* outing; (Zech~) go on a pub crawl (Brit. coll.); barhop (Amer.); **das ist 'ne ganz schöne ~** (ugs.) it's a fair *or* (Brit. coll.) fair old way [2] (feste Strecke) route; **die ~ Hamburg-Neapel** the run from Hamburg to Naples [3] (Tournee) tour; **auf ~ gehen** go on tour; **eine ~ durch Europa** a European tour [4] (ugs.: Methode) ploy; **die ~ zieht bei mir nicht** that [one] won't work with me; **etw. auf die sanfte/gemütliche ~ machen** get sth. by soft-soaping/take one's time doing sth.; **seine ~ kriegen/haben** (ugs.) get/be in one of one's moods; *s. auch* **krumm A 2** [5] (ugs.: Unternehmen) plan; **jmdm. die ~ vermasseln** (ugs.) put paid to sb.'s [little] plans [6] (Technik: Umdrehung) revolution; rev (coll.); **die Maschine kam schnell auf ~en** the machine/engine was soon running at full speed; **jmdn. auf ~en bringen** (ugs.) really get sb. going; (jmdn. böse machen) get sb. worked up; **auf vollen/höchsten ~en laufen** (ugs.) ‹*production, preparations, work, etc.*› be in full swing [7] *in* **in einer ~** (ugs.) the whole time

touren /'tu:rən/ *itr. V.* (Jargon) tour; **durch die Stadt ~:** tour the town

Touren-: **~rad** *das* roadster; **~ski** *der* touring ski; **~wagen** *der* (Motorsport) touring car; **~zahl** *die* (Technik) number of revolutions *or* (coll.) revs

Touri /'tu:ri/ *der;* **~s, ~s** (ugs. meist abwertend) tourist

Tourismus /tu'rɪsmʊs/ *der;* **~:** tourism *no art.*

Tourismus-: **~branche** *die* tourist trade; **~industrie** *die,* **~wirtschaft** *die* tourist industry

Tourist *der;* **~en, ~en** tourist

Touristen-: **~klasse** *die* tourist class; **~paradies** *das* tourist paradise; **~strom** *der* stream of tourists; **~visum** *das* tourist visa

Touristik *die;* **~:** tourism *no art.;* tourist industry *or* business

Touristin *die;* **~, ~nen** tourist

touristisch
A *Adj.* tourist *attrib*
B *adv.* **das Land ist ~ noch kaum erschlossen** the country is still scarcely developed as a tourist area

Tournedos /tʊrnə'do:/ *das;* **~** /tʊrnə'do:(s)/, **~s** tournedos

-tournee *die* … tour; **auf Europa~/Deutschland~:** on a European/German tour

Tournee /tʊr'ne:/ *die;* **~, ~s** *od.* **~n** /tʊr'ne:ən/ tour; **auf ~ sein/gehen** be/go on tour

Tower /'taʊɐ/ *der;* **~[s], ~s** (Flugw.) [control] tower

toxisch /'tɔksɪʃ/ *Adj.* toxic

Trab /tra:p/ *der;* **~[e]s** trot; **im ~:** at a trot; **im ~ reiten** trot; **in [den] ~ fallen** drop into a trot; **sich in ~ setzen** (ugs.) get going; get a move on (coll.); **jmdn. auf ~ bringen** (ugs.) make sb. get a move on; **jmdn. in ~ halten** (ugs.) keep sb. on the go (coll.)

Trabant /tra'bant/ *der;* **~en, ~en** [1] (Astron.) satellite [2] *Pl.* (fam. scherzh. veraltt.: Kinder) kids (coll.)

> **Trabant**
>
> A make of car produced in the former GDR. A *Trabant* or *Trabi* with its two-stroke engine and plastic body was a prized possession, and people had to wait for years to get one. After reunification, the *Trabant* came to symbolize the GDR era and has achieved cult status in Germany.

Trabanten·stadt *die* satellite town

traben *itr. V.; mit sein* (auch ugs.: laufen) trot

Traber *der;* **~s, ~:** trotter

Trab·rennen *das* trotting; (einzelne Veranstaltung) trotting race

Tracht /traxt/ *die;* **~, ~en** [1] (Volks~) traditional *or* national costume; (Berufs~) uniform; **die ~ der Nonnen** the nuns' dress *or* habit [2] *in* **eine ~ Prügel** a beating *or* thrashing; (als Strafe für ein Kind) a hiding [3] (Imkerei) yield

trachten *itr. V.* (geh.) strive (**nach** for, after); **all sein** *od.* **sein ganzes Trachten** all his striving *or* endeavours; *s. auch* **Leben 1**

Trachten-: **~anzug** *der: suit in the style of a traditional or national costume;* **~fest** *das: festival at which traditional or national costume is worn;* **~janker** *der* traditional Alpine jacket; **~kapelle** *die: band in traditional or national costume;* **~umzug** *der* procession in national *or* traditional costume

trächtig /'trɛçtɪç/ pregnant

Trächtigkeit *die;* **~, ~en** pregnancy

Track /trɛk/ *der;* **~s, ~s** (Jargon) track

Trader /'treɪdɐ/ *der;* **~s, ~,** **Traderin** *die;* **~, ~nen** (Börsenw.) trader

tradieren /tra'di:rən/ *tr. V.* (geh.) hand down, pass on ‹*ideas, customs, values, etc.*›

Tradierung *die;* **~, ~en** handing down

Tradition /tradi'tsjo:n/ *die;* **~, ~en** tradition; **~ sein/haben** be a tradition

Traditionalismus /traditsjona'lɪsmʊs/ *der;* **~** (geh.) traditionalism *no art.*

Traditionalist *der;* **~en, ~en, Traditionalistin** *die;* **~, ~nen** (geh.) traditionalist

traditionell /traditsjo'nɛl/
A *Adj.* traditional
B *adv.* traditionally

traditions-, Traditions-: **~bewusst, *~bewußt** **A** *Adj.* tradition-conscious; conscious of tradition *postpos.;* **B** *adv.* in a tradition-conscious way; **~marke** *die* traditional brand; (Auto) traditional make; **~reich** *Adj.* rich in tradition *postpos.*

traf /tra:f/ *1. u. 3. Pers. Sg. Prät. v.* **treffen**

träfe /'trɛ:fə/ *1. u. 3. Pers. Sg. Konjunktiv II v.* **treffen**

Trafik /tra'fɪk/ *die;* **~, ~en** (österr.) tobacconist's [shop]

Trafikant /trafi'kant/ *der;* **~en, ~en, Trafikantin** *die;* **~, ~nen** (österr.) tobacconist

Trafo /'tra:fo/ *der;* **~s, ~s** transformer

träg /trɛ:k/ ▸**träge**

Trag·bahre *die* stretcher

tragbar *Adj.* [1] portable [2] wearable ‹*clothes*› [3] (finanziell) supportable ‹*cost, debt, etc.*› [4] (erträglich, tolerierbar) bearable; tolerable; **er ist für die Partei nicht mehr ~:** the party can no longer tolerate him

träge /'trɛ:gə/
A *Adj.* [1] sluggish; (geistig) lethargic [2] (Physik) inert
B *adv.* ▸**träge A**: sluggishly; lethargically

Trage *die;* **~, ~n** [1] (Bahre) stretcher [2] (Traggestell) pannier

Trage·korb *der* pannier

tragen /tra:gn̩/
A *unr. tr. V.* [1] carry; **das Auto wurde aus der Kurve ge~** (fig.) the car went off the bend [2] (bringen) take; **vom Wasser/Wind ge~** (fig.) carried by water/[the] wind [3] (er~) bear ‹*fate, destiny*›; bear, endure ‹*suffering*› [4] (halten) hold; **einen/den linken Arm in der Schlinge ~:** have one's arm/one's left arm in a sling [5] (von unten stützen) support; **die Schwimmweste trägt dich** the life jacket will hold you up; **zum Tragen kommen** ‹*advantage, improvement, quality*› become noticeable; **ein solcher Boykott kann nur zum Tragen kommen, wenn …** such a boycott can be effective only if …; *s. auch* **tragend B 1-3** [6] (belastbar sein durch) be able to carry *or* take ‹*weight*›; **der Ast trägt dich nicht** the branch won't take your weight [7] (übernehmen, aufkommen für) bear, carry ‹*costs etc.*›; take ‹*blame, responsibility, consequences*›; (unterhalten, finanzieren) support; maintain, support ‹*school*›; **er trägt die Schuld** he is to blame; **die Versicherung trägt den Schaden** the insurance will pay for the damage; **die Organisation trägt sich selbst** the organization is self-supporting [8] (am Körper) wear ‹*clothes, wig, glasses, jewellery, etc.*›; have ‹*false teeth, beard, etc.*›; **man trägt [wieder] Hüte** hats are in fashion [again]; **getragene Kleider** second-hand clothes [9] (fig.: haben) have ‹*label etc.*›; have, bear ‹*title*›; bear, carry ‹*signature, inscription, seal*› [10] (hervorbringen) ‹*tree*› bear ‹*fruit*›; ‹*field*› produce ‹*crops*›; (fig.) yield ‹*interest*›; **gut/wenig ~** ‹*tree*› produce a good/poor crop; ‹*field*› produce a good/poor yield [11] (geh.: schwanger sein mit) be carrying; *s. auch* **Bedenken 2**; **getragen B, C**; **Sorge 3**
B *unr. itr. V.* [1] carry; **wir hatten schwer zu ~:** we were heavily laden; **schwer an etw.** (*Dat.*) **zu ~ haben** have difficulty carrying sth.; find sth. very heavy to carry; (fig.) find sth. hard to bear; **das Eis trägt noch nicht** the ice is not yet thick enough to skate/walk *etc.* on [2] (am Körper) **man trägt [wieder] kurz/lang** short/long skirts are in fashion [again] [3] **der Baum trägt gut** the tree produces a good crop; (in diesem Sommer) the tree has a lot of fruit on it [4] (trächtig sein) be carrying young; **eine ~de Sau/Kuh** a pregnant sow/cow [5] ([weit] reichen) ‹*voice*› carry; *s. auch* **tragend B 4**
C *unr. refl. V.* [1] **sich gut/schlecht** *usw.* **~** ‹*load*›

t

be easy/difficult *or* hard *etc.* to carry; **zu zweit trägt sich der Korb besser** two can carry the basket more easily **2** **der Mantel/Stoff trägt sich angenehm** the coat/material is pleasant to wear **3** *in* **sich mit etw. ~:** be contemplating sth.; **er trägt sich mit dem Gedanken** *od.* **der Absicht, auszuwandern** he is contemplating [the idea of] emigrating **4** (sich kleiden) dress

tragend
A *1. Part. von* **tragen**
B *Adj.* **1** (Stabilität gebend) load-bearing; supporting ‹*wall, column, function, etc.*› **2** (fig.: grundlegend) basic, main ‹*idea, motif*› **3** (fig.: wichtig, zentral) leading, major ‹*role, figure*› **4** (weithin hörbar) ‹*voice*› that carries [a long way]

Träger /ˈtrɛːgɐ/ *der;* **~s, ~** **1** porter; (Sänften~, Sarg~) bearer **2** (Zeitungs~) paper boy/girl; delivery boy/girl **3** (Bauw.) girder; [supporting] beam **4** (an Kleidung) strap; (Hosen~) braces *pl.* **5** (Inhaber) (eines Amts) holder; (eines Namens, Titels)bearer; (eines Preises) winner **6** (fig.: Urheber, treibende Kraft) moving force **7** (fig.: Unterhalter) **die Schule hat einen privaten ~:** the school is privately maintained; **~ der Arbeitslosenversicherung ist der Staat** unemployment insurance is financed *or* funded by the state **8** (fig.: einer Substanz, eines Erregers usw.) carrier **9** (Flugzeug~) carrier **10** (jmd., der etw. als Kleidung, Schmuck usw. trägt) wearer

Trägerin *die;* **~, ~nen** ▸**Träger 1, 2, 5, 6, 7, 8, 10**

träger-, Träger-: ~kleid *das* pinafore dress; **~los** *Adj.* strapless; **~rakete** *die* carrier vehicle *or* rocket; **~rock** *der* skirt with straps

Trägerschaft *die;* **~, ~en** (einer Schule) maintenance; **in freier ~ sein** be privately maintained

Trage-: ~tasche *die* carrier bag; **~zeit** *die* gestation [period]

trag-, Trag-: ~fähig *Adj.* able to take a load *or* weight *postpos.*; **eine ~fähige Mehrheit** (fig.) a workable majority; **~fähigkeit** *die* load- *or* weight-bearing capacity; **~fläche** *die* wing; (eines Boots) hydrofoil; **~flächenboot** *das* hydrofoil; **~flügel** *der* ▸**~fläche**; **~flügel·boot** *das* hydrofoil

Trägheit *die;* **~, ~en** **1** ▸**träge A 1**: sluggishness; lethargy **2** (Physik) inertia

Trägheits-: ~gesetz *das* (Physik) law of inertia; **~moment** *das* (Physik) moment of inertia

Tragik /ˈtraːgɪk/ *die;* **~:** tragedy

Tragiker *der;* **~s, ~:** tragedian

tragi-, Tragi- /tragi-/: **~komik** *die* tragicomedy; **~komisch** **A** *Adj.* tragicomic; **B** *adv.* tragicomically; **~komödie** *die* tragicomedy

tragisch /ˈtraːgɪʃ/
A *Adj.* tragic; **das ist nicht [so] ~** (ugs.) it's not the end of the world (coll.); **etw. ~ nehmen** take sth. to heart (coll.)
B *adv.* tragically; **der Film/die Tour endete ~:** the film had a tragic ending/the trip ended in tragedy

tragischer·weise *Adv.* tragically

Trag-: ~kraft ▸**~fähigkeit**; **~last** *die* load; **~luft·halle** *die* air hall

Tragöde /traˈgøːdə/ *der;* **~n, ~n** tragedian

Tragödie /traˈgøːdi̯ə/ *die;* **~, ~n** tragedy; **er macht immer gleich eine ~ daraus** (ugs.) he always acts as if it's the end of the world (coll.)

Tragödien·dichter *der* tragedian

Tragödin *die;* **~, ~nen** tragedienne

Trag-: ~sessel *der* sedan [chair]; **~weite** *die* consequences *pl.*; **von großer ~weite sein** have far-reaching consequences; **ein Ereignis von großer/weltpolitischer ~weite** an event of great consequence *or* moment/of moment in world politics; **~zeit** *die* gestation [period]

Trailer /ˈtreɪlɐ/ **~s, ~** (Film) trailer

Trainer /ˈtrɛːnɐ/ *der;* **~s, ~** **1** coach; trainer; (eines Schwimmers, Tennisspielers) coach; (einer Fußballmannschaft) manager **2** (Pferdesport) trainer

Trainer·bank *die; Pl.* **Trainerbänke** (Sport) trainer's bench

Trainerin *die;* **~, ~nen** ▸**Trainer**

trainieren
A *tr. V.* **1** train; coach; coach ‹*swimmer, tennis player*›; train ‹*horse*›; manage ‹*football team*›; exercise ‹*muscles etc.*›; **sein Gedächtnis ~** (fig.) train one's memory; **darauf trainiert sein, etw. zu tun** be trained to do sth.; **jmdn./ein Tier darauf ~, etw. zu tun** train sb./an animal to do sth.; **ein trainierter Schwimmer/Radfahrer/Bergsteiger** *usw.* a swimmer/cyclist/mountaineer *etc.* [who is] in training; **ein trainierter Körper** a body made fit by training **2** (üben, einüben) practise ‹*exercise, jump, etc.*› **3** (zu Trainingszwecken ausüben) **Fußball/Tennis ~:** do football/tennis training
B *itr. V.* train; (Motorsport) practise; **mit jmdm. ~** ‹*trainer*› coach sb.; ‹*player*› train with sb.

Training /ˈtrɛːnɪŋ/ *das;* **~s, ~s** (Fitness~, auch fig.: Ausbildung) training *no indef. art.*; (Motorsport, fig.) practice; **Radfahren ist ein gutes ~:** cycling is a good form of training *or* exercise; **sich einem strengen ~ unterziehen** submit oneself to a rigorous training programme; **er hat sich beim ~ verletzt** he injured himself in training/practice; **geistiges ~** (fig.) mental exercises *pl.*; **er hat das ~ der Mannschaft übernommen** he has taken over the coaching of the team *or* as coach to the team; **im ~ sein/bleiben** be/keep in training; *s. auch* **autogen**

Trainings-: ~anzug *der* track suit; **~hose** *die* track-suit bottoms *pl.*; **~jacke** *die* track-suit top; **~lager** *das; Pl.* **~~:** training camp; **~programm** *das* training programme; **~rückstand** *der* lack of training; **einen ~rückstand haben** be behind with one's training; **~runde** *die* (Rennsport) practice lap; **~schuh** *der* training shoe; trainer; **~stunde** *die* training session

Trakehner /traˈkeːnɐ/ *der;* **~s, ~** (Pferd) Trakehner

Trakt /trakt/ *der;* **~[e]s, ~e** section; (Flügel) wing

Traktat /trakˈtaːt/ *der od. das;* **~[e]s, ~e** **1** (Abhandlung) treatise **2** (religiöse Flugschrift) tract

Traktätchen /trakˈtɛːtçən/ *das;* **~s, ~** (abwertend) tract

traktieren *tr. V.* **1** set about ‹*person, thing*›; **jmdn. mit Ohrfeigen/Faustschlägen ~:** slap sb. round the face/punch sb. **2** (veralt.: bewirten) ply (**mit** with)

Traktion /trakˈtsi̯oːn/ *die;* **~, ~en** (Technik) traction

Traktor /ˈtraktɔr/ *der;* **~s, ~en** /-ˈtoːrən/ tractor

Traktorist *der;* **~en, ~en**, **Traktoristin** *die;* **~, ~nen** (regional) tractor driver

Tralala *das;* **~s, ~s** (ugs., meist abwertend) song and dance (coll.); **[viel] ~ machen** *od.* **veranstalten** make a [great] song and dance

trällern /ˈtrɛlɐn/ *itr., tr. V.* warble

Tram /traːm/ *die;* **~, ~s** *od. schweiz. das;* **~s, ~s** (bes. südd., schweiz.), **Tram·bahn** *die* (südd.) tram (Brit.); streetcar (Amer.)

Traminer /traˈmiːnɐ/ *der;* **~s, ~** **1** (Rebsorte) Traminer [grape] **2** (Weißwein) Traminer [white wine]

Tramp /trɛmp/ *der;* **~s, ~s** tramp; hobo (Amer.)

Trampel *der od. das;* **~s, ~** (ugs. abwertend) clumsy clot (Brit. sl.) *or* oaf

trampelig (ugs. abwertend)
A *Adj.* clumsy.
B *adv.* clumsily

Trampeligkeit *die;* **~** (ugs. abwertend) clumsiness

trampeln
A *itr. V.* **1** (aufstampfen) **[mit den Füßen] ~:** stamp one's feet **2** *mit sein* (abwertend: treten) trample (**auf** + *Akk.* on)
B *tr. V.* trample

Trampel-: ~pfad *der* [beaten] path; **~tier** *das* **1** (Kamel) Bactrian camel; **2** (salopp abwertend) clumsy clot (Brit. sl.) *or* oaf

trampen /ˈtrɛmpn̩/ *itr. V. mit sein* hitch-hike

Tramper *der;* **~s, ~, Tramperin** *die;* **~, ~nen** hitch-hiker

Trampolin /ˈtrampoliːn/ *das;* **~s, ~e** trampoline

Tramway /ˈtramve/ *die;* **~, ~s** (österr.) tram (Brit.); streetcar (Amer.)

Tran /traːn/ *der;* **~[e]s** **1** (vom Wal) train-oil; (von Fischen) fish oil **2** **im ~** (ugs.) befuddled; in a daze; (durch Alkohol, Drogen) stoned (sl.)

Trance /ˈtrãːs(ə)/ *die;* **~, ~n** trance; **in ~:** in a trance; **in ~ fallen** go into a trance

Trance·zustand *der* trance

Tranche /ˈtrãːʃ(ə)/ *die;* **~, ~n** **1** (Kochk.) thick slice **2** (Wirtsch.) tranche

Tränchen /ˈtrɛːnçən/ *das;* **~s, ~:** [little] tear

tranchieren *tr. V.* (Kochk.) carve

Tranchier·messer *das* carving knife

Träne /ˈtrɛːnə/ *die;* **~, ~n** tear; **~ traten ihr in die Augen** tears came into her eyes; **seine ~n trocknen** dry one's eyes; wipe away one's tears; **ihr kommen leicht die ~n** she cries easily; **~n lachen** laugh till one cries *or* till the tears run down one's cheeks; **in ~n aufgelöst sein** be in floods of tears; **in ~n zerfließen** dissolve in tears; **mit einer ~ im Knopfloch** (scherzh.) wiping away a tear (fig.); **jmdm./einer Sache keine ~ nachweinen** not shed any tears over sb./sth.

tränen *itr. V.* ‹*eyes*› water

Tränende Herz *das;* **Tränenden Herzens, Tränenden Herzen** bleeding heart; lyre-flower

tränen-, Tränen-: ~drüse *die* ▸❶ **S. 435** (Anat.) tear gland; **auf die ~drüsen drücken** (fig.) lay on the agony; **~erstickt** *Adj.* (geh.) **mit ~erstickter Stimme** in a voice choked with tears; **~gas** *das* tear gas; **~nass**, ***~naß** *Adj.* **~nasse Augen/Wangen** tear-stained eyes/cheeks; **~sack** *der* ▸❶ **S. 435** (Anat.) lachrymal sac; **~säcke [unter den Augen]** bags under the eyes; **~überströmt** *Adj.* tear-stained ‹*face*›

Tran·funzel *die* (ugs. abwertend) **1** (trübe Lampe) miserable lamp **2** (langweiliger Mensch) ponderous dimwit (coll.); (langsamer Mensch) slowcoach; slowpoke (Amer.)

tranig *Adj.* **1** (voller Tran) ‹*meat, fish*› full of train-oil **2** (wie Tran) ‹*taste*› like *or* of train-oil **3** (ugs. abwertend: langsam) sluggish; slow

Tranigkeit *die;* **~** (ugs. abwertend) sluggishness

trank /traŋk/ *1. u. 3. Pers. Sg. Prät. v.* **trinken**

Trank *der;* **~[e]s, Tränke** (geh.) drink; draught (liter.)

Tränke /ˈtrɛŋkə/ *die;* **~, ~n** watering place; (Gefäß) drinking trough

tränken *tr. V.* **1** (auch fig.) water **2** (sich voll saugen lassen) soak; **ein mit Hohn getränkter Brief** (fig.) a letter brimming with scorn

Tranquilizer /ˈtrɛŋkwɪlaizɐ/ *der;* **~s, ~** (Pharm.) tranquillizer

trans-, Trans- /trans-/: **~aktion** *die* transaction; **~alpin, ~alpinisch** *Adj.* transalpine; **~atlantisch** *Adj.* transatlantic; across the Atlantic *postpos.*

Transe /ˈtranzə/ *die;* **~, ~n** (ugs.) transvestite; trannie (coll.)

Trans-Europ-Express *der* Trans-Europe Express

Transfer /transˈfeːɐ̯/ *der;* **~s, ~s** (bes. Wirtsch., Sport) transfer

transferieren *tr. V.* (bes. Wirtsch., Sport) transfer (**auf** + *Akk.*, **in** + *Akk.*, **zu** to)

Transfer-: ~leistung *die* (Finanzw.) transfer; **~liste** *die* (Fußball) transfer list; **~zahlung** *die* **1** (Finanzw.) transfer payment; **2** (Sport) transfer fee

trans-, Trans-: ~formation *die* transformation; **~formations·grammatik** *die* (Sprachw.) transformational grammar; **~formator** /-fɔrˈmaːtɔr/ *der;* **~~s, ~en** /-ˈtoːrən/ transformer; **~formator-**

t

häuschen *das* transformer station; **~formieren** *tr. V.* transform (**in** + *Akk.* into, **auf** + *Akk.* to); **~fusion** *die* (Med.) transfusion

transgen *Adj.* transgenic

Transistor /tran'zɪstɔr/ *der;* **~s, ~en** /-'to:rən/ [1] (Elektronik) transistor [2] ▸ **~radio**

Transistor·radio *das* transistor radio

Transit[1] /*auch:* '--/ *der;* **~s, ~e** transit

Transit[2] /tran'zi:t, *auch:* 'tranzɪt/ *das;* **~s, ~s** transit visa

Transit·handel *der* transit trade

transitiv /'tranziti:f/ (Sprachw.)

A *Adj.* transitive

B *adv.* transitively

Transit·verkehr *der* transit traffic

transkribieren /transkri'bi:rən/ *tr. V.* (Sprachw.) transcribe

Transkription /transkrɪp'tsio:n/ *die;* **~, ~en** (Sprachw.) transcription

Trans-: ~literation /-lɪtera'tsio:n/ *die;* **~~, ~~en** (Sprachw.) transliteration; **~mission** *die* (Technik) transmission; **~missions·riemen** *der* transmission belt

transparent /transpa'rɛnt/ *Adj.* [1] transparent; (Licht durchlassend) translucent, diaphanous ‹*curtain, fabric, etc.*› [2] (fig.: verständlich) intelligible

Transparent *das;* **~[e]s, ~e** [1] (Spruchband) banner [2] (Bild) transparency

Transparenz *die;* **~** [1] transparency (also fig.) (von Gewebe, Porzellan usw.) translucence [2] (Verständlichkeit) intelligibility

Transpiration /transpira'tsio:n/ *die;* **~, ~en** [1] (geh.) perspiration [2] (Bot.) transpiration

transpirieren *itr. V.* (bes. Med.) perspire

Transplantation /transplanta'tsio:n/ *die;* **~, ~en** (Med.) transplant; (von Haut) graft

Transplantations·medizin *die* transplant medicine

transplantieren /transplan'ti:rən/ *tr. V.* (Med.) transplant ‹*organ, tissue*›; graft ‹*skin*›

Transponder /trans'pɔndɐ/ *der;* **~s, ~** (Elektrot.) transponder

transponieren /transpo'ni:rən/ *tr. V.* (Musik) transpose

Transport /trans'pɔrt/ *der;* **~[e]s, ~e** [1] (Beförderung) transportation; **beim** *od.* **auf dem ~:** during carriage [2] (beförderte Lebewesen od. Sachen) (mit dem Zug) trainload; (mit mehreren Fahrzeugen) convoy; (Fracht) consignment; shipment [3] (Technik) transport

transportabel /transpɔr'ta:bl̩/ *Adj.* transportable; mobile ‹*field kitchen*›; (tragbar) portable

Transport-: ~behälter *der* container; **~beton** *der* (Bauw.) ready-mixed concrete

Transporter *der;* **~s, ~** (Flugzeug) transport aircraft; (Auto) goods vehicle; (Schiff) cargo ship

Transporteur /-'tø:ɐ̯/ *der;* **~s, ~e. Transporteurin** *die;* **~, ~nen** carrier

transportfähig *Adj.* moveable

Transport·flugzeug *das* transport aircraft

transportieren

A *tr. V.* [1] transport ‹*goods, people*›; move ‹*patient*›; (fig.) convey ‹*feeling, information, knowledge*› [2] (Technik: weiterschieben) transport, wind on ‹*film*›

B *itr. V.* (Technik) ‹*camera*› wind on

Transport-: ~kosten *Pl.* carriage *sing.;* transport costs; **~mittel** *das* means *sing.* of transport; **~unter·nehmen** *das* haulage firm *or* contractor

Trans·sexualität *die* transsexuality

trans·sexuell

A *Adj.* transsexual.

B *adv.* ‹*live*› as a transsexual

Trans·uran *das* (Chemie, Physik) transuranic element

Tran·suse *die* (ugs. abwertend) ▸ **Tranfunzel 2**

Transvestit /transvɛs'ti:t/ *der;* **~en, ~en** transvestite

transzendent /transtsɛn'dɛnt/ *Adj.* [1] (Philos.) transcendent [2] (Math.) transcendental

transzendental /transtsɛndɛn'ta:l/ *Adj.* (Philos.) transcendental

Transzendental·philosophie *die* transcendental philosophy *no art.*

Transzendenz /transtsɛn'dɛnts/ *die;* **~** [1] transcendency; transcendent nature [2] (Philos.) transcendence

transzendieren *tr. V.* (geh.) transcend

Transzendierung *die;* **~, ~en** transcendence

Tran·tüte *die* (ugs. abwertend) ▸ **Tranfunzel 2**

trantütig (ugs. abwertend)

A *Adj.* ponderous; slow; plodding, slow-moving ‹*scene*›.

B *adv.* ponderously; (im Schneckentempo) at a snail's pace

Trapez /tra'pe:ts/ *das;* **~es, ~e** [1] (Geom.) trapezium (Brit.); trapezoid (Amer.) [2] (im Zirkus o. Ä.) trapeze

Trapez-: ~akt *der* trapeze act; **~künstler** *der,* **~künstlerin** *die* trapeze artist

Trapezoid /trapetso'i:t/ *das;* **~[e]s, ~e** (Geom.) trapezoid (Brit.); trapezium (Amer.)

Trappe /'trapə/ *die;* **~, ~n** bustard

trappeln /'trapl̩n/ *itr. V.; mit sein* patter [along]; ‹*feet*› patter; ‹*hoofs*› go clip-clop

Trapper /'trapɐ/ *der;* **~s, ~. Trapperin** *die;* **~, ~nen** trapper

Trappist /tra'pɪst/ *der;* **~en, ~en** Trappist

Trappisten-: ~käse *der* Trappist cheese; **~orden** *der* order of Trappists

Trappistin *die;* **~, ~nen** Trappistine

trapsen /'trapsn̩/ *itr. V.; mit sein* (ugs.) tramp; clump; *s. auch* **Nachtigall**

trara /tra'ra:/ *Interj.* tantara

Trara *das;* **~s** (ugs. abwertend) razzmatazz (coll.); **viel ~ um etw.** (*Akk.*) **machen** make a great song and dance about sth. (coll.)

Trass, *Traß /tras/ *der;* **Trasses, Trasse** (Geol.) trass

Trassant /tra'sant/ *der;* **~en, ~en, Trassantin** *die;* **~, ~nen** (Finanzw.) drawer

Trassat /tra'sa:t/ *der;* **~en, ~en, Trassatin** *die;* **~, ~nen** (Finanzw.) drawee

Trasse /'trasə/ *die;* **~, ~n** [1] (Verkehrsweg) [marked-out] route *or* line [2] (Damm) [railway/road] embankment

trat /tra:t/ *1. u. 3. Pers. Sg. Prät. v.* **treten**

Tratsch /tra:tʃ/ *der;* **~[e]s** (ugs. abwertend) gossip; tittle-tattle

tratschen *itr. V.* (ugs. abwertend) gossip; (schwatzen) chatter

Tratscherei *die;* **~, ~en** (ugs. abwertend) gossiping

Tratsch·tante *die* (ugs. abwertend) ▸ **Klatschtante**

Tratte /'tratə/ *die;* **~, ~n** (Finanzw.) bill [of exchange]

Trau·altar *der: in* **[mit jmdn.] vor den ~ treten** (geh.) enter into matrimony [with sb.]; **jmdn. zum ~ führen** (geh. veralt.) lead sb. to the altar

Träubchen /'trɔypçən/ *das;* **~s, ~:** little grape

Traube /'traubə/ *die;* **~, ~n** [1] (Beeren) bunch; (von Johannisbeeren o. Ä.) cluster [2] (Wein~) grape; **jmdm. sind die ~n zu sauer** (fig.) it's just sour grapes on sb.'s part [3] (Menschenmenge) bunch; cluster [4] (Bot.: Blütenstand) raceme

Trauben-: ~hyazinthe *die* grape hyacinth; **~kern** *der* grape pip; grape seed; **~kern·öl** *das* grapeseed oil; **~lese** *die* grape harvest; **~saft** *der* grape-juice; **~zucker** *der* glucose

trauen /'trauən/

A *itr. V.* **jmdm./einer Sache ~:** trust sb./sth.; **ich traue dem Braten nicht** (ugs.) I think something's up (coll.); it seems fishy to me (coll.); **trau, schau, wem!** make sure you know who you're dealing with; mind you're not taken for a ride (coll.); *s. auch* **Auge 1**

B *refl. V.* dare; **sich** (*Akk., selten Dat.*) **~, etw. zu tun** dare [to] do sth.; **du traust dich ja nicht!** you haven't the courage *or* nerve; **sich irgendwohin ~:** dare [to] go somewhere; **ich traue mich nicht in seine Nähe** I daren't go near him

C *tr. V.* (verheiraten) ‹*vicar, registrar, etc.*› marry; *s. auch* **kirchlich A 2, B; standesamtlich B**

Trauer /'trauɐ/ *die;* **~** [1] grief (**über** + *Akk.* over); (um einen Toten) mourning (**um** + *Akk.* for); **~ haben, in ~ sein** be in mourning; **in stiller/tiefer ~ X** (in Todesanzeigen) [much loved and] sadly mourned by X [2] (**~zeit**) [period of] mourning [3] (**~kleidung**) mourning

Trauer-: ~akt *der* memorial ceremony; (beim Begräbnis) funeral ceremony; **~arbeit** *die* (Psychol.) process of grieving; **~beflaggung** *die* flags *pl.* at half-mast; **~beflaggung anordnen** order flags to be flown at half-mast; **~fall** *der* bereavement; **~feier** *die* memorial ceremony; (beim Begräbnis) funeral ceremony; **~flor** *der* mourning band; black [crape] ribbon; **~gemeinde** *die* [congregation *sing.* of] mourners *pl.;* **~gottes·dienst** *der* funeral service; **~haus** *das* house of mourning; **~jahr** *das* year of mourning; **~karte** *die* [pre-printed] card of condolence; **~kleidung** *die* mourning clothes *pl.;* mourning; **~kloß** *der* (ugs. scherzh.) wet blanket; **~mantel** *der* (Zool.) Camberwell Beauty; mourning cloak [butterfly] (Amer.); **~marsch** *der* (Musik) funeral march; **~miene** *die* (ugs.) long face

trauern *itr. V.* [1] mourn; **um jmdn. ~:** mourn for sb.; **die ~den Hinterbliebenen** the bereaved [2] (Trauer tragen) be in mourning

Trauer-: ~rand *der* black border *or* edging; **~ränder unter den Nägeln haben** (fig. scherzh.) have black *or* grubby fingernails; **~rede** *die* funeral oration; **~schleier** *der* black veil; mourning veil; **~spiel** *das* tragedy; (fig. ugs.) deplorable business; **es ist doch ein ~spiel, dass ...** it's quite pathetic that ...; **~weide** *die* weeping willow; **~zeit** *die* period of mourning; **~zug** *der* funeral procession

Traufe /'traufə/ *die;* **~, ~n** eaves *pl.*

träufeln /'trɔyfl̩n/ *tr. V.* [let] trickle (**in** + *Akk.* into); drip ‹*ear drops etc.*›

Trauf·höhe *die* (Bauw.) eaves height

traulich /'traulɪç/

A *Adj.* cosy; **in ~er Runde** in a friendly *or* an intimate circle

B *adv.* cosily; (vertraut) intimately

Traulichkeit *die;* **~:** cosiness; (Vertrautheit) intimacy; friendliness

Traum /traum/ *der;* **~[e]s, Träume** /'trɔymə/ dream; **sie ist mir im ~ erschienen** she appeared to me in a dream; **wir denken nicht im ~ daran, hier wegzuziehen** we wouldn't dream of moving away from here; **nicht im ~ habe ich mit der Möglichkeit gerechnet, zu gewinnen** I didn't imagine in my wildest dreams that I could win; **Träume sind Schäume** (Spr.) dreams are but shadows; **Fliegen war schon immer sein ~:** he had always dreamed of flying; **der ~ ist ausgeträumt,** (ugs.) **aus [ist] der ~!** that's the end of 'that dream; 'that dream is over; *s. auch* **kühn 2**

Traum- dream ‹*house, hotel, job, etc.*›; ‹*house, hotel, woman*› of one's dreams; ideal, perfect ‹*couple, job*›

Trauma /'trauma/ *das;* **~s, Traumen** *od.* **~ta** ▸ ℹ **S. 439** (Psych., Med.) trauma

traum·artig

A *Adj.* dreamlike.

B *adv.* as in a dream

traumatisch (Psych., Med.)

A *Adj.* traumatic

B *adv.* traumatically

traumatisieren (Psych., Med.)

A *tr. V.* traumatize.

B *itr. V.* have a traumatizing effect

Traumatisierte *der/die; adj. Dekl.* traumatized person *or* (Psych.) subject; **durch Krieg ~:** those traumatized by war

Traum-: ~auto *das* dream car; **~beruf** *der* dream job; **~bild** *das* vision; (Wunschbild)

dream; (idealisiert) ideal; **∼deutung** *die* interpretation of dreams

träumen /ˈtrɔymən/
A *itr. V.* dream (**von** of, about); (unaufmerksam sein) [day]dream; **[schlaf gut und] träum süß** [sleep well and] sweet dreams; **träum nicht!** pay attention; stop daydreaming
B *tr. V.* dream; **etwas Schreckliches/Schönes ∼:** have a terrible/beautiful dream; **er träumte** *od.* (geh.) **ihm träumte, er sei ...** he dreamt that he was ...; **das hast du doch nur geträumt!** you must have imagined that; **ich hätte mir nie ∼ lassen, dass ...** I should never have imagined it possible that ...; I never imagined that ...

Traumen ▸ **Trauma**

Träumer *der;* **∼s, ∼:** dreamer

Träumerei *die;* **∼, ∼en** daydream; reverie

Traum·ergebnis *das* dream result

Träumerin *die;* **∼, ∼nen** dreamer

träumerisch
A *Adj.* dreamy; (sehnsüchtig) wistful
B *adv.* dreamily; (sehnsüchtig) wistfully

Traum-: **∼fabrik** *die* dream factory; **∼frau** *die* (ugs.) dream woman; woman of one's dreams

traumhaft
A *Adj.* 1 dreamlike 2 (ugs.: schön) marvellous; fabulous (coll.); **∼es Glück haben** have a fantastic piece of luck (coll.)
B *adv.* 1 as if in a dream 2 (ugs.: schön) fabulously (coll.); **eine ∼ eingerichtete Wohnung** a superbly furnished flat

traum-, Traum-: **∼haus** *das* dream house; **∼hochzeit** *die* dream wedding; fairytale wedding; **∼insel** *die* island paradise; **∼job** *der* dream job; **∼land** *das* 1 **ein ∼land für ...** a mecca *or* paradise for ...; 2 (Traumwelt) dreamland; **∼mann** *der* (ugs.) dream man; man of one's dreams; **∼paar** *das* ideal couple; perfect couple; **∼partner** *der,* **∼partnerin** *die* ideal partner; perfect partner; **∼prinz** *der* fairytale prince; Prince Charming; **∼prinzessin** *die* fairytale princess; **∼reise** *die* dream trip; **∼rolle** *die* dream part; **∼schiff** *das* floating paradise; **∼schloss** *das* dream palace; (fig.: Luftschloss) castle in the air; **∼sequenz** *die* dream sequence; **∼strand** *der* perfect beach; **sein ∼strand** the beach of his dreams; **∼tänzer** *der,* **∼tänzerin** *die* (abwertend) woolly-headed idealist; fantasizer; **∼verloren** **A** *Adj.* dreamy; **B** *adv.* in a dream; dreamily; **∼wandlerisch** *Adj.* somnambulistic; **mit ∼wandlerischer Sicherheit** with the sureness of a sleepwalker; with instinctive sureness; **∼welt** *die* dream world; **∼ziel** *das* dream destination

traurig /ˈtraurɪç/
A *Adj.* 1 sad; sad, sorrowful ‹*eyes, expression*›; unhappy ‹*childhood, youth*›; unhappy, painful ‹*duty*›; **ein ∼es Kapitel** (fig.) a sad story 2 (kümmerlich) sorry, pathetic ‹*state etc.*›; miserable ‹*result*›; pitiful, wretched ‹*conditions*›; down-at-heel ‹*area*›; **eine ∼e Berühmtheit/Rolle** an unfortunate notoriety/role
B *adv.* sadly

Traurigkeit *die;* **∼:** sadness; sorrow; **eine große/allgemeine ∼:** a great/general feeling of sadness

Trau-: **∼ring** *der* wedding ring; **∼schein** *der* marriage certificate

traut *Adj.* (geh.) 1 (heimelig) cosy; secure; **das ∼e Familienglück** happiness in the bosom of a/the family 2 (vertraut) familiar; close, intimate ‹*friend, family circle*›

Traute /ˈtrautə/ *die;* **∼** (ugs.) guts (coll.)

Trauung *die;* **∼, ∼en** wedding [ceremony]

Trau·zeuge *der,* **Trau·zeugin** *die* witness (*at wedding ceremony*)

Traveller·scheck /ˈtrɛvələʃɛk/ *der* traveller's cheque

Traverse /traˈvɛrzə/ *die;* **∼, ∼n** 1 (Technik) cross-beam 2 (Fechten) sideways movement to avoid opponent's attack

Travers·flöte /traˈvɛrs-/ *die* transverse flute

Travestie /travɛsˈtiː/ *die;* **∼, ∼n** travesty

Travestie·künstler *der,* **Travestie·künstlerin** *die* drag artist

Trebe /ˈtreːbə/ *die:* in **auf ∼ sein** (ugs.) be a runaway

Trebegänger /-gɛŋɐ/ *der;* **∼s, ∼, Trebegängerin** *die;* **∼, ∼nen** (ugs.) runaway

Treber *Pl.* 1 (Brauereiwesen) draff *sing.* 2 (Weinbau) marc *sing.*

Treck /trɛk/ *der;* **∼s, ∼s** train, column (*of refugees etc.*)

Trecker *der;* **∼s, ∼:** tractor

Treff[1] *das;* **∼s, ∼s** (Spielkartenfarbe) clubs *pl.*; *s. auch* **Pik**[2]

Treff[2] /trɛf/ *der;* **∼s, ∼s** (ugs.) 1 (Treffen) rendezvous; (bes. von mehreren Personen) get-together (coll.) 2 (Ort) meeting place

treffen
A *unr. tr. V.* 1 (erreichen [und verletzen/schädigen]) hit; ‹*punch, blow, object*› strike; **jmdn. am Kopf/ins Gesicht ∼:** hit *or* strike sb. on the head/in the face; **von einer Kugel tödlich getroffen** fatally wounded by a bullet; **vom Blitz getroffen** struck by lightning; **er fühlte sich von den Vorwürfen nicht getroffen** he did not consider that the reproaches applied to him; **ihn trifft keine Schuld** he is in no way to blame 2 (erraten) hit on; hit ‹*right tone*›; **du hast genau das Richtige getroffen** you've hit on just the right thing; (das stimmt haargenau) you've got it exactly right; **getroffen!** you've got it!; **mit dem Geschenk hast du seinen Geschmack getroffen/nicht getroffen** that present is just the sort of thing he likes/not the sort of thing he likes; **auf dem Foto ist er gut getroffen** the photo is a good likeness of him; that's a good photo of him 3 (erschüttern) affect [deeply]; (verletzen) hurt; **jmdn. tief** *od.* **schwer ∼:** affect sb. deeply; **es hat ihn in seinem Stolz getroffen** it hurt his pride 4 (schaden) hit; damage; **warum muss es immer mich ∼?** why does it always have to be me [who is affected *or* gets it]? 5 (begegnen) meet; **jmdn. zum Mittagessen ∼:** meet sb. for lunch; **ich traf ihn zufällig auf der Straße** I happened to run into him in the street; **ihre Blicke trafen sich** (fig.) their eyes met 6 (vorfinden) come upon, find ‹*anomalies etc.*›; **es gut/schlecht ∼:** be *or* strike lucky/be unlucky 7 (als Funktionsverb) make ‹*arrangements, choice, preparations, decision, etc.*›; **eine Vereinbarung** *od.* **Absprache ∼:** conclude an agreement
B *unr. itr. V.* 1 ‹*person, shot, etc.*› hit the target; **nicht ∼:** miss [the target]; **ins Schwarze ∼:** score a bullseye 2 *mit sein* **auf etw.** (*Akk.*) **∼:** come upon sth.; **auf Widerstand/Ablehnung/Schwierigkeiten ∼:** meet with *or* encounter resistance/rejection/difficulties; **auf jmdn./eine Mannschaft ∼** (Sport) come up against sb./a team
C *unr. refl. V.* 1 **sich mit jmdm. ∼:** meet sb. 2 (unpers.) **es trifft sich gut/schlecht** it is convenient/inconvenient

Treffen *das;* **∼s, ∼** 1 meeting; **ein ∼ alter Kameraden** a reunion of old comrades 2 (Sport) encounter; **ein faires/spannendes ∼:** a fair/exciting contest 3 (Milit. veralt.) encounter; **etw. ins ∼ führen** (fig. geh.) bring sth. into the attack

treffend
A *Adj.* apt; apposite ‹*remark*›; **ein ∼es Urteil** an accurate assessment
B *adv.* aptly; **kurz und ∼ sagte er ...** he said, short and to the point, ...

Treffer *der;* **∼s, ∼** 1 (Milit., Boxen, Fechten usw.) hit; (Schlag) blow; (Ballspiele) goal; **schwere ∼ an Kopf und Körper einstecken** (Boxen) take heavy blows *or* punches to the head and body; **er hatte auf zehn Schüsse acht ∼:** of his ten shots eight were on target 2 (Gewinn) win; (Los) winner

trefflich (geh.)
A *Adj.* excellent; splendid ‹*person*›; first-rate ‹*scholar*›
B *adv.* excellently; splendidly

treff-, Treff-: **∼punkt** *der* 1 (Stelle, Ort) meeting place; rendezvous; 2 (Geom.) point of incidence; (Schnittpunkt) point of intersection; **∼sicher** **A** *Adj.* with a sure aim *postpos.*, *not pred.*; accurate ‹*marksman*›; (fig.) accurate ‹*language, mode of expression*›; unerring ‹*judgement*›; **B** *adv.* (auch fig.) accurately; with unerring accuracy; **∼sicherheit** *die* ▸ **∼sicher A:** accuracy; sureness of aim; (fig.) accuracy; unerringness

Treib-: **∼anker** *der* (Seew.) sea anchor; **∼ball** *der* 1 (Spiel) [*informal*] *ball game played by two teams trying to throw the ball over the back line of the opposing team;* 2 (Badminton) drive; **∼eis** *das* drift-ice

treiben /ˈtraibn̩/
A *unr. tr. V.* 1 drive ‹*animals, people, leaves, etc.*›; (Fußball) dribble ‹*ball*›; **er ließ sich von der Strömung ∼:** he let himself be carried along by the current; **die Arbeit trieb ihm den Schweiß auf die Stirn** the effort brought the sweat to his brow; **die Preise in die Höhe ∼:** push *or* force up prices; **jmdn. in den Wahnsinn** *od.* **zur Raserei/zur Verzweiflung/in den Tod ∼:** drive sb. mad/to despair/to his/her death 2 (an∼) drive ‹*wheels etc.*›; **die ∼de Kraft [des Ganzen] ist ...** the moving spirit [behind the whole affair] is ...; **jmdn. zur Eile ∼:** make sb. hurry up 3 (einschlagen) drive ‹*nail, wedge, stake, etc.*› (**in** + *Akk.* into) 4 (durch Bohrung schaffen) drive, cut ‹*tunnel, gallery*› (**in** + *Akk.* into; **durch** through); sink ‹*shaft*› (**in** + *Akk.* into) 5 (durchpressen) force; press 6 (sich beschäftigen mit) go in for ‹*farming, cattle breeding, etc.*›; study ‹*French etc.*›; carry on, pursue ‹*studies, trade, craft*›; **viel Sport ∼:** do a lot of sport; go in for sport in a big way; **Handel ∼:** trade; **Unfug ∼:** get up to mischief; **Unsinn ∼:** mess *or* fool about; **was treibt ihr denn hier?** (ugs.) what are you up to *or* doing here?; **was habt ihr den ganzen Tag getrieben?** (ugs.) what did you do with yourself *or* get up to all day?; *s. auch* **Aufwand 2**; **Missbrauch 1**; **Scherz**; **Spionage**; **Spott** 7 (ugs. abwertend: in Verbindung mit „es") **es wüst/übel/toll ∼:** lead a dissolute/bad life/live it up; **es zu toll ∼:** overdo it; take things too far; **er hat es zu weit getrieben** he overstepped the mark; he went too far; **es [mit jmdm.] ∼** (ugs. verhüll.: koitieren) have it off [with sb.] (sl.) 8 (formen) beat ‹*metal, object*›; chase ‹*silver, gold*› 9 (Gartenbau) force ‹*plants*› 10 (aufgehen lassen) cause ‹*dough*› to rise
B *unr. itr. V.* 1 *meist, mit Richtungsangabe nur, mit sein* drift; **die Dinge ∼ lassen** (fig.) let things take their course; **sich ∼ lassen** (fig.) drift; go with the tide 2 (ugs.) (harntreibend sein) get the bladder going; (schweißtreibend sein) make you sweat; **ein ∼des Mittel** a diuretic/sudorific 3 (ausschlagen) ‹*tree, plant*› sprout

Treiben *das;* **∼s, ∼** 1 (Durcheinander) bustle; **in der Fußgängerzone herrscht ein lebhaftes ∼:** the pedestrian precinct is full of bustling activity; *s. auch* **närrisch A 3** 2 (Tun) activities *pl.*; doings *pl.*; (Machenschaften) wheelings and dealings *pl.* 3 (Jägerspr.) ▸ **Treibjagd**

Treiber *der;* **∼s, ∼** 1 (DV) driver 2 (Jägerspr.) beater

Treiberin *die;* **∼, ∼nen** (Jägerspr.) beater

Treib-: **∼gas** *das* 1 (für Motoren) liquefied petroleum gas; LPG; 2 (in Spraydosen) propellant; **∼gut** *das* flotsam; **∼haus** *das* hothouse; **∼haus·effekt** *der* greenhouse effect; **∼haus·gas** *das* greenhouse gas; **∼haus·luft** *die* hothouse atmosphere; (im Freien) sultry atmosphere; **∼holz** *das* driftwood; **∼jagd** *die* (Jägerspr.) battue; shoot (in which game is sent up by beaters); **eine ∼jagd auf kritische Journalisten** (fig.) a witch-hunt against critical journalists; **∼mittel** *das* 1 (Kochk.) raising agent; 2 (Chemie: für feste Stoffe) foaming agent; 3 ▸ **∼gas 2**; **∼netz** *das* drift net; **∼riemen** *der* (Technik) drive belt; **∼sand** *der* quicksand; **∼satz** *der* (Technik) [solid] rocket propulsion element; **∼schlag** *der* (Badminton, Golf, Tennis, Tischtennis) drive; **∼stoff** *der* fuel

treideln /ˈtraidl̩n/ *tr. V.* (veralt.) tow ‹*barge*› upstream

treife /ˈtraifə/ *Adj.* trefa; not kosher *pred.*

trekken /ˈtrɛkn̩/ *itr. V.*; *mit sein* trek

Trekking /ˈtrɛkɪŋ/ *das;* **∼s, ∼s** trekking

t

Trekking-: ~rad *das* trekking bike; **~tour** *die* trekking tour

Trema /'tre:ma/ *das;* **~s, ~s** *od.* **~ta** (Sprachw.) diaeresis

tremolieren *itr. V.* (Musik) play/sing with a tremolo

Tremolo /'tre:molo/ *das;* **~s, ~s** *od.* **Tremoli** (Musik) tremolo

Trenchcoat /'trentʃkoʊt/ *der;* **~[s], ~s** trench coat

Trend /trent/ *der;* **~s, ~s** trend (**zu** + *Dat.* towards); (Mode) vogue; **im ~ liegen** be in vogue

Trend·forscher *der,* **Trend·forscherin** *die* trend researcher

trendig
A *Adj.* trendy.
B *adv.* trendily

Trend-: ~scout /-skaut/ *der;* **~~s, ~~s** trend spotter; **~setter** *der,* **~setterin** *die* (bes. Werbejargon) trendsetter (*Gen.* in); **~sport** *der,* **~sportart,** *die* trend sport; **~wende** *die* change in trend

trendy /'trendi/
A *indekl. Adj.* trendy.
B *adv.* trendily

trennbar *Adj.* **1** (nicht fest zusammengesetzt) separable ‹*verb, prefix*› **2** (sich trennen lassend) **dieses Wort ist [nicht] ~:** this word can[not] be split *or* divided

trennen /'trenən/
A *tr. V.* **1** separate (**von** from); (abschneiden) cut off; sever ‹*head, arm*›; **der Krieg hatte die Familie getrennt** the war had split up the family; **das Kind von der Mutter ~:** take the child away from the mother; **das Futter aus der Jacke ~:** cut the lining out of the jacket; **nur noch wenige Tage ~ uns von den Ferien** the holidays are only a few days away **2** (auf~) unpick ‹*dress, seam*› **3** (teilen) divide ‹*word, parts of a room etc., fig.: people*›; **ein Zaun trennte die Grundstücke** a fence divided the plots from one another; a fence formed the boundary between the plots; **uns ~ Welten** (fig.) we are worlds apart; **„st" darf jetzt getrennt werden** 'st' can now be split *or* divided **4** (beim Telefon) **wir wurden getrennt** we were cut off **5** (zerlegen) separate ‹*mixture*› **6** (auseinander halten) differentiate *or* distinguish between; make a distinction between ‹*terms*›; **die Arbeit von der Freizeit ~:** keep work separate from leisure
B *itr. V.* (Rundf., Funkw.) **gut** *od.* **scharf ~** ‹*radio*› have good selectivity
C *refl. V.* **1** (voneinander weggehen) part [company]; (fig.) **die Mannschaften trennten sich 0:0** the game ended in a goalless draw; the two teams drew 0:0; **die Firma hat sich von ihm getrennt** the company has dispensed with his services **2** (eine Partnerschaft auflösen) ‹*couple, partners*› split up; **sich in Güte ~:** part on good terms; **sie hat sich von ihrem Mann getrennt** she has left her husband; *s. auch* **getrennt 3** (hergeben) **sich von etw. ~:** part with sth.

Trenn-: ~schärfe *die* (Rundf., Funkw.) selectivity; **~scheibe** *die* **1** glass partition; **2** (Schleifscheibe) cutting disc

Trennung *die;* **~, ~en 1** (von Menschen) separation (**von** from); **in ~ leben** have separated; **die ~ von Tisch und Bett** separation from bed and board; separation without divorce **2** (von Gegenständen) parting; **die ~ von allem irdischen Besitz** parting with all one's worldly goods **3** (von Wörtern) division **4** (von Begriffen) distinction (**von** between)

Trennungs-: ~linie *die* (auch fig.) dividing line; **~schmerz** *der* pain of separation; **~strich** *der* **1** hyphen; **2** (fig.) **einen ~strich ziehen** *od.* **machen** make a [clear] distinction; draw a [clear] line; **er zog einen ~strich zwischen sich und seiner Vergangenheit** he made a clean break with the past

Trenn·wand *die* partition

Trense /'trenzə/ *die;* **~, ~n 1** (Gebiss) snaffle bit **2** (Zaumzeug) snaffle

trepp- /trep-/: **~ab** *Adv.* down the stairs; **~auf** *Adv.* up the stairs

Treppchen *das;* **~s, ~ 1** small staircase **2** (Sportjargon) [winner's] rostrum

Treppe /'trepə/ *die;* **~, ~n 1** staircase; [flight *sing.* of] stairs *pl.;* (im Freien, auf der Bühne) [flight *sing.* of] steps *pl.;* **~n steigen** climb stairs; **eine ~ höher/tiefer** one floor *or* flight up/down; **die ~ hinauffallen** (fig. ugs.) rise in the world; **die ~ runtergefallen sein** (fig. ugs. scherzh.) have been to the sheep shearer's (joc.) **2** (in der Frisur) step

Treppen-: ~absatz *der* half landing; **~geländer** *das* banisters *pl.;* **~giebel** *der* (Archit.) stepped gable; **~haus** *das* stairwell; **das Licht im ~haus** the light on the staircase; **~lift** *der* stairlift; **~steigen** *das;* **~~s** climbing stairs *no art.;* **~stufe** *die* stair; (im Freien) step; **~witz** *der:* **ein ~witz der [Welt]geschichte** one of history's cruel ironies

Tresen /'tre:zn̩/ *der;* **~s, ~** (bes. nordd.) **1** (Theke) bar **2** (Ladentisch) counter

Tresor /tre'zo:ɐ̯/ *der;* **~s, ~e 1** safe **2** (~raum) strongroom

Tresse /'tresə/ *die;* **~, ~n** [strip of] braid; (Rangabzeichen) stripe

Trester /'trestɐ/ *Pl.* (Landw.) **1** (von Trauben) marc **2** (von Äpfeln o. Ä.) pomace

Trester·brannt·wein *der* marc

Tret-: ~boot *das* pedalo; **~eimer** *der* pedal bin

treten /'tre:tn̩/
A *unr. itr. V.* **1** *mit sein* (einen Schritt, Schritte machen) step (**in** + *Akk.* into, **auf** + *Akk.* on to); **ins Zimmer/in einen Laden ~:** enter the room/a shop; **ans Fenster ~:** go to the window; **zur Seite ~:** step *or* move aside; **von einem Fuß auf den anderen ~:** shift from one foot to the other; **der Schweiß ist ihm auf die Stirn ge~** (fig.) the sweat came to his brow; **der Fluss ist über die Ufer ge~** (fig.) the river has overflowed its banks; *s. auch* **Stelle 1 2** (seinen Fuß setzen) **auf etw.** (*Akk.*) **~** (absichtlich) tread on sth.; (unabsichtlich; meist mit sein) step *or* tread on sth.; **jmdm. auf den Fuß ~:** step/tread on sb.'s foot *or* toes; **auf das Gas[pedal]/die Bremse ~:** step on the accelerator/the brake; **kräftig in die Pedale ~:** pedal hard **3** *mit sein* (verblasst in Verbindungen mit Substantiven) **in jmds. Dienste ~:** enter sb.'s service; **in Kontakt** *od.* **Verbindung ~:** get in touch; **in den Ruhestand ~:** go into retirement; *s. auch* **Aktion 3; Ehestand; Hungerstreik; Streik 4** (ausschlagen) kick; **jmdm. an** *od.* **gegen das Schienbein ~:** kick sb. on the shin; **gegen die Tür ~:** kick the door
B *unr. tr. V.* **1** (Tritt versetzen) kick ‹*person, ball, etc.*›; **jmdn. in den Bauch ~:** kick sb. in the stomach; **eine Ecke ~** (Fußball) take a corner; **man muss ihn immer ~, damit er etwas tut** (fig.) you always have to give him a kick to make him do anything **2** (trampeln) trample, tread ‹*path*›; **sich** (*Dat.*) **einen Dorn in den Fuß ~:** get a thorn in one's foot; **sich** (*Dat.*) **den Lehm von den Schuhen ~:** stamp the mud off one's shoes **3** (mit dem Fuß niederdrücken) step on ‹*brake, pedal*›; operate ‹*bellows, clutch*›; **die Pedale ~:** pedal **4** (bei Geflügel: begatten) tread; mate with

Treter *der;* **~s, ~** (ugs., oft abwertend) casual shoe; casual

Tret-: ~kurbel *die* crank arm; crank; **~lager** *das* bottom bracket [bearing]; crank bearing; **~mine** *die* anti-personnel mine; **~mühle** *die* (fig. ugs. abwertend) treadmill; **in die ~mühle zurückkehren** return to the daily grind (coll.); **~roller** *der* pedal scooter

treu /trɔy/
A *Adj.* **1** (beständig) faithful, loyal ‹*friend, dog, customer, servant, etc.*›; faithful ‹*husband, wife*›; loyal ‹*ally, subject*›; (unbeirrt) staunch, loyal ‹*supporter*›; **jmdm. ~ sein/bleiben** be/remain true to sb.; **eine ~e Seele** a faithful *or* devoted soul; **jmdm. ~e Dienste leisten** serve sb. faithfully **2 sich selbst** (*Dat.*)**/seinem Glauben ~ bleiben** be true to oneself/one's faith; **seinen Grundsätzen ~ bleiben** stick to one's principles; **das Glück/der Erfolg ist ihm ~ geblieben** his luck has held out/success keeps coming his way; *s. auch* **Hand 6 3** (ugs.: ~herzig) ingenuous, trusting ‹*eyes, look*›
B *adv.* **1** (beständig) faithfully; loyally; **~ ergeben/sorgend** devoted; **jmdm. ~ ergeben sein** (veralt., sonst scherzh.) be utterly devoted to sb. **2** (ugs.: ~herzig) trustingly; **alles ~ und brav tun** do everything unquestioningly

Treu ▸ **Treue 1**

treu-, Treu-: ~bruch *der* **1 landesverräterischer ~bruch** (DDR Rechtsw.) state treason; **2** (hist.: Bruch der Lehnstreue) felony (Law Hist.); **~deutsch** *Adj.* (ugs., meist abwertend) typically German; **~doof** (ugs. abwertend) **A** *Adj.* gormlessly naïve (coll.); gormless (coll.); **B** *adv.* gormlessly (coll.) and naïvely

Treue *die;* **~ 1** loyalty; (von [Ehe]partnern) fidelity; **jmdm. ~ schwören** swear to be true *or* faithful to sb.; **jmdm. die ~ halten** keep faith with sb.; be loyal to sb.; **meiner Treu!** (veralt.) upon my word! (dated); **Treu und Glauben** (Rechtsw.) equity; **auf Treu und Glauben** (ugs.) in good faith **2** (Genauigkeit) accuracy

Treue: ~bruch *der* breach of faith; **~eid** ▸ **Treueid; ~gelöbnis** *das* pledge of loyalty; (von Ehepartnern) pledge of fidelity

Treu·eid *der* oath of allegiance; (hist.: im Lehnswesen) oath of fealty

Treue-: ~pflicht *die* (Rechtsw.) loyalty to one's employer; (des Arbeitgebers) loyalty to one's employee; **~prämie** *die* long-service bonus

treu·ergeben ▸ **treu B 1**

Treue·schwur *der* oath of loyalty *or* allegiance

treu-, Treu-: ~hand *die* **1** (Wirtschaft) German privatization agency; **2** (Rechtsw.) trusteeship; **~hand·anstalt** *die* (Wirtschaft) German privatization agency; **~händer** /-hendɐ/ *der;* **~~s, ~~, ~händerin** *die;* **~~, ~~nen** (Rechtsw.) trustee; **~händerisch A** *Adj.* fiduciary; **~händerische Übertragung** assignment on trust. **B** *adv.* on trust; **etw. ~händerisch verwalten** hold sth. in trust; **~herzig A** *Adj.* ingenuous; (naiv) naïve; (unschuldig) innocent; **B** *adv.* ingenuously; (naiv) naïvely; (unschuldig) innocently; **~herzigkeit** *die;* **~~:** ingenuousness; (Naivität) naivety; (Unschuld) innocence

treulich (veralt.)
A *Adj.* faithful
B *adv.* faithfully

treu-, Treu-: ~los A *Adj.* disloyal, faithless ‹*friend, person*›; unfaithful ‹*husband, wife, lover*›; **B** *adv.* faithlessly; **~losigkeit** *die;* **~~:** disloyalty; faithlessness; (von [Ehe]partnern) infidelity; **~sorgend** ▸ **treu B 1**

Trevira ⓌⓏ /tre'vi:ra/ *das;* **~:** Trevira ®

Triangel /'tri:aŋl/ *der; österr. das;* **~s, ~** (Mus.) triangle

Trias /'tri:as/ *die;* **~, ~ 1** (Geol.) Triassic; Trias **2** (geh.) trio; trinity

Trias·formation *die* (Geol.) Triassic system

Tri·athlet *der,* **Tri·athletin** *die* triathlete

Triathlon[1] /'tri:atlɔn/ *das* **~s** triathlon; **~ trainieren** train for the triathlon

Triathlon[2] *der;* **~s, ~s** triathlon

Tribun /tri'bu:n/ *der;* **~s** *od.* **~en, ~e[n]** (hist.) tribune

Tribunal /tribu'na:l/ *das;* **~s, ~e 1** tribunal **2** (im antiken Rom) tribune (*for the municipal authorities in the Forum Romanum*)

Tribüne /tri'by:nə/ *die;* **~, ~n** [grand]stand

Tribut /tri'bu:t/ *der;* **~[e]s, ~e 1** (hist.) tribute *no indef. art.* **2** (fig.) due; **einer Sache** (*Dat.*) **~ zollen** pay the price for sth.; **einen hohen ~ [an Menschenleben] fordern** take a heavy toll [of human lives]

Trichine /trɪ'çi:nə/ *die;* **~, ~n** trichina

trichinös /trɪçi'nø:s/ *Adj.* trichinous

Trichter /'trɪçtɐ/ *der;* **~s, ~ 1** funnel; **auf den [richtigen] ~ kommen** (fig. ugs.) get the message (coll.); *s. auch* **Nürnberger 2** (Granat~, Bomben~, Geogr.) crater

Trichter·mündung *die* estuary

Trick /trɪk/ *der;* **~s, ~s** trick; (fig.: List) ploy; **technische ~s** cunning techniques; **den ~ heraushaben** have got the knack

trick-, Trick-: ~betrüger *der,* **~betrügerin** *die* confidence trickster; **~film** *der* animated cartoon [film]; **~kiste** *die* (ugs.) repertoire of tricks/ploys; bag of tricks; **in die ~kiste greifen** dip into one's bag of tricks; **~reich** **A** *Adj.* wily; **B** *adv.* artfully; ‹*play*› trickily; **~reich geschlagene Bälle** cunningly hit shots

tricksen /ˈtrɪksn̩/ (ugs., bes. Sportjargon)
A *itr. V.* use tricks; work a fiddle (coll.); ‹*footballer*› play trickily
B *tr. V.* fiddle (coll.)

Trick·ski·laufen *das;* **~s** acrobatic *or* (Amer. sl.) hot-dog skiing *no art.*

Trick·technik *die* (Film) animation technology

Tricktrack /ˈtrɪktrak/ *das;* **~s, ~s** tric-trac

trieb /triːp/ *1. u. 3. Pers. Sg. Prät. v.* **treiben**

Trieb *der;* **~[e]s, ~e** **1** (innerer Antrieb) impulse; (Drang) urge; (Verlangen) [compulsive] desire **2** (Spross) shoot **3** (Technik: Übertragung) transmission; drive

trieb-, Trieb-: **~befriedigung** *die* [*esp.* sexual] gratification; **~fahrzeug** *das* ▸ **Triebwagen**; **~feder** *die* mainspring; (fig.) driving *or* motivating force; (Beweggrund) motive (+ *Gen.* behind); **~haft** **A** *Adj.* compulsive ‹*need, behaviour, action, etc.*›; carnal ‹*sensuality*›; **ein ~hafter Mensch** a person ruled by his/her [physical] impulses; **B** *adv.* compulsively; **~handlung** *die* compulsive act; (bei Tieren) instinctive act; **~kraft** *die* (bes. Soziol.) driving *or* motivating force; **~stoff** *der* (schweiz.) ▸ **Treibstoff**; **~täter** *der,* **~täterin** *die,* **~verbrecher** *der,* **~verbrecherin** *die: offender committing a crime in gratifying a compulsive desire;* (Sexualtäter) sexual offender; **~wagen** *der* (Eisenb.) railcar; **~werk** *das* engine

Trief·auge *das* watery eye; (eitrig) bleary *or* (Med.) blear eye

triefen /ˈtriːfn̩/ *unr. od. regelm. itr. V.* **1** *mit sein* (*fließen*) (in Tropfen) drip; (in kleinen Rinnsalen) trickle **2** (nass sein) be dripping wet; ‹*nose*› run; **~d nass** dripping wet; **von** *od.* **vor Fett/Nässe ~:** be dripping with fat/be dripping wet; **von** *od.* **vor Edelmut ~** (fig. iron.) be oozing with nobility

Trief·nase *die* runny nose

trief·nass, *trief·naß *Adj.* dripping wet

Triennale /triɛˈnaːlə/ *die;* **~, ~n** triennial festival; (Messe) triennial [trade] fair

triezen /ˈtriːtsn̩/ *tr. V.* (ugs.) torment; (plagen) pester; plague

triff /trɪf/ *Imperativ Sg. v.* **treffen**

trifft *3. Pers. Sg. Präsens v.* **treffen**

Trift /trɪft/ *die;* **~, ~en** **1** (Strömung) drift [current] **2** (Weide) common [*esp.* mountain] pasturage **3** (Weg) cattle track

triften *tr. V.* raft ‹*tree trunks*›

triftig
A *Adj.* good ‹*reason, excuse*›; valid, convincing ‹*motive, argument*›
B *adv.* convincingly

Triftigkeit *die;* **~:** validity

Trigonometrie /trigonomeˈtriː/ *die;* **~:** trigonometry *no art.*

trigonometrisch *Adj.* trigonometric; **~er Punkt** triangulation point

Trikot[1] /triˈkoː/ *der od. das;* **~s, ~s** (Stoff) cotton jersey

Trikot[2] *das;* **~s, ~** (ärmellos) singlet; (eines Tänzers) leotard; (eines Fußballspielers) shirt; **das gelbe ~** (Radsport) the yellow jersey

Trikotage /trikoˈtaːʒə/ *die;* **~, ~n** [cotton] jersey garments *pl.;* (Unterwäsche) cotton [jersey] underwear

Triller /ˈtrɪlɐ/ *der;* **~s, ~:** trill

trillern
A *itr. V.* (Musik) trill; (mit vielen T~ singen) ‹*bird, person*› warble
B *tr. V.* warble ‹*song*›

Triller·pfeife *die* police/referee's whistle

Trillion /trɪˈli̯oːn/ *die;* **~, ~en** quintillion

Trilogie /triloˈgiː/ *die;* **~, ~n** trilogy

Trimester /triˈmɛstɐ/ *das;* **~s, ~** (Hochschulw.) term

Trimm-dich-Pfad *der* keep-fit *or* trim trail

trimmen /ˈtrɪmən/ *tr. V.* **1** (durch Sport) get ‹*person*› into shape; **trimm dich durch Sport** keep fit with sport **2** **etw. auf alt/„Western" usw. ~:** do sth. up to look old/like the wild west *etc.* **3** (durch Scheren) clip ‹*dog*›; (durch Bürsten) groom ‹*dog*› **4** (Seew., Flugw.) trim ‹*ship, aircraft, cargo*›; stow ‹*barrels, bales, etc.*› properly; **Kohlen ~:** take on [a load of] coal

Trimm-: **~gerät** *das* exerciser; **~trab** *der* jogging *no art.*

Trinität /triniˈtɛːt/ *die;* **~** (christl. Rel.) Trinity

Trinitatis /triniˈtaːtɪs/ (*das*); **~, Trinitatis·fest** *das* Trinity Sunday *no art.*

trinkbar *Adj.* drinkable; **hast du was Trinkbares im Haus?** (ugs.) have you anything to drink in the house?

Trink-: **~becher** *der* beaker; (mit Henkel) mug; (hist.) drinking vessel; **~brunnen** *der* drinking fountain

trinken /ˈtrɪŋkn̩/
A *unr. itr. V.* drink; **in** *od.* **mit kleinen Schlucken/in großen Zügen ~:** drink in little sips/in big gulps; **lass mich mal [von dem Saft] ~:** let me have a drink [of the juice]; **jmdm. etw. zu ~ geben** give sb. sth. to drink; **was ~ Sie?** what are you drinking?; (was möchten Sie ~?) what would you like to drink?; **man merkte, dass er getrunken hatte** one could see that he had been drinking; **auf jmdn./etw. ~:** drink to sb./sth.; **ich trinke auf deine Gesundheit** I'll drink [to] your health; **das Trinken lassen** give up drink
B *unr. tr. V.* drink; **einen Kaffee/ein Bier** *usw.* **~:** have a coffee/beer *etc.;* **ich trinke keinen Tropfen [Alkohol]** I don't drink; I don't touch alcohol; **einen Schluck Wasser ~:** have a drink of water; **einen ~:** have a drink; **einen ~ gehen** (ugs.) go for a drink
C *refl. V.* **der Wein trinkt sich gut** the wine is pleasant to drink; **sich satt ~:** drink one's fill; **sich krank/zu Tode ~:** make oneself ill through drink/drink oneself to death

Trinker *der;* **~s, ~:** alcoholic; **ein heimlicher/starker ~:** a secret/heavy drinker

Trinkerei *die;* **~, ~en** drinking *no art.*

Trinker·heil·anstalt *die* drying-out clinic; detoxification centre

Trinkerin *die;* **~, ~nen** ▸ **Trinker**

trink-, Trink-: **~fest** *Adj.* **~fest sein** be able to hold one's drink; **ein ~fester Matrose** a sailor used to hard drinking; **~flasche** *die* [drinking] bottle; **~festigkeit** *die* ability to hold one's drink; **~freudig** *Adj.* fond of drinking *pred.;* **~gefäß** *das* drinking vessel (formal); **~gelage** *das* (oft scherzh.) drinking spree; **~geld** *das* tip; **wie viel ~geld gibst du ihm?** how much do you tip him?; how big a tip do you give him?; **~gewohnheiten** *Pl.* drinking habits; **~glas** *das; Pl.* **~gläser** [drinking] glass; tumbler; **~halle** *die* **1** (in einem Heilbad) pump room; **2** (Kiosk) refreshment kiosk; (größer) refreshment stall; **~halm** *der* [drinking] straw; **~horn** *das* (früher) drinking horn; **~kur** *die* drinking cure; (am Badeort) taking the waters; **~lied** *das* (veralt.) drinking song; **~milch** *die* low-fat pasteurized milk; **~schokolade** *die* drinking chocolate; **~sitten** *Pl.* ▸ **Trinkgewohnheiten**; **~spruch** *der* toast (**auf** + *Akk.* to); **einen ~spruch auf jmdn. ausbringen** propose a toast to sb.

Trinkwasser *das; Pl.* **~;** drinking water; **„kein ~"** 'not for drinking'

Trinkwasser-: **~aufbereitung** *die* purification of drinking water; **~brunnen** *der* well for drinking water; **~gewinnung** *die* drinking water extraction; **~leitung** *die* drinking water pipe; **~qualität** *die* drinking water quality; **~reservoir** *das* drinking water reservoir; **~verbrauch** *der* drinking water consumption; **~versorgung** *die* drinking water supply

Trio /ˈtriːo/ *das;* **~s, ~s** (Musik, fig.) trio

Triole /triˈoːlə/ *die;* **~, ~n** (Musik) triplet

Trio·sonate *die* (Musik) trio sonata

Trip /trɪp/ *der;* **~s, ~s** **1** (ugs.: Ausflug) trip; jaunt; (untertreibend:) **ein ~ in die Staaten** a little trip to the States **2** (Drogenjargon: Rausch) trip (coll.); **auf dem ~ sein** be tripping (coll.); **auf dem religiösen/anarchistischen** *usw.* **~ sein** (fig. ugs.) be going through a religious/anarchist *etc.* phase **3** (Drogenjargon: Dosis); fix (sl.); **~s werfen** *od.* **schmeißen** pop LSD (or other hallucinogen) (sl.)

Tripel-: triple ‹*fugue, concerto, etc.*›; **~allianz** Triple Alliance

trippeln /ˈtrɪpl̩n/ *itr. V.; mit sein* trip; ‹*child*› patter; (affektiert) mince

Trippel·schritt *der* short, rapid step; (affektiert) mincing step

Tripper /ˈtrɪpɐ/ *der;* **~s, ~** ▸ⓘ **S. 439** gonorrhoea; **sich** (*Dat.*) **einen ~ holen** (ugs.) get a dose of the clap (coarse)

Triptik ▸ **Triptyk**

Triptychon /ˈtrɪptyçɔn/ *das;* **~s, Triptychen** *od.* **Triptycha** (Kunstwiss.) triptych

Triptyk /ˈtrɪptʏk/ *das;* **~s, ~s** triptyque

trist /trɪst/ *Adj.* dreary; dismal

Tristheit *die;* **~:** dreariness

Tritons·horn /ˈtriːtɔns-/ *das* (Zool.) triton *or* trumpet shell

tritt /trɪt/ *Imperativ Sg. u. 3. Pers. Sg. Präsens v.* **treten**

Tritt *der;* **~[e]s, ~e** **1** (Aufsetzen des Fußes) step; (einmalig) [foot]step; **mit festem ~:** with a firm step *or* tread; *s. auch* **Schritt 1** **2** (Gleichschritt) **im ~ marschieren** march in step; **aus dem ~ geraten** *od.* **kommen** get out of step; **ohne ~, marsch!** break step!; **~ fassen** fall in step; (fig.: sich fangen) recover oneself **3** (Fuß~) kick; **jmdm. einen ~ versetzen** give sb. a kick; kick sb.; **einen ~ bekommen** *od.* **kriegen** (fig. ugs.) be given the push (Brit. coll.); get kicked out **4** (~brett) step **5** (Bergsteigen) (Halt für Füße) foothold; (im Eis) step **6** (Gestell) small stepladder; (in der Bibliothek) library steps *pl.* **7** (Jägerspr.: Abdruck) footprint

tritt-, Tritt-: **~brett** *das* step; (an älterem Auto) running-board; **~brett·fahrer** *der,* **~brett·fahrerin** *die* (fig. abwertend) ≈ free rider (Amer.); *person who profits from another's work;* **~fest** *Adj.* **1** non-slip ‹*shoes, surface*›; safe ‹*steps, path*›; **2** (strapazierfähig) hard-wearing ‹*carpet, lawn*›; **3** (mit sicherem Tritt) sure-footed (also fig.); **~festigkeit** *die* **1** (von Schuhen) resistance to slipping; **2** (Strapazierfähigkeit) hardwearing nature; **~leiter** *die* stepladder; **~sicher** **A** *Adj.* **1** safe, non-slip ‹*shoes, surface, steps*›; **2** sure-footed (also fig.); **B** *adv.* (mit sicherem Tritt) sure-footedly (also fig.); **~sicherheit** *die;* **~~** **1** (Beschaffenheit) resistance to slipping; non-slip quality; **2** (Verhalten) sure-footedness (also fig.); **~spur** *die* (von Mensch) footprint; (von Tier) track; (von Katze, Hund usw. auch) paw print

Triumph /triˈʊmf/ *der;* **~[e]s, ~e** triumph; **~e/einen großen ~ feiern** have a series of triumphs/a great triumph *or* success; be hugely successful/a huge success; **im ~:** in triumph

triumphal /triʊmˈfaːl/ *Adj.* **1** (begeisternd) triumphant ‹*success etc.*›; **~ sein** be a triumph **2** (mit Jubel) triumphal ‹*entry etc.*›; **jmdm. einen ~en Empfang bereiten** give sb. a hero's welcome

Triumphator /triʊmˈfaːtɔr/ *der;* **~s, ~en** /-ˈtoːrən/ **1** (hist.) triumphator **2** (geh.: Sieger) conquering hero

Triumph-: **~bogen** *der* (Archit.) triumphal arch; **~fahrt** *die* triumphant journey; (im Rennen usw.) triumphant progress; **~gefühl** *das* feeling of triumph; **~geschrei** *das* triumphant cheering *no indef. art.*

triumphieren *itr. V.* **1** (Genugtuung empfinden) exult; **~d** triumphant; exultant; **~d lachen** laugh triumphantly **2** (siegen) be triumphant *or* victorious; triumph (lit. or fig.) (**über** + *Akk.* over)

Triumph-: **~wagen** *der* (hist.) triumphal chariot (also fig.); **~zug** *der* (hist.) triumph; **im ~zug** (fig.) in a triumphal procession

Triumvirat /triʊmviˈraːt/ *das;* **~[e]s, ~e** (hist.) triumvirate

t

trivial /tri'vi̯a:l/
A *Adj.* **1** (platt) banal; trite; (unbedeutend) trivial **2** (alltäglich) humdrum ‹*life, career*›
B *adv.* (platt) banally; ‹*say etc.*› tritely; ‹*written*› in a banal style

trivialisieren *tr. V.* trivialize

Trivialität *die;* ~, ~en **1** (Plattheit, Alltäglichkeit) banality; triteness **2** (platte Äußerung) banality; (Gemeinplatz) commonplace [remark]

Trivial·roman *der* light [trashy] novel

Trochäus /trɔ'xɛ:ʊs/ *der;* ~, **Trochäen** (Verslehre) trochee

trocken /'trɔkn̩/
A *Adj.* **1** dry; **~en Auges** (geh.) dry-eyed; without shedding a tear; **etw. ~ bügeln/reinigen** dry-iron/dry-clean sth.; **sich ~ rasieren** use an electric razor; **noch ~ nach Hause kommen** get home without getting wet; **wieder auf dem Trock[e]nen sein** be on dry land *or* terra firma again; **auf dem Trock[e]nen sitzen** *od.* **sein** (ugs.) be completely stuck (coll.); (pleite sein) be skint (Brit. sl.); **~ sitzen** (ugs.) have nothing to drink **2** (ohne Zutat) **~es** *od.* (ugs.) **~ Brot essen** eat dry bread **3** (sachlich-langweilig) dry, factual ‹*account, report, treatise*›; bare ‹*words, figures*›; dull, dry ‹*person*› **4** (unverblümt) dry ‹*humour, remark, etc.*› **5** (dem Klang nach) dry ‹*laugh, cough, sound*›; sharp ‹*crack*›; clear ‹*acoustics*› **6** (Sportjargon, bes. Boxen, Fußball) sharp ‹*blow*›; snappy ‹*shot*›; **eine ~e Rechte** a straight right
B *adv.* **1** (sachlich-langweilig) ‹*speak, write*› drily, in a matter-of-fact way **2** (unverblümt) drily **3** (dem Klang nach) **das Gewehr knallte kurz und ~:** the rifle went off with a short, sharp report

trocken-, Trocken-: ~batterie *die* dry battery; **~beeren·auslese** *die: wine made from selected grapes left to dry on the vine at the end of the season;* **~blume** *die* dried flower; **~boden** *der* attic drying-room; **~dock** *das* dry dock; **~ei** *das* dried egg; **~eis** *das* dry ice; **~eis·nebel** *der* (Theater, Film) dry ice fog; **~|fallen** *unr. itr. V.; mit sein* (fachspr.) ‹*mud flats*› dry out and become visible [at low tide]; ‹*boat etc.*› be left high and dry [by the receding tide]; **~fäule** *die* dry rot; **~fisch** *der* dried fish; **~fleisch** *das* dried meat; **~|föhnen** *tr. V.* dry with a hair-dryer; **~früchte** *die Pl.* dried fruit *sing.*; **~futter** *das* (Landw.) dry fodder; **~gebiet** *das* (Geogr.) arid region; **~gestell** *das* (für Wäsche) clothes airer *or* -horse; **~haube** *die* [hood-type] hairdrier

Trockenheit *die;* ~, ~en **1** (auch fig.) dryness **2** (Dürreperiode) drought

trocken-, Trocken-: ~kurs *der* dry-skiing course; **~|legen** *tr. V.* **1** **ein Baby ~legen** change a baby's nappies (Brit.) *or* (Amer.) diapers; **2** (entwässern) drain ‹*marsh, pond, etc.*›; **~legung** *die;* ~~, ~~en draining; **~masse** *die* dry mass; **~mauer** *die* dry-stone wall; **~milch** *die* dried milk; **~obst** *das* ▸**Dörrobst**; **~periode** *die* dry period; **~rasen** *der* (fachspr.) arid grassland; **~rasierer** *der* (ugs.) **1** (Rasierapparat) electric razor; **2** (Person) user of an electric razor; **~raum** *der* drying room; **~|reiben** *unr. tr. V.* rub ‹*hair, child, etc.*› dry; wipe ‹*crockery, window, etc.*› dry; **~reifen** *der* dry-weather tyre; **~reinigung** *die* dry-cleaning; **~|rubbeln** *tr. V.* (bes. nordd.) rub dry; **~|schleudern** *tr. V.* spin-dry; **~schwimmen** *das* preparatory swimming exercises *pl.* [on land] (*for learners*); **~shampoo, ~shampoon** *das* dry shampoo; ***~|sitzen** ▸**trocken A 1**; **~spiritus** *der* solid fuel (*for camping-stove*); **~substanz** *die* ▸**Trockenmasse**; **~|tupfen** *tr. V.* dab dry; **~übung** *die* preliminary [swimming/skiing] exercise; (fig.) dry run; **~|wischen** *tr. V.* wipe dry; **~zeit** *die* dry season; **~zone** *die* (Geog.) arid zone

trocknen
A *itr. V.; meist mit sein* dry
B *tr. V.* dry; **die Kleider zum Trocknen aufhängen** hang up the clothes to dry

Trockner *der;* ~s, ~: drier; (Trockengestell) airer

Troddel /'trɔdl̩/ *die;* ~, ~n tassel

Trödel /'trø:dl̩/ *der;* ~s (ugs., oft abwertend) junk; (für den Flohmarkt) jumble

Trödelei *die;* ~, ~en (ugs. abwertend) dawdling *no pl.*

trödeln *itr. V.* **1** (ugs., oft abwertend) dawdle (**mit** over) **2** *mit sein* (ugs.: schlendern) saunter

Trödler *der;* ~s, ~, **Trödlerin** *die;* ~, ~nen **1** (ugs. abwertend) dawdler; slowcoach; slowpoke (Amer.) **2** (ugs.: Händler[in]) junk dealer; **etw. beim ~ kaufen** buy sth. from *or* at the junk shop

troff /trɔf/ *1. u. 3. Pers. Sg. Prät. v.* **triefen**

trog /tro:k/ *1. u. 3. Pers. Sg. Prät. v.* **trügen**

Trog *der;* ~[e]s, **Tröge** /'trø:gə/ (auch Geol.) trough

Troglodyt /troglo'dy:t/ *der;* ~en, ~en troglodyte; (fig. abwertend) caveman

Troika /'trɔyka/ *die;* ~, ~s troika; (fig.: Führungsgruppe) triumvirate

Troja /'tro:ja/ (*das*); ~s Troy

Trojaner *der;* ~s, ~, **Trojanerin** *die;* ~, ~nen Trojan

trojanisch *Adj.* Trojan; **das Trojanische Pferd** (Myth.; auch fig.) the Trojan Horse

Troll /trɔl/ *der;* ~[e]s, ~e (Myth.) troll

Troll·blume *die* globeflower

trollen (ugs.) *refl. V.* push off (coll.); **der Junge trollte sich in sein Zimmer** the boy took himself off to his room

Trolley·bus /'trɔli-/ *der* (bes. schweiz.) trolleybus

Trollinger /'trɔlɪŋɐ/ *der;* ~s, ~: Trollinger [grape/wine]

Trommel /'trɔml̩/ *die;* ~, ~n **1** (Schlaginstrument) drum; **die ~ für jmdn./etw. rühren** (ugs.) beat the drum for sb./sth. **2** (Behälter; Kabel~, Seil~) drum

Trommel-: ~bremse *die* (Technik) drum brake; **~fell** *das* **1** (bei ~n) drumhead; **2** (im Ohr) eardrum; **~feuer** *das* (Milit.; auch fig.) [constant] barrage

trommeln
A *itr. V.* **1** beat the drum; (als Beruf, Hobby usw.) play the drums **2** ([auf etw.] schlagen, auftreffen) drum (**auf** + *Akk.* on, **an** + *Akk.* against); **sie trommelte mit den Fäusten gegen die Tür** she hammered the door with her fists
B *tr. V.* **1** beat [out] ‹*march, rhythm, etc.*› **2** **jmdn. aus dem Bett/Schlaf ~:** get sb. out of bed/wake sb. up by hammering on the door

Trommel-: ~revolver *der* revolver; **~schlag** *der* drumbeat; **~schlägel, ~schlegel** *der,* **~stock** *der* drumstick; **~wirbel** *der* drum roll

Trommler *der;* ~s, ~, **Trommlerin** *die;* ~, ~nen drummer

Trompete /trɔm'pe:tə/ *die;* ~, ~n trumpet; **[eine Melodie] auf der ~ blasen** play [a tune on] the trumpet

trompeten
A *itr. V.* **1** play the trumpet; (fig.) ‹*elephant*› trumpet **2** (ugs. scherzh.: sich laut schnäuzen) blow one's nose like a foghorn
B *tr. V.* play ‹*piece*› on the trumpet; (fig.) proclaim ‹*news etc.*› loudly

Trompeten·stoß *der* blast on a/the trumpet

Trompeter *der;* ~s, ~, **Trompeterin** *die;* ~, ~nen ▸**❶ S. 113** trumpeter

Tropen *Pl.* tropics

Tropen- tropical

tropen-, Tropen-: ~arzt *der,* **~ärztin** *die* specialist in tropical medicine; **~fieber** *das* ▸**❶ S. 439** [falciparum] malaria (Med.); **~haus** *das* tropical house; **~helm** *der* sun helmet; **~holz** *das* tropical wood; **~institut** *das* institute of tropical diseases; **~klima** *das* tropical climate; **~krankheit** *die* tropical disease; **~koller** *der* tropical madness; **~medizin** *die* tropical medicine; **~mediziner** *der,* **~medizinerin** *die* specialist in tropical medicine; **~medizinisch** **A** *Adj.* ‹*research*› in tropical medicine; ‹*institute*› of tropical medicine; **B** *adv.* ‹*qualified, experienced*› in tropical medicine; ‹*relevant*› to tropical medicine; **~sturm** *der* tropical storm; **~tauglichkeit** *die* fitness for service/travel in the tropics; **~wald** *der* tropical forest

Tropf[1] /trɔpf/ *der;* ~[e]s, **Tröpfe** /'trœpfə/ (abwertend) twit (Brit. coll.); moron (coll.); **armer ~:** poor devil

Tropf[2] *der;* ~[e]s, ~e (Med.) drip; **am ~ hängen** be on a drip

Tröpfchen /'trœpfçən/ *das;* ~s, ~: droplet; (kleine Menge) drop; (scherzh.: Wein) **ein wahrhaft edles ~:** a really fine vintage

Tröpfchen·infektion *die* (Med.) droplet infection

tröpfchen·weise *Adv.* in small drops

tröpfeln /'trœpfl̩n/
A *itr. V.* **1** *mit sein* drip (**auf** + *Akk.* on to, **aus, von** from) **2** (unpers.) (ugs.: leicht regnen) **es tröpfelt** it's spitting [with rain]
B *tr. V.* let ‹*sth.*› drip (**in** + *Akk.* into, **auf** + *Akk.* on to)

tropfen
A *itr. V.; mit Richtungsangabe mit sein* drip; ‹*tears*› fall; **seine Nase tropft** his nose is running; (unpers.) **es tropft [vom Dach** *usw.***]** water is *or* it's dripping from the roof *etc.*; **es tropft** (es regnet) it's spitting [with rain]
B *tr. V.* let ‹*sth.*› drip (**in** + *Akk.* into, **auf** + *Akk.* on to); **jmdm. eine Tinktur auf die Wunde ~:** pour drops of a tincture into sb.'s wound

Tropfen *der;* ~s, ~ **1** drop; **ein paar ~ Parfüm** a few drops of perfume; **es regnet dicke ~:** the rain is falling in large drops *or* spots; **die ersten ~ fallen** the first spots [of rain] are falling; **er hat keinen ~ [Alkohol] getrunken** he hasn't touched a drop; **steter ~ höhlt den Stein** (Spr.) constant dropping wears away the stone (prov.); persistence gets there in the end; **ein ~ auf den heißen Stein sein** (fig. ugs.) be a drop in the ocean **2** **ein guter/edler ~:** a good/fine vintage

Tropfen·form *die* tear shape; **in ~:** tear-shaped *attrib.*

tropfen·weise *Adv.* drop by drop; a drop at a time

tropf-, Tropf-: ~infusion *die* (Med.) intravenous drip; **~nass, *~naß** *Adj.* dripping *or* soaking wet; **~stein·höhle** *die* limestone cave with stalactites and/or stalagmites

Trophäe /tro'fɛ:ə/ *die;* ~, ~n (hist., Jagd, Sport) trophy

Trophäen-: ~jagd *die* trophy hunting; **~jäger** *der,* **~jägerin** *die* trophy hunter (also Sport, fig.); **~sammlung** *die* (Jagdw.) trophy collection (also Sport, fig.)

tropisch
A *Adj.* tropical
B *adv.* tropically ‹*warm*›

Tropo·sphäre /tropo'sfɛ:rə/ *die;* ~ (Meteor.) troposphere

Tross, *Troß /trɔs/ *der;* **Trosses, Trosse** **1** (Milit.) baggage train **2** (Gefolge) retinue; (fig.: Zug) procession [of hangers-on]

Trosse /'trɔsə/ *die;* ~, ~n hawser (Naut.)

Trost /tro:st/ *der;* ~[e]s consolation; (bes. geistlich) comfort; **jmdm. ~ zusprechen** *od.* **spenden** comfort *or* console sb.; **jmdm. ein/kein ~ sein** be a/no comfort to sb.; **ein schwacher ~!** that's little *or* not much consolation; **in der Arbeit ~ suchen/finden** seek/find solace in work; **als ~:** as a consolation; **nicht [ganz** *od.* **recht] bei ~ sein** (ugs.) be out of one's mind; have taken leave of one's senses

trösten /'trø:stn̩/
A *tr. V.* comfort, console (**mit** with); **sie wollte sich nicht ~ lassen** she was not to be *or* refused to be comforted; she was inconsolable; **~de Worte** words of comfort; comforting words; **~d den Arm um jmdn. legen** put one's arm around sb. to comfort him/her; **etw. tröstet jmdn.** sth. is a comfort to sb.; **der Gedanke konnte ihn nicht ~:** the thought was no comfort to him
B *refl. V.* console oneself; **sich damit ~, dass ...** console oneself with the thought that ...; **sich mit einer anderen Frau ~:** find consolation with another woman

t

Tröster *der;* **~s, ~, Trösterin** *die;* **~, ~nen** comforter; (fig.: Sache) consolation

tröstlich *Adj.* comforting

trost-, Trost-: ~los *Adj.* [1] (ohne ~) hopeless; without hope *postpos.;* (verzweifelt) in despair *postpos.;* **mir war ~los zumute, ich fühlte mich ~los** I was in despair; [2] (deprimierend, öde) miserable, dreary ‹*time, weather, area, food, etc.*›; hopeless ‹*situation*›; **~losigkeit** *die;* **~~** [1] (einer Person, der Lage usw.) hopelessness; (Verzweiflung) despair; [2] (Öde) dreariness; **~pflaster** *das* (scherzh.) consolation; **~preis** *der* consolation prize; **~reich** [A] *Adj.* comforting; [B] *adv.* comfortingly; **~spender** *der,* **~spenderin** *die* (geh.) comforter; provider of comfort

Tröstung *die;* **~, ~en** comfort *no indef. art.;* **mit den ~en der Kirche versehen sterben** die after having received the last rites

Trost·wort *das; Pl.* **Trostworte** word of comfort

Trott /trɔt/ *der;* **~[e]s, ~e** [1] (Gangart) trot; **im ~ gehen** [go at a] trot [2] (leicht abwertend: Ablauf) routine; **in den alten ~ verfallen** fall back into the same old rut

Trottel *der;* **~s, ~** (ugs. abwertend) fool; wally (coll.)

trottelhaft (ugs. abwertend)
[A] *Adj.* bumbling ‹*idiot, person*›; oafish ‹*behaviour*›
[B] *adv.* oafishly

trottelig (ugs. abwertend)
[A] *Adj.* doddery; gaga *pred.* (sl)
[B] *adv.* in a feeble-minded *or* doddery way

Trotteligkeit *die;* **~** (ugs. abwertend) dodderiness; feeble-mindedness

trotten *itr. V.; mit sein* trot [along]; (freudlos) trudge

Trottoir /trɔ'to̯aːɐ̯/ *das;* **~s, ~e** *od.* **~s** pavement

trotz /trɔts/ *Präp. mit Gen., seltener mit Dat.* in spite of; despite; **~ Frost[s] und Schnee[s]** despite the frost and snow; **~ allem** *od.* **alledem** in spite of everything

Trotz *der;* **~es** defiance; (eines Pferdes) disobedience; (Oppositionsgeist) cussedness (coll.); contrariness; **jmdm./einer Sache zum ~:** in defiance of sb./sth.

Trotz·alter *das* difficult age

trotz·dem /*auch:* '-'-/
[A] *Adv.* nevertheless; **er tat es ~:** he did it all *or* just the same
[B] /-'-/ *Konj.* (ugs.) although; even though

trotzen *itr. V.* [1] (geh.: widerstehen) **jmdm./einer Sache ~** (auch fig.) defy sb./sth.; **Gefahren/der Kälte ~:** brave dangers/the cold [2] (trotzig sein) be contrary

Trotz·haltung *die* defiant attitude

trotzig
[A] *Adj.* defiant; (widerspenstig) contrary; bolshie (coll.); difficult ‹*child*›
[B] *adv.* defiantly

Trotzkismus /trɔts'kɪsmʊs/ *der;* **~:** Trotskyism *no art.*

Trotzkist *der;* **~en, ~en, Trotzkistin** *die;* **~, ~nen** Trotskyist

Trotz-: ~kopf *der* bolshie [little] so-and-so (coll.); **~köpfchen** *das* (fam. scherzh.) contrary little so-and-so (coll.); **~phase** *die* (Psych.) ▸ **~alter; ~reaktion** *die* act of defiance

Troubadour /'truːbaduːɐ̯/ *der;* **~s, ~e** *od.* **~s** (hist.) troubadour; (fig.: Schlagersänger) songster

Trouble /'trabl̩/ *der;* **~s** (ugs.) trouble; **~ haben wegen Drogen** be in trouble over drugs

Troubleshooter /'trablʃuːtɐ/ *der;* **~s, ~, Troubleshooterin** *die;* **~, ~nen** troubleshooter

trüb[e] /'tryːb(ə)/
[A] *Adj.* [1] (nicht klar) murky ‹*stream, water*›; cloudy ‹*liquid, wine, juice*›; (schlammig) muddy ‹*puddle*›; (schmutzig) dirty ‹*glass, window pane*›; dull ‹*eyes*›; **im Trüben fischen** (ugs.) fish in troubled waters [2] (nicht hell) dim ‹*light*›; dull, dismal ‹*day, weather*›; grey, overcast ‹*sky*›; dull, dingy ‹*red, yellow*› [3] (gedrückt) gloomy ‹*mood, voice, etc.*›; dreary ‹*time*›; *s. auch* **Tasse 1** [4] (unerfreulich) unfortunate, bad ‹*experience etc.*›; (zweifelhaft) dubious ‹*sources*›
[B] *adv.* [1] (nicht hell) ‹*shine, light*› dimly [2] (gedrückt) ‹*smile, look*› gloomily [3] (unerfreulich) **~ laufen** go badly

Trubel /'truːbl̩/ *der;* **~s** [hustle and] bustle; **sie stürzten sich in den dicksten ~:** they plunged into the thick of the hurly-burly; **im ~ der Ereignisse** (fig.) in the excitement of the moment; in the rush of events

trüben
[A] *tr. V.* [1] make ‹*liquid*› cloudy; cloud ‹*liquid*›; *s. auch* **Wässerchen 1** [2] (beeinträchtigen) dampen, cast a cloud over ‹*mood*›; mar ‹*relationship*›; cloud ‹*judgement*›; **jmds. Blick [für etw.] ~:** blind sb. [to sth.]
[B] *refl. V.* [1] ‹*liquid*› become cloudy; ‹*eyes*› become dull; ‹*sky*› darken [2] (sich verschlechtern) ‹*relationship*› deteriorate; ‹*awareness, memory, etc.*› become dulled *or* dim

Trübsal /'tryːpzaːl/ *die;* **~, ~e** (geh.) [1] (Leiden) affliction [2] (Kummer) grief; **~ blasen** (ugs.) mope (**wegen** over, about)

trüb-, Trüb-: ~selig [A] *Adj.* [1] (öde) dreary, depressing ‹*place, area, colour*›; dismal ‹*house*›; [2] (traurig) gloomy, melancholy ‹*thoughts, mood*›; gloomy, miserable ‹*face*›; [B] *adv.* (traurig) gloomily; **~seligkeit** *die:* [1] (Ödheit) dreariness; [2] (Traurigkeit) gloom; **~sinn** *der* melancholy; gloom; **~sinnig** [A] *Adj.* melancholy; gloomy; [B] *adv.* gloomily

Trübung *die;* **~, ~en** [1] clouding; (des Auges) dimming [2] (Beeinträchtigung) deterioration; (der Stimmung) dampening

trudeln /'truːdl̩n/ *itr. V.* [1] *mit sein* (rollen) roll; **auf die Erde ~:** flutter *or* twirl to the ground; **das Flugzeug geriet ins T~:** the plane went into a spin [2] (bes. berlin.: würfeln) play dice

Trüffel /'trʏfl̩/ *die;* **~, ~n** *od.* (ugs.) *der;* **~s, ~:** truffle

Trüffel·leber·wurst *die* liver sausage with truffles

trug /truːk/ *1. u. 3. Pers. Prät. v.* **tragen**

Trug *der;* **~[e]s** (geh.) deception (**um** over, concerning); *s. auch* **Lug**

Trug·bild *das* hallucination; illusion; (Bild der Fantasie) figment of the imagination

trüge /'tryːgə/ *1. u. 3. Pers. Sg. Konjunktiv II v.* **tragen**

trügen
[A] *unr. tr. V.* deceive; **dieses Gefühl hatte uns getrogen** this feeling had been a delusion; **wenn mich nicht alles trügt** unless I am very much mistaken
[B] *unr. itr. V.* be deceptive; ‹*feeling, deception*› be a delusion; *s. auch* **Schein 2**

trügerisch
[A] *Adj.* [1] deceptive; false ‹*hope, sign, etc.*›; treacherous ‹*ice*› [2] (veralt.: auf Betrug zielend) deceitful; **in ~er Absicht** with intent to deceive
[B] *adv.* [1] deceptively [2] (veralt.: auf Betrug zielend) deceitfully

Trug·schluss, ***Trug·schluß** *der* [1] wrong conclusion; (Irrtum) fallacy [2] (Musik) false *or* deceptive cadence

Truhe /'truːə/ *die;* **~, ~n** chest

Trumm /trʊm/ *das;* **~[e]s, Trümmer** /'trʏmɐ/ (bes. südd., österr., schweiz.) large lump; (großes Exemplar) whopper (coll.); **ein ~ von ...** a whopping great ... (coll.)

Trümmer /'trʏmɐ/ *Pl.* (eines Gebäudes) rubble *sing.;* (Ruinen) ruins; (eines Flugzeugs usw.) wreckage *sing.;* (kleinere Teile) debris *sing.;* **die Stadt lag in ~n** the town lay in ruins; **eine Stadt in ~ legen** reduce a town to rubble; flatten a town [completely]; **er stand vor den ~n seines Lebens** (fig.) he contemplated the ruins of what had once been his life

Trümmer-: ~berg *das* mountain *or* huge pile of rubble *or* debris; **~bruch** *der* (Med.) comminuted fracture; **~feld** *das* expanse of rubble; **~frau** *die* (hist.): *woman who cleared away rubble after World War II;* **~grund·stück** *das* bomb site; (nach einem Erdbeben) ruined site; **~haufen** *der* pile *or* heap of rubble; **der ~haufen seiner Ehe** (fig.) the ruins *pl.* of what had been his marriage; **~landschaft** *die* landscape of destruction; **~teil** *das* (von einem Gebäude) piece of rubble *or* debris; (von einem Flugzeug) piece of wreckage

Trumpf /trʊmpf/ *der;* **~[e]s, Trümpfe** /'trʏmpfə/ (auch fig.) trump [card]; (Farbe) trumps *pl.;* **was ist ~?** what are trumps?; **lauter ~** *od.* **Trümpfe haben** have nothing but trumps; **seinen [letzten] ~ ausspielen** (fig.) play one's [last] trump card; **alle Trümpfe in der Hand haben** (fig.) hold all the [trump] cards; **seine besten Trümpfe aus der Hand geben** (fig.) throw away one's greatest advantages; **einen ~ in der Hinterhand haben** (fig.) have a card up one's sleeve; **~ sein** (fig.) (das Nötigste sein) be what matters; be the order of the day; (Mode sein) be the in thing

Trumpf·ass, ***Trumpf·as** *das* ace of trumps

trumpfen *itr. V.* play a trump

Trumpf·karte *die* (auch fig.) trump card

Trunk /trʊŋk/ *der;* **~[e]s, Trünke** /'trʏŋkə/ (geh.) [1] (Getränk) drink; beverage (formal) [2] (das Trinken) **er ist dem ~ verfallen** he is a victim of the demon drink; **sich dem ~ ergeben** take to drink

trunken *Adj.* (geh.; auch fig.) drunk, intoxicated (**von, vor** + *Dat.* with); **jmdn. ~ machen** make sb. drunk; (fig.) intoxicate sb.

Trunkenbold /-bɔlt/ *der;* **~[e]s, ~e** (abwertend) drunkard

Trunkenheit *die;* **~** [1] drunkenness; **im Zustand der ~:** in a state of intoxication; in an intoxicated state; **~ am Steuer** drunken driving [2] (geh.: Begeisterung) [state of] intoxication

trunkieren *tr. V.* (DV) truncate

Trunk·sucht *die* alcoholism *no art.*

trunk·süchtig *Adj.* alcoholic; **~ sein** be an alcoholic

Trupp /trʊp/ *der;* **~s, ~s** troop; (von Arbeitern, Gefangenen) gang; (von Soldaten, Polizisten) detachment; squad

Trüppchen /'trʏpçən/ *das;* **~s, ~:** [small] group; (von Soldaten) small detachment

Truppe *die;* **~, ~n** [1] (Einheit der Streitkräfte) unit; **nicht von der schnellen ~ sein** (fig. ugs.) not be exactly a fast worker [2] *Pl.* (Soldaten) troops [3] (Streitkräfte) [armed] forces *pl.;* (Heer) army; **die kämpfende ~:** the front-line *or* combat troops *pl.;* **der Dienst bei der ~:** military service [4] (Gruppe von Schauspielern, Artisten) troupe; company; (von Sportlern) squad; (Mannschaft) team

Truppen-: ~abbau *der* reduction in the number of troops; **~abzug** *der* withdrawal of troops; troop withdrawal; **~aufmarsch** *der* build-up of troops; **massiver ~aufmarsch** massing of troops; **~besuch** *der* visit to the troops; **~bewegung** *die* troop movement; **~einsatz** *der* troop deployment; **~gattung** *die* arm [of the service]; corps; **~kontingent** *das* contingent of troops; **~konzentration** *die* massing of troops; **~parade** *die* military parade; **~präsenz** *die* military presence; **~reduzierung** *die* reduction in the number of troops; **~rückzug** *der* withdrawal of troops; **~stärke** *die* troop strength; number of troops; **~teil** *der* unit; **~transporter** *der* (Schiff, Flugzeug) troop carrier; (Kraftfahrzeug) personnel carrier; troop carrier; **~übungs·platz** *der* military training area; **~verband** *der* military unit; **ein internationaler ~verband** an international military force

Trust /trast/ *der;* **~[e]s, ~e** *od.* **~s** (Wirtsch.) trust

Trut- /'truːt-/: **~hahn** *der; Pl.* **~hähne** turkey [cock]; (als Braten) turkey; **~henne** *die* turkey [hen]

Trutz /trʊts/ *der;* **~es** (veralt.) resistance; **Schutz und ~:** protection and shelter

Trutz·burg *die* (hist.): *castle built to besiege an enemy castle*

trutzig (veralt.)
[A] *Adj.* massive, formidable ‹*wall, building*›
[B] *adv.* defiantly

Tschad /tʃat/ *(das) od. der;* **~s** Chad *no art.*

t

Tschador /tʃa'dɔr/ *der;* **~s, ~s** chador

Tschako /'tʃako/ *der;* **~s, ~s** (hist.) shako

tschau /tʃau̯/ (ugs.) ciao (coll.); so long (coll.)

Tscheche /'tʃɛçə/ *der;* **~n, ~n** ►❶ **S. 520** Czech

Tschechei *die;* **~** (ugs. veralt.) Czechoslovakia *no art.*

Tschechien *(das;)* **~s** Czech Republic

Tschechin *die;* **~, ~nen** ►❶ **S. 520** ►**Tscheche**

tschechisch ►❶ **S. 520,** ►❶ **S. 670**

A *Adj.* Czech

B *adv.* **~ sprechend** Czech-speaking; *s. auch* **deutsch; Deutsch; Deutsche²**

Tschechoslowakei /tʃɛçoslova'kai̯/ *die;* **~:** Czechoslovakia *no art.*

tschechoslowakisch *Adj.* Czechoslovak[ian]

Tschetschene /tʃe'tʃe:nə/ *der;* **~n, ~n** Chechen; **die ~n** the Chechen[s]

Tschetschenien /tʃe'tʃe:ni̯ən/ *das;* **~s** Chechenia; Chechnya

Tschetschenin /tʃe'tʃe:nɪn/ *die;* **~, ~nen** Chechen

tschetschenisch *Adj.* Chechen

Tschick /tʃɪk/ *der;* **~s, ~** (österr. ugs.) fag (Brit. coll.); (Zigarettenstummel) fag end (Brit. coll.)

tschilpen /'tʃɪlpn̩/ *itr. V.* chirp

Tschinelle /tʃi'nɛlə/ *die;* **~, ~n** (veralt., noch südd., österr.) cymbal

tschingderassabum /tʃɪŋdərasa'bʊm/ *Interj.* crash! crash! boom! boom! *(onomatopoeic for cymbals and drums)*

tschüs /tʃy:s/, **tschüss** /tʃʏs/ (ugs.) bye (coll.); so long (coll.)

Tsd. *Abk.* **= Tausend**

Tsetse·fliege /'tse:tse-/ *die* tsetse fly

T-Shirt /'ti:ʃø:t/ *das;* **~s, ~s** T-shirt

Tsunami /tsu'na:mi/ *der;* **~[s], ~s** tsunami

T-Träger *der* (Bauw.) T-girder

TU *Abk.* **= technische Universität**

Tuba /'tu:ba/ *die;* **~, Tuben** tuba

Tube /'tu:bə/ *die;* **~, ~n** tube; **eine ~ Zahnpasta** a tube of toothpaste; **auf die ~ drücken** (fig. ugs.) step on it (coll.); put one's foot down

Tuberkel·bazillus /tu'bɛrkl̩-/ *der* (Med.) tubercle bacillus

tuberkulös /tubɛrku'lø:s/ *Adj.* (Med.) tubercular

Tuberkulose /tubɛrku'lo:zə/ *die;* **~, ~n** ►❶ **S. 439** (Med.) tuberculosis *no art.*

Tuch /tu:x/ *das;* **~[e]s, Tücher** /'ty:çɐ/ *od.* **~e** **1** *Pl.* **Tücher** cloth; (Geschirr~) dishcloth; (Bade~) [bath] towel; (Kopf~, Hals~) scarf; **das rote ~ des Matadors** the matador's red cape; **ein rotes ~ für jmdn. sein** (ugs.) be like a red rag to a bull for sb.; make sb. see red **2** *Pl.* **~e** (Gewebe) cloth **3** *Pl.* **~e** (Seemannsspr.) ►**Segel~**

Tuchent /'tʊxn̩t/ *die;* **~, ~en** (österr.) feather bed

Tuch-: ~fühlung *die* (scherzh.) physical contact; (fig.: Kontakte) [close] contact; **auf** *od.* **mit ~fühlung** close together; **~händler** *der,* **~händlerin** *die* cloth merchant (esp. hist.); textile trader

Tüchlein *das;* **~s, ~:** [little] handkerchief

tüchtig /'tʏçtɪç/

A *Adj.* **1** efficient ‹*secretary, assistant, worker, etc.*›; (fähig) capable, competent (**in** + *Dat.* at); **freie Bahn dem Tüchtigen!** let ability win through **2** (von guter Qualität) excellent ‹*performance, piece of work, etc.*›; **~, ~!** (auch iron.) well done! **3** (ugs.: beträchtlich) sizeable ‹*piece, portion*›; big ‹*gulp*›; hearty ‹*eater, appetite*›; **eine ~e Tracht Prügel** a good hiding (coll.); **ein ~er Schrecken** quite a fright

B *adv.* **1** efficiently; (fähig) competently; **~ arbeiten** work hard **2** (ugs.: sehr) really ‹*cold, warm*›; ‹*snow, rain*› good and proper (coll.); ‹*eat*› heartily; **~ heizen** have the heating up good and high (coll.)

Tüchtigkeit *die;* **~** **1** efficiency; (Fähigkeit) ability; competence; (Fleiß) industry **2** **körperliche ~:** physical fitness

Tücke /'tʏkə/ *die;* **~, ~n** **1** (Hinterhältigkeit) deceit[fulness]; (List) guile; scheming *no indef. art.*; (fig.: des Schicksals) fickleness; **die ~ des Objekts** the perversity *or* (coll.) cussedness of inanimate objects; *s. auch* **List 2** **2** (hinterhältige Handlung) wile; ruse; (Betrug) deception **3** ([verborgene] Gefahr/Schwierigkeit) [hidden] danger/difficulty; (unberechenbare Eigenschaft) vagary; **seine ~n haben** ‹*engine, machine*› be temperamental; have its vagaries; ‹*mountain, river, course*› be treacherous

tuckern /'tukɐn/ *itr. V.; mit Richtungsangabe mit sein* chug

tückisch

A *Adj.* **1** (hinterhältig) wily; (betrügerisch) deceitful **2** (gefährlich) treacherous ‹*bend, slope, spot, etc.*›; (Gefahr signalisierend) menacing ‹*look, eyes*›

B *adv.* **1** (hinterhältig) craftily **2** (Gefahr signalisierend) menacingly

Tuff /tʊf/ *der;* **~s, ~e** (Geol.) **1** tuff **2** ►**Sinter**

Tuff·stein *der* tuff

Tüftel·arbeit *die* (ugs.) fiddly job

Tüftelei *die;* **~, ~en** (ugs.) **1** fiddling [about]; (geistig) racking one's brains **2** (tüftelige Arbeit) fiddly job

Tüfteler *der;* **~s, ~** ►**Tüftler**

tüfteln /'tʏftl̩n/ *itr. V.* (ugs.) fiddle (**an** + *Dat.* with); do finicky work (**an** + *Dat.* on); (geistig) rack one's brains, puzzle (**an** + *Dat.* over)

Tüftler *der;* **~s, ~, Tüftlerin** *die;* **~, ~nen** (ugs.) *person who likes finicky jobs/niggling problems;* (jmd., der gern Rätselspiele macht) puzzle freak (coll.)

Tugend /'tu:gn̩t/ *die;* **~, ~en** virtue; **auf dem Pfad der ~ wandeln** keep to the path of virtue *or* the straight and narrow

tugendhaft

A *Adj.* virtuous

B *adv.* virtuously; **~ leben** live a life of virtue

Tukan /'tu:kan/ *der;* **~s, ~e** toucan

Tüll /tʏl/ *der;* **~s, ~e** tulle

Tülle *die;* **~, ~n** (bes. nordd.) spout

Tüll-: ~gardine *die* net curtain; **~spitze** *die* tulle lace

Tulpe /'tʊlpə/ *die;* **~, ~n** **1** (Pflanze) tulip **2** (Glas) tulip glass

Tulpen-: ~baum *der* tulip tree; **~zwiebel** *die* tulip bulb

tumb /tʊmp/ *Adj.* (scherzh.) guileless; naïve; **~er Tor** simple Simon

Tumbheit *die;* **~** (scherzh.) guilelessness; ingenuousness

tummeln /'tʊml̩n/ *refl. V.* **1** (umhertollen) romp [about]; (im Wasser) splash about **2** (bes. westmd., österr., sich beeilen) stir one's stumps (coll.); get a move on (coll.)

Tummel·platz *der* (auch fig.) playground; **ein ~ der Linksradikalen** (fig.) a happy hunting ground for left-wing radicals

Tümmler /'tʏmlɐ/ *der;* **~s, ~** **1** (Delphin) bottle-nosed dolphin **2** (Taube) tumbler

Tumor /'tu:mɔr/ *der;* **~s, ~en** /tu'mo:rən/, *ugs. auch* **~e** /tu'mo:rə/ ►❶ **S. 439** (Med.) tumour

Tumor-: ~erkrankung *die* cancer; **~gewebe** *das* tumour tissue; **~patient** *der,* **~patientin** *die* tumour patient; **~therapie** *die* tumour therapy; **~wachstum** *das* tumour growth; **~zelle** *die* tumour *or* cancer cell; **~zentrum** *das* tumour centre; cancer centre

Tümpel /'tʏmpl̩/ *der;* **~s, ~:** pond

Tumult /tu'mʊlt/ *der;* **~[e]s, ~e** tumult; commotion; (Protest) uproar; **schwere ~e** serious disturbances

tumultuarisch /tumʊl'tu̯a:rɪʃ/ *Adj.* (geh.) turbulent; ‹*scenes*› of uproar

tun /tu:n/

A *unr. tr. V.* **1** (machen) do; **er tat, wie ihm befohlen** he did as he was told; **ich habe anderes zu ~, als hier herumzusitzen** I can't sit around here [all day], I've other things to do; **er tut nichts als meckern** (ugs.) he does nothing but moan; **ich weiß nicht, was ich ~ soll** I don't know what to do; **so etwas tut man nicht** that is just not done; **so tu doch etwas!** well, do something [about it], then!; **er hat sein Möglichstes getan** he did his [level] best; **du kannst ~ und lassen, was du willst** you can do just as you please; **was tust du hier/mit dem Messer?** what are you doing here/with that knife?; **dagegen kann man nichts ~:** there is nothing one can do about it; **es hat sich so ergeben, ohne dass ich etwas dazu getan hätte** it turned out that way without my having done anything [towards it]; **was ~?** what is to be done?; **was tut denn die tote Fliege in meiner Suppe?** what's that dead fly doing in my soup?; **man tut, was man kann** one does what one can; one tries one's best; **ich will sehen, was sich ~ lässt** I'll see what can be done; **was tut man nicht alles [...]!** the things I/you *etc.* do [...]!

2 (erledigen) do ‹*work, duty, etc.*›; **er tut nichts** he doesn't do a thing; **ich muss noch etwas [für die Schule] ~:** I've still got some [school] work to do; **tu's doch!** go on, do it!; **nach getaner Arbeit** when the work is/was done; **mit Geld/einer Entschuldigung** *usw.* **ist es nicht getan** money/an apology *etc.* is not enough; **es ~** (ugs. verhüll.: koitieren) do it (sl.); *s. auch* **Handschlag 2**

3 **[etwas] zu ~ haben** have something to do; **ich hatte dort zu ~/dort geschäftlich zu ~:** I had things/business to do there; **es mit jmdm./etw. zu ~ haben** be dealing with sb./sth.; **wir haben es mit einem gefährlichen Verbrecher zu ~:** we're up against a dangerous criminal; **er hat es mit dem Herzen zu ~** (ugs.) he's got heart trouble; **[es] mit jmdm. zu ~ bekommen** *od.* (ugs.) **kriegen** get into trouble with sb./sth.; **mit sich [selbst] zu ~ haben** have problems [of one's own]; **[etwas] mit etw./jmdm. zu ~ haben** be concerned with sth./have dealings with sb.; **er hat noch nie [etwas] mit der Polizei zu ~ gehabt** he has never been involved with the police; **mit etw. nichts zu ~ haben** have nothing to do with sth.; not be concerned with sth.; **er hat mit dem Mord nichts zu ~:** he had nothing to do with *or* was not involved in the murder; **mit Kunst hat das kaum etwas zu ~:** that has very little to do with art; **mit jmdm./etw. nichts zu ~ haben wollen** not want [to have] anything to do with sb./sth.; **es ist mir um dich/deine Gesundheit zu ~** (geh.) I'm concerned about you/your health

4 *nimmt die Aussage eines vorher gebrauchten Verbs auf* **ich riet ihm zu verschwinden, was er schleunigst tat** I advised him to disappear, which he did at the double *or* and he did so at the double; **es sollte am nächsten Tag regnen, und das tat es dann auch** it was expected to rain the next day, and it did [so]

5 *als Funktionsverb* make ‹*remark, catch, etc.*›; take ‹*step, jump*›; do ‹*deed*›; **einen Blick aus dem Fenster ~:** glance out of the window; (unpers.) **plötzlich tat es einen furchtbaren Knall** suddenly there was a dreadful bang

6 (bewirken) work, perform ‹*miracle*›; **seine Wirkung ~:** have its effect; **was tuts?, was tut das schon?** (ugs.) so what?; what does it matter?; **das tut nichts** it doesn't matter; *s. auch* **Sache 2**

7 (an~) **jmdm. etw. ~:** do sth. to sb.; **jmdm. einen Gefallen ~:** do sb. a favour; **er tut dir nichts** he won't hurt *or* harm you; **der Hund tut nichts** the dog doesn't bite

8 **es ~** (ugs.: genügen) be good enough; **die Schuhe ~ es noch einen Winter** the shoes will do for another winter

9 (ugs.: irgendwohin bringen) put; **Salz an** *od.* **in die Suppe ~:** put salt in *or* add salt to the soup; **den Kleinen zur Oma ~:** take the little boy to granny (coll.)

B *unr. itr. V.* **1** (ugs.: funktionieren) work; **die Kaffeemaschine tut nicht mehr** the coffee machine has had it (coll.)

2 **freundlich/geheimnisvoll ~:** pretend to be *or* (coll.) act friendly/act mysteriously; **vornehm ~:** act all genteel (coll.); **er tut [so], als ob** *od.* **als wenn** *od.* **wie wenn er nichts wüsste** he pretends not to know anything; **er tut nur so [als ob]** he's only pretending; **tu doch nicht so!** stop pretending!

C *unr. refl. V.* (unpers.) (geschehen) **es hat sich einiges getan** quite a bit has happened; **es tut sich nichts** there's nothing happening
D *Hilfsverb* **1** *betonend* (ugs.) **rechnen tut er gut** he's good at arithmetic; **kennen tue ich sie nicht** I don't know her; (in nicht korrektem Sprachgebrauch) **ich tu den Fleck einfach nicht wegkriegen** I simply can't get rid of the stain **2** *zur Umschreibung des Konjunktivs* (ugs.) **das täte mich interessieren/freuen** I'd be interested in/pleased about that

Tun *das;* **~s** action; activity; **unser nächtliches ~:** our nocturnal activities *pl.*; **jmds. ~ und Treiben** (geh.) [all] sb.'s doings

Tünche /ˈtʏnçə/ *die;* **~, ~n** **1** (Farbe) distemper; wash; **[weiße] ~:** whitewash **2** (abwertend: Oberfläche) veneer (fig.)

tünchen *tr.* (*auch itr.*) *V.* distemper; **weiß ~:** whitewash

Tundra /ˈtʊndra/ *die;* **~, Tundren** tundra

Tunell /tuˈnɛl/ *das;* **~s, ~s** (südd., österr., schweiz.) ▸ **Tunnel**

tunen /ˈtjuːnən/ *tr. V.* (Kfz-W.) tune

Tuner /ˈtjuːnɐ/ *der;* **~s, ~** **1** (Elektronik) tuner **2** (Kfz-W.) tuner; tuning expert

Tunesien /tuˈneːzi̯ən/ *(das);* **~s** Tunisia

Tunesier *der;* **~s, ~, Tunesierin** *die;* **~, ~nen** ▸ ❶ **S. 520** Tunisian

tunesisch *Adj.* ▸ ❶ **S. 520** Tunisian

Tun·fisch ▸ **Thunfisch**

Tu·nicht·gut *der;* **~** *od.* **~[e]s, ~e** good-for-nothing; ne'er-do-well

Tunika /ˈtuːnika/ *die;* **~, Tuniken** tunic; (hist.) tunica; tunic

Tunke /ˈtʊŋkə/ *die;* **~, ~n** (bes. ostmd.) sauce; (Bratensoße) gravy

tunken *tr. V.* (bes. ostmd.) dip; dip, dunk ‹*biscuit, piece of bread, etc.*›

tunlichst /ˈtuːnlɪçst/ *Adv.* (geh.) **1** (möglichst) as far as possible **2** (unbedingt) at all costs; **das hat in Zukunft ~ zu unterbleiben** this must not happen in future at any cost

Tunnel /ˈtʊnl̩/ *der;* **~s, ~** *od.* **~s** tunnel

Tunnel-: **~bau** *der* building of a/the tunnel; **~blick** *der* tunnel vision (also fig.)

tunnelieren *tr. V.* (österr.) tunnel through ‹*mountain etc.*›

Tunnel-: **~öffnung** *die* **1** (Ein-/Ausgang) mouth of a/the tunnel; **2** (Eröffnung) opening of the tunnel; **~projekt** *das* tunnel project; **~röhre** *die* tunnel tube; **~strecke** *die* stretch of tunnel; (einer Straße) stretch in a tunnel; **~system** *das* system of tunnels; **~wand** *die* wall of the tunnel; tunnel wall

Tunte /ˈtʊntə/ *die;* **~, ~n** **1** (ugs. abwertend: Frau) female **2** (salopp, auch abwertend: Homosexueller) queen (sl.)

tuntenhaft, tuntig
A *Adj.* **1** (ugs. abwertend: tantenhaft) prissy **2** (salopp abwertend: feminin) poofy (Brit. coll.)
B *adv.;* ▸ **A: 1** prissily **2** poofily (Brit. coll.)

Tuntigkeit *die;* **~** **1** (salopp abwertend: feminines Wesen) effeminacy; poofiness (Brit. coll.); **2** (ugs. abwertend: Tantenhaftigkeit) prissiness

Tüpfelchen /ˈtʏpfl̩çən/ *das;* **~s, ~:** dot; **das ~ auf dem i** the final touch

tüpfeln *tr. V.* stipple; (sprenkeln) speckle

tupfen /ˈtʊpfn̩/ *tr. V.* **1** dab; **sich** (*Dat.*) **den Schweiß von der Stirn ~:** dab the sweat from one's brow; **etw. auf etw.** (*Akk.*) **~:** dab sth. on to sth. **2** (mit T~ versehen) dot; **ein getupftes Kleid** a spotted dress

Tupfen *der;* **~s, ~:** dot; (größer) spot

Tupfer *der;* **~s, ~** **1** (ugs.) ▸ **Tupfen** **2** (Med.) swab

Tür /tyːɐ̯/ *die;* **~, ~en** door; (Garten~) gate; **an die ~ gehen** (öffnen) [go and] answer the door; **in der ~ stehen** stand in the doorway; **den Kopf zur ~ hereinstecken** put one's head round the door; **mach die ~ von außen zu!** (ugs.) out with you!; out you go!; **jmdm. die ~ einlaufen** *od.* **einrennen** (fig. ugs.) keep badgering sb.; **offene ~e einrennen** (fig.) be pushing at an open door; **jmdm. die ~ vor der Nase zuschlagen** (fig.) slam the door in sb.'s face; **einer Sache** (*Dat.*) **~ und Tor öffnen** (fig.) open the door *or* way to sth.; **hinter verschlossenen ~en** behind closed doors; **mit der ~ ins Haus fallen** (fig. ugs.) blurt out what one is after; **vor verschlossener ~ stehen** be locked out; **zwischen ~ und Angel** (fig. ugs.) in passing; **[ach,] du kriegst die ~ nicht zu!** (fig. ugs.) Good Lord!; well I never!; **jmdm. die ~ weisen** (fig. geh.) show sb. the door; **vor die ~ gehen** go outside; **jmdn. vor die ~ setzen** (fig. ugs.) chuck (coll.) *or* throw sb. out; **vor seiner eigenen ~ kehren** (fig. ugs.) set one's own house in order; **Pfingsten steht/die Sommerferien stehen vor der ~** (fig.) Whitsun is/the summer holidays are [just] coming up; **der Winter steht vor der ~** (fig.) winter is just around the corner

Tür·angel *die* door hinge

Turban /ˈtʊrbaːn/ *der;* **~s, ~e** turban

Turbine /tʊrˈbiːnə/ *die;* **~, ~n** (Technik) turbine

turbinen-, Turbinen-: **~antrieb** *der* turbine propulsion; **~flugzeug** *das* turbojet aircraft; **~getrieben** *Adj.* turbine-propelled ‹*ship, aircraft*›; turbine-driven ‹*generator*›

Tür·blatt *das* door; door leaf (as tech. term)

Turbo- /ˈtʊrbo-/ (Technik) turbo-

Turbo-Prop-Flugzeug *das* turboprop aircraft

turbulent /tʊrbuˈlɛnt/
A *Adj.* (auch Physik, Astron., Met.) turbulent; (allzu lebhaft) chaotic
B *adv.* (auch Physik, Astron., Met.) turbulently; (allzu lebhaft) chaotically; **bei uns/an den Devisenmärkten geht es ~ zu** things are chaotic [around] here/the exchange markets are in turmoil

Turbulenz /tʊrbuˈlɛnts/ *die;* **~, ~en** (auch Physik, Astron., Met.) turbulence *no pl.*

Tür·drücker *der;* **~s, ~** **1** doorknob **2** (Türöffner) [automatic] door-opener

Türen·schlagen *das;* **~s** slamming of doors (also fig.)

türen·schlagend
A *Adj.* door-slamming *attrib*
B *adv.* slamming the door [behind him/her *etc.*]

Turf /tʊrf/ (Pferdesport Jargon) turf

Tür-: **~flügel** *der* ▸ **Türblatt**; **~füllung** *die* door panel; **~glocke** *die* (fachspr., sonst veralt.) doorbell; **~griff** *der* door handle; **~hüter** *der*, **~hüterin** *die* (veralt.) doorkeeper; (fig.) gatekeeper (+ *Gen.*, **von** to)

Türke /ˈtʏrkə/ *der;* **~n, ~n** **1** ▸ ❶ **S. 520** Turk **2** (ugs.) **einen ~n bauen** tell a cock and bull story/cock and bull stories

Türkei *die;* **~:** Turkey *no art.*

türken *tr. V.* (ugs.) fake ‹*scene, letter, document, etc.*›; make up ‹*story, report*›

Türken·bund·lilie *die* turk's-cap lily

Türkin *die;* **~, ~nen** ▸ ❶ **S. 520** ▸ **Türke 1**

türkis /tʏrˈkiːs/ *indekl. Adj.* turquoise

Türkis[1] *der;* **~es, ~e** (Mineral.) turquoise

Türkis[2] *das;* **~** (Farbe) turquoise

türkis·blau *Adj., adv.* turquoise [blue]

türkisch *Adj.* ▸ ❶ **S. 520,** ▸ ❶ **S. 670** Turkish; **~er Honig** nougat; *s. auch* **deutsch**; **Deutsch**; **Deutsche**[2]

türkis-: **~farben** *Adj.* turquoise; **~grün** *Adj., adv.* turquoise [green]

Tür-: **~klingel** *die* doorbell; **~klinke** *die* door handle; **~klopfer** *der* door knocker; **~laibung** *die* (Archit., Bauw.) door jamb; (Sturz) door lintel

Turkologie /tʊrkoloˈgiː/ *die;* **~:** Turkish studies *pl., no art.*

Turk-: **~sprache** *die* Turkic language; **~volk** *das* Turkic people

Turm /tʊrm/ *der;* **~[e]s, Türme** /ˈtʏrmə/ **1** tower; (spitzer Kirch~) spire; steeple **2** (Schach) rook; castle **3** ▸ **Sprung~** **4** (hist.) ▸ **Schuld~**; **Hunger~** **5** (Milit.) turret

Turmalin /tʊrmaˈliːn/ *der;* **~s, ~e** (Mineral.) tourmaline

Turm·bau *der* building of a/the tower; **der ~ zu Babel** the building of the Tower of Babel

Türmchen /ˈtʏrmçən/ *das;* **~s, ~:** turret

türmen[1]
A *tr. V.* (stapeln) stack up; (häufen) pile up
B *refl. V.* be piled up; ‹*clouds*› gather

türmen[2] *itr. V.; mit sein* (salopp) scarper (Brit. coll.); do a bunk (Brit. coll.); beat it (coll.); **aus dem Knast ~:** do a bunk from prison

turm-, Turm-: **~falke** *der* kestrel; **~haube** *die* (Archit.) cupola; **~haus** *das* (Archit.) **1** (Wohnturm) tower house (esp. hist.); **2** (Hochhaus) tower [building]; **~hoch** **A** *Adj.* towering; **B** *adv.* **sich ~hoch stapeln** be piled high; **~hoch mit etw. beladen** piled high with sth.; **~spitze** *die* spire; **~springen** *das;* **~~s** high diving *no art.*; **~springer** *der*, **~springerin** *die* high diver; **~uhr** *die* tower clock; **~zimmer** *das* tower room

Turn·anzug *der* leotard

Turnaround /təːnəˈraʊ̯nt/ *der;* **~s, ~s** (Wirtsch.) turnaround

Turn·beutel *der* PE bag

turnen /ˈtʊrnən/
A *itr. V.* **1** (Sport) do gymnastics; (Schulw.) do gym *or* PE; **sie turnt gut** she's good at gymnastics *or* a good gymnast; (Schulw.) she's good at gym *or* PE; **er turnte am Reck/auf der Matte** he was doing *or* performing exercises *or* was working on the horizontal bar/the mat **2** *mit sein* (ugs.: klettern) clamber **3** (ugs.: herumklettern) clamber about
B *tr. V.* (Sport) do, perform ‹*exercise, routine*›

Turnen *das;* **~s** gymnastics *sing., no art.*; (Schulw.) gym *no art.*; PE *no art.*

Turner *der;* **~s, ~, Turnerin** *die;* **~, ~nen** gymnast

turnerisch
A *Adj.* gymnastic
B *adv.* gymnastically

Turn-: **~fest** *das* gymnastics festival; **~gerät** *das* gymnastics apparatus; **~halle** *die* gymnasium; **~hemd** *das* [gym] singlet; (für **~**unterricht) gym *or* PE vest; **~hose** *die* (mit langem Bein) gym trousers *pl.*; (mit kurzem Bein) gym shorts *pl.*; (für **~**unterricht) gym *or* PE shorts *pl.*

Turnier /tʊrˈniːɐ̯/ *das;* **~s, ~e** (auch hist.) tournament; (Reit~) show; (Tanz~) competition; **ein ~ reiten** ride in a tournament

Turnier-: **~chef** *der*, **~chefin** *die*, **~direktor** *der*, **~direktorin** *die*, **~leiter** *der*, **~leiterin** *die* tournament director, tournament manager; **~leitung** *die* tournament management; **~pferd** *das* show horse; **~sieg** *der* tournament win; **~sieger** *der*, **~siegerin** *die* tournament winner; **~tag** *der* day of the tournament; **~tanz** *der* **1** (Tanzsport) competitive ballroom dancing; **2** (Tanz) ballroom dance

Turn-: **~lehrer** *der*, **~lehrerin** *die* gym *or* PE teacher; **~schuh** *der* gym shoe; (Trainingsschuh) training shoe; trainer (coll.); **~schuh·generation** *die* youth of the '80s; **~stunde** *die* gym *or* PE lesson; **~übung** *die* gymnastics exercise; **~unterricht** *der* gym *no art.*; PE *no art.*

Turnüre /tʊrˈnyːrə/ *die;* **~, ~n** (Mode, hist.) bustle

Turnus /ˈtʊrnʊs/ *der;* **~, ~se** **1** regular cycle; **in einem 4-jährigen ~ stattfinden** take place on a four-year cycle; **er führt das Amt im ~ mit seinen Kollegen** he and his colleagues hold the office in rotation **2** (österr.) ▸ **Schicht 3**

turnus-: **~gemäß** **A** *Adj.* **die ~gemäße Ablösung des Vorsitzenden erfolgt im April** the chairmanship rotates in April; **B** *adv.* **er wird den Vorsitz ~gemäß am ersten Januar übernehmen** it will be his turn to take over the chair on 1 January; **~gemäß finden die Verhandlungen in X statt** it is the turn of X to host the negotiations; **~mäßig** **A** *Adj.* regular ‹*inspection, check, etc.*›; **B** *adv.* on a regular cycle; **~mäßig hat er morgen Nachtdienst** according to the rota he's on duty tomorrow night

Turn-: **~verband** *der* gymnastics association; **~verein** *der* gymnastics club; **~zeug** *das* gym kit; PE kit

Tür-: ~öffner *der* door-opener; **~öffnung** *die* doorway; **~pfosten** *der* doorpost; door jamb; **~rahmen** *der* doorframe; **~schild** *das* sign on a/the door; (Namensschild) nameplate; door plate; **~schloss, *~schloß** *das* door lock; **~schnalle** *die* (österr.) door handle; **~schwelle** *die* threshold; **~spalt** *der* crack [of the door]; **~spion** *der* ▸ **Spion 2**; **~steher** *der*, **~steherin** *die* doorkeeper; (Mann auch) doorman; **~sturz** *der* (Bauw.) lintel

turteln *itr. V.* 1 (scherzh.: zärtlich sein) bill and coo 2 (veralt.: gurren) coo

Turtel·taube /'tʊrtl-/ *die* turtle dove; (fig.) lovebird

Tür-: ~verkleidung *die* (Kfz.-W.) door trim; **~vorleger** *der* doormat

Tusch /tʊʃ/ *der;* **~[e]s, ~e** fanfare

Tusche *die;* **~, ~n** 1 Indian (Brit.) *or* (Amer.) India ink 2 (nordd., md.: Wasserfarbe) watercolour 3 (ugs.: Wimpern~) mascara

Tuschelei *die;* **~, ~en** 1 (das Tuscheln) whispering 2 (Äußerung) whisper

tuscheln /'tʊʃl̩n/ *itr., tr. V.* whisper

tuschen

A *tr. V.* 1 **etw. ~:** draw sth. in Indian (Brit.) *or* (Amer.) India ink/paint sth. in watercolours 2 **sich** (*Dat.*) **die Wimpern ~:** put one's mascara on

B *itr. V.* paint in watercolours

Tusch-: ~kasten *der* (nordd., md.) box of watercolours; **die ist der reinste ~kasten** (fig.) she's got all her warpaint on (coll. joc.); **~zeichnung** *die* pen-and-ink drawing

Tussi /'tʊsi/ *die;* **~, ~s** (salopp) female (derog.); (Mädchen) bird (sl.); chick (coll.)

tut /tu:t/ *Interj.* (Kinderspr.) beep; toot

Tütchen /'ty:tçən/ *das;* **~s, ~:** small bag

Tüte /'ty:tə/ *die;* **~, ~n** 1 bag; **~n kleben** *od.* **drehen** (fig. ugs.) be doing time; **das kommt nicht in die ~!** (fig. ugs.) not on your life! (coll.); no way! 2 (Eis~) cone; cornet 3 (ugs.: beim Alkoholtest) bag; **in die ~ blasen müssen** be breathalysed 4 (salopp: Person) jerk (coll.)

tuten /'tu:tn̩/ *itr. V.* hoot; ‹*siren,* [*fog*]*horn*› sound; **das Schiff tutet** the ship sounds its foghorn/hooter; **er wählte die Nummer, und es tutete** he dialled the number, and heard the ringing tone; **er tutete auf seiner Spielzeugtrompete** he tooted on his toy trumpet; *s. auch* **Ahnung 3**

Tüten·suppe *die* (ugs.) packet soup

Tutor /'tu:tɔr/ *der;* **~s, ~en** /tu'to:rən/, **Tutorin** *die;* **~, ~nen** (Päd.) 1 *senior student who helps beginners integrate into student life* 2 (Mentor) tutor

Tutorium /tu'to:ri̯ʊm/ *das;* **~, Tutorien** (Päd.) *seminar conducted by a postgraduate*

TÜV /tʏf/ *der;* **~** *Abk.* **= Technischer Überwachungsverein** ≈ MOT (Brit.); **ein Auto durch** *od.* **über den ~ bringen** ≈ get a car through its MOT

> **TÜV – Technischer Überwachungs-Verein**
>
> An independent organization responsible for testing the technical safety of vehicles and all types of machinery. Cars over three years old have to pass a *TÜV* safety and exhaust emission test every two years.

Tu·wort /'tu:-/ *das; Pl.* **Tuwörter** doing word

TV-: ~-Anstalt *die* television organization; **~-Auftritt** *der* TV appearance; appearance on TV; **~-Bild** *das* TV picture; **~-Duell** *das* TV [head-to-head] debate; **~-Film** *der* TV film; **~-Gelder** *Pl.* (bes. Fußball) TV rights fees; **~-Gerät** *das* TV set; **~-Interview** *das* TV interview; **~-Journalist** *der*, **~-Journalistin** *die* TV journalist; **~-Kamera** *die* TV camera; **~-Kanal** *der* TV channel; **~-Magazin** *das* [TV] magazine programme; **~-Moderator** *der*, **~-Moderatorin** *die* TV presenter; **~-Produktion** *die* TV production; **~-Produzent** *der*, **~-Produzentin** *die* ▸ ℹ **S. 113** (Person) TV producer; (Unternehmen) TV production company; **~-Programm** *das* TV schedule; **~-Rechte** *die Pl.* TV rights; **~-Sender** *der* TV station; **~-Serie** *die* ▸ **Fernsehserie**; **~-Show** *die* TV show; **~-Spot** *der* TV commercial; **~-Star** *der* TV star; **~-Station** *die* ▸ **TV-Sender**; **~-Studio** *das* TV studio; **~-Team** *das* TV crew; **~-Übertragung** *die* TV transmission; TV broadcast **~-Werbung** *die* TV advertising; **~-Zuschauer** *der*, **~-Zuschauerin** *die* [TV] viewer

Twen /tvɛn/ *der;* **~[s], ~s** twenty-to-thirty-year-old; **Mode für ~s** fashions for people in their 20s

Twist[1] /tvɪst/ *der;* **~[e]s, ~e** (Faden) twist

Twist[2] *der;* **~s, ~s** 1 (Tanz) twist; **~ tanzen** dance the twist 2 (Tennis) spin

twisten *itr. V.* twist; dance the twist

Tympanon /'tʏmpanɔn/ *das;* **~s, Tympana** (Archit.) tympanum

Typ /ty:p/ *der;* **~s, ~en** 1 type; **sie ist genau mein ~** (ugs.) she's just my type; **dein ~ wird verlangt** (salopp) you're wanted; **dein ~ ist hier nicht gefragt** (salopp) we don't want your sort here; **er ist ein dunkler/blonder ~:** he's dark/fair; **die beiden sind ganz verschiedene ~en** they're very different sorts of people 2 *Gen. auch* **~en** (ugs.: Mann) bloke (Brit. sl.); guy (coll.) 3 (Technik: Modell) (Auto) model; (Flugzeug) type 4 (bes. Philos.) type

Type /'ty:pə/ *die;* **~, ~n** 1 (Druck~, Schreibmaschinen~) type 2 (ugs.) (Person) type; sort; character; (seltsame Person) odd type *or* sort *or* character; **eine seltsame/originelle ~:** an odd sort *or* character/an oddball 3 (bes. österr.) ▸ **Typ 4** 4 (Fachspr.: Mehl~) grade

Typen-: ~hebel *der* typebar; **~rad** *das* daisy wheel; **~rad·schreib·maschine** *die* daisy wheel typewriter

Typhus /'ty:fʊs/ *der;* **~** ▸ ℹ **S. 439** typhoid [fever]

Typhus·epidemie *die* typhoid epidemic

typisch

A *Adj.* typical (**für** of)

B *adv.* typically; **das ist ~ Mann/Frau** that's just typical of a man/woman; **~ Gisela!** typical Gisela!; that's Gisela all over!

Typo·graph *der* ▸ ℹ **S. 113** typographer

Typographie /typogra'fi:/ *die;* **~, ~n** (Druckw.) typography

Typo·graphin *die;* **~, ~nen** ▸ ℹ **S. 113** typographer

typographisch (Druckw.)

A *Adj.* typographical

B *adv.* typographically

Typologie /typolo'gi:/ *die;* **~, ~n** (bes. Psych.) typology

typologisch (bes. Psych.)

A *Adj.* typological

B *adv.* typologically

Typo·skript *das; Pl.* **~e** typescript

Typus /'ty:pʊs/ *der;* **~, Typen** (auch Literaturw., bild. Kunst, Philos.) type

Tyrann /ty'ran/ *der;* **~en, ~en** (auch fig.) tyrant

Tyrannei *die;* **~, ~en** (auch fig.) tyranny

Tyrannen-: ~herrschaft *die* tyranny; tyrannical rule; **~mord** *der* tyrannicide

Tyrannin *die;* **~, ~nen** (auch fig.) tyrant

Tyrannis *die;* **~** (hist.) tyranny

tyrannisch

A *Adj.* tyrannical

B *adv.* tyrannically

tyrannisieren *tr. V.* tyrannize

tyrrhenisch /tʏ're:nɪʃ/ *Adj.* **Tyrrhenisches Meer** Tyrrhenian Sea

t

u, U /u:/ *das;* ~, ~: u/U; *s. auch* **a, A; X**
ü, Ü /y:/ *das;* ~, ~: u umlaut; *s. auch* **a, A**
U *Abk.* = **Umleitung**
u. *Abk.* = **und**
u. a. *Abk.* = **unter anderem**
u. ä. *Abk.* = **und ähnlich...**
u. Ä. *Abk.* = **und Ähnliches**
u. a. m. *Abk.* = **und andere[s] mehr** etc.
u. A. w. g., U. A. w. g. *Abk.* = **um Antwort wird gebeten** RSVP
UB *Abk.* = **Universitätsbibliothek**
U-Bahn *die* underground (Brit.); subway (Amer.); (bes. in London) tube

U-Bahn

Most large cities have a *U-Bahn* (*Untergrundbahn*) (underground railway network) that connects with an *S-Bahn* (*Schnellbahn* or *Stadtbahn*) (city and suburban railway). The same ticket can normally be used for both services.

U-Bahn-: **~hof** *der* underground station (Brit.); subway station (Amer.); (bes. in London) tube station; **~-Linie** *die* underground line; subway line (Amer.); **~-Netz** *das* underground network; subway network (Amer.); **~-Schacht** *der* underground station shaft; subway station shaft (Amer.); (U-Bahn-Tunnel) underground tunnel; subway tunnel (Amer.); **~-Station** *die* ▸**~hof**; **~-Strecke** *die* stretch of underground *or* (Amer.) subway line; **~-Tunnel** *der* underground tunnel; subway tunnel (Amer.); **~-Wagen** *der* underground carriage; subway car (Amer.); **~-Zug** *der* underground train; subway train (Amer.)

übel /'y:bl̩/
A *Adj.* **1** foul, bad, nasty ‹*smell, weather*›; bad, nasty ‹*headache, cold, taste*›; nasty ‹*situation, consequences*›; sorry ‹*state, affair*›; foul, (coll.) filthy ‹*mood*›; **nicht ~** (ugs.) not bad at all; **ein übles Ende nehmen** come to a bad end; **eine ~ riechende Substanz** an evil-smelling *or* foul-smelling substance **2** ▸**ⓘ S. 439** (unwohl) **jmdm. ist/wird ~:** sb. feels sick; **es kann einem ~ werden, wenn man so was hört** hearing that sort of thing is enough to make you sick **3** (verwerflich) bad; wicked; nasty, dirty ‹*trick*›; **ein übler Bursche** a bad sort (coll.) *or* lot; **in üble Gesellschaft geraten** fall in with a bad crowd
B *adv.* **1** **Wie geht's? — Danke, nicht ~:** How are things? — Not so bad, thanks; **nicht ~ Lust haben, etw. zu tun** have a good mind to do sth.; **etw. ~ aufnehmen** take sth. badly; **~ gelaunt sein** be in a bad mood; **er spielt nicht ~:** he plays pretty well **2** (nachteilig, schlimm) badly; **er ist ~ dran** he's in a bad way; **jmdm. etw. ~ nehmen** hold sth. against sb.; **etw. ~ nehmen** *od.* **vermerken** take sth. amiss; take offence at sth.; **nehmen Sie es [mir] bitte nicht ~, wenn ich ...** please don't take it amiss *or* be offended if I ...; **jmdm. ~ wollen** wish sb. ill; **~ wollend** malevolent; **jmdn. ~ zurichten** give sb. a working over (coll.) **3** (verwerflich) wickedly

Übel *das;* **~s, ~** **1** (Missstand, Ärgernis) evil; **zu allem ~:** on top of everything else; to make matters [even] worse; **ein notwendiges ~:** a necessary evil; **das kleinere ~:** the lesser evil; **das sind nur kleinere ~:** they are just minor annoyances *or* irritations **2** (veralt.: Krankheit) illness; malady **3** (veralt.: das Böse) evil *no art.*; **von** *od.* **vom ~ sein** be an evil

übel-: **~gelaunt** ▸**gelaunt, übel B 1**; **~gesinnt** ▸**gesinnt**

Übelkeit *die;* **~, ~en** ▸**ⓘ S. 439** nausea; **von einer plötzlichen ~ befallen werden** have a sudden feeling of nausea

übel-, Übel-: **~launig** **A** *Adj.* ill-humoured; ill-tempered; **B** *adv.* ill-humouredly; ill-temperedly; ***~|nehmen** ▸**übel B 2**; **~riechend** ▸**übel A 1**; **~stand** *der* evil; **~tat** *die* (geh.) evil *or* wicked deed; misdeed; **~täter** *der* wrongdoer; (Verbrecher) criminal; (Verantwortlicher) culprit; ***~|wollen** ▸**übel B 2**

üben /'y:bn̩/
A *tr. V.* **1** (auch itr.) practise; rehearse ‹*scene, play*›; practise on ‹*musical instrument*› **2** (trainieren, schulen) exercise ‹*fingers*›; train ‹*memory*›; **mit geübten Händen** with practised hands **3** (geh.: bekunden, tun) exercise ‹*patience, restraint, etc.*›; commit ‹*treason*›; take ‹*revenge, retaliation*›; **Kritik an etw.** (*Dat.*) **~:** criticize sth.
B *refl. V.* **sich in etw.** (*Dat.*) **~:** practise sth.; **sich in Geduld/Zurückhaltung ~** (geh.) exercise patience/restraint

über /'y:bɐ/
A *Präp. mit Dat.* **1** (Lage, Standort) over; above; (in einer Rangfolge) above; **das Bild hängt ~ dem Sofa** the picture hangs above the sofa; **~ jmdm. wohnen** live above sb.; **Nebel lag ~ der Wiese** fog hung over the meadow; **zehn Grad ~ Null/dem Gefrierpunkt** ten degrees above zero/freezing point; **sie trug eine Jacke ~ dem Kleid** she wore a jacket over her dress; **~ jmdm. stehen** (fig.) be above sb. **2** (während) during; **~ dem Lesen/der Arbeit einschlafen** fall asleep over one's book/magazine *etc.*/over one's work **3** (infolge) because of; as a result of; **~ der Aufregung vergaß ich, dass ...** in all the excitement I forgot that ...
B *Präp. mit Akk.* **1** (Richtung) over; (quer hinüber) across; **~ die Straße gehen** go across the road; cross the road; **~ Karlsruhe nach Stuttgart** via Karlsruhe to Stuttgart; **Tränen liefen ihr ~ die Wangen** tears ran down her cheeks; **ihr Rock reicht ~ die Knie** her skirt comes down to below the knee; **ein Wettlauf ~ eine Distanz von 5 000 Metern** a race over a distance of 5,000 metres; **er zog sich** (*Dat.*) **die Mütze ~ die Ohren** he pulled the cap down over his ears; **bis ~ die Knöchel im Schlamm versinken** sink up past one's ankles in mud; **es ist zwei Stunden ~ die Zeit** it should have happened two hours ago; (er/sie/es hat schon zwei Stunden Verspätung) he/she/it is two hours late; **Tennis/seine Tochter geht ihm ~ alles** tennis/his daughter means more to him than anything; **italienisches Essen geht ihm ~ alles** he loves Italian food more than anything else **2** (während) over; **~ Mittag** over lunchtime; **~ das Wochenende nach Hause fahren/zu Hause sein** go/be home for the weekend; **~ Wochen/Monate** for weeks/months; **~ Ostern/Weihnachten** over Easter/Christmas; **die ganze Zeit ~:** the whole time; **die Woche/den Sommer ~:** during the week/summer; **den ganzen Winter/Tag ~:** all winter/day long **3** (betreffend) about; **~ etw. reden/schreiben** talk/write about sth.; **ein Buch ~ die byzantinische Kunst** a book about *or* on Byzantine art; **ein Scheck/eine Rechnung ~ 1 000 Euro** a cheque/bill for 1,000 euros **4** **Kinder ~ 10 Jahre** children over ten [years of age] **5** **Gewalt ~ jmdn. haben** have power over sb.; **Wellingtons Sieg ~ Napoleon** Wellington's victory over Napoleon **6** **das geht ~ meine Kraft** that's too much for me; **jmdm. ~ den Verstand gehen** be beyond sb. **7** **sie macht Fehler ~ Fehler** she makes mistake after mistake; **er hat Schulden ~ Schulden** he's up to his ears in debt **8** (mittels, durch) through ‹*person*›; by ‹*post, telex, etc.*›; over ‹*radio, loudspeaker*›; **ich bin ~ die Autobahn gekommen** I came along the motorway; **etw. ~ alle Sender bringen/ausstrahlen** broadcast sth. on all stations **9** (geh. veralt.: bei Verwünschungen) on; **Schande/Fluch ~ ihn!** shame/a curse on him!
C *Adv.* **1** (mehr als) over **2** **~ und ~:** all over; **sie war ~ und ~ mit Schmutz bedeckt** she was covered all over in dirt
D *Adj.* (ugs.) **1** (überlegen) **jmdm. ~ sein** have the edge on sb. (coll.) **2** (übrig) left [over] **3** (zu viel, lästig) **das ist mir ~:** I'm fed up with it (coll.)

über-aktiv
A *Adj.* overactive
B *adv.* overactively

über-all /od. --'-/ *Adv.* **1** (an allen Orten) everywhere; **sie weiß ~ Bescheid** (auf allen Gebieten) she knows about everything **2** (bei jeder Gelegenheit) always

überall-: **~her** *Adv.* from all over the place; **~hin** *Adv.* everywhere

über-altert /y:bɐ'|altɐt/ *Adj.* **1** ‹*population*› containing a disproportionately high proportion of elderly people; **das Kabinett ist ~:** the cabinet has too many elderly members **2** (überholt) outdated; obsolete ‹*machine, vehicle, etc.*›

Über-alterung *die;* **~, ~en** **1** increase in the proportion of elderly people/workers/members *etc.* **2** ▸**überaltert 2**: outdatedness; obsolescence

überambitioniert (geh.)
A *Adj.* overambitious
B *adv.* overambitiously

Über-angebot *das* surplus (**an** + *Dat.* of); (Schwemme) glut (**an** + *Dat.* of)

über-ängstlich
A *Adj.* overanxious
B *adv.* overanxiously

über-anstrengen *tr. V.* overtax ‹*person, energy*›; strain ‹*eyes, nerves, heart*›; **sich ~:** overstrain *or* overexert oneself; **überanstreng dich nicht!** (iron.) don't strain yourself!

Über-anstrengung *die* over exertion; **~ der Augen/des Herzens** strain on the eyes/heart; **vermeiden Sie jede ~ der** *od.* **Ihrer Augen** avoid straining your eyes

über-antworten *tr. V.* (geh.) **1** (anvertrauen) **jmdn./etw. jmdm. ~:** entrust sb./sth. to sb.; **die Funde wurden dem Museum überantwortet** the finds were handed over to the museum **2** (ausliefern) **jmdn. dem Gericht ~:** hand sb. over to the courts

über-arbeiten
A *tr. V.* rework; revise ‹*text, edition*›
B *refl. V.* overwork

Über·arbeitung *die;* ~, ~en **1** reworking; (von Text, Manuskript, Ausgabe usw.) revision; (überarbeitete Fassung) revised version **2** (Überanstrengung) overwork

über·aus *Adv.* (geh.) extremely

über·backen *unr. tr. V.* **etw. mit Käse** *usw.* ~: top sth. with cheese *etc.* and brown it lightly [under the grill/in a hot oven]; **ein mit Käse ~er Auflauf** a soufflé au gratin

Über·bau *der; Pl.* ~e *od.* ~ten (Philos., Soziol.) superstructure

überbeanspruchen *tr. V.;* **ich überbeanspruche, überbeansprucht, überzubeanspruchen** put too great a strain on ‹*heart, circulation, etc.*›; strain ‹*nerves*›; overstrain, overstress ‹*material*›; overburden, overstretch ‹*facilities, services*›; overload ‹*machine*›; make excessive use of ‹*right, privilege*›; overtax ‹*person, body, strenght*›; (mit Arbeit) overwork ‹*person*›; (psychisch) put too great a strain on ‹*person*›

Über·beanspruchung *die* ▸**überbeanspruchen**: straining; overstraining; overstressing; overburdening; overloading; excessive use; overtaxing, overworking; **die ~ des Herzens führt zu ...** putting too great a strain on the heart leads to ...

über|behalten *unr. tr. V.* (ugs.) ▸**übrigbehalten**

Über·bein *das* ▸❶ **S. 439** (Med.) ganglion

über|bekommen *unr. tr. V.* (ugs.) **1** (satt bekommen) get fed up with (coll.) **2** **einen** *od.* **eins ~:** get a clout

überbelasten *tr. V.;* **ich überbelaste, überbelastet, überzubelasten** **1** overload **2** (zu stark in Anspruch nehmen) overburden ‹*person*›; place too much strain on ‹*bodily organ*›

Über·belastung *die* **1** overloading **2** (zu starke Inanspruchnahme) overburdening; **die ~ der Leber führt zu ...** placing too much strain on the liver leads to ...

über·belegt *Adj.* overcrowded; oversubscribed ‹*course*›

Über·belegung *die* overcrowding; **wegen der ~ des Kurses** because the course is/was oversubscribed

überbelichten *tr. V.;* **ich überbelichte, überbelichtet, überzubelichten** (Fot.) overexpose

Über·belichtung *die* (Fot.) overexposure

Über·beschäftigung *die* (Wirtsch.) overemployment

überbesetzt *Adj.* overstaffed ‹*company, civil service*›; overcrowded ‹*train*›, (fig.) ‹*market etc.*›

überbetonen *tr. V.;* **ich überbetone, überbetont, überzubetonen** overstress

überbetrieblich
A *Adj.* above company level *postpos.*; ‹*regulations*› applying to many firms
B *adv.* above company level

Über·bevölkerung *die* overpopulation

überbewerten *tr. V.;* **ich überbewerte, überbewertet, überzubewerten** overvalue; (überschätzen) overvalue; overrate; mark ‹*pupil, piece of work, gymnast, skater, etc.*› too high; **er warnte davor, diesen Faktor überzubewerten** he warned people not to attach too much significance to this factor

Über·bewertung *die* overvaluation; (Überschätzung) overvaluation; overrating

überbezahlen *tr. V.;* **ich überbezahle, überbezahlt, überzubezahlen** overpay

Über·bezahlung *die* overpayment

überbietbar *Adj.* **kaum noch ~ sein** take some beating; **das ist ein kaum ~es Beispiel für Intoleranz** as an example of intolerance that takes some beating

über·bieten *unr. tr. V.* **1** outbid (**um** by) **2** (übertreffen) surpass; outdo ‹*rival*›; break ‹*record*› (**um** by); exceed ‹*target*› (**um** by); **das ist kaum noch zu ~:** that takes some beating

über|bleiben *unr. itr. V.; mit sein* (ugs.) ▸**übrigbleiben**

Überbleibsel /-blaipsl/ *das;* ~s, ~: remnant; (einer Kultur) relic

über|blenden *tr. V.* (Rundf., Ferns., Film) dissolve

Überblendung *die* (Rundf., Ferns., Film) dissolve

Über·blick *der* **1** view; **einen guten ~ über etw.** (*Akk.*) **haben** have a good view over sth. **2** (Abriss) survey **3** (Einblick) overall view *or* perspective; **den ~ über etw.** (*Akk.*) **verlieren** lose track of sth.; **einen ~ über etw.** (*Akk.*) **gewinnen/haben** gain/have an overview of sth.

über·blicken *tr. V.* ▸**übersehen² 1, 2**

über·bordend *Adj.* exuberant

über|braten *unr. tr. V.* **jmdm. eins** *od.* **einen ~** (ugs.) belt sb. one

Über·breite *die:* **Transport/Ladung mit ~:** wide load; **~ haben** be over normal width

über·bringen *unr. tr. V.* deliver; convey ‹*greetings, congratulations*›

Über·bringer *der;* ~s, ~, **Über·bringerin** *die;* ~, ~nen bearer

über·brücken *tr. V.* **1** (veralt.) bridge ‹*river, ravine, etc.*› **2** (fig.) bridge ‹*gap, gulf*›; reconcile ‹*difference*›; **um die finanzielle Notlage zu ~, musste sie ...** to tide herself over the financial crisis, she had to ...

Überbrückung *die;* ~, ~en (fig.) bridging; (von Gegensätzen) reconciliation; **zur ~ der finanziellen Notlage musste sie ...** to tide herself over the financial crisis, she had to ...

Überbrückungs-: **~geld** *das* bridging allowance; **~hilfe** *die:* **jmdm. eine ~hilfe gewähren** give sb. interim financial help; **~kredit** *der* (Finanzw.) bridging loan

über·buchen *tr. V.* overbook

Überbuchung *die* overbooking

über·dachen *tr. V.* roof over; **überdacht** covered ‹*terrace, station platform, etc.*›

über·dauern *tr. V.* survive ‹*war, separation, hardship*›

Über·decke *die* cover; (auf einem Bett) bedspread

über|decken¹ *tr. V.* (ugs.) **jmdm. etw. ~:** cover sb. [up] with sth.

über|decken² *tr. V.* **1** (bedecken) cover **2** (verdecken) cover up

über·dehnen *tr. V.* overstretch; strain ‹*muscle*›

Überdehnung *die* overstretching; (von Muskel) straining; **eine ~** (eines Muskels) a strain

über·denken *unr. tr. V.* **etw. ~:** think sth. over

über·deutlich
A *Adj.* unusually clear
B *adv.* unusually clearly; with unusual clarity; **er hat mir ~ klargemacht, dass ...** he made it only too plain to me that ...

über·dies *Adv.* moreover; what is more

über·dimensional
A *Adj.* inordinately large ‹*spectacles, table, statue, etc.*›; inordinate ‹*love, influence*›
B *adv.* enormously ‹*enlarged*›

überdimensioniert *Adj.* inordinately large; oversized ‹*stadium*›; overblown ‹*project*›

überdosieren *tr. V.;* **ich überdosiere, überdosiert, überzudosieren: ein Medikament ~:** give/take too large a dose/doses of a medicine

Über·dosis *die* overdose

über·drehen *tr. V.* **1** overwind ‹*watch*›; overtighten ‹*screw, nut*› **2** (Technik) over-rev (coll.) ‹*engine*›; **einen Wagen ~:** over-rev (coll.) the engine of a car

überdreht *Adj.* (ugs.) wound up; (verrückt) crazy

Über·druck¹ *der; Pl.* **Überdrücke** excess pressure; **der Reifen hat ~:** the tyre is over-inflated

Über·druck² *der; Pl.* **Über·drucke** (Philat.) overprint

über·drucken *tr. V.* overprint

Überdruck·ventil *das* pressure-relief valve

Überdruss, *Überdruß /-drʊs/ *der;* **Überdrusses** surfeit (**an** + *Dat.* of); **etw. bis zum ~ tun** do sth. until one has wearied of it; **das habe ich schon bis zum ~ gehört!** I'm tired of hearing that

überdrüssig /-drysɪç/ *Adj.* **jmds./einer Sache ~ sein/werden** be/grow tired of sb./sth.

über·düngen *tr. V.* overfertilize ‹*soil, garden, etc.*›; **überdüngt sein** be overfertilized; ‹*river, lake, etc.*› contain too much fertilizer

Überdüngung *die* overfertilization

über·durchschnittlich
A *Adj.* above average
B *adv.* **sie ist ~ begabt** she is more than averagely gifted *or* talented; **er verdient ~ gut** he earns more than the average

über·eck *Adv.* across a/the corner; **die Decke liegt ~ auf dem Tisch** the tablecloth lies diagonally on the table

Über·eifer *der* overeagerness; (zu große Emsigkeit) overzealousness

über·eifrig
A *Adj.* overeager; (zu emsig) overzealous
B *adv.* overeagerly; (zu emsig) overzealously

über·eignen *tr. V.* **jmdm. etw. ~:** transfer sth. *or* make sth. over to sb.

Über·eignung *die* transfer (**an** + *Akk.* to)

über·eilen *tr. V.* rush; **übereilt** overhasty

Übereilung *die;* ~: excessive haste

über·einander *Adv.* **1** (räumlich) one on top of the other; **sie wohnen ~:** they live one above the other; **ihre Wohnungen liegen ~:** their flats (esp. Brit.) *or* (esp. Amer.) apartments are situated over each other; **Bretter ~ legen** lay planks one on top of the other; **die Enden des Tuchs ~ schlagen** fold the cloth in the middle so that it is edge to edge; **die Arme/Beine ~ schlagen** fold one's arms/cross one's legs; **mit ~ geschlagenen Armen** with [one's] arms folded **2** (fig.: voneinander) ‹*talk etc*› about each other; about one another

***übereinander|legen** *usw.* ▸**übereinander 1**

überein|kommen *unr. itr. V.; mit sein* agree; come to an agreement

Überein·kommen *das;* ~s, ~, **Übereinkunft** /-'ainkʊnft/ *die;* ~, **Übereinkünfte** agreement; **ein ~** *od.* **eine Übereinkunft treffen/erzielen** enter into *or* make an agreement/reach [an] agreement

überein|stimmen *itr. V.* **1** (einer Meinung sein) agree; **mit jmdm. in etw.** (*Dat.*) **~:** agree with sb. on sth.; **wir stimmen darin überein, dass ...** we are in agreement that ... **2** (sich gleichen) ‹*colours, styles*› match; ‹*figures, statements, reports, results*› tally, agree; ‹*views, opinions*› coincide; (Sprachw.: kongruieren) agree

übereinstimmend
A *Adj.* concurrent ‹*views, opinions, statements, reports*›
B *adv.* **sie stellten ~ fest, dass ...** they agreed in stating that ...; **wir sind ~ der Meinung, dass ...** we share the view that ...

Überein·stimmung *die* **1** (von Meinungen) agreement (**in** + *Dat.* on) **2** (Einklang, Gleichheit, Sprachw.: Kongruenz) agreement (*Gen.* between); **die ~ von** *od.* **zwischen Theorie und Praxis** the correspondence between theory and practice; **in ~ mit einem Vertrag stehen** be in accordance with a contract; **etw. mit etw. in ~ bringen** reconcile sth. with sth.

über·empfindlich
A *Adj.* oversensitive (**gegen** to); (Med.) hypersensitive (**gegen** to)
B *adv.* oversensitively; (Med.) hypersensitively

Über·empfindlichkeit *die* oversensitivity (**gegen** to); (Med.) hypersensitivity (**gegen** to)

übererfüllen *tr. V.;* **ich übererfülle, übererfüllt, überzuerfüllen** overfulfil

Über·erfüllung *die* overfulfilment

über|essen¹ *unr. tr. V.* **sich** (*Dat.*) **Hamburger/Nugat ~:** eat too many hamburgers/too much nougat

über·essen² *unr. refl. V.* **sich [an etw.** (*Dat.*)**] ~:** gorge oneself [on sth.]

U

über|fahren¹
A *unr. tr. V.* **jmdn. ~:** ferry *or* take sb. over
B *unr. itr. V.; mit sein* cross over

über·fahren² *unr. tr. V.* 1 run over 2 (übersehen u. weiterfahren) go through ‹*red light, stop signal, etc.*› 3 (hinwegfahren über) cross; go over ‹*crossroads*› 4 (ugs.: überrumpeln) **jmdn. ~:** catch *or* take sb. unawares

Über·fahrt *die* crossing (**über** + *Akk.* of)

Über·fall *der* attack (**auf** + *Akk.* on); (aus dem Hinterhalt) ambush (**auf** + *Akk.* on); (mit vorgehaltener Waffe) hold-up; (auf eine Bank o. Ä.) raid (**auf** + *Akk.* on); (fig. ugs.) surprise visit

überfallartig
A *Adj.* violent; (plötzlich) sudden; surprise *attrib*
B *adv.* suddenly; (wie [ein] Angreifer) like a raider/raiders

über·fallen *unr. tr. V.* 1 attack; raid ‹*bank, enemy position, village, etc.*›; (hinterrücks) ambush; (mit vorgehaltener Waffe) hold up; (fig.: besuchen) descend on; **jmdn. mit Wünschen/Fragen ~** (fig.) bombard sb. with requests/questions 2 (überkommen) ‹*tiredness, homesickness, fear*› come over; **ein Schauder überfiel mich** a shiver ran through me

über·fällig *Adj.* overdue

Überfall·kommando, (österr.) **Überfalls·kommando** *das* flying squad

über·fischen *tr. V.* overfish

Überfischung *die; ~, ~en* overfishing

über·fliegen *unr. tr. V.* 1 (hinwegfliegen über) fly over; overfly (formal) 2 (flüchtig lesen) skim [through]

Überflieger *der,* **Überfliegerin** *die* highflyer

über|fließen *unr. itr. V.; mit sein* ▸**überlaufen¹ 1, 2; sein Herz floss über** (fig.) his heart was full

über·flügeln *tr. V.* outshine; outstrip

Überflug·recht *das* overflying rights *pl.*

Über·fluss, *Über·fluß *der* abundance (**an** + *Dat.* of); (Wohlstand) affluence; **etw. im ~ haben** have sth. in abundance; **im ~ vorhanden sein** be in abundant *or* plentiful supply; **zu allem ~:** to cap *or* crown it all

Überfluss·gesellschaft, *Überfluß·gesellschaft *die* affluent society

über·flüssig *Adj.* superfluous; unnecessary ‹*purchase, words, work*›; (zwecklos) pointless; **~e Pfunde** (ugs. scherzh.) excess weight *sing.*; **~ zu erwähnen, dass ...** needless to say, ...

überflüssiger·weise *Adv.* unnecessarily; (sinnloserweise) pointlessly

über·fluten *tr. V.* (auch fig.) flood

Überflutung *die; ~, ~en* flooding; **~en** cases of flooding; floods

über·fordern *tr. V.* **jmdn. [mit etw.] ~:** overtax sb. [with sth.]; ask *or* demand too much of sb. [with sth.]; **mit diesem Posten ist er überfordert** this job is too much for him; he is not up to this job

Über·forderung *die* 1 **eine [körperliche] ~ für jmdn. sein** be too much for sb. [physically]; **eine intellektuelle ~ für jmdn. sein** ask *or* demand too much of sb. intellectually 2 (das Überfordern) overtaxing

über·frachten *tr. V.* overload; (fig.) overcharge

über·fragen *tr. V.* **da bin ich überfragt** I don't know the answer to that

über·fremden *tr. V.* **überfremdet werden/sein** ‹*language, culture, etc.*› be swamped [by foreign influences]; ‹*economy*› be dominated [by foreign firms/capital]; ‹*country*› be dominated [by foreign influences]

Über·fremdung *die; ~, ~en* domination [by foreign influences]; **eine amerikanische ~ des Marktes** domination of the market by American capital

über·fressen *unr. refl. V.* overeat; **der Hund/**(salopp) **sie hat sich an Schokolade ~:** the dog gorged itself/she gorged herself on chocolate

über·frieren *unr. itr. V.; mit sein* freeze over; **~de Nässe** black ice

Über·fuhr *die; ~, ~en* (österr.) ferry

über|führen¹ *tr. V.* 1 (an einen anderen Ort bringen) transfer; **der Tote wurde in seine Heimat übergeführt** the body of the dead man was brought back to his home town/country 2 (in einen anderen Zustand bringen) convert; **etw. in die Praxis ~:** give sth. practical application

über·führen² *tr. V.* 1 ▸**überführen¹ 1** 2 **jmdn. [eines Verbrechens] ~:** find sb. guilty [of a crime]; convict sb. [of a crime] 3 ▸**überführen¹ 2**

Über·führung *die* 1 transfer; **die ~ des Toten in seine Heimat** bringing back the body of the dead man to his home town/country 2 (eines Verdächtigen) conviction 3 (Brücke) bridge; (Hochstraße) overpass; (Fußgänger~) [foot-]bridge

Über·fülle *die* superabundance; **die ~ des Angebots** the excessive amount on offer

über·füllt *Adj.* crammed full, chock-full (coll.) (**von** with); (mit Menschen) overcrowded, packed (**von** with); oversubscribed ‹*course*›

Über·füllung *die* overcrowding; **„Wegen ~ geschlossen“** 'Full up'

Über·funktion *die* ▸❶ **S. 439** (Med.) hyperfunction

über·füttern *tr. V.* overfeed

Über·gabe *die* 1 handing over (**an** + *Akk.* to); (einer Straße, eines Gebäudes) opening; (von Macht) handing over; transfer 2 (Auslieferung an den Gegner) surrender (**an** + *Akk.* to)

Über·gang *der* 1 crossing 2 (Stelle zum Überqueren) crossing; (Bahn~) level crossing (Brit.); grade crossing (Amer.); (Fußgängerbrücke) footbridge; (an der Grenze, eines Flusses) crossing point 3 (Wechsel, Überleitung) transition (**zu, auf** + *Akk.* to); **ohne ~:** without any transition

übergangs-, Übergangs-: ~bestimmung *die* interim regulation; **~erscheinung** *die* transitional phenomenon; **~frist** *die* transitional period; **~geld** *das* (Med.) rehabilitation benefit; (bei Berufswechsel) transitional payment; **~los** **A** *Adj.* without any transition *postpos.*; **B** *adv.* without any transition; **~lösung** *die* interim *or* temporary solution; **~mantel** *der* coat for spring and autumn; **~periode** *die* transition period; **~phase** *die* transitional phase; **~regelung** *die* interim settlement; **~regierung** *die* transitional government; **~stadium** *das* transitional stage; **~weise** *Adv.* in the interim; (als Zwischenlösung) as an interim solution; **~zeit** *die* 1 transitional period; 2 (Frühling) spring; (Herbst) autumn; (Frühling und Herbst) spring and autumn

Über·gardine *die* curtain

über·geben
A *unr. tr. V.* 1 hand over; pass ‹*baton*›; **etw. den Flammen ~** (fig. geh.) consign sth. to the flames 2 (übereignen) transfer, make over (*Dat.* to) 3 (ausliefern) surrender (*Dat.*, **an** + *Akk.* to) 4 **eine Straße dem Verkehr ~:** open a road to traffic; **das neue Gemeindezentrum wurde seiner Bestimmung ~:** the new community centre was [officially] opened 5 (abgeben, überlassen) **er hat sein Amt ~:** he has handed over his position; **jmdm. etw. ~:** entrust sb. with sth.; **ich übergebe diese Angelegenheit meinem Anwalt** I am placing this matter in the hands of my lawyer
B *unr. refl. V.* (sich erbrechen) vomit

über|gehen¹ *unr. itr. V.; mit sein* 1 pass; **an jmdn./in jmds. Besitz ~:** become sb.'s property; *s. auch* **Fleisch 1** 2 **zu etw. ~:** go over to sth.; **dazu ~, etw. zu tun** go over to doing sth.; **zu einem anderen Thema ~:** move on to another subject 3 **in etw.** (*Akk.*) **~** (zu etw. werden) turn into sth.; **in Gärung/Verwesung ~:** begin to ferment/decompose; **ineinander ~** (sich vermischen) merge 4 **uns gingen die Augen über** we were overwhelmed by the sight 5 (Seemannsspr.) ‹*wave*› break over the side

über·gehen² *unr. tr. V.* 1 (nicht beachten) ignore; (nicht eingehen auf) **etw. [mit Stillschweigen] ~:** pass sth. over in silence 2 (auslassen, überspringen) skip [over] 3 (nicht berücksichtigen) pass over; **jmdn. bei der Beförderung ~:** pass sb. over for promotion; **jmdn. im Testament ~:** leave sb. out of one's will

über·genau
A *Adj.* over-meticulous
B *adv.* over-meticulously

über·genug *Adv.* more than enough

über·geordnet
A ▸**überordnen**
B *Adj.* higher ‹*authority, position, court*›; greater ‹*significance*›; superordinate ‹*concept*›; **einer Sache** (*Dat.*) **~ sein** ‹*authority, position, court*› be higher than sth.

Über·gepäck *das* (Flugw.) excess baggage

Über·gewicht *das* 1 ▸❶ **S. 315** excess weight; (von Person) overweight; **[5 kg] ~ haben** ‹*person*› be [5 kilos] overweight 2 (fig.) predominance; **das ~ [über jmdn./etw.] haben/gewinnen** be/become predominant [over sb./sth.]; **militärisches ~ haben/gewinnen** have/achieve military superiority 3 **das ~ bekommen** *od.* **kriegen** (ugs.) ‹*person*› overbalance

über·gewichtig *Adj.* overweight

über|gießen¹ *unr. tr. V.* **jmdm. etw. ~:** pour sth. over sb.

über·gießen² *unr. tr. V.* **etw. mit Wasser/Soße ~:** pour water/sauce over sth.; **sich mit etw. ~:** pour sth. over oneself; **von Licht übergossen sein** (fig.) be flooded with light

über·glücklich *Adj.* blissfully happy; (hoch erfreut) overjoyed

über·golden *tr. V.* gild; (fig. dichter.) ‹*sun*› bathe ‹*countryside*› in gold

über|greifen *unr. itr. V.* 1 (bes. beim Klavierspiel, Turnen) cross one's hands over 2 (sich ausdehnen) **auf etw.** (*Akk.*) **~:** spread to sth.; **auf** *od.* **in jmds. Machtbereich ~:** encroach on sb.'s area of authority

übergreifend *Adj.* predominant; (allumfassend) all-embracing

Über·griff *der* (unrechtmäßiger Eingriff) encroachment (**auf** + *Akk.* on); infringement (**auf** + *Akk.* of); (Angriff) attack (**auf** + *Akk.* on)

über·groß *Adj.* huge; enormous; overwhelming ‹*majority*›

Über·größe *die* outsize; **Kleider/Schuhe** *usw.* **in ~n** outsize dresses/shoes *etc.*

über|haben *unr. tr. V.* (ugs.) 1 (übergezogen haben) have ‹*coat, jacket, etc.*› on; be wearing ‹*coat, jacket, etc.*› 2 (satt haben) be fed up with (coll.) 3 (übrig haben) **etw. ~:** have sth. left [over]

überhand *in* **~ nehmen** get out of hand; ‹*attacks, muggings, etc.*› increase alarmingly; ‹*weeds*› run riot

***überhand|nehmen** ▸**überhand**

Über·hang *der* 1 (Überschuss) surplus (**an** + *Dat.* of) 2 (Fels~, Archit.) overhang

über|hängen¹ *unr. itr. V.; südd., österr., schweiz. mit sein* ‹*part of building*› overhang; ‹*branch*› hang over; ‹*rock face*› form an overhang

über|hängen² *tr. V.* **sich** (*Dat.*) **eine Jacke ~:** put a jacket round one's shoulders; **sich** (*Dat.*) **das Gewehr/die Tasche ~:** hang *or* sling the rifle/bag over one's shoulder

Überhang·mandat *das* (Politik): *seat won in addition to the number a party has gained through proportional representation*

über·hasten *tr. V.* rush; **überhastet handeln** act hastily *or* hurriedly

über·häufen *tr. V.* **jmdn. mit etw. ~:** heap *or* shower sth. on sb.; **jmdn. mit Ratschlägen/Vorwürfen ~:** bombard sb. with advice/pour reproaches on sb.

überhaupt
A *Adv.* 1 (insgesamt, im Allgemeinen) in general; **soweit es ~ Zweck hat** as far as there's any point in it at all; **~ fühlte er sich jetzt wohler** he felt better all round; **er ist ~ selten zu Hause** he's not at home much at all 2 (meist bei Verneinungen: gar) **~ nicht** not at all; **das ist ~ nicht wahr** that's not true at all; **~ keine Zeit haben** have no time at all; not have any time at all; **das kommt ~ nicht in Frage** it's quite *or* completely out of the question; **~ nichts** nothing at all; nothing what[so]ever; **wenn ~:** if at all; **wenn ~, dann komme ich**

U

morgen if I come at all, it will be tomorrow **3** (überdies, außerdem) besides **4** (besonders) particularly
B *Partikel* anyway; **wer sind Sie ~?** who are you anyway?; **wer hat dir das ~ gesagt?** who told you that anyway?; **was willst du hier ~?** what are you doing here anyway?; **wie konnte das ~ passieren?** how could it happen in the first place?; **das klingt verlockend, aber haben wir ~ Geld dafür?** that sounds tempting, but have we got the money for it?; **wissen Sie ~, mit wem Sie reden?** do you realize who you're talking to?

über·heben *unr. refl. V.* **1** ▸**verheben** **2** (überheblich sein) be arrogant

überheblich /-ˈheːplɪç/
A *Adj.* arrogant; supercilious ‹*grin*›
B *adv.* arrogantly; ‹*grin*› superciliously

Überheblichkeit *die;* **~:** arrogance

über·heizen *tr. V.* overheat

über·hitzen *tr. V.* (auch fig.) overheat

Überhitzung *die;* **~, ~en** (auch fig.) overheating

über·höhen *tr. V.* raise ‹*dyke, embankment, etc.*›; bank ‹*track, curve*›

überhöht /yːbɐˈhøːt/ *Adj.* (zu hoch) excessive

über|holen[1]
A *tr., itr. V.* **jmdn. ~:** ferry sb. across
B *itr. V.* (Seemannsspr.) keel over

über·holen[2]
A *tr. V.* **1** overtake (esp. Brit.); pass (esp. Amer.) **2** (übertreffen) outstrip **3** (wieder instand setzen) overhaul
B *itr. V.* overtake (esp. Brit.); pass (esp. Amer.)

Überhol-: ~manöver *das* overtaking (esp. Brit.) *or* (esp. Amer.) passing manoeuvre; **~spur** *die* overtaking lane (esp. Brit.); pass lane (esp. Amer.)

überholt *Adj.* (veraltet) outdated; **durch etw. ~ sein** have become outdated as a result of sth.

Überholung *die;* **~, ~en** overhaul; **der Wagen muss zur ~ in die Werkstatt** the car has to go into the garage for an overhaul

Überhol-: ~verbot *das* ban on overtaking; **„~verbot"** 'no overtaking' (esp. Brit.); 'no passing' (Amer.); **hier besteht ~verbot** overtaking is prohibited here; **~vorgang** *der* overtaking *no art.*; **während des ~vorgangs** while overtaking

über·hören *tr. V.* not hear; **das möchte ich überhört haben** I'll pretend I didn't hear that

Über-ich, Über-Ich *das* (Psych.) superego

über|interpretieren *tr., auch itr. V.* overinterpret

über·irdisch
A *Adj.* **1** (himmlisch) celestial; heavenly; (übernatürlich) supernatural; ethereal ‹*beauty*› **2** (veralt.) ▸**oberirdisch A**
B *adv.* **1** (himmlisch) celestially; (übernatürlich) supernaturally; ethereally ‹*beautiful*› **2** (veralt.) ▸**oberirdisch B**

über·kandidelt /-kandiːdl̩t/ *Adj.* (ugs.) affected

Über·kapazität *die* (Wirtsch.) overcapacity; **~en** overcapacity *sing.*

über|kippen *itr. V.; mit sein* tip over

über·kleben *tr. V.* **die alten Plakate mit neuen ~:** stick new posters over the old ones; **wir überklebten die Anschrift** we stuck something over the address; we covered the address by sticking something over it

über·klettern *tr. V.* climb over

über|kochen *itr. V.; mit sein* (auch fig. ugs.) boil over

über|kommen[1] *unr. itr. V.; mit sein* (Seemannsspr.) ‹*water*› wash over the deck; ‹*wave*› break over the side

über·kommen[2] *unr. tr. V.* **Mitleid/Ekel/Furcht überkam mich** I was overcome by pity/revulsion/fear; **ein Gefühl der Verlassenheit überkam sie** a feeling of desolation came over her

überkommen[3] *Adj.* (geh.) traditional

über·kompensieren *tr. V.;* (bes. Psych., Wirtsch.) **ich überkompensiere, überkompensiert, überzukompensieren** overcompensate for

überkonfessionell
A *Adj.* supradenominational
B *adv.* independently of denomination; ‹*understood*› across all denominations

über·kreuzen
A *tr. V.* ▸**kreuzen A 1**
B *refl. V.* cross; **sich ~de Linien** intersecting lines

über|kriegen *tr. V.* (ugs.) **jmdn./etw. ~:** get fed up with sb./sth. (coll.)

über·kronen *tr. V.* (Zahnmed.) crown

über·krusten *tr. V.* **das Salz hatte den Boden überkrustet** the ground was encrusted with salt *or* covered with a crust of salt; **von Dreck überkrustete Stiefel** boots caked with dirt

über·laden[1] *unr. tr. V.* (auch fig.) overload

überladen[2] *Adj.* over-ornate ‹*façade, style, etc.*›; overcrowded ‹*shop window*›

über·lagern *tr. V.* **1** overlie; (fig.) combine with; **sich ~:** combine; **von Sedimentschichten überlagertes Gestein** rock with overlying sedimentary strata; **sich ~de Gesteinsschichten** superimposed rock strata **2** (Physik) ‹*wave*› interfere with; ‹*force, field*› be superimposed on; **sich ~** ‹*waves*› interfere; ‹*forces, fields*› be superimposed

Über·lagerung *die* **1** superposition; (fig.) combination **2** (Physik) (von Wellen) interference; (von Kräften, Feldern) superposition

Überland- /*od.* --ˈ-/: **~bus** *der* country bus; **~leitung** *die* transmission line

über·lang *Adj.* unusually long

Über·länge *die:* **~ haben** be unusually long; **eine Ladung mit ~:** a long load; **„wegen ~ geänderte Anfangszeiten"** 'starting times changed due to the unusually long running time of the film'

über·lappen *tr. V.* (auch fig.) overlap

über|lassen[1] *unr. tr. V.* (ugs.) **etw. ~:** leave sth. over

über·lassen[2]
A *unr. tr. V.* **1** (geben) **jmdm. etw. ~:** let sb. have sth.; **er hat mir sein Auto übers Wochenende ~:** he let me use his car over the weekend; **er hat es mir billig ~:** he let me have it cheap **2** **jmdn. jmds. Fürsorge ~:** leave sb. in sb.'s care; **sich** (*Dat.*) **selbst ~ sein** be left to one's own devices **3** **etw. jmdm. ~** (etw. jmdn. entscheiden/tun lassen) leave sth. to sb.; **das bleibt [ganz] dir ~:** that's [entirely] up to you; **überlass das bitte mir** let that be my concern; let me worry about that; **jmdm. alle Arbeit ~:** leave sb. to do all the work; **etw. dem Zufall ~:** leave sth. to chance **4** **jmdn. seinem Kummer ~:** leave sb. to cope with his/her grief alone
B *unr. refl. V.* **sich der Leidenschaft/dem Gefühl/den Träumen** *usw.* **~:** abandon oneself to one's passions/emotions/dreams *etc.*

Überlassung *die;* **~, ~en** handing over, handover (**an** + *Akk.* to); (von Dienst, Daten) supply; (von Rechten) surrender

über·lasten *tr. V.* overload; overburden, overstretch ‹*facilities, authorities*›; put too great a strain on ‹*heart, circulation, etc.*›; strain ‹*nerves*›; overstress ‹*structure, material*›; overtax ‹*person*›; (mit Arbeit) overwork ‹*person*›; (psychisch) put too great a strain on ‹*person*›

Überlastung *die;* **~, ~en** ▸**überlasten:** overloading; overstretching; straining; overstressing; overtaxing; overworking; **die ständige ~ führte schließlich zu seinem Zusammenbruch** the continuous strain he was under led eventually to collapse

Über·lauf *der* (auch DV) overflow

über|laufen[1] *unr. itr. V.; mit sein* **1** ‹*liquid, container*› overflow **2** (auf die gegnerische Seite überwechseln) defect; ‹*partisan*› go over to the other side; **zum Feind/zu den Rebellen ~:** go over *or* desert to the enemy/the rebels

über·laufen[2] *unr. tr. V.* **1** (befallen) seize; **ein Frösteln/Schauer überlief mich, es überlief mich [eis]kalt** a cold shiver ran down my spine; **es überlief sie heiß** a hot flush came over her **2** (Sport: hinauslaufen über) run past **3** (Sport: umspielen) run through, beat ‹*defence*›

überlaufen[3] *Adj.* overcrowded; oversubscribed ‹*course, subject*›; **der Arzt ist sehr ~:** the doctor's list is very full

Über·läufer *der,* **Über·läuferin** *die* (auch fig.) defector

Überlauf·rohr *das* overflow pipe

über·laut
A *Adj.* too loud *pred.*; over-loud ‹*voice, laugh*›; ‹*engine*› too noisy *pred*
B *adv.* too loudly

über·leben
A *tr., auch itr. V.* survive; **das überleb ich nicht!** I'll never get over it!; **du wirst es schon** *od.* **wohl ~** (iron.) you'll survive; **jmdn. ~:** survive *or* outlive sb. (**um** by)
B *refl. V.* become outdated *or* outmoded; **sich überlebt haben** have become outdated; have had its day; **überlebt** outdated; out-of-date

Über·lebende *der/die; adj. Dekl.* survivor

überlebens-, Überlebens-: ~chance *die* chance of survival; **~fähig** *Adj.* capable of survival *postpos.*; **~fähigkeit** *die* ability to survive; **~frage** *die* question of survival; life-and-death question

über·lebens·groß *Adj.* larger than life-size

überlebens-, Überlebens-: ~kampf *der* struggle for survival; **~notwendig** *Adj.* essential for survival *postpos.*; vitally important; **~notwendig sein** be a matter of life and death; **~strategie** *die* survival strategy; **~training** *das* survival training; **ein ~training** a survival-training course; **~wichtig** *Adj.* vital for survival *postpos.*; **~wille** *der* will *or* determination to survive

über|legen[1]
A *tr. V.* **1** **jmdm. etw. ~:** put sth. over sb. **2** (ugs.: verhauen) **jmdn. ~:** put sb. over one's knee
B *refl. V.* lean over; ‹*ship*› list

über·legen[2]
A *tr. V.* consider; think over *or* about; **etw. noch einmal ~:** reconsider sth.; **das muss gut überlegt werden** that needs some careful consideration *or* thought; **es wäre zu ~, ob …** one might consider whether …; **es sich anders ~:** change one's mind; **wenn ich es mir recht überlege, …** now I come to think of it, …; **das hättest du dir auch vorher ~ können** you could have thought about that *or* given that some thought before
B *itr. V.* think; reflect; **überleg doch mal!** think about it!; **ohne zu ~** (unbedacht) without thinking; (spontan) without a moment's thought; **ohne lange zu ~:** without much reflection; **lass mich mal ~:** let me think; **lange hin und her ~:** agonize for ages; **ich habe hin und her überlegt** I've turned it over and over in my mind; **am Überlegen sein, ob …** be thinking over whether …

überlegen[3]
A *Adj.* **1** superior; clear, convincing ‹*win, victory*›; **jmdm. ~ sein** be superior to sb. (**an** + *Dat.* in); **zahlenmäßig ~ sein** be superior in numbers **2** (herablassend) supercilious; superior
B *adv.* **1** in a superior manner; ‹*play*› much the better: ‹*win, argue*› convincingly **2** (herablassend) superciliously; superiorly

Überlegenheit *die;* **~:** superiority

Überlegenheits·gefühl *das* feeling of superiority

überlegenswert *Adj.* worth considering *postpos.*; worthy of consideration *postpos.*

überlegt /yːbɐˈleːkt/
A *Adj.* carefully considered
B *adv.* in a carefully considered way

Überlegung *die;* **~, ~en** **1** thought; reflection; **nach reiflicher ~:** on careful consideration; **mit ~ handeln** act in a considered way; **einer ~ wert sein** be worth considering **2** (Gedanke) idea; **~en** (Gedankengang) thoughts; reflections; **~en zu etw. anstellen** give one's thoughts on sth.

über|leiten *itr. V.* **zum nächsten/zu einem neuen Thema ~** ‹*speaker*› move on to the next topic; **in etw.** (*Akk.*) **~:** lead into sth.; **in eine andere Tonart ~** ‹*player*› change key

Über·leitung *die* transition; **eine ~ zum nächsten Thema suchen** look for a way of moving on to the next subject

über·lesen *unr. tr. V.* overlook; miss

über·liefern *tr. V.* hand down; **überlieferte Sitten/Formen** *usw.* traditional customs/forms *etc.*; **in alten Chroniken ist überliefert, dass ...** it is recorded in ancient chronicles that ...

Über·lieferung *die* 1 (etw. Überliefertes) tradition; **schriftliche ~en** written records 2 (Brauch) tradition; custom 3 (das Überliefern) handing down

überlisten *tr. V.* outwit

überm *Präp. + Art.* = **über dem**

Über·macht *die* superior strength; (zahlenmäßig) superior numbers *pl.*; **in der ~ sein, die ~ haben** be superior in strength/numbers

über·mächtig
A *Adj.* 1 superior 2 (nicht mehr bezähmbar) overpowering ‹*desire, hatred, urge, etc.*›
B *adv.* **~ loderte das Feuer der Leidenschaft in ihnen** the fire of passion blazed uncontrollably in them; **es zog ihn ~ in die Ferne** he felt an overpowering desire to travel

über·malen *tr. V.* **etw. ~:** paint sth. over

über·mannen *tr. V.* overcome

Über·maß *das* excessive amount, excess (**an** + *Dat.* of); **ein ~ an Arbeit** *od.* **Arbeit im ~ haben** have an excessive amount of work *or* more than enough work; **etw. im ~ produzieren** produce sth. in excess; produce an excess of sth.

über·mäßig
A *Adj.* 1 excessive 2 (Musik) **ein ~es Intervall** an augmented interval
B *adv.* excessively; **~ viel essen** eat to excess *or* excessively; **nicht ~ attraktiv** not especially attractive; **man braucht sich nicht mal ~ zu beeilen** you don't even need to hurry overmuch

Über·mensch *der* superman

über·menschlich *Adj.* superhuman; **er hat Übermenschliches geleistet** he has achieved the almost impossible

über·mitteln *tr. V.* send; (als Mittler weitergeben) pass on, convey ‹*greetings, regards, etc.*›

Übermitt[e]lung *die* sending

über·morgen *Adv.* the day after tomorrow

über·müde *Adj.* overtired; exhausted

über·müden *tr. V.* overtire; **übermüdet** overtired; exhausted

Übermüdung *die;* **~:** overtiredness; exhaustion

Über·mut *der* high spirits *pl.*; **etw. aus [lauter]** *od.* **im ~ tun** do sth. out of [pure] high spirits; **~ tut selten gut** (Spr.) high spirits mustn't get out of hand

übermütig /'y:bɐmy:tɪç/
A *Adj.* high-spirited; in high spirits *pred.*; **in ~er Stimmung** high-spirited; in high spirits
B *adv.* high-spiritedly

Über·mutter *die* [dominant] mother figure

übern *Präp. + Art.* = **über den**

über·nächst... *Adj.* ▸ⓘ **S. 816 im ~en Jahr, ~es Jahr** the year after next; **~e Woche** the week after next; **am ~en Tag** two days later; the next day but one; **~en Montag** a week on Monday; Monday week; **er wohnt im ~en Haus** he lives in the next house but one *or* lives two doors away

über·nachten *itr. V.* stay overnight; **bei jmdm. ~:** stay *or* spend the night at sb.'s house/flat (esp. Brit.) *or* (esp. Amer.) apartment *etc.*; **im Hotel ~** stay the night at the hotel; **im Freien ~:** sleep in the open air

übernächtigt /y:bɐ'nɛçtɪçt/ *Adj.* ‹*person*› tired *or* worn out [through lack of sleep]; tired ‹*face, look, etc.*›

Übernachtung *die;* **~, ~en** overnight stay; **~ und Frühstück** bed and breakfast; **sechs ~en kosten ...** six nights cost ...

Übernachtungs-: ~gast *der* visitor staying the night; **~zahl** *die* number of overnight stays

Übernahme /'y:bɐna:mə/ *die;* **~, ~n** 1 (von Waren, einer Sendung) taking delivery *no art.*; (des Staffelstabs) receiving *no indef. art.*; (einer Idee, eines Themas, von Methoden) adoption, taking over *no indef. art.*; (einer Praxis, eines Geschäfts, der Macht) takeover; (von Wörtern, Ausdrücken) borrowing (**von** from); **er erklärt sich zur ~ der Kosten/des Falles bereit** he says he is prepared to meet the cost himself/to take on the case 2 (etw. Übernommenes) borrowing; (Sendung) re-broadcast; (Livesendung) relay

Übernahme-: ~schlacht *die* (Wirtsch.) takeover battle; **~versuch** *der* takeover attempt

über·national
A *Adj.* supranational
B *adv.* supranationally

über·natürlich *Adj.* supernatural

über·nehmen
A *unr. tr. V.* 1 take delivery of ‹*goods, consignment*›; receive ‹*relay baton*›; take over ‹*power, practice, business, building, school class*›; take on ‹*job, position, task, role, case, leadership*›; undertake to pay ‹*costs*›; **es ~, etw. zu tun** take on the job of doing sth.; **das lass mich ~:** let me do that; *s. auch* **Befehl 2**; **Bürgschaft 1**; **Garantie 1**; **Gewähr**; **Kommando 2**; **Steuer¹**; **Verantwortung 1**; **Verpflichtung 1** 2 (bei sich einstellen) take on ‹*staff*› 3 (Seemannsspr.: an Bord nehmen) take on board 4 (sich zu Eigen machen) adopt, take over ‹*ideas, methods, subject, etc.*› (**von** from); borrow ‹*word, phrase*› (**von** from); **eine Textstelle wörtlich ~:** use a passage verbatim; **das ZDF hat die Sendung vom britischen Fernsehen übernommen** the programme was re-transmitted/(als Livesendung) relayed from British television by ZDF 5 (österr. ugs.) ▸ **übertölpeln**
B *unr. refl. V.* overdo things *or* it; **er hat sich beim Training übernommen** he overdid things *or* it [while] training; **sich mit etw. ~:** take on too much with sth.; **übernimm dich nur nicht** (iron.) don't strain yourself!

Über·nutzung *die* overuse

über|ordnen *tr. V.* 1 **etw. einer Sache** (*Dat.*) **~:** give sth. precedence over sth. 2 **jmdn. jmdm. ~:** place sb. above sb.; *s. auch* **übergeordnet B**

über·örtlich (Amtsspr.)
A *Adj.* regional
B *adv.* regionally

über·parteilich
A *Adj.* non-party *attrib.*; **ein ~es Komitee** an all-party committee; **das Amt des Bundespräsidenten ist ~:** the office of Federal President is *or* stands above party politics
B *adv.* in a non-partisan way

über·pinseln *tr. V.* (ugs.) paint over

Über·produktion *die* (Wirtsch., Med.) overproduction

über·prüfbar *Adj.* checkable; **die Angaben waren nicht ~:** the details could not be checked

über·prüfen *tr. V.* 1 check (**auf** + *Akk.* for); check [over], inspect, examine ‹*machine, device*›; check, inspect, examine ‹*papers, luggage*›; review ‹*issue, situation, results*›; (Finanzw.) examine, inspect ‹*accounts, books*› 2 (überdenken) think over; consider; **etw. noch mal ~:** think sth. over again; reconsider sth.

Über·prüfung *die* 1 ▸ **überprüfen 1**: checking *no indef. art.* (**auf** + *Akk.* for); checking [over] *no indef. art.*; inspection; examination 2 (Kontrolle) check; (des Ausweises, der Geschäftsbücher) examination; inspection; (einer Lage, Frage, der Ergebnisse) review 3 (das Überdenken) consideration; **erneute ~:** reconsideration

über·pünktlich
A *Adj.* excessively punctual
B *adv.* more than punctually; with excessive punctuality

über·qualifiziert *Adj.* overqualified

über|quellen *unr. itr. V.; mit sein* 1 spill over 2 (zu voll sein) be brimming; **die Tribüne quoll von Zuschauern über** (fig.) the stand was overflowing with spectators

über·queren *tr. V.* cross; (schneiden) cut across; cross

Überquerung *die;* **~, ~en** crossing

über|ragen¹ *itr. V.* jut out; project

über·ragen² *tr. V.* 1 (hinausragen über) **jmdn./etw. ~:** tower above sb./sth.; **jmdn. um Kopfeslänge ~:** be a head taller than sb.; **der Berg überragt die Ebene** the mountain towers over the plain 2 (übertreffen) **jmdn. an etw.** (*Dat.*) **~:** be head and shoulders above sb. in sth.

überragend
A *Adj.* outstanding
B *adv.* outstandingly

überraschen *tr. V.* surprise; ‹*storm, earthquake*› take by surprise; (durch einen Angriff) take by surprise; catch unawares; **jmdn. beim Rauchen/Stehlen ~:** catch sb. smoking/stealing; **jmdn. überrascht ansehen** look at sb. in surprise; **überrascht tun** pretend to be surprised; **lassen wir uns ~:** let's wait and see; **vom Gewitter/vom Regen überrascht werden** be caught in the thunderstorm/caught [out] in the rain

überraschend
A *Adj.* surprising; surprise *attrib.* ‹*attack, visit*›; (unerwartet) unexpected
B *adv.* surprisingly; (unerwartet) unexpectedly; **die Nachricht kam ~:** the news came as a surprise

überraschender·weise *Adv.* surprisingly; (unerwartet) unexpectedly

Überraschung *die;* **~, ~en** surprise; **zu meiner [großen] ~:** to my [great] surprise; **für eine ~ sorgen** cause a surprise; **jmdm. eine kleine ~ mitbringen** bring sb. a little something as a surprise

Überraschungs-: ~coup *der* surprise coup; **~effekt** *der* surprise effect; **~erfolg** *der* unexpected success; surprise success; **~gast** *der* surprise guest; **~moment** *das* element of surprise; **~sieg** *der* surprise win; **~sieger** *der,* **~siegerin** *die* surprise winner

über|reagieren *itr. V.* overreact

Über·reaktion *die* overreaction

über·reden *tr. V.* persuade; **jmdn. ~, etw. zu tun** persuade sb. to do sth.; talk sb. into doing sth.; **jmdn. zum Mitmachen/zu einer Fahrt ~:** persuade sb. to take part/make a journey; talk sb. into taking part/making a journey; **ich habe mich zum Kauf eines neuen Autos ~ lassen** I was persuaded to buy *or* was talked into buying a new car

Überredung *die;* **~:** persuasion

Überredungs·kunst *die* powers *pl.* of persuasion

über·regional
A *Adj.* national ‹*newspaper, radio station*›; **eine Angelegenheit von ~er Bedeutung** a matter of more than just regional importance; **~e Veranstaltungen** events involving several regions
B *adv.* nationally; **~ bekannt werden** become known outside one's/its own region

über|regulieren *tr., auch itr. V.* over-regulate

Über·regulierung *die* over-regulation

über·reich
A *Adj.* lavish ‹*meal, decoration*›; abundant, very rich ‹*harvest*›; **~ an Bodenschätzen sein** be very rich in mineral resources; **eine an Ereignissen ~e Zeit** an extremely eventful time; **in ~em Maß vorhanden sein** be there in great quantity
B *adv.* **jmdn. ~ beschenken/belohnen** lavish gifts on sb./reward sb. lavishly; **~ verziert sein** be lavishly decorated

über·reichen *tr. V.* **[jmdm.] etw. ~:** present sth. [to sb.]

über·reichlich
A *Adj.* over-ample; **etw. ist in ~er Fülle vorhanden** there is an over abundance of sth.
B *adv.* over-amply

Überreichung *die;* **~:** presentation

über·reif *Adj.* over-ripe

U

über·reizen
A *tr. V.* **1** overtax ‹*person*›; overstrain ‹*eyes, nerves, etc.*›; **[nervlich] überreizt** overwrought **2** (bes. Skat) overbid ‹*hand*›
B *refl. V.* (bes. Skat) overbid

Überreiztheit *die;* ~ ▸ **überreizen A**: overtaxed/-strained/-wrought state

Über·reizung *die* ▸ **überreizen A**: overtaxing; overstraining; **ein Zeichen nervöser ~**: a sign of nervous strain

über·rennen *unr. tr. V.* **1** (Milit.) overrun **2** (umrennen) run down

über·repräsentiert *Adj.* over-represented

Über·rest *der* remnant; **~e** (eines Gebäudes) remains; ruins; (einer Mahlzeit) leftovers; **die sterblichen ~e** (geh. verhüll.) the mortal remains

Überroll·bügel *der* roll bar

über·rollen *tr. V.* **1** (Milit.) overrun; (fig.) overwhelm ‹*person*›; ‹*fashion, craze*› sweep through ‹*country*› **2** (hinwegrollen über) run down

über·rumpeln *tr. V.* **jmdn. ~**: take sb. by surprise; (bei einem Angriff) catch sb. unawares; take sb. by surprise; **jmdn. mit etw. ~**: surprise sb. with sth.; take sb. by surprise with sth.

Überrump[e]lung *die;* ~, **~en** surprise attack

über·runden *tr. V.* **1** (Sport) lap **2** (übertreffen) outstrip

übers *Präp. + Art.* **1** = **über das** **2** **~ Jahr** one year later

über·säen *tr. V.* strew (**mit** with); **mit etw. übersät sein** be strewn *or* scattered with sth.

übersät /y:bɐˈzɛ:t/ *Adj.* **mit** *od.* **von etw. ~ sein** be covered with sth.; (abwertend) be strewn with sth.; **mit** *od.* **von Sternen ~**: star-studded; studded with stars *postpos.*

über·sättigen *tr. V.* supersaturate ‹*solution*›; glut ‹*market*›; satiate ‹*public*›

über·säuern
A *tr. V.* over-acidify ‹*soil, river, lake, etc.*›; (Med.) cause excess acidity in ‹*stomach*›; **ein übersäuerter Magen** excess acidity in the stomach
B *itr. V.* (Med.) ‹*muscle, body*› produce too much acid

Über·säuerung *die* over-acidification; (das Übersäuertsein) excess acidity

Über·schall *der;* **~[e]s ~ fliegen/fahren** fly/drive at supersonic speeds

Überschall-: ~flugzeug *das* supersonic aircraft; **~geschwindigkeit** *die* supersonic speed

über·schatten *tr. V.* overshadow; cast its/their shadow over; (fig.) cast a shadow over

über·schätzen *tr. V.* overestimate; overrate ‹*writer, performer, book, performance, talent, ability*›

Über·schätzung *die* ▸ **überschätzen**: overestimation; overrating

überschaubar *Adj.* **eine ~e Menge/Zahl** a manageable quantity/number; **das sind ~e Größen** these are quantities one can grasp; **das Risiko ist nicht ~**: the risks cannot be calculated; **ein ~er Zeitraum/~es Gebiet** a reasonably short period/small area

über·schauen *tr. V.* ▸ **übersehen² 1, 2**

über|schäumen *itr. V.; mit sein* froth over; **~de Begeisterung** bubbling enthusiasm

über·schlafen *unr. tr. V.* sleep on ‹*matter, problem, etc.*›

Über·schlag *der* **1** rough calculation *or* estimate **2** (Turnen) handspring; (am Barren) forward roll **3** ▸ **Looping**

über|schlagen¹
A *unr. tr. V.* **die Beine ~**: cross one's legs; **mit übergeschlagenen Beinen** with [one's] legs crossed
B *unr. itr. V.; mit sein* ‹*wave*› break; ‹*spark*› jump

über·schlagen²
A *unr. tr. V.* **1** (auslassen) skip ‹*chapter, page, etc.*› **2** (ungefähr berechnen) calculate *or* estimate roughly; make a rough calculation *or* estimate of
B *unr. refl. V.* **1** go head over heels; ‹*car*› turn over; **sich vor Höflichkeit ~** (fig.) fall over oneself to be polite (coll.) **2** ‹*voice*› crack **3** ‹*events, reports, etc.*› come thick and fast; **die Gedanken überschlugen sich in meinem Kopf** the thoughts raced round and round in my head

überschlagen³ *Adj.* (bes. md.) lukewarm ‹*liquid*›; moderately warm ‹*room*›

überschlägig /-ʃlɛ:gɪç/
A *Adj.* [roughly] estimated; rough, approximate ‹*estimate*›
B *adv.* ‹*calculate, estimate*› roughly, approximately

über|schnappen *itr. V.; mit sein* **1** (ugs.: den Verstand verlieren) go crazy; go round the bend (coll.) **2** (ugs.: sich überschlagen) ‹*voice*› crack

über·schneiden *unr. refl. V.* ‹*lines, rays*› cross, intersect; (fig.) ‹*problems, areas of responsibility, events, etc.*› overlap

Überschneidung *die;* ~, **~en** ▸ **überschneiden**: intersection; (fig.) overlapping

über·schreiben *unr. tr. V.* **1** entitle; head ‹*chapter, section*› **2** (übertragen) **etw. jmdm.** *od.* **auf jmdn. ~**: transfer sth. to sb.; make sth. over to sb. **3** (DV) overwrite

Überschreibung *die* **1** (Übertragung) transfer (**in, auf** + *Akk.* to) **2** (DV) overwriting; **mehrere ~en** several overwrites

über·schreien *unr. tr. V.* shout down

über·schreiten *unr. itr. V.* **1** cross; (fig.) pass; **Überschreiten der Gleise verboten!** do not cross the line!; **er hat die Siebzig überschritten** (fig.) he is past seventy **2** (hinausgehen über) exceed ‹*authority, powers, budget, speed, limit, deadline, etc.*›; **das überschreitet jedes Maß** that's going too far; **die Grenzen des Erlaubten ~**: go beyond what is permissible

Über·schrift *die* heading; (in einer Zeitung) headline; (Titel) title

Über·schuh *der* overshoe; galosh *usu. pl.* (Brit.)

über·schuldet *Adj.* heavily indebted ‹*person, firm, country*›; heavily mortgaged ‹*house, property, etc.*›; **hoffnungslos ~ sein** ‹*person*› be hopelessly in debt

Überschuldung *die;* ~, **~en** heavy indebtedness

Über·schuss, *Über·schuß *der* surplus (**an** + *Dat.* of)

Überschuss·beteiligung *die* (Versicherungsw.) with-profits bonus

überschüssig /ˈy:bɐʃʏsɪç/ *Adj.* surplus

über|schütten¹ *tr. V.* (ugs.) spill

über·schütten² *tr. V.* cover; **jmdn./etw. mit Wasser ~**: throw water over sb./sth.; **jmdn. mit Vorwürfen/Lob/Ehrungen ~**: heap reproach/praise/honours on sb.; **jmdn. mit Fragen ~**: fire questions at sb.; **jmdn. mit Geschenken/Geld ~**: shower sb. with presents/lavish money on sb.

Überschwang *der;* **~[e]s** exuberance; **im ~ der Begeisterung** in one's exuberant enthusiasm; **im ~ der Gefühle** out of sheer exuberance

überschwänglich /-ʃvɛŋlɪç/
A *Adj.* effusive ‹*words, manner, etc.*›; wild ‹*joy, enthusiasm*›
B *adv.* effusively

Überschwänglichkeit *die;* **~**: effusiveness

über|schwappen *itr. V.; mit sein* ‹*liquid, container*› slop over

über·schwemmen *tr. V.* (auch fig.) flood; **von Touristen überschwemmt werden** (fig.) be flooded *or* swamped with tourists; **den Markt mit Waren ~** (fig.) flood *or* swamp the market/with goods

Überschwemmung *die;* ~, **~en** flood; (das Überschwemmen) flooding *no pl.;* **zu ~en führen** lead to flooding *or* floods

Überschwemmungs-: ~gebiet *das* flood area; **~gefahr** *die* danger of flooding; **~katastrophe** *die* disastrous floods *pl.*

***über·schwenglich** ▸ **überschwänglich**

***Überschwenglichkeit** ▸ **Überschwänglichkeit**

Über·see *in* **aus** *od.* **von ~**: from overseas; **in ~ leben** live overseas; **nach ~ auswandern** emigrate overseas; **Exporte/Post nach ~**: overseas exports/mail; **Besitzungen in ~**: overseas possessions

Übersee-: ~dampfer *der* ocean-going steamer; **~gebiet** *das* overseas territory; **Britische ~gebiete** British territories overseas; **~hafen** *der* international port; **~handel** *der* overseas trade

überseeisch /ˈy:bɐze:ɪʃ/ *Adj.* overseas

Übersee-: ~kabel *das* transoceanic cable; **~koffer** *der* cabin trunk; **~territorium** *das* overseas territory

übersehbar *Adj.* (abschätzbar) assessable; **der Schaden ist noch nicht ~**: the damage cannot yet be assessed

über|sehen¹ *unr. refl. V.* (ugs.) **sich** (*Dat.*) **etw. ~**: get fed up (coll.) *or* tired of seeing sth.; **diese Tapete habe ich mir übergesehen** I'm fed up with the sight of this wallpaper

über·sehen² *unr. tr. V.* **1** look out over; (fig.) survey ‹*subject*›; **man kann von hier die ganze Bucht ~**: you can look [right] out over the whole bay from here; **etw. gut** *od.* **leicht ~ können** have a good view of sth. **2** (abschätzen) assess ‹*damage, situation, consequences, etc.*› **3** (nicht sehen) overlook; miss; miss ‹*turning, signpost*›; **mit seinen roten Haaren ist er nicht zu ~**: you can't miss him with his red hair **4** (ignorieren) ignore

über·senden *unr.* (*auch regelm.*) *tr. V.* send; remit, send ‹*money*›; **die übersandten Waren sind fehlerhaft** the goods sent are faulty; **anbei übersende ich Ihnen ...** please find enclosed ...

Über·sendung *die* sending; (von Geld) remittance; sending

über·sensibel
A *Adj.* oversensitive
B *adv.* oversensitively

übersetzbar *Adj.* translatable; **schwer/leicht ~ sein** be difficult/easy to translate

über|setzen¹
A *tr. V.* ferry over
B *itr. V.; auch mit sein* cross [over]

über·setzen² *tr., itr. V.* (auch fig.) translate; **etw. ins Deutsche/aus dem Deutschen ~**: translate sth. into/from German

Über·setzer *der,* **Über·setzerin** *die;* ~, **~nen** ▸ **ⓘ S. 113** translator; *s. auch* **-in**

übersetzt *Adj.* **1** (bes. schweiz.: überhöht) excessive **2** (Technik) **hoch/niedrig ~ sein** have a high/low transmission ratio

Übersetzung *die;* ~, **~en** **1** translation **2** (Technik) transmission ratio

Übersetzungs-: ~büro *das* translation agency; **~fehler** *der* translation error

Über·sicht *die* **1** overall view, overview (**über** + *Akk.* of); **die ~ [über etw.** (*Akk.*)**] verlieren** lose track [of sth.] **2** (Darstellung) survey; (Tabelle) summary

über·sichtlich
A *Adj.* clear; ‹*crossroads*› which allows a clear view
B *adv.* clearly

Übersichtlichkeit *die;* **~**: clarity; (einer Kreuzung) clear layout

Übersichts·karte *die* outline map

über|siedeln¹, über·siedeln² *itr. V.; mit sein* move (**nach** to)

Über·sied[e]lung /*od.* --ˈ(-)-/ *die* move (**nach** to)

Über·siedler *der,* **Über·siedlerin** *die* migrant

über·sinnlich *Adj.* supersensory; (übernatürlich) supernatural

über·spannen *tr. V.* **1** (bespannen) cover **2** (zu stark spannen) over-tension, over-tighten ‹*string, cable*›; overdraw ‹*bow*›; over-tension ‹*spring*›; *s. auch* **Bogen 3** **3** (sich spannen über) span ‹*river, valley, etc.*›

überspannt *Adj.* exaggerated ‹*ideas, behaviour, gestures*›; extreme ‹*views*›; inflated ‹*demands, expectations*›

Über·spannung *die* overvoltage; excess voltage

U

über·spielen *tr. V.* **1** (hinweggehen über) cover up; cover up, gloss over ‹*mistake*›; smooth over ‹*difficult situation*› **2** (aufnehmen) **[auf ein Tonband] ~:** transfer ‹*record*› to tape; put ‹*record*› on tape; **[auf ein anderes Tonband] ~:** transfer to another tape **3** (Funkw., Ferns.) transfer **4** (Sport) outplay; **die Abwehr ~:** beat the defence

über·spitzen *tr. V.* **etw. ~:** push *or* carry sth. too far; **überspitzt ausgedrückt könnte man sagen, dass ...** to exaggerate, one might say that ...

Überspitzung *die; ~, ~en* exaggeration; (allzu verfeinert od. kompliziert) over-subtlety

über·sprechen *unr. tr. V.* **etw. ~:** talk *or* speak over sth.

über|springen¹ *unr. itr. V.; mit sein* **1** ‹*spark, fire*› jump across; **seine Begeisterung sprang auf uns alle über** (fig.) his enthusiasm communicated itself to all of us **2** (unvermittelt übergehen zu) **auf etw.** (*Akk.*) **~:** switch abruptly to sth.

über·springen² *unr. tr. V.* **1** jump ‹*obstacle*› **2** (auslassen) miss out; skip; **eine Klasse ~:** jump a class

über|sprudeln *itr. V.; mit sein* (auch fig.) bubble over (**von** with)

über·spülen *tr. V.* ‹*water, waves*› wash over; **bei Flut überspült** covered at high tide

über·staatlich *Adj.* supranational

über|stehen¹ *unr. itr. V.; südd., österr., schweiz. mit sein* jut out; project

über·stehen² *unr. tr. V.* come through ‹*danger, war, operation*›; get over ‹*illness*›; withstand ‹*heat, strain*›; ‹*boat*› weather, ride out ‹*storm*›; (überleben) survive; **das Schlimmste ist jetzt überstanden** we're/they're *etc.* over the worst; the worst is over; **nach überstandener Gefahr** when the danger was over; **das hätten wir** *od.* **das wäre überstanden** that's 'that over with

über·steigen *unr. tr. V.* **1** climb over **2** (fig.: hinausgehen über) exceed; **jmds. Fähigkeiten/Kräfte/Mittel ~:** be beyond sb.'s abilities/strength/means; **das übersteigt meinen Horizont** that's above my head

über·steigern *tr. V.* push up ‹*demands, speed*› too far *or* high; **ein übersteigertes Ehrgefühl** an exaggerated sense of honour

Über·steigerung *die* excessive increase; (einer Forderung) excessive pushing-up

über·stellen *tr. V.* (Amtsspr.) transfer ‹*convict*›; (an Gericht, Polizei) hand over (**an** + *Akk.* to)

Über·stellung *die* (Amtsspr.) handover (**an** + *Akk.* to); (in eine Klinik etc.) transfer (**in** + *Akk.* to)

über·steuern
A *tr. V.* (Elektrot.) overdrive
B *itr. V.* (Kfz-W.) ‹*vehicle*› oversteer

über·stimmen *tr. V.* outvote

über·strahlen *tr. V.* **1** (geh.) light up; illuminate; **Freude überstrahlte sein Gesicht** (fig.) his face lit up with joy **2** (fig.: in den Schatten stellen) outshine

überstrapazieren *tr. V.;* **ich überstrapaziere, überstrapaziert, überzustrapazieren** overtax ‹*person*›; overstrain ‹*nerves*›; make excessive demands on ‹*patience, willingness*›; treat ‹*car*› too roughly; **das Prinzip wird überstrapaziert** the principle is overworked

über·streichen *unr. tr. V.* paint over

über|streifen *tr. V.* **[sich** (*Dat.*)**] etw. ~:** slip sth. on

über|strömen¹ *itr. V.; mit sein* **1** (über den Rand strömen) overflow; **er strömt über vor Glück/Dankbarkeit** (fig.) he is brimming *or* bursting with happiness/gratitude **2** (geh.: übergehen) ‹*mood, feeling, etc.*› communicate itself, spread (**auf** + *Akk.* to)

über·strömen² *tr. V.* flood; **von Tränen/Blut überströmt [sein]** [be] streaming with tears/blood; **eine Welle des Glücks überströmte ihn** (fig.) a wave of happiness flooded over him

über|stülpen *tr. V.* pull on ‹*hat etc.*›

Über·stunde *die:* **er hat eine ~/drei ~n gearbeitet** he did one hour's/three hours' overtime; **~n machen** *od.* **leisten** *od.* (salopp) **schieben** do overtime

Überstunden·abbau *der* reduction of overtime

Überstunden·zuschlag *der* overtime supplement; **der ~ beträgt 50%** overtime is paid at time and a half

über·stürzen
A *tr. V.* rush; **nur nichts ~:** don't rush things; take it easy
B *refl. V.* rush; (rasch aufeinander folgen) ‹*events, news, etc.*› come thick and fast; **sich bei etw. ~:** rush sth.

überstürzt
A *Adj.* hurried ‹*escape, departure*›; overhasty ‹*decision*›
B *adv.* ‹*decide, act*› overhastily; ‹*depart*› hurriedly

über·tariflich
A *Adj.* **~e Bezahlung/Zulagen** payment/bonuses above agreed rates
B *adv.* **jmdn. ~ bezahlen** pay sb. above agreed rates

über·teuert *Adj.* over-expensive

über·titeln *tr. V.* **ein Werk** *usw.* **... ~:** give a work *etc.* the title ...

übertölpeln *tr. V.* dupe; con (coll.)

Übertölpelung *die; ~, ~en* duping; conning (coll.)

über·tönen *tr. V.* drown out

Über·topf *der* [decorative] outer pot

Übertrag /ˈyːbɐtraːk/ *der;* **~[e]s, Überträge** /-trɛːgə/ (bes. Buchf.) carry-over

über·tragbar *Adj.* transferable (**auf** + *Akk.* to); (auf etw. anderes anwendbar) applicable (**auf** + *Akk.* to); (übersetzbar) translatable; (ansteckend) communicable, infectious ‹*disease*›

Übertragbarkeit *die; ~:* transferability (**auf** + *Akk.* to); (von Krankheit) communicability (**auf** + *Akk.* to); (Anwendbarkeit) applicability (**auf** + *Akk.* to); **die leichte ~ einer Krankheit** the infectiousness of a disease; **die ~ von etw. in die Praxis** the possibility of putting sth. into practice

über·tragen
A *unr. tr. V.* **1** transfer (**auf** + *Akk.* to); transmit ‹*power, torque, etc.*› (**auf** + *Akk.* to); communicate ‹*disease, illness*› (**auf** + *Akk.* to); carry over ‹*subtotal*›; (auf etw. anderes anwenden) apply (**auf** + *Akk.* to); (übersetzen) translate; render; **ein Stenogramm in Langschrift ~:** write a piece of shorthand out in longhand; (mit der Schreibmaschine) type out a piece of shorthand; **eine Erzählung in Verse ~:** put a story into verse; **etw. ins reine** *od.* **in die Reinschrift ~:** make a fair copy of sth.; **etw. in ein Heft ~:** copy sth. out into a book; **seine Begeisterung** *usw.* **auf jmdn. ~:** communicate one's enthusiasm *etc.* to sb.; **etw. vom** *od.* **aus dem Englischen ins Deutsche ~:** translate sth. from English into German; **in ~er Bedeutung, im ~en Sinne** in a transferred sense **2** (senden) broadcast ‹*concert, event, match, etc.*›; (im Fernsehen) televise; **etw. direkt** *or* **live ~:** broadcast/televise sth. live; **etw. im Fernsehen ~:** televise sth. **3** (geben) **jmdm. Aufgaben/Pflichten** *usw.* **~:** hand over tasks/duties *etc.* to sb.; (anvertrauen) entrust sb. with tasks/duties *etc.*; **jmdm. ein Recht ~:** confer a right on sb. **4** (Med.: zu lange nicht gebären) **sie hat ihr Kind ~:** she had a post-term birth; **ein ~es Kind** a post-term infant
B *refl. V.* **sich auf jmdn. ~** ‹*disease, illness*› be communicated *or* be passed on to sb.; (fig.) ‹*enthusiasm, nervousness, etc.*› communicate itself to sb.

Über·träger *der,* **Über·trägerin** *die* (Med.) carrier

Übertragung *die; ~, ~en* **1** ▸ **übertragen A 1**: transference; transmission; communication; carrying over; application; translation; rendering; **die ~ einer Erzählung in Verse** putting a story into verse; **die ~ der Krankheit erfolgt über das Trinkwasser** the disease is spread through drinking water **2** (das Senden) broadcasting; (Programm, Sendung) broadcast; (im Fernsehen) televising/television broadcast **3** (von Aufgaben, Pflichten usw.) entrusting; (von Rechten) conferral **4** (Med.: eines Kindes) post-term birth

Übertragungs-: ~geschwindigkeit *die* **~rate** *die* ▸ **Übertragungsgeschwindigkeit;** (Elektrot.) transmission speed; **~recht** *das* (Ferns., Rundf.) broadcasting rights *pl.* (+ *Gen.*, **für** to); **~technik** *die* transmission technology; (Nachrichtentechnik) telecommunications technology; **~wagen** *der* outside broadcast vehicle; OB vehicle; **~weg** *der* **1** (Med.) transmission route; **2** (Nachrichtent., DV) transmission path

über·trainiert *Adj.* overtrained

über·treffen *unr. tr. V.* **1** surpass, outdo (**an** + *Dat.* in); break ‹*record*›; **jmdn. an Ausdauer ~:** be superior to sb. in stamina; **jmdn. an Fleiß/Intelligenz ~:** be more diligent/intelligent than sb.; **jmdn. in einem Fach/einem Sport ~:** be better than sb. at a subject/a sport; **in etw.** (*Dat.*) **nicht zu ~ sein** be unbeatable at sth.; **sich selbst ~:** excel oneself **2** (übersteigen) exceed; exceed, surpass ‹*expectations*›

über·treiben *unr. tr. V.* **1** *auch itr.* exaggerate **2** (zu weit treiben) overdo; take *or* carry too far; take *or* push ‹*claim, demand*› too far; **es mit etw. ~:** take *or* carry sth. too far; **man kann es auch ~:** you can take things *or* go too far

Übertreibung *die; ~, ~en* exaggeration; **er neigt zu ~en** he tends to exaggerate

über|treten¹ *unr. itr. V.; mit sein* **1** *auch mit haben* (Sport) step over the line/step out of the circle **2** (überwechseln) change sides; **zu einer anderen Partei ~:** join another party; switch parties; **[von der KPD] zur SPD ~:** switch [from the KPD] to the SPD; **zum Katholizismus/Islam ~:** convert to Catholicism/Islam **3** (gelangen) **in etw.** (*Akk.*) **~:** enter sth.

über·treten² *unr. tr. V.* break, contravene ‹*law*›; infringe, violate ‹*regulation, prohibition*›

Übertretung *die; ~, ~en* **1** ▸ **übertreten²**: breaking; contravention; infringement; violation **2** (Vergehen) misdemeanour

Übertretungs·fall *der:* **im ~[e]** (Amtsspr.) if the law is contravened; in the event of an infringement *or* a violation

übertrieben /-triːbn/
A *2. Part. v.* **übertreiben**
B exaggerated; (übermäßig) excessive ‹*care, thrift, etc.*›; **das finde ich reichlich ~:** I really think that's going too far
C *adv.* excessively

Über·tritt *der* change of allegiance, switch (**zu** to); (Rel.) conversion (**zu** to)

über·trumpfen *tr. V.* **1** (Kartenspiel) trump **2** (übertreffen) outdo

über·tünchen *tr. V.* cover with whitewash; (fig.) cover up

über·übermorgen *Adv.* in three days' time

Über·vater *der* [dominant] father figure

über|versorgen *tr. V.* overprovide (**mit** with); (Wirtsch.: beliefern) oversupply (**mit** with)

Über·versorgung *die* overprovision; (Wirtsch.: des Markts usw.) oversupply

übervölkern /-ˈfœlkɐn/ *tr. V.* overpopulate

Übervölkerung *die; ~:* overpopulation

über·voll *Adj.* overfull; overcrowded, packed ‹*room, train, tram, etc.*›; packed ‹*theatre, cinema*›

über·vorsichtig
A *Adj.* overcautious; excessively cautious
B *adv.* too cautiously

über·vor·teilen *tr. V.* cheat

über·wachen *tr. V.* watch, keep under surveillance ‹*suspect, agent, area, etc.*›; supervise ‹*factory, workers, process*›; control ‹*traffic*›; monitor ‹*progress, production process, experiment, patient*›; **die Polizei überwacht sein Telefon** the police are monitoring his telephone calls; **er überwacht jeden ihrer Schritte** he watches her every move

über·wachsen *unr. tr. V.* overgrow

Überwachung *die; ~, ~en* ▸ **überwachen**: surveillance; supervision; controlling; monitoring

U

Überwachungs-: ~kamera *die* security camera; surveillance camera; **~staat** *der* (abwertend) Big Brother state; **~system** *das* surveillance system

überwältigen /-ˈvɛltɪgn̩/ *tr. V.* ① overpower ② (fig.) ‹*sleep, emotion, fear, etc.*› overcome; ‹*sight, impressions, beauty, etc.*› overwhelm; **von Rührung überwältigt werden** be overcome with emotion

überwältigend
A *Adj.* overwhelming ‹*sight, impression, victory, majority, etc.*›; overpowering ‹*smell*›; stunning ‹*beauty*›; **das ist nicht [gerade] ~:** that isn't [exactly] anything to write home about (coll.)
B *adv.* stunningly ‹*beautiful*›; **das hat er ~ gespielt** he played that quite magnificently

über·wälzen *tr. V.* (bes. Wirtsch.) pass on ‹*costs etc.*› **(auf** + *Akk.* to); shift ‹*burden, blame, responsibility*› **(auf** + *Akk.* on to)

über|wechseln *itr. V.; mit sein* ① cross over **(auf** + *Akk.* to); **auf eine andere Spur ~:** change lanes; move to another lane ② (übertreten) change sides; **ins feindliche Lager/zur anderen Partei ~:** go over to the enemy/the other party; **von der SPD zur KPD ~:** switch from the SPD to the KPD ③ (mit etw. anderem beginnen) **zu etw. ~:** change over to sth.; **zu einem anderen Thema ~:** turn to another topic; **aufs Gymnasium ~:** go on to grammar school

über·weiden *tr. V.* overgraze

Über·weidung *die;* **~, ~en** overgrazing

über·weisen *unr. tr. V.* ① transfer ‹*money*› **(an, auf** + *Akk.* to); **er bekommt sein Gehalt [auf sein Konto] überwiesen** his salary is paid into his account ② (zu einem anderen Arzt schicken) refer **(an die** *Akk.* to); **jmdn. in die Klinik ~:** refer sb. to the clinic ③ (zuleiten) refer ‹*proposal*› **(an** + *Akk.* to); pass on ‹*file, application*› **(an** + *Akk.* to)

Über·weisung *die* ① transfer **(an, auf** + *Akk.* to) ② (Summe) remittance ③ (eines Patienten) referral **(an** + *Akk.* to) ④ ▸ **Überweisungsschein**

Überweisungs-: ~auftrag *der* (Bankw.) [credit] transfer order; **~formular** *das* (Bankw.) [credit] transfer form; **~schein** *der* (Med.) certificate of referral

Über·weite *die* outsize; **Röcke in ~n** outsize skirts

über|werfen¹ *unr. tr. V.* throw on ‹*clothes*›; **er warf dem Pferd eine Decke über** he threw a blanket over the horse

über·werfen² *unr. refl. V.* **sich mit jmdm. ~:** fall out with sb.; **sie haben sich überworfen** they have fallen out

über·wiegen
A *unr. itr. V.* predominate; **es überwog die Einsicht, dass ...** the recognition prevailed that ...
B *unr. tr. V.* ‹*advantages, disadvantages, etc.*› outweigh; ‹*emotion, argument*› prevail over

überwiegend
A /*auch* -ˈ--/ *Adj.* overwhelming; **der ~e Teil der Bevölkerung** the majority of the population
B *adv.* mainly

überwindbar *Adj.* surmountable; **schwer ~:** difficult to overcome

über·winden
A *unr. tr. V.* ① overcome ‹*resistance*›; overcome, surmount ‹*difficulty, obstacle, gradient*›; conquer ‹*capitalism, apartheid, etc.*›; overcome, get over ‹*fear, inhibitions, disappointment, grief*›; get past ‹*stage*› ② (aufgeben) overcome ‹*doubt, misgivings, reservations, suspicions*›; give up ‹*way of thinking, point of view*› ③ (geh.: besiegen) overcome; vanquish (literary)
B *unr. refl. V.* overcome one's reluctance; **sich [dazu] ~, etw. zu tun** bring oneself to do sth.; **ich konnte mich nur schwer [dazu] ~, es zu tun** I could hardly bring myself to do it; **dazu konnte ich mich nicht ~:** I could not bring myself to do that

Über·windung *die* ① ▸ **überwinden A 1:** overcoming; surmounting; conquest; getting over/past ② (Besiegung) overcoming; vanquishing (literary) ③ (das Sichüberwinden) **es war eine große ~ für ihn** it cost him a great effort; **das hat mich viel ~ gekostet** that was a real effort of will for me

über·wintern
A *itr. V.* [over]winter; spend the winter
B *tr. V.* overwinter ‹*plant*›

über·wölben *tr. V.* arch over

über·wuchern *tr. V.* overgrow

Über·wurf *der* ① (Umhang) wrap ② (österr.) ▸ **Zierdecke** ③ (Ringen) shoulder throw

über·würzen *tr., auch itr. V.* overseason

Über·zahl *die* majority; **in der ~ sein** be in the majority; ‹*army, enemy*› be superior in numbers

überzählig /-tsɛːlɪç/ *Adj.* surplus; spare; **einige Damen waren ~:** there were a few ladies too many

über·zeichnen *tr. V.* ① (Börsenw.) oversubscribe ② (zugespitzt darstellen) overdraw ‹*figure, character, etc.*›

Über·zeichnung ① (Börsenw.) oversubscription ② (zugespitzte Darstellung) overdrawn portrayal

Über·zeit *die* (schweiz.) overtime

überzeugen
A *tr. V.* convince; (umstimmen) persuade; convince; **jmdn. von etw. ~:** convince/persuade sb. of sth.
B *itr. V.* be convincing
C *refl. V.* convince *or* satisfy oneself; **sich persönlich** *od.* **mit eigenen Augen [von etw.] ~:** see [sth.] for oneself

überzeugend
A *Adj.* convincing; convincing, persuasive ‹*arguments, proof, words, speech*›
B *adv.* convincingly; ‹*argue, speak*› convincingly, persuasively

überzeugt *Adj.* ① convinced ② **von etw. ~ sein** (etw. hoch einschätzen) be convinced by sth.; **er ist sehr von sich [selbst] ~:** he's very sure of himself

Über·zeugung *die* ① convincing; (das Umstimmen) persuasion ② (feste Meinung) conviction; **der festen ~ sein, dass ...** be firmly convinced that ...; **zu der ~ kommen** *od.* **gelangen, dass ...** become convinced that ...; **meiner ~ nach ...** I am convinced that

Überzeugungs-: ~arbeit *die* propaganda work; **~kraft** *die* power[s] of persuasion; persuasiveness; **mit ~kraft reden** speak persuasively; **~täter** *der,* **~täterin** *die* (Rechtsspr.) offender who has acted on grounds of conscience

über|ziehen¹ *unr. tr. V.* ① pull on ‹*clothes*› ② **jmdn. eins** *od.* **ein paar ~** (ugs.) give sb. a clout

über·ziehen²
A *unr. tr. V.* ① **etw. mit etw. ~:** cover sth. with sth.; **die Torte mit Guss ~:** glaze the gateau; **die Betten frisch ~:** put clean sheets on the beds; change the sheets on the beds; **das Land mit Krieg ~** (fig.) spread war over the land ② overdraw ‹*account*› **(um** by); **sie hat ihr Konto [um 300 Euro] überzogen** she is [300 euros] overdrawn; **seinen Urlaub ~:** take too much time off; **die Mittagspause um 10 Minuten ~:** take an extra ten minutes over lunch; **die vorgesehene Sendezeit [um drei Minuten] ~:** overrun the programme time [by three minutes] ③ (übertreiben) overdo ‹*criticism etc.*›; **überzogene Leistungen/Erwartungen/Preiserhöhungen** *usw.* excessive payments/expectations/price increases *etc*
B *unr. itr. V.* ① overdraw one's account; go overdrawn ② (bei einer Sendung, einem Vortrag) overrun
C *unr. refl. V.* ‹*sky*› cloud over, become overcast

Überzieher *der;* **~s, ~** ① (veralt.: Herrenmantel) [light] overcoat ② (salopp: Kondom) johnny (Brit. sl.); rubber (sl.)

Über·ziehung *die* exceeding; (eines Zeitlimits) overrunning; (eines Kontos) overdrawing

Überziehungs-: ~kredit *der* (Finanzw.) overdraft facility; **~zins** *der* (Finanzw.) overdraft rate

überzüchtet /yːbɐˈtsʏçtət/ *Adj.* overbred; over-sophisticated ‹*engines, systems*›

über·zuckern *tr. V.* sugar

Überzug *der* ① (Beschichtung) coating ② (Bezug) cover

üblich /ˈyːplɪç/ *Adj.* usual; (normal) normal; (gebräuchlich) customary; **das ist hier so ~:** that's the accepted *or* (coll.) done thing here; **das ist nicht mehr ~:** that's no longer done (coll.); **wie ~:** as usual; **sie gebrauchte die ~e Ausrede** she used the same old excuse

üblicher·weise *Adv.* usually; generally

U-Boot *das* submarine; sub (coll.)

übrig /ˈyːbrɪç/ *Adj.* remaining *attrib.;* (ander...) other; **alle ~en Gäste sind bereits gegangen** all the other guests have already gone; **das/alles ~e erzähle ich dir später** I'll tell you the rest/all the rest later; **die/alle ~en** the/all the rest *or* others; **im ~en** besides; **ein ~es tun** (geh.) do one last thing; **es ist etwas ~:** there is some left; **es ist noch Suppe ~:** there is some soup left [over]; **ich habe noch Geld ~:** I [still] have some money left; (ich habe mehr Geld, als ich brauche) I [still] have some money to spare; **hast du vielleicht einen Euro [für mich] ~?** can you spare me a euro?; **für jmdn./etw. wenig/nichts ~ haben** have little/no time for sb./sth. (fig.); **etw. ~ behalten** have sth. left over; **~ bleiben** be left; remain; ‹*food, drink*› be left over; **ihm bleibt nichts [anderes** *od.* **weiter] ~, als zu ...** he has no [other] choice but to ...; there is nothing he can do but to ...; **~ lassen** + *Akk.* leave; leave ‹*food, drink*› over; **lasst mir etwas davon ~:** leave some of it for me; **zu wünschen ~ lassen** leave something to be desired; **sehr** *od.* **viel/nichts zu wünschen ~ lassen** leave much *or* (coll.) a lot/nothing to be desired

übrig-: *~|behalten ▸ **übrig**; ***~|bleiben** ▸ **übrig**

übrigens /ˈyːbrɪgn̩s/ *Adv.* by the way; incidentally

***übrig|lassen** ▸ **übrig**

Übung /ˈyːbʊŋ/ *die;* **~, ~en** ① exercise ② (das Üben, Geübtsein) practice; **das erfordert ~:** that takes practice; **das macht die ~, das ist alles nur ~:** it's [just] a question of practice; **etw. zur ~ tun** do sth. for practice; **außer ~ sein** be out of practice; **~/viel ~/keine ~ haben** have had some/a lot of (coll.)/no practice; **aus der ~ kommen** get out of practice; **in der ~ sein/bleiben** be/stay in practice; **~ macht den Meister** (Spr.) practice makes perfect (prov.) ③ (Lehrveranstaltung) class; seminar

übungs-, Übungs-: ~buch *das* book of exercises; (Lehrbuch) textbook with exercises; **~halber** *Adv.* for practice; **~munition** *die* (Milit.) blank ammunition; **~programm** *das* (Sport) training and practice programme; **~sache** *die:* **~sache sein** be a matter of practice; **~weise** *Adv.* for practice; **~zweck** *der:* **für ~zwecke, zu ~zwecken** for practice purposes

UdSSR *Abk.* **= Union der Sozialistischen Sowjetrepubliken** USSR

UEFA /uˈeːfa:/*die;* **~** (Fußball) UEFA

U-Eisen *das* channel iron

Ufer /ˈuːfɐ/ *das;* **~s, ~** ▸ **❶ S. 267** bank; (des Meers) shore; **ans ~ gespült werden** be washed ashore; **der Fluss trat über die ~:** the river burst its banks; **das sichere ~ erreichen** reach dry land; **das Haus liegt direkt am ~:** the house is right by the lake/river/sea

ufer-, Ufer-: ~befestigung *die* bank reinforcement; **~böschung** *die* [river/canal] embankment; **~los** *Adj.* limitless; boundless ‹*love, indulgence, etc.*›; endless ‹*discussions, talks, quarrel, subject*›; **ins Uferlose gehen** ‹*plans, ambitions, etc.*› know no bounds; **~promenade** *die* riverside walk; (am Meer) promenade; **~straße** *die* riverside/lakeside road; (am Meer) coast road

uff /ʊf/ *Interj.* oof; phew

UFO, Ufo /ˈuːfo/ *das;* **~[s], ~s** UFO

u-förmig, U-förmig *Adj.* U-shaped

UG *Abk.* **= Untergeschoss**

ℹ Uhrzeit

Wie viel Uhr ist es?, Wie spät ist es?
= What time is it?, What's the time?
Meine Uhr geht vor/nach
= My watch is fast/slow
Könnten Sie mir sagen, wie spät es ist?
= Could you tell me the time?
Es war soeben zehn Uhr
= It's just after *od.* just gone ten [o'clock]
Wie viel Uhr hast du?
= What time do you make it?
Es ist elf Uhr vorbei
= It's gone eleven [o'clock]
Nach meiner Uhr ist es fünf vor/zehn nach neun
= By my watch it's five to/ten past nine
Es ist gleich sieben
= It's coming up to seven

Im englischsprachigen Raum wird hauptsächlich die 12-Stunden-Uhr verwendet, mit den Zusätzen **a.m.** = ante meridiem = vor Mittag, also morgens, und **p.m.** = post meridiem = nach Mittag, also nachmittags oder abends. Der Ausdruck **o'clock** wird nur bei Uhrzeitangaben verwendet, die sich auf die volle Stunde beziehen. Danach steht statt a.m. bzw. p.m. **in the morning** bzw. **in the afternoon/evening**. Die 24-Stunden-Uhr wird meist nur beim Militär, in der Luftfahrt und für Fahrpläne benutzt. In der folgenden Aufstellung werden Beispiele ihrer hauptsächlich militärischen Form gegeben (jeweils nach dem Schrägstrich).

GESCHRIEBEN	GESPROCHEN
1 Uhr = 1.00 a.m./0100	***ein Uhr, eins*** one [a.m. *od.* in the morning]/one hundred hours
13 Uhr = 1.00 p.m./1300	***dreizehn Uhr, ein Uhr mittags*** one [p.m. *od.* in the afternoon]/thirteen hundred hours
2.05 Uhr = 2.05 a.m./0205	***fünf [Minuten] nach zwei, zwei Uhr fünf*** five past two [in the morning]/[o] two o five
14.05 Uhr = 2.05 p.m./1405	***vierzehn Uhr fünf*** five past two [in the afternoon]/fourteen o five
4.15 Uhr = 4.15 a.m./0415	***Viertel od. fünfzehn Minuten nach vier, vier Uhr fünfzehn*** four fifteen [a.m.], a quarter past four [in the morning]/[o] four fifteen
16.15 Uhr = 4.15 p.m./1615	***sechzehn Uhr fünfzehn*** four fifteen [p.m.], a quarter past four [in the afternoon]
5.30 Uhr = 5.30 a.m./0530	***halb sechs, fünf Uhr dreißig*** five thirty [a.m.], half past five [in the morning]/[o] five thirty
17.30 Uhr = 5.30 p.m./1730	***siebzehn Uhr dreißig*** five thirty [p.m.], half past five [in the afternoon]/seventeen thirty
7.45 Uhr = 7.45 a.m./0745	***Viertel od. fünfzehn Minuten vor acht, sieben Uhr fünfundvierzig*** seven forty-five [a.m.], a quarter to eight [in the morning]/[o] seven forty-five
19.45 Uhr = 7.45 p.m./1945	***neunzehn Uhr fünfundvierzig*** seven forty-five p.m., a quarter to eight [in the evening]/nineteen forty-five
0 Uhr, 24 Uhr = 12.00 [midnight]/0000, 2400*	***null Uhr, vierundzwanzig Uhr*** twelve [o'clock], [twelve] midnight/oo double o, twenty-four hundred hours*
12 Uhr = 12 [noon]/1200	***zwölf Uhr*** twelve [o'clock], [twelve] noon/twelve hundred hours

*Beim 24-Stunden-System zeigt 0000 = null Uhr den Tagesbeginn an, 2400 = vierundzwanzig Uhr das Tagesende.

Wann?

um + Uhrzeit = at + Uhrzeit

Er kam um acht Uhr
= He came at eight o'clock
Um wie viel Uhr wollen Sie frühstücken?
= [At] what time do you want breakfast?
um halb
= at half past
um halb neun
= at half past eight *od.* (*ugs.*) half eight
Punkt sechs, genau um sechs
= at six exactly, on the dot of six
gegen zehn
= at about ten
spätestens um zwölf
= at twelve at the latest
Es muss bis elf fertig sein
= It must be ready by eleven
Ich bin heute bis achtzehn Uhr hier
= I'll be here until six this evening
Ich bin erst um sechs dort
= I won't be there until six
von 13 bis 14 Uhr geschlossen
= closed from 1 to 2 p.m.
stündlich zur vollen Stunde
= every hour on the hour

Uganda /u'ganda/ *(das);* **~s** Uganda

Ugander /u'gandɐ/ *der;* **~s, ~, Uganderin** *die;* **~, ~nen** ▸ℹ **S. 520** Ugandan; *s. auch* **-in**

ugandisch *Adj.* ▸ℹ **S. 520** Ugandan

U-Haft *die* ▸**Untersuchungshaft**

Uhr /u:ɐ̯/ *die;* **~, ~en** ⓵ clock; (Armband~, Taschen~) watch; (Wasser~, Gas~) meter; (an Messinstrumenten) dial; gauge; **auf die** *od.* **nach der ~ sehen** look at the time; **ein Arbeiter, der dauernd auf die ~ sieht** a worker who is always clock-watching; **nach meiner ~:** by *or* according to my clock/watch; **jmds. ~ ist abgelaufen** (fig.) the sands of time have run out for sb.; **wissen, was die ~ geschlagen hat** (fig.) know what's what; know how things stand; **rund um die ~** (ugs.) round the clock ⓶ ▸ℹ **S. 729** (bei Uhrzeitangaben) **acht ~:** eight o'clock; **acht ~ dreißig** half past eight; 8.30 /eɪt'θɛ:tɪ/; **wie viel ~ ist es?** what's the time?; what time is it?; **um wie viel ~ treffen wir uns?** [at] what time shall we meet?; when shall we meet?

Uhr·armband *das* watch strap

Uhren·industrie *die* clock- and watchmaking industry

Uhr-: ~glas *das* watch glass; **~kette** *die* watch chain; **~macher,** *der,* **~macherin** *die* ▸ℹ **S. 113** watchmaker/clockmaker; **~werk** *das* clock/watch mechanism; **~zeiger** *der* clock/watch hand; **~zeigersinn** *der:* **im ~zeigersinn** clockwise; **entgegen dem ~zeigersinn** anticlockwise; **~zeit** *die* ▸ℹ **S. 729** time; **jmdn. nach der ~zeit fragen** ask sb. the time; **hast du [die] genaue ~zeit?** do you have the exact time?

Uhu /'u:hu/ *der;* **~s, ~s** eagle owl

Ukas /'u:kas/ *der;* **~ses, ~se** (scherzh.) edict

Ukraine /ukra̯i:nə/ *die;* **~:** Ukraine

Ukrainer *der;* **~s, ~, Ukrainerin** *die;* **~, ~nen** ▸ℹ **S. 520** Ukrainian

ukrainisch *Adj.* ▸ℹ **S. 670** Ukrainian; *s. auch* **deutsch**

Ukulele /uku'le:lə/ *die auch das;* **~, ~n** ukulele

UKW *Abk.* **= Ultrakurzwelle** VHF

UKW-Sender *der* VHF station; ≈ FM station

Ulan /u'la:n/ *der;* **~en, ~en** (hist.) uhlan

Ulk /ʊlk/ *der;* **~s, ~e** lark (coll.); (Streich) trick; [practical] joke; **etw. aus ~ sagen/tun** say/do sth. for fun *or* (coll.) for a laugh

ulken *itr. V.* clown *or* (coll.) lark about; **über jmdn./etw. ~:** make fun of sb./sth.

ulkig (ugs.)
A *Adj.* funny
B *adv.* in a funny way

Ulkus /'ʊlkʊs/ *das;* **~, Ulzera** /'ʊltsera/ ▸ℹ **S. 439** (Med.) ulcer

Ulme /'ʊlmə/ *die;* **~, ~n** ⓵ elm [tree] ⓶ (Holz) elm[wood]

Ultima Ratio /'ʊltima 'ra:tsi̯o/ *die;* **~ ~** (geh.) last resort

ultimativ /ʊltima'ti:f/
A *Adj.* ⓵ ‹demand› made as an ultimatum; **~en Charakter haben** constitute an ultimatum ⓶ ultimate; **die ~e Videoanlage** the ultimate video recorder *or* ultimate in video recorders
B *adv.* **etw. ~ fordern** demand sth. in [the form of] an ultimatum; **jmdn. ~ auffordern, etw. zu tun** give sb. an ultimatum to do sth.

Ultimatum /ʊlti'ma:tʊm/ *das;* **~s, Ultimaten** ultimatum; **[jmdm.] ein ~ stellen** give *or* set [sb.] an ultimatum

Ultimo /'ʊltimo/ *der;* **~s, ~s** last day of the month

U

ultra- 1 ultra-‹conservative, left-wing, modern, correct, critical, radical, fast, etc.›; extra-‹long, short, etc.› 2 (fachspr.) ultra‹short, violet, etc.›; **~rot** infrared

Ultra /ˈʊltra/ der; **~s, ~s** extremist

Ultra·kurz·welle /ʊltraˈkʊrtsvɛlə/ die 1 (Phys., Funkw., Rundf.) ultra-short wave 2 (Rundf.: Wellenbereich) very high frequency; VHF

Ultrakurzwellen·sender der very high frequency station; VHF station; ≈ FM station

ultra-, Ultra-: ~marin indekl. Adj. ultramarine; **~marin** das; **~~s** ultramarine; **~montan** Adj. (geh.) ultramontane; **~schall** /'---/ der (Physik, Med.) ultrasound

Ultraschall-: ~behandlung die (Med.) ultrasound therapy or treatment; (Technik) ultrasound treatment; **~untersuchung** die (Med.) ultrasound examination

ultra·violett Adj. (Physik) ultraviolet

Ulzera ▸**Ulkus**

um /ʊm/

A Präp. mit Akk. 1 (räumlich) [a]round; **um etw. herum** [a]round sth.; **um das Haus gehen** walk round the house; **das Rad dreht sich um seine Achse** the wheel turns on its axle; **um die Ecke** round the corner; **um sich schlagen** lash or hit out; **er warf mit Steinen um sich** he threw stones around or about; s. auch **greifen B 1**; **scharen B** 2 (zeitlich) (genau) at; (etwa) around [about]; **der Unterricht beginnt um acht [Uhr]** lessons start at eight [o'clock]; **um den 20. August [herum]** around [about] 20 August; **um die Mittagszeit [herum]** around midday 3 **Tag um Tag/Stunde um Stunde** day after day/hour after hour; **Meter um Meter/Schritt um Schritt** metre by metre/step by step 4 (bei Maß- u. Mengenangaben) by; **die Temperatur stieg um 5 Grad** the temperature rose [by] five degrees; **um 3 cm zu lang sein** be 3 cm too long; **um nichts/einiges/vieles besser sein** be no/somewhat/a lot better 5 (südd., österr.: bei Preisangaben) for

B Adv. 1 (etwa, ungefähr) around; about; **um [die] 10 Euro/50 Personen [herum]** around or about or round about 10 euros/50 people 2 (ugs.: vorüber, vorbei) over; **um sein** ‹time› be up

C Konj. 1 (final) **um ... zu** [in order] to; **um es gleich zu sagen, ich kann nicht lange bleiben** I'd better say straight away that I can't stay for long 2 (konsekutiv) **er ist groß genug/ist noch zu klein, um ... zu ...** he is big enough/is still too young to ...; **sie heirateten, um sich schon nach einem Jahr wieder scheiden zu lassen** they got married, only to get divorced again after just one year; s. auch **umso**

um|ackern tr. V. plough over

um|adressieren tr. V. redirect

um|ändern tr. V. change; alter; revise ‹text, novel›; alter ‹garment›

um|arbeiten tr. V. alter ‹garment›; revise, rework ‹text, novel, music›; **einen Roman zu einem Drama/Drehbuch ~:** adapt a novel for the stage/screen

Umarbeitung die; **~, ~en** (eines Kleidungsstücks) alteration; (eines Romans, Textes, Musikstücks) revision; reworking; (zu einem Drehbuch, Drama o. Ä.) adaptation

umarmen tr. V. embrace; put one's arms around; (an sich drücken) hug; **sie umarmten sich** they embraced/hugged; **sei umarmt [von deiner/deinem ...]** (als Briefschluss) lots of love [from ...]

Umarmung die; **~, ~en** ▸**umarmen**: embrace; hug

Um·bau der; Pl. **~ten** 1 rebuilding; reconstruction; (kleinere Änderung) alteration; (zu etw. anderem) conversion; (fig.: eines Systems, einer Verwaltung) reorganization; **„wegen ~[s] geschlossen“** 'closed for alterations'; **das Gebäude befindet sich im ~:** the building is being rebuilt/altered/converted 2 (das Umgebaute) ▸**a**: reconstruction/altered building/conversion

um|bauen¹ tr., auch itr. V. rebuild; reconstruct; (leicht ändern) alter; (zu etw. anderem) convert (**zu** into); (fig.) reorganize ‹system, administration, etc.›; **das Bühnenbild ~:** change the set; **wir bauen um** we're rebuilding/making alterations

um·bauen² tr. V. surround; **umbauter Raum** interior space

um|behalten unr. tr. V. keep ‹apron, scarf, etc.› on

um|benennen unr. tr. V. change the name of, rename ‹street, square, etc.›; **etw. in etw.** (Akk.) **~:** change the name of sth. to sth.; rename sth. sth.

um|beschreiben unr. tr. V. (Geom.) circumscribe

um|besetzen tr., auch itr. V. change ‹team›; recast ‹role, play›; reallocate ‹post, position›

um|bestellen itr. V. change the order

um|betten tr. V. 1 **jmdn. ~:** move sb. to another bed 2 (in ein anderes Grab legen) move or transfer ‹body› to another grave

um|biegen

A unr. tr. V. bend

B unr. itr. V.; mit sein turn; ‹path› bend, turn

um|bilden tr. V. reorganize, reconstruct ‹department etc.›; reshuffle ‹government, cabinet›; **etw. zu etw. ~** (Biol.) develop sth. into sth.

um|binden unr. tr. V. put on ‹tie, apron, scarf, etc.›

um|blasen unr. tr. V. blow over

um|blättern

A tr. V. turn [over] ‹page›

B itr. V. turn the page/pages

um|blicken refl. V. 1 look around; **sich nach allen Seiten ~:** look all around 2 (zurückblicken) [turn to] look back (**nach** at)

Umbra /ˈʊmbra/ die; **~** (Farbe) umber

um·branden tr. V. (geh.) surge around

um·brausen tr. V. roar around

um|brechen¹

A unr. tr. V. 1 bring down ‹telephone pole, tree, etc.› 2 (umpflügen) break up, turn over ‹land›; plough up ‹field›

B unr. itr. V.; mit sein collapse; fall down

um·brechen² unr. tr. V. (Druckw.) make up

um|bringen unr. tr. V. kill; **dieses Material ist nicht umzubringen** (fig. ugs.) this material is indestructible; **diese Packerei bringt mich fast um** (fig. ugs.) all this packing's nearly killing me (coll.); **sich vor Höflichkeit ~** (fig. ugs.) fall over oneself to be polite (coll.); **sich für jmdn. ~** (fig. ugs.) do everything for sb.

Um·bruch der 1 radical change; (Umwälzung) upheaval; **im ~ sein** be in a state of flux 2 (Druckw.) make-up; (Ergebnis) page proofs pl.

um|buchen

A tr. V. 1 change ‹flight, journey route› (**auf** + Akk. to) 2 (Finanzw.) transfer (**auf** + Akk. to)

B itr. V. change one's booking (**auf** + Akk. to)

Um·buchung die 1 change of booking; **eine ~ Ihres Fluges ist jederzeit möglich** you can change your flight at any time 2 (Finanzw.) transfer (**auf** + Akk. to)

um|datieren tr. V. change the date of; redate ‹contract, letter, etc.›

um|deklarieren tr. V. declare as something else; **etw. zu etw. ~:** alter the description of sth. to sth.

um|denken unr. itr. V. revise one's thinking; rethink; **ein Prozess des Umdenkens** a process of rethinking

um|deuten tr. V. reinterpret; give a new interpretation to

um|dichten tr. V. adapt, recast ‹poem, song, etc.›

um|disponieren itr. V. change one's arrangements; make new arrangements

um·drängen tr. V. crowd round; mob ‹actor, pop star, etc.›

um|drehen

A tr. V. turn round; turn over ‹coin, hand, etc.›; turn ‹key›; turn ‹pockets, bag, garment, sock, etc.› inside out; **jeden Euro** od. **jeden Cent [dreimal] ~** (ugs.) watch every penny; **einen Spion ~** (fig.) turn a spy

B refl. V. turn round; (den Kopf wenden) turn one's head; **sich nach jmdm. ~:** turn/turn one's head to look at sb.; **ein Mädchen, nach dem sich die Männer ~:** a girl who turns men's heads

C itr. V.; auch mit sein (ugs.: umkehren) turn back; (ugs.: wenden) turn round

Um·drehung die turn; (eines Motors usw.) revolution; rev (coll.); (eines Planeten) rotation

um·einander Adv. **sich ~ kümmern/sorgen** take care of/worry about each other or one another; **~ besorgt sein** be concerned about each other or one another; **sich ~ drehen** revolve around each other

um|erziehen tr. V. re-educate; **jmdn. zu etw. ~:** re-educate sb. to be or as sth.

Um·erziehung die re-education; **~ von Revolutionären zu Konformisten** re-education to turn revolutionaries into conformists

um|fahren¹ unr. tr. V. knock over or down

um·fahren² unr. tr. V. go round; make a detour round ‹obstruction, busy area›; (im Auto) drive or go round; (im Schiff) sail or go round; (auf einer Umgehungsstraße) bypass ‹town, village, etc.›

Umfahrungs·straße die (österr., schweiz.) ▸**Umgehungsstraße**

Um·fall der (ugs. abwertend) about-face; U-turn

um|fallen unr. itr. V.; mit sein 1 (umstürzen) fall over 2 (zusammenbrechen) collapse; **tot ~:** fall down dead; **~ wie die Fliegen** go down like flies; **ich falle vor Müdigkeit um** I'm just about ready to drop; **vor Hunger/Durst fast ~:** be faint with hunger/thirst; **vor Schreck fast ~:** nearly die with fright; nearly have a heart attack (coll.) 3 (ugs. abwertend: seine Meinung ändern) do an about-face; do a U-turn

Umfaller der; **~s, ~** (ugs.) 1 person who changes/changed his mind; (Abtrünniger) turncoat 2 (Umfall) change of mind; (Kehrtwendung) about-turn 3 (Umfallen) fall; (von Auto) overturn

Umfallerin die; **~, ~nen** (ugs. abwertend) person who changes/changed her mind; (Abtrünnige) turncoat

Um·fang der 1 circumference; (eines Quadrats usw.) perimeter; (eines Baums, Menschen usw.) girth; circumference; **er hat einen ganz schönen ~** (scherzh.) he has quite a girth 2 (Größe) size; **der Band hat einen ~ von 250 Seiten** the volume contains 250 pages or is 250 pages thick 3 (Ausmaß) extent; (von Wissen) range; extent; (einer Stimme) range; (einer Arbeit, Untersuchung) scope; **in vollem ~:** fully; completely; **in großem ~:** on a large scale

um·fangen unr. tr. V. (geh.) embrace; (fig.) ‹silence, warmth, etc.› envelop

umfänglich /ˈʊmfɛŋlɪç/ Adj. extensive; ‹case, parcel, etc.› of considerable size; voluminous, extensive ‹correspondence›

umfang·reich Adj. extensive; substantial ‹book›

um·fassen tr. V. 1 grasp; (umarmen) embrace; **jmds. Arme/Taille/Knie ~:** grasp or clasp sb. round the arms/waist/knees; **jmdn. umfasst halten** hold sb. in one's arms or in an embrace 2 (enthalten) contain; (einschließen) include; take in; span, cover ‹period› 3 (umgeben) enclose; surround 4 (Milit.: umzingeln) surround; encircle

umfassend

A Adj. full ‹reply, information, survey, confession›; extensive, wide, comprehensive ‹knowledge, powers›; broad ‹education›; extensive ‹preparations, measures›

B adv. ‹inform› fully

Um·fassung die enclosure

Um·feld das 1 (Psych., Soziol.) milieu 2 ▸**Umgebung 1**

um·flattern tr. V. flutter round

um·flechten unr. tr. V. put wicker round; **eine umflochtene Flasche** a wickered bottle; **eine mit Bast umflochtene Flasche** a raffia-covered bottle

um|fliegen¹ unr. itr. V.; mit sein (salopp) go flying (coll.)

um·fliegen² unr. tr. V. fly round

um·fließen unr. tr. V. flow round

U

um·fluten *tr. V.* wash round ‹*building, island, fig.: person*›; **umflutet sein** (von Wasser) be surrounded by water; (von Überschwemmung) be surrounded by floods; **umflutet von weißem Licht** flooded with white light

um|formen *tr. V.* **1** reshape; remodel; recast, revise ‹*poem, novel*›; transform ‹*person*› **2** (Elektrot.) convert

Um·former *der* (Elektrot.) converter

Um·formung *die* **1** ▸ **umformen 1**: reshaping; remodelling; recasting; revision; transformation **2** (Elektrot.) conversion

Um·frage *die* survey; (Politik) opinion poll; **eine ~ machen** *od.* **veranstalten** carry out a survey/conduct an opinion poll

Umfrage·ergebnis *das* [opinion] poll result

um·fried[ig]en *tr. V.* (geh.) ▸ **einfried[ig]en**

Umfried[ig]ung *die; ~, ~en* (geh.) ▸ **Einfried[ig]ung**

um|füllen *tr. V.* **etw. in etw.** (*Akk.*) **~:** transfer sth. into sth.; **der Kaffee muss umgefüllt werden** the coffee has to be put into another container

um|funktionieren *tr. V.* change the function of; **etw. zu etw. ~:** turn sth. into sth.

Um·gang *der* **1** (gesellschaftlicher Verkehr) contact; dealings *pl.*; **jmd. hat guten/schlechten ~:** sb. keeps good/bad company; **mit jmdm. ~ haben/pflegen** associate with sb.; **mit jmdm. keinen ~ haben** have nothing to do with sb.; **er ist kein ~ für dich!** he is not suitable *or* fit company for you **2** (das Umgehen) **den ~ mit Pferden lernen** learn how to handle horses; **im ~ mit Kindern erfahren sein** be experienced in dealing with children **3** (bild. Kunst, Archit.) gallery

umgänglich /ˈʊmɡɛŋlɪç/ *Adj.* (verträglich) affable; friendly; (gesellig) sociable

umgangs-, Umgangs-: ~formen *Pl.* manners *pl.*; **~sprache** *die* colloquial language; **die englische ~sprache** colloquial English; **~sprachlich** **A** *Adj.* colloquial; **B** *adv.* colloquially

um·garnen *tr. V.* beguile

um·geben *unr. tr. V.* **1** surround; ‹*hedge, fence, wall, etc.*› enclose; ‹*darkness, mist, etc.*› envelop **2** **etw. mit etw. ~:** surround sth. with sth.; (einfrieden) enclose sth. with sth.; **sich mit jmdm./etw. ~:** surround oneself with sb./sth.

Umgebung *die; ~, ~en* **1** surroundings *pl.*; (Nachbarschaft) neighbourhood; (eines Ortes) surrounding area; **die nähere/weitere ~ Mannheims** the immediate/broader environs *pl.* of Mannheim; **Wiesbaden und ~:** Wiesbaden and the surrounding area **2** (fig.) milieu; **jmds. nähere ~:** those *pl.* close to sb.; **das Kind braucht seine vertraute ~:** the child needs familiar faces around it

Um·gegend *die* (ugs.) surrounding area; **die ~ der Stadt** the area surrounding the town

um|gehen¹ *unr. itr. V.; mit sein* **1** (im Umlauf sein) ‹*list, rumour, etc.*› go round, circulate; ‹*illness, infection*› go round; **Angst geht in der Bevölkerung um** fear is spreading in the population **2** (spuken) **hier geht ein Gespenst um** this place is haunted; **im Schloss geht ein Gespenst um** a ghost haunts this castle; the castle is haunted **3** (behandeln) **mit jmdm. freundlich/liebevoll** *usw.* **~:** treat sb. kindly/lovingly *etc.*; **mit etw. sorgfältig/nachlässig** *usw.* **~:** treat sth. carefully/carelessly *etc.*; **er versteht es, mit Kindern umzugehen** he knows how to handle children; **er kann mit Geld nicht ~:** he can't handle money; **mit Pinsel und Farbe ~ können** be able to use a brush and paint **4** (verkehren) **mit jmdm. ~:** associate with sb. **5** **mit dem Plan/Gedanken ~, etw. zu tun** think of doing sth. **6** (bes. nordd.: einen Umweg machen) make a detour

um·gehen² *unr. tr. V.* **1** (herumgehen, -fahren um) go round; make a detour round ‹*obstruction, busy area*›; (auf einer Umgehungsstraße) bypass ‹*town, village, etc.*› **2** (vermeiden) avoid; avoid, get round ‹*problem, difficulty*›; evade ‹*question, issue*› **3** (nicht befolgen) get round, circumvent ‹*law, restriction, etc.*›; evade ‹*obligation, duty*›

umgehend
A *Adj.* immediate
B *adv.* immediately

Umgehung *die; ~, ~en* **1** **durch ~ der Innenstadt** by bypassing *or* avoiding the town centre **2** ▸ **umgehen² 3**: circumvention; evasion; **das ließe sich nur unter ~ der Bestimmung durchführen** that could only be done by circumventing the regulations **3** ▸ **Umgehungsstraße**

Umgehungs·straße *die* bypass

umgekehrt
A *Adj.* inverse ‹*ratio, proportion*›; reverse ‹*order*›; opposite ‹*sign*›; **es verhält sich** *od.* **ist genau ~:** the very opposite *or* reverse is true *or* the case
B *adv.* inversely ‹*proportional*›; **vom Englischen ins Deutsche und ~ übersetzen** translate from English into German and vice versa; **~ wirst du kaum erwarten können, dass ...** conversely you can hardly expect that ...

um|gestalten *tr. V.* reshape; remodel; redesign ‹*square, park, room, etc.*›; rework ‹*text, music, etc.*›; (reorganisieren) reorganize; (verändern) change; **der Garten wurde zu einem Park umgestaltet** the garden was turned into a park

um|gewöhnen *refl. V.* [re]adjust; get used to a/the change

Um·gewöhnung *die* [re]adjustment

um|gießen *unr. tr. V.* **1** **etw. ~:** pour sth. into another container/into bottles *etc.*; **etw. in etw.** (*Akk.*) **~:** pour sth. into sth. **2** (in eine andere Form gießen) recast

um·glänzen *tr. V.* (dichter.) **etw. ~:** bathe sth. in light

um|graben *unr. tr. V.* dig over

um·grenzen *tr. V.* ‹*wall, fence, etc.*› surround, enclose; (fig.) define; delimit

Umgrenzung *die; ~, ~en* **1** ▸ **umgrenzen**: surrounding; enclosing; (fig.) definition; delimitation **2** (Grenzlinie) boundary

um|gruppieren *tr. V.* rearrange

Um·gruppierung *die* rearrangement

um|gucken *refl. V.* (ugs.) ▸ **umsehen**

um|gürten *tr. V.* (veralt.) put on ‹*belt*›; **[sich** (*Dat.*)**] das Schwert ~:** gird on one's sword

um|haben *unr. tr. V.* **etw. ~:** have sth. on

um·halsen *tr. V.* embrace; **sie umhalsten sich** they embraced

Um·hang *der* cape

um|hängen *tr. V.* **1** **etw. ~:** hang sth. somewhere else; **die Bilder müssen umgehängt werden** the pictures must be changed around **2** **jmdm./sich einen Mantel/eine Decke ~:** drape a coat/blanket round sb.'s/one's shoulders; **sich** (*Dat.*) **ein Gewehr ~:** sling a rifle from one's shoulder; **sich** (*Dat.*) **einen Fotoapparat ~:** hang *or* sling a camera round one's neck; **jmdm. eine Medaille ~:** hang a medal round sb.'s neck

Umhänge·tasche *die* shoulder bag

um|hauen *unr. tr. V.* **1** (fällen) fell **2** (ugs.: niederwerfen) knock down; floor; **diese Hitze haut einen glatt um** (salopp) this heat is enough to knock you over (coll.); **schon ein Bier haut mich um** (salopp) just one beer's enough to put me under the table (coll.); **es hat mich fast umgehauen, als ich davon hörte** (salopp) I was flabbergasted when I heard

um·hegen *tr. V.* (geh.) care lovingly for; **sie umhegt die Kinder mit mütterlicher Liebe** she looks after the children with maternal love

um·her *Adv.* around; **weit ~:** all around

umher-: ▸ **herum-**

umhin|können *unr. itr. V.* **sie konnte nicht/kaum umhin, das zu tun** she had no/scarcely had any choice but to do it; (einem inneren Zwang folgend) she couldn't help/could scarcely help but do it

um|hören *refl. V.* keep one's ears open; (direkt fragen) ask around; **ich werde mich danach bei** *od.* **unter meinen Kollegen ~:** I'll ask around my workmates (Brit.) *or* (esp. Amer.) fellow workers

um·hüllen *tr. V.* wrap; (fig.) ‹*mist, fog, etc.*› shroud; **jmdn./etw. mit etw. ~:** wrap sb./sth. in sth.

um·jubeln *tr. V.* cheer

um·kämpfen *tr. V.* fight over ‹*position, village, etc.*›; contest ‹*victory*›; **ein heiß umkämpfter Sieg** a hotly contested victory

Umkehr /ˈʊmkeːɐ̯/ *die;* ~ (auch fig.) turning back; **zur ~ gezwungen werden** be forced to turn back

umkehr·bar *Adj.* reversible

um|kehren
A *itr. V.; mit sein* turn back; (fig. geh.: sich wandeln) change one's ways; **auf halbem Wege ~** (fig.) stop halfway
B *tr. V.* **1** turn upside down; turn over ‹*sheet of paper*›; (nach links drehen) turn ‹*garment etc.*› inside out; (nach rechts drehen) turn ‹*garment etc.*› right side out; **das ganze Haus [nach etw.] ~** (fig.) turn the whole house upside down [looking for sth.] **2** (ins Gegenteil verkehren) reverse; invert ‹*ratio, proportion*› **3** (Musik) invert **4** (Logik) convert ‹*proposition*›
C *refl. V.* be reversed; **der Magen kehrte sich ihm um** (fig.) his stomach turned over

Umkehr·film *der* (Fot.) reversal film

Umkehr·schluss *der* (Rechtsw.) argumentum e contrario; argument from the contrary

Umkehrung *die* **1** reversal **2** (Musik) inversion **3** (Logik) conversion

um|kippen
A *itr. V.; mit sein* **1** fall over; ‹*boat*› capsize, turn over; ‹*vehicle*› overturn **2** (ugs.: ohnmächtig werden) keel over **3** (ugs. abwertend) ▸ **umfallen 3** **4** (ugs.: umschlagen) ‹*wine*› go off **5** (Ökologie) ‹*river, lake*› reach the stage of biological collapse **6** (ugs.: ins Gegenteil umschlagen) ‹*mood*› turn; ‹*voice*› crack
B *tr. V.* tip over; knock over ‹*lamp, vase, glass, cup*›; capsize ‹*boat*›; turn ‹*boat*› over; overturn ‹*vehicle*›

um·klammern *tr. V.* clutch; clasp; **seine Hände umklammerten den Griff** his hands gripped *or* clasped the handle; **die Ringer/Boxer ~ sich** the wrestlers are locked together/the boxers are in a clinch; **etw./jmdn. fest umklammert halten** keep a firm grip on sth./clutch sb. tightly

Umklammerung *die; ~, ~en* clutch; clasp; (mit den Händen) clutch; grip; clasp; (Umarmung) firm embrace; (Boxen) clinch

um·klappbar *Adj.* fold-down ‹*seat*›; **~ sein** fold down

um|klappen
A *tr. V.* fold down
B *itr. V.; mit sein* (ugs.: ohnmächtig werden) keel over

Umkleide·kabine *die* changing cubicle

um|kleiden¹ (geh.)
A *refl. V.* change; change one's clothes
B *tr. V.* **jmdn. ~:** change sb.; change sb.'s clothes

um·kleiden² *tr. V.* cover

Umkleide·raum *der* changing room (Brit.); (im Theater) green room

um|knicken
A *itr. V.; mit sein* **1** **[mit dem Fuß] ~:** go over on one's ankle **2** ‹*tree, stalk, blade of grass, etc.*› bend; ‹*branch*› bend and snap; **umgeknickte Äste/Halme** snapped branches/bent straws
B *tr. V.* **1** (falten) fold ‹*page, sheet of paper*› over **2** (abknicken) bend over; break ‹*flower, stalk*›

um|kommen *unr. itr. V.; mit sein* **1** die; (bei einem Unglück, durch Gewalt) get killed; die; **ich komme um vor Hitze** (fig. ugs.) I'm dying in this heat (coll.); **ich komme um vor Hunger/Durst** (fig. ugs.) I'm dying of hunger/thirst (coll.); **vor Langeweile ~** (fig. ugs.) be bored to death (coll.); die of boredom (coll.) **2** (ungenießbar werden) ‹*food*› go off

umkränzen /ʊmˈkrɛntsn̩/ *tr. V.* garland; (fig.: umgeben) encircle

Um·kreis *der* **1** surrounding area; **im ~ von 5 km** within a radius of 5 km.; **der ~ der Stadt** the city's environs *pl. or* immediate surroundings *pl.*; **im [näheren] ~ der Stadt** in the [immediate] vicinity of the town; **aus dem ~ des Vorsitzenden hört man, ...** (fig.) one learns from those close to the chairman ... **2** (Geom.) circumcircle

um·kreisen *tr. V.* circle; ‹*spacecraft, satellite*› orbit; ‹*planet*› revolve [a]round; **seine Gedanken umkreisten das Thema** (fig.) he kept turning the matter over in his mind

um|krempeln *tr. V.* **1** (aufkrempeln) turn up ‹*cuff*›; roll up ‹*sleeve, trouser leg*› **2** **das ganze Haus [nach etw.] ~** (ugs.) turn the whole house upside down [looking for sth.] **3** (ugs.: von Grund auf ändern) **etw. ~:** give sth. a shake-up; **jmdn. ~:** [completely] change sb.

um|laden *unr. tr. V.* transfer ‹*goods etc.*›

Um·lage *die* share of the cost[s]; (bei einer Wohnung) share of the bill[s]; **die ~ beträgt 30 Euro pro Person** the cost is 30 euros per person

um·lagern *tr. V.* besiege

Um·land *das* surrounding area; **das ~ von Köln** the area around Cologne

um|lassen *unr. tr. V.* (ugs.) leave ‹*garment, watch, etc.*› on

Um·lauf *der* **1** rotation; **ein ~ [der Erde um die Sonne] dauert ein Jahr** one revolution [of the earth around the sun] takes a year **2** (Zirkulation) circulation; **in** *od.* **im ~ sein** ‹*magazine, report, etc.*› be circulating; ‹*coin, banknote*› be in circulation; **in ~ bringen** *od.* **setzen** circulate ‹*report, magazine, etc.*›; circulate, put about, start ‹*rumour*›; bring ‹*coin, banknote*› into circulation **3** (Rundschreiben) circular

Umlauf·bahn *die* (Astron., Raumf.) orbit; **etw. in eine ~ bringen** put sth. into orbit

um|laufen[1]

A *unr. tr. V.* knock over

B *unr. itr. V.; mit sein* **1** (rotieren) rotate; revolve; ‹*planet, satellite, etc.*› orbit **2** **~d** (ringsherum verlaufend) surrounding **3** (kursieren, zirkulieren) circulate

um·laufen[2] *unr. tr. V.* run around; ‹*planet, satellite, etc.*› orbit

Um·laut *der* (Sprachw.) umlaut

um|lauten *tr. V.* (Sprachw.) **ein umgelautetes a** an a umlaut; **das „a" wird hier umgelautet** the 'a' takes an umlaut in this case

um|legen *tr. V.* **1** (um einen Körperteil) put on; **jmdm. etw. ~:** put sth. on sb.; **sich** (*Dat.*) **etw. ~:** put sth. on; **jmdm. eine Stola/Decke ~:** put a stole round sb.'s shoulders/put a blanket round sb. **2** (auf den Boden, die Seite legen) lay down; flatten ‹*corn, stalks, etc.*›; (fällen) fell **3** (umklappen) fold down; turn down ‹*collar*›; turn up ‹*cuff*›; throw ‹*lever*›; turn over ‹*calendar-page*› **4** (ugs.: zu Boden werfen) floor, knock down ‹*person*› **5** (salopp: ermorden) **jmdn. ~:** do sb. in (sl.); bump sb. off (coll.) **6** (verlegen) transfer ‹*patient, telephone call*›; **den Termin ~:** change the date (**auf** + *Akk.* to) **7** (anteilmäßig verteilen) split, share ‹*costs*› (**auf** + *Akk.* between) **8** (derb: koitieren mit) lay (sl.)

um|leiten divert; re-route; divert ‹*river, stream*›

Um·leitung *die* diversion; re-routing; **die ~ fahren** take the diversion

um|lernen *itr. V.* **1** (beruflich) retrain; **auf Feinmechaniker ~:** retrain as a precision engineer **2** (seine Anschauungen ändern) learn to think differently

umliegend *Adj.* surrounding ‹*area, district*›; (nahe) nearby ‹*building*›

Um·luft *die* (Technik) recirculated air

um·mauern *tr. V.* surround with a wall; **ummauert** walled ‹*garden, town*›

um|melden *tr. V.* **sich ~:** report a change of address; **ein Auto ~:** inform the authorities of a change of ownership of a car/(am neuen Wohnort) of the new address of a car's owner

um|modeln *tr. V.* (ugs.) change ‹*house, flat*› round; refashion, alter ‹*jacket etc.*›

um|münzen *tr. V.* **etw. in etw.** (*Akk.*) **~:** convert sth. into sth.; **eine Niederlage in einen Sieg ~** (fig.: umdeuten) make a defeat out to be victory

um·nachtet *Adj.* (geh.) **[geistig] ~ sein** be [mentally] deranged

Umnachtung *die;* **~, ~en** (geh.) derangement; **im Zustand der ~, in geistiger ~:** in a state of mental derangement *or* insanity

um·nebeln *tr. V.* (fig.) cloud ‹*senses, glance*›; befog ‹*thoughts*›; **leicht umnebelt** slightly befuddled

um|organisieren *tr. V.* reorganize

um|orientieren *refl. V.* reorientate

Um·orientierung *die* reorientation

um|packen

A *itr. V.* repack

B *tr. V.* repack; **seine Sachen aus der Reisetasche in einen Koffer ~:** take one's things out of the holdall and pack them into a suitcase

um|pflanzen *tr. V.* transplant

um|pflügen *tr. V.* plough up

um|polen *tr. V.* (Elektrot.) reverse the polarity/connections of; (fig. ugs.: umwandeln) convert ‹*homosexual*›

um|pusten *tr. V.* (ugs.) blow over

um|quartieren *tr. V.* re-accommodate ‹*person*› (**in** + *Akk.* in); re-quarter, re-billet ‹*troops*› (**in** + *Akk.* in); move ‹*patient*›

um·rahmen *tr. V.* frame ‹*face etc.*›; **eine Feier mit Musik** *od.* **musikalisch ~** (fig.) begin and end a ceremony with music; give a ceremony a musical framework

Um|rahmung *die;* **~, ~en** **1** (das Umrahmen) bordering; **musikalische ~** (fig.) musical framework; music before and after **2** (Umrahmendes) border; (fig.) setting

um·randen *tr. V.* ring ‹*letter, error, etc.*›; border ‹*handkerchief, flower bed, etc.*›

umrändert /ʊmˈrɛndɐt/ *Adj.* **schwarz ~:** with a black border; **rot ~e Augen** red-rimmed eyes

Umrandung *die;* **~, ~en** **1** bordering **2** (Umrandendes) border; surround

um|räumen

A *tr. V.* rearrange

B *itr. V.* rearrange things

um|rechnen *tr. V.* convert (**in** + *Akk.* into); **Waren im Wert von umgerechnet 300 Euro** goods worth the equivalent of 300 euros

Um·rechnung *die* conversion (**in** + *Akk.* into)

Umrechnungs·kurs *der* exchange rate

um|reißen[1] *unr. tr. V.* pull ‹*mast, tree*› down; knock ‹*person*› down; ‹*wind*› tear ‹*tent etc.*› down

um·reißen[2] *unr. tr. V.* outline; summarize ‹*subject, problem, situation*›; **fest** *od.* **klar** *od.* **scharf umrissen** clearly defined ‹*programme*›; clear-cut ‹*ideas, views*›

um|rennen *unr. tr. V.* [run into and] knock down

um·ringen *tr. V.* surround; (in großer Zahl) crowd round

Um·riss, *Um·riß *der* (auch fig.) outline; **in Umrissen** in outline

um|rühren *tr.* (*auch itr.*) *V.* stir; **unter ständigem Umrühren** [while] stirring constantly

um·runden *tr. V.* go round ‹*lake, town*›; (Raumf.) orbit; (Seew.) round ‹*cape*›

um|rüsten

A *tr. V.* **1** (Technik) convert (**auf** + *Akk.* to, **zu** into) **2** (Milit.) **eine Armee [auf Atomwaffen] ~:** re-equip an army [with nuclear weapons]

B *itr. V.* re-equip; **auf etw.** (*Akk.*) **~:** change over to sth.

ums /ʊms/ *Präp. + Art.* **1** = **um das** **2** **~ Leben kommen** lose one's life; **ein Jahr ~ andere** (geh.) one year after another; year after year

um|satteln *itr. V.* (ugs.) change jobs; ‹*student*› change courses; **[von etw.] auf etw.** (*Akk.*) **~:** switch [from sth.] to sth.

Um·satz *der* turnover; (Verkauf) sales *pl.* (**an** + *Dat.* of); **~ machen** (ugs.) make money; **1 000 Euro ~ machen** turn over 1,000 euros

Umsatz-: ~beteiligung *die* share of the turnover; (eines Verkäufers) commission; **~steuer** *die* turnover *or* (Amer.) sales tax

um|säumen[1] *tr. V.* hem

um·säumen[2] *tr. V.* (fig.) surround

um|schalten

A *tr. V.* (auch fig.) switch [over] (**auf** + *Akk.* to); move ‹*lever*›

B *itr. V.* **1** (auch fig.) switch *or* change over (**auf** + *Akk.* to); **in den zweiten Gang ~:** change into second gear; **wir schalten jetzt ins Stadion um** now we're going over to the stadium **2** (umgeschaltet werden) **die Ampel schaltet [auf Grün] um** the traffic lights are changing [to green]

Umschalt-: ~hebel *der* [changeover] lever; **~taste** *die* shift key

Um·schau *die:* **[nach jmdm./etw.] ~ halten** look round *or* out [for sb./sth.]; **„Politische ~"** 'Political Review'

um|schauen *refl. V.* (bes. südd., österr., schweiz.) ▸ **umsehen**

um|schichten

A *tr. V.* **1** restack **2** (Wirtsch.) restructure ‹*investments*›; reinvest ‹*capital*›

B *refl. V.* (Soziol.) be restructured

um·schichtig

A *Adv.* ‹*work*› in shifts; **wir müssen ~ essen gehen** we have to eat on a rota basis

B *adj.* shift *attrib.* ‹*work*›; ‹*work*› in shifts; ‹*lunch break*› taken on a rota basis

Um·schichtung *die* ▸ **umschichten A, B:** restacking; (Wirtsch.) restructuring; reinvestment; (Soziol.) restructuring

um·schiffen *tr. V.* round ‹*headland, cape*›; steer clear of ‹*rocks, fig.: obstacle*›

Um·schlag *der* **1** cover **2** (Brief~) envelope **3** (Schutz~) jacket; (einer Broschüre, eines Heftes) cover **4** (Med.: Wickel) compress; (warm) poultice **5** (Hosen~) turn-up; (Ärmel~) cuff **6** (Veränderung) [sudden] change (*Gen.* in) **7** (Wirtsch.: Güter~) transfer; trans-shipment

Umschlag·bahnhof *der* transfer station

um|schlagen

A *unr. tr. V.* **1** (umklappen) turn up ‹*sleeve, collar, trousers*›; turn over ‹*page*› **2** (umladen, verladen) turn round, trans-ship ‹*goods*›

B *unr. itr. V.; mit sein* ‹*weather, mood*› change (**in** + *Akk.* into); ‹*wind*› veer [round]; ‹*voice*› break; ‹*wine*› go off; **ins Gegenteil ~:** change completely; become the opposite

Umschlage·tuch *das; Pl.* **Umschlagetücher** shawl

Umschlag-: ~hafen *der* port of trans-shipment; **~platz** *der* trans-shipment centre; **~tuch** *das* ▸ **Umschlagetuch**

um·schließen *unr. tr. V.* **1** ‹*river, wall*› surround; ‹*shell, husk, etc.*› enclose; ‹*hand, fingers, tentacles*› clasp, hold; **er umschloss sie mit beiden Armen** he put both arms around her **2** (einschließen, umzingeln) surround, encircle ‹*position, enemy*› **3** (zum Inhalt haben) embrace

um·schlingen *unr. tr. V.* **1** **jmdn./etw. [mit den Armen] ~:** put one's arms around sb./sth.; embrace sb./sth.; **sich umschlungen halten** hold one another in an embrace; **eng umschlungen** in a tight embrace *postpos.* **2** (sich schlingen um) twine [itself] round

Umschlingung *die;* **~, ~en** embrace; (einer Boa o. Ä.) grip

Um·schluss, *Um·schluß *der* (Rechtsw.) limited freedom of association (*for prisoners awaiting trial*)

um·schmeicheln *tr. V.* heap flattery on; (fig.) caress ‹*part of body*›

um|schmeißen *unr. tr. V.* (ugs.) ▸ **umwerfen 1, 2**

um|schnallen *tr. V.* **[sich** (*Dat.*)**] ~:** buckle on ‹*belt, sword*›; **jmdm./einem Tier etw. ~:** buckle *or* strap sth. on to sb./an animal

um|schreiben[1] *unr. tr. V.* **1** rewrite **2** (übertragen) transfer ‹*money, property*› (**auf** + *Akk.* to) **3** (transkribieren) transcribe

um·schreiben[2] *unr. tr. V.* **1** (in Worte fassen) describe; (definieren) define ‹*meaning, sb.'s task, etc.*›; (paraphrasieren) paraphrase ‹*word, expression*› **2** (Sprachw.) construct (**mit** with); **das Perfekt wird mit „sein" umschrieben** the perfect is conjugated with 'sein' **3** (mit einer Linie umgeben) outline; (andeuten) indicate; **umschrieben** (Med.) localized ‹*eczema etc.*›

Um·schreibung *die* **1** description; (Definition) definition; (Verhüllung) circumlocution (*Gen.* for) **2** ▸ **umschreiben**[2] **2**: construction; conjugation

Um·schrift *die* **1** (Sprachw.) transcription **2** (bes. Münzk.) circumscription

um|schulden *tr. (auch itr.) V.* (Finanzw.) convert ‹*loan*›; (mit längerer Laufzeit) reschedule ‹*loan, debt*›

Umschuldung *die;* ~, ~en (Finanzw.) loan conversion; (mit längerer Laufzeit) extension of credit; rescheduling [of a/the loan/loans]

um|schulen

A *tr. V.* **1** **ein Kind [auf eine andere Schule] ~:** transfer a child [to another school] **2** (beruflich) retrain; **jmdn. auf** *od.* **zum Monteur ~:** retrain sb. as a fitter

B *itr. V.* retrain (**auf** + *Akk.* as)

Umschulung *die* **1** transfer [to another school] **2** (beruflich) retraining *no pl.* (**auf** + *Akk.* as)

um|schütten *tr. V.* **1** pour [into another container]; decant ‹*liquid*› **2** (verschütten) spill

um·schwärmen *tr. V.* **1** swarm around; **von Moskitos umschwärmt werden** be besieged by mosquitoes **2** (fig.) flock around; **sie war sehr** *od.* **von vielen umschwärmt** she had many admirers

Um·schweif *der* circumlocution; **ohne ~e** without beating about the bush; **mach keine [langen] ~e!** get on with it!

um|schwenken *itr. V.; mit sein* **1** ‹*person, column*› swing round; ‹*wind*› veer [round] **2** (fig.) do an about-face

um·schwirren *tr. V.* buzz around

Um·schwung *der* **1** complete change; (in der Politik usw.) U-turn; volte-face **2** (Turnen) circle

um·segeln *tr. V.* sail round ‹*world, island, etc.*›; circumnavigate ‹*world*›; (fig.) negotiate ‹*obstacle etc.*›

um|sehen *unr. refl. V.* **1** look; **sich im Zimmer ~:** look [a]round the room; **sehen Sie sich ruhig um** (im Geschäft usw.) by all means have a look round; **du wirst dich noch ~!** (ugs.) you're in for a [nasty] shock; **sich nach etw. ~** (fig.) be looking *or* on the lookout for sth. **2** (zurücksehen) look round *or* back; **eine Frau, nach der sich alle Männer ~:** a woman who makes every man turn his head

***um|sein** ▸ **um B 2**

umseitig

A *Adj.* ‹*text, illustration, etc.*› overleaf

B *adv.* overleaf

umsetz·bar *Adj.* (fig.: umwandelbar) convertible (**in** + *Akk.* into); **der Vorschlag ist kaum in die Praxis ~:** the suggestion can scarcely be translated into practice

um|setzen

A *tr. V.* **1** move; (auf anderen Sitzplatz) move to another seat/other seats; (im Restaurant) move to another table; (auf anderen Posten, Arbeitsplatz usw.) move, transfer (**in** + *Akk.* to); (in andere Wohnung) rehouse (**in** + *Akk.* in); (umpflanzen) transplant ‹*bush etc.*›; (in anderen Topf) repot ‹*plant*› **2** (verwirklichen) implement ‹*plan*›; translate ‹*plan, intention, etc.*› into action *or* reality; realize ‹*ideas*›; **Erlebnisse in Literatur ~:** give experiences literary form; *s. auch* **Praxis 1**; **Tat 1** **3** (in Waren, Geld usw.) spend, dispose of ‹*money*›; **etw. in Geld/Bares ~:** turn sth. into money/cash; **Geld in Schnaps/Geschenke ~:** spend money on schnapps/presents **4** (Wirtsch.) turn over, have a turnover of ‹*x marks etc.*›; sell ‹*shares, goods*›

B *refl. V.* **1** (den Sitzplatz wechseln) move to another seat/other seats; change seats; (den Tisch wechseln) move to another table; change tables **2** (sich verwandeln) transform itself, (Physik) be converted (**in** + *Akk.* into)

Umsetzung *die;* ~, ~en **1** (auf einen anderen Posten) transfer (**in** + *Akk.* to); (in eine andere Wohnung) rehousing (**in** + *Akk.* in); (Umpflanzung) transplant[ing]; (in einen anderen Topf) repotting; **durch die ~ des Schülers** by moving the pupil [to another seat/desk] **2** (Verwirklichung) realization; (eines Plans) implementation; (Umformung) transformation (**in** + *Akk.* into); (bes. Technik, Physik) conversion (**in** + *Akk.* into); **chemische ~en** chemical changes **3** (Wirtsch.: Verkauf) turnover; sale

Um·sicht *die* circumspection; prudence

um·sichtig

A *Adj.* circumspect; prudent

B *adv.* circumspectly; prudently

um|siedeln

A *tr. V.* resettle; **nach X umgesiedelt werden** be moved to X

B *itr. V.; mit sein* move (**in** + *Akk.*, **nach** to); **in ein anderes Land ~:** settle in another country; emigrate

Um·siedler *der,* **Um·siedlerin** *die* resettled person; (freiwillig) resettler

Um·siedlung *die* resettlement; **seit meiner ~ aus der DDR in den Westen** since I moved to the West from the GDR

um|sinken *unr. itr. V.; mit sein* sink *or* fall to the ground

umso *Konj.* **je schneller der Wagen, ~ größer die Gefahr** the faster the car, the greater the danger; **je länger ..., ~ besser ...:** the longer ..., the better ...; **~ besser/schlimmer!** all the better/worse!; **~ mehr, als ...** (zumal, da ...) all the more so, as *or* since ...

um·sonst *Adv.* **1** (unentgeltlich) free; for nothing; **für ~** (ugs.) free, gratis, and for nothing (joc.); **~ sein** (ugs.) be free [of charge]; not cost anything; **das hast du nicht ~ getan!** (ugs.) you'll pay for that! **2** (vergebens) in vain **3** **nicht ~ hat er davor gewarnt** not for nothing did he warn of that

um·sorgen *tr. V.* care for; look after

um·spannen *tr. V.* **1** clasp ‹*hand, wrist, ankle, etc.*›; put one's hands round ‹*neck etc.*› **2** (fig.: einschieben) encompass ‹*subjects, period*›; **alles ~d** all-embracing

Umspann·werk *das* (Elektrot.) transformer station

um·spielen *tr. V.* **1** ‹*smile, light*› play about; ‹*waves*› lap about *or* around; ‹*skirt etc.*› swirl about *or* around **2** (Ballspiele) go round ‹*defender*›

um|springen *unr. itr. V.; mit sein* **1** ‹*wind*› veer round (**auf** + *Akk.* to); ‹*traffic light, fig.: mood*› change **2** (ugs. abwertend) **mit jmdm. grob/übel** *usw.* **~:** treat sb. roughly/badly *etc.*

um|spulen *tr. V.* rewind ‹*tape, film*›

um·spülen *tr. V.* wash round; **ein von den Wellen umspültes Riff** a reef washed by the waves

Um·stand *der* **1** (Gegebenheit) circumstance; (Tatsache) fact; **die näheren Umstände** the particular circumstances; (Einzelheiten) the details; **ein glücklicher ~:** a lucky *or* happy chance; **den Umständen entsprechend** as one would expect [in *or* under the circumstances]; **den Umständen entsprechend gut** (ugs.) as well as can be expected [given the circumstances]; **das kommt unter gar keinen Umständen in Frage** there is no question of that under any circumstances; **unter allen Umständen** whatever happens; **unter Umständen** possibly; **in anderen Umständen sein** (ugs.) be expecting; be in the family way (coll.) **2** (Aufwand) business; hassle (coll.); **macht keine [großen] Umstände** please don't go to any bother *or* trouble; **das macht gar keine Umstände** it's no bother *or* trouble at all

umstände·halber *Adv.* owing to circumstances; **„~ zu verkaufen"** 'forced to sell'; 'genuine reason for sale'

umständlich /ˈʊmʃtɛntlɪç/

A *Adj.* involved, elaborate ‹*procedure, method, description, explanation, etc.*›; elaborate, laborious ‹*preparation, check, etc.*›; awkward, difficult ‹*journey, job*›; (kompliziert) involved; complicated; (weitschweifig) long-winded; (Umstände machend) awkward, (coll.) pernickety ‹*person*›; **das ist mir zu ~:** that is too much trouble *or* (coll.) hassle [for me]; **es ist etwas ~, mit dem Auto dorthin zu kommen** getting there by car is rather awkward *or* rather a business

B *adv.* in an involved *or* roundabout way; (weitschweifig) ‹*explain etc.*› at great length *or* in a long-winded way; **sie drückt sich manchmal etwas ~ aus** she is sometimes rather long-winded; **er verabschiedete/entschuldigte sich ~:** he made a meal of saying 'goodbye'/'sorry'; **warum einfach, wenns auch ~ geht?** (iron.) why do things the easy way if you can make them difficult? (iron.)

umstands-, Umstands-: ~angabe, ~bestimmung *die* (Sprachw.) adverbial qualification; **~ergänzung** *die* (Sprachw.) adverbial complement; **~fürwort** *das* (Sprachw.) pronominal adverb; **~kleid** *das* maternity dress; **~kleidung** *die* maternity wear; **~krämer** *der,* **~krämerin** *die* (ugs. abwertend) fusspot (coll.); **~los** **A** *Adj.* straightforward; fuss-free; **B** *adv.* straightforwardly; without any fuss; **~moden** *Pl.* maternity styles; **~satz** *der* (Sprachw.) adverbial clause; **~wort** *das; Pl.* **~wörter** (Sprachw.) adverb

um·stehen *unr. tr. V.* stand round; surround

umstehend

A *Adj.* **1** standing round *postpos.*; **die ~en Personen, die Umstehenden** the bystanders **2** (umseitig) overleaf *postpos*

B *adv.* overleaf

um|steigen *unr. itr. V.* **1** change (**in** + *Akk.* [on] to); **nach Frankfurt ~:** change for Frankfurt **2** (fig. ugs.) change over, switch (**auf** + *Akk.* to)

um|stellen¹

A *tr. V.* **1** (anders stellen) rearrange, change round ‹*furniture, books, etc.*›; reorder ‹*words etc.*›; transpose ‹*two words*›; reshuffle ‹*team*› **2** (anders einstellen) reset ‹*lever, switch, points, clock*› **3** (ändern) change *or* switch over (**auf** + *Akk.* to)

B *refl. V.* adjust (**auf** + *Akk.* to); **er hat sich auf Rohkost umgestellt** he has changed his diet to raw fruit and vegetables

C *itr. V.* switch over (**auf** + *Akk.* to)

um·stellen² *tr. V.* surround

Um·stellung *die* ▸ **umstellen¹ A, B: 1** rearrangement; reordering; transposition; redeployment; reshuffle **2** resetting **3** changeover, switch (**auf** + *Akk.* to) **4** (das Sichumstellen) change; [re]adjustment

Umstieg *der;* ~[e]s, ~e changeover, switch (**auf** + *Akk.* to); (beruflich) career change

um|stimmen *tr. V.* (fig.: zu einer anderen Haltung bewegen) win ‹*person*› round; **er ließ sich nicht ~:** he was not to be persuaded; he refused to change his mind

um|stoßen *unr. tr. V.* **1** knock over **2** (rückgängig machen) reverse ‹*judgement, decision*›; change ‹*plan, decision*› **3** (zunichte machen) upset, wreck ‹*plan, theory*›

umstritten *Adj.* disputed; controversial ‹*bill, book, author, proposal, policy, etc.*›

um|strukturieren *tr. V.* restructure

um|stülpen *tr. V.* **1** turn inside out; (umkrempeln) turn *or* roll up ‹*trousers, sleeves, etc.*› **2** (auskippen) turn out, empty ‹*purse, bag, etc.*› **3** (umdrehen) turn upside down; (fig.) turn on its head

Um·sturz *der* coup

um|stürzen

A *tr. V.* overturn; knock over; (fig.) topple, overthrow ‹*political system, government*›

B *itr. V.* overturn; ‹*wall, building, chimney*› fall down

Umstürzler /ˈʊmʃtʏrtslɐ/ *der;* ~s, ~, **Umstürzlerin** *die;* ~, ~nen (abwertend) subversive agent

umstürzlerisch (abwertend)

A *Adj.* subversive

B *adv.* **sich ~ betätigen** engage in subversive activities

Umsturz·versuch *der* attempted coup

um|taufen *tr. V.* **jmdn.**/(ugs.) **etw. ~:** rename sb./sth.; change sb.'s name/the name of sth. (**auf** + *Akk.* to)

Um·tausch *der* exchange; **beim ~:** when exchanging goods/changing money; **reduzierte Ware ist vom ~ ausgeschlossen** sale

U

goods cannot be exchanged

um|tauschen *tr. V.* exchange ‹*goods, article*› (**gegen** for); change ‹*dollars, pounds, etc.*› (**in** + *Akk.* into)

um|topfen *tr. V.* repot ‹*plant*›

um·tosen *tr. V.* (geh.) surge around; **von etw. umtost** buffeted by sth.

Um|triebe *Pl.* (abwertend) [subversive] intrigues; subversion *sing.*

umtriebig (landsch.)
A *Adj.* busy
B *adv.* busily

Umtriebigkeit *die;* ~ (landsch.) [bustling] activity

Um·trunk *der* communal drink

UMTS-Handy *das* UMTS [mobile] phone

um|tun *unr. refl. V.* (ugs.) look [a]round; **sich nach etw. ~:** be on the lookout *or* looking for sth.

U-Musik *die* light music

um|verteilen *tr. V.* redistribute

Um·verteilung *die* redistribution

um|wälzen *tr. V.* 1 roll over; **~d** (fig.) revolutionary ‹*ideas, effect*›; epoch-making ‹*events*› 2 (zirkulieren lassen) circulate ‹*water, air*›

Umwälz·pumpe *die* circulating pump

Umwälzung *die;* **~, ~en** (fig.) revolution

um|wandeln
A *tr. V.* convert ‹*substance, building, etc.*› (**in** + *Akk.* into); commute ‹*sentence*› (**in** + *Akk.* to); (ändern) change; alter; **er ist wie umgewandelt** he is a changed man
B *refl. V.* be converted (**in** + *Akk.* into)

Um·wandlung *die* conversion (**in** + *Akk.* into); (einer Strafe) commutation (**in** + *Akk.* to); (der Gesellschaft usw.) transformation

um|wechseln *tr. V.* change ‹*marks, note, etc.*› (**in** + *Akk.* into)

Um·weg *der* detour; **auf einem ~ nach Hause fahren** go a long way round *or* make a detour to get home; **auf ~en** by a circuitous *or* roundabout route; (fig.) in a roundabout way; **auf dem ~ über** (+ *Akk.*) (fig.) [indirectly] via

Um·welt *die* 1 environment 2 (Menschen) people *pl.* around sb.; **meine/deine/seine ~:** those *pl.* around me/you/him

umwelt-, Umwelt-: ~allergie *die* environmental allergy; **~bedingt** *Adj.* caused by the *or* one's environment *postpos.*; **~belastung** *die* environmental pollution *no indef. art.*; **~bewusst**, ***~bewußt** *Adj.* environmentally conscious *or* aware; **~feindlich** A *Adj.* inimical to the environment *postpos.*; ecologically undesirable; B *adv.* in an ecologically undesirable way; ‹*drive, behave*› without regard for the environment; **~forschung** *die* 1 (Biol.) ecology; 2 (Soziol.) environmental studies *pl.*, *no art. or* science *no art.*; **~freundlich** A *Adj.* environment-friendly; ecologically desirable; B *adv.* in an ecologically desirable way; ‹*act*› with some regard for the environment; **~gift** *das* environmental poison; **~katastrophe** *die* environmental disaster; ecological disaster; **~kriminalität** *die* environmental crime; **~minister** *der*, **~ministerin** *die* environment minister; **~politik** *die* ecological policy; **~politisch** A *Adj.* environmental policy *attrib.*; ‹*speaker*› on environmental policy; B *adv.* with regard to environmental policy; **~schäden** *Pl.* environmental damage *sing.*; damage *sing.* to the environment; **~schädlich** A *Adj.* harmful to the environment *postpos.*; ecologically harmful; B *adv.* in an ecologically harmful way; **~schutz** *der* environmental protection *no art.*; conservation of the environment; **~schützer** *der;* **~~s, ~~, ~schützerin** *die;* **~~, ~~nen** environmentalist; conservationist; **~sünder** *der*, **~sünderin** *die* (ugs.) deliberate polluter of the environment; **~verschmutzung** *die* pollution [of the environment]

Umweltschutz

Most Germans feel individually responsible for the environment, especially after witnessing the dying of so many forests (**Waldsterben**). Households reuse packages and recycle their waste (**Recycling**). The *Bundesumweltministerium* (Ministry for the Environment) is responsible for all environmental matters. Its policy is based on the 'polluter must pay' principle, by which manufacturers are obliged to collect, sort, and recycle their waste, on the cooperation principle by which every individual is responsible for the environment, and the prevention principle which encourages manufacturers to develop environmentally friendly new products. Other focal points are a more efficient use of energy, a clean air and water programme, less road traffic and cleaner fuels, nature conservation, and soil protection.

um|wenden
A *regelm.* (*auch unr.*) *tr. V.;* 1 (auf die andere Seite) turn over ‹*page, joint, etc.*› 2 (in die andere Richtung) turn round ‹*vehicle, horse*› 3 (von innen nach außen) turn ‹*garment*› inside out
B *unr. od. regelm. refl. V.* turn round

um·werben *unr. tr. V.* court; woo; **viel umworben** much-courted

um|werfen *unr. tr. V.* 1 knock over; knock ‹*person*› down *or* over; (fig. ugs.: aus der Fassung bringen) bowl ‹*person*› over; stun ‹*person*›; (fig. ugs.: betrunken machen) knock ‹*person*› out (sl.); **das wirft selbst den stärksten Mann um!** it's more than even the strongest man can take 2 (fig. ugs.; umstoßen) knock ‹*plan*› on the head (coll.) 3 (umlegen, umhängen) throw *or* put sth. round sb.'s/one's shoulders

umwerfend (ugs.)
A *Adj.* fantastic (coll.); stunning (coll.)
B *adv.* fantastically [well] (coll.); brilliantly; **~ komisch** hilariously funny; **~ schön** stunningly beautiful (coll.)

Um·werfer *der* derailleur

um·wickeln *tr. V.* wrap; bind; (mit einem Verband) bandage; **etw. mit Schnur/Draht ~:** wind string/wire round sth.

um|widmen *tr. V.* (Verwaltung) re-designate (**in** + *Akk.*, **zu** as)

Um·widmung *die* (Verwaltung) re-designation (**in** + *Akk.* as)

um·wittern *tr. V.* (geh.) **von Gefahren/einem Geheimnis umwittert sein** be beset *or* fraught with danger/shrouded in mystery

umwohnend *Adj.* living in the neighbourhood *postpos.*

um·wölken /ʊmˈvœlkn̩/
A *refl. V.* (geh.) ‹*sky*› cloud over; (fig.) ‹*brow, look*› darken
B *tr. V.* shroud; veil

um|wühlen *tr. V.* churn *or* plough up

um·zäunen *tr. V.* fence round *or* off

Umzäunung *die;* **~, ~en** 1 (das Umzäunen) fencing round *or* off 2 (Zaun) fence, fencing (*Gen.* round)

um|ziehen
A *unr. itr. V.; mit sein* move (**an** + *Akk.*, **in** + *Akk.*, **nach** to)
B *unr. tr. V.* (umkleiden) **jmdn./sich ~:** change sb. *or* get sb. changed/change *or* get changed; **sich zum Essen ~:** change for dinner

um·zingeln /ʊmˈtsɪŋl̩n/ *tr. V.* surround; encircle

Umzingelung *die;* **~:** encirclement

Um·zug *der* 1 move; (von Möbeln) removal; **jmdm. beim ~ helfen** help sb. move; help with the removal 2 (Festzug) procession; (Demonstrationszug) demonstration

Umzugs·kosten *Pl.* removal costs

UN /uːˈɛn/ *Pl.* UN *sing.*

unabänderlich /ʊnlapˈɛndɐlɪç/
A *Adj.* unalterable; irrevocable ‹*decision*›; **sich in das Unabänderliche fügen** resign oneself to the inevitable
B *adv.* irrevocably; **das steht ~ fest** that is absolutely certain

unabdingbar /ʊnlapˈdɪŋbaːɐ̯/ *Adj.* 1 (geh.) indispensable 2 (Rechtsspr.) inalienable

unabhängig
A *Adj.* independent (**von** of); (unbeeinflusst) unaffected (**von** by); **sich ~ machen** go one's own way; ‹*colony*› become independent
B *adv.* independently (**von** of); **~ voneinander** independently [of one another]; separately; **es kostet 20 Cent, ~ von der Gesprächsdauer** it costs 20 cents irrespective *or* regardless of the length of the call; **~ davon, ob .../was .../wo ...** *usw.* irrespective *or* regardless of whether .../what .../where ... *etc.*

Unabhängigkeit *die* independence

Unabhängigkeits·erklärung *die* declaration of independence

unabkömmlich /ʊnlapˈkœmlɪç/ *Adj.* indispensable; **sie ist im Moment ~:** she is otherwise engaged

unablässig /ˈʊnlaplɛsɪç/
A *Adj.* incessant; constant ‹*repetition*›; unremitting ‹*effort*›
B *adv.* incessantly; constantly

unabsehbar
A *Adj.* 1 (fig.) incalculable, immeasurable ‹*extent, damage, etc.*›; **in ~er Ferne** (zeitlich) in the unforeseeable future; **auf ~e Zeit** far into the future 2 (noch nicht vorauszusehen) unforeseeable ‹*consequences*›
B *adv.* 1 incalculably; immeasurably 2 (in einem noch nicht erkennbaren Ausmaß) to an unforeseeable extent

unabsichtlich
A *Adj.* unintentional
B *adv.* unintentionally

unabweisbar
A *Adj.* irrefutable; absolute ‹*necessity*›
B *adv.* irrefutably; undeniably

unabwendbar *Adj.* inevitable

unachtsam
A *Adj.* 1 inattentive; **einen Augenblick ~ sein** let one's attention wander for a moment 2 (nicht sorgfältig) careless
B *adv.* (ohne Sorgfalt) carelessly

Unachtsamkeit *die;* **~** 1 inattentiveness 2 (mangelnde Sorgfalt) carelessness

unähnlich *Adj.* dissimilar; **jmdm./einer Sache ~ sein** be unlike sb./sth.

unanfechtbar *Adj.* incontestable

unangebracht *Adj.* inappropriate; misplaced

unangefochten *Adj.* unchallenged ‹*victor, leadership, etc.*›; (unbestritten) undisputed, unchallenged ‹*assertion, thesis*›; (Rechtsw.) uncontested ‹*verdict, will, etc.*›

unangemeldet *Adj.* 1 (unangekündigt) unexpected ‹*visit, guest*›; unauthorized ‹*demonstration*›; **~ kommen** come unannounced; **~ zum Arzt gehen** go to the doctor without an appointment 2 (nicht registriert) unregistered ‹*person, participant*›; unlicensed ‹*television set, radio*›

unangemessen
A *Adj.* unsuitable; inappropriate; unreasonable, disproportionate ‹*demand, claim, sentence, etc.*›
B *adv.* unsuitably; inappropriately; disproportionately ‹*high, low*›; **er reagierte völlig ~:** his reaction was out of all proportion; (unpassend) his reaction was entirely inappropriate

unangenehm
A *Adj.* unpleasant (+ *Dat.* for); (peinlich) embarrassing, awkward ‹*question, situation*›; **es ist mir sehr ~, dass ich mich verspätet habe** I am most upset about being late; **die Frage war ihm sichtlich ~:** he clearly found the question embarrassing; **~ werden** ‹*person*› get *or* turn nasty
B *adv.* unpleasantly; (peinlich) **die Frage schien ihn ~ zu berühren** the question appeared to embarrass him; **~ auffallen** make a bad impression

unangepasst, ***unangepaßt**
A *Adj.* nonconformist
B *adv.* in a nonconformist way

unangestrengt
A *Adj.* easy; effortless; (locker) easy-going
B *adv.* easily; effortlessly

u

unangetastet *Adj.* untouched

unangreifbar *Adj.* (auch fig.) unassailable; impregnable ‹*fortress*›; (unanfechtbar) irrefutable ‹*argument, thesis*›; incontestable ‹*judgement etc.*›

unannehmbar *Adj.* unacceptable

Unannehmlichkeit *die* trouble; **mit/durch etw. ~en bekommen** get [a lot of (coll.)] trouble with sth./as a result of sth.; **~en auf sich** (*Akk.*) **nehmen** take on unpleasant business; **jmdm. ~en bereiten** cause sb. [a lot of (coll.)] problems *or* difficulties

unansehnlich *Adj.* unprepossessing; plain ‹*girl*›

unanständig
A *Adj.* **1** improper; (anstößig) indecent ‹*behaviour, remark*›; dirty ‹*joke*›; rude ‹*word, song*› **2** (verwerflich) immoral
B *adv.* **1** improperly; **~ kurze Röcke** indecently short skirts **2** (verwerflich) immorally **3** (ugs.; unmäßig, allzu) disgustingly ‹*fat*›; indecently ‹*often*›; **~ viel essen** eat a disgusting amount

Unanständigkeit *die* **1** impropriety; indecency; (Obszönität) obscenity **2** (anstößige Handlung) impropriety; (anstößige Äußerung) obscenity; indecent remark **3** (Verwerflichkeit) immorality **4** (verwerfliche Handlung) immoral action

unantastbar *Adj.* inviolable

unappetitlich
A *Adj.* unappetizing; (fig.) unsavoury ‹*joke*›; unsavoury-looking ‹*person*›; disgusting ‹*washbasin, nails, etc.*›
B *adv.* unappetizingly

Unart *die* bad habit

unartig
A *Adj.* naughty
B *adv.* naughtily; ‹*behave*› badly

unartikuliert
A *Adj.* inarticulate; (fig.: nicht ausgedrückt) unexpressed ‹*feeling, thought, desire, etc.*›
B *adv.* inarticulately

unästhetisch
A *Adj.* unpleasant, unsavoury ‹*sight etc.*›; ugly ‹*building etc.*›; (abstoßend) disgusting
B *adv.* in an unsavoury/a disgusting way

unattraktiv
A *Adj.* unattractive
B *adv.* unattractively

unaufdringlich
A *Adj.* unassuming ‹*person*›; (fig.) unobtrusive, discreet ‹*music, décor, etc.*›; discreet ‹*perfume, colour, elegance, etc.*›
B *adv.* discreetly

unauffällig
A *Adj.* inconspicuous; unobtrusive ‹*scar, defect, skill, behaviour, surveillance, etc.*›; discreet ‹*signal, elegance*›; **sie ist eine eher ~e Erscheinung** she is not at all striking
B *adv.* inconspicuously; unobtrusively; ‹*behave, follow, observe, disappear, leave*› unobtrusively, discreetly

unauffindbar *Adj.* untraceable; **~ sein** *od.* **bleiben** be nowhere to be found

unaufgefordert *Adv.* without being asked; **~ eingesandte Manuskripte** unsolicited manuscripts

unaufgeklärt *Adj.* **1** unresolved ‹*misunderstanding*›; unsolved ‹*crime, mystery*› **2** (ignorant) unenlightened ‹*age, person*›; (sexualkundlich) ignorant of the facts of life *postpos.*

unaufgeregt
A *Adj.* calm
B *adv.* calmly

unaufhaltsam
A *Adj.* inexorable
B *adv.* inexorably

unaufhörlich
A *Adj.* constant; incessant; continuous ‹*rain*›
B *adv.* constantly; ‹*rain, snow*› continuously; **das Telefon klingelte ~:** the telephone was for ever ringing *or* never stopped ringing

unauflöslich *Adj.* irreconcilable ‹*contradiction etc.*›; indissoluble ‹*marriage, link*›

unaufmerksam
A *Adj.* inattentive (**gegenüber** to); careless ‹*driver*›
B *adv.* **sich seinen Gästen gegenüber ~ verhalten** not pay enough attention to one's guests

Unaufmerksamkeit *die* inattentiveness; (Fahrlässigkeit) carelessness

unaufrichtig *Adj.* insincere; **jmdm. gegenüber ~ sein** not be honest with sb.

Unaufrichtigkeit *die* **1** insincerity **2** (Handlung) insincere action

unaufschiebbar *Adj.* **es war ~:** it could not be put off *or* postponed

unausbleiblich *Adj.* inevitable; unavoidable

unausdenkbar *Adj.* unimaginable

unausgefüllt *Adj.* uncompleted, blank ‹*form*›; (fig.) unfulfilled ‹*person*›; unfilled ‹*time*›; empty ‹*life*›

unausgeglichen *Adj.* **1** (emotional) [emotionally] unstable ‹*person, behaviour*› **2** (Wirtsch.) ‹*balance of payments*› not in balance; unsettled ‹*account, debt*› **3** (unausgewogen) unbalanced ‹*report, relationship, etc.*›; unequal ‹*distribution*›; (ungleichmäßig) uneven, changeable ‹*climate*›

Unausgeglichenheit *die* **1** (eines Menschen) instability **2** (Wirtsch.) imbalance **3** (Unausgewogenheit) imbalance; (Ungleichmäßigkeit) unevenness; inconsistency

unausgegoren *Adj.* (abwertend) immature

unausgelastet
A *Adj.* **1** ‹*person*› without enough to do, with time on his/her hands; **~ sein** have time on one's hands **2** ‹*factory, machinery, rail system, waterway, etc.*› not working to capacity, with unused capacity; partly unused ‹*capacity*›; **~ sein** have unused capacity
B *adv.* without enough to do; **sich ~ fühlen** feel at a loose end

unausgereift *Adj.* immature ‹*work*›; not fully developed ‹*idea, proposal, method, etc.*›

unausgeschlafen *Adj.* **[völlig] ~ sein/aussehen** have not had/look as though one has not had [anything like] enough sleep; **~ zur Schule kommen** come to school tired through lack of sleep

unausgewogen
A *Adj.* unbalanced
B *adv.* in an unbalanced way

unauslöschlich
A *Adj.* (geh.) indelible ‹*impression*›; unforgettable ‹*experience*›
B *adv.* indelibly

unaussprechlich
A *Adj.* **1** inexpressible **2** (geh.: unbeschreiblich) indescribable ‹*misery, joy*›; unutterable ‹*misery, sorrow*›
B *adv.* (geh.) unutterably; indescribably; ‹*suffer, love*› beyond expression

unausstehlich
A *Adj.* unbearable ‹*person, noise, smell, etc.*›; insufferable ‹*person*›; intolerable ‹*noise, smell*›
B *adv.* unbearably; intolerably; insufferably ‹*stupid, curious*›

unausweichlich *Adj.* unavoidable; inevitable

unbändig /ˈʊnbɛndɪç/
A *Adj.* **1** boisterous ‹*person, horse, temperament*› **2** (überaus groß/stark) unbridled, unrestrained ‹*desire, longing, joy, merriment*›; unbridled, uncontrollable ‹*fury, hate, anger*›; ravenous ‹*hunger*›
B *adv.* **1** wildly **2** (sehr, äußerst) unrestrainedly; tremendously (coll.); **~ jubeln** *od.* **jauchzen, sich ~ freuen** jump for joy

unbar
A *Adj.* cashless
B *adv.* ‹*pay*› without using cash

unbarmherzig
A *Adj.* (auch fig.) merciless; remorseless, unsparing ‹*severity*›; (fig.) very severe ‹*winter, cold*›; **jmdm. gegenüber** *od.* **gegen jmdn. ~ sein** show sb. no mercy
B *adv.* mercilessly; without mercy

unbeabsichtigt
A *Adj.* unintentional
B *adv.* unintentionally

unbeachtet *Adj.* unnoticed; obscure ‹*existence*›; **~ leben** live in obscurity; **jmdn./etw. ~ lassen** not take any notice of sb./sth.

unbeanstandet
A *Adj.* **etw. ~ lassen** let sth. pass; **~ bleiben** be allowed to pass
B *adv.* without objection; **~ durch die Gütekontrolle gehen** be allowed to pass through quality control [without any problems]

unbeantwortet *Adj.* unanswered

unbearbeitet *Adj.* **1** undealt with *pred.*; which has/have not been dealt with *postpos.* **2** (roh) untreated ‹*wood, leather, metal*›; (unbestellt) uncultivated ‹*land, field*›; (nicht redigiert) unedited ‹*manuscript*›; (nicht verändert, adaptiert) unchanged, unadapted ‹*play, version*›

unbeaufsichtigt *Adj.* unsupervised ‹*child, animal*›; unattended ‹*baggage*›; **eine Kerze ~ lassen** leave a candle burning unattended

unbebaut *Adj.* **1** undeveloped ‹*site, land*› **2** (unbestellt) uncultivated ‹*land, area*›

unbedacht
A *Adj.* rash; thoughtless
B *adv.* rashly; thoughtlessly

unbedarft
A *Adj.* (ugs.) **1** inexpert; lay; **er ist literarisch [völlig/ziemlich] ~:** he has no/little idea about literature **2** (naiv) naïve; (dümmlich) gormless (coll.)
B *adv.* naïvely; (dümmlich) gormlessly (coll.)

unbedeckt *Adj.* uncovered; bare; **mit ~em Kopf** bare-headed

unbedenklich
A *Adj.* **1** harmless, safe ‹*substance, drug*›; ‹*state of health, situation*› giving no cause for concern; unobjectionable ‹*joke, plan, reading matter*›; **es ist nicht ganz ~:** it is to some extent open to objection **2** (hemmungslos, skrupellos) unthinking; unconsidered
B *adv.* without second thoughts

unbedeutend
A *Adj.* insignificant; minor ‹*artist, poet*›; slight, minor ‹*improvement, change, error*›
B *adv.* slightly

unbedingt
A *Adj.* **1** absolute ‹*trust, faith, reliability, secrecy, etc.*›; complete ‹*rest*› **2** (Physiol.) **~e Reflexe** unconditioned reflexes
B *Adv.* absolutely; (auf jeden Fall) whatever happens; **etw. ~ tun müssen/wollen** really *or* absolutely have to/be absolutely determined to do sth.; **der Brief muss ~ heute noch weg** the letter really must be posted today; **ich brauche ~ neue Reifen** I need new tyres whatever happens; I really have to have new tyres; **ich brauche jetzt ~ einen Schnaps** I've just got to have a schnapps; **nicht ~:** not necessarily; **nicht ~ nötig** not absolutely necessary; **~!** absolutely!; of course!

unbeeidigt *Adj.* (Rechtsw.) unsworn; **der Zeuge blieb ~:** the witness was not on *or* under oath

unbeeindruckt *Adj.* unimpressed

unbeeinflusst, *unbeeinflußt *Adj.* uninfluenced; **von jeder Propaganda ~:** not influenced by any propaganda *postpos.*

unbefahrbar *Adj.* **1** (für Landfahrzeuge) impassable **2** (für Wasserfahrzeuge) unnavigable; not navigable *pred.*

unbefangen
A *Adj.* **1** (ungehemmt) uninhibited; natural, uninhibited ‹*behaviour*›; **er ist anderen gegenüber ganz ~:** he is perfectly natural with other people **2** (unvoreingenommen) impartial
B *adv.* freely; without inhibition; ‹*behave*› naturally; **jmdm./einer Sache ~ gegenübertreten** approach sb./sth. with an open mind

Unbefangenheit *die* ▸**unbefangen A 1, 2**: uninhibitedness; naturalness; impartiality

unbefestigt *Adj.* **1** unmade, unsurfaced ‹*road*›; unstabilized ‹*bank*› **2** ‹*town*› without fortifications **3** (lose, nicht gebunden) unsecured

unbefleckt *Adj.* (geh.) undefiled; unsullied (literary); **die Unbefleckte Empfängnis** (christl. Rel.) the Immaculate Conception

unbefriedigend *Adj.* unsatisfactory

unbefriedigt *Adj.* dissatisfied (**von** with); unsatisfied ‹*need, curiosity, desire, etc.*›; (unausgefüllt) unfulfilled (**von** by); (sexuell) [sexually] unsatisfied *or* frustrated

unbefristet
A *Adj.* for an indefinite *or* unlimited period *postpos.*; indefinite ‹*strike*›; unlimited ‹*visa*›
B *adv.* for an indefinite *or* unlimited period

unbefugt
A *Adj.* unauthorized; **ein Unbefugter** an unauthorized person
B *adv.* without authorization

unbegabt *Adj.* ungifted; untalented; **für Sprachen ~ sein** have no talent for languages

unbegreiflich *Adj.* incomprehensible (+ *Dat.*, **für** to); incredible ‹*love, goodness, stupidity, carelessness, etc.*›; **auf ~e Weise** in a baffling *or* mysterious manner

unbegreiflicherweise *Adv.* inexplicably

unbegrenzt
A *Adj.* unlimited; **ein zeitlich ~er Vertrag** a contract with no time limit; **Kosten in ~er Höhe** costs up to an unlimited amount
B *adv.* ‹*stay, keep, etc.*› indefinitely; ‹*trust*› absolutely; **ich habe nicht ~ Zeit** I don't have unlimited time

unbegründet *Adj.* unfounded, groundless ‹*fear, accusation, suspicion*›

unbehaart *Adj.* hairless; bald ‹*head*›

Unbehagen *das* uneasiness, disquiet; (Sorge) concern (**an** + *Dat.* about); **etw. mit ~ feststellen/betrachten** note/watch sth. with concern; **ein leichtes körperliches ~:** a slight physical discomfort; **das bereitet mir ~:** it makes me feel uneasy

unbehaglich
A *Adj.* uneasy, uncomfortable ‹*feeling, atmosphere*›; uncomfortable ‹*thought, room*›; **mir war ~ zumute** I was *or* felt uneasy; **er/es war mir ~:** he/it made me feel uneasy *or* uncomfortable
B *adv.* uneasily; uncomfortably; **~ kühl** uncomfortably *or* unpleasantly cool

unbehandelt *Adj.* untreated; ‹*agenda item*› not dealt with

unbehauen *Adj.* unhewn

unbehelligt *Adj.* unmolested; (ohne Störung) ‹*read, work*› undisturbed, in peace; **er gelangte ~ von Journalisten in das Gebäude** he got into the building without being intercepted by journalists; **die Zollbeamten ließen uns ~ passieren** the customs let us through without stopping us

unbeherrscht
A *Adj.* uncontrolled; intemperate, wild ‹*reaction, behaviour, remark*›; **er ist ~:** he has no self-control
B *adv.* without any self-control

Unbeherrschtheit *die*; **~, ~en** [1] lack of self-control [2] (Handlung) uncontrolled fit; (Äußerung) wild outburst

unbehindert *Adj.* unhindered; unimpeded

unbeholfen
A *Adj.* clumsy; awkward
B *adv.* clumsily; awkwardly

unbeirrbar
A *Adj.* unwavering
B *adv.* unwaveringly; unswervingly

unbeirrt
A *Adj.* unwavering
B *adv.* without wavering

unbekannt
A *Adj.* [1] unknown; (nicht vertraut) unfamiliar; unidentified ‹*caller, donor, flying object*›; **das war mir bisher ~:** I didn't know that until now; **es ist mir nicht ~, dass ...** I am not unaware that ...; **sie ist hier ~:** she is not known here; **~e Täter** unknown *or* unidentified culprits; **„Empfänger ~"** 'not known at this address'; **eine ~e Größe** (Math.; auch scherzh.: Mensch) an unknown quantity; **ich bin hier ~** (ugs.) I'm a stranger here; **[Straf]anzeige gegen ~** (Rechtsw.) charge against person or persons unknown [2] (nicht vielen bekannt) little known; obscure ‹*poet, painter, etc.*›
B *adv.* **„Empfänger ~ verzogen"** 'moved'; 'address unknown'

Unbekannte[1] *der/die; adj. Dekl.* unknown *or* unidentified man/woman; (Fremde[r]) stranger; **er ist [hier/dem Fernsehpublikum] kein ~er [mehr]** he is no stranger [here/to television viewers]; **der große ~** (scherzh.) the mystery man *or* person

Unbekannte[2] *die; adj. Dekl.* (Math.; auch fig.) unknown

unbekannterweise *Adv.* **grüßen Sie ihn/sie ~ [von mir]** give him/her my regards, although we haven't met

unbekleidet *Adj.* without any clothes on *postpos.*; bare ‹*torso etc.*›; naked ‹*corpse*›

unbekümmert
A *Adj.* (unbeschwert) carefree; (ohne Bedenken, lässig) casual; **sie ist [ziemlich] ~:** she doesn't worry [much]; she is [pretty] unconcerned; **um etw. ~ sein** be unconcerned about sth.
B *adv.* [1] (unbeschwert) in a carefree way; without a care in the world; **~ leben** live a carefree life [2] (ohne Bedenken) without caring *or* worrying; **ganz** *od.* **völlig ~:** entirely unconcerned; without a second thought; **er raucht ~ weiter** he happily goes on smoking

Unbekümmertheit *die*; **~** [1] carefree manner *or* attitude; carefreeness [2] (Bedenkenlosigkeit) lack of concern

unbelastet *Adj.* [1] not under load *postpos.*; **im ~en Zustand** when not under load [2] (von Sorgen, Problemen usw.) free from care *or* worries *postpos.*; **von Sorgen ~:** free from worries [3] (ohne Schuld) **~ sein** have a clean record [4] (schuldenfrei) unmortgaged ‹*property, land*›

unbelebt *Adj.* [1] inanimate ‹*nature*›; (anorganisch) inorganic ‹*matter*› [2] (ohne Lebewesen) uninhabited; deserted; empty ‹*streets*›

unbeleckt *Adj.* (salopp) **von etw. ~ sein** not have a clue about sth. (coll.); **sie sind von jeder Kultur ~:** they are complete savages

unbelehrbar *Adj.* incorrigible; not accessible to reason *postpos.*; **er ist ~:** he will not learn

unbeleuchtet *Adj.* unlit ‹*street, corridor, etc.*›; ‹*vehicle*› without [any] lights

unbelichtet *Adj.* (Fot.) unexposed

unbeliebt *Adj.* unpopular (**bei** with)

Unbeliebtheit *die* unpopularity

unbemannt *Adj.* [1] unmanned [2] (scherzh.) (ohne Mann) husbandless (joc.); (ohne Freund) without a man *postpos.*

unbemerkt *Adj., adv.* unnoticed

unbemittelt *Adj.* penniless; impecunious; **nicht ganz ~:** not exactly penniless

unbenommen *Adj.* in **es ist/bleibt jmdm. ~, zu ...** sb. is/remains free *or* at liberty to ...; **dieses Recht bleibt Ihnen ~:** this remains your right

unbenutzbar *Adj.* unusable

unbenutzt *Adj.* unused

unbeobachtet *Adj.* unobserved; **in einem ~en Augenblick** *od.* **Moment** when no one is/was watching; **wenn er sich ~ fühlt** *od.* **glaubt** when he thinks no one is looking

unbequem
A *Adj.* [1] uncomfortable [2] (lästig) awkward, embarrassing ‹*question, opinion*›; awkward, troublesome ‹*politician etc.*›; unpleasant ‹*criticism, truth, etc.*›; **er wurde ihnen ~:** he became a nuisance *or* an embarrassment to them
B *adv.* uncomfortably

Unbequemlichkeit *die* [1] lack of comfort [2] (Lästigkeit) awkwardness [3] (etw., was unbequem ist) discomfort

unberechenbar
A *Adj.* unpredictable
B *adv.* unpredictably

unberechtigt
A *Adj.* [1] (ungerechtfertigt) unjustified [2] (unbefugt) unauthorized
B *adv.* [1] (unbefugt) without authorization [2] (ungerechtfertigt) without justification; unjustifiably ‹*expensive etc.*›

unberücksichtigt *Adj.* unconsidered; **etw. ~ lassen** leave sth. out of consideration; ignore sth.; **~ bleiben** not be considered; be ignored

unberufen[1] *Adj.* **in ~e Hände fallen** fall into the wrong hands

unberufen[2] *Interj.* **~ [toi, toi, toi]!** touch wood!; knock on wood! (Amer.)

Unberührbare *der/die; adj. Dekl.* (Rel.) untouchable

unberührt *Adj.* [1] untouched; virgin ‹*snow, forest, wilderness*›; **ein Stück ~er Natur** a stretch of unspoilt countryside [2] (geh.: jungfräulich) in the virgin state; **sie ist noch ~:** she is still a virgin [3] (unbeeindruckt) unmoved (**von** by); **die Nachricht ließ ihn ~:** he was unmoved by the news

Unberührtheit *die*; **~** [1] (natürlicher Zustand) unspoiled state [2] (geh.: Jungfräulichkeit) virginity [3] (das Unbeeindrucktsein) lack of emotion; impassivity

unbeschadet
A *Präp. mit Gen.* regardless of; notwithstanding
B *Adj.* (veralt.) ▸**unbeschädigt 1, 2**

unbeschädigt *Adj.* [1] undamaged [2] (veralt.: unverletzt) unharmed

unbescheiden *Adj.* presumptuous; **wenn ich mir die ~e Frage/Bitte erlauben darf** if you don't mind my asking; **ist es sehr ~, wenn ich Sie bitte ...?** I hope you don't mind my asking you ...

unbescholten *Adj.* respectable; (veralt.: keusch) chaste ‹*girl*›; **~ sein** (Rechtsspr.) have no [previous] convictions

Unbescholtenheit *die*; **~** ▸**unbescholten**: respectability; chastity; absence of [previous] convictions

unbeschrankt *Adj.* ‹*crossing*› without gates, with no gates

unbeschränkt
A *Adj.* unlimited; limitless ‹*possibilities, power*›; (hist.) absolute ‹*ruler*›; **die Teilnehmerzahl ist ~:** there is no limit on the number of participants
B *adv.* **für etw. ~ haften** have unlimited liability for sth.

unbeschreiblich
A *Adj.* indescribable; unimaginable ‹*fear, beauty*›; ‹*fear, beauty*› beyond description
B *adv.* indescribably ‹*beautiful*›; unbelievably ‹*busy*›; **~ viele Menschen** an incredible number of people; **sich ~ freuen** be overjoyed

unbeschrieben *Adj.* blank, empty ‹*piece of paper, page*›; *s. auch* **Blatt 2**

unbeschwert
A *Adj.* carefree
B *adv.* free from care; ‹*dance, play*› with a light heart

unbesehen
A *Adj.* unquestioning ‹*acceptance*›
B *adv.* without hesitation; **das glaube ich ~:** I don't doubt it for a moment

unbesetzt *Adj.* unoccupied; unfilled ‹*position, job*›; empty ‹*chair, bus*›

unbesiegbar *Adj.* invincible

unbesiegt *Adj.* undefeated ‹*army*›; unbeaten ‹*team, player*›

unbesonnen
A *Adj.* impulsive ‹*person, nature*›; unthinking ‹*remark*›; (übereilt) ill-considered, rash ‹*decision, action*›
B *adv.* ‹*act*› without thinking; (übereilt) rashly

unbesorgt *Adj.* unconcerned; **seien** *od.* **bleiben Sie ~!** don't [you] worry; you can set your mind at rest; **du darfst ~ nach Hause gehen** you can go home without worrying/with an easy mind

unbespielbar *Adj.* (Sport) unplayable ‹*pitch*›

unbespielt *Adj.* blank ‹*tape, cassette*›

unbeständig *Adj.* changeable, unsettled ‹*weather*›; erratic, inconsistent ‹*performance, person, etc.*›; inconstant, fickle ‹*lover etc.*›; (vergänglich) transitory ‹*love, luck*›

unbestätigt *Adj.* unconfirmed

unbestechlich *Adj.* [1] incorruptible [2] (fig.) uncompromising ‹*critic*›; incorruptible ‹*character*›; unerring ‹*judgement*›; unwavering ‹*honesty, love of truth*›

U

unbestimmbar *Adj.* unidentifiable ‹*plant, sound, colour, etc.*›; indeterminable ‹*age, distance*›; (Bot., Zool.) unclassifiable

unbestimmt
A *Adj.* 1 (nicht festgelegt) indefinite; indeterminate ‹*age, number*›; (ungewiss) uncertain; **auf ~e Zeit** for an indefinite period 2 (ungenau) vague 3 (Sprachw.) indefinite ‹*article, pronoun*›; non-finite ‹*verb form*›
B *adv.* (ungenau) vaguely

Unbestimmtheit *die* 1 (Ungenauigkeit) vagueness 2 (Ungewissheit) uncertainty

unbestreitbar
A *Adj.* indisputable; unquestionable
B *adv.* indisputably; unquestionably

unbestritten
A *Adj.* undisputed; **~ ist, dass ...** it is undisputed that ...; there is no disputing that ...
B *adv.* indisputably

unbeteiligt
A *Adj.* 1 (passiv, nicht mitwirkend) uninvolved; **~e Passanten/Zuschauer** passers-by/onlookers who are/were not involved; **ein Unbeteiligter** someone who is/was not involved; an outsider; (ein Unschuldiger) an innocent party 2 (gleichgültig) indifferent; detached ‹*manner, expression*›
B *adv.* with a detached *or* indifferent air; **~ dabeistehen** stand by without taking any interest in the proceedings

unbetont *Adj.* unstressed

unbeträchtlich
A *Adj.* insignificant; **nicht ~:** not inconsiderable
B *adv.* insignificantly; slightly; **nicht ~:** not inconsiderably

unbeugsam *Adj.* uncompromising; tenacious; indomitable, unshakeable ‹*will, pride*›; unwavering, resolute ‹*character*›

unbewacht *Adj.* unsupervised ‹*pupils, prisoners, etc.*›; unattended ‹*car park*›; **in einem ~en Moment** when no one is/was watching

unbewaffnet *Adj.* unarmed

unbewältigt *Adj.* unmastered, uncompleted ‹*task*›; unresolved ‹*conflict, problem*›; **unsere ~e Vergangenheit** the past with which we have not come to terms

unbeweglich *Adj.* 1 (bewegungslos) motionless; still ‹*air, water*›; fixed ‹*gaze, expression*›; **~ sitzen/stehen** sit/stand motionless 2 (starr) immovable, fixed ‹*part, joint, etc.*›; **~es Eigentum** real estate; **ein ~es Fest** an immovable feast 3 (nicht mobil) immobile 4 (schwerfällig) (geistig) ponderous; (körperlich) slow-moving; slow on one's feet *pred.*

unbewegt *Adj.* motionless; fixed ‹*expression*›

unbeweibt *Adj.* (ugs. scherzh.) wifeless

unbewiesen *Adj.* unproved

unbewohnbar *Adj.* uninhabitable; **ein Gebäude für ~ erklären** declare a building unfit for human habitation

unbewohnt *Adj.* uninhabited ‹*area*›; unoccupied ‹*house, flat*›

unbewusst, *unbewußt
A *Adj.* 1 unconscious 2 (ungewollt) unconscious, unintentional ‹*distortion, exaggeration, etc.*›
B *adv.* 1 unconsciously 2 (ungewollt) unconsciously; unintentionally

Unbewusste, *Unbewußte *das; adj. Dekl.* (Psych.) unconscious

unbezahlbar *Adj.* 1 (teuer) prohibitive; (zu teuer) prohibitively expensive ‹*article*› 2 (kostbar) priceless ‹*painting, china*›; **meine Sekretärin ist einfach ~** (ugs.) my secretary is worth her weight in gold

unbezahlt *Adj.* unpaid; ‹*goods etc.*› not [yet] paid for

unbezähmbar *Adj.* uncontrollable; insatiable ‹*hunger, thirst, curiosity*›

unbezwinglich *Adj.* 1 impregnable ‹*fortress*›; invincible ‹*enemy, opponent*› 2 (fig.: unbezähmbar) uncontrollable ‹*urge*›; insatiable ‹*hunger, thirst, curiosity, desire*›

Unbilden /ˈʊnbɪldn̩/ *Pl.* (geh.) rigours

Unbill /ˈʊnbɪl/ *die;* **~** (geh.) (Unrecht) wrong; injustice; (Beschwernis) rigours *pl.*

unblutig
A *Adj.* 1 bloodless 2 (Med.: nichtoperativ) non-surgical
B *adv.* 1 without bloodshed 2 (Med.: nichtoperativ) without [the need for] surgery

unbot·mäßig
A *Adj.* insubordinate; **~e Kritik** disrespectful criticism
B *adv.* insubordinately

Unbot·mäßigkeit *die* insubordination

unbrauchbar *Adj.* unusable; (untauglich) useless ‹*method, person*›; **~ machen** make ‹*machine*› unserviceable; put ‹*machine*› out of action; **er ist dafür ~:** he is no use for this

unbürokratisch
A *Adj.* unbureaucratic; **auf möglichst ~e Weise** with as little red tape as possible
B *adv.* unbureaucratically; without a great deal of red tape

unbuß·fertig *Adj.* impenitent; unrepentant

unchristlich
A *Adj.* 1 unchristian 2 **zu ~er Zeit** at an ungodly hour (coll.)
B *adv.* in an unchristian way

uncool (ugs.)
A *Adj.* uncool (coll.)
B *adv.* in an uncool way (coll.)

und /ʊnt/ *Konj.* 1 (nebenordnend) and; (folglich) [and] so; **das deutsche ~ das französische Volk** the German and French peoples; **zwei ~ drei ist fünf** two and *or* plus three makes five; **es wollte ~ wollte nicht gelingen** it simply *or* just wouldn't work; **es gibt Konservative ~ Konservative** there are conservatives and conservatives; **hoch ~ höher** higher and higher; **~ die anderen/ich?** [and] what about the others/about me?; **~ warum?** why [is that]?; **der ~ der** so-and-so; **zu der ~ der Zeit** at such-and-such a time; **so ~ so ist es gewesen** it was like this; **~?** and?; well?; **ich ~ tanzen?** what, me dance?; **der ~ arbeiten/arm?** what, him work/poor?; *s. auch* **na 1**; **ob¹ 3**; **wie A 3** 2 (unterordnend) (konsekutiv) **tu mir den Gefallen ~ komm mit** be so kind as to come too; **sei so gut ~ mach das Fenster zu** be so good as to shut the window; **warum bist du auch so leichtsinnig ~ schließt dein Fahrrad nicht ab?** why are you so careless as to leave your bicycle unlocked?; **es fehlte nicht viel, ~ der Deich wäre gebrochen** it wouldn't have taken much to breach the dyke; (konzessiv) **du musst es tun, ~ fällt es dir noch so schwer** you must do it however difficult you may find it; *s. auch* **wenn 3**

Undank *der* ingratitude; **nur ~ ernten** get no thanks; meet only with ingratitude; **~ ist der Welt Lohn** (Spr.) that's all the thanks you get

undankbar
A *Adj.* 1 ungrateful ‹*person, behaviour*› 2 (wenig lohnend) thankless ‹*task*›; unrewarding ‹*role, subject, job, etc.*›
B *adv.* ungratefully

undatiert *Adj.* undated

undefinierbar *Adj.* 1 indefinable 2 (nicht bestimmbar) unidentifiable; indeterminable ‹*feeling*›; indeterminate ‹*colour*›

undeklinierbar *Adj.* (Sprachw.) indeclinable

undenkbar *Adj.* unthinkable; inconceivable

undenklich *Adj.* **in vor ~er Zeit** *od.* **~en Zeiten** an eternity ago; **seit ~er Zeit** *od.* **~en Zeiten** since time immemorial

undeutlich
A *Adj.* unclear; indistinct; (ungenau) vague ‹*idea, memory, etc.*›
B *adv.* indistinctly; (ungenau) vaguely; **du schreibst zu ~:** you don't write clearly enough

undicht *Adj.* leaky; leaking; **~ werden** start to leak; develop a leak; **eine ~e Stelle** (auch fig.) a leak; **~e Fenster/Türen** windows/doors which do not fit tightly

undifferenziert
A *Adj.* 1 (geh.) indiscriminate ‹*criticism*›; ‹*criticism*› which fails to discriminate; overgeneralized, simplistic ‹*account*› 2 (Biol.) undifferentiated
B *adv.* (geh.) in an overgeneralized *or* indiscriminate way

Unding *das; in* **ein ~ sein** be preposterous *or* ridiculous

undiplomatisch
A *Adj.* undiplomatic
B *adv.* undiplomatically

undiszipliniert
A *Adj.* undisciplined; ‹*pupils, class*› lacking in discipline
B *adv.* in an undisciplined way

undogmatisch
A *Adj.* undogmatic
B *adv.* undogmatically

unduldsam
A *Adj.* intolerant
B *adv.* intolerantly

undurchdringlich *Adj.* 1 impenetrable; pitch-dark ‹*night*› 2 (undurchschaubar) inscrutable ‹*person, expression, mask*›

undurchführbar *Adj.* impracticable

undurchlässig *Adj.* impermeable; (wasserdicht) watertight; waterproof; (luftdicht) airtight

-undurchlässig *adj.* **licht~/wasser~/luft~:** lightproof/waterproof/airtight

undurchschaubar *Adj.* inscrutable ‹*person, plan, etc.*›; unfathomable ‹*cause, etc.*›; **für jmdn. ~ sein** be baffling to sb.

undurchsichtig *Adj.* 1 opaque ‹*glass*›; non-transparent ‹*fabric etc.*›; dense, impenetrable ‹*fog, mist*› 2 (fig.) unfathomable, inscrutable ‹*plan, intention, role*›; shady ‹*character, business*›

uneben *Adj.* uneven; (holprig) bumpy ‹*road, track*›

Unebenheit *die;* **~, ~en** 1 unevenness; (Holprigkeit) bumpiness 2 (unebene Stelle) lumpy *or* uneven patch

unecht *Adj.* 1 (falsch, imitiert) artificial ‹*fur, hair*›; false ‹*teeth*›; imitation ‹*jewellery, marble, etc.*›; (gefälscht) counterfeit ‹*notes*›; bogus, fake ‹*painting*› 2 (gespielt, vorgetäuscht) false, insincere ‹*friendliness, sympathy, smile, etc.*›; simulated ‹*enthusiasm, affection, etc.*› 3 (Math.) improper ‹*fraction*›

unehelich *Adj.* illegitimate ‹*child*›; unmarried ‹*mother*›; **~ geboren sein** be born out of wedlock

Unehre *die;* **~** (geh.) dishonour; **etw. macht jmdm. ~** *od.* **gereicht jmdm. zur ~:** sth. brings dishonour on sb.

unehrenhaft
A *Adj.* dishonourable
B *adv.* dishonourably; **er wurde ~ aus der Armee entlassen** (Milit.) he was given a dishonourable discharge from the army

unehrlich
A *Adj.* dishonest; **ein ~es Spiel treiben** play a double game
B *adv.* dishonestly; by dishonest means

Unehrlichkeit *die* 1 dishonesty 2 (Handlung) dishonest action

uneigennützig
A *Adj.* unselfish; selfless
B *adv.* unselfishly; selflessly; ‹*help*› from selfless motives

Uneigennützigkeit *die* unselfishness; selflessness

uneingeschränkt
A *Adj.* unlimited ‹*freedom, power, etc.*›; absolute ‹*trust, authority*›; unreserved ‹*praise, admiration, recognition*›
B *adv.* ‹*agree*› without reservation

uneingestanden
A *Adj.* unadmitted
B *adv.* without admitting it

uneingeweiht *Adj.* uninitiated

uneinig *Adj.* ‹*party*› divided by disagreement; **[sich** (*Dat.*)**] ~ sein** disagree; be in disagreement; **ich bin [mir] mit ihm darin ~:** I disagree with him on that

Uneinigkeit *die* disagreement (**in** + *Dat.* on)

uneinnehmbar *Adj.* impregnable

uneins *Adj.* **~ sein** be divided (**in** + *Dat.* on); ‹*persons, bodies*› be at variance *or* at cross purposes (**in** + *Dat.* over); **mit jmdm. ~ sein[, wie ...]** be unable to agree with sb. [how ...]; **er ist mit sich [selbst] ~:** he is undecided *or* cannot decide

uneitel
A *Adj.* modest; **nicht ~:** not lacking in vanity
B *adv.* modestly; **erstaunlich ~:** with an amazing modesty *or* lack of vanity

unempfänglich *Adj.* unreceptive (**für** to)

unempfindlich *Adj.* **1** insensitive (**gegen** to) **2** (nicht anfällig, immun) immune (**gegen** to, against) **3** (strapazierfähig) hard-wearing; (pflegeleicht) easy-care *attrib.*

unendlich
A *Adj.* infinite, boundless ‹*space, sea, expanse, fig.: love, care, patience, etc.*›; (zeitlich) endless; never-ending; (Math.) infinite ‹*number etc.*›; **das Unendliche** the infinite (Philos.); infinity (Math.); **sich im Unendlichen schneiden** (Math.) meet at infinity; **auf ~ stellen** (Fot.) focus ‹*lens*› on infinity; **bis ins Unendliche** (auch fig.) endlessly
B *adv.* infinitely ‹*lovable, sad*›; immeasurably ‹*happy*›; ‹*happy*› beyond measure; **~ langsam** with infinite slowness; **~ lang** endless; **~ groß/hoch** of infinite size/height *postpos.*; immensely (coll.) large/high; **sich ~ freuen** be tremendously pleased; **~ viele Menschen/Elemente** countless people/an infinite number of elements; **ein ~ ferner Punkt** (Math.) a point at an infinite distance; **~ klein** (Math.) infinitesimal

Unendlichkeit *die;* **~ 1** infinity *no def. art.*; (des Himmels/Ozeans) infinite expanse; boundlessness **2** (geh.: Ewigkeit) eternity *no def. art.*

unentbehrlich *Adj.* indispensable (*Dat.,* **für** to)

unentgeltlich /*od.* '---/
A *Adj.* free; **~ sein** be free of charge
B *adv.* free of charge; ‹*work*› for nothing, without pay

unentrinnbar (geh.)
A *Adj.* inescapable
B *adv.* inescapably

unentschieden
A *Adj.* **1** unsettled ‹*case, matter*›; undecided ‹*question*› **2** (Sport, Schach) drawn ‹*game, match*›; **bei ~em Spielausgang** if the game ends in a draw; **der Spielstand ist ~:** the scores are level **3** (unentschlossen) indecisive ‹*person*›
B *adv.* (Sport, Schach) **~ spielen** draw; **~ enden** end in a draw; **das Spiel steht 0 : 0 ~:** the game is a goalless draw [so far]

Unentschieden *das;* **~s, ~** (Sport, Schach) draw

unentschlossen *Adj.* **1** undecided **2** (entschlussunfähig) indecisive

Unentschlossenheit *die* **1** indecision *no def. art.* **2** (Entschlussunfähigkeit) indecisiveness

unentschuldbar
A *Adj.* inexcusable
B *adv.* inexcusably

unentschuldigt
A *Adj.* without giving any reason *postpos., not pred.*; **~es Fernbleiben vom Unterricht/Arbeitsplatz** absence from school/work
B *adv.* without giving any reason

unentwegt /*od.* --'-/
A *Adj.* **1** (beharrlich, ausdauernd) persistent ‹*fighter, champion, efforts*›; **ein paar Unentwegte** a few stalwarts **2** (unaufhörlich) constant; incessant
B *adv.* **1** (beharrlich) persistently **2** (unaufhörlich) constantly; incessantly

unentwirrbar
A *Adj.* inextricable ‹*tangle*›; ‹*threads, tangle*› that cannot be unravelled; (fig.) irredeemable ‹*muddle, chaos*›
B *adv.* inextricably

unerbittlich
A *Adj.* (auch fig.) inexorable; unsparing, unrelenting ‹*critic*›; relentless ‹*battle, struggle*›; implacable ‹*hate, enemy*›; **gegen jmdn. ~ sein** be completely unyielding towards sb.
B *adv.* (auch fig.) inexorably; relentlessly; **~ durchgreifen** take uncompromising action; **~ gegen jmdn./etw. vorgehen** take ruthless action against sb./sth.

unerfahren *Adj.* inexperienced

unerfindlich *Adj.* (geh.) unfathomable; inexplicable; **es ist mir ~, warum/wie** *usw.* **...** it is a mystery to me why/how *etc.* ...

unerforschlich *Adj.* (geh.) unfathomable; *s. auch* **Ratschluss**

unerforscht *Adj.* unexplored

unerfreulich
A *Adj.* unpleasant; bad ‹*news*›; **[etwas] Unerfreuliches** something unpleasant; (schlechte Nachricht) bad news
B *adv.* unpleasantly; **~ verlaufen** take a disagreeable course

unerfüllbar *Adj.* unrealizable

unergiebig *Adj.* (auch fig.) unproductive; (fig.: nicht lohnend) unrewarding ‹*work, subject*›

unergründlich *Adj.* unfathomable, inscrutable ‹*motive, mystery, etc.*›; inscrutable ‹*expression, smile*›

unerheblich
A *Adj.* insignificant; **nicht ~:** not inconsiderable; **es ist ~, ob ...** it is of no significance *or* importance whether ...
B *adv.* insignificantly; [very] slightly

unerhört
A *Adj.* **1** enormous, tremendous ‹*sum, quantity, etc.*›; incredible (coll.), phenomenal ‹*speed, effort, performance, increase*›; incredible (coll.), fantastic (coll.) ‹*splendour, luck*› **2** (abwertend: empörend) outrageous; scandalous
B *adv.* **1** (überaus) incredibly (coll.); **~ viel arbeiten** do a fantastic *or* incredible amount of work (coll.) **2** (abwertend: empörend) outrageously

unerkannt
A *Adj.* unrecognized; (nicht identifiziert) unidentified
B *adv.* without being recognized/identified

unerklärlich *Adj.* inexplicable; **es ist mir ~, wie das geschehen konnte** I simply cannot understand how that could happen

unerlässlich, *unerläßlich /ʊnlɛɐ̯'lɛslɪç/ *Adj.* indispensable; essential; **es ist ~, ... zu ...** it is essential *or* imperative to ...

unerlaubt
A *Adj.* ‹*entry, parking, absenteeism*› without permission; unauthorized ‹*parking, entry*›; (illegal) illegal ‹*act*›
B *adv.* without authorization *or* permission; (illegal) illegally; **der Schule** (*Dat.*) **~ fernbleiben** play truant

unerledigt *Adj.* not dealt with *postpos.*; ‹*work*› not done; unanswered ‹*mail, letters*›; unprocessed ‹*application*›

unermesslich, *unermeßlich
A *Adj.* (geh.) **1** (räumlich) immeasurable ‹*expanse, distance*›; boundless ‹*spaces*› **2** (mengen-, zahlenmäßig) immeasurable, immense ‹*wealth, fortune*›; **ins Unermessliche** beyond measure **3** (überaus groß) untold ‹*suffering, misery, damage*›; inestimable ‹*value, importance*›
B *adv.* immeasurably; ‹*rich*› beyond measure; **~ viel** an inestimable amount

unermüdlich
A *Adj.* tireless, untiring (**bei, in** + *Dat.* in)
B *adv.* tirelessly

unernst *Adj.* frivolous

unerotisch
A *Adj.* unerotic
B *adv.* unerotically

unerquicklich *Adj.* (geh.) unpleasant

unerreichbar
A *Adj.* **1** inaccessible; **in ~er Ferne** *od.* **Entfernung** so distant as to be beyond reach; **sie ist für ihn ~** (fig.) she is beyond his reach **2** (nicht kontaktierbar) unobtainable **3** (fig.) unattainable ‹*aim, ideal, accuracy, etc.*›
B *adv.* **1** (räumlich) inaccessibly **2** (fig.) unattainably

unerreicht *Adj.* unequalled ‹*record, achievement*›; **~ bleiben** remain unequalled; ‹*goal*› not be attained

unersättlich *Adj.* insatiable

unerschlossen *Adj.* unexploited, undeveloped ‹*area*›; unexploited, untapped ‹*market, resources, deposits*›

unerschöpflich *Adj.* inexhaustible; **ihre Geduld war ~:** there was no end to her patience

unerschrocken
A *Adj.* intrepid; fearless
B *adv.* intrepidly; fearlessly

unerschütterlich
A *Adj.* unshakeable; imperturbable ‹*calm, equanimity*›; tenacious ‹*fighter*›
B *adv.* unshakeably

unerschwinglich
A *Adj.* prohibitively expensive; prohibitive ‹*price*›; **für jmdn. ~ sein** be beyond sb.'s means
B *adv.* prohibitively ‹*expensive, high*›

unersetzlich *Adj.* irreplaceable; irretrievable, irrecoverable ‹*loss*›; irreparable ‹*harm, damage, loss of person*›

unersprießlich *Adj.* (geh.) unprofitable; unproductive

unerträglich /*od.* '----/
A *Adj.* unbearable ‹*pain, heat, person, etc.*›; intolerable ‹*situation, conditions, moods, etc.*›; **er/es ist mir ~:** I find him/it unbearable; I cannot stand him/it
B *adv.* unbearably

unerwähnt *Adj.* unmentioned; **völlig ~ bleiben** not be mentioned at all

unerwartet
A *Adj.* unexpected; **es war** *od.* **kam für alle ~:** it came as a surprise to everybody; **etwas Unerwartetes** something unexpected
B *adv.* unexpectedly

unerwidert *Adj.* unreturned ‹*visit*›; unrequited ‹*love*›; **~ bleiben** ‹*greetings*› receive no response

unerwünscht *Adj.* unwanted; unwelcome ‹*interruption, visit, visitor*›; undesirable ‹*side effects*›; **Sie sind hier ~:** you are not wanted *or* welcome here; **ein ~er Ausländer** an undesirable alien

unerzogen *Adj.* badly behaved

UNESCO /u'nɛsko/ *die;* **~:** UNESCO

unethisch
A *Adj.* unethical
B *adv.* unethically

unfähig *Adj.* **1** **~ sein, etw. zu tun** (ständig) be incapable of doing sth.; (momentan) be unable to do sth.; **er ist solch eines Verbrechens ~:** he is incapable of such a crime **2** (abwertend: inkompetent) incompetent

Unfähigkeit *die* **1** inability **2** (Inkompetenz) incompetence

unfair
A *Adj.* unfair (**gegen** to)
B *adv.* unfairly

Unfall *der* accident; **bei einem ~:** in an accident

unfall-, Unfall-: ~arzt *der,* **~ärztin** *die* casualty doctor; **zum ~arzt gehen** go to the doctor in the casualty department *or* casualty; **~flucht** *die* (Rechtsspr.) **wegen ~flucht** for failing to stop after [being involved in] an accident; **~flucht begehen** fail to stop after [being involved in] an accident; **~folge** *die* consequence *or* effect of an/the accident; **er starb an den ~folgen** he died as a result of the accident; **~frei A** *Adj.* accident-free; free from accidents *postpos.*; **B** *adv.* without an accident; **~gefahr** *die* risk of accidents/an accident; accident risk; **~kranken·haus** *das* accident *or* casualty hospital; **~opfer** *das* accident victim; **~rente** *die* disability pension (*paid by an accident insurance*); **~station** *die* accident *or* casualty department; **~stelle** *die* scene of an/the accident; **~tod** *der* accidental death; death in an accident; **~ursache** *die* cause of an/the accident; **~versicherung** *die* accident insurance; **~wagen** *der* **1** (Rettungswagen) incident vehicle; (Krankenwagen) ambulance; **2** (beschädigter Wagen) car [that has been] damaged in an/the accident

unfassbar, *unfaßbar
A *Adj.* incomprehensible; (unglaublich) incredible, unimaginable ‹*poverty, cruelty, etc.*›; **es ist mir ~, wie ...:** it is incomprehensible to me *or* I cannot understand how ...
B *adv.* incomprehensibly; incredibly, unimaginably ‹*cruel*›

unfehlbar *Adj.* infallible

Unfehlbarkeit *die;* **~:** infallibility

unfein
A *Adj.* ill-mannered, unrefined ‹*behaviour etc.*›; unrefined, coarse ‹*manner, word*›; bad ‹*manners*›; **das gilt als ~:** it's considered bad manners
B *adv.* ‹*behave*› badly, in an ill-mannered way

unfertig *Adj.* **1** unfinished ‹*manuscript, article, etc.*› **2** (fig.: unreif) immature

unfest (Sprachw.)
A *Adj.* separable
B *adv.* **~ zusammengesetzte Verben** separable [compound] verbs

Unflat /ˈʊnfla:t/ *der;* **~[e]s** (geh. veralt.) filth

unflätig /ˈʊnflɛ:tɪç/ (geh. abwertend)
A *Adj.* coarse ‹*behaviour, manners, speech, etc.*›; obscene ‹*expression, word, curse*›; dirty ‹*song*›
B *adv.* coarsely; obscenely

unflektiert *Adj.* (Sprachw.) uninflected

unflexibel
A *Adj.* inflexible
B *adv.* inflexibly

unflott
A *Adj. in* **nicht ~** (ugs.) not bad; (modisch, schick) quite with it (coll.)
B *adv.* **nicht ~:** not at all badly; **sie tanzt nicht ~** (ugs.) she's a pretty useful dancer (coll.)

unförmig
A *Adj.* shapeless ‹*lump, shadow, etc.*›; huge ‹*legs, hands, body*›; bulky, ungainly ‹*shape, shoes, etc.*›
B *adv.* **~ dick** fat and unshapely *or* bulky; **~ angeschwollen** swollen and unsightly

unfrankiert *Adj.* unstamped

unfrei
A *Adj.* **1** not free *pred.*; subject, dependent ‹*people*›; ‹*life*› of bondage *or* without liberty; **die Bauern waren noch ~** (hist.) the peasants were still serfs; **sich etwas ~ fühlen** feel a bit tied *or* unable to act freely **2** (gehemmt) inhibited **3** (keine Freiheit gewährend) restrictive ‹*education, regime*› **4** (Postw.) unstamped
B *adv.* (gehemmt) in an inhibited manner

Unfreie *der/die; adj. Dekl.* (hist.) serf

Unfreiheit *die* slavery *no art.*; bondage (esp. Hist./literary) *no art.*; **ein Leben in ~:** a life of bondage *or* without freedom

unfreiwillig
A *Adj.* involuntary; (erzwungen) enforced ‹*stay*›; (nicht beabsichtigt) unintended ‹*publicity, joke, humour*›
B *adv.* involuntarily; without wanting to; (unbeabsichtigt) unintentionally

unfreundlich
A *Adj.* **1** unfriendly (**zu, gegen** to); unkind ‹*words, remark*›; **ein ~er Akt** (Politik) an unfriendly *or* a hostile act **2** (fig.) unpleasant ‹*area, climate, environment*›; unpleasant, inclement ‹*weather, summer*›; cheerless ‹*room*›
B *adv.* in an unfriendly way

Unfreundlichkeit *die* **1** unfriendliness; **sie behandelte ihn mit einer solchen ~, dass ...** she treated him in such an unfriendly way that ... **2** (Handlung) unfriendly act; (Äußerung) unkind remark

Unfriede[n] *der* discord; **in ~ leben/auseinander gehen** live in a state of strife/part in hostility

unfrisiert *Adj.* ungroomed ‹*hair*›; **sie war ~:** she had not done her hair

unfruchtbar *Adj.* **1** infertile ‹*soil, field, land*›; **meine Anregungen fielen auf ~en Boden** (fig.) my suggestions fell on stony ground **2** (Biol.) infertile; sterile; **ein Tier ~ machen** sterilize *or* neuter an animal; **die ~en Tage der Frau** the days of infertility **3** (fig.) unfruitful, unproductive ‹*discussion, comparison, etc.*›; infertile ‹*years, period*›; ‹*idea*› which does not lead anywhere

Unfruchtbarkeit *die* **1** infertility **2** (Biol.) infertility; sterility **3** (fig.) unproductiveness

Unfug /ˈʊnfu:k/ *der;* **~[e]s** **1** [piece of] mischief; **allerlei ~ anstellen** get up to all kinds of mischief *or* (coll.) monkey business; **grober ~:** public nuisance; **was soll dieser ~?** what's this monkey business? (coll.); **lass diesen ~!** stop monkeying about (coll.) *or* making a nuisance of yourself **2** (Unsinn) nonsense

Ungar /ˈʊŋgar/ *der;* **~n, ~n, Ungarin** *die;* **~, ~nen** ▸ **S. 520** Hungarian; *s. auch* **-in**

ungarisch ▸ **S. 520,** ▸ **S. 670**
A *Adj.* Hungarian
B *adv.* in Hungarian; *s. auch* **deutsch**; **Deutsche²**

Ungarisch *das;* **~[s]** ▸ **S. 670** Hungarian; *s. auch* **Deutsch**

Ungarn *(das);* **~s** Hungary

ungastlich
A *Adj.* inhospitable
B *adv.* inhospitably

ungeachtet *Präp. mit Gen.* (geh.) notwithstanding; despite; **~ dessen, dessen ~:** nevertheless; notwithstanding [this]

ungeahnt
A *Adj.* unsuspected; (stärker) undreamt-of *attrib.*
B *adv.* unexpectedly

ungebärdig
A *Adj.* unruly ‹*child, horse, etc.*›; wild ‹*temperament, mountain stream, etc.*›
B *adv.* wildly

ungebeten
A *Adj.* uninvited; (nicht gern gesehen) unwelcome
B *adv.* uninvited

ungebeugt *Adj.* (Sprachw.) uninflected

ungebildet *Adj.* uneducated; **ein Ungebildeter** an uneducated person

ungeboren *Adj.* unborn

ungebräuchlich *Adj.* uncommon; rare; rarely used ‹*method, process*›

ungebraucht *Adj.* unused; mint ‹*stamp*›

ungebremst
A *Adj.* unchecked; unbridled ‹*optimism*›
B *adv.* ‹*spread, grow*› unchecked; ‹*continue, increase*› unabated; **~ kaufen** continue to buy without restraint

ungebrochen *Adj.* **1** (Physik) unrefracted ‹*rays, waves*› **2** (fig.) unbroken ‹*will, person*›; undiminished ‹*strength, courage*›

Ungebühr *die* (geh.) impropriety; **~ vor Gericht** (Rechtsspr.) contempt of court

ungebührlich (geh.)
A *Adj.* improper, unseemly ‹*behaviour*›; unreasonable ‹*demand*›
B *adv.* ‹*behave*› improperly; unreasonably ‹*high, long, etc.*›

ungebunden
A *Adj.* **1** unbound ‹*book etc.*› **2** (Literaturw.) **in ~er Rede** in prose **3** (frei von Bindungen) independent; without ties *postpos.*; (ohne Partner/Partnerin) unattached
B *adv.* **~ leben** live an independent life *or* a life without ties

ungedeckt *Adj.* **1** uncovered ‹*cheque, bill of exchange, etc.*›; unsecured ‹*bond*› **2** unlaid ‹*table*› **3** (ungeschützt) unprotected **4** (Ballspiele) unmarked ‹*player*›

Ungeduld *die* impatience

ungeduldig
A *Adj.* impatient
B *adv.* impatiently

ungeeignet *Adj.* unsuitable; (für eine Aufgabe, Stellung) unsuited (**für, zu** to, for)

ungefähr /ˈʊngəfɛ:ɐ̯/
A *Adj.* approximate; rough ‹*idea, outline*›
B *Adv.* approximately; roughly; (mit nachgestellter Zahl) about; roughly; **~ so** something like this; **so ~** (ugs.) more or less; **kannst du mir so ~ sagen, wie/wann** *usw.* **...?** can you give me some idea *or* a rough idea how/when *etc.* ...?; **wann wirst du ~ zurückkommen?** roughly *or* about when will you be back?; **wo ~ ...?** whereabouts ...?; **kannst du es ~ beschreiben?** can you give a rough description?; **ich kann es mir ~ vorstellen** I can imagine; **[wie] von ~:** [as if] by chance; **es kommt nicht von ~[, dass ...]** it's no accident [that ...]

ungefährdet *Adj.* safe; (gesichert) assured ‹*promotion etc.*›; ‹*play, swim, etc.*› in safety

ungefährlich
A *Adj.* safe; harmless ‹*animal, person, illness, etc.*›; **nicht ~ sein** be not without danger
B *adv.* safely

ungefällig
A *Adj.* disobliging, churlish (**gegenüber** to)
B *adv.* in a disobliging way; churlishly

ungefärbt *Adj.* **1** undyed ‹*wool, hair*›; ‹*food, drink*› without colouring matter **2** (fig.) unvarnished ‹*truth*›; uncoloured, undistorted ‹*account*›

ungefiltert *Adj.* unfiltered; (fig.: unzensiert) uncensored

ungefragt *Adj.* unasked

ungefüge *Adj.* (geh.) **1** cumbersome ‹*furniture*›; massive, bulky ‹*chunk, stature*›; massive ‹*wall, stone*›; ungainly ‹*person*› **2** (schwerfällig) ponderous ‹*style*›

ungehalten (geh.)
A *Adj.* annoyed (**über** + *Akk.*, **wegen** about); (entrüstet) indignant
B *adv.* indignantly; ‹*reply, say*› in an aggrieved tone

ungeheizt *Adj.* unheated

ungehemmt
A *Adj.* **1** uninhibited ‹*person*› **2** (uneingeschränkt) unrestricted, unimpeded ‹*movement*›; (fig.) unrestrained ‹*joy, anger, etc.*›
B *adv.* **1** without inhibition **2** (uneingeschränkt) ‹*develop*› unhindered, without hindrance; (fig.) ‹*cry, laugh, drink, etc.*› without restraint

ungeheuer
A *Adj.* enormous; immense; tremendous ‹*strength, energy, effort, enthusiasm, fear, success, pressure, etc.*›; vast, immense ‹*fortune, knowledge*›; (schrecklich) terrible (coll.), terrific (coll.) ‹*pain, rage*›; **ungeheure Ausgaben** an enormous amount of expense
B *adv.* tremendously; terribly (coll.) ‹*difficult, clever*›

Ungeheuer *das;* **~s, ~** (auch fig.) monster

ungeheuerlich
A *Adj.* monstrous; outrageous
B *adv.* (ugs.) terribly (coll.)

Ungeheuerlichkeit *die;* **~, ~en** **1** monstrous nature; outrageousness **2** (Vorgang) monstrous *or* outrageous thing

ungehindert *Adj.* unimpeded

ungehobelt
A *Adj.* **1** unplaned ‹*wood*› **2** (grob) uncouth
B *adv.* uncouthly

ungehörig
A *Adj.* improper ‹*behaviour*›; (frech) impertinent ‹*tone, answer*›
B *adv.* improperly; (frech) impertinently

ungehorsam *Adj.* disobedient (**gegenüber** to)

Ungehorsam *der* disobedience (**gegenüber** to)

ungehört *Adj.* unheard

Ungeist *der* (geh. abwertend) pernicious ideology

ungekämmt *Adj.* uncombed

ungekannt
A *Adj.* [previously] unknown
B *adv.* **~ lang/breit/einfach** of previously unknown length/width/simplicity *postpos.*

ungeklärt *Adj.* **1** unsolved ‹*question, problem*›; unknown ‹*cause*›; **die Angelegenheit ist noch ~:** the matter has yet to be cleared up **2** (ungereinigt) untreated ‹*sewage*›

ungekrönt *Adj.* (auch fig.) uncrowned

ungekündigt *Adj.* **in ~er Stellung** not under notice *postpos.*

ungekünstelt
A *Adj.* natural; unaffected
B *adv.* naturally; unaffectedly

ungekürzt *Adj.* unabridged ‹*edition, book*›; uncut ‹*film, speech*›

ungeladen *Adj.* **1** unloaded ‹*gun, camera*› **2** (nicht eingeladen) uninvited ‹*guest*›

ungelegen
A *Adj.* inconvenient, awkward ‹*time*›; ‹*visit etc.*› at an awkward *or* inconvenient time; **das kommt mir sehr ~/nicht ~:** that is very inconvenient *or* awkward/quite convenient for me
B *adv.* inconveniently; **komme ich ~?** have I come at an inconvenient *or* awkward time?

Ungelegenheit *die* inconvenience; **jmdm. große ~en machen** *od.* **bereiten** inconvenience sb. greatly

U

ungelegt *Adj. in* **kümmere dich nicht um ~e Eier** (ugs.) don't cross your bridges before you get to them

ungelenk
A *Adj.* clumsy; ungainly
B *adv.* clumsily

ungelenkig *Adj.* stiff-jointed

ungelernt *Adj.* unskilled

Ungelernte *der/die; adj. Dekl.* unskilled worker

ungeliebt *Adj.* unloved; (verhüll.: verhasst) hateful, odious ‹*task*›; odious ‹*school etc.*›

ungelogen *Adv.* (ugs.) honestly

ungelöscht *Adj.* (Chemie) unslaked ‹*lime*›

ungelöst *Adj.* (nicht geklärt) unsolved; unsettled ‹*quarrel, conflict*›

Ungemach *das;* **~[e]s** (geh. veralt.) trouble

ungemacht *Adj.* unmade

ungemein
A *Adj.* exceptional ‹*progress, popularity*›; tremendous ‹*advantage, pleasure*›
B *adv.* exceptionally; **~ fleißig** extraordinarily industrious; **das freut mich ~:** that pleases me no end (coll.)

ungemütlich
A *Adj.* [1] uninviting, cheerless ‹*room, flat*›; uncomfortable, unfriendly ‹*atmosphere*› [2] (unangenehm) unpleasant ‹*situation*›; **es wird jetzt ~:** things are getting nasty; **es wurde ihnen zu ~:** things got too unpleasant for them
B *adv.* uncomfortably ‹*furnished*›; **hier sitzt es sich ~:** it's not comfortable sitting here

ungenannt *Adj.* anonymous; **ein Ungenannter** an anonymous person

ungenau
A *Adj.* [1] inaccurate ‹*measurement, estimate, thermometer, translation, etc.*›; imprecise, inexact ‹*definition, formulation, etc.*›; (undeutlich) vague ‹*memory, idea, impression*› [2] (nicht sorgfältig) careless ‹*work, worker*›
B *adv.* [1] inaccurately; ‹*define*› imprecisely, inexactly; ‹*remember*› vaguely; **die Uhr geht ~:** the clock does not keep good time [2] (nicht sorgfältig) ‹*work*› carelessly

Ungenauigkeit *die* [1] inaccuracy; (einer Definition) imprecision; inexactness [2] (etwas Ungenaues) inaccuracy

ungenehmigt
A *Adj.* unauthorized
B *adv.* without authorization

ungeniert /ˈʊnʒeniːɐ̯t/
A *Adj.* free and easy; uninhibited; **er war ganz ~:** he was not at all embarrassed *or* concerned
B *adv.* openly; ‹*yawn*› unconcernedly; (ohne Scham) ‹*undress etc.*› without any embarrassment

ungenießbar *Adj.* [1] (nicht essbar) inedible; (nicht trinkbar) undrinkable [2] (fig. ugs.) unbearable ‹*person*›; **er ist heute ~:** he's in a foul mood today (sl.)

ungenügend
A *Adj.* inadequate; **die Note „ungenügend"/ein Ungenügend** (Schulw.) the/an 'unsatisfactory' [mark]
B *adv.* inadequately

ungenutzt, ungenützt *Adj.* unused; unexploited ‹*resource, energy*›; **eine Gelegenheit ~ vorübergehen lassen** let an opportunity slip *or* pass by

ungeöffnet *Adj.* unopened

ungeordnet
A *Adj.* disordered ‹*papers, thoughts, data, etc.*›; disorderly ‹*retreat, growth*›
B *adv.* in a disordered way

ungepflegt *Adj.* neglected ‹*garden, park, car, etc.*›; unkempt ‹*person, appearance, hair*›; uncared-for ‹*hands*›

ungeplant
A *Adj.* unplanned
B *adv.* without being planned; **~ hohe Steigerungen** increases that were not planned to be so large

ungeprüft
A *Adj.* unchecked
B *adv.* without checking

ungerade *Adj.* odd ‹*number*›

ungerecht
A *Adj.* unjust, unfair (**gegen, zu, gegenüber** to)
B *adv.* unjustly; unfairly

ungerechterweise *Adv.* unjustly; unfairly; **er verdient ~ genauso viel wie sie** he earns as much as she does, which is unfair

ungerechtfertigt *Adj.* unjustified; unwarranted

Ungerechtigkeit *die;* **~, ~en** injustice; **der Vorwurf der ~:** the reproach of being unjust; **so eine ~!** how unjust *or* unfair!

ungeregelt *Adj.* irregular; disorganized

ungereimt *Adj.* [1] (nicht stimmig) inconsistent; illogical; (ugs. abwertend: sinnlos, verworren) muddled [2] (reimlos) unrhymed

Ungereimtheit *die;* **~, ~en** (Unstimmigkeit) inconsistency; (ugs. abwertend: Unsinnigkeit, Verworrenheit) muddle

ungern *Adv.* reluctantly; **etw. ~ tun** not like *or* dislike doing sth.; **Würdest du das bitte tun? — Ungern** Would you do that, please? — I'd rather not

ungerufen *Adv.* without being called

ungerührt *Adj.* unmoved

ungesalzen *Adj.* unsalted

ungesättigt *Adj.* [1] (geh.) unsatisfied [2] (Chemie) unsaturated; **einfach/mehrfach ~e Fettsäuren** monounsaturated/polyunsaturated fats

ungesäuert *Adj.* unleavened ‹*bread*›

ungeschält *Adj.* unpeeled ‹*fruit*›; unstripped ‹*tree trunk*›; **~er Reis** paddy rice

ungeschehen *Adj. in* **etw. ~ machen** undo sth.

Ungeschick *das* clumsiness; **~ lässt grüßen!** (ugs.) butterfingers!

Ungeschicklichkeit *die;* **~, ~en** [1] clumsiness; ineptitude [2] (etwas Ungeschicktes) piece of clumsiness; (Fehler) clumsy mistake

ungeschickt
A *Adj.* clumsy; awkward ‹*movement, formulation, etc.*›; **technisch ~:** technically inept
B *adv.* clumsily; ‹*bow, express oneself, etc.*› awkwardly; **sich ~ anstellen** show a lack of skill; show oneself to be inept

ungeschlacht (geh.)
A *Adj.* [1] (unförmig, massig) huge and ungainly ‹*man, animal*›; huge, clumsy ‹*hands*›; clumsy, ungainly ‹*limbs, movement*›; massive ‹*building etc.*› [2] (grob, unkultiviert) coarse; uncouth
B *adv.* in an uncouth way

ungeschlagen
A *Adj.* unbeaten; undefeated
B *adv.* ‹*lead, win*› with an unbeaten record

ungeschlechtlich (Biol.)
A *Adj.* asexual
B *adv.* asexually

ungeschliffen
A *Adj.* [1] uncut ‹*diamond etc.*› [2] (fig. abwertend) unrefined ‹*behaviour, manners*›
B *adv.* (fig. abwertend) in an unrefined manner

ungeschmälert *Adj.* (geh.) undiminished; in full measure *postpos.*; (voll anerkannt) appreciated to the full *postpos.*

ungeschminkt
A *Adj.* [1] not made-up *pred.*; without make-up *postpos.* [2] (fig.) unvarnished ‹*truth*›; uncoloured ‹*account*›
B *adv.* without holding anything back; **jmdm. ~ seine Meinung sagen** give sb. one's honest opinion

ungeschoren *Adj.* [1] unshorn [2] (fig.) **~ bleiben** be left in peace; be spared; **~ davonkommen** get away with it; (ohne Schaden) get away unscathed

ungeschrieben *Adj.* unwritten

ungeschützt *Adj.* unprotected; (Wind und Wetter ausgesetzt) exposed

ungesehen *Adj.* unseen

ungesellig
A *Adj.* [1] unsociable [2] (Zool.) non-gregarious
B *adv.* (Zool.) non-gregariously

ungesetzlich
A *Adj.* unlawful; illegal
B *adv.* unlawfully; illegally

Ungesetzlichkeit *die* illegality

ungesichert *Adj.* [1] unsecured ‹*border, system, loan*›; [2] (nicht garantiert) not guaranteed; (unsicher) uncertain; **~e Beschäftigung** insecure employment

ungesittet
A *Adj.* uncivilized
B *adv.* in an uncivilized manner

ungestalt *Adj.* [1] (geh.) shapeless [2] (veralt.: missgestaltet) misshapen

ungestempelt *Adj.* unstamped ‹*licence etc.*›; uncancelled ‹*stamp*›

ungestillt *Adj.* (geh.) unquenched, unslaked ‹*thirst*›; unsatisfied, unsated ‹*curiosity, desire, greed*›

ungestört *Adj.* undisturbed; uninterrupted ‹*development*›; **~ arbeiten** work in peace *or* without interruption

ungestraft
A *Adj.* unpunished
B *adv.* with impunity

ungestüm /ˈʊngəʃtyːm/ (geh.)
A *Adj.* impetuous, tempestuous ‹*person, embrace, nature, etc.*›; wild ‹*imagination*›; violent, fierce ‹*wind*›; stormy ‹*sea*›
B *adv.* impetuously

Ungestüm *das;* **~[e]s** impetuosity

ungesühnt *Adj.* (geh.) unatoned

ungesund
A *Adj.* (auch fig.) unhealthy; (fig.: übermäßig) excessive ‹*ambition, activity*›; **Rauchen ist ~:** smoking is bad for you *or* for your health
B *adv.* unhealthily; **er lebt sehr ~:** he lives *or* leads a very unhealthy life

ungesüßt /ˈʊngəzyːst/ *Adj.* unsweetened

ungetan *Adj.* still to be done *postpos.*; **etw. ~ lassen** leave sth. undone

ungeteilt *Adj.* [1] undivided [2] (fig.) unrestricted, absolute ‹*power*›; undivided ‹*attention, interest*›; (einmütig) unanimous; universal ‹*approval, agreement, etc.*›

ungetreu *Adj.* (geh.) disloyal

ungetrübt *Adj.* unclouded, perfect ‹*happiness*›; unalloyed ‹*pleasure*›; unspoilt, perfect ‹*days, relationship*›; **seine Freude blieb nicht lange ~:** his pleasure did not long remain unsullied

Ungetüm /ˈʊngətyːm/ *das;* **~s, ~e** monster

ungeübt *Adj.* unpractised ‹*hand*›; **in etw. ~ sein** lack practice in sth.

ungewaschen *Adj.* unwashed

ungewiss, *ungewiß *Adj.* uncertain; **eine Fahrt ins Ungewisse** a journey into the unknown; **über etw.** (*Akk.*) **im Ungewissen sein** be uncertain *or* unsure about sth.; **jmdn. [über etw.** (*Akk.*)**] im Ungewissen lassen** leave sb. in the dark *or* keep sb. guessing [about sth.]

Ungewissheit, *Ungewißheit *die* uncertainty; **in ~ sein** be in a state of uncertainty

ungewöhnlich
A *Adj.* [1] unusual [2] (sehr groß) exceptional ‹*strength, beauty, ability, etc.*›; outstanding ‹*achievement, success*›
B *adv.* [1] (unüblich) ‹*behave*› abnormally, strangely [2] (enorm) exceptionally

ungewohnt
A *Adj.* unaccustomed ‹*exertion, heat, cold, load, etc.*›; unaccustomed, unusual ‹*sight, time*›; (nicht vertraut) unfamiliar ‹*method, work, surroundings, etc.*›; **sie sagte es mit ~er Schärfe** she said it with a sharpness [that was] unusual for her; **die Arbeit ist ihr** *od.* **für sie noch ~:** she is still not used to *or* familiar with the work
B *adv.* unusually

ungewollt
A *Adj.* unwanted; (unbeabsichtigt) unintentional; inadvertent
B *adv.* unintenionally; inadvertently

ungezählt *Adj.* [1] (unzählig) countless [2] (nicht gezählt) uncounted

Ungeziefer /ˈʊngətsiːfɐ/ *das;* **~s** vermin *pl.*

ungezogen
A *Adj.* naughty; badly behaved; bad ‹*behaviour*›;

(frech) cheeky; **zu jmdm. ~ sein** behave badly towards sb.; be cheeky to sb.
B *adv.* naughtily; ‹*behave*› badly

Ungezogenheit *die;* ~, **~en** **1** naughtiness; bad behaviour **2** (ungezogene Bemerkung) **~en** insolent remarks; **das ist eine ~:** that's very naughty/cheeky

ungezügelt
A *Adj.* unbridled
B *adv.* without restraint

ungezwungen
A *Adj.* natural, unaffected ‹*person, behaviour, cheerfulness*›; (nicht förmlich) informal, free and easy ‹*tone, conversation, etc.*›
B *adv.* ‹*behave*› naturally, unaffectedly; ‹*talk*› freely

Ungezwungenheit *die;* ~ ▸**ungezwungen A:** naturalness; unaffectedness; informality

ungiftig *Adj.* non-poisonous; non-toxic ‹*gas, substance*›

Unglaube[n] *der* **1** disbelief; incredulity **2** (Rel.) unbelief

unglaubhaft *Adj.* implausible

ungläubig
A *Adj.* **1** disbelieving; incredulous; **~er Thomas** doubting Thomas **2** (Rel.) unbelieving
B *adv.* incredulously; in disbelief

Ungläubige *der/die* (Rel.) unbeliever

unglaublich
A *Adj.* **1** incredible **2** (ugs.: sehr groß) incredible (coll.), fantastic (coll.) ‹*speed, amount, luck, etc.*›
B *adv.* (ugs.: äußerst) incredibly (coll.); (empörend) ‹*behave*› in an incredible fashion (coll.)

unglaubwürdig *Adj.* implausible; untrustworthy, unreliable ‹*witness etc.*›

ungleich
A *Adj.* **1** unequal; unequal, different ‹*sizes*›; odd, unmatching ‹*socks, gloves, etc.*›; (unähnlich) dissimilar ‹*characters etc.*›; odd ‹*couple*›; **a [ist] ~ b** (Math.) a is not equal to *or* does not equal b **2** (ungleichmäßig) uneven ‹*distribution etc.*›
B *adv.* **1** unequally; **~ geartet** of different dispositions **2** (ungleichmäßig) unevenly
C *Adv.* (mit Komparativ) far ‹*larger, more difficult*›; (unvergleichlich) incomparably ‹*better, more beautiful*›
D *Präp. mit Dat.* (geh.) unlike

Ungleich·behandlung *die* unequal treatment

Ungleichgewicht *das* imbalance

Ungleichheit *die* **1** inequality **2** (Unterschied) difference; dissimilarity

ungleichmäßig
A *Adj.* uneven
B *adv.* **1** unevenly **2** (verschieden) **~ lang** of different lengths

ungleichnamig *Adj.* **1** (Math.) ‹*fractions*› with different denominators **2** (Physik) opposite ‹*poles*›

Unglück *das;* **~[e]s, ~e** **1** (Unfall) accident; (Flugzeug~, Zug~) crash; accident; (Missgeschick) mishap; **das ist [doch] kein ~!** that's not a disaster; it doesn't really matter **2** (Not) misfortune; (Leid) suffering; distress; **jmdn. ins ~ stürzen** bring ruin *or* disaster on sb.; **sich ins ~ stürzen, in sein ~ rennen** rush headlong into disaster *or* to one's ruin; **es ist ein ~, dass ...** it is a real shame *or* a great pity that ... **3** (Pech) bad luck; misfortune; **~ haben** be unlucky; **das bringt ~:** that's unlucky; **zum ~:** unfortunately; **zu allem ~:** to make matters worse; **das ~ wollte es, dass ...** as luck would have it ...; **~ im Spiel, Glück in der Liebe** unlucky at cards, lucky in love **4** (Schicksalsschlag) misfortune; **ein ~ kommt selten allein** (ugs.) it never rains but it pours

unglücklich
A *Adj.* **1** (traurig) unhappy; unhappy, unrequited ‹*love*›; **er ist ~ darüber, dass ...** he is unhappy that ...; **mach dich nicht ~!** don't do it! **2** (nicht vom Glück begünstigt) unfortunate ‹*person*›; (bedauernswert, arm) hapless ‹*person, animal*›; **ich Unglücklicher/Unglückliche!** (geh.) poor me!; woe is me! (literary); **der/die Unglückliche** the unfortunate *or* poor man/woman **3** (ungünstig, ungeschickt) unfortunate ‹*moment, combination, meeting, etc.*›; unhappy ‹*end, choice, solution*›; unfortunate, unhappy ‹*coincidence, formulation*›; clumsy ‹*movement*›; (unverdient) unlucky ‹*defeat*›; **[bei** *od.* **in etw.** (*Dat.*)**] eine ~e Hand haben** get it wrong [when doing sth.]; **eine ~e Figur abgeben** cut a sorry figure
B *adv.* **1** unhappily; **~ verliebt sein** be unhappy in love **2** (ungünstig) unfortunately; (ungeschickt) unhappily, clumsily ‹*translated, expressed*›; **~ enden** come to an unfortunate end; ‹*love affair*› end unhappily; **er stürzte so ~, dass ...** he fell so awkwardly that ...; he had such a bad fall that ...

unglücklicherweise *Adv.* unfortunately

Unglücks·botschaft *die* bad news *sing.*; bad tidings *pl.*

unglück·selig *Adj.* **1** (bedauernswert) unfortunate, hapless ‹*person*› **2** (verhängnisvoll) unfortunate, fateful ‹*coincidence, combination*›; ill-starred, fateful ‹*time*›; fateful ‹*predilection*›

Unglücks-: ~fall *der* accident; **~maschine** *die* crashed aircraft; **~nacht** *die* the night of the accident; **~ort** *der* scene of the accident; **~rabe** *der* (ugs.) unlucky sort (coll.); luckless individual (coll.); **~reaktor** *der* reactor involved in the accident; **~stelle** *die* scene of an/the accident; **~tag** *der* day of the accident; (unglücklicher Tag) unhappy day; bad day; **~ursache** *die* cause of the accident; **~zahl** *die* unlucky number; **~zug** *der* crashed train

Ungnade *die:* in **[bei jmdm.] in ~** (*Akk.*) **fallen/in ~** (*Dat.*) **sein** fall/be out of favour [with sb.]

ungnädig
A *Adj.* bad-tempered; grumpy; (geh.: schlimm) unkind ‹*fate*›
B *adv.* in a bad-tempered way; grumpily

ungültig *Adj.* invalid; void (esp. Law); spoilt ‹*vote, ballot paper*›; disallowed ‹*goal*›; **~e Banknoten** banknotes which are not legal tender; **eine Ehe/ein Tor für ~ erklären** annul a marriage/disallow a goal

Ungunst *die* **1** (geh. veralt.) disfavour **2** **zu jmds. ~en** to sb.'s disadvantage **3** **zu ~en** ▸**zuungunsten**

ungünstig
A *Adj.* **1** unfavourable; unfavourable, poor ‹*climate, weather*›; (unglücklich) unfortunate ‹*consequence*›; unfortunate, bad ‹*shape, layout*›; (unvorteilhaft) unfavourable, unflattering ‹*light, perspective, impression*›; unflattering ‹*cut of dress*›; inconvenient ‹*position*›; (schädlich) harmful ‹*effect*› **2** (unpassend) inconvenient ‹*time*›; (ungeeignet) inappropriate, inconvenient ‹*time, place*›; unsuitable ‹*colour etc.*›
B *adv.* **1** unfavourably; badly ‹*designed, laid out*›; (unvorteilhaft) unflatteringly ‹*cut*›; **sich ~ auswirken** have a harmful effect **2** (unpassend, ungeeignet) inconveniently

ungut *Adj.* **1** uneasy ‹*feeling, premonition*›; negative ‹*impression, expectation*›; (unangenehm) unpleasant ‹*aftertaste, recollection, memories*› **2** in **nichts für ~!** no offence [meant]! (coll.)

unhaltbar *Adj.* **1** untenable ‹*thesis, statement, etc.*› **2** (unerträglich) unbearable, intolerable ‹*conditions, situation*› **3** (Ballspiele) unstoppable ‹*shot, goal, etc.*›

unhandlich *Adj.* unwieldy

Unheil *das* disaster; **~ anrichten** *od.* **stiften** wreak havoc

unheilbar
A *Adj.* incurable
B *adv.* incurably; **~ krank** suffering from an incurable disease *postpos.*; incurably ill

unheil·voll *Adj.* disastrous; (verhängnisvoll) fateful; ominous ‹*development*›

unheimlich
A *Adj.* **1** eerie ‹*story, figure, place, sound*›; eerie, uncanny ‹*feeling*›; **das/er ist mir ~:** it/he gives me an eerie feeling *or* (coll.) the creeps; **mir ist/wird [es] ~:** I have an eerie *or* uncanny feeling **2** (ugs.) (schrecklich) terrible (coll.) ‹*coward, idiot, hunger, headache, etc.*›; (enorm) terrific (coll.) ‹*fun, sum, amount, etc.*›
B *adv.* **1** eerily; uncannily **2** (ugs.; äußerst, sehr) terribly (coll.) ‹*fat, nice, etc.*›; terrifically (coll.) ‹*important, large*›; incredibly (coll.) ‹*quick, long*›; **~ viel** an incredible *or* a terrific amount (coll.); **es macht ~ Spaß** it's terrific fun (coll.)

unhöflich
A *Adj.* impolite
B *adv.* impolitely

Unhöflichkeit *die* impoliteness

Unhold, *der;* **~[e]s, ~e, Unholdin** *die;* **~, ~nen** **1** fiend; demon **2** (abwertend: böser Mensch) monster

unhörbar
A *Adj.* inaudible
B *adv.* inaudibly

unhygienisch
A *Adj.* unhygienic
B *adv.* unhygienically

uni /'yni/ *indekl. Adj.* plain, single-colour ‹*material etc.*›; plain ‹*tie*›

Uni /'ʊni/ *die;* **~, ~s** (ugs.) university

UNICE *Abk.* **= Union of Industrial and Employers' Confederations of Europe** UNICE

UNICEF /'u:nitsɛf/ *die;* **~:** UNICEF

uni·farben *Adj.* ▸**uni**

Uniform /'unifɔrm/ *die;* **~, ~en** uniform; **[Staats]bürger in ~:** soldier [in the Bundeswehr]; citizen in uniform; **die ~ ausziehen** (fig.) put aside one's uniform; leave the service

uniformieren *tr. V.* uniform; **uniformiert** in uniform *postpos.*; uniformed

Uniformierte *der/die; adj. Dekl.* man/woman in uniform; (Polizist) uniformed [police]man/woman

Unikat /uni'ka:t/ *das;* **~[e]s, ~e** ▸**Unikum 1**

Unikum /'u:nikʊm/ *das;* **~s, Unika** *od.* **~s** **1** (geh.) **ein ~ sein** be unique; **ein botanisches ~:** a unique botanical specimen **2** (ugs.: Original) [real] character

uninteressant *Adj.* **1** uninteresting; (nicht von Belang) of no interest *postpos.*; unimportant; **nicht ~:** quite interesting **2** (nicht lohnend, nicht attraktiv) untempting, unattractive ‹*offer*›; **[für jmdn.] ~ sein** be of no interest [to sb.]

uninteressiert *Adj.* uninterested; not interested (**an** + *Dat.* in); **er ist politisch völlig ~:** he is not at all interested in politics

Union /u'nio:n/ *die;* **~, ~en** union; **die ~** (Bundesrepublik Deutschland) the Union of Christian Democrats and Christian Socialists; the CDU and CSU

Unions·republik *die* republic [of the USSR]

unisono /uni'zo:no/ *Adv.* (Musik; auch fig.) in unison; (einmütig) unanimously

universal *Adj.* universal; all-embracing ‹*education*›

Universal-: ~erbe *der,* **~erbin** *die* sole heir; **~genie** *das* (fig.) universal genius; **~lexikon** *das* general encyclopedia

universell /univer'zɛl/
A *Adj.* universal
B *adv.* universally; **~ gebildet sein** have an all-embracing education

Universität /univerzi'tɛ:t/ *die;* **~, ~en** university; **die ~ Marburg, die Marburger ~:** the University of Marburg; Marburg University; **an der ~** ‹*meet, study, etc.*› at university; **auf die ~ gehen** (ugs.), **die ~ besuchen** go to university

Universitäts-: ~bibliothek *die* university library; **~buch·handlung** *die* university bookshop *or* (Amer.) bookstore; **„~buchhandlung C. F. Meyer"** 'C. F. Meyer, university booksellers'; **~dozent** *der,* **~dozentin** *die* university lecturer; **~klinik** *die* university hospital; **~stadt** *die* university town; **~studium** *das* study *no art.* at university

Universum /uni'vɛrzʊm/ *das;* **~s** universe

unkalkulierbar
A *Adj.* incalculable
B *adv.* incalculably

unkameradschaftlich
A *Adj.* uncomradely
B *adv.* in an uncomradely way

U

Unke /ˈʊnkə/ *die*; **~**, **~n** 1 fire-bellied toad 2 (ugs. abwertend: Schwarzseher[in]) Jeremiah; prophet of doom

unken *itr. V.* (ugs.) prophesy doom [and destruction] (joc.)

unkenntlich *Adj.* unrecognizable ‹*person, face*›; indecipherable ‹*writing, stamp*›

Unkenntlichkeit *die*; **~:** unrecognizable state; (einer Schrift, eines Stempels) indecipherable state; **bis zur ~ entstellt** disfigured to the point of being unrecognizable

Unkenntnis *die* ignorance; **~ auf einem Gebiet** ignorance of a subject; **etw. aus ~ tun** do sth. from *or* out of ignorance; **jmdn. [über etw.** (*Akk.*)**] in ~ lassen** leave sb. in ignorance [of sth.]; **~ schützt nicht vor Strafe** ignorance [of the law] is no excuse *or* defence

Unken·ruf *der* (fig.) prophecy of doom

unkeusch (geh.)
A *Adj.* unchaste
B *adv.* unchastely

Unkeuschheit *die* unchastity *no art.*

unklar *Adj.* 1 (undeutlich) unclear; indistinct; (fig.: unbestimmt) vague ‹*feeling, recollection, idea*› 2 (nicht klar verständlich) unclear 3 (nicht durchschaubar) unclear ‹*origin, situation, etc.*›; (ungewiss) uncertain ‹*outcome*›; **sich** (*Dat.*) **über etw.** (*Akk.*) **im Unklaren sein** be unclear *or* unsure about sth.; **ich bin mir noch im Unklaren, ob ...** I am still not sure *or* certain whether ...; **jmdn. über etw.** (*Akk.*) **im Unklaren lassen** keep sb. guessing about sth.

Unklarheit *die* 1 (Undeutlichkeit) lack of clarity; indistinctness 2 (Unverständlichkeit) lack of clarity (*Gen.* in) 3 (Undurchschaubarkeit, Ungewissheit) uncertainty; **es herrscht noch ~ darüber** it is still uncertain 4 (unklarer Punkt) unclear *or* outstanding point; **falls noch ~en bestehen** if anything is still unclear

unklug
A *Adj.* unwise
B *adv.* unwisely

unkollegial
A *Adj.* inconsiderate *or* unhelpful [to one's colleagues]; **er ist [sehr] ~:** he is not [at all] a good colleague
B *adv.* not ‹*behave*› like a good colleague

unkommentiert *Adj.* ‹*edition, pictures, etc.*› without any commentary; **er ließ Spekulationen einfach ~ abprallen** he just let the speculation bounce off without comment

unkompliziert
A *Adj.* uncomplicated, straightforward ‹*person, mechanism, etc.*›; straightforward, simple ‹*matter, case, problem*›; simple ‹*fracture*› (Med.)
B *adv.* ‹*express*› straightforwardly, simply

unkontrollierbar *Adj.* impossible to check *or* supervise *postpos.*; (nicht zu beherrschen) uncontrollable

unkontrolliert *Adj.* 1 unsupervised; ‹*route*› without checkpoints 2 (unbeherrscht) uncontrolled ‹*emotions, feelings, outburst*›; intemperate ‹*words*›

unkonventionell
A *Adj.* unconventional
B *adv.* unconventionally

unkonzentriert
A *Adj.* lacking in concentration *postpos.*; **du bist heute sehr ~:** you aren't concentrating today
B *adv.* without concentrating; **sie arbeitet sehr ~:** she doesn't concentrate at all on her work

Unkosten *Pl.* 1 [extra] expense *sing.*; expenses; **mit großen ~ verbunden sein** involve a great deal of expense; **sich in ~ stürzen** dig deep into one's pocket; [really] lash out (coll.); **sich in geistige ~ stürzen** (scherzh.) strain one's grey matter (coll.) 2 (ugs.: Ausgaben) costs; expenditure *sing.*

Unkosten·beitrag *der* contribution towards expenses

Unkraut *das* 1 weeds *pl.*; **~ vergeht nicht** (ugs. scherzh.) it would take a great deal to finish off his/her/our sort (coll.) 2 (Art) weed

Unkrautvernichtungs·mittel *das*, **Unkrautvertilgungs·mittel** *das* weedkiller

unkritisch
A *Adj.* uncritical
B *adv.* uncritically

unkultiviert *Adj.* uncultivated

unkündbar *Adj.* permanent ‹*position, contract*›; irredeemable ‹*loan*›; **er ist ~:** he cannot be given notice

unkundig *Adj.* (geh.) ignorant; **einer Sache** (*Gen.*) **~ sein** have no knowledge of sth.; **des Lesens/Schreibens/Deutschen ~:** unable to read/to write/to speak German

unlängst *Adv.* (geh.) not long ago; recently; **noch ~, ~ noch** only recently

unlauter *Adj.* (geh.) dishonest; **~er Wettbewerb** (Rechtsspr.) unfair competition

unleidlich
A *Adj.* tetchy
B *adv.* tetchily

unlesbar *Adj.* unreadable

unleserlich
A *Adj.* illegible
B *adv.* illegibly

unleugbar
A *Adj.* undeniable; indisputable
B *adv.* undeniably; indisputably

unliebsam
A *Adj.* unpleasant; **~es Aufsehen erregen** attract the wrong sort of attention
B *adv.* **er ist ~ aufgefallen** he made a bad impression

Unlogik *die* lack of logic; illogicality

unlogisch
A *Adj.* illogical
B *adv.* illogically

Unlust *die* (Widerwille) reluctance; (Lustlosigkeit) lack of enthusiasm; **mit ~:** with reluctance/without enthusiasm

unlustig
A *Adj.* listless; (ohne Begeisterung) unenthusiastic
B *adv.* listlessly; (ohne Begeisterung) unenthusiastically

unmännlich (abwertend)
A *Adj.* unmanly; (weibisch) effeminate
B *adv.* in an unmanly way

unmaßgeblich *Adj.* of no consequence *postpos.*; inconsequential; **nach meiner ~en Meinung** (scherzh.) in my humble opinion

unmäßig
A *Adj.* 1 (übermäßig, maßlos) immoderate; excessive; **~ im Essen/Trinken sein** eat/drink to excess; **~ in seinen Ansprüchen/Forderungen sein** make excessive claims/demands 2 (enorm) tremendous ‹*desire, thirst, fear, etc.*›
B *adv.* 1 (übermäßig, allzusehr) excessively; ‹*eat, drink*› to excess; **~ viel essen/Geld ausgeben** eat/spend far too much 2 (überaus, sehr) tremendously (coll.), terribly ‹*surprised, pleased, fond, etc.*›

Unmäßigkeit *die* immoderation *no art.*

Unmenge *die* mass; enormous number/amount; **eine ~ Geld/Bücher, eine ~ von** *od.* **an Geld/Büchern** an enormous amount of money/number of books; **er trinkt ~n [von] Tee** he drinks enormous quantities *or* (coll.) gallons of tea

Unmensch *der* brute; **ich bin/man ist ja kein ~** (ugs.) I'm not inhuman

unmenschlich
A *Adj.* 1 inhuman; brutal; subhuman, appalling ‹*conditions*› 2 (entsetzlich) terrible (coll.), appalling ‹*pain, heat, suffering, etc.*›
B *adv.* 1 in an inhuman way 2 (entsetzlich) appallingly (coll.)

unmerklich
A *Adj.* imperceptible
B *adv.* imperceptibly

unmissverständlich, ***unmißverständlich**
A *Adj.* 1 (eindeutig) unambiguous 2 (offen, direkt) blunt ‹*answer, refusal*›; unequivocal ‹*language*›
B *adv.* 1 (eindeutig) unambiguously 2 (offen, direkt) bluntly; unequivocally

unmittelbar
A *Adj.* 1 immediate ‹*vicinity, past, future*›; immediate, next-door ‹*neighbour etc.*›; **in ~er Strandnähe** right next to the beach; **aus ~er Nähe** ‹*shoot*› at close quarters, from point-blank range 2 (direkt) direct ‹*contact, connection, influence, etc.*›; immediate ‹*cause, consequence, predecessor, successor*›
B *adv.* 1 immediately; right ‹*behind, next to*›; **~ bevorstehen** be imminent; be almost upon us *etc.* 2 (direkt) directly; **ich fahre von dort ~ zum Bahnhof** I'll go straight from there to the station; **etw. ~ erleben** experience sth. at first hand

unmöbliert *Adj.* unfurnished

unmodern
A *Adj.* old-fashioned; (nicht modisch) unfashionable; **~ werden** go out of fashion
B *adv.* in an old-fashioned way; (nicht modisch) unfashionably

unmöglich
A *Adj.* 1 impossible; **ich verlange ja nichts Unmögliches [von dir]** I'm not asking [you] for the impossible; **es ist mir ~:** it is impossible for me; **du machst es ihm/mir ~[, zu ...]** you are making it impossible for him/me [to ...] 2 (ugs.: nicht akzeptabel, unangebracht) impossible ‹*person, behaviour, colour, ideas, place, etc.*›; **~ aussehen** look ridiculous; **jmdn./sich ~ machen** make a fool of sb./oneself; make sb./oneself look ridiculous; **sich bei jmdm. ~ machen** lose sb.'s respect 3 (ugs.: erstaunlich, seltsam) incredible; **an den ~sten Orten** in the most impossible *or* incredible places
B *adv.* (ugs.) ‹*behave*› impossibly; ‹*dress*› ridiculously; **~ angezogen sein** be wearing impossible clothes
C *Adv.* (ugs.: unter keinen Umständen) **ich/es** *usw.* **kann ~ ...** I/it *etc.* can't possibly ...; **mehr ist ~ zu erreichen** it's impossible to do any more; **das geht ~:** that's out of the question

Unmoral *die* immorality *no art.*

unmoralisch
A *Adj.* immoral
B *adv.* immorally

unmotiviert
A *Adj.* unmotivated
B *adv.* without reason; for no reason

unmündig *Adj.* 1 under-age; **~ sein** be under age *or* a minor 2 (fig.: geistig unselbstständig) dependent

Unmündigkeit *die*; **~** (fig.) dependence

unmusikalisch *Adj.* unmusical

Unmut *der* (geh.) displeasure; annoyance; **seinen ~ an jmdm. auslassen** take it out on sb.

unnachahmlich
A *Adj.* inimitable
B *adv.* inimitably

unnachgiebig *Adj.* intransigent; **in diesem Punkt ~ sein** be uncompromising in this respect; refuse to yield on this point

Unnachgiebigkeit *die* intransigence

unnachsichtig
A *Adj.* merciless; unmerciful; unrelenting ‹*severity*›
B *adv.* mercilessly; ‹*punish*› unmercifully

unnahbar *Adj.* unapproachable

unnatürlich
A *Adj.* unnatural; forced ‹*laugh*›; artificial ‹*material*›; ‹*death*› from unnatural causes; violent ‹*death*›
B *adv.* unnaturally; ‹*laugh*› in a forced way; ‹*speak*› affectedly; **er trinkt/schläft ~ viel** he drinks/sleeps an abnormal amount

Unnatürlichkeit *die* unnaturalness; (von Material) artificiality

unnormal
A *Adj.* abnormal
B *adv.* abnormally

unnötig
A *Adj.* unnecessary; needless, pointless ‹*heroism*›; **~ zu sagen, dass ...** needless to say ...
B *adv.* unnecessarily

unnütz
A *Adj.* useless ‹*stuff, person, etc.*›; pointless ‹*talk*›; wasted ‹*words*›; pointless, wasted ‹*expense, effort*›; vain ‹*attempt*›; **es ist ~, darüber zu streiten** it is no use arguing about it
B *adv.* (unnötig) needlessly

UNO /ˈu:no/ *die*: **die ~:** the UN

U

unökonomisch
A *Adj.* uneconomical
B *adv.* uneconomically; in an uneconomical way

unordentlich
A *Adj.* **1** untidy **2** (ungeregelt) disorderly ‹*life*›
B *adv.* untidily; ‹*tie, treat, etc.*› carelessly

Unordnung *die* disorder; mess; **so eine ~!** what a mess *or* muddle!; **in dem Zimmer herrschte eine fürchterliche ~:** the room was terribly untidy *or* in a terrible mess (coll.); **etw. in ~ bringen** muddle *or* mess sth. up; **in ~ geraten** get into a mess *or* muddle; (fig.) ‹*equilibrium*› become upset

unorthodox
A *Adj.* unorthodox
B in an unorthodox way

Unpaarhufer *der* (Zool.) odd-toed ungulate

unpaarig (Biol.)
A *Adj.* unpaired; azygous
B *adv.* dissimilarly

unparteiisch
A *Adj.* impartial
B *adv.* impartially

Unparteiische *der/die; adj. Dekl.* (Sport) ▸**Schiedsrichter 1**

unpassend
A *Adj.* inappropriate; unsuitable ‹*dress etc.*›
B *adv.* inappropriately; unsuitably ‹*dressed etc.*›

unpassierbar *Adj.* impassable

unpässlich, *unpäßlich /ˈʊnpɛslɪç/ *Adj.* indisposed

Unpässlichkeit, *Unpäßlichkeit *die;* **~, ~en** indisposition

Unperson *die* unperson

unpersönlich
A *Adj.* impersonal; distant, aloof ‹*person*›
B *adv.* impersonally; ‹*answer, write*› in impersonal terms

Unpersönlichkeit *die* impersonal nature

unpolitisch *Adj.* unpolitical; apolitical

unpopulär *Adj.* unpopular

unpraktisch
A *Adj.* unpractical
B *adv.* in an unpractical way

unproblematisch
A *Adj.* unproblematic; straightforward; **nicht ganz ~:** not without its problems
B *adv.* without any problems

unproduktiv
A *Adj.* unproductive
B *adv.* unproductively

unpünktlich
A *Adj.* **1** unpunctual ‹*person*› **2** (verspätet) late, unpunctual ‹*payment*›
B *adv.* late

Unpünktlichkeit *die* lateness; lack of punctuality

unqualifiziert
A *Adj.* **1** unqualified, unskilled ‹*person*›; unskilled ‹*work*› **2** (abwertend: nicht fundiert) inept ‹*remark, criticism*›
B *adv.* (abwertend) ineptly

unrasiert *Adj.* unshaven; **~ und fern der Heimat** (scherzh.) away from it all and looking pretty disreputable

Unrast *die* (geh.) restlessness

Unrat *der;* **~[e]s** (geh.) garbage (lit. or fig.); refuse (Brit.); **~ wittern** smell a rat (fig.)

unrationell
A *Adj.* inefficient
B *adv.* inefficiently

unrealistisch
A *Adj.* unrealistic
B *adv.* unrealistically

unrecht
A *Adj.* wrong; **auf ~e Gedanken kommen** get wicked ideas
B *adv.* wrongly; **jmdm. ~ tun** do sb. an injustice; do wrong by sb.

Unrecht *das;* **~[e]s** **1** **~ haben** be wrong; **~ bekommen** be shown to be in the wrong; **jmdm. ~ geben** disagree with sb. **2** wrong; **im ~ sein** be [in the] wrong; **sich ins ~ setzen** put oneself in the wrong; **ihm ist ein ~ geschehen** he has been wronged; **~ tun** do wrong; **zu ~:** wrongly; **nicht zu ~** (wohlbegründet) not without [good] reason

unrechtmäßig
A *Adj.* unlawful; illegal
B *adv.* unlawfully; illegally

Unrechts·regime *das* (abwertend) tyrannical regime

unredlich (geh.)
A *Adj.* dishonest
B *adv.* dishonestly

Unredlichkeit *die* **1** dishonesty **2** (Handlung) dishonest act

unreell *Adj.* unfair ‹*deal, price*›

unreflektiert
A *Adj.* (geh.) unthinking; (spontan) spontaneous ‹*tradition*›
B *adv.* without thinking; unthinkingly

unregelmäßig
A *Adj.* irregular
B *adv.* irregularly

Unregelmäßigkeit *die* irregularity

unregierbar *Adj.* ungovernable

Unregierbarkeit *die;* **~:** ungovernability

unreif *Adj.* **1** unripe **2** (nicht erwachsen) immature

Unreife *die* ▸**unreif 1, 2**: unripeness; immaturity

unrein *Adj.* **1** (auch fig.) impure; bad ‹*breath, skin*›; (nicht sauber) dirty, polluted ‹*water, air*›; unclear ‹*sound*› **2** (Rel.) unclean **3** **etw. ins Unreine schreiben** make a rough copy of sth.; write sth. [out] in rough; **ins Unreine sprechen** *od.* **reden** (ugs. scherzh.) talk off the top of one's head

Unreinheit *die* **1** ▸**unrein 1**: impurity; badness; dirtiness; polluted state; lack of clarity **2** **~en der Haut** skin disorders

unrentabel
A *Adj.* unprofitable
B *adv.* unprofitably

unrettbar
A *Adj.* unsavable; beyond hope *pred*
B *adv.* irretrievably ‹*lost*›

unrichtig
A *Adj.* incorrect; inaccurate
B *adv.* (fehlerhaft) incorrectly

Unrichtigkeit *die* **1** (das Unzutreffendsein) incorrectness; inaccuracy **2** (Fehlerhaftigkeit) incorrectness **3** (etw. Unzutreffendes, Fehler) inaccuracy

Unruh /ˈʊnruː/ *die;* **~, ~en** (Technik) balance [wheel] (*of clock*)

Unruhe *die* **1** (auch fig.) unrest; (Lärm) noise; commotion; (Unrast) restlessness; agitation; (Besorgnis) anxiety; disquiet; **unter den Zuschauern entstand ~:** the audience became restless **2** (Unfrieden) unrest; **~ stiften** stir up trouble **3** *Pl.* (Tumulte) disturbances; unrest *sing.*

Unruhe-: ~herd *der* seat of unrest; trouble spot; **~stifter** *der,* **~stifterin** *die* (abwertend) troublemaker

unruhig
A *Adj.* **1** restless; (besorgt) anxious; (nervös) agitated; jittery; (fig.) choppy ‹*sea*›; busy ‹*pattern*›; busy, eventful ‹*life*›; unsettled, troubled ‹*time*›; **er ist ein ~er Geist** he's a restless creature; **hier ist es mir zum Arbeiten viel zu ~:** there is too much going on [for me] to work here **2** (laut) noisy ‹*area etc.*› **3** (ungleichmäßig) uneven ‹*breathing, pulse, running, etc.*›; fitful ‹*sleep, motion*›; disturbed ‹*night*›; unsettled ‹*life*›
B *adv.* **1** restlessly; (besorgt) anxiously; **hier geht es sehr ~ zu** there is too much going on here **2** (ungleichmäßig) ‹*breathe, run*› unevenly; ‹*sleep*› fitfully

unrühmlich
A *Adj.* inglorious; ignominious
B *adv.* ignominiously

unrund *Adj.* (Technik) **1** not perfectly round *pred.* **2** (ungleichmäßig) uneven, rough ‹*running of engine*›

uns /ʊns/
A *Personalpron.* **1** *Akk. des Personalpron.* **wir** us **2** *Dat. des Personalpron.* **wir gib es ~:** give it to us; **gib ~ das Geld** give us the money; **wie geht es ~ heute?** (fam.) how are we today? (joc.); **kommst du zu ~?** are you coming to our place? (coll.); **Freunde von ~:** friends of ours; **von ~ aus** as far as we're concerned; **bei ~:** at our home *or* (coll.) place; (in der Heimat) where I/we live *or* come from; **bei ~ gegenüber, gegenüber von ~:** opposite us *or* our house
B *Reflexivpron. der 1. Pers. Pl.* **1** *refl.* ourselves; **wir schämen ~:** we are ashamed [of ourselves]; **wir waschen ~/~ die Hände** we are washing [ourselves]/our hands; **von ~ aus** (aus eigenem Antrieb) on our own initiative **2** *reziprok* one another; **wir kennen ~ schon** we know one another; we've met; **wir haben ~ gestritten** we had an argument *or* quarrel

unsachgemäß
A *Adj.* improper
B *adv.* improperly

unsachlich
A *Adj.* unobjective; **~ werden** lose one's objectivity
B *adv.* without objectivity

Unsachlichkeit *die* lack of objectivity

unsagbar, unsäglich /ʊnˈzɛːklɪç/ (geh.)
A *Adj.* indescribable; unutterable
B *adv.* indescribably; unutterably

unsanft
A *Adj.* rough; hard ‹*push, impact*›
B *adv.* roughly; **~ geweckt werden** be rudely awoken; **jmdn. ~ zurechtweisen** reprimand sb. curtly *or* rudely

unsauber
A *Adj.* **1** (schmutzig) dirty **2** (nachlässig) untidy, sloppy ‹*work, writing, etc.*› **3** (unklar) unclear ‹*sound*›; (ungenau) inexact, woolly ‹*definition*› **4** (unlauter) shady ‹*practice, deal, character, etc.*›; underhand, dishonest ‹*method, means, intention*›; (Sport: unfair) unsporting, unfair ‹*play*›
B *adv.* **1** (nachlässig) untidily; carelessly **2** (unklar) ‹*sing, play*› inaccurately **3** (Sport: unfair) unsportingly; unfairly

Unsauberkeit *die* **1** dirtiness; lack of cleanliness **2** (Nachlässigkeit) untidiness; sloppiness **3** (Unklarheit) lack of clarity; (Ungenauigkeit) woolliness **4** (Unehrlichkeit) shadiness; (Sport: Unfairness) unfairness

unschädlich *Adj.* harmless; **~ machen** render harmless, neutralize ‹*toxic substance, germ. etc.*›; put ‹*weapon, person*› out of action; render ‹*bomb etc.*› safe; (verhüll.: durch Tötung) eliminate ‹*person*›

unscharf
A *Adj.* **1** blurred, fuzzy ‹*photo, picture*› **2** (ungenau) woolly ‹*formulation*›; **die Grenzen sind ~:** there are no clear-cut borderlines **3** (ein ~es Bild ergebend) ‹*lens, optical instrument*› with poor definition; (falsch eingestellt) out-of-focus
B *adv.* **1** blurred; **durch diese Brille sehe ich alles ganz ~:** everything looks blurred *or* out of focus [to me] through these spectacles **2** (ungenau) unclearly

unschätzbar *Adj.* inestimable ‹*value etc.*›; invaluable ‹*service*›; priceless ‹*riches etc.*›

unscheinbar *Adj.* inconspicuous; nondescript; unspectacular ‹*plumage, blossom*›

unschicklich (geh.)
A *Adj.* unseemly; improper
B *adv.* improperly

unschlagbar *Adj.* unbeatable ‹*opponent, prices, etc.*›

Unschlitt /ˈʊnʃlɪt/ *das;* **~[e]s, ~e** (veralt.) tallow

unschlüssig *Adj.* undecided *pred.*; undecisive ‹*gesture, attitude*›; **ich bin [mir] noch ~, ob ...** I cannot decide whether ...

unschön
A *Adj.* **1** ugly; unattractive ‹*colour, voice*› **2** (unerfreulich, unfair) unpleasant, nasty ‹*business, incident, weather, conduct, etc.*›; ugly ‹*scene*›
B *adv.* **1** unattractively **2** (unfreundlich, unfair) badly

Unschuld *die* **1** innocence; **wegen erwiesener ~:** having been proved innocent; **seine Hände in ~ waschen** (fig.) wash one's hands in innocence **2** (Naivität) innocence; (Jungfräulichkeit) virginity; **in aller ~:** in all innocence;

U

eine ∼ vom Lande (ugs. scherzh.) a naïve country girl

unschuldig
A *Adj.* **1** innocent; **an etw.** (*Dat.*) **∼ sein** be not guilty of sth.; **er ist an dem Unfall völlig ∼:** he was in no way responsible for the accident **2** (unverdorben) innocent; **ein ∼es Mädchen** a virgin; **er/sie ist noch ∼:** he/she is still a virgin; **den Unschuldigen/die Unschuldige spielen** play the innocent
B *adv.* innocently

Unschulds-: ∼beteuerung *die* protestation of innocence; **∼lamm** *das* (spött.) little innocent; **sie sind auch keine ∼lämmer** they're no angels; **∼miene** *die* innocent expression; **mit ∼miene** with an air of innocence; **∼vermutung** *die* (Rechtsw.) assumption of innocence

unschwer *Adv.* (geh.) easily; without difficulty

unselbständig
A *Adj.* **1** dependent [on other people]; **sei doch nicht immer so ∼!** try to be a bit more independent! **2** (abhängig) [financially/economically] dependent; not self-supporting *pred.*; **∼e Arbeit** [paid] employment
B *adv.* **1** **[sehr] ∼ denken/handeln** not think [at all] for oneself *or* independently/not act [at all] on one's own *or* independently **2** (abhängig) **∼ beschäftigte Personen** *od.* **Beschäftigte** persons in employment; employed persons

Unselbständigkeit *die* **1** lack of independence **2** (Abhängigkeit) dependence

unselbstständig ▸**unselbständig**

Unselbstständigkeit ▸**Unselbständigkeit**

unselig *Adj.* (geh.) wretched ‹*fate, person, etc.*›; [extremely] unfortunate ‹*situation*›; ill-starred ‹*inheritance*›; (verhängnisvoll) disastrous ‹*journey, decision, etc.*›

unsensibel
A *Adj.* insensitive
B *adv.* insensitively

unser[1] /ˈʊnzɐ/ *Possessivpron. der 1. Pers. Pl.* our; **Vater ∼** (bibl.) Our Father; **das ist ∼s** *od.* (geh.) **∼es** *od.* (geh.) **das ∼e** that is ours; **sein Wagen stand neben ∼[e]m** *od.* **unsrem** his car was next to ours; **die Unseren** our family; **wir haben das Unsere getan** we have done our share *or* part

unser[2] *Gen. des Personalpronomens* **wir** (geh.) of us; **wir waren ∼ drei** there were three of us; **erbarme dich ∼!** have mercy upon us!; **in ∼ aller/beider Interesse** in the interest of all/both of us

unser·einer, unser·eins *Indefinitpron.* (ugs.) the likes of us *pl.*; our sort (coll.)

unserer·seits *Adv.* for our part

unseres·gleichen *indekl. Indefinitpron.* people *pl.* like us; *attr.* **Menschen ∼:** people like us

unseret·halben, unseret·wegen *Adv.* ▸**unsertwegen**

unseret·willen *Adv.* ▸**unsertwillen**

unserige *subst. Possessivpron.* ▸**unsrige**

unseriös (abwertend)
A *Adj.* **1** not [quite] the proper thing *pred.*; casual; ‹*appearance, manner*› **2** (niveaulos) low-quality ‹*newspaper*›; downmarket ‹*publisher*› **3** (unlauter) shady, dubious ‹*practice, deal*›; (unredlich) questionable, dishonest ‹*method etc.*›; (nicht reell) dubious ‹*firm, pseudo-scientist, faith healer*›; dishonest, shady ‹*business man*›
B *adv.* **1** ‹*behave, dress*› casually **2** (unlauter, unredlich) dishonestly; unfairly

unser·seits ▸**unsererseits**

unsers·gleichen ▸**unseresgleichen**

unsert·wegen *Adv.* **1** because of us; on our account **2** (was uns angeht) as far as we are concerned

unsert·willen *Adv. in* **um ∼:** for our sake[s]

unsicher
A *Adj.* **1** (gefährlich) unsafe; dangerous; (gefährdet) at risk *pred.*; insecure ‹*job*›; **einen Ort ∼ machen** (scherzh.) honour a place with one's presence (joc.); (sich vergnügen) have a good time in a place; (sein Unwesen treiben) get up to one's tricks in a place **2** (unzuverlässig) uncertain, unreliable ‹*method*›; unreliable ‹*source, person*› **3** (zögernd) uncertain, hesitant ‹*step*›; (zitternd) unsteady, shaky ‹*hand*›; (nicht selbstsicher) insecure; diffident; unsure of oneself *pred.*; **ich fühle mich ∼:** I don't feel sure of myself; **er ist im Rechnen noch ∼:** he still lacks confidence in arithmetic; **jmdn. ∼ machen** put sb. off his/her stroke **4** (keine Gewissheit habend) unsure; uncertain; **[sich** (*Dat.*)**] ∼ sein[, ob ...]** ‹*person*› be unsure *or* uncertain [whether ...] **5** (ungewiss) uncertain; **das ist mir zu ∼:** that's too uncertain *or* (coll.) dodgy for my liking
B *adv.* **1** (mit Schwierigkeiten) ‹*walk, stand, etc.*› unsteadily; **∼ fahren** drive without [much] confidence **2** (nicht selbstsicher) ‹*smile, look*› diffidently

Unsicherheit *die* **1** (Gefährlichkeit) dangerousness; (Gefahren) dangers *pl.* **2** (Unzuverlässigkeit) uncertainty; unreliability **3** (Zaghaftigkeit) unsureness; (der Schritte o. Ä.) unsteadiness **4** (fehlende Selbstsicherheit) insecurity; lack of [self-]confidence **5** (Ungewissheit) uncertainty **6** (der Arbeitsplätze) insecurity; (des Friedens) instability **7** (Unwägbarkeit) uncertainty

Unsicherheits·faktor *der* element of uncertainty

unsichtbar *Adj.* invisible (**für** to)

Unsinn *der* **1** nonsense; **rede doch keinen ∼!** don't talk nonsense *or* rubbish!; **es wäre ∼ zu glauben, ...** it would be ridiculous to believe ... **2** (Unfug) tomfoolery; fooling about *no art.*; **∼ machen** *od.* **treiben** mess *or* fool about; **mach [ja] keinen ∼:** don't do anything silly; no messing about

unsinnig
A *Adj.* **1** nonsensical ‹*statement, talk, etc.*›; absurd, ridiculous ‹*demand etc.*› **2** (ugs.: übermäßig) terrible (coll.) ‹*rage, fear, thirst, etc.*›
B *adv.* **1** foolishly; stupidly **2** (ugs.: übermäßig) insanely (coll.), terribly (coll.) ‹*expensive*›

Unsitte *die* bad habit; (allgemein verbreitet) bad practice

unsittlich
A *Adj.* indecent
B *adv.* indecently; **sich jmdm. ∼ nähern** make indecent advances to sb.

unsolid[e]
A *Adj.* **1** flimsy ‹*structure*›; shoddy ‹*work, repair*›; (fig.) superficial ‹*education*› **2** (ausschweifend) dissolute ‹*person, life*›
B *adv.* **1** flimsily ‹*made*›; shoddily ‹*executed*› **2** (ausschweifend) **∼ leben** live a dissolute life

unsortiert *Adj.* unsorted

unsozial
A *Adj.* unsocial ‹*policy, measure, rent, etc.*›; antisocial ‹*behaviour*›
B *adv.* unsocially; ‹*behave*› antisocially

unsportlich
A *Adj.* **1** unathletic ‹*person*› **2** (unfair) unsporting, unsportsmanlike ‹*behaviour, play*›
B *adv.* (unfair) in an unsporting way

unsr... ▸**unser**[1]

unsrer·seits ▸**unsererseits**

unsres·gleichen ▸**unseresgleichen**

unsrige /ˈʊnzrɪgə/ *Possessivpron.* (geh. veralt.) **der/die/das ∼:** ours; our one; **das ∼** *od.* **Unsrige** (unser Anteil) our share *or* part; (unser Besitz) what is/was ours; **die ∼n** *od.* **Unsrigen** our family *sing.*

unstatthaft *Adj.* inadmissible

unsterblich
A *Adj.* immortal; (fig.) undying ‹*love*›; **seine Kompositionen sind ∼** (fig.) his compositions will live for ever
B *adv.* (ugs.: außerordentlich) incredibly (coll.); **sich ∼ in jmdn. verlieben** fall madly in love with sb.; **sich ∼ blamieren** make a complete ass of oneself

Unsterbliche *der/die; adj. Dekl.* immortal

Unsterblichkeit *die* immortality

Unstern *der* (geh.) unlucky star; **unter einem ∼ stehen** be ill-starred

unstet (geh.)
A *Adj.* **1** (ruhelos) restless ‹*person, glance, thoughts, etc.*›; unsettled ‹*life*› **2** (unbeständig) vacillating ‹*person, nature*›; (labil) unstable ‹*person, character*›
B *adv.* (ruhelos) restlessly

unstimmig *Adj.* inconsistent [with the facts]; **[in sich] ∼:** inconsistent

Unstimmigkeit *die;* **∼, ∼en** **1** inconsistency **2** (etw. Unstimmiges) discrepancy **3** (Meinungsverschiedenheit) difference [of opinion]

unstreitig
A *Adj.* indisputable
B *adv.* indisputably

unstrittig
A *Adj.* **1** uncontentious **2** ▸**unstreitig A**
B *adv.* ▸**unstreitig B**

unstrukturiert
A *Adj.* unstructured
B *adv.* in an unstructured manner

Unsumme *die* vast *or* huge sum

Unsympath /ˈʊnzʏmpa:t/ *der;* **∼en, ∼en** (ugs.: oft scherzh.) unpleasant character

unsympathisch *Adj.* uncongenial, disagreeable ‹*person*›; unpleasant ‹*characteristic, nature, voice*›; **er ist mir ∼/nicht ∼:** I find him disagreeable/quite likeable; I don't like/I quite like him; **der Plan ist mir ∼:** the plan is not to my liking

unsystematisch
A *Adj.* unsystematic
B *adv.* unsystematically

untad[e]lig
A *Adj.* impeccable ‹*behaviour, reputation, etc.*›; irreproachable ‹*person, life*›
B *adv.* impeccably; irreproachably

Untat *die* misdeed; evil deed

untätig *Adj.* idle; **∼ herumsitzen/zusehen** sit around doing nothing/stand idly by

Untätigkeit *die* idleness; inactivity

untauglich *Adj.* **1** unsuitable ‹*applicant*›; **∼er Versuch** (Rechtsw.) attempt doomed to failure **2** (für Militärdienst) unfit [for service] *postpos.*

unteilbar *Adj.* **1** indivisible **2** (Math.: nicht dividierbar) prime ‹*number*›

unten /ˈʊntn̩/ *Adv.* **1** down; **hier/da ∼:** down here/there; **weiter ∼:** further down; **nach ∼** (auch fig.) downward; **der Weg nach ∼:** the way down; **mit dem Gesicht nach ∼:** face downwards; **von ∼:** from below; **∼ liegen** be down below; (darunter) lie underneath; **[im Bett] ∼ schlafen** sleep in the bottom **2** (im Gebäuden) (im Erdgeschoss) downstairs; (im Hochhaus) on the bottom floor; **nach ∼:** downstairs; **hier ∼:** down here; **der Aufzug fährt nach ∼/kommt von ∼:** the lift (Brit.) *or* (Amer.) elevator is going down/coming up **3** (am unteren Ende, zum unteren Ende hin) at the bottom; **nach ∼ [hin]** towards the bottom; **∼ [links] auf der Seite/im Schrank** at the bottom [left] of the page/cupboard; **in der dritten Zeile von ∼:** on the third line from the bottom; **die Abbildung ∼ links** the illustration bottom left; (als Bildunterschrift) **„∼ [rechts]"** 'below [right]'; (auf einem Karton o. Ä.) **„∼"** 'other side up'; **wo** *od.* **was ist [bei dem Karton] ∼?** which is the bottom [of the cardboard box]?; **sich ∼ herum waschen** wash one's nether regions *or* lower parts (joc.); **∼ am Tisch** (fig.) at the bottom of the table; **100 km weiter ∼ am Fluss** 100 km. further downstream; **zwei Häuser weiter ∼:** two houses further down [the road] **4** (an der Unterseite) underneath **5** (in einer Hierarchie, Rangfolge) **ziemlich weit/ganz ∼ auf der Liste** rather a long way down/right at the bottom of the list **6** ([weiter] hinten im Text) below; **weiter ∼:** further on; below; **wie ∼ angeführt** as stated below; **∼ erwähnt** *od.* **genannt** undermentioned (Brit.); mentioned below *postpos.*; **von den unten Genannten** of the undermentioned (Brit.); of those mentioned below; **∼ stehend** following; given below *postpos.* **7** (ugs.: im Süden) **∼ in Sizilien/im Süden** down in Sicily/in the south; **hier/dort ∼:** down here/there [in the south]; **weiter ∼:** further south

unten·drunter *Adv.* (ugs.) underneath [it/them]

unten-: ∼durch *Adv.* through underneath; *s. auch* **durch B 11**; **∼erwähnt, ∼genannt** ▸**unten 6**; **∼herum, ∼rum**

Adv. (ugs.) down below; **~stehend** ▸**unten 6**

unter /ˈʊntɐ/

A *Präp. mit Dat.* ① (Lage, Standort, Abhängigkeit, Unterordnung) under; **~ jmdm. wohnen** live below sb.; **~ der Devise ...** according to the motto ... ② (weniger, niedriger usw. als) **Mengen ~ 100 Stück** quantities of less than 100; *s. auch* **Durchschnitt 2**; **Gefrierpunkt**; **Preis 1**; **Wert 1** ③ (während) **~ Mittag/Tags/der Woche** (bes. südd.) at *or* around midday/during the day/during the week ④ (modal) **~ Angst/Tränen** in *or* out of fear/in tears; **~ Zittern** trembling; **~ dem Beifall der Menge** applauded by the crowd; *s. auch* **Aufbietung 1**; **Einbeziehung**; **Schmerz 1**; **Verwendung 1** ⑤ (aus einer Gruppe) among[st]; **~ anderem** among[st] other things; **einer ~ 40 Bewerbern** one of *or* among[st] 40 applicants ⑥ (zwischen) among[st]; **~ sich** by themselves; **~ uns gesagt** between ourselves *or* you and me ⑦ (Zustand) **~ Druck/Strom stehen** be under pressure/be live; *s. auch* **Dampf 1**; **leiden 1, 2** ⑧ **~ dem Datum des 1. März 1850** (veralt.) on 1 March 1850

B *Präp. mit Akk.* ① (Richtung, Ziel, Abhängigkeit, Unterordnung) under; **sich ~ einen Baum setzen** sit under a tree; **die Scheuer war bis ~ die Decke mit Heu gefüllt** the barn was full of hay right up to the roof ② (niedriger als) **~ null sinken** drop below zero ③ (zwischen) among[st]; **er geht zu wenig ~ Menschen** he has too little to do with people; **~ Strom/Dampf setzen** switch on/put under steam

C *Adv.* less than; **~ 30 [Jahre alt] sein** be under 30 [years of age]; **ein Kind von ~ 4 Jahren** a child of less than *or* under four years

unter... *Adj.* ① lower; bottom; (ganz unten) bottom; **das ~e/~ste Stockwerk** the lower/bottom storey; **das Unterste zuoberst kehren** (ugs.) turn everything upside down ② lower ‹*Rhine, Nile, etc.*› ③ (in der Rangfolge o. Ä.) lower; lesser ‹*authority*›; **die ~en Klassen der Schule** the junior classes *or* forms of the school ④ (der Oberfläche abgekehrt) **die ~e Seite [von etw.]** the bottom [of sth.]; **auf der ~en Seite** underneath

unter-, Unter-: ~abteilung *die* ① department; ② (Bot.) subdivision; **~arm** *der* ▸ⓘ **S. 435** forearm; **~art** *die* (Biol.) subspecies; **~bau** *der*; *Pl.* **~~ten** ① (Fundament) foundations *pl.*; ② (Grundlage, Basis) foundation; basis; ③ (Sockel) base; ④ (Straßenbau, Eisenb.) roadbed; **~bauch** *der* ▸ⓘ **S. 435** (Anat.) lower abdomen; **~belegt** *Adj.* undersubscribed; half-empty ‹*hotel, hospital, etc.*›; **~belegung** *die* undersubscription; **~belichten** *tr. V.* (Fot.); **ich ~belichte, ~belichtet, ~zubelichten** underexpose; **geistig ~belichtet sein** (fig. salopp) be a bit thick *or* (coll.) dim; **~belichtung** *die* (Fot.) underexposure; **~beschäftigung** *die* (Wirtsch.) underemployment; **~besetzt** *Adj.* understaffed; **~bett** *das* underblanket; **~bewerten** *tr. V.*; **ich ~bewerte, ~bewertet, ~zubewerten** undervalue; underrate; mark ‹*gymnast, skater*› too low; **der Euro wurde ~bewertet** the euro was undervalued; **~bewertung** *die* ▸**~bewerten**: undervaluation; underrating *no pl.*; **~bewusstsein**, ***~bewußtsein** *das* subconscious; **~bezahlen** *tr. V.*; **ich ~bezahle, ~bezahlt, ~zubezahlen** underpay; **~bezahlung** *die* underpayment; **~bieten** *unr. tr. V.* ① (weniger fordern) undercut (**um** by); **etw. ist [im Niveau] kaum noch zu ~bieten** (fig.) sth. is simply rock-bottom [in quality]; ② (bes. Sport) beat ‹*record*›; **jmds. Rekord ~bieten** be faster than sb.; **~binden** *unr. tr. V.* stop; **~bindung** *die* ending; stopping; **~bleiben** *unr. itr. V.*; *mit sein* **etw. ~bleibt** sth. does not occur *or* happen; **das hat zu ~bleiben!** this must stop

Unter·boden *der* (Kfz-W.) underside

Unterboden-: ~schutz *der* underseal; **~wäsche** *die* underbody wash; **der Wagen braucht eine ~wäsche** the underside of the car needs washing

unter·brechen *unr. tr. V.* interrupt; break ‹*journey, silence*›; interrupt, break off ‹*negotiations, studies*›; interrupt, cut off ‹*electricity supply*›; terminate ‹*pregnancy*›; **die Telefonverbindung ist unterbrochen worden** the telephone connection has been cut; **wir sind unterbrochen worden** (im Telefongespräch) we've been cut off

Unter·brechung *die* ▸**unterbrechen**: interruption; break (*Gen.* in); termination

unter·breiten *tr. V.* (geh.) present; **Vorschläge ~**: put suggestions *or* proposals forward

unter|bringen *unr. tr. V.* ① put; **sie konnten die Sachen nicht alle im Kofferraum ~**: they couldn't get *or* fit all the things in the boot (Brit.) *or* (Amer.) trunk; **er wusste nicht, wo er dieses Gesicht ~ sollte** (fig.) he knew the face but couldn't quite place it ② (beherbergen) put up; **die Kinder sind gut untergebracht** the children are well looked after ③ (ugs.) **jmdn. bei einer Firma/beim Film/als Lehrling ~**: get sb. a job in a company/in films/as an apprentice ④ (ugs.: einen Interessenten finden für) place

Unterbringung *die*; **~, ~en** accommodation *no indef. art.*

unter|buttern *tr. V.* (ugs.) ① (unterdrücken) push aside (fig.) ② (zusätzlich verbrauchen) use up

Unter·deck *das* lower deck

***unter·der·hand** ▸**Hand 6**

unter·dessen ▸**inzwischen**

Unter·druck *der*; *Pl.* **~drücke** (Physik, Technik) low pressure

unter·drücken *tr. V.* ① suppress; hold back ‹*comment, question, answer, criticism, etc.*›; **ein unterdrücktes Kichern** suppressed giggling ② (niederhalten) suppress ‹*revolution etc.*›; oppress ‹*minority etc.*›

Unter·drücker *der*, **Unter·drückerin** *die* (abwertend) oppressor

Unterdrückung *die*; **~, ~en** ① (das Unterdrücken) suppression ② (das Unterdrücktwerden, -sein) oppression

unter·durchschnittlich

A *Adj.* below average

B *adv.* below the average; **~ verdienen** have below average earnings; **~ häufig** with below average frequency

unter·einander *Adv.* ① (räumlich) one below the other; **~ liegen** lie *or* be one below *or* underneath the other ② (miteinander) among[st] ourselves/themselves *etc.*; **sie vertrugen sich gut ~**: they had a good relationship with each other; **die Leitungen ~ verbinden** join the wires together; **sich** (*Dat.*) **~ helfen** help each other *or* one another

***untereinander|liegen** *usw.* ▸**untereinander 1**

unter-, Unter-: ~entwickelt *Adj.* underdeveloped; **~ernährt** *Adj.* undernourished; suffering from malnutrition *postpos.*; **~ernährung** *die* malnutrition

unter-, Unter-: ~fahren *unr. tr. V.* drive *or* go under; **~fangen** **A** *unr. refl. V.* (geh.) ① (wagen) dare; venture; ② (sich erdreisten) have the audacity; **B** *unr. tr. V.* (Bauw.) underpin; **~fangen** *das*; **~~s** (geh.) venture; undertaking

unter|fassen *tr. V.* (ugs.) ① (einhaken) **jmdn. ~**: take sb.'s arm; **sie gingen untergefasst** they walked arm in arm ② (stützen) support

unter·fertigen *tr. V.* (Amtsspr.) sign

Unterfertiger *der*; **~s, ~, Unterfertigerin** *die*; **~, ~nen, Unterfertigte** *der/die*; *adj. Dekl.* (Amtsspr.) signatory

unter-, Unter-: ~fordern *tr. V.* **jmdn. [mit etw.] ~fordern** ask *or* demand too little of sb. [with sth.]; **~führen** *tr. V.* (Schrift- u. Druckw.) put ditto marks for; **~führung** *die* underpass; (für Fußgänger) subway (Brit.); [pedestrian] underpass (Amer.)

Unter·forderung *die* making too few demands; **schulische ~**: asking too little of pupils; **~ der Muskulatur** making too little use of the muscles

Unter·funktion *die* ▸ⓘ **S. 439** (Med.) hypofunction; **[eine] ~ der Schilddrüse** thyroid insufficiency

unter·füttern *tr. V.* ① line ‹*garment*› ② (unterlegen) **Fliesen mit einer Dämmschicht ~**: back tiles with a layer of insulating material

Unter·gang *der* ① (Sonnen~, Mond~ usw.) setting ② (von Schiffen) sinking ③ (das Zugrundegehen) decline; (plötzlich) destruction; (von Personen) downfall; (der Welt) end; **der ~ des Römischen Reiches** the fall of the Roman Empire; **er war ihr ~**: he was her ruin; **der Alkohol war ihr ~**: alcohol was the ruin of her *or* was her downfall; **vom ~ bedroht sein** be threatened by destruction; **etw. geht seinem ~ entgegen** sth. is heading for disaster; **etw. ist dem ~ geweiht** sth. is doomed

Untergangs·stimmung *die* feelings *pl.* of doom

unter·gärig /-gɛːrɪç/ *Adj.* bottom-fermented ‹*beer*›; bottom-fermenting ‹*yeast*›

unter·geben *Adj.* subordinate

Untergebene *der/die*; *adj. Dekl.* subordinate; **jmds. ~r sein** be subordinate to sb.; **die ~n des Königs** the subjects of the king

unter-, Unter-: ~|gehen *unr. itr. V.*; *mit sein* ① ‹*sun, star, etc.*› set; ‹*ship*› sink, go down; ‹*person*› drown, go under; (fig.) **sein Stern ist im Untergehen** his star is on the wane; **die Musik ging/seine Worte gingen in dem Lärm ~**: the music was/his words were drowned by *or* lost in the noise; **jmd. geht im Gedränge** *od.* **Gewühl ~**: sb. gets lost in the crowds; ② (zugrunde gehen) come to an end; **davon geht die Welt nicht ~**: it's not the end of the world; **~geordnet** **A** ▸**unterordnen**; **B** *Adj.* ① (weniger wichtig) secondary ‹*role, importance, etc.*›; subordinate ‹*position, post, etc.*›; ② (Sprachw.) subordinate; **~geschoss**, ***~geschoß** *das* basement; **~gestell** *das* ① (Fahrgestell) undercarriage; ② (salopp scherzh.: Beine) legs *pl.*; **~gewicht** *das* ▸ⓘ **S. 315** underweight; **[5 kg] ~gewicht haben** be [5 kilos] underweight; **~gewichtig** *Adj.* underweight

unter-, Unter-: ~gliedern *tr. V.* subdivide; **~gliederung** *die* subdivision; **~graben**[1] *unr. tr. V.* undermine (fig.); **~graben**[2] *unr. tr. V.* dig in; **~grenze** *die* lower limit; **~grund** *der* ① (bes. Landw.) subsoil; ② (Bauw.: Baugrund) foundation; ③ (Farbschicht) background; ④ (bes. Politik) underground; **in den ~grund gehen** go underground; **im ~grund** underground

Untergrund-: ~bahn *die* underground [railway] (Brit.); subway (Amer.); **mit der ~bahn fahren** travel on the *or* by underground (Brit.) *or* (Amer.) subway; **~bewegung** *die* (Politik) underground movement

untergründig *Adj.* hidden ‹*connection, sense*›

Untergrund·tätigkeit *die* unterground activity

unter-, Unter-: ~|haken *tr. V.* (ugs.) **jmdn. ~haken** take sb.'s arm; **mit jmdm. ~gehakt gehen** walk arm in arm with sb.; **sich ~haken** link arms; **~halb** **A** *Adv.* below; **weiter ~halb** further down; **~halb von** below; **B** *Präp. mit Gen.* below; **~halt** *der* ① living; ② (**~haltszahlung**) maintenance; ③ (Instandhaltung[skosten]) upkeep

unter|halten[1] *unr. tr. V.* (ugs.) hold underneath

unter·halten[2]

A *unr. tr. V.* ① (versorgen) support ② (instand halten) maintain ‹*building*› ③ (betreiben) run, keep ‹*car, hotel*› ④ (pflegen) maintain, keep up ‹*contact, correspondence*› ⑤ entertain ‹*guest, audience*›; **ein ~des Buch** an entertaining book

B *unr. refl. V.* ① talk; converse; **mit ihm kann man sich gut ~**: he is easy to talk to; one can have a pleasant conversation with him ② (sich vergnügen) enjoy oneself; **habt ihr euch gut ~?** did you have a good time?

unterhaltsam *Adj.* entertaining

unterhalts-, Unterhalts-: ~anspruch *der* maintenance claim; claim for maintenance; **~berechtigt** *Adj.* entitled to

U

maintenance *postpos.*; **~kosten** *Pl.* maintenance *sing.*; **~pflicht** *die* obligation to pay maintenance; **~pflichtig** *Adj.* obliged to pay maintenance *postpos.*; **~zahlung** *die* maintenance payment

Unterhaltung *die* 1 (Versorgung) support 2 (Instandhaltung) maintenance; upkeep; **etw. ist in der ~ sehr teuer** the maintenance *or* upkeep of sth. is very expensive 3 (Aufrechterhaltung) maintenance 4 (Gespräch) conversation 5 (Zeitvertreib) entertainment; **ich wünsche gute** *od.* **angenehme ~:** enjoy yourself/yourselves; **ich schreibe zu meiner eigenen ~ Geschichten** I write stories for my own enjoyment

Unterhaltungs-: ~elektronik *die* home electronics *sing., no art.* (*for entertainment purposes*); **~kosten** *Pl.* maintenance costs; (Kfz-W.) running costs; **~lektüre** *die* light reading *no art.*; **~literatur** *die* popular fiction; **~musik** *die* light music; **~sendung** *die* entertainment programme; **~wert** *der* entertainment value

unter·handeln *itr. V.* (bes. Politik) negotiate (**über** + *Akk.* on)

Unter·händler *der*, **Unter·händlerin** *die* (bes. Politik) negotiator

Unter·handlung *die* (bes. Politik) negotiation

Unter·haus *das* (Parl.) lower house *or* chamber; (in Großbritannien) House of Commons; Lower House

Unter·hemd *das* vest (Brit.); undershirt (Amer.)

unter·höhlen *tr. V.* 1 hollow out; erode 2 (untergraben) undermine (fig.)

Unter·holz *das* underwood; undergrowth

Unter·hose *die* (Herren~) [under]pants *pl.*; (Damen~) panties; knickers (Brit.); briefs *pl.*; **lange ~n** long underpants; long johns (coll.)

unter·irdisch
A *Adj.* underground; underground, subterranean ‹*river, spring, etc.*›
B *adv.* underground

unterjährig *Adv.* during the year

unter·jochen *tr. V.* subjugate

Unter·jochung *die*; **~:** subjugation

unter|jubeln *tr. V.* (ugs.) **jmdm. etw. ~:** palm sth. off on sb.

unter·kellern *tr. V.* **das Haus ist nicht unterkellert** the house doesn't have a cellar

unter-, Unter-: ~kiefer *der* lower jaw; **~klasse** *die* 1 (Biol.) subclass; 2 (Unterschicht) underclass; **~kleid** *das* [full-length] slip; **~kleidung** *die* underwear; **~|kommen** *unr. itr. V.; mit sein* 1 (Unterkunft finden) find accommodation; 2 (ugs.: eine Stelle finden) find *or* get a job; 3 (ugs.: Interesse finden) **er versuchte, mit seiner Story woanders ~zukommen** he tried to get his story accepted somewhere else; 4 (bes. südd., österr.: begegnen) **so etwas/ein solcher Dummkopf ist mir noch nicht ~gekommen** I've never come across 'anything like it/such a 'fool; **~kommen** *das*; **~~s, ~~:** accommodation *no indef. art.*; **~körper** *der* lower part of the body; **~|kriechen** *unr. itr. V.; mit sein* (ugs.) find shelter; **bei jmdm. ~kriechen** put up at sb.'s (coll.); **~|kriegen** *tr. V.* (ugs.) 1 (entmutigen, besiegen) bring *or* get down; **sich nicht ~kriegen lassen** not let things get one down; 2 ▸**unterbringen 1, 3**

unter-, Unter-: ~kühlen *tr. V.* **jmdn. ~kühlen** reduce sb.'s temperature [below normal]; **er war stark ~kühlt** he was suffering from hypothermia *or* exposure; **~kühlt** *Adj.* dry, factual ‹*style*›; cool ‹*person*›; icy ‹*tone*›; **~kühlung** *die* reduction of body temperature; **er musste mit ~kühlungen in ein Krankenhaus gebracht werden** he was taken to hospital suffering from exposure *or* hypothermia

Unterkunft /ˈʊntɐkʊnft/ *die*; **~, Unterkünfte** /...kʏnftə/ accommodation *no indef. art.*; lodging *no indef. art.*; **eine gute ~ haben** have good accommodation *or* lodgings; **~ und Frühstück** bed and breakfast; **~ und Verpflegung** board and lodging; **die Unterkünfte der Soldaten** the soldiers' quarters

Unter·lage *die* 1 (Schreib~, Matte o. Ä.) pad; (für eine Schreibmaschine usw.) mat; (unter einer Matratze, einem Teppich) underlay; (zum Schlafen usw.) base; **ich brauche eine feste ~ zum Schreiben** I need something to rest my paper on so that I can write; **sorgen Sie für eine gute ~** (ugs. scherzh.) make sure you've got something in your stomach 2 *Pl.* (Akten, Papiere) documents; papers

Unter·länge *die* descender

Unter·lass, *Unter·laß *der*: **in ohne ~:** incessantly

unter·lassen *unr. tr. V.* refrain from [doing]; **Zwischenrufe sind zu ~:** no heckling; **unterlass gefälligst diese Albernheiten** (ugs.) kindly stop being so silly; **warum haben Sie es ~, die Angelegenheit zu melden?** why did you omit *or* fail to report the matter?

Unterlassung *die*; **~, ~en** omission; failure; **~ der Deklination** (Sprachw.) omission of declensional inflexion

Unterlassungs-: ~klage *die* (Rechtsw.) application for a restrictive injunction; **~sünde** *die* (ugs.) sin of omission

Unter·lauf *der* ▸**i S. 267** lower reaches *pl.*

unter·laufen
A *unr. tr. V.; mit sein* 1 occur; **jmdm. ist ein Fehler/Irrtum ~:** sb. made a mistake 2 (ugs.: begegnen) ▸**unterkommen 4**
B *unr. tr. V.* 1 evade; get round 2 (bes. Fuß-, Handball) **einen Gegner ~:** charge an opponent who is in the air and knock him to the ground 3 *mit sein* ‹*skin tissue*› suffuse with blood; **das Auge war mit Blut** *od.* **blutig ~:** the eye was completely bloodshot

unter|legen¹ *tr. V.* 1 (unter etw. legen) put under[neath]; **jmdm. etw. ~:** put sth. under[neath] sb.; **einer Henne** (*Dat.*) **Eier [zum Brüten] ~:** set a hen [on eggs] 2 **einem Text einen anderen Sinn ~:** read another meaning into a text

unter·legen² *tr. V.* 1 (mit Stoff, Watte o. Ä.) underlay (**mit** with) 2 **einem Film Musik ~:** put music to a film; **einer Melodie einen Text ~:** put words to a tune

unter·legen³
A *2. Part. v.* **unterliegen**
B *Adj.* inferior; **jmdm. ~ sein** be inferior to sb. (**an** + *Dat.* in); **jmdm. zahlenmäßig ~ sein** be outnumbered by sb.

Unterlegene *der/die*; *adj. Dekl.* loser

Unterlegenheit *die*; **~, ~en** inferiority

Unterlegenheits·gefühl *das* feeling of inferiority

Unterleg·scheibe *die* washer

Unter-: ~leib *der* 1 ▸**i S. 435** (unterer Bauchteil) lower abdomen; 2 (verhüll.: weibliche Geschlechtsteile) pudenda; **~leibsschmerzen** *Pl.* abdominal pain *sing.*; **~lid** *das* ▸**i S. 435** lower [eye]lid

unter·liegen *unr. itr. V.* 1 *mit sein* (besiegt werden) lose; be beaten *or* defeated; **in einem Kampf ~:** lose a fight; **die unterlegene Mannschaft** the losing team 2 (unterworfen sein) be subject to; **es unterliegt keinem Zweifel, dass ...** there is *or* can be no doubt that ...; **einer Täuschung ~:** be mistaken *or* deceived

Unter·lippe *die* ▸**i S. 435** lower lip

unterm *Präp. + Art.* = **unter dem**

unter·malen *tr. V.* accompany; **etw. mit Musik ~:** accompany sth. with music

Unter·malung *die*; **~, ~en** accompaniment (*Gen.* to)

unter·mauern *tr. V.* 1 (mit Mauern stützen) underpin 2 (mit Argumenten, Fakten absichern) back up; support

Untermauerung *die*; **~, ~en** 1 underpinning; (Mauerwerk) foundation 2 (stützende Argumente) back-up; support

unter-, Unter-: ~|mengen *tr. V.* mix in; **~mensch** *der* (abwertend) 1 (brutaler Mensch) brute; 2 (ns.: minderwertiger Mensch) inferior person; subhuman creature; **~miete** *die* subtenancy; sublease; **bei jmdm. in** *od.* **zur ~miete wohnen** be sb.'s subtenant; lodge with sb.; **jmdn. in** *od.* **zur ~miete nehmen** sublet to sb.; **~mieter** *der*, **~mieterin** *die* subtenant; lodger

unterminieren /ʊntɐmiˈniːrən/ *tr. V.* undermine

unter|mischen *tr. V.* mix in

untern *Präp. + Art.* (ugs.) = **unter den**

unter·nehmen *unr. tr. V.* 1 (durchführen) undertake; make; make ‹*attempt*›; take ‹*steps*› 2 (Unterhaltsames machen, eingreifen) do; **viel zusammen ~:** do many things together; **etwas gegen die Missstände ~:** do something about the bad state of affairs

Unter·nehmen *das*; **~s, ~** 1 (Vorhaben) enterprise; venture; undertaking; (militärische Operation) operation 2 (Firma) enterprise; concern

unternehmend *Adj.* enterprising; active

Unternehmens-: ~berater *der*, **~beraterin** *die* ▸**i S. 113** management consultant; **~form** *die* form *or* type of enterprise; **~führung** *die*, **~leitung** *die* management; **~kultur** *die* corporate culture; company culture; **~philosophie** *die* corporate philosophy; company philosophy; **~pleite** *die* company bankruptcy; **~politik** *die* management policy; **~sprecher** *der*, **~sprecherin** *die* company spokesman/spokeswoman

Unternehmer *der*; **~s, ~, Unternehmerin** *die*; **~, ~nen** employer; (in der Industrie) industrialist

unternehmerisch
A *Adj.* entrepreneurial
B *adv.* ‹*think*› in an entrepreneurial *or* business-like way

Unternehmerschaft *die*; **~, ~en** employers *pl.*

Unternehmertum *das*; **~s** 1 employers *pl.* 2 (das Unternehmersein) enterprise *no art.*

Unternehmung *die*; **~, ~en** ▸**Unternehmen**

Unternehmungs·geist *der* spirit of enterprise; **er war voller ~:** he was full of initiative

unternehmungs·lustig *Adj.* active; **sie ist sehr ~:** she is always out doing things

unter-, Unter-: ~offizier *der* 1 non-commissioned officer; **~offizier vom Dienst** duty NCO; 2 ▸**i S. 44** (Dienstgrad) corporal; **~ordnen** A *tr. V.* subordinate; **jmdm./einem Ministerium ~geordnet sein** be [made] subordinate to sb./a ministry; B *refl. V.* **sich [anderen] nicht ~ordnen können** not be able to accept a subordinate role; **die Politik hat sich der Moral ~zuordnen** politics has to be subordinated to morality; **~ordnend** *Adj.* (Sprachw.) subordinating ‹*conjunction*›; **~ordnung** *die* 1 subordination; 2 (Sprachw.) hypotaxis; 3 (Biol.: ~gruppe) suborder; **~pfand** *das* (geh.) pledge (**für** of); **~|pflügen** *tr. V.* plough in *or* under; **~prima** *die* (Schulw. veralt.) eighth year (*of a Gymnasium*); **~primaner** *der*, **~primanerin** *die* (Schulw. veralt.) pupil in the eighth year (*of a Gymnasium*); **~privilegiert** *Adj.* (geh.) underprivileged; **~privilegierte** *der/die*; *adj. Dekl.* (geh.) underprivileged person; **die ~privilegierten** the underprivileged; **~punkt** *der* 1 subsidiary point; 2 (unter einem Buchstaben o. Ä.) dot underneath

unter·queren *tr. V.* cross under

unter·reden *refl. V.* (geh.) confer (**mit** with)

Unterredung *die*; **~, ~en** discussion; **er bat ihn um eine ~:** he asked to see him to discuss something [with him]

unter·repräsentiert *Adj.* under-represented

-unterricht *der*: **Geschichts-/Musik-** *usw.* **~:** history/music *etc.* teaching; (Unterrichtsstunde) history/music *etc.* lesson; *s. auch* **Englischunterricht**

Unterricht /ˈʊntɐrɪçt/ *der*; **~[e]s, ~e** instruction; (Schul~) teaching; (Schulstunden) classes *pl.*; lessons *pl.*; **der ~ ist beendet** classes *or* lessons are over; **jmdm. ~ [in Musik usw.] geben** give sb. [music *etc.*] lessons; teach sb. [music]; **bei jmdm. ~ [in Russisch] nehmen** have [Russian] lessons from sb.; **zu**

spät zum ~ kommen be late for class

unterrichten
A *tr. V.* [1] (lehren) teach; **er unterrichtet Englisch** he teaches Englisch; **sie unterrichtet ihre Kinder im Malen** she is teaching her children how to paint [2] (informieren) inform (**über** + *Akk.* of, about); **ich bin bestens/schlecht unterrichtet** I am fully/not well informed
B *itr. V.* (Unterricht geben) teach
C *refl. V.* (sich informieren) inform oneself (**über** + *Akk.* about)

unterrichtlich *Adj.* instructional ‹*purpose, problem*›; teaching ‹*success, work*›

unterrichts-, Unterrichts-: ~einheit *die* (Päd.) teaching unit; **~fach** *das* subject; **~frei** *Adj.* free ‹*day, hour*›; **der Samstag ist ~frei** there are no lessons on Saturday; **nächsten Samstag haben wir ~frei** there is no school this Saturday; **~methode** *die* teaching method; **~stoff** *der* subject matter; **~stunde** *die* lesson; period

Unterrichtung *die;* ~, **~en** instruction; (Information) information

Unter·rock *der* [1] [half] slip [2] ▸ **Unterkleid**

unter|rühren *tr. V.* stir in

unters *Präp.* + *Art.* = **unter das**

unter·sagen *tr. V.* forbid; prohibit; **der Arzt untersagte ihm, Alkohol zu trinken** the doctor ordered him not to drink any alcohol; **Rauchen ist strengstens untersagt** smoking is strictly prohibited

Unter·satz *der* ▸ **Untersetzer**

unter-, Unter-: ~schätzen *tr. V.* underestimate ‹*amount, effect, meaning, distance, etc.*›; underrate ‹*writer, performer, book, performance, talent, ability*›; **~schätzung** *die* underestimation; **~scheidbar** *Adj.* distinguishable; **~scheiden** A *unr. tr. V.* distinguish; **Weizen von Roggen nicht ~scheiden können** not be able to tell the difference between wheat and rye *or* tell wheat from rye; **die Zwillinge sind kaum zu ~scheiden** you can hardly tell the twins apart; B *unr. itr. V.* distinguish; differentiate; **zwischen Richtigem und Falschem ~scheiden** tell the difference between right and wrong; C *unr. refl. V.* differ (**durch** in, **von** from); **sich durch nichts ~scheiden** be in no way different; **sich dadurch ~scheiden, dass ...** differ in that ...; **in diesem Punkt ~scheiden sich die Parteien überhaupt nicht** on this point there is no difference at all between the parties; **~scheidung** *die* (Vorgang) differentiation; (Resultat) distinction

Unterscheidungs-: ~merkmal *das* distinguishing feature; **~vermögen** *das* ability to distinguish; discernment

unter-, Unter-: ~schenkel *der* ▸ ❶ **S. 435** shank; lower leg; **~schicht** *die* (Soziol.) lower class; **der ~schicht angehören** be a member of the lower classes *pl.*; **~|schieben¹** *unr. tr. V.* push under[neath]

unter·schieben² *unr. tr. V.* [1] (heimlich zuschieben) **jmdm. etw. ~:** foist sth. on sb. [2] (unterstellen) **jmdm. etw. ~:** attribute sth. falsely to sb.

Unter·schied *der;* **~[e]s, ~e** difference; **es lebe der kleine ~!** (ugs. scherzh.) vive la petite différence!; **das ist ein ~ wie Tag und Nacht** it's like the difference between black and white; **es ist [schon] ein [großer] ~, ob ...** it makes a [big] difference whether ...; **bei der Beurteilung der Schüler ~e machen** use different methods when assessing the pupils; **ohne ~ der Rasse/des Geschlechts** without regard to *or* discrimination against race/sex; **im ~ zu ihm/zum ~ von ihm** in contrast to him; **zwischen Arbeit und Arbeit ist noch ein ~** (ugs.) there is work and there is work (coll.)

unter·schieden *Adj.* different

unterschiedlich
A *Adj.* different; (uneinheitlich) variable; varying
B *adv.* **[sehr/ganz] ~:** in [very/quite] different ways; **~ hohe Erträge** yields of varying amount; **etw. sehr ~ einschätzen** give greatly varying estimates of sth.

Unterschiedlichkeit *die;* ~, **~en** difference (*Gen.* between); (Uneinheitlichkeit) variability

unterschieds·los
A *Adj.* uniform; equal ‹*treatment*›
B *adv.* ‹*treat*› equally; (ohne Benachteiligung) without discrimination

unter|schlagen¹ *unr. tr. V.* [1] cross ‹*legs*›; fold ‹*arms*› [2] ▸ **unterrühren**

unter·schlagen²
A *unr. tr. V.* embezzle, misappropriate ‹*money, funds, etc.*›; (unterdrücken) intercept ‹*letter*›; withhold, suppress ‹*fact, news, information, etc.*›
B *unr. itr. V.* **er hat ~:** he embezzled money

Unterschlagung *die;* ~, **~en** ▸ **unterschlagen²**: embezzlement; misappropriation; withholding; suppression; **~en begehen** embezzle sums of money/funds *etc.*

Unter·schlupf *der;* **~[e]s, ~e** shelter; (Versteck) hiding place; hideout

unter|schlupfen (südd.), **unter|schlüpfen** *itr. V.; mit sein* (ugs.) hide out; (Obdach finden) take shelter (**vor** + *Dat.* from)

unter·schneiden *unr. tr. V.* ([Tisch]tennis) chop

Unter·schnitt *der* ([Tisch]tennis) back spin; underspin

unter·schreiben
A *unr. itr. V.* sign; **mit vollem Namen ~:** sign one's full name
B *unr. tr. V.* sign; **diese Behauptung kann ich nicht ~** (fig. ugs.) I cannot subscribe to *or* approve this statement

unter·schreiten *unr. tr. V.* fall below; **wir haben die veranschlagten Summen/Kosten um 2 Prozent unterschritten** we stayed 2 per cent below the estimated amounts/costs

Unter·schrift *die* [1] signature; **seine ~ unter etw.** (*Akk.*) **setzen** put one's signature to sth.; sign sth. [2] (Bild~) caption

Unterschriften-: ~aktion *die* petition; **~liste** *die* list of signatures; **~mappe** *die* signature folder

unter·schriftlich *Adv.* by one's signature; **~ bestätigt** signed

unterschrifts-: ~berechtigt *Adj.* **~berechtigt sein** be authorized to sign; have power to sign; **~reif** *Adj.* ready to be signed *pred.*; **ein ~reifer Vertrag** a contract which is ready to be signed

unterschwellig /-ʃvɛlɪç/
A *Adj.* subliminal
B *adv.* subliminally

unter-, Unter-: ~see·boot *das* submarine; **~seite** *die* underside; (eines Stoffes) wrong side; **~sekunda** *die* (Schulw. veralt.) sixth year (*of a Gymnasium*); **~sekundaner** *der,* **~sekundanerin** *die* (Schulw. veralt.) pupil in the sixth year (*of a Gymnasium*); **~|setzen** *tr. V.* put underneath; **~setzer** *der* mat; (für Gläser) coaster; (für Bügeleisen) stand

untersetzt *Adj.* stocky

unter|sinken *unr. itr. V.; mit sein* sink

unter·spülen *tr. V.* undermine and wash away

unterst... ▸ **unter...**

Unter·stand *der* [1] (Schutzbunker) dugout [2] (Unterschlupf) shelter

unter|stehen¹ *unr. itr. V.; südd., österr., schweiz. mit sein* take shelter

unter|stehen²
A *unr. itr. V.* **jmdm. ~:** be subordinate *or* answerable to sb.; **jmdm. untersteht eine Abteilung** sb. is responsible for a department; **diese Ämter ~ dem Ministerium** these offices are under the control of *or* come under the ministry; **ständiger Kontrolle ~:** be under constant supervision
B *unr. refl. V.* dare; **untersteh dich!** [don't] you dare!; **was ~ Sie sich!** how dare you!

unter|stellen¹
A *tr. V.* [1] (zur Aufbewahrung) keep; store ‹*furniture*› [2] (unter etw.) put underneath
B *refl. V.* take shelter

unter·stellen² *tr. V.* [1] (jmdm. unterordnen, übertragen) **jmdm. ein Sachgebiet/eine Abteilung ~:** put sb. in charge of a subject/a department; **die Behörde ist dem Ministerium unterstellt** the office is under the ministry [2] (annehmen, vermuten) assume; suppose; **ich unterstelle [einmal], dass ...** I'll [first of all] assume that ... [3] (unterschieben) **jmdm. böse Absichten/ schlechte Motive** *usw.* **~:** insinuate *or* imply that sb.'s intentions/motives are bad; **was ~ Sie mir?** what are you trying to accuse me of?

Unter·stellung *die* [1] subordination (**unter** + *Akk.* to) [2] (falsche Behauptung) insinuation

unter·steuern *itr. V.* (Kfz-W.) understeer

unter·streichen *unr. tr. V.* [1] underline [2] (hervorheben) emphasize; **das kann ich nur ~!** I can only agree with that!

Unter·streichung *die;* ~, **~en** [1] underlining [2] (das Betonen) emphasizing

Unter-: ~strich *der* (DV) underscore; **~stufe** *die* (Schulw.) lower school

unter·stützen *tr. V.* (auch DV) support; **vom Staat unterstützte Einrichtungen** state-funded institutions; **das Mittel unterstützt den Heilungsprozess** the medicine promotes the healing process

Unter·stützung *die* [1] support; **der Plan fand bei vielen ~:** the plan was supported by many [2] (finanzielle Hilfe) allowance; (für Arbeitslose) [unemployment] benefit *no art.*; **staatliche ~:** state aid

Unterstützungs·empfänger *der,* **Unterstützungs·empfängerin** *die* person receiving [unemployment] benefit/an allowance

unter·suchen *tr. V.* [1] (zu erkennen suchen) examine [2] (überprüfen) test (**auf** + *Akk.* for) [3] (ärztlich) examine; **sich ärztlich ~ lassen** have a medical examination *or* check-up; **jmdn. auf seine Arbeitsfähigkeit [hin] ~:** test sb.'s fitness for work [4] (aufzuklären suchen) investigate; **einen Fall gerichtlich ~:** try a case [in court] [5] (durchsuchen) search (**auf** + *Akk.*, **nach** for)

Untersuchung *die;* ~, **~en** [1] ▸ **untersuchen**: examination; test; investigation; search [2] (wissenschaftliche Arbeit) study

Untersuchungs-: ~ausschuss, *~ausschuß *der* investigating committee; (für Unfälle usw.) committee of inquiry; **~ergebnis** *das* (der Polizei, des Gerichts) results *pl.* of an/the investigation; (Med.) results *pl.* of a/the test; **~gefängnis** *das* prison (*for people awaiting trial*); **~haft** *die* imprisonment *or* detention while awaiting trial; **jmdn. in ~haft nehmen** commit sb. for trial; **in ~haft sein** *od.* **sitzen** be held on remand; **~häftling** *der* prisoner awaiting trial; remand prisoner; **~kommission** *die* ▸ **~ausschuss**; **~zimmer** *das* examination room

unter·tags *Adv.* (bes. österr.) during the day

untertan /-ta:n/ *Adj.* **in sich** (*Dat.*) **jmdn./etw. ~ machen** (geh.) subjugate sb./dominate sth.; **jmdm./einer Sache ~ sein** (veralt.) be dominated by sb./be subject to sth.

Untertan *der;* **~s** *od.* **~en, ~en** (hist.) subject

Untertanen·geist *der* (abwertend) servile *or* subservient spirit

untertänig /-tɛ:nɪç/
A *Adj.* subservient; **Ihr ~ster Diener** (veralt.) your most obedient *or* humble servant
B *adv.* subserviently

Untertanin *die;* ~, **~nen** ▸ **Untertan**

unter·tariflich
A *Adj.* ‹*pay, wages, salaries, appointments*› below agreed rates; ‹*work*› paid less than the agreed rate
B *adv.* ‹*pay*› less than the agreed rate

Unter·tasse *die* saucer; **fliegende ~** (fig.) flying saucer

unter|tauchen
A *itr. V.; mit sein* [1] (im Wasser) dive [under] [2] (verschwinden) disappear [3] (unerkannt leben) disappear; go underground; **er musste vor der Gestapo [bei Freunden] ~:** he had [to seek

U

shelter with friends] to hide from the Gestapo
B *tr. V.* duck

Unter·teil *das od. der* bottom part

unter·teilen *tr. V.* 1 (aufteilen) divide 2 (einteilen, gliedern) subdivide

Unter·teilung *die;* ~, ~en [sub]division

Unter·temperatur *die* subnormal temperature of the body; **der Patient hat ~:** the patient's temperature is below normal

unter-, Unter-: ~tertia *die* (Schulw. veralt.) fourth year (*of a Gymnasium*); **~tertianer** *der,* **~tertianerin** *die* (Schulw. veralt.) pupil in the fourth year (*of a Gymnasium*); **~titel** *der* 1 subtitle; 2 (Bildunterschrift) caption; **~ton** *der; Pl.* **~töne** (auch Physik, Musik) undertone; **~tourig** /-tu:rıç/ (Technik) A *Adj.* ‹*driving*› with *or* at low revs (coll.). B *adv.* at low revs (coll.)

unter·treiben *unr. itr. V.* play things down

Untertreibung *die;* ~, ~en understatement

unter·tunneln *tr. V.* tunnel under; tunnel through *or* under ‹*mountain*›

unter-, Unter-: ~vermieten *tr., itr. V.* sublet; **~vermietung** *die* subletting; **~versichern** *tr. V.* under-insure; **~versicherung** *die* under-insurance; **~versorgen** *tr. V.* under-supply; **ärztlich ~versorgt sein** not be given proper medical treatment; **~versorgung** *die* under-supply (**mit** of); **die ~versorgung der Zellen mit Sauerstoff** the under-supply of the cells with oxygen

unter·wandern *tr. V.* infiltrate; **kommunistisch unterwandert** infiltrated by communists

Unter·wanderung *die* infiltration *no indef. art.*

unterwärts /ˈʊntɐvɛrts/ *Adv.* (ugs.) underneath

Unter·wäsche *die* underwear

Unter·wasser-: ~jagd *die* (Tauchsport) underwater harpooning; **~massage** *die* underwater massage

unterwegs *Adv.* 1 (auf dem Wege irgendwohin) on the *or* one's/its way; **er ist den ganzen Tag/geschäftlich viel ~:** he is away all day/a great deal on business; **bei ihr ist etwas Kleines ~** (ugs.) she is expecting [a happy event] 2 (auf, während der Reise) on the way; **sie waren vier Wochen ~:** they travelled for four weeks; the journey took them four weeks; **sie schickten eine Karte von ~:** they sent a card while they were away 3 (nicht zu Hause) out [and about]

unter·weisen *unr. tr. V.* (geh.) instruct (**in** + *Dat.* in)

Unter·weisung *die* instruction

Unter·welt *die;* ~ (griech. Myth., Verbrechermilieu) underworld

unter·weltlich *Adj.* underworld *attrib.*

unter·werfen
A *unr. tr. V.* 1 subjugate ‹*people, country*› 2 (unterziehen) subject (*Dat.* to); **jmds. Post einer genauen Kontrolle ~:** make a close scrutiny of sb.'s correspondence 3 (abhängig machen) **jmdm./einer Sache unterworfen sein** be subject to sb./sth.
B *unr. refl. V.* **sich [jmdm./einer Sache] ~:** submit [to sb./sth.]

Unterwerfung *die;* ~, ~en 1 (das Unterwerfen) subjugation (**unter** + *Akk.* to) 2 (das Sichunterwerfen) submission (**unter** + *Akk.* to)

unterwürfig /-vʏrfıç/ (abwertend)
A *Adj.* obsequious
B *adv.* obsequiously

Unterwürfigkeit *die;* ~ (abwertend) obsequiousness

unter·zeichnen
A *tr. V.* sign
B *refl. V.* (veralt.) sign

Unter·zeichner *der,* **Unter·zeichnerin** *die,* **Unterzeichnete** *der/die; adj. Dekl.* (Amtsspr.) signatory

Unterzeichnung *die* signing

Unter·zeug *das* (ugs.) underwear

unter|ziehen¹ *unr. tr. V.* 1 put ‹*underwear, jumper, etc.*› on underneath 2 (Kochk.: vermengen) fold in

unter·ziehen²
A *unr. refl. V.* **sich einer Sache** (*Dat.*) **~:** undertake sth.; **sich einer Operation** (*Dat.*) **~:** undergo *or* have an operation
B *unr. tr. V.* **etw. einer Untersuchung/Überprüfung/Reinigung** (*Dat.*) **~:** examine/check/clean sth.

Untiefe *die* 1 (seichte Stelle) shallow 2 (große Tiefe) depth

Untier *das* monster; **dieses ~ von einer Katze** (scherzh.) this beast of a cat

untilgbar *Adj.* (geh.) lasting; indelible ‹*impression, memory*›

Untote *der/die* zombie; (Vampir) vampire; **die ~n** the undead

untragbar *Adj.* unbearable; intolerable; **wirtschaftlich/finanziell ~:** no longer economically/financially viable

Untragbarkeit *die;* ~: intolerableness

untrainiert *Adj.* untrained; (nicht mehr trainiert) out of training *postpos.*

untrennbar *Adj.* inseparable

untreu *Adj.* 1 disloyal; **jmdm. ~ werden** be disloyal to sb.; **du bist uns ~ geworden** (scherzh.) you've abandoned us (joc.); **sich selbst ~ werden** be untrue to oneself; **seinen Grundsätzen ~ werden** abandon one's principles 2 (in der Ehe, Liebe) unfaithful; **jmdm. ~ werden** be unfaithful to sb.

Untreue *die* 1 disloyalty 2 (in der Ehe, Liebe) unfaithfulness 3 (Rechtsspr.: Veruntreuung) embezzlement

untröstlich *Adj.* inconsolable; **ich bin ~, dass ...** I am extremely sorry that ...

untrüglich *Adj.* unmistakable

untüchtig *Adj.* incompetent

Untugend *die* bad habit

untunlich *Adj.* (veralt.) impracticable; not sensible; (unklug) imprudent

untypisch
A *Adj.* untypical (**für** of)
B *adv.* unusually

unüberbietbar *Adj.* unparalleled

unüberbrückbar *Adj.* irreconcilable ‹*differences, contradictions*›

unüberhörbar *Adj.* unmistakable

unüberlegt
A *Adj.* rash
B *adv.* rashly

Unüberlegtheit *die;* ~, ~en 1 rashness 2 (unüberlegte Handlung) rash act

unüberschaubar ▸**unübersehbar A 2, B**

unübersehbar
A *Adj.* 1 (offenkundig) conspicuous; obvious 2 (sehr groß) enormous; immense
B *adv.* (sehr) extremely

unübersetzbar *Adj.* untranslatable

unübersichtlich
A *Adj.* unclear; confusing ‹*arrangement*›; blind ‹*bend*›; broken ‹*country etc.*›; (fig.) confused ‹*affair, matter, conditions, etc.*›
B *adv.* unclearly; confusingly ‹*arranged*›

Unübersichtlichkeit *die;* ~: **die ~ der Karte/des Geländes** the unclear map/broken country

unübertragbar *Adj.* non-transferable; not transferable *pred.*

unübertrefflich
A *Adj.* superb
B *adv.* superbly

unübertroffen *Adj.* unsurpassed

unüberwindbar, unüberwindlich *Adj.* insuperable, insurmountable ‹*problem, fear, mistrust, etc.*›; invincible ‹*opponent*›

unüblich *Adj.* not usual *or* customary *pred.*; unusual

unumgänglich *Adj.* [absolutely] necessary

Unumgänglichkeit *die;* ~: absolute necessity

unumkehrbar /*auch:* ˈ----/
A *Adj.* irreversible
B *adv.* irreversibly

unumschränkt /ˈʊnlʊmʃrɛŋkt/ *Adj.* absolute; **~ herrschen** have absolute rule

unumstritten *Adj.* undisputed

unumwunden /ˈʊnlʊmvʊndn̩/
A *Adj.* frank
B *adv.* frankly; openly

ununterbrochen
A *Adj.* incessant
B *adv.* incessantly

unveränderbar, unveränderlich *Adj.* unchangeable, unchanging ‹*law, principle*›; constant ‹*quantity etc.*›; permanent ‹*mark, scar*›; (nicht zu verändern) unalterable

Unveränderlichkeit *die;* ~ ▸**unveränderlich:** unchangeableness; unchangingness; constancy; permanence; unalterableness

unverändert *Adj.* unchanged ‹*appearance, weather, condition*›; unaltered, unrevised ‹*edition etc.*›; **in seinem Aussehen war er ~:** he had not changed in [his] appearance

unverantwortlich
A *Adj.* irresponsible
B *adv.* irresponsibly

Unverantwortlichkeit *die;* ~: irresponsibility

unverarbeitet *Adj.* 1 raw, unprocessed ‹*material*›; crude ‹*iron, oil, etc.*› 2 (nicht bewältigt) raw ‹*impression*›; raw, undigested ‹*thoughts*›

unveräußerlich *Adj.* 1 (geh.) inalienable ‹*rights, principles*› 2 (unverkäuflich) ‹*property*› not for sale

unverbaubar *Adj.* ‹*view*› that cannot be spoiled *or* obstructed

unverbesserlich *Adj.* incorrigible

unverbildet *Adj.* unspoiled

unverbindlich
A *Adj.* 1 (nicht bindend) not binding *pred.*; without obligation *postpos.*; ‹*information*› without guarantee of correctness 2 (zurückhaltend, reserviert) non-committal ‹*answer, words*›; detached, impersonal ‹*attitude, person*›
B *adv.* ‹*send, reserve*› without obligation

Unverbindlichkeit *die;* ~, ~en 1 (eines Angebots usw.) freedom from obligation; (einer Person) detached *or* impersonal manner; **die ~ der Auskunft** the fact that the information is not guaranteed correct 2 (unverbindliche Äußerung) non-committal remark

unverbleit *Adj.* unleaded

unverblümt /ʊnfɛɐ̯ˈbly:mt/
A *Adj.* blunt; undisguised, open ‹*distrust*›
B *adv.* bluntly

unverbraucht *Adj.* untouched; unspent ‹*energy*›; fresh ‹*air*›; **sie ist noch jung und ~:** she is still young and full of energy

unverbrüchlich /ʊnfɛɐ̯ˈbrʏçlıç/ *Adj.* (geh.) inviolable; steadfast

unverbürgt *Adj.* unconfirmed ‹*report, news, etc.*›

unverdächtig
A *Adj.* free from suspicion *postpos*
B *adv.* in a way that does/did not arouse suspicion

unverdaulich *Adj.* indigestible

unverdaut *Adj.* undigested

unverdient
A *Adj.* undeserved ‹*luck, praise*›; undeserved, unjust ‹*accusation, punishment, etc.*›
B *adv.* undeservedly

unverdientermaßen *Adv.* undeservedly

unverdorben *Adj.* unspoilt

Unverdorbenheit *die;* ~ (von Früchten, Speisen usw.) freshness; (sittliche ~) innocence

unverdrossen
A *Adj.* undeterred; (unverzagt) undaunted
B *adv.* **~ weitermachen** carry on undaunted

unverdünnt *Adj.* undiluted; **er trinkt Whisky ~:** he drinks whisky neat

unverehelicht *Adj.* (bes. Amtsspr.) unmarried

unvereinbar *Adj.* incompatible (**mit** with)

Unvereinbarkeit *die;* ~: incompatibility (**mit** with)

unverfälscht
A *Adj.* genuine; unadulterated ‹*wine etc.*›; pure

u

‹dialect›; unaltered ‹custom, text›
B *adv.* in pure/unaltered form

unverfänglich *Adj.* harmless

unverfroren
A *Adj.* insolent; impudent
B *adv.* insolently; impudently

Unverfrorenheit *die;* ~, ~en 1 insolence; impudence 2 (Äußerung, Handlung) insolent remark; impertinence

unvergänglich *Adj.* immortal ‹fame›; unchanging ‹beauty›; abiding ‹recollection›

Unvergänglichkeit *die* ▸ **unvergänglich**: immortality; unchangingness; abidingness

unvergessen *Adj.* unforgotten

unvergesslich, *unvergeßlich
A *Adj.* unforgettable; **dieses Erlebnis wird mir ~ bleiben** *od.* **sein** I shall never forget this experience
B *adv.* unforgettably

unvergleichbar *Adj.* incomparable (*Dat.* to, with)

unvergleichlich
A *Adj.* incomparable (*Dat.* to, with)
B *adv.* incomparably

unverhältnismäßig *Adv.* unusually

unverheiratet *Adj.* unmarried

unverhofft /ˈʊnfɛɐ̯hɔft/
A *Adj.* unexpected
B *adv.* unexpectedly; **~ kommt oft** (Spr.) always expect the unexpected

unverhohlen
A *Adj.* unconcealed
B *adv.* openly

unverhüllt
A *Adj.* 1 (ohne Umhüllung) uncovered 2 (unverhohlen) unconcealed
B *adv.* openly

unverkäuflich *Adj.* 1 (nicht zum Verkauf bestimmt) **~e Ausstellungsstücke** display items that are not for sale; **diese Vase ist ~:** this vase is not for sale; **~es Muster** free sample 2 (nicht absetzbar) unsaleable

unverkennbar
A *Adj.* unmistakable
B *adv.* unmistakably

unverkrampft
A *Adj.* relaxed
B *adv.* in a relaxed manner; **~ locker** free and easy

unverlangt
A *Adj.* unsolicited ‹manuscript, photograph›
B *adv.* **~ eingesandt** unsolicited

unvermählt *Adj.* (geh.) unmarried; unwedded

unvermeidbar *Adj.* unavoidable

unvermeidlich *Adj.* 1 (nicht vermeidbar) unavoidable; (spött.: obligatorisch) inevitable; **sich ins Unvermeidliche fügen** submit to *or* accept the inevitable 2 (sich als Folge ergebend) inevitable

unvermindert *Adj., adv.* undiminished

unvermittelt
A *Adj.* sudden; abrupt
B *adv.* suddenly; abruptly

Unvermögen *das* lack of ability; **jmds. ~, etw. zu tun** sb.'s inability to do sth.

unvermögend *Adj.* without means *postpos.*

unvermutet
A *Adj.* unexpected
B *adv.* unexpectedly

Unvernunft *die* stupidity

unvernünftig
A *Adj.* stupid; foolish
B *adv.* **er raucht/trinkt ~ viel** he smokes/drinks more than is good for him

unveröffentlicht *Adj.* unpublished

unverpackt *Adj.* unpacked; unwrapped

unverputzt *Adj.* unplastered

unverrichtet *Adj.* *in* **~er Dinge** without having achieved anything

unverrückbar
A *Adj.* unshakeable; immovable; unalterable ‹fact, truth›
B *adv.* unshakeably; immovably; **mein Entschluss steht ~ fest** my decision is absolutely final

unverschämt
A *Adj.* 1 (respektlos, impertinent) impertinent, impudent ‹person, manner, words, etc.›; barefaced, blatant ‹lie› 2 (ugs.: sehr groß) outrageous ‹price, luck, etc.›
B *adv.* 1 impertinently; impudently; ‹lie› barefacedly; blatantly 2 (ugs.: sehr) outrageously ‹expensive›; **du siehst ~ gut aus** you are looking disgustingly well (joc.)

Unverschämtheit *die;* ~, ~en 1 impertinence; impudence; (einer Lüge) barefacedness; blatancy 2 (Äußerung, Handlung) [piece of] impertinence; **das ist eine ~!** that's outrageous!

unverschleiert
A *Adj.* unveiled; (fig.) undisguised ‹criticism, attempt›; naked ‹terror›; unvarnished ‹truth›
B *adv.* (fig.) ‹portray, show› openly; candidly

unverschlossen *Adj.* unlocked; unsealed ‹letter›

unverschuldet *Adj.* **ein ~er Verkehrsunfall** an accident which happened through no fault of one's own; **eine ~e Notlage** a plight which is no fault of one's own

unverschuldetermaßen *Adv.* through no fault of one's own

unversehens *Adv.* suddenly

unversehrt *Adj.* unscathed; unhurt; (unbeschädigt) undamaged

Unversehrtheit *die;* ~: intactness; **körperliche ~:** freedom from bodily harm

unversöhnlich *Adj.* irreconcilable

Unversöhnlichkeit *die* irreconcilability

unversorgt *Adj.* ‹children, family, etc.› unprovided for

Unverstand *der* foolishness; stupidity; **so ein ~!** what foolishness *or* stupidity!

unverstanden *Adj.* misunderstood

unverständig *Adj.* without understanding *postpos.*; ignorant ‹child›

Unverständigkeit *die* lack of understanding

unverständlich *Adj.* incomprehensible; (undeutlich) unclear ‹pronunciation, presentation, etc.›; **es ist [mir] ~, warum er nicht kommt** I cannot *or* do not understand why he hasn't come

Unverständlichkeit *die* incomprehensibility

Unverständnis *das* lack of understanding

unverstellt *Adj.* normal ‹voice›; unfeigned, genuine ‹joy, passion, etc.›

unversteuert *Adj.* untaxed ‹earnings etc.›; duty-free ‹goods, cigarettes›

unversucht *in* **nichts ~ lassen** try everything; leave no stone unturned

unverträglich *Adj.* 1 (unbekömmlich) indigestible; unsuitable ‹medicine› 2 (streitsüchtig) quarrelsome 3 (nicht harmonierend) incompatible ‹blood groups, medicines, transplant tissue›

Unverträglichkeit *die* ▸ **unverträglich**: indigestibility; unsuitability; quarrelsomeness; incompatibility

unvertraut *Adj.* unfamiliar

unvertretbar *Adj.* unjustifiable

unverwandt
A *Adj.* fixed; steadfast ‹gaze›
B *adv.* fixedly; steadfastly; **jmdn. ~ anstarren** stare at sb. with a fixed gaze

unverwechselbar *Adj.* unmistakable; distinctive

Unverwechselbarkeit *die* distinctiveness

unverwundbar *Adj.* invulnerable

Unverwundbarkeit *die* invulnerability

unverwüstlich *Adj.* indestructible; (fig.) irrepressible ‹nature, humour›; robust ‹health›

Unverwüstlichkeit *die;* ~ ▸ **unverwüstlich**: indestructibility; irrepressible nature/humour; robustness

unverzagt *Adj.* undaunted

unverzeihlich *Adj.* unforgivable; inexcusable

unverzichtbar *Adj.* indispensable, essential ‹goods, requirements, etc.›; essential ‹measure›; inalienable ‹right›

unverzinslich (Bankw.) interest-free

unverzollt *Adj.* undeclared; **~e Ware** goods on which duty has not been paid

unverzüglich
A *Adj.* prompt; immediate
B *adv.* promptly; immediately

unvollendet *Adj.* unfinished

unvollkommen
A *Adj.* 1 imperfect 2 (unvollständig) incomplete ‹collection, account, etc.›
B *adv.* 1 imperfectly; **sie beherrscht diese Arbeit nur ~:** she does not have perfect *or* complete command of this work 2 (unvollständig) incompletely

Unvollkommenheit *die* 1 (Fehlerhaftigkeit) imperfectness 2 (Unvollständigkeit) incompleteness

unvollständig
A *Adj.* incomplete
B *adv.* **die Tatsachen nur ~ wiedergeben** give an incomplete rendering of the facts; **~ informiert sein** not be fully informed

Unvollständigkeit *die* incompleteness

unvorbereitet *Adj.* unprepared

unvoreingenommen
A *Adj.* unbiased; impartial
B *adv.* impartially

Unvoreingenommenheit *die* impartiality

unvorhergesehen
A *Adj.* unforeseen ‹difficulty, event, expenditure›; unexpected ‹visit›
B *adv.* **etw. kommt ganz ~:** sth. happens quite unexpectedly; **~ Besuch bekommen** have an unexpected visitor/unexpected visitors

unvorhersehbar *Adj.* unforeseeable

unvorschriftsmäßig
A *Adj.* contrary to *or* not in accordance with [the] regulations *postpos.*; **die ~e Anwendung eines Geräts** the improper use of a piece of equipment
B *adv.* contrary to [the] regulations; ‹use etc.› improperly; ‹park etc.› illegally

unvorsichtig
A *Adj.* careless; (unüberlegt) rash
B *adv.* carelessly; (unüberlegt) rashly

unvorsichtigerweise *Adv.* carelessly; (unüberlegt) without thinking

Unvorsichtigkeit *die* ▸ **unvorsichtig A**: 1 carelessness; rashness 2 (Handlung usw.) **eine ~ begehen** do sth. careless/rash; **die ~ begehen, ...** be careless/rash enough ...

unvorstellbar
A *Adj.* inconceivable; unimaginable
B *adv.* unimaginably; **~ leiden** suffer terribly

unvorteilhaft *Adj.* 1 (nicht attraktiv) unattractive ‹figure, appearance›; **das Kleid/die Frisur ist sehr ~ für dich** that dress/hairstyle doesn't suit you in the least 2 (ohne Vorteil) unfavourable, poor ‹purchase, exchange›; unprofitable ‹business›

unwägbar *Adj.* imponderable; incalculable ‹quantity, behaviour›

Unwägbarkeit *die;* ~, ~en 1 imponderability; (eines Verhaltens) incalculability; **wegen der ~ der Risiken** because of the incalculable risks 2 (etw. Unwägbares) uncertainty; imponderability

unwahr *Adj.* untrue

unwahrhaftig *Adj.* (geh.) untruthful

Unwahrheit *die* 1 untruthfulness 2 (Äußerung) untruth

unwahrscheinlich
A *Adj.* 1 (kaum möglich, unglaublich) improbable; unlikely; **es ist ~, dass er so spät noch kommt** it is unlikely that he'll come so late; **ich halte es für ~[, dass ...]** I think it [is] unlikely that ... 2 (ugs.: sehr viel) incredible (coll.)
B *adv.* (ugs.: sehr) incredibly (coll.); **er hat sich ~ gefreut** he was really thrilled (coll.)

Unwahrscheinlichkeit *die* improbability

unwandelbar (geh.)
A *Adj.* unwavering, steadfast ‹loyalty, love, friendship, attitude, etc.›; immutable ‹laws›
B *adv.* steadfastly

U

unwegsam *Adj.* [almost] impassable

unweiblich *Adj.* unfeminine

unweigerlich /ʊn'vaigɐlɪç/
A *Adj.* inevitable
B *adv.* inevitably

unweit
A *Präp. mit Gen.* not far from
B *Adv.* not far (**von** from)

Unwesen *das* dreadful state of affairs; **sein ~ treiben** (abwertend) be up to one's mischief *or* one's tricks

unwesentlich
A *Adj.* unimportant; insignificant
B *adv.* slightly; marginally

Unwetter *das* [thunder]storm

unwichtig *Adj.* unimportant; **Geld ist dabei ~:** the money is irrelevant; **etw. ist jmdm.** *od.* **für jmdn. ~:** sth. is unimportant *or* not important to sb.

Unwichtigkeit *die* 1 unimportance; lack of importance 2 (etw. Unwichtiges) unimportant thing; triviality

unwiderlegbar
A *Adj.* irrefutable
B *adv.* irrefutably

unwiderruflich
A *Adj.* irrevocable
B *adv.* irrevocably

unwidersprochen *Adj.* unchallenged

unwiderstehlich *Adj.* irresistible

Unwiderstehlichkeit *die;* **~:** irresistibility

unwiederbringlich (geh.)
A *Adj.* irretrievable
B *adv.* irretrievably

Unwiederbringlichkeit *die;* **~:** irretrievability

Unwille[n] *der* displeasure; indignation; **jmds. Unwillen erregen** *od.* **hervorrufen** incur sb.'s displeasure

unwillig
A *Adj.* indignant; angry; (widerwillig) unwilling; reluctant
B *adv.* indignantly; angrily; (widerwillig) unwillingly; reluctantly

unwillkommen *Adj.* unwelcome

unwillkürlich
A *Adj.* 1 spontaneous ‹*cry, sigh*›; instinctive ‹*reaction, movement, etc.*› 2 (Physiol.) involuntary ‹*movement etc.*›
B *adv.* 1 ‹*shout etc.*› spontaneously; ‹*react, move, etc.*› instinctively 2 (Physiol.) ‹*move etc.*› involuntarily

unwirklich (geh.)
A *Adj.* unreal
B *adv.* **seine Stimme klang ~ fern** his voice sounded distant and unreal

Unwirklichkeit *die;* **~, ~en** unreality

unwirksam *Adj.* ineffective

Unwirksamkeit *die* ineffectiveness

unwirsch
A *Adj.* surly; ill-natured
B *adv.* ill-naturedly

unwirtlich *Adj.* inhospitable; rough ‹*weather*›

Unwirtlichkeit *die;* **~:** inhospitableness; inhospitality; (des Wetters) roughness

unwirtschaftlich
A *Adj.* uneconomic ‹*procedure etc.*›; (nicht sparsam) uneconomical ‹*driving etc.*›
B *adv.* ‹*work, drive, etc.*› uneconomically

Unwirtschaftlichkeit *die* economic inefficiency; lack of economy; **der Betrieb musste wegen ~ geschlossen werden** the firm had to be closed down because it was uneconomic

Unwissen *das* ignorance

unwissend *Adj.* 1 (unerfahren) ignorant; innocent ‹*child*› 2 (unbewusst) unwitting; unknowing

Unwissenheit *die;* **~** 1 (Unkenntnis) ignorance; **~ schützt nicht vor Strafe** ignorance is no defence 2 (mangelndes Wissen) lack of education; (auf einem bestimmten Gebiet) lack of knowledge

unwissenschaftlich
A *Adj.* unscientific
B *adv.* unscientifically

Unwissenschaftlichkeit *die;* **~:** unscientific nature

unwissentlich
A *Adj.* unconscious
B *adv.* unknowingly; unwittingly

unwohl *Adv.* 1 ▸ **S. 439** (nicht wohl) unwell; **mir ist ~:** I don't feel well 2 (unbehaglich) uneasy; **mir ist ~ bei dem Gedanken** the thought makes me feel uneasy

Unwohlsein *das;* **~s** ▸ **S. 439** indisposition; **ein heftiges ~ überkam ihn** he suddenly felt very unwell

unwohnlich *Adj.* uncomfortable; unhomely

Unwucht *die;* **~, ~en** (Technik) imbalance

unwürdig *Adj.* 1 (verachtungswürdig) undignified ‹*person, behaviour*›; degrading ‹*treatment*› 2 (unangemessen) unworthy

Unzahl *die* huge *or* enormous number

unzählbar *Adj.* (auch Sprachw.) uncountable

unzählig
A *Adj.* innumerable; countless
B *adv.* **~ viele Besucher** a huge *or* an enormous number of visitors

***unzähligemal** ▸ **Mal**¹

unzähmbar *Adj.* untameable ‹*animal*›; (fig.) indomitable ‹*person*›

unzart
A *Adj.* indelicate
B *adv.* indelicately

Unze /'ʊntsə/ *die;* **~, ~n** ▸ **S. 315** ounce

Unzeit *die:* *in* **zur ~** (geh.) at an inopportune moment

unzeitgemäß *Adj.* anachronistic

unzensiert *Adj.* uncensored; (unbenotet) unmarked; ungraded (Amer.)

unzerbrechlich *Adj.* unbreakable

unzerkaut *Adj.* unchewed

unzerstörbar *Adj.* indestructible

Unzerstörbarkeit *die;* **~:** indestructibility

unzertrennlich *Adj.* inseparable

unziemlich *Adj.* (geh.) unseemly

unzivilisiert *Adj.* (abwertend) uncivilized

Unzucht *die* (veralt.) **das ist ~:** this is a sexual offence; **~ [mit jmdm.] treiben** fornicate [with sb.]; **~ mit Abhängigen/Kindern/Tieren** illicit sexual relations *pl.* with dependants/children/animals; **widernatürliche ~:** unnatural sexual act[s]; **gewerbsmäßige ~:** prostitution

unzüchtig
A *Adj.* obscene ‹*letter, gesture*›
B *adv.* ‹*touch, approach, etc.*› indecently; ‹*speak*› obscenely

unzufrieden *Adj.* dissatisfied; (stärker) unhappy

Unzufriedenheit *die* dissatisfaction; (stärker) unhappiness

unzugänglich *Adj.* inaccessible ‹*area, building, etc.*›; unapproachable ‹*character, person, etc.*›

Unzugänglichkeit *die;* **~** ▸ **unzugänglich**: inaccessibility; unapproachability

unzukömmlich /'ʊntsu:kœmlɪç/ *Adj.* (österr.) 1 (nicht zukommend) undeserved 2 (unzulänglich) inadequate

unzulänglich (geh.)
A *Adj.* insufficient; inadequate
B *adv.* insufficiently; inadequately

Unzulänglichkeit *die;* **~, ~en** 1 insufficiency; inadequacy 2 (etw. Unzulängliches) inadequacy; shortcoming

unzulässig *Adj.* inadmissible; undue ‹*influence, interference, delay*›; improper ‹*method, use, etc.*›

Unzulässigkeit *die* inadmissibility

unzumutbar *Adj.* unreasonable

Unzumutbarkeit *die;* **~, ~en** 1 (das Unzumutbarsein) unreasonableness 2 (etw. Unzumutbares) unreasonable demand

unzurechnungsfähig *Adj.* not responsible for one's actions *pred.;* (geistesgestört) of unsound mind *postpos.;* **für ~ erklärt werden** be certified insane

Unzurechnungs·fähigkeit *die* (Geistesgestörtheit) unsoundness of mind

unzureichend *Adj.* insufficient; inadequate

unzusammenhängend *Adj.* disconnected; incoherent ‹*words, ideas*›

unzustellbar *Adj.* (Postw.) undeliverable ‹*mail*›; **„falls ~, bitte zurück an Absender"** 'if undelivered, please return to sender'; **„~"** 'not known [at this address]'

unzuträglich *Adj. in* **jmdm./einer Sache ~ sein** (geh.) be detrimental to sb./sth.

Unzuträglichkeit *die;* **~:** detrimental effect; detrimentalness

unzutreffend *Adj.* inappropriate; inapplicable; (falsch) incorrect; **„Unzutreffendes bitte streichen"** 'please delete as appropriate'

unzuverlässig *Adj.* unreliable

Unzuverlässigkeit *die* unreliability

unzweckmäßig
A *Adj.* unsuitable; (unpraktisch) impractical
B *adv.* unsuitably; (unpraktisch) impractically

Unzweckmäßigkeit *die* ▸ **unzweckmäßig A**: unsuitability; impracticality

unzweideutig
A *Adj.* unambiguous; unequivocal; **etw. mit ~en Worten sagen** say sth. in no uncertain terms
B *adv.* unambiguously; unequivocally; **jmdm. ~ zu verstehen geben, dass ...** tell sb. in no uncertain terms that ...

Unzweideutigkeit *die* unambiguousness

unzweifelhaft
A *Adj.* unquestionable; undoubted
B *adv.* unquestionably; undoubtedly

Update /'apdeɪt/ *das;* **~s, ~s** (DV) update

üppig
A *Adj.* 1 (voll, dicht) lush, luxuriant ‹*vegetation*›; thick ‹*hair, beard*›; (fig.) sumptuous, opulent ‹*meal*›; rich ‹*colour*› 2 (rundlich, voll) full ‹*bosom, lips*›; voluptuous ‹*figure, woman*›
B *adv.* luxuriantly; (fig.) sumptuously

Üppigkeit *die;* **~** ▸ **üppig A**: lushness; luxuriance; thickness; sumptuousness; opulence; richness; fullness; voluptuousness

up to date /'ap tə 'deɪt/ up to date; **er ist modisch ~:** he wears fashionable clothes; he is fashionably dressed

Ur /u:ɐ̯/ *der;* **~[e]s, ~e** aurochs

Ur·abstimmung *die* [*esp.* strike] ballot

Ur·adel *der* ancient nobility

Ur·ahn[e] *der* 1 (Vorfahr) oldest known ancestor 2 (veralt.: Urgroßvater) great-grandfather

Ural *der;* **~[s]** Urals *pl.;* Ural Mountains *pl.*

ur·alt *Adj.* very old; ancient; **in ~en Zeiten** very long ago; **ein Märchen aus ~en Zeiten** a story of long, long ago

Uran /u'ra:n/ *das;* **~s** (Chemie) uranium

Uran·erz *das* uranium ore

Ur·angst *die* primeval fear

Uranus¹ /'u:ranʊs/ *der;* **~** (Astron.), **Uranus**² (*der*) (Myth.) Uranus *no def. art.*

ur·aufführen *tr. V.* première, give the first performance of ‹*play, concerto, etc.*›; première ‹*film*›; **uraufgeführt werden** ‹*film*› have its première

Ur·aufführung *die* première; first night *or* performance; (eines Films) première; first showing

urban /ʊr'ba:n/ *Adj.* (geh.) 1 (weltmännisch) urbane 2 (städtisch) urban

Urbanisation /ʊrbaniza'tsi̯o:n/ *die;* **~, ~en** urbanization

urbanisieren *tr. V.* urbanize

Urbanistik /ʊrba'nɪstɪk/ *die;* **~:** town planning and urban development *no art.;* (Studienfach) urban studies *pl., no art.*

Urbanität /ʊrbani'tɛ:t/ *die;* **~:** urbanity

urbar *in* **ein Stück Land/einen Sumpf/eine Wüste ~ machen** cultivate a piece of land/reclaim a swamp/desert

Urbarmachung *die;* **~** (von Land) cultivation; (von Sumpf, Wüste) reclamation

Ur·bevölkerung *die* native population; native inhabitants *pl.*

U

Ur·bild *das* 1 (Vorbild) archetype; prototype 2 (Inbegriff, Ideal) perfect example; epitome
urchig /ˈʊrçɪç/ *Adj.* (schweiz.) ▸ **urig**
Ur·christentum *das* early Christianity *no art.*
ur·christlich *Adj.* early Christian
ur·deutsch *Adj.* thoroughly *or* totally German
ur·eigen *Adj.* very own; **seine ~en Interessen** his own best interests
Ur·einwohner *der* native inhabitant; **die australischen ~**: the Australian Aborigines
Ur·einwohnerin *die* ▸ **Ureinwohner**
Ur·eltern *Pl.* original ancestors
Ur·enkel *der* great-grandson
Ur·enkelin *die* great-granddaughter
Ur·fassung *die* original version; original
Ur·fehde *die* (MA.) oath of truce
Ur·form *die* prototype
Ur·gemeinde *die* early Christian community
ur·gemütlich
A *Adj.* (ugs.) (behaglich) extremely cosy; (bequem) extremely comfortable
B *adv.* extremely cosily/comfortably
ur·germanisch *Adj.* proto-Germanic
Ur·geschichte *die* prehistory
ur·geschichtlich *Adj.* prehistoric
Ur·gesellschaft *die* primitive society
Ur·gestein *das* primitive *or* primary rocks *pl.*; **er ist politisches ~** (fig.) he is a founding father among politicians
Ur·gewalt *die* (geh.) elemental force
urgieren /ʊrˈgiːrən/ *tr., itr. V.* (bes. österr.) press; urge
Urgroß-: ~eltern *Pl.* great-grandparents; **~mutter** *die; Pl.* **~mütter** great-grandmother; **~vater** *der* great-grandfather
Ur·grund *der* basis; source; **der ~ alles Seins** the source of all being
Ur·heber *der;* **~s, ~, Ur·heberin** *die;* **~, ~nen** 1 (Initiator[in]) originator; initiator 2 (bes. Rechtsspr.: Verfasser[in]) author
Urheber·recht *das* copyright
urheber·rechtlich
A *Adj.* copyright *attrib*
B *adv.* **~ geschützt** copyright[ed]
Urheberschaft *die;* **~**: authorship
Ur·heimat *die* original home[land]
urig /ˈuːrɪç/ *Adj.* natural ‹*person*›; real ‹*beer*›; cosy ‹*pub*›; **sie ist einfach ~**: she is just different *or* an original
Urin /uˈriːn/ *der;* **~s, ~e** (Med.) urine; **etw. im ~ haben** (salopp) feel sth. in one's bones; have a gut feeling about sth.
Urinal /uriˈnaːl/ *das;* **~s, ~e** urinal
urinieren *itr. V.* urinate (**an** + *Akk.* against)
Urin·probe *die* urine sample
Ur·instinkt *der* basic instinct
Ur·kanton *der* original canton
Ur·kirche *die* early Church
Ur·knall *der* big bang
ur·komisch *Adj.* extremely funny; hilarious
Ur·kraft *die* elemental force
Ur·kunde *die;* **~, ~n** document; (Bescheinigung, Sieger~, Diplom~ usw.) certificate
Urkunden·fälschung *die* forgery *or* falsification of documents/of a/the document
urkundlich
A *Adj.* documentary
B *adv.* **~ erwähnt** mentioned in a document/in documents; **~ übereignen** transfer by deed
Urkunds·beamte *der,* **Urkunds·beamtin** *die* (Rechtsw.) registrar
-urlaub *der:* **Schweiz~/Österreich~** *usw.* holiday in Switzerland/Austria *etc.*; **Billig~/Neckermann~**: cheap *or* budget/Neckermann holiday
Urlaub *der;* **~[e]s, ~e** holiday[s] (Brit.); vacation; (bes. Milit.) leave; **~ haben** have a holiday/have leave; **[sich** (*Dat.*)**] ~ nehmen** take a holiday; **auf** *od.* **in** *od.* **im ~ sein** be on holiday/leave; **in ~ gehen/fahren** go on holiday; **unbezahlter ~**: unpaid leave; **~ von der Familie machen** have a holiday away from one's family; **sie machen ~**: they are on holiday; **sie ist noch nicht aus dem ~ zurück** she is still not back from holiday
urlauben *itr. V.* (ugs.) holiday; be/go on holiday
-urlauber *der:* **~s, ~: Sommer~/Winter~/Wochenend~**: summer/winter/weekend holidaymaker; **Billig~/Neckermann~**: person on a cheap *or* budget/Neckermann holiday; **Kreta~/Spanien~**: holidaymaker in *or* on Crete/in Spain
Urlauber *der;* **~s, ~**: holidaymaker
Urlauberin *die;* **~, ~nen** ▸ **Urlauber**
urlaubs-, Urlaubs-: ~anschrift *die* holiday address; **~anspruch** *der* holiday entitlement; **~foto** *das* holiday photo; **~geld** *das* holiday pay *or* money; (gespartes Geld) holiday money; **~gruß** *der* holiday greeting (**an** + *Akk.* to); **~lektüre** *die* holiday reading *no indef. art.*; **~ort** *der* holiday resort; **~pläne** *Pl.* holiday plans; **~reif** *Adj.* in **~reif sein** (ugs.) be ready for a holiday; **~reise** *die* holiday [trip]; **eine ~reise ans Meer/ins Gebirge machen** go on holiday to the seaside/go for a holiday in the mountains; **~reisende** *der/die* holidaymaker; **~schein** *der* (Milit.) [leave] pass; **~sperre** *die* 1 (Milit.) ban on leave; 2 (österr.) holiday closure; **~tag** *der* day of holiday; **zehn ~tage** ten days' holiday; **~vertretung** *die* holiday replacement; **er übernimmt die ~vertretung seines Chefs** he stands in *or* deputizes for his boss when the latter is on holiday; **~zeit** *die* 1 (Ferienzeit) holiday period *or* season; 2 (Zeit des eigenen Urlaubs) holiday
Ur·laut *der* elemental sound; (schrill) elemental cry
Ur·mensch *der* prehistoric *or* primitive man *no art., no pl.*; early hominid (as tech. term)
Ur·meter *das* (hist.) standard metre
Urne /ˈʊrnə/ *die;* **~, ~n** 1 urn 2 (Wahl~) [ballot] box; **zu den ~n gerufen werden** be called to the polls 3 (Verlosungs~) box; (Lostrommel) drum
Urnen-: ~feld *das* urnfield; **~fried·hof** *der* urn cemetery; cinerarium; **~grab** *das* urn grave
Urologe /uroˈloːgə/ *der;* **~n, ~n, Urologin** *die;* **~, ~nen** ▸ ❶ **S. 113** urologist
urologisch *Adj.* urological
Ur·oma *die* (fam.) great-granny (coll./child lang.)
Ur·opa *der* (fam.) great-grandpa (coll./child lang.)
ur·plötzlich
A *Adj.* extremely sudden
B *adv.* quite suddenly
Ur·quell *der* (geh.) [primary] source
Ur·sache *die* cause; **aus unbekannter ~**: for no apparent reason; for reasons *pl.* as yet unknown; **die ~ für etw.** the cause of sth.; the reason for sth.; **alle ~ haben, etw. zu tun** have every reason to do sth.; **keine ~!** don't mention it; you're welcome; **kleine ~, große Wirkung** (Spr.) great oaks from little acorns grow (prov.)
ur·sächlich *Adj.* causal; **in ~em Zusammenhang stehen** be causally related (**mit** to); **~ für etw. sein** be the cause of sth.
Ur·sächlichkeit *die;* **~, ~en** causality
Ur·schlamm *der,* **Ur·schleim** *der* primeval slime; **vom ~ an** (ugs.) from the very beginning
Ur·schrei *der* (Psych.) primal scream
Ur·schrift *die* original
ur·schriftlich *Adj.* original ‹*version etc.*›
Ur·schweiz *die the original Swiss Confederation with the three cantons of Schwyz, Uri and Unterwalden*
urschweizerisch *Adj.* typically Swiss
Ur·sendung *die* (Rundf.) first broadcast performance
Ur·sprache *die* 1 (Sprachw.: Grundsprache) protolanguage 2 (Originalsprache) original language; **in der ~**: in the original
Ur·sprung *der* origin; **vulkanischen ~s sein** be of volcanic origin; **seinen ~ in etw.** (*Dat.*) **haben** originate from sth.
ur·sprünglich
A *Adj.* 1 (anfänglich) original ‹*plan, price, form, material, etc.*›; initial ‹*reaction, trust, mistrust, etc.*› 2 (unverfälscht, natürlich) natural
B *adv.* 1 (anfänglich) originally; initially 2 (unverfälscht, natürlich) naturally
Ursprünglichkeit *die;* **~**: naturalness
Ursprungs·land *das* (einer Ware) country of origin (Commerc.); (einer Person) native land; (einer Bewegung, Sitte, Religion usw.) birthplace
urst /uːɐ̯st/
A *Adj.* great (coll.); brilliant (coll.)
B *adv.* (regional Jugendspr.) really
Urständ /ˈuːɐ̯ʃtɛnt/ *die:* in **[fröhliche] ~ feiern** be [coming] back with a vengeance
Ur·strom·tal *das* (Geol.) glacial valley
Ur·suppe *die* (Biol.) primordial soup
Urteil *das;* **~s, ~e** judgement; (Ansicht) opinion; (Strafe) sentence; (Gerichts~) verdict; **das ~ lautete auf 10 Jahre Freiheitsstrafe** the sentence was ten years' imprisonment; **über jmdn. das ~ sprechen** pass *or* pronounce judgement on sb.; **sich** (*Dat.*) **selbst das ~ sprechen** sentence oneself; **sich** (*Dat.*) **ein ~ bilden** form an opinion (**über** + *Akk.* about); **ein ~ über etw. fällen** pass *or* pronounce judgement on sth.
Ur·teilchen *das* ▸ **Quark**[2]
urteilen *itr. V.* form an opinion; judge; **nach etw. ~**: form an opinion *or* judge according to sth.; **nach seinem Äußeren zu ~**: to judge from his appearance; **über etw./jmdn. ~**: judge sth./sb.; give one's opinion on sth./sb.; **hart ~**: give a harsh opinion; judge harshly; **fachmännisch ~**: give an expert opinion; **~ Sie selbst** judge for yourself/yourselves
urteils-, Urteils-: ~begründung *die* opinion; reasons *pl.* for judgement; **~fähig** *Adj.* competent *or* able to judge *postpos.*; **~fähigkeit** *die* competence *or* ability to judge; **~findung** *die;* **~~, ~~en** (Rechtspr.) reaching a/the verdict *no art.*; **~kraft** *die* [power of] judgement; **~spruch** *der* judgement; (Strafe) sentence; (der Geschworenen) verdict; **~verkündung** *die* pronouncement of judgement; **~vermögen** *das* competence *or* ability to judge
Ur·text *der* original
Ur·tierchen *das* protozoan
urtümlich /ˈuːɐ̯tyːmlɪç/ *Adj.* natural ‹*landscape etc.*›; primitive ‹*culture etc.*›; (urweltlich) primeval ‹*plant, animal, landscape*›
Uruguay /uruˈgu̯aːi/ (*das*); **~s** Uruguay
Uruguayer /uruˈgu̯aːjɐ/ *der;* **~s, ~, Uruguayerin** *die;* **~, ~nen** Uruguayan
Ur·ur-: ~enkel *der* great-great-grandson; **~enkelin** *die* great-great-granddaughter; **~groß·mutter** *die* great-great-grandmother; **~groß·vater** *der* great-great-grandfather
Ur·väter·zeit *die* olden days *or* times *pl.*
Ur·vertrauen *das* (Päd., Psych.) sense of basic trust
Ur·viech *das* (salopp scherzh.) real character
Ur·vogel *der* (Paläont.) archaeopteryx
Ur·volk *das* original people
Ur·wald *der* primeval forest; **tropischer Urwald** tropical forest; jungle
ur·weltlich *Adj.* primeval
ur·wüchsig /ˈuːɐ̯vyːksɪç/ *Adj.* natural ‹*landscape, power*›; earthy ‹*language, humour*›
Urwüchsigkeit *die;* **~** ▸ **urwüchsig**: naturalness; earthiness
Ur·zeit *die* primeval times *pl.*; **vor ~en** in ages past; **seit ~en** since primeval times; (ugs.: seit längerer Zeit) since the year dot (coll.)
ur·zeitlich *Adj.* primeval
Ur·zelle *die* primeval cell; (fig.) initial germ

U̲r·zeugung *die* abiogenesis; spontaneous generation

U̲r·zustand *der* original state

USA /uːǀɛsǀ'aː/ *Pl.* USA

Usambara·veilchen /uzam'baːra-/ *das* African violet

Usance /y'zãːs/ *die;* ~, ~**n,** (schweiz.), **Usanz** /u'zants/ *die;* ~, ~**en** (bes. Kaufmannsspr.) practice

User /'juːzɐ/ *der;* ~**s,** ~, **U̲serin** *die;* ~, ~**nen** (bes. DV, Drogenjargon) user

usf. *Abk.* **= und so fort** etc.

Usurpator /uzʊr'paːtɔr/ *der;* ~**s,** ~**en** /...pa'toːrən/, **Usurpatorin** *die;* ~, ~**nen** usurper

usurpieren *tr. V.* usurp

Usus /'uːzʊs/ *der;* ~ (ugs.) custom; **das ist hier so ~:** that's the custom here

usw. *Abk.* **= und so weiter** etc.

Utensil /utɛn'ziːl/ *das;* ~**s,** ~**ien** /...i̯ən/ piece of equipment; ~**ien** equipment *sing.*

Uterus /'uːterʊs/ *der;* ~, **Uteri** [...ri] ▸ **❶ S. 435** (Anat.) uterus

Utilitarismus /utilita'rɪsmʊs/ *der;* ~ (Philos.) utilitarianism *no art.*

utilitaristisch *Adj.* utilitarian

Utopia /u'toːpi̯a/ *(das);* ~**s** Utopia

Utopie /uto'piː/ *die;* ~, ~**n** **1** (Idealvorstellung) utopian dream **2** (ideale Gesellschaftsform) utopia; (literarisches Werk) utopian *or* futuristic work

utopisch *Adj.* utopian

Utopist *der;* ~**en,** ~**en, Utopistin** *die;* ~, ~**nen** utopian dreamer; (Autor[in]) utopian [author]

utopistisch *Adj.* [absurdly] utopian

u. U. *Abk.* **= unter Umständen**

UV *Abk.* **= Ultraviolett** UV

ü̲ver·qualifiziert *Adj.* overqualified

UV-: ~-Filter *der* (Fot.) UV filter; ultraviolet filter; **~-Schutz** *der* UV protection; **~-Strahlen** *Pl.* UV rays; ultraviolet rays

Ü̲-Wagen *der* (Rundf., Ferns.) OB van or vehicle

u. Z. *Abk.* (bes. DDR) **= unserer Zeitrechnung** AD

Uz /uːts/ *der;* ~**es,** ~**e** (ugs.) joke

uzen *tr., itr. V.* (ugs.) tease; kid

U̲z·name *der* (ugs.) nickname

U

Vv

v, V /vau̯/ *das;* ~, ~: v/V; *s. auch* **a, A**
v. *Abk.* **= von** (in Familiennamen) von
V *Abk.* **= Volt** V
Vabanque·spiel /va'bã:k-/ *das* (geh.) dangerous *or* risky game
Vademekum /vade'me:kʊm/ *das;* ~s, ~s (geh. veralt.) vade mecum
vag /va:k/ ▸**vage**
Vagabund /vaga'bʊnt/ *der;* ~en, ~en (veralt.) vagabond
vagabundieren *itr. V.* **1** live as a vagabond/as vagabonds **2** *mit sein* (umherziehen) wander *or* travel around
Vagabundin *die;* ~, ~nen ▸**Vagabund**
Vagant /va'gant/ *der;* ~en, ~en goliard
Vaganten·dichtung *die* (Literaturw.) goliardic poetry *or* verse
vage
A *Adj.* vague
B *adv.* vaguely
Vagheit *die;* ~: vagueness
Vagina /va'gi:na/ *die;* ~, **Vaginen** ▸ℹ **S. 435** (Anat.) vagina
vaginal *Adj.* (Anat.) vaginal
vakant /va'kant/ *Adj.* vacant
Vakanz /va'kants/ *die;* ~, ~en (geh.) vacancy
Vakuum /'va:kuʊm/ *das;* ~s, **Vakua** /'va:kua/ *od.* **Vakuen** /...kən/ (bes. Physik, auch fig.) vacuum; **im ~:** in a vacuum
vakuum·verpackt *Adj.* vacuum-packed
Valentins·tag /'va:lɛnti:ns-/ *der* [St] Valentine's Day
Valenz /va'lɛnts/ *die;* ~, ~en **1** (Sprachw.) valency **2** (Chemie) valence; valency (Brit.)
Valet /va'lɛt/ *das;* ~s, ~s (veralt., noch scherzh.) farewell
valid /va'li:t/, **valide** /va'li:də/
A *Adj.* valid; (zuverlässig) reliable
B *adv.* validly; (zuverlässig) reliably
Valuta /va'lu:ta/ *die;* ~, **Valuten** (Wirtsch., Bankw.) foreign currency
Vamp /vɛmp/ *der;* ~s, ~s vamp
Vampir /'vampi:ɐ̯/ *der;* ~s, ~e **1** vampire **2** (Tier) vampire [bat]
Vampirin *die;* ~, ~nen ▸**Vampir 1**
Van /vɛn/ *der;* ~s, ~s (Kfz.-W.) MPV
Vandale *usw.:* ▸**Wandale**
Vanille /va'nɪljə/ *die;* ~: vanilla
Vanille-: **~eis** *das* vanilla ice cream; **~geschmack** *der* vanilla flavour; **Eis mit ~geschmack** vanilla-flavoured ice cream; **~pudding** *der* vanilla pudding; **~zucker** *der* vanilla sugar
Vanillin /vani'li:n/ *das;* ~s vanillin
variabel /va'ri̯a:bl̩/
A *Adj.* variable; **variable Geometrie** variable geometry
B *adv.* variably
Variabilität /vari̯abili'tɛ:t/ *die;* ~ (geh.) variability
Variable /va'ri̯a:blə/ *die; adj. Dekl.* (Math., Physik) variable
Variante /va'ri̯antə/ *die;* ~, ~n (geh.) variant; variation
Varianz /va'ri̯ants/ *die;* ~ (Math.) variance
Variation /varia'tsi̯o:n/ *die;* ~, ~en (auch Musik) variation (*Gen.*, **über, zu** on)
Varietät /vari̯e'tɛ:t/ *die;* ~, ~en (bes. Biol.) variety
Varieté, Varietee /vari̯e'te:/ *das;* ~s, ~s variety theatre; (Aufführung) variety show; **ins ~ gehen** go to a variety show
variieren *tr., itr. V.* vary
Vario·objektiv /'va:ri̯o-/ *das* (Fot.) zoom lens
Vasall /va'zal/ *der;* ~en, ~en (hist., auch fig. abwertend) vassal
Vasallen-: **~staat** *der* (abwertend) vassal state; **~treue** *die* (hist.) vassal's loyalty; loyalty as a vassal; (fig.) slavish loyalty
Väschen /'vɛ:sçən/ *das;* ~s, ~: [little] vase
Vase /'va:zə/ *die;* ~, ~n vase
Vasektomie /vazɛkto'mi/ *die;* ~, ~n (Med.) vasectomy
Vaseline /vaze'li:nə/ *die;* ~: Vaseline ®
Vasen·malerei *die* vase painting
vasomotorisch /vazomo'to:rɪʃ/ *Adj.* (Physiol.) vasomotor
Vater /'fa:tɐ/ *der;* ~s, **Väter** /'fɛ:tɐ/ **1** father; **er ist ~ von drei Kindern** he is the father of three children; **er ist ~ geworden** he has become a father; **ein werdender ~** (scherzh.) an expectant father (joc.); **grüßen Sie Ihren Herrn ~!** remember me to your father; **er ist ganz der ~:** he is just like his father; **er ist der [geistige] ~ dieser Idee** (fig.) he thought up this idea; this idea is his; **die Väter der amerikanischen Verfassung** (fig.) the [founding] fathers of the American constitution; **~ Staat** (scherzh.) the State; **~ Rhein** (dichter.) the Rhine; Father Rhine (literary); **Heiliger ~** (kath. Kirche) Holy Father; **ach, du dicker ~** (ugs.) oh my goodness!; oh heavens! **2** (Tier) sire **3** (Rel.) Father; **Gott ~:** God the Father
Väterchen /'fɛ:tɐçən/ *das;* ~s, ~: **1** (Koseform) daddy (coll.) **2** **[altes] ~:** little old man **3** **~ Frost** (scherzh.) Jack Frost
Vater-: **~figur** *die* father figure; **~freuden** *Pl.* **~freuden entgegensehen** (meist scherzh.) be expecting a happy event; be going to be a father; **~haus** *das* (geh.) parental home; **das ~haus verlassen** leave one's parents' house; **~land** *das* fatherland
vaterländisch /'--lɛndɪʃ/ *Adj.* (geh.) patriotic
vaterlands-, Vaterlands-: **~liebe** *die* (geh.) love of one's fatherland; patriotism; **~los** *Adj.* (abwertend) unpatriotic; **~verräter** *der* (abwertend) traitor to one's fatherland
väterlich /'fɛ:tɐlɪç/
A *Adj.* **1** (vom Vater) his/her *etc.* father's; (verallgemeinernd) the father's; (eines Vaters) paternal ‹*line, love, instincts, etc.*›; **das ~e Geschäft übernehmen** take over one's father's business; **die ~en Pflichten** the duties of a father **2** (fürsorglich) fatherly
B *adv.* in a fatherly way
väterlicherseits *Adv.* on the/his/her *etc.* father's side; **meine Großeltern ~:** my paternal grandparents; my grandparents on my father's side
Väterlichkeit *die;* ~: fatherliness; (väterliche Gefühle) fatherly feeling
vater-, Vater-: **~los** *Adj.* fatherless; **~los aufwachsen** grow up without a father; **~mord** *der* patricide; **~mörder** *der* **1** patricide; **2** (veralt. scherzh.: Stehkragen) choker [collar]; **~mörderin** *die* ▸**~mörder 1**
Vaterschaft *die;* ~, ~en fatherhood; (bes. Rechtsw.) paternity
Vaterschafts: **~klage** *die* paternity suit; **~test** *der* paternity test
Vater: **~stadt** *die* (geh.) home town; **~stelle** *die:* **bei** *od.* **an jmdm. ~stelle vertreten** take the place of a father to sb.; **~stolz** *der* fatherly pride; **~tag** *der* Father's Day *no def. art.*; **~tier** *das* (Landw.) sire; **~unser** *das;* ~~s, ~~: Lord's Prayer; **das ~unser sprechen** say the Lord's Prayer; **drei ~unser beten** say three Our Fathers
Vati /'fa:ti/ *der;* ~s, ~s (fam.) dad[dy] (coll.)
Vatikan /vati'ka:n/ *der;* ~s Vatican
vatikanisch *Adj.* Vatican
Vatikanstadt *die;* ~: Vatican City
V-Ausschnitt /'fau̯-/ *der* V-neck
VB *Abk.* **= Verhandlungsbasis: VB 7 800 Euro** 7,800 euros o.n.o. (Brit.)
VCD *Abk.* **= Verkehrsklub Deutschland**
v. Chr. *Abk.* **= vor Christus** ▸ℹ **S. 165** BC
VCS *Abk.* **= Verkehrsklub der Schweiz**
VEB *Abk.* (DDR) **= Volkseigener Betrieb**
Vegetarier /vege'ta:ri̯ɐ/ *der;* ~s, ~, **Vegetarierin** *die;* ~, ~nen vegetarian
vegetarisch
A *Adj.* vegetarian
B *adv.* **er isst** *od.* **lebt** *od.* **ernährt sich ~:** he is a vegetarian; he lives on a vegetarian diet
Vegetarismus *der;* ~: vegetarianism *no art.*
Vegetation /...'tsi̯o:n/ *die;* ~, ~en vegetation *no indef. art.*
vegetativ /vegeta'ti:f/ *Adj.* **1** (Biol.: ungeschlechtlich) vegetative **2** (Physiol., Biol.: unbewusst ablaufend) autonomic
vegetieren *itr. V.* (oft abwertend) vegetate; **am Rande der Existenz ~:** eke out a miserable existence
vehement /vehe'mɛnt/ (geh.)
A *Adj.* vehement
B *adv.* vehemently
Vehemenz /...'mɛnts/ *die;* ~ (geh.) vehemence
Vehikel /ve'hi:kl/ *das;* ~s, ~ **1** (oft abwertend: Auto) vehicle; **ein altes/klappriges ~:** an old crock (sl.) **2** (geh.: Ausdrucksmittel) vehicle
Veilchen /'fai̯lçən/ *das;* ~s, ~ **1** (Blume) violet; **wie ein ~ im Verborgenen blühen** be modesty itself; go unnoticed; *s. auch* **blau** **2** (ugs. scherzh.: blaues Auge) black eye; shiner (sl.)
veilchen-, Veilchen-: **~blau** *Adj.* violet; **~duft** *der* violet fragrance *or* scent; **~strauß** *der; Pl.* **~sträuße** bunch *or* bouquet of violets
Veits·tanz /'fai̯ts-/ *der* St Vitus's dance; **einen ~ kriegen** (ugs.) *od.* **aufführen** (fig.) kick up a terrible fuss
Vektor /'vɛktɔr/ *der;* ~s, ~en /-'to:rən/ (Math., Physik) vector
Vektor·rechnung *die* vector algebra; (im weiteren Sinne) vector analysis
velar /ve'la:ɐ̯/ (Sprachw.)
A *Adj.* velar
B *adv.* ‹*pronounce*› as a velar sound
Velar *der;* ~s, ~e, **Velar·laut** *der* (Phon.) velar sound
Velo /'ve:lo/ *das;* ~s, ~s (schweiz.) bicycle; bike (coll.)

Velo·taxi *das* velotaxi; pedicab

Velours¹ /və'lu:ɐ̯/ *der;* ~ /və'lu:ɐ̯s/, ~ /və'lu:ɐ̯s/ (Stoff) velour[s]

Velours² *das;* ~ /və'lu:ɐ̯s/, ~ /və'lu:ɐ̯s/, **Velours·leder** *das* suede

Vene /'ve:nə/ *die;* ~, ~n ▸❶ S. 435 (Anat.) vein

Venedig /ve'ne:dɪç/ *(das);* ~s ▸❶ S. 675 Venice

Venen·entzündung *die* phlebitis *no indef. art.*

venerisch /ve'ne:rɪʃ/ *Adj.* (Med.) venereal

Venezianer /vene'tsi̯a:nɐ/ *der;* ~s, ~, **Venezianerin** *die;* ~, ~nen ▸❶ S. 675 Venetian

venezianisch *Adj.* ▸❶ S. 675 Venetian

Venezolaner /venetso'la:nɐ/ *der;* ~s, ~, **Venezolanerin** *die;* ~, ~nen Venezuelan

venezolanisch *Adj.* Venezuelan

Venezuela /vene'tsu̯e:la/ *(das);* ~s Venezuela

Venia Legendi /'ve:ni̯a le'gɛndi/ *die;* ~ (geh.) *authorization to teach at university after habilitation*

venös *Adj.* (Med.) venous

Ventil /vɛn'ti:l/ *das;* ~s, ~e 1▸ valve; (fig.) outlet 2▸ (einer Orgel) pallet

Ventilation /vɛntila'tsi̯o:n/ *die;* ~, ~en ventilation

Ventilator /vɛnti'la:tɔr/ *der;* ~s, ~en /...la'to:rən/ ventilator

ventilieren *tr. V.* (geh.) consider

Venus¹ /'ve:nʊs/ *die;* ~ (Astron.), **Venus²** *(die)* (Myth.) Venus *no def. art.*

Venus·hügel *der* ▸❶ S. 435 (Anat.) mons Veneris

verabfolgen *tr. V.* (Papierdt. veralt.) ▸**verabreichen**

verabreden

A *tr. V.* arrange; **ein Erkennungszeichen** ~: agree on a sign to recognize each other by; **am verabredeten Ort** at the agreed place

B *refl. V.* **sich im Park/zum Tennis/für den folgenden Abend** ~: arrange to meet in the park/for tennis/next evening; **sich mit jmdm.** ~: arrange to meet sb.; **mit jmdm. verabredet sein** have arranged to meet sb.; (formell) have an appointment with sb.; (mit dem Freund/der Freundin) have a date with sb. (coll.)

Verabredung *die;* ~, ~en 1▸ (Absprache) arrangement; **eine** ~ **treffen** arrange to meet *or* a meeting; **wie auf** ~: as if by arrangement 2▸ (verabredete Zusammenkunft) appointment; **eine** ~ **absagen** call off a meeting *or* an engagement; **ich habe eine** ~: I am meeting sb.; (formell) I have an appointment; (mit meinem Freund/meiner Freundin) I have a date (coll.); **eine** ~ **für den Abend haben** have an engagement in the evening

verabreichen *tr. V.* administer ‹*medicine*›; give ‹*injection, thrashing*›

Verabreichung *die;* ~, ~en administration; administering

verabsäumen *tr. V.* (Papierdt.) neglect; omit

verabscheuen *tr. V.* detest; loathe

verabscheuenswürdig *Adj.* (geh.) detestable; loathsome

verabschieden

A *tr. V.* 1▸ say goodbye to; **sie wurde am Bahnhof verabschiedet** she was seen off at the station; **der Staatsgast wurde auf dem Bonner Flughafen verabschiedet** the official guest was given a farewell at the airport in Bonn 2▸ (aus dem Dienst) retire ‹*general, civil servant, etc.*› 3▸ (annehmen) adopt ‹*plan, budget*›; pass ‹*law*›

B *refl. V.* **sich [von jmdm.]** ~: say goodbye [to sb.]; (formell) take one's leave [of sb.]

Verabschiedung *die;* ~, ~en 1▸ leave-taking 2▸ (aus dem Dienst) retirement 3▸ (eines Plans, Etats) adoption; (eines Gesetzes) passing

verabsolutieren *tr. V.* make absolute

verachten *tr. V.* despise; **ihre Süßspeisen sind nicht zu** ~: her sweets are not to be scoffed at *or* (coll.) sneezed at

Verächter /fɛɐ̯'|ɛçtɐ/ *der;* ~s, ~, **Verächterin** *die;* ~, ~nen opponent; critic

verächtlich /fɛɐ̯'|ɛçtlɪç/

A *Adj.* 1▸ (abschätzig) contemptuous 2▸ (verachtenswürdig) contemptible; despicable; **jmdn./etw.** ~ **machen** disparage sb./sth.; run sb./sth. down

B *adv.* contemptuously

Verächtlichkeit *die;* ~: contempt; contemptuousness

Verächtlich·machung *die;* ~ (Papierdt.) disparagement

Verachtung *die;* ~: contempt; **seine** ~ **aller** *od.* **für alle Konventionen** his contempt for all forms of convention; **jmdn. mit** ~ **strafen** treat sb. with contempt

verachtungs·voll (geh.) ▸**verächtlich A 1, B**

veralbern *tr. V.* 1▸ (aufziehen) **jmdn.** ~: make fun of sb.; **willst du mich** ~? are you trying to make fun of me? 2▸ (verspotten) mock

verallgemeinern *tr., itr. V.* generalize

Verallgemeinerung *die;* ~, ~en generalization

veralten *itr. V.; mit sein* become obsolete; **veraltete Methoden/Wörter** obsolete *or* antiquated methods/obsolete *or* archaic words

Veranda /ve'randa/ *die;* ~, **Veranden** veranda; porch

veränderbar *Adj.* changeable; (Physik) variable; **nicht mehr** ~: unalterable

veränderlich *Adj.* 1▸ changeable ‹*weather*›; variable ‹*character, star*›; **das Barometer steht auf** ~: the barometer says 'changeable' 2▸ (veränderbar) variable

Veränderliche *die;* ~n, ~n (Math.) variable

Veränderlichkeit *die;* ~, ~en ▸**veränderlich**: changeability; variability

verändern

A *tr. V.* change; **der Bart verändert ihn stark** the beard makes him look very different

B *refl. V.* 1▸ (anders werden) change; **sich zu seinem Vorteil/Nachteil** ~: change for the better/worse; (nur im Aussehen) look better/worse 2▸ (die Stellung wechseln) **sich [beruflich]** ~: change one's job

Veränderung *die* change *(Gen.* in); **an etw.** *(Dat.)* **eine** ~ **vornehmen** change sth.; **berufliche** ~: change of job; **bei uns ist eine** ~ **eingetreten** our situation has changed

verängstigen *tr. V.* frighten; scare; **völlig verängstigt** terrified

verankern *tr. V.* fix ‹*tent, mast, pole, etc.*›; (mit einem Anker) anchor; (fig.) embody ‹*right etc.*›

Verankerung *die;* ~, ~en 1▸ (das Befestigen) fixing; (mit einem Anker) anchoring; (fig.) embodiment 2▸ (Halterung) anchorage; fixture

veranlagen *tr. V.* (Steuerw.) assess (**mit** at)

veranlagt *Adj.* **künstlerisch/praktisch/romantisch** ~ **sein** have an artistic bent/be practically minded/have a romantic disposition; **ein homosexuell** ~**er Mann** a man with homosexual tendencies

Veranlagung *die;* ~, ~en 1▸ [pre]disposition; **seine homosexuelle/künstlerische/praktische/romantische** ~: his homosexual tendencies *pl.*/artistic bent/practical nature/romantic disposition; **er hat eine** ~ **zur Fettsucht** he has a tendency towards obesity 2▸ (Steuerw.) assessment

veranlassen *tr. V.* 1▸ cause; induce; **was hat dich zu diesem Schritt/dieser Bemerkung veranlasst?** what caused *or* led you to take this step/make this remark?; **ich fühlte mich veranlasst einzugreifen** I felt obliged to intervene 2▸ (dafür sorgen, dass etw. getan wird) **etw.** ~: see to it that sth. is done *or* is carried out; **ich werde alles Weitere/das Nötige** ~: I will take care of *or* see to everything else/I will see [to it] that the necessary steps are taken

Veranlassung *die;* ~, ~en 1▸ reason, cause (**zu** for); **äußere** ~: outward reason 2▸ **auf jmds.** ~ **[hin]** on sb.'s orders

veranschaulichen *tr. V.* illustrate

Veranschaulichung *die;* ~, ~en illustration; **zur** ~: as an illustration/as illustrations

veranschlagen *tr. V.* estimate (**mit** at); **etw. zu hoch/niedrig** ~: overestimate/underestimate sth.

Veranschlagung *die;* ~, ~en estimate

veranstalten *tr. V.* 1▸ (stattfinden lassen) organize; hold, give ‹*party*›; hold ‹*auction*›; do ‹*survey*› 2▸ (ugs.: machen, aufführen) make ‹*noise, fuss*›

Veranstalter *der;* ~s, ~, **Veranstalterin** *die;* ~, ~nen organizer

Veranstaltung *die;* ~, ~en 1▸ (das Veranstalten) organizing; organization 2▸ (etw., was veranstaltet wird) event

Veranstaltungs·kalender *der* calendar of events; (für kürzeren Zeitraum) diary of events

verantworten

A *tr. V.* **etw.** ~: take responsibility for sth.; **ich kann das vor Gott/mir selbst/meinem Gewissen nicht** ~: I cannot be responsible for that before God/I cannot justify it to myself/I cannot square that with my conscience

B *refl. V.* **sich für etw.** ~: answer for sth.; **sich vor jmdm.** ~: answer to sb.; **sich vor Gericht für etw.** ~: answer to the courts for sth.; **der Angeklagte hat sich wegen Mordes zu** ~: the accused faces a charge of murder

verantwortlich *Adj.* responsible; **der** ~**e Redakteur** the managing editor; **der für den Einkauf** ~**e Mitarbeiter** the person responsible for purchasing; **ich fühle mich dafür** ~, **dass alles klappt** I feel responsible for making sure that everything goes off all right; **für etw.** ~ **zeichnen** be responsible for *or* in charge of sth.; **jmdm. [gegenüber]** ~ **sein** be responsible to sb.; **jmdn. für etw.** ~ **machen** hold sb. responsible for sth.; **die Verantwortlichen** those responsible

Verantwortlichkeit *die;* ~, ~en responsibility

Verantwortung *die;* ~, ~en 1▸ responsibility (**für** for); **die Eltern haben** *od.* **tragen die** ~ **für ihre Kinder** the parents have *or* bear the responsibility for their children; **die** ~ **für etw. übernehmen** take *or* accept [the] responsibility for sth.; **ich tue es auf deine** ~: you must take responsibility; on your own head be it; **in eigener** ~: on one's own responsibility; off one's own bat (Brit.); **jmdn. [für etw.] zur** ~ **ziehen** call sb. to account [for sth.]; **die Gruppe hat die** ~ **für den Anschlag übernommen** the group has accepted *or* admitted responsibility for the attack 2▸ (~sgefühl) sense of responsibility

verantwortungs-, Verantwortungs-: ~**bewusst**, *~**bewußt** *Adj.* responsible; **er handelt sehr** ~**bewusst** he acts in a very responsible manner; ~**bewusstsein**, *~**bewußtsein** *das,* ~**gefühl** *das* sense of responsibility; ~**los** *Adj.* irresponsible; ~**losigkeit** *die;* ~~: irresponsibility; ~**voll** *Adj.* responsible

veräppeln /fɛɐ̯'|ɛpl̩n/ *tr. V.* (ugs.) **jmdn.** ~: have (Brit. coll.) *or* (Amer. coll.) put sb. on; **willst du mich** ~? are you having (Brit. coll.) *or* (Amer. coll.) putting me on?

verarbeiten *tr. V.* 1▸ use; ~**de Industrie** processing industry; **im** *od.* **vom Gehirn verarbeitet** (fig.) processed by the brain; **etw. zu etw.** ~: make sth. into sth.; use sth. to make sth. 2▸ (verdauen) digest ‹*food*› 3▸ (geistig bewältigen) digest, assimilate ‹*film, experience, impressions*›; come to terms with ‹*disappointment*›

-verarbeitend *adj.* -processing

verarbeitet *Adj.* **gut/schlecht** *usw.* ~: well/badly *etc.* finished ‹*suit, dress, car, etc.*›

-verarbeitung *die* -processing

Verarbeitung *die;* ~, ~en 1▸ (das Verarbeiten) use 2▸ (Art der Fertigung) finish; **Schuhe in erstklassiger** ~: shoes with a first-class finish

verargen *tr. V.* (geh.) **jmdm. etw.** ~: hold sth. against sb.

verärgern *tr. V.* annoy; **verärgert wandte er sich ab** he turned away in annoyance

Verärgerung *die;* ~, ~en annoyance; **aus** ~ **über die verspätete Einladung nahm er an dem Empfang nicht teil** he did not attend

V

the reception, because he was annoyed about the late invitation

verarmen *itr. V.; mit sein* become poor *or* impoverished; **verarmte Provinzen/verarmter Adel** impoverished provinces/aristocracy

Verarmung *die;* **~:** impoverishment

verarschen *tr. V.* (derb) **jmdn. ~:** take the piss (coarse) *or* (Brit. coll.) mickey out of sb.; **willst du mich ~?** are you taking the piss (coarse) *or* (Brit. coll.) mickey?

verarzten *tr. V.* (ugs.) patch up (coll.) ‹*person*›; fix (coll.) ‹*wound, injury, etc.*›

verästeln /fɛɐ̯ˈ|ɛstl̩n/ *refl. V.* (auch fig.) branch out

Veräst[e]lung *die;* **~, ~en** (auch fig.) ramification

verätzen *tr. V.* corrode ‹*metal etc.*›; burn ‹*skin, face, etc.*›

Verätzung *die* corrosion; (der Haut) burn

verausgaben

A *tr. V.* (Papierdt.) spend

B *refl. V.* wear oneself out; **sie hat sich total verausgabt** (finanziell) she has completely spent out

veräußerlich *Adj.* (bes. Rechtsspr.) alienable; **nicht ~:** inalienable

veräußern *tr. V.* (bes. Rechtsspr.) dispose of, sell ‹*property*›; alienate ‹*right*›

Veräußerung *die* (bes. Rechtsspr.) (von Eigentum) disposal; sale; (eines Rechts) alienation

Veräußerungs·gewinn *der* gain on sale *or* disposal

Verb /vɛrp/ *das;* **~s, ~en** (Sprachw.) verb

Verba ▸ **Verbum**

verbacken *unr. tr. V.* use ‹*flour, butter, sugar, etc.*› [in baking]

verbal /vɛrˈbaːl/ *Adj.*

A (auch Sprachw.) verbal

B *adv.* verbally

Verbal·injurie *die;* **~** (auch Rechtsw.) verbal injury

verbalisieren *tr. V.* (geh.) verbalize

verballhornen /fɛɐ̯ˈbalhɔrnən/ *tr. V.* corrupt ‹*word, phrase*›

Verballhornung *die;* **~, ~en** misuse; corruption

Verbal-: ~phrase *die* (Sprachw.) verbal phrase; **~substantiv** *das* (Sprachw.) verbal noun

Verband *der* **1** (Binde) bandage; dressing; **einen ~ anlegen** apply a dressing **2** (von Vereinen, Clubs o. Ä.) association **3** (Milit.: vereinigte Truppenteile) unit **4** (Milit.: Fahrzeug~, Flugzeug~) formation **5** (Gruppe) group; unit

verbandeln (landsch.)

A *tr. V.* connect; (kombinieren) combine; **jmdn. mit jmdm. ~:** bring sb. and sb. together; **mit jmdm./etw. verbandelt sein** be [closely] associated with sb./sth.; **mit jmdm. geschäftlich verbandelt sein** have business ties with sb.; **mit einer Frau/einem Mann verbandelt sein** (eine sexuelle Beziehung haben) be having a relationship with a woman/a man

B *refl. V.* **sich [mit] jmdm. ~:** get together with sb.

Verband-: ~kasten *der* first-aid box; **~material** *das* dressing materials *pl.*; **~päckchen** *das* packet of dressings

Verbands·kasten *usw.* ▸ **Verbandkasten** *usw.*

Verband[s]·stoff *der* dressing [material]

Verband·zeug *das* first-aid things *pl.*

verbannen *tr. V.* (auch fig.) banish

Verbannte *der/die; adj. Dekl.* exile

Verbannung *die;* **~, ~en** banishment; exile; **in die ~ gehen** go into exile

Verbannungs·ort *der* place of exile

verbarrikadieren

A *tr. V.* barricade

B *refl. V.* barricade oneself

verbauen *tr. V.* **1** (versperren) obstruct; block; **jmdm./sich die Zukunft ~** (fig.) spoil sb.'s/one's prospects for the future **2** (abwertend: unschön bebauen) spoil **3** (zum Bauen verwenden) use; **sein ganzes Geld ~** (fig.) use [up] one's entire money for *or* on building

verbauern *itr. V.; mit sein* become a country bumpkin

verbeamten *tr. V.* make ‹*person*› a civil servant; (fig. abwertend) [over-]bureaucratize

verbeißen

A *unr. tr. V.* **1** (unterdrücken) suppress ‹*pain, laughter, anger, feelings*›; hold back ‹*tears etc.*› **2** (bes. Jägerspr.: beschädigen) bite; chew

B *refl. V.* **sich in etw. ~:** bite into sth.; ‹*dog*› sink its teeth into sth.; (fig.) get stuck into sth. (coll.)

verbellen *tr. V.* (Jägerspr.) **der Jagdhund verbellte den Bock** the hunting dog barked to show where the buck was

verbergen *unr. tr. V.* **1** (verstecken, auch fig.) hide; conceal; **jmdn. vor der Polizei verborgen halten** harbour sb.; **sich ~:** hide; **sein Gesicht in den Händen ~** bury *or* hide one's face in one's hands **2** (verheimlichen) hide; **jmdm. etw. ~, etw. vor jmdm. ~:** keep sth. from sb.; **ich will dir nicht ~, dass ...** I want you to know that ...; I want to make it clear that ...

verbessern

A *tr. V.* **1** improve ‹*machine, method, quality*›; improve [up]on, better ‹*achievement*›; beat ‹*record*›; reform ‹*schooling, world*› **2** (korrigieren) correct

B *refl. V.* **1** improve; **er hat sich im Skilauf stark verbessert** his skiing has improved a great deal **2** ([beruflich] aufsteigen) better oneself

Verbesserung *die* **1** improvement; **eine ~ der Lage** an improvement in the situation **2** (Korrektur) correction

verbesserungs·fähig *Adj.* capable of improvement *postpos.*; **es ist noch ~:** it could be improved [on]

Verbesserungs·vorschlag *der* suggestion for improvement

verbeugen *refl. V.* bow (**vor** + *Dat.* to)

Verbeugung *die;* **~, ~en** bow; **eine ~ vor jmdm. machen** bow to sb.

verbeulen *tr. V.* dent

verbiegen

A *unr. tr. V.* bend

B *unr. refl. V.* bend; buckle; **eine verbogene Wirbelsäule** a curved spine

Verbiegung *die* bending; buckling; (der Wirbelsäule) curvature

verbiestern /fɛɐ̯ˈbiːstɐn/ *tr. V.* (bes. nordd.: verwirren) confuse; bewilder

verbiestert *Adj.* (ugs.) grumpy

verbieten

A *unr. tr. V.* **1** forbid; **jmdm. etw. ~:** forbid sb. sth.; **du hast mir gar nichts zu ~:** you have no right to forbid me [to do] anything; **sie hat ihm das Haus verboten** she forbade him to enter the house; **der Arzt hat mir das Rauchen verboten** the doctor forbade me to smoke; **„Betreten des Rasens/Rauchen verboten!"** 'keep off the grass'/'no smoking'; **das verbietet mir mein Ehrgefühl** (fig.) my sense of honour prevents me from doing that; **das verbietet mir mein Geldbeutel** (fig. scherzh.) my resources don't run to that **2** (für unzulässig erklären) ban; **so viel Ignoranz müsste verboten werden** (scherzh.) such ignorance ought not to be allowed (joc.)

B *unr. refl. V.* **sich [von selbst] ~:** be out of the question

verbilden *tr. V.* bring up wrongly, miseducate ‹*person*›; **verbildeter Geschmack** (abwertend) misguided taste

verbilligen

A *tr. V.* bring down *or* reduce the cost of; bring down *or* reduce the price of, reduce ‹*goods*›; **verbilligte Butter/Waren** butter at a reduced price/reduced goods; **verbilligter Eintritt** reduced admission

B *refl. V.* become *or* get cheaper; ‹*goods*› come down in price, become *or* get cheaper

Verbilligung *die* (von Kosten) reduction; **eine ~ der Einfuhren** a reduction in the cost of imports; **zur ~ der Einfuhren** to reduce the cost of imports

verbimsen /fɛɐ̯ˈbɪmzn̩/ *tr. V.* (ugs.) bash; hit

verbinden

A *unr. tr. V.* **1** (bandagieren) bandage; dress; **jmdm./sich den Fuß ~:** bandage *or* dress sb.'s/one's foot; **jmdn./sich ~:** dress sb.'s/one's wounds **2** (zubinden) bind; **jmdm. die Augen ~:** blindfold sb.; **mit verbundenen Augen** blindfold[ed] **3** (zusammenfügen) join ‹*wires, lengths of wood, etc.*›; join up ‹*dots*› **4** (zusammenhalten) hold ‹*parts*› together **5** (in Beziehung bringen) connect (**durch** by); link ‹*towns, lakes, etc.*› (**durch** by); **ein paar ~de Worte sprechen** (fig.) say a few words as a link **6** (verknüpfen) combine ‹*abilities, qualities, etc.*›; **die damit verbundenen Anstrengungen/Kosten** *usw.* the effort/cost *etc.* involved **7** *auch itr.* (telefonisch) **jmdn. [mit jmdm.] ~:** put sb. through [to sb.]; **Moment, ich verbinde** one moment, I'll put you through; **falsch verbunden sein** have got the wrong number **8** *auch itr.* (in Bezug auf menschliche Beziehungen) **er war ihr freundschaftlich verbunden** he was bound to her by ties of friendship; **uns verbindet nichts mehr** nothing holds us together any longer; **gemeinsame Erlebnisse ~:** shared experiences draw people together **9** (assoziieren) associate (**mit** with) **10** (geh. veralt.) **jmdm. [für etw.] verbunden sein** be obliged to sb. [for sth.]

B *unr. refl. V.* **1** (zusammenkommen) (auch Chemie) combine (**mit** with) **2** (in Zusammenhang stehen) be connected *or* associated (**mit** with) **3** (sich zusammentun) join [together]; join forces; **sich zu einer Koalition ~:** join together *or* join forces to form a coalition *or* in a coalition **4** (in Gedanken) be associated (**mit** with); **mit dieser Melodie sind für mich schöne Erinnerungen verbunden** this tune has happy memories for me

verbindlich

A *Adj.* **1** (freundlich) friendly; (entgegenkommend) forthcoming; **eine ~e Verkäuferin** an obliging sales assistant; **~sten Dank!** (geh.) a thousand thanks **2** (bindend) obligatory; compulsory; binding ‹*agreement, decision, etc.*›

B *adv.* **1** (freundlich) in a friendly manner; (entgegenkommend) in a forthcoming manner **2** **~ zusagen** definitely agree; **jmdm. etw. ~ zusagen** make sb. a firm offer of sth.

Verbindlichkeit *die;* **~, ~en** **1** (Freundlichkeit) friendliness; (Entgegenkommen) forthcomingness **2** (verpflichtender Charakter) obligatory *or* compulsory nature; **rechtlich [gesehen] keine ~ haben** have no binding force in law **3** (freundliche Äußerung, Handlung) friendly remark/act; (entgegenkommende Äußerung, Handlung) forthcoming comment/gesture; **ein paar ~en sagen** say a few friendly words **4** (Pflicht) obligation; commitment **5** **~en** (Kaufmannsspr.: Schulden) liabilities (**gegen** to)

Verbindung *die* **1** (das Verknüpfen) linking **2** (Zusammenhalt) join; connection **3** (verknüpfende Strecke) link; **die kürzeste ~ zwischen zwei Punkten** the shortest line between two points **4** (Anschluss durch Telefon, Funk) connection; **keine ~ mit jmdm./einem Ort bekommen** not be able to get through to sb./a place; **unsere ~ wurde unterbrochen** we were cut off **5** (Verkehrs~) connection (**nach** to); **die ~ zur Außenwelt** connections *pl.* with the outside world **6** (Kombination) combination; **in ~ mit etw.** in conjunction with sth. **7** (Bündnis) association; **eheliche ~** (geh.) marriage; **eine ~ mit jmdm. eingehen** enter into association with sb.; (erotisch) begin a liaison with sb. **8** (Kontakt) contact; **sich mit jmdm. in ~ setzen, ~ mit jmdm. aufnehmen** get in touch *or* contact with sb.; contact sb.; **in ~ bleiben** keep in touch; **die ~ mit jmdm./etw. nicht abreißen lassen** not lose touch *or* contact with sb./sth.; **seine ~en spielen lassen** pull a few strings (coll.) **9** (Zusammenhang) connection; **jmdn. mit etw. in ~ bringen** connect sb. with sth. **10** (Studenten~) society; (für Männer) fraternity (Amer.); (für Frauen) sorority (Amer.); **eine schlagende ~:** a duelling society *or* (Amer.) fraternity **11** (das Zusammenfügen) joining **12** (das Zusammengefügtwerden) bonding **13** (bes. Chemie) (Stoff) compound; (Prozess) combination

V

Verbindungs-: ~frau *die* intermediary; (Agent) contact [woman] (**zu** with); **~linie** *die* 1 (verbindende Linie) connecting line; 2 (Milit.) communication line; line of communication; **~mann** *der; Pl.* **~männer** *od.* **~leute** intermediary; (Agent) contact [man] (**zu** with); **~offizier** *der* (Milit.) liaison officer; **~straße** *die* link road; **~stück** *das* connecting piece; **~student** *der,* **~studentin** *die* member of a students' society; *s. auch* **Verbindung 10**; **~tür** *die* connecting door

Verbiss, *Verbiß *der* (Jägerspr.) damage caused by browsing animals

verbissen
A *2. Part. v.* **verbeißen**
B *Adj.* 1 (hartnäckig) dogged; doggedly determined 2 (verkrampft) grim
C *adv.* 1 (hartnäckig) doggedly; with dogged determination 2 (verkrampft) grimly 3 (ugs.: engherzig) **etw. nicht so ~ sehen** not take sth. so seriously

Verbissenheit *die;* **~:** doggedness; dogged determination

verbitten *unr. refl. V.* **sich** (*Dat.*) **etw. ~:** refuse to tolerate sth.; **ich verbitte mir diesen Ton** I will not be spoken to in that tone of voice; **das möchte ich mir verbeten haben** I will not have it

verbittern *tr. V.* embitter; make bitter; **verbittert** embittered; bitter

Verbitterung *die;* **~, ~en** bitterness; embitterment

verblassen *itr. V.; mit sein* 1 (auch fig. geh.) fade 2 (die Leuchtkraft verlieren) ‹*star etc.*› fade, pale; ‹*sky*› grow dim; (fig.) pale; ‹*memory*› fade

verbläuen *tr. V.* (ugs.) bash *or* beat up; do over (sl.)

Verbleib *der;* **~[e]s** (geh.) 1 (Ort) whereabouts *pl.* 2 (das Verbleiben) staying; **ein weiterer ~:** a longer stay

verbleiben *unr. itr. V.; mit sein* 1 (sich einigen) **wie seid ihr denn nun verblieben?** what did you arrange?; **wir sind so verblieben, dass er sich bei mir meldet** we left it that he would contact me 2 (geh.: bleiben) remain; stay; **niemand wusste, wo Sie verblieben waren** nobody knew where you were; **im Amt ~:** remain *or* continue in office 3 (im Briefschluss) remain; **... verbleibe ich Ihr ...** ... I remain, Yours truly, ...; **ich verbleibe mit freundlichen Grüßen Ihr ...** I remain, Yours sincerely, ... 4 (übrig bleiben) remain; **etw. verbleibt jmdm.** sb. has sth. left

verbleichen *unr. od. regelm. itr. V.; mit sein* 1 (auch fig.) (blass werden) fade 2 (allmählich erlöschen) ‹*moon*› grow pale

verbleien /fɛɐ̯ˈblai̯ən/ *tr. V.* (Technik) lead ‹*petrol*›

verblenden *tr. V.* 1 blind; **ein verblendeter Revolutionär** a blind revolutionary 2 (Archit.: verkleiden) face ‹*wall, façade, etc.*›

Verblendung *die;* **~, ~en** 1 blindness 2 (bes. Archit.: Verkleidung) facing

***verbleuen** ▸ **verbläuen**

Verblichene /fɛɐ̯ˈblɪçənə/ *der/die; adj. Dekl.* (geh.) deceased; **unser teurer ~r** our dear departed brother/leader/friend *etc.*

verblöden *itr. V.; mit sein* 1 (veralt.: schwachsinnig werden) become feeble-minded 2 (ugs.: stumpfsinnig werden) become a zombie (coll.)

verblüffen /fɛɐ̯ˈblʏfn̩/ *tr. (auch itr.) V.* astonish; amaze; astound; (verwirren) baffle; **seine Offenheit verblüfft** his openness is astonishing; **ich war über seine Antwort verblüfft** I was taken aback by his answer

verblüffend
A *Adj.* astonishing; amazing; astounding
B *adv.* astonishingly; amazingly; astoundingly

Verblüffung *die;* **~, ~en** astonishment; amazement

verblühen *itr. V.; mit sein* (auch fig.) fade; **sie war schon verblüht** (geh.) her beauty had already faded

verblümt /fɛɐ̯ˈblyːmt/
A *Adj.* oblique
B *adv.* **sich ~ ausdrücken** express oneself in a roundabout *or* an oblique way

verbluten *itr. (auch refl.) V.; mit sein* bleed to death

verbocken *tr. V.* (ugs.) botch; bungle; make a botch-up of

verbohren *refl. V.* (ugs.) become obsessed (**in** + *Akk.* with)

verbohrt *Adj.* (abwertend) pigheaded; stubborn; obstinate; (unbeugsam) inflexible

Verbohrtheit *die;* **~** (abwertend) pigheadedness; stubbornness; obstinacy; (Unbeugsamkeit) inflexibility

verborgen[1] *tr. V.* lend out

verborgen[2]
A *2. Part. v.* **verbergen**
B *Adj.* 1 (abgelegen) secluded 2 (nicht sichtbar) hidden; **es wird ihm nicht ~ bleiben** he shall hear of it; (nicht entgehen) it will not escape his notice; **im Verborgenen** out of the public eye; **im Verborgenen blühen** flourish undetected

Verborgenheit *die;* **~** (Abgelegenheit) seclusion

Verbot *das;* **~[e]s, ~e** ban (*Gen.,* **von** on); **er hat gegen mein ausdrückliches ~ geraucht** he smoked although I had expressly forbidden him to do so; **trotz ärztlichen ~s** against doctor's orders

Verbots-: ~schild *das* 1 sign (*prohibiting sth.*); 2 (Verkehrsw.) prohibitive sign; **~tafel** *die* [large] sign (*prohibiting sth.*)

verbrämen /fɛɐ̯ˈbrɛːmən/ *tr. V.* 1 (einfassen) trim (**mit** with) 2 (verschleiern) dress up (fig.); **wissenschaftlich verbrämter Unsinn** nonsense dressed up as scientific fact

verbraten *unr. tr. V.* (salopp) blow (coll.) ‹*money*› (**für** on)

Verbrauch *der;* **~[e]s** 1 consumption; **die Seife ist sparsam im ~:** the soap is economical to use; **zum alsbaldigen ~ bestimmt** for immediate consumption 2 (verbrauchte Menge) consumption (**von, an** + *Dat.* of)

verbrauchen
A *tr. V.* 1 (verwenden) use; consume ‹*food, drink*›; use up ‹*provisions*›; spend ‹*money*›; consume, use ‹*fuel*›; (fig.) use up ‹*strength, energy*›; **das Auto verbraucht 10 Liter [auf 100 Kilometer]** the car does 10 kilometres to the litre 2 (verschleißen) wear out ‹*clothing, shoes, etc.*›; **die Luft in den Räumen ist verbraucht** the air in the rooms is stale
B *refl. V.* (sich abarbeiten) wear oneself out; **verbraucht aussehen** look worn out *or* exhausted

Verbraucher *der;* **~s, ~:** consumer

verbraucher-: ~feindlich A *Adj.* not in the interests of consumers *postpos.;* B *adv.* against the interests of consumers; **~freundlich** A *Adj.* consumer-friendly; B *adv.* in a consumer-friendly way

Verbraucherin *die;* **~, ~nen** consumer

Verbraucher-: ~preis *der* consumer price; **~schutz** *der* consumer protection

Verbraucherschutz·organisation *die* consumer protection organization

Verbrauchs·gut *das* consumer item; **Verbrauchsgüter** consumer goods

Verbrauch[s]·steuer *die* (Steuerw.) excise [tax]

verbrechen *unr. tr. V.* (scherzh.) **ich habe nichts verbrochen!** I haven't been up to *or* haven't done anything!; **was hast du verbrochen?** what have you been up to *or* been doing?; **wer hat dieses Gedicht verbrochen?** who's responsible for *or* who's the perpetrator of this poem?

Verbrechen *das;* **~s, ~** (auch Untat) crime (**an** + *Dat.,* **gegen** against)

Verbrechens·bekämpfung *die* combating of crime; combating crime *no art.;* **für die aktive ~:** for actively combating crime

Verbrecher *der;* **~s, ~:** criminal; **du kleiner ~!** (scherzh.) you little rascal!

Verbrecher-: ~album *das* (veralt.) ▸ **~kartei**; **~bande** *die* gang *or* band of criminals

Verbrecherin *die;* **~, ~nen** criminal

verbrecherisch *Adj.* criminal

Verbrecher-: ~jagd *die* (ugs.) chase after a/the criminal/criminals; **~kartei** *die* criminal records *pl.*; **~syndikat** *das* criminal syndicate

Verbrechertum *das;* **~s** criminality

verbreiten
A *tr. V.* 1 (bekannt machen) spread ‹*rumour, lies, etc.*›; **er verbreitete, dass ...** he spread it about that ...; **eine Nachricht über den Rundfunk ~:** broadcast an item of news on the radio 2 (weitertragen) spread ‹*disease, illness, etc.*›; disperse ‹*seeds, spores, etc.*› 3 (erwecken) radiate ‹*optimism, happiness, calm, etc.*›; spread ‹*fear*›; **ihre Gewalttaten verbreiteten überall Entsetzen** their deeds of violence horrified everyone
B *refl. V.* 1 (bekannt werden) ‹*rumour*› spread 2 (sich ausbreiten) ‹*smell, illness, religion, etc.*› spread 3 (häufig abwertend: sich äußern) go on (**über** + *Akk.* about)

verbreitern
A *tr. V.* widen; (fig.) broaden ‹*basis*›
B *refl. V.* widen out; get wider

Verbreiterung *die;* **~, ~en** 1 widening 2 (Stelle) widened section

verbreitet *Adj.* widespread; common ‹*misunderstanding, error, prejudice*›; widely used ‹*slogan, process*›; widely held ‹*view*›

Verbreitung *die;* **~, ~en** 1 ▸ **verbreiten A 1, 2, 3**: spreading; broadcasting; dispersal; radiation; **nicht für allgemeine ~ bestimmt** not [intended] for general circulation 2 (Ausbreitung) spread

Verbreitungs·gebiet *das* area of distribution; (einer Tierart) range

verbrennen
A *unr. itr. V.; mit sein* 1 burn; ‹*person*› burn to death; **die Dokumente sind verbrannt** the documents were destroyed by fire; **es riecht verbrannt** (ugs.) there's a smell of burning 2 (verkohlen) burn; **der Kuchen ist verbrannt** the cake got burnt 3 (ausdorren) scorch 4 (Chemie: sich umwandeln) be converted (**zu** into)
B *tr. V.* 1 (ins Feuer geben) burn; burn, incinerate ‹*rubbish*›; cremate ‹*dead person*› 2 ▸ⓘ **S. 439** (verletzen) burn; **sich** (*Dat.*) **an der heißen Suppe die Zunge ~:** burn *or* scald one's tongue on the hot soup; **sich** (*Dat.*) **den Mund** *od.* (derb) **das Maul** *od.* (salopp) **die Schnauze ~** (fig.) say too much; *s. auch* **Finger 2** 3 (ugs.: verbrauchen) use ‹*gas, electricity, etc.*› 4 (Chemie: umwandeln) convert

Verbrennung *die;* **~, ~en** 1 ▸ **verbrennen B 1**: burning; incineration; cremation 2 (Kfz-W.) combustion 3 ▸ⓘ **S. 439** (Wunde) burn

Verbrennungs-: ~anlage *die* incineration plant; incinerator; **~motor** *der* internal-combustion engine

verbriefen *tr. V.* attest

verbringen *unr. tr. V.* 1 spend ‹*time, holiday, weekend, year, etc.*› 2 (Papierdt.: bringen) take

verbrüdern *refl. V.* avow friendship and brotherhood; ‹*troops*› fraternize (**mit** with); (Politik) ally oneself/itself

Verbrüderung *die;* **~, ~en** avowal of friendship and brotherhood; (von Truppen) fraternization; (Politik) alliance

verbrühen *tr. V.* ▸ⓘ **S. 439** scald; **sich** (*Dat.*) **den Arm ~:** scald one's arm; **sich ~:** scald oneself

Verbrühung *die;* **~, ~en** 1 (das Verbrühen) scalding 2 (Wunde) scald

verbuchen *tr. V.* (Kaufmannsspr., Finanzw.) enter; (fig.) notch up ‹*success, score, etc.*›; **etw. auf einem Konto/im Haben ~:** credit sth. to an account/enter sth. on the credit side

verbuddeln *tr. V.* (ugs.) bury

Verbum /ˈvɛrbʊm/ *das;* **~s, Verben** *od.* (Sprachw. veralt.) **Verba** verb

verbummeln *tr. V.* (ugs., oft abwertend) 1 (verbringen) waste, fritter away ‹*time, day, afternoon, etc.*›; **sie wollten einmal einen ganzen Tag ~:** they wanted to spend a whole day lazing around doing nothing 2 (vergessen) forget [all]

V

about; clean forget; (verlieren) lose; (verlegen) mislay

Verbund der; ~[e]s, ~e 1 (Wirtsch.) association; **im ~ arbeiten** cooperate 2 (Technik) composite

Verbund·bau·weise die composite construction

verbünden /fɛɐ̯ˈbʏndn̩/ refl. V. form an alliance

Verbundenheit die; ~: closeness (**mit** to); (mit einem Ort, einer Tradition) attachment (**mit** to); **aus alter ~:** for the sake of old ties/attachments; **in herzlicher ~:** with deepest sympathy

verbündet Adj. **[miteinander] ~:** in alliance *postpos.*

Verbündete der/die; adj. Dekl. ally

Verbund-: **~glas** das (Technik) laminated glass; **~netz** das grid [system]; **~stein** der interlocking paving stone

verbürgen
A refl. V. (bürgen) vouch (**für** for); **sich für die Kosten ~:** accept liability for the costs
B tr. V. 1 (garantieren) guarantee; **verbürgte Rechte** established rights 2 *nur im Perf., Plusq. u. im 2. Part. gebr.* (authentisieren) verify; authenticate

verbürgerlichen
A itr. V.; *mit sein* become bourgeois
B tr. V. make bourgeois

verbüßen tr. V. serve ‹*sentence*›

Verbüßung die; ~: serving

verchromen tr. V. chromium-plate

Verdacht /fɛɐ̯ˈdaxt/ der; ~[e]s, ~e od. **Verdächte** /fɛɐ̯ˈdɛçtə/ suspicion; **mein ~ hat sich bestätigt/war begründet** my suspicion was confirmed/was well founded; **der ~ der Polizei fiel auf/richtete sich gegen ...** the police suspected ...; **ein ~ stieg in mir auf** I began to suspect something *or* to be suspicious; **er wurde wegen ~s der Steuerhinterziehung verhaftet** he was arrested on suspicion of tax evasion; **~ schöpfen** become suspicious; **jmdn. auf [einen] bloßen ~ hin verhaften lassen** have sb. arrested purely on suspicion; **wen hast du in ~?** who do you suspect?; **ich geriet in [den] ~, das Geld gestohlen zu haben** I was suspected of having stolen the money; **er ist über jeden ~ erhaben** he is above suspicion; **bei dem Patienten besteht ~ auf Meningitis** the patient is suspected of having meningitis; **etw. auf ~ tun** (ugs.) do sth. just in case

verdächtig /fɛɐ̯ˈdɛçtɪç/
A Adj. suspicious; **sich ~ machen** arouse suspicion; **er ist dringend der Tat ~:** he is strongly suspected of being the perpetrator
B adv. suspiciously

-verdächtig 1 (unter Verdacht stehend) suspected of ...; **mord~:** suspected of murder 2 (erwarten lassend) expected to ...; **ein hit~es Lied** a song expected to be a hit; **der medaillen~e Sportler** the sportsman expected to win a/the medal

Verdächtige der/die; adj. Dekl. suspect

verdächtigen tr. V. suspect (Gen. of)

Verdächtigte der/die; adj. Dekl. suspect

Verdächtigung die; ~, ~en suspicion

Verdachts·moment das incriminating factor

verdammen tr. V. 1 (verwerfen) condemn; (Rel.) damn ‹*sinner*›; **[Gott] verdamm mich!** damn it (coll.) 2 (zwingen) condemn (**zu** to); **das ist zum Scheitern verdammt** it is doomed to failure

verdämmern (geh.)
A itr. V.; *mit sein* fade
B tr. V. drowse away

Verdammnis die; ~ (christl. Theol.) damnation *no art.*

verdammt
A Adj. 1 (salopp abwertend) bloody (Brit. sl.); damned (coll.); **~ [noch mal** od. **noch eins]!** damn [it all] (coll.); bloody hell (Brit. sl.); **~ und zugenäht!** damn and blast [it]! (coll.); **so ein ~er Mist!** bloody hell (Brit. sl.) 2 (ugs.: sehr groß) **einen ~en Hunger haben** be damned hungry (coll.); **[ein] ~es Glück haben** be damn[ed] lucky (coll.)
B adv. (ugs.: sehr) damn[ed] (coll.) ‹*cold, heavy, beautiful, etc.*›; **ich musste mich ~ beherrschen** I had to keep a bloody good grip on myself (Brit. coll.)

Verdammte der/die; adj. Dekl. damned person/man/woman; **die ~n** the damned

Verdammung die; ~, ~en condemnation; damnation

verdammungs·würdig (geh.)
A Adj. damnable
B adv. damnably

verdampfen
A itr. V.; *mit sein* evaporate; vaporize; (fig.) ‹*anger*› abate; ‹*person*› make oneself scarce (coll.)
B tr. V. evaporate; vaporize

verdanken tr. V. **jmdm./einer Sache etw. ~:** owe sth. to sb./sth.; **ich verdanke meiner Frau wertvolle Anregungen** I have to thank my wife for valuable suggestions; **dass Sie bei uns sind, ~ wir ...** it is thanks *or* due to ... that you are here with us

verdarb /fɛɐ̯ˈdarp/ *1. u. 3. Pers. Sg. Prät. v.* **verderben**

verdaten tr. V. (DV) convert into data; (erfassen) store away on computer

verdattert /fɛɐ̯ˈdatɐt/ Adj. (ugs.) (überrascht) flabbergasted; (verwirrt) dazed; stunned; **~ dastehen** stand there flabbergasted/in a daze

verdauen /fɛɐ̯ˈdau̯ən/
A tr. V. (auch fig.) digest; (fig.) get over ‹*bad experience, shock, blow of fate*›; (Boxerjargon) take ‹*blow*›
B itr. V. digest [one's food]

verdaulich /fɛɐ̯ˈdaulɪç/ Adj. digestible

Verdaulichkeit die; ~: digestibility

Verdauung die; ~: digestion

Verdauungs-: **~beschwerden** Pl. digestive trouble *sing.*; **~spaziergang** der (ugs.) after-dinner walk; **~störung** die poor digestion *no pl.*; **~trakt** der ▸ **S. 435** (Anat.) digestive *or* alimentary tract

Verdeck das; ~[e]s, ~e top; hood (Brit.); (bei Kinderwagen) hood; **mit offenem ~ fahren** drive with the top *or* hood down

verdecken tr. V. 1 (nicht sichtbar sein lassen) hide; cover; **jmdm. die Sicht ~:** block sb.'s view 2 (verbergen) cover; conceal; (fig.) conceal ‹*intentions etc.*›

verdeckt
A Adj. concealed; (geheim) secret ‹*payment, surveillance, observation, etc.*›; (unter falscher Identität) undercover ‹*investigator, investigation, operation*›
B adv. (geheim) secretly; (unter falscher Identität) ‹*work, act, live, etc.*› under cover

verdenken unr. tr. V. **jmdm. etw. nicht ~ [können]** not [be able to] hold sth. against sb.; **kann man ihnen ~, dass sie ... hassen?** can one blame them for hating ...?

Verderb der; ~s 1 (von Lebensmitteln) spoilage 2 ▸ **Gedeih**

verderben
A unr. itr. V.; *mit sein* ‹*food, harvest*› go bad *or* off, spoil; **verdorbene Lebensmittel** food which has gone bad *or* off
B unr. tr. V. 1 (unbrauchbar machen) spoil; (stärker) ruin; **daran ist nichts mehr zu ~:** it's in a pretty sorry state anyway 2 (zunichte machen) ruin; spoil ‹*appetite, enjoyment, fun, etc.*›; **jmdm. die gute Laune ~:** spoil sb.'s good mood; **jmdm. den Abend ~:** ruin sb.'s evening 3 (geh.: negativ beeinflussen) corrupt; deprave; **er will es mit niemandem ~:** he tries to please everybody; he likes to keep in with everybody
C unr. refl. V. **sich** (Dat.) **den Magen/die Augen ~:** give oneself an upset stomach/ruin one's eyesight

Verderben das; ~s undoing; ruin; (Theol.) destruction; **sie sind ins/in ihr ~ gerannt** they rushed headlong towards ruin

verderben·bringend Adj. disastrous ‹*policy*›; deadly ‹*weapon, disease, etc.*›

Verderber der; ~s, ~, **Verderberin** die; ~, ~nen destroyer; **ein ~ der Jugend** a corrupter of youth

verderblich Adj. 1 perishable ‹*food*›; **leicht ~:** highly perishable 2 (unheilvoll) pernicious; (moralisch schädlich) corrupting; pernicious ‹*influence, effect, etc.*›

Verderblichkeit die; ~ ▸**verderblich**: perishableness; perniciousness; corrupting effect

verderbt Adj. 1 (geh. veralt.: verdorben) corrupt; depraved 2 (Literaturw.) illegible

Verderbtheit die; ~ (geh. veralt.: Verdorbenheit) corruptness; depravity

verdeutlichen tr. V. **etw. ~:** make sth. clear; (erklären) explain sth.; **etw. näher ~:** clarify sth. further

verdeutschen tr. V. 1 (veralt.: übersetzen) translate into German; (eindeutschen) Germanize ‹*name*› 2 (ugs.: erläutern) put ‹*facts etc.*› more plainly; translate ‹*instruction, officialese, etc.*› into everyday *or* ordinary language

verdichten
A refl. V. ‹*fog, smoke*› thicken, become thicker; (fig.) ‹*suspicion, rumour*› grow; ‹*feeling*› intensify
B tr. V. 1 (Physik, Technik) compress; (fig.) condense ‹*events etc.*› (**zu** into) 2 (ausbauen) increase the density of ‹*road network, public transport*›

verdicken
A refl. V. ‹*hard skin*› thicken, become thicker; (anschwellen) ‹*finger, jaw, etc.*› swell
B tr. V. thicken ‹*sauce*›; (gelieren lassen) cause ‹*fruit juice etc.*› to set

Verdickung die; ~, ~en 1 thickening; (Schwellung) swelling 2 (verdickte Stelle) (einer Arterie) thickened section; (Schwellung) swelling

verdienen
A tr. V. 1 (in Form von Geld) earn; **sauer/ehrlich verdientes Geld** hard-/honestly-earned money 2 (wert sein) deserve; **er verdient kein Vertrauen** he doesn't deserve to be trusted; **er hat es nicht besser/nicht anders verdient** he didn't deserve any better/anything else; **womit habe ich das verdient?** what have I done to deserve that?; **er hat die verdiente Strafe bekommen** he got the punishment he deserved
B itr. V. **beide Eheleute ~:** husband and wife are both wage earners *or* are both earning; **gut ~:** have a good income

Verdiener der; ~s, ~, **Verdienerin** die; ~, ~nen wage earner; **die Mutter ist die Verdienerin:** the mother is the breadwinner

Verdienst[1] der income; earnings *pl.*

Verdienst[2] das; ~[e]s, ~e merit; **sich** (Dat.) **etw. als** od. **zum ~ anrechnen** take the credit for sth.; **er hat sich** (Dat.) **große ~e um die Stadt erworben** he made a great contribution to the town

Verdienst-: **~aus·fall** der loss of earnings; **~kreuz** das: *national decoration awarded for service to the community*; **~orden** der order of merit

verdienst·voll
A Adj. 1 (lobenswert) commendable 2 (verdient) ‹*person*› of outstanding merit
B adv. (lobenswert) commendably

verdient
A Adj. 1 ‹*person*› of outstanding merit; **sich um etw. ~ machen** render outstanding services to sth. 2 (gerecht, zustehend) well-deserved
B adv. deservedly

verdientermaßen Adv. deservedly

Verdikt /vɛrˈdɪkt/ das; ~[e]s, ~e (geh.) verdict

verdingen unr. od. regelm. refl. V. (veralt.) go into service (**bei** with); go to work (**bei** for)

verdinglichen tr. V. (Philos.) reify

Verdinglichung die; ~, ~en (Philos.) reification

verdolmetschen tr. V. (ugs.) interpret, translate (Dat. for)

verdonnern tr. V. (salopp) sentence; **zu einem Bußgeld verdonnert werden** be ordered to pay a fine; **jmdn. dazu ~, etw. zu tun** order *or* make sb. do sth. [as a punishment]; **jmdn. zu einer Strafarbeit ~:** give sb. an imposition

verdoppeln
A tr. V. double; (fig.) double, redouble ‹*efforts etc.*›

V

B *refl. V.* double
Verdopp[e]lung *die;* ~, ~**en** doubling
verdorben /fɛɐ̯ˈdɔrbn̩/ *2. Part. v.* **verderben**
Verdorbenheit *die;* ~: depravity
verdorren /fɛɐ̯ˈdɔrən/ *itr. V.; mit sein* wither [and die]; ‹*meadow*› scorch
verdrängen *tr. V.* **1** (wegdrängen) drive out ‹*inhabitants*›; (fig.: ersetzen) displace; **das Schiff verdrängt 15 000 Tonnen** the ship displaces 15,000 tons; **jmdn. aus seiner Stellung** ~: oust sb. from his/her job **2** (Psych.) repress/(bewusst) suppress ‹*experience, desire, etc.*›
Verdrängung *die;* ~, ~**en** **1** ▸**verdrängen 1**: driving out; displacement; ousting **2** (Psych.) repression; (bewusst) suppression
Verdrängungs·wettbewerb *der* (Kaufmannsspr.) competition for markets
verdrecken (ugs. abwertend)
A *tr. V.* make filthy dirty
B *itr. V.; mit sein* get *or* become filthy dirty
verdrehen *tr. V.* **1** twist ‹*joint*›; roll ‹*eyes*›; **den Hals** ~: twist one's head round; **sich** (*Dat.*) **den Hals** ~: crick one's neck; **jmdm. das Handgelenk** ~: twist sb.'s wrist; *s. auch* **Kopf 5** **2** (ugs. abwertend: entstellen) twist ‹*words, facts, etc.*›; distort ‹*sense*›
verdreht *Adj.* (ugs. abwertend) crazy
Verdrehtheit *die;* ~ (ugs. abwertend) (Verrücktheit) craziness; (Verwirrung) confusion
verdreifachen *refl., tr. V.* treble; triple
verdreschen *unr. tr. V.* (ugs.) thrash
verdrießen /fɛɐ̯ˈdriːsn̩/ *unr. tr. V.* (geh.) irritate; annoy; **es sich nicht** ~ **lassen** (geh.) not be put off
verdrießlich
A *Adj.* **1** (missmutig) morose **2** (geh., veralt.: unangenehm) irksome ‹*task, matter, etc.*›
B *adv.* (missmutig) morosely
Verdrießlichkeit *die;* ~, ~**en** **1** (Missmut) moroseness **2** (unangenehmer Vorgang) irksome thing/matter *etc.*
verdross, ***verdroß** /fɛɐ̯ˈdrɔs/ *1. u. 3. Pers. Sg. Prät. v.* **verdrießen**
verdrossen
A *2. Part. v.* **verdrießen**
B *Adj.* (missmutig) morose; (missmutig und lustlos) sullen
C *adv.* (missmutig) morosely; (missmutig und lustlos) sullenly
Verdrossenheit *die;* ~ ▸**verdrossen B**: moroseness; sullenness
verdrücken (ugs.)
A *tr. V.* **1** (essen) polish off (coll.) **2** (verknautschen) crumple ‹*clothes*›
B *refl. V.* slip away
Verdruss, ***Verdruß** /fɛɐ̯ˈdrʊs/ *der;* **Verdrusses, Verdrusse** annoyance; (Unzufriedenheit) dissatisfaction; discontentment; **jmdm.** ~ **bereiten** annoy sb.
verduften *itr. V.; mit sein* **1** (Duft verlieren) ‹*coffee*› lose its aroma; ‹*aroma*› go **2** (salopp: sich entfernen) hop it (Brit. coll.); clear off (coll.)
verdummen
A *tr. V.* **jmdn.** ~: dull sb.'s mind
B *itr. V.; mit sein* become stultified
Verdummung *die;* ~ **1** **die** ~ **der Massen zum Ziel haben** be aimed at dulling the mind of the masses **2** (das Dummwerden) stultification
verdunkeln
A *tr. V.* **1** darken; (vollständig) black out ‹*room, house, etc.*› **2** (verdecken) darken; (fig.) cast a shadow on ‹*happiness etc.*› **3** (bes. Rechtsw.) obscure ‹*facts, situation, etc.*›
B *refl. V.* darken; grow darker; (fig.) ‹*expression etc.*› darken
Verdunkelung *die;* ~, ~**en** **1** (das Verdunkeln) darkening; (vollständig) blackout **2** (Vorrichtung) black out blind[s]/curtain[s] **3** (bes. Rechtsw.) obscuring; obscuration
Verdunkelungs·gefahr *die* (Rechtsw.) danger of suppression of evidence
Verdunklung *die;* ~, ~**en** ▸**Verdunkelung**

verdünnen *tr. V.* **1** dilute; (mit Wasser) water down; dilute; thin [down] ‹*paint etc.*› **2** (dünner machen) taper [off] ‹*stick etc.*› **3** (Militärjargon) reduce the number of ‹*troops etc.*› [in an/the area]
Verdünner *der;* ~**s**, ~, **Verdünnungs·mittel** *das* thinner; (in der Industrie) diluent
verdünnisieren *refl. V.* (salopp) clear off (coll.)
Verdünnung *die;* ~, ~**en** **1** dilution; (der Luft) rarefaction **2** (chem. Mittel) thinner
verdunsten
A *itr. V.; mit sein* evaporate
B *tr. V.* evaporate; ‹*plant*› transpire ‹*water*›
Verdunstung *die;* ~: evaporation
verdursten *itr. V.; mit sein* (auch fig.) die of thirst
verdüstern
A *tr. V.* darken; (fig. geh.) cast a shadow across
B *refl. V.* darken; grow dark; (fig.) darken
verdutzt /fɛɐ̯ˈdʊtst/ *Adj.* taken aback *pred.;* nonplussed; (verwirrt) baffled; ~ **hielt er inne** taken aback *or* nonplussed, he paused
Verdutztheit *die;* ~: bafflement
verebben *itr. V.; mit sein* (geh.) subside
veredeln *tr. V.* **1** (geh.) ennoble; improve ‹*taste*› **2** (Technik) refine; beneficiate ‹*coal*› **3** (Gartenbau) graft
Vered[e]lung *die;* ~, ~**en** **1** (geh.) ennoblement; (des Geschmacks) improvement **2** (Technik) refinement; (von Kohle) beneficiation **3** (Gartenbau) grafting
verehelichen *refl. V.* (Papierdt., veralt.) **sich jmdm.** ~: marry sb.; **Else Müller, verehelichte Meyer** Else Meyer, née Müller
Verehelichung *die;* ~, ~**en** (Papierdt., veralt.) marriage (**mit** to)
verehren *tr. V.* **1** (vergöttern) venerate; revere; **[sehr] verehrte Anwesende!** Ladies and Gentlemen; (in Briefanreden) **verehrte gnädige Frau!** [Dear] Madam; **verehrte Frau Müller!** Dear Frau Müller **2** (geh.: bewundern) admire; (ehrerbietig lieben) worship; adore **3** (scherzh.: schenken) give; **darf ich Ihnen dieses Buch** ~? may I make you a little gift of this book?
Verehrer *der;* ~**s**, ~, **Verehrerin** *die;* ~, ~**nen** admirer
Verehrung *die* **1** veneration; reverence **2** (Bewunderung) admiration
verehrungs·würdig *Adj.* admirable
vereidigen /fɛɐ̯ˈlaidɪɡn̩/ *tr. V.* swear in; **einen Zeugen vor Gericht** ~: swear in a witness; **jmdn. auf etw.** (*Akk.*) ~: make sb. swear to sth.; **ein vereidigter Sachverständiger** a sworn expert
Vereidigung *die;* ~, ~**en** swearing in
Verein *der;* ~**[e]s**, ~**e** **1** organization; (zur Förderung der Denkmalspflege usw.) society; (der Kunstfreunde usw.) association; society; (Sport~) club; (fig. ugs.) crowd (coll.); (kleiner) bunch (coll.) **2** **im** ~ **[mit]** in conjunction with; together with; **in trautem** ~ **[mit]** (scherzh.) in an unlikely twosome/group [with]

> **Verein**
>
> There are over 300,000 officially registered *Vereine* (clubs or associations) with their own constitution and by-laws. Millions of Germans belong to a club; nearly one in four is a member of a sports club, and there are around 15 million hiking-club members. Stamp collectors, marksmen, dog breeders, music fans, in fact those who follow any kind of activity or hobby, are soon organized into a *Verein*. Membership fees are usually low, and everybody is encouraged to socialize at club level.

vereinbar *Adj.* compatible (**mit** with); **nicht** ~: incompatible; **etw. ist mit etw. nur schwerlich** ~: it is difficult to reconcile sth. with sth.
vereinbaren *tr. V.* **1** (festlegen) agree; arrange ‹*meeting etc.*› **2** (harmonieren) **[nicht] zu** ~ **sein, sich [nicht]** ~ **lassen** be [in]compatible *or* [ir]reconcilable; **etw. mit etw. [nicht]** ~ **können** [not] be able to reconcile sth. with sth.

Vereinbarkeit *die;* ~, ~**en** compatibility; **die** ~ **von Familien- und Berufsleben** the compatibility of family life with *or* and working life
Vereinbarung *die;* ~, ~**en** **1** (das Festlegen) agreeing; (eines Termins usw.) arranging **2** (Abmachung) agreement; **eine** ~ **treffen** come to an agreement
vereinbarungs·gemäß
A *Adj.* as agreed/arranged *postpos*
B *adv.* as agreed/arranged
vereinen
A *tr. V.* **1** (zusammenfassen) unite; merge ‹*businesses*› (**zu** into) **2** (harmonisieren) reconcile **3** (besitzen) combine; **er vereint alle Kompetenzen in seiner Hand** he combines all responsibilities
B *refl. V.* **1** **sich zu gemeinsamem Handeln** ~: join forces **2** (vorhanden sein) combine; **in ihr** ~ **sich Geist und Anmut** in her, beauty and intellect are united
vereinfachen *tr. V.* simplify
Vereinfachung *die;* ~, ~**en** simplification
vereinheitlichen *tr. V.* standardize
Vereinheitlichung *die;* ~, ~**en** standardization
vereinigen
A *tr. V.* **1** (zusammenschließen) unite; merge ‹*businesses*› **2** (zusammenfassen) bring together; **alle Ämter sind in einer Person vereinigt** all offices are held by the same person; **die Mehrheit der Stimmen auf sich** ~: receive the majority of the votes
B *refl. V.* **1** (sich zusammenschließen) unite; ‹*organizations, firms*› merge; (fig.) be combined **2** (zusammentreffen) assemble (**zu** for); ‹*rivers*› meet, merge; **Fulda und Werra** ~ **sich zur Weser** the Fulda and the Werra meet and form the Weser **3** (geh.: sich paaren) couple
vereinigt *Adj.* **Vereinigte Arabische Emirate** United Arab Emirates; **Vereinigtes Königreich [Großbritannien und Nordirland]** United Kingdom [of Great Britain and Northern Ireland]; **Vereinigte Staaten [von Amerika]** United States *sing.* [of America]
Vereinigung *die* **1** (Rechtsw.) organization **2** (Zusammenschluss) uniting; (von Unternehmen) merging **3** (geh.: Koitus) union **4** (Zusammentreffen) assembly; (von Flüssen) meeting; merging
Vereinigungs-: ~**freiheit** *die* ▸**Koalitionsfreiheit**; ~**menge** *die* (Math.) union of sets
vereinnahmen *tr. V.* (Kaufmannsspr.) take; collect ‹*dividend*›; (fig.) monopolize
vereinsamen *itr. V.; mit sein* become [increasingly] lonely *or* isolated
Vereinsamung *die;* ~: loneliness; isolation
Vereins-: ~**freiheit** *die* freedom of association; ~**kamerad** *der,* ~**kameradin** *die* fellow club *etc.* member; ~**lokal** *das* club's *etc.* local pub (Brit.)/meeting room; ~**meier** *der;* ~~**s**, ~~ (ugs. abwertend) [real] clubman; enthusiast for club life; ~**meierei** *die* (ugs. abwertend) enthusiasm for club life; ~**sport** *der* club sport
vereinzeln *tr. V.* **1** (geh.) isolate **2** (Forstw., Landw.) thin out
vereinzelt
A *Adj.* occasional; isolated, occasional ‹*shower, outbreak of rain, etc.*›; **in** ~**en Fällen** in isolated cases
B *adv.* (zeitlich) occasionally; now and then; (örtlich) here and there
Vereinzelung *die;* ~, ~**en** isolation
vereisen
A *itr. V.; mit sein* freeze *or* ice over; ‹*wing*› ice up; ‹*lock*› freeze up; **eine vereiste Fahrbahn** an icy carriageway
B *tr. V.* (Med.) freeze
Vereisung *die;* ~, ~**en** **1** freezing *or* icing over; (einer Tragfläche) icing up; (eines Schlosses) freezing up **2** (Med.) freezing
vereiteln *tr. V.* thwart; prevent; thwart, foil ‹*attempt, plan, etc.*›; thwart, frustrate ‹*efforts, intentions, etc.*›

V

Vereitelung *die;* ~ ▸**vereiteln**: thwarting; prevention; foiling; frustrating

vereitern *itr. V.; mit sein* go septic; **vereitert sein** be septic; **dieser Zahn ist vereitert** this tooth has an abscess

Vereiterung *die* suppuration; (eines Zahns) abscess

verekeln *tr. V.* **jmdm. etw.** ~: put sb. off sth.

verelenden *itr. V.; mit sein* (geh., Soziol.) sink into poverty

Verelendung *die;* ~, ~en (geh., Soziol.) impoverishment

Verelendungs·theorie *die* (Soziol.) theory of the pauperization of the proletariat

verenden *itr. V.; mit sein* perish; die

verengen
A *refl. V.* narrow; become narrow; ‹*pupils*› contract; ‹*blood vessel*› constrict, become constricted
B *tr. V.* make narrower; narrow; restrict, narrow ‹*field of vision etc.*›; make ‹*circle, loop*› smaller

Verengung *die;* ~, ~en [1] (das [Sich]verengen) narrowing; (eines Blutgefäßes) constriction [2] (verengte Stelle) narrow part

vererben
A *tr. V.* [1] leave, bequeath ‹*property*› (*Dat.*, **an** + *Akk.* to); (fig.: schenken) bequeath (joc.) (*Dat.* to) [2] (Biol., Med.) transmit, pass on ‹*characteristic, disease*›; pass on ‹*talent*› (*Dat.*, **auf** + *Akk.* to)
B *refl. V.* (Biol., Med.) ‹*disease, tendency*› be passed on *or* transmitted (**auf** + *Akk.* to)

vererblich *Adj.* heritable ‹*goods, property*›

Vererbung *die;* ~, ~en (Biol., Med.) heredity *no art.*; **das ist** ~: it runs in the family

Vererbungs·lehre *die* genetics *sing., no art.*

verewigen
A *tr. V.* immortalize; (andauern lassen) perpetuate ‹*situation etc.*›; preserve ‹*text*› for posterity
B *refl. V.* (ugs.: Spuren hinterlassen) leave one's mark

verfahren[1]
A *unr. refl. V.* lose one's way
B *unr. tr. V.* use up ‹*petrol*›; **50 Euro mit dem Taxi** ~: spend 50 euros on a taxi/taxis
C *unr. itr. V.; mit sein* [1] (handeln) proceed [2] (umgehen) **mit jmdm./etw.** ~: deal with sb./sth.

verfahren[2] *Adj.* dead-end ‹*situation*›

Verfahren *das;* ~s, ~ [1] procedure; (Technik) process; (Methode) method [2] (Rechtsw.) proceedings *pl.*

Verfahrens-: ~**frage** *die* question *or* matter of procedure; procedural question *or* matter; ~**technik** *die* process engineering *no art.*; ~**weise** *die* procedure; method of proceeding; modus operandi

-verfall *der:* **Dollar-/Währungs**~: collapse of the dollar/currency; **Preis**~: collapse of prices

Verfall *der* [1] decay; dilapidation; (fig.: der Preise, einer Währung) collapse; **mit der Pensionierung begann sein gesundheitlicher** ~: on retirement his health started to deteriorate [2] (Auflösung) decline; **sittlicher** ~: moral degeneracy [3] (das Ungültigwerden) expiry

verfallen *unr. itr. V.; mit sein* [1] (baufällig werden) fall into disrepair; become dilapidated [2] (körperlich) ‹*strength*› decline; **der Kranke verfiel zusehends** the patient went into a rapid decline [3] (untergehen) ‹*empire*› decline; ‹*morals, morale*› deteriorate [4] (ungültig werden) expire [5] (hörig werden) **jmdm.** ~: become a slave; **einem Irrtum** ~: fall a victim to an error; **dem Alkohol** ~: become addicted to alcohol; **jmdm. ~ sein** be completely captivated by sb. [6] (geraten) **in einen Schlummer** ~: sink into a doze; **in den alten Fehler/Ton** ~: make the same old mistake/adopt the same old tone [7] (übergehen) **in seinen Dialekt** ~: lapse into one's dialect; **das Pferd verfiel in [einen] Trab** the horse broke into a trot [8] **auf jmdn./etw.** ~: think of sb./sth.; **auf einen sonderbaren Gedanken** ~: hit upon a strange idea; **warum seid ihr gerade auf uns** ~? what made you turn to us? [9] (zufallen) **dem Staat** ~: be forfeited to the state

Verfalls-: ~**datum** *das* use-by date; (ugs.: Mindesthaltbarkeitsdatum) best-before date; ~**erscheinung** *die* symptom of decline (*Gen.* in); (in der Sprache) sign of deterioration

verfälschen *tr. V.* distort, misrepresent ‹*statement, message*›; falsify, misrepresent ‹*facts, history, truth*›; falsify ‹*painting, banknote*›; adulterate ‹*wine, milk, etc.*›

Verfälschung *die* ▸**verfälschen**: distortion; misrepresentation; falsification; adulteration

verfangen
A *unr. refl. V.* get caught; (fig.) become entangled (**in** + *Dat.* in); **sich in Widersprüchen** ~ (fig.) contradict oneself
B *unr. itr. V.* have the desired effect; **wenig/nicht** ~: have little/no effect; **solche Tricks ~ bei mir nicht** such tricks cut no ice with me (coll.); such tricks won't get you/him *etc.* anywhere *or* won't work with me

verfänglich /fɛɐ̯ˈfɛŋlɪç/ *Adj.* awkward, embarrassing ‹*situation, question, etc.*›; incriminating ‹*evidence, letter, etc.*›

verfärben
A *refl. V.* change colour; ‹*washing*› become discoloured; ‹*leaves*› turn; **sich rot** ~: change colour to red/be stained red/turn red
B *tr. V.* discolour

Verfärbung *die* [1] (das [Sich]verfärben) change of colour [2] (verfärbte Stelle) discoloration; discoloured patch

verfassen *tr. V.* write; compose ‹*poetry*›; write, draw up ‹*document, law, etc.*›; draw up ‹*resolution*›

Verfasser *der;* ~s, ~, **Verfasserin** *die;* ~, ~nen writer; (eines Buchs, Artikels usw.) author; writer

Verfasserschaft *die;* ~: authorship

Verfassung *die* [1] (Politik) constitution [2] (Zustand) state [of health/mind]; **in guter/schlechter ~ sein** be in good/poor shape; **in bester** ~: on top form; **nicht in der ~ sein, Witze zu machen** not be in a joking mood; be in no mood to joke *or* to make jokes

verfassung·gebend *Adj.* constituent ‹*assembly, power, etc.*›

verfassungs-, Verfassungs-: ~**änderung** *die* constitutional amendment; ~**beschwerde** *die* (Rechtsw.) complaint about an infringement/infringements of the constitution (*committed by the State*); ~**bruch** *der* breach of the constitution; ~**feindlich** *Adj.* anti-constitutional; ~**gericht** *das* constitutional court; ~**konform** *Adj.* in conformity with the constitution; ~**mäßig** **A** *Adj.* constitutional; **B** *adv.* constitutionally; in accordance with a/the constitution; ~**rechtlich** **A** *Adj.* ‹*norms etc.*› of constitutional law; ‹*foundation*› in constitutional law; **aus ~rechtlicher Sicht** from the viewpoint of constitutional law; **B** *adv.* in terms of constitutional law; ‹*protected, guaranteed*› by constitutional law; ~**richter** *der*, ~**richterin** *die* judge of the Constitutional Court; ~**schutz** *der* [1] defence *or* protection of the constitution; [2] (Ämter) authorities responsible for the defence *or* protection of the constitution

verfaulen *itr. V.; mit sein* rot; (fig.) ‹*system, social order*› decay; (fig.: moralisch) degenerate

verfechten *unr. tr. V.* (eintreten für) advocate, champion ‹*theory, hypothesis, etc.*›; uphold ‹*view*›; (verteidigen) defend

Verfechter *der*, **Verfechterin** *die;* ~, ~nen advocate; champion

verfehlen *tr. V.* [1] (verpassen) miss ‹*train, person, etc.*› [2] (vorbeigehen) miss ‹*goal, target, etc.*›; **er hat seinen Beruf verfehlt** (fig.) he has missed his true vocation *or* is in the wrong job; **eine verfehlte Politik** (fig.) an unsuccessful policy; *s. auch* **Thema 1**

Verfehlung *die;* ~, ~en misdemeanour; (Rel.: Sünde) transgression

verfeinden *refl. V.* **sich ~ mit** make an enemy of; **verfeindet sein** be enemies; **sie hatten sich wegen einer Kleinigkeit verfeindet** they had fallen out over a trifling matter

verfeinern /fɛɐ̯ˈfainɐn/
A *tr. V.* improve; refine ‹*method, procedure, sense*›
B *refl. V.* improve; ‹*method, procedure, sense*› be refined

Verfeinerung *die;* ~, ~en [1] ▸**verfeinern A, B**: improvement; refinement; **etw. zur ~ tun** do sth. as a refinement [2] (etwas Verfeinertes) refinement

verfemen *tr. V.* (geh.) outlaw ‹*person, act*›; (verbieten) ban; (innerhalb einer Gruppe) ostracize ‹*person*›

Verfemte *der/die; adj. Dekl.* (geh.) outlaw; (fig.) ostracized person

verfertigen *tr. V.* produce; make; produce ‹*document*›

Verfertigung *die* production

verfestigen
A *tr. V.* harden; (verstärken) reinforce; strengthen
B *refl. V.* harden; (verstärkt werden) be reinforced *or* strengthened; (sich etablieren) become firmly established (**zu** + *Dat.* as)

Verfestigung *die* hardening; (Verstärkung) reinforcement; strengthening

verfetten *itr. V.; mit sein* become [too] fat

verfeuern *tr. V.* [1] burn; **alles Holz verfeuert haben** have used up all the wood [2] (verschießen) fire; **alle Munition war verfeuert** all the ammunition had been used up

verfilmen *tr. V.* [1] film; make a film of; **der Roman wird jetzt verfilmt** the novel is now being made into a film [2] (auf Mikrofilm aufnehmen) microfilm

Verfilmung *die;* ~, ~en [1] (das Verfilmen) filming [2] (Film) film [version]

verfilzen *itr. V.; mit sein* ‹*fabric, garment*› felt; become felted; ‹*hair*› become matted

verfinstern
A *tr. V.* obscure ‹*sun etc.*›
B *refl. V.* (auch fig.) darken

Verfinsterung *die;* ~, ~en darkening

verflachen
A *itr. V.; mit sein* ‹*ground*› flatten *or* level out, become flatter; ‹*water*› become shallow; (fig.) ‹*discussion*› become superficial *or* trivial
B *refl. V.* ‹*ground*› flatten *or* level out
C *tr. V.* flatten; level

verflechten *unr. tr. V.* interweave; intertwine; interlace; (verwickeln) involve; **[eng/innig] miteinander verflochten sein** (fig.) be [closely/intimately] interlinked

Verflechtung *die;* ~, ~en interconnection; (Verwicklung) involvement; **eine gegenseitige finanzielle** ~: a financial link-up

verfliegen
A *unr. refl. V.* ‹*pilot*› lose one's way; ‹*aircraft*› get off course
B *unr. itr. V.; mit sein* [1] (verschwinden) ‹*smoke*› disperse, vanish; ‹*scent, smell*› fade, disappear; ‹*mood, tiredness*› evaporate [2] (sich verflüchtigen) ‹*alcohol etc.*› evaporate [3] (vorübergehen) ‹*time*› fly by; ‹*anger*› pass

verfließen *unr. itr. V.; mit sein* [1] (verschwimmen) merge; ‹*colours*› run [2] (geh.: vergehen) go by; pass

verflixt /fɛɐ̯ˈflɪkst/ (ugs.)
A *Adj.* [1] (ärgerlich) awkward, unpleasant ‹*situation, business, etc.*› [2] (abwertend: verdammt) blasted (Brit.); blessed; confounded; **~ [noch mal]!, ~ noch eins!, ~ und zugenäht!** [damn and] blast (Brit. coll.) [3] (sehr groß) **er hat ~es Glück gehabt** he was damned lucky (coll.)
B *adv.* (sehr) damned (coll.); **das sieht ~ nach Betrug aus** that looks damned close to fraud (coll.)

verflossen
A *2. Part. v.* **verfließen**
B *Adj.* (ugs.) former; **seine ~e Freundin** his ex-girlfriend; **mein Verflossener/meine Verflossene** my ex (coll.)

verfluchen *tr. V.* curse

verflucht
A *Adj.* (salopp) [1] (verdammt) damned (coll.); bloody (Brit. sl.); **~ [noch mal]!, ~ und zugenäht!** (derb) damn [it] (coll.) [2] (sehr groß) **wir hatten ~es Glück/Pech** we were damned lucky/unlucky (coll.)
B *adv.* (sehr) damned (coll.)

verflüchtigen
A *tr. V.* (bes. Chemie) evaporate
B *refl. V.* [1] (in Gas übergehen) ‹*alcohol etc.*› evaporate [2] (sich auflösen) disperse; ‹*smell*› disappear;

V

(fig.) ‹fear, astonishment› subside; ‹cheerfulness, mockery› vanish; ‹time of youth› be dissipated 3 (ugs. scherzh.: sich davonmachen) make oneself scarce (coll.)

verflüssigen (bes. Chemie, Physik)
A tr. V. liquefy
B refl. V. liquefy; become liquid

Verflüssigung die; ~, ~en liquefaction

verfolgen tr. V. 1 pursue; hunt, track ‹animal›; **jmdn. auf Schritt und Tritt ~:** follow sb. wherever he/she goes; **der Gedanke daran verfolgte ihn** (fig.) the thought of it haunted him; **vom Pech verfolgt sein** (fig.) be dogged by bad luck; **jmdn. mit Blicken** od. **den Augen ~** (fig.) follow sb. with one's eyes 2 (bedrängen) plague; **jmdn. mit Bitten ~:** badger sb. with requests; **er verfolgte sie mit seiner Eifersucht** because he was jealous, he would not leave her in peace 3 (bedrohen) persecute; **politisch verfolgt sein** od. **werden** be a victim of political persecution 4 (folgen) follow ‹path etc.› 5 (zu verwirklichen suchen) pursue ‹policy, plan, career, idea, purpose, etc.› 6 (beobachten) follow ‹conversation, events, trial, developments, etc.› 7 **etw. [strafrechtlich] ~:** prosecute sth.

Verfolger der; ~s, ~, **Verfolgerin** die; ~, ~nen pursuer; (Häscher) persecutor

Verfolgte der/die; adj. Dekl. victim of persecution

Verfolgung die; ~, ~en 1 (das Hinterhereilen) pursuit; **die ~ aufnehmen** take up the chase 2 (Bedrohung) persecution 3 ▸ **verfolgen 5:** pursuance 4 **[strafrechtliche] ~:** prosecution

Verfolgungs-: **~jagd** die pursuit; chase; **~rennen** das (Radsport) pursuit race; **~wahn** der (Psych.) persecution mania

verformbar Adj. malleable; workable

verformen
A tr. V. 1 make ‹object› go out of shape; distort 2 (Technik) work ‹steel, plastic, etc.›
B refl. V. go out of shape; distort; become distorted

Verformung die distortion

verfrachten tr. V. transport; (mit dem Schiff) ship; **jmdn. ins Bett/in einen Streifenwagen ~** (fig.) bundle sb. into bed/into a patrol car

verfranzen /fɛɐ̯ˈfrantsn̩/ refl. V. 1 (Fliegerjargon) stray off course 2 (ugs.: sich verirren) lose one's way

verfremden tr. V. **[jmdm.] etw. ~:** make sth. [appear] unfamiliar [to sb.]; (Theaterw., Kunstw.) distance sth. [from sb.]

Verfremdung die; ~, ~en (Theaterw., Kunstw.) alienation; distancing

Verfremdungs·effekt der (Theaterw.) alienation or distancing effect

verfressen[1] unr. tr. V. (salopp) blow (coll.) ‹money› on food

verfressen[2] Adj. (salopp abwertend) piggish (coll.); greedy

Verfressenheit die; ~ (salopp abwertend) piggishness (coll.); greediness

verfroren Adj. 1 (durchgefroren) frozen; freezing cold 2 (leicht frierend) sensitive to the cold; **~ sein** feel the cold

verfrühen refl. V. arrive or come or be too early; **diese Maßnahme halte ich für verfrüht** I consider this measure to be premature

verfügbar Adj. available; **nicht ~:** unavailable

Verfügbarkeit die; ~: availability

verfügen
A tr. V. (anordnen) order; (dekretieren) decree; **in seinem Testament ~, dass ...** decree in one's will that ...
B itr. V. 1 (bestimmen) **über etw.** (Akk.) **[frei] ~ können** be free to decide what to do with sth.; **über jmdn. ~:** tell sb. what to do; **bitte ~ Sie über mich!** (geh.) I am at your disposal 2 (haben) **über etw.** (Akk.) **~:** have sth. at one's disposal; **über gute Beziehungen/große Erfahrung ~:** have good connections/great experience
C refl. V. (veralt., scherzh.: sich begeben) proceed

Verfügung die; ~, ~en 1 (Anordnung) order; (Dekret) decree; **eine ~ erlassen** issue a decree; **seine letztwilligen ~en** his last will and testament; **~en treffen** make provision sing.; **„~ von Todes wegen"** (Amtsspr.) 'Last Will and Testament'; s. auch **einstweilig** 2 (Disposition) **etw. zur ~ haben** have sth. at one's disposal; **jmdm. etw. zur ~ stellen** put sth. at sb.'s disposal; **sein Amt zur ~ stellen** offer to give up one's post or office; **jmdm. zur ~ stehen** be at sb.'s disposal; **sich zur ~ halten** hold oneself ready

Verfügungs·gewalt die power of disposal; **~ über etw.** (Akk.) **haben** (fig.) have power over sth.

verführbar Adj. **[leicht] ~:** easily tempted; easily influenced ‹child, young mind›

verführen
A tr. V. 1 (verleiten) tempt; **jmdn. zum Trinken ~:** encourage sb. to take up drinking; **jmdn. zu einem Bier ~** (scherzh.) tempt sb. to a beer 2 (sexuell) seduce
B itr. V. **zu etw. ~:** be a temptation to sth.

Verführer der seducer

Verführerin die seductress

verführerisch
A Adj. 1 (verlockend) tempting 2 (aufreizend) seductive
B adv. 1 (verlockend) temptingly 2 (aufreizend) seductively

Verführung die 1 temptation 2 (sexuell) seduction 3 (Reiz) enticement

verfüllen tr. V. (bes. Bergmannsspr.) backfill ‹old working›

verfüttern tr. V. 1 feed (+ Dat. to) 2 (verbrauchen) use [up] as animal/bird food

Vergabe die allocation; (eines Auftrages) placing; awarding; (eines Stipendiums, eines Preises) award

vergackeiern /fɛɐ̯ˈgak|ai̯ɐn/ tr. V. (salopp) **jmdn. ~:** pull sb.'s leg (coll.)

vergaffen refl. V. (ugs.) **sich in jmdn. ~:** fall for sb.

vergällen /fɛɐ̯ˈgɛlən/ tr. V. 1 (verderben) spoil ‹enjoyment etc.›; sour ‹life› 2 (bes. Chemie) denature; denaturalize

vergaloppieren refl. V. (ugs.) drop a clanger (coll.); (zu schnell vorgehen) fall over oneself

vergammeln (ugs.)
A itr. V.; mit sein ‹food› go bad
B tr. V. waste ‹time›; **den ganzen Sonntag im Bett ~:** idle away the whole of Sunday in bed

vergammelt Adj. (ugs. abwertend) scruffy (coll.); tatty (coll.); tatty (coll.), decrepit ‹vehicle›

vergangen /fɛɐ̯ˈgaŋən/
A 2. Part. v. **vergehen**
B Adj. 1 (vorüber, vorbei) bygone, former ‹times, years, etc.›; **die ~e Sitzung** the previous or last meeting 2 (letzt...) last ‹year, Sunday, week, etc.› 3 (ehemalig) former

Vergangenheit die; ~, ~en 1 (Zeit) past; **die jüngste ~:** the recent past; **etw. gehört der ~ an** sth. is a thing of the past; **einen Strich unter die ~ ziehen** let bygones be bygones 2 (Leben) past; (einer Stadt usw.) past; history; **eine Frau mit ~:** a woman with a past 3 (Grammatik) past tense

Vergangenheits-: **~bewältigung** die coming to terms with the past; **~form** die (Sprachw.) past tense

vergänglich /fɛɐ̯ˈgɛŋlɪç/ Adj. transient; transitory; ephemeral; **alles Irdische ist ~:** all earthly things will pass away

Vergänglichkeit die; ~: transience; transitoriness

vergären
A unr. od. regelm. tr. V. ferment (**zu** into)
B unr. od. regelm. itr. V.; mit sein (bes. Chemie) ferment

vergasen tr. V. 1 (bes. Physik) gasify 2 (töten) gas

Vergaser der; ~s, ~ (Kfz-W.) carburettor

vergaß /fɛɐ̯ˈgaːs/ 1. u. 3. Pers. Sg. Prät. v. **vergessen**

Vergasung die; ~, ~en 1 (von Kohle) gasification 2 (Tötung) gassing 3 **bis zur ~** (ugs.) ad nauseam

vergattern tr. V. (bes. Milit.) remind ‹soldier› of his duties; (fig.) reprimand; **jmdn. ~, etw. zu tun** (fig.) enjoin sb. to do sth.; **jmdn. zu Stillschweigen ~** (fig.) swear sb. to silence

vergeben unr. tr. V. 1 ▸ ❶ **S. 227** auch itr. (geh.: verzeihen) forgive; **jmdm. etw. ~:** forgive sb. [for] sth. 2 throw away ‹chance, goal, etc.›; **einen Elfmeter ~:** waste a penalty 3 (geben) place ‹order› (**an** + Akk. with); award ‹grant, prize› (**an** + Akk. to); **seine Töchter sind alle schon ~:** his daughters are all married [or engaged] already 4 **sich** (Dat.) **etwas/nichts ~:** lose/not lose face

vergebens
A Adv. in vain; vainly
B adj. **es war ~:** it was of or to no avail

vergeblich
A Adj. futile; vain, futile ‹attempt, efforts›; **alles Bitten/Zureden war ~:** all pleading/encouragement was of or to no avail; no amount of pleading/encouragement did any good
B adv. in vain; vainly

Vergeblichkeit die; ~: futility

Vergebung die; ~, ~en ▸ ❶ **S. 227** (geh.) forgiveness

vergegenständlichen tr. V. (bes. Philos.) reify; hypostatize

vergegenwärtigen /od. ---'---/ refl. V. **sich** (Dat.) **etw. ~:** imagine sth.; (erinnern) recall sth.

Vergegenwärtigung die; ~, ~en ▸ **vergegenwärtigen:** imagining; recalling

vergehen
A unr. itr. V.; mit sein 1 (verstreichen) ‹time› pass [by], go by; **es vergeht kein Tag, an dem er nicht anruft** not a day passes by without him ringing up (Brit.) or (coll.) phoning; **wie [doch] die Zeit vergeht!** how time flies! 2 (nachlassen) ‹pain› wear off, pass; ‹pleasure› fade; **ihr verging der Appetit** she lost her appetite 3 (sich verflüchtigen) ‹cloud, scent› disappear; ‹fog› lift 4 (geh.: sterben) pass away; die 5 (verschmachten) die (**vor** + Dat. of); **vor Sehnsucht ~:** pine away
B unr. refl. V. 1 (verstoßen) **sich gegen das Gesetz ~:** violate the law; **sich an fremdem Eigentum ~** (geh.) steal another's property 2 (sexuell) **sich an jmdm. ~:** commit indecent assault on sb.; indecently assault sb.

Vergehen das; ~s, ~: crime; (Rechtsspr.) offence

vergeigen tr. V. (ugs.) botch up ‹test, performance, etc.›; lose ‹game, match›

vergeistigt Adj. spiritual

vergelten unr. tr. V. repay (**durch** with); **jmdm. etw. ~:** repay sb. for sth.; **jmds. Freundlichkeit ~:** return sb.'s kindness; **eine Niederlage blutig ~:** take bloody revenge for a defeat; **vergelts Gott!** God bless you!

Vergeltung die 1 repayment 2 (Rache) revenge; **~ an jmdm./etw. üben** take revenge on sb./sth.; **die ~ eines Unrechts** the avenging of a wrong

Vergeltungs-: **~aktion** die retaliatory action; **~angriff** der retaliatory attack; **~maßnahme** die retaliatory measure; **~schlag** der retaliatory strike

vergesellschaften tr. V. socialize

Vergesellschaftung die; ~, ~en socialization

vergessen /fɛɐ̯ˈgɛsn̩/
A unr. tr. (auch itr.) V. forget; (liegen lassen) forget; leave behind; **seine Umgebung/sich völlig ~:** become totally engrossed; **er wird noch einmal seinen Kopf ~** (ugs.) he'd forget his head if it wasn't screwed on; **... und nicht zu ~ Tante Erna** ...: and not forgetting Aunt Erna; **das kannst du ~!** (ugs.) forget it!; you can forget about that!; **auf etw.** (Akk.) **~** (südd., österr.) forget sth.
B refl. V. (sich nicht beherrschen) forget oneself

Vergessenheit die; ~: oblivion; **in ~ geraten** fall into oblivion

vergesslich, *vergeßlich /fɛɐ̯ˈgɛslɪç/ Adj. forgetful

Vergesslichkeit, *Vergeßlichkeit *die;* **~:** forgetfulness

vergeuden /fɛɐ̯ˈgɔydn̩/ *tr. V.* waste; squander, waste ‹*money*›

Vergeudung *die;* **~, ~en** waste; squandering; **so eine ~!** what a waste!

vergewaltigen *tr. V.* 1 rape 2 (fig.) oppress ‹*nation, people*›; violate ‹*truth, conscience, law, language, etc.*›

Vergewaltigung *die;* **~, ~en** 1 rape 2 ▸**vergewaltigen 2**: oppression; violation

vergewissern /fɛɐ̯gəˈvɪsɐn/ *refl. V.* make sure (+ *Gen.* of); **der Lehrer vergewisserte sich durch Fragen, ob ...** the teacher ascertained by asking questions whether ...

Vergewisserung *die;* **~:** ascertainment; **nur zur ~:** just as a check

vergießen *unr. tr. V.* 1 (verschütten) spill 2 **Tränen ~:** shed tears; **viel Schweiß ~:** sweat blood (fig.); *s. auch* **Blut**

vergiften *tr. V.* ▸ℹ **S. 439** (auch fig.) poison

Vergiftung *die;* **~, ~en** ▸ℹ **S. 439** 1 (das Vergiften) poisoning; **~ durch Nahrungsmittel** food poisoning 2 (Erkrankung) poisoning; **~en behandeln** treat cases of poisoning; **an einer ~ sterben** die of poisoning

Vergil /verˈgiːl/ *(der)* Virgil

vergiss, *vergiß /fɛɐ̯ˈgɪs/ *Imperativ Sg. v.* **vergessen**

Vergiss·mein·nicht, *Vergiß·mein·nicht *das;* **~[e]s, ~[e]** forget-me-not

vergisst, *vergißt *2. u. 3. Pers. Sg. Präs. v.* **vergessen**

vergittern *tr. V.* put a grille on ‹*window etc.*›; (mit Stangen) put bars over ‹*window etc.*›; **ein vergittertes Fenster** a barred window

verglasen *tr. V.* glaze; **das Fenster neu ~:** put new glass in the window

Verglasung *die;* **~, ~en** 1 glazing 2 (Glasscheiben) panes *pl.* of glass

Vergleich *der;* **~[e]s, ~e** 1 comparison; **dieser ~ drängt sich einem geradezu auf** one cannot help making this comparison; **dieser ~ hinkt** this is a poor comparison; **das ist doch kein ~!** there is no comparison; **einen ~ anstellen** *od.* **ziehen** draw *or* make a comparison; **er hält dem ~ mit seinem Bruder nicht stand** he doesn't compare *or* stand comparison with his brother; **im ~ zu** *od.* **mit etw.** in comparison with sth.; compared with *or* to sth.; **etw. zum ~ heranziehen** use sth. by way of comparison 2 (Sprachw.) simile 3 (Rechtsw.) settlement; **einen ~ schließen** reach a settlement

vergleichbar *Adj.* comparable

Vergleichbarkeit *die;* **~:** comparability

vergleichen

A *unr. tr. V.* compare (**mit** with, to); **die Uhrzeit ~:** check that one has the correct time; **das ist [doch gar] nicht zu ~:** that [really] doesn't stand comparison *or* compare; **vergleiche Seite 77** compare page 77; **~de Literaturwissenschaft** comparative literature

B *unr. refl. V.* 1 **sich mit jmdm. ~:** compete with sb. 2 (Rechtsw.) reach a settlement; settle

vergleichs-, Vergleichs-: ~antrag *der* (Rechtsspr.) application for the initiation of composition proceedings; **~form** *die* (Sprachw.) comparative/superlative form; **~gruppe** *die* comparison group; **~kampf** *der* (Sport) friendly match; **~maßstab** *der* standard or yardstick of comparison; **~miete** *die* benchmark rent; **~möglichkeit** *die* opportunity for comparison; **~partikel** *die* (Sprachw.) comparative particle; **~verfahren** *das* (Rechtsw.) composition proceedings *pl.*; **~verwalter** *der,* **~verwalterin** *die* administrator in composition proceedings; **~weise** *Adv.* comparatively; **~wert** *der* (bes. Statistik) comparable value *or* figure; **~zahl** *die* comparable figure; **~zeitraum** *der* (bes. Statistik) comparable period

vergletschern *itr. V.; mit sein* become glaciated; **vergletschert** glaciated

verglimmen *unr. od. regelm. itr. V.; mit sein* ‹*fire etc.*› [die down and] go out; ‹*cigarette, embers*› go out

verglühen *itr. V.; mit sein* ‹*log, wick, fire, etc.*› smoulder and go out; ‹*glow of sunset*› fade; ‹*satellite, rocket, wire, etc.*› burn out

vergnügen /fɛɐ̯ˈgnyːgn̩/

A *refl. V.* enjoy oneself; have a good time; **sich beim Tanzen ~:** enjoy oneself dancing

B *tr. V.* amuse

Vergnügen *das;* **~s, ~:** pleasure; (Spaß) fun; **ein teueres ~** (ugs.) an expensive bit of fun (coll.); **ein kindliches ~ bei etw. empfinden** take a childlike pleasure *or* delight in sth.; **es ist mir ein ~:** it's a pleasure; **es war mir ein ~, Sie kennen zu lernen** it was a pleasure meeting you; **das ~ ist ganz meinerseits** *od.* **auf meiner Seite** the pleasure is all mine; **mit wem habe ich das ~?** with whom do I have the pleasure of speaking?; **etw. macht jmdm. [großes] ~:** sth. gives sb. [great] pleasure; sb. enjoys sth. [very much]; **sich ein ~ daraus machen, etw. zu tun** derive pleasure from doing sth.; **ich wünsche dir viel ~:** I hope you have a good time *or* enjoy yourself; **viel ~!** (auch iron.) have fun!; **mit [dem größten] ~:** with [the greatest of] pleasure; **etw. aus reinem ~** *od.* **nur zum ~ tun** do sth. just for the fun of it *or* for pleasure; **zu meinem ~:** to my great joy

vergnüglich

A *Adj.* amusing, entertaining ‹*play, programme*›

B *adv.* amusingly; entertainingly

vergnügt

A *Adj.* 1 (in guter Laune) cheerful; happy ‹*smile*›; merry ‹*group of people*› 2 (unterhaltsam) enjoyable

B *adv.* (in guter Laune) cheerfully; ‹*smile*› happily

Vergnügtheit *die;* **~:** cheerfulness

Vergnügung *die;* **~, ~en** 1 (Zeitvertreib) pleasure 2 (Veranstaltung) entertainment

vergnügungs-, Vergnügungs-: ~fahrt *die* pleasure trip; **~industrie** *die* entertainment industry; **~lokal** *das* bar providing entertainment; (Nachtlokal) nightclub; **~park** *der* amusement park; **~reise** *die* pleasure trip; **~steuer** *die* entertainment tax; **~sucht** *die* (oft abwertend) craving for pleasure; **~süchtig** *Adj.* pleasure-hungry; **~viertel** *das* pleasure district

vergolden *tr. V.* 1 gold-plate ‹*jewellery etc.*›; (mit Blattgold) gild ‹*statue, dome, etc.*›; (mit Gold bemalen) paint ‹*statue, dome, etc.*› gold; (fig.) ‹*evening sun*› bathe ‹*rooftops etc.*› in gold 2 (geh.: verklären) brighten up

vergönnen *tr. V.* grant; **es war ihm nicht vergönnt** it was not granted him

vergotten *tr. V.* deify

vergöttern /fɛɐ̯ˈgœtɐn/ *tr. V.* idolize

Vergötterung *die;* **~, ~en** idolization

vergöttlichen *tr. V.* (göttlich machen) deify; (als Gott verehren) worship [as God]

vergraben

A *unr. tr. V.* bury; **sein Gesicht in beide Hände** *od.* **in beiden Händen ~:** bury one's face in one's hands

B *unr. refl. V.* ‹*animal*› bury itself (**in** + *Akk. od. Dat.* in); (fig.) withdraw from the world; hide oneself away; **sich in die Arbeit/in seine Bücher ~** (fig.) bury oneself in one's work/books

vergrämen *tr. V.* 1 antagonize 2 (Jägerspr.) scare [off]

vergrämt *Adj.* careworn

vergraulen *tr. V.* (ugs.) put off; **jmdm. etw. ~:** put sb. off sth.

vergreifen *unr. refl. V.* 1 **sich im Ton/Ausdruck ~:** adopt the wrong tone/use the wrong expression; **sich in der Wahl seiner Mittel ~:** choose *or* select the wrong means 2 **sich an etw.** *(Dat.)* **~** (an fremdem Eigentum) misappropriate sth.; **sich an der Kasse ~:** put one's hand in the till (euphem.) 3 (tätlich werden) **sich an jmdm. ~:** assault sb.; (geschlechtlich missbrauchen) [indecently] assault sb.; **ich werde mich an der Maschine nicht ~** (ugs.) I'm not touching the machine 4 (danebengreifen) ‹*musician*› play a wrong note

vergreisen *itr. V.; mit sein* 1 go senile; **vergreist** senile 2 (überaltern) ‹*population*› age

Vergreisung *die;* **~** 1 senescence 2 (Überalterung) ageing

vergriffen

A *2. Part. v.* **vergreifen**

B *Adj.* out of print *pred.*

vergröbern /fɛɐ̯ˈgrøːbɐn/

A *tr. V.* coarsen

B *refl. V.* become coarser

Vergröberung *die;* **~, ~en** coarsening; **die Boulevardpresse arbeitet mit ~en** the popular press operates with crude generalizations

vergrößern /fɛɐ̯ˈgrøːsɐn/

A *tr. V.* 1 (erweitern) extend ‹*room, area, building, etc.*›; increase ‹*distance*›; **sein Repertoire ~:** extend *or* increase *or* enlarge one's repertoire 2 (vermehren) increase; **das Übel ~:** make the trouble worse 3 (größer reproduzieren) enlarge ‹*photograph etc.*›

B *refl. V.* 1 (größer werden) ‹*firm, business, etc.*› expand; **eine krankhaft vergrößerte Leber** a pathologically enlarged liver 2 (zunehmen) increase 3 (ugs.: durch Umzug) give oneself more space

C *itr. V.* ‹*lens etc.*› magnify

Vergrößerung *die;* **~, ~en** 1 ▸**vergrößern A, B**: extension; increase; enlargement; expansion 2 (Foto) enlargement; **in 100facher ~:** enlarged 100-fold

Vergrößerungs-: ~apparat *der* (Fot.) enlarger; **~glas** *das* magnifying glass; **~spiegel** *der* magnifying mirror

vergucken *refl. V.* (ugs.) 1 (sich verlieben) **sich in jmdn./etw. ~:** fall for sb./sth. (coll.) 2 (falsch sehen) be mistaken [about what one saw]

Vergünstigung *die;* **~, ~en** privilege

vergüten *tr. V.* 1 (erstatten) **jmdm. etw. ~:** reimburse sb. for sth.; **jmdm. seine Unkosten/Auslagen ~:** reimburse sb. for his/her costs/reimburse *or* refund sb.'s expenses 2 (bes. Papierdt.: bezahlen) remunerate, pay for ‹*work, services*›; **etw. ~:** pay for sth.

Vergütung *die;* **~, ~en** 1 (Rückerstattung) (von Unkosten) reimbursement; (von Auslagen) reimbursement; refunding 2 (Geldsumme) remuneration

verh. *Abk.* **= verheiratet** m.

verhackstücken *tr. V.* (ugs.) 1 (abwertend: kritisieren) ‹*critic etc.*› tear *or* pull to pieces 2 (nordd.: besprechen) discuss

verhaften *tr. V.* arrest; **Sie sind verhaftet** you are under arrest

verhaftet *Adj.* **einer Sache** *(Dat.)* **~ sein** be trapped in sth.

Verhaftete *der/die; adj. Dekl.* person under arrest; man/woman under arrest; arrested man/woman

Verhaftung *die;* **~, ~en** arrest

verhageln *itr. V.; mit sein* be destroyed by hail; *s. auch* **Petersilie**

verhaken

A *tr. V.* 1 (zuhaken) hook up 2 (in etw. haken) hook ‹*needle etc.*› (**in** + *Dat.* in)

B *refl. V.* ‹*person*› get hooked *or* caught up; ‹*zip*› get caught

verhallen *itr. V.; mit sein* ‹*sound*› die away; **[ungehört] ~** (fig.) ‹*call, words, etc.*› go unheard *or* unheeded

verhalten[1]

A *unr. refl. V.* 1 (reagieren) react; **sich still** *od.* **ruhig ~:** keep quiet; **ich verhielt mich abwartend** I decided to wait and see 2 (sich benehmen) behave 3 (beschaffen sein) be; **die Sache verhält sich nämlich so** this is how things stand *or* the matter stands 4 (im Verhältnis stehen) **a verhält sich zu b wie x zu y** a is to b as x is to y; **die beiden Größen ~ sich zueinander wie 1:10** the two values are in a ratio of 1:10

B *unr. tr. V.* 1 (geh.: zurückhalten) restrain, contain ‹*anger*›; restrain ‹*mockery*›; contain ‹*laughter*›; hold back ‹*tears, urine*› 2 (Reiten) ▸**parieren**[2] **3** 3 *auch itr.* (geh.) **[den Schritt] ~:** slow down; check one's pace; (stehen bleiben) stop

verhalten[2]

A *Adj.* 1 (unterdrückt) restrained; **mit ~em**

V

Tempo at a measured pace; **mit ~en Schritten** treading quietly; **mit ~em Atem** with bated breath **2** (dezent) restrained, subdued, muted ‹colours›; muted, soft ‹notes, voice, etc.› **3** (zurückhaltend) reserved; **eine ~e Fahrweise** a cautious way of driving

B *adv.* **1** (unterdrückt) in a restrained manner **2** (zurückhaltend) in a reserved manner; **~ fahren** drive cautiously **3** (dezent) ‹speak, play, etc.› softly

Verhalten *das;* ~s behaviour; (Vorgehen) conduct

verhaltens-, Verhaltens-: ~forschung *die* behavioural research *no art.;* (Ethologie) ethology *no art.;* **~gestört** *Adj.* (Psych.) ‹person, child› with a behavioural disorder; **~kodex** *der* code of conduct; (in der Wirtschaft) code of good practice; **~maßregel** *die* rule of conduct; **~maßregeln für den Notfall** rules governing emergencies; **~muster** *das* behaviour pattern; pattern of behaviour; **~störung** *die* (Psych.) behavioural disorder; **~therapie** *die* behavioural therapy; **~weise** *die* behaviour; **~weisen** behaviour patterns; patterns of behaviour

Verhältnis /fɛɐ̯ˈhɛltnɪs/ *das;* **~ses, ~se** **1** **ein ~ von drei zu eins** a ratio of three to one; **im ~ zu früher** in comparison with *or* compared to earlier times; **der Aufwand stand in keinem ~ zum Erfolg** the expenditure was out of all proportion to the result **2** (persönliche Beziehung) relationship (**zu** with); **zwischen uns** (*Dat.*) **herrscht ein vertrautes ~:** we are on intimate terms; **ein gutes ~ zu jmdm. haben** get on well with sb.; **er hat** *od.* **findet kein [rechtes] ~ zur Musik** he cannot relate to music **3** (ugs.: intime Beziehung) affair; relationship; **mit jmdm. ein ~ haben** have an affair with sb.; **ein ~ mit jmdm. beenden** break up with sb.; break off a relationship with sb. **4** (ugs.) (Geliebte) lady friend; (Geliebter) man **5** *Pl.* (Umstände) conditions; **in bescheidenen** *od.* **einfachen/gesicherten ~sen leben** live in modest circumstances/be financially secure; **aus bescheidenen** *od.* **einfachen ~sen kommen** come from a humble background; **sie kommt aus kleinen ~sen** she comes from a lower middle-class background; **über seine ~se leben** live beyond one's means

verhältnis-, Verhältnis-: ~gleichung *die* (Math.) proportion; **~mäßig** *Adv.* relatively; comparatively; **~wahl** *die* proportional representation; **~wahl·recht** *das* [system of] proportional representation; **~wort** *das; Pl.* **~wörter** (Sprachw.) preposition

verhandelbar *Adj.* negotiable

verhandeln

A *itr. V.* **1** negotiate (**über** + *Akk.* about) **2** (strafrechtlich) try a case; (zivilrechtlich) hear a case; **das Gericht verhandelt gegen die Terroristen** the court is trying the terrorists

B *tr. V.* **1** **etw. ~:** negotiate over sth. **2** (strafrechtlich) try ‹case›; (zivilrechtlich) hear ‹case›

Verhandlung *die* **1** (Besprechung) **~en** negotiations; **mit jmdm. in ~ stehen** be negotiating with sb.; be [involved *or* engaged] in negotiations *pl.* with sb.; **zu ~en bereit sein** be open to negotiation *sing.* **2** (strafrechtlich) trial; (zivilrechtlich) hearing; **die ~ gegen X** the trial of X

verhandlungs-, Verhandlungs-: ~basis *die* ▸ **~grundlage**; **~bereit** *Adj.* ready *or* willing to negotiate *pred.;* **~bereitschaft** *die* readiness *or* willingness to negotiate; **~gegen·stand** *der* subject for/under negotiation; **kein ~gegenstand sein** not be a matter for negotiation; **~grundlage** *die* basis for negotiation[s]; **~partner** *der,* **~partnerin** *die* opposite number [in the negotiations]; **die beiden ~partner** (die miteinander verhandeln) the two sides in the negotiations; **~tisch** *der* negotiating table; **~weg** *der:* in **auf dem ~weg** by negotiation

verhangen *Adj.* overcast

verhängen *tr. V.* **1** (zuhängen) cover (**mit** with) **2** (anordnen) impose ‹fine, punishment› (**über** + *Akk.* on); declare ‹state of emergency, state of siege›; (Sport) award, give ‹penalty etc.›

Verhängnis /fɛɐ̯ˈhɛŋnɪs/ *das;* **~ses, ~se** undoing; **jmdm. zum ~ werden** be sb.'s undoing; **das ~ brach über ihn herein** disaster overtook him

verhängnis·voll *Adj.* (unheilvoll) disastrous; fatal, disastrous ‹mistake, weakness, hesitation, etc.›; (schicksalsschwer) fateful

Verhängung *die;* **~, ~en** imposition; (des Ausnahme-, Belagerungszustandes) declaration

verharmlosen *tr. V.* play down

Verharmlosung *die;* **~, ~en** playing down

verhärmt /fɛɐ̯ˈhɛrmt/ *Adj.* careworn

verharren *itr. V.* (geh.) **1** (innehalten) remain; (plötzlich, kurz) pause **2** (beharren) **auf seinem Standpunkt ~:** persist in one's view; **in Resignation/Gleichgültigkeit ~:** remain resigned/indifferent

verharschen *itr. V.; mit sein* ‹snow› form a crust; ‹wound› form a scab

verhärten /fɛɐ̯ˈhɛrtn̩/

A *tr. V.* **1** (festigen) harden ‹material etc.› **2** (unbarmherzig machen) harden; make ‹person› hard

B *refl. V.* **1** (hart werden) ‹tissue› become hardened; ‹tumour› become scirrhous **2** (gefühllos werden) harden one's heart (**gegen** against); **die Fronten haben sich verhärtet** the positions of the opposing parties have become entrenched

Verhärtung *die;* **~, ~en** **1** hardening **2** (fig.) becoming hardened; **die ~ der Positionen auf beiden Seiten** the hardening of attitudes on both sides

verhaspeln *refl. V.* (ugs.) **1** (sich versprechen) stumble over one's words **2** (sich verwickeln) become *or* get tangled up

verhasst, *verhaßt *Adj.* hated; detested; **es war ihm ~:** he hated *or* detested it; **nichts ist mir so ~ wie ...** there is nothing I detest so much as ...

verhätscheln *tr. V.* (ugs.) pamper

Verhätschelung *die;* **~, ~en** (ugs.) pampering

Verhau /fɛɐ̯ˈhau̯/ *der od. das;* **~[e]s, ~e** **1** tangle of branches; (Dickicht) thicket **2** barrier [made of branches]; (bes. Milit.) entanglement

verhauen (ugs.)

A *unr. tr. V.* **1** (verprügeln) beat up; (als Strafe) beat; **jmdm. den Hintern ~:** give sb.'s bottom a good smack[ing] **2** (falsch machen) make a mess of; muck up (Brit. sl.)

B *unr. refl. V.* (sich verrechnen) make a mistake *or* slip; **sich bei etw. mächtig ~:** slip up badly in sth.

verheben *unr. refl. V.* do oneself an injury [while lifting sth.]

verheddern /fɛɐ̯ˈhɛdɐn/ *refl. V.* **1** (hängenbleiben) **sich in etw.** (*Dat.*) **~:** get tangled up in sth. **2** (sich verhaspeln) get muddled up

verheeren /fɛɐ̯ˈheːrən/ *tr. V.* devastate; lay waste [to]

verheerend *Adj.* **1** (katastrophal) devastating; disastrous **2** (ugs.: scheußlich) ghastly (coll.); dreadful (coll.)

Verheerung *die;* **~, ~en** devastation *no pl.;* **~[en] anrichten** cause devastation; wreak havoc

verhehlen *tr. V.* (geh.) conceal; hide; **jmdm. etw. ~:** conceal *or* hide sth. from sb.; **ich kann/will** *od.* **möchte [es] nicht ~, dass ...** there is no denying/I have no wish to deny that ...

verheilen *itr. V.; mit sein* ‹wound› heal [up]

verheimlichen *tr. V.* **[jmdm.] etw. ~:** keep sth. secret [from sb.]; conceal *or* hide sth. [from sb.]

Verheimlichung *die;* **~, ~en** concealment

verheiraten

A *refl. V.* get married; **sich mit jmdm. ~:** marry sb.; get married to sb.; **er ist mit seiner Firma/Gitarre verheiratet** (fig.) he has no time for anything except his company/guitar

B *tr. V.* (veralt.) marry (**mit, an** + *Akk.* to); **er hatte zwei Töchter zu ~:** he had two daughters to marry off

Verheiratete *der/die; adj. Dekl.* married person; married man/woman; **~** *Pl.* married people; married men/women

Verheiratung *die;* **~, ~en** marriage

verheißen *unr. tr. V.* (geh.; auch fig.) promise; **man verhieß ihm eine große Zukunft** a great future was predicted for him; **nichts Gutes ~:** not bode *or* augur well

Verheißung *die;* **~, ~en** (geh.) promise

verheißungs·voll

A *Adj.* promising; **ein ~er Anfang** a promising *or* an auspicious start

B *adv.* full of promise

verheizen *tr. V.* **1** burn; use as fuel **2** (abwertend: rücksichtslos einsetzen) burn out ‹athlete, skier, etc.›; use ‹troops› as cannon fodder; run ‹employee, subordinate, etc.› into the ground

verhelfen *unr. itr. V.* **jmdm./einer Sache zu etw. ~:** help sb./sth. to get/achieve sth.; **jmdm. zur Flucht/zum Sieg ~:** help sb. to escape/win

verherrlichen *tr. V.* glorify ‹war, violence, deed, etc.›; extol ‹virtues, leader, etc.›; celebrate ‹nature, freedom, peace, etc.›

Verherrlichung *die;* **~, ~en** ▸ **verherrlichen**: glorification; extolling; celebration

verhetzen *tr. V.* incite; stir up; **die verhetzten Massen** the inflamed masses

Verhetzung *die;* **~, ~en** incitement; stirring up

verheult /fɛɐ̯ˈhɔy̯lt/ *Adj.* (ugs.) ‹eyes› red from crying; ‹face› puffy *or* swollen from crying

verhexen *tr. V.* (auch fig.) bewitch; cast a spell on; **jmdn. in etw.** (*Akk.*) **~:** turn sb. into sth. [by magic]; **es ist wie verhext: kaum setze ich mich hin, klingelt das Telefon** there seems to be a jinx on me today: the moment I sit down, the telephone rings

verhindern *tr. V.* prevent; prevent, avert ‹war, disaster, etc.›; **es ließ sich nicht ~, dass er losfuhr** he couldn't be prevented from driving off; no one could stop him [from] driving off; **er ist [dienstlich] verhindert** he is prevented from coming [by business commitments]; he is unable to come [for business reasons]; **ein verhinderter Künstler/Schauspieler** (ugs.) a would-be artist/actor

Verhinderung *die;* **~, ~en** ▸ **verhindern**: prevention; averting

verhohlen /fɛɐ̯ˈhoːlən/ *Adj.* concealed; **kaum ~e Neugier** ill-concealed curiosity

verhöhnen /vɛrˈhøːnən/ *tr. V.* mock; deride; ridicule

verhohnepipeln /fɛɐ̯ˈhoːnəpiːpl̩n/ *tr. V.* (ugs.) send up (coll.)

Verhohnepipelung *die;* **~, ~en** send-up (coll.)

Verhöhnung *die;* **~, ~en** **1** mockery; ridiculing **2** (Äußerung) mocking remark

verhökern /fɛɐ̯ˈhøːkɐn/ *tr. V.* (salopp) flog (Brit. sl.)

Verhör /fɛɐ̯ˈhøːɐ̯/ *das;* **~[e]s, ~e** interrogation; questioning; (bei Gericht) examination; **jmdn. ins ~ nehmen** interrogate *or* question sb.; (fig.) grill *or* quiz sb.

verhören

A *tr. V.* (befragen) interrogate; question; (bei Gericht) examine

B *refl. V.* (falsch hören) mishear; hear wrongly; **Hier ist niemand. Du musst dich verhört haben** There's nobody here. You must have been hearing things

verhornen *itr. V.; mit sein* keratinize; ‹skin› become horny

verhüllen *tr. V.* **1** (verbergen) cover; (fig.) disguise; mask; **eine verhüllte Drohung** (fig.) a veiled threat **2** (umgeben) enshroud; **Wolken verhüllten die Bergspitzen** the mountain tops were veiled *or* shrouded in cloud

verhüllend *Adj.* (Literaturw.) euphemistic

Verhüllung *die;* **~, ~en** covering; (fig.) disguising

verhundertfachen *tr., refl. V.* increase a hundredfold

V

verhungern *itr. V.; mit sein* die of starvation; starve [to death]; **ich bin am Verhungern** (ugs.) I'm starving (fig. coll.); **Verhungernde** *Pl.* people starving to death; **verhungert aussehen** look half-starved

verhunzen /fɛɐ̯'hʊntsn̩/ *tr. V.* (ugs. abwertend) ruin; mess up; ruin ‹*landscape, townscape, etc.*›

verhüten *tr. V.* prevent; prevent, avert ‹*disaster*›; **der Himmel verhüte, dass ...** heaven forbid that ...; **~, dass jmd. etw. tut** prevent sb. [from] doing sth.

Verhüterli *das;* **~s, ~s** (ugs. scherzh.) French letter

verhütten *tr. V.* smelt

Verhüttung *die;* **~, ~en** smelting

Verhütung *die;* **~, ~en** prevention; (Empfängnis~) contraception

Verhütungs-: ~maßnahmen *Pl.* contraceptive precautions; **~mittel** *das* contraceptive

verhutzelt /fɛɐ̯'hʊtsl̩t/ *Adj.* (ugs.) wizened ‹*person, face*›; shrivelled ‹*fruit, plant*›

verifizieren /verifi'tsi:rən/ *tr. V.* verify

Verifizierung *die;* **~, ~en** verification

verinnerlichen *tr. V.* (Soziol., Psych.) internalize

verinnerlicht *Adj.* (vergeistigt) spiritualized; (introvertiert) introverted

Verinnerlichung *die;* **~, ~en** (Soziol., Psych.) internalization

verirren *refl. V.* [1] (abkommen) get lost; lose one's way; ‹*animal*› stray; **verirrte Gewehrkugeln** (fig.) stray bullets [2] (irgendwohin gelangen) stray (**in, an** + *Akk.* into)

Verirrung *die;* **~, ~en** aberration

veritabel /veri'ta:bl̩/ *Adj.* (geh.) veritable; real

verjagen *tr. V.* chase away; (fig.) dispel ‹*thoughts, cares, etc.*›; **jmdn. von Haus und Hof ~:** drive sb. out of house and home

verjähren /fɛɐ̯'jɛ:rən/ *itr. V.; mit sein* come under the statute of limitations; **dieses Verbrechen ist inzwischen verjährt** this crime was committed too long ago to be punishable now

Verjährung *die;* **~, ~en** limitation; **für Verbrechen wie Völkermord gibt es keine ~:** there is no statute of limitations for crimes like genocide

Verjährungs·frist *die* limitation period

verjazzen *tr. V.* play in a jazz style; jazz up

verjubeln *tr. V.* (ugs.) blow (coll.) ‹*money*›

verjüngen /fɛɐ̯'jʏŋən/

[A] *tr. V.* rejuvenate ‹*person, skin, etc.*›; (jünger aussehen lassen) make ‹*person*› look younger; recruit younger blood into ‹*team, company, etc.*›

[B] *refl. V.* (schmaler werden) taper; become narrower; narrow

Verjüngung *die;* **~, ~en** [1] (Jüngerwerden) rejuvenation; **eine ~ des Politbüros** a recruitment of younger blood into the politburo [2] (Schmalerwerden) tapering; narrowing

Verjüngungs·kur *die:* **ich fühle mich reif für eine ~:** I feel in need of being rejuvenated; **die neue Freundin wirkt auf ihn wie eine ~:** his new girlfriend has given him a new lease of life

verjuxen *tr. V.* (ugs.) [1] (verjubeln) blow (sl.) ‹*money*› [2] (verulken) poke fun at

verkabeln *tr. V.* connect up [by cable]

Verkabelung *die;* **~, ~en** installation of cables (*Gen.* in)

verkalken *itr. V.; mit sein* [1] ‹*tissue*› calcify, become calcified; ‹*arteries*› become hardened; ‹*bone*› thicken; ‹*pipe, kettle, coffee machine, etc.*› fur up [2] (ugs.: senil werden) become senile; **er ist schon ziemlich verkalkt** he is already pretty gaga (coll.)

verkalkulieren *refl. V.* [1] (falsch berechnen) miscalculate [2] (falsch einschätzen) miscalculate; make a miscalculation

Verkalkung *die;* **~, ~en** [1] ▸ **verkalken 1**: calcification; hardening; thickening; furring-up [2] (ugs.: Senilität) senility

verkannt /fɛɐ̯'kant/ *2. Part. v.* **verkennen**

verkanten

[A] *tr. V.* tilt; edge ‹*ski*›

[B] *itr., refl. V.* (sich festklemmen) get jammed

verkappt *Adj.* disguised; **~e Anarchisten** anarchists in disguise

verkarsten *itr. V.; mit sein* be karstified

Verkarstung *die;* **~, ~en** karstification

verkatert /fɛɐ̯'ka:tɐt/ *Adj.* (ugs.) hung-over (coll.); **~ aufwachen** wake up with a hang-over

Verkauf *der* [1] sale; (das Verkaufen) sale; selling; **zum ~ stehen** be [up] for sale; **etw. zum ~ anbieten** offer sth. for sale [2] (Kaufmannsspr.) sales *sing. or pl., no art.*

verkaufen

[A] *tr. V.* (auch fig.) sell (*Dat.*, **an** + *Akk.* to); **sie verkauft ihren Körper** she's a prostitute; **„zu ~"** 'for sale'

[B] *refl. V.* [1] ‹*goods*› sell; **sich schlecht/gut ~** ‹*goods*› sell badly/well [2] (ugs.: falsch kaufen) make a bad buy; **ich habe mich bei den Möbeln verkauft** the furniture was a bad buy

Verkäufer *der,* **Verkäuferin** *die* ▸ ❶ **S. 113** [1] seller; vendor (formal) [2] (Berufsbez.) sales *or* shop assistant; salesperson; (im Außendienst) salesman/saleswoman; salesperson

verkäuflich *Adj.* [1] (zum Verkauf geeignet) saleable; marketable; **schwer/leicht ~ sein** be hard/easy to sell [2] (zum Verkauf bestimmt) for sale *postpos.*; **dieses Mittel ist frei ~:** this medicine is available over the counter

verkaufs-, Verkaufs-: ~ausstellung *die* exhibition and sale of works; **~automat** *der* vending machine; **~förderung** *die* sales promotion; **~hit** *der* big seller; (am meisten verkauft) top seller; (Buch) best seller; **~leiter** *der,* **~leiterin** *die* sales manager; **~offen** *Adj.* **der offene Samstag** *od.* **Sonnabend** Saturday on which *or* when the shops are open all day; **~personal** *das* sales staff; **~preis** *der* retail price; **~schlager** *der* big seller; (Buch) best seller; **~stand** *der* stall

Verkehr *der;* **~s** [1] traffic; **den ~ regeln** regulate *or* control the [flow of] traffic; **etw. dem [öffentlichen] ~ übergeben** open sth. to public use; **aus dem ~ ziehen** take ‹*coin, banknote*› out of circulation; take ‹*product*› off the market; **jmdn. aus dem ~ ziehen** (ugs. scherzh.) put sb. out of circulation (joc.); **in [den] ~ bringen** put ‹*coin, banknote*› into circulation [2] (Kontakt) contact; communication; **diplomatischer ~:** diplomatic relations *pl.*; **keinen ~ mit jmdm. pflegen/den ~ mit jmdm. abbrechen** not/no longer associate with sb. [3] (Geschlechts~) intercourse

verkehren

[A] *itr. V.* [1] *auch mit sein* (fahren) run; ‹*aircraft*› fly; **der Dampfer verkehrt zwischen Hamburg und Helgoland** the steamer plies *or* operates *or* goes between Hamburg and Heligoland; **der Bus verkehrt alle 15 Minuten** the bus runs *or* goes every 15 minutes; there's a bus every 15 minutes [2] (in Kontakt stehen) **mit jmdm. ~:** associate with sb.; **wir ~ nur noch über unsere Anwälte/schriftlich miteinander** we only deal with each other through our solicitors/we only have written correspondence with each other [3] (zu Gast sein) **bei jmdm. ~:** visit sb. regularly; **in einem Lokal ~:** frequent a pub (Brit.); **in den besten Kreisen ~:** move in the best circles [4] (verhüll.: koitieren) have intercourse; **sexuell ~:** have sexual intercourse

[B] *tr. V.* (verdrehen) turn (**in** + *Akk.* into); **jmds. Absicht ~:** reverse sb.'s intentions; **den Sinn einer Aussage ins Gegenteil ~:** twist the meaning of a statement right round

[C] *refl. V.* (sich verwandeln) turn (**in** + *Akk.* into); **sich ins Gegenteil ~:** change to the opposite

verkehrs-, Verkehrs-: ~ader *die* traffic artery; **~ampel** *die* traffic lights *pl.*; **~amt** *das* tourist information office; **~anbindung** *die* [transport] connections *pl.* (**an** + *Akk.* to); **~arm** *Adj.* quiet ‹*road, time*›; **~aufkommen** *das* volume of traffic; **~beruhigt** *Adj.* (Verkehrsw.) **~beruhigte Zone, ~beruhigter Bereich** traffic-calmed area; **~beruhigung** *die* traffic calming; **~betrieb** *der* transport services *pl.*; **~büro** *das* tourist office; **~chaos** *das* traffic chaos *no indef. art.*; chaos *no indef. art.* on the roads; **~dichte** *die* traffic density; **~erziehung** *die* road safety training; **~flugzeug** *das* commercial aircraft; **~fluss, *~fluß** *der* flow of traffic; **~funk** *der* radio/television traffic reports service; **im ~funk** on the radio/television traffic reports service; **~gefährdung** *die* constituting *no art.* a hazard to other traffic; **eine ~gefährdung darstellen** be *or* constitute a hazard to other traffic; **~hindernis** *das* obstruction to traffic; **~insel** *die* traffic island; refuge; **~knotenpunkt** *der* [traffic] junction; **~kontrolle** *die* traffic check; **~lage** *die* [1] (Situation) traffic situation; [2] (Ortslage) situation with regard to road and rail links; **eine gute ~lage haben** be well situated with regard to road and rail links; **~lärm** *der* traffic noise; **~meldung** *die* traffic announcement *or* flash; **~minister** *der,* **~ministerin** *die* minister of transport; **~ministerium** *das* ministry of transport; **~mittel** *das* means of transport; **die öffentlichen ~mittel** public transport *sing.*; **~nachrichten** *Pl.* traffic news; **~netz** *das* transport system; **~opfer** *das* road accident *or* traffic accident victim; **~polizei** *die* traffic police *pl.*; **~polizist** *der* ▸ ❶ **S. 113** traffic policeman; **~polizistin** *die* ▸ ❶ **S. 113** traffic policewoman; **~regel** *die* traffic regulation; **~reich** *Adj.* busy ‹*crossing, street, etc.*›; **~rowdy** *der* road hog; **~schild** *das* traffic sign; road sign; **~service** *der* traffic reports service; **~sicher** *Adj.* roadworthy ‹*vehicle, condition*›; **~sicherheit** *die* road safety; (eines Fahrzeugs) roadworthiness; **~sprache** *die* lingua franca; **~stockung** *die* traffic hold-up; **~sünder** *der,* **~sünderin** *die* (ugs.) traffic offender; **~teilnehmer** *der,* **~teilnehmerin** *die* road user; **~tote** *der/die* person killed on the roads; **weniger ~tote** fewer deaths on the roads; **~unfall** *der* road accident; **~unterricht** *der* road safety instruction; **~verbindung** *die* transport link; **~verhältnisse** *Pl.* [1] (~verbindungen) transport links; [2] (~lage) traffic conditions; **~weg** *der* traffic route; **~widrig** [A] *Adj.* contrary to road traffic regulations *postpos.*; [B] *adv.* contrary to road traffic regulations; **~zeichen** *das* traffic sign; road sign

verkehrt

[A] *Adj.* wrong; **das ist gar nicht so ~:** that's not such a bad idea; **es ist sicher nicht ~, das zu tun** there's no harm in doing that; **an den Verkehrten/die Verkehrte kommen** *od.* **geraten** (ugs.) come to the wrong person

[B] *adv.* wrongly; **alles ~ machen** do everything wrong; **sich ~ verhalten** do the wrong thing; *s. auch* **herum 1**

Verkehrung *die;* **~, ~en** reversal; **eine ~ ins Gegenteil** a change to the opposite

verkeilen

[A] *tr. V.* wedge

[B] *refl. V.* become wedged (**in** + *Akk.* in); **sich ineinander ~:** become wedged together

verkennen *unr. tr. V.* fail to recognize; misjudge ‹*situation*›; fail to appreciate ‹*efforts, achievement, etc.*›; **es ist nicht zu ~, dass ...** it cannot be denied *or* is undeniable that ...; **ihre Absicht war nicht zu ~:** her intention was unmistakable; **ein verkanntes Genie** an unrecognized genius

Verkennung *die;* **~, ~en** ▸ **verkennen**: failure to recognize/appreciate; misjudgement; **in völliger ~ der Situation** completely misjudging the situation

verketten *refl. V.* become interlinked

Verkettung *die;* **~, ~en** (von Zufällen usw.) chain

verketzern *tr. V.* denounce

Verketzerung *die;* **~, ~en** denunciation

verkitschen *tr. V.* turn ‹*novel, film, etc.*› into kitsch; sentimentalize ‹*song, tune, etc.*›

verkitten *tr. V.* fill ‹*crack, hole, joint, etc.*›; put putty round ‹*window*›

verklagen *tr. V.* sue; take proceedings against; take to court; **eine Firma auf Schadenersatz ~:** sue a company for damages

verklammern *tr. V.* (Med.) close ‹*wound*› with a clamp/clamps

verklappen *tr. V.* dump ‹*waste*› [at sea]

Verklappung *die; ~, ~en* dumping [at sea]

verklären
A *tr. V.* (auch Rel.) transfigure
B *refl. V.* (auch fig.) be transfigured; ‹*eyes*› shine blissfully

verklärt
A *Adj.* transfigured, blissful ‹*expression, face, etc.*›
B *adv.* blissfully

Verklärung *die* transfiguration

verklausulieren /fɛɐ̯klauzu'li:rən/ *tr. V.* **1** (mit Klauseln versehen) hedge ‹*contract etc.*› with qualifying clauses **2** (verbergen) hedge ‹*admission of guilt etc.*› round with qualifications; **in verklausulierter Form** in a roundabout way

Verklausulierung *die; ~, ~en* **1** (das Verklausulieren) involved formulation **2** (Formulierung) qualification

verkleben
A *itr. V.; mit sein* stick together; **der Pinsel ist verklebt** the bristles of the brush are stuck together
B *tr. V.* **1** (zusammenkleben) stick ‹*eyelids, eyelashes*› together; **verklebte Hände/Haare** sticky hands/matted *or* sticky hair **2** (zukleben) seal up ‹*hole*›; **eine Wunde mit Heftpflaster ~:** cover a wound with sticking plaster **3** (festkleben) stick [down] ‹*floor covering etc.*›; **das Schaufenster mit Papier ~:** paper over the shop window **4** (verbrauchen) use up ‹*posters, rolls of wallpaper, etc.*›

verkleckern *tr. V.* (ugs.) spill

verkleiden *tr. V.* **1** disguise; (kostümieren) dress up; **sich ~:** disguise oneself/dress [oneself] up **2** (umhüllen, verdecken) cover; (verschalen) line; face ‹*façade*›

Verkleidung *die* **1** disguising; (das Kostümieren) dressing up **2** (Kostüm) (als Tarnung) disguise; (bei einer Party usw.) fancy dress **3** ▸**verkleiden 2**: covering; lining; facing **4** (Umhüllung) cover

verkleinern /fɛɐ̯'klainɐn/
A *tr. V.* **1** (kleiner machen) make smaller; reduce the size of; **den Abstand ~:** reduce *or* decrease the distance; **etw. in verkleinertem Maßstab darstellen** represent sth. on a smaller scale; scale sth. down **2** (verringern) reduce ‹*size, number, etc.*› **3** (schmälern) belittle ‹*person, achievements*›; minimize ‹*importance, significance*› **4** (kleiner reproduzieren) reduce ‹*photograph etc.*›
B *refl. V.* **1** (ugs.: sich einschränken) ‹*company etc.*› move to smaller premises; ‹*family etc.*› move to a smaller place **2** (kleiner werden) ‹*space, area, etc.*› become smaller **3** (sich verringern) ‹*number*› decrease, grow smaller; ‹*circle of friends*› grow smaller, shrink
C *itr. V.* ‹*lens etc.*› make things look *or* appear smaller

Verkleinerung *die; ~, ~en* reduction in size; making smaller; (des Formats, der Anzahl, des Maßstabs, durch eine Linse) reduction; (das Kleinerwerden) becoming smaller

Verkleinerungs·form *die* (Sprachw.) diminutive form

verkleistern *tr. V.* (ugs.) **1** (zukleben) fill ‹*crack, hole*›; (fig.) cover up **2** (zusammenkleben) make into a sticky mass

verklemmen *refl. V.* get *or* become stuck; ‹*door, window*› jam, get *or* become jammed

verklemmt
A *Adj.* inhibited
B *adv.* in an inhibited manner

Verklemmtheit *die; ~:* inhibitedness

verklickern *tr. V.* (salopp) **jmdm. etw. ~:** make sth. clear to sb.; spell sth. out to sb.; (erklären) explain sth. to sb. in every detail

verklingen *unr. itr. V.; mit sein* ‹*sound, voice, song, etc.*› fade away; (fig.) ‹*mood*› wear off

verklumpen *itr. V.; mit sein* ‹*gravy, sauce, etc.*› go lumpy

verknacken *tr. V.* (salopp) **jmdn. zu Gefängnis/einer Geldstrafe ~:** put sb. inside (sl.)/slap a fine on sb. (coll.); **er wurde zu 18 Monaten verknackt** he got 18 months; **er wurde wegen ein paar Brüchen verknackt** he was done for a couple of break-ins (sl.)

verknacksen /fɛɐ̯'knaksn̩/ *refl. V.* (ugs.) twist, sprain ‹*ankle, wrist*›; **sich** (*Dat.*) **den Fuß ~:** twist *or* sprain one's ankle

verknallen
A *tr. V.* (ugs.: verschießen) let off ‹*firework*›; use up ‹*ammunition*›; **zu Silvester werden unglaubliche Summen verknallt** incredible amounts of money are squandered on fireworks on New Year's Eve
B *refl. V.* (ugs.: sich verlieben) fall head over heels in love (**in** + *Akk.* with); **in jmdn. verknallt sein** be crazy about sb. (coll.)

verknappen
A *tr. V.* cut back [on] ‹*imports*›; **das würde das Wasser noch weiter ~:** that would create even more water shortages
B *refl. V.* run short

Verknappung *die; ~, ~en* cutting back (*Gen.* on); (der Liquidität) loss

verkneifen *unr. refl. V.* (ugs.) **1** **sich** (*Dat.*) **eine Frage/Bemerkung ~:** bite back a question/remark; **ich konnte mir das Lachen/ein Lächeln kaum ~:** I could hardly keep a straight face; I could hardly stop myself laughing/smiling **2** (verzichten) manage *or* do without; **es sich** (*Dat.*) **~, etw. zu tun** stop oneself doing sth.

verknicken *itr. V.* get bent; (verknittern) get creased; **verknickt** bent; (verknittert) creased

verkniffen
A *2. Part. v.* **verkneifen**
B *Adj.* strained ‹*expression*›; pinched ‹*mouth, lips*›
C *adv.* in a strained manner; **~ grinsen** force a grin

verknittern *tr. V.* crumple; **ein verknittertes Gesicht** (fig.) a wrinkled face

verknöchern /fɛɐ̯'knœçɐn/ *itr. V.; mit sein* ‹*person*› become fossilized

verknorpeln *itr. V.; mit sein* (Med.) become cartilaginous

Verknorpelung *die; ~, ~en* cartilaginification

verknoten
A *tr. V.* **1** (verknüpfen) tie; knot; **zwei Fäden [miteinander] ~:** tie two threads together **2** (festbinden) tie (**an** + *Akk.* to)
B *refl. V.* become knotted

verknüpfen
A *tr. V.* **1** (knoten) tie; knot; **die beiden Fäden miteinander ~:** tie *or* knot the two threads together **2** (zugleich tun) combine **3** (in Beziehung setzen) link; (unwillkürlich) associate
B *refl. V.* be associated

Verknüpfung *die; ~, ~en* **1** ▸**verknüpfen A**: tying; knotting; combination; linking; association **2** (Knoten) knots *pl.*

verknusen /fɛɐ̯'knu:zn̩/ *in* **jmdn./etw. nicht ~ können** (ugs.) not be able to stick (sl.) *or* stand sb./sth.

verkochen
A *itr. V.; mit sein* **1** (verdampfen) boil away **2** (breiig werden, zerfallen) boil down to a pulp
B *tr. V.* boil (**zu** + *Dat.* to make)

verkohlen[1]
A *itr. V.* char; become charred
B *tr. V.* burn ‹*wood*› to charcoal; char

verkohlen[2] *tr. V.* (ugs.) ▸**veräppeln**

verkommen[1] *unr. itr. V.; mit sein* **1** (verwahrlosen) go to the dogs; (moralisch, sittlich) go to the bad; ‹*child*› go wild; **im tiefsten Elend ~:** sink deeper and deeper into poverty **2** (verfallen) ‹*building etc.*› go to rack and ruin, fall into disrepair, become dilapidated; ‹*garden*› run wild; ‹*area*› become run down **3** (herabsinken) degenerate (**zu** into) **4** (verderben) ‹*food*› go bad; ‹*wine, beer*› go off

verkommen[2]
A *2. Part. v.* **~**[1]
B *Adj.* depraved; **ein ~es Subjekt** a dissolute character

Verkommenheit *die; ~:* depravity

verkomplizieren *tr. V.* complicate

verkonsumieren *tr. V.* (ugs.) get through; consume

verkoppeln *tr. V.* couple; ‹*spacecraft*› link up

Verkoppelung *die; ~, ~en* coupling; (von Flugkörpern) link-up

verkorken
A *tr. V.* cork [up]
B *itr. V.; mit sein* (Bot.) suberize

verkorksen /fɛɐ̯'kɔrksn̩/ (ugs.)
A *tr. V.* make a mess of; mess up; **eine verkorkste Gesellschaft** a screwed-up society (sl.)
B *refl. V.* **sich** (*Dat.*) **den Magen ~:** upset one's stomach

verkörpern
A *tr. V.* **1** (als Schauspieler) play [the part of] **2** (bilden) embody; ‹*person*› embody, personify
B *refl. V.* be embodied (**in** + *Dat.* in)

Verkörperung *die; ~, ~en* embodiment; (Mensch) embodiment; personification

verkosten *tr. V.* **1** (bes. österr.: kosten) try; taste **2** (prüfend schmecken) taste ‹*wine*›

verköstigen /fɛɐ̯'kœstɪgn̩/ *tr. V.* feed; provide with meals

Verköstigung *die; ~, ~en* **1** feeding; **die ~ der Kinder** the provision of the children with meals **2** (Kost) foods; meals *pl.*

verkrachen *refl. V.* (ugs.) fall out

verkracht *Adj.* failed; **er war ein ~er Student** he had been a failure at university/college; *s. auch* **Existenz 3**

verkraftbar *Adj.* manageable

verkraften *tr. V.* cope with; **sie hat dieses Erlebnis nie verkraftet** she's never come to terms with this experience

verkrallen *refl. V.* dig one's fingers (**in** + *Akk.* into); (festhalten) cling (**in** + *Akk./Dat.* to)

verkramen *tr. V.* (ugs.) mislay

verkrampfen *refl. V.* ‹*muscle*› become cramped; ‹*person*› go tense, tense up; **verkrampft sitzen/lächeln** sit tensed up/smile tensely

Verkrampfung *die; ~, ~en* tenseness; tension

verkratzen *tr. V.* scratch; **sich** (*Dat.*) **die Beine ~:** scratch one's legs

verkrebst /fɛɐ̯'kre:pst/ *Adj.* (ugs.) cancerous

verkriechen *unr. refl. V.* ‹*animal*› creep [away]; ‹*person*› hide [oneself away]; **sich unter die** *od.* **der Bank ~:** crawl *or* creep under the bench; **sich ins Bett ~** (ugs.) crawl into bed (coll.); **am liebsten hätte ich mich [in den hintersten Winkel] verkrochen** I'd have liked to crawl away and hide in a corner; I wished the ground would open and swallow me up

verkrümeln *refl. V.* (ugs.: sich entfernen) slip off *or* away

verkrümmen
A *refl. V.* double up; ‹*spine*› become curved
B *tr. V.* bend ‹*finger etc.*›

verkrümmt *Adj.* bent ‹*person*›; crooked ‹*finger*›; curved ‹*spine*›

Verkrümmung *die* crookedness; **~ der Wirbelsäule** curvature of the spine

verkrüppeln
A *itr. V.; mit sein* ‹*tree*› become stunted; **verkrüppelt** stunted
B *tr. V.* cripple ‹*person*›; **verkrüppelte Arme/Füße** deformed arms/crippled feet

Verkrüppelung *die; ~, ~en* deformity

verkrusten *itr. V.; mit sein* form a crust; ‹*wound*› form a scab; **mit Blut verkrustet** encrusted with blood

verkühlen *refl. V.* catch a chill

Verkühlung *die* chill

verkümmern *itr. V.; mit sein* **1** ‹*person, animal*› go into a decline; ‹*plant etc.*› become stunted; ‹*muscle, limb*› waste away, atrophy; **seelisch ~** ‹*person*› become emotionally stunted **2** ‹*talent, emotional life, etc.*› wither away; ‹*strength*› decline, fade; ‹*relationship*› become less close; ‹*trade, initiative*› dwindle

Verkümmerung *die; ~, ~en* ▸**verkümmern 2**: withering away; declining; fading; becoming less close; dwindling

verkünden *tr. V.* announce; pronounce ‹*judgement*›; promulgate ‹*law, decree*›; ‹*sign, omen*› presage; **die Menschenrechte ~:** proclaim the rights of man; **seine Miene verkündete nichts Gutes** (fig.) his expression did not augur well

verkündigen *tr. V.* (geh.) **1** (predigen) preach **2** (bekannt machen) announce; proclaim; (mit Nachdruck sagen) announce **3** (ankündigen) ‹*sign, omen*› presage

Verkündigung *die* **1** (das Predigen) preaching **2** (Bekanntmachung) announcement; proclamation **3** (das Wort Gottes) word of God; **die kirchliche ~:** the Church's message

Verkündung *die;* **~, ~en** announcement; (von Urteilen) pronouncement; (von Gesetzen, Verordnungen) promulgation

verkuppeln *tr. V.* pair off (**mit** with)

verkürzen

A *tr. V.* **1** (verringern) reduce; (abkürzen) shorten; **die Linie erscheint verkürzt** this line appears foreshortened **2** (abbrechen) cut short ‹*stay, life*›; put an end to, end ‹*suffering*›; **verkürzte Arbeitszeit** reduced *or* shorter working hours *pl.* **3** **sich** (*Dat.*) **die Zeit ~:** while away the time; make the time pass more quickly; **jmdm. die Winterabende ~:** help sb. while away the winter evenings

B *refl. V.* (kürzer werden) become shorter; shorten; ‹*perspective*› become foreshortened

C *itr. V.* (Ballspiele) close the gap (**auf** + *Akk.* to)

Verkürzung *die* ▸**verkürzen A 1, 2**: shortening; reduction; foreshortening; cutting short; ending; **eine ~ der Arbeitszeit** a reduction in working hours; **starkes Rauchen hat eine ~ der Lebenserwartung um ... zur Folge** heavy smoking reduces life expectancy by ...

verlachen *tr. V.* laugh at; **etw. als Unsinn ~:** ridicule sth. as nonsense

verladen *unr. tr. V.* **1** (laden) load **2** (ugs.: betrügen) **jmdn. ~:** take sb. for a ride (coll.); con sb. (sl.); (Ballspiele) out-trick sb.

Verlade·rampe *die* loading platform

Verladung *die* loading

Verlag /fɛɐ̯ˈlaːk/ *der;* **~[e]s, ~e** publishing house *or* firm; publisher's; **in welchem ~ ist das Buch erschienen?** who published the book?; who is the publisher of the book?

verlagern

A *tr. V.* shift ‹*weight, centre of gravity*›; (an einen anderen Ort) move; (fig.) transfer; shift ‹*emphasis*›

B *refl. V.* (auch fig.) shift; ‹*area of high/low pressure etc.*› move

Verlagerung *die* moving; **eine ~ des Schwergewichts** (fig.) a shift in emphasis

Verlags-: ~anstalt *die* publishing house *or* firm; firm of publishers; **~buchhändler** *der,* **~buchhändlerin** *die* publisher; **~gruppe** *die* publishing group; **~haus** *das* publishing house *or* firm; **~programm** *das* [publisher's] list; **~wesen** *das* publishing *no art.*

verlanden *itr. V.; mit sein* silt up

Verlandung *die* silting up

verlangen

A *tr. V.* **1** (fordern) demand; (wollen) want; **man kann von ihm nicht ~, dass er alles bezahlt** one can't ask *or* expect him to pay everything; **das ist zu viel verlangt** that's asking too much; that's too much to expect; **du verlangst Unmögliches** you're asking the impossible; **die Firma verlangt [von den Bewerbern] EDV-Kenntnisse** the company asks for [applicants with] a knowledge of computers; **die Rechnung ~:** ask for the bill; **von jedem wird Pünktlichkeit verlangt** everyone is required *or* expected to be punctual **2** (nötig haben) ‹*task etc.*› require, call for ‹*patience, knowledge, experience, skill, etc.*›; **diese Aufgabe verlangt den ganzen Menschen** this task makes demands of the whole person **3** (gebieten) ‹*situation, decency*› demand **4** (berechnen) charge; **sie verlangte 200 Euro von ihm** she charged him 200 euros; **wie viel verlangst du dafür?** how much are you asking for it? **5** (sehen wollen) ask for, ask to see ‹*passport, driving licence, etc.*› **6** (am Telefon) ask for; ask to speak to; **du wirst am Telefon verlangt** you're wanted on the phone **7** *unpers.* (geh.) **es verlangt mich, ihn noch einmal zu sehen** I long *or* yearn to see him again

B *itr. V.* (geh.) **1** (bitten) **nach einem Arzt/Priester** *usw.* **~:** ask for a doctor/priest *etc.*; **nach einem Glas Wasser ~:** ask for a glass of water **2** (sich sehnen) **nach jmdm./etw. ~:** long for sb./sth.

Verlangen *das;* **~s, ~** **1** (Bedürfnis) desire (**nach** for); **ein starkes ~ nach Schokolade haben** *od.* **verspüren** have a craving for chocolate **2** (Forderung) demand; **auf ~:** on request; **auf jmds. ~:** at sb.'s request

verlängern /fɛɐ̯ˈlɛŋɐn/

A *tr. V.* **1** (länger machen) lengthen, make longer ‹*skirt, sleeve, etc.*›; extend ‹*flex, cable, road, etc.*›; *s. auch* **Arm 1; Rücken 1** **2** (länger gültig sein lassen) renew ‹*passport, driving licence, etc.*›; extend, renew ‹*contract*› **3** (länger dauern lassen) extend, prolong ‹*stay, life, suffering, etc.*› (**um** by); **ein verlängertes Wochenende** a long weekend **4** (verdünnen) add water *etc.* to ‹*sauce, gravy, etc.*› (*to make it go further*) **5** (Ballspiele) touch ‹*cross, corner kick, etc.*› on

B *refl. V.* **1** (länger werden) become longer; ‹*stay, life, suffering, etc.*› be prolonged (**um** by) **2** (länger gültig bleiben) ‹*contract etc.*› be extended

C *itr. V.* (Ballspiele) touch [the ball] on; **mit dem Kopf ~:** head [the ball] on

Verlängerung *die;* **~, ~en** **1** ▸**verlängern A 1-3**: lengthening; renewal; extension; prolongation **2** (Ballspiele) extra time *no indef. art.*; (nachgespielte Zeit) injury time *no indef. art.*; **in der/nach ~:** in/after extra time **3** (Teilstück) extension

Verlängerungs·schnur *die* extension lead *or* (Amer.) cord

verlangsamen

A *tr. V.* **die Fahrt** *od.* **das Tempo/seine Schritte ~:** reduce speed/slacken one's pace; slow down

B *refl. V.* slow down; ‹*pace*› slacken

Verlangsamung *die;* **~, ~en** slowing down; (des Tempos) slackening; **zu einer ~ des Tempos gezwungen sein** be forced to slow down

Verlass, *Verlaß *der: in* **auf jmdn./etw. ist [kein] ~:** sb./sth. can[not] be relied *or* depended [up]on; **auf ihn ist kein ~:** you can't rely *or* depend on him

verlassen[1]

A *unr. refl. V.* (vertrauen) rely, depend (**auf** + *Akk.* on); **er verlässt sich darauf, dass du kommst** he's relying on you to come; **darauf kannst du dich ~/worauf du dich ~ kannst** you can depend on *or* be sure of that

B *unr. tr. V.* **1** leave; **die Patientin konnte das Bett ~:** the patient was able to get up **2** (sich trennen von) desert; abandon; forsake; leave, desert ‹*wife, family, etc.*›; **Großvater hat uns für immer ~** (verhüll.) grandfather has been taken from us (euphem.); **und da/dann verließen sie ihn** (ugs.) and after that I/he *etc.* was at a loss; **der Mut/alle Hoffnung hatte mich ~** (fig.) my courage/all hope had deserted me

verlassen[2]

A *2. Part. v.* **~[1]**

B *Adj.* deserted ‹*street, square, village, etc.*›; empty ‹*house*›; (öd) desolate ‹*region etc.*›; **einsam und ~:** all alone; **~ daliegen** be deserted

Verlassenheit *die;* **~:** desertedness; (Öde) desolation; **ein Gefühl von ~:** a feeling of desolation

verlässlich, *verläßlich /fɛɐ̯ˈlɛslɪç/

A *Adj.* reliable; reliable, dependable ‹*person*›

B *adv.* reliably

Verlässlichkeit, *Verläßlichkeit *die;* **~:** reliability; (eines Menschen) reliability; dependability

verlästern *tr. V.* malign

Verlaub /fɛɐ̯ˈlaup/ *der: in* **mit ~** (geh.) with your permission; **mit ~ [gesagt** *od.* **zu sagen]** if you will pardon *or* forgive my saying so

Verlauf *der;* **~[e]s, Verläufe** course; **im ~e des Sommers/ihrer Rede** during *or* in the course of the summer/her speech; **der glückliche ~ der Revolution** the fortunate outcome of the revolution

verlaufen

A *unr. itr. V.; mit sein* **1** (sich erstrecken) run **2** (ablaufen) ‹*test, rehearsal, etc.*› go; ‹*party etc.*› go off; **es ist alles gut ~:** everything went [off] well; **die Untersuchung ist ergebnislos ~:** the investigation yielded no results **3** ‹*butter, chocolate, etc.*› melt; ‹*make-up, ink*› run

B *unr. itr.* (*auch refl.*) *V.; mit sein* (sich verlieren) ‹*track, path*› disappear (**in** + *Dat.* in)

C *unr. refl. V.* **1** (sich verirren) get lost; lose one's way **2** (auseinander gehen) ‹*crowd etc.*› disperse **3** (abfließen) ‹*floods*› subside

Verlaufs·form *die* (Sprachw.) progressive *or* continuous form

verlausen *itr. V.; mit sein* become infested with lice; **verlaust** louse-ridden; infested with lice *postpos.*

verlautbaren

A *tr. V.* announce [officially]; **offen ~:** state openly; **die Ärzte verlautbarten, dass ...** the doctors issued a bulletin to the effect that ...

B *itr. V.; mit sein* (geh.) become known; **es verlautbarte, der Staatschef sei krank** it was reported *or* said that the head of state was ill

Verlautbarung *die;* **~, ~en** announcement; (inoffizielle Meldung) [unofficial] report

verlauten

A *tr. V.* announce; **er hütete sich davor, ein Wort davon zu ~:** he was careful not to say a word about it

B *itr. V.; mit sein* be reported; **wie verlautet** according to reports; **aus amtlicher Quelle verlautet, dass ...** official reports say that ...; **über ihr Privatleben ließ sie nichts ~:** she let nothing be known about her private life

verleasen /fɛɐ̯ˈliːsn̩/ *tr. V.* lease (**an** + *Akk.* to)

verleben *tr. V.* **1** (verbringen) spend **2** (ugs.: verbrauchen) spend ‹*money*› on everyday needs

verlebendigen *tr. V.* make ‹*text, past, etc.*› come alive; imbue ‹*portrait, figure*› with life

verlebt *Adj.* dissipated

verlegen[1]

A *tr. V.* **1** (nicht wieder finden) mislay **2** (verschieben) postpone (**auf** + *Akk.* until); (vor~) bring forward (**auf** + *Akk.* to); **einen Termin ~:** alter an appointment **3** (verlagern) move; transfer ‹*patient*›; **die Handlung ins 18. Jahrhundert ~:** transpose *or* shift the action to the 18th century **4** (legen) lay ‹*cable, pipe, carpet, etc.*› **5** (versperren) block, bar ‹*way etc.*›; block off ‹*retreat*›; **jmdm. den Weg ~:** block *or* bar sb.'s way **6** (veröffentlichen) publish

B *refl. V.* (sich ausrichten) take up ‹*subject, activity, occupation, etc.*›; resort to ‹*guesswork, flattery, silence, lying, etc.*›; **sich auf eine andere Taktik ~:** change [one's] tactics; resort to a different tactic

verlegen[2]

A *Adj.* **1** embarrassed **2** **um etw. ~ sein** (etw. nicht zur Verfügung haben) be short of sth.; (etw. benötigen) be in need of sth.; **nicht/nie um Worte/eine Ausrede ~ sein** not/never be at a loss for words/an excuse

B *adv.* in embarrassment

Verlegenheit *die;* **~, ~en** **1** (Befangenheit) embarrassment; **in ~ geraten** get *or* become embarrassed; **jmdn. in ~ bringen** embarrass sb. **2** (Unannehmlichkeit) embarrassing situation; **in finanzieller ~ sein** be in financial difficulties; be financially embarrassed; **ich bin nie in die ~ gekommen** I've never been in that embarrassing situation

Verlegenheits·lösung *die* makeshift solution

Verleger *der;* **~s, ~, Verlegerin** *die;* **~, ~nen** ▸ℹ **S. 113** publisher; *s. auch* **-in**

verlegerisch

A *Adj.* publishing; **~e Kenntnisse** knowledge of publishing; **~e Anstrengungen** efforts on the part of the publishers

B *adv.* from the publishing standpoint

Verlegung *die;* **~, ~en** **1** (Verschiebung) postponement; (Vor~) bringing forward *no art.*; **um eine ~ des Termins bitten** ask to change the

V

appointment [2] ▸**verlegen**[1] **A 3**: moving; transfer; transposition; shifting [3] (von Kabeln, Rohren, Teppichen usw.) laying

verleiden *tr. V.* **jmdm. etw. ~**: spoil sth. for sb.

Verleih *der;* **~[e]s, ~e** [1] (das Verleihen) hiring out; (von Autos) renting *or* hiring out [2] (Unternehmen) hire firm *or* company; (Film~) distribution company; (Video~) video library; (Auto~) rental *or* hire firm

verleihen *unr. tr. V.* [1] hire out; rent *or* hire out ‹*car*›; (umsonst) lend [out] [2] (überreichen) award; bestow, confer ‹*award, honour*›; **jmdm. einen Orden/Titel ~**: decorate sb./confer a title on sb.; **jmdm. die Ehrenbürgerrechte ~**: give sb. the freedom of the city/town [3] (verschaffen) give; lend; **er verlieh seinen Worten mit Drohungen Nachdruck** he used threats to lend weight to his words

Verleiher *der;* **~s, ~**, **Verleiherin** *die;* **~, ~nen** hirer; (Film~) distributor

Verleihung *die;* **~, ~en** [1] ▸**verleihen 1**: hiring out; renting out; lending [out] [2] ▸**verleihen 2**: awarding; bestowing; conferring; (Zeremonie) award; conferment; bestowal

verleimen *tr. V.* glue

verleiten *tr. V.* **jmdn. dazu ~, etw. zu tun** lead *or* induce sb. to do sth.; (verlocken) tempt *or* entice sb. to do sth.; **jmdn. zum Trinken/Stehlen ~**: lead sb. into drinking/stealing; **sich zu voreiligen Schlussfolgerungen ~ lassen** allow oneself to be led into drawing hasty conclusions

Verleitung *die:* **sie beschuldigte ihn der ~ zum Meineid** she accused him of inducing *or* encouraging her to commit perjury; **das wäre ~ zum Diebstahl** it would be encouraging theft

verlernen *tr. V.* forget; **das Kochen ~**: forget how to cook; **sie hat das Lachen verlernt** (fig.) she has forgotten how to laugh

verlesen[1]

A *unr. tr. V.* read out

B *unr. refl. V.* (falsch lesen) make a mistake/mistakes in reading; **er hat sich wohl ~**: he must have read it wrongly

verlesen[2]

A *2. Part. v.* **~**[1]

B *unr. tr. V.* (auslesen) sort ‹*fruit, vegetables*›

Verlesung *die;* **~, ~en** reading out

verletzbar *Adj.* **leicht ~ sein** be easily hurt

Verletzbarkeit *die;* **~: seine ~ war groß** he was very easily hurt; **sie kannte meine ~**: she knew how easily I could be hurt

verletzen /fɛɐ̯ˈlɛt͜sn̩/ *tr. V.* [1] ▸**i S. 439** (beschädigen) injure; (durch Schuss, Stich) wound; **ich habe mich am Kopf/mir das Bein verletzt** I injured *or* hurt my head/leg [2] (kränken) hurt, wound ‹*person, feelings*›; **verletzte Eitelkeit/verletzter Stolz** injured *or* wounded vanity/pride; **eine ~de Bemerkung** a wounding remark; **sich in seinem Stolz verletzt fühlen** feel that one's pride has been hurt *or* has taken a blow [3] (verstoßen gegen) violate; infringe; infringe ‹*regulation*›; break ‹*agreement, law*›; **das Wahlgeheimnis ~**: breach the secrecy of the vote; **den guten Geschmack ~**: offend against good taste [4] (eindringen in) violate ‹*frontier, airspace, etc.*›

verletzlich *Adj.* vulnerable; (empfindlich) sensitive

Verletzlichkeit *die;* **~**: vulnerability; (Empfindlichkeit) sensitivity

Verletzte *der/die; adj. Dekl.* injured person; casualty; (durch Schuss, Stich) wounded person; **die ~n** the injured/wounded; the casualties; **bei dem Unfall gab es einen Toten und zwei ~**: one person died and two were injured in the accident; **es gab keine ~n bei der Demonstration** nobody was hurt during the demonstration

Verletzung *die;* **~, ~en** [1] ▸**i S. 439** (Wunde) injury; **eine ~ am Knie haben** have an injury to one's knee *or* an injured knee [2] (Kränkung) hurting; wounding [3] ▸**verletzen 3**: violation; infringement; breaking [4] (Grenz~, Luftraum~ usw.) violation

verleugnen *tr. V.* deny; disown ‹*friend, relation*›; **er kann seine Herkunft nicht ~**: it is obvious where he comes from; **sich selbst ~**: go against *or* betray one's principles

Verleugnung *die* denial; (eines Freundes, Verwandten) disownment

verleumden /fɛɐ̯ˈlɔymdn̩/ *tr. V.* slander; (schriftlich) libel

Verleumder *der;* **~, ~**, **Verleumderin** *die;* **~, ~nen** slanderer; (schriftlich) libeller

verleumderisch *Adj.* slanderous; (in Schriftform) libellous

Verleumdung *die;* **~, ~en** [1] slander; (in Schriftform) libelling [2] (Bemerkung usw.) slander; (in Schriftform) libel

Verleumdungs·kampagne *die* smear campaign

verlieben *refl. V.* fall in love (**in** + *Akk.* with); **ein verliebtes Pärchen** a pair of lovers; **jmdm. verliebte Blicke zuwerfen** make eyes at sb.; **er ist ganz verliebt in seine Idee** (fig.) he is infatuated with his idea; **zum Verlieben sein/aussehen** (ugs.) be/look perfectly sweet

Verliebte *der/die; adj. Dekl.* lover; **die beiden ~n** the [two] lovers

Verliebtheit *die;* **~**: being *no art.* in love; **die ~ dauerte bei ihr nur drei Wochen** she was only in love for three weeks; **in ihrer ~ hatte sie …** being so much in love, she had …

verlieren /fɛɐ̯ˈliːrən/

A *unr. tr. V.* lose; ‹*plant, tree*› lose, shed ‹*leaves*›; **sich** (*Dat.*) **verloren vorkommen** feel lost; **für jmdn./etw. verloren sein** be lost to sb./sth.; **die Katze verliert Haare** the cat is moulting; **nichts [mehr] zu ~ haben** have nothing [more] to lose; **jmdn./etw. verloren geben** give sb./sth. up for lost; **das hat hier nichts verloren** it has no business to be here

B *unr. itr. V.* lose; **an etw.** (*Dat.*) **~**: lose sth.; **sie hat an Reiz verloren** she has lost some of her attraction; **bei jmdm. ~**: become less highly regarded by sb.

C *unr. refl. V.* [1] (weniger werden) ‹*enthusiasm*› subside; ‹*reserve etc.*› disappear [2] (entschwinden) vanish; ‹*sound*› die away [3] (sich verirren) lose one's way; get lost [4] (sich hingeben) **er war in Gedanken verloren** he was lost in thought [5] (abschweifen) digress; **sich in Detailschilderungen ~**: digress into detailed descriptions

Verlierer *der;* **~s, ~**, **Verliererin** *die;* **~, ~nen** loser; **ein schlechter ~**: a bad loser; **der ~ des Autoschlüssels** the person who has lost the car key

Verlierer·straße *die* (bes. Sport Jargon) **auf der ~ sein** be facing defeat; (fig.) ‹*Aktien*› be on the way down; **jmdn. auf die ~ bringen** start sb. on the road to defeat; **sie landen auf der ~**: they end up the losers (also fig.)

Verlies /fɛɐ̯ˈliːs/ *das;* **~es, ~e** dungeon

verlinken (DV)

A *itr. V.* link (**zu, auf** + *Akk.* to)

B *tr. V.* link (**mit** to)

verloben

A *refl. V.* become *or* get engaged, (arch.) become betrothed (**mit** to); **verlobt sein** be engaged

B *tr. V.* (veralt.) **jmdn. mit jmdm. ~**: betroth sb. to sb. (arch.)

Verlöbnis /fɛɐ̯ˈløːpnɪs/ *das;* **~ses, ~se** (geh.) engagement, (arch.) betrothal (**mit** to)

Verlobte *der/die; adj. Dekl.* **mein ~r** my fiancé *or* (arch.) betrothed; **meine ~**: my fiancée *or* (arch.) betrothed; **die ~n** the engaged *or* (arch.) betrothed couple

Verlobung *die;* **~, ~en** engagement; betrothal (arch.); (Feier) engagement party

Verlobungs·anzeige *die* engagement announcement

verlocken *tr. V.* (geh.) tempt; entice; **der See verlockt zum Baden** the lake tempts *or* entices one to bathe in it

verlockend *Adj.* tempting; enticing; **das Wetter war nicht gerade ~**: the weather wasn't exactly enticing

Verlockung *die* temptation; enticement; **der ~ widerstehen** resist the temptation

verlogen /fɛɐ̯ˈloːɡn̩/ (abwertend)

A *Adj.* lying, mendacious ‹*person*›; false ‹*morality, phrases, romanticism, etc.*›; insincere ‹*compliment*›

B *adv.* mendaciously; falsely

Verlogenheit *die;* **~, ~en** (eines Menschen) mendacity; (einer Moral, Romantik, von Phrasen usw.) falseness; (von Komplimenten) insincerity

verlohnen (geh.)

A *refl.* (*auch itr.*) *V.* be worth while; **es verlohnt sich nicht, das zu tun** it is not worth [while] doing that

B *tr.* (*od. veralt. itr.*) *V.* **das verlohnt die**/ (veralt.) **der Mühe nicht** it is not worth the trouble

verlor /fɛɐ̯ˈloːɐ̯/ *1. u. 3. Pers. Sg. Prät. v.* **verlieren**

verloren

A *2. Part. v.* **verlieren**

B *Adj.* lost; **[eine] ~e Mühe** a wasted effort; **Lass uns aufhören! Die Sache ist ~**: Let's give up! It's hopeless; **er ist ~**: that's the end of him now; **ohne meine Brille bin ich ~** (fig.) I'm lost without my glasses; **~e Eier** poached eggs; **der ~e Sohn** (bibl.) the Prodigal Son

C **~ gehen** (abhanden kommen) get lost; (nicht gewonnen werden) ‹*war, battle, etc.*› be lost; **deine Postkarte muss wohl verloren gegangen sein** your postcard must have got lost *or* gone astray; **durch diesen Umweg ging uns/ging viel Zeit verloren** we lost a lot of time/a lot of time was lost by this detour; **ein verloren gegangenes Buch** a lost book; a book that has gone missing; **an dir ist ein Künstler verloren gegangen** you ought to have been an artist; you would have made a good artist

Verlorenheit *die;* **~**: loneliness; isolation

verlöschen *unr. itr. V.; mit sein* ‹*light, fire, etc.*› go out; ‹*comet, shooting star*› die

verlosen *tr. V.* raffle

Verlosung *die;* **~, ~en** raffle; draw; (Ziehung) draw; (Vorgang) raffling

verlottern /fɛɐ̯ˈlɔtɐn/ *itr. V.; mit sein* (abwertend) ‹*building, town, area, etc.*› become run-down; ‹*person*› go to seed; ‹*firm, business*› go downhill, go to the dogs

Verlust *der;* **~[e]s, ~e** loss (**an** + *Dat.* of); **bei ~**: in the case *or* event of loss; **schwere ~e erleiden** ‹*army etc.*› suffer heavy losses *or* casualties; **etw. mit ~ verkaufen** sell sth. at a loss

Verlust·geschäft *das* loss-making deal *or* transaction; **sonst mache ich ein ~**: otherwise I'll be making a loss

verlustieren *refl. V.* (scherzh.) amuse oneself; **wir haben uns auf der Party verlustiert** we had fun *or* enjoyed ourselves at the party; **sich mit jmdm. im Bett ~**: have a good time in bed with sb.

verlustig *Adj.* **in einer Sache** (*Gen.*) **~ gehen** (Papierdt.) lose sth.; (verwirken) forfeit *or* lose sth.

verlust-, Verlust-: ~liste *die* list of casualties and losses; (fig.) casualty list; **~meldung** *die* casualty report; **~reich** *Adj.* [1] (mit vielen Toten) ‹*battle etc.*› involving heavy losses; [2] (mit finanziellen ~en) heavily loss-making ‹*product, project, etc.*›

vermachen *tr. V.* **jmdm. etw. ~**: leave *or* bequeath sth. to sb.; (fig.: schenken, überlassen) give sth. to sb.; let sb. have sth.

Vermächtnis /fɛɐ̯ˈmɛçtnɪs/ *das;* **~ses, ~se** [1] (Rechtspr.: Legat) bequest; legacy; (fig.) legacy [2] (letzter Wille) last wish

vermählen /fɛɐ̯ˈmɛːlən/ (geh.)

A *refl. V.* **sich [jmdm.** *od.* **mit jmdm.] ~**: marry *or* wed [sb.]; (fig.) be wedded (**mit** to); **frisch vermählt** newly married

B *tr. V.* (veralt.) **seine Tochter mit jmdm. ~**: marry one's daughter to sb.; give one's daughter to sb. in marriage

Vermählte *der/die; adj. Dekl.*; (geh.) bridegroom/bride; **die ~n** the bride and bridegroom; **die beiden frisch ~n** the newly-married couple; the newly-weds (coll.)

Vermählung *die;* **~, ~en** (geh.) [1] marriage; wedding [2] (Fest) wedding ceremony

vermaledeit /fɛɐ̯maleˈdait/ *Adj.* (ugs. veralt.) damned; blasted (Brit.)

vermännlichen *tr. V.* masculinize

vermarkten *tr. V.* [1] (als Ware verkaufen) exploit commercially [2] (Wirtsch.) market ‹*goods etc.*›

Vermarktung *die;* ~, ~**en** [1] commercial exploitation [2] (Wirtsch.) marketing

vermasseln /fɛɐ̯ˈmasl̩n/ *tr. V.* (salopp) [1] (verderben) muck up (Brit. sl.); mess up; ruin [2] (verhauen) make a cock-up (Brit. sl.) *or* mess of ‹*exam etc.*›

Vermassung *die;* ~, ~**en** (abwertend) loss of individuality

vermauern *tr. V.* [1] (zumauern) wall up ‹*entrance*›; brick up ‹*hole, window, etc.*› [2] (verbrauchen) use up ‹*bricks, sand, etc.*› in building a/the wall *etc.*

vermehren
A *tr. V.* (größer machen) increase (**um** by)
B *refl. V.* [1] (größer werden) increase [2] (sich fortpflanzen) reproduce; ‹*bacterium, virus*› multiply

vermehrt
A *Adj.* increased
B *adv.* increasingly; ~ **auftreten** occur with increasing frequency

Vermehrung *die;* ~, ~**en** [1] increase (*Gen.* in) [2] (Fortpflanzung) reproduction; (von Bakterien, Viren) multiplying

vermeidbar *Adj.* avoidable; **die Niederlage wäre** ~ **gewesen** the defeat could have been avoided

vermeiden *unr. tr. V.* avoid; **es lässt sich nicht** ~: it is unavoidable; **es** ~, **etw. zu tun** avoid doing sth.; **er hatte gehofft, dass der Krieg zu** ~ **sei** he had hoped that war could be avoided; **ein Gegentor** ~: avoid conceding a goal

Vermeidung *die;* ~, ~**en** avoidance

vermeinen *tr. V.* (geh.) think; **er vermeinte, ihre Stimme zu hören** he thought he heard her voice

vermeintlich /fɛɐ̯ˈmaintlɪç/
A *Adj.* supposed
B *adv.* supposedly

vermelden *tr. V.* report; ‹*report*› announce

vermengen
A *tr. V.* [1] (mischen) mix (**miteinander** together) [2] (durcheinander bringen) mix up; confuse
B *refl. V.* (sich mischen) mingle

vermenschlichen *tr. V.* anthropomorphize

Vermenschlichung *die;* ~, ~**en** anthropomorphization

Vermerk /fɛɐ̯ˈmɛrk/ *der;* ~**[e]s**, ~**e** note; (amtlich) remark; (Stempel) stamp; (im Kalender) entry

vermerken *tr. V.* [1] (notieren) make a note of; note [down]; (in Akten, Wachbuch usw.) record; **das sei aber nur am Rande vermerkt** but that is only by the way [2] (feststellen) note; *s. auch* **übel B 2**

vermessen[1]
A *unr. tr. V.* measure; survey ‹*land, site*›
B *unr. refl. V.* [1] (falsch messen) measure wrongly [2] (geh.: sich anmaßen) **sich** ~, **etw. zu tun** presume *or* have the presumption to do sth.; **wie konnte er sich** ~**!** what presumption!

vermessen[2] *Adj.* (geh.) presumptuous; **darf ich so** ~ **sein anzunehmen, dass ...** may I be so bold as to assume that ...

Vermessenheit *die;* ~, ~**en** (geh.) presumption; presumptuousness; **das ist eine große** ~ **von dir** that is very presumptuous of you

Vermesser *der;* ~**s**, ~, **Vermesserin** *die;* ~, ~**nen** [land] surveyor

Vermessung *die* measurement; (Land~) surveying

vermiesen *tr. V.* (ugs.) **jmdm. etw.** ~: spoil sth. for sb.; **jmdm. die Laune/das Vergnügen** ~: spoil sb.'s mood/enjoyment

vermieten *tr.* (*auch itr.*) *V.* rent [out], let [out] ‹*flat, room, etc.*› (**an** + *Akk.* to); hire [out] ‹*boat, car, etc.*›; **wir** ~ **auch an Studenten** we also rent *or* let to students; **„Zimmer zu** ~**"** 'room to let'

Vermieter *der* landlord

Vermieterin *die* landlady

Vermietung *die;* ~, ~**en** ▸**vermieten**: renting [out]; letting [out]; hiring [out]

vermindern
A *tr. V.* reduce; decrease; reduce, lessen ‹*danger, stress*›; lessen ‹*admiration, ability*›; lower ‹*resistance*›; reduce ‹*debt*›
B *refl. V.* decrease; ‹*influence, danger*› decrease, diminish; ‹*resistance*› diminish

vermindert *Adj.* [1] ~**e Zurechnungsfähigkeit** (Rechtsw.) diminished responsibility [2] (Mus.) diminished

Verminderung *die* ▸**vermindern A**: reduction; decreasing; lessening; lowering; **eine** ~ **der Einnahmen** a decrease in revenues

verminen *tr. V.* mine

vermischen
A *tr. V.* mix (**miteinander** together); blend ‹*teas, tobaccos, etc.*›; **Wahres und Erdachtes miteinander** ~: mingle truth and fiction
B *refl. V.* mix; (fig.) mingle; ‹*races, animals*› interbreed; **unter der Rubrik „Vermischtes"** under the heading 'Miscellaneous'

Vermischung *die* ▸**vermischen**: mixing; blending; (fig.) mingling

vermissen *tr. V.* [1] (sich sehnen nach) miss [2] (nicht haben) **ich vermisse meinen Ausweis** my identity card is missing; **nach dem Brand wurde er vermisst** he was unaccounted for after the fire; **ich vermisse in deiner Küche einen Kühlschrank** I notice that you do not have a fridge in your kitchen; **etw.** ~ **lassen** lack sth.; be lacking in sth.; **er gilt als** *od.* **ist vermisst** (fig.) he is listed as a missing person; **der vermisste Soldat** the missing soldier; **man hat dich in der Vorlesung vermisst** your absence from the lecture was noticed

Vermisste, *Vermißte *der/die; adj. Dekl.* missing person

Vermissten·anzeige, *Vermißten·anzeige *die:* ~ **[von jmdm.] erstatten** report sb. [as] missing

vermittelbar *Adj.* [1] (in Bezug auf Arbeitsplätze) **sie sind** ~: they can be found a job; **schwer** ~**e Jugendliche** young people who are difficult to place in a job; ~**e Arbeitsplätze** fillable vacancies [2] (sich weitergeben lassend) communicable; (verständlich) comprehensible; **schwer** ~: difficult to put across; **es ist der Bevölkerung nicht** ~: it cannot be explained in terms the public will understand

vermitteln
A *itr. V.* mediate, act as [a] mediator (**in** + *Dat.* in); ~**d eingreifen** act as [a] mediator; ~**de Worte** conciliating words
B *tr. V.* [1] (herbeiführen) arrange; negotiate ‹*transaction, ceasefire, compromise*› [2] (besorgen) **jmdm. eine Stelle** ~: find sb. a job; find a job for sb.; **jmdm. ein Haus** ~: locate a house for sb. [3] (als Mittler tätig sein für) **das Arbeitsamt vermittelt die Arbeitskräfte an die Firmen** the job centre (Brit.) *or* (Amer.) employment office places workers with firms [4] (weitergeben) impart ‹*knowledge, insight, values, etc.*›; communicate, pass on ‹*message, information, etc.*›; convey, give ‹*feeling*›; pass on ‹*experience*›; **jmdm. ein genaues Bild von etw.** ~: convey a precise picture of sth. to sb.; **jmdm. Bildung** ~: educate sb.

vermittels[t] *Präp. mit Gen.* (Papierdt.) by means of; ~ **eines Wörterbuchs** with the help of a dictionary

Vermittler *der;* ~**s**, ~, **Vermittlerin** *die;* ~, ~**nen** [1] (Mittler[in]) mediator [2] (Träger[in]) ▸**vermitteln B 4**: imparter; communicator; conveyer [3] (von Berufs wegen) agent; **der** ~ **eines Geschäfts** the negotiator of a transaction

Vermittler·rolle *die* role of mediator

Vermittlung *die;* ~, ~**en** [1] (Schlichtung) mediation; **seine** ~ **anbieten** offer to mediate [2] ▸**vermitteln B 1**: arrangement; negotiation; **durch die** ~ **eines Beamten** through the good offices of an official [3] (das Besorgen) **die** ~ **einer Stelle** finding a job for sb.; **die** ~ **eines Hauses für jmdn.** locating a house for sb. [4] ▸**vermitteln B 4**: imparting; communicating; passing on; conveying [5] (Telefonzentrale) exchange; (in einer Firma) switchboard; (Telefonist) operator

Vermittlungs-: ~ausschuss, *~ausschuß *der* mediation committee [between the two houses of parliament]; **~gebühr** *die* commission

vermöbeln *tr. V.* (ugs.) beat up; (als Strafe) thrash

vermodern *itr. V.; mit sein* decay; rot

vermöge *Präp. mit Gen.* (geh.) by virtue of

vermögen *unr. tr. V.* (geh.) **etw. zu tun** ~: be able to do sth.; be capable of doing sth.; **er vermochte [es] nicht, mich zu überzeugen** he was not able to convince me; **wir werden alles tun, was wir [zu tun]** ~: we will do everything we can; **wer vermöchte zu sagen, ob ...** who can say whether ...; **er vermochte nichts dagegen** he could do nothing to prevent it

Vermögen *das;* ~**s**, ~ [1] (geh.: Fähigkeit) ability [2] (Besitz) fortune; **er hat** ~: he has money; he is a man of means; **das kostet ja ein** ~ (ugs.) it costs a fortune; **sein ganzes** ~: all his money

vermögend *Adj.* wealthy; well-off; **sie ist eine** ~**e Frau** she is a woman of means *or* a wealthy woman

Vermögens-: ~abgabe *die* capital levy; **~bildung** *die:* (wider) *creation of wealth by participation of employees in savings and share-ownership schemes;* **~steuer** *die* wealth tax

Vermögen·steuer *die* ▸**Vermögenssteuer**

vermögens-, Vermögens-: ~verhältnisse *Pl.* financial circumstances; **~verwalter** *der,* **~verwalterin** *die* asset manager; **~werte** *Pl.* investments; **~wirksam A** *Adj.* ‹*saving*› under the employee's savings scheme; **~wirksame Leistungen** employer's contributions to employees' savings schemes; **B** *adv.* ‹*invest*› profitably

vermummen /fɛɐ̯ˈmʊmən/ *tr. V.* [1] (einhüllen) wrap up [warmly] [2] (verbergen) disguise; **vermummte Jugendliche** masked youths

Vermummung *die;* ~, ~**en** [1] **zur** ~ **hatten wir ...** in order to disguise ourselves we had ...; ~ **soll unter Strafe gestellt werden** wearing a mask is to be made a punishable offence [2] (Kleidung) disguise

Vermummungs·verbot *das* ban on wearing masks [during demonstrations]

vermurksen *tr. V.* (ugs.) mess up; muck up (Brit. sl.)

vermuten *tr. V.* suspect; **das ist zu** ~: that is what one would suppose *or* expect; we may assume that; **die Untersuchung lässt** ~, **dass ...** the investigation leads one to suppose that ...; **ich vermute/vermutete ihn in der Bibliothek** I suspect *or* presume he is/supposed *or* presumed he was in the library

vermutlich
A *Adj.* probable; probable, likely ‹*result*›; **der** ~**e Täter** the suspect
B *Adv.* presumably; (wahrscheinlich) probably; **[ja,]** ~: [yes,] I suppose so

Vermutung *die;* ~, ~**en** supposition; (Verdacht) suspicion; **es liegt die** ~ **nahe, dass ...** it seems a likely supposition that ...; there are grounds for supposing that ...; **die** ~ **haben, dass ...** presume *or* suppose that ...

vernachlässigen *tr. V.* [1] neglect [2] (unberücksichtigt lassen) ignore; disregard

Vernachlässigung *die;* ~, ~**en** neglect; (das Nichtberücksichtigen) disregard; **unter** ~ **dieser Erkenntnisse** ignoring these perceptions

vernageln *tr. V.* nail up, cover ‹*hole etc.*›; **mit Brettern vernagelt** boarded up

vernähen *tr. V.* [1] stitch [up] ‹*tear, wounds*›; **den Faden gut** ~: sew the thread in firmly [2] (beim Nähen verbrauchen) use up ‹*thread, material*›

vernarben *itr. V.; mit sein* [form a] scar; heal (lit. or fig.)

Vernarbung *die*; ~, ~**en** formation of a scar; **die ~ der Wunde dauerte Wochen** the wound took weeks to form a scar

vernarren *refl. V.* **sich in jmdn./etw. ~:** become besotted *or* infatuated with sb./sth.; **in jmdn./etw. vernarrt sein** be infatuated with *or* (coll.) crazy about sb./be crazy (coll.) about sth.

Vernarrtheit *die*; ~, ~**en** infatuation (**in** + *Akk.* with)

vernaschen *tr. V.* 1 (für Süßigkeiten ausgeben) spend on sweets (Brit.) *or* (Amer.) candy 2 (salopp: geschlechtlich verkehren mit) lay ‹*girl*› (sl.) 3 (salopp: bezwingen, ausschalten) wipe the floor with (coll.) ‹*opponent, competitors*›

vernebeln *tr. V.* shroud ‹*area*› in fog; (mit Rauch) cover ‹*area*› with a smokescreen; (fig.) obscure ‹*facts*›; **jmdm. das Gehirn ~** (fig.) ‹*alcohol*› befuddle sb.'s brain

Vernebelung *die*; ~, ~**en** shrouding in fog/smoke; (fig.: des Kopfes) befuddling; clouding; (der Tatsachen) obscuration

vernehmbar *Adj.* (geh.) audible

vernehmen *unr. tr. V.* 1 (geh.: hören, erfahren) hear; **über seine Absichten nichts ~ lassen** not say anything *or* keep quiet about one's intentions 2 (verhören) question; (vor Gericht) examine

Vernehmen *das*: *in* **dem/allem ~ nach** from what/all that one hears; **sicherem ~ nach** according to reliable sources

vernehmlich
A *Adj.* [clearly] audible
B *adv.* audibly; **laut und ~:** loud and clear

Vernehmung *die*; ~, ~**en** questioning; (vor Gericht) examination

vernehmungsfähig *Adj.* in a condition *or* fit to be questioned/examined *postpos.*

verneigen *refl. V.* (geh.) bow (**vor** + *Dat.* to, (literary) before)

Verneigung *die*; ~, ~**en** (geh.) bow

verneinen *tr.* (*auch itr.*) *V.* 1 say 'no' to ‹*question*›; answer ‹*question*› in the negative; **er verneinte [es]** he said 'no'; **eine ~de Antwort** a negative answer; an answer in the negative; **er schüttelte ~d den Kopf** he shook his head to say 'no' 2 (ablehnen) reject 3 (Sprachw.) negate

Verneinung *die*; ~, ~**en** 1 **~ einer Frage** negative answer to a question 2 (Ablehnung) rejection 3 (Sprachw.) negation

Verneinungs-: **~fall** *der*: *in* **im ~falle** (Papierdt.) should the answer be in the negative; **~wort** *das*; *Pl.* **~wörter** (Sprachw.) negative [word]

vernetzen *tr. V.* (Chemie, Technik) interlink

vernichten *tr. V.* destroy; exterminate ‹*pests, vermin*›

vernichtend
A *Adj.* crushing ‹*defeat*›; shattering ‹*blow*›; (fig.) devastating ‹*criticism*›; devastating, withering ‹*glance*›
B *adv.* **den Feind ~ schlagen** inflict a crushing defeat on the enemy

Vernichtung *die*; ~, ~**en** destruction; (von Schädlingen) extermination

Vernichtungs-: **~lager** *das* extermination camp; **~potenzial** *das* destructive potential; **~waffe** *die* weapon of annihilation

verniedlichen *tr. V.* trivialize ‹*matter, situation, etc.*›; play down ‹*guilt, error*›

Verniedlichung *die*; ~, ~**en** trivialization

Vernissage /vɛrnɪ'sa:ʒə/ *die*; ~, ~**n** (geh.) private view (*of contemporary artist's exhibition*)

Vernunft /fɛɐ̯'nʊnft/ *die*; ~: reason; **gegen alle [Regeln der] ~:** contrary to all [dictates of] common sense; **ohne ~ handeln** act rashly *or* without thinking; **~ annehmen, zur ~ kommen** see reason; come to one's senses; **jmdn. zur ~ bringen** make sb. see reason

vernunft-, Vernunft-: **~begabt** *Adj.* rational; **~ehe** *die*, **~heirat** *die* marriage of convenience

vernünftig /fɛɐ̯'nʏnftɪç/
A *Adj.* 1 sensible; **es wäre das ~ste gewesen, zu ...** the most sensible thing would have been to ...; **mit ihm kann man kein ~es Wort reden** one can't have a sensible conversation with him 2 (ugs.: ordentlich, richtig) decent; **einen ~en Beruf lernen** learn a proper trade
B *adv.* 1 sensibly; **über etw.** (*Akk.*) **~ diskutieren** have a sensible discussion about sth. 2 (ugs.: ordentlich, richtig) ‹*talk, eat*› properly; ‹*dress*› sensibly

vernünftigerweise *Adv.* sensibly; **etw. ~ tun** ‹*person*› have the [good] sense to do sth.

Vernunft·mensch *der* [purely] rational person

vernunft·widrig
A *Adj.* irrational
B *adv.* irrationally

veröden
A *itr. V.*; *mit sein* 1 (menschenleer werden) become deserted; **verödet** deserted ‹*houses, streets, etc*› 2 (unfruchtbar werden) ‹*land*› become barren *or* desolate
B *tr. V.* (Med.) treat ‹*varicose veins*› by injection

Verödung *die*; ~, ~**en** ▸ **veröden**: desertion; desolation; (Med.) injection treatment

veröffentlichen *tr. V.* publish

Veröffentlichung *die*; ~, ~**en** publication

verordnen *tr. V.* **[jmdm. etw.] ~:** prescribe [sth. for sb.]; **der Arzt hat mir Bettruhe verordnet** the doctor ordered me to stay in bed

Verordnung *die* 1 prescribing; prescription 2 (Direktive) directive

verorten *tr. V.* (bes. Soziol.) place; locate

Verortung *die*; ~, ~**en** (bes. Soziol.) placing; location

verpachten *tr. V.* lease

Verpächter *der*; ~**s**, ~: landlord; lessor (Law)

Verpächterin *die*; ~, ~**nen** landlady; lessor (Law)

Verpachtung *die*; ~, ~**en** leasing

verpacken *tr. V.* pack; wrap up ‹*present, parcel*›; **etw. als Geschenk ~:** gift-wrap sth.

Verpackung *die* 1 packing 2 (Umhüllung) packaging *no pl.*; wrapping

Verpackungs·material *das* packaging [material]

verpassen *tr. V.* 1 miss ‹*train, person, entry (Mus.), chance, etc.*› 2 (ugs.: geben) **jmdm. etw. ~:** give sb. sth.; **jmdm. eins ~:** clout sb. one (coll.)

verpatzen *tr. V.* (ugs.) make a mess of; muck up (Brit. sl.); botch ‹*job*›; **du hast mir alles verpatzt** you've spoilt it all for me; **eine verpatzte Gelegenheit** a wasted opportunity

verpeilen *tr. V.* (Jugendspr.) 1 (vergessen) forget; **ich hab's total verpeilt** I clean forgot 2 (nicht hinbekommen) mess up (coll.)

verpeilt (Jugendspr.) *Adj.*, *adv.* (durch Drogen) stoned (sl.); out of his/her head *pred.* (sl.); (verrückt) crazy

verpennen (salopp)
A *itr. V.* oversleep
B *tr. V.* 1 (vergessen) forget 2 (verschlafen) sleep through ‹*morning etc.*›

verpennt *Adj.* (salopp) half asleep *pred.*; (fig.) dozy ‹*place*›; **total ~:** in a complete sleepy daze

verpesten *tr. V.* (abwertend) pollute

Verpestung (abwertend) *die*; ~, ~**en** pollution

verpetzen *tr. V.* (abwertend) **jmdn. [beim Lehrer** *usw.*] **~:** tell *or* (coll.) split on sb. [to the teacher *etc.*]

verpfänden *tr. V.* pawn ‹*article*›; mortgage ‹*house*›; (fig.) pledge ‹*word, honour*›

Verpfändung *die* pawning; (von Hausbesitz) mortgaging; mortgage

verpfeifen *unr. tr. V.* (ugs. abwertend) grass *or* split on ‹*person*› (coll.) (**bei** to); sing about ‹*plan etc.*› (sl.)

verpflanzen *tr. V.* 1 transplant ‹*tree, bush*›; (fig.) uproot and move ‹*person*› 2 (Med.) transplant ‹*heart etc.*›; graft ‹*skin*›

Verpflanzung *die*; ~, ~**en** 1 transplanting 2 (Med.) transplant[ing]; (von Haut) graft

verpflegen *tr. V.* cater for; feed; **sich selbst ~:** cater for oneself; **nur kalt/im Heim verpflegt werden** only be served cold food/be served one's food in the hostel

Verpflegung *die*; ~, ~**en** 1 catering *no indef. art.* (*Gen.* for) 2 (Nahrung) food; **Unterkunft und ~:** board and lodging

Verpflegungs·kosten *Pl.* cost *sing.* of food *or* meals

verpflichten
A *tr. V.* 1 oblige; commit; (festlegen, binden) bind; (durch Eid) swear; **jmdn. auf die Verfassung ~:** make sb. swear *or* promise to uphold the constitution; **zur Verschwiegenheit verpflichtet** sworn to secrecy; **der Kauf des ersten Bandes verpflichtet zur Abnahme des gesamten Werkes** purchase of the first volume is a commitment *or* obliges one to take the complete work; **sich verpflichtet fühlen[, etw. zu tun]** feel obliged [to do sth.]; **das verpflichtet dich zu nichts** that doesn't commit you to anything; **jmdm. verpflichtet sein** be indebted to sb.; **ich bin Ihnen zu Dank verpflichtet** I am indebted *or* obliged to you 2 (einstellen, engagieren) engage ‹*actor, manager, etc.*›; (Sport) sign ‹*player*›; **jmdn. ans Stadttheater/nach Berlin ~:** take sb. on *or* engage sb. at the Municipal Theatre/for Berlin
B *refl. V.* undertake; promise; **sich zu einer Zahlung ~:** commit oneself to making a payment; **sich vertraglich ~:** sign a contract; bind oneself by contract; **sich bei der Bundeswehr auf 8 Jahre ~:** sign on with the [Federal] Armed Forces for eight years

Verpflichtung *die*; ~, ~**en** 1 obligation; commitment; **eine ~ übernehmen** take on an obligation *or* a commitment; **[finanzielle] ~en** [financial] commitments; liabilities; **dienstliche/gesellschaftliche** *usw.* **~en** official/social *etc.* commitments; **ich habe keine anderweitigen ~en** I am not otherwise engaged; I have no other engagements 2 (Engagement) engaging; engagement; (Sport: eines Spielers) signing

verpfuschen *tr. V.* (ugs.) make a mess of; muck up (Brit. sl.); **sich** (*Dat.*) **das Leben/die Karriere ~:** make a mess of one's life/career

verpickelt *Adj.* covered in pimples *postpos.*

verpissen *refl. V.* (salopp) piss off (Brit. sl.); beat it (coll.)

verplanen *tr. V.* 1 (falsch planen) get the plans wrong for 2 (festlegen, einteilen) book ‹*person, time*› up; commit ‹*money, reprint*›; **er hat sein Geld/seine Freizeit schon verplant** his money is already fully committed/his spare time is fully booked

verplappern *refl. V.* (ugs.) blab (coll.); let the cat out of the bag

verplaudern
A *tr. V.* chat away ‹*time*›; spend ‹*time*› chatting
B *refl. V.* go on chatting too long

verplempern /fɛɐ̯'plɛmpɐn/ (ugs.)
A *tr. V.* fritter away
B *refl. V.* fritter away one's time/opportunities

verplomben *tr. V.* seal

Verplombung *die*; ~, ~**en** 1 sealing 2 (Plombe) seal

verpönt *Adj.*: scorned; (tabu) taboo

verpoppen *tr. V.* popularize; (aufmöbeln) jazz up

verprassen *tr. V.* squander, (coll.) blow ‹*money, fortune*›

verprellen *tr. V.* alienate

verproviantieren
A *tr. V.* supply with food *or* provisions
B *refl. V.* stock up [with food *or* provisions]

verprügeln *tr. V.* beat up; (zur Strafe) thrash

verpuffen *itr. V.*; *mit sein* go phut; (fig.) fizzle out; ‹*joke*› fall flat

verpulvern *tr. V.* (ugs.) blow (coll.) ‹*money*›; (allmählich) fritter away ‹*money*›

verpuppen *refl. V.* (Zool.) pupate

Verputz *der* plaster; (auf Außenwänden) rendering; (Rauputz) roughcast

verputzen *tr. V.* 1 (mit Putz versehen) plaster; render ‹*outside wall*›; (mit Rauputz) roughcast

V

[2] (ugs.: aufessen) polish off (coll.) ‹*food*›

Verputzer *der;* **~s, ~, Verputzerin** *die;* **~, ~nen** plasterer

verqualmen
A *itr. V.; mit sein* ‹*cigar, cigarette*› go out
B *tr. V.* (ugs. abwertend) fill ‹*room*› with smoke; **verqualmt** smoke-filled

verquält /fɛɐ̯'kvɛ:lt/ *Adj.* tormented; in torment *or* agony *pred.*

verquatschen (ugs.)
A *tr. V.* natter away (coll.) ‹*time*›; spend ‹*time*› nattering (coll.)
B *refl. V.* blab (coll.); let the cat out of the bag

verquer
A *Adj.* [1] (schief) angled, crooked ‹*position*› [2] (absonderlich) weird, outlandish ‹*idea*›
B *adv.* [1] (schief) at an angle; crookedly [2] (absonderlich) ‹*behave*› weirdly [3] **jmdm. geht etw./alles ~:** sth./everything is going wrong for sb.

verquicken /fɛɐ̯'kvɪkn̩/ *tr. V.* combine

Verquickung *die;* **~, ~en** combination

verquirlen *tr. V.* mix [with a whisk]; whisk

verquollen /fɛɐ̯'kvɔlən/ *Adj.* swollen

verrammeln *tr. V.* barricade

verramschen *tr. V.* (ugs. abwertend) ▸**verschleudern 1**

verrannt /fɛɐ̯'rant/ *Adj.* obsessed

Verrat *der;* **~[e]s** betrayal (**an** + *Dat.* of); **~ begehen** (Politik) commit [an act of] treason; **~ an jmdm. begehen** betray sb.

verraten
A *unr. tr. V.* [1] betray ‹*person, cause*›; betray, give away ‹*secret, plan, etc.*› (**an** + *Akk.* to); **wer hat dir das Versteck ~?** who told you about the hiding place?; **~ und verkauft sein** be well and truly in the soup *or* sunk (coll.) [2] (ugs.: mitteilen) **jmdm. den Grund** *usw.* **~:** tell sb. the reason *etc.* [3] (erkennen lassen) show, betray ‹*feelings, surprise, fear, etc.*›; show ‹*influence, talent*› [4] (zu erkennen geben) give ‹*person*› away
B *unr. refl. V.* [1] ‹*person*› give oneself away [2] (sich zeigen) show itself; be revealed

Verräter /fɛɐ̯'rɛ:tɐ/ *der;* **~s, ~:** traitor (*Gen.*, **an** + *Dat.* to)

Verräterei *die;* **~, ~en** treachery

Verräterin *die;* **~, ~nen** traitress

verräterisch *Adj.* [1] treacherous ‹*plan, purpose, act, etc.*› [2] (erkennen lassend) telltale, giveaway ‹*look, gesture*›; **die Röte in ihrem Gesicht war ~:** her red face gave her away

verrauchen
A *itr. V.; mit sein* ‹*smoke, cloud, etc.*› clear [away], disappear; (fig.) ‹*anger etc.*› blow over, subside
B *tr. V.* spend ‹*money*› on smoking

verräuchern *tr. V.* fill with smoke; **verräuchert** smoke-filled; smoky

verraucht *Adj.* smoke-filled; smoky

verrauschen *itr. V.; mit sein* die *or* fade [away]

verrechnen
A *tr. V.* include, take into account ‹*amount etc.*›; (gutschreiben) credit ‹*cheque etc.*› to another account
B *refl. V.* (auch fig.) miscalculate; make a mistake/mistakes

Verrechnung *die* settlement (**mit** by means of); **„nur zur ~"** (Bankw.) 'not negotiable'; 'a/c payee [only]'

Verrechnungs-: ~einheit *die* (Wirtsch.) clearing unit; **~scheck** *der* (Wirtsch., Bankw.) crossed cheque

verrecken *itr. V.; mit sein* (salopp) die [a miserable death]; **das tu ich ums Verrecken nicht** there's no way I'll do that

verregnen *itr. V.; mit sein* be spoilt *or* ruined by rain; **verregnet** rainy, wet ‹*spring, summer, holiday, etc.*›; ‹*harvest*› spoilt by rain

verreiben *unr. tr. V.* rub in

verreisen *itr. V.; mit sein* go away; **verreist sein** be away

verreißen *unr. tr. V.* [1] (ugs.) tear ‹*book, play, etc.*› to pieces [2] (ugs.: beim Lenken) **den Wagen/die Lenkung/das Steuer ~:** snatch at the steering; (als Ausweichmanöver) swerve

verrenken /fɛɐ̯'rɛŋkn̩/ *tr. V.* [1] (verletzen) dislocate; **sich** (*Dat.*) **den Fuß ~:** twist one's ankle [2] (biegen) **sich** *od.* **seine Glieder ~:** go into *or* perform contortions

Verrenkung *die;* **~, ~en** [1] (Verletzung) dislocation [2] (Biegung des Körpers) contortion; **~en machen** go into *or* perform contortions

verrennen *unr. refl. V.* get on the wrong track *or* off course; **sich in etw.** (*Akk.*) **~:** become obsessed with sth.

verrenten *tr. V.* (Amtsspr.) retire [on a pension]

Verrentung *die;* **~, ~en** (Amtsspr.) retirement [on a pension]

verrichten *tr. V.* perform ‹*work, duty, etc.*›; **seine Notdurft ~:** relieve oneself

Verrichtung *die* carrying out; performance; **gute ~!** (scherzh. wenn jmd. zur Toilette geht) have fun!; **die täglichen ~en** one's daily tasks

verriegeln *tr. V.* bolt

Verriegelung *die;* **~, ~en** [1] (das Verriegeln) bolting [2] (Vorrichtung) bolt mechanism; (Schloss) lock

verringern /fɛɐ̯'rɪŋɐn/
A *tr. V.* reduce
B *refl. V.* decrease

Verringerung *die;* **~:** reduction; decrease (*Gen.*, **von** in)

verrinnen *unr. itr. V.; mit sein* [1] (versickern) seep away [2] (geh.: verstreichen) pass [by]; ‹*year, month*› elapse, pass

Verriss, *Verriß *der* (ugs.) damning review *or* criticism (**über** + *Akk.* of)

verrocken *tr. V.* produce a rock arrangement of ‹*piece*›

verrohen
A *tr. V.* brutalize
B *itr. V.; mit sein* become brutal

Verrohung *die;* **~, ~en** brutalization

verrosten *itr. V.; mit sein* rust; **verrostet** rusty

verrotten *itr. V.; mit sein* rot; ‹*building etc.*› decay

verrucht /fɛɐ̯'ru:xt/ *Adj.* [1] (veralt.: ruchlos) despicable [2] (scherzh.: verworfen) disreputable, seedy ‹*quarter etc.*›

Verruchtheit *die;* **~** [1] despicableness [2] (scherzh.: Verworfenheit) disreputableness; seediness

verrücken *tr. V.* move; shift

verrückt (ugs.)
A *Adj.* [1] mad; **~ werden** go mad *or* insane; **jmdn. ~ machen** drive sb. mad; **mach dich doch nicht ~!** don't get yourself into a state!; **du bist wohl ~!** you must be mad *or* crazy!; **bei diesem Lärm kann man ja ~ werden!** this noise is enough to drive you mad *or* (coll.) round the bend; **wie ~:** like mad *or* crazy (coll.); **ich werde ~!** I'll be blowed (sl.) *or* (coll.) damned; **~ spielen** (salopp) ‹*person*› act crazy (coll.); ‹*car, machine, etc.*› play up; ‹*watch, weather*› go crazy [2] (überspannt, ausgefallen) crazy ‹*idea, fashion, prank, day, etc.*›; **so was Verrücktes!** what a crazy idea! [3] (begierig, geil) crazy; **sie macht die Männer ~:** she drives men crazy [with desire]; **auf jmdn.** *od.* **nach jmdm./auf etw.** (*Akk.*) **~ sein** be crazy (coll.) *or* mad about sb./sth.
B *adv.* crazily; ‹*behave*› crazily *or* like a madman; ‹*paint, dress, etc.*› in a mad *or* crazy way

Verrückte *der/die; adj. Dekl.* (ugs.) madman/madwoman; lunatic

Verrücktheit *die;* **~, ~en** [1] madness; insanity; (Überspanntheit) craziness [2] (irre Handlung) act of madness; folly; (überspannte Idee) crazy idea

Verrückt·werden *das* (ugs.) *in* **zum ~ sein** be enough to drive you mad *or* (coll.) round the bend; **es ist zum ~ mit ihm** he's enough to drive anyone scatty (Brit. coll.)

Verruf *der: in* **in ~ kommen** *od.* **geraten** fall into disrepute; **jmdn./etw. in ~ bringen** bring sb./sth. into disrepute

verrufen *Adj.* disreputable

verrühren *tr. V.* stir together; mix

verrunzelt *Adj.* wrinkled

verrußen
A *itr. V.; mit sein* become sooty; ‹*sparking plug*› soot up; **verrußt** sooty; (von Ruß bedeckt) covered in soot *postpos*
B *tr. V.* make sooty

verrutschen *itr. V.* slip

Vers /fɛrs/ *der;* **~es, ~e** verse; (Zeile) line; **~e schreiben** *od.* (ugs.) **schmieden** write verse *or* poetry; **etw. in ~e setzen** *od.* **bringen** put sth. into verse; **ein Epos in ~en** a verse epic; **sich** (*Dat.*) **einen ~ auf etw.** (*Akk.*)**/darauf machen** (fig.) make sense of sth./put two and two together

versachlichen *tr. V.* make [more] objective

Versachlichung *die;* **~: zur ~ der Diskussion beitragen** help to make the discussion more objective

versacken *itr. V.; mit sein* (ugs.) [1] sink [2] (fig.) ▸**versumpfen 2, 3**

versagen
A *itr. V.* fail; ‹*machine, engine*› stop [working], break down; **ihre Stimme versagte** her voice failed
B *tr. V.* (geh.) (nicht gewähren) **jmdm./sich etw. ~:** deny *or* refuse sb. sth./deny oneself sth.; **ein Kind blieb ihr versagt** a child was denied her; **es war ihm versagt, das mitzuerleben** circumstances did not allow him to witness it; **ich konnte es mir nicht ~, darauf zu antworten** I could not refrain from answering; *s. auch* **Dienst 4**
C *refl. V.* **sich jmdm. ~:** refuse to give oneself *or* surrender to sb.

Versagen *das;* **~s** failure; **menschliches ~:** human error

Versagens·angst *die* fear of failure

Versager *der;* **~s, ~, Versagerin** *die;* **~, ~nen** failure

Versagung *die;* **~, ~en** refusal

versalzen
A *unr. tr. V.* [1] put too much salt in/on; **die Suppe ist ~:** there is too much salt in the soup; the soup is too salty [2] (fig. ugs.) spoil; **jmdm. etw. ~:** spoil sth. for sb.; *s. auch* **Suppe**
B *itr. V.; mit sein* (bes. Ökologie; Bodenk.) become salty

versammeln
A *tr. V.* assemble; gather [together]; **seine Leute um sich ~:** gather one's people around one
B *refl. V.* assemble; (weniger formell) gather; **sich um jmdn./etw. ~:** gather round sb./sth.; **vor versammelter Belegschaft sprechen** speak to the assembled staff; *s. auch* **Mannschaft 3**

Versammlung *die* [1] meeting; (Partei~) assembly; (unter freiem Himmel, bes. politisch) rally; **auf einer ~ sprechen** speak at a meeting/rally [2] (Gremium) assembly; **gesetzgebende/verfassunggebende ~:** legislative/constituent assembly [3] (das Sichversammeln) assembly; bringing together *no art.*

Versammlungs-: ~freiheit *die* freedom of assembly; **~lokal** *das* meeting place

Versand *der;* **~[e]s** [1] dispatch; **zum ~ fertig machen** prepare for dispatch [2] (Abteilung) dispatch department [3] (ugs.: ~haus) mail order firm

Versand·buch·handel *der* mail order trade

versanden *itr. V.; mit sein* [1] fill with sand; ‹*harbour etc.*› silt up; (mit Sand bedeckt werden) be covered with sand [2] (fig. ugs.) peter *or* fizzle out

Versand-: ~geschäft *das,* **~handel** *der* mail order business; **~haus** *das* mail order firm; **~haus·katalog** *der* mail order catalogue; **~kosten** *Pl.* dispatch costs; carriage *sing.*; (Post u. Verpackung) postage and packing

Versatz-: ~amt *das* (südd., österr.) pawnshop; **~stück** *das* [1] (Theater) [movable] piece of scenery; set piece; [2] (fig.) cliché; hackneyed idea; [3] (österr.: Pfand) security

versaubeuteln *tr. V.* (ugs.) [1] (verderben) mess up [2] (verlieren, verlegen) lose; mislay

versauen *tr. V.* (salopp) [1] (verschmutzen) mess up; make mucky (coll.) [2] (verderben) foul up (coll.)

versauern *itr. V.; mit sein* (ugs.) waste away; stagnate

V

versaufen
A *unr. tr. V.* (salopp) drink one's way through
B *unr. itr. V.; mit sein* **1** (ugs.: ertrinken) drown **2** (Bergmannsspr.) flood

versäumen *tr. V.* **1** (verpassen) miss; lose ‹*time, sleep*›; **da hast du nichts/nicht viel versäumt** you didn't miss anything/miss much; **den versäumten Schlaf nachholen** catch up on lost sleep **2** (vernachlässigen, unterlassen) neglect ‹*duty, task*›; **das Versäumte/Versäumtes nachholen** make up for *or* catch up on what one has neglected *or* failed to do; **er versäumte [es] nicht, X zu erwähnen** he did not omit *or* fail to mention X

Versäumnis *das;* **~ses, ~se** omission; **die ~se der Eltern gegenüber ihren Kindern** the parents' sins of omission towards their children

verschachern *tr. V.* (abwertend) sell off

verschachtelt *Adj.* higgledy-piggledy ‹*streets, town*›; **ein ~er Satz** (fig.) an encapsulated sentence

verschaffen *tr. V.* **jmdm. Arbeit/Geld/Unterkunft** *usw.* **~:** provide sb. with work/money/accommodation *etc.*; get sb. work/money/accommodation *etc.*; **sich** (*Dat.*) **etw. ~:** get hold of sth.; obtain sth.; **sich** (*Dat.*) **Respekt ~:** gain respect; **sich Gewissheit ~:** make sure *or* certain; **es verschaffte mir die Möglichkeit, zu ...** it gave me the opportunity to ...; **was verschafft mir die Ehre?** (iron.) to what do I owe this honour?

verschalen *tr. V.* line ‹*wall, shaft, etc.*› [with boards]; (bedecken) board up ‹*window, hole*›

verschalten *tr. V.* (Elektrot.) connect; **etw. zu einem Netzwerk ~:** connect sth. to form a network

Verschalung *die;* **~, ~en** **1** (das Verschalen) lining; boarding; (eines Fensters) boarding up **2** (Produkt) lining; (aus Brettern) boarding

verschämt /fɛɐ̯ˈʃɛːmt/
A *Adj.* bashful
B *adv.* bashfully

verschandeln *tr. V.* (ugs.) spoil; ruin; **das Gebäude verschandelt die Landschaft** the building is a blot on the landscape

Verschandelung *die;* **~, ~en** (ugs.) ruination *no indef. art.*; **eine solche ~ der Gegend** ruining the area like this

verschanzen
A *refl. V.* (Milit.) take up a [fortified] position; (in einem Graben) entrench oneself; dig [oneself] in; (in einem Gebäude) barricade oneself (**in** + *Dat.* into); **sich in seinem Büro/hinter einer Zeitung ~** (fig.) take refuge in one's office/take cover *or* hide behind a newspaper; **sich hinter einer Ausrede/seiner Müdigkeit ~** (fig.) hide behind an excuse/use one's tiredness as an excuse
B *tr. V.* (Milit.) fortify

Verschanzung *die;* **~, ~en** (Milit.) fortification; (in Gräben) entrenchment

verschärfen
A *tr. V.* **1** (steigern) intensify ‹*conflict, difference, desire, etc.*›; increase, step up ‹*pace, pressure*› **2** (strenger machen) tighten ‹*law, control, restriction, etc*›; make ‹*penalty*› more severe **3** (verschlimmern) make ‹*unemployment etc.*› worse; aggravate ‹*situation, crisis, etc.*›
B *refl. V.* **1** (sich steigern) ‹*pace, pressure, etc.*› increase; ‹*pain, tension, conflict, difference*› intensify **2** (sich verschlimmern) get worse

verschärft
A *Adj.* **1** (gesteigert) increased ‹*pressure*›; intensified ‹*conflict*›; more intense ‹*training*› **2** (strenger) tighter, stricter ‹*control, check, restriction*›; more severe ‹*reprimand, punishment*› **3** (schlimmer geworden) aggravated
B *adv.* (strenger) more strictly

Verschärfung *die;* **~, ~en** ▸**verschärfen A 1-3**: intensification; increase; tightening; greater severity; aggravation; worsening

verscharren *tr. V.* bury (just below the surface); bury ‹*person*› in a shallow grave

verschätzen
A *refl. V.* **sich in etw.** (*Dat.*) **~:** misjudge sth.; **wenn du dich da mal nicht verschätzt!** unless you've got it all wrong!
B *tr. V.* misjudge

verschauen *refl. V.* (österr. ugs.) ▸**vergucken 1**

verschaukeln *tr. V.* (ugs.) **jmdn. ~:** take sb. for a ride (coll.)

verscheiden *unr. itr. V.; mit sein* (geh.) pass away

verscheißen (derb)
A *unr. tr. V.* cover with shit (coarse); **verschissene Unterhosen** shitty (coarse) underpants
B *unr. itr. V.* in **bei jmdm. verschissen haben** (fig.) have had it as far as sb. is concerned (coll.)

verscheißern *tr. V.* (derb) **jmdn. ~:** have (Brit. coll.) *or* (Amer. coll.) put sb. on; **du willst mich wohl ~!** pull the 'other one[, it's got bells on] (sl.)

verschenken
A *tr. V.* **1** give away; **etw. an jmdn. ~:** give sth. to sb. **2** (ungewollt vergeben) waste ‹*space*›; give away ‹*points*›; **den Sieg ~:** throw away one's chance of winning
B *refl. V.* (geh.) **sich [an jmdn.] ~:** throw oneself away [on sb.]

verscherbeln /fɛɐ̯ˈʃɛrbl̩n/ *tr. V.* (ugs.) flog (Brit. sl.) (*Dat.,* **an** + *Akk.* to)

verscherzen *refl. V.* **sich** (*Dat.*) **etw. ~:** lose *or* forfeit sth. [through one's own folly]

verscheuchen *tr. V.* chase away (lit. or fig.); (durch Erschrecken) frighten *or* scare away

verscheuern *tr. V.* (ugs.) flog (Brit. sl.) (*Dat.,* **an** + *Akk.* to)

verschicken *tr. V.* **1** ▸**versenden** **2** **jmdn. zur Kur/an die See** *usw.* **~:** send sb. away to take a cure/to the seaside *etc.*

Verschickung *die* **1** ▸**Versendung** **2** (zur Erholung) sending away [for health reasons] *no indef. art.*

verschiebbar *Adj.* **1** movable; (verstellbar) adjustable **2** (aufschiebbar) which can be put off *postpos., not pred.*

Verschiebe·bahnhof *der* marshalling yard

verschieben
A *unr. tr. V.* **1** shift; move; **die Grenze wurde um 5 km nach Süden verschoben** the boundary was moved five kilometres to the south *or* further south; **die Perspektive/das ganze Bild ~** (fig.) alter *or* change the perspective/the whole picture **2** (aufschieben) put off, postpone (**auf** + *Akk.* till); **etw. um eine Woche/auf unbestimmte Zeit ~:** postpone sth. for a week/indefinitely; *s. auch* **besorgen 3** **3** (ugs.: illegal verkaufen) traffic in ‹*goods*›; (beiseite schaffen) move illegally; **Waren/Devisen ins Ausland ~:** smuggle goods/currency to a foreign country
B *unr. refl. V.* **1** get out of place; (rutschen) slip; (Geol.) ‹*continent etc.*› shift; **das Kräfteverhältnis hat sich verschoben** (fig.) the balance of power has shifted **2** (erst später stattfinden) be postponed (**um** for); ‹*start*› be put back *or* delayed (**um** by)

Verschiebung *die* **1** movement; (fig.: Änderung) alteration, shift (*Gen.* in); **die ~ der Kontinente** (Geol.) the continental shift **2** (zeitlich) postponement **3** (ugs.: illegaler Handel) trafficking (**von** in); (ins Ausland) smuggling

verschieden
A *2. Part. v.* **verscheiden**
B *Adj.* **1** (nicht gleich) different (**von** from); **er hat zwei ~e Socken an** he is wearing two odd socks *or* two socks that don't match; **das ist von Fall zu Fall/von Land zu Land ~:** that varies from one case to another/from country to country **2** (vielfältig) various; **auf ~e Weise** in various ways; **die ~sten ...** all sorts of ...; **die ~sten Theorien** the most diverse theories; **in den ~sten Farben** in the most varied colours; in a whole variety of colours; **die ~en ...** the various ... **3** *allein stehend* **Verschiedene** various people; **Verschiedene der Anwesenden** several of those present; **Verschiedenes** various things *pl.*; **„Verschiedenes"** 'miscellaneous'; (Tagesordnungspunkt) 'any other business'
C *adv.* differently; **~ groß** of different sizes *postpos.*; different-sized; ‹*people*› of different heights; **~ schwer/lang** of different weights/lengths *postpos.*

verschieden·artig
A *Adj.* different in kind *pred.*; (mehr als zwei) diverse; **~e Werkzeuge** tools of various [different] kinds; **~e Mittel anwenden** use various different means
B *adv.* diversely; (auf verschiedene Weise) in various different ways; **sehr ~ interpretiert werden** be subjected to very diverse interpretations

Verschiedenartigkeit *die;* **~:** difference in nature; (unter mehreren) diversity; **die ~ der beiden Systeme** the different nature of the two systems

***verschiedene·mal** ▸**Mal**[1]

verschiedenerlei *unbest. Gattungsz.; indekl.:* **1** *attr.* various different **2** *allein stehend* various different things; **~ Käse** various different kinds of cheese

verschieden·farbig
A *Adj.* different-coloured; of different colours *postpos*
B *adv.* ‹*paint etc*› in different colours

Verschiedenheit *die;* **~, ~en** difference; dissimilarity; (unter mehreren) diversity; (Unterschied) difference

verschiedentlich *Adv.* on various occasions

verschießen
A *unr. tr. V.* **1** (als Geschoss verwenden) fire ‹*shell, cartridge, etc.*› **2** (verbrauchen) use up ‹*ammunition*›; **verschossene/nicht verschossene Patronen** spent/unspent *or* live cartridges; *s. auch* **Pulver 2** **3** **einen Strafstoß ~** (Fußball) miss with a penalty
B *unr. refl. V.* (ugs.) **[in jmdn.] verschossen sein** be madly in love [with sb.] (coll.)
C *unr. itr. V.; mit sein* (verblassen) fade

verschiffen *tr. V.* ship ‹*goods, coal*›; transport ‹*troops, emigrants, etc.*› by ship

Verschiffung *die;* **~, ~en** shipment; (von Personen) transportation [by ship]

verschimmeln *itr. V.; mit sein* go mouldy; **verschimmelt** mouldy

verschlafen[1]
A *unr. itr.* (*auch refl.*) *V.* oversleep
B *unr. tr. V.* **1** (schlafend verbringen) sleep through ‹*morning, journey, etc.*›; **sein halbes Leben ~:** doze away half one's life **2** (versäumen) sleep through ‹*concert*›; not wake up in time for ‹*appointment*›; not wake up in time to catch ‹*train, bus*›; (einschlafen und versäumen) fall asleep and miss **3** (ugs.: vergessen) forget about ‹*appointment etc.*›

verschlafen[2] *Adj.* **1** half asleep **2** (fig.: ruhig, langweilig) sleepy ‹*town, village*›

Verschlag *der* shed; (angebaut) lean-to; (für Kaninchen) hutch

verschlagen[1] *unr. tr. V.* **1** **[jmdm.] die Seite ~:** lose sb.'s place *or* page; **die Seite ~** (im eigenen Buch) lose one's place *or* page **2** **jmdm. den Appetit ~:** rob sb. of his/her appetite; **jmdm. die Sprache** *od.* **Rede/den Atem ~:** leave sb. speechless/take sb.'s breath away **3** (Ballspiele) mishit ‹*ball*› **4** **das Leben/Schicksal hat ihn nach X ~** the vagaries of life caused/fate caused him to end up in X; **vom Sturm an eine Küste ~ werden** be driven on to a coast by the gale; **es hat ihn nach Berlin ~:** he landed [up] *or* ended up in Berlin

verschlagen[2]
A *Adj.* **1** (abwertend: gerissen) sly; shifty **2** (bes. nordd.: lauwarm) lukewarm; tepid
B *adv.* (abwertend: gerissen) slyly; shiftily

Verschlagenheit *die;* **~** (abwertend) slyness; shiftiness

verschlammen *itr. V.* become *or* get muddy; ‹*ditch, river*› silt up; **verschlammt** muddy

verschlampen (ugs., bes. südd.)
A *tr. V.* succeed in losing (iron.)
B *itr. V.; mit sein* (abwertend) ‹*person*› let oneself go; ‹*house etc.*› get into a bad state; **verschlampt** slovenly; in a slovenly state *postpos.*

verschlanken *tr. V.* (Wirtschaftsjargon) trim [down], reduce ‹*production etc.*›

V

verschlechtern
A tr. V. make worse
B refl. V. get worse; deteriorate; **sich [finanziell/wirtschaftlich** usw.**] ~:** be worse off [financially/economically etc.]; **er hat sich verschlechtert** he is worse off [now]

Verschlechterung die; ~, ~en worsening, deterioration (Gen. in); **der Wohnungswechsel bedeutet für ihn keine ~:** his change of flat (esp. Brit.) or (esp. Amer.) apartment leaves him no worse off

verschleiern
A tr. V. 1 veil; (fig.) cover, veil ‹sky, moon, etc.›; obscure ‹view›; cloud ‹consciousness›; **Dunst verschleierte die Berge** (fig.) a veil of mist hid the mountains; **Tränen verschleierten ihre Augen** od. **ihr den Blick** (fig.) she could scarcely see through her tears; her vision was blurred by tears 2 (fig.: verbergen) draw a veil over, cover up ‹deception, facts, scandal, etc.›; hide ‹intentions›
B refl. V. ‹vision etc.› become blurred; ‹sky› cloud over

verschleiert
A Adj. veiled; misty ‹vision etc.›; fogged ‹photograph›; **mit ~er Stimme** in a husky voice; (vor Rührung) in a voice choked with emotion
B adv. **ohne Brille sieht er [alles] nur ~:** without [his] glasses he sees everything as in a mist

Verschleierung die; ~, ~en 1 veiling; **ohne ~:** without a veil 2 (fig.: von Sachverhalten, Motiven) covering up

Verschleierungs·taktik die cover-up tactics pl.

verschleifen unr. tr. V. smooth; (fig.) slur ‹consonants, vowels›

verschleimt Adj. congested with phlegm postpos.

Verschleimung die; ~, ~en mucous congestion

Verschleiß /fɛɐ̯'ʃlais/ der; ~es, ~e 1 (Abnutzung) wear no indef. art.; wear and tear sing., no indef. art; **der Auspuff unterliegt einem sehr hohen/raschen ~:** the exhaust is subject to a great deal of wear and tear/does not last very long; **einen höheren ~ haben** wear more rapidly; have a higher rate of wear 2 (Verbrauch) consumption (**an** + Dat. of); **einen hohen ~ an etw.** (Dat.) **haben** use up a large amount of sth.; **sie hat einen unheimlichen ~ an Männern** (ugs. scherzh.) she gets through men at an incredible rate (coll.) 3 (österr. veralt.: Vertrieb) sale; retailing

verschleißen
A unr. itr. V.; mit sein wear out
B unr. tr. V. 1 wear out; (fig.) run down, ruin ‹one's nerves, one's health›; use up ‹energy, ability, etc.›; **verschlissen** worn ‹material, suit, etc.›; worn out ‹machine parts etc.›; **sich ~:** wear oneself out; use up all one's energy (**bei** on) 2 (ugs. scherzh.: verbrauchen) get through ‹men friends, cleaning-women, etc.›
C unr. (auch regelm.) tr. V. (österr. veralt.: verkaufen) sell; retail

Verschleißer der; ~s, ~, **Verschleißerin** die; ~, ~nen (österr. veralt.) retailer

Verschleiß·erscheinung die sign of wear; (an einem Menschen) sign of wear and tear or exhaustion

verschleppen tr. V. 1 carry off ‹valuables, animals›; take away ‹person›; (bes. nach Übersee) transport ‹convicts, slaves, etc.›; **in die Sklaverei verschleppt werden** be carried off into slavery 2 (weiterverbreiten) carry, spread ‹disease, bacteria, mud, etc.› 3 (verzögern) delay; (in die Länge ziehen) draw out 4 (unbehandelt lassen) let ‹illness› drag on [and get worse]; **verschleppte Krankheit** illness aggravated by neglect

Verschleppung die; ~, ~en ▸**verschleppen:** 1 carrying off; transportation 2 carrying; spreading 3 delaying; drawing out 4 aggravation by neglect

verschleudern tr. V. 1 (billig verkaufen) sell dirt cheap; (mit Verlust) sell at a loss 2 (abwertend: verschwenden) squander

verschließbar Adj. 1 closable; **[luftdicht] ~:** sealable ‹container etc.› 2 (abschließbar) lockable ‹suitcase, drawer, etc.›

verschließen
A unr. tr. V. 1 close ‹package, tin, pores, mouth, etc›; close up ‹blood vessel, aperture, etc.›; stop ‹bottle›; put a/the bung in ‹barrel›; (mit einem Korken) cork bottle ; **hermetisch verschlossen** hermetically sealed; **etw. luftdicht ~:** make sth. airtight; put an airtight seal on sth.; **die Augen/Ohren [vor etw.** (Dat.)**] ~** (fig.) close one's eyes or be blind/turn a deaf ear or be deaf [to sth.] 2 (abschließen) lock ‹door, cupboard, drawer, etc.›; lock up ‹house etc.›; s. auch **Tür** 3 (wegschließen) lock away (**in** + Dat. od. Akk. in) 4 (versperren) bar ‹way etc.›; **viele berufliche Möglichkeiten blieben ihm verschlossen** many possible professions remained barred or closed to him
B unr. refl. V. 1 **sich jmdm. ~:** be closed to sb.; ‹person› shut oneself off from sb.; **er verschloss sich** he shut up like a clam; **der tiefere Sinn verschloss sich ihm** the deeper meaning remained obscure to him; s. auch **verschlossen B** 2 in **sich einer Sache** (Dat.) **~:** close one's mind to sth.; (ignorieren) ignore sth.

verschlimmbessern tr. V. (ugs. scherzh.) make worse with so-called corrections

Verschlimmbesserung die; ~, ~en (ugs. scherzh.) so-called correction (which is wrong); **das ist eine ~!** that so-called correction has made things worse

verschlimmern
A tr. V. make worse; aggravate ‹state of health›
B refl. V. get worse; worsen; ‹position, conditions› deteriorate, worsen

Verschlimmerung die; ~, ~en worsening

verschlingen
A unr. tr. V. 1 [inter]twine ‹threads, string, etc.› (**zu** into); **miteinander ~:** intertwine ‹threads, ropes, etc.› 2 (essen, fressen) devour ‹food›; (fig.) devour, consume ‹novel, money, etc.›; **jmdn. mit den Augen ~:** devour sb. with one's eyes; **die tobende See verschlang das Schiff** the raging sea engulfed the ship
B unr. refl. V. **sich ineinander ~:** become entwined or intertwined; s. auch **verschlungen**

verschlissen 2. Part. v. **verschleißen B**

verschlossen
A 2. Part. v. **verschließen**
B Adj. (wortkarg) taciturn, tight-lipped; (zurückhaltend) reserved

Verschlossenheit die; ~: taciturnity; (Zurückhaltung) reserve

verschlucken
A tr. V. 1 swallow ‹food, bone, word, etc.›; (fig.) absorb, deaden ‹sound›; absorb, eliminate ‹rays› 2 (fig.: unterdrücken) choke back ‹anger, tears›; hold back ‹remark›
B refl. V. choke; **er verschluckte sich beim Essen/Lachen** he choked over his food/with laughing

verschludern tr. V. (ugs. abwertend)
A tr. V. 1 (verlieren) lose; (verlegen) mislay 2 (vergeuden) waste ‹material›; throw away ‹money› 3 (verderben) ruin, mess up ‹exercise book›
B itr. V. go to rack and ruin

verschlungen
A 2. Part. v. **verschlingen**
B Adj. entwined ‹ornamentation›; winding ‹path etc.›; **er saß mit ~en Armen da** he sat there with arms folded

Verschluss, *Verschluß der 1 (am BH, an Schmuck usw.) fastener; fastening; (an Taschen, Schmuck) clasp; (an Schuhen, Gürteln) buckle; (am Schrank, Fenster, Koffer usw.) catch; (an Flaschen) top; (Stöpsel) stopper; (Schraub~) [screw] top; [screw] cap; (Tank~) cap 2 (einer Feuerwaffe) breechblock 3 (einer Kamera) shutter 4 (Med.: einer Arterie) blockage; occlusion 5 in **unter ~ sein/bleiben** be under lock and key; **etw. unter ~ halten** keep sth. under lock and key or locked away

verschlüsseln tr. V. [en]code; (bes. DV) encrypt

Verschlüsselung die; ~, ~en [en]coding

Verschluss-, *Verschluß-: ~kappe die top; cap; **~laut** der (Sprachw.) stop; **~sache** die [item of] confidential information; **~sachen** confidential information sing.

verschmachten itr. V.; mit sein (geh.) fade away (**vor** + Dat. from); (vor Sehnsucht) pine away

verschmähen tr. V. (geh.) spurn; **verschmähte Liebe** unrequited love

verschmälern
A tr. V. narrow; make narrower (**um** by)
B refl. V. narrow; become narrower

verschmausen tr. V. (ugs. scherzh.) dig or tuck into (coll.); (aufessen) eat up

verschmelzen
A unr. tr. V. 1 fuse ‹metals›; (fig.) fuse, merge (**zu** into, to form); **Kupfer und Zink zu Messing ~:** fuse copper and zinc to make brass 2 (verschweißen) weld together ‹metal parts›
B unr. itr. V.; mit sein ‹metals, cells› fuse; (fig.) ‹firms, images, towns, etc.› merge (**zu** into, to form); **zu einem Ganzen ~:** blend into one

Verschmelzung die; ~, ~en 1 fusing, fusion (lit. or fig.) (**zu** into); (von Städten, Firmen usw.) merging, merger (**zu** into, to form) 2 (Verschweißung) weld

verschmerzen tr. V. get over ‹defeat, disappointment›

verschmieren tr. V. 1 smear ‹window etc.›; (beim Schreiben) mess up ‹paper›; scrawl all over ‹page› 2 (verteilen) spread ‹butter etc.›; smudge ‹ink› 3 (verbrauchen) use up ‹butter, oil, plaster, etc.› 4 (zuschmieren) fill [in] ‹crack, hole, etc.›

verschmitzt /fɛɐ̯'ʃmɪtst/
A Adj. mischievous; roguish
B adv. mischievously; roguishly

Verschmitztheit die; ~: mischievousness; roguishness

verschmoren itr. V.; mit sein (ugs.) burn; **es riecht verschmort** there's a smell of burning or a burnt smell

verschmust /fɛɐ̯'ʃmu:st/ Adj. (ugs.) ‹child, cat, etc.› that always wants to be cuddled; **er ist [sehr] ~:** he always wants to be cuddled

verschmutzen
A itr. V.; mit sein ‹material› get dirty; ‹river etc.› become polluted
B tr. V. dirty, soil ‹carpet, clothes›; pollute ‹air, water, etc.›

Verschmutzung die; ~, ~en 1 (der Umwelt) pollution 2 (von Stoffen, Teppichen usw.) soiling 3 (Schmutz) dirt no pl.; **~en** [cases pl. of] soiling sing.

verschnaufen itr. (auch refl.) V. have or take a breather

Verschnauf·pause die breather; rest; **eine ~ einlegen** have or take a breather

verschneiden unr. tr. V. 1 (durch Schneiden verderben) cut ‹hair, roses, etc.› all wrong; ruin ‹wood, material, film› by bad/wrong cutting 2 (mischen) blend ‹rum, whisky, etc.› 3 (kastrieren) castrate, geld ‹animal›

verschneit Adj. snow-covered attrib.; covered with snow postpos.

-verschnitt der: **ein James-Bond-Verschnitt** a second-rate James Bond

Verschnitt der; ~[e]s, ~e 1 (das Mischen) blending 2 (Mischung) blend (**aus** of); (fig., meist abwertend) mixture; combination 3 (Abfall) waste; (von Holz usw.) offcuts pl.

verschnörkelt Adj. ornate

Verschnörkelung die; ~, ~en ornamentation; (Schnörkel) flourish

verschnupft /fɛɐ̯'ʃnʊpft/
A Adj. 1 suffering from a cold postpos.; **[ganz] ~ sein** have a [bad] cold 2 (fig. ugs.: gekränkt) peeved (coll.)
B adv. in a peeved way (coll.); peevishly

verschnüren tr. V. tie up (**zu** into)

Verschnürung die; ~, ~en 1 (das Verschnüren) tying up 2 (Schnur) string

verschollen /fɛɐ̯'ʃɔlən/ Adj. missing; **er ist ~:** he has disappeared; (wird vermisst) he is missing; **sie ließ ihren Mann für ~ erklären** she had her husband declared missing, presumed

V

dead; **er galt seit langem als ~:** for a long time it had been thought he had disappeared

verschonen *tr. V.* spare; **von etw. verschont bleiben** be spared by sth.; escape sth.; **jmdn. mit etw. ~:** spare sb. sth.

verschönen *tr. V.* brighten up

verschönern /fɛɐ̯ˈʃøːnɐn/ *tr. V.* brighten up

Verschönerung *die; ~, ~en* brightening up; beautification (joc.)

Verschonung *die* sparing; **er flehte um ~ seines Lebens/der Kinder** he pleaded that his life/the children be spared

verschorfen *itr. V.; mit sein* form a scab; **eine verschorfte Wunde** a wound with a scab

verschrammen

A *tr. V.* scratch

B *itr. V.; mit sein* scratch; get scratched

verschränken /fɛɐ̯ˈʃrɛŋkn̩/ *tr. V.* fold ‹*arms*›; cross ‹*legs*›; clasp ‹*hands*›; **mit verschränkten Armen/Händen** with one's arms folded/hands clasped

Verschränkung *die; ~, ~en* ▸**verschränken**: folding; crossing; clasping

verschrauben *tr. V.* screw on; **[miteinander] ~:** screw together

Verschraubung *die; ~, ~en* [1] (das Verschrauben) screwing [together] [2] (Schraubverbindung) screw fixing

verschrecken *tr. V.* frighten *or* scare [off *or* away]

verschreiben

A *unr. tr. V.* [1] (verbrauchen) use up ‹*paper, ink, pencils, etc.*› [2] (Med.: verordnen) prescribe ‹*medicine, treatment, etc.*›; **jmdm. ein Medikament ~:** prescribe a medication for sb.; **sich** (*Dat.*) **etw. für** *od.* **gegen sein Rheuma ~ lassen** get the doctor to prescribe sth. for one's rheumatism [3] *in* **sich/seine Seele dem Teufel ~:** give oneself/sell one's soul to the devil [4] (falsch schreiben) write incorrectly *or* wrongly

B *unr. refl. V.* [1] (einen Fehler machen) make a slip of the pen; **sich beim Datum ~:** make a mistake when writing the date [2] (sich widmen) **sich einer Sache** (*Dat.*) **~:** devote oneself to sth.

Verschreibung *die; ~, ~en* prescription; **mit der ~ von Pillen allein ist es nicht getan** it is not enough simply to prescribe pills

verschreibungs·pflichtig *Adj.* available only on prescription *postpos.*

verschrie[e]n /fɛɐ̯ˈʃriː[ə]n/ *Adj.* notorious (**wegen** for); **als etw. ~ sein** have the reputation of being sth. (**bei** with)

verschroben /fɛɐ̯ˈʃroːbn̩/

A *Adj.* eccentric, cranky ‹*person*›; cranky, weird ‹*ideas*›

B *adv.* eccentrically; weirdly

Verschrobenheit *die; ~, ~en* eccentricity

verschrotten *tr. V.* scrap

Verschrottung *die; ~, ~en* scrapping

verschrumpeln *itr. V.; mit sein* (ugs.) go shrivelled; **verschrumpelt** shrivelled

verschüchtern *tr. V.* intimidate; **verschüchtert** timid; (adverbial) timidly

verschulden

A *tr. V.* be to blame for ‹*accident, death, etc.*›; (Fußball usw.) give away ‹*goal, corner*›; **sein Unglück selbst ~:** have only oneself to blame for one's misfortune

B *refl. V.* get into debt; **er hat sich dafür hoch ~ müssen** he had to borrow heavily to do that; **sich auf Jahre hinaus ~:** incur debts/a debt that will take years to pay off

Verschulden *das; ~s* guilt; **durch eigenes/fremdes ~:** through one's own/someone else's fault; **ohne mein ~:** through no fault of my own

verschuldet *Adj.* [1] in debt *postpos.* (**bei** to); **hoch ~:** deeply in debt [2] (belastet) mortgaged; **hoch ~:** heavily mortgaged

Verschuldung *die; ~, ~en* indebtedness *no pl.*; **die hohe ~ des Staates** the state's heavy debts *pl.*

Verschulung *die; ~, ~en* organization on school lines

verschusselt *Adj.* (ugs.) ▸**schusselig**

verschütt *in* **~ gehen** (ugs.) do a vanishing trick *or* disappearing act (coll.); (salopp: umkommen) go for a burton (Brit. sl.)

verschütten *tr. V.* [1] spill [2] (begraben) bury ‹*person*› [alive]; submerge, bury ‹*road etc.*›; (fig.) submerge; **die verschütteten Bergleute** the trapped miners; **ein Verschütteter** one of those buried/trapped; **die Verschütteten** those buried/trapped; **verschüttete Erinnerungen** memories buried in the subconscious

***verschütt|gehen** ▸**verschütt**

verschwägert /fɛɐ̯ˈʃvɛːɡɐt/ *Adj.* related by marriage *postpos.*

verschweigen *unr. tr. V.* conceal ‹*truth etc.*›; (verheimlichen) keep quiet about; **jmdm. etw. ~:** hide *or* conceal sth. from sb.; **du verschweigst mir doch etwas** you're keeping something from me; *s. auch* **verschwiegen B**

verschweißen *tr. V.* weld [together]; **etw. mit etw. ~:** weld sth. to sth.

verschwenden *tr. V.* waste (**an** + *Akk.* on); **du verschwendest deine Worte** you are wasting your breath; **sie verschwendete keinen Blick an ihn** she did not give him a single glance

Verschwender *der; ~s, ~,* **Verschwenderin** *die; ~, ~nen* (von Geld) spendthrift; (von Dingen) wasteful person

verschwenderisch

A *Adj.* [1] wasteful, extravagant ‹*person*›; ‹*life*› of extravagance [2] (üppig) lavish; sumptuous

B *adv.* [1] wastefully, extravagantly; **sie geht ~ mit ihrem Geld um** she is lavish *or* extravagant with her money [2] (üppig) lavishly; sumptuously

Verschwendung *die; ~, ~en* wastefulness; extravagance; **so eine ~!** what a waste!; **~ von Steuergeldern** waste *or* squandering of taxpayers' money

Verschwendungs·sucht *die* love of extravagance; squandermania (coll.)

verschwiegen

A *2. Part. v.* **verschweigen**

B *Adj.* [1] (diskret) discreet; *s. auch* **Grab** [2] (still, einsam) secluded ‹*place, bay*›; quiet ‹*restaurant etc.*›; **auf dem ~en Örtchen** (ugs. scherzh.) in the smallest room (joc.)

Verschwiegenheit *die; ~:* secrecy; (Diskretion) discretion; *s. auch* **Siegel 2**

verschwimmen *unr. itr. V.; mit sein* blur; become blurred; **die Zeilen/Buchstaben verschwammen mir vor den Augen** the lines/letters swam in front of my eyes; **ineinander/in eins ~:** merge into one another/into one; *s. auch* **verschwommen B**

verschwinden *unr. itr. V.; mit sein* [1] disappear; vanish; ‹*pain, spot, etc.*› disappear, go [away]; **seine Zahnschmerzen sind von selbst verschwunden** his toothache went away *or* stopped of its own accord; **die Maus verschwand in ihrem Loch** *od.* **in ihr Loch** the mouse disappeared into its hole; **es ist besser, wir ~/lass uns hier ~:** we'd better/let's make ourselves scarce (coll.); **verschwinde [hier]!** off with you!; go away!; hop it! (coll.); **ich muss mal ~** (ugs. verhüll.) I have to pay a visit (coll.) *or* (Brit. coll.) spend a penny; **der Müll muss hier ~:** this rubbish must be removed; **jmdn. ~ lassen** take sb. away; (in einer Anstalt usw.) put sb. away; (ermorden) eliminate sb.; do away with sb.; **etw. ~ lassen** (wegzaubern) ‹*conjuror*› make sth. disappear *or* vanish; (stehlen) help oneself to sth. (coll.); (verstecken) hide sth.; (unterschlagen, beiseite schaffen) dispose of sth.; **Zigaretten in seiner Tasche/Karten in seinem Ärmel ~ lassen** slip cigarettes into one's pocket/cards up one's sleeve [2] (verborgen sein) **unter etw.** (*Dat.*) **~:** disappear under sth.; be hidden by sth. [3] **neben jmdm./etw. ~** (sehr klein wirken) be dwarfed by sb./sth.; (unbedeutend wirken) pale into insignificance beside sb./sth.

verschwindend

A *Adj.* tiny

B *adv.* **~ klein** tiny; minute; **~ wenig** a tiny amount

verschwistert /fɛɐ̯ˈʃvɪstɐt/ *Adj.* **[miteinander] ~ sein** (Bruder u. Schwester sein) be brother and sister; (Brüder u. Schwestern sein) be brothers and sisters; (Brüder/Schwestern sein) be brothers/sisters

verschwitzen *tr. V.* [1] make ‹*shirt, dress, etc.*› sweaty; **verschwitzt** sweaty; **total verschwitzt** soaked in sweat *or* perspiration [2] (ugs.: vergessen) forget; **ich habe es völlig verschwitzt** I clean forgot

verschwollen /fɛɐ̯ˈʃvɔlən/ *Adj.* swollen

verschwommen

A *2. Part. v.* **verschwimmen**

B *Adj.* blurred ‹*photograph, vision*›; blurred, hazy ‹*outline*›; vague, woolly ‹*idea, concept, formulation, etc.*›; vague ‹*hope*›

C *adv.* ‹*express, formulate, refer*› vaguely; ‹*remember*› hazily; **ich sehe alles ganz ~:** everything looks blurred to me

Verschwommenheit *die; ~, ~en* ▸**verschwommen B**: blurring; haziness; vagueness; woolliness

verschworen

A *2. Part. v.* **verschwören**

B *Adj.* [1] (fest zusammenhaltend) sworn; **ein ~er Haufen** a band of blood brothers [2] *in* **einer Idee/Sache** (*Dat.*) *usw.* **~ sein** be dedicated to an idea/a cause *etc.*

verschwören *unr. refl. V.* [1] conspire, plot (**gegen** against); **alles scheint sich gegen uns verschworen zu haben** (fig.) everything seems to have conspired against us [2] (sich verschreiben) **sich jmdm./einer Sache ~:** dedicate *or* devote oneself to sb./sth.; *s. auch* **verschworen**

Verschworene *der/die; adj. Dekl.,* **Verschwörer** *der; ~s, ~,* **Verschwörerin** *die; ~, ~nen* conspirator

verschwörerisch

A *Adj.* conspiratorial

B *adv.* conspiratorially

Verschwörung *die; ~, ~en* conspiracy; plot

Verschwörungs·theorie *die* conspiracy theory

versehen

A *unr. tr. V.* [1] (ausstatten) provide; equip ‹*car, factory, machine, etc.*› [2] (ausüben, besorgen) perform ‹*duty etc.*›; **bei jmdm. den Haushalt ~:** keep house for sb. [3] (innehaben) hold ‹*post, job*› [4] (kath. Kirche) administer the last rites *or* sacraments to ‹*dying person*›

B *unr. refl. V.* [1] (einen Fehler machen) make a slip; slip up [2] *in* **ehe man sich's versieht** before you know where you are; **ehe ich mich's versah** before I knew what was happening

Versehen *das; ~s, ~:* oversight; slip; **aus ~:** by mistake; inadvertently

versehentlich

A *Adv.* by mistake; inadvertently

B *adj.* inadvertent

versehrt /fɛɐ̯ˈzeːɐ̯t/ *Adj.* disabled

Versehrte *der/die; adj. Dekl.* disabled person; **die ~n** the disabled

Versehrten·sport *der* sport *no art.* for the disabled

verselbständigen *refl. V.* become independent; **sich zu einer eigenen wissenschaftlichen Disziplin ~:** become an independent scientific discipline

Verselbständigung *die; ~, ~en* gaining *or* achievement of independence

verselbstständigen ▸**verselbständigen**

Verselbstständigung ▸**Verselbständigung**

versemmeln *tr. V.* (Jargon Sport) mess up (coll.); botch

versenden *unr.* (*auch regelm.*) *tr. V.* send ‹*letter, parcel*›; send out ‹*invitations*›; dispatch ‹*goods*›

Versendung *die* ▸**versenden**: sending; sending out; dispatch

versengen *tr. V.* scorch; singe ‹*hair*›

versenkbar *Adj.* (Technik) foldaway ‹*sewing machine*›; telescopic ‹*aerial*›

versenken

A *tr. V.* [1] sink ‹*ship*›; sink, dump ‹*waste*›; lower ‹*body, coffin*›; **das eigene Schiff ~:** scuttle one's ship [2] (verschwinden lassen) lower, retract

V

‹*aerial, rostrum, etc.*›; sink ‹*nail, rivet*› [flush]; countersink ‹*screw*›; **die Hände in die Taschen ~:** sink one's hands [deep] into one's pockets
B *refl. V.* (fig.) **sich in etw.** (*Akk.*) **~:** immerse oneself *or* become engrossed in sth.; **sich in den Anblick von etw. ~:** lose oneself in the contemplation of sth.

Versenkung *die* 1 ▸ **versenken A 1, 2:** sinking; dumping; lowering; scuttling; retraction; countersinking 2 (fig.: das Sichversenken) immersion, absorption (**in** + *Akk.* in); **mystische ~:** mystic contemplation 3 (Theater) trap; **in der ~ verschwinden** (fig. ugs.) vanish from the scene; sink into oblivion; **aus der ~ auftauchen** (fig. ugs.) re-emerge on the scene

Vers·epos *das* epic poem

Verse·schmied *der*, **Verse·schmiedin** *die* (scherzh., abwertend) rhymester; poetaster

versessen /fɛɐ̯ˈzɛsn̩/ *Adj.* **auf jmdn./etw. ~ sein** be dead keen on *or* crazy about sb./sth. (coll.); **auf peinlichste Genauigkeit ~:** obsessed with scrupulous accuracy; **darauf ~ sein, etw. zu tun** be dying to do sth.

versetzen
A *tr. V.* 1 move; transfer, move ‹*employee*›; (auf einen anderen Platz) move ‹*pupil*› [to another seat]; (in die nächsthöhere Klasse) move ‹*pupil*› up, (Amer.) promote ‹*pupil*› (**in** + *Akk.* to); (umpflanzen) transplant, move ‹*plant*›; (fig.) transport (**in** + *Akk.* to); **sich ins vorige Jahrhundert versetzt fühlen** (fig.) be taken back to the last century 2 (nicht geradlinig anordnen) stagger; **versetzt angeordnet sein** be staggered 3 (verpfänden) pawn 4 (verkaufen) sell 5 (ugs.: vergeblich warten lassen) stand ‹*person*› up (coll.) 6 (vermischen) mix 7 (erwidern) retort 8 **etw. in Bewegung/Tätigkeit ~:** set sth. in motion/operation; **jmdn. in Erstaunen/Unruhe/Angst/Begeisterung ~:** astonish sb./make sb. uneasy/frighten sb./fill sb. with enthusiasm; **jmdn. in die Lage ~, etw. zu tun** put sb. in a position to do sth.; **jmdm. einen Stoß/Fußtritt/Schlag** *usw.* **~:** give sb. a push/kick/deal sb. a blow *etc.*; **jmdm. eine** *od.* **eins ~** (ugs.) belt sb. one (coll.)
B *refl. V.* **sich an jmds. Stelle** (*Akk.*) *od.* **in jmds. Lage** (*Akk.*) **~:** put oneself in sb.'s position *or* place; **sich in jmdn. ~:** put oneself in sb.'s shoes *or* position

Versetzung *die*; **~, ~en** 1 moving; (einer Pflanze) transplanting; (eines Schülers) moving up, (Amer.) promotion (**in** + *Akk.* to); (eines Angestellten) transfer; move; (fig.) transporting 2 (Verpfändung) pawning 3 (Verkauf) selling; sale 4 (das Mischen) mixing; *s. auch* **Ruhestand**

Versetzungs-: ~konferenz *die*: (Schulw.) *staff meeting to discuss moving pupils to higher classes*; **~zeugnis** *das* (Schulw.) end-of-year report (*confirming pupil's move to a higher class*)

verseuchen *tr. V.* (auch fig.) contaminate; **radioaktiv ~:** contaminate with radioactivity

Verseuchung (auch fig.) *die*; **~, ~en** contamination

Vers·fuß *der* (Verslehre) [metrical] foot

Versicherer *der*; **~s, ~, Versicherin** *die*; **~, ~nen** insurer

versichern
A *tr. V.* 1 (als wahr hinstellen) assert, affirm ‹*sth.*›; **etw. hoch und heilig/eidesstattlich ~:** swear blind to sth./attest sth. in a statutory declaration; **jmdm. etw.** *od.* (geh.) **jmdn. einer Sache** (*Gen.*) **~:** assure sb. of sth.; **jmdm.** *od.* (geh.) **jmdn. ~, dass ...** assure sb. that ...; **seien Sie versichert, dass ...** (geh.) you may rest assured that ... 2 (vertraglich schützen) insure (**bei** with); **sein Leben ist hoch/mit 50 000 Euro versichert** his life is assured *or* insured for a large sum/50,000 euros
B *refl. V.* (geh.) 1 **sich jmds./einer Sache ~:** make sure *or* certain of sb./sth. 2 (veralt.: sich bemächtigen) **sich einer Sache** (*Gen.*) **~:** seize sth.

Versicherte *der/die*; *adj. Dekl.* insured [person]

Versicherung *die* 1 (Beteuerung) assurance; **eine eidesstattliche ~:** a statutory declaration 2 (Schutz durch Vertrag) insurance; (Vertrag) insurance [policy] (**über** + *Akk.* for); (ugs.: Beitrag, Prämie) insurance [premium]; **eine ~ abschließen** take out an insurance [policy] 3 (Gesellschaft) insurance [company]

versicherungs-, Versicherungs-: ~agent *der*, **~agentin** *die* ▸ⓘ **S. 113** insurance broker; **~beitrag** *der* insurance premium; **~betrug** *der* insurance fraud; **~fall** *der* event giving rise to a claim; **~gesellschaft** *die* insurance company; **~karte** *die* 1 (Sozialversicherung) insurance *or* contribution card; 2 (Kfz.-Versicherung) **die grüne ~karte** the green card; **~kauffrau** *die* insurance saleswoman; **~kaufmann** *der* insurance salesman; **~mathematiker** *der*, **~mathematikerin** *die* actuary; **~nehmer** *der*; **~~s, ~~, ~nehmerin** *die*; **~~, ~~nen** policy holder; **~pflichtig** *Adj.* 1 (Sozialversicherung) ‹*person*› liable for [insurance] contributions; ‹*earnings*› subject to [insurance] contributions; 2 (individuell) subject to compulsory insurance *postpos.*; **~police** *die*, **~schein** *der* insurance policy; **~schutz** *der* insurance cover; **~summe** *die* sum insured; **~vertreter** *der*, **~vertreterin** *die* ▸ⓘ **S. 113** insurance agent

versickern *itr. V.*; *mit sein* 1 ‹*river etc.*› drain *or* seep away 2 (fig.: enden) ‹*conversation*› fade away; ‹*money*› drain away

versieben *tr. V.* (ugs.) 1 (verlegen) mislay 2 (verderben) ruin; waste ‹*chance*›

versiegeln *tr. V.* 1 seal; **jmdm. den Mund** *od.* **die Lippen ~** (fig.) seal sb.'s lips; silence sb. 2 (lackieren, überziehen) seal ‹*floor, paintwork, etc.*›

Versiegelung *die*; **~, ~en** 1 (das Versiegeln) sealing 2 (Siegel) seal 3 (Schutzschicht) protective coating; seal

versiegen *itr. V.*; *mit sein* (geh.) dry up; run dry; ‹*tears*› cease [to flow]; (fig.) peter out; ‹*energy*› run out; **sein nie ~der Humor** his inexhaustible fund of humour

versiert /vɛrˈziːɐ̯t/ *Adj.* experienced [and knowledgeable]; **in etw.** (*Dat.*) **~ sein** be well versed in sth.

Versiertheit *die*; **~:** experience (**in** + *Dat.* in); (Wissen) knowledge (**in** + *Dat.* of)

versifft /fɛrˈzɪft/ *Adj.* (ugs.) filthy

versilbern *tr. V.* 1 silver-plate; (dichter.) silver 2 (ugs.: verkaufen) turn into cash; flog (Brit. sl.)

versinken *unr. itr. V.*; *mit sein* 1 sink; **im Schlamm/Schnee ~:** sink into the mud/snow; **in den Wellen ~:** sink beneath the waves; **im Moor ~:** be sucked into the bog; **ich wäre am liebsten im Erdboden versunken** I wished the ground would [open and] swallow me up; **die Stadt versank im Dunkel** (fig. geh.) darkness descended over the town; **eine versunkene Kultur** (fig.) a long-vanished civilization 2 (fig.) **~ in** (+ *Akk.*) become immersed in *or* wrapped up in ‹*memories, thoughts*›; subside, lapse into ‹*melancholy, silence, etc.*›; **in Gedanken versunken, nickte er** deep *or* lost in thought, he nodded; **er war ganz in ihren Anblick versunken** he was completely absorbed in looking at her

versinnbildlichen *tr. V.* symbolize

Versinnbildlichung *die*; **~, ~en** symbolic representation

Version /vɛrˈzi̯oːn/ *die*; **~, ~en** version

versippt *Adj.* related by marriage *postpos.* (**mit** to)

versklaven *tr. V.* enslave

Versklavung *die*; **~, ~en** enslavement

Vers·maß *das* metre

versnoben *itr. V.*; *mit sein* (abwertend) become snobbish; turn into a snob; **versnobt** snobbish

versoffen /fɛɐ̯ˈzɔfn̩/
A *2. Part. v.* **versaufen**
B *Adj.* (salopp abwertend) boozy (coll.)

versohlen *tr. V.* (ugs.) belt ‹*person, backside, etc.*›; **er muss mal ordentlich versohlt werden** he needs a good hiding (coll.)

versöhnen /fɛɐ̯ˈzøːnən/
A *refl. V.* **sich [miteinander] ~:** become reconciled; make it up; **sich mit jmdm. ~:** make it up with sb.; **sich mit seinem Schicksal ~:** come to terms with one's fate
B *tr. V.* 1 reconcile; **jmdn. mit jmdm. ~:** reconcile sb. with sb.; **jmdn. mit seinem Schicksal ~:** reconcile sb. to his/her fate 2 (besänftigen) placate; appease

versöhnlich
A *Adj.* 1 conciliatory 2 (erfreulich) positive; optimistic
B *adv.* 1 in a conciliatory way; ‹*say*› in a conciliatory tone 2 (erfreulich) ‹*end*› positively, optimistically

Versöhnlichkeit *die*; **~** 1 conciliatory nature 2 (Erfreulichkeit) positive nature; optimism

Versöhnung *die*; **~, ~en** 1 reconciliation 2 (das Besänftigen) appeasement; **zu ihrer ~:** in order to placate her

Versöhnungs·fest *das* (jüd. Rel.) Day of Atonement

versonnen
A *Adj.* dreamy; (in Gedanken versunken) lost in thought *postpos*
B *adv.* dreamily; (in Gedanken) lost in thought

Versonnenheit *die*; **~;** dreaminess

versorgen *tr. V.* 1 supply; **jmdn. mit etw. ~:** supply *or* provide sb. with sth.; **danke, ich bin noch versorgt** I still have plenty, thank you; **seid ihr da drüben noch alle [mit Getränken] versorgt?** have you all got enough to drink over there?; are we looking after you over there?; **hast du den Hund/die Blumen schon versorgt?** have you fed the dog/watered the flowers?; **ich muss mich für die Reise mit Lesestoff ~:** I must get myself something to read on the journey; **das Gehirn ist nicht ausreichend mit Blut versorgt** the blood supply to the brain is not sufficient 2 (unterhalten, ernähren) provide for ‹*children, family*›; **er hat eine Familie zu ~:** he has a family to support *or* provide for; **versorgt sein** be provided for 3 (sorgen für) look after; attend to, see to ‹*heating, garden, etc.*›; **er versorgt sich selbst** he looks after himself; he does his own housework; **sie versorgt ihn** *od.* **versorgt ihm den Haushalt** she keeps house for him; **jmdn. ärztlich ~:** give sb. medical care; (kurzzeitig) give sb. medical attention

Versorger *der*; **~s, ~, Versorgerin** *die*; **~, ~nen** 1 breadwinner; provider 2 (Unternehmen) supplier

Versorgung *die*; **~, ~en** 1 supply[ing]; **die ~ einer Stadt/eines Gebiets/eines Organs mit etw.** the supply of sth. to a town/an area/an organ; **die ~ der Insel erfolgt auf dem Luftwege** the island is supplied by air; supplies reach the island by air; **die ~ des Hundes/der Blumen übernehmen** see to the feeding of the dog/watering of the flowers 2 (Unterhaltung, Ernährung) support[ing]; **zur ~ einer Familie ausreichen** be enough to provide for *or* support a family; **die ~ der Kriegerwitwen/der pensionierten Beamten** making provision for war widows/retired civil servants 3 (Bedienung, Pflege) care; **die ~ des Haushalts** the housekeeping; **die ~ der Heizung/des Gartens** seeing *or* attending to the heating/garden; **die ~ der Heimbewohner ist gut** the people living in the home are well looked after; **ärztliche ~:** medical care *or* treatment; (kurzzeitig) medical attention; **die ~ der Wunde** the treatment of the wound 4 (Bezüge) maintenance; (Sozialhilfe) benefit

Versorgungs-: ~anspruch *der* entitlement to benefit/maintenance; **~ausgleich** *der* (Rechtsw.) maintenance settlement; **~lage** *die* supply situation (**bei** with regard to); **~lücke** *die* gap in provision; (Rentenlücke) pension gap; **~netz** *das* supply network *or* grid

verspachteln *tr. V.* 1 fill, put filler in ‹*holes, cracks*› 2 (ugs.: aufessen) scoff (coll.)

verspannen
A *refl. V.* ‹*muscle*› tense up; **verspannt** taut ‹*muscle*›; (völlig verkrampft) seized-up ‹*back*›
B *tr. V.* brace ‹*mast etc.*›

V

Verspannung *die* 1 ▸ⓘ **S. 439** (Med.: der Muskulatur) tension 2 (eines Mastes o. Ä.) bracing; (Seile) stays *pl.*

verspäten *refl. V.* be late; **ich habe mich leider etwas/[um] fünf Minuten verspätet** I am unfortunately a little/five minutes late

verspätet *Adj.* late ‹*arrival, rose, butterfly*›; belated ‹*greetings, thanks*›; **~ eintreffen** *od.* **ankommen** arrive late

Verspätung *die;* **~, ~en** lateness; (verspätetes Eintreffen) late arrival; **[fünf Minuten] ~ haben** be [five minutes] late; **eine fünfminütige ~:** a five-minute delay; **mit [fünfminütiger] ~ abfahren/ankommen** leave/arrive [five minutes] late; **seine** *od.* **die ~ aufholen** make up the lost time; **mit dreimonatiger ~:** three months late

verspeisen *tr. V.* (geh.) consume; partake of

verspekulieren

A *refl. V.* make a bad speculation; back the wrong horse (fig.); **wenn du gedacht hast, ich vergesse das, hast du dich verspekuliert** (ugs.) if you thought I would forget about it, you've got another think coming (coll.)

B *tr. V.* lose through speculation

versperren *tr. V.* 1 block ‹*road, entrance*›; obstruct ‹*view*›; **jmdm. den Weg/die Sicht ~:** block sb.'s path/block *or* obstruct sb.'s view 2 (bes. österr.: abschließen) lock

verspiegeln *tr. V.* 1 cover ‹*wall*› with mirrors 2 (beschichten) cover with a reflective surface

verspielen

A *tr. V.* 1 gamble away; (fig.: vertun, verwirken) squander, throw away ‹*opportunity, chance*›; forfeit ‹*right, credibility, sb.'s trust, etc*› 2 (spielend verbringen) spend ‹*hours, day*› playing

B *itr. V.* **in [bei jmdm.] verspielt haben** (ugs.) have had it [so far as sb. is concerned] (coll.)

C *refl. V.* play a wrong note/wrong notes

verspielt

A *Adj.* (auch fig.) playful; fanciful, fantastic ‹*form, design, etc.*›; **das Kleid ist/wirkt etwas zu ~:** the dress is/seems a little too fanciful

B *adv.* playfully (lit. or fig.); ‹*dress, designed*› fancifully, fantastically

verspießern *itr. V.; mit sein* (abwertend) become typically bourgeois

verspinnen *unr. tr. V.* spin ‹*wool*› (**zu** into)

versponnen

A *2. Part. v.* **verspinnen**

B *Adj.* eccentric, odd ‹*person*›; odd, weird ‹*idea*›

Versponnenheit *die;* **~:** eccentricity; oddness; (einer Idee) weirdness

verspotten *tr. V.* mock; ridicule

Verspottung *die;* **~, ~en** mocking; ridiculing

versprechen

A *unr. tr. V.* 1 promise; **jmdm. etw. ~:** promise sb. sth.; **was er verspricht, hält er auch** he keeps his promises; **versprich [mir], pünktlich zu sein** *od.* **dass du pünktlich bist** promise [me] you will be on time; **sich jmdm. ~** (veralt.) promise oneself to sb.; **seine Miene/sein Blick versprach nichts Gutes** his expression/glance was ominous 2 **sich** (*Dat.*) **etw. von etw./jmdm. ~:** hope for sth. *or* to get sth. from sth./sb.; **ich würde mir nicht zu viel davon ~:** I wouldn't set my hopes too high

B *unr. refl. V.* make a slip/slips of the tongue; **ich habe mich nur versprochen** it was just a slip of the tongue [on my part]

Versprechen *das;* **~s, ~:** promise; **jmdm. das ~ geben, etw. zu tun** promise sb. *or* give sb. a promise to do sth.

Versprecher *der;* **~s, ~:** slip of the tongue; **ein freudscher ~:** a Freudian slip

Versprechung *die;* **~, ~en** promise

versprengen *tr. V.* 1 (bes. Milit.) disperse; scatter; **versprengte Soldaten** soldiers who have/had lost contact with their units 2 (verspritzen) sprinkle ‹*water*›

verspritzen *tr. V.* 1 spray; **darüber ist schon viel Tinte verspritzt worden** (fig.) a lot of ink has been spilt over that 2 (bespritzen) spatter ‹*windscreen, coat, etc.*›

versprühen *tr. V.* spray; **Funken ~:** send out a shower of sparks; **Geist** *od.* **Witz ~** (fig.) show sparkling wit; scintillate

verspüren *tr. V.* feel; **Lust/keine Lust zu etw./Verlangen/kein Verlangen nach etw. ~:** have *or* feel a desire/no desire for sth.

verstaatlichen *tr. V.* nationalize

Verstaatlichung *die;* **~, ~en** nationalization

verstädtern /fɛɐ̯ˈʃtɛːtɐn/ *itr. V.; mit sein* become urbanized

Verstädterung *die;* **~, ~en** urbanization

Verstand *der;* **~[e]s** (Fähigkeit zu denken) reason *no art.;* (Fähigkeit, Begriffe zu bilden) mind; (Vernunft) [common] sense *no art.;* **Tiere haben keinen ~:** animals do not have the power *or* faculty of reason; **der menschliche ~:** the human mind; **mein** *od.* **der ~ sagt mir, dass ...** reason *or* common sense tells me that ...; **wenn du deinen ~ gebraucht hättest** if you had used your brain *or* had been thinking; **er hat einen klaren ~:** he has a lucid mind; **ich hätte ihm mehr ~ zugetraut** I thought he would have had more sense; **er musste all seinen ~ zusammennehmen** he had to summon up all his mental powers *or* rack his brains; **manchmal zweifle ich an seinem ~:** I sometimes doubt his sanity; **bei klarem ~ bleiben** keep one's mental faculties; **~ und Vernunft** understanding and reason; **~ und Gefühl** head and heart; **das schreckliche Erlebnis hat ihren ~ verwirrt** the terrible experience threw her mind into confusion; **ich verliere noch den ~:** I'll go out of my mind; **hast du denn den ~ verloren** (ugs.) have you taken leave of your senses?; are you out of your mind?; **du bist wohl nicht [ganz] bei ~!** (ugs.) you must be out of your mind!; **das geht über meinen ~:** that's beyond me; **der Schmerz hat ihn um den ~ gebracht** the pain drove him out of his mind; **seinen ~ versaufen** (salopp) drink oneself stupid; **etw. mit ~ trinken/essen/rauchen** really savour sth. [while drinking/eating/smoking it]; *s. auch* **Glück 1; Sinn 7**

verstandes-, Verstandes-: ~kraft *die* mental *or* intellectual powers *pl.;* **~mäßig A** *Adj.* rational; intellectual ‹*inferiority, superiority*›; **B** *adv.* rationally; intellectually ‹*inferior, superior*›; **~mensch** *der* rational person

verständig /fɛɐ̯ˈʃtɛndɪç/

A *Adj.* sensible; intelligent

B *adv.* sensibly; intelligently

verständigen /fɛɐ̯ˈʃtɛndɪɡn̩/

A *tr. V.* notify, inform (**von, über** + *Akk.* of)

B *refl. V.* 1 make oneself understood; **sich mit jmdm. ~:** communicate with sb. 2 (sich einigen) **sich [mit jmdm.] über/auf etw.** (*Akk.*) **~:** come to an understanding *or* reach agreement [with sb.] about *or.* on sth.

Verständigkeit *die;* **~:** understanding; intelligence

Verständigung *die;* **~, ~en** 1 notification 2 (das Sichverständlichmachen) communication *no art.;* **wegen des Lärms war eine ~ praktisch unmöglich** because of the noise, it was almost impossible to make oneself understood 3 (Einigung) understanding; **eine Politik der ~:** a policy of rapprochement; **über diesen Punkt kam es zu keiner ~:** no agreement was reached on this point

Verständigungs-: ~bereitschaft *die* readiness to come to an understanding; **~schwierigkeit** *die* difficulty of communication

verständlich

A *Adj.* 1 comprehensible; (deutlich) clear ‹*pronunciation, presentation, etc.*›; **[leicht] ~:** easily understood; **schwer ~:** difficult to understand; (bei Lärm) difficult to make out; **sich ~ machen** make oneself understood; **sich seinen Zuhörern ~ machen** get [one's message] across to one's listeners; **jmdm. etw. ~ machen** make sth. clear to sb. 2 (begreiflich, verzeihlich) understandable; **seine Verärgerung ist mir durchaus ~:** I can fully understand his annoyance

B *adv.* comprehensibly; in a comprehensible way; (deutlich) ‹*speak, express oneself, present*› clearly

verständlicher·weise *Adv.* understandably

Verständlichkeit *die;* **~:** comprehensibility; clarity

Verständnis *das;* **~ses, ~se** understanding; **dem Leser das ~ erleichtern** make it easier for the reader to understand; **ein ~ für Kunst/Musik** an appreciation of *or* feeling for art/music; **ich habe volles ~ dafür, dass ...** I fully understand that ...; **für so etwas habe ich kein ~:** I have no time for that kind of thing; **für die Unannehmlichkeiten bitten wir um [Ihr] ~:** we ask for your forbearance *or* we apologize for the inconvenience caused

verständnis-, Verständnis-: ~innig A *Adj.* knowing, meaningful ‹*glance*›; **B** *adv.* knowingly; meaningfully; **~los A** *Adj.* uncomprehending; **der modernen Kunst steht er völlig ~los gegenüber** he has no understanding of *or* feeling for modern art at all; **B** *adv.* uncomprehendingly; **~losigkeit** *die;* **~~:** incomprehension; **voller ~losigkeit** uncomprehendingly; with a complete lack of understanding; **~voll A** *Adj.* understanding; **B** *adv.* understandingly

verstärken

A *tr. V.* 1 strengthen; **die Socken sind an den Fersen verstärkt** the socks have reinforced heels 2 (zahlenmäßig) reinforce ‹*troops, garrison, etc.*› (**um** by); enlarge, augment ‹*orchestra, choir*› (**um** by); **die Truppen auf 1 500 Mann ~:** bring the troops up to a strength of 1,500 men 3 (intensiver machen) intensify, increase ‹*effort, contrast*›; strengthen, increase ‹*impression, suspicion*›; (größer machen) increase ‹*pressure, voltage, effect, etc.*›; (lauter machen) amplify ‹*signal, sound, guitar, etc.*›

B *refl. V.* increase; *s. auch* **verstärkt**

Verstärker *der;* **~s, ~:** amplifier

verstärkt

A *Adj.* 1 increased; (größer) greater ‹*efforts, vigilance, etc.*›; **in ~em Maße** to a greater *or* increased extent 2 (zahlenmäßig) enlarged, augmented ‹*orchestra, choir, etc.*›; reinforced (Mil.) ‹*unit*›

B *adv.* to an increased extent

Verstärkung *die;* **~, ~en** 1 strengthening 2 (zahlenmäßig) reinforcement (esp. Mil.); (eines Orchesters usw.) enlargement 3 (Intensivierung, Zunahme) increase (*Gen.* in); (der Lautstärke) amplification; **zur ~ einer Sache** (*Gen.*) to increase/amplify sth. 4 (zusätzliche Person[en]) reinforcements *pl.* 5 (verstärkendes Element) reinforcement

verstauben *itr. V.; mit sein* get dusty; gather dust (lit. or fig.); *s. auch* **verstaubt**

verstäuben /fɛɐ̯ˈʃtɔybn̩/ *tr. V.* spray ‹*insecticide etc.*›

verstaubt *Adj.* dusty; covered in dust *postpos.;* (fig. abwertend) old-fashioned; outmoded

verstauchen *tr. V.* ▸ⓘ **S. 439** sprain; **sich** (*Dat.*) **den Fuß/die Hand ~:** sprain one's ankle/wrist

Verstauchung *die;* **~, ~en** ▸ⓘ **S. 439** sprain

verstauen *tr. V.* pack (**in** + *Dat. od. Akk.* in[to]); (bes. im Boot/Auto) stow (**in** + *Dat. od. Akk.* in); **etw. auf dem Boden/in einem** *od.* **einen Schrank ~:** put *or* (coll.) stash sth. away in the loft/a cupboard; **etw. in der Hosentasche ~:** stuff sth. into one's trouser pocket; **er verstaute seine Familie im Auto** (scherzh.) he packed his family into the car

Versteck *das;* **~[e]s, ~e** hiding place; (eines Flüchtlings, Räubers usw.) hideout; **~ spielen** play hide-and-seek; **[vor jmdm./voreinander** *od.* **mit jmdm./miteinander] ~ spielen** (fig.) hide *or* keep things [from sb./one another]

verstecken

A *tr. V.* hide (**vor** + *Dat.* from); **jmdn. versteckt halten** keep sb. hidden; **das Haus war in einem Wäldchen versteckt** the house was tucked away in a small wood

B *refl. V.* **sich [vor jmdm./etw.] ~:** hide [from sb./sth.]; **sich versteckt halten** be [in] hiding; (versteckt bleiben) remain in hiding; **ich möchte**

bloß wissen, wo sich meine Brille schon wieder versteckt hat I should love to know where my glasses have got to; **sich vor** *od.* **neben jmdm. nicht zu ~ brauchen** *od.* **nicht ~ müssen** (fig.) not need to fear comparison with sb.; **das ist eine Leistung, mit der er sich nicht ~ muss** it is a performance of which he has no need to be ashamed; **sich vor** *od.* **neben jmdm. ~ müssen** (fig.) not be able to compare with sb.; not be a patch on sb. (coll.); **sich hinter seinem Chef/seinen Vorschriften** *usw.* **~** (fig.) use one's boss (coll.)/one's rules and regulations to hide behind; *s. auch* **versteckt**

Verstecken *das;* **~s** hide-and-seek *no art.*

Versteck·spiel *das* game of hide-and-seek; (fig.) charade; pretence

versteckt *Adj.* hidden; concealed ‹*polemics*›; veiled ‹*threat*›; (heimlich) secret ‹*malice, activity, etc.*›; disguised ‹*foul*›; (verstohlen) furtive ‹*glance, smile*›

verstehen

A *unr. tr. V.* [1] (wahrnehmen) understand; make out; **ich konnte ihn bei dem Lärm nicht ~:** I couldn't make out what he was saying because of the noise; **man versteht [vor Lärm] sein eigenes Wort nicht** one cannot hear oneself speak; **er war am Telefon gut/schlecht/kaum zu ~:** it was easy/difficult/barely possible to understand *or* make out what he was saying on the telephone [2] *auch itr.* (begreifen, interpretieren) understand; **das musst du schon ~:** you must understand *or* see that; **ich verstehe** I understand; I see; **[ich habe] verstanden** understood; I've got it; **wir ~ uns schon** we understand each other; we see eye to eye; **das verstehe [nun] einer!** what is one supposed to make of that?; **du bleibst hier, verstanden** *od.* **verstehst du!** you stay here, understand!; **jmdm. etw. zu ~ geben** give sb. to understand sth.; **das ist in dem Sinne** *od.* **so zu ~, dass ...** it is supposed to mean that ...; **wie soll ich das ~?** how am I to interpret that?; what am I supposed to make of that?; **jmdn./etw. falsch ~:** misunderstand sb./sth.; **versteh mich bitte richtig** *od.* **nicht falsch** please don't misunderstand me *or* get me wrong; **wenn ich [es] recht verstehe** if I understand rightly; **falsch verstandene Loyalität** misunderstood loyalty; **etw. unter etw.** (*Dat.*) **~:** understand sth. by sth.; **was ~ Sie darunter?** what do you think that means?; **jmdn./sich als etw. ~:** see sb./oneself as sth.; consider sb./oneself to be sth.; **er will sich als Christ verstanden wissen** he wants to be seen as *or* to be considered a Christian; *s. auch* **Bahnhof**; **Spaß 2** [3] (beherrschen, wissen) **es ~, etw. zu tun** know how to do sth.; **er versteht zu genießen** he knows how to enjoy himself *or* things; **er versteht eine Menge von Autos** he knows a lot about cars; he is quite an expert on cars; **davon verstehe ich nichts/nicht viel** I don't know anything/know much about it

B *unr. refl. V.* [1] **sich mit jmdm. ~:** get on with sb.; **sie ~ sich** they get on well together [2] (selbstverständlich sein) **das versteht sich [von selbst]** that goes without saying; **versteht sich!** (ugs.) of course! [3] (Kaufmannsspr.: gemeint sein) **der Preis versteht sich einschließlich Mehrwertsteuer** the price is inclusive of VAT [4] **sich auf Pferde/Autos** *usw.* (*Akk.*) **~:** know what one is doing with horses/cars; know all about horses/cars; **er versteht sich aufs Dichten** he knows how to write poetry [5] **sich zu etw. ~** (veralt.) agree [reluctantly] to sth.

versteifen

A *tr. V.* [1] stiffen ‹*collar, part of body, etc.*› [2] (Bauw.: abstützen) shore up ‹*wall, house, excavation, etc.*›; brace ‹*fence*›

B *itr. V.; mit sein* stiffen [up]; become stiff

C *refl. V.* [1] stiffen [up]; become stiff [2] *in* **sich auf etw.** (*Akk.*) **~:** insist on sth.

Versteifung *die;* **~, ~en** [1] stiffening [2] (Bauw.) shoring [up]

versteigen *unr. refl. V.* [1] (sich verirren) get lost [while climbing]; (nicht mehr herunterkönnen) get stuck; get into difficulties [2] **sich zu einer Behauptung/zu Angriffen gegen jmdn.** *usw.* **~:** have the presumption to make an assertion/attacks on sb. *etc.*; **wie konnte ich mich zu solcher Schwärmerei ~?** how could I get so carried away?; *s. auch* **versteigen B**

versteigern *tr. V.* auction; **etw. ~ lassen** put sth. up for auction; **auf einer Auktion meistbietend versteigert werden** be sold to the highest bidder at an auction

Versteigerung *die* [1] auction *no indef. art.*; **zur ~ kommen** *od.* **gelangen** (Amtsspr.) be auctioned [2] (Veranstaltung) auction; **auf einer ~:** at an auction

versteinern

A *itr. V.; mit sein* ‹*plant, animal*› fossilize, become fossilized; ‹*wood etc.*› petrify, become petrified; (fig. geh.) ‹*person*› go rigid; ‹*expression, face*› harden, become stony; **sie blieb [wie] versteinert stehen** she stopped in her tracks, as rigid as a statue

B *refl. V.* (geh.) ‹*face, features*› harden

Versteinerung *die;* **~, ~en** [1] (das Versteinern) fossilization; (von Holz) petrification [2] (Fossil) fossil

verstellbar *Adj.* adjustable

verstellen

A *tr. V.* [1] (falsch platzieren) misplace; put [back] in the wrong place [2] (anders einstellen) adjust ‹*seat etc.*›; alter [the adjustment of] ‹*mirror etc.*›; reset ‹*alarm clock, points, etc.*›; **der Sitz lässt sich in der Höhe ~:** the seat can be adjusted for height [3] (versperren) block, obstruct ‹*entrance, exit, view, etc.*›; **er verstellte mir den Weg** he blocked my path; he stood in my way; **[jmdm.] den Blick für etw. ~** (fig.) obscure sb.'s view of sth. [4] (zur Täuschung verändern) disguise, alter ‹*voice, handwriting*›

B *refl. V.* [1] (seine Einstellung, Position verändern) alter; (so, dass es falsch eingestellt ist) get out of adjustment [2] (sich anders geben als man ist) pretend; play-act; **sich vor jmdm. ~:** pretend to sb.

Verstellung *die* play-acting; pretence; (der Stimme, Schrift) disguising; alteration

Verstellungs·kunst *die* [art of] play-acting *no pl.*

versteppen *itr. V.; mit sein* become steppe

versterben *unr. itr. V.; mit sein* (geh.) die; pass away; **mein verstorbener Mann** my late husband; *s. auch* **Verstorbene**

versteuern *tr. V.* pay tax on

verstiegen

A *2. Part. v.* **versteigen**

B *Adj.* whimsical ‹*idealist, person*›; extravagant, fantastic ‹*idea, expectation, etc.*›; wild ‹*dream, desire*›

Verstiegenheit *die;* **~, ~en** [1] extravagance [2] (etw. Verstiegenes) extravagant *or* fantastic idea/remark

verstimmen

A *tr. V.* [1] (Musik) put ‹*instrument*› out of tune [2] (schlecht gelaunt machen) put ‹*person*› in a bad mood; (verärgern) annoy

B *refl. V.* get *or* go out of tune

verstimmt *Adj.* [1] (Musik) out of tune *pred.* [2] (verärgert) put out, peeved, disgruntled (**über** + *Akk.* by, about); **ein ~er Magen** an upset stomach

Verstimmung *die* disgruntled *or* bad mood; **eine leichte ~ hinterlassen** leave a slight sense of annoyance

verstockt

A *Adj.* obdurate; stubborn

B *adv.* obdurately; stubbornly

Verstocktheit *die;* **~:** obduracy; stubbornness

verstohlen /fɛɐ̯ˈʃtoːlən/

A *Adj.* furtive; surreptitious

B *adv.* furtively; surreptitiously

verstolpern *tr. V.* (Sportjargon) stumble and miss ‹*ball, chance, etc.*›

verstopfen

A *tr. V.* block; **verstopft sein** ‹*pipe, drain, jet, nose, etc.*› be blocked (**durch, von** with); (Med.: keinen Stuhlgang haben) be constipated; **die vielen Autos ~ die Altstadt** the large number of cars causes congestion in the old quarter

B *itr. V.; mit sein* become blocked

Verstopfung *die;* **~, ~en** ▸ **i S. 439** (Med.: Stuhl~) constipation

verstorben /fɛɐ̯ˈʃtɔrbn̩/ *2. Part. v.* **versterben**

Verstorbene *der/die; adj. Dekl.* (geh.) deceased

verstören *tr. V.* distress

verstört *Adj.* distraught; **einen ~en Eindruck machen** appear distraught *or* distressed

Verstörtheit *die;* **~:** distressed *or* distraught state; distress

Verstoß *der* violation, infringement (**gegen** of); **~ gegen die Etikette/den guten Geschmack** breach of etiquette/offense against good taste

verstoßen

A *unr. tr. V.* disown; **aus dem Elternhaus ~ werden** be turned out of one's parents' house; **ein Verstoßener** an outcast

B *unr. itr. V.* **gegen etw. ~:** infringe *or* contravene sth.; **gegen die Etikette/den guten Geschmack ~:** commit a breach of etiquette/offend against good taste

Verstoßung *die;* **~, ~en** disowning; (aus dem Elternhaus) turning out

verstrahlen *tr. V.* [1] radiate [2] (radioaktiv verseuchen) contaminate with radiation

Verstrebung *die;* **~, ~en** struts *pl.*; (einzelne Strebe) strut

verstreichen

A *unr. tr. V.* [1] (verteilen) apply, put on ‹*paint*›; spread ‹*butter etc.*› [2] (verbrauchen) use [up] ‹*paint*› [3] (zustreichen) fill ‹*hole, crack*›

B *unr. itr. V.; mit sein* (geh.) ‹*time*› pass [by]

verstreuen *tr. V.* [1] (verteilen) scatter; put down ‹*bird food, salt*›; (unordentlich) strew; **seine Kleider lagen im ganzen Zimmer verstreut** his clothes were scattered *or* strewn all over the room; **verstreute Gehöfte/Aufsätze** isolated *or* scattered farms/isolated essays [2] (versehentlich) spill

verstricken

A *tr. V.* [1] (verbrauchen) use ‹*wool*› [in knitting] [2] (geh.: verwickeln) **jmdn. in etw.** (*Akk.*) **~:** involve sb. in sth.; draw sb. into sth.; **in etw.** (*Akk.*) **verstrickt [sein]** [be] mixed up *or* involved in sth.

B *refl. V.* [1] (falsch stricken) make a mistake/mistakes [in knitting] [2] (fig.) **sich in etw.** (*Akk.*) **~:** become entangled *or* caught up in sth.

Verstrickung *die;* **~, ~en** involvement (**in** + *Akk.* in)

verströmen *tr. V.* exude

verstrubbeln *tr. V.* (ugs.) tousle

verstümmeln *tr. V.* mutilate; (fig.) garble ‹*report*›; chop, mutilate ‹*text*›; mutilate, do violence to ‹*name*›; **sich selbst ~:** maim oneself

Verstümmelung *die;* **~, ~en** mutilation; (Selbst~) self-mutilation; (fig.: einer Meldung usw.) garbling

verstummen *itr. V.; mit sein* (geh.) fall silent; ‹*music, noise, conversation*› cease; (allmählich) die *or* fade away; (fig.) ‹*rumour, question*› go away; **er verstummte vor Schreck** he broke off, terrified; **jmdn. zum Verstummen bringen** silence sb.; **jeder Zweifel verstummte** (fig.) every doubt was stilled

Versuch *der;* **~[e]s, ~e** [1] attempt; **beim ~, etw. zu tun** in attempting to do sth.; **er hat es gleich beim ersten ~ geschafft** he made it *or* succeeded at the first attempt; **er hat schon mehrmals den ~ gemacht zu ...** he has already made several attempts to ...; **das käme auf einen ~ an** we'll have to try it and see; **einen ~ wäre es wert** it's worth a try; **ich will noch einen letzten ~ mit ihm/damit machen** I'd like to give him/it one more try [2] (Experiment) experiment (**an** + *Dat.* on); (Probe) test [3] (literarisches Produkt) attempt; **seine ersten lyrischen/literarischen ~e** his first attempts at poetry/literature; **„~ über das Schöne"** 'Essay on Beauty' [4] (Rugby) try; **einen ~ erzielen** *od.* **legen** score a try

versuchen

A *tr. V.* [1] try; attempt; **versuchs doch!** (drohend) just you try!; (ermunternd) just try it!; **es mit jmdm./etw. ~:** give sb./sth. a try; **es bei**

jmdm. ~: try sb.; **versuchter Mord** (Rechtsspr.) attempted murder; **lass mich mal ~, ob ...** (ugs.) let me [try and] see if ...; *s. auch* **Glück 1** **2** (auch bibl.: in Versuchung führen) tempt; **versucht sein, etw. zu tun** be tempted to do sth. **B** *tr., itr. V.* (probieren) **den Kuchen/von dem Kuchen ~:** try the cake/some of the cake **C** *refl. V.* **sich in/an etw.** (*Dat.*)**/auf einem Instrument/als etw. ~:** try one's hand at sth./at playing an instrument/at being sth.

Versucher *der;* **~s, ~, Versucherin** *die;* **~, ~nen** tempter

versuchs-, Versuchs-: ~anordnung *die* set-up for an/the experiment/for experiments; **~anstalt** *die* research institute; **~ballon** *der* **1** (Met.) sounding balloon; **2** (fig.) try-out; (Gerücht, Vorschlag usw.) feeler; **einen ~ballon [auf]steigen lassen** fly a kite (fig.); put out feelers (fig.); **~gelände** *das* testing ground; (für nukleare Waffen usw.) test site; **~kaninchen** *das* (fig.) guinea pig; **~person** *die* (bes. Med., Psych.) test *or* experimental subject; **~reihe** *die* series of experiments; (mit Waffen, Bomben) series of tests; **~stadium** *das* experimental stage; **~tier** *das* experimental animal; **~weise** **A** *Adv.* on a trial basis; as an experiment; **B** *adj.* experimental; **~zweck** *der* experimental purpose; **zu ~zwecken gehaltene Tiere** animals kept for experiments

Versuchung *die;* **~, ~en** temptation; **jmdn. in ~ führen** lead sb. into temptation (esp. Rel.); put sb. in the way of temptation; **in ~** (*Akk.*) **kommen** *od.* **geraten[, etw. zu tun]** be *or* feel tempted [to do sth.]

versumpfen *itr. V.* **1** become marshy *or* boggy; **versumpft** marshy; boggy **2** (ugs. abwertend: verwahrlosen) go to seed *or* to the dogs **3** (ugs.; lange bleiben und trinken) stay out late boozing (coll.)

versündigen *refl. V.* **sich an jmdm./etw. ~:** sin against sb./sth.; **sich an seiner Gesundheit ~:** abuse one's health; **versündige dich nicht!** (als Antwort) what a [wicked] thing to say/do!

Versunkenheit *die;* **~** (geh.) [state of] contemplation; deep meditation; **in seiner ~ hatte er ihr Kommen gar nicht bemerkt** he was so deep in thought *or* so engrossed that he had not noticed her coming

versüßen *tr. V.* **jmdm./sich etw. ~** (fig.) make sth. more pleasant for sb./oneself; (erträglicher machen) make sth. more bearable for sb./oneself

vertäfeln *tr. V.* panel

Vertäfelung *die;* **~, ~en** panelling

vertagen
A *tr. V.* adjourn ‹*meeting, debate, etc.*› (**auf** + *Akk.* until); postpone ‹*decision, verdict*› (**auf** + *Akk.* until)
B *refl. V.* ‹*court*› adjourn; ‹*meeting*› be adjourned

vertändeln *tr. V.* (auch Sport) fritter away ‹*time, chance*›

vertäuen /fɛɐ̯ˈtɔyən/ *tr. V.* (Seemannsspr.) moor

vertauschen *tr. V.* **1** exchange; switch; reverse, switch ‹*roles*›; reverse, transpose ‹*poles*›; **etw. mit** *od.* **gegen etw. ~:** exchange sth. for sth.; **die Kanzel mit dem Ministersessel ~:** exchange the pulpit for a ministerial post; **die Buchstaben eines Wortes ~:** transpose *or* switch round the letters in a word **2** (verwechseln) mix up

Vertauschung *die;* **~, ~en** **1** exchange; (von Buchstaben, Polen usw.) transposition; (von Rollen) reversal; switching **2** (Verwechslung) mixing up; **eine ~:** a mix-up

Vertäuung *die;* **~, ~en** (Seemannsspr.) mooring

verteidigen /fɛɐ̯ˈtaidɪgn̩/
A *tr. V.* defend; **der Angeklagte wird sich selbst ~:** the accused will conduct his own defence
B *itr. V.* (Ballspiele) defend; (Verteidiger sein) be a defender

Verteidiger *der;* **~s, ~, Verteidigerin,** *die;* **~, ~nen** **1** (auch Sport) defender; **[als] ~ spielen** (Sport) play as a defender **2** (Rechtsw.) defence counsel

Verteidigung *die;* **~, ~en** (auch Sport, Rechtsw.) defence; **zur ~ seiner Meinung/der Stadt bereit sein** be ready to defend one's opinion/the town; **jmdn. in die ~ drängen** force sb. on [to] the defensive

Verteidigungs-: ~bereitschaft *die* readiness to defend; **~bündnis** *das* defensive alliance; **~drittel** *das* (Eishockey) defence zone; **~haushalt** *der* defence budget; **~minister** *der,* **~ministerin** *die* minister of defence; **~ministerium** *das* ministry of defence; **~rede** *die* (vor Gericht) speech for the defence; (Apologie) apologia; **~waffe** *die* defensive weapon

verteilen
A *tr. V.* **1** (austeilen) distribute, hand out ‹*exercise books, leaflets, prizes, etc.*› (**an** + *Akk.* to, **unter** + *Akk.* among); share [out], distribute ‹*money, food*› (**an** + *Akk.* to, **unter** + *Akk.* among); allocate ‹*work*›; cast, allocate ‹*parts*›; **Karten an die Spieler ~:** deal out cards to the players; **ein Drama mit verteilten Rollen lesen** read a play with each part allocated to a different person **2** (an verschiedene Plätze bringen) distribute ‹*weight etc.*› (**auf** + *Akk.* over); spread ‹*cost*› (**auf** + *Akk.* among); distribute, spread out ‹*cushions etc.*›; **Flüchtlinge auf drei Lager ~:** divide up refugees and send them to three camps **3** (verstreichen, verstreuen, verrühren usw.) distribute, spread ‹*butter, seed, dirt, etc.*›
B *refl. V.* **1** spread out **2** (sich ausbreiten, verteilt sein) be distributed (**auf** + *Akk.* over)

Verteiler *der;* **~s, ~** **1** (Person) distributor **2** (Technik: Zündverteiler) distributor **3** (Bürow.) distribution list; **„~"** 'copies to'

Verteilerin *die;* **~, ~nen** ▸ **Verteiler 1**

Verteiler·schlüssel *der* (Bürow.) distribution list

Verteilung *die* distribution; (der Rollen, der Arbeit) allocation; **etw. zur ~ bringen** (Papierdt.) distribute sth.; **zur ~ kommen** *od.* **gelangen** (Papierdt.) be distributed

Verteilungs·kampf *der* (Jargon) fight over a/the share-out

vertelefonieren *tr. V.* (ugs.) spend ‹*time*› telephoning *or* on the phone; spend ‹*money*› on telephoning

verteuern
A *tr. V.* make ‹*goods*› more expensive
B *refl. V.* become more expensive; **die Lebenshaltung verteuert sich** the cost of living is going up

Verteuerung *die* increase *or* rise in price; **die ~ des Kaffees** the increase in the price of coffee

verteufeln *tr. V.* condemn; denigrate

verteufelt
A *Adj.* (ugs.) **1** (verzwickt) extremely tricky ‹*situation, business*› **2** (äußerst) fiendish ‹*thirst, pain, etc*›
B *adv.* (ugs.) damned; fiendishly ‹*cold*›; terribly (coll.) ‹*similar*›; **~!** damn!

Verteufelung *die;* **~, ~en** condemnation; denigration

verticken *tr. V.* (ugs.) peddle, flog (Brit. coll.) (**an** + *Akk.* to)

vertiefen
A *tr. V.* **1** deepen (**um** by); make deeper; **eine vertiefte Stelle** a depression; a hollow **2** (intensivieren) deepen ‹*knowledge, understanding, love*›; deepen, strengthen ‹*dislike, friendship, collaboration, etc.*›; **ein vertieftes Verständnis** a deeper understanding
B *refl. V.* **1** deepen; become deeper **2** (sich konzentrieren) **sich ~ in** (+ *Akk.*) bury oneself in ‹*book, work, etc.*›; become deeply involved in ‹*conversation*›; **in etw.** (*Akk.*) **vertieft sein** be engrossed *or* absorbed in sth.; **in Gedanken vertieft** deep in thought **3** (intensiver werden) ‹*friendship*› deepen; ‹*relations*› become closer; ‹*hate, conflict*› deepen, become more intense

Vertiefung *die;* **~, ~en** **1** deepening; (von Freundschaft, Abneigung) deepening; strengthening; (von Zusammenarbeit, Beziehungen) strengthening; (von Wissen) consolidation; reinforcement; (von Hass, Konflikten) intensification **2** (in Gedanken) absorption (**in** + *Akk.* in) **3** (Mulde) depression; hollow

vertieren *itr. V.; mit sein* become brutalized; **vertiert** brutalized

vertikal /vɛrtiˈkaːl/
A *Adj.* vertical; **in ~er Richtung** vertically
B *adv.* vertically

Vertikale *die;* **~, ~n** **1** (Linie) vertical line **2** (Lage) **die ~:** the vertical *or* perpendicular; **etw. in die ~ bringen** *od.* **bewegen** move sth. into a vertical position

Vertiko /ˈvɛrtiko/ *das, auch der;* **~s, ~s** *small decorated cabinet with a drawer and display shelf on top*

vertilgen *tr. V.* **1** (vernichten) exterminate ‹*vermin*›; kill off ‹*weeds*› **2** (ugs.: verzehren) devour, (joc.) demolish ‹*food*›

Vertilgung *die;* **~, ~en** **1** (von Ungeziefer) extermination; (von Unkraut) killing off **2** (ugs.: das Verzehren) demolition (joc.)

Vertilgungs·mittel *das* (gegen Unkraut) weed-killer; (gegen Insekten) pesticide

vertippen
A *refl. V.* **1** make a typing mistake/typing mistakes; (auf der Rechenmaschine, dem Tastentelefon usw.) press the wrong number **2** (im Lotto, Toto, bei Vorhersagen) get it wrong
B *tr. V.* mistype ‹*word*›; type ‹*word, letter*› wrongly; (auf der Rechenmaschine, dem Tastentelefon usw.) get ‹*number*› wrong

vertonen *tr. V.* set ‹*text, poem*› to music; set, write the music to ‹*libretto*›; add sound to ‹*slides*›; add a soundtrack to ‹*film*›

Vertonung *die;* **~, ~en** **1** setting [to music]; **die ~ eines Librettos** writing the music to a libretto; **die ~ von Dias/eines Films** adding sound to slides/a soundtrack to a film **2** (Werk) setting

vertrackt /fɛɐ̯ˈtrakt/ *Adj.* (ugs.) **1** complicated, involved ‹*situation, business, etc.*›; tricky, intricate ‹*job*› **2** (ärgerlich) confounded; infuriating; **das ~e Gefühl haben, dass ...** have a nasty feeling that ...

Vertracktheit *die;* **~, ~en** (ugs.) **1** complexity **2** (Ärgerlichkeit) maddening *or* infuriating nature

Vertrag *der;* **~[e]s, Verträge** /...trɛːgə/ contract; (zwischen Staaten) treaty; **mündlicher ~:** verbal agreement; **laut ~:** according to the terms of the contract; **ein ~ auf drei Jahre** a three-year contract; **jmdn. unter ~ nehmen** contract sb.; put sb. under contract; **[bei jmdm.] unter ~ stehen** be under contract [to sb.]; **der ~ von Rom** the Treaty of Rome

vertragen
A *unr. tr. V.* **1** endure; tolerate (esp. Med.); (aushalten, leiden können) stand; bear; take ‹*joke, criticism, climate, etc.*›; **die Pflanze verträgt keinen Zug/kann Sonne ~:** the plant will not tolerate draughts/can tolerate some sun; **Rauch/Lärm/Belastungen/Aufregung schlecht ~:** not be able to stand too much smoke/noise/strain/excitement; **das Klima [nicht] gut ~:** [not] be able to take the climate; **ich vertrage keinen Kaffee/kein fettes Essen** coffee/fatty food disagrees with me; **den Wein/das Medikament habe ich gut ~:** I was able to drink the wine/take the medicine with no ill effects; **sie verträgt dieses Medikament schlecht/nicht** this medicine doesn't really agree with her/does not agree with her at all; **ich könnte jetzt einen Whisky ~** (ugs.) I could do with *or* wouldn't say no to a whisky; **er verträgt eine Menge [Alkohol]/nichts/nicht viel** (ugs.) he can hold a lot of drink (coll.)/can't hold his drink/can't hold much drink; **er verträgt keine Kritik/keinen Spaß** he cannot take criticism/a joke; **ich kann alles ~, nur nicht das** I can put up with anything but not that; **die Sache verträgt keinen Aufschub** (geh.) the matter brooks no delay **2** (landsch.: abtragen) wear out
B *unr. refl. V.* **1** **sich mit jmdm. ~:** get on *or* along with sb.; **sich gut [miteinander] ~:** get on well together; **er verträgt sich mit keinem** he never gets on with anybody; **sie ~ sich wieder** they are friends again; they have made it up; **wir wollen uns wieder ~:** let's make it up *or* let bygones be bygones; **so Kinder, nun vertragt euch wieder** come on children, stop

squabbling and call a truce; *s. auch* **Pack**[2] 2 (passen) **sich mit etw. ~:** go with sth.; **die Farben ~ sich nicht [miteinander]** the colours do not go together; **wie verträgt sich das mit seinen christlichen Überzeugungen** how does this square with his Christian convictions?; **so ein Verhalten verträgt sich nicht mit seinem liberalen Anspruch** such behaviour is not consistent with his liberal pretensions

vertraglich
A *Adj.* contractual
B *adv.* contractually; by contract

verträglich /fɛɐ̯ˈtrɛːklɪç/ *Adj.* 1 digestible ‹*food*›; **leicht/schwer ~:** easily digestible/indigestible; **ein gut ~es Medikament** a drug which has no side effects 2 (umgänglich) good-natured; easy to get on with *pred.*

Verträglichkeit *die;* **~, ~en** 1 digestibility; **die ~ eines Medikaments** a drug's lack of side effects 2 (Umgänglichkeit) good nature

vertrags-, Vertrags-: ~abschluss, ***~abschluß** *der* completion of [a/the] contract; **~bruch** *der* breach of contract; **~brüchig** *Adj.* in breach of contract *postpos.;* **~brüchig werden/sein** be in breach of contract

vertrag·schließend *Adj.* contracting

vertrags-, Vertrags-: ~entwurf *der* draft contract/treaty; **~gemäß** *adv.* as per contract; as stipulated in the contract; **~händler** *der,* **~händlerin** *die* authorized *or* appointed dealer; **~partei** *die* party to a/the contract; contracting party; **~partner** *der,* **~partnerin** *die* party to a/the contract; **unser ~partner** our contractual partner; **~schluss,** ***~schluß** *der* ▸**~abschluss**; **~spieler** *der,* **~spielerin** *die* (Fußball) semi-professional (*under contract to a club*); **~werk** *das* major agreement; (international) treaty; **~werkstatt** *die* authorized garage

vertrauen *itr. V.* **jmdm./einer Sache ~:** trust sb./sth.; **auf etw.** (*Akk.*) **~:** [put one's] trust in sth.; **auf sein Glück ~:** trust to luck; **ich vertraue darauf, dass ...** I am confident *or* have confidence that ...; **auf Gott ~:** put one's trust in God

Vertrauen *das;* **~s** trust; confidence; **~ zu jmdm./etw. haben/fassen** have/come to have confidence in sb./sth.; trust/come to trust sb./sth.; **er hat kein ~ zu sich selbst** he has no confidence in himself *or* self-confidence; **er hat mein volles ~:** I have complete confidence in him; **jmdm. [sein] ~ schenken** put one's trust in sb.; **jmdm. das** *od.* **sein ~ entziehen** withdraw the trust *or* confidence one has/had [placed] in sb.; **jmds. ~ enttäuschen/erschüttern** betray sb.'s trust/destroy sb.'s confidence [in one]; **das Parlament sprach dem Kanzler das ~ aus** parliament passed a vote of confidence in the Chancellor; **sein ~ in jmdn./etw. setzen** put *or* place one's trust in sb./sth.; **sein** *od.* **das ~ zu jmdm. verlieren** lose confidence in sb.; **im ~ [gesagt]** [strictly] in confidence; between you and me; **im ~ auf etw.** (*Akk.*) trusting to *or* in sth.; **im ~ darauf, dass ...** trusting that ...; **ein Mann seines ~s** a man whom he trusts; **jmdn. ins ~ ziehen** take sb. into one's confidence

vertrauen·erweckend *Adj.* inspiring *or* that inspires confidence *postpos.;* **einen ~en Eindruck machen** inspire confidence [by one's/it's appearance]; look trustworthy

vertrauens-, Vertrauens-: ~arzt *der,* **~ärztin** *die* independent examining doctor (*working for health service, health insurance, etc.*); **~beweis** *der* show of confidence (**für** in); **~bildend** *Adj.* **~bildende Maßnahmen** measures designed to build up trust; **~bruch** *der* breach of trust; (wenn man Vertrauliches weitersagt) breach of confidence; **~frage** *die* (Parl.) question of confidence; **die ~frage stellen** ask for a vote of confidence; **~frau** *die* 1 spokeswoman (*Gen.* for); representative; 2 (in der Gewerkschaft) [union] representative; (in einer Fabrik o. Ä.) shop steward; **~krise** *die* crisis of confidence; **~lehrer** *der,* **~lehrerin** *die* (Schulw.) liaison teacher (liaising between staff and pupils); **~mann** *der* 1 *Pl.* **~männer** *od.* **~leute** spokesman (*Gen.* for); representative; 2 *Pl.* **~leute** (in der Gewerkschaft) [union] representative; (in einer Fabrik o. Ä.) shop steward; **~person** *die* person in a position of trust; **~sache** *die* matter *or* question of trust; **~sache sein** be a matter *or* question of trust; **~selig** *Adj.* all too trustful *or* trusting; **~seligkeit** *die* excessive trustfulness; **~stellung** *die* position of trust; **~verhältnis** *das* relationship based on trust; **~voll** A *Adj.* trusting ‹*relationship*›; ‹*collaboration, cooperation*› based on trust; (zuversichtlich) confident; B *adv.* trustingly; (zuversichtlich) confidently; **sich ~voll an jmdn. wenden** turn to sb. with complete confidence; **~würdig** *Adj.* trustworthy; **~würdigkeit** *die* trustworthiness

vertrauern *tr. V.* (geh.) spend ‹*time*› in grieving

vertraulich
A *Adj.* 1 confidential 2 (freundschaftlich, intim) familiar ‹*manner, tone, etc.*›; intimate ‹*mood, conversation, whisper*›; **er wird gleich ~:** he gets familiar straight away
B *adv.* 1 confidentially; in confidence 2 (freundschaftlich, intim) in a familiar way; familiarly

Vertraulichkeit *die;* **~, ~en** 1 confidentiality 2 (vertrauliche Information) confidence 3 (distanzloses Verhalten) familiarity; (Intimität) intimacy 4 (vertrauliche Handlung) act of familiarity; (Äußerung) familiar remark

verträumen *tr. V.* [day]dream away ‹*time*›

verträumt
A *Adj.* dreamy; **sie ist zu ~:** she lives too much in a world of dreams
B *adv.* dreamily; idyllically ‹*situated*›

Verträumtheit *die;* **~:** dreaminess; (idyllischer Charakter) idyllic nature

vertraut /fɛɐ̯ˈtraut/ *Adj.* 1 close ‹*friend etc.*›; intimate ‹*circle, conversation, etc.*›; **sie sind sehr/ein wenig ~ miteinander** they are very close/quite friendly; **mit jmdm. ~ werden** become very friendly *or* close friends with sb.; **auf ~em Fuße** on intimate terms 2 (bekannt) familiar; **jmdm. ~ sein/werden** be/become familiar to sb.; **er ist mit Pferden ~:** he knows about horses; **mit etw. gut/wenig ~ sein** be well acquainted/have little knowledge of sth.; **jmdn./sich mit etw. ~ machen** familiarize sb./oneself with sth.; **mit diesem Gedanken solltest du dich ~ machen** you should get used to this idea

Vertraute *der/die; adj. Dekl.* close friend; **enger ~r** intimate friend

Vertrautheit *die;* **~** ▸**vertraut**: closeness; intimacy; familiarity

vertreiben *unr. tr. V.* 1 drive out (**aus** of); (wegjagen) drive away ‹*animal, smoke, clouds, etc.*› (**aus** from); **aus der Heimat vertrieben werden** be driven out of *or* expelled from one's homeland; **die vertriebenen Juden** the exiled *or* expelled Jews; **von Haus und Hof vertrieben werden** be turned out of house and home; **jmdn. aus seinem Amt ~:** oust sb. from office; **jmdn. [von seinem Platz] ~:** take sb.'s seat; **bleiben Sie doch ruhig sitzen, ich wollte Sie nicht ~:** please don't get up, I didn't mean to take your place *or* chase you away; **die Müdigkeit/Sorgen ~** (fig.) fight off tiredness/drive troubles away; *s. auch* **Zeit 1** 2 (verkaufen) sell

Vertreibung *die;* **~, ~en** driving out; (das Wegjagen) driving away; (aus dem Amt) ousting; (aus der Heimat) expulsion

vertretbar *Adj.* defensible ‹*risk etc.*›; tenable, defensible ‹*standpoint*›; justifiable ‹*costs*›

vertreten
A *unr. tr. V.* 1 stand in *or* deputize for ‹*colleague etc.*›; ‹*teacher*› cover for ‹*colleague*›; **er lässt sich von seinem Staatssekretär ~:** he is sending his permanent secretary as his representative 2 (eintreten für, repräsentieren) represent ‹*person, firm, interests, constituency, country, etc.*›; (Rechtsw.) act for ‹*person, prosecution, etc.*›; **er lässt sich durch einen Anwalt ~:** he is getting a lawyer to act for him; **den Fall vertritt Rechtsanwalt Müller** the lawyer defending the case is Müller; **~ sein** be represented (**mit, durch** by); (anwesend sein) be present; **schwach/stark ~:** poorly/well represented 3 (einstehen für, verfechten) support ‹*point of view, principle*›; hold ‹*opinion*›; advocate ‹*thesis etc.*›; pursue ‹*policy*›; **er vertritt den Standpunkt** *od.* **die Meinung, dass ...** he takes *or* holds the view that ...; **etw. zu ~ haben** be responsible for sth. 4 **jmdm. den Weg ~:** bar sb's way
B *unr. refl. V.* **sich** (*Dat.*) **den Fuß ~:** twist one's ankle; **sich** (*Dat.*) **die Füße** *od.* **Beine ~** (ugs.: sich Bewegung verschaffen) stretch one's legs

Vertreter *der;* **~s, ~** 1 (Stell~) deputy; stand-in; (eines Arztes) locum (coll.) 2 ▸ **S. 113** (Interessen~, Repräsentant) representative; (Handels~) sales representative; commercial traveller; **ein ~ für Staubsauger** a traveller in vacuum cleaners; **Hoher ~ in für die GASP** High Representative of the CFSP 3 (Verfechter, Anhänger) supporter; advocate 4 (ugs. abwertend: Kerl, Bursche) **du bist ein übler/sauberer ~!** you're a nasty piece of work (coll.)/a fine one! (iron.)

Vertreterin *die;* **~, ~nen** ▸**Vertreter 1-3**

Vertretung *die;* **~, ~en** 1 deputizing; **jmds. ~ übernehmen** stand in *or* deputize for sb.; ‹*doctor*› act as locum for sb. (coll.); **in ~ von Herrn N.** in place of *or* standing in for Mr. N.; **in ~ unterschreiben** sign as a proxy; **in ~ M. Schmidt** (am Schluss eines Briefes usw.) p.p. M. Schmidt 2 (Vertreter[in]) deputy; stand-in; (eines Arztes) locum (coll.); **ich brauche für morgen eine ~:** I need somebody to take my place *or* stand in for me tomorrow; (als Lehrer) I need cover for tomorrow 3 (Delegierte[r]) representative; (Delegation) delegation; **eine diplomatische ~:** a diplomatic mission; **die deutsche ~** (Sport) the German team *or* squad 4 (Handels~) [sales] agency; (Niederlassung) agency; branch 5 (Interessen~) representation 6 (Verfechtung) advocacy

Vertretungs·stunde *die* (Schulw.) cover lesson

vertretungs·weise *Adv.* as a [temporary] replacement *or* stand-in

Vertrieb *der* 1 sale; marketing 2 (Abteilung) sales [department]

Vertriebene *der/die; adj. Dekl.* expellee [from his/her homeland]

Vertriebs-: ~gesellschaft *die* sales *or* marketing company; **~kanal** *der* sales channel; **~weg** *der* sales medium

vertrimmen *tr. V.* (ugs.) wallop (coll.)

vertrinken *unr. tr. V.* spend ‹*money*› on drink

vertrocknen *itr. V.; mit sein* dry up; (fig.) ‹*person*› wither, shrivel up

vertrödeln *tr. V.* (ugs. abwertend) dawdle away, waste ‹*time*›

vertrösten *tr. V.* put ‹*person*› off (**auf** + *Akk.* until)

Vertröstung *die* prevarication

vertrotteln *itr. V.; mit sein* go gaga (coll.); **vertrottelt** gaga

vertun
A *unr. tr. V.* waste; **die Mühe war vertan** it was a waste of effort
B *unr. refl. V.* (ugs.) make a slip; **wenn du dich da mal nicht vertust!** I think you're a bit wide of the mark there

vertuschen *tr. V.* hush up ‹*scandal etc.*›; keep ‹*truth etc.*› secret

Vertuschung *die;* **~, ~en** hushing up; **eine ~:** a hush-up *or* cover-up

verübeln *tr. V.* **jmdm. eine Äußerung** *usw.* **~:** take sb.'s remark *etc.* amiss; **Sie werden es mir nicht ~, wenn ich ...** I hope you won't take it amiss *or* mind if I ...; **das kann man ihm kaum ~:** one can hardly blame him for that

verüben *tr. V.* commit ‹*crime etc.*›; **Streiche ~:** get up to pranks

verulken *tr. V.* (ugs.) make fun of; take the mickey out of (Brit. coll); **du willst mich wohl ~!** you're pulling my leg (coll.)

verunfallen *itr. V.; mit sein* (Amtsspr., bes. schweiz.) have an accident

V

Verunfallte *der/die; adj. Dekl.* (Amtsspr., bes. schweiz.) accident victim

verunglimpfen /fɛɐ̯ˈlʊnglɪmpfn̩/ *tr. V.* (geh.) denigrate ‹*person, etc.*›; sully ‹*honour, name, memory*›

Verunglimpfung *die;* ~, ~**en** (geh.) ▸ **verunglimpfen**: denigration; sullying

verunglücken *itr. V.; mit sein* **1** have an accident; ‹*car etc.*› be involved in an accident; **mit dem Auto/Flugzeug ~:** be in a car/an air accident *or* crash; **beim Segeln ~:** have a sailing accident *or* an accident while sailing; **der verunglückte Fahrer** the driver involved in the accident **2** (scherzh.: misslingen) go wrong; ‹*attempt*› fail; ‹*cake, sauce, etc.*› be a disaster; **verunglückt** unsuccessful

Verunglückte *der/die; adj. Dekl.* accident victim; casualty

verunklaren, (bes. Schweiz) **verunklären** *tr. V.* make unclear

verunmöglichen /*od.* --ˈ---/ *tr. V.* (bes. schweiz.) **[jmdm.] etw. ~:** make sth. impossible [for sb.]

verunreinigen
A *tr. V.* **1** pollute; contaminate ‹*water, milk, flour, oil*›; ~**de Stoffe** pollutants/contaminants **2** (geh.: beschmutzen) dirty, soil ‹*clothes, floor, etc.*›; (durch Fäkalien) foul ‹*pavement etc.*›
B *refl. V.* (verhüll.) soil oneself

Verunreinigung *die* **1** pollution; (von Wasser, Milch, Mehl, Öl) contamination **2** (Stoff) pollutant/contaminant **3** (von Kleidern, Fußböden usw.) soiling; (von Straßen usw.) fouling

verunsichern *tr. V.* **jmdn. ~:** make sb. feel unsure *or* uncertain; (sodass er sich gefährdet fühlt) undermine sb.'s sense of security; **verunsichert** insecure; (nicht selbstsicher) unsure of oneself

Verunsicherung *die* **1** (das Verunsichern) **die argumentative ~ der Richter** making the judges uncertain by means of argument; **zur ~ der Bevölkerung dienen** serve to undermine the people's sense of security **2** (Unsicherheit) [feeling of] insecurity

verunstalten /fɛɐ̯ˈlʊnʃtaltn̩/ *tr. V.* disfigure; **du verunstaltest dich mit dieser Frisur** this hairstyle spoils your looks *or* makes you look terrible

Verunstaltung *die;* ~, ~**en** disfigurement

veruntreuen *tr. V.* embezzle

Veruntreuung *die;* ~, ~**en** embezzlement

verunzieren *tr. V.* spoil the look of

verursachen *tr. V.* cause; **es hat ihm viel Arbeit verursacht** it caused *or* gave him a great deal of work

Verursacher *der;* ~**s**, ~, **Verursacherin** *die;* ~, ~**nen** cause; person responsible; **der ~ des Unfalls** the person responsible for the accident

Verursacher·prinzip *das: principle that the person who causes damage must bear the cost*

Verursachung *die;* ~: causing

verurteilen *tr. V.* **1** pass sentence on; sentence; **jmdn. zu Gefängnis** *od.* **einer Haftstrafe/drei Monaten Haft ~:** sentence sb. to imprisonment/to three months' imprisonment; **jmdn. zu einer Geldstrafe ~:** impose a fine on sb.; **jmdn. zum Tode ~:** sentence *or* condemn sb. to death; **jmdn. wegen Diebstahl** *usw.* **~:** sentence sb. for theft *etc.*; **der zum Tode Verurteilte** the condemned man; **zum Scheitern verurteilt sein** (fig.) be condemned to failure *or* bound to fail; **zum Schweigen verurteilt sein** (fig.) be condemned to silence **2** (fig.; negativ bewerten) condemn ‹*behaviour, action*›

Verurteilte *der/die; adj. Dekl.* convicted man/woman

Verurteilung *die;* ~, ~**en** **1** sentencing; **eine ~ zu fünf Jahren Zuchthaus** a sentence of five years' imprisonment **2** (fig.) condemnation

veruzen *tr. V.* (ugs.) ▸ **verulken**

Verve /ˈvɛrvə/ *die;* ~ (geh.) enthusiasm; verve; **mit ~:** enthusiastically

vervielfachen
A *tr. V.* greatly increase; (multiplizieren) multiply ‹*number*›; **wir müssen unsere Anstrengungen ~:** we must redouble our efforts
B *refl. V.* multiply [several times]; (fig.) ‹*efforts*› be redoubled

Vervielfachung *die;* ~, ~**en** multiplication; (fig.: der Anstrengungen) redoubling

vervielfältigen *tr. V.* duplicate, make copies of ‹*document etc.*›

Vervielfältigung *die;* ~, ~**en** **1** duplicating; copying **2** (Kopie) copy

Vervielfältigungs·zahlwort *das* (Sprachw.) multiplicative

vervollkommnen /fɛɐ̯ˈfɔlkɔmnən/
A *tr. V.* perfect
B *refl. V.* become perfected

Vervollkommnung *die;* ~, ~**en** perfecting; (Zustand) perfection

vervollständigen
A *tr. V.* complete; (vollständiger machen) make ‹*library etc.*› more complete
B *refl. V.* become complete/more complete

Vervollständigung *die;* ~, ~**en** completion/making more complete

verwachsen[1] *Adj.* deformed

verwachsen[2] *unr. itr. V.; mit sein* **1** ‹*wound, scab*› heal [up *or* over] **2** (zusammenwachsen) grow together (**mit** with); **zu etw. ~:** grow together to form sth.; grow into sth. **3** (fig.) grow closer (**mit** to); **zu einer Gemeinschaft ~:** grow into a community; **sich mit seiner Umwelt ~ fühlen** feel at one with one's environment

Verwachsung *die;* ~, ~**en** deformity

verwackeln (ugs.)
A *tr. V.* make ‹*picture*› blurred; **verwackelt** blurred; shaky
B *itr. V.; mit sein* turn out blurred

verwählen *refl. V.* misdial; dial the wrong number

verwahren
A *tr. V.* **1** keep [safe]; (verstauen) put away [safely] **2** (gefangen halten) detain, hold ‹*person*›
B *refl. V.* protest

verwahrlosen *itr. V.; mit sein* **1** get in a bad state; ‹*house, building*› fall into disrepair, become dilapidated; ‹*garden, hedge*› grow wild, become overgrown; ‹*person*› let oneself go, (coll.) go to pot; **etw. ~ lassen** neglect sth.; allow sth. to get in a bad state; **verwahrlost** neglected; overgrown ‹*hedge, garden*›; dilapidated ‹*house, building*›; unkempt ‹*person, appearance, etc.*›; (in der Kleidung) ragged ‹*person*› **2** (sittlich ~) fall into bad ways; **[sittlich] verwahrlost** depraved

Verwahrlosung *die;* ~ (eines Gebäudes) dilapidation; (einer Person) advancing decrepitude; (sittliche ~) decline into depravity; **[Zustand der] ~:** state of dilapidation/decrepitude/depravity

Verwahrung *die* **1** keeping [in a safe place]; **etw. in ~ geben/nehmen/haben** give/take sth. into safe keeping/hold sth. in safe keeping; **jmdm. etw. in ~ geben** give sth. to sb. for safe keeping **2** (Arrest) detention *no def. art.* **3** (Einspruch, Protest) protest

verwaisen *itr. V.* be orphaned; become an orphan; **verwaist** orphaned ‹*child*›; (fig.) lonely, deserted ‹*person, place*›; unoccupied ‹*house*›; vacant ‹*professorship*›

verwalken *tr. V.* (ugs.) ▸ **vertrimmen**

verwalten *tr. V.* **1** (betreuen) administer, manage ‹*estate, property, etc.*›; run, look after ‹*house*›; hold ‹*money*› in trust **2** (leiten) run, manage ‹*hostel, kindergarten, etc.*›; (regieren) administer ‹*area, colony, etc.*›; govern ‹*country*›; **die Kanalinseln ~ sich selbst** the Channel Islands are self-governing **3** (versehen) hold ‹*office*›; carry out, perform ‹*task, duty*› **4** (bürokratisch beherrschen) **eine verwaltete Gesellschaft** a bureaucratized society

Verwalter *der;* ~**s**, ~, **Verwalterin** *die;* ~, ~**nen** administrator; (eines Amts usw.) manager; (eines Nachlasses) trustee

Verwaltung *die;* ~, ~**en** **1** (Betreuung, Leitung) administration; management; **etw. unter staatliche ~ stellen** put sth. under State control; **in eigener ~:** under one's own control **2** (eines Gebiets) administration; (eines Landes) government; **unter britischer ~:** under British administration *or* rule **3** (eines Amtes) tenure; (einer Aufgabe) performance **4** (Organ, Behörde, Apparat) administration; (eines Betriebes) management; **die öffentliche/staatliche ~:** the public/state authority

Verwaltungs-: ~apparat *der* administrative machine; **~beamte** *der,* **~beamtin** *die* administrative official; administrator; **~bezirk** *der* administrative district; **~gebühr** *die* administrative charge *or* fee; **~gericht** *das* administrative court; **~kosten** *Pl.* administrative costs; **~organ** *das* administrative organ; **~rat** *der* **1** governing body; administrative council; **2** (schweiz. Wirtsch.) board of directors

verwamsen /fɛɐ̯ˈvamzn̩/ *tr. V.* (ugs.) wallop (coll.) ‹*child*›

verwandelbar *Adj.* convertible

verwandeln
A *tr. V.* **1** convert (**in** + *Akk.*, **zu** into); (völlig verändern) transform (**in** + *Akk.*, **zu** into); **er ist/ich fühlte mich wie verwandelt** he's/I felt a different person *or* transformed; **das Sofa lässt sich in ein Bett ~:** the sofa can be converted into a bed; **der Prinz wurde in einen Frosch verwandelt** the prince was turned *or* transformed into a frog **2** (Ballspiele) score from ‹*corner, free kick*›; convert ‹*penalty*›
B *refl. V.* **sich in etw.** (*Akk.*) *od.* **zu etw. ~:** turn *or* change into sth.; (bei chemischen Vorgängen usw.) be converted into sth.; **die Raupe verwandelt sich in einen Schmetterling** the caterpillar metamorphoses into a butterfly
C *itr. V.* (Ballspiele) **er verwandelte [zum 2:0]** he scored [to make it 2-0]

Verwandlung *die;* ~, ~**en** **1** (das Verwandeln) conversion (**in** + *Akk.*, **zu** into); (völlige Veränderung) transformation (**in** + *Akk.*, **zu** into) **2** (das Sichverwandeln) transformation; (Metamorphose) metamorphosis

Verwandlungs·künstler *der,* **Verwandlungs·künstlerin** *die* quick-change artist

verwandt[1] /fɛɐ̯ˈvant/ *2. Part. v.* **verwenden**

verwandt[2] *Adj.* **1** (auch fachspr.) related (**mit** to); **mit jmdm.** *od.* (schweiz.) **jmdm. ~ sein** be related to sb. **2** (fig.: ähnlich) similar ‹*views, ideas, forms*›

Verwandte *der/die; adj. Dekl.* relative; relation

Verwandten·besuch *der* (Besuch bei Verwandten) visit to relatives; (Besuch von Verwandten) visit from *or* by relatives; **einen ~ machen** visit relatives; **wir erwarten ~:** we are expecting relatives

Verwandtschaft *die;* ~, ~**en** **1** relationship (**mit** to); (fig.; Ähnlichkeit) affinity; **zwischen ihnen besteht keine ~:** they are not related [to one another] **2** (Verwandte) relatives *pl.*; relations *pl.*; **die ganze ~:** all one's relatives; **eine große ~ haben** have a large number of relatives; **zur ~ gehören** be one of the family

verwandtschaftlich
A *Adj.* family ‹*ties, relationships, etc.*›
B *adv.* **~ miteinander verbunden sein** be related [to each other]

Verwandtschafts-: ~grad *der* degree of relationship; **~verhältnis** *das* family relationship; **in einem ~verhältnis zu jmdm. stehen** be related to sb.

verwanzen
A *itr. V.; mit sein* **verwanzt** bug-ridden
B *tr. V.* (fig.) bug

verwarnen *tr. V.* warn, caution (**wegen** for)

Verwarnung *die;* ~, ~**en** warning; caution

verwaschen *Adj.* **1** washed out, faded ‹*jeans, material, inscription, etc.*› **2** (blass) washy, watery ‹*colour*›; blurred ‹*lines, contours*› **3** (fig.) wishy-washy ‹*idea, formulation*›

verwässern *tr. V.* (auch fig.) water down; **verwässert schmecken** taste watery

Verwässerung *die* (auch fig.) watering down

verweben
A *tr. V.* **1** weave with; use [for weaving] **2** *auch*

unr. **[miteinander] ~:** interweave ‹*threads*›; **etw. in etw.** (*Akk.*) **~** (auch fig.) weave sth. into sth.; **mit etw. verwoben** (fig.) bound *or* caught up with sth.
B *unr. refl. V.* (dichter.) **sich [zu etw.] ~:** become interwoven [to form *or* into sth.]

verwẹchselbar *Adj.* mistakable (**mit** for); **leicht ~:** easily confused (**mit** with)

verwẹchseln *tr. V.* **1** **[miteinander] ~:** confuse ‹*two things/people*›; **du musst da irgendetwas ~:** you must be getting mixed up; **er verwechselt immer rechts und links** he always gets mixed up between *or* mixes up right and left; **etw. mit etw./jmdn. mit jmdm. ~:** mistake sth. for sth./sb. for sb.; confuse sth. with sth./sb. with sb.; **Entschuldigung, ich habe Sie [mit jemandem] verwechselt/ich habe die Tür[en] verwechselt** sorry, I thought you were *or* I mistook you for somebody else/I've got the wrong door; **jmdm. zum V~ ähnlich sehen** be the spitting image of sb.; **leicht mit etw. zu ~ sein** be easily confused with sth.; **nicht zu ~ mit ...** not to be confused with ... **2** (vertauschen) mix up; **jemand hat meinen Regenschirm verwechselt** somebody has taken my umbrella by mistake

Verwẹchslung *die;* **~, ~en** **1** [case of] confusion; mistake; **um ~en auszuschließen** to avoid any possibility of confusion **2** (Vertauschung) mixing up; **eine ~:** a mix-up

verwegen
A *Adj.* daring; (auch fig.) audacious
B *adv.* (auch fig.) audaciously

Verwegenheit *die;* **~, ~en** **1** daring; (auch fig.) audacity **2** (Tat) act of daring

verwehen
A *tr. V.* **1** (zudecken) cover [over] ‹*track, path*›; **der Wind verwehte die Spur im Sand** the wind covered up the track in the sand; **vom Schnee verweht** covered in snow **2** (wegwehen) blow away; scatter; **vom Winde verweht** (fig.) gone with the wind
B *itr. V.; mit sein* (geh.) **im Wind ~:** drift away *or* be lost on the wind

verwehren *tr. V.* **jmdm. etw. ~:** refuse *or* deny sb. sth.; **jmdm. ~, etw. zu tun** bar sb. from doing sth.; (verbieten) forbid sb. to do sth.; **es verwehrt uns die Sicht** (fig.) it obstructs our view

Verwehung *die;* **~, ~en** [snow]drift

verweichlichen
A *itr. V.; mit sein* grow soft; **ein verweichlichter Mensch** a weakling
B *tr. V.* make soft; **ein verweichlichter Junge** a mollycoddled boy

Verweichlichung *die;* **~, ~en** **1** (Vorgang) **die ~ der Jugendlichen verhindern** prevent young people from becoming soft **2** (Zustand) softness; **eine solche Lebensweise führt zur ~:** this way of life makes one soft

Verweigerer *der;* **~s, ~, Verweigerin** *die;* **~, ~nen** **1** rebel; dissident **2** (des Kriegsdienstes usw.) objector (*Gen.* to)

verweigern
A *tr. V.* refuse; **jmdm. die Erlaubnis/eine Hilfeleistung ~:** refuse sb. permission/assistance; **„Annahme verweigert"** 'delivery refused'; **die Aussage/einen Befehl/die Nahrungsaufnahme ~:** refuse to make a statement/to obey an order/to take food; **den Kriegsdienst ~:** refuse to do military service; be a conscientious objector; **[jmdm.] den Gehorsam ~:** refuse to obey [sb.]; **ein Hindernis ~** (Pferdesport) refuse at a jump
B *refl. V.* object; refuse to cooperate; **sich jmdm./einer Sache ~:** refuse to accept sb./sth.; **sich der Gesellschaft ~:** contract out of society; **sich jmdm. [sexuell] ~** (geh.) refuse [to have sexual intercourse with] sb.
C *itr. V.* **1** (ugs.: den Kriegsdienst ~) refuse [to do military service]; be a conscientious objector **2** (Pferdesport) refuse

Verweigerung *die;* **~, ~en** refusal; (Protest) protest; **~ des Kriegsdienstes** refusal to do military service; conscientious objection

Verweigerungs·haltung *die* rejectionist stance

Verweil·dauer *die* length of stay; time spent (*Gen.* by); **die ~ der Speisen im Magen** the period during which food remains in the stomach

verweilen *itr. V.* (geh.) stay; (länger als nötig) linger; **verweile doch** tarry awhile (literary); **bei einem Thema/Gedanken ~** (fig.) dwell on a theme/thought

verweint /fɛɐ̯'vaint/ *Adj.* tear-stained ‹*face*›; ‹*eyes*› red with tears *or* from crying; ‹*person*› with a tear-stained face; **sie sah ~ aus/war ~:** she looked as if she had been crying/she had a tear-stained face

Verweis *der;* **~es, ~e** **1** reference (**auf** + *Akk.* to); (Quer~) cross reference **2** (Tadel) reprimand; rebuke; **jmdm. einen ~ erteilen** *od.* **aussprechen** reprimand *or* rebuke sb.

verweisen *unr. tr. V.* **1** **jmdn./einen Fall** *usw.* **an jmdn./etw. ~** (auch Rechtsspr.) refer sb./a case *etc.* to sb./sth. **2** (wegschicken) **jmdn. von der Schule/aus dem Saal ~:** expel sb. from the school/send sb. out of the room; **jmdn. des Landes ~:** exile *or* (Hist.) banish sb.; **einen Spieler vom Platz ~:** send a player off [the field] **3** (Sport) **jmdn. auf den zweiten Platz ~:** relegate sb. to *or* push sb. into second place **4** *auch itr.* (hinweisen) **[jmdn.] auf etw.** (*Akk.*) **~:** refer [sb.] to sth.; (durch Querverweis) cross-refer [sb.] to sth.

verwẹlken *itr. V.; mit sein* ‹*flower, leaf*› wilt; (fig.) ‹*fame*› fade; **verwelkt** wilted ‹*flowers*›; withered ‹*hands, face*›; (fig.) faded ‹*beauty*›

verwẹltlichen
A *tr. V.* secularize
B *itr. V.; mit sein* (geh.) become worldly *or* secularized

Verwẹltlichung *die;* **~, ~en** secularization

verwẹndbar *Adj.* usable (**zu, für** for); **es ist mehrfach ~:** it has several uses *or* applications

Verwẹndbarkeit *die;* **~:** usability

verwẹnden
A *unr. od. regelm. tr. V.* **1** use (**zu, für** for); **ich kann es nicht mehr ~** *od.* **zu nichts mehr ~:** it is no use to me any more; **jmdn./etw. als etw. ~:** use *or* employ sb./sth. as sth. **2** (aufwenden) spend ‹*time*› (**auf** + *Akk.* on); **viel Energie/Mühe auf etw.** (*Akk.*) **~:** put a lot of energy/effort into sth.; **du solltest mehr Sorgfalt auf deine Schularbeiten ~:** you should take more care with *or* over your school work
B *unr. od. regelm. refl. V.* (geh.) **sich [bei jmdm.] für jmdn./etw. ~:** intercede [with sb.] for sb./use one's influence [with sb.] on behalf of sth.

Verwẹndung *die;* **~, ~en** **1** use; **bei ~ dieses Materials** when using this material; **~ finden** be used; **unter ~ einer Sache** (*Gen.*) *od.* **von etw.** using sth.; **~/keine ~ für etw. haben** have a/no use for sth.; **etw. in ~ nehmen** (österr.) put sth. into use *or* service **2** (geh.: Fürbitte) intercession

verwẹndungs-, Verwẹndungs-: ~fähig *Adj.* employable; (als Soldat usw.) fit for service *postpos.*; **~möglichkeit** *die* [possible] application *or* use; **~weise** *die* application; **es hängt von der ~weise ab** it depends how it is used; **~zweck** *der* application; purpose; **„~zweck"** (auf Zahlkarten usw.) 'as payment for'

verwẹrfen
A *unr. tr. V.* **1** reject; dismiss ‹*thought*›; **etw. als unsittlich ~:** condemn sth. as [being] immoral; **einen Antrag/Vorschlag** *usw.* **~:** reject *or* turn down an application/suggestion *etc.* **2** (Rechtsw.) dismiss ‹*appeal, action*›; overturn, quash ‹*judgement*› **3** (geh., bibl.: verstoßen) reject ‹*person, people*›
B *unr. refl. V.* **1** (sich verziehen) warp **2** (Geol.) fault **3** (Kartenspiel) put down the wrong cards/card

verwẹrflich (geh.)
A *Adj.* reprehensible
B *adv.* reprehensibly

Verwẹrflichkeit *die;* **~** (geh.) reprehensibility; reprehensible *or* despicable nature

Verwẹrfung *die;* **~, ~en** (Geol.) fault

verwertbar *Adj.* utilizable; usable

Verwertbarkeit *die;* **~:** usability; **etw. auf seine ~ untersuchen** examine sth. to see if it can/could be utilized

verwerten *tr. V.* utilize, use (**zu** for); make use of, exploit ‹*suggestion, experience, knowledge, etc.*›; put ‹*idea*› into practice; (bes. kommerziell) exploit ‹*idea, invention, place, etc.*›; **es ist noch zu ~:** it can still be put to good use

Verwertung *die* utilization; use; (bes. kommerziell) exploitation

verwesen *itr. V.; mit sein* decompose

verweslich *Adj.* decomposable

verwẹstlichen *itr. V.; mit sein* become westernized

Verwẹstlichung *die;* **~:** westernization

Verwesung *die;* **~:** decomposition; **in ~ übergehen** start to decompose

verwẹtten *tr. V.* spend ‹*money*› on betting; **seinen Kopf für etw. ~:** bet anything on sth.

verwịchsen *tr. V.* (ugs.) beat ‹*person*› up; (zur Strafe) give ‹*person*› a hiding (coll.)

verwịckeln
A *refl. V.* **1** get tangled up *or* entangled **2** (sich verfangen) **sich in etw.** (*Akk. od. Dat.*) **~:** get caught [up] in sth.; **sich in Widersprüche ~** (fig.) tie oneself up in contradictions
B *tr. V.* involve; **in etw.** (*Akk.*) **verwickelt werden/sein** get/be mixed up *or* involved in sth.

verwịckelt
A *Adj.* involved; complicated
B *adv.* in an involved *or* a complicated way

Verwịcklung *die;* **~, ~en** complication

verwiegen *unr. refl. V.* get the weight wrong

verwịldern *itr. V.* **1** ‹*garden*› become overgrown, go wild; ‹*domestic animal*› go wild, return to the wild; ‹*plant*› go *or* grow wild **2** (unkultiviert werden) ‹*person*› turn wild; (verwahrlosen) go to seed; let oneself go

verwịldert *Adj.* **1** overgrown ‹*garden*›; ‹*animal, plant*› which has gone wild **2** (unkultiviert) unkempt, dishevelled ‹*person, appearance, etc.*›; (ungehobelt) uncouth ‹*person*›; (ausschweifend) morally decadent ‹*person, society*›

Verwịlderung *die;* **~, ~en** **1** return to the wild [state]; **die ~ des Gartens schreitet weiter fort** the garden is continuing to get more and more overgrown **2** (geh.: von Menschen) reversion to a primitive state; **die ~ der Sitten** moral decadence

verwịnden *unr. tr. V.* (geh.) get over

verwịnkelt *Adj.* [narrow and] winding ‹*street, corridor*›; ‹*flat, old quarter*› full of nooks and crannies

verwịrken *tr. V.* (geh.) forfeit

verwịrklichen
A *tr. V.* realize ‹*dream*›; realize, put into practice ‹*plan, proposal, idea, etc.*›; carry out ‹*project, intention*›
B *refl. V.* **1** ‹*hope, dream*› be realized *or* fulfilled **2** (sich voll entfalten) **sich [selbst] ~:** realize one's [full] potential; fulfil oneself

Verwịrklichung *die;* **~, ~en** realization; (eines Wunsches, einer Hoffnung) fulfilment; **er begann mit der ~ seines Plans** he started to put his plan into practice; **jmdm. bei der ~ eines Projekts helfen** help sb. carry out a project

verwịrren
A *tr. V.* entangle, tangle up ‹*thread etc.*›; tousle, ruffle ‹*hair*›
B *tr.* (*auch itr.*) *V.* confuse; bewilder; **jmds. Geist ~** (geh.) upset sb.'s mental balance; **das verwirrt [den Zuhörer] nur** it is only confusing [for the listener]; **verwirrt** confused; bewildered; **„Träume ich?", dachte er verwirrt** 'Am I dreaming?' he thought in confusion *or* bewilderment; **~d** bewildering; **~d viele Möglichkeiten** a bewildering number of possibilities
C *refl. V.* ‹*thread etc.*› become entangled; ‹*hair*› become tousled *or* ruffled; ‹*person, mind*› become confused; (fig.: kompliziert werden) become confused *or* complicated

Verwịrr·spiel *das* deliberate confusion *no indef. art.*; **ein ~ mit jmdm. treiben** use intentionally confusing tactics on sb.; **zu einem ~ für jmdn. werden** confuse sb. completely

V

Verwirrtheit *die;* **~:** [state of] confusion *or* bewilderment

Verwirrung *die;* **~, ~en** confusion; **jmdn. in ~ bringen** make sb. confused *or* bewildered; **in ~ geraten** become confused *or* bewildered; **im Zustand geistiger ~:** in a disturbed *or* confused mental state

verwirtschaften *tr. V.* squander ‹*money*› by mismanagement

verwischen
A *tr. V.* smudge ‹*signature, writing, etc.*›; smear ‹*paint*›; **alle Spuren ~** (fig.) cover up all [one's] tracks
B *refl. V.* become blurred

verwissenschaftlichen *tr. V.* make ‹*teaching, life*› highly scientific; put ‹*research, procedure*› on a scientific basis

verwittern *itr. V.; mit sein* weather

Verwitterung *die;* **~, ~en** weathering

verwitwet /fɛɐ̯'vɪtvət/ *Adj.* widowed; **Frau Meier, ~e Schmidt** Mrs Meier, the widow of the late Mr Schmidt

verwohnen *tr. V.* ruin, make a mess of ‹*house, flat*›; **das Zimmer sieht verwohnt aus** the room looks badly knocked about

verwöhnen /fɛɐ̯'vøːnən/ *tr. V.* spoil; **~ Sie sich mit einer Tasse X-Kaffee!** treat yourself to a cup of X coffee; **das Schicksal hat ihn nicht gerade verwöhnt** (fig.) fate has not exactly smiled upon him

verwöhnt *Adj.* spoilt; (anspruchsvoll) discriminating; ‹*taste, palate*› of a gourmet

Verwöhnung *die;* **~:** spoiling

verworfen /fɛɐ̯'vɔrfn̩/
A *2. Part. v.* **verwerfen**
B *Adj.* (geh.) depraved ‹*person*›; dastardly ‹*act*›

Verworfenheit *die;* **~:** depravity

verworren /fɛɐ̯'vɔrən/ *Adj.* confused, muddled ‹*ideas, situation, etc.*›; confused ‹*sound*›

Verworrenheit *die;* **~:** confused nature; confusion

verwundbar *Adj.* open to injury *pred.;* (fig.) vulnerable; **eine sehr ~e Stelle treffen** (fig.) touch a very sensitive spot

Verwundbarkeit *die* vulnerability

verwunden¹ *2. Part. v.* **verwinden**

verwunden² *tr. V.* ▸❶ **S. 439** wound; injure; (fig. geh.) wound ‹*person, feelings, etc.*›

verwunderlich *Adj.* surprising

verwundern
A *tr. V.* **1** surprise; (erstaunen) astonish; **verwundert** surprised/astonished (**über** + *Akk.* at); *adv.* in surprise *or* wonderment/astonishment **2** *in* **zu/nicht zu ~ sein** be surprising/not surprising; be a/no wonder
B *refl. V.* be surprised (**über** + *Akk.* at); (erstaunt sein) be astonished (**über** + *Akk.* at)

Verwunderung *die;* **~:** surprise; (Staunen) astonishment; **jmdn. in ~ setzen** surprise/astonish sb.

Verwundete *der/die; adj. Dekl.* wounded person; casualty; **die ~n** the wounded

Verwundung *die;* **~, ~en** ▸❶ **S. 439** **1** wounding **2** (Wunde, Verletzung) wound

verwunschen *Adj.* enchanted; bewitched

verwünschen *tr. V.* **1** curse **2** (veralt.) ▸**verzaubern 1**

verwünscht *Adj.* **1** (vermaledeit) accursed; wretched **2** (verzaubert) enchanted; bewitched

Verwünschung *die;* **~, ~en** **1** (das Verfluchen) cursing **2** (Fluch) curse; oath **3** (veralt.) ▸**Verzauberung 1**

verwurschteln /fɛɐ̯'vʊrʃtl̩n/, **verwursteln** (ugs.)
A *tr. V.* get ‹*thing*› in a muddle *or* a tangle
B *refl. V.* get in a muddle *or* a tangle

verwursten *tr. V.* turn into sausage; (fig.) use as grist to the mill

verwurzelt *Adj.* [deeply] rooted; **fest ~** (auch fig.) deep-rooted; **in etw.** (*Dat.*) **~ sein** have one's roots in sth.; (in der Tradition, im Glauben usw.) be [deeply] rooted in *or* committed to sth.

Verwurzelung *die;* **~:** deep-rootedness (**mit, in** + *Dat.* in); **trotz seiner ~ in der Tradition** although deeply rooted in tradition

verwüsten *tr. V.* devastate

Verwüstung *die;* **~, ~en** devastation; **die ~en des Krieges** the ravages of war

verzagen *itr. V.; mit sein od. haben* despair; lose heart; **verzagt sein** be despondent

Verzagtheit *die;* **~:** despondency; despair

verzählen *refl. V.* miscount; **ich verzähle mich dauernd** I keep losing count

verzahnen *tr. V.* connect up (**mit** to); (fig.) link, dovetail (**mit** with); **miteinander verzahnt** (fig.) interconnected

Verzahnung *die;* **~, ~en** connection; (fig.) link

verzanken *refl. V.* (ugs.) **sich [mit jmdm. wegen etw.] ~:** fall out [with sb. over sth.]

verzapfen *tr. V.* **1** (landsch.: zapfen) pull, draw ‹*beer etc.*› **2** (Tischlerei) tenon **3** (ugs. abwertend) **Blödsinn** *od.* **Mist ~:** come out with *or* produce rubbish

verzärteln /fɛɐ̯'tsɛːɐtl̩n/ *tr. V.* mollycoddle

Verzärtelung *die;* **~:** mollycoddling

verzaubern *tr. V.* **1** cast a spell on; bewitch; **jmdn. in etw.** (*Akk.*) **~:** transform sb. into sth.; **eine verzauberte Prinzessin** a bewitched princess **2** (fig.) enchant

Verzauberung *die;* **~, ~en** **1** casting of a/the spell (*Gen.* on) **2** (fig.) enchantment

verzehnfachen *tr., refl. V.* increase tenfold

Verzehr /fɛɐ̯'tseːɐ̯/ *der;* **~[e]s** consumption; **zum alsbaldigen ~ bestimmt** for immediate consumption

Verzehr·bon *der* meal voucher; (für Getränke) drinks voucher

verzehren
A *tr. V.* (auch fig. geh.) consume; ‹*illness etc.*› exhaust, debilitate ‹*person*›; consume, drain [away] ‹*strength*›; **der Gram verzehrt sie** she is consumed with grief
B *refl. V.* (geh.) ‹*energy etc.*› be consumed; ‹*person*› eat one's heart out; **sich [in Sehnsucht] nach jmdm. ~:** pine away for sb.; **sich in ohnmächtiger Wut ~:** be consumed with *or* by helpless rage

Verzehr·zwang *der* obligation to order (*in a restaurant*)

verzeichnen *tr. V.* **1** (falsch zeichnen) draw wrongly **2** (aufführen) list; (eintragen) enter; (registrieren) record; **der Ort ist auf der Karte nicht verzeichnet** the place is not [marked] on the map; **das Wörterbuch verzeichnet das Wort nicht** the dictionary does not list *or* include the word; **große Erfolge/Verluste zu ~ haben** have scored great successes/suffered great losses; **Fortschritte/Erfolge sind nicht zu ~:** no progress was made/there were no successes **3** (fig. geh.: zur Kenntnis nehmen) note **4** *auch itr.* (Optik) ‹*lens*› distort

Verzeichnis /fɛɐ̯'tsaiçnɪs/ *das;* **~ses, ~se** list; (Register) index; **ein ~ der lieferbaren Titel** a list *or* catalogue of available titles

verzeihen *unr. tr., itr. V.* ▸❶ **S. 227** forgive; (entschuldigen) excuse ‹*behaviour, remark, etc.*›; **jmdm. [etw.] ~:** forgive sb. [sth. *or* for sth.]; **es sei dir verziehen, ich will es [dir] ~:** you are *or* shall be forgiven; **ich kann es mir nicht ~, dass ich das nicht verhindert habe** I can't *or* I'll never forgive myself for not preventing it; **das ist nicht zu ~:** that's unforgivable/inexcusable; **kannst du mir noch einmal ~?** (auch iron.) can you ever forgive me?; **~ Sie [bitte] die Störung** pardon the intrusion; [please] excuse me for disturbing you; **~ Sie [bitte], können Sie mir sagen ...?** excuse me, could you tell me ...?

verzeihlich *Adj.* forgivable; excusable; **kaum ~:** almost unforgivable

Verzeihung *die;* **~** ▸❶ **S. 227** forgiveness; **~, können Sie mir sagen, ...?** excuse me, could you tell me ...?; **~!** sorry!; **jmdn. um ~ bitten** apologize to sb.; **ich bitte vielmals um ~:** I do apologize *or* [do] beg your pardon

verzerren
A *tr. V.* **1** contort ‹*face etc.*› (**zu** into) **2** (zerren, überdehnen) **sich** (*Dat.*) **einen Muskel/eine Sehne ~:** pull *or* strain a muscle/tendon **3** (akustisch, optisch) distort ‹*sound, image*›; **etw. verzerrt darstellen** (fig.) present a distorted account *or* picture of sth.; **seine Stimme klang verzerrt** his voice sounded distorted
B *itr. V.* ‹*loudspeaker, mirror, etc.*› distort
C *refl. V.* ‹*face, features*› become contorted (**zu** into)

Verzerrung *die;* **~, ~en** **1** (des Gesichts usw.) contortion **2** (eines Muskels usw.) strain; pull **3** (des Klangs, eines Bildes, der Realität usw.) distortion

verzetteln¹
A *tr. V.* fritter away ‹*time, money*›; dissipate ‹*energy*›
B *refl. V.* dissipate one's energies; try to do too many things at once

verzetteln² *tr. V.* (auf Zettel schreiben) put ‹*words etc.*› on slips

Verzettelung *die;* **~, ~en** (auf Zettel) transfer to slips

Verzicht /fɛɐ̯'tsɪçt/ *der;* **~[e]s, ~e** **1** renunciation (**auf** + *Akk.* of); **ich bin zum ~ auf meinen Anteil bereit** I am prepared to give up my share; **auf etw.** (*Akk.*) **~ leisten** (geh.) renounce sth. **2** (auf Reichtum, ein Amt usw.) relinquishment (**auf** + *Akk.* of)

verzichtbar *Adj.* dispensable; (nicht nötig) unnecessary

verzichten *itr. V.* do without; **~ auf** (+ *Akk.*) (auskommen ohne) do without; (sich enthalten) refrain *or* abstain from; (aufgeben) give up ‹*share, smoking, job, etc.*›; renounce ‹*inheritance*›; renounce, relinquish ‹*right, privilege*›; (opfern) sacrifice ‹*holiday, salary*›; **wenn es nicht mehr für alle reicht, verzichte ich freiwillig** if there isn't enough for everybody I will gladly go without; **auf weitere Ansprüche ~:** waive *or* relinquish further claims; **auf den Thron ~:** renounce one's right to the throne; **auf einen Ministersessel ~:** refuse a ministerial post; **ich verzichte auf deine Hilfe/Ratschläge** I can do without *or* you can keep your help/advice; **[nein danke,] ich verzichte** not for me[, thanks]; **darauf möchte ich nicht [mehr] ~:** I wouldn't be without it now; **darauf kann ich ~** (iron.) I can do without that; **auf eine Strafanzeige ~:** not bring a charge; **ich könnte dazu noch einiges sagen, aber ich will darauf ~:** I could add a few things to that, but I will refrain; **auf eine förmliche Vorstellung ~:** dispense with a formal introduction

Verzicht[s]·erklärung *die* waiver; disclaimer

verziehen¹ *2. Part. v.* **verzeihen**

verziehen²
A *unr. tr. V.* **1** screw up ‹*face, mouth, etc.*›; **er verzog sein Gesicht zu einer Grimasse/zu einem spöttischen Lächeln** he pulled a face *or* grimaced/put on a derisive smile; *s. also* **Miene** **2** (schlecht erziehen) spoil; **so ein verzogener Bengel!** what a badly brought up *or* spoilt brat! **3** (Ballspiele) mishit ‹*ball*› **4** (Landw.) thin out ‹*seedlings etc.*›
B *unr. refl. V.* **1** twist; be contorted; **sein Gesicht verzog sich zu einer Grimasse** his face twisted *or* screwed itself into a grimace **2** (aus der Form geraten) go out of shape; ‹*wood*› warp; **ein verzogener Rahmen** a distorted frame; **total verzogen sein** be completely out of shape **3** (wegziehen) ‹*clouds, storm*› move away, pass over; ‹*fog, mist*› disperse **4** (ugs.: weggehen) take oneself off; **ich verziehe mich jetzt [ins Bett]** I'm off to bed now; **verzieh dich!** (salopp) clear (coll.) *or* (coll.) push off
C *unr. itr. V.; mit sein* move [away]; **„Empfänger [unbekannt] verzogen"** 'no longer at this address'

verzieren *tr. V.* decorate

Verzierung *die;* **~, ~en** decoration; **überflüssige ~en** superfluous ornamentation *sing.*; **brich dir [bloß/nur] keine ~ ab!** (fig. ugs.) don't make [such] a fuss!

verzinsen
A *tr. V.* pay interest on ‹*sum, capital, etc.*›; **etw. mit 6% ~:** pay 6% interest on sth.
B *refl. V.* **sich [mit 6%] ~:** yield *or* bear [6%] interest

verzinslich *Adj.* bearing *or* yielding interest *postpos., not pred.* (**mit, zu** at a rate of)

V

Verzinsung *die;* ~, ~**en** [payment of] interest (*Gen.* on)

verzögern
A *tr. V.* **1** delay (**um** by) ; delay, postpone ‹*departure etc.*›; **den Baubeginn um zwei Jahre ~:** put back the start of building work [by] two years **2** (verlangsamen) slow down
B *refl. V.* be delayed (**um** by)
C *itr. V.* slow down; decelerate

Verzögerung *die;* ~, ~**en** **1** delaying; delay (*Gen.* in) **2** (Verlangsamung) slowing down; (Technik) deceleration **3** (Verspätung) delay; hold-up

Verzögerungs·taktik *die* delaying tactics *pl.*

verzollen *tr. V.* pay duty on

Verzollung *die;* ~, ~**en** payment of duty (*Gen.* on)

verzücken *tr. V.* (geh.) enrapture; send into ecstasies; **verzückt** enraptured; in rapture; (ekstatisch) ecstatic; **mit verzückter Miene** with a look of ecstasy [on his/her face]

verzuckern *tr. V.* **1** sugar ‹*almonds*›; (kandieren) candy ‹*fruit*› **2** (fig.) ▸ **versüßen**

Verzückung *die;* ~: ecstasy; rapture; **in ~ geraten** go into ecstasies

Verzug *der;* ~**[e]s** **1** delay; **~ der Zahlung** delay in payment; late payment; **[mit etw.] im ~ sein/in ~ kommen** *od.* **geraten** be/fall behind [with sth.]; **jmdn./etw. in ~ bringen** delay sb./sth.; hold sb. up/put sth. back; **ohne ~:** without delay **2** **es ist Gefahr im ~** (ugs.) danger is imminent

Verzugs·zinsen *Pl.* interest *sing.* on arrears *or* for late payment

verzurren *tr. V.* lash down [securely]; tie up [securely] ‹*parcel*›

verzweifeln *itr. V.; meist mit sein* despair; **über etw./jmdn. ~:** despair at sth./of sb.; **am Leben/an den Menschen ~:** despair of life/humanity; **es ist zum V~!** it's enough to drive you to despair; **es ist zum V~ mit dir** you're enough to drive anyone to despair

verzweifelt
A *Adj.* **1** despairing ‹*person, animal*›; **~ sein** be in despair *or* full of despair; **ich bin [ganz] ~** (ratlos) I'm at my wit's end **2** desperate ‹*situation, attempt, effort, struggle, etc*›
B *adv.* **1** (entmutigt) despairingly **2** (sehr angestrengt) desperately

Verzweiflung *die;* ~: despair; **etw. aus ~ tun** do sth. out of despair; **jmdn. zur ~ treiben/bringen** drive sb. to despair

Verzweiflungs·tat *die* act of despair

verzweigen *refl. V.* branch [out]; **ein weit verzweigtes System/Netz** (fig.) a widely branching system/network; **das Unternehmen ist stark verzweigt** (fig.) the firm is very diversified

Verzweigung *die;* ~, ~**en** **1** branching **2** (schweiz.) (Gabelung) fork; (Kreuzung) crossroads *sing.*; (Autobahn~) intersection

verzwickt /fɛɐ̯ˈtsvɪkt/ *Adj.* (ugs.) tricky; complicated

Vesper /ˈfɛspɐ/ *die;* ~, ~**n** **1** vespers *pl.*; **in die** *od.* **zur ~ gehen** go to vespers **2** *auch das;* ~**s,** ~ (südd.: Zwischenmahlzeit) snack; **~ machen** have a snack

Vesper·brot *das* (südd.) sandwiches *pl.*

vespern (bes. südd.)
A *itr. V.* have a snack
B *tr. V.* **etw. ~:** have a snack of sth.

Vestibül /vɛstiˈbyːl/ *das;* ~**s,** ~**e** (veralt.) vestibule

Vesuv /veˈzuːf/ *der;* ~**s** Vesuvius

Veteran /veteˈraːn/ *der;* ~**en,** ~**en, Veteranin** *die;* ~, ~**nen** (auch fig.) veteran

Veterinär /veteriˈnɛːɐ̯/ *der;* ~**s,** ~**e, Veterinärin** *die;* ~, ~**nen** veterinary surgeon

Veterinär·medizin *die* ▸ **Tiermedizin**

Veto /ˈveːto/ *das;* ~**s,** ~**s** veto; **ein ~ gegen etw. einlegen** veto sth.

Veto·recht *das* right of veto

Vetter /ˈfɛtɐ/ *der;* ~**s,** ~**n** cousin

Vettern·wirtschaft *die* (abwertend) nepotism

Vexier·bild /vɛˈksiːɐ̯-/ *das* puzzle picture

v-förmig, V-förmig /ˈfau̯-/ *Adj.* V-shaped

V-Frau /ˈfau̯-/ *die* contact [woman]; (Informantin) informer

vgl. *Abk.* **= vergleiche** cf.

v.H. *Abk.* **= vom Hundert** per cent

VHB *Abk.* **= Verhandlungsbasis: ~ 800 Euro** 800 euros o.n.o. (Brit.)

VHS *Abk.* **= Volkshochschule**

via /ˈviːa/ *Präp.* via

Viadukt /vi̯aˈdʊkt/ *das od. der;* ~**[e]s,** ~**e** viaduct

Vibraphon /vibraˈfoːn/ *das;* ~**s,** ~**e** (Musik) vibraphone

Vibration /vibrəˈtsi̯oːn/ *die;* ~, ~**en** vibration

Vibrato /viˈbraːto/ *das;* ~**s,** ~**s** *od.* **Vibrati** (Musik) vibrato

Vibrator *der;* ~**s, Vibratoren** vibrator

vibrieren /viˈbriːrən/ *itr. V.* vibrate; ‹*voice*› quiver, tremble

video-, Video- /ˈviːdeo-/ video

Video *das;* ~**s,** ~**s** (ugs.) video

Video-: ~**aufzeichnung** *die* video recording; ~**band** *das; Pl.* ~**bänder** videotape; ~**clip** *der* video; ~**film** *der* video [film]; ~**gerät** *das* video machine; (*nur für Wiedergabe*) video player; ~**kamera** *die* video camera; ~**kassette** *die* video cassette; ~**konferenz** *die* videoconference; ~**kunst** *die* video art; ~**künstler** *der,* ~**künstlerin** *die* video artist; ~**recorder,** ~**rekorder** *der* video recorder; ~**technik** *die* video technology *no art.* ~**text** *der* videotex[t]

Videothek /vi:deoˈteːk/ *die;* ~, ~**en** **1** (Sammlung) video library **2** (Laden) video hire shop *or* store

Video-: ~**überwachung** *die* video surveillance; ~**verleih** *der* video hire; (Firma) video hire company

Viech /fiːç/ *das;* ~**[e]s,** ~**er** **1** (ugs.: Tier) creature **2** (derb abwertend: Mensch) bastard (coll.)

Viecherei *die;* ~, ~**en** (ugs.) hard grind *or* slog

Vieh /fiː/ *das;* ~**[e]s** **1** (Nutztiere) livestock *sing. or pl.*; **jmdn. wie ein Stück ~ behandeln** treat sb. like an animal **2** (Rind~) cattle *pl.* **3** ▸ **Viech**

Vieh-: ~**bestand** *der* stocks *pl.* of animals/cattle; **wie hoch ist der ~bestand dieses Betriebs?** how much livestock does this farm have?; ~**futter** *das* animal/cattle feed *or* fodder; ~**händler** *der,* ~**händlerin** *die* livestock/cattle dealer; ~**hirt** *der* herdsman; (von Rindern) cowherd ~**hirtin** *die* herdswoman; (von Rindern) cowherd

viehisch
A *Adj.* **1** (abwertend: brutal) brutish **2** (ugs.: immens) terrible (coll.) ‹*fear, stupidity, pain*›
B *adv.* **1** (abwertend) ‹*beat, torment*› brutally **2** (ugs.) ‹*hurt*› like hell (coll.); **~ kalt** perishing cold (coll.)

Vieh-: ~**markt** *der* livestock/cattle market; ~**salz** *das* rock salt; (als Streusalz) road salt; ~**stall** *der* cowshed; ~**tränke** *die* cattle trough; ~**treiber** *der,* ~**treiberin** *die* [cattle] drover; ~**waggon** *der* cattle truck; ~**wirtschaft** *die* livestock farming *no art.*; ~**zeug** *das* (ugs.) **1** (Kleinvieh) animals *pl.*; **2** (abwertend: lästige Tiere) creatures *pl.*; ~**zucht** *die* [live]stock/cattle breeding *no art.*; ~**züchter** *der,* ~**züchterin** *die* [livestock/cattle breeder

viel /fiːl/
A *Indefinitpron. u. unbest. Zahlw.* **1** *Sg.* a great deal of; a lot of (coll.); **so/wie/nicht/zu ~:** that/how/not/too much; **wie ~ auch immer** however much; **seine dauernden Besuche werden mir allmählich zu ~:** his constant visits are getting me down (coll.;) **was zu ~ ist, ist zu ~:** enough is enough; there must be a limit; ~**[es]** (~e Dinge, vielerlei) much; **er weiß ~es, aber nicht alles** he knows a great deal, but not everything; **ich kann mich an ~es nicht mehr erinnern** there's much I can't remember; **der ~e Regen** all the rain; **sein ~es Geld** all his money; **gleich ~ Geld/Wasser** the same amount of money/water; **gleich ~ verdienen** earn the same; **in ~er Hinsicht** *od.* **Beziehung** in many respects; **um ~es jünger** a great deal younger; **das ist ein bisschen [sehr] ~!** that's rather too much; **~ Erfreuliches** a great many pleasant things; **er hat in ~em recht** he is right on many points; **er ist nicht ~ über fünfzig** he is not much more than *or* much over fifty **2** *Pl.* many; **gleich ~[e]** the same number of; **wie ~[e]** how many; **zu ~[e]** too many; **~e hundert** many hundreds of; **die ~en Bäume/Menschen/Probleme** all the trees/people/problems; **seine ~en Kinder** all his children; ~**e** (~e Menschen) many people; **das wissen nicht ~e** not many people know that; **das wissen ~e nicht** many people don't know that
B *Adv.* **1** (oft, lange) a great deal; a lot (coll.); **man redet ~ vom Fortschritt** there is much *or* (coll.) a lot of talk of progress; **er spielt ~ Golf** he plays a lot of golf; **er fährt [nicht] ~ Rad** he does[n't do] a lot of cycling; **~ befahren** busy, much-used ‹*road*›; **~ beschäftigt** very busy; **~ besucht** much-frequented ‹*restaurant, etc.*›; much-visited ‹*resort, museum, etc.*›; **~ gekauft** widely bought; **~ gelesen** widely read; **~ gepriesen** much-praised; **~ geschmäht** much-maligned; much-abused; **ein ~ gefragter Artikel** an article that is in great demand *or* much in demand; **einmal zu ~:** once too often **2** (wesentlich) much; a great deal; a lot (coll.); **~ zu viel** far *or* much too much; **~ zu wenig** far too little; **es geht ihm sehr ~ besser** he is very much better; **~ mehr/weniger** much more/less; **~ zu klein** much too small

viel-, Viel-: ~**befahren** *usw.* ▸ **viel B 1**; ~**deutig** /-dɔy̯tɪç/ **A** *Adj.* ambiguous; **B** *adv.* ambiguously; ~**deutigkeit** *die;* ~~: ambiguity; ~**eck** *das* polygon; ~**ehe** *die* polygamy *no art.*

vielerlei *indekl. unbest. Gattungsz.* **1** *attr.* many different; all kinds *or* sorts of **2** *subst.* all kinds *or* sorts of things

vieler·orts *Adv.* in many places

viel-, Viel-: ~**fach** **A** *Adj.* **1** multiple; **die ~fache Menge** many times the amount; **ein ~facher Millionär** a multimillionaire; **er ist ~facher Weltmeister** he has been world champion many times over; **auf ~fachen Wunsch unserer Zuschauer** at the request of many of our viewers; **2** (~fältig) manifold; many kinds of; **B** *adv.* many times; (ugs.: oft) often; frequently; **ein ~fach geäußerter Wunsch** a wish many times expressed; ~**fache** *das; adj. Dekl.* **1** **ein ~faches** many times the amount/number; **die Preise werden ein ~faches von dem betragen, was ...** the prices will be many times greater than ...; **um ein ~faches** many times over; **um ein ~faches schneller/teurer** many times faster/more expensive; **2** (Math.) multiple; ~**falt** *die;* ~~: diversity; wide variety; ~**fältig** /-fɛltɪç/ **A** *Adj.* many and diverse; **B** *adv.* in many different ways; ~**farbig,** (österr.) ~**färbig** *Adj.* multicoloured; ~**flach** *das;* ~~**[e]s,** ~~**e** polyhedron; ~**flieger** *der,* ~**fliegerin** *die* (ugs.) frequent flyer; ~**fraß** *der;* ~~**es,** ~~**e** **1** (ugs.: Mensch) glutton; [greedy-]guts *sing.* (sl.); **2** (Tier) wolverine; ~**gefragt** *usw.* ▸ **viel B 1**; ~**gestaltig** *Adj.* varied *or* diversified in form *postpos.*; **~gestaltig sein** be varied *or* diversified in form; have many different forms; ~**götterei** /-gœtəˈrai̯/ *die;* ~~: polytheism *no art.*

vielleicht /fiˈlai̯çt/
A *Adv.* **1** perhaps; maybe; **~ kommt er morgen** perhaps *or* maybe he will come tomorrow; he might come tomorrow; **du hast dich ~ geirrt** perhaps you were wrong; you may have been mistaken; **~, dass alles nur ein Missverständnis war** perhaps it was all just a misunderstanding; **hast du den Schirm ~ im Büro liegen lassen?** could it be that you left your umbrella in the office? **2** (ungefähr) perhaps; about; **ein Mann von ~ fünfzig Jahren** a man of perhaps *or* about fifty
B *Partikel* **1** **kannst du mir ~ sagen, ...?** could

V

you possibly tell me ...?; **hast du ~ meinen Bruder gesehen?** have you seen my brother by any chance? 2 (wirklich) really; **ich war ~ aufgeregt** I was terribly excited *or* as excited as anything (coll.); **du bist ~ ein Blödmann!** what a stupid idiot you are! (coll.) 3 (ich bitte dringend, dass ...) **~ hilfst du mir mal!** would you mind helping me! 4 (etwa) **ist das ~ eine Lösung?** is that supposed to be a solution?; **ist das ~ dein Ernst?** you don't mean that, do you?

viel-, Viel-: ~mals *Adv.* **ich bitte ~mals um Entschuldigung** I'm very sorry; I do apologize; **sie lässt ~mals grüßen** she sends her best regards *or* wishes; **danke ~mals** thank you very much; many thanks; **~männerei** /-mɛnəˈrai/ *die;* ~~: polyandry *no art.*; **~mehr** /od. -ˈ-/ *Konj. u. Adv.* rather; (im Gegenteil) on the contrary; **~sagend** A *Adj.* meaningful; B *adv.* meaningfully; **~schichtig** *Adj.* multi-layered; (fig.: komplex) complex; **~schreiber** *der,* **~schreiberin** *die* (abwertend) [over-]prolific writer; **~seitig** A *Adj.* versatile ‹*person*›; varied ‹*work, programme, etc.*›; **auf ~seitigen Wunsch** by popular request; **diese Küchenmaschine ist sehr ~seitig** this food processor has many uses; B *adv.* **~seitig begabt sein** be versatile; **sich ~seitig verwenden lassen** have many uses; **~seitigkeit** *die;* ~~ ▸ **~seitig** A: versatility; variedness; **Kombiwagen sind vor allem wegen ihrer ~seitigkeit so beliebt** estate cars are popular above all because of their many uses; **~sprachig** Adj. multilingual; polyglot; **~staaterei** /-ʃtaːtəˈrai/ *die;* ~~ ▸ **Partikularismus**; **~stimmig** A *Adj.* many-voiced; **ein ~stimmiger Chor** a choir of many voices; B *adv.* in many voices; **~versprechend** A *Adj.* [very] promising; B *adv.* [very] promisingly; **~völker·staat** /ˈ-ˈ---/ *der* multinational state; **~weiberei** /-vaibəˈrai/ *die;* ~~: polygyny *no art.*; polygamy *no art.*; **~zahl** *die* large number; multitude

vier /fiːɐ̯/ *Kardinalz.* ▸ⓘ **S. 29,** ▸ⓘ **S. 729,** ▸ⓘ **S. 826** four; **alle ~e von sich strecken** (ugs.) put one's feet up; **auf allen ~en** (ugs.) on all fours; *s. auch* **acht**

Vier *die;* ~, **~en** four; **eine ~ schreiben/bekommen** (Schulw.) get a D; *s. auch* **Acht¹; Zwei**

vier-, Vier- (*s. auch* **acht-, Acht-**): **~achser** *der;* ~~, ~~: four-axle vehicle; **~achsig** (Technik) four-axle *attrib.*; **vierachsig sein** have four axles; **~achtel·takt** /ˈ-ˈ---/ *der* (Musik) four-eight time; **~augen·gespräch** *das* (ugs.) private talk *or* discussion; **~beiner** *der;* ~~s, ~~ (ugs.) four-legged friend; **~beinig** *Adj.* four-legged; **~blättrig** *Adj.* four-leaf *attrib.*; four-leaved; **~eck** *das* quadrilateral; (Rechteck) rectangle; (Quadrat) square; **~eckig** *Adj.* quadrilateral; (rechteckig) rectangular; (quadratisch) square

Vierer *der;* **~s,** ~ 1 (Rudern) four 2 (ugs.: im Lotto) four winning numbers *pl.* 3 (ugs.: Ziffer, beim Würfeln) four 4 (landsch.: Schulnote) D 5 (ugs.: Autobus) [number] four 6 (Golf) foursome

Vierer·bob *der* four-man bob

viererlei *Gattungsz.; indekl.* 1 *attr.* four kinds *or* sorts of; four different ‹*sorts, kinds, sizes, possibilities*› 2 *subst.* four [different] things

vier·fach *Vervielfältigungsz.* fourfold; quadruple; **der ~e Olympiasieger** quadruple Olympic winner; *s. auch* **achtfach**

Vier·fache *das;* **~n;** *adj. Dekl.* **um das ~:** fourfold; by four times the amount; **die Preise sind um das ~ gestiegen** the prices have quadrupled *or* increased four times; **sie verlangen das ~ des normalen Tarifs** they are demanding four times the normal rate; *s. auch* **Achtfache**

vier-, Vier-: ~farben·druck /ˈ-ˈ---/ *der; Pl.* **~~e** 1 (Verfahren) four-colour printing *no art.* 2 (einzelnes Stück) four-colour print; **~farb[en]·stift** *der* four-colour pen; **~flach** *das;* ~~[e]s, ~~, **~flächner** /-flɛçnɐ/ *der;* ~~s, ~~ (Math.) tetrahedron; **~füßer** /-fyːsɐ/ *der;* ~~s, ~~ (Zool.) quadruped; **~füßig** *Adj.* 1 four-legged; 2 (Verslehre) tetrameter; **~füßig sein** be a tetrameter; **~gang·getriebe** *das* (Technik) four-speed gearbox; **~geschossig** *Adj., adv.* ▸ **vierstöckig**; **~händig** /-hɛndɪç/ A *Adj.* **~händiges Klavierspiel üben** practise piano duets *or* duets on the piano; B *adv.* ‹*play*› as a duet; **~händig Klavier spielen** play a duet/duets on the piano; **~hundert** *Kardinalz.* ▸ⓘ **S. 826** four hundred; **~jährig** *Adj.* (4 Jahre alt) four-year-old *attrib.*; four years old *pred.*; (4 Jahre dauernd) four-year *attrib.*; *s. auch* **achtjährig**; **~jährlich** A *Adj.* four-yearly; *s. auch* **achtjährlich**; B *adv.* every four years

Vierkant-: ~eisen *das* square iron; **~holz** *das* squared timber; **~schlüssel** *der* square-section key

vier·köpfig *Adj.* four-headed ‹*monster*›; ‹*family, staff*› of four

Vierling *der;* **~s, ~e** quadruplet

vier-, Vier-: ~mal *Adv.* four times; *s. auch* **achtmal**; **~malig** *Adj.* **nach ~maliger Aufforderung** at the fourth request; after being asked four times; *s. auch* **achtmalig**; **~master** *der;* ~~s, ~~: four-master; **~motorig** *Adj.* four-engined ‹*aircraft etc.*›; **~rad·antrieb** *der* (Kfz-W.) four-wheel drive; **~räd[e]rig** /-rɛːd[ə]rɪç/ *Adj.* four-wheeled; **~raum·wohnung** *die* ▸ **Vierzimmerwohnung**; **~schrötig** /-ʃrøːtɪç/ *Adj.* thickset; **~seitig** *Adj.* 1 four-sided ‹*figure, object, etc.*›; four-page *attrib.* ‹*letter, article, etc.*›; 2 (zwischen ~ Beteiligten) quadripartite ‹*agreement, talks, etc.*›; **~sitzer** *der;* ~~s, ~~: four-seater; **~spänner** /-ʃpɛnɐ/ *der;* ~~s, ~~: four-in-hand; **~spännig** A *Adj.* four-horse ‹*coach, carriage, etc.*›; B *adv.* with a team of four horses; **~spurig** A *Adj.* four-lane ‹*road, motorway*›; **~spurig sein** have four lanes; B *adv.* **~spurig befahrbar sein** have all four lanes open; **eine Straße ~spurig ausbauen** widen a road into four lanes; **~stellig** *Adj.* four-figure *attrib.*; *s. auch* **achtstellig**; **~sterne·general** /ˈ-----/ *der* (Militärjargon) four-star general; **~sterne·hotel** /ˈ-ˈ---/ *das* four-star hotel; **~stimmig** A *Adj.* four-part ‹*harmony, song, etc.*›; four-voice ‹*choir, group*›; B *adv.* **etw. ~stimmig singen** sing sth. in four voices; **~stöckig** *Adj.* four-storey; *s. auch* **achtstöckig**; **~stündig** *Adj.* four-hour *attrib.*; *s. auch* **achtstündig**

viert /fiːɐ̯t/ *in* **wir waren zu ~:** there were four of us; **zu ~ verreisen** go away *or* on holiday in a foursome; *s. auch* **acht²**

viert... *Ordinalz.* ▸ⓘ **S. 165,** ▸ⓘ **S. 826** fourth; *s. auch* **acht...**

vier-, Vier-: ~tägig *Adj.* four-day *attrib.*; *s. auch* **achttägig**; **~takter** *der;* ~~s, ~~ (Auto) car with a four-stroke engine; (Motor) four-stroke engine; **~takt·motor** *der* (Kfz-W.) four-stroke engine; **~tausend** *Kardinalz.* ▸ⓘ **S. 826** four thousand

Vierte *der/die; adj. Dekl.* fourth; *s. auch* **Achte**

vier-: ~teilen *tr. V.* quarter; **~teilig** *Adj.* four-part ‹*serial, documentary, etc.*›; **~teilig sein** be in four parts

viertel /ˈfɪrtl̩/ *Bruchz.* ▸ⓘ **S. 729,** ▸ⓘ **S. 826** quarter; **ein ~ Pfund/eine ~ Million** a quarter of a pound/million; **drei ~ Liter** three quarters of a litre; **um ~/drei ~ acht** (landsch.) at [a] quarter past seven; at [a] quarter to eight; **die Flasche ist drei ~ leer** the bottle is three-quarters empty

Viertel¹ /ˈfɪrtl̩/ *das* (*schweiz. meist der*); **~s,** ~ ▸ⓘ **S. 729,** ▸ⓘ **S. 826** quarter; **ein ~ Leberwurst** (ugs.) a quarter of liver sausage; **ein ~ Wein** (ugs.) a quarter-litre of wine; **~ vor/nach eins** [a] quarter to/past one; *s. auch* **akademisch A**

Viertel² *die;* ~, ~ (Musik) crotchet (Brit.;) quarter (Amer.)

viertel-, Viertel-: ~drehung *die* quarter turn; **~finale** *das* (Sport) quarter-final; **sich für das ~finale qualifizieren** qualify for the quarter-finals; **~jahr** *das* three months *pl.*; **~jährlich** A *Adj.* quarterly; B *adv.* quarterly; every three months; **~kreis** *der* quadrant; **~liter** *der* quarter of a litre; **~note** *die* (Musik) crotchet (Brit.); quarter note (Amer.); **~pause** *die* crotchet rest (Brit.); quarter rest (Amer.); **~pfund** *das* quarter [of a] pound; **~pfünder** *der* **~pfünders, ~pfünder** quarter-pounder; **~stunde** *die* quarter of an hour; **~stündig** *Adj.* quarter-of-an-hour; fifteen-minute; **~stündlich** A *Adj.* quarter-hourly; every quarter of an hour *postpos.*; B *adv.* every quarter of an hour; **~ton** *der; Pl.* **~töne** (Musik) quarter tone

***vierte·mal, *vierten·mal** ▸ **Mal¹**

viertens /ˈfiːɐ̯tn̩s/ *Adv.* fourthly; *s. auch* **zweitens**

Viertonner *der;* **~s,** ~: four-tonner

viertürig /-tyːrɪç/ *Adj.* four-door *attrib.*; **~ sein** have four doors

Vierung *die;* ~, **~en** (Archit.) crossing

Vier·viertel·takt /ˈ-ˈ--/ *der* (Musik) four-four time

Vierwaldstätter See, (schweiz.:) **Vierwaldstättersee** *der* Lake Lucerne

vier·wöchig *Adj.* four-week [-long]

vier- /ˈfɪr-/: **~zehn**: *Kardinalz.* ▸ⓘ **S. 29,** ▸ⓘ **S. 729,** ▸ⓘ **S. 826** fourteen; *s. auch* **achtzehn**; **~zehnjährig** *Adj.* (14 Jahre alt) fourteen-year-old *attrib.*; fourteen years old *pred.*; (14 Jahre dauernd) fourteen-year *attrib.*

vierzehnt... /ˈfɪr-/ *Ordinalz.* ▸ⓘ **S. 165** fourteenth; *s. auch* **acht...**

vier- /ˈfɪr-/: **~zehn·tägig** *Adj.* two-week; **unser ~zehntägiger Urlaub** our two-week *or* two weeks' *or* fortnight's holiday; **~zehn·täglich** A *Adj.* fortnightly; B *adv.* fortnightly; every two weeks

vierzig /ˈfɪrtsɪç/ *Kardinalz.* ▸ⓘ **S. 29,** ▸ⓘ **S. 826** forty; *s. auch* **achtzig**

vierziger /ˈfɪrtsɪɡɐ/ *indekl. Adj.* **die ~ Jahre** the forties; *s. auch* **achtziger**

Vierziger¹ *der;* **~s,** ~ 1 (40-jähriger) forty-year-old 2 (ugs.: Autobus) number forty 3 (Wein) '40's vintage

Vierziger² *die;* ~, ~ (ugs.) 1 (Briefmarke) forty-cent/centime *etc.* stamp 2 (Glühbirne) 40-watt bulb

Vierziger³ *Pl.* forties; *s. auch* **Achtziger³**

Vierzigerin /ˈ----/ *die;* ~, **~nen** forty-year-old

Vierziger·jahre /ˈ---ˈ--/ *Pl.* ▸ⓘ **S. 29,** ▸ⓘ **S. 165** forties *pl.*

vierzig·jährig /ˈfɪrtsɪç-/ *Adj.* (40 Jahre alt) forty-year-old *attrib.*; forty years old *pred.*; (40 Jahre dauernd) forty-year *attrib.*

vierzigst... /ˈfɪrtsɪçst.../ *Ordinalz.* ▸ⓘ **S. 826** fortieth; *s. auch* **acht...**

Vierzig·stunden·woche *die* forty-hour week

vier-, Vier-: ~zimmer·wohnung *die* four-room flat (esp. Brit.) *or* (esp. Amer.) apartment; **~zylinder** *der* (ugs.) four-cylinder; **~zylinder·motor** *der* four-cylinder engine

Vietnam /vi̯ɛtˈnam/ *(das);* **~s** Vietnam

Vietnamese /vi̯ɛtnaˈmeːzə/ *der;* **~n, ~n,** **Vietnamesin,** *die;* ~, **~nen** Vietnamese

vietnamesisch ▸ⓘ **S. 670**

A *Adj.* Vietnamese

B *adv.* **wir waren ~ essen** we went to a Vietnamese restaurant *or* for a Vietnamese meal; *s. auch* **deutsch; Deutsch; Deutsche²**

Vietnamisierung *die;* ~: Vietnamization

Vietnam·krieg *der* Vietnam war

vif /viːf/ (veralt.)

A *Adj.* lively; brisk

B *adv.* briskly

Vigil /viˈgiːl/ *die;* ~, **~ien** (kath. Kirche) vigil

Vignette /vɪnˈjɛtə/ *die;* ~, **~n** vignette

V

Vignette

In order to be able to use Austrian and Swiss motorways, all vehicles must display a sticker on the windscreen called a *Vignette*. These stickers are usually valid for one year, but foreign tourists in Austria can buy stickers for a period of 10 days or two months. The sticker can be bought at all Austrian border crossings and petrol stations.

Vikar /vi'ka:ɐ̯/ *der;* **~s, ~e, Vikarin** *die;* **~, ~nen** 1 (kath. Kirche) locum tenens 2 (ev. Kirche) ≈ [trainee] curate

Viktimologie /vɪktimologi:/ *die;* **~:** victimology *no art.*

Viktoria /vɪk'to:ri̯a/ *(die)* Victoria

viktorianisch
A *Adj.* Victorian
B *adv.* in a Victorian manner

Villa /'vɪla/ *die;* **~, Villen** villa

Villen·viertel *das* exclusive residential district

Vinaigrette /vinɛ'grɛtə/ *die;* **~, ~n** vinaigrette [dressing]

Viola /'vi̯o:la/ *die;* **~, Violen** (Musik) viola

violett /vi̯o'lɛt/ purple; violet

Violett *das;* **~s, ~e** *od. ugs.* **~s** purple; violet; (im Spektrum) violet

Violine /vi̯o'li:nə/ *die;* **~, ~n** (Musik) violin

Violinist *der;* **~en, ~en, Violinistin,** *die;* **~, ~nen** violinist

Violin-: ~konzert *das* violin concerto; **~schlüssel** *der* treble clef

Violon·cello /vi̯olɔn'tʃɛlo/ *das* violoncello

Viper /'vi:pɐ/ *die;* **~, ~n** viper; adder

viral /vi'ra:l/ *Adj.* (Med.) viral; **~es Marketing** (DV) viral marketing

Viren ▸**Virus**

Viren-: ~scanner *der* (DV) virus scanner; **~schutz** *der* (DV, Med.) virus protection

Virologe *der;* **~n, ~n** ▸🛈 **S. 113** virologist

Virologie /virolo'gi:/ *die;* **~:** virology *no art.*

Virologin *die;* **~, ~nen** ▸🛈 **S. 113** virologist

virtuell /vɪr'tu̯ɛl/
A *Adj.* 1 potential 2 (DV, Optik) virtual ‹*memory, image;*› **~e Wirklichkeit** virtual reality
B *adv.* virtually

virtuos /vɪr'tu̯o:s/
A *Adj.* virtuoso ‹*performance etc.*›
B *adv.* in a virtuoso manner

Virtuose /vɪr'tu̯o:zə/ *der;* **~n, ~n, Virtuosin** *die;* **~, ~nen** virtuoso

Virtuosität *die;* **~:** virtuosity

virulent /viru'lɛnt/ *Adj.* (Med., geh.) virulent

Virus /'vi:rʊs/ *das;* **~, Viren** /'vi:rən/ virus

Virus·infektion *die* ▸🛈 **S. 439** virus infection

Visa ▸**Visum**

Visage /vi'za:ʒə/ *die;* **~, ~n** (salopp abwertend) mug (coll.); (Miene) expression

vis-a-vis, vis-à-vis /viza'vi:/
A *Präp. mit Dat.* opposite
B *Adv.* opposite; **~ von etw./jmdm.** opposite sth./sb.

Visavis /viza'vi:/ *das;* **~** /viza'vi:(s)/, **~** /viza 'vi:s/ **mein ~:** the person opposite me; **jmdn. zum ~ haben** have sb. opposite one

Visen ▸**Visum**

Visier /vi'zi:ɐ̯/ *das;* **~s, ~e** 1 (am Helm) visor; **das ~ herunterlassen** (fig.) put up one's guard; **mit offenem ~ kämpfen** (fig.) fight out in the open 2 (an der Waffe) backsight; **jmdn. ins ~ nehmen** (fig. ugs.) start to keep close tabs on sb.

visieren *itr. V.* take aim

Vision /vi'zi̯o:n/ *die;* **~, ~en** vision

visionär /vizi̯o'nɛ:ɐ̯/
A *Adj.* visionary
B *adv.* in a visionary manner

Visite /vi'zi:tə/ *die;* **~, ~n** 1 round; **~ machen** do one's round; **um 10 Uhr war ~:** at 10 o'clock, the doctor did his round 2 (veralt.: Besuch) visit; **zu einer ~:** on a visit

Visiten·karte *die* visiting card; **diese gepflegten Grünanlagen sind eine gute ~ für die Stadt** these well-tended parks and gardens are a good advertisement for the town; **seine ~ hinterlassen** (fig.) leave one's visiting card (joc.)

Visit·karte *die* (österr.) ▸**Visitenkarte**

viskos /vɪs'ko:s/, **viskös** /vɪs'kø:s/ *Adj.* (Chemie) viscous

Viskose /vɪs'ko:zə/ *die;* **~** (Chemie) viscose

Viskosität *die;* **~** (Chemie) viscosity

visuell /vi'zu̯ɛl/ (geh.)
A *Adj.* visual
B *adv.* visually

Visum /'vi:zʊm/ *das;* **~s, Visa** /'vi:za/ *od.* **Visen** /'vi:zn̩/ visa

Visum·zwang *der* visa requirement

vital /vi'ta:l/
A *Adj.* 1 (voller Energie) vital; energetic; vigorous; **~ sein** be full of life *or* vigour 2 (wichtig) vital
B *adv.* (voller Energie) energetically

Vitalität *die;* **~:** vitality

Vitamin /vita'mi:n/ *das;* **~s, ~e** 1 vitamin 2 **~ B** (ugs. scherzh.) connections *pl.*; **etw. durch ~ B kriegen** get sth. through knowing the right people

vitamin-, Vitamin-: ~arm *Adj.* ‹*food, diet, etc.*› low in vitamins; **~gehalt** *der* vitamin content; **~mangel** *der* vitamin deficiency; **~reich** *Adj.* rich in vitamins *postpos.*; vitamin-rich; **~stoß** *der* large dose of vitamins; **~tablette** *die* vitamin tablet *or* pill

Vitrine /vi'tri:nə/ *die;* **~, ~n** display case; showcase; (Möbel) display cabinet

Vivi·sektion /vivi-/ *die* (bes. Med.) vivisection *no art.*

vivi·sezieren *tr. V.* (bes. Med.) vivisect

Vize /'fi:tsə/ *der;* **~s, ~s** (ugs.) number two (coll.)

Vize- /'vi:tsə/: **~kanzler** *der,* **~kanzlerin** *die* vice-chancellor; **~könig** *der* viceroy; **~meister** *der,* **~meisterin** *die* (Sport) runner-up; **~präsident** *der,* **~präsidentin** *die* vice-president

Vlies /fli:s/ *das;* **~es, ~e** fleece

V-Mann /'fau̯-/ *der;* **~[e]s, V-Männer** *od.* **V-Leute** contact [man]; (Informant) informer

Vogel /'fo:gl̩/ *der;* **~s, Vögel** /'fø:gl̩/ 1 bird; **friss, ~, oder stirb!** (ugs.) [you can] like it or lump it! (coll.); **der ~ ist ausgeflogen** (ugs.) the bird has flown; **[mit etw.] den ~ abschießen** (ugs.) take the biscuit [with sth.] (coll.); **einen ~ haben** (salopp) be off one's rocker *or* head (coll.); **jmdm. den ~ zeigen** tap one's forehead at sb. *(as a sign that one thinks he/she is stupid)* 2 (salopp, oft scherzh.: Mensch) character; **ein seltsamer** *od.* **komischer ~:** an odd bird *or* character 3 (Fliegerspr.: Flugzeug) machine

Vogel-: ~bauer *das od. der* birdcage; **~beer·baum** *der* rowan [tree]; mountain ash; **~beere** *die* rowan berry

Vögelchen /'fø:gl̩çən/ *das;* **~s, ~:** little *or* small bird

Vogel-: ~dreck *der* (ugs.) bird droppings *pl.*; **~ei** *das* bird's egg

Vögelei *die;* **~, ~en** (derb) screwing (coarse)

vogel-, Vogel-: ~flug *der* flight of the birds; **~frei** *Adj.* (hist.) outlawed; **jmdn./etw. für ~frei erklären** outlaw sb./sth.; **~futter** *das* bird food; **~grippe** *die* bird flu; **~häuschen** *das* bird house; **~käfig** *der* birdcage; **~kunde** *die* ornithology *no art.*

vögeln /'fø:gln/ *tr., itr. V.* (derb) screw (coarse); **jmdn./mit jmdm. ~:** screw sb.

Vogel-: ~nest *das* bird's nest; **~perspektive** *die* bird's-eye view; **Manhattan aus der ~perspektive** a bird's-eye view of Manhattan; **~scheuche** *die* scarecrow; **~schutz** *der* protection of birds; **~-Strauß-Politik** /--'----/ *die* head-in-the-sand policy; **~-Strauß-Politik treiben** pursue a policy of burying one's head in the sand; **~warte** *die* ornithological institute; **~zug** *der* bird migration

Vogesen /vo'ge:zn̩/ *Pl.* Vosges [Mountains]

Vöglein /'fø:glai̯n/ *das;* **~s, ~:** little bird

Vogt /fo:kt/ *der;* **~[e]s, Vögte** /'fø:ktə/ (hist.) (eines Gutes, einer Burg usw.) steward; (Land~) governor

Vogtei /fo:k'tai̯/ *die;* **~, ~en** (hist.) ▸**Vogt**: (Amt) stewardship; governorship; (Sitz) steward's office; governor's residence

Vögtin /'fø:ktɪn/ *die;* **~, ~nen** ▸**Vogt**

Voicemail /'vɔy̯smeɪl/ *die;* **~, ~s** voicemail

Voice·recorder /'vɔy̯s-/ *der* voice recorder

Vokabel /vo'ka:bl̩/ *die;* **~, ~n** *od. österr. auch das;* **~s, ~:** word; vocabulary item; **~n** vocabulary *sing.*; vocab *sing.* (Sch. coll.)

Vokabel·heft *das* vocabulary *or* (coll.) vocab book

Vokabular *das;* **~s, ~e** vocabulary

vokal *Adj.* (Musik) vocal

Vokal /vo'ka:l/ *der;* **~s, ~e** (Sprachw.) vowel

Vokal·ensemble *das* vocal ensemble

Vokalisation *die;* **~, ~en** (Musik) vocalization

vokalisch (Sprachw.)
A *Adj.* vocalic; **mit ~em Anlaut** beginning with a vowel
B *adv.* **~ auslauten** end in *or* with a vowel

Vokalismus *der;* **~** (Sprachw.) vocalism

Vokalist *der;* **~en, ~en, Vokalistin** *die;* **~, ~nen** vocalist

Vokal·musik *die* vocal music

Vokativ /'vo:kati:f/ *der;* **~s, ~e** (Sprachw.) vocative

Volant /vo'lã:/ *der, schweiz., österr. meist das;* **~s, ~s** 1 (an Kleidungsstücken) flounce 2 (Lenkrad) steering wheel

Voliere /vo'li̯e:rə/ *die;* **~, ~n** aviary

Volk /fɔlk/ *das;* **~[e]s, Völker** /'fœlkɐ/ 1 people; **das ~ der Kurden** the Kurdish people; **das irische und das deutsche ~:** the Irish and German peoples 2 (Bevölkerung) people *pl.*; (Nation) people *pl.*; nation; **im ~e** among the people; **das ~ befragen** ask the people *or* nation; **das arbeitende/unwissende ~:** the working people/the ignorant masses *pl.* 3 (einfache Leute) people *pl.*; **ein Mann aus dem ~:** a man of the people; **dem ~ aufs Maul schauen** listen to the way the ordinary man speaks 4 (ugs.: Leute) people *pl.*; **viel junges ~:** many young people; **sich unters ~ mischen** go among the people; **etw. unters ~ bringen** make sth. [known to the] public 5 (Gruppe) lot; crowd (coll.); **die Spatzen sind ein freches ~** (fig.) sparrows are a cheeky lot 6 (Bienen~) colony

Völkchen /'fœlkçən/ *das;* **~s, ~:** lot; crowd (coll.)

völker-, Völker-: ~ball *der: ball game in which two teams try to get the other side's players out by hitting them with a ball;* **~bund** *der* League of Nations; **~familie** *die* (geh.) family of nations; **~freundschaft** *die* international friendship *no art.*; **~kunde** *die* ethnology *no art.*; **~kundler** *der;* **~~s, ~~, ~kundlerin** *die;* **~~, ~~nen** ethnologist; **~mord** *der* genocide; **~recht** *das* international law *no art.*; **~rechtlich** A *Adj.* ‹*issue, problem, etc.*› of international law; **~rechtliche Verträge** agreements in *or* under international law; **die ~rechtliche Anerkennung eines Staates** the recognition of a state under international law; B *adv.* ‹*settle*› in accordance with international law; ‹*control, regulate*› by international law; ‹*recognize*› under international law; **~rechts·widrig** *Adj., adv.* contrary to international law *postpos.*

Völkerschaft *die;* **~, ~en** people; (Volksstamm) tribe

völker-, Völker-: ~verbindend ‹*idea, event*› which brings nations together; **der ~verbindende Charakter des Sports** the ability of sport to bring nations together; **~verständigung** *die* international understanding; understanding between nations; **~wanderung** *die* 1 (hist.) migration of peoples; völkerwanderung; 2 (ugs.) mass migration; (Zug) mass progression

völkisch *Adj.* (veralt., bes. ns.) national

volk·reich *Adj.* heavily populated

V

volks-, Volks-: ~abstimmung *die* plebiscite; **~armee** *die* People's Army; **~armist** /-armɪst/ *der;* **~~, ~~, ~armistin** *die;* **~~, ~~nen** member of the People's Army; **~aufstand** *der* national uprising; **~ausgabe** *die* (veralt.) popular edition; **~befragung** *die* (Politik) referendum; **~begehren** *das* (Politik) petition for a referendum; **~belustigung** *die* public entertainment; **~brauch** *der* popular custom; **~bücherei** *die* public library; **~demokratie** people's democracy; **~deutsche** *der/die* ethnic German; **~dichtung** *die* (Literaturw.) folk literature *no indef. art.;* **eine ~dichtung** a piece of folk literature; **~eigen** *Adj.* (DDR) publicly *or* nationally owned; **~er Betrieb** publicly *or* nationally owned company; **~eigentum** *das* (DDR) national[ly owned] property; **~einkommen** *das* (Wirtsch.) national income; **~empfinden** *das:* **das [gesunde] ~empfinden** popular sentiment *or* opinion; **~entscheid** *der* (Politik) referendum; **~etymologie** *die* (Sprachw.) folk *or* popular etymology; **~feind** *der,* **~feindin** *die* enemy of the people; **~fest** *das* public festival; (Jahrmarkt) fair; **~front** *die* (Politik) popular front; **~gemeinschaft** *die* (bes. ns.) national community; **~gemurmel** *das* (ugs. scherzh.) mutterings *pl.;* **~genosse** *der,* **~genossin** *die* (ns.) national comrade; **~gerichts·hof** *der* (ns.) People's Court; **~gesundheit** *die* public health; **~glaube[n]** *der* (Volksk.) popular belief; **~gruppe** *die* ethnic group; (Minderheit) ethnic minority; **~held** *der,* **~heldin** *die* folk hero; **~hochschule** *die* adult education centre; **ein Kurs an der ~hochschule** an adult education class; **~initiative** *die* (schweiz. Politik) petition for a referendum; **~kammer** *die* (DDR) **die ~kammer** the Volkskammer; the People's Chamber; **~kunde** *die* folklore; **~kundler** *der;* **~~s, ~~, ~kundlerin** *die;* **~~, ~~nen** folklorist; **~kundlich** *Adj.* folkloric; **~kundliche Bücher** books on folklore; **~kunst** *die* folk art; **~lied** *das* folk song; **~märchen** *das* folk tale; **~masse** *die* **1** **die ~massen** the people; the masses; **2** (versammeltes Volk) crowd [of people]; **~medizin** *die* folk medicine *no art.;* **~mund** *der:* **im ~mund wird das … genannt** in the vernacular it is called …; **~musik** *die* folk music; **~nahrungs·mittel** *das* staple food; **~partei** *die* people's party; **~polizei** *die* (DDR) People's Police; **~polizist** *der* (DDR) People's Policeman; member of the People's Police; **~polizistin** *die* (DDR) member of the People's Police; **~rede** *die* (veralt.) public address *or* speech; **~reden halten** (ugs. abwertend) make a long speech; **halt keine ~reden!** no speechifying! (coll.); no long speeches!; **~republik** *die* People's Republic; **die ~republik China** the People's Republic of China; **~schicht** *die* social class; **~schule** *die* **1** (Bundesrepublik Deutschland und Schweiz veralt.) *school providing basic primary and secondary education;* **2** (österr.) primary school; **~schüler** *der,* **~schülerin** *die* pupil at a 'Volksschule'; **~schul·lehrer** *der,* **~schul·lehrerin** *die* teacher at a 'Volksschule'; **~seele** *die* soul of the people; **die russische ~seele** the soul of the Russian people; **~seuche** *die* national epidemic; **~souveränität** *die* (Politik) sovereignty of the people; **~sprache** *die* vernacular [language]; **~stamm** *der* tribe; **~stück** *das* (Theater) folk play; **~sturm** *der:* (ns.) *German territorial army created towards the end of World War II to help defend the fatherland;* **~tanz** *der* folk dance; **~tracht** *die* traditional costume; (eines Landes) national costume; **~trauer·tag** *der* (Bundesrepublik Deutschland) national remembrance day; **~tribun** *der* (hist.) tribune [of the people]

> **Volkshochschule (VHS)**
>
> A local adult education centre that can be found in every German town. The *VHS* offers low-cost daytime and evening classes in a wide range of subjects, including crafts, languages, music, and exercise.

Volkstum *das;* **~:** national character; (Traditionen) national customs and traditions

volkstümlich /'fɔlksty:mlɪç/

A *Adj.* popular; **ein ~er Politiker** a politician of the people *or* with the common touch; **der ~e Name einer Pflanze** the vernacular name of a plant; **~e Preise** popular prices; **eine ~e Einführung** an introduction readily comprehensible to the layman; **sich ~ geben** act the man/woman of the people

B *adv.* **~ schreiben** write in terms readily comprehensible to the layman

volks-, Volks-: ~verdummung *die* (ugs. abwertend) deliberate deception of the public; **~verhetzung** *die* incitement of the people; **~vermögen** *das* (Wirtsch.) national wealth; **~versammlung** *die* **1** public meeting; **2** (Parlament) national assembly; **~vertreter** *der,* **~vertreterin** *die* representative of the people; **~vertretung** *die* representative body of the people; **~wahl** *die* (DDR Politik) general election; **~weise** *die* folk tune; **~weisheit** *die* old saying; **~wirt** *der,* **~wirtin** *die* economist; **~wirtschaft** *die* national economy; (Fach) economics *sing., no art.;* **~wirtschaftler** *der;* **~~s, ~~, ~wirtschaftlerin** *die;* **~~, ~~nen** economist; **~wirtschaftlich** **A** *Adj.* economic; **B** *adv.* economically; **~wirtschafts·lehre** *die* economics *sing., no art.;* **~wohl** *das* welfare *or* well-being of the people; **~zählung** *die* [national] census; **~zorn** *der* public anger; **~zugehörigkeit** *die* ethnic origin

voll /fɔl/

A *Adj.* **1** full; **der Saal ist ~ Menschen** the room is full of people; **ein Korb ~ [roter] Äpfel** a basket full of [red] apples; **~ von** *od.* **mit etw. sein** be full of sth.; **das Glas ist halb ~:** the glass is half full; **beide Hände ~ haben** have both hands full; **~ [von] Dankbarkeit sein** be full of *or* filled with gratitude; **~ Güte/Tatkraft sein** be full of goodness/vigour; **den Kopf ~ haben** (ugs.) be preoccupied (**mit** with); **der Saal ist brechend/gestopft ~** (ugs.) the room is jam-packed (coll.); **die Straßen lagen ~ Schnee** (ugs.) the streets were deep in snow; **jeder bekam einen Korb ~:** everybody received a basketful; **mit ~en Backen kauen** eat with bulging cheeks; **aus dem Vollen schöpfen** draw on abundant *or* plentiful resources; **aus dem Vollen leben** *od.* **wirtschaften** live off *or* on the fat of the land; **~e Pulle** *od.* **~[es] Rohr** (salopp) ‹*drive*› flat out; **das Radio auf ~e Pulle drehen** (salopp) turn the radio on full blast (coll.); **~ laufen** fill up; **etw. ~ laufen lassen** fill sth. [up]; **sich ~ laufen lassen** (salopp.) get completely paralytic *or* canned (Brit. sl.); **~ schlagen** (Seemannsspr.) **become swamped; ~ pumpen** + *Akk.* pump up ‹*tyre;*› fill up ‹*reservoir*›; **sich mit Tabletten ~ pumpen** (fig. ugs.) pump oneself full of tablets; **~ schmieren** + *Akk.* (beschmutzen) smear; (abwertend: beschreiben, bemalen) scrawl/draw all over ‹*wall etc.*›; fill ‹*exercise book etc.*› with scrawl; **die Mauern mit Parolen ~ schmieren** scrawl *or* daub slogans all over the walls; **etw. ~ laden** load sth. up completely; **~ geladen** fully laden; **etw. ~ füllen** fill sth. up; **etw. ~ gießen** fill sth. [up]; **den Teppich/sich** (*Dat.*) **die Hose mit Wein ~ gießen** (ugs.) spill wine all over the carpet/one's trousers; **etw. ~ machen** fill sth. up; (ugs.: beschmutzen) get *or* make sth. dirty; **[sich (*Dat.*)] die Hosen ~ machen** mess one's pants; **um das Maß ~ zu machen** (fig.) to crown *or* cap it all; **etw. ~ packen** pack sth. full; **etw. ~ pfropfen** cram sth. full; **mit etw. ~ gepfropft sein** be crammed full of sth.; **das Zimmer ~ qualmen** (ugs.) fill the room with smoke; **sich** (*Dat.*) **den Bauch [mit etw.] ~ schlagen** (salopp) stuff oneself *or* one's face [with sth.] (sl.); **etw. ~ schreiben** fill sth. [with writing]; **jmdn/etw. ~ spritzen** splash/spray water *etc.* all over sb./sth.; **jmdn./etw. mit etw. ~ spritzen** splash/spray sth. all over sb./sth.; **etw. ~ stopfen** stuff *or* cram sth. full; **jmdn. mit Fakten ~ stopfen** (ugs.) pump sb. full of facts; **etw. ~ tanken** fill sth. up; **bitte ~ tanken** fill it up, please; **sich ~ fressen** ‹*animal*› eat its fill; (derb) ‹*person*› stuff oneself *or* one's face (sl.); **~ gefressen sein** (derb) ‹*person*› be stuffed (sl.); **sich ~ saufen** (salopp) get completely plastered (sl.); **sich ~ saugen** ‹*leech*› suck itself full (*mit* of); ‹*sponge*› become saturated (*mit* with); **sich ~ stopfen** (ugs.) stuff oneself *or* one's face; **er hat sich** (*Dat.*) **die Hosen ~ geschissen** he filled his pants; **er hat den ganzen Teppich ~ gepinkelt** he peed all over the carpet; **soll ich dir dein Glas noch mal ~ schenken?** do you want a refill?; can I give you a refill?; *s. auch* **Lob; Mund**

2 (salopp: betrunken) plastered (sl.); canned (Brit. sl.)

3 (üppig) full ‹*figure, face, lip*›; thick ‹*hair*›; ample ‹*bosom*›; **im Gesicht ~er geworden sein** have filled out *or* be fuller in the face

4 (ganz, ~ständig) full; complete ‹*seriousness, success*›; **etw. mit ~em Recht tun** be quite right to do sth.; **einen ~en Tag/Monat warten** wait a full *or* whole day/month; **in ~er Fahrt** at full speed; **in ~em Gange sein** be in full swing; **die ~ Wahrheit** the full *or* whole truth; **mit dem ~en Namen unterschreiben** sign one's full name *or* one's name in full; **das Dutzend ist ~:** it's a round dozen; **~es/~stes Verständnis für jmdn. haben** have full/the fullest understanding for sb.; **~e Gewissheit über etw.** (*Akk.*) **haben** be completely certain about sth.; **der Mond ist ~:** the moon is full; **jmdn. nicht für ~ nehmen** not take sb. seriously; **in die Vollen gehen** (ugs.) go all out; **etw. ~ machen** (vervollständigen) complete sth.; **das Dutzend ~ machen** make up a round dozen; *s. auch* **Brust 1; Hals 2; Kehle 1**

5 (kräftig) full, rich ‹*taste, aroma*›; rich ‹*voice*›

6 ▸ **S. 729** (ugs.: bei Uhrzeitangaben) **die Uhr schlug ~:** the clock struck the hour; **fünf nach ~:** five past the hour

B *adv.* **1** (völlig, ganz) fully; **~ und ganz** completely; **etw. ~ auslasten** make full use of sth.; **~ verantwortlich für etw. sein** be wholly responsible *or* bear full responsibility for sth.; **~ arbeiten** (ugs.) work full-time; **er ist mir ~ in die Seite gefahren** (salopp) he drove straight into my side

2 (kräftig) richly; **~ klingen** have a full, rich sound; *s. auch* **voller**

***volladen** ▸ **voll A 1**

Voll·akademiker *der,* **Voll·akademikerin** *die* university graduate

voll·auf /od. '-–/ *Adv.* completely; fully; **~ genügen/reichen** be quite enough

***vollaufen** ▸ **voll A 1**

voll-, Voll-: ~automatisch **A** *Adj.* fully automatic; **B** *adv.* fully automatically; **~bad** *das* bath; **~bart** *der* full beard; **~bärtig** *Adj.* ‹*man*› with a full beard; **~beschäftigung** *die* (Wirtsch.) full employment *no art.;* **~besitz** *der:* **im ~besitz seiner [geistigen und körperlichen] Kräfte sein** be in full possession of one's [mental and physical] faculties; **~bild** *das* (Med.) complete picture; **~blut** *das* **1** thoroughbred; **2** (Med.) whole blood; **~blut-** true; **er ist ein ~blutpolitiker/~blutschauspieler** he is a true politician/actor *or* a politician/actor through and through; **~blüter** /-bly:tɐ/ *der;* **~~s, ~~:** thoroughbred; **~blütig** *Adj.* thoroughbred ‹*horse*›; (fig.) full-blooded ‹*person*›; **~bremsung** *die:* **eine ~bremsung machen** put the brakes full on; **~bringen** /-'-–/ *unr. tr. V.* (geh.) accomplish; achieve; **es ist ~bracht** (bibl.) it is finished; **~busig** /-bu:zɪç/ full-bosomed; buxom; **~dampf** *der* (Seemannsspr.) full steam; **mit ~dampf** at full steam *or* speed; (fig. ugs.) flat out

Völle·gefühl /'fœlə-/ *das* feeling of fullness

voll·enden

A *tr. V.* complete; finish; **mit vollendetem** *od.* **dem vollendeten 16. Lebensjahr** on reaching the age of 16 *or* completing one's sixteenth year; **vollendeter Mord/Landesverrat** consummated murder/treason; **sein Leben ~** (fig. geh. verhüll.) pass away; depart this life; *s. auch* **vollendet**

B *refl. V.* (geh.) (seinen Abschluss finden) ‹*process, transformation, etc.*› reach its conclusion; (vollkommen

V

werden) reach [its] completion

vollendet
A *Adj.* accomplished ‹*performance*›; perfect ‹*gentleman, host, manners, reproduction*›; **~e Gegenwart/Vergangenheit/Zukunft** (Sprachw.) perfect/pluperfect/future perfect; *s. auch* **Tatsache**
B *adv.* ‹*play*› in an accomplished manner; **~ schön sein** be perfectly beautiful

vollends /ˈfɔlɛnts/ *Adv.* completely; **~ für Behinderte ist das unzumutbar** for disabled people in particular *or* especially it is unreasonable

Voll·endung *die* **1** completion; **kurz vor der ~ stehen** be nearing completion; **mit/nach ~ des 65. Lebensjahres** on reaching the age of 65 *or* completing one's sixty-fifth year **2** (geh.: Krönung) culmination **3** (Vollkommenheit) perfection

voller *indekl. Adj.* full of; (erfüllt von) full of; filled with; **sein Anzug war ~ Flecken** his suit was covered with stains; **ein Leben ~ Arbeit** a life full of *or* filled with work; **~ Widersprüche sein** be full of contradictions

Völlerei /fœləˈrai/ *die;* **~, ~en** (abwertend) gluttony *no pl., no art.*

volley /ˈvɔli/ *Adv.* (bes. Fußball, Tennis) on the volley

Volley·ball *der* volleyball

voll-, Voll-: ~fett *Adj.* full-fat; ***~|fressen** ▸**voll A 1**; **~führen** /-ˈ--/ *tr. V.* perform, execute ‹*somersault, movement*›; perform ‹*dance, deed*›; ***~|füllen** ▸**voll A 1**; **~gas** *das:* ▸**ⓘ S. 310 ~gas geben** put one's foot down; **~gas fahren** drive flat out; **mit ~gas** at full throttle; ***~|gießen** ▸**voll A 1**; **~gummireifen** *der* solid rubber tyre; **~idiot** *der,* **~idiotin** *die* (salopp abwertend) complete idiot (coll.)

völlig /ˈfœlɪç/
A *Adj.* complete; total
B *adv.* completely; totally; **du hast ~ recht** you are absolutely right; **das ist ~ unmöglich** that is absolutely impossible; **mit etw. ~ einverstanden sein** be in complete agreement with sth.

voll-, Voll-: ~inhaltlich **A** *Adj.* complete; full; **B** *adv.* fully; **~jährig** *Adj.* of age *pred.*; **~jährig werden** come of age; attain one's majority; **sie hat zwei ~jährige Kinder** she has two children who are of age; **~jährigkeit** *die;* **~~:** majority *no art.*; **~jurist** *der,* **~juristin** *die* [fully-]qualified lawyer (*who has attained the qualifications necessary to become a judge*); **~kasko·versicherung** *die* fully comprehensive insurance; **~klimatisiert** *Adj.* fully air-conditioned

voll·kommen
A *Adj.* **1** /-ˈ-- od. ˈ---/ (vollendet) perfect **2** /ˈ---/ (vollständig) complete; total
B /ˈ---/ *adv.* completely; totally

Vollkommenheit *die;* **~:** perfection

voll-, Voll-: ~korn·brot *das* wholemeal (Brit.) *or* (Amer.) wholewheat bread; ***~|machen** ▸**voll A1, 4**; **~macht** *die;* **~~, ~~en** **1** authority; **jmdm. [die] ~macht geben/erteilen** give/grant sb. power of attorney; **seine ~macht[en] überschreiten** exceed one's authority; **in ~macht** per procurationem; **2** (Urkunde) power of attorney; **~mast** *Adv.* (Seemannsspr.) full mast; **auf ~mast** at full mast; **~mast flaggen** hoist a flag/flags to full mast; **~matrose** *der* able-bodied seaman; **~milch** *die* full-cream milk; **~milch·schokolade** *die* full-cream milk chocolate; **~mond** *der* full moon; **es ist/wir haben heute ~mond** there is a full moon tonight; **bei ~mond** at full moon; **~mond·gesicht** *das* (ugs.) moon face; **~mundig** **A** *Adj.* **1** (~ im Geschmack) full-bodied ‹*wine, flavour, etc.*›; **2** (abwertend: wichtigtuerisch) pompous; **B** *adv.* (abwertend: wichtigtuerisch) pompously; **~narkose** *die* (Med.) general anaesthetic; **unter ~narkose** under a general anaesthetic; ***~|packen** ▸**voll A 1**; **~pension** *die* full board *no art.*; **~profi** *der* (ugs.) real pro (coll.); ***~pfropfen** ▸**voll A 1**; ***~|pumpen** ▸**voll A 1**; ***~|qualmen** ▸**voll A 1**; **~rausch** *der:* **sich** (*Dat.*) **einen ~rausch antrinken** get completely drunk; **etw. im ~rausch tun** do sth. while completely drunk; **~reif** *Adj.* fully ripe; ***~|saufen** ▸**voll A 1**; ***~|saugen** ▸**voll A 1**; ***~|schlagen** ▸**voll A 1**; **~schlank** *Adj.* with a fuller figure *postpos., not pred.*; **ein Modell für ~schlanke Damen** a model for the fuller figure; **~schlank sein** have a fuller figure; ***~|schmieren** ▸**voll A 1**; ***~|schreiben** ▸**voll A 1**; **~sperrung** *die* (Verkehrsw.) complete closure; ***~|spritzen** ▸**voll A 1**; **~ständig** **A** *Adj.* complete; full ‹*text, address, etc.*›; **nicht ~ständig** incomplete; **B** *adv.* completely; ‹*list*› in full; **~ständigkeit** *die;* **~~:** completeness; **der ~ständigkeit halber** for the sake of completeness; ***~|stopfen** ▸**voll A 1**; **~streckbar** /-ˈ--/ *Adj.* (Rechtsw.) enforceable; implementable ‹*sentence*›; **~strecken** /-ˈ--/ *tr. V.* enforce ‹*penalty, fine, law*›; carry out ‹*sentence*› (**an** + *Dat.* on); **die ~streckende Gewalt** the executive [power]; **ein Testament ~strecken** execute a will; **~strecker** /-ˈ--/ *der,* **~streckerin** *die;* **~~, ~~nen** (des Gesetzes) enforcer; (eines Testaments) executor; **~streckung** /-ˈ--/ *die;* **~~, ~~en** ▸**vollstrecken**: enforcement; carrying out; execution

Vollstreckungs·befehl *der* (Rechtsw.) enforcement order; writ of execution

voll-, Voll-: *~|tanken ▸**voll A 1**; **~tönend** **A** *Adj.* sonorous; **B** *adv.* sonorously; **~treffer** *der* direct hit; **ein ~treffer sein** (fig.) hit the bullseye; **~trunken** *Adj.* completely *or* blind drunk; **in ~trunkenem Zustand** in a state of total inebriation; **~trunkenheit** *die* total inebriation *or* intoxication; **~verb** *das* (Sprachw.) full verb; **~versammlung** *die* general meeting; **~waise** *die* orphan; **~weib** *das* (ugs.) [real] stunner (coll.); **~wert·ernährung** *die* wholefood diet; **~wertig** *Adj.* full ‹*job, member*›; [fully] adequate ‹*replace ment, substitute, nourishment, diet*›; **~wert·kost** *die* wholefoods *pl.*; **~zählig** /-tsɛːlɪç/ *Adj.* complete; **wir bitten um ~zähliges Erscheinen** we request everyone to attend; **sie waren ~zählig erschienen** they had turned out in full strength; **als wir ~zählig [versammelt] waren** when everyone was present; **~zeit** *die* full-time work; **[in] ~zeit arbeiten** work full-time; **~zeit·beschäftigt** *Adj.* employed *or* working full-time *postpos.*; **~zeit·beschäftigte** *der/die* full-time employee; **~zeit·beschäftigung** *die* full-time employment *no. art.*; **~zeit·job** *der* (ugs.) full-time job; **~zeit·kraft** *die* full-time employee; **~zeit·kräfte** *Pl.* full-time staff *sing.*; **~zeit·stelle** *die* full-time post

voll·ziehen
A *unr. tr. V.* carry out ‹*instruction, action, will*›; carry out ‹*sentence*› (**an** + *Dat.* on); execute, carry out ‹*order*›; perform ‹*sacrifice, ceremony, sexual intercourse*›; **die Ehe ~:** consummate the marriage; **die ~de Gewalt** the executive [power];
B *unr. refl. V.* take place; **in ihm hatte sich eine Wandlung ~zogen** a change had come over him *or* taken place in him

Voll·zug *der* ▸**vollziehen A**: carrying out; execution; performance; consummation

Vollzugs-: ~anstalt *die* penal institution; **~beamte** *der,* **~beamtin** *die* [prison] warder; **~meldung** *die: report that an instruction has been carried out*

Volontär /volɔnˈtɛːɐ̯/ *der;* **~s, ~e** trainee (receiving a low salary in return for training)

Volontariat /volɔntaˈriaːt/ *das;* **~[e]s, ~e** **1** (Zeit) period of training **2** (Stelle) traineeship; *s. auch* **Volontär**

Volontärin *die;* **~, ~nen** ▸**Volontär**

volontieren *itr. V.* work as a trainee (**bei** with); *s. auch* **Volontär**

Volt /vɔlt/ *das;* **~** *od.* **~[e]s, ~** (Physik, Elektrot.) volt

Volte /ˈvɔltə/ *die;* **~, ~n** **1** (beim Kartenspiel) sleight of hand; **die** *od.* **eine ~ schlagen** (fig.) do a volte-face *or* an about-turn **2** (Reiten, Fechten) volte

voltigieren /vɔltiˈʒiːrən/ *itr. V.* perform acrobatics on horseback

Volt·meter *das;* **~s, ~** (Elektrot.) voltmeter

Volumen /voˈluːmən/ *das;* **~s, ~** ▸**ⓘ S. 582** volume

Volumen-: ~gewicht *das* ▸**Volumgewicht**; **~prozent** *das* ▸**Volumprozent**

Volum·gewicht *das* weight per [unit] volume

voluminös /voluminøːs/ *Adj.* voluminous; bulky ‹*tome*›

Volum·prozent *das* per cent by volume

vom /fɔm/ *Präp. + Art.* **1** = **von dem** **2** (räumlich) from the; **links/rechts ~ Eingang** to the left/right of the entrance; **~ Stuhl aufspringen** jump up out of one's chair **3** (zeitlich) **~ Morgen bis zum Abend** from morning till night; **~ ersten Januar an** [as] from the first of January **4** (zur Angabe der Ursache) **das kommt ~ Rauchen/Alkohol** that comes from smoking/drinking alcohol; **müde ~ Arbeiten/wund ~ Liegen** tired from working/sore from lying; **jmdn. ~ Sehen kennen** know sb. by sight

Vom·hundert·satz *der* percentage

von /fɔn/ *Präp. mit Dat.* **1** (räumlich) from; **nördlich/südlich ~ Mannheim** to the north/south of Mannheim; **rechts/links ~ mir** on my right/left; **~ hier an** *od.* (ugs.) **ab** from here on[ward]; **~ Mannheim aus** from Mannheim; **etw. ~ etw. [ab]wischen/[ab]brechen/[ab]reißen** wipe/break/tear sth. off sth.; *s. auch* **aus B 3**; **her 1**; **vorn[1]** **2** ▸**ⓘ S. 165** (zeitlich) from; **~ jetzt an** *od.* (ugs.) **ab** from now on; **~ heute/morgen an** [as] from today/tomorrow; starting today/tomorrow; **~ Kindheit an** from *or* since childhood; **in der Nacht ~ Freitag auf** *od.* **zu Samstag** during Friday night *or* the night of Friday to Saturday; **das Brot ist ~ gestern** it's yesterday's bread; *s. auch* **her 2**; **klein A 2**; **Mal[1]** **3** (anstelle eines Genitivs) of; **ein Stück ~ dem Kuchen** a slice of the cake; **acht ~ hundert/zehn** eight out of a hundred/ten; **ein Teufel ~ einem Vorgesetzten** a devil of a boss (coll.); **die Stimme ~ Caruso** (ugs.) Caruso's voice **4** (zur Angabe des Urhebers, der Ursache, beim Passiv) by; **der Roman ist ~ Fontane** the novel is by Fontane; **müde ~ der Arbeit sein** be tired from work[ing]; **etw. ~ seinem Taschengeld kaufen** buy sth. with one's pocket money; **sie hat ein Kind ~ ihm** she has a child by him; *s. auch* **wegen B** **5** (zur Angabe ~ Eigenschaften) of; **eine Fahrt ~ drei Stunden** a three-hour drive; **Kinder [im Alter] ~ vier Jahren** children aged four; **~ bester Qualität** of the best quality; **ein Mann/eine Frau ~ Charakter** a man/woman of character; **~ größter Bedeutung/Wichtigkeit sein** be of the utmost importance **6** (bestehend aus) of; **ein Ring ~ Gold** a ring of gold **7** (als Adelsprädikat) von; **Alexander ~ Humboldt** Alexander von Humboldt; **mit einer ~ verheiratet sein** (ugs.) be married to a woman with a title **8** (in Bezug auf) **er ist ~ Beruf Lehrer** he is a teacher by profession; **klein ~ Statur sein** be small in stature; *s. auch* **her 3** **9** (über) about; **~ diesen Dingen spricht man besser nicht** it's better not to speak of such things *s. auch* **Haus 7**; **davon**; **wovon**

von·einander *Adv.* from each other *or* one another; **sich ~ trennen** separate *or* part from each other; **sie sind ~ enttäuscht** they are disappointed in each other *or* in one another; **sie halten viel ~:** they think highly of each other

vonnöten /fɔnˈnøːtn̩/ *Adj. in* **~ sein** be necessary

vonseiten *Präp. + Gen.* **~ der Direktion** from the management side

vonstatten /fɔnˈʃtatn̩/ *Adv. in* **~ gehen** proceed; **der Umzug kann am 15. Juni ~ gehen** the removal can go ahead on 15 June

Voodoo /ˈvuːdu/ *der;* **~:** voodoo

Vopo[1] /ˈfoːpo/ *der;* **~s, ~s** (ugs.) ▸**Volkspolizist**

Vopo[2] *die;* **~** (ugs.) ▸**Volkspolizei**

vor /foːɐ̯/
A *Präp. mit Dat.* **1** (räumlich) in front of; (weiter

V

vorn) ahead of; in front of; (nicht ganz so weit wie) before; (außerhalb) outside; **~ einem Hintergrund von ...** against a background of ...; **zwei Schritte ~ jmdm. gehen** walk two paces ahead of *or* in front of sb.; **kurz/200 m ~ der Abzweigung** just/200 m. before the turn-off; **~ der Stadt/den Toren der Stadt** outside the town/the gates of the town; **etw. ~ sich haben** (fig.) have sth. before one; **das liegt noch ~ mir** (fig.) I still have that to come *or* have that ahead of me [2] ▸ⓘ **S. 729** (zeitlich) before; **~ Christus** before Christ; B C; **es ist fünf [Minuten] ~ sieben** it is five [minutes] to seven [3] (bei Reihenfolge, Rangordnung) before; **knapp ~ jmdm. siegen** win just ahead *or* in front of sb. [4] (in Gegenwart von) before; in front of; **etw. ~ Zeugen erklären** state sth. before *or* in the presence of witnesses; **sie tanzte ~ ausverkauftem Haus** she danced before *or* to a full house [5] (aufgrund von) with; **~ Freude strahlen** beam with joy; **~ Kälte zittern** shiver with cold; **~ Hunger/Durst umkommen** die of hunger/thirst; **~ Arbeit/Schulden nicht mehr aus und ein wissen** not know which way to turn for work/debts [6] **~ fünf Minuten/10 Jahren/Wochen** *usw.* five minutes/ten years/weeks ago; **heute/gestern/morgen ~ einer Woche** a week ago today/yesterday/tomorrow

[B] *Präp. mit Akk.* in front of; **keinen Schritt ~ die Tür tun** *od.* **setzen** not set foot outside the door; **er fuhr bis ~ die Haustür** he drove right up to the front door; **~ sich hin** to oneself; **still ~ sich hin arbeiten** work away quietly; *s. auch* **davor**; **wovor**

[C] *Adv.* (voran) forward; **Freiwillige ~!** volunteers to the front!; **~ und zurück** backwards and forwards

vor·ab *Adv.* beforehand

Vorab·druck *der; Pl.* **~e** [1] preprinting [2] (gedruckter Text) preprint

Vor·abend *der* [1] evening before; (fig.) eve; **das war am ~:** that was the evening before [2] (Ferns.) early evening; **am ~:** in the early evening

Vorabend-: ~programm *das* (Ferns.) early evening schedule; **~serie** *die* (Ferns.) early evening series; (Fortsetzungsgeschichte) early evening serial

Vor·ahnung *die* premonition; presentiment; **dunkle/schlimme ~en** dark forebodings

vor·an /fo'ran/

[A] *Adv.* (vorwärts) forward[s]

[B] *Präp. mit Dat., nachgestellt* ahead; first; **dem Festzug ~:** at the head of the parade; **allem ~:** first and foremost

voran-: ~|bringen *unr. tr. V.* make progress with ‹*work, project, etc.*›; **die Sache des Friedens ~bringen** advance *or* further the cause of peace; **jmdn./etw. ein gutes Stück ~bringen** bring sb./sth. a good step further; **~|gehen** *unr. itr. V.; mit sein* [1] go first *or* ahead; **jmdm. ~gehen** go ahead of sb.; **[jmdm.] mit gutem Beispiel ~gehen** (fig.) set [sb.] a good example; [2] (Fortschritte machen) make progress; **rasch/nur schleppend ~gehen** make rapid/only slow progress; **es geht mit der Arbeit/dem Schreiben nicht [so recht] ~:** the work/writing is not making [much] progress; [3] ▸**vorausgehen 2**; **~|kommen** *unr. itr. V.; mit sein* [1] make headway; **gut ~kommen** make good headway *or* progress; [2] (Fortschritte machen) make progress; **die Arbeit kommt gut/nicht ~:** the work is making good progress *or* coming along well/not making any progress; **beruflich ~kommen** get on in one's job

Vor·ankündigung *die* advance announcement; **ohne ~:** without any advance *or* prior notice

Vor·anmeldung *die* booking; (für einen Kursus) registration

voran-: ~|schreiten *unr. itr. V.; mit sein* (geh.) [1] lead the way; [2] (fortschreiten) progress; advance; **~|stellen** *tr. V.* place *or* put first; **dem Buch ist eine Einleitung ~gestellt** the book starts *or* begins with an introduction; **~|treiben** *unr. tr. V.* push ahead

Vor·anzeige *die* advance announcement

Vor·arbeit *die* preliminary work *no pl.*

vor|arbeiten

[A] *itr. V.* put in some hours in advance; **einen Tag/zwei Tage ~:** work a day/two days in advance

[B] *refl. V.* work one's way forward; **sich auf den zweiten Platz ~:** work one's way up to second place

Vor·arbeiter *der* foreman

Vor·arbeiterin *die* forewoman

vor·aus

[A] /-'-/ *Präp. mit Dat., nachgestellt* in front; **jmdm. weit ~ sein** be a long way in front *or* far ahead of sb.; **jmdm./seiner Zeit ~ sein** (fig.) be ahead of sb./one's time

[B] *Adv.* [1] **im Voraus** /'--/ in advance [2] (Seemannsspr.) ahead; **Volldampf ~!** full steam ahead!

voraus-, Voraus-: ~|ahnen *tr. V.* have a presentiment of; **~ahnen, dass ...** have a presentiment that ...; **~|berechnen** *tr. V.* (auch fig.) calculate in advance; **~|bestimmen** *tr. V.* determine in advance; **~|eilen** *itr. V.; mit sein* hurry on ahead; **jmdm. ~eilen** hurry on ahead of sb.; **~|fahren** *unr. itr. V.; mit sein:* ▸**vorfahren 3**; **~|gehen** *unr. itr. V.; mit sein* [1] go [on] ahead; **ihm geht der Ruf ~, sehr streng zu sein** (fig.) he has the reputation of being very strict; [2] (zeitlich) **einem Ereignis ~gehen** precede an event; **dem Entschluss gingen lange Überlegungen ~:** the decision was preceded by *or* followed lengthy deliberations; **~gegangene Misserfolge** previous failures; **wie im Vorausgehenden bereits dargestellt worden ist** as has already been shown above; **~|haben** *unr. tr. V.* **jmdm./einer Sache etw. ~haben** have the advantage of sth. over sb./sth.; **er hat ihm [an diplomatischem Geschick] viel/nichts ~:** he has a great/no advantage over him [with regard to diplomatic skill]; **~|laufen** *unr. itr. V.; mit sein* run on ahead *or* in front; **~|planen** [A] *itr. V.* plan ahead; [B] *tr. V.* **etw. ~planen** plan sth. in advance; **~sage** *die* ▸**Vorhersage**; **~|sagen** *tr. V.* predict; **jmdm. die Zukunft ~sagen** foretell *or* predict sb.'s future; **~|schauen** *itr. V.* look ahead; **~schauende Planung/Politik** foresighted planning/policy; **~|schicken** *tr. V.* [1] send [on] ahead; [2] (einleitend sagen) say first; **ich muss folgendes ~schicken** I must start *or* begin by saying the following; **~sehbar** *Adj.* foreseeable; **~|sehen** *unr. tr. V.* foresee; **das war [doch] ~zusehen/ließ sich nicht ~sehen** that was foreseeable/unforeseeable; **~|setzen** *tr. V.* [1] (als gegeben ansehen) assume; **etw. als bekannt ~setzen** assume sth. is known; **er setzte stillschweigend/als selbstverständlich ~, dass ...** he took it for granted that ...; **Ihr Einverständnis ~setzend** assuming *or* provided that you agree; **~gesetzt, [dass] ...** provided [that] ...; [2] (erfordern) require ‹*skill, experience, etc.*›; presuppose ‹*good organization, planning, etc.*›; **~setzung** *die;* **~~, ~~en** [1] (Annahme) assumption; (Prämisse) premise; [2] (Vorbedingung) prerequisite; **unter der ~setzung, dass ...** on condition *or* on the pre-condition that ...; **etw. zur ~setzung haben/machen** have sth. as/make sth. a pre-condition *or* prerequisite; **er hat die besten ~setzungen für den Job** he has the best qualifications for the job; **~sicht** *die* foresight; **aller ~sicht nach** in all probability; **in weiser ~sicht** (scherzh.) with great foresight; **~sichtlich** [A] *Adj.* anticipated; expected; [B] *adv.* probably; **der Abflug wird sich ~sichtlich verzögern** the departure is expected to be delayed; **~zahlung** *die* advance payment

vor|backen *unr. tr. V.* pre-bake; (im Voraus backen) bake beforehand

Vor·bau *der; Pl.* **~ten** [1] porch [2] (salopp scherzh.: Busen) [well-developed] bust [3] *s.* **Lenkervorbau**

vor|bauen *itr. V.* make provision; **der kluge Mann baut vor** (Spr.) a wise man makes provision for the future; **um vorzubauen, habe ich gleich gesagt, dass ...** to avoid any problems, I said straight away that ...

Vor·bedacht *der:* **in mit** *od.* (seltener) **aus ~:** intentionally; deliberately

Vor·bedingung *die* [pre]condition; **~en stellen** set preconditions

Vorbehalt /'fo:ɐ̯bahalt/ *der;* **~[e]s, ~e** reservation; **etw. nur unter ~ tun** do sth. only with reservations; **unter dem ~, dass ...** with the reservation that ...; **ohne ~:** unreservedly; without reservation

vor|behalten *unr. tr. V.* reserve; **sich** (Dat.) **etw. ~:** reserve oneself sth.; reserve sth. [for oneself]; **sich** (Dat.) **das Recht ~, etw. zu tun** reserve the right to do sth.; **„Änderungen ~"** 'subject to alterations'; **alle Rechte ~** (Druckw.) all rights reserved; **jmdm. ~ sein/bleiben** ‹*decision*› be left [up] to sb.; ‹*discovery, revision work, etc.*› be left to sb.; **die ersten Sitzreihen waren den Ehrengästen ~:** the first rows of seats were reserved for the guests of honour

vorbehaltlich *Präp. mit Gen.* (Papierdt.) subject to

vorbehalt·los

[A] *Adj.* unreserved; unconditional

[B] *adv.* unreservedly; without reservation[s]

vor·bei *Adv.* [1] (räumlich) past; by; **der Wagen war schon [an uns] ~:** the car was already past [us] *or* had already gone past *or* by [us]; **an etw.** (Dat.) **~:** past sth.; **[wieder] ~!** missed [again]! [2] ▸ⓘ **S. 729** (zeitlich) past; over; (beendet) finished; over; **es ist acht Uhr ~** (ugs.) it is past *or* gone eight o'clock; **~ ist ~:** what's past is past; *s. auch* **aus B 1**

vorbei-: ~|bringen *unr. tr. V.* (ugs.) drop off; drop round with; **kannst du mir das Buch heute Abend ~bringen?** can you drop the book off at my place this evening?; **~|dürfen** *unr. itr. V.* (ugs.) be allowed past *or* by; **an jmdm./etw. ~dürfen** be allowed past *or* by sb./sth.; **darf/dürfte ich mal bitte ~?** can/could I come *or* get past *or* by, please?; **~|fahren** [A] *unr. itr. V.; mit sein* [1] drive/ride past; pass; **an jmdm. ~fahren** drive/ride past *or* pass sb.; [2] (ugs.: einen kurzen Besuch machen) **[bei jmdm./der Post] ~fahren** drop in (coll.) [at sb.'s/at the post office]; [B] *tr. V.* (ugs.) **kannst du mich schnell beim Bahnhof ~fahren?** can you just run me to the station?; (absetzen) can you just drop me off at the station?; **~|führen** *itr. V.* ‹*path, road, etc.*› go *or* run past; **an etw.** (Dat.) **~führen** go *or* run past sth.; **daran führt kein Weg ~** (fig.) there's no getting around it; **~|gehen** *unr. itr. V.; mit sein* [1] pass; go past; **an jmdm./etw. ~gehen** pass *or* go past sb./sth.; **der Schuss/Schlag ist [am Ziel] ~gegangen** the shot/blow missed [its mark *or* target]; **an der Wirklichkeit ~gehen** (fig.) miss the truth; **im Vorbeigehen** (auch fig.) in passing; [2] (ugs.: einen kurzen Besuch machen) **[bei jmdm./der Post] ~gehen** drop in (coll.) [at sb.'s/at the post office]; [3] (vergehen) pass; **keine Gelegenheit ~gehen lassen** not let an *or* let no opportunity slip *or* pass; [4] (Sport) **an jmdm. ~gehen** pass *or* go past *or* overtake sb.; **~|kommen** *unr. itr. V.; mit sein* [1] pass; **an etw.** (Dat.) **~kommen** pass sth.; [2] (ugs.: einen kurzen Besuch machen); **[bei jmdm.] ~kommen** drop in (coll.) [at sb.'s]; [3] (~gehen, -fahren können) get past *or* by; **daran kommt man nicht ~** (fig.) there's no getting around *or* away from that; **~|können** *unr. itr. V.* (ugs.) be able to get past *or* by; **~|lassen** *unr. tr. V.* (ugs.) let past *or* by; **jmdn. an etw.** (Dat.) **~lassen** let sb. past *or* by sth.; **~|marschieren** *itr. V.; mit sein* march past; **an jmdm./etw. ~marschieren** march past sb./sth.; **~|mogeln** [A] *refl. V.* **sich an etw.** (Dat.) **~mogeln** fiddle *or* (coll.) finagle one's way round sth.; [B] *tr. V.* **etw. an jmdm./etw. ~mogeln** get sth. past sb./sth. [by a fiddle]; **~|müssen** *unr. itr. V.* (ugs.) have to pass *or* go past; **an jmdm./etw. ~müssen** have to pass *or* go past sb./sth.; **~|planen** *itr. V.* **an etw.** (Dat.) **~planen** plan without regard to sth.; **~|rauschen** *itr. V.; mit sein* (ugs.) ‹*car, bus, train*› whoosh past (coll.); ‹*person*› sweep past; **das ist alles an mir regelrecht ~gerauscht** (fig.) it all just passed me by; **~|reden** *itr. V.* **an etw.** (Dat.) **~reden** talk round sth. without getting to the point; **am Wesentlichen**

V

~**reden** miss the essential point; **aneinander ~reden** talk at cross purposes; **~|schießen** A *unr. itr. V.* [1] (danebenschießen) miss; **[am Ziel] ~schießen** miss [the target]; [2] *mit sein* (~fahren, -fliegen) ‹*car etc.*› shoot past; **an jmdm./etw. ~schießen** shoot past sb./sth.; B *unr. tr. V.* **den Ball am Tor ~schießen** shoot wide of the goal; **~|schrammen** *itr. V.; mit sein* (ugs.) **an etw.** (*Dat.*) **~schrammen** just miss *or* escape sth.; **~|ziehen** *unr. itr. V.; mit sein* pass by; (überholen) pass; go past; overtake; **an jmdm./etw. ~ziehen** pass by sb./sth.; (jmdn./etw. überholen) pass *or* go past *or* overtake sb.

vor·belastet *Adj.* handicapped (**durch** by); **erblich ~ sein** have an inherited defect

Vor·bemerkung *die* preliminary remark

vor|bereiten *tr. V.* [1] prepare; **jmdn./sich auf** *od.* **für etw. ~:** prepare sb./oneself for sth.; **sich [in Latein] nicht vorbereitet haben** not be prepared [in Latin]; **auf diese Reaktion war ich nicht vorbereitet!** I was unprepared for that reaction! [2] (die Vorarbeiten machen für) prepare for; **ein Fest/eine Reise ~:** prepare for *or* make preparations for a party/trip

Vor·bereitung *die;* **~, ~en** preparation; **~en [für** *od.* **zu etw.] treffen** make preparations for sth.; **in ~ sein** be in preparation

Vorbereitungs·zeit *die* preparatory period; **zwei Jahre ~, eine ~ von zwei Jahren** two years preparation time

Vor·besitzer *der,* **Vor·besitzerin** *die* previous owner

Vor·besprechung *die* [1] preliminary discussion[s *pl.*] [2] (Rezension) advance review

vor|bestellen *tr. V.* order in advance

Vor·bestellung *die* advance order

vor·bestimmt *Adj.* predestined

vor·bestraft *Adj.* (Amtsspr.) with a previous conviction/previous convictions *postpos., not pred.*; **[zweimal/mehrfach] ~ sein** have [two/several] previous convictions

Vor·bestrafte *der/die; adj. Dekl.* person with a previous conviction/previous convictions

vor|beten
A *itr. V.* lead the prayer/prayers
B *tr. V.* [1] **jmdm. das Vaterunser** *usw.* **~:** say the Lord's Prayer *etc.* [aloud] to sb. [2] (ugs.) reel off ‹*list, text, explanation, etc.*›

Vorbeuge·haft *die* preventive custody

vor|beugen
A *tr. V.* bend ‹*head, upper body*› forward; **sich ~:** lean *or* bend forward
B *itr. V.* **einer Sache** (*Dat.*) *od.* **gegen etw. ~:** prevent sth.; **einer Gefahr ~:** avert a danger; **~de Maßnahmen** preventive measures; **Vorbeugen ist besser als Heilen** (Spr.) prevention is better than cure (prov.)

Vor·beugung *die* prevention (**gegen** of); **zur ~:** as a preventive

Vorbeugungs·maßnahme *die* preventive measure

Vor·bild *das* model; **jmdm. als ~ dienen** serve sb. as a model; **jmdm. ein gutes ~ sein** be a good example to sb.; set sb. a good example; **sich** (*Dat.*) **jmdn./etw. zum ~ nehmen** take sb. as a model *or* model oneself on sb./take sth. as a model

Vorbild·funktion *die:* **eine ~ haben** be there to set an example

vor·bildlich
A *Adj.* exemplary
B *adv.* in an exemplary way *or* manner

Vor·bildung *die:* **die nötige/theoretische ~ besitzen** have the necessary knowledge and training/the theoretical background; **über eine mangelhafte ~ verfügen** have inadequate knowledge and training; have an inadequate background

vor|bohren *tr. V.* pre-drill

Vor·bote *der,* **Vor·botin** *die* harbinger

vor|bringen *unr. tr. V.* say; **eine Frage/Forderung/ein Anliegen ~:** ask a question/make a demand/express a desire; **Argumente ~:** present *or* state arguments; **Beweise ~:** produce evidence; **dagegen lässt sich viel ~:** there's much to be said against it

vor·christlich *Adj.* pre-Christian; **das dritte ~e Jahrhundert** the third century before Christ

Vor·dach *das* canopy

vor|datieren *tr. V.* [1] postdate ‹*cheque, letter, etc.*› [2] (zurückdatieren) antedate

vor|dem /*od.* '-/ *Adv.* [1] (geh.: zuvor) before [2] (veralt.: früher) in [the] olden days

Vor·denker *der,* **Vor·denkerin** *die* (Politikjargon) guiding intellectual force

vorder... /'fɔrdɐ.../ *Adj.* front; **die ~en Reihen** the front rows; **die ~sten Reihen** the rows at the very front; **der Vordere Orient** the Middle East

vorder-, Vorder-: **~achse** *die* front axle; **~ansicht** *die* front view; **~asien** (*das*) the Middle East; the Near East; **~bein** *das* foreleg; **~eingang** *der* front entrance; **~front** *die* [front] facade; front (also fig.); **~gebäude** *das* front building; **~grund** *der* foreground; **im ~grund stehen** (fig.) be prominent *or* to the fore; **bei seiner Entscheidung standen diese Überlegungen im ~grund** (fig.) these considerations were uppermost in his mind when taking his decision; **etw. in den ~grund stellen** *od.* **rücken** (fig.) give priority to sth.; place special emphasis on sth.; **in den ~grund treten** *od.* **rücken** (fig.) come to the fore; **sich in den ~grund spielen** *od.* **schieben** *od.* **drängen** (fig.) push oneself forward; **~gründig** /-grʏndɪç/ A *Adj.* superficial; B *adv.* superficially; **~hand** *Adv.* for the time being; for the present; **~haus** *das* house facing the street/square *etc.*; **~huf** *der* front hoof; **~leute** *Pl.* [1] ▸**Vordermann**; [2] (einer Fraktion o. Ä.) leaders

Vorder·indien (*das*) the Indian Peninsula

vorder-, Vorder-: **~lader** *der;* **~~s, ~~** (Waffenkunde) muzzle-loader; **~lastig** *Adj.* bow-heavy ‹*ship*›; nose-heavy ‹*aircraft*›; **~lauf** *der* (Jägerspr.) foreleg; **~mann** *der; Pl.* **~männer,** (selten auch) **~leute** person in front; **ihr/sein ~mann** the person in front of her/him; **jmdn. auf ~mann bringen** (ugs.) lick sb. into shape; **den Garten/Haushalt auf ~mann bringen** (ugs.) get the garden/house shipshape; **~pfote** *die* front paw; **~rad** *das* front wheel; **~rad·antrieb** *der* front-wheel drive; **~reifen** *der* front tyre; **~seite** *die* front; (einer Münze, Medaille) obverse; **~sitz** *der* front seat

vorderst... ▸**vorder...**

Vorder-: **~steven** *der* (Seemannsspr.) stem; **~teil** *das od. der* front [part]; **~zahn** *der* front tooth

vor|drängen *refl. V.* push [one's way] forward *or* to the front; (fig.) push oneself forward; **sich bis an etw.** (*Akk.*) **~:** push [one's way] forward to sth.; **sich an der Kasse/in der Schlange ~:** push to the front at the checkout/push to the front of the queue *or* (Amer.) line

vor|dringen *unr. itr. V.; mit sein* push forward; advance; **in den Weltraum ~:** push forward into space; **bis zu jmdm. ~** (fig.) reach sb.; get as far as sb.

vor·dringlich
A *Adj.* [1] priority *attrib.* ‹*treatment*›; **eine ~e Angelegenheit** a matter of priority [2] (dringlich) urgent; **unser ~stes Anliegen ist es, ...** our main *or* overriding concern is ...
B *adv.* [1] as a matter of priority [2] as a matter of urgency

Vor·druck *der; Pl.* **~e** form

vor·ehelich *Adj.* premarital

vor·eilig
A *Adj.* rash
B *adv.* rashly; **~ den Schluss ziehen, dass ...** jump to the conclusion that ...

vor·einander *Adv.* [1] one in front of the other [2] (einer dem anderen gegenüber) opposite each other; face to face; **Geheimnisse ~ haben/Gefühle ~ verbergen** have secrets/hide feelings from each other; **Hochachtung/Furcht ~ haben** have great respect for each other/be afraid of each other

vor·eingenommen *Adj.* prejudiced; biased; **für/gegen jmdn. ~ sein** be prejudiced in sb.'s favour/against sb.; **jmdm. gegenüber ~ sein** be prejudiced towards sb.

Vor·eingenommenheit *die;* **~, ~en** prejudice; bias; **politische ~:** political bias

vor|einstellen *tr. V.* preset ‹*time, code, temperature, station*›; pre-adjust ‹*device*›

Vor·einstellung *die* (DV) default

vorenthalten *unr. tr. V.;* **ich enthalte vor** (*od. seltener:* **vorenthalte**), **vorenthalten, vorzuenthalten: jmdm. etw. ~:** withhold sth. from sb.; **jmdm. eine Nachricht ~:** keep *or* withhold news from sb.

Vor·entscheidung *die* preliminary decision; **mit diesem Tor war eine ~ gefallen** this goal decided the course of the match

vor·erst /*od.* -'-/ *Adv.* for the present; for the time being

Vor·essen *das* (schweiz.) stew

vor|exerzieren *tr. V.* (ugs.) demonstrate

vor·fabriziert *adj.* pre-fabricated; (fig.) ready-made ‹*opinion, solution*›

Vorfahr /-fa:ɐ̯/ *der;* **~en** *od. selten* **~s, ~en, Vorfahre** *der;* **~n, ~n** forefather; ancestor

vor|fahren *unr. itr. V.; mit sein* [1] (ankommen) drive/ride up; **vor dem Hotel/Haus ~:** drive/ride up outside the hotel/house [2] (weiter nach vorn fahren) ‹*person*› drive *or* move forward; ‹*car*› move forward [3] (vorausfahren) drive *or* go on ahead

Vorfahrin *die;* **~, ~nen** [female] ancestor

Vor·fahrt *die* (Verkehrsw.) right of way; **„~ beachten/gewähren!"** 'give way'; **weil er die ~ nicht beachtete** because he failed to give way; **jmdm. die ~ nehmen** fail to give way to sb.

Vorfahrt[s]-: **~schild** *das* (Verkehrsw.) right of way sign; **~straße** *die* main road; **~zeichen** *das* (Verkehrsw.) ▸**~schild**

Vor·fall *der* [1] incident; occurrence [2] ▸❶ **S. 439** (Med.) prolapse

vor|fallen *unr. itr. V.; mit sein* [1] (sich ereignen) happen; occur; **ist etwas [Besonderes] vorgefallen?** has anything [special] happened? [2] (nach vorn fallen) fall forward

vor|feiern *tr., itr. V.* celebrate early *or* ahead of time

Vor·feld *das* [1] (eines Flughafens) apron [2] (Basketball) front court [3] (fig.) **im ~:** in advance; **im ~ des Parteitages** in the run-up to the party conference

Vor·film *der* supporting film

vor|finden
A *unr. tr. V.* find
B *unr. refl. V.* be to be found

vor|flunkern *tr. V.* (ugs.) **jmdm. ~, dass ...** spin sb. a yarn that ...; **sie flunkerte ihm irgendetwas vor** she told him some fib or other

Vor·form *die* early form

Vor·frau *die* (ugs.) woman in charge; (einer Partei) leader

Vor·freude *die* anticipation; **voller ~ auf etw.** (*Akk.*) **sein** be full of [happy] anticipation of sth.

Vor·frühling *der* early spring

vor|fühlen *itr. V.* **bei jmdm. ~:** sound sb. out; **ich habe bei ihnen vorgefühlt, was ...** I sounded them out about *or* as to what ...

vor|führen *tr. V.* [1] bring forward; **jmdn. dem Richter ~:** bring sb. before the judge; **er wurde zur Vernehmung vorgeführt** he was brought for questioning [2] (zeigen) show; **wann führst du uns deinen Freund vor?** when are you going to introduce your boyfriend to us? [3] (demonstrieren) demonstrate; **jmdm. etw. ~:** demonstrate sth. to sb. [4] (darbieten) show ‹*film, slides, etc.*›; present ‹*circus act, programme*›; perform ‹*play, trick, routine*›

Vorführ·gerät *das* (Projektor) projector

Vor·führung *die* [1] bringing forward; **der Richter ordnete die ~ des Gefangenen an** the judge ordered the prisoner to be brought forward [2] (das Zeigen) showing; exhibiting [3] (das Demonstrieren) demonstration [4] (das

V

Darbieten) ▸**vorführen 4**: showing; presentation; performance [5] (Veranstaltung) ▸**vorführen 4**: show; presentation; performance

Vorführ·wagen *der* demonstration car *or* model

Vor·gabe *die* [1] (Sport) handicap [2] (Richtlinie) guideline

Vorgabe·zeit *die* (Wirtsch.) [target] time for the job/project *etc.*

Vor·gang *der* [1] occurrence; event; **chemische/physikalische** *usw.* **Vorgänge** chemical/physical *etc.* processes [2] (Amtsspr.) file; **der ~ XY** the file on XY

Vor·gänger /-gɛŋɐ/ *der;* **~s, ~, Vor·gängerin** *die;* **~, ~nen** (auch fig.) predecessor

Vor·garten *der* front garden

vor|gaukeln *tr. V.* **jmdm. ~, dass ...** lead sb. to believe that ...; **jmdm. eine heile Welt ~:** lead sb. to believe in a perfect *or* an ideal world

vor|geben *unr. tr. V.* [1] (vortäuschen) pretend [2] (Sport) **jmdm. eine Runde/50 m/15 Punkte ~:** give sb. a lap [start]/[a start of] 50 m/[a lead of] 15 points [3] (im Voraus festlegen) set in advance; **vorgegebene Normen/Werte** predetermined standards/preset values; **ein vorgegebenes Programm** a preset programme

Vor·gebirge *das* promontory

vor·geblich *Adj.; adv.* ▸**angeblich**

vor·geburtlich

[A] *Adj.* antenatal

[B] *adv.* before birth

vor·gedruckt *Adj.* pre-printed

vor·gefasst, *vor·gefaßt *Adj.* preconceived

vor·gefertigt *Adj.* ▸**vorfabriziert**

Vor·gefühl *das* presentiment; **im ~ solchen Glücks** in anticipation of such happiness

vor|gehen *unr. itr. V.; mit sein* [1] (ugs.: nach vorn gehen) go forward; **an die Tafel/zum Altar ~:** go up to the blackboard/the altar [2] (vorausgehen) go on ahead; **jmdn. ~ lassen** let sb. go first [3] ‹*clock*› be fast; *s. auch* **nachgehen 4** [4] (einschreiten) **gegen jmdn./etw. ~:** take action against sb./sth.; **gesetzlich gegen jmdn./etw. ~:** take legal action *or* proceedings against sb./sth.; **mit etw./mit Strenge gegen jmdn./etw. ~:** use sth. on/take strict measures against sb./sth. [5] (verfahren) proceed [6] (sich abspielen) happen; go on; **was geht hier vor?** what is happening *or* going on here?; **in jmdm. ~:** go on inside sb.; **mit ihm war eine Veränderung vorgegangen** there had been a change in him; a change had taken place in him [7] (Vorrang haben) have priority; come first; **allem anderen ~:** have priority *or* take precedence over everything else

Vor·gehen *das;* **~s** action

vor·gelagert *Adj.* **die [der Küste] ~en Inseln** the offshore islands; the islands situated off the coast

vor·genannt *Adj.* (Amtsspr.) aforementioned; aforesaid

Vor·geplänkel *das* preliminary skirmishing *no indef. art.*

Vor·gericht *das* ▸**Vorspeise**

Vor·geschichte *die* [1] prehistory *no art.* [2] (Begebenheiten) history

vor·geschichtlich *Adj.* prehistoric

Vor·geschmack *der* foretaste

vor·geschritten *Adj.* (geh.) late ‹*hour*›; advanced ‹*age*›

Vor·gesetzte *der/die; adj. Dekl.* superior

Vor·gespräch *das* preliminary discussion

vor·gestern *Adv.* the day before yesterday; **~ Mittag/Abend/früh** the day before yesterday at midday/the evening before last/the morning of the day before yesterday; **er ist von ~** (ugs.) he is old-fashioned *or* behind the times; **Ansichten/Konventionen von ~** (ugs.) old-fashioned *or* outdated views/conventions

vor·gestrig *Adj.* of the day before yesterday *postpos.*

vor|glühen *tr., itr. V.* (Kfz-W.) preheat

vor|greifen *unr. itr. V.* [1] **jmdm. [bei** *od.* **in/mit etw.] ~:** anticipate sb. *or* jump in ahead of sb. [in/with sth.]; **einer Sache** (*Dat.*) **~:** anticipate sth. [2] (in einer Erzählung) jump ahead

Vor·griff *der* anticipation (**auf** + *Akk.* of); (bei einer Erzählung) jump *or* leap ahead (**auf** + *Akk.* to); **im ~ auf etw.** (*Akk.*) in anticipation of sth.

vor|haben *unr. tr. V.* intend; (geplant haben) plan; **er hat eine Reise vor** *od.* **er hat vor, eine Reise zu machen** he intends going on a journey/plans to go on a journey; **hast du heute Abend etwas vor?** have you anything planned *or* any plans for this evening?; are you doing anything this evening?; **wenn du nichts Besseres vorhast** if you have nothing better to do; **er hat Großes mit seinem Sohn vor** he has great plans for his son

Vor·haben *das;* **~s, ~** (Plan) plan; (Projekt) project

Vor·halle *die* (eines Tempels) portico; (Eingangshalle) entrance hall; (eines Theaters, Hotels) foyer

vor|halten

[A] *unr. tr. V.* [1] hold up; **sich** (*Dat.*) **etw. ~:** hold sth. [up] in front of oneself; **jmdn. mit vorgehaltener Schusswaffe bedrohen** threaten sb. at gunpoint; *s. auch* **Hand 6** [2] (zum Vorwurf machen) **jmdm. etw. ~:** reproach sb. for sth.

[B] *unr. itr. V.* (ugs., auch fig.) last

Vor·haltungen *Pl.* **jmdm. [wegen etw.] ~ machen** reproach sb. [for sth.]

Vor·hand *die* [1] (Sport, bes. Tennis) forehand; *s. auch* **Rückhand** [2] (beim Pferd) forehand [3] (Kartenspiel) lead; **in der ~ sein** have the lead

vorhanden /-'handn̩/ *Adj.* existing; (verfügbar) available; **~ sein** exist *or* be in existence/be available; **ein Vorratsraum ist hier leider nicht ~:** unfortunately there is no storeroom here; **von dieser Sorte ist noch genügend ~:** there's still plenty of this sort left

Vorhanden·sein *das;* **~s** existence

Vor·hang *der* (auch Theater) curtain; **viele Vorhänge bekommen** (Theater) get a large number of curtain calls; *s. auch* **eisern A1**

Vorhänge·schloss, *Vorhänge·schloß *das* padlock

Vorhang-: ~stange *die* curtain rod; **~stoff** *der* curtain material; curtaining

Vor·haut *die* ▸🅘 **S. 435** foreskin; prepuce

vor|heizen *tr. V.* put the heating on in ‹*room etc.*› [to warm it up in advance]; **im vorgeheizten Ofen** in a preheated oven

vor·her *od.* -'-/ beforehand; (davor) before; **am Abend ~:** [on] the evening before; [on] the previous evening; **das ist drei Wochen ~ passiert** it happened three weeks earlier *or* before

vorher-, Vorher-: ~|bestimmen *tr. V.* determine in advance; predetermine; **alles ist vom Schicksal/von Gott ~bestimmt** everything is foreordained by fate/preordained by God; **~bestimmung** *die* predetermination; (Prädestination) predestination; **~|gehen** *unr. itr. V.; mit sein* **in den ~gehenden Wochen** in the preceding weeks; in the weeks before; **wie im Vorhergehenden erläutert** as explained above

vorherig /od. '---/ *Adj.* prior ‹*notice, announcement, warning*›; previous ‹*discussion, agreement*›; **um ~e Bezahlung bitten** request payment in advance

Vor·herrschaft *die* supremacy; dominance

vor|herrschen *itr. V.* predominate; **die ~de Meinung/der ~de Geschmack** the predominant *or* prevailing opinion/taste

vorher-, Vorher-: ~sage *die* prediction; (des Wetters) forecast; **~|sagen** *tr. V.* predict; forecast ‹*weather*›; **~sehbar** *Adj.* ▸**voraussehbar**; **~|sehen** *unr. tr. V.* ▸**voraussehen**

vor|heucheln *tr. V.* **[jmdm.] etw. ~:** feign sth. [to sb.]; **er heuchelte ihr Liebe vor** he pretended to love her

vor·hin /od. -'-/ *Adv.* a short time *or* while ago; **sie ist ~ erst angekommen** she has only just arrived; **das ist der Junge von ~** (ugs.) that's the boy who we saw a short time ago *or* just now

***vor·hinein, Vor·hinein** *in* **im ~** (bes. österr.) in advance

Vor·hof *der* [1] ▸🅘 **S. 435** (Anat.) atrium [2] (vorderer Hof) forecourt; **für uns war es schon der ~ zur Seligkeit** (fig.) to us it was almost perfect bliss

Vor·hölle *die* (kath. Rel.) limbo *no art.*

Vor·hut *die;* **~, ~en** advance guard; (fig.) vanguard

vorig *Adj.* [1] ▸🅘 **S. 165** last [2] (schweiz.) (übrig) left over *postpos.;* (verfügbar) spare; **etw. ~ lassen** leave sth. over; **~e Zeit haben** have some spare time

vor·industriell *Adj.* pre-industrial

Vor·jahr *das* previous year

Vorjahres·monat *der* (bes. Wirtsch.) **der ~:** the same month the previous year; (voriges Jahr) the same month last year

vor·jährig *Adj.* of the previous year

vor|jammern *tr. V.* (ugs.) **jmdm. etw. ~:** moan *or* whine to sb. about sth.

Vor·kämpfer *der,* **Vor·kämpferin** *die* pioneer; **ein ~ der Freiheit** a pioneering champion of freedom

vor|kauen *tr. V.* (fig. ugs.) spell out; **jmdm. etw. ~:** spell sth. out for sb.; spoon-feed sth. to sb.

Vor·kaufs·recht *das* (Rechtsw.) right of first refusal

Vorkehr /-ke:ɐ/ *die;* **~, ~en** (schweiz.) precaution

Vorkehrungen *Pl.* precautions; **~ [gegen etw.] treffen** take precautions [against sth.]

Vor·kenntnis *die* background knowledge

vor|knöpfen *tr. V.* (ugs.) **sich** (*Dat.*) **jmdn. [ordentlich/kräftig] ~:** give sb. a [proper/good] talking-to (coll.)

vor|kochen *tr. V.* pre-cook; (im Voraus kochen) cook beforehand

vor|kommen *unr. itr. V.; mit sein* [1] (sich ereignen) happen; **dass mir so etwas nicht wieder vorkommt!** I hope I never experience anything like that again; **so etwas ist mir noch nie vorgekommen** nothing like that has ever happened to me before [2] (vorhanden sein) occur; **das Tier/die Pflanze kommt nur im Gebirge vor** the animal/plant is found only in the mountains; **in einer Erzählung ~** ‹*character, figure*› appear in a story [3] (erscheinen) seem; **das Lied kommt mir bekannt vor** I seem to know the song; **es kam mir [so] vor, als ob ...** I felt *or* it seemed as if ...; **du kommst dir wohl schlau vor** I suppose you think you're clever; **das kommt dir nur so vor** it just seems like that to you; **ich komme mir überflüssig vor** I feel [as if I am] superfluous; **wie kommst du mir eigentlich vor?** (ugs.) who do you think you are? [4] (ugs.: nach vorne kommen) come forward; **an die Tafel ~:** come up to the blackboard [5] (her~) come out; **hinter/unter etw.** (*Dat.*) **~:** come out from behind/under sth.; **unter dem Schnee ~** ‹*flower*› come up out of the snow

Vorkommen *das;* **~s, ~** [1] (das Auftreten) occurrence; (einer Krankheit) incidence [2] (Geol.: Lagerstätte) deposit

Vorkommnis /-kɔmnɪs/ *das;* **~ses, ~se** incident; occurrence

vor|kosten *tr. V.* sample in advance

Vor·kriegszeit *die* pre-war period

vor|laden *unr. tr. V.* summon; summon, subpoena ‹*witness*›

Vor·ladung *die* summons; **eine ~ vor Gericht** a summons to appear in court; **eine gerichtliche/polizeiliche ~:** a court/police summons; **die ~ eines Zeugen beantragen** apply for a witness to be summoned *or* subpoenaed

Vor·lage *die* [1] ▸**vorlegen A1**: presentation; showing; production; submission; tabling; introduction; **gegen ~ einer Sache** (*Gen.*) on production *or* presentation of sth. [2] (Entwurf) draft; (Gesetzentwurf) bill [3] (Muster) pattern; (Modell) model; **~n zum Stricken** knitting patterns; **etw. von einer ~ abschreiben** copy

V

sth.; **etw. als ~ benutzen** use sth. as a model; **nach einer/ohne ~ zeichnen** draw from/without a model **4** (Ballspiele, bes. Fußball) forward pass; **eine ~ geben/schlagen** make a forward pass; lay the ball forward **5** (Skisport) vorlage; forward lean **6** (Kaufmannsspr.) advance; **[für etw.] in ~ treten** advance the money [for sth.]

Vor·land *das* **1** (vor einem Gebirge) foothills *pl.* **2** (Deich~) foreshore

vor|lassen *unr. tr. V.* **1** (ugs.: den Vortritt lassen) **jmdn. ~:** let sb. go first *or* in front **2** (empfangen) admit; let in

Vor·lauf *der* **1** (Sport) [preliminary] heat **2** (bes. DDR: eines Projekts) preliminary work; groundwork **3** (bei Kassettenspieler etc.) fast forward; **das Band im [schnellen] ~ umspulen** fast-forward the tape

vor|laufen *unr. itr. V.; mit sein* (ugs.) **1** (ugs.: nach vorn laufen) run forward **2** ▸**vorauslaufen**

Vor·läufer *der,* **Vor·läuferin** *die* precursor; forerunner

vor·läufig

A *Adj.* temporary; provisional ‹*diagnosis, settlement, result, successor*›; interim ‹*order, agreement*›

B *adv.* for the time being; for the present; **jmdn. ~ festnehmen** detain sb. temporarily; take sb. into temporary custody

Vor·lauf·zeit *die* (Wirtsch.: eines Projekts) lead time

vor·laut

A *Adj.* forward

B *adv.* forwardly

vor|leben *tr. V.* **jmdn. etw. ~:** set sb. an example of sth. [in the way one lives]

Vor·leben *das* past life; past

Vorlege-: ~besteck *das* [set of] serving cutlery; **~gabel** *die* serving fork; **~löffel** *der* serving spoon

vor|legen

A *tr. V.* **1** present; show, produce ‹*certificate, identity card, etc.*›; show ‹*sample*›; submit ‹*evidence*›; table, introduce ‹*parliamentary bill*›; (veröffentlichen) publish **2** **jmdm./sich eine Frage ~:** pose sb./oneself a question **3** (anbringen vor) **eine Kette/einen Riegel ~:** put a chain on *or* across/a bolt across **4** (geh.: aufgeben) serve ‹*food*›; **jmdm. etw. ~:** serve sb. with sth.; serve sth. to sb. **5** (bes. Fußball) **jmdm./sich den Ball ~:** lay the ball on for sb./tap the ball on **6** **ein scharfes Tempo ~:** set a fast pace

B *refl. V.* lean forward

Vorleger *der;* **~s, ~** (vor der Badewanne, dem Waschbecken) mat; (vor dem Bett) rug

Vor·leistung *die* advance concession

vor|lesen *unr. tr., itr. V.* read aloud *or* out; read ‹*story, poem, etc.*› aloud; **jmdm. [etw.] ~:** read [sth.] to sb.; **lies schon vor!** read it out!; read out what it says!; **aus seinen Werken ~:** read from one's works

Vor·lesung *die* lecture; (~sreihe) series *or* course of lectures

Vorlesungs·verzeichnis *das* lecture timetable

vor·letzt... *Adj.* ▸❶ **S. 816** last but one; next to last; penultimate ‹*page, episode, etc.*›; **mein ~es Exemplar** my last copy but one; my next to last copy; **~es Mal** the time before last; **im ~en Jahr/Sommer** the year/summer before last; **seit ~er Woche** since the week before last

vorlieb *in* **mit jmdm./etw. ~ nehmen** put up with sb./sth.; (sich begnügen) make do with sb./sth.

Vor·liebe *die* preference; [special] fondness *or* liking; **eine ~ für jmdn./etw. haben** be fond of sb./be fond of *or* partial to sth.; **etw. mit ~ tun** particularly like doing sth.

***vorlieb|nehmen** ▸**vorlieb**

vor|liegen *unr. itr. V.* **1** **jmdm. ~** ‹*application, complaint, plans, etc.*› be with sb.; **das Beweismaterial liegt dem Gericht vor** the evidence is before *or* has been submitted to the court; **die Ergebnisse liegen uns noch nicht vor** we do not have the results yet; **die mir ~de Ausgabe/~den Ergebnisse** the edition/results in front of me; **im ~den Fall, in ~dem Fall** in the present case **2** (bestehen) be [present]; exist; ‹*symptom*› be present; ‹*book*› be available; **gegen ihn liegt nichts vor** there is nothing against him; **hier liegt ein Irrtum/Missverständnis vor** there is a mistake/misunderstanding here; **ein Verschulden des Fahrers liegt nicht vor** the driver is/was not to blame **3** *südd., österr., schweiz. mit sein* (ugs.: vorgelegt sein) ‹*chain, bolt, etc.*› be on *or* across

vor|lügen *unr. tr. V.* (ugs.) **jmdm. etwas ~:** lie to sb.; **er hat uns vorgelogen, dass er die Prüfung bestanden habe** he lied to us, pretending he had passed the examination

vorm /fo:ɐ̯m/ *Präp. + Art.* **1** = **vor dem** **2** (räumlich) in front of the **3** (zeitlich, bei Reihenfolge, Rangordnung) before the; **~ Frühstück** before breakfast

vor|machen *tr. V.* (ugs.) **1** (vorführen) **jmdm. etw. ~:** show sb. sth.; **ihm macht niemand was vor** there is no one better than him; no one can teach him anything **2** (vortäuschen) **jmdm. etwas ~:** kid (coll.) *or* fool sb.; **mir kannst du nichts ~:** you can't kid (coll.) *or* fool me; **wir wollen uns nichts ~:** let's not kid (coll.) *or* fool ourselves; **mach mir doch nichts vor** don't try and kid me (coll.); **der lässt sich von keinem was ~:** he's nobody's fool; *s. auch* **Dunst 2; X**

Vor·macht *die* supremacy *no art.*

Vormacht·stellung *die* [position of] supremacy *no art.*; **sich** (*Dat.*) **eine ~ sichern** secure [a position of] supremacy

vormalig /-ma:lɪç/ *Adj.* former

vormals /-ma:ls/ *Adv.* formerly

Vor·mann *der* foreman

Vor·marsch *der* (auch fig.) advance; **auf dem** *od.* **im ~ sein** ‹*army*› be advancing *or* on the advance; (fig.) ‹*ideas, new development, etc.*› be gaining ground

Vor·märz *der* (*hist.*): *period in German history from 1815 until the March 1848 revolution*

vor|merken *tr. V.* make a note of; **ein Zimmer ~ lassen** reserve a room; **ich habe Sie für den Kurs/für Montag vorgemerkt** I've put you down for the course/for Monday

Vor·mieter *der,* **Vor·mieterin** *die* previous tenant

***vor·mittag** ▸**Vormittag**

Vor·mittag *der* morning; **am [späten] ~:** [late] in the morning; **am frühen ~:** during the first part of the morning; **heute/morgen/Freitag ~:** this/tomorrow/Friday morning

vor·mittäglich *Adj.* morning

vor·mittags *Adv.* ▸❶ **S. 729** in the morning

Vormittags·stunde *die* morning hour

Vor·monat *der* previous *or* preceding month

Vor·mund *der;* **~[e]s, ~e** *od.* **Vormünder, Vormundin** *die;* **~, ~nen** guardian; **einen Vormund bestellen** appoint a guardian; **ich brauche keinen Vormund** (fig.) I don't need anyone telling me what to do

Vormundschaft *die;* **~, ~en** guardianship; **die ~ über** *od.* **für jmdn. übernehmen** become sb.'s guardian; **jmdn. unter jmds. ~ stellen** place sb. under sb.'s guardianship

Vormundschafts·gericht *das: court dealing with matters of guardianship*

vorn[1] /'fɔrn/ *Adv.* at the front; **das Zimmer liegt nach ~ [raus]** (ugs.) the room faces the front; **~ am Haus/in der Schlange** at the front of the house/queue *or* (Amer.) line; **ganz ~ sitzen** sit right at the front; **das Kleid wird ~ zugeknöpft** the dress buttons up at the front *or* in front; **~ im Bild** in the foreground of the picture; **nach ~ schauen** look in front *or* to the front; **nach ~ gehen/kommen** go/come to the front; **~ im Buch** at the front of the book; **[gleich] da ~:** [just] over there; **weiter ~:** up ahead; a bit further on; **der Wind/Schlag kam von ~:** the wind/blow came from the front; **noch einmal von ~ anfangen** start afresh; start from the beginning again; **es geht wieder von ~ los** it is starting all over again; **von ~ bis hinten** (ugs.) from beginning to end; **das ist von ~ bis hinten gelogen** it's all lies from beginning to end

vorn[2] /fo:ɐ̯n/ *Präp. + Art.* (ugs.) = **vor den**

Vor·name *der* first *or* Christian name

vorne *Adv.* ▸**vorn**[1]

vorne·dran *Adv.* (ugs.) in front; at the front; (beim Rennen führend) in the lead; (vor allem) first and foremost

vornehm /'fo:ɐ̯ne:m/

A *Adj.* **1** (nobel) noble ‹*character, behaviour, gesture, etc.*›; **~e Gesinnung** noble-mindedness **2** (der Oberschicht angehörend, kultiviert) distinguished; **zur ~en Welt/Gesellschaft/zu den ~en Kreisen gehören** be part of high society; **~e Blässe/~es Getue** genteel pallor/behaviour **3** (von adliger Herkunft) noble **4** (elegant) exclusive ‹*district, hotel, restaurant, resort*›; elegant ‹*villa, clothes*›; elegant, distinguished ‹*appearance*› **5** **~st...** (geh.: vorrangig) primary ‹*duty, task, function, source of income, etc.*›

B *adv.* **1** (nobel) nobly **2** (elegant) elegantly

vor|nehmen *unr. tr. V.* **1** **sich** (*Dat.*) **etw. ~:** plan sth.; **sich** (*Dat.*) **~, etw. zu tun** plan to do sth.; **sich** (*Dat.*) **~, mit dem Rauchen aufzuhören** resolve to give up smoking **2** (ugs.: sich beschäftigen mit) get busy with; **nimm dir ein Buch vor und lies!** pick up a book and read! **3** (ugs.: zur Rede stellen) **sich jmdn. ~:** give sb. a talking-to (coll.) **4** (durchführen) carry out, make ‹*examination, search, test*›; perform ‹*action, ceremony*›; make ‹*correction, change, division, choice, selection*›; take ‹*measurements*›

Vornehmheit *die;* **~** ▸**vornehm A 1-4**: nobility; exclusivity; elegance; **seine ~ beeindruckte sie** she was impressed by his distinguished manner; **die ~ seiner Erscheinung** his distinguished appearance

vornehmlich *Adv.* (geh.) above all; primarily

Vornehm·tuerei /od. ----'-/ *die;* **~** (abwertend) affectation

vor|neigen *tr., refl. V.* lean forward; **in vorgeneigter Haltung** bent forward

vorne·weg *Adv.* ▸**vorweg**

vorn-: ~herein *in* **von** *od.* (schweiz.) **zum** *od.* **im ~herein** from the start *or* outset *or* beginning; **~über** *Adv.* forwards

vornüber|fallen *unr. itr. V.; mit sein* fall forwards

Vor·ort *der* suburb

Vorort·zug *der* suburban train

Vor·platz *der* forecourt

Vor·posten *der* (Milit., auch fig.) outpost

vor|preschen *itr. V.; mit sein* (fig.) rush ahead

Vor·programm *das* supporting programme

vor|programmieren *tr. V.* (auch fig.) pre-programme

vor|ragen *itr. V.* project; jut out

Vor·rang *der* **1** **[den] ~ [vor jmdm./etw.] haben** have priority *or* take precedence [over sb./sth.]; **jmdn. mit ~ bedienen** give sb. priority service; **jmdm./einer Sache den ~ geben** give sb./sth. priority **2** (bes. österr.: Vorfahrt) right of way

vorrangig /-raŋɪç/

A *Adj.* priority *attrib.* ‹*treatment, task, objective*›; **~ sein** be a matter of priority *or* of prime importance; **von ~er Bedeutung** of prime *or* utmost importance; **jmds. ~es Anliegen/Ziel sein** be sb.'s primary concern/goal; **zu den ~sten Aufgaben gehören** be one of the prime *or* most important tasks

B *adv.* **jmdn. ~ behandeln** give sb. priority treatment; **etw. ~ erledigen** deal with sth. as a matter of priority

Vorrang·stellung *die* position of prime importance; (eines Landes) supremacy

Vor·rat *der* supply, stock (**an** + *Dat.* of); **etw. auf ~ kaufen/herstellen** stock up with *or* on sth./produce stocks of sth.; **ein ~ an Witzen** (fig.) a stock of jokes; **solange der ~ reicht** while stocks last

vorrätig /-rɛ:tɪç/ *Adj.* in stock *postpos.*; **etw. ~ haben** have sth. in stock; **etw. nicht ~ haben** be out of [stock of] sth.

V

Vorrats-: ~kammer *die* pantry; larder; **~keller** *der* cellar storeroom; **~raum** *der* storeroom

Vor·raum *der* anteroom

vor|rechnen *tr. V.* **jmdm. etw. ~:** work sth. out *or* calculate sth. for sb.; **jmdm. seine Fehler ~** (fig.) enumerate sb.'s mistakes

Vor·recht *das* privilege

Vor·rede *die* **1** (Vorwort) preface; foreword **2** (einleitende Worte) introductory remarks *pl.*; **sich nicht lange bei** *od.* **mit der ~ aufhalten** not take long over the introductions

Vor·redner *der*, **Vor·rednerin** *die* previous speaker; **mein ~:** the previous speaker

vor|reiten *unr. itr. V.; mit sein* ride on ahead

Vor·reiter *der*, **Vor·reiterin** *die:* **den Vorreiter/die Vorreiterin machen, ~ sein** lead the way

Vorreiter·rolle *die* pioneering role

Vor·richtung *die* device

vor|rücken
A *tr. V.* move forward; advance ‹*chess piece*›
B *itr. V.; mit sein* move forward; (Milit.) advance; **mit dem Turm ~** (Schach) advance the rook; **auf den 5. Platz ~:** move up to fifth place; **zu vorgerückter Stunde** (geh.) at a late hour

Vor·ruhestand *der* early retirement

Vor·ruheständler *der*, **Vor·ruheständlerin** *die* early retiree; person who has taken early retirement

Vor·ruhestands·regelung *die* regulation enabling employees to take early retirement

Vor·runde *die* (Sport) preliminary *or* qualifying round

vors *Präp. + Art.* **1** = **vor das 2** in front of the; **jmdm. ~ Auto laufen** run in front of sb.'s car

vor|sagen *tr. V.* **1** *auch itr.* **jmdm. [die Antwort] ~:** tell sb. the answer; (flüsternd) whisper the answer to sb. **2** (aufsagen) recite; **sich** (*Dat.*) **etw. ~:** recite sth. to oneself

Vor·saison *die* start of the season; early [part of the] season

Vor·satz *der* intention; **den ~ fassen, etw. zu tun** resolve to do sth.; make a resolution to do sth.; **den ~ haben, etw. zu tun** intend to do sth.; have the intention of doing sth.; **mit ~:** with intent; **der Weg zur Hölle ist mit guten Vorsätzen gepflastert** (Spr.) the road to hell is paved with good intentions (prov.)

Vorsatz·blatt *das* (Buchw.) endpaper

vorsätzlich /-zɛtslɪç/
A *Adj.* intentional; deliberate; wilful ‹*murder, arson, etc.*›
B *adv.* intentionally; deliberately

Vor·schau *die* preview

Vor·schein *der:* in **etw. zum ~ bringen** reveal sth.; bring sth. to light; **zum ~ kommen** appear; (entdeckt werden) come to light; **sie griff in ihre Tasche und brachte eine Tüte zum ~:** she delved into her pocket and produced a bag; **wieder zum ~ kommen** reappear

vor|schieben
A *unr. tr. V.* **1** push ‹*bolt*› across; *s. auch* **Riegel 1 2** (nach vorn schieben) push forward; **den Kopf/die Schultern ~:** stick one's head forward/put one's shoulders forward; **die Unterlippe ~:** stick out one's bottom lip **3** (für sich handeln lassen) **jmdn. ~:** use sb. as a front man **4** (als Vorwand nehmen) use as a pretext *or* excuse; **die Verabredung war nur vorgeschoben** the appointment was only an excuse
B *unr. refl. V.* push forward; ‹*air mass, glacier*› advance

vor|schießen *unr. tr. V.* **jmdm. Geld ~:** advance sb. money

vor|schlafen *unr. itr. V.* (ugs.) stock up on sleep

Vorschlag *der* suggestion; proposal; **das ist ein** *od.* **das nenn ich einen ~!** what a good *or* (coll.) great suggestion *or* idea!; **auf ~ von ...** at the suggestion of ...; **ein ~ zur Güte** (scherzh.) a conciliatory proposal

vor|schlagen *unr. tr. V.* **[jmdm.] etw. ~:** suggest *or* propose sth. [to sb.]; **jmdn. für/als etw. ~:** propose sb. for/as sth.

Vorschlag·hammer *der* sledgehammer

vor|schmecken *itr. V.* **der Knoblauch schmeckt vor** there is too strong a taste of garlic; it tastes too strongly of garlic; **das Gewürz soll nicht ~:** [the flavour of] the spice should not stand out

vor·schnell *Adj., adv.* ▸ **voreilig**

vor·schreiben *unr. tr. V.* stipulate, lay down, set ‹*conditions*›; lay down ‹*rules*›; prescribe ‹*dose*›; **er wollte uns ~, was wir zu tun hätten** he wanted to tell us *or* dictate to us what to do; **ich lasse mir [von dir] nichts ~:** I won't be told what to do [by you]; I won't be dictated to [by you]; **das Gesetz schreibt vor, dass ...** the law lays down *or* provides that ...; **wie es der Brauch vorschreibt** as custom dictates *or* demands; **die vorgeschriebene Geschwindigkeit/Zahl/Dosis** the prescribed speed/number/dose

Vor·schrift *die* instruction; order; (gesetzliche od. amtliche Bestimmung) regulation; **ich lasse mir von dir keine ~en machen** I won't be told what to do by you; I won't be dictated to by you; **das ist ~:** that's/those are the regulations; **das verstößt** *od.* **ist gegen die ~:** it's against the rules *or* regulations; **die Medizin nach ~ einnehmen** take the medicine as directed; **Dienst nach ~ machen** work to rule

vorschrifts·mäßig
A *Adj.* correct; proper
B *adv.* correctly; properly

Vor·schub *der:* in **jmdm./einer Sache ~ leisten** encourage sb./encourage *or* promote *or* foster sth.

Vorschul·alter *das* preschool age

Vor·schule *die* nursery school

Vorschul·erziehung *die* preschool education

vor·schulisch *Adj.* preschool

Vor·schuss, *Vor·schuß *der* advance; **er bekam 500 Euro ~:** he received an advance of 500 euros

Vorschuss·lorbeeren, *Vorschuß·lorbeeren *Pl.* premature praise *sing.*

vor|schützen *tr. V.* plead as an excuse; **wichtige Geschäfte/Krankheit ~:** pretend one has important business/feign illness; **Unwissenheit ~:** plead ignorance; *s. auch* **Müdigkeit**

vor|schwärmen *tr. V.* **jmdm. von jmdm./etw. ~:** rave about sb./sth. to sb. (coll.)

vor|schweben *itr. V.* **jmdm. schwebt etw./jmd. vor** sb. has sth./sb. in mind

vor|schwindeln *tr. V.* (ugs.) **jmdm. ~, dass ...** kid sb. that ... (coll.); **sie wollte den anderen nichts ~:** she didn't want to kid the others (coll.)

vor|sehen
A *unr. tr. V.* **1** (planen) plan; **wie vorgesehen** as planned; **die Eröffnung ist für den 21. März vorgesehen** the opening is scheduled *or* planned for 21 March **2** (einsetzen, verwenden wollen) **etw. für/als etw. ~:** intend sth. for/as sth.; **die Gelder sind für den Neubau einer Schule vorgesehen** the money is earmarked for the building of a school; **jmdn. für/als etw. ~:** designate sb. for/as sth. **3** (festlegen) ‹*law, plan, contract, etc.*› provide for
B *unr. refl. V.* (sich in Acht nehmen) **sich [vor jmdm./etw.] ~:** be careful [of sb./sth.]; **sieh dich vor dem Hund vor** be careful of *or* mind the dog; **sieh dich vor, dass du nicht krank wirst** be careful *or* take care you don't become ill

Vorsehung *die;* **~:** Providence *no art.*

vor|setzen *tr. V.* **1** (nach vorn setzen) move forward; **den rechten/linken Fuß ~:** put one's right/left foot forward; **sich ~** (ugs.) come/go and sit at the front **2** (zu essen, trinken geben) **jmdm. etw. ~:** serve sb. sth.; (fig.) serve *or* dish sb. up sth.

Vor·sicht *die* care; (bei Risiko, Gefahr) caution; care; (Umsicht) circumspection; caution; **hier ist ~ geboten/nötig** caution/care is advisable/needed here; **alle ~ außer Acht lassen** throw [all] caution to the winds; **zur ~:** as a precaution; to be on the safe side; **er ist mit ~ zu genießen** (ugs.) you should be wary of *or* careful with him; **was er sagt, ist mit ~ zu genießen** (ugs.) what he says should be taken with caution; **~!** be careful!; watch *or* look out!; **„~, Glas"** 'glass — handle with care'; **„~, bissiger Hund"** 'beware of the dog'; **~ an der Bahnsteigkante** stand back from the edge of the platform; **„~, Stufe!"** 'mind the step!'; **„~, Steinschlag"** 'danger, falling rocks'; **„~, frisch gestrichen"** 'wet paint'; **~ ist die Mutter der Porzellankiste** (ugs.), **~ ist besser als Nachsicht** (ugs. scherzh.) better safe than sorry

vorsichtig /-zɪçtɪç/
A *Adj.* careful; (bei Risiko, Gefahr) cautious; careful; (umsichtig) circumspect; cautious; guarded ‹*remark, hint, question, optimism*›; cautious, conservative ‹*estimate*›; **sei ~!** be careful!; take care!
B *adv.* carefully; with care; **~ optimistisch** guardedly *or* cautiously optimistic; **etw. ~ andeuten** hint at sth. cautiously; **~ geschätzt** at a conservative estimate

vorsichts·halber *Adv.* as a precaution; to be on the safe side

Vorsichts·maßnahme *die* precautionary measure; precaution

Vor·silbe *die* [monosyllabic] prefix

vor|singen
A *unr. tr. V.* **[jmdm.] etw. ~:** sing sth. [to sb.]; **ich singe euch die erste Strophe vor** I'll sing you the first verse
B *unr. itr. V.* **1** **[jmdm.] ~:** sing [to sb.]; **wenn er ~ soll** when he has to sing in public *or* in front of people **2** (zur Prüfung) have *or* take a singing test; **bei der Oper ~:** audition for *or* have an audition with the opera company

vor·sintflutlich *Adj.* (ugs.) antiquated

Vor·sitz *der* chairmanship; **den ~ haben** *od.* **führen** be the chairman; be in the chair; (im Gericht) preside over the trial; **er hat** *od.* **führt bei der Tagung den ~:** he is chairing the conference; **den ~ übernehmen** (eines Vereins) take over the chairmanship *or* presidency; (bei einer Tagung, Sitzung) take the chair; **unter dem ~ von ...** under the chairmanship of ...

vor|sitzen *unr. itr. V.* **einer Versammlung/Kommission** (*Dat.*) **~:** chair a *or* preside over a meeting/commission

Vorsitzende *der/die; adj. Dekl.* chair[person]; (bes. Mann) chairman; (Frau auch) chairwoman

Vor·sorge *die* precautions *pl.*; (für den Todesfall, Krankheit, Alter) provisions *pl.*; (Vorbeugung) prevention; **~ treffen** take precautions (**gegen** against)/make provisions (**für** for); **für den Fall einer Krankheit ~ treffen** make provisions in case of illness; **~ treffen, dass ...** take precautions/make provisions so that ...

vor|sorgen *itr. V.* **für etw. ~:** make provisions for sth.; provide for sth.

Vorsorge·untersuchung *die* (Med.) medical check-up

vorsorglich
A *Adj.* precautionary ‹*measure, check-up, etc.*›
B *adv.* as a precaution; to be on the safe side

Vor·spann *der* (Film, Ferns.) opening credits *pl.*

Vor·speise *die* starter; hors d'oeuvre

vor|spiegeln *tr. V.* **jmdm. ~, dass ...** delude sb. into believing that ...; **er spiegelte ihnen eine Notlage vor** he deluded them into believing *or* led them to believe that he was in a plight; **Unwissenheit/Krankheit ~:** feign ignorance/illness

Vor·spiegelung *die:* **das ist [eine] ~ falscher Tatsachen** these are falsehoods presented as if they were facts; **unter ~ falscher Tatsachen** under false pretences

Vor·spiel *das* **1** (Theater) prologue; (Musik) prelude **2** (vorm Geschlechtsakt) foreplay **3** (als Prüfung) practical examination; (bei Bewerbungen) audition

vor|spielen
A *tr. V.* **1** **jmdm. ein Musikstück/eine Szene ~:** play a piece of music to *or* for sb./act out *or* perform a scene for *or* in front of sb. **2** (vorspiegeln) **jmdm. etw. ~:** feign sth. to sb.; **spiel uns doch nichts vor!** don't try and fool us!;

V

jmdm. Theater/eine Komödie ~: put on an act for sb.
B *itr. V.* **1** **jmdm. ~:** play to *or* for sb.; **einer Jury ~:** perform in front of a jury **2** (bei einer Bewerbung) audition, have an audition (**bei** for); **jmdn. ~ lassen** audition sb.

Vor·sprache *die* (österr.) visit (**bei** to)

vor|sprechen
A *unr. tr. V.* **1** (zum Nachsprechen) **jmdm. etw. ~:** pronounce *or* say sth. first for sb.; **einem Zeugen den Eid ~:** say the oath for the witness to repeat **2** (zur Prüfung) recite
B *unr. itr. V.* **1** (zur Prüfung) recite one's examination piece; (bei Bewerbungen) audition; **am Staatstheater ~:** audition for the State Theatre; **jmdn. ~ lassen** audition sb. **2** (einen Besuch machen) **bei jmdm. [in einer Angelegenheit] ~:** call on sb. about a matter; **bei** *od.* **auf einer Behörde ~:** call at an office

vor·springen *unr. itr. V.; mit sein* **1** (ugs.) **hinter einem Auto ~:** jump out from behind a car **2** (weit hervorstehen) jut out; project; **ein ~des Kinn** a prominent chin

Vor·sprung *der* **1** (vorspringender Teil) projection; (Fels~) ledge **2** (räumlicher, zeitlicher Vorteil) lead; **einen [knappen] ~ [vor jmdm.] haben** have a [slight] lead [over sb.]; be [slightly] ahead [of sb.]; **jmdm. einen ~ geben** give sb. a start; **jmdm. zehn Schritte/einen zehnminütigen ~ geben** give sb. ten paces'/ten minutes' start

vor|spulen *tr. V.* wind forward ‹*tape, video*›

Vor·stadt *die* suburb; **in der ~ wohnen** live in the suburbs

vor·städtisch *Adj.* suburban

Vor·stand *der* **1** (leitendes Gremium) (einer Firma) board [of directors]; (eines Vereins, einer Gesellschaft) executive committee; (einer Partei) executive; **im ~ sein** be on the board/executive committee/executive **2** (Leiter) chairman

Vorstands-: ~chef *der,* **~chefin** *die* chairman/chairwoman [of the board]; **~etage** *die* management floor; **~mitglied** *das* ▸**Vorstand 1**: member of the board; board member; member of the executive committee; member of the executive; **~posten** *der* position *or* place on the board; **~sprecher** *der,* **~sprecherin** *die* board spokesman/-woman; spokesman/-woman for the board; **~vorsitz** *der* chairmanship [of the board]; **~vorsitzende** *der/die* chairman/chairwoman [of the board]

vor|stehen *unr. itr. V.* **1** (her~) ‹*house, roof, etc.*› project, jut out; ‹*teeth, chin*› stick out; ‹*cheek-bones*› be prominent; **~de Zähne/Augen** buck teeth *or* projecting teeth/bulging eyes **2** (geh.: leiten) **einer Institution/dem Haushalt ~:** be the head of an institution/the household; **einem Geschäft/einer Abteilung ~:** be in charge of *or* run a business/department

vorstehend *Adj.* above *attrib.* ‹*explanation, remarks, etc.*›; **im Vorstehenden** above; **das Vorstehende** the above

Vorsteher *der;* **~s, ~:** head; (einer Schule) headmaster; (einer Gemeinde) chairman; (eines Klosters) abbot

Vorsteher·drüse *die* ▸ⓘ **S. 435** prostate [gland]

Vorsteherin *die;* **~, ~nen** head; (einer Schule) headmistress; (eines Klosters) abbess

Vorsteh·hund *der* pointer; (langhaarig) setter

vorstell·bar *Adj.* conceivable; imaginable; **es ist durchaus/[nur] schwer ~, dass ...** it is quite/scarcely conceivable that ...

vor|stellen
A *tr. V.* **1** (nach vorn stellen) put ‹*leg, foot, etc.*› out *or* forward; **die Uhr [um eine Stunde] ~:** put the clock forward [one hour] **2** (bekannt machen mit; auch fig.) introduce; **jmdn./sich jmdm. ~:** introduce sb./oneself to sb. **3** (bei Bewerbung) **sich ~:** come/go for [an] interview; **sich beim Personalleiter ~:** go for an interview with the personnel director **4** (darstellen) represent; **er stellt etwas vor** (ugs.) (sieht gut aus) he looks good; (gilt als Persönlichkeit) he is somebody **5** (zur Untersuchung) **sich dem Arzt ~:** go to see the doctor
B *refl. V.* **1** **sich** (*Dat.*) **etw. ~:** imagine sth.; **stell dir vor, wir würden gewinnen** imagine we won; **ja, stell dir vor!** just imagine!; **ich habe mir das Wochenende ganz anders vorgestellt** the weekend was not at all what I had imagined; **ich kann ihn mir gut als Lehrer ~:** I can easily imagine *or* see him as a teacher; **was haben Sie sich** (*Dat.*) **als Preis vorgestellt?** what price did you have in mind?; **man stelle sich** (*Dat.*) **bitte einmal vor, dass ...** just imagine that ...; **das muss man sich** (*Dat.*) **[ein]mal ~!** just imagine *or* picture it! **2** **sich** (*Dat.*) **unter etw.** (*Dat.*) **etw. ~:** understand sth. by sth.; **darunter kann ich mir nichts ~:** it doesn't mean anything to me

vorstellig /ˈfoːɐ̯ʃtɛlɪç/ *Adj. in* **bei jmdm./etw. ~ werden** (Papierdt.) approach sb./sth.

Vor·stellung *die* **1** (Begriff) idea; **jmdm. eine ~ von etw. geben** give sb. an idea of sth.; **sich** (*Dat.*) **von jmdm./etw. eine ~ machen** picture sb./sth.; **er macht sich** (*Dat.*) **keine ~ [davon], welche Mühe das kostet** he has no idea how much effort that costs; **das entspricht ganz/nicht meinen ~en** that is exactly/not what I had in mind **2** (Fantasie) imagination; **das geht über alle ~ hinaus** it is unimaginable **3** (Aufführung) performance; (im Kino) showing; **eine starke/schwache ~ geben** (fig.) perform well/badly **4** (das Bekanntmachen) introduction **5** (Präsentation) presentation **6** (bei einer Bewerbung) interview; **zur ~ kommen** come for [an] interview

Vorstellungs-: ~gespräch *das* interview; **~kraft** *die* [powers *pl.* of] imagination; **~vermögen** *das* ▸**~kraft**

Vor·steuer *die* input tax

Vor·stopper *der,* **Vor·stopperin** *die* (Fußball) central defender

Vor·stoß *der* advance; **einen ~ in ein Gebiet/in den Weltraum unternehmen** push forward *or* advance into an area/venture into space; **einen ~ bei der Geschäftsleitung unternehmen** (fig.) make an approach to management

vor|stoßen *unr. itr. V.; mit sein* advance; push forward; **in den Weltraum ~:** venture into space

Vor·strafe *die* (Rechtsw.) previous conviction

Vorstrafen·register *das* ▸**Strafregister**

vor|strecken *tr. V.* **1** stretch ‹*arm, hand*› out; stick out ‹*stomach*›; **den Kopf/Hals ~:** crane one's neck forward **2** (auslegen) advance ‹*money, sum*›

vor|streichen *unr. tr. V.* **etw. ~:** give sth. an undercoat; undercoat sth.

Vor·stufe *die* preliminary stage

vor|stürmen *itr. V.; mit sein* rush *or* charge forward

Vor·tag *der* day before; previous day; **am ~ der Prüfung** the day before *or* on the eve of the examination

vor|tanzen
A *tr. V.* **der Tanzlehrer tanzte ihnen den Foxtrott vor** the dancing teacher showed them *or* demonstrated how to dance the foxtrot
B *itr. V.* demonstrate one's dancing ability; **jmdm. ~:** dance in front of sb.

vor|tasten *refl. V.* (auch fig.) feel one's way forward

vor|täuschen *tr. V.* feign ‹*interest, illness, etc.*›; simulate ‹*reality etc.*›; fake ‹*crime*›

Vor·täuschung *die* ▸**vortäuschen**: feigning; simulation; faking; **unter ~ falscher Tatsachen** under false pretences

Vor·teil /*od.* ˈfɔrtail/ *der* **1** advantage; **~e und Nachteile einer Sache gegeneinander abwägen** weigh up the pros and cons *or* the advantages and disadvantages of sth.; **einen ~ aus etw. ziehen** derive an *or* some advantage from sth.; benefit from sth.; **auf seinen [eigenen] ~ bedacht sein** have an eye to the main chance *or* to one's own interests; **jmdm. gegenüber im/sehr im ~ sein** have an/a great advantage over sb.; **[für jmdn.] von ~ sein** be advantageous [to sb.]; **sich zu seinem ~ verändern** change for the better **2** (Fußball, Hockey, Rugby usw.) advantage; **~ gelten lassen, auf ~ erkennen** ‹*referee*› play advantage **3** (Tennis) advantage; **~ Aufschläger** ad in

vorteilhaft
A *Adj.* advantageous
B *adv.* advantageously; **sich auf etw.** (*Akk.*) **~ auswirken** have a favourable *or* beneficial effect on sth.; **sich ~ kleiden** wear clothes that suit one

Vorteil[s]nahme *die* (Rechtsspr.) acceptance of advantage

Vortrag /-traːk/ *der;* **~[e]s, Vorträge** /-trɛːɡə/ **1** (Rede) talk; (wissenschaftlich) lecture; **einen ~ halten** give a talk/lecture **2** (Darbietung) presentation; performance; (eines Gedichts) recitation; rendering

vor|tragen *unr. tr. V.* **1** (darbieten) perform ‹*gymnastic routine etc.*›; sing ‹*song*›; perform, play ‹*piece of music*›; recite ‹*poem*› **2** (darlegen) present ‹*case, matter, request, demands*›; lodge, make ‹*complaint*›; express ‹*wish, desire*›; **ich habe ihm die Gründe für meinen Entschluss vorgetragen** I told him the reasons for my decision

Vortragende *der/die; adj. Dekl.* speaker; (bei wissenschaftlichem Vortrag) lecturer

Vortrags-: ~reihe *die* series of lectures/talks; **~reise** *die* lecture tour

vor·trefflich
A *Adj.* excellent; splendid; superb ‹*singer, player, swimmer, etc.*›; **~ schmecken** taste excellent *or* superb
B *adv.* excellently; splendidly; ‹*sing, play, swim, etc.*› superbly; **sich ~ für etw. eignen** be perfectly *or* excellently suited for sth.

Vortrefflichkeit *die;* **~:** excellence

vor|treiben *unr. tr. V.* drive ‹*tunnel, shaft*›

vor|treten *unr. itr. V.; mit sein* step forward

Vor·tritt *der* **1** **jmdm. den ~ lassen** (auch fig.) let sb. go first; **Damen haben den ~:** ladies first **2** (schweiz.) ▸**Vorfahrt**

Vor·trupp *der* advance guard; (fig.) vanguard

vor|turnen *tr. V.* **[jmdm.] eine Übung ~:** perform a gymnastic exercise [in front of sb.]; (zur Nachahmung) demonstrate a gymnastic exercise [to sb.]

Vor·turner *der,* **Vor·turnerin** *die* demonstrator [gymnast]

vorüber *Adv.* **1** (zeitlich) over; **~ sein** be over; ‹*pain*› be gone; ‹*danger*› be past; **die Gelegenheit ist noch nicht ~:** the opportunity has not yet passed *or* is still there; **das ist aus und ~** (ugs.) that is [all] over and done with **2** (räumlich) past; **an etw.** (*Dat.*) **~:** past sth.

vorüber|gehen *unr. itr. V.; mit sein* **1** go *or* walk past; pass by; **an jmdm./etw. ~:** go past sb./sth.; pass sb./sth.; (achtlos) pass sb./sth. by; **im V~:** in passing; (fig.: nebenbei) in a trice **2** (fig.) **an jmdm./etw. ~:** ignore sb./sth.; **die Krise ist an uns** (*Dat.*) **vorübergegangen** the crisis passed us by *or* left us untouched; *s. auch* **Kelch 1**; **spurlos B** **3** (vergehen) pass; ‹*pain*› go; ‹*storm*› pass, blow over; **das geht vorüber** (ugs.) (tröstend) it'll pass; (scherzh. iron.) that won't last long; **eine Gelegenheit ~ lassen** let an opportunity slip; miss an opportunity

vorübergehend
A *Adj.* temporary; passing ‹*interest, infatuation*›; brief ‹*illness, stay*›
B *adv.* temporarily; (auf kurze Zeit) for a short time; briefly

Vor·urteil *das* bias; (voreilige Schlussfolgerung) prejudice (**gegen** against, towards); **gegen etw. ~e haben** *od.* (geh.) **hegen** be biased/prejudiced against *or* towards sth.

vorurteils-, Vorurteils-: ~frei, ~los
A *Adj.* open-minded; **B** *adv.* open-mindedly; **~losigkeit** *die;* **~~:** open-mindedness

Vor·väter *Pl.* forefathers

Vor·vergangenheit *die* (Sprachw.) pluperfect

Vor·verkauf *der* advance sale of tickets; advance booking; **Karten im ~ besorgen** buy tickets in advance; **im ~ kosten die Karten 20 Euro** the tickets cost 20 euros if bought in advance

Vorverkaufs·kasse *die* advance ticket office; (im Theater) box office

V

vor|verlegen *tr. V.* ① (zeitlich) bring forward (**auf** + *Akk.* to; **um** by) ② (räumlich) move forward; (Milit.) push forward ‹*front, position*›

vor·veröffentlichen *tr. V.* arrange advance publication of; **vorveröffentlicht werden** appear in advance publication

Vor·verurteilung *die* condemnation in advance of trial

vor·vor·gestern *Adv.* (ugs.) three days ago; the day before the day before yesterday

vor|wagen *refl. V.* dare to go forward *or* (Mil.) advance; **sich zu weit ~:** venture too far forward; (fig.) stick one's neck out too far (coll.)

Vor·wahl *die* ① (Politik) preliminary election; (in den USA) primary ② (Fernspr.) dialling code

Vor·wahlkampf *der* (Politik) advance election campaign

Vorwähl·nummer *die* (Fernspr.) dialling code

Vorwand *der;* **~[e]s, Vorwände** pretext; (Ausrede) excuse; **etw. zum ~ nehmen** use sth. as a pretext/an excuse; **unter dem ~, dass ...** giving as one's pretext that ...

vor|wärmen *tr. V.* warm ‹*bed, room, teapot, etc.*› beforehand; (bes. Technik) preheat ‹*air, oven, etc.*›

vor|warnen *tr. V.* **jmdn. ~:** give sb. advance warning; warn sb. [in advance]; **vorgewarnt sein** be forewarned

Vor·warnung *die* [advance] warning; **~ geben** give an early *or* advance warning

vor·wärts *Adv.* forwards; (weiter) onwards; (mit der Vorderseite voran) facing forwards; **~ marsch!** (Milit.) forward, march!; **~!** (weiter!) come on!; **den Wagen ~ einparken** park the car nose first; **ein Schritt ~** (auch fig.) a step forwards; **mach mal [etwas] ~!** (ugs.) get a move on! (coll.); **eine Rolle/ein Salto ~:** a forward roll/somersault; **das Buch kenne ich ~ und rückwärts** I know the book inside out; **~ gehen** (fig.) make progress; **mit der Arbeit will es nicht ~ gehen** the work just isn't getting anywhere; **~ kommen** (fig.) make progress; (im Beruf, Leben) get on *or* ahead; **~ bringen** + *Akk.* advance ‹*plan, process, cause*›; allow ‹*person*› to make progress

vorwärts-, Vorwärts-: ***~|bringen** ▸ **vorwärts**; **~gang** *der* forward gear; ***~|gehen** ▸ **vorwärts**; ***~|kommen** ▸ **vorwärts**; **~strategie** *die* strategy of attack; **~verteidigung** *die* (Milit.) forward defence

Vor·wäsche *die* prewash

Vorwasch·gang *der* prewash programme

vor·weg *Adv.* ① (vorher) beforehand; **um es ~ zu sagen, ...** let me say right away ... ② (voraus) in front; ahead; **~ marschieren** march at the head of the column ③ (vor allem) above all

Vor·weg *der: in* **im ~[e]** in anticipation

Vorwegnahme *die;* **~:** anticipation

vorweg|nehmen *unr. tr. V.* anticipate; **um das Ergebnis vorwegzunehmen, ...** to come straight to the result ...

Vor·wehe *die* (Med.) early contraction

vor·weihnachtlich
A *Adj.* pre-Christmas
B *adv.* **~ gestimmt** in a pre-Christmas mood; **~ dekoriert** adorned with Christmas decorations

Vor·weihnachtszeit *die* pre-Christmas period

vor|weisen *unr. tr. V.* produce; **~ können, vorzuweisen haben** (fig.) possess ‹*knowledge, experience, etc.*›

vor|werfen *unr. tr. V.* ① (zum Vorwurf machen) **jmdm. etw. ~:** reproach sb. with sth.; (beschuldigen) accuse sb. of sth.; **jmdm. ~, etw. getan zu haben** reproach sb. with *or* accuse sb. of doing *or* having done sth.; **jmdm. Parteilichkeit/Rücksichtslosigkeit ~:** accuse sb. of being biased/careless; **ich habe mir nichts vorzuwerfen** I've nothing to reproach myself for; **sie haben sich** (*Dat.*) **[gegenseitig] nichts vorzuwerfen** one is as bad as the other ② (hinwerfen) **etw. den Tieren [zum Fraß] ~:** throw sth. to the animals [as food] ③ (nach vorn werfen) throw ‹*head, ball, etc.*› forward

Vor·werk *das* ① (veralt.: eines Guts) outlying farm ② (hist.: einer Festung) outworks *pl.*

vor|wiegen *unr. itr. V.* predominate

vor·wiegend *Adv.* mainly

Vor·wissen *das* previous *or* existing knowledge; (über einen bestimmten Sachverhalt) foreknowledge; prior knowledge

Vor·witz *der* bumptiousness; (eines Kindes) pertness; (Anmaßung) presumption; (Neugier) excessive curiosity

vor·witzig
A *Adj.* bumptious; pert ‹*child*›; (anmaßend) presumptuous ‹*speech etc.*›; (neugierig) curious
B *adv.* (anmaßend) presumptuously

vor|wölben
A *tr. V.* push out ‹*stomach etc.*›
B *refl. V.* bulge; ‹*curtain, sail*› billow [out]; **vorgewölbt** puffed-out ‹*chest*›; pouting ‹*lips*›

Vor·wort *das; Pl.* **~e** foreword; preface

Vor·wurf *der* reproach; (Beschuldigung) accusation; **jmdm. etw. zum ~ machen** reproach sb. with sth.; **jmdm. [wegen etw.] einen ~/Vorwürfe machen** reproach sb. [for sth.]; **sich** (*Dat.*) **[wegen etw.] [bittere] Vorwürfe machen** reproach *or* blame oneself [bitterly] [for sth.]; **..., sagte er mit leisem ~ [in der Stimme]** ..., he said in a tone of gentle reproach

vorwurfs·voll
A *Adj.* reproachful
B *adv.* reproachfully

vor|zählen *tr. V.* **[jmdm.] Geld** usw. **~:** count out money *etc.* for sb.

Vor·zeichen *das* ① (Omen) omen ② (Math.) [algebraic] sign; **unter anderen/mit veränderten ~** (fig.) under different/changed conditions ③ (Musik) sharp/flat [sign]; (für Tonart) key signature

vor|zeichnen *tr. V.* ① make a preparatory sketch for ‹*picture etc.*› ② (zur Nachahmung) **jmdm. etw ~:** draw sth. for sb. to copy ③ (im Voraus festlegen) lay down, set out ‹*policy etc.*›; (vorschreiben) prescribe ‹*path*›

vorzeigbar *Adj.* presentable

vor|zeigen *tr. V.* produce, show ‹*passport, ticket, etc.*›; show ‹*hands, fingernails*›

Vorzeige-: ~objekt *das* (ugs.) showpiece; **~projekt** *das* (ugs.) showpiece project; **~unternehmen** *das* (ugs.) showpiece enterprise

Vor·zeit *die* prehistory; **in grauer ~:** in the dim and distant past

vorzeitig
A *Adj.* premature ‹*birth, death, ageing*›; early ‹*retirement*›
B *adv.* prematurely; **~ pensioniert werden** be retired early

Vorzeitigkeit *die;* **~** (Sprachw.) anteriority

vor·zeitlich *Adj.* prehistoric

Vor·zensur *die* ① preliminary censorship ② (Schulw.) classwork mark (*to be combined with examination marks in deciding the final grading*)

vor|ziehen *unr. tr. V.* ① (lieber mögen) prefer; (bevorzugen, besser behandeln) favour, give preference to ‹*person*›; **etw. einer Sache** (*Dat.*) **~:** prefer sth. to sth.; **ich ziehe ihn seinem Bruder vor** I prefer him to *or* like him better than his brother; **das jüngste Kind wird oft [den anderen] vorgezogen** the youngest child is often given preference [over the others] ② (zuziehen) draw ‹*curtain*› ③ (vorverlegen) bring forward ‹*date*› (**um** by); **der Arzt hat mich vorgezogen** (ugs.) the doctor gave me priority; **vorgezogene Wahlen** early elections ④ (nach vorn ziehen) pull forward; (Milit.) move ‹*troops*› forward

Vor·zimmer *das* ① outer office; anteroom ② (österr.: Diele) hall

Vorzimmer·dame *die* receptionist

Vor·zug *der* ① preference (**gegenüber** over); **jmdm./einer Sache den ~ geben** prefer sb./sth.; (Vorrang) give precedence to sb./sth.; **den ~ haben** be preferred/take precedence ② (gute Eigenschaft) good quality; merit; (Vorteil) advantage ③ (österr. Schulw.: Auszeichnung) distinction ④ (Vorrecht, Vergünstigung) privilege

vorzüglich /foːɐ̯ˈtsyːklɪç/
A *Adj.* excellent; first-rate; (in Briefen) **mit ~er Hochachtung** (veralt.) yours faithfully; your obedient servant (dated); **~ schmecken** taste excellent
B *adv.* excellently; **~ speisen** have an excellent meal

Vorzüglichkeit *die;* **~, ~en** excellence

vorzugs-, Vorzugs-: ~aktie *die* (Wirtsch.) preference share; **~milch** *die* best quality milk; **~weise** *Adv.* (hauptsächlich) primarily; (besonders) especially; particularly; (am liebsten) preferably

Vota, Voten ▸ **Votum**

votieren /voˈtiːrən/ *itr. V.* (geh.) vote

Votiv·bild *das* votive picture

Votum /ˈvoːtʊm/ *das;* **~s, Vota** *od.* **Voten** ① vote ② (geh.: Urteil) judgement

Voyeur/voaˈjøːɐ̯/ *der;* **~s, ~e** voyeur

Voyeurin *die;* **~, ~nen** voyeuse; voyeur

VP *Abk.* (DDR) **= Volkspolizei**

VR *Abk.* **= Volksrepublik**

vulgär /vʊlˈgɛːɐ̯/
A *Adj.* vulgar
B *adv.* in a vulgar way; **er drückt sich sehr ~ aus** he uses very vulgar language

Vulgarität /vʊlgariˈtɛːt/ *die;* **~, ~en** vulgarity

Vulgär·latein *das* vulgar Latin

Vulkan /vʊlˈkaːn/ *der;* **~s, ~e** volcano; **wie auf einem ~ leben** be sitting on a powder keg; *s. auch* **Tanz 1**

Vulkan-: ~ausbruch *der* volcanic eruption; **~insel** *die* volcanic island

vulkanisch *Adj.* volcanic

Vulkanisier·anstalt *die* (veralt.) vulcanizing plant

vulkanisieren *tr. V.* vulcanize

Vulkanismus *der;* **~:** volcanism *no art.*

Vulkanologe *der;* **~n, ~n, Vulkanologin** *die;* **~, ~nen** volcanologist

Vulva /ˈvʊlva/ *die;* **~, Vulven** vulva

v. u. Z. *Abk.* **= vor unserer Zeit[rechnung]** BC

VWL *Abk.* **= Volkswirtschaftslehre**

Ww

w, W /ve:/ *das;* **~s,** **~:** w/W *s. auch* **a, A**
W *Abk.* 1 **= West, Westen** ▸ℹ **S. 363** W 2 **= Watt** W
WAA *Abk.* **= Wiederaufbereitungsanlage**
Waadt /va[:]t/ *die;* **~, Waadt·land** *das* Vaud *no art.*
Waage /ˈva:gə/ *die;* **~, ~n** 1 [pair *sing.* of] scales *pl.;* (Gold~, Apotheker~ usw.) balance; (Brücken~) weighbridge; **etw. mit der ~ wiegen** weigh sth. on the scales; **er bringt 80 kg auf die ~** (ugs.) he tips the scales at 80 kilos; **sich** (*Dat.*) *od.* **einander die ~ halten** balance out; balance one another; *s. auch* **Zünglein 2** 2 (Astrol., Astron.) **[die] ~:** Libra; **er ist [eine] ~:** he is a Libra *or* Libran
waage-, Waage-: ~balken *der* balance *or* scale beam; **~recht** A *Adj.* horizontal; B *adv.* horizontally; **~rechte** *die; adj. Dekl.* 1 (Linie) horizontal line; horizontal; 2 (Lage) horizontal position; **in der ~n** horizontal; level; (flach liegend) flat
waag·recht ▸ **waagerecht**
Waag·schale *die* scale pan; **etw. in die ~schale werfen** (fig.) bring sth. to bear
wabb[e]lig /ˈvab(ə)lɪç/ *Adj.* (ugs.) wobbly; flabby ‹*muscles, flesh*›
Wabe /ˈva:bə/ *die;* **~, ~n** honeycomb
Waben·honig *der* comb honey
wabern *itr. V.* (geh.) 1 ‹*smoke, mist, cloud*› swirl, drift; ‹*steam*› billow; (fig.) fluctuate 2 (flackern, lodern) ‹*flames etc.*› flicker
wach /vax/
A *Adj.* 1 awake; **in ~em** *od.* **im ~en Zustand** in a state of wakefulness; **jmdn. ~ machen** wake sb. up; **jmdn. ~ küssen** wake sb. with a kiss; **sich ~ halten** stay awake; **er wurde früh ~:** he woke up early; **~ halten** (+ *Akk.*) keep ‹*interest, memory, etc.*› alive 2 (aufmerksam, rege) alert ‹*mind, eyes, etc.*›; attentive ‹*audience*›; lively, keen ‹*interest*›; **mit ~em Verstand** with an alert *or* lively mind
B *adv.* alertly; attentively
Wach-: ~ablösung *die* changing of the guard/watch; **eine politische ~ablösung** (fig.) a change of political leadership; **~boot** *das* patrol boat; **~dienst** *der* (Milit.) guard *or* sentry duty; (Seew.) watch [duty]; **~dienst haben** (Milit.) be on guard *or* sentry duty; (Seew.) be on watch; have the watch
Wache /ˈvaxə/ *die;* **~, ~n** 1 (Wachdienst) (Milit.) guard *or* sentry duty; (Seew.) watch [duty]; (Seew.: Zeitabschnitt) watch; **~ haben** *od.* **halten** (Milit.) be on guard *or* sentry duty; (Seew.) be on watch; have the watch; **~ schieben** (ugs.) do sentry duty; **~ gehen** (Seemannsspr.) do watch duty; **~ stehen** (Milit.) stand on guard; (Ausschau halten) keep lookout 2 (Wächter) guard; (Milit.: Posten) sentry; **eine ~ aufstellen** post a guard/sentry 3 (Mannschaft) (Milit.) guard; (Seew.) watch 4 (Wachlokal) guardroom; (Gebäude) guardhouse; (Polizei~) police station
wachen *itr. V.* 1 (geh.: wach sein) be awake 2 (um jmdn. zu betreuen) **bei jmdm. ~:** stay up at sb.'s bedside; sit up with sb. 3 **über etw.** (*Akk.*) **~:** watch over *or* keep an eye on sth.; (über~) supervise sth.; **er wachte darüber, dass ...** he watched carefully to ensure that ...
wach-, Wach-: ~habend *Adj.* **~habender Offizier** (Milit.) duty officer; (Seew.) officer of the watch; **~habende** *der/die; adj. Dekl.* (Milit.) person on guard; guard; (Seew.) watch; **~|halten** ▸ **wach A 1**
Wachheit *die;* **~:** alertness; (Scharfsinn) acuity
wach-, Wach-: ~hund *der* guard dog; watchdog; **~koma** *das* (Med.) waking coma; **~küssen** *tr. V.* wake[n] with a kiss; **etw. ~küssen** (fig.) bring sth. back to life; **~lokal** *das* (Milit.) guardroom; **~mann** *der; Pl.* **~männer** *od.* **~leute** ▸ℹ **S. 113** 1 watchman; 2 (österr.: Polizist) policeman; **~mannschaft** *die* (Milit.) guard detachment
Wacholder /vaˈxɔldɐ/ *der;* **~s, ~** 1 juniper 2 (Schnaps) *spirit from juniper berries;* ≈ gin
Wacholder-: ~beere *die* juniper berry; **~schnaps** *der* ▸ **Wacholder 2**
wach-, Wach-: ~posten *der* (Milit.) guard; sentry; **~|rufen** *unr. tr. V.* awaken, rouse ‹*enthusiasm, ambition, etc.*›; evoke, bring back ‹*memory, past*›; **~|rütteln** *tr. V.* rouse *or* shake ‹*person*› out of his/her apathy; stir ‹*conscience*›
Wachs /vaks/ *das;* **~es, ~e** wax; **er wurde weich wie ~:** he became really amenable; **~ in jmds. Hand** *od.* **Händen sein** (fig.) be like wax in sb.'s hands
Wachs·abdruck *der; Pl.* **Wachsabdrücke** wax impression
wachsam /ˈvaxza:m/
A *Adj.* watchful; vigilant; **sei ~!** be on your guard!
B *adv.* vigilantly
Wachsamkeit *die;* **~:** vigilance
Wachs-: ~bild *das* wax relief; **~bohne** *die* wax bean
wachsen[1] *unr. itr. V.; mit sein* 1 grow; ‹*shadow*› lengthen; ‹*building*› rise; **sich** (*Dat.*) **einen Bart ~ lassen** grow a beard; **sich** (*Dat.*) **die Haare/die Fingernägel ~ lassen** let one's hair/fingernails grow long; **hoch gewachsen** tall; **ein schlank gewachsener Mann** a slimly-built man; **er ist mit** *od.* **an seiner Verantwortung gewachsen** (fig.) he has grown with his responsibilities 2 (fig.: allmählich entstehen) evolve [naturally]; **eine gewachsene Stadt** a city which has evolved naturally; **eine gewachsene Ordnung** an organic order 3 (fig.: größer werden) grow; ‹*wealth, danger, etc.*› grow, increase; ‹*flood, tide*› rise; ‹*tension, excitement, anger, astonishment*› grow, mount
wachsen[2] *tr. V.* wax; (polieren) wax-polish
wächsern /ˈvɛksɐn/ *Adj.* (geh.: bleich) waxen
Wachs-: ~figur *die* waxwork; wax figure; **~figuren·kabinett** *das* waxworks *sing. or pl.;* waxworks museum; **wir waren im ~figurenkabinett** we went to see the waxworks; **~kerze** *die* wax candle; **~malerei** *die* encaustic; **~mal·kreide** *die* wax crayon
Wach·soldat *der,* **Wach·soldatin** *die* 1 sentry 2 (eines Garderegiments) Guard
Wachs·papier *das* waxed paper
wächst /vɛkst/ *2. u. 3. Pers. Sg. Präsens v.* **wachsen**
Wachs·tafel *die* wax tablet
Wach·stube *die* 1 (Milit.) guardroom 2 (Polizeiwache) duty room
Wachs·tuch *das* 1 *Pl.* **~e** (Material) oilcloth 2 *Pl.* **Wachs·tücher** (Tischtuch) oilcloth tablecloth
Wachstum /ˈvakstu:m/ *das;* **~s** growth; **im ~ zurückgeblieben** stunted ‹*tree etc.*›; underdeveloped ‹*person*›
wachstums-, Wachstums-: ~branche *die* (Wirtsch.) growth industry; **~fördernd** *Adj.* promoting growth *postpos.;* **~fördernd wirken** promote growth; **~hemmend** *Adj.* inhibiting growth *postpos.;* **~hemmend wirken** inhibit growth; **~hormon** *das* growth hormone; **~markt** *der* (Wirtsch.) growth market; **~potenzial** *das* (Wirtsch.) potential for growth; **~prognose** *die* (Wirtsch.) growth forecast; **~rate** *die* (bes. Wirtsch.) growth rate; **~schub** *der* (Wirtsch.) increase in growth; **~störung** *die* growth disorder
wachs·weich *Adj.* 1 as soft as butter *postpos.* 2 (fig.: ängstlich, gefügig) [weak and] submissive
Wacht /vaxt/ *die;* **~, ~en** (geh.) guard *or* sentry duty; **~ haben** *od.* **halten** be on guard *or* sentry duty
***Wächte** ▸ **Wechte**
Wachtel /ˈvaxtl̩/ *die;* **~, ~n** quail
Wächter /ˈvɛçtɐ/ *der;* **~s, ~:** guard; (Leib~) bodyguard; (Nacht~, Turm~) watchman; (Park~) [park]-keeper; (fig.) guardian
Wächterin *die;* **~, ~nen** ▸ **Wächter**
Wacht-: ~meister *der* ▸ℹ **S. 44** 1 (Dienstgrad der Polizei) constable (Brit.); patrolman (Amer.); 2 (ugs.: Polizist) policeman; (als Anrede) **Herr ~meister** officer; 3 (Milit. hist.) sergeant; **~meisterin** *die* ▸ℹ **S. 44** 1 (Dienstgrad der Polizei) constable (Brit.); patrolwoman (Amer.); 2 (ugs.: Polizistin) policewoman; **~posten** *der* ▸ **Wachposten**
Wach·traum *der* daydream; waking dream
Wach[t]·turm *der* watchtower
Wach- und Schließ·gesellschaft *die* property security company
Wach-: ~zimmer *das* (österr.) [police] duty room; **~zustand** *der* waking state
wackelig
A *Adj.* 1 (nicht stabil) wobbly ‹*chair, table, etc.*›; loose ‹*tooth*›; shaky, rickety ‹*structure*›; rickety ‹*car, furniture*› 2 (ugs.: kraftlos, schwach) frail ‹*person*›; frail, doddery ‹*old person*›; **~ auf den Beinen sein** be a bit shaky on one's feet 3 (fig. ugs.: gefährdet, bedroht) dodgy (Brit. coll.) ‹*business*›; insecure, shaky ‹*job*›; **er steht in der Schule/in Latein ziemlich ~:** things are dodgy for him at school (Brit. coll.)/his Latin is somewhat shaky
B *adv.* **~ stehen** be wobbly; (nicht fest gefügt sein) be shaky/rickety
Wackel·kandidat *der,* **Wackel·kandidatin** *die* uncertain prospect; (in seiner/ihrer Haltung schwankend) waverer
Wackel·kontakt *der* (Elektrot.) loose connection
wackeln /ˈvakl̩n/ *itr. V.* 1 wobble; ‹*post etc.*› move about; ‹*tooth etc.*› be loose; ‹*house, window, etc.*› shake; **mit dem Kopf/den Ohren/den Hüften ~:** waggle *or* wag one's head/ears/wiggle one's hips; **der Hund wackelte mit dem Schwanz** the dog wagged its tail 2 *mit sein* (ugs.: gehen) ‹*person*› totter 3 (ugs.: gefährdet, bedroht sein) ‹*job, government*› be insecure; ‹*firm*› be in a dodgy (Brit. coll.) *or* shaky state
Wackel·peter *der;* **~s, ~** (ugs.) wobbly jelly

wacker /'vakɐ/ (veralt.)
A *Adj.* **1** (rechtschaffen) upright; decent; (iron.) trusty; worthy **2** (tüchtig) good; **ein ~er Zecher/Esser** a hearty drinker/eater **3** (tapfer, mutig) valiant
B *adv.* **1** (tapfer) valiantly; **sich ~ halten/schlagen** put up a good show **2** (tüchtig) ‹*eat, drink, etc.*› heartily

Wacker·stein *der* (veralt.) lump of rock

wacklig /'vaklıç/ ▸**wackelig**

Wade /'va:də/ *die;* **~, ~n** ▸❶ **S. 435** (Anat.) calf

Waden-: ~bein *das* ▸❶ **S. 435** (Anat.) fibula; **~krampf** *der* ▸❶ **S. 439** cramp in one's calf; **einen ~krampf bekommen** get cramp in one's calf; **~wickel** *der* leg compress

Waffe /'vafə/ *die;* **~, ~n** **1** (auch fig.) weapon; (Feuerwaffe) firearm; **~n tragen** bear arms; **der Kriegsdienst mit der ~:** service under arms; **unter ~n stehen** *od.* **sein** be under arms; **jmdn. zu den ~n rufen** call sb. to arms; **zu den ~n rufen** issue a call to arms; **die ~n strecken** lay down one's arms; (fig.) give up the struggle; **jmdn. mit seinen eigenen ~n schlagen** (fig.) defeat sb. with his own arguments **2** (veralt.: Waffengattung) arm [of the service]

Waffel /'vafl/ *die;* **~, ~n** **1** waffle; (dünne ~, Eis~) wafer **2** (Eistüte) cone

Waffel·eisen *das* waffle iron

waffen-, Waffen-: ~arsenal *das* arsenal [of weapons]; (Versteck) cache of arms; **~besitz** *der* possession of a firearm/firearms; **~bruder** *der* (geh.) brother- *or* comrade-in-arms; **~gang** *der* (geh.) engagement; (fig.) clash; **~gattung** *die* **1** (Truppengattung) arm [of the service]; **2** (Teilstreitkraft) armed service; **~gesetz** *das* weapons control law; **~gewalt** *die* armed force; **mit ~gewalt** by force of arms; **~handel** *der* arms trade; arms trading; **~händler** *der,* **~händlerin** *die* arms dealer; **~kammer** *die* (Milit.) armoury; **~kontrolle** *die* arms control; **~lager** *das* arsenal; **~narr** *der,* **~närrin** *die* (ugs.) gun freak (coll.); **~rock** *der* (veralt.) tunic; **~ruhe** *die* ceasefire; **~schein** *der* firearms licence; **~schmied** *der* armourer; **~schmiede** *die* (geh.) armoury; **~schmuggel** *der* gun-running; **~-SS** *die* (ns.): *armed divisions of the SS;* Waffen-SS; **~starrend** *Adj.* (geh.) armed to the teeth *postpos.;* **~still·stand** *der* armistice; [permanent] ceasefire; **~stillstands·abkommen** *das* armistice agreement; **~stillstands·linie** *die* ceasefire line; **~technik** *die* arms technology *no art.*

wägbar /'vɛ:kba:ɐ̯/ *Adj.* **nicht ~:** imponderable; **ein kaum ~es Risiko** a risk which it is barely possible to gauge

Wage·mut *der* daring; audacity

wage·mutig *Adj.* daring; audacious

wagen /'va:gn̩/
A *tr. V.* risk; **[es] ~, etw. zu tun** dare to do sth.; **einen Versuch/eine Wette ~:** dare to make an attempt/a bet; risk an attempt/a bet; **eine Bitte/Behauptung ~:** venture a request/statement; **wer nicht wagt, der nicht gewinnt** (Spr.), **frisch gewagt ist halb gewonnen** (Spr.) nothing ventured, nothing gained; *s. auch* **gewagt B**
B *refl. V.* **sich irgendwohin/nicht irgendwohin ~:** venture somewhere/not dare to go somewhere; **sich an etw.** (*Akk.*) **~:** dare to tackle sth.; venture to tackle sth.

wägen /'vɛ:gn̩/ *unr. od. regelm. tr. V.* **1** ▸**wiegen¹ B** **2** (geh.: ab~) weigh up ‹*pros and cons etc.*›

Wagen *der;* **~s, ~** **1** (PKW) car; (Omnibus) bus; (LKW) truck; lorry (Brit.); (Liefer~) van **2** (Pferde~) cart; (Kutsche) coach; carriage; (Plan~) wagon; (Zirkus~, Wohn~) caravan (Brit.); trailer (esp. Amer.); **der Große ~** (Astron.) the Plough; the Big Dipper (Amer.); (Ursa Major) the Great Bear; **der Kleine ~** (Astron.) the Little Dipper (Amer.); (Ursa Minor) the Little Bear; **jmdm. an den ~ fahren** (fig. ugs.) give sb. what for (coll.); pitch into sb. (coll.); **sich [nicht] vor jmds. ~** (*Akk.*) **spannen lassen** (fig. ugs.) not let sb. lead one by the nose **3** (Eisenbahn~) (Personen~) coach; carriage; (Güter~) truck; wagon; car (Amer.); (Straßenbahn~) car **4** (Kinder~, Puppen~) pram (Brit.); baby carriage (Amer.); (Sport~) pushchair (Brit.); stroller (Amer.) **5** (Hand~) handcart **6** (Einkaufs~) [shopping] trolley **7** (Schreibmaschinen~) carriage **8** (Servier~, Tee~) trolley

Wagen-: ~burg *die* **1** (hist.) [defensive] circle of wagons; **2** *urban, gypsy-style encampment;* **~heber** *der* jack; **~ladung** *die* truckload; lorryload (Brit.); **~park** *der* vehicle pool; **~pflege** *die* car care; **~plane** *die* tarpaulin; **~rad** *das* cartwheel; **~rennen** *das* (hist.) chariot race; **~schlag** *der* (geh.) ▸**~tür**; **~schmiere** *die* cart grease; **~tür** *die* **1** (einer Kutsche) carriage door; **2** (eines Autos) car door; **~wäsche** *die* car wash

Waggon /va'gɔŋ, *südd., österr.:* va'go:n/ *der;* **~s, ~s,** *südd., österr.:* **~s, ~e** **1** (Güterwagen) wagon; truck (Brit.); car (Amer.) **2** (veralt.: Personenwagen) carriage; coach

waggon·weise *Adv.* by the wagonload

waghalsig
A *Adj.* daring; risky ‹*speculation*›; (leichtsinnig) reckless ‹*driver, rider*›
B *adv.* daringly; ‹*speculate*› riskily; (leichtsinnig) recklessly

Wagnerianer /va:gnə'rja:nɐ/ *der;* **~s, ~, Wagnerianerin** *die;* **~, ~nen** Wagnerian

wagnerianisch *Adj.* Wagnerian

Wagnis /'va:knıs/ *das;* **~ses, ~se** daring exploit *or* feat; (Risiko) risk

Wahl /va:l/ *die;* **~, ~en** **1** choice; **eine/seine ~ treffen** make a/one's choice; **jmdm. die ~ lassen** let sb. choose; **es gibt/mir bleibt** *od.* **ich habe keine [andere] ~:** there is/I have no choice *or* alternative; **vor die ~ gestellt, nach A oder B zu fahren** faced with the choice between going to A or B; **es stehen drei Menüs zur ~:** there are three set meals to choose from; **die ~ fiel auf ihn** the choice fell on him; **in die engere ~ kommen** be shortlisted *or* put on the shortlist (Brit.); **das Mädchen seiner ~** (geh.) his intended; **wer die ~ hat, hat die Qual** (Spr.) it's agonizing to have to choose **2** (in ein Gremium, Amt usw.) election; **die ~[en] zum Bundestag vom 6. März** the election[s] [to the Bundestag] of 6 March; **in Hessen ist ~** *od.* **sind ~en** there are elections in Hessen; **ich werde nicht zur ~ gehen** I am not going to vote; **sich zur ~ stellen** stand *or* (Amer.) run for election; **jmdn. zur ~ vorschlagen** suggest sb. as a candidate; nominate sb.; **seine ~ zum Präsidenten** his election as President *or* to the Presidency; **geheime ~:** secret ballot **3** (Güteklasse) **erste/zweite/dritte ~:** best/second/third quality; **die Socken sind zweite ~:** the socks are seconds

Wahl- *in* **~berliner/~bayer** *usw.* (scherzh.) Berliner/Bavarian *etc.* by adoption

Wahl-: ~alter *das* voting age; **~ausgang** *der* election result

wählbar *Adj.* **1** eligible for election *postpos.;* **diese Partei ist für mich einfach nicht ~:** I just couldn't vote for this party **2** (passiv wahlberechtigt) eligible to stand for election *postpos.*

wahl-, Wahl-: ~benachrichtigung *die* polling card; **~berechtigt** *Adj.* eligible *or* entitled to vote *postpos.;* **~berechtigte** *der/die; adj. Dekl.* person entitled to vote; **~beteiligung** *die* turnout; **die ~beteiligung lag bei 81%** there was an 81% turnout; **~betrug** *der* electoral fraud; **~bezirk** *der* ward

wählen /'vɛ:lən/
A *tr. V.* **1** choose; (aus~) select ‹*station, programme, etc.*›; **seine Worte [sorgfältig/genau] ~:** choose one's words [carefully]; **sich** (*Dat.*) **jmdn. zum Vorbild ~:** take sb. as one's model; model oneself on sb.; *s. auch* **gewählt B, C** **2** (Fernspr.) dial ‹*number*› **3** (durch Stimmabgabe) elect; **jmdn. ins Parlament/in den Vorstand ~:** elect sb. to Parliament/to the board; **jmdn. zum Vorsitzenden ~:** elect sb. as chairman **4** (stimmen für) vote for ‹*party, candidate*›
B *itr. V.* **1** choose; **zwischen zwei Möglichkeiten** (*Dat.*) **~:** choose between two possibilities; **haben Sie schon gewählt?** (im Lokal) are you ready to order? **2** (Fernspr.) dial **3** (stimmen) vote; **konservativ/grün ~:** vote Conservative/for the Greens; **wann wird in Hessen gewählt?** when are the elections in Hessen?

Wähler *der;* **~s, ~:** voter

Wähler·auftrag *der* mandate [given by the electorate]

Wahl·ergebnis *das* election result

Wählerin *die;* **~, ~nen** voter

Wähler·initiative *die* **1** voters' campaign **2** (Gruppe) voters' action group

wählerisch *Adj.* choosy; particular (**in** + *Dat.* about); **er war in seiner Ausdrucksweise nicht sehr ~:** his choice of vocabulary was not exactly refined

Wählerschaft *die;* **~, ~en** electorate; **die ~ der SPD** the SPD's voters *pl.;* those who vote for the SPD

Wähler-: ~stimme *die* vote; **~verzeichnis** *das* electoral register *or* roll

wahl-, Wahl-: ~fach *das* (Schulw.) optional subject; **~frei** *Adj.* optional; **~gang** *der* ballot; **~geheimnis** *das* secrecy *or* confidentiality of the ballot; **~geschenk** *das* pre-election bonus; **~gesetz** *das* electoral law; **~heimat** *die* adopted country/place of residence; **~helfer** *der,* **~helferin** *die* **1** election worker; **2** (Helfer[in] im Wahlkampf) supporter (*at election time*); **~kabine** *die* polling booth; **~kampf** *der* election campaign; **~kreis** *der* constituency; **~leiter** *der,* **~leiterin** *die* returning officer (Brit.); election official (Amer.); **~liste** *die* list of candidates; **~lokal** *das* polling station; **~los** **A** *Adj.* indiscriminate; random; **B** *adv.* indiscriminately; at random; **~los durcheinander** ‹*eat, drink, read*› in any *or* (coll.) any old order; **~mann** *der; Pl.* **~männer** elector (elected by and representing other voters); **~möglichkeit** *die* choice; (Alternative) alternative; **~nacht** *die* election night; **~niederlage** *die* election defeat; **~periode** *die* legislative period; (eines Amtsträgers) term in office; **~pflicht** *die* compulsory voting; **~plakat** *das* election poster; **~programm** *das* election manifesto; **~propaganda** *die* election propaganda; **~recht** *das* **1** **[aktives] ~recht** right to vote; (einer Gruppe) franchise; **[passives] ~recht** right to stand [as a candidate] for election; **2** (Rechtsvorschriften) electoral law; **~rede** *die* election speech

Wähl·scheibe *die* (Fernspr.) dial

wahl-, Wahl-: ~schein *der* voting permit (*esp. for postal voter*); **~schlappe** *die* [heavy] election defeat; **~sieg** *der* election victory; **~spruch** *der* motto; **~system** *das* electoral system; **~tag** *der* election day; polling day; **~urne** *die* ballot box; **~verfahren** *das* electoral procedure; **~verhalten** *das* voting habits *pl.;* **~versammlung** *die* election meeting; **~versprechen** *das* election promise; **~verteidiger** *der,* **~verteidigerin** *die* (Rechtsw.) *defence lawyer chosen by the defendant;* **~verwandtschaft** *die* (geh.) feeling of affinity; **~volk** *das* electorate; **~vorschlag** *der* nomination; **~weise** *Adv.* as desired; to choice; **~weise ... oder ...** either ... or ... [as desired]; **~wiederholung** *die* (Fernspr.) redial

Wahn /va:n/ *der;* **~[e]s** **1** mania **2** (Täuschung) delusion; **sie ließ ihn in diesem ~:** she let him go on believing this; **er ist in dem ~ befangen** *od.* **lebt in dem ~, dass ...** he is labouring under the delusion that ...

wähnen /'vɛ:nən/ *tr. V.* (geh.) think [mistakenly]; imagine; **jmdn. in Sicherheit** *od.* **sicher ~:** imagine *or* think sb. is safe

wahn-, Wahn-: ~idee *die* ▸**~vorstellung**; **~sinn** *der* **1** insanity; madness; **jmdn. in den ~sinn treiben** drive sb. insane; **in ~sinn** *od.* **dem ~sinn verfallen** go insane; **2** (ugs.: Unvernunft) madness; lunacy; **das ist ja ~sinn!** that's just crazy!; **3** (salopp) **~sinn!** incredible! (coll.); amazing!; **dieser Film ist einfach ~sinn** this film is just fantastic (coll.);

~sinnig A *Adj.* 1 (geistesgestört) insane; mad; **~sinnig werden** go insane; **du machst mich noch ~sinnig!** (ugs.) you're driving me round the bend (coll.); **wie ~sinnig** (ugs.) like mad *or* crazy (coll.); **ich werde ~sinnig!** (ugs.) fantastic! (coll.); 2 (ugs.: ganz unvernünftig) mad; crazy; **so etwas ~sinniges!** what a crazy idea!; 3 (ugs.: groß, heftig, intensiv) terrific (coll.) ‹*effort, speed, etc.*›; terrible (coll.) ‹*fright, job, pain*›. B *adv.* (ugs.) incredibly (coll.); terribly (coll.); **ich habe ~sinnig viel zu tun** I'm terribly *or* terrifically busy (coll.)

Wahnsinnige *der/die; adj. Dekl.* maniac; madman/madwoman

Wahnsinnig·werden *in* **es ist zum ~/zum ~ mit ihm** it's/he's enough to drive you round the bend *or* up the wall (coll.)

Wahn·sinns-: **~idee** *die* 1 crazy idea (coll.); 2 (salopp: großartige Idee) great *or* fantastic idea (coll.); **~tat** *die* insane act; act of madness

wahn-, Wahn-: **~vorstellung** *die* delusion; **~witz** *der* lunacy; insanity; **~witzig** A *Adj.* 1 insane; 2 (ugs.: allzu groß, stark usw.) insane, lunatic ‹*speed*›; terrible (coll.), awful ‹*pain*›. B *adv.* (ugs.) insanely (coll.) ‹*fast, expensive*›; incredibly (coll.) ‹*high*›; ‹*hurt*› like hell (coll.)

wahr /vaːɐ̯/

A *Adj.* 1 true; **[das] ist ja gar nicht ~!** that's just not true!; **davon ist kein Wort ~:** there isn't a word of truth in it; **nicht ~?** *translation depends on preceding verb form;* **du hast Hunger, nicht ~?** you're hungry, aren't you?; **nicht ~, er weiß es doch?** he does know, doesn't he?; **du hast es vergessen, nicht ~?** you've forgotten it, haven't you?; **das darf [doch] nicht ~ sein!** I don't believe it!; **etw. ~ machen** carry sth. out; **so ~ ich hier stehe** as surely as I stand here; **so ~ mir Gott helfe** so help me God; **was ~ ist, muss ~ bleiben** facts are facts; **das ist schon gar nicht mehr ~** (ugs.) that was donkey's years ago (coll.); **daran ist etwas Wahres** there's a grain of *or* some truth in that 2 (wirklich) real ‹*reason, motive, feelings, joy, etc.*›; actual ‹*culprit*›; (echt) true, real ‹*friend, friendship, love, art*›; (regelrecht) veritable ‹*miracle*›; **es war eine ~e Pracht** it was really *or* truly magnificent; **im ~sten Sinne des Wortes** in the truest sense of the word; **das ist nicht das Wahre** (ugs.) it's not exactly ideal; it's not quite the thing; **das ist doch das einzig Wahre** (ugs.) that's just what the doctor ordered (coll.); *s. auch* **Jakob**.
B *adv.* **~ sprechen** (geh.) speak true (literary)

wahren *tr. V.* (geh.) preserve, maintain ‹*balance, equality, neutrality, etc.*›; maintain, assert ‹*authority, right*›; keep ‹*promise, secret*›; (verteidigen) defend, safeguard ‹*interests, rights, reputation*›; **Anstand ~:** observe the proprieties; *s. auch* **Distanz 2**; **Form 5**; **Gesicht**[1] **1**; **Schein 2**

währen /ˈvɛːrən/ *itr. V.* (geh.) last; **ein lange ~der Prozess** a process of long duration; **immer ~:** perpetual; eternal, everlasting ‹*bliss, friendship, memory*›; **der immer ~de Kalender** the perpetual calendar; **was lange währt, wird endlich gut** (Spr.) it will be/was worth it in the end

während /ˈvɛːrənt/

A *Konj.* 1 (zeitlich) while 2 (adversativ) whereas
B *Präp. mit Gen.* during; (über einen Zeitraum von) for; **~ des ganzen Tages** all day [long]

während·dem (ugs.), **während·des** (geh.), **während·dessen** *Adv.* in the meantime; meanwhile

wahr|haben *unr. tr. V. in* **etw. nicht ~ wollen** not want to admit sth.

wahrhaft (geh.)
A *Adj.* true; genuine
B *adv.* truly

wahrhaftig
A *Adj.* (geh.) truthful ‹*person*›; (wahr) true, truthful ‹*statement*›; **der ~e Gott** the true God; **~er Gott!** good God!
B *adv.* really; genuinely; **das habe ich nicht gewollt, ~ nicht!** I didn't want that, really I didn't!; **wirklich und ~:** really and truly

Wahrhaftigkeit *die;* ~ (geh.) truthfulness

Wahrheit *die;* ~, **~en** truth; **die ~ eines Berichts** the accuracy *or* faithfulness of an account; **in ~:** in truth; in reality; **die ~ sagen** *od.* (geh.) **sprechen** tell *or* speak the truth; **um der ~ willen ...** to be truthful ...

wahrheits-, Wahrheits-: **~beweis** *der* proof of truth; **~findung** *die;* ~~, ~~**en** (Rechtsw.) ascertainment of the truth; **~gehalt** *der* truth; **~gemäß** A *Adj.* truthful; accurate ‹*information*›; B *adv.* truthfully; **~getreu** A *Adj.* truthful; faithful, accurate ‹*account*›; B *adv.* truthfully; ‹*portray*› faithfully, accurately; **~liebe** *die* love of truth; **~liebend** *Adj.* honest

wahrlich *Adv.* (geh.) really; truly; **~, ich sage euch: ...** (bibl.) verily I say unto you, ...

wahrnehmbar *Adj.* perceptible; (hörbar) audible

wahr|nehmen *unr. tr. V.* 1 (mit den Sinnen erfassen) perceive; discern; (spüren) feel; detect ‹*sound, smell*›; (bemerken) notice; be aware of; (erkennen, ausmachen) make out; discern; detect, discern ‹*atmosphere, undertone*›; **er nimmt alles, was um ihn herum vorgeht, genau wahr** he takes in everything going on around him 2 (nutzen) take advantage of ‹*opportunity*›; exploit ‹*advantage*›; exercise ‹*right*›; **die Vorfahrt ~:** exercise one's right of way 3 (vertreten) look after ‹*sb.'s interests, affairs*› 4 (erfüllen, ausführen) carry out, perform ‹*function, task, duty*›; fulfil ‹*responsibility*›

Wahrnehmung *die;* ~, **~en** 1 perception; (eines Sachverhalts) awareness; (eines Geruchs, eines Tons) detection 2 (Nutzung) (eines Rechts) exercise; (einer Gelegenheit, eines Vorteils) exploitation 3 (Vertretung) representation; **in ~ von jmds. Interessen** in sb's interest 4 (einer Funktion, Aufgabe, Pflicht) performance; execution; (einer Verantwortung) fulfilment

Wahrnehmungs·vermögen *das* faculty of perception

wahr·sagen, wahr|sagen
A *itr. V.* **ich wahrsage/sage wahr, gewahrsagt/wahrgesagt, zu wahrsagen/wahrzusagen** tell fortunes; **sich** (*Dat.*) **[von jmdm.] ~ lassen** have one's fortune told [by sb.]; **aus den Karten/den Handlinien ~:** read the cards/palms
B *tr. V.* predict, foretell ‹*future*›; **sie hat ihm gewahrsagt, dass er ...** she predicted that he ...

Wahrsager *der;* **~s, ~:** fortune teller

Wahrsagerei *die;* ~: fortune telling *no def. art.*

Wahrsagerin *die;* ~, **~nen** fortune teller

Wahrsagung *die;* ~, **~en** prediction

währschaft /ˈvɛːɐ̯ʃaft/ *Adj.* (schweiz.) durable ‹*material*›; solid ‹*roof*›; wholesome ‹*food*›; strong ‹*coffee*›; reliable ‹*workman*›

wahrscheinlich
A *Adj.* probable; likely; **~ klingen** sound plausible; **wenig ~:** not very likely; **das halte ich für das Wahrscheinlichste** I think that's the most likely answer; **nicht im Bereich des Wahrscheinlichen liegen** be beyond the bounds of probability
B *adv.* probably

Wahrscheinlichkeit *die;* ~, **~en** probability (also Math.); likelihood; **mit einiger/hoher** *od.* **großer ~:** quite/very probably; **aller ~ nach** in all probability

Wahrscheinlichkeits-: **~grad** *der* degree of probability; **~rechnung** *die* (Math.) probability calculus

Wahrung *die;* ~: preservation; maintenance; (eines Versprechens, Geheimnisses) keeping; (von Interessen, Rechten, Ruf) defence; safeguarding; **die ~ des Anstandes** the observation of the proprieties

Währung *die;* ~, **~en** ▸ⓘ **S. 299** currency

Währungs-: **~block** *der; Pl.* **~blöcke** currency bloc; **~einheit** *die* currency unit; monetary unit; **~reform** *die* currency reform; **~reserve** *die* currency reserve; **~schlange** *die* (Wirtsch.) [EC] currency snake; **~system** *das* currency system; **~union** *die* currency union; **~, Wirtschafts- und Sozialunion** social, economic, and currency union

Wahr·zeichen *das* symbol; (einer Stadt, einer Landschaft) [most famous] landmark

Waise /ˈvaizə/ *die;* ~, **~n** orphan; **er/sie ist ~:** he/she is an orphan

Waisen-: **~haus** *das* orphanage; **~kind** *das* orphan; **~knabe** *der* (veralt.) orphaned boy; **gegen jmdn. der reinste ~knabe sein** (ugs.) be a mere novice compared to sb.; **~rente** *die* orphan's [social] benefit

Wal /vaːl/ *der;* **~[e]s, ~e** whale

Wald /valt/ *der;* **~[e]s, Wälder** /ˈvɛldɐ/ wood; (größer) forest; **die Tiere des ~es** the animals of the forest; **im ~ spazieren gehen** go walking in the woods; **viel ~:** a great deal of woodland; **in/durch ~ und Feld** *od.* **Flur** in/through woods and fields; **ein ~ von Masten/Antennen** (fig.) a forest of masts/aerials; **ich glaub, ich steh im ~** (salopp) I don't believe this!; you can't be serious!; **den ~ vor [lauter] Bäumen nicht sehen** (fig.) not see the wood for the trees; **wie man in den ~ hineinruft, so schallt es heraus** (Spr.) you are treated as you treat others

Wald-: **~ameise** *die* wood ant; **~arbeiter** *der,* **~arbeiterin** *die* ▸ⓘ **S. 113** forestry worker; **~bestand** *der* forests *pl.;* (Fläche) area of forest; **~brand** *der* forest fire

Wäldchen /ˈvɛltçən/ *das* copse; spinney

Wald·einsamkeit *die* (dichter.) woodland solitude

Wald·erdbeere *die* wild strawberry

Waldes-: **~rauschen** *das;* **~~s** (dichter.) forest murmurs *pl.;* **~saum** *der* (dichter.) edge of the woods/forest

Wald-: **~frevel** *der* ▸**Forstfrevel**; **~gebiet** *das* forest area; **~geist** *der* woodland sprite; **~gott** *der* (Myth.) forest god; **~göttin** *die* (Myth.) forest goddess; **~horn** *das* French horn; (Jagdhorn) [large] hunting horn

waldig *Adj.* wooded

Wald-: **~land** *das* woodland; **~lauf** *der:* **[einen] ~lauf machen** go jogging through the woods; **~lehr·pfad** *der* woodland nature trail; **~meister** *der* (Bot.) woodruff

Waldorf- /ˈvaldɔrf/: **~salat** *der* (Kochk.) Waldorf salad; **~schule** *die* Rudolf Steiner school

> **Waldorfschule**
>
> An increasingly popular type of private school originally founded by the Austrian anthroposophist Rudolf Steiner in the 1920s. The main aim of these schools is to develop pupils' creative and cognitive abilities through music, art, and crafts.

wald-, Wald-: **~rand** *der* edge of the woods *or* the forest; **~reich** *Adj.* densely wooded; **~schrat** *der* hobgoblin; woodland gnome; **~spaziergang** *der* walk in the woods; **~sterben** *das;* **~~s** forest dieback; death of the forest (*as a result of pollution*); **~stück** *das* piece of woodland; **~tier** *das* forest *or* woodland animal

> **Waldsterben**
>
> *Waldsterben* (the death of forests) is due mainly to pollution from factories and cars. By 1996 over half of Germany's trees were damaged. The threat to forests has strengthened Germany's ecological political movement, *die Grünen*.

Wald-und-Wiesen- ▸**Feld-Wald-und-Wiesen-**

Waldung *die;* ~, **~en** forest

Wald·weg *der* forest path; (für Fahrzeuge) forest track

Wales /weɪlz/ *(das);* **~'** Wales

Wal-: **~fang** *der* whaling *no def. art.;* **auf ~fang gehen/sein** go/be whaling; **~fänger** *der* ▸ⓘ **S. 113** whaler; **~fisch** *der* (ugs.) whale

Walhall, Walhalla /valˈhal(a)/ *(das);* **~s** Valhalla

W

Waliser /va'li:zɐ/ *der;* ~**s,** ~ ▸❶ **S. 520** Welshman

Waliserin *die;* ~, ~**nen** ▸❶ **S. 520** Welshwoman

walisisch /va'li:zɪʃ/ ▸❶ **S. 520,** ▸❶ **S. 670**

A *Adj.* Welsh; **das Walisische** Welsh

B *adv.* **etw.** ~ **aussprechen** pronounce sth. the Welsh way

walken /'valkn̩/ *tr. V.* full ‹*cloth*›; roll ‹*sheet metal*›; tumble ‹*leather*›

***Walkie-talkie, Walkie-Talkie** /'wɔ:ki 'tɔ:ki/ *das;* ~**s,** ~**s** walkie-talkie

Walkman Ⓦⓩ /'wɔkmən/ *der;* ~**s, Walkmen** /'wɔkmən/ Walkman ®; personal stereo

Walküre /val'ky:rə/ *die;* ~, ~**n** (nord. Myth., fig.) Valkyrie

Wall /val/ *der;* ~**[e]s, Wälle** /'vɛlə/ earthwork; embankment; rampart (esp. Mil.); (fig.) wall

Wallach /'valax/ *der;* ~**[e]s,** ~**e** gelding

wallen *itr. V.* **1** (brodeln) boil; **der Zorn brachte sein Blut zum Wallen** (fig. geh.) anger made his blood boil **2** (geh.: aufgewühlt sein) ‹*sea, waves*› seethe, churn **3** *mit Richtungsangabe mit sein* (geh.) ‹*mist, steam*› swirl **4** ~**des Haar**/~**de Gewänder** (geh.) flowing hair/robes

wall-, Wall-: ~**fahren** *itr. V.; mit sein* make a pilgrimage; ~**fahrer** *der,* ~**fahrerin** *die* pilgrim; ~**fahrt** *die* pilgrimage; **eine** ~**fahrt machen** go on a pilgrimage

Wall·fahrts-: ~**kirche** *die* pilgrimage church; ~**ort** *der* place of pilgrimage

Wall·graben *der* moat

Wallis /'valɪs/ *das;* ~: Valais; **im/aus dem** ~: in/from Valais

Wallone /va'lo:nə/ *der;* ~**n,** ~**n** Walloon

Wallonien /va'lo:niən/ *(das);* ~**s** Wallonia

Wallonin *die;* ~, ~**nen** Walloon

wallonisch *Adj.* ▸❶ **S. 670** Walloon

Wallung *die;* ~, ~**en** ▸❶ **S. 439** **1** (geh.) **in** ~ **sein** be seething *or* churning; **in** ~ **geraten** start to seethe *or* churn; **in** ~ **bringen** make ‹*sea, water, etc.*› churn **2** (fig. geh.) **er** *od.* **sein Blut war/geriet in** ~: he *or* his blood was seething/began to seethe; (vor Leidenschaft) his feelings were in turmoil *or* inflamed/became inflamed; **jmdn.** *od.* **jmds. Blut in** ~ **bringen** (vor Wut, Ärger) make sb.'s blood boil; (vor Leidenschaft) inflame sb. *or.* sb.'s feelings **3** (Med.) ▸**Hitzewallung**

Walm·dach /'valm-/ *das* hipped roof

Wal·nuss, *Wal·nuß /'valnʊs/ *die* walnut

Walnuss·baum, *Walnuß·baum *der* walnut tree

walnuss·groß, *walnuß·groß *Adj.* walnut-sized

Walpurgis·nacht /val'pʊrgɪs-/ *die* Walpurgis Night *no art.*

Wal·ross, *Wal·roß /'valrɔs/ *das; Pl.* ~**rosse** walrus

Wal·statt *die* (dichter. veralt.) field of battle; **auf der** ~ **bleiben** (veralt.) fall in battle

walten /'valtn̩/

A *itr. V.* (geh.) **1** ‹*good sense, good spirit*› prevail; ‹*peace, silence, harmony, etc.*› reign; **rohe Kräfte haben hier gewaltet** brutal forces have been at work here; **Vorsicht/Gnade/Milde/Strenge** *usw.* ~ **lassen** exercise caution/mercy/leniency/rigour *etc.*; **Vernunft** ~ **lassen** be reasonable **2** (veralt.: das Regiment führen) rule (**über** + *Akk.* over); *s. auch* **Amt 2, schalten B 4**

B *tr. V. in* **das walte Gott** (geh.)/(salopp scherzh.) **Hugo** may God grant that this be so/I hope to God it is

Walz *die;* ~ ▸**Walze 5**

Walze /'valtsə/ *die;* ~, ~**n** **1** roller; (Straßen~) [road] roller; (Schreib~) platen; (Tiefdruck~) gravure cylinder **2** (eines mechanischen Musikinstruments) barrel; (hist.: eines Phonographen) cylinder; **er spielt immer wieder die alte** ~ (ugs.) he always comes out with the same old story **3** (Geom.) cylinder **4** (Walzwerk) rolling mill **5** (veralt.) **auf der** ~ **sein/auf die** ~ **gehen** be on/take to the road; **ein Handwerksbursche auf der** ~: an itinerant journeyman

walzen

A *tr. V.* roll ‹*field, road, steel, etc.*›

B *itr. V.* (veralt., scherzh.) **1** *mit Richtungsangabe mit sein* (Walzer tanzen) waltz **2** *mit sein* (reisen) rove; (zu Fuß) hike

wälzen /'vɛltsn̩/

A *tr. V.* **1** roll ‹*round object*›; heave ‹*heavy object*›; (drehen) roll ‹*person etc.*› over; (fig.) shove ‹*blame, responsibility*› (**auf** + *Akk.* on); **die Arbeit auf jmdn.** ~: lumber sb. with the work **2** (ugs.: studieren) pore over ‹*books etc.*› **3** (Kochk.: wenden) **etw. in Mehl** *usw.* ~: toss sth. in flour *etc.* **4** (ugs.: diskutieren, nachdenken über) mull over ‹*plans, problem, etc.*›

B *refl. V.* roll; (auf der Stelle) roll about *or* around; (im Krampf, vor Schmerzen) writhe around; **sich schlaflos im Bett** ~: toss and turn in bed, unable to sleep; **sich vor Lachen** ~ (ugs.) fall about laughing; **Menschenmengen wälzten sich durch die Straßen** crowds of people thronged through the streets

Walzen·dynamo *der* tread-driven dynamo

walzen·förmig *Adj.* cylindrical

Walzer *der;* ~**s,** ~: waltz; **kannst du** ~ **tanzen?** can you waltz?

Wälzer *der;* ~**s,** ~ (ugs.) hefty tome

Walzer-: ~**musik** *die* waltz music; ~**takt** *der* waltz time

Walz-: ~**stahl** *der* rolled steel; ~**straße** *die* (Technik) roll train; ~**werk** *das* rolling mill

Wampe /'vampə/ *die;* ~, ~**n** (ugs. abwertend) pot belly

Wams /vams/ *das;* ~**es, Wämser** /'vɛmzɐ/ **1** (hist.: Untergewand zur Rüstung) gambeson **2** (veralt.: Jacke) doublet

wand *1. u. 3. Pers. Sg. Prät. v.* **winden**

Wand /vant/ *die;* ~, **Wände** /'vɛndə/ **1** wall; (Trenn~) partition; **die eigenen vier Wände** one's own four walls; **..., dass die Wände wackeln** (ugs.) ... almost fit to raise the roof (coll.); **jmdn. an die** ~ **stellen** (verhüll. ugs.) put sb. up against a wall (euphem.); **da kann man die Wände hochgehen** (fig.) it's enough to drive you up the wall (coll.); **jmdn. an die** ~ **drücken** (fig.) push sb. into the background; **jmdn. an die** ~ **spielen** (fig.) outclass sb.; (durch Manöver ausschalten) outmanoeuvre sb.; **bei ihm redet man gegen eine** ~ (fig.) talking to him is like talking to a brick wall; **sie wohnen** ~ **an** ~: they live next door to one another; they are neighbours; **die Wände haben Ohren** (ugs.) walls have ears **2** (bewegliche Trenn~) screen; **spanische** ~: folding screen **3** (eines Behälters, Schiffs) side; (eines Zeltes) wall; side; (Biol.) septum; (Anat.) wall **4** (Fels~) face; wall **5** (Wolken~) bank of cloud

Wandale /van'da:lə/ *der;* ~**n,** ~**n, Wandalin** *die;* ~, ~**nen** **1** (hist.) Vandal **2** (fig.) vandal

Wandalismus /vanda'lɪsmʊs/ *der;* ~: vandalism

Wand·behang *der* wall hanging

Wandel /'vandl̩/ *der;* ~**s** change; **im** ~ **der Zeiten/der Jahrhunderte** through the ages/over the centuries

Wandel·anleihe *die* (Bankw.) convertible loan

wandelbar *Adj.* changeable; variable ‹*size, number*›

Wandel-: ~**gang** *der* promenade; (im Theater) foyer; ~**halle** *die* lobby; (im Theater) foyer

wandeln

A *refl. V.* change (**in** + *Akk.* into)

B *tr. V.* (verändern) change; **etw. in etw.** (*Akk.*) ~ (geh.) change *or* turn sth. into sth.

C *itr. V.; mit sein* (geh.) stroll; *s. auch* **Leiche; Lexikon 1**

Wander-: ~**ameise** *die* army ant; ~**ausstellung** *die* touring exhibition; ~**bühne** *die* touring company; ~**bursche** *der* journeyman (travelling from place to place); ~**düne** *die* wandering dune

Wanderer *der;* ~**s,** ~ **1** walker; (der weite Wege zurücklegt) rambler; hiker **2** (dichter.: Reisender) traveller

Wander-: ~**falke** *der* peregrine falcon; ~**gewerbe** *das* itinerant trade; ~**heuschrecke** *die* migratory locust

Wanderin *die;* ~, ~**nen** ▸**Wanderer**

Wander-: ~**jahr** *das* year of travel; (eines Handwerkers) journeyman year; ~**karte** *die* rambler's [path] map; ~**kleidung** *die* rambling *or* hiking clothes *pl.;* ~**leben** *das* unsettled life; (von Nomaden) nomadic life; ~**lied** ramblers' *or* hikers' song

wandern /'vandɐn/ *itr. V.; mit sein* **1** hike; ramble; (ohne Angabe des Ziels) go hiking *or* rambling **2** (ugs.: gehen) wander (lit. or fig.); (fig.) ‹*glance, eyes, thoughts*› roam, wander **3** (ziehen, reisen) travel; (ziellos) roam; ‹*exhibition, circus, theatre*› tour, travel; ‹*animal, people, tribe*› migrate; (fig.) ‹*cloud, star*› drift; ~**de Stämme** nomadic tribes **4** (sich verlagern) ‹*glacier, dune, island*› move, shift; (innerhalb des Körpers) ‹*kidney etc.*› be displaced; ‹*foreign body*› migrate **5** (ugs.: befördert werden) land; **in den Papierkorb/Müll** *usw.* ~: land *or* be thrown in the waste-paper basket/rubbish bin *etc.* **6** (fig.: weitergegeben werden) be handed *or* passed on

Wander-: ~**niere** *die* ▸❶ **S. 439** (Med.) floating kidney; ~**pokal** *der* challenge cup; ~**prediger** *der* itinerant preacher; ~**ratte** *die* brown rat

Wanderschaft *die;* ~: travels *pl.;* **die Zeit der** ~: the years *pl.* of travel; **auf [der]** ~ **sein/auf [die]** ~ **gehen** be on/set off on one's travels; **ein Handwerksbursche auf [der]** ~: a travelling *or* an itinerant journeyman

Wander·schuh *der* hiking shoe

Wanders·mann *der; Pl.* **Wanders·leute** (veralt.) wayfarer

Wander-: ~**stock** *der* staff; ~**tag** *der* day's hike (*for a class or school*)

Wanderung *die;* ~, ~**en** **1** hike; walking tour; (sehr lang) trek; **eine** ~ **machen** go on a hike/tour/trek **2** (Zool., Soziol.) migration

Wanderungs·bewegung *die* (Soziol.) migration; migratory movement

Wander-: ~**verein** *der* ramblers' association; ~**vogel** *der* **1** (ugs.: begeisterter Wanderer) keen hiker; **2** *in* **der** ~**vogel** (hist.) *ramblers' association, founded 1895, precursor of the German youth movement;* **3** (Mitglied) member of the *Wandervogel;* ~**weg** *der* footpath (*constructed for ramblers*); ~**zirkus** *der* travelling circus

Wand-: ~**gemälde** *das* mural; ~**haken** *der* [wall] hook; ~**kalender** *der* calendar; ~**lampe** *die,* ~**leuchte** *die* wall light

Wandlung *die;* ~, ~**en** **1** change; (grundlegend) transformation **2** (kath. Rel.) transubstantiation; (in der Messe) consecration of the bread and wine

wandlungs·fähig *Adj.* adaptable

Wand·malerei *die* mural painting; wall painting; (Bild) mural; wall painting

Wandrer *der;* ~**s,** ~ ▸**Wanderer**

Wandrerin *die;* ~, ~**nen** ▸**Wanderin**

Wand-: ~**schirm** *der* folding screen; ~**schrank** *der* wall cupboard *or* (Amer.) closet; (Einbauschrank) built-in cupboard *or* (Amer.) closet; (für Kleidung) built-in wardrobe *or* (Amer.) closet; ~**spiegel** *der* wall mirror; ~**tafel** *die* [wall] blackboard

wandte /'vantə/ *1. u. 3. Pers. Prät. v.* **wenden**

Wand-: ~**teller** *der* wall [display] plate; ~**teppich** *der* wall hanging; tapestry; ~**uhr** *die* wall clock

Wandung *die;* ~, ~**en** (von Gefäßen usw.) side; (von Organen) wall

Wand-: ~**verkleidung** *die* (außen) facing; (innen) wall covering; (Täfelung) wall panelling; ~**zeitung** *die* wall newspaper

Wange /'vaŋə/ *die;* ~, ~**n** **1** ▸❶ **S. 435** (geh.) cheek; ~ **an** ~: cheek to cheek; **ihm stieg das Blut in die** ~**n** the blood rose to his cheeks **2** (Technik) cheek; (einer Treppe) stringer; (einer Leiter) stile

Wangen·kuss, *Wangen·kuß *der:* **jmdm. einen** ~ **geben** kiss sb's cheek

Wankel·motor *der* Wankel engine

Wankel·mut *der* (geh.) vacillation

wankelmütig /-my:tɪç/ *Adj.* (geh.) vacillating

wanken /'vaŋkn̩/ *itr. V.* **1** (schwanken) sway; ‹*person*› totter; (unter einer Last) stagger; **ins**

W

Wanken geraten *od.* **kommen** begin to sway/totter; **nicht ~ und nicht weichen** (geh.) not budge an inch **2** *mit sein* (unsicher gehen) stagger; totter; **~den Schrittes** (geh.) with unsteady gait **3** (geh.: bedroht sein) ‹*government, empire, etc.*› totter; **ins Wanken geraten** begin to totter; ‹*theory, faith, etc.*› become shaky; **ins Wanken bringen** make ‹*monarchy, government, etc.*› totter; shake ‹*resolve, faith*› **4** (geh.: unsicher sein/werden) ‹*person*› waver, vacillate; **[in etw.** (*Dat.*)**] ~d werden** begin to waver *or* vacillate [in sth.]; **jmdn. ~d machen** make sb. waver

wann /van/ *Adv.* ▸ⓘ **S. 729** when; **~ kommst du morgen?** when *or* [at] what time are you coming tomorrow?; **~ ist dieses Jahr Ostern?** when *or* on what date does Easter fall this year?; **seit ~ wohnst du dort?** how long have you been living there?; **seit ~ sind Delphine Fische/bin ich dein Laufbursche?** (iron.) since when have dolphins been fish/have I been your errand boy?; **bis ~ kann ich noch anrufen?** until when *or* how late can I still phone?; **von ~ an ...?** from when ...?; **von ~ bis ~ gilt es?** for what period is it valid?; **bis ~ ist das Essen fertig?** [by] when will the food be ready?; **ich weiß nicht, ~:** I don't know when; **du kannst kommen, ~ du willst** you can come when[ever] you like; **~ [auch] immer** (geh.) whenever

Wanne *die;* **~, ~n** bath[tub]; (Öl~) sump; (Fot.) [wash] tank; **in die ~ steigen** get into the bath

Wannen·bad *das* bath

Wanst /vanst/ *der;* **~[e]s, Wänste** /ˈvɛnstə/ (ugs. abwertend) belly; (dicker Bauch) potbelly; **sich den ~ voll schlagen** stuff oneself (coll.)

Want /vant/ *die;* **~, ~en** (Schiffbau) shroud

Wanze /ˈvant͜sə/ *die;* **~, ~n** (Bett~, Abhör~) bug (coll.)

Wappen /ˈvapn̩/ *das;* **~s, ~:** coat of arms; **~ oder Zahl?** heads or tails?

Wappen-: ~feld *das* (Her.) quarter; **~kunde** *die* heraldry *no art.*; **~schild** *der od. das* (Her.) shield; **~spruch** *der* motto; **~tier** *das* heraldic beast

wappnen *refl. V.* (geh.) **1** forearm oneself; **sich gegen etw. ~:** prepare [oneself] for sth.; **[gegen etw.] gewappnet sein** be forearmed [against sth.]

war /vaːɐ̯/ *1. u. 3. Pers. Sg. Prät. v.* **sein**

Waran /vaˈraːn/ *der;* **~s, ~e** (Zool.) monitor lizard

warb /varp/ *1. u. 3. Pers. Sg. Prät. v.* **werben**

ward /vart/ (geh.) *1. u. 3. Pers. Sg. Prät. v.* **werden**

Ware /ˈvaːrə/ *die;* **~, ~n** **1** **~[n]** goods *pl.* **2** (einzelne ~) article; commodity (Econ., fig.); (Erzeugnis) product; **neue ~ bekommen** receive new stock; **die Händler preisen ihre ~n an** the traders are vaunting the excellence of their wares; **heiße ~** (ugs.) hot goods **3** (Kaufmannsspr.: Stoff) material

Waren-: ~an·gebot *das* supply [of goods]; (Sortiment) range of goods; **~annahme** *die* **1** acceptance of goods; **„keine ~annahme"** no deliveries; **2** (Annahmestelle) goods reception; **„~annahme"** 'goods in'; **~aufzug** *der* goods lift (Brit.) *or* (Amer.) elevator; **~ausfuhr** *die* export of goods; **~ausgabe** *die* **1** issue of goods; **2** (Ausgabestelle) goods collection point; **~begleit·schein** *der* (Zollw.) [customs] bond note; **~bestand** *der* stock; **~börse** *die* (Wirtsch.) commodity exchange; **~einfuhr** *die* import of goods; **~haus** *das* department store; **~korb** *der* (Statistik) basket of goods; **~lager** *das* (einer Fabrik o. Ä.) stores *pl.*; (eines Geschäftes) stockroom; (größer) warehouse; (Bestand) stocks *pl.*; **~muster** *das,* **~probe** *die* sample; **~sendung** *die* (Postw.) parcel containing samples (*sent at a special rate*); **~test** *der* product test; **~umsatz** *der* turnover of goods; **~umschlag** *der* volume of goods handled; **~zeichen** *das* trade mark

warf /varf/ *1. u. 3. Pers. Sg. Prät. v.* **werfen**

warm /varm/; **wärmer** /ˈvɛrmɐ/, **wärmst ...** /ˈvɛrmst.../

A *Adj.* **1** warm; hot ‹*meal, food, bath, spring*›; hot, warm ‹*climate, country, season, etc.*›; **~e Küche** hot food; **das Essen ~ machen/stellen** heat up the food/keep the food warm *or* hot; **im Warmen sitzen/ins Warme kommen** sit in/come into the warm; **~ halten** ‹*coat, blanket, etc.*› keep one warm; **etw. ~ halten** keep sth. warm; **sich** (*Dat.*) **jmdn. ~ halten** (fig. ugs.) keep on the right side of sb.; **mir ist/wird ~:** I feel warm/I'm getting warm; (zu ~) I feel hot/I'm getting hot; **den Motor ~ laufen lassen** warm up the engine; **~ laufen/sich ~ laufen** warm up; **„~"** (auf Wasserhahn) 'hot'; **~e Miete** ▸**Warmmiete** **2** (herzlich) warm ‹*sympathy, appreciation, words, etc.*›; (lebhaft) enthusiastic ‹*agreement*›; keen, lively ‹*interest*›; **[mit jmdm./etw.] ~ werden** (ugs.) warm [to sb./sth.]; **mir wurde ganz ~ ums Herz** (geh.) I felt a warm glow [of emotion] **3** (salopp abwertend: homosexuell) gay (coll.); queer (sl.); **ein ~er Bruder** (salopp abwertend) a queer (sl.); a fag (Amer. sl. derog.)

B *adv.* warmly; **~ essen/duschen** have a hot meal/shower; **~ sitzen/schlafen** sit/sleep in the warm; **sich ~ anziehen/zudecken** dress up/cover oneself up warmly

warm-, Warm-: ~blut *das: cross between heavy and light breeds;* ≈ cross-bred horse; **~blüter** /-blyːtɐ/ *der;* **~~s, ~~** (Zool.) warm-blooded creature; **~blütig** /-blyːtɪç/ *Adj.* (Zool.) warm-blooded

Warme *der; adj. Dekl.* (salopp abwertend) queer (sl.); fag (Amer. sl. derog.)

Wärme /ˈvɛrmə/ *die;* **~:** warmth; (Hitze; auch Physik) heat; **wir haben drei Grad ~:** it is three degrees above zero; **spezifische ~** (Physik) specific heat

wärme-, Wärme-: ~austauscher *der;* **~~s, ~~** (Technik) heat-exchanger; **~belastung** *die* **1** (Ökologie) thermal pollution; **2** (Technik) thermal stress; **~beständig** *Adj.* heat-resistant; **~bild·kamera** *die* thermal imaging camera; **~dämmend** *Adj.* insulating [against heat loss]; **~einheit** *die* thermal unit; **~energie** *die* thermal energy; **~gewitter** *das* (Met.) heat thunderstorm; **~grad** *der* **1** *Pl.* degrees above zero; **wir hatten ~grade** the temperature was above zero; **2** (Temperatur) temperature; **~haushalt** *der* **1** (der Erde) heat balance; **2** (des Körpers) heat regulation; **~isolation** *die* thermal insulation; **~kraftwerk** *das* thermal power station; **~lehre** *die* (Physik) theory of heat; (Thermodynamik) thermodynamics *sing., no art.*

wärmen

A *tr. V.* warm; (auf~) warm up ‹*food, drink*›; **jmdn./sich/sich [gegenseitig] ~:** warm sb./oneself/each other up

B *itr. V.* be warm; (warm halten) keep one warm; **die Sonne wärmt kaum noch** the sun has hardly any warmth now

Wärme-: ~pumpe *die* (Technik) heat pump; **~speicher** *der* thermal store; **~strahlung** *die* thermal radiation; **~technik** *die* heat technology *no art.*; **~verlust** *der* heat loss

Wärm·flasche *die* hot-water bottle

warm-, Warm-: ~front *die* (Met.) warm front; **~|halten** ▸**warm A 1**; **~halte·platte** *die* hotplate; **~herzig** **A** *Adj.* warm-hearted; **B** *adv.* warm-heartedly; **~herzigkeit** *die;* **~~:** warm-heartedness; warmth; **~|laufen** ▸**warm A 1**; **~luft** *die* warm air; **~miete** *die* (ugs.) rent inclusive of heating; **es kostet 500 Euro ~miete** the rent, inclusive of heating, is 500 euros

wärmstens /ˈvɛrmstn̩s/ *Adv.* **~ empfehlen** warmly recommend

Warm·wasser *das* hot water

Warm·wasser-: ~bereiter *der;* **~~s, ~~:** water heater; boiler; **~heizung** *die* hot-water heating; **~versorgung** *die* hot-water supply

Warn-: ~blink·anlage *die* (am Bahnübergang) flashing warning lights *pl.*; (am Kfz) hazard warning lights *pl.*; **~blinker** *der* (ugs.) hazard warning lights *pl.*; **~blink·leuchte** *die* flashing warning light; **~dreieck** *das* (Kfz-W.) hazard warning triangle

warnen /ˈvarnən/ *tr.* (*auch itr.*) *V.* warn **(vor +** *Dat.* of, about); **jmdn. [davor] ~, etw. zu tun** warn sb. against doing sth.; **vor dem Betreten des Eises wird gewarnt** you are warned to beware of thin ice; **die Polizei warnt vor Nebel/vor Taschendieben** the police have issued a fog warning/a warning against pickpockets; **ich bin jetzt gewarnt** I have been warned; I know now to be careful; **ein ~des Beispiel** a cautionary example; **er hob ~d den Zeigefinger** he raised an admonitory finger

Warn-: ~kreuz *das* (Verkehrsw.) warning cross; **~lampe** *die* warning light; **~ruf** *der* **1** warning shout; **2** (eines Tiers) warning cry; **~schild** *das* warning sign; **~schuss,** ***~schuß** *der* warning shot; **~signal** *das* warning signal; **~streik** *der* token strike; **~system** *das* warning system

Warnung *die;* **~, ~en** warning **(vor +** *Dat.* of, about); **lass dir das eine ~ sein!** let that be a warning to you!; **das ist meine letzte ~:** that's the last warning I shall give you; I shan't warn you again

Warn·zeichen *das* warning sign; (Schall~, Leuchtzeichen) warning signal

Warschau /ˈvarʃau/ (*das*); **~s** ▸ⓘ **S. 675** Warsaw

Warschauer ▸ⓘ **S. 675**

A *der;* **~s, ~:** citizen of Warsaw; (geborener ~) native of Warsaw

B *indekl. Adj.* Warsaw

Warschauerin *die;* **~, ~nen** ▸**Warschauer A**

Warte /ˈvartə/ *die;* **~, ~n** (geh.) **[hohe] ~:** vantage point; (fig.: Standpunkt) **von jmds. ~ aus [gesehen]** [seen] from sb.'s standpoint

Warte-: ~frau *die* (veralt.) [*esp.* toilet] attendant; **~frist** *die* ▸**~zeit 2**; **~halle** *die* waiting room; (Flugw.) departure lounge; **~häuschen** *das* passenger shelter; (an Bushaltestelle) bus shelter; **~liste** *die* waiting list; **auf ~liste** (Flugw.) on standby

warten /ˈvartn̩/

A *itr. V.* wait **(auf +** *Akk.* for); **warte mal!** wait a moment!; just a moment!; **na warte!** (ugs.) just you wait!; **„bitte ~!"** 'wait'; (am Telefon) 'hold the line please'; **da kannst du lange ~!** (iron.) you'll have a long wait; you'll be lucky (iron.); **auf sich ~ lassen** take one's/its time; **nicht lange auf sich ~ lassen** not be long in coming; **das lange Warten war völlig umsonst gewesen** the long wait had been all for nothing; **wir wollen mit dem Essen ~, bis alle da sind** we'll hold the meal until everybody's here; **sie wollen mit dem Heiraten noch [etwas] ~:** they want to wait a little before getting married; **darauf habe ich schon lange gewartet** (iron.) I've seen that coming [for a long time]; **auf dich/den haben wir gerade noch gewartet** (iron.) you were/he was all we needed; **Sie können [gleich] drauf ~:** you might as well wait for it; **so lange ~/mit etw. ~, bis es zu spät ist** leave it/leave sth. until it's too late

B *tr. V.* service ‹*car, machine, etc.*›

Wärter /ˈvɛrtɐ/ *der;* **~s, ~** ▸ⓘ **S. 113** attendant; (Tier~, Zoo~, Leuchtturm~) keeper; (Kranken~) orderly; (Gefängnis~) warder; (Schranken~) crossing keeper

Warte·raum *der* waiting room

Wärter·häuschen *das* attendant's hut; (Schranken~) crossing-keeper's hut

Wärterin *die;* **~, ~nen** ▸ⓘ **S. 113** ▸**Wärter**

Warte-: ~saal *der* waiting room; **~schleife** *die* (Flugw.) turning loop; **~zeit** *die* **1** wait; **nach einer ~zeit von einer Stunde** after waiting for an hour; **2** (festgesetzte Frist) waiting period; **~zimmer** *das* waiting room

-wärts /-vɛrt͜s/ *adv.* ‹*north-, south-, up-, down-, etc.*›wards; **seit~:** sideways

Wartung *die;* **~, ~en** service; (das Warten) servicing; (Instandhaltung) maintenance; **der Wagen muss zur ~:** the car has to go to be serviced *or* go for servicing

wartungs·frei *Adj.* maintenance-free

W

warum /va'rʊm/ *Adv.* why; **~ nicht?** why not?; **~ nicht gleich so?** why not do that in the first place?; **nach dem Warum fragen** ask the reason why

Warze /'vartsə/ *die;* **~, ~n** [1] wart [2] (Brust~) nipple

Warzen-: ~hof *der* ▸ⓘ **S. 435** (Anat.) nipple areola; **~schwein** *das* warthog

warzig *Adj.* warty

was /vas/

[A] *Interrogativpron. Nom. u. Akk. u. (nach Präp.) Dat. Neutr.; s. auch (Gen.)* **wessen A 2** what; **~ kostet das?** what *or* how much does that cost?; **~ ist er [von Beruf]?** what's his job?; **[das ist] gut, ~?** (ugs.: nicht?) not bad, eh?; **~ ist?, ~ denn?** (~ ist denn los?) what is it?; what's up?; **~ denn, willst du etwa schon gehen?** you're not going already, are you?; **ach ~!** (ugs.) oh, come on!; of course not!; **für ~ brauchst du es?** (ugs.) what do you need it for?; **mit ~ beschäftigt er sich?** (ugs.) how does he occupy his time?; **~ der alles weiß!** what a lot he knows!; **~ es [nicht] alles gibt!** (Ding) what will they think of next?; (Ereignis) the things people will do!; **und ~ nicht alles** (ugs.) and so on ad infinitum; **~ [auch] immer** whatever; **~ für ein .../~ für ...** what sort *or* kind of ...; **~ für ein Auto hat er?,** (ugs.) **~ hat er für ein Auto?** what kind of car has he got?; **~ für Möglichkeiten haben wir?** (ugs.) what possibilities do we have?; **Hast du den Apfel gegessen? — Was fürn Apfel?** (ugs.) Did you eat the apple? — What apple?; **~ für ein Unsinn/Glück/gemeiner Kerl!** (ugs.) what nonsense/luck/(coll.) what a mean so-and-so!; **Wars ein Sturm? — Und ~ für einer!** Was it a storm? — Not half! (coll.) *or* And then some! (coll.)

[B] *Relativpron. Nom. u. Akk. u. (nach Präp.) Dat. Neutr.; s. auch (Gen.)* **wessen B 2** [1] **[das,] ~:** what; **alles, ~ ...** everything *or* all that ...; **alles, ~ ich weiß** all [that] I know; **das Beste, ~ du tun kannst** the best thing that you can do; **das, ~ du nicht mehr brauchst** the things *pl. or* what you no longer need; **~ er nicht kennt, [das] isst er nicht** he won't eat anything he doesn't know; **vieles/manches/nichts/dasselbe/etwas, ~ ...** much/many things/nothing/the same one/something that ...; **~ mich betrifft/das anbelangt, [so] ...** as far as I'm/that's concerned, ...

[2] *weiterführend* which; **er hat zugesagt, ~ mich gefreut hat** he agreed, which pleased me; **es hat geregnet, ~ uns aber nicht gestört hat** it rained, but that didn't bother us

[3] (ugs.: wer) **~ ein ganzer Kerl ist, [der] wehrt sich** anyone worth his salt will put up a fight

[4] (landsch.: derjenige, der/diejenige, die) **~ unser Vater ist, der sagt immer ...** our father always says ...

[5] (landsch.: der, die, das) **die Frieda, ~ unsere Jüngste ist** Frieda, who is our youngest

[C] *Indefinitpron. Nom. u. Akk. u. (nach Präp.) Dat. Neutr.* (ugs.) [1] (etwas) something; (in Fragen, Verneinungen) anything; **er hat kaum ~ gesagt** he hardly said anything *or* a thing; **ist ~?** is anything wrong?; **wenn er ~ gesehen hätte ...** if he had seen anything; **haben die ~ miteinander?** is there something between them?; **so ~:** such a thing; something like that; **nein, so ~!** you don't say!; **so ~ könnte mir nicht passieren** nothing like that could happen to me; **gibt es hier so ~ wie'n Klo?** there isn't a loo (Brit.) *or* (Amer.) john here, is there? (coll.); **er ist so ~ wie'n Professor** he's a professor *or* something of the sort; **so ~ Dummes/Ärgerliches!** how stupid/annoying!; **gibt es ~ Neues?** Is there any news?; **aus ihm wird mal/wird nie ~:** he'll make something of himself/he'll never come to anything; **das will ~ heißen** that really means something

[2] (ein Teil) some; **ich bekomme auch ~:** I get some too

[3] (landsch.: ein wenig) a little; a bit; **noch ~ Geld/Milch** some more money/milk; **~ lauter** a bit louder

[D] *Adv.* (ugs.) [1] (warum, wozu) why; what ... for; **~ stehst du hier herum?** what are you standing around here for?

[2] (wie) how; **~ hast du dich verändert!** how you've changed; **lauf, ~ du kannst!** run as fast as you can!

[3] (inwiefern) **~ kümmerts dich?** what does it matter to you?

wasch-, Wasch-: ~aktiv *Adj.* detergent; **~anlage** *die* washing plant; (Autowaschanlage) car wash; (Scheibenwaschanlage) windscreen washer; **~anleitung** *die* washing instructions *pl.*; **~automat** *der* washing machine

wasch·bar *Adj.* washable

Wasch-: ~bär *der* raccoon; **~becken** *das* washbasin; **~benzin** *das* cleaning fluid (*with petrol base*); **~beton** *der* exposed aggregate concrete; **~brett** *das* washboard; **~brett·bauch** *der* (ugs.) washboard stomach

Wäsche /'vɛʃə/ *die;* **~, ~n** [1] (zu waschende Textilien) washing; (für die Wäscherei) laundry; **jmdm. die ~ machen** do sb.'s washing; **schmutzige ~ waschen** (fig.) wash [one's] dirty linen in public [2] (Unterwäsche) underwear; **dumm/verdutzt aus der ~ gucken** (ugs.) look stupid/flabbergasted; **jmdm. an die ~ gehen/wollen** (salopp) go for sb./try to get at sb. [3] (das Waschen) washing *no pl.*; (einmalig) wash; **bei/nach der ersten ~:** when washed for the first time/after the first wash; **in der ~ sein** be in the wash; **etw. in die** *od.* **zur ~ tun** put sth. in the wash; **bei uns ist heute große ~:** we're doing a big wash today [4] (Waschanlage) washing plant

Wäsche·beutel *der* laundry bag

wasch·echt *Adj.* [1] colour-fast ‹*textile, clothes*›; fast ‹*colour*› [2] (fig.: echt) genuine; pukka (coll.)

Wäsche-: ~garnitur *die* set of underwear; **~klammer** *die* clothes peg (Brit.); clothespin (Amer.); **~korb** *der* laundry basket; (für nasse ~) clothes basket; **~leine** *die* clothes line

waschen

[A] *unr. tr. V.* [1] wash; **sich ~:** wash [oneself]; have a wash; **jmdm./sich die Hände/das Gesicht** *usw.* **~:** wash sb.'s/one's hands/face *etc.*; **Wäsche ~:** do the/some washing; **sich ge~ haben** (fig. ugs.) be quite something [2] (fig. ugs.) launder ‹*money*›

[B] *unr. itr. V.* do the washing

Wäsche·puff *der* linen basket (Brit.), clothes hamper (Amer.) (*with upholstered lid*)

Wäscherei *die;* **~, ~en** laundry

Wäscherin *die;* **~, ~nen** laundrywoman

Wäsche-: ~schleuder *die* spin dryer; **~spinne** *die* rotary clothes drier; **~ständer** *der* clothes airer; **~tinte** *die* marking ink; **~trockner** *der* [1] (Maschine) tumble-drier; [2] (Gestell) clothes airer; **~zeichen** *das* linen mark

wasch-, Wasch-: ~frau *die* washerwoman; **~gang** *der* washing cycle; **~gelegenheit** *die* washing facilities *pl.*; **~hand·schuh** *der* flannel mitt (Brit.); shower/bath mitt (Amer.); **~küche** *die* [1] laundry room; [2] (ugs.: dichter Nebel) pea-souper; **~lappen** *der* [1] [face] flannel; washcloth (Amer.); [2] (ugs. abwertend) (Weichling) softie (coll.); (Feigling) sissy; **~lauge** *die* soapy water; soapsuds *pl.*; **~maschine** *die* washing machine; **~maschinen·fest** *Adj.* machine washable; **~mittel** *das* detergent; **~muschel** *die* (österr.) washbasin; **~programm** *das* washing programme; **~pulver** *das* washing powder; **~raum** *der* washing room; **~salon** *der* launderette; laundromat (Amer.); **~schüssel** *die* washing bowl; **~straße** *die* [automatic] car wash

wäscht /vɛʃt/ *3. Pers. Sg. Präsens v.* **waschen**

Wasch-: ~tag *der* washday; **~tisch** *der* washstand

Waschung *die;* **~, ~en** (Rel., Med.) ablution

Wasch-: ~wasser *das* washing water; **~weib** *das* (salopp abwertend: Klatschbase) gossip; **~zettel** *der* (Buchw.) blurb; **~zeug** *das* washing things *pl.*; **~zwang** *der* (Psych.) obsession with washing oneself

Wasser /'vasɐ/ *das;* **~s, ~/Wässer** /'vɛsɐ/ [1] water; **ins ~ gehen** enter the water; (zum Schwimmen) go for a swim; (verhüll.: sich ertränken) drown oneself; **warst du schon im ~?** have you been in the water?; (zum Schwimmen) have you been for a swim?; **sich über ~ halten** (auch fig.) keep one's head above water (lit. or fig.); **direkt am ~:** right by the water; (am Meer) right by the sea; **ein Boot zu ~ lassen** put out *or* launch a boat; **auflaufendes/ablaufendes ~:** incoming/outgoing tide; **unter ~ stehen** be under water; be flooded; **etw. unter ~ setzen** flood sth.; **zu ~:** by sea; **ihre Überlegenheit zu ~:** their naval superiority; **der Transport zu ~:** transport by water; **~ treten** paddle (*for therapeutic purposes*); (strampeln) tread water [2] (fig.) **ins ~ fallen** fall through; **das ~ steht ihm bis zum Hals** he's up to his neck in trouble; (verschuldet sein) he's up to his eyes in debt; **reinsten ~s** par excellence; **bis dahin fließt noch viel ~ den Bach** *od.* **Fluss** *od.* **Rhein** *usw.* **hinunter** a lot of water will have flowed under the bridge by then; **nahe am ~ gebaut haben** (ugs.) be rather weepy *or* tearful; **mit allen ~n gewaschen sein** know all the tricks; **jmdm. das ~ abgraben** pull the carpet from under sb.'s feet; leave sb. high and dry; **~ ziehen** (ugs.) ‹*stockings, socks*› be at half mast; **~ hat keine Balken** (Spr.) you must either sink or swim; **stille ~ sind tief** (Spr.) still waters run deep (prov.); **die kochen auch nur mit ~** (ugs.) they're no different from the rest of us; **bei ~ und Brot sitzen** be doing time [in prison]; **jmdm. nicht das ~ reichen können** not be able to hold a candle to sb.; not be a patch on sb. (coll.); *s. auch* **Mühle 1** [3] *Pl.* **Wässer** (Mineral~, Tafel~) mineral water; (Heil~) water [4] *Pl.* **die ~ des Ganges** (geh.) the waters of the Ganges [5] *Pl.* **~** (Gewässer) **ein fließendes/stehendes ~:** a moving/stagnant stretch of water [6] (Schweiß) sweat; (Urin) water; urine; (Speichel) saliva; (Gewebsflüssigkeit) fluid; **~ lassen** pass water; **sein ~ abschlagen** (salopp) have a slash (sl.); **ihm lief das ~ im Mund[e] zusammen** his mouth watered; **~ in den Beinen haben** have fluid in one's legs; *s. auch* **Blut**; **Rotz 1** [7] *Pl.* **Wässer** (Lösung, Lotion usw.) lotion; (Mund~) mouthwash; (Duft~) scent; (Kölnisch ~) cologne

wasser-, Wasser-: ~abweisend *Adj.* water-repellent; **~ader** *die* [underground] watercourse; **~arm** *Adj.* ‹*area*› suffering from a water shortage; **~aufbereitung** *die* water treatment; **~bad** *das* (Kochk.) bain-marie; **~ball** *der* [1] beachball; [2] (Spiel) water polo; **~baller** *der;* **~~s, ~~, ~ballerin** *die;* **~~, ~~nen** water polo player; **~bau** *der* hydraulic engineering *no art.*; **~becken** *das* pool; (~tank) water tank; **~bett** *das* waterbed; **~büffel** *der* water buffalo; **~burg** *die* moated castle

Wässerchen /'vɛsɐçən/ *das;* **~s, ~** [1] **er sieht aus, als könnte er kein ~ trüben** (fig.) he looks as though butter wouldn't melt in his mouth [2] ▸**Wasser 7** [3] (scherzh.: Wodka) vodka

wasser-, Wasser-: ~dampf *der* steam; **~dicht** *Adj.* [1] waterproof ‹*clothing, watch, etc.*›; watertight ‹*container, seal, etc.*›; [2] (fig. ugs.) watertight ‹*alibi, contract*›; **~druck** *der; Pl.* **~drücke** water pressure; **~eimer** *der* bucket; **~eis** *das* [1] frozen water; water ice; [2] (Speiseeis) water ice; **~fahrzeug** *das* vessel; watercraft; **~fall** *der* waterfall; **reden wie ein ~fall** (ugs.) talk non-stop; **~farbe** *die* watercolour; **~fläche** *die* expanse of water; **~flasche** *die* water bottle; **~floh** *der* water flea; **~flugzeug** *das* seaplane; **~führend** *Adj.* water-bearing; **~gehalt** *der* water content; **~gekühlt** *Adj.* water-cooled; **~glas** *das* [1] (Gefäß) glass; tumbler; *s. auch* **Sturm 1**; [2] (Chemie) water glass; **~glätte** *die:* **bei ~glätte** in wet and slippery conditions; **~graben** *der* [1] ditch; (um eine Burg) moat; [2] (Reiten, Leichtathletik) water jump; **~hahn** *der; Pl.* **~hähne,** *fachspr.* **~~en** water tap; faucet (Amer.); **~haushalt** *der* [1] (Physiol.) water balance; [2] (Ökologie, Bodenk.) hydrologic balance; **~hose** *die* (Met.) waterspout; **~huhn** *das* coot

wässerig /'vɛsərɪç/ ▸**wässrig**

wasser-, Wasser-: ~kasten *der* water tank; (im WC) cistern; **~kessel** *der* kettle; **~kopf** *der* ▸❶ **S. 439** hydrocephalus (Med.); **der ~kopf der Bürokratie** (fig.) excessive bureaucracy; **~kraft** *die* water power; **~kraftwerk** *das* hydroelectric power station; **~kreislauf** *der* water cycle; **~krug** *der* water jug; **~kühlung** *die* water-cooling system; **mit ~kühlung** water-cooled; **~lache** *die* puddle [of water]; **~lauf** *der* watercourse; (Bach) stream; **~leiche** *die* (ugs.) body of a drowned person; **~leitung** *die* [1] water pipe; (Hauptleitung) water main; **unter der/die ~leitung** (ugs.) under the tap; **die ~leitung aufdrehen/zudrehen** (ugs.) turn the tap on/off; [2] (Aquädukt) aqueduct; **~linie** *die* (Schifffahrt) waterline; **~loch** *das* waterhole; **~mann** *der* [1] (Myth.) merman; [2] (Astron., Astrol.) **[der] ~mann** Aquarius; [3] (Astrol.: Mensch) Aquarian; **~masse** *die* mass *or* torrent of water; **~melone** *die* watermelon; **~messer** *der;* **~s, ~~:** water meter; **~mühle** *die* watermill

wassern *itr. V.; mit sein* (Flugw., Zool.) land [on the water]; (Raumf.) splash down

wässern /ˈvɛsɐn/

A *tr. V.* [1] (einweichen) soak; (Phot.) wash ‹*negative, print*› [2] (bewässern) water

B *itr. V.* (geh.) water; **eine ~de Wunde** a suppurating wound

wasser-, Wasser-: ~nixe *die* (Myth.) water nymph; **~oberfläche** *die* surface of the water; **~pfeife** *die* hookah; water pipe; **~pflanze** *die* aquatic plant; **~pistole** *die* water pistol; **~pumpe** *die* water pump; **~rad** *das* waterwheel; **~ratte** *die* [1] water rat; [2] (ugs. scherzh.) keen swimmer; (Kind) water baby; **~rohr** *das* water pipe; **~rohrbruch** *der* burst pipe; **~säule** *die* head of water; **~schaden** *der* water damage *no pl., no indef. art.;* (durch Überschwemmung) flood damage *no pl., no indef. art.;* **~scheide** *die* (Geogr.) watershed; **~scheu** *Adj.* scared of water; **~schlange** *die* water snake; **~schlauch** *der* [water] hose; **~schloss,** ***~schloß** *das* (mit ~graben) moated [residential] castle; (an einem kleinen See o. Ä.) [residential] castle set on a lake; **~schutz·gebiet** *das* water conservation area; **~schutzpolizei** *die* river/lake police; **~ski**[1] *der* waterski; **~ski fahren** waterski; **~ski**[2] *das;* **~skis** waterskiing *no art.;* **~speier** *der;* **~~s, ~~:** (Archit.) gargoyle; **~spiegel** *der* [1] (Oberfläche) surface [of the water]; [2] (Niveau) water level; **~spiele** *Pl.* waterworks *pl.;* **~sport** *der* water sport *no art.;* **~sportler** *der,* **~sportlerin** *die* water sports enthusiast; **~spülung** *die* flush; flushing system; **~stand** *der* water level; **~stands·anzeiger** *der* water gauge; **~stands·meldung** *die* water level report (*on the radio*); **~stelle** *die* watering place

Wasser·stoff *der* hydrogen

Wasser·stoff-: ~bombe *die* hydrogen bomb; **~per·oxid, ~per·oxyd, ~super·oxid, ~super·oxyd** *das* (Chemie) hydrogen peroxide

Wasser-: ~strahl *der* jet of water; **~straße** *die* waterway; **~sucht** *die* ▸❶ **S. 439** (Med.) dropsy; **~tank** *der* water tank; **~temperatur** *die* water temperature; **~tiefe** *die* depth of the water; **bei einer ~tiefe von nur 0,50 m** when the water is/was only 0.5 m deep; **~träger** *der,* **~trägerin** *die* water carrier; (fig.) dogsbody (coll.); **~treten** *das;* **~~s** treading water *no art.;* **~tropfen** *der* drop of water; **~turm** *der* water tower; **~uhr** *die* [1] water clock; [2] (volkst.: ~messer) water meter; **~verbrauch** *der* water consumption; **~verdunster** *der;* **~~s, ~~:** humidifier; **~verschmutzung** *die* water pollution; **~versorgung** *die* water supply; **~vogel** *der* waterbird; aquatic bird; **~vorkommen** *das* occurrence of water; **riesige ~vorkommen** huge water resources; **~vorrat** *der* water reserves *pl.;* water supply; **~waage** *die* spirit level; **~weg** *der* water route; **auf dem ~weg** by water; **~welle** *die* shampoo and set; **~werfer** *der* water cannon; **~werk** *das* waterworks *sing.;* **~wirtschaft** *die* water management; **~zähler** *der* water meter; **~zeichen** *das* watermark

wässrig, *wäßrig /ˈvɛs(ə)rɪç/ *Adj.* [1] watery; *s. auch* **Mund** [2] (Chemie) aqueous ‹*solution*›

waten /ˈvaːtn̩/ *itr. V.; mit sein* wade

Waterkant /ˈvaːtɐkant/ *die;* ~ (nordd.) [North German] coast

watscheln /ˈvatʃl̩n/ *itr. V.; mit sein* waddle

Watschen /ˈvaːtʃn̩/ *die;* **~, ~** (bayr., österr. ugs.) ▸ **Ohrfeige**

Watt[1] /vat/ *das;* **~[e]s, ~en** mudflats *pl.*

Watt[2] *das;* **~s, ~** (Technik, Physik) watt; **die Glühlampe hat 100 ~:** it is a 100-watt lightbulb

Watte /ˈvatə/ *die;* **~, ~n** cotton wool; (als Polsterung) wadding

Watte·bausch *der* wad of cotton wool

Watten·meer *das* tidal shallows *pl.* (*covering mudflats*)

wattieren *tr. V.* wad; (gesteppt) quilt ‹*garment*›; pad ‹*shoulder etc.*›

wattiert *Adj.* quilted; padded ‹*shoulder etc., envelope*›

Watt·sekunde *die* (Physik, Technik) joule; watt-second

Wat·vogel *der* (Zool.) wading bird; wader

wau, wau /vau̯, vau̯/ *Interj.* (Kinderspr.) bow-wow; woof-woof

Wauwau *der;* **~s, ~s** (Kinderspr.) bow-wow (child lang.)

WC *Abk. engl.* **watercloset** toilet; WC

WC-Becken *das* toilet bowl

WDR *Abk.* **Westdeutscher Rundfunk** West German Radio

Web /ˈwɛp/ *das;* **~s** (DV) Web; **im ~ surfen** surf the Web

Web- /ˈwɛp-/ **: ~cam** /-kæm/ *die;* **~~, ~~s** (DV) Webcam; **~dokument** *das* (DV) Web document

weben /ˈveːbn̩/

A *regelm.* (*geh., fig. auch unr.*) *tr., itr. V.* weave

B *unr. refl. V.* (geh.) ‹*legend*› be woven (**um** around)

Weber *der;* **~s, ~** ▸❶ **S. 113** weaver

Weberei *die;* **~, ~en** [1] weaving *no art.* [2] (Betrieb) weaving mill

Weberin *die;* **~, ~nen** ▸❶ **S. 113** weaver

Weber·knecht *der* (Zool.) daddy-long-legs

Web·fehler *der* flaw [in the weave]

Web·kamera /ˈwɛp-/ *die* (DV) Webcamera

Web·kante *die* selvage

Web- /ˈwɛp-/ **: ~master** *der;* **~~s, ~~** (DV) Webmaster; **~seite** *die* (DV) web page; **~site** /-sai̯t/ *die;* **~, ~s** (DV) Web site

Web·stuhl *der* loom

Web·surfer /ˈwɛp-/ *der,* **Websurferin** *die* Web surfer

Wechsel /ˈvɛksl̩/ *der;* **~s, ~** [1] (das Auswechseln) change; (Geld~) exchange; (Ballspiele) (Seiten~) changeover; (Spieler~) substitution; **fliegender ~** (Handball, Eishockey) substitution without stopping play [2] (Aufeinanderfolge) alternation; **der ~ der Jahreszeiten** the rotation *or* succession of the seasons; **im ~:** alternately; (bei mehr als zwei) in rotation; **im ~ mit ...** alternating with ...; **in täglichem/regelmäßigem ~:** in daily/regular rotation; **im ~ der Zeiten/Jahre/Jahreszeiten** over the ages/years/through the changing seasons [3] (das Überwechseln) move; (Sport) transfer [4] (Bankw.) bill of exchange (**über** + *Akk.* for) [5] (ugs. veralt.: monatliches Unterhaltsgeld) monthly allowance [6] (Jägerspr.) game path

Wechsel-: ~bad *das:* **ein ~bad nehmen, ~bäder machen** dip one's feet/arms *etc.* in alternate hot and cold water; **~balg** *der Pl.* **~bälge** *od.* **~bälger** changeling; **~beziehung** *die* interrelation; **in [einer] ~beziehung zueinander** *od.* **miteinander stehen** be interrelated; **~dienst** *der* shift work; **im ~dienst arbeiten** work shifts; **~fälle** *Pl.* vicissitudes; ups and downs (coll.); **~geld** *das* ▸❶ **S. 299** change; **~gesang** *der* antiphonal chant; (Art des Gesangs) antiphony *no art.*

wechsel·haft *Adj.* changeable

Wechsel-: ~jahre *Pl.* change of life *sing.;* menopause *sing.;* **in die ~jahre kommen** reach the menopause; **die ~jahre des Mannes** the male menopause; **~kasse** *die* office issuing change; **~kurs** *der* ▸❶ **S. 299** exchange rate

wechseln

A *tr. V.* [1] change ‹*subject, socks, job, doctor, etc.*›; **das Hemd ~:** change one's shirt; **die Wohnung ~:** move home; **ein Hemd/ein Paar Socken zum Wechseln** a spare shirt/pair of socks; *s. auch* **Besitzer 1** [2] ([aus]tauschen) exchange ‹*letters, words, glances, etc.*›; **mit jmdm. den Platz ~:** change places with sb.; **sie wechselten die Plätze** they changed places; *s. auch* **Ring 1** [3] ▸❶ **S. 299** (um~) change ‹*money, note, etc.*› (**in** + *Akk.* into); **kannst du mir 100 Euro ~?** can you change 100 euros for me?; **einen Hunderter in fünf Zwanziger/einen Schein in Münzen/Euros in Franken ~:** change a hundred for five twenties/a note into coins/euros into francs

B *itr. V.* [1] (sich ändern) change; **auf Rot ~** ‹*traffic light*› change to red; **mit ~dem Erfolg** with varying success; **~de Bewölkung, ~d wolkig** *od.* **bewölkt** (bei Wettervorhersagen) variable cloud; **Wind aus ~den Richtungen** wind variable [2] *mit sein* (über~) move; (Jägerspr.) ‹*game*› change its habitat; **über die Grenze ~:** get across the frontier [3] ([sich] ab~) alternate; (aufeinander folgen) succeed one another; **Geschlechtsverkehr mit [häufig] ~den Partnern** sexual intercourse with frequent changes of partner [4] (herausgeben) **ich kann nicht ~:** I haven't any change

wechsel-, Wechsel-: ~objektiv *das* (Fot.) interchangeable lens; **~rahmen** *der* picture frame (*with a removable back*); **~schicht** *die* alternating shift; **in ~schicht arbeiten** work alternate shifts; **~schritt** *der* changeover step; **~seitig A** *Adj.* mutual; **~seitiger Zusammenhang** interconnection; **~seitige Abhängigkeit** interdependence; **B** *adv.* mutually; **sich ~seitig beeinflussen** influence each other; **~seitigkeit** *die;* **~~, ~~en** reciprocity; **~spiel** *das* interplay; **das ~spiel des Zufalls** (geh.) the vagaries *pl.* of chance; **~ständig** *Adj.* (Bot.) alternate ‹*leaves*›; **~strom** *der* (Elektrot.) alternating current; **~stube** *die* bureau de change; **~voll** *Adj.* chequered ‹*history*›; **ein ~volles Leben/Schicksal** a life full of vicissitudes; **~wähler** *der,* **~wählerin** *die* (Politik) floating voter; **~warm** *Adj.* (Zool.) cold-blooded; **~weise** *Adv.* alternately; **~wirkung** *die* interaction

Wechsler /ˈvɛkslɐ/ *der;* **~s, ~** (bibl.) money changer

Wechte /ˈvɛçtə/ *die;* **~, ~n** [snow] cornice

Weck·dienst *der* [telephone] alarm call service

wecken /ˈvɛkn̩/ *tr. V.* [1] **jmdn. [aus dem Schlaf] ~:** wake sb. [up]; **der Kaffee weckte seine Lebensgeister** (fig.) the coffee revived his spirits [2] (fig.: hervorrufen) arouse, awaken ‹*interest, curiosity*›; arouse ‹*anger*›; awaken ‹*desire, misgiving*›

Wecken[1] *das;* **~s** morning call; (Mil.) reveille

Wecken[2] *der;* **~s, ~** (südd., österr.) [1] (Brötchen) oblong roll [2] (Brot) oblong loaf

Wecker *der;* **~s, ~** [1] alarm clock; **jmdm. auf den ~ gehen** *od.* **fallen** (ugs.) get on sb.'s nerves [2] (ugs.: Uhr) big fat watch

Weck·glas (Wz) *das; Pl.* **Weckgläser** preserving jar

Weck·ruf *der* morning call

Wedel *der;* **~s, ~** [1] (Staub~) feather duster [2] (Palm~, Farn~) [palm/fern] frond

wedeln

A *itr. V.* [1] ‹*tail*› wag; **[mit dem Schwanz] ~** ‹*dog*› wag its tail; (winken) **mit der Hand/einem Tuch ~:** wave one's hand/a handkerchief [2] *mit Richtungsangabe mit sein* (Ski) wedel

B *tr. V.* **Krümel vom Tisch ~:** flap crumbs off the table

weder /ˈveːdɐ/ *Konj.* **~ A noch B** neither A nor B

W

ℹ Wegbeschreibung

Die Fragen

1. ***Wie komme ich zum Bahnhof?*** = How do I get to the station?
2. ***Wie kommt man am besten zum Museum?*** = Which is the best way to the museum?
3. ***Geht es hier zum White Hart Hotel?*** = Am I right for the White Hart Hotel?
4. ***Wo ist hier die nächste Bank?*** = Where is the nearest bank?
5. ***Gibt es hier in der Nähe eine Apotheke?*** = Is there a chemist's near here?
6. ***Wie weit ist es zum Krankenhaus?*** = How far is it to the hospital?
7. ***Können Sie mir sagen, wo es hier ein gutes Restaurant gibt?*** = Can you direct me to a good restaurant?

Die Antworten

1. ***Gehen Sie die erste Straße rechts, dann die zweite links, dann immer nur geradeaus bis zur Kreuzung. Biegen Sie rechts ein und dann sehen Sie den Bahnhof vor sich*** = Take the first turning on the right, then the second on the left, then go straight on as far as the junction. Turn right and you will see the station in front of you
2. ***Am besten, Sie gehen hier an der Ampel über die Straße, dann die Gasse entlang, die links am Theater vorbeiführt. Sie kommen dann gegenüber vom Museum heraus*** = The best way is to cross over here at the lights and go down the alleyway along the left side of the theatre. You will come out opposite the museum
3. ***Nein, Sie sind zu weit gegangen/gefahren. Gehen/Fahren Sie zurück zur Kreuzung und biegen Sie links ab. Das Hotel liegt etwa hundert Meter weiter auf der rechten Seite*** = No, you've come too far. Go back to the crossroads and turn left, you'll find the hotel about a hundred yards further on on the right
4. ***Am Marktplatz ist eine Filiale von Barclays. Biegen Sie dort drüben rechts ein, Sie kommen dann nach ein paar hundert Metern zum Marktplatz*** = There is a branch of Barclays on the market place, which is a couple of hundred yards along that turning over there on the right
5. ***In der nächsten Straße links ist eine, allerdings nur eine kleine. Falls Sie eine größere brauchen, müssen Sie mit der Linie 11 ins Zentrum fahren*** = There's one in the next street on the left, but it's only small. If you want a bigger one you'll have to take the number 11 bus into the centre
6. ***Es liegt etwa zwei Kilometer von hier an der Hauptstraße nach Cardiff. Am besten nehmen Sie ein Taxi, die Busse fahren nämlich nicht sehr oft*** = It's about a mile and a half from here on the main Cardiff road. You'd best take a taxi as the buses aren't very frequent
7. ***Tut mir Leid, ich bin auch fremd hier*** = Sorry, I'm a stranger here myself

weg /vɛk/ *Adv.* 1 ▸ℹ **S. 224** away; (verschwunden, ~gegangen) gone; **~ sein** be away; (~gegangen) be gone; **er ist schon seit einer Stunde ~:** he left an hour ago; **~ sein** (fig. ugs.) (eingeschlafen sein) have dropped off; (bewusstlos sein) be out [cold]; **er war sofort ~:** he was out like a light; **[von jmdm./etw.] ~ sein** (fig. ugs.) be knocked sideways [by sb./sth.] (coll.); **[immer] ~ damit!** [let's] chuck it away (coll.); **~ mit dir!** away *or* off with you!; **~ da!** get away from there!; **Hände ~ [von meiner Kamera]!** hands off [my camera]!; **Kopf ~!** move your head!; **[nur] ~ von hier!, nichts wie ~!** let's hop it (sl.); let's make ourselves scarce (coll.); **und ~ ist/war er, und schon ist/war er ~:** and he is/was gone; **weit ~:** far away; a long way away; **weit ~ von der Schule** a long way from the school; **100 Meter von der Straße ~:** 100 metres from the road; *s. auch* **Fenster** 2 **von ... ~** (ugs.: unmittelbar von) straight off *or* from; **von der Schule ~ eingezogen werden** be conscripted straight from school 3 **über einen Schock/Schrecken** *usw.* **~ sein** (ugs.) have got over a shock/fright *etc.*

Weg /veːk/ *der;* **~[e]s, ~e** 1 (Fuß~) path; (Feld~) track; **„kein öffentlicher ~"** 'no public right of way'; **am ~[e]** by the wayside; **er kennt hier ~ und Steg** (geh.) he knows every inch of this area
2 (Zugang) way; (Passage, Durchgang) passage; **sich** (*Dat.*) **einen ~ durch etw. bahnen** clear a path *or* way through sth.; **jmdm. im ~[e] stehen** *od.* (auch fig.) **sein** be in sb.'s way; **einer Sache** (*Dat.*) **im ~[e] stehen** (fig.) stand in the way of sth.; **sich** (*Dat.*) **selbst im ~[e] stehen** (fig.) be one's own worst enemy; **geh [mir] aus dem ~[e]** get out of the *or* my way; **jmdm. aus dem ~[e] gehen** (fig.) keep out of sb's way; avoid sb.; **einer Gefahr/Situation/Diskussion** *usw.* **aus dem ~[e] gehen** (fig.) keep clear of a danger/avoid a situation/discussion *etc.*; **jmdn./etw. aus dem ~[e] räumen** (fig.) get rid of sb./sth.; **jmdm. den ~ abschneiden** head sb. off; **jmdm. den ~ versperren, sich jmdm. in den ~ stellen, jmdm. in den ~ treten** block sb.'s path
3 ▸ℹ **S. 800** (Route, Verbindung) way; route; **[jmdn.] nach dem ~ fragen** ask [sb.] the way; **wir haben denselben ~:** we're going the same way; **wohin/woher des ~[e]s?** (veralt., scherzh.) wither goest/whence comest thou? (arch./joc.); **des ~es kommen** (geh.) draw near; approach; **seines ~es** *od.* **seiner ~e gehen** (geh.) go on one's way; **eigene** *od.* **seine eigenen ~e gehen** (fig.) go one's own way; **das liegt auf dem/meinem ~:** that's on the/my way; **er ist mir über den ~ gelaufen** (fig. ugs.) I ran *or* bumped into him; **jmdm. nicht über den ~ trauen** (fig.) not trust sb. an inch; **neue ~e beschreiten** *od.* **gehen** (fig.) break new ground; **den ~ der Tugend verlassen** leave the path of virtue; **den ~ des geringsten Widerstands gehen** take the line of least resistance; **hier trennen sich unsere ~e** (auch fig.) this is where we part company; **seinen ~ machen** (fig.) make one's way [in the world]
4 ▸ℹ **S. 224** (Strecke, Entfernung) distance; (Gang) walk; (Reise) journey; **es sind 2 km/10 Minuten ~:** it is a distance of two kilometres/it is ten minutes' walk; **zwei Stunden ~:** two hours' journey; **er hat noch einen weiten ~ vor sich** (*Dat.*) he still has a long way to go; **den ~ abkürzen** take a short cut; **auf dem kürzesten ~:** by the shortest route; **auf halbem ~[e]** (auch fig.) halfway; **sich auf den ~ machen** set off; **jmdm. einen guten Ratschlag mit auf den ~ geben** (fig.) give sb. some good advice for his/her future life; **etw. in die ~e leiten** get sth. under way; **jmdn. auf seinem letzten ~ begleiten** (geh.) accompany sb. on his/her last journey; **auf dem besten ~ sein, etw. zu tun** (meist iron.) be well on the way towards doing sth.; **er ist** *od.* **befindet sich auf dem ~[e] der Besserung** he's on the road to recovery; **viele ~e führen nach Rom** (Spr.) all roads lead to Rome
5 (ugs.: Besorgung) errand; **einen ~ machen** do *or* run an errand; **jmdm. einen ~ abnehmen** run an errand for sb.
6 (Methode) way; (Mittel) means; **ich sehe keinen anderen ~:** I can't see any alternative; **auf diesem ~[e]** by this means; in this way; **auf schnellstem ~[e]** as speedily as possible; **auf legalem/diplomatischem ~[e]** through legal/diplomatic channels; **auf friedlichem/gütlichem ~[e]** by peaceful/amicable means; **auf schriftlichem ~[e]** by letter; **auf kaltem ~[e]** (ugs.) without bothering about the niceties
7 **zu ~e** ▸**zuwege**

Weg·bereiter *der;* **~s, ~, Wegbereiterin** *die;* **~, ~nen** forerunner; **er war ein Wegbereiter des Sozialismus** he helped pave the way for socialism

weg-: ~|blasen *unr. tr. V.* blow away; **wie ~geblasen sein** have vanished; **~|bleiben** *unr. itr. V.*; *mit sein* 1 (nicht kommen) stay away; (nicht nach Hause kommen) stay out; 2 (ugs.: aussetzen) ⟨*engine*⟩ stop; ⟨*electricity*⟩ go off; **mir blieb die Luft ~:** I was left gasping; 3 (ugs.: ~gelassen werden) be left out; **~brechen** *unr. itr. V.*; *mit sein* disappear; **es ist uns ein wichtiger Markt weggebrochen** we have lost an important market; **~|bringen** *unr. tr. V.* 1 take away; (zur Reparatur, Wartung usw.) take in; 2 (ugs., bes. südd.) ▸**~kriegen**; **~|denken** *unr. tr. V.* **sich** (*Dat.*) **etw. ~denken** imagine sth. is not there; **er ist aus unserem Team nicht [mehr] ~zudenken** I/we can't imagine our team without him; **~|diskutieren** *tr. V.* **es lässt sich nicht ~diskutieren** its existence cannot be argued away; **~|drehen** *tr. V., refl. V.* turn away; **~|dürfen** *unr. itr. V.* be allowed to go away; (ausgehen dürfen) be allowed to go out; **ich darf hier nicht ~:** I can't leave here

Wege·geld *das* 1 mileage charge 2 (veralt.: Straßenzoll) road toll

Wegelagerei *die;* **~:** highway robbery

Wegelagerer *der;* **~s, ~:** highwayman

Wegelagerin *die;* **~, ~nen** highwaywoman

wegen
A *Präp. mit Gen., in bestimmten Fällen auch mit Dat./mit endungslosem Nomen* 1 (zur Angabe einer Ursache, eines Grundes) because of; owing to; **~ des schlechten Wetters,** (geh.) **des schlechten Wetters ~:** because of the bad weather; **[nur] ~ Peter/**(ugs.) **euch** all because of Peter/you; **~ Hochwasser[s]** owing to flooding; **von Berufs ~:** for professional reasons; **~ mir** (ugs., bes. südd.) because of me; (was mich betrifft) as far as I'm concerned; **~ Umbau[s] geschlossen** closed for alterations; **~ Mangel[s] an Beweisen** owing to lack of evidence 2 (zur Angabe eines Zwecks, Ziels) for [the sake of]; **~ einer Tagung nach X fahren** go to X for a conference; **er ist ~ dringender Geschäfte verreist** he's away on urgent business 3 (um ... willen) for the sake of; **~ der Kinder/**(ugs.) **dir** for the children's/your sake 4 (bezüglich) about; regarding; **ich habe ~ morgen noch eine Frage** I've another question about tomorrow
B *in* **von ~!** (ugs.) you must be joking!; **von ~ lauwarm/billig!** lukewarm/cheap? not on your life!

Wege·netz *das* network of paths

Wegerich /ˈveːgərɪç/ *der;* **~s, ~e** (Bot.) plantain

Weges·rand *der* (geh.) **am ~:** by the wayside

weg-, Weg-: ~|essen *unr. tr. V.* eat up; **jmdm. alles ~essen** eat up all sb.'s food; **~|fahren** A *unr. itr. V.*; *mit sein* 1 leave; (im Auto) drive off; (losfahren) set off; **wann seid ihr in Kiel ~gefahren?** when did you leave Kiel?; 2 (irgendwohin fahren) go away. B *unr. tr. V.* drive away; (mit dem Handwagen/Boot/Schubkarren) take away; **~fahr·sperre** *die* (Kfz.-W.) immobilizer; **~fall** *der* ending; (Einstellung) discontinuation; **in ~fall kommen** (Papierdt.) be

W

discontinued; ~|**fallen** *unr. itr. V.; mit sein* to be discontinued; (nicht mehr zutreffen) ‹*reason*› no longer apply; (~gelassen werden) be omitted; ~|**fegen** *tr. V.* (auch fig.) sweep away; ~|**fliegen** *unr. itr. V.; mit sein* fly away; (~geschleudert-/~geblasen werden) fly off; ~|**führen** *tr., itr. V.* lead away; **das führt vom Thema ~:** this takes us away from the subject

Weg·gab[e]lung *die* fork [in the path/road]

Weg·gang *der* departure

weg|geben *unr. tr. V.* [1] **etw. zur Reparatur ~:** take sth. to be repaired; **ich gebe meine Wäsche weg** I send my washing to the laundry [2] (verschenken) give away

Weg·gefährte *der,* **Weg·gefährtin** *die* (auch fig.) fellow-traveller

weg-: ~|**gehen** *unr. itr. V.* [1] leave; (ugs.: ausgehen) go out; (ugs.: ~ziehen) move away; **von jmdm. ~gehen** leave sb.; **geh ~!** go away!; **geh mir [bloß] ~ damit!** (ugs.) you can keep that!; [2] (verschwinden) ‹*spot, fog, etc.*› go away; [3] (sich entfernen lassen) ‹*stain*› come out; [4] (ugs.: verkauft werden) sell; ~|**gießen** *unr. tr. V.* pour away; ~|**gucken** *itr. V.* ▸ ~**sehen**; ~|**haben** *unr. tr. V.* (ugs.) [1] have got rid of ‹*dirt, stain, etc.*›; **etw. ~haben wollen** want to get rid of sth.; [2] (bekommen haben) have got ‹*punishment, cold, etc.*›; **einen ~haben** (betrunken sein) have had one too many (coll.); (nicht bei Verstand sein) be off one's rocker (coll.); *s. auch* **Fett 1**; **Teil 2**; [3] (können, wissen) **in Literatur/auf einem Gebiet [et]was ~haben** know a thing or two about literature/on a subject; [4] (begriffen haben) **er hatte es sofort ~:** he immediately got the hang of it (coll.); *s. auch* **Ruhe 6**; ~|**holen** (ugs.) [A] *tr. V.* take away; [B] *refl. V.* **sich** (*Dat.*) **was ~holen** catch something; ~**hören** *itr. V.* not listen; **er konnte nicht ~hören** he couldn't help listening; ~|**jagen** *tr. V.* chase away; ~|**kippen** [A] *tr. V.* (ugs.) [1] (weggießen) pour away; [2] ([aus]trinken) knock back (coll.); [B] *itr. V.; mit sein* (salopp: ohnmächtig werden) pass out; ~|**kommen** *unr. itr. V.; mit sein* [1] get away; (~gehen können) manage to go out; **mach, dass du [hier] ~kommst!** (ugs.) come on, hop it! (coll.); make yourself scarce! (coll.); [2] (abhanden kommen) go missing; [3] **gut/schlecht** *usw.* **[bei etw.] ~kommen** (ugs.) come off well/badly *etc.* [in sth.]; [4] (ugs.: davon ~kommen) get off; [5] (ugs.) ▸ **hinwegkommen**; [6] (ugs.: loskommen) **von jmdm. ~kommen** get away from sb.; **vom Rauchen ~kommen** give up smoking; ~|**können** *unr. itr. V.* [1] be able to leave *or* get away; (ausgehen können) be able to go out; [2] (~geworfen werden können) **die Zeitung kann ~:** the paper can be thrown away

Weg·kreuz *das* wayside cross

weg-: ~|**kriegen** *tr. V.* get rid of ‹*cold, pain, etc.*›; get out, get rid of ‹*stain*›; shift, move ‹*stone, tree trunk*›; **er ist von seinem Spielzeug kaum ~zukriegen** you can hardly tear him away from his toys; ~|**lassen** *unr. tr. V.* [1] **jmdn. ~lassen** let sb. go; (ausgehen lassen) let sb. go out; [2] (auslassen) leave out; omit; **die Soße ~lassen** do without the sauce; give the sauce a miss; ~|**laufen** *unr. itr. V.; mit sein* run away (**von, vor** + *Dat.* from); **von zu Hause ~laufen** run away from home; **seine Frau ist ihm ~gelaufen** (ugs.) his wife has gone *or* run off and left him (coll.); **die Arbeit läuft [dir] nicht ~** (ugs.) the work will keep; ~|**legen** *tr. V.* (beiseite legen) put aside; (an seinen Platz legen) put away; (aus der Hand legen) put down; ~|**leugnen** *tr. V.* (ugs.) deny ‹*sth.*› out of existence; ~|**loben** *tr. V.* **jmdn. ~loben** get rid of sb. by singing his/her praises; ~|**locken** *tr. V.* lure away; **jmdn. von jmdm./aus** *od.* **von etw. ~locken** lure sb. away from sb./sth.; ~|**machen** (ugs.) [A] *tr. V.* get rid of; remove ‹*wart*›; delete ‹*comma etc.*›; **[sich** (*Dat.*)**] ein Kind ~machen lassen** (salopp) get rid of a baby (*before birth*); [B] *itr. V.; mit sein* (landsch.: ~ziehen) go off; ~|**müssen** *unr. itr. V.* [1] have to leave; (loskommen müssen) have to get away; **ich muss kurz ~:** I've got to go out for a short while; [2] (entfernt werden müssen) have to be removed; ‹*furniture etc.*› have to be moved; (~gebracht werden müssen) ‹*letter etc.*› have to go; (~geworfen werden müssen) have to be thrown away; **du musst da ~:** you'll have to move; **der Diktator muss ~:** the dictator must go; ~|**nehmen** *unr. tr. V.* [1] (entfernen) take away; remove; move ‹*head, arm*›; **nimm die Finger da ~!** [keep your] fingers off!; **[das/etwas] Gas ~nehmen** take one's foot off/ease up on the accelerator; [2] (entziehen, entwenden) **jmdm. etw. ~nehmen** take sth. away from sb.; (einem Besitzer) **er hat mir das Buch ~genommen** he's taken my book; **dem Freund die Freundin ~nehmen** pinch one's friend's girlfriend (coll.); **jmdm. den Turm** *usw.* **~nehmen** (Schachspiel) take sb.'s rook *etc.*; **du nimmst mir das [ganze] Licht ~:** you're in my light; [3] (beanspruchen, einnehmen) take up ‹*space, time*›; ~|**packen** *tr. V.* put away; ~|**pusten** *tr. V.* [1] (ugs.) blow away; (fig.) clear away ‹*doubts*›; **wie weggepustet sein** have vanished completely; be all gone; [2] (salopp: erschießen) blow away (coll.); ~|**putzen** *tr. V.* [1] clean off ‹*marks etc.*›; [2] (ugs.: aufessen, trinken) polish off (coll.)

Weg·rand *der* wayside; **Blumen/Gasthöfe am ~:** wayside flowers/inns

weg-: ~|**rationalisieren** *tr. V.* cut ‹*staff, jobs*› as part of a rationalization programme; ~|**räumen** *tr. V.* clear away ‹*dishes, rubbish, snow, etc.*›; remove ‹*obstacles, difficulties*›; (an seinen Platz tun) tidy *or* put away; ~|**reden** *tr. V.* **etw. ~reden** talk sth. away; ~|**rennen** *unr. itr. V.; mit sein* (ugs.) run away (**vor** + *Dat.* from); ~|**retuschieren** *tr. V.* **etw. ~retuschieren** remove sth. by retouching; **jmdn. ~retuschieren** (fig.) airbrush sb. out; ~|**rutschen** *itr. V.; mit sein* [1] slip *or* slide [away]; (fig.) stray from the straight and narrow; **[hinten] ~rutschen** ‹*car*› break away [at the back]; [2] (ugs.: wegrücken) move away; ~|**schaffen** *tr. V.* get rid of; (~räumen) clear away; (~bringen) take away; ~|**schauen** *itr. V.* (bes. südd., österr., schweiz.) look away; ~|**scheren** *refl. V.* clear off (coll.); ~|**schicken** *tr. V.* [1] send off ‹*letter, parcel*›; [2] send ‹*person*› away; ~|**schieben** *unr. tr. V.* push away; ~|**schleichen** *unr. itr., refl. V.; itr. mit sein* creep away; ~|**schleppen** [A] *tr. V.* [1] (~tragen) carry *or* lug off *or* away; [2] (abschleppen) tow ‹*car, rig, etc.*› away; [B] *refl. V.* drag oneself away; ~|**schließen** *unr. tr. V.* lock away; ~|**schmeißen** *unr. tr. V.* (ugs.) chuck away (coll.); ~|**schnappen** *tr. V.* (ugs.) **jmdm. etw. ~schnappen/vor der Nase ~schnappen** snatch sth. away from sb./from under sb.'s nose; **jmdm. die Freundin ~schnappen** pinch sb.'s girlfriend (coll.); ~|**schütten** *tr. V.* pour away; ~|**sehen** *unr. itr. V.* [1] look away; [2] (ugs.) ▸ **hinwegsehen**; ~|**sollen** *unr. itr. V.* **er soll jetzt ~:** he is to *or* should leave now; **diese Sachen sollen ~:** these things are to go; **das Plakat soll ~:** the poster is to be removed; ~|**sperren** *tr. V.* [1] (landsch.: wegschließen) lock away; [2] (einsperren) lock up; ~|**spülen** *tr. V.* [1] wash away; [2] (ugs.: spülen) wash up; ~|**stecken** *tr. V.* [1] put away; [2] (fig. ugs.: hinnehmen) take, accept ‹*blow*›; swallow ‹*insult*›; **einen ~stecken** (derb) have a poke (coarse); ~|**stellen** *tr. V.* put away; move ‹*car*› out of the way; (beiseite stellen) put aside; ~|**stoßen** *unr. tr. V.* push *or* shove away

Weg·strecke *die* stretch [of road]; (Entfernung) distance

weg-: ~|**tragen** *unr. tr. V.* carry away; ~|**treten** [A] *unr. tr. V.* kick away; [B] *unr. itr. V.; mit sein* step away; (zurücktreten) step back; (Milit.) dismiss; **~getreten!** (Milit.) dismiss!; **[etwas] ~getreten sein** (fig. ugs.) be [somewhat] distracted; ~|**tun** *unr. tr. V.* (ugs.) [1] put away; [2] (~werfen) throw away

wegweisend *Adj.* pioneering; **~ sein/werden** show the way forward (**für** to)

Wegweiser *der;* **~s, ~** [1] signpost [2] (fig.: Buch) guide

weg-: ~|**werfen** *unr. tr. V.* (auch fig.) throw away; **das ist doch ~geworfenes Geld** (ugs.) that's money down the drain (coll.); ~**werfend** *Adj.* dismissive ‹*gesture, remark*›

Weg·werf-: ~**flasche** *die* disposable *or* non-returnable bottle; ~**gesellschaft** *die* (abwertend) throwaway society; ~**mentalität** *die* (abwertend) use-and-throw-away attitude

weg-: ~|**wischen** *tr. V.* wipe away; (fig.) erase ‹*memory*›; dispel ‹*fear, doubt*›; dismiss ‹*objection*›; ~|**wollen** *unr. itr. V.* want to go *or* leave; (loskommen wollen) want to get away; (ausgehen wollen) want to go out; (verreisen wollen) want to go away; ~|**zaubern** *tr. V.* spirit away; **wie ~gezaubert sein** have vanished into thin air

Weg·zehrung *die* (geh.) provisions *pl.* for the journey

weg-: ~|**zerren** *tr. V.* drag away; ~|**ziehen** [A] *unr. tr. V.* pull away; pull *or* draw back ‹*curtain*›; pull off ‹*blanket*›; **jmdm. den Stuhl ~ziehen** pull away sb.'s chair [from under him/her]; [B] *unr. itr. V.; mit sein* [1] (umziehen) move away; **aus X ~ziehen** leave X; move from X; [2] (wandern) ‹*animals, nomads, etc.*› leave [on their migration]

Weg·zug *der* move; **nach ihrem ~ aus Berlin** after moving [away] from Berlin

weh[1] /ve:/ *Interj.* (veralt.) **o ~:** alas; **~ mir!** woe is me! (arch.)

weh[2] *Adj.* [1] (ugs.: schmerzend) sore; **einen ~en Finger haben** have a sore *or* bad finger [2] (geh.: schmerzlich) painful; **ein ~es Lächeln** a sad smile [3] (geh.: schmerzlich) **ihr ist ~ ums Herz** her heart aches; she is sore at heart; **ein ~es Gefühl** an aching feeling; *s. auch* **wehtun**

Weh *das;* **~[e]s** (geh.) sorrow; grief

wehe /ˈveːə/ *Interj.* woe betide you/him *etc.*; **~ [dir], wenn du ...** woe betide you if you ...

Wehe[1] *die;* **~, ~n** contraction; **die ~n setzten ein** the contractions started; she went into labour; **~n haben** have contractions; **in den ~n liegen** be in labour

Wehe[2] *die;* **~, ~n** drift

wehen

[A] *itr. V.* [1] (blasen) blow [2] (flattern) flutter; **ihre Haare wehten im Wind** her hair was blowing about in the wind; **mit ~den Rockschößen** with coat-tails flapping [3] *mit sein* ‹*leaves, snowflakes, scent*› waft

[B] *tr. V.* blow

weh-, Weh-: ~**klage** *die* (geh.) lamentation; ~**klagen** *itr. V.* (geh.) lament; **über etw.** (*Akk.*) **~klagen** lament *or* bewail sth.; ~**leidig** (abwertend) [A] *Adj.* [1] (überempfindlich) soft; **sei nicht so ~leidig!** don't be so soft *or* such a sissy; [2] (weinerlich) whining *attrib.*; **ein ~leidiges Gesicht machen** look sorry for oneself; [B] *adv.* self-pityingly; (weinerlich) whiningly; ~**mut** *die;* **~~** (geh.) melancholy *or* wistful nostalgia; ~**mütig** [A] *Adj.* melancholically *or* wistfully nostalgic; [B] *adv.* with melancholy *or* wistful nostalgia

wehmuts·voll (geh.) ▸ **wehmütig**

Wehr[1] *die;* **~, ~en** [1] *in* **sich [gegen jmdn./etw.] zur ~ setzen** make a stand [against sb./sth.]; resist [sb./sth.] [2] ▸ **Feuerwehr** [3] ▸ **Wehrmacht**

Wehr[2] *das;* **~[e]s, ~e** weir

Wehr-: ~**beauftragte** *der/die: parliamentary commissioner for the armed forces;* ~**bereichs·kommando** *das* military district command

Wehr·dienst *der* military service *no art.*; **zum ~ einberufen werden** be called up; **seinen ~ ableisten** do one's military service

Wehrdienst

Compulsory military service for young men in Germany (9 months), Switzerland (3 months), and Austria (6 months). Young Germans are generally called up when they are 18 or 19, although there are certain exemptions. Conscientious objectors may apply to do **Zivildienst** instead.

wehr·dienst-, Wehr·dienst-: ~**pflichtig** *Adj.* ▸ **wehrpflichtig**; ~**verweigerer** *der* conscientious objector; ~**verweigerung** *die* conscientious objection

W

wehren
A *refl. V.* **1** (körperlich Widerstand leisten) defend oneself; put up a fight; **sich tapfer/mit aller Kraft ~:** defend oneself *or* resist bravely/with all one's might; *s. auch* **Haut 1** **2** (sich verwahren) **sich gegen etw. ~:** fight against sth.; **gegen so etwas weiß ich mich zu ~:** I know how to deal with that sort of thing **3** (sich sträuben) **sich [dagegen] ~, etw. zu tun** resist having to do sth.
B *itr. V.* (geh.: einschreiten gegen) **jmdm./einer Sache ~:** fight sb./fight [against] sth.
C *tr. V.* (geh. veralt.) ▸ **verwehren**

wehr-, Wehr-: ~ersatzdienst *der* ▸ **Ersatzdienst**; **~erziehung** *die* (bes. DDR) defence education; **~experte** *der*, **~expertin** *die* defence expert; **~fähig** *Adj.* fit for military service *postpos.*; **~gang** *der* (hist.) battlemented parapet; **~haft** *Adj.* **1** (fähig, sich zu verteidigen) able to defend oneself *postpos.*; **2** (befestigt) fortified; **~kirche** *die* fortified church; **~kraft** *die* military strength; **~kraft·zersetzung** *die* (Milit., bes. ns.) undermining of military strength; **~los** *Adj.* defenceless; **jmdm./einer Sache ~los ausgeliefert sein** be defenceless against sb./sth.; **~losigkeit** *die*; **~~:** defencelessness; **~macht** *die* armed forces *pl.*; **~mann** *der* **1** *Pl.* **~männer** *od.* **~leute** ▸ **Feuerwehrmann**; **2** (schweiz.: Soldat) soldier; **~pass**, ***~paß** *der* service record [book]; **~pflicht** *die* military service; conscription; **die allgemeine ~pflicht** compulsory military service; **~pflichtig** *Adj.* liable for military service *postpos*; **~pflichtige** *der/die*; *adj. Dekl.* person liable for military service; **~sold** *der* military pay; **~übung** *die* reserve duty [re]training exercise

weh|tun *unr. itr. V.* ▸ⓘ **S. 439** (ugs.) hurt; **mir tut der Magen/Kopf/Rücken weh** my stomach/head/back is aching *or* hurts; **mir tut der Hals weh** my throat is sore; **jmdm./sich ~:** hurt sb./oneself

Weh·weh *das*; **~s, ~s** (Kinderspr.) hurt; **hast du ein ~?** have you hurt yourself?

Wehwehchen *das*; **~s, ~:** little complaint

Weib /vaip/ *das*; **~[e]s, ~er** **1** (veralt.: weibliches Wesen, ugs.: Frau) woman; female (derog.); **sie ist ein tolles ~:** she's a bit of all right (coll.) **2** (veralt., noch scherzh.: Ehefrau) wife; **~ und Kind [haben]** [have a] wife and family; **er nahm sie zum ~[e]** he took her for his wife

Weibchen *das*; **~s, ~** **1** (weibliches Tier) female **2** (abwertend: Frau) female; **er degradiert sie zum ~:** he reduces her to the role of dumb female **3** (veralt., noch fam. scherzh.: Ehefrau) little woman (joc.)

Weiber-: ~feind *der* woman-hater; misogynist; **~geschichten** *Pl.* (salopp) affairs; **~held** *der* (ugs.) ladykiller; **~wirtschaft** *die* (abwertend) **das ist ja hier die reinste ~wirtschaft** the whole place seems to be run by women *or* females

weibisch (abwertend)
A *Adj.* womanish; effeminate
B *adv.* womanishly; effeminately

weiblich
A *Adj.* **1** female **2** (für die Frau typisch) feminine **3** (Sprachw.) feminine ‹*noun, declension, gender*›; (Verslehre) female ‹*rhyme*›
B *adv.* femininely

Weiblichkeit *die*; **~** **1** (weibliche Art) femininity **2** (Gesamtheit der Frauen) women *pl.*; **die holde ~** (veralt.) the fair sex

Weibs-: ~bild *das* **1** (ugs.) woman; **2** (salopp abwertend) female; **~stück** *das* (salopp abwertend) bitch (sl.)

weich /vaiç/
A *Adj.* **1** (auch fig.) soft; soft, mellow ‹*sound, voice*›; **ein ~es** *od.* **~ gekochtes Ei** a soft-boiled egg; **ein Ei ~ kochen** soft-boil an egg; **ein ~es Herz** *od.* **Gemüt haben** be soft-hearted; **~ werden** (ugs.) soften; weaken; **jmdn. ~ machen** (ugs.) soften sb. up **2** (nicht scharf u. streng) soft, gentle ‹*features*›; gentle ‹*mouth, face*›
B *adv.* softly; ‹*brake*› gently; **~ landen** *od.* **aufsetzen** make a soft landing; *s. auch* **betten A 1**

Weich·bild *das*: **wir nähern uns dem ~ der Stadt** we're approaching the outskirts of the town; **noch im ~ der Stadt liegen** be still just in[side] the town

Weiche[1] *die*; **~, ~n** **1** (Flanke) flank **2** (Weichheit) softness

Weiche[2] *die*; **~, ~n** points *pl.* (Brit.); switch (Amer.); **die ~ stellen** set the points; **die ~n [für etw.] stellen** (fig.) set the course [for sth.]

weichen[1]
A *itr. V.*; *mit sein* (weich werden) soak
B *tr. V.* (ein~) soak

weichen[2] *unr. itr. V.*; *mit sein* **1** (sich entfernen) move; **nicht von jmds. Seite ~:** not move from *or* leave sb.'s side; **das Blut wich aus ihrem Gesicht** (geh.) the blood drained from her face **2** (Platz machen) **vor jmdm./einer Sache ~:** give way to sb./sth.; **dem Feind ~:** retreat from the enemy; **vor jmdm./etw. zur Seite ~:** step *or* move out of the way of sb./sth.; **die Bäume sind dem Neubau gewichen** the trees have gone to make room for the new building; **die Spannung wich großer Erleichterung** (fig.) [the] tension gave way to great relief; *s. auch* **wanken 1** **3** (nachlassen) subside; **die Angst/Spannung wich von ihm** the fear/tension left him

Weichen·steller *der*; **~s, ~:** pointsman (Brit.); switchman (Amer.)

Weichen·stellerin *die*; **~, ~nen** pointswoman (Brit.); switchwoman (Amer.)

Weichen·stellung *die* decisive measure setting the way ahead

weich·gekocht ▸ **weich A 1**

Weichheit *die*; **~** **1** (auch fig.) softness; (eines Tons, der Stimme) mellowness; **die ~ seines Gemüts** (fig.) his soft-heartedness **2** ▸ **weich A 2**: softness; gentleness

weich-, Weich-: ~herzig **A** *Adj.* soft-hearted; **B** *adv.* soft-heartedly; **~herzigkeit** *die*; **~~:** soft-heartedness; **~holz** *das* softwood; **~käse** *der* soft cheese

weichlich
A *Adj.* soft; (ohne innere Festigkeit) weak
B *adv.* softly

Weichling *der*; **~s, ~e** (abwertend) weakling

weich-, Weich-: *~|machen ▸ **weich A 1**; **~macher** *der* (Chemie, Technik) plasticizer; **~schalig** *Adj.* soft-shelled ‹*crustacean*›; soft-skinned ‹*fruit*›

Weichsel /ˈvaiksl̩/ *die*; **~:** Vistula

Weichsel·kirsche *die* (landsch.) ▸ **Sauerkirsche**

Weich-: ~spüler *der*; **~~s, ~~** (Werbespr.), **~spülmittel** *das* [fabric] softener; **~teile** *Pl.* ▸ⓘ **S. 435** **1** (Anat.) soft parts; **2** (ugs.: Genitalien) privates; **~tier** *das* mollusc; **~zeichner** *der* (Fot.) soft-focus lens

Weide[1] /ˈvaidə/ *die*; **~, ~n** willow

Weide[2] *die*; **~, ~n** pasture; **auf der ~ sein** be at pasture; **die Kühe auf die** *od.* **zur ~ treiben** drive the cows to pasture

Weide-: ~fläche *die* pasture; **~land** *das* pasture[land]; grazing land

weiden
A *itr., tr. V.* graze
B *refl. V.* **1** (geh.: sich erfreuen) **er** *od.* **sein Auge weidete sich an dem herrlichen Anblick** he feasted his eyes on the glorious sight **2** (abwertend: schadenfroh beobachten) gloat over; revel in; **sich an jmds. Schmerz** (*Dat.*) **~:** gloat over sb.'s pain

Weiden-: ~baum *der* willow tree; **~gerte** *die* willow rod; (zum Korbflechten) osier; (kleiner) wicker; **~kätzchen** *das* willow catkin

Weide-: ~platz *der* pasture; **~wirtschaft** *die* pastoral farming *no art.*

weidlich *Adv.* **etw. ~ ausnutzen** make full use of sth.; **sich ~ über etw. lustig machen** have a good laugh at sth.; **sie mussten sich ~ plagen** they really had to slave away

Weid·mann *der* (geh.) huntsman; hunter

weid·männisch
A *Adj.* hunting, huntsman's *attrib.* ‹*expression, terminology, customs*›
B *adv.* in the manner of a huntsman; like a huntsman

Weidmanns·heil *Interj.* good hunting

Weid·werk *das* [art of] hunting

weid·wund *Adj.* **ein ~ geschossenes Tier** an animal shot in the belly [and fatally wounded]

weigern /ˈvaigɐn/
A *refl. V.* refuse; **sich ~, etw. zu tun** refuse to do sth.
B *tr. V.* (veralt.: ver~) **jmdm. etw. ~:** refuse *or* deny sb. sth.

Weigerung *die*; **~, ~en** refusal

Weih·bischof *der* (kath. Kirche) suffragan bishop

Weihe[1] *die*; **~, ~n** **1** (Rel.: Einweihung) consecration; dedication **2** (kath. Kirche: Priester~, Bischofs~) ordination; **die niederen/höheren ~n** (hist.) the minor/major orders **3** (geh.: Erhabenheit) solemnity

Weihe[2] *die*; **~, ~n** (Zool.) harrier

weihen *tr. V.* **1** (Rel.: durch Weihe heiligen) consecrate **2** (kath. Kirche: ordinieren) ordain; **jmdn. zum Priester/Bischof ~:** ordain sb. priest/consecrate sb. bishop **3** (Rel.: durch Weihe zueignen) dedicate (*Dat.* to) **4** (geh.: preisgeben) **dem Tod[e]/dem Untergang geweiht sein** be doomed to die/to fall **5** (geh.: widmen) dedicate

Weiher *der*; **~s, ~** (bes. südd.) [small] pond

Weihe·stätte *die* (geh.) holy place

weihe·voll *Adj.* (geh.) solemn

Weih-: ~gabe *die* (bes. kath. Kirche) votive offering; **~nacht** *die* (geh.) ▸ **Weihnachten**

weihnachten *itr. V.* (unpers.) **es weihnachtet bereits/es fängt an zu ~:** Christmas has already started/Christmas is starting

Weihnachten *das*; **~, ~** ▸ⓘ **S. 331** Christmas; **frohe** *od.* **fröhliche** *od.* **gesegnete ~!** Merry *or* Happy Christmas!; **grüne ~:** Christmas without snow; **zu** *od.* (bes. südd.) **an/über ~:** at *or* for/over Christmas

> **Weihnachten**
>
> Christmas is a family event in Germany, and preparations begin with the **Adventskranz**. Christmas decorations are generally still very traditional — no garlands or balloons — with fir branches, candles and wooden Christmas figurines, which can be bought at the **Weihnachtsmarkt**. Typical Christmas baking includes *Stollen* or *Christstollen* (a rich fruit bread), *Lebkuchen* (spicy honey biscuits made from a recipe that goes back to the Middle Ages), and lots of biscuits in the shape of stars, bells, etc. The decorated Christmas tree should only be seen by the children on *Heiligabend* (Christmas Eve), when presents are given out. The *erster Weihnachtstag* (Christmas Day) is a public holiday in Germany, Austria, and Switzerland. It tends to be a quiet day for family get-togethers, often with a traditional lunch of goose or carp. The *zweiter Weihnachtstag* (Boxing Day) is also a public holiday; in Austria and Switzerland it is called *Stephanstag* (St Stephen's Day).

weihnachtlich
A *Adj.* Christmassy
B *adv.* **~ geschmückt/gedeckt sein** be decorated/set for Christmas; **ihr war ~ zumute** she was in a Christmassy mood

Weihnachts-: ~abend *der* Christmas Eve; **~baum** *der* Christmas tree; **~einkauf** *der* Christmas purchase; **~einkäufe** Christmas shopping *sing.*; **~feier** *die* Christmas party; **~feiertag** *der*: **der erste/zweite ~feiertag** Christmas Day/Boxing Day; **~ferien** *Pl.* Christmas holidays; **~fest** *das* ▸ⓘ **S. 331** Christmas; **~gans** *die* Christmas goose; **~gebäck** *das* Christmas biscuits *pl.* (Brit.) *or* (Amer.) cookies *pl.*; **~geld** *das* Christmas bonus; **~geschäft** *das* Christmas trade; **~geschenk** *das* Christmas present *or* gift; **~geschichte** *die* Christmas story; **~gratifikation** *die* Christmas bonus; **~karte** *die* Christmas card; **~lied** *das* Christmas carol; **~mann** *der* **1** Father Christmas; Santa Claus; **2** (ugs.: Dummkopf) silly idiot (coll.); **~markt** *der* Christmas fair; **~spiel** *das*

W

(Literaturw.) nativity play; **~stern** *der* 1▸ Christmas star; 2▸ (Pflanze) poinsettia; **~stollen** *der* Christmas Stollen; **~tag** *der* ▸**~feiertag**; **~zeit** *die* Christmas time; **in der ~zeit** at Christmas time

Weihnachtsmarkt

During the weeks of Advent, these Christmas markets take place in most German towns, selling Christmas decorations, handmade toys and crib figures, traditional Christmas biscuits, and mulled wine to sustain the shoppers.

Weih-: ~rauch *der* incense; **jmdm. ~rauch streuen** (geh.) eulogize sb.; **~wasser** *das* (kath. Kirche) holy water; **~wasser·becken** *das* (kath. Kirche) stoup

weil /vail/ *Konj.* because

weiland *Adv.* (veralt.) (vormals) formerly; (einst) once

Weilchen *das;* **~s** little while

Weile *die;* ~: while; **eine ganze** *od.* (geh.) **geraume ~**: a good while; **eine ~ dauern** take a while; **vor einer ~**: a while ago; **damit hat es noch [gute] ~** (geh.) there is still [plenty of] time; *s. auch* **Ding¹ 3**; **eilen A 1**

weilen *itr. V.* (geh.) (ver~) stay; (sein) be; **zu Besuch bei jmdm. ~**: be on a visit to sb.; be visiting sb.; **er weilt nicht mehr unter uns** (*Dat.*) *od.* **unter den Lebenden** (verhüll.) he is no longer among *or* with us

Weiler *der;* **~s, ~**: hamlet

Weimarer Republik *die* Weimar Republic

Wein /vain/ *der;* **~[e]s, ~e** 1▸ wine; **im ~ ist** *od.* **liegt Wahrheit** (Spr.) in vino veritas; **jmdm. reinen ~ einschenken** (fig.) tell sb. the truth; **neuen ~ in alte Schläuche füllen** (fig.) pour new wine into old bottles (prov.) 2▸ (Reben) vines *pl.*; **wilder ~**: Virginia creeper 3▸ (~trauben) grapes *pl.*

Wein

Germany, Switzerland, and Austria are wine-producing countries, best known for their white wines. Germany's main wine regions are Franconia, the Rhineland-Palatinate, the Moselle area and Baden-Württemberg. Rhine wine (or hock) is sold in tall brown bottles and wine from the Moselle in green bottles; Franconian *Bocksbeutel* comes in wide, bulbous bottles. There are two categories of German wine, the cheap *Tafelwein* (table wine) and the superior *Qualitätswein* (quality wine). The best wines are designated *Qualitätswein mit Prädikat*. *Sekt* is a champagne-like sparkling wine. In August and September there are festivals in German wine towns and villages. Austria grows red and white wines, mainly in the Burgenland, in Styria and around the Neusiedler See where the **Heurige** is celebrated. More than a third of the total area of grape cultivation is devoted to *Grüner Veltliner*, a full-bodied, fruity white wine. Wines from Switzerland are mostly drunk locally and are produced in the Thurgau region. The Swiss reputation rests with their spirits, such as *Kirsch, Pflümli, Mirabelle*, and *Enzian*.

Wein-: ~[an]bau *der* wine-growing *no art.*; **~bauer** *der;* **~~n, ~~n, ~bäuerin** *die* winegrower; **~beere** *die* 1▸ grape; 2▸ (südd., österr., schweiz.: Rosine) raisin; **~beißer** *der;* **~~s, ~~** (österr.) 1▸ (Gebäck) iced ginger biscuit; 2▸ (~kenner) wine connoisseur; **~beißerin** *die;* **~~, ~~nen** ▸**Weinbeißer 2**; **~berg** *der* vineyard; **~berg·schnecke** *die* [edible] snail; **~brand** *der* brandy

weinen

A *itr. V.* cry; (aus Trauer, Kummer) cry; weep; **um jmdn. ~**: cry *or* weep for sb.; **über jmdn./etw. ~**: cry over *or* about sb./sth.; **vor Glück/Wut ~**: cry with happiness/anger; **vor Freude ~**: cry *or* weep for *or* with joy; **es ist zum Weinen** it's enough to make you weep; **es ist zum Weinen mit dir** (ugs.) you're enough to make anyone weep; **leise ~d abziehen** (fig. ugs.) leave with one's tail between one's legs

B *tr. V.* shed ‹*tears*›; **sich** (*Dat.*) **die Augen rot ~**: make one's eyes red with crying; **sich in den Schlaf ~**: cry oneself to sleep

weinerlich

A *Adj.* tearful; weepy; **ein ~es Gesicht machen** look on the verge of tears *or* as if one is about to cry

B *adv.* tearfully

wein-, Wein-: ~essig *der* wine vinegar; **~fass**, ***~faß** *das* wine barrel *or* cask; **~flasche** *die* wine bottle; **~garten** *der* vineyard; **~gegend** *die* winegrowing region; **~geist** *der* ethyl alcohol; ethanol; **~glas** *das* wineglass; **~gut** *das* vineyard; **~händler** *der,* **~händlerin** *die* ▸❶ **S. 113** wine merchant; **~handlung** *die* wine merchant's; **~hauer** *der,* **~hauerin** *die;* **~~, ~~nen** (österr.) winegrower; **~jahr** *das* vintage; **~karte** *die* wine list; **~keller** *der* window cellar; **~kenner** *der,* **~kennerin** *die* wine connoisseur; **~königin** *die* wine queen (*representing a particular wine region for the year*); **~krampf** *der* crying fit; fit of crying; **~küfer** *der* cellarman; **~küferin** *die* cellarwoman; **~laub** *das* vine leaves *pl.*; **~lese** *die* grape harvest; **~lokal** *das* wine bar; **~probe** *die* wine tasting [session]; **~rebe** *die* 1▸ grapevine; 2▸ (Ranke) [grapevine] shoot; **~rot** *Adj.* wine-red; wine-coloured; **~schaum·creme** *die* (Kochk.) zabaglione; **~selig** *Adj.* merry on *or* with wine *pred.*; **in ~seliger Stimmung sein** be merry on *or* with wine; **~stein** *der* cream of tartar; **~stock** *der; Pl.* **~stöcke** [grape]vine; **~straße** *die* wine route; **~stube** *die* wine bar; **~traube** *die* grape; **~trinker** *der,* **~trinkerin** *die* wine drinker; **~verkoster** *der,* **~~s, ~~, ~verkosterin** *die;* **~~, ~~nen** wine taster

Weinstube

A cosy wine bar which offers a wide choice of wines and usually also serves a few dishes which are considered to go well with wine. A *Weinstube* tends to be more upmarket than an ordinary pub, or else fairly rustic, especially in wine-growing areas.

weise /'vaizə/

A *Adj.* wise; **ein Weiser** a wise man; **die drei Weisen aus dem Morgenland** the three Wise Men from the East

B *adv.* wisely

-weise (bei Mengen- und Maßangaben) by the ...; **kilo~/meter~/liter~/eimer~** *usw.* by the kilo/metre/litre/bucketful *etc.*; in kilos/metres/litres/bucketfuls *etc.*; **monats~/wochen~/stunden~**: by the month/week/hour; **paar~**: in pairs

Weise *die;* **~, ~n** 1▸ (Art, Verfahren) way; **auf diese/andere ~**: this way/ [in] another way; **auf die eine oder andere ~**: in one way or another; **auf meine ~**: in my own way; **auf geheimnisvolle ~**: in a mysterious manner; mysteriously; **in gewisser ~**: in certain respects; **in keiner ~**: in no way 2▸ (Melodie) tune; melody

weisen

A *unr. tr. V.* 1▸ (geh.: zeigen) show; **jmdm. etw. ~**: show sb. sth.; *s. auch* **Tür** 2▸ (ver~) **jmdn. aus dem Zimmer ~**: send sb. out of the room; **jmdn. aus dem Land/von der Schule ~**: expel sb. from the country/from the school; **etw. von sich ~** (fig.) reject sth.; *s. auch* **Hand 6**; **Schranke 2**

B *unr. itr. V.* (irgendwohin zeigen) point; **mit der Hand auf etw.** (*Akk.*) **~**: point to sth.; **nach Norden ~**: point North; **eine Idee, die in die Zukunft weist** a forward-looking idea

Weisheit *die;* **~, ~en** 1▸ wisdom; **die ~ mit Löffeln gefressen haben** (ugs.) know it all; know all the answers; **er hat die ~ [auch] nicht mit Löffeln gefressen** (ugs.) he is not all that bright; **der ~ letzter Schluss** the answer to everything; **mit seiner ~ am Ende sein** be at one's wit's end 2▸ (Erkenntnis) wise insight; (Spruch) wise saying; **deine ~en kannst du für dich behalten** (spött.) you can keep your pearls of wisdom to yourself

Weisheits·zahn *der* ▸❶ **S. 435** wisdom tooth

weis|machen *tr. V.* (ugs.) **das kannst du mir nicht ~!** you can't expect me to swallow that!; **du willst mir doch nicht ~, dass ...?** you're not trying to make me believe *or* (coll.) to kid me that ...; **er lässt sich** (*Dat.*) **nichts ~**: you can't fool him; he's not to be fooled; **das kannst du anderen ~!** tell that to the marines (coll.)

weiß¹ /vais/ *1. u. 3. Pers. Sg. Präsens v.* **wissen**

weiß²

A *Adj.* 1▸ white; **~e Ostern/Weihnachten** Easter with snow/white Christmas; **das Weiße Meer** the White Sea; **Weißer Sonntag** (christl. Kirche) Low Sunday; **der ~e Sport** tennis; **er/sie ist ~ geworden** his/her hair has turned white; *s. auch* **Fleck 2**; **Haus 1**; **Tod**; **Weste** 2▸ (Kaufmannsspr.) unbranded ‹*product*›

B *adv.* white; **~ gepunktet** with white dots *postpos., not pred.*; **~ glühend** white-hot

Weiß *das;* **~[es], ~**: white

weis-, Weis-: ~sagen *tr. V.* 1▸ *auch itr.* (prophezeien) prophesy; foretell; 2▸ (ahnen lassen) forebode; **~sager** *der;* **~~s, ~~**: prophet; **~sagerin** *die;* **~~, ~~nen** prophetess; **~sagung** *die;* **~~, ~~en** prophecy

weiß-, Weiß-: ~bier *das:* wheat beer; weiss beer; *light, highly effervescent, top-fermented beer made from wheat and barley;* **~blech** *das* tin plate; **~blond** *Adj.* ash-blond/-blonde; **~brot** *das* white bread; **ein ~brot** a white loaf; **~buch** *das* (Politik) White Paper; **~burgunder** *der* white burgundy; **~dorn** *der; Pl.* **~~e** hawthorn

Weiße¹ *die;* **~, ~n** 1▸ whiteness 2▸ ▸**Berliner¹ A**

Weiße² *der/die; adj. Dekl.* white; white man/woman

Weiße-Kragen-Kriminalität *die* white-collar crime *no art.*

weißeln (südd., österr., schweiz.), **weißen** *tr. V.* paint white; (tünchen) whitewash

weiß-, Weiß-: ~gardist *der* (hist.) member of the White Guard; **~glühend** ▸**weiß² B**; **~glut** *die* white heat; **jmdn. [bis] zur ~glut bringen** *od.* **reizen** *od.* **treiben** (ugs.) make sb. livid (Brit. coll.); **~gold** *das* white gold; **~haarig** *Adj.* white-haired; **~haarig sein** have white hair; **~herbst** *der* ≈ rosé wine; **~käse** *der* (bes. nordd.) ▸**Quark**; **~kohl** *der,* (bes. südd., österr.) **~kraut** *das* white cabbage

weißlich *Adj.* whitish

Weiß-: ~macher *der* whitener; **~russland**, ***~rußland** (*das*) White Russia

weißt *2. Pers. Sg. Präsens v.* **wissen**

weiß-, Weiß-: ~tanne *die* silver fir; **~wal** *der* white whale; **~wand·reifen** *der* whitewall tyre; **~|waschen** *unr. tr. V.* (ugs.) **jmdn./sich ~waschen** clear sb.'s/one's name; **~wein** *der* white wine; **~wurst** *die* veal sausage

Weisung *die;* **~, ~en** 1▸ (geh., sonst Amtsspr.) instruction; (Direktive) directive; **auf** *od.* **nach ~ [von jmdm.]** on *or* in accordance with [sb.'s] instructions; **~ geben/erhalten/haben, etw. zu tun** give/receive/have instructions to do sth. 2▸ (Rechtsw.) [court] order; **jmdm. die ~ erteilen, etw. zu tun** order sb. to do sth.

weisungs-, Weisungs-: ~befugnis *die* authority to issue instructions/directives; **~gebunden** *Adj.* subject to instructions/directives *postpos.*; **~gemäß** *Adv.* in accordance with instructions; as instructed

weit /vait/

A *Adj.* 1▸ ▸❶ **S. 800** (räumlich ausgedehnt) wide; (fig.) broad ‹*concept*›; **in die ~e Welt ziehen** go out into the big wide world; **~e Kreise** *od.* **Teile der Bevölkerung** (fig.) large *or* broad sections of the population; **im ~eren Sinn** (fig.) in the broader sense; **das Weite suchen** (fig.) take to one's heels; *s. auch* **Feld 5**

2▸ (locker sitzend) wide; **jmdm. zu ~ sein** ‹*clothes*› be too loose on sb.; **einen Rock [in der Taille] ~er machen** let out a skirt [at the waist]

3▸ (streckenmäßig ausgedehnt, lang) long ‹*way*›; **einen ~en Blick [über die Gegend] haben** have a wide view [over the area]

B *adv.* 1▸ (räumlich ausgedehnt) **~ geöffnet** wide open; **~ bekannt** widely known; **~ gereist** widely travelled; **~ verbreitet** widespread;

W

common; common ‹plant, animal›; ~ verzweigt extensive ‹network›; ‹firm› with many [different] branches; eine ~ verzweigte Verwandtschaft haben have numerous branches in one's family; ~ herumgekommen sein have got around a good deal; have travelled widely; ~ und breit war niemand zu sehen there was no one to be seen anywhere; den besten Fisch ~ und breit kriegst du in diesem Restaurant this restaurant has the best fish for miles around

2 ▸ ❶ S. 224, ▸ ❶ S. 800 (streckenmäßig ausgedehnt, lang) far; ~er further; farther; am ~esten [the] furthest or farthest; es ist noch ~: it is still a long way; sehr ~ gehen walk a very long way; hast du es ~? do you have far to go?; ~ [entfernt od. weg] wohnen live a long way away or off; live far away; zwei Häuser ~er wohnen live two houses further or farther on; 15 km ~ [von hier] 15 km. away [from here]; 5,80 Meter ~ springen jump [a distance of] 5.80 metres; von ~em od. Weitem from a distance; von ~ her from far away; es würde zu ~ führen, das alles jetzt zu analysieren it would be too much to analyse it all now; das geht zu ~ (fig.) that is going too far; etw. zu ~ treiben, es mit etw. zu ~ treiben (fig.) overdo sth.; carry sth. too far; mit etw. [nicht] ~ kommen (fig.) [not] get far with sth.; so ~, so gut so far, so good; ~ blickend ▸ weitblickend; ~ gehend ▸ weitgehend; ~ reichend ▸ weitreichend; s. auch entfernt 1; hersein 3

3 (zeitlich entfernt) ~ nach Mitternacht well past midnight; ~ zurückliegen be a long way back or a long time ago

4 (in der Entwicklung) far; sehr ~ mit etw. sein have got a long way with sth.; wie ~ seid ihr? how far have you got?; wir wollen es gar nicht erst so ~ kommen lassen we do not want to let it come to that; so ~ ist es schon mit dir gekommen? have things come to that with you?; er wird es einmal ~ bringen he will go far one of these days; ~ fortgeschritten od. gediehen sein be far advanced

5 (~aus) far; jmdn. ~ übertreffen surpass sb. by far or by a long way; bei ~em by far; by a long way; bei ~em nicht! not by a long way!; bei ~em nicht so gut wie ... nowhere near as good as ...; das ist bei ~em od. Weitem nicht alles that's not all by a long way; bei ~em od. Weitem hübscher als ... far prettier than ...; etw. bei ~em od. Weitem übertreffen far exceed sth.; s. auch gefehlt B; weiter

-weit Adj., adv. europa~/hessen~: throughout Europe/Hessen postpos.

weit-, Weit-: ~ab Adv. far away; ~aus Adv. far ‹better, worse, etc.›; der ~aus beste od. ~aus der beste Reiter by far or far and away the best rider; ~bekannt ▸ weit B1; ~blick der far-sightedness; politischen ~blick haben be politically far-sighted; ihm fehlt der ~blick he lacks vision; ~blickend Adj. far-sighted

Weite die; ~, ~n 1 (räumliche Ausdehnung) expanse 2 (bes. Sport: Entfernung) distance 3 (eines Kleidungsstückes) width 4 (Größe, Durchmesser) width

weiten
A tr. V. widen
B refl. V. widen; ‹pupil› dilate; (fig.) ‹chest› swell

weiter Adv. 1 ▸ weit B 2 further; farther; halt, nicht ~! stop, don't go any further; ~! go on!; er hat immer ~ gelacht/geschwatzt he carried on laughing/chattering; nur immer ~ so! keep it up!; und so ~: and so on; und so ~ und so fort and so on and so forth 3 (~hin, anschließend) then; was geschah ~? what happened then or next? 4 (außerdem, sonst) ~ nichts, nichts ~: nothing more or else; ~ weiß ich nichts von der Sache that's all I know about it; ich brauche ~ nichts I don't need anything else; there's nothing else I need; er wollte ~ nichts als ... all he wanted was ...; Was ist los? — Ach, nichts ~: What's the matter — Oh, nothing in particular; das macht ~ nichts od. ist nicht ~ schlimm it isn't that important; it doesn't really matter; wenn es ~ nichts ist if that's all

weiter... Adj. (zusätzlich) further; ~e zwei Jahre warten wait a further two years or two more years; ohne ~e Umstände without any fuss; die ~e Entwicklung abwarten await further developments; im ~en Verlauf zeigte sich, dass ... it later became clear that ...; bis auf ~es od. Weiteres for the time being; „bis auf ~es od. Weiteres geschlossen" 'closed until further notice'; des Weiteren (geh.) furthermore; s. auch ohne A 3

weiter-, Weiter-: ~|arbeiten itr. V. continue or carry on working; ~|bestehen unr. itr. V. continue to exist; ~|bilden tr. V. ▸ fortbilden; ~bildung die ▸ Fortbildung; ~|bringen unr. tr. V. die Diskussion/Auskunft/sein Ratschlag brachte uns nicht ~bringen: the discussion/information/his advice did not get us any further [forward]; ~|entwickeln tr., refl. V. develop [further]; er hat sich im letzten Jahr auffallend ~entwickelt he has matured noticeably in the last year; ~entwicklung die [further] development; ~|erzählen tr. V. 1 continue telling; 2 (~sagen) pass on; erzähl das nicht ~: don't tell anyone; ~|fahren unr. itr. V.; mit sein continue [on one's way]; (~reisen) travel on; ~fahrt die continuation of one's journey; angenehme ~fahrt! enjoy the rest of your journey; auf der ~fahrt nach X trafen wir ... continuing our journey to X we met ...; ~flug der connecting flight; onward flight; auf unserem ~flug as we continued our flight; Passagiere zum ~flug nach New York passengers continuing on to New York; ~|führen A tr. V. 1 (fortführen) continue; 2 (voranbringen) das führt uns nicht ~: that does not get us any further or anywhere; B itr. V. continue; ~führende Schulen secondary schools; ~gabe die 1 passing on; 2 (Sport) pass; ~|geben unr. tr. V. 1 pass on; 2 (Sport) pass; ~|gehen unr. itr. V.; mit sein 1 go on; bitte ~gehen, nicht stehen bleiben! please move along or keep moving, don't stop!; 2 (sich fortsetzen, noch nicht aufhören) continue; go on; der Weg geht nicht ~: the path does not go any further; die Geschichte/Sache geht ~: there's more to come; das Leben geht ~: life goes on; so kann es nicht ~gehen it cannot go on like this; so kann es mit uns nicht ~gehen we cannot go on like this; wie soll es denn nun ~gehen? what is going to happen now?; ~|helfen unr. itr. V. jmdm. [mit etw.] ~helfen help sb. [with sth.]; ~hin Adv. 1 (immer noch) still; 2 (künftig) in future; etw. ~hin tun continue to do sth. [in future]; 3 (außerdem) in addition; ~|kommen unr. itr. V.; mit sein 1 get further; mach, dass du ~kommst (ugs.) clear off (coll.); 2 (Fortschritte machen) make progress or headway; im Leben/Beruf ~kommen get on in life/one's career; ~|können unr. itr. V. (ugs.) 1 be able to go on; geradeaus können wir nicht ~: we can't go or get any further straight on; 2 (bei einer Aufgabe) nicht ~können get stuck; be unable to go on; ~|laufen unr. itr. V.; mit sein 1 (~gehen) walk on; carry on walking; 2 (in Betrieb bleiben, auch fig.) keep going; 3 (fortgeführt werden) continue; ‹agreement, insurance› run; ~|leben itr. V. 1 (am Leben bleiben) go on living; 2 (seine Existenz fortsetzen) continue or carry on one's life; 3 (nach dem Tod fortleben) live on; ~|leiten tr. V. pass on ‹news, information, etc.›; forward ‹letter, parcel, etc.›; ~|machen (ugs.) A itr. V. carry on; go on; ~machen! (Milit.) carry on; as you were; B tr. V. etw. ~machen carry on with sth.; ~|müssen unr. itr. V. (ugs.) have to be on one's way; ich muss ~: I must be on my way; ~|qualifizieren A refl. V. improve one's qualifications; B tr. V. jmdn. ~qualifizieren improve sb.'s qualifications; ~|reden itr. V. go on or carry on talking; sie ließ mich nicht ~reden she would not let me carry on [with what I was saying]; ~|reichen tr. V. pass on; ~reise die ▸ ~fahrt

weiters Adv. (österr.) ▸ ferner

weiter-: ~|sagen tr. V. pass on; sag es nicht ~: don't tell anyone; ~|schicken tr. V. forward; send on; send ‹person› on; ~|sehen unr. itr. V. see; morgen werden wir ~sehen we'll see what we can do tomorrow; ~|spielen tr., itr. V. 1 go on or carry on playing; der Schiedsrichter ließ ~spielen the referee allowed play to continue; 2 (Sport: abspielen) pass; ~|sprechen unr. itr. V. go on or carry on speaking or talking; ~|suchen itr. V. go on searching or looking (nach for); ~|tragen unr. tr. V. 1 continue to carry; carry further; etw. nach X ~tragen carry sth. on to X; 2 spread ‹disease, rumour›

Weiterungen Pl. complications; difficulties

weiter-, Weiter-: ~|verarbeiten tr. V. process; ~verarbeitung die processing; ~|verbreiten tr. V. spread [further]; (weitergeben) pass on; disseminate ‹information, news›; ~|vererben A tr. V. bequeath; pass on; B refl. V. be passed on [to others]; ~|verfolgen tr. V. follow up ‹clue, case, etc.›; continue to follow ‹developments, events, etc.›; pursue further ‹idea, line of thought, etc.›; ~|verhandeln itr. V. continue to negotiate; ~verkauf der resale; nicht zum ~verkauf bestimmt not for resale; ~|verkaufen tr. V. resell; ~|vermitteln tr. V. 1 (weitergeben) pass on; 2 (an eine andere Stelle vermitteln) place ‹workers› in other jobs; ~|verwenden tr. V. continue to use; ~|wissen unr. itr. V. 1 nicht [mehr] ~wissen be at one's wit's end; 2 (bei einem Rätsel, einer Aufgabe usw.) be stuck; ~|wollen unr. itr. V. (ugs.) want to go on; das Pferd wollte nicht ~: the horse would not go any further; ~|zahlen tr., auch itr. V. continue or go on paying; continue to pay; das Gehalt wird ~gezahlt the salary continues to be paid; ~|ziehen unr. itr. V.; mit sein move on

weitest·möglich (Papierdt.)
A Adj. greatest possible
B adv. as far as possible

weit-, Weit-: ~gehend A Adj. extensive, wide, sweeping ‹powers›; far-reaching ‹support, concessions, etc.›; wide ‹support, agreement, etc.›; general ‹renunciation›. B adv. to a large or great extent; ~gereist ▸ weit B1; ~her Adv. (geh.) from afar; ~herzig A Adj. generous; liberal ‹interpretation›; B adv. generously; ‹interpret› liberally; ~hin Adv. 1 (~ umher) for miles around; 2 (~gehend) to a large or great extent; ~läufig A Adj. 1 (ausgedehnt) extensive; (geräumig) spacious; 2 (entfernt) distant; 3 (ausführlich) lengthy; long-winded; B adv. 1 (ausgedehnt) spaciously; 2 (entfernt) distantly; 3 (ausführlich) at length; long-windedly; ~maschig Adj. wide-meshed; ~räumig A Adj. spacious ‹room, area, etc.›; wide ‹gap, space›; B adv. spaciously; etw. ~räumig umfahren give sth. a wide berth; ~reichend A Adj. 1 long-range; 2 (umfangreich und gewichtig) far-reaching ‹importance, consequences›; sweeping ‹changes, powers›; extensive ‹relations, influence›; ~reichende Freiheiten a large or great degree of freedom; B adv. extensively; to a large extent; ~schuss, *~schuß der (Sport) long-range shot; ~schweifig A Adj. long-winded; B adv. long-windedly; ~sicht die far-sightedness; ~sichtig A Adj. long-sighted; (fig.) far sighted; B adv. (fig.) far-sightedly; ~sichtigkeit die; ~~: long-sightedness; (fig.) far-sightedness; ~springen unr. itr. V.; mit sein; nur im Inf. u. Part. gebr. (Sport) do the long jump (Brit.) or broad jump (Amer.); ~sprung der (Sport) long jump (Brit.); broad jump (Amer.); ~verbreitet ▸ weit B 1; ~verzweigt ▸ weit B 1; ~winkelobjektiv das wide-angle lens

Weizen /ˈvaitsn̩/ der; ~s wheat

Weizen-: ~bier das ▸ Weißbier; ~brot das wheat bread; ein ~brot a wheat loaf; a loaf of wheat bread; ~keim der wheat germ no pl.; ~keim·öl das wheatgerm oil; ~mehl das wheat flour

welch /vɛlç/
A Interrogativpron. 1 (bei Wahl aus einer unbegrenzten Menge) what; aus ~em Grund? for what reason?; ~e Folgen wird das haben? what will be the consequences of that?; um ~e Zeit? [at] what time? 2 (bei Wahl aus einer begrenzten Menge) (adj.) which; (subst.) which one;

W

an ~em Tag/in ~em Jahr? on which day/in which year?; **~e Folgen auch immer** whatever the consequences; **~er/~e/~es auch immer** whichever one; **~er/~e/~es von [den] beiden** which of the two 3 (geh.: was für ein) what a; (oft unflektiert) **~ reizendes Geschöpf!** what a charming creature!; **~ ein Zufall/Glück!** what a coincidence/how fortunate!

B *Relativpron.* (bei Menschen) who; (bei Sachen) which; (unflektiert, Papierdt.) **X, Y und Z, ~ Letztere/Letzterer/Letzteres ...** X, Y, and Z, the latter of whom/which ...

C *Indefinitpron.* some; **ich habe keine Seife — hast du ~e?** I have no soap — have you any?; **es gibt ~e, die behaupten, dass ...** (ugs.) there are some [people] *or* those who claim that ...

welcher·art *Adv.* what kind of; **es ist gleichgültig, ~ seine Überlegungen waren** it's irrelevant what his considerations were

welcher·lei *indekl. Interrogativadj.* whatever

Welfe /ˈvɛlfə/ *der;* **~n, ~n** (hist.) Guelph

welk /vɛlk/ *Adj.* withered ‹*skin, hands, etc.*›; wilted ‹*leaves, flower*›; limp ‹*lettuce*›; shrivelled ‹*breasts*›; **sein Gesicht sah ~ aus** his face looked old and tired

welken *itr. V.; mit sein* ‹*plant, flower*› wilt; (fig.) ‹*beauty*› fade; ‹*woman*› age

Well·blech *das* corrugated iron

Wellblech·dach *das* corrugated-iron roof

Welle /ˈvɛlə/ *die;* **~, ~n** 1 ▸❶ **S. 374** (auch fig.) wave; **sein Grab in den ~n finden** (geh.) go to *or* find a watery grave; **grüne ~** (Verkehrsw.) linked *or* synchronized traffic lights; **grüne ~ bei 70 km/h** traffic lights phased *or* synchronized for 70 km per hour; **[hohe] ~n schlagen** (fig.) cause a [major] stir; **die weiche ~** (fig. ugs.) the soft approach *or* line 2 (im Haar) wave; **sich** (*Dat.*) **~n legen lassen** have one's hair waved 3 (Physik) wave; (Rundf.: Frequenz) wavelength 4 (Technik) shaft 5 (wellenförmige Erhebung) undulation 6 (Gymnastik) circle

wellen

A *tr. V.* (wellig formen) wave ‹*hair*›; corrugate ‹*iron, metal*›

B *refl. V.* 1 (wellig sein) ‹*hair*› be wavy; ‹*ground, carpet*› undulate; ‹*stairs*› be uneven 2 (wellig werden) ‹*carpet, stairs*› become uneven

wellen-, Wellen-: ~bad *das* artificial wave pool; **~bereich** *der* (Rundf.) waveband; **~berg** *der* crest [of a/the wave]; **~brecher** *der* breakwater; **~förmig** A *Adj.* wavy ‹*line, outline, seam, etc.*›; wavelike ‹*motion, movement, etc.*›; B *adv.* ‹*be propagated*› in the form of waves *or* as waves; **~gang** *der* swell; **ein starker/leichter ~gang** a strong/light swell; **bei starkem ~gang** in heavy seas; **~länge** *die* (Physik) wavelength; **[mit jmdm.] auf der gleichen ~länge liegen** (fig. ugs.) be on the same wavelength [as sb.]; **~linie** *die* wavy line; **~reiten** *das* surfing *no art.*; **~sittich** *der* budgerigar; **~tal** *das* trough [of a/the wave]

Well·fleisch *das* boiled belly pork

Well·horn·schnecke *die* whelk

wellig *Adj.* wavy ‹*hair*›; undulating ‹*scenery, hills, etc.*›; uneven ‹*surface, track, etc.*›

Well·pappe *die* corrugated cardboard

Welpe /ˈvɛlpə/ *der;* **~n, ~n** (Hund) whelp; pup; (Wolf, Fuchs) whelp; cub

Wels /vɛls/ *der;* **~es, ~e** catfish

welsch /vɛlʃ/ *Adj.* 1 (schweiz.) **die ~e Schweiz** French[-speaking] Switzerland 2 (veralt.: romanisch) Latin 3 (veralt. abwertend: fremdländisch) foreign

Welschland *das;* **~[e]s** (schweiz.) French[-speaking] Switzerland;

welsch-, Welsch-: ~schweizer *der* (schweiz.) French[-speaking] Swiss [man]; **~schweizerin** *die* (schweiz.) French[-speaking] Swiss [woman/girl]; **~schweizerisch** *Adj.* (schweiz.) French Swiss

Welt /vɛlt/ *die;* **~, ~en** 1 world; **auf der ~:** in the world; **in der ganzen ~ bekannt sein** be known worldwide *or* all over the world; **eine Reise um die ~:** a round-the-world tour; **die schönste Frau der ~:** the most beautiful woman in the world; **in seiner eigenen ~ leben** live in a world of one's own; **die Alte/Neue ~:** the Old/New World; **die Dritte/Vierte ~:** the Third/Fourth World; **zwölf Euro, das ist doch nicht die ~!** (ugs.) twelve euros, that's not the earth! (coll.); **nicht die ~ kosten** (ugs.) not cost the earth (coll.); **die ~ ist klein** *od.* **ein Dorf** (scherzh.) it's a small world; **davon geht die ~ nicht unter** (ugs.) it's not the end of the world; **auf die** *od.* **zur ~ kommen** be born; **auf der ~ sein** have been born; **aus aller ~:** from all over the world; **nicht aus der ~ sein** (ugs.) not be at the other end of the earth; **in aller ~:** throughout the world; all over the world; **in alle ~:** all over the world; **um nichts in der ~, nicht um alles in der ~:** not for anything in the world *or* on earth; **um alles in der ~** (ugs.) for heaven's sake; **die ganze ~** (fig.) the whole world; **so etwas hat die ~ noch nicht gesehen** (fig. ugs.) it is/was incredible *or* fantastic (coll.); **alle ~** (fig. ugs.) the whole world; everybody; **vor aller ~** (fig. ugs.) in front of everybody; **eine verkehrte ~:** a topsy-turvy world; **mit sich und der ~ zufrieden sein** be content with life; **aus der ~ schaffen** resolve ‹*problem, dispute, etc.*›; **Kinder in die ~ setzen** (ugs.) have children; **Gerüchte in die ~ setzen** start rumours; **wer/was/wo/warum in aller ~ ...?** (ugs.) who/what/where/why on earth ...?; **er/sie ist nicht von dieser ~** (geh.) he/she is not of this world; **zur ~ bringen** bring into the world; give birth to; **eine Dame/ein Mann von ~:** a woman/man of the world; **die gelehrte ~:** the world of scholars; **die vornehme ~:** high society; *s. auch* **Brett 4**; **nobel A 2** 2 (~all) universe; (Planetensystem) planetary system; (Sternensystem) galaxy; **uns trennen ~en** (fig.) we are worlds apart

Die Welt

A national daily newspaper which was founded in 1946 and is published in Hamburg. It has a large business section and is considered to be right-wing in its views.

welt-, Welt-: ~abgeschieden *Adj.* remote; **~all** *das* universe; cosmos; **~anschaulich** A *Adj.* ideological; B *adv.* ideologically; **~anschauung** *die* world view; Weltanschauung; **~atlas** *der* atlas of the world; **~ausstellung** *die* world fair; **~bank** *die* World Bank; **~bekannt** *Adj.* known all over the world *pred.*; world-famous ‹*artist, author, etc.*›; **~berühmt** *Adj.* world-famous; **~best...** *Adj.* world's best *attrib.*; best ... in the world; **der/die ~beste** the world champion; **~bestleistung** *die* (Sport) world record; **~bestzeit** *die* (Sport) world record time; **~bevölkerung** *die* world population; **~bewegend** A *Adj.* world-shaking; **nicht ~bewegend sein** (ugs. spött.) be nothing to write home about (coll.); B *adv.* **er spielt nicht [gerade] ~bewegend** (ugs. spött.) his playing isn't [exactly] anything to write home about (coll.); **~bild** *das* world view; conception of the world; **~bürger** *der,* **~bürgerin** *die* citizen of the world; cosmopolite

Welten·bummler *der,* **Welten·bummlerin** *die* globetrotter

Welt·erfolg *der* worldwide success

Welter·gewicht *das* welterweight

welt-, Welt-: ~erschütternd ▸ **~bewegend**; **~flucht** *die* withdrawal from the world; **~fremd** A *Adj.* unworldly; B *adv.* unrealistically; **~frieden** *der* world peace; **~geist** *der* (Philos.) world spirit; **~geistliche** *der* (kath. Kirche) secular priest; **~geltung** *die* international standing; **~gericht** *das* (Rel.) Last Judgement; **~geschichte** *die* 1 world history *no art.*; **in der ~geschichte umherreisen** (ugs. scherzh.) travel around all over the place; 2 (Werk) history of the world; **~geschichtlich** A *Adj.* **ein ~geschichtliches Ereignis, ein Ereignis von ~geschichtlicher Bedeutung** an important event in world history; B *adv.* **~geschichtlich gesehen** *od.* **betrachtet** [viewed] from the point of view of world history; **~gesundheits·organisation** *die* World Health Organization; **~gewandt** *Adj.* sophisticated; **~handel** *der* world trade; **~handels·organisation** *die* World Trade Organization; **~herrschaft** *die* world domination; **~hilfs·sprache** *die* international auxiliary language; **~hit** *der* worldwide hit; **ein ~hit werden** become a hit all over the world; **~karte** *die* map of the world; **~kind** *das* (dichter.) worldling; **~klasse** *die* world class; **~klasse sein, zur ~klasse gehören** be world-class; **~klug** A *Adj.* worldly-wise; B *adv.* in a worldly-wise manner; **~krieg** *der* world war; **der Erste/Zweite ~krieg** the First/Second World War; World War I/II; **~kugel** *die* globe

weltlich *Adj.* 1 (irdisch, sinnlich) worldly 2 (nicht geistlich) secular

welt-, Welt-: ~literatur *die* world literature *no art.*; **~macht** *die* world power; **~mann** *der* man of the world; **~männisch** /-mɛnɪʃ/ A *Adj.* sophisticated; B *adv.* in a sophisticated manner; **~marke** *die* international make; **~markt** *der* (Wirtsch.) world market; **~meer** *das* ocean; **die sieben ~meere** the seven seas; **~meister** *der,* **~meisterin** *die* world champion; **die Mannschaft ist ~meister** the team are world champions; **~meisterschaft** *die* world championship; **die ~meisterschaft im Fußball** the [football] World Cup; **~meister·titel** *der* world title; **~musik** *die* world music; **~offen** A *Adj.* 1 (aufgeschlossen) open-minded; 2 (für alle ~ offen) open to the world *postpos.*; B *adv.* open-mindedly; **~öffentlichkeit** *die:* **die Meinung der ~öffentlichkeit** world opinion; **an die ~öffentlichkeit appellieren** make an appeal to the people of the world; **~ordnung** *die* world order; **~politik** *die* world politics *pl.*; **~politisch** A *Adj.* **~politische Auswirkungen/Bedeutung haben** have an effect on world politics/be important in world politics; **das ~politische Klima** the climate in world politics; B *adv.* in terms of *or* from the point of view of world politics

Welt·raum *der* space *no art.*

Weltraum-: ~bahnhof *der* launch site [for space missions]; **~fahrer** *der,* **~fahrerin** *die* space traveller; **~fahrt** *die* space travel *no art.*; **~station** *die* space station; **~teleskop** *das* space telescope

welt-, Welt-: ~reich *das* empire; **~reise** *die* world tour; **eine ~reise machen** go round the world; **~reisende** *der/die* globetrotter; **~rekord** *der* world record; **~rekordler** *der,* **~rekordlerin** *die* world record holder; **~religion** *die* world religion; **~revolution** *die* world revolution; **~ruf** *der* worldwide reputation; **~ruf haben** have a worldwide reputation; **von ~ruf** with a worldwide reputation *postpos., not pred.*; **~schmerz** *der* world-weariness; Weltschmerz; **~sicherheits·rat** *der* (Pol.) [United Nations] Security Council; **~sicht** *die* view of the world; world view; **~sprache** *die* world language; **~stadt** *die* cosmopolitan city; **~städtisch** A *Adj.* cosmopolitan; B *adv.* in a cosmopolitan manner; **~städtisch anmuten** make a cosmopolitan impression; **sich ~städtisch geben** put on cosmopolitan airs; **~star** *der* international star; **~um·segler** *der,* **~um·seglerin** *die* circumnavigator of the globe; **~umspannend** *Adj.* global; **~untergang** *der* end of the world; **~untergangs·stimmung** *die* mood of black despair; (in der Natur) **es herrschte ~untergangsstimmung** it was as if the end of the world were approaching; **~uraufführung** *die* world première; **~verbesserer** *der;* **~~s, ~~,** **~verbesserin** *die;* **~~, ~~nen** (iron.) **ein ~verbesserer/eine ~verbesserin** someone who thinks he/she can set the world to rights; **~währungs·fonds** *der* International Monetary Fund; **~weit** A *Adj.* worldwide; B *adv.* throughout *or* all over the world; **~wirtschaft** *die* world economy; **~wirtschafts·gipfel** *der* (Politik) world economic summit; ~**wirtschafts·krise** *die* world economic crisis; ~**wunder** *das:* **die sieben ~wunder** the Seven Wonders of the World; **etw. wie ein ~wunder anstaunen** stare at sth. as if it were from another planet; ~**zeit·uhr** *die* clock showing times around the world

wem /veːm/ *Dat. von* **wer**

A *Interrogativpron.* to whom; who ... to; **~ hast du das Buch geliehen?** to whom did you lend the book?; who did you lend the book to?; **mit/von/zu ~:** with/from/to whom; who ... with/from/to

B *Relativpron.* the person to whom ...; the person who ... to; **~ der Schal gehört** the person to whom the scarf belongs; the person the scarf belongs to; **~ so etwas nicht selbst passiert ist** anyone to whom this has never happened; **~ es auch [immer]** *od.* **~ immer es passiert ist** (geh.) whoever it was it happened to

C *Indefinitpron.* (ugs.: jemandem) to somebody *or* someone; **gehört das ~?** does this belong to anybody?; **telefoniert sie mit ~?** is she on the phone to somebody?

Wem·fall *der* dative [case]

wen /veːn/ *Akk. von* **wer**

A *Interrogativpron.* whom; who; **an/für ~:** to/for whom ...; who ... to/for; **an ~ schreibst du?** to whom are you writing?; who are you writing to?; **~ von ihnen kennst du?** which [one] of these do you know?

B *Relativpron.* the person whom; **~ das nicht überzeugt** anyone who is not convinced by that; **~ [auch] immer** (geh.) whoever; no matter whom

C *Indefinitpron.* (ugs.: jemanden) somebody; someone; **suchst du ~?** are you looking for somebody?

Wende[1] *die;* ~, ~**n** **1** (Veränderung) change; **eine ~ zum Besseren/Schlechteren** a change for the better/worse **2** *in* **um die ~ des Jahrhunderts** at the turn of the century **3** (Turnen) front vault **4** (Seemannsspr.) turn

Wende[2] *der;* ~**n**, ~**n** Wend

Wende

This word can refer to any major political or social change or turning point, but it is used especially to refer to the collapse of Communism in 1989, which was symbolized by the fall of *die Mauer* (the Berlin wall) and eventually led to the **Wiedervereinigung** in 1990.

Wende·hals *der* (ugs. abwertend) turncoat; renegade

Wende·kreis *der* **1** (Geogr.) tropic; **der nördliche ~, der ~ des Krebses** the Tropic of Cancer; **der südliche ~, der ~ des Steinbocks** the Tropic of Capricorn **2** (Kfz-W.) turning circle

Wendel *die;* ~, ~**n** (Technik) coil

Wendel·treppe *die* spiral staircase

Wende-: ~**manöver** *das* turning manoeuvre; ~**marke** *die* (Sport) turning mark

wenden[1]

A *tr., auch itr. V.* (auf die andere Seite) turn [over]; toss ‹*pancake, cutlet, etc.*›; (in die entgegengesetzte Richtung) turn [round]; **einen Mantel ~:** turn a coat inside out; **bitte ~!** please turn over; *s. auch* **drehen A 1**

B *itr. V.* **1** turn [round] **2** (Seemannsspr.) tack

C *refl. V.* **sich zum Besseren/Schlechteren ~:** take a turn for the better/worse; **das Glück hat sich gewendet** (geh.) his/her *etc.* luck has turned; *s. auch* **Blatt 5**

wenden[2]

A *unr.* (*auch regelm.*) *tr. V.* **1** (in eine andere Richtung drehen) turn; **den Kopf ~:** turn one's head; **keinen Blick von jmdm. ~:** not take one's eyes off sb.; **er wandte seine Schritte nach links** (geh.) he turned his steps to the left **2** (geh.: auf~) spend; **viel Zeit/Geld an** *od.* **auf etw.** (*Akk.*) **~:** spend a great deal of time/money on sth.; **viel Mühe an** *od.* **auf etw.** (*Akk.*) **~:** take a great deal of trouble over sth.

B *unr.* (*auch regelm.*) *refl. V.* **1** ‹*person*› turn; **das Glück hat sich von ihm gewandt** *od.* **gewendet** (fig. geh.) his good fortune deserted him **2** (sich richten) **sich an jmdn. [um Rat/Hilfe] ~:** turn to sb. [for advice/help]; **sich mit einer Bitte an jmdn. ~:** ask a favour of sb.; **ich habe mich schriftlich dorthin gewandt** I've written there; **an wen soll ich mich ~?** whom should I approach?; **sich an eine höhere Instanz/die richtige Adresse ~:** go to a higher authority/the right address; **das Buch wendet sich an junge Leser** (fig.) the book is addressed to *or* intended for young readers; **sich gegen jmdn./etw. ~:** oppose sb./sth. **3** (geh.: sich anschicken) **sich zum Gehen/zur Flucht ~:** get ready *or* prepare to go/flee

Wende-: ~**platz** *der* turning area; ~**punkt** *der* turning point; (Geom.: einer Kurve) point of inflexion

wendig

A *Adj.* **1** agile; nimble; manoeuvrable ‹*vehicle, boat, etc.*› **2** (gewandt) astute

B *adv.* **1** (beweglich) agilely; nimbly **2** (gewandt) astutely

Wendigkeit *die;* ~ **1** agility; nimbleness; (eines Flugzeugs) manoeuvrability **2** (Gewandtheit) astuteness

Wendin *die;* ~, ~**nen** ▸**Wende**[2]

Wendung *die;* ~, ~**en** **1** (Änderung der Richtung) turn; **eine ~ um 180°** a 180° turn **2** (Veränderung) change; **eine unerwartete/entscheidende ~:** an unexpected/decisive turn of events; **eine ~ zum Besseren/Schlechteren** a turn for the better/worse **3** (Biegung) bend **4** (Rede~) expression

Wen·fall *der* accusative [case]

wenig /ˈveːnɪç/

A *Indefinitpron. u. unbest. Zahlw.* **1** *Sg.* little; **sie besitzt nur ~ Schmuck** she owns only a little *or* doesn't own much jewellery; **das ~e Geld reicht nicht aus** this small amount of money is not enough; **~ Zeit/Geld haben** not have much *or* have little time/money; **das ist ~:** that isn't much; **dazu kann ich ~ sagen** I can't say much about that; **nicht ~ Mühe/Arbeit/Zeit kosten** take quite a lot of effort/work/time; **zu ~:** too little; **zu ~ Zeit/Geld haben** not have enough time/money; **ein Exemplar/50 Euro zu ~:** one copy too few/50 euros too little; **nur ~es** only a little; **um [ein] ~es älter** (veralt.) a little older **2** *Pl.* a few; **es sind nur noch ~e Wochen bis ...** there are only a few weeks to go until ...; **bis auf ~e/mit ~en Ausnahmen** apart from/with a few exceptions; **nur ~ Leute waren unterwegs** only a few people were about; **~ Chancen haben, etw. zu tun** have little chance of doing sth.; **sie hatte ~ Bücher/Freunde** she had few books/friends; **mit ~en Worten** in a few words; **die ~en, die davon wussten** the few who knew about it; **nur ~e haben teilgenommen** only a few took part; **einer von** *od.* **unter ~en** one of only a few; **nicht ~e** quite a few

B *Adv.* little; **nur ~ besser** only a little better; **er war ~ erbaut** he was not particularly pleased; **wir waren nicht ~ erstaunt/erfreut** we were more than a little astonished/pleased; **~ mehr** not much more; **das ist ~ nett von ihr** that is not very nice of her; **ein ~:** a little; **ein ~ zusammensitzen/ausruhen** sit together for a little while/rest a little; **das nützt [mir] ~:** it won't do [me] much good; **ich komme nur ~ in die Stadt** I don't often get into town; **wir gehen ~ ins Theater** we don't go much to the theatre; **zu ~ schlafen/sich zu ~ bewegen** get too little or not get enough sleep/exercise

weniger

A *Komp. von* **wenig;** *Indefinitpron. u. unbest. Zahlw.* (+ *Sg.*) less; (+ *Pl.*) fewer; **immer ~:** less and less; **du wirst [ja] immer ~** (ugs.) you're wasting away

B *Komp. von* **wenig;** *Adv.* less; **es kommt ~ auf Quantität als auf Qualität an** quantity is less important than quality; **~ schön als praktisch** more practical than attractive; **das ist ~ angenehm/erfreulich/schön** that is not very pleasant/pleasing/nice; **nichts ~ als ...** nothing less than ...; **je mehr ich darüber nachdenke, umso ~ überzeugt es mich** the more I think about it, the less it convinces me; *s. auch* **mehr A**

C *Konj.* less; **fünf ~ drei** five, take away three

Wenigkeit *die;* ~**:** small amount; **meine ~** (scherzh.) yours truly

wenigst...

A *Sup. von* **wenig;** *Indefinitpron. u. unbest. Zahlw.* least; **damit habe ich die ~e Arbeit** *od.* **am ~sten Arbeit** that gives me the least work; **am ~en** least; **sie hat am ~en [geschenkt] bekommen** she received the fewest presents; **in den ~en Fällen/für die ~en Menschen** in very few cases/for very few people; **nur die ~en** only very few; **das ~e, was wir tun können** the least we can do; **das ist noch das ~e, ...** worse still, ...

B *Sup. von* **wenig;** *Adv.* **am ~en** the least; **das hätte ich am ~en erwartet** that's the last thing I should have expected; **das konnte sie am ~en leiden** it was what she hated most

wenigstens *Adv.* at least

wenn /vɛn/ *Konj.* **1** (konditional) if; **außer ~:** unless; **und [selbst] ~:** even if; **~ es sein muss, komme ich mit** If I have to, I'll come along; **~ es nicht anders geht** if there's no other way; **~ du schon rauchen musst** if you 'must smoke; **~ nicht, dann nicht** if not, it doesn't matter; **~ das Wörtchen ~ nicht wär[, wär mein Vater Millionär]** (scherzh.) if only, if only **2** (temporal) when; **jedes Mal,** *od.* **immer, ~:** whenever; **~ du dich erst einmal eingearbeitet hast ...** once you've got used to the work ... **3** (konzessiv) **~ ... auch** even though; **~ es auch schwer ist** even though it is hard; **und ~ es [auch] noch so spät ist ...** no matter how late it is ...; however late it is ...; **[und] ~ auch!** (ugs.) even so; all the same **4** (in Wunschsätzen) if only; **~ ich doch** *od.* **nur** *od.* **bloß wüsste, ob ...** if only I knew whether ...; **~ er doch käme!** if only he would come

Wenn *das;* ~**s**, ~ *od.* (ugs.) ~**s: das ~ und Aber, die ~[s] und Aber[s]** the ifs and buts

wenn·gleich *Konj.* (geh.) even though; although

wenn·schon *Adv.* **~ [nicht] ..., dann ...** even if [not] ..., then ...; **[na** *od.* **und] ~!** (ugs.) so what?; **~, dann ...** if that's how it is, then ...; **~, dennschon** (ugs.) if you're going to do something, you may as well do it properly; no half measures!

Wenzel[1] /ˈvɛntsl̩/ (*der*) Wenceslas

Wenzel[2] *der;* ~**s**, ~ (Kartenspiele) jack; knave

wer /veːɐ̯/ *Nom. Mask. u. Fem.; s. auch* (*Gen.*) **wessen;** (*Dat.*) **wem;** (*Akk.*) **wen**

A *Interrogativpron.* who; **~ alles ist dabei gewesen?** which people were there?; who was there?; **~ von ...** which of; **~ weiß wie viel/wie oft/wie lange** *usw.* who knows how much/how often/how long *etc.;* **~ da?** (Milit.) who goes there?; **was glaubt er eigentlich, ~ er ist?** who does he think he is?

B *Relativpron.* the person who; (jeder, der) anyone *or* anybody who; **~ es auch [immer]** *od.* **~ immer es getan hat** (geh.) whoever did it

C *Indefinitpron.* (ugs.: jemand) someone; somebody; (in Fragen, Konditionalsätzen) anyone; anybody; **ist da ~?** is anyone there?; **hat ~ nach mir gefragt?** did anyone ask for me?; **~ sein** be somebody

Werbe-: ~**abteilung** *die* advertising *or* publicity department; ~**agentur** *die* advertising agency; ~**aktion** *die* advertising campaign; ~**banner** *das* **1** advertising banner; **2** (DV) banner advertisement; ~**block** *der; Pl.* ~**blöcke** commercial break; ~**einnahme** *die* advertising revenue; ~**feldzug** *der* advertising campaign; ~**fernsehen** *das* television commercials *pl.;* ~**film** *der* advertising *or* promotional *or* publicity film; ~**fläche** *die* advertising surface; ~**funk** *der* radio commercials *pl.;* ~**gag** *der* publicity gimmick (coll.); ~**geschenk** *das* [promotional] free gift; ~**kampagne** *die* ▸~**feldzug;** ~**leiter** *der,* ~**leiterin** *die* advertising manager

werben /ˈvɛrbn̩/

A *unr. itr. V.* **1** advertise; **für etw. ~:** advertise sth.; **für eine Partei ~:** canvass for a party

2 (geh.: sich bemühen) ~ **um** try to enlist ‹*subscribers, helpers, etc.*›; recruit ‹*soldier, mercenary, etc.*›; **um Wählerstimmen ~:** seek to attract votes; **um jmds. Gunst/Freundschaft ~:** court sb.'s favour/friendship; **um eine Frau ~:** court a woman
B *unr. tr. V.* attract ‹*readers, customers, etc.*›; recruit ‹*soldiers, volunteers, members, staff, etc.*›

werbe-, Werbe-: ~pause *die* (Ferns.) commercial break; **~schrift** *die* prospectus; advertising brochure; **~sendung** *die* mailshot; **ich will keine ~sendungen bekommen** I don't want any junk mail; **~slogan** *der* advertising slogan; **~spot** *der* commercial; advertisement; ad (coll.); **~sprache** *die* advertising jargon; **~spruch** *der* advertising slogan; **~text** *der* advertising copy *no pl.*; **~texter** *der*, **~texterin** *die* ▸**i S. 113** advertising copywriter; **~träger** *der* advertising medium; **~trommel** *die*: *in* **[für jmdn./etw.] die ~trommel rühren** *od.* **schlagen** beat *or* thump the drum [for sb./sth.]; **~verbot** *das* advertising ban; **~vertrag** *der* advertising contract; **~wirksam** **A** *Adj.* effective ‹*advertisement etc.*›; **~wirksam sein** be good publicity *or* a good advertisement; **dieser Slogan ist wenig ~wirksam** this slogan is not very effective publicity *or* not a very effective advertisement; **B** *adv.* effectively ‹*worded etc.*›

Werbung *die*; **~, ~en** 1 (Reklame, Propaganda) advertising; **für etw. ~ machen** advertise sth.; **für ein neues Buch/einen Kandidaten viel ~ machen** give a lot of publicity to a new book/a candidate 2 ▸**Werbeabteilung** 3 (geh.: Bemühen um jmds. Gunst) courtship *no pl.*

Werbungs·kosten *Pl.* (Steuerw.) advertising costs

Werde·gang *der* 1 (Laufbahn) career 2 (Entwicklungsgang) development

werden /'ve:ɐ̯dn̩/
A *unr. itr. V.; mit sein; 2. Part.* **geworden** 1 become; get; **älter ~:** get *or* grow old[er]; **du bist aber groß/schlank geworden!** you've grown so tall/slim; **wahnsinnig** *od.* **verrückt ~:** go mad; **gut ~:** turn out well; **das muss anders ~:** things have to change; **wach ~:** wake up; **rot ~:** go *or* turn red; **das Wetter wurde schlechter** the weather got worse; **er ist 70 [Jahre alt] geworden** he has had his 70th birthday *or* has turned 70; **heute soll es/wird es heiß ~:** it's supposed to get/it's going to be hot today; **mir wird übel/heiß/schwindelig** I feel sick/I'm getting hot/dizzy; **Arzt/Professor ~:** become a doctor/professor; **was willst du einmal ~?** what do you want to be when you grow up?; **Vater ~:** become a father; **Erster/Letzter ~:** be *or* come first/last; **das Kind wird ein Junge** the baby is going to be a boy; **was soll das ~?** what is that going to be?; **eine ~de Mutter** a mother-to-be; an expectant mother
2 (sich entwickeln) **zu etw. ~:** become sth.; **das Wasser wurde zu Eis** the water turned into ice; **was soll aus dir ~?** what is to become of you?; **aus Liebe wurde Hass** love turned into hate; **aus ihm ist nichts/etwas geworden** he hasn't got anywhere/has got somewhere in life; **daraus wird nichts ~:** nothing will come of it/that!; **Von wegen! Daraus wird nichts!** You must be joking! No chance!
3 (unpers.) (sich einem bestimmten Zeitpunkt nähern) **es wird [höchste] Zeit** it is [high] time; **es wird ein Jahr, seit ...** it will be a year since ...; **es wird 10 Uhr** it is nearly 10 o'clock; **es wird Tag/Nacht** day is dawning/night is falling; **es wird Herbst** autumn is coming
4 (entstehen) come into existence; **es werde Licht!** (bibl.) let there be light!; **jeder Tag, den Gott ~ lässt** every day that God gives *or* grants us; **was nicht ist, [das] kann noch ~:** things can change; **im Werden sein** be coming into being
5 (ugs.) **sind die Fotos [etwas] geworden?** have the photos turned out [well]?; **wirds bald?** (ugs.) hurry up!; **was soll nur ~?** what's going to happen now? **nicht mehr** *od.* **wieder ~** (salopp) flip one's lid (coll.); **ich werd nicht mehr** *od.* **wieder!** (salopp) well, I'm blowed! (sl.)
6 (geh. veralt.: widerfahren) **ihm soll [sein] Recht ~:** he shall have justice
B *Hilfsverb; 2. Part.* **worden** 1 (zur Bildung des Futurs) **wir ~ uns um ihn kümmern** we will take care of him; **dem werd ichs zeigen!** (ugs.) I'll show him (coll.); **dir werd ich helfen!** (ugs.) I'll give you what for (coll.); **wer wird denn gleich weinen!** you're not going to cry, are you?; **Sie ~ entschuldigen** (ugs.) excuse me[, please]; **es wird gleich regnen** it is going to rain any minute; **wir ~ nächste Woche in Urlaub fahren** we are going on holiday next week
2 (als Ausdruck der Vermutung) **es wird um die 80 Euro kosten** it will cost around 80 euros; **sie ~ [wohl] im Garten sein** they are probably in the garden; **er wird doch nicht [etwa] krank sein?** he wouldn't be ill, would he?; **sie wird schon wissen, was sie tut** she must know what she's doing
3 (zur Bildung des Passivs) **du wirst gerufen** you are being called; **er wurde gebeten** he was asked; **ihm wurde gesagt** he was told; **es wurde gelacht/gesungen/getanzt** there was laughter/singing/dancing; **jetzt wird aber geschlafen!** right, it's time to go to sleep now!; **unser Haus wird renoviert** our house is being renovated
4 (zur Umschreibung des Konjunktivs) **was würdest du tun?** what would you do?; **würdest du bitte etwas für mich besorgen?** would you mind getting something for me?; **ich würde kommen** I would come

Wer·fall *der* nominative [case]

werfen /'vɛrfn̩/
A *unr. tr. V.* 1 throw; drop ‹*bombs*›; **die Tür ins Schloss ~:** slam the door shut; **jmdn. aus dem Saal ~** (fig. ugs.) throw sb. out of the hall; **eine Frage in die Debatte ~** (fig.) throw *or* inject a question into the debate; **neue Waren auf den Markt ~** (fig.) bring new products on to the market; **Bilder an die Wand ~** (fig.) project pictures on the wall; **einen kurzen Blick in den Spiegel/in die Zeitung ~** (fig.) cast a glance in the mirror/at the paper 2 (ruckartig bewegen) throw; **den Kopf in den Nacken ~:** throw *or* toss one's head back; **die Arme in die Höhe ~:** throw one's arms up 3 (erzielen) throw; **eine Sechs ~:** throw a six; **ein Tor ~** (Handball, Wasserball) shoot *or* throw a goal 4 (Ringen, Judo: nieder~) throw, floor ‹*opponent*› 5 (bilden) **Falten ~:** wrinkle; crease; **Blasen ~:** bubble; **[einen] Schatten ~:** cast [a] shadow 6 (gebären) give birth to
B *unr. itr. V.* 1 throw; **mit etw. [nach jmdm.] ~:** throw sth. [at sb.]; **mit Geld/Fremdwörtern/Schimpfwörtern** *usw.* **um sich ~** (fig.) throw [one's] money around/bandy foreign words about/bandy curses *etc.* about 2 (Junge kriegen) give birth; ‹*dog, cat*› litter
C *unr. refl. V.* 1 throw oneself; **sich vor einen Zug ~:** throw oneself under a train; **sich jmdm. in die Arme/zu Füßen ~:** throw oneself into sb.'s arms/at sb.'s feet; **sich auf eine neue Aufgabe ~** (fig.) throw oneself into a new task; **sich in die** *od.* **seine Kleider ~** (fig.) throw on one's clothes 2 (sich verziehen) buckle; ‹*wood*› warp

Werfer *der*; **~s, ~, Werferin** *die*; **~, ~nen** thrower; (Baseball) pitcher; (Cricket) bowler

Werft /vɛrft/ *die*; **~, ~en** shipyard; dockyard; (Flugw.) hangar

Werft·arbeiter *der*, **Werft·arbeiterin** *die* shipyard worker

Werg /vɛrk/ *das*; **~[e]s** tow

werk-, Werk- (Betrieb) ▸**werk[s]-, Werk[s]-:**

Werk /vɛrk/ *das*; **~[e]s, ~e** 1 (Arbeit) work; **am ~[e] sein** be at work; **sich ans ~ machen, ans ~ gehen** set to *or* go to work; **ins ~ setzen** carry out ‹*attack, strategy, etc.*›; put ‹*agreement, plan, etc.*› into effect; set ‹*arrangements, events*› in motion; **zu ~e gehen** (geh.) proceed 2 (Tat) work; **~e der Nächstenliebe** works of charity; **das ist dein ~!** that is your doing *or* handiwork; **du tätest ein gutes ~, wenn ...** (scherzh.) you would be doing me/him/us *etc.* a favour if ... 3 (geistiges, künstlerisches Erzeugnis) work; **ein neues ~ beginnen** begin a new piece of work 4 (Betrieb, Fabrik) factory; plant; works *sing. or pl.*; (Belegschaft) works *sing. or pl.*; **ab ~:** ex works 5 (Trieb~) mechanism; **das ~ einer Uhr/Orgel** the works *pl.* of a clock/organ

Werk·bank *die*; *Pl.* **Werkbänke** workbench

werkeln *itr. V.* 1 (bes. südd., österr.) work 2 (herumbasteln) potter around *or* about

werken *itr. V.* work

Werken *das*; **~s** (Schulw.) handicraft

werk-, Werk-: ~getreu **A** *Adj.* faithful to the spirit of the original *postpos.*; **eine ~getreue Inszenierung** a production which is/was faithful to the original; **B** *adv.* ‹*stage, present, produce*› in a manner faithful to the original; **~lehrer** *der*, **~lehrerin** *die* [handi]craft teacher; **~meister** *der* foreman; **~meisterin** *die* forewoman

Werk[s]-: ~angehörige *der/die* factory *or* works employee; **~arzt** *der*, **~ärztin** *die* factory *or* works doctor; **~bücherei** *die* factory *or* works library

Werk·schutz *der* 1 factory *or* works security 2 (Personen) factory *or* works security service

werk[s]-, Werk[s]-: ~eigen *Adj.* factory- *or* company-owned; **~fahrer** *der*, **~fahrerin** *die* (Motorsport) works driver; **~gelände** *das* factory *or* works premises *pl.*; **~halle** *die* workshop; **~kantine** *die* works canteen; **~leitung** *die* factory *or* works management; **~spionage** *die* industrial espionage

Werk-: ~statt *die*, **~stätte** *die* workshop; (Kfz-W.) garage; **~stoff** *der* material; **~stoffprüfung** *die* testing of materials; material testing; **~stück** *das* workpiece; **~verkehr** *der* works transport

Werk[s]·wohnung *die* company-owned flat (esp. Brit.) *or* (esp. Amer.) apartment

werk-, Werk-: ~tag *der* working day; workday; **~tags** *Adv.* on weekdays; **~tätig** *Adj.* working; **~tätige** *der/die; adj. Dekl.* worker; **die Zahl der ~tätigen** the number of people in work; **~treue** *die* faithfulness to the original; **~unterricht** *der* [handi]craft instruction *no art.*; (Unterrichtsstunde) [handi]craft lesson; *s. auch* **Englischunterricht**; **~verzeichnis** *das* (Musik) catalogue of works; **~zeug** *das* 1 (auch fig.) tool; 2 (Gesamtheit) tools *pl.*

Werkzeug-: ~kasten *der* toolbox; **~macher** *der*, **~macherin** *die* tool maker; **~maschine** *die* machine tool

Wermut /'ve:ɐ̯mu:t/ *der*; **~[e]s, ~s** 1 (Pflanze) wormwood 2 (Wein) vermouth

Wermut·bruder *der* (ugs. abwertend) wino (coll.)

Wermuts·tropfen *der* (geh.) drop of bitterness

Wermut·wein *der* vermouth

wert /ve:ɐ̯t/ *Adj.* 1 (geh.) esteemed; (als Anrede) **~e Genossen!** my dear comrades; **Ihr ~es Schreiben** (Kaufmannsspr. veralt.) your esteemed letter; **wie ist Ihr ~er Name, bitte?** (geh.) may I have your name, please? 2 ▸**i S. 299** *in* **etw. ~ sein** be worth sth.; **das ist nichts ~:** this is worth nothing *or* worthless; **der Teppich ist sein Geld nicht ~:** the carpet is not worth the money; **jmds./einer Sache ~ sein** deserve sb./sth.; **das ist nicht der Erwähnung ~:** this is not worth mentioning; **Berlin ist immer eine Reise ~:** Berlin is always worth a visit; **jmdn./etw. einer Sache** (*Gen.*) **[für] ~ erachten** (geh.) consider sb./sth. worthy of sth.; *s. auch* **Rede 3**

Wert *der*; **~[e]s, ~e** 1 (Preis) value; **im ~ steigen/fallen** increase/decrease in value; **an ~ gewinnen/verlieren** gain/lose in value; **im ~[e] von ...** worth ...; **etw. unter [seinem] ~ verkaufen** sell sth. for less than its value 2 (positive Bedeutung) value; **einer Sache** (*Dat.*) **großen ~ beimessen** attach great value to sth.; **sich** (*Dat.*) **seines [eigenen] ~es bewusst sein** be conscious of one's own importance; **das hat [doch] keinen ~!** (ugs.: ist sinnlos) there's no point; **~ auf etw.** (*Akk.*) **legen** set great store by *or* on sth. 3 (Zahlen~) value; (als Ergebnis) result 4 *Pl.* (~sachen) valuable objects; objects of value 5 (Briefmarke)

W

denomination [6] Pl. (~papiere) securities

wert-, Wert-: **~arbeit** *die* high-quality workmanship; **~beständig** *Adj.* of lasting value *postpos.*; stable ‹*currency, investment, etc.*›; **~beständig bleiben/sein** retain its value; **~brief** *der* (Postw.) registered letter

Werte-: **~gemeinschaft** *die* community of values; **~kanon** *der* canon of values

werten *tr., itr. V.* [1] judge; assess; **etw. als besondere Leistung ~:** rate sth. as a special achievement; **etw. als Erfolg/Misserfolg ~:** regard sth. as *or* consider sth. a success/failure; **etw. hoch/gering ~:** rate sth. highly/not rate sth. very highly; **diese Leistung kann nicht hoch genug gewertet werden** this achievement cannot be regarded highly enough; **etw. kritisch/moralisch ~:** judge sth. critically/from a moral point of view [2] (Sport) **etw. hoch/niedrig ~:** award high/low points to sth.; **der schlechteste Sprung wird nicht gewertet** the worst jump is not counted

Werte-: **~ordnung** *die* system of values; **~system** *das* system of values; **~verfall** *der* decline in values; **~wandel** *der* change in values

wert·frei
[A] *Adj.* detached; impartial; neutral ‹*term*›
[B] *adv.* with detachment; impartially

Wert·gegenstand *der* valuable object; object of value; **Wertgegenstände** valuables

-wertig (Chemie, Sprachw.) -valent; **zwei~/drei~:** bivalent/trivalent

Wertigkeit *die;* **~, ~en** (Chemie, Sprachw.) valency (Brit.); valence (Amer.)

wert-, Wert-: **~konservativ** *Adj.* with conservative values *postpos.*; **~konservativ sein** hold conservative values; **~los** *Adj.* worthless; valueless; **~marke** *die* stamp; (Essenmarke usw.) ticket; **~maßstab** *der* standard [of value]; **~mindernd** [A] *Adj.* value-reducing; depreciating ‹*effect*›; [B] *adv.* with a depreciating *or* value-reducing effect; **~minderung** *die* depreciation; reduction in value; **~objekt** *das* article of value; **~orientiert** *Adj.* value-oriented; value-centred; **~paket** *das* (Postw.) registered parcel; **~papier** *das* (Wirtsch.) security; **~papier·börse** *die* stock exchange; **~papier·geschäft** *das* (Wirtsch.) ▸ **Effektengeschäft**; **~sache** *die* valuable item *or* object; **~sachen** valuables; **~schätzung** *die* (geh.) esteem; high regard; **~schöpfung** *die* (Wirtsch.) added value; **~sendung** *die* (Postw.) registered item; **~steigerung** *die* appreciation; increase in value; **~stoff** *der* reusable material; (recycelbar) recyclable material; **~system** *das* system of values; value system

Wertstofftonne
▸ Recycling

Wertung *die;* **~, ~en** judgement; (Sport) **er erreichte ~en über 16** he was given scores [of] over 16; **noch in der ~ sein** be still in the competition/race *etc.*

Wertungs·richter *der,* **Wertungs·richterin** *die* (Sport) points judge

wert-, Wert-: **~urteil** *das* value judgement; **~verlust** *der* loss of value; depreciation; **~voll** *Adj.* valuable; (moralisch) estimable ‹*person, quality*›; **~vorstellung** *die* [concept *sing.* of] values *pl.*; **~zeichen** *das* stamp; **~zuwachs** *der* appreciation [in value]

Wer·wolf *der* (Myth.) werewolf

wes /vɛs/ *Gen. v.* **wer** (veralt.) ▸ **wessen**; *s. auch* **Brot 1**; **Geist 3**

Wesen /ˈveːzn̩/ *das;* **~s, ~** [1] (Natur) nature; (Art, Charakter) character; nature; **ein freundliches/kindliches ~ haben** have a friendly/childlike nature *or* manner; **von liebenswürdigem ~ sein** have a pleasant nature [2] (Mensch) creature; soul; **ein weibliches/männliches ~:** a woman *or* female/a man *or* male [3] (Lebe~) being; creature; **es war kein menschliches ~ zu sehen** there was not a [living] soul in sight; **ein höheres ~:** a higher being; **das höchste ~:** the Supreme Being [4] (Philos.) essence [5] (veralt.: Tun u. Treiben) hustle and bustle; **sein ~ treiben** ‹*child*› romp *or* play around; ‹*ghost*› be abroad, go around; ‹*thief*› be at work; **viel ~s/kein ~ [aus** *od.* **um** *od.* **von etw.] machen** (ugs.) make a lot of fuss/not make a fuss [about sth.]

wesenhaft (geh.)
[A] *Adj.* intrinsic
[B] *adv.* intrinsically

wesens-, Wesens-: **~art** *die* nature; character; **~eigen** *Adj.* characteristic; **jmdm./einer Sache ~eigen sein** be characteristic of sb./sth.; **~fremd** *Adj.* foreign to sb.'s/sth.'s nature *postpos.*; **~gemäß** *Adj.* **etw. ist jmdm. [nicht] ~gemäß** sth. is [not] in keeping with sb.'s nature; **~merkmal** *das* essential feature; **~verwandt** *Adj.* who are similar in character *or* nature *postpos., not pred.*; **~verwandt sein** be similar in character *or* nature; **~zug** *der* trait; characteristic

wesentlich
[A] *Adj.* fundamental (**für** to); **sich auf das Wesentliche beschränken** limit oneself to [the] essentials; **von ~er Bedeutung** of considerable importance; **im Wesentlichen** essentially
[B] *adv.* (weit, um vieles) considerably; much; **es wäre mir ~ lieber, wenn wir ...** I would much rather we ...; **sich von etw. ~ unterscheiden** be very *or* considerably different from sth.; **nichts ~ Neues enthalten** contain nothing substantially new

Wes·fall *der* genitive [case]

wes·halb *Adv.* ▸ **warum**

Wesir /veˈziːɐ̯/ *der;* **~s, ~e** vizier

Wespe /ˈvɛspə/ *die;* **~, ~n** wasp

Wespen-: **~nest** *das* wasp's nest; **in ein ~nest stechen** (fig. ugs.) stir up a hornets' nest; **sich in ein ~nest setzen** (fig.) bring a hornets' nest [down] about one's ears; **~stich** *der* wasp sting; **~taille** *die* wasp waist

wessen *Gen. von* **wer** *u.* **was**
[A] *Interrogativpron.* [1] (*von* **wer**) whose [2] (*von* **was**) **~ wird er beschuldigt?** what is he accused of?; **~ hat er sich schuldig gemacht** what is he guilty of?
[B] *Relativpron.* [1] (*von* **wer**) **~ er gedachte, war seine Mutter** the person [whom] he was thinking about was his mother [2] (*von* **was**) **[das,] ~ er sich rühmt, ist ...** what he prides himself on his ...

wessent·wegen *Interrogativadv.* (geh.) on whose account; because of whom

wessent·willen *Interrogativadv. in* **um ~** (geh.) for whose sake

Wessi /ˈvɛsi/ *der;* **~s, ~s** (ugs.) Westerner; West German

Wessi

A colloquial and sometimes derogatory term for someone from West Germany, as opposed to an **Ossi**. The expression *Besserwessi*, a pun on *Besserwisser* (know-all), is used by East Germans to describe a *Wessi* who thinks he knows it all.

Wessiland *(das);* **~s** (salopp, bes. berlin.) West Germany

West[1] /vɛst/ ▸ ❶ **S. 363** [1] (bes. Seemannsspr., Met.: Richtung) west [2] (westliches Gebiet, Politik) West; *s. auch* **Ost**[1] **2** [3] *einem Subst. nachgestellt* (westlicher Teil, westliche Lage) West; *s. auch* **Süd**[1] **3**

West[2] *der;* **~[e]s, ~e** (Seemannsspr.) westerly; (dichter.) west wind

West·afrika *(das)* West Africa

West-Berlin, Westberlin *(das)* West Berlin

West·berliner
[A] *der* West Berliner
[B] *indekl. Adj.* West Berlin

West·berlinerin *die* ▸ **Westberliner A**

west-, West-: **~besuch** *der* (ugs.) visitor/visitors *pl.* from West Germany; **~besuch haben** have a visitor/visitors from West Germany; **~deutsch** [A] *Adj.* [1] (Politik) West German; [2] (Geogr.) Western German; [B] *adv.* in a Western German manner; **~deutsche** *der/die* [1] (Politik) West German; [2] (Geogr.) Western German; **~deutschland** *(das)* [1] (Politik) West Germany; [2] (Geogr.) Western Germany

Westdeutsche Allgemeine Zeitung (WAZ)

Germany's highest-circulation serious national paper. It was founded in 1948 and is published in Essen, catering mainly for the densely populated Ruhr area.

Weste /ˈvɛstə/ *die;* **~, ~n** waistcoat (Brit.); vest (Amer.); **eine schuss-** *od.* **kugelsichere ~:** a bulletproof vest; **eine weiße** *od.* **reine** *od.* **saubere ~ haben** (ugs.) have a clean record; **jmdm. etw. unter die ~ jubeln** (fig. ugs.) shift *or* push sth. on to sb.

Westen *der;* **~s** ▸ ❶ **S. 363** [1] (Richtung) west; **nach ~:** westwards; to the west; **im/aus** *od.* **von** *od.* **vom ~:** in/from the west; *s. auch* **Norden 1** [2] (Gegend) West; **im ~:** in the West; **der Wilde ~:** the Wild West; *s. auch* **Norden 2** [3] (Geogr.) **der ~:** the West [4] (Politik) **der ~** (Westeuropa u. die USA) the West; (die [alte] BRD) the West; West Germany

Westen·tasche *die* waistcoat (Brit.) *or* (Amer.) vest pocket; **etw. wie seine ~ kennen** (ugs.) know sth. like the back of one's hand *or* inside out

Westentaschen·format *das: in* **in** *od.* **im ~:** pocket-size[d] ‹*calculator etc.*›; (ugs. spött. fig.) small-time ‹*politician etc.*›; tinpot ‹*dictator*›

Western *der;* **~[s], ~:** western

West·europa *(das)* Western Europe

west·europäisch *Adj.* West[ern] European; **W~e Union** Western European Union; **~e Zeit** Greenwich Mean Time

Westfale /-ˈfaːlə/ *der;* **~n, ~n** Westphalian

Westfalen *(das);* **~s** Westphalia

Westfälin /-ˈfɛːlɪn/ *die;* **~, ~nen** Westphalian

westfälisch *Adj.* Westphalian; **der Westfälische Friede** (hist.) the Treaty of Westphalia; *s. auch* **deutsch**; **Deutsch 1**; **badisch**

west-, West-: **~fernsehen** *das* (ugs.) West German television; **~flanke** *die* (Milit., Geogr.) western flank; (Met.) western edge; **~geld** *das* (ugs.) West German money; **~germanisch** *Adj.* West Germanic; **~gote** *der,* **~gotin** *die* West Goth; Visigoth; **~hang** *der* western slope

West·indien *(das)* the West Indies *pl.*

west·indisch *Adj.* West Indian

West·küste *die* west[ern] coast

Westler *der;* **~s, ~, Westlerin** *die;* **~, ~nen** (ugs.) West German

westlich
[A] *Adj.* ▸ ❶ **S. 363** [1] (im Westen) western; **15 Grad ~er Länge** 15 degrees west [longitude]; **das ~e Frankreich** western France; **~st** westernmost; **der ~ste Punkt** the most westerly point [2] (nach, aus dem Westen) westerly [3] (aus dem Westen kommend, für den Westen typisch) Western, [4] (Politik) Western; *s. auch* **östlich A 4**
[B] *adv.* westwards; **~ von ...** [to the] west of ...
[C] (Präp. mit Gen.) [to the] west of

west-, West-: **~mächte** *Pl.* (Politik) Western powers; **~mark** *die; Pl.* **~~** (ugs.) West German mark; **~nordwest**[1] /--ˈ-/ (Seemannsspr., Met.) west-north-west; *s. auch* **Nord**[1] **1**; **~nordwest**[2] /--ˈ-/ *der* (Seemannsspr.) west-north-wester[ly]; **~nordwesten** /--ˈ--/ *der* west-north-west; *s. auch* **Norden 1**; **~östlich** [A] *Adj.* west-to-east; from west to east *postpos.* [B] *adv.* [from] west to east

West·preußen *(das)* West Prussia

west-, West-: **~reise** *die* (ugs.) trip to the West; **~seite** *die* western side; **~sender** *der* (ugs.) radio station in the West; **~südwest**[1] /--ˈ-/ (Seemannsspr., Met.) west-south-west; *s. auch* **Nord**[1] **1**; **~südwest**[2] /--ˈ-/ *der* (Seemannsspr.) west-south-wester[ly]; **~südwesten** /--ˈ--/ *der* west-south-west; *s. auch* **Norden 1**; **~teil** *der* western part; **~wall** *der* (hist.) Siegfried Line; **~wärts** *Adv.* ▸ ❶ **S. 363** [1] (nach Westen) [to the] west; [2] (im Westen) in the west; **~wind** *der* west[erly]

W

wind; **~zone** *die* (hist.) Western zone

wes·wegen *Adv.* ▸ **warum**

Wett-: ~annahme *die* betting office; bookmaker's; **~bewerb** *der;* **~~[e]s, ~~e** **1** competition; **in einem ~bewerb siegen** win a competition; **sehr gut im ~bewerb liegen** have a good chance of winning the competition; **außer ~bewerb laufen** run as an unofficial competitor; **2** (Wirtsch.: Konkurrenz, Konkurrenten) competition *no indef. art.;* **unlauterer ~bewerb** (Rechtsw.) unfair competition; **~bewerber** *der,* **~bewerberin** *die* competitor

wettbewerbs-, Wettbewerbs-: ~bedingung *die* competition condition; **~bedingungen** conditions *or* terms of a/the competition; **~behörde** *die* competition authority; **~beitrag** *der* competition entry; **~beschränkung** *die* (Wirtsch.) restraint of trade; **~druck** *der* ▸ **Konkurrenzdruck**; **~fähig** *Adj.* competitive; **~fähigkeit** *die* competitiveness; **~feindlich** **A** *Adj.* detrimental to competition *postpos.;* anti-competitive ‹*agreement, practice*›; **B** *adv.* to the detriment of competition; **~hüter** *der,* **~hüterin** *die* competition regulator; **~kommissar** *der,* **~kommissarin** *die* competition commissioner; **~nachteil** *der* competitive disadvantage; **~recht** *das* competition law; antitrust law (Amer.); **~rechtlich** **A** *Adj.* relating to competition law *or* (Amer.) antitrust law *postpos.;* **B** *adv.* with regard to competition law *or* (Amer.) antitrust law; **~regeln** *die Pl.* competition rules; **~teilnehmer** *der,* **~teilnehmerin** *die* contestant; competitor; **~verzerrend** **A** *Adj.* distorting competition *postpos.;* **B** *adv.* in a way that distorts competition; **~verzerrung** *die* (Wirtsch.) distortion of competition; **~vorteil** *der* competitive advantage; **~widrig** **A** *Adj.* anti-competitive; **B** *adv.* anti-competitively

Wett·büro *das* betting office; bookmaker's

Wette /ˈvɛtə/ *die;* **~, ~n** bet; **die ~ ging um 100 Euro** the bet was 100 euros; **was gilt die ~?** how much do you want to bet?; what do you bet?; **eine ~ [mit jmdm.] abschließen** make a bet [with sb.]; **[ich gehe] jede ~ [ein], dass ...** I bet you anything [you like] that ...; **mit jmdm. um die ~ laufen** *od.* **rennen** race sb.; **die Jungen schwammen um die ~:** the boys raced each other at swimming; **um die ~ arbeiten/singen** (fig.) try to outdo each other at hard work/singing

Wett·eifer *der* competitiveness

wett·eifern *itr. V.* **mit jmdm. [um etw.] ~:** compete with sb. [for sth.]; **miteinander ~:** compete with each other

wetten

A *itr. V.* bet; **mit jmdm. ~:** have a bet with sb.; **mit jmdm. um etw. ~:** bet sb. sth.; **auf etw.** (*Akk.*) **~:** bet on sth.; put one's money on sth.; **[wollen wir] ~?** [do you] want to bet?; **~ [dass]?** (ugs.) you can bet on it; it's a dead cert (Brit. sl.) *or* (Amer. coll.) sure-fire thing; **ich wette hundert zu eins, dass ...** (ugs.) I'll bet [you] a hundred to one that ...; **so haben wir nicht gewettet** (ugs.) that was not the deal *or* not what we agreed; **auf Platz/Sieg ~:** make a place bet/bet on a win

B *tr. V.* **10 Euro ~:** bet 10 euros

Wetter[1] *das;* **~, ~** **1** weather; **bei jedem ~:** in all weathers; **es ist schönes ~:** the weather is good *or* fine; **was haben wir heute für ~?** what's the weather like today?; **falls das ~ es zulässt** weather permitting; **nach dem ~ sehen** see what the weather is like; **bei solchem ~ jagt man keinen Hund vor die Tür** the weather is/was not fit for a dog to be out in; **ein ~ zum Eierlegen** (salopp) fantastic *or* marvellous weather (coll.); **bei jmdm. gut ~ machen** (fig. ugs.) get on the right side of sb.; butter sb. up; **um gut[es] ~ bitten** (fig. ugs.) try to make it up **2** (Un~) storm; **alle ~!** (veralt.) by Jove! **3** *Pl.* (Bergbau) **schlagende ~:** firedamp

Wetter[2] *der;* **~s, ~:** better

wetter-, Wetter-: ~amt *das* meteorological office; **~aussichten** *Pl.* weather outlook *sing.;* **~bedingt** **A** *Adj.* ‹*accident, delay, etc.*› due to the weather; **B** *adv.* due to the weather; **~bedingungen** *die Pl.* weather conditions; **~bericht** *der* weather report; (Voraussage) weather forecast; **~besserung** *die* improvement in the weather; **~beständig** *Adj.* weatherproof

Wetterchen *das;* **~s** (ugs.) fantastic (coll.) *or* lovely weather

wetter-, Wetter-: ~dienst *der* weather *or* meteorological service; **~fahne** *die* weathervane; **~fest** *Adj.* weather-resistant; **~fleck** *der* (österr.) weatherproof cape; **~frosch** *der* **1** (ugs.) *tree frog kept as a means of predicting the weather;* **2** (scherzh.) weatherman; **~fühlig** *Adj.* sensitive to [changes in] the weather *postpos.;* **~fühligkeit** *die;* **~~:** sensitivity to [changes in] the weather; **~gegerbt** *Adj.* tanned by the weather *postpos.;* weather-beaten; **~gott** *der* weather god; **~hahn** *der; Pl.* **~hähne** weathercock

Wetterin *die;* **~, ~nen** better

wetter-, Wetter-: ~karte *die* weather chart; weather map; **~kunde** *die* meteorology *no art.;* **~lage** *die* weather situation; (fig.) situation; climate; **~lampe** *die* (Bergbau) safety lamp; **~leuchten** *itr. V.* (unpers.) **es ~leuchtet** there is summer lightning; **es begann zu ~leuchten** flashes of [summer] lightning began to appear; **~leuchten** *das;* **~~s** sheet (esp. summer) lightning *no indef. art.;* (fig.) first ominous signs *pl.;* **~mantel** *der* ▸ **Regenmantel**

wettern *itr. V.* (ugs.: schimpfen) curse; **gegen** *od.* **über etw./jmdn. ~:** loudly denounce sth./sb.

wetter-, Wetter-: ~prognose *die* weather forecast; **~regel** *die* saying about the weather; **~satellit** *der* weather satellite; **~schacht** *der* (Bergbau) ventilation shaft; **~scheide** *die* weather *or* meteorological divide; **~seite** *die* windward side; side exposed to the weather; **~station** *die* weather station; **~sturz** *der* sudden fall in temperature; **~umschlag** *der* change in the weather; **~umschwung** *der* sudden change in the weather; **~verhältnisse** *Pl.* weather conditions; **~vorhersage** *die* weather forecast; **~warte** *die* weather station; **~wendisch** *Adj.* (abwertend) capricious; unpredictable

wett-, Wett-: ~fahrt *die* race; **eine ~fahrt machen** have a race; **~kampf** *der* competition; **jmdn. zum ~kampf auffordern** challenge sb. to a contest; **~kämpfer** *der,* **~kämpferin** *die* competitor; **~lauf** *der* race; **einen ~lauf machen** run a race; **ein ~lauf mit der Zeit/dem Tod** (fig.) a race against time/with death; **~läufer** *der,* **~läuferin** *die* runner; **~|machen** *tr. V.* (ugs.) **1** (ausgleichen) make up for; **etw. durch etw. ~machen** make up for sth. with sth.; (wieder gutmachen) make good ‹*loss, mistake, etc.*›; **2** (sich erkenntlich zeigen für) do something in return for; **~rennen** *das* (auch fig.) race; **ein ~rennen machen** have *or* run a race; **~rüsten** *das;* **~~s** arms race; **~schwimmen** *das* swimming contest; **~streit** *der* contest; (fig.) conflict; **mit jmdm./etw. in ~streit liegen/treten** be competing/compete with sb./sth.; **~streiten** *unr. itr. V.; nur im Inf. gebr.* compete

wetzen /ˈvɛtsn̩/

A *tr. V.* sharpen; whet; **der Vogel wetzt seinen Schnabel an einem Stein** the bird rubs its beak on a stone

B *itr. V.; mit sein* (ugs.) dash

Wetz-: ~stahl *der* steel; **~stein** *der* whetstone

WEU *Abk.* **= Westeuropäische Union** WEU

WEZ *Abk.* **= Westeuropäische Zeit** GMT

WG *Abk.* **= Wohngemeinschaft**

WGB *Abk.* **= Weltgewerkschaftsbund** WFTU

Whiskey /ˈvɪski/ *der;* **~s, ~s** whiskey; [American/Irish] whisky

Whisky /ˈvɪski/ *der;* **~s, ~s** whisky; **ein ~ mit Eis/[mit] Soda** whisky on the rocks/and soda

Whist /vɪst/ *das;* **~[e]s** whist

wich /vɪç/ *1. u. 3. Pers. Sg. Prät. v.* **weichen**

Wichs /vɪks/ *der;* **~es, ~e,** (österr.:) *die;* **~, ~en** (Studentenspr.) **in [vollem/voller] ~ erscheinen** appear in full regalia *or* full [gala] dress

Wichse *die;* **~, ~n** (ugs.) **1** (Schuhcreme) [shoe] polish **2** (Schläge) a hiding (coll.); **dann kriegst du** *od.* **dann gibts ~:** you'll get a good hiding (coll.)

wichsen

A *tr. V.* (ugs.) **1** polish **2** (landsch.: schlagen) **jmdn. ~:** give sb. a good hiding (coll.); **jmdm. eine ~:** box sb.'s ears

B *itr., tr. V.* (derb: masturbieren) wank (Brit. coarse); jerk off (coarse)

Wichser *der;* **~s, ~** (derb) wanker (Brit. coarse)

Wicht /vɪçt/ *der;* **~[e]s, ~e** **1** (fam.: kleines Kind) little rascal *or* imp (joc.) **2** (abwertend: männliche Person) [insignificant] creature; **armer ~:** poor devil

Wichtel *der;* **~s, ~** **1** ▸ **Wichtelmännchen** **2** (bei den Pfadfinderinnen) brownie

Wichtel·männchen *das* gnome; (Kobold) goblin

wichtig /ˈvɪçtɪç/ *Adj.* important; **nimm die Sache nicht so ~:** don't take the matter so seriously; **es ist mir ~ zu wissen, ob ...** it is important to me to know if ...; **nichts Wichtigeres zu tun haben[, als ...]** (auch iron.) have nothing better to do [than ...]; **das Wichtigste ist, dass du schweigst** the most important thing is that you remain silent; **Wichtiges zu tun haben** have important things to do; **sich ~ machen** *od.* **tun** (ugs. abwertend) be full of one's own importance; **sich mit etw. ~ machen** be pompous about sth.; **sich** (*Dat.*) **~ vorkommen** (ugs. abwertend) be full of oneself; **sich sehr ~ nehmen** (ugs.) be full of self-importance

Wichtigkeit *die;* **~:** importance; **einer Sache** (*Dat.*) **[große/besondere] ~ beimessen** *od.* **beilegen** attach [great/particular] importance to sth.

Wichtigtuer /-tuːɐ/ *der;* **~s, ~** (ugs. abwertend) pompous ass

Wichtigtuerei *die;* **~, ~en** (ugs. abwertend) pomposity; pompousness *no pl.*

Wichtigtuerin *die;* **~, ~nen** ▸ **Wichtigtuer**

wichtigtuerisch

A *Adj.* self-important; pompous

B *adv.* in a self-important manner; ‹*behave, act*› pompously

Wicke /ˈvɪkə/ *die;* **~, ~n** vetch; (im Garten) sweet pea

Wickel *der;* **~s, ~:** compress; **jmdm. einen ~ machen** put a compress on sb.; **jmdn. am** *od.* **beim ~ haben/nehmen** (fig. ugs.) have/grab sb. by the scruff of his/her neck

Wickel-: ~gamasche *die* puttee; **~kind** *das* baby; infant; **~kommode** *die* baby's changing table

wickeln *tr. V.* **1** (schlingen) wind; **Wolle zu einem Knäuel ~:** wind wool into a ball; **etw. auf/um etw.** (*Akk.*) **~:** wind sth. on to sth./round sth. **2** (eindrehen) **sich/jmdm. die Haare ~:** put one's/sb.'s hair in curlers *or* rollers **3** (ein~) wrap; **etw./jmdn./sich in etw.** (*Akk.*) **~:** wrap sth./sb./oneself in sth.; **er hat sich [fest] in seinen Mantel gewickelt** he wrapped his coat tightly [a]round himself **4** (windeln) **ein Kind ~:** change a baby's nappy; **der Kleine ist frisch gewickelt** the baby has had his nappy changed **5** (bandagieren) bandage **6** (aus~) unwrap; **etw./jmdn./sich aus etw. ~:** unwrap sth./sb./oneself from sth.; **das Buch aus dem Papier ~:** take the book out of the wrapping paper **7** (ab~) unwind ‹*thread, wool, etc.*› (**von** from) **8** *in* **schief** *od.* **falsch gewickelt sein** (ugs.) be very much mistaken

Wickel-: ~rock *der* wrapover skirt; **~tisch** *der* baby's changing table

Wicklung *die;* **~, ~en** (Elektrot.) winding

Widder /ˈvɪdɐ/ *der;* **~s, ~** **1** (Tier) ram **2** (Astron., Astrol.) Aries; **sie/er ist [ein] ~:** she/he is [an] Aries

wider /ˈviːdɐ/ *Präp. mit Akk.* 1 (geh., veralt.) against 2 (geh.: entgegen) contrary to; **~ [alles] Erwarten** contrary to [all] expectations; **~ besseres Wissen/alle Vernunft** against one's better knowledge/all reason; **~ Willen** against one's will

wider-, Wider-: ~borstig A *Adj.* unruly, unmanageable ‹*hair*›; (fig.) rebellious, contrary ‹*person*›; unruly, rebellious, contrary ‹*child*›; **sich ~borstig zeigen** be rebellious; B *adv.* rebelliously; contrarily; **~borstigkeit** *die; ~~, ~~en* 1 rebelliousness; contrariness; 2 (Äußerung) contrary remark; (Handlung) contrary act; **~fahren** /--'--/ *unr. itr. V.; mit sein* (geh.) **etw. ~fährt jmdm.** sth. happens to sb.; **jmdm. ~fährt eine große Freude/ein schweres Leid** sb. experiences great joy/great sorrow; **ihm ist [ein] Unrecht ~fahren** he has been done an injustice; **jmdm. Gerechtigkeit ~fahren lassen** see that justice is done to sb.; **~haken** *der* barb; **~hall** *der* echo; (fig.) **[bei jmdm.] ~hall finden** meet with a [positive] response [from sb.]; **großen ~hall finden** meet with a wide response; **~|hallen** *itr. V.* echo; resound (**von** with); **der Schuss hallte von den Bergwänden ~:** the shot echoed from the mountainsides; **~legen** /--'--/ *tr. V.* **etw. ~legen** refute *or* disprove sth.; **jmdn. ~legen** prove sb. wrong; **~legung** /--'--/ *die; ~~, ~~en* refutation

widerlich (abwertend)
A *Adj.* 1 (Ekel erregend) revolting; repulsive; **~ schmecken/riechen** taste/smell revolting 2 (höchst unsympathisch, kaum erträglich) repugnant, repulsive ‹*person, behaviour, etc.*›; awful ‹*headache etc.*›
B *adv.* 1 (Ekel erregend) revoltingly 2 (verabscheuungswürdig) ‹*behave, act*› in a repugnant *or* repulsive manner 3 (unangenehm) awfully ‹*cold, hot, sweet, etc.*›

Widerlichkeit *die; ~, ~en* (abwertend) 1 repulsiveness 2 (Äußerung/Handlung) revolting remark/action

Widerling *der; ~[e]s, ~e* (abwertend) repulsive creature

widern /ˈviːdɐn/ *tr., itr. V.* (veralt.) ▸ **ekeln B**

wider-, Wider-: ~natürlich *Adj.* unnatural; **~part** *der; ~~[e]s, ~~e* (geh.) adversary; **jmdm. ~part bieten** resist sb.; **~raten** /--'--/ *unr. itr. V.* (geh. veralt.) **jmdm. ~raten, etw. zu tun** advise sb. against doing sth.; **~rechtlich** A *Adj.* illegal; unlawful; **~rechtliches Betreten eines Geländes/Gebäudes** trespass[ing] on a property/unlawful *or* illegal entry to a building; B *adv.* illegally; unlawfully; **~rechtlichkeit** *die* illegality; unlawfulness; **~rede** *die* 1 argument; contradiction; **keine ~rede!** don't argue!; no arguing!; **ohne ~rede** without [any] argument *or* protest; 2 ▸ **Gegenrede 1**; **~rist** *der* (Zool.) withers *pl.*; **~ruf** *der* (einer Aussage) retraction; (eines Befehls, einer Anordnung, Erlaubnis usw.) revocation; withdrawal; **[bis] auf ~ruf** until revoked *or* cancelled; **~rufen** /--'--/ *unr. tr., auch itr. V.* retract, withdraw ‹*statement, claim, confession, etc.*›; revoke, cancel ‹*order, permission, etc.*›; repeal ‹*law*›; **~ruflich** A *Adj.* revocable ‹*permission, power of attorney*›; B *adv.* until further notice; **~sacher** *der; ~~s, ~~,* **~sacherin** *die; ~~, ~~nen* (geh.) adversary; opponent; **~schein** *der* (geh.) reflection; **~setzen** /--'--/ *refl. V.* **sich jmdm./einer Sache ~setzen** oppose sb./sth.; **sich einer Aufforderung ~setzen** refuse to comply with a demand; **~setzlich** /*od.* --'--/ A *Adj.* rebellious; **sich ~setzlich zeigen** be rebellious; B *adv.* rebelliously; **~setzlichkeit** /*od.* --'--/ *die; ~~, ~~en* 1 (Haltung) rebelliousness; 2 (Handlung) rebellious action; **~sinn** *der* absurdity; **~sinnig** *Adj.* absurd; **~spenstig** /-ʃpɛnstɪç/ A *Adj.* unruly; rebellious; wilful; unruly, unmanageable ‹*hair*›; stubborn ‹*horse, mule, etc.*›; B *adv.* wilfully; rebelliously; **~spenstigkeit** *die; ~~, ~~en* 1 (Haltung) unruliness; rebelliousness; wilfulness; (von Haaren) unruliness; unmanageableness; (von Pferden usw.) stubborness; 2 (Handlung) unruly *or* rebellious *or* wilful behaviour *no pl.*; **~|spiegeln** /--'--/ A *tr. V.* reflect; (als Spiegelbild) mirror; (fig.) reflect; B *refl. V.* be reflected; (als Spiegelbild) be mirrored; (fig.) be reflected; **~sprechen** *unr. itr. V.* 1 (Einwände erheben) contradict; **jmdm./einer Sache/sich [selbst] ~sprechen** contradict sb./sth./oneself; **der Betriebsrat hat der Entlassung ~sprochen** the works committee has opposed the dismissal; 2 (im Gegensatz stehen zu) contradict, be inconsistent with ‹*facts, truth, etc.*›; **sich** (*Dat.*) **~sprechende Aussagen/Nachrichten** conflicting statements/news reports; **~spruch** *der* 1 (Widerrede, Protest) opposition; protest; **es erhob sich allgemeiner ~spruch** there was a general protest; **nicht den geringsten ~spruch dulden** not tolerate the slightest argument; **auf ~spruch stoßen** meet with opposition *or* protests; **etw. ohne ~spruch hinnehmen** accept sth. without argument; 2 (etw. Unvereinbares) contradiction; **ein ~spruch in sich** (*Dat.*) **[selbst] sein** be a contradiction in terms; **sich** (*Akk.*) **in ~sprüche verwickeln** get entangled *or* caught up in contradictions; **in ~spruch zu** *od.* **mit etw. stehen** contradict sth.; be contradictory to sth.; **in ~spruch zu etw. geraten** come into conflict with sth.; 3 (Philos.) contradiction; **~sprüchlich** A *Adj.* contradictory ‹*news, statements, etc.*›; inconsistent ‹*behaviour, attitude, etc.*›; B *adv.* **er verhielt sich sehr ~sprüchlich** his behaviour was very inconsistent; **~sprüchlichkeit** *die; ~~, ~~en* 1 (Eigenschaft) contradictoriness; inconsistency; 2 (Äußerung, Handlung) contradiction; **~spruchs·los** A *Adj.* unprotesting; uncontradicting; B *adv.* without opposition *or* protest

Wider·stand *der* 1 resistance (**gegen** to); **jmdm./einer Sache ~ leisten** resist sb./sth.; put up resistance to sb./sth.; **an jmds. ~** (*Dat.*) **scheitern** collapse in the face of sb.'s resistance; **bei jmdm. auf ~ stoßen** meet with *or* encounter resistance from sb.; **zum bewaffneten ~ aufrufen** call [people] to arms 2 (Hindernis) opposition; **allen Widerständen zum Trotz** despite all opposition; *s. auch* **Weg 3** 3 (Widerstandbewegung) **der ~:** the Resistance 4 (Mech., Elektrot.) resistance; (Elektrot.: Schaltungselement) resistor

widerständig
A *Adj.* combative; **gegen etw. ~ werden** take a stand against sth.
B *adv.* combatively

Widerständler *der,* **Widerständlerin** *die* resistance member; (Protestierende[r]) protester

widerstands-, Widerstands-: ~bewegung *die* resistance movement; **~fähig** *Adj.* robust; resistant ‹*material etc.*›; hardy ‹*animal, plant*›; **~fähig gegen** *od.* **gegenüber etw. sein** be resistant to sth.; **~fähigkeit** *die* robustness; (von Material usw.) resistance; (von Tier, Pflanze) hardiness; **~fähigkeit gegen etw.** resistance to sth.; **~kämpfer** *der,* **~kämpferin** *die* resistance fighter; **~kraft** *die* resistance; **~los** A *Adj.* without resistance *postpos.*; B *adv.* without resistance

wider-, Wider-: ~stehen *unr. itr. V.* 1 (nicht nachgeben) **[jmdm./einer Sache] ~stehen** resist [sb./sth.]; 2 (standhalten) **jmdm./einer Sache ~stehen** withstand sb./sth.; **~streben** *itr. V.* 1 (zu~ sein) **etw. ~strebt jmdm.** sb. dislikes *or* detests sth.; **das ~strebt meinem Taktgefühl** that goes against my sense of tact; **es ~strebt jmdm., etw. zu tun** sb. dislikes doing sth. *or* is reluctant to do sth.; 2 (geh.: sich ~setzen) **einer Sache** (*Dat.*) **~streben** oppose sth.; **~d nachgeben/einwilligen** give in/agree reluctantly; **~streben** *das; ~~s* reluctance; **trotz anfänglichem ~streben** after some initial reluctance; **~streit** *der* conflict; **in** *od.* **im ~streit mit etw. leben/stehen** be/live in conflict with sth.; **~streitend** *Adj.* conflicting; **~wärtig** /-vɛrtɪç/ (abwertend) A *Adj.* 1 (unangenehm) disagreeable, unpleasant ‹*conditions, situation, etc.*›; 2 (ekelhaft, abscheulich) revolting, repugnant ‹*smell, taste, etc.*›; objectionable, offensive ‹*person, behaviour, attitude, etc.*›; **das ist mir ~wärtig** I find that offensive *or* objectionable; **~wärtig riechen/schmecken** smell/taste revolting; B *adv.* ‹*behave, act, etc.*› in an objectionable *or* offensive manner; **~wärtigkeit** *die; ~~, ~~en* 1 offensiveness; objectionableness; repulsiveness; 2 (Umstand) disagreeable *or* unpleasant circumstance; **~wille** *der* aversion (**gegen** to); **einen ~willen gegen jmdn./etw. haben** *od.* **empfinden** have/experience an aversion to sb./sth.; **etw. mit ~willen essen/tun** eat sth. with distaste/do sth. with reluctance *or* reluctantly; **~willig** A *Adj.* (unwillig) reluctant; unwilling; B *adv.* reluctantly; unwillingly; **etw. nur ~willig tun** do sth. only with reluctance; **~wort** *das; Pl.* **~~e: ~worte geben** answer back; **etw. ohne [ein] ~wort tun** do sth. without argument *or* protest; **keine ~worte dulden** not tolerate any argument; **keine ~worte!** no arguments!

widmen /ˈvɪtmən/
A *tr. V.* 1 (zueignen) **jmdm. ein Buch/Gedicht/eine Sinfonie** *usw.* **~:** dedicate a book/poem/symphony *etc.* to sb. 2 (verwenden für/auf) **etw. jmdm./einer Sache ~:** devote sth. to sb./sth.; **jmdm./einer Sache seine Liebe/Aufmerksamkeit ~:** give sb./sth. one's love/attention
B *refl. V.* (sich beschäftigen mit) **sich jmdm./einer Sache ~:** attend to sb./sth.; (ausschließlich) devote oneself to sb./sth.; **heute kann ich mich dir ganz ~:** I can devote myself to you entirely today

Widmung *die; ~, ~en* dedication (**an** + *Akk.* to)

widrig /ˈviːdrɪç/ *Adj.* unfavourable, adverse ‹*wind, circumstances, fate, etc.*›

widrigen·falls *Adv.* (bes. Amtsspr.) otherwise

Widrigkeit *die; ~, ~en* adversity

wie
A *Interrogativadv.* 1 (auf welche Art u. Weise) how; **~ heißt er/das?** what is his/its name?; what is he/that called?; **~ [bitte]?** [I beg your] pardon?; (entrüstet) I beg your pardon!; **~ war das?** (ugs.) what was that?; what did you say?; **~ meinen?** (scherzh.) [I beg your] pardon?; **~ kommt es, dass ...?** how is it that ...?; **~ das?** (ugs.) how did that come about?; **~ käme ich denn dazu?** why should I?
2 (durch welche Merkmale gekennzeichnet) **~ war das Wetter?** what was the weather like?; how was the weather?; **~ ist dein neuer Chef?** what is your new boss like? (coll.); how is your new boss? (coll.); **~ geht es ihm?** how is he?; **~ war es in Spanien?** what was Spain like?; what was it like in Spain?; **~ findest du das Bild?** what do you think of the picture?; **~ gefällt er dir?** how do you like him?; **~ wärs mit ...** how about ...; **~ wäre es, wenn du dir die Schuhe putztest?** how about [you] cleaning your shoes?; **Gott, ~ du aussiehst!** God, just look at yourself!
3 (in welchem Grade) how; **~ lange/groß/hoch/oft?** how long/big/high/often?; **~ sehr haben wir uns das gewünscht!** how badly we wanted that!; **~ spät ist es?** what time is it?; **~ alt bist du?** how old are you?; **~ er läuft!** how fast he runs!; **und ~!** and how! (coll.)
4 (ugs.: nicht wahr) **das hat dir Spaß gemacht, ~?** you enjoyed that, didn't you?; **das ärgert dich wohl, ~?** that does annoy you, doesn't it?
B *Relativadv.* **[die Art,] ~ er es tut** the way *or* manner in which he does it; **die Preise steigen in dem Maße, ~ die Löhne erhöht werden** prices are rising at the same rate as wages; **~ man es auch [immer] macht, es ist ihr nie recht** whatever you do *or* whichever way you do it she's never happy with it; **~ er das wieder geschafft hat!** he's done it again — how does he manage it?
C *Konj.* 1 *Vergleichspartikel* as; **[so] ... ~ ...** as ... as ...; **das Buch ist so unterhaltend ~ lehrreich** the book is as entertaining as it is instructive; **er kam so schnell ~ möglich** he came as quickly as possible; **~ gewöhnlich** *od.* **üblich/immer** as usual/always; **ein Mann ~ er** a man like him; **es geht dir [so] ~ mir** you're like me; **er macht es [genauso] ~ du** he does it [just] like you [do]; **~ durch ein Wunder** as if by a miracle; **er kann spielen ~ kein Zweiter** no one can touch him when it comes to playing; **ich fühlte mich ~ ...** I felt as if I were ...; **„N" ~ „Nordpol"** N for November

W

[2] (zum Beispiel) like; such as; **Entwicklungsländer ~ [zum Beispiel] Somalia oder Tansania** developing countries such as Somalia or Tanzania [for example]; **~ folgt** as follows; **~ schon der Name sagt** as the name already implies; **~ wenn** as if *or* though

[3] (und, so~) as well as; both; **Männer ~ Frauen** men as well as women; both men and women

[4] (temporal: als) **~ ich an seinem Fenster vorbeigehe, höre ich ihn singen** as I pass by his window I hear him singing; **~ ich die Tür öffne, steht doch tatsächlich Christine vor mir** when I open the door, who is standing there but Christine

[5] (ugs.: außer) **wir hatten nichts ~ Ärger [damit]** we had nothing but trouble [with it]; **nichts ~ hin!** come on, let's go!; *s. auch* **nichts**

[6] (nicht standardsprachlich: als) than

Wiedehopf /ˈviːdəhɔpf/ *der;* **~[e]s, ~e** hoopoe

wieder /ˈviːdɐ/ *Adv.* [1] again; **etw. ~ aufbauen** reconstruct *or* rebuild sth.; **etw. ~ aufbereiten** (Kerntechnik) reprocess sth.; **~ aufführen** + *Akk.* revive ‹*play*›; rerun, reshow ‹*film*›; **~ aufnehmen** + *Akk.* resume; take up ‹*subject, idea*› again; re-establish ‹*relations, contact*›; **ein Verfahren ~ aufnehmen** (Rechtsspr.) reopen a case; **jmdn. ~ aufrichten** give fresh heart to sb.; **~ auftauchen** turn up again; **~ beleben** + *Akk.* revive, resuscitate ‹*person*›; revive, resurrect ‹*friendship, custom, etc.*›; **etw. ~ entdecken** rediscover sth.; **jmdn./etw. ~ erkennen** recognize sb./sth.; **er war kaum ~ zu erkennen** he was almost inrecognizable; **etw. ~ eröffnen** reopen sth.; **jmdn. ~ erwecken** revive sb.; bring back *or* restore sb. to life; **etw. ~ erwecken** (fig.) revive *or* reawaken sth.; **~ finden** + *Akk.* find again; regain ‹*composure, dignity, courage, etc.*›; **die Handschuhe haben sich ~ gefunden** the gloves have been found; **jmdn./etw. ~ sehen** see sb./sth. again; **etw. ~ tun** do sth. again; **ein Land ~ vereinigen** reunify a country; **etw. ~ verwenden** reuse sth.; **jmdn. ~ wählen** re-elect sb.; **je/nie ~:** ever/never again; **~ mal** *od* **mal ~ ins Kino gehen** go to the cinema again some time; **immer ~,** (geh.) **~ und ~:** again and again; time and [time] again; **es regnet schon ~:** it's raining again; **das Buch ist ~ ein Bestseller** the book is another best seller; **nie ~ Krieg!** no more war!; **wie du ~ aussiehst!** just look at yourself again!; **was ist denn jetzt schon ~ los?** what's happened 'now?; **alles ist ~ beim Alten** everything is back as it was before; **etw. ~ an seinen Platz zurückstellen** put sth. back in its place; **ich bin gleich ~ da** I'll be right back (coll.); I'll be back in a minute; **willst du schon ~ gehen?** are you going already?; **gib es ihm ~ zurück** (ugs.) give it back to him! [2] **einige ..., andere ... und ~ andere ...** some ..., others ..., and yet others ...; **das ist ~ etwas anderes** that is something else again [3] (andererseits, anders betrachtet) **das ist auch ~ wahr** that's true enough; **da hast du auch ~ Recht** you're right there; **so schlimm ist es auch ~ nicht** it's not as bad as all that [4] (meinerseits, deinerseits usw.) in turn [5] (auch) likewise; also [6] (ugs.: noch) **wie heißt er ~?** what's his name again?; **wo/wann war das [gleich] ~?** where/when was that again?

wieder-, Wieder-: ~aufbau *der* reconstruction; rebuilding; **der wirtschaftliche ~aufbau** economic recovery; **~auf|bauen** ▸ **wieder 1**; **~auf|bereiten** ▸ **wieder 1**; **~aufbereitung** *die* recycling; (bes. Kerntechnik) reprocessing; **~aufbereitungs·anlage** *die* recycling plant; (Kerntechnik) reprocessing plant; **~auf|führen** ▸ **wieder 1**; **~aufführung** *die* (eines Theaterstücks) revival; (eines Films) rerun; **~aufnahme** *die* [1] resumption; (von Beziehungen) re-establishment; **die ~aufnahme eines Verfahrens** (Rechtsspr.) the resumption *or* reopening of proceedings; [2] (als Mitglied) readmittance; [3] (eines Theaterstücks) revival; **~aufnahme·verfahren** *das* (Rechtsspr.) retrial; **~auf|nehmen, ~auf|richten** ▸ **wieder 1**; **~aufrüstung** *die* rearmament; ***~auf|tauchen** ▸ **wieder 1**

wieder-, Wieder-: ~beginn *der* recommencement; resumption; **~|bekommen** *unr. tr. V.* get back; **du bekommst es ~:** you'll get it back; **~|beleben** ▸ **wieder 1**; **~belebungs·versuch** *der* attempt at resuscitation; **bei jmdm. ~belebungsversuche machen** attempt to revive *or* resuscitate sb.; **~|beschaffen** *tr. V.* recover; (ersetzen) replace; **jmdm. etw. ~beschaffen** recover/replace sth. for sb.; **~bewaffnung** *die* rearmament; **~|bringen** *unr. tr. V.* bring back; **~eingliederung** *die* reintegration; **~einsetzung** *die* reinstatement; **~|entdecken** ▸ **wieder 1**; **~entdeckung** *die* rediscovery; **~|erkennen** ▸ **wieder 1**; **~|erobern** *tr. V.* recapture ‹*territory*›; regain ‹*position, title, etc.*›; **~eroberung** *die* ▸ **~erobern**: recapture; regaining; **~|eröffnen** ▸ **wieder 1**; **~eröffnung** *die* reopening; **~|erwecken, ~|finden** ▸ **wieder 1**; **~gabe** *die* [1] (Darstellung, Schilderung) report; account; [2] (Übersetzung) rendering; [3] (Reproduktion; in Ton u. Bild) reproduction; [4] (Aufführung) rendition; **~|geben** *unr. tr. V.* [1] (zurückgeben) give back; return; [2] (berichten) report; give an account of; (~holen) repeat; (ausdrücken) express; (zitieren) quote; **etw. gekürzt ~geben** give a shortened version of sth.; [3] (übersetzen) render; [4] (darstellen) portray; depict; **die Gebirge sind auf der Landkarte in Braun ~gegeben** the mountains are shown in brown on the map; [5] (hörbar, sichtbar machen) reproduce; **~geburt** *die* [1] (Rel.) reincarnation; [2] (christl. Rel., fig. geh.) rebirth; **~|gewinnen** *unr. tr. V.* recover ‹*lost item, money, etc.*›; regain ‹*composure, equilibrium, etc.*›

wieder·gut|machen ▸ **gutmachen 1**

Wiedergutmachung *die;* **~, ~en** [1] reparation; **die ~ des Unrechts fordern** demand that the injustice be made good [2] (Leistung) compensation

wieder|haben *unr. tr. V.* (auch fig.) have back

wieder-, Wieder-: ~her|stellen *tr. V.;* **ich stelle wieder her** [1] re-establish ‹*contact, peace*›; [2] (reparieren) restore ‹*building*›; [3] (~ gesund machen) **jmdn. ~herstellen** restore sb. to health; get sb. on his/her feet again; **~herstellung** *die* [1] re-establishment; [2] (~instandsetzung) restoration; [3] (Genesung) recovery; **bis zu seiner völligen ~herstellung** until he has completely recovered *or* is fully restored to health; **~holbar** *Adj.* repeatable; **das ist nicht ~holbar** it cannot be repeated; **~holen** [A] *tr. V.* [1] repeat; replay ‹*football match*›; retake ‹*penalty kick*›; resit, retake ‹*exam*›; **eine Wahl ~holen** hold an election again; rehold an election; [2] (nochmals sagen) repeat, reiterate ‹*question, demand, offer, etc.*›; [3] (repetieren) revise ‹*lesson, vocabulary, etc.*›; [B] *refl. V.* [1] (~ dasselbe sagen) repeat oneself; [2] (erneut geschehen) happen again; [3] (~kehren) be repeated; recur

wieder|holen *tr. V.* fetch *or* get back

wiederholt

[A] *Adj.* repeated; **zum ~en Male** yet again

[B] *adv.* repeatedly

Wiederholung *die;* **~, ~en** [1] repetition; (eines Fußballspiels usw.) replay; (eines Freistoßes, Elfmeters usw.) retaking; (einer Sendung) repeat; (einer Aufführung) repeat performance; **eine ~ der Wahl ist notwendig** the election must be held again *or* reheld [2] (des Schuljahrs, einer Prüfung usw.) repeating; **eine ~ der Prüfung ist nicht möglich** it is not possible to resit *or* retake the exam [3] (von Fragen, Forderungen, Angeboten usw.) repetition; reiteration [4] (von Lernstoff) revision

Wiederholungs-: ~fall *der:* *in* **im ~fall** (bes. Amtsspr.) in the event of [any] recurrence; **~täter** *der,* **~täterin** *die* (Kriminologie) habitual offender; **~zahlwort** *das* (Sprachw.) multiplicative; **~zeichen** *das* (Musik) repeat sign

Wieder·hören *das:* *in* **[auf] ~!** goodbye! (*at end of telephone call*)

Wieder·instandsetzung *die* reconstruction

wieder-, Wieder-: ~|käuen /-kɔyən/ [A] *itr. V.* ruminate; chew the cud; [B] *tr. V.* [1] chew again; [2] (fig. abwertend) rehash; **~käuer** *der;* **~~s, ~~:** ruminant; **~kehr** *die;* **~~** (geh.) [1] (Rückkehr) return; [2] (~holung) recurrence; (Jahrestag) anniversary; **~|kehren** *itr. V.; mit sein* (geh.) [1] (zurückkehren) return; [2] (sich noch einmal ereignen) come again; **eine nie ~kehrende Gelegenheit** a chance that will never come again; the chance of a lifetime; [3] (sich wiederholen) be repeated; recur; **~|kommen** *unr. itr. V.; mit sein* [1] (zurückkommen) return; come back; [2] (noch einmal kommen) come back *or* again; [3] (sich noch einmal ereignen) ‹*opportunity, past*› come again; **~|kriegen** *tr. V.* (ugs.) ▸ **~bekommen**; **~kunft** /-kʊnft/ *die;* **~~** (geh.) return; **die ~kunft Christi** the Second Coming of Christ; **~schauen** *das:* *in* **[auf] ~schauen!** (südd., österr.) goodbye!; **~|sehen** *unr. tr. V.* see again; **sich ~sehen** see each other *or* meet again; **~sehen** *das;* **~~s, ~~:** reunion; **~sehen mit Berlin/der Heimat** return to Berlin/one's homeland; **sie stießen auf ein baldiges ~sehen an** they drank to seeing each other again soon; **~sehen macht Freude** (scherzh.) I'd like to have it back some time; **[auf] ~sehen!** goodbye!; **jmdm. Auf ~sehen sagen** say goodbye to sb.; **[auf] ~sehen nächsten Monat/in London** goodbye until we meet again next month/in London

Wiedersehens·freude *die* pleasure of seeing sb./each other again

wieder-, Wieder-: ~täufer *der* (Rel.) anabaptist; ***~|tun** ▸ **wieder 1**; **~um** *Adv.* [1] (erneut) again; [2] (andererseits) on the other hand; **so weit würde ich ~um nicht gehen** I wouldn't, however, go that far; [3] (meiner-, deinerseits usw.) in turn; **~|vereinigen** ▸ **wieder 1**; **~vereinigung** *die* reunification; **~verheiratung** *die* remarriage; **~|verwenden** ▸ **wieder 1**; **~verwendung** *die* reuse; **~vorlage** *die* (bes. Amtsspr.) **zur ~vorlage** for resubmission; to be resubmitted; **~wahl** *die* re-election; **sich zur ~wahl stellen** stand *or* run for re-election; **~|wählen** ▸ **wieder 1**

> **Wiedervereinigung**
>
> This is the German word for the reunification of Germany which officially took place on 3 October 1990, when the former GDR was incorporated into the Federal Republic. The huge financial and social costs of reunification are still being felt throughout Germany.

Wiege /ˈviːgə/ *die;* **~, ~n** (auch fig.) cradle; **seine ~ stand in Sachsen** (geh.) he was born in Saxony; his birthplace was in Saxony; **es ist ihm nicht an der ~ gesungen worden, dass ...** he would never have dreamt *or* could never have foreseen that ...; **eine solche Karriere ist ihm nicht an der ~ gesungen worden** he would never have dreamt of such a career; **von der ~ an** (geh.) from the day he/she was born; **von der ~ bis zur Bahre** (scherzh.) from the cradle to the grave

Wiege·messer *das* chopping knife (*with curved blade used by rocking to and fro*)

wiegen[1] ▸ **ⓘ S. 315**

[A] *unr. itr. V.* weigh; **was** *od.* **wie viel wiegst du?** how much do you weigh?; what weight *or* how heavy are you?; **schwer ~** (fig.) carry weight

[B] *unr. tr. V.* weigh; **etw. gut/knapp ~:** weigh sth. generously/short; **gewogen und zu leicht befunden** (fig.) weighed [in the balance] and found wanting

wiegen[2]

[A] *tr. V.* [1] (schaukeln, hin u. her bewegen) rock; shake ‹*head*› (in doubt); **die Hüften ~:** sway one's hips; **einen ~den Gang haben** have a rolling gait [2] (zerkleinern) chop [up] (*with a Wiegemesser*)

[B] *refl. V.* ‹*boat, cradle, etc.*› rock; ‹*person, branch, etc.*› sway; **sich in den Hüften ~:** sway one's hips; **sich in der Hoffnung ~, dass ...** cherish *or* nurture the hope that ...

W

Wiegen-: ∼fest *das* (geh.) birthday; **∼lied** *das* lullaby; cradle song

wiehern /ˈviːɐn/ *itr. V.* 1▸ whinny; (lauter) neigh 2▸ (fig. ugs.) **vor Lachen ∼:** roar with laughter; **[das ist ja] zum ∼!** that's a scream! (coll.); **sich ∼d auf die Schenkel schlagen** slap one's thigh with a bellow of laughter; **∼des Gelächter** uproarious laughter

Wien /viːn/ *(das)*; **∼s** ▸❶ **S. 675** Vienna

Wiener¹ *der*; **∼s, ∼** ▸❶ **S. 675** Viennese

Wiener² *Adj.* Viennese; **∼ Würstchen** wiener; frankfurter; **∼ Schnitzel** Wiener schnitzel; **der ∼ Kongress** the Congress of Vienna; **die ∼ Sängerknaben/Philharmoniker** the Vienna Boys' Choir/Vienna Philharmonic

Wiener³ *die*; **∼, ∼:** wiener [sausage]

Wienerin *die*; **∼, ∼nen** Viennese

wienerisch *Adj.* ▸❶ **S. 675** Viennese; **das Wienerische** the Viennese dialect

wienern *tr. V.* (ugs.) polish; shine

wies /viːs/ *1. u. 3. Pers. Sg. Prät. v.* **weisen**

Wiese /ˈviːzə/ *die*; **∼, ∼n** meadow; (Rasen) lawn; **auf der grünen ∼** (fig.) out in the [open] country

Wiesel /ˈviːzl̩/ *das*; **∼s, ∼:** weasel; **wie ein ∼ laufen** run like a hare; *s. auch* **flink A**

wiesel·flink
A *Adj.* nimble
B *adv.* quick as a flash

wieseln *itr. V.; mit sein* scurry

Wiesen-: ∼blume *die* meadow flower; **∼grund** *der* (geh.) meadowland; **∼schaum·kraut** *das* lady's smock

wie·so *Interrogativadv.* why

***wie·viel** ▸**viel A1, 2, Uhr 2, Seite 3**

wie·viel·mal /od. ˈ-ˈ-/ *Interrogativadv.* how many times

wievielt /od. ˈ-ˈ-/ *in* **zu ∼ [wart ihr]?** how many [of you were there]?

wievielt... /od. ˈ-ˈ-/ *Interrogativadj.* ▸❶ **S. 165**, ▸❶ **S. 826 zum ∼en Mal bitte ich dich das nun?** how many times *or* how often have I asked you?; **als ∼er Läufer ist er durchs Ziel gekommen?** in what position did he finish?; **die ∼e Querstraße ist das von hier aus?** how many turnings is that from here?; **der ∼e Band?** which number volume?; **beim ∼en Versuch hat es geklappt?** how many attempts did it take?; **der ∼e ist heute?** what is the date today?; **am ∼en?** [on] what date?

wie·weit *Interrogativadv.* to what extent; how far

wie·wohl *Konj.* (geh. veralt.) although

Wigwam /ˈvɪkvam/ *der*; **∼s, ∼s** wigwam

Wikinger /ˈviːkɪŋɐ/ *der*; **∼s, ∼, Wikingerin** *die*; **∼, ∼nen** Viking

wild /vɪlt/
A *Adj.* 1▸ wild; rugged, wild ‹*countryside, area, etc.*›; untouched, uncultivated ‹*land, soil*›; wild, unruly ‹*hair, beard, etc.*›; **Geranien kommen ∼ vor** geraniums grow wild; **∼e Triebe** rank shoots; **∼es Fleisch** (Med.) proud flesh; **∼ lebende Tiere** wild animals; animals living in the wild; **∼ wachsende Pflanzen** wild plants 2▸ (nicht [behördlich] genehmigt, nicht angemeldet) unauthorized; illegal; **∼e Taxis** unlicensed taxis; **∼es Parken** illegal parking; **in ∼er Ehe leben** (veralt.) live in sin; **∼er Streik** wildcat strike 3▸ (heftig, gewaltig) wild ‹*panic, flight, passion, desire, etc.*›; fierce ‹*battle, anger, determination, look*›; **∼ auf etw.** (Akk.) **sein** (ugs.) be mad *or* crazy about sth. (coll.); **∼ auf jmdn.** *od.* **nach jmdm. sein** (ugs.) be mad *or* crazy *or* wild about sb. (coll.); *s. auch* **Jagd 5** 4▸ (wütend) furious ‹*cursing, shouting, etc.*›; **∼ werden** get furious; **jmdn. ∼ machen** make sb. furious; infuriate sb.; **den ∼en Mann spielen** (ugs.) get heavy (coll.) 5▸ (unbändig, ungestüm) wild, unruly ‹*child*› 6▸ (maßlos, wüst) wild ‹*speculation, claim, rumour, accusation*›; vile ‹*oaths, curses*›; **halb so** *od.* **nicht so ∼ sein** (ugs.) not be as bad as all that (coll.) 7▸ (primitiv) savage; wild; (abwertend: unzivilisiert) uncivilized; **ein ∼er Haufen** a pack of savages; **der wilde Mann** (Myth.) the wild man of the woods
B *adv.* 1▸ wildly; **die Haare hingen ihr ∼ ins Gesicht** her hair hung wildly about her face; **alles ging ∼ durcheinander** everything was in chaos; **∼ bewegtes Wasser** turbulent water; **∼ entschlossen sein** (ugs.) be absolutely determined; **wie ∼ um sich schlagen** hit out *or* lash out wildly; **wie ∼** (ugs.) like mad (coll.) 2▸ (ordnungswidrig) illegally; **∼ zelten/bauen** camp/build in an unauthorized place

Wild *das*; **∼[e]s** 1▸ (Tiere, Fleisch) game 2▸ (einzelnes Tier) [wild] animal

Wild-: ∼bach *der* mountain torrent; **∼bahn** *die*: *in* **in freier ∼bahn** in the wild; **∼bret** /-brɛt/ *das*; **∼s** (geh.) game; **∼dieb** *der*, **∼diebin** *die* poacher

Wilde *der/die*; *adj. Dekl.* savage; **wie ein ∼r/eine ∼/die ∼n** (ugs.) like a mad thing/like mad things (coll.)

Wild·ente *die* wild duck

Wilderei *die*; **∼, ∼en** poaching *no pl., no art.*

Wilderer *der*; **∼s, ∼, Wilderin** *die*; **∼, ∼nen** poacher

wildern
A *itr. V.* 1▸ poach; go poaching 2▸ ‹*cat, dog*› kill game
B *tr. V.* poach

wild-, Wild-: ∼fang *der* wild creature; **er ist ein kleiner ∼fang** he is a wild little thing; **sie war ein richtiger ∼fang** she was a real tomboy; **∼fremd** *Adj.* completely strange; **∼fremder Mensch/∼fremde Leute** complete stranger/strangers; **∼gans** *die* wild goose; **∼gehege** *das* game enclosure

Wildheit *die*; **∼:** wildness; (eines Volkes usw.) savageness

wild-, Wild-: ∼hüter *der*, **∼hüterin** *die* ▸❶ **S. 113** gamekeeper; **∼katze** *die* wild cat; **∼lebend** ▸**wild A1**; **∼leder** *das* suede; **∼ledern** *Adj.* suede

Wildnis *die*; **∼, ∼se** wilderness

wild-, Wild-: ∼park *der* game park; **∼pferd** *das* wild horse; **∼pflanze** *die* wild plant; **∼romantisch** *Adj.* wild and romantic; romantically wild; **∼sau** *die* wild sow; **∼schaden** *der* damage *no pl., no indef. art.* caused by game; **∼schwein** *das* wild boar; **∼tier** *das* wild animal; **∼wachsend** ▸**wild A1**; **∼wasser** *das; Pl.* **∼∼:** mountain torrent; **∼wasser·rennen** *das* wild-water racing; (einzelne Veranstaltung) wild water race; **∼wechsel** *der* 1▸ (Weg, Pfad) game path; 2▸ (Vorgang) game crossing; **∼west** /-ˈvɛst/ *in* **in/aus** *usw.* **∼west** in/from *etc.* the Wild West; **∼west·film** *der* western; Wild West film; **∼wuchs** *der* rank growth

Wilhelm /ˈvɪlhɛlm/ *(der)* William; **∼ der Eroberer** William the Conqueror; *s. auch* **Friedrich ∼**

wilhelminisch /vɪlhɛlˈmiːnɪʃ/ *Adj.* Wilhelminian

will /vɪl/ *1. u. 3. Pers. Sg. Präsens v.* **wollen**

Wille *der*; **∼ns** will; (Wunsch) wish; (Absicht) intention; **der ∼ zur Macht** the will to power; **guter/böser ∼:** goodwill/ill will; **es war kein böser ∼ von mir** there was no ill will intended; **etw. aus freiem ∼n tun** do sth. of one's own free will; **seinen ∼n durchsetzen** get one's own way; **sie hat den festen ∼n, es zu tun** she firmly intends to do it; **er hat seinen eigenen ∼n** he has a mind of his own; **sie ist voll guten ∼ns** she is very well-intentioned; **lass ihm seinen ∼n** let him have his way; **beim besten ∼n nicht** not with the best will in the world; **wo ein ∼ ist, ist auch ein Weg** (Spr.) where there's a will, there's a way (prov.); **letzter ∼:** will; last will and testament (formal); **mit ∼n** intentionally; **ich musste wider ∼n lachen** I couldn't help laughing; **jmdm. zu ∼n sein** (geh.) do sb.'s bidding; **sie war ihm zu ∼n** (veralt.) she let him have his way with her

willen *Präp. mit Gen. in* **um jmds./einer Sache ∼:** for sb.'s/sth.'s sake

Willen *der*; **∼s** ▸**Wille**

willen·los
A *Adj.* will-less; **völlig ∼ sein** have no will of one's own
B *adv.* will-lessly

Willenlosigkeit *die*; **∼:** lack of will

willens *Adj. in* **∼ sein, etw. zu tun** (geh.) be willing to do sth.; **ich bin nicht ∼, es zu tun** I have no intention of doing it

willens-, Willens-: ∼akt *der* act of will; **∼anstrengung** *die* effort of will; **unter größter ∼anstrengung** by a huge effort of will; **∼bildung** *die*: **die politische ∼bildung** the formulation of political demands and objectives; **∼erklärung** *die* (bes. Rechtsw.) declaration of intent; **∼freiheit** *die* freedom of will; **∼kraft** *die* will power; strength of will; **∼schwach** *Adj.* weak-willed; **∼schwäche** *die* weakness of will; **∼stark** *Adj.* strong-willed; **∼stärke** *die* strength of will

willentlich /ˈvɪləntlɪç/
A *Adj.* deliberate
B *adv.* deliberately; on purpose

willfahren /od. ˈ---/ *itr. V.* (geh.) **ich willfahre, willfahrt** *od.* **gewillfahrt, zu willfahren: [jmdm.] ∼:** obey [sb.]; do sb.'s bidding; **jmds. Bitte** *(Dat.)* **∼:** comply with sb.'s request

willfährig /ˈvɪlfɛːrɪç *od.* -ˈ--/ *Adj.* compliant; **jmdm. ∼ sein** submit to sb.'s will; **sich** *(Dat.)* **jmdn. ∼ machen** make sb. submit to one's will

Willfährigkeit /od. -ˈ---/ *die*; **∼** (geh.) compliance

Williams Christ·birne /ˈvɪljamz ˈkrɪst-/ *die* Bartlett pear

willig
A *Adj.* willing; obedient ‹*horse*›; *s. auch* **Geist¹ 1**
B *adv.* willingly

will·kommen *Adj.* welcome; **jmdm. ∼ sein** be welcome to sb.; **∼ zu Hause/in Mannheim!** welcome home/in Mannheim!; **jmdn. ∼ heißen** welcome sb.; **ich möchte Sie herzlich ∼ heißen** a very warm welcome to you

Will·kommen *das od.* (selten) *der*; **∼s, ∼:** welcome; **jmdm. ein herzliches ∼ bereiten** *od.* **bieten** give sb. a warm welcome

Willkommens-: ∼gruß *der* welcome; **∼trunk** *der* welcoming drink

Will·kür *die*; **∼:** arbitrary use of power; (einer Entscheidung, Handlung o. Ä.) arbitrariness; **jmds. ∼** *(Dat.)* **preisgegeben** *od.* **ausgeliefert sein** be at sb.'s mercy; **das ist die reine ∼:** that is purely arbitrary

Willkür-: ∼akt *der* arbitrary act; **∼herrschaft** *die* tyranny

willkürlich
A *Adj.* arbitrary; (vom Willen gesteuert) voluntary ‹*muscle, movement, etc.*›
B *adv.* arbitrarily; (vom Willen gesteuert) voluntarily

Willkür·maßnahme *die* arbitrary measure

wimmeln /ˈvɪml̩n/ *itr. V.* 1▸ (sich bewegen) **Insekten/Ratten ∼ dort** the place is swarming with insects/rats 2▸ (voll sein) **von Menschen ∼:** be teeming *or* swarming with people; **von Fischen/Läusen/Ungeziefer ∼:** be teeming with fish/swarming with lice/vermin; **in dem Artikel wimmelt es von Fehlern** the article is teeming with mistakes

wimmern /ˈvɪmɐn/ *itr. V.* whimper; **zum Wimmern [sein]** (ugs.) [be] simply pathetic

Wimpel /ˈvɪmpl̩/ *der*; **∼s, ∼:** pennant

Wimper /ˈvɪmpɐ/ *die*; **∼, ∼n** 1▸ [eye]lash; **ohne mit der ∼ zu zucken** without batting an eyelid 2▸ (Biol.) cilium

Wimpern:- ∼schlag *der* flick of the eyelid; blink; (fig.: Augenblick) blink of an eye; **[um] einen ∼schlag voraus/zurück/schneller** a fraction ahead/behind/faster; **∼tusche** *die* mascara

Wimper·tierchen *das* ciliate; infusorian

Wind /vɪnt/ *der*; **∼[e]s, ∼e** 1▸ wind; **bei ∼ und Wetter** in all weathers; **[schnell] wie der ∼:** like the wind 2▸ (fig.) **hier weht [jetzt] ein schärferer/anderer/frischer ∼** (ugs.) things have tightened up a lot here [now]/things are different here [now]/there's a much fresher feel to the place [now]; **wissen/merken, woher der ∼ weht** (ugs.) know/notice which way the wind's blowing; **∼ machen** (ugs.) brag; **viel ∼ um etw. machen** (ugs.) make a great fuss about sth.; **∼ von etw. bekommen** *od.* **kriegen** (ugs.) get wind of sth.; **jmdm. den**

~ aus den Segeln nehmen (ugs.) take the wind out of sb.'s sails; **sich** (*Dat.*) **den ~ um die Nase** *od.* **Ohren wehen lassen** (ugs.) see a bit of life *or* the world; **gegen den/mit dem ~ segeln** swim against/with the tide; **etw. in den ~ schlagen** turn a deaf ear *or* pay no heed to sth.; **in den ~ reden** waste one's breath; **alle Appelle waren in den ~ gesprochen** all appeals were in vain; **in alle [vier] ~e** in all directions; **ihre Kinder sind in alle ~e zerstreut** her children are scattered to the four corners of the earth; **sein Mäntelchen nach dem ~e hängen** be a trimmer; **wer ~ sät, wird Sturm ernten** (Spr.) sow the wind and reap the whirlwind (prov.) **3** (Blähung) wind; **einen ~ fahren lassen** break wind

Wind-: ~beutel *der* **1** (Gebäck) cream puff; **2** (abwertend: Person) frivolous and irresponsible person; **~bö[e]** *die* gust of wind

Winde *die;* **~, ~n** **1** (Technik) winch **2** (Bot.) bindweed; convolvulus

Wind·ei *das* wind egg; (fig. abwertend) dud

Windel /ˈvɪndl̩/ *die;* **~, ~n** nappy (Brit.); diaper (Amer.); **damals lagst du noch in [den] ~n** you were still in nappies then; **noch in den ~n liegen** *od.* **stecken** (fig.) ‹*project etc.*› still be in its infancy

Windel·höschen *das* nappy pants *pl.*

windeln *tr. V.* **ein Baby ~:** put a baby's nappy (Brit.) *or* (Amer.) diaper on

windel·weich *Adj.* (ugs.) soft; **jmdn. ~ schlagen** *od.* **hauen** beat the living daylights out of sb. (coll.)

winden[1]

A *unr. tr. V.* **1** (geh.) make ‹*wreath, garland*›; **Blumen zu einem/in einen Kranz ~:** bind flowers into a wreath; make a wreath out of flowers; **etw. um etw. ~:** wind sth. around sth.; **jmdm. etw. aus der Hand ~:** wrest sth. from sb.'s hand **2** (mit einer Winde bewegen) winch

B *unr. refl. V.* **1** ‹*plant, tendrils*› wind (**um** around); ‹*snake*› coil [itself], wind itself (**um** around) **2** (sich krümmen) writhe; **sich vor Schmerzen/in Krämpfen ~:** writhe in pain/convulsions; **sich vor Verlegenheit ~:** squirm with embarrassment; **sich vor Lachen ~:** fall about laughing; **sich ~ wie ein Aal** (fig.) try to wriggle out of it **3** (sich schlängeln) ‹*path, river*› wind [its way]; **sich durch etw. ~:** wind one's/its way through sth.

winden[2] *itr. V.; unpers.* **es windet** it's windy

Windes·eile *die* in **in** *od.* **mit ~:** in next to no time; **sich in ~ verbreiten** spread like wildfire

wind-, Wind-: ~fang *der* porch; **~geschützt** *Adj.* sheltered from the wind *postpos.;* sheltered; **diese Pflanzen müssen ~geschützt stehen** these plants must be kept sheltered from the wind; **~geschwindigkeit** *die* wind speed; **~harfe** *die* wind harp; aeolian harp; **~hauch** *der* breath of wind; **~hose** *die* (Met.) whirlwind; **~hund** *der* **1** greyhound; **Afghanischer ~hund** Afghan hound; **2** (ugs. abwertend) careless and unreliable sort (coll.)

windig *Adj.* **1** windy **2** (ugs. abwertend) shady; dubious ‹*excuse, morality*›; empty ‹*words, talk, hope*›

Wind-: ~jacke *die* windcheater (Brit.); windbreaker (Amer.); **~jammer** *der; Pl.* **~~s, ~:** (Seemannsspr.) windjammer; **~kanal** *der* **1** (Technik) wind tunnel; **2** (an der Orgel) wind trunk; **~licht** *das; Pl.* **~~er** table lantern (*with candle in glass container*); **~mühle** *die* windmill; **gegen** *od.* **mit ~mühlen kämpfen** (fig.) tilt at windmills; **~mühlen·flügel** *der* windmill sail; **~park** *der* wind farm; **~pocken** *Pl.* ▸ⓘ **S. 439** chickenpox *sing.;* **~rad** *das* **1** wind wheel; **2** ▸**~rädchen**; **~rädchen** *das* windmill; **~richtung** *die* wind direction; **~rose** *die* compass card

Winds·braut *die* (dichter.) gale; (Wirbelwind) whirlwind

wind-, Wind-: ~schatten *der* lee; **~schief** *Adj.* (oft abwertend) crooked; **~schlüpfig**, **~schnittig** *Adj.* streamlined; **~schutz·scheibe** *die* windscreen (Brit.); windshield (Amer.); **~spiel** *das* [small] greyhound; **~stärke** *die* force of the wind; **~stärke 7/9** *usw.* wind force 7/9 *etc.;* **~still** *Adj.* windless; still; **es war völlig ~still** there was no wind at all; **ein ~stilles Plätzchen** a sheltered spot; a spot out of the wind; **~stille** *die* calm; **es herrschte völlige ~stille** there was no wind at all; **~stoß** *der* gust of wind; **~surfer** *der,* **~surferin** *die* windsurfer; **~surfing** *das* windsurfing *no art.*

Windung *die;* **~, ~en** **1** (Krümmung) bend; (eines Flusses) meander; (des Darms, Gehirns) convolution **2** (spiralförmiger Verlauf) spiral; (einer Spule o. Ä.) winding **3** (schlangenartige Bewegung) wriggling

Wind·zug *der* breeze

Wingert /ˈvɪŋɐt/ *der;* **~s, ~e** (westmd., schweiz.) ▸**Weinberg**

Wink /vɪŋk/ *der;* **~[e]s, ~e** **1** (Zeichen) sign; (mit dem Kopf) nod **2** (Hinweis) hint; (Ratschlag) tip; hint; (an die Polizei) tip-off; **ein ~ mit dem Zaunpfahl** (scherzh.) a strong hint

winke *in:* **~, ~ machen** (Kindersprache) wave

Winkel /ˈvɪŋkl̩/ *der;* **~s, ~** **1** (Math.) angle; **toter ~:** blind spot **2** (Ecke; auch fig.) corner; **in allen Ecken und ~n suchen** search every nook and cranny **3** (Ort) corner; spot **4** (Werkzeug) [carpenter's] square; (T-förmig) T-square **5** (milit. Rangabzeichen) chevron **6** (**~eisen**) angle iron

winkel-, Winkel-: ~advokat *der,* **~advokatin** *die* (abwertend) shady lawyer; **~eisen** *das* (Technik) angle iron; **~förmig** *Adj.* angled; **~funktion** *die* (Math.) trigonometrical function; **~halbierende** *die; adj. Dekl.* (Math.) bisector of a/the angle

winkelig *Adj.* twisty ‹*streets*›; **ein ~es Haus** a house full of odd corners

Winkel-: ~maß *das* measure of angle; **~messer** *der;* **~~s, ~~:** protractor; **~schleifer** *der* angle grinder; **~zug** *der* shady trick *or* move

winken

A *itr. V.* **1** wave; **jmdm. ~:** wave to sb.; **mit etw. ~:** wave sth.; **mit dem Kopf ~:** nod [one's head] **2** (auffordern heranzukommen) **jmdm. ~:** beckon sb. over; **einem Taxi ~:** hail a taxi **3** (in Aussicht stehen) **etw. winkt jmdm.** sth. is in prospect for sb.; **dem Sieger winkt eine Flasche Sekt** the winner will receive a bottle of champagne

B *tr. V.* **1** (heran**~**) beckon; **jmdn. zu sich ~:** beckon sb. over [to one]; **der Polizist winkte den Wagen zur Seite** the policeman waved the car over [to the side] **2** (signalisieren) signal

Winker *der;* **~s, ~:** trafficator; indicator

winklig *Adj.* ▸**winkelig**

winseln /ˈvɪnzl̩n/ *itr. V.* **1** ‹*dog*› whimper **2** (abwertend) whine; **um Gnade/sein Leben ~:** whine and beg for mercy/one's life

Winter /ˈvɪntɐ/ *der;* **~s, ~** ▸ⓘ **S. 395** winter; **über den ~:** over [the] winter; *s. auch* **Frühling**

winter-, Winter-: ~abend *der* winter['s] evening; **~anfang** *der* beginning of winter; **am 22. Dezember ist ~anfang** 22 December is the first day of winter; **~depression** *die* winter depression; **~einbruch** *der* onset of winter; **~fahr·plan** *der* winter timetable; **~fell** *das* winter coat; **~fest** *Adj.* **1** winter *attrib.* ‹*clothing*›; **ein ~festes Haus** a house that can withstand the rigours of winter; **2** ▸**~hart**; **~frucht** *die* ▸**~getreide**; **~garten** *der* conservatory; **~getreide** *das* (Landw.) winter grain; **~halb·jahr** *das:* **während des ~halbjahrs/im ~halbjahr** from October to March; **~hart** *Adj.* (Bot.) hardy; **~hilfswerk** *das:* (ns.) *relief organization in Nazi Germany providing clothes, fuel, food, etc. for the needy;* **~jasmin** *der* winter jasmine; **~kleid** *das* **1** (auch fig.) winter dress; **2** (Zool.) winter coat; (von Vögeln) winter plumage; **~kleidung** *die* winter clothes *pl. or* clothing; **~landschaft** *die* winter landscape

winterlich ▸ⓘ **S. 395**

A *Adj.* wintry; winter *attrib.* ‹*clothing, break*›

B *adv.* **~ kalt/öde** cold/bare and wintry; **~ warm angezogen** dressed in warm winter clothes

Winter-: ~luft *die* winter air; **~mantel** *der* winter coat; **~mode** *die* winter fashions *pl.;* (eines Modehauses) winter collection; **~monat** *der* winter month; **~nacht** *die* winter['s] night; **~olympiade** *die* Winter Olympics *pl.;* **~quartier** *das* **1** (Milit.) winter quarters *pl.;* **2** (Zool.) wintering grounds *pl.;* **~reifen** *der* winter tyre; **~ruhe** *die* (Zool.) winter dormancy; **~ruhe halten** have a period/periods of winter inactivity

winters *Adv.* in winter

Winter-: ~saat *die* (Landw.) (Saatgut) winter seed; (Pflanzen) young winter corn; **~sachen** *Pl.* winter things; **~saison** *die* winter season

Winters·anfang *der* ▸**Winteranfang**

Winter-: ~schlaf *der* (Zool.) hibernation; **~schlaf halten** hibernate; **~schlussverkauf**, ***~schlußverkauf** *der* winter sale[s *pl.*]; **~schuh** *der* winter shoe; **~semester** *das* winter semester; **~sonne** *die* winter sun; **~sonnenwende** *die* winter solstice; **~speck** *der* (ugs. scherzh.) winter flab (coll.); **~spiele** *Pl.* Winter Games; **die Olympischen ~spiele** the Winter Olympics; **~sport** *der* winter sports *pl.;* **in den ~sport fahren** go on a winter sports holiday; **~sport·gebiet** *das* winter sports area; **~sportler** *der* winter sportsman; **~sportlerin** *die* winter sportswoman; **~sport·ort** *der* winter sports resort

Winters·zeit *die* ▸**Winterzeit**

Winter-: ~tag *der* winter['s] day; **~urlaub** *der* winter holiday; **~wetter** *das* winter weather; **~zeit** *die* wintertime; **zur ~zeit** in [the] wintertime

Winzer /ˈvɪntsɐ/ *der;* **~s, ~, Winzerin** *die;* **~, ~nen** ▸ⓘ **S. 113** winegrower

winzig /ˈvɪntsɪç/

A *Adj.* tiny; tiny, minute ‹*portion, writing*›

B *adv.* **er schreibt ~:** he has tiny *or* minute writing; **~ klein** tiny; minute

Winzigkeit *die;* **~, ~** **1** tininess; minuteness **2** (Kleinigkeit) tiny thing; triviality

Winzling /ˈvɪntslɪŋ/ *der;* **~s, ~e** tiny person/animal/thing; **er/sie/es ist ein ~:** he/she/it is a tiny little thing

Wipfel /ˈvɪpfl̩/ *der;* **~s, ~:** treetop

Wippe /ˈvɪpə/ *die;* **~, ~n** see-saw

wippen *itr. V.* bob up and down; (hin und her) bob about; (auf einer Wippe) see-saw; **er ließ das Kind auf den Knien ~:** he bounced the child [up and down] on his knees; **er wippte in den Knien** he bobbed up and down, bending at the knees; **mit dem Fuß ~:** jiggle one's foot up and down; **mit dem Schwanz ~:** jerk its tail up and down

wir /viːɐ/ *Personalpron.; 1. Pers. Pl. Nom.* we; **~ beide** *od.* **beiden** we two; the two of us; **sie weiß mehr als ~:** she knows more than we do; she knows more than us (coll.); **nicht nur ~ würden profitieren** we shouldn't be the only ones to profit; **Wer hat das getan? — Wir nicht!** Who did it? — It wasn't us! *or* We didn't!; **Wer kommt mit? — Wir!** Who's coming? — We are!; **Wer ist es? — Wir sinds!** Who is it? — It's us!; **wie fühlen ~ uns heute?** (zu einem Patienten) how are we feeling today?; *s. auch* (*Gen.*) **unser**; (*Dat.*) **uns**; (*Akk.*) **uns**

wirb /vɪrp/ *Imperativ Sg. v.* **werben**

Wirbel /ˈvɪrbl̩/ *der;* **~s, ~** **1** (kreisende Bewegung) (im Wasser) whirlpool; vortex; (in der Luft) whirlwind; (kleiner) eddy; (von Rauch, beim Tanz) whirl; **alles drehte sich in einem ~ um ihn** everything was whirling round him; **ein ~ der Leidenschaft** (fig.) a whirlpool of passions **2** (Trubel) hurly-burly; **der ~ der Ereignisse** the whirl of events **3** (Aufsehen) fuss; **um jmdn./etw. ~ machen** make a fuss about sb./sth. **4** ▸ⓘ **S. 435** (Anat.) vertebra

5 (Haar~) crown; (vorne) cowlick 6 (Trommel~) [drum] roll 7 (Musik, bei Streichinstrumenten) tuning peg

Wirbellose *Pl.; adj. Dekl.* (Zool.) invertebrates

wirbeln

A *itr. V.* 1 *mit sein* whirl; ‹*water, snowflakes*› swirl; **jmdm. durch den Kopf ~** (fig.) ‹*thoughts*› race through sb.'s head 2 *auch mit sein* (in kreisender Bewegung sein) ‹*propeller, wheel, etc.*› whirl 3 (einen Wirbel schlagen) ‹*drum*› roll; ‹*drummer*› beat a roll

B *tr. V.* swirl ‹*leaves, dust*›; whirl ‹*dancer*›

Wirbel-: ~säule *die* ▸ⓘ **S. 435** (Anat.) vertebral column; spinal column; **~sturm** *der* cyclone; **~tier** *das* (Zool.) vertebrate; **~wind** *der* whirlwind; (fig., meist scherzh.) bundle of energy

wirbt /vɪrpt/ *3. Pers. Sg. Präsens v.* **werben**

wird /vɪrt/ *3. Pers. Sg. Präsens v.* **werden**

wirf /vɪrf/ *Imperativ Sg. v.* **werfen**

wirft *3. Pers. Sg. Präsens v.* **werfen**

wirken /ˈvɪrkn̩/

A *itr. V.* 1 (eine Wirkung haben) have an effect; **wirkt die Tablette schon?** is the tablet beginning to take effect yet?; **es wirkte erst nach einer Stunde** it only took effect after an hour; **schmerzstillend/einschläfernd ~:** have a pain-killing/soporific effect; **gegen etw. ~:** be effective against sth.; **bei jmdm. ~:** have an effect on sb.; **seine Worte wirkten ermutigend** his words were encouraging; **ihre Heiterkeit wirkte ansteckend** her cheerfulness was infectious; **lassen Sie die Farben und Klänge auf sich ~:** let the colours and sounds sink in; **Sauerstoff wirkt dabei als Katalysator** oxygen acts as a catalyst 2 (erscheinen) seem; appear; **neben ihm wirkt sie ausgesprochen klein** she seems decidedly small beside him; **sie wirkt sehr nett** she seems very nice; **er wirkt auf mich sehr sympathisch** I find him very congenial 3 (beeindrucken) ‹*person*› make an impression (**auf** + *Akk.* on); ‹*picture, design, etc.*› be effective 4 (tätig sein) work; **da wirkt ein verborgener Mechanismus** a hidden mechanism is operating there

B *tr. V.* 1 (geh.: be~, vollbringen) bring about; do ‹*good, harm*›; *s. auch* **Wunder 1** 2 (Textilw.) knit

Wirker *der;* **~s, ~:** knitter

Wirkerei *die;* **~, ~en** 1 (Herstellung) knitting 2 (Betrieb) knitwear factory

Wirkerin *die;* **~, ~nen** knitter

wirklich

A *Adj.* real; actual, real ‹*event, incident, state of affairs*›; real, true ‹*friend*›

B *Adv.* really; (in der Tat) actually; really; **nein, ~?** no, really?; **er ist es ~:** it really is him; **~ und wahrhaftig** really and truly

Wirklichkeit *die;* **~, ~en** reality; **~ werden** become a reality; ‹*dream*› come true; **in ~:** in reality; **auf den Boden der ~ zurückkehren** come back down to earth (fig.)

wirklichkeits-, Wirklichkeits-: ~fern A *Adj.* unrealistic; **B** *adv.* unrealistically; **~form** *die* (Sprachw.) indicative; **~fremd A** *Adj.* unrealistic; **er ist ~fremd** he is out of touch with reality; **B** *adv.* unrealistically; **~getreu A** *Adj.* faithful; **B** *adv.* faithfully; **~nah A** *Adj.* realistic; **B** *adv.* realistically; **~sinn** *der* sense of realism

wirksam /ˈvɪrkza:m/

A *Adj.* effective; **mit dem 1. Juli ~ werden** (Amtsspr.) take effect from 1 July

B *adv.* effectively

Wirksamkeit *die;* **~:** effectiveness

Wirk·stoff *der* active agent

Wirkung *die;* **~, ~en** 1 effect (**auf** + *Akk.* on); **ohne ~ bleiben** have no effect; **seine ~ verfehlen** fail to have the desired effect; **seine ~ tun** ‹*drug, medicine, etc.*› take effect; ‹*treatment, therapy*› be effective; **mit ~ vom 1. Juli** (Amtsspr.) with effect from 1 July 2 (Physik) action

wirkungs-, Wirkungs-: ~bereich *der* 1 area of activity; **sie fühlte sich in ihrem häuslichen ~bereich wohl** she felt quite happy in her domestic domain; 2 (Milit.) range; **~dauer** *die:* **eine kurze/lange ~dauer haben** be effective for a short/long period; **~feld** *das* sphere of activity; **~grad** *der* effectiveness; (Technik) efficiency; **~los A** *Adj.* ineffective; **B** *adv.* ineffectively; **~losigkeit** *die;* **~~:** ineffectiveness; **~mechanismus** *der* mode of action; **~stätte** *die* (geh.) workplace; **~voll A** *Adj.* effective; **B** *adv.* effectively; **~weise** *die* (eines Wirkstoffs) mode of action; **die ~weise eines Mechanismus/ökonomischer Gesetze** the way a mechanism works/economic laws operate

Wirk·waren *Pl.* knitwear *sing.;* (Strümpfe, Socken) hosiery *sing.*

wirr /vɪr/

A *Adj.* 1 (unordentlich) tousled ‹*hair, beard*›; tangled ‹*ropes, roots*›; **ein ~es Durcheinander** a chaotic muddle 2 (unklar, verwirrt) confused; muddled, confused ‹*thoughts*›; **mir war ~ im Kopf** my head was reeling

B *adv.* 1 (unordentlich) **das Haar hing ihr ~ ins Gesicht** her tousled hair hung over her face; **alles lag ~ durcheinander** everything lay in a chaotic muddle 2 (verworren) **sie träumte ~:** she had confused dreams; **~ reden** talk in a confused way 3 (verwirrt) in confusion

Wirren *Pl.* turmoil *sing.*

Wirr·kopf *der* (abwertend) muddle-headed person; **ein ~ sein** be muddle-headed

wirr·köpfig

A *Adj.* muddle-headed

B *adv.* muddle-headedly

Wirrnis /ˈvɪrnɪs/ *die;* **~, ~se** (geh.) confusion; **die ~se der Revolution** the chaos *sing.* of the revolution

Wirrsal /ˈvɪrza:l/ *das;* **~[e]s, ~e** *od.* **die; ~, ~e** (geh.) ▸**Wirrnis**

Wirrwarr /-var/ *der;* **~s** chaos; (von Stimmen) clamour; (von Meinungen) welter; (von Haaren, Wurzeln, Vorschriften) tangle

Wirsing /ˈvɪrzɪŋ/ *der;* **~s, Wirsing·kohl** *der* savoy [cabbage]

Wirt /vɪrt/ *der;* **~[e]s, ~e** 1 landlord; *s. auch* **Rechnung** 2 (Biol.) host

Wirtel /ˈvɪrtl̩/ *der;* **~s, ~** ▸**Spinnwirtel**

Wirtin *die;* **~, ~nen** landlady

Wirtschaft *die;* **~, ~en** 1 economy; (Geschäftsleben) commerce and industry; **in die ~ gehen** become a business man/woman; **die freie ~:** the free market economy 2 (Gast~) public house (Brit.); pub (Brit.); bar (Amer.) 3 (Haushalt) household; **jmdm. die ~ führen** keep house for sb. 4 (ugs. abwertend: Unordnung) mess; shambles *sing.* 5 (landwirtschaftlicher Betrieb) [small] farm 6 (das Haushalten) housekeeping

wirtschaften

A *itr. V.* 1 **mit dem Geld gut ~:** manage one's money well; **mit Verlust/Gewinn ~:** run at a loss/profit; **wenn weiter so gewirtschaftet wird wie bisher** if things continue to be run as they have been up to now 2 (sich zu schaffen machen) busy oneself

B *tr. V.* **eine Firma konkursreif/in den Ruin ~:** bring a company to the brink of bankruptcy/ruin a company; **er hat den Hof zugrunde gewirtschaftet** he brought the farm to rack and ruin

Wirtschafter *der;* **~s, ~** 1 (Wirtsch.: Unternehmer) entrepreneur; (Industrieller) industrialist 2 (in landwirtschaftlichem Betrieb) farm manager

Wirtschafterin *die;* **~, ~nen** 1 ▸**Wirtschafter** 2 (Haushälterin) housekeeper

Wirtschaftler *der;* **~s, ~, Wirtschaftlerin** *die;* **~, ~nen** 1 ▸**Wirtschaftswissenschaftler** 2 ▸**Wirtschafter 1**

wirtschaftlich

A *Adj.* 1 (die Wirtschaft betreffend) economic 2 (finanziell) financial 3 (sparsam, rentabel) economical

B *adv.; s. Adj.* **1, 2, 3** economically; financially

Wirtschaftlichkeit *die;* **~:** economic viability

wirtschafts-, Wirtschafts-: ~abkommen *das* economic agreement; **~aufschwung** *der* economic upturn; **~ausschuss** *der* economic committee; **~- und Finanzauschuss** (EU) Economic and Finance Committee; **~berater** *der,* **~beraterin** *die* economic adviser; **~beziehungen** *Pl.* economic relations; **~block** *der; Pl.* **~blöcke** economic bloc; **~buch** *das* ▸**Haushaltsbuch**; **~faktor** *der* economic factor; **~flüchtling** *der* economic refugee; **~form** *die* economic system; **~forschung** *die* economics research; **~führer** *der,* **~führerin** *die* leading figure in commerce and industry; **~führung** *die* (eines Landes) management of the economy; (eines Betriebs) financial management; **~gebäude** *Pl.* domestic offices; **~geld** *das* ▸**Haushaltsgeld**; **~gemeinschaft** *die* economic community; **~geographie** *die* economic geography *no art.;* **~gymnasium** *das: grammar school placing emphasis on economics, law, and business studies;* **~hilfe** *die* economic aid *no indef. art.;* **~hochschule** *die* business school *or* college; **~ingenieur** *der,* **~ingenieurin** *die* industrial engineer; **~jahr** *das* ▸**Geschäftsjahr**; **~kapitän** *der,* **~kapitänin** *die* captain of industry; **~krieg** *der* economic war; (Kriegsführung) economic warfare; **~kriminalität** *die* economic crime *no art.;* **~krise** *die* economic crisis; **~lage** *die* economic situation; **~leben** *das* economic life; (Geschäftsleben) business life; **ein Mann aus dem ~leben** a man from the business world; **~lenkung** *die* economic control; **~minister** *der,* **~ministerin** *die* minister for economic affairs; **~ministerium** *das* ministry of economic affairs; **~ordnung** *die* economic system; **~politik** *die* economic policy; **~politisch A** *Adj.* relating to economic policy *postpos.;* economic policy *attrib.* ‹*measures, decisions*›; **B** *adv.* from the point of view of economic policy; **~prüfer** *der,* **~prüferin** *die* ▸ⓘ **S. 113** auditor; **~recht** *das* commercial law; **~spionage** *die* industrial espionage; **~standort** *der* ▸**Standort 3**; **~system** *das* economic system; **~teil** *der* business section; **~union** *die* economic union; **~- und Währungsunion** Economic and Monetary Union; **~verband** *der* employers' association; **~wachstum** *das* economic growth; **~wissenschaft** *die* economics *no art.;* economic science *no art.;* **~wissenschaftler** *der,* **~wissenschaftlerin** *die* ▸ⓘ **S. 113** economist; **~wunder** *das* (ugs.) economic miracle; **~zeitung** *die* financial newspaper; **~zweig** *der* economic sector

Wirtschaftswunder

The German economic miracle was the result of the country's rapid reconstruction after the Second World War and its successful economic recovery. It boomed in the decades after 1950.

Wirts-: ~haus *das* pub (Brit.); (mit Unterkunft) inn; pub (Brit.); **~leute** *Pl.* landlord and landlady; **~organismus** *der* (Biol.) host organism; **~pflanze** *die* (Biol.) host plant; **~stube** *die* bar; **~tier** *das* (Biol.) host animal; **~zelle** *die* (Biol.) host cell

Wisch /vɪʃ/ *der;* **~[e]s, ~e** (salopp abwertend) piece *or* bit of paper

wischen

A *itr., tr. V.* wipe; **etw. von etw. ~:** wipe sth. off *or* from sth.; **er wischte sich** (*Dat.*) **die Stirn** he wiped his brow; **sich** (*Dat.*) **den Schlaf aus den Augen ~:** wipe the sleep from one's eyes; **mit der Hand/einem Lappen über den Tisch ~:** wipe the table with one's hand/a cloth; **versehentlich mit dem Ärmel über die Zeichnung ~:** accidentally brush one's sleeve across the drawing; **Staub ~:** do the dusting; dust; **jmdm. eine ~** (ugs.) give sb. a clout round the face

B *itr. V.; mit sein* (huschen) ‹*person*› slip; ‹*mouse, lizard*› scurry; ‹*cat*› dart

Wischer *der;* **~s, ~** ▸**Scheibenwischer**

Wischiwaschi /vɪʃiˈvaʃi/ *das;* **~s** (salopp abwertend) wish-wash

Wisch-: ~lappen *der,* **~tuch** *das; Pl.* **~tücher** cloth

Wisent /ˈvi:zɛnt/ *der;* **~s, ~e** wisent; aurochs

W

Wismut /ˈvɪsmu:t/ *das;* **~[e]s** bismuth

wispern /ˈvɪspɐn/ *itr., tr. V.* whisper

wiss-, *wiß-, Wiss-, *Wiß-: ~begier, ~begierde *die* thirst for knowledge; **~begierig** *Adj.* eager for knowledge; ‹*child*› eager to learn

wissen /ˈvɪsn̩/

A *unr. tr. V.* know; **ich weiß [es]** I know; **ich weiß [es] nicht** I don't know; **etw. genau ~:** know sth. for certain; **ich weiß [mir] keinen anderen Rat/kein größeres Vergnügen, als ...** I can't think of anything other/I know of no greater pleasure than ...; **soviel ich weiß** as far as I know; **ich weiß ein gutes Lokal** I know [of] a good pub (Brit.); **er weiß es nicht anders** he knows no better; **er weiß immer alles besser** he always knows better; **ich wüsste nicht, dass ich dich um deinen Rat gebeten hätte** I am not aware of having asked your advice; **nicht, dass ich wüsste** not so far as I know; not that I know of; **ich möchte nicht ~, wieviel das gekostet hat** I hardly dare think how much it cost; **woher soll ich das ~?** how should I know?; **weißt du [was], wir fahren einfach dorthin** I'll tell you what, let's just go there; **jmdn. etw. ~ lassen** let sb. know sth.; **ein ~der Blick/ein ~des Lächeln** a knowing look/smile; **nicht mehr weiter ~:** not know what to do next; **was weiß ich** (ugs.) I don't know; **man kann nie ~** (ugs.) you never know; **gewusst, wie!** (ugs.) it's easy when you know how; **was ich nicht weiß, macht mich nicht heiß** (Spr.) what I don't know doesn't hurt me; **von jmdm./etw. nichts [mehr] ~ wollen** want to have nothing [more] to do with sb./sth.; **jmd. will es ~** (ugs.) sb. wants to put himself/herself to the test; **er tut, als sei es wer weiß wie wichtig** (ugs.) he behaves as if it were incredibly important (coll.); **dies und noch wer weiß was alles** (ugs.) this and heaven knows what else [too]; **ich hätte wer weiß was darum gegeben** (ugs.) I'd have given almost anything for it; **ich weiß sie in Sicherheit/glücklich** (geh.) I know she's safe/happy; **ich wusste ihn in Gefahr** (geh.) I knew him to be in danger; **ich wollte diese Äußerung nicht als Vorwurf verstanden ~** (geh.) I didn't mean what I said to be taken as a reproach; **sich zu benehmen ~:** know how to behave oneself; **er wusste zu berichten, dass ...** he was able to report that ...; **ich weiß nichts mit ihm anzufangen** he isn't my type of person; **Sie müssen ~, dass ...** (erklärend) I should tell you that ...; **ich weiß ihren Namen nicht mehr** I can't remember her name; **weißt du noch, wie arm wir damals waren?** do you remember how poor we were then?; *s. auch* **Glocke 1**; **Gott 1, 2**; **Stunde 1**

B *unr. itr. V.* **von etw./um etw. ~:** know about sth.; **ich weiß von nichts** I don't know anything about it

Wissen *das;* **~s** knowledge; **ein großes ~ haben** be very knowledgeable; **meines/unseres ~s** to my/our knowledge; **ohne jmds. ~:** without sb.'s knowledge; **mit jmds. ~:** with sb.'s knowledge; **wider** *od.* **gegen besseres ~:** against one's better judgement; **nach bestem ~ und Gewissen** to the best of one's knowledge and belief; **~ ist Macht** (Spr.) knowledge is power (prov.)

Wissenschaft *die;* **~, ~en** science; **die ~ hat ...** science has ...; **in der ~ tätig sein** be a scientist; **etw. ist eine ~ für sich** (ugs.) there's a real art to sth.

Wissenschafter *der;* **~s, ~, Wissenschafterin** *die;* **~, ~nen** (österr. u. schweiz.), **Wissenschaftler** *der;* **~s, ~, Wissenschaftlerin** *die;* **~, ~nen** ▸ⓘ S. 113 academic; (Natur~) scientist

wissenschaftlich

A *Adj.* scholarly; (natur~) scientific; **~er Assistent** ≈ assistant lecturer; **~er Rat** ≈ lecturer; assistant professor (Amer.)

B *adv.* in a scholarly manner; (natur~) scientifically; **das ist ~ nicht haltbar** that is not scientifically tenable; **~ arbeiten** (als Wissenschaftler tätig sein) work as a scholar/scientist

Wissenschaftlichkeit *die;* **~** ▸**wissenschaftlich**: scholarliness; scientific rigour; **die ~ einer Untersuchung infrage stellen** question whether a piece of research has been conducted in a proper scholarly/scientific manner

wissenschafts-, Wissenschafts-: ~betrieb *der* (ugs.) academic activity; (in den Naturwissenschaften) scientific activity; **~gläubig** **A** *Adj.* with a belief in science *postpos.*; **~gläubig sein** believe in science; **B** *adv.* believing in science; with a belief in science; **~gläubigkeit** *die* belief *or* faith in science; **~theorie** *die* philosophy of science

wissens-, Wissens-: ~drang *der,* **~durst** *der* thirst for knowledge; **~gebiet** *das* area *or* field of knowledge; **~lücke** *die* gap in sb's knowledge; **~stand** *der* state of knowledge; **~vermittlung** *die* transmission of knowledge; **zeitgemäße ~vermittlung** the modern way to pass on knowledge; **~wert** *Adj.* **~wert sein** be worth knowing; **eine ~werte Tatsache** a fact worth knowing; **das Buch enthält viel ~wertes** the book contains a great deal of valuable and interesting information

wissentlich /ˈvɪsn̩tlɪç/

A *Adj.* deliberate

B *adv.* knowingly; deliberately

witschen /ˈvɪtʃn̩/ *itr. V.; mit sein* (ugs.) slip

wittern /ˈvɪtɐn/

A *itr. V.* sniff the air

B *tr. V.* get wind of; scent; (fig.: ahnen) sense

Witterung *die;* **~, ~en** 1 (Wetter) weather *no indef. art* 2 (Jägerspr.) (Geruchssinn) sense of smell; (Geruch) scent; **~ nehmen, die ~ aufnehmen** pick up the scent; **~ von etw. bekommen** (auch fig.) get wind of sth. 3 (Spürsinn) **eine/keine ~ für etw. haben** have a/no instinct for sth.

witterungs-, Witterungs-: ~bedingt *Adj.* caused by the weather *postpos.*; **~einfluss, *~einfluß** *der* effect of the weather; **~umschlag** *der* change in the weather; **~verhältnisse** *Pl.* weather conditions

Witwe /ˈvɪtvə/ *die;* **~, ~n** widow; **~ werden** be widowed; **grüne ~** (ugs. scherzh.) *suburban housewife left alone at home during the day while her husband is at work*

Witwen-: ~rente *die* widow's pension; **~schaft** *die;* **~~:** widowhood; **~schleier** *der* widow's veil; **~tröster** *der* (ugs. scherzh.) skirt-chaser (coll.) with a preference for widows; **~verbrennung** *die* suttee

Witwer *der;* **~s, ~:** widower; **~ werden** be widowed

Witwerschaft *die;* **~:** widowhood

Witz /vɪts/ *der;* **~es, ~e** 1 joke; **~e reißen** (ugs.) crack jokes; **das ist der [ganze] ~:** that's the whole point; **der ~ ist nämlich der, dass ...** the thing about it is that ...; **ich mache keine ~e** I'm not joking; **das soll wohl ein ~ sein** you/he *etc.* must be joking; **mach keine ~e!** come off it! (coll.) 2 (Geist, Esprit, veralt.: Klugheit) wit; **mit ~:** wittily

Witz-: ~blatt *das* humorous magazine; **~blatt·figur** *die* joke figure; **~bold** /-bɔlt/ *der;* **~~[e]s, ~~e** joker; (der jmdm. einen Streich spielt) practical joker; prankster

Witzelei *die;* **~, ~en** 1 teasing 2 (witzelnde Bemerkung) joke

witzeln /ˈvɪtsl̩n/ *itr. V.* joke (**über** + *Akk.* about)

Witz·figur *die* 1 (in Witzen) joke character 2 (ugs. abwertend) figure of fun; **du ~!** you clown!

witzig

A *Adj.* 1 (spaßig) funny; amusing 2 (ugs.: seltsam) funny; odd 3 (einfallsreich) imaginative

B *adv.; s. Adj.* **1, 2, 3** amusingly; oddly; imaginatively

Witzigkeit *die;* **~** 1 wit; **von umwerfender ~ sein** be hilariously funny 2 ▸**Witz 2**

witz·los

A *Adj.* 1 (ohne Witz) dull 2 (ugs.: sinnlos) pointless

B *adv.* (ohne Witz) unimaginatively

WM *Abk.* **= Weltmeisterschaft**

WNW *Abk.* **= Westnordwest[en]** ▸ⓘ **S. 363** WNW

wo /vo:/

A *Adv.* 1 (interrogativ) where; **~ gibts denn so was!** (ugs.) who ever heard of such a thing!; *s. auch* **ach A 5**; **hindenken** 2 (relativisch) where; (temporal) when; **überall, ~:** wherever; **~ immer er auch sein mag** wherever he may be 3 (indefinit) (ugs.) somewhere; **wenn du ihn ~ sehen solltest** if you should see him anywhere

B *Konj.* 1 (da, weil) seeing that 2 (obwohl) although; when 3 (falls) **~ möglich** if possible; **~ nicht ..., so doch ...** if not ..., then ...

wo·anders *Adv.* somewhere else; elsewhere; **sie ist mit ihren Gedanken ganz ~:** she's miles away (coll.)

wob /vo:p/ *1. u. 3. Pers. Sg. Prät. v.* **weben**

wo·bei *Adv.* 1 (interrogativ) **~ hast du sie ertappt?** what did you catch her doing?; **~ ist es kaputtgegangen?** how did it get broken? 2 (relativisch) **er gab sechs Schüsse ab, ~ einer der Täter getötet wurde** he fired six shots — one of the criminals was killed; **so viel zu den Statistiken, ~ [aber] zu beachten ist, dass ...** that concludes our remarks on the statistics, though it should be noted that ...; **sie sagte nein, ~** (indem) **sie vermied, mich anzusehen** she said 'no', avoiding looking at me as she did so; *NB The word occurs in North German coll. usage in two parts, e.g.* **wo hast du sie bei ertappt?**

Woche /ˈvɔxə/ *die;* **~, ~n** ▸ⓘ **S. 816** week; **in dieser/der nächsten/der letzten ~:** this/next/last week; **heute in/vor einer ~:** a week today/a week ago today; **zweimal die** *od.* **in der ~:** twice a week

> **Die Woche**
>
> A relatively new weekly newspaper which was founded in 1993 and is published in Hamburg. It is less comprehensive and easier to read than **Die Zeit**, but is also an important opinion leader with a liberal outlook offering background information, analyses, and reports.

Wochen-: ~bett *das:* **im ~bett liegen** be lying in; **im ~bett sterben** die soon after childbirth; **~blatt** *das* weekly

Wochenend-: ~arbeit *die* weekend work; **~ausflug** *der* weekend trip; **~ausgabe** *die* weekend edition; **~beilage** *die* weekend supplement

Wochen·ende *das* weekend; **schönes ~!** have a nice weekend!

Wochenend-: ~haus *das* weekend house; **~seminar** *das* weekend seminar; **~ticket** *das* weekend ticket; **~trip** *der* weekend trip

wochen-, Wochen-: ~fluss, *~fluß *der* (Med.) lochia; **~karte** *die* weekly season ticket; **~lang** **A** *Adj.* lasting weeks *postpos.*; **B** *adv.* for weeks [on end]; **~lohn** *der* weekly wages *pl.*; **~markt** *der* weekly market; **~schau** *die* (bes. früher) weekly newsreel; **~schrift** *die* weekly; **~stunde** *die* (Schulw.) period per week; **~tag** *der* ▸ⓘ **S. 816** weekday (*including Saturday*); **welcher ~tag ist heute?** what day of the week is it?; **~tags** *Adv.* on weekdays [and Saturdays]

wöchentlich /ˈvœçn̩tlɪç/

A *Adj.* weekly

B *adv.* weekly; **es werden ~ ca. 50 Briefe beantwortet** some fifty letters are answered every week; **~ einmal** once a week; **wir treffen uns ~:** we meet once a week

-wöchentlich

A *Adj.* -weekly

B *adv.* every ... weeks; *s. auch* **achtwöchentlich**

wochen·weise *Adv.* for a week at a time

Wochen·zeitung *die* weekly newspaper

-wöchig /-vœçɪç/ 1 (... Wochen alt) ... -week-old; **ein achtwöchiges Kind** an eight-week-old baby 2 (... Wochen dauernd) ... week's/weeks'; ... -week; **eine vierwöchige Kur** a four-week course of treatment; **mit dreiwöchiger Verspätung** three weeks late

W

ℹ Wochentage

Deutsch	Englisch	Abkürzung
Sonntag	Sunday	Sun
Montag	Monday	Mon
Dienstag	Tuesday	Tues
Mittwoch	Wednesday	Wed
Donnerstag	Thursday	Thurs
Freitag	Friday	Fri
Samstag	Saturday	Sat

Es ist zu beachten, dass im englischsprachigen Raum die Woche am Sonntag beginnt und am Samstag endet.

Wann?

Wie beim Datum wird *am* + Wochentag mit **on** übersetzt (ohne **the**). Dieses **on** kann nicht ausgelassen werden.

Ich fahre [am] Mittwoch nach Kairo
= I am going to Cairo on Wednesday

Selbstverständlich wird aber, wenn es sich um einen bestimmten, näher beschriebenen Tag handelt, ein Artikel eingesetzt.

am letzten Sonntag vor Pfingsten
= on the last Sunday before Whitsun

Es geschah an einem verregneten Montag
= It happened on a wet Monday

Aber:

Eines [schönen] Samstags trafen wir uns im Zoo
= One [fine] Saturday we met at the zoo

Wiederholtes

Hier fällt das **on** vor **every, most** und **some** weg. Vor der Pluralform (**Mondays, Fridays** usw.) fehlt das **on** im amerikanischen Englisch, wird aber im britischen Englisch meist nicht weggelassen.

Ich fahre freitags/jeden Freitag nach Hause
= I go home [on] Fridays/every Friday

jeden zweiten Donnerstag
= every other Thursday

jeden dritten Montag
= every third Monday

fast jeden Samstag
= almost every Saturday, most Saturdays

manchmal am Mittwoch
= sometimes on a Wednesday, some Wednesdays

ab und zu am Freitag
= occasionally on a Friday, on the occasional *od.* odd Friday

Vergangenes und Künftiges

letzten Donnerstag
= last Thursday

am vorangehenden Donnerstag
= [on] the preceding Thursday

vorletzten Donnerstag
= [on] the Thursday before last

Donnerstag vor einer Woche
= a week ago on Thursday

Ich werde sie [am] nächsten od. kommenden Montag sehen
= I will see her next Monday *od.* this [coming] Monday

Ich habe sie am [darauf] folgenden Montag gesehen
= I saw her the following *od.* the next Monday

übernächsten Montag
= the Monday after next

Montag in einer Woche
= a week on Monday

ab Samstag
= from Saturday [on]

Es muss bis Freitag fertig sein
= It must be ready by Friday

Tageszeiten

[am] Montagmorgen, Montag früh
= on Monday morning

[am] Dienstagmittag
= midday on Tuesday

[am] Mittwochnachmittag
= on Wednesday afternoon

[am] Donnerstagabend
= on Thursday evening; (*am späten Abend*) on Thursday night

Freitagnacht
= on Friday night

Und wenn es regelmäßig geschieht:

montagmorgens
= on Monday mornings

dienstagmittags
= midday on Tuesdays

mittwochnachmittags
= on Wednesday afternoons

donnerstagabends
= on Thursday evenings; (*am späten Abend*) on Thursday nights

freitagnachts
= on Friday nights

Heute

Welchen Tag haben wir heute?
= What day is it today?

Heute ist Dienstag
= It's Tuesday [today]

Adjektive und Zusammensetzungen

Im Englischen gibt es keine Adjektive, die dem deutschen *sonntäglich, sonntägig* usw. entsprächen. Man verwendet das Substantiv, mit oder ohne **'s:**

sein sonntäglicher Spaziergang
= his [regular] Sunday walk

ein sonntägiger Spaziergang
= a Sunday walk, a walk on a Sunday

ein Sonntagsfahrer
= a Sunday driver

die Sonntagszeitungen
= the Sunday papers

Vergleich aber:

die Zeitung von Dienstag
= Tuesday's paper

Ferner:

die Züge am Montag
= Monday's trains

die Schulstunden am Mittwoch
= Wednesday's lessons

Wöchnerin /ˈvœçnərɪn/ *die;* **~, ~nen** woman who has just given birth; puerpera (Med.)

Wöchnerinnen·station *die* maternity ward

Wodka /ˈvɔtka/ *der;* **~s, ~s** vodka

wo·durch *Adv.* **1** (interrogativ) how; **~ unterscheidet sie sich von den anderen?** in what way is she different from the others? **2** (relativisch) as a result of which; **alles, ~ er sich verletzt fühlen könnte** anything that might offend him; *s. auch* **wobei** *NB*

wo·fern *Konj.* (veralt.) provided that

wo·für *Adv.* **1** (interrogativ) for what; **~ brauchst du es?** what do you need it for?; **~ hältst du mich?** what do you take me for?; **~ interessierst du dich?** what are you interested in? **2** (relativisch) for which; **er ist nicht das, ~ er sich ausgibt** he's not what he claims to be; *s. auch* **wobei** *NB*

wog /voːk/ *1. u. 3. Pers. Sg. Prät. v.* **wiegen**

Woge /ˈvoːgə/ *die;* **~, ~n** (auch fig.) wave; **die ~n glätten** (fig.) pour oil on troubled waters

wo·gegen
A *Adv.* **1** (interrogativ) against what; what ... against; **~ ist sie allergisch?** what is she allergic to? **2** (relativisch) against which; which ... against; **..., ~ nichts einzuwenden ist** to which there is no objection; *s. auch* **wobei** *NB*
B *Konj.* whereas

wogen /ˈvoːgn̩/ *itr. V.* (geh.) ‹sea› surge; (fig.) ‹corn› wave; ‹crowd› surge; ‹battle› rage; **mit ~dem Busen** (fig.) with heaving bosom

wo·her *Adv.* **1** (interrogativ) where ... from; **~ weißt du das?** how do you know that?; **~ kennst du ihn?** where do you know him from?; **[ach] ~ denn!, ach ~!** (ugs.) good heavens, no!; not at all!; **~ bist du so braun?** how did you get so brown? **2** (relativisch) where ... from; *s. auch* **wobei** *NB*

wohin *Adv.* **1** (interrogativ) where [... to]; **~ damit?** (ugs.) where shall I put it/them?; **~ so spät/eilig?** where are you/is he *etc.* going so late/in such a hurry? **2** (relativisch) where; **er ging ins Zimmer, ~ ihm die anderen folgten** he went into the room, and the others followed him in **3** (indefinit) **ich muss mal ~** (ugs. verhüll.) I've got to pay a visit *or* a call (euphem.); *s. auch* **wobei** *NB*

wo·hinein *Adv.* ▸ **worein**

wo·hingegen *Konj.* whereas

wo·hinter *Adv.* **1** (interrogativ) behind what; what ... behind; **~ habt ihr euch versteckt?** what did you hide behind? **2** (relativisch) behind which; *s. auch* **wobei** *NB*

wohl /voːl/
A *Adv.* **1** (gesund) well; **jmdm. ist nicht ~, jmd. fühlt sich nicht ~:** sb. does not feel well **2** (behaglich) at ease; happy; **es sich ~ sein lassen** spoil oneself; **mir ist nicht recht ~ bei der Sache** the whole thing makes me a bit uneasy; **lass es dir ~ ergehen!** enjoy yourself!; **leb ~!/leben Sie ~!** farewell!; **~ oder übel** whether I/you *etc.* want to or not **3** (durchaus) well; **ich bin mir dessen ~ bewusst** I'm quite *or* perfectly conscious of that **4** (ungefähr) about; **~ 100 Gäste** 100 or so guests; about 100 guests **5** (veralt.: gewiss) **sehr ~[, der** *od.* **mein Herr]** certainly [, sir]; very good [, sir] **6** (geh.: gut) well; **er tat es, ~ wissend, dass ...** he did it knowing full well that ...; **~ ausgewogen** well-balanced; **~ bedacht** well-considered; [carefully] considered ‹reply, judgement›; well *or* carefully thought-out ‹plan›; **~ bedacht vorgehen** proceed in a carefully considered way *or* with careful consideration; **~ begründet** well-founded; (berechtigt) well-justified; **~ bekannt** well-known; **~ beraten** well-advised; **~ beleibt** corpulent; **~ dosiert** carefully measured; **~ durchdacht** carefully thought-out; **~**

geordnet well-ordered; **~ überlegt** well-considered; carefully considered ‹*decision*›; **~ versehen** well-provided (**mit** with); **~ verwahrt** safely stored; (unter Verschluss) safely locked away; **~ temperiert** ‹*room*› at a pleasant temperature; ‹*wine*› at the correct temperature; **das ~ temperierte Klavier** the Well-Tempered Clavier **7** (jedoch) **..., ~ aber ...** but ...; however ...; **hier gibt es keine Ratten, ~ aber Mäuse** there are no rats here, but there are mice **8** (geh.) **~ dem, der ...!** happy the man who ...; **~ dir, dass du das nicht machen musst** count yourself lucky not to have to do that; **jmdm. ~ tun** show sb. kindness; **es tut ihm ~:** it does him good; **jmdm. ~ wollen** wish sb. well **9** (zwar) **~ versprach ich hinzugehen, aber ...** I may have promised to go, but ...

B *Partikel* **1** (vermutlich) probably; **er wird ~ bald kommen** I imagine he'll come soon; **~ kaum** hardly; **du bist ~ nicht recht bei Verstand?** have you taken leave of your senses?; **dir ist ~ schlecht?** aren't you feeling well?; **was/warum/wie ~?** but what/why/how?; **na** *od.* **ja, was/warum/wie ~?** need you ask what/why/how?; **das mag ~ sein** that may well be; **es wird ~ gleich Schluss sein** I imagine it's nearly over; **das wird ~ so sein** that's probably the case; **ich habe ~ nicht recht gehört** I don't think I could have heard right **2** (verstärkend) **wirst du ~ herkommen!** will you come here!; **siehst du ~!** there, you see!; **man wird doch ~ fragen dürfen** there's nothing wrong in asking, is there?

Wohl *das;* **~[e]s** welfare; well-being; **das allgemeine/öffentliche ~:** the public good; **zu jmds. ~:** for sb.'s benefit *or* good; **auf jmds. ~ trinken** drink sb.'s health; **[auf] dein ~!** your health!; **zum ~!** cheers!; **das ~ und Weh[e]** (geh.) the weal and woe

wohl-, Wohl-: ~an /-ˈ-/ *Interj.* (veralt.) [well,] come now; **~anständig** (veralt.) **A** *Adj.* respectable; proper ‹*behaviour*›; **B** *adv.* respectably; ‹*behave*› properly; **~auf** /-ˈ-/ *Adj.* (geh.) **~auf sein** be well *or* in good health; **~ausgewogen, ~bedacht** ▸**wohl A 6**; **~befinden** *das* well-being; **~begründet** ▸**wohl A 6**; **~behagen** *das* sense of well-being; **mit ~behagen** with a sense of well-being; **etw. mit ~behagen essen** eat sth. with relish; **~behalten** *Adj.* safe and well ‹*person*›; undamaged ‹*thing*›; ***~bekannt, ~beleibt, ~beraten** ▸**wohl A 6**; **~bestallt** *Adj.* (geh.) well-established; **~dosiert** ▸**wohl A 6**; **~durchdacht** ▸**wohl A 6**; **~ergehen** *das* ▸**~befinden**; **~erzogen** *Adj.* well brought-up; **~erzogenheit** *die;* **~~** (geh.) good upbringing; (gute Manieren) good manners *pl.*; **~fahrt** *die* **1** (geh.: **~ergehen**) welfare; **2** (öffentliche Fürsorge) **von der ~fahrt betreut werden** be looked after by the welfare services; **von der ~fahrt leben** (ugs.) live on welfare

Wohlfahrts-: ~marke *die* (Postw.) charity stamp; **~pflege** *die* social welfare *no art.*; **~staat** *der* welfare state

wohl-, Wohl-: ~feil A *Adj.* **1** (preiswert) inexpensive; **2** (geistlos, platt) trite; **B** *adv.* cheaply; **etw. ~feil verkaufen/erstehen** sell/buy sth. cheap; **~geboren** *Adj.* (veralt.) **Euer ~geboren** Your Honour; **Seiner ~geboren** to His Honour; **~gefallen** *das* pleasure; **sein ~gefallen an jmdm. haben** have a great liking for sb.; **an etw.** (*Dat.*) **~gefallen finden** take pleasure in sth.; **sich in ~gefallen auflösen** (scherzh.) (ein gutes Ende finden) end well; ‹*difficulties, misunderstandings*› be cleared up; (entzweigehen, auseinander fallen) ‹*clothes, book, etc.*› fall apart; (verschwinden) vanish into thin air; **~gefällig A** *Adj.* **1** (**~gefallen** ausdrückend) ‹*smile, look*› of pleasure; **2** (veralt.: angenehm) pleasing; agreeable; **B** *adv.* **1** (mit **~gefallen**) with pleasure; **2** (veralt.: angenehm) **die Speisen ~gefällig darreichen** serve the food in a way that is pleasing *or* agreeable to the eye; **~geformt** *Adj.* well-formed; **~gefühl** *das* sense of well-being; **~gelitten** *Adj.* (geh.) well-liked; **~gemerkt** *Adv.* please note; mark you; **~gemut** /-gəmu:t/ (geh.) **A** *Adj.* cheerful; **B** *adv.* cheerfully; **~genährt** *Adj.* (meist spött.) well-fed; **~geordnet** ▸**wohl A 6**; **~geraten** *Adj.* (geh.) fine *attrib.* ‹*child*›; successful ‹*piece of work, translation, etc.*›; **ihre Kinder sind ~geraten** their children have turned out well; **~geruch** *der* (geh.) pleasant *or* agreeable aroma; (von Blumen) agreeable fragrance; **alle ~gerüche Arabiens** (scherzh. od. iron.) all the perfumes of Arabia; **~gesetzt** *Adj.* (geh.) well-turned ‹*compliment*›; well-chosen ‹*words*›; well-worded ‹*speech*›; **~gesinnt** *Adj.* well-disposed; **jmdm./einer Sache ~gesinnt sein** be well-disposed towards sb./sth.; **der Wettergott war uns nicht ~gesinnt** the weather was unkind to us; **~gestalt** (veralt.), **~gestaltet** *Adj.* (geh.) well-shaped; well-proportioned ‹*body*›; **~getan A** *2. Part. v.* **~tun; B** *Adj. in* **~getan sein** (veralt.) be well done; **~habend** *Adj.* prosperous; **~habenheit** *die;* **~~:** prosperity

wohlig

A *Adj.* pleasant; agreeable; (gemütlich) cosy

B *adv.* ‹*sigh, purr, etc.*› with pleasure; ‹*stretch oneself*› luxuriously

wohl-, Wohl-: ~klang *der* (geh.) melodious *or* pleasing sound; **~klingend** *Adj.* (geh.) melodious; **~laut** *der* (geh.) ▸**~klang**; **~leben** *das* (geh.) good living; **~meinend** *Adj.* (geh.) well-meaning; **~proportioniert** *Adj.* (geh.) well-proportioned; **~riechend** *Adj.* (geh.) fragrant; **~schmeckend** *Adj.* (geh.) delicious; **~sein** *das:* **[zum] ~sein!** your health!; **~stand** *der* prosperity; **zu ~stand gelangen** achieve a degree of prosperity; **bei dir ist wohl der ~stand ausgebrochen!** (scherzh.) have you won the pools *or* something?

Wohlstands-: ~gesellschaft *die* (abwertend) affluent society; **~kriminalität** *die* (Rechtsspr.) crime characteristic of the affluent society; **~müll** *der* (abwertend) refuse produced by the affluent society

wohl-, Wohl-: ~tat *die* **1** (gute Tat) good deed; (Gefallen) favour; **jmdm. eine ~tat erweisen** do sb. a good turn; **auf die ~taten anderer angewiesen sein** be dependent on the kindness of others; **2** (Genuss) blissful relief; **~täter** *der* benefactor; **~täterin** *die* benefactress; **~tätig** *Adj.* charitable; **~tätigkeit** *die* charity; charitableness

Wohltätigkeits-: ~basar *der* charity bazaar; **~konzert** *das* charity concert; **~veranstaltung** *die* charity event

wohl-, Wohl-: ~temperiert ▸**wohl A 6**; **~tuend A** *Adj.* agreeable; **eine ~tuende Wirkung haben** have a beneficial effect; **B** *adv.* agreeably; **~|tun, *~überlegt** ▸**wohl A 6**; **~verdient** *Adj.* well-earned, well-deserved ‹*reward, honour, success, etc.*›; well-deserved ‹*punishment, fate*›; **~verhalten** *das* good behaviour *no indef. art.*; **~versehen** ▸**wohl A6**; **~verstanden** *Adv.* (geh.) ▸**~gemerkt**; **~verwahrt** ▸**wohl A 6**; **~weislich** /-vaislɪç/ *Adv.* deliberately; ***~|wollen** ▸**wohl A 6**; **~wollen** *das;* **~~s** goodwill; **jmdn. mit ~wollen betrachten** regard sb. benevolently; **~wollend A** *Adj.* benevolent; favourable ‹*judgement, opinion*›; **B** *adv.* benevolently; ‹*judge, consider*› favourably

Wohn-: ~anhänger *der* caravan; trailer (Amer.); **~anlage** *die* residential estate; **~bau** *der; Pl.* **~~ten** residential building; **~bereich** *der* living rooms *pl.*; (eines Zimmers) living area; **~bezirk** *der* **1** residential district; **2** (DDR) district; **~block** *der; Pl.* **~~s,** *od.* **~blöcke** residential block; **~container** *der* Portakabin®[-style home]

wohnen *itr. V.* live; (kurzfristig) stay; (fig. dichter.) dwell; **sie ~ sehr hübsch** they have a lovely home; (der Lage nach) they live in a lovely spot; **ich wohne in der Leibnizstraße 7** I live/am staying at [number] 7 Leibnizstrasse; **wo ~ Sie?** where do you live/where are you staying?

wohn-, Wohn-: ~fläche *die* living space; **eine Wohnung mit 50 m² ~fläche** a flat (esp. Brit.) *or* (esp. Amer.) apartment with 50 sq.m. floor area; **~gebäude** *das* residential building; **~gebiet** *das,* **~gegend** *die* residential area; **~geld** *das* housing benefit; **~gemeinschaft** *die* group sharing a flat (esp. Brit.) *or* (esp. Amer.) apartment/house; **unsere ~gemeinschaft** the group who share our flat (esp. Brit.) *or* (esp. Amer.) apartment/house; **in einer ~gemeinschaft leben** live in a shared flat (esp. Brit.) *or* (esp. Amer.) apartment/house; share a flat (esp. Brit.) *or* (esp. Amer.) apartment/house; **in diesem Haus wohnt eine studentische ~gemeinschaft/wohnen nur ~gemeinschaften** a group of students is sharing this house/the flats (esp. Brit.) *or* (esp. Amer.) apartments in this house are all shared; **~haft** *Adj.* resident (**in** + *Dat.* in); **~haus** *das* [dwelling] house; **~heim** *das* (für Alte, Behinderte) home; (für Obdachlose, Lehrlinge) hostel; (für Studenten) hall of residence; **~komplex** *der* residential complex; **~küche** *die* combined kitchen and living room; **~kultur** *die* style of home furnishing; **~lage** *die:* **unsere ~lage ist optimal** our house/flat (esp. Brit.) *or* (esp. Amer.) apartment is ideally situated; **in ruhiger/guter ~lage** in a quiet/good area; **~landschaft** *die* (bes. Werbesprache): *arrangement of furniture etc. to give an impressive 'landscape' effect*

wohnlich

A *Adj.* homely

B *adv.* **~ eingerichtet** furnished in a homely way

Wohnlichkeit *die;* **~:** homeliness

Wohn-: ~mobil *das;* **~~s, ~~e** motor home; motor caravan; **~ort** *der* place of residence; **~park** *der* landscaped residential estate; **~raum** *der* **1** living room; **2** (**~**fläche) living space; **~raum·mangel** *der* housing shortage; **~siedlung** *die* residential estate; (mit gleichartigen Häusern) housing estate; **~silo** *der od. das* (abwertend) [anonymous] tower block *or* high-rise block; **~sitz** *der* place of residence; domicile (formal); **seinen ~sitz in Hamburg haben** live *or* (formal) be domiciled in Hamburg; **ohne festen ~sitz** of no fixed abode; **ohne festen ~sitz sein** have no fixed abode; **~sitzlose** *der/die; adj. Dekl.* homeless person; **~stube** *die* (landsch.) living room

Wohnung *die;* **~, ~en 1** flat (esp. Brit.); apartment (esp. Amer.); (Wohneinheit); home; dwelling (formal) **2** (Unterkunft) lodging; **freie ~ haben** have free lodging; **~ nehmen** (veralt.) take up residence

Wohnungs-: ~amt *das* housing department; **~bau** *der* housing construction; **der soziale ~bau** (Amtsspr.) public-sector house-building; **~einrichtung** *die* home furnishings [and equipment]; **~inhaber** *der,* **~inhaberin** *die* occupant (*of a dwelling*); **~mangel** *der* housing shortage; **~markt** *der* housing market; **~miete** *die* rent; **~not** *die* housing crisis; serious housing shortage; **~schlüssel** *der* key to the flat (esp. Brit.) *or* (esp. Amer.) apartment; **~suche** *die* search for a flat (esp. Brit.) *or* (esp. Amer.) apartment; **auf ~suche sein** be flat-hunting; **~suchende** *der/die; adj. Dekl.* person looking for a flat (esp. Brit.) *or* (esp. Amer.) apartment; **~tausch** *der* flat-swap (coll.); exchange of flats (esp. Brit.) *or* (esp. Amer.) apartments; **~tür** *die* door of the flat (esp. Brit.) *or* (esp. Amer.) apartment

Wohnung-: ~suche ▸**Wohnungssuche**; **~suchende** ▸**Wohnungssuchende**

Wohnungs·wechsel *der* move to a new flat (esp. Brit.) *or* (esp. Amer.) apartment

Wohn-: ~verhältnisse *Pl.* living conditions; **~viertel** *das* residential district; **~wagen** *der* caravan; trailer (Amer.); **~zimmer** *das* **1** living room; **2** (Einrichtung) set of living room furniture

wölben /ˈvœlbn̩/

A *tr. V.* curve; arch ‹*brows, shoulders*›; cup ‹*hand*›; bend ‹*metal*›; vault, arch ‹*roof, ceiling*›; **eine gewölbte Decke** a vaulted ceiling; **die Brust ~:** swell out one's chest

B *refl. V.* curve; ‹*sky, bridge, ceiling*› arch; ‹*chest*› swell; ‹*stomach, muscles*› bulge; ‹*metal*› bend; **eine gewölbte Stirn** a domed forehead

Wölbung *die;* ~, ~**en** curve; (einer Decke, des Himmels) arch; vault; (von Augenbrauen) arch; (eines Bauches, Muskels) bulge

Wolf /vɔlf/ *der;* ~**[e]s, Wölfe** /ˈvœlfə/ **1** wolf; **ein ~ im Schafspelz sein** (fig.) be a wolf in sheep's clothing; **mit den Wölfen heulen** (fig. ugs.) run with the pack; **unter die Wölfe geraten** (fig.) be ruthlessly exploited **2** (ugs.: Fleisch~) mincer; **jmdn. durch den ~ drehen** (fig. salopp) put sb. through the mill **3** (volkst.: Wundsein) intertrigo *no art. (Med.); soreness caused by the rubbing of areas of the skin against each other;* **sich** *(Dat.)* **einen ~ laufen** make oneself sore between the legs through walking too much

Wölfin /ˈvœlfɪn/ *die;* ~, ~**nen** [wolf] bitch

wölfisch *Adj.* wolfish; ravenous ‹*hunger*›

Wölfling /ˈvœlflɪŋ/ *der;* ~**s,** ~**e** Cub

Wolfram /ˈvɔlfram/ *das;* ~**s** (Chemie) tungsten

Wolfs-: ~**hund** *der* (volkst.) Alsatian [dog]; **Irischer ~hund** Irish wolfhound; ~**hunger** *der* (ugs.) ravenous hunger; **ich habe einen ~hunger!** I'm ravenous!; ~**kind** *das* (Myth.) wolf child; ~**milch** *die* (Bot.) spurge; ~**rachen** *der* (volkst.) cleft palate; ~**spinne** *die* wolf spider

Wolfsmilch·gewächs *das* euphorbia

Wolga /ˈvɔlga/ *die;* ~ ▸ⓘ **S. 267** Volga

Wölkchen /ˈvœlkçən/ *das;* ~**s,** ~: small cloud

Wolke /ˈvɔlkə/ *die;* ~, ~**n** (auch Mineral.) cloud; **'ne ~ sein** (berlin. salopp) be fantastic (coll.); **auf ~n** *od.* **in den ~n schweben** (fig.) have one's head in the clouds; **aus allen ~n fallen** (fig. ugs.) be completely stunned; **eine ~ von Tüll** billows of tulle

wolken-, Wolken-: ~**bank** *die; Pl.* ~**bänke** bank of cloud; ~**bildung** *die* formation of cloud; **es wird zu stärkerer ~bildung kommen** it will become very cloudy *or* overcast; ~**bruch** *der* cloudburst; ~**bruch·artig** *Adj.* torrential; ~**decke** *die* [unbroken] cloud *no indef. art.;* **die ~decke riss auf** the clouds broke; ~**feld** *das* (Met.) cloud field; ~**fetzen** *der* wisp of cloud; ~**kratzer** *der* skyscraper; ~**kuckucks·heim** *das* cloud cuckoo land; **im ~kuckucksheim** in cloud cuckoo land; ~**los** *Adj.* cloudless; ~**schleier** *der* veil of cloud; ~**verhangen** *Adj.* overcast; ~**wand** *die* wall of cloud

wolkig *Adj.* **1** (auch Fot., Chemie, Mineral.) cloudy **2** (unklar, verschwommen) vague; vague, hazy ‹*idea, concept*›

Woll·decke *die* [woollen] blanket

Wolle /ˈvɔlə/ *die;* ~, ~**n** **1** wool; (fig.: Haar) hair; **in der ~ gefärbt** dyed-in-the-wool; **sich in die ~ kriegen** (fig. ugs.) quarrel (**wegen** over); **sich in der ~ haben** *od.* **liegen** (fig. ugs.) be at loggerheads **2** (Jägerspr.) hair; (von Hasen, Kaninchen) fur

wollen[1] *Adj.* woollen

wollen[2]

A *unr. Modalverb; 2. Part.* ~ **1 etw. tun ~** (den Wunsch haben, etw. zu tun) want to do sth.; (die Absicht haben, etw. zu tun) be going to do sth.; **wir wollten gerade gehen** we were just about to go; **das Buch habe ich immer lesen ~:** I've always wanted to read that book; **ich will lieber zu Hause bleiben** I'd rather stay at home; **was will man da machen?** (ugs.) what can you do?; **ohne es zu ~:** without intending to; **ich wollte Sie fragen, ob ...** I wanted to ask you if ...; **wenn Sie bitte Platz nehmen ~:** would you like to take a seat/take your seats?; **~ Sie mich entschuldigen?** would you excuse me?; **wenn ich mich darum auch noch kümmern wollte, ...** if I were to see to that as well, then ...; **na gut, ich will [mal] nicht so sein** (ugs.) all right, I don't want to be awkward; **dann will ich nichts gesagt haben** (ugs.) I take it all back; **das will ich meinen!** (ugs.) I absolutely agree; **wir ~ sehen** we'll see
2 (in Aufforderungen) **man wolle bitte darauf achten, dass ...** please note that ...; **wollt ihr Ruhe geben/damit aufhören!** (ugs.) will you be quiet/stop that!; **~ Sie bitte so freundlich sein und das heute noch erledigen** would you be so kind as to do it today
3 (in Bezug auf bezweifelte Behauptungen) **er will ein Dichter sein** he claims to be a poet; **sie will es [nicht] gesehen haben** she claims [not] to have seen it
4 (sich in der gewünschten Weise verhalten) **die Wunde will nicht heilen** the wound [just] won't heal; **der Motor wollte nicht anspringen** the engine wouldn't start; **es will nicht gelingen** it just won't work; **es will mir nicht einleuchten, dass ...** I can't really see that ...
5 (müssen) **etw. will getan sein** sth. needs *or* (coll.) has got to be done; **das will gelernt sein** it has to be learned
6 (einen bestimmten Zweck, eine bestimmte Funktion haben) be intended to; **die Aktion will die Leute über ... aufklären** the purpose of the campaign is to inform people about ...
7 das will nichts heißen/nicht viel sagen that doesn't mean anything/much

B *unr. itr. V.* **1 du musst nur ~, dann geht es auch** you only have to want to enough *or* have the will, then it's possible; **ob du willst oder nicht** whether you want to or not; **ganz wie du willst** just as you like; **wenn du willst, könnten wir ...** if you want [to], we could ...; **du kannst es halten, wie du willst** you can do just as you like; **das ist, wenn man so will, ...** that is, if you like, ...; **[na] dann ~ wir mal!** (ugs.) [right,] let's get started!
2 (ugs.: irgendwohin zu gehen wünschen) **ich will nach Hause/ans Meer** I want to go home/to go to the seaside; **ich will hier raus** I want to get out of here; **zu wem ~ Sie?** whom do you want to see?; **er wollte zum Theater** he wanted to become an actor
3 *verneint* (ugs.: funktionieren) **der Motor will nicht** the engine won't go; **seine Beine/Gelenke/Augen ~ nicht mehr** his legs/joints/eyes just aren't up to it any more

C *unr. tr. V.* **1** want; **das wollte ich nicht** I didn't mean to do that; **das habe ich nicht gewollt** I never meant that to happen; **~, dass jmd. etw. tut** want sb. to do sth.; **er will nicht, dass du ihm hilfst** he doesn't want you to help him; **er wollte nur euer Bestes** he only wanted what's best for you; **er will es nicht anders** he wouldn't have it any other way; **da ist nichts [mehr] zu ~** (ugs.) there's nothing we/you *etc.* can do about it; **was du nicht willst, dass man dir tu, das füg auch keinem anderen zu** (Spr.) do as you would be done by (prov.); **ich wollte, er wäre hier/es wäre vorbei** I wish he were here/it were over
2 (ugs.: zum Gedeihen brauchen) need
3 (ugs.: schaden) **jmdm. nichts ~ können** be unable to harm sb.; **was kann sie mir schon ~?** what can she do to me?

Woll·gras *das* cotton grass

wollig *Adj.* woolly

Woll-: ~**jacke** *die* woollen cardigan; ~**kleid** *das* woollen dress; ~**knäuel** *das* ball of wool; ~**mütze** *die* woollen cap; ~**pullover** *der* woollen pullover *or* sweater; ~**sachen** *Pl.* woollen things; woollies (coll.); ~**socke** *die* woollen sock; ~**stoff** *der* woollen cloth; ~**strumpf** *der* woollen stocking; (Kniestrumpf) woollen sock

Wollust /ˈvɔlʊst/ *die;* ~, **Wollüste** /ˈvɔlʏstə/ (geh.) lust; (Sinnlichkeit) sensuality; (großes Vergnügen) delight; **etw. mit wahrer ~ tun** take great delight in doing sth.

wollüstig /ˈvɔlʏstɪç/ (geh.)
A *Adj.* lustful; (sinnlich) sensual
B *Adj.* lustfully; (sinnlich) sensually

wo·mit *Adv.* **1** (interrogativ) **~ schreibst du?** what do you write with?; (more formal) with what do you write?; **~ habe ich das verdient?** what have I done to deserve that? **2** (relativisch) **~ du schreibst** which *or* that you write with; (more formal) with which you write; **~ ich nicht sagen will, dass ...** by which I don't mean to say that ...; **~ er nicht gerechnet hatte, war ...** what he had not reckoned with was ...; **~ du es auch machst, ...** whatever you do it with ...; *s. auch* **wobei** *NB*

wo·möglich *Adv.* possibly

wo·nach *Adv.* **1** (interrogativ) after what; what ... after; **~ suchst du?** what are you looking for?; **~ riecht es?** what does it smell of?; **~ richtet ihr euch?** what do you go by?; **~ verlangte er?** what did he ask for? **2** (relativisch) after which; which ... after; **alles, ~ er verlangte** all he asked for; **etwas, ~ sie sich sehnte** something she longed for; **eine Vorschrift, ~ ...** a regulation according to which ...; *s. auch* **wobei** *NB*

Wonderbra /ˈwandəbra:/ *der;* ~**[s],** ~**s** Wonderbra ®

Wonne /ˈvɔnə/ *die;* ~, ~**n** (geh.) bliss *no pl.;* ecstasy; (etw., was Freude macht) joy; delight; **es war eine ~, ihr zuzuhören** she was a joy *or* delight to listen to; **das Kind ist ihre ganze ~:** the child is her great joy; **es ist eine wahre ~:** it's sheer delight; **Würdest du helfen? — Aber mit ~!** (scherzh.) Would you help? — Of course, I'd be delighted!

Wonne-: ~**monat** (geh.), ~**mond** (veralt.) *der* May *no art.;* **im ~monat [Mai]** in the merry month of May; ~**proppen** *der* (ugs. scherzh.) chubby cherub

wonnig *Adj.* sweet

woran /voˈran/ *Adv.* **1** (interrogativ) **~ hast du dich verletzt?** what did you hurt yourself on?; **~ hat sie sich gelehnt?** what did she lean against?; **man weiß nicht, ~ man ist** you don't know where you are; **~ ist sie gestorben?** what did she die of?; **~ denkst du?** what are you thinking of? **2** (relativisch) **nichts, ~ man sich verletzen/lehnen könnte** nothing one could hurst oneself on/one could lean against; **alles, ~ er sich erinnern konnte** everything he could remember

worauf /voˈrauf/ **1** (interrogativ) **~ sitzt er?** what is he sitting on?; **~ wartest du?** what are you waiting for?; **~ will er hinaus?** what is he getting at? **2** (relativisch) **es gab nichts, ~ er sich hätte setzen können** there was nothing for him to sit on; **etwas, ~ ich schreiben kann** something to write on; **etwas, ~ man sich verlassen kann** something one can rely on; **etwas, ~ ich Sie hinweisen sollte, ist ...** something I ought to point out to you is ...; **das Einzige, ~ es jetzt ankommt** the only thing that matters now; **es gab nichts, ~ er sich hätte freuen können** there was nothing for him to look forward to **3** (relativisch: ~hin) whereupon

worauf·hin *Adv.* **1** (interrogativ) **~ hat er das getan?** what made him do it?; what was the cause of his doing it? **2** (relativisch) whereupon

woraus /voˈraus/ *Adv.* **1** (interrogativ) **~ ist das Zitat?** where is the quotation from?; **~ trinken wir den Wein?** what shall we drink the wine from?; **~ ist das Gewebe?** what is the fabric made of?; **~ schließt du das?** what do you infer that from? **2** (relativisch) **es gab nichts, ~ wir den Wein hätten trinken können** there was nothing for us to drink the wine out of; **es gab nichts, ~ sie Werkzeuge machen konnten** there was nothing for them to make tools from; **..., ~ ich schließe, dass ...** ... from which I conclude that ...

worden /ˈvɔrdn̩/ *2. Part. v.* **werden B**

worein /voˈrain/ *Adv.* **1** (interrogativ) in what; what ... in **2** (relativisch) in which; which ... in; **..., ~ sie sich schickte** ..., to which she resigned herself; ..., which she resigned herself to

worin /voˈrɪn/ *Adv.* **1** (interrogativ) in what; what ... in; **~ willst du es verschicken?** what do you want to send it in?; **ich weiß nicht, ~ der Unterschied liegt** I don't know what the difference is **2** (relativisch) in which; which ... in; **..., ~ ich mit dir übereinstimme** ..., which I agree with you on

Workaholic /wəːkəˈhɔlɪk/ *der;* ~**s,** ~**s** workaholic

Workflow /ˈwəːkfloʊ/ *der od. das;* ~**s,** ~**s** workflow

Work·shop /ˈwəːkʃɔp/ *der;* ~**s,** ~**s** workshop

World·cup /ˈwəːldkap/ *der* (Sport) World Cup

Wort /vɔrt/ *das;* **∼[e]s, Wörter** /ˈvœrtɐ/ *od.* **∼e** 1 *Pl.* **Wörter,** *auch:* **∼e** word; **∼ für ∼:** word for word; € **1 000 (in ∼en: tausend)** € 1,000 (in words: one thousand); **in des ∼es wahrster Bedeutung, im wahrsten Sinne des ∼es** in the truest sense of the word; **Liebe ist ein großes ∼:** love is a big word; **das treffende** *od.* **passende ∼:** the right word
2 *Pl.* **∼e** (Äußerung) word; **zwischen uns ist kein böses ∼ gefallen** not a harsh word has passed between us; **das ist das erste ∼, das ich [davon] höre** that's the first I've heard of it; **mir fehlen die ∼e** I'm lost for words; **davon ist kein ∼ wahr** not a word of it is true; **darüber ist kein ∼ gefallen** not a word was said about it; **spar dir deine ∼e!** don't waste your breath!; **in ∼ und Tat** in word and deed; **eine Sprache in ∼ und Schrift beherrschen** have a written and spoken command of a language; **das ∼ an jmdn. richten** address sb.; **ein paar ∼e sprechen** say a few words; **ein ∼ mit jmdm. sprechen** have a word with sb.; **bei ihm ist jedes zweite ∼ Geld** he's always talking about money; **nicht viele ∼e machen** not beat about the bush; **ich verstehe kein ∼:** I don't understand a word [of it]; **auf ein ∼!** (veralt.) can I have a word with you?; **auf jmds. ∼e hören** listen to what sb. says; **etw. in ∼e fassen** put sth. into words; **mit einem ∼:** in a word; **mit anderen ∼en** in other words; **ich glaube dir aufs ∼:** I can well believe it; **jmdn. [nicht] zu ∼ kommen lassen** [not] let sb. get a word in; **kein ∼ mehr!** not another word!; **etw. mit keinem ∼ erwähnen** not say a word about sth.; not mention sth. at all; **man versteht sein eigenes ∼ nicht** you could not hear yourself speak; **die ∼e gut zu setzen wissen** (geh.) have a way with words; **jmdm. aufs ∼ folgen** *od.* **gehorchen** obey sb.'s every word; **dein ∼ in Gottes Ohr!** let's hope you're right!; **ein ∼ gab das andere** one thing led to another; **hast du [da noch] ∼e?** what do you say to that?; **das ist das letzte/mein letztes ∼:** that's the/my last word on the matter; **[immer] das letzte ∼ haben wollen/müssen** want to have/have to have the last word; **Dr. Meyer hat das ∼:** it's Dr Meyer's turn to speak; **das ∼ ergreifen** *od.* **nehmen** start to speak; **das ∼ führen** be the main speaker; **das große ∼ haben** *od.* **führen** talk big; **jmdm. das ∼ geben** *od.* **erteilen/entziehen** call upon sb. to speak/to finish speaking; **jmdm. das ∼ verbieten** forbid sb. to speak; **einer Sache das ∼ reden** (geh.) speak out in favour of sth.; **für jmdn. ein [gutes] ∼ einlegen** put in a [good] word for sb.; **jmdm. das ∼ aus dem Munde nehmen** take the words out of sb.'s mouth; **jmdm. das ∼ im Munde herumdrehen** twist sb.'s words; **kein ∼/kein weiteres ∼ über etw.** *(Akk.)* **verlieren** not spend time discussing sth./not say another word about sth.; **jmdm. ins ∼ fallen** interrupt sb.; **ums ∼ bitten** ask to speak; **sich zu ∼ melden** indicate one's wish to speak
3 *Pl.* **∼e** (Spruch) saying; (Zitat) quotation; **geflügelte ∼e** well-known sayings and quotations; **das bekannte ∼ Schillers** the well-known quotation from Schiller
4 *Pl.* **∼e** (geh.: Text) words *pl.*; **in ∼ und Bild** in words and pictures; **das geschriebene/gedruckte ∼:** the written/printed word
5 *Pl.* **∼e** (Versprechen) word; **[sein] ∼ halten** keep one's word; **sein ∼ brechen** break one's word; **jmdm. sein ∼ [auf etw.** *(Akk.)***] geben** give sb. one's word [on sth.]; **auf mein ∼!** I give you my word; **jmdn. beim ∼ nehmen** take sb. at his/her word; **[bei jmdm.] im ∼ sein** have made a promise [to sb.]
6 (christl. Rel., Theol.) Word

wort-, Wort-: ∼art *die* (Sprachw.) part of speech; **∼bedeutung** *die* word meaning; meaning of a/the word; **∼bildung** *die* (Sprachw.) word formation; **∼bruch** *der* breaking one's word *no art.*; **∼brüchig** *Adj.* **∼brüchig werden** break one's word

Wörtchen /ˈvœrtçən/ *das;* **∼s, ∼:** little word; **noch ein ∼ mit jmdm. zu reden haben** (ugs.) have a bone to pick with sb.; **[bei** *od.* **in etw.** *(Dat.)***] ein ∼ mitzureden haben** (ugs.) have some say [in sth.]

Wörter-: ∼buch *das* dictionary; **∼verzeichnis** *das* word index

wort-, Wort-: ∼familie *die* (Sprachw.) word family; **∼feld** *das* (Sprachw.) word field; **∼fetzen** *Pl.* scraps of conversation; **∼forschung** *die* lexicology *no art.*; **∼führer** *der,* **∼führerin** *die* spokesman/spokeswoman; spokesperson; **sich zum ∼führer einer Gruppe/Sache machen** make oneself the spokesman of a group/cause; **∼gefecht** *das* battle of words; **∼geklingel** *das* (abwertend) fine-sounding verbiage; **∼geplänkel** *das* banter *no indef. art.*; **∼geschichte** *die* etymology *no art.*; **∼getreu** A *Adj.* word-for-word; B *adv.* word for word; **∼gewaltig** A *Adj.* powerfully eloquent; B *adv.* with powerful eloquence; **∼gewandt** A *Adj.* eloquent; B *adv.* eloquently; **∼gottes·dienst** *der* (christl. Kirche): *service centred on the sermon and readings from the Scriptures;* **∼gut** *das* vocabulary; **∼hülse** *die* (abwertend) [empty] cliché; **∼inhalt** *der* (Sprachw.) word meaning; meaning of a/the word; **∼karg** A *Adj.* taciturn ‹*person*›; laconic ‹*reply, greeting, etc.*›; **ein ∼karger Mann** a man of few words; B *adv.* taciturnly; ‹*reply, greet, etc.*› laconically; **∼kargheit** *die* ▸ **∼karg**: taciturnity; laconicism; **∼klauberei** /-klaubəˈrai/ *die;* **∼∼, ∼∼en** quibbling; **solche ∼klaubereien ändern nichts an der Tatsache, dass ...** such quibbles do not alter the fact that ...; **∼laut** *der* wording; **im [vollen] ∼laut** verbatim

Wörtlein *das;* **∼s, ∼** ▸ **Wörtchen**

wörtlich /ˈvœrtlɪç/
A *Adj.* 1 (wortgetreu) word-for-word; *s. auch* **Rede 5** 2 (der eigentlichen Bedeutung entsprechend) literal
B *adv.* 1 (wortgetreu) word-for-word; ‹*copy, repeat*› verbatim, word-for-word; **das hat sie ∼ gesagt** those were her very words 2 (der eigentlichen Bedeutung entsprechend) literally

wort-, Wort-: ∼los A *Adj.* silent; wordless; unspoken ‹*agreement, understanding*›; B *adv.* without saying a word; **∼mächtig** A *Adj.* eloquent; B *adv.* eloquently; **∼meldung** *die:* **gibt es noch ∼meldungen?** does anyone else wish to speak?; **es liegen keine weiteren ∼meldungen vor** no one else wishes to speak; **∼reich** A *Adj.* 1 (mit vielen ∼en) verbose; 2 (reich im ∼schatz) **eine ∼reiche Sprache** a language with a rich vocabulary; B *adv.* (mit vielen ∼en) verbosely; ‹*apologize, thank*› profusely; **∼schatz** *der* vocabulary; **∼schöpfung** *die* 1 word-coining *no art.*; 2 (∼) neologism; new coinage; **∼schwall** *der* torrent of words; **∼sinn** *der* sense of a word/the word[s]; **∼spiel** *das* play on words; (mit ähnlich klingenden Wörtern) pun; play on words; **∼stamm** *der* (Sprachw.) stem of a/the word; **∼stellung** *die* (Sprachw.) word order; **∼streit** *der* ▸ **∼gefecht**; **∼ungetüm** *das* overlong monstrosity of a word; **∼wahl** *die* choice of word; **∼wechsel** *der* exchange of words; **mit jmdm. einen ∼wechsel haben** exchange words with sb.; **∼witz** *der* pun; **∼wörtlich** A *Adj.* word-for-word; B *adv.* word for word; **etw. ∼wörtlich nehmen** take sth. literally

worüber *Adv.* 1 (interrogativ) over what ...; what ... over; **∼ bist du gestolpert?** what did you trip over?; **∼ lachst du?** what are you laughing about? 2 (relativisch) over which; which ... over; **es gibt nichts, ∼ wir sprechen könnten** we have nothing to talk about

worum *Adv.* 1 (interrogativ) around what; what ... around; **∼ bat er?** what did he ask for?; **∼ geht es denn?** what is it about then? 2 (relativisch) around which; which ... around; **alles, ∼ er bat** everything he asked for

worunter *Adv.* 1 (interrogativ) under what; what ... under; **∼ leidet er?** what is he suffering from? 2 (relativisch) under which; which ... under; **etwas, ∼ er besonders leidet, ist ...** something he particularly suffers from is ...

wo·selbst *Adv.* (veralt.) where

Wotan /ˈvo:tan/ *(der)* Wotan

wo·von *Adv.* 1 (interrogativ) from where; where ... from; **∼ soll er leben?** what is he supposed to live on?; **∼ redest du?** what are you talking about?; **∼ ist er müde/krank?** what has made him tired/ill? 2 (relativisch) from which; which ... from; **das, ∼ er sprach** what he was talking about; *s. auch* **wobei** *NB*

wo·vor *Adv.* 1 (interrogativ) in front of what; what ... in front of; **∼ stand er?** what was he standing in front of?; **∼ hast du Angst?** what are you afraid of? 2 (relativisch) in front of which; which ... in front of; **das, ∼ er sie gewarnt hatte** what he had warned her about; **das einzige, ∼ ich Angst habe** the only thing I am afraid of; *s. auch* **wobei** *NB*

wo·zu *Adv.* 1 (interrogativ) to what; what ... to; (wofür) what ... for; **∼ brauchst du das Geld?** what do you need the money for?; **∼ hast du dich entschlossen?** what have you decided [on]?; **∼ hat sie ihn gezwungen?** what did she force him to do?; **∼ diese Umstände?** why all this fuss?; **∼ denn?** (zu welchem Zweck) what for?; (als Ausdruck der Ablehnung) why should I/you *etc.?;* **weißt du, ∼ das gut sein soll?** do you know what the point of it is supposed to be? 2 (relativisch) **dann habe ich gebügelt, ∼ ich keine Lust hatte** then I did some ironing, which I had no inclination to do; **∼ du dich auch entschließt** whatever you decide on; **er will studieren, ∼ er allerdings das Abitur braucht** he wants to go to university but for that he needs the Abitur; *s. auch* **wobei** *NB*

Wrack /vrak/ *das;* **∼[e]s, ∼s** *od.* **∼e** wreck; (fig.: Mensch) [physical] wreck; **ein seelisches/nervöses ∼** (fig.) a mental/nervous wreck

wrang /vraŋ/ *1. und 3. Pers. Sg. Prät. v.* **wringen**

Wrasen /ˈvra:zn̩/ *der;* **∼s, ∼** (nordd.) steam

wringen /ˈvrɪŋən/ *unr. tr. V.* (bes. nordd.) wring

WS *Abk.* = **Wintersemester**

WSV *Abk.* = **Winterschlussverkauf**

WSW *Abk.* = **Westsüdwest[en]** ▸ **S. 363** WSW

WTO *Abk.* = **World Trade Organization** WTO

Wucher /ˈvu:xɐ/ *der;* **∼s** profiteering; (beim Verleihen von Geld) usury; **18 Prozent Zinsen: das ist ja ∼!** 18 per cent interest: that's extortionate!; **[mit etw.] ∼ treiben** profiteer [on sth.]; (beim Verleihen von Geld) charge an extortionate rate/extortionate rates of interest [on sth.]

Wucher·blume *die* chrysanthemum

Wucherer *der;* **∼s, ∼, Wucherin** *die;* **∼, ∼nen** profiteer; (beim Verleihen von Geld) usurer

wuchern *itr. V.* 1 *auch mit sein* (stark wachsen) ‹*plants, weeds, etc.*› proliferate, run wild; (fig.) be rampant; **eine ∼de Geschwulst** a cancerous tumour; **krebsartig ∼** (fig.) grow like a cancer; **eine ∼de Fantasie** (fig.) an imagination that runs wild 2 (Wucher treiben) **[mit etw.] ∼:** profiteer [on sth.]; (beim Verleihen von Geld) lend [sth.] at extortionate interest rates

Wucher·preis *der* extortionate price

Wucherung *die;* **∼, ∼en** growth

Wucher·zins *der; Pl.* **∼en** extortionate rate of interest

wuchs /vu:ks/ *1. u. 3. Pers. Sg. Prät. v.* **wachsen**

Wuchs *der;* **∼es** 1 (Wachstum) growth 2 (Gestalt) stature; **klein/groß von ∼ sein** ‹*person*› be small/tall in stature

Wucht /vʊxt/ *die;* **∼** 1 force; (von Schlägen) power; weight; **mit voller ∼:** with full force; **mit voller ∼ zuschlagen** hit with all one's might 2 *in* **eine ∼ sein** (salopp) be absolutely fantastic (coll.) 3 (bes. ostmd.: Schläge) beating; (als Strafe für Kind) hiding (coll.); beating

wuchten *tr. V.* heave

wuchtig
A *Adj.* 1 (voller Wucht) powerful; mighty 2 (schwer, massig) massive
B *adv.* powerfully

Wühl·arbeit *die* (fig.) subversive activities *pl.;* subversion

wühlen /ˈvy:lən/
A *itr. V.* 1 (graben) dig; (mit der Schnauze, dem Schnabel) root **(nach** for); ‹*mole*› tunnel, burrow; **er**

wühlte in ihren Locken he tousled her hair [2] (ugs.: suchen) rummage [around] (**nach** for) [3] (fig.: Wühlarbeit leisten) engage in subversive activities *or* subversion (**gegen** against) [4] (ugs.: schwer arbeiten) graft (Brit. coll.); slave away
B *tr. V.* burrow; tunnel out ‹*burrow*›
C *refl. V.* **sich in etw.** (*Akk.*)/**durch etw. ~:** burrow into/through sth.; **die Autos wühlten sich durch den Schlamm** the cars churned their way through the mud

Wühler *der;* **~s,** ~ [1] (Zool.) cricetine [2] (fig.: Subversiver) subversive [3] (ugs.: fleißig Arbeitender) grafter (Brit. coll.)

Wühlerin *die;* **~, ~nen** ▸**Wühler 2, 3**

Wühl-: ~maus *die* one of the Microtinae (*the voles and lemmings*); (Kleine ~maus) European pine vole; (Schermaus) European water vole; **~tisch** *der* (ugs.) bargain counter

Wulst /vʊlst/ *der;* **~[e]s, Wülste** /ˈvʏlstə/ *od.* **~e** [1] bulge; (Fett~) roll of fat; (an einer Flasche, einem Reifen) bead [2] (Heraldik) wreath [3] (Archit.) torus

wulstig *Adj.* bulging; thick ‹*lips*›

wumm /vʊm/ *Interj.* boom

wummern /ˈvʊmɐn/ *itr. V.* ‹*machine, engine*› hum; **mit den Fäusten gegen etw. ~:** drum one's fists against sth.

wund /vʊnt/ *Adj.* ▸ⓘ **S. 439** sore; **sich ~ laufen** walk until one's feet are sore; **sich ~ liegen** get bedsores (**an** + *Dat.* on); **sich** (*Dat.*) **den Rücken ~ liegen** get bedsores on one's back; **ich habe mir die Finger ~ geschrieben** (ugs.) I've worn my fingers to the bone with all that writing; *s. auch* **Fuß 2**; **Punkt 4**; **reiben A 1**

Wund-: ~arzt *der* (hist.) surgeon; **~brand** *der* ▸ⓘ **S. 439** (Med.) gangrene

Wunde *die;* **~, ~n** wound; **alte ~n wieder aufreißen** (fig.) open up old wounds; **der Krieg hat dem Land tiefe ~n geschlagen** (fig.) the war has left deep scars on the country; *s. auch* **Salz**

***wunder, Wunder**[1] (ugs.) *in* (ugs.) **er denkt, er sei ~ wer** he thinks he's really something; **sie glaubt, sie sei ~ wie klug** she thinks she's ever so *or* oh so clever (coll.); **er glaubt, ~ was geleistet zu haben** he thinks he's achieved something fantastic (coll.); **ich dachte, ~ was es da alles zu sehen gibt** I thought there would be all sorts of fantastic things to see; **er bildet sich ~ was darauf ein** he's terribly pleased with himself about it (coll.)

Wunder[2] *das;* **~s, ~** [1] miracle; **~ tun** work *or* perform miracles; **~ wirken** (fig. ugs.) work wonders; **o ~!** wonders will never cease!; **ein/kein ~ sein** (ugs.) be a/no wonder; **was ~, wenn ...?** small *or* no wonder that ...; **er wird sein blaues ~ erleben** (ugs.) he's in for a nasty shock [2] (etw. Außergewöhnliches, Erstaunliches) wonder; **~ an ...** (*Dat.*) a miracle of ...; **ein technisches ~:** a technological marvel

wunderbar
A *Adj.* [1] (übernatürlich erscheinend) miraculous; **das grenzt ans Wunderbare** it's bordering on the miraculous; **auf ~e Weise** miraculously [2] (sehr schön, herrlich) wonderful; marvellous
B *adv.* [1] (sehr schön, herrlich) wonderfully; marvellously [2] (ugs.: sehr) wonderfully

wunder-, Wunder-: ~ding *das; Pl.* **~~e** amazing thing; (ugs.: Gegenstand) wonder; **~doktor** *der* (spött.) miracle-working doctor; **~glaube** *der* belief in miracles; **~gläubig** *Adj.* ‹*person*› who believes in miracles; **~gläubig sein** believe in miracles; **~heiler** *der;* **~~s, ~~,** **~heilerin** *die;* **~~, ~~nen** faith healer; **~heilung** *die* miraculous cure; **~hübsch** **A** *Adj.* wonderfully pretty; **B** *adv.* quite beautifully; **~kerze** *die* sparkler; **~kind** *das* child prodigy; **~knabe** *der* boy prodigy; **~lampe** *die* magic lamp; **~land** *das* wonderland

wunderlich
A *Adj.* strange; odd
B *adv.* strangely; oddly

Wunderlichkeit *die;* **~, ~en** [1] strangeness; oddness [2] (etwas Wunderliches) oddity

Wunder·mittel *das* miracle cure (**gegen** for)

wundern
A *tr. V.* surprise; **mich wundert** *od.* **es wundert mich, dass ...** I'm surprised that ...; **es würde** *od.* **sollte mich [nicht] ~, wenn ...** I should [not] be surprised *or* it would [not] surprise me if ...
B *refl. V.* **sich über jmdn./etw. ~:** be surprised at sb./sth.; **du wirst dich [noch mal] ~** (ugs.) you're in for a shock; you've got a surprise in store; **ich muss mich doch sehr über dich ~:** I really am surprised at you

wunder|nehmen *unr. tr. V.* (geh.) **etw. nimmt jmdn. wunder** sth. surprises sb.

wunders ▸**Wunder**[1]

wundersam (geh.)
A *Adj.* strange
B *adv.* **ihr wurde ~ zumute** she had a strange feeling

wunder-, Wunder-: ~schön **A** *Adj.* simply beautiful; (herrlich) simply wonderful; **B** *adv.* quite beautifully; (einwandfrei) perfectly; **~tat** *die* miracle; **~täter** *der,* **~täterin** *die* miracle worker; **~tätig** *Adj.* miraculous; **~tier** *das* strange and wonderful animal; **~tüte** *die* surprise packet; **~voll** **A** *Adj.* wonderful; marvellous; **B** *adv.* wonderfully; marvellously; **~waffe** *die* superweapon; **~welt** *die* wonderworld; **~werk** *das* marvel

wund-, Wund-: ~fieber *das* ▸ⓘ **S. 439** (Med.) traumatic fever; wound fever; **~infektion** *die* ▸ⓘ **S. 439** (Med.) wound infection; ***~|liegen** ▸**wund**; **~mal** *das; Pl.* **~~e** (bes. Rel.) scar; **die ~male Christi** Christ's stigmata; **~pflaster** *das* sticking plaster; **~rand** *der* (Med.) edge of a/the wound; **~rose** *die* ▸ⓘ **S. 439** (Med.) St Anthony's fire; erysipelas (Med.); **~sein** *das* ▸ⓘ **S. 439** soreness; **~starrkrampf** *der* ▸ⓘ **S. 439** (Med.) tetanus

Wunsch /vʊnʃ/ *der;* **~[e]s, Wünsche** /ˈvʏnʃə/ [1] wish (**nach** to have); (Hoffen, Sehnen) desire (**nach** for); **sich** (*Dat.*) **einen ~ erfüllen/versagen** grant/deny oneself something one wants; **haben Sie [sonst] noch einen ~?** will there be anything else?; **jmds. ~ und Wille sein** be something sb. most earnestly desires; **auf jmds. ~:** at sb.'s wish; **auf allgemeinen ~ [hin]** in response to popular demand; **alles geht** *od.* **läuft nach ~:** everything's going as we want/he wants *etc.*; **dein ~ ist mir Befehl** (scherzh.) your wish is my command; **der ~ ist der Vater des Gedankens** (scherzh.) the wish is father to the thought; *s. auch* **fromm 3** [2] *Pl.* ▸ⓘ **S. 331** (zu bestimmten Anlässen) wishes; **mit den besten/herzlichsten Wünschen** with best/warmest wishes; **beste Wünsche zum Geburtstag** many happy returns of the day

wünschbar *Adj.* (bes. schweiz.) desirable

Wunsch-: ~bild *das* desired ideal; **~denken** *das* wishful thinking

Wünschel- /ˈvʏnʃl-/: **~rute** *die* divining rod; **~rutengänger** *der,* **~rutengängerin** *die* diviner

wünschen /ˈvʏnʃn/ *tr. V.* [1] **sich** (*Dat.*) **etw. ~:** want sth.; (im Stillen) wish for sth.; **jmdm. Erfolg/nichts Gutes/den Tod ~:** wish sb. success/no good/wish sb. dead; **er wünschte sich** (*Dat.*) **ein Rad zum Geburtstag** he asked for a cycle for his birthday; **du darfst dir [von mir] etwas ~:** you can have a present [from me] — what would you like?; **sich** (*Dat.*) **jmdn. als** *od.* **zum Freund ~:** want to have sb. as a friend; **alles, was du dir nur ~ kannst** everything you could wish for; **er war so, wie man sich** (*Dat.*) **einen Lehrer wünscht** he was just as one would want a teacher to be; **was wünschst du dir?** what would you like?; **ich wünschte, du wärest hier** I wish you were here; **jmdn. weit fort ~:** wish sb. far away; **ich wünschte mich auf eine einsame Insel** I wished I were on a desert island [2] ▸ⓘ **S. 331** (in formelhaften Wünschen) wish; **jmdm. alles Gute/frohe Ostern ~:** wish sb. all the best/a happy Easter; **jmdm. gute Nacht ~:** wish *or* bid sb. good night; **sie wünschte ihm gute Besserung** she said she hoped he would soon get better [3] *auch itr. V.* (begehren) want; **was ~ Sie?, Sie ~?** (von einem Bediensteten gesagt) yes, madam/sir?; (von einem Kellner gesagt) what would you like?; (von einem Verkäufer gesagt) can I help you?; **er wünscht, dass du gehst** he wants you to go; **ganz, wie Sie ~:** just as you like; **solange Sie es ~:** as long as you wish *or* like; **ich wünsche das nicht** I do not wish it; **dein Chef wünscht dich zu sprechen** your boss would like to speak to you; **etw. lässt [viel]/lässt nichts zu ~ übrig** sth. leaves a great deal/nothing to be desired; **es verlief alles wie gewünscht** everything went as we/he *etc.* had wanted; *s. auch* **gewünscht**

wünschens·wert *Adj.* desirable

wunsch-, Wunsch-: ~form *die* (Sprachw.) ▸**Optativ**; **~gegner** *der,* **~gegnerin** *die* (bes. Sport) ideal opponent; **~gemäß** **A** *Adv.* as desired; (einer Bitte gemäß) as requested; **B** *adj.* **die ~gemäße Ausführung eines Auftrags** the performance of a task as desired/requested; **~kind** *das* wanted child; **~konzert** *das* request concert; (im Rundfunk) request programme; **~los** **A** *Adj.* [perfectly] contented; perfect ‹*happiness*›; **B** *adv.* **~los glücklich sein** be perfectly contented; **~satz** *der* (Sprachw.) optative sentence; **~traum** *der* wishful dream; (unrealistisch) pipe dream; **~vorstellung** *die* wishful notion; **~zettel** *der* list of things one would like; (zum Geburtstag o. Ä.) list of presents one would like

wupp /vʊp,/ **wupp·dich, wupps** *Interj.* (ugs.) woomph (coll.)

wurde /ˈvʊrdə/ *1. u. 3. Pers. Sg. Prät. v.* **werden**

würde /ˈvʏrdə/ *1. u. 3. Pers. Sg. Konjunktiv II v.* **werden**

Würde *die;* **~, ~n** [1] dignity; **seine ~ bewahren** preserve one's dignity; **sich in seiner ~ verletzt fühlen** feel that one's dignity has been affronted; **etw. mit ~ tragen** bear sth. with dignity; (scherzh.) bear up well in spite of sth.; **unter jmds. ~ sein** be beneath sb.'s dignity; **unter aller ~ sein** be beneath contempt [2] (Rang) rank; (Amt) office; (Titel) title; (Auszeichnung) honour; **die ~ eines Professors** the title of professor; **zu höchsten ~n gelangen** attain high office

würde·los
A *Adj.* undignified; (schimpflich) disgraceful
B *adv.* in an undignified way; (schimpflich) disgracefully

Würdelosigkeit *die;* **~** ▸**würdelos**: lack of dignity; disgracefulness

Würden·träger *der,* **Würden·trägerin** *die* dignitary

würde·voll
A *Adj.* dignified
B *adv.* with dignity

würdig
A *Adj.* [1] (würdevoll) dignified [2] (wert) worthy; suitable ‹*occasion*›; **jmds./einer Sache [nicht] ~ sein** [not] be worthy of sb./sth.; **sich jmds./einer Sache [nicht] ~ erweisen** *od.* **zeigen** prove oneself [not] worthy of sb./sth.
B *adv.* [1] (würdevoll) with dignity; ‹*dressed*› in a dignified manner [2] (angemessen) worthily; ‹*celebrate*› in a/the appropriate manner; **jmdn. ~ zu vertreten wissen** make a worthy deputy for sb.

würdigen *tr. V.* [1] (anerkennen, beachten) recognize; (schätzen) appreciate; (lobend hervorheben) acknowledge; **etw. zu ~ wissen** appreciate sth. [2] (für wert halten) **jmdn. einer Sache** (*Gen.*) **~:** deem sb. worthy of sth.; **jmdn. keines Blickes/keiner Antwort ~:** not deign to look at/answer sb.

Würdigkeit *die;* **~** [1] (Würde) dignity [2] (Wert) worth

Würdigung *die;* **~, ~en** ▸**würdigen 1**: recognition; appreciation; acknowledgement; **in ~ einer Sache** (*Gen.*) in recognition of sth.

Wurf /vʊrf/ *der;* **~[e]s, Würfe** /ˈvʏrfə/ [1] throw; (beim Baseball) pitch; (beim Kegeln) bowl; (gezielt aufs Tor) shot [2] (das Werfen) throwing/pitching/bowling; **zum ~ ausholen** draw

W

back one's arm ready to throw; **beim ~:** when throwing/pitching/bowling **3** (Zool.) litter **4** (gelungenes Werk) successful work; success; **mit dieser Erfindung ist ihm ein großer ~ gelungen** this invention has been a great success for him

Wurf·bahn *die* trajectory

Würfel /ˈvʏrfl̩/ *der;* **~s, ~ 1** (auch Math.) cube; **Gemüse/Fleisch in ~ schneiden** dice vegetables/meat **2** (Spiel~) dice; die (formal); **die ~ sind gefallen** (fig.) the die is cast

Würfel·becher *der* dice cup

Würfel·muster *das* check pattern

würfeln

A *itr. V.* throw the dice; (mit Würfeln spielen) play dice; **du bist mit Würfeln dran** it's your turn to throw; **hast du schon gewürfelt?** have you already thrown *or* had your throw?; **um etw. ~:** play dice for sth.; **darum ~, wer anfangen soll** throw a/the dice to see who should start

B *tr. V.* **1** throw **2** (in Würfel schneiden) dice ‹*vegetables, meat*›

Würfel-: ~spiel *das* **1** (Glücksspiel) dice; (einzelne Partie) game of dice; **2** (Brettspiel) dice game; **~zucker** *der* cube sugar; lump sugar

Wurf-: ~geschoss, ***~geschoß** *das* missile; **~kreis** *der* (Sport) throwing circle; **~scheibe** *die* discus; **~sendung** *die* ▸ **Postwurfsendung**; **~speer** *der,* **~spieß** *der* (hist.) spear; **~taube** *die* (Schießsport) clay pigeon; **~tauben·schießen** *das;* **~~s** (Schießsport) clay-pigeon shooting *no art.*

Würge-: ~engel *der* (bes. christl. Rel.) Angel of Death; **~griff** *der* (auch fig.) stranglehold; **~mal** *das; Pl.* **~~e** *od.* **~mäler** strangle *or* strangulation mark

würgen /ˈvʏrgn̩/

A *tr. V.* **1** strangle; throttle; (fig.) ‹*tie, collar*› strangle; **~de Angst** (fig.) choking fear **2** (ugs.: zwängen) **etw. in etw.** (*Akk.*) **~:** stuff sth. into sth.

B *itr. V.* **1** (Brechreiz haben) retch **2** (mühsam schlucken) **an etw.** (*Dat.*) **~:** have to force sth. down; *s. auch* **hängen² A 4**

Würger *der;* **~s, ~ 1** strangler **2** (Zool.) shrike

Würgerin *die* ▸ **Würger 1**

Wurm¹ /vɔrm/ *der;* **~[e]s, Würmer** /ˈvʏrmɐ/ worm; (Made) maggot; **von Würmern befallen sein** have worms/be maggoty; **da ist** *od.* **sitzt der ~ drin** (fig. ugs.) there's something wrong there; **jmdm. die Würmer aus der Nase ziehen** (fig. ugs.) get sb. to spill the beans (fig. sl.); **den ~** *od.* **Würmer baden** (ugs. scherzh.) be fishing

Wurm² *das;* **~[e]s, Würmer** (fam.) little mite

wurmen *tr., auch itr. V.* (ugs.) **jmdn. ~:** rankle with sb.; **so was wurmt [einen] schon** that sort of thing rankles

Wurm·fort·satz *der* ▸ ❶ **S. 435** (Anat.) appendix

wurmig *Adj.,* **wurm·stichig** *Adj.* worm-eaten; (madig) maggoty

Wurscht /vʊrʃt/ (ugs.) *in* **jmdm. ist jmd./etw. ~:** sb. doesn't care about sb./sth.; **das ist mir vollkommen** *od.* **völlig ~:** I couldn't care less about that; **ach, mir ist alles ~!** oh, what do I care!

wurscht·egal *Adj.* (ugs.) ▸ **wurstegal**

Wurst /vʊrst/ *die;* **~, Würste** /ˈvʏrstə/ **1** sausage; **es geht um die ~** (fig. ugs.) the crunch has come; **mit der ~ nach der Speckseite** *od.* **dem Schinken werfen** (fig. ugs.) use a sprat to catch a mackerel (fig. coll.) **2** (wurstähnliches Gebilde) roll; **den Teig zu einer ~ formen** roll the dough into a sausage shape; **eine ~ machen** (fam.) do a big one (child lang.) **3** (ugs.) ▸ **Wurscht**

Wurst·brot *das* open sausage sandwich; (mit Streichwurst) open meat-spread sandwich; (zusammengeklappt) sausage/meat-spread sandwich

Würstchen /ˈvʏrstçən/ *das;* **~s, ~ 1** [small] sausage; **Frankfurter/Wiener ~:** frankfurter/wienerwurst; **heiße ~:** hot sausages **2** (ugs., oft abwertend) nobody; (hilfloser Mensch) poor soul; **ein armes ~:** a poor soul **3** **[ein] ~ machen** (Kinderspr.) do [poo]poos (child lang.)

Würstchen·bude *die* sausage stand

wurst·egal *Adj.* (ugs.) *in* **~ sein** not matter in the slightest; **das ist mir ~:** I couldn't care less [about that]

Wurstel /ˈvʊrstl̩/ *der;* **~s, ~** (bayr., österr.) clown

Würstel /ˈvʏrstl̩/ *das;* **~s, ~** (bes. österr.) sausage

Wurstelei *die;* **~, ~en** (ugs. abwertend) pottering about *no pl.*

wursteln *itr. V.* (ugs.)

A potter; **an etw.** (*Dat.*) **~:** potter about with sth.

B *refl. V.* **sich durchs Leben ~:** muddle [along] through life

Wurst-: ~finger *der* podgy finger; **~haut** *die* sausage skin

wurstig (ugs.)

A *Adj.* couldn't-care-less *attrib.* ‹*attitude, behaviour, reply*›; **er ist ein ~er Typ** *od.* **ist ~:** he couldn't care less about anything

B *adv.* in a couldn't-care-less way

Wurstigkeit *die;* **~** (ugs.) couldn't-care-less attitude

Wurst-: ~salat *der: piquant salad with pieces of sausage, onion rings, boiled eggs and/or cheese;* **~suppe** *die* sausage soup; **~waren** *Pl.* sausages; **~zipfel** *der* end of a/the sausage

württembergisch /ˈvʏrtəmbɛrgɪʃ/ *Adj.* of/from Württemberg; *s. auch* **badisch**

Würze /ˈvʏrtsə/ *die;* **~, ~n 1** (Gewürz) spice; seasoning **2** (Aroma) aroma; (fig.) spice; *s. auch* **Kürze 3**

Wurzel /ˈvʊrtsl̩/ *die;* **~, ~n 1** (auch fig.) root; **~[n] fassen** take root; **~n schlagen** take root; (fig.: heimisch werden) put down roots; **ich stehe hier schon so lange, dass ich bald ~n schlage** (scherzh.) I've been standing here so long I'll soon grow roots; **seine ~n in etw.** (*Dat.*) **haben** (fig.) have its roots in sth.; **die ~ allen Übels** (fig.) the root of all evil; **das Übel an der ~ fassen** *od.* **packen** (fig.) strike at the root of the problem; **etw. mit der ~ ausrotten** (fig.) eradicate sth. completely **2** ▸ ❶ **S. 826** (Math.) root; **~n ziehen** calculate roots; **aus einer Zahl die ~ ziehen** extract the [square] root of a number; **die dritte ~ aus** *od.* **von 8** the cube root of 8 **3** (bes. nordd.) carrot **4** (der Hand) wrist; (des Fußes) ankle; (eines Nagels, der Nase) root **5** (Sprachw.) root

Wurzel-: ~ballen *der* root ball; **~behandlung** *die* (Zahnmed.) root treatment; **~bürste** *die* stiff brush; (zum Scheuern) [stiff] scrubbing brush *or* (Amer.) scrub brush

Würzelchen /ˈvʏrtsl̩çən/ *das;* **~s, ~:** rootlet

Wurzel·haut·entzündung *die* ▸ ❶ **S. 439** (Med.) periodontitis *no indef. art.*

wurzelig *Adj.* full of roots *postpos.*

Wurzel·knolle *die* tuber

wurzel·los *Adj.* without roots *postpos.;* (auch fig.) rootless

Wurzel·losig·keit *die;* **~:** lack of roots; (fig.) rootlessness

wurzeln *itr. V.* **1** (Wurzeln schlagen) take root; **flach ~:** have shallow roots; **das Misstrauen wurzelt tief in ihm** (fig.) his mistrust is deep-rooted **2** **in etw.** (*Dat.*) **~** (seinen Ursprung haben in) be rooted in sth.; (verursacht sein durch) have its roots in sth.

Wurzel-: ~spross, ***~sproß** *der* (Bot.) root sucker; **~stock** *der; Pl.* **~stöcke 1** (Bot.) rootstock; rhizome; **2** (eines Baumes) stump and roots *pl.;* **~werk** *das* roots *pl.*

würzen /ˈvʏrtsn̩/ *tr. V.* season; (fig.) spice; **Humor würzt das Leben** (fig.) humour is the spice of life

würzig

A *Adj.* tasty; full-flavoured ‹*beer, wine*›; aromatic ‹*fragrance, smell, tobacco*›; tangy ‹*air*›; (scharf) spicy

B *adv.* **sie kocht nicht ~ genug** she doesn't use enough seasoning

Würzigkeit *die;* **~** ▸ **würzig A**: tastiness; full flavour; aromatic fragrance; tanginess; spiciness

wusch /vu:ʃ/ *1. u. 3. Pers. Sg. Prät. v.* **waschen**

Wuschel·haar *das* (ugs.) frizzy *or* fuzzy hair

wuschelig *Adj.* (ugs.) frizzy; fuzzy

Wuschel·kopf *der* (ugs.) **1** (Haar) shock *or* mop of frizzy *or* fuzzy hair **2** (Mensch) frizzy-haired *or* fuzzy-haired man/girl *etc.;* man/girl *etc.* with frizzy *or* fuzzy hair

wuscheln /ˈvʊʃl̩n/ *tr., itr. V.* tousle; **in jmds. Haar ~:** tousle sb.'s hair

wuselig *Adj.* (bes. südd., md.) busy; bustling

wuseln /ˈvu:zl̩n/ *itr. V.* (bes. südd., md.) **1** *mit sein* (sich flink bewegen) scurry **2** (sich beschäftigen) bustle around

wusste, ***wußte** /ˈvʊstə/ *1. und 3. Pers. Sg. Prät. v.* **wissen**

wüsste, ***wüßte** /ˈvʏstə/ *1. und 3. Pers. Sg. Konjunktiv II v.* **wissen**

wüst /vy:st/

A *Adj.* **1** (öde) desolate **2** (unordentlich) chaotic; tangled, tousled ‹*hair, beard, etc.*›; wild ‹*appearance*›; **ein ~es Durcheinander herrschte dort** it was utter chaos *or* an utter shambles there **3** (abwertend: wild, ungezügelt) wild; furious ‹*fight, shoot-out*› **4** (abwertend: unanständig) rude; coarse ‹*oath, abuse*› **5** (abwertend: furchtbar, abscheulich) terrible; foul (sl.), terrible (coll.) ‹*weather*›

B *adv.* **1** (unordentlich) chaotically; **das Haar hing ihr ~ ins Gesicht** her hair straggled down over her face **2** (abwertend: wild, ungezügelt) wildly; **sie habens ~ getrieben** they had a wild time **3** (abwertend: unanständig) ‹*swear, abuse sb.*› coarsely **4** (abwertend: furchtbar, abscheulich) terribly; **sie haben ihn ~ zugerichtet** they really knocked him about

Wust /vu:st/ *der;* **~[e]s** (abwertend) jumble; (fig.) welter; **ein ~ von Daten/Vorschriften** a mass of data/regulations

Wüste *die;* **~, ~n** desert; (Eis~) waste; (fig.) wasteland; **jmdn. in die ~ schicken** (ugs.) give sb. the push (coll.)

wüsten *itr. V.* **mit etw. ~:** squander sth.

Wüsten·bildung *die* desertification

Wüstenei *die;* **~, ~en 1** (Einöde) waste land **2** (scherzh.: Unordnung) shambles *sing.;* chaos *no indef. art.*

Wüsten-: ~fuchs *der* fennec; **~gebiet** *das* desert area; **~klima** *das* desert climate; **~landschaft** *die* desert landscape; **~region** *die* desert region; **~sand** *der* desert sand[s *pl.*]; **~schiff** *das* (dichter.) ship of the desert; **~staat** *der* desert state; **~wind** *der* desert wind

Wüstling *der;* **~s, ~e** (abwertend) lecher; debauchee

Wut /vu:t/ *die;* **~:** rage; fury; **auf jmdn. eine ~ haben** be furious with sb.; **seine ~ an jmdm. auslassen** vent one's rage *or* fury on sb.; **in ~ geraten** *od.* **kommen** get furious; **jmdn. in ~ bringen** infuriate sb.; **eine ~ im Bauch haben** (ugs.) be livid (Brit. coll.)

Wut-: ~anfall *der* fit of rage; **~ausbruch** *der* outburst of rage *or* fury

wüten /ˈvy:tn̩/ *itr. V.* (auch fig.) rage; (zerstören) wreak havoc

wütend

A *Adj.* **1** furious; angry ‹*voice, mob*›; **auf** *od.* **über jmdn. ~ sein** be furious with sb.; **er war ~ auf sie, weil sie ihn warten ließ** he was furious with her for keeping him waiting; **über etw.** (*Akk.*) **~ sein** be furious about sth. **2** (sehr groß, heftig) raging ‹*pain, hatred, etc.*›; fierce ‹*proponent, defender*›

W

B *adv.* **1** furiously; in a fury **2** (heftig) furiously

wut·entbrannt
A *Adj.* infuriated; furious
B *adv.* in a fury

Wüterich /ˈvyːtərɪç/ *der;* **~s, ~e** (abwertend) hot-tempered person; (Gewaltmensch) brute

wut·schnaubend
A *Adj.* snorting with rage *pred*
B *adv.* snorting with rage

Wutz /vʊts/ *die;* **~, ~en** *od.* **der; ~en, ~en** (bes. westmd.) pig

WWU *Abk.* **= Wirtschafts- und Währungsunion** EMU

Wz *Abk.* **= Warenzeichen** TM; ®

W

x, X /ıks/ *das;* **~, ~:** x/X; **Herr/die Stadt X** Mr X/the town of X; **jmdm. ein X für ein U vormachen** (fig.) dupe sb.; **er lässt sich** (*Dat.*) **kein X für ein U vormachen** you can't fool him; he's not easily fooled; *s. auch* **a, A**

x *unbest. Zahlwort* (ugs.) umpteen (coll.)

x-Achse *die* (Math.) x-axis

Xanthen /ksan'teːn/ *das;* **~s** (Chem.) xanthene

Xanthippe /ksan'tıpə/ *die;* **~, ~n** (abwertend) harridan

X-Beine *Pl.* knock knees; **~ haben** have knock knees; be knock-kneed

x-beinig *Adj.* knock-kneed

x-beliebig *Adj.* (ugs.) **irgendein ~er/irgendeine ~e/irgendein ~es** any old (coll. attrib.); **jeder ~e Ort** any old place (coll.); **der Ort ist ~:** any old place will do (coll.); **denk dir eine ~e Zahl** think of a number, any old number (coll.); **irgendwelche ~en Leute** just anybody; **ich tue das nicht für jeden x-Beliebigen** I don't do it for just anybody

X-Chromosom *das* (Biol.) X-chromosome

Xenon /'kseːnɔn/ *das;* **~s** (Chem.) xenon

Xenon-: ~licht *das* (Kfz.-W.) xenon lights *pl.*; **~scheinwerfer** *der* xenon headlight

xenophob /kseno'foːp/

A *Adj.* xenophobic.

B *Adv.* xenophobically

Xenophobie *die;* **~, ~n** xenophobia

x-fach

A *Vervielfältigungsz.* **die ~e Menge** (Math.) x times the amount; (ugs.) umpteen times the amount (coll.)

B *adv.* (ugs.) **~ erprobt sein** have been tested umpteen times (coll.) *or* any number of times

x-fache, *X-fache *das;* **~n: das ~ einer Zahl** (Math.) X times a number; **das ~ seines normalen Einkommens** (ugs.) umpteen times his normal income (coll.)

X-Haken *der* picture hook

x-mal *Adv.* (ugs.) umpteen times (coll.); any number of times

X-Strahlen *Pl.* (Physik) X-rays

x-t... *Ordinalz.* ▸ⓘ **S. 826** **1** (Math.) xth **2** (ugs.) umpteenth (coll.)

***x-te·mal, *x-ten·mal** ▸**Mal**[1]

Xylophon /ksylo'foːn/ *das;* **~s, ~e** xylophone

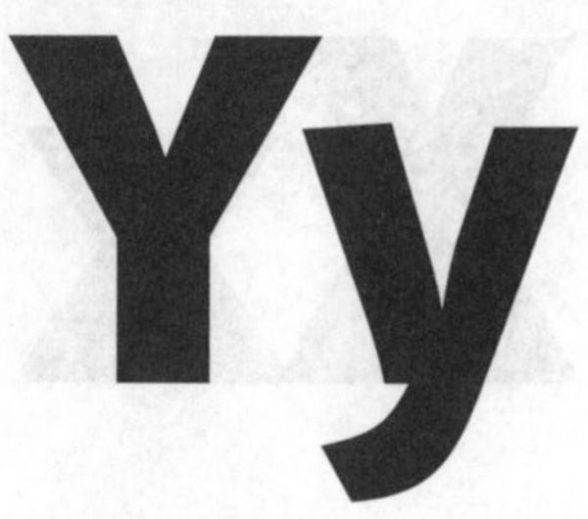

y, Y /ˈʏpsilɔn/ *das;* **~, ~:** y/Y; *s. auch* **a, A**
y-Achse *die* (Math.) y-axis
Yacht ▸ **Jacht**
Yakuza¹ /jaˈkuːza/ *die;* **~:** yakuza
Yakuza² *der;* **~s, ~s** yakuza [clan member]
Yankee /ˈjɛnki/ *der;* **~s, ~s** (oft abwertend) Yankee (Brit. coll.); Yank (Brit. coll.)
Y-Chromosom *das* (Biol.) Y-chromosome
Yen /jɛn/ *der;* **~[s], ~[s]** ▸ ❶ **S. 299** yen
Yeti /ˈjeːti/ *der;* **~s, ~s** yeti
Yoga ▸ **Joga**
Yogi[n] ▸ **Jogi[n]**
Youngster /ˈjaŋstə/ *der;* **~s, ~[s]** (Sport) youngster
Yo-Yo /joˈjoː *od.* ˈjoːˈjoː/ *das;* **~s, ~s** yo-yo
Yo-Yo-Effekt *der* yo-yo effect
Ypsilon /ˈʏpsilɔn/ *das;* **~[s], ~s** y, Y; (im griechischen Alphabet) upsilon
Ysop /ˈiːzɔp/ *der;* **~s, ~e** hyssop
Yucca /ˈjʊka/ *die;* **~, ~s** yucca

Zz

z, Z /tsɛt/ *das;* ~, ~: z/Z; *s. auch* **a, A**

zach /tsax/ *Adj.* (bes. ostmd.) timid

zack /tsak/ *Interj.* (salopp) **~! ~!** (beeil dich) get a move on! (coll.); make it snappy! (coll.); **bei ihm muss alles ~, ~ gehen** he likes things done at the double; **und ~, ~ wars fertig** and in a flash it was done

Zack *in* **auf ~ sein** (ugs.) (tüchtig sein) be on the ball (coll.) *or* one's toes; (funktionieren) be in good shape; **jmdn./etw. auf ~ bringen** (ugs.) knock sb./sth. into shape (coll.)

Zacke *die;* ~, ~n point; (eines Bergkamms, eines Diagramms) peak; (einer Säge, eines Kamms) tooth; (einer Gabel, Harke) prong

zacken *tr. V.* serrate; pink ⟨*cloth, seam, hem*⟩; **mit gezacktem Rand** with a serrated edge

Zacken *der;* ~s, ~ 1 ▸**Zacke** 2 (fig.) **sich** (*Dat.*) **keinen ~ aus der Krone brechen** (ugs.) not lose face; **dir bricht kein ~ aus der Krone, wenn du mithilfst!** (ugs.) it wouldn't hurt you to help out; **einen [kleinen] ~ [in der Krone] haben** (ugs.) be [a bit] tipsy

zackig
A *Adj.* 1 (gezackt) jagged; (mit kleinen, regelmäßigen Zacken) serrated 2 (schneidig) dashing; smart; rousing ⟨*music*⟩; brisk ⟨*orders, tempo*⟩; lively ⟨*organization*⟩
B *adv.* 1 (gezackt) jaggedly 2 (schneidig) smartly; ⟨*play music*⟩ rousingly; **…, aber mach ein bisschen ~!** …, and make it snappy! (coll.)

zag /tsa:k/ (geh.)
A *Adj.* timid; (fig.) tentative ⟨*hope*⟩
B *adv.* timidly; (fig.) tentatively

zagen *itr. V.* (geh.) hesitate (**vor** + *Dat.* in the face of); **zögern und ~:** keep hesitating; **~d** hesitant[ly]

zaghaft
A *Adj.* timid; (zögernd) hesitant; tentative
B *adv.* timidly; (zögernd) hesitantly; tentatively

Zaghaftigkeit *die;* ~: timidity; (Zögern) hesitancy

Zagheit *die;* ~ (geh.) timidity

zäh /tsɛ:/
A *Adj.* 1 (fest) tough; heavy ⟨*dough, soil*⟩; (dickflüssig) glutinous; viscous ⟨*oil*⟩ 2 (schleppend) sluggish, dragging ⟨*conversation*⟩ 3 (widerstandsfähig) tough ⟨*person*⟩ 4 (beharrlich) tenacious; tough ⟨*negotiations*⟩; dogged ⟨*resistance*⟩; **mit ~em Fleiß** by dint of sheer hard work
B *adv.* 1 (schleppend) sluggishly 2 (beharrlich) tenaciously; ⟨*resist*⟩ doggedly

***Zäheit** ▸**Zähheit**

zäh·flüssig *Adj.* glutinous; viscous ⟨*oil*⟩; thick ⟨*soup*⟩; heavy ⟨*dough*⟩; (fig.: langsam) slow-moving ⟨*traffic*⟩; **die Verhandlungen waren ~** (fig.) the negotiations were hard going

Zäh·flüssigkeit *die* glutinousness; (von Öl) viscosity; (von Soße, Suppe) thickness

Zähheit *die;* ~: 1 (Festigkeit) toughness; (des Teigs, Bodens) heaviness; (Dickflüssigkeit) glutinousness; (von Öl) viscosity 2 (schleppendes Tempo) sluggishness 3 (Widerstandsfähigkeit) toughness; (der Konstitution) robustness 4 (Beharrlichkeit) tenacity; (des Widerstands) doggedness

Zähigkeit *die;* ~ 1 (Widerstandsfähigkeit) toughness 2 (Beharrlichkeit) tenacity; **mit ~:** tenaciously

Zahl /'tsa:l/ *die;* ~, ~en ▸ⓘ **S. 826** number; (Ziffer) numeral; (Zahlenangabe, Geldmenge) figure; **er nannte keine ~en** he did not give any figures; **in die/aus den roten ~en kommen** go into/get out of the red; **in den roten/schwarzen ~en** in the red/black; **mit ~en umgehen können** be good with figures; **[fünf/sieben] an der ~:** [five/seven] in number; **in großer ~:** in great numbers; **Leiden ohne** *od.* (veralt.) **sonder ~:** suffering beyond measure

Zahl·adjektiv *das* numeral adjective

zahlbar *Adj.* (Kaufmannsspr.) payable

zählbar *Adj.* countable

zählebig *Adj.* hardy ⟨*plant, animal*⟩; **ein ~es Vorurteil** a prejudice which dies hard

zahlen
A *tr. V.* ▸ⓘ **S. 299** 1 pay ⟨*price, amount, rent, tax, fine, etc.*⟩ (**an** + *Akk.* to); **jmdm. 200 Euro ~, 200 Euro an jmdn. ~:** pay sb. 200 euros; **einen hohen Preis ~** (auch fig.) pay a high price 2 (ugs.: für eine Dienstleistung) pay for ⟨*taxi, repair, etc.*⟩; **jmdm. etw. ~:** pay for sth. for sb.; **zahlst du mir ein Bier?** will you buy me a beer?
B *itr. V.* pay; **er will nicht ~:** he won't pay [up]; **er zahlt noch an seinem Auto** he is still paying off his car; **in Dollar** *od.* **mit Dollars ~:** pay in dollars; **~ bitte!** (im Lokal) [can I/we have] the bill, please!; **die Firma zahlt gut/schlecht** the firm pays well/badly

zählen /'tsɛ:lən/
A *itr. V.* 1 count; **ich zähle bis drei** I'll count up to three 2 (geh.: vorhanden sein) **nach Tausenden/Millionen ~:** number thousands/millions 3 (gehören) **zu einer Gruppe** *usw.* **~:** be one of *or* belong to a group *etc.*; **diese Tage zählten zu den schönsten seines Lebens** these days were among *or* were some of the most wonderful in his life 4 (gültig/wichtig sein) count; **die Pause zählt nicht als Arbeitszeit** the break does not count as working time; **bei ihm** *od.* **für ihn zählt nur Erfolg** for him the only thing that counts is success 5 (vertrauen) **auf jmdn./etw. ~:** count on sb./sth.
B *tr. V.* 1 count; **Geld auf den Tisch ~:** count money out on to the table 2 (geh.: eine bestimmte Anzahl haben) number; **die Stadt zählt 500 000 Einwohner** the town has 500,000 inhabitants; **er zählt 90 Jahre** he is 90 years of age; **seine Tage sind gezählt** (fig.) his/its days are numbered 3 (als zugehörig betrachten) **jmdn. zu seinen Freunden ~:** count sb. among one's friends 4 (wert sein) be worth 5 (werten) **das Tor wurde nicht gezählt** the goal was not counted *or* didn't count

zahlen-, Zahlen-: ~angabe *die* figure (**über** + *Akk.*, **zu** for); **~angaben schwanken zwischen …** figures given vary between …; **~code** *der* number code; **~folge** *die* sequence *or* series of numbers; **~gedächtnis** *das* memory for figures; **~kolonne** *die* column of figures; **~kombination** *die* combination (*for a lock*); **~lotterie** *die*, **~lotto** *das: lottery in which entrants guess which set of figures will be drawn at random from a fixed sequence of numbers;* **~mäßig** A *Adj.* numerical; B *adv.* numerically; **~material** *das* figures *pl.*; **~mystik** *die* numerology *no art.*; **~reihe** *die* sequence of numbers; **~schloss**, ***~schloß** *das* combination lock; **~spiel** *das* numbers game; **~spielerei** *die* playing with figures *no art.*; **~werk** *das* set of figures

Zähler *der;* ~s, ~ 1 (Messgerät) meter 2 (Math.) numerator

Zähler·stand *der* meter reading; **den ~ ablesen** read the meter

zahl-, Zahl-: ~grenze *die* fare stage; **~karte** *die* (Postw.) paying-in slip; **~kellner** *der,* **~kellnerin** *die: waiter/waitress to whom payment is made;* **~los** *Adj.* countless; innumerable

Zahl·meister *der,* **Zahl·meisterin** *die* ▸ⓘ **S. 113** (auch fig.) paymaster; (auf Schiffen) purser

zahl·reich
A *Adj.* numerous; large ⟨*family, group, audience*⟩; **seine ~e Nachkommenschaft** his numerous descendants
B *adv.* in large numbers

Zahl·tag *der* pay day

Zahlung *die;* ~, ~en ▸ⓘ **S. 299** payment; **etw. in ~ nehmen/geben** (Kaufmannsspr.) take/give sth. in part exchange; take sth. as a trade-in/trade sth. in

Zählung *die;* ~, ~en counting; **eine ~:** a count

zahlungs-, Zahlungs-: ~anweisung *die: postal order paid by the postman to the payee in person;* **~aufforderung** *die* notice to pay; demand for payment; **~aufschub** *der* deferment of payment; **~bedingungen** *Pl.* (Wirtsch.) terms of payment; **~befehl** *der* (Rechtsspr. veralt.) order to pay; **~bilanz** *die* (Wirtsch.) balance of payments; **~empfänger** *der,* **~empfängerin** *die* payee; **~erleichterung** *die* easy terms *pl.*; **~erinnerung** *die* (Amtsspr.) reminder [of payment]; **~fähig** *Adj.* solvent; **~fähigkeit** *die* solvency; **~frist** *die* period for payment; credit period; **~kräftig** *Adj.* (ugs.) affluent; **~mittel** *das* means of payment; **~termin** *der* date for payment (**für** of); **~unfähig** *Adj.* insolvent; **~unfähigkeit** *die* insolvency; **~verkehr** *der* payments *pl.*; transactions *pl.*; **~weise** *die* method of payment (*Gen.* for); **~willig** *Adj.* prepared to pay *postpos.*; **~ziel** *das* (Kaufmannsspr.) ▸**~frist**

Zähl·werk *das* counter

Zahl-: ~wort *das; Pl.* **~wörter** (Sprachw.) numeral; **~zeichen** *das* numeral

zahm /tsa:m/
A *Adj.* (auch fig.) tame
B *adv.* (auch fig.) tamely

zähmen /'tsɛ:mən/ *tr. V.* 1 (auch fig.) tame; subdue ⟨*forces of nature*⟩ 2 (geh.) restrain ⟨*curiosity, impatience, etc.*⟩

Zähmung *die;* ~, ~en taming

Zahn /tsa:n/ *der;* ~[e]s, **Zähne** /'tsɛ:nə/ 1 ▸ⓘ **S. 435** tooth; (Raubtier~) fang; (an einer Briefmarke usw.) serration; **Zähne** (an einer Briefmarke usw.) perforations; **sich** (*Dat.*) **einen ~ ziehen lassen** have a tooth out; **die dritten Zähne** (scherzh.) dentures 2 (fig.) **der ~ der Zeit** (ugs.) the ravages *pl.* of time; **der ~ der Zeit hat an diesem Haus genagt** (ugs.) time has left its mark on this house; **jmdm. diesen** *od.* **den ~ ziehen** (ugs.) put paid to this idea [of sb.'s] (coll.); **[jmdm.] die Zähne zeigen** (ugs.) show [sb.] one's teeth; **die Zähne zusammenbeißen** (ugs.) grit one's teeth; **sich** (*Dat.*) **an**

ℹ Zahlen

Kardinalzahlen = Cardinal numbers

0 (*null*) = nought (*bes. brit.*), zero[1]
1 (*eins, ein...*) = one
2 (*zwei*) = two
3 (*drei*) = three
4 (*vier*) = four
5 (*fünf*) = five
6 (*sechs*) = six
7 (*sieben*) = seven
8 (*acht*) = eight
9 (*neun*) = nine
10 (*zehn*) = ten
11 (*elf*) = eleven
12 (*zwölf*) = twelve
13 (*dreizehn*) = thirteen
14 (*vierzehn*) = fourteen
15 (*fünfzehn*) = fifteen
16 (*sechzehn*) = sixteen
17 (*siebzehn*) = seventeen
18 (*achtzehn*) = eighteen
19 (*neunzehn*) = nineteen
20 (*zwanzig*) = twenty
21 (*einundzwanzig*) = twenty-one
22 (*zweiundzwanzig*) = twenty-two
30 (*dreißig*) = thirty
40 (*vierzig*) = forty
50 (*fünfzig*) = fifty
60 (*sechzig*) = sixty
70 (*siebzig*) = seventy
80 (*achtzig*) = eighty
90 (*neunzig*) = ninety
100 (*[ein]hundert*) = a *od.* one hundred[2]
101 (*[ein]hundert[und]eins, [ein]hundert[und]ein...*)
= a *od.* one hundred and one (*brit.*), a *od.* one hundred one (*amerik.*)
555 (*fünfhundert[und]fünfundfünfzig*) = five hundred and fifty-five (*brit.*), five hundred fifty-five (*amerik.*)
1 000 (*[ein]tausend*) = a *od.* one thousand
1 001 (*[ein]tausend[und]eins, [ein]tausend[und]ein...*)
= a *od.* one thousand and one (*brit.*), a *od.* one thousand one (*amerik.*)
1 200 (*[ein]tausendzweihundert* od. *zwölfhundert*) = one thousand two hundred, twelve hundred
100 000 (*[ein]hunderttausend*) = a *od.* one hundred thousand
1 000 000 (*eine Million*) = a *od.* one million
3 536 000 (*drei Millionen fünfhundertsechsunddreißigtausend*) = three million[3] five hundred and thirty-six (*brit.*) *od.* (*amerik.*) five hundred thirty-six thousand
1 000 000 000 (*eine Milliarde*) = a *od.* one billion, a *od.* one thousand million
1 000 000 000 000 (*eine Billion*) = a *od.* one trillion, a *od.* one million million

Anmerkungen

[1] 'Nought' wird hauptsächlich im britischen Englisch, 'zero' dagegen im amerikanischen Englisch für die Ziffer 0 verwendet. Wenn man eine Zahl ausspricht, die eine Null enthält, sagt man entweder 'oh' oder (besonders im amerikanischen Sprachraum) 'zero':

Die Vorwahl für London (Mitte) ist 020 7
= The code for central London is 020 7 (oh-two-oh-seven *od.* (*bes. amerik.*) zero-two-zero-seven)
der Peugeot 406
= the Peugeot 406 (four-oh-six)
Sie haben 4:0 gewonnen
= They won 4-0 (four-nil *od.* (*amerik.*) four-zero)
Den ersten Satz gewann sie 6:0
= She won the first set 6-0 (six-love)
Tiefsttemperaturen um 4 Grad unter Null
= Temperatures falling to *od.* (*bes. amerik.*) Lows around 4 degrees below zero

[2] **one** sagt man statt **a**, wenn man die Genauigkeit der Ziffer betonen will; **a hundred** (und **a thousand, a million** usw.) ist aber viel häufiger, vor allem bei zusammengesetzten Zahlen (z.B. **a hundred and twenty**).

[3] Wie bei **hundred** und **thousand** verwendet man die Pluralform **millions** nicht in Zahlen, da **million** hier kein Substantiv ist; das gilt auch für unbestimmte Zahlwörter:

einige/ein paar Millionen [Pfund]
= several/a couple of million [pounds]

millions kommt nur in ungenauen Ausdrücken vor, wie etwa:

Man kann Millionen von Pfund/Dollar verdienen
= One can earn millions [of pounds/dollars]
Hunderte von Millionen
= hundreds of millions

Brüche = Fractions

½	a half	1½	one and a half
⅓	a third	5⅔	five and two thirds
¼	a quarter	2¾	two and three quarters
⅕	a fifth	4⅘	four and four fifths
⅛	an eighth	8⅞	eight and seven eighths
1/32	one thirty-second	10/71	ten seventy-firsts

Zur Bildung der Brüche dienen also die (substantivisch gebrauchten) Formen der Ordinalzahlen.

zwei Drittel des Weges
= two thirds of the distance
drei Viertel aller Offiziere
= three quarters of all officers

Nach dem Bruch folgt bei Maßeinheiten **of a**, und die Einheit steht dementsprechend im Singular.

ein Viertelliter
= a quarter of a litre
fünf achtel Meilen
= five eighths of a mile
sechs Hundertstelsekunden
= six hundredths of a second

Dezimalzahlen = Decimal numbers

0,1	=	0.1 (point one oh *od.* (*brit.*) nought *od.* (*amerik.*) zero point one)
0,015	=	0.015 ([oh] point oh *od.* (*brit.*) [nought] point nought *od.* (*amerik.*) [zero] point zero one five)
1,43	=	1.43 (one point four three)
11,70	=	11.70 (eleven point seven oh)
12,$\bar{3}$	=	12.$\bar{3}$ (twelve point three recurring)

▶

jmdm./etw. die Zähne ausbeißen (ugs.) get nowhere with sb./sth.; **lange Zähne machen, mit langen Zähnen essen** (ugs.) make a face over one's food; **jmdn. auf den ~ fühlen[, ob ...]** (ugs.) sound sb. out [to see whether ...]; **bis an die Zähne bewaffnet** armed to the teeth; **etw. mit Zähnen und Klauen verteidigen** (ugs.) defend sth. tooth and nail **3** (ugs.: Geschwindigkeit) **einen ganz schönen ~ drauf haben** be going like the clappers (Brit. coll.); **mit einem höllischen ~:** at a hell of a lick (coll.); **einen ~ zulegen** (ugs.) get a move on (coll.) **4** (Jugendspr. veralt.) piece *or* bit of skirt (sl.); **ein steiler ~:** a piece of hot stuff (coll.)

Zahnarzt *der* ▸ℹ **S. 113** dentist; (mit chirurgischer Ausbildung) dental surgeon

zahnarzt-, Zahnarzt-: ~besuch *der* visit to the dentist; **~helfer** *der*, **~helferin** *die* ▸ℹ **S. 113** dental assistant

Zahnärztin *die* ▸**Zahnarzt**

Z

▸ ⓘ Zahlen (Fortsetzung)

Ordinalzahlen = Ordinal numbers

***1.* (*erst...*)** = 1st (first)
***2.* (*zweit...*)** = 2nd (second)
***3.* (*dritt...*)** = 3rd (third)
***4.* (*viert...*)** = 4th (fourth)
***5.* (*fünft...*)** = 5th (fifth)
***6.* (*sechst...*)** = 6th (sixth)
***7.* (*sieb[en]t...*)** = 7th (seventh)
***8.* (*acht...*)** = 8th (eighth)
***9.* (*neunt...*)** = 9th (ninth)
***10.* (*zehnt...*)** = 10th (tenth)
***11.* (*elft...*)** = 11th (eleventh)
***12.* (*zwölft...*)** = 12th (twelfth)
***13.* (*dreizehnt...*)** = 13th (thirteenth)
***14.* (*vierzehnt...*)** = 14th (fourteenth)
***15.* (*fünfzehnt...*)** = 15th (fifteenth)
***16.* (*sechzehnt...*)** = 16th (sixteenth)
***17.* (*siebzehnt...*)** = 17th (seventeenth)
***18.* (*achtzehnt...*)** = 18th (eighteenth)
***19.* (*neunzehnt...*)** = 19th (nineteenth)
***20.* (*zwanzigst...*)** = 20th (twentieth)
***21.* (*einundzwanzigst...*)** = 21st (twenty-first)
***22.* (*zweiundzwanzigst...*)** = 22nd (twenty-second)
***30.* (*dreißigst...*)** = 30th (thirtieth)
***40.* (*vierzigst...*)** = 40th (fortieth)
***50.* (*fünfzigst...*)** = 50th (fiftieth)
***60.* (*sechzigst...*)** = 60th (sixtieth)
***70.* (*siebzigst...*)** = 70th (seventieth)
***80.* (*achtzigst...*)** = 80th (eightieth)
***90.* (*neunzigst...*)** = 90th (ninetieth)
***100.* ([*ein*]*hundertst...*)** = 100th ([*one*] *hundredth)*
***101.* ([*ein*]*hundert*[*und*]*erst...*)** = 101st ([one] hundred and first (*brit.*), [one] hundred first (*amerik.*))
***555.* (*fünfhundert*[*und*]*fünfundfünfzigst...*)** = 555th (five hundred and fifty-fifth (*brit.*), five hundred fifty-fifth (*amerik.*))
***1 000.* ([*ein*]*tausendst...*)** = 1,000th ([one] thousandth)
***1 001.* ([*ein*]*tausend*[*und*]*erst...*)** = 1,001st (one thousand and first (*brit.*), one thousand first (*amerik.*))
***1 200.* ([*ein*]*tausendzweihundertst... od. zwölfhundertst...*)**
= 1,200th (one thousand two hundredth, twelve hundredth)
***100 000.* ([*ein*]*hunderttausendst...*)** = 100,000th ([one] hundred thousandth*)*
***1 000 000.* (*millionst...*)** = 1,000,000th ([one] millionth)
***3 536 000.* (*drei Millionen fünfhundertsechsunddreißigtausendst...*)**
= 3,536,000th (three million five hundred and thirty-six (*brit.*) *od.* (*amerik.*) five hundred thirty-six thousandth)
***1 000 000 000.* (*milliardst...*)** = 1,000,000,000th ([one] billionth, [one] thousand millionth)
***1 000 000 000 000.* (*billionst...*)** = 1,000,000,000,000th ([one] trillionth, one million millionth)

Rechnen

7 + 3 = 10 (seven plus three is *od.* equals ten)
10 – 3 = 7 (ten minus three is *od.* equals seven)
10 x 3 = 30 (ten times three is *od.* equals thirty)
30 ÷ 3 = 10 (thirty divided by three is *od.* equals ten)

Potenzen = Powers

3^2 = *drei hoch zwei* = three squared
3^3 = *drei hoch drei* = three cubed
3^{10} = *drei hoch zehn* = three to the power of ten
$\sqrt{25}$ = [*Quadrat*]*wurzel aus fünfundzwanzig*
= the square root of twenty-five

Siehe auch ◻ **Altersangaben, Datum, Entfernung, Fläche, Geld, Gewichte, Höhe und Tiefe, Länge und Breite, Rauminhalt, Temperaturen, Uhrzeit**

zahnärztlich
A *Adj.* dental ‹*treatment etc.*›; **~er Befund** dentist's findings *pl*
B *adv.* **jmdn. ~ behandeln** give sb. dental treatment; **~ empfohlen** recommended by dentists

Zahnarzt·praxis *die* dental practice

Zahn-: ~behandlung *die* dental treatment; **~bein** *das* (Biol.) dentine; **~belag** *der* [dental] plaque; **~bürste** *die* toothbrush; **~creme** *die* ▸▸ **pasta**

zähne-, Zähne-: ~fletschend *Adj.* baring its/their teeth *postpos.*; (knurrend) snarling; **~klappern** *das*; **~~s** chattering teeth *pl.*; *s. auch* **heulen 2**; **~klappernd** *Adj.* with chattering teeth *postpos.*; **~knirschend** *adv.* gnashing one's teeth; cursing silently; **~knirschend nachgeben** give in with bad grace *or* under protest

zahnen *itr. V.* ‹*baby*› be teething

zahn-, Zahn-: ~ersatz *der* denture; **~fäule** *die* tooth decay; dental caries (Med.); **~fleisch** *das* ▸ⓘ **S. 435** gum; (als Ganzes) gums *pl.*; **auf dem ~fleisch gehen** (fig. ugs.) be absolutely knackered (Brit. coll.); be tuckered [out] (Amer. coll.); **~fleisch·bluten** *das*; **~~s** bleeding gums *pl.*; **~füllung** *die* filling; **~gold** *das* dental gold; **~hals** *der* neck of a/the tooth; **~heilkunde** *die* dentistry *no art.*; **~implantat** *das* (Zahnmed.) tooth implant; **~klinik** *die* dental clinic; **~kranz** *der* **1** sprocket [wheel]; **2** (~kranzpaket) rear sprocket [cluster]; **~krone** *die* crown [of a/the tooth]; **~laut** *der* (Sprachw.) dental; **~los** *Adj.* toothless; **~lücke** *die* gap in one's teeth; **~medizin** *die* dentistry *no art.*; **~mediziner** *der*, **~medizinerin** *die* ▸ⓘ **S. 113** dental specialist; (Forscher) dental researcher; **~pasta** /-pasta/ *die*; **~~**, **~pasten** toothpaste; **~pasta·tube** *die* toothpaste tube; **~pflege** *die* dental care; **~prothese** *die* dentures *pl.*; [set *sing.* of] false teeth *pl.*; **~pulver** *das* tooth powder; **~putz·becher** *der* tooth mug; **~rad** *das* gearwheel; (für Ketten) sprocket; **~rad·bahn** *die* rack railway; **~reihe** *die* row of teeth; **~riemen** *der* (Technik) toothed belt; **~schmelz** *der* [tooth] enamel;

Z

~schmerzen *Pl.* ▸ⓘ **S. 439** toothache *sing.*; **~seide** *die* dental floss; **~spange** *die* [tooth] brace; **~stein** *der* tartar; **~stocher** *der;* **~~s, ~~:** toothpick; **~stumpf** *der* [tooth] stump; **~technik** *die* dental technology; **~techniker** *der,* **~technikerin** *die* ▸ⓘ **S. 113** dental technician; **~technisch** **A** *Adj.* (*nicht präd.*) dental technology ‹*work*›; ‹*examination*› by means of dental technology; dental ‹*laboratory, equipment*›; **B** *adv.* ‹*produce, restore*› by means of dental technology; **~verfall** *der* tooth decay; dental decay; **~wal** *der* toothed whale; **~weh** *das* (ugs.) toothache; **~wurzel** *die* root of a/the tooth

Zähre /ˈtsɛːrə/ *die;* **~, ~n** (dichter. veralt.) tear[drop]

Zaire /zaˈiːr/ *(das);* **~s** Zaire

Zairer /zaˈiːrɐ/ *der;* **~s, ~, Zairerin** *die;* **~, ~nen** Zairean

Zampano /ˈtsampano/ *der;* **~s, ~s** golden boy; **er ist ein richtiger ~:** everything just falls into his lap

Zander /ˈtsandɐ/ *der;* **~s, ~:** zander

Zange /ˈtsaŋə/ *die;* **~, ~n** [1] (Werkzeug) pliers *pl.*; (Eiswürfel~, Wäsche~, Zucker~) tongs *pl.*; (Geburts~) forceps *pl.*; (Kneif~) pincers *pl.*; (Loch~) punch; **eine ~:** a pair of pliers/tongs/forceps/pincers/a punch; **jmdn. in die ~ nehmen** (fig. ugs.) put the screws on sb.; (Fußballjargon) crowd sb. out; **jmdn. in der ~ haben** (fig. ugs.) have sb. where one wants him/her [2] (bei Tieren) pincer

Zangen·geburt *die* forceps delivery

Zank /tsaŋk/ *der;* **~[e]s** squabble; row; **[um** *od.* **über etw.** (*Akk.*)**] in ~ geraten** start squabbling [over sth.]

Zank·apfel *der* bone of contention

zanken

A *refl.* (*auch itr.*) *V.* squabble, bicker (**um** *od.* **über** + *Akk.* over)

B *itr. V.* (bes. ostmd.: schimpfen) **[mit jmdm.] ~:** scold [sb.]

Zänkerei *die;* **~, ~en** [minor] squabbling *no pl. or* squabbles *pl.*

zänkisch *Adj.* quarrelsome

Zapf·anlage *die* beer pump

Zäpfchen /ˈtsɛpfçən/ *das;* **~s, ~** [1] suppository [2] ▸ⓘ **S. 435** (Anat.) uvula

Zäpfchen-r, Zäpfchen-R *das* (Sprachw.) uvular r

zapfen /ˈtsapfn̩/ *tr. V.* tap, draw ‹*beer, wine*›; **kannst du mir zwei Pils ~?** can you draw me two Pils?

Zapfen *der;* **~s, ~** [1] (Bot.) [pine/fir] cone [2] (Stöpsel) bung [3] (Eis~) icicle [4] (Holzverarb.) tenon

Zapfen·streich *der* (Milit.) [1] (Signal) last post (Brit.); taps *pl.* (Amer.); **der Große ~:** the tattoo [2] (Ende der Ausgehzeit) time for return to barracks

Zapfer *der;* **~s, ~:** barman

Zapferin *die;* **~, ~nen** barmaid

Zapf-: ~hahn *der;* *Pl.* **~hähne,** *fachspr.* **~~en** tap; **~pistole** *die* [petrol] pump nozzle; **~säule** *die* petrol pump (Brit.); gasoline pump (Amer.); **~stelle** *die* (mit Wasser) [drinking] fountain; (Hahn) tap; (mit Brennstoff) refuelling pont; (Tankstelle) petrol station; gas station (Amer.)

zappelig *Adj.* (ugs.) [1] wriggly; fidgety ‹*child*› [2] (nervös) jittery (coll.)

zappeln /ˈtsapl̩n/ *itr. V.* wriggle; ‹*child*› fidget; **mit den Beinen/Armen ~:** wave one's legs/arms about; **jmdn. ~ lassen** (fig. ugs.) keep sb. on tenterhooks; (im Unklaren lassen) keep sb. guessing

Zappelphilipp *der;* **~s, ~e** *od.* **~s** (ugs.) fidgety child; fidget

zappen /ˈzɛpn̩/ (ugs.)

A *itr. V.* zap (coll.)

B *refl. V.* zap (coll.); **sich durch die Frühstückssendungen/zwanzig Kanäle ~:** zap through the breakfast programmes/twenty channels

zappen·duster /ˈtsapn̩ˈduːstɐ/ *Adj.* (ugs.) pitch-dark; **es ist ~** (fig.) things look black *or* hopeless

Zar /tsaːɐ̯/ *der;* **~en, ~en** (hist.) Tsar

Zaren·reich *das* (hist.) tsardom

Zarewitsch /tsaˈreːvɪtʃ/ *der;* **~[e]s, ~e** (hist.) Tsarevitch

Zarge /ˈtsargə/ *die;* **~, ~n** [1] (Rahmen) frame [2] (eines Saiteninstruments) side wall; rib

Zarin *die;* **~, ~nen** (hist.) Tsarina

Zarismus *der;* **~** (hist.) tsarism *no art.*

zaristisch *Adj.* (hist.) tsarist

zart /tsaːɐ̯t/

A *Adj.* [1] delicate; soft ‹*skin*›; tender ‹*bud, shoot*›; fragile, delicate ‹*china*›; fine ‹*silk, lace*›; delicate, frail ‹*health, constitution, child*›; **im ~en Alter von sechs Jahren** (geh.) at the tender age of six; **das ist nichts für ~e Seelen** *od.* **Gemüter** it is not at all suitable for sensitive souls [2] (weich) tender ‹*meat, vegetables*›; soft ‹*filling*›; fine ‹*biscuits*› [3] (leicht) gentle ‹*kiss, touch*›; delicate ‹*colour, complexion, fragrance, etc.*›; soft ‹*pastel colours*›; soft, gentle ‹*voice, sound, tune*› [4] (einfühlsam, zärtlich) tender ‹*care, feelings*› [5] (zurückhaltend) delicate ‹*reference*›; gentle ‹*hint*›; faint ‹*smile*›

B *adv.* [1] (empfindlich) delicately [2] (leicht) delicately ‹*coloured, fragrant*›; ‹*kiss, touch*› gently [3] (zärtlich, einfühlsam) tenderly [4] (zurückhaltend) ‹*hint*› gently; ‹*smile*› faintly

zart-, Zart-: ~besaitet *Adj.* highly sensitive; **~bitter** *Adj.* plain ‹*chocolate*›; **~blau** *Adj.* pale blue; **~fühlend** **A** *Adj.* tactful; **B** *adv.* tactfully; **~gefühl** *das* tact; delicacy of feeling

Zartheit *die;* **~** [1] delicacy; (der Haut) softness; (von Porzellan) fragility; (von Spitzen, Seide) fineness; (der Gesundheit, Konstitution, eines Kindes) delicateness; (Sensibilität) sensitivity [2] (von Fleisch, Gemüse) tenderness [3] (Leichtheit) (eines Kusses, einer Berührung) gentleness; (einer Farbe, des Teints, eines Dufts) delicacy; (der Stimme, des Tons, einer Melodie) softness; gentleness [4] (Zärtlichkeit) tenderness [5] (Zurückhaltung) delicacy

zärtlich /ˈtsɛːɐ̯tlɪç/

A *Adj.* [1] tender; loving; **~ werden** (verhüll.) start petting [2] (geh.: fürsorglich) loving; caring

B *adv.* [1] (liebevoll) tenderly; lovingly [2] (geh.: fürsorglich) lovingly; caringly

Zärtlichkeit *die;* **~, ~en** [1] (Zuneigung) tenderness; affection [2] (Liebkosung) caress; **es kam zu ~en zwischen ihnen** they became intimate; **~en austauschen** become intimate [3] (Fürsorglichkeit) loving care

zart·rosa *Adj.* pale pink

Zaster /ˈtsastɐ/ *der;* **~s** (salopp) dough (coll.)

Zäsur /tsɛˈzuːɐ̯/ *die;* **~, ~en** [1] (Verslehre, Musik) caesura [2] (geh.) (Einschnitt) break; (Wendepunkt) turning point

Zauber /ˈtsaubɐ/ *der;* **~s, ~** [1] (auch fig.) magic; (magische Handlung) magic trick; (Bann) [magic] spell; **einen großen ~ auf jmdn. ausüben** have a great fascination for sb.; **er ist ihrem ~ erlegen** he has fallen under her spell; **der ~ des Verbotenen** the fascination of what is forbidden; *s. auch* **faul A 3** [2] (ugs. abwertend: Aufheben) fuss; **ich halte nichts von dem ganzen ~:** the whole palaver means nothing to me (coll.) [3] (ugs.: Zeug) stuff

Zauber·buch *das* book of magic spells

Zauberei *die;* **~, ~en** [1] (das Zaubern) magic [2] (Zaubertrick) magic trick

Zauberer *der;* **~s, ~:** magician

zauber-, Zauber-: ~flöte *die:* **„Die ~flöte"** 'The Magic Flute'; **~formel** *die* magic spell; (fig.: Patentlösung) magic formula; panacea; **~haft** **A** *Adj.* enchanting; delightful; **B** *adv.* enchantingly; delightfully; **~hand** *die:* **wie durch** *od.* **von ~hand** as though by magic

Zauberin *die;* **~, ~nen** [1] sorceress [2] (Zauberkünstlerin) conjuror

zauberisch (geh.)

A *Adj.* [1] (traumhaft) magical [2] (bezaubernd) enchanting

B *adv.* [1] (traumhaft) magically [2] (bezaubernd) enchantingly

zauber-, Zauber-: ~kraft *die* magic[al] *or* supernatural powers *pl.*; **~kräftig** *Adj.* with magic properties *postpos., not pred.*; **ein ~kräftiger Trank** a magic potion; **~kunst** *die* [1] magic *no art.*; (eines Bühnenkünstlers) magic *no art.*; conjuring *no art.*; [2] (magische Fähigkeit) magic; **~künstler** *der,* **~künstlerin** *die* conjuror; magician; **~lehrling** *der* apprentice sorcerer; **Goethes „~lehrling"** Goethe's 'The Sorcerer's Apprentice'; **~mittel** *das* magic method; magic formula; (Heilmittel) magic cure (**gegen** for)

zaubern

A *itr. V.* [1] (Zauberkraft ausüben) do magic; **ich kann doch nicht ~!** (ugs.) I can't work miracles [2] (Zaubertricks ausführen) do conjuring tricks

B *tr. V.* (auch fig.) conjure; conjure up ‹*palace, horse, etc.*›; **eine Taube aus dem Hut ~:** produce a dove out of a hat; **ein vorzügliches Essen auf den Tisch ~** (fig.) conjure up an excellent meal

Zauber-: ~spruch *der* magic spell; **~stab** *der* magic wand; **~trank** *der* magic potion; **~trick** *der* conjuring trick; **~welt** *die* magic world (also fig.); **~wort** *das;* *Pl.* **~~e** magic word (also fig.)

Zauderer *der;* **~s, ~, Zauderin** *die;* **~, ~nen** waverer; ditherer

zaudern /ˈtsaudɐn/ *itr. V.* (geh.) delay; **mit etw. ~:** delay in doing sth.; **zu lange ~:** procrastinate for too long

Zaum /tsaum/ *der;* **~[e]s, Zäume** /ˈtsɔymə/ [1] bridle [2] (geh.) **jmdn./etw. im ~ halten** keep sb./sth. in check *or* under control; **sich/seine Zunge im ~ halten** restrain *or* control oneself/control one's tongue; **seine Gefühle/Leidenschaften im ~ halten** control one's feelings/passions

zäumen /ˈtsɔymən/ *tr. V.* bridle ‹*horse*›

Zaum·zeug *das* bridle

Zaun /tsaun/ *der;* **~[e]s, Zäune** /ˈtsɔynə/ fence; **einen Streit/Krieg vom ~ brechen** (fig.) suddenly start a quarrel/war

Zaun-: ~gast *der* onlooker; **~könig** *der* (Zool.) wren; **~pfahl** *der* fence post; *s. auch* **Wink 2**; **~winde** *die* (Bot.) hedge bindweed

Zausel *der;* **~s, ~** (landsch. abwertend) fellow; **ein alter ~:** an old buffer (coll.)

zausen /ˈtsauzn̩/ *tr. V.* (auch fig.) ruffle; ruffle, tousle ‹*hair*›

z. B. *Abk.* **= zum Beispiel** e.g.

z. b. V. *Abk.* **= zur besonderen Verwendung**

ZDF *Abk.* **= Zweites Deutsches Fernsehen** Second German Television Channel

ZDF — Zweites Deutsches Fernsehen

The second German public TV channel, which was founded in 1961 and broadcasts the *Zweites Programm* with entertainment, news, information, and a limited amount of advertising.

Zebra /ˈtseːbra/ *das;* **~s, ~s** (Zool.) zebra

Zebra·streifen *der* zebra crossing (Brit.); pedestrian crossing

Zebu /ˈtseːbu/ *der od. das;* **~s, ~s** (Zool.) zebu

Zech·bruder *der* (ugs. abwertend) [1] drinking pal (coll.) [2] (Trinker) boozer (coll.); tippler

Zeche *die;* **~, ~n** [1] (Rechnung) bill (Brit.); check (Amer.); **eine hohe ~ machen** run up a large bill; **die ~ prellen** (ugs.) leave without paying [the bill]; **die ~ bezahlen müssen** (fig.) have to foot the bill *or* pay the price [2] (Grube) pit; mine

zechen /ˈtsɛçn̩/ *itr. V.* (veralt., scherzh.) tipple

Zecher *der;* **~s, ~, Zecherin** *die;* **~, ~nen** (veralt., scherzh.) tippler

Zech-: ~gelage *das* (veralt., scherzh.) drinking bout; **~genosse** *der,* **~genossin** *die* (veralt., scherzh.) drinking companion; **~kumpan** *der,* **~kumpanin** *die* (ugs. abwertend) drinking pal (coll.); **~preller** *der;* **~~s, ~~:** *person who leaves without paying the bill;* bill-dodger; **~prellerei** *die;* **~~, ~~en** *leaving without paying the bill;* bill-dodging; **~prellerin** *die;* **~~, ~~nen** ▸ **~preller**; **~tour** *die* (ugs.) pub crawl (Brit. coll.); **eine ~tour unternehmen** go on a pub crawl (Brit. coll.); barhop (Amer. coll.)

Zecke /ˈt̮sɛkə/ *die;* ~, ~n (Zool.) tick

Zeder /ˈt̮seːdɐ/ *die;* ~, ~n cedar

Zedern·holz *das* cedarwood

Zeh /t̮seː/ *der;* ~s, ~en, **Zehe** *die;* ~, ~n [1] ▸❶ S. 435 toe; **jmdm. auf die ~en treten** (auch fig.) tread on sb.'s toes [2] (Knoblauchzehe) clove

Zehen-: **~nagel** *der* ▸❶ S. 435 toenail; **~spitze** *die:* ▸❶ S. 435 **auf ~spitzen** on tiptoe; **sich auf die ~spitzen stellen** stand on tiptoe

zehn /t̮seːn/ *Kardinalz.* ▸❶ S. 29, ▸❶ S. 729, ▸❶ S. 826 ten; *s. auch* **acht**[1]

Zehn *die;* ~, ~en ten; *s. auch* **Acht**[1] **1, 4, 5, 7**

zehn-, Zehn- *s. auch* **acht-, Acht-**: **~cent·stück** *das* ten-cent piece; **~eck** *das* decagon; **~eckig** *Adj.* decagonal; **~ender** *der;* ~~s, ~~ (Jägerspr.) ten-pointer

Zehner *der;* ~s, ~ [1] (ugs.: Geldschein, Münze) ten [2] (ugs.: Autobus) number ten [3] (Math.) ten; **die ~ addieren** add up the tens [4] (Sprungturm) ten-metre platform; *s. auch* **Achter 4**

Zehner·karte *die* ticket for ten trips/visits *etc.*

zehnerlei *Gattungsz.; indekl.* [1] *attr.* ten kinds *or* sorts of; ten different ‹*sorts, sizes, etc.*› [2] *subst.* ten [different] things

Zehner-: **~pack** *der* pack of ten; **~packung** *die* packet of ten; **~stelle** *die* (Math.) **in der ~stelle** in the tens; **~system** *das* (Math.) ▸**Dezimalsystem**; **~ziffer** *die* (Math.) figure in the tens

Zehn·euro·schein *der* ten-euro note

zehn·fach *Vervielfältigungsz.* tenfold; **die ~e Menge** ten times the quantity; *s. auch* **achtfach**

Zehnfache *das; adj. Dekl.* **das ~:** ten times as much; **um ein ~s/um das ~:** ten times; *s. auch* **Achtfache**

zehn-, Zehn-: **~finger·system** *das* touch [-typing] system; **im ~fingersystem schreiben** touch-type; **~flach** *das;* ~~[e]s, ~~e, **~flächner** *der;* ~~s, ~~ (Math.) decahedron; **~jahres·feier**, **~jahr·feier** *die* tenth anniversary celebration; **~jährig** *Adj.* (10 Jahre alt) ten-year-old *attrib.;* ten years old *postpos.;* (10 Jahre dauernd) ten-year *attrib.; s. auch* **achtjährig**; **~jährlich** A *Adj.* ten-yearly; B *adv.* every ten years; *s. auch* **achtjährlich**; **~kampf** *der* (Sport) decathlon; **~kämpfer** *der* decathlete; **~mal** *Adv.* ten times; **und wenn du dich ~mal langweilst** it doesn't matter 'how bored you are; *s. auch* **achtmal**; **~malig** *Adj.* **nach ~maligem Läuten** after ringing ten times; *s. auch* **achtmalig**; **~seitig** *Adj.* ten-sided; ten-page *attrib.* ‹*letter, article, etc.*›; **~stöckig** *Adj.* ten-storey ‹*building*›; *s. auch* **achtstöckig**

zehnt /t̮seːnt/ *in* **wir waren zu ~:** there were ten of us; *s. auch* **acht**[2]

zehnt... *Ordinalz.* ▸❶ S. 165, ▸❶ S. 826 tenth; *s. auch* **acht...**

zehn-: **~tägig** *Adj.* (10 Tage alt) ten-day-old *attrib.;* (10 Tage dauernd) ten-day *attrib.; s. auch* **achttägig**; **~tausend** *Kardinalz.* ▸❶ S. 826 ten thousand; **die oberen ~tausend** (fig.: die vornehmen Leute) the élite of society

Zehnte[1] *der;* ~n, ~n (hist.) tithe

Zehnte[2] *der/die; adj. Dekl.* tenth; *s. auch* **Achte**

zehn·teilig *Adj.* ten-piece ‹*tool set etc.*›; ten-part ‹*serial*›; *s. auch* **achtteilig**

zehntel /ˈt̮seːnt̮l/ *Bruchz.* ▸❶ S. 826 tenth; *s. auch* **achtel**

Zehntel *das* (*schweiz. meist der*); ~s, ~: ▸❶ S. 826 tenth

Zehntel-: **~liter** *der* tenth of a litre; **~sekunde** *die* tenth of a second

***zehnte·mal**, ***zehnten·mal** ▸**Mal**[1]

zehntens *Adv.* tenthly

Zehn·tonner *der;* ~s, ~: ten-tonner

zehren /ˈt̮seːrən/ *itr. V.* [1] (leben) **von etw. ~:** live on *or* off sth.; **von Erinnerungen** *usw.* **~** (fig.) sustain oneself on memories *etc.* [2] (geh.: schwächen) drain sb.'s strength; take it out of sb. [3] (zusetzen) **an jmdm./jmds. Kräften ~:** wear sb. down/sap sb.'s strength

Zehr·geld *das* (veralt.) money for the journey

Zeichen /ˈt̮saiçn̩/ *das;* ~s, ~ [1] (Gebärde) sign; (Laut, Wink) signal; **das ~ zum Angriff** the signal to attack; **jmdm. ein ~ geben** signal to sb.; **zum ~, dass ...** to show that ...; as a sign that ...; **zum** *od.* **als ~ ihrer Versöhnung** as a sign *or* token of their reconciliation [2] (Markierung) mark; (Waren~) [trade] mark; (am Briefkopf) reference; **sein ~ unter ein Schriftstück setzen** initial a document; **seines/ihres ~s** (veralt., scherzh.) by trade/profession; **[ein] ~ setzen** set an example; point the way [3] (Symbol) sign; (Chemie, Math., auf Landkarten usw.) symbol; (DV) character; (Satz~) punctuation mark; (Musik) accidental; **das ~ des Kreuzes** the sign of the cross [4] (An~) sign; indication; (einer Krankheit) sign; symptom; **ein ~ dafür, dass ...** a [sure] sign that ...; **wenn nicht alle ~ trügen** unless I am very much mistaken; **es geschehen noch ~ und Wunder** wonders will never cease (iron.); **die ~ der Zeit erkennen** see which way the wind's blowing (fig.) [5] (Tierkreis~) sign [of the zodiac]; **ich bin im ~ des Krebses** *usw.* **geboren** I was born under the sign of Cancer *etc.;* **im** *od.* **unter dem ~ von etw. stehen** (geh.) be much influenced by sth.

zeichen-, Zeichen-: **~block** *der; Pl.* **~blöcke** *od.* ~~s sketch pad; **~brett** *das* drawing board; **~dreieck** *das* set square; **~erklärung** *die* legend; **~feder** *die* drawing pen; **~folge** *die* sequence of signs; (DV) character string; **~haft** (geh.) A *Adj.* symbolic; B *adv.* symbolically; **~heft** *das* drawing book; **~kette** *die* (DV) character string; **~kohle** *die* charcoal (in stick form); **~kunst** *die* [1] [art of] drawing; graphic art; [2] *Pl.* drawing skills; **~lehrer** *der*, **~lehrerin** *die* drawing teacher; **~papier** *das* drawing paper; **~satz** *der* (DV) set of symbols; (DV) character set; **~setzung** *die;* ~~, ~~en punctuation; **~sprache** *die* sign language; **~stift** *der* drawing pencil; **~system** *das* system of signs; **~tisch** *der* drawing board; **~trick** *der* (ugs.) cartoons *pl.;* **~trick·figur** *die* cartoon character; **~trick·film** *der* animated cartoon; **~trick·serie** *die* cartoon series; **~unterricht** *der* drawing lessons *pl.;* (Schulfach) art *no art.; s. auch* **Englischunterricht**; **~winkel** *der* set square

zeichnen

A *tr. V.* [1] (malen, darstellen) draw; (fig.) portray ‹*character*›; **ein Bild von dem Geschehen ~** (fig.) describe what happened [2] (markieren) **das Fell ist schön/auffallend gezeichnet** the fur has beautiful/striking markings; **er war vom Alter/von der Krankheit gezeichnet** (fig.) age/sickness had left its mark on him; **ein vom Tode Gezeichneter** (fig. geh.) a man already bearing the mark of death [3] (bes. Kaufmannsspr.) sign ‹*cheque*›; subscribe for ‹*share, loan*›

B *itr. V.* [1] draw; **ich zeichne schon länger daran** I have been working on this drawing for quite a while [2] (bes. Kaufmannsspr.: unterschreiben) sign; **für etw. [verantwortlich] ~** (fig.) be responsible for sth.

Zeichnen *das;* ~s drawing; **technisches ~:** technical drawing

Zeichner *der;* ~s, ~, **Zeichnerin** *die;* ~, ~nen [1] ▸❶ S. 113 graphic artist; (Technik) draughtsman/-woman [2] (Kaufmannsspr.) subscriber

zeichnerisch

A *Adj.* ‹*fault*› of draughtsmanship; ‹*talent*› as a draughtsman/-woman *or* for drawing; **exakte ~e Wiedergabe** exact portrayal in a drawing

B *adv.* **~ begabt sein** have a talent for drawing; **etw. ~ darstellen** make a drawing of sth.

Zeichnung *die;* ~, ~en [1] drawing; (fig.: von Figuren) portrayal [2] (bei Tieren und Pflanzen) markings *pl.* [3] (Kaufmannsspr.) subscription

zeichnungs·berechtigt *Adj.* (Kaufmannsspr.) with signatory powers *postpos.;* **~ sein** have signatory powers

Zeige·finger *der* index finger; forefinger; **der erhobene ~** (fig.) the wagging *or* monitory finger

zeigen /ˈt̮saign̩/

A *tr. V.* point; **[mit dem Finger/einem Stock] auf jmdn./etw. ~:** point [one's finger/a stick] at sb./sth.; **nach Norden/zwölf ~:** point [to the] north/to twelve o'clock

B *tr. V.* show; **jmdm. etw. ~:** show sb. sth.; show sth. to sb.; **jmdm. sein Zimmer ~:** show sb. to his/her room; **dem werd ichs ~!** (ugs.) I'll show him!; **er hat es allen seinen Konkurrenten gezeigt** (ugs.) he showed all his competitors just how it was done; **zeig mal, was du kannst** show [us] what you can do

C *refl. V.* [1] (sich sehen lassen) appear; **er zeigt sich selten in der Öffentlichkeit** he is rarely seen in public; **mit ihr kann man sich überall ~:** you can take her anywhere; **er wollte sich von seiner besten Seite ~:** he wanted to show himself to advantage [2] (sich erweisen) prove to be; **es wird sich ~, wer daran schuld war** time will tell who was responsible; **es hat sich gezeigt, dass ...** it turned out that ...; **sich als etw. ~:** prove *or* turn out to be sth.

Zeiger *der;* ~s, ~: pointer; (Uhr~) hand

Zeige·stock *der; Pl.* **~stöcke** pointer

Zeig·finger *der* (schweiz.) ▸**Zeigefinger**

zeihen /ˈt̮saiən/ *unr. tr. V.* (geh.) **jmdn. einer Sache** (*Gen.*) **~:** indict sb. of sth.

Zeile /ˈt̮sailə/ *die;* ~, ~n [1] line; **jmdm. ein paar ~n schreiben** drop sb. a line; **vielen Dank für Ihre ~:** many thanks for your letter; **mit zwei ~n Abstand** with double spacing; **zwischen den ~n lesen** (fig.) read between the lines [2] (Reihe) row; (des Fernsehbildes) line

Zeilen-: **~abstand** *der* [line] spacing; (in gedrucktem Text) leading; **~bau·weise** *die* ribbon development; **~gieß·maschine** *die* Linotype (P) machine; **~honorar** *das* payment by the line; **~sprung** *der* (Verslehre) enjambement

-zeilig /-t̮sailɪç/ -line; **zwei~ sein** have two lines

Zeisig /ˈt̮saizɪç/ *der;* ~s, ~e (Zool.) siskin

zeit /t̮sait/ *Präp. mit Gen. in* **~ meines** *usw.*/**unseres** *usw.* **Lebens** all my *etc.* life/our *etc.* lives

Zeit *die;* ~, ~en [1] time *no art.;* **im Laufe der ~:** in the course of time; **mit der ~:** with time; in time; (allmählich) gradually; **die ~ arbeitet für/gegen jmdn.** time is on sb.'s side/is against sb.; **die ~ heilt alle Wunden** (Spr.) time is a great healer; **kommt ~, kommt Rat** (Spr.) take your time and you'll find an answer; **keine ~ verlieren dürfen** have no time to lose; **die ~ drängt** time is pressing; there is [precious] little time; **~ ist Geld** (Spr.) time is money (prov.); **sich** (*Dat.*) **die ~ [mit etw.] vertreiben** pass the time [with/doing sth.]; **jmdm. ~/drei Tage** *usw.* **~ lassen** give sb. time/three days *etc.;* **sich** (*Dat.*) **~ lassen** *od.* **nehmen** take one's time; **sich** (*Dat.*) **für jmdn./etw. ~ nehmen** make time for sb./sth.; **etw. hat ~, mit etw. hat es ~:** there's no hurry about sth.; **auf ~ spielen** (Sportjargon) play for time; **eine ~ lang** for a while *or* a time; *s. auch* **nachtschlafend**; **sparen**; **stehlen**; **totschlagen**

[2] (~punkt) time; **ihre/seine ~ ist gekommen** (geh. verhüll.) her/his time has come; **außer der ~, außerhalb der üblichen ~:** at an unusual time; **seit der** *od.* **dieser ~:** since that time; **um diese ~:** at this time; **vor der ~:** prematurely; early; **zu jeder ~:** at any time; **zur rechten ~:** at the right time; **wer nicht kommt zur rechten ~, der muss essen, was übrig bleibt** (Spr.) the early bird catches the worm (prov.); **zu welcher ~?** at what time?; when?; **zu bestimmten ~en** at certain times; **alles zu seiner ~:** all in good time; **es ist/wird [langsam] ~** *od.* **ist an der ~:** it's time/[just] about time; **es ist [aller]höchste ~[, dass wir uns wehren]** it's high time [we fought back]; **von ~ zu ~:** from time to time; **zur ~** ▸**zurzeit**

[3] (~abschnitt, Lebensabschnitt) time; period; (Geschichtsabschnitt) age; period; **die schönste ~**

Z

des Lebens *od.* **im Leben** the best time of one's life; **er hat ~en, in denen ...** he has times *or* periods when ...; **die erste ~:** at first; **auf ~:** temporarily; **ein Vertrag auf ~:** a fixed-term contract; **ein Zug der ~:** a feature of the times; **mit der ~ gehen** move with the times; **der Geist der ~:** the spirit of the age; **die ~, als es noch kein Telefon gab** the days *pl.* before there were telephones; **andere ~en, andere Sitten** things are different now; **in früheren ~en** in former times; in the old days; **zu meiner ~:** in my day; **in der nächsten ~, in nächster ~:** in the near future; **für alle ~:** for ever; for all time; **in der letzten** *od.* **in letzter** *od.* **in jüngster ~:** recently; **zu allen ~en** always; at all times; **zu keiner ~:** at no time; never; **hier bin ich die längste ~ gewesen** (ugs.) I've been here for long enough; **seit ewigen ~en** (ugs.) for ages (coll.); **seit undenklichen ~en** from time immemorial; **vor ~en** (dichter.) long ago; in days gone by; **zu ~en von jmdm./etw.** in sb.'s day/at the time of sth.; *s. auch* **lieb A 4**

4 (Sport: ~raum) time; **gute ~en laufen** do good times; **die ~ bei etw. stoppen** time sth. 5 (Sport: Wettbewerbsdauer) **einen Vorsprung über die ~ bringen** retain one's lead until the end of the game; **über die ~ kommen** (Boxen) go the distance

6 (Sprachw.) tense

Die Zeit

Germany's 'heaviest' weekly newspaper is published in Hamburg and is considered essential reading for academics and intellectuals. Former **Bundeskanzler** Helmut Schmidt is a joint editor. The paper offers in-depth analysis of current issues in politics, society, culture, and the arts.

zeit-, Zeit-: **~abschnitt** *der* period; **~abstand** *der* interval; **~alter** *das* age; era; **~angabe** *die* 1 statement regarding time; **er konnte keine genaue ~angabe machen** he could not be precise about the time; 2 (Sprachw.) expression of time; **~ansage** *die* (im Radio) time check; (am Telefon) speaking clock; **~arbeit** *die* (Wirtsch.) temporary work; work as a temp (coll.); **~arbeit machen** temp; **~arbeiter** *der,* **~arbeiterin** *die* (Wirtsch.) temporary worker; **~arbeits·firma** *die* ▸**Zeitarbeitsunternehmen**; **~arbeits·unternehmen** *das* temping agency; **~aufwand** *der:* **viel ~aufwand erfordern** take up a great deal of time; **den ~aufwand verringern** reduce the time needed; **~bedingt** *Adj.* arising from prevailing circumstances *postpos.*; (vorübergehend) temporary; **~begriff** *der* concept of time; **~bestimmung** *die* (Sprachw.) expression of time; **~bombe** *die* (auch fig.) time bomb; **~budget** *das* time budget; **~dauer** *die* duration; **~dokument** *das* contemporary document; **~druck** *der* pressure of time; **unter ~druck** under pressure; **unter ~druck stehen/in ~druck kommen** be/become pressed for time; be/come under pressure [of time]; **~einteilung** *die* timing; **mit seiner ~einteilung nie zurechtkommen** never succeed in organizing one's time properly

Zeiten-: **~folge** *die* (Sprachw.) sequence of tenses; **~wende** *die* turning point in history

zeit-, Zeit-: **~erfassung** *die* time-recording; **~erscheinung** *die* transient phenomenon; **~ersparnis** *die* time-saving; **das bedeutete keine ~ersparnis** it did not save any time; **~fahren** *das;* **~~s** (Radsport) time trial; **~faktor** *der* time factor; **~fenster** *das* time window; **~form** *die* (Sprachw.) tense; **in der ~form der Gegenwart** in the present tense; **~gebunden** *Adj.* characteristic of its/their time *postpos.*; **~gebunden sein** be an expression *or* a reflection of its/their time; **~gefühl** *das* sense of time; **~geist** *der* spirit of the age; **~gemäß** *Adj.* (modern) up-to-date; (aktuell) topical ‹*theme*›; contemporary ‹*views*›; (in der Vergangenheit) in keeping with the period *postpos.*; **~genosse** *der,* **~genossin** *die* 1 contemporary; 2 (Mitmensch) fellow man/woman; **ein seltsamer ~genosse** a strange individual (coll.); **prominente ~genossen waren anwesend** leading figures [of the day] were present; **~genossenschaft** *die* contemporaneity; (Zeitgenossen) contemporaries *pl.*; **~genössisch** /-gənœsɪʃ/ *Adj.* contemporary; **~geschehen** *das:* **das [aktuelle] ~geschehen** current events *pl.*; **~geschichte** *die* 1 **die ~geschichte** the modern age; our age; 2 (Disziplin) contemporary history *no art.*; **~geschichtlich** **A** *Adj.* 1 (zeitlich) contemporary ‹*source etc.*›; 2 (fachlich) **~geschichtlicher Unterricht** contemporary-history teaching; **B** *adv.* 1 historically; 2 (fachlich) from the point of view of contemporary history; **~geschmack** *der* contemporary taste; **~gewinn** *der* ▸**~ersparnis**; **~gleich** **A** *Adj.* 1 (Sport) ‹*runners etc.*› with the same time; 2 ▸**gleichzeitig A**; **B** *adv.* ▸**gleichzeitig B**; **~gründe** *Pl.* time reasons; **~historiker** *der,* **~historikerin** *die* contemporary historian; **~historisch** *Adj., adv.* ▸**zeitgeschichtlich**; **~horizont** *der* time horizon

zeitig *Adj., adv.* early

zeitigen *tr. V.* (geh.) produce, yield ‹*result, success, etc.*›; provoke, precipitate ‹*uproar*›

zeit-, Zeit-: **~karte** *die* (Verkehrsw.) season ticket; **~konto** *das* time and attendance account *or* record; **~kritik** *die* appraisal *or* analysis of contemporary issues; **~kritisch** **A** *Adj.* ‹*essay, article, film*› analysing contemporary issues; **~kritische Themen** contemporary issues; **B** *adv.* ‹*examine*› in the light of contemporary issues; ***~lang** ▸**Zeit 1**; **~läuf[t]e** /-lɔyf(t)ə/ *Pl.* (geh.) times; **über alle ~läuf[t]e hinweg** for all time; **~lebens** *Adv.* all one's life

zeitlich

A *Adj.* 1 ‹*length, interval*› in time; chronological ‹*order, sequence*›; **in großem/kurzem ~en Abstand** at long/short intervals 2 (Rel.) temporal; **das Zeitliche segnen** (verhüll.) pass on (euphem.); (scherzh.) come to grief

B *adv.* 1 with regard to time; **ich kann es ~ nicht einrichten** I can't fit it in time-wise (coll.); **wenn es der Beruf ~ erlaubt** if one's job leaves enough time

zeit-, Zeit-: **~limit** *das* time limit; **~lohn** *der* (Wirtsch.) time-work rate; (Stundenlohn) hourly rate; **~los** **A** *Adj.* timeless; classic ‹*fashion, shape*›; **B** *adv.* timelessly; **~los eingerichtet** furnished in a classic *or* timeless style; **~losigkeit** *die;* **~~:** timelessness; **~lupe** *die* (Film) slow motion; **~lupen·tempo** *das:* **in im ~lupentempo** at a crawl; at a snail's pace; **~management** *das* time management; **~mangel** *der* lack of time; **aus ~mangel, wegen ~mangel[s]** owing to lack of time; **~maschine** *die* time machine; **~maß** *das* speed; (von Musik usw.) tempo; **~messer** *der;* **~~s, ~~:** timepiece; **~messung** *die* 1 time measurement; 2 (Chronologie) chronology; **~nah[e]** **A** *Adj.* topical ‹*play etc.*›; ‹*teaching, syllabus*› relevant to the present day; **B** *adv.* topically; **~nehmer** *der;* **~~s, ~~, ~nehmerin** *die;* **~~, ~~nen** timekeeper; **~not** *die* **in ~not geraten** *od.* **kommen** become pressed for time; **in ~not machte er einen falschen Zug** (Schach) in time pressure he made a wrong move; **~plan** *der* schedule; **~punkt** *der* moment; **zum jetzigen ~punkt** at the present moment; at this point in time; **~raffer** *der;* **~~s, ~~:** (Film) timelapse; **etw. im ~raffer zeigen** show sth. speeded up; **~raubend** *Adj.* time-consuming; **~raum** *der* period; **über einen ~raum von fünf Tagen** for a period of five days; **~rechnung** *die* calendar; **vor unserer ~rechnung** BC; before Christ; **unserer/christlicher ~rechnung** AD; Anno Domini; **~reise** *die* journey through time; (rückwärts) journey back in time (also fig.); **~schrift** *die* magazine; (bes. wissenschaftlich) journal; periodical; **~soldat** *der,* **~soldatin** *die: soldier serving for a fixed period;* **~spanne** *die* period; **~springen** *das;* **~~s, ~~** (Pferdesport) jumping against the clock; **~strafe** *die* (Sport) sending off for a specified time; (im Eishockey) penalty; **~strömung** *die* prevailing trend; **~takt** *der* 1 (Fernspr.) call rate; **im ~takt** on a time basis; 2 (Zeitabstand) [time] interval; (Verkehrsw.) service interval; **~typisch** *Adj.* typical of the time *postpos.*; **~umstände** *Pl.* prevailing circumstances; **die damaligen ~umstände** the circumstances prevailing at the time; **~umstellung** *die* 1 changing the clocks; 2 (das Sichumstellen) adjusting *no art.* to a/the different time

Zeitung *die;* **~, ~en** [news]paper; **[die] ~ lesen** read the paper; **bei einer ~ arbeiten** work for a newspaper; **er ist von der ~** (ugs.) he's from the press; **eine Anzeige in die ~ setzen** put an advertisement in the paper

Zeitungs-: **~abonnement** *das* newspaper subscription; **~annonce** *die,* **~anzeige** *die* newspaper advertisement; **~artikel** *der* newspaper article; **~ausschnitt** *der* newspaper cutting; **~austräger** *der,* **~austrägerin** *die* newspaper deliverer; **~bericht** *der* newspaper report; **~ente** *die* (ugs.) false [newspaper] report; canard; **~frau** *die* newspaper seller; (Austrägerin) newspaper deliverer; **~inserat** *das* newspaper advertisement; **~interview** *das* newspaper interview; **~kiosk** *der* newspaper kiosk; **~leser** *der,* **~leserin** *die* newspaper reader; **~meldung** *die* newspaper report; **~notiz** *die* newspaper item; **~papier** *das* 1 (alte Zeitung[en]) newspaper; 2 (unbedruckt) newsprint; **~redaktion** *die* newspaper's editorial office; **~ständer** *der* newspaper rack; **~träger** *der,* **~trägerin** *die* ▸**~austräger**; **~verkäufer** *der,* **~verkäuferin** *die* newspaper seller; news vendor; **~verlag** *der* newspaper publisher; **~verleger** *der,* **~verlegerin** *die* ▸**❶ S. 113** newspaper publisher; **~wissenschaft** *die* (Hochschulw.) journalistic studies *pl., no art.*

zeit-, Zeit-: **~unterschied** *der* time difference; **~verlust** *der* loss of time; **ohne/trotz ~verlust** without/in spite of losing time; **den ~verlust aufholen** make up for lost time; **~verschiebung** *die* time change; time difference; **~verschwendung** *die* waste of time; **[reine** *od.* **pure] ~verschwendung sein** be a [pure *or* complete] waste of time; **~vertrag** *der* fixed-term contract; **~vertreib** *der;* **~~[e]s, ~~e** pastime; **zum ~vertreib** to pass the time; **~verzögerung** *die* delay; **die ~verzögerung, mit der der Körper reagiert** the time lag before the body reacts; **~verzug** *der* ▸**Verzug 1**; **~vorgabe** *die* time allowance; (Sport) target time; (Zeitlimit) time limit; **die ~vorgabe für das Projekt** the scheduled duration of the project; **an der ~vorgabe scheitern** (Sport) fail to make the qualifying time; **~weilig** **A** *Adj.* temporary; **B** *adv.* 1 (vorübergehend) temporarily; for a time; 2 (gelegentlich) occasionally; at times; **~weise** *Adv.* 1 (gelegentlich) occasionally; at times; (von ~ zu ~) from time to time; **~weise Regen** occasional rain; 2 (vorübergehend) for a time; for a while; **~wende** *die* 1 **vor/nach der ~wende** BC/AD; before Christ/Anno Domini; **um die ~wende** about the time of the birth of Christ; 2 ▸**Zeitenwende**; **~wert** *der* current value; **~wort** *das; Pl.* **~wörter** (Sprachw.) verb; **~zeichen** *das* (Rundf., Funkw.) time signal; **~zeuge** *der,* **~zeugin** *die* contemporary witness; **~zone** *die* time zone; **~zünder** *der* time fuse

zelebrieren /tsele'bri:rən/ *tr. V.* 1 (kath. Kirche) celebrate ‹*mass*›; conduct ‹*service, wedding*› 2 (feierlich ausführen) make ‹*meal, event, etc.*› into a ritual 3 (ehren) honour

Zelebrität /tselebri'tɛ:t/ *die;* **~, ~en** (geh.) celebrity

Zelle /'tsɛlə/ *die;* **~, ~n** cell; (Telefon~) [telephone booth *or* (Brit.) box; **die [kleinen] grauen ~n** (scherzh.) one's grey matter *sing.*

Zeller *der;* **~s** (österr. ugs.) celeriac

Zell-: **~gewebe** *das* (Biol.) cell tissue; **~gift** *das* (Biol., Med.) cytotoxin; **~haufen** *der* (Biol.) morula; **~kern** *der* (Biol.) cell nucleus;

~kultur *die* (Biol., Med.) cell culture

Zellophan /tsɛlo'fa:n/ *das;* **~s** cellophane

Zell-: ~stoff *der* [1] cellulose; [2] (Material) cellulose wadding; **~teilung** *die* (Biol.) cell division; **~tod** *der* (Biol., Med.) cell death; **programmierter ~tod** programmed cell death; **~typ** *der* (Biol.) cell type

Zellulitis /tsɛlu'li:tɪs/ *die;* **~, Zellulitiden** /tsɛluli'ti:dn/ ▸ⓘ **S. 439** (Med.) cellulitis

Zelluloid /tsɛlu'lɔyt/ *das;* **~[e]s** celluloid

Zellulose /tsɛlu'lo:zə/ *die;* **~, ~n** cellulose

Zell-: ~wand *die* (Biol.) cell wall; **~wolle** *die* rayon

Zelt /tsɛlt/ *das;* **~[e]s, ~e** tent; (Fest~) marquee; (Zirkus~) big top; **das himmlische ~** (fig. dichter.) the canopy of heaven (literary); **seine ~e irgendwo aufschlagen** (fig.) settle down somewhere; **seine ~e abbrechen** (fig.) up sticks (coll.); decamp

zelten *itr. V.* camp; **wir waren ~:** we went camping; **„Zelten verboten"** 'no camping'

Zelt-: ~lager *das* camp; **~pflock** *der* tent peg; **~plane** *die* tarpaulin; **~platz** *der* camping site; campsite

Zement /tse'mɛnt/ *der;* **~[e]s, ~e** cement

Zement·boden *der* concrete floor

zementieren *tr. V.* [1] cement; **zementierte Wege** concrete paths [2] (fig.: festlegen) make ‹*division, situation, etc.*› permanent; **weiter zementiert werden** ‹*prejudice, opinion*› become further entrenched

Zen /zɛn/ *das;* **~[s], Zen-Buddhismus** *der* (Rel.) Zen [Buddhism] *no art.*

Zenit /tse'ni:t/ *der;* **~[e]s** zenith; **im ~ stehen** be at its zenith; **er stand im ~ seines Ruhms** (fig. geh.) he was at the peak of his fame

zensieren /tsɛn'zi:rən/

A *tr. V.* [1] (Schulw.) mark, (Amer.) grade ‹*essay etc.*› [2] (der Zensur unterziehen) censor ‹*article, film, etc.*›

B *itr. V.* (Schulw.) **streng/milde ~:** mark *or* (Amer.) grade severely/leniently

Zensierung *die;* **~, ~en** (Schulw.) marking; grading (Amer.)

Zensor /'tsɛnzɔr/ *der;* **~s, ~en** /tsɛn'zo:rən/ censor

Zensur /tsɛn'zu:ɐ/ *die;* **~, ~en** [1] (Schulw.: Note) mark; grade (Amer.); **~en austeilen** (fig.) mete out praise and blame (literary) [2] (Kontrolle) censorship [3] (Geom.) censors *pl.*

zensurieren *tr. V.* (österr.) ▸ **zensieren A 2**

Zentaur /tsɛn'tauɐ/ *der;* **~en, ~en** (Myth.) centaur

Zenti- /tsɛnti-/: **~gramm** /--'gram/ *das* centigram; **~liter** /--'li:tɐ/ *der, auch: das* ▸ⓘ **S. 582** centilitre; **~meter** /--'me:tɐ/ *der, auch: das* ▸ⓘ **S. 454** centimetre; **~meter·maß** *das* [centimetre] measuring tape

Zentner /'tsɛntnɐ/ *der;* **~s, ~** ▸ⓘ **S. 315** [1] centner; metric hundredweight [2] (österr., schweiz.) centner; 100 kilograms

zentner-, Zentner-: ~gewicht *das* centner *or* fifty-kilogram weight; (fig.: große Last) massive weight; **~last** *die* hundredweight load; **ihr fiel eine ~last vom Herzen** (fig.) that was a load off her mind; **~schwer** **A** *Adj.* weighing over a hundredweight *postpos., not pred.*; (äußerst schwer) massively heavy; **B** *adv.* **~schwer auf jmdm. lasten** (fig.) weigh heavily on sb.; **~weise** *Adv.* by the hundredweight

zentral /tsɛn'tra:l/

A *Adj.* central

B *adv.* centrally

Zentral·abitur *das* (Schulw.) *centrally organized Abitur within a Bundesland, with uniform question-setting and marking*

Zentral·afrikanische Republik *die* Central African Republic

Zentral·bank *die; Pl.* **~en** (Finanzw.) central bank

zentral·beheizt *Adj.* centrally heated; (durch Fernwärme) heated by a district heating system

Zentrale *die;* **~, ~n** [1] (zentrale Stelle) head *or* central office; (der Polizei, einer Partei) headquarters *sing. or pl.*; (Funk~) control centre; (fig.: Mittelpunkt) centre; **das Gehirn ist die ~ für das Nervensystem** the brain is the control centre of the nervous system [2] (Telefon~) [telephone] exchange; (eines Hotels, einer Firma o. Ä.) switchboard [3] (Geom.) line passing through the centres of two circles

Zentral-: ~einheit *die* (DV) central processing unit; **~heizung** *die* central heating

Zentralisation /tsɛntraliza'tsio:n/ *die;* **~, ~en** centralization

zentralisieren *tr. V.* centralize

Zentralisierung *die;* **~, ~en** centralization

Zentralismus *der;* **~:** centralism *usu. no art.*

zentralistisch

A *Adj.* centralist

B *adv.* centralistically

Zentral-: ~komitee *das* Central Committee; **~nerven·system** *das* ▸ⓘ **S. 435** (Anat.) central nervous system; **~organ** *das* official organ; **~speicher** *der* (DV) main memory

Zentren ▸ **Zentrum**

zentrieren

A *tr. V.* centre (**um** on)

B *refl. V.* **sich um etw. ~:** be centred around sth.

Zentrierung *die;* **~, ~en** centring

zentrifugal /tsɛntrifu'ga:l/ (Physik)

A *Adj.* centrifugal

B *adv.* centrifugally

Zentrifugal·kraft *die* (Physik) centrifugal force

Zentrifuge *die;* **~, ~n** centrifuge

zentripetal /tsɛntripe'ta:l/ (Physik)

A *Adj.* centripetal

B *adv.* centripetally

Zentripetal·kraft *die* (Physik) centripetal force

Zentri·winkel /'tsɛntrivɪŋkl/ *der* (Geom.) central angle

Zentrum /'tsɛntrʊm/ *das;* **~s, Zentren** centre; **im ~:** at the centre; (im Stadt~) in the town/city centre; **im ~ des öffentlichen Interesses stehen** (fig.) be the focus of public interest

Zephir /'tse:fɪr/ *der;* **~s, ~e** (dichter. veralt.) zephyr

Zeppelin /'tsɛpəli:n/ *der;* **~s, ~e** Zeppelin

Zepter /'tsɛptɐ/ *das, auch: der;* **~s, ~:** sceptre; **das ~ übernehmen** (fig.) take the helm; **das ~ führen** *od.* (scherzh.) **schwingen** (fig.) wield the sceptre

zerbeißen *unr. tr. V.* bite in two; ‹*flea, mosquito, etc.*› bite ‹*person etc.*› all over

zerbersten *unr. itr. V.; mit sein* burst apart; **zerborstene Mauern** smashed walls

zerbomben *tr. V.* bomb to pieces; destroy by bombing; **zerbombt** bombed ‹*streets, houses*›

zerbrechen

A *unr. itr. V.; mit sein* break [into pieces]; smash [to pieces]; ‹*glass*› shatter; (fig.) ‹*marriage, relationship*› break up; **an seinem Kummer ~** (fig. geh.) be broken down by grief

B *unr. tr. V.* break; smash, shatter ‹*dishes, glass*›

zerbrechlich *Adj.* [1] fragile; **„Vorsicht, ~!"** 'fragile; handle with care' [2] (zart, schwach) frail

Zerbrechlichkeit *die;* **~** [1] fragility [2] (Zartheit, Schwachheit) frailty

zerbröckeln

A *itr. V.; mit sein* (auch fig.) crumble away

B *tr. V.* break into small pieces

zerbröseln

A *itr. V.; mit sein* crumble

B *tr. V.* crumble up

zerdehnen *tr. V.* [1] (dehnen) stretch [out of shape] [2] (verlängern) draw out ‹*plot, scenes*›; drawl ‹*word, vowel*›

zerdeppern /tsɛɐ'dɛpɐn/ *tr. V.* (ugs.) smash ‹*window, china, glass*›

zerdrücken *tr. V.* [1] (zerquetschen) mash ‹*potatoes, banana*› [2] (zusammendrücken) squash ‹*fly etc.*›; stub out ‹*cigarette*›; **eine Träne ~** (fig. spöttisch) shed a tear [3] (ugs.: zerknittern) crease ‹*clothes*›

Zeremonie /tseremo'ni:/ *die;* **~, ~n** ceremony; (fig.) ritual

Zeremoniell /tseremo'niɛl/ *das;* **~s, ~e** ceremonial

Zeremonien·meister *der* master of ceremonies

Zeremonien·meisterin *die* master of ceremonies; mistress of ceremonies (rare)

zerfahren

A *Adj.* distracted; scrappy ‹*play*›

B *adv.* distractedly; ‹*play*› scrappily, without concentration

Zerfall *der;* **~[e]s, Zerfälle** [1] disintegration; (eines Organismus, fig.: der Moral) breakdown; (einer Leiche) decomposition; (eines Gebäudes) decay [2] (Kernphysik) decay

zerfallen[1] *unr. itr. V.; mit sein* [1] (auch fig.) disintegrate (**in** + *Akk.*, **zu** into); ‹*building*› fall into ruin, decay; ‹*corpse*› decompose, decay; **~de Mauern/Ruinen** crumbling walls/ruins; **zu Staub ~:** crumble into dust; **Moral und Kultur waren ~** (fig.) morals and culture had broken down *or* fallen into decay [2] (unterteilt sein) **in Phasen/Teile** *usw.* **~:** be divided into phases/parts *etc.* [3] (Kernphysik) decay

zerfallen[2] *Adj.* **mit jmdm. ~ sein** have fallen out with sb.; **mit sich und der Welt ~ sein** be at odds with oneself and the world

Zerfalls·produkt *das* (bes. Kernphysik) decay product

zerfasern *itr. V.; mit sein* fray

zerfetzen *tr. V.* [1] (zerstören) rip *or* tear to pieces; rip *or* tear up ‹*letter etc.*› (**in** + *Akk.* into); (fig.) tear apart ‹*body, limb*› [2] (kritisieren) tear ‹*book, play, etc.*› to pieces *or* shreds

zerfleddern *tr. V.* wear out ‹*book etc.*›; **das Buch ist zerfleddert** the book is falling apart

zerfleischen *tr. V.* tear ‹*person, animal*› limb from limb; **sich ~** (auch fig.) tear each other apart; ‹*country*› tear itself apart

Zerfleischung *die;* **~, ~en** tearing apart *no art.*

zerfließen *unr. itr. V.; mit sein* [1] (schmelzen) melt [away]; **in** *od.* **vor Mitleid ~** (fig.) dissolve with pity; **das Geld ist ihr unter den Händen zerflossen** the money ran through her fingers (fig.) [2] (auseinander fließen) ‹*paint, ink*› run; ‹*shapes*› dissolve; **~de Konturen/Grenzen** blurred outlines/limits

zerfransen

A *itr. V.; mit sein* fray

B *tr. V.* fray; (zerreißen) tear

zerfressen *unr. tr. V.* [1] (fressen) eat away; ‹*moth etc.*› eat holes in; **von Motten ~:** moth-eaten [2] (zersetzen) corrode ‹*metal*›; eat away ‹*bone*›; **Kummer/Eifersucht zerfrisst ihm das Herz** (fig.) he is consumed with grief/jealousy

zerfurchen *tr. V.* [1] rut ‹*track etc.*› [2] furrow ‹*brow, face*›

zergehen *unr. itr. V.; mit sein* melt; (in Wasser, im Mund) ‹*tablet etc.*› dissolve; **auf der Zunge ~:** melt in the mouth

zergliedern *tr. V.* [1] dissect ‹*plant, animal, corpse*› [2] analyse ‹*behaviour, process, etc.*›; **Sätze ~:** parse sentences

Zergliederung *die* [1] dissection [2] (Analyse) analysis; (von Sätzen) parsing

zergrübeln *refl. V.* **sich** (*Dat.*) **den Kopf** *od.* **das Hirn ~:** rack one's brains

zerhacken *tr. V.* chop up (**zu** into); (in Wut) hack to pieces

zerhauen *unr. tr. V.* chop up

zerkauen *tr. V.* chew [up]

zerkleinern /tsɛɐ'klainɐn/ *tr. V.* chop up ‹*vegetables, meat, wood*›; (zerkauen) chew up ‹*food*›; (zermahlen) crush ‹*rock etc.*›

Zerkleinerung *die;* **~, ~en** chopping up; (Zerkauung) chewing; (Zermahlung) crushing

zerklüftet *Adj.* fissured ‹*landscape*›; craggy ‹*mountains*›; deeply indented ‹*coastline*›

zerknallen

A *itr. V.; mit sein* burst [with a bang]

B *tr. V.* burst ‹*bag etc.*› [with a bang]

zerknautschen *tr. V.* (ugs.) crumple

zerknicken

A *tr. V.* snap

Z

B *itr. V.; mit sein* snap
zerknirscht
A *Adj.* remorseful
B *adv.* remorsefully
Zerknirschung *die;* ~: remorse
zerknittern *tr. V.* crease; crumple; **ein zerknittertes Gesicht** a wrinkled face
zerknüllen *tr. V.* crumple up [into a ball]
zerkochen
A *itr. V.; mit sein* get overcooked; **zu Brei** ~: cook to a pulp; **zerkocht** overcooked
B *tr. V.* overcook
zerkratzen *tr. V.* scratch
zerkrümeln
A *tr. V.* crumble up
B *itr. V.; mit sein* break into crumbs; crumble
zerlassen *unr. tr. V.* (Kochk.) melt
zerlegen *tr. V.* **1** (auseinander nehmen) dismantle; take to pieces; strip, dismantle ‹*engine*›; **etw. in seine Bestandteile** ~: reduce sth. to its component parts; **einen Lichtstrahl in die Farben des Spektrums** ~: split up a ray of light into the colours of the spectrum **2** (zerschneiden) cut up ‹*animal, meat*›; carve ‹*joint*›; dissect ‹*corpse*›
zerlesen *unr. tr. V.* read ‹*book etc.*› again and again until it looks worn out; **ein [völlig] ~es Exemplar** a well-thumbed copy
zerlumpt *Adj.* ragged ‹*clothes, person*›; ~ **sein** ‹*clothes*› be in tatters, be torn; ~ **herumlaufen** go about in rags
zermahlen *unr. tr. V.* grind
zermalmen /tsɛɐ̯ˈmalmən/ *tr. V.* crush
zermartern *refl. V.* **in sich** (*Dat.*) **den Kopf** *od.* **das Hirn** ~: rack one's brains
zermürben *tr. V.* wear ‹*person*› down; **~d** wearing; trying
Zermürbung *die* wearing down *no art.*; (Milit.) attrition
Zermürbungs·krieg *der* war of attrition
zernagen *tr. V.* gnaw away
zerpflücken *tr. V.* **1** pick ‹*flower, lettuce, etc.*› apart **2** (fig.: kritisch analysieren) pull ‹*play, book, etc.*› to pieces; destroy ‹*alibi, reputation*›
zerplatzen *itr. V.; mit sein* burst; **vor Wut** ~ (fig.) explode [with anger]
zerquetschen *tr. V.* crush; mash ‹*potatoes*›; **es kostet 20 Euro und ein paar Zerquetschte** (ugs.) it costs 20 euros and a bit
zerraufen *tr. V.* tousle ‹*hair*›
Zerr·bild *das* distorted image
zerreden *tr. V.* talk over and over; do *or* flog ‹*subject*› to death (coll.)
zerreiben *unr. tr. V.* crush ‹*spices, paint colours, etc.*›; grind ‹*corn*›; (fig.) crush, wipe out ‹*enemy*›
zerreißen
A *unr. tr. V.* **1** (auseinander reißen) tear up; (in kleine Stücke) tear to pieces; ‹*animal*› tear ‹*prey*› limb from limb; dismember ‹*prey*›; break ‹*thread*›; **ich könnte ihn ~!** I could tear him limb from limb!; **sich [fast]** ~ **[um jmdn.]** [nearly] kill oneself [for sb. *or* to help sb.]; **ich kann mich nicht** ~: I can't be in two places at once; **Schüsse zerrissen die Stille** shots rent the silence **2** (beschädigen) tear ‹*stocking, trousers, etc.*› (**an** + *Dat.* on)
B *unr. itr. V.; mit sein* **1** (auseinander gehen) ‹*thread, string, rope*› break; **die Bande zwischen ihnen waren zerrissen** (fig.) the bonds between them had parted; **ihre Nerven war zum Zerreißen gespannt** her nerves were stretched to breaking point **2** (kaputtgehen) ‹*paper, cloth, etc.*› tear; **zerrissene Kleider/Schuhe** ragged clothes/worn-out shoes
Zerreiß·probe *die* acid test
zerren /ˈtsɛrən/
A *tr. V.* **1** drag; **etw. an die Öffentlichkeit** ~ (fig.) drag sth. into the limelight **2** **sich** (*Dat.*) **einen Muskel/eine Sehne** ~: pull a muscle/tendon
B *itr. V.* **an etw.** (*Dat.*) ~: tug *or* pull at sth.
zerrinnen *unr. itr. V.* melt; (fig.) ‹*time, years*› pass; **seine Hoffnungen/Träume/Pläne zerrannen [in nichts]** (geh.) his hopes/dreams vanished/plans came to nothing; **jmdm. unter den Händen/Fingern** ~: slip through sb.'s fingers
zerrissen /tsɛɐ̯ˈrɪsn̩/
A *2. Part. v.* **zerreißen**
B *Adj.* **[innerlich]** ~: at odds with oneself
Zerrissenheit *die;* ~: inner turmoil
Zerr·spiegel *der* distorting mirror
Zerrung *die;* ~, **~en** pulled muscle; (Sehnen~) pulled tendon
zerrupfen *tr. V.* tear to bits
zerrütten /tsɛɐ̯ˈrʏtn̩/ *tr. V.* ruin ‹*health*›; shatter ‹*nerves*›; ruin, wreck ‹*marriage*›; **aus zerrütteten Familienverhältnissen stammen** come from a broken home; **die Finanzen sind zerrüttet** the finances are in a disastrous state
Zerrüttung *die;* ~, **~en** (der Gesundheit) ruining; (der Nerven) shattering; (einer Ehe) [irretrievable] breakdown; (einer Familie) break-up
Zerrüttungs·prinzip *das* (Rechtsw.) principle of irretrievable breakdown (*of a marriage*)
zersägen *tr. V.* saw up
zerschellen *itr. V.; mit sein* be dashed *or* smashed to pieces
zerschlagen[1]
A *unr. tr. V.* smash ‹*plate, windscreen, etc.*›; smash up ‹*furniture*›; (fig.) smash ‹*spy ring etc.*›; crush ‹*enemy, attack*›; break up ‹*cartel*›
B *unr. refl. V.* ‹*plan, deal*› fall through
zerschlagen[2] *Adj.* worn out; whacked (Brit. coll.); tuckered [out] (Amer. coll.); shattered (Brit. coll.)
Zerschlagung *die;* ~, **~en** smashing; destruction; (eines Gegners, Widerstands) crushing; **die** ~ **der Kartelle** the breaking up of cartels
zerschlissen *Adj.* worn out; worn-out *attrib.*; threadbare ‹*clothes, upholstery, curtains, carpets, etc.*›
zerschmelzen *unr. itr. V.; mit sein* (auch fig.) melt
zerschmettern *tr. V.* smash; shatter ‹*glass, leg, bone*›; (fig.) crush ‹*army, enemy*›
zerschneiden *unr. tr. V.* **1** (schneiden) cut; (in Stücke) cut up; (in zwei Teile) cut in two; carve ‹*joint*›; **von tiefen Furchen zerschnitten** deeply rutted **2** (verletzen) cut [into] ‹*skin etc.*›
zerschnippeln *tr. V.* (ugs.) cut up *or* snip into small pieces
zerschunden /tsɛɐ̯ˈʃʊndn̩/ *Adj.* covered in scratches *postpos.*
zersetzen
A *tr. V.* **1** (auflösen) corrode ‹*metal*›; decompose ‹*organism*› **2** (untergraben) subvert ‹*ideals*›; undermine ‹*morale*›; **~de Schriften** subversive writings
B *refl. V.* decompose; ‹*wood, compost*› rot
Zersetzung *die;* ~, **~en** **1** ▸ **zersetzen B**: decomposition; rotting **2** ▸ **zersetzen A 2**: subversion; undermining
Zersetzungs·prozess, ***Zersetzungs·prozeß** *der* process of decomposition
zersiedeln *tr. V.* (Amtsspr.) overdevelop ‹*area*›; spoil ‹*area*› by overdevelopment
Zersied[e]lung *die* overdevelopment
zerspalten *unr.* (*auch regelm.*) *tr. V.* (auch fig.) split [up]; (Chemie) break down ‹*compounds*› (**in** + *Akk.* into)
zersplittern
A *itr. V.; mit sein* ‹*wood, bone*› splinter; ‹*glass*› shatter; **das Land war in viele Kleinstaaten zersplittert** the country was fragmented into many small states
B *tr. V.* splinter; shatter ‹*glass*›
zersprengen *tr. V.* **1** (sprengen) blow up; (in Stücke) blow to pieces **2** (auseinander treiben) scatter ‹*army*›
zerspringen *unr. itr. V.; mit sein* **1** shatter; (Sprünge bekommen) crack; (fig.) ‹*heart*› burst (**vor** + *Dat.* with); **der Kopf wollte mir** ~ **vor Schmerzen** my head was splitting; I had a splitting headache **2** (geh.: zerreißen) ‹*string etc.*› break
zerstampfen *tr. V.* **1** (zerkleinern) pound, crush ‹*spices etc.*›; mash ‹*potatoes*› **2** (beschädigen) trample down ‹*field etc.*›
zerstäuben *tr. V.* spray
Zerstäuber *der;* **~s,** ~: atomizer
zerstechen *unr. tr. V.* **1** (stechen) sting all over; ‹*mosquitoes*› bite all over **2** (beschädigen) jab holes in ‹*cushion etc.*›; puncture, slit ‹*tyre*›; **ihre Venen sind ganz zerstochen** her veins are covered in needle marks
zerstieben *unr.* (*auch regelm.*) *itr. V.; mit sein* (geh.) scatter; ‹*crowd*› disperse; (fig.) ‹*sadness, nightmare*› vanish; **in alle Winde** ~: disappear without trace
zerstörbar *Adj.* destructible; **leicht** ~ **sein** be easily destroyed *or* broken
zerstören *tr. V.* destroy; ‹*hooligan*› smash up, vandalize ‹*telephone box etc.*›; (fig.) ruin ‹*landscape, health, life*›; dash, destroy ‹*hopes, dreams*›; wreck, destroy ‹*marriage*›; **durch ein Feuer/Erdbeben zerstört** destroyed in *or* by a fire/an earthquake; **~de Gewalt** destructive power; **zerstörte Städte** ruined cities
Zerstörer *der;* **~s,** ~ **1** (Schiff) destroyer **2** (Person) destroyer; wrecker; (Rowdy) vandal
Zerstörerin *die;* ~, **~nen** ▸ **Zerstörer 2**
zerstörerisch
A *Adj.* destructive
B *adv.* ~ **wirken** have a destructive effect
Zerstörung *die* destruction; (durch Rowdys) smashing up; vandalization; (der Gesundheit, Existenz) ruin[ation]; (einer Ehe) wrecking; destruction; (von Hoffnungen) dashing; destruction
Zerstörungs·wut *die* destructive frenzy
zerstoßen *unr. tr. V.* crush ‹*berries etc.*›; (im Mörser) pound, crush ‹*peppercorns etc.*›
zerstreiten *unr. refl. V.* **sich mit jmdm.** ~: fall out with sb.; **untereinander zerstritten sein** be at loggerheads
zerstreuen
A *tr. V.* **1** scatter; (auseinander treiben) disperse ‹*crowd*›; (fig.) **zerstreut liegende Gehöfte** scattered farms; **in alle Welt zerstreut** scattered to the four winds **2** (unterhalten) **jmdn./sich** ~: entertain sb./oneself; (ablenken) take sb.'s/one's mind off things; **sich ein wenig** ~: enjoy oneself a little; **sich mit** *od.* **durch etw.** ~: pass the time with sth. **3** (beseitigen) allay ‹*fear, doubt, suspicion*›; dispel ‹*worry, concern*›
B *refl. V.* disperse; (schneller) scatter
zerstreut
A *Adj.* distracted; (vergesslich) absent-minded; **ein ~er Professor** (ugs. scherzh.) an absent-minded professor
B *adv.* absent-mindedly
Zerstreutheit *die;* ~: absent-mindedness
Zerstreuung *die;* ~, **~en** diversion; (Unterhaltung) entertainment; ~ **suchen** look for a distraction [to take one's mind off things]
zerstückeln *tr. V.* break ‹*sth.*› up into small pieces; (zerschneiden) cut *or* chop sth. up into small pieces; dismember ‹*corpse*›
Zerstückelung *die;* ~, **~en** breaking up; (Zerschneidung) cutting *or* chopping up; (einer Leiche) dismembering
zerteilen
A *tr. V.* divide into pieces; (zerschneiden) cut into pieces; cut up; **das Schiff zerteilte die Wellen** (fig.) the ship sliced through the waves
B *refl. V.* part
zerteppern /tsɛɐ̯ˈtɛpɐn/ ▸ **zerdeppern**
Zertifikat /tsɛrtifiˈkaːt/ *das;* **~[e]s, ~e** certificate; ~ **Deutsch als Fremdsprache** diploma in German as a foreign language
zertrampeln *tr. V.* trample all over ‹*flower bed etc.*›; trample ‹*child etc.*› underfoot
zertrennen *tr. V.* take apart; unpick ‹*dress*›
zertreten *unr. tr. V.* stamp on; stamp out ‹*cigarette, match*›; stamp on, crush ‹*insect*› underfoot
zertrümmern *tr. V.* smash; smash, shatter ‹*glass*›; smash up ‹*furniture*›; wreck ‹*car, boat*›; reduce ‹*building, city*› to ruins
Zervelat·wurst /tsɛrvəˈlaːt-/ *die* cervelat [sausage]
zerwühlen *tr. V.* churn up ‹*bedclothes, soil*›; make a mess of, tousle ‹*hair*›
Zerwürfnis /tsɛɐ̯ˈvʏrfnɪs/ *das;* **~ses, ~se** (geh.) quarrel; dispute; (Bruch) rift

zerzausen *tr. V.* ruffle; ruffle, tousle ‹*hair*›; **zerzaust aussehen** look dishevelled; **vom Wind zerzauste Bäume** windswept trees

Zeter *das: in* ~ **und Mord[io] schreien** (ugs.) scream blue murder (coll.); raise hell (coll.)

zetern /ˈtseːtɐn/ *itr. V.* (abwertend) (schimpfen) scold [shrilly]; (sich beklagen) moan (**über** + *Akk.* about); **gegen den Sittenverfall** ~: declaim against the decay of morals

Zettel /ˈtsɛtl̩/ *der;* ~**s,** ~: slip *or* piece of paper; (mit einigen Zeilen) note; (Bekanntmachung) notice; (Formular) form; (Kassen~) receipt; (Hand~) leaflet; (Stimm~) [ballot] paper

Zettel-: ~**kasten** *der* index on slips of paper; ~**wirtschaft** *die* (ugs. abwertend) jumble of bits of paper

Zeug /tsɔyk/ *das;* ~**[e]s,** ~**e** 1 (ugs., oft abwertend: Sachen) stuff; **fürchterliches** ~ **träumen** dream awful things; **sie hat** *od.* **in ihr steckt das** ~ **zu etw.** (fig.) she has what it takes to be sth. *or* has the makings of sth.; **was das** ~ **hält** (fig. ugs.) for all one's worth; ‹*drive*› hell for leather; **sich [für jmdn./etw. mächtig** *od.* **tüchtig] ins** ~ **legen** (fig.) do one's utmost [for sb./sth.] 2 (ugs.: Unsinn) **dummes/albernes** ~ (Gerede) nonsense; rubbish; **dummes** ~ **machen** mess about 3 (Kleidung) things *pl.*; **jmdm. etwas am** ~ **flicken** (ugs.) pin something on sb. 4 (veralt.: Tuch) cloth

Zeuge /ˈtsɔygə/ *der;* ~**n,** ~**n** witness; ~ **von etw. sein/werden** be a witness to sth.; witness sth.; ~ **der Anklage/Verteidigung** (Rechtsw.) witness for the prosecution/defence; **die** ~**n Jehovas** the Jehovah's Witnesses; **die Ruinen sind** ~**n der Vergangenheit** (fig.) the ruins bear witness to the past

zeugen[1] *itr. V.* give evidence; testify; **von etw.** ~ (fig.) testify to sth.; (zeigen) display sth.; **das zeugt nicht gerade für seine Uneigennützigkeit** (fig.) that doesn't say much for his unselfishness

zeugen[2] *tr. V.* procreate; ‹*man*› father ‹*child*›; (fig.) engender; bring about; **Kinder** ~: reproduce; have children

Zeugen·aussage *die* testimony; witness's statement

Zeugenschaft *die;* ~: testimony

Zeugen-: ~**stand** *der* witness box (Brit.); witness stand (Amer.); ~**vernehmung** *die* examination of the witness/witnesses

Zeug·haus *das* (bes. Milit. hist.) armoury

Zeugin *die;* ~, ~**nen** witness

Zeugnis *das;* ~**ses,** ~**se** 1 (Schulw.) report; ~ **der Reife** ▸**Abitur**~ 2 (Arbeits~) reference; testimonial; **ich kann ihm nur das beste** ~ **ausstellen** (fig.) I can't speak too highly of him 3 (Gutachten) certificate 4 (geh.: Beweis) evidence; ~**se einer früheren Kulturstufe** evidence *or* testimony of an earlier stage of civilization 5 (veralt.: Aussage) testimony; **falsches** ~ **ablegen** bear false witness

> **Zeugnis der allgemeinen Hochschulreife**
> ▸ Abitur

Zeugs *das;* ~ (ugs. abwertend) stuff; (einzelne Dinge) things *pl.*

Zeugung *die;* ~, ~**en** procreation; (eines Kindes) fathering

zeugungs-, Zeugungs-: ~**akt** *der* act of procreation *or* reproduction; ~**fähig** *Adj.* fertile; ~**fähigkeit** *die* fertility

Zeus (*der*) Zeus

ZGB *Abk.* (DDR, Schweiz) = **Zivilgesetzbuch**

z. Hd. *Abk.* = **zu Händen; zu Handen** (österr.) attn.

Zibebe /tsiˈbeːbə/ *die;* ~, ~**n** (österr., südd.) sultana

Zichorie /tsɪˈçoːri̯ə/ *die;* ~: chicory

Zicke /ˈtsɪkə/ *die;* ~, ~**n** 1 (Ziege) she goat; nanny goat 2 (Schimpfwort) ▸**Ziege 2** 3 *Pl.* (ugs.: Dummheiten) stupid tricks; monkey business (coll.); ~**n machen** mess about; (Schwierigkeiten machen) make trouble; **mach bloß keine** ~**n!** none of your monkey business! (coll.)

zickig (ugs. abwertend)
A *Adj.* prim; (prüde) prudish
B *adv.* primly; (prüde) prudishly

Zicklein *das;* ~**s,** ~: kid

Zick·zack *der;* ~**[e]s,** ~**e** zigzag; **im** ~: in a zigzag; **sie fuhren im** ~ **durch den Verkehr** they zigzagged through the traffic

Zickzack·kurs *der* zigzag line; **im** ~: in a zigzag [line]

Ziege /ˈtsiːɡə/ *die;* ~, ~**n** 1 goat 2 (Schimpfwort: Frau) **dumme** *od.* **blöde** ~: stupid cow (sl. derog.); **eingebildete** ~: stuck-up female (derog.)

Ziegel /ˈtsiːɡl̩/ *der;* ~**s,** ~ 1 brick 2 (Dach~) tile

Ziegel·dach *das* tiled roof

Ziegelei *die;* ~, ~**en** brickworks *sing.*

ziegel·rot *Adj.* brick-red

Ziegel·stein *der* brick

Ziegen-: ~**bart** *der* goat's beard; (ugs.: Spitzbart) goatee beard; ~**bock** *der* he- *or* billy goat; ~**käse** *der* goat's cheese; ~**leder** *das* goatskin; ~**milch** *die* goat's milk; ~**peter** *der;* ~**s,** ~ (ugs.) mumps *sing.*

zieh /tsiː/ *1. u. 3. Pers. Sg. Prät. v.* **zeihen**

Zieh-: ~**brunnen** *der* draw-well; ~**eltern** *Pl.* (veralt.) foster-parents

ziehen /ˈtsiːən/
A *unr. tr. V.* 1 pull; (sanfter) draw; (zerren) tug; (schleppen) drag; **jmdn. an sich** ~: draw sb. to one; **jmdn. am Ärmel** ~: pull sb. by the sleeve; **sie zogen ihn mit Gewalt ins Auto** they dragged him into the car by force; **er zog die Knie bis unters Kinn** he drew his knees up under his chin; **das Auto nach rechts/links** ~: pull the car over to the left/right; **das Flugzeug nach oben/unten** ~: put the plane into a climb/descent; **die Rollläden nach oben** ~: roll up the shutters; **ein Hemd** *usw.* **durchs Wasser** ~: give a shirt *etc.* a quick rinse; **die Gardinen vor das Fenster** ~: draw the curtains [across the window]; **Perlen auf eine Schnur** ~: thread pearls/beads on to a string; **den Hut ins Gesicht** ~: pull one's hat down over one's face; **einen Pullover über das Hemd** ~: put a pullover on over one's shirt; ~ **und ablegen** (DV) drag and drop
2 (fig.) **es zog ihn zu ihr/zu dem Ort** he felt drawn to her/to the place; **es zog ihn in die Ferne** he felt an urge to travel; **alle Blicke auf sich** ~: attract *or* capture all the attention; **jmds. Zorn/Unwillen** *usw.* **auf sich** ~: incur sb.'s anger/displeasure *etc.*; **etw. nach sich** ~: result in sth.; entail sth.; **gewisse Folgen nach sich** ~: have certain consequences
3 (heraus~) pull out ‹*nail, cork, organ-stop, etc.*›; extract ‹*tooth*›; take out, remove ‹*stitches, splinter*›; draw ‹*cord, sword, pistol*›; **den Ring vom Finger** ~: pull *or* take one's ring off one's finger; **den Hut** ~: raise *or* (dated) doff one's hat; **etw. aus der Tasche** ~: take sth. out of one's pocket; (aus Automaten) **Zigaretten/Süßigkeiten** *usw.* ~: get cigarettes/sweets *etc.* from a slot machine; **die [Quadrat]wurzel** ~ (Math.) extract the square root
4 (dehnen) stretch ‹*elastic etc.*›; stretch out ‹*sheets etc.*›; *s. auch* **Blase 1**; **Faden**[1]
5 (Gesichtspartien bewegen) make ‹*face, grimace*›; **die Augenbrauen nach oben** ~: raise one's eyebrows; **die Stirn in Falten** ~: wrinkle *or* knit one's brow; (missmutig) frown; **die Mundwinkel nach unten** ~: pull down the corners of one's mouth
6 (bei Brettspielen) move ‹*chessman etc.*›
7 (einatmen) **Luft durch die Nase** ~: breathe *or* draw in air; **er zog den Rauch in die Lungen** he inhaled the smoke [into his lungs]
8 (zeichnen) draw ‹*line, circle, arc, etc.*›
9 (anlegen) dig ‹*trench*›; build ‹*wall*›; erect ‹*fence*›; put up ‹*washing line*›; run, lay ‹*cable, wires*›; draw ‹*frontier*›; trace ‹*loop*›; follow ‹*course*›; **sich** (*Dat.*) **einen Scheitel** ~: make a parting [in one's hair]
10 (auf~) grow ‹*plants, flowers*›; breed ‹*animals*›; **den Burschen werde ich mir noch** ~ (ugs.) I'll knock the lad into shape yet (coll.)
11 (verblasst; auch als Funktionsverb) draw ‹*lesson, conclusion, comparison*›; *s. auch* **Konsequenz 1**; **Rechenschaft**; **Verantwortung 1**
12 (herstellen) make ‹*candles*›; draw ‹*wire, pipes*›
13 (spannen) mount ‹*picture*› (**auf** + *Akk.* to); fit ‹*string*› (**auf** + *Akk.* to)
14 (beim Sprechen) draw out ‹*vowel*›
15 (in sich aufnehmen) ‹*plant*› draw [up] ‹*water, nourishment*› (**aus** from); (gewinnen) extract ‹*oil, ore*› (**aus** from); **Profit/Nutzen aus etw.** ~ (fig.) derive profit/benefit from sth.
16 (Finanzw.) **einen Wechsel auf jmdn.** ~: draw a bill on sb.
17 (schlagen) **jmdm. etw. über den Kopf** ~: hit sb. over the head with sth.
18 (Waffenkunde) rifle ‹*barrel*›
B *unr. itr. V.* 1 (reißen) pull; **an etw.** (*Dat.*) ~: pull on sth.; **der Hund zieht an der Leine** the dog is straining at the leash; **an einem** *od.* **am gleichen** *od.* **an demselben Strang** *od.* **Strick** ~ (fig.) be pulling in the same direction
2 (funktionieren) ‹*stove, pipe, chimney*› draw; **ausgezeichnet/nicht richtig** ~ (Kfz-W.) ‹*car, engine*› pull really well/not pull properly
3 *mit sein* (um~) move (**nach, in** + *Akk.* to); **aufs Land** ~: move [out] into the country; **zu jmdm.** ~: move in with sb.
4 *mit sein* (gehen) go; (marschieren) march; (umherstreifen) roam; rove; (fortgehen) go away; leave; ‹*fog, clouds*› drift; **durch etw.** ~: pass through sth.; **in den Krieg** ~: go *or* march off to war; **an die Front** ~: move up to the front; **jmdn. ungern** ~ **lassen** be sorry to see sb. go; **die Schwalben** ~ **nach Süden** the swallows are flying southwards
5 (saugen) draw; **an einer Zigarette/Pfeife** ~: draw on a cigarette/pipe; **an einem Strohhalm** ~: suck at a straw; **lass mich mal an deiner Zigarette** ~: let me have a puff of your cigarette
6 ‹*tea, coffee*› draw
7 (Kochk.) simmer
8 (unpers.) **es zieht [vom Fenster her]** there's a draught [from the window]; **es zieht mir an den Beinen** there's a draught round my legs
9 (ugs.: ankommen) sell; ‹*trick*› work; **das zieht bei mir nicht** that won't wash *or* won't cut any ice with me (coll.)
10 (schmerzen) **es zieht [mir] im Rücken** I've got backache; ~**de Schmerzen** aches; **ein leichtes/starkes Ziehen im Bauch** a slight/intense stomach ache
C *unr. refl. V.* 1 (sich erstrecken) ‹*road*› run, stretch; ‹*frontier*› run; **eine Narbe zog sich über sein ganzes Gesicht** there was a scar right across his face; **der Weg** *o. Ä.* **zieht sich** (ugs.) the journey *etc.* goes on and on
2 (sich ver~) warp; get out of shape

Zieher *der;* ~**s,** ~, **Zieherin** *die;* ~, ~**nen** (salopp) pickpocket

Zieh-: ~**harmonika** *die* piano accordion; ~**kind** *das* (veralt.) foster-child; ~**mutter** *die; Pl.* ~**mütter** (veralt.) foster-mother

Ziehung *die;* ~, ~**en** draw; **die** ~ **des Hauptgewinns** the draw for the main prize

Zieh·vater *der* 1 (veralt.) foster-father 2 (fig.) sponsor; patron

Ziel /tsiːl/ *das;* ~**[e]s,** ~**e** 1 (Punkt, Ort) destination; **am** ~ **der Reise angelangen** reach the end of one's journey; reach one's destination; **mit unbekanntem** ~ **abreisen** leave for an unknown destination 2 (Sport) finish; (~linie) finishing line; (Pferderennen) finishing post; **im** ~: at the finish; **das** ~ **erreichen** finish; **als Erster das** ~ **erreichen** *od.* **durchs** ~ **gehen** finish first; cross the finishing line first; ‹*horse*› be first past the [finishing] post 3 (~scheibe; auch Milit.) target; **[weit] über das** ~ **[hinaus]schießen** (fig. ugs.) go over the top; overstep the mark 4 (Zweck) aim; goal; **sein** ~ **erreichen** achieve one's objective *or* aim; **[das]** ~ **unserer Bemühungen ist es, ... zu ...** the object of our efforts is to ...; **mit dem** ~, **etw. zu tun** with the aim of doing sth.; **sich** (*Dat.*) **ein** ~ **setzen** *od.* **stecken** set oneself a goal; **sich** (*Dat.*) **etw. zum** ~ **setzen** set oneself *or* take sth. as one's aim; **etw. zum** ~ **haben** have sth. as one's/its goal; **Beharrlichkeit führt zum** ~: if at first you don't succeed, try, try, and try again 5 (Ende) **einer Sache** (*Dat.*) **ein** ~ **setzen** put an end to sth.

ziel-, Ziel-: ~bahnhof *der* destination; **~band** *das; Pl.* **~bänder** (Sport) finishing tape; **~bewusst**, ***~bewußt** A *Adj.* purposeful; determined; **sehr ~bewusst sein** know exactly where one is going; B *adv.* purposefully; determinedly

zielen *itr. V.* 1 (mit einer Waffe) aim (**auf** + *Akk.*, **nach** at); **genau ~:** take careful aim; **ein gut gezielter Schuss/Wurf** an accurate *or* well-aimed shot/throw; *s. auch* **gezielt** 2 (sich richten) **auf jmdn./etw. ~** ‹*reproach, plan, efforts, etc.*› be aimed at sb./sth.

zielend *Adj.* (Sprachw.) transitive

ziel-, Ziel-: ~erreichung *die* achievement of goals; **~fernrohr** *das* telescopic sight; **~foto** *das* (Sport) photograph of a/the finish; photo-finish photograph; **~führend** A *Adj.* (erfolgreich) successful; (gezielt) targeted ‹*action, therapy*›; (sinnvoll) useful; helpful; B *adv.* successfully; (sinnvoll) usefully; **~genau** A *Adj.* extremely accurate; (gezielt) precisely targeted ‹*attack, treatment, aid, measure*›; pinpoint ‹*landing*›; B *adv.* with pinpoint accuracy; ‹*promote, assist*› in a precisely targeted manner; **~gerade** *die* (Sport) finishing straight; **~gerichtet** A *Adj.* purposeful; B *adv.* purposefully; **~gruppe** *die* target group; **~gruppen·gerecht** A *Adj.* adapted *or* geared to the [needs of the] target group *postpos.*; B *adv.* with the right touch for the target group; **~kamera** *die* (Sport) photo-finish camera; **~linie** *die* (Sport) finishing line; **~los** A *Adj.* aimless; B *adv.* aimlessly; **~losigkeit** *die;* **~~:** aimlessness; **~orientiert** A *Adj.* goal-oriented; purposeful; B *adv.* with a clear goal/clear goals in view; purposefully; **~richter** *der,* **~richterin** *die* finish judge; **~scheibe** *die* (auch fig.) target (*Gen.* for); **~setzung** *die;* **~~, ~en** aims *pl.*; objectives *pl.*; **~sicher** A *Adj.* 1 (treffsicher) accurate; 2 (~gerichtet) decisive, purposeful ‹*steps*›; confident ‹*grip*›; B *adv.* 1 (treffsicher) accurately; 2 (~gerichtet) decisively; (zuversichtlich) confidently; **~sicherheit** *die* accuracy; **~sprache** *die* (Sprachw.) target language; **~strebig** A *Adj.* 1 purposeful; 2 (energisch) single-minded ‹*person*›; B *adv.* 1 purposefully; 2 (energisch) single-mindedly; **~strebigkeit** *die;* **~~** ▸**~strebig**: 1 purposefulness; 2 single-mindedness; **~wahl** *die* (Fernspr.) one-touch dialling

ziemen /'tsi:mən/ (veralt.)

A *refl. V.* be seemly; **das ziemt sich einfach nicht** that just is not done (coll.)

B *itr. V.* **jmdm./einer Sache ~:** befit sb./sth.; be fitting for sb./sth.

Ziemer *der;* **~s, ~** ▸**Ochsenziemer**

ziemlich

A *Adj.* (ugs.) fair, sizeable ‹*quantity, number*›; **eine ~e Frechheit/Weile** quite a cheek/while; **mit ~er Lautstärke** quite loudly; **er kommt mit ~er Sicherheit** he is more or less certain to come; **ich weiß mit ~er Sicherheit, dass …** I am fairly *or* reasonably certain that …

B *adv.* 1 quite; fairly; (etwas intensiver) pretty; **du kommst ~ spät** you're rather late; **~ viele Leute** quite a few people 2 (ugs.: fast) pretty well; more or less; **er ist so ~ in meinem Alter** he's more or less my age

ziepen /'tsi:pn/ (bes. nordd.)

A *itr. V.* **es ziepte ihr im Kreuz** she had a twinge in her back

B *tr. V.* tweak (**an** + *Dat.* by); **jmdn. an den Haaren ~:** give sb.'s hair a tug

Zier /tsi:ɐ/ *die;* **~** (veralt.) ▸**Zierde**

***Zierat** ▸**Zierrat**

Zierde *die;* **~, ~n** (auch fig.) ornament; embellishment; **zur ~:** as decoration; **jmdm. zur ~ gereichen** (fig.) be a credit to sb.; **[die] ~ des Landes** (fig.) the pride of the nation; **eine ~ des Landes** (fig.) one of the country's jewels

Zier·decke *die* ornamental bedspread

zieren

A *tr. V.* (geh.) adorn; decorate ‹*room*›

B *refl. V.* be coy; (sich bitten lassen) need some coaxing *or* pressing; **zier dich nicht so!** don't make such a fuss!; don't be so coy!

Ziererei *die;* **~, ~en** (abwertend) coyness *no indef. art., no pl.*; (Zögern) hedging *no indef. art., no pl.*; (Pose) posturing *no indef. art.*

Zier-: ~fisch *der* ornamental fish; **~garten** *der* ornamental garden; (Blumengarten) flower garden; **~leiste** *die* [decorative] moulding; (an der Decke) cornice; (am Auto) trim

zierlich

A *Adj.* dainty; delicate; petite, dainty ‹*woman, figure*›

B *adv.* daintily; delicately

Zierlichkeit *die;* **~:** daintiness; delicateness; (einer Frau, Gestalt) petiteness; daintiness

Zier·pflanze *die* ornamental plant

Zierrat /'tsi:ra:t/ *der;* **~[e]s, ~e** (geh.) ornament[ation]; **bloßer ~ sein** be purely ornamental; **reich an ~en** richly decorated *or* ornamented

Zier-: ~stich *der* (Handarb.) ornamental stitch; **~strauch** *der* ornamental shrub

Ziffer /'tsɪfɐ/ *die;* **~, ~n** 1 (Zahlzeichen) numeral; (in einer mehrstelligen Zahl) digit; figure; **arabische/römische ~n** Arabic/Roman numerals 2 (Unterabschnitt) subsection; clause

Ziffer·blatt *das* dial; face

-zig, zig /tsɪç/ *unbest. Zahlwort* (ugs.) umpteen (coll.)

Zigarettchen *das;* **~s, ~** (ugs.) ciggy (coll.)

Zigarette /tsiga'rɛtə/ *die;* **~, ~n** cigarette

Zigaretten-: ~asche *die* cigarette ash; **~automat** *der* cigarette machine; **~etui** *das* cigarette case; **~kippe** *die* cigarette end; **~länge** *die* (ugs.) *in* **auf** *od.* **für eine ~länge** just for a smoke; **~papier** *das* cigarette paper; **~pause** *die* (ugs.) break for a smoke; **~raucher** *der,* **~raucherin** *die* cigarette smoker; **~schachtel** *die* cigarette packet; **~spitze** *die* cigarette holder

Zigarillo /tsiga'rɪlo/ *der od. das;* **~, ~s** cigarillo; small cigar

Zigarre /tsi'garə/ *die;* **~, ~n** 1 cigar 2 (ugs.: Rüffel) telling-off; rocket (Brit. coll.); **jmdm. eine ~ verpassen** give sb. a dressing down *or* (Brit. coll.) rocket

Zigarren-: ~abschneider *der* cigar cutter; **~asche** *die* cigar ash; **~raucher** *der,* **~raucherin** *die* cigar smoker; **~stummel** *der* cigar stub

Zigeuner /tsi'gɔynɐ/ *der;* **~s, ~, Zigeunerin** *die;* **~, ~nen** 1 gypsy 2 (ugs.: Tramp) vagabond

Zigeuner-: ~kapelle *die* gypsy band; **~musik** *die* gypsy music; **~primas** *der* leading fiddle player [of a gypsy band]; **~schnitzel** *das* (Kochk.): *veal or pork escalope in a spicy sauce with green peppers, tomato, etc.*; **~sprache** *die* Romany [language]

zig·mal *Adv.* (ugs.) umpteen times (coll.)

zigst… ▸ⓘ **S. 826** (ugs.) umpteenth (coll.)

zig·tausend *unbest. Zahlwort* (ugs.) umpteen thousand (coll.)

Zikade /tsi'ka:də/ *die;* **~, ~n** (Zool.) cicada

Zimbal /'tsɪmbal/ *das;* **~s, ~e** *od.* **~s** (Musik) cimbalom

Zimbel /'tsɪmbl/ *die;* **~, ~n** (Musik) cymbal

Zimmer /'tsɪmɐ/ *das;* **~s, ~:** room; **auf/in sein ~ gehen** go to one's room

Zimmer-: ~antenne *die* indoor aerial *or* (Amer.) antenna; **~arbeit** *die* carpentry *no indef. art.*; **~arbeiten** carpentry work *sing.*; **~brand** *der* room fire; **~decke** *die* ceiling

Zimmerer *der;* **~s, ~, Zimmerin** *die;* **~, ~nen** carpenter

Zimmer-: ~flucht *die* suite [of rooms]; **~hand·werk** *das* carpentry *no art.*; **~kellner** *der* room waiter; **~kellnerin** *die* room waitress; **~lautstärke** *die* domestic listening level; **das Radio auf ~lautstärke stellen** turn the radio down to a reasonable volume [so as not to disturb the neighbours]; **~linde** *die* African hemp; **~mädchen** *das* chambermaid; **~mann** *der; Pl.* **~leute** carpenter; **~meister** *der,* **~meisterin** *die* master carpenter

zimmern

A *tr. V.* make ‹*shelves, coffin, etc.*›

B *itr. V.* do carpentry; **an einem Regal ~:** be making a bookshelf

Zimmer-: ~nummer *die* room number; **~pflanze** *die* house plant; indoor plant; **~suche** *die* room-hunt; **bei der ~suche** when room-hunting; **auf ~suche sein** be looking for a room; **~temperatur** *die* room temperature; **~theater** *das* studio theatre; **~vermittlung** *die* accommodation office

zimperlich /'tsɪmpɐlɪç/ (abwertend)

A *Adj.* timid; (leicht angeekelt) squeamish; (prüde) prissy; (übertrieben rücksichtsvoll) overscrupulous; **sei nicht ~ mit ihnen** don't go easy on them

B *s. Adj.:* timidly; squeamishly; prissily; overscrupulously; **die Polizei ging nicht gerade ~ mit ihr um** the police didn't exactly treat her with kid gloves

Zimperlichkeit *die;* **~, ~en** (abwertend) timidity; (Neigung zum Ekel) squeamishness; (Prüderie) prissiness; (übertriebene Rücksicht) overscrupulousness; excessive scruples *pl.*

Zimt /tsɪmt/ *der;* **~[e]s, ~e** 1 cinnamon 2 (ugs. abwertend: Zeug) rubbish; **so ein ~!** what a load of rubbish! (coll.)

Zimt-: ~stange *die* cinnamon stick; **~ziege** *die* (Schimpfwort: Frau) cow (sl. derog.)

Zink[1] /tsɪŋk/ *das;* **~[e]s** zinc

Zink[2] *der;* **~[e]s, ~en** (Musik) cornetto

Zink-: ~blech *das* zinc [sheet]; **~blende** *die* zinc blende

Zinke *die;* **~, ~n** prong; (eines Kammes) tooth; (Holzverarb.) dovetail

zinken *tr. V.* (ugs.) mark ‹*cards*›

Zinken *der;* **~s, ~** 1 (Gaunerspr.) [crook's/beggar's] secret sign *or* mark 2 (ugs. scherzh.: Nase) conk (coll.)

Zink-: ~leim·verband *der* (Med.) Unna's paste dressing; **~salbe** *die* (Med.) zinc oxide ointment

Zinn /tsɪn/ *das;* **~[e]s** 1 (Metall) tin 2 (Gegenstände) pewter[ware]

Zinne *die;* **~, ~n** 1 merlon; **~n** battlements 2 (schweiz.: Dachterrasse) roof terrace

Zinn·figur *die* pewter figure; (Zinnsoldat o. Ä.) tin figure;

Zinnie /'tsɪnjə/ *die;* **~, ~n** (Bot.) zinnia

Zinn·kraut *das* common horsetail

Zinnober /tsɪ'no:bɐ/ *der;* **~s, ~** 1 cinnabar 2 *österr.: das;* **~s** (~rot) vermilion 3 (*salopp abwertend*) (wertloses Zeug) junk; rubbish; (Unsinn) twaddle; **~ machen** make a big fuss

zinnober·rot *Adj.* vermilion

Zinn-: ~soldat *der* tin soldier; **~teller** *der* pewter plate

Zins /tsɪns/ *der;* **~es, ~en** *od.* **~e** 1 *Pl.* **~en** (Geld) interest; **~en tragen** *od.* **bringen** earn interest; **zu 8% ~en** at 8% interest; **bei einem ~ von 8%** at 8% interest; **die ~en sind gestiegen** interest rates have gone up; **jmdm. etw. mit ~en** *od.* **mit ~ und ~eszins zurückzahlen** (fig.) make sb. pay dearly for sth. 2 *Pl.* **~e** (südd., österr., schweiz.: Mietzins) rent

Zins·erhöhung *die* increase in the rate of interest

Zinses·zins *der; Pl.* **~en** compound interest

zins-, Zins-: ~fuß *der* interest rate; **~günstig** (Finanzw.) A *Adj.* at a favourable rate of interest *postpos.*; low-interest ‹*credit, loan*›; high-interest, high-yield ‹*savings scheme, investment, etc.*›; B *adv.* at a favourable rate of interest; **~los** A *Adj.* interest-free; B *adv.* free of interest; **~pflichtig** *Adj.* liable to interest *postpos.*; **… ist ~pflichtig** interest is payable on …; **~politik** *die* policy on interest rates; **~rechnung** *die* calculation of interest; **~satz** *der* interest rate; **~senkung** *die* reduction of interest rates

Zionismus /tsio'nɪsmʊs/ *der;* **~:** Zionism *no art.*

Zionist *der;* **~en, ~en, Zionistin,** *die;* **~, ~nen** Zionist

zionistisch *Adj.* Zionist

Zip-Datei /'zɪp-/ *die* (DV) zip file

Zipfel /ˈtsɪpfl/ *der;* **~s, ~** (einer Decke, eines Tischtuchs, Handtuchs usw.) corner; (Wurst~, eines Halstuchs) [tail] end; (einer ~mütze) point; (Spitze eines Sees usw.) tip

zipfelig *Adj.* uneven ‹*hem*›; ‹*coat, skirt*› with an uneven hem

Zipfel·mütze *die* [long-]pointed cap

Zipp Ⓦᵹ /tsɪp/ *der;* **~s, ~s** (österr.) zip

zippen /ˈzɪpn̩/ *tr. V.* (DV) zip

Zipperlein /ˈtsɪpɐlain/ *das;* **~** (ugs. veralt.) gout

Zipp·verschluss, *Zipp·verschluß *der* (österr.) zip fastener

Zirbel- /ˈtsɪrbl̩/: **~drüse** *die* (Biol.) pineal gland; **~kiefer** *die* Swiss [stone] pine; arolla pine

Zirconium (fachspr.) ▸ **Zirkonium**

zirka /ˈtsɪrka/ *Adv.* about; approximately

Zirkel /ˈtsɪrkl̩/ *der;* **~s, ~** **1** (Gerät) [pair *sing.* of] compasses *pl.* **2** (Kreis, Gruppe; beim Pferdesport) circle **3** ▸ **Zirkeldefinition**; **Zirkelschluss**

Zirkel-: ~definition *die* circular definition; **~kasten** *der* compasses case

zirkeln
A *tr. V.* (genau abmessen) measure out precisely; **gezirkelt** precisely laid out; **er zirkelte den Ball genau in die linke obere Ecke** (Fußballjargon) he placed the ball with precision in the top left-hand corner
B *itr. V.* (ugs.: sehr genau arbeiten) try to get things just right

Zirkel·schluss, *Zirkel·schluß *der* circular argument

Zirkonium /tsɪrˈkoːni̯ʊm/ *das;* **~s** zirconium

zirkular /tsɪrkuˈlaːɐ̯/ (Physik, Fot.)
A *Adj.* circular
B *adv.* circularly

Zirkulation /tsɪrkulaˈtsi̯oːn/ *die;* **~, ~en** **1** circulation **2** (Fechten) circular parry

zirkulieren *itr. V.; auch mit sein* circulate

Zirkumflex /tsɪrkʊmˈflɛks/ *der;* **~es, ~e** (Sprachw.) circumflex

Zirkus /ˈtsɪrkʊs/ *der;* **~, ~se** **1** circus **2** (ugs.) (Trubel) hustle and bustle; (Krach) to-do; rumpus (coll.); (Umstände) **mach nicht so einen ~!** don't make such a fuss!

Zirkus-: ~direktor *der,* **~direktorin** *die* circus director; **~kuppel** *die* roof of the big top; **~nummer** *die* circus act; **zu einer ~nummer werden** (fig.) turn into a farce; **~pferd** *das* circus horse; **~vorstellung** *die* circus performance; **~zelt** *das* big top

zirpen /ˈtsɪrpn̩/ *itr. V.* chirp

Zirren ▸ **Zirrus**

Zirrhose /tsɪˈroːzə/ *die;* **~, ~n** ▸ⓘ **S. 439** (Med.) cirrhosis

Zirrus /ˈtsɪrʊs/ *der;* **~, ~** *od.* **Zirren, Zirrus·wolke** *die* (Met.) cirrus [cloud]

zirzensisch /tsɪrˈtsɛnzɪʃ/ *Adj.* circus *attrib.*

zisalpin /tsɪs|alˈpiːn/ *Adj.* cisalpine

Zischelei *die;* **~, ~en** whispering

zischeln /ˈtsɪʃl̩n/ *tr. V.* whisper angrily

zischen /ˈtsɪʃn̩/
A *itr. V.* **1** hiss; ‹*hot fat*› sizzle **2** *mit sein* hiss; (ugs.: flitzen) whizz
B *tr. V.* **1** (zischend sprechen) hiss **2** **ein Bier/einen ~** (ugs.) knock back a beer (coll.)/knock one back (coll.)

Zisch·laut *der* (Sprachw.) sibilant

Ziseleur /tsizeˈløːɐ̯/ *der;* **~s, ~e, Ziseleurin** *die* engraver

Ziselier·arbeit *die* engraving; (von Gold, Silber) chasing *no indef. art.;* (Produkt) piece of engraved/chased work

ziselieren /tsizeˈliːrən/ *tr., itr. V.* engrave; chase ‹*gold, silver*›

Ziselierung *die;* **~, ~en** engraving; (von Gold, Silber) chasing

Zisterne /tsɪsˈtɛrnə/ *die;* **~, ~n** [underground] tank *or* cistern

Zisterzienser /tsɪstɛrˈtsi̯ɛnzɐ/ *der;* **~s, ~, Zisterzienserin** *die;* **~, ~nen** Cistercian [monk/nun]

Zisterzienser·orden *der* Cistercian order

Zitadelle /tsitaˈdɛlə/ *die;* **~, ~n** citadel

Zitat /tsiˈtaːt/ *das;* **~[e]s, ~e** quotation (**aus** from); **falsches ~:** misquotation

Zitaten-: ~sammlung *die* collection of quotations; **~schatz** *der* store of quotations

Zither /ˈtsɪtɐ/ *die;* **~, ~n** zither

Zither·spieler *der,* **Zither·spielerin** *die* zither player

zitieren /tsiˈtiːrən/ *tr., itr. V.* **1** quote (**aus, nach** from); (Rechtspr.: anführen) cite; **..., ich zitiere: „...“** ... and I quote: '...'; (wie er usw. sich ausdrückt) '...', as he *etc.* puts it; **falsch ~:** misquote **2** (vorladen, rufen) summon (**vor** before, **zu** to)

Zitronat /tsitroˈnaːt/ *das;* **~[e]s** candied lemon peel

Zitrone /tsiˈtroːnə/ *die;* **~, ~n** lemon; **jmdn. ausquetschen wie eine ~** (ugs.) (ausfragen) pump sb.; (ausbeuten) bleed sb. dry

zitronen-, Zitronen-: ~falter *der* brimstone butterfly; **~gelb** *Adj.* lemon yellow; **~gras** *das* lemon grass; **~limonade** *die* lemonade; **~melisse** *die* lemon balm; **~presse** *die* lemon squeezer; **~saft** *der* lemon juice; **~säure** *die* (Chemie) citric acid; **~schale** *die* lemon peel

Zitrus /ˈtsiːtrʊs/ *der;* **~:** citrus

Zitrus·frucht /ˈtsiːtrʊs-/ *die* citrus fruit

Zitter-: ~aal *der* electric eel; **~gras** *das* quaking grass

zittern /ˈtsɪtɐn/ *itr. V.* **1** tremble (**vor** + *Dat.* with); (vor Kälte) shiver; ‹*needle, arrow, leaf, etc.*› quiver; (flimmern) ‹*air*› shimmer; (beben) ‹*walls, windows*› shake; **mit ~der Stimme** in a trembling *or* quavering voice **2** (Angst haben) tremble; quake; **vor jmdm./etw. ~:** be terrified of sb./sth.; **er zittert vor der Prüfung** he's scared stiff (coll.) about the exam; **mit Zittern und Zagen** in fear and trembling; **um jmdn./etw. ~:** be very worried about sb./sth.; **für jmdn. ~:** be anxious for sb. **3** *mit sein* (salopp: gehen) **nach Hause ~:** slope off home (coll.)

Zitter-: ~pappel *die* aspen; **~partie** *die* (Sportjargon, auch fig.) nail-biting affair; **~rochen** *der* torpedo ray

zittrig
A *Adj.* shaky; doddery ‹*old man*›
B *adv.* shakily

Zitze /ˈtsɪtsə/ *die;* **~, ~n** teat

Zivi /ˈtsiːvi/ *der;* **~s, ~s** (ugs.) ▸ **Zivildienstleistende**

zivil /tsiˈviːl/
A *Adj.* **1** civilian ‹*life, population*›; non-military ‹*purposes*›; civil ‹*aviation, marriage, law, defence*›; *s. auch* **Ersatzdienst** **2** (annehmbar) decent; reasonable
B *adv.* decently; reasonably

Zivil *das;* **~s** **1** civilian clothes *pl.;* **Polizist in ~:** plain-clothes policeman **2** (schweiz.: Familienstand) marital status

Zivil-: ~beruf *der* civilian profession *or* job; **~bevölkerung** *die* civilian population; **~courage** *die* courage of one's convictions; **~diener** *der* (österr.) ▸ **Ersatzdienstleistende**; **~dienst** *der* ▸ **Ersatzdienst**; **~dienst·leistende** *der; adj. Dekl.,* **~dienstler** /-diːnstlɐ/ *der;* **~~s, ~~** (ugs.) ▸ **Ersatzdienstleistende**; **~ehe** *die* civil marriage; **~flughafen** *der* civil airport; **~gericht** *das* civil court; **~gesetz·buch** (schweiz., DDR) civil code

> **Zivildienst**
>
> Community service which recognized conscientious objectors in Germany, Austria, and Switzerland can choose to carry out instead of **Wehrdienst**. It lasts longer than *Wehrdienst* and usually involves caring for children, the elderly, the disabled, or the sick.

Zivilisation /tsiviliza'tsi̯oːn/ *die;* **~, ~en** civilization; **eine hohe/niedrige ~:** a high/low level of civilization; **fortschreitende ~:** progressively increasing degree of civilization

Zivilisations·krankheit *die* disease of modern civilization *or* society

zivilisations·müde *Adj.* weary of modern civilization *postpos.*

zivilisatorisch /tsivilizaˈtoːrɪʃ/
A *Adj.* ‹*development, level, standard*› of civilization
B *adv.* with regard to civilization

zivilisieren *tr. V.* civilize

zivilisiert
A *Adj.* civilized
B *adv.* in a civilized way

Zivilist *der;* **~en, ~en** civilian

Zivil-: ~kammer *die* (Rechtsw.) *chamber for civil matters;* **~klage** *die* (Rechtsw.) private action *or* prosecution; **~kleidung** *die* civilian clothes *pl;* **~leben** *das* civilian life; **~luftfahrt** *die* civil aviation; **~person** *die* civilian; **~prozess, *~prozeß** *der* (Rechtsw.) civil action; **~prozess·ordnung, *~prozeß·ordnung** *die* (Rechtsw.) civil procedure; **~recht** *das* civil law; **~richter** *der,* **~richterin** *die* civil judge; **~sache** *die* (Rechtsw.) civil case; **~schutz** *der* civil defence; **~trauung** *die* civil wedding; **~verfahren** *das* (Rechtsw.) civil proceedings *pl.*

ZK *Abk.* **= Zentralkomitee**

Zloty /ˈzlɔti/ *der;* **~s, ~s** zloty

Znüni /ˈtsnyːni/ *der od. das;* **~s, ~** (schweiz.) mid-morning snack

Zobel /ˈtsoːbl̩/ *der;* **~s, ~:** sable

Zobel·pelz *der* sable [fur]

zockeln /ˈtsɔkl̩n/ ▸ **zuckeln**

Zofe /ˈtsoːfə/ *die;* **~, ~n** (hist.) lady's maid

Zoff /tsɔf/ *der;* **~s** (ugs.) rowing (coll.); squabbling; **~ machen** cause trouble; **mit jmdm. ~ haben** have a set-to with sb.

zoffen /ˈtsɔfn̩/ *refl V.* (ugs.) row, have a row (**um, über** + *Akk.* over)

zog *1. u. 3. Pers. Sg. Prät. v.* **ziehen**

zögerlich /ˈtsøːgəlɪç/
A *Adj.* hesitant; tentative
B *adv.* hesitantly; tentatively

zögern *itr. V.* hesitate; **ich zögere nicht zu behaupten, dass ...** I have no hesitation in saying that ...; **mit der Antwort ~:** hesitate before answering; **mit der Abreise ~:** delay one's departure; **ohne zu ~:** without hesitation; **nach einigem Zögern** after a moment's hesitation; **~d vorangehen** proceed hesitantly

Zögling /ˈtsøːklɪŋ/ *der;* **~s, ~e** (veralt.) boarding pupil; boarder

Zölibat /tsøliˈbaːt/ *das od. der;* **~[e]s, ~e** celibacy *no art.*

Zoll[1] /tsɔl/ *der;* **~[e]s, Zölle** /ˈtsœlə/ **1** (Abgabe) [customs] duty; **auf dieser Ware liegt kein/ein hoher ~:** there is no duty/a high rate of duty on this article; **die Zölle senken** reduce rates of duty *or* [customs] tariffs **2** (hist.: Benutzungsgebühr) toll; **~ erheben** charge a toll **3** (Behörde) customs *pl.*

Zoll[2] *der;* **~[e]s, ~** ▸ⓘ **S. 454** inch; **ein Nagel von 2 ~:** a two-inch nail; **von 4 ~ Durchmesser** 4 inches in diameter; **keinen ~ nachgeben** *od.* **weichen** (fig.) not give *or* budge an inch; **jeder ~** *od.* **~ für ~ ein Gentleman** (fig.) every inch a gentleman

zoll-, Zoll-: ~abfertigung *die* customs clearance; **die ~abfertigung passieren** go through custom; **bei der ~abfertigung** at the customs; **~amt** *das* customs house *or* office; **~ausland** *das: region outside one's own customs area;* **~beamte** *der,* **~beamtin** *die* ▸ⓘ **S. 113** customs officer; **~breit** *Adj.* inch-wide; **~breit** *der;* **~~, ~~: keinen ~breit zurückweichen** (fig.) not budge an inch

zollen *tr. V.* (geh.) **jmdm. etw. ~:** accord sb. sth.; **jmdm. Respekt/Bewunderung ~:** show sb. respect/admiration; **jmdm. Lob ~:** bestow praise upon sb.; **jmdm. Anerkennung ~:** give sb. recognition; **jmdm. Beifall ~:** applaud sb.; **jmdm./einer Sache Tribut ~:** pay tribute to sb./sth.

zoll-, Zoll-: ~erklärung *die* customs declaration; **~fahndung** *die* customs investigation; **~formalität** *die* customs formality;

Z

~frei A *Adj.* duty-free; free of duty *pred.*; B *adv.* free of duty; **~gebiet** *das* customs area; **sich auf britischem ~gebiet befinden** be in the British customs area; **~grenz·bezirk** *der* frontier area under customs surveillance; **~grenze** *die* limit of a/the customs area; **~inland** *das* domestic customs area; **~kontrolle** *die* customs examination *or* check; **zur ~kontrolle gehen** go to customs for clearance

Zöllner /ˈt͜sœlnɐ/ *der;* **~s, ~, Zöllnerin** *die;* **~, ~nen** [1] (ugs. veralt.) customs officer [2] (hist.: Steuereintreiber) tax collector; (bibl.) publican

zoll-, Zoll-: ~pflichtig *Adj.* dutiable; **~schranke** *die* customs barrier; **~station** *die,* **~stelle** *die* customs post; **~stock** *der* folding rule; **~union** *die* customs union; **~verein** *der* (hist.) **der Deutsche ~verein** the German customs union; the Zollverein

Zombie /ˈt͜sɔmbi/ *der;* **~[s], ~s** zombie

Zone /ˈt͜so:nə/ *die;* **~, ~n** [1] zone; (für Telefongespräche) charge zone; (für öffentlichen Nahverkehr) fare zone [2] **die ~** (ugs. veralt.) East Germany

Zonen-: ~grenze *die* [1] **die ~grenze** (ugs. veralt.) the East German border; [2] (hist.: zwischen Besatzungszonen) zonal frontier; **~rand·gebiet** *das* area along the East German border; **~zeit** *die* zone time

Zoo /tso:/ *der;* **~s, ~s** zoo; **im/in den ~:** at/to the zoo

Zoo·handlung *die* pet shop

Zoologe /tsooˈlo:gə/ *der;* **~n, ~n** ▸ⓘ **S. 113** zoologist

Zoologie *die;* **~:** zoology *no art.*

Zoologin *die;* **~, ~nen** ▸ⓘ **S. 113** zoologist

zoologisch
A *Adj.* zoological; **~er Garten** zoological gardens *pl.*; **~er Bedarf** *pet foods and accessories pl*
B *adv.* zoologically; **~ interessiert/beschlagen** interested in/knowledgeable about zoology

Zoom¹ /zu:m/ *das;* **~s, ~s** (Film, Fot.: Objektiv) zoom

Zoom² *der;* **~s, ~s** (Film: Aufnahme) zoom shot

zoomen /ˈzu:mn̩/ *itr. V.* (Film) zoom (**auf +** *Akk.* in on)

Zoom·objektiv *das* (Film, Fot.) zoom lens

Zoo-: ~tier *das* zoo animal; **~wärter** *der,* **~wärterin** *die* ▸ⓘ **S. 113** zookeeper

Zopf /t͜sɔpf/ *der;* **~[e]s, Zöpfe** /ˈt͜sœpfə/ [1] plait; (am Hinterkopf) pigtail; **sich** (*Dat.*) **Zöpfe flechten** plait one's hair [into pigtails]; **falscher ~:** false braid; **einen alten ~ abschneiden** (fig.) put an end to an antiquated custom *or* practice [2] (Backwerk) plait

Zopf·band *das; Pl.* **Zopfbänder** pigtail ribbon

Zöpfchen /ˈt͜sœpfçən/ *das;* **~s, ~:** small plait/pigtail

Zopf-: ~muster *das* cable pattern; **~spange** *die* hairslide (Brit.), barrette (esp. Amer.) (*for a pigtail*); **~stil** *der* (*Kunstwiss.*): *plain style of the late 18th century;* **~zeit** *die* (Kunstwiss.) age of the Zopfstil

Zorn /t͜sɔrn/ *der;* **~[e]s** anger; (stärker) wrath; fury; **ihn packte der ~:** he flew into a rage; **einen ~ auf jmdn. haben** (ugs.) be furious with sb.; **jmds. ~ erregen** anger sb.; **der ~ der Götter** the wrath of the Gods; **vor ~ kochen** be boiling with rage; **gerechter ~:** righteous anger; **im ~:** in a rage; in anger

Zorn-: ~ader *die:* **in jmdm. schwillt die ~ader** (geh.) sb. flies into a rage; **~ausbruch** *der* angry outburst; fit of rage

Zornes-: ~ader ▸**Zornader**; **~falte** *die* (geh.) vertical line [on the brow]; angry furrow; **~röte** *die* (geh.) **in jmdm. die ~röte ins Gesicht treiben** make sb. flush with anger; **jmdm. steigt die ~röte ins Gesicht** sb. flushes with anger

zornig
A *Adj.* furious; **~ über etw.** furious about sth.; **~ auf** *od.* **über jmdn.** furious with sb.
B *adv.* furiously

Zorn·röte *die* ▸**Zornesröte**

Zote /ˈt͜so:tə/ *die;* **~, ~n** dirty joke

Zoten·reißer *der;* **~s, ~, Zoten·reißerin** *die;* **~, ~nen** (abwertend) teller of dirty jokes

zotig
A *Adj.* smutty; dirty ‹*joke*›
B *adv.* smuttily

Zotte /ˈt͜sɔtə/ *die;* **~, ~n** [1] (Haarbüschel) shaggy tuft [of hair] [2] ▸ⓘ **S. 435** (Anat.) villus

Zottel /ˈt͜sɔtl̩/ *die;* **~, ~n** (ugs.) [1] ▸**Zotte 1** [2] *Pl.* (abwertend: Haare) shaggy locks

Zottel·haar *das* (ugs.) shaggy *or* unkempt hair

zottelig
A *Adj.* shaggy
B *adv.* **die Haare hingen ihr ~ ins Gesicht** her hair hung shaggily over her face

Zottel·kopf *der* (ugs.) [1] (Frisur) shaggy hair [2] (Person) shaggy-haired type

zotteln *itr. V.; mit sein* (ugs.) saunter; amble

Zottel·trab *der* jogtrot

zottig *Adj.* shaggy

ZPO *Abk.* **= Zivilprozessordnung**

Z-Soldat *der* (Militärjargon) ▸**Zeitsoldat**

Ztr. *Abk.* **= Zentner** cwt.

zu /t͜su:/
A *Präp. mit Dat.* [1] (Richtung) to; **zu ... hin** towards ...; **er kommt zu mir** (besucht mich) he is coming to my place
[2] (zusammen mit) with; **zu dem Käse gab es Wein** there was wine with the cheese; **das passt nicht zu Bier/zu dem Kleid** that doesn't go with beer/with that dress
[3] (Lage) at; **zu beiden Seiten** on both sides; **zu seiner Linken** (geh.) on his left; **es ist zu Wasser und zu Lande zu erreichen** it can be reached by water and overland; **er kam zu dieser Tür herein** he came in by this door; **der Dom zu Speyer** (veralt.) Speyer Cathedral; **er wurde zu Köln geboren** (veralt.) he was born in Cologne; **das Gasthaus zu den drei Eichen** the Three Oaks Inn; **der Graf zu Mansfeld** the Count of Mansfeld
[4] (zeitlich) at; **zu Weihnachten** at Christmas; **was schenkst du ihnen zu Weihnachten?** what will you give them for Christmas?; **er will zu Ostern verreisen** he wants to go away for Easter; **zu Anfang des Jahres** at the beginning of the year; **zu dieser Stunde** at this time; **zu meiner Zeit** in my day; *s. auch* **Lebzeiten**
[5] (Art u. Weise) **zu meiner Zufriedenheit/Überraschung** to my satisfaction/surprise; **zu seinem Vorteil/Nachteil** to his advantage/disadvantage; **zu niedrigen Preisen** at low prices; **zu Deutsch** (fig.) in plain German; in words of one syllable; (bei Mengenangaben o. Ä) **zu Dutzenden/zweien** by the dozen/in twos; **sie sind zu einem Drittel/zu 50% arbeitslos** a third/50% of them are jobless; **zu einem großen Teil** largely; to a large extent
[6] (ein Zahlenverhältnis ausdrückend) **ein Verhältnis von 3 zu 1** a ratio of 3 to 1; **das Ergebnis war 2 zu 1** the result was 2-1 *or* 2 to 1
[7] (einen Preis zuordnend) at; for; **Stoff zu zwanzig Euro der Meter** cloth at *or* for twenty euros a metre; **fünf Briefmarken zu fünfzig [Cent]** five 50-cent stamps
[8] (eine Zahlenangabe zuordnend) **ein Fass zu zehn Litern** a ten-litre barrel; **Portionen zu je einem Pfund** portions weighing a pound each
[9] (Zweck) for; **zu einer weiteren Behandlung nach X fahren** go to X for further treatment; **sie sagte das zu seiner Beruhigung** she said it to allay his fears; **Stoff zu einem Kleid** material for a dress
[10] (Ziel, Ergebnis) into; **zu etw. werden** turn into sth.; **die Kartoffeln zu einem Brei zerstampfen** mash the potatoes into a purée; **das hat ihn zu meinem Freund gemacht** that made him my friend; **zu Staub zerfallen** crumble into dust
[11] (über) about; on; **sich zu etw. äußern** comment on sth.; **zu welchem Thema spricht er?** what is he going to speak about?; **was sagst du zu meinem Vorschlag?** what do you say to my proposal?
[12] (gegenüber) **freundlich/hässlich zu jmdm. sein** be friendly/nasty to sb.; **Liebe zu jmdm. empfinden** have feelings of love towards sb.; *s. auch* **zum**; **zur**
B *Adv.* [1] (allzu) too; **zu sehr** too much; **er ist zu alt, um diese Reise zu unternehmen** he is too old to undertake this journey; **das ist ja zu schön/komisch!** that's really wonderful/hilarious!; that's too wonderful/hilarious for words!
[2] *nachgestellt* (Richtung) towards; **der Grenze zu** towards the border; **dem Fenster zu stand ein Polizist** a policeman stood over towards the window
[3] (ugs.) **~ sein** ‹*door, window*› be shut; ‹*shop*› have shut; (fig.: betrunken sein) be tight (coll.); **Augen/Tür zu!** shut your eyes/the door!
[4] (ugs.: Aufforderung) **nur zu!** (fang/fangt an!) get going!; get down to it!; (mach/macht weiter!) get on with it!; **dort gehst du richtig, nur zu!** you're going the right way, just keep going!; **Wir sind fertig. — Na, dann zu!** We're ready. — Right, let's go!
C *Konj.* [1] (mit Infinitiv) to; **ich bat ihn zu helfen** I asked him to help; **du hast zu gehorchen** you must obey; **was gibts da zu lachen?** what is there to laugh about?; **er ist heute nicht zu sprechen** he is not available today; **die Wände sind noch zu streichen** the walls still have to be painted; **das ist nicht zu glauben** it is unbelievable; **Haus zu verkaufen/vermieten** house for sale/to let
[2] (mit 1. Part.) **die zu gewinnenden Preise** the prizes to be won; **die zu erledigende Post** the letters *pl.* to be dealt with

zu·aller·erst *Adv.* first of all; (hauptsächlich) above all else

zu·aller·letzt *Adv.* last of all

zu|arbeiten *itr. V.* **jmdm. ~:** assist sb. [with preparatory work]

zu|bauen *tr. V.* [1] develop, build on ‹*land*› [2] (ugs.: versperren) block ‹*entrance, door*›; obstruct ‹*view*›

Zubehör /ˈt͜su:bəhø:ɐ̯/ *das;* **~[e]s, ~e** *od. schweiz.* **~den** accessories *pl.*; (eines Staubsaugers, Mixers o. Ä.) attachments *pl.*; (Ausstattung) equipment; **mit allem ~:** with all accessories *pl.*; fully equipped ‹*workshop, kitchen, etc.*›

zu|beißen *unr. itr. V.* bite; **einen Hund ärgern, bis er zubeißt** tease a dog until he bites one

zu|bekommen *unr. tr. V.* get ‹*suitcase, door, etc.*› shut; get the top on ‹*bottle*›; get ‹*clothes, buttons*› done up; manage to repair ‹*leak*›; manage to mend ‹*hole*›

Zuber /ˈtsuˈbɐ/ *der;* **~s, ~** (bes. südd.) tub

zu|bereiten *tr. V.* prepare ‹*meal, food, cocktail, etc.*›; make up ‹*medicine, ointment*›; (kochen) cook ‹*fish, meat, etc.*›

Zu·bereitung *die;* **~, ~en** preparation; (von Arznei) making up; (Kochen) cooking

zu|betonieren *tr. V.* concrete over; cover in concrete

Zu·bett·gehen *das;* **~s vorm/beim ~:** before/on going to bed

zu|bewegen
A *tr. V.* **etw. auf jmdn./etw. ~:** move sth. towards sb./sth.
B *refl. V.* **sich auf etw. ~:** move towards sth.

zu|billigen *tr. V.* **jmdm. etw. ~:** grant *or* allow sb. sth.; **jmdm. ~, dass er in gutem Glauben gehandelt hat** accept that sb. acted in good faith; **dem Angeklagten mildernde Umstände ~:** allow the accused's plea of extenuating circumstances

Zu·billigung *die;* **~, ~en** granting; allowing; **er wurde unter ~ mildernder Umstände für schuldig befunden** he was found guilty but with extenuating circumstances

zu|binden *unr. tr. V.* tie [up]

zu|blinzeln *itr. V.* **jmdm. ~:** wink at sb.

zu|bringen *unr. tr. V.* [1] (verbringen) spend [2] (landsch.) ▸**zubekommen**

Z

ℹ zu, zum, zur

Wohin? = to

Sie gehen zur Schule/zur Arbeit
= They are going to school/to work

Es ist zu beachten, dass bei diesen Ausdrücken im Englischen kein Artikel verwendet wird.

Beim Modalverb mit *zu* darf **go** im Englischen nicht fehlen:

Er will morgen zu ihr
= He wants to go and see her tomorrow

Ich muss zum Arzt
= I must go to the doctor's *od.* go to see the doctor

Aber:

Er geht zum Militär/Theater
= He is going into the army/the theatre

Adverbiale Zusätze wie *hin, hinaus, herüber* usw. verlangen andere Übersetzungen:

zur Küste hin
= towards the coast

zur Tür herein/hinaus
= in through/out of the door

Sie sah zu mir herüber/zum Himmel hinauf
= She looked across at me/up at the sky

Beim übertragenen Gebrauch, der eine ***Verwandlung*** kennzeichnet, verwendet man oft auch **into:**

Das Wasser wurde zu Eis
= The water turned [in]to ice

Der Junge war zu einem Mann geworden
= The boy had grown into a man

Die Zutaten zu einem Brei verrühren
= Mix the ingredients [in]to a paste

Das machte ihn zum Märtyrer
= This made him into a martyr

Aber:

Ich machte/ernannte ihn zu meinem Vertreter
= I made/appointed him my representative

Wenn man ein ***Verhältnis*** beschreiben will, sagt man auch **to:**

in einem Verhältnis von drei zu eins
= in a ratio of three to one

Beim Spielstand aber wird das **to** meist ausgelassen, außer wenn die Worte 'goals', 'points', 'games', 'sets' usw. verwendet werden:

Das Ergebnis war zwei zu null
= The final score was two-nil *od.* two goals/points *etc.* to nil

Wo? Wann? Wieviel? = at

1. Ort

Ich bleibe zu Hause
= I am staying at home

Er lag zu ihren Füßen
= He lay at her feet

Zu ebener Erde haben wir fünf Zimmer
= We have five rooms at ground level *od.* on the ground floor

Aber:

zu beiden Seiten
= on both sides

zu meiner Linken
= on my left

2. Zeit

zu Anfang/Ende des Jahres
= at the beginning/end of the year

Zu Ostern/Zum Wochenende wollen wir verreisen
= We want to go away at *od.* for Easter/the weekend

Sie bekommen es zu gegebener Zeit
= You will get it at the appropriate time

***Er kam zu später Stunde* (geh.)**
= He came at a late hour

Aber:

Es tritt zum 1. Januar in Kraft
= It comes into force on January 1st

Es muss [bis] zum 31. August fertig werden
= It must be finished by August 31st

zu diesem Anlass
= on this occasion

zum ersten/letzten Mal
= for the first/last time

3. Preis

Sie verkaufen alles zu niedrigsten Preisen
= They sell everything at rock-bottom prices

Kartoffeln zu 50 Cent das Pfund
= Potatoes at *od.* for 50 cents a pound

Aber:

sechs Briefmarken zu sieben Schilling
= six seven schilling stamps

Was ist der Zweck? = for

Zu diesem Zweck gibt es einen Notruf
= There is an emergency line for this purpose

Sie fährt zu einer Besprechung nach Berlin
= She is going to Berlin for a meeting

Das haben wir nur zum Spaß gemacht
= We only did it for fun

das Öl zum Schmieren der Nockenwelle
= the oil for lubricating the camshaft

Hier verwendet man auch **to** + Infinitiv:

Zum Lesen braucht er eine Brille
= He needs spectacles for reading *od.* to read with

etwas zum Schreiben
= something to write with

ein paar Worte zur Beruhigung
= a few words to set your mind at rest

Aber:

ein paar Worte zur Einführung/Erklärung
= a few words by way of introduction/explanation

Wenn es sich um den Anlass für ein Geschenk oder dergleichen handelt, sagt man auch **for:**

Er hat es mir zu Weihnachten/zum Geburtstag geschenkt
= He gave it to me for Christmas/my birthday

Zum 30. Jubiläum überreichte ihm die Firma eine Uhr
= For *od.* On the occasion of his 30th anniversary the firm presented him with a clock

Womit zusammen? = with

Diese Bluse kannst du zu dem Rock tragen
= You can wear this blouse with that skirt

Zum Essen gab es Rotwein
= There was red wine with the meal

Worüber? = on

Es gibt mehrere Bücher zu diesem Thema
= There are several books on this subject

Was meinen Sie zu dieser Entwicklung?
= What is your opinion on this development?

Zu·bringer *der;* **~s, ~** (Verkehrsw.) **1** (Straße) access *or* feeder road **2** (Verkehrsmittel) shuttle; (Flughafenbus o. Ä.) courtesy bus

Zu·brot *das* bit extra *or* on the side; **er ist auf ein ~ angewiesen** he is forced to earn a bit on the side

zu|buttern *tr., itr. V.* (ugs.) chip in (coll.)

Zucchetto /tsu'kɛto/ *der;* **~s, Zucchetti** (schweiz.), **Zucchino** /tsu'ki:no/ *der;* **~s, Zucchini** courgette (Brit.); zucchini (Amer.)

Zucht /tsʊxt/ *die;* **~, ~en** **1** (*Züchtung*) (von Tieren) breeding; (von Pflanzen) cultivation; breeding; (von Bakterien, Perlen) culture **2** (**~ergebnis**) (von Tieren) breed; (von Pflanzen) variety; strain; (von Bakterien) culture; strain; **ein Pferd aus deutscher ~:** a German-bred horse; **Pflanzen/Tiere aus meiner ~:** plants which I have grown/animals which I have bred **3** (Einrichtung) breeding establishment; (für Pferde) stud; (für Pflanzen) plant breeding establishment **4** (geh.: Disziplin) discipline; **für ~ und Ordnung sorgen** keep order; **jmdn. in strenge ~ nehmen** take sb. firmly in hand

Zucht-: **~bulle** *der* breeding bull; **~eber** *der* breeding boar

züchten /'tsʏçtn/ *tr. V.* (auch fig.) breed; cultivate ‹*plants*›; culture ‹*bacteria, pearls*›

Züchter *der;* **~s, ~, Züchterin,** *die;* **~, ~nen** breeder; (von Pflanzen) grower [of new varieties]; plant breeder

Zucht·haus *das* **1** (Gefängnis) [long-stay] prison; penitentiary (Amer.) **2** (Strafe) [severest form of] imprisonment; imprisonment in a penitentiary (Amer.); (mit Zwangsarbeit) penal servitude (hist.)

Zuchthäusler /-hɔyslɐ/ *der;* **~s, ~, Zuchthäuslerin** *die;* **~, ~nen** (veralt.) convict

Zuchthaus·strafe *die* [severe] prison sentence; sentence to a penitentiary (Amer.); **eine lebenslange ~:** life imprisonment; a life sentence

Zucht·hengst *der* stud horse; breeding stallion

züchtig (veralt.)
A *Adj.* demure
B *adv.* demurely

züchtigen /'tsʏçtɪgn/ *tr. V.* (geh.) beat; thrash; (fig.: bestrafen) castigate

Züchtigung *die;* **~, ~en** (geh.) beating; thrashing; (fig.: Bestrafung) castigation; **körperliche ~:** corporal punishment

zucht·los (veralt.)
A *Adj.* undisciplined; (unzüchtig) licentious
B *adv.* without discipline; in an undisciplined way; (unzüchtig) licentiously

Zuchtlosigkeit *die;* **~, ~en** (veralt.) **1** lack of discipline; (Unzüchtigkeit) licentiousness **2** (Verhalten) impropriety

Zucht-: **~perle** *die* cultured pearl; **~tier** *das* breeding animal

Züchtung *die;* **~, ~en** **1** (das Züchten) breeding; (von Pflanzen) cultivation **2** (Zuchtergebnis) strain

zuck /tsʊk/ ▸ **ruck, zuck**

zuckeln /'tsʊkln/ *itr. V.; mit sein* saunter; amble; (schleppend) trail; ‹*cart etc.*› trundle

Zuckel·trab *der* (ugs.) jogtrot

zucken *itr. V.; mit Richtungsangabe mit sein* twitch; ‹*body, arm, leg, etc.*› jerk; (vor Schreck) start; ‹*flames*› flicker, flare up; ‹*light, lightning*› flicker, flash; ‹*whip*› flick (**nach** at); ‹*dragonfly*› flick; ‹*clock-hand*› jerk; **er zuckte zur Seite** he jumped to one side; **mit der Hand ~:** jerk one's hand; **mit den Achseln/Schultern ~:** shrug one's shoulders; **er ertrug den Schmerz, ohne auch nur zu ~:** he bore the pain without even flinching; **es zuckte in seinem Gesicht/um ihren Mund** his face twitched/there was a twitch around her mouth

zücken /ˈtsʏkn̩/ *tr. V.* draw ‹*sword, dagger, knife*›; (scherzh.) take out, produce ‹*wallet, notebook, camera, etc.*›

Zucker *der;* **~s, ~** [1] sugar; **~ sein** (fig. salopp) be fabulous (coll.) [2] (Medizinjargon) ▸**Blutzuckerspiegel** [3] (ugs.: ~krankheit) diabetes; **~ haben** be a diabetic

Zucker·bäcker *der,* **Zucker·bäckerin** *die* (veralt., bes. südd., österr.) confectioner

Zuckerbäcker·stil *der* (Archit.) wedding cake style

Zucker·brot *das: in* **mit ~ und Peitsche** with a carrot and a stick

zucker-, Zucker-: ~dose *die* sugar bowl; **~erbse** *die* edible-podded *or* mangetout pea; **~fabrik** *die* sugar factory; **~guss, *~guß** *der* icing; **~hut** *der* sugar loaf; **~krank** *Adj.* diabetic; **~kranke** *der/die* diabetic; **~krankheit** *die* diabetes

Zuckerl *das;* **~s, ~[n]** (südd., österr.) sweet (Brit.); candy (Amer.); (fig.) sweetener; enticement

Zucker-: ~lecken *das* ▸**Honiglecken**; **~lösung** *die* sugar solution; (sirupartig) syrup

zuckern *tr. V.* sugar

zucker-, Zucker-: ~puppe *die* (ugs.) sweet little thing; sweetie (coll.); **~rohr** *das* sugar cane; **~rübe** *die* sugar beet; **~schlecken** *das* ▸**Honiglecken**; **~stange** *die* stick of rock; **~streuer** *der* sugar caster; **~süß** **A** *Adj.* as sweet as sugar *postpos.*; beautifully sweet; (fig. abwertend) saccharine, sugary ‹*picture, smile, etc.*›; **B** *adv.* **~süß lächeln** (fig. abwertend) give a saccharine *or* sugary smile; **~wasser** *das* sugar water; **~watte** *die* candyfloss; **~werk** *das* (veralt.) ▸**Zuckerzeug**; **~würfel** *der* sugar cube; **~zange** *die* sugar tongs *pl.*; **~zeug** *das* (veralt.) sweet things *pl.*; confectionery

zuckrig *Adj.* sugary

Zuckung *die;* **~, ~en** twitch; **letzte ~en** death throes

Zu·decke *die* (ugs.) cover

zu|decken *tr. V.* cover up; cover [over] ‹*well, ditch*›; **sich ~:** tuck oneself up; **gut/warm zugedeckt** well/warmly tucked up

zu·dem *Adv.* (geh.) moreover; furthermore

zu|denken *unr. tr. V.* (geh.) **jmdm. etw. ~:** intend sth. for sb.

zu|diktieren *tr. V.* **jmdm. etw. ~:** impose sth. on sb.

zu|drehen
A *tr. V.* [1] (abdrehen) turn off ‹*tap, heating, water, gas*›; (schließen) screw ‹*valve, container*› shut [2] (zuwenden) **jmdm. den Kopf/Rücken ~:** turn one's head towards/one's back on sb.
B *refl. V.* **sich jmdm./etw. ~:** turn to *or* towards sb./sth.

zu·dringlich
A *Adj.* pushy (coll.), pushing ‹*person, manner*›; (sexuell) importunate ‹*person, manner*›; prying ‹*glance*›; **er wurde ~:** he began to force his attentions on her/me/*etc*
B *adv.* importunately

Zu·dringlichkeit *die;* **~, ~en** [1] pushiness (coll.); (in sexueller Hinsicht) importunate manner [2] (Handlung) **~en** insistent advances *or* attentions

zu|dröhnen *refl. V.* (Jargon) get plastered (sl.); (mit Drogen) get stoned (sl.)

zu|drücken
A *tr. V.* press shut; push ‹*door*› shut; **er drückte ihr die Gurgel** *od.* **Kehle zu** he choked *or* throttled her; **sie drückte ihm** (dem Toten) **die Augen zu** she closed his eyes
B *itr. V.* press

zu|eignen *tr. V.* (geh.) **jmdm. etw. ~:** dedicate sth. to sb.

Zu·eignung *die;* **~, ~en** dedication

zu|eilen *itr. V.; mit sein* **auf jmdn./etw. ~:** hurry *or* rush towards sb./sth.

zu·einander *Adv.* to one another; (zusammen) together; **~ finden** come together; (fig.: sich einigen) find common ground; **~ halten** stick together; **~ kommen** meet up; get together; **~ stehen** stand by one another; stick together; **Liebe ~ empfinden** have feelings of love towards one another; **gut/schlecht ~ passen** ‹*things*› go well together/not match; ‹*people*› be well-/ill-suited

***zueinander|finden** *usw.:* ▸**zueinander**

zu|erkennen *unr. tr. V.* **jmdm. ein Recht ~:** grant sb. a right; **jmdm. eine Entschädigung/einen Preis ~:** award sb. compensation/a prize; **jmdm. einen Titel ~:** confer a title on sb.

Zuerkennung *die;* **~, ~en** (eines Rechts) granting; (einer Entschädigung, eines Preises) award; (eines Titels) conferring

zu·erst *Adv.* [1] first; **ich muss ~ einmal etwas essen** I must have something to eat first; **er war ~ da** he was here first; he was the first to come; **wer ~ kommt, wird ~ bedient** first come, first served; **mit dem Kopf ~ ins Wasser springen** jump into the water head first [2] (anfangs) at first; to start with [3] (erstmals) first; for the first time

Zu·erwerb *der* ▸**Nebenerwerb**

Zuerwerbs·betrieb *der* (Landw.): *holding which does not provide an adequate income without supplementation from non-agricultural work*

zu|fächeln *tr. V.* **jmdm. etw. ~:** waft sth. towards sb.; **jmdm./sich Kühlung ~:** fan sb./oneself

zu|fahren *unr. itr. V.; mit sein* [1] (sich zubewegen) **auf jmdn./etw. ~:** head towards sb./sth.; (zusteuern) drive at *or* aim for sb./sth.; **auf jmdn./etw. zugefahren kommen** come towards sb./sth. [2] (ugs.: los-, weiterfahren) get a move on (coll.); **fahr zu!** step on it! (coll.)

Zu·fahrt *die* [1] access [for vehicles]; **die ~ zum Stadion erfolgt über die B 27** the stadium is approached along the B 27 [2] (Straße, Weg) access road; (zum Haus) driveway

Zufahrts·straße *die* access road; **~ zur Innenstadt** road leading to the town centre

Zu·fall *der* chance; (zufälliges Zusammentreffen von Ereignissen) coincidence; **es war [ein] reiner ~:** it was pure chance *or* coincidence; **der ~:** chance; **es ist kein ~, dass ...** it is no accident that ...; **durch ~:** by chance *or* accident; **ich habe durch ~ gesehen, wo sie es versteckt hat** I happened to see where she hid it; **dass wir uns dort begegneten, war ~:** our meeting there was a coincidence; **das ist aber ein ~/was für ein ~!** what a coincidence!; **der ~ wollte es, dass das Seil riss** by a stroke of fate *or* as chance would have it, the rope broke; **der ~ hat uns dorthin geführt** fate led us there; **etw. dem ~ überlassen** leave sth. to chance; **das verdankt er nur einem ~:** he owes it to chance

zu|fallen *unr. itr. V.; mit sein* [1] (sich schließen) ‹*door etc.*› slam shut; ‹*eyes*› close; **ihm fielen [vor Müdigkeit] die Augen zu** his eyelids were drooping [with tiredness] [2] (zuteil werden, zukommen) **jmdm. ~** ‹*task*› fall to sb.; ‹*prize, inheritance*› go to sb.; **ihm fällt alles nur so zu** everything just drops into his lap; **die Verantwortung fällt ihm zu** the responsibility is his

zu·fällig
A *Adj.* accidental; chance *attrib.* ‹*meeting, acquaintance*›; random ‹*selection*›; **~e Ereignisse/Prozesse** (Math.) random events/processes
B *adv.* by chance; **ich bin ~ hier vorbeigekommen** I just happened to be passing; **wissen Sie ~, wie spät es ist?** (ugs.) do you by any chance know the time?; **~ habe ich den Brief bei mir** as it happens, I have the letter on me; **es ist nicht ~ so, dass ...** it is no accident *or* coincidence that ...

zufälliger·weise *Adv.* ▸**zufällig B**

Zu·fälligkeit *die* [1] accidental nature; fortuitousness; (des Zusammentreffens von Ereignissen) coincidental nature [2] (zufälliges Ereignis) coincidence; chance occurrence

Zufalls-: ~ auswahl *die* random selection; **~bekanntschaft** *die* chance acquaintance; **~ergebnis** *das* chance result; **~fund** *der* chance find; **~generator** *der* random generator; **~größe** *die* (Math.) ▸**~variable**; **~prinzip** *das* random principle; **~produkt** *das* fluke; (Ergebnis) random result; **~treffer** *der* fluke; **~variable** *die* (Math.) random variable; **~zahl** *die* (Math.) random number; **~ziffer** *die* (Math.) random digit

zu|fassen *itr. V.* [1] (zugreifen) make a snatch *or* grab [2] (ugs.) ▸**zupacken 2**

zu|faxen *tr.V.* **jmdm. etw. ~:** fax sth. to sb.; fax sb. sth.; **etw. zugefaxt erhalten** receive sth. by fax

zu|fliegen *unr. itr. V.; mit sein* [1] **auf jmdn./etw. ~:** fly towards sb./sth.; **es kam auf mich zugeflogen** it came flying towards me [2] (geflogen kommen) **jmdm. ~** ‹*bird*› fly into sb.'s house; **ihm fliegen die Herzen zu** (fig.) all hearts surrender to his charms; **ihr fliegt in der Schule alles nur so zu** (fig.) school work comes easily to her; **die Einfälle fliegen ihm nur so zu** (fig.) he is never short of inspiration [3] (ugs.: zufallen) ‹*door, window, etc.*› slam shut

zu|fließen *unr. itr. V.; mit sein* [1] **einer Sache** (*Dat.*) **~:** flow towards sth.; (in etw. hineinfließen) flow into sth. [2] (zukommen) **jmdm./einer Sache ~** ‹*money etc.*› go to sb./sth.

Zu·flucht *die* refuge (**vor** + *Dat.* from); (vor Unwetter o. Ä.) shelter (**vor** + *Dat.* from); **[seine] ~ zu etw. nehmen** (fig.) resort to sth.

Zufluchts-: ~ort *der,* **~stätte** *die* place of refuge; sanctuary

Zu·fluss, *Zu·fluß *der* [1] (das Zufließen) inflow; supply; (fig.) influx [2] (Gewässer) feeder stream/river

zu|flüstern *tr. V.* **jmdm. etw. ~:** whisper sth. to sb.

zu·folge *Präp. mit Dat.; nachgestellt* according to; **sein Vorschlag, dem ~ das Haus versteigert werden soll** his proposal that the house should be put up for auction

zu·frieden
A *Adj.* contented; (befriedigt) satisfied; **mit etw. ~ sein** be satisfied with sth.; **bist du jetzt ~?** are you satisfied [now]?; **ein ~es Gesicht machen** look contented *or* satisfied; **wir können ~ sein** we can't complain; **sich ~ geben** be satisfied; **sich mit etw. nicht ~ geben wollen** refuse to accept sth.; **damit gebe ich mich nicht ~:** I cannot accept that; **jmdn. ~ stellen** satisfy sb.; **jmdn./etw. ~ lassen** leave sb./sth. alone; **lass mich damit ~!** stop going on at me about it! (coll.); **ich bin es ~** (veralt.) it's all right with me
B *adv.* contentedly

***zufrieden|geben** ▸**zufrieden A**

Zufriedenheit *die;* **~:** contentment; (Befriedigung) satisfaction; **zu meiner vollen ~:** to my complete satisfaction

***zufrieden|lassen, *zufrieden|stellen** ▸**zufrieden A**

zufriedenstellend
A *Adj.* satisfactory
B *adv.* satisfactorily

zu|frieren *unr. itr. V.; mit sein* freeze over

zu|fügen *tr. V.* [1] **jmdm. etw. ~:** inflict sth. on sb.; **jmdm. Schaden/[ein] Unrecht ~:** do sb. harm/an injustice; **jmdm. eine Beleidigung/Kränkung ~:** insult/hurt sb.; *s. auch* **wollen** [2] (hin~) **etw. einer Sache** (*Dat.*) **~:** add sth. to sth.

Zufuhr /ˈtsu:fu:ɐ̯/ *die;* **~, ~en:** supply; (Material) supplies *pl.*; **die ~ milder Meeresluft** the stream of mild sea air

zu|führen
A *itr. V.* **auf etw.** (*Akk.*) **~:** lead towards sth.
B *tr. V.* [1] (zuleiten) **einer Sache** (*Dat.*) **etw. ~:** supply sth. to sth.; supply sth. with sth.; **dem Motor Kraftstoff ~:** supply fuel to the engine; supply the engine with fuel [2] (bringen) **einer Firma Kunden/einer Partei Mitglieder ~:** bring new customers to a firm/new members to a party; **die Stute dem Hengst ~:** bring the mare to the stallion; **etw. seiner eigentlichen**

Bestimmung ~: devote sth. to its proper purpose; **jmdn. der gerechten Strafe ~:** give sb. the punishment that he/she deserves

Zu-Fuß-Gehen *das;* **~s** walking

Zug /tsuːk/ *der;* **~[e]s, Züge** /ˈtsyːgə/ **1** (Bahn) train; (Straßenbahn) tram (Brit.); streetcar (Amer.) *(consisting of two or more cars);* (Last~) truck *or* (Brit.) lorry and trailer; **ich nehme lieber den ~** *od.* **fahre lieber mit dem ~:** I prefer to go by train *or* rail; **jmdn. vom ~ abholen/zum ~ bringen** meet sb. off/take sb. to the train; **jmdn. in den ~ setzen** (ugs.) put sb. on the train **2** (Gespann von ~tieren) team; **ein ~ Ochsen** a team *or* yoke of oxen **3** (Kolonne) column; (Um~) procession; (Demonstrations~) march; (Vogelschar) flock **4** (das Ziehen) pull; traction (Phys.); (fig.) **das ist der ~ der Zeit** this is the modern trend *or* the way things are going; **die Sache hat einen ~ ins Lächerliche** there's something ridiculous about it; **dem ~ des Herzens folgen** follow the promptings of one's heart **5** (Vorrichtung) pull; (einer Posaune) slide **6** (Wanderung) migration; (Streif~, Beute~, Diebes~) expedition **7** (beim Brettspiel) move; **du bist am ~:** it's your move; **etw. ~ um ~ erledigen** (fig.) deal with sth. step by step; **Leistung/Erfüllung ~ um ~** (Rechtsw.) simultaneous performance; **zum ~e kommen** (fig.) get a chance **8** (Schluck) swig (coll.); mouthful; (großer Schluck) gulp; **einen tiefen ~ [von etw.] nehmen** take a big gulp *or* (literary) deep draught [of sth.]; **das Glas auf einen** *od.* **in einem ~ leeren** empty the glass at one go; **einen Roman in einem ~ durchlesen** (fig.) read a novel at one sitting; **er hat einen guten ~** (ugs.) he can really knock it back (coll.); **etw. in vollen Zügen genießen** (fig.) enjoy sth. to the full **9** (beim Rauchen) pull; puff; drag (coll.) **10** (Atem~) breath; **in tiefen** *od.* **vollen Zügen** in deep breaths; **in den letzten Zügen liegen** (ugs.) be at death's door; (fig. scherzh.) *‹car, engine, machine›* be at its last gasp; *‹project etc.›* be on the last lap **11** (~luft; beim Ofen) draught; **im ~ sitzen** sit in a draught; **der Kamin hat einen schlechten/guten ~:** the fire draws badly/well **12** (Gesichts~) feature; trait; (Wesens~) characteristic; trait; **seine Züge** his features; **in ihrem Gesicht lag ein ~ von Strenge** there was a hint of severity in her face; **die Stadt trägt noch dörfliche Züge** the town still has something of the village about it; **das ist ein charakteristischer ~ an ihm** it is a characteristic of his; **das war kein schöner ~ von ihr** that did her no credit **13** (landsch.: Schublade) drawer **14** (Bewegung eines Schwimmers/Ruderers) stroke **15** (ugs.: Disziplin) discipline; **jmdn. gut im ~ haben** have sb. well trained *or* under control; **in etw.** *(Dat.)* **ist ~** (ugs.) sth. has punch; **~ in etw.** *(Akk.)* **bringen** get sth. organized **16** (Milit.: Einheit) platoon **17** (Schulw.: Zweig) side **18** (Höhen~) range; chain; **die Züge des Odenwalds** the hills of the Odenwald **19** (Abluftrohr) flue **20** (Schrift~; Strich) stroke; **mit klaren Zügen geschrieben** written in a clear hand; **in großen/groben Zügen** (fig.) in broad outline

Zu·gabe *die* **1** (Geschenk) [free] gift **2** (im Konzert, Theater) encore **3** (das Zugeben) addition; **unter sparsamer ~ von Wasser** adding water sparingly

Zug·abteil *das* [train] compartment (Brit.)

Zu·gang *der* **1** (Weg) access; (Eingang) entrance **2** (das Betreten, Hineingehen) access; **~ verboten!** no admittance!; **er hat jederzeit ~ zum Chef** he can see the boss (coll.) at any time **3** (fig.) access; **~ zu jmdm./etw. finden** be able to relate to sb./sth. **4** (das Hinzukommen) (von Personen) intake; (von Patienten) admission; (Zuwachs) increase **(von** in) **5** (Person, Sache) (Patient) new admission; (Soldat) new recruit; (Buch) [new] accession; (Ware) new stock item

zu·gange *in* **irgendwo/mit jmdm./einer Sache ~ sein** (ugs.) be busy *or* occupied somewhere/with sb./sth.

zugänglich /ˈtsuːgɛŋlɪç/ *Adj.* **1** (Zugang bietend) accessible; (geöffnet) open; **schwer ~:** difficult to reach *pred.*; **die Zimmer sind von der Terrasse her ~:** the rooms can be reached from the terrace **2** (zur Verfügung stehend) available *(Dat.,* **für** to); (verständlich) accessible *(Dat.,* **für** to); **schwer ~es Material** material that is difficult to obtain **3** (aufgeschlossen) approachable *‹person›*; **für neue Ideen** *usw.* **~ sein** be amenable *or* receptive to new ideas *etc;* **allem Schönen** *od.* **für alles Schöne ~ sein** respond to all that is beautiful

Zugänglichkeit *die;* **~ 1** accessibility; **schlechte ~:** difficulty of access **2** (Aufgeschlossenheit) receptiveness **(gegenüber** to)

Zugangs·berechtigung *die* entitlement to access; (zum Eintritt) entry permit; (zum Studium) entry qualification **(zu** for)

Zug-: ~anschluss, *~anschluß *der* [train] connection; **~begleiter** *der* **1** (Schaffner) guard; **2** (Faltblatt) train schedule leaflet; **~begleiterin** *die* ▸ **~begleiter 1**; **~brücke** *die* drawbridge

zu·geben *unr. tr. V.* **1** (hinzufügen) add *(Dat.* to); **[jmdm.] etw. ~:** give [sb.] sth. as an extra; **der Sänger gab noch ein Lied zu** the singer sang another song as an encore **2** (gestehen, zugestehen) admit; admit, confess *‹guilt, complicity›*; admit to, confess to *‹deed, crime›*; **sie gab zu, es gestohlen zu haben** she admitted stealing it *or* having stolen it; **ich gebe zu, dass ich mich geirrt habe** I admit [that] I was wrong; **gibs doch endlich zu!** come on, admit it!; **du wirst mir ~** *od.* **du wirst doch ~ müssen, dass ...** you have to admit that ...; **es war, zugegeben, viel Glück dabei** true, there was a lot of luck involved **3** (erlauben) allow; permit; **er wollte nicht ~, dass ich allein reise** he would not allow me to *or* let me travel alone

zu·gegebener·maßen *Adv.* admittedly

zu·gegen *Adj. in* **~ sein** (geh.) be present

zu|gehen *unr. itr. V.; mit sein* **1** (sich nähern) **auf jmdn./etw. ~:** approach sb./sth.; **sie sollten endlich aufeinander ~** (fig.) they should try to come together at last; **dem Ende ~:** be coming to an end; **es geht auf Weihnachten zu** it is coming up to Christmas; **er geht schon auf die Achtzig zu** he is coming up to eighty **2** (ugs.: vorangehen) get a move on (coll.); step on it (coll.) **3** (Amtsspr.) **jmdm. ~:** be sent to sb.; **jmdm. etw. ~ lassen** send sth. to sb. **4** *unpers.* (geschehen, verlaufen) **hier/dort geht es ... zu** things are ... here/there; **ich weiß, wie es zugegangen ist** I know what went on; **auf dem Fest ging es fröhlich zu** it was very jolly at the party; **es müsste seltsam ~, wenn das nicht gelänge** something remarkable would have to happen for that not to succeed; **es geht nicht mit rechten Dingen zu** there is something fishy going on (coll.) **5** (ugs.: sich schließen) close; shut **6** (ugs.: sich schließen lassen) **die Tür/der Knopf geht nicht zu** the door will not shut/the button will not fasten; **der Reißverschluss geht schwer zu** the zip is difficult to do up **7** ▸ **zulaufen 5**

Zu·geherin *die;* **~, ~nen, Zu·geh·frau** *die* (bes. südd., österr.) cleaning lady; (Haushaltshilfe) home help

zu|gehören *itr. V.* (geh.) **jmdm./einer Sache ~:** belong to sb./sth.

zu·gehörig *Adj.* belonging to it/them *postpos., not pred.*; (begleitend) accompanying; **der Kreis und die ~en Gemeinden** the district and the communities belonging to it; **einer Sache** *(Dat.)* **~:** belonging to sth.; **sich jmdm./einer Sache** *(Dat.)* **~ fühlen** have a feeling of belonging [to sb./sth.]

Zugehörigkeit *die;* **~:** belonging **(zu** to); (Mitgliedschaft) membership **(zu** of)

Zugehörigkeits·gefühl *das* sense of belonging

zu·geknöpft *Adj.* (fig. ugs.) tight-lipped; (nicht zugänglich) unapproachable

Zügel /ˈtsyːgl̩/ *der;* **~s, ~ 1** rein; **ein Pferd am ~ führen** lead a horse by the reins; **einem Pferd in die ~ fallen** stop a horse by seizing the reins **2** (fig.) **die ~ [fest] in der Hand haben** be [firmly] in control; have things [firmly] under control; **die ~ straffer anziehen** tighten up on things; **jmdm./seiner Fantasie** *usw.* **~ anlegen** clamp down on sb./curb one's imagination *etc.*; **die ~ schießen lassen** let things take their course; **die ~ schleifen lassen** *od.* **lockern** slacken the reins

zügel·los (fig.)

A *Adj.* unrestrained; unbridled *‹rage, passion›*; limitless *‹ambition›*; frantic *‹rush, retreat›*; **ein ~es Leben führen** live a life of licentious indulgence

B *adv.* without restraint; **~ leben** live a life of licentious indulgence

Zügellosigkeit *die;* **~, ~en** lack of restraint; (Unzüchtigkeit) licentiousness

zügeln *tr. V.* **1** rein [in] *‹horse›* **2** (fig.) curb, restrain *‹feeling, desire, curiosity, etc.›*; **sich ~:** restrain oneself

Zügelung *die;* **~, ~en** curbing; restraining

Zu·gereiste *der/die; adj. Dekl.* newcomer

zu|gesellen *refl. V.* **sich jmdm./einer Sache ~:** join sb./sth.

Zu·geständnis *das* concession **(an** + *Akk.* to)

zu|gestehen *unr. tr. V.* **1** (anerkennen) grant *‹right, claim, share, etc.›*; allow *‹discount, commission, time›*; **jmdm. ~, etw. zu tun** give sb. permission to do sth. **2** (zugeben) admit; concede; **du wirst mir ~ müssen, dass ...** you have to admit that ...

zu·getan

A *2. Part. v.* **zutun**

B *Adj. in* **jmdm. [herzlich] ~ sein** (geh.) be [very] attached to sb.; **den schönen Künsten ~ sein** have a penchant for the fine arts

Zu·gewinn *der* gain **(an** + *Dat.* in)

Zugewinn·gemeinschaft *die* (Rechtsw.): *separate property with equal division of property acquired after marriage*

Zu·gezogene *der/die; adj. Dekl.* newcomer

zug·fest *Adj.* tensile *‹steel etc.›*; **sehr ~ sein** have great tensile strength

Zug·führer *der,* **Zug·führerin** *die* **1** (Eisenb.) guard **2** (Milit.) platoon sergeant

zu|gießen *unr. tr., itr. V.* add *(Dat.* to); **darf ich [dir] ~?** may I top you up (Brit. coll.) *or* (Amer. coll.) put a top on it?

zugig *Adj.* draughty, (im Freien) windy *‹corner etc.›*

zügig /ˈtsyːgɪç/

A speedy; rapid; **mit ~er Geschwindigkeit, in ~er Fahrt** at a good *or* brisk speed

B *adv.* speedily; rapidly

Zügigkeit *die;* **~:** speediness; rapidity

Zug·kraft *die* **1** (Physik) (verformend) tensile force; (beschleunigend) traction force **2** (fig.) attraction

zug·kräftig *Adj.* effective *‹publicity›*; powerful *‹argument›*; convincing *‹evidence›*; influential *‹name›*; catchy *‹title, slogan›*; **ein ~er Schauspieler/Film** an actor who/film which is a big draw; **~ sein** *‹film, actor, etc.›* be a big draw

zu·gleich *Adv.* at the same time; **er ist Maler und Dichter ~:** he is both a painter and a poet

Zug-: ~luft *die* draught; **~luft [ab]bekommen** be in a draught; **~maschine** *die* tractor; (von Sattelzug) tractor [unit]; **~nummer** *die* **1** ▸ **Zugpferd 2**; **2** (Eisenb.) train number; **~personal** *das* train crew; **~pferd** *das* **1** (Pferd) draughthorse; **2** (fig.: Attraktion) big draw; crowd-puller; **3** (treibende Kraft) dynamo; **~pflaster** *das* (Med.) cantharidal plaster

zu|greifen *unr. itr. V.* **1** take hold; **er kann nicht richtig ~:** he cannot grasp things properly; **rasch ~:** make a quick grab **2** (sich bedienen) help oneself; (fig.: handeln) take action; **er sah seine Chance und griff zu** (fig.) he saw his chance and acted at once **3** (fleißig arbeiten) **[hart** *od.* **kräftig] ~:** [really] knuckle down to it; **wenn viele Hände mit ~:** when plenty of people lend a hand

Zu·griff *der* **1** grasp; **sich dem ~ der Polizei entziehen** escape the clutches of the police **2** (Zugang) access **(auf** + *Akk.* to)

Zugriffs·recht *das* access rights *pl.* **(auf** + *Akk.* to); (Option) option **(auf** + *Akk.* on); **das erste ~:** the first option

Z

zu·grunde *Adv. in* **1** ~ **gehen** (sterben) die (**an** + *Dat.* of); (zerstört werden) be destroyed (**an** + *Dat.* by); ‹*marriage*› founder (**an** + *Dat.* owing to); ‹*person*› go under; (finanziell) be ruined; ‹*company*› go to the wall; **an sich selbst ~ gehen** destroy oneself; ~ **richten** destroy; (finanziell) ruin ‹*company, person*› **2** **etw. ~ legen** use sth. as a basis; **etw. einer Sache** (*Dat.*) ~ **legen** base sth. on sth.; **etw. liegt einer Sache ~:** sth. is based on sth.; **das diesem Urteil ~ liegende Gesetz** the law which gives rise to this verdict

Zugrunde·legung *die;* ~: **unter** *od.* **bei ~ dieser Umstände** on the basis of these facts

Zugs- (österr.) ▸**Zug-**

Zug-: ~schaffner *der,* **~schaffnerin** *die* ticket inspector; **~telefon** *das* train telephone; **~tier** *das* draught animal

zu|gucken *itr. V.* (ugs.) ▸**zusehen**

Zug·unglück *das* train crash

zu·gunsten

A *Präp. mit Gen.* in favour of; **eine Sammlung ~ der Flutopfer** a collection for the flood victims

B *Adv.* ~ **von** in favour of

zu·gut *in* **etw. ~ haben** (schweiz., südd.) be owed sth.; **du hast [bei mir] 10 Euro ~:** you've got ten euros to come [from me]

zu·gute *Adv. in* **jmdm. seine Jugend/Unerfahrenheit** *usw.* ~ **halten** (geh.) take sb.'s youth/inexperience *etc.* into consideration; make allowances for sb.'s youth/inexperience *etc.;* **sich** (*Dat.*) **etwas/viel auf etw.** (*Akk.*) ~ **tun** *od.* **halten** (geh.) be proud/very proud of sth.; **jmdm./einer Sache ~ kommen** stand sb./sth. in good stead; **jmdm. etw. ~ kommen lassen** let sb. have the benefit of *or* let sb. benefit from sth.

Zug-: ~verbindung *die* **1** (Eisenbahnverbindung) rail *or* (Amer.) railroad service; **2** (~anschluss) [train] connection; **~verkehr** *der* rail *or* (Amer.) railroad traffic; **~vogel** *der* migratory bird; **~zeit** (Zool.) *die* period of migration; **~zwang** *der* **1** (fig.) pressure to take action; **unter ~zwang stehen, in ~zwang sein** be under pressure to take action; **jmdn. in ~zwang bringen** put sb. under pressure; **2** (Schach) zugzwang

zu|haben *unr. itr. V.* (ugs.) **1** ‹*shop, office*› be shut *or* closed; **wir haben montags zu** we are closed on Mondays **2** (zubekommen haben) **endlich hat sie den Koffer/Reißverschluss zu** at last she's managed to shut the suitcase/do up the zip

zu|haken *tr. V.* hook up; do up the hooks on

zu|halten

A *unr. tr. V.* hold closed; (nicht öffnen) keep closed; **jmdm./sich die Augen/den Mund** *usw.* ~**:** put one's hand[s] over sb.'s/one's eyes/mouth *etc.;* **sich** (*Dat.*) **die Nase ~:** hold one's nose

B *itr. V.* **auf etw.** (*Akk.*) ~**:** head for sth.

Zuhälter /ˈt͡suːhɛltɐ/ *der;* **~s, ~:** pimp

Zuhälterei *die;* ~: pimping; (Rechtsw.) living off the earnings of prostitution

Zuhälterin *die;* **~, ~nen** procuress

zu·handen

A *Adj.* **jmdm. ~ sein** be available to sb.; be at sb.'s disposal

B *Präp. mit Gen.* (österr., schweiz.) ~ **Herrn B** for the attention of Herr B

C *Adv.* (österr., schweiz.) ~ **von Herrn B** for the attention of Herr B

zu|hängen *tr. V.* cover ‹*window, cage*›

zu|hauen

A *unr. itr. V.* **1** (ugs.) bang *or* slam ‹*door, window*› shut **2** (behauen) hew into shape

B *unr. itr. V.* (ugs.) hit *or* strike out

zu·hauf *Adv.* (geh.) in great numbers

zu·hause *Adv.* (österr., schweiz.) ▸**daheim**

Zu·hause *das;* **~s** home

zu|heilen *itr. V.; mit sein* heal [over]

Zuhilfenahme /t͡suˈhɪlfənaːmə/ *die;* ~: utilization; **ohne/unter ~ einer Sache** (*Gen.*)**/von etw.** without/with the aid of sth.

zu·hinterst *Adv.* right at the back; ~ **in der Schublade/auf dem Regal** right at the back of the drawer/of the shelf

zu|hören *itr. V.* **jmdm./einer Sache ~:** listen to sb./sth.; **nun hör mal zu** now listen; (leicht drohend) now [you] listen here; **er kann gut ~:** he's a good listener

Zu·hörer *der,* **Zu·hörerin** *die* listener; **sie merkte, dass sie einen ~ hatte** she noticed that somebody was listening

Zuhörerschaft *die;* ~: audience

zu·innerst *Adv.* (geh.) deep down; in one's heart of hearts; ~ **aufgewühlt** moved to the depths of one's soul

zu|jubeln *itr. V.* **jmdm. ~:** cheer sb. [on]

Zu·kauf *der* additional purchase/purchases; ~ **an Grund und Boden** purchase of more land

zu|kehren *tr. V.* turn (*Dat.* to); **jmdm. den Rücken/das Gesicht ~:** turn one's back on sb./one's face towards sb.

zu|klappen

A *tr. V.* close; fold ‹*penknife*› shut; (mit Wucht) slam ‹*lid*› shut

B *itr. V.; mit sein* ‹*window, lid, etc.*› click to *or* shut; (mit Wucht) slam shut

zu|kleben *tr. V.* **1** (verschließen) seal ‹*letter, envelope*› **2** (bekleben) cover

zu|kleistern *tr. V.* (ugs.) paste over ‹*crack*›; gum up ‹*skin*›; (fig.) paper over ‹*problems*›

zu|klinken *tr. V.* [click] shut

zu|knallen (ugs.)

A *tr. V.* slam

B *itr. V.; mit sein* slam

zu|kneifen *unr. tr. V.* squeeze ‹*eye[s]*› shut; shut ‹*eye[s]*› tight; shut ‹*mouth*› tightly

zu|knöpfen *tr. V.* button up

zu|knoten *tr. V.* knot; tie up

zu|kommen *itr. V.; mit sein* **1** (sich nähern) **auf jmdn. ~:** approach sb.; (zu jmdm. kommen) come up to sb.; **er/der Stier/das Auto kam direkt auf mich zu** he/the bull/the car came straight towards me; **er ahnte nicht, was noch auf ihn ~ sollte** (fig.) he had no idea what he was in for; **die Dinge auf sich ~ lassen** (fig.) take things as they come; **wir werden in der Angelegenheit noch auf Sie ~:** we shall be coming back to you on this matter **2** (geh.) (zuteil/übermittelt werden) **jmdm. ~:** reach sb.; ‹*inheritance*› come to sb.; **jmdm. etw. ~ lassen** (schicken) send sb. sth.; (schenken) give sb. sth.; **jmdm./einer Sache Pflege/Aufmerksamkeit ~ lassen** devote care/attention to sth. **3** (gebühren) **jmdm. kommt etw. zu/nicht zu** sb. is entitled/not entitled to sth.; sb. has a right/no right to sth.; (etw. ist jmdm. angemessen/nicht angemessen) sth. befits/does not befit sb.; **dir kommt diese Entscheidung nicht zu** this decision is not up to you; this is not your decision **4** (beizumessen sein) **dieser Entdeckung kommt große Bedeutung zu** great significance must be attached to this discovery

zu|korken *tr. V.* cork

zu|kriegen *tr. V.* (ugs.) ▸**zubekommen**

Zukunft /ˈt͡suːkʊnft/ *die;* **~, Zukünfte** /ˈt͡suːkynftə/ **1** future; **das wird die ~ lehren** time will tell; **für alle ~:** for all time; **~/keine ~ haben** have a/no future; **in naher/ferner ~:** in the near *or* immediate/distant future; **in ~:** in future; **einer Sache** (*Dat.*) **gehört die ~:** the future belongs to sth.; **seine [politische] ~ schon hinter sich** (*Dat.*) **haben** (scherzh.) be over the hill [politically]; **mit/ohne ~:** with/without a future; **ich wünsche Ihnen alles Gute für Ihre weitere ~:** I wish you all the best for the future **2** (Grammatik) future [tense]; **erste** *od.* **unvollendete/zweite** *od.* **vollendete ~:** future/future perfect [tense]

zu·künftig

A *Adj.* future

B *Adv.* in future

Zukünftige *der/die; adj. Dekl.* (ugs.) **mein ~r/meine ~:** my husband/wife-to-be; my intended (joc.)

zukunfts-, Zukunfts-: ~angst *die* fear of the future; **~aufgabe** *die* task for the future; **~aussichten** *Pl.* prospects for the future; **~bezogen** **A** *Adj.* relating to the future *postpos.;* **~bezogen sein** relate to the future; **B** *adv.* ‹*work, live*› with a view to the future; **~branche** *die* industry of the future; **~chance** *die* chance *or* hope for the future; **~erwartung** *die* future expectations *pl.;* **~fähig** **A** *Adj.* with a future *postpos.;* sustainable ‹*energy, supply, policy, development, etc.*›; **B** *adv.* ‹*reform, rebuild sth.*› so that it has a future; **~fähigkeit** *die* ability to survive; (einer Politik, Entwicklung, der Energieversorgung) sustainability; **~fonds** *der* fund for forward development; **~forscher** *der,* **~forscherin** *die* futurologist; **~forschung** *die* futurology *no art.;* **~gerichtet** *Adj., adv.* ▸**zukunftsorientiert**; **~hoffnung** *die* hope for the future; **~investition** *die* investment for the future; **~markt** *der* market with a future; market of the future; **~modell** *das* model for the future; **~musik** *die* (fig.) *in* **~musik sein** be very much in the future; (als utopisch anzusehen sein) be pie in the sky; **~orientiert** **A** *Adj.* forward-looking ‹*person, policy, concept, solution, etc.*›; future-oriented ‹*research, technology, etc.*›; **B** *adv.* ‹*think, plan, develop*› with an eye to the future; **~perspektive** *die* prospects *pl.* for the future; future prospects *pl.;* **~potenzial** *das* potential for the future; future potential; **~prognose** *die* [future] prognosis; **~programm** *das* future programme; forward programme; **~projekt** *das* project for the future; **~roman** *der* novel set in the future; **~sicher** **A** *Adj.* with an assured future *postpos.;* **~sicher sein** have an assured future; **etw. ~sicher machen** safeguard the future of sth.; **B** *adv.* with an assured future; **~sicherung** *die* safeguarding *no art.* the future; **etwas für die ~sicherung tun** do something to secure *or* safeguard the future; **~technologie** *die* technology of the future; **~trächtig** *Adj.* with a promising future *postpos.;* **~trächtig sein** have a promising future; **~vision** *die* vision of the future

zukunft[s]·weisend *Adj.* forward-looking; pointing the way forward *postpos.*

zu|lächeln *itr. V.* **jmdm./sich ~:** smile at sb./each other

zu|lachen *itr. V.* **jmdm. ~:** give sb. a friendly laugh

Zulage *die* (vom Arbeitgeber) extra pay *no indef. art.;* additional allowance *no indef. art.;* (vom Staat) benefit

***zu·lande** ▸**Land 5**

zu|langen *itr. V.* **1** (ugs.: sich bedienen) tuck in (coll.) **2** (ugs.: zupacken) [really] knuckle down to it

zu|länglich (geh.)

A *Adj.* adequate

B *adv.* adequately

zu|lassen *unr. tr. V.* **1** (erlauben, dulden) allow; permit; **solches Unrecht darf man nicht ~:** such injustice must not be permitted; **ich lasse keine Ausnahme zu** I do not allow *or* permit any exceptions; **das lässt nur einen/keinen anderen Schluss zu** that permits of *or* allows only one/no other conclusion **2** (teilnehmen lassen) admit; **jmdn. bei etw. ~:** admit sb. to sth. **3** (mit einer Erlaubnis, Lizenz usw. versehen) **jmdn. als Arzt ~:** register sb. as a doctor; **eine Partei ~** (Politik) permit a party to exist; **der Anwalt ist beim Amtsgericht Mannheim zugelassen** the lawyer is registered to practise at Mannheim district court; **jmdn. zum Studium/zum Studium der Medizin ~:** accept sb. at university/to study medicine; **jmdn. zu einer Prüfung ~:** allow *or* permit sb. to take an examination; **der Bulle ist zur Zucht zugelassen** the bull is registered for breeding **4** (zur Benutzung, zur Anwendung, zum Verkauf usw. freigeben) allow; permit; **ein Medikament ~:** approve a medicine [for sale]; **für den öffentlichen Verkehr/für Autobahnen [nicht] zugelassen sein** [not] be authorized for use on public highways/motorways (Brit.) *or* (Amer.) freeways **5** (Kfz-W.) register ‹*vehicle*›; **auf jmdn./jmds. Namen zugelassen sein** be registered in sb.'s name **6** (geschlossen lassen) leave closed *or* shut; leave ‹*letter*› unopened; leave ‹*collar, coat*› fastened [up]

zu·lässig *Adj.* permissible; admissible ‹*appeal*›; **~e [Höchst]geschwindigkeit** [maximum] permissible speed; [upper] speed limit

Zulässigkeit *die;* **~:** permissibility; (einer Berufung) admissibility

Zulassung *die;* **~, ~en** 1 (Erlaubnis, Lizenz) **~ als Arzt** registration as a doctor; **~ zur Teilnahme/zur Prüfung beantragen** apply for permission to attend/to take *or* (Brit.) sit an examination; **ihm ist die ~ zum Studium/zum Medizinstudium erteilt worden** he has been accepted at university/to study medicine 2 (Freigabe) approval; authorization 3 (Kfz-W.) registration 4 (Kfz-W. ugs.) ▸ **Kraftfahrzeugschein**

zulassungs·pflichtig *Adj.* liable *or* subject to registration *postpos.*

Zulassungs·stelle *die* vehicle registration office

zu·lasten

A *Präp. mit Gen.* **die Kosten gehen ~ des Käufers/der Staatskasse** the costs are borne by the purchaser/the public purse

B *Adv. in* **~ von: dies muss ~ von Millionen Arbeitnehmern gehen** the cost of this must be borne by millions of workers; **hässliche Verallgemeinerungen ~ von Minderheiten** nasty generalizations at the expense of minorities

Zu·lauf *der* 1 **[großen** *od.* **starken** *od.* **viel] ~ haben** ‹*shop, restaurant, etc.*› enjoy a large clientele, be very popular; ‹*doctor, lawyer*› have a large practice, be very much in demand; **mehr** *od.* **größeren ~ haben** ‹*shop, restaurant, etc.*› enjoy an increased clientele, be more popular; ‹*doctor, lawyer*› have a larger practice, be more in demand; **der ~ war so groß, dass das Gastspiel verlängert werden musste** the guest performance was so popular that its run had to be extended 2 (zulaufende Menge) inflow 3 (Rohr, Leitung) intake

zu|laufen *unr. itr. V.; mit sein* 1 **auf jmdn./etw. ~** (auch fig.) run towards sb./sth.; **auf jmdn./etw. zugelaufen kommen** come running towards sb./sth.; **einer Sache** (*Dat.*) **~** (geh.) run towards sth. 2 **jmdm. ~** ‹*cat, dog, etc.*› adopt sb. as a new owner; **ein zugelaufener Hund** a stray dog that has adopted us/them *etc.* 3 (hin~) ‹*water etc.*› run in; **warmes Wasser ~ lassen** run [some] warm water in 4 (sich verjüngen) taper; **spitz/konisch/keilförmig ~:** taper to a point 5 (ugs.: schnell laufen) get one's skates on (Brit. sl.); get a move on (coll.)

zu|legen

A *refl. V.* **sich** (*Dat.*) **etw. ~:** get oneself sth.; **er hat sich einen Bart zugelegt** (ugs.) he has grown a beard; **sich einen Künstlernamen ~:** adopt a pseudonym

B *itr. V.* (ugs.) 1 (sein Tempo steigern) step on it (coll.) 2 (wachsen, stärker werden) ‹*sales, output, turnover, etc.*› increase; **der Dollar hat [um vier Eurocent] zugelegt** the dollar has risen [four eurocents]; **sie könnten bei Neuwahlen ~:** they could improve their position if there were fresh elections

C *tr. V.* (ugs.) add; **wenn meine Eltern noch 100 Euro ~, kann ich mir das Fahrrad kaufen** if my parents put in a hundred euros, I can afford the bicycle; **einen Schritt**/(ugs.:) **Zahn ~:** get a move on (coll.)

zu·leid[e] *in* **jmdm. etwas/nichts ~ tun** hurt *or* harm sb./not [do anything to] hurt *or* harm sb.; *s. auch* **Fliege 1**

zu|leiten *tr. V.* 1 feed; supply; supply ‹*nourishment*›; feed ‹*signal*›; channel ‹*sewage*› 2 (zukommen lassen) send; forward

Zu·leitung *die* 1 supply 2 (Übersendung, Zustellung) sending; forwarding 3 (Rohr, Kabel usw.) feed line

zu·letzt *Adv.* 1 (zum Schluss, nach allem anderen) last [of all]; **~ liest du es noch einmal durch** finally, read it through again; **an sich selbst denkt sie immer ~:** she always thinks of herself last; **sich** (*Dat.*) **etw. für ~ aufheben** save sth. till last 2 (als Letzter/Letzte/Letztes) last; **er kommt immer ~:** he always comes last; he is always [the] last; **das ~ geborene Kind** the child born last 3 (fig.: am wenigsten) least of all; **darauf wäre ich ~ gekommen** that's the last thing I should have thought of; **nicht ~:** not least 4 (das letzte Mal) last; **ich habe ihn ~ gestern Abend gesehen** I last saw him yesterday evening 5 (schließlich, am Ende) in the end; **bis ~:** [right up] to *or* until the end

zu·liebe *Adv.* **jmdm./einer Sache ~:** for sb.'s sake/for the sake of sth.

Zu·liefer·betrieb *der* supplier (*Gen.* to)

Zulieferer *der;* **~s, ~, Zulieferin** *die;* **~, ~nen** supplier

Zuliefer: ~firma *die* supplier; **~industrie** *die* supply industry

zu|liefern *tr. V.* 1 supply (*Dat.* to); 2 (liefern) deliver (*Dat.* to)

Zu·lieferung *die* 1 supply; 2 (Lieferung) delivery [of goods]

zu|löten *tr. V.* solder; solder up ‹*hole*›

Zu·luft *die* (Technik) incoming air

zum /tsʊm/ *Präp. + Art.* 1 = **zu dem** 2 (räumlich: Richtung) to the; **ein Fenster ~ Hof** a window on to *or* facing the yard; **~ Hof liegen** face the yard; **wo geht es ~ Stadion?** which is the way to the stadium? 3 (räumlich: Lage) **etw. ~ Fenster hinauswerfen** throw sth. out of the window; **die Gaststätte „Zum Lamm"** the 'Lamb Inn' 4 (Zusammengehörigkeit, Hinzufügung) **Milch ~ Tee/Sahne ~ Kuchen nehmen** take milk with [one's] tea/have cream with one's cake 5 (zeitlich) at the; **spätestens ~ 15. April** by 15 April at the latest; **~ Schluss/richtigen Zeitpunkt** at the end/the right moment 6 (Zweck) **ein Gerät ~ Schneiden** an instrument for cutting [with]; **hol dir was ~ Schreiben** get something to write with; **~ Spaß/Vergnügen** for fun/pleasure; **~ Lesen braucht er eine Brille** he needs glasses for reading; **~ Schutz** as *or* for protection; **etw. ~ Essen/Lesen** (österr.) sth. to eat/read; **~ Schwimmen gehen** go swimming 7 (Folge) **~ Nachteil des Kunden** to the disadvantage of the customer; **~ Ärger/Leidwesen seines Vaters** to the annoyance/sorrow of his father; **~ Nutzen der Allgemeinheit** for the benefit of the general public; **es ist ~ Verrücktwerden** it is enough to drive you mad; **das ist gar nicht ~ Lachen** it's no laughing matter; (in Bezug auf etwas Sichtbares) it's nothing to laugh at 8 (sonstige Verwendungen) **jmdn. ~ Direktor ernennen/~ Kanzler wählen** appoint sb. director/elect sb. chancellor; **~ Dieb werden** become a thief; **sich** (*Dat.*) **etw. ~ Ziel setzen** set oneself sth. as a goal; **~ Ersten, ~ Zweiten, ~ Dritten!** (bei Versteigerung) going, going, gone!; **~ Funk/Fernsehen/Film wollen** want to go *or* get into radio/television/films

zu|machen

A *tr. V.* close; shut; fasten, do up ‹*dress*›; seal ‹*envelope, letter*›; turn off ‹*tap*›; put the top on ‹*bottle*›; (stilllegen) close *or* shut down ‹*factory, mine, etc.*›; **den Laden ~** (ugs.: auflösen) shut up shop; **ich habe kein Auge zugemacht** I didn't sleep a wink

B *itr. V.* 1 close; shut; **der Laden hat zugemacht** (ugs.) the place has closed down 2 (ugs., bes. nordd.: sich beeilen) get a move on (coll.)

zu·mal

A *Adv.* especially; particularly; **~ da ...** especially *or* particularly since ...

B *Konj.* especially *or* particularly since

zu|marschieren *itr. V.; mit sein* **auf jmdn./etw. ~:** march towards sb./sth.

zu|mauern *tr. V.* wall *or* brick up

zu·meist *Adj.* in the main; for the most part

zu|messen *unr. tr. V.* (geh.) 1 (zuteilen) **jmdm. seine Essensration ~:** issue sb. with his food ration; **ihm war nur eine kurze Zeit für seine Lebensarbeit zugemessen** (fig.) he was only allotted a few short years for his life's work 2 ▸ **beimessen**

zumindest *Adv.* at least; **so schien es ~:** at least, that is how it seemed; **~ hätte er sich entschuldigen müssen** he should at least have apologized

zumutbar *Adj.* reasonable; **das ist ihm kaum/durchaus/nicht ~:** one can scarcely/quite well/not expect that of him; **das ist ihr körperlich nicht ~:** that is asking too much of her physically; **im Rahmen des Zumutbaren** within the bounds of what is reasonable

Zumutbarkeit *die;* **~:** reasonableness

zu·mute *Adj. in* **jmdm. ist unbehaglich/elend** *usw.* **~:** sb. feels uncomfortable/wretched *etc.*; **mir war merkwürdig ~:** I had a peculiar *or* strange feeling; **mir wurde ganz komisch ~:** I felt quite funny; a funny feeling came over me; **ich kann mir gut vorstellen, wie dir ~ ist** I can well imagine how you feel; **mir war nicht danach ~:** I didn't feel like it *or* in the mood; **mir war nicht nach Lachen/Ironie ~:** I did not feel in the mood for laughing/irony; **mir war zum Weinen ~:** I felt like crying

zu|muten *tr. V.* 1 (abverlangen) **jmdm. etw. ~:** expect *or* ask sth. of sb.; **willst du mir etwa ~, dass ich die ganze Zeit herumsitze und warte?** do you expect me to *or* are you asking me to sit around here the whole time and wait?; **diesen kleinen Umweg können wir ihm schon ~:** I do not think this small detour would be asking too much of him; **diese Arbeit möchte ich ihm nicht ~:** I would not like to ask him to do this work *or* impose this work on him; **das ist ihm durchaus/nicht zu~:** it is perfectly reasonable to/one cannot expect *or* ask that of him; **seinem Körper/seinem Wagen zu viel ~:** overtax oneself physically/ask too much of one's car; **sich** (*Dat.*) **etw. ~:** undertake sth.; **sich zu viel ~:** take on too much; overdo it 2 (antun) **jmdm. etw. ~:** expect sb. to put up with sth.; **diesen Lärm können wir den Nachbarn nicht ~:** we cannot expect the neighbours to put up with this noise; **so eine winzige Schrift kann man keinem ~:** nobody can be expected to read such tiny writing; **diesen Anblick wollte ich ihm nicht ~:** I wanted to spare him this sight

Zumutung *die;* **~, ~en** 1 (Ansinnen) unreasonable demand; imposition; **eine ~ sein** be unreasonable; **etw. als [eine] ~ empfinden** consider sth. unreasonable 2 (Belästigung) imposition; **etw. ist [einfach] eine ~:** sth. is [simply *or* just] too much; **eine ~ für jmdn. sein** be an imposition on sb.; **der Film/die Schauspielerin war eine ~:** the film/actress was appalling; **das Essen war eine ~:** the meal was an affront

zu·nächst

A *Adv.* 1 (als Erstes) first; (anfangs) at first; **~ einmal** first; **~ ..., zum Zweiten ..., zum Dritten ..., schließlich ...** firstly *or* in the first place *or* for one thing ..., secondly ..., thirdly ..., lastly ... 2 (im Moment, vorläufig) for the moment; for the time being

B *Präp. + Dat.* (geh.) next to; **jmdm./einer Sache ~:** next to sb./sth.

zu|nageln *tr. V.* nail up; **etw. mit Brettern ~:** board sth. up

zu|nähen *tr. V.* sew up; *s. auch* **verdammt A 1; verflixt A 2**

Zunahme /ˈtsuːnaːmə/ *die;* **~, ~n** increase (*Gen.*, **an** + *Dat.* in)

Zu·name *der* surname; last name

Zünd·blättchen *das* percussion cap

zündeln /ˈtsʏndl̩n/ *itr. V.* (bes. südd., österr.; auch fig.) play with fire

zünden /ˈtsʏndn̩/

A *tr. V.* ignite ‹*gas, fuel, etc.*›; detonate ‹*bomb, explosive device, etc.*›; let off ‹*fireworks*›; fire ‹*rocket*›

B *itr. V.* ‹*rocket, engine*› fire; ‹*candle, lighter, match*› light; ‹*gas, fuel, explosive*› ignite; (fig.) arouse enthusiasm; **bei ihm hat es gezündet** (ugs.) he's cottoned *or* caught on (coll.); the penny's dropped (coll.); **der ~de Funke** (auch fig.) the igniting spark

zündend *Adj.* (fig.) stirring, rousing ‹*speech, song, effect, tune, etc.*›; exciting ‹*rhythm*›

Zunder /ˈtsʊndɐ/ *der;* **~s** 1 tinder; **trocken wie ~:** dry as tinder; tinder-dry 2 (fig. ugs.) *in* **jmdm. ~ geben** lay into sb. (coll.); **~ kriegen** get it in the neck (coll.)

Zünder *der;* **~s, ~** 1 (Waffent.) igniter; (für Bombe, Mine) detonator 2 *Pl.* (österr.) matches

Zünd-: ~holz *das* (bes. südd., österr.) match; **~holz·schachtel** *die* (bes. südd., österr.) matchbox; **~hütchen** *das;* **~~s, ~~:** percussion cap; **~kabel** *das* (Kfz-W.) ignition lead; (*from coil to distributor*) coil lead; (*from distributor to plugs*) plug lead; **~kapsel** *die* ▸**Sprengkapsel**; **~kerze** *die* spark[ing] plug; **~plättchen** *das* percussion cap; **~schloss**, ***~schloß** *das* (Kfz-W.) ignition [lock]; **der Schlüssel steckt im ~schloss** the key is in the ignition; **~schlüssel** *der* (Kfz-W.) ignition key; **~schnur** *die* fuse; **~spule** *die* spark coil; **~stoff** *der* (fig.) fuel for conflict; **zum ~stoff eines Konflikts werden** become the trigger for a conflict; **die Rede enthält einigen ~stoff** the speech contains some explosive material

Zündung *die;* **~, ~en** 1 ▸**zünden A**: ignition; detonation; letting off; firing 2 (Kfz-W.: Anlage) ignition; **die ~ einstellen** adjust the timing

Zünd·verteiler *der* (Kfz-W.) distributor

Zünd·zeitpunkt *der* (Kfz-W.) ignition time; **den ~ einstellen/verstellen** set/alter the ignition timing

zu|nehmen
A *unr. itr. V.* 1 increase (**an** + *Dat.* in); ‹*moon*› wax; **an Größe/Länge** *usw.* **~:** increase in size/length *etc.*; **an Erfahrung/Macht ~:** gain [in] experience/power; **in ~dem Maße** to an increasing extent *or* degree; increasingly; **mit ~dem Alter** with advancing age; **die Tage nehmen zu** the days are drawing out *or* getting longer 2 ▸❶ **S. 315** (schwerer werden) put on *or* gain weight; **er hat [um] ein Kilo zugenommen** he has put on *or* gained a kilo
B *unr. tr.* (*auch itr.*) *V.* (Handarb.) increase

zunehmend *Adv.* increasingly; **sich ~ vergrößern/verschlechtern** get increasingly bigger/worse

zu|neigen
A *itr. V.* incline *or* be inclined towards; **ich neige mehr dieser Ansicht/Auffassung zu** I tend *or* incline more towards this view
B *refl. V.* 1 (geh.: sich angezogen fühlen von) be *or* feel drawn to; **er ist ihr sehr/in Liebe zugeneigt** he is attracted to *or* fond of her/is drawn to her by feelings of love and affection; **der den Künsten zugeneigte Fürst** the prince, who is/was fond of the arts 2 (sich neigen nach) **jmdm./einer Sache ~:** lean towards sb./sth.; **sich dem/seinem Ende ~** (fig.) draw to a close

Zu·neigung *die;* **~, ~en** affection; **[eine] starke ~ zu jmdm. haben/empfinden** have/feel [a] strong *or* deep affection for *or* towards sb.; **~ zu jmdm. fassen** become fond of sb.

Zunft /tsʊnft/ *die;* **~, Zünfte** /ˈtsʏnftə/ (hist.) guild; **die ~ der Bäcker** the bakers' guild; **die ~ der Journalisten** (scherzh.) the journalistic fraternity; **zu welcher ~ gehört er?** (scherzh.) what does he do for a living?

zünftig /ˈtsʏnftɪç/
A *Adj.* 1 (ugs.) proper; **eine ~e Tracht Prügel/Ohrfeige** a good thrashing/box on the ears; **er sieht richtig ~ aus in seiner Tracht** he really looks the genuine article in his costume; **ein ~es Bier trinken** drink a decent beer 2 (hist.) guild *attrib.* ‹*craftsman, traditions, etc.*›
B *adv.* (ugs.) properly; **~ Skat spielen** have a decent game of skat

Zunge /ˈtsʊŋə/ *die;* **~, ~n** 1 ▸❶ **S. 435** tongue; **einen bitteren Geschmack auf der ~ haben** have a bitter taste in one's mouth; **dem Hund hing die ~ heraus** the dog's tongue was hanging out; **[jmdm.] die ~ herausstrecken** put one's tongue out [at sb.]; **auf der ~ zergehen** melt in one's mouth; **mit der ~ anstoßen** (ugs.) lisp 2 (fig.) **mit schwerer ~:** with a thick tongue; in a slurred voice; **eine spitze** *od.* **scharfe/lose ~ haben** have a sharp/loose tongue; **mit doppelter** *od.* **gespaltener ~ sprechen** (geh.) be two-faced; **böse ~n behaupten, dass ...** malicious gossip has it that ...; malicious tongues are saying that ...; **seine ~ hüten** *od.* **zügeln** *od.* **im Zaum halten** guard *or* mind one's tongue; **der Wein hatte ihm die ~ gelöst** the wine had loosened his tongue; **ich musste mir auf die ~ beißen** I had to bite my tongue; **lieber beiße ich mir die ~ ab** (ugs.) I would bite my tongue off first; **der Name liegt mir auf der ~:** the name is on the tip of my tongue; **etw. auf der ~ haben** have sth. on the tip of one's tongue; **sich** (*Dat.*) **die ~ abbrechen** tie one's tongue in knots; **bei dem Namen bricht man sich** (*Dat.*) **die ~ ab** that name is a real tongue-twister; **jmdm. leicht** *od.* **glatt von der ~ gehen** trip easily off sb.'s tongue; **Liebe ist ein Wort, das mir nur schwer von der ~ geht** I find it difficult to say the word 'love'; **er ließ den Namen/das Wort auf der ~ zergehen** he rolled the name/word around his tongue; **mit [heraus]hängender ~:** with [one's/its] tongue hanging out; **er hat eine feine** *od.* **verwöhnte ~** (fig.) he has a delicate palate 3 (eines Blasinstruments) reed; (einer Orgel) tongue; (einer Waage) needle; pointer; (eines Schuhs) tongue 4 (geh.: Sprache) tongue

züngeln /ˈtsʏŋl̩n/ *itr. V.* 1 ‹*snake etc.*› dart its tongue in and out 2 *mit Richtungsangabe mit sein* ‹*flame*› flicker; dart; ‹*water*› lick; **die Flammen züngelten aus dem Dach** tongues of flame leapt up out of the roof

zungen-, Zungen-: ~brecher *der* (ugs.) tongue-twister; **~fertig A** *Adj.* eloquent; **B** *adv.* eloquently; **~fertigkeit** *die* eloquence; **~kuss**, ***~kuß** *der* French kiss; **~piercing** *das* 1 tongue-piercing; 2 (Schmuck) tongue stud; **~schlag** *der* way *or* manner of speaking; **ein falscher ~schlag** a slip of the tongue; **~spitze** *die* tip of the tongue; **~spitzen-r, ~spitzen-R** *das* (Sprachw.) apical R; **~wurst** *die* tongue sausage

Zünglein /ˈtsʏŋlai̯n/ *das;* **~s, ~** 1 [little] tongue 2 (einer Waage) [small] needle *or* pointer; **das ~ an der Waage sein** (fig.) tip the scales

zu·nichte *Adj.* in **etw. ~ machen** ruin sth.; **jmds. Hoffnungen ~ machen** shatter *or* dash sb.'s hopes; **jmds. Anstrengungen/Pläne ~ machen** ruin *or* wreck sb.'s efforts/plans; **~ werden/sein** be ruined/shattered *or* dashed/ruined *or* wrecked

zu|nicken *itr. V.* **jmdm./sich ~:** nod to sb./one another

zu·nutze *Adj.* in **sich** (*Dat.*) **etw. ~ machen** (nutzen) make use of sth.; (ausnutzen) take advantage of sth.

zu·oberst *Adv.* [right] on [the] top; **ganz ~:** right on [the] top; on the very top; *s. auch* **unter... 1**

zuordenbar *Adj.* 1 relatable; **einander ~e Elemente** elements that can be related to each other 2 (sich zurechnen lassend) assignable; **einer Sache** (*Dat.*) **~ sein** be classifiable as sth.

zu|ordnen *tr. V.* 1 relate (*Dat.* to); **einem Bild ein Wort ~:** relate a word to a picture; **einer Sache** (*Dat.*) **eine Zahl/einen Wert ~:** assign a number/value to sth. 2 (zurechnen) **jmdn./etw. einer Sache** (*Dat.*) **~:** classify sb./sth. as belonging to sth.; **Organismen, die sich den Tieren ~ lassen** organisms which can be classified as animals 3 (zuweisen) assign (*Dat.* to) 4 (beimessen) attribute, attach (*Dat.* to)

Zu·ordnung *die* 1 relating; **die ~ x→y** (Math.) the relation x→y 2 (Zurechnung) classification 3 (Zuweisung) assigning, assignment (*Dat.* to)

zu|packen *itr. V.* 1 grab it/them; **fest ~ können** be able to grab things and grip them tightly; **der Hund stellte den Dieb und packte zu** the dog caught the thief and sank its teeth into him; **bei dem günstigen Angebot habe ich zugepackt** (fig.) the offer was a good one and I jumped at it 2 (fig.: energisch ans Werk gehen) knuckle down to it; **er hat eine sehr ~de Art** he has a very vigorous, purposeful manner

zu·pass, ***zu·paß** in **jmdm. ~ kommen** come [to sb.] at just the right time *or* moment

zu|passen *tr. V.* **jmdm. den Ball ~:** pass the ball to sb.

zupfen /ˈtsʊpfn̩/
A *itr. V.* **an etw.** (*Dat.*) **~:** pluck *or* pull at sth.; **sich** (*Dat.*) **am Ohrläppchen ~:** pull [at] one's ear lobe; **an einer Gitarre/an den Saiten ~:** pluck a guitar/the strings
B *tr. V.* 1 **etw. aus/von** *usw.* **etw. ~:** pull sth. out of/from *etc.* sth.; **sie zupfte ihm ein paar Fusseln vom Pullover** she pulled *or* picked a few pieces of fluff off his pullover 2 (aus~) pull out; pluck ‹*eyebrows*›; pull up ‹*weeds*› 3 pluck ‹*string, guitar, tune*› 4 **jmdn. am Ärmel/Bart ~:** pull *or* tug [at] sb.'s sleeve/beard

Zupf-: ~geige *die* (veralt.) guitar; **~instrument** *das* plucked [string] instrument

zu|pflastern *tr. V.* pave over

zu|pressen *tr. V.* press shut

zu|prosten *itr. V.* **jmdm. ~:** drink sb.'s health; raise one's glass to sb.

zur /tsuːɐ̯/ *Präp.* + *Art.* 1 = **zu der** 2 (räumlich, fig.: Richtung) to the; **~ Schule/Arbeit gehen** go to school/work; **ein Fenster ~ Straße** a window on to the street; **~ Straße liegen** face the street; **wo geht es ~ Post?** which is the way to the post office? 3 (räumlich: Lage) **~ Tür hereinkommen** come [in] through the door; **~ Rechten** to *or* on the right; **die Gaststätte „Z~ Rose"** the 'Rose Inn' 4 (Zusammengehörigkeit, Hinzufügung) **~ Hasenkeule empfehle ich einen Rotwein** I recommend a red wine with the haunch of hare 5 (zeitlich) at the; **~ Stunde/Zeit** at the moment; at present; **~ Adventszeit** at Advent time; **~ Jahreswende** at New Year; **rechtzeitig ~ Buchmesse** in [good] time for the book fair 6 (Zweck) **ein Gerät ~ Zerkleinerung von Gemüse** a device for chopping up vegetables; **~ Entschuldigung** by way of [an] excuse; **~ Inspektion in die Werkstatt müssen** have to go in for a check-up 7 (Folge) **~ vollen Zufriedenheit ihres Chefs** to the complete satisfaction of her boss; **~ allgemeinen Erheiterung** to everybody's amusement 8 (sonstige Verwendungen) **sie wurde ~ Direktorin ernannt/~ Präsidentin gewählt** she was appointed director/elected president; **~ Diebin werden** become a thief; **die Wahlen ~ Knesseth** elections to the Knesset

zu·rande in **mit etw. ~ kommen** (ugs.) [not] able to cope with sth.; **mit jmdm. [nicht] ~ kommen** (ugs.) [not] get on with sb.

zu·rate in **mit sich ~ gehen** give the matter a lot of thought; **jmdn./etw. ~ ziehen** consult sb./sth.

zu|raten *unr. itr. V.*; **ich würde/kann dir nur ~:** I would advise you to do so/I can only recommend it; **auf jmds. Z~ [hin]** on sb.'s advice *or* recommendation; **ich möchte [dir] weder zu- noch abraten** I should not like to advise you one way or the other

zu|raunen *tr. V.* **jmdm. etw. ~:** whisper sth. to sb.

Zürcher /ˈtsʏrçɐ/
A *indekl. Adj.* Zurich *attrib*
B *der;* **~s, ~:** inhabitant/native of Zurich; **er ist ~:** he is from Zurich; *s. auch* **Kölner**

zürcherisch *Adj.* Zurich *attrib.*; **~ sein** ‹*area:*› belong to *or* be part of Zurich

zu|rechnen *tr. V.* 1 (zuordnen) **jmdn./etw. einer Sache** (*Dat.*) **~:** class sb./sth. as belonging to sth.; **solche Wörter rechnen wir den Adverbien zu** such words are classed as adverbs 2 (anlasten, zuschreiben) **jmdm. etw. ~:** attribute *or* ascribe sth. to sb.; **die Folgen hast du dir selbst zuzurechnen:** you've only got yourself to blame for the consequences 3 (hinzufügen) **etw. einer Sache** (*Dat.*) **~:** add sth. to sth.

zurechnungs·fähig *Adj.* 1 sound of mind *pred.* 2 (Rechtsw.: schuldfähig) responsible [for one's actions]

Zurechnungs·fähigkeit *die* 1 soundness of mind 2 (Rechtsw.: Schuldfähigkeit) responsibility [for one's actions]

zurecht-, Zurecht-: ~|biegen *unr. tr. V.* bend into shape; **er wird die Sache schon wieder ~biegen** (fig.) he will get things

Z

straightened out *or* sorted out again; **im Internat werden sie den Jungen schon ∼biegen** (fig.) they will soon lick the boy into shape at boarding school; **∼|finden** *unr. refl. V.* find one's way [around]; **sich in einem Fahrplan/Kursbuch ∼finden** find one's way around a timetable; **er findet sich im Leben/in der Welt nicht [mehr] ∼:** he is not able to cope with life/the world [any longer]; **∼|kommen** *unr. itr. V.; mit sein* **1** get on (**mit** with); **wir kommen gut miteinander ∼:** we get on well [with each other]; **mit etw. ∼kommen** cope with sth.; **ich komme auch ohne Geschirrspülmaschine/mit meinem Gehalt [ganz gut] ∼:** I manage *or* cope *or* get on [very well] without a dishwasher/on my salary; **mit einem Problem/den Kindern ∼kommen** cope with *or* handle a problem/the children; **2** (ugs.: rechtzeitig kommen) come in time; **∼|legen** *tr. V.* **1** lay out [ready]; **jmdm. etw. ∼legen** lay sth. out ready for sb.; **sich** (*Dat.*) **den Ball ∼legen und schießen** spot the ball and shoot; **2** (fig.) get ready; prepare; **sich** (*Dat.*) **ein Gegenargument/eine Erwiderung ∼gelegt haben** have a counter-argument/reply ready; **∼|machen** *tr. V.* (ugs.) **1** (vorbereiten) get ready; **2** (herrichten) do up; **3** **jmdn./sich ∼machen** get sb. ready/get [oneself] ready; (schminken) make sb. up/put on one's make-up; **sich** (*Dat.*) **die Haare ∼machen** do one's hair; **∼|rücken** *tr. V.* put *or* set ‹*chair, crockery, etc.*› in place; straighten ‹*tie*›; adjust ‹*spectacles, hat, etc.*›; (fig.: richtig stellen, korrigieren) put straight; **jmdm. einen Stuhl ∼rücken** put *or* set a chair in place for sb.; *s. auch* **Kopf 1**; **∼|schneiden** *unr. tr. V.* cut to size/shape; trim ‹*fringe, beard, hedge*›; (herstellen) cut out (**aus** of); **∼|setzen** **A** *tr. V.* adjust ‹*spectacles, hat, etc.*›; **B** *refl. V.* settle oneself; **∼|stellen** *tr. V.* put *or* set ‹*chair, crockery, etc.*› in place; **∼|stutzen** *tr. V.* trim ‹*hedge, beard, hair etc.*›; **jmdn./etw. ∼stutzen** (fig.) sort *or* straighten sb. out/get *or* knock sth. into shape; **∼|weisen** *unr. tr. V.* rebuke; reprimand ‹*pupil, subordinate, etc.*›; **∼weisung** *die* ▸ **∼weisen**: rebuke; reprimand

zu|reden *itr. V.* **jmdm. ∼:** persuade sb.; (ermutigen) encourage sb.; **jmdm. gut ∼:** encourage sb.; **gutes Z∼:** persuasion; **erst nach langem Zureden** only after a great deal of persuasion

zu·reichend (geh.) ▸ **zulänglich**

zu|reiten

A *unr. tr. V.* break [in] ‹*horse*›

B *unr. itr. V.; mit sein* **auf jmdn./etw. ∼:** ride towards sb./sth.; **auf jmdn./etw. zugeritten kommen** come riding towards sb./sth.

Zürich /ˈtsyːrɪç/ (*das*); **∼s** ▸ⓘ **S. 675** Zurich

zürich·deutsch

A *Adj.* Zurich-German

B *adv.* in Zurich German; *s. auch* **deutsch**; **Deutsch**

Zürich·see *der*; **∼s** Lake [of] Zurich

zu|richten *tr. V.* **1** (verletzen) injure; **sie haben ihn übel zugerichtet** they [really] knocked him about; **übel zugerichtet** badly injured **2** (beschädigen) make a mess of **3** (landsch.: zubereiten, vorbereiten) prepare; (Technik: zuschneiden) cut to size/shape **4** (Lederherstellung, Kürschnerei, Textilind.) dress, finish ‹*leather, fur, etc.*› **5** (Druckw.) make ready

zu|riegeln *tr. V.* bolt

zürnen /ˈtsʏrnən/ *itr. V.* (geh.) **jmdm. ∼:** be angry with sb.

zurren /ˈtsʊrən/ *tr. V.* (Seemannsspr.) lash down

Zur·schau·stellung *die* exhibition; display

zu·rück *Adv.* **1** back; **ich bin gleich [wieder] ∼:** I'll be right back (coll.); **sei bitte zum Essen ∼:** please be back in time for lunch/dinner *etc;* **einen Schritt ∼ machen** take a step backwards; **∼!** get *or* go back!; **„∼ an Absender"** 'return to sender'; **... und 10 Cent ∼:** ... and 10 cents change; *s. auch* **Dank 1**; **hin 4**; **Natur 1** **2** (weiter hinten; auch fig.) behind; **[mit etw.] ∼ sein** (fig.: im Rückstand) be behind [with sth.]

Zurück *das:* in **es gibt [für jmdn.] kein ∼ [mehr]** there is no going back [for sb.]

zurück-, Zurück-: **∼|begleiten** *tr. V.* **jmdn. ∼begleiten** accompany sb. back; **∼|behalten** *unr. tr. V.* **1** keep [back]; retain; **2** (nicht mehr loswerden) be left with ‹*scar, heart defect, etc.*›; **∼|bekommen** *unr. tr. V.* get back; **Sie bekommen noch 10 Euro ∼:** you get 10 euros change; **er bekommt es von mir [doppelt] ∼** (fig.) I'll pay him back [twice over]; **∼|beordern** *tr. V.* order back; **∼|besinnen** *unr. refl. V.* **sich auf etw.** (*Akk.*) **∼besinnen** remember sth.; think back to sth.; **∼|beugen** **A** *tr. V.* bend back; **B** *refl. V.* lean *or* bend back; **∼|bilden** *refl. V.* (Biol.) **1** ‹*swelling*› go down; ‹*uterus*› contract; ‹*symptoms*› disappear; (atrophieren) ‹*limb, organ, etc.*› atrophy; **2** (im Laufe der Stammesentwicklung) ‹*limb, organ*› be lost; **∼|blättern** *itr. V.* turn back the pages; **auf Seite 7 ∼blättern** turn back to page 7; **∼|bleiben** *unr. itr. V.; mit sein* **1** remain *or* stay behind; **2** (nicht mithalten) lag behind; (fig.) fall behind; **hinter den Erwartungen ∼bleiben** fall short of expectations; **in seiner Entwicklung ∼bleiben** ‹*child*› be retarded *or* backward in its development; **3** (bleiben) remain; **von der Krankheit ist [bei ihm] nichts ∼geblieben** the illness has left no lasting effects [on him]; **4** (wegbleiben) stay *or* keep back; *s. auch* **zurückgeblieben**; **∼|blenden** *itr. V.* (Film; auch fig.) flash back; **in/auf etw.** (*Akk.*) **∼blenden** flash back to sth.; **∼|blicken** *itr. V.* **1** look back (**auf** + *Akk.* at); (sich umblicken) look back *or* round; **2** (fig.) **auf etw.** (*Akk.*) **∼blicken** look back on sth.; **∼|bringen** *unr. tr. V.* **1** (wieder herbringen) bring back; return; (wieder hinbringen) take back; return; **jmdn. ins Leben/in die Wirklichkeit ∼bringen** (fig.) bring sb. back to life/reality; **2** (ugs.: ∼werfen) set back; **∼|datieren** *tr. V.* antedate, backdate ‹*letter, cheque, etc.*›; antedate ‹*event, artefact, etc.*›; **∼|denken** *unr. itr. V.* think back (**an** + *Akk.* to); **so weit ich ∼denken kann** as far as I can remember *or* recall; **∼|drängen** *tr. V.* force back; drive back ‹*enemy*›; **den Drogenmissbrauch ∼drängen** (fig.) fight drug abuse; **∼|drehen** *tr. V.* **1** turn back; turn down ‹*heating, volume, etc.*›; **das Rad der Geschichte ∼drehen** (fig.) turn back the wheel of history; **2** (rückwärts drehen) turn backwards; **∼|dürfen** *unr. itr. V.* be allowed [to go] back *or* to return; **das Fleisch darf nicht in die Kühltruhe ∼:** the meat must not go back in the freezer; **∼|eilen** *itr. V.; mit sein* hurry back; **∼|erbitten** *unr. tr. V.* (geh.) **etw. ∼erbitten** ask for sth. to be returned; **etw. von jmdm. ∼erbitten** ask sb. to return sth.; **∼|erhalten** *unr. tr. V.* (geh.) be given back; get back; **anliegend erhalten Sie Ihre Bewerbungsunterlagen ∼:** please find enclosed your application, which we are returning to you; **∼|erinnern** *refl. V.* **sich an etw.** (*Akk.*) **∼erinnern** remember *or* recall sth.; **∼|erlangen** *tr. V.* (geh.) regain; **∼|erobern** *tr. V.* win back ‹*votes, majority, etc.*›; regain ‹*power, position, etc.*›; recapture ‹*territory, town, etc.*›; **∼|erstatten** *tr. V.* refund; **jmdm. etw. ∼erstatten** refund sth. to sb.; **∼|erwarten** *tr. V.* **jmdn. ∼erwarten** expect sb. back; **∼|fahren** **A** *unr. itr. V.; mit sein* **1** go back; return; (als Autofahrer) drive back; (mit dem Fahrrad, Motorrad usw.) ride back; **2** (nach hinten fahren) go back[wards]; **3** (∼weichen) start back; (entsetzt) recoil; **B** *unr. tr. V.* **1** **jmdn./etw. ∼fahren** drive sb./sth. back; **2** (Technikjargon) reduce the output of ‹*power plant, refinery, etc.*›; cut back ‹*delivery, production, budget, etc.*›; **∼|fallen** *unr. itr. V.; mit sein* **1** fall back; **2** (nach hinten fallen) fall back[wards]; **3** (fig.: in Rückstand geraten) fall behind; **4** (fig.: auf einen niedrigeren Rang) drop (**auf** + *Akk.* to); **5** (fig.: in einen früheren Zustand) **in etw.** (*Akk.*) **∼fallen** fall back into sth.; **in den alten Trott ∼fallen** slip back into the old routine; **6** (fig.) **an jmdn. ∼fallen** ‹*property*› revert to sb.; **7** (fig.) **auf jmdn. ∼fallen** ‹*actions, behaviour, etc.*› reflect [up]on sb.; **deine Gemeinheiten werden eines Tages auf dich [selbst] ∼fallen** your meanness will recoil [up]on you one day; **∼|faxen** *tr., itr. V.* fax back; **jmdm. etw. ∼faxen** fax sth. back to sb.; **∼|finden** *unr. itr. V.* find one's way back; **∼|fliegen** **A** *unr. itr. V.; mit sein* fly back; **B** *unr. tr. V.* **jmdn./etw. ∼fliegen** fly sb./sth. back; **∼|fließen** *unr. itr. V.; mit sein* flow back; **∼|fordern** *tr. V.* **etw. ∼fordern** ask for sth. back; (nachdrücklicher) demand sth. back; **∼|fragen** *itr. V.* answer with a question; **„...?", fragte er ∼:** '...?', he asked in return; **∼|führen** **A** *tr. V.* **1** **jmdn. ∼führen** take sb. back; **2** (∼bewegen) **etw. ∼führen** move sth. back; return sth.; **3** **etw. auf etw.** (*Akk.*) **∼führen** (auf Ursprung) trace sth. back to sth.; (auf Ursache) attribute sth. to sth.; put sth. down to sth.; (auf einfachere Form) reduce sth. to sth.; **B** *itr. V.* lead back; **es führt kein anderer Weg ∼:** there is no other way back; **∼|geben** **A** *unr. tr. V.* **1** give back; return; hand in ‹*driver's licence, membership card*›; return ‹*goods, unused ticket, etc.*›; relinquish ‹*mandate, office, etc.*›; take back ‹*defective goods*›; give back ‹*freedom*›; **jmdm. etw. ∼geben** give sth. back to sb.; return sth. to sb.; **2** (erwidern) reply; **B** *unr. tr.* (*auch itr.*) *V.* (Ballspiele) **1** return ‹*ball, puck, service, pass, throw*›; **[den Ball] an jmdn. ∼geben** return the ball to sb.; **2** (nach hinten geben) **[den Ball] ∼geben** pass the ball back; **∼geblieben** **A** *2. Part. v.* **∼bleiben;** **B** *Adj.* retarded; **∼|gehen** *unr. itr. V.; mit sein* **1** go back; return; (sich ∼bewegen) ‹*pick-up arm, indicator, needle, etc.*› return; **2** (nach hinten gehen) go back; ‹*enemy*› retreat; **in die Geschichte/bis in die Jahre meiner Kindheit ∼gehen** (fig.) go back into history/to the years of my childhood; **3** (verschwinden) ‹*bruise, ulcer*› disappear; ‹*swelling, inflammation*› go down; ‹*pain*› subside; **4** (sich verringern) decrease; go down; ‹*fever*› abate; ‹*flood*› subside; ‹*business*› fall off; **5** (∼geschickt werden) be returned *or* sent back; **ein Essen ∼gehen lassen** send a meal back; **6** **auf jmdn. ∼gehen** (jmds. Werk sein) go back to sb.; (von jmdm. abstammen) originate from *or* be descended from sb.; **der Name geht auf ein lateinisches Wort ∼:** the name comes from a Latin word; **7** (sich ∼bewegen lassen) ‹*lever etc.*› go back; **∼|gewinnen** *unr. tr. V.* **1** win back; regain ‹*confidence, title, strength, freedom, etc.*›; **2** (Wirtsch.) reclaim, recover ‹*raw materials etc.*›; **∼gezogen** **A** *2. Part. v.* **∼ziehen;** **B** *Adj.* secluded; **C** *adv.* **∼gezogen leben** lead a withdrawn life; (an abgelegenem Ort) live a secluded life; **∼gezogenheit** *die;* **∼∼:** seclusion; **∼|greifen** *unr. itr. V.* **auf jmdn./etw. ∼greifen** fall back on sb./sth.; **∼|haben** *unr. tr. V.* have back; **hast du es inzwischen ∼?** have you got it back yet?; **ich will es ∼haben** I want it back; **∼|halten** **A** *unr. tr. V.* **1** **jmdn. ∼halten** hold sb. back; **eine dringende Angelegenheit hielt mich in Köln ∼:** an urgent matter kept *or* detained me in Cologne; **er war durch nichts ∼zuhalten** there was no stopping him; nothing would stop him; **2** (am Vordringen hindern) keep back ‹*crowd, mob, etc.*›; **3** (behalten) withhold ‹*news, letter, parcel, etc.*›; **4** (nicht austreten lassen) hold back ‹*tears etc.*›; **sein Wasser ∼halten** hold one's water; **5** (von etw. abhalten) **jmdn. ∼halten** stop sb.; **jmdn. von etw. ∼halten** keep sb. from sth.; **jmdn. davon ∼halten, etw. zu tun** stop sb. doing sth.; keep sb. from doing sth.; **B** *unr. refl. V.* **1** (sich zügeln, sich beherrschen) restrain *or* control oneself; **2** (nicht aktiv werden) **sich in einer Diskussion ∼halten** keep in the background in a discussion; **C** *unr. itr. V.* **mit etw. ∼halten** (etw. nicht äußern) keep sth. to oneself; **∼haltend** **A** *Adj.* **1** reserved; subdued, muted ‹*colour*›; **2** (kühl, reserviert) cool, restrained ‹*reception, response*›; **3** (Wirtsch.: schwach) slack ‹*demand*›; **4** (sparsam) **mit etw. ∼haltend** ‹*person*› who is/was sparing with sth.; sparing with sth. *pred.;* **B** *adv.* **1** ‹*behave*› with reserve *or* restraint; **eine ∼haltend gemusterte Tapete** a wallpaper with a subdued pattern; **2** (kühl, reserviert) coolly; **das Publikum/Bonn reagierte ∼haltend** the public's response was cool/Bonn's response was cautious; **sich ∼haltend zu etw. äußern** be cautious in one's comments on sth.; **∼haltung** *die* **1** reserve; **∼haltung üben** (geh.) exercise restraint; **sich** (*Dat.*) **∼haltung auferlegen** (geh.) adopt an attitude of reserve; **2** (Kühle, Reserviertheit) coolness; reserve; **ein Buch mit ∼haltung aufnehmen** give a book a cool reception; **3** (Wirtsch.: geringe Kaufbereitschaft) caution; **∼|holen** *tr. V.*

1 fetch back; get back ‹money›; bring back ‹satellite, missile›; **jmdn. ~holen** bring sb. back; 2 (~rufen) call back; **~|kämmen** *tr. V.* comb back; backcomb; **seine ~gekämmten Haare** his backcombed hair; **~|kaufen** *tr. V.* buy back; repurchase; **~|kehren** *itr. V.; mit sein* return; come back (**von, aus** from); **zu jmdm. ~kehren** return *or* go back to sb.; **~|klappen** *tr. V.* tip back ‹seat›; lift back ‹lid›; fold back ‹flap›; **~|kommen** *unr. itr. V.; mit sein* 1 come back; return; ‹letter› come back, be returned; 2 (~gelangen) get back; 3 **~kommen auf** (+ *Akk.*) come back to ‹subject, question, point, etc.›; **auf ein Angebot ~kommen** come back on an offer; 4 (ugs.: ~befördert werden) go back; **~|können** *unr. itr. V.* be able to go back *or* return; **nicht ans Ufer ~können** not be able to get back to the bank; **jetzt können wir nicht mehr ~** (fig.) there's no going *or* turning back now; **~|kriegen** *tr. V.* ▸ **~bekommen**; **~|lassen** *unr. tr. V.* 1 leave; 2 (~kehren lassen) **jmdn. ~lassen** allow sb. to return; let sb. return; **~|lassung** *die;* **~~: unter ~lassung einer Sache/jmds.** leaving sth./sb. behind; **~|laufen** *unr. itr. V.; mit sein* 1 run back; 2 (ugs.: ~gehen) come/go back; 3 (sich ~bewegen) run back; **das Tonband ~laufen lassen** run the tape back; **~|legen** **A** *tr. V.* 1 put back; 2 (nach hinten beugen) lean *or* lay ‹head› back; 3 (reservieren) put aside, keep (*Dat.*, **für** for); 4 (sparen) put away; put by; 5 (hinter sich bringen) cover ‹distance›; **B** *refl. V.* lie back; (sich ~lehnen, ~neigen) lean back; **~|lehnen** *refl. V.* lean back; **~|liegen** *unr. itr. V.* 1 **das Ereignis/das liegt einige Jahre ~:** the event took place/that was several years ago; **in den ~liegenden Jahren** in the past [few] years; 2 (bes. Sport) be behind; **mit 2:3 Toren ~liegen** be 3-2 behind; **~|melden** *refl. V.* report back (**bei** to); **~|müssen** *unr. itr. V.* 1 have to go back *or* return; 2 (~befördert werden müssen) have to go back; **~|nehmen** *unr. tr. V.* 1 take back; 2 (widerrufen) take back; **ich nehme alles ~ [und behaupte das Gegenteil** (scherzh.)**]** I take it all back; 3 (rückgängig machen) revoke, rescind ‹decision, ban, etc.›; withdraw ‹complaint, legal action›; **einen Zug ~nehmen** (Brettspiele) take a move back; **~|pfeifen** *unr. tr. V.* 1 whistle ‹dog› back; 2 (fig. salopp) **jmdn. ~pfeifen** call sb. off; **~|prallen** *itr. V.; mit sein* 1 bounce back (**von** off); ‹bullet› ricochet (**von** from); 2 (fig.) start back; (entsetzt) recoil; **~|rechnen** *itr. V.* reckon back; **~|reichen** **A** *tr. V.* hand back; **B** *itr. V.* go back (**in** + *Akk.* to); **~|rollen** **A** *tr. V.* 1 roll back; 2 (nach hinten rollen) roll back[wards]; **B** *itr. V.; mit sein* 1 roll back; 2 (nach hinten rollen) roll back [wards]; **~|rudern** *itr. V.; mit sein* 1 row back; 2 (ugs.: einen Rückzieher machen) back down; **~|rufen** **A** *unr. tr. V.* 1 call back; recall ‹ambassador›; **jmdn. ins Leben ~rufen** (fig.) bring sb. back to life; 2 (anrufen) call *or* (Brit.) ring back; 3 **jmdm./sich etw. ins Gedächtnis** *od.* **in die Erinnerung ~rufen** remind sb. of sth./call sth. to mind; 4 (als Antwort, nach hinten rufen) call *or* shout back; 5 (Wirtsch.) recall ‹defective goods, car, etc.›; **B** *unr. itr. V.* (anrufen) call *or* (Brit.) ring back; **~|schalten** *itr. V.* 1 switch *or* turn back; 2 (beim Autofahren) change down; **~|schaudern** *itr. V.; mit sein* shrink back (**vor** + *Dat.* from); **~|schauen** *itr. V.* (bes. südd., österr., schweiz.) ▸ **~blicken**; **~|scheuen** *itr. V.; mit sein* ▸ **~schrecken²**; **~|schicken** *tr. V.* send back; **~|schieben** *unr. tr. V.* 1 push back; draw back ‹bolt, curtains›; 2 (nach hinten schieben) push back[wards]; **~|schlagen** **A** *unr. tr. V.* 1 (nach hinten schlagen) fold back ‹cover, hood, etc.›; turn down ‹collar›; (zur Seite schlagen) pull *or* draw back ‹curtains›; 2 (durch einen Schlag ~befördern) hit back; (mit dem Fuß) kick back; 3 (zum Rückzug zwingen, abwehren) beat off, repulse ‹enemy, attack›; **B** *unr. itr. V.* 1 hit back; ‹enemy› strike back, retaliate; 2 *mit sein* ‹pendulum› swing back; ‹starting handle› kick back; ‹wave› crash back; 3 **auf etw.** (*Akk.*) **~schlagen** (fig.) have repercussions on sth.; **~|schneiden** *unr. tr. V.* cut back ‹plant, shoot, etc.›; **~|schrauben** *tr. V.* reduce ‹demand, wage, consumption, etc.›; lower ‹expectations›; **~|schrecken¹** *tr. V.* **jmdn. ~schrecken** deter sb.; **~|schrecken²** *regelm., veralt. unr. itr. V.; mit sein* 1 shrink back; recoil; 2 **vor etw.** (*Dat.*) **~schrecken** (fig.) shrink from sth.; **er schreckt vor nichts ~:** he will stop at nothing; **~|sehnen** *refl. V.* **sich nach der Geborgenheit seines Elternhauses ~sehnen** long to return to the security of one's parents' home; **sich zu jmdm./nach Italien ~sehnen** long to be back with sb./in Italy; **~|senden** *unr. od. regelm. tr. V.* (geh.) ▸ **~schicken**; **~|setzen** **A** *tr. V.* 1 put back; 2 (nach hinten setzen) move back; 3 (~fahren) move back; reverse; back; 4 (benachteiligen) **jmdn. ~setzen** neglect sb.; **sich ~gesetzt fühlen** feel neglected; **B** *refl. V.* 1 sit down again (**an** + *Akk.* at); 2 (sich weiter nach hinten setzen) move back; **C** *itr. V.* (~fahren) move back[wards]; reverse; back; **~setzung** *die;* **~~, ~~en** neglect; (Kränkung) insult; slight; **~|spielen** *tr. V.* (Ballspiele) **den Ball ~spielen** pass *or* play the ball back; **~|springen** *unr. itr. V.; mit sein* 1 jump back; ‹indicator needle etc.› spring back; ‹ball› bounce back; 2 (nach hinten springen) jump back[wards]; 3 (weiter hinten liegen) be set back; **~|spulen** *tr. V.* wind back; **~|stecken** **A** *tr. V.* 1 put back; 2 (nach hinten stecken) move back; **B** *itr. V.* (ugs.) lower one's sights; **~|stehen** *unr. itr. V.* 1 stand back; be set back; 2 (fig.: übertroffen werden) be left behind; **hinter jmdm. ~stehen** take second place to sb.; 3 (fig.: verzichten) miss out; **~|stellen** **A** *tr. V.* 1 put back; 2 (nach hinten stellen) move back; 3 (niedriger einstellen) turn down ‹heating›; put back ‹clock›; 4 (reservieren) put aside, keep (*Dat.*, **für** for); 5 (vorläufig befreien) **jmdn. vom Wehrdienst ~stellen** defer sb.'s military service; defer sb. (Amer.); **sollen wir ihn schon einschulen oder noch ~stellen lassen?** shall we start him at school now or delay it a while?; 6 (aufschieben) postpone; defer; 7 (hintanstellen) put aside ‹reservations, doubts, etc.›; 8 (österr.: ~geben) return; **B** *refl. V.* go *or* get back; **stell dich an deinen Platz ~!** get back in *or* go back to your place!; **~|stoßen** **A** *unr. tr. V.* 1 push back; 2 (von sich stoßen) push away; **B** *unr. itr. V.; mit sein* ▸ **~setzen C**; **~|streifen** *tr. V.* pull back; pull up ‹sleeve›; **~|stufen** *tr. V.* downgrade (**in** + *Akk.* to); **~|treten** *unr. itr. V.* 1 *mit sein* step back; **bitte von der Bahnsteigkante ~treten** please stand back from the edge of the platform; 2 *mit sein* (von einem Amt) resign; step down; ‹government› resign; **als Vorsitzender/von einem Amt ~treten** step down as chairman/resign from an office; 3 *mit sein* (von einem Vertrag, einer Vereinbarung usw.) withdraw (**von** from); back out (**von** of); 4 *mit sein* (fig.: in den Hintergrund treten) become less important; fade in importance; **hinter/gegenüber etw.** (*Dat.*) **~treten** take second place to sth.; **~|tun** *unr. tr. V.* put back; **~|übersetzen** *tr. V.* translate back; **~|verfolgen** *tr. V.* trace back; **~|verlangen** *tr. V.* demand back; **~|versetzen** **A** *tr. V.* 1 move *or* transfer back; 2 (fig.) take *or* transport back; **B** *refl. V.* think oneself back (**in** + *Akk.* to); **~|weichen** *unr. itr. V.; mit sein* draw back (**vor** + *Dat.* from); back away; (~schrecken) shrink back, recoil (**vor** + *Dat.* from); **er wich keinen Schritt/Zentimeter ~:** he stood his ground; **~|weisen** *unr. tr. V.* 1 send back; **jmdn. an der Grenze ~weisen** turn sb. back at the frontier; 2 (abweisen, nicht akzeptieren) reject ‹proposal, question, demand, application, etc.›; turn down, refuse ‹offer, request, invitation, help, etc.›; turn away ‹petitioner, unwelcome guest›; 3 (sich verwahren gegen) repudiate ‹accusation, claim, etc.›; **~weisung** *die* ▸ **~weisen 1—3**: sending back; turning back; rejection; turning down; refusal; turning away; repudiation; **~|wenden** *unr. od. regelm. tr. u. refl. V.* turn back; **~|werfen** **A** *unr. tr. V.* 1 throw back; **den Kopf/sein Haar ~werfen** throw *or* toss one's head back/toss one's hair back; 2 (reflektieren) reflect ‹light, sound›; 3 (Milit.) repulse ‹enemy›; 4 (fig.: in einer Entwicklung) set back; **B** *unr. refl. V.* throw oneself back; **~|wirken** *itr. V.* react (**auf** + *Akk.* [up]on); **~|wollen** **A** *unr. itr. V.* want to go back; **B** *unr. tr. V.* (ugs.) **etw. ~wollen** want sth. back; **~|zahlen** *tr. V.* pay back; **~|ziehen** **A** *unr. tr. V.* 1 pull back; draw back ‹bolt, curtains, one's hand, etc.›; **es zieht ihn in die Heimat/zu ihr ~** (fig.) he is drawn back to his homeland/to her; 2 (abziehen, ~beordern) withdraw, pull back ‹troops›; withdraw, recall ‹ambassador›; 3 (rückgängig machen) withdraw; cancel ‹order, instruction›; 4 (wieder aus dem Verkehr ziehen) withdraw ‹coin, stamp, etc.›; **B** *unr. refl. V.* withdraw (**aus, von** from); ‹troops› withdraw, pull back; **sich von** *od.* **aus der Politik/aus dem Showgeschäft/aus dem Berufsleben ~ziehen** retire from politics/show business/professional life; **sich aufs Land/in sein Zimmer ~ziehen** retreat to the country/retire to one's room; *s. auch* **zurückgezogen**; **C** *unr. itr. V.; mit sein* go back; return; **~|zucken** *itr. V.; mit sein* flinch; (erschrocken) start back; **mit der Hand ~zucken** jerk one's hand away

Zu·ruf *der* shout; **durch ~ wählen/abstimmen** vote by acclamation

zu|rufen *unr. tr. V.* **jmdm. etw. ~:** shout sth. to sb.

zur·zeit *Adv.* at the moment; at present

Zu·sage *die* 1 (auf eine Einladung hin) acceptance; (auf eine Stellenbewerbung hin) offer 2 (Versprechen) promise; undertaking; **jmdm. die** *od.* **seine ~ geben, etw. zu tun** promise sb. that one will do sth.; **ich kann Ihnen keine ~n machen** I cannot make you any promises

zu|sagen

A *itr. V.* 1 (auf eine Einladung hin) **[jmdm.] ~/fest ~:** accept/give sb. a firm acceptance 2 (auf ein Angebot hin) accept; **sie haben fest zugesagt** (auf eine Stellenbewerbung hin) they made me/him *etc.* a firm offer [of a job] 3 (gefallen) **jmdm. ~:** appeal to sb.

B *tr. V.* 1 promise; **jmdm. etw. ~:** promise sb. sth.; **sein Kommen ~:** promise to come; **jmdm. sein Kommen ~:** promise sb. that one will come 2 ▸ **Kopf 1**

zusammen /tsu'zamən/ *Adv.* together; **mit jmdm. ~ sein** (zusammenleben) be *or* live with sb.; **wir bestellten uns ~ eine Flasche Wein** we ordered a bottle of wine between us; **wir haben ~ ein Auto** we own a car between us; **alle/alles ~:** all together; **ihr seid alle ~ Feiglinge!** (ugs.) you're cowards, the whole lot of you (coll.); **guten Abend/schöne Ferien** *usw.* **~!** (ugs.) good evening/have a good holiday, everyone *or* all of you!; **er verdient mehr als alle anderen ~:** he earns more than the rest of us/them put together

zusammen-, Zusammen-: ~arbeit *die* cooperation *no indef. art.*; **~|arbeiten** *itr. V.* cooperate; work together; (kollaborieren) collaborate; **mit ihm könnte ich nicht ~arbeiten** I could not work with him; **~|ballen** **A** *tr. V.* **[zu einem Klumpen] ~ballen** make into a ball; **B** *refl. V.* mass together; **dunkle Wolken ballten sich ~:** dark clouds loomed; **~ballung** *die;* **~~, ~~en** concentration; **eine ~ballung von Städten** a conglomeration of towns; **~|bauen** *tr. V.* assemble; put together; **~|beißen** *unr. tr. V.* **die Zähne ~beißen** clench one's teeth together; *s. auch* **Zahn 2**; **~|bekommen** *unr. tr. V.* 1 get together, raise ‹money, rent, etc.›; manage to collect ‹signatures›; 2 (~gesetzt/~gebaut usw. bekommen) get together; 3 (fig. ugs.) remember; **~|betteln** *tr. V.* **sich** (*Dat.*) **etw. ~betteln** manage to collect sth. by begging; **~|binden** *unr. tr. V.* tie together; **jmdm. die Hände auf dem Rücken ~binden** tie sb.'s hands behind his/her back; **sich** (*Dat.*) **das Haar ~binden** tie one's hair; **~|bleiben** *unr. itr. V.; mit sein* stay together; **~|brauen** **A** *tr. V.* (ugs.) concoct ‹drink›; **B** *refl. V.* (fig.) ‹storm, bad weather, trouble, etc.› be brewing; ‹disaster› loom; **da braut sich was ~:** there's something brewing there; **~|brechen** *unr. itr. V.; mit sein* 1 (einstürzen) collapse; 2 (zu Boden sinken) ‹person, animal› collapse; (fig.) ‹person› break down; **nervlich ~brechen** have a nervous breakdown; 3) (fig.) collapse; ‹*order, communications, system, telephone network*› break down; ‹*theory*› collapse, break down; ‹*traffic*› come to a standstill, be paralysed; ‹*attack, front, resistance*› crumble; **für ihn brach eine Welt ~:** his whole world collapsed; **~|bringen** *unr. tr. V.* 1) bring together; bring ‹*chemicals*› into contact with each other; **die Ziege mit einem Bock ~bringen** put the nanny goat together with a billy goat; **jmdn. mit jmdm. ~bringen** bring sb. together with sb.; 2) (ugs., bes. südd.) ▸ **~bekommen**; **~bruch** *der* 1) (eines Menschen) collapse; (psychisch, nervlich) breakdown; **dem ~bruch nahe sein** be near to collapse/breakdown; 2) (fig.) ▸ **~brechen 3**: collapse; breakdown; crumbling; **es kam zu einem ~bruch des Verkehrs** traffic came to a standstill *or* was paralysed; **~|drängen** A *tr. V.* push together; herd ‹*crowd*› together; (fig.) condense ‹*story, report, facts, etc.*›; B *refl. V.* crowd together; (fig.) be concentrated (**auf** + *Akk.* into); **~|drücken** *tr. V.* 1) press together; (komprimieren) compress ‹*gas*›; 2) (zerdrücken) crush; **~|fahren** A *unr. itr. V.; mit sein* 1) collide (**mit** with); **zwei Autos sind ~gefahren** two cars have collided [with each other]; 2) (~zucken) start; jump; B *unr. tr. V.* (ugs.) smash up ‹*vehicle*›; run over ‹*person, animal*›; **~fall** *der* coincidence; **~|fallen** *unr. itr. V.; mit sein* 1) collapse; **in sich ~fallen** (auch fig.) collapse; ‹*fire*› die down; **das ganze Lügengebäude fiel in sich ~** (fig.) the whole tissue of lies fell apart; 2) (~sinken, schrumpfen) **[in sich] ~fallen** ‹*cake*› sink [in the middle]; ‹*froth, foam, balloon, etc.*› collapse; 3) ‹*person*› become emaciated; 4) (zeitlich) **[zeitlich] ~fallen** coincide; fall at the same time; 5) (räumlich) coincide; **~|falten** *tr. V.* fold up; **~|fassen** *tr. V.* 1) put together; **einzelne Verbände in einer Dachorganisation ~fassen** bring individual associations together in one umbrella organization; 2) (in eine kurze Form bringen) summarize; **etw. in einem Satz ~fassen** sum sth. up *or* summarize sth. in one sentence; **~fassend kann man sagen ...** to sum up *or* in summary, one can say ...; **~fassung** *die* ▸ **~fassen 1, 2**: putting together; bringing together; summary; **~|fegen** *tr. V.* (bes. nordd.) sweep together; **~|finden** *unr. refl. V.* 1) get together; 2) (~treffen) meet up; **~|flicken** *tr. V.* 1) (auch fig.) patch up; 2) ▸ **~stoppeln**; **~|fließen** *unr. itr. V.; mit sein* ‹*rivers, streams*› flow into each other, join up; (fig.) ‹*colours*› run together; ‹*sounds*› blend together; **~fluss**, ***~fluß** *der* ▸ ❶ **S. 267** confluence; **~|fügen** A *tr. V.* fit together; **was Gott ~gefügt hat, das soll der Mensch nicht scheiden** what therefore God hath joined together, let not man put asunder; B *refl. V.* fit together; **sich zu einem Ganzen ~fügen** fit together to form a whole; **~|führen** *tr. V.* bring together; **getrennte Familien wieder ~führen** reunite divided families; **~|gehen** *unr. itr. V.; mit sein* 1) (sich verbünden, sich ~tun) join forces (**mit** with); (fusionieren) ‹*firms*› merge; 2) (~passen) go together; 3) (ugs.: ~laufen, ~fließen usw.) join up; meet; 4) (ugs.: sich ~fügen, verbinden usw. lassen) fit together; meet; **~|gehören** *itr. V.* belong together; **~gehörig** *Adj.* [closely] related *or* connected ‹*subjects, problems, etc.*›; matching *attrib.* ‹*pieces of tea service, cutlery, etc.*›; **die ~gehörigen Teile/Fotos** the parts/photographs which belong together; **~gehörigkeit** *die;* **~~: tiefe ~gehörigkeit mit jmdm. fühlen** have a deep sense *or* feeling of unity with sb.; **die beiden verbindet ein starkes Gefühl der ~gehörigkeit** the two of them are joined by a strong sense *or* feeling of belonging together; **~gehörigkeits·gefühl** *das* sense *or* feeling of belonging together; **~genommen** *Adj.* **alle diese Dinge ~genommen** all these things together; **~gewürfelt** *Adj.* oddly assorted; **ein bunt ~gewürfelter Haufen** a motley collection of people; **~|haben** *unr. tr. V.* (ugs.) have got together; **~halt** *der* cohesion; **keinen/einen guten ~halt haben** have no/good cohesion; **~|halten** A *unr. tr. V.* 1) hold together; 2) (beisammenhalten) keep together; **sein Geld ~halten** be careful with one's money; B *unr. itr. V.* 1) hold together; 2) (fig.) ‹*friends, family, etc.*› stick together; **~hang** *der* connection; (einer Geschichte, Rede) coherence; (Kontext) context; **was er sagte, hatte keinen ~hang** what he said was incoherent; **in [keinem] ~hang mit etw. stehen** be [in no way] connected with sth.; **die historischen/gesellschaftlichen ~hänge kennen** know the historical/social context; **etw. mit etw. in ~hang bringen** connect sth. with sth.; make a connection between sth. and sth.; **im ~hang mit ...** in connection with ...; **etw. aus dem ~hang lösen/reißen** take sth. out of [its] context; **~|hängen** *unr. itr. V.* 1) be joined [together]; **in ~hängenden Sätzen** in coherent sentences; **~hängender Text** continuous text; **~hängend erzählen** relate in a coherent manner; 2) (fig.) **mit etw. ~hängen** (zu etw. eine Beziehung haben) be related to sth.; (durch etw. [mit] verursacht sein) be the result of sth.; **das hängt damit ~, dass ...** that is connected with *or* has to do with the fact that ...; **die damit ~hängenden Fragen** the related issues; **~hang·los** A *Adj.* incoherent, disjointed ‹*speech, story, etc.*›; **~hanglos nebeneinander stehen** stand disconnectedly side by side; B *adv.* ‹*speak*› incoherently; **~|hauen** *unr. tr. V.* (ugs.) 1) (zerschlagen) smash up; 2) (verprügeln) **jmdn. ~hauen** beat sb. up; 3) (abwertend: nachlässig anfertigen) knock together ‹*furniture*›; knock off (coll.) ‹*homework, task, etc.*›; **~|heften** *tr. V.* 1) staple together; (Buchbinderei) stitch together; 2) (Schneiderei) tack *or* baste together; **~|kauern** *refl. V.* huddle [up]; **sich ängstlich ~kauern** cower; **~|kaufen** *tr. V.* buy; **~|kehren** *tr. V.* (bes. südd.) ▸ **~fegen**; **~klappbar** *Adj.* folding; **~klappbar sein** fold up; **~|klappen** A *tr. V.* 1) fold up; 2) (~schlagen) **die Hacken/Absätze ~klappen** click one's heels; B *itr. V.; mit sein* (ugs.) collapse; **~|klauben** *tr. V.* (südd., österr.) gather together; **~|kleben** *tr., itr. V.* stick together; **~|kneifen** *unr. tr. V.* press ‹*lips*› together; screw ‹*eyes*› up; **~|knüllen** *tr. V.* crumple up; (fest) screw up; **~|kommen** *unr. itr. V.; mit sein* 1) meet; **mit jmdm. ~kommen** meet sb.; 2) (zueinander kommen; auch fig.) get together; 3) (~treffen, gleichzeitig auftreten) occur *or* happen together; **heute kommt bei mir aber auch alles ~!** (ugs.) everything's going wrong at once today!; 4) (sich summieren, sich sammeln) accumulate; **da werden schon so an die 50 Leute ~kommen** there are sure to be getting on for 50 people there altogether; **~|koppeln** *tr. V.* couple together; dock ‹*spacecraft*›; **~|krachen** *itr. V.; mit sein* (ugs.) 1) collapse with a crash; **er ist mit dem Stuhl ~gekracht** he crashed to the floor with the chair; 2) (~stoßen) ‹*vehicles*› crash [into each other], collide [with each other]; **mit einem Auto ~krachen** crash *or* collide with a car; **~|krampfen** *refl. V.* ‹*hands*› clench; ‹*stomach, chest*› tighten; **es krampfte sich in mir alles ~:** I tensed up inside; **~|kratzen** *tr. V.* (ugs.) scrape together ‹*money, savings, etc.*›; **~|kriegen** *tr. V.* (ugs.) ▸ **~bekommen**; **~|krümmen** *refl. V.* double up; writhe

Zusammenkunft /tsuˈzamənkʊnft/ *die;* **~, Zusammenkünfte** /...kʏnftə/ meeting

zusammen-: **~|läppern** *refl. V.* (ugs.) mount up; **~|laufen** *unr. itr. V.; mit sein* 1) ‹*people, crowd*› gather, congregate; 2) (~fließen) ‹*rivers, streams*› flow into each other, join up; 3) (sich sammeln) ‹*water, oil, etc.*› collect; 4) (sich vereinigen) converge; (Geom.) intersect; 5) (ineinander laufen) ‹*colours*› run together; **~|leben** *itr. V.* live together; **~|leben** *das* living together *no art.*; **das eheliche/menschliche ~leben** married life/man's social existence; **~|legen** A *tr. V.* 1) put *or* gather together; 2) (~falten) fold [up]; 3) (miteinander verbinden) amalgamate, merge ‹*classes, departments, etc.*›; combine ‹*events*›; 4) put ‹*patients, guests, etc.*› together [in the same room]; 5) (aneinander legen) fold ‹*hands, arms*›; B *itr. V.* club together; pool our/your/their money; **~|leimen** glue *or* stick together; **~|lesen** *unr. tr. V.* gather; **~|nähen** *tr. V.* 1) sew together; **etw. mit etw. ~nähen** sew sth. to sth.; 2) (durch Nähen reparieren) sew up; **~|nehmen** A *unr. tr. V.* 1) summon *or* muster up ‹*courage, strength, understanding*›; 2) collect ‹*thoughts, wits*›; *s. auch* **~genommen**; B *unr. refl. V.* get *or* take a grip on oneself; **nimm dich ~!** pull yourself together!; **~|packen** A *tr. V.* pack up; (~ verpacken) pack up together; B *itr. V.* pack up; **~|passen** *itr. V.* ‹*colours, clothes, furniture*› go together; ‹*persons*› be suited to each other; **mit etw. ~passen** go with sth.; **~|fantasieren** *refl. V.* (ugs.) **sich** (*Dat.*) **etw. ~fantasieren** dream up sth.; invent sth.; (im Fieber) imagine

Zusammenprall *der;* **~[e]s, ~e** collision; (fig.) clash

zusammen-, Zusammen-: **~|prallen** *itr. V.; mit sein* collide (**mit** with); (fig.) clash; **~|pressen** *tr. V.* 1) squeeze; (komprimieren) compress ‹*gas*›; 2) (aneinander pressen) press ‹*lips, hands*› together; **~|raffen** *tr. V.* gather up ‹*possessions, papers, etc.*›; bundle up ‹*clothes*›; **~|rasseln** *itr. V.; mit sein* (ugs.) ▸ **~krachen 2**; **~|rechnen** *tr. V.* add up; **einen Betrag mit einem anderen ~rechnen** add one amount to another; **~|reimen** *refl. V.* (ugs.) 1) **sich** (*Dat.*) **etw. ~reimen** work sth. out [for oneself]; **ich kann mir das nur so ~reimen** that's the only way I can make sense of it; 2) (~passen, ~gehören) **wie reimt sich das ~?** how does that tally?; **~|reißen** *unr. refl. V.* (ugs.) ▸ **~nehmen B**; **~|ringeln** *refl. V.* ‹*snake*› coil itself up; **~|rollen** A *tr. V.* roll up; B *refl. V.* ‹*cat, dog, etc.*› curl up; ‹*hedgehog*› roll [itself] up [into a ball]; **~|rotten** *refl. V.* (abwertend) ‹*crowds, groups, etc.*› band together; ‹*youths*› gang together *or* up; (in Aufruhr) form a mob; **~rottung** *die;* **~~, ~~en** (abwertend) gathering; **auf der Straße kam es zu ~rottungen** mobs [of hooligans] gathered in the street; **~|rücken** A *tr. V.* move ‹*chairs, tables, etc.*› together; B *itr. V.; mit sein* (auch fig.) move closer together; **~|rufen** *unr. tr. V.* call together; **~|sacken** *itr. V.; mit sein* (ugs.) 1) (einstürzen) **[in sich] ~sacken** collapse; 2) (zu Boden sinken) ‹*person*› collapse; 3) (eine schlaffe Haltung annehmen) **[in sich] ~sacken** slump; **~|scharen** *refl. V.* gather; **~schau** *die* survey; **aus der ~schau beider ergibt sich ...** looking at *or* viewing the two together shows ...; **~|scheißen** *unr. tr. V.* (salopp) **jmdn. ~scheißen** tear sb. off a strip (coll.); **~|schlagen** A *unr. tr. V.* 1) strike *or* bang together; clap ‹*hands*› [together]; **die Hacken ~schlagen** click one's heels; 2) (verprügeln) beat up; 3) (zertrümmern) smash up *or* to pieces; 4) (~falten) fold up; B *unr. itr. V.; mit sein* **über jmdm./etw. ~schlagen** engulf sb./sth.; (fig.) ‹*disaster, misfortune*› overtake sb./sth.; **~|schließen** A *unr. refl. V.* join together; ‹*firms*› merge, amalgamate; **sich im Kampf für/gegen etw. ~schließen** unite in the struggle for/against sth.; B *unr. tr. V.* lock together; **~schluss**, ***~schluß** *der* joining together; union; (von Firmen) merger; amalgamation; **~|schmelzen** *unr. itr. V.; mit sein* melt [away]; (fig.) ‹*supplies, savings, etc.*› dwindle (**auf** + *Akk.* to); **~|schneiden** *unr. tr. V.* (Film, Ferns., Rundf.: kürzen) cut; **~|schnüren** *tr. V.* 1) tie up (**zu** in); 2) (einschnüren) lace in ‹*waist*›; **der Anblick schnürte mir das Herz ~** (geh.) the sight tore at my heart[strings]; **~|schrecken** *unr. od. regelm. itr. V.; mit sein* start; jump; **~|schreiben** *unr. tr. V.* 1) write together; 2) (abwertend: verfassen) dash off ‹*report, letter, etc.*›; **was für einen Unsinn hast du denn da ~geschrieben!** what a lot of rubbish you've written there; **~schreibung** *die* writing together *or* as one word; **beachten Sie bitte die ~schreibung solcher Bezeichnungen** please remember that such terms are written together *or* as one word; **~|schrumpfen** *itr. V.; mit sein* shrivel [up]; (fig.) dwindle; **~|schustern** *tr. V.* (ugs. abwertend) cobble together; **~|schweißen** *tr. V.* weld together; **etw. mit etw. ~schweißen** weld sth. to sth.; **die Gefahr hat sie noch enger ~geschweißt** (fig.) the danger forged even stronger bonds between them; ***~|sein** ▸ **zusammen**; **~sein** *das* 1) being together *no art.*; 2) (Treffen) get-together; **~|setzen**

Z

A *tr. V.* **1** put together; **Steine zu einem Mosaik ~:** put stones together to make a mosaic; **2** (herstellen) make; **ein ~gesetztes Wort/Verb** a compound word/verb; **3** (~bauen, ~montieren) assemble; put together; **4** (beieinander sitzen lassen) seat *or* put together; **jmdn. mit jmdm. ~:** seat *or* put sb. next to sb.; **B** *refl. V.* **1** **sich aus etw. ~:** be made up *or* composed of sth.; **wie setzt sich das Gremium ~?** how is the committee made up?; **2** (sich zueinander setzen) sit together; **sich mit jmdm. ~:** sit next to sb.; **3** (zu einem Gespräch) get together; **~setzung** *die;* **~~, ~~en** **1** putting together; **2** (Aufbau) composition; **„~setzung: ..."** (als Aufschrift auf Medikamentenpackung) 'ingredients: ...'; **3** (Sprachw.) compound; **~|sinken** *unr. itr. V.; mit sein* **1** **[in sich] ~sinken** collapse; ‹*fire*› die down; ‹*dough*› sink; **2** (zu Boden sinken) **[in sich] ~sinken** slump to the ground; (eine schlaffe Haltung einnehmen) slump; **ohnmächtig/tot ~sinken** collapse in a faint/fall down dead; **~|sitzen** *unr. itr. V.* **1** sit together; **mit jmdm. ~sitzen** sit next to sb.; **2** (miteinander verbunden sein) be joined together; **~|sparen** *tr. V.* save up; **sich** (*Dat.*) **ein Auto/Fahrrad ~sparen** save up and buy a car/bicycle; **~spiel** *das* **1** (von Musikern) ensemble playing; (von Darstellern) ensemble acting; (einer Mannschaft) teamwork; **2** (fig.) interplay; **~|spielen** *itr. V.* **1** play together; ‹*actors*› act together; **mit jmdm. ~spielen** play/act with sb.; **2** (fig.) ‹*forces, influences, etc.*› work together, combine; **~|stauchen** *tr. V.* **1** compress; **2** (fig. ugs.) **jmdn. ~stauchen** tear sb. off a strip (coll.); **~|stecken** **A** *tr. V.* **1** fit together; join up ‹*extension cables*›; **2** (mit einer Nadel, Spange usw.) pin together; *s. auch* **Kopf 1**; **B** *itr. V.* (ugs.) be together; **~|stehen** *unr. itr. V.* **1** stand together; **mit jmdm. ~stehen** stand with sb.; **2** (fig.: ~halten) stand by one another; **~|stellen** **A** *tr. V.* **1** put together; **2** (aus einzelnen Teilen gestalten) put together ‹*programme, film, book, menu, exhibition, team, delegation*›; draw up ‹*list, timetable*›; compile ‹*report, broadcast*›; work out ‹*route, tour*›; make up ‹*bouquet, flower arrangement*›; **3** (in einer Übersicht, Liste usw.) draw together; compile ‹*facts, data*›; **4** (kombinieren) combine; **B** *refl. V.* stand together; **~stellung** *die* **1** ▸**~stellen A 2**: putting together; drawing up; compilation; working out; making up; **2** (Übersicht) survey; (von Tatsachen, Daten) compilation; **3** (Kombination) combination; **~|stimmen** *itr. V.* **1** ‹*instruments*› harmonize; ‹*colours, furniture*› match, go together; **mit etw. ~stimmen** go with sth.; **2** (stimmig sein) agree (**mit** with); **~|stoppeln** *tr. V.* (abwertend) cobble together; **~stoß** *der* collision; (fig.) clash (**mit** with); **bei dem ~stoß [der beiden Züge]** in the collision [between the two trains]; **~|stoßen** *unr. itr. V.; mit sein* collide (**mit** with); **wir stießen mit den Köpfen ~:** we banged *or* bumped our heads; **~|strömen** *itr. V.; mit sein* **1** ‹*rivers, streams*› flow into one another, join up; **2** (~laufen, ~kommen) congregate; **~|stückeln** *tr. V.* (ugs.) patch together; **~|stürzen** *itr. V.; mit sein* collapse; ‹*mine shaft, roof*› cave in, collapse; **~|suchen** *tr. V.* collect bit by bit; hunt out ‹*information*› bit by bit; **~|tragen** *unr. tr. V.* collect; **~|treffen** *unr. itr. V.; mit sein* **1** meet; **mit jmdm. ~treffen** meet sb.; **2** (zeitlich) coincide; **~treffen** *das* **1** meeting; **2** **ein merkwürdiges ~treffen von Zufällen** a peculiar set of coincidences; **~|treiben** *unr. tr. V.* herd together; **~|treten** *unr. itr. V.; mit sein* meet (**zu** for); ‹*parliament*› assemble; **~|trommeln** *tr. V.* (ugs.) round up; **~|tun** (ugs.) **A** *unr. tr. V.* put together; **B** *unr. refl. V.* get together (**mit** with); **~|wachsen** *unr. itr. V.; mit sein* grow together; join [up]; ‹*bones*› knit together; (fig.) ‹*towns*› merge into one; **~gewachsen sein** be joined; ‹*bones*› have knitted together; **~|werfen** *unr. tr. V.* (ugs.) lump together; **~|wirken** *itr. V.* combine; **~|würfeln** *tr. V.* throw together; **~|zählen** *tr. V.* add up; **~|ziehen** **A** *unr. tr. V.* **1** draw *or* pull together; draw *or* pull ‹*noose, net*› tight; **die Brauen ~ziehen** knit one's brows; **die Säure zieht einem den Mund ~:** the sourness makes you pucker up your mouth; **2** (konzentrieren) mass ‹*troops, police*›; **3** (addieren) add up *or* together; (~fassen) simplify ‹*mathematical expression*›; **B** *unr. refl. V.* **1** ‹*skin, muscle, heart*› contract; ‹*face*› tighten up; ‹*wound*› close up; **2** ▸▸**~brauen B**; **C** *unr. itr. V.; mit sein* move in together; **mit jmdm. ~ziehen** move in with sb.; **~|zimmern** *tr. V.* (ugs.) knock together; (fig. abwertend) cobble together; **~|zucken** *itr. V.; mit sein* start; jump

Zu̲·satz *der* **1** addition; **unter ~ von etw.** while adding sth.; **ohne ~ von ...** without the addition of ...; without adding ... **2** (Zugesetztes, Additiv) additive **3** (zusätzlicher Teil) addition; (zu einem Vertrag) rider; additional clause; (Nachtrag) addendum; (zu einem Brief) postscript; (zu einem Testament) codicil

Zu̲satz-: ~angebot *das* additional offering; **~ausbildung** *die* supplementary course; **~belastung** *die* additional charge; **~bremsleuchte** *die* (Kfz-W.) high-level brake light; **~funktion** *die* additional function; **~gerät** *das* add-on; (kleines) attachment; **~geschäft** *das* additional business; **~information** *die* supplementary information; additional information; **~kosten** *Pl.* supplementary costs; additional costs; **~leistung** *die* extra

zusätzlich /ˈt̮suːzɛt̮slɪç/

A *Adj.* additional;

B *adv.* in addition

Zu̲satz-: ~nutzen *der* additional benefit; **~qualifikation** *die* additional qualification; **~rente** *die* supplementary pension; **~stoff** *der* additive; **~studium** *das* supplementary course; **~versicherung** *die* additional *or* supplementary insurance; **~versorgung** *die* supplementary benefit; **~vorsorge** *die* additional pension provision; **~zahl** *die* bonus number

zu̲schaltbar *Adj.* that can be switched on [as required] *postpos.* (also fig.); **etw. ist ~:** sth. can be switched on [as required] (also fig.)

zu̲|schalten

A *tr. V.* **1** switch on; bring in, engage ‹*rear wheels*›; **2** (Funk, Ferns.) patch in ‹*person, images, etc.*›.

B *refl. V.* (Funk, Ferns.) switch on (*Dat.* for); **sich [per Satellit] ~ lassen** be linked *or* connected by satellite

zu·scha̲nden *Adv.* **in etw. ~ machen** wreck *or* ruin sth.; **ein Auto ~ fahren/ein Pferd ~ reiten** wreck a car/ruin a horse by bad riding; **~ werden** be wrecked *or* ruined

zu̲|schanzen *tr. V.* (ugs.) **jmdm./sich etw. ~:** wangle sth. for sb./oneself (coll.)

zu̲|schauen *itr. V.* (südd., österr., schweiz.) ▸**zusehen**

Zu̲·schauer *der,* **Zu̲·schauerin** *die;* **~s, ~nen** spectator; (im Theater, Kino) member of the audience; (an einer Unfallstelle) onlooker; (Fernseh~) viewer; **die ~:** the spectators; the crowd *sing.;* (im Theater, Kino) the audience *sing.;* (an einer Unfallstelle) the onlookers; (Fernseh~) the audience *sing.;* the viewers

Zu̲schauer-: ~interesse *das* audience interest; (Ferns.) interest among viewers; **~rang** *der* block of seats; **die ~ränge** the rows of spectators; **~raum** *der* auditorium; (beim Gericht) public gallery; **~rekord** *der* attendance record; (Film, Ferns.) audience record; **~schnitt** *der* (Sport) average attendance; **~tribüne** *die* grandstand; **~zahl** *die* (bes. Ferns.) audience [numbers]; (Sport) attendance

zu̲|schaufeln *tr. V.* fill in [with a shovel/shovels]

zu̲|schicken *tr. V.* send; **jmdm. etw. ~:** send sth. to sb.; send sb. sth.; **sich** (*Dat.*) **etw. ~ lassen** send for sth.

zu̲|schieben *unr. tr. V.* **1** push ‹*drawer, door*› shut; **den Riegel ~:** put the bolt across **2** (fig.: zuweisen) **jmdm. die Schuld/Verantwortung ~:** lay the blame/responsibility on sb.

zu̲|schießen

A *unr. tr. V.* **1** **jmdm. den Ball ~:** kick *or* pass the ball to sb. **2** (als Zuschuss geben) contribute (**zu** towards); **Geld zu etw. ~:** contribute [money] *or* put money towards sth.; **jmdm. 200 Euro ~:** give sb. 200 euros towards it

B *unr. itr. V.; mit sein* **auf jmdn./etw. zugeschossen kommen** come shooting towards sb.

Zu̲·schlag *der* **1** additional *or* extra charge; (für Nacht-, Feiertagsarbeit, Arbeitserschwernisse) additional *or* extra payment; **der Intercity-Zug kostet [5 Euro] ~:** you have to pay a supplement [of 5 euros] on an intercity train **2** (Eisenb.) supplement ticket **3** (bei einer Versteigerung) acceptance of a/the bid; **der ~ erfolgt an Herrn X** *od.* **wird Herrn X erteilt** the lot is knocked down to Mr X *or* goes to Mr X **4** (bei Ausschreibung eines Auftrags) acceptance of a/the tender; **jmdm. den ~ für etw. geben** give sb. the contract for sth.; **den ~ bekommen** *od.* **erhalten** get the contract

zu̲|schlagen

A *unr. tr. V.* **1** bang or slam ‹*door, window, etc.*› shut; close ‹*book*›; (heftig) slam ‹*book*› shut **2** **jmdm. etw. ~** (bei einer Versteigerung) knock sth. down to sb.; (bei Ausschreibung eines Auftrags, durch Gerichtsbeschluss) award sth. to sb. **3** (angliedern) annex (*Dat.* to) **4** (als Zuschlag erheben) add on; **das Porto wird dem Preis zugeschlagen** the price does not include postage

B *unr. itr. V.* **1** *mit sein* ‹*door, trap*› slam *or* bang shut **2** (einen Schlag führen) throw a blow/blows; (losschlagen) hit *or* strike out; (fig.) ‹*army, police, murderer*› strike; **er schlug kräftig zu** he threw a powerful blow; **schlag doch zu!** [go on,] hit it/me/him *etc.* **3** (salopp: zugreifen) jump at it; (beim Essen) have a good nosh-up (coll.); (beim Trinken) knock it back (coll.)

zu̲schlag·pflichtig /-ˈpflɪçtɪç/ *Adj.* (Eisenb.) ‹*train*› on which on supplement is payable

Zu̲schlag·stoff *der* (Hüttenw.) flux; (Bauw.) aggregate

zu̲|schließen

A *unr. tr. V.* lock

B *unr. itr. V.* lock up

zu̲|schnappen *itr. V.* **1** *mit sein* snap shut **2** (zubeißen) snap; **der Hund schnappt zu, wenn man ihn neckt** if you tease him the dog will snap at you

zu̲|schneiden *unr. itr. V.* cut out ‹*material etc.*› (**zu, für** for); saw ‹*plank, slat*› to size; cut out ‹*dress, jacket*›; **auf jmdn./etw. zugeschnitten sein** (fig.) be tailor-made for sb./sth.; **auf jmds. Geschmack zugeschnitten** geared to sb.'s taste

zu̲|schneidern *tr. V.* tailor; **neu ~:** refashion; **etw. auf jmdn./etw. ~:** tailor sth. to fit sb./sth. (also fig.)

zu̲|schneien *itr. V.; mit sein* snow in *or* up

Zu̲·schnitt *der* **1** (von Kleidung) cut; (fig.) character; (Format) calibre **2** (*das Zuschneiden*) (von Kleidung) cutting [out]; (von Platten usw.) sawing to size

zu̲|schnüren *tr. V.* tie up; **sich** (*Dat.*) **die Schuhe ~:** tie *or* do up one's shoes; *s. auch* **Kehle**

zu̲|schrauben *tr. V.* screw the lid *or* top on ‹*jar, flask*›; screw ‹*lid, top*› on

zu̲|schreiben *unr. tr. V.* **1** **jmdm./einem Umstand etw. ~:** attribute sth. to sb./a circumstance; **jmdm. das Verdienst/die Schuld an etw.** (*Dat.*) **~:** credit sb. with/blame sb. for sth.; **das hast du dir selbst zu~:** you only have yourself to blame [for this]; **jmdm./einer Sache eine Eigenschaft ~:** ascribe a characteristic *or* quality to sb./sth.; credit sb./sth. with a quality **2** (überschreiben) **einem Konto eine Summe ~:** transfer a sum to an account

Zu̲·schrift *die* letter; (auf eine Anzeige) reply

zu·schu̲lden *Adv.* **sich** (*Dat.*) **[irgend]etw. ~ kommen lassen** do [any] wrong

Zu̲·schuss, ***Zu̲·schuß** *der* contribution (**zu** towards); (regelmäßiger ~) allowance; **[staatlicher] ~:** state subsidy (**für, zu** towards); **ich gebe dir einen kleinen ~:** I'll give you something towards it

Z

Zu̲schuss·betrieb, *Zu̲schuß·betrieb *der* subsidized concern
zu̲|schustern *tr. V.* (ugs.) **1** **jmdm. einen Posten** *usw.* **~:** organize a job *etc.* for sb. **2** (zuschießen) contribute (**zu** towards)
zu̲|schütten
A *tr. V.* **1** fill in ‹*ditch etc.*› **2** (ugs. hinzufügen) pour on, add ‹*water etc.*›.
B *refl. V.* (ugs.) get plastered (sl.)
zu̲|sehen *unr. itr. V.* **1** watch; **jmdm. [bei einem Spiel/beim Arbeiten** *usw.*] **~:** watch sb. [playing a game/working *etc.*]; **bei näherem Zusehen** on closer examination; if you look more closely; **vom [bloßen] Zusehen** [simply] by watching; **er musste ~, wie sein Haus niederbrannte** he had to stand by and watch his house burn down; **wir dürfen diesem Unrecht nicht tatenlos ~:** we cannot stand idly by and allow this injustice **2** (dafür sorgen, sich darum bemühen) make sure; see to it; **sieh zu, dass ...** see that ...; make sure that ...; **er soll ~, wie er das hinkriegt** he'll just have to manage somehow; **sieh zu, wo du bleibst!** you're on your own
zusehends /ˈt͜suːzeːənt͜s/ *Adv.* visibly
Zu̲·seher *der,* **Zu̲·seherin** *die* (österr.) ▸**Zuschauer**
***zu̲·sein** ▸**zu B 3**
zu̲|senden *unr. od. regelm. tr. V.* ▸**zuschicken**
Zu̲·sendung *die* **1** (das Zusenden) sending; **ich bitte um ~ des Vertrages** I would ask that the contract be sent to me **2** (Zugesandtes) (Brief) letter; (Paket) parcel; (Warensendung) consignment
zu̲|setzen
A *tr. V.* **1** **[zu] einem Stoff etw. ~:** add sth. to a substance **2** (zuzahlen) pay out; **er hat nichts [mehr] zu~** (fig.) he has no strength left in him
B *itr. V.* (ugs.) **jmdm. ~** (jmdn. angreifen) go for sb.; (beim Verhör) grill sb.; (jmdn. bedrängen) pester *or* badger sb.; ‹*mosquitoes etc.*› plague sb.; ‹*illness, heat*› take a lot out of sb.; ‹*death, divorce*› be a heavy blow for sb.; **einer Sache** (*Dat.*) **~** (beschädigen) damage sth.
zu̲|sichern *tr. V.* **jmdm. etw. ~:** promise sb. sth.; assure sb. of sth.
Zu̲·sicherung *die* promise; assurance
zu̲|sperren (südd., österr.)
A *tr. V.* lock
B *itr. V.* lock up
Zu̲·spiel *das* (Ballspiele) passing; (einzelner Spielzug) pass
zu̲|spielen
A *itr. V.* (Ballspiele) pass
B *tr. V.* **1** (Ballspiele) **jmdm. den Ball ~:** pass the ball to sb. **2** (fig.: zukommen lassen) **der Presse Informationen ~:** leak information to the press
zu̲|spitzen
A *tr. V.* **1** sharpen to a point **2** (fig.: verschärfen) aggravate ‹*position, crisis*›; intensify ‹*competition, conflict, etc.*› **3** (fig.: pointieren) make ‹*question, answer*› pointed
B *refl. V.* become aggravated
Zu̲·spitzung *die;* **~, ~en** **1** (fig.: Verschärfung) aggravation; (der Konkurrenz, eines Konflikts) intensification **2** (fig.: Pointierung) pointed emphasis
zu̲|sprechen
A *unr. tr. V.* **1** **er sprach ihr Trost/Mut zu** his words gave her comfort/courage; **sich** (*Dat.*) **selbst Mut ~:** give oneself courage **2** (zuerkennen) **jmdm. ein Erbe** *usw.* **~:** award sb. an inheritance *etc.*; **die Kinder der Mutter/dem Vater ~:** award custody of the children to the mother/father **3** (zuschreiben) **jmdm./einer Sache etw. ~:** ascribe sth. to sb./sth.
B *unr. itr. V.* **1** (zureden) **jmdm. ermutigend/tröstend** *usw.* **~:** speak encouragingly/comfortingly to sb. **2** (geh.) **dem Essen/den Getränken ~:** partake of the food/drinks
Zu̲·spruch *der* (geh.) **1** (Zureden) words *pl.*; **Worte des ~s** (tröstend) words of comfort; (ermutigend) words of encouragement **2** (Anklang) **[bei jmdm.] ~ finden** be popular [with sb.]
Zu̲·stand *der* **1** condition; (bes. abwertend) state; **in rohem/gefrorenem ~:** in the raw/frozen state; raw/frozen; **in flüssigem ~:** in liquid form; **in betrunkenem ~:** while under the influence of alcohol; **in bewusstlosem ~:** in a state of unconsciousness; unconscious; **geistiger/gesundheitlicher ~:** state of mind/health; **der ~ des Patienten** the patient's condition; **er war in einem schlimmen ~:** he was in a bad way; **Zustände kriegen** *od.* **bekommen** (ugs.) have a fit (coll.) **2** (Stand der Dinge) state of affairs; situation; **Zustände** conditions; **das sind ja [schöne] Zustände!** that's a fine state of affairs!; these are fine goings-on!; **das ist doch kein ~!** that just won't do (coll.); *s. auch* **Rom**
zu·sta̲nde *in* **~ bringen** + *Akk.* manage to do; [manage to] bring about ‹*agreement, coalition, etc.*›; **~ kommen** come into being; (geschehen) take place; **es wollte kein Gespräch ~ kommen** it was impossible to get a conversation going
zu̲·ständig *Adj.* **1** appropriate, proper, relevant ‹*authority, office, etc.*›; **das ~e Gericht** the court of jurisdiction; **von ~er Seite** by the proper authority; **[für etw.] ~ sein** (verantwortlich) be responsible [for sth.]; (kompetent) be competent [to deal with sth.]; ‹*court*› have jurisdiction [in sth.]; **dafür sind wir nicht ~:** it's not our responsibility/we are not competent to decide that **2** (österr. Amtsspr.) **nach Wien ~ sein** be domiciled in Vienna
Zu̲ständigkeit *die;* **~, ~en** (Verantwortlichkeit) responsibility; (Kompetenz) competence; (eines Gerichts) jurisdiction
Zu̲ständigkeits·bereich *der* (Verantwortlichkeit) area of responsibility; (Kompetenz) range of competence; **das fällt in den ~ des Innenministeriums** it is within the responsibility/competence of the Ministry of the Interior
Zu̲stands-: ~passiv *das* (Sprachw.) passive of condition; **~verb** *das* (Sprachw.): *verb describing a state*
zu·sta̲tten *Adv. in* **jmdm./einer Sache ~ kommen** be a help *or* be useful to sb./for sth.; (von Vorteil sein) be of advantage to sb./sth.
zu̲|stecken *tr. V.* **1** pin up ‹*tear*›; pin together ‹*curtains etc.*› **2** (heimlich geben) **jmdm. etw. ~:** slip sb. sth.
zu̲|stehen *unr. itr. V.* **etw. steht jmdm. zu** sb. is entitled to sth.; **ein Urteil über ihn steht mir nicht zu** it is not for me to judge him
zu̲|steigen *unr. itr. V.; mit sein* get on; **ist noch jemand zugestiegen?** (im Bus) any more fares, please?; (im Zug) ≈ tickets, please!
zu̲|stellen *tr. V.* **1** block ‹*entrance, passage, etc.*› **2** (bringen) deliver ‹*letter, parcel, etc.*›; **jmdm. etw. ~:** deliver sth. to sb.; (zuschicken) send sb. sth.; **jmdm. ein Schriftstück ~:** serve a writ on sb.
Zu̲·steller *der;* **~s, ~,** **Zu̲·stellerin** *die;* **~, ~nen** **1** deliverer **2** (Postbote/-botin) postman/postwoman
Zu̲·stellung *die* delivery; (Zusendung) submission
zu̲|steuern
A *itr. V.; mit sein* **auf jmdn./etw. ~:** head for sb./sth.; **einer Sache** (*Dat.*) **~:** head for sth.
B *tr. V.* **1** **etw. auf jmdn./etw. ~:** steer *or* drive sth. towards sb./sth. **2** (ugs.) ▸**beisteuern**
zu̲|stimmen *itr. V.* agree; **jmdm. [in einem Punkt] ~:** agree with sb. [on a point]; **~d nicken** nod in agreement; **einer Sache** (*Dat.*) **~:** agree to sth.; **einem Gesetzentwurf ~** ‹*parliament*› pass *or* approve a bill; **dem kann ich nur ~:** I quite agree
Zu̲·stimmung *die* (Billigung) approval (**zu** of); (Einverständnis) agreement (**zu** to, with); (Plazet) consent (**zu** to); **[allgemeine] ~ finden** meet with [general] approval; **die ~ der Eltern** the parents' consent; **jmdm. seine ~ zu etw. geben** give sb. one's consent to *or* for sth.; **nicht ohne/nur mit jmds. ~:** not without/only with the agreement *or* consent of sb.
zu̲|stopfen *tr. V.* **1** plug, stop up ‹*hole, crack*›; plug ‹*ears*› **2** (mit Nadel und Faden) darn, mend ‹*hole*›
zu̲|stöpseln *tr. V.* **1** put a stopper in ‹*bottle*›; (mit Korken); put a cork in, cork ‹*bottle*› **2** put a plug in ‹*basin*›; plug ‹*drain etc.*›
zu̲|stoßen
A *unr. tr. V.* push ‹*door etc.*› shut; (mit dem Fuß, heftig) kick ‹*door etc.*› shut
B *unr. itr. V.* **1** strike out; (mit einem Messer usw.) make a stab; stab; ‹*snake etc.*› strike **2** *mit sein* **jmdm. ~:** happen to sb.; **wenn mir etwas zustößt** if anything should happen to me
zu̲|streben *itr. V.; mit sein* **einer Sache** (*Dat.*) *od.* **auf etw.** (*Akk.*) **~:** make for sth.; (fig.) strive for *or* aim at sth.
Zu̲·strom *der* **1** (von Luft, fig.: Geld usw.) flow **2** (von Menschen) influx; stream; **starken** *od.* **großen ~ haben** have a great influx of people
zu̲|stürmen *itr. V.; mit sein* **auf jmdn./etw. ~:** charge towards sb./sth.
zu̲|stürzen *itr. V.; mit sein* **auf jmdn./etw. ~/zugestürzt kommen** rush/come rushing towards sb./sth.; (direkt heran) rush/come rushing up to sb./sth.
zu|ta̲ge *Adv. in:* **~ kommen** *od.* **treten** become visible (lit. or fig.); ‹*stream*› come to the surface; (ans Licht kommen) ‹*documents etc.*› come to light, be revealed; ‹*story*› come out, be made public; (fig.: erkennbar werden) become evident; ‹*differences etc.*› come into the open; **etw. ~ bringen** *od.* **fördern** (aus der Tasche usw.) produce sth.; (fig.: erkennbar machen) bring sth. to light; reveal sth.; **offen** *od.* **klar ~ liegen** be perfectly clear *or* evident
Zu̲·tat *die* ingredient
zu·te̲il *Adv.* (geh.) *in* **jmdm./einer Sache ~ werden** be granted *or* accorded to sb./sth.; **ihm wurde die Ehre ~, die Ansprache halten zu dürfen** he was accorded the honour of giving the address; **jmdm. etw. ~ werden lassen** accord sb. sth.; bestow sth. on sb.; **einer Sache** (*Dat.*) **mehr Aufmerksamkeit ~ werden lassen** devote more attention to sth.
zu̲|teilen *tr. V.* **1** **jmdm. jmdn./etw. ~:** allot *or* assign sb./sth. to sb. **2** (als Ration) **jmdm. seine Portion ~:** mete out his/her share to sb.; **den Kindern das Essen ~:** ration *or* share out the food to the children; **die zugeteilte Menge** the allocated amount
Zu̲·teilung *die* **1** allotting, assigning (**an** + *Akk.* to) **2** (als Ration) sharing out, allocation (**an** + *Akk.* to); (eines Mandats, Quartiers) allocation, assignment (**an** + *Akk.* to); **es gab Fleisch nur auf ~:** meat was only to be had on rations **3** (Ration) allocation, ration (**an** + *Dat.* of)
zu̲teilungs·reif *Adj.* (Wirtsch.) mature
zu·ti̲efst *Adv.* profoundly; **~ verletzt** deeply hurt *or* offended
zu̲|tragen
A *unr. refl. V.* (geh.) take place; occur
B *unr. tr. V.* **jmdm. etw. ~:** carry sth. to sb. (fig.: mitteilen) report sth. to sb.; **jmdm. Nachrichten/Gerüchte** *usw.* **~:** pass on news/rumours *etc.* to sb.
Zu̲·träger *der,* **Zu̲·trägerin** *die* informer
zuträglich /ˈt͜suˈtrɛːklɪç/ *Adj.* healthy ‹*climate*›; **jmdm./einer Sache ~ sein** be good for sb./sth.; be beneficial to sb./sth.
Zu̲träglichkeit *die;* **~:** beneficial effect; (des Klimas) healthiness
zu̲|trauen *tr. V.* **jmdm. etw. ~:** believe sb. [is] capable of [doing] sth.; **den Mut hätte ich ihm gar nicht zugetraut** I should never have thought he had the courage; **ich hätte ihm mehr Taktgefühl zugetraut** I should have thought he had more tact; **ihm ist alles zu~:** I wouldn't put anything past him; **das hätte ich ihm nicht zugetraut** I should never have thought it of him; **das ist ihm [durchaus] zu~:** I could [well] believe it of him; **sich** (*Dat.*) **etw. ~:** think one can do *or* is capable of doing sth.; **trau dir nicht zu viel zu** don't take on too much; don't overdo it; **er traut sich** (*Dat.*) **zu wenig zu** he has too little self-confidence
Zu̲trauen *das;* **~s** confidence, trust (**zu** in); **~ zu sich selbst** self-confidence
zu̲traulich
A *Adj.* trusting; trustful

Z

B *adv.* trustingly; trustfully

Zutraulichkeit *die;* ~: trust[fulness]

zu|treffen *unr. itr. V.* **1** be correct; **der Vorwurf trifft zu** the reproach is justified **2** **auf** *od.* **für jmdn./etw.** ~: apply to sb./sth.

zutreffend

A *Adj.* **1** correct; (treffend) accurate; **es ist** ~, **dass ...** it is correct *or* the case that ... **2** (geltend) applicable; relevant; **Zutreffendes bitte ankreuzen** please mark with a cross where applicable

B *adv.* correctly; (treffend) accurately

zu|treiben *unr. itr. V.; mit sein* **jmdm./einer Sache** ~, **auf jmdn./etw.** ~ (auch fig.) be carried along *or* drift towards sb./sth.

zu|trinken *unr. itr. V.* **jmdm.** ~: raise one's glass and drink to sb.

Zu·tritt *der* entry; admittance; **„kein ~", „~ verboten"** 'no entry'; 'no admittance'; **jmdm. den ~ verweigern** refuse sb. admission; ~ **[zu etw.] haben** have access [to sth.]

zu|tun *unr. tr. V.* **kein Auge** ~: not sleep a wink

Zu·tun *das;* ~s *in* **ohne jmds.** ~: without sb.'s being involved; **es geschah ohne mein** ~: I had nothing to do with it

zu·ungunsten

A *Präp. mit Gen.* to the disadvantage of

B *Adv.* ~ **von** to the disadvantage of

zu·unterst *Adv.* right at the bottom; *s. auch* **ober... 1**

zuverlässig /ˈt̮suːfɛɐ̯lɛsɪç/

A *Adj.* reliable; (verlässlich) dependable ‹*person*›

B *adv.* **1** reliably; **er arbeitet sehr** ~: he is a very reliable worker **2** (mit Gewissheit) ‹*confirm*› with certainty; ‹*know*› for sure, for certain

Zuverlässigkeit *die;* ~: reliability; (Verlässlichkeit) dependability

Zuversicht /ˈt̮suːfɛɐ̯zɪçt/ *die;* ~: confidence

zuversichtlich

A *Adj.* confident; **sich** ~ **geben** express one's confidence

B *adv.* confidently

Zuversichtlichkeit *die;* ~: confidence

***zuviel** ▸ **viel; gut A 1; kriegen A 1; sagen A 3**

Zu·viel *das;* ~s excess (**an** + *Dat.* of)

zu·vor *Adv.* before; **tags/im Jahr** ~: the day/year before

zu·vorderst *Adv.* right at the front

zuvörderst /t̮suˈfœrdɐst/ *Adv.* (veralt.) first and foremost

zuvor|kommen *unr. itr. V.; mit sein* **1** **jmdm.** ~: beat sb. to it; get there first **2** **einer Sache** (*Dat.*) ~: anticipate *or* forestall sth.

zuvorkommend

A *Adj.* obliging; (höflich) courteous

B *adv.* obligingly; (höflich) courteously

Zuvorkommenheit *die;* ~: courteousness; courtesy

-zuwachs *der* increase in ‹*income, capital, exports, votes, expenditure, productivity, population, etc.*›; **Lohn-/Gehalts~:** wage/salary increase

Zu·wachs *der;* ~**es, Zuwächse** /ˈt̮suːvɛksə/ increase (*Gen.*, **an** + *Dat.* in); ~ **an Besuchern/Mitgliedern** increase in the number of visitors/members; **wirtschaftlicher** ~: economic growth; **die Familie hat** ~ **bekommen** there has been an addition to the family; **der Mantel ist auf** ~ **genäht** the coat has been made [on the large side] to allow room to grow into

zu|wachsen *unr. itr. V.; mit sein* **1** ‹*wound*› heal [over] **2** (bewachsen/überwachsen werden) become overgrown; **mit etw. zugewachsen sein** be overgrown with sth. **3** (zuteil werden) **jmdm./einer Sache** ~: fall *or* be granted to sb./sth.

Zuwachs·rate *die* (bes. Wirtsch.) growth rate

Zu·wanderer *der,* **Zu·wanderin** *die* immigrant

zu|wandern *itr. V.; mit sein* immigrate

Zu·wanderung *die* immigration

Zuwanderungs·gesetz *das* immigration law

zu|warten *itr. V.* wait

zu·wege *Adv. in* **etw.** ~ **bringen** [manage to] achieve sth.; **gut/schlecht** ~ **sein** (ugs.) be in good shape/a bad way

zu·weilen *Adv.* (geh.) now and again; at times

zu|weisen *unr. tr. V.* **jmdm. etw.** ~: allocate *or* allot sb. sth.

zu|wenden

A *unr. od. regelm. refl. V.* **1** **sich jmdm./einer Sache** ~ (auch fig.) turn to sb./sth.; (sich widmen) devote oneself to sb./sth.: **2** (geh.: gehen) **er wandte sich dem Ausgang zu** he moved towards the exit

B *unr. od. regelm. tr. V.* **1** **jmdm./einer Sache etw.** ~: turn sth. to[wards] sb./sth.; **jmdm. den Rücken** ~: turn one's back on sb. **2** (geben, zuteil werden lassen) **jmdm. Geld** ~: give *or* donate money to sb.

Zu·wendung *die* **1** (Aufmerksamkeit) [loving] attention *or* care **2** (Geldgeschenk) gift of money; (Unterstützung) [financial] contribution; (Geldspende) donation; **auf ~en angewiesen sein** be dependent on financial support *sing. or* contributions

***zu·wenig** ▸ **wenig; viel B 2**

zu|werfen *unr. tr. V.* **1** slam ‹*door, lid*› **2** **jmdm. etw.** ~: throw sth. to sb.; throw sb. sth.; **jmdm. einen bösen/giftigen Blick** ~: look daggers at sb.; *s. auch* **Ball 1; Blick 1; Kusshand**

zuwider

A *Adj.* **1** **jmdm.** ~ **sein** be repugnant to sb.; **Spinat ist mir äußerst** ~: I absolutely detest spinach **2** (geh.: nicht förderlich) **jmdm./einer Sache** (*Dat.*) ~ **sein** ‹*circumstances, weather, etc.*› be against sb./sth.

B *Präp. mit Dat.; nachgestellt* contrary to *attrib.*

zuwider-, Zuwider-: ~**|handeln** *itr. V.* **dem Gesetz/einer Vorschrift** *usw.* ~**handeln** contravene *or* infringe the law/a regulation *etc.*; **einer Anordnung/einem Verbot ~handeln** defy an instruction/a ban; ~**handelnde** *der/die; adj. Dekl.* offender; ~**|laufen** *unr. itr. V.; mit sein* **einer Sache** (*Dat.*) ~**laufen** go against *or* run counter to sth.

zu|winken *itr. V.* **jmdm./einander** ~: wave to sb./one another

zu|zahlen *tr. V.* pay ‹*five euros etc.*› extra; **einen Betrag** ~: pay an additional sum

zu|zählen *tr. V.* **1** (dazurechnen) add on **2** (zurechnen) **etw. einem Gebiet/Zeitalter** ~: assign sth. to an area/era

zu·zeiten *Adv.* (geh.) ▸ **zuweilen**

zu|ziehen

A *unr. tr. V.* **1** pull ‹*door*› shut; draw ‹*curtain*›; pull *or* draw ‹*knot, net*› tight; do up ‹*zip*› **2** call in ‹*expert, specialist*›

B *unr. refl. V.* **1** **sich** (*Dat.*) **eine Krankheit/Infektion** ~: catch an illness/contract an infection; **sich** (*Dat.*) **einen Schädelbruch** ~: sustain a fracture of the skull; **sich** (*Dat.*) **jmds. Zorn/Vorwürfe** ~: incur sb.'s anger/reproaches **2** (sich schließen) ‹*knot, noose*› tighten, get tight

C *unr. itr. V.; mit sein* move here *or* into the area

Zu·zug *der* **1** influx **2** (Genehmigung) settlement permit

zuzüglich /ˈt̮suːt̮syːklɪç/ *Präp. mit Gen.* plus; **400 Euro** ~ **[der] Heizungskosten** 400 euros plus *or* not including heating

Zuzugs·genehmigung *die* settlement permit

zu|zwinkern *itr. V.* **jmdm.** ~: wink at sb.

zwacken /ˈt̮svakn̩/ *tr., auch itr. V.* (ugs.) ▸ **zwicken**

zwang /t̮svaŋ/ *1. u. 3. Pers. Sg. Prät. v.* **zwingen**

Zwang *der;* ~**[e]s, Zwänge** /ˈt̮svɛŋə/ **1** compulsion; **unter** ~ **handeln** act under duress; **Kinder ohne** ~ **erziehen** bring children up without constraint; **auf jmdn.** ~ **ausüben** exert pressure on sb.; force sb.'s hand; **der** ~ **der Verhältnisse** the force of circumstance[s]; **soziale Zwänge** social constraints; the constraints of society; **unmittelbarer** ~ (Rechtsspr.) direct coercion; **das ist freiwilliger** ~ (iron.) it's voluntary but compulsory **2** (unwiderstehlicher Drang) irresistible urge; **aus einem** ~ **[heraus] handeln** act under a compulsion *or* on an irresistible impulse **3** (Beschränkung) constraint; compulsion; **sich** (*Dat.*) ~ **antun** *od.* **auferlegen** restrain oneself; exercise self-restraint; **tu dir keinen** ~ **an!** feel free!; don't force yourself! (iron.); **ohne [jeden]** ~: without any constraint; ‹*speak*› [quite] freely *or* openly **4** (Pflicht, Verpflichtung) obligation; **es besteht kein** ~ **zur Teilnahme/zum Kauf** there is no obligation to take part/to buy anything

zwängen /ˈt̮svɛŋən/

A *tr. V.* squeeze; **Bücher in seine Aktentasche** ~: cram books into one's briefcase

B *refl. V.* squeeze [oneself]

zwanghaft

A *Adj.* **1** compulsive; (als Ausdruck einer Zwangsneurose) obsessive; ~**e Vorstellung** obsession **2** ▸ **gezwungen B**

B *adv.* **1** compulsively **2** ▸ **gezwungen C**

zwanglos

A *Adj.* **1** informal; casual, free and easy ‹*behaviour*› **2** (unregelmäßig) haphazard ‹*arrangement*›; **in ~er Folge** at irregular intervals

B *adv.* **1** informally; freely; **es ging dort ziemlich** ~ **zu** things were pretty free and easy there **2** (unregelmäßig) haphazardly ‹*arranged*›

Zwanglosigkeit *die;* ~ **1** informality **2** (Unregelmäßigkeit) haphazard *or* casual manner

zwangs-, Zwangs-: ~**abgabe** *die* compulsory charge; ~**anleihe** *die* (Wirtsch.) compulsory loan; ~**arbeit** *die* forced labour; ~**arbeiter** *der,* ~**arbeiterin** *die* forced labourer; ~**ehe** *die* forced marriage (also fig.); ~**ernähren** *tr. V.* force-feed; ~**ernährung** *die* force-feeding *no indef. art.*; ~**evakuieren** *tr. V.* evacuate forcibly; ~**geld** *das* (Rechtsw.) compulsory fine; ~**handlung** *die* (Psych.) compulsive act; ~**herrschaft** *die* tyranny; despotism; ~**jacke** *die* straitjacket; ~**lage** *die* predicament; **jmdn. in eine ~lage bringen** put sb. in a predicament; ~**läufig** /-lɔyfɪç/ **A** *Adj.* inevitable; **B** *adv.* inevitably; ~**läufigkeit** *die;* ~~, ~~**en** inevitability; ~**maßnahme** *die* coercive measure; sanction; ~**mitgliedschaft** *die* compulsory membership; ~**mittel** *das* means of compulsion; ~**neurose** *die* (Psych.) compulsion *or* obsessive-compulsive neurosis; ~**pause** *die* compulsory break; ~**pfand** *das* compulsory deposit; ~**|räumen** *tr. V.* compulsorily clear; (mit Gewalt) forcibly clear; ~**räumung** *die* [enforced] eviction; ~**rekrutieren** *tr. V.* (Milit.) forcibly recruit; ~**sterilisieren** *tr. V.* compulsorily sterilize; subject to compulsory sterilization; ~**umsiedeln** *tr. V.* forcibly resettle ‹*people*›; ~**urlaub** *der* (ugs.) compulsory leave; **Arbeiter in den ~urlaub entlassen** *od.* **schicken** lay off workers temporarily; ~**vereinigen** *tr. V.* forcibly unite; ~**vereinigung** *die* enforced union; ~**verheiraten** *tr. V.* **jmdn. [an jmdn.] ~verheiraten** force sb. to marry [sb.]; ~**verpflichten** *tr. V.* conscript; ~**versetzen** *tr. V.* forcibly transfer; ~**versteigern** *tr. V., nur im Inf. u. Part.* (Rechtsw.) put up for compulsory auction; ~**versteigerung** *die* (Rechtsw.) compulsory auction; ~**verwalten** *tr. V.* (Rechtsw.) place in administration; ~**verwalter** *der,* ~**verwalterin** *die* (Rechtsw.) administrator; ~**verwaltung** *die* (Rechtsw.) administration; ~**vollstreckung** *die* (Rechtsw.) [compulsory] execution; ~**vorstellung** *die* (Psych.) obsession; ~**weise** **A** *Adv.* compulsorily; (mit Gewalt) by force; **B** *adj.* compulsory; enforced ‹*evacuation etc.*›; ~**weise Ernährung** force-feeding

zwanzig /ˈt̮svant̮sɪç/ *Kardinalz.* ▸ **S. 29,** ▸ **S. 729,** ▸ **S. 826** twenty; *s. auch* **achtzig**

Zwanzig *die;* ~, ~**en** twenty

Zwanzig·cent·stück *das* twenty-cent piece

zwanziger *indekl. Adj.* **die** ~ **Jahre** the twenties; *s. auch* **achtziger**

Zwanziger[1] *der;* ~**s,** ~ **1** (20-Jähriger) twenty-year-old; (Mann von 20 bis 29) man in his twenties **2** (Geldschein) twenty-euro/-franc/-dollar *etc.* note; *s. auch* **Achtziger**[1] **2, 3**

Zwanziger² *die;* ~, ~ (ugs.: Briefmarke) twenty-cent/centime *etc.* stamp

Zwanziger³ *Pl.* twenties; **die goldenen** *od.* **wilden** ~: the roaring twenties; **in den** ~**n sein** be in one's twenties

Zwanziger·jahre *Pl.* ▸❶ **S. 29**, ▸❶ **S. 165** twenties

Zwanzig·euro·schein *der* twenty-euro note

zwanzig·jährig *Adj.* (20 Jahre alt) twenty-year-old *attrib.*; (20 Jahre dauernd) twenty-year *attrib.*; *s. auch* **achtjährig**

zwanzigst... *Ordinalz.* ▸❶ **S. 165**, ▸❶ **S. 826** twentieth; *s. auch* **acht...**; **achtzigst...**

zwar /tsvaːɐ̯/ *Adv.* [1] admittedly; **ich war** ~ **dabei, habe aber trotzdem nichts gesehen** I was indeed *or* I 'was there, but I didn't see anything; **ich weiß es** ~ **nicht genau, aber ...** I'm not absolutely sure [I admit,] but ... [2] *in* **und** ~: to be precise; **er ist Zahnarzt, und** ~ **ein guter** he is a dentist, and a good one at that; **ich komme heute, und** ~ **um fünf Uhr** I'm coming today, at five o'clock [to be precise]; **verschwinde hier, und** ~ **sofort!** clear off (coll.), and I mean now!

Zweck /tsvɛk/ *der;* ~**[e]s**, ~**e** [1] purpose; **zu diesem** ~: for this purpose; **zum** ~ **der Fortbildung** for the purposes of further education; **was ist der** ~ **Ihrer Reise?** what is the purpose of your journey?; **seinen** ~ **erfüllen** serve its purpose; **Geld für einen guten/wohltätigen** ~: money for a good cause/for a charity; **das ist [nicht] der** ~ **der Übung** (ugs.) that is [not] the object *or* point of the exercise; *s. auch* **heiligen 1**; **Mittel 1** [2] (Sinn) point; **es hat keinen/wenig** ~ **[, das zu tun]** it's pointless *or* there is no point/there is little *or* not much point [in doing that]; **ohne [jeden] Sinn und** ~: completely pointless

zweck-, Zweck-: ~**bau** *der; Pl.* ~~**ten** functional building; ~**bestimmung** *die* function; ~**bindung** *die* (Finanzw.) earmarking [for a purpose]; ring-fencing; ~**bündnis** *das* alliance of convenience; ~**dienlich** [A] *Adj.* appropriate; helpful, relevant ‹*information etc.*›; **wäre es nicht** ~**dienlicher, wenn ...?** wouldn't it be more to the point if ...?; [B] *adv.* ~**dienlich verwendet werden** be used for an appropriate purpose; ~**ehe** *die* marriage of convenience (fig.); ~**entfremden** *tr. V.* use for another purpose; (durch Umbau) convert sth. to another use; (für den falschen ~) misuse; **etw. als etw.** ~**entfremden** use sth. as sth.; **die Gelder sind** ~**entfremdet [verwendet] worden** the money has been diverted from its proper use; ~**entfremdung** *die* use/conversion for another purpose; (von Geldern) diversion [from its proper use]; ~**entsprechend** [A] *Adj.* appropriate; suitable; [B] *adv.* appropriately; ~**frei** [A] *Adj.* ‹*research*› without any specific purpose; pure ‹*science*›; [B] *adv.* without any specific purpose; ~**gebunden** *Adj.* (Finanzw.) [to be used] for a specified purpose; ring-fenced; ~**gemeinschaft** *die* partnership of convenience; ~**gerichtet** [A] *Adj.* with a purpose in view *postpos.*; ~**gerichtet sein** have a purpose in view; [B] *adv.* with a purpose in view

zweckhaft
[A] *Adj.* purposeful; **nicht** ~ **sein** have no purpose
[B] *adv.* purposefully; with purpose

zweck-, Zweck-: ~**los** *Adj.* pointless; ~**losigkeit** *die;* ~~: pointlessness; ~**mäßig** [A] *Adj.* appropriate; expedient ‹*behaviour, action*›; functional ‹*building, fittings, furniture*›; [B] *adv.* appropriately ‹*arranged, clothed*›; ‹*act*› expediently; ‹*equip, furnish*› functionally; ~**mäßigkeit** *die* appropriateness; (einer Handlung) expediency; (eines Gebäudes) functionalism; ~**optimismus** *der* expedient optimism; ~**propaganda** *die* [calculated *or* targeted] propaganda

zwecks *Präp. mit Gen.* (Papierdt.) for the purpose of; ~ **Heirat** with a view to marriage

Zweck·verband *der* administration union; *association of local councils co-operating to fulfil a particular function*

zweck·voll *Adj.*; *adv.* ▸**zweckmäßig**

zweck·widrig
[A] *Adj.* inappropriate; improper ‹*use*›
[B] *adv.* inappropriately; ‹*use*› improperly

zwei /tsvai̯/ *Kardinalz.* ▸❶ **S. 29**, ▸❶ **S. 729**, ▸❶ **S. 826** two; **wir** ~: we two; the two of us; **sie gehen** ~ **und** ~ *od.* **zu** ~**en nebeneinander** they are walking in pairs; **sie waren/kamen zu** ~**en** there were two of them/two of them came; **für** ~ **essen/arbeiten** eat enough for two/do the work of two people; **dazu gehören immer noch** ~! (ugs.) it takes two [to do that]!; **das ist so sicher, wie** ~ **mal** ~ **vier ist** (ugs.) it's as sure as eggs is eggs (coll.); *s. auch* **acht¹**

Zwei *die;* ~, ~**en** [1] (Zahl) two [2] (Schulnote) B; **eine** ~ **schreiben/bekommen** get a B; **er hat die Prüfung mit** ~ **bestanden** he got a B in the examination; *s. auch* **Acht¹ 1, 4, 5, 7**

zwei-, Zwei- *s. auch* **acht-, Acht-**: ~**ad[e]rig** *Adj.* (Elektrot.) two-core; ~**atomig** *Adj.* (Chemie, Physik) diatomic; ~**bändig** *Adj.* two-volume; ~**beiner** *der;* ~~**s**, ~~, ~**beinerin** *die;* ~~, ~~**nen** (scherzh.) human [being]; ~**bett·zimmer** *das* twin-bedded room; ~**cent·stück** *das* two-cent piece; ~**deutig** /-dɔy̯tɪç/ [A] *Adj.* [1] ambiguous; equivocal ‹*smile*›; [2] (fig.: schlüpfrig) suggestive ‹*remark, joke*›; ‹*novel, film, etc.*› full of double entendre; [B] *adv.* [1] ambiguously; ‹*smile*› equivocally; [2] (fig.: schlüpfrig) suggestively; ~**deutigkeit** *die;* ~~, ~~**en** [1] ambiguity; (fig.: Schlüpfrigkeit) suggestiveness; [2] (zweideutige Äußerung) ambiguity; (schlüpfrige Äußerung) double entendre; ~**dimensional** /-dimɛnzi̯onaːl/ [A] *Adj.* two-dimensional; [B] *adv.* two-dimensionally; in two dimensions; ~**drittel·mehrheit** *die* two-thirds majority; ~**ein·halb** *Bruchz.* ▸❶ **S. 826** two and a half

Zweier *der;* ~**s**, ~ [1] (ugs. Schulnote) **einen** ~ **haben/schreiben** get a B [2] (ugs.: Münze) two-cent piece [3] (Ruderboot) pair; **im** ~ **ohne Steuermann** in the coxless pairs [4] (Golf) twosome; (Wettkampf) single; twosome

zweierlei *Gattungsz.; indekl.* [1] *attr.* two sorts *or* kinds of; two different ‹*sizes, kinds, etc.*›; odd ‹*socks, gloves*›; **mit** ~ **Maß messen** use double standards; **auf** ~ **Art** in two different ways [2] *subst.* two [different] things; **es ist** ~, **ob man es sagt oder [ob man es] auch tut** it is one thing to say it and another [thing] to do it; **Ordnung und Ordnung sind** ~: there is order and order

Zweier·team *das* team of two

zwei-, Zwei-: ~**euro·stück** *das* two-euro piece; ~**fach** *Vervielfältigungsz.* double; (~mal, um den Faktor 2) twice; **die** ~**fache Menge/Länge** double *or* twice the amount/length; **in** ~**facher Vergrößerung/Verkleinerung** enlarged to twice its size/reduced to half-size; **der** ~**fache Vater** the father of two; **in** ~**facher Hinsicht** in two respects; ~**fach gesichert** double-locked; ~**fach gegen die Vorschriften verstoßen** infringe the regulations in two ways; **etw.** ~**fach vergrößern/verkleinern** enlarge sth. to twice its size/reduce sth. to half-size; *s. auch* **achtfach**; ~**fache** *das; adj. Dekl.* **das** ~**fache kosten** cost twice as much; cost double [the amount]; **ein Foto um das** ~**fache vergrößern** enlarge a photo to twice its size; *s. auch* **Achtfache**; ~**familien·haus** *das* two-family house; duplex (esp. Amer.); ~**farbig** [A] *Adj.* two-coloured; two-tone ‹*scarf, paintwork, etc.*›; [B] *adv.* in two colours

Zweifel /ˈtsvai̯fl̩/ *der;* ~**s**, ~: doubt (**an** + *Dat.* about); **in** ~ **geraten**, ~ **bekommen** become doubtful; **ich habe keinen** ~ **daran/[gewisse]** ~ **daran, dass ...** I am in no doubt that/in some doubt whether ...; **ich habe da so meine** ~ *od.* **bin [mir] darüber im** ~: I have my doubts about that; **ich bin mir noch im** ~, **ob ...** I am still uncertain whether ...; **etw. in** ~ **ziehen** question sth.; **[für jmdn.] außer** ~ **stehen** be beyond doubt [as far as sb. is concerned]; **über jeden** *od.* **allen** ~ **erhaben sein** be beyond any shadow of a doubt; **er ließ keinen** ~ **daran, dass ...** he left no doubt [in anyone's mind] that ...; **jmdn. [über etw.** (*Akk.*)**] [nicht] im** ~ **lassen** leave sb. in [no] doubt [about sth.]; **daran** *od.* **darüber besteht kein** ~, **daran gibt es keinen** ~: there is no doubt about it; **mir kommen** ~: I am beginning to have my doubts; **kein** ~, **...** there is/was no doubt about it, ...; **ohne** ~: without [any] doubt; **im** ~: in case of doubt; if in doubt

zweifelhaft *Adj.* [1] doubtful [2] (fragwürdig) dubious; (suspekt) suspicious

zweifel·los *Adv.* undoubtedly; without [any] doubt

zweifeln *itr. V.* doubt; **wenn man zweifelt** if one is in doubt *or* has any doubts; **an jmdm./etw.** ~: doubt sb./sth.; have doubts about sb./sth.; **man hat lange daran gezweifelt** it has long been in doubt *or* uncertain; ~ **daran, dass ...**, ~, **ob ...** doubt whether ...; **er hat nie daran gezweifelt, dass ...** he never doubted that ...; **daran ist nicht zu** ~: there can be no doubt about it

zweifels-, Zweifels-: ~**fall** *der* case of doubt; doubtful *or* problematic case; **im** ~**fall[e]** in case of doubt; if in doubt; ~**frei** [A] *Adj.* definite; ~**frei sein** be beyond doubt; [B] *adv.* beyond [any] doubt; ~**ohne** *Adv.* undoubtedly; without doubt

zwei·flammig *Adj.* two-burner ‹*cooker*›

Zweifler *der;* ~**s**, ~, **Zweiflerin** *die;* ~, ~**nen** doubter

zweiflerisch
[A] *Adj.* doubtful; (skeptisch) sceptical
[B] *adv.* doubtfully; (skeptisch) sceptically

zweiflüg[e]lig *Adj.* two-winged

Zwei·fronten·krieg *der* war on two fronts; **einen** ~ **führen** (fig.) fight on two fronts

Zweig /tsvai̯k/ *der;* ~**[e]s**, ~**e** [1] [small] branch; (meist ohne Blätter) twig; **auf keinen grünen** ~ **kommen** (ugs.) not get anywhere; (finanziell) not become well off [2] (einer Familie) branch [3] (Unterabteilung, Branche) (einer Wissenschaft usw.) branch; (eines Gymnasiums usw.) side

Zweig·betrieb *der* subsidiary; (Filiale) branch

zwei-, Zwei-: ~**geschlechtig** *Adj.* (Biol.) hermaphroditic; bisexual; ~**geschossig** *Adj., adv.* ▸~**stöckig**; ~**gespann** *das* [1] pair of horses/oxen; [2] (Wagen) carriage and pair; [3] (fig.) duo; two-man band; ~**gestrichen** *Adj.* (Musik) two-line ‹*octave*›; **das** ~**gestrichene A** the A two above middle C; **das** ~**gestrichene C** the C above middle C; ~**geteilt** *Adj.* divided; divided in two *postpos.*

Zweig·geschäft *das* branch

zwei·gleisig
[A] *Adj.* two-track; double-track; (fig.) two-way ‹*therapy, treatment*›
[B] *adv.* [1] ‹*run*› on two tracks; **eine Strecke** ~ **ausbauen** add a second track [to a section] [2] (fig.) ~ **fahren** follow a dual-track policy

Zweig-: ~**stelle** *die* branch [office]; ~**werk** *das* subsidiary plant

zwei·händig /-hɛndɪç/
[A] *Adj.* two-handed
[B] *adv.* ‹*hold on, catch ball, etc.*› with both hands; ‹*type, play*› with two hands

Zweiheit *die;* ~ (geh.) duality

zwei-, Zwei-: ~**höck[e]rig** *Adj.* two-humped; ~**hundert** *Kardinalz.* ▸❶ **S. 826** two hundred; ~**jährig** *Adj.* [1] (~ Jahre alt) two-year-old *attrib.*; (~ Jahre dauernd) two-year *attrib.*; [2] (Bot.) biennial ‹*plant*›; *s. auch* **achtjährig**; ~**jährlich** [A] *Adj.* two-yearly *attrib.*; biennial; *s. auch* **achtjährlich**; [B] *adv.* every two years; biennially; ~**kammer·system** *das* (Politik) bicameral system; ~**kampf** *der* [1] single combat; (Duell) duel; **jmdn. im** ~**kampf töten** kill sb. in single combat/a duel; [2] (Sport) man-to-man tussle; duel; ~**keim·blättrig** *Adj.* (Bot.) dicotyledonous

Zweiklassen-: ~**gesellschaft** *die* two-class society; ~**medizin** *die* two-tier health service

zwei-, Zwei-: ~**köpfig** *Adj.* [1] two-headed; [2] (aus ~ Personen bestehend) two-person *attrib.*;

Z

of two [people] *postpos.*; **~kreis·bremse** *die* (Kfz-W.) dual-circuit braking system; **~mal** *Adv.* twice; **das wird er sich** (*Dat.*) **~mal überlegen** he'll think twice about that; *s. auch* **achtmal**; **~malig** *Adj.* **nach ~maligem Versuch** after trying twice; after two tries; *s. auch* **achtmalig**; **~monats·schrift** *die* bimonthly [periodical]; **~motorig** *Adj.* twin-engined; **~parteien·system** *das* two-party system; **~phasen·strom** *der* (Physik, Elektrot.) two-phase current; **~phasig** *Adj.* (Physik, Elektrot.) two-phase; **~-plus-vier-Gespräche** *Pl.* (Politik) two plus four talks; **~polig** *Adj.* (Physik, Elektrot.) double-pole; two-core ‹*cable*›; two-pin ‹*plug, socket*›; **~rad** *das* two-wheeler; **~räd[e]rig** *Adj.* two-wheeled; **~raum·wohnung** *die* ▸**Zweizimmerwohnung**; **~reiher** *der* double-breasted suit/coat/jacket; **~reihig** A *Adj.* 1 in two rows *postpos.*; double ‹*chain*›; 2 (mit ~ Knopfreihen) double-breasted ‹*suit, coat*›; B *adv.* in two rows

Zweisamkeit *die*; ~, **~en** togetherness; partnership

zwei-, Zwei-: **~schläfrig** *Adj.* double ‹*bed*›; **~schneidig** *Adj.* double-edged; **ein ~schneidiges Schwert** (fig.) a double-edged sword; **~seitig** A *Adj.* 1 double-sided; two-sided; 2 (~ Seiten lang) two page ‹*letter, article, etc.*›; 3 (bilateral) bilateral ‹*treaty, agreement, etc.*›; B *adv.* 1 on two *or* both sides; **~seitig tragbar** reversible ‹*anorak, coat*›; 2 (bilateral) bilaterally; **~silbig** A *Adj.* two-syllable *attrib.*; B *adv.* ‹*pronounced*› as two syllables; **~sitzer** *der*; **~~s**, **~~**: two-seater; **~sitzig** *Adj.* two-seater *attrib.*; **~spaltig** A *Adj.* two-column; *s. auch* **achtspaltig**; B *adv.* ‹*printed, set*› in two columns; **~spänner** *der*; **~~s**, **~~**: carriage and pair; **~spännig** A *Adj.* drawn by two horses *postpos.*; B *adv.* **~spännig fahren** drive [in] a carriage and pair; **~sprachig** A *Adj.* bilingual; ‹*sign*› in two languages; B *adv.* bilingually; ‹*written*› in two languages; ‹*published*› in a bilingual edition; **~sprachigkeit** *die*; **~~**: bilingualism; **~spurig** A *Adj.* 1 two-lane ‹*road, motorway*›; (Eisenb.) double-track ‹*railway*›; 2 two-track ‹*vehicle*›; 3 two- *or* twin-track ‹*recording*›; B *adv.* 1 in two lanes; **~spurig ausbauen** make ‹*road*› dual carriage-way; dual ‹*road*›; widen ‹*railway*› to two tracks; 2 ‹*record*› on two tracks; **~stellig** *Adj.* two-figure *attrib.* ‹*number, sum*›; **~stellige Stimmenverluste** loss of more than 10% of votes; **~stimmig** A *Adj.* two-part *attrib.*; B *adv.* in two parts; **~stöckig** A *Adj.* two-storey *attrib.*; **~stöckig sein** have two storeys *or* floors; **ein ~stöckiges Bett** a bunk bed; B *adv.* ‹*build*› two storeys high; **~strahlig** *Adj.* twin-engined ‹*jet aircraft*›; **~stündig** *Adj.* two-hour *attrib.*; (Schulw.) double period *attrib.* ‹*test, examination*›; **nach ~stündiger Wartezeit** after waiting for two hours; **~stündlich** A *Adj.* two-hourly *attrib.*; B *adv.* every two hours

zweit /ˈt͜svait/ *in* **wir waren zu ~**: there were two of us; **sie sind zu ~ verreist** the two of them went away together; **sie schlafen je zu ~ in den Zimmern** they sleep two to a room; **zu ~ lebt man billiger als allein** two can live cheaper than one; *s. auch* **acht**[2]

zweit... *Ordinalz.* ▸ⓘ **S. 165**, ▸ⓘ **S. 826** 1 second; **jeder ~e Einwohner** every other *or* second inhabitant; **jeder Zweite** every other one 2 (zweitbest...) second; **~er Klasse fahren/liegen** travel second-class/be in a second-class hospital bed 3 (ander..., weiter...) second; other; **ich habe noch einen ~en** I have a second one; (als Ersatz) I have a spare; **wie kein Zweiter** as no one else can; like nobody else; **ein ~er Al Capone** (fig.) a second Al Capone; *s. auch* **erst...**

zwei-, Zwei-: **~tägig** *Adj.* (2 Tage alt) two-day-old *attrib.*; (2 Tage dauernd) two-day *attrib.*; *s. auch* **achttägig**; **~täglich** A *Adj.* **in ~täglichem Wechsel** on a two-day rota; B *adv.* every two days; **~takter** *der*; **~~s**, **~~** (Kfz-W.) 1 (Motor) two-stroke engine; 2 (ugs.: Fahrzeug) two-stroke; **~takt·motor** *der* (Kfz-W.) two-stroke engine

zweit·ältest ... *Adj.* second oldest; **der/die Zweitälteste** the second oldest

zwei·tausend *Kardinalz.* ▸ⓘ **S. 165**, ▸ⓘ **S. 826** two thousand

Zwei·tausender *der*: *mountain more than two thousand metres high*

Zweit·ausfertigung *die* [second] copy; duplicate

zweit·best... *Adj.* second best; **der/die Zweitbeste** the second best

Zwei·teiler *der*; **~s**, **~** 1 (Badeanzug, Kleid) two-piece; (Kostüm, Anzug) two-piece suit 2 (Ferns.) two-part film/programme

zwei·teilig *Adj.* two-piece ‹*suit, bathing suit, suite, etc.*›; two-part ‹*film, programme*›; two-volume ‹*dictionary, novel*›; *s. auch* **achtteilig**

Zwei·teilung *die* division (**in** + *Akk.* into)

***zweite·mal, *zweiten·mal** ▸**Mal**[1]

zweitens *Adv.* secondly; in the second place

Zweite[r]-Klasse-Abteil *das* second-class compartment

zweit-, Zweit-: **~frisur** *die* wig; **~größt...** *Adj.* second biggest *or* largest; **~häufigst...** *Adj.* second most frequent; **~höchst...** *Adj.* second highest; **~job** *der* second job; **~klassig** A *Adj.* second-rate; **als ~klassig behandelt werden** be treated as a second-class citizen/as second-class citizens; B *adv.* **die Mannschaft hat nur ~klassig gespielt** the team's performance was second-rate; **~klassigkeit** *die*; **~~** (Sport, abwertend) second-rate status; **~klässler**, ***~kläßler** *der*; **~~s**, **~~**, **~klässlerin**, ***~kläßlerin** *die*; **~~**, **~~nen** (südd., schweiz.) pupil in second class of primary school; second-year pupil; **~längst...** *Adj.* second longest; **~liga** *die* (bes. Sport) second division (also fig.): **~liga·spiel** *das* (Sport) second-division game; **~ligist** *der*; **~~en**, **~~en**, **~ligistin** *die*; **~~**, **~~nen** (Sport) second-division club; **~mächtigst...** *Adj.* second most powerful; **~platzierte** *der*/*die*; *adj. Dekl.* (Sport) runner-up; **~rangig** /-raŋıç/ *Adj.* 1 (nicht vordringlich) of secondary importance *postpos.*; **von ~rangiger Bedeutung sein** be of secondary importance; 2 (~klassig) second-rate; **~schlechtest...** *Adj.* second worst; **~schlüssel** *der* second *or* spare key; **~schnellst...** *Adj.* second fastest; **~stärkst...** *Adj.* second strongest; **~stimme** *die* second vote; **~studium** *das* second course of study

zwei·türig *Adj.* two-door ‹*car*›; ‹*room*› with two doors

zweit-, Zweit-: **~verwertung** *die* recycling; reuse; **~wagen** *der* second car; **~wichtigst...** *Adj.* second most important; **~wohnsitz** *der* second residence (form.); **~wohnung** *die* second home

zwei-, Zwei-: **~viertel·takt** /-ˈfırtl̩-/ *der* (Musik) two-four time; **im ~vierteltakt** in two-four time; **~wertig** *Adj.* 1 (Chemie) bivalent; 2 (Sprachw.) two-place *attrib.*; **~wöchentlich** A *Adj.* fortnightly; B *adv.* every fortnight *or* two weeks; *s. auch* **achtwöchentlich**; **~wöchig** *Adj.* (zwei Wochen alt) two-week-old *attrib.*; (2 Wochen dauernd) two-week *attrib.*; fortnight's *attrib.*; **~zeiler** *der*; **~~s**, **~~**: couplet; **~zeilig** *Adj.* two-line *attrib.*; (Maschinenschreiben) **in ~zeiligem Abstand** double-spaced; **~zeiliger Leerraum** double-spacing; **~zimmer·wohnung** /-ˈ----/ *die* two-room flat (esp. Brit.) *or* (esp. Amer.) apartment; **~zügig** *Adj.* ‹*school*› with two main subject areas

Zwerch·fell /ˈt͜svɛrç-/ *das* ▸ⓘ **S. 435** (Anat.) diaphragm

zwerchfell·erschütternd
A *Adj.* side-splitting; screamingly funny
B *adv.* side-splittingly, screamingly ‹*funny*›

Zwerg /t͜svɛrk/ *der*; **~[e]s**, **~e** 1 dwarf 2 (Garten~) gnome 3 (abwertend: unbedeutender Mensch) [little] squirt (coll.); wretch

zwergenhaft *Adj.* dwarfish

Zwerg·huhn *das* bantam

Zwergin *die*; **~**, **~nen** dwarf

zwerg-, Zwerg-: **~pudel** *der* miniature *or* toy poodle; **~schule** *die* single-class school; **~staat** *der* miniature state; **~wuchs** *der* (Biol.) dwarfism *no art.*; stunted growth *no art.*; **~wüchsig** /-vyːksıç/ *Adj.* (Biol.) dwarf-like ‹*race, people*›; dwarf, miniature ‹*tree, plant*›

Zwetsche /ˈt͜svɛt͜ʃə/ *die*; **~**, **~n** 1 damson plum 2 (Baum) damson plum [tree]

Zwetschen-: **~baum** *der* damson plum tree; **~kern** *der* plum stone; **~kuchen** *der* plum flan; **~mus** *das* plum purée; **~schnaps** *der*, **~wasser** *das*; *Pl.* **~wässer** plum brandy

Zwetschge /ˈt͜svɛt͜ʃgə/ *die*; **~**, **~n** (bes. südd., schweiz.) ▸**Zwetsche**

Zwetschken·knödel /ˈt͜svɛt͜ʃkn̩-/ *der* (Kochk.) plum dumpling

Zwickel /ˈt͜svıkl̩/ *der*; **~s**, **~** 1 (Schneiderei) gusset 2 (Archit.) spandrel; (einer Kuppel) pendentive 3 (salopp) ▸**Zweimarkstück**

zwicken /ˈt͜svıkn̩/
A *tr., auch itr. V.* (bes. südd., österr.) 1 pinch; **jmdm.** *od.* **jmdn. in den Arm ~**: pinch sb.'s arm 2 (plagen) **jmdn. ~**: give sb. twinges; **es zwickte und zwackte ihn überall** he had twinges *or* little aches and pains all over
B *itr. V.* ‹*trousers, skirt*› pinch

Zwicker *der*; **~s**, **~**: pince-nez

Zwick·mühle *die* 1 double mill 2 (fig.: Dilemma) dilemma; **in der ~ sitzen** *od.* **sein** *od.* **stecken** be in a dilemma

Zwie·back /ˈt͜sviːbak/ *der*; **~[e]s**, **~e** *od.* **Zwiebäcke** /ˈt͜sviːbɛkə/ rusk; (unzählbar) rusks *pl.*

Zwiebel /ˈt͜sviːbl̩/ *die*; **~**, **~n** 1 onion; (Blumen~) bulb 2 (ugs. scherzh.: Taschenuhr) pocket watch; turnip (sl.) 3 (ugs. scherzh.: Haarknoten) bun

Zwiebel-: **~kuchen** *der* (Kochk.) onion pie; **~muster** *das* onion pattern

zwiebeln *tr. V.* (ugs.) keep on at ‹*person*›; give ‹*person*› a hard time

Zwiebel-: **~ring** *der* onion ring; **~schale** *die* onion skin; **~suppe** *die* onion soup; **~turm** *der* onion tower

zwie-, Zwie-: **~fach** *Adj.*; *adv.* (veralt.) ▸**zweifach**; **~fältig** *Adj.*; *adv.* (veralt.) ▸**zweifach**; **~gespräch** *das* (geh.) dialogue; **~laut** *der* (Sprachw.) diphthong; **~licht** *das* 1 (Dämmerlicht) twilight; 2 (Mischung von Dämmer- und Kunstlicht) half-light (*that is unpleasant for the eye*); 3 **ins ~licht geraten** (fig.) become suspect; ‹*person*› come under suspicion; **~lichtig** *Adj.* shady; dubious; **~spalt** *der*; **~~[e]s**, **~~e** *od.* **~spälte** /-ʃpɛltə/ 1 ([innerer] Widerspruch) [inner] conflict; **in einen ~spalt geraten** get into a state of conflict; 2 (Kluft) rift; split; **~spältig** /-ʃpɛltıç/ *Adj.* conflicting ‹*mood, feelings*›; discordant ‹*impression*›; (widersprüchlich) contradictory ‹*nature, attitude, person, etc.*›; **~spältigkeit** *die*; **~~**: conflicting *or* contradictory nature; **~sprache** *die* (geh.) dialogue; **mit jmdm./etw. ~sprache halten** commune with sb./sth.; **~tracht** *die* (geh.) discord; **~tracht säen** sow the seeds of discord

Zwille /ˈt͜svılə/ *die*; **~**, **~n** (nordd.) 1 ▸**Astgabel** 2 (Schleuder) catapult

Zwilling /ˈt͜svılıŋ/ *der*; **~s**, **~e** 1 twin 2 *Pl.* (Astrol.) Gemini; the Twins; **er/sie ist [ein] ~**: he/she is a Gemini

Zwillings-: **~bruder** *der* twin brother; **~geburt** *die* twin birth; **~paar** *das* pair of twins; **~schwester** *die* twin sister; **~turm** *der* twin tower

Zwing·burg *die* fortress, stronghold (*for the subjugation of the population*)

zwingen /ˈt͜svıŋən/
A *unr. tr. V.* 1 force; **jmdn. zu etw. ~, jmdn. [dazu] ~, etw. zu tun** force *or* compel sb. to do sth.; make sb. do sth.; **jmdn. zu einem Geständnis ~**: force sb. into a confession *or* to make a confession; **sich zu etw. gezwungen sehen** find oneself forced *or* compelled to do sth.; **man kann ihn nicht dazu ~**: he can't be forced *or* made to do it 2 (geh.) **jmdn.**

Z

in/auf *usw.* **etw.** (*Akk.*) **~:** force sb. into/on to *etc.* sth.

B *unr. refl. V.* force oneself; **sich [dazu] ~, etw. zu tun** force oneself to do sth.; **sich zum Schreiben/Essen ~:** force oneself to write/make oneself eat; *s. auch* **gezwungen B, C**

zwingend *Adj.* compelling ‹*reason, logic*›; conclusive ‹*proof, argument*›; imperative, absolute ‹*necessity*›

Zwinger *der;* **~s, ~** [1] (Hunde~) kennel; (ganze Anlage, auch Zucht) kennels *pl.* [2] (Gehege) compound; enclosure; (für Bären) bear pit

zwinkern /ˈtsvɪŋkɐn/ *itr. V.* **[mit den Augen] ~:** blink; (als Zeichen) wink; **jmdn. ~d ansehen** wink at sb.; look at sb. with a wink

zwirbeln /ˈtsvɪrbl̩n/ *tr. V.* twirl; twist

Zwirn /tsvɪrn/ *der;* **~[e]s, ~e** [strong] thread *or* yarn

Zwirns·faden *der* [strong] thread

zwischen /ˈtsvɪʃn̩/ *Präp. mit Dat./Akk.* [1] (räumlich, zeitlich, fig.) between [2] (räumlich: unter, inmitten) among[st]

zwischen-, Zwischen-: ~akt *der* interlude; **~akt·musik** *die* incidental music; (einzelnes Stück) entr'acte; **~applaus** *der* spontaneous applause (during a performance); **~aufenthalt** *der* stopover; **~bemerkung** *die* interjection; **~bericht** *der* interim report; **~bescheid** *der* provisional notification; (Entscheidung) interim decision; **~bilanz** *die* (Wirtsch.) interim balance; (fig.) provisional appraisal; **~blutung** *die* (Med.) intermenstrual *or* mid-cyclical bleeding; **~buch·handel** *der* wholesale book trade; **~deck** *das* (Schiffbau) [1] 'tween-deck; [2] (Raum) 'tween-decks *sing.*; **im ~deck** 'tween-decks; **~decke** *die* (Bauw.) false ceiling; **~ding** *das* ▸**Mittelding**; **~drin** /-ˈ-/ *Adv.* (ugs.) ▸**~durch 1**; **~durch** /-ˈ-/ *Adv.* [1] (zeitlich) between times; (~ zwei Zeitpunkten) in between; (von Zeit zu Zeit) from time to time; (in der ~zeit) in the mean time; **das mache ich mal irgendwann ~durch** I'll fit that in whenever I have time; **iss nicht so viel ~durch** don't eat so much between meals; [2] (räumlich) here and there; **~eis·zeit** *die* interglacial period; **~ergebnis** *das* interim result; (einer Untersuchung) interim findings *pl.*; (Sport) latest score; **~examen** *das* ▸**~prüfung**; **~fall** *der* incident; **es kam zu schweren/blutigen ~fällen** there were serious/violent incidents; **~finanzierung** *die* (Bankw.) bridging finance; **~frage** *die* question; **jmdm. eine ~frage stellen** interrupt sb. to ask a question; **~gas** *das* (Kfz-W.) **~gas geben** *od.* **mit ~gas schalten** double-declutch; **~gericht** *das* (Kochk.) entrée (Brit.); **~geschoss**, ***~geschoß** *das* mezzanine; **~größe** *die* intermediate size; (bei Schuhen) half-size; **~handel** *der* (Wirtsch.) intermediate trade; (Großhandel) wholesale trade; (~händler) middleman; **~händler** *der* (Wirtsch.) middleman; (fig.) go-between; **~hirn** *das* ▸ⓘ **S. 435** (Anat.) diencephalon; **~hoch** *das* (Met.) ridge of high pressure; **~kiefer[knochen]** *der* ▸ⓘ **S. 435** (Anat.) intermaxillary; premaxilla; **~kriegs·zeit** *die* period between the wars; inter-war years *pl.*; **~lager** *das* temporary *or* interim storage facility; **~lagern** *tr. V.* store temporarily; **~lagerung** *die* interim storage; temporary storage; **~|landen** *itr. V.*; *mit sein* **in X ~landen** land in X on the way; **~landung** *die* stopover; **~lauf** *der* (Sport) [intermediate] heat; **~lösung** *die* interim solution; **~mahlzeit** *die* snack [between meals]; **~menschlich A** *Adj.* interpersonal ‹*relations*›; ‹*contacts*› between people; **B** *adv.* on a personal level; **~musik** *die* musical interlude; **~produkt** *das* (bes. Wirtsch.) intermediate product; **~prüfung** *die* intermediate examination; **~raum** *der* space; gap; (Lücke) gap; **eine Zeile ~raum lassen** leave a space of one line; (Maschinenschreiben) double-space; **~reich** *das* (geh.) twilight world; **~ruf** *der* interruption; **viele ~rufe** a great deal of heckling *sing.*; **~rufer** *der*, **~ruferin** *die* heckler; **~runde** *die* (Sport) intermediate round; **~satz** *der* (Sprachw.) parenthetic clause; parenthesis; **~|schalten** *tr. V.* (Elektrot.) insert ‹*resistance, amplifier, etc.*› in a circuit; **~schritt** *der* intermediate step; **~spiel** *das* (Musik-, Theaterstück) intermezzo; (in einem Solokonzert/Gesangsstück) linking passage; (fig.) interlude; **~spurt** *der* (Sport) spurt; burst [of speed]; **~staatlich** *Adj.* international; **~stadium** *das* intermediate stage; **~stand** *der* interim position; (~stadium) intermediate stage; **~station** *die* [1] stop; stopping place; [2] (~aufenthalt) stop; **dort machten wir einen Tag ~station** we stopped there for a day; **~stecker** *der* (Elektrot.) adaptor; **~stopp** *der* ▸**Zwischenaufenthalt**; **~stück** *das* connecting *or* middle piece; (Verbindungsstück) connector; (Adapter) adaptor; **~stufe** *die* intermediate stage; **~summe** *die* subtotal; **~text** *der* linking text; **~ton** *der; Pl.* **~töne** shade; nuance; (fig.) nuance; **~tür** *die* connecting door; **~wand** *die* dividing wall; partition; **~wirt** *der* (Biol., Med.) intermediate host; **~zeit** *die* [1] interim; (länger) intervening period; **in der ~zeit** in the mean time; [2] (Sport) split time; **~zeitlich** *Adv.* (bes. Amtsspr.) in the mean time; **~zeugnis** *das* (Schulw.) intermediate report; (Arbeitswelt) [intermediate] performance appraisal; **~ziel** *das* intermediate goal

Zwist /tsvɪst/ *der;* **~[e]s, ~e** (geh.) strife *no indef. art.*; (Fehde) feud; dispute; **in** *od.* **im ~ leben** live in a state of strife; **den alten ~ begraben** bury the hatchet

Zwistigkeit *die;* **~, ~en** (geh.) dispute

zwitschern /ˈtsvɪtʃɐn/
A *itr.* (*auch tr.*) *V.* chirp
B *tr. V.* **in einen ~** (salopp) have a drink

Zwitter /ˈtsvɪtɐ/ *der;* **~s, ~** (Biol., Med.) hermaphrodite; **ein ~ aus A und B** (fig.) a cross between A and B

Zwitter·stellung *die* ambiguous position

zwittrig *Adj.* (Biol., Med.) hermaphroditic

zwo /tsvoː/ *Kardinalz.* ▸ⓘ **S. 826** (ugs.; bes. zur Verdeutlichung) ▸**zwei**

zwölf /tsvœlf/ *Kardinalz.* ▸ⓘ **S. 29**, ▸ⓘ **S. 729**, ▸ⓘ **S. 826** twelve; **~ Uhr mittags/nachts** [twelve o'clock] midday/midnight; **es ist fünf [Minuten] vor ~** (fig.) we are on the brink; *s. auch* **acht**[1]

zwölf-, Zwölf- twelve-; *s. auch* **acht-, Acht-**

Zwölf *die;* **~, ~en** twelve; *s. auch* **Acht**[1] **1, 5, 7**

Zwölf-: ~eck *das* (Geom.) dodecagon; **~ender** *der;* **~~s, ~~:** [1] (Jägerspr.) royal [stag]; [2] (scherzh. veralt.) *soldier with twelve years service*

Zwölfer *der;* **~s, ~:** twelve; *s. auch* **Achter 3, 4**

zwölferlei *Gattungsz.; indekl.* [1] *attr.* twelve sorts *or* kinds of; twelve different ‹*sorts, sizes, etc.*› [2] *subst.* twelve [different] things

zwölf-, Zwölf-: ~fach *Vervielfältigungsz.* twelvefold; **die ~fache Menge** twelve times the quantity; *s. auch* **achtfach**; **~fache** *das; adj. Dekl.;* **das ~fache** twelve times as much; **um ein ~faches** *od.* **um das ~fache** twelve times; *s. auch* **Achtfache**; **~finger·darm** *der* ▸ⓘ **S. 435** (Anat.) duodenum; **~fingerdarm·geschwür** *das* ▸ⓘ **S. 439** (Med.) duodenal ulcer; **~hundert** *Kardinalz.* ▸ⓘ **S. 826** one thousand two hundred; twelve hundred; **~jährig** *Adj.* (12 Jahre alt) twelve-year-old *attrib.*; twelve years old *pred.*; (12 Jahre dauernd) twelve-year *attrib.*; *s. auch* **achtjährig**; **~kampf** *der* (Turnen) twelve-exercise event; **~mal** *Adv.* twelve times; *s. auch* **achtmal**; **~meilen·zone** /-ˈ----/ *die* twelve-mile zone

zwölft /tsvœlft/ *in* **wir waren zu ~:** there were twelve of us; *s. auch* **acht**[2]

zwölft... *Ordinalz.* ▸ⓘ **S. 165**, ▸ⓘ **S. 826** twelfth; *s. auch* **acht...**

zwölf·tausend *Kardinalz.* twelve thousand

zwölf·teilig *Adj.* twelve-piece ‹*set*›; twelve-part ‹*serial etc.*›; *s. auch* **achtteilig**

zwölftel *Bruchz.* ▸ⓘ **S. 826** twelfth; *s. auch* **achtel**

Zwölftel *das* (*schweiz. meist der*) **~s, ~** ▸ⓘ **S. 826** twelfth

***zwölfte·mal, *zwölften·mal** ▸**Mal**[1]

zwölftens *Adv.* twelfthly

Zwölf·ton·musik *die* twelve-tone music

zwot... /tsvoːt.../ *Ordinalz.* (ugs.; bes. bei Datumsangaben) ▸**zweit...**

zwotens *Adv.* (ugs.) secondly

Zyan /tsy̆aːn/ *das;* **~s** (Chemie) cyanogen

Zyanid /tsy̆aˈniːt/ *das;* **~s, ~e** (Chemie) cyanide

Zyan·kali *das;* **~s** (Chemie) potassium cyanide

Zyklen ▸**Zyklus**

zyklisch /ˈtsyːklɪʃ/
A *Adj.* cyclic[al]
B *adv.* cyclically; as a cycle

Zykloide /tsykloˈiːdə/ *die;* **~, ~n** (Math.) cycloid

Zyklon /tsyˈkloːn/ *der;* **~s, ~e** (Met.) cyclone

Zyklop /tsyˈkloːp/ *der;* **~en, ~en** (griech. Myth.) Cyclops

Zyklopen·mauer *die* (Archäol., Bauw.) Cyclopean wall

zyklothym /tsykloˈtyːm/ *Adj.* (Psych., Med.) cyclothymic

Zyklotron /ˈtsyːklotroːn/ *das;* **~s, ~s** *od.* **~e** (Kernphysik) cyclotron

Zyklus /ˈtsyːklʊs/ *der;* **~, Zyklen** (auch Math.) cycle

Zylinder /tsiˈlɪndɐ/ *der;* **~s, ~** [1] (Geom., Technik) cylinder; (einer Lampe) chimney [2] (Hut) top hat

Zylinder-: ~hut *der* top hat; **~kopf** *der* cylinder head

zylindrisch
A *Adj.* cylindrical
B *adv.* cylindrically

Zyniker *der;* **~s, ~, Zynikerin** *die;* **~, ~nen** cynic

zynisch /ˈtsyːnɪʃ/
A *Adj.* cynical
B *adv.* cynically

Zynismus *der;* **~, Zynismen** [1] cynicism [2] (Äußerung) cynical remark

Zypern /ˈtsyːpɐn/ (*das*); **~s** Cyprus

Zyprer /ˈtsyːprɐ/ *der;* **~s, ~, Zyprerin** *die;* **~, ~nen** Cypriot

Zypresse /tsyˈprɛsə/ *die;* **~, ~n** cypress

Zypriot /tsypriˈoːt/ *der;* **~en, ~en, Zypriotin** *die;* **~, ~nen** ▸ⓘ **S. 520** Cypriot

zypriotisch, zyprisch *Adj.* ▸ⓘ **S. 520** Cypriot

Zyste /ˈtsʏstə/ *die;* **~, ~n** ▸ⓘ **S. 439** (Med.) cyst

Zytologie /tsytoloˈgiː/ *die;* **~** (Biol.) cytology *no art.*

z. Z., z. Zt. *Abk.* **= zur Zeit**

Z

Correspondence
Musterbriefe

Holidays and travel plans

Holiday postcard

- Beginnings (informal): *Lieber* here because it's a man; if it's a woman, use e.g. *Liebe Elke*.

  To two people, repeat *Liebe(r)*: *Lieber Hans, liebe Elke*.

  To a family: *Liebe Schmidts, Liebe Familie Schmidt*, or just *Liebe Leute*.

  - On postcards – as on most personal letters – German speakers do not put their address at the top, but just the name of the place and the date.

- Address: Note that the title (*Herrn, Frau*) stands on the line above the name. *Herr* always has an n on the end in addresses.

  When writing to a couple:
  Herrn und Frau
  Hans Schmidt und Elke Schmidt
  or:
  Herrn Hans Schmidt
  Frau Elke Schmidt

  If they have different surnames:
  Herrn und Frau
  Hans Schmidt und Elke Morris

  The house number comes after the street name.

  The postcode comes before the place, and if you're writing from outside the country put a *D-* for Germany, *A-* for Austria or *CH-* for Switzerland in front of it.

Heidelberg, den 6. 8. 2005

Lieber Hans!

Einen schönen Gruß aus Alt-Heidelberg! Wir sind erst zwei Tage hier, aber schon sehr angetan von der Stadt und ihrer Umgebung, trotz der vielen Touristen. Allerdings ist es ziemlich schwül. Wir waren gestern Abend in einem Konzert im Schlosshof, eine wunderbare Stimmung! Und dann die herrliche Aussicht auf Altstadt und Neckar von der Terrasse. Morgen machen wir eine Bootsfahrt, dann geht's am Donnerstag wieder nach Hause. Hoffentlich ist deine Mutter inzwischen wieder gesund.

Bis bald

Max und Sophie

Herrn
Hans Matthäus
Brucknerstr. 26
91052 Erlangen

- Endings (informal): *Herzlich* or *Herzlichst, Herzliche Grüße*; more affectionately: *Alles Liebe; Bis bald* = See you soon.

- If more than one person signs the card or letter, *dein(e)* etc. has to be repeated:

  Alles Liebe
  deine Oma und dein Opa
  eure Steffi und euer Rolf
  dein Peter, dein Hans

Ferien und Reisepläne

Postkarte aus dem Urlaub

- Anrede: sehr einfach auf Postkarten, immer *Dear* und der Vorname, der im englischen Sprachraum viel häufiger verwendet wird. Die Anrede kann auch entfallen.

- Meist keine Ortsangabe, wenn der Ort aus dem Inhalt oder dem Bild auf der Postkarte klar hervorgeht. Datum – in den USA verwendet man die Reihenfolge Monat, Tag, Jahr, wenn das Datum mit Ziffern angegeben ist – in diesem Fall also 8.6.2005.

- Adresse: Die Anrede (*Mr, Mrs, Miss, Ms*) steht direkt vor dem Namen auf der gleichen Zeile.

  Das Haus hat oft einen Namen anstelle einer (oder zusätzlich zur) Hausnummer, die übrigens vor dem Straßennamen steht.

  Es folgen (in GB) Ortschaft, meist auch Grafschaft, dann Postleitzahl (*postcode*), alles jeweils auf einer eigenen Zeile; in den USA Ortschaft und Postleitzahl (*zipcode*), mit dem auf zwei Buchstaben abgekürzten Namen des Staates davor:

  John Splaine Jr.
1067 Blackwall Avenue
Studio City
CA 91604
USA

6.8.2005

Dear John,

Greetings from old Heidelberg! Got here **1** a couple of days ago, but already in love with the place (in spite of all the tourists). It's pretty sultry though. Last night we went to a concert in the castle courtyard, very atmospheric. And a terrific view of the river and the old town from the terrace. Tomorrow we're taking a boat trip, and then on Thursday we head for home. Hope **1** your mother's fully recovered by now.

See you soon,

Mark and Juliet

Mr J. Roberts
The Willows
49 North Terrace
Kings Barton
Nottinghamshire
NG8 4LQ
England

- Schlussformel:
  All the best, Best wishes, oder einfach *Yours*; auch *Love* (*from*), wenn man den Adressaten näher steht.
  Etwas formeller: *With best wishes.*

1 Telegrammstil: die Angabe der Person entfällt auf Postkarten oft.

Enquiry to a tourist office

Verkehrsverein Heidelberg e.V.
Friedrich-Ebert-Anlage 2
69117 Heidelberg

Silvia Sommer
Tannenweg 23
48149 Münster

24. April 2005

Hotels und Pensionen in Heidelberg

Sehr geehrte Damen und Herren,

würden Sie mir bitte freundlicherweise eine Liste der Hotels und Pensionen (der mittleren Kategorie) am Ort zusenden?

Ich wäre Ihnen dankbar, wenn Sie mir auch Informationen über Busfahrten zu den Sehenswürdigkeiten der Umgebung in der zweiten Augusthälfte schicken könnten.

Mit freundlichen Grüßen

Silvia Sommer

- A simple business-style letter. The recipient's address is on the left and the sender's name and address on the right, with the date below.

  Note that the sender's full address is also given on the back of the envelope (or on the front, top left).
- This is the standard formula for starting a business letter addressed to a firm or organization, and not to a particular person.
- *Mit freundlichen Grüßen* is the standard ending for a formal or business letter; another possibility is *Mit besten Grüßen*.

Asking for a theatre programme listing

GEORG DORN
PEINER LANDSTRAẞE 78
31135 HILDESHEIM

12. Mai 2005

Hotel Stetter
z. H. Frau Schmidt
Gartenstr. 32
26122 Oldenburg

Sehr geehrte Frau Schmidt,

meine Frau und ich werden in der Woche vom 19. bis 25. Juli in Ihrem Hause zu Gast sein (Reservierung vom 27. 4.) und möchten Sie um eine kleine Gefälligkeit bitten: Würden Sie so freundlich sein und uns einen Spielplan des Staatstheaters sowie Informationen über Reservierungsmöglichkeiten besorgen? Sollten Sie dazu nicht in der Lage sein, so teilen Sie uns doch bitte mit, an welche Stelle wir uns wenden können.

Wir freuen uns sehr auf unseren Aufenthalt bei Ihnen.

Mit freundlichen Grüßen

Georg Dorn

- The sender's name and address can be either on the left with the date on the right, or on the right with the date underneath. A letterhead is usually in the middle with the date on the right.
- If you have been in contact with a particular person or a person's name has been recommended to you, follow the organization's name with "for the attention of ...": *z. H.* (= *zu Händen*) *Frau Schmidt* or *z. H. Herrn Schmidt*. You then start the letter with: *Sehr geehrte Frau Schmidt* or *Sehr geehrter Herr Schmidt*.
- In German all women are addressed as *Frau* (the equivalent of both Mrs and Ms) in letters.

Anfrage an ein Fremdenverkehrsbüro

Am Grün 28
A-9026 Klagenfurt
Austria

4th May 2005

The Manager
Regional Tourist Office
3 Virgin Road
Canterbury
CT1 3AA

Dear Sir or Madam,

Please send me a list of hotels and guest houses in Canterbury in the medium price range.

I would also like details of coach trips to local sights in the second half of August.

Yours sincerely

Bruno Angermeyer

- Oben auf dem Brief steht die Adresse, aber nicht der Name des Absenders.
- Diese Anrede verwendet man, wenn der Name des Adressaten nicht bekannt ist. Es wäre hier auch möglich, *The Manager* wegzulassen und das Tourist Office anzuschreiben; in diesem Fall könnte der Brief auch mit *Dear Sirs* anfangen.
- *Yours sincerely* ist der übliche Briefschluss für Geschäftsbriefe sowie für persönliche Briefe an Leute, die man nicht sehr gut kennt. *Yours faithfully* ist etwas altmodisch und wird nur noch für sehr formelle Geschäftsbriefe verwendet, vor allem in Rechtssachen.

Bitte um Zusendung eines Theaterspielplans

3 CORK ROAD
DUBLIN 55
IRELAND
TEL: (1) 3432255

23/5/05

Ms A. Smith
Plaza Hotel
Old Bromwood Lane
Victoria
London

Dear Ms Smith,

My wife and I have booked a room in your hotel for the week beginning 9th July 2005. We would be very grateful if you could send us the theatre listings for that week, along with some information on how to book tickets in advance. If you are unable to provide this information, could you please advise us on where we could get it from? We are looking forward to our visit very much.

Yours sincerely,

Ryan Friel

Mr RYAN FRIEL

- Im Englischen werden Frauen in Briefen meist mit *Ms* statt *Miss* oder *Mrs* angeredet.
- Am Schluss des Briefes kann der Name des Absenders/der Absenderin mit dem Titel (*Mr, Mrs, Ms* etc.) angegeben werden, um klar zu machen, wie er/sie angeredet werden möchte.

Booking a hotel room

Hotel Goldener Pflug
Ortsstraße 7
69235 Steinbach

Tobias Schwarz
Gartenstr. 19
76530 Baden-Baden

16. Juli 2005

Sehr geehrte Damen und Herren,

Ich wurde durch die Broschüre „Hotels und Pensionen im Naturpark Odenwald (Ausgabe 2005)" auf Ihr Hotel aufmerksam.

Ich möchte für mich und meine Frau für die Zeit vom 2. bis 11. August (neun Nächte) ein ruhiges Doppelzimmer mit Dusche **1** reservieren, sowie ein Einzelzimmer für unseren Sohn.

Falls Sie für diese Zeit etwas Passendes haben, informieren Sie mich doch bitte über den Preis und darüber, ob Sie eine Anzahlung wünschen.

Mit freundlichen Grüßen

Tobias Schwarz

1 Alternative: *mit Bad.*

Booking a campsite

Camilla Stumpf
Saalgasse 10
60311 Frankfurt

Camping am See
Frau Bettina Sattler
Auweg 6-10
87654 Waldenkirchen

Frankfurt, den 16.04.2005

Sehr geehrte Frau Sattler,

Ihr Campingplatz wurde mir von Herrn Stephan Seidel empfohlen, der schon mehrmals bei Ihnen war. **1** *Ich würde nun gerne vom 18. bis 25. Juli mit zwei Freunden eine Woche bei Ihnen verbringen. Könnten Sie uns bitte einen Zeltplatz* **2** *möglichst in unmittelbarer Nähe des Sees* **3** *reservieren?*

Würden Sie mir freundlicherweise mitteilen, ob Sie meine Reservierung annehmen können und ob Sie eine Anzahlung wünschen?

Außerdem wäre ich Ihnen dankbar für eine kurze Wegbeschreibung von der Autobahn.

Mit vielem Dank im Voraus und freundlichen Grüßen

Camilla Stumpf

- For a business letter to a particular person, use *Sehr geehrte(r)* and the name. (If this letter were to a man, it would start *Sehr geehrter Herr Sattler.*)

1 Or if you have found the campsite in a guide, say e.g.: *Ich habe Ihre Anschrift dem ADAC-Campingführer 2004 entnommen.*

2 Or if you have a caravan: *einen Stellplatz für einen Wohnwagen.*

3 Alternatives: *in schattiger/geschützter Lage.*

Hotelzimmerreservierung

The Manager
Torbay Hotel
Dawlish
Devon
EX37 2LR

35 Prince Edward Road
Oxford OX7 3AA

Tel. 01865 322435
23rd April 2005

Dear Sir or Madam,

I saw your hotel listed in the Inns of Devon guide for last year, and wish to reserve a double (or twin-bedded) room with shower **1** in a quiet position from August 2nd -11th (nine nights), also a single room for our son.

If you have anything suitable for this period please let me know the price and whether you require a deposit.

Yours sincerely

Charles Fairhurst

1 Alternativen: *with bath, with en suite bathroom.*

Campingplatzreservierung

22 Daniel Avenue
Caldwood
Leeds LS8 7RR
Tel. 01132 998767

25th April 2005

Mr Joseph Vale
Lakeside Park
Rydal
Cumbria
LA22 9RZ

Dear Mr Vale

Your campsite was recommended to me by James Dallas, who knows it from several visits. **1**
I and two friends would like to come for a week from July 18th to 25th. Could you please reserve us a pitch for one tent, **2** *preferably close to the shore.* **3**

Please confirm the booking and let me know if you require a deposit. Would you also be good enough to send me instructions on how to reach you from the motorway.

Yours sincerely

Frances Good

■ Die Adresse (aber nicht der Name) des Absenders steht oben in der Mitte (oder auch rechts). Die Angabe der Telefonnummer weist darauf hin, dass man telefonisch benachrichtigt werden kann oder möchte.

1 Oder falls Sie den Campingplatz einem Führer entnommen haben, etwa: *I found your site in the Tourist Board's list/the Good Camper's Guide* etc.

2 Oder falls Sie einen Wohnwagen haben: *a caravan pitch.*

3 Andere Möglichkeiten: *in a shady/sheltered spot.*

Cancelling a reservation

Herrn
Hans Knauer
Gasthaus Sonnenblick
Hauptstr. 6
D-94066 Bad Füssing
Germany

Aberdeen, den 2.6.2005

Sehr geehrter Herr Knauer,

leider muss ich meine/unsere Reservierung für die Woche vom 14. bis 20. August **1** rückgängig machen. Wegen unvorhergesehener Umstände **2** muss ich/müssen wir auf meinen/unseren Urlaub verzichten.

Es tut mir aufrichtig leid, **3** dass ich so spät abbestellen muss, und ich hoffe, dass Sie deswegen keine Unannehmlichkeiten haben.

Mit freundlichen Grüßen

Robert McDonald

1 Or: *für die Zeit vom 14. bis 20. August* etc.

2 Or more precisely: *Durch den überraschenden Tod meines Vaters/die Krankheit meines Mannes* etc.

3 Or: *Ich bedaure sehr* etc.

Cancelling a hotel booking

Tobias Schwarz
Gartenstr. 19
76530 Baden-Baden

16. Juli 2005

Hotel Deutscher Hof
Hauptstr. 102
68293 Mannheim

Stornierung meiner Zimmerreservierung
(bestätigt mit Schreiben vom 7.7.05)

■ The subject line gives a reference to any previous correspondence. This reference usually includes the last letter, its date, and possibly a reference number.

Sehr geehrte Damen und Herren,

zu meinem Bedauern sehe ich mich genötigt, meine Reservierung für die Zeit vom 2. bis 18. August rückgängig zu machen.

Würden Sie so freundlich sein, den von mir angezahlten Betrag (100,00 EUR) auf mein Ihnen bekanntes Konto zurückzuüberweisen?

Mit bestem Dank im Voraus und freundlichen Grüßen

■ This is a polite way of ending a letter in which the recipient has been asked to do something – usually an administrative task or a favour.

If you need written confirmation:
Für eine schriftliche Bestätigung wäre ich Ihnen dankbar.
or *Schon jetzt vielen Dank für Ihre schriftliche Bestätigung.*

Ihr

Tobias Schwarz

Stornierung einer Reservierung

Mrs J. Warrington
Downlands
Steyning
West Sussex
BN44 6LZ

Wernerstr. 17
49835 Wietmarschen
Germany

July 20th 2005

Dear Mrs Warrington,

Unfortunately I have to cancel my/our reservation for the week of August 14th. 1 Due to unforeseen circumstances 2 I/we have had to abandon my/our holiday plans.

I very much regret having to cancel 3 [at such a late stage] and hope it does not cause you undue inconvenience.

Yours sincerely

Elke Nordrup

1 Oder: *for the period from August 14th to 20th.*

2 Oder genauer: *Owing to my father's sudden death/my husband's illness* etc.

3 Oder : *I am really* or *genuinely sorry that I have to cancel* etc.

Stornierung einer Hotelzimmerreservierung

Message for: The Manager, The Black Bear Hotel
Address: 14 Valley Road, Dorchester
Fax Number: (01305) 367492
From: Ulrike Fischer
Date: 16 March 2005
Number of pages including this page: 1

Sonnenblickallee 61
80339 München
Germany

Dear Sir or Madam,

I am afraid that I must cancel my booking for August 2nd-18th. I would be very grateful if you could confirm the cancellation and return my £50.00 deposit at your earliest convenience.

■ Eine Stornierung per Fax oder E-Mail sollte man sich brieflich bestätigen lassen.

Yours faithfully,

Ulrike Fischer

Personal and social correspondence

Invitation

Hamm, den 22.4.2005

Liebe Jennie,

wäre es möglich, dass du **1** in den Sommerferien zu uns kommst? Katrin und Niko würden sich riesig freuen (ich und mein Mann natürlich auch). Wir planen eine Reise zum Bodensee Ende Juli/Anfang August, du **1** könntest gerne mitfahren. Es ist wirklich sehr schön dort unten.
Wir werden wahrscheinlich zelten – hoffentlich hast du **1** nichts dagegen!

Schreib bald, ob das für dich **1** in Frage kommt.

Herzliche Grüße

Monika Pfortner

■ Beginning: if you put a comma after the name on the first line (which is usual), the letter proper should start with a small letter.

1 *du, dich, dein* etc.: although many people still write these with a capital in letters, this is not necessary. But the formal *Sie, Ihnen, Ihr* must always have a capital.

Irene Brinkmann Stefan Hopf

Wir heiraten am Samstag, den 23. April 2005 um 14 Uhr in der Pfarrkirche Landsberg.

Goethestraße 12
Landsberg

Ulrichsweg 4
Altötting

■ Invitations to parties are usually by word of mouth, while for weddings, announcements are usually sent out.

Invitation (formal)

Dr. Heinrich und Frau Gertrud Brinkmann geben die bevorstehende Vermählung ihrer Tochter Irene mit Stefan Hopf bekannt.

Die Trauung findet am Samstag, dem 23. April 2005, um 14 Uhr in der Pfarrkirche Landsberg statt.

Sehr geehrte Frau Gustav,
sehr geehrter Herr Gustav,

am Donnerstag, den 5. Mai 2005 heiratet unsere Tochter Christa. Sie haben ihre Vermählungsanzeige sicher bereits erhalten. Wir als Brauteltern möchten Sie nun ganz persönlich zur Feier einladen, denn Sie haben viele Jahre als Freunde des Hauses den Lebensweg unserer Tochter begleitet. Bitte machen Sie uns die Freude und nehmen Sie an ihrer Hochzeit teil.

Ursula und Dieter Zimmermann

u.A.w.g.

The bride's parents often send separate invitations to close friends and relatives, inviting them personally to the wedding. ■

When *u.A.w.g.* (= *um Antwort wird gebeten*) or a telephone number is added, the sender expects a reply. ■

Private Korrespondenz

Einladung

35 Winchester Drive
Stoke Gifford
Bristol
BS34 8PD

May 10th 2005

Dear Klaus,

Is there any chance of your coming to stay with us in the summer holidays? Roy and Debbie would be delighted if you could (as well as David and me, of course). We hope to go to North Wales at the end of July/beginning of August, and you'd be very welcome to come too. It's really beautiful up there. We'll probably take tents – I hope that's OK by you.

Let me know as soon as possible if you can manage it.

All best wishes

Rachel Hemmings

- Die Absenderadresse befindet sich oben auf dem Brief selbst, entweder rechts oder in der Mitte, darunter das Datum.
- Das Datum im Englischen hat viele Formen: *May 10, 10 May, May 10th, 10th May* sind alle möglich und gleichermaßen richtig. In den USA verwendet man die Reihenfolge Monat, Tag, Jahr, wenn das Datum in Ziffern angegeben wird – in diesem Fall also 05/10/2005.

Please come to Jennifer's 40th birthday party from 8 o'clock on 23rd September at 12 Parkhurst Gardens, SW4.

Buffet and disco RSVP 020 8323 1279

- Mit der Angabe der Telefonnummer oder dem Hinweis *RSVP* (= *répondez s'il vous plaît*) signalisiert man, dass eine Zu- oder Absage erwartet wird.

Einladung (förmlich)

Mr and Mrs Peter Thompson
request the pleasure of your company
at the marriage of their daughter

Hannah Louise
to
Steven David Warner

at St. Mary's Church, Little Bourton
on Saturday 23rd July 2005 at 2 p.m.
and afterwards at the
Golden Cross Hotel, Billing

R.S.V.P. *23 Santers Lane*
Little Bourton
Northampton
NN6 1AZ

- Bei einer Hochzeit wird gewöhnlich zur Trauungszeremonie und zu einem anschließenden Empfang eingeladen. Freunde können auch eine „Evening Invitation" erhalten, die sich nur auf eine Party nach dem Empfang bezieht.

Replying to an invitation

Edinburgh, den 2.5.2005

Liebe Frau Pfortner,

recht herzlichen Dank für Ihre **1** liebe Einladung. Da ich noch keine festen Pläne für die Sommerferien habe, möchte ich sie sehr gerne annehmen. Allerdings darf ich nicht mehr als vier bis fünf Tage weg sein, da es meiner Mutter nicht sehr gut geht. Sie **1** müssen mir sagen, was ich mitbringen soll (außer Edinburgh Rock!). Ist es sehr warm am Bodensee? Kann man im See schwimmen?

Natürlich habe ich nichts gegen Zelten. Auch hier in Schottland bei Wind und Regen macht es mir Spaß!

Ich freue mich auf ein baldiges Wiedersehen.

Herzliche Grüße **2**

Jennie Stewart

1 Since this is a letter from a younger person writing to the mother of a friend, she uses the formal *Sie* form and possessive *Ihr* (always with capitals), and writes to her as *Frau Pfortner*. On the other hand it was quite natural for Frau Pfortner to use the *du* form to her.

2 This informal ending is normally used when you know the person you are writing to but the relationship is not very close. You could also finish the letter with:

Mit den besten Grüßen
Mit freundlichen Grüßen
Herzlichst
Es grüßt Sie

or, more affectionately:

Alles Liebe
Bis bald
Mit bestem Dank
Dein(e)

Accepting a wedding invitation

Sehr geehrte Frau Heiner,
sehr geehrter Herr Heiner,

vielen Dank für die Einladung zur Hochzeit Ihrer Tochter.

Es freut uns sehr, dass Sie uns zu den Freunden Ihrer Familie zählen, und wir werden selbstverständlich gerne kommen.

Mit den besten Grüßen

Lotte und Franz Dernbach

Useful phrases for accepting/refusing an invitation

- Herzlichen Dank für die Einladung [zum Abendessen/zu deiner Party]. Ich werde bestimmt kommen und freue mich schon sehr darauf./ Leider kann ich nicht kommen, weil …
- (***Formal:***) Ich bedanke mich für Ihre freundliche Einladung [zum Abendessen/zum Empfang/zur Hochzeit Ihrer Tochter], die ich gerne annehme/ die ich leider nicht annehmen kann[, da ich schon anderweitig verpflichtet bin].

Antwort auf eine Einladung (informell)

Mozartstraße 5
32756 Detmold
Germany

2 May 2005

Dear Mrs Hemmings,

Many thanks for your letter and kind invitation. Since I don't have anything fixed yet for the summer holidays, I'd be delighted to come. However I mustn't be away for more than four or five days since my mother hasn't been very well.

You must let me know what I should bring. How warm is it in North Wales? Can one swim in the sea? Camping is fine as far as I'm concerned, we take our tent everywhere.

Looking forward to seeing you again soon,

Yours **1**

Klaus

1 Andere Möglichkeiten, einen Brief an Bekannte zu schließen, sind:

Best wishes
All the best
Take care

oder, bei Verwandten und guten Freunden:

Love (from)
Lots of love

Dank für eine Einladung zur Hochzeit

Schillerstraße
35041 Marburg
Germany

22/8/05

Dear Joe,

Thanks for your letter. I was delighted to hear that you two are getting married, and I'm sure you'll be very happy together. I will do my best to come to the wedding, it'd be such a shame to miss it.

I think your plans for a small wedding sound just the thing, and I feel honoured to be invited. I wonder if you have decided where you are going for your honeymoon yet? I look forward to seeing you both soon. Beate sends her congratulations.

Best wishes,

Erik

Formulierungshilfen für Zusagen/Absagen

Many thanks for the invitation [to dinner/to your party]. I'd love to come and I'm really looking forward to it/Unfortunately I can't come because… *(coll.)*

Antwort auf eine Einladung (förmlich)

Greenacres
Westway
Balsall Common
West Midlands
CV7 8RR

Richard Willis has great pleasure in accepting Mr and Mrs Peter Thompson's kind invitation to the marriage of their daughter Hannah Louise to Steven Warner at St. Mary's Church, Little Bourton, on Saturday 23rd July.

- Man wiederholt die Details von der Einladung, etwas vereinfacht.
- Im Falle einer Absage ist es oft höflicher, einen Brief zu schreiben.

Christmas and New Year Wishes

On a card:

Frohe Weihnachten und viel Glück im neuen Jahr

A bit more formal: Ein gesegnetes Weihnachtsfest und die besten Wünsche zum neuen Jahr

A bit less formal: Fröhliche Weihnachten und einen guten Rutsch

In a letter:

■ On most personal letters German speakers don't put their address at the top, but just the name of the place and the date

Würzburg, den 20.12.2005

Liebe Karin, lieber Ferdinand,

euch und euren Kindern wünschen wir von Herzen frohe Weihnachten und ein glückliches neues Jahr. Wir hoffen, es geht euch allen gut, und dass wir uns bald mal wieder sehen werden. Es kommt uns so vor, als hätten wir uns eine Ewigkeit nicht gesehen.

Das vergangene Jahr war für uns sehr ereignisreich. Thomas hatte im Sommer einen Unfall mit dem Fahrrad und brach sich den Arm und das Schlüsselbein. Sabine hat das Abitur gerade noch bestanden und ist jetzt an der Uni in Erlangen, studiert Sport. Der arme Michael ist im Oktober arbeitslos geworden und sucht immer noch nach einer Stelle.

Ihr müsst unbedingt vorbeikommen, wenn ihr das nächste Mal in der Gegend seid. Ruft doch einfach ein paar Tage vorher an, damit wir etwas ausmachen können.

Mit herzlichen Grüßen **1**

eure Gabi und Michael

1 Alternative endings:

Es grüßen euch
Mit den besten Grüßen
Mit den besten Wünschen für euch und eure Kinder

Greetings and congratulations

For a birthday
Herzliche Grüße/Herzlichen Glückwunsch/Alles Gute zum Geburtstag

For Easter
Frohe *od.* Fröhliche Ostern/Ein frohes Osterfest

For an exam
Viel Erfolg bei der bevorstehenden Prüfung/Alles Gute zum Abitur

For a house move
Viel Glück im neuen Heim

For an illness
Gute Besserung!

For a wedding
Dem glücklichen Paar viel Freude am Hochzeitstag [und viel Glück im künftigen gemeinsamen Leben]

Congratulations
Herzlichen Glückwunsch/Herzliche Glückwünsche/Ich gratuliere/Wir gratulieren [herzlichst] zum neuen Baby/zur bestandenen Prüfung.

Ich habe mich sehr über deinen Erfolg bei der Prüfung gefreut. Das hast du gut gemacht!

Ich habe/Wir haben mit großer Freude von deiner/eurer bevorstehenden Vermählung gehört. Herzlichen Glückwunsch und alles Gute für die Zukunft!

Weihnachts- und Neujahrsgrüße

Auf einer Karte:

[Best wishes for a] Happy Christmas and a Prosperous New Year

All best wishes for Christmas and the New Year

Wishing you every happiness this Christmas and in the New Year

■ Auch bei privaten Briefen gibt der Absender seine Adresse oben rechts (oder oben in der Mitte) auf dem Brief an. Darunter steht das Datum.

In einem Brief:

44 Louis Gardens
London NW6 4GM

December 20th 2005

Dear Peter and Claire,

First of all, a very happy Christmas and all the best for the New Year to you and the children. **1** We hope you're all well **2** and that we'll see you again soon. It seems ages since we last met up.

We've had a very eventful year. Last summer Gavin came off his bike and broke his arm and collarbone. Kathy scraped through her A levels and is now at Sussex doing European Studies. Poor Tony was made redundant in October and is still looking for a job.

Do come and see us next time you are over this way. Just give us a ring a couple of days before so we can fix something.

All best wishes

Tony and Ann

1 Oder (vor allem, wenn die Kinder älter sind): *to you and the family*.

2 Informeller: *flourishing*.

Glückwünsche und Gratulationen

Zum Geburtstag
Many happy returns [of the day]
Happy Birthday
All good *or* best wishes for your birthday

Zu Ostern
[Best wishes for a] Happy Easter

Zu einer Prüfung
Every success in your [forthcoming] exams
All good wishes for your A-levels/GCSEs

Zum Umzug
Every happiness in your new home

Bei einem Krankheitsfall
Get well soon!
All best wishes for a speedy recovery

Zu einer Hochzeit
Every good wish to the happy couple/to the bride and bridegroom on their wedding day [and in the years to come]

Gratulation
Congratulations/Many congratulations/ I /We congratulate you [most sincerely] on the [arrival of the] new baby/on passing the exam.

I was delighted to hear of your success in the exam. Well done!

I/We have just heard the wonderful news of your forthcoming marriage and offer you my/our sincerest *or* heartiest congratulations and best wishes for your future happiness.

The world of work

Replying to a job advertisement

David Baker
67 Whiteley Avenue
St George
Bristol
BS5 6TW

Softwarehaus WSO GmbH
Personalabteilung
Kanalstr. 75
D-75757 Pforzheim

Bristol, den 26.2.2005

Ihre Stellenanzeige im Tagblatt vom 23.2.2005

Sehr geehrte Damen und Herren, **1**

ich interessiere mich für die von Ihnen im Tagblatt vom 23. Februar ausgeschriebene Stelle eines Computergrafikers und würde mich freuen, wenn Sie mir nähere Informationen zuschicken könnten. **2**

Derzeit bin ich bei der Firma Wondersoft Ltd in Bristol tätig, aber mein Vertrag läuft schon Ende des Monats aus, **3** und ich möchte gerne in Deutschland arbeiten. Wie Sie meinem Lebenslauf entnehmen können, verfüge ich über ausgezeichnete Sprachkenntnisse sowie die geforderten Qualifikationen und einschlägige Berufserfahrung.

Zu einem Vorstellungsgespräch stehe ich jederzeit ab dem 6. März zur Verfügung. Sie können mich ab diesem Datum unter der folgenden Adresse in Deutschland erreichen:

bei Gerber
Rudolfstr. 22
81925 München
Tel. (089) 460 99 507

Ich freue mich darauf, von Ihnen zu hören. **4**

Mit freundlichen Grüßen

David Baker

Anlage: Lebenslauf **5**

1 Correct if the letter is addressed to the personnel department, but if it is addressed to the personnel manager (*An den Personalleiter, …*) the letter begins: *Sehr geehrter Herr XY* or *Sehr geehrte Frau XY*.

2 Or if you have enough details and want to apply for the job right away: *und möchte mich um diese Stellung bewerben.* Or: *hiermit bewerbe ich mich auf Ihre Anzeige im Tagblatt vom 23.02.2005 für die Stelle als Computergrafiker.*

3 Or if you are unemployed: *Derzeit bin ich arbeitslos, …*

4 Or: *Ihre Antwort erwarte ich mit Interesse.*

5 Make sure that you enclose all the certificates mentioned in the advertisement.

Die Berufswelt

Bewerbung auf eine Stellenanzeige hin

Humboldtweg 16
60247 Frankfurt a. M.
Germany
Tel. (069) 724 689

13th February 2005

The Personnel Manager **1**
Patterson Software plc
Milton Estate
Bath BA6 8YZ

Dear Sir or Madam, **2**

I am interested in the post of programmer advertised in the Guardian of 12th February and would be grateful if you could send me further particulars. **3**

I am currently working for the Sempo Corporation in Frankfurt, but my contract finishes at the end of the month, and I would like **4** to come and work in the UK. As you can see from my CV (enclosed), I have an excellent command of English and also the required qualifications and experience.

I will be available for interview any time after 6th March, from which date I can be contacted at the following address in the UK:

c/o Lewis
51 Dexter Road
London N7 6BW
Tel. 0207 607 5512

I look forward to hearing from you. **5**

Yours sincerely

Rita Steinmüller

Encl. **6**

1 Den Brief so addressieren, wenn in der Anzeige kein Name vorkommt; aber wenn es z.B. heißt *Reply to Angela Summers*, dann *Ms Angela Summers …*

2 Wenn der Name bekannt ist, dann *Dear Ms Summers, Dear Mr Wright etc.*

3 Oder falls Sie schon genügend Informationen haben und sich gleich bewerben wollen: *and would like to apply for this position.*

4 Oder falls Sie arbeitslos sind: *I am currently unemployed and would like …*

5 Oder: *Thanking you in anticipation.*

6 Prüfen Sie, ob Sie alle Unterlagen beigelegt haben, die das Unternehmen in seiner Anzeige verlangt.

Curriculum Vitae (CV) or (*Amer.*) Résumé

Lebenslauf

David Baker
67 Whiteley Avenue
St George
Bristol
BS5 6TW
Großbritannien

Tel. +44 (0)117 945 3421

geboren am 30.06.1973 in London, ledig [1]

Ausbildung

1990 GCSE in 7 Fächern (ungefähr = mittlere Reife), John Radcliffe School, Croydon

1992 A Levels in Mathematik, Höherer Mathematik, Informatik, Deutsch (ungefähr = Abitur), Croydon Sixth Form College

1993 Teilzeitarbeit in München, Abendkurse an der VHS

1993-97 University of Aston, Birmingham, BSc in Informatik

Berufstätigkeit

08/97 - 08/2000 Traineeausbildung, anschließend Softwareentwickler bei IBM

seit 09/2000 Programmierer bei Wondersoft plc, Bristol

Entwicklung von Programmen für die Industrie; Schwerpunkt: Grafiksoftware

Besondere Kenntnisse

Fremdsprachen: Deutsch (fließend), Französisch (gut)

[1] Or: *verheiratet (mit einem Kind/zwei Kindern etc.); geschieden (mit einem Kind/zwei Kindern etc.)*

When applying for a job in Germany, photocopies of certificates and diplomas for qualifications gained must accompany the application.

Attach a photograph of yourself to the top right-hand corner of the application form or your CV. Make sure that your name and address are on the back of the photograph.

Depending on your age, qualifications, experience and interests, you could add further sections to your CV:

Jetzige Position	*Direktionssekretärin*
Fortbildung	*1997-1998: Abendlehrgang* *Abschluss: gepr. Sekretärin*

Lebenslauf

CURRICULUM VITAE [1]

Name:	Rita Steinmüller
Address:	Humboldtweg 16 60247 Frankfurt a. M. Germany
Telephone:	+49 (0)69 724 689
Nationality:	German
Date of Birth:	11/3/1979
Marital status:	Single [2]

Education:

1997-2001	Degree Course in Information Technology at Stuttgart University
1990-1997	Theodor-Heuss-Gymnasium, Eichborn Abitur examination (approx. A Level) in Mathematics, Physics, Economics and English

Employment:

2001-present	Program development engineer with Sempo-Informatik, Frankfurt, specializing in computer graphics
2000-2001	Trainee programmer with Oregon Germany, Rüsselsheim

Further skills:

Languages:	German (mother tongue), English (fluent spoken and written), French (good)
Interests:	Travel (many trips to the UK), chess, tennis
References: [3]	Mr J Byers-Ellis Manager, Retail Outlets Division Delicatessen International Riverside House 22 Charles Street, London EC7X 4JJ [As my present employer is not yet aware of this application, please inform me before contacting him] Dr Margaret McIntosh Director of Studies University of Essex Business School Colchester CR3 5SA

[1] Oder (Amer.): *RÉSUMÉ*

[2] Oder: *Married (with one/two/three* etc. *children), Divorced (with one/two/three* etc. *children)*

[3] Wenn man sich in Großbritannien oder den USA um eine Stelle bewirbt, legt man keine Zeugnisse bei, sondern gibt frühere Arbeitgeber, Vorgesetzte oder Tutoren als Referenz an.

▸872

Accepting a job

Oliver Zahn
Hansastr. 43
26723 Emden

31. März 2005

Werbeagentur
Fissler & Partner
Großkopfstr. 44
30303 Hannover

Sehr geehrter Herr Fissler,

ich freue mich sehr, dass Sie sich dafür entschieden haben, die freie Stelle in Ihrem Team durch mich neu zu besetzen. Ich nehme Ihr Angebot hiermit gerne an.

Ich kann, wie ich Ihnen bereits bei unserem Gespräch sagte, am ersten August beginnen, früher allerdings leider wirklich nicht.

Würden Sie mir bitte noch mitteilen, wann genau ich mich am ersten August bei Ihnen einfinden soll?

Ich freue mich sehr auf die Arbeit bei Ihnen.

Mit freundlichen Grüßen

Ihr

Oliver Zahn

Refusing a job

Christoph Höfer
Weidengrund 7
58515 Lüdenscheid

5. November 2005

Frau Ursula Jaspers
Zahntechnik GmbH
Am Hang 21
33333 Bielefeld

Sehr geehrte Frau Jaspers,

ich möchte mich ganz herzlich dafür bedanken, dass Sie mir die Stelle, um die ich mich bei Ihnen beworben habe, anbieten.

Zu meinem Bedauern muss ich Ihr freundliches Angebot nun aber doch ablehnen, da mein derzeitiger Arbeitgeber mir völlig überraschend ein Angebot gemacht hat, das so attraktiv war, dass ich es trotz allem nicht ausschlagen mochte.

Ich hoffe, Sie haben ein wenig Verständnis für meine Entscheidung.

Mit freundlichen Grüßen

Christoph Höfer

Thanking for a reference

Jens Kettler
Kieselstr.
41472 Neuss

30. April 05

Herrn
Volker Grimm
Turnerstraße 54
51515 Köln

Lieber Herr Grimm,

ich möchte mich ganz herzlich bei Ihnen bedanken. Sie haben mir bei meiner Bewerbung um eine Redakteursstelle beim „Kunstmagazin" durch Ihr Empfehlungsschreiben sehr geholfen. **1**

Ich nehme an, dass es auch Sie freuen wird zu hören, dass man mir den Posten angeboten hat und dass ich bereits in drei Wochen beginnen werde. Ich bin so froh, dass es nun endlich einmal geklappt hat und würde mich am liebsten gleich morgen in die Arbeit stürzen.

Noch einmal ganz herzlichen Dank! **2**

Mit herzlichem Gruß

Ihr
Jens Kettler

Resigning from a post

Walter Schreiber
Fördestraße 25
24944 Flensburg

3. Oktober 2005

Frau Dr. Elfriede Singer

Liebe Frau Singer,

mit diesem Brief möchte ich Ihnen mitteilen, dass ich mein Arbeitsverhältnis mit Wirkung zum 31. Oktober kündige.

Der Entschluss ist mir nicht leicht gefallen, da ich mich bei der Arbeit in Ihrer Redaktion immer sehr wohl gefühlt habe - bis es am Anfang dieses Jahres zu den bekannten Veränderungen an der Spitze des Verlages kam.

Seither ist es mir aber beim besten Willen nicht mehr möglich, mich in der Redaktion so einzubringen, wie Sie es von Ihren Mitarbeitern erwarten können und wie ich es unter anderen Umständen auch liebend gern täte.

Ich hoffe, dass Sie Verständnis für meinen Schritt haben.

Mit besten Grüßen

Ihr Walter Schreiber

1 Or: *Ich bin Ihnen sehr dankbar für die große Hilfe, die Sie mir bei meiner Bewerbung um ... waren.*

2 Or: *Ich bin Ihnen sehr dankbar für die viele Mühe, die Sie sich (meinetwegen) gemacht haben.*
Or: *Haben Sie herzlichen Dank für Ihre wertvolle Hilfe.*

Annahme eines Stellenangebots

16 Muddy Way
Wills
Oxon
OX23 9WD
Tel: 01865 767543

Your ref : TT/99/HH — 4 July 2005

Mr M Flynn
Mark Building
Plews Drive
London
NW4 9PP

Dear Mr Flynn,

I was delighted to receive your letter offering me the post of Senior Designer, which I hereby accept.

I confirm that I will be able to start on 31 July but not, unfortunately, before that date. Can you please inform me where and when exactly I should report on that day? I very much look forward to becoming a part of your design team.

Yours sincerely,

Nicholas Plews

Ablehnung eines Stellenangebots

4 Manchester St
London
NW6 6RR
Tel: 020 8334 5343

Your ref : 099/PLK/001 — 9 July 2005

Ms J Jamieson
Vice-President
The Nona Company
98 Percy St
YORK
YO9 6PQ

Dear Ms Jamieson,

I am very grateful to you for offering me the post of Instructor. I shall have to decline this position, however, with much regret, as I have accepted a permanent post with my current firm.

I had believed that there was no possibility of my current position continuing after June, and the offer of a job, which happened only yesterday, came as a complete surprise to me.

I apologize for the inconvenience to you.

Yours sincerely,

J D Salam

Dank für ein Empfehlungsschreiben

The Stone House
Wallop
Cambs
CB13 9RQ

8/9/05

Dear Capt. Dominics,

I would like to thank you for writing a reference to support my recent application for the job as an assistant editor on the Art Foundation Magazine. **1**

I'm sure you'll be pleased to know that I was offered the job and should be starting in three weeks' time. I am very excited about it and can't wait to start.

Many thanks once again, **2**

Yours sincerely,

Molly (Valentine)

Kündigung des Arbeitsverhältnisses

Editorial Office

Modern Living Magazine
22 Salisbury Road, London W3 9TT
Tel: 020 7332 4343 Fax: 020 7332 4354

To: Ms Ella Fellows — 6 June 2005
General Editor.

Dear Ella,

I am writing to you, with great regret, to resign my post as Commissioning Editor with effect from the end of August.

As you know, I have found the recent management changes increasingly difficult to cope with. It is with great reluctance that I have come to the conclusion that I can no longer offer my best work under this management.

I wish you all the best for the future,

Yours sincerely,

Elliot Ashford-Leigh

1 Oder: *Thank you very much for writing such a good reference, which has greatly helped me with my application for …*

2 Oder: *I greatly appreciate all the trouble you have taken (on my behalf).*
Oder: *Please accept my warmest thanks for your valuable assistance.* (formell)

▸874

Enquiring about work

Joseph Bauer
Gotenstraße
81925 München

30.04.05

Frau [1]
Marianne Lösch
Fremdspracheninstitut
Langenbrücker Straße 65
91019 Erlangen

Bewerbung

Sehr geehrte Frau Lösch,

von meinem Kollegen Fritz Langenberg, der bis vor kurzem bei Ihnen beschäftigt war, weiß ich, dass Sie im kommenden September neue Mitarbeiter einstellen wollen. [2]

Ich bin derzeit als Lehrer für Deutsch als Fremdsprache beim Goethe-Institut beschäftigt. Da mein Vertrag jedoch auf Ende Juni dieses Jahres befristet ist, suche ich nach einem neuen Betätigungsfeld.

Wie Sie meinem Lebenslauf entnehmen können, bringe ich die notwendigen Qualifikationen sowie einschlägige Berufserfahrung mit.

Zu einem Vorstellungsgespräch stehe ich ab dem 22. Juni jederzeit zur Verfügung. Sie können mich ab diesem Datum unter der folgenden Adresse erreichen:

bei Gerber
Voltastraße 67
91056 Erlangen
Tel.: (09131) 786546

Mit freundlichen Grüßen

Anlage

Joseph Bauer

[1] The recipient's basic title (*Frau, Herrn*) is on a separate line. Titles like *Dr., Prof.* etc. are on the same line as the name.

[2] Or, if you don't have a specific name to refer to: *durch Zufall habe ich erfahren, dass …*
Or: *ich wende mich an Sie in der Hoffnung, dass Sir mir eventuell eine Stelle anbieten können.*

To a university about admission as a research student

Thomas Emmler
Donaustr. 56
91052 Erlangen

11.11.05

Herrn
Prof. Dr. Helmut Schulte
Institut für Komparatistik
Petersstraße 54
28282 Bremen

Sehr geehrter Herr Professor Schulte,

ich wende mich auf Anraten von Herrn Dr. Michael Wagner in Erlangen, der dort meine Magisterarbeit betreut hat, an Sie.

Ich würde gerne an Ihr Institut kommen, um bei Ihnen zu promovieren. Eine Übersicht über meine bisherige Forschungstätigkeit, eine Skizze der mir vorschwebenden Dissertation sowie ein Lebenslauf liegen diesem Schreiben bei.

Ich würde mich sehr freuen, wenn Sie bereit wären, mich als Doktoranden anzunehmen. Um mein Vorhaben finanzieren zu können, werde ich gegebenenfalls ein Stipendium der Deutschen Forschungsgemeinschaft beantragen. [1]

Ich freue mich darauf, von Ihnen zu hören, und verbleibe mit freundlichen Grüßen [2]

Ihr

Thomas Emmler

Anlagen

[1] You could add: *In der Anlage finden Sie meinen Lebenslauf und ein Empfehlungsschreiben.*

A letter of recommendation is especially useful if you are applying for a position as a trainee and have no other professional qualifications.

[2] Or: *In der Hoffnung auf eine positive Antwort verbleibe ich mit*

Asking for a reference

Torsten Kruse
Franzstr. 53
47441 Moers

28.11.05

Herrn
Dr. Karsten Matern
Lessingstraße 20
47474 Moers

Sehr geehrter Herr Dr. Matern,

wie Sie ja wissen, ist meine derzeitige Anstellung befristet und wird in etwa drei Monaten auslaufen.

Ich habe mich daher beim Verlag Köpke in Herten um eine Stelle als Korrektor beworben und mir erlaubt, Sie als Referenz anzugeben.

Ich hoffe, dass Sie die Freundlichkeit haben, ein paar Zeilen zu schreiben, falls man Sie darum bitten sollte. Mit ein wenig Glück könnte ich beim Verlag Köpke endlich eine Dauerstellung finden und ich danke Ihnen schon heute für Ihre Hilfe.

Mit freundlichem Gruß

Ihr

Torsten Kruse

Giving a reference

Dr. Adalbert Fiedler
Zeppelinstr. 43
70193 Stuttgart

14. August 2005

Produktdesign GmbH
Neckarstr. 70
71717 Ludwigsburg

Ihr Schreiben vom 5. August

Sehr geehrte Damen und Herren,

ich freue mich über die Gelegenheit, Frau Luise Gebhard bei ihrer Bewerbung um die Stelle einer Designerin in Ihrem Hause zu unterstützen.

Während ihres Studiums habe ich Frau Gebhard als eine herausragende Studentin kennnen gelernt. Sie hat originelle und spannende Ideen - die sie auch umzusetzen weiß. Ihre Magisterarbeit, die ich betreut habe, ist exzellent.

Frau Gebhard ist eine angenehme, fleißige und verlässliche Frau, und ich kann sie ohne jede Einschränkung empfehlen.

Mit freundlichem Gruß

Dr. A. Fiedler

Blindbewerbung

23 Ave Rostand
7500 Paris
France

6th May 2005

Ms J Allsop
Lingua School
23 Handle St
London SE3 4ZK

Dear Ms Allsop,

I understand that you are planning to appoint extra staff this September. **1** I am currently teaching German as a Foreign Language at the Goethe Institut in Paris.

You will see from my CV (enclosed) that I have appropriate qualifications and experience. I will be available for interview after the 22nd June, and may be contacted after that date at the following address:

c/o Lewis
Dexter Road
London NE2 6KQ
Tel: 070 2335 6978

Yours sincerely,

Steffi Newmann

Encl.

1 Oder: *I believe that you may have a vacancy …*

Oder: *I understand that there is a position available within your company for …*

Bewerbung um einen Studienplatz

43 Wellington Villas
York
YO6 93E

2.2.05

Dr T Benjamin,
Department of Fine Art
University of Brighton
Falmer Campus
Brighton
BN3 2AA

Dear Dr Benjamin,

I have been advised by Dr Kate Rellen, my MA supervisor in York, to apply to do doctoral studies in your department.

I enclose details of my current research and also my tentative Ph.D. proposal, along with my up-to-date curriculum vitae, and look forward to hearing from you. I very much hope that you will agree to supervise my Ph.D. If you do, I intend to apply to the Royal Academy for funding.

I enclose my CV and a letter of recommendation. **1**

Yours sincerely, **2**

Alice Nettle

Encls.

1 Referenzen sind besonders wichtig, wenn man sich um einen Studienplatz oder eine Praktikantenstelle bewirbt.

2 Oder als Briefschluss:
I look forward to hearing from you.
Yours sincerely,

Bitte um ein Empfehlungsschreiben

8 Spright Close
Kelvindale
Glasgow GL2 0DS
Tel: 0141-357 6857

23rd February 2005

Dr M Mansion
Department of Civil Engineering
University of East Anglia

Dear Dr Mansion,

As you may remember, my job here at Longiron & Co is only temporary. I have just applied for a post as Senior Engineer with Bingley & Smith in Glasgow and have taken the liberty of giving your name as a referee.

I hope you will not mind sending a reference to this company should they contact you. With luck, I should find a permanent position in the near future, and I am very grateful for your help.

With best regards,

Yours sincerely,

Helen Lee

Empfehlungsschreiben

DEPT OF DESIGN

University of Hull
South Park Drive
Hull HL5 9UU
Tel: 01482 934 5768
Fax: 01482 934 5766

Your ref. DD/44/34/AW 5/3/05

Dear Sirs,

Mary O'Donnel. Date of birth 21-3-75

I am glad to be able to write most warmly in support of Ms O'Donnel's application for the post of Designer with your company.

During her studies, Ms O'Donnel proved herself to be an outstanding student. Her ideas are original and exciting, and she carries them through - her MSc thesis was an excellent piece of work. She is a pleasant, hard-working and reliable person and I can recommend her without any reservations.

Yours faithfully,

Dr AA Jamal

The world of work

Asking for an estimate

Karl Esser
Karlstraße 23
23554 Lübeck

Firma
Anton Schmidt
Am Graben 8
23456 Lübeck

30.07.05

Sehr geehrter Herr Schmidt,

in dem in meiner oben stehenden Adresse genannten Haus, das ich kürzlich erworben und bezogen habe, sind die Fensterrahmen erneuerungsbedürftig. Ich möchte Sie bitten, mir ein entsprechendes Angebot zu unterbreiten.

Wenn Sie so freundlich sein wollen, mich kurz anzurufen, können wir einen Termin vereinbaren, sodass Sie sich die Fenster zunächst ansehen können.

Mit freundlichen Grüßen

Karl Esser

Karl Esser

Asking for work to be undertaken

Manfred Scherer
Brahmsbogen 33
06124 Halle

12.09.05

Firma
Sanitär Grimmig
Kanalstraße 25
06060 Halle

Ihr Schreiben vom 09.09.05

Sehr geehrte Damen und Herren,

ich bin mit Ihrem Kostenvoranschlag einverstanden und möchte Ihnen nun den Auftrag erteilen, den verrosteten Heizkörper zu ersetzen.

Bitte teilen Sie mir mit, wann Sie die Arbeiten ausführen können, damit ich es einrichten kann, dass ich zu der Zeit im Hause bin.

Mir würde es am besten an einem Mittwoch- oder Donnerstagnachmittag passen.

Mit freundlichen Grüßen

Manfred Scherer

Complaining about quality of work

Helmut Sommer
Dolberger Str. 21
59077 Hamm

28. April 2005

Fa.
Klaus & Söhne
Bahnhofstraße 7
59078 Hamm

Sehr geehrte Damen und Herren,

wie ich Ihnen bereits telefonisch mitgeteilt habe, bin ich mit der Ausführung Ihrer Arbeiten am Freisitz meines Hauses keineswegs zufrieden. In dem betonierten Bereich zeigen sich bereits jetzt große Risse und in dem gepflasterten Teil haben sich etliche Steine gelockert oder gesenkt. Abgesehen von der ästhetischen Seite ist es momentan geradezu gefährlich, den Bereich zu betreten. Ich bitte Sie daher mit Nachdruck, umgehend für Abhilfe zu sorgen. Ihre Rechnung werde ich selbstverständlich erst begleichen, wenn dies zu meiner vollen Zufriedenheit erfolgt ist.

Mit freundlichen Grüßen

Helmut Sommer

Useful phrases:

Making an enquiry

Ihrer Anzeige in … entnehmen wir, dass …
Bitte senden Sie uns nähere Angaben über …
Wir bitten um Ihr Angebot.
Durch Ihre Anzeige im „Wertmarkt" sind wir auf Ihr Produkt aufmerksam geworden.

Replying to an enquiry

Mit Bezug auf Ihre Anfrage vom …
Wir danken Ihnen für Ihre Anfrage vom …
Vielen Dank für Ihr Interesse an unseren …

Replying to an order

Ihre Bestellung vom 3.12.2005
Wir danken Ihnen für Ihre Bestellung.

Delivery

Unsere Lieferzeit beträgt …
Wir erwarten Ihre Lieferung.

Placing an order

Anbei unsere Bestellung Nr. …

Payment

In der Anlage übersenden wir Ihnen einen Scheck über …
Die Lieferung ist kostenfrei.
Wir mussten Sie bereits viermal an die Begleichung der Rechnung vom … erinnern, die bis zum 15.12.2005 zahlbar war.

Apologizing

Wir bedauern sehr, dass …
Zu unserem Bedauern können wir nicht …
Entschuldigen Sie bitte das Versehen.
Ich hoffe, dass Sie Verständnis für die Verzögerung haben.
Sicher können Sie verstehen, dass uns keine andere Wahl blieb.

Anfrage an einen Handwerksbetrieb

'Pond Cottage'
Marsh Road
Cambridge
CB2 9EE

01223 456454

Message for: Shore Builders Ltd
Address: 667, Industrial Drive, Cambridge CB12 9RR
Fax Number: (01223) 488322

From: T H Meadows
Date: June 21st 2005
Number of pages including this page: 1

Dear Sirs.

I have just purchased the above cottage in which several window frames are rotten. I would be glad if you could call and give me a written estimate of the cost of replacement (materials and labour).
Please telephone before calling.

Yours faithfully,

T H Meadows

Auftrag an einen Handwerksbetrieb

The Garden House
Willow Road
Hereford

Tel: 01432 566885

9th September 2005

Rouche Building Co
33 Hangar Lane
Hereford

Dear Sirs,

I accept your estimate of £195 for replacing the rusty window frame.

Please would you phone to let me know when you will be able to do the work, as I will need to take time off to be there.

A Wednesday or Thursday afternoon would suit me best.

Yours faithfully,

Steven Hartwell

Reklamation an einen Handwerksbetrieb

112 Victoria Road
Chelmsford
Essex CM1 3JJ
Tel: 01621 33433

28th April 2005

Allan Deal Builders
35 Green St
Chelmsford
Essex CM3 4RT

ref. WL/45/LPO

Dear Sirs,

I confirm my phone call, complaining that the work carried out by your firm on our patio last week is not up to standard. Large cracks have already appeared in the concrete area and several of the slabs in the paved part are unstable. Apart from anything else, the area is now dangerous to walk on.

Please send someone round this week to re-do the work. In the meantime I am of course withholding payment.

Yours faithfully,

W. Nicholas Cotton

Formulierungshilfen:

Anfragen
We see from your advertisement in …
Please send us details of …

Antwort auf Anfragen
In response to your enquiry of …
Thank you for your enquiry of …
Thank you for your interest in our …

Antwort auf Bestellung
Your order of …
Thank you for your order of …

Lieferungen
Please allow … days/weeks for delivery.
We await confirmation of your order.

Bestellungen
Please find our order (no. …) enclosed.

Bezahlung
Please find enclosed a cheque for …
Carriage is free of charge.
This is our fourth reminder concerning settlement of our invoice dated …, which was due for payment on …

Entschuldigung
We are very sorry that …
Regretfully we are unable to …
We owe you an apology.
Please accept our apologies for the delay.
We are sure you will understand that we had no alternative.

Using the telephone

Answering the telephone

German speakers usually say their surname (and often their full name) when they answer the phone. It is considered impolite just to say *Hallo*.

Andrea Meier.
Guten Tag, Frau Meier, hier spricht Susanne Schmidt.

Meier.
Guten Tag, spreche ich mit Frau Andrea Meier?
Am Apparat.
Hier ist Susanne Schmidt.

In a work situation, the person who answers the phone gives the name of the company and possibly the department, and their full name.

Guten Morgen, Reisebüro Sonnenhut, Sie sprechen mit Anna Keller.

Sich melden und vorstellen

Im englischsprachigen Raum meldet man sich am privaten Telefon meist nur mit *hello*.

Hello.
Hi, Nick, it's Julie.

Hello.
Hello, is that Emma?
Speaking.
Oh, hello. This is James.

Firmenangestellte dagegen melden sich mit dem Namen der Firma, möglicherweise der Abteilung, und dem eigenen (Vor)namen.

Good afternoon, Modern Living Magazine, Joanna speaking, how may I help you?

Asking for someone, leaving a message

When you call a friend at home:

Hallo, Anna hier. Kann ich bitte mit Susi sprechen?

Susi ist gerade nicht da. Kann ich ihr etwas ausrichten?

Ja, kannst du sie bitten, mich anzurufen?

or:

Nein, ich rufe später nochmal an.

When you call a company:

Guten Tag, hier spricht Frank Phillip. Bitte verbinden Sie mich mit Herrn Müller.

Herr Müller ist zur Zeit leider nicht im Haus. Möchten Sie ihm eine Nachricht hinterlassen?

Ja, gerne. Der Termin nächsten Freitag muss leider verschoben werden. Können Sie ihn bitten, mich zurückzurufen, um einen neuen Termin auszumachen?

or:

Nein, danke. Können Sie mir sagen, wann er wieder im Haus ist?

or:

Nein, ich rufe später zurück.

Jemanden am Telefon verlangen, Nachrichten entgegennehmen

Wenn man jemanden zu Hause anruft:

Hello, this is Amy. Can I speak to Susan, please.

Susan's not in at the moment. Can I take a message?

Yes, can you ask her to call me?

oder:

No, thank you, I'll call again later.

Wenn man bei einer Firma anruft:

Good afternoon, this is Frank Phillip. Can you put me through to James Miller, please.

Mr Miller is not in the office today. Would you like to leave a message for him?

Yes, please. Next Friday's meeting has been postponed. Could you ask him to call me to arrange a new time?

oder:

No, thank you. Can you tell me when he will be back in the office?

oder:

No, thank you, I'll call back later.

Leaving a message on the answerphone

Hier spricht Frank Phillip. Dies ist eine Nachricht für Hans Müller. Es ist Freitag morgen, 10 Uhr, und ich muss Sie dringend wegen des Vertrags mit Simcom sprechen, es gibt einige interessante Entwicklungen. Rufen Sie mich bitte so bald wie möglich zurück, meine Handynummer ist ....

Einen Text auf den Anrufbeantworter sprechen

Hello, this is a message for James Miller. It's 10 am Friday, this is Frank Phillip. I need to speak to you urgently about the deal with Simcom, as there have been some new developments. Could you please call me on my mobile, the number is ...

Number please

Verbinden Sie mich bitte mit der Telefonzentrale.

Welche Nummer wünschen Sie?

Alle Leitungen sind besetzt.

Legen Sie bitte auf.

Der Teilnehmer antwortet nicht.

Es ist besetzt.

Kein Anschluss unter dieser Nummer.

Ich komme nicht durch.

Können Sie mich bitte mit Frankfurt 794003 verbinden?

Welche Nummer möchten Sie?

Could you put me through to the switchboard?

What number are you calling?

All lines are engaged *or* (*Amer.*) busy.

Please replace the receiver.

There is no reply.

It's engaged *or* (*Amer.*) busy.

The number you have called has not been recognized.

I can't get through.

Could you get me Frankfurt 794003, please?

Am Telefon

Ich hätte gern die Nummer des Reisebüros Sonnenhut in München.	Can you give me the number of the Sonnenhut travel agency in Munich?
Können Sie mich bitte mit der Auskunft verbinden?	Could you put me through to directory enquiries (*Brit.*), directory information (*Amer.*) ?
Er steht nicht im Telefonbuch; er hat eine Geheimnummer.	He is ex-directory (*Brit.*), unlisted (*Amer.*).
Ich habe mich verwählt.	I've dialled the wrong number.
Könnten Sie bitte Ihre Nummer hinterlassen, damit er Sie zurückrufen kann?	Could you leave your number so he can ring you back?

Common phrases used on the phone	Was man am Telefon sagt
Wer ist am Apparat?	Who's calling?
Ich verbinde Sie.	I'll put you through.
Bitte bleiben Sie am Apparat.	Hold the line please.
Es meldet sich niemand.	There's no reply.
Frau Neubert ist am Apparat.	Mrs Neubert is on the phone.
Sie spricht gerade auf der anderen Leitung.	She's on the other line.
Die Verbindung ist sehr schlecht, ich kann Sie kaum verstehen.	This is a very bad line, I can hardly hear you.
Wir sind unterbrochen worden.	We were cut off.
Versuchen Sie doch, ihn über sein Handy zu erreichen.	Try him on his mobile.
Auf Wiederhören.	Goodbye.

Useful words and phrases	Formulierungshilfen
Das ist ein Ortsgespräch.	It's a local call.
ein Ferngespräch führen	to make a long-distance call
Telefonate vom Festnetz zum Handy sind teuer.	Calls from land lines to mobiles are expensive.
gebührenfreie Gespräche	free calls
Telefontarife	call charges
Kennzahlen für Auslandsgespräche	country codes for international calls
Ich möchte ein R-Gespräch nach Dublin anmelden.	I want to make a reverse-charge call (*Brit.*), collect call (*Amer.*), to a Dublin number.
die Telefonkarte	phone card
das schnurlose Telefon	cordless phone
das Mobiltelefon, das Handy	mobile phone, mobile
freecall, gebührenfreie Hotline	freephone line, hot line
Infos unter freecall 8080.	For information call freephone 8080.
ein Handy mit Internetzugang	a mobile phone with Internet access
Sie können eine Nachricht auf dem automatischen Anrufbeantworter hinterlassen.	You can leave a message on the answering machine.
Hier spricht der automatische Anrufbeantworter.	This is a recorded message.
Bitte sprechen Sie nach dem Piepton.	Please speak after the tone.
der Nebenanschluss, die Nebenstelle	extension
Apparat 12	extension 12
eine SMS an jemanden senden	to send a text message to somebody, to text somebody

SMS (electronic text messaging)

The basic principles governing German SMS abbreviations are similar to those governing English SMS. Certain words or syllables are represented by letters or numbers that sound the same. Most punctuation is usually omitted, umlauts are rarely used, and there are no strict rules about upper and lower case. For example 'viele Grüße' can be 'vlg'. Sentences are shortened by leaving out certain letters – 'bist du noch wach?' might read 'bidunowa'. Often just the initial letter of a word is used, as in 'ff' for 'Fortsetzung folgt'. Many English abbreviations have made it into German text messages. For example '4u' (for you) is often used for 'für dich'. New abbreviations are added all the time to SMS chat.

As in English, emoticons are very popular, and some of the more established ones are included in the table below.

Glossary of German SMS abbreviations

Abbreviation	Meaning
8ung	Achtung
ads	alles deine Schuld
akla?	alles klar?
aws	auf Wiedersehen
bb	bis bald
bda	bis dann
bidunowa?	bist du noch wach?
braduhi?	brauchst du Hilfe?
bs	bis später
dad	denke an dich
d	der
div	danke im Voraus
dubido	du bist doof
ff	Fortsetzung folgt
g	grinsen
g&k	Gruß und Kuss
gn8	gute Nacht
gngn	geht nicht, gibts nicht
hahu	habe Hunger
hdl	habe dich lieb
hdos	halt die Ohren steif
hegl	herzlichen Glückwunsch
ild	ich liebe dich
jon	jetzt oder nie
katze?	kannst du tanzen?
ko5mispä	komme 5 Minuten später
l8er	later = später
lg	liebe Grüße
lidumino	liebst du mich noch?
mamima	mail mir mal
mumidire	muss mit dir reden
n8	Nacht
nfd	nur für dich
pg	Pech gehabt
rumian	ruf mich an
sfh	Schluss für heute
siw	soweit ich weiß
sms	schreib mir schnell
sz	schreib zurück
tabu	tausend Bussis
vegimini	vergiss mich nicht
vlg	viele Grüße
vv	viel Vergnügen
wamaduheu?	was machst du heute?
waudi	warte auf dich
we	Wochenende
zdom?	zu dir oder zu mir?

Emoticons

<table>
<tr><td>:-)</td><td>lächeln, glücklich</td></tr>
<tr><td>:-))</td><td>sehr glücklich</td></tr>
<tr><td>:-|</td><td>Stirnrunzeln</td></tr>
<tr><td>:-e</td><td>enttäuscht</td></tr>
<tr><td>:-(</td><td>unglücklich, traurig</td></tr>
<tr><td>:-((</td><td>sehr unglücklich</td></tr>
<tr><td>:-></td><td>sarkastisch</td></tr>
<tr><td>%-)</td><td>verwirrt</td></tr>
<tr><td>:~(or :'-(</td><td>weinen</td></tr>
<tr><td>;-)</td><td>zwinkern</td></tr>
<tr><td>|-o</td><td>müde</td></tr>
<tr><td>:-\</td><td>skeptisch</td></tr>
<tr><td>:-D</td><td>lachen</td></tr>
<tr><td>:-<></td><td>erstaunt</td></tr>
<tr><td>:-p</td><td>rausgestreckte Zunge</td></tr>
<tr><td>:-O</td><td>schreien</td></tr>
<tr><td>O:-)</td><td>Engel</td></tr>
<tr><td>:-* or :-x</td><td>Kuss</td></tr>
<tr><td>:-o</td><td>Schock</td></tr>
<tr><td>@}-,-'–</td><td>Rose</td></tr>
</table>

SMS (elektronische Textmitteilungen über das Handy)

SMS ist die englische Abkürzung für "Short Message Service", was sich als "Kurznachrichtendienst" übersetzen lässt. Das Verschicken einer englischen SMS funktioniert genauso wie das Senden einer deutschen SMS-Nachricht. Die Regeln sind die gleichen und man gibt Abkürzungen, auch SMS-Kürzel oder Akronyme genannt, über die Handytasten ein. Im Englischen gibt es zahllose Abkürzungen, die es erlauben, viele Informationen mit wenigen Zeichen und Zahlen zu übermitteln. Zum Beispiel: 2L8 = 'too late'. Für die meisten Nachrichten tippt man nur die Anfangsbuchstaben jedes Wortes ein, zum Beispiel: ttyl = 'talk to you later' oder fyi = 'for your information'. Erfahrene SMS-Sender verständigen sich problemlos und billig über ein Kauderwelsch aus Abkürzungen.

So genannte Emoticons oder Smileys, witzige Symbole, die mit ein paar Punkten, Klammern und Strichen die Gefühle des Senders ausdrücken, werden besonders gern per SMS versendet. In der Tabelle unten sind ein paar lustige Beispiele.

Verzeichnis von englischen SMS-Abkürzungen

Abkürzung	Bedeutung
adn	any day now
afaik	as far as I know
atb	all the best
b	be
b4	before
b4n	bye for now
bbl	be back late(r)
bcnu	be seeing you
bfn	bye for now
brb	be right back
btw	by the way
bwd	backward
c	see
cu	see you
cul8r	see you later
f2f	face to face
f2t	free to talk
fwd	forward
fwiw	for what it's worth
fyi	for your information
gal	get a life
gr8	great
h8	hate
hand	have a nice day
hak	hugs and kisses
hth	hope this helps
ic	I see
iluvu	I love you
imho	in my humble opinion
imo	in my opinion
iow	in other words
jic	just in case
jk	just kidding
kit	keep in touch
kwim	know what I mean?

Abkürzung	Bedeutung
l8	late
l8r	later
lol	lots of luck/ laughing out loud
mob	mobile
msg	message
myob	mind your own business
ne	any
ne1	anyone
no1	no one
oic	oh, I see
otoh	on the other hand
pcm	please call me
pls	please
ppl	people
r	are
rofl	rolling on the floor, laughing
ru	are you
ruok	are you OK?
sit	stay in touch
som1	someone
spk	speak
thkq	thank you
ttyl	talk to you later
tx	thanks
u	you
ur	you are
w/	with
wan2	want to
wan2 tlk	want to talk?
werv u bin	where have you been?
wknd	weekend
wot	what
wu	what's up?

Abkürzung	Bedeutung
x	kiss
xlnt	excellent
xoxoxo	hugs and kisses
yr	your
2	to, too
2day	today
2l8	too late
2moro	tomorrow
2nite	tonight
3sum	threesome
4	for

Emoticons

:-)	smiling, happy face
:-))	very happy face
:-|	frowning
:-e	disappointed
:-(	unhappy, sad face
:-((	very unhappy face
:->	sarcastic
%-)	confused
:~(or **:'-(**	crying
;-)	winking happy face
|-o	tired, asleep
:-	sceptical
:-D	big smile, laughing face
:-<>	amazed
X=	fingers crossed
:-p	tongue sticking out
:-O	shouting
O:-)	angel
:-* or **:-x**	big kiss!
:-o	shocked face
@}-,-'—	a rose

E-mail E-Mail

Sending an e-mail

The illustration shows a typical interface for sending e-mail.

E-mails normally take the form of a simple letter, especially when you don't know the recipient or contact them for the first time:

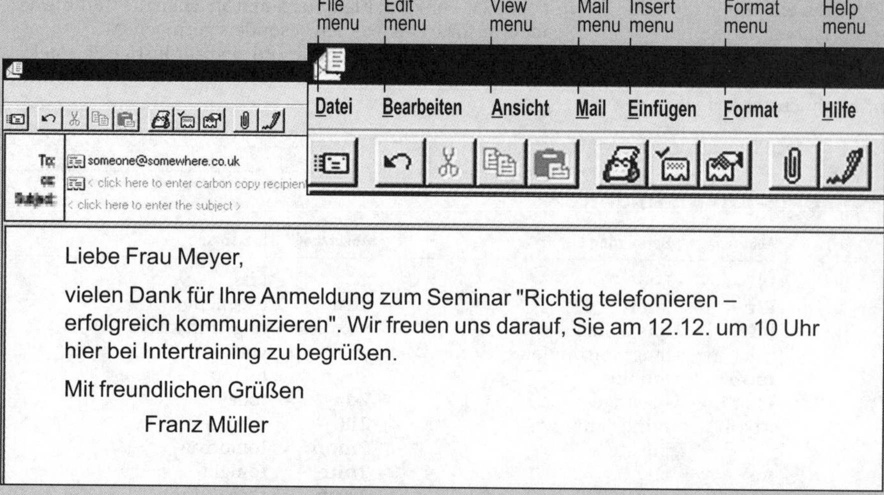

When sending routine e-mails to friends and colleagues, you do not have to address them by name or use formal endings:

Die nächste Besprechung findet am Freitag, 15.7., um 10 Uhr statt. E

Das Verschicken von E-Mails

Die Abbildung zeigt eine typische Oberfläche zum Verschicken von E-Mails.

E-Mails werden in der Form eines einfachen Briefs abgefasst, besonders wenn man den Empfänger nicht kennt oder zum ersten Mal Kontakt aufnimmt:

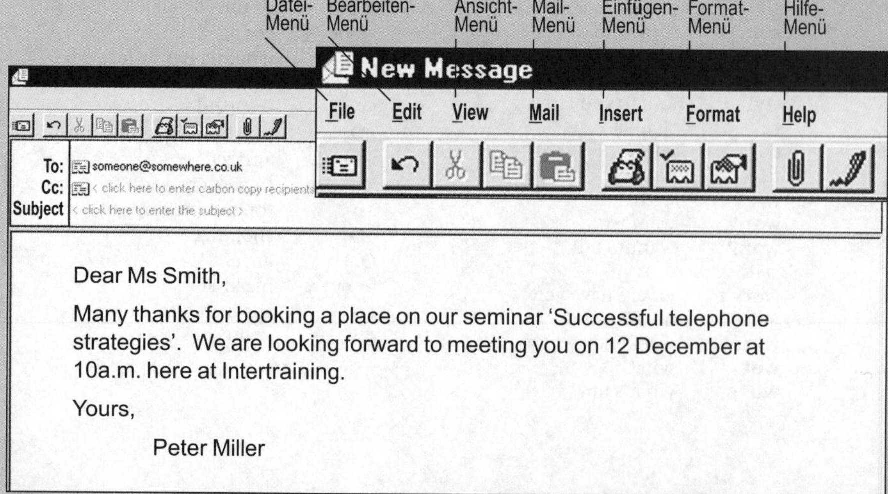

Bei E-Mails an Freunde und Kollegen können Anrede und Briefschluss ganz wegfallen, der Stil ist formlos:

The date for the next departmental meeting is Friday 14th at 10 am. E.

Englisch–deutsches Wörterverzeichnis
English–German Dictionary

Aa

A¹, a¹ /eɪ/ *n., pl.* **As** *or* **A's** **1** (letter) A, a, *das;* **from A to Z** von A bis Z; **A road** Straße 1. Ordnung; ≈ Bundesstraße, *die* **2** **A** (Mus.) A, a, *das;* **A sharp** ais, Ais, *das;* **A flat** as, As, *das* **3** (example) A, a; **if A says to B: ...:** wenn A zu B sagt: ... **4** (Naut.) **A 1** in erstklassigem Zustand **5** **A 1** (coll.) eins a (ugs.); **I'm feeling absolutely A 1** ich fühle mich eins a (ugs.) *od.* erstklassig **6** (paper size) **A1, A2, A3,** *etc.* [DIN] A1, A2, A3 *usw.;* **a pad of A4 [paper]** ein [DIN-]A4-Block **7** (Sch., Univ.: mark) Eins, *die;* **he got an A [in French]** er bekam [in Französisch] „sehr gut" *od.* eine Eins

a² /ə, *stressed* eɪ/ *indef. art.* **1** ein/eine/ein; **he is a gardener/a Frenchman** er ist Gärtner/Franzose; **she did not say a word** sie sagte kein Wort; *see also* **many A 2; quite; such A 1** **2** (per) pro; **£40 a year** 40 Pfund pro Jahr; **it's 20p a pound** es kostet 20 Pence das Pfund; **two a penny** zwei Stück [für] einen Penny; **six a side** sechs auf jeder Seite

A² *abbr.* **1** = **answer** **2** = **ampere** A

AA *abbr.* **1** (Brit.) = **Automobile Association** *britischer Automobilklub* **2** = **anti-aircraft** Flugabwehr-; Fla-; **AA gun** Flak, *die* **3** = **Alcoholics Anonymous**

A & E *abbr.* = **accident and emergency**

AB *abbr.* **1** = **able seaman** **2** (Amer. Univ.) = **Bachelor of Arts**

aback /əˈbæk/ *adv.* **be taken ~:** erstaunt sein (**by** über + *Akk.*); **I've never seen her so taken ~:** ich habe sie noch nie so betroffen gesehen

abacus /ˈæbəkəs/ *n., pl.* **~es** *or* **abaci** /ˈæbəsaɪ/ Abakus, *der*

abandon /əˈbændən/

A *v.t.* **1** (forsake) verlassen ‹*Ort*›; verlassen, im Stich lassen ‹*Person*›; aussetzen ‹*Kind, Tier*›; aufgeben ‹*Prinzip*›; stehen lassen ‹*Auto*›; aufgeben, fallen lassen ‹*Gedanken, Plan*›; **~ hope** die Hoffnung aufgeben; **~ ship** das Schiff verlassen; **~ ship!** alle Mann von Bord! **2** (surrender) **~ sth. to the enemy** etw. dem Feind übergeben *od.* überlassen **3** (yield) **~ oneself to sth.** sich einer Sache (*Dat.*) hingeben **4** (give up) ablegen ‹*Gewohnheit*›; abbrechen ‹*Spiel*›; sich trennen von ‹*Reichtümern, Besitz*›; hingeben (geh.) ‹*Reichtum, Geld und Gut*›

B *n., no pl.* Unbekümmertheit, *die;* Ungezwungenheit, *die;* **with ~:** unbekümmert; ungezwungen

abandoned /əˈbændənd/ *adj.* **1** (deserted) verlassen, ausgesetzt ‹*Kind, Tier*›; **~ property** herrenloses Gut **2** (profligate) verworfen, verkommen ‹*Person*›; lasterhaft ‹*Benehmen*›

abandonment /əˈbændənmənt/ *n., no pl.* **1** (giving up) (of right, claim) Preisgabe, *die;* Abtretung, *die;* (of plan, property) Aufgabe, *die* **2** (carefreeness) Zwanglosigkeit, *die;* Unbekümmertheit, *die* **3** (self-surrender) Sichgehenlassen, *das;* Hingabe, *die* (**to** an + *Akk.*)

abase /əˈbeɪs/ *v.t.* demütigen, erniedrigen ‹*Person*›; **~ oneself** sich erniedrigen

abashed /əˈbæʃt/ *adj.* beschämt; verlegen; **feel ~:** beschämt sein; **be ~ [by sth.]** sich [durch etw.] aus der Fassung bringen lassen

abate /əˈbeɪt/ *v.i.* [an Stärke *od.* Intensität] abnehmen; nachlassen; ‹*Zorn, Eifer, Sturm:*› abflauen, nachlassen

abatement /əˈbeɪtmənt/ *n., no pl.* Abnahme, *die;* Nachlassen, *das;* (of a nuisance) Beseitigung, *die; see also* **noise abatement; smoke abatement**

abattoir /ˈæbətwɑː(r)/ *n.* Schlachthof, *der;* ([part of] building) Schlachthaus, *das*

abbess /ˈæbɪs/ *n.* Äbtissin, *die*

abbey /ˈæbɪ/ *n.* **1** Abtei, *die* **2** (church) Abteikirche, *die;* **the A~** (Brit.) die Abteikirche von Westminster

abbot /ˈæbət/ *n.* Abt, *der*

abbreviate /əˈbriːvɪeɪt/ *v.t.* abkürzen ‹*Wort usw.*›; **~ 'Saint' to 'St'** Saint mit St. abkürzen

abˈbreviated dialling *n., no pl.* (Teleph.) Kurzwahl, *die*

abbreviation /əbriːvɪˈeɪʃn/ *n.* (of word etc.) Abkürzung, *die*

ABC /eɪbiːˈsiː/ *n.* **1** (alphabet) Abc, *das;* **as easy as ~:** kinderleicht **2** (fig.: rudiments) Abc, *das;* Einmaleins, *das*

> **ABC - American Broadcasting Company**
>
> Eine der größten amerikanischen Fernsehanstalten; gehört jetzt zur Walt Disney Company. Der Medienkonzern wurde 1943 als Rundfunkgesellschaft gegründet.

abdicate /ˈæbdɪkeɪt/ *v.t.* abdanken; **~ [the throne]** auf den Thron verzichten; dem Thron entsagen (geh.); **~ one's rights** auf seine Rechte verzichten

abdication /æbdɪˈkeɪʃn/ *n.* (by monarch) Abdankung, *die;* Thronverzicht, *der;* **the ~ of his rights** der Verzicht auf seine Rechte

abdomen /ˈæbdəmən/ *n.* (Anat.) Bauch, *der;* Unterleib, *der;* Abdomen, *das* (fachspr.)

abdominal /æbˈdɒmɪnl/ *adj.* (Anat.) Bauch-; Abdominal- (fachspr.)

abduct /əbˈdʌkt/ *v.t.* entführen

abduction /əbˈdʌkʃn/ *n.* Entführung, *die*

abeam /əˈbiːm/ *adv.* (Naut.) querab; dwars; **~ of the ship** dwarsschiffs

Aberdeen /ˈæbədiːn/ *n.* **~ [Angus]** Angusrind, *das;* **~ [terrier]** Scotchterrier *od.* Schottische Terrier, *der*

Aberdonian /æbəˈdəʊnɪən/

A *adj.* aus Aberdeen; Aberdeener

B *n.* Aberdeener, *der*/Aberdeenerin, *die*

aberrant /əˈberənt/ *adj.* abweichend, (bes. fachspr.) anomal ‹*Verhalten, Exemplar*›

aberration /æbəˈreɪʃn/ *n.* **1** (straying, lit. or fig.) Abweichung, *die;* (deviation) Abweichung, *die;* Anomalie, *die* (bes. fachspr.); (lapse, moral slip) Verirrung, *die;* **mental ~[s** *pl.*] geistige Verirrung **2** (Optics, Astron.) Aberration, *die*

abet /əˈbet/ *v.t.,* **-tt-** (support) helfen (+ *Dat.*); unterstützen; **aid and ~:** Beihilfe leisten (+ *Dat.*); **aiding and ~ting [a criminal]** (Law) Beihilfe [bei einem Verbrechen]

abeyance /əˈbeɪəns/ *n.* **1** (suspension) **be in/fall into ~:** zeitweilig außer Kraft sein/treten **2** (Law) **be in ~** ‹[*Adels*]*titel:*› [vorübergehend] abgeschafft sein

abhor /əbˈhɔː(r)/ *v.t.,* **-rr-** hassen; (loathe) verabscheuen

abhorrence /əbˈhɒrəns/ *n.* **1** *no pl.* (loathing) Abneigung, *die* (**of** gegen); Abscheu, *der* (**of** vor + *Dat.*); **hold sth. in ~:** einen Abscheu vor etw. (*Dat.*) haben **2** (detested thing) Gräuel, *der*

abhorrent /əbˈhɒrənt/ *adj.* (disgusting) abscheulich ‹*Benehmen, Gedanke, Person*›; **be ~ to sb.** jmdm. zuwider sein

abide /əˈbaɪd/

A *v.i.* **1** **~ by** befolgen ‹*Gesetz, Regel, Vorschrift*›; [ein]halten ‹*Versprechen*› **2** (continue) fortdauern; fortbestehen; (remain) bleiben; verweilen (geh.)

B *v.t.* (coll.: tolerate) ertragen; **I can't ~ dogs** ich kann Hunde nicht ausstehen

abiding /əˈbaɪdɪŋ/ *attrib. adj.* bleibend, beständig ‹*Liebe*›; dauerhaft ‹*Verbindung, Freundschaft*›

ability /əˈbɪlɪtɪ/ *n.* **1** (capacity) Können, *das;* Fähigkeit, *die;* **have the ~ to do sth.** etw. können *od.* (geh.) vermögen; **make use of one's ~** *or* **abilities** seine Fähigkeiten einsetzen; **have the ~ to type/do shorthand** Maschine schreiben können/Kurzschrift beherrschen *od.* können; **to the best of my ~:** soweit es in meinen Kräften steht **2** *no pl.* (cleverness) Intelligenz, *die;* **she is a girl of great ~:** sie ist ein sehr intelligentes Mädchen; **it depends on his ~ at school** es hängt von seinen Leistungen in der Schule ab **3** (talent) Begabung, *die;* Talent, *das;* Anlagen *Pl.;* **he shows** *or* **has great musical ~:** er ist musikalisch sehr begabt; **she has a natural ~ for teaching** sie hat eine natürliche Begabung zur Lehrerin

ability: ~ level *n.* Kenntnisstand, *der;* **cater for all ~ levels** den Fähigkeiten jedes Einzelnen gerecht werden; **~ range** *n.* Wissensskala, *die;* **a wide/narrow ~ range** eine große/kleine Bandbreite des Wissens

abject /ˈæbdʒekt/ *adj.* **1** (miserable) elend; erbärmlich; **in the most ~ poverty** in bitterster Armut **2** (self-abasing, submissive) unterwürfig

abjectly /ˈæbdʒektlɪ/ *adv.* **1** (miserably) erbärmlich **2** (submissively) unterwürfig

abjectness /ˈæbdʒektnɪs/ *n., no pl.* **1** (misery) Erbärmlichkeit, *die* **2** (submissiveness) Unterwürfigkeit, *die*

abjuration /æbdʒʊəˈreɪʃn/ *n.* (of belief, religion) Abschwören, *das*

abjure /əbˈdʒʊə(r)/ *v.t.* abschwören (+ *Dat.*) ‹*Glauben, Religion*›; sich lossagen von ‹*Theorie, Weltanschauung*›

ablative /ˈæblətɪv/ (Ling.)

A *adj.* Ablativ-; **~ case** Ablativ, *der*

B *n.* Ablativ, *der; see also* **absolute 3**

ablaut /ˈæblaʊt/ *n.* (Ling.) Ablaut, *der*

ablaze /əˈbleɪz/ *pred. adj.* in Flammen; **be ~:** in Flammen stehen; (fig.) glühen (**with** vor + *Dat.*); **be ~ with light** hell erleuchtet sein

able /ˈeɪbl/ *adj.* **1** **be ~ to do sth.** etw. tun können; **I'd love to come but I don't know if I'll be ~ [to]** ich würde sehr gern kommen, aber ich weiß nicht, ob es mir möglich sein wird; **I think you'd be better/more ~ to do it than I would** ich glaube, Sie sind eher dazu in der Lage als ich **2** (competent) fähig; tüchtig; (talented) begabt; fähig

able: ~-bodied /ˈeɪblbɒdɪd/ *adj.* kräftig; stark; tauglich ‹*Soldat, Matrose*›; **~ 'seaman** *n.* Vollmatrose, *der*

ablution /əˈbluːʃn/ *n., usu. in pl.* **1** (ceremony) Waschung, *die;* Ablution, *die* (Rel.); (joc.: washing) Wäsche, *die;* **perform one's ~s** sich waschen **2** *in pl.* (Brit.) sanitäre Anlagen

ably /ˈeɪblɪ/ *adv.* geschickt; gekonnt

abnormal /æbˈnɔːml/ *adj.* **1** (deviant) abnorm ‹*Gestalt, Größe*›; a[b]normal ‹*Interesse, Verhalten*›;

mentally/physically ~: geistig/physisch anomal *od.* krank 2 (irregular) ungewöhnlich; a[b]normal

abnormality /æbnɔːˈmælɪtɪ/ *n.* 1 (deviation) Abnormität, *die;* Anomalie, *die* 2 (irregularity) Ungewöhnlichkeit, *die;* Regelwidrigkeit, *die;* Abnormität, *die*

abnormally /æbˈnɔːməlɪ/ *adv.* (untypically) ungewöhnlich; abnorm; (unusually) ungewöhnlich

Abo /ˈæbəʊ/ *n., pl.* **~s** (Austral. sl. derog.) Eingeborene, *der/die*

aboard /əˈbɔːd/

A *adv.* (on or in ship etc.) an Bord; **a bus with 30 passengers ~:** ein Bus mit 30 Fahrgästen; **all ~!** alle Mann an Bord!; (bus, train) alle[s] einsteigen!

B *prep.* an Bord; **~ an ocean liner** an Bord eines Überseedampfers; **~ the bus/train** im Bus/Zug; **~ ship** an Bord

abode /əˈbəʊd/ *n.* (formal/joc.: dwelling place) Wohnstätte, *die;* Bleibe, *die;* **of no fixed ~:** ohne festen Wohnsitz

abolish /əˈbɒlɪʃ/ *v.t.* abschaffen; abschaffen, aufheben ‹*Gesetz*›

abolishment /əˈbɒlɪʃmənt/, **abolition** /æbəˈlɪʃn/ *ns.* Abschaffung, *die;* (of law) Abschaffung, *die;* Aufhebung, *die;* (of slavery) Abschaffung, *die;* Abolition, *die*

abolitionist /æbəˈlɪʃənɪst/ *n.* Abolitionist, *der; attrib.* abolitionistisch

ˈA-bomb *n.* Atombombe, *die*

abominable /əˈbɒmɪnəbl/ *adj.* abscheulich; scheußlich; widerwärtig; **the A~ Snowman** der Schneemensch; der Yeti

abominably /əˈbɒmɪnəblɪ/ *adv.* abscheulich; scheußlich; widerwärtig

abominate /əˈbɒmɪneɪt/ *v.t.* verabscheuen

abomination /əbɒmɪˈneɪʃn/ *n.* 1 *no pl.* (abhorrence) Abscheu, *der* (**of** vor + *Dat.*) 2 (object of disgust) Abscheulichkeit, *die*

aboriginal /æbəˈrɪdʒɪnl/

A *adj.* 1 einheimisch ‹*Pflanze, Tier, Bevölkerung*›; **the ~ inhabitants of this region** die Ureinwohner *od.* die Urbevölkerung dieser Region 2 (in Australia) **A~ tribes** Aboriginesstämme; **A~ customs** Brauchtum der Aborigines

B *n.* Ureinwohner, *der;* (in Australia) **A~:** [australischer] Ureinwohner

aborigine /æbəˈrɪdʒɪnɪ/ *n.* Ureinwohner, *der;* Urbewohner, *der;* (in Australia) **A~:** [australischer] Ureinwohner

abort /əˈbɔːt/

A *v.i.* 1 (Med.) eine Fehlgeburt haben; abortieren (Med.) 2 (fail) misslingen; scheitern

B *v.t.* 1 (Med.) **~ a baby** eine Schwangerschaftsunterbrechung durchführen; [ein Baby] abtreiben; **~ a woman** bei einer Frau eine Schwangerschaftsunterbrechung durchführen 2 (fig.: end) vorzeitig beenden; abbrechen ‹*Projekt, Unternehmen*› 3 (Aeronaut., Astronaut.) abbrechen; aufgeben ‹*Rakete*›

abortion /əˈbɔːʃn/ *n.* 1 (deliberate) Schwangerschaftsunterbrechung, *die;* Abtreibung, *die;* **have/get an ~:** die Schwangerschaft unterbrechen lassen; **back-street ~:** illegale Abtreibung (durch Engelmacherin) 2 (involuntary) Frühod. Fehlgeburt, *die;* Abort, *der* (Med.) 3 (monstrosity) Missgeburt, *die*

abortionist /əˈbɔːʃənɪst/ *n.* abtreibender Arzt/abtreibende Ärztin; **back-street ~:** Engelmacherin, *die*/Engelmacher, *der* (ugs.)

aˈbortion pill *n.* Abtreibungspille, *die*

abortive /əˈbɔːtɪv/ *adj.* misslungen ‹*Plan*›; fehlgeschlagen ‹*Versuch*›; **be ~:** ein Fehlschlag sein

abound /əˈbaʊnd/ *v.i.* 1 (be plentiful) reichlich *od.* in Hülle und Fülle vorhanden sein *od.* da sein 2 **~ in sth.** an etw. (*Dat.*) reich sein; **the English language ~s in idioms** die englische Sprache ist reich an Redensarten; **~ with** voll sein von; wimmeln von ‹*Lebewesen*›

about /əˈbaʊt/

A *adv.* 1 (all around) rings[her]um; (here and there) überall; **all ~:** ringsumher; **strewn/littered ~ all over the room** überall im Zimmer verstreut; **there must be some kitchen utensils ~:** irgendwo müssen hier ein paar Küchengeräte herumliegen 2 (near) **be ~:** da sein; hier sein; **is John ~?** ist John da?; **there was nobody ~:** es war niemand da 3 **be ~ to do sth.** gerade etw. tun wollen; im Begriff sein, etw. zu tun; (intend) beabsichtigen, etw. zu tun; **I was just ~ to go shopping when …:** ich wollte gerade einkaufen gehen, als … 4 (active) **be out and ~:** aktiv sein; etwas unternehmen; **be up and ~:** auf sein (ugs.) 5 ▸ ❶ **p. 894,** ▸ ❶ **p. 1001** (approximately) ungefähr; **[at] ~ 5 p.m.** ungefähr um *od.* gegen 17 Uhr; **Here I am! — And ~ time too!** (coll.) Hier bin ich. — Langsam wird es auch Zeit!; **it's ~ time somebody told him a thing or two** (coll.) langsam wird es Zeit, dass ihm mal jemand die Meinung sagt; **I've had [just] ~ enough of this** (coll.) ich habe [endgültig] genug *od.* (salopp) die Nase voll davon 6 (round) herum; rum (ugs.); **the battery is the wrong way ~:** die Batterie ist falsch [herum] eingebaut; **~ turn!,** (Amer.) **~ face!** (Mil.) kehrt!; *see also* **about-turn** 7 (in rotation) **[week and] week ~:** in wöchentlichem Wechsel; **[turn and] turn ~:** abwechselnd; **we take turn ~ at [the] cooking** wir wechseln uns mit dem Kochen ab

B *prep.* 1 (all around) um [… herum]; **there was litter lying ~ the park/streets** überall im Park/auf den Straßen lag der Abfall herum; **walk ~ the garden** im Garten herumgehen; **man ~ town** ▸ **town** 1 2 (with) **have sth. ~ one** etw. [bei sich] haben; **have you got a match ~ you?** haben Sie vielleicht ein Streichholz?; *see also* **wit¹** 2 3 (concerning) **a talk/an argument/a question ~ sth.** ein Gespräch über etw. (*Akk.*)/Streit wegen etw./eine Frage zu etw.; **talk/laugh ~ sth.** über etw. (*Akk.*) sprechen/lachen; **cry ~ sth.** wegen etw. weinen; **know ~ sth.** von etw. wissen; **what was it ~?** worum ging es?; **what is/was all that ~?** worum geht/ging es denn?; *see also* **do¹** A 2; **what** E 1 4 (occupied with) **be ~ sb.'s business** für jmdn. arbeiten *od.* tätig sein; **what are you/is he ~?** was hast du/hat er vor?; was führst du/führt er im Schilde?; **mind what you're ~:** pass auf!; sieh dich vor!; sei vorsichtig!; **be quick/brief ~ it** beeil dich!; (in speaking) fasse dich kurz!; **while you're ~ it** da Sie gerade dabei sind. *See also* **go about** B

about-ˈface, about-ˈturn

A *ns.* (lit. or fig.) Kehrtwendung, *die*

B *vs. i.* kehrtmachen; **~!** kehrt!

above /əˈbʌv/

A *adv.* 1 (position) oben; oberhalb; (higher up) darüber; (on top) oben; (upstream) weiter oben; **up ~:** oben; droben (bes. südd.); **from ~:** von oben [herab]; **~ right** rechts oben; oben rechts 2 (direction) nach oben; hinauf; (upstream) stromauf[wärts] 3 (earlier in text) weiter oben; **see ~, p. 123** siehe oben, S. 123 4 (upstairs) (position) oben; (direction) nach oben; **the flat/floor ~:** die Wohnung/das Stockwerk *od.* die Etage darüber *od.* über uns/ihnen *usw.;* **on the floor ~:** eine Etage höher 5 (in heaven) [droben] im Himmel; **from ~:** vom Himmel [herab *od.* hoch]

B *prep.* 1 (position) über (+ *Dat.*); (upstream from) oberhalb (+ *Gen.*); **my brother is head and shoulders ~ me** mein Bruder ist zwei Köpfe größer als ich; (fig.) mein Bruder ist mir haushoch überlegen; **~ the general noise was heard …:** durch den allgemeinen Lärm hindurch konnte man … hören; **~ oneself** (in high spirits) übermütig; aufgekratzt (ugs.); (conceited) größenwahnsinnig (ugs.); **~ board** einwandfrei; korrekt; *see also* **average** A 1; **ground¹** A 1, 2; **head** A 2; **par** 1, 4 2 (direction) über (+ *Akk.*); **the sun rose ~ the horizon** am Horizont ging die Sonne auf 3 (more than) über (+ *Akk.*); **will anyone go ~ £2,000?** bietet jemand mehr als 2 000 Pfund?; **he valued honour ~ life** er stellte die Ehre über das Leben; **be ~ criticism/suspicion/reproach** über jede Kritik/jeden Verdacht/allen Vorwurf erhaben sein; **that's ~ me** das ist mir zu hoch (ugs.); **you ought to be ~ all that at your age** du solltest in deinem Alter über so etwas stehen (ugs.); **~ all [else]** vor allem; insbesondere; *see also* **over** A 7; **station** A 4 4 (ranking higher than) über (+ *Dat.*); **she's in the class ~ me** sie ist eine Klasse über mir *od.* höher als ich

C *adj.* (earlier) obig ‹*Erklärung, Aufzählung, Ziffern*›; (**~mentioned**) oben genannt

D *n.* **the ~:** das Obige; (person[s]) der/die Obengenannte/die Obengenannten

above: ~ board *pred. adj.* einwandfrei; korrekt; **~-mentioned** /əˈbʌvmenʃnd/, **above-named** /əˈbʌvneɪmd/ *adjs.* oben genannt; oben erwähnt

abracadabra /æbrəkəˈdæbrə/ *n.* Abrakadabra, *das;* Hokuspokus, *der*

abrade /əˈbreɪd/ *v.t.* (scrape off) abschaben; abschürfen ‹*Haut*›

abrasion /əˈbreɪʒn/ *n.* 1 (Med.) Abschürfung, *die* 2 (graze) Hautabschürfung, *die*

abrasive /əˈbreɪsɪv/

A *adj.* 1 scheuernd; Scheuer-; (scratchy) kratzig 2 (fig.: harsh) aggressiv; herausfordernd ‹*Ton*›; **an ~ remark** eine barsche Bemerkung

B *n.* Scheuermittel, *das;* Schleifmittel, *das* (Technik)

abreast /əˈbrest/ *adv.* 1 nebeneinander; Seite an Seite; **walk/ride three ~:** zu dritt nebeneinander gehen/fahren 2 (fig.) **keep ~ of** *or* **with sth.** sich über etw. (*Akk.*) auf dem Laufenden halten

abridge /əˈbrɪdʒ/ *v.t.* 1 (condense) kürzen 2 (curtail) einschränken; beschneiden ‹*Rechte, Freiheiten, Privilegien*›

abridg[e]ment /əˈbrɪdʒmənt/ *n.* 1 (shortening) Kürzung, *die* 2 (summary) (of text) Kurzfassung, *die;* (of book) Epitome, *die* (Literaturw.); Abriss, *der*

abroad /əˈbrɔːd/ *adv.* 1 (overseas) im Ausland; (direction) ins Ausland; **have you ever been ~?** waren Sie schon mal im Ausland?; **are you going ~?** fahren Sie ins Ausland?; **from ~:** aus dem Ausland 2 (widely) in alle Richtungen; **the news was spread ~ that …:** überall verbreitete sich die Nachricht, dass …; (at large) **there is a rumour ~ that …:** es geht ein Gerücht um, dass …

abrogate /ˈæbrəgeɪt/ *v.t.* annullieren ‹*Vertrag*›; aufheben, außer Kraft setzen ‹*Gesetz, Vorschrift*›

abrogation /æbrəˈgeɪʃn/ *n., no pl.* ▸ **abrogate:** Annullierung, *die;* Aufhebung, *die;* Außerkraftsetzung, *die*

abrupt /əˈbrʌpt/ *adj.* 1 (sudden) abrupt, plötzlich ‹*Ende, Abreise, Wechsel*›; **come to an ~ halt** ‹*Fahrzeug:*› plötzlich *od.* abrupt anhalten 2 (disconnected) zusammenhanglos ‹*Schreibstil*› 3 (brusque) schroff, barsch ‹*Art, Ton*› 4 (steep) jäh, steil ‹*Abhang*›; stark ‹*Gefälle*›; (fig.) plötzlich ‹*Zunahme, Abnahme, Anstieg*›

abruptly /əˈbrʌptlɪ/ *adv.* 1 (suddenly) abrupt; plötzlich 2 (disconnectedly) zusammenhanglos; unzusammenhängend 3 (brusquely) schroff; barsch 4 (steeply) jäh; steil; (fig.) plötzlich ‹*zunehmen, abnehmen*›

abruptness /əˈbrʌptnɪs/ *n., no pl.* ▸ **abrupt:** 1 Plötzlichkeit, *die* 2 Zusammenhanglosigkeit, *die* 3 Schroffheit, *die;* Barschheit, *die* 4 Steilheit, *die;* Jähe, *die* (veralt.); (fig.) Plötzlichkeit, *die*

ABS *abbr.* = **anti-lock brake** *or* **braking system** ABS

abscess /ˈæbsɪs/ *n.* (Med.) Abszess, *der*

abscond /əbˈskɒnd/ *v.i.* 1 (depart) sich entfernen; [heimlich] verschwinden (ugs.) 2 (flee) flüchten; fliehen

abseil /ˈæbseɪl, ˈæbzaɪl/ (Mount.)

A *v.i.* abseilen

B *n.* Abseilen, *das*

absence /ˈæbsəns/ *n.* 1 Abwesenheit, *die;* (from work) Fernbleiben, *das;* **his ~s from school** sein Fehlen in der Schule; **how long was your ~ from home?** wie lange waren Sie von zu Hause fort?; **~ makes the heart grow fonder** Abwesenheit verstärkt die Zuneigung; *see also* **leave¹** 2 2 (lack) **the ~ of sth.** der Mangel an etw. (*Dat.*); das Fehlen von etw.; **in the ~ of concrete evidence** mangels konkreter Beweise 3 **~ [of mind]** Geistesabwesenheit, *die;* Zerstreutheit, *die*

absent
A /'æbsənt/ *adj.* **1** abwesend; **be ~:** nicht da sein; **be ~ from school/work** in der Schule/ am Arbeitsplatz fehlen; **for all those ~ from the last meeting** für alle, die beim letzten Treffen nicht anwesend waren; **he's ~ on leave** er ist auf Urlaub; **be ~ without leave** sich unerlaubt entfernt haben; **~ voter** Briefwähler, *der*/-wählerin, *die* **2** (lacking) **be ~:** fehlen **3** (abstracted) geistesabwesend; zerstreut
B /əb'sent/ *v. refl.* **~ oneself [from sth.]** [einer Sache (*Dat.*)] fernbleiben

absentee /æbsən'ti:/ *n.* Fehlende, *der/die;* Abwesende, *der/die;* **there were a few ~s** ein paar fehlten; **~ landlord** nicht auf seinem Gut lebender Gutsherr

absen'tee ballot *n.* (Amer.) Briefwahl, *die*

absenteeism /æbsən'ti:ɪzm/ *n., no pl.* [häufiges] Fernbleiben; (without good reason) Krankfeiern, *das* (ugs.)

absen'tee rate *n.* Abwesenheitsrate, *die*

absently /'æbsəntlɪ/ *adv.* [geistes]abwesend

absent-minded /æbsənt'maɪndɪd/ *adj.* geistesabwesend; (habitually) zerstreut

absent-mindedly /æbsənt'maɪndɪdlɪ/ *adv.* geistesabwesend

absent-mindedness /æbsənt'maɪndɪdnɪs/ *n., no pl.* Geistesabwesenheit, *die;* (habitual) Zerstreutheit, *die*

absinth /'æbsɪnθ/ *n.* **1** (liqueur) **~[e]** Absinth, *der* **2** (essence) Wermutextrakt, *der* **3** (Bot.: wormwood) Wermut, *der*

absolute /'æbsəlu:t, 'æbsəlju:t/ *adj.* **1** (complete, not relative) absolut; unumstößlich ‹*Beweis, Tatsache*›; unbestreitbar ‹*Tatsache*›; ausgemacht ‹*Lüge, Schurkerei, Skandal*›; (unconditional) fest ‹*Versprechen*›; streng ‹*Verpflichtung*›; **~ alcohol** reiner Alkohol; *see also* **zero A 3** **2** (unrestricted) absolut ‹*Monarchie, Herrscher*›; uneingeschränkt ‹*Macht*›; unumschränkt ‹*Herrscher*›; **~ majority** absolute Mehrheit **3** (Ling.) absolut ‹*Verb*›; (uninflected) ungebeugt; unflektiert; **ablative ~:** Ablativus absolutus, *der;* **accusative/genitive/nominative ~:** absoluter Akkusativ/Genitiv/Nominativ; **~ construction** absolute Konstruktion **4** (Philos.) absolut; **the ~:** das Absolute

absolutely /'æbsəlu:tlɪ, 'æbsəlju:tlɪ/ *adv.* **1** absolut; strikt ‹*ablehnen*›; völlig ‹*verrückt*›; entschieden ‹*bestreiten*›; ausgesprochen ‹*kriminell, schlimm, ekelhaft*›; **you're ~ right!** du hast völlig Recht **2** (positively) regelrecht; **~ fabulous/gorgeous** echt toll (ugs.); **I say ~ no** ich sage entschieden nein; **~ not!** auf keinen Fall! **3** (unconditionally) mit absoluter Sicherheit ‹*behaupten, glauben, beweisen*›; strikt ‹*sich weigern*› **4** (without qualification, independently) absolut **5** (Ling.) absolut **6** /æbsə'lu:tlɪ/ (coll.: yes indeed) hundertprozentig (ugs.)

absolute: ~ 'pitch *n.* (Mus.) (ability) absolutes Gehör; (standard) absolute Tonhöhe; **~ temperature** *n.* (Phys.) absolute Temperatur

absolution /æbsə'lu:ʃn, æbsə'lju:ʃn/ *n.* **1** (release) Lossprechung, *die* (**from** von); (forgiveness of wrongdoing) Vergebung, *die* **2** (Relig.) (forgiveness) Vergebung, *die;* (release) Erlass, *der* (**from** *Gen.*); **the priest pronounced ~:** der Priester erteilte [die] Absolution

absolutism /'æbsəlu:tɪzm, 'æbsəlju:tɪzm/ *n., no pl.* (Polit.) Absolutismus, *der*

absolutist /æbsə'lu:tɪst/ *adj.* absolutistisch

absolve /əb'zɒlv/ *v.t.* **1** (release) **~ from** entbinden von ‹*Pflichten*›; vergeben ‹*Sünde, Verbrechen*›; lossprechen von ‹*Schuld*›; (Relig.) Absolution erteilen (+ *Dat.*) **2** (acquit) freisprechen (Rechtsw.)

absorb /əb'sɔ:b, əb'zɔ:b/ *v.t.* **1** aufsaugen ‹*Flüssigkeit*›; aufnehmen ‹*Flüssigkeit, Nährstoff, Wärme*›; resorbieren (Med.); absorbieren (fachspr.); (fig.) in sich aufnehmen ‹*Wissen*›; **~ a price increase** Mehrkosten auffangen **2** (reduce in strength) absorbieren; abfangen ‹*Schlag, Stoß*› **3** (incorporate) absorbieren ‹*Chemikalie*›; eingliedern, integrieren ‹*Abteilung, Gemeinde*›; inkorporieren (Rechtsw.) ‹*Gemeinde*›; **be ~ed by** *or* **into the crowd** von der Menge verschluckt werden **4** (consume) aufzehren ‹*Kraft, Zeit, Vermögen*›; aufnehmen ‹*Importe, Arbeitskräfte*› **5** (engross) ausfüllen ‹*Person, Interesse, Gedanken*›

absorbed /əb'sɔ:bd, əb'zɔ:bd/ *adj.* versunken; **be/get ~ in sth.** in etw. (*Akk.*) vertieft sein/ sich in etw. (*Akk.*) vertiefen; **be/get ~ in sb.** von jmdm. gefangen genommen sein/werden; **he's totally ~ in his work** er geht völlig in seiner Arbeit auf; **be/get ~ by sth./sb.** von etw./jmdm. [völlig] in Anspruch genommen sein/werden

absorbency /əb'sɔ:bənsɪ, əb'zɔ:bənsɪ/ *n.* Saugfähigkeit, *die*

absorbent /əb'sɔ:bənt, əb'zɔ:bənt/
A *adj.* saugfähig; absorbierend (fachspr.); **~ cotton** (Amer.) Watte, *die*
B *n.* (substance) Absorbens (Chemie, Med.); (material) absorbierendes Material

absorbing /əb'sɔ:bɪŋ, əb'zɔ:bɪŋ/ *adj.* faszinierend

absorption /əb'sɔ:pʃn, əb'zɔ:pʃn/ *n.* **1** (incorporation, physical process) Absorption, *die* (fachspr.); Resorption, *die* (Med.) **2** (of department, community) Integration, *die;* (of effort) Aufnahme, *die;* (of goods) Abnahme, *die* **3** (engrossment) (in reading, watching) Versunkenheit, *die;* **their ~ in each other** ihr vollkommenes Aufgehen ineinander

ab'sorption spectrum *n.* Absorptionsspektrum, *das*

abstain /əb'steɪn/ *v.i.* **1** enthaltsam sein; **~ from sth.** sich einer Sache (*Gen.*) enthalten **2** **~ [from voting]** sich der Stimme enthalten

abstainer /əb'steɪnə(r)/ *n.* **1** Antialkoholiker, *der;* Abstinenzler, *der* **2** (in vote) **an ~** *jmd., der sich der Stimme enthält*

abstemious /əb'sti:mɪəs/ *adj.*, **abstemiously** /əb'sti:mɪəslɪ/ *adv.* enthaltsam

abstemiousness /əb'sti:mɪəsnɪs/ *n., no pl.* Enthaltsamkeit, *die*

abstention /əb'stenʃn/ *n.* **1** Enthaltung, *die;* **~ from sex** sexuelle Enthaltsamkeit **2** **~ from the vote/from voting** Stimmenthaltung, *die;* **how many ~s were there?** wie viele Personen enthielten sich der Stimme?

abstinence /'æbstɪnəns/ *n.* **1** (abstaining) Abstinenz, *die;* **total ~:** völlige Abstinenz **2** (moderation) Entsagung, *die*

abstinent /'æbstɪnənt/ *adj.* abstinent

abstract
A /'æbstrækt/ *adj.* abstrakt; **~ noun** (Ling.) Abstraktum, *das;* **the ~:** das Abstrakte; **in the ~:** abstrakt; **~ expressionism** ▸ **action painting**
B *n.* **1** (summary) Zusammenfassung, *die;* Abstract, *das* (fachspr.); (of book) Inhaltsangabe, *die* **2** (idea) Abstraktum, *das* **3** (Art) abstraktes [Kunst]werk
C /æb'strækt/ *v.t.* **1** (remove) wegnehmen; (euphem.: steal) entwenden, (ugs.) stibitzen (**from** aus) **2** (summarize) zusammenfassen ‹*Bericht, Referat*›

abstracted /æb'stræktɪd/ *adj.*, **abstractedly** /æb'stræktɪdlɪ/ *adv.* [geistes]abwesend

abstraction /æb'strækʃn/ *n.* **1** (removal) Entnahme, *die;* (euphem.: stealing) Entwendung, *die* **2** *no pl.* (absence of mind) Geistesabwesenheit, *die;* Zerstreutheit, *die* **3** (idea) Abstraktion, *die;* **he talks in ~s** er spricht in abstrakten Begriffen

abstractly /'æbstræktlɪ/ *adv.* abstrakt

abstractness /'æbstræktnɪs/ *n., no pl.* Abstraktheit, *die*

abstractor /æb'stræktə(r)/ *n.: Verfasser[in] von Abstracts*

abstruse /æb'stru:s/ *adj.*, **abstrusely** /æb'stru:slɪ/ *adv.* abstrus

abstruseness /æb'stru:snɪs/ *n., no pl.* Abstrusität, *die*

absurd /əb'sɜ:d/ *adj.* absurd; (ridiculous) lächerlich; **the theatre of the ~:** das absurde Theater

absurdity /əb'sɜ:dɪtɪ/ *n.* Absurdität, *die*

absurdly /əb'sɜ:dlɪ/ *adv.* lächerlich; **he is ~ afraid of ...:** er hat eine krankhafte Angst vor (+ *Dat.*) ...

ABTA *abbr.* (Brit.) **= Association of British Travel Agents** *Vereinigung der britischen Reiseveranstalter*

abundance /ə'bʌndəns/ *n.* **1** **[an] ~ of sth.** eine Fülle von etw.; **an ~ of love/energy** ein Übermaß an Liebe/Energie (*Dat.*); **in ~:** in Hülle und Fülle **2** (profusion) Überfluss, *der* **3** (wealth) Reichtum, *der*

abundant /ə'bʌndənt/ *adj.* reich ‹*Auswahl*›; übergroß ‹*Interesse, Begeisterung*›; **an ~ supply of fish/fruit** Fisch/Obst im Überfluss; **~ proof/reason** mehr als genug Beweise/Gründe; **be ~:** reichlich vorhanden sein; **~ in** reich an (+ *Dat.*)

abundantly /ə'bʌndəntlɪ/ *adv.* reichlich; **I made it ~ clear that ...:** ich habe es mehr als deutlich zum Ausdruck gebracht, dass ...

abuse
A /ə'bju:z/ *v.t.* **1** (misuse) missbrauchen ‹*Macht, Recht, Autorität, Vertrauen*›; (maltreat) peinigen, quälen ‹*Tier*›; schaden (+ *Dat.*) ‹*Motor*›; **sexually ~:** sexuell missbrauchen **2** (insult) beschimpfen
B /ə'bju:s/ *n.* **1** (misuse) Missbrauch, *der* **2** (unjust or corrupt practice) Missstand, *der* **3** (insults) Beschimpfungen *Pl.;* **a term of ~:** ein Schimpfwort

abuser /ə'bju:zə(r)/ *n.* **1** (misuser, maltreater) Missbraucher, *der*/Missbraucherin, *die* **2** (of rights) Verletzer, *der*/Verletzerin, *die*

abusive /ə'bju:sɪv/ *adj.* beleidigend; **~ language** Beleidigungen; Beschimpfungen; **become** *or* **get ~:** ausfallend werden

abut /ə'bʌt/
A *v.i.*, **-tt-:** **1** (border) **~ on** grenzen an (+ *Akk.*) **2** (end) **~ on/against** stoßen *od.* angrenzen an (+ *Akk.*); (rest) **~ on** ruhen auf (+ *Dat.*)
B *v.t.* **1** (border on) angrenzen an (+ *Akk.*) **2** (end on) anstoßen an (+ *Akk.*)

abutment /ə'bʌtmənt/ *n.* Widerlager, *das*

abysmal /ə'bɪzml/ *adj.* **1** (bottomless) unergründlich ‹*Tiefe*›; (fig.) grenzenlos ‹*Unwissenheit*› **2** (coll.: bad) katastrophal (ugs.)

abysmally /ə'bɪzməlɪ/ *adv.* katastrophal

abyss /ə'bɪs/ *n.* (lit. or fig.) Abgrund, *der;* **the ~ of space/the sea** die unendliche Tiefe des Weltraums/der See

Abyssinia /æbɪ'sɪnɪə/ *pr. n.* (Hist.) Abessinien (*das*)

a/c *abbr.* **= account**

AC *abbr.* (Electr.) **= alternating current** Ws

acacia /ə'keɪʃə/ *n.* (Bot.) Akazie, *die;* **[false] ~:** Robinie, *die*

academe /'ækədi:m/ *n.* (literary) Akademie, *die;* (university) Alma Mater, *die;* **the grove[s] of A~:** die akademischen Gefilde

academia /ækə'di:mɪə/ *n., no pl.* die akademische Welt

academic /ækə'demɪk/
A *adj.* **1** (scholarly) akademisch; wissenschaftlich ‹*Fach, Studium*›; **an ~ person/thinker** ein Theoretiker; **he's better on the ~ side** das Theoretische liegt ihm mehr **2** (of university etc.) akademisch; **~ year** Universitätsjahr, *das* **3** (abstract, formal) akademisch
B *n.* Wissenschaftler, *der*/Wissenschaftlerin, *die;* (scholar) Gelehrte, *der/die*

academical /ækə'demɪkl/
A *adj.* akademisch
B *n. in pl.* (Brit. dated) akademische Tracht

academically /ækə'demɪkəlɪ/ *adv.* **1** (intellectually) wissenschaftlich; **be ~ very able** große intellektuelle Fähigkeiten haben **2** (educationally) **~ [speaking]** was die akademische Ausbildung betrifft

academician /əkædə'mɪʃn/ *n.* Akademiemitglied, *das*

academy /ə'kædəmɪ/ *n.* **1** (society) Akademie, *die;* **Royal A~ [of Arts]** *Akademie der Künste in Großbritannien* **2** (school) höhere Bildungsanstalt; (college) Akademie, *die*

acanthus /ə'kænθəs/ *n.* (Bot.) Akanthus, *der;* Bärenklau, *die od. der*

ACAS /'eɪkæs/ *abbr.* (Brit.) **= Advisory Conciliation and Arbitration Service** *staatliche Schlichtungsstelle*

accede /æk'si:d/ *v.i.* 1 (assent) zustimmen (**to** *Dat.*) 2 beitreten (**to** *Dat.*) ‹*Abkommen, Bündnis*›; antreten ‹*Amt*›; ~ **[to the throne]** den Thron besteigen

accelerate /ək'seləreɪt/
A *v.t.* beschleunigen; erhöhen ‹*Geschwindigkeit, Notwendigkeit*›
B *v.i.* sich beschleunigen; ‹*Auto[fahrer], Läufer:*› beschleunigen; ‹*Autofahrer:*› Gas geben (ugs.)

accelerated 'learning *n., no pl.* beschleunigtes Lernen

acceleration /əkselə'reɪʃn/ *n.* Beschleunigung, *die;* **the ~ of economic growth** das verstärkte wirtschaftliche Wachstum

accelerator /ək'seləreɪtə(r)/ *n.* 1 (Motor Veh.) ~ **[pedal]** Gas[pedal], *das* 2 (Phys.) Beschleuniger, *der*

ac'celerator key *n.* (Computing) Schnelltaste, *die*

accent
A /'æksənt/ *n.* 1 (prominence by stress) Akzent, *der;* (mark) Akzent, *der;* Akzentzeichen, *das* 2 ▸ⓘ **p. 1277** (pronunciation) Akzent, *der;* (note in sb.'s voice) Unterton, *der* 3 *in pl.* (speech) Ton[fall], *der* 4 (Mus.) Akzent, *der* 5 (rhythmical stress) Betonung, *die* 6 (emphasis) Akzent, *der;* **the ~ is on ...:** der Akzent liegt auf (+ *Dat.*) ... 7 (distinctive character) Gepräge, *das* 8 (contrasting detail) [Farb]akzent, *der*
B /ək'sent/ *v.t.* (stress, lit. or fig.) betonen; (mark) mit Akzent[en] versehen

accentuate /ək'sentjʊeɪt/ *v.t.* betonen; vertiefen ‹*Eindruck, Erinnerung, Feindschaft*›; verstärken ‹*Schmerz, Kummer*›

accentuation /əksentjʊ'eɪʃn/ *n.* Betonung, *die*

accept /ək'sept/ *v.t.* 1 ▸ⓘ **p. 908** (be willing to receive) annehmen; aufnehmen ‹*Mitglied*›; (take formally) entgegennehmen ‹*Dank, Spende, Auszeichnung*›; übernehmen ‹*Verantwortung, Aufgabe*›; (agree to) annehmen ‹*Vorschlag, Plan, Heiratsantrag, Einladung*›; ~ **sb. for a job/school** jmdm. eine Einstellungszusage geben/jmdn. in eine Schule aufnehmen; ~ **sb. for a course** jmdn. in einen Lehrgang aufnehmen; ~ **sb. on to the staff** jmdn. in die Belegschaft aufnehmen; ~ **sb. into the Church/the family** jmdn. in die Kirche/in die Familie aufnehmen; **get sth. ~ed** dafür sorgen, dass etw. angenommen wird; ~ **sth. for publication** etw. zur Veröffentlichung annehmen 2 (approve) akzeptieren; **he is ~ed in the best circles** er ist in den besten Kreisen eingeführt; ~ **sb. as a member of the group** jmdn. als Mitglied der Gruppe anerkennen 3 (acknowledge) akzeptieren; **it is ~ed that ...:** es ist unbestritten, dass ...; **an ~ed fact** eine anerkannte Tatsache; **an ~ed opinion** eine verbreitete Ansicht; ~ **sb. for what he is** jmdn. so nehmen, wie er ist 4 (believe) ~ **sth. [from sb.]** [jmdm.] etw. glauben 5 (heed) beherzigen ‹*Rat, Warnung*› 6 (tolerate) hinnehmen; ~ **losing a job** sich mit einer Kündigung abfinden; **he won't ~ that** er wird das nicht ohne weiteres hinnehmen 7 (Commerc.) annehmen ‹*Scheck*›

acceptability /əkseptə'bɪlɪtɪ/ *n., no pl.* Annehmbarkeit, *die;* (of salary, price, risk) Angemessenheit, *die;* (agreeableness) Annehmlichkeit, *die*

acceptable /ək'septəbl/ *adj.* 1 (suitable, reasonable) akzeptabel; **damaged banknotes are not ~:** beschädigte Banknoten können nicht angenommen werden 2 (agreeable) annehmbar ‹*Preis, Gehalt*›; angenehm ‹*Person*›; **would the salary be ~ to you?** wäre das Gehalt annehmbar für Sie?

acceptably /ək'septəblɪ/ *adv.* 1 (suitably, agreeably) angenehm ‹*nahe, wenig*›; **be ~ priced** nicht zu teuer sein 2 (reasonably) vernünftig; **she sings ~ well** sie singt ganz akzeptabel 3 (adequately) hinreichend

acceptance /ək'septəns/ *n.* 1 (willing receipt) Annahme, *die;* (of gift, offer) Annahme, *die;* Entgegennahme, *die;* (of duty, responsibility) Übernahme, *die;* (in answer) Zusage, *die;* (welcome) Aufnahme, *die;* (agreement) Annahme, *die;* Zustimmung, *die* (**of** zu); **[letter of] ~:** schriftliche Zusage, *die;* **she gave her ~ to his proposal of marriage** sie gab ihm ihr Jawort 2 *no pl.* (approval) Billigung, *die* 3 *no pl.* (acknowledgement) Anerkennung, *die;* (of excuse, explanation) Annahme, *die;* **that fact has gained general ~:** diese Tatsache wird allgemein anerkannt 4 *no pl.* (heeding) Beachtung, *die* 5 *no pl.* (toleration) (of a fact) Hinnahme, *die;* (of behaviour) Duldung, *die* 6 (Commerc.: [engagement to honour] bill etc.) Akzept, *das*

ac'ceptance trial *n.* Abnahmetest, *der*

access /'ækses/
A *n.* 1 *no pl., no art.* (entering) Zutritt, *der* (**to** zu); (by vehicles) Einfahren, *das* (**into** in + *Akk.*); **this doorway is the only means of ~:** diese Tür ist der einzige Zugang; **'no entry except for ~'** „Anlieger[verkehr] frei" 2 (admission) **gain** *or* **obtain** *or* **get ~:** Einlass finden 3 *no pl.* (opportunity to use or approach) Zugang, *der* (**to** zu); **the father has ~ to the children** der Vater hat ein Recht zum Umgang mit den Kindern; **she was not allowed ~ to her personal file** man verweigerte ihr die Einsichtnahme in ihre Personalakte 4 (accessibility) **easy/difficult of ~:** leicht/schwer zugänglich 5 (way [in]) Zugang, *der;* (road) Zufahrt, *die;* (door) Eingang, *der*
B *v.t.* (Computing) ~ **the file/drive** *etc.* auf die Datei/das Laufwerk *usw.* zugreifen

accessary /ək'sesərɪ/
A *n.* ▸ **accessory B 4**
B *adj.* beteiligt (**to** an + *Dat.*)

'access code *n.* Zugangscode, *der*

accessibility /əksesɪ'bɪlɪtɪ/ *n., no pl.* 1 (reachability) **the easy ~ of the beach** der leichte Zugang zum Strand 2 (approachability, availability, understandability) Zugänglichkeit, *die*

accessible /ək'sesɪbl/ *adj.* 1 (reachable) **[more] ~ [to sb.]** [besser] erreichbar [für jmdn.] 2 (available, open, understandable) zugänglich (**to** für)

accession /ək'seʃn/ *n.* 1 Amtsantritt, *der;* (to position, estate) Übernahme, *die* (**to** *Gen.*); ~ **to the throne** Thronbesteigung, *die* 2 (being added) Zugang, *der* 3 (thing added) **new ~s to the library** Neuerwerbungen der Bibliothek 4 (joining, also EU) Beitritt, *der* (**to** zu); *attrib.* ~ **country** Beitrittsland, *das;* ~ **language** Beitrittssprache, *die*

accessory /ək'sesərɪ/
A *adj.* ~ **[to sth.]** zusätzlich [zu etw.]
B *n.* 1 (accompaniment) Extra, *das* 2 *in pl.* (attachments) Zubehör, *das;* **one of the accessories** eines der Zubehörteile 3 (dress article) Accessoire, *das* 4 ~ **[to a crime]** Mittäter [bei einem Verbrechen]; ~ **before the fact** Anstifter, *der;* ~ **after the fact** Begünstiger, *der*

access: ~ point *n.* 1 (to river, hiking trail) Zugang, *der;* 2 (Computing) Zugangspunkt, *der;* **the role of libraries as ~ points to the Internet** die Rolle von Bibliotheken als Zugangsorten zum Internet; ~ **provider** *n.* (Computing) Zugangsanbieter, *der*/-anbieterin, *die;* ~ **road** *n.* Zufahrtsstraße, *die;* ~ **television** *n., no pl.* offenes Fernsehen; ~ **time** *n.* (Computing) Zugriffszeit, *die*

accidence /'æksɪdəns/ *n.* (Ling.) Formenlehre, *die*

accident /'æksɪdənt/ *n.* 1 (unlucky event) Unfall, *der;* **road ~:** Verkehrsunfall, *der;* **meet with/have an ~:** einen Unfall erleiden/haben; ~ **rate** Unfallziffer, *die* 2 (chance) Zufall, *der;* (unfortunate chance) Unglücksfall, *der;* **by ~:** zufällig; **by an** *or* **some ~ of fate** durch eine Laune des Schicksals 3 (mistake) Versehen, *das;* **by ~:** versehentlich 4 (mishap) Missgeschick, *das;* **chapter of ~s** (coll.) Pechsträhne, *die;* **have a chapter of ~s** vom Pech verfolgt sein; **~s will happen** das kommt schon mal vor

accidental /æksɪ'dentl/
A *adj.* (fortuitous) zufällig; (unintended) unbeabsichtigt; ~ **death** Tod durch Unfall
B *n.* (Mus.) Akzidens, *das* (fachspr.); Vorzeichen, *das*

accidentally /æksɪ'dentəlɪ/ *adv.* (by chance) zufällig; (by mistake) versehentlich

Accident and E'mergency Department *n.* Unfallstation, *die;* Notaufnahme[station], *die*

accident: ~ figures *n. pl.* Unfallzahlen *Pl.;* ~ **insurance** *n.* Unfallversicherung, *die;* **~-prone** *adj.* **~-prone person** Unfäller, *der* (Psych.); **he was the most ~-prone of the children** er hatte von den Kindern immer die meisten Unfälle; **he's such an ~-prone boy** mit dem Jungen ist aber auch immer irgendwas (ugs.)

acclaim /ə'kleɪm/
A *v.t.* (welcome) feiern; (hail as) ~ **sb. king** jmdn. zum König ausrufen
B *n., no pl.* 1 (welcome) Beifall, *der* 2 (approval) Anerkennung, *die*

acclamation /æklə'meɪʃn/ *n.* 1 *no pl.* (approval of plan or proposal) Beifall, *der* 2 *usu. in pl.* (shouting) Beifallsbekundung, *die*

acclimatisation, acclimatise ▸ **acclimatiz-**

acclimatization /əklaɪmətaɪ'zeɪʃn/ *n.* (lit. or fig.) Akklimatisation, *die*

acclimatize /ə'klaɪmətaɪz/ *v.t.* (lit. or fig.) akklimatisieren; ~ **sth./sb. to sth.** etw./jmdn. an etw. (*Akk.*) gewöhnen; ~ **oneself, get** *or* **become ~d** sich akklimatisieren; ~ **oneself** *or* **get** *or* **become ~d to sth.** sich an etw. (*Akk.*) gewöhnen

accolade /'ækəleɪd, ækə'leɪd/ *n.* (gesture) Akkolade, *die;* (fig.) (praise) **~[s]** Lob, *das;* (approval, acknowledgement) Anerkennung, *die*

accommodate /ə'kɒmədeɪt/ *v.t.* 1 (lodge) unterbringen; (hold, have room for) Platz bieten (+ *Dat.*) 2 (oblige) gefällig sein (+ *Dat.*)

accommodating /ə'kɒmədeɪtɪŋ/ *adj.* (obliging) zuvorkommend; (compliant) entgegenkommend

accommodatingly /ə'kɒmədeɪtɪŋlɪ/ *adv.* (obligingly) zuvorkommend

accommodation /əkɒmə'deɪʃn/ *n.* 1 *no pl.* (lodgings) Unterkunft, *die;* **can you provide us with [some] ~ for the night?** können Sie uns ein Nachtquartier besorgen?; **~ is very expensive in Oxford** Wohnungen/Zimmer sind in Oxford sehr teuer; **there is a lack of good hotel ~ in this town** in dieser Stadt fehlt es an guten Hotels; **student ~ is getting more expensive** Studentenunterkünfte *od.* -wohnungen werden [immer] teurer 2 (space) **there is ~ for 500 people in this auditorium** in diesem Auditorium haben 500 Personen Platz 3 *in pl.* (Amer.: lodgings) Unterkunft, *die*

accommo'dation address *n.* Gefälligkeitsadresse, *die*

accompaniment /ə'kʌmpənɪmənt/ *n.* 1 (lit. or fig.; also Mus.) Begleitung, *die* 2 (thing) Begleiterscheinung, *die*

accompanist /ə'kʌmpənɪst/ *n.* (Mus.) Begleiter, *der*/Begleiterin, *die*

accompany /ə'kʌmpənɪ/ *v.t.* (go along with; also Mus.) begleiten; **the ~ing booklet** die beiliegende Broschüre

accomplice /ə'kʌmplɪs, ə'kɒmplɪs/ *n.* Komplize, *der*/Komplizin, *die*

accomplish /ə'kʌmplɪʃ, ə'kɒmplɪʃ/ *v.t.* (perform) vollbringen ‹*Tat*›; erfüllen ‹*Aufgabe*›; (complete) vollenden ‹*Kunstwerk, Bauwerk*›; (achieve) erreichen; verwirklichen ‹*Ziel, Wunsch*›

accomplished /ə'kʌmplɪʃt, ə'kɒmplɪʃt/ *adj.* fähig; **he is an ~ speaker/dancer** er ist ein erfahrener Redner/vollendeter Tänzer

accomplishment /ə'kʌmplɪʃmənt, ə'kɒmplɪʃmənt/ *n.* 1 *no pl.* (completion) Vollendung, *die;* (of deed) Ausführung, *die;* (of task) Erfüllung, *die;* (of aim) Verwirklichung, *die* 2 (achievement) Leistung, *die;* (skill) Fähigkeit, *die*

accord /ə'kɔ:d/
A *v.i.* ~ **[with sth.]** [mit etw.] übereinstimmen
B *v.t.* (formal: grant) ~ **sb. sth.** jmdm. etw. gewähren
C *n.* 1 (volition) **of one's own ~:** aus eigenem Antrieb; von selbst; **of its own ~:** von selbst 2 (harmonious agreement) Übereinstimmung, *die;* **with one ~:** geschlossen 3 (harmony) Harmonie, *die;* **be in ~ with** harmonieren mit

4 (treaty) Übereinkunft, *die*

accordance /ə'kɔ:dəns/ *n.* **in ~ with** in Übereinstimmung mit; gemäß (+ *Dat.*)

according /ə'kɔ:dɪŋ/ *adv.* **1** **~ as** (depending on how) je nachdem wie; (depending on whether) je nachdem ob **2** **~ to** nach; **act ~ to the rules** sich an die Regeln halten; **~ to how** je nachdem wie; **~ to him** (opinion) seiner Meinung nach; (account) nach seiner Aussage; **~ to circumstances/the season** den Umständen/der Jahreszeit entsprechend

accordingly /ə'kɔ:dɪŋlɪ/ *adv.* (as appropriate) entsprechend; (therefore) folglich

accordion /ə'kɔ:dɪən/ *n.* Akkordeon, *das;* **~ pleats** Plisseefalten

accost /ə'kɒst/ *v.t.* ansprechen

account /ə'kaʊnt/

A *v.t.* (consider) halten für; ansehen als

B *n.* **1** (Finance) (reckoning) Rechnung, *die;* (statement) Auflistung, *die;* Aufstellung, *die;* (invoice) Rechnung, *die;* **money of ~** (Finance) Rechnungseinheit, *die;* **~ rendered** ▸ **render 5**; **keep ~s/the ~s** Buch/die Bücher führen; **settle** *or* **square ~s with sb.** (lit. or fig.) mit jmdm. abrechnen; **on ~:** auf Rechnung; a conto; **on one's [own] ~:** auf eigene Rechnung; auf eigenes Risiko; (fig.) von sich aus **2** (at bank, shop) Konto, *das;* **an ~ with** *or* **at a bank** ein Konto bei einer Bank; **pay sth. into one's ~:** etw. auf sein Konto einzahlen; **draw sth. out of one's ~:** etw. von seinem Konto abheben; **on ~:** auf Rechnung; **joint ~:** gemeinsames Konto; Gemeinschaftskonto, *das* **3** (statement of facts) Rechenschaft, *die;* **give** *or* **render an ~ for sth.** über etw. (*Akk.*) Rechenschaft ablegen; **call sb. to ~:** jmdn. zur Rechenschaft ziehen; **give a good ~ of oneself** seinen Mann stehen **4** (consideration) **take ~ of sth., take sth. into ~:** etw. berücksichtigen; **take no ~ of sth./sb., leave sth./sb. out of ~:** etw./jmdn. unberücksichtigt lassen *od.* nicht berücksichtigen; **don't change your plans on my ~:** ändert nicht meinetwegen eure Pläne; **on ~ of** wegen; **on no ~, not on any ~:** auf [gar] keinen Fall **5** (importance) **of some/little/no ~:** von/von geringer/ohne Bedeutung **6** (performance) Interpretation, *die* **7** (report) **an ~ [of sth.]** ein Bericht [über etw. (*Akk.*)]; **give a full ~ of sth.** ausführlich über etw. (*Akk.*) berichten *od.* Bericht erstatten; **by** *or* **from all ~s** nach allem, was man hört **8** (advantage) **turn sth. to [good] ~:** aus etw. Nutzen *od.* Vorteil ziehen

Phrasal verb

• **~ for** *v.t.* **1** (give reckoning) Rechenschaft *od.* Rechnung ablegen über (+ *Akk.*) **2** (explain) erklären; **I can't ~ for that** ich kann mir das nicht erklären **3** (represent in amount) ausmachen; ergeben **4** (kill, destroy, capture) zur Strecke bringen

accountability /əkaʊntə'bɪlɪtɪ/ *n., no pl.* Verantwortlichkeit, *die* (**to** gegenüber)

accountable /ə'kaʊntəbl/ *adj.* verantwortlich; (explicable) erklärlich; **be ~ to sb.** jmdm. Rechenschaft schuldig sein; **be ~ for sth.** für etw. verantwortlich sein

accountancy /ə'kaʊntənsɪ/ *n., no pl.* Buchhaltung, *die*

accountant /ə'kaʊntənt/ *n.* ▸**i** **p. 1260** [Bilanz-]buchhalter, *der*/[Bilanz]buchhalterin, *die; see also* **chartered accountant**

account: ~ executive *n.* Kundenbetreuer, *der*/-betreuerin, *die;* **~ holder** *n.* Kontoinhaber, *der*/-inhaberin, *die*

accounting /ə'kaʊntɪŋ/ *n.* **1** *no pl.* (Finance) Buchführung, *die* **2** (explanation) **there's no ~ for it** das ist nicht zu erklären; **there's no ~ for taste[s]** über Geschmack lässt sich [nicht] streiten

account: ~ manager *n.* Accountmanager, *der*/-managerin, *die;* **~ number** *n.* Kontonummer, *die*

accoutrement /ə'ku:trəmənt/ (*Amer.:* **accouterment** /ə'ku:təmənt/) *n.* Requisit, *das*

accredit /ə'kredɪt/ *v.t.* **1** (vouch for) bestätigen **2** (send as representative) **be ~ed to sb.** bei jmdm. akkreditiert sein

accreditation /əkredɪ'teɪʃn/ *n., no pl.* Akkreditierung, *die;* (of institution, organization) Anerkennung, *die*

accredited /ə'kredɪtɪd/ *adj.* anerkannt ‹*Schule, Anstalt, Buch, Regierung*›; akkreditiert ‹*Botschafter, Diplomat*›; zugelassen ‹*Journalist*›

accretion /ə'kri:ʃn/ *n.* **1** (combination) Verschmelzung, *die* **2** (growth) Wachstum, *das;* (of power) Anwachsen, *das*

accrual /ə'kru:əl/ *n.* (Bookk.) **1** (of interest) Auflaufen, *das* **2** (accrued amount) ausstehender Posten

accrue /ə'kru:/ *v.i.* ‹*Zinsen:*› auflaufen; **~ to sb.** ‹*Macht, Ansehen:*› jmdm. zuwachsen; ‹*Reichtümer, Einnahmen:*› jmdm. zufließen

accrued /ə'kru:d/ *adj.* anfallend ‹*Ausgaben, Gewinne*›; aufgelaufen ‹*Schulden, Zinsen*›; entstanden ‹*Vorteile, Kontakte*›

accumulate /ə'kju:mjʊleɪt/

A *v.t.* (gather) sammeln; machen, (fachspr.) akkumulieren ‹*Vermögen*›; (in a pile) zusammentragen; (along the way) einsammeln; (produce) einbringen ‹*Zinsen, Gewinne, Undank, Kritik*› (**for sb.** jmdm.); **it's amazing how much stuff you ~ in the space of a year** es ist erstaunlich, wie viel Zeug sich bei einem in einem Jahr so ansammelt

B *v.i.* ‹*Menge, Staub:*› sich ansammeln; ‹*Schnee, Geld:*› sich anhäufen; ‹*Schlamm:*› sich absetzen

accumulation /əkju:mjʊ'leɪʃn/ *n.* [An]sammeln, *das;* (being accumulated) Anhäufung, *die;* (growth) Zuwachs, *der* (**of** an + *Dat.*); (mass) Menge, *die*

accumulator /ə'kju:mjʊleɪtə(r)/ *n.* **1** (Electr.) Akkumulator, *der;* Akku, *der* (ugs.); Sammler, *der* **2** (bet) Kumulativwette, *die*

accuracy /'ækjʊrəsɪ/ *n.* Genauigkeit, *die*

accurate /'ækjʊrət/ *adj.* genau; akkurat (geh.); (correct) richtig; getreu ‹*Wiedergabe*›; **the description of the man turned out to be completely ~:** die Beschreibung des Mannes erwies sich als völlig korrekt; **is the clock ~?** geht die Uhr richtig *od.* genau?

accurately /'ækjʊrətlɪ/ *adv.* (precisely) genau; exakt; (correctly) richtig; korrekt; (faithfully) getreu; genau; **the landscape is represented ~:** die Landschaft ist naturgetreu dargestellt

accursed, (arch.) **accurst** /ə'kɜ:st/ *adj.* **1** (ill-fated) verflucht; verwünscht **2** (involving misery) unselig **3** (coll.: detestable) verflixt (ugs.); verdammt (ugs.)

accusation /ækju:'zeɪʃn/ *n.* **1** (accusing) Anschuldigung, *die* (**of** gegen); Anklage, *die* (Rechtsw.); (being accused) Beschuldigung, *die* **2** (charge) Vorwurf, *der;* **make an ~/make ~s about sb./sth.** eine Anschuldigung/Anschuldigungen gegen jmdn./wegen etw. vorbringen

accusative /ə'kju:zətɪv/ (Ling.)

A *adj.* Akkusativ-; akkusativisch; **~ case** Akkusativ, *der*

B *n.* Akkusativ, *der*

accusatory /ə'kju:zətərɪ/ *adj.* anklagend ‹*Blick, Stimme, Schweigen*›

accuse /ə'kju:z/ *v.t.* (charge) beschuldigen; bezichtigen (geh.); (Law) (indict) anklagen; **~ sb. of cowardice** jmdm. Feigheit vorwerfen; **what are you accusing me of?** wessen beschuldigt *od.* bezichtigt ihr mich?; was werft ihr mir vor?; **the children were ~d of stealing apples** die Kinder wurden beschuldigt, Äpfel gestohlen zu haben; **~ sb. of theft/murder** jmdn. wegen Diebstahl[s]/Mord[es] anklagen; jmdn. des Diebstahls/Mordes anklagen (geh.); **the ~d** der/die Angeklagte/die Angeklagten

accuser /ə'kju:zə(r)/ *n.* Ankläger, *der*/Anklägerin, *die*

accusing /ə'kju:zɪŋ/ *adj.* anklagend; **point an ~ finger at sb.** (lit. or fig.) anklagend mit dem Finger auf jmdn. zeigen

accusingly /ə'kju:zɪŋlɪ/ *adv.* anklagend; (reproachfully) vorwurfsvoll

accustom /ə'kʌstəm/ *v.t.* **~ sb./sth. to sth.** jmdn./etw. an etw. (*Akk.*) gewöhnen; **~ sb. to doing sth.** jmdn. daran gewöhnen, etw. zu tun; **grow/be ~ed to sth.** sich an etw. (*Akk.*) gewöhnen/an etw. (*Akk.*) gewöhnt sein; **I'm not ~ed to being called rude names** ich bin nicht gewohnt, dass man mich beschimpft

accustomed /ə'kʌstəmd/ *attrib. adj.* gewohnt; üblich

ace /eɪs/

A *n.* **1** (Cards, Tennis) Ass, *das;* **~ of trumps/diamonds** Trumpf-/Karoass, *das* **2** (fig.) **an ~ up one's sleeve** ein Trumpf in der Hand; **play one's ~:** seinen Trumpf ausspielen; **hold all the ~s** alle Trümpfe auf *od.* in der Hand haben **3** (champion, outstanding person) Ass, *das;* (pilot) erfolgreicher Kampfflieger **4** (hair's breadth) **he was within an ~ of doing it/of winning** er hätte es um ein Haar getan/hätte um ein Haar gewonnen

B *adj.* (coll.) klasse (ugs.); spitze (ugs.)

acerbic /ə'sɜ:bɪk/ *adj.* scharf ‹*Worte, Kritik, Zunge*›; rau ‹*Umgangston, Temperament*›

acerbity /ə'sɜ:bɪtɪ/ *n., no pl.* ▸ **acerbic**: Schärfe, *die;* Rauheit, *die*

acetate /'æsɪteɪt/ *n.* (Chem.) Acetat, *das;* **~ fibre/silk** Acetatfaser/-seide, *die*

acetic /ə'si:tɪk/ *adj.* (Chem.) essigsauer; **~ acid** Essigsäure, *die*

acetone /'æsɪtəʊn/ *n.* Aceton, *das*

acetylene /ə'setɪli:n/ *n.* Acetylen, *das*

acetylene 'burner *n.* Acetylenbrenner, *der*

ache /eɪk/

A *v.i.* **1** ▸**i** **p. 1231** schmerzen; wehtun; **whereabouts does your leg ~?** wo tut [dir] das Bein weh?; **I'm aching all over** mir tut alles weh; **her heart ~s with love** (fig.) das Herz tut ihr weh vor Liebe **2** (fig.: long) **~ for sb./sth.** sich nach jmdm./etw. verzehren; **~ to do sth.** darauf brennen, etw. zu tun

B *n.* ▸**i** **p. 1231** Schmerz, *der;* **~s and pains** Wehwehchen, *die*

achievable /ə'tʃi:vəbl/ *adj.* (accomplishable) durchführbar; (attainable) erreichbar ‹*Ziel, Standard*›

achieve /ə'tʃi:v/ *v.t.* zustande bringen; ausführen ‹*Aufgabe, Plan*›; erreichen ‹*Ziel, Standard, Absicht*›; herstellen, herbeiführen ‹*Frieden, Harmonie*›; erzielen ‹*Rekord, Leistung, Erfolg*›; erfüllen ‹*Zweck*›; finden ‹*Seelenfrieden*›; es bringen zu, erlangen ‹*Berühmtheit, Anerkennung*›; erlangen ‹*gutes Aussehen*›; **he ~d great things** er hat Großes geleistet; **he's ~d what he set out to do** er hat erreicht, was er sich (*Dat.*) vorgenommen hat; **he'll never ~ anything [in life]** er wird es [im Leben] nie zu etwas bringen

achievement /ə'tʃi:vmənt/ *n.* **1** *no pl.* ▸ **achieve**: Zustandebringen, *das;* Ausführung, *die;* Erreichen, *das;* Herstellung, *die;* Herbeiführung, *die;* Erzielen, *das;* Erfüllung, *die;* Finden, *das;* Erlangen, *das;* **the task is impossible of ~:** die Aufgabe ist undurchführbar; **for these people ~ is measured in terms of money** für diese Leute wird Erfolg am Geld gemessen **2** (thing accomplished) Leistung, *die;* Errungenschaft, *die*

achiever /ə'tʃi:və(r)/ *n.* Erfolgsmensch, *der;* (woman) Erfolgsfrau, *die*

Achilles /ə'kɪli:z/ *pr. n.* Achilles (*der*); *see also* **heel[1] A 1; tendon**

achy /'eɪkɪ/ *adj.* **feel ~:** Schmerzen haben; **I feel ~ all over** mir tut alles weh

acid /'æsɪd/

A *adj.* **1** (sour) sauer; (fig.: biting) bissig **2** (Chem., Agric., Geol.) sauer ‹*Reaktion, Lösung, Boden, Gesteine*›

B *n.* **1** Säure, *die* **2** (sl.: LSD) Acid, *das*

acid: ~ drop *n.* (Brit.) saurer *od.* saures Drops; **~-free** *adj.* säurefrei ‹*Papier*›; **~ head** *n.* (sl.) Säurekopf, *der* (salopp); LSD-Schlucker, *der* (salopp); **~ house** *n.* Acidhouse, *das; attrib.* **~ house music/party** Acidhousemusik, *die*/-party, *die*

acidic /ə'sɪdɪk/ *adj.* **1** (sour) säuerlich; (fig.) bissig **2** (Chem., Agric., Geol.) sauer

acidity /ə'sɪdɪtɪ/ *n.* Säure, *die;* Acidität, *die* (fachspr.); Säuregrad, *der;* (excessive) Übersäuerung, *die;* (fig.) Bissigkeit, *die*

acidly /'æsɪdlɪ/ *adv.* (fig.) bissig

acidosis /æsɪ'dəʊsɪs/ *n., pl.* **acidoses** /æsɪ'dəʊsi:z/ (Med.) Acidose, *die*

acid: ~ **rain** *n.* saurer Regen; ~ **snow** *n.* saurer Schnee; ~ **test** *n.* Goldprobe, *die;* (fig.) Feuerprobe, *die*

acknowledge /əkˈnɒlɪdʒ/ *v.t.* **1** (admit) zugeben, eingestehen ‹*Tatsache, Notwendigkeit, Fehler, Schuld*›; (accept) sich bekennen zu ‹*einer Verantwortung, Pflicht, Schuld*›; anerkennen ‹*Schulden*›; (take notice of) grüßen ‹*Person*›; (recognize) anerkennen ‹*Autorität, Recht, Forderung, Notwendigkeit*›; **an ~d expert** ein anerkannter Fachmann; ~ **sb./sth. [as** *or* **to be] sth.** jmdn./etw. als etw. anerkennen; **he was ~d [as] the world's greatest living poet** er galt als der Welt größter lebender Dichter; ~ **sb. [as] capable of doing sth.** jmdn. für fähig halten, etw. zu tun **2** (express thanks for) sich erkenntlich zeigen für ‹*Dienste, Bemühungen, Gastfreundschaft*›; erwidern ‹*Gruß*› **3** (confirm receipt of) bestätigen ‹*Empfang, Bewerbung*›; ~ **a letter** den Empfang eines Briefes bestätigen

acknowledg[e]ment /əkˈnɒlɪdʒmənt/ *n.* **1** (admission of a fact, necessity, error, guilt) Eingeständnis, *das;* (acceptance of a responsibility, duty, debt) Bekenntnis, *das* (**of** zu); (recognition of authority, right, claim) Anerkennung, *die* **2** (thanks, appreciation) (of services, friendship) Dank, *der* (**of** für); (of greetings) Erwiderung, *die;* **a grateful ~ of the services you have rendered to the community** eine dankbare Anerkennung Ihrer Verdienste um die Gemeinschaft **3** (confirmation of receipt) Bestätigung [des Empfangs/einer Bewerbung]; **letter of ~:** Bestätigungsschreiben, *das* **4** (author's) Danksagung, *die;* **'~s'** „Dank"

acme /ˈækmɪ/ *n.* Gipfel, *der;* Höhepunkt, *der*

acne /ˈæknɪ/ *n.* ▸ℹ **p. 1231** (Med.) Akne, *die*

acolyte /ˈækəlaɪt/ *n.* **1** (Eccl.) Ministrant, *der;* Messdiener, *der* **2** (fig.: follower) Gefolgsmann, *der*

aconite /ˈækənaɪt/ *n.* (Bot.) Eisenhut, *der;* Sturmhut, *der;* Akonit, *das* (fachspr.)

acorn /ˈeɪkɔːn/ *n.* Eichel, *die*

acoustic /əˈkuːstɪk/ *adj.* **1** akustisch **2** (Mus.) ~ **guitar** Konzertgitarre, *die;* (in pop, folk, etc.) akustische Gitarre

acoustically /əˈkuːstɪkəlɪ/ *adv.* akustisch

acoustics /əˈkuːstɪks/ *n. pl.* **1** (properties) Akustik, *die;* akustische Verhältnisse *Pl.* **2** *constr. as sing.* (science) Akustik, *die*

ACP States *n. pl.* AKP-Staaten *Pl.*

acquaint /əˈkweɪnt/ *v.t.* ~ **sb./oneself with sth.** jmdn./sich mit etw. vertraut machen; **be ~ed with sb.** mit jmdm. bekannt sein

acquaintance /əˈkweɪntəns/ *n.* **1** *no pl.* Vertrautheit, *die;* ~ **with sb.** Bekanntschaft mit jmdm.; **a passing ~:** eine flüchtige Bekanntschaft; **make the ~ of sb.** jmds. Bekanntschaft machen; jmdn. kennen lernen **2** (person) Bekannte, *der/die*

aˈcquaintance rape *n.* Vergewaltigung durch einen Bekannten

acquiesce /ækwɪˈes/ *v.i.* einwilligen (**in** in + *Akk.*); (under pressure) sich fügen; **you must not ~ in everything [they say]** du darfst nicht allem zustimmen [,was sie sagen]

acquiescence /ækwɪˈesəns/ *n.* **1** *no pl.* (acquiescing) Einwilligung, *die* (**in** in + *Akk.*); (state) Ergebenheit, *die* **2** (assent) Zustimmung, *die*

acquiescent /ækwɪˈesənt/ *adj.* fügsam; ergeben

acquire /əˈkwaɪə(r)/ *v.t.* **1** sich (*Dat.*) anschaffen ‹*Gegenstände*›; (gain) erwerben ‹*Land, Besitz, Wohlstand, Kenntnisse*›; sammeln ‹*Erfahrungen*›; ernten ‹*Lob*› **2** (take on) annehmen ‹*Tonfall, Farbe, Aussehen, Gewohnheit*›; **last year the orchestra ~d a new leader** letztes Jahr erhielt das Orchester einen neuen Konzertmeister; **I have ~d a few unwanted pounds** ich habe leider ein paar Pfund[e] zugenommen; **~d characteristics** (Biol.) erworbene Eigenschaften; ~ **the habit of smoking** sich (*Dat.*) das Rauchen angewöhnen; ~ **a taste for sth.** Geschmack an etw. (*Dat.*) gewinnen; **this wine is an ~d taste** an diesen Wein muss man sich erst gewöhnen

acquired ˈimmune deficiency syndrome *n.* (Med.) erworbenes Immunschwächesyndrom

acquirement /əˈkwaɪəmənt/ *n.* ▸ **acquisition 1**

acquis /æˈkiː/ *n.* (EU) ~ **[communautaire]** Acquis communautaire, *der*

acquisition /ækwɪˈzɪʃn/ *n.* **1** (of goods, wealth, land) Erwerb, *der;* (of knowledge) Aneignung, *die;* Erwerb, *der;* (of attitude, habit) Annahme, *die* **2** (thing) Anschaffung, *die*

acquisitive /əˈkwɪzɪtɪv/ *adj.* raffsüchtig; ~ **instinct** Sammeltrieb, *der;* **the ~ society** die nach Besitz strebende Gesellschaft

acquisitiveness /əˈkwɪzɪtɪvnɪs/ *n., no pl.* Raffgier, *die*

acquit /əˈkwɪt/ *v.t.*, **-tt-: 1** (Law) freisprechen; ~ **sb. of sth.** jmdn. von etw. freisprechen; **he was ~ted on all three charges** er wurde in allen drei Anklagepunkten freigesprochen **2** (discharge) ~ **oneself of** erfüllen ‹*Pflichten*›; ~ **oneself well** seine Sache gut machen; **if you ~ yourself well in the test** wenn du in der Prüfung gut abschneidest

acquittal /əˈkwɪtl/ *n.* **1** (Law) Freispruch, *der* **2** (performance) Erfüllung, *die;* Erledigung, *die*

acre /ˈeɪkə(r)/ *n.* **1** ▸ℹ **p. 911** (measure) Acre, *der;* ≈ Morgen, *der* **2** *in pl.* (land) Grund und Boden, *der;* **broad ~s** weites Land

acreage /ˈeɪkərɪdʒ/ *n.* **what is the ~ of your estate?** wie viel Land *od.* wie viele Morgen hat Ihr Gut?; **a farm of small ~:** ein Hof mit kleiner Anbaufläche

acrid /ˈækrɪd/ *adj.* beißend ‹*Geruch, Dämpfe, Rauch*›; bitter ‹*Geschmack*›

acrimonious /ækrɪˈməʊnɪəs/ *adj.* bitter; aggressiv ‹*Haltung*›; bissig ‹*Bemerkung*›; erbittert ‹*Streit, Diskussion*›

acrimoniously /ækrɪˈməʊnɪəslɪ/ *adv.* bitter; erbittert ‹*angreifen*›

acrimony /ˈækrɪmənɪ/ *n., no pl.* Bitterkeit, *die;* (of attitude) Aggressivität, *die;* (of comment, criticism, etc.) Bissigkeit, *die;* (of argument, discussion) Erbitterung, *die*

acrobat /ˈækrəbæt/ *n.* ▸ℹ **p. 1260** (lit. or fig.) Akrobat, *der*/Akrobatin, *die;* **a mental/intellectual ~:** ein Geistesakrobat

acrobatic /ækrəˈbætɪk/ *adj.* (lit. or fig.) akrobatisch

acrobatics /ækrəˈbætɪks/ *n., no pl.* Akrobatik, *die;* **mental ~:** Gehirnakrobatik, *die*

acronym /ˈækrənɪm/ *n.* Akronym, *das;* Initialwort, *das*

across /əˈkrɒs/

A *adv.* **1** (to intersect) [quer] darüber **2** (from one side to the other) darüber; (in crossword puzzle) waagerecht; (from here to there) hinüber; **go ~ to the enemy** (fig.) zum Feind übergehen; **measure** *or* **be 9 miles ~:** 9 Meilen breit sein **3** (on the other side) drüben; ~ **there/here** [da] drüben/hier drüben; ~ **from** gegenüber von; **just ~ from us there is a little shop** bei uns ist gleich gegenüber ein kleiner Laden **4** *with verbs* (towards speaker) herüber-; (away from speaker) hinüber-; **swim ~:** herüber-/hinüberschwimmen

B *prep.* **1** (crossing) über (+ *Akk.*); **right ~ the field** quer über das Feld; **a double yellow line ~ an entrance** eine gelbe Doppellinie vor einer Einfahrt **2** (from one side to the other of) über (+ *Akk.*); **we went ~ the Atlantic** wir überquerten den Atlantik; **protest meetings ~ Canada** Protestversammlungen in ganz Kanada; ~ **the board** pauschal; **a pay rise ~ the board** eine pauschale *od.* generelle Lohnerhöhung **3** (on the other side of) auf der anderen Seite (+ *Gen.*); ~ **the ocean/river** jenseits des Meeres/Flusses

aˈcross-the-board *adj.* pauschal; **an ~ pay rise** eine pauschale *od.* generelle Lohnerhöhung

acrostic /əˈkrɒstɪk/ *n.* Akrostichon, *das*

acrylamide /əˈkrɪləmaɪd/ *n.* (Chem.) Acrylamid, *das*

acrylic /əˈkrɪlɪk/

A *adj.* aus Acryl *nachgestellt;* Acryl-; ~ **paint/fibre** Acrylfarbe, *die*/Acrylfaser, *die*

B *n.* Acryl, *das*

act /ækt/

A *n.* **1** (deed) Tat, *die;* (official action) Akt, *der;* **an ~ of God** höhere Gewalt; **an ~ of mercy** ein Gnadenakt; **an ~ of kindness** ein Akt *od.* Zeichen der Güte; **an ~ of folly** eine Dummheit; **Acts [of the Apostles]** (Bibl.) *constr. as sing.* Apostelgeschichte, *die* **2** (process) **be in the ~ of doing sth.** gerade dabei sein, etw. zu tun; **he was caught in the ~ [of stealing]** er wurde [beim Stehlen] auf frischer Tat ertappt; **they were caught in the [very] ~:** sie wurden in flagranti ertappt **3** (in a play) Akt, *der;* Aufzug, *der* (geh.); **a five-~ play** ein Drama in fünf Akten; **a one-~ play** ein Einakter **4** (theatre performance) Akt, *der;* Nummer, *die;* (performer) Darsteller, *der*/Darstellerin, *die;* **the ~ consisted of four jugglers** die Truppe bestand aus vier Jongleuren; **get in on the ~** (fig. coll.) ins Geschäft einsteigen; mitmischen (ugs.); **he/she will be a hard ~ to follow** (fig.) das macht ihm/ihr so leicht keiner nach; **get one's ~ together** (coll.) sich am Riemen reißen (ugs.) **5** (pretence) Theater, *das;* Schau, *die* (ugs.); **it's all an ~ with her** sie tut nur so; **put on an ~** (coll.) eine Schau abziehen (ugs.); Theater spielen; **get in on the ~** (coll.) in das Geschäft einsteigen; mitmischen (ugs.) **6** (decree) Gesetz, *das;* **Act of Parliament** Parlamentsakte, *die*

B *v.t.* **1** (perform) spielen ‹*Stück*› **2** (play role of) spielen ‹*Rolle*›; **he's a famous film producer and really ~s the part** (fig.) er ist ein berühmter Filmproduzent und benimmt sich auch so; *see also* **fool¹ A 2**

C *v.i.* **1** (perform actions) handeln; reagieren; ~ **upon the instructions you were given** folgen Sie den Anweisungen wie gegeben; ~ **[up]on sb.'s advice** jmds. Rat[schlag] (*Dat.*) folgen; ~ **quickly** schnell reagieren *od.* handeln **2** (behave) sich verhalten; (function) ~ **as sb.** als jmd. fungieren *od.* tätig sein; ~ **as sth.** als etw. dienen **3** (perform special function) ‹*Person:*› handeln; ‹*Gerät, Ding:*› funktionieren; ‹*Substanz, Mittel:*› wirken; ~ **for** *or* ~ **on behalf of sb.** für jmdn. *od.* in jmds. Auftrag tätig werden; jmdn. vertreten; ~ **to prevent sth.** ‹*Vorrichtung, Gerät:*› zur Verhütung von etw. dienen **4** (perform play etc.; lit. or fig.) spielen; schauspielern (ugs.); **she wants to ~ on stage/in films** sie will zum Theater/Film **5** (have effect) ~ **on sth.** auf etw. (*Akk.*) wirken *od.* einwirken

Phrasal verbs

- ~ **ˈout** *v.t.* **1** vorspielen, nachmachen ‹*Bewegungen, Handlung*› **2** (Psych.) abreagieren ‹*Spannung, Ärger*›
- ~ **ˈup** *v.i.* (coll.) Theater machen (ugs.); ‹*Auto, Magen:*› Zicken machen (ugs.), verrückt spielen (salopp); **the kids have been ~ing up like mad today** die Kinder haben heute total verrückt gespielt (salopp)

ACT *abbr.* **= American College Test** amerikanische College-Aufnahmeprüfung

> **ACT – American College Test**
>
> Ein Test, den Studierende in fast allen Staaten der USA bestehen müssen, um an einem College zugelassen zu werden. Der Test wird normalerweise am Ende der **high school** abgelegt und deckt eine Reihe von Kernfächern einschließlich Englisch und Mathematik ab.

acting /ˈæktɪŋ/

A *adj.* (temporary) stellvertretend; (in charge) geschäftsführend; amtierend

B *n., no pl.* (Theatre etc.) die Schauspielerei; **she's studying ~:** sie ist auf der Schauspielschule; **an ~ career** eine Karriere als Schauspieler; **she does a lot of ~ in her spare time** sie spielt in ihrer Freizeit viel Theater

action /ˈækʃn/ *n.* **1** (doing sth.) Handeln, *das;* **what kind of ~ do you think is necessary?** welche Schritte *od.* Maßnahmen halten Sie für notwendig?; **his quick ~ saved the boy's life** sein schnelles Eingreifen rettete dem Jungen das Leben; **a man of ~:** ein Mann der Tat; **take ~:** Schritte *od.* etwas unternehmen; Maßnahmen ergreifen; **see sth. in ~:** etw. in Betrieb sehen; **put a plan into ~:** einen Plan in die Tat umsetzen; **come into ~:** in die Tat umgesetzt werden; **put sth. out of ~:** etw. außer Betrieb setzen; **be/be put out of ~:** außer Betrieb sein/gesetzt werden; **a film full of ~:** ein Film mit viel Handlung **2** (effect) **the ~ of salt on ice** die Wirkung von Salz auf Eis **3** (act) Tat, *die;* **she is impulsive in her ~s** sie handelt sehr impulsiv **4** (Theatre) Handlung, *die;* Geschehen, *das;* **where the ~ is** (coll.) wo was los ist (ugs.); **hey, man, where's the ~?** (coll.) du, sag mal, wo ist hier was los? (ugs.); **get a piece of the ~** (coll.) mitmachen **5** (legal process) [Gerichts]verfahren, *das;* **bring an ~ against sb.** eine Klage *od.* ein Verfahren gegen jmdn. anstrengen **6** (fighting) Gefecht, *das;* Kampf, *der;* **he died in ~:** er ist [im Kampf] gefallen; **go into ~:** Kampfhandlungen aufnehmen; **we all went into ~** (fig.) wir machten uns alle an die Arbeit **7** (movement) Bewegung, *die;* (mechanism) Mechanismus, *der;* (of piano, organ) Mechanik, *die*

actionable /'ækʃənəbl/ *adj.* [gerichtlich] verfolgbar *od.* strafbar

action: ~ committee, ~ group *ns.* [Eltern-/Bürger- *usw.*]initiative, *die;* **~-packed** *adj.* spannend ‹*Buch, Roman*›; **an ~-packed film** ein Film mit viel Aktion; **an ~-packed holiday** ein Aktivurlaub; **~ painting** *n.* Actionpainting, *das;* abstrakter Expressionismus; **~ plan** *n.* Aktionsplan, *der;* **~ point** *n.* Erledigungspunkt, *der;* **~ 'replay** *n.* Wiederholung [in Zeitlupe]; **~ stations** *n. pl.* (Mil.; also fig.) Stellung, *die;* **go to ~ stations** Stellung beziehen; **~ stations!** in die Stellungen!

activate /'æktɪveɪt/ *v.t.* **1** in Gang setzen ‹*Vorrichtung, Mechanismus*›; auslösen ‹*Mechanismus*› **2** (Chem., Phys.) aktivieren; **~d carbon** *or* **charcoal** Aktivkohle, *die*

activation /æktɪ'veɪʃn/ *n.* Aktivierung, *die*

active /'æktɪv/ *adj.* **1** aktiv; wirksam ‹*Kraft, Mittel*›; praktisch ‹*Gebrauch, Versuch, Kenntnisse*›; tätig ‹*Vulkan*›; rege ‹*Verstand, Gesellschaft*›; **a very ~ child** ein sehr lebhaftes Kind; **take an ~ interest in sth.** reges Interesse an etw. (*Dat.*) zeigen; regen Anteil an etw. (*Dat.*) nehmen; **take an ~ part in sth.** sich aktiv an etw. (*Dat.*) beteiligen; **he's still ~ as an author** er arbeitet noch als Schriftsteller; **maintain an ~ knowledge of current affairs** im politischen Tagesgeschehen auf dem Laufenden bleiben; **~ carbon** Aktivkohle, *die;* **on ~ service** *or* (Amer.) **duty** (Mil.) im aktiven Dienst; *see also* **list[1] A 1** **2** (Ling.) aktiv[isch]; **~ voice** Aktiv, *das*

actively /'æktɪvlɪ/ *adv.* aktiv; **be ~ engaged in sth.** intensiv mit etw. beschäftigt sein; **be ~ interested in sth.** ein reges Interesse an etw. (*Dat.*) zeigen

activeness /'æktɪvnɪs/ *n., no pl.* Aktivität, *die;* (of mind) Regsamkeit, *die;* (of person) Regheit, *die*

activism /'æktɪʌɪzm/ *n., no pl.* Aktivismus, *der*

activist /'æktɪvɪst/ *n.* Aktivist, *der*/Aktivistin, *die*

activity /æk'tɪvɪtɪ/ *n.* **1** *no pl.* Aktivität, *die;* **military ~:** militärischer Einsatz; **~ in the field of reform** reformerische Aktivitäten **2** (exertion) aktive Tätigkeit; rege [Mit]arbeit **3** *usu. in pl.* (action) Aktivität, *die;* (occupation) Betätigung, *die;* **she has so many social activities** sie ist gesellschaftlich so aktiv; **classroom activities** schulische Tätigkeiten; **outdoor activities** Betätigung an der frischen Luft; **a new sporting ~:** eine neue Sportart; **~ holiday** Aktivurlaub, *der;* **some activities offered by the youth centre** einige Veranstaltungen des Jugendzentrums

actor /'æktə(r)/ *n.* **1** Schauspieler, *der* **2** ► **actress**

Actors' Studio

Ein Institut in New York zur Fortbildung von Schauspielern. Die Werkstatt, in der sich die Schauspieler erproben konnten, wurde 1947 von Elia Kazan, Robert Lewis und Cheryl Crawford gegründet. Unter der Leitung von Lee Strasberg wurde im *Actors' Studio* eine neuartige Methode der Schauspielkunst gelehrt. *Method acting* stützte sich in starkem Maße auf eine reiche Palette schauspielerischen Ausdrucks. Mit Schülern wie Marlon Brando und Rod Steiger, Paul Newman, Marilyn Monroe und vielen anderen berühmten Stars ging das *Actors' Studio* in die Filmgeschichte ein.

actress /'æktrɪs/ *n.* Schauspielerin, *die*

actual /'æktʃʊəl/ *adj.* **1** (real) eigentlich, tatsächlich ‹*Lage, Gegebenheiten*›; wirklich ‹*Name, Gegenstand*›; konkret ‹*Beispiel*›; **what was the ~ time of his arrival?** wann genau ist er angekommen?; **what is the ~ position now?** wie ist eigentlich der Stand der Dinge?; **it's an ~ fact** das ist eine Tatsache *od.* ein Faktum; **in ~ fact** tatsächlich; **no ~ crime was committed** es wurde kein eigentliches Verbrechen begangen **2** (current) derzeitig; **the ~ situation** der gegenwärtige Stand der Dinge

actual bodily 'harm *n.* (Law) leichte Körperverletzung

actuality /æktʃʊ'ælɪtɪ/ *n.* Wirklichkeit, *die;* Realität, *die;* **the ~ of the situation** die reale *od.* wirkliche Lage; **in ~:** in Wirklichkeit; **when her dream became an ~:** als ihr Traum Wirklichkeit wurde

actualize /'æktʃʊəlaɪz/ *v.t.* umsetzen

actually /'æktʃʊəlɪ/ *adv.* (in fact) eigentlich; (by the way) übrigens; (believe it or not) sogar; **~, to tell you the truth ...:** also, um die Wahrheit zu sagen, ...; **~, I must be going** ich muss jetzt wirklich gehen; **I'm ~ quite capable of looking after myself** im Übrigen bin ich gut in der Lage, für mich selbst zu sorgen; **he ~ had the cheek to suggest ...:** er hatte tatsächlich die Unverfrorenheit, vorzuschlagen ...

actuarial /æktʃʊ'eərɪəl/ *adj.* versicherungsmathematisch

actuary /'æktʃʊərɪ/ *n.* ►**i** **p. 1260** Versicherungsmathematiker, *der;* Aktuar, *der*

actuate /'æktʃʊeɪt/ *v.t.* (activate) antreiben ‹*Maschine*›; in Bewegung setzen ‹*Vorgang*›; auslösen ‹*Mechanismus, Reaktion*›

actuation /æktʃʊ'eɪʃn/ *n.* (of machine) Antrieb, *der;* (of mechanism) Auslösen, *das*

acuity /ə'kjuːɪtɪ/ *n., no pl.* Schärfe, *die;* **visual ~:** Sehschärfe, *die;* **mental/intellectual ~:** Scharfsinn, *der;* **~ of judgement** Urteilskraft, *die;* **interpret sth. with great ~:** etw. mit großer Scharfsinnigkeit interpretieren

acumen /'ækjʊmen/ *n.* Scharfsinn, *der;* **business ~:** Geschäftssinn, *der;* **political ~:** politische Klugheit

acupressure /'ækjʊpreʃə(r)/ *n.* (Med.) Akupressur, *die*

acupuncture /'ækjʊpʌnktʃə(r)/ *n.* (Med.) Akupunktur, *die*

acupuncturist /'ækjʊpʌŋktʃərɪst/ *n.* ►**i** **p. 1260** Akupunkteur, *der*/Akupunkteurin, *die*

acute /ə'kjuːt/ *adj.*, **~r** /ə'kjuːtə(r)/, **~st** /ə'kjuːtɪst/ **1** (penetrating) scharf ‹*Kritik*›; genau ‹*Beobachtung*›; wach ‹*Bewusstsein*› **2** (Geom.) **~ angle** spitzer Winkel **3** (Med.) akut ‹*Krankheit, Stadium*› **4** (critical) akut ‹*Gefahr, Knappheit, Situation, Mangel*› **5** (keen) fein ‹*Geruchssinn*›; heftig ‹*Schmerz*› **6** (Ling.) **~ accent** Akut, *der* **7** (sharp) scharf ‹*Schneide*›; fein ‹*Spitze*›

acutely /ə'kjuːtlɪ/ *adv.* **1** (penetratingly) genau[estens] ‹*sich bewusst sein, durchdenken, beobachten*› **2** (Med.) akut; **he is ~ ill with pneumonia** er hat eine akute Lungenentzündung **3** (critically) äußerst; (keenly) äußerst; überaus; intensiv ‹*fühlen*›

acuteness /ə'kjuːtnɪs/ *n., no pl.* **1** (of criticism) Schärfe, *die;* (of observation) Genauigkeit, *die;* (of understanding) Scharfsinn, *der* **2** (Med.) Akutheit, *die* **3** (of pain, sensation) Heftigkeit, *die* **4** (of sense, hearing, etc.) Feinheit, *die* **5** (of cutting edge) Schärfe, *die;* (of point) Feinheit, *die*

ad /æd/ *n.* (coll.) Annonce, *die;* Inserat, *das;* **small ad** Kleinanzeige, *die;* **TV ads** Werbespots im Fernsehen

AD *abbr.* ►**i** **p. 1047** = **Anno Domini** n. Chr.

adage /'ædɪdʒ/ *n.* Sprichwort, *das*

adagio /ə'dɑːdʒjəʊ/ (Mus.)

A *adv.* adagio

B *adj.* Adagio-; langsam; ruhig

C *n., pl.* **~s** Adagio, *das*

Adam /'ædəm/ *pr. n.* (first man) Adam (*der*); **he doesn't know me from ~:** er hat keine Ahnung, wer ich bin

adamant /'ædəmənt/ *adj.* unnachgiebig; **be ~ that ...:** darauf bestehen, dass ...

Adam's 'apple *n.* Adamsapfel, *der*

adapt /ə'dæpt/

A *v.t.* **1** (adjust) anpassen (**to** *Dat.*); umbauen ‹*Auto*›; variieren ‹*Frisur, Kleidung*›; umstellen ‹*Maschine*› (**to** auf + *Akk.*); **this room can easily be ~ed to individual tastes** dieses Zimmer lässt sich leicht auf den persönlichen Geschmack abstimmen; **your eyes will quickly ~ themselves to the dark** deine Augen werden sich schnell an die Dunkelheit gewöhnen; **~ oneself to sth.** sich an etw. (*Akk.*) gewöhnen; **this furnace can be ~ed to take coal or oil** dieser Ofen lässt sich auf Kohle oder Öl einstellen; **be ~ed for doing sth.** darauf eingestellt sein, etw. zu tun **2** (modify) adaptieren, bearbeiten ‹*Text, Theaterstück*›; **~ed for TV by ...:** für das Fernsehen bearbeitet von ...; **~ sth. from sth.** etw. nach etw. bearbeiten

B *v.i.* **1** ‹*Tier, Auge:*› sich anpassen (**to** an + *Akk.*) **2** (to surroundings, circumstances) sich gewöhnen (**to** an + *Akk.*)

adaptability /ədæptə'bɪlɪtɪ/ *n., no pl.* (to way of life or environment) Anpassungsfähigkeit, *die* (**to** *or* **for** an + *Akk.*)

adaptable /ə'dæptəbl/ *adj.* anpassungsfähig; vielseitig ‹*Maschine*›; flexibel ‹*Planung*›; **be ~ to** *or* **for sth.** an etw. (*Akk.*) angepasst werden können

adaptation /ædəp'teɪʃn/ *n.* **1** *no pl.* Anpassung, *die* (**to** an + *Akk.*); (of garment) Veränderung, *die;* (of system, machine) Umstellung, *die* (**to** auf + *Akk.*) **2** (version) Adap[ta]tion, *die;* (of story, text) Bearbeitung, *die* **3** (Biol.) Adaptation, *die;* Anpassung, *die*

adaptor (**adapter**) /ə'dæptə(r)/ *n.* (device) Adapter, *der;* **a four-socket ~:** eine Vierfachsteckdose

ADC *abbr.* (Mil.) = **aide-de-camp**

add /æd/

A *v.t.* hinzufügen (**to** *Dat.*); hinzufügen, anfügen ‹*weitere Worte*›; beisteuern ‹*Ideen, Vorschläge*› (**to** zu); dazusetzen ‹*Namen, Zahlen*›; **~ two and two** zwei und zwei zusammenzählen; **~ two numbers together** zwei Zahlen addieren; **~ the flour to the liquid** geben Sie das Mehl in die Flüssigkeit; **we have ~ed a number of new books to our collection** wir haben unsere Sammlung um ein paar neue Bücher erweitert

B *v.i.* **~ to** vergrößern ‹*Schwierigkeiten, Einkommen*›; verbessern ‹*Ruf*›; **~ [together] to give** *or* **make the desired amount** zusammen den gewünschten Betrag ergeben

Phrasal verb

• **~ 'up**

A *v.i.* **1** **these figures ~ up to 30** diese Zahlen ergeben zusammen[gezählt] 30; **these things ~/it ~s up** (fig. coll.) all diese Dinge summieren sich/das summiert sich alles; **~ up to sth.** (fig.) auf etw. hinauslaufen **2** (make sense) einen Sinn ergeben

B *v.t.* zusammenzählen

added /'ædɪd/ *attrib. adj.* zusätzlich; **~ to this** außerdem; obendrein

addendum /ə'dendəm/ *n., pl.* **addenda** /ə'dendə/ (thing to be added) Nachtrag, *der;* Addendum, *das* (veralt.); (addition) Zusatz, *der; in pl.* (in book etc.) Addenda *Pl.*

adder /'ædə(r)/ *n.* (Zool.) Kreuzotter, *die*

addict

A /ə'dɪkt/ *v.t.* **be ~ed** süchtig sein; **become ~ed [to sth.]** [nach etw.] süchtig werden; **be ~ed**

to alcohol/smoking/drugs alkohol-/nikotin-/drogensüchtig sein
B /'ædɪkt/ *n.* Süchtige, *der/die;* (fig. coll.) [begeisterte] Anhänger, *der*/Anhängerin, *die;* **become an ~:** süchtig werden; **drug/heroin ~s** Drogen-/Heroinsüchtige *Pl.;* **a TV ~** (fig. coll.) ein Fernsehnarr

addiction /ə'dɪkʃn/ *n.* Sucht, *die;* (fig. coll.) Fimmel, *der* (ugs.); **an ~ to sth.** die Sucht nach etw.; **~ to heroin** Heroinsucht, *die*

addictive /ə'dɪktɪv/ *adj.* **be ~:** süchtig machen; (fig. coll.) zu einer Sucht werden

'adding machine *n.* Rechenmaschine, *die*

addition /ə'dɪʃn/ *n.* **1▸** *no pl.* Hinzufügen, *das;* (of ingredient) Dazugeben, *das;* (adding up) Addieren, *das;* (process) Addition, *die;* **in ~:** außerdem; **in ~ to** zusätzlich zu **2▸** (thing added) Ergänzung, *die* (**to** zu); **we are expecting a new ~ to our family** wir erwarten Familienzuwachs

additional /ə'dɪʃənl/ *adj.* zusätzlich; **~ details** weitere Einzelheiten

additionality /ædɪʃə'nælɪtɪ/ *n., no pl.* (EU) Additionalität, *die*

additionally /ə'dɪʃənəlɪ/ *adv.* außerdem

additive /'ædɪtɪv/
A *n.* Zusatz, *der*
B *adj.* zusätzlich; (to be added) weiter

addled /'ædld/ *adj.* **1▸** (rotten) verdorben; faul **2▸** (muddled) verwirrt ‹*Gedanken*›; benebelt ‹*Kopf*›

'add-on
A *n.* (accessory) Zubehörteil, *das;* (for electrical appliance) Zusatzgerät, *das;* (addition) Zusatz, *der*
B *adj.* **~ accessory** Zubehörteil, *das;* (for electrical appliance) Zusatzgerät, *das;* **sth. can be bought as an ~ feature/accessory for sth.** etw. ist als Zubehör zu einer Sache erhältlich

address /ə'dres/
A *v.t.* **1▸** **~ sth. to sb./sth.** etw. an jmdn./etw. richten; **you must ~ your complaint to ...:** richten Sie Ihre Beschwerde an (+ *Akk.*) ...; **~ oneself to sb./sth.** sich an jmdn./etw. wenden **2▸** ▸**❶ p. 1287** (mark with ~) adressieren (**to** an + *Akk.*); mit Anschrift versehen **3▸** (speak to) anreden ‹*Person*›; sprechen zu ‹*Zuhörern*›; **~ sb. as sth.** jmdn. mit etw. *od.* als etw. anreden **4▸** (give attention to) angehen ‹*Problem*› **5▸** (apply) **~ oneself to sth.** sich zu etw. anschicken
B *n.* **1▸** ▸**❶ p. 1287** (on letter or envelope) Adresse, *die;* Anschrift, *die;* (place of residence) Wohnsitz, *der;* **of no fixed ~:** ohne festen Wohnsitz **2▸** (speech) Ansprache, *die;* Rede, *die* **3▸** (Computing) Adresse, *die* **4▸** *in pl.* (arch.: courteous approach) Werben, *das;* **pay one's ~es to sb.** (arch.) jmdm. den Hof machen

ad'dress book *n.* Adressenbüchlein, *das*

addressee /ædre'si:/ *n.* Adressat, *der*/Adressatin, *die;* Empfänger, *der*/Empfängerin, *die*

ad'dress label *n.* Adressenaufkleber, *der*

adduce /ə'dju:s/ *v.t.* anführen

adenoids /'ædɪnɔɪdz/ *n. pl.* (Med.) Rachenmandel- *od.* Nasenpolypen *Pl.;* Rachenmandelwucherungen *Pl.*

adept /'ædept, ə'dept/
A *adj.* geschickt (**in, at** in + *Dat.*)
B *n.* Kenner, *der*/Kennerin, *die;* Meister, *der*/Meisterin, *die*

adequacy /'ædɪkwəsɪ/ *n., no pl.* **1▸** (sufficiency) Adäquatheit, *die;* Angemessenheit, *die* **2▸** (suitability) Eignung, *die* **3▸** (bare sufficiency) Zulänglichkeit, *die* **4▸** (proportionateness) **the ~ of sth. to sth.** die Angemessenheit einer Sache für etw.

adequate /'ædɪkwət/ *adj.* **1▸** (sufficient) ausreichend; angemessen ‹*Bezahlung, Wohnraum*› **2▸** (barely sufficient) hinreichend; zulänglich; **my grant is ~ and no more** mein Stipendium reicht gerade so aus **3▸** (suitable) angemessen; **he couldn't find ~ words** ihm fehlten die richtigen *od.* passenden Worte **4▸** (proportionate) **~ [to sth.]** einer Sache (*Dat.*) angemessen

adequately /'ædɪkwətlɪ/ *adv.* **1▸** (sufficiently) ausreichend; **are you ~ prepared for your exam?** haben Sie sich auf die Prüfung in ausreichender Weise vorbereitet?; **these children are not ~ nourished** diese Kinder sind unterernährt **2▸** (barely sufficiently) hinreichend; zulänglich **3▸** (suitably) angemessen ‹*gekleidet, qualifiziert usw.*›

adhere /əd'hɪə(r)/ *v.i.* **1▸** (stick) haften, (by glue) kleben (**to** an + *Dat.*); **~ [to each other]** ‹*zwei Dinge:*› zusammenkleben **2▸** (give support) **~ to sth./sb.** an jmdn./einer Sache festhalten; **~ to a party/policy** eine Partei/Politik unterstützen **3▸** (keep) **~ to** festhalten an (+ *Dat.*) ‹*Programm, Brauch, Gewohnheit*›; sich halten an (+ *Akk.*) ‹*Abmachung, Versprechen, Regel*›; **we must ~ strictly to the schedule** wir müssen uns genau an den Zeitplan halten

adherence /əd'hɪərəns/ *n., no pl.* **1▸** (to party, leader, policy) Unterstützung, *die* (**to** *Gen.*) **2▸** (to programme, agreement, promise, schedule) Einhalten, *das* (**to** *Gen.*); (to decision, tradition, principle) Festhalten, *das* (**to** an + *Dat.*); (to rule) Befolgen, *das* (**to** *Gen.*)

adherent /əd'hɪərənt/ *n.* Anhänger, *der*/Anhängerin, *die*

adhesion /əd'hi:ʒn/ *n.* **1▸** *no pl.* (sticking) Haften, *das* (**to** an + *Dat.*); (by glue) Kleben, *das* (**to** an + *Dat.*) **2▸** *no pl.* (support) Unterstützung, *die* (**to** *Gen.*); (to agreement) Einhalten, *das* (**to** *Gen.*)

adhesive /əd'hi:sɪv/
A *adj.* (adherent) klebrig; gummiert ‹*Briefmarke, Umschlag*›; Klebe‹*band, -schicht*›; **be ~:** kleben/gummiert sein; **~ plaster** Heftpflaster, *das; see also* **tape A 1**
B *n.* Klebstoff, *der;* Klebemittel, *das*

ad hoc /æd 'hɒk/
A *adv.* ad hoc
B *adj.* Ad-hoc-

adieu /ə'dju:/
A *int.* adieu; leb/lebt wohl; **we bid** *or* **wish you ~:** leb/lebt wohl
B *n., pl.* **~s** *or* **~x** /ə'dju:z/ Adieu *od.* Lebewohl, *das*

ad infinitum /æd ɪnfɪ'naɪtəm/ *adv.* ad infinitum (geh.); ohne Ende

adipose /'ædɪpəʊs/ *adj.* adipös (fachspr.); verfettet; **~ tissue** Fettgewebe, *das*

adjacent /ə'dʒeɪsənt/ *adj.* angrenzend; Neben-; **~ to** (position) neben (+ *Dat.*); (direction) neben (+ *Akk.*); **he sat in the ~ room** er saß im Zimmer nebenan

adjectival /ædʒɪk'taɪvəl/ *adj.* (Ling.) adjektivisch; **~ endings** Adjektivendungen

adjective /'ædʒɪktɪv/ *n.* (Ling.) Adjektiv, *das;* Eigenschaftswort, *das*

adjoin /ə'dʒɔɪn/
A *v.t.* grenzen an (+ *Akk.*); **the room ~ing ours** das Zimmer neben unserem
B *v.i.* aneinander grenzen; nebeneinander liegen; **an ~ing field** ein angrenzendes *od.* benachbartes Feld; **in the ~ing room** im Zimmer daneben *od.* nebenan

adjourn /ə'dʒɜ:n/
A *v.t.* (break off) unterbrechen; (put off) aufschieben
B *v.i.* (suspend proceedings) sich vertagen; **let's ~ to the sitting room/pub** begeben wir uns ins Wohnzimmer/(ugs.) in die Kneipe

adjournment /ə'dʒɜ:nmənt/ *n.* (suspending) (of court) Vertagung, *die;* (of meeting) Unterbrechung, *die*

adjudge /ə'dʒʌdʒ/ *v.t.* (pronounce) **~ sb./sth. [to be] sth.** jmdn./etw. für etw. erklären *od.* befinden

adjudicate /ə'dʒu:dɪkeɪt/ *v.i.* (in court, tribunal) als Richter tätig sein; (in contest) Preisrichter sein (**at** bei, in + *Dat.*)

adjudication /ədʒu:dɪ'keɪʃn/ *n.* **1▸** (judging) Beurteilung, *die;* **expert ~:** Expertenmeinung, *die* **2▸** (decision) Entscheidung, *die*

adjudicator /ə'dʒu:dɪkeɪtə(r)/ *n.* Schiedsrichter, *der*/Schiedsrichterin, *die;* (in contest) Preisrichter, *der*/Preisrichterin, *die*

adjunct /'ædʒʌŋkt/ *n.* **1▸** Anhängsel, *das;* (effect) Neben- *od.* Begleiterscheinung, *die* **2▸** (Ling.) Adjunkt, *das*

adjuration /ædʒʊə'reɪʃn/ *n.* (formal) [inständige] Bitte; Beschwörung, *die*

adjure /ə'dʒʊə(r)/ *v.t.* (formal) inständig bitten; beschwören

adjust /ə'dʒʌst/
A *v.t.* **1▸** richtig [an]ordnen ‹*Gegenstände, Gliederung*›; ändern ‹*Gegebenheiten*›; zurechtmachen ‹*Frisur*›; zurechtrücken ‹*Hut, Krawatte*›; (regulate) regulieren, regeln ‹*Geschwindigkeit, Höhe usw.*›; [richtig] einstellen ‹*Gerät, Mechanismus, Bremsen, Vergaser, Motor, Zündung*›; (adapt) entsprechend ändern ‹*Plan, Bedingungen*›; angleichen ‹*Gehalt, Lohn, Zinsen*›; **~ sth. [to sth.]** etw. [an etw. (*Akk.*)] anpassen *od.* [auf etw. (*Akk.*)] einstellen; **please ~ your watches** bitte stellen Sie Ihre Uhren richtig; **'do not ~ your set'** „Störung" **2▸** (assess) berechnen ‹*Schaden*›; regulieren ‹*Versicherungsansprüche*›; eichen ‹*Maß, Gewicht*›
B *v.i.* **~ [to sth.]** sich [an etw. (*Akk.*)] gewöhnen *od.* anpassen; ‹*Gerät, Maschine usw.:*› sich [auf etw. (*Akk.*)] einstellen lassen; **the eye soon ~s to the dark** das Auge gewöhnt sich schnell an die Dunkelheit; **~ to new conditions/a requirement** sich auf neue Verhältnisse/eine Forderung einstellen

adjustable /ə'dʒʌstəbl/ *adj.* einstellbar (**to** auf + *Akk.*); verstellbar, justierbar ‹*Gerät*›; regulierbar ‹*Temperatur*›

adjustment /ə'dʒʌstmənt/ *n.* **1▸** (of layout, plan) Ordnung, *die;* (of things) Anordnung, *die;* (of device, engine, machine) Einstellung, *die;* (of hair, clothing) Zurechtmachen, *das;* (to situation, lifestyle) Anpassung, *die* (**to** an + *Akk.*); (of eye) Adaption, *die;* Gewöhnung, *die;* **some ~s are necessary on your car engine** an Ihrem Motor muss einiges neu *od.* richtig eingestellt werden; **she made a few minor ~s to her manuscript** sie brachte an ihrem Manuskript ein paar kleinere Korrekturen an **2▸** (of insurance claim, damage) Schadensfestsetzung, *die* **3▸** (settlement) (of claims or damages) Regulierung, *die* **4▸** (device) Einstellvorrichtung, *die*

adjutant /'ædʒʊtənt/ *n.* **1▸** (Mil.) Adjutant, *der* **2▸** (Ornith.) **~ [bird]** Indischer Marabu

ad lib /æd 'lɪb/ *adv.* zwanglos, nach Belieben

ad-lib
A *adj.* (unprepared, improvised) Stegreif-, improvisiert ‹*Rede, Vortrag*›; **give an ~ rendering** improvisieren
B *v.i.*, **-bb-** (coll.) improvisieren

Adm. *abbr.* **= admiral** Adm.

adman /'ædmæn/ *n., pl.* **admen** /'ædmen/ Werbe-, Reklamefachmann, *der*

admin /'ædmɪn/ *n.* (coll.) Verwaltung, *die;* **an ~ problem** ein Verwaltungsproblem

administer /əd'mɪnɪstə(r)/ *v.t.* **1▸** (manage) verwalten; führen ‹*Geschäfte, Regierung*›; regieren ‹*Land*› **2▸** (give, apply) spenden ‹*Trost*›; leisten, gewähren ‹*Hilfe, Unterstützung*›; austeilen, verabreichen ‹*Schläge, Prügel*›; verabreichen, geben ‹*Medikamente*›; spenden, geben ‹*Sakramente*›; anwenden ‹*Disziplinierungsmaßnahmen*›; **~ justice [to sb.]** [über jmdn.] Recht sprechen; **~ punishment to sb.** jmdn. bestrafen; **~ an oath to sb.** jmdn. vereidigen; jmdm. einen Eid abnehmen; **~ treatment to sb.** jmdn. behandeln

administrate /əd'mɪnɪstreɪt/ *v.t.* ▸**administer 1**

administration /ədmɪnɪ'streɪʃn/ *n.* **1▸** (management, managing) Verwaltung, *die* **2▸** (giving, applying) (of sacraments) Spenden, *das;* Geben, *das;* (of discipline) Anwendung, *die;* (of medicine) Verabreichung, *die;* (of aid, relief) Gewährung, *die;* **~ of justice** Rechtspflege, *die;* **~ of an oath** Eidesabnahme, *die* **3▸** (ministry, government) Regierung, *die;* (Amer.: period of office) Amtszeit, *die* **4▸** (Law) **~ of the estate** Nachlassverwaltung, *die*

administrative /əd'mɪnɪstrətɪv/ *adj.* Verwaltungs-; administrativ ‹*Angelegenheit, Geschick, Fähigkeit*›; **~ work** Verwaltungsarbeit, *die;* **an ~ job** ein Verwaltungsposten

administrative 'law *n., no pl.* Verwaltungsrecht, *das*

administrator /əd'mɪnɪstreɪtə(r)/ *n.* ▸**❶ p. 1260** **1▸** (manager) Administrator, *der;*

Verwalter, *der;* (sb. capable of organizing) Organisator, *der* 2 (performing official duties) Verwaltungsbeamte/-angestellte, *der* 3 (of deceased person's estate) Verwalter, *der;* Testamentsvollstrecker, *der*

admirable /'ædmərəbl/ *adj.* bewundernswert; erstaunlich; (excellent) vortrefflich; ausgezeichnet

admirably /'ædmərəblɪ/ *adv.* bewundernswert; erstaunlich; (excellently) vortrefflich

admiral /'ædmərəl/ *n.* 1 ▸ⓘ **p. 1634** Admiral, *der;* **A~ of the Fleet** (Brit.) Großadmiral, *der* 2 (butterfly) **red ~:** Admiral, *der*

Admiralty /'ædmərəltɪ/ *n.* **~ [Board]** (Hist.) *britisches Marineministerium*

admiration /ædmə'reɪʃn/ *n., no pl.* 1 Bewunderung, *die* **(of, for** für) 2 (object of **~**) **be the ~ of sb.** von jmdm. bewundert werden

admire /əd'maɪə(r)/ *v.t.* bewundern **(for** wegen)

admirer /əd'maɪərə(r)/ *n.* Bewunderer, *der*/Bewunderin, *die;* (suitor) Verehrer, *der*/Verehrerin, *die*

admiring /əd'maɪərɪŋ/ *adj.,* **admiringly** /əd'maɪərɪŋlɪ/ *adv.* bewundernd

admissibility /ədmɪsɪ'bɪlɪtɪ/ *n., no pl.* Zulässigkeit, *die*

admissible /əd'mɪsɪbl/ *adj.* 1 akzeptabel ‹*Plan, Vorschlag*›; erlaubt, zulässig ‹*Abweichung, Schreibung*› 2 (Law) zulässig; **that is not ~ evidence** das ist kein vor Gericht zugelassener Beweis *od.* zugelassenes Beweisstück

admission /əd'mɪʃn/ *n.* 1 (entry) Zutritt, *der;* **~ to university** Zulassung [zum Studium] an einer Universität; **~ costs** *or* **is 50p** der Eintritt kostet 50 Pence; **charge for ~:** Eintrittspreis, *der* 2 (charge) Eintritt, *der* 3 (confession) Eingeständnis, *das* **(of, to** *Gen.*); **by** *or* **on one's own ~:** nach eigenem Eingeständnis

admission: ~ charge, ~ fee, ~ price *ns.* Eintrittspreis, *der;* **~ money** *n.* Eintrittsgeld, *das;* **~s tutor** *n.* für Zulassungen zuständiger Dozent/zuständige Dozentin; **~ ticket** *n.* Eintrittskarte, *die*

admit /əd'mɪt/

A *v.t.,* **-tt-:** 1 (let in) hinein-/hereinlassen; **persons under the age of 16 not ~ted** kein Zutritt für Jugendliche unter 16 Jahren; **~ sb. to a school/club** jmdn. in eine Schule/einen Klub aufnehmen; **'this ticket ~s two'** „Eintrittskarte für zwei Personen"; **be ~ted to hospital** ins Krankenhaus eingeliefert werden 2 (accept as valid) **if we ~ that argument/evidence** wenn wir davon ausgehen, dass dieses Argument zutrifft/dass diese Beweise erlaubt sind 3 (acknowledge) zugeben; eingestehen; **~ sth. to be true** zugeben *od.* eingestehen, dass etw. wahr ist; **~ to being guilty/drunk** zugeben, schuldig/betrunken zu sein 4 (have room for) Platz bieten (+ *Dat.*)

B *v.i.,* **-tt-:** **~ of sth.** etw. zulassen *od.* erlauben

admittance /əd'mɪtəns/ *n.* Zutritt, *der;* **no ~ [except on business]** Zutritt [für Unbefugte] verboten

admittedly /əd'mɪtɪdlɪ/ *adv.* zugegeben[ermaßen]; **~ he is very young** zugegeben, er ist sehr jung

admixture /əd'mɪkstʃə(r)/ *n.* 1 *no pl.* (mixing) [Ver]mischen, *das;* Vermengen, *das* 2 (ingredient) Zusatz, *der;* Beimischung, *die*

admonish /əd'mɒnɪʃ/ *v.t.* ermahnen; (reproach) ermahnen; tadeln

admonishment /əd'mɒnɪʃmənt/, **admonition** /ædmə'nɪʃn/ *ns.* Ermahnung, *die;* (reproach) Ermahnung, *die;* Tadel, *der*

ad nauseam /æd 'nɔ:zɪæm, æd 'nɔ:sɪæm/ *adv.* bis zum Überdruss

ado /ə'du:/ *n., no pl., no art.* **without more** *or* **with no further ~:** ohne weiteres Aufhebens

adobe /ə'dəʊbɪ, ə'dəʊb/ *n.* (brick) Adobe, *der;* ungebrannter Lehmziegel

adolescence /ædə'lesns/ *n., no art.* die Zeit des Erwachsenwerdens; die Adoleszenz (Med.)

adolescent /ædə'lesnt/

A *n.* Heranwachsende, *der/die*

B *adj.* heranwachsend ‹*Person*›; pubertär ‹*Benehmen*›

adopt /ə'dɒpt/ *v.t.* 1 adoptieren; aufnehmen ‹*Tier*›; **we ~ed a refugee family** wir übernahmen die Patenschaft für eine Flüchtlingsfamilie 2 (take over) annehmen, übernehmen ‹*Kultur, Sitte*›; annehmen ‹*Glaube, Religion*› 3 (take up) übernehmen, sich aneignen ‹*Methode*›; einnehmen ‹*Standpunkt, Haltung*›; **that's not the right attitude to ~:** das ist nicht die richtige Einstellung 4 (approve) annehmen; billigen; **the meeting ~ed the motion** die Versammlung stimmte dem Antrag zu

adoption /ə'dɒpʃn/ *n.* 1 Adoption, *die* 2 (taking over) (of culture, custom) Annahme, *die;* Übernahme, *die;* (of belief) Annahme, *die* 3 (taking up) (of method) Aneignung, *die;* Übernahme, *die;* (of point of view) Einnahme, *die* 4 (approval) Annahme, *die*

a'doption agency *n.* Adoptionsagentur, *die*

adoptive /ə'dɒptɪv/ *adj.* adoptiert; **~ son/mother** Adoptivsohn, *der*/-mutter, *die*

adorable /ə'dɔ:rəbl/ *adj.,* **adorably** /ə'dɔ:rəblɪ/ *adv.* bezaubernd; hinreißend

adoration /ædə'reɪʃn/ *n.* 1 Verehrung, *die* 2 (worship of gods etc.) Anbetung, *die*

adore /ə'dɔ:(r)/ *v.t.* 1 innig *od.* über alles lieben; **his adoring girlfriend/fans** seine schmachtende Freundin/schmachtenden Fans 2 (coll.: like greatly) **~ sth.** für etwas schwärmen; **~ doing sth.** etw. sehr, sehr gern *od.* (ugs.) für sein Leben gern tun 3 (worship) anbeten ‹*Götter usw.*›

adorn /ə'dɔ:n/ *v.t.* schmücken; **~ oneself** sich schön machen

adornment /ə'dɔ:nmənt/ *n.* 1 *no pl.* Verschönerung, *die* 2 (ornament) Verzierung, *die;* **~s** Schmuck, *der*

adrenal /ə'dri:nl/ (Anat.)

A *adj.* **~ glands** Nebennieren *Pl.*

B *n.* Nebenniere, *die*

adrenalin, (Amer. ®) /ə'drenəlɪn/ *n.* (Physiol., Med.) Adrenalin, *das*

Adriatic /eɪdrɪ'ætɪk/ *pr. n.* **~ [Sea]** Adriatisches Meer; Adria, *die*

adrift /ə'drɪft/ *pred. adj.* 1 **be ~:** treiben; **cut a boat ~:** die Halteleine eines Bootes durchschneiden 2 (fig.: exposed) verloren; preisgegeben; **turn sb. ~:** jmdn. sich (*Dat.*) selbst überlassen

adroit /ə'drɔɪt/ *adj.* geschickt; gewandt; **be ~ at sth./doing sth.** gewandt *od.* geschickt in etw. (*Dat.*) sein

adroitly /ə'drɔɪtlɪ/ *adv.* geschickt; gewandt

adroitness /ə'drɔɪtnɪs/ *n., no pl.* Geschicklichkeit, *die;* Gewandtheit, *die*

ADSL *abbr.* (Teleph.) **= asymmetric digital subscriber line** ADSL

adulation /ædjʊ'leɪʃn/ *n., no pl.* (praise) Beweihräucherung, *die;* (admiration of person) Vergötterung, *die*

adult /'ædʌlt, ə'dʌlt/

A *adj.* erwachsen ‹*Person*›; reif ‹*Verhalten*›; ausgewachsen ‹*Tier, Pflanze*›; **this play is suitable only for ~ audiences** dieses Stück ist nur für Erwachsene geeignet; **an ~ film/book** *etc.* ein Film/Buch *usw.* [nur] für Erwachsene; **behave in an ~ manner** sich wie ein Erwachsener benehmen

B *n.* Erwachsene, *der/die;* **'~s only'** „Nur für Erwachsene"; **~ education** Erwachsenenbildung, *die*

adulterate /ə'dʌltəreɪt/ *v.t.* verunreinigen; panschen ‹*Wein, Milch*›

adulteration /ədʌltə'reɪʃn/ *n.* Verunreinigung, *die;* (of wine, milk) Panschen, *das*

adulterer /ə'dʌltərə(r)/ *n.* Ehebrecher, *der*

adulteress /ə'dʌltərɪs/ *n.* Ehebrecherin, *die*

adulterous /ə'dʌltərəs/ *adj.* ehebrecherisch

adultery /ə'dʌltərɪ/ *n., no pl.* Ehebruch, *der*

adulthood /'ædʌlthʊd, ə'dʌlthʊd/ *n., no pl.* Erwachsenenalter, *das;* **reach ~:** erwachsen werden

adumbrate /'ædəmbreɪt/ *v.t.* (formal) 1 (outline) umreißen; skizzieren 2 (suggest faintly) andeuten 3 (foreshadow) ankündigen

advance /əd'vɑ:ns/

A *v.t.* 1 (move forward) vorrücken lassen 2 (put forward) vorbringen ‹*Plan, Meinung, These*› 3 (bring forward) vorverlegen ‹*Termin*› 4 (promote) befördern 5 (further) fördern; **~ one's own interests** [nur] die eigenen Interessen verfolgen 6 (pay before due date) vorschießen; **~ sb. a week's pay** jmdm. einen Wochenlohn [als] Vorschuss geben; (loan) **the bank ~d me two thousand pounds** die Bank lieh mir zweitausend Pfund 7 (increase) erhöhen

B *v.i.* 1 (move forward; also Mil.) vorrücken; ‹*Prozession:*› sich vorwärts bewegen; **~ towards sb./sth.** ‹*Person:*› auf jmdn./etw. zugehen; **he ~d towards me** er kam auf mich zu 2 (fig.: make progress) Fortschritte machen; vorankommen 3 (increase) steigen

C *n.* 1 (forward movement) Vorrücken, *das;* (fig.: progress) Fortschritt, *der;* **any ~ on £30?** [bietet] jemand mehr als 30 Pfund? 2 *usu. in pl.* (personal overture) Annäherungsversuch, *der* 3 (payment beforehand) Vorauszahlung, *die;* (on salary) Vorschuss, *der* **(on** auf + *Akk.*); (loan) Darlehen, *das* 4 **in ~:** im Voraus; **be in ~ of one's age** seiner Zeit voraus sein; **send sb./sth. in ~:** jmdn./etw. vorausschicken

ad'vance booking *n.* (for a film, play) [vorherige] Kartenreservierung; (of a table in a restaurant) [vorherige] Tischreservierung

advanced /əd'vɑ:nst/ *adj.* fortgeschritten; **he has ~ ideas** er hat Ideen, die seiner Zeit voraus sind; **be ~ in years** in fortgeschrittenem Alter sein; **~ level** ▸ **A level**; **~ studies** weiterführende Studien; **~ supplementary level** ▸ **AS level**

advance: ~ guard *n.* (lit. or fig.) Vorhut, *die;* **~ man** *n.* (Amer.) vorausgeschickter Mitarbeiter

advancement /əd'vɑ:nsmənt/ *n., no pl.* 1 (promotion) Aufstieg, *der* 2 (furtherance) Förderung, *die*

advance: ~ 'notice *n.* **a week's ~ notice** Benachrichtigung eine Woche [im] Voraus; **give sb. ~ notice of sth.** jmdn. im Voraus von etw. in Kenntnis setzen; **~ 'payment** *n.* Vorauszahlung, *die*

advantage /əd'vɑ:ntɪdʒ/ *n.* 1 (better position) Vorteil, *der;* **give sb. an ~ over sb.** für jmdn. einen Vorteil gegenüber jmdm. bedeuten *od.* ein Vorteil gegenüber jmdm. sein; **gain an ~ over sb.** sich (*Dat.*) einen Vorteil gegenüber jmdm. verschaffen; **have an ~ over sb.** jmdm. gegenüber im Vorteil sein; **take [full/unfair] ~ of sth.** etw. [voll/unfairerweise] ausnutzen; **take ~ of sb.** jmdn. ausnutzen; (euphem.: seduce) jmdn. missbrauchen; **don't let them take ~ of you** lass dich nicht von ihnen ausnutzen; **have the ~ of sb.** [jmdm. gegenüber] in der besseren Position sein; **we shall show our range of products to ~:** wir werden unser Sortiment vorteilhaft ausstellen; **be seen to better ~:** vorteilhafter aussehen 2 (benefit) Vorteil, *der;* **'ability to type [would be] an ~'** „Schreibmaschinenkenntnisse von Vorteil"; **it could be done/we could do it with ~:** es wäre von Vorteil, wenn es getan würde/wenn wir es täten; **be to one's ~:** für jmdn. von Vorteil sein; **something to your ~:** etwas, was für dich von Vorteil ist; **turn sth. to [one's] ~:** etw. ausnutzen 3 (Tennis) Vorteil, *der;* **~ in/out** Vorteil Aufschläger/Rückschläger

advantageous /ædvən'teɪdʒəs/ *adj.* vorteilhaft ‹*Verfahren, Übereinkunft*›; günstig ‹*Lage*›; **be [mutually] ~:** [für beide Seiten] von Vorteil sein; **be ~ to sb.** für jmdn. von Vorteil sein

advantageously /ædvən'teɪdʒəslɪ/ *adv.* **we could ~ discuss this** es wäre von Vorteil, wenn wir das besprächen; **be ~ placed** günstig gelegen sein; **compare ~ with sth.** gegenüber etw. günstig abschneiden

advent /'ædvənt/ *n., no pl.* 1 (of thing) Beginn, *der;* Anfang, *der;* **before the ~ of the railways** vor dem Aufkommen der Eisenbahn 2 *no art.* **A~** (season) Advent, *der*

adventitious /ædvən'tɪʃəs/ *adj.* zufällig

adventure /əd'ventʃə(r)/ *n.* Abenteuer, *das;* **in a spirit of ~:** voller Abenteuerdrang

a

ad'venture: ~ **holiday** *n.* Abenteuerurlaub, *der;* **they organize ~ holidays** sie bieten Abenteuerurlaub an; ~ **park** *n.* Erlebnispark, *der;* ~ **'playground** *n.* (Brit.) Abenteuerspielplatz, *der*

adventurer /əd'ventʃərə(r)/ *n.* Abenteurer, *der;* (derog.: speculator) Glücksritter, *der*

adventuress /əd'ventʃərɪs/ *n.* Abenteu[r]erin, *die*

adventurism /əd'ventʃərɪzm/ *n., no pl.* Abenteuerlust, *die;* Wagemut, *der;* (Polit.) Abenteuerpolitik, *die*

adventurous /əd'ventʃərəs/ *adj.* 1 (venturesome) abenteuerlustig; ~ **spirit** Abenteurergeist, *der* 2 (filled with adventures) abenteuerlich 3 (enterprising) kühn

adverb /'ædvɜ:b/ *n.* (Ling.) Adverb, *das;* Umstandswort, *das;* ~ **of time/place** Zeit-/Ortsadverb, *das*

adverbial /əd'vɜ:bɪəl/ *adj.* (Ling.) adverbial

adverbially /əd'vɜ:bɪəlɪ/ *adv.* (Ling.) adverbial

adversarial /ædvə'seərɪəl/ *adj.* 1 (involving conflict) konfliktär 2 (Law) auf dem Verhandlungsgrundsatz beruhend ‹*System*›; nach dem Verhandlungsgrundsatz durchgeführt ‹*Prozess*›

adversary /'ædvəsərɪ/ *n.* (enemy) Widersacher, *der*/Widersacherin, *die;* (opponent) Kontrahent, *der*/Kontrahentin, *die*

adverse /'ædvɜ:s/ *adj.* 1 (hostile) ablehnend (**to** gegenüber); **an ~ response** eine abschlägige Antwort 2 (unfavourable) ungünstig ‹*Bedingung, Entwicklung*›; negativ ‹*Bilanz, Urteil*›; nachteilig ‹*Auswirkung*›; **developments ~ to our interests** für unsere Interessen nachteilige Entwicklungen 3 (contrary) widrig ‹*Wind, Umstände*›

adversely /'ædvɜ:slɪ/ *adv.* 1 (hostilely) ablehnend 2 (unfavourably) nachteilig

adversity /əd'vɜ:sɪtɪ/ *n.* 1 *no pl.* Not, *die;* **in ~:** in der Not; in Notzeiten 2 *usu. in pl.* (misfortune) Widrigkeit, *die*

advert /'ædvɜ:t/ (Brit. coll.) ▸ **advertisement**

advertise /'ædvətaɪz/

A *v.t.* werben für ‹*Güter, Waren*›; (by small ad) inserieren ‹*Auto, Haus*›; ausschreiben ‹*Stelle*›; ~ **one's intentions** seine Absichten bekannt geben; ~ **one's presence** seine Anwesenheit bekannt machen

B *v.i.* werben; (in newspaper) inserieren; annoncieren; ~ **on television** Werbung im Fernsehen machen; ~ **for sb./sth.** jmdn./etw. [per Inserat] suchen

advertisement /əd'vɜ:tɪsmənt/ *n.* Anzeige, *die;* **TV ~:** Fernsehspot, *der;* **classified ~:** Kleinanzeige, *die;* **his behaviour is not a good ~ for the firm** (fig.) sein Verhalten ist für das Unternehmen keine gute Reklame

advertiser /'ædvətaɪzə(r)/ *n.* (in newspaper) Inserent, *der*/Inserentin, *die;* (on radio, TV) Auftraggeber/Auftraggeberin [der Werbesendung]

advertising /'ædvətaɪzɪŋ/ *n., no pl., no indef. art.* Werbung, *die;* ~ **agency/campaign/industry** Werbeagentur, *die*/-kampagne, *die*/-branche, *die*

Advertising 'Standards Authority *n.* (Brit.) *Werbeaufsichtsbehörde*

advice /əd'vaɪs/ *n.* 1 *no pl., no indef. art.* (counsel) Rat, *der;* **seek ~ from sb.** bei jmdm. Rat suchen; **my ~ to you would be ...:** ich würde dir raten ...; **he doesn't listen to ~:** er hört nicht auf Ratschläge; **on sb.'s ~:** auf jmds. Rat (*Akk.*) hin; **a piece of ~:** ein Rat[schlag]; **give sb. a piece** *or* **bit** *or* **word of ~:** jmdm. einen guten Rat geben; **if you ask** *or* **want my ~:** wenn du meinen Rat hören willst; **take ~ [from sb.]** [jmdn.] um Rat fragen; **take sb.'s ~:** jmds. Rat (*Dat.*) folgen; **take legal ~:** sich juristisch beraten lassen 2 (formal notice) Bescheid, *der;* Avis, *der od. das* (Kaufmannsspr.)

advisability /ədvaɪzə'bɪlɪtɪ/ *n., no pl.* Ratsamkeit, *die;* **consider the ~ of doing sth.** erwägen, ob es ratsam ist, etw. zu tun

advisable /əd'vaɪzəbl/ *adj.* ratsam

advise /əd'vaɪz/

A *v.t.* 1 (offer advice to) beraten; **please ~ me** bitte geben Sie mir einen Rat; ~ **sb. to do sth.** jmdm. raten, etw. zu tun; ~ **sb. not to do** *or* **against doing sth.** jmdm. abraten, etw. zu tun; **what would you ~ me to do?** wozu würdest du mir raten? 2 (recommend) ~ **sth.** zu etw. raten 3 (inform) unterrichten, informieren (**of** über + *Akk.*); **keep me ~d** halten Sie mich auf dem Laufenden

B *v.i.* raten; ~ **on sth.** bei etw. beraten; **please ~:** erbitte Rat

advised /əd'vaɪzd/ *adj.* **[well-]~:** wohl überlegt; **be well/better ~** ‹*Person:*› wohl beraten/besser beraten sein

advisedly /əd'vaɪzɪdlɪ/ *adv.* bewusst

adviser, advisor /əd'vaɪzə(r)/ *n.* Berater, *der*/Beraterin, *die*

advisory /əd'vaɪzərɪ/ *adj.* beratend; ~ **committee** Beratungsausschuss, *der;* **in an ~ capacity** in beratender Funktion

advocaat /ædvə'kɑ:t/ *n.* Eierlikör, *der*

advocacy /'ædvəkəsɪ/ *n., no pl.* **sb.'s ~ of sth.** jmds. Engagement *od.* Eintreten für etw.

advocate

A /'ædvəkət/ *n.* ▸ⓘ **p. 1260** (of a cause) Befürworter, *der*/Befürworterin, *die;* Fürsprecher, *der*/Fürsprecherin, *die;* (for a person) Fürsprecher, *der*/Fürsprecherin, *die;* (Law: professional pleader) [Rechts]anwalt, *der*/[Rechts]anwältin, *die;* **A~ General** (EU) Generalanwalt, *der;* **Faculty of A~s** [schottische] Anwaltskammer, *die;* **Lord A~:** [schottische] Generalstaatsanwalt, *der*

B /'ædvəkeɪt/ *v.t.* 1 (recommend) befürworten; empfehlen; ~ **a policy** für eine Politik eintreten; ~ **that ...:** dafür plädieren, dass ... 2 (defend) verteidigen; eintreten für

advt. *abbr.* = **advertisement**

adze (*Amer.:* **adz**) /ædz/ *n.* Dechsel, *die*

Aegean /i:'dʒi:ən/ *pr. n.* ~ **[Sea]** Ägäisches Meer; Ägäis, *die*

aegis /'i:dʒɪs/ *n.* 1 (auspices) **under the ~ of sb./sth.** unter der Ägide (geh.) *od.* Schirmherrschaft von jmdm./etw. 2 (protection) Schutz, *der*

Aeneid /'i:nɪɪd/ *n.* Äneis, *die*

aeon /'i:ən/ *n.* (age) Äon, *der* (geh.)

aerate /'eəreɪt/ *v.t.* 1 (charge with gas) [mit Kohlendioxid] anreichern; **~d water** kohlensaures Wasser 2 (Agric., Hort.) durchlüften

aerial /'eərɪəl/

A *adj.* 1 (in the air) Luft-; ~ **root** Luftwurzel, *die;* ~ **cableway** *or* **ropeway** *or* **railway** Seilbahn, *die* 2 (atmospheric) atmosphärisch 3 (Aeronaut.) Luft-; ~ **bombardment** Bombardierung [aus der Luft]; ~ **photograph/photography** Luftaufnahme, *die*/Luftaufnahmen; ~ **spraying** Besprühung aus der Luft

B *n.* Antenne, *die*

aero- /eərə/ *in comb.* Aero-

aerobatic /eərə'bætɪk/ *adj.* aerobatisch

aerobatics /eərə'bætɪks/ *n.* 1 *no pl.* Kunstflug, *der;* Aerobatik, *die* 2 *pl.* (feats of flying skill) fliegerische Kunststücke

aerobic /eə'rəʊbɪk/ *adj.* aerob (Biol.)

aerobics /eə'rəʊbɪks/ *n., no pl.* Aerobic, *das*

aerodrome /'eərədrəʊm/ *n.* (Brit. dated) Aerodrom, *das* (veralt.); Flugplatz, *der*

aerody'namic *adj.* aerodynamisch

aerody'namics *n., no pl.* Aerodynamik, *die*

aero-engine /'eərəʊendʒɪn/ *n.* (Aeronaut.) Flug[zeug]motor, *der*

'aerofoil *n.* Tragfläche, *die;* Tragflügel, *der* (fachspr.); (on car) Heckspoiler, *der*

aerogenerator /'eərəʊdʒenəreɪtə(r)/ *n.* Windgenerator, *der*

'aerogram[me] ▸ **air letter**

aeronautic /eərə'nɔ:tɪk/, **aeronautical** /eərə'nɔ:tɪkl/ *adj.* aeronautisch

aeronautics /eərə'nɔ:tɪks/ *n., no pl.* Aeronautik, *die*

aeroplane /'eərəpleɪn/ *n.* (Brit.) Flugzeug, *das*

aerosol /'eərəsɒl/ *n.* 1 (spray) Spray, *der od. das;* (container) ~ **[spray]** Spraydose, *die* 2 (system of particles) Aerosol, *das*

aerospace /'eərəspeɪs/ *n., no pl., no art.* Erdatmosphäre und Weltraum; (technology) Luft- und Raumfahrt, *die*

aesthete /'i:sθi:t/ *n.* Ästhet, *der*/Ästhetin, *die*

aesthetic /i:s'θetɪk/

A *adj.* ästhetisch; schöngeistig ‹*Person, Epoche*›

B *n.* **the Hegelian ~:** die hegelsche Ästhetik

aesthetically /i:s'θetɪkəlɪ/ *adv.* ästhetisch

aestheticism /i:s'θetɪsɪzm/ *n., no pl.* Ästhetizismus, *der*

aesthetics /i:s'θetɪks/ *n., no pl.* Ästhetik, *die*

aether ▸ **ether 2**

aetiology /i:tɪ'ɒlədʒɪ/ *n.* (Med., Philos.) Ätiologie, *die*

AF *abbr.* = **audio frequency**

afar /ə'fɑ:/ *adv.* ~ **[off]** weit fort; in weiter Ferne; **from ~:** aus der Ferne

AFC *abbr.* (Brit.) = **Association Football Club** *Fußballverein*

affability /æfə'bɪlɪtɪ/ *n., no pl.* Freundlichkeit, *die;* **the boss's back-slapping ~:** die joviale Leutseligkeit des Chefs

affable /'æfəbl/ *adj.* freundlich; **he is on ~ terms with everyone** er versteht sich mit allen gut

affably /'æfəblɪ/ *adv.* freundlich

affair /ə'feə(r)/ *n.* 1 (concern, matter) Angelegenheit, *die;* **it's not my ~:** es geht mich nichts an; **that's 'his ~:** das ist seine Sache; **the Dreyfus ~:** die Dreyfus-Affäre 2 *in pl.* (everyday business) Geschäfte *Pl.;* [tägliche] Arbeit; (business dealings) Geschäfte *Pl.;* **state of ~s** Lage, *die; see also* **current A 3**; **foreign 3**; **state A 4** 3 (love ~) Affäre, *die;* **have an ~ with sb.** eine Affäre *od.* ein Verhältnis mit jmdm. haben 4 (occurrence) Geschichte, *die* (ugs.); Angelegenheit, *die* 5 (coll.: thing) Ding, *das;* **our house is a tumbledown ~:** unser Haus ist eine Bruchbude (ugs.) 6 ~ **of honour** Ehrenhandel, *der*

affect[1] /ə'fekt/ *v.t.* (pretend to have) nachahmen; imitieren; (pretend to feel or do) vortäuschen; spielen; **the boy ~ed indifference** der Junge tat so, als sei es ihm gleichgültig; ~ **to do sth.** vorgeben, etw. zu tun

affect[2] *v.t.* 1 (produce effect on) sich auswirken auf (+ *Akk.*); **damp had ~ed the spark plugs** Feuchtigkeit hatte die Zündkerzen in Mitleidenschaft gezogen; **plant growth is ~ed by the amount of rainfall** das Wachstum der Pflanzen wird von der Niederschlagsmenge beeinflusst 2 (emotionally) betroffen machen; **be ~ed by sth.** von etw. betroffen sein 3 ‹*Vorschrift:*› betreffen; ‹*Krankheit:*› infizieren ‹*Person*›; befallen ‹*Pflanze*›

affectation /æfek'teɪʃn/ *n.* 1 (studied display) Verstellung, *die;* (artificiality) Affektiertheit, *die* 2 *no pl.* (pretence) ~ **of sth.** Vortäuschung von etw.

affected /ə'fektɪd/ *adj.* affektiert; gekünstelt ‹*Sprache, Stil*›

affectedly /ə'fektɪdlɪ/ *adv.* affektiert

affectedness /ə'fektɪdnɪs/ *n., no pl.* Affektiertheit, *die*

affecting /ə'fektɪŋ/ *adj.* rührend; ergreifend

affectingly /ə'fektɪŋlɪ/ *adv.* in ergreifender Weise; rührend

affection /ə'fekʃn/ *n.* 1 (kindly feeling) Zuneigung, *die;* **have** *or* **feel ~ for sb./sth.** für jmdn. Zuneigung empfinden/an etw. (*Dat.*) hängen; **gain** *or* **win sb.'s ~s** jmds. Zuneigung gewinnen; **she was held in great ~ by many people** viele hatten sie in ihr Herz geschlossen; **have a place in sb.'s ~s** einen festen Platz in jmds. Herzen einnehmen; **lots of love and ~** (close of letter) alles Liebe und Gute 2 (Med.: illness) Affektion, *die*

affectionate /ə'fekʃənət/ *adj.* anhänglich ‹*Person, Kind, [Haus]tier*›; liebevoll ‹*Umarmung*›; zärtlich ‹*Lächeln, Erinnerung*›; **your ~ son** (in letter) Dein dich liebender Sohn

affectionately /ə'fekʃənətlɪ/ *adv.* liebevoll; **yours ~:** viele Grüße und Küsse

affidavit /æfɪ'deɪvɪt/ *n.* (Law) **[sworn] ~:** eidesstattliche Versicherung; **swear an ~:** eine eidesstattliche Versicherung abgeben

affiliate /ə'fɪlɪeɪt/
A *v.t.* **1** (attach) **be ~d to** *or* **with sth.** an etw. (*Akk.*) angegliedert *od.* angeschlossen sein; **the organization is not politically ~d** die Organisation ist politisch nicht gebunden **2** (adopt) aufnehmen ‹*Mitglied*›; angliedern ‹*Vereinigung*›; **be an ~d member of an organization** einer Organisation angeschlossen sein
B *n.* (person) assoziiertes Mitglied; (organization) Zweigorganisation, *die;* Affiliation, *die* (Wirtsch.)

affiliation /əfɪlɪ'eɪʃn/ *n.* Angliederung, *die* (**to, with** an + *Akk.*); **~ order** (Brit. Law Hist.) *gerichtliche Feststellung der Vaterschaft und Festsetzung der Unterhaltsverpflichtung für ein nichteheliches Kind*

affinity /ə'fɪnɪtɪ/ *n.* **1** (relationship) Verwandtschaft, *die* (**to** mit) **2** (liking) Neigung, *die* (**for** zu); **feel an ~ to** *or* **for sb./sth.** sich zu jmdm./etw. hingezogen fühlen **3** (structural resemblance) Affinität, *die;* Verwandtschaft, *die;* (fig.) Verwandtschaft, *die* (**with, to** mit); **the ~ of sth. to** *or* **with sth.** die Affinität von etw. zu etw.

affinity 'credit card *n.* Affinity-Karte, *die*

affirm /ə'fɜːm/
A *v.t.* (assert) bekräftigen ‹*Absicht*›; beteuern ‹*Unschuld*›; (state as a fact) bestätigen; **~ sth. to sb.** jmdm. etw. versichern
B *v.i.* (Law) *ohne religiöse Beteuerung schwören*

affirmation /æfə'meɪʃn/ *n.* **1** (of intention) Bekräftigung, *die;* (of fact) Bestätigung, *die;* (of quality) Versicherung, *die* **2** (Law) eidesstattliche Erklärung

affirmative /ə'fɜːmətɪv/
A *adj.* affirmativ; bestätigend ‹*Erklärung*›; bejahend, zustimmend ‹*Antwort*›; **~ vote** Jastimme, *die*
B *n.* Bejahung, *die;* **answer in the ~:** bejahend antworten; **the answer is in the ~:** die Antwort ist „ja" *od.* positiv

affirmative 'action *n.* (esp. Amer.) positive Diskriminierung (fachspr.); Bevorzugung, *die*

affirmatively /ə'fɜːmətɪvlɪ/ *adv.* **answer ~:** bejahend antworten

affix
A /ə'fɪks/ *v.t.* **1** (fix) **~ sth. to sth.** etw. an etw. (*Dat.*) befestigen; **the stamp had not been properly ~ed to the letter** die Marke war nicht richtig auf den Brief geklebt worden **2** (impress) aufdrücken; **~ one's stamp/seal upon sth.** seinen Stempel/sein Siegel auf etw. (*Akk.*) drücken **3** (add) beifügen; **~ one's signature [to sth.]** seine Unterschrift [unter etw. (*Akk.*)] setzen
B /'æfɪks/ *n.* (Ling.) Affix, *das*

afflict /ə'flɪkt/ *v.t.* (physically) plagen; (mentally) quälen; peinigen; **be ~ed with sth.** von etw. befallen sein

affliction /ə'flɪkʃn/ *n.* **1** *no pl.* (distress) Bedrängnis, *die;* **endure sorrow and ~:** Kummer und Leid ertragen **2** (cause of distress) Leiden, *das;* **bodily ~s** körperliche Gebrechen

affluence /'æfluəns/ *n., no pl.* **1** (wealth) Reichtum, *der* **2** (plenty) Überfluss, *der*

affluent /'æfluənt/*adj.* (wealthy) reich; **the ~ society** die Überflussgesellschaft

afford /ə'fɔːd/ *v.t.* **1** sich (*Dat.*) leisten; **be able to ~ sth.** sich (*Dat.*) etw. leisten können; **be able to ~:** aufbringen können ‹*Geld*›; erübrigen können ‹*Zeit*›; **be able to ~ to do sth.** es sich (*Dat.*) leisten können, etw. zu tun; **sb. can ill ~ sth.** jmd. kann sich (*Dat.*) etw. kaum leisten **2** (provide) bieten; gewähren ‹*Schutz*›; bereiten ‹*Vergnügen*›; **~ sb. sth.** jmdm. etw. bieten/gewähren/bereiten

affordable /ə'fɔːdəbl/ *adj.* erschwinglich

afforest /ə'fɒrɪst/ *v.t.* aufforsten

afforestation /əfɒrɪ'steɪʃn/ *n.* Aufforstung, *die*

affray /ə'freɪ/ *n.* Schlägerei, *die*

affront /ə'frʌnt/
A *v.t.* (insult) beleidigen; (offend) kränken; vor den Kopf stoßen (ugs.)
B *n.* (insult) Affront, *der* (geh.) (**to** gegen); Beleidigung, *die* (**to** *Gen.*); (offence) Kränkung, *die* (**to** *Gen.*)

Afghan /'æfgæn/ ▸ **p. 1277**, ▸ **p. 1345**
A *adj.* afghanisch; *see also* **English A**
B *n.* **1** (person) Afghane, *der*/Afghanin, *die* **2** (language) Afghanisch, *das; see also* **English B 1**

Afghan 'hound *n.* Afghane, *der*

Afghanistan /æf'gænɪstɑːn/ *pr. n.* Afghanistan (*das*)

aficionado /əfɪsjə'nɑːdəʊ/ *n., pl.* **~s** Liebhaber, *der*/Liebhaberin, *die*

afield /ə'fiːld/ *adv.* **far ~** (direction) weit hinaus; (place) weit draußen; **we didn't go farther ~ than ...:** wir gingen nicht weiter hinaus als bis zu ...; **from as far ~ as ...:** von so weit her wie ...; **go too far ~** (fig.) sich zu weit entfernen

afire /ə'faɪə(r)/ *pred. adj.* **[set] ~:** in Brand [setzen *od.* stecken]; **be ~:** in Flammen stehen

aflame /ə'fleɪm/ *pred. adj.* **be ~:** in Flammen stehen

afloat /ə'fləʊt/ *pred. adj.* **1** (floating) über Wasser; flott ‹*Schiff*›; **get a boat ~:** ein Boot flottmachen; **stay ~** (also fig.) sich über Wasser halten **2** (at sea) auf See; **be ~:** auf dem Meer treiben **3** (awash) **be ~:** unter Wasser stehen

afoot /ə'fʊt/ *pred. adj.* **1** (astir) auf den Beinen **2** (under way) im Gange; **set ~:** in Gang setzen; aufstellen ‹*Plan*›; **plans were ~ to ...:** es gab Pläne, zu ...; **there's trouble ~:** es gibt Ärger

aforementioned /əfɔːmenʃnd/, **aforesaid** /ə'fɔːsed/ *adjs.* oben erwähnt *od.* genannt

aforethought /ə'fɔːθɔːt/ *adj.* **with malice ~:** mit Vorbedacht

a fortiori /eɪ fɔːtɪ'ɔːraɪ/ *adv.* erst recht

afoul /ə'faʊl/ *adv.* (Amer.) verwickelt (**of** in + *Akk.*); **fall** *or* **run ~ of sth.** sich in etw. (*Akk.*) verwickeln; (fig.) mit etw. in Konflikt geraten

afraid /ə'freɪd/ *pred. adj.* **[not] be ~ [of sb./sth.]** [vor jmdm./etw.] [keine] Angst haben; **be ~ lest ...:** befürchten, dass ...; **be ~ to do sth.** Angst davor haben, etw. zu tun; **be ~ of doing sth.** Angst haben, etw. zu tun; **I'm ~ [that] we must assume that ...:** leider müssen wir annehmen, dass ...; **I'm ~ so/not** ich fürchte ja/nein

afresh /ə'freʃ/ *adv.* von neuem; **every word has been translated ~:** jedes Wort ist neu übersetzt worden

Africa /'æfrɪkə/ *pr. n.* Afrika (*das*); *see also* **black A 3**

African /'æfrɪkən/ ▸ **p. 1345**
A *adj.* afrikanisch; **sb. is ~:** jmd. ist Afrikaner/Afrikanerin
B *n.* Afrikaner, *der*/Afrikanerin, *die*

African A'merican *n.* Afroamerikaner, *der*/-amerikanerin, *die*

> **African American**
>
> Dies ist in den USA zur Zeit der gebräuchlichste Begriff für Amerikaner afrikanischer Abstammung.

African 'violet *n.* (Bot.) Usambaraveilchen, *das*

Afrikaans /æfrɪ'kɑːns/ *n.* ▸ **p. 1277** Afrikaans, *das; see also* **English B 1**

Afrikaner /æfrɪ'kɑːnə(r)/ *n.* ▸ **p. 1345** Afrika[a]nder, *der*/Afrika[a]nderin, *die*

Afro /'æfrəʊ/
A *adj.* Afro-; **~ look** Afrolook, *der*
B *n., pl.* **~s** Afrolook, *der*

Afro- /'æfrəʊ/ *in comb.* afro-/Afro-

Afro-A'merican
A *adj.* afroamerikanisch
B *n.* Afroamerikaner, *der*/-amerikanerin, *die*

Afro-Carib'bean
A *adj.* afrokaribisch
B *n.* Mensch afrokaribischer Herkunft *od.* Abstammung

> **Afro-Caribbean**
>
> Dies ist in Großbritannien und den USA zur Zeit der gebräuchlichste Begriff für Menschen afrikanischer Herkunft, die in der Karibik leben oder aus der Karibik kommen.

aft /ɑːft/ *adv.* (Naut., Aeronaut.) achtern; **go ~:** nach achtern gehen

after /'ɑːftə(r)/
A *adv.* **1** (later) danach; **two days ~:** zwei Tage danach *od.* später; **soon/shortly ~:** bald/kurz danach *od.* darauf; **long ~:** lange danach **2** (behind) hinterher
B *prep.* **1** ▸ **p. 1001** (following in time) nach; **~ six months** nach sechs Monaten; **~ you** nach Ihnen; **~ you with the salt** (coll.) kann ich das Salz nach dir haben?; **time ~ time** wieder und wieder; **day ~ day** Tag für Tag; **it is a quarter ~ ten o'clock** (Amer.) es ist Viertel nach zehn **2** (behind) hinter (+ *Dat.*); (in pursuit of) **be/shout ~ sb.** hinter jmdm. her sein/herrufen; **what are you ~?** was suchst du denn?; (to questioner) was willst du wirklich wissen?; **she's only ~ his money** sie ist nur hinter seinem Geld her **3** (about) **ask ~ sb./sth.** nach jmdm./etw. fragen **4** (next in importance to) nach **5** (in spite of) nach; **~ all** schließlich; **so you've come ~ all!** du bist also doch gekommen!; **I think I'll have a beer ~ all** ich glaube, ich trinke doch ein Bier; **so we took the train ~ all** wir haben den Zug schließlich doch genommen **6** (as a result of) **~ what has happened** nach dem, was geschehen ist; **~ seeing that film/reading that book** nach diesem Film/diesem Buch **7** (in allusion to, in imitation of) nach; **named ~:** benannt nach; **a picture ~ Rubens** ein Bild nach Rubens
C *conj.* nachdem
D *adj.* **1** (later) später; **in ~ years** in späteren Jahren **2** (Naut.) Achter-

after: ~birth *n.* Nachgeburt, *die;* **~care** *n., no pl.* (after hospital stay) Nachsorge, *die;* (after prison sentence) Resozialisierung, *die;* **~-'dinner speaker** *n.* Tischredner, *der;* **~-'dinner speech** *n.* Tischrede, *die;* **~-effect** *n., usu. in pl.* Nachwirkung, *die;* **~glow** *n.* **1** (of light) Nachschein, *der;* (of sunset) Abendrot, *das;* **2** (of pleasure) [wohliges] Nachgefühl (geh.); **in the ~glow of [the] victory** im Hochgefühl nach dem Sieg; **~life** *n.* Leben nach dem Tod

aftermath /'ɑːftəmæθ, 'ɑːftəmɑːθ/ *n., no pl.* Nachwirkungen *Pl.;* **the ~ of the war** die Folgen *od.* Auswirkungen des Krieges; **in the ~ of sth.** nach etw.

afternoon /ɑːftə'nuːn/ *n.* ▸ **p. 1001**, ▸ **p. 1048**, ▸ **p. 1189** Nachmittag, *der; attrib.* Nachmittags-; **this/tomorrow ~:** heute/morgen Nachmittag; **during the ~:** im Laufe des Nachmittags; **[early/late] in the ~:** am [frühen/späten] Nachmittag; (regularly) [früh/spät] nachmittags; **at three in the ~:** um drei Uhr nachmittags; **on Monday ~s/~:** Montag nachmittags/[am] Montagnachmittag; **one ~:** eines Nachmittags; **~s, of an ~:** nachmittags; **the other ~:** neulich nachmittags; **~, all!** (coll. greeting) Tag, zusammen!; *see also* **good A 13**

afters /'ɑːftəz/ *n. pl.* (Brit. coll.) Nachtisch, *der*

after: ~-sales service *n.* Kundendienst, *der;* **~-school** *adj.* ‹*Unternehmungen, Erholung usw.*› nach der Schule; **~-school child care** Nachmittagskinderbetreuung, *die;* **~-school job/club** Freizeitjob, *der*/-klub, *der;* **~shave** *n.* Aftershave, *das;* **~shock** *n.* Nachbeben, *das;* **~taste** *n.* Nachgeschmack, *der;* **~thought** *n.* nachträglicher Einfall; nachträgliche Idee; **be added as an ~thought** erst später hinzukommen

afterwards /'ɑːftəwədz/ (*Amer.:* **afterward** /'ɑːftəwəd/) *adv.* danach

again /ə'gen, ə'geɪn/ *adv.* **1** (another time) wieder; **see a film ~:** einen Film noch einmal sehen; **play/sing a tune ~:** eine Melodie noch einmal spielen/singen; **not ~!** nicht schon wieder!; **~ and ~, time and [time] ~:** immer wieder; **back ~:** wieder zurück; **go back there ~:** wieder dorthin gehen; **as much ~:** noch einmal so viel; **half as much/many ~:** noch einmal halb so viel/so viele; **come ~**

a

ℹ Age

How old?

How old is she?*, *What age is she?
= Wie alt ist sie?
She is forty** [**years old**] or (more formal) **forty years of age
= Sie ist vierzig [Jahre alt]
He has just turned sixty
= Er ist gerade sechzig geworden
at the age of twenty
= im Alter von zwanzig Jahren, mit zwanzig
Life begins at forty
= Mit vierzig fängt das Leben an
a man of fifty** or **aged fifty
= ein fünfzigjähriger Mann, ein Fünfzigjähriger
a girl of ten
= ein zehnjähriges Mädchen
***a thirty-year-old** [**man**]*
= ein Dreißigjähriger
***a thirty-year-old** [**woman**]*
= eine Dreißigjährige
an eighty-year-old pensioner
= ein achtzigjähriger Rentner
They have an eight-year-old and a five-year-old
= Sie haben ein achtjähriges und ein fünfjähriges Kind

Older and younger

I'm older than you (are)
= Ich bin älter als du
She's younger than him** or **than he is
= Sie ist jünger als er
He's four years older than me** or (more formal) **four years my senior
= Er ist vier Jahre älter als ich

You are twenty years younger than her** or (more formal) **twenty years her junior
= Du bist zwanzig Jahre jünger als sie
They are the same age
= Sie sind gleich alt *or* gleichaltrig
She is (exactly) the same age as John
= Sie ist [genau] so alt wie John

Approximate ages

He's about fifty
= Er ist ungefähr fünfzig *or* um die fünfzig
She's just over sixty
= Sie ist etwas über sechzig
He's nearly seventy** or **just under seventy
= Er ist fast *or* bald siebzig
He's getting on for seventy
= Er geht auf die siebzig zu *or* wird bald siebzig
She's in her sixties
= Sie ist in den Sechzigern
He's in his late/early sixties
= Er ist Ende/Anfang sechzig
Jane's in her mid-forties
= Jane ist Mitte vierzig
He's still a teenager** or **in his teens
= Er ist noch ein Teenager *or* in den Teenagerjahren
Her son's just ten
= Ihr Sohn ist gerade zehn geworden
She's barely twelve
= Sie ist noch keine zwölf Jahre alt
games for the under-twelves
= Spiele für Kinder unter 12 Jahren
only for the over-eighties
= nur für Leute über achtzig

(coll.: would you say that ~?) wie bitte? **2** (besides) **[there] ~:** außerdem **3** (on the other hand) **[then/there] ~:** andrerseits

against /əˈgenst, əˈgeɪnst/ *prep.* **1** (in opposition to, to the disadvantage of, in contrast to) gegen; **those ~ the motion** diejenigen, die gegen den Antrag sind; **as ~:** gegenüber; **be ~ sb.'s doing sth.** dagegen sein, dass jmd. etw. tut **2** (into collision with, in contact with) gegen; **lean sth. ~ sth.** etw. gegen etw. lehnen **3** (in preparation for) gegen; **protect sth. ~ frost** etw. vor Frost schützen; **save money ~ a rainy day** Geld für schlechte Zeiten sparen; **be warned ~ sth./doing sth.** vor etw. (*Dat.*) gewarnt werden/davor gewarnt werden, etw. zu tun **4** (in return for) gegen; **rate of exchange ~ the dollar** Wechselkurs des Dollar

agape /əˈgeɪp/ *adj.* **with mouth ~:** mit offenem Mund; **be ~** ‹*Person:*› den Mund aufsperren (**with** vor)

agaric /ˈægərɪk/ *n.* (Bot.) Blätterpilz, *der*

agate /ˈægət/ *n.* (Min.) Achat, *der*

agave /əˈgeɪvɪ/ *n.* (Bot.) Agave, *die*

age /eɪdʒ/

A *n.* **1** ▸ℹ **p. 894** Alter, *das;* **the boys' ~s are 7, 6, and 3** die Jungen sind 7, 6 und 3 Jahre alt; **what ~ are you?, what is your ~?** wie alt bist du?; **at the ~ of** im Alter von; **at what ~:** in welchem Alter; **be six years of ~:** sechs Jahre alt sein; **children of six years of ~ and under** Kinder [im Alter] von sechs Jahren und darunter; **when I was your ~:** als ich so alt war wie du; **he looks his ~:** man sieht ihm sein Alter an; **come of ~:** mündig *od.* volljährig werden; (fig.) den Kinderschuhen entwachsen; **be over ~:** die vorgeschriebene Altersgrenze überschritten haben; **be/look under ~:** zu jung sein/aussehen; **she's now of an ~ when she ...:** sie ist jetzt in dem Alter, in dem sie ...; **be** *or* **act your ~** (coll.) sei nicht so kindisch **2** (advanced ~) Alter, *das;* **her ~ is catching up with her** sie merkt jetzt doch, dass sie alt wird; **her face was wrinkled with ~:** ihr Gesicht war vom Alter zerfurcht; **~ before beauty** (joc.) Alter vor Schönheit **3** (generation) Generation, *die* **4** (great period) Zeitalter, *das;* **wait [for] ~s** *or* **an ~ for sb./sth.** (coll.) eine Ewigkeit auf jmdn./etw. warten; **take/be ~s** *or* **an ~** (coll.) eine Ewigkeit dauern; **she took ~s looking for the book** (coll.) sie suchte eine Ewigkeit nach dem Buch; **I'll be ~s yet** (coll.) ich brauche noch eine Ewigkeit

B *v.t.* **1** altern lassen; altern (selten); **sth. ~s sb./sth. prematurely** etw. lässt jmdn./etw. frühzeitig alt werden **2** (mature) reifen lassen; altern (fachspr)

C *v.i.* altern

'age bracket *n.* Altersstufe, *die;* **children in the 9–13 ~:** Kinder im Alter von 9–13 Jahren

aged

A *adj.* **1** /eɪdʒd/ ▸ℹ **p. 894 be ~ five** fünf Jahre alt sein; **a boy ~ five** ein fünfjähriger Junge **2** /eɪdʒd/ (matured) gealtert ‹*Wein, Käse, Brandy*› **3** /ˈeɪdʒɪd/ (elderly) bejahrt

B /ˈeɪdʒɪd/ *n. pl.* **the ~:** die alten Menschen

age: ~ difference *n.* Altersunterschied, *der;* **~ discrimination** *n., no pl.* Altersdiskriminierung, *die;* **~ gap** *n.* Alterskluft, *die;* **~ group** *n.* Altersgruppe, *die*

ageism /ˈeɪdʒɪzm/ *n., no pl.* Diskriminierung aufgrund des Alters

ageist /ˈeɪdʒɪst/ *adj.* das Alter diskriminierend

ageless /ˈeɪdʒlɪs/ *adj.* nicht alternd ‹*Person*›; (eternal) zeitlos

age: ~ limit *n.* Altersgrenze, *die;* **~-long** *adj.* jahrhundertelang

agency /ˈeɪdʒənsɪ/ *n.* **1** (action) Handeln, *das;* **through/by the ~ of sth.** durch [die Einwirkung von] etw.; **through/by the ~ of sb.** durch jmds. Vermittlung **2** (business establishment) Geschäftsstelle, *die;* (news/advertising ~) Agentur, *die;* (United Nations department) (major) Sonderorganisation, *die;* (minor) Unterorganisation, *die*

agency 'nurse *n.: von einer Agentur vermittelte Krankenschwester*

agenda /əˈdʒendə/ *n.* (lit. or fig.) Tagesordnung, *die;* Agenda, *die;* **[be] on the ~:** auf der Tagesordnung *od.* Agenda [stehen]; **six items on the ~:** sechs Tagesordnungspunkte; **be high on the ~:** obenan *od.* ganz oben auf der Tagesordnung *od.* Agenda stehen; **have a hidden ~:** heimliche Absichten hegen *od.* verfolgen

agent /ˈeɪdʒənt/ *n.* **1** [treibende] Kraft; (Ling.) Agens, *das;* **be a free ~:** sein eigener Herr sein **2** (substance) Mittel, *das;* **an oxidizing ~:** ein Oxidationsmittel **3** (one who acts for another) Vertreter, *der*/Vertreterin, *die* **4** (spy) Agent, *der*/Agentin, *die*

agent provocateur /ɑːʒɑ̃ prɒvɒkəˈtɜː(r)/ *n., pl.* **agents provocateurs** /ɑːʒɑ̃ prɒvɒkəˈtɜː(r)/ Agent provocateur, *der*

age: ~-old *adj.* uralt; **~ range** *n.* Altersstufe, *die;* **teach English across a very large ~ range** Schüler der verschiedensten Altersstufen in Englisch unterrichten; *see also* **age bracket**

agglomerate /əˈglɒməreɪt/ *v.t.* agglomerieren

agglomeration /əglɒməˈreɪʃn/ *n.* (mass) Agglomeration, *die* (bes. fachspr.); Anhäufung, *die*

aggrandizement /əˈgrændɪzmənt/ *n., no pl.* Vergrößerung, *die;* (of power, influence) Ausdehnung, *die;* **his personal ~:** die Glorifizierung seiner Person

aggravate /ˈægrəveɪt/ *v.t.* **1** verschlimmern ‹*Krankheit, Zustand, Situation*›; verschärfen ‹*Streit*› **2** (coll.: annoy) aufregen; ärgern; **be ~d by sth.** sich über etw. (*Akk.*) ärgern *od.* aufregen

aggravating /ˈægrəveɪtɪŋ/ *adj.* (coll.) ärgerlich; lästig ‹*Kind, Lärm*›

aggravation /ægrəˈveɪʃn/ *n., no pl.* **1** Verschlimmerung, *die;* (of dispute) Verschärfung, *die* **2** (coll.: annoyance) Ärger, *der*

aggregate

A /ˈægrɪgət/ *n.* **1** (sum total) Gesamtmenge, *die;* (assemblage) Ansammlung, *die;* **in the ~:** in seiner/ihrer Gesamtheit **2** (Building) [Beton]zuschlag, *der* **3** (Geol.) Aggregat, *das*

B *adj.* (collected into one) zusammengefügt; (collective) gesamt; **the ~ amount** der Gesamtbetrag

C /ˈægrɪgeɪt/ *v.t.* **1** verbinden ‹*Material, Stoff*› (**into** zu); ansammeln ‹*Reichtum*› **2** (unite) vereinigen; (coll.: amount to) sich [insgesamt] belaufen auf (+ *Akk.*); **audiences aggregating 7 million** insgesamt 7 Millionen Zuhörer/Zuschauer

aggregation /ægrɪˈgeɪʃn/ *n.* Ansammlung, *die;* Aggregation, *die* (bes. fachspr.)

aggression /əˈgreʃn/ *n.* **1** *no pl.* Aggression, *die* **2** (unprovoked attack) Angriff, *der* **3** *no pl.* (Psych.) Aggression, *die*

aggressive /əˈgresɪv/ *adj.* aggressiv; angriffslustig ‹*Kämpfer*›; heftig ‹*Angriff*›

aggressive ac'counting *n., no pl.* aggressive Bilanzierung; *attrib.* **~ methods** aggressive Bilanzierungsmethoden

aggressively /əˈgresɪvlɪ/ *adv.* aggressiv, herausfordernd ‹*handeln, reagieren*›; (forcefully) aggressiv, wirkungsvoll, dynamisch ‹*verkaufen, anbieten*›; **the product was marketed ~:** die Werbung für das Produkt hatte Biss

aggressiveness /əˈgresɪvnɪs/ *n., no pl.* Aggressivität, *die*

aggressor /əˈgresə(r)/ *n.* Aggressor, *der*

aggrieve /əˈgriːv/ *v.t.* **1** (treat unfairly) ungerecht behandeln; **feel [oneself] much ~d at** *or* **over sth.** sich durch etw. ungerecht behandelt fühlen **2** **~d** (resentful) verärgert; (offended) gekränkt

aggro /ˈægrəʊ/ *n., no pl.* (Brit. sl.) Zoff, *der* (ugs.); Krawall, *der;* **they are looking for ~:** sie suchen Streit

aghast /əˈgɑːst/ *pred. adj.* (horrified) bestürzt, erschüttert (**at** über + *Akk.*); (terrified) erschrocken (**at** über + *Akk.*); **we stood ~ as ...:** wir standen wie versteinert, als ...

agile /'ædʒaɪl/ *adj.* beweglich; agil (geh.); flink, behänd[e] ‹*Bewegung*›

agility /ə'dʒɪlɪtɪ/ *n., no pl.:* ▸ **agile**: Beweglichkeit, *die;* Flinkheit, *die;* Behändigkeit, *die;* **mental ~:** geistige Behändigkeit *od.* Beweglichkeit

agitate /'ædʒɪteɪt/

A *v.t.* 1 (shake) schütteln; (stir up) aufrühren 2 (disturb) beunruhigen; erregen

B *v.i.* **~ for/against sth.** für/gegen etw. agitieren

agitation /ædʒɪ'teɪʃn/ *n.* 1 (shaking) Schütteln, *das;* (stirring up) Aufrühren, *das* 2 (emotional disturbance) Erregung, *die* 3 (campaign) Agitation, *die*

agitator /'ædʒɪteɪtə(r)/ *n.* 1 Agitator, *der* 2 (device) Rührwerk, *das*

AGM *abbr.* **= Annual General Meeting** JHV

agnostic /æg'nɒstɪk/

A *adj.* agnostizistisch

B *n.* Agnostiker, *der*/Agnostikerin, *die*

agnosticism /æg'nɒstɪsɪzm/ *n., no pl.* Agnostizismus, *der*

ago /ə'gəʊ/ *adv.* **ten years ~:** vor zehn Jahren; **[not] long ~:** vor [nicht] langer Zeit; **that was a long while ~:** das war vor langer Zeit; **how long ~ is it that ...?** wie lange ist es her, dass ...?; **no longer ~ than last Sunday** nicht vor letztem Sonntag; (only last Sunday) erst letzten Sonntag

agog /ə'gɒg/ *pred. adj.* gespannt (**for** auf + *Akk.*); **be ~ to hear the news** gespannt darauf sein, die Neuigkeiten zu hören

agonize /'ægənaɪz/

A *v.i.* 1 (suffer agony) Todesqualen erleiden 2 (fig.: struggle) ringen; **~ over sth.** sich (*Dat.*) den Kopf über etw. (*Akk.*) zermartern

B *v.t.* quälen; **an ~d scream** ein qualerfüllter Schrei; **an agonizing wait** (fig.) eine qualvolle Wartezeit

agony /'ægənɪ/ *n.* Todesqualen *Pl.;* **suffer ~/agonies** Todesqualen erleiden; **die in ~:** qualvoll sterben; **in an ~ of indecision/anticipation** (fig.) in qualvoller Unentschlossenheit/Erwartung; **death ~, last ~:** Agonie, *die;* Todeskampf, *der*

agony: ~ aunt *n.* (coll.) Briefkastentante, *die* (ugs. scherzh.); **~ column** *n.* (Brit. coll.) 1 *Zeitungsspalte für private Mitteilungen* („Persönliches"); 2 (advice column) *Spalte für die „Briefkastentante"*

agoraphobia /ægərə'fəʊbɪə/ *n.* (Psych.) Agoraphobie, *die;* Platzangst, *die*

agoraphobic /ægərə'fəʊbɪk/ *adj.* (Psych.) an Agoraphobie *od.* Platzangst leidend; **be ~:** an Agoraphobie *od.* Platzangst leiden

agrarian /ə'greərɪən/ *adj.* Agrar-; (relating to agricultural matters) agrarisch

agree /ə'gri:/

A *v.i.* 1 (consent) einverstanden sein; **~ to** *or* **with sth./to do sth.** mit etw. einverstanden sein/damit einverstanden sein, etw. zu tun; **we can only ~ to differ** *or* **disagree** wir können nur darin übereinstimmen, dass wir nicht übereinstimmen 2 (hold similar opinion) einer Meinung sein; **they ~d [with me]** sie waren derselben Meinung [wie ich]; **~ with sb. about** *or* **on sth./that ...:** jmdm. in etw. (*Dat.*) zustimmen/jmdm. darin zustimmen, dass ...; **I ~:** stimmt; **I couldn't ~ more** ich bin völlig deiner Meinung; **do you ~ with what I say?** stimmst du darin mit mir überein? 3 (reach similar opinion) **~ on sth.** sich über etw. (*Akk.*) einigen; **we could not ~ on how ...:** wir konnten uns nicht darüber einigen, wie ... 4 (harmonize) übereinstimmen; **sth. ~s with sth.** etw. stimmt mit etw. überein; **make ~:** zur Übereinstimmung bringen; **~ closely** weitgehend übereinstimmen 5 (suit) **~ with sb.** ‹*Essen:*› jmdm. bekommen 6 (Ling.) übereinstimmen

B *v.t.* 1 (reach agreement about) vereinbaren 2 (consent to) **~ sth.** einer Sache (*Dat.*) zustimmen

agreeable /ə'gri:əbl/ *adj.* 1 (pleasing) angenehm ‹*Überraschung, Person, Abend, Stimme*›; erfreulich ‹*Anblick*› 2 (willing to agree) **be ~ [to sth.]** [mit etw.] einverstanden sein

agreeableness /ə'gri:əbəlnɪs/ *n., no pl.* **the ~ of his company** seine angenehme Gesellschaft; **the ~ of the taste/climate** der angenehme Geschmack/das angenehme Klima

agreeably /ə'gri:əblɪ/ *adv.* angenehm; **~ surprised** angenehm überrascht; **we were ~ entertained** wir wurden auf angenehme Weise *od.* nett unterhalten

agreed /ə'gri:d/ *adj.* einig; vereinbart ‹*Summe, Zeit*›; **be ~ that .../about sth.** sich (*Dat.*) darüber einig sein, dass .../sich (*Dat.*) über etw. (*Akk.*) einig sein; **it was ~ that ...:** man war sich (*Dat.*) darüber einig, dass ...; **~!** einverstanden!

agreement /ə'gri:mənt/ *n.* 1 Übereinstimmung, *die;* (mutual understanding) Übereinkunft, *die;* **be in ~ [about sth.]** sich (*Dat.*) [über etw. (*Akk.*)] einig sein; **I'm in ~ with what you say** ich stimme darin mit dir überein; **enter into an ~:** eine Übereinkunft treffen; **come to** *or* **reach an ~ with sb. [about sth.]** mit jmdm. eine Einigung [über etw. (*Akk.*)] erzielen 2 (treaty) Abkommen, *das* 3 *no pl., no indef. art.* (state of harmony) Übereinstimmung, *die* 4 (Law) Abkommen, *das;* Vertrag, *der;* **legal ~:** rechtliche Vereinbarung 5 (Ling.) Übereinstimmung, *die*

agribusiness /'ægrɪbɪznɪs/ *n.* ≈ Agrarindustrie, *die*

agrichemical /'ægrɪkemɪkl/ *n.* Agrochemikalie, *die*

agricultural /ægrɪ'kʌltʃərl/ *adj.* landwirtschaftlich; **~ worker** Landarbeiter, *der*

agriculturalist /ægrɪ'kʌltʃərəlɪst/ ▸ **agriculturist**

agriculture /'ægrɪkʌltʃə(r)/ *n.* Landwirtschaft, *die*

agriculturist /ægrɪ'kʌltʃərɪst/ *n.* ▸ⓘ **p. 1260** Landwirtschaftsexperte, *der;* (farmer) Landwirt, *der*

agrimony /'ægrɪmənɪ/ *n.* (Bot.) Odermennig, *der*

agriproduct /'ægrɪprɒdʌkt/ *n.* Agrarprodukt, *das*

agronomist /ə'grɒnəmɪst/ *n.* Agronom, *der*/Agronomin, *die*

agronomy /ə'grɒnəmɪ/ *n., no pl.* Agronomie, *die*

aground /ə'graʊnd/ *pred. adj.* auf Grund gelaufen; **go** *or* **run ~:** auf Grund laufen

ague /'eɪgju:/ *n.* ▸ⓘ **p. 1231** 1 *no pl.* (arch.: fever) Wechselfieber, *das* (veralt.) 2 (shivering fit) Schüttelfrost, *der*

ah /ɑ:/ *int.* ach; (of pleasure) ah

aha /ɑ:'hɑ:/ *int.* aha

ahead /ə'hed/ *adv.* 1 (further forward in space) voraus; **the way ~ was blocked** der Weg vor uns/ihnen *usw.* war versperrt; **~ of sb./sth.** vor jmdm./etw.; **right** *or* **straight ~ of us** (directly in line) genau vor uns (*Dat.*); **keep going straight ~** (straight forwards) gehen Sie immer geradeaus 2 (fig.) **be ~ of the others** den anderen voraus sein; **be ~ on points** nach Punkten führen; **get ~:** vorwärts kommen 3 (further forward in time) **~ of us lay three days of intensive training** vor uns lagen drei Tage intensives Training; **Britain is eight hours ~ of Los Angeles** in Großbritannien ist es acht Stunden später als in Los Angeles; **finish ~ of schedule** *or* **time** früher als geplant fertig werden; **get home ~ of sb.** eher *od.* früher nach Hause kommen als jmd.; **we've got ~ of ourselves** (fig.) wir sind zu schnell vorgegangen; **there is no point in looking too far ~:** es hat keinen Sinn, zu weit in die Zukunft zu planen

ahoy /ə'hɔɪ/ *int.* (Naut.) ahoi

AI *abbr.* 1 **= artificial intelligence** KI 2 **= artificial insemination** KB

aid /eɪd/

A *v.t.* 1 **~ sb. [to do sth.]** jmdm. helfen[, etw. zu tun]; **~ed by** unterstützt von; *see also* **abet** 2 (promote) fördern

B *n.* 1 *no pl.* (help) Hilfe, *die;* **come to sb.'s ~,** **go to the ~ of sb.** jmdm. zu Hilfe kommen; **with the ~ of sth./sb.** mithilfe einer Sache (*Gen.*)/mit jmds. Hilfe; mithilfe von etw./jmdm.; **in ~ of sb./sth.** zugunsten von jmdm./etw.; **what's [all] this in ~ of?** (coll.) wozu soll das [Ganze *od.* alles] gut sein?; *see also* **foreign aid** 2 (source of help) Hilfsmittel, *das* (**to** für)

'aid agency *n.* Hilfsagentur, *die;* (aid organization) Hilfsorganisation, *die*

aide /eɪd/ *n.* 1 ▸ **aide-de-camp** 2 (assistant) Berater, *der*/Beraterin, *die*

aide-de-camp /eɪddə'kɑ̃:/ *n., pl.* **aides-de-camp** /eɪddə'kɑ̃:/ (Mil.) Adjutant, *der*

aide-mémoire /'eɪdmemwɑ:(r)/ *n.* (aid to memory) Gedächtnisstütze, *die*

aid: ~ package *n.* Hilfspaket, *das;* **~ plan** *n.* Hilfsplan, *der;* **~ programme** *n.* Hilfsprogramm, *das*

Aids /eɪdz/ *n., no pl., no art.* ▸ⓘ **p. 1231** Aids (*das*); *attrib.* **~ awareness** Aidsbewusstsein, *das;* **~ baby** Aidsbaby, *das;* **~ education** Aidsaufklärung, *die;* **~ test** Aidstest, *der;* **~ victim** Aidsopfer, *das;* **~ virus** Aidsvirus, *der,* (fachspr.) *das*

'Aids-related *adj.* **~ disease/illness** durch Aids hervorgerufene Krankheit

aid: ~ station *n.* 1 (on battlefield) Erste-Hilfe-Posten, *der;* 2 (in race) Hilfstation, *die;* **~ worker** *n.* [humanitärer] Helfer/[humanitäre] Helferin; Mitarbeiter[in] einer Hilfsorganisation

aikido /'aɪkɪdəʊ/ *n.* (Sport) Aikido, *das*

ail /eɪl/ *v.t.* (arch.: trouble) plagen; **what ~s him?** was ist mit ihm?

aileron /'eɪlərɒn/ *n.* (Aeronaut.) Querruder, *das*

ailing /'eɪlɪŋ/ *adj.* (sickly) kränklich

ailment /'eɪlmənt/ *n.* Gebrechen, *das;* **minor ~:** leichte Erkrankung

aim /eɪm/

A *v.t.* ausrichten ‹*Schusswaffe, Rakete*›; **~ sth. at sb./sth.** etw. auf jmdn./etw. richten; **that remark was not ~ed at you** (fig.) diese Bemerkung war nicht gegen Sie gerichtet; **~ a blow/shot/book at sb.** nach jmdm. schlagen/auf jmdn. schießen/ein Buch nach jmdm. werfen

B *v.i.* 1 zielen; **~ at sth./sb.** auf etw./jmdn. zielen; **~ high/wide** [zu] hoch/[zu] weit zielen; **~ high** (fig.) sich (*Dat.*) ein hohes Ziel stecken *od.* setzen 2 (intend) **~ to do sth.** *or* **at doing sth.** beabsichtigen, etw. zu tun; **please ~ to be back by 4 p.m.** versuche bitte, bis 16 Uhr zurück zu sein; **~ at** *or* **for sth.** (fig.) etw. anstreben; **I'm not quite sure what you're ~ing at** (fig.) ich weiß nicht recht, worauf Sie hinauswollen

C *n.* 1 Ziel, *das;* **his ~ was true** er hatte genau gezielt; **take ~ [at sth./sb.]** [auf etw./jmdn.] zielen; **take ~ at the target** das Ziel anvisieren 2 (purpose) Ziel, *das*

AIM *abbr.* **= Alternative Investment Market**

aimless /'eɪmlɪs/ *adj.* ziellos ‹*Leben, Aktivität*›; sinnlos ‹*Vorhaben, Beschäftigung*›

aimlessly /'eɪmlɪslɪ/ *adv.* ziellos

aimlessness /'eɪmlɪsnɪs/ *n.* Ziellosigkeit, *die*

ain't /eɪnt/ (coll.) 1 **= am not, is not, are not;** ▸ **be** 2 **= has not, have not;** ▸ **have B**

air /eə(r)/

A *n.* 1 Luft, *die;* **take the ~:** [frische] Luft schöpfen (geh.); **be in the ~** (fig.) (be spreading) ‹*Gerücht, Idee:*› in der Luft liegen; (be uncertain) ‹*Plan, Projekt:*› in der Luft hängen; **be up in the ~** ‹*Plan, Projekt:*› in der Luft hängen; **be walking on ~** (fig.) wie auf Wolken schweben (ugs.); **by ~:** mit dem Flugzeug; **travel by ~:** fliegen; **send a letter by ~:** einen Brief mit *od.* per Luftpost schicken; **from the ~:** aus der Vogelperspektive 2 (breeze) Lüftchen, *das* 3 (Radio, Telev.) **be/go on the ~:** senden; ‹*Programm, Sendung:*› gesendet werden; **be/go off the ~:** nicht/nicht mehr senden; ‹*Programm:*› beendet sein/werden 4 (appearance) **there was an ~ of absurdity about the whole exercise** die ganze Übung hatte etwas Absurdes; **his newspaper stories have the ~ of fiction** seine Zeitungsgeschichten haben etwas Fiktives 5 (bearing) Auftreten, *das;* (facial expression) Miene, *die;* **~s and graces** Allüren *Pl.* (abwertend); **give oneself** *or* **put on ~s** sich aufspielen 6 (Mus.) Melodie, *die*

B *v.t.* 1 (ventilate) lüften ‹*Zimmer, Matratze, Klei-*

a

dung› [2] (finish drying) nachtrocknen ‹Wäsche› [3] (parade) zur Schau tragen [4] (make public) [öffentlich] darlegen
[C] v.i. (be ventilated) lüften

air: ~ 'ambulance n. Flugambulanz, die; **~ bag** n. (Motor Veh.) Airbag, der; **side ~ bag** Seitenairbag, der; **~bed** n. Luftmatratze, die; **~borne** adj. **~borne bacteria** in der Luft befindliche Bakterien; **~borne freight** Luftfracht, die; **~borne troops** Luftlandetruppen Pl.; **be ~borne** sich in der Luft befinden; **become ~borne** sich in die Luft erheben; **~ brake** n. Druckluftbremse, die; (flap) Luftbremse, die; **~ brick** n. Lüftungsstein, der (Bauw.); **~ bridge** n. (at airport) Fluggastbrücke, die; **~brush** n. Spritzpistole, die; **~ bubble** n. Luftblase, die; **~burst** n. Explosion in der Luft; Luftexplosion, die; **~ bus** n. Airbus, der; **~-conditioned** adj. klimatisiert; **~ conditioner** n. Klimaanlage, die; **~ conditioning** n., no pl. Klimatisierung, die; (system) Klimaanlage, die; **~-cooled** adj. luftgekühlt; **~ corridor** n. (Aeronaut.) Luftkorridor, der; **~ cover** n. Deckung aus der Luft

aircraft /'eəkrɑːft/ n., pl. same Luftfahrzeug, das; (aeroplane) Flugzeug, das

aircraft: ~ carrier n. (Navy) Flugzeugträger, der; **~ noise** n. Fluglärm, der

air: ~ crash n. Flugzeugabsturz, der; **~ crew** n. Besatzung, die; Flugpersonal, das; **~ cushion** n. [1] Luftkissen, das; [2] **~ -cushion vehicle** Luftkissenfahrzeug, das; **~ disaster** Flugzeugkatastrophe, die; **~ display** n. Flugschau, die

Airedale /'eədeɪl/ n. Airedaleterrier, der

airer /'eərə(r)/ n. Wäscheständer, der

air: ~ ex'clusion zone n. Flugverbotszone, die; **~ fare** n. Flugpreis, der; **~ ferry** n. (~craft) [im Pendelluftverkehr eingesetztes] Flugzeug; (service) Pendelluftverkehr, der; **~field** n. Flugplatz, der; **~ filter** n. Luftfilter, der od. das; **~foil** (Amer.) ▸ **aerofoil**; **~ force** n. Luftstreitkräfte Pl.; Luftwaffe, die; **~frame** n. (Aeronaut.) Flugwerk, das; **~ freight terminal** n. Luftfrachtterminal, der od. das; **~ freshener** n. Lufterfrischer, der; Luftverbesserer, der; **~ gap** Luftspalt, der; (layer) Luftschicht, die; **~ guitar** n. (coll.) Luftgitarre, die; **~gun** n. Luftgewehr, das; **~head** n. (coll.) Hohlkopf, der; attrib. hohlköpfig; **~ hostess** n. **▸❶ p. 1260** Stewardess, die

airily /'eərɪlɪ/ adv. (flippantly) leichthin

airiness /'eərmɪs/ n., no pl. (flippancy) Unbekümmertheit, die

airing /'eərɪŋ/ n. Auslüften, das; **these clothes need a good ~:** diese Kleider müssen gründlich gelüftet werden; **give a problem an ~** (fig.) ein Problem an die Öffentlichkeit bringen; attrib. **~ cupboard** Trockenschrank, der

air: ~ kiss n. Luftkuss, der; **blow sb. an ~ kiss** jmdm. einen Luftkuss zuwerfen od. schicken; **~-kiss** v.t. **~-kiss sb./sb.'s cheek** jmdm. einen Luftkuss geben

airless /'eəlɪs/ adj. stickig ‹Zimmer, Büro›; windstill ‹Nacht›

air: ~ letter n. Luftpostleichtbrief, der; Aerogramm, das; **~lift** [A] n. Luftbrücke, die (**of** für); [B] v.t. auf dem Luftweg od. über eine Luftbrücke transportieren; **~line** n. Fluggesellschaft, die; Fluglinie, die; attrib. **~line pilot ▸❶ p. 1260** [für eine Fluggesellschaft fliegender] Pilot; **~ liner** n. Verkehrsflugzeug, das; **~lock** n. [1] (stoppage) Luftblase, die; [2] (of spacecraft etc.) Luftschleuse, die; **~ mail** n. Luftpost, die; **by ~ mail** mit od. per Luftpost; **~mail** v.t. mit od. per Luftpost befördern; **~mail letter** n. Luftpostbrief, der; **~man** /'eəmən/ n., pl. **~men** /'eəmən/ Flieger, der; **~ mile** n. Flugmeile, die; **~-minded** adj. am Fliegen interessiert; **~miss** n. (Aeronaut.) Beinahezusammenstoß, der; **~ pistol** n. Luftpistole, die; **~plane** (Amer.) ▸ **aeroplane**; **~ play** n., no pl. (Radio) Radiopräsenz, die; **the record receives** or **gets no/a great deal of ~play** die Platte wird [überhaupt] nicht/wird sehr häufig im Radio gespielt; **~ pocket** n. (Aeronaut.) Luftloch, das; **~ pollution** n. Luftverschmutzung, die; **~port** n. Flughafen, der; attrib. **~port tax** Flughafengebühr, die; **~ power** n. Schlagkraft der Luftwaffe; **~ pressure** n. Luftdruck, der; **~ pump** n. Luftpumpe, die; **~ quality** n. Luftqualität, die; **~ rage** n. Flugkoller, der; ausfälliges Fluggastverhalten; **~ raid** n. Luftangriff, der; attrib. **~-raid precautions** Luftschutz, der; **~-raid shelter** Luftschutzraum, der; **~-raid siren** Luftschutzsirene, die; **~-raid warden** Luftschutzwart, der; **~ rifle** n. Luftgewehr, das; **~screw** n. (Aeronaut.) Luftschraube, die (Technik); **~-sea 'rescue** n. Seenotrettungseinsatz aus der Luft; **~ship** n. Luftschiff, das; **~ show** n. Flugschau, die; **~sick** adj. luftkrank; **~sickness** n. Luftkrankheit, die; **~space** n. Luftraum, der; **~ speed** n. (Aeronaut.) Eigengeschwindigkeit, die; **~stream** n. (Meteorol.) Luftströmung, die; **~ strike** n. Luftschlag, der; **~strip** n. Start-und-Lande-Bahn, die; **~ terminal** n. [Air]terminal, der od. das; **~ ticket** n. Flugticket, das; **~tight** adj. luftdicht; **~time** n. Sendezeit, die; **~-to-~** adj. Luft-Luft-; **~-to-~ refuelling** Betanken in der Luft; **~ traffic** n. (Aeronaut.) Flugverkehr, der; attrib. **~-traffic control** (Aeronaut.) Flugsicherung, die; **~-traffic controller ▸❶ p. 1260** (Aeronaut.) Fluglotse, der; **~ travel** n., no pl. Fliegen, das; Reisen mit dem Flugzeug; **the growth in** or **of ~ travel** die Zunahme der Flugreisen; **transatlantic ~ travel** Transatlantikflüge Pl; **~ traveller** n. Flugreisende, der/die; **~ war** n. Luftkrieg, der; **~waves** n. pl. Äther, der; **~way** n. [1] (Aeronaut.) Luftstraße, die; [2] (Anat.) Luftröhre, die; [3] (ventilation shaft) Lüftungsschacht, der; **~woman** n. Fliegerin, die; **~worthy** adj. (Aeronaut.) lufttüchtig

airy /'eərɪ/ adj. [1] luftig ‹Büro, Zimmer›; windig ‹Küste› [2] (poet.: lofty) **the ~ mountain** der in luftige Höhen hinaufragende Berg [3] (superficial) vage; (flippant) leichtfertig

airy-fairy /eərɪ'feərɪ/ adj. (coll.) aus der Luft gegriffen ‹Plan›; versponnen ‹Idee, Vorstellung›

aisle /aɪl/ n. Gang, der; (lateral section of church) Seitenschiff, das; **have the audience rolling in the ~s** (coll.) das Publikum dazu bringen, dass es sich vor Lachen kugelt; **walk down the ~ with sb.** (fig.) mit jmdm. vor den Traualtar treten

aitch /eɪtʃ/ n. H, h, das; **drop one's ~es** das h [im Anlaut] nicht aussprechen

Aix-la-Chapelle /eɪkslɑːʃæ'pel/ pr. n. **▸❶ p. 1643** Aachen (das)

ajar /ə'dʒɑː(r)/ pred. adj. **be** or **stand [slightly] ~:** einen [winzigen] Spaltbreit offen stehen; **leave ~:** offen lassen

a.k.a. abbr. **= also known as** al.

akimbo /ə'kɪmbəʊ/ adv. **with arms ~:** die Arme in die Seite gestemmt

akin /ə'kɪn/ pred. adj. [1] verwandt; **look ~:** sich (Dat.) ähnlich sehen [2] (fig.) ähnlich; **be ~ to sth.** einer Sache (Dat.) ähnlich sein

à la /ɑː lɑː/ prep. à la; **~ russe** /ɑː lɑː 'ruːs/ auf russische Art

alabaster /'æləbɑːstə/
[A] n. Alabaster, der
[B] adj. alabastern; **an ~ sculpture** eine Alabasterskulptur

à la carte /ɑː lɑː 'kɑːt/
[A] adv. à la carte
[B] adj. **the ~ menu** das Menü à la carte

alack /ə'læk/ int. (arch.) o weh; **~-a-day** ach und weh

alacrity /ə'lækrɪtɪ/ n., no pl. Eilfertigkeit, die; **accept with ~:** mit [großer] Bereitwilligkeit annehmen

Aladdin's /ə'lædɪnz/: **~ cave** n.: Ort, an dem man Kostbarkeiten in großer Fülle findet; **~ lamp** n. Aladins Wunderlampe

à la mode /ɑː lɑː 'məʊd/ adj. [1] in Mode; à la mode (veralt.); **be ~:** Mode sein [2] (Cookery) in Wein geschmort [3] (Amer. Gastr.) **pie ~:** Kuchen mit Eis

alarm /ə'lɑːm/
[A] n. [1] Alarm, der; **give** or **raise the ~:** Alarm schlagen [2] (fear) Angst, die; (uneasiness) Besorgnis, die; **jump up in ~:** erschreckt aufspringen; **spread ~ and despondency** allgemeine Angst und Mutlosigkeit erzeugen [3] (mechanism) Alarmanlage, die; (of ~ clock) Weckmechanismus, der; (signal) Warnsignal, das; **sound the ~:** die Alarmanlage betätigen [4] ▸ **alarm clock**
[B] v.t. [1] (make aware of danger) aufschrecken; (call into action) alarmieren [2] (cause anxiety to) beunruhigen

a'larm: ~ bell n. Alarmglocke, die; Warnsignal, das; **the ~ bells started ringing [in my head]** (fig.) in meinem Kopf fing ein rotes Lämpchen an zu leuchten; **~ call** n. Weck[an]ruf, der; **~ clock** n. Wecker, der

alarming /ə'lɑːmɪŋ/ adj. alarmierend

alarmingly /ə'lɑːmɪŋlɪ/ adv. in alarmierendem Maße

alarmist /ə'lɑːmɪst/
[A] n. Panikmacher, der
[B] adj. ‹Reden, Behauptungen› von Panikmachern

alarum /ə'lɑːrəm/ n. **~s and excursions** (joc.) Lärm und Getümmel

alas /ə'læs, ə'lɑːs/
[A] int. ach
[B] adv. (unfortunately) leider Gottes

Alaska /ə'læskə/ [1] pr. n. Alaska (das) [2] n. (Cookery) **baked ~:** ≈ Überraschungsomelett, das; Omelette surprise, die

Albania /æl'beɪnɪə/ pr. n. Albanien (das)

Albanian /æl'beɪnɪən/ **▸❶ p. 1277, ▸❶ p. 1345**
[A] adj. albanisch; **sb. is ~:** jmd. ist Albaner/Albanerin; see also **English A**
[B] n. [1] (person) Albaner, der/Albanerin, die [2] (language) Albanisch, das; see also **English B 1**

albatross /'ælbətrɒs/ n. (Ornith., Golf) Albatros, der

albedo /æl'biːdəʊ/ n. (Astron.) Albedo, die

albeit /ɔːl'biːɪt/ conj. (literary) wenn auch; obgleich (geh.)

albino /æl'biːnəʊ/ n., pl. **~s** Albino, der

Albion /'ælbɪən/ n. (literary/poet.) Albion, das; **perfidious ~:** das perfide Albion

album /'ælbəm/ n. [1] Album, das [2] (record, set of records) Album, das; **four-record ~:** Kassette mit vier Langspielplatten [3] (record holder) Kassette, die

albumen /'ælbjʊmɪn/ n. [1] Albumen, das; Eiweiß, das [2] (Bot.) Nährgewebe, das

alchemist /'ælkəmɪst/ n. Alchimist, der; Alchemist, der

alchemy /'ælkəmɪ/ n., no pl. (lit. or fig.) Alchimie, die; Alchemie, die

alcohol /'ælkəhɒl/ n. Alkohol, der

'alcohol-free adj. alkoholfrei

alcoholic /ælkə'hɒlɪk/
[A] adj. alkoholisch; **~ smell/taste** Alkoholgeruch, der/-geschmack, der; **~ stupor** Vollrausch, der
[B] n. Alkoholiker, der/Alkoholikerin, die

Alcoholics A'nonymous n. die Anonymen Alkoholiker

alcoholism /'ælkəhɒlɪzm/ n., no pl. Alkoholismus, der; Trunksucht, die

alcopop /'ælkəʊpɒp/ n. Alcopop, der od. das

alcove /'ælkəʊv/ n. Alkoven, der; (in garden wall, hedge) Nische, die

aldehyde /'ældɪhaɪd/ n. (Chem.) Aldehyd, der; (acetaldehyde) Acetaldehyd, der

alder /'ɔːldə(r)/ n. (Bot.) Erle, die; **~ buckthorn** Faulbaum, der

alderman /'ɔːldəmən/ n., pl. **aldermen** /'ɔːldəmən/ [1] Stadtrat, der; Alderman, der; Ratsherr, der (veralt.) [2] (Amer., Austral.) gewähltes Mitglied einer Stadtverwaltung

ale /eɪl/ n. [1] Ale, das [2] (Hist.) Bier, das

aleatoric /eɪlɪə'tɔːrɪk/, **aleatory** /'eɪlɪətərɪ/ adjs. aleatorisch

'alehouse n. (Hist.) [Bier]schenke, die

alert /ə'lɜːt/
[A] adj. [1] (watchful) wachsam; **be ~ for trouble** auf der Hut sein; **be ~ to sth.** mit etw. rechnen [2] (physically lively) lebhaft; (mentally lively) aufgeweckt; (attentive) **the ~ listener** der aufmerksame Zuhörer

B *n.* 1 (warning) Alarmsignal, *das* 2 (state of preparedness) Alarmbereitschaft, *die;* **air-raid ~:** Fliegeralarm, *der;* **be on the ~ [for/against sth.]** [vor etw. (*Dat.*)] auf der Hut sein

C *v.t.* alarmieren; **~ sb. [to sth.]** jmdn. [vor etw. (*Dat.*)] warnen

alertly /əˈlɜːtlɪ/ *adv.* aufmerksam

alertness /əˈlɜːtnɪs/ *n., no pl.* Wachsamkeit, *die;* **~ of mind** geistige Beweglichkeit

A level /ˈeɪ levl/ *n.* (Brit. Sch.) 1 ≈ Abitur, *das;* Abschluss der Sekundarstufe II; **take one's ~s** ≈ das Abitur machen 2 *attrib.* ≈ Abitur-; **~ French** ≈ Französisch als Abiturfach; **~ papers** ≈ Abiturarbeiten

A level – Advanced level

Ein Examen, das von vielen Schülern in England und Wales, üblicherweise im letzten Jahr der weiterführenden Schule, abgelegt wird. Die Abschlussnoten (*grades*) werden in jedem Fach einzeln vergeben. Schüler, die ein Hochschulstudium (*higher education*) anstreben, absolvieren in der Regel drei bis vier *A levels* und werden von den Universitäten und anderen Institutionen entsprechend ihren Abschlussnoten, besonders in den für ihr Studienfach relevanten Fächern, ausgewählt. Siehe auch **AS level**.

alexandrine /ælɪgˈzændrɪn/ *n.* (Pros.) Alexandriner, *der*

alfalfa /ælˈfælfə/ *n.* (Bot.) Luzerne, *die;* Alfalfa, *die*

alfresco /ælˈfreskəʊ/

A *adv.* im Freien

B *adj.* ‹*Unterhaltung, Essen*› im Freien

alga /ˈælgə/ *n., pl.* **~e** /ˈældʒiː, ˈælgiː/ (Bot.) Alge, *die*

algebra /ˈældʒɪbrə/ *n.* (Math.) Algebra, *die*

algebraic /ældʒɪˈbreɪɪk/ *adj.* (Math.) algebraisch

Algeria /ælˈdʒɪərɪə/ *pr. n.* Algerien (*das*)

Algerian /ælˈdʒɪərɪən/ ▸ⓘ **p. 1345**

A *adj.* algerisch; **sb. is ~:** jmd. ist Algerier/Algerierin

B *n.* Algerier, *der*/Algerierin, *die*

Algiers /ælˈdʒɪəz/ *pr. n.* ▸ⓘ **p. 1643** Algier (*das*)

algorithm /ˈælgərɪðm/ *n.* (Math., Computing) Algorithmus, *der*

alias /ˈeɪlɪəs/

A *adv.* alias

B *n.* 1 angenommener Name; (of criminal) falscher Name 2 (Computing) Alias, *das*

alibi /ˈælɪbaɪ/ *n.* Alibi, *das;* (coll.: excuse) Ausrede, *die*

Alice /ˈælɪs/ *n.* **an ~-in-Wonderland situation** eine völlig groteske Situation

alien /ˈeɪlɪən/

A *adj.* 1 (strange) fremd; **be ~ to sb.** jmdm. fremd sein 2 (foreign) ausländisch; (from another world) außerirdisch 3 (repugnant) **be ~ to sb.** jmdm. zuwider sein 4 (contrary) **cruelty was ~ to her nature** Grausamkeit lag ihr völlig fern; **fascism is ~ to our democratic beliefs** der Faschismus steht in krassem Gegensatz zu unserer demokratischen Überzeugung

B *n.* 1 (Admin.: foreigner) Ausländer, *der*/Ausländerin, *die* 2 (a being from another world) Außerirdische, *der/die*

alienate /ˈeɪlɪəneɪt/ *v.t.* 1 (estrange) befremden ‹*Person*›; zerstören ‹*Zuneigung*›; verlieren ‹*Unterstützung*›; **his gaffes have ~d many of his supporters** durch seine Ausrutscher hat er sich (*Dat.*) viele seiner Anhänger entfremdet; **feel ~d from society** sich der Gesellschaft entfremdet fühlen 2 (Law: divert) entziehen (**from** *Dat.*)

alienation /eɪlɪəˈneɪʃn/ *n., no pl.* 1 Entfremdung, *die* 2 (Theatre) Verfremdung, *die*

alight[1] /əˈlaɪt/ *v.i.* 1 aussteigen; **~ from a vehicle** aus einem Fahrzeug aussteigen; **~ from a horse** von einem Pferd absitzen 2 ‹*Vogel:*› sich niedersetzen; ‹*Flugzeug, Schneeflocken:*› landen

alight[2] *pred. adj.* (on fire) **be/catch ~:** brennen; **set sth. ~:** etw. in Brand setzen; **the upper storey was well ~:** das obere Stockwerk brannte lichterloh

align /əˈlaɪn/ *v.t.* 1 (place in a line) ausrichten; **the posts must be ~ed** die Pfosten müssen in einer Linie ausgerichtet werden 2 (bring into line) in eine Linie bringen; **~ the wheels** (Motor Veh.) die Spur einstellen

alignment /əˈlaɪnmənt/ *n.* 1 Ausrichtung, *die;* **in/out of ~:** [genau] ausgerichtet/nicht richtig ausgerichtet; **the wheels are in/out of ~** (Motor Veh.) die Spur ist richtig/falsch eingestellt 2 (Polit.) Gruppierung, *die;* Ausrichtung, *die*

alike /əˈlaɪk/

A *pred. adj.* ähnlich; (indistinguishable) [völlig] gleich

B *adv.* gleich; in gleicher Weise; **winter and summer ~:** Sommer wie Winter; **all of us ~ are concerned, this concerns us all ~:** es geht uns alle gleichermaßen an

alimentary /ælɪˈmentərɪ/ *adj.* Nahrungs-; alimentär (Med.); **~ organ/system** Verdauungsorgan/-system, *das*

alimentary caˈnal *n.* (Anat.) Verdauungskanal, *der*

alimentation /ælɪmənˈteɪʃn/ *n., no pl.* (formal) Ernährung, *die*

alimony /ˈælɪmənɪ/ *n.* Unterhaltszahlung, *die*

alive /əˈlaɪv/ *pred. adj.* 1 lebendig; lebend; **stay ~:** am Leben bleiben; **if I'm still ~ in thirty years' time** wenn ich in dreißig Jahren noch am Leben bin; **any man ~:** jeder x-Beliebige; **no man ~:** kein Mensch auf der ganzen Welt; **man ~!** (coll. dated) Menschenskind!; **keep one's hopes ~:** nicht die Hoffnung verlieren; **keep sb.'s hopes ~:** jmdn. noch hoffen lassen; **the issue is still ~:** die Angelegenheit ist immer noch offen; **come ~:** wieder aufleben; ‹*Ereignis:*› wieder lebendig werden 2 (aware) **be ~ to sth.** sich (*Dat.*) einer Sache (*Gen.*) bewusst sein; **he's always ~ to new ideas** er ist neuen Ideen gegenüber immer aufgeschlossen 3 (brisk) rege; munter; **be ~ and kicking** gesund und munter sein; **look ~!** ein bisschen munter! 4 (swarming) **be ~ with sth.** von etw. wimmeln

alkali /ˈælkəlaɪ/ *n., pl.* **~s** *or* **~es** (Chem.) Alkali, *das;* **~ metal** Alkalimetall, *das*

alkaline /ˈælkəlaɪn/ *adj.* (Chem.) alkalisch; **~ earth** Erdalkali, *das;* alkalische Erde

all /ɔːl/

A *attrib. adj.* 1 (entire extent or quantity of) ganz; **~ England** ganz England; **~ day** den ganzen Tag; **~ the snow/milk/food** der ganze *od.* aller Schnee/die ganze *od.* alle Milch/das ganze *od.* alles Essen; **~ the family** die ganze Familie; **for ~ that** trotz allem; **~ his life** sein ganzes Leben; **~ my money** all mein Geld; mein ganzes Geld; **stop ~ this noise/shouting!** hör mit dem Krach/Geschrei auf!; **what's ~ this noise/shouting about?** was soll der [ganze] Krach/das [ganze] Geschrei?; **thank you for ~ your hard work** danke für all deine Anstrengungen; **get away from it ~:** einmal von allem abschalten; **that says it ~:** das sagt alles

2 (entire number of) alle; **~ the books** alle Bücher; **~ my books** all[e] meine Bücher; **in ~ our houses** in allen unseren Häusern; **where are ~ the glasses?** wo sind all die Gläser *od.* (ugs.) die ganzen Gläser?; **~ ten men** alle zehn Männer; **we ~ went to bed** wir gingen alle schlafen; **aren't we ~?** trifft das nicht für uns alle zu?; **~ you children can stay here** ihr Kinder könnt alle hier bleiben; **~ the others** alle anderen; **~ those present** alle Anwesenden; **be ~ things to ~ men** es allen recht machen [wollen]; **~ Goethe's works** sämtliche Werke Goethes; **why he of ~ people?** warum ausgerechnet er?; **of ~ the nitwits!** so ein Schwachkopf!; **~ manner of things** alles Mögliche; **~ manner of sausages** die verschiedensten Wurstsorten; **people of ~ ages** Menschen jeden Alters; **with ~ her faults** trotz all ihrer Fehler; **A~ Fools' Day** der 1. April; **A~ Saints' Day** Allerheiligen; **A~ Souls' Day** Allerseelen

3 (any whatever) jeglicher/jegliche/jegliches

4 (greatest possible) **in ~ innocence** in aller Unschuld; **with ~ speed** so schnell wie möglich. *See also* **four B 3**; **kind A 1**; **that B 1**; **time A 1, 2, 6**; **way A 1**

B *n.* 1 (~ persons) alle; **~ present** alle Anwesenden; **one and ~:** [alle] ohne Ausnahme; **goodbye, one and ~!** Wiedersehen, alle zusammen!; **~ and sundry** Krethi und Plethi; **~ of us** wir alle; **the happiest/most beautiful of ~:** der/die Glücklichste/die Schönste unter allen; **the best pupils of ~:** die besten Schüler [von allen]; **most of ~:** am meisten; **he ran fastest of ~:** er lief am schnellsten

2 (every bit) **~ of it/the money** alles/das ganze *od.* alles Geld

3 **~ of** (as much as) **be ~ of seven feet tall** gut sieben Fuß groß sein

4 (~ things) alles; **~ that I possess** alles, was ich besitze; **~ I need is the money** ich brauche nur das Geld; **not ~ of the missing antiques have been recovered** nicht alle [der] fehlenden Antiquitäten sind wieder gefunden worden; **when ~ is said and done** alles in allem; **~ is lost** alles ist verloren; **~ is not lost** es ist nicht alles verloren; **he wants ~ or nothing** er will alles oder nichts; **it's ~ or nothing** es geht ums Ganze; **that is ~:** das ist alles; **it is not ~ it might be** es lässt zu wünschen übrig; **the most beautiful of ~:** der/die/das Schönste von allen; **most of ~:** am meisten; **for ~ you say, I still like her** trotz allem, was du sagst, mag ich sie immer noch; **give one's ~:** sein Letztes geben; **lose one's ~:** sein ganzes Hab und Gut verlieren; **it was ~ but impossible** es war fast unmöglich; **it was ~ I could do not to laugh** ich konnte mir das Lachen kaum verbeißen; **~ in ~:** alles in allem; **sb.'s ~ in ~:** jmds. Ein und Alles; **it's ~ the same** *or* **~ one to me** es ist mir ganz egal *od.* völlig gleichgültig; **that's ~ very well** *or* **fine** das ist alles schön und gut; **sth. and ~:** mitsamt etw.; **can I help you at ~?** kann ich Ihnen irgendwie behilflich sein?; **I do not know at ~:** ich weiß wirklich nicht; **I do not care at ~:** es ist mir völlig gleich; **you are not disturbing me at ~:** du störst mich nicht im Geringsten; **were you surprised at ~?** warst du denn überrascht?; **if you go to Venice at ~:** wenn du überhaupt nach Venedig fährst; **is he there at ~?** ist er überhaupt da?; **he is not stupid at ~:** er ist keineswegs dumm; **he is not at ~ stupid** er ist gar nicht *od.* überhaupt nicht dumm; **she has no talent at ~:** sie hat gar *od.* überhaupt kein Talent; **nothing at ~:** gar nichts; **not at ~ happy/well** überhaupt nicht glücklich/gesund; **not at ~!** überhaupt nicht!; (acknowledging thanks) gern geschehen!; nichts zu danken!; **if at ~:** wenn überhaupt; **in ~:** insgesamt; *see also* **time A 3**

5 (Sport) **two [goals] ~:** zwei zu zwei; (Tennis) **thirty ~:** dreißig beide

C *adv.* ganz; **~ but** fast; **he ~ but fell down** er wäre fast heruntergefallen; **dressed ~ in white** ganz in Weiß [gekleidet]; **~ the better/worse [for that]** um so besser/schlimmer; **I feel ~ the better for it** das hat mir wirklich gut getan; **~ the more reason to do sth.** um so mehr sollte man etw. tun; **~ at once** (suddenly) plötzlich; (simultaneously) alle[s] zugleich; **~ too soon** allzu schnell; **go ~ serious** (coll.) ganz ernst werden; **be ~ ˈfor sth.** (coll.) sehr für etw. sein; **her latest play is ~ about ...:** in ihrem jüngsten Stück geht es um ...; **be ~ ˈin** (exhausted) total *od.* völlig erledigt sein (ugs.); **go ~ out [to do sth.]** alles daransetzen[, etw. zu tun]; **be ~ ready [to go]** (coll.) fertig [zum Weggehen] sein (ugs.); **sth. is ~ right** etw. ist in Ordnung; (tolerable) etw. ist ganz gut; **did you get home ~ right?** sind Sie gut nach Hause gekommen?; **I'm ~ right** mir geht es ganz gut; **work out ~ right** gut gehen; klappen (ugs.); **that's her, ~ right** das ist sie, ganz recht; **yes, ~ right** ja, gut; **is it ~ right if I go in?** kann ich reingehen?; **it's ~ right for you/him** *etc.*, **but ...** (coll.) es passt dir/ihm *usw.*, aber ...; **it's ~ right by** *or* **with me** das ist mir recht; **lie ~ round the room** überall im Zimmer herumliegen; **it was agreed ~ round that ...:** alle waren [damit] einverstanden, dass ...; **order drinks ~ round** Getränke für alle bestellen; **better ~ round** in jeder Hinsicht besser; **be ~ there** (coll.) voll da sein (ugs.); **I don't think he's ~ there** (coll.) ich glaube, er ist nicht ganz da

a

(ugs.); ~ **the same** trotzdem; **it's ~ the same to me** es ist mir einerlei; **if it's ~ the same to you** wenn du nichts dagegen hast; **the A~ Blacks** (coll.) *die neuseeländische Rugbynationalmannschaft*

Allah /ˈælə/ *pr. n.* Allah *(der)*

all: ~-A'merican *adj.* **the ~-American football team** die beste Footballmannschaft der ganzen USA; **the ~-American boy** der typisch amerikanische Junge; **~-around** (Amer.) ▸ **~-round**

allay /əˈleɪ/ *v.t.* **1** vermindern; trüben, dämpfen ‹*Freude, Glück*›; zerstreuen ‹*Besorgnis, Befürchtungen*› **2** (alleviate) stillen ‹*Hunger, Durst*›; lindern ‹*Schmerz*›

all: ~-'clear *n.* Entwarnung, *die;* **sound the ~-clear** entwarnen; **~-day** *adj.* ganztägig ‹*Ausflug, Versammlung*›

allegation /ælɪˈgeɪʃn/ *n.* Behauptung, *die;* **make ~s against sb.** Beschuldigungen gegen jmdn. erheben; **reject all ~s of corruption** jeglichen Vorwurf der Korruption zurückweisen

allege /əˈledʒ/ *v.t.* ~ **that …:** behaupten, dass …; ~ **criminal negligence** den Vorwurf grober Fahrlässigkeit erheben

alleged /əˈledʒd/ *adj.*, **allegedly** /əˈledʒɪdlɪ/ *adv.* angeblich

allegiance /əˈliːdʒəns/ *n.* Loyalität, *die* (**to** gegenüber); **swear ~ to king and country** dem König und dem Vaterland Treue schwören; **oath of ~:** Treueeid, *der;* **some supporters changed their ~ from Liverpool to Everton** einige Fans sind von Liverpool zu Everton umgeschwenkt

allegorical /ælɪˈgɒrɪkl/ *adj.* allegorisch

allegory /ˈælɪgərɪ/ *n.* Allegorie, *die;* (emblem) Sinnbild, *das*

allegro /æˈleɪgrəʊ, æˈlegrəʊ/ (Mus.)
A *adv.* allegro
B *n., pl.* **~s** Allegro, *das*

all-e'lectric *adj.* vollelektrisch; **our house is ~:** in unserem Haus ist alles elektrisch

'all-embracing *adj.* alles umfassend

Allen key ® /ˈælən kiː/ *n.* Inbusschlüssel, *der* (Wz)

allergen /ˈælədʒən/ *n.* (Med.) Allergen, *das*

allergic /əˈlɜːdʒɪk/ *adj.* allergisch (**to** gegen)

allergy /ˈælədʒɪ/ *n.* **1** (Med.) Allergie, *die* (**to** gegen) **2** (fig. coll.) **have an ~ to sth.** auf etw. (*Akk.*) allergisch reagieren

'allergy clinic *n.* Allergieklinik, *die*

alleviate /əˈliːvɪeɪt/ *v.t.* abschwächen

alleviation /əliːvɪˈeɪʃn/ *n., no pl.* Abschwächung, *die*

alley[1] /ˈælɪ/ *n.* **1** [schmale] Gasse; (between flower beds or gardens) Pfad, *der;* (avenue) Allee, *die;* **be up sb.'s ~** (coll.) jmds. Fall sein (ugs.); **this problem is just** *or* **right up his ~** (coll.) für dieses Problem ist er genau der Richtige **2** (skittle ~) Bahn, *die*

alley[2] ▸ **ally**[2]

'alleyway Gasse, *die*

'all-fired (Amer. coll.) *adj., adv.* verdammt

alliance /əˈlaɪəns/ *n.* Bündnis, *das;* (league) Allianz, *die;* **~ with other groups would increase our influence** ein Bündnis mit anderen Gruppen würde unseren Einfluss vergrößern; **in ~ with sb./sth.** im Verein mit jmdm./etw.

> **Alliance Party (Northern Ireland)**
> Eine politische Partei in Nordirland, deren Ziel es ist, ein Ende des Konflikts zwischen extremen religiösen Gruppen zu bewirken, indem sie Menschen mit gemäßigten Ansichten beider Seiten zusammenführt.

allied /ˈælaɪd/ *adj.* **be ~ to** *or* **with sb./sth.** mit jmdm./etw. verbündet sein; **German is more closely ~ to English than to French** das Deutsche ist mit dem Englischen enger verwandt als mit dem Französischen; **the A~ Powers** die Alliierten

alligator /ˈælɪgeɪtə(r)/ *n.* (Zool.) Alligator, *der;* (skin) Krokodilleder, *das*

'alligator clip *n.* Krokodilklemme, *die*

all: ~-important *adj.* entscheidend; **~-in** *adj.* Pauschal-; **it costs £350 ~-in** es kostet 350 Pfund alles inklusive; **~-in wrestling** Freistilringen, *das*

alliteration /əlɪtəˈreɪʃn/ *n.* Stabreim, *der;* Alliteration, *die*

alliterative /əˈlɪtərətɪv/ *adj.* stabreimend; alliterierend

'all-night *adj.* die ganze Nacht dauernd ‹*Sitzung*›; nachts durchgehend geöffnet ‹*Gaststätte*›

allocate /ˈæləkeɪt/ *v.t.* zur Verfügung stellen ‹*Geld, Mittel*›; **~ sth. to sb./sth.** jmdm./einer Sache etw. zuweisen *od.* zuteilen

allocation /æləˈkeɪʃn/ *n.* Verteilung, *die;* (ration) Zuteilung, *die*

allot /əˈlɒt/ *v.t.*, **-tt-: ~ sth. to sb.** jmdm. etw. zuteilen; **you will be ~ted fifty pounds** es werden Ihnen fünfzig Pfund bewilligt; **we ~ted two hours to the task** wir haben zwei Stunden für diese Arbeit vorgesehen; **~ shares** Aktien ausgeben

allotment /əˈlɒtmənt/ *n.* **1** Zuteilung, *die* **2** (Brit.: plot of land) Gartenparzelle, *die;* ≈ Schrebergarten, *der* **3** (share) Anteil, *der*

all: ~-out *attrib. adj.* mit allen [verfügbaren] Mitteln *nachgestellt;* **~-over** *attrib. adj.* **~-over tan** nahtlose Bräune

allow /əˈlaʊ/
A *v.t.* **1** (permit) **~ sth.** etw. erlauben *od.* zulassen *od.* (förmlicher) gestatten; **~ sb. to do sth.** jmdm. erlauben, etw. zu tun; **be ~ed to do sth.** etw. tun dürfen; **will you be ~ed to?** darfst du?; **~ sb./oneself sth.** jmdm./sich etw. erlauben; **sb. is ~ed sth.** jmdm. ist etw. erlaubt; **~ sth. to happen** zulassen, dass etw. geschieht; **~ yourself to be convinced** lassen Sie sich überzeugen; **~ sb. in/out/past/through** jmdn. hinein-/hinaus-/vorbei-/durchlassen; **you are not ~ed in/out/past/through** Sie dürfen nicht hinein/hinaus/vorbei/durch; **~ sb. a discount/5% interest** jmdm. Rabatt/5% Zinsen geben **2** (agree) zugeben **3** (Law) bestätigen ‹*Anspruch*›; **~ the appeal** der Berufung (*Dat.*) stattgeben **4** (Sport) **the referee ~ed the goal** der Schiedsrichter gab das Tor
B *v.i.* **~ of sth.** etw. zulassen *od.* erlauben; **~ for sth.** etw. berücksichtigen; **we started very early, to ~ for delays** wir begannen sehr früh, um etwaige Verzögerungen auffangen zu können

allowable /əˈlaʊəbl/ *adj.* zulässig

allowance /əˈlaʊəns/ *n.* **1** Zuteilung, *die;* (money for special expenses) Zuschuss, *der;* **your luggage ~ is 44 kg.** Sie haben 44 kg Freigepäck; **tax ~:** Steuerfreibetrag, *der;* **clothing ~:** Kleidergeld, *das* **2** **make ~s for sth./sb.** etw./jmdn. berücksichtigen; **make ~ for errors** eventuelle Fehler einkalkulieren **3** (Commerc.) Ermäßigung, *die*

alloy
A /ˈælɔɪ/ *n.* Legierung, *die;* (inferior metal added) unedles Metall; *attrib.* **~ steel** Sonderstahl, *der*
B /əˈlɔɪ/ *v.t.* legieren; (debase) geringhaltiger machen

all: ~-points bulletin *n.* (Amer.) Fahndungsaufruf, *der;* **~-'powerful** *adj.* allmächtig; **~-purpose** *adj.* Universal-; Allzweck-; **~-risks** *attrib. adj.* **an ~-risks insurance** eine alle gängigen Risiken abdeckende Versicherung; **~-round** *adj.* Allround-; **~-round vision** Rundumsicht, *die;* **~-'rounder** *n.* Allroundtalent, *das;* (Sport) Allroundspieler, *der*/-spielerin, *die;* **~-seater** /ˈɔːlsiːtə(r)/ (Brit.) **A** *adj.* **~-seater stadium** [reines] Sitzplatzstadion; **B** *n.* [reines] Sitzplatzstadion; **~spice** *n.* Pimentbaum, *der;* (berry) Piment, *der;* **~-terrain bike** *n.* Gelände[fahr]rad, *das;* ATB[-Fahrrad], *das* (fachspr.); **~-terrain vehicle** *n.* ATV, *das* (fachspr.); Geländefahrzeug, *das;* **~-ticket** *adj.* **~-ticket game** *etc.* Spiel *usw.*, zu dem es nur Karten im Vorverkauf gibt; Spiel *usw.* ohne Tageskasse/Abendkasse; **~-time** *adj.* **~-time record** absoluter Rekord; **~-time favourites** *or* **greats** unvergessene Publikumslieblinge; **~-time high/low** höchster/niedrigster Stand aller Zeiten

allude /əˈljuːd, əˈluːd/ *v.i.* **~ to sth./sb.** sich auf etw./jmdn. beziehen; (covertly) auf etw./jmdn. anspielen

'all-up weight *n.* (Brit.: of aircraft) Fluggewicht, *das;* (of ship, train) Gesamtgewicht, *das*

allure /əˈljʊə(r)/
A *v.t.* locken; (fascinate) faszinieren; **~ sb. to do sth.** jmdn. dazu verlocken, etw. zu tun; **~d by thoughts of stardom** durch die Aussicht auf eine glänzende Karriere verlockt
B *n., no pl.* Verlockung, *die;* (personal charm) Charme, *der*

allurement /əˈljʊəmənt/ *n.* Verlockung, *die;* (charm) **she displayed all her ~s** sie ließ all ihre Reize spielen

alluring /əˈljʊərɪŋ/ *adj.* verlockend; **an ~ appeal** eine Verlockung

allusion /əˈljuːʒn, əˈluːʒn/ *n.* **1** Hinweis, *der;* **in an ~ to** unter Bezugnahme auf (+ *Akk.*) **2** (covert reference) Anspielung, *die* (**to** auf + *Akk.*)

allusive /əˈljuːsɪv, əˈluːsɪv/ *adj.* voller Anspielungen; **be ~ to sth.** auf etw. (*Akk.*) anspielen

alluvial /əˈluːvɪəl/ *adj.* (Geol.) angeschwemmt; **~ soil** Alluvialboden, *der*

all: ~-weather *attrib. adj.* Allwetter-; **~-wheel drive** *n.* (Amer.) Allradantrieb, *der*

ally[1]
A /əˈlaɪ, ˈælaɪ/ *v.t.* **~ oneself with sb./sth.** sich mit jmdm./etw. verbünden; *see also* **allied**
B /ˈælaɪ/ *n.* Verbündete, *der/die;* **my old friend and ~:** mein alter Freund und Kampfgefährte; **the Allies** die Alliierten

ally[2] /ˈælɪ/ *n.* (besonders schöne) Murmel (*aus Alabaster od. Glas*)

Alma Mater /ælmə ˈmeɪtə(r), ælmə ˈmɑːtə(r)/ *n.* Alma Mater, *die*

almanac /ˈɔːlmənæk, ˈɒlmənæk/ *n.* Almanach, *der*

almighty /ɔːlˈmaɪtɪ/
A *adj.* **1** allmächtig; **the A~:** der Allmächtige; **God A~!** (coll.) großer Gott!; **he acts as if he were God A~:** er tut, als ob er der liebe Gott selber wäre **2** (coll.: very great, hard, etc.) mächtig
B *adv.* (coll.) mächtig

almond /ˈɑːmənd/ *n.* **1** Mandel, *die;* **sweet/bitter ~:** Süß-/Bittermandel, *die;* **~ eyes** Mandelaugen **2** (tree) Mandelbaum, *der*

almoner /ˈɑːmənə(r)/ *n.* (Brit. dated) Sozialbetreuer, *der*/-betreuerin, *die* (*eines Krankenhauses*)

almost /ˈɔːlməʊst/ *adv.* fast; beinahe; **she ~ fell** sie wäre fast gefallen

alms /ɑːmz/ *n., no pl.* (Hist.) Almosen, *das*

'almshouse *n.* Armenhaus, *das*

aloe /ˈæləʊ/ *n.* **1** Aloe, *die* **2** *in pl.* (Pharm.) Aloe, *die;* Aloesaft, *der*

aloft /əˈlɒft/ *adv.* **1** (position) (literary) hoch droben (dichter.); (Naut.) [oben] in der Takelage *od.* im Rigg **2** (direction) (literary) empor (dichter.); (Naut.) in die Takelage; in das Rigg; **go ~:** in die Takelage *od.* in das Rigg klettern; aufentern (Seemannsspr.)

alone /əˈləʊn/
A *pred. adj.* allein; alleine (ugs.); **be [all] ~:** [ganz] allein sein; **she likes to be ~ sometimes** manchmal ist sie gern [für sich] allein; **when his parents died he was left ~ [in the world]** als seine Eltern starben, stand er ganz allein da; **he was not ~ in the belief that …:** er stand nicht allein mit der Überzeugung, dass …
B *adv.* allein; **you ~ can help me** nur du *od.* du allein kannst mir helfen; **the problem/money was his ~:** es war einzig und allein sein Problem/Geld; **this fact ~:** schon allein dies; **go it ~:** es im Alleingang tun

along /əˈlɒŋ/
A *prep.* **1** (position) entlang (+ *Dat.*); **~ one side of the street** auf der einen Straßenseite; **all ~ the wall** die ganze *od.* an der ganzen Mauer entlang **2** (direction) entlang (+ *Akk.*); **walk ~ the riverbank/street** am Ufer *od.* das Ufer/die Straße entlanglaufen; **creep ~ a wall** eine Mauer *od.* an einer Mauer entlangschleichen
B *adv.* **1** (onward) weiter; **he came running ~:**

er kam herbei- *od.* angelaufen; **leaves carried ~ by the wind** vom Wind fortgetragenes Laub; **he saw the train steaming ~ in the distance** er sah den Zug in der Ferne vorbei- *od.* vorüberdampfen; **the snake was slithering ~ in the tall grass** die Schlange glitt durch das hohe Gras **2** (with one) **bring/take sb./sth. ~:** jmdn./etw. mitbringen/mitnehmen **3** (there) **I'll be ~ shortly/as soon as I can** ich komme gleich/sobald ich kann **4** **all ~:** die ganze Zeit [über]

alongside /əlɒŋˈsaɪd/
A *adv.* daneben; längsseits (Seemannsspr.); **~ the quay** am Kai; **~ of** (esp. Amer.) ▸ **B**
B *prep.* (position) neben (+ *Dat.*); längsseits (Seemannsspr.) (+ *Gen.*); (direction) neben (+ *Akk.*); längsseits heran an (Seemannsspr.) (+ *Akk.*); (fig.) neben (+ *Dat.*); **work ~ sb.** mit jmdm. zusammen arbeiten/(fig.) zusammenarbeiten

aloof /əˈluːf/
A *adv.* abseits; **stand ~ from the others** abseits der anderen stehen; **hold ~ from sb.** sich von jmdm. fern halten; sich abseits von jmdm. halten; **keep ~:** Distanz wahren; **keep ~ from sb.** sich von jmdm. absondern *od.* fern halten
B *adj.* distanziert; reserviert

aloofness /əˈluːfnɪs/ *n., no pl.* Reserviertheit, *die;* Distanz[iertheit], *die*

aloud /əˈlaʊd/ *adv.* laut; **read [sth.] ~:** [etw.] vorlesen; **think ~:** laut denken

alp /ælp/ *n.* (mountain) Berg, *der;* (pasture) Alp, *die; see also* **Alps**

alpaca /ælˈpækə/ *n.* **1** (Zool.) Alpaka, *das* **2** (wool) Alpaka, *das;* Alpakawolle, *die;* (fabric) Alpaka, *der*

alpenhorn /ˈælpənhɔːn/ *n.* Alphorn, *das*

alpenstock /ˈælpənstɒk/ *n.* Bergstock, *der*

alpha /ˈælfə/ *n.* **1** (letter) Alpha, *das;* **the A~ and Omega** das A und O **2** (Sch., Univ.: mark) Eins, *die*

alphabet /ˈælfəbet/ *n.* Alphabet, *das;* Abc, *das;* **the phonetic/Cyrillic ~:** das phonetische/kyrillische Alphabet

alphabetical /ælfəˈbetɪkl/ *adj.* alphabetisch; **in ~ order** in alphabetischer Reihenfolge; alphabetisch geordnet

alphabetically /ælfəˈbetɪkəlɪ/ *adv.* alphabetisch; nach dem Alphabet

alphabetize /ˈælfəbetaɪz/ *v.t.* alphabetisieren; nach dem Alphabet ordnen

alpha male *n.* Alphatier, *das*

alphanumeric /ælfənjuːˈmerɪk/ *adj.* (Computing) alphanumerisch

alpha: ~ particle *n.* (Phys.) Alphateilchen, *das;* **~ ray** *n.* (Phys.) Alphastrahl, *der*

alpine /ˈælpaɪn/
A *adj.* **1** alpin; Hochgebirgs-; **~ region/climate/vegetation** Hochgebirgsregion, *die*/-klima, *das*/alpine Vegetation; **~ flowers** Alpen-, Gebirgsblumen; **~ garden** Alpengarten, *der;* Alpinum, *das;* **~ skiing/event** alpiner Skisport/Wettbewerb **2** **A~:** Alpen-
B *n.* (Bot.) Alpenblume, *die;* [Hoch]gebirgspflanze, *die*

Alpinist, alpinist /ˈælpɪnɪst/ *n.* Alpinist, *der*/Alpinistin, *die*

Alps /ælps/ *pr. n. pl.* **the ~:** die Alpen

already /ɔːlˈredɪ/ *adv.* schon; **it's ~ 8 o'clock** *or* **8 o'clock ~:** es ist schon 8 Uhr; **He's here. — A~?** Er ist hier. — Schon [so früh]?; **she's ~ got ten children** sie hat schon *od.* bereits zehn Kinder

Alsace /ælˈsæs/ *pr. n.* Elsass, *das;* **~-Lorraine** Elsass-Lothringen (*das*)

Alsatian /ælˈseɪʃn/
A *adj.* elsässisch
B *n.* **1** (person) Elsässer, *der*/Elsässerin, *die* **2** (dog) [deutscher] Schäferhund

also /ˈɔːlsəʊ/ *adv.* auch; (moreover) außerdem; **I'm going, and John is ~ going** *or* **John is going ~:** ich gehe, und John geht auch *od.* ebenfalls; **he's writing a book and ~ translating one** er schreibt ein Buch und übersetzt auch *od.* außerdem eines; **he's writing and ~ translating a book** er schreibt ein Buch und übersetzt es auch

ˈalso-ran *n.* **be an ~** ⟨*Hund, Pferd:*⟩ [immer nur] hintere Plätze/einen hinteren Platz belegen; **he remained an ~ all his life** (fig.) er kam sein ganzes Leben lang auf keinen grünen Zweig (ugs.)

altar /ˈɔːltə(r), ˈɒltə(r)/ *n.* **1** (Communion table) Altar, *der;* **lead sb. to the ~** (fig.) jmdn. zum Traualtar führen **2** (for sacrifice) Opferstätte, *die;* Opfertisch, *der*

ˈaltarpiece *n.* Altarbild, -gemälde, *das*

alter /ˈɔːltə(r), ˈɒltə(r)/
A *v.t.* **1** (change) ändern; verändern ⟨*Stadt, Wohnung*⟩; **That's wrong. It will have to be ~ed** Das ist falsch. Es muss geändert werden; **have a dress ~ed** ein Kleid ändern lassen **2** (Amer.: castrate, spay) sterilisieren
B *v.i.* sich verändern; **he has ~ed a lot since then** (in appearance) er hat sich seitdem stark verändert; (in character) er hat sich seitdem sehr geändert

alteration /ɔːltəˈreɪʃn, ɒltəˈreɪʃn/ *n.* Änderung, *die;* (of text) Abänderung, *die;* (of house) Umbau, *der;* **without any ~s** ohne jede Änderung; **we're having some ~s done to the house** wir bauen um

altercation /ɔːltəˈkeɪʃn, ɒltəˈkeɪʃn/ *n.* Auseinandersetzung, *die;* Streiterei, *die*

alter ego /æltər ˈegəʊ, æltər ˈiːgəʊ/ *n., pl.* **~s** Alter Ego, *das* (geh.)

alternate
A /ɔːlˈtɜːnət, ɒlˈtɜːnət/ *adj.* **1** (in turn) sich abwechselnd; **John and Mary come on ~ days** John und Mary kommen abwechselnd einen um den anderen Tag; (together) John und Mary kommen jeden zweiten Tag; **she goes shopping and goes to work on ~ Saturdays** sie geht abwechselnd jeden zweiten Samstag arbeiten und einkaufen; **~ leaves** (Bot.) wechselständige Blätter; **~ angles** (Math.) Wechselwinkel *Pl.* **2** (esp. Amer.) ▸ **alternative A**
B *n.* **1** (deputy) Vertreter, *der*/Vertreterin, *die* **2** (substitute) Alternative, *die*
C /ˈɔːltəneɪt, ˈɒltəneɪt/ *v.t.* abwechseln lassen; **she has only two summer dresses, so she ~s them** sie hat nur zwei Sommerkleider, deshalb trägt sie sie abwechselnd; **he ~s his days off and** *or* **with his working days** er hat abwechselnd einen Tag frei und geht einen Tag zur Arbeit
D *v.i.* sich abwechseln; alternieren (fachspr.)

alternately /ɔːlˈtɜːnətlɪ, ɒlˈtɜːnətlɪ/ *adv.* abwechselnd

ˈalternating current *n.* (Electr.) Wechselstrom, *der*

alternation /ɔːltəˈneɪʃn, ɒltəˈneɪʃn/ *n.* Wechsel, *der;* **~ of generations** (Biol.) Generationswechsel, *der*

alternative /ɔːlˈtɜːnətɪv, ɒlˈtɜːnətɪv/
A *adj.* alternativ; Alternativ-; **~ possibility** Ausweich- *od.* Alternativmöglichkeit, *die;* **~ suggestion** Alternativ- *od.* Gegenvorschlag, *der;* **~ route** Alternativstrecke, *die;* (to avoid obstruction etc.) Ausweichstrecke, *die;* **we'll try to get you on an ~ flight** wir werden versuchen, Ihren Flug umzubuchen; **the ~ society** die alternative Gesellschaft
B *n.* **1** (choice) Alternative, *die;* Wahl, *die;* **if I had the ~:** wenn ich vor die Wahl *od.* Alternative gestellt würde; wenn ich vor der Wahl *od.* Alternative stünde; **we have no ~ [but to ...]** wir haben keine andere Wahl[, als zu ...]; **that left me** *or* **I was left with no ~:** mir blieb keine andere Wahl **2** (possibility) Möglichkeit, *die;* **we have two ~s: either we press forward or we turn back** wir haben zwei Möglichkeiten: weiterzufahren oder umzukehren; **there is no [other] ~:** es gibt keine Alternative *od.* andere Möglichkeit; **what are the ~s?** welche Alternativen gibt es?

alternative: ~ coˈmedian *n.* ≈ Kabarettist, *der*/Kabarettistin, *die;* **~ ˈcomedy** *n.* ≈ Kabarett, *das;* **~ ˈenergy** *n.* alternative Energie; *attrib.* **~ energy sources** alternative Energiequellen; **~ ˈfuel** *n.* Alternativkraftstoff, *der* (*für Verbrennungsmotoren*); **~ inˈvestment market** *n.* Alternativer Investmentmarkt

alternatively /ɔːlˈtɜːnətɪvlɪ, ɒlˈtɜːnətɪvlɪ/ *adv.* oder aber; **or ~:** oder aber auch

alternative: ~ ˈmedicine *n.* Alternativmedizin, *die;* **~ techˈnology** *n.* alternative Technologie

alternator /ˈɔːltəneɪtə(r), ˈɒltəneɪtə(r)/ *n.* (Electr.) Wechselstromgenerator, *der*

although /ɔːlˈðəʊ/ *conj.* obwohl; **~ quite clever, he still makes mistakes** obwohl er ziemlich klug ist, macht er trotzdem *od.* doch Fehler

altimeter /ˈæltɪmiːtə(r)/ *n.* Höhenmesser, *der*

altitude /ˈæltɪtjuːd/ *n.* ▸ **p. 1208** (height) Höhe, *die;* **what is our ~?** wie hoch sind wir?; **at what ~ are we flying?** wie hoch *od.* in welcher Höhe fliegen wir?; **from this ~:** aus dieser Höhe; **what is the ~ of ...?** wie hoch liegt ...?; **at an ~ of 2,000 ft.** ≈ in einer Höhe von 600 Metern; **at high ~:** in großer Höhe; **gain/lose ~:** [an] Höhe gewinnen/verlieren

Alt key /ˈɔːlt kiː/ *n.* (Computing) Alt-Taste, *die*

alto /ˈæltəʊ/ *n., pl.* **~s** (Mus.) (voice, part) Alt, *der;* (male singer) Alt, *der;* Altist, *der;* Altsänger, *der;* (female singer) Alt, *der;* Altistin, *die;* Altsängerin, *die; attrib.* **~ saxophone/clarinet** Altsaxophon, *das*/Altklarinette, *die;* **~ clef** Altschlüssel, *der*

altogether /ɔːltəˈgeðə(r)/
A *adv.* völlig; (on the whole) im Großen und Ganzen; (in total) insgesamt; **not ~ [true/convincing]** nicht ganz [wahr/überzeugend]
B *n.* **in the ~** (coll.) im Evas-/Adamskostüm

altruism /ˈæltrʊɪzm/ *n., no pl.* Altruismus, *der;* Uneigennützigkeit, *die*

altruist /ˈæltrʊɪst/ *n.* Altruist, *der* (geh.)

altruistic /æltrʊˈɪstɪk/ *adj.*, **altruistically** /æltrʊˈɪstɪkəlɪ/ *adv.* altruistisch; uneigennützig

alum /ˈæləm/ *n.* (Chem.) Alaun, *der*

alumina /əˈluːmɪnə/ *n.* Aluminiumoxyd, (fachspr.) -oxid, *das;* Tonerde, *die*

aluminium /æljʊˈmɪnɪəm/ *n.* (Brit.) Aluminium, *das; attrib.* **~ foil** Alufolie, *die*

aluminize /əˈluːmɪnaɪz/ *v.t.* aluminieren

aluminum /əˈluːmɪnəm/ (Amer.) ▸ **aluminium**

alumna /əˈlʌmnə/ *n., pl.* **~e** /əˈlʌmniː/ Absolventin, *die*

alumnus /əˈlʌmnəs/ *n., pl.* **alumni** /əˈlʌmnaɪ/ Absolvent, *der;* **we are both alumni of Harvard** wir sind beide ehemalige Harvard-Studenten

alveolar /ælˈvɪələ(r), ælvɪˈəʊlə(r)/ *adj.* **1** (Anat.) **~ ridge** Alveolarfortsatz, *der* **2** (Phonet.) alveolar; Alveolar-

always /ˈɔːlweɪz, ˈɔːlwɪz/ *adv.* (at all times) immer; (repeatedly) ständig; [an]dauernd (ugs.); (whatever the circumstances) jederzeit; **he ~ comes on Monday** er kommt immer am Montag; **he is ~ making fun of other people** er macht sich dauernd *od.* ständig über andere lustig; **don't worry, I can ~ sleep on the floor** keine Sorge, ich kann jederzeit *od.* ohne weiteres auf dem Fußboden schlafen; **you can ~ come by train if you prefer** ihr könnt ja auch mit der Bahn kommen, wenn euch das lieber ist

alyssum /ˈælɪsəm/ *n.* (Bot.) Steinkraut, *das*

Alzheimer's disease /ˈæltshaɪmez dɪziːz/ *n.* ▸ **p. 1231** Alzheimerkrankheit, *die*

am ▸ **be**

a.m. /eɪˈem/ ▸ **p. 1001**
A *adv.* vormittags; **[at] one/four ~:** [um] ein/vier Uhr nachts *od.* morgens *od.* früh; **[at] five/eight ~:** [um] fünf/acht Uhr morgens *od.* früh; **[at] nine ~:** [um] neun Uhr morgens *od.* früh *od.* vormittags; **[at] ten/eleven ~:** [um] zehn/elf Uhr vormittags
B *n.* Vormittag, *der;* **Monday/this ~:** Montagvormittag/heute Vormittag

AM *abbr.* **= amplitude modulation** AM

amalgam /əˈmælgəm/ *n.* **1** (lit. or fig.: mixture) Mischung, *die* **2** (alloy) Amalgam, *das*

amalgamate /əˈmælgəmeɪt/
A *v.t.* vereinigen; verschmelzen (geh.); amalgamieren (geh.) ⟨*Rassen*⟩; zusammenlegen ⟨*Abteilungen*⟩; fusionieren ⟨*Firmen*⟩

a

a

B *v.i.* sich vereinigen; ‹*Firmen*:› fusionieren; ‹*Abteilungen*:› zusammengelegt werden

amalgamation /əmælgəˈmeɪʃn/ *n.* **1** (action) Vereinigung, *die;* (of races) Verschmelzung, *die* (geh.); Amalgamierung, *die* (geh.); (of firms) Fusion, *die;* (of departments) Zusammenlegung, *die* **2** (result) Vereinigung, *die;* **his 'theory' is an ~ of various ideas** seine „Theorie" besteht aus einer Mischung *od.* (geh.) ist ein Amalgam der verschiedensten Ideen

amanuensis /əmænjʊˈensɪs/ *n., pl.* **amanuenses** /əmænjʊˈensiːz/ Sekretär, *der*

amaryllis /æməˈrɪlɪs/ *n.* (Bot.) **1** (plant of genus A~) Amaryllis, *die* **2** (plant of related genus) Amaryllisgewächs, *das*

amass /əˈmæs/ *v.t.* [ein]sammeln; **what a lot of books you have ~ed over the years!** was für eine Menge Bücher sich bei dir während der Jahre angesammelt *od.* angehäuft hat!; **~ a [large] fortune** ein [großes] Vermögen anhäufen

amateur /ˈæmətə(r)/ *n.* **1** (non-professional) Amateur, *der* **2** (derog.: trifler) Amateur, *der;* Dilettant, *der* **3** *attrib.* Amateur-; Laien-; **~ actor/theatre** Amateur- *od.* Laienschauspieler/Amateur- *od.* Laientheater; **when he retired he took up ~ photography/writing** als Rentner fing er an zu fotografieren/schriftstellern

amateurish /ˈæmətərɪʃ/ *adj.* (derog.) laienhaft; amateurhaft

amateurishness /ˈæmətərɪʃnɪs/ *n.* Dilettantismus, *der*

amateurism /ˈæmətərɪzm/ *n., no pl.* Amateursport, *der;* (as qualifying principle) Amateurstatus, *der*

amatory /ˈæmətərɪ/ *adj.* erotisch; Liebes-; **~ poems/letters/affairs** Liebesgedichte/-briefe/-affären; **~ advances** amouröse Avancen (geh.)

amaze /əˈmeɪz/ *v.t.* verblüffen; verwundern; **be ~d [by sth.]** [über etw. (*Akk.*)] verblüfft *od.* verwundert sein

amazement /əˈmeɪzmənt/ *n., no pl.* Verblüffung, *die;* Verwunderung, *die*

amazing /əˈmeɪzɪŋ/ *adj.* (remarkable) erstaunlich; (astonishing) verblüffend; **'~ value'** „sensationell günstig"

amazingly /əˈmeɪzɪŋlɪ/ *adv.* **1** *as sentence-modifier* (remarkably) erstaunlicherweise; (astonishingly) verblüffenderweise **2** erstaunlich; **~ stupid** außerordentlich *od.* (ugs.) selten dumm

Amazon[1] /ˈæməzən/ *pr. n.* ▸**i** **p. 1491 the ~:** der Amazonas *od.* (veralt.) Amazonenstrom

Amazon[2] *n.* **1** (Mythol.: female warrior) Amazone, *die* **2** (fig.) Mannweib, *das* (abwertend); Amazone, *die* (veralt.)

ambassador /æmˈbæsədə(r)/ *n.* **1** ▸**i** **p. 1260,** ▸**i** **p. 1634** Botschafter, *der*/Botschafterin, *die;* (on particular mission) Sonderbotschafter, *der;* Gesandte, *der* (hist.); **~ to a country/court** Botschafter in einem Land/an einem Hof **2** (messenger) Abgesandte, *der/die;* Beauftragte, *der/die*

ambassadorial /æmbæsəˈdɔːrɪəl/ *adj.* Botschafter-; eines/des Botschafters *nachgestellt;* (of envoy) Gesandten-; eines/des Gesandten *nachgestellt*

amber /ˈæmbə(r)/

A *n.* **1** Bernstein, *der* **2** (traffic light) Gelb, *das;* **when the ~ is flashing** bei gelbem Blinklicht

B *adj.* Bernstein-; aus Bernstein *nachgestellt;* (colour) bernsteinfarben; gelb ‹*Verkehrslicht*›

ambergris /ˈæmbəgrɪs, ˈæmbəgriːs/ *n.* Amber, *der;* Ambra, *die*

ambiance /ɑ̃bɪˈɑ̃s/ ▸ **ambience**

ambidexterity /æmbɪdeksˈterɪtɪ/ ▸ **ambidextrousness**

ambidextrous /æmbɪˈdekstrəs/ *adj.* beidhändig; ambidexter (fachspr.)

ambidextrously /æmbɪˈdekstrəslɪ/ *adv.* beidhändig

ambidextrousness /æmbɪˈdekstrəsnɪs/ *n., no pl.* Beidhändigkeit, *die*

ambience /ˈæmbɪəns/ *n.* Ambiente, *das* (geh.); Milieu, *das;* Atmosphäre, *die;* **the ~ of the theatre** das Ambiente des Theaters; das Theatermilieu; die Theateratmosphäre

ambient /ˈæmbɪənt/ *adj.* Umgebungs-; **~ pressure/air** Umgebungsdruck, *der*/-luft, *die*

ambiguity /æmbɪˈgjuːɪtɪ/ *n.* Zweideutigkeit, *die;* Doppelsinnigkeit, *die* (geh.); (having several meanings) Mehrdeutigkeit, *die;* Ambiguität, *die* (Sprachw.)

ambiguous /æmˈbɪgjʊəs/ *adj.* zweideutig; doppelsinnig (geh.); (with several meanings) mehrdeutig; ambig (Sprachw.); nicht eindeutig klassifizierbar ‹*Pflanze, Tier*›; **her smile was ~:** ihr Lächeln war zweideutig

ambiguously /æmˈbɪgjʊəslɪ/ *adv.* zweideutig; doppelsinnig (geh.); (with several meanings) mehrdeutig; ambig (Sprachw.); **smile ~:** zweideutig lächeln

ambiguousness /æmˈbɪgjʊəsnɪs/ *n., no pl.* Zweideutigkeit, *die;* Doppelsinnigkeit, *die* (geh.); (having several meanings) Mehrdeutigkeit, *die*

ambit /ˈæmbɪt/ *n.* Gebiet, *das;* Bereich, *der;* **the ~ of sb.'s experience/competence** jmds. Erfahrungs-/Kompetenz- *od.* Zuständigkeitsbereich

ambition /æmˈbɪʃn/ *n.* Ehrgeiz, *der;* (aspiration) Ambition, *die;* Wunsch, *der;* **you can never fulfil every ~:** man kann nie all seine Ambitionen verwirklichen

ambitious /æmˈbɪʃəs/ *adj.* ehrgeizig; ambitioniert (geh.) ‹*Person*›; **she was very ~ for him to succeed** ihr ganzer Ehrgeiz war es, dass er Erfolg hatte; **be ~ to do sth.** von dem Ehrgeiz erfüllt sein, etw. zu tun

ambitiously /æmˈbɪʃəslɪ/ *adv.* voller Ehrgeiz; von Ehrgeiz erfüllt

ambitiousness /æmˈbɪʃəsnɪs/ *n., no pl.* Ehrgeiz, *der;* ehrgeiziges Streben; **the ~ of his proposal/the new project** das Ehrgeizige an seinem Plan/an dem neuen Projekt

ambivalence /æmˈbɪvələns/ *n., no pl.* Ambivalenz, *die*

ambivalent /æmˈbɪvələnt/ *adj.* ambivalent

amble /ˈæmbl/

A *v.i.* **1** ‹*Reiter*:› im Passgang reiten; ‹*Pferd*:› im Passgang gehen; (ride at easy pace) im Schritt reiten **2** (fig.: walk slowly) schlendern; gemütlich gehen

B *n.* **1** Passgang, *der* **2** (fig.) Schlendern, *das*

ambrosia /æmˈbrəʊzɪə/ *n., no pl.* Ambrosia, *die*

ambulance /ˈæmbjʊləns/ *n.* **1** (vehicle) Krankenwagen, *der;* Ambulanz, *die;* (Mil.) Sanitätswagen, *der;* Sanka, *der* (bes. Soldatenspr.) **2** (Mil.: mobile hospital) Feldlazarett, *das;* Ambulanz, *die*

ambulance: ~ chaser *n.* (esp. Amer.) *Anwalt oder sein Agent, der Unfallopfer dazu überredet, auf Schadenersatz zu klagen;* **~ driver** *n.* ▸**i** **p. 1260** Fahrer eines/des Krankenwagens; **~ man** *n.* ▸**i** **p. 1260** Sanitäter, *der;* **~ service** *n.* Rettungsdienst, *der;* **~ worker** *n.* ▸**i** **p. 1260** Sanitäter, *der*/Sanitäterin, *die*

ambulant /ˈæmbjʊlənt/ *adj.* gehfähig ‹*Patient*›; ambulant ‹*Behandlung*›

ambush /ˈæmbʊʃ/

A *n.* (concealment) Hinterhalt, *der;* (troops concealed) im Hinterhalt liegende Truppe; **lie in ~** (lit. or fig.) im Hinterhalt liegen; **arrange an ~:** einen Überfall aus dem Hinterhalt führen

B *v.t.* [aus dem Hinterhalt] überfallen

ameba /əˈmiːbə/ (Amer.) ▸ **amoeba**

ameliorate /əˈmiːlɪəreɪt/ *v.t.* verbessern

amelioration /əmiːlɪəˈreɪʃn/ *n.* [Ver]besserung, *die*

ameliorative /əˈmiːlɪərətɪv/ *adj.* verbessernd; bessernd ‹*Einfluss*›; **~ measures/effect** Verbesserungsmaßnahmen *Pl.*/-effekt, *der*

amen /ɑːˈmen, eɪˈmen/

A *int.* amen; **say '~' to sth.** Ja und Amen zu etw. sagen

B *n.* Amen, *das*

amenability /əmiːnəˈbɪlɪtɪ/ *n., no pl.* **1** (responsiveness) Zugänglichkeit, *die* (**to** für) **2** (of phenomenon etc.) Unterworfenheit, *die* (**to** unter + *Akk.*)

amenable /əˈmiːnəbl/ *adj.* **1** (responsive) zugänglich, aufgeschlossen ‹*Person*› (**to** *Dat.*); **he simply isn't ~ to reason/advice** er ist Vernunftgründen/Ratschlägen einfach nicht zugänglich; **~ to kindness** für Freundlichkeit empfänglich **2** (subject) unterworfen ‹*Sache*› (**to** *Dat.*); **be ~ to the laws of nature/rules of grammar** den Naturgesetzen/Regeln der Grammatik unterworfen sein *od.* gehorchen

amend /əˈmend/ *v.t.* (correct) berichtigen; (improve) abändern, ergänzen ‹*Gesetzentwurf, Antrag*›; ändern ‹*Verfassung*›; [ver]bessern ‹*Situation*›

amendment /əˈmendmənt/ *n.* (to motion) Abänderungsantrag, *der;* (to bill) Änderungsantrag, *der;* (to Constitution) Änderung, *die* (**to** *Gen.*); Amendement, *das* (Dipl.); (of situation) [Ver]besserung, *die*

amends /əˈmendz/ *n. pl.* **make ~ [to sb.]** es [bei jmdm.] wieder gutmachen; **make ~ for sth.** etw. wieder gutmachen

amenity /əˈmiːnɪtɪ/ *n.* **1** *no pl.* (pleasantness) Annehmlichkeiten *Pl.* **2** (pleasant feature) (of residence) Attraktivität, *die;* Wohnqualität, *die;* (of locality) Attraktivität, *die;* Reiz, *der;* **the amenities of a town** die kulturellen und Freizeiteinrichtungen einer Stadt; **social amenities** öffentliche Freizeiteinrichtungen; **with every ~, including showers, central heating, etc.** mit allem Komfort inklusive Duschen, Zentralheizung usw.

amenity: ~ bed *n.* (Brit.) ≈ Privatbett [in einem öffentlichen Krankenhaus]; **~ centre** *n.* Freizeitzentrum, *das*

America /əˈmerɪkə/ *pr. n.* **1** Amerika (*das*) **2** **the ~s** Nord-, Süd- und Mittelamerika

American /əˈmerɪkən/ ▸**i** **p. 1277,** ▸**i** **p. 1345**

A *adj.* amerikanisch; **sb. is ~:** jmd. ist Amerikaner/Amerikanerin; **~ English** amerikanisches Englisch; **~ studies** Amerikanistik, *die; see also* **English A; legion 2**

B *n.* **1** (person) Amerikaner, *der*/Amerikanerin, *die* **2** (language) Amerikanisch, *das; see also* **English B 1**

> **American dream**
>
> Der Glaube, dass Amerika das Land unbegrenzter Möglichkeiten ist, in dem jeder sein Leben erfolgreich gestalten kann. Für Minderheiten und Einwanderer bedeutet der Traum weitgehende Toleranz und Anspruch auf eigene freie Lebensgestaltung. Der *American dream* verkörpert eine optimistische allgemeine Grundhaltung mit auf Erfolg gerichtetem Denken und Handeln.

> **American eagle**
>
> Der Weißkopf-Seeadler, der im Schnabel ein gelbes Band mit dem lateinischen Wahlspruch 'e pluribus unum' (aus mehreren eines) hält, ist seit 1782 das amerikanische Wappentier. Der Adler trägt ein Pfeilbündel mit 13 Pfeilen als Symbol des Krieges und als Friedenssymbol einen Ölzweig in den Fängen. Auf der Brust trägt der Adler einen Schild mit roten und weißen Streifen ähnlich denen der Staatsflagge.

American: ~ 'football *n.* Football, *der;* **~ 'Indian** ▸**i** **p. 1345** **A** *n.* Indianer, *der*/Indianerin, *die;* **B** *adj.* indianisch

> **American Indian**
>
> ▸ Native American.

Americanisation, Americanise ▸ **Americaniz-**

Americanism /əˈmerɪkənɪzm/ *n.* **1** (Ling.) Amerikanismus, *der* **2** (attachment) Amerikanertum, *das*

Americanization /əmerɪkənaɪ'zeɪʃn/ *n.* 1 Amerikanisierung, *die* 2 (naturalization) Einbürgerung [in Amerika]

Americanize /ə'merɪkənaɪz/ *v.t.* 1 amerikanisieren 2 (naturalize) [in Amerika] einbürgern

American Legion

Größter Verband ehemaliger Kriegsteilnehmer in den USA. Er wurde 1919 in Paris gegründet und hat rund drei Millionen Mitglieder. Von seiner Zentrale in Indianapolis, Indiana, tritt er für den sozialen Schutz der Kriegsveteranen ein.

American: ~ 'organ *n.* (Mus.) amerikanische Orgel; **~ plan** *n.* (Amer. Hotel Managem.) Vollpension, *die*

American Revolution

Die Loslösung der 13 britischen Kolonien in Nordamerika vom Mutterland. Sie begann im April 1775 in Lexington (Massachusetts), als Soldaten beider Seiten zusammentrafen und jemand einen Schuss abgab. Der Krieg, der auf diesen Schuss folgte, war von entscheidender Bedeutung für die Zukunft des britischen Weltreichs und Amerikas und führte nach dem Unabhängigkeitskrieg (1775-83) zur Gründung der USA als Bundesstaat.

American studies

Die Wissenschaft von Gesellschaft, Kultur, Sprache und Literatur der USA. Seit den 40er Jahren ist Amerikanistik ein Fachgebiet an verschiedenen Universitäten. Ursprünglich war sie ein Teil der Anglistik.

America's Cup

Bedeutendster Wettbewerb des Hochseesegelns, um einen 1851 gestifteten Pokal. Er findet meist alle drei oder vier Jahre statt und wurde fast immer von den Amerikanern gegen Herausforderer aus Großbritannien, Australien und Neuseeland erfolgreich verteidigt. Neuseeland gewann 1995 und 2000, die Schweiz 2003.

Amerindian /æmə'rɪndɪən/ ▸ⓘ **p. 1345**
A *adj.* indianisch; **~ languages** Indianersprachen; **~ peoples** Indianer *Pl*
B *n.* Indianer, *der*/Indianerin, *die*

amethyst /'æmɪθɪst/ *n.* Amethyst, *der*

AMEX /'æmeks/ *abbr.* **= American Stock Exchange** A.S.E.

amiability /eɪmɪə'bɪlɪtɪ/ *n.*, *no pl.* ▸ **amiable**: Umgänglichkeit, *die;* Freundlichkeit, *die;* Entgegenkommen, *das*

amiable /'eɪmɪəbl/ *adj.* umgänglich; freundlich ‹*Person*›; entgegenkommend ‹*Haltung*›; **be in an ~ mood** gut gelaunt sein

amiably /'eɪmɪəblɪ/ *adv.* freundlich; **be ~ disposed towards sb./sth.** jmdm./einer Sache wohlgesinnt sein

amicability /æmɪkə'bɪlɪtɪ/ *n.*, *no pl.* Freundschaftlichkeit, *die*

amicable /'æmɪkəbl/ *adj.* freundschaftlich ‹*Gespräch, Beziehungen*›; gütlich ‹*Einigung*›; friedlich ‹*Lösung*›; **~ relations with one's neighbours** ein freundnachbarliches Verhältnis

amicably /'æmɪkəblɪ/ *adv.* in [aller] Freundschaft; **get on ~ with one's neighbours** mit seinen Nachbarn gut auskommen

amid /ə'mɪd/ *prep.* inmitten; (fig.: during) bei; **~ the fighting** mitten im Gefecht

amidships /ə'mɪdʃɪps/ (*Amer.:* **amidship** /ə'mɪdʃɪp/) *adv.* (position) mittschiffs; Mitte Schiff (Seemannsspr.); (direction) [nach] mittschiffs; **hit sb. ~** (fig. coll.) jmdn. in den Bauch schlagen/treffen

amidst /ə'mɪdst/ ▸ **amid**

amino acid /əmi:nəʊ 'æsɪd/ *n.* (Chem.) Aminosäure, *die*

Amish /'ɑ:mɪʃ, 'eɪmɪʃ, 'æmɪʃ/ *adj.* Amisch; **the ~ Mennonites** die Amischen

Amish

Die Amischen sind eine christliche Gruppe, die sich unter dem schweizerischen Ältesten Jakob Ammann von den Mennoniten trennte und nach Amerika auswanderte. Sie siedelten sich im 17. und 18. Jahrhundert in Pennsylvania an und haben die Sprache und Lebensart ihrer Vorfahren bewahrt. Sie führen ein einfaches Leben und sind überwiegend Farmer. Aus religiösen Gründen verzichten sie auf Autos, landwirtschaftliche Maschinen, Telefon und Elektrizität und sind gegen jede technische Entwicklung. Ihre Kleidung ist durch Tradition und Vorschrift bestimmt: Frauen tragen dunkle Kleider, schwarze Kapotthüte oder weiße Häubchen, Männer tragen schwarze, breitkrempige Hüte.

amiss /ə'mɪs/
A *pred. adj.* 1 (wrong) verkehrt; falsch; **is anything ~?** stimmt irgendetwas nicht?; ist irgendetwas nicht in Ordnung? 2 (out of place) fehl am Platz[e]; unangebracht
B *adv.* **take sth. ~:** etw. übel nehmen; **come** *or* **go ~:** ungelegen kommen; **a glass of wine would not come** *or* **go ~:** ein Glas Wein wäre nicht verkehrt

amity /'æmɪtɪ/ *n.* Freundschaft, *die;* gutes Einvernehmen

ammeter /'æmɪtə(r)/ *n.* (Electr.) Amperemeter, *das;* Strommesser, *der*

ammo /'æməʊ/ *n.*, *no pl.* (Mil. coll.) Muni, *die* (Milit. ugs.)

ammonia /ə'məʊnɪə/ *n.* Ammoniak, *das; attrib.* **~ water** Salmiakgeist, *der;* Ammoniaklösung, *die*

ammonite /'æmənaɪt/ *n.* (Palaeont.) Ammonit, *der*

ammunition /æmjʊ'nɪʃn/ *n.*, *no pl.*, *no indef. art.* (lit. or fig.) Munition, *die*

amnesia /æm'ni:zɪə/ *n.* (Med.) Amnesie, *die;* Gedächtnisschwund, *der*

amnesty /'æmnɪstɪ/ *n.* Amnestie, *die;* **grant an ~ to sb.** jmdn. amnestieren; **they were released under an ~:** sie wurden im Rahmen einer Amnestie freigelassen

Amnesty International

Eine internationale Hilfsorganisation, die 1961 in London gegründet wurde. Die Organisation setzt sich für politische Gefangene ein und hat rund eine Million Mitglieder in über 162 Ländern. Sie organisiert Demonstrationen, Appelle, Protestbriefe und Benefizveranstaltungen. Amnesty International erhielt 1977 den Friedensnobelpreis.

amniocentesis /æmnɪəʊsen'ti:sɪs/ *n.* (Med.) Fruchtwasserentnahme, *die*

amniotic fluid /æmnɪɒtɪk 'flu:ɪd/ *n.*, *no pl.* (Physiol.) Fruchtwasser, *das*

amoeba /ə'mi:bə/ *n.*, *pl.* **~s** *or* **~e** /ə'mi:bi:/ (Zool.) Amöbe, *die*

amok /ə'mɒk/ *adv.* **run ~:** Amok laufen

among[st] /ə'mʌŋ(st)/ *prep.* 1 unter (+ *Dat.*; *seltener:* + *Akk.*); **~ us/you/friends** unter uns/euch/Freunden; **~ other things** unter anderem; **~ others** unter anderen 2 (in/into the middle of, surrounded by) zwischen (+ *Dat./Akk.*); **hide ~ the bushes** sich im Gebüsch verstecken; **~ tall trees** inmitten hoher Bäume; **she was sitting ~ her children** sie saß im Kreise ihrer Kinder; **there are some weeds ~ the flowers** zwischen den Blumen wächst Unkraut; **a village ~ the hills** ein Dorf in den Bergen; **I saw him ~ the crowd** ich habe ihn in der Menge gesehen 3 (in the practice or opinion of, in the number of) unter (+ *Dat.*); **~ men/scientists** unter Männern/Wissenschaftlern; **who is the tallest ~ you?** wer ist der größte von *od.* (geh.) unter euch?; **I count him ~ my friends** ich zähle ihn zu meinen Freunden; **that painting is reckoned ~ his best works** das Bild zählt zu seinen besten Werken 4 (between) unter (+ *Dat.*; *seltener:* + *Akk.*); **share the sweets ~ yourselves** teilt euch die Bonbons; **we only have five pounds ~ us** wir haben zusammen nur fünf Pfund; **he distributed his wealth ~ the poor** er verteilte sein Vermögen an die *od.* unter die *od.* unter den Armen 5 (reciprocally) **they often quarrel ~ themselves** sie streiten oft miteinander; sie streiten sich oft; **we often disagree ~ ourselves** wir sind [untereinander] oft verschiedener Meinung 6 (jointly) **~ you/them** *etc.* gemeinsam; zusammen

amoral /eɪ'mɒrəl/ *adj.* amoralisch

amorous /'æmərəs/ *adj.* verliebt; amourös ‹*Abenteuer, Beziehung*›; **~ glances** verliebte Blicke; **~ advances** Annäherungsversuche *Pl.;* amouröse Avancen *Pl.* (veralt., scherzh.); **an ~ novel/poem** ein Liebesroman/-gedicht

amorously /'æmərəslɪ/ *adv.* verliebt

amorousness /'æmərəsnɪs/ *n.*, *no pl.* Verliebtheit, *die*

amorphous /ə'mɔ:fəs/ *adj.* 1 (shapeless, unorganized) formlos; amorph ‹*Masse*›; (fig.) chaotisch ‹*Stil*› 2 (Min., Chem.) amorph

amortization /əmɔ:taɪ'zeɪʃn/ *n.* (Finance) 1 (of assets) Abschreibung, *die* 2 (of debt, mortgage) Tilgung, *die;* Amortisation, *die*

amortize /ə'mɔ:taɪz/ *v.t.* (Finance) abschreiben ‹*Vermögenswerte*›; tilgen, amortisieren ‹*Schuld, Hypothek*›

amount /ə'maʊnt/
A *v.i.* **~ to sth.** sich auf etw. (*Akk.*) belaufen; (fig.) auf etw. (*Akk.*) hinauslaufen; einer Sache (*Dat.*) gleichkommen; **the cost/debts/fees/profits ~ed to ...:** die Kosten/Schulden/Gebühren/Gewinne beliefen sich auf ... (*Akk.*); **all these arguments/proposals don't ~ to much** diese Argumente/Vorschläge bringen alle nicht viel; **my savings don't ~ to very much** meine Ersparnisse sind nicht gerade groß; **what this all ~s to is that ...:** zusammenfassend kann man sagen, dass ...
B *n.* 1 (total) Betrag, *der;* Summe, *die;* (full significance) volle Bedeutung *od.* Tragweite 2 **the ~ of a bill** die Höhe einer Rechnung 3 (quantity) Menge, *die;* **an ~ of rain/patience** eine Menge Regen/Geduld; **large ~s of money** beträchtliche Geldsummen; **a tremendous ~ of** (coll.) wahnsinnig viel (ugs.); **no ~ of money will make me change my mind** und wenn man mir noch so viel Geld gibt: Meine Meinung werde ich nicht ändern; **no ~ of talking will settle the matter** so viel wir auch darüber reden, wir werden zu keinem Ergebnis kommen; *see also* **any A 5**

amour /ə'mʊə(r)/ *n.* Affäre, *die;* Liebschaft, *die*

amour propre /æmʊə 'prɒpr/ *n.*, *no pl.* (self-esteem) Ehrgefühl, *das;* Selbstachtung, *die*

amp /æmp/ *n.* 1 (Electr.) Ampere, *das* 2 (coll.: amplifier) Verstärker, *der*

ampere /'æmpeə(r)/ *n.* (Electr.) Ampere, *das*

ampersand /'æmpəsænd/ *n.* Et-Zeichen, *das*

amphetamine /æm'fetəmɪn, æm'fetəmi:n/ *n.* Amphetamin, *das*

amphibian /æm'fɪbɪən/
A *adj.* 1 (Zool.) amphibisch; **~ animal** amphibisches Lebewesen; Amphibie, *die;* Lurch, *der* 2 (Mil.) ▸ **amphibious 2**
B *n.* 1 (Zool.) Amphibie, *die;* Lurch, *der* 2 (vehicle) Amphibienfahrzeug, *das*

amphibious /æm'fɪbɪəs/ *adj.* 1 (Biol.) amphibisch; **toads are ~:** Kröten sind Amphibien 2 (operating on land or water) amphibisch; zu Lande und zu Wasser einsetzbar; **~ vehicle/tank/aircraft** Amphibienfahrzeug, *das*/-panzer, *der*/-flugzeug, *das;* **~ warfare/operations/forces** amphibische Kriegsführung/Operationen/Streitkräfte

amphitheatre (*Amer.:* **amphitheater**) /'æmfɪθɪətə(r)/ *n.* 1 Amphitheater, *das* 2 (Geog.: hollow) Kessel, *der* 3 (fig.: arena) Schauplatz, *der*

amphora /'æmfərə/ *n.*, *pl.* **~e** /'æmfəri:/ *or* **~s** Amphora, Amphore, *die*

ample /'æmpl/ *adj.*, **~r** /'æmplə(r)/, **~st** /'æmplɪst/ 1 (spacious) weitläufig ‹*Garten, Räume*›; groß ‹*Ausdehnung*›; (extensive, abundant) reichhaltig ‹*Mahl, Bibliographie*›; ausführlich, umfassend ‹*Behandlung eines Themas*›; weit reichend, umfassend ‹*Vollmachten, Machtbefugnisse*› 2 (enough) **~ room/food** reichlich Platz/zu essen; **this hall is ~ in size for the party** dieser Saal bietet reichlich Platz für die Feier 3 (stout) üppig ‹*Busen*›; stattlich ‹*Erscheinung*›

amplification /æmplɪfɪ'keɪʃn/ *n.* [1] (Phys.) Verstärkung, *die* [2] (enlargement) weitere *od.* zusätzliche Erläuterungen [3] (of knowledge, wisdom, etc.) Erweiterung, *die;* Vertiefung, *die*

amplifier /'æmplɪfaɪə(r)/ *n.* Verstärker, *der*

amplify /'æmplɪfaɪ/
A *v.t.* [1] verstärken ‹*Ton*› [2] (enlarge on) weiter ausführen, näher *od.* ausführlicher erläutern ‹*Erklärung, Bericht*› [3] (enhance) erweitern, vertiefen ‹*Wissen, Kenntnisse*›
B *v.i.* auf Einzelheiten (*Akk.*) eingehen; **~ on sth.** etw. näher erläutern

amplitude /'æmplɪtju:d/ *n.* [1] (Electr.) Amplitude, *die;* Schwingungsweite, *die;* **~ modulation** Amplitudenmodulation, *die* [2] (Phys.) Amplitude, *die;* größte Ausschlagweite [3] *no pl.* (breadth) Breite, *die;* Weite, *die;* (abundance) Fülle, *die;* (wide range) Breite, *die*

amply /'æmplɪ/ *adv.* (spaciously, abundantly) reichlich ‹*breit, belohnen*›; zur Genüge ‹*zeigen, demonstrieren*›

ampoule /'æmpu:l/ *n.* Ampulle, *die*

amputate /'æmpjʊteɪt/ *v.t.* amputieren

amputation /æmpjʊ'teɪʃn/ *n.* Amputation, *die*

amputee /æmpjʊ'ti:/ *n.* Amputierte, *der/die*

Amtrak ® /'æmtræk/*n.*: *amerikanische Eisenbahngesellschaft*

> **Amtrak**
>
> *Amtrak*, die 1970 gegründete amerikanische Aktiengesellschaft, heißt offiziell *National Railroad Passenger Corporation*. Die verstaatlichte Gesellschaft, eine Fusion von mehreren privaten Eisenbahngesellschaften für den Personenverkehr zwischen Großstädten innerhalb der USA, wird von der Regierung subventioniert. Trotz eines Streckennetzes von fast 45 000 km werden die Züge von nur einem Prozent der Amerikaner benutzt.

amuck /ə'mʌk/ ► **amok**

amulet /'æmjʊlɪt/ *n.* (lit. or fig.) Amulett, *das*

amuse /ə'mju:z/ *v.t.* [1] (interest) unterhalten; **keep a child ~d** ein Kind richtig beschäftigen; **~ oneself with sth.** sich mit etw. beschäftigen; **~ oneself by doing sth.** sich (*Dat.*) die Zeit damit vertreiben, etw. zu tun [2] (make laugh or smile) belustigen; amüsieren; **be ~d by** *or* **at sth.** sich über etw. (*Akk.*) amüsieren

amusement /ə'mju:zmənt/ *n.* Belustigung, *die;* (pastime) Freizeitbeschäftigung, *die;* **all the ~s on offer at the seaside** das gesamte Freizeitangebot am Meer; **in the ~s** in der Spielhalle

a'musement arcade *n.* Spielhalle, *die*

amusing /ə'mju:zɪŋ/ *adj.*, **amusingly** /ə'mju:zɪŋlɪ/ *adv.* amüsant

an /ən, *stressed* æn/ *indef. art. see also* **a²**: ein/eine/ein; **an elephant/Englishman** ein Elefant/Engländer; **an hour/historical play** eine Stunde/ein historisches Stück; **an LP** eine LP

anabolic steroid /ænəbɒlɪk 'stɪərɔɪd, ænəbɒlɪk 'sterɔɪd/ *n.* (Physiol.) anaboles Steroid; Anabolikum, *das*

anachronism /ə'nækrənɪzm/ *n.* Anachronismus, *der*

anachronistic /ənækrə'nɪstɪk/ *adj.* anachronistisch; zeitwidrig

anaconda /ænə'kɒndə/ *n.* (Zool.) Anakonda, *die*

anaemia /ə'ni:mɪə/ *n.*, *no pl.* ►**i** **p. 1231** (Med.) Blutarmut, *die;* Anämie, *die; see also* **pernicious**

anaemic /ə'ni:mɪk/ *adj.* (Med.) blutarm; anämisch; (fig.) blutleer; saft- und kraftlos

anaerobic /æneə'rəʊbɪk/ *adj.* (Biol.) anaerob

anaesthesia /ænɪs'θi:zɪə/ *n.* (Med.) (absence of sensation) Empfindungslosigkeit, *die;* Anästhesie, (fachspr.) Anaesthesia, *die;* (artificially induced) Narkose, *die;* **general ~:** [Voll]narkose, *die;* Allgemeinanästhesie, *die* (fachspr.); **local ~:** örtliche Betäubung; Lokalanästhesie, *die* (fachspr.)

anaesthetic /ænɪs'θetɪk/
A *adj.* (Med.) anästhetisch; betäubend
B *n.* Anästhetikum, *das;* **give sb. an ~:** jmdm. eine Narkose geben; (local) jmdn. betäuben; **be under an ~:** in Narkose liegen; **general ~:** Narkotikum, *das;* Narkosemittel, *das;* **local ~:** Lokalanästhetikum, *das*

anaesthetist /ə'ni:sθətɪst/ *n.* ►**i** **p. 1260** (Med.) Anästhesist, *der*/Anästhesistin, *die;* Narkose[fach]arzt, *der*/-ärztin, *die*

anaesthetization /əni:sθətaɪ'zeɪʃn/ *n.* Betäubung, *die;* (fig.) Abstumpfung, *die* (**to** gegenüber)

anaesthetize /ə'ni:sθətaɪz/ *v.t.* narkotisieren; betäuben; anästhesieren (fachspr.); (fig.) abstumpfen (**to** gegenüber); **become ~d to sth.** (fig.) gegenüber etw. abstumpfen

anagram /'ænəgræm/ *n.* Anagramm, *das*

anagrammatic /ænəgrə'mætɪk/, **anagrammatical** /ænəgrə'mætɪkl/ *adj.* anagrammatisch

anal /'eɪnl/ *adj.* [1] (Anat.) anal; Anal-; After-; **~ region** Analbereich, *der;* **~ canal** Afterkanal, *der* [2] (Psych.) **~ stage** anale Phase; **~ eroticism** Analerotik, *die*

analgesia /ænæl'dʒi:zɪə/ *n.* (Med.) Analgesie, *die*

analgesic /ænæl'dʒi:sɪk/ (Med.)
A *adj.* analgetisch
B *n.* Analgetikum, *das*

analog (Amer.) ► **analogue**

analogical /ænə'lɒdʒɪkl/ *adj.* [1] analog; Analogie-; **~ reasoning** Analogiedenken, *das* [2] (expressing analogy) metonymisch ‹*Wort, Ausdruck*›

analogous /ə'næləgəs/ *adj.* vergleichbar; analog; **be ~ to sth.** einer Sache (*Dat.*) entsprechen

analogously /ə'næləgəslɪ/ *adv.* analog

analogue /'ænəlɒg/ *n.* Entsprechung, *die;* Analogon, *das* (geh.); **~ computer** Analogrechner, *der;* **~ watch** Analoguhr, *die*

analogy /ə'nælədʒɪ/ *n.* [1] (agreement; also Ling.) Analogie, *die* [2] (similarity) Parallele, *die;* Analogie, *die;* **draw an ~ between/with** eine Parallele ziehen zwischen (+ *Dat.*)/zu [3] (Logic) Analogie, *die;* **use an argument by ~/argue by ~:** einen Analogieschluss/Analogieschlüsse ziehen

analysable /'ænəlaɪzəbl/ *adj.* analysierbar; zerlegbar ‹*Satz*›

analyse /'ænəlaɪz/ *v.t.* [1] analysieren; kritisch untersuchen ‹*Literatur*› [2] (Chem.) untersuchen (**for** auf + *Akk.*) [3] (Ling.) [zer]gliedern [4] (Psych.) analysieren (fachspr.); psychoanalytisch behandeln; **get ~d** sich einer [Psycho]analyse unterziehen

analysis /ə'nælɪsɪs/ *n.*, *pl.* **analyses** /ə'nælɪsi:z/ [1] Analyse, *die;* (Chem., Med.: of sample) Untersuchung, *die;* (statement) Analyse, *die;* [Lage]beurteilung, *die;* **in the final** *or* **last** *or* **ultimate ~:** letzten Endes [2] (Math.) Analysis, *die* [3] (Psych.) Analyse, *die*

analyst /'ænəlɪst/ *n.* ►**i** **p. 1260** [1] Laboratoriumsingenieur, *der;* Laborfachmann, *der* (ugs.) [2] (Econ., Polit., etc.) Experte, *der;* Fachmann, *der* [3] (Psych.) Analytiker, *der*/Analytikerin, *die*

analytic /ænə'lɪtɪk/ *adj.* analytisch

analytical /ænə'lɪtɪkl/ *adj.* [1] analytisch ‹*Methode, Sprache, Begabung*› [2] **~ geometry** analytische Geometrie

analytically /ænə'lɪtɪkəlɪ/ *adv.* analytisch

analyze (Amer.) ► **analyse**

anapaest (*Amer.:* **anapest**) /'ænəpi:st/ *n.* (Pros.) Anapäst, *der*

anaphora /ə'næfərə/ *n.* (Lit.) Anapher, *die*

anarchic /ə'nɑ:kɪk/, **anarchical** /ə'nɑ:kɪkl/ *adj.* anarchisch; (anarchistic) anarchistisch

anarchism /'ænəkɪzm/ *n.*, *no pl.* Anarchismus, *der*

anarchist /'ænəkɪst/ *n.* Anarchist, *der*/Anarchistin, *die*

anarchistic /ænə'kɪstɪk/ *adj.* anarchistisch

anarchy /'ænəkɪ/ *n.*, *no pl.* Anarchie, *die;* (fig.: disorder) Chaos, *das*

anathema /ə'næθəmə/ *n.* [1] *no pl.*, *no art.* (detested thing) ein Gräuel; **be ~ to sb.** jmdm. verhasst *od.* ein Gräuel sein [2] *no pl.*, *no art.* (accursed thing) **be ~:** verflucht sein [3] (curse of God) Fluch, *der;* (curse of Church) Anathema, *das;* Kirchenbann, *der*

anathematize /ə'næθəmətaɪz/
A *v.t.* verdammen; verfluchen; ‹*Kirche, Papst:*› in den Bann tun
B *v.i.* fluchen

anatomical /ænə'tɒmɪkl/ *adj.*, **anatomically** /ænə'tɒmɪkəlɪ/ *adv.* anatomisch

anatomist /ə'nætəmɪst/ *n.* Anatom, *der;* (dissector) Anatomiegehilfe, *der;* (fig.) Sezierer, *der;* Analytiker, *der*

anatomize /ə'nætəmaɪz/ *v.t.* sezieren

anatomy /ə'nætəmɪ/ *n.*, *no pl.* [1] Anatomie, *die;* (dissection) Sektion, *die* [2] (joc.: body) Anatomie, *die* (scherzh.); **a certain part of his ~:** ein bestimmter Körperteil [3] (fig.: analysis) Anatomie, *die;* Analyse, *die*

ANC *abbr.* **= African National Congress** ANK

ancestor /'ænsestə(r)/ *n.* Vorfahr, *der;* Ahn[e], *der;* (fig.) Ahn[e], *der*

ancestral /æn'sestrəl/ *adj.* angestammt ‹*Grundbesitz, Land*›; **~ portraits** Ahnenbilder

ancestry /'ænsestrɪ/ *n.* [1] (lineage) Abstammung, *die;* Herkunft, *die* [2] (ancestors) Vorfahren *Pl.* [3] *no pl.* (ancient descent) Familientradition, *die*

anchor /'æŋkə(r)/
A *n.* Anker, *der;* **lie at ~:** vor Anker liegen; **come to** *or* **cast** *or* **drop ~:** vor Anker gehen; **weigh ~:** den Anker lichten; *see also* **drag B 5**
B *v.t.* [1] verankern; vor Anker legen; (secure) befestigen (**to** an + *Dat.*) [2] (fig.) **be ~ed to sth.** an etw. (*Akk.*) gefesselt sein
C *v.i.* ankern

anchorage /'æŋkərɪdʒ/ *n.* [1] (place for anchoring) Ankerplatz, *der;* Ankergrund, *der* (geh.) [2] (anchoring, lying at anchor) Ankern, *das* [3] (fig.) [Rück]halt, *der*

anchorite /'æŋkəraɪt/ *n.* (lit. or fig.) Einsiedler, *der*

anchor: ~man *n.* [1] (Sport) (in tug-of-war) hinterster *od.* letzter Mann; (in relay race) Schlussläufer, *der;* (Mountaineering) Seilletzte, *der;* **he is the ~man of the company** (fig.) er ist die Stütze der Firma; [2] ►**i** **p. 1260** (Telev., Radio) Moderator, *der;* Redakteur im Studio, *der;* **~ ring** *n.* Ankerring, *der*

anchovy /'æntʃəvɪ, æn'tʃəʊvɪ/ *n.* An[s]chovis, *die;* Sardelle, *die*

anchovy: ~ 'pear *n.* An[s]chovisbirne, *die;* **~ 'toast** *n.* Toast mit An[s]chovispaste

ancien régime /ɑ̃sjɛ̃ reɪ'ʒi:m/ *n.*, *pl.* **anciens régimes** /ɑ̃sjɛ̃ reɪ'ʒi:m/ Ancien Régime, *das;* (fig.) alte Regierungsform

ancient /'eɪnʃənt/
A *adj.* [1] (belonging to past) alt; (pertaining to antiquity) antik; **~ Rome/Greece** das alte *od.* antike Rom/Griechenland; **in ~ times** im Altertum; **~ history** Alte Geschichte, *die* ; **that's ~ history, everybody knows it** (fig.) das ist längst ein alter Hut (ugs.), jeder weiß das; **the ~ Greeks** die alten Griechen; **A~ Greek** Altgriechisch, *das;* **~ Egypt** Altägypten (*das*) [2] (old) alt; historisch ‹*Gebäude usw.*›; **~ monument** (Brit. Admin.) [offiziell anerkanntes] historisches Denkmal; [offiziell anerkannte] historische Stätte
B *n.* [1] **the ~s** Menschen der Antike; (authors) die Schriftsteller der Antike [2] **the A~ of Days** (literary) der Allvater [3] (arch.: old man) Alte, *der*

anciently /'eɪnʃəntlɪ/ *adv.* in alten Zeiten; (in antiquity) in der Antike; im Altertum

ancillary /æn'sɪlərɪ/
A *adj.* [1] (auxiliary) **be ~ to sth.** für etw. Hilfsdienste leisten; **be ~ to medicine** eine Hilfswissenschaft der Medizin sein [2] (subordinate) zweitrangig; **~ industries** Zulieferindustrien; **~ services** Hilfeleistungen; **~ worker** Hilfskraft, *die;* **~ subject** Nebenfach, *das;* **a network of ~ roads** ein Netz von Verbindungsstraßen
B *n.* (Brit.) Hilfskraft, *die*

and /ənd, *stressed* ænd/ *conj.* [1] und; **two hundred ~ forty** zweihundert[und]vierzig; **a knife,**

fork, ~ spoon Messer, Gabel und Löffel; **there are books ~ books** es gibt Bücher und Bücher; es gibt sone Bücher und solche (salopp); **two ~ two are four** zwei und zwei ist *od.* sind vier; **[by] two ~ two** in Zweierreihen; **~/or** und/oder **2** *expr. condition* und; **take one more step ~ I'll shoot** noch einen Schritt, und ich schieße; **do that ~ you'll regret it** wenn du das tust, wirst du es noch bedauern **3** *expr. continuation* und; **she cried ~ cried** sie weinte und weinte; **he tried ~ tried to open it** er versuchte immer wieder, es zu öffnen; **for weeks ~ weeks/years ~ years** wochen-/jahrelang; **for miles ~ miles** meilenweit; **better ~ better** immer besser

andante /æn'dæntɪ/ (Mus.)
A *adv.* andante; gemessen
B *adj.* ruhig
C *n.* Andante, *das*

Andean /æn'di:ən/ *adj.* (Geog.) Anden-

Andes /'ændi:z/ *pr. n. pl.* Anden *Pl.*

andiron /'ændaɪən/ *n.* Feuerbock, *der*

Andorra /æn'dɔ:rə/ *pr. n.* Andorra *(das)*

Andrew /'ændru:/ *pr. n.* (as name of saint) Andreas *(der)*

androgynous /æn'drɒdʒɪnəs/ *adj.* (Biol.) zwittrig

android /'ændrɔɪd/ *n.* Android[e], *der*

anecdotal /'ænɪkdəʊtl/ *adj.* anekdotisch; anekdotenhaft

anecdote /'ænɪkdəʊt/ *n.* Anekdote, *die;* **he is never without a witty ~:** er ist nie um eine witzige Geschichte verlegen

anemia, anemic (Amer.) ▸ **anaem-**

anemometer /ænɪ'mɒmɪtə(r)/ *n.* (Meteorol.) Anemometer, *das;* Windmesser, *der*

anemone /ə'nemənɪ/ *n.* Anemone, *die;* (pasque flower) Kuhschelle, *die; see also* **sea anemone; wood anemone**

aneroid /'ænərɔɪd/ *adj.* **~ barometer** Aneroidbarometer, *das*

anesthesia *etc.* (Amer.) ▸ **anaesthesia** *etc.*

anew /ə'nju:/ *adv.* **1** aufs Neue; erneut; **let's start ~:** fangen wir noch einmal von vorne an **2** (in a new form) neu; **he decided to start life ~ in Australia** er beschloss, in Australien ein neues Leben zu beginnen

angel /'eɪndʒl/ *n.* **1** (lit. or fig.) Engel, *der;* **evil ~:** böser Geist; **good ~:** guter Engel; **be on the side of the ~s** (fig.) auf der Seite der Guten stehen; **be an ~ and ...** (coll.) sei so lieb und ...; *see also* **guardian angel** **2** (Commerc. coll.) Finanzier, *der*

angel: ~ cake *n., no pl.* Biskuitkuchen, *der;* **~ fish** *n.* Kaiserfisch, *der;* Engelfisch, *der*

angelic /æn'dʒelɪk/ *adj.* **1** (of angel[s]) Engels- **2** (like angel[s]) engelhaft; engelgleich (geh.); **an ~ child** ein Kind wie ein Engel; **she looked ~:** sie sah wie ein Engel aus

angelica /æn'dʒelɪkə/ *n.* **1** (Bot., Cookery, Med.) Angelika, *die;* Engelwurz, *die* **2** (candied) kandierte Angelika

angelus /'ændʒɪləs/ *n.* (RC Ch.) Angelus, *der od. das;* **~ bell** Angelusläuten, *das*

anger /'æŋgə(r)/
A *n., no pl.* (wrath) Zorn, *der* (**at** über + *Akk.*); (fury) Wut, *die* (**at** über + *Akk.*); **be filled with ~:** erzürnt/wütend sein; **in [a moment of] ~:** im Zorn/in der Wut
B *v.t.* verärgern; (infuriate) erzürnen (geh.)/wütend machen; **be ~ed by sth.** über etw. (*Akk.*) verärgert/erzürnt/wütend sein

angina [pectoris] /æn'dʒaɪnə ('pektərɪs)/ *n., no pl.* ▸ **p. 1231** (Med.) Angina Pectoris, *die*

angle[1]
A *n.* **1** (Geom.) Winkel, *der;* **acute/obtuse/right ~:** spitzer/stumpfer/rechter Winkel; **at an ~ of 60°** im Winkel von 60°; **at an ~:** schief; **at an ~ to the wall** schräg zur Wand **2** (corner) Ecke, *die;* (recess) Winkel, *der* **3** (direction) Perspektive, *die;* Blickwinkel, *der;* (fig.) Gesichtspunkt, *der;* Aspekt, *der;* **the photo isn't taken from a flattering ~:** die Aufnahme ist aus einem unvorteilhaften [Blick]winkel gemacht; **the committee examined the matter from various ~s** der Ausschuss prüfte die Angelegenheit von verschiedenen Seiten; **looking at it from a commercial ~:** aus kaufmännischer Sicht betrachtet
B *v.t.* **1** [aus]richten **2** (coll.: bias) färben ‹*Nachrichten, Formulierung*›
C *v.i.* [im Winkel] abbiegen; **the road ~s sharply to the left** die Straße biegt scharf nach links ab

angle[2] *v.i.* angeln; (fig.) **~ for sth.** sich um etw. bemühen; **~ for compliments** nach Komplimenten fischen; **~ for an opportunity** eine Gelegenheit suchen

Angle /'æŋgl/ *n.* Angehöriger/Angehörige des Volksstammes der Angeln; **the ~s** die Angeln

'angle brackets *n. pl.* spitze Klammern

angled /'æŋgəld/ *adj.* (angular) eckig ‹*Form, Figur*›; (placed obliquely) schief; (fig.) tendenziös, gefärbt ‹*Bericht, Kommentar*›; **acute-/obtuse-/right-~:** spitz-/stumpf-/rechtwinklig

angle: ~ dozer /'æŋgldəʊzə(r)/ *n.* Seitenräumer, *der;* **~ grinder** *n.* Winkelschleifer, *der;* (with cutting disc) Flex, *die;* **~ iron** *n.* Winkeleisen, *das;* **~-parking** *n., no pl.* Schrägparken, *das*

angler /'æŋglə(r)/ *n.* **1** Angler, *der*/Anglerin, *die* **2** **~[fish]** Angler, *der;* Seeteufel, *der*

Anglican /'æŋglɪkən/
A *adj.* anglikanisch
B *n.* Anglikaner, *der*/Anglikanerin, *die*

Anglicanism /'æŋglɪkənɪzm/ *n., no pl.* Anglikanismus, *der*

Anglicism /'æŋglɪsɪzm/ *n.* **1** (word or idiom) Anglizismus, *der* **2** (Englishness) englische Eigenart

Anglicize /'æŋglɪsaɪz/ *v.t.* anglisieren

angling /'æŋglɪŋ/ *n.* Angeln, *das*

Anglist /'æŋglɪst/ *n.* Anglist, *der*/Anglistin, *die*

Anglistics /æŋ'glɪstɪks/ *n., no pl.* Anglistik, *die*

Anglo- /æŋgləʊ/ *in comb.* anglo-/Anglo-; **he's an ~Cypriot** er ist Zyprer britischer Herkunft

Anglo-A'merican ▸ **p. 1345**
A *adj.* angloamerikanisch; **an ~ agreement** ein englisch-/britisch-amerikanischer Vertrag
B *n.* Angloamerikaner, *der*/Angloamerikanerin, *die*

Anglo-'Catholic
A *n.* Anglokatholik, *der*/Anglokatholikin, *die*
B *adj.* anglokatholisch

Anglo-'French
A *adj.* englisch-/britisch-französisch; (Ling.) anglofranzösisch; anglonormannisch
B *n.* (Ling.) Anglonormannisch, *das;* Anglofranzösisch, *das*

Anglo-'German *adj.* englisch-/britisch-deutsch

Anglo-'Indian ▸ **p. 1345**
A *adj.* angloindisch
B *n.* Anglo-Inder, *der*/Anglo-Inderin, *die*

Anglo-'Irish
A *adj.* angloirisch
B *n. pl.* **the ~:** die Angloiren

Anglomania /æŋgləʊ'meɪnɪə/ *n.* Anglomanie, *die*

Anglo-'Norman
A *adj.* anglonormannisch
B *n.* (dialect) Anglonormannisch, *das*

Anglophile /'æŋgləʊfaɪl/
A *n.* Anglophile, *der/die*
B *adj.* anglophil

Anglophobia /æŋgləʊ'fəʊbɪə/ *n.* Anglophobie, *die*

anglophone /'æŋgləʊfəʊn/
A *adj.* anglophon
B *n.* Anglophone, *der/die*

Anglo-'Saxon ▸ **p. 1345**
A *n.* Angelsachse, *der*/Angelsächsin, *die;* (language) Angelsächsisch, *das;* (Amer. coll.: English) Englisch, *das*
B *adj.* angelsächsisch; (Amer. coll.: English) englisch

Angola /æŋ'gəʊlə/ *pr. n.* Angola *(das)*

Angolan /æŋ'gəʊlən/ ▸ **p. 1345**
A *adj.* angolanisch; **sb. is ~:** jmd. ist Angolaner/Angolanerin
B *n.* Angolaner, *der*/Angolanerin, *die*

angora /æŋ'gɔ:rə/ *n.* Angora‹*katze, -ziege, -kaninchen*›; **~ [wool]** Angorawolle, *die;* Mohair, *der*

angrily /'æŋgrɪlɪ/ *adv.* verärgert; (stronger) zornig

angry /'æŋgrɪ/ *adj.* **1** böse; verärgert ‹*Person, Stimme, Geste*›; (stronger) zornig; wütend; **be ~ at** *or* **about sth.** wegen etw. böse sein; **he was ~ at being asked** er war verärgert darüber, dass man ihn fragte; **be ~ with** *or* **at sb.** mit jmdm. *od.* auf jmdn. böse sein; sich über jmdn. ärgern; **be in an ~ mood** schlechter Laune *od.* böse sein; **get ~:** böse werden; **get** *or* **make sb. ~:** jmdn. verärgern; (stronger) jmdn. wütend machen **2** (fig.) drohend, bedrohlich ‹*Wolke, Himmel*› **3** (inflamed and painful) böse, schlimm ‹*Riss, Wunde*›; **an ~ red** eine entzündliche Röte

angst /æŋst/ *n.* neurotische Angst; (remorse) Schuldgefühl, *das*

anguish /'æŋgwɪʃ/ *n., no pl.* Qualen *Pl.;* **he shuddered with ~:** er erschauerte vor Schmerz

anguished /'æŋgwɪʃt/ *adj.* qualvoll; gequält ‹*Herz, Gewissen*›

angular /'æŋgjʊlə(r)/ *adj.* **1** (having angles) eckig ‹*Gebäude, Struktur, Gestalt*› **2** (lacking plumpness, stiff) knochig ‹*Körperbau*›; kantig ‹*Gesicht*› **3** (measured by angle) angular; winklig; **~ momentum** (Phys.) Drehimpuls, *der;* Drall, *der;* **~ motion** (Phys.) Kreisbewegung, *die;* **~ velocity** (Phys.) Winkelgeschwindigkeit, *die;* (Electr.) Kreisfrequenz, *die;* (Mech.) Umlauf- *od.* Drehgeschwindigkeit, *die*

angularity /æŋgjʊ'lærɪtɪ/ *n., no pl.* Eckigkeit, *die;* **the ~ of his handwriting** seine eckige Handschrift

anhydride /æn'haɪdraɪd/ *n.* (Chem.) Anhydrid, *das*

anhydrous /æn'haɪdrəs/ *adj.* (Chem.) [kristall-]wasserfrei; nichtwässrig

aniline /'ænɪli:n, 'ænɪlaɪn, 'ænɪlɪn/ *n.* Anilin, *das;* **~ dye** künstlicher Farbstoff, *der;* (made from ~) Anilinfarbstoff, *der*

animal /'ænɪməl/
A *n.* **1** Tier, *das;* (quadruped) Vierbeiner, *der;* (any living being) Lebewesen, *das;* **domestic ~:** Haustier, *das; see also* **kingdom 4** **2** (fig. coll.) **there is no such ~ as a 'typical' criminal** so etwas wie den „typischen" Verbrecher gibt es gar nicht; **that's a queer sort of ~:** das ist 'ne Sorte für sich (ugs.) **3** (fig.: ~ instinct; brute) Tier, *das;* **don't be such an ~!** benimm dich doch mal wie ein Mensch!
B *adj.* **1** tierisch; **~ behaviour/breeding** Tierverhalten, *das*/Tierzucht, *die* **2** (from ~s) tierisch ‹*Produkt, Klebstoff, Öl*› **3** (carnal, sexual) körperlich ‹*Bedürfnisse, Triebe, Wünsche*›; tierisch, animalisch ‹*Veranlagung, Natur*›

animalcule /ænɪ'mælkju:l/ *n.* Mikroorganismus, *der*

animal: ~ 'hospital *n.* Tierklinik, *die;* **A~ Libe'ration Front** *n.* Tierbefreiungsfront, *die;* **~ lover** *n.* Tierfreund, *der*/-freundin, *die;* **~ pro'tectionist** *n.* Tierschützer, *der*/-schützerin, *die;* **~ 'rights** *n. pl.* Tierrechte *Pl.; attrib.* **~ rights activist** [militanter] Tierrechtler *der*/[militante] Tierrechtlerin *die;* **~ rights campaigner** Tierrechtler *der*/-rechtlerin *die;* **~ rights supporter** Tierrechtler, *der*/-rechtlerin, *die;* **~ 'testing** *n. no pl.* Tierversuche *Pl.*

animate
A /'ænɪmeɪt/ *v.t.* **1** (enliven) beleben **2** (inspire) anregen; (to do sth. mischievous) animieren; **~ sb. with enthusiasm** jmdn. mit Begeisterung erfüllen; **he was ~d by a passion for truth** er war von einer leidenschaftlichen Wahrheitsliebe beseelt **3** (breathe life into) mit Leben erfüllen
B /'ænɪmət/ *adj.* beseelt ‹*Leben, Körper*›; belebt ‹*Objekt, Welt*›; lebendig ‹*Seele*›

animated /'ænɪmeɪtɪd/ *adj.* lebhaft ‹*Diskussion, Unterhaltung, Ausdruck, Gebärde*›; lebendig ‹*Darstellung*›; **~ cartoon** Zeichentrickfilm, *der*

animatedly /'ænɪmeɪtɪdlɪ/ *adv.* lebhaft

animation /ænɪ'meɪʃn/ *n.* **1** *no pl.* Lebhaftigkeit, *die* **2** (Cinemat.) Animation, *die*

animator /'ænɪmeɪtə(r)/ *n.* ▸ **p. 1260** (Cinemat.) Animator, *der*/Animatorin, *die*

animatronic /ænɪmə'trɒnɪk/ *adj.* animatronisch

animatronics /ænɪmə'trɒnɪks/ *n.* **1** *no pl.* Animatronik, *die* **2** *constr. as pl.* (effects) animatronische Effekte; ~ **figures** animatronische Figuren

animism /'ænɪmɪzm/ *n., no pl.* (Relig.) Animismus, *der*

animist /'ænɪmɪst/ *n.* Animist, *der*/Animistin, *die*

animosity /ænɪ'mɒsɪtɪ/ *n.* Animosität, *die* (geh.), Feindseligkeit, *die* (**against, towards**) gegen)

anion /'ænaɪən/ *n.* (Phys.) Anion, *das*

anise /'ænɪs/ *n.* (Bot.) Anis, *der*

aniseed /'ænɪsi:d/ *n.* Anis[samen], *der*

anisette /ænɪ'zet/ *n.* Anislikör, *der;* Anisette, *der*

ankle /'æŋkl/ *n.* ▸ℹ **p. 951** (joint) Fußgelenk, *das;* (part of leg) Knöchelgegend, *die;* Fessel, *die*

ankle: ~-deep *adj.* knöcheltief; ~ **sock** *n.* Socke, *die;* (esp. for children) Söckchen, *das*

anklet /'æŋklɪt/ *n.* **1** Fußkettchen, *das* **2** (Amer.) ▸ **ankle sock**

annalist /'ænəlɪst/ *n.* Annalist, *der*

annals /'ænəlz/ *n. pl.* (lit. or fig.) Annalen *Pl.;* **in the ~ of human history** in der Geschichte *od.* in den Annalen der Menschheit

Anne /æn/ *pr. n.* (Hist., as name of ruler, saint, etc.) Anna *(die)*

anneal /ə'ni:l/ *v.t.* ausglühen ‹*Stahl*›; kühlen ‹*Glas*›

annelid /'ænəlɪd/ *n.* (Zool.) Ringelwurm, *der*

annex

A /ə'neks/ *v.t.* **1** (add) angliedern (**to** *Dat.*); anbauen ‹*Gebäude*›; (append) anfügen ‹*Bemerkungen*› (**to** *Dat.*) **2** (incorporate) annektieren ‹*Land, Territorium*›; (coll.: take without right) sich (*Dat.*) unter den Nagel reißen (ugs.) ‹*Gegenstände*› **3** (attach) (as an attribute) zuschreiben (**to** *Dat.*); verbinden (**to** mit); (as a condition) verbinden (**to** mit); (as a consequence) binden, knüpfen (**to** an + *Akk.*)

B /'æneks/ *n.* (supplementary building) Anbau, *der;* Annexbau, *der* (selten); (built-on extension) Erweiterungsbau, *der;* (appendix) (to document) Zusatz, *der;* Annex, *der* (geh.); (to treaty) Anhang, *der;* Annex, *der* (geh.)

annexation /ænɪk'seɪʃn/ *n.* **1** (of land) Annexion, *die;* Annektierung, *die* **2** (as an attribute) Verknüpfung, *die* (**to** mit)

annexe ▸ **annex B**

annihilate /ə'naɪəleɪt/ *v.t.* **1** vernichten ‹*Armee, Flotte, Bevölkerung, Menschheit*›; zerstören ‹*Stadt, Land*› **2** (fig.) zunichte machen; am Boden zerstören ‹*Person*›

annihilation /ənaɪə'leɪʃn/ *n.* **1** ▸ **annihilate**: Vernichtung, *die;* Zerstörung, *die;* (fig.) Verderben, *das;* Untergang, *der;* **the party's ~:** der Untergang der Partei **2** (Phys.) Paarvernichtung, *die*

anniversary /ænɪ'vɜ:sərɪ/ *n.* Jahrestag, *der;* **wedding ~:** Hochzeitstag, *der;* **the university celebrated its 500th ~:** die Universität feierte ihr 500jähriges Jubiläum *od.* Bestehen; **the ~ of Shakespeare's birth** [die Wiederkehr von] Shakespeares Geburtstag; **the ~ of his death** sein Todestag

Anno Domini /ænəʊ 'dɒmɪnaɪ/

A *adv.* ▸ℹ **p. 1047** nach Christi Geburt; ~ **62** [im Jahre] 62 nach Christi Geburt

B *n.* (coll.) das Alter

annotate /'ænəteɪt/ *v.t.* kommentieren; mit Anmerkungen versehen

annotation /ænə'teɪʃn/ *n.* (act) Kommentierung, *die;* (comment) Anmerkung, *die*

announce /ə'naʊns/ *v.t.* bekannt geben; ansagen ‹*Programm*›; (over Tannoy etc.) durchsagen; (in newspaper) anzeigen ‹*Heirat usw.*›; (make known the approach of; fig.: signify) ankündigen

announcement /ə'naʊnsmənt/ *n.* Bekanntgabe, *die;* (over Tannoy etc.) Durchsage, *die;* **they made an ~ over the radio that ...:** sie gaben im Radio bekannt, dass ...; **did you read the ~ of his death in the paper?** haben Sie seine Todesanzeige in der Zeitung gelesen?

announcer /ə'naʊnsə(r)/ *n.* ▸ℹ **p. 1260** Ansager, *der*/Ansagerin, *die;* Sprecher, *der*/Sprecherin, *die*

annoy /ə'nɔɪ/ *v.t.* **1** ärgern; **his late arrival ~ed me** ich habe mich über sein spätes Kommen geärgert; **her remarks ~ everybody** ihre Bemerkungen sind allen lästig **2** (harass) schikanieren

annoyance /ə'nɔɪəns/ *n.* Verärgerung, *die;* (nuisance) Plage, *die;* **[much] to my/his ~:** [sehr] zu meiner/seiner Verärgerung; **a look of ~:** ein Blick der Verärgerung; **having a pub next door to one's house is a constant ~:** wenn man eine Kneipe nebenan hat, ist das ein ständiges Ärgernis

annoyed /ə'nɔɪd/ *adj.* **be ~ [at** *or* **with sb./sth.]** ärgerlich [auf *od.* über jmdn./über etw.] sein; **be ~ to find that ...:** sich darüber ärgern, dass ...; **he got very ~:** er hat sich darüber sehr geärgert

annoying /ə'nɔɪɪŋ/ *adj.* ärgerlich; lästig ‹*Gewohnheit, Person*›; **the ~ part of it is that ...:** das Ärgerliche daran *od.* was einen daran ärgert ist, dass ...

annual /'ænjʊəl/

A *adj.* **1** (reckoned by the year) Jahres-; ~ **income/subscription/rent/turnover/production/leave/salary** Jahreseinkommen, *das*/-abonnement, *das*/-miete, *die*/-umsatz, *der*/-produktion, *die*/-urlaub, *der*/-gehalt, *das;* ~ **rainfall** jährliche Regenmenge **2** (recurring yearly) [all]jährlich ‹*Ereignis, Feier*›; Jahres‹*bericht,-hauptversammlung*› **3** (Bot.) einjährig, (fachspr.) annuell ‹*Pflanze*›; ~ **ring** (Bot.) Jahresring, *der*

B *n.* **1** (Bot.) einjährige Pflanze **2** (Bibliog.) Jahrbuch, *das;* Jahresschrift, *die;* (of comic etc.) Jahresalbum, *das*

annually /'ænjʊəlɪ/ *adv.* (per year) jährlich; (once a year) [all]jährlich

annuity /ə'nju:ɪtɪ/ *n.* (grant, sum payable) Jahresrente, *die;* (investment) Rentenversicherung, *die*

annul /ə'nʌl/ *v.t.,* **-ll-** (abolish) annullieren, für ungültig erklären ‹*Gesetz, Vertrag, Ehe, Testament*›; auflösen ‹*Vertrag*›

annular /'ænjʊlə(r)/ *adj.* ringartig; ringförmig

annulment /ə'nʌlmənt/ *n.* (of law, treaty, marriage, will) Annullierung, *die;* (of treaty also) Auflösung, *die*

Annunciation /ənʌnsɪ'eɪʃn/ *n.* **1** (Eccl.) **the ~:** Mariä Verkündigung; **Feast of the ~:** Fest der Verkündigung Mariä **2** **a~** (formal/arch.) Ankündigung, *die*

annunciator /ə'nʌnsɪeɪtə(r)/ *n.* (indicator) [elektrische] Anzeige

annus mirabilis /ænəs mɪ'rɑ:bɪlɪs/ *n., no pl.* Wunderjahr, *das;* wundersames Jahr

anode /'ænəʊd/ *n.* (Electr.) Anode, *die*

anodize /'ænədaɪz/ *v.t.* anodisieren; **anodizing** anodische Behandlung

anodyne /'ænədaɪn/

A *adj.* (Med.) schmerzstillend; analgetisch (fachspr.); (fig.) wohltuend; (soothing) einlullend; **the ~ aspects of modern life** die Segnungen des modernen Lebens (iron.)

B *n.* (Med.) Schmerzmittel, *das;* Analgetikum, *das*

anoint /ə'nɔɪnt/ *v.t.* (esp. Relig.) salben; ~ **sb. king** jmdn. zum König salben

anomalous /ə'nɒmələs/ *adj.* **1** (abnormal) anomal, anormal ‹*Lage, Verhältnisse, Zustand*›; ungewöhnlich ‹*Situation, Anblick*› **2** (Ling.: irregular) unregelmäßig

anomalously /ə'nɒmələslɪ/ *adv.* **1** außergewöhnlich **2** (Ling.) unregelmäßig ‹*deklinieren, konjugieren*›

anomaly /ə'nɒməlɪ/ *n.* Anomalie, *die;* Absonderlichkeit, *die;* (exception) Ausnahme, *die*

anon /ə'nɒn/ *adv.* **1** (arch./literary: soon) bald **2** (coll.: later) später; **more of that ~!** mehr davon später!; **see you ~:** bis später [dann]

anon. /ə'nɒn/ *abbr.* = **anonymous [author]** anon.

anonymity /ænə'nɪmɪtɪ/ *n.* Anonymität, *die*

anonymous /ə'nɒnɪməs/ *adj.* anonym

anonymously /ə'nɒnɪməslɪ/ *adv.* anonym; **he phoned ~:** er machte einen anonymen Anruf; **he dresses rather ~:** er kleidet sich sehr unauffällig

anorak /'ænəræk/ *n.* Anorak, *der*

anorexia /ænə'reksɪə/ *n.* Anorexie, *die* (Med.); Appetitlosigkeit, *die;* Magersucht, *die* (volkst.); ~ **nervosa** /ænəreksɪə nɜ:'vəʊsə/ nervöse Anorexie (Med.); Anorexia nervosa, *die* (Med.)

anorexic /ænə'reksɪk/

A *adj.* anorektisch (fachspr.); magersüchtig; **be ~:** an Anorexie (Med.) *od.* Magersucht leiden;

B *n.* Anorektiker, *der*/Anorektikerin, *die* (fachspr.); Magersüchtige, *der/die;* **he/she is an ~:** er/sie leidet an Magersucht

another /ə'nʌðə(r)/

A *pron.* **1** (additional) noch einer/eine/eins; ein weiterer/eine weitere/ein weiteres; **yet ~:** noch einer/eine/eins; **one thing leads to ~:** eines ergibt sich aus dem anderen; **We have lots of apples. Please have ~:** Wir haben eine ganze Menge Äpfel. Nimm dir doch noch einen; **send a copy to the customer and keep ~ for reference** schicken Sie eine Kopie an den Kunden, und eine weitere nehmen Sie für unsere Unterlagen; **there's one school in the neighbourhood already and ~ [which is] being built** es gibt schon eine Schule in der Gegend, und eine zweite ist gerade im Bau **2** (counterpart) wieder einer/eine/eins; **such ~:** noch so einer/so eine/so eins **3** (Brit. Law) **X versus Y and ~:** X gegen Y und andere **4** (different) ein anderer/eine andere/ein anderes; **she ran off with/married ~:** sie brannte mit einem anderen durch (ugs.)/heiratete einen anderen; **making a mistake is one thing, but lying deliberately is quite ~:** einen Fehler zu machen ist eine Sache, aber absichtlich zu lügen ist ganz etwas anderes; **they said one to ~:** sie sagten zueinander; **in one way or ~:** so oder so; irgendwie; **for one reason or ~:** aus irgendeinem Grund; **A. N. Other** (Brit.) N. N.; *see also* **one A 6, C 2**

B *adj.* **1** (additional) noch einer/eine/eins; ein weiterer/eine weitere/ein weiteres; **give me ~ chance** gib mir noch [einmal] eine Chance; **after ~ six weeks** nach weiteren sechs Wochen; ~ **100 pounds** weitere 100 Pfund; **he didn't say ~ word** er sagte nichts mehr; **he hasn't ~ day to live** er hat keinen Tag länger zu leben; **he hasn't ~ penny left** er hat keinen Cent mehr; **it'll take ~ few years** es wird noch ein paar Jahre [länger] dauern **2** (a person like) ein neuer/eine neue/ein neues; ein zweiter/eine zweite/ein zweites; ~ **Chaplin** ein neuer *od.* zweiter Chaplin **3** (different) ein anderer/eine andere/ein anderes; **ask ~ person** fragen Sie jemand anderen *od.* anders; ~ **time, don't be so greedy** sei beim nächsten Mal nicht so gierig; **I'll do it ~ time** ich tu's ein andermal; **[and] [there's] ~ thing** [und] noch etwas; **it's one thing to make a request, ~ thing to order** zu bitten ist eine Sache, zu befehlen eine andere; **that's quite ~ problem** das ist wieder ein anderes Problem; ~ **place** (Brit. Parl.) die andere Kammer [dieses Parlaments]; *see also* **tomorrow 1**

anschluss /'ænʃlʊs/ *n.* (Hist.) Anschluss, *der;* **the ~ of Austria by Germany** der Anschluss Österreichs [an Deutschland]

answer /'ɑ:nsə(r)/

A *n.* **1** (reply) Antwort, *die* (**to** auf + *Akk.*); (reaction) Reaktion, *die;* **I tried to phone him, but there was no ~:** ich habe versucht, ihn anzurufen, aber es hat sich niemand gemeldet; **do you have any ~ to the accusations made against you?** haben Sie irgendetwas auf die Anschuldigungen gegen Sie zu erwidern?; **there is no ~ to that** dem ist nichts mehr hinzuzufügen; **by way of [an] ~:** als Antwort; **in ~ to sth.** als Antwort *od.* Reaktion auf etw. (*Akk.*); **he always has an ~ [ready]** er hat immer eine Antwort parat; **make ~** (formal) [eine] Antwort geben **2** (to problem) Lösung, *die* (**to** *Gen.*); (to calculation) Ergebnis, *das;* **have** *or* **know all the ~s** (coll.) alles wissen

B *v.t.* **1** beantworten ‹*Brief, Frage*›; antworten auf (+ *Akk.*) ‹*Frage, Hilferuf, Einladung, Inserat*›; (react to) erwidern ‹*Geste, Schlag*›; (respond to) eingehen auf (+ *Akk.*) ‹*Angebot, Vorschlag*›; eingehen auf (+ *Akk.*), erfüllen ‹*Bitte*›; sich stellen zu ‹*Beschuldigung*›; erhören ‹*Gebet*›; erfüllen

‹*Wunsch*›; **~ sb.** jmdm. antworten; **~ me!** antworte [mir]!; **~ a question** eine Frage beantworten; auf eine Frage antworten 2▸ **~ the door/bell** an die Tür gehen 3▸ (be satisfactory for) genügen (+ *Dat.*); entsprechen (+ *Dat.*); **the flat ~ed his purpose very well** die Wohnung entsprach *od.* genügte seinen Anforderungen vollauf; *see also* **telephone A**

C *v.i.* 1▸ (reply) antworten; **~ to sth.** sich zu etw. äußern 2▸ (be responsible) **~ for sth.** für etw. die Verantwortung übernehmen; **~ to sb.** jmdm. [gegenüber] Rechenschaft ablegen; **one day you will have to ~ for your crimes** eines Tages wirst du dich für deine Verbrechen verantworten müssen; **he has a lot to ~ for** er hat vieles zu verantworten 3▸ (correspond) **~ to a description** einer Beschreibung (*Dat.*) entsprechen 4▸ (be satisfactory) **~ for a purpose/intention** sich für einen Zweck/ein Vorhaben eignen 5▸ **~ to the name of ...:** auf den Namen ... hören

Phrasal verb

• **~ 'back** *v.i.* widersprechen; Widerworte haben (ugs.); **he's always ready to ~ back** er gibt einem gern Kontra (ugs.); **don't ~ back!** keine Widerworte!

answerable /'ɑːnsərəbl/ *adj.* (responsible) **be ~ to sb.** jmdm. [gegenüber] verantwortlich sein; **be ~ for sb./sth.** für jmdn./etw. verantwortlich sein

answering: ~ machine *n.* (Teleph.) Anrufbeantworter, *der*; **~ service** *n.* (Teleph.) Fernsprechauftragsdienst, *der*

'answerphone (Brit.) ▸ **answering machine**

ant /ænt/ *n.* Ameise, *die*; **white ~:** Termite, *die*; weiße Ameise (volkst.); **have ~s in one's pants** (coll.) nicht stillsitzen können

antacid /ænt'æsɪd/

A *n.* Antazidum, *das*

B *adj.* Magensäure bindend

antagonism /æn'tægənɪzm/ *n.* Feindseligkeit, *die* (**towards, against** gegenüber); (between two) Antagonismus, *der* (geh.); **the ~ between the two families** die Feindschaft zwischen den beiden Familien

antagonist /æn'tægənɪst/ *n.* Gegner, *der*/Gegnerin, *die*; (in debate etc.) Kontrahent, *der*/Kontrahentin, *die*

antagonistic /æntægə'nɪstɪk/ *adj.* feindlich ‹*Mächte, Prinzipien*›; feindselig ‹*Kritik*›; antagonistisch, gegensätzlich ‹*Interessen*›; **be ~ towards sth.** gegen etw. eingestellt sein; **be ~ towards sb.** jmdn. anfeinden

antagonize /æn'tægənaɪz/ *v.t.* 1▸ (evoke hostility or enmity of) sich (*Dat.*) zum Feind machen; vor den Kopf stoßen (ugs.) 2▸ (counteract) entgegenwirken (+ *Dat.*); **~ one another** sich gegenseitig bekämpfen

Antarctic /ænt'ɑːktɪk/

A *adj.* antarktisch; **~ explorer** Antarktisforscher, *der*/-forscherin, *die*; **~ Circle/Ocean** südlicher Polarkreis/Südpolarmeer, *das*

B *pr. n.* **the ~:** die Antarktis

Antarctica /ænt'ɑːktɪkə/ *pr. n.* die Antarktis

ante /'æntɪ/

A *n.* (in poker etc.) Einsatz, *der*; **up the ~** (fig. coll.) den Einsatz erhöhen

B *v.t.* setzen; **~ [up] £10** 10 Pfund setzen; **can you ~ up £1,000 to buy this plot of land?** können Sie 1000 Pfund zum Kauf dieses Grundstücks aufbringen?

'anteater *n.* (Zool.) Ameisenfresser, *der*

antecedent /æntɪ'siːdənt/

A *adj.* vorher-, vorausgehend ‹*Faktoren, Elemente, Prinzipien*›; **be ~ to sth.** einer Sache (*Dat.*) vorausgehen

B *n.* 1▸ (preceding event) früherer Umstand; vorangegangenes Ereignis; (preceding thing) Vorläufer, *der* 2▸ *in pl.* (past history) **sb.'s ~s** jmds. Vorleben

antechamber /'æntɪtʃeɪmbə(r)/ *n.* Vorzimmer, *das*

antedate /æntɪ'deɪt/ *v.t.* 1▸ (precede) voraus-, vorangehen (+ *Dat.*) 2▸ (give earlier date to) zurückdatieren

antediluvian /æntɪdɪ'luːvɪən, æntɪdɪ'luːvɪən/ *adj.* (lit. or fig.) vorsintflutlich

antelope /'æntɪləʊp/ *n.* 1▸ (Zool.) Antilope, *die* 2▸ (leather) Antilopenleder, *das*

antenatal /æntɪ'neɪtl/ *adj.* 1▸ (concerning pregnancy) Schwangerschafts-; Schwangeren-; **~ care** Schwangerenfürsorge, *die*; **~ clinic** Klinik für werdende Mütter 2▸ (before birth) vorgeburtlich; prä- *od.* antenatal (fachspr.)

antenna /æn'tenə/ *n.* 1▸ *pl.* **~e** /æn'teniː/ (Zool.) Fühler, *der*; Antenne, *die* (fachspr.) 2▸ *pl.* **~s** (tech, Amer.: aerial) Antenne, *die*

antepenultimate /æntɪpɪ'nʌltɪmət/ *adj.* drittletzt...

ante-post /æntɪ'pəʊst/ *adj.* (Horseracing) **~ betting** Wetten vor dem Renntag

anterior /æn'tɪərɪə(r)/ *adj.* 1▸ (to the front) vorder...; **be in an ~ position** vorn sein 2▸ (formal: prior) früher...; **be ~ to sth.** einer Sache (*Dat.*) vorausgehen

anteroom /'æntɪruːm, 'æntɪrʊm/ *n.* Vorraum, *der*; (waiting room) Warteraum, *der*

antheap /'ænthiːp/ *n.* Ameisenhaufen, *der*; Ameisenhügel, *der*; **this human ~** (fig.) dieses Menschengewimmel

anthem /'ænθəm/ *n.* 1▸ (Eccl. Mus.) Chorgesang, *der* 2▸ (song of praise) Jubel-, Preisgesang, *der* (geh.); Hymne, *die*; *see also* **national anthem**

anther /'ænθə(r)/ *n.* (Bot.) Staubbeutel, *der*

anthill /'ænthɪl/ ▸ **antheap**

anthologist /æn'θɒlədʒɪst/ *n.* Herausgeber, *der*/Herausgeberin, *die* [einer Anthologie/von Anthologien]

anthology /æn'θɒlədʒɪ/ *n.* (of poetry, prose, songs) (by different writers) Anthologie, *die*; (by one writer) Auswahl, *die*

anthracite /'ænθrəsaɪt/ *n.* Anthrazit, *der*

anthrax /'ænθræks/ *n.*, *no pl.*, *no indef. art.* ▸❶ **p. 1231** (Med., Vet. Med.) Milzbrand, *der*; Anthrax, *der* (fachspr.)

anthropocentric /ænθrəpə'sentrɪk/ *adj.* anthropozentrisch

anthropoid /'ænθrəpɔɪd/

A *adj.* 1▸ (manlike) menschenähnlich; anthropoid; **~ ape** Menschenaffe, *der* 2▸ (coll. derog.: apelike) affenartig (abwertend)

B *n.* Anthropoid[e], *der*; Menschenaffe, *der*

anthropological /ænθrəpə'lɒdʒɪkl/ *adj.* anthropologisch

anthropologist /ænθrə'pɒlədʒɪst/ *n.* ▸❶ **p. 1260** Anthropologe, *der*/Anthropologin, *die*

anthropology /ænθrə'pɒlədʒɪ/ *n.*, *no pl.* Anthropologie, *die*

anthropomorphic /ænθrəpə'mɔːfɪk/ *adj.* anthropomorphisch

anthropomorphism /ænθrəpə'mɔːfɪzm/ *n.*, *no pl.* Anthropomorphismus, *der*

anti /'æntɪ/

A *prep.* gegen; **be ~ sth.** gegen etw. sein; Gegner von etw. sein

B *adj.* ablehnend; **young people are all so ~ these days** die jungen Leute heutzutage sind gegen alles *od.* lehnen einfach alles ab

C *n.* Gegner, *der*; Widersacher, *der*

anti- /æntɪ/ *pref.* anti-/Anti-

anti: ~-a'bortion *attrib. adj.* **~-abortion protester** Abtreibungsgegner, *der*/Abtreibungsgegnerin, *die*; **~-abortion protest/law** Protest/Gesetz gegen Abtreibung; **~-abortion demonstration/movement** Antiabtreibungsdemonstration, *die*/-bewegung, *die*; **~-abortionist** /æntɪə'bɔːʃənɪst/ *n.* Abtreibungsgegner, *der*/-gegnerin, *die*; **~-'aircraft** *adj.* (Mil.) Flugabwehr-; **~-aircraft gun** Flak, *die*; **~-aircraft battery** Flakbatterie, *die*; **~-a'partheid** *adj.* Antiapartheid‹*bewegung, -gruppe usw.*›

antibiotic /æntɪbaɪ'ɒtɪk/

A *adj.* antibiotisch

B *n.* Antibiotikum, *das*

'antibody *n.* (Physiol.) Antikörper, *der*

antic /'æntɪk/ *n.* (trick) Mätzchen, *das* (ugs.); (of clown) Possen, *der*

Antichrist /'æntɪkraɪst/ *n.* Antichrist, *der*

anticipate /æn'tɪsɪpeɪt/ *v.t.* 1▸ (expect) erwarten; (foresee) voraussehen; **~ rain/trouble** mit Regen/Ärger rechnen 2▸ (discuss or consider before due time) vorwegnehmen; antizipieren 3▸ (forestall) **~ sb./sth.** jmdm./einer Sache zuvorkommen

anticipation /æntɪsɪ'peɪʃn/ *n.*, *no pl.* Erwartung, *die*; **in ~ of sth.** in Erwartung einer Sache (*Gen.*); **she was looking forward to the event with ~:** sie sah dem Ereignis erwartungsvoll entgegen; **thanking you in ~:** Ihnen im Voraus dankend

anticipatory /æn'tɪsɪpətərɪ/ *adj.* vorwegnehmend

anti'clerical *adj.* antiklerikal; kirchenfeindlich

anticli'mactic *adj.* [auf enttäuschende Weise] abfallend; **the film has an ~ ending** der Film hat ein enttäuschendes Ende

anti'climax *n.* 1▸ (ineffective end) Abstieg, *der*; Abfall, *der* 2▸ (Lit.) Antiklimax, *die*

anti'clockwise

A *adv.* gegen den Uhrzeigersinn

B *adj.* gegen den *od.* entgegen dem Uhrzeigersinn *nachgestellt*; linksläufig (Technik); **in an ~ direction** gegen den *od.* entgegen dem Uhrzeigersinn

anti-com'petitive *adj.* wettbewerbswidrig

anticor'rosive *adj.* Rostschutz-

anti'cyclone *n.* (Meteorol.) Hochdruckgebiet, *das*; Antizyklone, *die* (Met.)

antidepressant /æntɪdɪ'presənt/ *n.* (Med.) Antidepressivum, *das*

antidote /'æntɪdəʊt/ *n.* Gegengift, -mittel, *das* (**for, against** gegen); (fig.) Gegenmittel, *das* (**to** gegen)

'antifreeze *n.* Gefrierschutzmittel, *das*; Frostschutzmittel, *das*

antigen /'æntɪdʒən/ *n.* (Physiol.) Antigen, *das*

anti'glare *adj.* blendfrei; Antiblend‹*filter, -beschichtung*›; **~ protection** Blendschutz, *der*

antiglobalization /æntɪgləʊbəlaɪ'zeɪʃn/ *n.*, *no pl.* Antiglobalisierung, *die*

'anti-hero *n.* Antiheld, *der*

anti'histamine *n.* (Med.) Antihistamin[ikum], *das*

anti-in'flammatory

A *n.* entzündungshemmendes Mittel; Antiphlogistikum, *das* (fachspr.)

B *adj.* entzündungshemmend; antiphlogistisch (fachspr.)

anti-in'flationary *adj.* antiinflationär

'antiknock *n.* (Motor Veh.) Antiklopfmittel, *das*

Antilles /æn'tɪliːz/ *pr. n. pl.* Antillen *Pl.*

'anti-lock *adj.* Antiblockier-; **~ brake** *or* **braking system** Antiblockiersystem, *das*

antimacassar /æntɪmə'kæsə(r)/ *n.* Schonbezug, *der*

'antimatter *n.* (Phys.) Antimaterie, *die*

anti-'missile *adj.* Antiraketen-; **~ defence system** Raketenabwehrsystem, *das*

antimony /'æntɪmənɪ/ *n.* Antimon, *das*

antinomy /æn'tɪnəmɪ/ *n.* Antinomie, *die*

'anti-novel *n.* Antiroman, *der*

anti'nuclear *adj.* Anti-Atom[kraft]-

'antiparticle *n.* (Phys.) Antiteilchen, *das*

antipathetic /æntɪpə'θetɪk/, **antipathetical** /æntɪpə'θetɪkl/ *adj.* 1▸ (averse, opposed) **be ~ to sb./sth.** jmdm./einer Sache abgeneigt sein; eine Antipathie gegen jmdn./etw. haben 2▸ (arousing antipathy) **be ~ to sb.** jmdm. zuwider sein

antipathy /æn'tɪpəθɪ/ *n.* Antipathie, *die*; Abneigung, *die*; **~ to** *or* **for sb./sth.** Abneigung gegen jmdn./etw.

anti-person'nel *adj.* gegen Menschen gerichtet; **~ bomb** Splitterbombe, *die*; **~ mine** Schützenmine, *die*

antiperspirant /æntɪ'pɜːspɪrənt/

A *adj.* schweißhemmend; **~ spray** Deodorantspray, *der od. das*

B *n.* Antitranspirant, *das*

antiphonal /æn'tɪfənəl/ *adj.* (Eccl. Mus.) **~ singing** Wechselgesang, *der*

antipodal /æn'tɪpədl/ *adj.* (Australasian) australisch und ozeanisch

antipodean /æntɪpəˈdiːən/ *adj.* ▸ **antipodal**

antipodes /ænˈtɪpədiːz/ *n. pl.* entgegengesetzte *od.* antipodische Teile der Erde; (Australasia) Australien und Ozeanien

ˈantipope *n.* (Hist.) Gegenpapst, *der*

antiquarian /æntɪˈkweərɪən/

A *adj.* **1** (of antiquity) antik; Altertums-; **~ research** Altertumsforschung, *die;* **~ writings** antike Schriften; **~ society** Gesellschaft für Altertumsforschung **2** **~ bookshop** *or* **bookseller's** Antiquariat, *das;* Antiquariatsbuchhandlung, *die;* **~ bookseller** ▸**i** **p. 1260** Antiquar, *der;* Antiquariatsbuchhändler, *der*

B *n.* (collector) Antiquitätensammler, *der*

antiquarianism /æntɪˈkweərɪənɪzm/ *n., no pl.* Liebhaberei für Altertümer; Altertümelei, *die* (auch abwertend)

ˈantiquark *n.* (Phys.) Antiquark, *das*

antiquary /ˈæntɪkwərɪ/ ▸ **antiquarian B**

antiquated /ˈæntɪkweɪtɪd/ *adj.* (old-fashioned) antiquiert; veraltet; (out of date) überholt

antique /ænˈtiːk/

A *adj.* **1** antik ‹*Möbel, Schmuck usw.*›; (as an **~**) antiquarisch ‹*Wert, Bedeutung*›; **furniture of ~ design** Möbel im antiken Stil **2** (existing since old times) antik ‹*Philosophie, Literatur, Kultur, Volk, Kunst, Ideen*›; (antiquated) altertümlich ‹*Sprache, Ansicht, Verhalten*›

B *n.* ▸**i** **p. 1260** Antiquität, *die; attrib.* **~ dealer** Antiquitätenhändler, *der/*-händlerin, *die;* **~ shop** Antiquitätenladen, *der*

antiquity /ænˈtɪkwɪtɪ/ *n.* **1** *no pl.* (ancientness) Alter, *das;* **a city/law/fossil of great ~:** eine uralte Stadt/ein uraltes Gesetz/Fossil **2** *no pl., no art.* (old times) Altertum, *das;* Antike, *die;* (the ancients) Antike, *die;* **in ~:** im Altertum; in der Antike **3** *in pl.* (ancient relics) Altertümer *Pl.;* (ancient customs) altertümliche Bräuche

anti-ˈroll bar ▸ **roll bar**

antirrhinum /æntɪˈraɪnəm/ *n.* (Bot.) Löwenmaul, *das*

anti-ˈSemite *n.* Antisemit, *der/*-semitin, *die;* Judenfeind, *der/*-feindin, *die*

anti-Seˈmitic *adj.* antisemitisch; judenfeindlich

anti-Semitism /æntɪˈsemɪtɪzm/ *n., no pl.* Antisemitismus, *der;* Judenhass, *der*

antiˈsepsis *n., no pl.* (Med.) Antisepsis, *die*

antiˈseptic

A *adj.* **1** antiseptisch; keimtötend **2** (scrupulously clean) aseptisch; keimfrei; (sterile) keimfrei; steril; (fig.: unfeeling) gefühllos

B *n.* Antiseptikum, *das*

anti-ˈsmoking *adj.* Antirauch[er]‹*gesetz, -kampagne*›

antiˈsocial *adj.* **1** asozial **2** (unsociable) ungesellig ‹*Person*›; unwirtlich ‹*Ort*›

antisocial beˈhaviour order *n.* (Brit.) Verfügung gegen antisoziales Verhalten

antiˈstatic *adj.* antistatisch

anti-ˈtank gun *n.* (Mil.) Panzerabwehrkanone, *die*

anti: ~-ˈterrorist *attrib. adj.* antiterroristisch; **~-ˈtheft** *attrib. adj.* Antidiebstahl-

antithesis /ænˈtɪθəsɪs/ *n., pl.* **antitheses** /ænˈtɪθəsiːz/ **1** (thing) Gegenstück, *das* (**of, to** zu); **these two concepts are the ~ of each other** diese beiden Begriffe sind Gegensätze **2** (state) Gegensatz, *der;* (Rhet.: contrast of ideas) Antithese, *die;* **stand in ~ to sth.** einer Sache (*Dat.*) antithetisch gegenüberstehen; **the ~ of** *or* **between two things** der Gegensatz zwischen zwei Dingen

antithetic /æntɪˈθetɪk/, **antithetical** /æntɪˈθetɪkl/ *adj.* **1** (opposite) gegensätzlich; (consisting of opposites) antithetisch; **be ~ to sth.** zu einer Sache im Gegensatz stehen **2** (Rhet.) antithetisch

antiˈtoxin *n.* (Med.) Antitoxin, *das*

antiˈtrust *adj.* (esp. Amer.) Kartell-; Antitrust-; **~trust law** Kartellgesetz, *das*

antiˈvirus *attrib. adj.* (Computing) Antivirus-; **~virus software** Antivirensoftware, *die*

antivivisectionism /æntɪvɪvɪˈsekʃənɪzm/ *n., no pl.* Ablehnung der Vivisektion

antivivisectionist /æntɪvɪvɪˈsekʃənɪst/ *n.* Vivisektionsgegner, *der/*-gegnerin, *die*

anti-ˈwar *adj.* Antikriegs‹*demonstration, -bewegung*›

antler /ˈæntlə(r)/ *n.* (branch of horn) Geweihsprosse, *die;* (horn) Stange, *die* (Jägerspr.); **a pair of ~s** ein Geweih *od.* (Jägerspr.) Gehörn

antonym /ˈæntənɪm/ *n.* Antonym, *das;* Gegen[satz]wort, *das*

antonymous /ænˈtɒnɪməs/ *adj.* antonym

Antwerp /ˈæntwɜːp/ *pr. n.* ▸**i** **p. 1643** Antwerpen (*das*)

anus /ˈeɪnəs/ *n.* (Anat.) After, *der;* Anus, *der*

anvil /ˈænvɪl/ *n.* (also Anat.) Amboss, *der*

anxiety /æŋˈzaɪətɪ/ *n.* **1** (state) Angst, *die;* (concern about future) Sorge, *die* (**about** wegen); **anxieties** Sorgen *Pl.;* **cause sb. ~:** jmdm. Angst/Sorgen machen **2** (desire) Verlangen, *das* (**for** nach); **his ~ to do sth.** sein Verlangen danach, etw. zu tun

anxious /ˈæŋkʃəs/ *adj.* **1** (troubled) besorgt; **days of ~ waiting** Tage bangen Wartens; **be ~ about sth./sb.** um etw./jmdn. besorgt sein; **we were all so ~ about you** wir haben uns (*Dat.*) alle solche Sorgen um Sie gemacht **2** (eager) sehnlich; **be ~ for sth.** ungeduldig auf etw. (*Akk.*) warten; **have an ~ desire to do sth.** ängstlich darauf bedacht sein, etw. zu tun; **he is ~ to please** er ist bemüht zu gefallen; **he is ~ to learn another language** er will unbedingt noch eine Sprache lernen **3** (worrying) **an ~ time** eine Zeit banger Sorge; **two ~ days of waiting** zwei Tage bangen Wartens

anxiously /ˈæŋkʃəslɪ/ *adv.* **1** besorgt **2** (eagerly) sehnsüchtig; **always ~ eager to help** immer eifrig darauf bedacht, zu helfen

any /ˈenɪ/

A *adj.* **1** (some) [irgend]ein/eine; **have you ~ wool/~ statement to make?** haben Sie Wolle/[irgend]eine Erklärung abzugeben?; **if you have ~ difficulties** wenn du irgendwelche Schwierigkeiten hast; **not ~:** kein/keine; **that isn't ~ way to behave** das ist keine Art, sich zu benehmen; **without ~:** ohne jeden/jede/jedes; **if you've ~ spare time** *or* **time to spare** wenn du Zeit hast *od.* hättest; **we haven't ~ time to lose** wir haben keine Zeit zu verlieren; **have you ~ idea of the time?** hast du eine Ahnung, wie spät es ist?; **~ news of Peter yet?** schon was von Peter gehört? **2** (one) ein/eine; **there isn't ~ hood on this coat** dieser Mantel hat keine Kapuze; **a book without ~ cover** ein Buch ohne Deckel **3** (all) jeder/jede/jedes; **to avoid ~ delay** um jede Verzögerung zu vermeiden **4** (every) jeder/jede/jedes; **~ and every** jeder/jede/jedes beliebige; **~ fool knows that!** das weiß doch jedes Kind!; **~ time** *or* **on ~ occasion [when] I went there** jedes Mal *od.* immer, wenn ich dorthin ging; **[at] ~ time** jederzeit; **[at] ~ time of day** zu jeder Tageszeit **5** (whichever) jeder/jede/jedes [beliebige]; **choose ~ book/~ books you like** suchen Sie sich (*Dat.*) irgendein Buch/irgendwelche Bücher aus; **choose ~ two numbers** nimm zwei beliebige Zahlen; **do it ~ way you like** machen Sie es, wie immer Sie wollen; **cook the meat [in] ~ way/[for] ~ length of time you wish** kochen Sie das Fleisch, wie/so lange Sie wollen; **visit us [at] ~ time** besuchen Sie uns, wann [immer] Sie wollen; **~ day/minute [now]** jeden Tag/jede Minute; **[at] any time [now]** jederzeit; **~ moment now the bomb will explode** die Bombe wird jeden Moment explodieren; **you can count on him ~ time** (coll.) du kannst dich jederzeit auf ihn verlassen; **I'd prefer Mozart ~ day** (coll.) ich würde Mozart allemal (ugs.) *od.* jederzeit vorziehen; **not [just] ~ house** nicht irgendein beliebiges Haus; **take ~ amount you wish** nehmen Sie, so viel Sie wollen; **~ amount of** jede Menge (ugs.); **the room was filled with ~ amount of decorations/~ number of film stars** das Zimmer war reich geschmückt/in dem Zimmer war ein Heer von Filmstars; *see also* **case¹ 1; old A 4; rate A 6** **6** (an appreciable) ein nennenswerter/eine nennenswerte/ein nennenswertes; **she didn't stay ~ length of time** sie ist nicht sehr lange geblieben; **he couldn't walk ~ distance without feeling exhausted** er konnte keine längere Strecke gehen, ohne sich erschöpft zu fühlen; **if he drinks ~ amount he gets roaring drunk** wenn er einmal etwas mehr trinkt, ist er gleich sternhagelvoll (salopp)

B *pron.* **1** (some) *in condit., interrog., or neg. sentence* (replacing sing. n.) einer/eine/ein[e]s; (replacing collect. n.) welcher/welche/welches; (replacing pl. n.) welche; **not ~:** keiner/keine/kein[e]s/*Pl.* keine; **without ~:** ohne; **I need to buy some sugar, we haven't got ~ at the moment** ich muss Zucker kaufen, wir haben im Augenblick keinen; **Here are some sweets. Would you like ~?** Hier sind ein paar Bonbons. Möchtest du welche?; **they ate all the cake and didn't leave ~ for us** *or* **without leaving ~ for us** sie haben den ganzen Kuchen gegessen und uns nichts übrig gelassen; **hardly ~:** kaum welche/etwas; **Tea? No, I don't want ~ at the moment, thanks** Tee? Nein danke, im Moment nicht; **not known to ~ except ...:** keinem *od.* niemandem bekannt außer ...; **Here is a list of the books I need. Do you have ~ of them in stock?** Hier ist eine Liste mit den Büchern, die ich brauche. Haben Sie [irgend]welche davon vorrätig?; **I haven't seen ~ of my friends for years** ich habe seit Jahren keinen von meinen Freunden gesehen; **is there ~ of that cake left?** ist noch etwas [von dem] Kuchen übrig?; **is there ~ of you who would be willing to help?** wäre irgendjemand von Ihnen bereit zu helfen?; **he is not having ~ of it** (fig. coll.) er will nichts davon wissen **2** (no matter which) irgendeiner/irgendeine/irgendein[e]s/irgendwelche *Pl.;* **you have to pick a number between 1 and 10, ~ you like** du musst eine Zahl zwischen 1 und 10 ziehen, irgendeine; **you can choose three books, ~ you like** Sie können sich (*Dat.*) drei Bücher aussuchen, egal welche; **Which numbers? — A~ between 1 and 10** Welche Zahlen? — Irgendwelche zwischen 1 und 10

C *adv.* **do you feel ~ better today?** fühlen Sie sich heute [etwas] besser?; **if it gets ~ colder** wenn es noch kälter wird; **he didn't seem ~ [the] wiser after that** danach schien er auch nicht klüger zu sein; **I can't wait ~ longer** ich kann nicht [mehr] länger warten; **the occasional jokes do not make the book ~ [the] less boring** durch die gelegentlichen Witze wird das Buch keineswegs interessanter; **I don't feel ~ [the] better** mir ist kein bisschen wohler; **not ~ too happy about it** nicht gerade glücklich darüber; *see also* **more A 1, C 4, 9**

ˈanybody *n. & pron.* **1** (whoever) jeder; **~ and everybody** jeder Beliebige **2** (somebody) [irgend]jemand; **how could ~ be so cruel?** wie kann man nur so grausam sein?; **there wasn't ~ willing to help** es war niemand bereit zu helfen; **there's never ~ at home when I phone** es ist nie jemand zu Hause, wenn ich anrufe; **I've never seen ~ who ...:** ich habe noch keinen gesehen, der ...; **he is a match for ~ with his strength** bei seiner Kraft kann er sich mit jedem *od.* jedermann messen; **~ but** jeder[mann] außer; **The score is 1 : 1. It's ~'s match now** Es steht 1 : 1. Das Spiel ist jetzt offen; **what will happen is ~'s guess** was geschehen wird, [das] weiß keiner; **he's not [just] ~:** er ist nicht [einfach] irgendwer **3** (important person) jemand; wer (ugs.); **everybody who was ~ was there** alles, was Rang und Namen hatte, war da

ˈanyhow *adv.* **1** ▸ **anyway** **2** (haphazardly) irgendwie; **he dresses ~:** er kleidet sich ohne Überlegung; **the furniture was arranged ~:** die Möbel waren wahllos irgendwo hingestellt; **all ~:** ganz unordentlich

ˈanyone ▸ **anybody**

ˈanyplace (Amer. coll.) ▸ **anywhere**

ˈanything

A *n. & pron.* **1** (whatever thing) was [immer]; alles, was; **you may do ~ you wish** Sie können [alles] tun, was Sie möchten; **~ and everything** alles Mögliche **2** (something) irgendetwas; **is there ~ wrong with you?** fehlt Ihnen

[irgend] etwas?; **have you done ~ silly?** hast du [irgend]etwas Dummes gemacht?; **can we do ~ to help you?** können wir Ihnen irgendwie helfen?; **I don't want ~ [further] to do with him** ich möchte nichts [mehr] mit ihm zu tun haben; **I've never seen ~ like it in my life** ich habe noch nie in meinem Leben so etwas gesehen; **he can hardly see ~ without his glasses** ohne seine Brille kann er kaum etwas sehen **3** (a thing of any kind) alles; **~ like that** so etwas; **as ... as ~** (coll.) wahnsinnig ... (ugs.); **not for ~ [in the world]** um nichts in der Welt; **I will do ~ in my power to help you** ich werde alles tun, was in meiner Macht steht, um Ihnen zu helfen; **the temperature is ~ from 30 to 40 degrees** die Temperatur liegt irgendwo zwischen 30 und 40 Grad; **~ but** (~ except) alles außer; (far from) alles andere als; **Cheap? The house was ~ but!** Billig war das Haus? Von wegen!; **prices are rising like ~** (coll.) die Preise steigen wie nur was *od.* wie verrückt (ugs.); **we don't want [just] ~:** wir wollen nicht einfach irgendetwas [Beliebiges]
B *adv.* **not ~ like as ... as** keineswegs so ... wie

'anyway *adv.* **1** (in any case, besides) sowieso; **we wouldn't accept your help ~:** wir würden von Ihnen sowieso keine Hilfe annehmen **2** (at any rate) jedenfalls; **~, I must go now** wie dem auch sei, ich muss jetzt gehen

'anywhere
A *adv.* **1** (in any place) (wherever) überall, wo; wo [immer]; (somewhere) irgendwo; **can you see my bag ~?** siehst du meine Tasche irgendwo?; **the price could be ~ between £30 and £40** der Preis könnte irgendwo zwischen 30 Pfund und 40 Pfund liegen; **not ~ near as ... as** (coll.) nicht annähernd so ... wie; **~ but ...:** überall, außer ...; überall, nur nicht ...; **[just] ~:** überall; **not just ~:** nicht überall **2** (to any place) (wherever) wohin [auch immer]; (somewhere) irgendwohin; **have you ever been ~ by plane?** sind Sie je mit dem Flugzeug [irgendwohin] geflogen?; **I wouldn't go ~ near that island again** ich würde nicht wieder auch nur in die Nähe der Insel fahren; **~ but ...:** überallhin, außer ...; überallhin, nur nicht ...; **[just] ~:** [einfach] irgendwohin
B *pron.* **if there's ~ you'd like to see** wenn es irgendetwas gibt, was du sehen möchtest; **have you found ~ to live yet?** haben Sie schon eine Wohnung gefunden?; **is there ~ we can stay for the night?** können wir hier irgendwo übernachten?; **there's never ~ open for milk after 6 p.m.** nach 18 Uhr kann man nirgends mehr Milch bekommen; **~ but ...:** überall, außer ...; **[just] ~:** irgendein x-beliebiger Ort; **from ~ hot** von irgendwo, wo es warm ist; **from ~ in the world** aus aller Welt

AOB *abbr.* **= any other business** Sonstiges

aorta /eɪˈɔːtə/ *n.* (Anat.) Aorta, *die*

apace /əˈpeɪs/ *adv.* (arch./literary) rasch; geschwind (veralt.)

apart /əˈpɑːt/ *adv.* **1** (separately) getrennt; **with one's legs ~:** mit gespreizten Beinen; **a few problems ~:** einige Probleme ausgenommen; **~ from ...** (except for) außer ...; bis auf ... (+ *Akk.*); (in addition to) außer ...; **everybody ~ from one person** alle außer einem; **a race ~:** ein Volk für sich **2** (into pieces) auseinander; **he took the engine ~:** er nahm den Motor auseinander; **the toy came ~ in his hands** das Spielzeug zerbrach in seinen Händen; **take ~** (fig.) (criticize) auseinander nehmen (ugs.) ‹*Theaterstück, Theoretiker, Politiker*›; (analyse) zergliedern; (coll.: defeat) vernichtend schlagen; **take a poem/play/book ~:** ein Gedicht/Stück/Buch zergliedern *od.* [im Einzelnen] analysieren **3** **~ [from]** (to a distance) weg [von]; (at a distance) **ten kilometres ~:** zehn Kilometer voneinander entfernt; **they have moved far ~ from each other** sie sind weit voneinander weggezogen; **they are miles** *or* **worlds ~ [from each other] in their tastes** zwischen ihren Geschmäckern liegen Welten

apartheid /əˈpɑːteɪt/ *n., no pl., no art.* Apartheid, *die;* (fig.) Diskriminierung, *die*

apartment /əˈpɑːtmənt/ *n.* **1** (room) Apartment, *das;* Appartement, *das;* **~s** (in a mansion etc.) Räume *Pl.;* Räumlichkeiten *Pl.* **2** (esp. Amer.) Wohnung, *die;* **~ block** Wohnhaus, *das;* **~ house** Appartementhaus, *das*

apathetic /æpəˈθetɪk/ *adj.* apathisch (**about** gegenüber); (not feeling emotion) gleichgültig

apathetically /æpəˈθetɪkəlɪ/ *adv.* apathisch; (without emotion) gleichgültig

apathy /ˈæpəθɪ/ *n., no pl.* Apathie, *die* (**about** gegenüber); (lack of emotion) Gleichmut, *der*

APB *abbr.* (Amer.) **= all-points bulletin**

ape /eɪp/
A *n.* **1** (tailless monkey) [Menschen]affe, *der;* (monkey) Affe, *der;* **man is descended from the ~s** der Mensch stammt vom Affen ab **2** (imitator) Nachahmer, *der;* Nachäffer, *der* (abwertend) **3** (apelike person) Affe, *der;* **go ~** (coll.) verrückt werden (ugs.); durchdrehen (ugs.)
B *v.t.* nachahmen; nachäffen (abwertend)

apelike /ˈeɪplaɪk/ *adj.* wie ein Affe *nachgestellt*

Apennines /ˈæpɪnaɪnz/ *pr. n. pl.* Apenninen *Pl.*

aperçu /æpɜːˈsjuː/ *n.* **1** (summary) kurzer Überblick (**of** über + *Akk.*) **2** (insight) Aperçu, *das*

aperient /əˈpɪərɪənt/ (Med.)
A *adj.* abführend; **this preparation is mildly/strongly ~:** dieses Präparat ist ein schwaches/starkes Abführmittel
B *n.* Abführmittel, *das*

aperitif /əˈperɪtiːf, əperɪˈtiːf/ *n.* Aperitif, *der*

aperture /ˈæpətʃə(r)/ *n.* **1** (opening) Öffnung, *die* **2** (Optics, Photog., etc.) Blende, *die*

apex /ˈeɪpeks/ *n., pl.* **~es** *or* **apices** /ˈeɪpɪsiːz/ (tip) Spitze, *die;* (of heart, lung, etc.) Spitze, *die;* Apex, *der* (fachspr.); (fig.) Gipfel, *der;* Höhepunkt, *der*

APEX /ˈeɪpeks/ *abbr.* **= Advance Purchase Excursion** *reduzierter Flugtarif bei Vorauszahlung*

apfelstrudel /ˈæpfəlstruːdl/ *n.* Apfelstrudel, *der*

aphasia /əˈfeɪzɪə/ *n.* (Med.) Aphasie, *die*

aphelion /æpˈhiːlɪən/ *n., pl.* **aphelia** /æpˈhiːlɪə/ (Astron.) Aphel, *das;* **at ~:** im Aphel

aphid /ˈeɪfɪd/ *n.* (Zool.) Blattlaus, *die*

aphorism /ˈæfərɪzm/ *n.* (pithy statement) Aphorismus, *der;* (maxim) Maxime, *die*

aphoristic /æfəˈrɪstɪk/ *adj.* aphoristisch

aphrodisiac /æfrəˈdɪzɪæk/ (Med.)
A *adj.* aphrodisisch
B *n.* Aphrodisiakum, *das*

apiarist /ˈeɪpɪərɪst/ *n.* ▸ **i** **p. 1260** Bienenzüchter, *der;* Imker, *der*

apiary /ˈeɪpɪərɪ/ *n.* Bienenhaus, *das*

apices *pl. of* **apex**

apiece /əˈpiːs/ *adv.* je; **we took two bags ~:** wir nahmen je zwei Beutel; **they cost a penny ~:** die kosten einen Penny das Stück; **books/five books at £1 ~:** jedes Buch ein Pfund/fünf Bücher zu je einem Pfund

apish /ˈeɪpɪʃ/ *adj.* **1** (apelike) affenartig **2** (imitative) sklavisch [nachahmend] **3** (silly) affig (ugs.)

aplenty /əˈplentɪ/ *adv.* in [Hülle und] Fülle

aplomb /əˈplɒm/ *n.* Sicherheit [im Auftreten]; Aplomb, *der* (geh.)

apnoea /æpˈniːə/ *n.* (Med.) Apnoe, *die*

apocalypse /əˈpɒkəlɪps/ *n.* **1** (event) Apokalypse, *die* **2** (Relig.) (revelation) Offenbarung, *die;* (book) Apokalypse, *die;* Offenbarung, *die*

apocalyptic /əpɒkəˈlɪptɪk/ *adj.* **1** (dramatic) apokalyptisch **2** (Relig.) (of revelation) apokalyptisch; (of book) Offenbarungs-; der Offenbarung *nachgestellt*

Apocrypha /əˈpɒkrɪfə/ *n.* (Bibl.) Apokryphen *Pl.*

apocryphal /əˈpɒkrɪfl/ *adj.* **1** (of doubtful origin) apokryph; zweifelhaft; (invented) apokryph; unecht **2** (of the Apocrypha) apokryph

apogee /ˈæpədʒiː/ *n.* **1** (highest point) Höhepunkt, *der;* Gipfel[punkt], *der* **2** (Astron.) Apogäum, *das;* Erdferne, *die*

apolitical /eɪpəˈlɪtɪkl/ *adj.* apolitisch; unpolitisch

Apollo /əˈpɒləʊ/ *pr. n.* Apoll[o], *der*

apologetic /əpɒləˈdʒetɪk/ *adj.* **1** entschuldigend; **~ words** Worte der Entschuldigung; **an ~ person** jmd., der sich dauernd entschuldigt; **he wrote a very ~ letter** er schrieb einen Brief, in dem er sich vielmals entschuldigte; **he was most ~ about ...:** er entschuldigte sich vielmals für ... **2** (diffident) zaghaft ‹*Lächeln, Ton*›; zurückhaltend, bescheiden ‹*Wesen, Art*›

apologetically /əpɒləˈdʒetɪkəlɪ/ *adv.* **1** entschuldigend; **he wrote very ~ to say that he ...:** er schrieb mit großem Bedauern, dass er ... **2** (diffidently) zaghaft; bescheiden

apologetics /əpɒləˈdʒetɪks/ *n. sing. or pl.* Apologetik, *die*

apologia /æpəˈləʊdʒɪə/ *n.* Apologie, *die*

apologist /əˈpɒlədʒɪst/ *n.* Apologet, *der*/Apologetin, *die*

apologize /əˈpɒlədʒaɪz/ *v.i.* **1** ▸ **i** **p. 908** sich entschuldigen; **~ to sb. for sth./sb.** sich bei jmdm. für etw./jmdn. entschuldigen **2** (defend one's actions) sich rechtfertigen

apology /əˈpɒlədʒɪ/ *n.* **1** ▸ **i** **p. 908** Entschuldigung, *die;* **make an ~ [to sb.] for sth.** sich für etw. [bei jmdm.] entschuldigen; **an ~ to sb. for sth.** eine Entschuldigung bei jmdm. für etw.; **you owe him an ~/he deserves an ~ from you** Sie müssen sich bei ihm entschuldigen; **please accept our apologies** wir bitten vielmals um Entschuldigung; **she was full of apologies for her mistake** sie entschuldigte sich vielmals für ihren Fehler **2** (defence) Rechtfertigung, *die* **3** (poor substitute) **an ~ for a ...:** ein erbärmliches Exemplar von ...; **what's this ~ for a meal?** was ist denn das für eine kärgliche *od.* armselige Mahlzeit?

apoplectic /æpəˈplektɪk/ *adj.* apoplektisch; **~ stroke** *or* **fit** Schlaganfall, *der*

apoplexy /ˈæpəpleksɪ/ *n.* Apoplexie, *die* (fachspr.); Schlaganfall, *der;* **a fit of ~:** ein Schlaganfall

apostasy /əˈpɒstəsɪ/ *n.* Apostasie, *die*

apostate /əˈpɒsteɪt/
A *n.* Abtrünnige, *der/die;* Renegat, *der;* Apostat, *der* (Rel.)
B *adj.* abtrünnig; [von einer Partei/Glaubensrichtung] abgefallen

a posteriori /eɪ pɒsterɪˈɔːraɪ/
A *adv.* a posteriori
B *adj.* aposteriorisch

apostle /əˈpɒsl/ *n.* (lit. or fig.) Apostel, *der;* **the A~s** die [zwölf] Apostel; **A~s' Creed** Apostolisches Glaubensbekenntnis; Apostolikum, *das* (fachspr.)

apostolic /æpəˈstɒlɪk/ *adj.* apostolisch

apostrophe /əˈpɒstrəfɪ/ *n.* **1** (sign) Apostroph, *der;* Auslassungszeichen, *das* **2** (Rhet.: exclamatory passage) Apostrophe, *die*

apostrophize /əˈpɒstrəfaɪz/ *v.t.* apostrophieren

apothecary /əˈpɒθɪkərɪ/ *n.* **1** (arch.) Apotheker, *der*/Apothekerin, *die* **2** **apothecaries' measure/weight** Apothekermaß/-gewicht, *das*

apotheosis /əpɒθɪˈəʊsɪs/ *n., pl.* **apotheoses** /əpɒθɪˈəʊsiːz/ **1** (ultimate point) Gipfelpunkt, *der;* Apotheose, *die* (geh.) **2** (deification) Apotheose, *die* (auch fig.); Vergöttlichung, *die*

app. *abbr.* **1** **= appendix** Anh. **2** (Computing) **= application**

appal (*Amer.:* **appall**) /əˈpɔːl/ *v.t.*, **-ll-** (dismay) entsetzen; (terrify) erschrecken; **your behaviour ~s me!** ich bin entsetzt über dein Benehmen!; **obscenity ~s her** sie empört sich über Obszönitäten

appalling /əˈpɔːlɪŋ/ *adj.* (dismaying) entsetzlich; (terrifying) schrecklich; (coll.: very bad) fürchterlich; scheußlich

apparatchik /æpəˈrɑːtʃɪk/ *n., pl.* **~s** *or* **~i** /æpəˈrɑːtʃɪkiː/ Apparatschik, *der*

apparatus /æpəˈreɪtəs/ *n.* (equipment) Gerät, *das;* (gymnastic ~) Geräte *Pl.;* (machinery, lit. or fig.) Apparat, *der;* **a piece of ~:** ein Apparat

apparel /əˈpærəl/
A *n.* Kleidung, *die;* Gewänder *Pl.* (geh.)
B *v.t.*, (Brit.) **-ll-** (arch.) gewanden (veralt.); kleiden (auch fig.)

apparent /əˈpærənt/ *adj.* **1** (clear) offensichtlich ‹*Ziel, Zweck, Wirkung, Begeisterung, Interesse*›;

a

ℹ Apologizing

Fairly formal

I owe you an apology or ***I must apologize for accusing you wrongly***
= Ich muss mich bei Ihnen entschuldigen, dass ich Sie fälschlich beschuldigt habe

Please accept my humble apology
= Ich bitte vielmals um Entschuldigung

I take back all that I said and apologize unreservedly
= Ich nehme alles zurück und bitte tausendmal um Entschuldigung

I greatly or ***very much regret that I have had to disappoint you***
= Ich bedaure sehr, dass ich Sie enttäuschen musste

I must ask you to forgive or ***excuse my mistake***
= Ich muss Sie für meinen Fehler um Verzeihung bitten

Please excuse my oversight
= Bitte entschuldigen Sie mein Versehen

Please forgive me for being so late with these birthday wishes
= Bitte entschuldigen Sie, dass diese Geburtstagswünsche so verspätet eintreffen

I must apologize for the delay in replying to your letter
= Ich muss mich entschuldigen, dass ich Ihren Brief erst so spät beantworte

I am sorry or ***I regret to have to inform you that ...***
= Ich muss Ihnen leider mitteilen, dass ..., Ich bedaure, Ihnen mitteilen zu müssen, dass ...

Less formal

I really am sorry that I've let you down
= Es tut mir aufrichtig Leid, dass ich dich im Stich gelassen habe

I'm sorry to be such a nuisance
= Tut mir Leid, dass ich dir so viel Mühe mache

***Sorry!* (e.g. when you bump into someone)**
= Entschuldigung!

Sorry to bother you, but can you tell me ...
= Entschuldigung, wenn ich störe, aber können Sie mir sagen ...

I'm sorry, but or ***Unfortunately I'll have to go now***
= Leider muss ich jetzt gehen

Sorry, but I can't help
= Tut mir Leid, da kann ich nicht helfen

Don't be cross that I haven't written before
= Sei mir nicht böse *or* Nimm es mir nicht übel, dass ich nicht früher geschrieben habe

Forgive me! It was all a stupid misunderstanding
= Verzeih! Es war alles nur ein dummes Missverständnis

offenbar ‹*Bedeutung, Wahrheit*›; **it soon became ~ that ...:** es zeigte sich bald, dass ...; **the meaning was/became clearly ~ to all of us** die Bedeutung war/wurde uns allen deutlich klar; **heir ~:** recht- *od.* gesetzmäßiger Erbe; **he is the heir ~ to the throne** er ist der rechtmäßige Thronfolger 2 (seeming) scheinbar; **be only ~:** nur scheinbar sein; **this was only the ~ truth** das schien nur die Wahrheit zu sein

apparently /əˈpærəntlɪ/ *adv.* 1 (clearly) offensichtlich; offenbar 2 (seemingly) scheinbar; **he was not asleep, but only ~ so** er schien nur zu schlafen

apparition /æpəˈrɪʃn/ *n.* 1 (appearance) [Geister]erscheinung, *die* 2 (ghost) Gespenst, *das*

appeal /əˈpiːl/
A *v.i.* 1 (Law etc.) Einspruch erheben *od.* einlegen (**to** bei); **~ to a court** bei einem Gericht Berufung einlegen; **~ against sth.** gegen etw. Einspruch/Berufung einlegen; **~ from a judgement** gegen ein Urteil Berufung einlegen 2 (refer) **~ to** verweisen auf ‹*Erkenntnisse, Tatsachen*› 3 (make earnest request) **~ to sb. for sth./to do sth.** jmdn. um etw. ersuchen/jmdn. ersuchen, etw. zu tun; **I ~ to you to give generously** ich appelliere an Sie *od.* ich ersuche Sie, großzügig zu spenden 4 (address oneself) **~ to sb./sth.** an jmdn./etw. appellieren; **this type of music ~s to the senses rather than the intellect** solche Musik spricht eher das Gefühl an als den Verstand 5 (be attractive) **~ to sb.** jmdm. zusagen; **how does that ~?** könnte dir das gefallen?; **this music does not ~ to their tastes** diese Musik ist nicht ihr Geschmack 6 (Cricket) Einspruch erheben
B *v.t.* überweisen ‹*Sache, Fall usw.*›
C *n.* 1 (Law etc.) Einspruch, *der* (**to** bei); (to higher court) Berufung, *die* (**to** bei); **an ~ against** *or* **from a judgement** Berufung gegen eine Entscheidung; **lodge an ~ with sb.** bei jmdm. Einspruch/Berufung einlegen; **acquittal on ~:** Freispruch in der Berufung; **right of ~:** Einspruchs-/Berufungsrecht, *das;* **there is no ~ against this decision** gegen diese Entscheidung gibt es keine Einspruchs-/Berufungsmöglichkeit; **Court of A~:** Berufungsgericht, *das;* Appellationsgericht, *das* (veralt.) 2 (attraction) Reiz, *der;* Anziehungskraft, *die;* **the ~ of the music is to the senses rather than the intellect** die Musik spricht eher das Gefühl an als den Verstand; **a Rolls Royce has a certain class ~:** ein Rolls Royce ist etwas für Standesbewusste 3 (imploring request) Appell, *der;* Aufruf, *der;* **an ~ to sb. for sth.** eine Bitte an jmdn. um etw.; **make an ~ to sb.** eine dringende Bitte an jmdn. richten; an jmdn. appellieren 4 (reference) Berufung, *die;* Verweisung, *die;* **make an ~ to sth.** sich auf etw. (*Akk.*) berufen; auf etw. (*Akk.*) verweisen 5 (Cricket) Einspruch, *der*

appealable /əˈpiːləbl/ *adj.* gerichtlich anfechtbar; appellabel (veralt.)

appealing /əˈpiːlɪŋ/ *adj.* 1 (imploring) flehend 2 (attractive) ansprechend ‹*Farbe, Geschichte, Stil*›; verlockend ‹*Essen, Idee*›; reizvoll ‹*Haus, Beruf, Baustil*›; angenehm ‹*Stimme, Charakter*›

appealingly /əˈpiːlɪŋlɪ/ *adv.* ansprechend

appear /əˈpɪə(r)/ *v.i.* 1 (become visible, be seen, arrive) erscheinen; ‹*Licht, Mond:*› auftauchen; ‹*Symptom, Darsteller:*› auftreten; (present oneself) auftreten; (Sport) spielen; **he was ordered to ~ at the police station/before the court** er wurde zum Polizeirevier geladen/vom Gericht vorgeladen; **he ~ed in court charged with murder** er stand wegen Mordes vor Gericht 2 (occur) vorkommen; ‹*Irrtum:*› vorkommen, auftreten; ‹*Ereignis:*› vorkommen, eintreten; (be manifest) ‹*Einstellung, Meinung:*› sich zeigen 3 (seem) **~ [to be] ...:** scheinen ... [zu sein]; **try to ~ relaxed** versuch, entspannt zu erscheinen; **you could at least ~ to be interested** du könntest zumindest so tun, als ob du interessiert wärest; **~ to do sth.** scheinen, etw. zu tun; **she only ~s to be asleep** es hat nur den Anschein, als schlafe sie 4 (be published) erscheinen; herauskommen

appearance /əˈpɪərəns/ *n.* 1 (becoming visible) Auftauchen, *das;* (of symptoms) Auftreten, *das;* (arrival) Erscheinen, *das;* (of performer, speaker, etc.) Auftritt, *der;* **make an** *or* **one's ~:** erscheinen; **make a public ~:** in der Öffentlichkeit auftreten; **put in an ~:** sich sehen lassen 2 (look) Äußere, *das;* **outward ~:** äußere Erscheinung; **~s** Äußerlichkeiten *Pl.;* **the house had a shabby ~:** das Haus hatte ein schäbiges Aussehen; **his ~ of being nervous** sein nervöses Auftreten; **to judge by ~s, to all ~s** allem Anschein nach; **for the sake of ~s, to keep up ~s** um den Schein zu wahren 3 (semblance) Anschein, *der;* **~s to the contrary, ...:** entgegen allem Anschein ...; **~s can be deceptive** der Schein trügt 4 (occurrence) Auftreten, *das;* Vorkommen, *das* 5 (publication) Veröffentlichung, *die;* Erscheinen, *das*

appease /əˈpiːz/ *v.t.* 1 (make calm) besänftigen; (Polit.) beschwichtigen 2 (soothe) lindern ‹*Leid, Schmerz, Not*›; mildern ‹*Beunruhigung, Erregung*›; (satisfy) befriedigen ‹*Verlangen, Lust*›; stillen ‹*Hunger, Durst*›

appeasement /əˈpiːzmənt/ *n.* ► **appease**: Besänftigung, *die;* Beschwichtigung, *die;* Linderung, *die;* Milderung, *die;* Befriedigung, *die;* Stillen, *das*

appellant /əˈpelənt/ (Law)
A *n.* Berufungskläger, *der*/-klägerin, *die;* Appellant, *der* (veralt.)
B *adj.* Berufungs-; Appellations- (veralt.)

appellate /əˈpelət/ *adj.* (Law) Berufungs-; Appellations- (veralt.); **~ judge/hearing** Berufungsrichter, *der*/-verfahren, *das*

appellation /æpəˈleɪʃn/ *n.* (name, nomenclature) Bezeichnung, *die;* (way of addressing) Anrede, *die*

append /əˈpend/ *v.t.* **~ sth. to sth.** etw. an etw. (*Akk.*) anhängen; (add) etw. einer Sache (*Dat.*) anfügen; **~ one's signature to a document** seine Unterschrift unter ein Dokument setzen

appendage /əˈpendɪdʒ/ *n.* 1 Anhängsel, *das;* (addition) Anhang, *der;* **he feels as if he has become a mere ~ to the household** er fühlt sich im Haus nur noch als fünftes Rad am Wagen 2 (accompaniment) Zu-, Beigabe, *die* (**to** zu)

appendectomy /æpenˈdektəmɪ/, **appendicectomy** /əpendɪˈsektəmɪ/ *ns.* (Med.) Blinddarmoperation, *die* (volkst.); Appendektomie, *die* (fachspr.)

appendices *pl. of* **appendix**

appendicitis /əpendɪˈsaɪtɪs/ *n.* ► ℹ **p. 1231** Blinddarmentzündung, *die* (volkst.); Appendizitis, *die* (fachspr.)

appendix /əˈpendɪks/ *n., pl.* **appendices** /əˈpendɪsiːz/ *or* **~es** 1 Anhang, *der* (**to** zu) 2 ► ℹ **p. 951** (Anat.) **[vermiform]** /ˈvɜːmɪfɔːm/ **~:** Blinddarm, *der* (volkst.); Wurmfortsatz [des Blinddarms]

appertain /æpəˈteɪn/ *v.i.* **~ to sth.** (relate) sich auf etw. (*Akk.*) beziehen; (belong) zu etw. gehören; (be appropriate) zu etw. dazugehören

appetite /ˈæpɪtaɪt/ *n.* 1 (for food) Appetit, *der* (**for** auf + *Akk.*); **~ for sex** Lust auf Sex 2 (fig.: desire) Verlangen, *das* (**for** nach); **~ for knowledge** Wissensdrang, *der;* Wissensdurst, *der;* **~ for life** Lebenshunger, *der;* Lebensgier, *die*

appetizer /ˈæpɪtaɪzə(r)/ *n.* Appetitanreger, *der;* (on menu) Vorspeise, *die;* **act as an/be an ~:** appetitanregend wirken

appetizing /ˈæpɪtaɪzɪŋ/ *adj.* appetitlich ‹*Anblick, Speise, Geruch*›; appetitanregend ‹*Getränk, Geschmack*›

appetizingly /ˈæpɪtaɪzɪŋlɪ/ *adv.* appetitanregend

applaud /əˈplɔːd/
A *v.i.* applaudieren; [Beifall] klatschen
B *v.t.* applaudieren (+ *Dat.*); Beifall spenden (+ *Dat.*); (approve of, welcome) billigen ‹*Entschluss*›; (praise) loben, anerkennen ‹*Versuch, Bemühungen*›

applause /əˈplɔːz/ *n.* Applaus, *der;* (praise) Lob, *das;* Anerkennung, *die;* **give ~:** Applaus *od.* Beifall spenden; **get ~:** Applaus *od.* Beifall ernten

apple /ˈæpl/ *n.* Apfel, *der;* **the ~ of sb.'s eye** (fig.) jmds. Liebling

apple: ~ 'brandy *n.* Apfelschnaps, *der;* **~ cart** *n.* **upset the ~ cart** (fig.) die Pferde *od.* Gäule scheu machen (ugs.); **~-'green A** *adj.* apfelgrün; **B** *n.* Apfelgrün, *das;* **~jack** (Amer.) ► **~ brandy; ~ 'pie** *n.* gedeckte Apfeltorte; *attrib.* **~ pie bed** *Bett, in dem das Betttuch aus Scherz so gefaltet ist, dass man die Beine nicht ausstrecken kann;* **in ~ pie order** picobello (ugs.); tadellos in Ordnung; **~ 'sauce** *n.* Apfelmus, *das*

applet /ˈæplɪt/ *n.* (Computing) Applet, *das*

'apple tree *n.* Apfelbaum, *der*

appliance /ə'plaɪəns/ *n.* (utensil) Gerät, *das;* (aid) Hilfsmittel, *das;* (fire engine) Feuerlöschfahrzeug, *das*

applicability /æplɪkə'bɪlɪtɪ/ *n.* [1] Anwendbarkeit, *die* (**to** auf + *Akk.*) [2] (appropriateness) Eignung, *die* (**to** für)

applicable /'æplɪkəbl, ə'plɪkəbl/ *adj.* [1] anwendbar (**to** auf + *Akk.*) [2] (appropriate) geeignet; angebracht; zutreffend ‹*Fragebogenteil usw.*›; **the ~ documents** die entsprechenden Unterlagen

applicant /'æplɪkənt/ *n.* Bewerber, *der*/Bewerberin, *die* (**for** um); (claimant) Antragsteller, *der*/Antragstellerin, *die*

application /æplɪ'keɪʃn/ *n.* [1] (putting) Auftragen, *das* (**to** auf + *Akk.*); (administering) Anwendung, *die;* (of heat, liquids) Zufuhr, *die;* (employment; of rule etc.) Anwendung, *die;* **the ~ of new technology** der Einsatz neuer Technologien; **this rule is of** *or* **has universal ~:** diese Regel beansprucht allgemeine Gültigkeit [2] (request) Bewerbung, *die* (**for** um); (for passport, licence, etc.) Antrag, *der* (**for** auf + *Akk.*); **~ form** Antragsformular, *das;* **available on ~:** auf Anfrage erhältlich; **~ for a passport** Antrag auf Erteilung eines Passes [3] (diligence) Fleiß, *der* (**to** bei); (with enthusiasm) Eifer, *der* (**to** für) [4] (Med.: lotion, poultice, etc.) Mittel, *das* [5] (Computing) Applikation, *die*

applicator /'æplɪkeɪtə(r)/ *n.* Applikator, *der*

appliqué /æ'pli:keɪ/
A *n.* Applikationsstickerei, *die*
B *adj.* appliziert

apply /ə'plaɪ/
A *v.t.* [1] anlegen ‹*Verband*›; auftragen ‹*Creme, Paste, Farbe*› (**to** auf + *Akk.*); zuführen ‹*Wärme, Flüssigkeit*› (**to** *Dat.*); **~ the brakes** bremsen; die Bremse betätigen; **~ gentle pressure to the tube** drücken Sie leicht auf die Tube; **~ pressure to sb.** (fig.) jmdn. unter Druck setzen [2] (make use of) anwenden; **applied linguistics/mathematics** angewandte Sprachwissenschaft/Mathematik [3] (devote) richten, lenken ‹*Gedanken, Überlegungen, Geist*› (**to** auf + *Akk.*); verwenden ‹*Zeit, Energie*› (**to** auf + *Akk.*); **~ oneself [to sth.]** sich (*Dat.*) Mühe geben [mit etw.]; sich [um etw.] bemühen; **~ oneself to a task** sich an eine Aufgabe machen
B *v.i.* [1] (have relevance) zutreffen (**to** auf + *Akk.*); (be valid) gelten; **things which don't ~ to us** Dinge, die uns nicht betreffen [2] (address oneself) **~ [to sb.] for sth.** [jmdn.] um etw. bitten *od.* (geh.) ersuchen; (for passport, licence, etc.) [bei jmdm.] etw. beantragen; (for job) sich [bei jmdm.] um etw. bewerben

appoint /ə'pɔɪnt/ *v.t.* [1] (fix) bestimmen; festlegen ‹*Zeitpunkt, Ort*›; **~ that ...** (formal) anordnen, dass ... [2] (choose for a job) einstellen; (assign to office) ernennen; **~ sb. [to be** *or* **as] sth./to do sth.** jmdn. zu etw. ernennen/jmdn. dazu berufen, etw. zu tun; **~ sb. to sth.** jmdn. in etw. (*Akk.*) einsetzen; **he was ~ed governor** er wurde zum Gouverneur bestellt *od.* ernannt; **~ sb. one's heir** jmdn. als seinen Erben einsetzen

appointed /ə'pɔɪntɪd/ *adj.* [1] (fixed) vereinbart; verabredet [2] **well/badly ~:** gut/schlecht ausgestattet *od.* eingerichtet ‹*Zimmer usw.*›

appointee /əpɔɪn'ti:/ *n.* Ernannte, *der/die;* Berufene, *der/die*

appointment /ə'pɔɪntmənt/ *n.* [1] (fixing) Festlegung, *die;* Festsetzung, *die* [2] (assigning to office) Ernennung, *die;* Berufung, *die;* (Law) Verfügung, *die* (**of** über + *Akk.*); (being assigned to office) Ernennung, *die* (**as** zum/zur); (to job) Einstellung, *die;* **~ to a position** Berufung auf einen Posten; **by ~ to Her Majesty the Queen, makers of fine confectionery** königlicher Hoflieferant für feines Konfekt [3] (office) Stelle, *die;* Posten, *der;* **a teaching ~:** eine Stelle als Lehrer/Lehrerin [4] (arrangement) Termin, *der;* **dental ~:** Termin beim Zahnarzt; **make an ~ with sb.** sich (*Dat.*) von jmdm. einen Termin geben lassen; **by ~:** nach Anmeldung; mit Voranmeldung [5] *usu. in pl.* (equipment etc.) Ausstattung, *die*

apportion /ə'pɔ:ʃn/ *v.t.* [1] (allot) **~ sth. to sb.** jmdm. etw. zuteilen [2] (portion out) [gleichmäßig] verteilen (**among** an + *Akk.*); aufteilen (**among** unter + *Akk.*)

apportionment /ə'pɔ:ʃnmənt/ *n.* [1] (allotting) Zuteilung, *die* (**to** an + *Akk.*) [2] (portioning out) Verteilung, *die* (**among** an + *Akk.*); Aufteilung, *die* (**among** unter + *Akk.*)

apposite /'æpəzɪt/ *adj.* (appropriate) passend; geeignet; (well chosen) treffend; **~ to sth.** zutreffend auf etw. (*Akk.*); **these remarks are very ~ to the matter** diese Bemerkungen treffen die Sache genau

appositely /'æpəzɪtlɪ/ *adv.* (appropriately) in passender *od.* geeigneter Weise

appositeness /'æpəzɪtnɪs/ *n., no pl.* (appropriateness) Angemessenheit, *die*

apposition /æpə'zɪʃn/ *n.* (Ling.) Apposition, *die;* **in ~ [to sth.]** in Apposition [zu etw.]

appraisal /ə'preɪzl/ *n.* (evaluation) Bewertung, *die;* (of property) Taxierung, *die;* Schätzung, *die;* **what ~ do you give/what is your ~ of the situation?** wie beurteilen Sie die Situation?

appraise /ə'preɪz/ *v.t.* (evaluate) bewerten; (value) schätzen; taxieren; **~ the extent of the damage** das Ausmaß des Schadens abschätzen

appreciable /ə'pri:ʃəbl/ *adj.* (perceptible) nennenswert ‹*Unterschied, Einfluss*›; spürbar ‹*Veränderung, Wirkung, Erfolg*›; merklich ‹*Verringerung, Anstieg*›; (considerable) beträchtlich; erheblich

appreciably /ə'pri:ʃəblɪ/ *adv.* (perceptibly) spürbar ‹*verändern*›; merklich ‹*sich unterscheiden*›; (considerably) beträchtlich; erheblich

appreciate /ə'pri:ʃɪeɪt, ə'pri:sɪeɪt/
A *v.t.* [1] ([correctly] estimate value or worth of) [richtig] einschätzen; (understand) verstehen; (be aware of) sich (*Dat.*) bewusst sein (+ *Gen.*); (be receptive to) Gefallen finden an (+ *Dat.*); **~ that/what ...:** verstehen, dass/was ... [2] (be grateful for) anerkennen; schätzen; (enjoy) genießen; **I'd really ~ that** das wäre sehr nett von dir; **a stamped addressed envelope would be ~d** bitte einen frankierten Rückumschlag beilegen
B *v.i.* im Wert steigen

appreciation /əpri:ʃɪ'eɪʃn, əpri:sɪ'eɪʃn/ *n.* [1] ([right] estimation) [richtige] Einschätzung; (understanding) Verständnis, *das* (**of** für); (awareness) Bewusstsein, *das;* (sensitivity) Sinn, *der* (**of** für) [2] (gratefulness) Dankbarkeit, *die;* (enjoyment) Gefallen, *das* (**of** an + *Dat.*); **in grateful ~ of** *or* **for your help** in dankbarer Anerkennung Ihrer Hilfe [3] (rise in value) Wertsteigerung, *die* [4] (review) [positive] Kritik; Würdigung, *die*

appreciative /ə'pri:ʃətɪv/ *adj.* [1] **be ~ of sth./sb.** (aware of) fähig sein, etw./jmdn. [richtig] einzuschätzen; **she is very ~ of music** sie hat viel Sinn für Musik [2] (grateful) dankbar (**of** für); (approving) anerkennend

apprehend /æprɪ'hend/ *v.t.* [1] (arrest) festnehmen; fassen [2] (perceive) wahrnehmen; vernehmen ‹*Stimme, Geräusch*›; einsehen ‹*Wahrheit*›; (understand) erfassen; begreifen [3] (anticipate) vorausahnen; befürchten ‹*Unglück*›

apprehension /æprɪ'henʃn/ *n.* [1] (arrest) Festnahme, *die;* Verhaftung, *die* [2] (uneasiness) Besorgnis, *die* [3] (conception) Auffassung, *die;* Ansicht, *die* (**of** über + *Akk.*); (understanding) Verständnis, *das*

apprehensive /æprɪ'hensɪv/ *adj.* (uneasy) besorgt; **~ of sth.** besorgt wegen etw.; **be ~ of doing sth.** ein ungutes Gefühl haben, etw. zu tun; **be ~ that ...:** befürchten, dass ...; **~ for sb./sb.'s safety** besorgt um jmdn./jmds. Sicherheit

apprehensively /æprɪ'hensɪvlɪ/ *adv.* (uneasily) besorgt

apprehensiveness /æprɪ'hensɪvnɪs/ *n.* Besorgnis, *die* (**of** wegen); **~ that ...:** Sorge, dass ...; **~ for sb./sb.'s safety** Besorgtheit um jmdn./jmds. Sicherheit

apprentice /ə'prentɪs/
A *n.* (learner) Lehrling, *der* (**to** bei); (to a painter) Schüler, *der* (**to** *Gen.*); (beginner) Neuling, *der;* Anfänger, *der;* (jockey) angehender Jockey
B *v.t.* in die Lehre geben (**to** bei); **be ~d [to sb.]** [bei jmdm.] in der Lehre sein *od.* in die Lehre gehen; **become ~d** eine Lehre beginnen

apprenticeship /ə'prentɪsʃɪp/ *n.* (training) Lehre, *die* (**to** bei); (learning period) Lehrzeit, *die;* Lehrjahre *Pl.;* **serve an/one's ~:** eine/seine Lehre machen; (fig.) ein/sein Volontariat machen

apprise /ə'praɪz/ *v.t.* unterrichten; in Kenntnis setzen; **~ sb. of sth.** jmdn. über etw. (*Akk.*) *od.* von etw. unterrichten; **be ~d of sth.** über etw. (*Akk.*) unterrichtet sein

appro /'æprəʊ/ *n.* (Brit.) **on ~** (Commerc. coll.) **= on approval;** ▸ **approval 2**

approach /ə'prəʊtʃ/
A *v.i.* (in space) sich nähern; näher kommen; ‹*Soldaten:*› [her]anrücken; ‹*Sturm usw.:*› aufziehen; (in time) nahen; **the train now ~ing platform 1** der auf Gleis 1 einfahrende Zug; **the time is fast ~ing when you will have to ...:** es wird nicht mehr lange dauern und du musst ...
B *v.t.* [1] (come near to) sich nähern (+ *Dat.*); (set about) herangehen an (+ *Akk.*); angehen ‹*Problem, Aufgabe, Thema*› [2] (be similar to) verwandt sein (+ *Dat.*) [3] (approximate to) nahe kommen (+ *Dat.*); **the temperature/weight ~es 100 °C/50 kg** die Temperatur/das Gewicht beträgt nahezu 100 °C/50 kg; **a performance ~ing perfection** eine an Perfektion grenzende Aufführung; **few writers can ~ Shakespeare** wenige Dichter reichen an Shakespeare heran [4] (appeal to) sich wenden an (+ *Akk.*) [5] (attempt to influence) herantreten an (+ *Akk.*) [6] (make advances to) sich heranmachen an (+ *Akk.*)
C *n.* [1] [Heran]nahen, *das;* (treatment) Herangehensweise, *die* (**to** an + *Akk.*); Ansatz, *der* (**to** zu); (attitude) Einstellung, *die* (**to** gegenüber); **a new ~:** eine neue Sicht [2] (similarity) Ähnlichkeit, *die* (**to** mit) [3] (approximation) Annäherung, *die;* **some sort of ~ to a timetable** ein ungefährer Zeitplan [4] (appeal) Herantreten, *das* (**to** an + *Akk.*); **make an ~ to sb. concerning sth.** wegen etw. an jmdn. herantreten; sich wegen etw. an jmdn. wenden [5] (attempt to influence) Vorstoß, *der* (**to** bei) [6] (advance) Annäherungsversuche; **make ~es to sb.** Annäherungsversuche bei jmdm. machen [7] (access) Zugang, *der;* (road) Zufahrtsstraße, *die;* (fig.) Zugang, *der* [8] (Aeronaut.) Landeanflug, *der;* Approach, *der*

approachability /əprəʊtʃə'bɪlɪtɪ/ *n.* [1] (friendliness) Umgänglichkeit, *die;* (receptiveness) Empfänglichkeit, *die* [2] (accessibility) Zugänglichkeit, *die*

approachable /ə'prəʊtʃəbl/ *adj.* [1] (friendly) umgänglich; (receptive) empfänglich [2] (accessible) zugänglich; erreichbar

ap'proach road *n.* Zufahrtsstraße, *die*

approbation /æprə'beɪʃn/ *n.* (sanction) Genehmigung, *die;* (Relig.) Approbation, *die;* (approval) Zustimmung, *die;* Einverständnis, *das;* **meet with/get sb.'s ~:** jmds. Zustimmung finden

appropriate
A /ə'prəʊprɪət/ *adj.* (suitable) geeignet (**to, for** für); (peculiar) eigen (**to** *Dat.*); **I feel it is ~ on such an occasion to say a few words** ich halte es für angebracht, bei einem solchen Anlass ein paar Worte zu sagen; **a style ~ to a man of his age and importance** ein Stil, der einem Mann in seinem Alter und seiner Stellung entspricht; **the ~ authority** die zuständige Behörde
B /ə'prəʊprɪeɪt/ *v.t.* [1] (take possession of) sich (*Dat.*) aneignen; sich bemächtigen (+ *Gen.*); (take to oneself) **~ sth. [to oneself]** etw. in [seinen] Besitz nehmen; etw. mit Beschlag belegen [2] (reserve) **~ sth. [to/for sth.]** etw. [zu/für etw.] bestimmen

appropriately /ə'prəʊprɪətlɪ/ *adv.* gebührend; passend ‹*dekoriert, gekleidet, genannt*›

appropriateness /ə'prəʊprɪətnɪs/ *n., no pl.* Angemessenheit, *die;* (of remarks, words) Angebrachtheit, *die*

appropriate tech'nology *n.* angepasste Technologie

appropriation /əprəʊprɪ'eɪʃn/ *n.* Besitzergreifung, *die;* (taking to oneself) Aneignung, *die;* In-Beschlag-Nehmen, *das;* (reservation) Bestimmung, *die*

a

approval /əˈpruːvl/ *n.* 1 (sanctioning) (of plan, project, expenditure) Genehmigung, *die;* (of proposal, reform, marriage) Billigung, *die;* (agreement) Zustimmung, *die;* Einwilligung, *die* (**for** in + *Akk.*); **letter of ~:** Genehmigungsschreiben, *das* 2 (esteem) Lob, *das;* Anerkennung, *die;* **does the plan meet with your ~?** findet der Plan Ihre Zustimmung?; **murmurs of ~:** zustimmendes Gemurmel; **on ~** (Commerc.) zur Probe; (to view) zur Ansicht

approve /əˈpruːv/

A *v.t.* 1 (sanction) genehmigen ‹*Plan, Projekt, Ausgaben*›; billigen ‹*Vorschlag, Reform, Heirat*›; (commend) loben; anerkennen; **~d hotel** empfohlenes Hotel; **~d school** (Brit. Hist.) Erziehungsheim, *das;* Besserungsanstalt, *die* (veralt.) 2 (find good) gutheißen; für gut halten

B *v.i.* **~ of** billigen; zustimmen (+ *Dat.*) ‹*Plan*›; einverstanden sein mit ‹*Tätigkeiten, Gewohnheiten, Verhalten*›; **they don't ~ of her going out with boys** sie sind nicht damit einverstanden, dass sie mit Jungen ausgeht

approving /əˈpruːvɪŋ/ *adj.* zustimmend, beipflichtend ‹*Worte*›; anerkennend, bewundernd ‹*Blicke*›

approvingly /əˈpruːvɪŋlɪ/ *adv.* ▸ **approving**: zustimmend; anerkennend

approx. /əˈprɒks/ *abbr.* = **approximately** ca.

approximate

A /əˈprɒksɪmət/ *adj.* (fairly correct) ungefähr *attr.;* **the figures given here are only ~:** dies hier sind nur ungefähre Zahlen

B /əˈprɒksɪmeɪt/ *v.t.* 1 (make similar) **~ sth. to sth.** etw. einer Sache (*Dat.*) anpassen 2 (come near to) nahe kommen (+ *Dat.*); annähernd erreichen (+ *Akk.*)

C *v.i.* **sth. ~s to sth.** etw. gleicht einer Sache (*Dat.*) annähernd

approximately /əˈprɒksɪmətlɪ/ *adv.* (roughly) ungefähr; (almost) fast; **the answer is ~ correct** die Antwort stimmt ungefähr; **very ~:** ganz grob

approximation /əprɒksɪˈmeɪʃn/ *n.* 1 Annäherung, *die* (**to** an + *Dat.*); Angleichung, *die* (**to** an + *Dat.*) 2 (estimate) Annäherungswert, *der;* **at** *or* **as a rough ~ I'd say ...:** grob geschätzt würde ich sagen ...

appurtenances /əˈpɜːtɪnənsɪz/ *n. pl.* 1 (belongings, appendages) Zubehör, *das;* **he had all the ~ of 'the good life'** er hatte alles, was zum „guten Leben" gehört; **... and all the ~:** ... mit allem Zubehör 2 (accessories) Attribute

Apr. *abbr.* = **April** Apr.

APR *abbr.* = **annualized percentage rate** Jahreszinssatz, *der*

après-ski /æpreɪˈskiː/ *n., no pl.* Après-Ski, *der; attrib.* Après-Ski-

apricot /ˈeɪprɪkɒt/

A *n.* 1 (fruit, tree) Aprikose, *die; attrib.* **~ jam** Aprikosenmarmelade, *die;* **~ brandy** Apricot-Brandy, *der;* Aprikosenlikör, *der* 2 (colour) Aprikosenfarbe, *die;* Apricot, *das*

B *adj.* aprikosenfarben

April /ˈeɪprəl/ *n.* ▸ⓘ **p. 1047** April, *der; attrib.* **~ fool** April[s]narr, *der;* **make an ~ fool of sb.** jmdn. in den April schicken; **'~ fool!'** „April, April!"; **~ Fool's Day** der 1. April; **~ showers** typisches Aprilwetter; *see also* **August**

a priori /eɪ praɪˈɔːraɪ/

A *adv.* von vornherein; a priori (Philos.)

B *adj.* apriorisch

apron /ˈeɪprən/ *n.* 1 (garment) Schürze, *die;* **be tied to sb.'s ~ strings** jmdm. an der Schürze *od.* am Schürzenzipfel hängen 2 (on airfield) Vorfeld, *das* 3 (Theatre) **~ [stage]** Vorbühne, *die*

apropos /æprəˈpəʊ, ˈæprəpəʊ/

A *adv.* 1 (to the purpose) passend; (just when wanted) zur Hand 2 **~ of** (in respect of) in Bezug auf (+ *Akk.*); hinsichtlich (+ *Gen.*) 3 (incidentally) apropos; übrigens; da wir gerade davon sprechen

B *adj.* passend; treffend ‹*Bemerkung*›

C *prep.* (coll.) apropos

apse /æps/ *n.* (Archit.) Apsis, *die*

apt /æpt/ *adj.* 1 (suitable) passend ‹*Ausdruck, Geschenk*›; angemessen ‹*Reaktion*›; treffend ‹*Zitat, Bemerkung*› 2 (tending) **be ~ to do sth.** dazu neigen, etw. zu tun 3 (quick-witted) begabt (**at** für); **be ~ at doing sth.** eine Gabe dafür haben, etw. zu tun

aptitude /ˈæptɪtjuːd/ *n.* 1 (propensity) Neigung, *die;* (ability) Begabung, *die;* **linguistic ~:** Sprachbegabung, *die;* **learning ~:** Lernfähigkeit, *die; attrib.* **~ test** Eignungstest, *der* 2 (suitability) Eignung, *die*

aptly /ˈæptlɪ/ *adv.* passend; **~ chosen words** treffend gewählte Worte

aptness /ˈæptnɪs/ *n., no pl.* 1 (suitability) Angemessenheit, *die;* **the ~ of his replies** die Treffsicherheit seiner Antworten 2 (tendency) Neigung, *die* 3 (quick-wittedness) Begabung, *die* (**at** für)

ˈaquajogging *n., no pl.* Aquajogging, *das*

aqualung /ˈækwəlʌŋ/ *n.* Tauchgerät, *das*

aquamarine /ækwəməˈriːn/

A *n.* 1 (colour) Aquamarin, *das* 2 (stone) Aquamarin, *der*

B *adj.* aquamarin[farben]

aquaplane /ˈækwəpleɪn/

A *v.i.* 1 ‹*Reifen:*› aufschwimmen; ‹*Fahrzeug:*› [durch Aquaplaning] ins Rutschen geraten 2 (use ~) Wasserski laufen

B *n.* Monoski, *der;* Wasserski, *der*

aquaplaning /ˈækwəpleɪnɪŋ/ *n., no pl.* 1 (sliding) Aquaplaning, *das* 2 (Sport) Wasserski, *das*

aqua regia /ækwə ˈriːdʒɪə/ *n.* (Chem.) Königswasser, *das;* Goldscheidewasser, *das*

aquarelle /ækwəˈrel/ *n.* (technique) Aquarellmalerei, *die;* (product) Aquarell, *das*

Aquarian /əˈkweərɪən/ *n.* (Astrol.) Wassermann, *der*

aquarium /əˈkweərɪəm/ *n., pl.* **~s** *or* **aquaria** /əˈkweərɪə/ Aquarium, *das*

Aquarius /əˈkweərɪəs/ *n.* (Astrol., Astron.) der Wassermann; der Aquarius; *see also* **Aries**

aquatic /əˈkwætɪk/

A *adj.* 1 aquatisch; Wasser-; **~ plant/bird** Wasserpflanze, *die*/-vogel, *der* 2 (Sport) Wassersport-; **~ sports** Wassersportarten

B *n.* 1 (plant) Wasserpflanze, *die;* (animal) Wassertier, *das* 2 *in pl.* (Sport) Wassersport, *der*

aquatint /ˈækwətɪnt/ *n.* (technique) Aquatinta, *die;* (product) Aquatintaarbeit, *die*

aqueduct /ˈækwɪdʌkt/ *n.* Aquädukt, *der od. das*

aqueous /ˈeɪkwɪəs, ˈækwɪəs/ *adj.* (containing water, watery) wässerig; wässrig; aquatisch (fachspr.); **~ vapour/content** Wasserdampf/-gehalt, *der*

aqueous ˈhumour *n.* (Anat.) Kammerwasser, *das;* Humor aquosus (fachspr.)

aquifer /ˈækwɪfə(r)/ *n.* (Geol.) Wasser führende Schicht

aquilegia /ækwɪˈliːdʒɪə/ *n.* (Bot.) [Gemeine] Akelei

aquiline /ˈækwɪlaɪn/ *adj.* adlerartig; Adler-; **~ eye/nose** Adlerauge, *das*/-nase, *die*

Arab /ˈærəb/

A *adj.* ▸ⓘ **p. 1345** arabisch; **~ horse** Araber, *der*

B *n.* 1 ▸ⓘ **p. 1345** Araber, *der*/Araberin, *die;* **desert ~:** Beduine, *der* 2 (Arabian horse) Araber, *der* 3 **street arab** Betteljunge, *der*

arabesque /ærəˈbesk/ *n.* 1 Arabeske, *die* 2 (Ballet) Arabesque, *die*

Arabia /əˈreɪbɪə/ *pr. n.* Arabien (*das*)

Arabian /əˈreɪbɪən/

A *adj.* arabisch; **the ~ Nights** Tausendundeine Nacht

B *n.* Araber, *der*/Araberin, *die*

Arabic /ˈærəbɪk/

A *adj.* arabisch; **gum a~** Gummiarabikum, *das;* **a~ numerals** arabische Ziffern; *see also* **English A**

B *n.* ▸ⓘ **p. 1277** Arabisch, *das; see also* **English B 1**

arabis /ˈærəbɪs/ *n.* (Bot.) Gänsekresse, *die*

Arab-Isˈraeli *attrib. adj.* ▸ⓘ **p. 1345** arabisch-israelisch

Arabist /ˈærəbɪst/ *n.* Arabist, *der*/Arabistin, *die*

arable /ˈærəbl/

A *adj.* bebaubar, landwirtschaftlich nutzbar ‹*Land*›; **~ land** (cultivated) Ackerland, *das;* **~ crops** landwirtschaftliche Nutzpflanzen

B *n.* Ackerland, *das*

Araby /ˈærəbɪ/ *pr. n.* (poet.) Arabien (*das*)

arachnid /əˈræknɪd/ *n.* (Zool.) Spinnentier, *das;* **the ~s** die Spinnentiere *od.* (fachspr.) Arachn[o]iden

Araldite ® /ˈærəldaɪt/ *n.* Araldit, *das* (Wz)

Aramaic /ærəˈmeɪɪk/ ▸ⓘ **p. 1277**

A *adj.* aramäisch

B *n.* Aramäisch, *das*

araucaria /ærɔːˈkeərɪə/ *n.* (Bot.) Araukarie, *die*

arbiter /ˈɑːbɪtə(r)/ *n.* (judge) Richter, *der;* (arbitrator) Vermittler, *der;* (controller) Herr, *der,* (geh.) Gebieter, *der* (**of** über + *Akk.*)

arbitrage /ˈɑːbɪtrɑːʒ/ *n.* (St. Exch.) Arbitrage, *die*

arbitrarily /ˈɑːbɪtrərɪlɪ/ *adv.* 1 (at random) willkürlich; arbiträr (geh.); (capriciously) aus einer Laune heraus 2 (unrestrainedly) rücksichtslos 3 (despotically) willkürlich

arbitrariness /ˈɑːbɪtrərɪnɪs/ *n., no pl.* 1 (randomness) Willkür, *die;* Willkürlichkeit, *die;* Arbitrarität, *die* (geh.); (capriciousness) Launenhaftigkeit, *die* 2 (unrestrainedness) Rücksichtslosigkeit, *die* 3 (despotism) Willkür, *die*

arbitrary /ˈɑːbɪtrərɪ/ *adj.* 1 (random) willkürlich; arbiträr; (capricious) launenhaft; launisch ‹*Idee*› 2 (unrestrained) rücksichtslos ‹*Vorgehen, Bestrafung, Wesen, Haltung*› 3 (despotic) willkürlich; **~ rule** Willkürherrschaft, *die*

arbitrate /ˈɑːbɪtreɪt/

A *v.t.* schlichten, beilegen ‹*Streit*›; **~ a difference of opinion** eine Meinungsverschiedenheit beseitigen

B *v.i.* **~ [upon sth.]** [in einer Sache] vermitteln *od.* als Schiedsrichter fungieren; **~ between parties** zwischen Parteien vermitteln

arbitration /ɑːbɪˈtreɪʃn/ *n.* Vermittlung, *die;* (in industry) Schlichtung, *die;* **go to ~:** einen Schlichter anrufen *od.* einschalten; ‹*Konflikt:*› einem Schlichter vorgelegt werden; **take sth. to ~:** etw. einem Schlichter vorlegen

arbitrator /ˈɑːbɪtreɪtə(r)/ *n.* (mediator) Vermittler, *der;* (in industry) Schlichter, *der;* (arbiter) Schiedsrichter, *der;* (judge) Richter, *der*

arbor[1] /ˈɑːbə(r)/ *n.* (axle) Welle, *die;* Spindel, *die;* (Amer.: tool holder) Dorn, *der;* Aufsteckhalter, *der;* Träger, *der*

arbor[2] (Amer.) ▸ **arbour**

Arbor Day /ˈɑːbə deɪ/ *n.* (Amer., Austral.) Tag des Baumes

arboreal /ɑːˈbɔːrɪəl/ *adj.* (of trees) Baum-; (inhabiting trees) Baum-; auf Bäumen lebend; **be ~:** auf Bäumen leben

arboretum /ɑːbəˈriːtəm/ *n., pl.* **arboreta** /ɑːbəˈriːtə/ *or* **~s** Arboretum, *das;* Baumgarten, *der*

arboriculture /ˈɑːbərɪkʌltʃə(r)/ *n., no pl.* Baumzucht, *die*

arbor vitae /ɑːbə ˈvaɪtiː, ɑːbə ˈviːtaɪ/ *n.* (Bot.) Lebensbaum, *der*

arbour /ˈɑːbə(r)/ *n.* (Brit.) Laube, *die*

arbutus /ɑːˈbjuːtəs/ *n.* Arbutus, *der;* Erdbeerbaum, *der;* **trailing ~** (Amer.) kriechende Heide

arc /ɑːk/ *n.* 1 [Kreis]bogen, *der* 2 (Electr.) Lichtbogen, *der;* **~ lamp, ~ light** Lichtbogenlampe, *die;* **~ welding** Lichtbogen-, Elektroschweißung, *die*

arcade /ɑːˈkeɪd/ *n.* Arkade, *die;* **shopping ~:** Einkaufspassage, *die*

Arcadian /ɑːˈkeɪdɪən/ *adj.* arkadisch

arcane /ɑːˈkeɪn/ *adj.* geheimnisvoll; undurchschaubar; **an ~ secret** ein verborgenes Geheimnis

arch[1] /ɑːtʃ/

A *n.* Bogen, *der;* (curvature; of foot) Wölbung, *die;* (of bridge) Bogen, *der;* Joch, *das;* (vault) Gewölbe, *das*

B *v.i.* sich wölben; ‹*Ast, Glied:*› sich biegen

C *v.t.* 1 (furnish with ~) mit Bogen versehen; **~ed gateway** Torbogen, *der;* **~ed in the Gothic manner** mit gotischem/gotischen Bogen 2 (form into ~) beugen ‹*Rücken, Arm*›; **the cat ~ed its back** die Katze machte einen Buckel

arch[2] *adj.* schelmisch; kokett

ℹ Area (square measure)

1 square inch (sq in.)	= *6,45 cm²* (sechs Komma vier fünf Quadratzentimeter)	
144 square inches	= *1 square foot (sq ft)*	= 929 cm²
9 square feet	= *1 square yard (sq yd)*	= 0,836 m² (null Komma acht drei sechs Quadratmeter)
4,840 square yards	= *1 acre*	= 0,4 ha (null Komma vier Hektar)
640 acres	= *1 square mile*	= 2,59 km² (zwei Komma fünf neun Quadratkilometer)

What is the area of the room?
= Wie viel Quadratmeter hat das Zimmer?
The area of the room is 180 square feet
= Das Zimmer hat 16,72 Quadratmeter [Fläche]
2,000 square feet of office space
≈ 186 Quadratmeter Bürofläche
He farms 1,000 acres [of land]
≈ Er bewirtschaftet 400 Hektar [Land]
a farm of 1,000 acres
≈ ein 400 Hektar großer Bauernhof, ein Bauernhof von 400 Hektar
an area of about 40 square miles
≈ eine Fläche von etwa 100 Quadratkilometern

arch- *pref.* Erz-; **~villain** Erzschurke, *der;* Erzgauner, *der*

archaeological /ɑːkɪəˈlɒdʒɪkl/ *adj.* archäologisch; **~ dig** [Aus]grabung, *die*

archaeologist /ɑːkɪˈɒlədʒɪst/ *n.* ▸ℹ **p. 1260** Archäologe, *der*/Archäologin, *die;* Altertumsforscher, *der*/-forscherin, *die*

archaeology /ɑːkɪˈɒlədʒɪ/ *n.* Archäologie, *die;* Altertumskunde, *die;* **marine/industrial ~:** Unterwasser-/Industriearchäologie, *die*

archaic /ɑːˈkeɪɪk/ *adj.* (out of use) veraltet; archaisch; (antiquated) altertümlich; überholt ‹*Methode, Gesetz*›; **an ~ typewriter** (coll.) eine museumsreife *od.* vorsintflutliche Schreibmaschine

archaically /ɑːˈkeɪɪkəlɪ/ *adv.* (in out-of-use style) altertümlich, (deliberately) altertümelnd ‹*sich ausdrücken, schreiben*›

archaism /ˈɑːkeɪɪzm/ *n.* Archaismus, *der*

archangel /ˈɑːkeɪndʒl/ *n.* Erzengel, *der*

archˈbishop *n.* ▸ℹ **p. 1634** Erzbischof, *der*

archˈbishopric *n.* 1▸ (office) Amt des Erzbischofs 2▸ (diocese) Erzbistum, *das*

archˈdeacon *n.* Archi-, Erzdiakon, *der*

archˈdeaconry, archˈdeaconship *ns.* Archidiakonat, *das od. der*

archˈdiocese ▸ **archbishopric 2**

archˈduchess *n.* (Hist.) Erzherzogin, *die*

archˈduke *n.* (Hist.) Erzherzog, *der*

arch-ˈenemy *n.* (chief enemy) Erzfeind, *der;* (the Devil) ▸ **arch-fiend**

archeology *etc.* (*Amer.*) ▸ **archaeology** *etc.*

archer /ˈɑːtʃə(r)/ *n.* 1▸ Bogenschütze, *der* 2▸ (Astrol.) **the A~:** der Schütze; **under the sign of the A~:** im Zeichen des Schützen

ˈarcherfish *n.* Schützenfisch, *der*

archery /ˈɑːtʃərɪ/ *n., no pl.* Bogenschießen, *das*

archetypal /ˈɑːkɪtaɪpl/ *adj.* (original) archetypisch (geh.); (typical) typisch; prototypisch; **he was the ~ film director** er war der Prototyp des Regisseurs

archetype /ˈɑːkɪtaɪp/ *n.* (original) Urfassung, *die;* Archetyp, *der;* (typical specimen) Prototyp, *der;* Archetyp, *der*

arch-ˈfiend *n.* Erzfeind, *der;* Satan, *der*

archiepiscopal /ɑːkɪɪˈpɪskəpl/ *adj.* erzbischöflich

archiepiscopate /ɑːkɪɪˈpɪskəpət/ ▸ **archbishopric 1**

Archimedes /ɑːkɪˈmiːdiːz/ *n.* **~ˈ principle** (Phys.) das Archimedische Prinzip

archipelago /ɑːkɪˈpeləgəʊ/ *n., pl.* **~s** *or* **~es** Archipel, *der;* (islands) Inselgruppe, *die;* (sea) Inselmeer, *das*

architect /ˈɑːkɪtekt/ *n.* 1▸ ▸ℹ **p. 1260** (designer) Architekt, *der*/Architektin, *die;* Baumeister, *der* (geh.); **naval ~:** Schiffskonstrukteur, *der;* Schiffbauer, *der; see also* **landscape architect** 2▸ (maker, creator) Schöpfer, *der;* (fig.) Urheber, *der;* **the ~ of one's own fate/fortune** seines [eigenen] Glückes Schmied

architectonic /ɑːkɪtekˈtɒnɪk/ *adj.* 1▸ architektonisch 2▸ (constructive) schöpferisch ‹*Fähigkeiten, Kraft*›

architectural /ɑːkɪˈtektʃərl/ *adj.* architektonisch; **~ style** Baustil, *der*

architecture /ˈɑːkɪtektʃə(r)/ *n.* 1▸ Architektur, *die;* Baukunst, *die* (geh.); (style) Bauweise, *die;* Architektur, *die;* **naval/railway/bridge ~:** Schiff[s]-/Eisenbahn-/Brückenbau, *der* 2▸ (structure, lit. or fig.) Konstruktion, *die* 3▸ (Computing) [System]architektur, *die*

architrave /ˈɑːkɪtreɪv/ *n.* (beam) Architrav, *der;* Epistylion, *das;* (moulding) Archivolte, *die*

archival /ɑːˈkaɪvəl/ *adj.* archivalisch

archive /ˈɑːkaɪv/
A *n.* 1▸ *usu. in pl.* (historical documents or records) Archiv, *das.* 2▸ (Computing) Archiv, *das*
B *v.t.* (also Computing) archivieren

ˈarchive file *n.* (Computing) Archivdatei, *die*

archivist /ˈɑːkɪvɪst/ *n.* ▸ℹ **p. 1260** Archivar, *der*/Archivarin, *die*

archly /ˈɑːtʃlɪ/ *adv.* schelmisch; kokett

archness /ˈɑːtʃnɪs/ *n., no pl.* Schalkhaftigkeit, *die;* (of woman) Koketterie, *die*

arch-ˈtraitor *n.* Erzverräter, *der*

ˈarchway *n.* (vaulted passage) Gewölbegang, *der;* Tunnel, *der;* (arched entrance) Durchgang, *der;* Torbogen, *der*

Arctic /ˈɑːktɪk/
A *adj.* 1▸ arktisch; **~ Circle/Ocean** nördlicher Polarkreis/Nordpolarmeer, *das* 2▸ **a~** (coll.: very cold) arktisch
B *pr. n.* **the ~:** die Arktis
C *n.* (Amer.: overshoe) hoher Überschuh

arctic: ~ ˈfox *n.* Polarfuchs, *der;* **~ ˈtern** *n.* Küstenseeschwalbe, *die*

ˈarc welder *n.* Lichtbogenschweißgerät, *das*

ardency /ˈɑːdənsɪ/ *n., no pl.* Eifer, *der* (**in** bei); (of feeling, desire, etc.) Leidenschaftlichkeit, *die;* Heftigkeit, *die;* (of admiration, prayer, belief, poem) Inbrunst, *die*

Ardennes /ɑːˈden/ *pr. n. pl.* Ardennen *Pl.*

ardent /ˈɑːdənt/ *adj.* 1▸ (eager) begeistert ‹*Anhänger, Theaterbesucher, Interesse, Gefolgsmann*›; (fervent) glühend ‹*Bewunderer, Leidenschaft*›; hitzig ‹*Temperament, Wesen*›; brennend ‹*Wunsch*›; feurig ‹*Rede, Liebhaber*›; leidenschaftlich ‹*Gedicht, Liebesbrief, Anbetung*›; innigst, (geh.) inbrünstig ‹*Hoffnung, Liebe*›

ardently /ˈɑːdəntlɪ/ *adv.* (eagerly) begeistert; (fervently) glühend; **hope ~:** inbrünstig (geh.) *od.* inständig hoffen

ardour (*Brit.; Amer.:* **ardor**) /ˈɑːdə(r)/ *n.* (warm emotion) Leidenschaft, *die;* (passionate emotion) Inbrunst, *die* (geh.); (fervour) Eifer, *der;* **~ for reform/learning** Reformeifer, *der*/Wissensdurst, *der*

arduous /ˈɑːdjʊəs/ *adj.* schwer, anstrengend ‹*Aufgabe, Arbeit, Unterfangen*›; hart ‹*Arbeit, Tag, Zeit*›; beschwerlich ‹*Reise, Aufstieg, Fahrt*›

arduously /ˈɑːdjʊəslɪ/ *adv.* (laboriously) beschwerlich

arduousness /ˈɑːdjʊəsnɪs/ *n., no pl.* (difficulty) Mühe, *die;* Beschwerlichkeit, *die*

are¹ /ɑː(r)/ *n.* Ar, *das*

are² ▸ **be**

area /ˈeərɪə/ *n.* 1▸ ▸ℹ **p. 911** (surface measure) Flächenausdehnung, *die;* **the floor ~ is 15 square metres** der Fußboden hat eine Fläche von 15 Quadratmetern; **what is the ~ of your farm?** wie groß ist Ihr Hof? 2▸ (region) Gelände, *das;* (of wood, marsh, desert) Gebiet, *das;* (of city, country) Gegend, *die;* (of skin, wall, etc.) Stelle, *die;* **a poor ~ of the town** eine arme Gegend der Stadt; **it happened in this ~:** es ereignete sich hier in der Nähe; **in the Hamburg ~:** im Hamburger Raum; **in the ~ of ...** (fig.) um ... herum; **an ~ of ground** ein Grundstück *od.* Gelände *od.* Areal 3▸ (defined space) Bereich, *der;* **parking/picnic/sports ~:** Park-/Picknick-/Sportplatz, *der;* **no-smoking ~:** Nichtraucherzone, *die* 4▸ (subject field) Gebiet, *das;* **in the ~ of electronics/medicine** auf dem Gebiet *od.* im Bereich der Elektronik/Medizin 5▸ (scope) Raum, *der;* **~ of choice** Wahlmöglichkeiten *Pl.;* **~ of responsibility** Verantwortungsbereich, *der* 6▸ (sunken court) Vorhof, *der*

area: ~ code *n.* (Amer. Teleph.) Gebietsvorwahl[nummer], *die;* **~ manager** *n.* Gebietsleiter, *der*/-leiterin, *die;* **~way** (Amer.) ▸ **area 6**

areca /ˈærɪkə, əˈriːkə/ *n.* Arekapalme, *die; attrib.* **~ nut** Arekanuss, *die*

arena /əˈriːnə/ *n.* (at circus, bullfight) Arena, *die;* (in equestrianism) Dressurviereck, *das;* (fig.: scene of conflict) Bühne, *die;* Schauplatz, *der;* (fig.: sphere of action) Bereich, *der;* **the political ~:** die politische Arena; **enter the ~** (fig.) die Arena betreten; auf den Plan treten; **~ stage** Arenabühne, *die;* **~ theatre** Arenatheater, *das*

aren't /ɑːnt/ (coll.) = **are not;** ▸ **be**

areola /əˈriːələ/ *n., pl.* **~e** /əˈriːəliː/ (Anat.) (of nipple) Warzenhof, *der;* (*of eye*) *an die Pupille grenzender Teil der Iris*

argent /ˈɑːdʒənt/ (esp. Her.)
A *n.* Silber, *das*
B *adj.* silbern

Argentina /ɑdʒənˈtiːnə/ *pr. n.* Argentinien (*das*)

Argentine /ˈɑːdʒəntaɪn/
A *pr. n.* **the ~:** Argentinien (*das*)
B *adj.* argentinisch

Argentinian /ɑːdʒənˈtɪnɪən/ ▸ℹ **p. 1345**
A *adj.* argentinisch; **sb. is ~:** jmd. ist Argentinier/Argentinierin
B *n.* Argentinier, *der*/Argentinierin, *die*

argillaceous /ɑːdʒɪˈleɪʃəs/ *adj.* (Geol.) tonig

argle-bargle /ɑːglˈbɑːgl/ ▸ **argy-bargy**

argon /ˈɑːgɒn/ *n.* (Chem.) Argon, *das*

argonaut /ˈɑːgənɔːt/ *n.* 1▸ (Zool.) Papierboot, *das* 2▸ **A~** (Mythol.) Argonaut, *der*

argosy /ˈɑːgəsɪ/ *n.* (Hist./poet.: merchant vessel) Handelsschiff, *das*

argot /ˈɑːgəʊ/ *n.* Argot, *das od. der;* **thieves' ~:** Rotwelsch, *das;* **that class/group has its own ~:** diese Klasse/Gruppe hat ihren eigenen Jargon *od.* Slang

arguable /ˈɑːgjʊəbl/ *adj.* 1▸ fragwürdig ‹*Angelegenheit, Punkt*›; **it's ~ whether ...:** es ist noch die Frage, ob ... 2▸ **it is ~ that ...** (can reasonably be argued that) man kann sich auf den Standpunkt stellen, dass ...

arguably /ˈɑːgjʊəblɪ/ *adv.* möglicherweise

argue /ˈɑːgjuː/
A *v.t.* 1▸ (maintain) **~ that ...:** die Ansicht vertreten, dass ... 2▸ (treat by reasoning) darlegen ‹*Grund, Standpunkt, Fakten*›; **I don't want to ~ the point now** lassen wir für den Moment diesen Punkt noch ungeklärt; **~ sth. away** etw. wegdiskutieren 3▸ (persuade) **~ sb. into doing sth.** jmdn. dazu überreden, etw. zu tun; **~ sb. out of doing sth.** [es] jmdm. ausreden, etw. zu tun 4▸ (prove) **~ sb. [to be] sb./sth.** der Beweis dafür sein, dass jmd. jmd./etw. ist 5▸ (indicate) **~ sth.** von etw. zeugen
B *v.i.* **~ with sb.** sich mit jmdm. streiten; **~ against sb.** jmdm. widersprechen; **~ for/against sth.** für/gegen etw. eintreten; sich für/gegen etw. aussprechen; **~ about sth.** sich über/um etw. (*Akk.*) streiten; **none of your**

arguing! keine Widerrede!

argument /ˈɑːgjʊmənt/ *n.* [1] (reason) Begründung, *die;* **~s for/against sth.** Argumente für/gegen etw. [2] *no pl.* (reasoning process) Argumentieren, *das;* **the powers of logical ~:** das Vermögen, logisch zu argumentieren; **assume sth. for ~'s sake** etw. rein theoretisch annehmen [3] (debate) Auseinandersetzung, *die;* **get into an ~/get into ~s with sb.** mit jmdm. in Streit geraten [4] (summary) Kurzfassung, *die;* Zusammenfassung, *die* [5] (Math.) Argument, *das*

argumentation /ɑːgjʊmenˈteɪʃn/ *n.* [1] *no pl.* (reasoning) Argumentieren, *das;* **his powers of ~:** seine Fähigkeit, zu argumentieren [2] (debate) Gezänk, *das*

argumentative /ɑːgjʊˈmentətɪv/ *adj.* [1] (fond of arguing) widerspruchsfreudig; (quarrelsome) streitlustig; streitsüchtig [2] (logical) argumentativ

Argus /ˈɑːgəs/ *n.* [1] (butterfly) Augenfalter, *der* [2] (Ornith.) Arguspfau, *der*

argy-bargy /ɑːdʒɪˈbɑːdʒɪ/ (joc.)
A *n.* Hickhack, *der od. das* (ugs.); Streiterei, *die*
B *v.i.* sich herumstreiten (ugs.) (**about** über + *Akk.*)

aria /ˈɑːrɪə/ *n.* (Mus.) Arie, *die*

Arian[1] /ˈeərɪən/ *n.* (Astrol.) Widder, *der*

Arian[2] ▸ **Aryan**

arid /ˈærɪd/ *adj.* [1] (dry; also fig.) trocken ‹*Klima, Land*› [2] (barren) dürr; karg [3] (Geog.) arid; **~ zone** Trockengürtel, *der*

aridity /əˈrɪdɪtɪ/ *n., no pl.* [1] (dryness of land, heat; also fig.) Trockenheit, *die;* (Geog.) Aridität, *die* [2] (barrenness) Kargheit, *die*

aridness /ˈærɪdnɪs/ ▸ **aridity**

Aries /ˈeəriːz/ *n.* (Astrol., Astron.) der Widder; der Aries; **under [the sign of] ~, the Ram** im Zeichen des Aries *od.* des Widders; **he/she is an ~:** er/sie ist [ein] Widder; **first point of ~:** Frühlingspunkt, *der;* Widderpunkt, *der*

aright /əˈraɪt/ *adv.* recht ‹*hören, sich erinnern*›

arise /əˈraɪz/ *v.i.,* **arose** /əˈrəʊz/, **arisen** /əˈrɪzn/ [1] (originate) entstehen; (present itself) auftreten; ‹*Gelegenheit:*› sich bieten; **a crisis has ~n in Turkey** in der Türkei ist es zu einer Krise gekommen; **new hopes have** *or* **hope has ~n that ...:** man hat wieder Hoffnung geschöpft, dass ... [2] (result) **~ from** *or* **out of sth.** von etw. herrühren [3] ‹*Sonne, Nebel:*› aufsteigen; ‹*Sturm:*› anschwellen [4] (Hist.: stand up) **~, Sir Robert!** erhebt euch, Sir Robert!

aristocracy /ærɪˈstɒkrəsɪ/ *n.* Aristokratie, *die;* (fig.) **an ~ of ...:** eine Elite von ...

aristocrat /ˈærɪstəkræt/ *n.* Aristokrat, *der*/Aristokratin, *die;* **an ~ among wines** (fig.) ein besonders edler Wein

aristocratic /ærɪstəˈkrætɪk/ *adj.* [1] aristokratisch; Aristokraten-; adelig; Adels- [2] (grand) exklusiv ‹*Luxus, Pracht etc.*›; (distinguished) vornehm ‹*Aussehen, Auftreten*›; (refined) kultiviert; fein ‹*Manieren, Sitten*›; (stylish, fine) edel ‹*Qualität, Geschmack, Gesichtszüge, Wein, Möbel*›

aristocratically /ærɪstəˈkrætɪkəlɪ/ *adv.* aristokratisch

Aristotelian /ærɪstəˈtiːlɪən/ *adj.* aristotelisch

Aristotle /ˈærɪstɒtl/ *pr. n.* Aristoteles (*der*)

arithmetic[1] /əˈrɪθmətɪk/ *n.* [1] (science) Arithmetik, *die* [2] (computation) Rechnen, *das;* **mental ~:** Kopfrechnen, *das;* **there are several mistakes in your ~:** du hast dich mehrmals verrechnet

arithmetic[2] /ærɪθˈmetɪk/, **arithmetical** /ærɪθˈmetɪkl/ *adj.* arithmetisch; **arithmetical progression** arithmetische Progression; (sequence/series) arithmetische Folge/Reihe

ark /ɑːk/ *n.* **sth. looks as if it came [straight] out of the ~:** etw. sieht vorsintflutlich aus; *see also* **Noah's ark**

arm[1] /ɑːm/ *n.* [1] ▸ⓘ **p. 951** (limb) Arm, *der;* **~ in ~ [with each other]** Arm in Arm; **[be] at ~'s length [from]** auf Armeslänge [entfernt sein von]; **keep sb. at ~'s length** (fig.) eine gewisse Distanz zu jmdm. wahren; **as long as sb.'s ~** (fig.) ellenlang; **cost sb. an ~ and a leg** (fig.) jmdn. eine Stange Geld kosten (ugs.); **on sb.'s ~:** an jmds. Arm (*Dat.*); **under one's ~:** unter dem Arm; **a babe** *or* **a child in ~s** ein kleines Kind; **in sb.'s ~s** in jmds. Armen; **fall into each other's ~s** sich (*Dat.*) in die Arme fallen; **take sb. in one's ~s** jmdn. in die Arme nehmen *od.* (geh.) schließen; **the lovers were found dead in each other's ~s** die beiden Liebenden wurden eng umschlungen tot aufgefunden; **with open ~s** (lit. or fig.) mit offenen Armen; **within ~'s reach** (lit. or fig.) in Reichweite; **be within ~'s reach of safety** fast in Sicherheit sein [2] (sleeve) Ärmel, *der;* (of chair) Armlehne, *die* [3] (branch) Ast, *der* [4] (~-like thing) Arm, *der* [5] (military grouping) Waffengattung, *die. See also* **arms**

arm[2] *v.t.* [1] (furnish with weapons) bewaffnen; mit Waffen ausrüsten ‹*Schiff*› [2] (furnish with tools etc.) ausrüsten; bewaffnen (fig.); **~ oneself with sth.** sich mit etw. wappnen; **~ed with all advantages/virtues** mit allen Vorteilen/Tugenden ausgestattet [3] scharf machen ‹*Bombe usw.*›. *See also* **arms**

armada /ɑːˈmɑːdə/ *n.* Armada, *die*

armadillo /ɑːməˈdɪləʊ/ *n., pl.* **~s** (Zool.) Gürteltier, *das*

Armageddon /ɑːməˈgedən/ *n.* Armageddon, *das* (geh.)

armament /ˈɑːməmənt/ *n.* [1] (weapons etc.) **~[s]** Kriegsgerät, *das* [2] (force) Streitmacht, *die* [3] *no pl.* (process) (of persons) Bewaffnung, *die;* (of boat) Ausrüstung, *die*

armature /ˈɑːmətʃə(r)/ *n.* [1] (Biol.: defensive covering) Schutzkleid, *das* [2] (sculptor's framework) Knebel, *der;* Reiter, *der* [3] (Magn., Electr.) Anker, *der*

arm: ~band *n.* Armbinde, *die;* **~ candy** *n.* (coll.) attraktive *od.* aparte Begleitung; **~chair A** *n.* Sessel, *der;* **B** *adj.* **~chair politician/strategist** politischer Amateur/Amateurstratege, *der;* **~chair critic** Hobby- *od.* Amateurkritiker, *der;* **~chair travel** Reisen in der Fantasie

armed /ɑːmd/ *adj.* bewaffnet; mit Geschützen bestückt ‹*Schiff*›; **~ forces** Streitkräfte *Pl.;* **~ neutrality** bewaffnete Neutralität

-armed *adj. in comb.* (with arms) mit ... Armen; (with sleeves) -ärm[e]lig; **long-/brown-~:** mit langen/braunen Armen; **two-~:** zweiarmig

Armenia /ɑˈmiːnɪə/ *pr. n.* Armenien (*das*)

Armenian /ɑːˈmiːnɪən/ ▸ⓘ **p. 1277,** ▸ⓘ **p. 1345**
A *adj.* armenisch; **sb. is ~:** jmd. ist Armenier/Armenierin; *see also* **English A**
B *n.* [1] (person) Armenier, *der*/Armenierin, *die* [2] (language) Armenisch, *das; see also* **English B 1**

armful /ˈɑːmfʊl/ *n.* **an ~ of fruit** ein Arm voll Obst; **with an ~ of gifts** mit einem Arm voll Geschenken; **flowers by the ~:** ganze Arme voll Blumen

ˈarmhole *n.* Armloch, *das*

armistice /ˈɑːmɪstɪs/ *n.* (cessation from hostilities; also fig.) Waffenstillstand, *der;* (short truce) Waffenruhe, *die;* **A~ Day** *Gedenktag des Endes des 1. Weltkriegs*

armless /ˈɑːmlɪs/ *adj.* (without arms) ohne Arme; armlos; (without sleeves) ohne Ärmel; ärmellos

armlet /ˈɑːmlɪt/ *n.* (band) Armbinde, *die;* (bracelet) Armring, *der;* Armreif, *der*

ˈarmlock *n.* (Wrestling) Armschlüssel, *der*

armor (Amer.) ▸ **armour**

armorer (Amer.) ▸ **armourer**

armorial /ɑːˈmɔːrɪəl/ *adj.* Wappen-; heraldisch; **~ bearings** Wappen, *das;* Wappenschild, *der*

armory (Amer.) ▸ **armoury**

armour /ˈɑːmə(r)/ (Brit.)
A *n.* [1] *no pl.* (Hist.) Rüstung, *die;* **suit of ~:** Harnisch, *der* [2] *no pl.* (steel plates) Panzerung, *die;* Panzer, *der* [3] *no pl.* (~ed vehicles) Panzerfahrzeuge [4] (steel plate) **~ [plate]** Panzerplatte, *die;* Panzerblech, *das;* **~-clad** gepanzert; Panzer- [5] *no pl.* (protective covering) Panzer, *der*
B *v.t.* (furnish with protective cover) ausrüsten; armieren ‹*Kabel*›; (toughen) panzern ‹*Glas*›; (with steel plates) verkleiden; **~ed car/train** gepanzerter Wagen/Zug; Panzerwagen/-zug, *der;* **~ed cable** bewehrtes *od.* armiertes Kabel; **~ed division** Panzerdivision, *die;* **~ed glass** Panzerglas, *das*

armourer /ˈɑːmərə(r)/ *n.* (Brit.) [1] (maker of arms) Waffentechniker, *der*/-technikerin, *die;* Waffenschmied, *der* (hist.) [2] (official in charge of arms) Waffenmeister, *der*/-meisterin, *die*

armoury /ˈɑːmərɪ/ *n.* (Brit.) [1] (array of weapons) Waffenarsenal, *das;* (fig.) Arsenal, *das;* **one of the strongest weapons in the British ~:** eine der stärksten britischen Waffen [2] (arsenal) [Waffen]arsenal, *das;* Waffenkammer, *die* [3] (Amer.: drill hall) Exerzierhalle, *die*

arm: ~pit *n.* Achselhöhle, *die;* **~rest** *n.* Armlehne, *die*

arms *n. pl.* [1] (weapons) Waffen; **possession/export of ~:** Waffenbesitz, *der*/-export, *der;* **small ~:** Handfeuerwaffen; **bear ~** (be armed) bewaffnet sein; (serve as soldier) Waffen tragen; **in ~:** bewaffnet; **lay down one's ~:** die Waffen niederlegen; **take up ~:** zu den Waffen greifen; **under ~:** bewaffnet; unter Waffen; **be up in ~ about sth.** (fig.) wegen etw. in Harnisch *od.* aufgebracht sein [2] (heraldic device) Wappen, *das;* (inn sign) **'The King's/Waterman's Arms'** ≈ „Zum König/Fährmann"; *see also* **coat of arms**

arms: ~ control *n.* Rüstungskontrolle, *die; attrib.* Rüstungskontroll-; **~ dealer** *n.* Waffenhändler, *der*/-händlerin, *die;* **~ dump** *n.* Waffendepot, *das;* Waffenlager, *das;* **~ embargo** *n.* Waffenembargo, *das;* **~ limitation** *n.* Rüstungsbegrenzung, *die; attrib.* Rüstungsbegrenzungs-; **~ manufacturer** *n.* Waffenhersteller, *der*/-herstellerin, *die;* **~ race** *n.* Rüstungswettlauf, *der;* **~ reduction** *n.* Abrüstung, *die; attrib.* Abrüstungs-; **~ trade** *n.* Waffenhandel, *der*

army /ˈɑːmɪ/ *n.* [1] (fighting force) Heer, *das;* **standing ~:** stehendes Heer; **mercenary ~:** Söldnerheer, *das;* **Napoleon's ~:** die Armee Napoleons [2] *no pl., no indef. art.* (military profession) Militär, *das;* **be in the ~:** beim Militär sein; **go into** *or* **join the ~:** zum Militär gehen; (as a career) die Militärlaufbahn einschlagen; **leave the ~:** aus dem Militärdienst ausscheiden [3] (large number) Heer, *das;* **an ~ of workmen/officials/ants** ein Heer von Arbeitern/Beamten/Ameisen

army: ~ corps *n.* Armeekorps, *das;* **A~ List** *n.* (Brit.) Rangliste des Heeres; **~ ˈsurplus store** *n.* Armeeladen, *der;* Militärladen, *der*

arnica /ˈɑːnɪkə/ *n.* Arnika, *die*

aroma /əˈrəʊmə/ *n.* (fragrance) Duft, *der*

aromatherapist /ərəʊməˈθerəpɪst/ *n.* ▸ⓘ **p. 1260** Aromatherapeut, *der*/-therapeutin, *die*

aromatherapy /ərəʊməˈθerəpɪ/ *n., no pl.* Aromatherapie, *die*

aromatic /ærəˈmætɪk/
A *adj.* (fragrant) aromatisch (auch Chem.); duftend ‹*Blütenblätter, Nelken usw.*›; (pleasant) angenehm würzig
B *n.* Duftstoff, *der*

arose ▸ **arise**

around /əˈraʊnd/
A *adv.* [1] (on every side) **[all] ~:** überall; **he waved his arms ~:** er ruderte mit den Armen; **all ~ there was nothing but trees** ringsumher *od.* ringsherum gab es nichts als Bäume [2] (round) herum; **come ~ to sb.'s house** bei jmdm. vorbeikommen; **show sb. ~:** jmdn. herumführen; **pass the hat ~:** den Hut herumgehen lassen; **have to get ~ to doing sth.** [endlich] einmal daran denken müssen, etw. zu tun; **look ~, have a look ~:** sich [ein bisschen] umsehen *od.* umschauen [3] (coll.: near) in der Nähe; **have you seen my hat ~?** hast du irgendwo meinen Hut gesehen?; **we'll always be ~ when you need us** wir werden immer da sein, wenn du uns brauchst [4] (coll.: in existence) vorhanden; **there's not/you don't see much leather ~ these days** zur Zeit gibt es/sieht man nur wenig Leder [5] (in various places) **ask/look ~:** herumfragen/-schauen;

travel ~ within England in England herumreisen; **he's been** ~ (fig.) er ist viel herumgekommen. *See also* **go around**; **hang around**

B *prep.* **1** um [… herum]; rund um; **they had their arms** ~ **each other** sie hielten sich umschlungen; **darkness closed in** ~ **us** die Dunkelheit umfing uns (geh.) *od.* schloss uns ein; **he wore a coat** ~ **his shoulders** er hatte einen Mantel um die Schultern gelegt **2** (here and there in) **we went** ~ **the town** wir gingen durch die Stadt; ~ **the garden you'll find …:** im Garten findet man … **3** (here and there near) ~ **London** um London herum **4** (round) um [… herum]; ~ **the back of the house** (position) hinter dem Haus; (direction) hinter das Haus **5** (approximately at) ~ **3 o'clock** ungefähr um 3 Uhr; gegen 3 Uhr; **I saw him somewhere** ~ **the station** ich habe ihn irgendwo am Bahnhof gesehen **6** (approximately equal to) etwa; ungefähr; **sth. [costing]** ~ **£2** etw. für um die *od.* ungefähr 2 Pfund

arousal /əˈraʊzl/ *n.* **1** (awakening) Aufwachen, *das* **2** (excitement, also sexual) Erregung, *die;* (calling into existence) (of interest, enthusiasm) Erweckung, *die;* (of hatred, passion) Erregung, *die*

arouse /əˈraʊz/ *v.t.* **1** (awake) [auf]wecken; ~ **sb. from his sleep** jmdn. aus dem Schlaf reißen **2** (excite) erregen; (call into existence) erwecken ‹*Interesse, Begeisterung*›; erregen ‹*Hass, Leidenschaften usw.*›; **be sexually ~d by sth./sb.** durch etw./jmdn. sexuell erregt werden; ~ **suspicion** Verdacht erregen

arpeggio /ɑːˈpedʒɪəʊ/ *n., pl.* **~s** (Mus.) Arpeggio, *das*

arr. *abbr.* **1** (Mus.) = **arranged by** Arr. **2** = **arrives** Ank.

arrack /ˈærək/ *n.* Arrak, *der*

arraign /əˈreɪn/ *v.t.* (indict) vor Gericht bringen, anklagen (**for** wegen); (accuse) beschuldigen; ~ **sb. for sth.** jmdm. die Schuld an etw. (*Dat.*) geben

arraignment /əˈreɪnmənt/ *n.* (indictment) Anklageerhebung, *die;* (accusation) Beschuldigung, *die;* **the** ~ **of them, their** ~**:** die Anklageerhebung gegen sie

arrange /əˈreɪndʒ/

A *v.t.* **1** (order) anordnen; (adjust) in Ordnung bringen; **the seating was ~d so that …:** die Sitzreihen waren so angeordnet, dass … **2** (Mus., Radio, etc.: adapt) bearbeiten **3** (settle beforehand) ausmachen, vereinbaren ‹*Termin*›; ~ **the catering for a party** sich um Essen und Trinken für eine Feier kümmern **4** (plan) planen ‹*Urlaub*›; aufstellen ‹*Stundenplan*›; **don't** ~ **anything for next Saturday** nimm dir für nächsten Sonnabend nichts vor **5** (resolve) beilegen; ins Reine bringen ‹*Beziehungen*›

B *v.i.* **1** (plan) sorgen (**for** für); ~ **for sb./sth. to do sth.** veranlassen *od.* dafür sorgen, dass jmd./etw. etw. tut; **can you** ~ **to be at home when …?** kannst du es so einrichten, dass du zu Hause bist, wenn …?; ~ **about sth.** etw. in die Wege leiten; **she ~d about getting him a work permit** sie leitete alles in die Wege, damit er eine Arbeitserlaubnis bekam **2** (agree) **they ~d to meet the following day** sie verabredeten sich für den nächsten Tag; ~ **with sb. about sth.** sich mit jmdm. über etw. (*Akk.*) einigen; ~ **with sb. about doing sth.** sich mit jmdm. darüber einigen, etw. zu tun

arrangement /əˈreɪndʒmənt/ *n.* **1** (ordering, order) Anordnung, *die;* (thing ordered) Arrangement, *das;* **seating** ~**:** Anordnung der Sitze **2** (Mus., Radio, etc.: adapting, adaptation) Bearbeitung, *die;* Arrangement, *das;* **a guitar** ~**:** eine Bearbeitung *od.* ein Arrangement für Gitarre **3** (settling beforehand) Vereinbarung, *die;* Übereinkunft, *die;* (of plans) Aufstellung, *die;* **by** ~**:** nach Vereinbarung *od.* Absprache **4** *in pl.* (plans) Vorkehrungen; **make ~s** Vorkehrungen treffen; **we have made ~s for you to be picked up from the airport** wir haben veranlasst, dass Sie vom Flughafen abgeholt werden; **holiday ~s** Urlaubsvorbereitungen; **~s about security** Sicherheitsvorkehrungen **5** (agreement) Vereinbarung, *die;* **make an** ~ **to do sth.** vereinbaren *od.* die Vereinbarung treffen, etw. zu tun; **the** ~ **is that …:** die Vereinbarung lautet, dass … **6** (resolution) Einigung, *die;* **make an** ~**:** eine Einigung erzielen; **I'm sure we can come to some** ~ **about …:** wir können uns sicher irgendwie einigen über (+ *Akk.*) …

arrant /ˈærənt/ *adj.* Erz‹*lump, -schurke, -lügner, -feigling*›; dreist ‹*Lüge, Missbrauch, Anmaßung*›; unverhüllt ‹*Grobheit, Heuchelei, Begierde*›; ~ **nonsense** barer Unsinn

arras /ˈærəs/ *n.* A[r]razzo, *der*

array /əˈreɪ/

A *v.t.* (formal: dress) kleiden; schmücken; ~ **sb. in sth.** jmdn. in etw. (*Akk.*) kleiden *od.* (geh.) hüllen; ~ **sth. with sth.** etw. mit etw. schmücken

B *n.* (ordered display) Reihe, *die*

arrears /əˈrɪəz/ *n. pl.* (debts) Schulden *Pl.;* Rückstände *Pl.;* (remainder) **there were huge** ~ **of work to be done/letters to be answered** es war noch eine Menge Arbeit aufzuholen/es mussten noch zahlreiche Briefe beantwortet werden; **the work on the building is badly in** ~**:** man ist mit den Arbeiten an dem Gebäude beträchtlich in Verzug [geraten]; **be in** ~ **with sth.** mit etw. im Rückstand sein; **be paid in** ~**:** rückwirkend bezahlt werden

arrest /əˈrest/

A *v.t.* **1** (stop) aufhalten; zum Stillstand bringen ‹*Fluss*›; ~ **judgement** (Law) ein/das Urteil aufheben **2** (seize) verhaften, (temporarily) festnehmen ‹*Person*›; beschlagnahmen ‹*Sache*› **3** (catch) erregen ‹*Aufmerksamkeit, Interesse*›; (catch attention of) fesseln; faszinieren

B *n.* **1** (stoppage) Stillstand, *der;* ~ **of judgement** (Law) Aussetzung des/eines Verfahrens; **cardiac** ~**:** Herzstillstand, *der* **2** (legal apprehension) (of person) Verhaftung, *die;* (temporary) Festnahme, *die;* (of thing) Beschlagnahme, *die;* **under** ~**:** festgenommen; **he was put under police/military** ~**:** er wurde in Polizeigewahrsam genommen/unter Arrest gestellt

arrestable /əˈrestəbl/ *adj.* **be an** ~ **act/offence** ein Grund zur Festnahme sein

arˈrest warrant *n.* Haftbefehl, *der*

arris /ˈærɪs/ *n.* (Archit.) [Dach]grat, *der*

arrival /əˈraɪvl/ *n.* **1** Ankunft, *die;* (fig.: at decision etc.) Gelangen, *das* (**at** zu); (of mail etc.) Eintreffen, *das;* (coming) Kommen, *das;* Nahen, *das;* **it marked his** ~ **in the literary world** damit hat er sich in der literarischen Welt etabliert; **'A~'** „Ankunft"; **~s hall** Ankunftshalle, *die* **2** (appearance) Auftauchen, *das;* **the** ~ **of buds in springtime** das Sprießen der Knospen im Frühling **3** (person) Ankömmling, *der;* (thing) Lieferung, *die;* **new** ~ (coll.: newborn baby) Neugeborene, *das;* **how's the new** ~**?** (coll.) wie gehts dem neuen Erdenbürger?; **new ~s** Neuankömmlinge; **late ~s at the theatre** verspätet eintreffende Theaterbesucher

arrive /əˈraɪv/ *v.i.* **1** ankommen; **when do we** ~ **at Frankfurt?** wann kommen wir in Frankfurt an? ~ **at a conclusion/an agreement** zu einem Schluss/einer Einigung kommen; **we've ~d at stalemate** wir sind in eine Sackgasse geraten; **the train is just arriving** der Zug läuft gerade ein **2** (establish oneself) es schaffen; arrivieren (geh.); **with this book he ~d** mit diesem Buch hat er es geschafft **3** (be brought) eintreffen; (coll.: be born) ankommen; **what time does the mail usually** ~**?** wann kommt die Post normalerweise? **4** (come) ‹*Stunde, Tag, Augenblick:*› kommen; **the time has ~d when …:** jetzt ist der Zeitpunkt gekommen, wo …

arrogance /ˈærəgəns/ *n., no pl.* Arroganz, *die;* (presumptuousness) Anmaßung, *die;* Überheblichkeit, *die*

arrogant /ˈærəgənt/ *adj.* arrogant; (presumptuous) überheblich; anmaßend

arrogantly /ˈærəgəntlɪ/ *adv.* arrogant; penetrant ‹*überlegen, stolz*›; (presumptuously) anmaßend; überheblich; anmaßenderweise ‹*behaupten, verlangen*›

arrogate /ˈærəgeɪt/ *v.t.* (claim) ~ **sth. to oneself** etw. für sich in Anspruch nehmen; sich (*Dat.*) etw. anmaßen

arrow /ˈærəʊ/

A *n.* (missile) Pfeil, *der;* (pointer) [Hinweis-, Richtungs]pfeil, *der;* **as straight as an** ~**:** schnurgerade

B *v.t.* mit einem Pfeil/mit Pfeilen markieren

arrow: ~head *n.* **1** Pfeilspitze, *die;* **2** (Bot.) Pfeilkraut, *das;* ~ **key** *n.* (Computing) Cursortaste, *die;* Pfeiltaste, *die;* **~root** *n.* **1** (plant) Pfeilwurz, *die;* **2** (starch) Arrowroot, *das* (*Stärkemehl*)

arse[1] /ɑːs/ *n.* (coarse) Arsch, *der* (derb); **move your** ~**!** sei nicht so lahmarschig! (derb)

Phrasal verb

• ~ **aˈbout,** ~ **around** *v. i.* (Brit. coarse) herumalbern (ugs.); herumblödeln (ugs.)

arse[2] ▸ **ass**[1] **B**

arse: ~hole *n.* (coarse) Arschloch, *das* (derb); **~-licking** *n., no pl.* (coarse) Arschkriecherei, *die* (derb); Schleimscheißerei, *die* (derb)

arsenal /ˈɑːsənl/ *n.* (store) [Waffen]arsenal, *das;* Waffenlager, *das;* (fig.) Arsenal, *das*

arsenic /ˈɑːsənɪk/ *n.* (Chem.) **1** Arsenik, *das* **2** (element) Arsen, *das*

arson /ˈɑːsn/ *n.* Brandstiftung, *die*

arsonist /ˈɑːsənɪst/ *n.* Brandstifter, *der*/Brandstifterin, *die*

art /ɑːt/ *n.* **1** Kunst, *die;* **the ~s** ▸ **fine art 3** **2** (skill, skilled activity) Kunst, *die;* **works of** ~**:** Kunstwerke *Pl.;* ~ **needlework/music/film** künstlerische Handarbeit/Kunstmusik/Kunstfilm; **~s and crafts** Kunsthandwerk, *das;* Kunstgewerbe, *das;* **he is a master of his** ~**:** er ist ein Meister [in] seiner Kunst; **translation is an** ~**:** Übersetzen ist eine Kunst **3** *in pl.* (branch of study) Geisteswissenschaften; **he's an ~s student** er studiert Geisteswissenschaften; **faculty of ~s** philosophische Fakultät; **he has an ~s degree** er hat das Abschlussexamen der philosophischen Fakultät [gemacht]; **Bachelor/Master of Arts** Bakkalaureus/Magister der philosophischen Fakultät **4** (knack) Kunst, *die;* (stratagem) Kunstgriff, *der;* Kniff, *der* (ugs.); **an** ~ **in itself** eine Kunst für sich **5** (cunning) List, *die*

art: ~ **collection** *n.* Kunstsammlung, *die;* ~ **collector** *n.* Kunstsammler, *der;* ~ **college** ▸ ~ **school**

art deco /ɑːt ˈdekəʊ/ *n., no pl.* Art déco, *der u. das*

artefact /ˈɑːtɪfækt/ *n.* Artefakt, *das*

arterial /ɑːˈtɪərɪəl/ *adj.* **1** (of artery) arteriell **2** (principal) Haupt-; ~ **road** Hauptverkehrsstraße, *die*

arteriosclerosis /ɑːtɪərɪəʊskləˈrəʊsɪs/ *n., pl.* **arterioscleroses** /ɑːtɪərɪəʊskləˈrəʊsiːz/ ▸ⓘ **p. 1231** (Med.) Arteriosklerose, *die* (fachspr.); Arterienverkalkung, *die*

artery /ˈɑːtərɪ/ *n.* **1** ▸ⓘ **p. 951** (Anat.) Schlagader, *die;* Arterie, *die* (bes. fachspr.) **2** (fig.: road etc.) [Haupt]verkehrsader, *die*

artesian /ɑːˈtiːzɪən, ɑːˈtiːʒən/ *adj.* ~ **well** artesischer Brunnen

ˈart form *n.* (form of composition) Kunstform, *die;* [Kunst]gattung, *die;* (medium of expression) Kunst[form], *die*

artful /ˈɑːtfl/ *adj.* schlau; raffiniert; ~ **dodger** Schlawiner, *der*

artfully /ˈɑːtfəlɪ/ *adv.* schlau; raffiniert

artfulness /ˈɑːtflnɪs/ *n., no pl.* Schlauheit, *die;* Raffiniertheit, *die*

art: ~ **gallery** *n.* Kunstgalerie, *die;* ~ **house** *n.* **1** (building) Programmkino, *das;* Arthaus, *das;* **2** (genre) Arthausfilm, *der;* **~-house** *adj.* Arthaus-; **~-house film** Arthausfilm, *der; künstlerisch anspruchsvoller Film*

arthritic /ɑːˈθrɪtɪk/ (Med.)

A *adj.* arthritisch; **she's got** ~ **joints in her fingers** sie hat Arthritis in den Fingergelenken

B *n.* Arthritiker, *der*/Arthritikerin, *die*

arthritis /ɑːˈθraɪtɪs/ *n.* ▸ⓘ **p. 1231** (Med.) Arthritis, *die* (fachspr.); Gelenkentzündung, *die*

arthropod /ˈɑːθrəpɒd/ *n.* (Zool.) Gliederfüßler, *der;* **the ~s** die Arthropoden

Arthur /ˈɑːθə(r)/ *pr. n.* **King** ~**:** König Artus

a

artic /ɑːˈtɪk/ *n.* (coll.) Zug, *der* (ugs.); Sattelschlepper, *der* (ugs.)

artichoke /ˈɑːtɪtʃəʊk/ *n.* **[globe] ~:** Artischocke, *die;* **Jerusalem ~:** Topinambur, *der;* (edible part) Topinamburwurzel, *die*

article /ˈɑːtɪkl/
A *n.* **1** (of constitution, treaty) Artikel, *der;* (of creed) Glaubensartikel, *der;* (of indictment) [Anklage]punkt, *der;* (of agreement) [Vertrags]punkt, *der;* (of the law) Paragraph, *der;* (in dictionary etc.) Eintrag, *der;* **~s [of association]** Satzung, *die;* **~s of apprenticeship/employment** Lehr-/Arbeitsvertrag, *der;* **~ of faith** (fig.) Glaubensbekenntnis, *das* (fig.) **2** (in magazine, newspaper) Artikel, *der;* (in technical journal) Beitrag, *der;* Aufsatz, *der* **3** (Ling.) Artikel, *der;* Geschlechtswort, *das;* **definite/indefinite ~:** bestimmter/unbestimmter Artikel **4** (particular part, thing) Artikel, *der;* **woollen ~s [of clothing]** Wollsachen; **an ~ of furniture/clothing** ein Möbel-/Kleidungsstück; **an ~ of value** ein Wertgegenstand
B *v.t.* in die Lehre geben (**to** bei); **be ~d to sb.** bei jmdm. in der Lehre sein

articled /ˈɑːtɪkld/ *adj.* **~ clerk** (Law) Rechtspraktikant, *der*/-praktikantin, *die;* ≈ Rechtsreferendar, *der*/-referendarin, *die*

articulate
A /ɑːˈtɪkjʊlət/ *adj.* **1** (clear) verständlich **2** (eloquent) redegewandt; **be ~/not very ~:** sich gut/nicht sehr gut ausdrücken [können] **3** (jointed) gegliedert; Glieder-; (distinctly joined) aus Einzelgliedern; mit Gelenken
B /ɑːˈtɪkjʊleɪt/ *v.t.* **1** *usu. in pass.* durch Gelenke/ein Gelenk verbinden; **~d lorry** Sattelzug, *der;* Sattelschlepper, *der* (ugs.) **2** (pronounce) [deutlich] aussprechen; (utter, express) artikulieren; in Worte fassen
C *v.i.* **1** (speak distinctly) artikuliert sprechen; deutlich sprechen; **~ clearly** klar und deutlich sprechen **2** (speak) sprechen **3** (form a joint) **~ with sth.** mit etw. ein Gelenk bilden

articulately /ɑːˈtɪkjʊlətlɪ/ *adv.* **1** (clearly) klar; deutlich **2** (coherently) klar; **he expresses himself very ~:** er drückt sich sehr klar aus

articulateness /ɑːˈtɪkjʊlətnɪs/ *n., no pl.* (clarity) Deutlichkeit, *die;* (coherence) Klarheit, *die*

articulation /ɑːtɪkjʊˈleɪʃn/ *n.* **1** (clear speech) deutliche Aussprache; **his ~ is good** er hat eine deutliche Aussprache **2** (coherent speech) flüssige Ausdrucksweise; (act of speaking) Artikulation, *die;* [Laut]bildung, *die*

artifact (Amer.) ▸ **artefact**

artifice /ˈɑːtɪfɪs/ *n.* **1** (cunning) List, *die;* Raffinement, *das* (geh.) **2** (device) Trick, *der;* List, *die*

artificial /ɑːtɪˈfɪʃl/ *adj.* **1** (not natural) künstlich; Kunst-; (not real) unecht; imitiert; (**~ly** produced) künstlich; Kunst-; synthetisch [hergestellt]; **~ sweetener** Süßstoff, *der;* **~ limb** Prothese, *die;* **~ eye** Glasauge, *das* **2** (affected, insincere) gekünstelt; unecht; **she's ~ and two-faced** sie verstellt sich; **~ politeness** gekünstelte *od.* gespielte Höflichkeit; **she wore an ~ smile for the cameras** für die Fotografen setzte sie ein einstudiertes Lächeln auf; **her ~ enthusiasm** ihre gespielte Begeisterung

artificial: ~ 'aid *n.* [künstliches] Hilfsmittel; **~ ho'rizon** *n.* Kreiselhorizont, *der;* **~ insemi'nation** *n.* künstliche Befruchtung; (of animal) künstliche Besamung; **~ in'telligence** *n.* künstliche Intelligenz

artificiality /ɑːtɪfɪʃɪˈælɪtɪ/ *n., no pl.* **1** (unnaturalness) Künstlichkeit, *die* **2** (unreality) Unechtheit, *die* **3** (affectedness) Affektiertheit, *die;* Geziertheit, *die;* (formality) Förmlichkeit, *die;* (insincerity) Gekünsteltheit, *die*

artificial: ~ 'kidney ▸ **kidney machine**; **~ 'language** *n.* Kunstsprache, *die*

artificially /ɑːtɪˈfɪʃəlɪ/ *adv.* **1** (unnaturally) künstlich; unnatürlich; **the food has been ~ flavoured** die Lebensmittel sind mit künstlichem Geschmacksstoff versetzt; **~ produced diamonds/pearls** synthetische Diamanten/künstliche Perlen **2** (affectedly, insincerely) affektiert; geziert

artificialness /ɑːtɪˈfɪʃəlnɪs/ ▸ **artificiality**

artificial respi'ration *n.* künstliche Beatmung

artillery /ɑːˈtɪlərɪ/ *n.* Artillerie, *die*

artilleryman /ɑːˈtɪlərɪmən/ *n., pl.* **artillerymen** /ɑːˈtɪlərɪmən/ Artillerist, *der*

artisan /ˈɑːtɪzn, ɑːtɪˈzæn/ *n.* [Kunst]handwerker, *der*

artist /ˈɑːtɪst/ *n.* ▸ **❶ p. 1260** **1** (exponent of a fine art) Künstler, *der*/Künstlerin, *die;* (fig.) Künstler, *der*/Künstlerin, *die;* Könner, *der*/Könnerin, *die;* **he's an ~ in words/rhetoric** er ist ein Wort-/Redekünstler; **she's an ~ in cookery** sie ist eine Kochkünstlerin; **he's a real ~ at his job** er ist ein echter Könner seines Fachs **2** ▸ **artiste**

artiste /ɑːˈtiːst/ *n.* Artist, *der*/Artistin, *die;* Künstler, *der*/Künstlerin, *die;* **circus ~s** Zirkusartisten *Pl.*

artistic /ɑːˈtɪstɪk/ *adj.* **1** (of art) Kunst-; künstlerisch; **~ movements such as Expressionism** Kunstrichtungen, zum Beispiel der Expressionismus; **the ~ world** die Welt der Kunst **2** (of artists) Künstler-; künstlerisch; **~ circles** Künstlerkreise **3** (made with art) kunstvoll; Kunst-; **~ designs** kunstvolle Muster; **a truly ~ piece of poetry/writing** ein dichterisches/schriftstellerisches Kunstwerk **4** (naturally skilled in art) künstlerisch veranlagt *od.* begabt; **she's quite ~:** sie ist künstlerisch ziemlich begabt; **have ~ leanings** künstlerische Neigungen haben **5** (appreciative of art) kunstverständig; **~ sense** Kunstverständnis, *das*

artistically /ɑːˈtɪstɪkəlɪ/ *adv.* **1** (in art) künstlerisch; in der Kunst; (from an artist's viewpoint) künstlerisch [gesehen] **2** (with art) kunstvoll ‹*geschmückt, gestaltet*› **3** künstlerisch ‹*begabt, veranlagt*›; **be ~ interested/appreciative** an Kunst interessiert sein/einen Sinn für Kunst haben

artistry /ˈɑːtɪstrɪ/ *n., no pl.* **1** (artistic pursuit) künstlerisches Schaffen **2** (artistic ability) künstlerische Fähigkeit[en]; künstlerisches Geschick; (artistic quality) Kunst, *die;* künstlerischer Wert

artless /ˈɑːtlɪs/ *adj.* **1** (guileless) arglos; **~ piety** schlichte Frömmigkeit **2** (simple) schmucklos; schlicht; **~ beauty/grace** natürliche Schönheit/Anmut

artlessly /ˈɑːtlɪslɪ/ *adv.* **1** (guilelessly) arglos **2** (simply) schmucklos; schlicht

artlessness /ˈɑːtlɪsnɪs/ *n., no pl.* **1** (guilelessness) Arglosigkeit, *die* **2** (simplicity) Schmucklosigkeit, *die;* Schlichtheit, *die*

art: ~ nouveau /ɑː nuːˈvəʊ/ *n.* Jugendstil, *der;* **~ paper** *n.* Kunstdruckpapier, *das;* **~ room** *n.* Kunstsaal, *der*

Arts and Crafts Movement

Eine englische Bewegung zur Reform des Kunsthandwerks in der zweiten Hälfte des 19. Jahrhunderts. Die Bewegung ging von William Morris (1834-96) aus, der mit John Ruskin (1819-1900) und anderen Architekten und Malern eine Gesellschaft zur Herstellung kunsthandwerklicher Gegenstände gründete, um der zunehmend industriellen Massenproduktion entgegenzuwirken. Während der *Industrial Revolution* (industrielle Revolution) wurden mehr und mehr Gebrauchsgegenstände, oft mit minderwertigem Ergebnis, maschinell hergestellt. Ziel der Arts-and-Crafts-Bewegung war es, die mittelalterliche Handwerksstruktur mit sozialistischen Gemeinschaftsvorstellungen zu verbinden.

'arts centre *n.* Kunstzentrum, *das*

art school *n.* Kunsthochschule, *die;*

Arts Council

Eine der vier Organisationen (je eine in England, Schottland, Wales und Nordirland) zur Förderung von Kunst und Kultur innerhalb Großbritanniens. Zuwendungen aus öffentlichen Mitteln ▸▸▸

▸▸▸ werden an kulturelle Einrichtungen und Festspiele vergeben. Der *Arts Council* von Großbritannien, der 1946 gegründet wurde, subventioniert Theater, Orchester, Ausstellungen, Festivals, sowie einzelne Künstler und Schriftsteller mit dem Ziel, Kunst und Kultur zu unterstützen und breiteren Kreisen zugänglich zu machen.

art: ~ student *n.* Kunststudent, *der*/-studentin, *die;* **~ theft** *n.* Kunstraub, *der;* **~work** *n.* Bildmaterial, *das*

arty /ˈɑːtɪ/ *adj.* (coll.) auf Künstler machend; **he's an ~ type** er ist so ein Künstlertyp; **~ furniture** auf Kunst gemachte Möbel; **an ~ design** ein pseudokünstlerisches Muster; **~-crafty** (joc.) auf Kunstgewerbe gemacht

arum /ˈeərəm/ *n.* (Bot.) Aronstab, *der;* **~ lily** Zimmercalla, *die*

Aryan /ˈeərɪən/
A *adj.* indogermanisch; arisch (veralt.)
B *n.* (person) Arier, *der*/Arierin, *die* (bes. ns.); Indogermane, *der*/Indogermanin, *die*

as /əz, *stressed* æz/
A *adv. in main sentence* (in same degree) **as ... [as ...]** so ... [wie ...]; **as soon as possible** so bald wie möglich; **almost as tall as ...:** fast so groß wie ...; **half as much** halb soviel; **you know as well as I do that ...:** Sie wissen genauso gut wie ich, dass ...; **they did as much as they could** sie taten, was sie konnten; **as good a ... [as ...]** ein so guter ... [wie ...]/eine so gute ... [wie ...]/ein so gutes ... [wie ...]
B *rel. adv. or conj. in subord. clause* **1** *expr. degree* **[as** *or* **so] ... as ...:** [so ...] wie ...; **as ... as possible** so ... wie möglich; **as ... as you can** so ...[, wie] Sie können; **come as quickly as you can** kommen Sie, so schnell Sie können; **quick as a flash** blitzschnell; **as recently as [this morning]** erst [heute Morgen]; **as early as [tomorrow]** schon *od.* bereits *od.* gleich [morgen]
2 (though) **... as he** *etc.* **is/was** obwohl er *usw.* ... ist/war; **intelligent as she is/was, ...:** obwohl sie ziemlich intelligent ist/war, ...; **safe as it might be, ...:** obwohl es vielleicht ungefährlich ist, ...
3 (however much) **try as he might/would, he could not concentrate** sosehr er sich auch bemühte, er konnte sich nicht konzentrieren; **push/strain/pull as he might/would, ...:** wie sehr er auch drückte/sich anstrengte/zog, ...
4 *expr. manner* wie; **as you may already have heard, ...:** wie Sie vielleicht schon gehört haben, ...; **as we are all well aware, ...:** wie wir alle sehr wohl wissen, ...; **as we had hoped/expected ...:** wie erhofft/erwartet, ...; **as it were** sozusagen; gewissermaßen; **as you were!** Kommando zurück!
5 *expr. time* als; während; **as and when** wann immer; **as we climbed the stairs** als wir die Treppe hinaufgingen; **as we were talking** während wir uns unterhielten; **he knew her as a teenager** er kannte sie schon, als sie noch ein Teenager war
6 *expr. reason* da; **as we're now all assembled** da wir jetzt vollzählig sind
7 *expr. result* **so ... as to ...** so ... zu; **would you be so kind as to help us?** würden Sie so freundlich sein und uns helfen?
8 *expr. purpose* **so as to ...** um ... zu ...
9 *expr. illustration* wie [z. B.]; **industrial areas, as the north-east of England for example** Industriegebiete wie z. B. der Nordosten Englands
C *prep.* **1** (in the function of) als; **as an artist** als Künstler; **speaking as a parent, ...:** als Mutter/Vater ...
2 (like) wie; **he's treated as an outcast** er wird wie ein Ausgestoßener behandelt; **they regard him as a fool** sie halten ihn für einen Dummkopf
D *rel. pron.* (which) **fool as he was he did not notice the obvious dangers** dumm, wie er war, sah er die Gefahren nicht; **as is our custom** wie immer; **they danced, as was the custom there** sie tanzten, wie es dort Sitte war; **he was shocked, as were we all** er war wie wir alle schockiert; **it was him/the earthquake as did it** (uneducated) er ists gewesen/das

ℹ As

When used as a preposition or conjunction to mean *like*, the usual translation is **wie:**

as usual
= wie gewöhnlich

as explained below
= wie unten erklärt

as so often
= wie so oft

as you may have heard
= wie Sie vielleicht gehört haben

as was the custom there
= wie es dort Sitte war

Note also:

a coat the same colour as mine
= ein Mantel in derselben Farbe wie meiner

a writer such as Dickens
= ein Schriftsteller wie Dickens

However if the sense is *in the manner of* or *in the function of*, the translation is **als** (note that *a*/*an* is not translated):

dressed as a sailor
= als Matrose gekleidet

He works as an engineer
= Er arbeitet als Ingenieur

my duty as a father
= meine Pflicht als Vater

In comparisons (*as ... as ...*) the first *as* is translated by **so,** but this is often omitted in set similes:

She is as old as my mother
= Sie ist so alt wie meine Mutter

This car is not as fast as yours
= Dieses Auto ist nicht so schnell wie deins

He is not as good a cook as you
= Er ist kein so guter Koch wie du

He is as wily as a fox
= Er ist schlau wie ein Fuchs

Where a verb such as *can*/*could* or *want*/*like* comes after the *as*, **wie** is usually omitted:

Come as quickly as you can
= Komm, so schnell du kannst

Take as much as you like
= Nimm, so viel du willst

And where the sense of *as ... as* is the same as *however*, the translation is *wie ... auch:*

As fast as we rowed* (= However fast we rowed), *the others rowed faster
= Wie schnell wir auch ruderten, die anderen ruderten schneller

For the conjunction in time expressions, the translations are **als** (with the sense of *when*) or **während** (with the sense of *while*):

As I stepped into the house, I heard her voice
= Als ich in das Haus hineintrat, hörte ich ihre Stimme

As we were talking, the doorbell rang
= Während wir uns unterhielten, klingelte es

And expressing a reason with the sense of *since*, the translation is **da:**

As I am going to London I can take it with me
= Da ich nach London fahre, kann ich es mitnehmen

Erdbeben wars; **the same as ...:** der-/die-/dasselbe wie ...; **such as** wie zum Beispiel; **they enjoy such foreign foods as ...:** sie essen gern ausländische Lebensmittel wie ...

E **as far** ▸ **far A 4; as for ...:** was ... angeht *od.* betrifft *od.* anbelangt; **as from ...:** von ... an; **you will receive a pension as from your 60th birthday** vom 61. Lebensjahr an bekommen Sie Rente; **you are dismissed as from today** Sie sind mit sofortiger Wirkung entlassen; **as [it] is** wie die Dinge liegen; wie es aussieht; **I'll take the dress as it is** ich nehme das Kleid, wie es ist; **the place is untidy enough as it is** es ist schon liederlich genug[, wie es jetzt ist]; **as of ...:** von ... an; **as of 31 December annually** am 31. 12. jeden Jahres; **as to** hinsichtlich (+ *Gen.*); **nothing further was mentioned as to holiday plans** von Urlaubsplänen wurde nichts weiter gesagt; **as was** wie es einmal war; **Miss Tay as was** das frühere Fräulein Tay; **as yet** bis jetzt; noch; **as yet the plan is only under discussion** der Plan wird noch diskutiert

a.s.a.p. *abbr.* **= as soon as possible**

asbestos /æz'bestɒs, æs'bestɒs/ *n.* **1** (fabric) Asbest, *der* **2** (mineral) Amiant, *der*

asbestosis /æzbes'təʊsɪs, æsbes'təʊsɪs/ *n., no pl.* ▸ℹ **p. 1231** (Med.) Asbestose, *die* (fachspr.); Staublungenerkrankung, *die;* **suffer from ~:** eine Staublunge haben

ASBO /'æzbəʊ/ *abbr.* (Brit.) **= antisocial behaviour order**

ascend /ə'send/

A *v.i.* **1** (go up) hinaufgehen *od.* -steigen; (climb up) hinaufklettern; (by vehicle) hinauffahren; (come up) heraufkommen; **the lift ~ed** der Aufzug fuhr nach oben; **Christ ~ed into heaven** Christus fuhr auf gen Himmel (geh.); **~ in the lift** mit dem Aufzug hinauffahren **2** (rise) [höher-]steigen; aufsteigen; **the helicopter ~ed slowly** der Hubschrauber stieg langsam höher **3** (slope upwards) ‹*Hügel, Straße:*› ansteigen; **the stairs ~ very steeply** die Treppe ist sehr steil **4** (in quality, rank, etc.) aufsteigen **5** (in pitch) höher werden

B *v.t.* **1** (go up) hinaufsteigen, hinaufgehen ‹*Treppe, Leiter, Berg*›; **~ a rope** an einem Seil hochklettern **2** (come up) **we saw a fireman ~ing the ladder towards us** wir sahen einen Feuerwehrmann die Leiter heraufsteigen **3** (go along) hinauffahren ‹*Straße*› **4** **~ the throne** den Thron besteigen

ascendancy /ə'sendənsɪ/ *n., no pl.* beherrschender Einfluss; Vorherrschaft, *die;* **gain/have the ~ over sb.** die Vorherrschaft über jmdn. gewinnen/haben

ascendant /ə'sendənt/ *n.* **1** (Astrol.) Aszendent, *der* **2** **in the ~:** im Aufsteigen begriffen; **his popularity was now firmly in the ~:** seine Beliebtheit nahm beständig zu

ascension /ə'senʃn/ *n.* **1** (going up) Auffahrt, *die;* **right ~** (Astron.) Rektaszension, *die* **2** **[the] A~** (Relig.) [Christi] Himmelfahrt

A'scension Day *n.* Himmelfahrtstag, *der*

ascent /ə'sent/ *n.* **1** (going up, rise; also fig.) Aufstieg, *der;* **our ~ in the lift/up the hill** unsere Auffahrt mit dem Lift/unser Aufstieg den Berg hinauf **2** (way; also fig.) Aufstieg, *der* **3** (slope) Steigung, *die* **4** (steps) Aufgang, *der*

ascertain /æsə'teɪn/ *v.t.* feststellen; ermitteln ‹*Fakten, Daten*›

ascertainable /æsə'teɪnəbl/ *adj.* feststellbar; zu ermittelnd ‹*Fakten, Daten*›

ascertainment /æsə'teɪnmənt/ *n., no pl.* Feststellung, *die;* (of facts, data) Ermittlung, *die;* (of information) Beschaffung, *die*

ascetic /ə'setɪk/

A *adj.* asketisch

B *n.* **1** Asket, *der*/Asketin, *die* **2** (Relig. Hist.) Eremit, *der;* Klausner, *der*

ascetically /ə'setɪkəlɪ/ *adv.* asketisch

asceticism /ə'setɪsɪzm/ *n., no pl.* Askese, *die*

ASCII /'æskɪ/ *abbr.* (Computing) **= American Standard Code for Information Interchange** ASCII, *der*

ascorbic acid /ə'skɔ:bɪk æsɪd/ *n., no pl.* Askorbinsäure, *die*

ascribe /ə'skraɪb/ *v.t.* zuschreiben (**to** *Dat.*); **~ sth. to sth./sb.** (regard as belonging) etw. einer Sache/jmdm. zuschreiben; (attribute, impute) etw. auf etw./jmdn. zurückführen

ascription /ə'skrɪpʃn/ *n.* ▸ **ascribe:** Zuschreiben, *das;* Zurückführen, *das*

asepsis /eɪ'sepsɪs/ *n., no pl.* **1** (absence of sepsis) Asepsis, *die;* Keimfreiheit, *die* (fachspr.) **2** (aseptic method) Aseptik, *die* (fachspr.); keimfreie Wundbehandlung

aseptic /eɪ'septɪk/ *adj.* aseptisch

asexual /eɪ'sekʃʊəl/ *adj.* **1** (without sexuality) asexuell **2** (Biol.: without sex) asexual; ungeschlechtig; **~ reproduction** ungeschlechtliche Vermehrung

asexually /eɪ'seksjʊəlɪ/ *adv.* (Biol.) ungeschlechtlich

ash[1] /æʃ/ *n.* **1** (tree) Esche, *die* **2** (wood) Eschenholz, *das. See also* **mountain ash**

ash[2] *n.* **1** (powdery residue) Asche, *die;* **layer of ~:** Ascheschicht, *die;* **cigarette ~:** Zigarettenasche, *die;* **sweep up the ~[es]** die Asche auffegen **2** *in pl.* (remains) Asche, *die;* **in ~es** in Schutt und Asche; *see also* **sackcloth** **3** (Cricket) **the Ashes** *Trophäe für den Gewinner einer Serie von Vergleichswettkämpfen zwischen den Mannschaften Englands und Australiens*

ashamed /ə'ʃeɪmd/ *adj., usu. pred.* beschämt; **we were ~:** wir schämten uns *od.* waren beschämt; **be ~ [of sb./sth.]** sich [jmds./einer Sache wegen] schämen; **you ought to be ~ of yourselves for telling lies** ihr solltet euch schämen zu lügen; **be/feel ~ for sb./sth.** sich für jmdn./etw. schämen; **be ~ to do sth.** sich schämen, etw. zu tun; **I'm ~ to have to say/admit that I told a white lie** ich muss leider *od.* zu meiner Schande zugeben, dass ich eine Notlüge erzählt habe; **he was not ~ to stand up and say that ...:** er schämte sich nicht, aufzustehen und zuzugeben, dass ...

ash: ~ bin *n.* Mülleimer, *der;* **~ blonde** **A** *adj.* aschblond; **B** *n.* Aschblonde, *der/die;* **~can** (Amer.) ▸ **~ bin**

ashen /'æʃn/ *adj.* **1** (ash-coloured) aschfarben; aschfahl ‹*Gesicht*›; **~ grey** aschgrau **2** (of ashes) aus Asche; Asche-

ashore /ə'ʃɔ:(r)/ *adv.* (position) an Land; am Ufer; (direction) an Land; ans Ufer; **go/be ~:** an Land gehen/sein

'ashpan *n.* Aschkasten, *der*

ashram /'æʃrəm/ *n.* Ashram, *das od. der*

ash: ~tray *n.* Aschenbecher, *der;* **~ tree** ▸ **ash**[1] **1; Ash 'Wednesday** *n.* Aschermittwoch, *der;* **~wood** ▸ **ash**[1] **2**

Asia /'eɪʃə/ *pr. n.* Asien (*das*); **~ 'Minor** Kleinasien (*das*)

Asian /'eɪʃən, 'eɪʒən/, **Asiatic** /eɪʃɪ'ætɪk, eɪʒɪ-/

A *adj.* asiatisch

B *n.* Asiat, *der*/Asiatin, *die*

Asian A'merican *n.* Amerikaner, *der*/Amerikanerin, *die* [ost]asiatischer Abstammung

Asian American

Dies ist zur Zeit der gebräuchlichste Begriff für einen Amerikaner asiatischer, besonders fernöstlicher Abstammung.

aside /ə'saɪd/

A *adv.* beiseite; zur Seite; **stand ~!** treten Sie zur Seite!; **I pulled the curtain ~:** ich zog den Vorhang zur Seite; **~ from sb./sth.** außer jmdm./etw.; **take sb. ~:** jmdn. beiseite nehmen

B *n.* **1** (in a play) Apart, *das;* Beiseitesprechen, *das* **2** (incidental remark) [beiläufige] Bemerkung

asinine /'æsɪnaɪn/ *adj.* (stupid) dämlich; **don't be so ~:** sei kein Esel

asininity /æsɪ'nɪnɪtɪ/ *n.* Dämlichkeit, *die*

ask /ɑ:sk/

A *v.t.* **1** fragen; **~ [sb.] a question** [jmdm.] eine Frage stellen; **~ sb.'s name** nach jmds. Namen fragen; **~ sb. [sth.]** jmdn. [nach etw.] fragen; **I was ~ed some awkward questions by the boss** der Chef stellte mir einige unangenehme Fragen; **~ sb. about sth.** jmdn. nach etw. fragen; **I ~ you!** (coll.) ich muss schon sagen!; **if you ~ 'me** (coll.) [also,] wenn du mich fragst; **~ me another** (coll.) frag mich was Leichteres (ugs.) **2** (seek to obtain) **~ sth.** um etw. bitten; **~ sb.'s advice on sth.** jmdn. wegen etw. um Rat fragen; **how much are you**

~ing for that car? wie viel verlangen Sie für das Auto?; ~ a favour of sb., ~ sb. a favour jmdn. um einen Gefallen bitten; ~ sb. to do sth. jmdn. [darum] bitten, etw. zu tun; you have only to ~: du brauchst es nur zu sagen; ~ a lot of sb. viel von jmdm. verlangen; it's ~ing a lot es ist viel verlangt; it's yours for the ~ing du kannst es gern haben **3** (invite) einladen; ~ sb. to dinner jmdn. zum Essen einladen; ~ sb. out jmdn. einladen; the boss ~ed me up to his office der Chef hat mich gebeten, in sein Büro hinaufzukommen
B *v.i.* you may well ~: du hast allen Grund zu fragen; ~ after sb./sth. nach jmdm./etw. fragen; ~ after sb.'s health fragen, wie es jmdm. [gesundheitlich] geht; ~ for sth./sb. etw./jmdn. verlangen; ~ for it (coll.: invite trouble) es herausfordern; es so *od.* nicht anders haben wollen; *see also* trouble A 1

askance /ə'skæns, ə'skɑ:ns/ *adv.* **1** (sideways) von der Seite **2** (suspiciously) look ~ [at sb./sth.] [über jmdn./etw.] befremdet sein

askew /ə'skju:/
A *adv.* schief; (awry) the wind had blown all her clothes ~: der Wind hatte ihre ganze Kleidung in Unordnung gebracht
B *pred. adj.* schief; (awry) in Unordnung

'asking price *n.* Angebotspreis, *der*

asleep /ə'sli:p/ *pred. adj.* **1** (lit. or fig.) schlafend; (euphem.: dead) entschlafen (geh.); be/lie ~: schlafen; he seems to be ~: er scheint zu schlafen; fall ~: einschlafen; has the government fallen ~? (fig.) schläft die Regierung?; the old man fell ~ (euphem.) der alte Mann schlief [für immer] ein **2** (numb) eingeschlafen ‹*Arm, Bein*›

A'S level *n.*

AS level — Advanced Supplementary level

Ein Abschlussexamen in einem bestimmten Fach, das im vorletzten oder letzten Jahr der *secondary school* von vielen Schülern in England und Wales abgelegt wird. Ein AS level liegt zwischen einem **GCSE** und einem **A level** und zählt für den Zugang zur Universität halb so viele Punkte wie ein A level. Viele Studierende legen eine Mischung aus *A levels* und *AS levels* ab.

asocial /eɪ'səʊʃl/ *adj.* (antisocial) asozial; (not social) ungesellig; asozial; (inconsiderate) rücksichtslos

asp /æsp/ *n.* (Zool.) (Vipera aspis) Aspisviper, *die;* (Naja haje) Uräusschlange, *die*

asparagus /ə'spærəgəs/ *n.* Spargel, *der;* ~ fern (Bot.) Asparagus, *der*

aspect /'æspekt/ *n.* **1** Aspekt, *der* **2** (expression) Gesichtsausdruck, *der;* (appearance) [physical] ~: Erscheinungsbild, *das* **3** (position looking in a given direction) Lage, *die;* (front) Seite, *die;* have a southern ~: nach Süden liegen **4** (Ling., Astrol.) Aspekt, *der*

aspectual /æ'spektjʊəl/ *adj.* (Ling.) aspektisch

aspen /'æspən/ *n.* (Bot.) Espe, *die*

asperity /æ'sperɪtɪ/ *n., no pl.* **1** (harshness) Schroffheit, *die* **2** (roughness) Rauheit, *die*

aspersion /ə'spɜ:ʃn/ *n.* Verunglimpfung, *die;* cast ~s on sb./sth. jmdn./etw. in den Schmutz ziehen

asphalt /'æsfælt/
A *n.* Asphalt, *der*
B *v.t.* asphaltieren

asphyxia /æ'sfɪksɪə/ *n., no pl.* (Med.) Asphyxie, *die* (fachspr.); schwere Atemstörung; Erstickung, *die*

asphyxiate /æ'sfɪksɪeɪt/ (Med.)
A *v.t.* ersticken; be ~d by sth. an etw. (*Dat.*) ersticken
B *v.i.* ersticken

asphyxiation /æsfɪksɪ'eɪʃn/ *n.* (Med.) Erstickung, *die;* death by ~: Erstickungstod, *der*

aspic /'æspɪk/ *n.* (jelly) Aspik, *der*

aspidistra /æspɪ'dɪstrə/ *n.* (Bot.) Schusterpalme, *die;* Aspidistra, *die* (fachspr.)

aspirant /ə'spaɪərənt, 'æspərənt/
A *adj.* aufstrebend
B *n.* Aspirant, *der*/Aspirantin, *die;* Bewerber, *der*/Bewerberin, *die*

aspirate
A /'æspərət/ *adj.* (Phonet.) aspiriert; behaucht
B *n.* (Phonet.) Aspirata, *die;* behauchter [Verschluss]laut
C /'æspəreɪt/ *v.t.* **1** (Phonet.) aspirieren **2** (draw by suction) absaugen

aspiration /æspə'reɪʃn/ *n.* **1** Streben, *das;* Aspiration, *die* (geh.); your ~[s] for *or* after success dein Streben nach Erfolg; have ~s to sth. nach etw. streben **2** (Phonet.) Aspiration, *die;* Behauchung, *die*

aspire /ə'spaɪə(r)/ *v.i.* ~ to *or* after sth. nach etw. streben; ~ to be sth. danach streben, etw. zu sein; I once ~d to be an actor ich wollte einmal [unbedingt] Schauspieler werden

aspirin /'æspərɪn/ *n.* (Med.) Aspirin Ⓦⓩ, *das;* Kopfschmerztablette, *die*

aspiring /ə'spaɪərɪŋ/ *adj.* aufstrebend

ass[1] /æs/
A *n.* (Zool.; also fig.) Esel, *der;* make an ~ of oneself sich blamieren
B *v.i.* (coll.) ~ about *or* around herumalbern (ugs.)

ass[2] (Amer.) ▸ arse[1]

assail /ə'seɪl/ *v.t.* **1** angreifen **2** (fig.) in Angriff nehmen ‹*Hindernis, Aufgabe*›; ~ sb. with questions/insults jmdn. mit Fragen/Beleidigungen überschütten; I was ~ed with doubts mich überkamen Zweifel; the noise ~ed our ears der Lärm dröhnte in unseren Ohren

assailant /ə'seɪlənt/ *n.* Angreifer, *der*/Angreiferin, *die*

assassin /ə'sæsɪn/ *n.* **1** Mörder, *der*/Mörderin, *die* **2** (Hist.) Assassine, *der*

assassinate /ə'sæsɪneɪt/ *v.t.* ermorden; be ~d einem Attentat zum Opfer fallen

assassination /əsæsɪ'neɪʃn/ *n.* Mord, *der* (of an + *Dat.*); *attrib.* ~ attempt Attentat, *das* (on auf + *Akk.*); *see also* character assassination

assault /ə'sɔ:lt/
A *n.* **1** Angriff, *der;* (fig.) Anschlag, *der;* (euphem.: rape) Vergewaltigung, *die;* verbal ~s verbale Angriffe **2** (Mil.) Sturmangriff, *der; attrib.* ~ craft Sturmboot, *das;* ~ course Hindernisstrecke, *die;* Hindernisparcours, *der* **3** (Law) [Androhung einer] Tätlichkeit; *see also* battery 2
B *v.t.* **1** (lit. or fig.) angreifen; (euphem.: rape) vergewaltigen; missbrauchen (geh.) **2** (Mil.) stürmen; angreifen

assay /ə'seɪ/
A *n.* **1** Probe, *die;* A~ Office [*amtliches*] *Labor für die Analyse von Edelmetallen o. Ä.* **2** (Chem.) Analyse, *die*
B *v.t.* **1** prüfen ‹*Metall, Erz*› **2** (Chem.) analysieren **3** (show on ~) enthalten

assemblage /ə'semblɪdʒ/ *n.* **1** (of things, persons) Ansammlung, *die* **2** (process) (bringing together) Zusammentragen, *das;* (fitting together) Zusammensetzen, *das*

assemble /ə'sembl/
A *v.t.* **1** zusammentragen ‹*Beweise, Material, Sammlung*›; zusammenrufen ‹*Menschen*›; a team was ~d, and work began ein Team wurde zusammengestellt, und die Arbeit begann **2** (fit together) zusammenbauen
B *v.i.* sich versammeln

assembly /ə'semblɪ/ *n.* **1** (coming together, meeting, deliberative body) Versammlung, *die;* (in school) (*tägliche Versammlung aller Schüler und Lehrer zur*) Morgenandacht **2** (fitting together) Zusammenbau, *der;* Montage, *die* **3** (assembled unit) Einheit, *die*

as'sembly line *n.* Fließband, *das;* work/be produced on an ~: am Fließband arbeiten/produziert werden

as'sembly-line worker *n.* Fließbandarbeiter, *der*/-arbeiterin, *die*

assent /ə'sent/
A *v.i.* zustimmen; ~ to sth. einer Sache (*Dat.*) zustimmen
B *n.* Zustimmung, *die;* royal ~: Zustimmung des Königs/der Königin; by common ~: nach allgemeiner Auffassung

assert /ə'sɜ:t/ *v.t.* **1** geltend machen; ~ oneself sich durchsetzen **2** (declare) behaupten; beteuern ‹*Unschuld*›

assertion /ə'sɜ:ʃn/ *n.* **1** Geltendmachen, *das* **2** (declaration) Behauptung, *die;* ~ of innocence Unschuldsbeteuerung, *die;* make an ~: eine Behauptung aufstellen

assertive /ə'sɜ:tɪv/ *adj.* energisch ‹*Person*›; bestimmt ‹*Ton, Verhalten*›; fest ‹*Stimme*›; (dogmatic) rechthaberisch

assertiveness /ə'sɜ:tɪvnɪs/ *n., no pl.* Bestimmtheit, *die;* (dogmatism) Rechthaberei, *die*

as'sertiveness training *n.* Selbstsicherheitstraining, *die*

assess /ə'ses/ *v.t.* **1** (evaluate) einschätzen; beurteilen **2** (value) schätzen; taxieren **3** (fix amount of) festsetzen ‹*Steuer, Bußgeld usw.*› (at auf + *Akk.*) **4** (tax) veranlagen

assessment /ə'sesmənt/ *n.* **1** (evaluation) Einschätzung, *die;* Beurteilung, *die* **2** (valuation) Schätzung, *die;* Taxierung, *die* **3** (fixing amount of damages or fine) Festsetzung, *die;* (of tax) Veranlagung, *die* **4** (tax to be paid) Steuerbescheid, *der*

assessor /ə'sesə(r)/ *n.* ▸❶ p. 1260 **1** (tax inspector) ≈ Finanzbeamte, *der*/Finanzbeamtin, *die* **2** (adviser to judge) (*als Beisitzer fungierender*) Sachverständiger

asset /'æset/ *n.* **1** Vermögenswert, *der;* my [personal] ~s mein [persönlicher] Besitz **2** (fig.) (useful quality) Vorzug, *der* (to für); (person) Stütze, *die;* (thing) Hilfe, *die*

'asset-stripping *n., no pl.* (Commerc.) *Ankauf unrentabler Unternehmen, von denen einzelne Teile gewinnbringend weiterverkauft werden*

asseverate /ə'sevəreɪt/ *v.t.* (formal) beteuern

asseveration /əsevə'reɪʃn/ *n.* (formal) Beteuerung, *die*

assiduity /æsɪ'dju:ɪtɪ/ *n.no pl.* Gewissenhaftigkeit, *die*

assiduous /ə'sɪdjʊəs/ *adj.* gewissenhaft; we made ~ efforts wir unternahmen alle Anstrengungen

assiduously /ə'sɪdjʊəslɪ/ *adv.* gewissenhaft

assiduousness /ə'sɪdjʊəsnɪs/ ▸ assiduity

assign /ə'saɪn/
A *v.t.* **1** (allot) ~ sth. to sb. jmdm. etw. zuweisen **2** (appoint) zuteilen; ~ sb. to a job/task jmdn. mit einer Arbeit/Aufgabe betrauen; ~ sb. to do sth. jmdn. damit betrauen, etw. zu tun; ~ sb. to a post jmdn. auf einen Posten berufen **3** (specify) festsetzen ‹*Zeit, Datum, Grenzwert*› **4** (ascribe) angeben; ~ a cause to sth. einen Grund für etw. angeben; ~ an event to a date ein Ereignis einer Zeit zuschreiben
B *n.* (Law) Rechtsnachfolger, *der*

assignable /ə'saɪnəbl/ *adj.* **1** (allottable) zuteilbar; be ~ to sb. jmdm. zugeteilt werden können **2** (specifiable) bestimmbar **3** (ascribable) angebbar

assignation /æsɪg'neɪʃn/ *n.* **1** (appointment) sb.'s ~ to a job/task jmds. Betrauung mit einer Arbeit/Aufgabe; sb.'s ~ to a post jmds. Berufung auf einen Posten **2** (allotment) Zuteilung, *die;* (of property) Übereignung, *die* **3** (attribution) Zuordnung, *die* **4** (illicit lovers' meeting) Stelldichein, *das; attrib.* ~ house (Amer.) Bordell, *das*

assignee /æsaɪ'ni:/ *n.* **1** (agent) Bevollmächtigte, *der/die* **2** ▸ assign B

assignment /ə'saɪnmənt/ *n.* **1** (allotment) Zuteilung, *die;* (of property) Übereignung, *die;* (document) Übereignungsurkunde, *die* **2** (task) Aufgabe, *die;* (Sch. and Univ.) Arbeit, *die;* Aufgabe, *die* **3** (attribution) (of date) Bestimmung, *die;* (of reason, cause) Aufgabe, *die*

assimilate /ə'sɪmɪleɪt/ *v.t.* **1** (make like) angleichen; ~ sth. with *or* to sth. etw. an etw. (*Akk.*) angleichen **2** (absorb) (Biol.) assimilieren **3** (fig.) aufnehmen ‹*Informationen, Einflüsse usw.*› **4** (Ling.) angleichen

assimilation /əsɪmɪ'leɪʃn/ *n.* **1** (making or becoming like) Angleichung, *die* (to, with an + *Akk.*) **2** (Biol.: absorbing) Assimilation, *die* **3** (fig.) (of information, influences, etc.) Aufnahme, *die;* (of people) Integration, *die* 4) (Ling.) Assimilation, *die*

assist /ə'sɪst/

A *v.t.* (help) helfen (+ *Dat.*); voranbringen ‹*Vorgang, Prozess*›; **~ sb. to do** *or* **in doing sth.** jmdm. helfen, etw. zu tun; **~ sb. with sth.** jmdm. bei etw. helfen

B *v.i.* 1) (help) helfen; **~ with sth./in doing sth.** bei etw. helfen/helfen, etw. zu tun 2) (take part) mitarbeiten; **~ in sth.** an etw. (*Dat.*) mitarbeiten; **~ in an operation** bei einer Operation assistieren

assistance /ə'sɪstəns/ *n., no pl.* Hilfe, *die;* **give ~ to sb.** jmdm. behilflich sein; jmdm. helfen; **be of ~ [to sb.]** [jmdm.] behilflich sein; [jmdm.] helfen

assistant /ə'sɪstənt/ ▸ⓘ **p. 1260**

A *n.* (helper) Helfer, *der*/Helferin, *die;* (subordinate) Mitarbeiter, *der*/Mitarbeiterin, *die;* (of professor, artist) Assistent, *der*/Assistentin, *die;* (in shop) Verkäufer, *der*/Verkäuferin, *die*

B *attrib. adj.* **~ manager** stellvertretender Geschäftsführer; **~ editor** Redaktionsassistent, *der;* **~ professor** (Amer.) ≈ Assistenzprofessor, *der*

assisted 'suicide *n.* Beihilfe zur Selbsttötung; assistierter Suizid

assizes /ə'saɪzɪz/ *n. pl.* (Brit. Law Hist.) *regelmäßige Gerichtstage in den verschiedenen Grafschaften*

associate

A /ə'səʊʃɪət, ə'səʊsɪət/ *n.* 1) (partner) Partner, *der*/Partnerin, *die;* Kompagnon, *der;* (colleague) Kollege, *der*/Kollegin, *die;* (companion) Gefährte, *der*/Gefährtin, *die* (geh.); Kamerad, *der*/Kameradin, *die;* (of gangster) Komplize, *der*/Komplizin, *die* 2) (subordinate member) außerordentliches Mitglied

B *adj.* ▸ⓘ **p. 1260** beigeordnet; (allied) verwandt; außerordentlich ‹*Mitglied usw.*›; **~ professor** (Amer.) ≈ außerordentlicher Professor

C /ə'səʊʃɪeɪt, ə'səʊsɪeɪt/ *v.t.* 1) (join) in Verbindung bringen; **be ~d** in Verbindung stehen 2) (connect in the mind) in Verbindung bringen; assoziieren (Psych.); **~ sth. with sth.** etw. mit etw. assoziieren (Psych.) *od.* verbinden 3) **~ oneself with sth.** sich einer Sache (*Dat.*) anschließen

D *v.i.* **~ with sb.** mit jmdm. verkehren *od.* Umgang haben; (for common purpose) sich zusammenschließen

associateship /ə'səʊʃɪətʃɪp, ə'səʊsɪətʃɪp/ *n.* außerordentliche Mitgliedschaft

association /əsəʊsɪ'eɪʃn/ *n.* 1) (organization) Verband, *der;* Vereinigung, *die;* **an ~ of residents** eine Vereinigung von Anwohnern; **articles** *or* **deeds of ~:** Satzung, *die* 2) (mental connection) Assoziation, *die;* **~ of ideas** Gedankenassoziation, *die;* **have ~s for sb.** bei jmdm. Assoziationen hervorrufen 3) **A~ football** (Brit.) Fußball, *der* 4) (connection) Verbindung, *die* 5) (contact with people) Kontakt, *der;* (cooperation) Zusammenarbeit, *die;* **business ~:** geschäftliche Zusammenarbeit

associ'ation agreement *n.* (EU) Assoziierungsabkommen, *das*

associative /ə'səʊʃɪətɪv, ə'səʊsɪətɪv/ *adj.* assoziativ

assonance /'æsənəns/ *n.* (Pros.) Assonanz, *die*

assorted /ə'sɔːtɪd/ *adj.* gemischt ‹*Bonbons, Sortiment*›; **cardigans of ~ kinds** verschiedenerlei Strickjacken; **an ~ bunch of people** ein zusammengewürfelter Haufen Leute; *see also* **ill-assorted**

assortment /ə'sɔːtmənt/ *n.* Sortiment, *das;* **a good ~ of hats [to choose from]** eine gute Auswahl an Hüten; **an ~ of ideas** eine Reihe von Ideen; **an odd ~ of players** eine seltsame Mischung von Spielern

Asst. *abbr.* **= Assistant** Ass.

assuage /ə'sweɪdʒ/ *v.t.* stillen; (soothe) besänftigen ‹*Person, Ärger*›; lindern ‹*Schmerz, Sorge*›

assume /ə'sjuːm/ *v.t.* 1) voraussetzen; ausgehen von; **~ sb.'s innocence** von jmds. Unschuld ausgehen; jmds. Unschuld voraussetzen; **he's not so stupid as we ~d him to be** er ist nicht so dumm, wie wir angenommen haben 2) (undertake) übernehmen ‹*Amt, Pflichten*› 3) (take on) annehmen ‹*Namen, Rolle*›; gewinnen ‹*Aspekt, Bedeutung*›; **under an ~d name** unter einem Decknamen

assuming /ə'sjuːmɪŋ/ *adj.* 1) **~ that ...:** vorausgesetzt, dass ... 2) (presumptuous) anmaßend

assumption /ə'sʌmpʃn/ *n.* 1) Annahme, *die;* **going on the ~ that ...:** vorausgesetzt, dass ... 2) (undertaking) Übernahme, *die;* **~ of power/office** Macht-/Amtsübernahme, *die* 3) (simulation) Vortäuschung, *die;* (of look, air) Aufsetzen, *das;* **with an ~ of indifference** mit scheinbarer Gleichgültigkeit 4) **the A~** (Relig.) Mariä Himmelfahrt

assurance /ə'ʃʊərəns/ *n.* 1) Zusicherung, *die;* **I give you my ~ that ...:** ich versichere Ihnen, dass ...; **I can give you no ~ that ...:** ich kann Ihnen nicht versprechen, dass ... 2) *no pl.* (self-confidence) Selbstsicherheit, *die* 3) *no pl.* (certainty) Sicherheit, *die* 4) *no pl.* (Brit.: insurance) Versicherung, *die*

assure /ə'ʃʊə(r)/ *v.t.* 1) versichern (+ *Dat.*); **you're safe now, I ~ you** ich versichere dir, du bist jetzt in Sicherheit; **~ sb. of sth.** jmdn. einer Sache (*Gen.*) versichern (geh.) 2) (convince) **~ sb./oneself** jmdn./sich überzeugen 3) (make certain or safe) gewährleisten 4) (Brit.: insure) versichern

assured /ə'ʃʊəd/ *adj.* gesichert ‹*Tatsache*›; gewährleistet ‹*Erfolg*›; **be ~ of sth.** sich (*Dat.*) einer Sache (*Gen.*) sicher sein

assuredly /ə'ʃʊərɪdlɪ/ *adv.* gewiss; gewisslich (geh., veralt.)

Assyrian /ə'sɪrɪən/ ▸ⓘ **p. 1277**, ▸ⓘ **p. 1345**

A *adj.* assyrisch

B *n.* Assyrer, *der*/Assyrerin, *die*

aster /'æstə(r)/ *n.* Aster, *die;* **China ~:** Sommeraster, *die*

asterisk /'æstərɪsk/

A *n.* Sternchen, *das;* Asteriskus, *der* (Druckw.)

B *v.t.* mit einem Sternchen versehen

astern /ə'stɜːn/ *adv.* (Naut., Aeronaut.) achtern; (towards the rear) achteraus; **~ of sth.** hinter etw. (*Dat.*); **full speed ~!** volle Kraft zurück!; **go ~:** achteraus fahren; **fall ~:** achteraus sacken

asteroid /'æstərɔɪd/ *n.* (Astron.) Asteroid, *der*

asthma /'æsmə/ *n.* ▸ⓘ **p. 1231** (Med.) Asthma, *das*

asthmatic /æs'mætɪk/ (Med.)

A *adj.* asthmatisch

B *n.* Asthmatiker, *der*/Asthmatikerin, *die*

astigmatism /ə'stɪgmətɪzm/ *n.* (Med., Optics) Astigmatismus, *der*

astir /ə'stɜː(r)/ *pred. adj.* in Bewegung; (out of bed) auf den Beinen; (excited) in Aufruhr

astonish /ə'stɒnɪʃ/ *v.t.* erstaunen; **you ~ me** (iron.) wer hätte das gedacht; **he was ~ed to hear that ...:** er war erstaunt zu hören, dass ...

astonishing /ə'stɒnɪʃɪŋ/ *adj.* erstaunlich

astonishingly /ə'stɒnɪʃɪŋlɪ/ *adv.* erstaunlich; *as sentence-modifier* **~ [enough], no one has yet ...** erstaunlicherweise hat noch niemand ...

astonishment /ə'stɒnɪʃmənt/ *n., no pl.* Erstaunen, *das;* **in utter ~:** äußerst erstaunt

astound /ə'staʊnd/ *v.t.* verblüffen; [sehr] überraschen; **you ~ me** (iron.) das überrascht mich aber sehr

astounding /ə'staʊndɪŋ/ *adj.* erstaunlich

astrakhan /æstrə'kæn/ *n.* (fleece, cloth) Astrachan, *der*

astral /'æstrəl/ *adj.* astral; **~ body** Astralleib, *der;* **~ spirits** Sterngeister

astray /ə'streɪ/

A *adv.* in die Irre; **sb. goes ~:** jmd. verirrt sich; **sth. goes ~** (is mislaid) etw. wird verlegt; (is lost) etw. geht verloren; **lead ~:** irreführen; **go/lead ~** (fig.) in die Irre gehen/führen; (into sin) vom rechten Weg abkommen/abbringen

B *pred. adj.* **be ~:** sich verirrt haben; (fig.: be in error) sich irren; ‹*Rechnung:*› abwegig sein

astride /ə'straɪd/

A *adv.* rittlings ‹*sitzen*›; breitbeinig ‹*stehen*›; **with one's legs ~:** mit gespreizten Beinen; **~ of sth.** rittlings auf etw. (*Dat./Akk.*)

B *prep.* 1) rittlings auf (+ *Dat.*) 2) (extending across) zu beiden Seiten (+ *Gen.*)

astringency /ə'strɪndʒənsɪ/ *n., no pl.* Schärfe, *die;* (of wine, fruit) Säure, *die;* (severity) Schärfe, *die;* (of judgement) Strenge, *die*

astringent /ə'strɪndʒənt/

A *adj.* 1) herb, streng ‹*Geruch, Geschmack*›; stechend, beißend ‹*Geruch*›; sauer ‹*Obst, Wein*› 2) (styptic) adstringierend (Med.); blutstillend 3) (severe) scharf; beißend; streng ‹*Urteil*›

B *n.* Adstringens, *das*

astro- /æstrəʊ/ *in comb.* astro-/Astro-

astrologer /ə'strɒlədʒə(r)/ *n.* ▸ⓘ **p. 1260** Astrologe, *der*/Astrologin, *die*

astrological /æstrə'lɒdʒɪkl/ *adj.* astrologisch

astrology /ə'strɒlədʒɪ/ *n., no pl.* Astrologie, *die*

astronaut /'æstrənɔːt/ *n.* ▸ⓘ **p. 1260** Astronaut, *der*/Astronautin, *die*

astronautical /æstrə'nɔːtɪkl/ *adj.* astronautisch; **~ research** Weltraumforschung, *die;* **~ engineering** Raumfahrttechnik, *die*

astronautics /æstrə'nɔːtɪks/ *n., no pl.* Astronautik, *die;* Raumfahrt, *die*

astronomer /ə'strɒnəmə(r)/ *n.* ▸ⓘ **p. 1260** Astronom, *der*/Astronomin, *die*

astronomical /æstrə'nɒmɪkl/ *adj.,* **astronomically** /æstrə'nɒmɪkəlɪ/ *adv.* (lit. or fig.) astronomisch

astronomy /ə'strɒnəmɪ/ *n., no pl.* Astronomie, *die*

astrophysical /æstrəʊ'fɪzɪkl/ *adj.* astrophysikalisch

astrophysicist /æstrəʊ'fɪzɪsɪst/ *n.* ▸ⓘ **p. 1260** Astrophysiker, *der*/Astrophysikerin, *die*

astrophysics /æstrəʊ'fɪzɪks/ *n., no pl.* Astrophysik, *die*

astute /ə'stjuːt/ *adj.* scharfsinnig ‹*Beobachter, Bemerkung*›; (skilful) geschickt

astutely /ə'stjuːtlɪ/ *adv.* scharfsinnig ‹*bemerken, entscheiden*›; (skilfully) geschickt

astuteness /ə'stjuːtnɪs/ *n., no pl.* Scharfsinnigkeit, *die;* (skill) Geschick, *das*

asunder /ə'sʌndə(r)/ *adv.* (literary) auseinander; **tear sth. ~:** etw. zerreißen

asylee /æsaɪ'liː/ *n.* Asylant, *der*/Asylantin, *die*

asylum /ə'saɪləm/ *n.* 1) Asyl, *das;* **grant sb. ~:** jmdm. Asyl gewähren; **seek ~:** um Asyl bitten *od.* nachsuchen; **political ~:** politisches Asyl; *attrib.* **~ seeker** Asylsuchende, *der/die* 2) (Hist.: mental ~) [Irren]anstalt, *die* (veralt.)

asymmetric /æsɪ'metrɪk, eɪsɪ'metrɪk/, **asymmetrical** /æsɪ'metrɪkl, eɪsɪ'metrɪkl/ *adj.* asymmetrisch; unsymmetrisch; **~ bars** (Sport) Stufenbarren, *der*

asymmetry /æ'sɪmɪtrɪ, eɪ'sɪmɪtrɪ/ *n.* Asymmetrie, *die*

asynchronous /eɪ'sɪŋkrənəs/ *adj.* asynchron; **~ motor** Asynchronmotor, *der*

at /ət, *stressed* æt/ *prep.* 1) *expr. place* an (+ *Dat.*); **at the station** am Bahnhof; **at the baker's/butcher's/grocer's** beim Bäcker/Fleischer/Kaufmann; **at the chemist's** in der Apotheke/Drogerie; **at the supermarket** im Supermarkt; **at my mother's** bei meiner Mutter; **at home** zu Hause; **at the party** auf der Party; **at the office/hotel** im Büro/Hotel; **at school** in der Schule; **at Dover** in Dover 2) ▸ⓘ **p. 1001** *expr. time* **at Christmas/Easter/Whitsun** [zu *od.* an] Weihnachten/Ostern/Pfingsten; **at six o'clock** um sechs Uhr; **at midnight** um Mitternacht; **at midday** am Mittag; mittags; **at dawn** im Morgengrauen; **at [the age of] 40** mit 40; im Alter von 40; **at this/the moment** in diesem/im Augenblick *od.* Moment; **at any time** jederzeit; **at irregular intervals** in unregelmäßigen Abständen; **at the first attempt** beim ersten Versuch 3) *expr. price* **at £2.50 [each]** zu *od.* für [je] 2,50 Pfund; **petrol is charged at 15p per mile** die Benzinkosten werden mit 15 Pence pro Meile berechnet 4) **she's still 'at it** sie ist immer noch dabei; **while we're/you're** *etc.* **'at it** wenn wir/du *usw.* schon dabei sind/bist *usw.*; **so while I was 'at it,...:** und wo *od.* da ich schon dabei war...; **at that** (at that point)

ℹ At

Where?

an + dative describes position:

at the corner of the street = an der Straßenecke

at the royal court = am königlichen Hof

at the side = an der Seite

But note

at the top/bottom = oben/unten

at the front/back = vorne/hinten

at the top of the pile = oben auf dem Stapel

at the bottom of page 4 = auf Seite 4 unten

at the back of the house = (*inside*) hinten im Haus; (*outside*) hinterm Haus

When referring to someone's house or shop, **bei** + dative is used:

at my uncle's = bei meinem Onkel

at the Robinsons = bei Robinson

at the baker's = beim Bäcker

at Woolworth's = bei Woolworth

Note that there is usually no article with a name.

In the case of buildings, **an** indicates the general area (including outside), while **in** is used for the inside:

***They are at the theatre* (i.e. inside)** = Sie sind im Theater

***We met at the theatre* (i.e. inside/just outside)** = Wir trafen uns im/amTheater

bei is also often used for a place of work:

He works at the bank = Er arbeitet bei der Bank

but in the case of most offices and shops it is **in:**

at the bookshop = in der Buchhandlung

at the supermarket = im Supermarkt

at the office = im Büro

at the travel agent's = im Reisebüro

Cf. also

at school = in der Schule

at university = auf der Universität

at a party = auf einer Party

With place names, use **in:**

You have to change at Cologne = Sie müssen in Köln umsteigen

When?

With an actual time, *at* is translated by **um:**

at 9 a.m. = um 9 Uhr (morgens)

at 9 p.m. = um 9 Uhr abends *or* 21 Uhr

at midday/midnight = um zwölf Uhr mittags/um Mitternacht

But note

at a late hour = zu später Stunde

at night = bei Nacht

at sunrise/sunset = bei Sonnenaufgang/Sonnenuntergang

With the main church festivals, *at* is either not translated or **zu** (or in South Germany **an**) is used:

She's coming at Christmas/Easter = Sie kommt [zu *or* an] Weihnachten/Ostern

Cf. also

at (5 minute) intervals = in Abständen (von 5 Minuten)

at this moment = in diesem Augenblick

at any moment or at any time = jederzeit

How old?

at (the age of) sixty = im Alter von sechzig

too old at forty = mit vierzig schon zu alt

at her age = in ihrem Alter

How much?

Expressing price, the translation is **zu:**

two pounds at fifty pence a pound = zwei Pfund zu fünfzig Pence das Pfund

six oranges at 30p each = sechs Orangen zu 30 Pence das Stück

at the same price = zum gleichen Preis

With superlatives

She was at her most charming = Sie zeigte sich von ihrer charmantesten Seite

I am not at my best in the morning = Morgens bin ich nicht gerade in Höchstform

This is an example of Czech music at its most captivating = Das ist eines der reizvollsten Beispiele tschechischer Musik

---

dabei; (at that provocation) daraufhin; (moreover) noch dazu; (nevertheless) trotzdem; **this is where it's at** (coll.) da ist was los (ugs.)

atavism /'ætəvɪzm/ *n.* Atavismus, *der*

atavistic /ætə'vɪstɪk/ *adj.* atavistisch

ataxia /ə'tæksɪə/ *n., no pl.* (Med.) Ataxie, *die;* **locomotor ~:** lokomotorische Ataxie

ate ▸ **eat**

atheism /'eɪθɪɪzm/ *n., no pl.* Atheismus, *der*

atheist /'eɪθɪɪst/ *n.* Atheist, *der*/Atheistin, *die*

Athenian /ə'θi:nɪən/
A *adj.* athenisch; **the ~ people** die Athener; **~ history** die Geschichte Athens
B *n.* Athener, *der*/Athenerin, *die*

Athens /'æθɪnz/ *pr. n.* ▸ℹ **p. 1643** Athen (*das*)

atherosclerosis /æθərəʊsklə'rəʊsɪs/ *n., pl.* **atheroscleroses** /æθərəʊsklə'rəʊsi:z/ (Med.) Atherosklerose, *die*

athlete /'æθli:t/ *n.* Athlet, *der*/Athletin, *die;* Sportler, *der*/Sportlerin, *die;* (runner, jumper) Leichtathlet, *der*/Leichtathletin, *die;* **~'s foot** ▸ℹ **p. 1231** (Med.) Athletenfuß, *der* (fachspr.); Fußpilz, *der*

athletic /æθ'letɪk/ *adj.* sportlich; (robust) athletisch; **~ sports** Leichtathletik, *die;* **any reasonably ~ person** jeder einigermaßen sportliche Mensch; **the goalkeeper made an ~ save** der Torwart zeigte eine Glanzparade

athletically /æθ'letɪkəlɪ/ *adv.* sportlich; athletisch ‹*gebaut*›

athleticism /æθ'letɪsɪzm/ *n., no pl.* Sportlichkeit, *die*

athletics /æθ'letɪks/ *n., no pl.* **1** Leichtathletik, *die* **2** (Amer.: physical sports) Sport, *der*

at-'home *n.* (dated) *festgesetzter Tag, an dem man zu festgesetzter Zeit zwanglos Gäste empfängt;* Jour fixe, *der* (veralt.)

athwart /ə'θwɔ:t/
A *adv.* **1** (literary: from side to side) quer (**to** zu) **2** (Naut.) dwars
B *prep.* **1** (literary: from side to side of) quer über (+ *Dat./Akk.*) **2** (Naut.) dwars zu

a'tishoo /ə'tɪʃu:/
A *int.* hatschi
B *n.* Niesen, *das*

Atlantic /ət'læntɪk/
A *adj.* atlantisch; **~ Ocean** Atlantischer Ozean; **~ coast** Atlantikküste, *die*
B *pr. n.* Atlantik, *der*

atlas /'ætləs/ (also Anat.) Atlas, *der;* **~ of the world** Weltatlas, *der*

ATM *abbr.* **= automated teller machine**

atmosphere /'ætməsfɪə(r)/ *n.* **1** (lit. or fig.) Atmosphäre, *die;* **the ~ of the Earth** die Erdatmosphäre **2** (air in a place) Luft, *die*

atmospheric /ætmə'sferɪk/ *adj.* **1** atmosphärisch; **~ moisture** Luftfeuchtigkeit, *die* **2** (fig.: evocative) stimmungsvoll

atmospherics /ætmə'sferɪks/ *n. pl.* (Radio) atmosphärische Störungen

atoll /'ætɒl, ə'tɒl/ *n.* Atoll, *das*

atom /'ætəm/ *n.* **1** Atom, *das* **2** (fig.) **not an ~ of truth** kein Körnchen Wahrheit; **not a single ~ of evidence** nicht der Schatten eines Beweises

'atom bomb ▸ **atomic bomb**

atomic /ə'tɒmɪk/ *adj.* (Phys.) Atom-

atomic: ~ 'bomb *n.* Atombombe, *die;* **~ 'energy** *n., no pl.* Atomenergie, *die;* **~ 'mass** ▸ **~ weight; ~ 'number** *n.* (Phys., Chem.) Kernladungszahl, *die;* Ordnungszahl, *die;* **~ 'particle** *n.* atomares Teilchen; **~ 'physics** *n., no pl.* Atomphysik, *die;* **~ 'power** *n., no pl.* Atomkraft, *die;* **~ 'warfare** *n., no pl.* Atomkrieg, *der;* **~ 'weight** *n.* (Phys., Chem.) Atomgewicht, *das*

atomization /ætəmaɪ'zeɪʃn/ *n.* Atomisierung, *die;* (of liquid) Zerstäubung, *die*

atomize /'ætəmaɪz/ *v.t.* atomisieren; zerstäuben ‹*Flüssigkeit*›

atomizer /'ætəmaɪzə(r)/ *n.* Zerstäuber, *der*

atonal /eɪ'təʊnl, ə'təʊnl/ *adj.* (Mus.) atonal

atone /ə'təʊn/ *v.i.* es wieder gutmachen; **~ for sth.** etw. wieder gutmachen

atonement /ə'təʊnmənt/ *n.* **1** (atoning) Buße, *die;* (reparation) Wiedergutmachung, *die;* **make ~ for sth.** für etw. Buße tun **2** (Relig.) Versöhnung, *die;* **Day of A~:** Versöhnungsfest, *das;* Jom Kippur, *der;* **the A~:** das Sühneopfer [Christi]

atonic /ə'tɒnɪk/ *adj.* (Phonet., Pros.) unbetont; atonisch (veralt.)

atop /ə'tɒp/
A *adv.* obendrauf; **~ of sth.** [oben] auf etw. (*Dat./Akk.*)
B *prep.* [oben] auf (+ *Dat./Akk.*)

at-'risk *adj.* gefährdet; Risiko‹*gruppe, -patient*›; **the ~ register** das Register gefährdeter Kinder

atrium /'eɪtrɪəm/ *n., pl.* **atria** /'eɪtrɪə/ *or* **~s** **1** (Anat.) Vorhof, *das* (fachspr.) **2** (Archit., Roman Ant.) Atrium, *das*

atrocious /ə'trəʊʃəs/ *adj.* grauenhaft; scheußlich ‹*Wetter, Benehmen*›

atrociously /ə'trəʊʃəslɪ/ *adv.* grauenhaft; scheußlich ‹*sich benehmen*›

atrocity /ə'trɒsɪtɪ/ *n.* **1** *no pl.* (extreme wickedness) Grauenhaftigkeit, *die* **2** (atrocious deed) Gräueltat, *die* (geh.); Grausamkeit, *die* **3** (coll.: repellent thing) Widerwärtigkeit, *die*

atrophy /'ætrəfɪ/
A *n.* **1** (Med.) Atrophie, *die;* Verkümmerung, *die;*

muscular ~: Muskelatrophie, *die* (Med.); Muskelschwund, *der* [2] (emaciation) Abmagerung, *die;* (fig.) Verfall, *der*

B *v.i.* atrophieren (Med.); verkümmern

atropine /ˈætrəpɪn, ˈætrəpi:n/ *n.* (Med.) Atropin, *das*

ˈat sign *n.* At-Zeichen, *das;* Klammeraffe, *der* (ugs.)

attach /əˈtætʃ/

A *v.t.* [1] (fasten) befestigen (**to** an + *Dat.*); anhängen ‹*Wagen*› (**to** an + *Dat.*); **please find ~ed a copy of the letter** beigeheftet ist eine Kopie des Briefes [2] (join) **~ oneself to sth./sb.** sich einer Sache/jmdm. anschließen [3] (assign) **be ~ed to sth.** einer Sache (*Dat.*) zugeteilt sein; **is there a car ~ed to the job?** ist die Stelle mit einem Dienstwagen verbunden?; **the research unit is ~ed to the university** die Forschungsabteilung ist der Universität (*Dat.*) angegliedert [4] (fig.: ascribe) zuschreiben; **~ no blame to sb.** jmdm. keine Schuld geben; **I can't ~ a name to that face** ich kann diesem Gesicht keinen Namen zuordnen [5] (attribute) beimessen; **~ importance/meaning to sth.** einer Sache (*Dat.*) Gewicht/Bedeutung beimessen [6] (Law) pfänden ‹*Eigentum*›; festnehmen ‹*Person*›

B *v.i.* **no blame ~es to sb.** jmdn. trifft keine Schuld; **suspicion ~es to sb.** der Verdacht fällt auf jmdn.

attachable /əˈtætʃəbl/ *adj.* [1] **be ~ to sth.** an etw. (*Dat.*) befestigt werden können [2] (Law) pfändbar ‹*Gut, Ware*›

attaché /əˈtæʃeɪ/ *n.* Attaché, *der;* **cultural/military/press/naval ~:** Kultur-/Militär-/Presse-/Marineattaché, *der*

atˈtaché case *n.* Diplomatenkoffer, *der*

attached /əˈtætʃt/ *adj.* (emotionally) **be ~ to sb./sth.** an jmdm./etw. hängen; **become ~ to sb./sth.** jmdn./etw. lieb gewinnen

attachment /əˈtætʃmənt/ *n.* [1] (act or means of fastening) Befestigung, *die;* **the ~ of a recording device to a telephone** der Anschluss eines Aufnahmegerätes an ein Telefon [2] (accessory) Zusatzgerät, *das;* **blender ~:** Mixaufsatz, *der* [3] (ascribing) Zuordnung, *die* [4] (attribution) Beimessung, *die* [5] (affection) Anhänglichkeit, *die* (**to** an + *Akk.*); **his ~ to that party** seine Sympathie für diese Partei; **have an ~ for sb.** an jmdm. hängen [6] (Law) Pfändung, *die* [7] (Computing) Anhang, *der;* Attachment, *das*

attack /əˈtæk/

A *v.t.* [1] angreifen; (ambush, raid) überfallen; (fig.: criticize) attackieren; **a woman was ~ed and raped** eine Frau wurde überfallen und vergewaltigt [2] (affect) ‹*Krankheit:*› befallen [3] (start work on) in Angriff nehmen; **she ~ed the washing-up** sie machte sich an den Abwasch [4] (take action against) vorgehen gegen [5] (act harmfully on) angreifen ‹*Metall, Oberfläche*›

B *v.i.* angreifen; **~ in strength** in großer Zahl angreifen

C *n.* [1] (on enemy) Angriff, *der;* (on person) Überfall, *der;* (fig.: criticism) Attacke, *die;* Angriff, *der;* **air ~:** Luftangriff, *der;* **be under ~:** angegriffen werden; **come under ~ from all directions** (fig.) von allen Seiten attackiert *od.* angegriffen werden [2] (start) Inangriffnahme, *die* (**on** *Gen.*); **make a spirited ~ on sth.** etw. beherzt in Angriff nehmen [3] (of illness, lit. or fig.) Anfall, *der;* **the girls got an ~ of the giggles** die Mädchen mussten furchtbar kichern [4] (Sport) Angriff, *der* [5] (Mus.) [präziser] Einsatz; (on piano) Anschlag, *der;* Attacke, *die* (Jazz)

attack: ~ aircraft *n.* Kampfflugzeug, *das;* **~ alarm** *n.* Personenalarm, *der*

attacker /əˈtækə(r)/ *n.* (also Sport) Angreifer, *der*/Angreiferin, *die*

atˈtack helicopter *n.* Kampfhubschrauber, *der*

attacking /əˈtækɪŋ/ *adj.* offensiv ‹*Spielweise, Spieler*›; angreifend ‹*Truppen*›

attain /əˈteɪn/*v.t.* erreichen ‹*Ziel, Wirkung*›; **~ power** an die Macht gelangen; **the author ~ed his ambition** der Autor erreichte sein Ziel; **she ~ed her hope** ihre Hoffnung erfüllte sich

attainability /əteɪnəˈbɪlɪtɪ/ *n., no pl.* Erreichbarkeit, *die*

attainable /əˈteɪnəbl/ *adj.* erreichbar ‹*Ziel*›; realisierbar ‹*Hoffnung, Ziel*›

attainder /əˈteɪndə(r)/ *n.* (Hist.) Verlust von Recht und Besitz (*als Folge eines Todesurteils oder der Ächtung*)

attainment /əˈteɪnmənt/ *n.* [1] *no pl.* Verwirklichung, *die;* **be impossible of ~:** unmöglich zu erreichen sein [2] (thing attained) Leistung, *die*

atˈtainment target *n.* (Educ.) Leistungsziel, *das*

attar /ˈætə(r)/ *n.* Rosenöl, *das;* Attar, *der* (veralt.)

attempt /əˈtempt/

A *v.t.* [1] versuchen; **~ to do sth.** versuchen, etw. zu tun [2] (try to accomplish) sich versuchen an (+ *Dat.*); (try to conquer) angreifen; **candidates should ~ 5 out of 10 questions** die Kandidaten sollten 5 von 10 Fragen zu beantworten versuchen

B *n.* Versuch, *der;* **make an ~ at sth.** sich an etw. (*Dat.*) versuchen; **make an ~ to do sth.** den Versuch unternehmen, etw. zu tun; **he will make an ~ on the 800 m record tonight** er wird heute Abend einen Rekordversuch über 800 m unternehmen; **make an ~ on sb.'s life** ein Attentat *od.* einen Mordanschlag auf jmdn. verüben

attend /əˈtend/

A *v.i.* [1] (give care and thought) aufpassen; (apply oneself) **~ to sth.** auf etw. (*Akk.*) achten; (deal with sth.) sich um etw. kümmern; **everyone had their own tasks to ~ to** jeder musste sich um seine eigenen Aufgaben kümmern *od.* sich seinen eigenen Aufgaben widmen [2] (be present) anwesend sein; **~ at sth.** bei etw. anwesend sein; **the chiropodist ~s on Wednesdays** der Fußpfleger ist [immer] mittwochs da [3] (wait) bedienen; aufwarten (veralt.); **~ on sb.** jmdn. bedienen; jmdm. aufwarten (veralt.)

B *v.t.* [1] (be present at) teilnehmen an (+ *Dat.*); (go regularly to) besuchen; **his lectures are well ~ed** seine Vorlesungen werden gut besucht [2] (follow as a result from) sich ergeben aus; **be ~ed by sth.** etw. zur Folge haben [3] (accompany) verbunden sein mit; **may good luck ~ you** (formal) möge das Glück dir hold sein (geh.) [4] (wait on) bedienen; aufwarten (veralt.) (+ *Dat.*) [5] ‹*Arzt:*› behandeln

attendance /əˈtendəns/ *n.* [1] (being present) Anwesenheit, *die;* (going regularly) Besuch, *der* (**at** *Gen.*); **regular ~ at school** regelmäßiger Schulbesuch; **your ~ record is very poor** Sie haben reichlich oft gefehlt [2] (number of people present) Teilnehmerzahl, *die;* **there was only a small ~ for sth.** etw. wurde nur schwach besucht; **~s at churches are declining** die Zahl der Kirchenbesucher geht zurück [3] **be in ~:** anwesend sein; **the ladies in ~:** die anwesenden Damen; **in close ~:** in unmittelbarer Nähe. *See also* **dance B 1**

attendance: ~ allowance *n.* (Brit.) *Sozialversicherungsleistung für Personen, die die Pflege einer pflegebedürftigen Person besorgen;* **~ centre** *n.* (Brit.) Jugendarrestanstalt (in der Freizeitarrest verbüßt wird)

attendant /əˈtendənt/

A *n.* [1] ▸ⓘ **p. 1260** (person providing service) **[lavatory] ~:** Toilettenmann, *der*/Toilettenfrau, *die;* **[cloakroom] ~:** Garderobenmann, *der*/Garderobenfrau, *die;* **museum ~:** Museumswärter, *der* [2] (member of entourage) Begleiter, *der*/Begleiterin, *die*

B *adj.* begleitend; **~ circumstances** Begleitumstände; **its ~ problems/risks** die damit verbundenen Probleme/Risiken; **be ~ upon sth.** (formal) mit etw. verbunden sein

attender /əˈtendə(r)/ *n.* (person present) Anwesende, *der/die;* **regular ~s will know ...:** wer regelmäßig teilnimmt, wird wissen, ...

attention /əˈtenʃn/

A *n.* [1] *no pl.* Aufmerksamkeit, *die;* **your careful ~ would be much appreciated** ich wäre Ihnen dankbar, wenn Sie gut aufpassen würden; **pay ~ to sb./sth.** jmdn./etw. beachten; **pay ~!** gib Acht!; pass auf!; **hold sb.'s ~:** jmds. Interesse wach halten; **attract [sb.'s] ~:** [jmdn.] auf sich (*Akk.*) aufmerksam machen; **catch sb.'s ~:** jmds. Aufmerksamkeit erregen; **bring sth. to sb.'s ~:** jmds. Aufmerksamkeit auf etw. (*Akk.*) lenken; jmdn. auf etw. (*Akk.*) aufmerksam machen; **call** *or* **draw sb.'s ~ to sb./sth.** jmds. Aufmerksamkeit auf jmdn./etw. lenken; jmdn. auf jmdn./etw. aufmerksam machen; **~ Miss Jones** (on letter) zu Händen [von] Miss Jones [2] *no pl.* (consideration) **give sth. one's personal ~:** sich einer Sache (*Gen.*) persönlich annehmen; **we are giving your enquiry our fullest ~:** wir bearbeiten Ihre Anfrage mit der größten Sorgfalt [3] *in pl.* (ceremonious politeness) Aufmerksamkeit, *die;* **show sb. little ~s** jmdm. kleine Aufmerksamkeiten erweisen; **pay [one's] ~s to sb.** jmdm. den Hof machen (veralt.) [4] (Mil.) Grundstellung, *die;* Habachtstellung, *die;* **stand to ~:** stillstehen; strammstehen

B *int.* [1] Achtung!; **~ all shipping** Achtung! An alle Schiffe! [2] (Mil.) stillgestanden!

atˈtention deficit disorder *n.* Aufmerksamkeitsdefizitsyndrom, *das*

attentive /əˈtentɪv/ *adj.* [1] (paying attention) aufmerksam; **be ~ to sth.** auf etw. (*Akk.*) achten [2] (heedful) **be more ~ to one's studies** sich gewissenhafter seinen Studien widmen; **be [more] ~ to sb.'s warnings** auf jmds. Warnungen hören [3] (assiduous) aufmerksam; **he was very ~ to the ladies** er war den Damen gegenüber sehr aufmerksam *od.* zuvorkommend

attentively /əˈtentɪvlɪ/ *adv.* aufmerksam

attentiveness /əˈtentɪvnɪs/ *n., no pl.* Aufmerksamkeit, *die*

attenuate /əˈtenjʊeɪt/ *v.t.* [1] (make thin) dünn machen; dünnflüssig machen ‹*Öl*› [2] (reduce, lit. or fig.) abschwächen; dämpfen ‹*Schall, Ton*› [3] (Electr.) [ab]schwächen; dämpfen ‹*Welle, Schwingung*›

attenuation /ətenjʊˈeɪʃn/ *n.* ▸ **attenuate 1, 2, 3:** Verdünnung, *die;* Abschwächung, *die;* Dämpfung, *die*

attest /əˈtest/

A *v.t.* (certify validity of) bestätigen; beglaubigen ‹*Unterschrift, Urkunde*›

B *v.i.* (bear witness) **~ to sth.** etw. bezeugen; (fig.) von etw. zeugen

attestation /ætɪˈsteɪʃn/ *n.* Bestätigung, *die*

attic *n.* [1] (storey) Dachgeschoss, *das;* oberstes Stockwerk [2] (room) Dachboden, *der;* (habitable) Dachkammer, *die;* Mansarde, *die*

Attic /ˈætɪk/

A *adj.* attisch; **~ dialect** attischer Dialekt

B *n.* attischer Dialekt

attire /əˈtaɪə(r)/

A *n., no pl.* Kleidung, *die*

B *v.t.* kleiden; **be ~d in sth.** in etw. (*Akk.*) gekleidet sein; **~ oneself** sich kleiden

attitude /ˈætɪtju:d/ *n.* [1] (posture, way of behaving) Haltung, *die;* **in a defensive/threatening ~:** in abwehrender/drohender Haltung; **strike an ~:** eine Haltung einnehmen [2] (mode of thinking) **~ [of mind]** Einstellung, *die* (**to[wards]** zu) [3] (Aeron.) Fluglage, *die*

attitudinize /ætɪˈtju:dɪnaɪz/ *v.i.* sich in Szene setzen

attn. *abbr.* **= for the attention of** z. H[d].

attorney /əˈtɜ:nɪ/ *n.* ▸ⓘ **p. 1260** [1] (legal agent) Bevollmächtigte, *der/die;* **power of ~:** Vollmacht, *die* [2] (Amer.: lawyer) [Rechts]anwalt, *der*/[Rechts]anwältin, *die; see also* **district attorney**

Attorney-ˈGeneral *n., pl.* **Attorneys-General** *oberster Justizbeamter bestimmter Staaten;* ≈ Generalbundesanwalt, *der;* (in USA) ≈ Justizminister, *der*

attract /əˈtrækt/ *v.t.* [1] (draw) anziehen; auf sich (*Akk.*) ziehen ‹*Interesse, Blick, Kritik*›; ‹*Köder, Attraktion:*› anlocken; **the party launched a publicity campaign to ~ new members** die Partei startete eine Werbekampagne, um neue Mitglieder zu gewinnen [2] (arouse pleasure in) anziehend wirken auf (+ *Akk.*); **what ~s me about the girl** was ich an dem Mädchen anziehend finde [3] (arouse interest in) reizen (**about** an + *Dat.*); **I am ~ed by that idea** der Gedanke reizt mich

a

attractant /ə'træktənt/ *n.* Lockmittel, *das*

attraction /ə'trækʃn/ *n.* 1 Anziehung, *die;* (force, lit. or fig.) Anziehung[skraft], *die;* **I cannot see the ~ of going to horror films** ich kann nichts Besonderes daran finden, in Gruselfilme zu gehen; **the possibility of promotion has little ~ for me** die Möglichkeit, befördert zu werden, reizt mich nur wenig 2 (fig.: thing that attracts) Attraktion, *die;* (charm) Verlockung, *die;* Reiz, *der* 3 (Ling.) Attraktion, *die*

attractive /ə'træktɪv/ *adj.* 1 anziehend; **~ power/force** Anziehungskraft, *die* 2 (fig.) attraktiv; reizvoll ‹*Vorschlag, Möglichkeit, Idee*›

attractively /ə'træktɪvlɪ/ *adv.* reizvoll

attractiveness /ə'træktɪvnɪs/ *n., no pl.* Attraktivität, *die*

attributable /ə'trɪbjʊtəbl/ *adj.* **be ~ to sb./sth.** jmdm./einer Sache zuzuschreiben sein; **this comment is not ~:** dieser Kommentar muss anonym bleiben

attribute

A /'ætrɪbju:t/ *n.* 1 (quality) Attribut, *das;* Eigenschaft, *die;* **punctuality is not one of her ~s** Pünktlichkeit ist nicht gerade eine ihrer Stärken 2 (symbolic object) Attribut, *das* 3 (Ling.) Attribut, *das*

B /ə'trɪbju:t/ *v.t.* (ascribe, assign) zuschreiben (**to** *Dat.*); (refer) zurückführen (**to** auf + *Akk.*)

attribution /ætrɪ'bju:ʃn/ *n.* (ascribing, assigning) Zuordnung, *die* (**to** *Dat.*); (referring) Zurückführung, *die* (**to** auf + *Akk.*)

attributive /ə'trɪbjʊtɪv/ *adj.*, **attributively** /ə'trɪbjʊtɪvlɪ/ *adv.* (Ling.) attributiv

attrition /ə'trɪʃn/ *n., no pl.* 1 (wearing down) Zermürbung, *die;* **war of ~** (lit. or fig.) Zermürbungskrieg, *der* 2 (friction, abrasion) Abrieb, *der*

attune /ə'tju:n/ *v.t.* 1 (bring into accord) aufeinander abstimmen 2 (fig.: make accustomed) gewöhnen (**to** an + *Akk.*); **be ~d to sth.** auf etw. (*Akk.*) eingestellt sein

atypical /eɪ'tɪpɪkl, ə'tɪpɪkl/ *adj.* atypisch; untypisch

aubergine /'əʊbəʒi:n/ *n.* Aubergine, *die*

aubrietia /ɔ:'bri:ʃə/ *n.* (Bot.) Blaukissen, *das;* Aubrietie, *die* (fachspr.)

auburn /'ɔ:bən/ *adj.* rötlich braun

auction /'ɔ:kʃn/

A *n.* 1 Auktion, *die;* Versteigerung, *die;* **sell sth. by ~:** etw. durch Versteigerung verkaufen; **be put up for ~:** zur Versteigerung kommen; versteigert werden; **Dutch ~:** Abschlag, *der* 2 (Cards) Bieten, *das*

B *v.t.* versteigern

auctioneer /ɔ:kʃə'nɪə(r)/ *n.* ▸ⓘ **p. 1260** Auktionator, *der*/Auktionatorin, *die*

auction: ~ house *n.* Auktionshaus, *das;* **~ sale** *n.* Auktion, *die;* Versteigerung, *die*

audacious /ɔ:'deɪʃəs/ *adj.* (daring) kühn; verwegen; (impudent) dreist

audaciously /ɔ:'deɪʃəslɪ/ *adv.* (daringly) kühn; (impudently) dreist

audacity /ɔ:'dæsɪtɪ/ *n., no pl.* 1 (daringness) Kühnheit, *die;* Verwegenheit, *die* 2 (impudence) Dreistigkeit, *die*

audibility /ɔ:dɪ'bɪlɪtɪ/ *n.* Hörbarkeit, *die*

audible /'ɔ:dɪbl/ *adj.* hörbar; **every word was ~ through the wall** man konnte jedes Wort durch die Wand hören; **the child's voice was scarcely ~:** die Stimme des Kindes war kaum zu hören

audibly /'ɔ:dɪblɪ/ *adv.* hörbar; **whisper sth. quite ~:** etw. recht vernehmlich flüstern

audience /'ɔ:dɪəns/ *n.* 1 (listeners, spectators) Publikum, *das;* **cinema/concert ~s have increased** die Zahl der Kino-/Konzertbesucher hat zugenommen 2 (formal interview) Audienz, *die* (**with** bei); **private ~:** Privataudienz, *die* 3 (readers) Publikum, *das;* Leserkreis, *der*

audio /'ɔ:dɪəʊ/ *adj.* Ton-; **~ frequency** Tonfrequenz, *die;* **~ range** Hörbereich, *der;* **~ equipment** Audioanlage, *die*

audio: ~book *n.* Hörbuch, *das;* **~ cassette** *n.* Audiokassette, *die;* Tonkassette, *die;* **~ engineer** *n.* Toningenieur, *der*/-ingenieurin, *die;* **~ stream** *n.* Audiostream, *der;* **~ tape** *n.* Tonband, *das;* (recording) Tonbandaufnahme, *die;* **make an ~ tape of a conversation** ein Gespräch [auf Tonband] aufzeichnen *od.* aufnehmen; **~tape** A *n.* ▸ **audio tape;** B *v.t.* [auf Tonband] aufzeichnen *od.* aufnehmen; **~ typist** *n.* ▸ⓘ **p. 1260** Phonotypist, *der*/-typistin, *die;* **~-'visual** *adj.* audiovisuell (fachspr.)

audit /'ɔ:dɪt/

A *n.* **~ [of the accounts]** Rechnungsprüfung, *die* (Wirtsch.); **the ~ of the firm's books** die Revision der Firmengeschäftsbücher

B *v.t.* 1 prüfen 2 (Amer.: attend) als Gasthörer belegen

audition /ɔ:'dɪʃn/

A *n.* (singing) Probesingen, *das;* (dancing) Vortanzen, *das;* (acting) Vorsprechen, *das;* **~s are being held today** heute ist Probesingen/Vortanzen/Vorsprechen

B *v.i.* (sing) vorsingen; probesingen; (dance) vortanzen; (act) vorsprechen; **~ for a part** für eine Rolle vorsprechen

C *v.t.* vorsingen/vortanzen/vorsprechen lassen

auditor /'ɔ:dɪtə(r)/ *n.* ▸ⓘ **p. 1260** Buchprüfer, *der*/-prüferin, *die;* Rechnungsprüfer, *der*/-prüferin, *die*

auditorium /ɔ:dɪ'tɔ:rɪəm/ *n., pl.* **~s** *or* **auditoria** /ɔ:dɪ'tɔ:rɪə/ Zuschauerraum, *der*

auditory /'ɔ:dɪtərɪ/ *adj.* 1 (concerned with hearing) Gehör-; auditiv (Med.) 2 (received by the ear) akustisch; auditiv (Med.)

au fait /əʊ 'feɪ/ *pred. adj.* vertraut (**with** mit); au fait (geh.); (up to date) auf dem Laufenden

Aug. *abbr.* **= August** Aug.

Augean /ɔ:'dʒi:ən/ *adj.* überaus schmutzig; **~ stables** (lit. or fig.) Augiasstall, *der*

auger /'ɔ:gə(r)/ *n.* (for wood) Handbohrer, *der;* Stangenbohrer, *der;* (for soil) Erdbohrer, *der*

aught[1] /ɔ:t/ *n., no pl., no art.* (arch./poet.) [irgend-]etwas

aught[2] ▸ **ought**[2]

augment

A /ɔ:g'ment/ *v.t.* verstärken ‹*Armee*›; verbessern ‹*Einkommen*›; aufstocken ‹*Fonds, finanzielle Mittel*›; **~ed interval** (Mus.) übermäßiges Intervall

B *v.i.* zunehmen; ‹*Reserven:*› zunehmen, anwachsen; ‹*Lärm:*› zunehmen, anschwellen

augmentation /ɔ:gmən'teɪʃn/ *n., no pl.* 1 (enlargement) Erweiterung, *die;* (of funds, finances) Aufstockung, *die;* (growth) Anstieg, *der;* Zunahme, *die* 2 (Mus.) Augmentation, *die*

au gratin ▸ **gratin**

augur /'ɔ:gə(r)/

A *n.* 1 (Roman Ant.) Augur, *der* 2 (soothsayer) Augur, *der* (geh.)

B *v.t.* 1 (portend) bedeuten; versprechen ‹*Erfolg*› 2 (foretell) prophezeien (**of, for** *Dat.*)

C *v.i.* **~ well/ill for sth./sb.** ein gutes/schlechtes Zeichen für etw./jmdn. sein

augury /'ɔ:gjʊrɪ/ *n.* Vorzeichen, *das*

august /ɔ:'gʌst/ *adj.* 1 (venerable) ehrwürdig; (noble) erlaucht 2 (majestic) großartig; eindrucksvoll

August /'ɔ:gəst/ *n.* ▸ⓘ **p. 1047** August, *der;* **in ~:** im August; **last/next ~:** letzten/nächsten August; **the first of/on the first of ~** *or* **on ~ [the] first** der erste/am ersten August; **1st ~** (as date on document) 1. August; **every ~:** jeden August; jedes Jahr im August; **an ~ day** ein Augusttag; **from ~ to October** von August bis Oktober

Augustine[1] /ɔ:'gʌstɪn/ *pr. n.* Augustinus (*der*)

Augustine[2] *n.* Augustiner, *der*

Augustinian /ɔ:gʌ'stɪnɪən/

A *adj.* Augustinisch ‹*Lehre*›; **~ monk** Augustinermönch, *der*

B *n.* (monk) Augustiner, *der*

auk /ɔ:k/ *n.* (Ornith.) Alk, *der*

auld /ɔ:ld/ *adj.* (Scot.) ▸ **old; for ~ lang syne** um der guten, alten Zeiten willen

au naturel /əʊ nætjə'rel/ *adv., pred. adj.* (Gastr.) nature; au naturel

aunt /ɑ:nt/ *n.* Tante, *die;* **A~ Sally** *Wurfspiel [auf dem Jahrmarkt], bei dem mit Stöcken oder Bällen auf eine Holzfigur geworfen wird;* (target doll) ≈ Schießbudenfigur, *die;* (fig.) Zielscheibe, *die* (fig.); **my sainted ~!** (esp. Brit. coll.) du liebe Güte!

auntie, aunty /'ɑ:ntɪ/ *n.* (coll.) Tantchen, *das;* (with name) Tante, *die;* **do you love A~ Betty?** magst du die liebe Tante Betty?

au pair /əʊ 'peə(r)/

A *n.* Aupairmädchen, *das*

B *adj.* **~ girl** Aupairmädchen, *das*

aura /'ɔ:rə/ *n., pl.* **~e** /'ɔ:ri:/ *or* **~s** 1 (atmosphere, Med.) Aura, *die;* **have an ~ about one** von einer Aura umgeben sein; **an ~ of mystery** eine Aura des Geheimnisvollen 2 (subtle emanation) Aura, *die;* Fluidum, *das*

aural /'ɔ:rl/ *adj.* akustisch; aural (Med.)

aureola /ɔ:'ri:ələ/, **aureole** /'ɔ:rɪəʊl/ *n.* (Art) Aureole, *die;* (around head) Nimbus, *der*

auricle /'ɔ:rɪkl/ *n.* 1 (external ear) Ohrmuschel, *die;* Auricula, *die* (Med.) 2 (Anat.: of heart) Atrium, *das* (fachspr.); Vorhof, *der;* Herzohr, *das* 3 (Bot.) Blattöhrchen, *das;* Aurikel, *die*

auricular /ɔ:'rɪkjʊlə(r)/ *adj.* 1 (of the ear) Ohr-; aurikular (Med.); (by the ear) akustisch; **~ confession** (Relig.) Ohrenbeichte, *die* 2 (Anat.: of auricle of heart) Vorhof-

auriferous /ɔ:'rɪfərəs/ *adj.* (Geol.) goldhaltig

aurora /ɔ:'rɔ:rə/ *n., pl.* **~s** *or* **~e** /ɔ:'rɔ:ri:/ Polarlicht, *das;* **~ borealis** /bɔ:rɪ'eɪlɪs/ Nordlicht, *das;* **~ australis** /ɔ:'streɪlɪs/ Südlicht, *das*

auscultation /ɔ:skəl'teɪʃn/ *n., no pl.* (Med.) Auskultation, *die* (fachspr.); Abhorchen, *das*

auspice /'ɔ:spɪs/ *n.* 1 *in pl.* **under the ~s of sb./sth.** unter jmds./einer Sache Auspizien (geh.) *od.* Schirmherrschaft 2 (sign) Auspizium, *das* (geh.); Vorzeichen, *das;* **under favourable ~s** unter günstigen Auspizien (geh.) *od.* Vorzeichen

auspicious /ɔ:'spɪʃəs/ *adj.* 1 (favourable) günstig; viel versprechend ‹*Anfang*› 2 (fortunate) glückhaft (geh.); glücklich

auspiciously /ɔ:'spɪʃəslɪ/ *adv.* 1 (favourably) viel versprechend 2 (fortunately) glücklich

Aussie /'ɒzɪ, 'ɒsɪ/ (coll.)

A *adj.* australisch

B *n.* 1 Australier, *der*/Australierin, *die* 2 (Australia) Australien (*das*)

austere /ɒ'stɪə(r), ɔ:'stɪə(r)/ *adj.* 1 (morally strict, stern) streng; unbeugsam ‹*Haltung*› 2 (severely simple) karg 3 (ascetic) asketisch ‹*Leben*›

austerely /ɒ'stɪəlɪ, ɔ:'stɪəlɪ/ *adv.* 1 (morally, strictly, sternly) streng 2 (severely simply) karg; **~ simple** karg und schlicht 3 (ascetically) asketisch ‹*leben*›

austereness /ɒ'stɪənɪs, ɔ:'stɪənɪs/ ▸ **austerity 1, 2**

austerity /ɒ'sterɪtɪ, ɔ:'sterɪtɪ/ *n.* 1 *no pl.* (moral strictness) Strenge, *die* 2 *no pl.* (severe simplicity) Kargheit, *die* 3 *no pl.* (lack of luxuries) wirtschaftliche Einschränkung; Austerity, *die* (Wirtsch.) 4 *in pl.* (deprivations) Entbehrungen; (for religious reasons) Entsagungen

Australasia /ɒstrə'leɪʃə, ɔ:strə'leɪʃə/ *pr. n.* Australien und der südwestliche Pazifik

Australasian /ɒstrə'leɪʃn, ɔ:strə'leɪʃn/ *adj.* **~ peoples/cultures** Völker/Kulturen Australiens und des südwestlichen Pazifiks; **~ region** australische Region (Zool.)

Australia /ɒ'streɪlɪə, ɔ:'streɪlɪə/ *pr. n.* Australien (*das*)

Australian /ɒ'streɪlɪən, ɔ:'streɪlɪən/ ▸ⓘ **p. 1345**

A *adj.* australisch; **~ bear** Beutelbär, *der;* Koala, *der;* **sb. is ~:** jmd. ist Australier/Australierin; **~ [National] Rules football** *australische Art des Football*

B *n.* Australier, *der*/Australierin, *die*

Austria /'ɒstrɪə, 'ɔ:strɪə/ *pr. n.* Österreich (*das*); **~-Hungary** (Hist.) Österreich-Ungarn (*das*)

Austrian /'ɒstrɪən, 'ɔ:strɪən/ ▸ⓘ **p. 1345**

A *adj.* österreichisch; **sb. is ~:** jmd. ist Österreicher/Österreicherin

B *n.* Österreicher, *der*/Österreicherin, *die*

Austro-Hungarian /ɒstrəʊhʌŋ'geərɪən, ɔ:strəʊhʌŋ'geərɪən/ *adj.* (Hist.) österreichisch-ungarisch

autarchy /ˈɔːtɑːkɪ/ *n., no pl.* 1 ▸ **autocracy** 2 ▸ **autarky**

autarky /ˈɔːtɑːkɪ/ *n., no pl.* Autarkie, *die*

authentic /ɔːˈθentɪk/ *adj.* (reliable; also Mus.) authentisch; (genuine) authentisch; echt; berechtigt ‹Anspruch›; unverfälscht ‹Akzent›

authentically /ɔːˈθentɪkəlɪ/ *adv.* (genuinely) **his accent was ~ upper-class** er sprach im unverfälschten Tonfall der Oberschicht

authenticate /ɔːˈθentɪkeɪt/ *v.t.* authentifizieren; **~ sth.** die Echtheit einer Sache (*Gen.*) bestätigen; **~ information/a report** eine Information/einen Bericht bestätigen; **I succeeded in authenticating my claim** es gelang mir, meinen Anspruch zu beweisen

authentication /ɔːθentɪˈkeɪʃn/ *n., no pl.* Bestätigung der Echtheit; (of information, report) Bestätigung, *die*

authenticity /ɔːθenˈtɪsɪtɪ/ *n., no pl.* Echtheit, *die;* Authentizität, *die;* (of claim) Berechtigung, *die;* (of information, report) Zuverlässigkeit, *die*

author /ˈɔːθə(r)/

A *n.* 1 ▸ⓘ **p. 1260** (writer) Autor, *der*/Autorin, *die;* (profession) Schriftsteller, *der*/Schriftstellerin, *die;* **the ~ of the book/article** der Autor *od.* Verfasser des Buches/Artikels; **the ~s of the 19th century** die Autoren *od.* Schriftsteller des 19. Jahrhunderts 2 (originator) Vater, *der*

B *v.t.* (write) verfassen

authoress /ˈɔːθərɪs/ *n.* ▸ⓘ **p. 1260** Autorin, *die*

authoring /ˈɔːθərɪŋ/ *n., no pl.* (Computing) Authoring, *das* (fachspr.); *attrib.* **~ software/system** Autorensoftware, *die*/Autorensystem, *das*

authorisation, authorise ▸ **authoriz-**

authoritarian /ɔːθɒrɪˈteərɪən/

A *adj.* autoritär

B *n.* autoritäre Person; **be an ~:** autoritär sein

authoritarianism /ɔːθɒrɪˈteərɪənɪzm/ *n., no pl.* Autoritarismus, *der;* autoritäre Einstellung

authoritative /ɔːˈθɒrɪtətɪv/ *adj.* 1 (recognized as reliable) autoritativ; maßgebend; zuverlässig ‹Bericht, Information›; (official) amtlich 2 (commanding) Respekt einflößend

authoritatively /ɔːˈθɒrɪtətɪvlɪ/ *adv.* 1 (reliably) zuverlässig ‹berichten›; (officially) offiziell; **he talked ~ about his specialist field** er sprach als Fachmann über sein Spezialgebiet 2 (commandingly) mit Bestimmtheit

authoritativeness /ɔːˈθɒrɪtətɪvnɪs/ *n., no pl.* 1 (reliability) Zuverlässigkeit, *die;* (official nature) amtlicher Charakter 2 (commanding quality) Bestimmtheit, *die;* (of person) entschiedenes Auftreten; **the ~ of his manner** seine Respekt einflößende Art

authority /ɔːˈθɒrɪtɪ/ *n.* 1 *no pl.* (power) Autorität, *die;* (delegated power) Befugnis, *die;* **have the/no ~ to do sth.** berechtigt *od.* befugt/nicht befugt sein, etw. zu tun; **you have my ~:** Sie haben meine Zustimmung; **have/exercise ~ over sb.** Weisungsbefugnis gegenüber jmdm. haben; **on one's own ~:** in eigener Verantwortung; **[be] in ~:** verantwortlich [sein]; **be under sb.'s ~:** jmdm. unterstehen; **those in ~:** die Verantwortlichen 2 (person having power) Autorität, *die;* (body having power) **the authorities** die Behörde[n]; **the highest legal ~:** die höchste rechtliche Instanz 3 (expert, book, quotation) Autorität, *die;* (evidence) Quelle, *die;* **what is your ~ for your assertion?** worauf stützt du deine Behauptung?; **on the ~ of Darwin** nach Darwin; **have it on the ~ of sb./sth. that ...:** durch jmdn./etw. wissen, dass ...; **have it on good ~ that ...:** aus zuverlässiger Quelle wissen, dass ... 4 *no pl.* (weight of testimony) Autorität, *die;* **give** *or* **add ~ to sth.** einer Sache (*Dat.*) Gewicht verleihen 5 *no pl.* (power to influence) Autorität, *die* 6 *no pl.* (masterfulness) Souveränität, *die*

authorization /ɔːθəraɪˈzeɪʃn/ *n.* Genehmigung, *die;* Autorisation, *die;* **obtain/give ~:** die Genehmigung einholen/erteilen

authorize /ˈɔːθəraɪz/ *v.t.* 1 (give authority to) ermächtigen; bevollmächtigen; autorisieren; **~ sb. to do sth.** jmdn. ermächtigen, etw. zu tun; **entry is permitted only to ~d personnel** Unbefugten ist der Zutritt verboten 2 (sanction) genehmigen; **~ sth.** etw. genehmigen; einer Sache (*Dat.*) zustimmen; **the A~d Version** *engl. Fassung der Bibel von 1611*

authorship /ˈɔːθəʃɪp/ *n., no pl.* (origin) Autorschaft, *die;* **of unknown ~:** von einem unbekannten Autor *od.* Verfasser

autism /ˈɔːtɪzm/ *n., no pl.* (Psych., Med.) Autismus, *der*

autistic /ɔːˈtɪstɪk/ *adj.* (Psych., Med.) autistisch

auto /ˈɔːtəʊ/ *n., pl.* **~s** (Amer. coll.) Auto, *das*

auto- /ɔːtəʊ/ *in comb.* auto-/Auto-

autobahn /ˈɔːtəbɑːn/ *n., pl.* **~s** *or* **~en** /ˈɔːtəbɑːnən/ [deutsche] Autobahn

autobi'ographer *n.* Autobiograph, *der*/Autobiographin, *die*

autobio'graphic, autobio'graphical *adj.* autobiographisch

autobi'ography *n.* Autobiographie, *die*

autocade /ˈɔːtəʊkeɪd/ (Amer.) ▸ **motorcade**

autoclave /ˈɔːtəkleɪv/ *n.* Autoklav, *der*

autocracy /ɔːˈtɒkrəsɪ/ *n.* Autokratie, *die*

autocrat /ˈɔːtəkræt/ *n.* Autokrat, *der*

autocratic /ɔːtəˈkrætɪk/ *adj.* autokratisch

'autocross *n., no pl.* Autocross, *das*

Autocue ® /ˈɔːtəʊkjuː/ *n.* Teleprompter (Wz), *der*

'autofocus *n., no pl.* (Photog.) Autofokus, *der*

autogenic /ɔːtəʊˈdʒenɪk/ *adj.* autogen; **~ training** autogenes Training

autogenous /ɔːˈtɒdʒɪnəs/ *adj.* (Med., Industry) autogen; **~ welding** autogene Schweißung; Autogenschweißen, *das*

'autogiro *n., pl.* **~s** Autogiro, *das*

autograph /ˈɔːtəgrɑːf/

A *n.* 1 (signature) Autogramm, *das* 2 (manuscript) Autograph, *das;* (signed document) **the original ~:** das Original

B *v.t.* 1 (sign) signieren 2 (write with one's own hand) mit eigener Hand schreiben

autogyro ▸ **autogiro**

auto-im'mune *adj.* (Med.) autoimmun; **~ response** Autoimmunantwort, *die*

automat /ˈɔːtəmæt/ *n.* (Amer. Hist.: cafeteria) Automatenrestaurant, *das*

automate /ˈɔːtəmeɪt/ *v.t.* automatisieren

automated 'teller machine *n.* Geldautomat, *der*

automatic /ɔːtəˈmætɪk/

A *adj.* automatisch; **~ weapons** automatische Waffen; Schnellfeuerwaffen; **~ writing** automatisches Schreiben; **~ gear system, ~ transmission** Automatikgetriebe, *das;* **his reaction was completely ~:** er reagierte ganz automatisch; **disqualification is ~ after two false starts** die Disqualifikation erfolgt automatisch nach zwei Fehlstarts; **~ pilot** ▸ **autopilot**

B *n.* (weapon) automatische Waffe; (vehicle) Fahrzeug mit Automatikgetriebe; (tool, apparatus) Automat, *der*

automatically /ɔːtəˈmætɪkəlɪ/ *adv.* automatisch

automation /ɔːtəˈmeɪʃn/ *n., no pl.* Automation, *die;* (automatic control) Automatisierung, *die;* automatische Steuerung

automatism /ɔːˈtɒmətɪzm/ *n., no pl.* (Biol., Med., Psych.) Automatismus, *der*

automaton /ɔːˈtɒmətən/ *n., pl.* **~s** *or* **automata** /ɔːˈtɒmətə/ Automat, *der*

automobile /ˈɔːtəməbiːl/ *n.* (Amer.) Auto, *das*

automotive /ɔːtəˈməʊtɪv/ *adj.* Kraftfahrzeug-; **~ industry** Auto[mobil]industrie, *die;* **~ workers** Arbeiter in der Auto[mobil]industrie; **~ products** Erzeugnisse der Auto[mobil]industrie

autonomic /ɔːtəˈnɒmɪk/ *adj.* 1 (Physiol.) autonom; unbedingt ‹Reflex› 2 ▸ **autonomous**

autonomous /ɔːˈtɒnəməs/ *adj.* (also Philos.) autonom

autonomy /ɔːˈtɒnəmɪ/ *n., no pl.* (also Philos.) Autonomie, *die;* **~ of action** autonomes Handeln

'autopilot *n.* Autopilot, *der;* **[fly] on ~:** mit Autopilot [fliegen]

autopsy /ˈɔːtɒpsɪ, ɔːˈtɒpsɪ/ *n.* (post-mortem) Autopsie, *die;* Obduktion, *die;* (fig.) Manöverkritik, *die*

auto: ~save (Computing) A *n.* automatisches Speichern; B *v.t.* automatisch speichern; **~-suggestion** *n.* Autosuggestion, *die;* **~timer** *n.* [automatische] Schaltuhr; **~wind** /ˈɔːtəʊwaɪnd/ *n.* automatischer Filmtransport; *attrib.* **~wind camera** Kamera mit automatischem Filmtransport; **~zoom** *n.* 1 (zoom lens) Autozoomobjektiv, *das;* 2 *no pl.* (adjusting facility) Autozoom, *der; attrib.* **~zoom camera** Kamera mit Autozoom

autumn /ˈɔːtəm/ *n.* ▸ⓘ **p. 1515** (lit. or fig.) Herbst, *der;* **in ~ 1969, in the ~ of 1969** im Herbst 1969; **in early/late ~:** im Frühherbst/Spätherbst; **last/next ~:** letzten/nächsten Herbst; **~ is a beautiful time of the year** der Herbst ist eine schöne Jahreszeit; **~ weather/fashions** Herbstwetter, *das*/Herbstmoden

autumnal /ɔːˈtʌmnl/ *adj.* (lit. or fig.) herbstlich; (blooming or maturing in autumn) Herbst-; **~ flower** Herbstblume, *die*

autumn 'crocus *n.* Herbstzeitlose, *die*

auxiliary /ɔːgˈzɪljərɪ/

A *adj.* 1 (helping) Hilfs-; auxiliar (fachspr.); **be ~ to sth.** etw. unterstützen *od.* fördern; **~ troops** Hilfstruppen 2 (subsidiary) zusätzlich; Zusatz- 3 (Ling.) **~ verb** Hilfsverb, *das*

B *n.* 1 ▸ⓘ **p. 1260** Hilfskraft, *die;* **medical ~:** ärztliches Hilfspersonal 2 *in pl.* (Mil.) Hilfstruppen 3 (Ling.) Hilfsverb, *das*

AV *abbr.* = **Authorized Version;** ▸ **authorize 2**

avail /əˈveɪl/

A *n., no pl., no art.* Nutzen, *der;* **be of no ~:** nichts nützen; nutzlos *od.* vergeblich sein; **to no ~:** vergebens; **of what ~ is it ...?** was nützt es ...?

B *v.i.* 1 (be of profit) etwas nützen *od.* fruchten; **it will not ~:** es wird nichts nützen *od.* fruchten 2 (afford help) helfen

C *v.t.* nützen; **it will ~ you nothing** es wird dir nichts nützen

D *v. refl.* **~ oneself of sth.** von etw. Gebrauch machen; **~ oneself of an opportunity** eine Gelegenheit nutzen

availability /əveɪləˈbɪlɪtɪ/ *n., no pl.* Vorhandensein, *das;* **the ~ of sth.** die Möglichkeit, etw. zu bekommen; **I'll find out about the ~ of tickets** ich werde mich erkundigen, ob Karten zu bekommen sind; **the likely ~ of spare parts** die voraussichtliche Lieferbarkeit von Ersatzteilen; **the ~ of accommodation** das Zimmer-/Wohnungsangebot

available /əˈveɪləbl/ *adj.* 1 (at one's disposal) verfügbar; **make sth. ~ to sb.** jmdm. etw. zur Verfügung stellen; **be ~:** zur Verfügung stehen 2 (capable of use) gültig ‹Fahrkarte, Angebot› 3 (obtainable) erhältlich; lieferbar ‹Waren›; verfügbar ‹Unterkunft, Daten›; **have sth. ~:** etw. zur Verfügung haben; **nobody was ~ for comment** niemand stellte sich für einen Kommentar zur Verfügung

avalanche /ˈævəlɑːnʃ/

A *n.* (lit. or fig.) Lawine, *die*

B *v.i.* **mud ~d down** eine Lawine von Schlamm stürzte herab

avant-garde /ævɑ̃ˈgɑːd/

A *adj.* avantgardistisch

B *n.* Avantgarde, *die*

avarice /ˈævərɪs/ *n., no pl.* Geldgier, *die;* Habsucht, *die;* **~ for sth.** (fig.) Gier nach etw.

avaricious /ævəˈrɪʃəs/ *adj.* geldgierig; habsüchtig; (fig.) gierig (**for** nach); **~ for power** machtgierig

Ave. *abbr.* = **Avenue**

Ave [Maria] /ˈɑːveɪ (məˈriːə)/ *n.* Ave[-Maria], *das*

avenge /əˈvendʒ/ *v.t.* rächen; **be ~d/~ oneself on sb.** sich an jmdm. rächen; **be ~d for sth.** sich für etw. rächen

avenger /əˈvendʒə(r)/ *n.* Rächer, *der*/Rächerin, *die* (geh.)

avenue /ˈævənjuː/ *n.* (broad street) Avenue, *die;* Boulevard, *der;* (tree-lined road; Brit.: approach to country house) Allee, *die;* (fig.) Weg, *der* (**to** zu); **~ of approach** Zugang, *der;* **all ~s of escape**

were closed jeder Ausweg war versperrt; *see also* **explore 2**

aver /əˈvɜː(r)/ *v.t.*, **-rr-** beteuern

average /ˈævərɪdʒ/

A *n.* **1** Durchschnitt, *der;* **the ~ is about ...:** der Durchschnitt liegt bei [ungefähr] ...; **on [the** *or* **an] ~:** im Durchschnitt; durchschnittlich; im Schnitt (ugs.); **above/below ~:** über/unter dem Durchschnitt; **law of ~s** Wahrscheinlichkeitsgesetz, *das* **2** (arithmetic mean) Mittelwert, *der;* **batting ~** (Baseball, Cricket) Durchschnittsleistung als Schlagmann; **bowling ~** (Cricket) Durchschnittsleistung als Werfer **3** (Insurance) Havarie, *die;* **~ adjustment** Dispache, *die*

B *adj.* **1** durchschnittlich; **~ speed** durchschnittliche Geschwindigkeit; Durchschnittsgeschwindigkeit, *die;* **he is of ~ height** er ist mittelgroß **2** (mediocre) durchschnittlich; mittelmäßig

C *v.t.* **1** (find the ~ of) den Durchschnitt ermitteln von **2** (amount on ~ to) durchschnittlich betragen; **the planks ~d three metres in length** die Bretter waren durchschnittlich drei Meter lang; **these things ~ themselves out** so etwas gleicht sich aus **3** (do on ~) einen Durchschnitt von ... erreichen; **she ~s four novels a year** sie schreibt durchschnittlich vier Romane im Jahr; **the train ~d 90 mph** der Zug fuhr im Durchschnitt mit 144 Kilometern pro Stunde

D *v.i.* **~ out at** im Durchschnitt betragen

averagely /ˈævərɪdʒlɪ/ *adv.* durchschnittlich

averse /əˈvɜːs/ *pred. adj.* **be ~ to** *or* **from sth.** einer Sache (*Dat.*) abgeneigt sein; **be ~ to** *or* **from doing sth.** abgeneigt sein, etw. zu tun

aversion /əˈvɜːʃn/ *n.* **1** *no pl.* (dislike) Abneigung, *die;* Aversion, *die;* **have/take an ~ to** *or* **from sth.** eine Abneigung *od.* Aversion gegen etw. haben/bekommen; *attrib.* **~ therapy** (Psych.) Aversionstherapie, *die* **2** (object) **be sb.'s ~:** jmdm. ein Gräuel sein; **my pet ~ is ...:** ein besonderer Gräuel ist mir ...

avert /əˈvɜːt/ *v.t.* **1** (turn away) abwenden ‹*Blick, Gesicht, Aufmerksamkeit*› **2** (prevent) abwenden ‹*Katastrophe, Schaden, Niederlage*›; verhüten ‹*Unfall*›; verhindern ‹*Fehlschlag*›

avian flu /eɪvɪən ˈfluː/ *n.* Geflügelpest, *die*

aviary /ˈeɪvɪərɪ/ *n.* Vogelhaus, *das;* Aviarium, *das*

aviation /eɪvɪˈeɪʃn/ *n.*, *no pl.*, *no art.* **1** (operating of aircraft) Luftfahrt, *die; attrib.* **~ fuel** Flugbenzin, *das* **2** (aircraft manufacture) Flugzeugbau, *der; attrib.* **~ industry** Flugzeugindustrie, *die;* Luftfahrtindustrie, *die*

aviator /ˈeɪvɪeɪtə(r)/ *n.* ▸**i** **p. 1260** Flieger, *der*/Fliegerin, *die*

avid /ˈævɪd/ *adj.* (enthusiastic) begeistert; passioniert; **be ~ for sth.** (eager, greedy) begierig auf etw. (*Akk.*) sein

avidity /əˈvɪdɪtɪ/ *n.*, *no pl.* (enthusiasm) Begeisterung, *die;* (greed) Begierde, *die*

avidly /ˈævɪdlɪ/ *adv.* (enthusiastically) eifrig; begeistert ‹*annehmen*›; (greedily) begierig

avionics /eɪvɪˈɒnɪks/ *n.* **1** *no pl.* Bordelektronik, *die;* Avionik, *die* **2** *constr. as pl.* (systems) Bordelektr[on]ik, *die;* Avionik, *die*

avis /æˈviː/ *n.* (EU) Avis, *der*

avocado /ævəˈkɑːdəʊ/ *n.*, *pl.* **~s:** **~ [pear]** Avocado[birne], *die;* (tree) Avocado, *die*

avocation /ævəˈkeɪʃn/ *n.* (formal) Nebenbeschäftigung, *die*

avocet /ˈævəset/ *n.* (Ornith.) Säbelschnäbler, *der*

avoid /əˈvɔɪd/ *v.t.* **1** (keep away from) meiden ‹*Ort*›; **~ an obstacle/a cyclist** einem Hindernis/Radfahrer ausweichen; **~ the boss when he's in a temper** geh dem Chef aus dem Weg, wenn er schlechte Laune hat **2** (refrain from) vermeiden; **~ doing sth.** vermeiden, etw. zu tun; **you can hardly ~ seeing her** du wirst kaum umhinkönnen, sie zu sehen **3** (escape) vermeiden; **they wore masks to ~ recognition** sie trugen Masken, um nicht erkannt zu werden

avoidable /əˈvɔɪdəbl/ *adj.* vermeidbar; **if it is [at all] ~:** wenn es sich [irgend] vermeiden lässt

avoidance /əˈvɔɪdəns/ *n.*, *no pl.* Vermeidung, *die;* **the ~ of accidents** das Vermeiden von Unfällen; die Unfallverhütung; **~ of death duties** Umgehung der Erbschaftssteuer

avoirdupois /ævədjʊˈpɔɪz/

A *adj.* Avoirdupois-

B *n.* **1** Avoirdupois, *das* **2** (joc.: bodily weight) Gewicht, *das*

avow /əˈvaʊ/ *v.t.* bekennen; **~ oneself [to be] sth.** sich als etw. bekennen; **an ~ed opponent/supporter** ein erklärter Gegner/Befürworter

avowal /əˈvaʊəl/ *n.* Bekenntnis, *das;* **on your own ~:** wie Sie selbst erklärt haben

avowedly /əˈvaʊɪdlɪ/ *adv.* erklärtermaßen

avuncular /əˈvʌŋkjʊlə(r)/ *adj.* onkelhaft

aw /ɔː/ *int. expr. remonstrance, commiseration* oh; *expr. disgust* bah; **aw, bad luck!** so ein Pech!

AWACS /ˈeɪwæks/ *abbr.* **= Airborne Warning and Control Systems** AWACS

await /əˈweɪt/ *v.t.* erwarten; **disaster ~s us if ...:** uns erwartet eine Katastrophe, wenn ...; **the long ~ed visit** der lang ersehnte Besuch

awake /əˈweɪk/

A *v.i.*, **awoke** /əˈwəʊk/, **awoken** /əˈwəʊkn/ (lit. or fig.) erwachen; **we awoke to the sound of rain on the windows** als wir erwachten, hörten wir den Regen gegen die Fenster prasseln; **one day I shall ~ to find myself a rich man** eines Tages werde ich aufwachen und ein reicher Mann sein; **~ to sth.** einer Sache (*Gen.*) gewahr werden; **when she awoke to her surroundings** als sie gewahr wurde, wo sie sich befand

B *v.t.*, **awoke, awoken** (lit. or fig.) wecken; **~ sb. to sth.** (fig.) jmdm. etw. bewusst machen; **be awoken to sth.** (fig.) einer Sache (*Gen.*) gewahr werden

C *pred. adj.* (lit. or fig.) wach; **wide ~:** hellwach; **lie ~:** wach liegen; **be ~ to sth.** (fig.) sich (*Dat.*) einer Sache (*Gen.*) bewusst sein

awaken /əˈweɪkn/

A *v.t.* (esp. fig.) ▸ **awake B**

B *v.i.* (esp. fig.) ▸ **awake A**

awakening /əˈweɪknɪŋ/ *n.* Erwachen, *das;* **a rude ~** (fig.) ein böses Erwachen

award /əˈwɔːd/

A *v.t.* (grant) verleihen, zuerkennen ‹*Preis, Auszeichnung*›; zusprechen ‹*Sorgerecht, Entschädigung*›; gewähren ‹*Zahlung, Gehaltserhöhung*›; **~ sb. sth.** jmdm. etw. verleihen/zusprechen/gewähren; **sb. is ~ed sth.** jmdm. wird etw. verliehen/zugesprochen/gewährt; **he was ~ed the prize** der Preis wurde ihm zuerkannt; **the referee ~ed a penalty [to Arsenal]** der Schiedsrichter erkannte auf Strafstoß [für Arsenal]

B *n.* **1** (judicial decision) Schiedsspruch, *der* **2** (payment) Entschädigung[ssumme], *die;* (grant) Stipendium, *das;* **make an ~ to sb.** jmdm. finanzielle Unterstützung gewähren **3** (prize) Auszeichnung, *die;* Preis, *der*

a'ward-winning *adj.* preisgekrönt

aware /əˈweə(r)/ *adj.* **1** *pred.* (conscious) **be ~ of sth.** sich (*Dat.*) einer Sache (*Gen.*) bewusst sein; **be ~ that ...:** sich (*Dat.*) [dessen] bewusst sein, dass ...; **what made you ~ that ...?** woran bemerkten Sie, dass ...?; **the patient was ~ of everything going on around him** der Patient bekam alles mit, was um ihn herum vorging; **as far as I am ~:** soweit ich weiß; **not that I am ~ of** nicht, dass ich wüsste **2** (well-informed) informiert

awareness /əˈweənɪs/ *n.*, *no pl.* (consciousness) Bewusstsein, *das;* **raise public ~ of sth.** etw. der Öffentlichkeit zu Bewusstsein bringen; etw. ins allgemeine Bewusstsein bringen

awash /əˈwɒʃ/ *pred. adj.* auf gleicher Höhe mit dem Wasserspiegel; **be ~** (flooded) unter Wasser stehen; (fig.) **be ~ with money** im Geld schwimmen

away /əˈweɪ/

A *adv.* **1** (at a distance) entfernt; **~ in the distance** weit in der Ferne; **two feet ~ [from sth.]** zwei Fuß entfernt [von etw.]; **play ~** (Sport) auswärts spielen; **Christmas is still months ~:** bis Weihnachten dauert es noch Monate **2** (to a distance) weg; fort; **get ~ from it all** ▸ **all A 1**; **~ with you/him!** weg *od.* fort mit dir/ihm!; **throw sth. ~:** etw. wegwerfen *od.* fortwerfen; **~ we go!** los gehts! **3** (absent) nicht da; **be ~ on business** geschäftlich außer Haus sein; **be ~ [from school] with a cold** wegen einer Erkältung [in der Schule] fehlen; **he's ~ in France/on holiday** er ist zur Zeit in Frankreich/im Urlaub **4** (towards or into non-existence) **die/fade ~:** verhallen; **gamble one's money ~:** sein Geld verspielen; **drink the evening ~:** den Abend mit Trinken verbringen; **the water has all boiled ~:** das ganze Wasser ist verkocht; **idle one's time ~:** seine Zeit vertrödeln **5** (constantly) unablässig; **work ~ on sth.** ohne Unterbrechung an etw. (*Dat.*) arbeiten; **laugh ~ at sth.** unablässig über etw. (*Akk.*) lachen; **they were singing ~:** sie sangen aus voller Kehle **6** (without delay) gleich ‹*fragen usw.*›; **fire ~** (lit. or fig.) losschießen (ugs.)

B *adj.* (Sport) auswärts *präd.;* Auswärts-; **the next match is ~:** das nächste Spiel ist auswärts; **~ match** Auswärtsspiel, *das;* **~ team** Gastmannschaft, *die*

awe /ɔː/

A *n.* Ehrfurcht, *die* (**of** vor + *Dat.*); **be** *or* **stand in ~ of sb.** jmdn. fürchten; (feel respect) Ehrfurcht vor jmdm. haben; **hold sb. in ~:** jmdn. ehrfürchtig respektieren

B *v.t.* Ehrfurcht einflößen (+ *Dat.*); **be ~d by sth.** sich von etw. beeindrucken *od.* einschüchtern lassen; **be ~d into silence** beeindruckt *od.* eingeschüchtert schweigen; **in an ~d voice** mit ehrfurchtsvoller Stimme

aweigh /əˈweɪ/ *pred. adj.* (Naut.) aus dem Grund

'awe-inspiring *adj.* Ehrfurcht gebietend

awesome /ˈɔːsəm/ *adj.* **1** überwältigend; eindrucksvoll ‹*Schweigen*›; übergroß ‹*Verantwortung*› **2** (coll.: wonderful, excellent) geil (ugs.)

awe: ~stricken, ~struck *adj.* [von Ehrfurcht] ergriffen; ehrfurchtsvoll ‹*Ausdruck, Staunen*›

awful /ˈɔːfl/ *adj.* **1** furchtbar; fürchterlich; **too ~ for words** (coll.) unbeschreiblich schlecht; **be an ~ lot better/worse** (coll.) ein ganzes Stück besser/schlechter sein; **not an ~ lot better/worse** (coll.) nicht gerade viel besser/schlechter; **an ~ lot of money/people** (coll.) ein Haufen Geld/Leute (ugs.); **an ~ long time/way** (coll.) eine furchtbar lange Zeit/ein furchtbar weiter Weg **2** (commanding reverence) Ehrfurcht gebietend; (solemnly impressive) eindrucksvoll; **~ silence** feierliche Stille

awfully /ˈɔːfəlɪ, ˈɔːflɪ/ *adv.* furchtbar; **not ~** (coll.) nicht besonders; **thanks ~** (coll.) tausend Dank

awfulness /ˈɔːflnɪs/ *n.*, *no pl.* **1** (terribleness) Furchtbarkeit, *die* **2** (impressive solemnity) [eindrucksvolle *od.* Ehrfurcht gebietende] Feierlichkeit

awhile /əˈwaɪl/ *adv.* eine Weile; **not yet ~:** so bald nicht

awkward /ˈɔːkwəd/ *adj.* **1** (ill-adapted for use) ungünstig; **be ~ to use** unhandlich sein; **the parcel is ~ to carry** das Paket ist schlecht zu tragen **2** (clumsy) unbeholfen; **be at an ~ age** in einem schwierigen Alter sein **3** (embarrassing, embarrassed) peinlich; **feel ~:** sich unbehaglich fühlen **4** (difficult) schwierig, unangenehm ‹*Person*›; ungünstig ‹*Zeitpunkt*›; schwierig, peinlich ‹*Lage, Dilemma*›; *see also* **customer 2**

awkwardly /ˈɔːkwədlɪ/ *adv.* **1** (badly) ungünstig ‹*geformt, angebracht*› **2** (clumsily) ungeschickt, unbeholfen ‹*gehen, sich ausdrücken*›; ungeschickt, unglücklich ‹*fallen, sich ausdrücken*› **3** (embarrassingly) peinlicherweise; (embarrassedly) peinlich berührt; betreten **4** (unfavourably) ungünstig ‹*gelegen*›

awkwardness /ˈɔːkwədnɪs/ *n.*, *no pl.* ▸ **awkward: 1** Unhandlichkeit, *die;* **the ~ of the design puts me off** das ungünstige Design stößt mich ab **2** Unbeholfenheit, *die* **3** Peinlichkeit, *die;* **a moment of ~:** ein peinlicher Augenblick **4** (of person) unangenehmes Wesen; (of situation, position) Schwierigkeit, *die*

awl /ɔːl/ *n.* Ahle, *die;* Pfriem, *der*

a

awn /ɔːn/ *n.* (Bot.) Granne, *die*

awning /ˈɔːnɪŋ/ *n.* (on wagon) Plane, *die;* (on house) Markise, *die;* (of tent) Vordach, *das;* (on ship) Sonnensegel, *das*

awoke, awoken ▸ **awake**

AWOL /ˈeɪwɒl/ *adj.* (Mil.) unerlaubt von der Truppe entfernt; **go ~:** sich unerlaubt von der Truppe entfernen

awry /əˈraɪ/

A *adv.* schief; **your coat has pulled your scarf [all] ~:** deine Jacke hat deinen Schal ganz verzogen; **go ~** (fig.) schiefgehen (ugs.); ‹*Plan:*› fehlschlagen

B *pred. adj.* schief; unordentlich; **your tie is all ~:** deine Krawatte sitzt ganz schief; **our clothes were all ~:** unsere Kleidung war völlig in Unordnung; **now our plans are utterly ~** (fig.) nun sind unsere Pläne völlig fehlgeschlagen

axe (Amer.: **ax**) /æks/

A *n.* **1** Axt, *die;* Beil, *das;* **have an ~ to grind** (fig.) sein eigenes Süppchen kochen (ugs.) **2** (fig.: reduction) **the ~:** radikale Kürzung; Rotstift, *der;* **on which sector will the ~ fall next?** welcher Sektor wird als nächster dem Rotstift zum Opfer fallen? *See also* **take A 6**

B *v.t.* (reduce) [radikal] kürzen; (eliminate) [radikal] einsparen ‹*Stellen*›; (dismiss) entlassen; (abandon) aufgeben ‹*Projekt*›

axes *pl. of* **axe, axis**

axial /ˈæksɪəl/ *adj.* axial; Achsen-; Axial-

axil /ˈæksɪl/ *n.* (Bot.) Blattachsel, *die;* (of tree) Winkel zwischen Ast und Stamm

axiom /ˈæksɪəm/ *n.* Axiom, *das*

axiomatic /æksɪəˈmætɪk/ *adj.* axiomatisch; **I have taken it as ~ that ...:** ich gehe von dem Grundsatz aus, dass ...

axis /ˈæksɪs/ *n., pl.* **axes** /ˈæksiːz/ **1** Achse, *die;* **~ of rotation** Rotationsachse, *die* **2** (Polit.) Achse, *die;* **the A~** (Hist.) die Achse; **the A~ powers** (Hist.) die Achsenmächte **3** (Bot.) Sprossachse, *die* **4** (Anat., Physiol.) Axis, *der*

axle /ˈæksl/ *n.* Achse, *die*

ˈaxle grease *n.* Wagenschmiere, *die*

ayatollah /aɪəˈtɒlə/ *n.* Ajatollah, *der*

aye[1] /aɪ/

A *adv.* **1** (in voting; arch./dial.) ja; **answer ~:** mit Ja antworten **2** (Naut.) **~, ~, sir!** jawohl, Herr Kapitän!/Admiral! *etc*

B *n.* (answer) Ja, *das;* (vote) Jastimme, *die;* **the ~s have it** die Mehrheit ist dafür

aye[2] /eɪ/ *adv.* (arch.: ever) all[e]zeit (veralt.); **for ~:** auf ewig

azalea /əˈzeɪlɪə/ *n.* (Bot.) Azalee, *die*

Azerbaijan /æzəbaɪˈdʒɑːn/ *pr. n.* Aserbaidschan (*das*); Aserbeidschan (*das*)

azimuth /ˈæzɪməθ/ *n.* (Astron.) Azimut, *der*

Azores /əˈzɔːz/ *pr. n. pl.* Azoren *Pl.*

Aztec /ˈæztek/ ▸ⓘ **p. 1277**, ▸ⓘ **p. 1345**

A *adj.* aztekisch

B *n.* **1** (person) Azteke, *der*/Aztekin, *die* **2** (language) Aztekisch, *das*

azure /ˈæʒjə(r), ˈeɪʒjə(r)/

A *n.* **1** (sky blue) Azur[blau], *das* **2** (Her.) Blau, *das* **3** (literary: unclouded sky) Azur, *der*

B *adj.* **1** (sky-blue) azurblau; azurn **2** (Her.) blau

Bb

B, b /biː/ *n., pl.* **Bs** *or* **B's** **1** (letter) B, b, *das;* **B road** Straße 2. Ordnung; ≈ Landstraße, *die;* **B film** *or* (Amer.) **movie** Vorfilm, *der* **2** **B** (Mus.) H, h, *das;* **B flat** B, b, *das* **3** (example) B, b (ohne Artikel) **4** **B** (Sch., Univ.: mark) Zwei, *die;* **he got a B** er bekam „gut" *od.* eine Zwei

b. *abbr.* **1** = **born** geb. **2** (Cricket) = **bowled by** ausgeschlagen durch Tortreffer von

B. *abbr.* **1** (Univ.) = **Bachelor** **2** = **bishop** Bisch.; (Chess) L **3** (on pencil) = **black** B

BA *abbr.* **1** (Univ.) = **Bachelor of Arts;** *see also* **BSc** **2** = **British Academy** *geisteswissenschaftliche akademische Institution in Großbritannien* **3** = **British Association** *naturwissenschaftliche akademische Institution in Großbritannien*

baa /bɑː/
A *n.* Blöken, *das*
B *v.i.,* **~ed** *or* **~'d** /bɑːd/ mähen; blöken

BAA *abbr.* = **British Airports Authority** *britische Flughafenbehörde*

'baa-lamb *n.* (child lang.) Bählämmchen, *das;* Bählamm, *das*

baba /ˈbɑːbɑː/ *n.* **[rum]** **~:** [Rum]baba, *das; mit Rumsirup getränktes Gebäck*

babble /ˈbæbl/
A *v.i.* **1** (talk incoherently) stammeln; **~ [away** *or* **on]** ‹*Baby:*› [vor sich (*Akk.*) hin] lallen *od.* plappern **2** (talk foolishly) [dumm] schwatzen; **a babbling idiot** ein dummer Schwätzer **3** (talk excessively) **~ away** *or* **on** quasseln (ugs.) **4** (murmur) ‹*Bach:*› plätschern
B *v.t.* **1** (divulge foolishly) ausplaudern; **~ sth. to sb.** etw. bei jmdm. ausplaudern **2** (utter incoherently) stammeln
C *n.* **1** (incoherent speech) Gestammel, *das;* (childish or foolish speech) Gelalle, *das* **2** (confused sound of voices) **~ [of voices]** Stimmengewirr, *das* **3** (murmur of water) Geplätscher, *das*

babbler /ˈbæblə(r)/ *n.* **1** (chatterer, teller of secrets) Plaudertasche, *die* **2** (Ornith.) Timalie, *die*

babe /beɪb/ *n.* **1** (inexperienced person) Anfänger, *der*/Anfängerin, *die;* **be a ~:** noch nicht trocken hinter den Ohren sein (ugs.) **2** (guileless person) Lamm, *das;* **~s in the wood** hilflose Lämmchen **3** (coll.: young woman) Kleine, *die* (ugs.); **I love you, ~:** ich liebe dich, Kleines **4** (young child) kleines Kind; **as innocent as a newborn ~:** unschuldig wie ein neugeborenes Kind; *see also* **mouth A 1**

babel /ˈbeɪbl/ *n.* **1** (noisy medley) **~ of voices** [lautes] Stimmengewirr **2** (scene of confusion) Durcheinander, *das* **3** (confusion of languages) babylonisches Sprachgewirr; **the Tower of B~:** der Turm zu Babel

baboon /bəˈbuːn/ *n.* (Zool.) Pavian, *der;* (fig. derog.: person) Neandertaler, *der;* Halbaffe, *der*

babushka /bəˈbʊʃkə/ *n.* Kopftuch, *das*

baby /ˈbeɪbɪ/
A *n.* **1** Baby, *das;* **have a ~/be going to have a ~:** ein Kind bekommen; **she is having a ~ in May** sie bekommt im Mai ein Kind; **she has a young ~:** sie hat ein kleines Baby; **mother and ~ are doing fine** Mutter und Kind sind wohlauf; **a ~ boy/girl** ein kleiner Junge/ein kleines Mädchen; **throw out** *or* **away the ~ with the bathwater** (fig.) das Kind mit dem Bade ausschütten; **be left holding** *or* **carrying the ~** (fig.) die Sache ausbaden müssen (ugs.); der Dumme sein (ugs.); **leave sb. carrying the ~** (fig.) jmdn. die Sache ausbaden lassen (ugs.); **it's your/his** *etc.* **~** (fig.) das ist dein/sein *usw.* Bier (ugs.); **reference books are Jones's ~:** um Nachschlagewerke muss sich Jones kümmern **2** (youngest member) Jüngste, *der/die;* (male also) Benjamin, *der;* **the ~ of the family** das Küken der Familie **3** (childish person) **be a ~:** sich wie ein kleines Kind benehmen **4** (young animal) Junge, *das;* **~ bird/giraffe** junger Vogel/junge Giraffe; Vogeljunge, *das*/Giraffenjunge, *das* **5** (small thing) **be a ~:** winzig sein; **~ [car]** Miniauto, *das;* Kleinwagen, *der;* **~ [bottle]** Miniflasche, *die* **6** (coll.: sweetheart) Schatz, *der;* (in pop song also) Baby, *das* **7** (coll.: person) Typ, *der;* (thing) Ding, *das* (ugs.); **this ~** (the speaker himself) unsereiner (ugs.)
B *v.t.* wie ein kleines Kind behandeln; (be easy on) mit Samthandschuhen anfassen

baby: ~ alarm *n.* Babyfon(Wz), *das;* **~ battering** *n., no pl.* Misshandlung eines Babys; **~ boom** *n.* Babyboom, *der;* **~-bouncer** *n.: federnd aufgehängter Sitz für Kleinkinder, in dem sie durch Wippen ihre Beine kräftigen sollen;* **~ buggy** *n.* (Amer.) Kinderwagen, *der;* **~ car** ▸ **baby A 5;** **~ carriage** *n.* (Amer.) Kinderwagen, *der;* **~ clothes** *n. pl.* Babykleidung, *die;* **~-doll** *adj.* **~-doll pyjamas/nightdress** Babydoll, *das;* **~ face** *n.* **1** (face) Kindergesicht, *das;* **2** (person) Milchgesicht, *das* (leicht abwertend); **~ food** *n.* Babynahrung, *die;* **~ 'grand** *n.* (Mus.) Stutzflügel, *der*

babyhood /ˈbeɪbɪhʊd/ *n., no pl.* frühe Kindheit

babyish /ˈbeɪbɪɪʃ/ *adj.* kindlich ‹*Aussehen*›; kindisch ‹*Benehmen, Person*›; **don't be so ~:** benimm dich nicht wie ein kleines Kind

baby: ~-minder *n.* Tagesmutter, *die;* **~ powder** *n.* Babypuder, *der;* **~ seat** *n.* Babysitz, *der;* Kindersitz, *der;* **~ shower** *n.* (Amer.) Babyparty, *die* (*mit Verteilung von Geschenken an die werdende Mutter*); **~sit** *v.i., forms as* **sit A** babysitten (ugs.); auf das Kind/die Kinder aufpassen; **she ~sits for us** sie kommt zu uns zum Babysitten; **~sitter** *n.* Babysitter, *der;* **~sitting** *n.* Babysitting, *das;* **~-snatch** *v.i.* ▸ **cradle-snatch;** **~-snatcher** *n.* **1** Kindesentführer, *der;* **2** ▸ **cradle-snatcher 2;** **~-snatching** *n.* **1** Kindesentführung, *die;* **2** ▸ **cradle-snatching 2;** **~-talk** *n.* Babysprache, *die;* **~ walker** *n.* Laufstuhl, *der;* **~ wipe** *n.* Baby[feucht]tuch, *das*

baccalaureate /bækəˈlɔːrɪət/ *n.* Bakkalaureat, *das*

baccarat /ˈbækərɑː/ *n.* Bakkarat, *das*

Bacchanalia /bækəˈneɪlɪə/ *n. pl.* **1** (drunken revelry) Bacchanal, *das* (geh.) **2** (Greek and Roman Ant.) Bacchanalien *Pl.*

Bacchanalian /bækəˈneɪlɪən/ *adj.* bacchantisch

baccy /ˈbækɪ/ *n.* (Brit. coll.) Tabak, *der*

bachelor /ˈbætʃələ(r)/ *n.* **1** (unmarried man) Junggeselle, *der* **2** (Univ.) Bakkalaureus, *der;* Bachelor, *der;* **B~ of Arts/Science** Bakkalaureus der philosophischen Fakultät/der Naturwissenschaften

bachelor: ~ flat *n.* Junggesellenwohnung, *die;* **~ girl** *n.* Junggesellin, *die*

bachelorhood /ˈbætʃələhʊd/ *n., no pl.* Junggesellendasein, *das*

bacillary /bəˈsɪlərɪ/ *adj.* (Biol., Med.) bazillär

bacillus /bəˈsɪləs/ *n., pl.* **bacilli** /bəˈsɪlaɪ/ (Biol., Med.) **1** (rod-shaped bacterium) Bazillus, *der* **2** (pathogenic bacterium) Bakterie, *die*

back /bæk/
A *n.* **1** ▸ℹ **p. 951** (of person, animal) Rücken, *der;* **stand ~ to ~:** Rücken an Rücken stehen; **as soon as my ~ was turned** (fig.) sowie ich den Rücken gedreht hatte; **behind sb.'s ~** (fig.) ▸ **behind B 2;** **be on one's ~:** [auf dem Rücken] liegen; (fig.: be ill) im Bett liegen; flachliegen (salopp); auf der Nase liegen (ugs.); **turn one's ~ on sb.** jmdm. den Rücken zuwenden; (fig.: abandon sb.) jmdn. im Stich lassen; **turn one's ~ on sth.** (fig.) etw. vernachlässigen; sich um etw. nicht kümmern; **don't turn your ~ on this chance** lass dir diese Chance nicht entgehen; **get** *or* **put sb.'s ~ up** (fig.) jmdn. wütend machen; **be glad to see the ~ of sb./sth.** (fig.) froh sein, jmdn./etw. nicht mehr sehen zu müssen; **have one's ~ to the wall** (fig.) mit dem Rücken zur Wand stehen; **be at sb.'s ~** (fig.) (in support) hinter jmdm. stehen; (in pursuit) jmdm. auf den Fersen sein; **with sb. at one's ~** (fig.) gefolgt von jmdm.; **get off my ~** (fig. coll.) lass mich zufrieden; **have sb./sth. on one's ~** (fig.) jmdn./etw. am Hals haben (ugs.); **put one's ~ into sth.** (fig.) sich für etw. mit allen Kräften einsetzen; **you're not exactly putting your ~ into this work** (fig.) du strengst dich bei dieser Arbeit nicht genug an; *see also* **break A 3, B 2**
2 (outer or rear surface) Rücken, *der;* (of vehicle) Heck, *das;* **the car went into the ~ of me** (coll.) das Auto ist mir hinten reingefahren (ugs.); **with the ~ of one's hand** mit dem Handrücken; **know sth. like the ~ of one's hand** (fig.) etw. wie seine Westentasche kennen; **the ~ of one's/the head** der Hinterkopf; **the ~ of the leg** (below knee) die Wade
3 (of book) (spine) [Buch]rücken, *der;* (final pages) Ende, *das;* **at the ~ [of the book]** hinten [im Buch]
4 (of dress) Rücken, *der;* (of knife) [Messer]rücken, *der*
5 (more remote part) hinterer Teil; **at the ~ [of sth.]** hinten [in etw. (*Dat.*)]; im hinteren Teil [von etw.]
6 (inside car) Rücksitz, *der;* Fond, *der* (seltener); (of chair) [Rücken]lehne, *die;* (of material) linke Seite; (of house, cheque) Rückseite, *die;* (**~** wall) Rückseite, *die;* Rückwand, *die;* **~ to front** verkehrt rum; **please get to the ~ of the queue** bitte, stellen Sie sich hinten an; **we squeezed five people into the ~ [of the car]** wir zwängten fünf Personen auf die Rücksitze [des Wagens]; **the coat hook was on the ~ of the door** der Kleiderhaken befand sich hinten an der Tür; **there's something at the ~ of my mind** ich habe da noch etwas im Hinterkopf; **in ~ of sth.** (Amer.) hinter etw. (*Dat.*); *see also* **beyond C**
7 (Sport) (player) Verteidiger, *der;* (position) **he played at ~ this week** diese Woche hat er als Verteidiger gespielt
8 (of ship) Kiel, *der*
B *adj., no comp.; superl.* **~most** /ˈbækməʊst/ **1** (situated behind) hinter...; **from the ~most of the three lines** von der hintersten der drei Linien
2 (overdue) rückständig ‹*Lohn, Steuern*›
3 (remote) abgelegen ‹*Ort, Straße*›
4 (reversed) **~ motion** Rückwärtsbewegung, *die;* **~ flow** Rückfluss, *der*
C *adv.* **1** (to the rear) zurück; **step ~:** zurücktre-

ten; **play ~** (Cricket) zurücktreten, um zu schlagen
[2] (behind) zurück; weiter hinten; **we passed a pub two miles ~:** wir sind vor zwei Meilen an einem Pub vorbeigefahren; **~ and forth** hin und her; **~ of sth.** (Amer.) hinter etw. (*Dat.*)
[3] (at a distance) **the house stands a long way ~ from the road** das Haus steht weit von der Straße zurück
[4] (to original position, home) [wieder] zurück; **I got my letter ~:** ich habe meinen Brief zurückbekommen; **the journey ~:** die Rückfahrt/der Rückflug; **there and ~:** hin und zurück
[5] (in the past) zurück; **go a long way ~:** weit zurückgehen; **a week/month ~:** vor einer Woche/vor einem Monat
[7] (in return) zurück; **I got a letter ~:** er/sie hat mir wiedergeschrieben
D *v.t.* [1] (assist) unterstützen ‹*Person, Sache*›
[2] (bet on) wetten *od.* setzen auf (+ *Akk.*) ‹*Pferd, Gewinner, Favorit*›; **~ the wrong/right horse** (lit. or fig.) aufs falsche/richtige Pferd setzen (ugs.); **~ X to beat Y** darauf wetten, dass X gegen Y gewinnt; **the horse which is most heavily ~ed** das Pferd, auf das am meisten gesetzt wurde
[3] (cause to move ~) zurücksetzen [mit] ‹*Fahrzeug*›; rückwärts gehen lassen ‹*Pferd*›; **how did you manage to ~ the car into that lamp post?** wie hast du es nur fertig gebracht, rückwärts gegen den Laternenpfahl zu fahren?; **~ water** rückwärts rudern
[4] (put or act as a ~ to) [an der Rückseite] verstärken
[5] (endorse) indossieren ‹*Wechsel, Scheck*›
[6] (lie at the ~ of) **~ sth.** hinten an etw. (*Akk.*) grenzen
[7] (Mus.) begleiten
E *v.i.* zurücksetzen; ‹*Wind:*› [sich] gegen den Uhrzeigersinn drehen; **~ into/out of sth.** rückwärts in etw. (*Akk.*)/aus etw. fahren; **~ on to sth.** hinten an etw. (*Akk.*) grenzen; **~ and fill** (Amer.) sich hin und her bewegen; (fig.) schwanken

Phrasal verbs

- **~ a'way** *v.i.* zurückweichen; (fig.) zurückschrecken
- **~ 'down** *v.i.* (fig.) nachgeben; einen Rückzieher machen (ugs.); *see also* **back-down**
- **~ 'off ▸ ~ away**
- **~ 'out** *v.i.* rückwärts herausfahren; (fig.) einen Rückzieher machen (ugs.); **~ out of sth.** (fig.) von etw. zurücktreten
- **~ 'up**

A [1] *v.t.* unterstützen; untermauern ‹*Anspruch, Geschichte, These*› [2] (Computing) sichern ‹*Daten, Dokumente*›; **~ up a file on to a floppy disk** von einer Datei eine Sicherungskopie auf Diskette machen
B *v.i.* [1] ‹*Wasser:*› sich [auf]stauen [2] (reverse) zurücksetzen [3] (Amer.: form queue of vehicles) sich stauen. *see also* **back-up**

back: ~ache *n., no pl.* ▸ ℹ **p. 1231** Rückenschmerzen *Pl.*; **~ 'bench** *n.* (Brit. Parl.) hintere Sitzreihe; **a ~-bench MP** ein Parlamentsabgeordneter [aus den hinteren Reihen]; **~-bencher** /bæk'bentʃə(r)/ *n.* (Brit. Parl.) [einfacher] Abgeordneter/[einfache] Abgeordnete; (derog.) Hinterbänkler, *der* (abwertend); **~biter** *n.* Verleumder, *der*/Verleumderin, *die*; **~biting** *n.* Verleumdung, *die*; Hetzerei, *die* (ugs.); **~blocks** *n. pl.* (Austral., NZ) ≈ Hinterland, *das; dünn besiedeltes, abgelegenes Land im Landesinneren*; **~ boiler** *n.* (Brit.) (hinter dem Ofen o. Ä. angebrachter) Boiler; **~bone** *n.* Wirbelsäule, *die*; Rückgrat, *das* (auch fig.); (Amer.: of book) [Buch]rücken, *der*; **to the ~bone** (fig.) durch und durch; **~-breaking** *adj.* äußerst mühsam; gewaltig ‹*Anstrengung*›; **~-breaking work** Knochenarbeit, *die*; **~ 'burner** *n.* **put sth. on the ~ burner** (fig. coll.) etw. zurückstellen; **~chat** *n., no pl.* (coll.) [freche] Widerrede; **none of your ~chat!** keine Widerrede!; **~cloth** *n.* (Brit. Theatre) Prospekt, *der*; **~comb** *v.t.* zurückkämmen; **~ copy ▸ ~ number**; **~date** *v.t.* zurückdatieren (**to** auf + *Akk.*); **~ 'door** *n.* Hintertür, *die* (auch fig.); **~-door** *adj.* (fig.) Hintertreppen- (abwertend); **~-down** *n.* (coll.) Rückzieher, *der* (ugs.); **~drop ▸ ~cloth**

> **backbencher**
>
> Ein einfacher Abgeordneter im britischen Parlament, der für kein bestimmtes politisches Ressort verantwortlich ist. *Backbenchers* sitzen auf den Bänken hinter den Ministern der Regierungspartei oder hinter den Ministern des Schattenkabinetts.

backer /'bækə(r)/ *n.* Geldgeber, *der*; (of horse) Wetter, *der*

back: ~fill *v.t.* [wieder] auffüllen; **~fire** **A** /'--/ *n.* Fehlzündung, *die*; **B** /-'-/ *v.i.* knallen; (fig.) fehlschlagen; **it ~fired on me/him** *etc.* der Schuss ging nach hinten los (ugs.); **~-formation** *n.* (Ling.) (word) rückgebildetes Wort; (action) Rückbildung, *die*

backgammon /'bækgæmən/ *n.* (game) Backgammon, *das*; ≈ Tricktrack, *das*; ≈ Puff, *das*

background *n.* [1] (lit. or fig.) Hintergrund, *der*; (social status) Herkunft, *die*; (education) Ausbildung, *die*; (experience) Erfahrung, *die*; **be in the ~** im Hintergrund stehen; **he comes from a poor ~:** er stammt aus ärmlichen Verhältnissen; **against this ~:** vor diesem Hintergrund; *attrib.* **~ heating** *Heizung, die automatisch für eine erträgliche Zimmertemperatur sorgt*; **~ music** Hintergrundmusik, *die* [2] **~ [information]** Hintergrundinformation, *die* [3] (Radio) Störgeräusch, *das*

backgrounder /'bækgraʊndə(r)/ *n.* (Amer.) Hintergrundinformationen *Pl.*

background: ~ 'processing *n., no pl.* (Computing) Hintergrundverarbeitung, *die*; **~ 'reading** *n., no pl.* vertiefende Lektüre; **~ task** *n.* (Computing) Hintergrundaktion, *die*

back: ~hand (Tennis etc.) **A** *adj.* Rückhand-; **B** *n.* Rückhand, *die*; **~handed** /bæk 'hændɪd/ *adj.* [1] **~handed slap** Schlag mit dem Handrücken; **~handed stroke** (Tennis) Rückhandschlag, *der*; [2] (fig.) indirekt; zweifelhaft ‹*Kompliment*›; **~hander** /bæk'hændə(r)/ *n.* [1] (stroke) Rückhandschlag, *der* (Tennis usw.); (blow) Schlag [mit dem Handrücken]; [2] (coll.: bribe) Schmiergeld, *das*; **~heel** **A** *n.* Hackenschuss, *der*; **B** *v.t.* mit der Hacke schießen *od.* treten

backhoe loader /'bækhəʊ ləʊdə(r)/ *n.* (Brit.) Baggerlader, *der*

backing /'bækɪŋ/ *n.* [1] (material) Rückenverstärkung, *die*; **leather ~:** Rückseite aus Leder; **the silver ~ of a mirror** die silberne Beschichtung eines Spiegels [2] (support) Unterstützung, *die*; **the President has a large ~:** der Präsident kann sich auf eine große Anhängerschaft stützen [3] (betting) **there was much ~ of the favourite** es wurden viele Wetten auf den Favoriten abgeschlossen [4] (Mus.: accompaniment) Begleitung, *die*

'backing track *n.* [aufgezeichnete] Begleitung

back: ~ issue ▸ ~ number; **~lash** *n.* Rückstoß, *der*; (excessive play in machine) Spiel, *das*; (fig.) Gegenreaktion, *die*; **a right-wing ~lash** eine Gegenbewegung nach rechts

backless /'bæklɪs/ *adj.* rückenfrei ‹*Kleid*›

back: ~list *n.* Verzeichnis der lieferbaren Titel; Backlist, *die* (Verlagsw.); **~log** *n.* Rückstand, *der*; **~log of work** Arbeitsrückstand, *der*; **a large ~log of unfulfilled orders** ein großer Überhang an unerledigten Aufträgen; **~lot** *n.* (Cinemat.) Backlot[gelände], *das*; **~marker** *n.* [1] (lagging behind other competitors) Schlusslicht, *das* (ugs. fig.); [2] *jmd., der ohne Vorgabe od. mit dem größten Handicap startet*; **~ number** *n.* [1] (of periodical, magazine) alte Nummer; [2] (fig. coll.) **these methods are a [real] ~ number** diese Methoden sind [reichlich] rückständig; **~ office** *n.* Backoffice, *das*; **~-of-the-'envelope** *adj.* ungenau, überschlägig ‹*Berechnung*›; grob ‹*Schätzung*›; **~pack** **A** *n.* Rucksack, *der*; **B** *v.i.* mit dem Rucksack [ver]reisen; **~packer** *n.* Rucksackreisende, *der/die*; Rucksacktourist, *der*/-touristin, *die*; (hiker) Wanderer, *der*/Wanderin, *die* mit Rucksack; **~packing** *n., no pl.* das [Ver-]reisen mit dem Rucksack; (hiking) das Wandern mit dem Rucksack; *attrib.* ‹*Reise usw.*› mit dem Rucksack; **~ pass** *n.* (Footb.) Rückpass, *der*; **~ passage** *n.* (Anat. coll.) After, *der*; **~ pay** *n.* ausstehender Lohn/ausstehendes Gehalt; **he was reinstated with ~ pay** er wurde wieder eingestellt und erhielt eine Lohn-/Gehaltsnachzahlung; **she was awarded £7,850 in ~ pay** sie erhielt eine Nachzahlung von £7,850; **~-'pedal** *v.i.* [1] die Pedale rückwärts treten; (brake) mit dem Rücktritt bremsen; [2] (fig.) einen Rückzieher machen (ugs.); **~rest** *n.* Rückenlehne, *die*; **~ 'room** *n.* Hinterzimmer, *das*; **in the ~ room** (fig.) hinter verschlossenen Türen; *attrib.* **~room boys** (coll.) Experten im Hintergrund (*bes. Wissenschaftler, die an Geheimprojekten arbeiten*); **~scratcher** *n.* Rückenkratzer, *der*; **~scratching** *n., no pl.* (fig. coll.) **[mutual] ~scratching** Klüngelei, *die* (abwertend); **~ 'seat** *n.* Rücksitz, *der*; (in bus, coach) hinterer Sitzplatz; **take a ~ seat** (fig.) in den Hintergrund treten; **be in the ~ seat** (fig.) im Hintergrund stehen; *attrib.* **~-seat driver** *besserwisserischer Beifahrer, der immer dazwischenredet*; (fig.) Neunmalkluge, *der/die*; **~side** *n.* Hinterteil, *das* (ugs.); Hintern, *der* (ugs.); **get [up] off one's ~side** seinen Hintern heben (ugs.); **~sight** *n.* Visier, *das*; **~slapping** *adj.* (fig.) plump-vertraulich; **~slash** *n.* umgekehrter Schrägstrich; **~slider** *n.* Abtrünnige, *der/die*; **~space** *v.i.* die Rücktaste betätigen; **~spin** *n., no pl.* Rückwärtsdrall, *der*; Backspin, *der*; **~'stage** **A** *adj.* hinter der Bühne; **~stage activities** (fig.) Aktivitäten hinter den Kulissen; **B** *adv.* [1] **go ~stage** hinter die Bühne gehen; **wait ~stage for the artist** hinter der Bühne auf den Künstler warten; [2] (fig.) hinter den Kulissen; **~'stair[s] ▸ ~-door**; **~'stairs** *n. pl.* Hintertreppe, *die*; **~stitch** **A** *v.t. & i.* steppen; **B** *n.* Steppstich, *der*; *attrib.* **~stitch seam** Steppnaht, *die*; **~ street** kleine Seitenstraße; **from the ~ streets of Naples** ≈ aus den Hinterhöfen Neapels; *see also* **abortion 1**; **abortionist**; **~stroke** *n.* (Swimming) Rückenschwimmen, *das*; **do** *or* **swim the ~stroke** rückenschwimmen; **~ talk** (Amer.) ▸ **~chat**; **~-to-back** **A** *adj.* [1] (Brit.) **~-to-back houses** Doppelreihenhäuser *Pl.*; [2] (consecutive) unmittelbar aufeinander folgend; **B** *n.* (Brit.: house) Doppelreihenhaus, *das*; **C** *adv.* [1] (with backs touching) mit den Rückseiten aneinander; **they sat on the ground ~-to back** sie saßen Rücken an Rücken auf dem Boden; [2] (consecutively) [direkt] nacheinander; **~-to-'basics** *adj.* durch eine Rückbesinnung auf das Elementare gekennzeichnet; **~track** *v.i.* wieder zurückgehen; (fig.) eine Kehrtwendung machen; **~-up** *n.* [1] (support) Unterstützung, *die*; **a racing driver needs a large ~-up crew** ein Rennfahrer muss eine große Crew hinter sich haben; [2] (reserve) Reserve, *die*; **~-up supplies** Vorräte für den Bedarfs- *od.* Notfall; **~-up [copy]** (Computing) Sicherungskopie, *die*; [3] (Amer.: queue of vehicles) Stau, *der*; **a ~-up of cars** eine Autoschlange; **~-up light** *n.* (Amer.) Rückfahrscheinwerfer, *der*; **~ vowel** *n.* (Phonet.) Hinterzungenvokal, *der*

backward /'bækwəd/
A *adj.* [1] (directed to rear) rückwärts gerichtet; Rückwärts-; **~ movement** Rückwärtsbewegung, *die*; **the ~ slant to his handwriting** seine nach links geneigte Handschrift [2] (reluctant, shy) zurückhaltend; **be ~ in coming forward** (joc.) sich zurückhalten [3] (slow, retarded) zurückgeblieben ‹*Kind*›; (underdeveloped) rückständig, unterentwickelt ‹*Land, Region*›; **~ in sth.** in etw. (*Dat.*) zurückgeblieben
B *adv.* ▸ **backwards**

'backward-looking *adj.* rückwärts gewandt

backwardness /'bækwədnɪs/ *n., no pl.* (of child) Zurückgebliebenheit, *die*; (of country, region) Rückständigkeit, *die*; **the child's ~ in school** dass das Kind in der Schule zurückgeblieben ist/war

backwards /'bækwədz/ *adv.* [1] nach hinten; **the child fell [over] ~ into the water** das Kind fiel rückwärts ins Wasser; **bend** *or* **fall** *or* **lean**

b

over ~ to do sth. (fig. coll.) sich zerreißen, um etw. zu tun (ugs.) **2** (oppositely to normal direction) rückwärts; **~ and forwards** (to and fro, lit. or fig.) hin und her **3** (into a worse state) **go ~:** sich verschlechtern; **under his leadership the country is going ~:** unter seiner Führung verschlechtert sich die Lage des Landes **4** (into past) **look ~:** an frühere Zeiten denken **5** (reverse way) rückwärts; von hinten nach vorn; **you're doing everything ~:** du machst ja alles verkehrt herum; **know sth. ~:** etw. in- und auswendig kennen

back: ~wash *n.* Rückstrom, *der* (**from** *Gen.*); (fig.) Auswirkungen *Pl.;* **in the ~wash of** (fig.) als Folge von; **~water** *n.* totes Wasser; (fig.) Kaff, *das* (ugs. abwertend); **this town is too much of a ~water** diese Stadt ist zu provinziell; **~woods** *n. pl.* abgelegene Wälder; unerschlossene Waldgebiete; (fig.) hinterste Provinz; **~woodsman** *n.* ≈ Waldbewohner, *der;* (uncouth person) Hinterwäldler, *der* (spött.); **~'yard** *n.* Hinterhof, *der;* (Amer.: garden) Garten, *der* [hinter dem Haus]; **in one's own ~ yard** (fig.) vor der eigenen Haustür

bacon /'beɪkn/ *n.* [Frühstücks]speck, *der;* **~ and eggs** Eier mit Speck; **bring home the ~** (fig. coll.) es schaffen; (der Ernährer sein) die Brötchen verdienen (ugs.); **save one's ~** (fig.) die eigene *od.* seine Haut retten

bacteria *pl. of* **bacterium**

bacterial /bæk'tɪərɪəl/ *adj.* bakteriell

bactericide /bæk'tɪərɪsaɪd/ *n.* Bakterizid, *das*

bacteriological /bæktɪərɪə'lɒdʒɪkl/ *adj.* bakteriologisch; **~ warfare** Bakterienkrieg, *der*

bacteriologist /bæktɪərɪ'ɒlədʒɪst/ *n.* Bakteriologe, *der*/Bakteriologin, *die*

bacteriology /bæktɪərɪ'ɒlədʒɪ/ *n.* Bakteriologie, *die*

bacterium /bæk'tɪərɪəm/ *n., pl.* **bacteria** /bæk'tɪərɪə/ Bakterie, *die*

Bactrian camel /bæktrɪən 'kæml/ *n.* Trampeltier, *das*

bad /bæd/

A *adj.,* **worse** /wɜːs/, **worst** /wɜːst/ **1** schlecht; (rotten) schlecht, verdorben ‹*Fleisch, Fisch, Essen*›; faul ‹*Ei, Apfel*›; (unpleasant) schlecht, unangenehm ‹*Geruch*›; **do a ~ job on sth.** bei etw. schlecht arbeiten; **sth. gives sb. a ~ name** etw. trägt jmdm. einen schlechten Ruf ein; **sb. gets a ~ name** jmd. kommt in Verruf; **she is in ~ health** sie hat eine angegriffene Gesundheit; **she has a ~ complexion** sie hat einen unreinen Teint; **be ~ at doing sth.** etw. nicht gut können; **be a ~ liar** ein schlechter Lügner sein; **[some] ~ news** schlechte *od.* schlimme Nachrichten; **~ breath** Mundgeruch, *der;* **he is having a ~ day** er hat einen schwarzen Tag; **it is a ~ business** (fig.) das ist eine schlimme Sache; **in the ~ old days** in den schlimmen Jahren; **not ~** (coll.) nicht schlecht; nicht übel; **not so ~** (coll.) gar nicht so schlecht *od.* übel; **things weren't so ~** (coll.) es war alles nicht so schlimm; **sth. is not a ~ idea** etw. ist keine schlechte Idee; **not half ~** (coll.) [gar] nicht schlecht; **sth. is too ~** (coll.) etw. ist ein Jammer; **too ~!** (coll.) so ein Pech! (auch iron.); **go ~:** schlecht werden; **in a ~ sense** im schlechten Sinne; **it is ~ for you** es ist schlecht für dich; es schadet dir **2** (wicked) schlecht; (immoral) schlecht; verdorben; unmoralisch ‹*Buch, Heft*›; (naughty) ungezogen, böse ‹*Kind, Hund*› **3** (offensive) **[use] ~ language** Kraftausdrücke [benutzen] **4** (in ill health) **she's ~ today** es geht ihr heute schlecht; **have a ~ arm/finger** einen schlimmen Arm/Finger haben (ugs.); **I have a ~ pain** ich habe schlimme Schmerzen; **be in a ~ way** in schlechtem Zustand sein **5** (serious) schlimm, böse ‹*Sturz, Krise*›; schwer ‹*Fehler, Krankheit, Unfall, Erschütterung*›; hoch ‹*Fieber*›; schrecklich ‹*Feuer*› **6** (regretful) **a ~ conscience** ein schlechtes Gewissen; **feel ~ about sth./not having done sth.** etw. bedauern/bedauern, dass man etw. nicht getan hat; **I feel ~ about him/her** ich habe seinetwegen/ihretwegen ein schlechtes Gewissen **7** (worthless) wertlos, ungedeckt ‹*Scheck*›; (counterfeit) falsch ‹*Münze, Banknote*›; **a ~ debt** eine uneinbringliche Schuld (Wirtsch.).

See also **book A 1**; **egg[1]**; **form A 8**; **hat 2**; **lot 3**; **luck 1**; **patch A 1**; **penny 3**; **temper A 1**; **worse A**; **worst A**

B *n.* **1** (debit) **be £100 to the ~:** mit 100 Pfund in der Kreide stehen (ugs.) **2** (ruin) **go to the ~:** auf die schiefe Bahn geraten. *see also* **worse C**

C *adv.* (Amer. coll.) ▸ **badly**

baddish /'bædɪʃ/ *adj.* ziemlich schlecht

baddy /'bædɪ/ *n.* (coll.) Schurke, *der;* **the goodies and the baddies** die Guten und die Bösen (oft iron.)

bade ▸ **bid A 3, 4, 5**

badge /bædʒ/ *n.* **1** (as sign of office, membership, support) Abzeichen, *das;* (larger) Plakette, *die* **2** (symbol) Symbol, *das* **3** (thing revealing quality or condition) Kennzeichen, *das*

badger /'bædʒə(r)/

A *n.* Dachs, *der*

B *v.t.* **~ sb. [into doing/to do sth.]** jmdm. keine Ruhe lassen[, bis er/sie etw. tut]; **~ sb. with questions** jmdn. mit Fragen löchern (ugs.); **don't ~ her out of her wits!** mach sie nicht verrückt! (ugs.)

'badger baiting *n.* Dachshetze, *die*

bad 'hair day *n.* (Amer. coll.) Tag, an dem die Frisur einfach nicht sitzen will; (fig.) schlechter Tag; **I'm having a ~:** heute geht bei mir alles schief

badinage /'bædɪnɑːʒ/ *n.* Spöttelei, *die*

'bad lands *n. pl.* (Amer.) Badlands *Pl.*

badly /'bædlɪ/ *adv.,* **worse** /wɜːs/, **worst** /wɜːst/ **1** schlecht **2** (seriously) schwer ‹*verletzt, beschädigt*›; sehr ‹*schief sein, knarren*›; **he hurt himself ~:** er hat sich (*Dat.*) schwer verletzt; **he has got it ~:** es hat ihn schlimm erwischt (ugs.); **be ~ beaten** schwer verprügelt werden (ugs.); (in game, battle) vernichtend geschlagen werden **3** (urgently) dringend; **want sth. [so] ~:** sich (*Dat.*) etw. [so] sehr wünschen **4** (coll.: regretfully) **feel ~ about sth.** etw. [sehr] bedauern; **I don't feel too ~ about it** es macht mir nicht so viel aus. *See also* **worse B**; **worst B**

'bad man *n.* Bösewicht, *der*

badminton /'bædmɪntən/ *n.* Federball, *der;* (als Sport) Badminton, *das*

'bad-mouth *v.t.* (coll.) in *od.* durch den Dreck ziehen (salopp)

badness /'bædnɪs/ *n., no pl.* ▸ **bad 1, 2**: Schlechtigkeit, *die;* Verdorbenheit, *die;* Ungezogenheit, *die;* **the ~ in him** seine innere Schlechtigkeit

bad-tempered /bæd'tempəd/ *adj.* griesgrämig

BAe *abbr.* = **British Aerospace** *britisches Unternehmen, das Flugzeuge und Raumschiffe herstellt*

baffle /'bæfl/

A *v.t.* **1** (perplex) **~ sb.** jmdm. unverständlich sein; jmdn. vor ein Rätsel stellen **2** (stop progress of) aufhalten

B *n.* **~ [plate]** Prallfläche, *die* (Technik); **~ [board]** (of loudspeaker) Schallwand, *die*

baffled /'bæfld/ *adj.* verwirrt; **be ~:** vor einem Rätsel stehen

bafflement /'bæflmənt/ *n.* Verwirrung, *die*

baffling /'bæflɪŋ/ *adj.* rätselhaft

bag /bæg/

A *n.* **1** Tasche, *die;* (sack) Sack, *der;* (hand~) [Hand]tasche, *die;* (of plastic) Beutel, *der;* (small paper ~) Tüte, *die;* **a ~ of cement** ein Sack Zement; **with ~ and baggage** (fig.) mit Sack und Pack; **be a ~ of bones** (fig.) nur Haut und Knochen sein; **[whole] ~ of tricks** (fig.) Trickkiste, *die* (ugs.); **have exhausted one's [whole] ~ of tricks** sein Pulver verschossen haben (ugs.); **leave sb. holding the ~** (Amer. fig.) jmdm. den schwarzen Peter zuschieben; **his nomination is in the ~** (fig. coll.) er hat die Nominierung in der Tasche (ugs.); **freedom was as good as in the ~** (coll.) die Freiheit war so gut wie gewonnen; *see also* **cat 1**; **mixed bag** **2** (Hunting: amount of game) Jagdbeute, *die;* Strecke, *die* (Jägerspr.) **3** *in pl.* (coll.: large amount) **~s of** jede Menge (ugs.) **4** *in pl.* (Brit. dated: trousers) Hose, *die* **5** (puffiness) **have ~s under** *or* **below one's eyes** Tränensäcke haben **6** (sl. derog.: woman) **[old] ~:** alte Schlampe (ugs. abwertend) **7** (coll.: current interest, activity) **what's your ~?** auf was stehst du [zur Zeit]? (ugs.)

B *v.t.,* **-gg- 1** (put in sacks) in Säcke füllen; einsacken (fachspr.); (put in plastic ~s) in Beutel füllen; (put in small paper ~s) in Tüten füllen; eintüten (fachspr.) **2** (Hunting) erlegen, erbeuten ‹*Tier*› **3** (claim possession of) sich (*Dat.*) schnappen (ugs.); (Brit. Sch. coll.: claim) **~s I go first!** erster!

bagatelle /bægə'tel/ *n.* **1** (trifle) Nebensächlichkeit, *die* **2** (Mus.) Bagatelle, *die* (fachspr.); kurzes Musikstück

bagel /'beɪgl/ *n. hartes, ringförmiges Hefegebäck*

bagful /'bægfʊl/ *n.* ▸ **bag A 1: a ~ of** ein Sack [voll]/eine Tasche/ein Beutel/eine Tüte [voll]

baggage /'bægɪdʒ/ *n.* **1** Gepäck, *das;* **mental/cultural ~** (fig.) geistiges/kulturelles Rüstzeug; *see also* **bag A 1** **2** (Mil.) Gepäck, *das* **3** (dated derog.: woman) Stück, *das* (ugs. abwertend)

baggage: ~ allowance *n.* Freigepäck, *das;* **be over/within one's ~ allowance** Übergepäck/kein Übergepäck haben; **~ car** *n.* (Amer.) Gepäckwagen, *der;* **~ carousel** *n.* Gepäckkarussell, *das;* **~ check** *n.* Gepäckkontrolle, *die;* (Amer.: ticket) Gepäckschein, *der;* **~ hall** *n.* Gepäckhalle, *die;* **~ handler** *n.* Gepäckverlader, *der*/-verladerin, *die;* **~ handling** *n., no pl.* Gepäckverladung, *die; attrib.* Gepäckverladungs-; **~ reclaim** *n.* Gepäckausgabe, *die;* **~ room** *n.* (Amer.) Gepäckaufbewahrung, *die;* **~ tag** *n.* (Amer.) Kofferanhänger, *der*

bagginess /'bægɪnɪs/ *n., no pl.* Schlaffheit, *die;* **the ~ of these old trousers** die Ausgebeultheit dieser alten Hose

baggy /'bægɪ/ *adj.* weit [geschnitten] ‹*Kleid*›; schlaff [herabhängend] ‹*Haut*›; (through long use) ausgebeult ‹*Hose*›

Baghdad /bæg'dæd/ *pr. n.* ▸ ❶ **p. 1643** Bagdad (*das*)

bag: ~lady *n.* (coll.) Obdachlose (*die ihre Habseligkeiten in einer Tasche ständig mit sich herumträgt*); **~man** /'bægmən/ *n., pl.* **~men** /-mən/ (esp. Amer. coll.) ≈ Geldkurier, *der;* **~pipe[s]** *n.* Dudelsack, *der;* **~piper** *n.* Dudelsackpfeifer, *der*

baguette /bæ'get/ *n.* Baguette, *die;* [französisches] Stangenweißbrot

bah /bɑː/ *int.* bah

Bahamas /bə'hɑːməz/ *pr. n. pl.* **the ~:** die Bahamainseln

Bahamian /bə'heɪmɪən/

A *adj.* bahamisch

B *n.* Bahamer, *der*/Bahamerin, *die*

bail[1] /beɪl/

A *n.* **1** Sicherheitsleistung, *die* (Rechtsw.); (financial) Kaution, *die;* (personal) Bürgschaft, *die;* **grant sb. ~:** jmdm. die Freilassung gegen Kaution bewilligen; **give sb. ~ on payment of the sum of ...:** jmdn. gegen eine Kaution in Höhe von ... freilassen; **be [out] on ~:** gegen Kaution auf freiem Fuß sein; **the judge refused ~ to the accused** der Richter lehnte es ab, den Angeklagten gegen Kaution freizulassen; **put** *or* **release sb. on ~:** jmdn. gegen Kaution freilassen; **forfeit one's** *or* (coll.) **jump** *or* (coll.) **skip [one's] ~:** die Kaution verfallen lassen [und nicht vor Gericht erscheinen] **2** (person[s] acting as surety) Bürge, *der;* **go** *or* **stand ~ for sb.** für jmdn. Bürge sein

B *v.t.* **1** (entrust) anvertrauen **2** (release) gegen Kaution freilassen **3** (go ~ for) bürgen für; **~ sb. out** jmdn. gegen Bürgschaft freibekommen; (fig.) jmdn. aus der Klemme helfen (ugs.)

bail[2] *n.* (Cricket) Querstab, *der*

bail[3] *v.t.* (scoop) **~ [out]** ausschöpfen

Phrasal verb

• **~ out** *v.i.* (Aeronaut.) ‹*Pilot:*› abspringen *od.* (Fliegerspr.) aussteigen

bailey /'beɪlɪ/ *n.* (wall) Burgmauer, *die;* (outer court) Zwinger, *der;* (inner court) Burghof, *der;* **the Old B~:** das Old Bailey (*oberster Strafgerichtshof für London*)

Old Bailey

Der Name für das Hauptstrafgericht von London in England, vor das nur die schwersten Straftaten kommen. Das Gerichtsgebäude steht auf dem Grund des Newgate-Gefängnisses, das dort im 12. Jahrhundert erbaut wurde. Auf der Kuppel des *Old Bailey* steht Justitia, Sinnbild der Gerechtigkeit, mit dem Schwert in einer Hand und der Waage in der anderen.

'Bailey bridge *n.* Bailey-Brücke, *die* (*Brücke aus vorgefertigten Teilen, die in kurzer Zeit errichtet werden kann*)

bailiff /'beɪlɪf/ *n.* ▸ℹ **p. 1260** 1 ≈ Justizbeamte, *der;* (performing distraints) Gerichtsvollzieher, *der;* (serving writs) Gerichtsbote, *der* (veralt.) 2 (agent of landlord) Verwalter, *der;* Vogt, *der* (hist.) 3 (Amer. Admin.: court official) ≈ Gerichtsbeamte, *der*

bailiwick /'beɪlɪwɪk/ *n.* 1 (Hist.) Amtsbezirk eines Bailiffs; Vogtei, *die* 2 (coll. area of activity or interest) Reich, *das* (fig.)

bairn /beən/ *n.* (Scot./N. Engl./literary) Kind, *das*

bait[1] /beɪt/

A *v.t.* 1 mit einem Köder versehen ‹*Falle*›; beködern ‹*Angelhaken*› 2 (torment with dogs) **~ sth. [with dogs]** die Hunde auf etw. (*Akk.*) hetzen 3 (fig.: torment) herumhacken auf (+ *Dat.*) (ugs.); (in playful manner) necken; **~ sb. with questions** jmdn. mit Fragen zusetzen (ugs.)

B *n.* (lit. or fig.) Köder, *der;* **live ~:** lebender Köder; **rise to** *or* **take the ~** (fig.) anbeißen

bait[2] ▸ **bate**[2]

baize /beɪz/ *n.* (Textiles) Fries, *der*

bake /beɪk/

A *v.t.* 1 (cook) backen; **~d apple** Bratapfel, *der;* **~d beans** gebackene Bohnen [in Tomatensoße]; **~d potato** [in der Schale] gebackene Kartoffel 2 (harden) brennen ‹*Ziegel, Keramik*›; ausdörren ‹*Erde, Boden, Land*›

B *v.i.* 1 backen; gebacken werden; (fig.: be hot) **I'm baking!** mir ist wahnsinnig heiß! (ugs.) 2 (be hardened) ‹*Ziegel, Keramik:*› gebrannt werden; ‹*Boden, Erde:*› ausdorren

C *n.* (Amer.: party) Party[, bei der Gebackenes gegessen wird]

bake: ~apple *n.* (Can.) [getrocknete] Moltebeere; **~house** *n.* Backstube, *die*

bakelite /'beɪkəlaɪt/ *n.* Bakelit, *das*

baker /'beɪkə(r)/ *n.* ▸ℹ **p. 1260** Bäcker, *der;* **at the ~'s** beim Bäcker; in der Bäckerei; **go to the ~'s** zum Bäcker *od.* zur Bäckerei gehen; **a ~'s dozen** 13 Stück

bakery /'beɪkərɪ/ *n.* Bäckerei, *die*

'bake sale *n.* (Amer.) Verkauf von Selbstgebackenem und Bastelarbeiten

baking /'beɪkɪŋ/ *adv.* **it's ~ hot today, isn't it?** eine Hitze wie im Backofen ist das heute, nicht wahr?

baking: ~ dish *n.* Auflaufform, *die;* **~ potato** *n.* große Kartoffel (*zum Backen*); **~ powder** *n.* Backpulver, *das;* **~ sheet** *n.* Backblech, *das;* **~ soda** *n.* Natron, *das;* **~ tin** *n.* Backform, *die;* **~ tray** *n.* Kuchenblech, *das*

Balaclava /bælə'klɑːvə/ *n.* **~ [helmet]** Balaklavamütze, *die* (*Wollmütze, die Kopf und Hals bedeckt und nur das Gesicht frei lässt*)

balalaika /bælə'laɪkə/ *n.* Balalaika, *die*

balance /'bæləns/

A *n.* 1 (instrument) Waage, *die;* **~ [wheel]** Unruh, *die* 2 **the B~** (Astrol.) die Waage; *see also* **archer 2** 3 (fig.) **be** *or* **hang in the ~:** in der Schwebe sein; **the prisoners' lives are in the ~:** das Leben der Gefangenen ist bedroht 4 (even distribution) Gleichgewicht, *das;* (correspondence) Übereinstimmung, *die;* (due proportion) ausgewogenes Verhältnis; **strike a ~ between** den Mittelweg finden zwischen (+ *Dat.*); **the ~ of sb.'s mind** jmds. seelisches Gleichgewicht; **~ of power** ▸ **power A 6; upset the ~ of nature** das natürliche Gleichgewicht stören 5 (counterpoise) Gegengewicht, *das;* Ausgleich, *der* 6 (steady position) Gleichgewicht, *das;* **keep/lose one's ~:** das Gleichgewicht halten/verlieren; (fig.) sein Gleichgewicht bewahren/verlieren; **off [one's] ~** (lit. or fig.) aus dem Gleichgewicht; **throw sb. off [his] ~** (lit. or fig.) jmdn. aus dem Gleichgewicht werfen 7 (preponderating weight or amount) Bilanz, *die;* **the ~ of evidence appears to be in his favour** die Beweise zu seinen Gunsten scheinen zu überwiegen 8 (Bookk.: difference) Bilanz, *die;* (state of bank account) Kontostand, *der;* (statement) Auszug, *der;* **on ~** (fig.) alles in allem 9 (Econ.) **~ of payments** Zahlungsbilanz, *die;* **~-of-payments deficit** Zahlungsbilanzdefizit, *das;* **~ of trade** Handelsbilanz, *die* 10 (surplus amount) **~ [in hand]** Überschuss, *der;* **you may keep the ~:** der Rest ist für Sie 11 (remainder) Rest, *der*

B *v.t.* 1 (weigh up) abwägen; **~ sth. with** *or* **by** *or* **against sth. else** etw. gegen etw. anderes abwägen 2 (bring into or keep in ~) balancieren; auswuchten ‹*Rad*›; **~ oneself** balancieren 3 (equal, neutralize) ausgleichen; **~ each other, be ~d** sich (*Dat.*) die Waage halten 4 (make up for, exclude dominance of) ausgleichen 5 (Bookk.) bilanzieren

C *v.i.* 1 (be in equilibrium) balancieren; **do these scales ~?** ist diese Waage im Gleichgewicht?; **balancing act** (lit. or fig.) Balanceakt, *der* 2 (Bookk.) ausgeglichen sein; bilanzieren (Kaufmannsspr.)

balanced /'bælənst/ *adj.* ausgewogen; ausgeglichen ‹*Person, Team, Gemüt*›

'balance sheet *n.* (Bookk.) Bilanz, *die*

Balaton /'bælətɒn/ *pr. n.* **Lake ~:** der Plattensee

balcony /'bælkənɪ/ *n.* Balkon, *der;* (Amer. Theatre: dress circle) erster Rang

bald /bɔːld/ *adj.* 1 kahl ‹*Person, Kopf*›; kahlköpfig, glatzköpfig ‹*Person*›; **he is ~:** er ist kahl[köpfig] *od.* hat eine Glatze; **go ~:** eine Glatze bekommen 2 (plain) einfach, schmucklos ‹*Stil, Rede, Prosa*›; schlicht ‹*Appell*›; knapp, nackt ‹*Behauptung*› 3 (coll.: worn smooth) abgefahren ‹*Reifen*›

'bald eagle *n.* Weißkopf-Seeadler, *der*

balderdash /'bɔːldədæʃ/ *n., no pl., no indef. art.* Unsinn, *der;* dummes Zeug (ugs.)

bald-'headed *adj.* glatzköpfig; kahlköpfig

balding /'bɔːldɪŋ/ *adj.* mit beginnender Glatze *nachgestellt;* **be ~:** kahl werden

baldly /'bɔːldlɪ/ *adv.* unverhüllt; offen; knapp und klar ‹*zusammenfassen, umreißen*›; **simply and ~:** schlicht und einfach; **to put it ~:** um es geradeheraus zu sagen

baldness /'bɔːldnɪs/ *n., no pl.* ▸ **bald 1, 2:** Kahlheit, *die;* Einfachheit, *die;* Schlichtheit, *die;* Knappheit, *die*

'baldpate *n.* (Ornith.) Amerikanische Pfeifente

baldric /'bɔːldrɪk/ *n.* (Hist.) Bandelier, *das*

baldy /'bɔːldɪ/ *n.* (coll. derog.) Glatzkopf, *der* (ugs.); Kahlkopf, *der* (ugs.)

bale[1] /beɪl/

A *n.* Ballen, *der*

B *v.t.* (pack) in Ballen verpacken; zu Ballen binden ‹*Heu*›

bale[2] ▸ **bail**[3]

Balearic Islands /bælɪ'ærɪk aɪləndz/ *pr. n. pl.* Balearen *Pl.*

baleful /'beɪlfl/ *adj.* unheilvoll; (malignant) böse

balefully /'beɪlfəlɪ/ *adv.* unheilvoll; (malignantly) böse

balk (esp Amer.) ▸ **baulk**

Balkan /'bɔːlkn/

A *adj.* Balkan-

B *n. pl.* **the ~s** der Balkan; die Balkanländer

Balkanize /'bɔːlkənaɪz/ *v.t.* balkanisieren

ball[1] /bɔːl/

A *n.* 1 Ball, *der;* (sphere) Kugel, *die;* **the animal rolled itself into a ~:** das Tier rollte sich [zu einer Kugel] zusammen 2 (Sport, incl. Golf, Polo) Ball, *der;* (Billiards etc., Croquet) Kugel, *die;* **the ~ is in your court** (fig.) jetzt bist du am Zug (fig.); **have the ~ at one's feet** (fig.) alle Möglichkeiten *od.* Chancen haben; **keep one's eye on the ~** (fig.) die Sache im Auge behalten; **keep the ~ rolling** (fig.) die Sache in Schwung halten; **start the ~ rolling** (fig.) den Anfang machen; **be on the ~** (fig. coll.) voll da sein (salopp); (be alert) auf Zack sein (ugs.); **play ~:** Ball spielen; (fig. coll.: cooperate) mitmachen; **play ~ with sb.** mit jmdm. Ball spielen; (fig. coll.: cooperate) mit jmdm. zusammenarbeiten 3 (missile) Kugel, *die* 4 (round mass) Kugel, *die;* (of wool, string, fluff, etc.) Knäuel, *das;* **two ~s of wool** zwei Wollknäuel *od.* Knäuel Wolle; **~ of clay** Lehmklumpen, *der* 5 (Anat.: rounded part) Ballen, *der;* **~ of the hand/foot** Hand-/Fußballen, *der* 6 *in pl.* (coarse: testicles) Eier *Pl.* (derb); **~s!** (fig.) Scheiß! (salopp abwertend); *constr. as sing.* **make a ~s of sth.** (fig.) bei etw. Scheiße bauen (derb)

B *v.t.* zusammenballen; zerknüllen ‹*Papier*›; ballen ‹*Faust*›

Phrasal verb

• **~ 'up** (Brit.) ▸ **balls up**

ball[2] *n.* (dance) Ball, *der;* **give a ~:** einen Ball geben *od.* veranstalten; **have [oneself] a ~** (fig. coll.) sich riesig amüsieren (ugs.); **open the ~:** den Ball eröffnen; (fig.) den Tanz beginnen

ballad /'bæləd/ *n.* 1 Lied, *das;* (narrative) Ballade, *die;* Lied, *das* 2 (poem) Ballade, *die*

balladry /'bælədrɪ/ *n., no pl.* Balladendichtung, *die*

ball and 'socket joint *n.* Kugelgelenk, *das*

ballast /'bæləst/ *n.* 1 Ballast, *der;* **be in ~:** auf Ballastfahrt sein (Seemannsspr.) 2 (fig.: sth. that gives stability) stabilisierender Faktor 3 (coarse stone etc.) Schotter, *der*

ball: ~ 'bearing *n.* (Mech.) Kugellager, *das;* **~boy** *n.* Balljunge, *der;* **~ clay** *n.* (Amer. Min.) Pfeifenton, *der;* **~cock** *n.* Schwimmer[regel]ventil, *das* (Technik); **~ control** *n., no pl.* Ballführung, *die*

ballerina /bælə'riːnə/ *n.* ▸ℹ **p. 1260** Ballerina, *die;* **prima ~:** Primaballerina, *die*

ballet /'bæleɪ/ *n.* Ballett, *das*

'ballet dancer *n.* Balletttänzer, *der*/-tänzerin, *die*

balletic /bə'letɪk/ *adj.* ballettös

ballet: ~ school *n.* Ballettschule, *die;* **~ shoe** *n.* Ballettschuh, *der*

ball: ~ game *n.* 1 Ballspiel, *das;* 2 (Amer.) Baseballspiel, *das;* **a whole new ~ game** (fig. coll.) eine ganz neue Geschichte (ugs.); **a different ~ game** (fig. coll.) eine andere Sache; **~girl** *n.* Ballmädchen, *das*

ballistic /bə'lɪstɪk/ *adj.* ballistisch; **~ missile** ballistische Rakete; **go ~** (*fig. coll.*) ausrasten (salopp)

ballistics /bə'lɪstɪks/ *n., no pl.* Ballistik, *die*

ball: ~ joint ▸ **ball and socket joint; ~ lightning** *n.* Kugelblitz, *der*

balloon /bə'luːn/

A *n.* 1 Ballon, *der;* **hot-air ~:** Heißluftballon, *der;* **when the ~ goes up** (fig.) wenn es losgeht (ugs.) 2 (toy) Luftballon, *der* 3 (coll.: in strip cartoon etc.) Sprechblase, *die* 4 (drinking glass) **~ [glass]** Schwenker, *der;* Schwenkglas, *das*

B *v.i.* 1 sich blähen 2 (travel in ~) im Ballon fahren

C *v.t.* (hit, kick) hoch in die Luft schlagen

balloon: ~ angioplasty /'ændʒɪəplæstɪ/ *n., no pl.* (Med.) Ballonangioplastie, *die* (fachspr.); Katheterdilatation, *die;* Ballondilatation, *die;* **~ 'catheter** *n.* (Med.) Ballonkatheter, *der;* **~ 'tyre** *n.* Ballonreifen, *der*

ballot /'bælət/

A *n.* 1 (voting) Abstimmung, *die;* **[secret] ~:** geheime Wahl; **hold** *or* **take a ~:** abstimmen 2 (vote) Stimme, *die;* **cast one's ~:** seine Stimme abgeben 3 (ticket, paper) Stimmzettel, *der*

B *v.i.* abstimmen; **~ for sb./sth.** für jmdn./etw. stimmen

C *v.t.* abstimmen lassen; eine Abstimmung vornehmen bei

ballot: ~ box *n.* Wahlurne, *die;* **~-box stuffing** *n., no pl.* (Amer.) Wahlfälschung, *die;* Wahlmanipulation, *die;* **~ paper** *n.* Stimmzettel, *der*

ball: ~park *n.* (Amer.) Baseballfeld, *das;* **your estimate is not in the right ~park** (fig.) mit deiner Schätzung liegst du völlig falsch (ugs.); **~ estimate/figure** Schätzung, *die*/Schätzwert, *der;* **~ pen, ~point, ~point 'pen** *ns.* Kugelschreiber, *der;* **~ pool** *n.* Ballpool, *der;* **~room** *n.* Tanzsaal, *der;* **~room 'dancing** *n.* Gesellschaftstanz, *der*

balls 'up *v.t.* (coarse) Scheiße bauen bei (derb)

balls-up /'bɔːlzʌp/ (coarse) *n.* Scheiß, *der* (salopp abwertend); **make a ~ of sth.** bei etw. Scheiße bauen (derb)

'ball-tampering *n., no pl.: die Manipulierung der Balloberfläche beim Kricketspiel*

bally /'bælɪ/ (Brit. dated euphem.) *adj., adv.* verdammt (salopp)

ballyhoo /bælɪ'huː/ *n.* 1 (publicity) [Reklame-]rummel, *der* (ugs.); **create a great deal of ~ over sth.** einen großen Rummel um etw. veranstalten (ugs.) 2 (nonsense) Geschrei, *das* (abwertend)

balm /bɑːm/ *n.* 1 (lit. or fig.) Balsam, *der* 2 (fragrance) [aromatischer] Duft 3 (tree) Balsambaum, *der* 4 (herb) Melisse, *die;* **~ of Gilead** Gileadbalsam, *der*

balmy /'bɑːmɪ/ *adj.* 1 (yielding balm) Balsam liefernd 2 (fragrant) wohlriechend; balsamisch (geh.) 3 (soft, mild) mild 4 (Amer. or dated coll.: crazy) bescheuert (salopp)

baloney ▸ **boloney 1**

balsa /'bɔːlsə, 'bɒlsə/ *n.* 1 (tree) Balsabaum, *der* 2 (wood) **~[wood]** Balsaholz, *das*

balsam /'bɔːlsəm, 'bɒlsəm/ *n.* 1 (lit. or fig.; also Med., Chem.) Balsam, *der;* **Canada ~:** Kanadabalsam, *der* 2 (tree) Balsambaum, *der* 3 (plant of genus Impatiens) Springkraut, *das;* (garden flower) Gartenbalsamine, *die;* (touch-me-not) Rührmichnichtan, *das*

balsam 'fir *n.* Balsamtanne, *die*

balsamic vinegar /bælsæmɪk 'vɪnɪgə(r)/ *n.* Balsamessig, *der*

Balt /bɔːlt, bɒlt/ *n.* Balte, *der*/Baltin, *die*

Baltic /'bɔːltɪk, 'bɒltɪk/

A *pr. n.* Ostsee, *die*

B *adj.* baltisch; **~ coast** Ostseeküste, *die;* **the ~ Sea** die Ostsee; **the ~ States** das Baltikum

baluster /'bæləstə(r)/ *n.* 1 (pillar) Baluster, *der;* Docke, *die* 2 (post) Geländerpfosten, *der;* (balustrade) Balustrade, *die*

balustrade /bælə'streɪd/ *n.* Balustrade, *die*

bamboo /bæm'buː/ *n.* 1 (stem) Bambus, *der;* Bambusrohr, *das* 2 (grass) Bambus, *der; attrib.* **~ curtain** (Polit.) Bambusvorhang, *der;* **~ shoots** Bambussprossen

bamboozle /bæm'buːzl/ *v.t.* (coll.) 1 (mystify) verblüffen 2 (cheat) reinlegen (ugs.); **~ sb. into doing sth.** jmdn. [durch Tricks] dazu bringen, etw. zu tun; jmdn. so reinlegen, dass er etw. tut; **~ sb. out of sth.** jmdm. etw. abluchsen (salopp)

ban /bæn/

A *v.t.,* **-nn-** verbieten; **~ sb. from doing sth.** jmdm. verbieten, etw. zu tun; **he was ~ned from driving/playing** er erhielt Fahr-/Spielverbot; **~ sb. from a place** jmdm. die Einreise/den Zutritt *usw.* verbieten; **~ sb. from a pub/the teaching profession** jmdm. Lokalverbot erteilen/jmdn. vom Lehrberuf ausschließen

B *n.* Verbot, *das;* **place a ~ on sth.** etw. mit einem Verbot belegen; **the ~ placed on these drugs** das Verbot dieser Drogen; **lift the ~ on sth.** das Verbot einer Sache (*Gen.*) aufheben

banal /bə'nɑːl, bə'næl/ *adj.* banal

banality /bə'nælɪtɪ/ *n.* Banalität, *die*

banana /bə'nɑːnə/ *n.* 1 (fruit) Banane, *die;* **a hand of ~s** eine Hand Bananen (fachspr.); **go ~s** (Brit. coll.) verrückt werden (salopp); überschnappen (ugs.) 2 (plant) Bananenstaude, *die*

banana: ~ republic *n.* (derog.) Bananenrepublik, *die* (abwertend); **~ skin** *n.* Bananenschale, *die;* **~ 'split** *n.* Bananensplit, *das*

band /bænd/

A *n.* 1 Band, *das;* **a ~ of light/colour** ein Streifen Licht/Farbe 2 (range of values) Bandbreite, *die* (fig.); **income ~:** ≈ Gehaltsstufe, *die* 3 (of frequency or wavelength) **long/medium ~:** Langwellen-/Mittelwellenband, *das;* **high-frequency ~:** Hochfrequenzbereich, *der* 4 (organized group) Gruppe, *die;* (of robbers, outlaws, etc.) Bande, *die;* **B~ of Hope** (Brit.) *Organisation jugendlicher Abstinenzler* 5 (of musicians) [Musik]kapelle, *die;* (pop group, jazz ~) Band, *die;* Gruppe, *die;* (dance ~) [Tanz]kapelle, *die;* (military ~) Militärkapelle, *die;* (brass ~) Blaskapelle, *die;* **if** *or* **when the ~ begins to play** (fig. coll.) wenn es ernst wird 6 *in pl.* (part of legal, clerical, or academic dress) Beffchen, *das* 7 (Amer.: ring round bird's leg) Beringung, *die* 8 (Amer.) (herd) Herde, *die;* (of birds, insects) Schwarm, *der. See also* **beat A 4**

B *v.t.* 1 **~ sth.** ein Band um etw. machen 2 (form into a league) vereinigen 3 (mark with stripes) bändern; **~ed** (Biol.) Streifen-; gestreift

C *v.i.* **~ together [with sb.]** sich [mit jmdm.] zusammenschließen

bandage /'bændɪdʒ/

A *n.* (for wound, fracture) Verband, *der;* (for fracture, as support) Bandage, *die;* (for blindfolding) Binde, *die*

B *v.t.* verbinden ‹[*offene*] *Wunde usw.*›; bandagieren ‹[*verstauchtes*] *Gelenk usw.*›

'Band Aid ® *n.* ≈ Hansaplast (Wz), *das*

bandanna /bæn'dænə/ *n.* Bandanatuch, *das*

b. & b. /biː ən 'biː/ *abbr.* = **bed & breakfast**

'bandbox *n.* Bandschachtel, *die* (veralt.); ≈ Hutschachtel, *die*

bandicoot /'bændɪkuːt/ *n.* 1 (Ind.: rat) Bandikutratte, *die* 2 (Austral.: marsupial) Bandikut, *der;* Beuteldachs, *der*

bandit /'bændɪt/ *n.* Bandit, *der*

banditry /'bændɪtrɪ/ *n.* Banditen[un]wesen, *das*

'bandmaster *n.* Kapellmeister, *der*

bandolier (**bandoleer**) /bændə'lɪə(r)/ *n.* Schultergürtel, *der;* Bandelier, *das* (veralt.)

'bandsaw *n.* Bandsäge, *die*

bandsman /'bændzmən/ *n., pl.* **bandsmen** /'bændzmən/ Mitglied der/einer Kapelle/Band

band: ~stand *n.* Musikertribüne, *die;* (circular) Konzertpavillon, *der;* **~wagon** *n.* Wagen der Musikkapelle; **climb** *or* **jump on [to] the ~wagon** (fig.) auf den fahrenden Zug aufspringen (fig.); **~width** *n.* (Communications) Bandbreite, *die*

bandy¹ /'bændɪ/ *v.t.* 1 (toss to and fro) hin- und herspielen 2 (fig.) herumerzählen (ugs.) ‹*Geschichte*›; **be bandied from mouth to mouth** von Mund zu Mund gehen; **insults were being bandied about** Beschimpfungen flogen hin und her 3 (discuss) **~ about** hin und her diskutieren 4 (exchange) wechseln; **they were ~ing blows** sie tauschten Schläge aus; **don't ~ words with me** ich wünsche keine Diskussion

bandy² *adj.* krumm; **he has ~ legs** *or* **is ~-legged** er hat O-Beine (ugs.); **~-legged person** o-beinige Person (ugs.)

bane /beɪn/ *n.* Ruin, *der;* **he is the ~ of my life** er ist der Nagel zu meinem Sarg (ugs.)

bang¹ /bæŋ/

A *v.t.* 1 knallen (ugs.); schlagen; zuknallen (ugs.), zuschlagen ‹*Tür, Fenster, Deckel*›; **~ one's head on** *or* **against the ceiling** mit dem Kopf an die Decke knallen (ugs.) *od.* schlagen; **I could ~ their heads together** (fig.) ich könnte ihre Köpfe gegeneinander schlagen; **she ~ed down the receiver** sie knallte den Hörer auf die Gabel (ugs.); **he ~ed the nail in** er haute den Nagel rein (ugs.); *see also* **brick wall** 2 (sl.: copulate with) bumsen (salopp)

B *v.i.* 1 (strike) **~ [against sth.]** [gegen etw.] schlagen *od.* (ugs.) knallen; **~ at the door** gegen die Tür hämmern 2 (make sound of blow or explosion) knallen; ‹*Kanonen:*› donnern; ‹*Trommeln:*› dröhnen; **~ away at sth.** auf etw. (*Akk.*) ballern (ugs.); **~ shut** zuknallen (ugs.); zuschlagen; **a door is ~ing somewhere** irgendwo schlägt eine Tür

C *n.* 1 (blow) Schlag, *der;* **give your radio a good ~:** hau mal kräftig gegen dein Radio (ugs.) 2 (noise) Knall, *der;* **the party went off with a ~** (fig.) die Party war eine Wucht (ugs.). *see also* **big bang**; **whimper A**

D *adv.* 1 (with impact) mit voller Wucht 2 (explosively) **go ~** ‹*Gewehr, Feuerwerkskörper:*› krachen; **the balloon went ~ and exploded** der Ballon explodierte mit einem lauten Knall 3 **~ goes sth.** (fig.: sth. ends suddenly) aus ist es mit etw.; **~ went £50** 50 Pfund waren weg 4 **~ off** (coll.: immediately) sofort; **answer ~ off** wie aus der Pistole geschossen antworten (ugs.) 5 (coll.: exactly) genau; **you are ~ on time** du bist pünktlich auf die Minute (ugs.); **~ on [the] target** genau richtig; **~ on** genau *od.* gerade

E *int.* peng

bang²

A *v.t.* (esp. Amer.) gerade abschneiden ‹*Haare*›

B *n. in pl.* (esp. Amer.: fringe) Pony, *der*

banger /'bæŋə(r)/ *n.* (coll.) 1 (sausage) Würstchen, *das* 2 (firework) Kracher, *der* (ugs.) 3 (car) Klapperkiste, *die* (ugs.)

Bangladesh /bæŋglə'deʃ/ *pr. n.* Bangladesch (*das*)

Bangladeshi /bæŋglə'deʃɪ/ ▸**ⓘ p. 1345**

A *adj.* bangalisch

B *n.* Bangali, *der/die*

bangle /'bæŋgl/ *n.* Armreif, *der*

'bang-up *adj.* (Amer. coll.: first-class) klasse (ugs.)

banian ▸**banyan**

banish /'bænɪʃ/ *v.t.* verbannen (**from** aus); bannen ‹*Furcht*›

banishment /'bænɪʃmənt/ *n.* Verbannung, *die* (**from** aus)

banister /'bænɪstə(r)/ *n.* 1 (uprights and rail) [Treppen]geländer, *das* 2 *usu. in pl.* (upright) Geländerpfosten, *der*

banjo /'bændʒəʊ/ *n., pl.* **~s** *or* **~es** Banjo, *das*

bank¹ /bæŋk/

A *n.* 1 (slope) Böschung, *die* 2 ▸**ⓘ p. 1491** (at side of river) Ufer, *das* 3 (elevation in bed of sea or river) Bank, *die* 4 (mass) **a ~ of clouds/fog** eine Wolken-/Nebelbank; **a ~ of snow** eine Schneewehe 5 (artificial slope) Überhöhung, *die* (Verkehrsw.)

B *v.t.* 1 (build higher) überhöhen (Verkehrsw.) 2 (heap) **~ [up]** aufschichten; **~ [up] the fire with coal** Kohlen auf das Feuer schichten 3 in die Kurve legen ‹*Flugzeug*›

C *v.i.* 1 (rise) **~ [up]** ‹*Rauch, Wolken:*› sich aufschichten 2 ‹*Flugzeug:*› sich in die Kurve legen

bank²

A *n.* 1 (Commerc., Finance) Bank, *die;* **the B~** (Brit.) die Bank von England; **cry/laugh all the way to the ~** (fig. coll.) sich für seinen Erfolg entschuldigen (iron.)/aus seiner Freude über seinen Erfolg keinen Hehl machen 2 (Gaming) Bank, *die. See also* **blood bank**; **bottle bank**

B *v.i.* 1 (keep ~) Bankier sein 2 (keep money) **~ at/with ...:** ein Konto haben bei ... 3 **~ on sth.** (fig.) auf etw. (*Akk.*) zählen

C *v.t.* zur Bank bringen

bank³ *n.* 1 (row) Reihe, *die* 2 (tier) **~ [of oars]** Ruderreihe, *die*

bankable /'bæŋkəbl/ *adj.* bankfähig; (fig.) erfolgversprechend

bank: ~ account *n.* Bankkonto, *das;* **~ balance** *n.* Kontostand, *der;* **~ bill** *n.* (Brit.) Bankakzept, *der;* (Amer.: **~note**) Banknote, *die;* **~ book** *n.* Sparbuch, *das;* **~ card** *n.* Scheckkarte, *die;* **~ charges** *n. pl.* Kontoführungskosten *Pl.;* **~ clerk** *n.* ▸**ⓘ p. 1260** Bankangestellte, *der/die;* **~ draft** *n.* Bankakzept, *das*

banker /'bæŋkə(r)/ *n.* ▸**ⓘ p. 1260** (Commerc., Finance) Bankier, *der;* Banker, *der* (ugs.)

banker's: ~ card ▸ **bank card**; **~ draft** ▸ **~ draft**; **~ 'order** ▸ **order A 15**

bank 'holiday *n.* 1 Bankfeiertag, *der* 2 (Brit.: public holiday) Feiertag, *der*

banking /'bæŋkɪŋ/ *n., no pl.* Bankwesen, *das;* **a career in ~:** die Banklaufbahn; *attrib.* **~ hours** Schalterstunden *Pl.;* Öffnungszeiten *Pl.* (*der Bank*); **new ~ arrangements** neue Bankverhältnisse

'banking hours *n. pl.* Banköffnungszeiten *Pl.*

bank: ~ loan *n.* Bankdarlehen, *das;* **take out a ~ loan** bei einer Bank einen Kredit *od.* ein Darlehen aufnehmen; **~ manager** *n.* ▸**ⓘ p. 1260** Zweigstellenleiter [einer/der Bank]; **~note** *n.* Banknote, *die;* Geldschein, *der;* **~ raid** *n.* Banküberfall, *der;* **~ rate** *n.* Diskontsatz, *der;* **~ robber** *n.* Bankräuber, *der;* **~roll** **A** *n.* finanzielle Mittel *Pl.;* **B** *v.t.*

finanziell unterstützen

Bank of England

Die *Bank of England* ist die Zentralnotenbank Großbritanniens mit dem alleinigen Recht auf Notenausgabe in England und Wales. Die Bank berät die Regierung in Finanzfragen und ist die Geschäftsbank der Regierung und anderer Banken. Die *Bank of England* wurde 1694 als private Aktienbank gegründet und 1946 verstaatlicht. Sie wird von einem Direktorium geleitet, dessen Mitglieder von der Regierung ernannt werden. Seit 1997 kann die *Bank of England* selbstständig Zinssätze festlegen.

bankrupt /ˈbæŋkrʌpt/
A *n.* [1] (Law) Gemeinschuldner, *der;* **become a ~:** Gemeinschuldner werden; **be declared a ~:** zum Gemeinschuldner erklärt werden [2] (insolvent debtor) Bankrotteur, *der*
B *adj.* [1] bankrott; **go ~:** in Konkurs gehen; Bankrott machen; bankrottieren (veralt.) [2] (fig.) **morally ~:** moralisch bankrott (fig.)
C *v.t.* bankrott machen

bankruptcy /ˈbæŋkrʌptsɪ/ *n.* Konkurs, *der;* Bankrott, *der;* **go into ~:** in Konkurs gehen; Bankrott machen; *attrib.* **~ proceedings** Konkursverfahren, *das*

bank: ~ statement *n.* Kontoauszug, *der;* **~ teller** *n.* Kassierer, *der*/Kassiererin, *die;* **~ transfer** *n.* Banküberweisung, *die*

banner /ˈbænə(r)/
A *n.* [1] (flag, ensign; also fig.) Banner, *das;* **join** *or* **follow the ~ of** dem Banner (+ *Gen.*) folgen [2] (on two poles) Spruchband, *das;* Transparent, *das* [3] (sth. used as symbol) Symbol, *das*
B *adj.* [1] (conspicuous) **~ headline** Balkenüberschrift, *die* [2] (Amer.: pre-eminent) herausragend

ˈbanner advert *n.* Werbebanner, *der*

bannister ▸ **banister**

bannock /ˈbænək/ *n.* (Scot., N. Engl.) *rundes, flaches Brot*

banns /bænz/ *n. pl.* Aufgebot, *das;* **publish/put up the ~:** das Aufgebot verkünden/aushängen; **forbid the ~:** Einspruch [gegen die Eheschließung] erheben

banquet /ˈbæŋkwɪt/
A *n.* Bankett, *das* (geh.)
B *v.i.* [1] [festlich] tafeln (geh.); bankettieren (veralt.); **~ing hall** Bankettsaal, *der* [2] (carouse) zechen (geh.)

banshee /ˈbænʃiː/ *n.* (Ir., Scot.) Banshee, *die* (Myth.); ≈ Weiße Frau

bantam /ˈbæntəm/ *n.* Zwerg-, Bantamhuhn, *das*

ˈbantamweight *n.* (Boxing etc.) Bantamgewicht, *das;* (person also) Bantamgewichtler, *der*

banter /ˈbæntə(r)/
A *n.* [1] heiterer Spott [2] (remarks) Spöttelei, *die* (**on** über + *Akk.*); (joking back and forth) spöttisches Geplänkel
B *v.t.* aufziehen (**about** mit)
C *v.i.* spötteln

Bantu /bænˈtuː/
A *n.* [1] *pl. same or* **~s** Bantu, *der/die* [2] (language group) Bantu, *das;* Bantusprachen
B *adj.* Bantu-

Bantustan /bæntʊˈstɑːn/ *n.* (S. Afr.) Bantuheimatland, *das*

banyan /ˈbænɪən/ *n.* (Bot.) **~ [tree]** Banyanbaum, *der*

baobab /ˈbeɪəbæb/ *n.* (Bot.) Baobab, *der;* Affenbrotbaum, *der*

BAOR *abbr.* **= British Army of the Rhine** Britische Rheinarmee

bap /bæp/ *n.* ≈ Brötchen, *das*

baptise ▸ **baptize**

baptism /ˈbæptɪzm/ *n.* Taufe, *die;* **~ is the first sacrament** die Taufe ist das erste Sakrament; **~ of fire** (fig.) Feuertaufe, *die;* **~ of blood** (fig.) Bluttaufe, *die* (Rel.)

baptismal /bæpˈtɪzml/ *adj.* Tauf-; ‹*Wiedergeburt, Reinigung*› durch die Taufe; **~ certificate** Taufschein, *der;* **~ name** Taufname, *der*

Baptist /ˈbæptɪst/
A *n.* [1] Baptist, *der*/Baptistin, *die* [2] **John the ~:** Johannes der Täufer
B *adj.* **the ~ Church/a ~ chapel** die Kirche/eine Kapelle der Baptisten

baptize /bæpˈtaɪz/ *v.t.* taufen; **be ~d a Catholic/Protestant** katholisch/protestantisch getauft werden; **what name were you ~d by?** auf welchen Namen wurden Sie getauft?

bar¹ /bɑː(r)/
A *n.* [1] (long piece of rigid material) Stange, *die;* (shorter, thinner also) Stab, *der;* (of gold, silver) Barren, *der;* **a ~ of soap** ein Stück Seife; **a ~ of chocolate** ein Riegel Schokolade; (slab) eine Tafel Schokolade [2] (Sport) Stab, *der;* (of high ~) [Reck]stange, *die;* (of parallel ~s) [Barren]holm, *der;* (cross~) [Sprung]latte, *die;* **high** *or* **horizontal ~:** Reck, *das;* **parallel ~s** Barren, *der* [3] (heating element) Heizelement, *das* (Elektrot.) [4] (band) Streifen, *der;* (on medal) silberner Querstreifen; (Her.) Balken, *der* [5] (rod, pole) Stange, *die;* (of cage, prison) Gitterstab, *der;* **behind ~s** (in prison) hinter Gittern; (into prison) hinter Gitter [6] (barrier, lit. or fig.) Barriere, *die* (**to** für); **a ~ on recruitment/promotion** ein Einstellungs-/Beförderungsstopp [7] (for refreshment) Bar, *die;* (counter) Theke, *die* [8] (Law: place at which prisoner stands) ≈ Anklagebank, *die;* **the prisoner at the ~:** der/die Angeklagte; **be judged at the ~ of public opinion** (fig.) sich vor dem der öffentlichen Meinung verantworten müssen [9] (Law: barristers, particular court) Gerichtshof, *der;* **be called to the ~:** als Anwalt vor höheren Gerichten zugelassen werden; **be called within the ~:** zum Anwalt der Krone ernannt werden; **the B~:** die höhere Anwaltschaft; **the inner ~:** die Anwaltschaft der Krone; **the outer ~** *die Anwälte, die nicht Anwälte der Krone sind;* **he was reading for the ~:** er bereitete sich auf die Zulassung als Anwalt vor höheren Gerichten vor [10] (Mus.) Takt, *der;* **~[-line]** Taktstrich, *der* [11] (sandbank, shoal) Barre, *die;* Sandbank, *die*
B *v.t.*, **-rr-** [1] (fasten) verriegeln; **~red window** vergittertes Fenster [2] (keep) **~ sb. in/out** jmdn. ein-/aussperren [3] (obstruct) sperren ‹*Straße, Weg*› (**to** für); **~ sb.'s way** jmdm. den Weg versperren [4] (prohibit, hinder) verbieten; **~ sb. from doing sth.** jmdn. daran hindern, etw. zu tun [5] (not consider) unberücksichtigt lassen [6] (mark) mit Streifen versehen; **~red [with colourful stripes]** [bunt]gestreift; **~red with brown** braun gestreift [7] (Law) ausschließen
C *prep.* abgesehen von; **~ any accidents** falls nichts passiert; **~ none** ohne Einschränkung; **bet two to one ~ one** (Racing) zwei zu eins auf alle außer einem wetten

bar² *n.* (Meteorol., Phys.) Bar, *das*

barb /bɑːb/
A *n.* [1] Widerhaken, *der;* (fig.) Gehässigkeit, *die;* **~s of ridicule** gehässige Spötteleien [2] (of fish) Bartfaden, *der;* Bartel, *die* [3] (of feather) Fahne, *die*
B *v.t.* mit Widerhaken versehen

Barbadian /bɑːˈbeɪdɪən/ ▸ⓘ p. 1345
A *adj.* barbadisch; **sb. is ~:** jmd. ist Barbadier/Barbadierin
B *n.* Barbadier, *der*/Barbadierin, *die*

Barbados /bɑːˈbeɪdəʊz, bɑːˈbeɪdɒs/ *pr. n.* Barbados (*das*)

barbarian /bɑːˈbeərɪən/
A *n.* (lit. or fig.) Barbar, *der*
B *adj.* (lit. or fig.) barbarisch; **a ~ king** ein Barbarenkönig

barbaric /bɑːˈbærɪk/ *adj.* barbarisch

barbarically /bɑːˈbærɪkəlɪ/ *adv.* barbarisch

barbarism /ˈbɑːbərɪzm/ *n.* [1] *no pl.* (absence of civilization) Barbarei, *die* [2] (Ling.) Barbarismus, *der* [3] (instance of cruelty) [barbarische] Grausamkeit

barbarity /bɑːˈbærɪtɪ/ *n.* [1] *no pl.* Grausamkeit, *die;* **he treats criminals with ~:** er behandelt Verbrecher äußerst barbarisch [2] (instance) Barbarei, *die*

barbarous /ˈbɑːbərəs/ *adj.* barbarisch

barbarously /ˈbɑːbərəslɪ/ *adv.* auf barbarische Art und Weise; barbarisch

barbarousness /ˈbɑːbərəsnɪs/ *n., no pl.* Rohheit, *die*

Barbary ˈape *n.* (Zool.) Magot, *der;* Berberaffe, *der*

barbecue /ˈbɑːbɪkjuː/
A *n.* [1] (party) Grillparty, *die;* Barbecue, *das* [2] (food) Grillgericht, *das;* Barbecue, *das; attrib.* **~ sauce** Grillsoße, *die;* Barbecuesoße, *die* [3] (fireplace with frame) Grill, *der* [4] (frame) Grill, *der;* Bratrost, *der;* Barbecue, *das*
B *v.t.* grillen

barbed /bɑːbd/ *adj.* [1] (having barbs) ‹*Angelhaken, Pfeil*› mit Widerhaken [2] (hurtful) spitz ‹*Bemerkung*›; scharf ‹*Kritik*›

barbed ˈwire *n.* Stacheldraht, *der; attrib.* **~ fence** Stacheldrahtzaun, *der*

barbel /ˈbɑːbl/ *n.* [1] (Zool.) Barbe, *die* [2] (filament) Bartfaden, *der;* Bartel, *der*

ˈbarbell *n.* Hantel, *die*

barber /ˈbɑːbə(r)/ *n.* ▸ⓘ p. 1260 Friseur, *der;* Barbier, *der* (veralt.); **go to the ~'s** zum Friseur gehen; **~'s pole** *spiralig rot und weiß gestreifter Stab als Ladenschild des Friseurs*

barberry /ˈbɑːbərɪ/ *n.* [1] (shrub) Berberitze, *die;* Sauerdorn, *der* [2] (berry) Berberitzenbeere, *die;* Sauerdornbeere, *die*

barber: ~-shop *n.* (Amer.) **~-shop harmony** Barbershopharmonie, *die; vokale Harmonik mit paralleler Stimmführung;* **~-shop singing/quartet** Barbershopgesang, *der*/-quartett, *das;* **~'s shop** *n.* (Brit.) Friseursalon, *der*

barbican /ˈbɑːbɪkən/ *n.* (Hist.) Barbakane, *die;* Torvorwerk, *das*

barbiturate /bɑːˈbɪtjʊrət/ *n.* (Chem.) Barbiturat, *das*

barcarole /bɑːkəˈrəʊl/, **barcarolle** /bɑːkəˈrɒl/ *n.* (Mus.) Barkarole, *die*

Barcelona /bɑːsɪˈləʊnə/ *pr. n.* ▸ⓘ p. 1643 Barcelona (*das*); **~ nut** Barcelonanuss, *die* (*eine Haselnusssorte*)

bar: ~ chart *n.* Stabdiagramm, *das;* **~ code** *n.* Strichcode, *der;* **~-coded** /ˈbɑːkəʊdɪd/ *adj.* mit Strichcode *nachgestellt;* **~-coded label** Strichcode-Etikett, *das;* **~ code reader** *n.* Strichcodelesegerät, *das*

bard /bɑːd/ *n.* Barde, *der;* **the B~ [of Avon]** Shakespeare

bardic /ˈbɑːdɪk/ *adj.* (arch./literary) bardisch (veralt.)

bare /beə(r)/
A *adj.* [1] nackt; **expose a ~ back to the sun** den nackten Rücken der Sonne aussetzen; **walk with** *or* **in ~ feet** barfuß gehen; **in one's ~ skin** nackt [und bloß] [2] (hatless) **with one's head ~:** ohne Hut [3] (leafless) kahl [4] (unfurnished) kahl; nackt ‹*Boden*› [5] (unconcealed) **lay ~ sth.** etw. aufdecken [6] (unadorned) nackt, ungeschminkt ‹*Wahrheit, Tatsache*›; grob ‹*Skizze*›; nackt, kahl ‹*Wand*›; *see also* **bone A 1** [7] (empty) leer [8] (scanty) knapp ‹*Mehrheit*›; [sehr] gering ‹*Menge, Teil*› [9] (mere) äußerst ‹*Notwendige*›; nur gering ‹*Möglichkeit*›; bloß ‹*Gedanke*›; **the ~ necessities of life** das zum Leben Notwendigste [10] (without tools) **do sth. with one's ~ hands** etw. mit den *od.* seinen bloßen Händen tun [11] (unprovided with) **~ of sth.** ohne etw.; **the land was ~ of any vegetation** das Land war völlig vegetationslos
B *v.t.* [1] (uncover) entblößen ‹*Kopf, Arm, Bein*›; ziehen ‹*Schwert*›; bloßlegen ‹*Draht eines Kabels*›; **~ one's back to the sun** seinen Rücken der Sonne aussetzen [2] (reveal) blecken ‹*Zähne*›; **she ~d her heart to him** (fig.) sie schüttete ihm ihr Herz aus

bare: ~back **A** *adj.* ‹*Reiter, Reiten*› auf ungesatteltem Pferd; **B** *adv.* ohne Sattel; **~faced** *adj.*, **~faced[ly]** /beəˈfeɪsɪd(lɪ)/ *adv.* (fig.) unverhüllt; **~foot** **A** *adj.* barfüßig; **he is ~foot** er ist barfuß *od.* barfüßig; **~foot doctor** Barfußarzt, *der;* **B** *adv.* barfuß; **~handed** /beəˈhændɪd/ **A** *adj.* **he was ~handed** (without gloves) er trug keine Handschuhe; (without weapon) er war unbewaffnet; **B** *adv.* mit bloßen Händen; **~headed** /beəˈhedɪd/ **A** *adj.* **he was ~headed** er trug keine Kopfbedeckung; **B** *adv.* ohne Kopfbedeckung; **~-legged** *adj.* mit bloßen Beinen

barely /ˈbeəlɪ/ *adv.* [1] (only just) kaum; knapp ‹*vermeiden, entkommen*› [2] (scantily) karg

bare-ˈmidriff *adj.* taillenfrei ‹*Kleid*›

'**bar end** *n.* Lenkerhörnchen, *das*

bareness /'beənɪs/ *n., no pl.* ▸ **bare A 3, 4, 6**: Kahlheit, *die;* Nacktheit, *die;* Kargheit, *die*

'**barfly** *n.* (coll.) Kneipenhocker, *der*/-hockerin, *die* (ugs.)

bargain /'bɑːgɪn/

A *n.* **1** (agreement) Abmachung, *die;* **an unequal ~:** ein ungleicher Handel; **into the ~,** (Amer.) **in the ~:** darüber hinaus; **make** *or* **strike a ~ to do sth.** sich darauf einigen, etw. zu tun; **I'll make a ~ with you** ich mache dir ein Angebot; **they got the best of the ~:** sie haben den besseren Teil bekommen; **a ~'s a ~:** was einmal abgemacht ist, gilt **2** (thing acquired) Kauf, *der;* **a good/bad ~:** ein guter/schlechter Kauf **3** (thing offered cheap) günstiges Angebot; (thing acquired cheaply) guter Kauf; **a definite ~:** ein absolutes Sonderangebot. *See also* **best C 5; hard A 1**

B *v.i.* **1** (discuss) handeln; **~ for** *or* **on sth.** um etw. handeln **2** **~ for** (expect): **more than one had ~ed for** mehr, als man erwartet hatte; **~ for sth.** mit etw. rechnen

C *v.t.* **~ away** sich (*Dat.*) abhandeln lassen

bargain: ~ 'basement *n.* Untergeschoss mit Sonderangeboten; **~ 'break** *n.* Schnäppchenreise, *die* (ugs.); **~ counter** *n.* Tisch mit Sonderangeboten; **~ hunter** *n.* Schnäppchenjäger, *der*/-jägerin, *die*

bargaining /'bɑːgɪnɪŋ/ *n.* Handel, *der;* (negotiating) Verhandlungen; *attrib.* **~ position** Verhandlungsposition, *die;* **~ power** Verhandlungsmacht, *die;* **~ counter** (fig.) Trumpf [für Verhandlungen]; *see also* **collective bargaining**

bargain: ~ offer *n.* Sonderangebot, *das;* **~ price** *n.* Sonderpreis, *der*

barge /bɑːdʒ/

A *n.* **1** Kahn, *der;* **freight/cargo ~:** Fracht-/Lastkahn, *der* **2** (for State occasions) Prunkschiff, *das* (veralt.)

B *v.i.* **1** (lurch) **~ into sb.** jmdn. anrempeln; **~ against sth.** gegen etw. taumeln; **~ about the house** im Haus herumtoben **2** **~ in** (intrude) hineinplatzen/hereinplatzen (ugs.); **he ~d in on us** er platzte bei uns herein (ugs.)

'**bargeboard** *n.* Giebelbrett, *das*

bargee /bɑː'dʒiː/(Brit.), **bargeman** (esp. Amer.) *ns.* ▸ℹ **p. 1260** Flussschiffer, *der*

'**bargepole** *n.* Stake, *die* (nordd.); **I wouldn't touch him/that** *etc.* **with [the end of] a ~!** (fig.) ich würde ihn/das *usw.* nicht mit der Beißzange anfassen! (ugs.)

'**bar graph** *n.* Stabdiagramm, *das*

baritone /'bærɪtəʊn/ (Mus.)

A *n.* Bariton, *der;* (voice, part also) Baritonstimme, *die*

B *adj.* **~ voice** Baritonstimme, *die*

barium /'beərɪəm/ *n.* (Chem.) Barium, *das; attrib.* **~ meal** Kontrastbrei, *der* (*mit Bariumsulfat*)

bark[1] /bɑːk/

A *n.* **1** (of tree) Borke, *die;* Rinde, *die* **2** (for tanning, dyeing) [Gerber]lohe, *die*

B *v.t.* **1** (abrade) aufschürfen **2** (strip ~ from) entrinden

bark[2]

A *n.* (lit. or fig.) Bellen, *das;* **his ~ is worse than his bite** (fig.) er ist nicht so bissig, wie er tut; ≈ Hunde, die bellen, beißen nicht

B *v.i.* **1** (lit. or fig.) bellen; **~ at sb.** jmdn. anbellen; **be ~ing up the wrong tree** auf dem Holzweg sein **2** (speak loudly and curtly) brüllen **3** (Amer.: act as tout) den Ausrufer machen

C *v.t.* **1** bellen **2** (bellow) **~ [out] orders to sb.** jmdm. Befehle zubrüllen

bark[3] *n.* (poet.: ship) Schiff, *das*

'**barkeep** (Amer.), '**barkeeper** *n.* Barkeeper, *der;* (owner) Wirt, *der*

barker /'bɑːkə(r)/ *n.* Ausrufer, *der*

barley /'bɑːlɪ/ *n.* Gerste, *die; see also* **pearl barley**

barley: ~corn *n.* (grain) Gerstenkorn, *das;* **~ sugar** *n.* Gerstenzucker, *der;* **~ water** *n.* Gerstenwasser, *das* (veralt.)

bar: ~maid *n.* ▸ℹ **p. 1260** (Brit.) Bardame, *die;* **~man** /'bɑːmən/ *n., pl.* **~men** /'bɑːmən/ ▸ℹ **p. 1260** Barmann, *der;* Schankkellner, *der*

bar mitzvah /bɑː'mɪtzvə/ *n.* **1** (boy) Bar-Mizwa, *der* **2** (ceremony) Bar-Mizwa, *die*

barmy /'bɑːmɪ/ *adj.* (coll.: crazy) bescheuert (salopp)

barn /bɑːn/ *n.* **1** (Brit.: for grain etc.) Scheune, *die;* (Amer.: for implements etc.) Schuppen, *der;* (Amer.: for animals) Stall, *der* **2** (derog.) [großer, hässlicher] Schuppen

barnacle /'bɑːnəkl/ *n.* **1** (Zool.) Rankenfüßer, *der* **2** **~ [goose]** Weißwangengans, *die*

barn: ~ dance *n.* ≈ Schottische, *der;* **~ door** *n.* Scheunentor, *das;* **be as big as a ~ door** (fig.) nicht zu verfehlen sein

barney /'bɑːnɪ/ *n.* (coll.) Krach, *der* (ugs.); **have a ~:** Krach haben (ugs.)

barn: ~ owl *n.* Schleiereule, *die;* **~storm** *v.i.* durch die Provinz ziehen *od.* tingeln; **~stormer** *n.* tingelnder Schauspieler; (Amer.: politician) Politiker [im Wahlkampf in der Provinz]; (Amer.: aviator) [Kunstflug]pilot [auf Tournee durch die Provinz]; **~storming** /'bɑːnstɔːmɪŋ/ *adj.* mitreißend; **~yard** *n.* Wirtschaftshof, *der*

barograph /'bærəgrɑːf/ *n.* Barograph, *der*

barometer /bə'rɒmɪtə(r)/ *n.* (lit. or fig.) Barometer, *das*

barometric /bærə'metrɪk/ *adj.* barometrisch; **~ pressure** Luftdruck, *der*

baron /'bærn/ *n.* ▸ℹ **p. 1634** **1** (holder of title) Baron, *der;* Freiherr, *der* **2** (powerful person) Papst, *der* (fig.); **press ~:** Pressezar, *der;* **coal/oil ~:** Kohlen-/Ölmagnat, *der* **4** (Hist.: holder of land) Baron, *der* **4** (Brit.: joint of meat) **~ of beef** [ungeteiltes] Lendenstück; Baron, *der* (Kochk.)

baroness /'bærənɪs/ *n.* ▸ℹ **p. 1634** Baronin, *die;* Freifrau, *die*

baronet /'bærənɪt/ *n.* Baronet, *der*

baronetcy /'bærənɪtsɪ/ *n.* Stand/Titel eines Baronets

baronial /bə'rəʊnɪəl/ *adj.* freiherrlich

barony /'bærənɪ/ *n.* Baronie, *die;* Baronat, *das*

baroque /bə'rɒk/

A *n.* Barock, *das*

B *adj.* **1** barock; **~ painting/literature** Barockmalerei/-literatur, *die;* **~ painter/writer** Maler/Schriftsteller des Barock **2** (grotesque) barock

barouche /bə'ruːʃ/ *n.* (Hist.) Kalesche, *die*

barque /bɑːk/ *n.* Bark, *die*

barrack

A *v.i.* buhen (ugs.)

B *v.t.* ausbuhen (ugs.)

barrack: ~-room 'lawyer *n.* Feldwebeltyp, *der* (abwertend); **~ 'square** *n.* Kasernenhof, *der*

barracks /'bærəks/ *n. pl., often constr. as sing.* **1** (for soldiers) Kaserne, *die* **2** (for temporary housing) Baracke, *die* **3** (plain, dull building) Kaserne, *die*

barracouta /bærə'kuːtə/ *n., pl. same or* **~s** Atun, *der*

barracuda /bærə'kuːdə/ *n., pl. same or* **~s** Barrakuda, *der;* Pfeilhecht, *der*

barrage /'bærɑːʒ/ *n.* **1** (Mil.) Sperrfeuer, *das;* (fig.) **a ~ of questions/insults** ein Bombardement von Fragen/Beleidigungen **2** (dam) Talsperre, *die;* Staustufe, *die*

'**barrage balloon** *n.* Sperrballon, *der*

barramundi /bærə'mʌndɪ/ *n.* (Zool.) Barramundi, *der*

barre /bɑː(r)/ *n.* (Ballet) Stange, *die*

barrel /'bærl/ *n.* **1** (vessel) Fass, *das;* (of metal, for oil, fuel, tar, etc.) Tonne, *die;* Fass, *das;* (measure) Barrel, *das;* **be over a ~** (fig.) in der Klemme sitzen (ugs.); **have sb. over a ~** (fig.) jmdn. in der Zange haben (ugs.); **scrape the ~** (fig.) das Letzte zusammenkratzen (ugs.) **2** (revolving cylinder) Walze, *die* **3** (of pump) Stiefel, *der;* (of engine boiler) Trommel, *die;* (of pen or pencil) Schaft, *der* **4** (of gun) Lauf, *der;* (of cannon etc.) Rohr, *das*

barrel: ~-chested /'bærltʃestɪd/ *adj.* **a ~-chested man** ein Mann mit einem breiten, gewölbten Brustkorb; **~house** *n.* (Amer.) Kneipe, *die; attrib.* **~house music** [einfache, laute] Jazzmusik; **~-organ** *n.* (Mus.) Leierkasten, *der;* Drehorgel, *die;* **~ vault** *n.* (Archit.) Tonnengewölbe, *das*

barren /'bærn/

A *adj.* **1** unfruchtbar ‹*Land, Tier, Pflanze*›; gelt (Jägerspr., Landw.) ‹*Wild, Ziege, Rind*› **2** (meagre, unproductive) nutzlos ‹*Handlung, Arbeit*›; mager ‹*Ergebnis*›; unfruchtbar ‹*Periode, Beziehung*›; fruchtlos ‹*Diskussion*›; **be ~ of results** wenig Erfolg haben

B *n.* (esp. Amer.) **~[s]** Ödland, *das*

barrenness /'bærnnɪs/ *n., no pl.* **1** Unfruchtbarkeit, *die* **2** ▸ **barren 2**: Nutzlosigkeit, *die;* Magerkeit, *die;* Unfruchtbarkeit, *die;* Fruchtlosigkeit, *die*

barrette /bə'ret/ *n.* (Amer.) Haarspange, *die*

barricade /bærɪ'keɪd/

A *n.* Barrikade, *die*

B *v.t.* verbarrikadieren

barrier /'bærɪə(r)/ *n.* **1** (fence) Absperrung, *die;* Barriere, *die;* (at railway, frontier) Schranke, *die* **2** (gate of railway station) Sperre, *die* **3** (obstacle, lit. or fig.) Barriere, *die;* **a ~ to progress** ein Hindernis für den Fortschritt; **break the class ~:** die Klassenschranken durchbrechen; *see also* **sound barrier**

barrier: ~ cream *n.* Schutzcreme, *die;* **~ method** *n.* Barrieremethode, *die;* **~ reef** *n.* Barrier- *od.* Wallriff, *das*

barring /'bɑːrɪŋ/ *prep.* außer im Falle (+ *Gen.*); **~ accidents** falls nichts passiert; **~ the possibility of rain** falls es nicht vielleicht regnet

barrister /'bærɪstə(r)/ *n.* ▸ℹ **p. 1260** **1** (Brit.) **~[-at-law]** Barrister, *der;* ≈ [Rechts]anwalt/-anwältin vor höheren Gerichten **2** (Amer.: lawyer) [Rechts]anwalt, *der*/-anwältin, *die*

barroom /'bɑːruːm/ *n.* (Amer.) Bar, *die*

barrow[1] /'bærəʊ/ *n.* **1** Karre, *die;* Karren, *der* **2** ▸ **wheelbarrow**

barrow[2] *n.* (Archaeol.) Hügelgrab, *das*

'**barrow boy** *n.* ▸ℹ **p. 1260** (Brit.) Straßenhändler, *der*

bar ~ 'sinister *n.* (Her.) Bastardfaden, *der;* **~ snack** *n.* Imbiss, *der;* Snack, *der* (*an der Bar*)

Bart. *abbr.* = **baronet**

'**bartender** *n.* ▸ℹ **p. 1260** Barkeeper, *der;* Schankkellner, *der*

barter /'bɑːtə(r)/

A *v.t.* [ein]tauschen; **~ sth. for sth. [else]** etw. für *od.* gegen etw. [anderes] [ein]tauschen; **~ away sth.** etw. verspielen (fig.)

B *v.i.* Tauschhandel treiben; **they ~ed for cigarettes with books and clothes** sie tauschten Bücher und Kleidung gegen Zigaretten

C *n.* Tauschhandel, *der*

barytes /bə'raɪtiːz/ *n.* (Min.) Baryt, *der*

basal /'beɪsl/ *adj.*(Med., Biol.) basal; **~ cell** Basalzelle, *die; see also* **metabolism**

basalt /'bæsɔːlt, bə'sɔːlt/ *n.* Basalt, *der*

bascule /'bæskjuːl/ *n.* Baskule, *die* (veralt.); **~ bridge** Klappbrücke, *die*

base[1] /beɪs/

A *n.* **1** (of lamp, pyramid, wall, mountain, microscope) Fuß, *der;* (of cupboard, statue) Sockel, *der;* (fig.) (support) Basis, *die;* Fundament, *das;* (principle) Ausgangsbasis, *die;* (main ingredient) Grundbestandteil, *der;* (of make-up) Grundlage, *die;* (Photog.: support for film etc.) Unterlage, *die;* (Ling.: root) Wurzel, *die;* (Ling.: primary morpheme) Stamm, *der;* **shake the very ~ of sth.** (fig.) etw. in seinen Grundfesten erschüttern; **glue has a flour ~:** die Grundsubstanz von Leim ist Mehl; **a sauce which has a tomato ~:** eine Soße auf Tomatenbasis (Kochk.) **2** (Mil.) Basis, *die;* Stützpunkt, *der* **3** (Baseball) Mal, *das;* **get to first ~** (fig. coll.) [wenigstens] etwas erreichen; **he didn't get to first ~ with her** er konnte bei ihr überhaupt nicht landen (ugs.); **be off ~** (fig. coll.) falsch liegen (ugs.) **4** (Archit.) Basis, *die* **5** (Geom.) Basis, *die;* (of triangle also) Grundlinie, *die;* (of solid also) Grundfläche, *die* **6** (Chem.) Base, *die* **7** (Surv.) Basis, *die* **8** (Math.: number) Basis, *die;* Grundzahl, *die* **9** (Bot., Zool.) Basis, *die;* (of leaf) Blattgrund, *der* **10** (Her.) Schildfuß, *der*

B *v.t.* **1** **~ sth. on sth.** etw. auf etw. (*Dat.*) aufbauen; ~ **one's hopes on sth.** seine Hoffnung auf etw. (*Akk.*) gründen; **be ~d on sth.** sich auf etw. (*Akk.*) gründen; **a book ~d on newly discovered papers** ein Buch, das auf neu entdeckten Dokumenten basiert **2** *in pass.* (have chief station or means) **be ~d in Paris** (permanently) in Paris sitzen; (temporarily) in Paris sein; **a submarine ~d on Malta** ein U-Boot, das seinen Stützpunkt auf Malta hat; **computer-~d accountancy** Buchführung über Computer; **land-~d forces** landgestützte Streitkräfte **3** ~ **oneself on** sich stützen auf (+ *Akk.*)

base² *adj.* **1** (without moral principles, ignoble) niederträchtig; niedrig ‹*Beweggrund*›

baseball /ˈbeɪsbɔːl/ *n.* Baseball, *der*

ˈbaseball cap *n.* Baseballkappe, *die;* Baseballmütze, *die*

base: ~ board *n.* (Amer.) Fußleiste, *die;* **~born** *adj.* (arch.) von niederer Herkunft; (illegitimate) unehelich; ~ **camp** *n.* Basislager, *das;* ~ **ˈcoin** *n.* entwertete Münze; ~ **hit** *n.* (Baseball) *Schlag, der dem Schlagmann ermöglicht, das erste Mal zu erreichen;* ~ **jump, BASE jump A** *n.* Basejump, *der;* **B** *v.i.* Basejumping machen *od.* betreiben; ~ **jumper, BASE jumper** *n.* Basejumper, *der*/-jumperin, *die;* ~ **jumping, BASE jumping** *n., no pl.* Basejumping, *das*

baseless /ˈbeɪslɪs/ *adj.* unbegründet

baselessly /ˈbeɪslɪslɪ/ *adv.* grundlos

baselessness /ˈbeɪslɪsnɪs/ *n., no pl.* Haltlosigkeit, *die*

base: ~line *n.* Grundlinie, *die;* **~load** *n.* (Electr.) Grundlast, *die*

basely /ˈbeɪslɪ/ *adv.* niederträchtig

baseman /ˈbeɪsmən/ *n., pl.* **basemen** /ˈbeɪsmən/ (Baseball) Malspieler, *der*

basement /ˈbeɪsmənt/ *n.* Souterrain, *das;* Kellergeschoss, *das;* (esp. in department store) Untergeschoss, *das;* Tiefgeschoss, *das; attrib.* **a ~ flat** (esp. Brit.) eine Souterrain- *od.* Kellerwohnung

base ˈmetal *n.* unedles Metall

baseness /ˈbeɪsnɪs/ *n., no pl.* Niedrigkeit, *die;* Niederträchtigkeit, *die*

ˈbase rate *n.* **1** (Finance) Eckzins, *der* **2** (wage) Grundlohn, *der*

bases¹ /ˈbeɪsɪz/ *pl. of* **base¹**

bases² /ˈbeɪsiːz/ *pl. of* **basis**

base: ~ station *n.* (Teleph.) Basisstation, *die;* ~ **unit** *n.* **1** (in measure) Basiseinheit, *die;* Grundeinheit, *die;* **2** (of device) Grundeinheit, *die;* (of telephone) Basisstation, *die;* **3** (piece of furniture) Grundelement, *das*

bash /bæʃ/

A *v.t.* [heftig] schlagen; ~ **one's head against sth.** sich (*Dat.*) den Kopf [heftig] an etw. (*Dat.*) anschlagen; ~ **sth. in** etw. einschlagen; **the car was badly ~ed in** *or* **up** das Auto war völlig verbeult; ~ **sb. up** jmdn. zusammenschlagen; **he was badly ~ed up** er wurde schlimm zusammengeschlagen; *see also* **queer-bashing**; **union-bashing**

B *n.* **1** [heftiger] Schlag **2** (coll.: attempt) Versuch, *der;* **have a ~ at sth.** etw. [mal] probieren *od.* versuchen **3** (coll.: party) Fete, *die* (ugs.)

bashful /ˈbæʃfl/ *adj.* **1** (shy) schüchtern **2** (shamefaced) verschämt

bashfully /ˈbæʃfəlɪ/ *adv.* ▸ **bashful**: schüchtern; verschämt

bashfulness /ˈbæʃflnɪs/ *n., no pl.* ▸ **bashful**: Schüchternheit, *die;* Verschämtheit, *die*

basic /ˈbeɪsɪk/ *adj.* **1** (fundamental) grundlegend; ~ **structure/principle/element/vocabulary** Grundstruktur, *die*/-prinzip, *das*/-bestandteil, *der*/-wortschatz, *der;* **be ~ to sth.** wesentlich für etw. sein; **have a ~ knowledge of sth.** Grundkenntnisse einer Sache (*Gen.*) haben; ~ **problem/reason/issue** Hauptproblem, *das*/-grund, *der*/-sache, *die* **2** (standard minimum) ~ **wages/salary** Grundlohn, *der*/Grundgehalt, *das;* **the length of a ~ working day is 8 hours** ein normaler Arbeitstag dauert 8 Stunden **3** (Chem., Geol.) basisch. *See also* **basics**

basically /ˈbeɪsɪkəlɪ/ *adv.* im Grunde; grundsätzlich ‹*übereinstimmen*›; (mainly) hauptsächlich

basic: ~ ˈdye *n.* (Chem.) basischer Farbstoff; **B~ ˈEnglish** *n.* Basic English, *das; auf einem sehr einfachen Grundwortschatz beruhendes Englisch;* ~ **ˈindustry** *n.* wichtiger Industriezweig

basics /ˈbeɪsɪks/ *n. pl.* **stick to the ~:** beim Wesentlichen bleiben; **the ~ of maths/cooking** die Grundlagen der Mathematik/das Abc der Kochkunst; **go** *or* **get back to ~** (when learning) sich [zuerst] Grundkenntnisse aneignen; (return to moral values) wieder auf die [moralischen] Grundwerte zurückkommen; **he doesn't understand the ~ of honesty** er weiß überhaupt nicht, was Ehrlichkeit ist

basic ˈslag *n.* Thomasschlacke, *die* (Hüttenw.); (finely ground) Thomasmehl, *das* (Landw.)

basidium /bəˈsɪdɪəm/ *n., pl.* **basidia** /bəˈsɪdɪə/ (Bot.) Basidie, *die;* Sporenständer, *der*

basil /ˈbæzɪl/ *n.* (Bot.) **[sweet] ~:** Basilikum, *das;* **bush ~:** Buschbasilikum, *das*

basilica /bəˈzɪlɪkə/ *n.* (Archit., Eccl.) Basilika, *die*

basilisk /ˈbæzɪlɪsk/ *n.* (Mythol., Zool.) Basilisk, *der;* ~ **stare** (fig.) Basiliskenblick, *der*

basin /ˈbeɪsn/ *n.* **1** Becken, *das;* (wash~) Waschbecken, *das;* (bowl) Schüssel, *die* **2** (depression) Becken, *das;* (artificial) Bassin, *das;* Becken, *das;* (valley) [Tal]kessel, *der* **3** (of river etc.) Becken, *das;* **the ~ of the Amazon, the Amazon ~:** das Amazonasbecken **4** (harbour) [Hafen]becken, *das*

basinful /ˈbeɪsnfʊl/ *n.* **ten ~s of water** zehn Schüsseln [voll] Wasser; **have had a ~ of sth.** (fig. coll.: more than enough) von etw. die Nase voll haben (ugs.)

basis /ˈbeɪsɪs/ *n., pl.* **bases** /ˈbeɪsiːz/ **1** (ingredient) Grundbestandteil, *der* **2** (foundation, principle, common ground) Basis, *die;* Grundlage, *die;* **rest on a ~ of conjecture** sich auf Vermutungen gründen; **meet on a purely friendly ~:** einander auf rein freundschaftlicher Basis begegnen; **on a first come first served ~:** nach dem Prinzip „Wer zuerst kommt, mahlt zuerst" **3** (beginning) Ausgangspunkt, *der*

bask /bɑːsk/ *v.i.* **1** sich [wohlig] wärmen; sich aalen (ugs.); ~ **in the sun** sich sonnen; sich in der Sonne aalen (ugs.) **2** (fig.) sich sonnen (**in** in + *Dat.*)

basket /ˈbɑːskɪt/ *n.* **1** Korb, *der;* (smaller, for bread etc.) Körbchen, *das;* (of chip pan) Drahteinsatz, *der;* **wire ~:** Drahtkorb, *der* **2** (quantity) **a ~ [full] of plums/apples** ein Korb [voll] Pflaumen/Äpfel; **sell ~s of sth.** [ganze] Körbe voll etw. verkaufen; etw. körbeweise verkaufen **3** (protection for hand) Korb, *der;* (Fencing) Glocke, *die* **4** (Basketball) Korb, *der;* **make** *or* **score a ~:** einen Korb werfen **5** (Econ.) ~ **of currencies** Währungskorb, *der*

basket: ~ball *n.* Basketball, *der;* ~ **case** *n.* (coll.) Schwerbeschädigte ohne Arme und Beine; (fig.) hoffnungsloser Fall; ~ **chair** *n.* Korbsessel, *der*

basketful /ˈbɑːskɪtfʊl/ ▸ **basket 2**

basketry /ˈbɑːskɪtrɪ/ ▸ **basketwork**

basket: ~ weave *n.* Panamabindung, *die* (Weberei); **~work** *n., no pl.* (art) Korbflechterei, *die;* (collectively) Korbwaren; **a piece of ~work** ein Korbgeflecht; **~work is his hobby** Korbflechten ist sein Hobby

basking ˈshark *n.* Riesenhai, *der*

Basle /bɑːl/ ▸ⓘ **p. 1643**

A *pr. n.* Basel (*das*)

B *attrib. adj.* Baseler

Basque /bæsk, bɑːsk/

A *adj.* ▸ⓘ **p. 1277**, ▸ⓘ **p. 1345** baskisch; **the ~ Country** das Baskenland

B *n.* **1** ▸ⓘ **p. 1277**, ▸ⓘ **p. 1345** Baske, *der*/Baskin, *die;* (language) Baskisch, *das* **2** **b~** (bodice) Schößchenjacke, *die*

bas-relief /ˈbæsrɪliːf/ *n.* (Art) Basrelief, *das*

bass¹ /beɪs/ (Mus.)

A *adj.* Bass-; ~ **voice** Bassstimme, *die*

B *n.* **1** Bass, *der;* (voice, part) Bass, *der;* Bassstimme, *die;* (singer) Bassist, *der;* Bass, *der* **2** (double ~) [Kontra]bass, *der;* (~ guitar) Bass, *der* **3** **figured** *or* **thorough ~:** Generalbass, *der;* (theory) Generalbasslehre, *die; see also* **ground¹**

bass² /bæs/ *n., pl. same or* **~es** (Zool.) Barsch, *der;* (Perca fluviatilis) [Fluss]barsch, *der*

bass³ /bæs/ *n.* (fibre) Bast, *der*

bass/beɪs/: ~ **clef** *n.* (Mus.) Bassschlüssel, *der;* ~ **drum** *n.* große Trommel

basset /ˈbæsɪt/ *n.* ~ **[hound]** Basset, *der*

bass guiˈtar /beɪs/ *n.* Bassgitarre, *die*

bassinet /bæsɪˈnet/ *n.* Korbwiege, *die*

bassist /ˈbeɪsɪst/ *n.* Bassist, *der*/Bassistin, *die*

basso /ˈbæsəʊ/ *n., pl.* **~s** *or* **bassi** /ˈbæsiː/ (Mus.) Basso, *der*

bassoon /bəˈsuːn/ *n.* (Mus.) Fagott, *das*

bassoonist /bəˈsuːnɪst/ *n.* (Mus.) Fagottist, *der*/Fagottistin, *die*

bass: ~ player *n.* Bassist, *der*/Bassistin, *die;* ~ **viol** /beɪs ˈvaɪəl/ *n.* Gambe, *die;* Kniegeige, *die* (veralt.); (Amer.: double ~) Bassgeige, *die;* Kontrabass, *der*

bast /bæst/ *n.* Bast, *der*

bastard /ˈbɑːstəd/

A *adj.* **1** unehelich **2** (hybrid) verfälscht ‹*Sprache, Stil*› **3** (Bot., Zool.) Bastard-

B *n.* **1** uneheliches Kind; unehelicher Sohn/uneheliche Tochter; Bastard, *der* (hist.) **2** (sl.) (disliked person) Schweinehund, *der* (derb); Mistkerl, *der* (derb); (disliked thing) Scheißding, *das* (derb); **you old ~!** (in friendly exclamation) alter Schwede! (salopp); **the poor ~!** (unfortunate person) das arme Schwein! (ugs.)

bastardize /ˈbɑːstədaɪz/ *v.t.* bastardisieren

bastard: ~ title *n.* (Printing) Schmutztitel, *der;* ~ **wing** *n.* (Zool.) Afterflügel, *der*

bastardy /ˈbɑːstədɪ/ *n., no pl.* uneheliche Herkunft; Unehelichkeit, *die*

baste¹ /beɪst/ *v.t.* (stitch) heften; reihen

baste² *v.t.* **1** [mit Fett/Bratensaft] begießen ‹*Fleisch*› **2** (thrash, cudgel) prügeln

bastion /ˈbæstɪən/ *n.* Bastei, *die;* (fig.) Bastei, *die;* Bastion, *die;* Bollwerk, *das*

bat¹ /bæt/ *n.* (Zool.) Fledermaus, *die;* **blind as a ~** (fig.) blind wie ein Maulwurf; **have ~s in the belfry** (fig. coll.) einen Dachschaden haben (ugs.); **sb. drives like a ~ out of hell** (sl.) jmd. fährt, als ob der Teufel hinter ihm her wäre (ugs.)

bat²

A *n.* **1** (Sport) Schlagholz, *das;* (for table tennis) Schläger, *der;* **do sth. off one's own ~** (fig.) etw. auf eigene Faust tun; **carry one's ~** (Cricket) *als Schlagmann während eines Durchgangs nicht ausscheiden;* **right off the ~** (Amer. fig.) sofort **2** (act of using ~) Schlag, *der* **3** *usu. in pl.* (implement to guide aircraft) Kelle, *die* **4** (batsman) Schlagmann, *der*

B *v.i.*, **-tt- 1** (Sport) schlagen **2** (coll.: move) ~ **around the town** in der Stadt rummachen (ugs.)

C *v.t.*, **-tt- 1** schlagen **2** (Baseball) ~ **in two runs** zwei Läufe holen (ugs.)

bat³ *v.t.*, **-tt-:** ~ **one's eyelids** [mit den Augenlidern] blinzeln *od.* zwinkern; **he never ~ted an eyelid** *or* (Amer.) **eye** (fig.: betrayed no emotion) er hat nicht mit der Wimper gezuckt; **without ~ting an eyelid** *or* (Amer.) **eye** (fig.) ohne mit der Wimper zu zucken

batch /bætʃ/ *n.* **1** (of loaves) Schub, *der* **2** (of people) Gruppe, *die;* Schwung, *der* (ugs.); (of letters, books, files, papers) Stapel, *der;* Schwung, *der* (ugs.); (of rules, regulations) Bündel, *das*

batch: ~ file *n.* (Computing) Stapeldatei, *die;* ~ **ˈprocessing** *n.* (Computing) Schub-, Stapelverarbeitung, *die;* ~ **production** *n.* Stapelfertigung, *die*

bate *n.* (Brit. dated coll.) Rage, *die* (ugs.); **be in a [terrible] ~:** [schrecklich] in Rage sein; **get/fly into a ~:** in Rage geraten

bated /ˈbeɪtɪd/ *adj.* **with ~ breath** mit angehaltenem *od.* (geh.) verhaltenem Atem

bath /bɑːθ/

A *n., pl.* **~s** /bɑːðz/ **1** Bad, *das;* **have** *or* **take a ~:** ein Bad nehmen **2** (vessel) **~[tub]** Badewanne, *die;* **room with ~:** Zimmer mit Bad **3** *usu. in pl.* (building) Bad, *das;* **[swimming] ~s** Schwimmbad, *das* **4** **Order of the B~** (Brit.) Orden vom Bade

B *v.t. & i.* baden

b

bath: B~ 'brick *n.* Putzstein, *der;* **B~ 'bun** *n.* ≈ Rosinenbrötchen mit Zuckerguss; **~ cap** *n.* Badekappe, *die;* Bademütze, *die;* **~ chair** *n.* Rollstuhl, *der;* **~ cube** *n. pl.* Badesalzwürfel, *der*

bathe /beɪð/

A *v.t.* **1** baden **2** (moisten) baden ‹*Wunde, Körperteil*›; **~d with** *or* **in sweat** schweißüberströmt ‹*Gesicht, Person*›; in Schweiß gebadet ‹*Person*›; **~d with** *or* **in tears** tränenüberströmt **3** (envelop) **sunlight ~d the gardens** Sonne lag über den Gärten (geh.); **~d in sunlight** von der Sonne beschienen

B *v.i.* baden; **go bathing** baden gehen

C *n.* Bad, *das* (*im Meer usw.*); **take** *or* **have a ~:** baden; ein Bad nehmen

bather /'beɪðə(r)/ *n.* **1** Badende, *der/die* **2** *in pl.* (Austral.: garment) Badeanzug, *der*

bathetic /bə'θetɪk/ *adj.* bathisch (geh.)

bathing /'beɪðɪŋ/ *n.* Baden, *das;* **'~ prohibited'** „Baden verboten!"

bathing: ~ beach *n.* Badestrand, *der;* **~ beauty, ~ belle** *ns.* Badenixe, *die;* **~ cap** *n.* Badekappe, *die;* Bademütze, *die;* **~ costume** *n.* Badeanzug, *der;* **~-machine** *n.* (Hist.) Badekarren, *der;* **~ suit** *n.* Badeanzug, *der;* **~ trunks** *n. pl.* Badehose, *die*

'bath mat *n.* Badematte, *die*

bathos /'beɪθɒs/ *n., no pl.* (Lit., Rhet.) Bathos, *das* (geh.); Umschlag ins Triviale; (anticlimax) Antiklimax, *die* (Stilk.)

bath: ~robe *n.* Bademantel, *der;* **~room** *n.* Badezimmer, *das;* **~ salts** *n. pl.* Badesalz, *das;* **~time** *n.* Badezeit, *die;* **~ towel** *n.* Badetuch, *das;* **~tub** ▸ **bath A 2;** **~water** *n.* Badewasser, *das; see also* **baby A 1**

batik /'bætɪk, bə'ti:k/ *n.* Batik, *der od. die*

batiste /bə'ti:st/

A *n.* Batist, *der*

B *adj.* batisten; **~ dress/blouse** Batistkleid, *das*/Batistbluse, *die*

batman /'bætmən/ *n., pl.* **batmen** /'bætmən/ (Mil.) [Offiziers]bursche, *der*

baton /'bætn/ *n.* **1** (staff of office) Stab, *der;* Baton, *der* (veralt.); **Field Marshal's ~:** Marschallstab, *der* **2** (truncheon) Schlagstock, *der* **3** (Mus.) Taktstock, *der;* **conductor's ~:** Dirigentenstab, *der* **4** (for relay race) [Staffel]stab, *der;* Staffelholz, *das*

bats /bæts/ *pred. adj.* (coll.) bekloppt (salopp); **go ~:** überschnappen (ugs.)

batsman /'bætsmən/ *n., pl.* **batsmen** /'bætsmən/ (Sport) Schlagmann, *der;* **~'s wicket** *für den Schlagmann günstige Spielbahn*

battalion /bə'tæljən/ *n.* (lit. or fig.) Bataillon, *das;* **~s of** (fig.) ganze Bataillone von; **God is for the big ~s** Gott ist mit dem Stärkeren

batten /'bætn/

A *n.* **1** (piece of timber) Latte, *die* **2** (Naut.) Latte, *die* **3** (bar, strip of wood) Leiste, *die*

B *v.t.* (Naut.) **~ down** [ver]schalken ‹*Luke*›

batter¹ /'bætə(r)/

A *v.t.* **1** (strike) einschlagen auf (+ *Akk.*); **~ down/in** einschlagen; **~ sth. to pieces** etw. zerschmettern *od.* in Stücke schlagen; **he ~ed his head against the wall** er schlug seinen Kopf gegen die Wand **2** (attack with artillery) beschießen; bombardieren (Milit. veralt.); **~ down** zusammenschießen **3** (fig.: handle severely) bombardieren; **~ sb. into exhaustion** jmdn. völlig zermürben **4** (bruise, damage) übel zurichten; ramponieren (ugs.); **~ed baby** misshandeltes Baby; **~ed wife** misshandelte Ehefrau; geschlagene Frau; **~ed wives' home** Frauenhaus, *das;* **~ed by the gales** vom Sturm stark beschädigt

B *v.i.* heftig klopfen; **they ~ed at** *or* **against the door** sie hämmerten gegen die Tür

batter² *n.* (Cookery) [Back]teig, *der;* (for pancake) [Eierkuchen]teig, *der;* (for waffle) [Waffel]teig, *der*

batter³ *n.* (Baseball) Schlagmann, *der*

battering ram /'bætərɪŋ ræm/ *n.* Rammbock, *der*

battery /'bætərɪ/ *n.* **1** (series; also Mil., Electr.) Batterie, *die;* **a ~ of specialists** (fig.) eine ganze Reihe von Spezialisten; *see also* **recharge A 2** (Law) **[assault and] ~:** tätlicher Angriff **3** (series) **a ~ of tests** eine Testreihe **4** (Baseball) *Werfer und Fänger* **5** (Agric.) Legebatterie, *die*

battery: ~ charger *n.* Batterieladegerät, *das;* **~ 'chicken** *n.* Batteriehuhn, *das;* **~ 'farming** *n., no pl.* Batteriehaltung, *die;* **~ 'hen** *n.* Batteriehuhn, *das;* **~-operated** *adj.* batteriebetrieben

batting /'bætɪŋ/ *n.* (Sport) Schlagen, *das; see also* **average A 2**

battle /'bætl/

A *n.* **1** (fight) Schlacht, *die;* **the ~ at Amman** die Schlacht bei Amman; **they went out to ~:** sie zogen in die Schlacht; **do** *or* **give ~:** kämpfen; **join ~ with sb.** jmdm. eine Schlacht liefern; **die in ~:** [in der Schlacht] fallen; *see also* **pitch¹ B 6.** **2** (fig.: contest) Kampf, *der;* **~ for life** Kampf ums Überleben; **~ of words** Wortgefecht, *das;* **~ of ideas/wits** Wettstreit der Ideen/geistiger Wettstreit; **sth./that is half the ~:** mit etw./damit ist schon viel gewonnen; *see also* **fight B 3**

B *v.i.* **~ with** *or* **against sth.** mit *od.* gegen etw. kämpfen; **~ for sth.** für etw. kämpfen

C *v.t.* **1** kämpfen gegen **2** **~ one's way through the crowd** sich durch die Menge kämpfen

battle: ~axe *n.* Streitaxt, *die;* (coll.: woman) Schreckschraube, *die* (ugs. abwertend); **~-cruiser** *n.* (Navy) Schlachtkreuzer, *der;* **~ cry** *n.* Schlachtruf, *der*

battle: ~dress *n.* (Mil.) (for general service) Arbeitsanzug, *der;* (for field service) Kampfanzug, *der;* **~ fatigue** *n.* Frontkoller, *der* (ugs.); Frontneurose, *die;* **~field, ~ground** *ns.* Schlachtfeld, *das;* **~-lines** *n. pl.* Kampflinien

battlement /'bætlmənt/ *n., usu. in pl.* **1** Zinne, *die* **2** (roof) mit Zinnen bewehrtes Dach

battlemented /'bætlməntɪd/ *adj.* mit Zinnen bewehrt

battle: ~ 'royal *n.* [heftiger] Kampf (auch fig.); (everyone for himself) Kampf jeder gegen jeden; **~ship** *n.* Schlachtschiff, *das;* **~ stations** *n. pl.* (esp. Amer.) [Kampf]stellungen; **~ stations!** in die Stellungen!; **~-weary** *adj.* kampfesmüde

batty /'bætɪ/ *adj.* (coll.) bekloppt (salopp); **go** *or* **become ~:** überschnappen (ugs.)

'batwing sleeve *n.* Fledermausärmel, *der*

bauble /'bɔ:bl/ *n.* **1** (trinket) Flitter, *der;* **little ~s** kleine, wertlose Schmuckstücke **2** (toy) Spielzeug, *das;* **dolls and other ~s** Puppen und anderes Spielzeug **3** (Hist.: jester's emblem) Narrenzepter, *das* **4** (worthless thing) Talmi, *der;* **be a ~/be ~s** Talmi sein

baud *n., pl. same or* **bauds** (Computing) Baud, *das*

baulk /bɔ:k, bɔ:lk/

A *n.* **1** (ridge) Rain, *der* **2** (timber beam) Balken, *der* **3** (tie beam) Binderbalken, *der* (Bauw.); ≈ Dachbalken, *der* **4** (hindrance) Hindernis, *das* **(to** für) **5** *no indef. art.* (*Billiards*) *markierte Fläche auf dem Billardtisch, wo die Kugel nicht direkt gespielt werden darf* **6** (Baseball) *Art Foul des Werfers*

B *v.t.* **1** [be]hindern; **they were ~ed in their plan/undertaking** *etc.* ihr Plan/Unternehmen *usw.* wurde blockiert; **they were ~ed of their prey** sie wurden um ihre Beute gebracht **2** (avoid) ausweichen (+ *Dat.*) ‹*Person, Gespräch*›; sich entziehen (+ *Dat.*) ‹*Verantwortung, Aufgabe, Gespräch*›

C *v.i.* sich sträuben (**at** gegen); ‹*Pferd:*› scheuen (**at** vor + *Dat.*)

bauxite /'bɔ:ksaɪt/ *n.* (Min.) Bauxit, *der*

Bavaria /bə'veərɪə/ *pr. n.* Bayern *(das)*

Bavarian /bə'veərɪən/ ▸ **i p. 1277, ▸ i p. 1345**

A *adj.* bay[e]risch; **sb. is ~:** jmd. ist Bayer/Bayerin

B *n.* **1** (person) Bayer, *der*/Bayerin, *die* **2** (dialect) Bay[e]risch[e], *das;* Bairisch[e], *das*

bawdily /'bɔ:dɪlɪ/ *adv.* zweideutig, (stronger) obszön ‹*lachen, schreiben*›

bawdiness /'bɔ:dɪnɪs/ *n., no pl.* ▸ **bawdy A:** Zweideutigkeit, *die;* Obszönität, *die*

bawdy /'bɔ:dɪ/

A *adj.* zweideutig, (stronger) obszön ‹*Witz, Geschichte, Sprache*›; obszön ‹*Person*›

B *n.* Zweideutigkeit, *die;* (stronger) Obszönität, *die*

bawl /bɔ:l/

A *v.t.* brüllen; **~ sth. at sb.** jmdm. etw. zubrüllen; **~ sb. out** (coll.) jmdn. zusammenstauchen (ugs.)

B *v.i.* brüllen; **~ out to sb.** nach jmdm. brüllen; **~ at sb.** jmdn. anbrüllen

bay¹ *n.* (of sea) Bucht, *die;* (larger also) Golf, *der;* **the B~ of Bengal** der Golf von Bengalen; **Hudson's B~:** die Hudsonbai; **the B~ of Pigs** die Schweinebucht

bay² *n.* **1** (division of wall) Joch, *das* (Archit.) **2** (space in room) Erker, *der* **3** (recess, compartment) Lagerraum, *der;* (in barn) Banse, *die* **4** (in bus station) Haltestelle, *die;* (of railway line) ≈ Nebengleis, *das;* (platform) *Bahnsteig an einem Nebengleis; see also* **loading bay; parking bay; sickbay**

bay³

A *n.* (bark) Gebell, *das;* Gelaut, *das* (Jägerspr.); **at ~:** gestellt; **be at ~** (fig.) mit dem Rücken zur Wand stehen (fig.); **hold** *or* **keep sb./sth. at ~** (fig.) jmdn./etw. vom Leib halten; **stand at ~** (fig.) sich [den Verfolgern] stellen

B *v.i.* bellen; **~ at sb./sth.** jmdn./etw. anbellen

C *v.t.* anbellen

bay⁴ /beɪ/ *n.* (Bot.) Lorbeer[baum], *der*

bay⁵

A *adj.* braun ‹*Pferd*›

B *n.* Braune, *der*

bay: ~berry *n.* Pimentbaum, *der;* **~leaf** *n.* (Cookery) Lorbeerblatt, *das*

bayonet /'beɪənɪt/

A *n.* Bajonett, *das;* Seitengewehr, *das;* **with fixed ~s** mit aufgepflanzten Bajonetten

B *v.t.* mit dem Bajonett *od.* Seitengewehr aufspießen; **~ sb. to death** jmdn. mit dem Bajonett erstechen

bayonet: ~ fitting *n.* Bajonettfassung, *die;* **~ plug** *n.* Stecker mit Bajonettverschluss *od.* -fassung; **~ socket** *n.* Steckdose mit Bajonettfassung

bay: ~ 'rum *n.* Pimentöl, *das;* **~ 'window** *n.* Erkerfenster, *das*

bazaar /bə'zɑ:(r)/ *n.* (oriental market) Basar, *der;* (large shop) Kaufhaus, *das;* Basar, *der* (DDR); (sale) [Wohltätigkeits]basar, *der*

bazooka /bə'zu:kə/ *n.* (Mil.) Bazooka, *die;* (smaller) Panzerfaust, *die*

BB *abbr.* **1** (Amer.) (size of pellet) BB; *attrib.* **~ gun** Luftgewehr, *das* **2** (Brit.) (grade of pencil lead) 2B

BBC *abbr.* **= British Broadcasting Corporation** BBC, *die*

> **BBC – British Broadcasting Corporation**
>
> Eine der wichtigsten britischen Fernseh- und Rundfunkanstalten. Sie erhielt 1927 die *Royal Charter*, das königliche Privileg, finanziert sich über Fernsehgebühren, nicht über Werbeeinnahmen, und ist zur unparteiischen Berichterstattung verpflichtet.

bbl. *abbr.* **= barrels** (esp. of oil)

BBQ *abbr.* **= barbecue**

BBS *abbr.* (Computing) **= bulletin board system**

BC *abbr.* ▸ **i p. 1047 = before Christ** v. Chr.; (bes. DDR) v. u. Z.

BD *abbr.* **= Bachelor of Divinity** Bakkalaureus der Theologie; *see also* **BSc**

BDS *abbr.* **= Bachelor of Dental Surgery** Bakkalaureus der Zahnheilkunde; *see also* **BSc**

be /bi:/ *v., pres. t.* **I am** /əm/, *stressed* æm/, *neg.* (coll.) **ain't** /eɪnt/, **he is** /ɪz/, *neg.* (coll.) **isn't** /'ɪznt/; **we are** /ə(r)/, *stressed* ɑ:(r)/, *neg.* (coll.) **aren't** /ɑ:nt/; *p. t.* **I was** /wəz, *stressed* wɒz/, *neg.* (coll.) **wasn't** /'wɒznt/, **we were** /wə(r), *stressed* wɜ:(r), weə(r)/, *neg.* (coll.) **weren't** /wɜ:nt, weənt/; *pres. p.* **being** /'bi:ɪŋ/; *p. p.* **been** /bɪn, *stressed* bi:n/

A *copula* **1** *indicating quality or attribute* sein; **she'll be ten next week** sie wird nächste Woche zehn; **she is a mother/an Italian** sie ist Mutter/Italienerin; **being a Frenchman, he naturally took an interest in politics** als Franzose interessierte er sich natürlich für Politik; **not being a cat lover, I kept well away** da ich nicht gerade ein Katzenfreund bin, hielt ich

mich fern; **he is being nice to them/sarcastic** er ist nett zu ihnen/jetzt ist er sarkastisch; **he has always been lazy** er ist schon immer faul gewesen; **be sensible!** sei vernünftig!
2 *in exclamations* **was she pleased!** war sie [vielleicht] froh!; **isn't he stupid!** ist er nicht [wirklich] dumm!; **aren't you a big boy!** was bist du schon für ein großer Junge!
3 **will be** *indicating supposition* **[I dare say] you'll be a big boy by now** du bist jetzt sicher schon ein großer Junge; **you'll be relieved to hear that** du wirst erleichtert sein, das zu hören
4 *indicating physical or mental welfare or state* sein; sich fühlen; **be ill/unwell** krank sein/sich nicht wohl fühlen; **I am well** es geht mir gut; **I am hot** mir ist heiß; **I am freezing** mich friert; es friert mich; **how are you/is she?** wie gehts (ugs.)/geht es ihr?
5 *identifying the subject* **he is the person I was speaking of** er ist es, von dem ich sprach; **it is the 5th today** heute haben wir den Fünften; **who's that?** wer ist das?; **it is she, it's her** sie ists; **it is Joe who came** Joe ist gekommen; **if I were you** wenn ich du *od.* an deiner Stelle wäre
6 *indicating profession, pastime, etc.* **be a teacher/a footballer** Lehrer/Fußballer sein; **she wants to be a surgeon** sie möchte Chirurgin werden
7 *with possessive* **it is/was hers** es ist/war ihrs; es gehört/gehörte ihr; **this book is your uncle's** dieses Buch gehört deinem Onkel
8 *indicating intended recipient* **it's for you** es ist für dich
9 (cost) kosten; **how much are those eggs?** was kosten die Eier da?; **that will be 76p** das macht 76 Pence
10 (equal) sein; **two times three is six, two threes are six** zweimal drei ist *od.* sind *od.* gibt sechs; **sixteen ounces is a pound** sechzehn Unzen sind *od.* ergeben ein Pfund
11 (constitute) ausmachen; bilden; **London is not England** London ist nicht [gleich] England
12 (mean) bedeuten; **he was everything to her** er bedeutete ihr alles; **seeing is believing** was man [selbst] sieht, glaubt man
13 (represent) darstellen; stehen für; bedeuten; **let x be 3** [angenommen] x sei 3
B *v.i.* 1 (exist) [vorhanden] sein; existieren; **can such things be?** kann es so etwas geben?; kann es so etwas vorkommen?; **I think, therefore I am** ich denke, also bin ich; **there is/are ...:** es gibt ...; **there are no such things** es gibt nichts dergleichen; so etwas gibt es nicht; **once upon a time there was a princess** es war einmal eine Prinzessin; **to be or not to be** Sein oder Nichtsein; **the powers that be** die maßgeblichen Stellen; die da oben (ugs.); **for the time being** vorläufig; **Miss Jones that was** das frühere Fräulein Jones; **be that as it may** wie dem auch sei
2 (remain) bleiben; **I shan't be a moment** *or* **second** ich komme gleich; noch eine Minute; **she has been in her room for hours** sie ist schon seit Stunden in ihrem Zimmer; **let it be** lass es sein; **let him/her be** lass ihn/sie in Ruhe
3 (attend) sein; **is he here?** ist er hier?
4 *indicating position in space or time* **he's upstairs** er ist oben; **how long has he been here?** wie lange ist er schon hier?
5 (be situated) sein; **Hungary is in the heart of Europe** Ungarn liegt im Herzen Europas; **the chair is in the corner** der Stuhl steht *od.* ist in der Ecke; **here you are** (on arrival) da bist du/da seid ihr [ja]; (on giving sb. sth.) so, bitte!
6 (happen, occur, take place) stattfinden; sein; **where will the party be?** wo ist die Party?; wo findet die Party statt?
7 (go, come) **be off with you!** geh/geht!; **I'm off** *or* **for home** ich gehe jetzt nach Hause; **she's from Australia** sie stammt *od.* ist aus Australien; **are you for London?** wollen Sie nach London?; sind Sie auf dem Weg nach London?; **be on one's way** unterwegs *od.* auf dem Wege sein
8 (on visit etc.) sein; **have you [ever] been to London?** bist du schon einmal in London gewesen?; **has anyone been?** ist jemand da gewesen?; **has the postman been?** war der Briefträger *od.* die Post schon da?
9 **be for/against sth./sb.** für/gegen etw./jmdn. sein; **How kind she is. She's been and tidied the room** (coll.) Wie nett sie ist. Sie hat doch wirklich das Zimmer aufgeräumt; **the children have been at the biscuits** die Kinder waren an den Keksen (ugs.); **I've been into this matter** ich habe mich mit der Sache befasst
C *v. aux.* 1 *forming passive* werden; **the child was found** das Kind wurde gefunden; **German is spoken in this shop** in diesem Geschäft wird Deutsch gesprochen
2 *forming continuous tenses, active* **he is reading** er liest [gerade]; er ist beim Lesen; **I am leaving tomorrow** ich reise morgen [ab]; **the train was departing when I got there** der Zug fuhr gerade ab, als ich ankam
3 *forming continuous tenses, passive* **the house is/was being built** das Haus wird/wurde [gerade] gebaut *od.* ist/war im Bau
4 *expr. obligation* **be to** sollen; **I am to inform you** ich soll Sie unterrichten; **you are to report to the police** Sie sollen sich bei der Polizei melden; **he is to clean the house thoroughly** er soll das ganze Haus gründlich putzen; **he is to be admired** er ist zu bewundern
5 *expr. arrangement* **the Queen is to arrive at 3 p.m.** die Königin soll um 15 Uhr eintreffen; **he is to be there** er soll dort sein; **I am to go** ich soll gehen
6 *expr. possibility* **the car is for sale** das Auto ist zu verkaufen; **it was not to be seen** es war nicht zu sehen; **there was nothing to be seen** es war nichts zu sehen; **I was not to be sidetracked** ich ließ mich nicht ablenken
7 *expr. destiny* **they were never to meet again** sie sollten sich nie wieder treffen
8 *expr. condition* **if I were to tell you that ..., were I to tell you that ...** wenn ich dir sagen würde, dass ...
9 (arch.) *forming past tenses of verbs of motion* sein; **the sun is set** die Sonne ist untergegangen; **Christ is risen** (Relig.) Christ[us] ist auferstanden *od.* (dichter. veralt.) erstanden; **the prisoner is fled** der Gefangene ist geflohen;
D **bride-/husband-to-be** zukünftige Braut/zukünftiger Ehemann; **mother-/father-to-be** werdende Mutter/werdender Vater; **the be-all and end-all** das A und O

beach /biːtʃ/
A *n.* Strand, *der;* **on the ~:** am Strand; *attrib.* **~ area** Strandzone, *die;* **~ hat/suit/shoe** Strandhut/-anzug/-schuh, *der*
B *v.t.* auf [den] Strand setzen ‹*Schiff usw.*›; ans Ufer ziehen ‹*Boot, Wal*›

beach: ~ball *n.* Wasserball, *der;* **~comber** /ˈbiːtʃkəʊmə(r)/ *n.* 1 Strandgutsammler, *der;* 2 (wave) große Brandungswelle; **~head** *n.* (Mil.) Brückenkopf, *der;* **~ hut** *n.* Strandhütte, *die;* **~ umbrella** *n.* Strandschirm, *der;* **~ volleyball** *n.* Beachvolleyball, *der od. das;* **~wear** *n.* Strandkleidung, *die*

beacon /ˈbiːkn/ *n.* 1 Leucht-, Signalfeuer, *das;* (Naut.) Leuchtbake, *die* 2 (Brit.) (hill) leicht sichtbarer Hügel (*für ein Signalfeuer*) 3 (lighthouse, tower, etc.) Leuchtfeuer, *das* 4 (radio station) Funkfeuer, *das* 5 (signal light) Signalleuchte, *die;* (for aircraft) Landelicht, *das* 6 (fig.) Leitstern, *der*

bead /biːd/
A *n.* 1 Perle, *die;* **~s** Perlen *Pl.;* Perlenkette, *die;* **tell one's ~s** den Rosenkranz beten; **~s of dew** Tautropfen *od.* (geh.) -perlen; **~s of perspiration** *or* **sweat** Schweißtropfen *od.* -perlen
2 (gunsight) Kornspitze, *die;* Korn, *das;* **draw a ~ on sb./sth.** auf jmdn./etw. zielen 3 (tyre edge) ▸ **beading 3**
B *v.t.* mit Perlen/perlenartiger Verzierung versehen

beading /ˈbiːdɪŋ/ *n.* 1 Perlenstickerei, *die* 2 (Archit.) Perl- *od.* Rundstab, *der;* Abdeckstab, *der* 3 (tyre edge) Wulst, *der od. die*

beadle /ˈbiːdl/ *n.* ▸ℹ **p. 1260** (Brit.) (Hist.: of church) Kirchendiener, *der;* (with more responsibility, esp. Scot.) Küster, *der;* (of university) Pedell, *der*

beady /ˈbiːdɪ/ *adj.* **~ eyes** Knopfaugen; **those ~ eyes of hers don't miss anything** ihrem wachsamen Blick entgeht nichts; **I've got my ~ eye on you** ich lasse dich nicht aus den Augen

ˈbeady-eyed *adj.* mit Knopfaugen *nachgestellt;* (watchful) mit wachen Augen *nachgestellt*

beagle /ˈbiːgl/ *n.* Beagle, *der*

beak[1] /biːk/ *n.* Schnabel, *der;* (of turtle, octopus) Mundwerkzeug, *das;* (fig.: large, hooked nose) Hakennase, *die;* Zinken, *der* (salopp)

beak[2] *n.* (Brit. dated coll.) 1 (magistrate, judge) Kadi, *der* (ugs.) 2 (schoolmaster) Pauker, *der*

beaked /biːkt/ *adj.* geschnäbelt

beaker /ˈbiːkə(r)/ *n.* 1 (cup) Becher, *der* 2 (Chem.) Becherglas, *das*

ˈbe-all ▸ **be D**

beam /biːm/
A *n.* 1 (timber etc.) Balken, *der* 2 (ray etc.) [Licht-]strahl, *der;* **~ of light** Lichtstrahl, *der;* **the car's headlamps were on full ~:** die Scheinwerfer des Wagens waren aufgeblendet
3 (Aeronaut., Mil., etc.: guide) Peil- *od.* Leitstrahl, *der;* (course) **come in on the ~:** auf dem Peil- *od.* Leitstrahl ein- *od.* anfliegen; **be off ~** (fig. coll.) danebenliegen (ugs.); **be on the ~** (fig. coll.) richtig liegen (ugs.) 4 (smile) Strahlen, *das.*
5 (Naut.) (ship's breadth) [größte] Schiffsbreite; (side of ship) [Schiffs]seite, *die;* **~s** Decksbalken; **on the ~:** querschiffs; **on the port ~:** backbords; **broad in the ~** (fig. coll.) breithüftig
6 (in balance) Waagebalken, *der*
B *v.t.* (broadcast) aussenden; ausstrahlen ‹*Wellen, Licht, Rundfunkprogramm*›
C *v.i.* 1 (shine) strahlen; glänzen; **the sun ~ed down** die Sonne strahlte vom Himmel
2 (smile) strahlen; **~ at sb.** jmdn. anstrahlen

ˈbeam-ends *n. pl.* **the ship is on her ~:** das Schiff liegt auf der Seite; **be on one's ~** (fig.) pleite (ugs.) *od.* in großer Geldnot sein

beaming /ˈbiːmɪŋ/ *adj.* strahlend

bean /biːn/
A *n.* 1 Bohne, *die;* **full of ~s** (fig. coll.) putzmunter (ugs.); quietschlebendig (ugs.); **he hasn't [got] a ~** (fig. coll.) er hat keinen roten Heller (ugs.); **not worth a ~** (coll.) nicht die Bohne *od.* keinen Pfifferling wert (ugs.); *see also* **old A 4**; **spill**[1] **A 2** 2 (Amer. coll.: head) Birne, *die* (fig. salopp)
B *v.t.* (Amer. coll.: hit) **~ sb.** jmdn. eins auf die Birne geben (salopp)

bean: ~bag *n.* 1 *mit Bohnen gefülltes Säckchen zum Spielen;* 2 (cushion) Knautschsessel, *der;* **~burger** *n.* Gemüseburger, *der;* **~ counter** *n.* (derog.) Zahlenverdreher, *der*/-verdreherin, *die* (ugs.); Erbsenzähler, *der*/-zählerin, *die* (ugs.); **~ curd** *n.* Soja[bohnen]quark, *der;* **~ feast** *n.* (Brit. coll.) Gelage, *das*

beanie /ˈbiːnɪ/ *n.* **~ [cap]** Beaniemütze, *die*

beano /ˈbiːnəʊ/ *n., pl.* **~s** (Brit. coll.) Gelage, *das*

bean: ~pole *n.* (lit. or fig.) Bohnenstange, *die;* **~sprout** *n.* Sojabohnenkeim, *der;* **~stalk** *n.* Bohnenstängel, *der;* **~stick** *n.* Bohnenstange, *die*

bear[1] /beə(r)/ *n.* 1 Bär, *der;* **be like a ~ with a sore head** (coll.) ein richtiger Brummbär sein (ugs.) 2 (fig.) Tollpatsch, *der* (ugs.) 3 (Astron.) **Great/Little B~:** Großer/Kleiner Bär 4 (St. Exch.) Baissier, *der*

bear[2]
A *v.t.,* **bore** /bɔː(r)/, **borne** /bɔːn/ 1 (carry) tragen ‹*Waffe, Last*›; mitgebracht haben, mit sich führen ‹*Geschenk, Botschaft*›; **I was borne along by the fierce current** die starke Strömung trug mich mit [sich]; **be borne in upon sb.** jmdm. klar werden; jmdm. zu[m] Bewusstsein kommen
2 (endure, tolerate) ertragen, erdulden ‹*Schmerz, Kummer*›; *with neg.* ertragen, aushalten ‹*Schmerz*›; ausstehen, leiden ‹*Geruch, Lärm*›; **he couldn't ~ the misery** er konnte das Elend nicht ertragen; **I can't ~ watching her eat** ich kann ihr beim Essen einfach nicht zusehen; **I can't ~ salami** ich kann Salami einfach nicht ausstehen
3 (sustain) tragen, aushalten ‹*Gewicht*›; tragen, übernehmen ‹*Verantwortlichkeit, Kosten*›; auf sich (*Akk.*) nehmen ‹*Schuld*›

b

4 (show) tragen ‹*Wappen, Inschrift, Unterschrift*›; aufweisen, zeigen ‹*Merkmal, Spuren, Ähnlichkeit, Verwandtschaft*›; ~ **a resemblance** *or* **likeness to sb.** Ähnlichkeit mit jmdm. haben
5 (be known by) tragen, führen ‹*Namen, Titel*›
6 (be fit for, be able to stand up to) vertragen; **it does not ~ repeating** *or* **repetition** das lässt sich unmöglich wiederholen; (is not important) es lohnt sich nicht, das zu wiederholen; **his language won't ~ repeating** man kann seine [gemeinen] Ausdrücke gar nicht wiederholen; **it will not ~ scrutiny** es hält einer Überprüfung nicht stand; **it does not ~ thinking about** daran darf man gar nicht denken; ~ **comparison with sth.** den *od.* einen Vergleich mit etw. aushalten; einem *od.* dem Vergleich mit etw. standhalten
7 (have in the mind) hegen ‹*Hass, Liebe*›; ~ **sb. a grudge** *or* **a grudge against sb.** jmdm. gegenüber nachtragend sein; ~ **sb. malice** *or* **malice towards sb.** jmdm. grollen; einen Groll auf jmdn. hegen; ~ **sth. in mind** an etw. (*Akk.*) denken; etw. nicht vergessen; ~ **in mind that …:** vergiss nicht, dass …; merk dir, dass …
8 (give birth to) gebären ‹*Kind, Junges*›; *see also* **born**
9 (produce) tragen ‹*Blumen, Früchte usw.*›; bringen, tragen ‹*Zinsen*›; **his efforts bore no result** (fig.) seine Bemühungen hatten *od.* brachten keinen Erfolg; ~ **fruit** (fig.) Früchte tragen (geh.)
10 (bring sth. needed) leisten ‹*Hilfe*›; ~ **witness** *or* **testimony to sth.** von etw. zeugen *od.* Zeugnis ablegen; ~ **sb. company** jmdm. Gesellschaft leisten; ~ **a hand** helfen; ~ **a hand in an undertaking** bei einem Vorhaben helfen
11 ~ **oneself well/with dignity** (behave) sich gut betragen *od.* benehmen/Würde zeigen

B *v.i.*, **bore, borne** **1** **the path ~s [to the] left** der Weg führt [nach] links; **he bore right** er hielt sich [nach] rechts
2 **bring to ~:** aufbieten ‹*Kraft, Energie*›; ausüben ‹*Druck*›; **bring one's influence to ~:** seinen Einfluss geltend machen

Phrasal verbs
- ~ **a'way** *v.t.* wegtragen; davontragen ‹*Preis usw.*›; **be borne away** fort- *od.* davongetragen werden
- ~ **'down**

A *v.t.* niederdrücken; überwältigen ‹*Feind*›; **be borne down by the weight of …:** von der Last (+ *Gen.*) gebeugt sein
B *v.i.* ~ **down on sb./sth.** auf jmdn./etw. zusteuern; sich jmdm./einer Sache schnell nähern; ‹*Schiff:*› auf jmdn./etw. zu- *od.* lossegeln; ‹*Wagen:*› auf jmdn./etw. zufahren *od.* -steuern
- ~ **'off** ▸ ~ **away**
- ~ **on** ▸ ~ **upon**
- ~ **'out** *v.t.* **1** hinaustragen **2** (fig.) bestätigen ‹*Bericht, Erklärung*›; ~ **sb. out** jmdm. Recht geben; ~ **sb. out in sth.** jmdn. in etw. (*Dat.*) bestätigen
- ~ **'up**

A *v.t.* halten; [unter]stützen
B *v.i.* **1** durchhalten; ausharren (geh.); ~ **up well under sth.** etw. gut ertragen **2** (Naut.) abfallen
- ~ **upon** *v.t.* (relate to) sich beziehen auf (+ *Akk.*); Bezug haben auf (+ *Akk.*); im Zusammenhang stehen mit
- ~ **with** *v.t.* ~ **with sb./sth.** mit jmdm./etw. Nachsicht haben; ~ **with sth. for the time being** etw. vorübergehend auf sich (*Akk.*) nehmen; **if you'll ~ with me a little longer** wenn Sie sich vielleicht noch einen Moment gedulden wollen

bearable /ˈbeərəbl/ *adj.* zum Aushalten *nachgestellt*; erträglich ‹*Situation, Beruf*›

bear: ~-baiting *n., no pl.* (Hist.) Bärenhatz, *die;* **~ cub** *n.* Bärenjunge, *das*

beard /bɪəd/
A *n.* **1** Bart, *der;* **full ~:** Vollbart, *der;* **small pointed ~:** Spitzbart, *der* **2** (Bot.) Grannen
B *v.t.* trotzen (+ *Dat.*); Trotz bieten (+ *Dat.*); ~ **the lion in his den** (fig.) sich in die Höhle des Löwen wagen

bearded /ˈbɪədɪd/ *adj.* bärtig; **be ~:** einen Bart haben; **a ~ gentleman** ein Herr mit Bart

bearer /ˈbeərə(r)/ *n.* **1** (carrier) Träger, *der*/Trägerin, *die;* (of letter, message, cheque, banknote) Überbringer, *der*/Überbringerin, *die;* **cheque to ~:** Inhaberscheck, *der;* **payable to ~:** zahlbar an Überbringer *od.* Inhaber ‹*Scheck*›; **I am the ~ of glad tidings** ich bringe euch eine frohe Botschaft **2** **the ~ of shares/bonds** der Aktionär/Obligationär; *attrib.* ~ **share/bond** Inhaberaktie/Inhaberschuldverschreibung, *die*

bear: ~ garden *n.* (fig.) Tollhaus, *das* (fig.); **~ hug** *n.* kräftige Umarmung

bearing /ˈbeərɪŋ/ *n.* **1** (behaviour) Verhalten, *das;* Gebaren, *das* (geh.); (deportment) [Körper]haltung, *die* **2** (endurance) Ertragen, *das;* Erdulden, *das;* **beyond** *or* **past [all] ~:** unerträglich; nicht zum Aushalten **3** (relation) Zusammenhang, *der;* Bezug, *der;* **consider sth. in all its ~s** etw. in seiner ganzen Tragweite betrachten; **have some/no ~ on sth.** relevant/irrelevant *od.* von Belang/belanglos für etw. sein **4** (significance) Bedeutung, *die;* [tieferer] Sinn; **the ~ of a remark** die Bedeutung *od.* der Sinn einer Bemerkung **5** (Mech. Engin.) Lager, *das* **6** (compass ~) Lage, *die;* Position, *die;* **take a compass ~:** den Kompasskurs feststellen; **get one's ~s** sich orientieren; (fig.) sich zurechtfinden; **I have lost my ~s** (lit. or fig.) ich habe die Orientierung verloren

bearish /ˈbeərɪʃ/ *adj.* **1** brummig; unfreundlich **2** (St. Exch.) baissierend; auf Baisse spekulierend ‹*Kapitalanleger*›

bear: ~ market *n.* (St. Exch.) Markt mit fallenden Preisen; Baissemarkt, *der;* **~skin** *n.* **1** Bärenfell, *das;* Bärenhaut, *die;* **2** (Mil.) Bärenfellmütze, *die*

beast /biːst/ *n.* Tier, *das;* (quadruped) Vierbeiner, *der;* (ferocious, wild) Bestie, *die;* (fig.: brutal person) roher, brutaler Mensch; Bestie, *die* (abwertend); (disliked person) Scheusal, *das* (abwertend); **it was a ~ of a winter** das war ein scheußlicher Winter; **man and ~:** Mensch und Tier

beastliness /ˈbiːstlɪnɪs/ *n., no pl.* (coll.) Scheußlichkeit, *die*

beastly /ˈbiːstlɪ/ *adj., adv.* (coll.) scheußlich; (unkind, malicious) gemein

beat /biːt/
A *v.t.*, **~, beaten** /ˈbiːtn/ **1** (strike repeatedly) schlagen ‹*Trommel, Rhythmus, Eier, Teig*›; klopfen ‹*Teppich*›; hämmern ‹*Gold, Silber usw.*›; ~ **the dust out of a carpet/cushion** einen Teppich/ein Polster ausklopfen; ~ **a path through sth.** sich (*Dat.*) einen Weg durch etw. bahnen; ~ **one's breast** (lit. or fig.) sich (*Dat.*) an die Brust schlagen; ~ **its chest** ‹*Affe:*› sich (*Dat.*) gegen die Brust trommeln; ~ **some sense into sb.** jmdm. Vernunft einprügeln; ~ **the bounds** (Brit.) die Grenzen der Gemarkung abgehen; ~ **one's brains** sich (*Dat.*) den Kopf zerbrechen; ~ **it** (coll.) sich verdrücken (ugs.); ~ **it!** (coll.) hau ab! (ugs.); verschwinde! **2** (hit) schlagen; [ver]prügeln; **be ~en to death** totgeschlagen *od.* -geprügelt werden **3** (defeat) schlagen ‹*Mannschaft, Gegner*›; (surmount) in den Griff bekommen ‹*Inflation, Arbeitslosigkeit, Krise*›; ~ **the deadline** den Termin noch einhalten **4** (surpass) brechen ‹*Rekord*›; übertreffen ‹*Leistung*›; **hard to ~:** schwer zu schlagen; **you can't ~** *or* **nothing ~s French cuisine** es geht [doch] nichts über die französische Küche; ~ **that!** das soll mal einer nachmachen!; ~ **everything** (coll.), ~ **the band** (Amer. coll.) alles in den Schatten stellen; ~ **sb. to it** jmdm. zuvorkommen; **can you ~ it?** ist denn das zu fassen? **5** (circumvent) umgehen; ~ **the system** sich gegen das bestehende System durchsetzen **6** (perplex) **it ~s me how/why …:** es ist mir ein Rätsel, wie/warum … **7** ~ **time** den Takt schlagen **8** *p.p.* **~: I'm ~** (coll.: exhausted) ich bin geschafft (ugs.) *od.* erledigt (ugs.). *See also* **beaten B**
B *v.i.*, **~, beaten** **1** (throb) ‹*Herz:*› schlagen, klopfen; ‹*Puls:*› schlagen; **my heart seemed to stop ~ing** ich dachte, mir bleibt das Herz stehen **2** ‹*Sonne:*› brennen (**on** auf + *Akk.*); ‹*Wind, Wellen:*› schlagen (**on** auf + *Akk.*, **against** gegen); ‹*Regen, Hagel:*› prasseln, trommeln (**against** gegen) **3** ~ **about the bush** um den [heißen] Brei herumreden (ugs.) **4** (knock) klopfen, pochen (**at** an + *Dat.*) **5** (Naut.) kreuzen
C *n.* **1** (stroke, throbbing) Schlag, *der;* Schlagen, *das;* (rhythm) Takt, *der;* **his heart missed a ~:** ihm stockte das Herz; ~ **[music]** Beat, *der;* Beatmusik, *die* **2** (Mus.) Schlag, *der;* (of metronome, baton) Taktschlag, *der* **3** (Phys.) Schwebung, *die* **4** (of policeman, watchman) Runde, *die;* (habitual round) übliche Runde; (area) Revier, *das;* **be off sb.'s [usual] ~** (fig.) nicht in jmds. Fach schlagen **5** **did you ever see the ~ of that?** (Amer. coll.) hast du so etwas schon mal gesehen? **6** (Amer. Journ.: scoop) Knüller, *der* (ugs.)

Phrasal verbs
- ~ **a'bout** *v.i.* [herum]suchen
- ~ **'back** *v.t.* zurückschlagen ‹*Feind*›
- ~ **'down**

A *v.i.* ‹*Sonne:*› herniederbrennen; ‹*Regen:*› niederprasseln
B *v.t.* **1** einschlagen ‹*Tür*› **2** (in bargaining) herunterhandeln
- ~ **'in** *v.t.* einschlagen; demolieren (ugs.)
- ~ **'off** *v.t.* abwehren, zurückschlagen ‹*Angriff*›
- ~ **'out** *v.t.* heraushämmern ‹*Rhythmus, Melodie*›; aushämmern ‹*Metall*›; ausschlagen ‹*Feuer*›
- ~ **'up** *v.t.* **1** zusammenschlagen ‹*Person*›; schlagen ‹*Sahne usw.*› **2** (attract) anwerben ‹*Rekruten*›

beaten /ˈbiːtn/
A ▸ **beat A, B**
B *adj.* **1** **a ~ track** *or* **path** ein Trampelpfad; **off the ~ track** (remote) weit abgelegen; weitab vom Schuss (ugs.); **he has always kept to the ~ track** (fig.) er ist immer in den gewohnten Bahnen geblieben; **go off the ~ track** (fig.) vom üblichen Weg abweichen **2** (hammered) gehämmert ‹*Silber, Gold*› **3** (exhausted, dejected) erschöpft, (ugs.) erledigt ‹*Person*›

beater /ˈbiːtə(r)/ *n.* **1** (Cookery) Rührbesen, *der* **2** (Hunting) Treiber, *der* **3** (carpet ~) [Teppich]klopfer, *der*

beatific /biːəˈtɪfɪk/ *adj.* beglückend; (blissful) beglückt, selig ‹*Lächeln*›

beatification /bɪætɪfɪˈkeɪʃn/ *n.* (Relig.) Seligsprechung, *die;* Beatifikation, *die*

beatify /bɪˈætɪfaɪ/ *v.t.* (Relig.) selig sprechen; beatifizieren

beating /ˈbiːtɪŋ/ *n.* **1** (punishment) **a ~:** Schläge *Pl.;* Prügel *Pl.;* **a good ~:** eine gehörige Tracht Prügel (ugs.) **2** (defeat) Niederlage, *die;* **give sb. a good ~:** jmdm. eine schwere Niederlage zufügen; **take** *or* **get a [sound] ~:** eine [schwere] Niederlage hinnehmen [müssen] **3** (surpassing) **take some/a lot of ~:** nicht leicht zu übertreffen sein/seinesgleichen suchen

beatitude /bɪˈætɪtjuːd/ *n.* **1** (blessedness) [Glück]seligkeit, *die* **2** *in pl.* Seligpreisungen

beatnik /ˈbiːtnɪk/ *n.* Beatnik, *der*

'beat-up *adj.* (coll.) ramponiert (ugs.)

beau /bəʊ/ *n., pl.* **~x** /bəʊz/ *or* **~s** (dated) **1** (boyfriend) Galan, *der* (veralt.); Verehrer, *der* **2** (fop) Beau, *der* (geh.); Dandy, *der* (geh.)

Beaufort scale /ˈbəʊfət skeɪl/ *n.* (Meteorol.) Beaufortskala, *die*

Beaujolais /ˈbəʊʒəleɪ/ *n.* Beaujolais, *der*

beaut /bjuːt/ (Austral., NZ, & Amer. sl.)
A *n.* Prachtexemplar, *das;* (woman) Schönheit, *die*
B *adj.* klasse (ugs.)

beauteous /ˈbjuːtɪəs/ *adj.* (poet.) wunderschön; herrlich

beautician /bjuːˈtɪʃn/ *n.* ▸ℹ **p. 1260** Kosmetiker, *der*/Kosmetikerin, *die*

beautification /bjuːtɪfɪˈkeɪʃn/ *n.* Verschönerung, *die;* (of the body) Schönheitspflege, *die*

beautiful /ˈbjuːtɪfl/ *adj.* [ausgesprochen] schön; wunderschön ‹*Augen, Aussicht, Blume, Kleid, Morgen, Musik, Schmuck*›; (enjoyable, impressive) großartig; **the B~ People** die Hippies; **small is ~:** klein ist schön

beautifully /ˈbjuːtɪfəlɪ/ *adv.* wunderbar; (coll.: very well) prima (ugs.); (coll.: very) wunderbar, schön ‹*weich, warm*›; **you did [that] ~:** du hast es prima gemacht

beautify /ˈbjuːtɪfaɪ/ *v.t.* verschönern; schöner machen; (adorn) [aus]schmücken; ~ **oneself** sich schönmachen (ugs.)

beauty /ˈbjuːtɪ/ *n.* **1** *no pl.* Schönheit, *die;* (of action, response) Eleganz, *die;* (of idea, simplicity, sacrifice) Größe, *die;* **~ is only skin deep** man kann nicht nach dem Äußeren urteilen; **be a thing of ~:** wunderschön sein **2** (person or thing) Schönheit, *die;* (animal) wunderschönes Tier; **she is a real ~:** sie ist wirklich eine Schönheit; **B~ and the Beast** die Schöne und das Tier; **They've just bought a new car. It's a ~:** Sie haben sich (*Dat.*) gerade einen neuen Wagen gekauft. Er ist wunderbar **3** (exceptionally good specimen) Prachtexemplar, *das;* **that last goal was a ~:** dieses letzte Tor war ein richtiges Bilderbuchtor **4** (beautiful feature) Schöne, *das;* **her eyes are her great ~:** das Schöne an ihr sind ihre Augen; **the ~ of it/of living in California** das Schöne *od.* Gute daran/am Leben in Kalifornien

beauty: ~ competition, ~ contest *ns.* Schönheitswettbewerb, *der;* **~ cream** *n.* Schönheitscreme, *die;* **~ parlour ▸ ~ salon; ~ queen** *n.* Schönheitskönigin, *die;* **~ salon** *n.* Schönheitssalon, *der;* Kosmetiksalon, *der;* **~ spot** *n.* Schönheitsfleck, *der;* (patch) Schönheitspflästerchen, *das;* (place) schönes Fleckchen [Erde]; **a local ~ spot** ein Ausflugsziel am Ort; **~ treatment** *n.* Schönheitsbehandlung, *die*

beaux *pl. of* **beau**

beaver /ˈbiːvə(r)/

A *n.* **1** *pl. same or* **~s** Biber, *der;* Biberratte, *die;* **eager ~** (fig. coll.) Übereifrige, *der/die;* (esp. at school) Streber, *der*/Streberin, *die* **2** (fur) Biber[pelz], *der*

B *v.i.* (Brit.) **~ away** schuften (ugs.); eifrig arbeiten (**at** an + *Dat.*)

beaver: ~board ® *n., no pl.* (Amer.) Hartfaserplatte, *die;* **~ lamb** *n.* Biberlamm, *das*

becalmed /bɪˈkɑːmd/ *adj.* **be ~:** in einer Flaute *od.* Windstille treiben

became ▸ become

because /bɪˈkɒz/

A *conj.* weil; **one of the reasons why she stopped is ~ she was tired** einer der Gründe, warum sie aufhörte, ist, dass sie müde war; **he is popular ~ handsome** er ist beliebt, weil er gut aussieht; **that is ~ you don't know German** das liegt daran, dass du kein Deutsch kannst

B *adv.* **~ of** wegen (+ *Gen.*); **don't come just ~ of me** nur meinetwegen brauchen Sie nicht zu kommen; **~ of which he ...:** weswegen er ...

beck[1] /bek/ *n.* (dial.: brook) [Wild]bach, *der*

beck[2] *n.* **be at sb.'s ~ and call** jmdm. zur Verfügung stehen; **have sb. at one's ~ and call** jmdn. zur Verfügung haben; ganz über jmdn. verfügen können

beckon /ˈbekn/

A *v.t.* **1** winken; **~ sb. in/over** jmdn. herein-/herbei- *od.* herüberwinken **2** (fig.: invite) locken; rufen

B *v.i.* **1** **~ to sb.** jmdm. winken *od.* ein Zeichen geben; jmdn. zu sich winken **2** (fig.: be inviting) locken

become /bɪˈkʌm/

A *copula, forms as* **come** werden; **~ a politician/dentist** Politiker/Zahnarzt werden; **~ a hazard/nuisance/rule** zu einem Risiko/zu einer Plage/zur Regel werden; **~ popular/angry** beliebt/böse werden; **~ accustomed** *or* **used to sb./sth.** sich an jmdn./etw. gewöhnen

B *v.i., forms as* **come** werden; **what has ~ of him?** was ist aus ihm geworden?; **what is to ~ of you?** was soll bloß aus dir werden?

C *v.t., forms as* **come** **1** ▸ **befit** **2** (suit) **~ sb.** jmdm. stehen; zu jmdm. passen

becoming /bɪˈkʌmɪŋ/ *adj.* **1** (fitting) schicklich (geh.); geziemend (geh.); **it is not ~ for a young lady to ...:** es ziemt sich für eine junge Dame nicht, zu ... **2** (flattering) vorteilhaft, kleidsam ‹*Hut, Kleid, Frisur*›

becquerel /ˈbekərel/ *n.* (Phys.) Becquerel, *das*

bed /bed/

A *n.* **1** Bett, *das;* (without bedstead) Lager, *das;* **they talked together till ~** (coll.) sie unterhielten sich, bis sie ins Bett gingen; **he's very fond of his ~:** er liegt gerne im Bett; **be/lie in ~:** im Bett sein/liegen; **~ and board** (lodging) Unterkunft und Verpflegung; (marital relations) Tisch und Bett; **~ and breakfast** Zimmer mit Frühstück; **a ~ and breakfast place** eine Frühstückspension; **get into/out of ~:** ins *od.* zu Bett gehen/aufstehen; **go to ~:** zu *od.* ins Bett gehen; **go to ~ with sb.** (fig.) mit jmdm. ins Bett gehen (ugs.); **make the ~:** das Bett machen; **put sb. to ~:** jmdn. zu *od.* ins Bett bringen; **put a [news]paper to ~** (fig.) eine Zeitung in Druck geben; **life isn't a** *or* **is no ~ of roses** (fig.) das Leben ist kein reines Vergnügen; **his life isn't exactly a ~ of roses** (fig.) er ist nicht gerade auf Rosen gebettet; **~ of sickness** (literary) Krankenlager, *das* (geh.); **have got out of ~ on the wrong side** (fig.) mit dem linken Fuß zuerst aufgestanden sein; **as you make your ~ so you must lie on it** (prov.) wie man sich bettet, so liegt man; **take to one's ~:** sich krank ins Bett legen; **be confined to ~:** ans Bett gefesselt sein (fig.) **2** (flat base) Unterlage, *die;* (of machine) Bett, *das;* (of road, railway, etc.) Unterbau, *der;* Kies-/Schotterbett, *das;* (of billiard table) Schieferplatte (*die mit grünem Kammgarntuch bespannt ist*) **3** (in garden) Beet, *das* **4** (of sea, lake) Grund, *der;* Boden, *der;* (of river) Bett, *das* **5** (layer) Schicht, *die* **6** (of oysters etc.) Bank, *die*

B *v.t.,* **-dd-** **1** (plant) setzen ‹*Pflanze, Sämling*› **2** (coll.: have sex with) beschlafen ‹*Frau*›

Phrasal verbs

- **~ ˈdown**

A *v.t.* mit Streu versorgen ‹*Pferd usw.*›; **the troops were ~ded down in a barn** die Soldaten wurden über Nacht in einer Scheune einquartiert

B *v.i.* kampieren

- **~ ˈin** *v.t.* einlassen
- **~ ˈout** *v.t.* auspflanzen ‹*Pflanzen*›

BEd /biː ˈed/ *abbr.* **= Bachelor of Education** Bakkalaureus der Erziehungswissenschaften; *see also* **BSc**

> **bed and breakfast**
>
> Überall in Großbritannien sieht man Schilder mit der Aufschrift *Bed & Breakfast* oder *B&B*. Sie weisen auf Privathäuser hin, die Unterkunft zu meist recht niedrigen Preisen anbieten, wobei im Zimmerpreis das Frühstück mit eingeschlossen ist. Die Gäste erhalten normalerweise ein üppiges traditionelles Frühstück mit Fruchtsaft, Müsli, warmem Essen – dazu gehört vor allem *bacon and eggs* (Spiegelei mit Speck) – und Toast und Marmelade.

bedazzle /bɪˈdæzl/ *v.t.* **1** blenden **2** (confuse) verwirren

bed: ~bug *n.* [Bett]wanze, *die;* **~chamber** *n.* **1** (arch.) Schlafgemach, *das* (veralt.); Schlafzimmer, *das;* **2** **the Royal Bedchamber** das königliche Schlafgemach; **Lady/Gentleman of the Bedchamber** königliche Hofdame/königlicher Kammerjunker; **~clothes** *n. pl.* Bettzeug, *das;* **turn down** *or* **back the ~clothes** das Bett aufdecken

beddable /ˈbedəbl/ *adj.* (coll.) **be ~:** was fürs Bett sein (ugs.)

bedding /ˈbedɪŋ/ *n., no pl., no indef. art.* **1** Matratze und Bettzeug; (for animal) Streu, *das* **2** (Geol.) Lagerung, *die;* Schichtung, *die*

ˈbedding plant *n.* Freilandpflanze, *die*

beddy-byes /ˈbedɪbaɪz/ *n.* (child lang.) Heiabett, *das* (Kinderspr.); Heia, *die* (Kinderspr.); **off to ~:** ab in die Heia *od.* ins Heiabett

bedeck /bɪˈdek/ *v.t.* schmücken; **~ oneself** sich aufputzen (abwertend); **~ed with flags** mit Fahnen geschmückt; fahnengeschmückt

bedevil /bɪˈdevl/ *v.t.,* (Brit.) **-ll-** **1** (spoil) verderben; durcheinander bringen ‹*System*› **2** (plague, afflict) heimsuchen; **that family is ~led by bad luck** diese Familie ist vom Pech verfolgt **3** (torment) quälen; peinigen (geh.); **~ sb.'s life** jmdm. das Leben zur Hölle machen

bed: ~fellow *n.* Bettgenosse, *der*/-genossin, *die;* **make** *or* **be strange ~fellows** (fig.) ‹*Personen:*› ein merkwürdiges Gespann sein; ‹*Staaten, Organisationen:*› eine eigenartige Kombination sein; **~head** *n.* Kopfende des Bettes; **~jacket** *n.* Bettjacke, *die*

bedlam /ˈbedləm/ *n.* Chaos, *das;* Durcheinander, *das;* **absolute ~:** ein totales Chaos *od.* Durcheinander; **it is [like] ~ in here** hier geht es zu wie im Irrenhaus

ˈbedlinen *n.* Bettwäsche, *die*

bedouin /ˈbeduːɪn/ *n., pl. same* Beduine, *der*/Beduinin, *die*

bed: ~pan *n.* Bettschüssel, *die;* Bettpfanne, *die;* **~plate** *n.* Grundplatte, *die;* Bodenplatte, *die;* **~post** *n.* Bettpfosten, *der*

bedraggled /bɪˈdrægld/ *adj.* [nass und] verschmutzt *od.* schmutzig

bed: ~ rest *n.* Bettruhe, *die;* **~ridden** *adj.* bettlägerig; **~rock** *n.* Felssohle, *die;* (fig.) Basis, *die;* Fundament, *das;* **get** *or* **reach down to ~rock** (fig.) zum Kern der Sache kommen; einer Sache (*Dat.*) auf den Grund gehen; **~ roll** *n.* zusammengerolltes Bettzeug; **~room** *n.* Schlafzimmer, *das; attrib.* **~room comedy/farce** Schlafzimmerkomödie, *die;* **~room scene** Bettszene, *die;* **she has ~room eyes** sie hat einen Schlafzimmerblick (ugs.); **a two-~room[ed] house** ein Haus mit zwei Schlafzimmern; **~room community/town/suburb** Schlafstadt, *die;* **~ setˈtee** *n.* Bettcouch, *die;* **~side** *n.* Seite des Bettes, *die;* **be at the ~side** am Bett sein; **~side table/lamp** Nachttisch, *der*/Nachttischlampe, *die;* **~side reading** Bettlektüre, *die;* **a ~side book** ein Buch als Bettlektüre; **have a good ~side manner** ‹*Arzt:*› gut mit Kranken umgehen können; **~sit, ~ˈsitter** *ns.* (coll.), **~ˈsitting room** *n.* (Brit.) Wohnschlafzimmer, *das;* **~socks** *n. pl.* Bettsocken; **~sore** *n.* wundgelegene Stelle; **get ~sores** sich wundliegen; **~spread** *n.* Tagesdecke, *die;* **~stead** /ˈbedsted/ *n.* Bettgestell, *das;* **~straw** *n.* (Bot.) **[Our Lady's] ~straw** Echtes Labkraut; **~table** *n.* Krankentisch, *der;* **~time** *n.* Schlafenszeit, *die;* **at ~time** vor dem Zubettgehen; **it's past the children's ~time** die Kinder müssten schon im Bett sein; **will you have it finished by ~time?** bist du vor dem Schlafengehen damit fertig?; *attrib.* **a ~time story** eine Gutenachtgeschichte; **a novel that makes good ~time reading** ein Roman, den man gut vor dem Einschlafen lesen kann

beduin ▸ bedouin

ˈbed-wetting *n., no pl.* Bettnässen, *das*

bee /biː/ *n.* **1** Biene, *die;* **she's such a busy ~** (fig.) sie ist so ein fleißiges Mädchen; **as busy as a ~** (fig.) bienenfleißig; **have a ~ in one's bonnet** (fig.) einen Fimmel *od.* Tick haben (ugs.); **she thinks she's the ~'s knees** (fig. coll.) sie hält sich für die Größte (ugs.) **2** (Amer.) (meeting) *nachbarliche Versammlung zu gemeinsamer Arbeit;* (party) Fest, *das; see also* **spelling bee**

Beeb /biːb/ *n.* (Brit. coll.) **the ~:** die BBC

beech /biːtʃ/ *n.* **1** (tree) Buche, *die;* (Austral.) Scheinbuche, *die* **2** (wood) Buche, *die;* Buchenholz, *das; attrib.* buchen

beech: ~-marten *n.* Steinmarder, *der;* **~-mast** *n.* Bucheckern *Pl.;* **~-nut** *n.* [Buch]ecker, *die;* **~wood ▸ beech 2**

ˈbee-eater *n.* (Ornith.) Bienenfresser, *der*

beef /biːf/

A *n.* **1** *no pl.* Rindfleisch, *das;* Rind, *das* **2** *no pl.* (coll.: muscles) Muskeln; **have plenty of ~:** sehr muskulös sein; **there's a great deal of ~ on him** er ist ganz schön mit Muskeln bepackt (ugs.) **3** *usu. in pl.* **beeves** /biːvz/ *or* (Amer.) **~s** (ox) Mastrind, *das* **4** *pl.* **~s** (coll.: complaint) Meckerei, *die* (ugs.)

B *v.t.* **~ up** stärken

C *v.i.* (coll.) meckern (ugs.) (**about** über + *Akk.*)

beef: ~burger *n.* Beefburger, *der;* **~cake** *n.* (coll.) Muskeln *Pl.;* Bizeps, *der* (ugs.); **~ cattle** *n. pl.* Mastrinder; **~eater** *n.* (Brit.) Beefeater, *der;* **~steak** *n.* Beefsteak, *das; attrib.* **~steak fungus** Leberpilz, *der;* **~ ˈtea** *n.* Kraftbrühe, *die;* Fleischbrühe, *die*

beefy /ˈbiːfɪ/ *adj.* **1** (like beef) wie Rindfleisch *nachgestellt;* Rindfleisch- **2** (coll.: muscular) muskulös; (fleshy) massig

bee: ~hive *n.* Bienenstock, *der;* (rounded) Bienenkorb, *der;* (fig.: scene of activity) Taubenschlag,

b

der; (hairstyle) toupierte Hochfrisur; **~-keeper** *n.* ▸❶ **p. 1260** Imker, *der*/Imkerin, *die;* Bienenzüchter, *der*/-züchterin, *die;* **~-keeping** *n., no pl.* ▸❶ **p. 1260** Imkerei, *die;* Bienenhaltung, *die;* Bienenzucht, *die;* **~line** *n.* **make a ~line for sth./sb.** schnurstracks auf etw./jmdn. zustürzen

been ▸ **be**

beep /biːp/
A *n.* Piepton, *der;* (of car horn) Tuten, *das*
B *v.i.* piepen; ‹*Signalhorn:*› hupen; **~ at sb.** jmdn. anhupen; **a ~ing sound** ein Piepton
C *v.t.* (esp. Amer.) ▸ **bleep C**

beeper /ˈbiːpə(r)/ *n.* Piepser, *der*

beer /bɪə(r)/ *n.* Bier, *das;* **order two ~s** zwei Bier bestellen; **brew various ~s** verschiedene Biere *od.* Biersorten brauen; **life is not all ~ and skittles** (fig.) das Leben ist kein reines Vergnügen; **small ~:** Dünnbier, *das* (ugs.); (fig.: trifles) Nebensächlichkeiten *Pl.;* Kleinigkeiten *Pl.;* **that firm's turnover is only small ~:** der Umsatz dieser Firma ist kaum der Rede wert; **he is only small ~:** er hat nichts zu sagen

beer: ~ barrel *n.* Bierfass, *das;* **~ belly** *n.* (coll.) Bierbauch, *der* (ugs.); **~ bottle** *n.* Bierflasche, *die;* **~ can** *n.* Bierdose, *die;* **~ cellar** *n.* Bierkeller, *der;* **~ crate** *n.* Bierkasten, *der;* **~ drinker** *n.* Biertrinker, *der;* **~ engine** *n.* Bierpumpe, *die;* **~ garden** *n.* Biergarten, *der;* **~ glass** *n.* Bierglas, *das;* **~ hall** *n.* Bierhalle, *die;* **~house** *n.* (Brit.) Bierschenke, *die;* Bierstube, *die;* **~ making** *n., no pl.* Brauerei, *die;* **~ mat** *n.* Bierdeckel, *der;* Bieruntersetzer, *der;* **~ money** *n.* Geld für Getränke; **~ mug** *n.* Bierkrug, *der;* **~ pump** ▸ **~ engine;** **~-swilling** *adj.* (coll.) biersaufend (salopp); **~ tent** *n.* Bierzelt, *das*

beery /ˈbɪərɪ/ *adj.* **1** ‹*Person*› mit Bierfahne; **~ taste/smell** Biergeschmack, *der*/Biergeruch, *der* **2** (tipsy) bierselig

beestings /ˈbiːstɪŋz/ *n. pl.* (Agric.) Biestmilch, *die*

beeswax /ˈbiːzwæks/ *n.* Bienenwachs, *das*

beet /biːt/ *n.* Rübe, *die;* **red ~:** rote Bete *od.* Rübe; **white ~:** weiße Rübe; Wasserrübe, *die; attrib.* **~ sugar** Rübenzucker, *der*

beetle¹ /ˈbiːtl/ *n.* (insect) Käfer, *der*

beetle² *n.* (tool) Holzhammer, *der;* (machine) Kalander, *der*

beetle³ *v.i.* **1** ‹*Brauen:*› vorstehen; ‹*Felsen:*› überhängen, vorstehen **2** **~ along/off/past** (coll.) ‹*Mensch:*› entlangpesen/abhauen/vorbeirennen (ugs.); ‹*Auto:*› entlang-/weg-/vorbeibrummen (ugs.)

beetle: ~-browed /biːtlˈbraʊd/ *adj.* finster aussehend; **~ ˈbrows** *n. pl.* buschige [vorstehende] Augenbrauen; **~-crusher** *n.* Quadratlatschen, *der*

ˈbeetroot *n.* rote Beete *od.* Rübe

beeves ▸ **beef A 3**

befall /bɪˈfɔːl/
A *v.i., forms as* **fall B** sich begeben (geh.); geschehen
B *v.t., forms as* **fall B** widerfahren (+ *Dat.*)

befit /bɪˈfɪt/ *v.t.,* **-tt-** (be seemly for) sich ziemen *od.* gebühren für (geh.); **it ill ~s you to do that** es steht Ihnen schlecht an, das zu tun; **she behaved as ~ted a lady** sie benahm sich, wie es sich für eine Dame gebührte

befitting /bɪˈfɪtɪŋ/ *adj.* gebührend (geh.); schicklich ‹*Benehmen*› (geh.)

befog /bɪˈfɒg/ *v.t.,* **-gg-:** **1** (confuse) verwirren; ‹*Drogen, Alkohol:*› benebeln, umnebeln **2** (obscure) verunklaren ‹*Sachverhalt, Thema*›

before /bɪˈfɔː(r)/
A *adv.* **1** (of time) vorher; zuvor; **the day ~:** am Tag zuvor; **long ~:** lange vorher *od.* zuvor; **not long ~:** kurz vorher; **our friendship is less close than ~:** unsere Freundschaft ist nicht mehr so eng wie früher *od.* vorher; **the noise continued as ~:** der Lärm ging nach wie vor weiter; **you should have told me so ~:** das hättest du mir vorher *od.* früher *od.* eher sagen sollen; **I've seen that film ~:** ich habe den Film schon [einmal] gesehen; **I've heard that ~:** das habe ich schon einmal gehört; **I wish I had known that ~:** hätte ich das nur früher gewusst; **I'll give it to you on your birthday and not ~:** ich gebe es dir an deinem Geburtstag und nicht eher **2** (ahead in position) vor[aus] **3** (arch.: in front) voran; **go/ride ~:** voran- *od.* vorausgehen/-reiten
B *prep.* **1** ▸❶ **p. 1047** (of time) vor; **the day ~ yesterday** vorgestern; **the year ~ last** vorletztes Jahr; **the year ~ that** das Jahr davor; **the time ~ that** das vorige Mal; **old/die ~ one's time** frühzeitig gealtert/sterben; **it was [well] ~ my time** das war [lange] vor meiner Zeit; **since ~ the operation/war** schon vor der Operation/dem Krieg; **~ now** vorher; früher; **~ Christ** vor Christus; vor Christi Geburt; **he got there ~ me** er war vor mir da; **~ then** vorher; **~ long** bald; **~ leaving, he phoned/I will phone** bevor er wegging, rief er an/bevor ich weggehe, rufe ich an; **~ tax** brutto; vor [Abzug (*Dat.*) der] Steuern **2** (position) vor (+ *Dat.*); (direction) vor (+ *Akk.*); **~ my very eyes** vor meinen Augen; **go ~ a committee/court of law** vor einen Ausschuss/ein Gericht kommen; **be brought/appear ~ the judge** vor den Richter gebracht werden/vor dem Richter erscheinen **3** (under the action of) vor (+ *Dat.*); **sail ~ the wind** vor dem Wind segeln; *see also* **carry A 1** **4** (awaiting) **have one's future/life ~ one** seine Zukunft/sein Leben noch vor sich (*Dat.*) haben; (confronting) **the matter ~ us** das uns (*Dat.*) vorliegende Thema; die Sache, die uns (*Akk.*) betrifft; **the task ~ us** die Aufgabe, die vor uns (*Dat.*) liegt; **the problem ~ them** das Problem, vor dem sie stehen/standen **5** (ahead of in sequence) vor (+ *Dat.*); **he puts work ~ everything** die Arbeit ist ihm wichtiger als alles andere; **~ all else she is a teacher** in erster Linie ist sie Lehrerin; **~ everything else** (as most important) vor allem; vor allen Dingen; **ladies ~ gentlemen** Damen haben [den] Vortritt **6** (rather than) vor; **death ~ dishonour** lieber tot als ehrlos; **right ~ might** Macht darf nicht vor Recht gehen
C *conj.* **1** bevor; **it'll be ages ~ I finish this** es wird eine Ewigkeit dauern, bis ich damit fertig bin; **shortly/long ~ I met you** kurz/lange bevor ich dich kennen lernte **2** (rather than) bevor; ehe

beforehand /bɪˈfɔːhænd/
A *adv.* vorher; (in anticipation) im Voraus; **I found out about it ~:** ich habe es schon vorher herausgefunden; **whereas five minutes ~ it had been sunny, ...:** während die Sonne vor fünf Minuten noch geschienen hatte, …
B *pred. adj.* **be ~ with** (early) vorzeitig tun; (premature, overhasty) voreilig sein mit

befoul /bɪˈfaʊl/ *v.t.* (formal) **1** verschmutzen ‹*Gebäude*›; verpesten ‹*Luft*› **2** (fig.) beschmutzen ‹*Namen*›; vergiften ‹*Atmosphäre*›

befriend /bɪˈfrend/ *v.t.* **1** (act as a friend to) sich anfreunden mit **2** (help) sich annehmen (+ *Gen.*)

befuddle /bɪˈfʌdl/ *v.t.* **1** (make drunk) benebeln **2** (confuse) verwirren; konfus machen

beg /beg/
A *v.t.,* **-gg-** **1** betteln um; erbetteln ‹*Lebensunterhalt*› **2** (ask earnestly) bitten; **he ~ged her not to go** er bat sie, doch nicht zu gehen; **she ~ged to come with us** sie bat darum, mit uns kommen zu dürfen; **~ that sth. be done** darum bitten, dass etw. getan wird; **I ~ to inform you that ...** (formal) ich erlaube mir, Sie davon in Kenntnis zu setzen, dass … (geh.); **I ~ to differ** da bin ich [aber] anderer Meinung; **~ sb. for sth.** jmdn. um etw. bitten **3** (ask earnestly for) **~ sth.** um etw. bitten; **~ sth. of sb.** etw. von jmdm. erbitten; **~ a favour [of sb.]** [jmdn.] um einen Gefallen bitten; **~ forgiveness** um Verzeihung bitten; **~ leave** *or* **permission to do sth.** um Erlaubnis bitten, etw. tun zu dürfen; *see also* **pardon A 2** **4** **~ the question** (evade difficulty) der Frage (*Dat.*) ausweichen
B *v.i.,* **-gg-** **1** ‹*Bettler:*› betteln (**for** um); ‹*Hund:*› Männchen machen; betteln; **a ~ging letter** ein Bettelbrief; **go ~ging** keinen Abnehmer finden **2** (ask earnestly) bitten (**for** um); **~ of sb. to do sth.** jmdn. [darum] bitten, etw. zu tun; **~ off** sich entschuldigen [lassen]

began ▸ **begin**

begat ▸ **beget**

beget /bɪˈget/ *v.t.,* **begot** /bɪˈgɒt/ *or* (arch.) **begat** /bɪˈgæt/, **begotten** /bɪˈgɒtn/ **1** (arch.: procreate) zeugen; **God's only begotten son** Gottes eingeborener Sohn **2** (literary: cause) zeugen; gebären (geh.)

beggar /ˈbegə(r)/
A *n.* **1** Bettler, *der*/Bettlerin, *die;* **~s can't be choosers** (prov.) man kann es sich (*Dat.*) eben nicht immer aussuchen **2** (coll.: person) Arme, *der/die;* **poor ~:** armer Teufel; **a poor old ~:** ein armer alter Mann; **be a lucky/lazy/cheeky ~:** ein Glückspilz/Faulpelz/frecher Kerl sein (ugs.)
B *v.t.* **1** an den Bettelstab bringen; arm machen **2** **~ description** jeder Beschreibung spotten; **~ belief** nicht zu glauben *od.* zu fassen sein

beggarly /ˈbegəlɪ/ *adj.* erbärmlich; erbarmungswürdig ‹*Person*›; (fig.) erbärmlich; (ungenerous) engherzig ‹*Einstellung*›; armselig ‹*Bezahlung*›

beggary /ˈbegərɪ/ *n., no pl.* [Bettel]armut, *die;* **be reduced to ~:** bettelarm werden

begin /bɪˈgɪn/
A *v.t.,* **-nn-, began** /bɪˈgæn/, **begun** /bɪˈgʌn/ **1** **~ sth.** [mit] etw. beginnen; **~ a new bottle** eine neue Flasche anbrechen; **she began life in a small village** sie verbrachte ihre ersten Lebensjahre in einem kleinen Dorf; **~ school** in die Schule kommen; eingeschult werden; **when do you ~ your retirement?** wann gehen Sie in Pension?; **~ doing** *or* **to do sth.** anfangen *od.* beginnen, etw. zu tun; **I began to slip** ich kam ins Rutschen; **I am ~ning to get annoyed** so langsam werde ich ärgerlich **2** **not ~ to do sth.** (coll.: make no progress towards doing sth.): **the film does not ~ to compare with the book** der Film lässt sich nicht annähernd mit dem Buch vergleichen; **she didn't even ~ to grasp it** sie hat es nicht einmal ansatzweise verstanden; **the authorities couldn't even ~ to assess the damage** die Behörden konnten den Schaden nicht einmal grob abschätzen
B *v.i.* **-nn-, began, begun** anfangen; beginnen (oft geh.); **when the world began** als die Erde entstand; **~ning student** (Amer.) Anfänger, *der*/Anfängerin, *die;* **~ning next month** vom nächsten Monat an; **~ at the beginning** von vorne anfangen; **~ [up]on sth.** etw. anfangen; **~ with sth./sb.** bei *od.* mit etw./jmdm. anfangen *od.* beginnen; **to ~ with** zunächst *od.* zuerst einmal; **it is the wrong book, to ~ with** das ist schon einmal das falsche Buch

beginner /bɪˈgɪnə(r)/ *n.* Anfänger, *der*/Anfängerin, *die;* **~'s luck** Anfängerglück, *das*

beginning /bɪˈgɪnɪŋ/ *n.* ▸❶ **p. 1047** Anfang, *der;* Beginn, *der;* **at** *or* **in the ~:** am Anfang; **at the ~ of February/the month** Anfang Februar/des Monats; **myths about the ~ of the world** Mythen über die Entstehung der Welt; **at the ~ of the day** zu Beginn des Tages; **from ~ to end** von Anfang bis Ende; von vorn bis hinten; **from the [very] ~:** [ganz] von Anfang an; **have its ~s in sth.** seine Anfänge *od.* seinen Ursprung in etw. (*Dat.*) haben; **small ~s** kleine Anfänge; **[this is] the ~ of the end** [das ist] der Anfang vom Ende; **go back to the ~:** wieder von vorne anfangen; **make a ~ with sth.** mit etw. anfangen

begone /bɪˈgɒn, bɪˈgɔːn/ *v.i. in imper. and inf. only* (arch.) **~!** fort!; hinweg! (veralt.); **tell sb. to ~:** jmdm. sagen, dass er sich fortmachen solle

begonia /bɪˈgəʊnɪə/ *n.* (Bot.) Begonie, *die;* Schiefblatt, *das*

begorra /bɪˈgɒrə/ *int.* (Ir.) Jesses

begot, begotten ▸ **beget**

begrudge /bɪˈgrʌdʒ/ *v.t.* **1** (envy) **~ sb. sth.** jmdm. etw. missgönnen; **I don't ~ their buying a car** ich gönne ihnen, dass sie sich (*Dat.*) ein Auto kaufen **2** (give reluctantly) **I ~ the time/money I have to spend** es tut mir leid um die Zeit/das Geld **3** (be dissatisfied with) **~ doing sth.** etw. ungern tun; **he did not ~ the fact that ...:** er war nicht darüber verärgert, dass …

b

beguile /bɪˈgaɪl/ *v.t.* **1** (delude) betören; verführen; ~ **sb. into doing sth.** jmdn. dazu verführen, etw. zu tun; **be ~d by sb./sth.** sich von jmdm./etw. täuschen lassen **2** (cheat) betrügen; ~ **sb. [out] of sth.** jmdn. um etw. betrügen; ~ **sb. into doing sth.** jmdn. verleiten, etw. zu tun **3** (charm) bezaubern **4** (literary: help pass pleasantly) sich (*Dat.*) [angenehm] vertreiben ‹*Zeit*›

beguiling /bɪˈgaɪlɪŋ/ *adj.* verführerisch; betörend ‹*Einfluss*›; verlockend ‹*Zeitvertreib*›

begun ▸ **begin**

behalf /bɪˈhɑːf/ *n., pl.* **behalves** /bɪˈhɑːvz/: **on** *or* (Amer.) **in ~ of sb./sth.** (as representing sb./sth.) für jmdn./etw.; (more formally) im Namen von jmdm./etw.; **on** *or* (Amer.) **in sb.'s/my ~** (for sb.'s/my benefit) zugunsten von jmdm./zu meinen Gunsten; **don't fret on my ~:** mach dir meinetwegen keine Sorgen

behave /bɪˈheɪv/

A *v.i.* **1** sich verhalten; sich benehmen; **how do you ~ under stress?** wie verhältst du dich bei Stress?; **he ~s more like a friend to them** er behandelt sie mehr wie Freunde; **~ well/badly** sich gut/schlecht benehmen *od.* betragen; **~ well/badly towards sb.** jmdn. gut/schlecht behandeln; **my car hasn't been behaving too well of late** mein Auto hat mir in letzter Zeit ziemlich viel Ärger gemacht; **well/badly/nicely ~d** brav/ungezogen/lieb (ugs.) **2** (do what is correct) brav sein; sich benehmen; sich betragen

B *v. refl.* **~ oneself** sich benehmen; **~ yourself!** benimm dich!

behavior *etc.* (*Amer.*) ▸ **behaviour** *etc.*

behaviour /bɪˈheɪvjə(r)/ *n.* **1** Verhalten, *das* (**towards** gegenüber); Benehmen, *das* (**towards** gegenüber); (of child) Betragen, *das;* **be on one's good/best ~:** sein bestes Benehmen an den Tag legen; **put sb. on his/her best ~:** jmdm. raten, sich gut zu benehmen; **his ~ towards her** sein Verhalten ihr gegenüber **2** (of ship) Seeverhalten, *das;* (of machine) Eigenschaften *Pl.;* (of substance) Verhalten, *das* **3** (Psych.) Verhalten, *das; attrib.* **~ therapy** Verhaltenstherapie, *die*

behavioural /bɪˈheɪvjərl/ *adj.* Verhaltens-; **~ similarities** Ähnlichkeiten im Verhalten

behavioural 'science *n.* Verhaltensforschung, *die*

behaviourism /bɪˈheɪvjərɪzm/ *n., no pl.* (Psych.) Behaviorismus, *der*

behaviourist /bɪˈheɪvjərɪst/ *n.* (Psych.) Behaviorist, *der*/Behavioristin, *die*

behead /bɪˈhed/ *v.t.* enthaupten, köpfen ‹*Person*›

beheld ▸ **behold**

behest /bɪˈhest/ *n., no pl.* (literary) **at sb.'s ~:** auf jmds. Geheiß (*Akk.*)

behind /bɪˈhaɪnd/

A *adv.* **1** (at rear of sb./sth.) hinten; **from ~:** von hinten; **be ~:** dahinter sein; **the person ~:** der Hintermann; **come from ~:** von hinten kommen; (fig.) aufholen; **he glanced ~ before moving off** er schaute nach hinten, bevor er losfuhr; **you go ahead and we'll follow on ~:** geh du vor, und wir kommen hinterher; **the church tower and the mountain ~:** der Kirchturm und der Berg dahinter **2** (further back) **[be] miles ~:** kilometerweit [zurückliegen]; **[be] years/weeks ~:** Jahre/Wochen im Rückstand *od.* Verzug [sein]; **leave sb. ~:** jmdn. zurücklassen; (move faster) jmdn. hinter sich (*Dat.*) lassen; **fall ~:** zurückbleiben; (fig.) in Rückstand geraten; **lag ~:** zurückbleiben; (fig.) im Rückstand sein; **be ~:** hinten sein; (be late) im Verzug sein **3** (in arrears) **be/get ~ with one's payments/rent** mit seinen Zahlungen/der Miete *usw.* im Rückstand *od.* Verzug sein/in Rückstand *od.* Verzug geraten **4** (remaining after one's departure) **leave sth. ~:** etw. zurücklassen; **he left his gloves ~ by mistake** er ließ seine Handschuhe versehentlich liegen; er vergaß seine Handschuhe; **stay ~:** dableiben; (as punishment) nachsitzen

B *prep.* **1** (at rear of, on other side of; fig.: hidden by) hinter (+ *Dat.*); **he stepped out from ~ the wall** er trat hinter der Mauer hervor; **he came from ~ her/a bush** er kam von hinten/er kam hinter einem Busch hervor; **one ~ the other** hintereinander; **the person ~ him** sein Hintermann; **~ sb.'s back** (fig.) hinter jmds. Rücken (*Dat.*); **what was ~ his words?** was verbirgt sich hinter seinen Worten? **2** (towards rear of) hinter (+ *Akk.*); **I don't want to go ~ his back** ich will nicht hinter seinem Rücken handeln; **put ~ one** vergessen; **put the past ~ one** einen Strich unter die Vergangenheit ziehen; **look ~ the facade** (fig.) hinter die Fassade blicken **3** (further back than) hinter (+ *Dat.*); **they were miles ~ us** sie lagen meilenweit hinter uns (*Dat.*) zurück; **be ~ the times** nicht auf dem Laufenden sein; **fall ~ sb./sth.** hinter jmdm./etw. zurückfallen; **lag ~ sb./sth.** hinter jmdm./etw. bleiben **4** (past) hinter (+ *Dat.*); **my youth is now ~ me** meine Jugend liegt jetzt hinter mir; **all that trouble is ~ me** ich habe den ganzen Ärger hinter mir **5** (later than) **be/run ~ schedule** im Rückstand *od.* Verzug sein; **~ time** im Rückstand *od.* Verzug **6** (in support of) hinter (+ *Dat.*); **I'm right ~ you in all you do** ich stehe hinter dir in allem, was du tust; **the man ~ the project** der Mann, der hinter dem Projekt steht; **he has a lot of money ~ him** er verfügt über viel Geld **7** (in the tracks of) hinter (+ *Dat.*); **he followed ~ her on his bike** er fuhr ihr mit dem Fahrrad hinterher **8** (remaining after departure of) **she left nothing ~ her but an old photograph** sie hinterließ nichts als eine alte Fotografie

C *n.* (buttocks) Hintern, *der* (ugs.); Hinterteil, *das* (ugs.)

behindhand /bɪˈhaɪndhænd/ *pred. adj.* **1** **be/get ~ with one's payments/rent** mit seinen Zahlungen/der Miete im Rückstand *od.* Verzug sein/in Rückstand *od.* Verzug geraten; **I am getting ~ in my work** ich komme mit meiner Arbeit in Verzug; **the farmers are ~ with their harvesting** die Bauern sind mit der Ernte zurück *od.* im Rückstand **2** (arch.: unaware of recent events, behind the times) zurück; **she is about twenty years ~ in her style of dress/taste in music** sie hinkt der Mode/dem Musikgeschmack etwa zwanzig Jahre hinterher

behold /bɪˈhəʊld/ *v.t.*, **beheld** /bɪˈheld/ (arch./literary) **1** erblicken (geh.) **2** *in imper.* siehe/sehet!

beholden /bɪˈhəʊldn/ *pred. adj.* **be ~ to sb. [for sth.]** jmdm. [für etw.] verpflichtet *od.* verbunden sein

beholder /bɪˈhəʊldə(r)/ *n.* (arch./literary) Betrachter, *der;* Beschauer, *der;* **beauty is in the eye of the ~:** schön ist, was gefällt

behove /bɪˈhəʊv/ *v.t. impers.* (arch./literary) **it ~s sb. to do sth.** es [ge]ziemt *od.* schickt sich für jmdn., etw. zu tun (geh.); **it ill ~s sb. to do sth.** es steht jmdm. schlecht an, etw. zu tun (geh.)

beige /beɪʒ/

A *n.* Beige, *das*

B *adj.* beige

being /ˈbiːɪŋ/

A *pres. part. of* **be**

B *n.* **1** *no pl., no art.* (existence) Dasein, *das;* Leben, *das;* Existenz, *die;* **in ~:** bestehend; **bring sth. into ~:** etw. einführen; **call into ~:** ins Leben rufen; **come into ~:** entstehen; **when the new system comes into ~:** wenn das neue System eingeführt wird **2** (living creature or entity) Wesen, *das;* Geschöpf, *das;* **the Supreme B~:** das höchste Wesen **3** (nature, essence) Sein, *das;* **my very ~ cried out in protest** mein Innerstes schrie aus Protest auf

bejewelled (*Amer.:* **bejeweled**) /bɪˈdʒuːəld/ *adj.* mit Edelsteinen geschmückt; juwelengeschmückt

belabour (*Brit.; Amer.:* **belabor**) /bɪˈleɪbə(r)/ *v.t.* **1** (beat) einschlagen auf (+ *Akk.*); (fig.) überhäufen **2** ▸ **labour C**

belated /bɪˈleɪtɪd/ *adj.* verspätet

belatedly /bɪˈleɪtɪdlɪ/ *adv.* verspätet; nachträglich

belay /bɪˈleɪ, *Mount. also* ˈbiːleɪ/

A *v.t.* belegen ‹*Tau, Seil*›; (Mount.) anseilen; **~ing pin** (Naut.) Belegklampe, *die*

B *n.* (Mount.) Selbstsicherung, *die;* (rock) Felskopf, *der*

bel canto /bel ˈkæntəʊ/ *n.* (Mus.) Belcanto, Belkanto, *der*

belch /beltʃ/

A *v.i.* heftig aufstoßen; rülpsen (ugs.); **flames ~ed forth from the furnace** Flammen schlugen aus dem Ofen

B *v.t.* ausstoßen ‹*Rauch, Flüche usw.*›; [aus]speien ‹*Asche*›; **the car exhaust was ~ing clouds of smoke** aus dem Auspuff quollen Rauchschwaden

C *n.* Rülpser, *der* (ugs.)

beleaguer /bɪˈliːgə(r)/ *v.t.* (lit. or fig.) belagern

belfry /ˈbelfrɪ/ *n.* Glockenturm, *der;* (bell space) Glockenstube, *die*

Belgian /ˈbeldʒən/ ▸ⓘ **p. 1345**

A *n.* Belgier, *der*/Belgierin, *die*

B *adj.* belgisch; **sb. is ~:** jmd. ist Belgier/Belgierin

Belgium /ˈbeldʒəm/ *pr. n.* Belgien (*das*)

Belgrade /belˈgreɪd/ *pr. n.* ▸ⓘ **p. 1643** Belgrad (*das*)

belie /bɪˈlaɪ/ *v.t.*, **belying** /bɪˈlaɪɪŋ/ (fail to fulfil) enttäuschen ‹*Versprechen, Vorstellung*›; (give false notion of) hinwegtäuschen über (+ *Akk.*) ‹*Tatsachen, wahren Zustand*›; (fail to justify) nicht gerecht werden (+ *Dat.*) ‹*einer Erwartung, Theorie*›; (fail to corroborate) im Widerspruch stehen zu

belief /bɪˈliːf/ *n.* **1** Vertrauen, *das;* Glaube[n], *der;* **have great ~ in sth.** großes Vertrauen zu etw. haben; **~ in sth.** Glaube an etw. (*Akk.*); **beyond** *or* **past ~:** unglaublich; **it is my ~ that ...:** ich bin der Überzeugung, dass ...; **in the ~ that ...:** in der Überzeugung, dass ...; **to the best of my ~:** meines Wissens **2** (Relig.) Glaube[n], *der*

believable /bɪˈliːvəbl/ *adj.* glaubhaft; glaubwürdig

believe /bɪˈliːv/

A *v.i.* **1** **~ in sth.** (put trust in truth of) an etw. (*Dat.*) glauben; **I ~ in him** ich vertraue ihm; **I ~ in free medical treatment for all** ich bin für die kostenlose ärztliche Behandlung aller; **I don't ~ in going to the dentist** ich halte nicht viel von Zahnärzten **2** (have faith) glauben (**in** an + *Akk.*) ‹*Gott, Himmel usw.*› **3** (suppose, think) glauben; denken; **I ~ so/not** ich glaube schon/nicht; **Mr Smith, I ~:** Herr Smith, nehme ich an

B *v.t.* **1** **~ sth.** etw. glauben; **I ~d his words** ich glaubte seinen Worten; **I can well ~ it** das glaub ich gerne; **if you ~ that, you'll ~ anything** wers glaubt, wird selig (ugs. scherzh.); **[I] don't ~ a word of it** [ich] glaube kein Wort [davon]; **don't you ~ it** glaub das [ja] nicht; **~ it or not** ob du es glaubst oder nicht; **would you ~ [it]** (coll.) stell dir mal vor (ugs.); **I'd never have ~d it of her** das hätte ich ihr nie zugetraut; **~ sb.** jmdm. glauben; **I don't ~ you** das glaube ich dir nicht; **they would have us ~ that ...:** sie wollen uns glauben machen, dass ...; **~ [you] me** glaub/glaubt mir!; **I [can] ~ you** ich kann es dir nachfühlen; **I couldn't ~ my eyes/ears** ich traute meinen Augen/Ohren nicht **2** (be of opinion that) glauben; der Überzeugung sein; **she ~d it to be wrong** sie hielt es für falsch; **he is ~d to be in the London area** man vermutet ihn im Raum London; **people ~d her to be a witch** die Leute hielten sie für eine Hexe; **make ~ [that ...]** so tun, als ob ...

believer /bɪˈliːvə(r)/ *n.* **1** Gläubige, *der/die* **2** **be a great** *or* **firm ~ in sth.** viel von etw. halten; **I'm a firm ~ in being strict with children** ich bin sehr für eine strenge Kindererziehung; **I'm no great ~ in taking exercise** ich halte nicht viel von körperlicher Bewegung

Belisha beacon /bəliːʃə ˈbiːkn/ *n.* (Brit.) *gelbes Blinklicht an Zebrastreifen*

belittle /bɪˈlɪtl/ *v.t.* herabsetzen; schlecht machen; schmälern ‹*Erfolg, Verdienste, Rechte*›; **don't ~ yourself** mach dich nicht schlechter, als du bist

belittlement /bɪˈlɪtlmənt/ *n.* Herabsetzung, *die;* Schlechtmachen, *das*

bell /bel/

A *n.* **1** Glocke, *die;* (smaller) Glöckchen, *das;* (device giving ~-like sound) Klingel, *die;* **clear as a**

~: glockenklar; (understandable) [ganz] klar und deutlich; **sound as a ~:** kerngesund ‹*Person*›; völlig intakt ‹*Gerät, Gegenstand*›; **the ~ has gone** es hat geläutet *od.* geklingelt; **there's the ~:** es läutet *od.* klingelt; **was that the ~?** hat es geläutet *od.* geklingelt? [2] (Boxing) Gong, *der* [3] (Naut.) **one ~/eight ~s** ein Glas/acht Glasen [4] (Bot.) Glöckchen, *das;* Kelch, *der*
B *v.t.* **~ the cat** (fig.) der Katze (*Dat.*) die Schelle umhängen (ugs.)

belladonna /belə'dɒnə/ *n.* [1] (Bot.) Belladonna, *die;* (drug) Atropin, *das* [2] **~ lily** Belladonnalilie, *die* (*südafrik. Amaryllis*)

bell: ~-bottomed *adj.* ausgestellt; **~boy** *n.* (Amer.) [Hotel]boy, *der;* [Hotel]page, *der;* **~-buoy** *n.* (Naut.) Glockenboje, *die*

belle /bel/ *n.* Schönheit, *die;* Schöne, *die;* **~ of the ball** Ballkönigin, *die*

belles-lettres /bel'letr/ *n. pl.* schöngeistige Literatur; Belletristik, *die*

bell: ~flower *n.* Glockenblume, *die;* **~hop** (Amer.) ▸ **bellboy**

bellicose /'belɪkəʊs/ *adj.* kriegerisch, kriegslustig ‹*Stimmung, Nation*›; streitsüchtig ‹*Person*›

belligerence /bɪ'lɪdʒərəns/, **belligerency** /bɪ'lɪdʒərənsɪ/ *n., no pl.* Kriegslust, *die;* (of person) Kampfeslust, *die;* Streitlust, *die*

belligerent /bɪ'lɪdʒərənt/
A *adj.* kriegslustig, kriegerisch, kampflustig ‹*Nation*›; streitlustig ‹*Person, Benehmen*›; aggressiv ‹*Rede*›; **~ powers** Krieg führende Mächte
B *n.* (nation) Krieg führendes Land; (person) Streitende, *der/die*

bellow /'beləʊ/
A *v.i.* ‹*Tier, Person:*› brüllen; **~ at sb.** jmdn. anbrüllen; **~ for sth./sb.** lauthals nach etw./jmdm. schreien
B *v.t.* **~ out** brüllen ‹*Befehl*›; grölen ‹*Lied*›
C *n.* Brüllen, *das*

bellowing /'beləʊɪŋ/ *n.* Gebrüll, *das*

bellows /'beləʊz/ *n. pl.* [1] Blasebalg, *der;* (Mus.) Bälge *Pl.;* **a pair of ~:** ein Blasebalg [2] (Phot.) Balgen, *der*

bell: ~ pull *n.* Glockenzug, *der;* Klingelzug, *der;* **~ push** *n.* Klingeltaster, *der* (fachspr.); Klingel, *die;* **~-ringer** *n.* Glöckner, *der;* **~-ringing** *n.* Glockenläuten, *das;* **~ rope** *n.* Glockenseil, *das;* **~-shaped** *adj.* glockenförmig; **~ tent** *n.* Rundzelt, *das;* **~ tower** *n.* Glockenturm, *der;* **~wether** *n.* Leithammel, *der*

belly /'belɪ/
A *n.* Bauch, *der;* (womb) Leib, *der;* (stomach) Magen, *der;* **go ~ up** (coll.: go bankrupt) Pleite gehen (ugs.)
B *v.t.* blähen; **the wind bellied [out] the sails** der Wind blähte die Segel
C *v.i.* **~ [out]** ‹*Segel:*› sich blähen, schwellen

belly: ~ache **A** *n.* Bauchschmerzen *Pl.;* Bauchweh, *das* (ugs.); **B** *v.i.* (coll.) jammern (**about** über + *Akk.*); **~aching** *n.* (coll.) Gejammer, *das* (ugs.); **~ button** *n.* (coll.) Bauchnabel, *der;* **~ dance** *n.* Bauchtanz, *der;* **~ dancer** *n.* Bauchtänzerin, *die;* **~flop** (coll.) **A** *n.* Bauchklatscher, *der;* **B** *v.i.* einen Bauchklatscher machen

bellyful /'belɪfʊl/ *n.* **a ~ of food** eine ordentliche Portion Essen (ugs.); **have had a ~ of sth.** (fig.) von etw. die Nase voll haben (ugs.)

belly: ~ landing *n.* (Aeronaut.) Bauchlandung, *die;* **~ laugh** *n.* dröhnendes Lachen; **he gave a great ~ laugh** er lachte lauthals los

belong /bɪ'lɒŋ/ *v.i.* [1] (be rightly assigned) **~ to sb.** jmdm. gehören; **~ to sth.** zu etw. gehören; **power ~s to the workers** (as slogan) alle Macht den Arbeitern [2] **~ to** (be member of) **~ to a club/party** einem Verein/einer Partei angehören; **she ~s to a trade union/the club** sie ist Mitglied einer Gewerkschaft/des Vereins; **~ to a church/the working class/another generation** einer Kirche/der Arbeiterklasse/einer anderen Generation (*Dat.*) angehören [3] (be rightly placed) **feel that one doesn't ~:** das Gefühl haben, fehl am Platze zu sein *od.* dass man nicht dazugehört; **he doesn't really ~ anywhere** er ist nirgendwo wirklich zu Hause; **a sense of ~ing** ein Zugehörigkeitsgefühl; **where does this ~?** wo gehört das hin?; **the cutlery ~s in this drawer** das Besteck gehört in diese Schublade; **~ outside** nach draußen gehören; **~ together** zusammengehören; **this item doesn't ~ under this heading** dieser Punkt fällt nicht unter diese Rubrik

belongings /bɪ'lɒŋɪŋz/ *n. pl.* Habe, *die;* Sachen *Pl.;* **personal ~:** persönlicher Besitz; persönliches Eigentum; **all our ~:** unsere gesamte Habe; unser ganzes Hab und Gut

beloved /bɪ'lʌvɪd/
A *adj.* geliebt; lieb; teuer; **be ~** /bɪ'lʌvd/ **by** *or* **of sb.** von jmdm. geliebt werden; jmdm. lieb und teuer sein; **in ~ memory of my husband, in memory of my ~ husband** in treuem Angedenken an meinen geliebten *od.* teuren Mann
B *n.* Geliebte, *der/die;* **my ~** (iron.) mein Lieber/meine Liebe; **dearly ~** (Relig.) liebe Brüder und Schwestern im Herrn; liebe Gemeinde

below /bɪ'ləʊ/
A *adv.* [1] (position) unten; unterhalb; (lower down) darunter; (downstream) weiter unten; **it is on the shelf ~:** es ist auf dem [Regal]brett darunter; **down ~:** unten; drunten (bes. südd.); **from ~:** von unten [herauf]; **~ left** links unten; unten links [2] (direction) nach unten; hinunter; hinab (geh.); (downstream) stromab[wärts]; **if you glance ~:** wenn Sie nach unten blicken *od.* (geh.) hinabblicken [3] (later in text) unten; **see [p. 123] ~:** siehe unten[, S. 123]; **as described in detail ~:** wie [weiter] unten ausführlich beschrieben; **please sign ~:** bitte hier unterschreiben; **a photo with a caption ~:** ein Foto mit einer Bildunterschrift [4] (downstairs) (position) unten; (direction) nach unten; (Naut.) unter Deck; **go ~:** unter Deck gehen; **the flat/floor ~:** die Wohnung/das Stockwerk *od.* die Etage darunter *od.* unter uns/ihnen *usw.;* **on the floor ~:** eine Etage tiefer [5] (~ zero) **ten/twenty ~:** zehn/zwanzig Grad unter Null [6] (Relig.) **on earth ~:** [hier] auf Erden; **here ~:** hienieden (geh.)
B *prep.* [1] (position) unter (+ *Dat.*); unterhalb (+ *Gen.*); (downstream from) unterhalb (+ *Gen.*); **down ~ us was a huge abyss** tief unter uns war ein riesiger Abgrund; **his hair is well ~ shoulder level** sein Haar reicht bis weit über die Schultern; *see also* **average A 1**; **par 1, 4** [2] (direction) unter (+ *Akk.*); **the sun sank ~ the horizon** die Sonne ging am Horizont unter; **he went ~ deck** (Naut.) er ging unter Deck [3] (ranking lower than) unter (+ *Dat.*); **she's in the class ~ me** sie ist eine Klasse unter mir *od.* tiefer als ich; **~-zero temperatures** Temperaturen unter Null; **the temperature is well ~ zero** die Temperatur liegt weit unter Null; **~ the breadline** unter dem Existenzminimum [4] (unworthy of) **it is ~ him** es ist unter seiner Würde

below-the-'line *adj.* (in accounts) unter dem Strich *nachgestellt;* **~ marketing** Below-the-Line-Marketing, *das* (fachspr.)

belt /belt/
A *n.* [1] Gürtel, *der;* (for carrying tools, weapons, ammunition, etc.) Gurt, *der;* (on uniform) Koppel, *das;* **he wears both ~ and braces** (fig.) er sichert etw. doppelt und dreifach; er glaubt, doppelt genäht hält besser; **hit below the ~** (lit. or fig.) unter die Gürtellinie schlagen; **under one's ~** ‹*Essen usw.*› im Bauch; **with a couple of drinks under his ~:** mit ein paar Drinks intus (ugs.); **with all those qualifications under his ~:** mit all den Zeugnissen in der Tasche; *see also* **tighten A 1** [2] (strip) Gurt, *der;* (of colour, trees) Streifen, *der;* (region) Gürtel, *der;* **industrial ~:** Industrierevier, *das;* **~ of warm air/low pressure** Warmluft-/Tiefdruckgürtel, *der;* **coal/oil ~:** Kohlerevier, *das*/Ölgebiet, *das* [3] (of machine gun cartridges) Gurt, *der* [4] (Mech. Engin.: drive ~) Riemen, *der* [5] (coll.: heavy blow) Schlag, *der;* **give sb. a ~:** jmdm. eine runterhauen (ugs.)
B *v.t.* (hit) schlagen; **I'll ~ you [one]** (coll.) ich hau dir eine runter (ugs.)
C *v.i.* (coll.) **~ up/down the motorway** über die Autobahn rasen; **he ~ed off as fast as his legs would carry him** er rannte davon, so schnell er konnte

Phrasal verbs
- **~ along** *v.i.* (coll.) rasen (ugs.)
- **~ out** *v.t.* (coll.) schmettern; voll herausbringen ‹*Rhythmus*›; (on piano) hämmern
- **~ 'up** *v.i.* [1] (Amer. coll., Brit. coll. joc.: put seat~ on) sich anschnallen; sich angurten [2] (Brit. coll.: be quiet) die Klappe halten (salopp)

belter /'beltə(r)/ *n.* (coll.) [1] (impressive thing) Hammer, *der* (ugs.); **a ~ of a day** ein hammermäßiger Tag (ugs.) [2] (loud song) Knaller, *der* (ugs.); Hammerhit, *der* (ugs.) [3] (singer) Röhre, *die;* **blues/rock ~:** Blues-/Rockröhre, *die*

belting /'beltɪŋ/ *n.* [1] **give sb. a [good] ~** (coll.) jmdm. eine [ordentliche] Tracht Prügel verabreichen (ugs.) [2] (material) Gürtelstoff, *der;* (of leather) Riemenleder, *das*

'belt-tightening *n., no pl.* Gürtel-enger-Schnallen, *das; attrib.* **~ measures** drastische Sparmaßnahmen; **a round of ~:** eine Kürzungsrunde

belying ▸ **belie**

bemoan /bɪ'məʊn/ *v.t.* beklagen

bemuse /bɪ'mju:z/ *v.t.* verwirren; (stupefy) verblüffen

bemused /bɪ'mju:zd/ *adj.* verwirrt

bemusement /bɪ'mju:zmənt/ *n., no pl.* Verwirrung, *die*

bench /bentʃ/ *n.* [1] Bank, *die;* (seat across boat) Ducht, *die;* (Sport: for reserves) Reservebank, *die;* Ersatzbank, *die* [2] (work table) Werkbank, *die;* (gold or silversmith's) Werkbrett, *das;* (carpenter's) Hobelbank, *die;* (in laboratory) [Labor]tisch, *der* [3] (Law) **on the ~:** auf dem Richterstuhl; **he was given a seat on the ~:** er wurde zum Richter ernannt [4] (office of judge) Richteramt, *das;* **be raised to the B~:** zum Richter ernannt werden [5] (lawcourt) **Queen's/King's B~** (Brit.) *Abteilung des obersten Gerichts, die sich mit Kriminalfällen befasst* [6] (Brit. Parl.) Bank, *die;* Reihe, *die; see also* **back bench**; **crossbench**; **front bench**

bench: ~mark *n.* Höhenmarke, *die;* (fig.) Maßstab, *der;* Fixpunkt, *der;* **~marking** *n., no pl.* Benchmarking, *das* (fachspr.); Leistungsvergleich, *der;* **~ 'seat** *n.* Sitzbank, *die;* **~ test** *n.* Test auf dem Prüfstand

bend[1] /bend/
A *n.* [1] (bending) Beuge, *die;* Beugung, *die;* **a ~ of the body/the knee** eine Rumpf-/Kniebeuge [2] (curve) (in road) Kurve, *die;* **there is a ~ in the road** die Straße macht eine Kurve; **a ~ in the river** eine Flussbiegung; **be round the ~** (fig. coll.) spinnen (ugs.); verrückt sein (ugs.); **go round the ~** (fig. coll.) überschnappen (ugs.); durchdrehen (ugs.); **drive sb. round the ~** (fig. coll.) jmdn. wahnsinnig *od.* verrückt machen (ugs.) [3] ▸ **i p. 1231** **the ~s** (Med. coll.) Taucherkrankheit, *die*
B *v.t.,* **bent** /bent/ [1] (force out of straightness) biegen; verbiegen ‹*Nadel, Messer, Eisenstange, Ast*›; spannen ‹*Bogen*›; beugen ‹*Arm, Knie*›; anwinkeln ‹*Arm, Bein*›; krumm machen ‹*Finger*›; **~ sth. at an angle** etw. umbiegen; **~ sth. back/forward/up/down** etw. nach hinten/vorne/oben/unten biegen; **'please do not ~'** (on envelope) „bitte nicht knicken!“; **~ sth. back into shape** etw. zurückbiegen; etw. wieder in Form biegen; **~ the law** (fig.) das Gesetz beugen; *see also* **rule A 1** [2] (fix) **be bent on sth.** zu etw. entschlossen sein; auf etw. (*Akk.*) versessen *od.* erpicht sein; **~ one's energies on sth.** (dated) seine ganze Kraft auf etw. (*Akk.*) verwenden; **~ oneself to sth.** sich auf etw. (*Akk.*) konzentrieren [3] (direct) **we must ~ our steps home** wir müssen unsere Schritte heimwärts lenken (geh.); **he bent his mind to the problem** er dachte ernst über das Problem nach; **~ sb.'s ear** (coll.) jmdn. voll quatschen (ugs.) [4] (force to submit) unterwerfen; gefügig machen; **~ sb. to one's will** sich (*Dat.*) jmdn. gefügig machen [5] (Naut.) festmachen; befestigen ‹*Tau*›
C *v.i.,* **bent** [1] sich biegen; sich krümmen; ‹*Äste:*› sich neigen; **the road ~s** die Straße macht eine Kurve; **the road ~s for two miles** die Straße ist auf zwei Meilen kurvenreich; **the river ~s/~s in and out** der Fluss macht eine Biegung/schlängelt sich; **catch sb. ~ing**

(fig. coll.) jmdn. [in einer peinlichen Lage] erwischen **2** (bow) sich bücken; (fig.) sich beugen; **~ to** *or* **before sb.** (fig.) sich jmdm. beugen

Phrasal verbs

- **~ 'down** *v.i.* sich bücken; sich hinunterbeugen
- **~ 'over** *v.i.* sich nach vorn beugen; sich bücken; *see also* **backwards 1**

bend² *n.* **1** (Naut.) Knoten, *der;* Schlinge, *die* **2** (Her.) Schrägbalken, *der;* **~ sinister** schräglinker Balken; Schräglinksbalken, *der*

bendable /ˈbendəbl/ *adj.* biegbar

bended /ˈbendɪd/ *adj.* **on ~ knee[s]** auf [den] Knien

bender /ˈbendə(r)/ *n.* (coll.) Besäufnis, *das* (salopp)

bendy /ˈbendɪ/ *adj.* (coll.) **1** biegsam **2** (winding) gewunden ‹*Pfad, Straße*›

beneath /bɪˈniːθ/

A *prep.* **1** (unworthy of) **~ sb.** jmds. unwürdig; unter jmds. Würde (*Dat.*); **~ sb.'s dignity** unter jmds. Würde (*Dat.*); **marry ~ one** nicht standesgemäß heiraten; unter seinem Stand heiraten; **~ contempt** verachtenswert; unter aller Kritik **2** (under) unter (+ *Dat.*)

B *adv.* darunter

Benedictine

A *n.* **1** /benɪˈdɪktɪn/ (monk/nun) Benediktiner, *der*/Benediktinerin, *die* **2** ® /benɪˈdɪktiːn/ (liqueur) Benediktiner, *der*

B *adj.* Benediktiner-

benediction /benɪˈdɪkʃn/ *n.* (Relig.) Benediktion, *die;* Segnung, *die;* **pronounce/say the ~** (before meal) um den Segen Gottes bitten; (after meal) das Dankgebet sprechen *od.* sagen

benefaction /benɪˈfækʃn/ *n.* (formal) (gift) Spende, *die;* (endowment) Schenkung, *die;* Stiftung, *die*

benefactor /ˈbenɪfæktə(r)/ *n.* Wohltäter, *der;* (patron) Stifter, *der;* Gönner, *der*

benefactress /ˈbenɪfæktrɪs/ *n.* Wohltäterin, *die;* (patroness) Stifterin, *die;* Gönnerin, *die*

benefice /ˈbenɪfɪs/ *n.* (Eccl.) Benefizium, *das*

beneficence /bɪˈnefɪsəns/ *n.* (formal) Mildtätigkeit, *die;* (active kindness) Güte, *die*

beneficent /bɪˈnefɪsənt/ *adj.* (formal) (showing active kindness) gütig; (doing good) wohltätig; mildtätig

beneficial /benɪˈfɪʃl/ *adj.* **1** nutzbringend; nützlich; vorteilhaft ‹*Einfluss*›; günstig ‹*Klima*›; **be ~ to sth./sb.** zum Nutzen von etw./jmdm. sein; **a good night's sleep is very ~:** ein guter Schlaf ist sehr erholsam **2** (Law) nutznießerisch; **~ owner** Nießbraucher, *der*

beneficially /benɪˈfɪʃəlɪ/ *adv.* ▸ **beneficial 1:** nutzbringend; nützlich; vorteilhaft; günstig

beneficiary /benɪˈfɪʃərɪ/ *n.* Nutznießer, *der*/Nutznießerin, *die*

benefit /ˈbenɪfɪt/

A *n.* **1** Vorteil, *der;* Vorzug, *der* (geh.); **be of ~ to sb./sth.** jmdm./einer Sache von Nutzen sein; **have the ~ of** den Vorteil *od.* (geh.) Vorzug (+ *Gen.*) haben; **derive ~ from sth., get some ~ from sth.** aus etw. Nutzen ziehen; von etw. profitieren; **not get much ~ from sth.** wenig Nutzen aus etw. ziehen; nicht viel von etw. profitieren; **did you get much ~ from your holiday?** hat dir der Urlaub viel genützt?; **without the ~ of** ohne das Zutun (+ *Gen.*); **with the ~ of** mithilfe (+ *Gen.*); **to sb.'s ~:** zu jmds. Nutzen; **for sb.'s ~:** in jmds. Interesse (*Dat.*); im Interesse von jmdm.; **for the ~ of sth.** im Interesse einer Sache (*Gen.*); **for the ~ of future generations** im Interesse künftiger Generationen; **for the ~ of anyone who/all those who ...** (iron.) allen/all denen zuliebe, die ... (iron.); **give sb. the ~ of the doubt** im Zweifelsfall zu jmds. Gunsten entscheiden; **give sb. the ~ of sth.** jmdm. etw. zugute kommen lassen (iron.) **2** (allowance) Beihilfe, *die;* **social security ~:** Sozialhilfe, *die;* Hilfe zum Lebensunterhalt (Amtsspr.); **supplementary ~** (Brit.) zusätzliche Hilfe zum Lebensunterhalt; **unemployment ~:** Arbeitslosenunterstützung, *die;* **sickness ~:** Krankengeld, *das;* **disablement ~:** Invalidenrente, *die;* **child ~** (Brit.) Kindergeld, *das;* **maternity ~:** Mutterschaftsgeld, *das;* *attrib.* **~ club** *or* **society** Versicherungsverein auf Gegenseitigkeit **3** **~ [performance/match/concert]** Benefizveranstaltung, *die*/-spiel, *das*/-konzert, *das* **4** **without ~ of clergy** (dated joc.) ohne kirchlichen Segen

B *v.t.* **~ sb./sth.** jmdm./einer Sache nützen *od.* gut tun; **these facilities/discoveries have ~ed the area/humanity** diese Einrichtungen/Entdeckungen sind dem Gebiet/der Menschheit zugute gekommen *od.* haben dem Gebiet/der Menschheit Nutzen gebracht

C *v.i.* **~ by/from sth.** von etw. profitieren; aus etw. Nutzen ziehen; **~ from experience** aus Erfahrung lernen; **how do I/will my son ~?** was habe ich/hat mein Sohn davon?

'benefits package *n.* geldwerte Leistungen

'benefit tourism *n., no pl.* Sozialhilfetourismus, *der*

Benelux /ˈbenɪlʌks/ *pr. n.* **the ~ countries** die Beneluxländer

benevolence /bɪˈnevələns/ *n., no pl.* (desire to do good) Güte, *die;* (of ruler) Milde, *die;* (of despot, the authorities) Wohlwollen, *das*

benevolent /bɪˈnevələnt/ *adj.* **1** (desiring to do good) gütig; mild ‹*Herrscher*›; wohlwollend ‹*Behörde, Despot*›; **~ despotism** aufgeklärter Absolutismus **2** *attrib.* (charitable) wohltätig, mildtätig ‹*Institution, Verein*› **3** (kind and helpful) hilfsbereit; **a ~ smile/air** ein gütiges Lächeln/gütiger Gesichtsausdruck

benevolently /bɪˈnevələntlɪ/ *adv.* gütig ‹*lächeln*›

Bengali /beŋˈgɔːlɪ/ ▸ⓘ **p. 1277,** ▸ⓘ **p. 1345**

A *n.* **1** (person) Bengale, *der*/Bengalin, *die* **2** (language) Bengali, *das*

B *adj.* bengalisch

benighted /bɪˈnaɪtɪd/ *adj.* unwissend, (ugs.) unbedarft ‹*Person*›; rückständig ‹*Land*›; finster ‹*Gegend, Zeitalter*›

benign /bɪˈnaɪn/ *adj.* **1** (gracious, gentle) gütig ‹*Person, Aussehen, Verständnis*›; wohlwollend ‹*Person, Verhalten*›; (mild) mild, heilsam ‹*Klima, Sonne*›; (fortunate) günstig ‹*Stern, Einfluss, Ergebnis, Aspekt*› **2** (Med.) gutartig, (fachspr.) benigne ‹*Tumor*›

benignity /bɪˈnɪgnɪtɪ/ *n., no pl.* **1** Wohlwollen, *das* **2** (Med.) Gutartigkeit, *die*

benignly /bɪˈnaɪnlɪ/ *adv.* gütig; wohlwollend

bent¹ /bent/

A ▸ **bend¹ B, C**

B *n.* Neigung, *die;* Hang, *der;* Schlag, *der;* **have a ~ for sth.** einen Hang zu etw. *od.* eine Vorliebe für etw. haben; **those with** *or* **of an artistic ~:** Menschen mit einer künstlerischen Ader *od.* Veranlagung; **follow one's ~:** seiner Neigung *od.* seinen Neigungen folgen

C *adj.* **1** krumm; gebogen **2** (Brit. coll.: corrupt) link (salopp); nicht ganz sauber (salopp) ‹*Händler usw.*› **3** (Brit. coll. offensive: homosexual) schwul (ugs.); andersrum *präd.* (ugs.)

bent² *n.* (Bot.) Straußgras, *das;* (stiff flower stalk) Halm, *der;* (heath) Heide, *die*

benumb /bɪˈnʌm/ *v.t.* **1** gefühllos machen ‹*Glieder*›; **~ed** gefühllos; **~ed with cold** starr vor Kälte **2** (fig.: stupefy) lähmen; betäuben ‹*Sinne, Gefühle*›; **he was ~ed with grief** er war vor Kummer gelähmt

Benzedrine ® /ˈbenzɪdriːn/ *n.* (Med.) Benzedrin, *das*

benzene /ˈbenziːn/ *n.* (Chem.) Benzol, *das;* **~ ring** Benzolring, *der*

benzine /ˈbenziːn/ *n.* Leichtbenzin, *das*

bequeath /bɪˈkwiːð/ *v.t.* **1** **~ sth. to sb.** jmdm. etw. vermachen *od.* hinterlassen **2** (fig.) überliefern ‹*Märchen, Legende, Zeugnisse*›; vererben ‹*Tradition*›

bequest /bɪˈkwest/ *n.* Legat, *das* (**to** an + *Akk.*); **make a ~ to sb. of sth.** jmdm. etw. vermachen

berate /bɪˈreɪt/ *v.t.* schelten

bereave /bɪˈriːv/ *v.t.* **~ A of B** B (*Dat.*) A nehmen; **be ~d [of sb.]** jmdn. verlieren; **a disaster ~d him of his father** er hat seinen Vater durch ein Unglück verloren; **the ~d** der/die Hinterbliebene/die Hinterbliebenen;

bereavement /bɪˈriːvmənt/ *n.* Trauerfall, *der;* **he sympathized with her in her ~:** er sprach ihr sein Beileid aus; **on account of their recent ~:** aufgrund ihres Trauerfalles

bereavement: ~ counselling, (Amer.) **~ counseling** *n., no pl.* Trauerberatung, *die;* **~ counsellor,** (Amer.) **~ counselor** *n.* Trauerberater, *der*/-beraterin, *die*

bereft /bɪˈreft/ *pred. adj.* **be ~ of sth.** etw. verloren haben

beret /ˈbereɪ, ˈberɪ/ *n.* Baskenmütze, *die;* (as military headdress) Barett, *das*

bergamot /ˈbɜːgəmɒt/ *n.* **1** (tree) Bergamotte, *die;* Bergamottenbaum, *der* **2** (perfume) Bergamottparfüm, *das* **3** (herb) Zitronenminze, *die;* Pfefferminze, *die;* *attrib.* **~ oil** Bergamottöl, *das*

beriberi /berɪˈberɪ/ *n.* ▸ⓘ **p. 1231** (Med.) Beriberi, *die*

berk /bɜːk/ *n.* (Brit. sl.) Dussel, *der* (ugs.); Spinner, *der* (ugs.); Blödmann, *der* (salopp)

Berlin /bɜːˈlɪn/ ▸ⓘ **p. 1643**

A *pr. n.* Berlin (*das*)

B *attrib. adj.* Berliner; (Ling.) berlinisch

Berliner /bɜːˈlɪnə(r)/ *n.* Berliner, *der*/Berlinerin, *die*

Bermuda /bəˈmjuːdə/ *pr. n.* die Bermudainseln; **the ~s** die Bermudas; **~s, ~ shorts** Bermudashorts

Berne /bɜːn/ ▸ⓘ **p. 1643**

A *pr. n.* Bern (*das*)

B *attrib. adj.* Berner

berry /ˈberɪ/ *n.* Beere, *die; see also* **brown A**

berserk /bəˈsɜːk, bəˈzɜːk/ *adj.* rasend; **go ~:** durchdrehen (ugs.); **he went ~ with an axe** er wütete mit einem Beil

berth /bɜːθ/

A *n.* **1** (adequate space) Seeraum, *der* (der für ein Schiff erforderlich ist); **give the rocks a wide ~:** Abstand zu den Felsen halten; gut frei von den Felsen halten (fachspr.); **give sb./sth. a wide ~** (fig.) jmdm./einer Sache aus dem Weg gehen; einen großen Bogen um jmdn./etw. machen **2** (ship's place at wharf) Liegeplatz, *der* **3** (sleeping place) (in ship) Koje, *die;* Kajütenbett, *das;* (in train) Schlafwagenbett, *das;* (in aircraft) Sleeper, *der;* **a 4-~ caravan** ein Vierpersonenanhänger **4** (coll.: job) Stelle, *die;* **find a cushy ~:** eine bequeme Stelle *od.* einen bequemen Job finden

B *v.t.* festmachen ‹*Schiff*›

C *v.i.* ‹*Schiff:*› festmachen, anlegen

beryl /ˈberɪl/ *n.* Beryll, *der*

beryllium /bɪˈrɪlɪəm/ *n.* (Chem.) Beryllium, *das*

beseech /bɪˈsiːtʃ/ *v.t.,* **besought** /bɪˈsɔːt/ *or* **~ed** (literary) flehen um, (geh.) erflehen ‹*Gnade, Vergebung*›; anflehen ‹*Person*›; **~ sb. to do sth.** jmdn. anflehen *od.* inständig bitten, etw. zu tun; **~ sb. for sth.** jmdn. um etw. anflehen; **I ~ you** ich flehe dich an

beseeching /bɪˈsiːtʃɪŋ/ *adj.,* **beseechingly** /bɪˈsiːtʃɪŋlɪ/ *adv.* flehend; flehentlich (geh.)

beset /bɪˈset/ *v.t., forms as* **set A** heimsuchen; plagen; ‹*Probleme, Zweifel, Versuchungen:*› bedrängen; **sth. is ~ with troubles** etw. steckt voller Schwierigkeiten/Probleme; **~ by doubts** von Zweifeln geplagt; **~ting sin** Untugend, *die*

beside /bɪˈsaɪd/ *prep.* **1** (close to) neben (+ *Dat.*); an (+ *Dat.*); **~ the sea/lake** am Meer/See; **walk ~ the river** am Fluss entlanggehen; **sit/stand ~ sb.** neben jmdm. sitzen/stehen; **sit down/go and stand ~ sb.** sich neben jmdn. setzen/stellen **2** (compared with) neben (+ *Dat.*) **3** (wide of) weit entfernt von ‹*Problem, Frage*›; **be ~ the point** nichts damit zu tun haben **4** **~ oneself with joy/grief** außer sich vor Freude/Kummer

besides /bɪˈsaɪdz/

A *adv.* außerdem; **he was a historian ~:** er war außerdem noch Historiker; **do/say sth. [else] ~:** sonst noch etw. tun/sagen; **~, we don't need it** außerdem brauchen wir es nicht; **whatever she may have done ~:** was sie sonst noch getan haben mag

B *prep.* außer; **~ us [there were others]** außer

uns [waren noch andere da]; ~ **my husband and me** außer meinem Mann und mir; ~ **which, he was late** und obendrein *od.* außerdem kam er zu spät; **he said nothing ~ that** er sagte weiter *od.* sonst nichts

besiege /bɪˈsiːdʒ/ *v.t.* (lit. or fig.) belagern; **be ~d with letters/offers/requests/enquiries** mit Briefen/Angeboten/Bitten/Anfragen überschüttet *od.* überhäuft werden

besieger /bɪˈsiːdʒə(r)/ *n.* Belagerer, *der*

besmear /bɪˈsmɪə(r)/ *v.t.* verschmieren; **~ed with blood** blutverschmiert

besmirch /bɪˈsmɜːtʃ/ *v.t.* (lit. or fig.) beschmutzen (geh.); besudeln (geh.) ~ **sb.'s name** jmds. Namen besudeln *od.* beflecken

besom /ˈbiːzəm/ *n.* [Reisig]besen, *der*

besotted /bɪˈsɒtɪd/ *adj.* **be ~ by** *or* **with sb.** in jmdn. vernarrt sein; **be ~ by** *or* **with the idea that ...:** von der Idee besessen sein, dass ...; ~ **with alcohol** berauscht *od.* benommen vom Alkohol

besought ▸ **beseech**

bespatter /bɪˈspætə(r)/ *v.t.* bespritzen; vollspritzen

bespeak /bɪˈspiːk/ *v.t.*, *forms as* **speak B** (formal) **1)** (be evidence of) zeugen von; verraten **2)** (reserve) reservieren; vorbestellen

bespectacled /bɪˈspektəkld/ *adj.* bebrillt

bespoke /bɪˈspəʊk/
A ▸ **bespeak**
B *attrib. adj.* ~ **overcoat** maßgeschneiderter Mantel; ~ **boots** Stiefel nach Maß; ~ **tailor** Maßschneider, *der*

bespoken ▸ **bespeak**

best /best/
A *adj. superl. of* **good 1)** best...; **be ~ [of all]** am [aller]besten sein; **the ~ thing about it was ...:** das Beste daran war ...; **the ~ thing to do is to apologize** das Beste ist, sich zu entschuldigen; **the very ~ people** die feinen Leute; **may the ~ man win!** auf dass der Beste gewinnt!
2) (most advantageous) best...; günstigst...; **which** *or* **what is the ~ way?** wie ist es am besten *od.* günstigsten?; **it's ~ to travel via Paris** am besten fährt man über Paris; **think it ~ to do sth.** es für das Beste halten, etw. zu tun; **do as you think ~** *or* **what you think is ~:** mach, was du für richtig hältst
3) (greatest) größt...; **the ~ part of the day/money** der größte Teil des Tages/Geldes; **[for] the ~ part of an hour** fast eine ganze Stunde
B *adv. superl. of* **well² B** am besten; **like sth. ~ of all** etw. am liebsten mögen; **as ~ we could** so gut wir konnten; **as ~ you can** so gut es geht; **you know ~:** Sie müssen es [am besten] wissen; **you'd ~ be going now** am besten gehen Sie jetzt; **he is ~ known for his etchings** er ist vor allem für seine Kupferstiche bekannt; **he is the person ~ able to do it/to cope** er ist der Fähigste, um das zu tun/damit fertig zu werden; **I was not ~ pleased to discover that ...** (iron.) ich war gar nicht begeistert, als ich entdeckte, dass ... (iron.)
C *n.* **1) the ~:** der/die/das Beste; **the wine was not of the ~:** der Wein war nicht von der besten Qualität; **their latest record is their ~:** ihre letzte Platte ist die beste
2) (clothes) beste Sachen; Sonntagskleider *Pl.*; **wear one's [Sunday] ~:** seine Sonntagskleider tragen; sich in Schale werfen (ugs.)
3) play the ~ of three [games] um zwei Gewinnsätze spielen; **the ~ of it is ...** (also iron.) das Beste daran ist ...; der Witz dabei ist ... (iron.); **get** *or* **have the ~ of it** gut damit fahren; gut dabei wegkommen; **get the ~ out of sth./sb.** das Beste aus etw./jmdm. herausholen; **that's the ~ of having a car** das ist das Beste an einem Auto; **he is not in the ~ of health** es geht ihm nicht sehr gut; **bring out the ~ in sb.** jmds. beste Seiten zum Vorschein bringen; **all the ~!** alles Gute!
4) the ~ *pl.* die Besten; **they are the ~ of friends** sie sind die besten Freunde; **with the ~ of intentions** in bester Absicht; **from the ~ of motives** aus den edelsten Motiven [heraus]; **get six of the ~** (coll.) Prügel beziehen; verdroschen werden (ugs.); **[sb. is] one of the ~** (coll.) [jmd. ist] ein feiner Kerl; **she can down a pint of beer/play tennis with the ~ of them** (coll.) beim Biertrinken/Tennisspielen macht ihr keiner was vor (ugs.)
5) at ~: bestenfalls; **be at one's ~:** in Hochform sein; **an example of modern architecture at its ~:** eines der gelungensten Beispiele moderner Architektur; **[even] at the ~ of times** schon normalerweise; **it is [all] for the ~:** es ist [doch] nur zum Guten; **he did it [all] for the ~:** er hat es [doch] nur gut gemeint; **hope for the ~:** das Beste hoffen; **do one's ~:** sein Bestes *od.* Möglichstes tun; **he is doing his ~ to ruin me** (iron.) er tut sein Möglichstes, mich zu ruinieren; **do the ~ you can** machen Sie es so gut Sie können; **it's not good, but it's the ~ I can do** es ist nicht gut, aber mehr kann ich nicht tun; **look one's ~:** möglichst gut aussehen; **make the ~ of oneself** das Beste aus sich machen; **make the ~ of it/things** das Beste daraus machen; **make the ~ of a bad job** *or* **bargain** (coll.) das Beste daraus machen; **to the ~ of one's ability** nach besten Kräften; so gut man kann; **to the ~ of my belief/knowledge** meines Wissens; **she wants/has the ~ of everything** sie will immer nur/hat von allem das Beste
D *v.t.* (Sport) schlagen; (outwit) übervorteilen

best: ~-before date *n.* Mindesthaltbarkeitsdatum, *das;* **~-dressed** *attrib. adj.* bestgekleidet; ~ **'end** *n.* (Gastr.) Filet, *das;* ~ **'friend** *n.* bester Freund/beste Freundin; **be ~ friends with sb.** sehr gute mit jmdm. befreundet sein; **~-hated** *attrib. adj.* (iron.) bestgehasst (iron.)

bestial /ˈbestɪəl/ *adj.* (of or like a beast) tierisch; (brutish, barbarous) barbarisch; (savage) brutal; (depraved) bestialisch; tierisch

bestiality /bestɪˈælɪtɪ/ *n., no pl.* **1)** Bestialität, *die;* (savagery) Brutalität, *die* **2)** (sex with animals) Sodomie, *die*

bestir /bɪˈstɜː(r)/ *v. refl.*, **-rr-** sich aufraffen

best: ~-kept *attrib. adj.* bestgepflegt; bestgehütet ‹*Geheimnis*›; **the ~-kept village in England** das schönste Dorf Englands; **~-known** *attrib. adj.* bekanntest...; **~-laid** *attrib. adj.* bestüberlegt ‹*Pläne*›; **~-loved** *attrib. adj.* meistgeliebt; ~ **'man** *n.* Trauzeuge, *der* (*des Bräutigams*)

bestow /bɪˈstəʊ/ *v.t.* verleihen ‹*Titel*›; schenken ‹*Gunst, Wohlwollen*›; zuteil werden lassen ‹*Ehre, Segnungen*›; ~ **sth. [up]on sb.** jmdm. etw. verleihen/schenken/zuteil werden lassen

bestowal /bɪˈstəʊəl/ *n.* Verleihung, *die* (**[up]on** an + *Akk.*); (of land) Schenkung, *die*

'best-quality *attrib. adj.* der Spitzenklasse *nachgestellt;* erstklassig

bestride /bɪˈstraɪd/ *v.t.*, *forms as* **stride C** sich rittlings setzen auf (+ *Akk.*); (position) rittlings sitzen auf (+ *Dat.*) ‹*Mauer, Bank*›

best: ~ 'seller *n.* Bestseller, *der;* (author) Bestsellerautor, *der;* **~-selling** *attrib. adj.* meistverkauft ‹*Schallplatte*›; **~-selling book/novel** Bestseller, *der;* **a ~-selling author/novelist** ein Bestsellerautor

bet /bet/
A *v.t.*, **-tt-**, ~ *or* **~ted 1)** wetten; **I ~ him £10** ich habe mit ihm um 10 Pfund gewettet; **he ~ £10 on that horse** er hat 10 Pfund auf das Pferd gesetzt **2)** (coll.: be confident) wetten; **I ~ he's late** wetten, dass er zu spät kommt?; **[I] ~ you I know where he got it from** wetten, dass ich weiß, woher er es hat?; **[you can] ~ your life** darauf kannst du Gift nehmen (ugs.); **[I] ~ you [anything]** ich gehe jede Wette darauf ein; **I'll ~ he tells them he's swum the Channel** ich wette, er erzählt ihnen, dass er den Kanal durchschwommen hat; ~ **[you] I 'can** und ob ich kann; **you '~ [I am/he will** *etc.*] und ob; allerdings
B *v.i.*, **-tt-**, ~ *or* **~ted 1)** wetten (**for** um); ~ **on sth.** auf etw. (*Akk.*) setzen **2)** (coll.: be confident) **the shops will be closed, I'll ~:** ich wette, die Geschäfte sind geschlossen; **[do you] want to ~?** [wollen wir] wetten? *See also* **boot¹ A 1**; **bottom B 2**
C *n.* **1)** Wette, *die;* (sum) Wetteinsatz, *der;* **make** *or* **have a ~ with sb. on sth.** mit jmdm. über etw. (*Akk.*) wetten; **accept** *or* **take a ~ on sth.** eine Wette auf etw. (*Akk.*) eingehen; **lay a ~ on sth.** auf etw. (*Akk.*) wetten **2)** (fig. coll.: choice) Tipp, *der;* **be a bad/good/safe ~:** ein schlechter/guter/sicherer Tipp sein; **it's a fair ~ that ...:** du kannst ziemlich sicher sein, dass ...; **be sb.'s best ~:** das Beste sein; **my ~ is that ...:** ich wette, dass ...

beta /ˈbiːtə/ *n.* **1)** (letter) Beta, *das* **2)** (Sch., Univ.: mark) Zwei, *die*

beta-blocker /ˈbiːtəblɒkə(r)/ *n.* (Med.) Beta[rezeptoren]blocker, *der*

betake /bɪˈteɪk/ *v. refl.*, *forms as* **take A** (arch./literary) sich begeben; ~ **oneself somewhere** sich irgendwohin begeben

beta: ~ particle *n.* (Phys.) Betateilchen, *das;* ~ **ray** *n.* (Phys.) Betastrahl, *der;* ~ **test** *n.* (Computing) Betatest, *der;* **~-test** *v.t.* (Computing) einem Betatest unterziehen; betatesten (fachspr.); ~ **tester** *n.* (Computing) Betatester, *der*/-testerin, *die;* ~ **version** *n.* (Computing) Betaversion, *die*

betel /ˈbiːtl/ *n.* (Bot.) Betel, *der;* ~ **nut** Betelnuss, *die*

bête noire /beɪt ˈnwɑː(r)/ *n.*, *pl.* **bêtes noires** /beɪt ˈnwɑː(r)/ Gräuel, *der*

bethink /bɪˈθɪŋk/ *v. refl.*, **bethought** /bɪˈθɔːt/ (arch./literary) sich besinnen

betide /bɪˈtaɪd/ (literary)
A *v.t.* geschehen (+ *Dat.*) (veralt., geh.); **woe ~ you if ...:** wehe dir, wenn ...; **whatever ~s you** was Ihnen auch immer geschieht
B *v.i.* geschehen

betoken /bɪˈtəʊkn/ *v.t.* (literary) **1)** (be an indication or a warning of) ankündigen ‹*Frühjahr, Krieg*› **2)** (suggest) hindeuten auf (+ *Akk.*)

betony /ˈbetənɪ/ *n.* (Bot.) Ziest, *der*

betook ▸ **betake**

betray /bɪˈtreɪ/ *v.t.* **1)** verraten (**to** an + *Akk.*); missbrauchen ‹*jmds. Vertrauen*›; ~ **oneself** sich verraten; ~ **the fact that ...:** verraten, dass ... **2)** (lead astray) fehlleiten

betrayal /bɪˈtreɪəl/ *n.* Verrat, *der;* ~ **of one's friends/country** Verrat an seinen Freunden/seinem Vaterland; **an act of ~:** ein Verrat; **a ~ of trust** ein Vertrauensbruch

betroth /bɪˈtrəʊð/ *v.t.* (arch.) versprechen (veralt.); **be ~ed to sb.** jmdm. versprochen sein (veralt.)

betrothal /bɪˈtrəʊðl/ *n.* (dated) Verlöbnis, *das*

betrothed /bɪˈtrəʊðd/ (dated)
A *adj.* versprochen (veralt.)
B *n.* Anverlobter, *der*/Anverlobte, *die* (veralt.)

better /ˈbetə(r)/
A *adj.* ▸ **i p. 1231** *compar. of* **good A** besser; **I have something ~ to do** ich habe etwas Besseres zu tun; **do you know of anything ~?** kennst du etwas Besseres?; **that's ~:** so ists schon besser; **~ and ~:** immer besser; **~ still, let's phone** oder noch besser: Rufen wir doch an; **be much ~** (recovered) sich viel besser fühlen; **he is much ~ today** es geht ihm heute schon viel besser; **get ~** (recover) besser werden; **I am/my ankle is getting ~:** mir/meinem Knöchel geht es besser; **so much the ~:** umso besser; **she is none the ~ for it** das hat ihr nichts genützt; **she is much the ~ for having been to university** es hat ihr sehr genützt, dass sie studiert hat; **my ~ feelings/nature** mein besseres Ich; **be ~ than one's word** mehr tun, als man versprochen hat; **my/his ~ half** (joc.) meine/seine bessere Hälfte (scherzh.); **the ~ part of sth.** (greater part) der größte Teil einer Sache (*Gen.*); **[for] the ~ part of an hour** fast eine ganze Stunde; **he is no ~ than a criminal** er kommt einem Kriminellen gleich; **she's no ~ than she should be** (euphem.) sie ist auch nicht gerade eine Heilige; **on ~ acquaintance** bei näherer Bekanntschaft; *see also* **all C**
B *adv. compar. of* **well² B 1)** (in a ~ way) besser; **I hope you do ~ in future** hoffentlich haben Sie in Zukunft mehr Glück; (by your own efforts) ich hoffe, dass Sie es in Zukunft besser machen werden **2)** (to a greater degree) mehr; **the ~ to do sth.** um etw. besser tun zu können; **you cannot do ~ than ...:** das Beste,

was du tun kannst, ist ...; **I like Goethe ~ than Schiller** ich mag Goethe lieber als Schiller; **he is ~ liked than Carter** er ist beliebter als Carter **3) he would do ~ to ask first** er sollte lieber *od.* besser zuerst fragen **4) know ~ than ...:** es besser wissen als ...; **you ought to know ~ than to ...:** du solltest es besser wissen und nicht ... **5) go one ~ [than sb.],** (Amer.) **go sb. one ~:** jmdn. überbieten **6) you'd ~ not tell her** Sie erzählen es ihr besser nicht; **I'd ~ begin by introducing myself** ich stelle mich besser zuerst einmal vor; **I'd ~ be off now** ich gehe jetzt besser; **hadn't you ~ ask first?** sollten Sie nicht besser zuerst fragen?; **I promise I'll clear up after the party — You'd ~!** Ich verspreche, dass ich nach der Party aufräume — Das will ich aber auch hoffen. *See also* **better off**

C *n.* **1)** Bessere, *das;* **we hope for ~:** wir erhoffen uns (*Dat.*) mehr; **get the ~ of sb./sth.** jmdn./etw. unterkriegen (ugs.); **exhaustion got the ~ of him** seine Erschöpfung machte ihm schwer zu schaffen; **be a change for the ~:** eine vorteilhafte Veränderung sein; **for ~, for worse** in Freud und Leid; **for ~ or for worse** was immer daraus werden wird; **I thought ~ of it** ich habe es mir anders überlegt **2)** *in pl.* Leute, die höher stehen; **one's ~s** Leute, die über einem stehen *od.* die einem überlegen sind

D *v.t.* **1)** (surpass) übertreffen **2)** (improve) verbessern; **~ oneself** (rise socially) sich verbessern

'better-class *attrib. adj.* (dated) besser, feiner ‹*Leute*›; vornehm ‹*Vorort, Familie*›

betterment /'betəmənt/ *n., no pl.* Verbesserung, *die*

better: **~ 'off** *adj.* **1)** (financially) [finanziell] besser gestellt; **2) he is ~ off than I am** ihm geht es besser als mir; **be ~ off than sb.** besser als jmd. dran sein (ugs.); **be ~ off without sth./sb.** ohne etw./jdmn. besser dran sein; **~-quality** *attrib. adj.* qualitativ besser; **~-than-average** *attrib. adj.* überdurchschnittlich [gut/viel]; **earn a ~-than-average income** überdurchschnittlich viel verdienen

betting /'betɪŋ/

A *n., no pl.* Wetten, *das;* **there was heavy ~ on that horse** auf das Pferd wurde sehr viel gesetzt; **what's the ~ it rains?** (fig.) ob es wohl regnen wird?

B *attrib. adj.* Wett-; **I'm not a ~ man** ich wette nicht

betting: **~ office, ~ shop** *ns.* Wettbüro, *das;* **~ slip** *n.* Wettschein, *der;* Wettzettel, *der*

between /bɪ'twi:n/

A *prep.* **1)** (position) zwischen (+ *Dat.*); (direction) zwischen (+ *Akk.*); **it is not far ~ the two places** die beiden Orte liegen nicht weit auseinander; **~ then and now** zwischen damals und jetzt; **~ now and the end of term** bis zum Ende des Trimesters; **there's nothing to choose ~ them** sie unterscheiden sich durch nichts; **[in] ~:** zwischen **2)** (amongst) unter (+ *Dat.*); **the work was divided ~ the volunteers** die Arbeit wurde zwischen den Freiwilligen aufgeteilt; **~ ourselves, ~ you and me** unter uns (*Dat.*) gesagt; **that's [just] ~ ourselves** das bleibt aber unter uns (*Dat.*) **3)** (by joint action of) **~ them/the four of them they succeeded in dislodging the stone** gemeinsam/zu viert gelang es ihnen, den Stein zu lösen; **we ate it up ~ us** wir haben es zusammen *od.* gemeinsam aufgegessen **4)** (shared by) **~ us we had 40p** wir hatten zusammen 40 Pence; **we had three tents ~ the five of us** wir hatten drei Zelte für uns fünf; **there is nothing ~ us** wir haben nichts miteinander; **it's all over ~ us** es ist aus zwischen uns (*Dat.*) (ugs.)

B *adv.* **[in] ~:** dazwischen; (in time) zwischendurch; **the space ~:** der Zwischenraum

between: **~times, ~whiles** *advs.* in der Zwischenzeit

betwixt /bɪ'twɪkst/

A *prep.* (arch./poet.) zwischen

B *adv.* **1)** (arch./poet.) dazwischen **2) ~ and between** (coll.) zwischen beiden

bevel /'bevl/

A *n.* (slope) Schräge, *die; attrib.* **~ edge** Schrägkante, *die;* **~ gear** Kegelradgetriebe, *das*

B *v.t.,* (Brit.) **-ll-** abschrägen

beverage /'bevərɪdʒ/ *n.* (formal) Getränk, *das*

bevy /'bevɪ/ *n.* (of people) Schar, *die;* (of things) Batterie, *die*

bewail /bɪ'weɪl/ *v.t.* beklagen; (lament) bejammern

beware /bɪ'weə(r)/ *v.t. & i.; only in imper. and inf.* **~ [of] sth./sb.** sich vor jmdm./etw. hüten *od.* in Acht nehmen; **~ of doing sth.** sich davor hüten, etw. zu tun; **'~ of black ice/falling masonry'** „Vorsicht, Glatteis/herabfallendes Mauerwerk!"; **'~ of pickpockets'** „vor Taschendieben wird gewarnt": **'~ of the dog'** „Vorsicht, bissiger Hund!"; **~ [of] how ...** darauf Acht geben, wie ...

bewilder /bɪ'wɪldə(r)/ *v.t.* verwirren; **be ~ed by sth.** durch *od.* von etw. verwirrt werden/sein

bewildering /bɪ'wɪldərɪŋ/ *adj.* verwirrend

bewilderment /bɪ'wɪldəmənt/ *n., no pl.* Verwirrung, *die;* **in total ~:** völlig verwirrt

bewitch /bɪ'wɪtʃ/ *v.t.* verzaubern; verhexen; (fig.) bezaubern

bewitching /bɪ'wɪtʃɪŋ/ *adj.* bezaubernd

bewitchingly /bɪ'wɪtʃɪŋlɪ/ *adv.* bezaubernd; **smile ~ at sb.** jmdn. mit einem bezaubernden Lächeln ansehen

beyond /bɪ'jɒnd/

A *adv.* **1)** (in space) jenseits; (on other side of wall, mountain range, etc.) dahinter; **the world ~:** das Jenseits **2)** (in time) darüber hinaus **3)** (in addition) daneben; außerdem; **and nothing ~:** und weiter nichts *od.* nichts weiter

B *prep.* **1)** (at far side of) jenseits (+ *Gen.*); **when we get ~ the river, we'll stop** wenn wir den Fluss überquert haben, machen wir Halt **2)** (later than) nach; **she never looks** *or* **sees ~ the present** sie sieht *od.* blickt nie über die Gegenwart hinaus; **I shan't wait ~ an hour/~ 6 o'clock** ich warte nicht länger als eine Stunde/nicht länger als bis 6 Uhr **3)** (out of reach, comprehension, range) über ... (+ *Akk.*) hinaus; **it's [far** *or* (coll.) **way] ~ me/him** *etc.* (too difficult) das ist mir/ihm *usw.* [bei weitem] zu schwer; (incomprehensible) das ist mir/ihm *usw.* [völlig] unverständlich; **be ~ the power of anyone's imagination** jedermanns Vorstellungsvermögen (*Akk.*) übersteigen; **your work is ~ all praise** Ihre Arbeit kann man nicht genug loben; **~ reproach** tadellos; **that is ~ my powers/competence** das liegt nicht in meiner Macht/überschreitet meine Befugnisse; **be ~ sb.'s capabilities/understanding** jmds. Fähigkeiten/Begriffsvermögen (*Akk.*) übersteigen **4)** (surpassing, exceeding) mehr als; **I succeeded ~ my wildest hopes** mein Erfolg übertraf meine kühnsten Hoffnungen; **they're living ~ their means** sie leben über ihre Verhältnisse **5)** (more than) weiter als; **he can't yet walk ~ a few steps** er kann noch nicht weiter als ein paar Schritte gehen; *see also* **joke A 1 6)** (besides) außer; **there's nothing you can do ~ writing to him regularly** Sie können nichts weiter tun, als ihm regelmäßig [zu] schreiben; **~ this/that** weiter

C *n.* **the B~:** das Jenseits; **at the back of ~:** am Ende der Welt

b.f.[1] /bi: 'ef/ *n.* (Brit. euphem.) = **bloody fool** Blödmann, *der* (salopp)

b.f.[2] *abbr.* (Bookk.) = **brought forward** Übertrag

BFPO *abbr.* = **British Forces Post Office** *Postdienst der britischen Streitkräfte*

b.h.p. *abbr.* (Mech. Engin.) = **brake horsepower**

biannual /baɪ'ænjʊəl/ *adj.* halbjährlich

biannually /baɪ'ænjʊəlɪ/ *adv.* zweimal jährlich

bias /'baɪəs/

A *n.* **1)** (tendency) Neigung, *die;* **have a ~ towards** *or* **in favour of sth./sb.** etw./jmdn. bevorzugen; **have a ~ against sth./sb.** gegen etw./jmdn. eingenommen sein; **be of** *or* **have a conservative ~:** konservativ eingestellt sein **2)** (prejudice) Voreingenommenheit, *die;* **be without ~:** unvoreingenommen sein **3)** (Statistics) systematischer Fehler; Bias, *das* (fachspr.) **4)** (Dressmaking) schräger Schnitt; **cut on the ~:** schräg zum Fadenlauf schneiden; *attrib.* **~ binding** Schrägband, *das*

B *v.t.,* **-s-** *or* **-ss-** beeinflussen; **be ~ed towards** *or* **in favour of sth./sb.** für etw./jmdn. eingestellt sein; **they are ~ed in favour of women** sie bevorzugen Frauen; **be ~ed against sth./sb.** gegen etw./jmdn. voreingenommen sein; **a ~ed account** eine gefärbte *od.* tendenziöse Darstellung; **a ~ed jury/judge** befangene Geschworene/ein befangener Richter/eine befangene Richterin

biathlon /baɪ'æθlən/ *n.* (Sport) Biathlon, *das*

bib /bɪb/*n.* **1)** (for baby) Lätzchen, *das* **2)** (of apron etc.) Latz, *der;* **put on one's best ~ and tucker** (joc.) sich in Schale werfen (ugs.).

Bible /'baɪbl/ *n.* **1)** (Christian) Bibel, *die* **2)** (of other religion) heiliges Buch; (fig.: authoritative book) Bibel, *die*

Bible: **~ class** *n.* Bibelstunde, *die;* **~ 'oath** *n.* Eid auf die Bibel

biblical /'bɪblɪkl/ *adj.* biblisch; Bibel-

bibliographer /bɪblɪ'ɒgrəfə(r)/ *n.* ▸ⓘ **p. 1260** Bibliograph, *der*/Bibliographin, *die*

bibliographic /bɪblɪə'græfɪk/, **bibliographical** /bɪblɪə'græfɪkl/ *adj.* bibliographisch

bibliography /bɪblɪ'ɒgrəfɪ/ *n.* **1)** (list) Bibliographie, *die;* Schriftenverzeichnis, *das* **2)** (study) Bibliographie, *die*

bibliophile /'bɪblɪəfaɪl/ *n.* Bibliophile, *der/die*

bibulous /'bɪbjʊləs/ *adj.* (formal) trunksüchtig

bicarb /'baɪkɑ:b/ *n.* (coll.) Natron, *das*

bicarbonate /baɪ'kɑ:bəneɪt/ *n.* **1)** (Cookery) **~ [of soda]** Natron, *das* **2)** (Chem.) doppeltkohlensaures Natrium

bicentenary /baɪsen'ti:nərɪ, baɪsen'tenərɪ/, **bicentennial** /baɪsen'tenɪəl/

A *adjs.* Zweihundertjahr-; **~ celebrations** Zweihundertjahrfeier, *die*

B *ns.* Zweihundertjahrfeier, *die*

biceps /'baɪseps/ *n.* **1)** (Anat.) Bizeps, *der* **2)** (muscularity) Muskeln *Pl.;* Bizeps, *der* (ugs.)

bicker /'bɪkə(r)/ *v.i.* zanken; streiten; **~ with sb. about** *or* **over sth.** sich mit jmdm. um etw. zanken *od.* streiten

bickering /'bɪkərɪŋ/ *n.* Gezänk, *das;* Zankerei, *die* (ugs.)

bicky /'bɪkɪ/ (*pl.* **-ies**) (coll.) Keksel, *das* (ugs.)

bicycle /'baɪsɪkl/

A *n.* Fahrrad, *das; attrib.* Fahrrad-; **ride a ~:** [mit dem] Fahrrad fahren; Rad fahren; **by ~:** mit dem [Fahr]rad

B *v.i.* Rad fahren; **he ~s to work** er fährt mit dem Fahrrad zur Arbeit

bicycle: **~ chain** *n.* Fahrradkette, *die;* **~ clip** *n.* Hosenklammer, *die;* **~ courier** *n.* Fahrradkurier, *der*/-kurierin, *die;* **~ kick** *n.* (Football) Fallrückzieher, *der;* **~ lane** *n.* (reserved for cyclists) Radfahrstreifen, *der;* (with priority for cyclists) Schutzstreifen, *der* [für Radfahrer]; **~ messenger** *n.* Fahrradkurier, *der*/-kurierin, *die;* **~ path** *n.* [Fahr]radweg, *der;* **~ pump** *n.* Fahrradpumpe, *die;* **~ rack** *n.* Fahrradständer, *der;* **~ shed** *n.* Fahrradschuppen, *der;* (*überdachter*) Fahrradstand, *der;* **~ track** *n.* [Fahr]radweg, *der*

bid /bɪd/

A *v.t.* **1) -dd-,** ~ (at auction) bieten; **what am I ~?** was höre ich?; was wird geboten?; **~ up the price** den Preis in die Höhe treiben **2) -dd-,** ~ (Cards) reizen **3) -dd-, bade** /bæd, beɪd/ *or* **~, bidden** /'bɪdn/ *or* ~ (arch./poet.: command) heißen (geh.); **~ sb. do sth.** jmdn. etw. tun heißen; **do as you are ~[den]** tu, was man dich geheißen hat **4) -dd-, bade** *or* **~, bidden** *or* ~ (invite) einladen; **he bade her be seated** er bat sie, Platz zu nehmen **5) -dd-, bade** *or* **~, bidden** *or* **~: ~ sb. welcome** jmdn. willkommen heißen; **~ sb. goodbye** sich von jmdm. verabschieden; **~ sb./** (coll.) **sth. farewell, ~ farewell to sb./** (coll.) **sth.** jmdm./einer Sache Lebewohl sagen; **~ sb. good day** jmdm. einen guten Tag wünschen

B *v.i.,* **-dd-, ~ 1)** werben (**for** um); **the Presi-**

b

dent is ~ding for re-election der Präsident bewirbt sich um die Wiederwahl; **~ fair to be sth.** etw. zu werden versprechen 2) (at auction) bieten 3) (Cards) bieten; reizen

C *n.* 1) (at auction) Gebot, *das;* **make a ~ of £90 for sth.** 90 Pfund für etw. bieten 2) (fig.: attempt) Versuch, *der;* **make a ~ for sth.** sich um etw. bemühen; **he made a strong ~ for the Presidency** er griff nach dem Präsidentenamt; **in his absence they made a ~ for power** in seiner Abwesenheit versuchten sie, die Macht an sich (*Akk.*) zu reißen; **a ~ for fame and fortune** ein Versuch, berühmt und reich zu werden; **the prisoner made a ~ for freedom** der Gefangene versuchte, die Freiheit zu erlangen; **his ~ to save the crew failed** sein Versuch, die Besatzung zu retten, scheiterte 3) (Cards) Ansage, *die;* **make no ~:** passen; **it's your ~:** Sie bieten!

biddable /'bɪdəbl/ *adj.* (obedient) fügsam

bidden ► **bid A 3, 4, 5**

bidder /'bɪdə(r)/ *n.* Bieter, *der*/Bieterin, *die;* **the highest ~:** der/die Höchstbietende

bidding /'bɪdɪŋ/ *n., no pl.* 1) (at auction) Steigern, *das;* Bieten, *das;* **open the ~:** das erste Gebot machen; **~ was brisk** es wurde lebhaft *od.* rege geboten; *see also* **force B 9** 2) (command) Geheiß, *das* (geh.); **at sb.'s ~:** auf jmds. Geheiß (*Akk.*); **do sb.'s ~:** tun, was einem von jmdm. befohlen wird 3) (Cards) Bieten, *das;* Reizen, *das*

bidding: ~ prayer *n.* Bittgebet, *das;* **~ war** *n.* (Commerc.) Bieterkrieg, *der*

bide /baɪd/

A *v.t.* **~ one's time** den rechten Augenblick abwarten

B *v.i.* (arch./dial.: remain) ausharren; **~ awhile** *or* (Scot.) **a wee** ein Weilchen warten

bidet /'bi:deɪ/ *n.* Bidet, *das*

bidirectional /baɪdɪ'rekʃənl, baɪdaɪ'rekʃənl/ *adj.* bidirektional

biennial /baɪ'enɪəl/

A *adj.* 1) (lasting two years) zweijährig; bienn (fachspr.), zweijährig ‹*Pflanze*› 2) (once every two years) zweijährlich

B *n.* (Bot.) zweijährige Pflanze; Bienne, *die* (fachspr.)

biennially /baɪ'enɪəlɪ/ *adv.* alle zwei Jahre

bier /bɪə(r)/ *n.* Totenbahre, *die*

biff /bɪf/ (coll.)

A *n.* Klaps, *der* (ugs.); **he gave her a ~ on the head** er haute ihr auf den Kopf

B *v.t.* hauen; **he ~ed me on the head with a book** er hat mir ein Buch auf den Kopf geknallt (ugs.)

bifocal /baɪ'fəʊkl/ (Optics)

A *adj.* Bifokal-

B *n. in pl.* Bifokalgläser *Pl.*

bifurcate /'baɪfəkeɪt/ (formal)

A *v.i.* sich gabeln

B *v.t.* gabelförmig teilen

bifurcation /baɪfə'keɪʃn/ *n.* (formal) (division) Aufspaltung, *die;* (point) Gabelung, *die;* (branch) Zweig, *der*

big /bɪg/

A *adj.* 1) (in size) groß; schwer, heftig ‹*Explosion, Zusammenstoß*›; schwer ‹*Unfall, Niederlage*›; hart ‹*Konkurrenz*›; reichlich ‹*Mahlzeit*›; **earn ~ money** das große Geld verdienen; **he is a ~ man/she is a ~ woman** (tall) er/sie ist eine lange Latte (ugs.); (fat) er/sie ist wohlbeleibt; **she is a ~ girl** (joc.: busty) sie hat einen ganz schönen Balkon (ugs.); **the ~ expense of moving house** die hohen Umzugskosten; **~ words** geschraubte Ausdrücke (*see also* **7**); **in a ~ way** (coll.) im großen Stil; **he fell in love with her in a ~ way** er verliebte sich heftig in sie; **carry/wield a ~ stick** (fig.) den großen Knüppel schwingen (ugs.) 2) (of largest size, larger than usual) groß ‹*Appetit, Zehe, Buchstabe*›; **Conservatism with a ~ C** (fig.) Konservati[vi]smus par excellence *od.* in Reinkultur 3) **~ger** (worse) schwerer; **the ~ger the crime the more severe the penalty** je schwerer das Verbrechen, desto härter die Strafe; **~gest** (worst) größt...; **he is the ~gest liar/idiot** er ist der größte Lügner/Idiot 4) (grown up, elder) groß; **you're ~ enough to know better** du bist groß *od.* alt genug, um es besser zu wissen 5) (important) groß; wichtig ‹*Nachricht, Entscheidung*›; **the ~ story in the papers today is ...:** das Hauptthema in den Zeitungen von heute ist ...; **a ~ man** ein wichtiger Mann (*see also* **1**); **the B~ Three/Four** *etc.* die Großen Drei/Vier *usw.* 6) (coll.: outstanding) groß ‹*Augenblick, Chance*›; **what's the ~ hurry?** warum die große Eile? 7) (boastful) angeberisch (ugs.); großspurig (ugs.); **get** *or* **grow/be too ~ for one's boots** *or* **breeches** (coll.) größenwahnsinnig werden/sein (ugs.); **~ talk** Großsprecherei, *die;* **~ talker** Großsprecher, *der*/Grosprecherin, *die;* **~ words** große Worte (*see also* **1**) 8) (coll.: generous) großzügig; nobel (oft iron.); **that's ~ of you** (iron.) wie nobel! 9) (coll.: keen) **be ~ on sth.** großen Wert auf etw. (*Akk.*) legen 10) (coll.: popular) **be ~** ‹*Schauspieler, Popstar:*› gut ankommen. *See also* **idea 5**

B *adv.* groß; **come/go over ~:** groß ankommen (ugs.) (**with** bei); **talk ~:** groß daherreden (ugs.); **think ~:** im großen Stil planen

bigamist /'bɪgəmɪst/ *n.* Bigamist, *der*/Bigamistin, *die*

bigamous /'bɪgəməs/ *adj.* bigamistisch

bigamy /'bɪgəmɪ/ *n.* Bigamie, *die*

big: ~ band *n.* (Mus.) Bigband, *die;* **~ 'bang** *n.* Urknall, *der;* **Big Ben** *n.* Big Ben (*der*); *Glocke/Uhr im Turm des Parlamentsgebäudes in London;* **Big 'Brother** *n.* der Große Bruder; **~ 'business** *n.* das Großkapital; **~ 'cheese** *n.* (coll.: person) hohes Tier (ugs.); **~ 'deal** ► **deal¹ C 1**; **~ 'dipper** *n.* 1) (Brit.: at fair) Achterbahn, *die;* 2) (Astron.) ► **dipper 4**; **~ end** *n.* (Motor Veh.) Pleuelfuß, *der;* **~ game** *n.* Großwild, *das; attrib.* **~-game hunting** Großwildjagd, *die;* **~ government** *n.* Big Government *das;* **~head** *n.* (coll.) Fatzke, *der* (ugs. abwertend); **~-'headed** *adj.* (coll.) eingebildet; **~-'hearted** *adj.* großherzig

bight /baɪt/ *n.* 1) (loop) Schlaufe, *die* 2) (curve) (in coast) Bucht, *die;* (in river) Krümmung, *die;* Schleife, *die*

> **Big Issue**
>
> Eine Zeitung, die von Obdachlosen in vielen größeren und kleineren Städten in Großbritannien verkauft wird. Die Artikel haben oft ein sehr gutes Niveau, sie behandeln hauptsächlich soziale Themen oder Aspekte der Stadtkultur. Die Verkäufer kaufen die Zeitungen von einer zentralen Stelle und verkaufen sie zu einem festgelegten Preis. Den Gewinn dürfen sie behalten.

big: ~ mouth *n.* (fig. coll.) **have a ~ mouth** ein Schwätzer/eine Schwätzerin sein (ugs.); **~mouth** *n.* (coll.) **be a ~mouth** ein Angeber/eine Angeberin sein (ugs.); **~ 'name** *n.* (person) Größe, *die;* **~ 'noise** *n.* (coll.) hohes Tier (ugs.)

bigot /'bɪgət/ *n.* bornierter Mensch; (Relig.) bigotter Mensch

bigoted /'bɪgətɪd/ *adj.* borniert; (Relig.) bigott

bigotry /'bɪgətrɪ/ *n.* Borniertheit; (Relig.) Bigotterie, *die*

big: ~ shot ► **~ noise**; **~ time** *n.* **be in the ~ time** (coll.) eine große Nummer sein (ugs.); **make it [in]to** *or* **hit the ~ time** (sl.) groß herauskommen (ugs.); **~ 'top** *n.* Zirkuszelt, *das;* **~ 'wheel** *n.* 1) (at fair) Riesenrad, *das;* 2) (coll.: person) hohes Tier (ugs.); **~wig** *n.* (coll.) hohes Tier (ugs.)

bijou /'bi:ʒu:/*adj.* (esp. Brit.) exquisit ‹*Haus, Wohnung*›

bike /baɪk/ (coll.)

A *n.* (bicycle) Rad, *das;* (motorcycle) Maschine, *die*

B *v.i.* (by bicycle) Rad fahren; radeln (ugs., bes. südd.); mit dem Fahrrad fahren; (by motorcycle) [mit dem] Motorrad fahren

bike: ~ courier ► **~ messenger**; **~ lane** (esp. Amer.) ► **bicycle lane**; **~ messenger** *n.* ►ℹ **p. 1260** (on motorbike) Motorradkurier, *der*/Motorradkurierin, *die;* (on bicycle) Fahrradkurier, *der*/Fahrradkurierin, *die;* **~ path** (esp. Amer.) ► **bicycle path**

biker /'baɪkə(r)/ *n.* (cyclist) Radfahrer, *der*/Radfahrerin, *die;* Biker, *der* (Jargon); (motorcyclist) Motorradfahrer, *der*/Motorradfahrerin, *die;* Biker, *der* (Jargon)

bike: ~ rack *n.* ► **bicycle rack**; **~ shed** *n.* ► **bicycle shed**

bikini /bɪ'ki:nɪ/ *n.* Bikini, *der;* **~ briefs** Slip, *der*

bikky ► **bicky**

bilateral /baɪ'lætərl/ *adj.* bilateral

bilaterally /baɪ'lætərəlɪ/ *adv.* bilateral; **the two countries agreed ~ on disarmament** beide Länder einigten sich darauf abzurüsten

bilberry /'bɪlbərɪ/ *n.* Blau-, Heidelbeere, *die*

bile /baɪl/ *n.* 1) (Physiol.) Gallenflüssigkeit, *die;* **~ duct** Gallengang, *der* 2) (Med.) Gallenleiden, *das* 3) (fig.: peevishness) Verdrießlichkeit, *die;* Übellaunigkeit, *die*

bilge /bɪldʒ/ *n.* 1) Bilge, *die* 2) (filth) angesammelter Schmutz im Kielraum; (fig. coll.: nonsense) Quatsch, *der;* Unsinn, *der*

bilge: ~-keel *n.* Kimm- *od.* Bilge[n]kiel, *der;* **~-water** *n.* Bilge[n]wasser, *das*

bilingual /baɪ'lɪŋgwəl/ *adj.* zweisprachig; bilingual (fachspr.) ‹*Person*›; bilinguisch (fachspr.) ‹*Buch, Ausgabe*›

bilingualism /baɪ'lɪŋgwəlɪzm/ *n., no pl.* Bilingualismus, *der;* Zweisprachigkeit, *die*

bilious /'bɪljəs/ *adj.* (Med.) Gallen-; biliös (fachspr.); (fig.: peevish) verdrießlich; **~ attack** Gallenanfall, *der;* Gallenkolik, *die;* **a ~ green** ein unappetitliches Grün

biliousness /'bɪljəsnɪs/ *n., no pl.* Gallenbeschwerden *Pl.;* Gallenleiden, *das;* (fig.) Reizbarkeit, *die;* Verdrießlichkeit, *die*

bilk /bɪlk/ *v.t.* (coll.) 1) (evade payment to) prellen ‹*Gläubiger, Kellner usw.*› 2) (evade payment of) nicht bezahlen ‹*Schuld, Rechnung usw.*›; **~ payment** nicht bezahlen *od.* Zahlung unterlassen 3) (cheat) betrügen; **~ sb. of sth.** jmdn. um etw. betrügen

bill¹ /bɪl/

A *n.* 1) (of bird) Schnabel, *der* 2) (promontory) Landzunge, *die* 3) (Naut.: point of anchor fluke) Spitze, *die*

B *v.i.* ‹*Vögel:*› schnäbeln; ‹*Personen:*› sich liebkosen; **~ and coo** ‹*Vögel:*› schnäbeln und gurren; ‹*Personen:*› [miteinander] turteln

bill²

A *n.* 1) (Parl.) Gesetzentwurf, *der;* Gesetzesvorlage, *die* 2) (note of charges) Rechnung, *die;* **could we have the ~, please?** wir möchten zahlen; **a ~ for £100** eine Rechnung über 100 Pfund (*Akk.*); (amount) **a large ~:** eine hohe Rechnung; **a ~ of £100** eine Rechnung von 100 Pfund 3) (poster) Plakat, *das;* **'[stick] no ~s'** „Plakate ankleben verboten" 4) (programme) Programm, *das;* **what's on the ~?** was steht auf dem Programm?; **top the ~, be top of the ~:** der Star [des Abends *usw.*] sein; **~ of fare** Speisekarte, *die;* (fig.) [bunter] Programmreigen 5) ►ℹ **p. 1332** (Amer.: banknote) Banknote, *die;* [Geld]schein, *der;* **a 50-dollar ~:** ein Fünfzigdollarschein 6) **~ [of exchange]** (Commerc.) Wechsel, *der;* Tratte, *die* (fachspr.) 7) **~ of health** Gesundheitsattest *od.* -zeugnis, *das;* **give sb./sth. a clean ~ of health** (fig.) jmdm./einer Sache ein gutes/einwandfreies Zeugnis ausstellen; **~ of lading** Konnossement, *das;* Seefrachtbrief, *der;* **~ of quantities** (Brit.) Kostenvoranschlag, *der* (*Aufstellung der Kosten/Dimensionen eines Bauwerks*); **~ of sale** Kaufvertrag, *der;* Verkaufsurkunde, *die*

B *v.t.* 1) (announce) ankündigen; **he is ~ed to appear next week at the Palace Theatre** er soll nächste Woche im Palace Theatre auftreten 2) (advertise) durch Anschlag bekannt machen *od.* bekannt geben 3) (charge) eine Rechnung ausstellen (+ *Dat.*); **~ sb. for sth.**

jmdm. etw. in Rechnung stellen *od.* berechnen

Bill of Rights

In den Vereinigten Staaten von Amerika ist die *Bill of Rights* der Grundrechtkatalog, der seit 1791 in Kraft ist und aus den ersten zehn Änderungen der Verfassung besteht. Zum Beispiel garantiert die erste Verfassungsänderung (*First Amendment*) Glaubensfreiheit, Freiheit der Meinungsäußerung und Pressefreiheit. Die zweite Änderung (*Second Amendment*) gibt allen Bürgern das Recht, eine Schusswaffe zu besitzen (allerdings sind jetzt viele der Ansicht, dass dieses Recht eingeschränkt werden sollte). Nach der berühmten fünften Änderung (*Fifth Amendment*) darf ein Angeklagter die Aussage gegen sich selbst verweigern.

Die englische *Bill of Rights* ist das Staatsgrundgesetz von 1689 und die Grundlage für die parlamentarische Regierungsform in Großbritannien. Das Gesetz klärt die Frage der Machtverteilung zwischen König, Ministern und Parlament, die jedoch erst im 18. und frühen 19. Jahrhundert zugunsten des Parlaments entschieden wurde.

'billboard *n.* Anschlagbrett, *das od.* -tafel, *die;* Plakattafel, *die;* Reklametafel, *die*

billet¹ /'bɪlɪt/ (esp. Mil.)
A *n.* Quartier, *das;* Unterkunft, *die*
B *v.t.* unterbringen, einquartieren (**with, on** bei; **in** in + *Dat.*)

billet² *n.* **1** (of wood) Holzscheit, -klotz, *der* **2** (bar) kleine Metallstange **3** (Archit.) Spannkeil, *der*

billet-doux /bɪlɪ'du:/ *n., pl.* **billets-doux** /bɪlɪ'du:z/ Liebesbrief, *der;* Billetdoux, *das* (veralt.)

bill: ~fold *n.* (Amer.) Brieftasche, *die;* **~head** *n.* gedrucktes Rechnungsformular; **~hook** *n.* Hippe, *die*

billiard/'bɪljəd/: **~ ball** *n.* Billardkugel, *die;* Billardball, *der;* **~ cue** *n.* Queue, *das;* Billardstock, *der;* **~ player** *n.* Billardspieler, *der*/-spielerin, *die;* **~ room** *n.* Billardzimmer, *das*

billiards /'bɪljədz/ *n.* Billard[spiel], *das;* **a game of ~:** eine Partie Billard; **bar ~** (Brit.) *Billardspiel, bei dem die Löcher, in die die Kugeln gespielt werden müssen, nicht an den Seiten, sondern über die Tischplatte verteilt sind*

'billiard table *n.* Billardtisch, *der*

billion /'bɪljən/ *n.* ▸**ⓘ p. 1358** Milliarde, *die*

billionaire /bɪljə'neə(r)/ *n.* Milliardär, *der*

billionth /'bɪlɪənθ/
A *adj.* milliardst...
B *n., no pl.* Milliardstel, *das*

billow /'bɪləʊ/
A *n.* **1** (surging mass) Masse, *die;* **~ of smoke** Rauchwolke, *die;* **~ of fog** Nebelschwaden, *der;* **a ~ of flame** eine Feuerwalze **2** (arch.: wave) Woge, *die;* **~s** (poet.: sea) Wogen *Pl.* (dichter.)
B *v.i.* ‹*Ballon, Segel:*› sich [auf]blähen; ‹*See, Meer:*› wogen, sich [auf]türmen; ‹*Rauch:*› in Schwaden aufsteigen; ‹*Kleid, Vorhang:*› sich bauschen

billowy /'bɪləʊɪ/ *adj.* wogend ‹*See, Kornfeld*›; gebläht ‹*Segel*›; in Schwaden ziehend ‹*Rauch*›; bauschig ‹*Rock*›

bill: ~poster, ~sticker *ns.* ▸**ⓘ p. 1260** Plakat[an]kleber, *der*

billy¹ /'bɪlɪ/ *n.* (pot) Kochgeschirr, *das*

billy² *n.* **1** ▸ **billy goat 2** **~ [club]** (Amer.) [Gummi]knüppel, *der*

'billycan ▸ **billy¹**

'billy goat *n.* Ziegenbock, *der*

billy-o /'bɪlɪəʊ/ *n.* (coll.) **like ~:** wie verrückt (ugs.); **they are fighting like ~:** sie prügeln sich wie die Wilden (ugs.)

bimbo /'bɪmbəʊ/ *n.* (coll. derog.) Puppe, *die* (salopp)

bimetallic /baɪmɪ'tælɪk/ *adj.* bimetallisch; **~ strip** Bimetall, *das;* Bimetallstreifen, *der*

bimonthly /baɪ'mʌnθlɪ/
A *adj.* **1** (two-monthly) zweimonatlich; alle zwei Monate erscheinend ‹*Zeitschrift*›/stattfindend ‹*Treffen, Ereignis*› **2** (twice-monthly) zweimal im Monat erscheinend ‹*Zeitschrift*›/stattfindend ‹*Treffen, Ereignis*›
B *adv.* **1** (two-monthly) alle zwei Monate **2** (twice monthly) zweimal im Monat

bin /bɪn/ *n.*
A **1** (for storage) Behälter, *der;* (for coal) Kohlenkasten, *der;* (for fruit) [Obst]kiste, *die;* (for bread) Brotkasten, *der;* (for wine) Weinregal, *das* **2** (for rubbish) (inside house) Abfalleimer, *der;* Mülleimer, *der;* (outside house) Mülltonne, *die;* (in public place) Abfallkorb, *der*
B *v.t.* (coll.) wegschmeißen (ugs.)

binary /'baɪnərɪ/
A *adj.* **1** binär; zweizählig; **~ system** binäres System **2** (Math.) **~ digit** binäre Ziffer; Dualzahl, *die;* **~ number** binäre Zahl **3** (Biol.) **~ fission** äquale Zellteilung **4** (Mus.) **~ form** zweiteilige Form; **~ measure** gerader Takt **5** (Astron.) **~ star** Doppelstern, *der* **6** (Chem.) **~ compound** binäre Verbindung; Zweifachverbindung, *die*
B *n.* (Astron.) Doppelstern, *der*

binaural /bɪ'nɔ:rl/ *adj.* (Audio) binaural ‹*Übertragung usw.*›

'bin bag *n.* Müllbeutel, *der*

bind /baɪnd/
A *v.t.*, **bound** /baʊnd/ **1** (tie) fesseln ‹*Person, Tier*›; (bandage) wickeln, binden ‹*Glied, Baum*›; verbinden ‹*Wunde*› (**with** mit); **he was bound hand and foot** er war/wurde an Händen und Füßen gefesselt; **they bound the animal's legs together** sie fesselten das Tier an den Beinen; **~ sb. to sth.** jmdn. an etw. (*Akk.*) fesseln *od.* binden; **~ sth. to sth.** etw. an etw. (*Akk.*) binden **2** (fasten together) zusammenbinden; (fig.: unite) verbinden **3** **~ books** Bücher binden **4** **be bound up with sth.** (fig.) eng mit etw. verbunden *od.* verknüpft sein; eng mit etw. zusammenhängen **5** (oblige) **~ sb./oneself to sth.** jmdn./sich an etw. (*Akk.*) binden; **this agreement ~s us** wir sind an diese Abmachung gebunden; **be bound to do sth.** (required) verpflichtet sein, etw. zu tun; **be bound by law** von Gesetzes wegen verpflichtet sein; **be bound to secrecy** zur Verschwiegenheit verpflichtet sein; *see also* **honour A 4** **6** **be bound to do sth.** (certain) etw. ganz bestimmt tun; **it is bound to rain** es wird bestimmt *od.* sicherlich regnen **7** **I'm bound to say that ...** (feel obliged) ich muss schon sagen, dass ...; ich fühle mich verpflichtet zu sagen, dass ...; **I'm bound to agree** ich glaube, ich stimme überein **8** (constipate) verstopfen **9** (Cookery) binden **10** (indenture) durch Lehrvertrag binden ‹*Lehrling*›; **he was bound [apprentice] for 3 years** er ging drei Jahre in die Lehre **11** (Law) **~ sb. over [to keep the peace]** jmdn. verwarnen *od.* rechtlich verpflichten[, die öffentliche Ordnung zu wahren]; **I'll be bound** (fig.) ganz gewiss; auf mein Wort **12** (encircle) **~ one's hair with flowers** sich (*Dat.*) Blumen ins Haar binden **13** (edge) einfassen ‹*Stoffkante usw.*› (**with** mit)
B *v.i.*, **bound** **1** (cohere) binden; ‹*Lehm, Ton:*› fest *od.* hart werden; ‹*Zement:*› abbinden **2** (be restricted) blockieren; ‹*Kolben:*› sich festfressen; **the window frame ~s easily** der Fensterrahmen verklemmt sich leicht **3** (coll.: complain) meckern (ugs.) (**about** über + *Akk.*)
C *n.* **1** (coll.: nuisance) **be a ~:** recht lästig sein; **what a ~!** wie unangenehm *od.* lästig! **2** **be in a ~** (coll.) in einer Klemme sitzen (ugs.) **3** (Mus.) Bindebogen, *der;* Bindungszeichen, *das;* Bindung, *die*

binder /'baɪndə(r)/ *n.* **1** (for papers) Hefter, *der;* (for magazines) Mappe, *die* **2** (substance) Bindemittel, *das;* Binder, *der* **3** (book~) Buchbinder, *der*/-binderin, *die* **4** (Agric.) [Mäh]binder, *der;* Bindemäher, *der*

bindery /'baɪndərɪ/ *n.* Buchbinderei, *die*

binding /'baɪndɪŋ/
A *adj.* bindend, verbindlich ‹*Vertrag, Abkommen*› (**on** für)
B *n.* **1** (cover of book) [Buch]einband, *der* **2** (edge) (of carpet, material, etc.) [Einfass]band, *das;* Besatz, *der* **3** (on ski) Bindung, *die*

bindweed /'baɪndwi:d/ *n.* (Bot.) Winde, *die*

'bin end *n.* Restflasche, *die*

binge /bɪndʒ/
A *n.* (coll.: drinking bout) Sauferei, *die* (salopp); **go/be out on a ~:** auf Sauftour gehen/sein (salopp)
B *v.i.* **~ on sth.** (on food) sich mit etw. voll fressen; (on drink) sich mit etw. voll laufen lassen

binge: ~ drinker *n.* Quartalssäufer, *der*/-säuferin, *die* (ugs.); **~ drinking** *n., no pl.* Quartalssaufen, *das* (Med. Jargon); **~ eating** *n., no pl.* Heißhungeressen *das;* **suffer from a ~ eating disorder** von Fressattacken *od.* Essanfällen heimgesucht werden

bingo /'bɪŋgəʊ/
A *n., no pl.* Bingo, *das;* **~ hall** Bingohalle, *die*
B *int.* peng; zack

bin: ~ liner *n.* Müllbeutel, *der;* **~man** /'bɪnmæn/ *n., pl.* **-men** /-men/ (Brit. coll.) Müllman, *der*

binnacle /'bɪnəkl/ *n.* (Naut.) Kompasshaus, *das*

binocular /bɪ'nɒkjʊlə(r)/
A *adj.* binokular
B *n.* in *pl.* **[pair of] ~s** Fernglas, *das;* Binokular, *das*

bint /bɪnt/ *n.* (coll. derog.) Weib[stück], *das*

bio- /baɪəʊ/ *in comb.* Bio-; Lebens-

bio'active *adj.* bioaktiv; biologisch aktiv

bio'chemical *adj.* biochemisch

bio'chemist *n.* ▸**ⓘ p. 1260** Biochemiker, *der*/Biochemikerin, *die*

bio'chemistry *n., no pl.* Biochemie, *die*

biocidal /baɪə'saɪdl/ *adj.* biozid; **~ agent** Biozid, *das*

biocide /'baɪəsaɪd/ *n.* Biozid, *das*

biocom'patible *adj.* biokompatibel; bioverträglich

biocom'puter *n.* Biocomputer, *der*

biocom'puting *n., no pl.* Biocomputing, *das*

'biocontrol *n.* **1** *no pl.* (control of pests) biologische Schädlingsbekämpfung **2** (organism) [Bio-]kontrollorganismus, *der;* **~s** Nutzorganismen; Nützlinge

biode'gradable *adj.* biologisch abbaubar

biode'grade *v.i.* sich biologisch abbauen

biodi'versity *n., no pl.* biologische Vielfalt

'bioenergy *n., no pl.* **1** (renewable energy) Bioenergie, *die* **2** **~ [healing]** Heilung durch Bioenergie

bioengi'neering *n.* **1** Biotechnik, *die;* **a ~ process** ein biotechnisches Verfahren **2** (genetic engineering) Gentechnologie, *die*

bio'ethics *n.* Bioethik, *die*

'biofeedback *n., no pl.* Biofeedback, *das*

'biofilm *n.* Biofilm, *der*

'biofuel *n.* Biobrennstoff, *der;* (for vehicle) Biokraftstoff, *der*

'biogas *n.* Biogas, *das*

bio'genesis *n., no pl.* Biogenese, *die*

biogenic /baɪə'dʒenɪk/ *adj.* biogenetisch

biographer /baɪ'ɒgrəfə(r)/ *n.* ▸**ⓘ p. 1260** Biograph, *der*/Biographin, *die*

biographic /baɪə'græfɪk/, **biographical** /baɪə'græfɪkl/ *adj.* biographisch

biography /baɪ'ɒgrəfɪ/ *n.* Biographie, *die;* (branch of literature) biographische Literatur

'biohazard *n.* Biogefahr, *die*

bioinfor'matics *n., no pl.* Bioinformatik, *die*

biological /baɪə'lɒdʒɪkl/ *adj.* biologisch

biological: ~ 'clock *n.* biologische Uhr; **~ con'trol** *n.* biologische Schädlingsbekämpfung

biologically /baɪə'lɒdʒɪkəlɪ/ *adv.* biologisch

biological: ~ 'parent *n.* biologischer Elternteil; **~ parents** biologische Eltern; **~ 'shield** *n.* biologischer Schild; **~ 'warfare** *n., no pl.* biologische Kriegführung; Bakterienkrieg, *der;* **~ 'waste** *n., no pl.* Bioabfall, *der;* Biomüll, *der;* biologischer Abfall

biologist /baɪ'ɒlədʒɪst/ *n.* ▸**ⓘ p. 1260** Biologe, *der*/Biologin, *die*

biology /baɪ'ɒlədʒɪ/ *n., no pl.* Biologie, *die*

biolumi'nescence *n., no pl.* Biolumineszenz, *die*

'biomarker *n.* Biomarker, *der*

b

'**biomass** *n.* Biomasse, *die*
biome'chanics *n., no pl.* Biomechanik, *die*
biometric /baɪə'metrɪk/, **biometrical** /baɪə'metrɪkl/ *adj.* biometrisch
bionic /baɪ'ɒnɪk/ *adj.* bionisch
bionics /baɪ'ɒnɪks/ *n., no pl.* Bionik, *die*
bio'physical *adj.* biophysikalisch
bio'physics *n., no pl.* Biophysik, *die*
biopic /'baɪəʊpɪk/ *n.* (coll.) Filmbiographie, *die*
biopsy /'baɪɒpsɪ/ *n.* Biopsie, *die*
'**bioregion** *n.* Bioregion, *die*
'**biorhythm** *n.* Biorhythmus, *der*
BIOS /'baɪɒs/ *n.* (Computing) = **Basic Input-Output System** BIOS, *das*
'**biosafety** *n., no pl.* Biosicherheit, *die;* biologische Sicherheit; *attrib.* ~ **protocol** Protokoll über die biologische Sicherheit
bioscope /'baɪəskəʊp/ *n.* (S. Afr.) Filmtheater, *das;* Kino, *das*
biose'curity *n., no pl.* Biosicherheit, *die;* biologische Sicherheit; *attrib.* ~ **measures** Maßnahmen zur Erhaltung der biologischen Sicherheit
'**biosensor** *n.* Biosensor, *der*
'**biosphere** *n.* Biosphäre, *die*
'**biosphere reserve** *n.* Biosphärenreservat, *das*
bio'synthesis *n., no pl.* Biosynthese, *die*
biotech /'baɪəʊtek/ *n., no pl.* Biotechnologie, *die; attrib.* ~ **company/industry** Biotechfirma, *die*/Biotechindustrie, *die;* ~ **product** biotechnisches Produkt
biotech'nologist *n.* Biotechnologe, *der*/-technologin, *die*
biotech'nology *n.* Biotechnologie, *die*
bio'terrorism *n., no pl.* Bioterrorismus, *der*
bio'terrorist *n.* Bioterrorist, *der*/-terroristin, *die*
biotope /'baɪətəʊp/ *n.* Biotop, *der od. das*
bipartisan /baɪpɑ:tɪ'zæn, baɪ'pɑ:tɪzæn/ *adj.* Zweiparteien-
bipartite /baɪ'pɑ:taɪt/ *adj.* (having two parts) zweiteilig; (involving two parties) zweiseitig ‹*Dokument, Abkommen*›
biped /'baɪped/ *n.* Bipede, *der;* Zweifüßer, *der*
biplane /'baɪpleɪn/ *n.* Doppeldecker, *der*
birch /bɜ:tʃ/
A *n.* **1** (tree) Birke, *die* **2** ▸ **birch rod**
B *v.t.* mit der Rute züchtigen
birch: ~ **bark** *n.* Birkenrinde, *die;* ~ **rod** *n.* [Birken]rute, *die*
bird /bɜ:d/ *n.* **1** Vogel, *der;* **the ~ is** *or* **has flown** (fig.) der Vogel ist ausgeflogen (fig.); **~s of a feather flock together** (prov.) Gleich und Gleich gesellt sich gern (Spr.); **it's [strictly] for the ~s** (coll.) das kannste vergessen (salopp); **get the ~** (Brit. coll.: be booed etc.) ausgepfiffen werden; **give sb. the ~** (boo sb.) jmdn. auspfeifen; **kill two ~s with one stone** (fig.) zwei Fliegen mit einer Klappe schlagen; **a ~ in the hand is worth two in the bush** (prov.) ein Spatz in der Hand ist besser als eine Taube auf dem Dach (Spr.); **like a ~** (without difficulty or hesitation) einfach so; **a little ~ told me** mein kleiner Finger sagt mir das; **tell sb. about the ~s and the bees** (euphem.) jmdm. erzählen, wo die kleinen Kinder herkommen; *See also* **prey A 1** **2** (sl.: girl) Mieze, *die* (salopp) **3** (coll.: person) Vogel, *der* (ugs.); **a queer ~:** ein komischer Kauz *od.* Vogel **4** *no art.* (sl.: imprisonment) Knast, *der* (ugs.); **do ~:** Knast schieben (salopp). *See also* **early bird**
bird: ~ **bath** *n.* Vogelbad, *das;* **~brained** *adj.* (coll.) **1** (stupid) gehirnamputiert (salopp); **~brained person** Mensch mit einem Spatzenhirn (salopp); **2** (flighty) flatterhaft; **~cage** *n.* Vogelkäfig, *der;* Vogelbauer, *das od. der;* ~ **call** *n.* Vogelruf, *der;* (instrument) Lockpfeife, *die;* ~ **fancier** *n.* Vogelfreund, *der*/-freundin, *die;* (breeder) Vogelzüchter, *der*/-züchterin, *die;* ~ **flu** *n.* Vogelgrippe, *die*
birdie /'bɜ:dɪ/
A *n.* **1** Vögelchen, *das* **2** (Golf) Birdie, *das;* ein Schlag unter Par
B *v.t.* einen Schlag unter Par spielen

bird: **~lime** *n.* Vogelleim, *der;* ~ **of 'paradise** *n.* Paradiesvogel, *der;* ~ **of 'passage** *n.* (lit. or fig.) Zugvogel, *der;* ~ **sanctuary** *n.* Vogelschutzgebiet, *das;* ~ **scarer** /'bɜ:dskeərə(r)/*n.* (person) Vogelvertreiber, *der*/-vertreiberin, *die;* (device) Vogelschreckanlage, *die;* **~seed** *n.* Vogelfutter, *das;* **~'s-eye** *n.* (Bot.) Gamander- Ehrenpreis, *der;* **~'s-eye 'view** *n.* Vogelperspektive, *die;* **have/get a ~'s-eye view of sth.** (lit. or fig.) etw. aus der Vogelperspektive sehen; **~'s nest** *n.* Vogelnest, *das;* **~'s nest soup** Schwalbennestersuppe, *die;* ~ **strike** *n.* Kollision von Flugzeug und Vogel; ~ **table** *n.* Futterstelle für Vögel; **~watcher** *n.* Vogelbeobachter, *der*/-beobachterin, *die;* **~-watching** *n., no pl., no indef. art.* das Beobachten von Vögeln
biretta /bɪ'retə/ *n.* (Eccl.) Birett, *das*
Biro ® /'baɪrəʊ/ *n., pl.* **~s** Kugelschreiber, *der;* Kuli, *der* (ugs.)
birth /bɜ:θ/ *n.* **1** Geburt, *die;* **at the/at ~:** bei der Geburt; **[deaf] from** *or* **since ~:** von Geburt an [taub]; **date and place of ~:** Geburtsdatum und -ort; **land of my ~:** Land meiner Väter (geh.); **give ~** ‹*Frau:*› entbinden; gebären (geh.); ‹*Tier:*› jungen; werfen; **she gave ~ prematurely** sie hatte eine Frühgeburt; **give ~ to a child** von einem Kind entbunden werden; ein Kind gebären (geh.) *od.* zur Welt bringen **2** (coming into existence) (of movement, fashion, etc.) Aufkommen, *das;* (of party, company) Gründung, *die;* (of nation) Geburt, *die;* (of new era) Anbruch, *der;* Geburt, *die;* **the ~ of an idea** die Geburt einer Idee; **give ~ to sth.** etw. entstehen lassen **3** (parentage) Geburt, *die;* Abkunft, *die* (geh.); **of good/low** *or* **humble ~:** aus gutem Hause *od.* guter Familie/von niedriger Abstammung; **of high ~:** von hoher Geburt; [von] edler Abkunft (geh.); **be a German by ~:** Deutsche[r] von Geburt sein; [ein] gebürtiger Deutscher/[eine] gebürtige Deutsche sein; **sb.'s right by ~:** jmds. angeborenes Recht
birth: ~ **certificate** *n.* Geburtsurkunde, *die;* ~ **control** *n.* Geburtenkontrolle *od.* -regelung, *die;* **~day** *n.* ▸ℹ **p. 1189** Geburtstag, *der;* **when is your ~day?** wann haben Sie Geburtstag?; *attrib.* **~day card** Geburtstagskarte, *die;* **~day party** Geburtstagsfeier, *die;* (with music and dancing) Geburtstagsparty, *die;* (children's) Kindergeburtstag, *der;* **~day present** Geburtstagsgeschenk, *das;* **~day honours** (Brit.) Titel- und Ordensverleihungen *Pl.* (*am offiziellen Geburtstag des britischen Monarchen*); **[be] in his/her ~day suit** (coll. joc.: naked) im Adams-/Evaskostüm [sein]
'**birthing pool** /'bɜ:θɪŋ/ *n.* Gebärwanne, *die*
birth: **~mark** *n.* Muttermal, *das;* ~ **parent** *n.* leiblicher Elternteil; ~ **parents** leibliche Eltern; **~place** *n.* Geburtsort, *der;* (house) Geburtshaus, *das;* **~rate** *n.* Geburtenrate *od.* -ziffer, *die;* **~right** *n.* Geburtsrecht, *das;* (right of first-born) Erstgeburtsrecht, *das;* **~stone** *n.* Monatsstein, *der;* **~weight** *n.* Geburtsgewicht, *das*
biscuit /'bɪskɪt/
A *n.* **1** (Brit.) Keks, *der;* **coffee and ~s** Kaffee und Gebäck; **~ tin** Keksdose, *die* **2** (Amer.: roll) [weiches] Brötchen **3** (colour) Beige, *das* **4** (pottery) Biskuit, *das. see also* **take A 3**
B *adj.* beige
bisect /baɪ'sekt/ *v.t.* (into halves) in zwei Hälften teilen; halbieren; (into two) in zwei Teile teilen
bisection /baɪ'sekʃn/ *n.* (into halves) Halbierung, *die;* (into two) Zweiteilung, *die*
bisector /baɪ'sektə(r)/ *n.* Halbierende, *die*
bisexual /baɪ'seksjʊəl/
A *adj.* **1** (attracted to both sexes) bisexuell **2** (Biol.) zwittrig; doppelgeschlechtig
B *n.* Bisexuelle, *der/die*
bisexuality /baɪseksjʊ'ælɪtɪ/ *n., no pl.* ▸ **bisexual A:** Bisexualität, *die;* Zwittrigkeit, *die;* Doppelgeschlechtigkeit, *die*
bish /bɪʃ/ *n.* (Brit. dated coll.) Fehler, *der*
bishop /'bɪʃəp/ *n.* **1** ▸ℹ **p. 1634** (Eccl.) Bischof, *der; as voc.* Herr Bischof **2** (Chess) Läufer, *der*

bishopric /'bɪʃəprɪk/ *n.* **1** (office) Bischofsamt, *das;* Bischofswürde, *die* **2** (diocese) Bistum, *das;* Diözese, *die*
bismuth /'bɪzməθ/ *n.* (Chem., Med.) Wismut, *das*
bison /'baɪsn/ *n.* (Zool.) **1** (buffalo) Bison, *der* **2** (European ~) Wisent, *der*
bisque /bɪsk/ **1** (porcelain) Biskuit, *das* **2** (Gastr.) Fischcremesuppe, *die*
bistort /'bɪstɔ:t/ *n.* (Bot.) Wiesenknöterich, *der*
bistro /'bi:strəʊ/ *n., pl.* **~s** Bistro, *das*
bit[1] *n.* **1** (piece) Stück, *das;* (smaller) Stückchen, *das;* **a little ~:** ein kleines Stückchen; **a ~ of cheese/wood/coal/sugar** ein bisschen *od.* etwas Käse/ein Stück Holz/etwas Kohle/ein bisschen *od.* etwas Zucker; **a ~ of trouble/luck** ein wenig Ärger/Glück; **the best ~s** die besten Teile; **it cost quite a ~:** es kostete ziemlich viel; **have a ~ of cheek** ein bisschen frech sein; **a ~ of all right** (coll.) gar nicht übel (ugs.); **a ~ [of stuff]** (coll.: woman) ein netter *od.* toller Käfer (ugs.); **~ by ~:** Stück für Stück; (gradually) nach und nach; **smashed to ~s** in tausend Stücke zersprungen; **sb./sth. is blown to ~s** jmd. wird zerrissen/etw. wird in die Luft gesprengt; **he was thrilled to ~s** (coll.) er hat sich wahnsinnig gefreut (ugs.); **~s and bobs** Krimskrams, *der* (ugs.); Kram, *der* (ugs.); **~s and pieces** Verschiedenes; **do one's ~:** seinen Teil tun *od.* dazu beitragen; (fair share also) das Seine tun; **not a** *or* **one ~** (not at all) überhaupt nicht; **sb./sth. is not a ~ of use** jmd. ist zu nichts zu gebrauchen/mit etw. kann man überhaupt nichts anfangen; **it is not a ~ of use complaining** es hat überhaupt keinen Sinn, sich zu beklagen; **not a ~ of it** ganz im Gegenteil; **he is every ~ as clever as you are** er ist genauso schlau wie du **2** **a ~** (somewhat): **a ~ tired/late/too early** ein bisschen müde/spät/zu früh; **a little ~, just a ~:** ein klein bisschen; **quite a ~:** um einiges ‹*besser, stärker, hoffnungsvoller*›; **with a ~ more practice** mit etwas mehr Übung **3** **a ~ of** (rather): **be a ~ of a coward/bully** ganz schön feige *od.* ein ziemlicher Feigling sein/den starken Mann markieren (ugs.); **every politician has to be a ~ of a showman** jeder Politiker muss auch etwas von einem Schauspieler an sich (*Dat.*) haben; **a ~ of a disappointment** eine ganz schöne Enttäuschung **4** (Brit.) **~s of furniture** [armselige] Möbel; **~s of children** kleine Kinder **5** (short time) **[for] a ~:** eine Weile; **a little ~, just a ~:** ein klein bisschen; **wait a ~ longer** noch ein Weilchen warten **6** (short distance) **a ~:** ein Stückchen; **a ~ closer** ein bisschen näher; **a little ~, just a ~:** ein kleines Stückchen **7** (coin) Münze, *die;* **sixpenny/threepenny ~** (Brit. Hist.) Sixpence-/Dreipencestück, *das* **8** (Amer.: $12\frac{1}{2}$ cents) **two ~s** 25 Cent; **four/six ~s** 50/75 Cent
bit[2] /bɪt/ *n.* **1** (for horse) Gebiss, *das;* Gebissstange, *die;* **take the ~ between one's teeth** (fig.) aufmüpfig werden (ugs.) **2** (of drill) [Bohr]einsatz, *der;* Bohrer, *der;* (of key) [Schlüssel]bart, *der;* (of soldering iron) Lötkolben[kopf], *der*
bit[3] *n.* (Computing) Bit, *das*
bit[4] ▸ **bite A, B**
bitch /bɪtʃ/
A *n.* **1** (dog) Hündin, *die;* (vixen) Füchsin, *die* **2** (sl. derog.: woman) Miststück, *das;* Schlampe, *die* (*salopp*); *see also* **son** **3** (coll.: grumble) **have a ~ about sth.** über etw. (*Akk.*) meckern (ugs.)
B *v.i.* (coll.) meckern (ugs.) (**about** über + *Akk.*)
bitchy /'bɪtʃɪ/ *adj.* (coll.) gemein; gehässig; **be/get ~ about sb.** gehässige Bemerkungen über jmdn. machen/anfangen, gehässige Bemerkungen über jmdn. zu machen
bite /baɪt/
A *v.t.,* **bit** /bɪt/, **bitten** /'bɪtn/ beißen; (sting) ‹*Moskito usw.:*› stechen; **~ one's nails** an den Nägeln kauen; (fig.) wie auf Kohlen sitzen; **~ one's lip** (lit. or fig.) sich (*Dat.*) auf die Lippen beißen; **he won't ~ you** (fig. coll.) er wird dich schon nicht beißen; **once bitten twice shy** (prov.) einmal und nie wieder!; **~ the hand that feeds one** (fig.) sich [seinem Gönner gegenüber] undankbar zeigen; **~ the bullet** (fig.) in den sauren Apfel beißen (ugs.); **~ the dust** (fig.) daran glauben müssen (ugs.); **be bitten with an idea** von einer Idee besessen sein; **what's**

biting *or* **bitten you/him?** (fig. coll.) was ist mit dir/ihm los?; was hast du/hat er denn?

B *v.i.*, **bit, bitten** **1** beißen; (sting) stechen; ‹*Rad:*› fassen, greifen; ‹*Schraube:*› fassen; (take bait, lit. or fig.) anbeißen **2** **~ at sth.** nach etw. schnappen **3** (have an effect) sich auswirken; greifen

C *n.* **1** (act) Biss, *der;* (piece) Bissen, *der;* (wound) Bisswunde, *die;* (by mosquito etc.) Stich, *der;* **he took a ~ of the apple** er biss in den Apfel; **can I have a ~?** darf ich mal [ab]beißen?; **take one ~ at a time** immer nur einen Bissen auf einmal nehmen; **put the ~ on [sb.]** (Amer. coll.) jmdn. unter Druck setzen **2** (food) Happen, *der;* Bissen, *der;* **I haven't had a ~ [to eat] since breakfast** ich habe seit dem Frühstück nichts mehr gegessen; **have a ~ to eat** eine Kleinigkeit essen; **come and have a ~ to eat** komm und iss eine Kleinigkeit (ugs.) **3** (taking of bait) [An]beißen, *das;* **I haven't had a ~ all day** es hat den ganzen Tag noch keiner angebissen; **wait for a ~:** darauf warten, dass einer *od.* ein Fisch anbeißt **4** (incisiveness) Bissigkeit, *die;* Schärfe, *die;* **we need new laws that will have more ~:** wir brauchen neue Gesetze, die besser greifen **5** (Dent.) Biss, *der;* normale Bissstellung

Phrasal verbs

- **~ 'back** *v.t.* **~ sth. back** etw. unterdrücken; **~ back one's words/a remark** sich (*Dat.*) seine Worte/eine Bemerkung verkneifen
- **~ 'off** *v.t.* abbeißen; **the dog bit off the man's ear** der Hund hat dem Mann ein Ohr abgebissen; **~ sb.'s head off** (fig.) jmdm. den Kopf abreißen; **~ off more than one can chew** (fig.) sich (*Dat.*) zu viel zumuten; sich übernehmen

biter /ˈbaɪtə(r)/ *n.* **the ~ bit** mit den eigenen Waffen geschlagen; (in deception also) der betrogene Betrüger; **it's a case of the ~ bit** wer andern eine Grube gräbt, fällt selbst hinein (Spr.)

'bite-size *adj.* mundgerecht

biting /ˈbaɪtɪŋ/ *adj.* (stinging) beißend; schneidend ‹*Kälte, Wind*›; (sarcastic) scharf ‹*Angriff, Worte*›; beißend ‹*Kritik*›; bissig, sarkastisch ‹*Bemerkung, Kommentar*›

bit: ~map (Computing) **A** *n.* Bitmap, *die od. das; attrib.* Bitmap-; **~ graphics** Raster- *od.* Pixelgraphik, *die;* **B** *v.t.*, **-pp-** als Bitmap *od.* im Rasterrgraphikformat darstellen; **~ part** *n.* kleine Rolle; **~ rate** *n.* (Electronics) Bitrate, *die*

bitten ▸ **bite A, B**

bitter /ˈbɪtə(r)/

A *adj.* **1** bitter; **~ orange** (Bot.) Pomeranze, *die;* **~ lemon** (drink) Bitter lemon, *das* **2** (fig.) scharf, heftig ‹*Antwort, Bemerkung, Angriff*›; bitter ‹*Kampf, Kälte, Enttäuschung, Tränen*›; verbittert ‹*Person*›; erbittert ‹*Feind*›; scharf, bitterkalt ‹*Wind, Wetter*›; streng ‹*Winter*›; **~ experience** bittere Erfahrung; **to the ~ end** bis zum bitteren Ende; **be/feel ~ [about sth.]** [über etw. (*Akk.*)] bitter *od.* verbittert sein. *see also* **pill 2**

B *n.* **1** (Brit.: beer) bitteres Bier (*halbdunkles, obergäriges Bier*) **2** *in pl.* (flavoured alcohol) Magenbitter, *der*

bitterly /ˈbɪtəlɪ/ *adv.* bitterlich ‹*weinen, sich beschweren*›; bitter ‹*erwidern*›; erbittert ‹*kämpfen, sich widersetzen*›; scharf ‹*kritisieren*›; **~ cold** bitterkalt; **he ~ resented the unfounded accusations** er war äußerst erbittert über die unbegründeten Beschuldigungen; **be ~ opposed to sth.** ein erbitterter Gegner einer Sache (*Gen.*) sein

bittern /ˈbɪtən/ *n.* (Ornith.) Rohrdommel, *die*

bitterness /ˈbɪtənɪs/ *n., no pl.* Bitterkeit, *die;* (of reply, remark, attack) Schärfe, *die;* Heftigkeit, *die;* (of person) Verbitterung, *die;* (of wind) bittere Kälte

bitter-'sweet *adj.* (lit. or fig.) bittersüß

bitty /ˈbɪtɪ/ *adj.* zusammengestoppelt (abwertend); zusammengestückelt

bitumen /ˈbɪtjʊmən/ *n.* Bitumen, *das*

bituminous /bɪˈtju:mɪnəs/ *adj.* bituminös; **~ coal** Stein- *od.* Fettkohle, *die;* Bituminit, *das*

bivalve /ˈbaɪvælv/

A *adj.* **1** (Zool.) zweischalig ‹*Muschel*›; zweiklappig ‹*Schale*› **2** (Biol.) zweiklappig ‹*Frucht*›

B *n.* (Zool.) Muschel, *die*

bivouac /ˈbɪvʊæk/

A *n.* Biwak, *das;* Lager, *das*

B *v.i.*, **-ck-** biwakieren; im Freien übernachten

bi-weekly /baɪˈwi:klɪ/

A *adj.* **1** (two-weekly) zweiwöchentlich; alle zwei Wochen erscheinend ‹*Zeitschrift*›/stattfindend ‹*Treffen, Ereignis*› **2** (twice-weekly) zweimal in der Woche erscheinend ‹*Zeitschrift*›/stattfindend ‹*Treffen, Ereignis*›

B *adv.* **1** (two-weekly) alle zwei Wochen **2** (twice weekly) zweimal in der Woche

biz /bɪz/ *n.* (coll.) Geschäft, *das*

bizarre /bɪˈzɑ:(r)/ *adj.* bizarr; (eccentric) exzentrisch; (grotesque, irregular) grotesk

bk. *abbr.* = **book** Bch.

blab /blæb/ (coll.)

A *v.i.*, **-bb-** quatschen (abwertend)

B *v.t.*, **-bb-** ausplaudern

black /blæk/

A *adj.* **1** schwarz; (very dark) dunkel; (dirty) **as ~ as coal** *or* **ink** kohlrabenschwarz; *see also* **face A 1** **2** (dark-clothed) schwarz [gekleidet] **3** **B~** (dark-skinned) schwarz; **B~ man/woman/child** Schwarze, *der*/Schwarze, *die*/schwarzes Kind; **B~ people** Schwarze *Pl.*; **B~ Africa** Schwarzafrika (*das*) **4** (looking gloomy) düster; **things look ~:** es sieht böse *od.* düster aus; **~ clouds** dunkle Wolken **5** (wicked) schwarz ‹*Gedanken*›; **he is not as ~ as he is painted** er ist nicht so schlecht, wie er dargestellt wird **6** (angry) **get some ~ looks** finster angesehen werden; **give sb. a ~ look** jmdn. finster ansehen **7** (dismal) **a ~ day** ein schwarzer Tag; **be in a ~ mood** deprimiert sein; **~ despair** tiefe Verzweiflung **8** (macabre) schwarz ‹*Witz, Humor*› **9** (not to be handled) bestreikt ‹*Lastwagen, Schiff*›

B *n.* **1** (colour) Schwarz, *das;* (in roulette) Noir, *das* **2** **B~** (person) Schwarze, *der/die* **3** (credit) **[be] in the ~:** in den schwarzen Zahlen [sein] **4** (Snooker) schwarze Kugel **5** (**~** clothes) **dressed in ~:** schwarz gekleidet

C *v.t.* **1** (blacken) schwärzen; **~ sb.'s eye** jmdm. ein blaues Auge machen; **~ one's face** sich schwarz anmalen; **~ one's shoes** seine Schuhe wichsen **2** (declare **~**) bestreiken ‹*Betrieb*›; boykottieren ‹*Arbeit*›

Phrasal verb

- **~ 'out**

A *v.t.* verdunkeln

B *v.i.* das Bewusstsein verlieren. *See also* **blackout**

black: ~ and 'blue *pred. adj.* grün und blau; **~ and 'white** **A** *pred. adj.* (in writing) schwarz auf weiß; (Cinemat., Photog., etc.) schwarzweiß; (fig.: comprising only opposite extremes) Schwarz-weiß-; **B** *n.* **[sth. is there/down] in ~ and white** (in writing) [etw. steht] schwarz auf weiß [geschrieben]; **this film is in ~ and white** dieser Film ist in schwarzweiß; **see/portray** *etc.* **things in ~ and white** (fig.) schwarzweiß malen; **~-and-white** *attrib. adj.* Schwarz-weiß-; **~ 'art** *n.* schwarze Kunst, *die;* Magie, *die;* **~ball** *v.t.* stimmen gegen; **~ 'beetle** *n.* (Zool.) Küchenschabe, *die;* **~berry** /ˈblækbərɪ/ *n.* Brombeere, *die;* **go ~berrying** Brombeeren pflücken gehen; **~bird** *n.* Amsel, *die;* **~board** *n.* [Wand]tafel, *die;* **~board jungle** *n.* Schulchaos *das;* **~ 'books** *n. pl.* **be in sb.'s ~ books** bei jmdm. schlecht angeschrieben sein; **~ 'box** *n.* (flight recorder) Flugschreiber, *der;* (apparatus with concealed mechanism) Black box, *die;* **~ 'bread** *n.* Schwarzbrot, *das;* **~buck** *n.* (Zool.) Hirschziegenantilope, *die;* **~ 'cap** *n.* (Brit. Law Hist.) *gefaltetes Tuch aus schwarzer Seide, das der Richter früher auf dem Kopf trug, wenn er ein Todesurteil verkündete;* **~cap** *n.* (Ornith.) Mönchsgrasmücke, *die;* **~cock** *n.* (Ornith.) Birkhahn, *der;* **B~ Country** *n.* (Brit.) *Industriegebiet von Staffordshire und Warwickshire;* **~'currant** *n.* schwarze Johannisbeere; **B~ 'Death** *n.* schwarzer Tod; **~ 'earth** *n.* (Geol.) Schwarzerde, *die;* Tschernosjom, *der od. das* (fachspr.); **~ e'conomy** *n.* Schattenwirtschaft, *die*

blacken /ˈblækn/ *v.t.* **1** (make dark[er]) verfinstern ‹*Himmel*›; (make black[er]) schwärzen; **the ancient buildings were ~ed by centuries of smoke and grime** die alten Bauwerke waren durch die Jahrhunderte rauch- und rußgeschwärzt **2** (fig.: defame) verunglimpfen; **~ sb.'s [good] name** jmds. [guten] Namen beschmutzen; **~ the picture** schwarz malen

black: ~ 'eye *n.* **1** (bruised) blaues Auge (fig.); Veilchen, *das* (ugs.); **2** (dark) **~ eyes** schwarze Augen; **~-eyed** *adj.* schwarzäugig; **be ~-eyed** schwarze Augen haben; **~-face** *n.* (sheep) Schaf mit schwarzem Gesicht; **~fly** *n.* (Zool.) **1** (aphid) Blattlaus, *die;* **2** (thrips) Schwarze Fliege; **B~ 'Forest** *pr. n.* Schwarzwald, *der;* **B~ Forest 'gateau** *n.* Schwarzwälder [Kirschtorte], *die;* **B~ Friar** *n.* Dominikaner, *der;* **~ 'frost** ▸ **frost A 1**; **~ grouse** *n.* (Ornith.) Birkhuhn, *das*

blackguard /ˈblægɑ:d/ *n.* (dated) Schurke, *der;* Lump, *der*

blackguardly /ˈblægɑ:dlɪ/ *adj.* (dated) gemein

black: ~head *n.* **1** (Ornith.) Bergente, *die;* **2** (pimple) Mitesser, *der;* **~ 'hole** *n.* (Astron.) schwarzes Loch; **~ 'ice** *n.* Glatteis, *das*

blacking /ˈblækɪŋ/ *n.* schwarze Schuhcreme

blackish /ˈblækɪʃ/ *adj.* schwärzlich

black: ~jack *n.* **1** (flag) schwarze Piratenflagge; **2** (Amer.: bludgeon) Totschläger, *der;* **3** (Cards) Vingt-[et-]un, *das;* **4** (vessel) lederner (außen mit Teer überzogener) Trinkbecher; **~lead** /ˈblækled/ **A** *n.* Graphit, *der;* **B** *v.t.* schwärzen; **~leg** **A** *n.* **1** (Brit.: strike-breaker) Streikbrecher, *der*/-brecherin, *die;* **2** (swindler) *jmd., der bei Pferderennen od. anderen Glücksspielen falsch spielt;* **B** *v.i.* Streikbrecher/-brecherin sein; **~ 'letter** *n.* (Gothic type) gotische Schrift; (Schwabacher type) Schwabacher [Schrift], *die;* (Fraktur) Fraktur, *die;* **~ list** *n.* schwarze Liste; **~list** *v.t.* auf die schwarze Liste setzen

blackly /ˈblæklɪ/ *adv.* **1** (darkly, gloomily) düster **2** (angrily) finster

black: ~mail **A** *v.t.* erpressen; **~mail sb. into doing sth.** jmdn. durch Erpressung dazu zwingen, etwas zu tun; **B** *n.* Erpressung, *die;* **sheer/emotional ~mail** glatte/psychologische Erpressung; **~mailer** /ˈblækmeɪlə(r)/ *n.* Erpresser, *der*/Erpresserin, *die;* **B~ Maria** /blæk məˈraɪə/ *n.* grüne Minna (ugs.); **~ 'mark** *n.* (fig.) Makel, *der;* **a ~ mark against sb.** ein Makel, der an jmdm. haftet; **~ 'market** *n.* schwarzer Markt; **~ marketeer** /blæk mɑ:kɪˈtɪə(r)/ *n.* Schwarzhändler, *der*/-händlerin, *die;* **~ 'mass** *n.* (Satanist mass) schwarze Messe; **B~ 'Nationalism** *n., no pl.* schwarzer Nationalismus

blackness /ˈblæknɪs/ *n., no pl.* **1** (black colour) Schwärze, *die;* **the ~ of the sky** das Schwarz des Himmels **2** (darkness) Finsternis, *die;* (fig.: wickedness) Abscheulichkeit, *die*

'blackout *n.* **1** Verdunkelung, *die;* (Theatre, Radio) Blackout, *der;* **news ~:** Nachrichtensperre, *die* **2** (Med.) **I had a ~:** ich verlor das Bewusstsein

'blackout curtain *n.* Verdunklungsvorhang, *der*

black: ~ 'pudding *n.* Blutwurst, *die;* **B~ 'Rod** *n.* (Brit. Parl.) *Zeremonienmeister des britischen Oberhauses;* **B~ 'Sea** *pr. n.* Schwarze Meer, *das;* **~ 'sheep** *n.* (lit. or fig.) schwarzes Schaf; **~shirt** *n.* (Polit.) Schwarzhemd, *das;* **~smith** *n.* ▸ **i p. 1260** Schmied, *der;* **~ spot** *n.* (fig.) schwarzer Fleck; (dangerous) Gefahrenstelle, *die;* **~ 'tea** *n.* schwarzer Tee; **~thorn** *n.* (Bot.) Schwarzdorn, *der;* **~ 'tie** *n.* schwarze Fliege (*zur Smokingjacke getragen*); **~top** *n.* (esp. Amer. Road Constr.) Schwarzdecke, *die;* **~ 'velvet** *n.* (drink) *Mixgetränk mit Champagner und Starkbier;* **~ 'widow** *n.* (Zool.) Schwarze Witwe

bladder /ˈblædə(r)/ *n.* ▸ **i p. 951** (Anat., Zool., Bot.) Blase, *die*

'bladderwrack *n.* (Bot.) Blasentang, *der*

blade /bleɪd/ *n.* **1** (of sword, knife, dagger, razor, plane) Klinge, *die;* (of chisel, scissors, shears) Schneide, *die;* (of saw, oar, paddle, spade, propeller) Blatt, *das;* (of paddle wheel, turbine) Schaufel, *die* **2** (of grass etc.) Spreite, *die* **3** (dated: young man) zackiger, schneidiger Bursche (veralt.)

blah /blɑː/, **blah-blah** /ˈblɑːblɑː/ *n.* (coll.) Blabla, *das*

blahs /blɑːz/ *n. pl.* (Amer. coll.) Frust, *der* (ugs.)

Blairite /ˈbleəraɪt/

A *n.* Blair-Anhänger, *der*/-Anhängerin, *die*

B *adj.* Blair-‹*Politik usw.*›

blame /bleɪm/

A *v.t.* 1 (hold responsible) ~ **sb. [for sth.]** jmdm. die Schuld [an etw. (*Dat.*)] geben; **always get ~d for sth.** immer an etw. (*Dat.*) schuld sein sollen; **don't ~ me [if ...]** geben Sie nicht mir die Schuld[, wenn ...]; ~ **sth. [for sth.]** etw. [für etw.] verantwortlich machen; **be to ~ [for sth.]** an etw. (*Dat.*) schuld sein; ~ **sth. on sb./sth.** jmdn./etw. für etw. verantwortlich machen 2 (reproach) ~ **sb./oneself** jmdm./sich Vorwürfe machen; **I don't ~ you/him** (coll.) ich kann es Ihnen/ihm nicht verdenken; **who can ~ her?** wer kann es ihr verdenken?; **don't ~ yourself** machen Sie sich (*Dat.*) keine Vorwürfe; **have only oneself to ~:** die Schuld bei sich selbst suchen müssen; **blaming oneself never helps** Selbstvorwürfe helfen nichts

B *n.* 1 (responsibility) Schuld, *die;* **lay** *or* **put the ~ on sb. [for sth.]** jmdm. [an etw. (*Dat.*)] die Schuld geben; **bear the ~ [for sth.]** die Schuld [an etw. (*Dat.*)] tragen; **get the ~:** die Schuld bekommen; **take the ~ [for sth.]** die Schuld [für etw.] auf sich (*Akk.*) nehmen 2 (censure) Tadel, *der*

blameable /ˈbleɪməbl/ *adj.* tadelnswert

blameless /ˈbleɪmlɪs/ *adj.*, **blamelessly** /ˈbleɪmlɪslɪ/ *adv.* untadelig

blameworthy /ˈbleɪmwɜːðɪ/ *adj.* tadelnswert

blanch /blɑːnʃ/

A *v.t.* 1 (whiten) bleichen; abziehen ‹*Mandeln*›; (make pale) erbleichen lassen 2 (Cookery: scald) blanchieren; überbrühen

B *v.i.* (grow pale) bleich werden

blancmange /bləˈmɒnʒ/ *n.* Flammeri, *der*

blanco /ˈblæŋkəʊ/ (Mil.)

A *n., no pl.* weißes Mittel zum Wachsen

B *v.t.* [weiß] wachsen

bland /blænd/ *adj.* (gentle, suave) verbindlich; freundlich ‹*Art, Stimmung*›; (mild) mild ‹*Luft*›; (not irritating, not stimulating) mild ‹*Medizin, Nahrung*›; (unexciting) farblos

blandish /ˈblændɪʃ/ *v.t.* (flatter) schmeicheln (+ *Dat.*); (cajole) beschwatzen

blandishment /ˈblændɪʃmənt/ *n.* (flattery) Schmeichelei, *die;* (cajolery) Beschwatzen, *das;* (allurement) Verlockung, *die*

blandly /ˈblændlɪ/ *adv.* (gently) verbindlich; (mildly) mild

blandness /ˈblændnɪs/ *n., no pl.;* ▸ **bland**: Verbindlichkeit, *die;* Freundlichkeit, *die;* Milde, *die;* Farblosigkeit, *die*

blank /blæŋk/

A *adj.* 1 leer; kahl ‹*Wand, Fläche*› 2 (empty) frei; **leave a ~ space** Platz frei lassen 3 (fig.) leer, ausdruckslos ‹*Gesicht, Blick*›; **look ~:** ein verdutztes Gesicht machen; **give sb. a ~ look** jmdn. verdutzt ansehen

B *n.* 1 (space) Lücke, *die;* **my mind was a ~:** ich hatte ein Brett vor dem Kopf; **his memory was a ~:** er hatte keinerlei Erinnerung 2 (document with ~s) Vordruck, *der* 3 (lottery ticket) Niete, *die;* **draw a ~:** eine Niete ziehen; (fig.) kein Glück haben 4 (domino) *Dominostein mit ein od. zwei Leerfeldern* 5 (cartridge) Platzpatrone, *die* 6 (Num.) Schrötling, *der* 7 (dash) Lücke, *die;* (euphemism) Gedankenstrich, *der;* Punkt, Punkt, Punkt

blank: ~ **'cartridge** *n.* Platzpatrone, *die;* ~ **'cheque** *n.* Blankoscheck, *der;* (fig.) Blankovollmacht, *die;* **give sb. a ~ cheque** (fig.) jmdm. freie Hand *od.* eine Blankovollmacht geben

blanket /ˈblæŋkɪt/

A *n.* 1 Decke, *die;* **wet '~** (fig.) Trauerkloß, *der* (ugs.); **be born on the wrong side of the ~** (fig. dated) unehelich geboren sein 2 (thick layer) Decke, *die;* **a ~ of snow** eine Schneedecke; **a ~ of fog/cloud** eine Nebel-/Wolkendecke 3 (Printing) Gummituch, *das*

B *v.t.* 1 (cover) zudecken 2 (stifle) ersticken

C *adj.* umfassend; ~ **agreement** Pauschalabkommen, *das;* ~ **term** Allerweltswort, *das*

'blanket stitch *n.* Festonstich, *der*

blankety /ˈblæŋkɪtɪ/ *adj.* (euphem.) ~ **[blank]** verflixt (ugs.); **what the ~ blank ...?** was zum Kuckuck ...? (ugs.); **call sb./sth. a ~ blank** jmdn./etw. zum Kuckuck wünschen (ugs.)

blankly /ˈblæŋklɪ/ *adv.* verdutzt

blankness /ˈblæŋknɪs/ *n., no pl.* 1 (of surface etc.) Leere, *die;* **the ~ of the wall** die kahle Wand 2 (expressionlessness) Ausdruckslosigkeit, *die;* **the ~ of his expression** sein nichts sagender Gesichtsausdruck

blank 'verse *n.* (Pros.) Blankvers, *der*

blanquette /blɑ̃ˈket/ *n.* (Cookery) [Kalbs]frikassee, *das*

blare /bleə(r)/

A *v.i.* ‹*Lautsprecher:*› plärren; ‹*Trompete:*› schmettern

B *v.t.* ~ **[out]** [hinaus]plärren ‹*Worte*›; [hinaus]schmettern ‹*Melodie*›

C *n.* (of loudspeaker, radio, voice) Plärren, *das;* (of trumpet, trombone) Schmettern, *das*

blarney /ˈblɑːnɪ/*n., no pl.* (cajoling) Schmeichelei, *die;* (nonsense) Geschwätz, *das.*

blasé /ˈblɑːzeɪ/ *adj.* blasiert

blaspheme /blæsˈfiːm/ *v.i.* lästern

blasphemous /ˈblæsfəməs/ *adj.* lästerlich, blasphemisch ‹*Bemerkung, Eid, Fluch*›

blasphemy /ˈblæsfəmɪ/ *n.* Blasphemie, *die;* ~ **is a sin** Gotteslästerung ist eine Sünde

blast /blɑːst/

A *n.* 1 (of explosion) Druckwelle, *die;* (coll.: explosion) Explosion, *die* 2 (gust) **a ~ [of wind]** ein Windstoß 3 (sound) Tuten, *das;* **he gave a ~ on his trumpet** er ließ seine Trompete erschallen; **give a ~ of the horn** einmal ins Horn stoßen 4 (Metallurgy etc.: air current) Gebläseluft, *die;* **at full ~** (fig.) auf Hochtouren *Pl.* 5 (coll.: reprimand) Standpauke, *die* (ugs.)

B *v.t.* 1 (blow up) sprengen ‹*Felsen*›; (coll.: kick) donnern ‹*Fußball*› 2 (wither) verdorren lassen 3 (curse) ~ **you/him!** zum Teufel mit dir/ihm!

C *v.i.* (coll.: shoot) **start ~ing away** drauflosschießen (**at** auf + *Akk.*);

D *int.* **[oh] ~!** [oh] verdammt!

(Phrasal verb)

- ~ **'off** *v.i.* abheben; *see also* **blast-off**

blasted /ˈblɑːstɪd/ *adj.* (damned) verdammt (salopp); verflucht (salopp)

blast: ~ **furnace** *n.* Hochofen, *der;* **~-hole** *n.* Sprengloch, *das;* **~-off** *n.* Abheben, *das;* ~ **wave** *n.* [Explosions]druckwelle, *die*

blatancy /ˈbleɪtənsɪ/ *n., no pl.* ▸ **blatant**: Eklatanz, *die;* Offensichtlichkeit, *die;* Unverhohlenheit, *die;* Unverfrorenheit, *die*

blatant /ˈbleɪtənt/ *adj.* 1 (flagrant) eklatant; offensichtlich 2 (unashamed) unverhohlen; unverfroren ‹*Lüge*›

blatantly /ˈbleɪtəntlɪ/ *adv.* ▸ **blatant**: eklatant; offensichtlich; unverhohlen; unverfroren

blather /ˈblæðə(r)/

A *v.i.* schwafeln (ugs. abwertend)

B *n., no pl.* Geschwafel, *das* (ugs. abwertend)

blaze[1] /bleɪz/

A *n.* 1 (conflagration) Feuer, *das;* **it took hours to put out the ~:** es dauerte Stunden, bis das Feuer *od.* der Brand gelöscht war 2 (display) **a ~ of lights** ein Lichtermeer; **a ~ of colour** eine Farbenpracht; ein Farbenmeer 3 (fig.: full light) Glanz, *der;* **in a ~ of glory** mit Glanz und Gloria 4 (coll.) **go to ~s!** scher dich zum Teufel! (salopp); **like ~s** wie verrückt (ugs.) ‹*arbeiten, rennen usw.*›; **what the ~s [are you doing]?** was zum Teufel [machst du da]? (salopp); **how the ~s am I supposed to ...?** wie zum Teufel soll ich ...?

B *v.i.* 1 (burn) brennen; **the house was already blazing when the firemen arrived** das Haus stand schon in Flammen als die Feuerwehr ankam; **a blazing fire** ein hell loderndes Feuer; **the blazing sun** die glühende Sonne; **a blazing hot day** ein glühend heißer Tag 2 (be brilliantly lighted) [er]strahlen; ‹*Schnee:*› glänzen 3 (emit light) strahlen; **the spotlight ~d down on them** der Scheinwerfer strahlte sie an 4 (fig.: with anger etc.) ‹*Augen:*› glühen; **a blazing row** ein heftiger Streit

(Phrasal verbs)

- ~ **a'way** *v.i.* 1 (shoot) [drauf]losschießen (**at** auf + *Akk.*) 2 (work) loslegen (**at** mit)
- ~ **'up** *v.i.* 1 (burst into ~) aufflammen 2 (in anger) aufbrausen

blaze[2]

A *n.* (on animal's head) Blesse, *die;* (on tree) Markierung, *die*

B *v.t.* markieren, kennzeichnen ‹*Baum, Weg, Pfad*›; ~ **a trail** einen Weg markieren; ~ **a** *or* **the trail** (fig.) den Weg bahnen

blaze[3] *v.t.* (proclaim) verkünden; ~ **sth. abroad** etw. ausposaunen (ugs.)

blazer /ˈbleɪzə(r)/ *n.* Blazer, *der*

blazing 'star *n.* (Amer. Bot.) Prachtscharte, *die*

blazon /ˈbleɪzn/ *v.t.* 2 (display, report) verkünden 1 (Her.) blasonieren ‹*Wappen*›

bleach /bliːtʃ/

A *v.t.* bleichen ‹*Wäsche, Haar, Knochen*›

B *v.i.* bleichen

C *n.* (substance) Bleichmittel, *das;* (process) Bleiche, *die*

bleaching /ˈbliːtʃɪŋ/: ~ **agent** *n.* Bleichmittel, *das;* ~ **powder** *n.* Bleichpulver, *das*

bleak[1] /bliːk/ *adj.* 1 (bare) öde ‹*Landschaft, Berg, Insel, Ebene, Hügel*›; karg ‹*Zimmer*› 2 (chilly) rau; kalt ‹*Wetter, Tag*› 3 (unpromising) düster; ~ **prospect[s]** trübe Aussichten

bleak[2] *n.* (Zool.) Ukelei, *der*

bleakly /ˈbliːklɪ/ *adv.* 1 düster ‹*anschauen*› 2 kalt ‹*wehen*›

bleakness /ˈbliːknɪs/ *n., no pl.* 1 (of prospect) Düsterkeit, *die* 2 (of weather) Kälte, *die*

bleary /ˈblɪərɪ/ *adj.* trübe ‹*Augen*›; **look ~-eyed** verschlafen aussehen; einen verschleierten Blick haben

bleat /bliːt/

A *v.i.* ‹*Schaf, Kalb:*› blöken; ‹*Ziege:*› meckern; (fig.) jammern; (plaintively) meckern

B *v.t.* ~ **[out]** herunterplärren ‹*Entschuldigungen, Klagen*›

C *n.* ▸ **A**: Blöken, *das;* Geblök, *das;* Meckern, *das;* (fig.) Gejammer, *das* (ugs.); (plaintive) Gemecker, *das* (ugs.)

bled ▸ **bleed**

bleed /bliːd/

A *v.i.*, **bled** /bled/ bluten

B *v.t.*, **bled** 1 (draw blood from, lit. or fig.) zur Ader lassen; ~ **sb. white** (fig.) jmdn. den letzten Cent kosten (ugs.); ‹*Erpresser:*› jmdn. bis aufs Hemd ausziehen (ugs.) 2 (extract fluid, air, etc. from) entlüften ‹*Bremsen, Heizkörper*›

bleeder /ˈbliːdə(r)/ *n.* 1 (Brit. sl: unpleasant person) Scheißer, *der* (derb) 2 (coll.: haemophiliac) Bluter, *der*

bleeding /ˈbliːdɪŋ/

A *n.* (loss of blood) Blutung, *die*

B *adj.* (Brit. sl: damned) Scheiß-; **don't stand there the whole ~ time doing nothing!** steh da nicht die ganze Zeit so blöd rum, ohne was zu tun! (salopp)

C *adv.* (Brit. sl) ~ **awful** total beschissen (derb); **I don't ~ care!** das ist mir scheißegal! (salopp); **don't be ~ stupid!** sei doch nicht so saublöd! (salopp)

bleeding 'heart *n.* 1 (Bot.) Tränendes Herz; Flammendes Herz 2 (coll.: person) mitfühlende Seele

bleep /bliːp/

A *n.* Piepen, *das;* Piepton, *der;* **two faint ~s** zwei schwache Piepser

B *v.i.* ‹*Geigerzähler, Funksignal:*› piepen

C *v.t.* ~ **sb.** jmdn. über seinen Kleinempfänger *od.* (ugs.) Piepser rufen

bleeper /ˈbliːpə(r)/ *n.* Kleinempfänger, *der;* Piepser, *der* (ugs.)

blemish /ˈblemɪʃ/

A *n.* 1 (stain) Fleck, *der;* (on fruit) Stelle, *die* 2 (defect, lit. or fig.) Makel, *der;* **be without a ~:** makellos sein; **her only ~ was her quick temper** ihr einziger Fehler war ihr aufbrausendes Wesen

B *v.t.* 1 (spoil) verunstalten 2 (fig.) ~ **sth.** einer Sache (*Dat.*) schaden

blench /blenʃ/ *v.i.* zurückschrecken

blend /blend/
A *v.t.* **1** (mix) mischen ‹*Whisky-, Tee-, Tabaksorten*› **2** (combine harmoniously) vermischen
B *v.i.* **1** sich mischen lassen; **pink does not ~ with orange** Rosa verträgt sich nicht mit Orange; **~ in with/into sth.** [gut] zu etw. passen/mit etw. verschmelzen **2** ‹*Whisky-, Tee-, Tabaksorten:*› sich [harmonisch] verbinden
C *n.* (mixture) Mischung, *die*

blender /ˈblendə(r)/ *n.* **1** (person) [Ver]mischer, *der* **2** (apparatus) Mixer, *der;* Mixgerät, *das*

Blenheim /ˈblenɪm/ *pr. n.* **the Battle of ~:** die Schlacht von Höchstädt

bless /bles/ *v.t.* **1** (consecrate, pronounce blessing on) segnen; **be ~ with sth.** (also iron.) mit etw. gesegnet sein; **she did not have a penny to ~ herself with** (fig. dated) sie besaß keinen Cent *od.* (ugs.) keinen roten Heller; **they have been ~ed with a son** sie wurden mit einem Sohn gesegnet; **[God] ~ you** Gottes Segen; (as thanks) das ist sehr lieb von dir/Ihnen; (to person sneezing) Gesundheit!; **goodbye and God ~:** Wiedersehen, [und] mach's/macht's gut!; **~ you, I wouldn't dream of it** mein Gott, ich denke gar nicht daran; **~ me!, I'm blest!, ~ my soul!** du meine Güte! (ugs.); **~ me if it isn't Sid** ja das ist doch Sid! **2** (call holy) preisen; (attribute one's good fortune to) **they ~ed their stars/guardian angel that ...:** sie priesen dankbar das Glück/ihren Schutzengel dafür, dass ...

blessed/ˈblesɪd, *pred.* blest/ *adj.* **1** (revered) heilig ‹*Gott, Mutter Maria*›; (in Paradise) selig; (RC Ch.: beatified) selig **3** *attrib.* (euphem.: cursed) verdammt (salopp)

blessing /ˈblesɪŋ/ *n.* **1** (declaration or bestowal of divine favour, grace at table) Segen, *der;* **do sth. with sb.'s ~** (fig.) etw. mit jmds. Segen tun (ugs.); **give sb./sth. one's ~** (fig.) jmdm./etw. seinen Segen geben (ugs.) **2** (fig.: welcome thing) Segen, *der;* **what a ~!** welch ein Segen!; **count one's ~s** dankbar sein; **be a ~ in disguise** sich schließlich doch noch als Segen erweisen; *see also* **mixed blessing**

blest *adj.* (arch./literary) ▸ **blessed 1**

blether /ˈbleðə(r)/
A *v.i.* schwafeln (ugs.); sülzen (ugs.); **go on ~ing** weiterschwafeln *od.* -sülzen
B *n.* Geschwafel, *das;* Gesülze, *das* (ugs.)

blew ▸ **blow¹ A, B**

blight /blaɪt/
A *n.* **1** (plant disease) Brand, *der;* (fig.: malignant influence) Fluch, *der;* Geißel, *die;* **fascism — a ~ on the twentieth century** Faschismus—ein Fluch des zwanzigsten Jahrhunderts **2** (fig.: unsightly urban area) Schandfleck, *der*
B *v.t.* **1** (affect with ~) **be ~ed** von Brand befallen werden/sein **2** (spoil) beeinträchtigen ‹*Schönheit*›; überschatten ‹*Freude, Leben*›; (frustrate) zunichte machen ‹*Hoffnung*›; **a ~ed area** eine heruntergekommene Gegend

blighter /ˈblaɪtə(r)/ *n.* (Brit. coll.) **1** **the poor ~:** der arme Kerl **2** (derog.) Lümmel, *der* (abwertend); (thing) Mistding, *das* (salopp)

blimey /ˈblaɪmɪ/ *int.* (Brit. sl.) Mensch (salopp)

blimp /blɪmp/ *n.* **1** (Brit.) **[Colonel] B~:** *Personifikation des stockkonservativen Engländers* **2** (airship) Blimp, *der;* unstarres Kleinluftschiff

blimpish /ˈblɪmpɪʃ/ *adj.* reaktionär

blind /blaɪnd/
A *adj.* **1** blind ‹*Person, Tier*›; **a ~ man/woman** ein Blinder/eine Blinde; **[be] as ~ as a bat** stockblind [sein] (ugs.); **~ in one eye** auf einem Auge blind; **go** *or* **become ~:** blind werden; erblinden; **turn a ~ eye [to sth.]** (fig.) [bei etw.] ein Auge zudrücken **2** (Aeronaut.) **~ landing/flying** Blindlandung, *die*/Blindflug, *der* **3** (without foresight) blind; **a ~ policy** eine kurzsichtige *od.* unbesonnene Politik **4** (unreasoning) blind ‹*Vorurteil, Weigerung, Gehorsam, Vertrauen*› **5** (oblivious) **be ~ to sth.** blind gegenüber etw. sein **6** (reckless) blind ‹*Hast*›; rasend ‹*Geschwindigkeit*› **7** (not ruled by purpose) blind ‹*Wut, Zorn*›; dunkel ‹*Instinkt*›; kopflos ‹*Panik*› **8** (impossible to see round) unübersichtlich ‹*Kurve*› **9** (walled up) blind ‹*Tür, Fenster*› **10** **a ~** (coll.: any whatever): **he doesn't do a ~ thing [to help her]** er rührt keinen Finger[, um ihr zu helfen]; **not a ~ bit of** überhaupt kein/keine; **it didn't do a ~ bit of good** es hat überhaupt nichts genützt; **you didn't take a ~ bit of notice** du hast dich überhaupt nicht darum gekümmert
B *adv.* **1** blindlings; **the pilot had to fly/land ~:** der Pilot musste blind fliegen/landen **2** (completely) **~ drunk** stockbetrunken (ugs.); **swear ~:** hoch und heilig versichern **3** (Cookery) **bake sth. ~:** etw. blind backen
C *n.* **1** (screen) Jalousie, *die;* (made of cloth) Rollo, *das;* (of shop) Markise, *die* **2** (Amer. Hunting: hide) Jagdschirm, *der* **3** (pretext) Vorwand, *der;* (cover) Tarnung, *die;* **be a ~ for sth.** als Tarnung für etw. dienen **4** *pl.* **the ~:** die Blinden *Pl.;* **it's [a case of] the ~ leading the ~** (fig.) das ist, wie wenn ein Blinder einen Lahmen [spazieren] führt
D *v.t.* (lit. or fig.) blenden; **be ~ed** (accidentally) das Augenlicht verlieren; **~ sb. to the fact that ...:** jmdn. gegenüber der Tatsache blind machen, dass ...; **he was ~ed by his infatuation** er war von seiner eigenen Verliebtheit geblendet *od.* verblendet; **~ sb. with science** jmdn. mit großen Worten beeindrucken

blind: ~ ˈalley *n.* (lit. or fig.) Sackgasse, *die;* **~ ˈcorner** *n.* unübersichtliche Kurve; **~ ˈdate** *n.* Verabredung mit einem/einer Unbekannten

blinder /ˈblaɪndə(r)/ *n.* **1** **play a ~** (Sport) sich selbst übertreffen **2** *usu. in pl.* (Amer.: blinker) Scheuklappe, *die*

ˈblindfold
A *v.t.* die Augen verbinden (+ *Dat.*); **the conjuror asked to be ~ed** der Zauberer bat darum, ihm die Augen zu verbinden
B *adj.* mit verbundenen Augen *nachgestellt;* **he was ~ all the time** er hatte die ganze Zeit die Augen verbunden; **I could do that ~** (fig.) das könnte ich mit verbundenen Augen [tun]
C *n.* Augenbinde, *die*

blind ˈgut *n.* (Anat.) Blinddarm, *der*

blinding /ˈblaɪndɪŋ/ *adj.* blendend ‹*Licht, Sonnenlicht, Blitz*›; grell ‹*Strahl*›; **a ~ headache** rasende Kopfschmerzen *Pl.*

blindly /ˈblaɪndlɪ/ *adv.* [wie] blind; wie ein Blinder; (fig.) blindlings

blind man's ˈbuff *n.* Blindekuh *o. Art.*

blindness /ˈblaɪndnɪs/ *n., no pl.* **1** Blindheit, *die* **2** (lack of foresight) Blindheit, *die* (**to** gegenüber); (unreasonableness) Verblendung, *die*

blind: ~ side *n.* (Rugby) ungeschützte Seite; (fig.) schwache Seite (fig.); **~ spot** *n.* (Anat.) blinder Fleck; (Motor Veh.) toter Winkel; (fig.: weak spot) schwacher Punkt; **~ ˈtest** *n.* Blindversuch, *der;* **~worm** *n.* (Zool.) Blindschleiche, *die*

blink /blɪŋk/
A *v.i.* **1** blinzeln **2** (shine intermittently) blinken; (shine momentarily) aufblinken
B *v.t.* **~ back/away one's tears** seine Tränen blinzelnd zurückhalten; **~ one's eyes** mit den Augen zwinkern
C *n.* **1** (blinking) Blinzeln, *das;* **he gave one or two ~s** er blinzelte ein paarmal **2** (intermittent light) Blinken, *das;* (momentary gleam) Aufblinken, *das* **3** (coll.) **be on the ~:** kaputt sein (ugs.)

blinker /ˈblɪŋkə(r)/
A *n. in pl.* Scheuklappen; **have/put ~s on** (lit. or fig.) Scheuklappen tragen/anlegen
B *v.t.* Scheuklappen anlegen (+ *Dat.*); **this horse has to be ~ed** dieses Pferd muss Scheuklappen tragen; **be ~ed** (fig.) borniert sein

blinking /ˈblɪŋkɪŋ/ (Brit. coll. euphem.)
A *adj.* verflixt (ugs.); **it's a ~ nuisance** das ist verdammt ärgerlich (ugs.)
B *adv.* verflixt (ugs.); **I don't ~ [well] care** das kümmert mich verflixt wenig; **it's ~ raining** verflixt [und zugenäht], es regnet

blip /blɪp/ *n.* **1** (minor deviation from trend) Delle, *die* **2** (Radar: image) Echozeichen, *das*

bliss /blɪs/ *n.* (joy) [Glück]seligkeit, *die;* Glück, *das;* (gladness) Freude, *die;* **his idea of ~:** seine Vorstellung vom Glücklichsein

blissful /ˈblɪsfl/ *adj.* [glück]selig; **~ ignorance** (iron.) selige Unwissenheit

blissfully /ˈblɪsfəlɪ/ *adv.* **~ happy** glückselig; **be ~ unaware** *or* **ignorant [of sth.]** (iron.) in seliger Unwissenheit [von etw.] sein

blister /ˈblɪstə(r)/
A *n.* (on skin, plant, metal, paintwork) Blase, *die*
B *v.t.* Blasen hervorrufen auf (+ *Dat.*) ‹*Metall, Anstrich, Haut*›
C *v.i.* ‹*Haut, Pflanze:*› Blasen bekommen; ‹*Metall, Anstrich:*› Blasen werfen

blistering /ˈblɪstərɪŋ/ *adj.* **a ~ attack** ein erbitterter Angriff; **a ~ criticism** eine ätzende Kritik; **a ~ pace** ein mörderisches Tempo

ˈblister pack *n.* Klarsichtpackung, *die*

blithe /blaɪð/ *adj.* **1** (poet.: joyous) fröhlich; heiter **2** (casual) unbekümmert

blithely /ˈblaɪðlɪ/ *adv.* **~ ignore sth.** sich unbekümmert über etw. (*Akk.*) hinwegsetzen

blithering /ˈblɪðərɪŋ/ *adj.* (coll.) **1** (utter) total; völlig; **a ~ idiot** ein alter Idiot (salopp) **2** (senselessly talkative) quatschig (salopp) ‹*Kommentator, Journalist*›

BLitt /bi: ˈlɪt/ *abbr.* **= Bachelor of Letters** Bakkalaureus der Literaturwissenschaften; *see also* **BSc**

blitz /blɪts/ (coll.)
A *n.* **1** (Hist.) Luftangriff, *der* (**on** auf + *Akk.*); **during the [London] ~:** während der Luft- *od.* Bombenangriffe [auf London] **2** (fig.: attack) Großaktion, *die* (fig.); **have a ~ on one's room** in seinem Zimmer gründlich sauber machen
B *v.t.* [schwer] bombardieren

blizzard /ˈblɪzəd/ *n.* Schneesturm, *der*

bloat /bləʊt/
A *v.t.* aufblähen; **dead bodies ~ed by the water** vom Wasser aufgedunsene Leichen
B *v.i.* aufschwellen; aufschwemmen

bloated /ˈbləʊtɪd/ *adj.* **1** (having overeaten) aufgedunsen; **I feel ~:** ich bin voll (ugs.) **2** **be ~ with pride/wealth** aufgeblasen sein/im Geld schwimmen

bloater /ˈbləʊtə(r)/ *n.* Bückling, *der*

blob /blɒb/ *n.* **1** (drop) Tropfen, *der;* (small mass) Klacks, *der* (ugs.); (of butter etc.) Klecks, *der* **2** (spot of colour) Fleck, *der*

bloc /blɒk/ *n.* (Polit.) Block, *der;* **the Eastern ~/Eastern ~ countries** (Hist.) der Ostblock/die Ostblockstaaten; **the Western ~ [countries]** (Hist.) die westlichen Staaten; **the anti-EU ~:** der Anti-EU-Block

block /blɒk/
A *n.* **1** (large mass of concrete or stone, building stone) Block, *der* **2** (large piece) Klotz, *der;* **~ of wood** Holzklotz, *der* **3** (building) [Häuser]block, *der;* **~ of flats/offices** Wohnblock, *der*/Bürohaus, *das* **4** (Amer.: area between streets) Block, *der;* **on this/our ~:** in diesem/unserem Block; **six ~s away** sechs Blocks weiter **5** (for beheading on) Richtblock, *der;* (for hammering on, for mounting horse from) Klotz, *der;* (toy building brick) Bauklotz, *der;* **be a chip off the old ~:** ganz der Vater sein; **be on the ~** (Amer.) zur Versteigerung angeboten werden **6** (for chopping on) Hackklotz, *der* **7** (large quantity) Masse, *die;* **a ~ of shares** ein Aktienpaket; **a ~ of seats** mehrere nebeneinander liegende Sitze; **in the cheapest ~ of seats** im billigsten Block **8** (pad of paper) Block, *der* **9** (obstruction) Verstopfung, *die* **10** (coll.: head) **knock sb.'s ~ off** jmdm. eins überziehen (salopp) **11** (mental barrier) **a mental ~:** eine geistige Sperre; Mattscheibe *o. Art.* (salopp); **a psychological ~:** ein psychologischer Block **12** (pulley) Block, *der;* **~ and tackle** Flaschenzug, *der* **13** (Athletics) Startblock, *der* **14** (Printing) Klischee, *das*
B *v.t.* **1** (obstruct) blockieren, versperren ‹*Tür, Straße, Durchgang, Sicht*›; verstopfen ‹*Rohr, Nase, Abfluss*›; blockieren, verhindern ‹*Fortschritt*›; abblocken ‹*Ball, Torschuss*› **2** (Commerc.) einfrieren ‹*Investitionen, Guthaben*›; **~ed currency** nicht frei konvertierbare Währung **3** (emboss) prägen

Phrasal verbs

- **~ ˈin** *v.t.* ausfüllen ‹*Umrisse, Zeichnung*›; abdecken ‹*Kamin, Fenster usw.*›
- **~ ˈoff** *v.t.* [ab]sperren ‹*Straße*›; blockieren ‹*Rohr, Verkehr*›
- **~ ˈout** *v.t.* ausschließen ‹*Licht, Lärm*›; retuschieren ‹*Foto*›; abdecken ‹*Matrize, Schablone*›
- **~ ˈup** *v.t.* verstopfen; versperren, blockieren ‹*Eingang*›

b

blockade /blɒˈkeɪd/
A n. Blockade, *die*
B *v.t.* blockieren

blockage /ˈblɒkɪdʒ/ *n.* Block, *der;* (of pipe, gutter) Verstopfung, *die*

block: **~board** *n.* Tischlerplatte, *die;* **~ ˈbooking** *n.* Gruppenbuchung, *die;* **~buster** *n.* [1] (bomb) [große] Fliegerbombe; [2] (fig.) Knüller, *der* (ugs.); **~ ˈcapital** *n.* Blockbuchstabe, *der;* **~ diagram** *n.* Blockdiagramm, *das;* **~ ˈgrant** *n.* Pauschalsubvention, *die;* **~head** *n.* Dummkopf, *der* (abwertend); **~ heater** *n.* Nachtspeicherheizung, *die;* **~house** *n.* Blockhaus, *das*

blocking: **~ minority** *n.* Sperrminorität, *die;* **~ software** *n., no pl.* (Computing) Blockiersoftware, *die*

block: **~ ˈletters** *n. pl.* Blockschrift, *die;* **~ ˈvote** *n.* Stimmenblock, *der*

blog /blɒg/ (Computing)
A *n.* Blog, *das* (Jargon)
B *v.i.* ein Weblog unterhalten; (visit weblogs) Weblogs besuchen; bloggen (Jargon)

blogger /ˈblɒgə(r)/ *n.* (author of a weblog) Weblogautor, *der*/-autorin, *die*

blogging /ˈblɒgɪŋ/ *n., no pl.* (Computing) Bloggen, *das;* Webloggen, *das*

bloke /bləʊk/ *n.* (Brit. coll.) Typ, *der* (ugs.)

blokeish /ˈbləʊkɪʃ/ *adj.* (Brit. coll.) männlich; Macho‹*image*›; Männer‹*Arbeit*›

blond /blɒnd/ ▸ **blonde A**

blonde /blɒnd/
A *adj.* blond ‹*Haar, Person*›; hell ‹*Teint*›
B *n.* Blondine, *die*

blood /blʌd/
A *n.* [1] ▸❶ **p. 951** Blut, *das;* **sb.'s ~ boils** (fig.) jmd. ist in Rage; **it makes my ~ boil** es bringt mich in Rage; **sb.'s ~ turns** *or* **runs cold** (fig.) jmdm. erstarrt das Blut in den Adern; **draw first ~** (lit. or fig.) den ersten Treffer erzielen; **be after** *or* **out for sb.'s ~** (fig.) es auf jmdn. abgesehen haben; **taste ~** (fig.) Blut lecken; **it's like getting ~ out of** *or* **from a stone** das ist fast ein Ding der Unmöglichkeit; **[a policy of] ~ and iron** Blut und Eisen; **~ is thicker than water** (prov.) Blut ist dicker als Wasser; **his ~ is up** er ist in Rage; **do sth. in cold ~:** etw. kaltblütig tun; **[there is] bad ~ [between them]** [es gibt] böses Blut [zwischen ihnen]; **fresh** *or* **new ~:** frisches Blut; **young ~:** Nachwuchs, *der;* **sth. is in sb.'s ~:** etw. liegt jmdm. im Blut [2] (race) Blut, *das;* Geblüt, *das* (geh.); **of noble ~:** von edlem Geblüt
B *v.t.* an Blut gewöhnen ‹*Spürhund*›; (fig.) **he was ~ed in the Battle of Leipzig** er bestand seine Feuertaufe in der Völkerschlacht bei Leipzig

blood: **~ and ˈthunder** *n.* Mord und Totschlag; *attrib.* **~-and-thunder stories** Schauer- und-Schund-Geschichten; **~ bank** *n.* Blutbank, *die;* **~bath** *n.* Blutbad, *das;* **~ brother** *n.* (by birth) leiblicher Bruder; (by ceremony) Blutsbruder, *der;* **~ cell** *n.* Blutkörperchen, *das;* **~ clot** *n.* Blutgerinnsel, *das;* **~ count** *n.* Blutbild, *das;* **carry out a ~ count** das Blutbild bestimmen; **~-curdling** *adj.* Grauen erregend; **~ donor** ▸ **donor 2**; **~ feud** *n.* Blutrache, *die;* **~ group** *n.* Blutgruppe, *die;* **~ heat** *n.* Körpertemperatur, *die;* **~hound** *n.* Bluthund, *der*

bloodless /ˈblʌdlɪs/ *adj.* [1] (without bloodshed) unblutig; **a ~ coup** ein unblutiger Staatsstreich [2] (without blood, pale) blutleer [3] (cold, ruthless) gefühllos

blood: **~letting** *n., no pl.* (Med. Hist.; also fig.) Aderlass, *der;* **~lust** *n.* Blutgier, *die;* **~ money** *n.* Blutgeld, *das;* **~ orange** *n.* Blutorange, *die;* **~ poisoning** *n., no pl.* Blutvergiftung, *die;* **~ pressure** *n.* Blutdruck, *der;* **~ ˈpudding** *n.* ≈ Blutwurst, *die;* **~-red** *adj.* blutrot; **~ relation** *n.* Blutsverwandte, *der/die;* **~ sample** *n.* Blutprobe, *die;* **~shed** *n.* Blutvergießen, *das;* **~shot** *adj.* blutunterlaufen; **~ sports** *n. pl.* Hetzjagd, *die;* **~stain** *n.* Blutfleck, *der;* **~stained** *adj.* (lit. or fig.) blutbefleckt; **~stock** *n.* Vollblutpferde *Pl.;* **~stone** *n.* Blutstein, *der;* **~stream** *n.* Blutstrom, *der;* **~sucker** *n.* (leech) Blutegel, *der;* (fig.: extortioner) Blutsauger, *der;* **~ sugar** *n.* Blutzucker, *der* (Med.); **~ test** *n.* Blutprobe, *die;* **~thirsty** *adj.* blutdürstig (geh.); blutrünstig; **~ transfusion** *n.* Bluttransfusion, *die;* **~ vessel** *n.* Blutgefäß, *das*

bloody /ˈblʌdɪ/
A *adj.* [1] blutig; (running with blood) blutend; (like blood) blutrot; (loving bloodshed) blutrünstig; **give sb. a ~ nose** (lit., or fig. coll.) jmdm. eins auf die Nase geben [2] (sl.: damned) verdammt (salopp); **you ~ fool!** du Vollidiot! (salopp); **~ hell!** verdammt noch mal! (salopp) [3] (Brit.) *as intensifier* (sl.) einzig; **he didn't leave me a ~ penny** er ließ mir keinen roten Heller; **that/he is a ~ nuisance** das ist vielleicht ein Mist (salopp)/der geht einem vielleicht *od.* ganz schön auf den Wecker (ugs.)
B *adv.* [1] (sl.: damned) verdammt (salopp); **don't be so ~ stupid!** sei doch nicht so verdammt blöde! [2] (Brit.) *as intensifier* (sl.) verdammt (salopp); **not ~ likely!** denkste! (salopp); **I don't ~ [well] like it!** ich kann das, verdammt noch mal, nicht leiden!
C *v.t.* (make ~) blutig machen; (stain with blood) mit Blut beflecken

bloody: **B~ ˈMary** *n.* Bloody Mary, *der od. die* (*ein Cocktail*); **~-ˈminded** *adj.* stur (ugs.)

bloom /bluːm/
A *n.* [1] Blüte, *die;* **be in ~:** in Blüte stehen; **have come into ~:** blühen [2] (on fruit) Flaum, *der;* (flush) rosige Gesichtsfarbe [3] (prime) Blüte, *die;* **in the ~ of youth** in der Blüte der Jugend; **come into ~:** erblühen
B *v.i.* blühen; (fig.: flourish) in Blüte stehen

bloomer /ˈbluːmə(r)/ *n.* (Brit.) [1] (coll.: error) Schnitzer, *der* [2] (loaf) Langbrot, *das*

bloomers /ˈbluːməz/ *n. pl.* [1] (dated) [Damen]pumphose, *die;* (coll.: knickers) Schlüpfer, *der* [2] (Hist.: costume) weite Damenhose (*zum Radfahren*)

blooming /ˈbluːmɪŋ/ (Brit. coll. euphem.)
A *adj.* verflixt (ugs.); **oh, you ~ idiot!** du Trottel! (ugs.)
B *adv.* verflixt (ugs.)

blooper /ˈbluːpə(r)/ *n.* (Amer. coll.) [peinlicher] Fehler, *der;* Patzer, *der* (ugs.); **make** *or* **pull a ~:** einen Bock schießen (ugs.)

blossom /ˈblɒsəm/
A *n.* [1] (flower) Blüte, *die* [2] *no pl., no indef. art.* (mass of flowers) Blüte, *die;* Blütenmeer, *das* (geh.); **be in ~:** in [voller] Blüte stehen *od.* sein; **have come into ~:** blühen
B *v.i.* [1] blühen; **the trees ~ed early this year** die Baumblüte begann dieses Jahr schon früh [2] (fig.) blühen; ‹*Mensch:*› aufblühen; erblühen (geh.); **~ [out] into a statesman/poet** sich zu einem Staatsmann/Dichter entwickeln

blot /blɒt/
A *n.* [1] (spot of ink) Tintenklecks, *der;* (stain) Fleck, *der;* (blemish) Makel, *der;* Schandfleck, *der;* **a ~ on the landscape** (lit. or fig.) ein Schandfleck in der Landschaft [2] (fig.) Makel, *der;* **a ~ on sb.'s character** ein Fleck auf jmds. weißer Weste (fig.); *see also* **escutcheon**
B *v.t.*, **-tt-:** [1] (dry) ablöschen ‹*Tinte, Schrift, Papier*› [2] (spot with ink) beklecksen; verklecksen; (fig.: disgrace) beflecken ‹*Namen, guten Ruf*›; **~ one's copybook** (fig. coll.) sich unmöglich machen

Phrasal verb

• **~ ˈout** *v.t.* [1] (obliterate) einen Klecks machen auf (+ *Akk.*); unleserlich machen ‹*Schrift*› [2] (obscure) verdecken ‹*Sicht*›; **thick smoke/fog ~ted out the enemy ship/the mountains** dichter Rauch/Nebel verdeckte [die Sicht auf] das feindliche Schiff/die Berge [3] auslöschen ‹*Erinnerung*›

blotch /blɒtʃ/ *n.* (on skin) Fleck, *der;* (patch of ink etc.) Klecks, *der*

blotchy /ˈblɒtʃɪ/ *adj.* (skin) fleckig; (with wet blotches) verkleckst

blotter /ˈblɒtə(r)/ *n.* [1] Schreibunterlage, *die* [2] (Amer.) (record book) Kladde, *die;* (Police: record of arrests) [Polizei]register, *das*

ˈblotting paper *n.* Löschpapier, *das*

blotto /ˈblɒtəʊ/ *pred. adj.* (coll.) [sternhagel]voll (salopp)

blouse /blaʊz/ *n.* Bluse, *die*

blow¹ /bləʊ/
A *v.i.*, **blew** /bluː/, **blown** /bləʊn/ [1] ‹*Wind:*› wehen; ‹*Sturm:*› blasen; ‹*Luft:*› ziehen; **there is a gale ~ing out there** es stürmt draußen; **the wind blew in gusts** es wehte ein böiger Wind; der Wind war böig; **there's a draught ~ing** es zieht; **cold air blew down every corridor** auf allen Gängen war es kalt und zugig
[2] (exhale) blasen; **~ on one's tea to cool it** in den Tee pusten, um ihn abzukühlen; **~ on one's hands to warm them** in die Hände hauchen, um sie zu wärmen; **~ hot and cold** (fig.) einmal hü und einmal hott sagen
[3] (puff, pant) ‹*Person:*› schwer atmen, schnaufen; ‹*Tier:*› schnaufen
[4] (eject air and water) ‹*Wal:*› spritzen
[5] (be sounded by ~ing) geblasen werden; ‹*Trompete, Flöte, Horn, Pfeife usw.:*› ertönen
[6] (be driven by ~ing) geblasen *od.* geweht werden; ‹*Blätter, Schneeflocken, Seifenblasen:*› [durch die Luft] fliegen; **a few leaves blew along the road** einige Blätter wirbelten *od.* (dichter.) tanzten die Straße entlang
[7] (melt) ‹*Sicherung, Glühfaden:*› durchbrennen
B *v.t.*, **blew, blown** (*see also* **13**): [1] (breathe out) [aus]blasen, ausstoßen ‹*Luft, Rauch*›
[2] (send by ~ing) **~ sb. a kiss** jmdm. eine Kusshand zuwerfen
[3] (drive by ~ing) treiben ‹*Blätter, Schnee, Staub usw.*›
[4] (make by ~ing) blasen ‹*Glas*›; machen ‹*Seifenblasen*›
[5] (sound) blasen ‹*Trompete, Flöte, Horn, Pfeife usw.*›; **~ one's own trumpet** (fig.) sein Eigenlob singen
[6] (send jet of air at) anblasen ‹*Feuer*›; (gently) anhauchen
[7] (clear) ausblasen ‹*Ei*›; **~ one's nose** sich (*Dat.*) die Nase putzen; [sich] schnäuzen (geh.)
[8] (send flying) schleudern; **~ sth. to pieces** etw. in die Luft sprengen; **it ~s your mind** (coll.) da flippst du aus (ugs.); **this dope will ~ your mind** (coll.) der Stoff hier haut voll rein (salopp); **~ one's top** *or* (Amer.) **stack** (coll.) in die Luft gehen (ugs.)
[9] (cause to melt) durchbrennen lassen ‹*Sicherung, Glühlampe*›; durchhauen (ugs.) ‹*Sicherung*›
[10] (break into) sprengen, aufbrechen ‹*Tresor, Safe*›; aufbrechen ‹*Schloss*›
[11] (coll.: reveal) verraten ‹*Plan, Komplizen*›; *see also* **cover A 9**; **gaff²**
[12] **be ~n** (out of breath) erschöpft sein
[13] *p. t., p. p.* **~ed** (coll.: curse) **[well,] I'm** *or* **I'll be ~ed** ich werde verrückt! (salopp); **I'll be ~ed if I'll do it!** ich denk' nicht [im Traum] dran, das zu tun (ugs.); **well, I'll be ~ed if it isn't old Sid!** Mensch[enskind], wenn das nicht der alte Sid ist! (ugs.); **~ you, Jack!** du kannst mich mal gern haben! (salopp); **~ you, Jack, I'm all right** [das ist] dein Pech *od.* Problem *od.* Bier (ugs.); **~!** [so ein] Mist! (ugs.); **~ the expense** es ist doch Wurscht, was es kostet (ugs.)
[14] (coll.: squander) verpulvern, verplempern (ugs.) ‹*Geld, Mittel, Erbschaft*›; **he blew all his winnings on gambling** er hat seinen ganzen Gewinn verspielt; **he blew all his money on women** er hat sein ganzes Geld für Frauen ausgegeben; **~ it** (lose opportunity) es vermasseln (salopp)
C *n.* [1] (wind) Sturm, *der*
[2] (inhaling of fresh air) **we went outside for a ~:** wir gingen raus, um etwas frische Luft zu schnappen (ugs.)
[3] (~ing of instrument) **he gave a loud/long ~ on his trumpet** er ließ einen lauten/langen Trompetenstoß erschallen
[4] (~ing of nose) **he gave his nose a [good] ~:** er schnäuzte sich [gründlich] (geh.); **have a good ~:** putz dir mal ordentlich die Nase

Phrasal verbs

• **~ aˈway**
A *v.i.* wegfliegen
B *v.t.* [1] wegblasen [2] (esp. Amer. coll.: shoot dead) umblasen (ugs.) [3] (coll.: defeat utterly) vernichtend schlagen; (Football, Tennis, etc.) vom Platz fegen (ugs.) [4] (coll.: disprove) wegfegen ‹*Meinung, Vorschlag*›; über den Haufen werfen (ugs.) ‹*Theorie*› [5] (coll.: impress) anmachen (ugs.); **be ~n away by sb./sth.** von jmdm./etw. [hin

und] weg sein (ugs.); **we were ~n away by the news** die Neuigkeiten haben uns umgehauen (ugs.)

• **~ 'down**

A *v.i.* umgeblasen werden

B *v.t.* umblasen

• **~ 'in**

A *v.t.* zum Einsturz bringen ‹*Haus, Mauer*›; **the gale blew the windows in** der Sturm drückte die Fenster ein

B *v.i.* **1** ‹*Luft:*› hereinkommen; ‹*Staub:*› hereingeweht werden **2** (coll.: enter) hereinschneien; hereinplatzen

• **~ 'off**

A *v.i.* **1** weggeblasen werden **2** (Brit. sl.: break wind) pup[s]en (fam.)

B *v.t.* wegblasen; ‹*Explosion:*› wegreißen

• **~ 'out**

A *v.t.* **1** (extinguish) ausblasen ‹*Kerze, Lampe*› **2** (by explosion) **the explosion blew all the windows out** durch die Explosion flogen alle Fensterscheiben raus; **~ sb.'s/one's brains out** jmdm./sich eine Kugel durch den Kopf jagen (ugs.)

B *v.i.* ‹*Reifen:*› platzen; ‹*Kerze, Lampe:*› ausgeblasen werden

C *v. refl.* ‹*Sturm:*› sich legen. *See also* **blow-out**

• **~ 'over**

A *v.i.* umgeblasen werden; ‹*Streit, Sturm:*› sich legen; **wait till the whole thing ~s over** (fig.) warte, bis sich die Sache gelegt hat

B *v.t.* umblasen

• **~ 'up**

A *v.t.* **1** (shatter) [in die Luft] sprengen **2** (inflate) aufblasen ‹*Ballon*›; aufpumpen ‹*Reifen*› **3** (coll.: reprove) in der Luft zerreißen (ugs.) **4** (coll.: enlarge) vergrößern ‹*Foto, Seite*› **5** (coll.: exaggerate) hochspielen, aufbauschen ‹*Ereignis, Bericht*›

B *v.i.* **1** (explode) explodieren **2** (arise suddenly) ‹*Krieg, Konflikt, Sturm:*› ausbrechen **3** (lose one's temper) [vor Wut] explodieren (ugs.); in die Luft gehen (ugs.). *See also* **blow-up**

blow² *n.* **1** (stroke) Schlag, *der;* (with axe) Hieb, *der;* (jolt, push) Stoß, *der;* **in** *or* **at one ~** (lit. or fig.) mit einem Schlag; **come to ~s** handgreiflich werden; **a ~-by-~ description/account** eine Beschreibung/ein Bericht in allen Einzelheiten; **strike a ~ for sb./sth.** (fig.) jmdm./einer Sache einen großen Dienst erweisen; **strike a ~ against sb./sth.** (fig.) jmdm./einer Sache einen [schweren] Schlag versetzen **2** (disaster) [schwerer] Schlag, *der* (fig.) (**to** für); Schicksalsschlag, *der;* Tiefschlag, *der;* **come as** *or* **be a ~ to sb.** ein schwerer Schlag für jmdn. sein; **suffer a ~:** einen Schock erleiden

blow: ~ drier, ~ dryer *n.* Haartrockner, *der;* Föhn, *der;* **~-dry** *v.t.* fönen

blower /'bləʊə(r)/ *n.* **1** (apparatus) Gebläse, *das* **2** (Brit. coll.: telephone) **on the ~:** an der Strippe; **get on the ~:** sich an die Strippe hängen; **I spoke to him on the ~ yesterday** ich habe gestern mit ihm telefoniert

blow: ~fish *n.* Kugelfisch, *der;* **~fly** *n.* Schmeißfliege, *die;* **~hole** *n.* **1** (Zool.) Atemloch, *das;* Spritzloch, *das;* **2** (Metallurgy) Abzugsloch, *das;* **~ job** *n.* (coarse) Blasmusik, *die* (fig. vulg.); **give sb. a ~ job** jmdm. einen blasen (vulg.); **~lamp** *n.* Lötlampe, *die*

blown ▸ **blow¹ A, B**

blow: ~-out *n.* **1** (burst tyre) Reifenpanne, *die;* **2** (coll.: meal) feudales Essen (ugs.); **we had a good ~-out** wir sind richtig feudal essen gewesen (ugs.); **~pipe** *n.* (weapon) Blasrohr, *das;* (tool) Lötrohr, *das* (Chemie); (Glass-blowing) Glasmacherpfeife, *die;* **~torch** (Amer.) ▸ **~lamp; ~-up** *n.* (coll.: enlargement) Vergrößerung, *die*

blowsy, blowzy /'blaʊzɪ/ *adj.* schlampig [und rotbäckig]

blowy /'bləʊɪ/ *adj.* windig; (windswept) stürmisch

blub /blʌb/ *v.i.,* **-bb-** (coll.) heulen (ugs.); plärren (ugs.)

blubber /'blʌbə(r)/

A *n.* **1** (whale-fat) Walspeck, *der* **2** (coll.: weeping) Geplärr[e], *das* (ugs.); Heulen, *das* (ugs.)

B *v.i.* (coll.: weep) heulen (ugs.); plärren (ugs.)

bludgeon /'blʌdʒn/

A *n.* Knüppel, *der*

B *v.t.* niederknüppeln; **~ sb. to death** jmdm. [mit einem Knüppel] totschlagen

blue¹ /blu:/

A *adj.* **1** blau; **be ~ with cold/rage** blau gefroren/rot vor Zorn sein; *see also* **face A 1** **2** (depressed) **be/feel ~:** niedergeschlagen sein/sich bedrückt *od.* deprimiert fühlen **3** (Brit. Polit.: conservative) konservativ; ≈ schwarz (ugs.) **4** (pornographic) pornographisch; Porno-; **~ film** *or* **movie** Porno[film], *der;* **~ jokes** unanständige Witze

B *n.* **1** (colour) Blau, *das* **2** (blueness) Bläue, *die* **3** (Snooker) blaue Kugel **4** (~ clothes) **dressed in ~:** blau gekleidet; **the boys in ~** (Brit. coll.: police) die Blauen (ugs.) **5** (Brit. Univ.) **be a/get a** *or* **one's ~:** die Universität bei Sportwettkämpfen vertreten haben/vertreten **6** (sky) Himmelsblau, *das;* **out of the ~** (fig.) aus heiterem Himmel (ugs.); völlig unerwartet (ugs.); **disappear into the ~** (fig.) sich in nichts auflösen **7** (Polit.: Conservative) Konservative, *der/die;* ≈ Schwarze, *der/die* (ugs.) **8** (butterfly) Bläuling, *der* **9** **the ~s** (melancholy) Niedergeschlagenheit; **have the ~s** niedergeschlagen *od.* deprimiert sein; **get the ~s** schwermütig *od.* melancholisch werden **10** **the ~s** (Mus.) der Blues; **play/sing the ~s** Blues spielen/singen; **play a ~s** einen Blues spielen

blue² *v.t.* (Brit. coll.: squander) verpulvern, verplempern ‹*Geld, Erbe*›

blue: ~ baby *n.* (Med.) blausüchtiger Säugling; **~bell** *n.* (campanula) [blaue Wiesen]glockenblume, *die;* (wild hyacinth) Sternhyazinthe, *die;* **~berry** /blu:bərɪ/ *n.* Heidelbeere, *die;* Blaubeere, *die;* **~bird** *n.* (of N. Amer.) Elfenblauvogel, *der;* (of S. and S.E. Asia) Rotkehlhüttensänger, *der;* **~ 'blood** *n.* blaues Blut; **~-'blooded** *adj.* blaublütig; **~ book** *n.* **1** (Brit. Parl.) Blaubuch, *das;* **2** (Amer. Polit.) *eine Art Who's Who;* **~bottle** *n.* **1** (Zool.) Schmeißfliege, *die;* **2** (Bot.) Kornblume, *die;* **~ 'cheese** *n.* Blauschimmelkäse, *der;* Edelpilzkäse, *der;* **~ 'chip** *n.* (Poker) blaue Spielmarke, *die;* **~-chip share** *n.* (St. Exch.) erstklassiges Wertpapier; Blue chip, *der* (fachspr.); **~-'collar** *adj.* **~-collar worker** Arbeiter, *der/*Arbeiterin, *die;* **~-collar union** Arbeitergewerkschaft, *die;* **~-eyed** *adj.* blauäugig; **be ~-eyed** blaue Augen haben; **~-eyed 'boy** *n.* (fig. coll.) Goldjunge, *der;* **~fish** *n.* Blaubarsch, *der;* **~ 'fit** *n.* (coll.) **have a ~ fit** Zustände kriegen (ugs.); **~ 'flag** (for beach cleanliness) blaue Flagge; *attrib.* **~-flag beach** blauer Strand; **~ grass** *n.* (Amer.: Poa pratensis) Wiesenrispengras, *das;* **~ gum** *n.* (Bot.) Blaugummibaum, *der;* Fieberbaum, *der;* **~jacket** *n.* (fig. coll.) Blaujacke, *die* (ugs.); **~ 'jeans** *n. pl.* Blue jeans *Pl.;* **~ law** *n.* (Amer.) Sonntagsschutzgesetz, *das;* **~ 'moon** *n.* **once in a ~ moon** alle Jubeljahre (ugs.); **~ 'mould** *n.* essbare Schimmelpilze *Pl.;* **~ 'murder** *n.* **cry** *or* **scream ~ murder** (coll.) Zeter und Mordio schreien (ugs.)

blueness /'blu:nɪs/ *n., no pl.* Bläue, *die*

blue: ~ 'pencil *n.* (fig.) blauer Farbstift; ≈ Rotstift, *der;* **~-'pencil** *v.t.* mit dem Rotstift gehen an ‹*Text*›; zensieren ‹*Nachricht*›; **B~ 'Peter** *n.* (Naut.) Blauer Peter; **~print** *n.* **1** Blaupause, *die;* **2** (fig.) Plan, *der;* Entwurf, *der;* **~ 'ribbon** *n.* **1** (ribbon of the Garter) das blaue Band des Hosenbandordens; **2** (distinction) höchste Auszeichnung; erster Preis; **~ 'rinse** *n.* Blauspülung, *die;* **~-'rinse brigade** *n.* ältere Damen [mit blaugespültem Haar]; **~-sky** *adj.* (creative, visionary) schöpferisch ‹*Denken*›; kreativ ‹*Forschung*›; ungetrübt ‹*Optimismus*›; **~-sky thinker** Schöpfergeist, *der* (geh.); **~stocking** *n.* Blaustrumpf, *der;* **she was too much of a ~stocking** sie war zu blaustrümpfig; **~ 'streak** *n.* (coll.) **he ran like a ~ streak** er rannte wie ein geölter Blitz (ugs.); **~throat** *n.* (Ornith.) Blaukehlchen, *das;* **~ tit** *n.* (Ornith.) Blaumeise, *die;* **~ 'water** *n.* hohe See; **~ 'whale** *n.* Blauwal, *der*

bluff¹ /blʌf/

A *n.* (act) Täuschungsmanöver, *das;* Bluff, *der* (ugs.); **it's nothing but a ~:** das ist bloß [ein] Bluff; *see also* **call B 3**

B *v.i. & t.* bluffen (ugs.)

bluff²

A *n.* (headland) Kliff, *das;* Steilküste, *die;* (inland) Steilhang, *der*

B *adj.* **1** (abrupt, blunt, frank, hearty) raubeinig (ugs.) **2** (perpendicular) steil; schroff ‹*Felswand, Abhang, Küste*›; breit ‹*Schiffsbug*›

bluffness /'blʌfnɪs/ *n., no pl.* Raubeinigkeit, *die* (ugs.)

bluish /'blu:ɪʃ/ *adj.* bläulich

blunder /'blʌndə(r)/

A *n.* [schwerer] Fehler; **make a ~:** einen [schweren] Fehler machen; einen Bock schießen (ugs.)

B *v.i.* **1** (make mistake) einen [schweren] Fehler machen **2** (move blindly) tappen; **he ~ed about the darkened room/down the corridor** er tappte in dem dunklen Zimmer umher/den Flur entlang

blunderbuss /'blʌndəbʌs/ *n.* (Arms Hist.) Donnerbüchse, *die* (veralt.)

blunt /blʌnt/

A *adj.* **1** stumpf; **a ~ instrument** ein stumpfer Gegenstand **2** (outspoken) direkt; unverblümt; **he was quite ~ about his opinion/dislike** er machte aus seiner Meinung/Abneigung überhaupt keinen Hehl **3** (uncompromising) glatt (ugs.) ‹*Ablehnung*›

B *v.t.* **~ [the edge of]** stumpf machen ‹*Messer, Schwert, Säge*›; dämpfen ‹*Begeisterung, Mut*›; mildern ‹*Trauer, Enttäuschung*›; **~ the edge of one's appetite** sich (*Dat.*) den Appetit verderben

bluntly /'blʌntlɪ/ *adv.* **1** (outspokenly) direkt, unverblümt ‹*sprechen, antworten*› **2** (uncompromisingly) glatt ‹*ablehnen*›

bluntness /'blʌntnɪs/ *n., no pl.* ▸ **blunt A:** Stumpfheit, *die;* Direktheit, *die;* Unverblümtheit, *die;* **he was shocked by the ~ of her refusal** ihre glatte Absage hat ihn regelrecht schockiert (ugs.)

blur /blɜ:(r)/

A *v.t.,* **-rr-** **1** (smear) verwischen, verschmieren ‹*Schrift, Seite*› **2** (make indistinct) verwischen ‹*Schrift, Farben, Konturen*›; **become ~red** ‹*Farben, Schrift:*› verwischt werden **3** (dim) trüben ‹*Sicht, Wahrnehmung*›; **my vision is ~red** ich sehe alles verschwommen; mir [ver-]schwimmt alles vor [den] Augen; **her eyes were ~red by tears** ihre Augen schwammen in Tränen

B *n.* **1** (smear) [verschmierter] Fleck, *der* **2** (dim image) verschwommener Fleck

blurb /blɜ:b/ *n.* Klappentext, *der;* Waschzettel, *der*

blurry /'blɜ:rɪ/ *adj.* verschwommen

blurt /blɜ:t/ *v.t.* hervorstoßen ‹*Worte, Beschimpfung*›; **~ sth. out** mit etw. herausplatzen (ugs.)

blush /blʌʃ/

A *v.i.* **1** erröten (geh.); rot werden; **make sb. ~:** jmdn. erröten (geh.) *od.* rot werden lassen **2** (be ashamed) sich schämen (**at** bei)

B *n.* **1** (reddening) Erröten, *das* (geh.); **spare sb.'s ~es** jmdn. nicht in Verlegenheit bringen **2** (rosy glow) Röte, *die;* **the ~ of dawn** (literary) der rosige Schimmer der Morgenröte **3** (glance) **at [the] first ~:** auf den ersten Blick

blusher /'blʌʃə(r)/ *n.* Rouge, *das*

bluster /'blʌstə(r)/

A *v.i.* **1** ‹*Person:*› sich aufplustern (ugs.) **2** ‹*Wind:*› tosen, brausen

B *v.t.* **~ one's way out of sth.** etw. lautstark abstreiten; **you can't ~ your way out of this one** diesmal kannst du dich nicht großartig aus der Affäre ziehen

C *n.* **1** (talk, threats) Schreierei, *die* (ugs.); Geschrei, *das* (abwertend) **2** (blowing of wind) Tosen, *das;* Brausen, *das*

blustery /'blʌstərɪ/ *adj.* stürmisch ‹*Wetter, Wind*›

BM *abbr.* **1** ▸ **MB** **2** **= British Museum** Britisches Museum

BMA *abbr.* **= British Medical Association**

BMus /bi:'mʌz/ *abbr.* **= Bachelor of Music** Bakkalaureus der Musik; *see also* **BSc**

BMX *abbr.* **= bicycle moto-cross** BMX; **~ [bike]** BMX-Rad, *das*

BO *abbr.* (coll.) = **body odour** Körpergeruch, *der*

boa /ˈbəʊə/ *n.* [1] (Zool.) Boa, *die;* (python) Riesenschlange, *die* [2] (garment) Boa, *die*

boa constrictor /ˈbəʊə kənstrɪktə(r)/ *n.* Boa constrictor, *die;* (python) Riesenschlange, *die*

boar /bɔː(r)/ *n.* [1] (male pig) Eber, *der* [2] (wild) Keiler, *der*

board /bɔːd/
A *n.* [1] Brett, *das;* **as flat as a ~:** flach; ‹*Frau*› flach wie ein Bügelbrett; **bare ~s** bloße Dielen [2] (black~) Tafel, *die* [3] (notice~) Schwarzes Brett [4] (in game) Brett, *das* [5] (spring~) [Sprung]brett, *das* [6] (material) Spanplatte, *die* [7] (meals) Verpflegung, *die;* **~ and lodging** Unterkunft und Verpflegung; **full ~:** Vollpension, *die* [8] (Admin. etc.) Amt, *das;* Behörde, *die;* **gas/water/electricity ~:** Gas-/Wasser-/Elektrizitätsversorgungsgesellschaft, *die;* **~ [of examiners]** [Prüfungs]kommission, *die;* **~ of inquiry** Untersuchungsausschuss, *der;* **~ of trustees** Kuratorium, *das;* **~ [of interviewers]** Gremium, *das* (*zur Auswahl von Bewerbern*); (Univ.) Berufungskommission, *die;* **~ of trade** (Amer.) Handelskammer, *die* [9] (Commerc., Industry) **~ [of directors]** Vorstand, *der;* (supervisory ~) Aufsichtsrat, *der;* (in public body) Verwaltungsrat, *der;* **chairman of the ~:** Vorstands-/Aufsichtsrats-/Verwaltungsratsvorsitzende, *der/die* [10] (Naut., Aeronaut., Transport) **on ~:** an Bord; **on ~ the ship/plane** an Bord des Schiffes/Flugzeugs; **on ~ the train/bus** im Zug/Bus; **go on ~ the train/bus** in den Zug/Bus einsteigen; **take sb. on ~** (fig. coll.) jmdn. aufnehmen; **take sth. on ~** (fig. coll.: accept) etw. annehmen [11] **go by the ~:** ins Wasser fallen; **your high principles will have to go by the ~:** du musst deine hohen Grundsätze über Bord werfen. *See also* **above B 1**; **across B 2**; **tread C 1**
B *v.t.* [1] ▸ **~ up** [2] (go on ~) **~ the ship/plane** an Bord des Schiffes/Flugzeugs gehen; **~ the train/bus** in den Zug/Bus einsteigen [3] (come alongside) längsseits herankommen an (+ *Akk.*); (force one's way on ~) entern
C *v.i.* [1] (lodge) [in Pension] wohnen (**with** bei) [2] (~ an aircraft) an Bord gehen; **'flight L 5701 now ~ing [at] gate 15'** „Passagiere des Fluges L 5701 bitte zum Flugsteig 15"
(Phrasal verbs)
• **~ 'out**
A *v.i.* in Pension wohnen
B *v.t.* in Pension geben
• **~ 'up** *v.t.* mit Brettern vernageln

boarder /ˈbɔːdə(r)/ *n.* [1] (lodger) Pensionsgast, *der* [2] (Sch.) Internatsschüler, *der*/-schülerin, *die;* Interne, *der/die* (veralt.) [3] (Naut.) Enterer, *der*

ˈboard game *n.* Brettspiel, *das*

boarding /ˈbɔːdɪŋ/: **~ house** *n.* Pension, *die;* **~ kennel** *n.* Hundepension, *die;* **~ party** *n.* Enterkommando, *das;* **~ pass** *n.* Bordkarte, *die;* **~ school** *n.* Internat, *das*

board: ~ meeting *n.* Vorstands-/Aufsichtsrats-/Verwaltungsratssitzung, *die;* **~room** *n.* Sitzungssaal, *der;* (fig.: top management) Vorstandsetage, *die;* **~sailing** ▸ **windsurfing**; **~walk** *n.* [1] (Amer.: along waterfront) Bohlenweg, *der;* [2] (across marshy ground etc.) Holzsteg, *der*

boast /bəʊst/
A *v.i.* prahlen (**of, about** mit); **that's nothing to ~ about** das ist kein Grund zum Prahlen
B *v.t.* prahlen mit; (possess) sich rühmen (+ *Gen.*); **our school ~s a fine playing field** unsere Schule nennt einen sehr schönen Sportplatz ihr Eigen
C *n.* [1] Prahlerei, *die;* **his favourite ~ is that ...:** am liebsten prahlt er damit, dass ... [2] (cause of pride) Stolz, *der*

boaster /ˈbəʊstə(r)/ *n.* Aufschneider, *der*/Aufschneiderin, *die* (ugs.)

boastful /ˈbəʊstfl/ *adj.* prahlerisch; großspurig ‹*Erklärung, Behauptung*›; **~ stories** Angebergeschichten (ugs.)

boastfully /ˈbəʊstfəlɪ/ *adv.* großspurig; **talk ~ of sth.** mit etw. prahlen

boastfulness /ˈbəʊstfəlnɪs/ *n., no pl.* Großspurigkeit, *die*

boat /bəʊt/
A *n.* [1] Boot, *das;* **ship's ~:** Beiboot, *das;* **go by ~:** mit dem Schiff fahren; **push the ~ out** (fig. coll.) ein Fass aufmachen (ugs.); **be in the same ~** (fig.) im gleichen Boot sitzen; *see also* **burn**[1] **B 1**; **miss B 4**; **rock**[2] **A 2** [2] (ship) Schiff, *das*
B *v.i.* **go ~ing** eine Bootsfahrt machen

boat: ~ deck *n.* Bootsdeck, *das;* **~ drill** *n.* Bootsmanöver, *das*

boater /ˈbəʊtə(r)/ *n.* [1] (person) Bootsfahrer, *der*/-fahrerin, *die* [2] (hat) steifer Strohhut; Kreissäge, *die* (ugs.)

boatful /ˈbəʊtfʊl/ *n.* Bootsladung, *die*

boat: ~hook *n.* Bootshaken, *der;* **~house** *n.* Bootshaus, *das;* **~ lift** *n.* Schiffshebewerk, *das;* **~load** *n.* Bootsladung, *die;* **~man** /ˈbəʊtmən/ *n., pl.* **~men** /ˈbəʊtmən/ [1] (hiring) Bootsverleiher, *der;* [2] (providing transport) Bootsführer, *der;* **~ people** *n. pl.* Boatpeople *Pl.;* Bootsflüchtlinge; **~ race** *n.* Regatta, *die;* **the B~ Race** die Oxford-Cambridge-Regatta; **~swain** /ˈbəʊsn/ *n.* Bootsmann, *der;* **~swain's chair** Bootsmannsstuhl, *der;* **~ train** *n.* Zug mit Schiffsanschluss

Boat Race

Seit 1829 findet jährlich (meist am Samstag vor Ostern) ein Ruderrennen auf der Themse in London statt. Das Achterrennen wird von den Rudermannschaften der Universitäten Oxford und Cambridge ausgetragen. Im Gegensatz zu anderen sportlichen Universitätswettbewerben wird dieses Ruderrennen landesweit im Fernsehen übertragen.

bob[1] /bɒb/
A *v.i.,* **-bb-** [1] **~ [up and down]** sich auf und nieder bewegen; (jerkily) auf und nieder schnellen; ‹[*Pferde*]*schwanz:*› [auf und nieder] wippen; **the poppies ~bed in the breeze** der Mohn wiegte sich im Wind [hin und her]; **a cork was ~bing on the waves** ein Korken tanzte auf den Wellen [auf und nieder]; **~ up** hochschnellen [2] (curtsy) knicksen
B *n.* (curtsy) Knicks, *der*

bob[2]
A *n.* [1] (weight) Gewicht, *das* [2] (hairstyle) Bubikopf, *der*
B *v.t.,* **-bb-** kurz schneiden ‹*Haar*›; **wear one's hair ~bed** einen Bubikopf tragen

bob[3] *n., pl. same* (Brit. coll.)(Hist./coll.: shilling) Schilling, *der;* (fig.) **she's got** *or* **she's worth a few ~, she's not short of a ~ or two** sie hat schon ein paar Euro

bob[4] *n.* (coll.) **~'s your uncle** die Sache ist geritzt (ugs.); fertig ist der Lack (ugs.)

bob[5] *n.* (~sled) Bob, *der*

bobbin /ˈbɒbɪn/ *n.* Spule, *die*

ˈbobbin lace *n.* Klöppelspitze, *die*

bobble /ˈbɒbl/ *n.* Pompon, *der;* Bommel, *die* (bes. nordd.)

bobby /ˈbɒbɪ/ *n.* (Brit. coll.) Bobby, *der* (ugs.); Schupo, *der* (ugs. veralt.)

bobby: ~ pin *n.* (Amer.) Haarklemme, *die;* **~ socks** *n. pl.* (Amer.) Söckchen; **~-soxer** /ˈbɒbɪsɒksə(r)/ *n.* (Amer. dated coll.) Backfisch, *der*

ˈbobcat *n.* (Amer.) [Rot]luchs, *der*

bob: ~sled, ~sleigh *ns.* Bob[schlitten], *der;* **~stay** *n.* (Naut.) Wasserstag, *das*

bock /bɒk/ *n.* Bock[bier], *das*

bod /bɒd/ *n.* (Brit. coll.) Mensch, *der;* **~s** Leute; **odd ~:** seltsamer Typ (ugs.)

bode /bəʊd/
A *v.i.* **~ ill/well** nichts Gutes/einiges erhoffen lassen
B *v.t.* (portend) bedeuten; **~ no good** nichts Gutes ahnen lassen

bodega /bəˈdiːgə/ *n.* Bodega, *die*

bodge /bɒdʒ/ *v.t.* (Brit. coll.) hinpfuschen (ugs. abwertend); zusammenpfuschen (ugs. abwertend); **it's a ~d repair** die Reparatur ist Pfusch

bodhran /ˈbaʊrɑːn/ *n.* (Irish drum) Bodhran, *die*

bodice /ˈbɒdɪs/ *n.* (part of dress) Oberteil, *das;* (undergarment, part of dirndl) Mieder, *das*

ˈbodice-ripper /ˈbɒdɪsrɪpə(r)/ *n.* (coll.) Verführungsschnulze, *die*

-bodied /bɒdɪd/ *in comb.* von ... Körperbau; **big-~:** von großem, schwerem Körperbau

bodiless /ˈbɒdɪlɪs/ *adj.* körperlos ‹*Gespenst*›; **a ~ head** ein Kopf ohne Rumpf

bodily /ˈbɒdɪlɪ/
A *adj.* körperlich; organisch ‹*Krankheit*›; **~ harm** Körperverletzung, *die;* **~ needs** leibliche Bedürfnisse; **~ organs** Körperorgane
B *adv.* **he lifted her ~:** er hob sie einfach hoch; **the audience rose ~:** das Publikum stand geschlossen auf

bodkin /ˈbɒdkɪn/ *n.* [1] (needle) Durchziehnadel, *die* [2] (Hist.: hairpin) lange Haarnadel [3] (tool) Ahle, *die*

body /ˈbɒdɪ/
A *n.* [1] ▸ⓘ **p. 951** (of person) Körper, *der;* Leib, *der* (geh.); (of animal) Körper, *der;* **bend one's ~ forward** den Oberkörper nach vorne beugen; **the ~ of Christ** der Leib Christi; **enough to keep ~ and soul together** genug, um am Leben zu bleiben; **do sth. ~ and soul** etw. mit aller Kraft tun [2] (corpse) Leiche, *die;* Leichnam, *der* (geh.); **over my dead ~!** nur über meine Leiche [3] (coll.: person) Mensch, *der;* (woman also) Person, *die;* **she/he is a very kind ~:** sie ist ein sehr netter Mensch/er ist ein sehr netter Kerl [4] (group of persons) Gruppe, *die;* (having a particular function) Organ, *das;* (military force) [Truppen]verband, *der;* **government ~:** staatliche Einrichtung; **charitable ~:** Wohltätigkeitsorganisation, *die;* **student ~:** Studentenschaft, *die;* **in a ~:** geschlossen [5] (mass) **a huge ~ of water** große Wassermassen [6] (main portion) Hauptteil, *der* [7] (Motor Veh.) Karosserie, *die;* (Railw.) Aufbau, *der;* (aircraft fuselage) Rumpf, *der* [8] (collection) Sammlung, *die;* **a ~ of knowledge** ein Wissensschatz; **a ~ of facts** Tatsachenmaterial, *das* [9] (of soup or gravy) Substanz, *die;* (of wine) Körper, *der;* **have no ~:** nicht sehr gehaltvoll sein/nicht sehr viel Körper haben. *See also* **corporate 1**; **foreign 4**; **heavenly 2**; **politic A 3**
B *v.t.* **~ sth. forth** etw. verkörpern *od.* versinnbildlichen

body: ~ armour, (Amer.) **ˈbody armor** kugel- *od.* schusssicherer [Schutz]anzug; Panzeranzug, *der;* (waistcoat) kugel- *od.* schusssichere Weste; Panzerweste, *die;* **~ art** *n.* [1] (~ decoration) Körperkunst, *die;* Body-Art, *die;* [2] (Art) Body-Art, *die;* **~ bag** *n.* Leichensack, *der;* **~ blow** *n.* Körperstoß, *der* (Boxen); (fig.) schwerer Schlag; **~board** *n.* Bodyboard, *das;* **~boarder** *n.* Bodyboarder, *der*/Bodyboarderin, *die;* **~boarding** *n., no pl.* Bodyboarding, *das;* **~ builder** *n.* Bodybuilder, *der*/Bodybuilderin, *die;* **~building A** *n., no pl.* Bodybuilding, *das;* **B** *adj.* **~building food** Aufbaukost, *die;* **~ clock** ▸ **biological clock**; **~ colour** *n.* Deckfarbe, *die;* **~ count** *n.* Opferzahl, *die;* [An]zahl der Todesopfer; **~ double** *n.* Körperdouble, *das;* **~ fascism** *n., no pl.* Körperfaschismus, *der;* **~ fat** *n.* Körperfett, *das;* **~ fluids** *n. pl.* Körperflüssigkeiten; **~guard** *n.* ▸ⓘ **p. 1260** (single) Leibwächter, *der;* (group) Leibwache, *die;* **~ hair** *n.* Körperhaar, *das;* **~ heat** *n.* [1] (body temperature) Körpertemperatur, *die;* [2] (heat) Körperwärme, *die;* **~ language** *n.* Körpersprache, *die;* **~ odour** *n.* Körpergeruch, *der;* **~ part** *n.* Körperteil, *der;* **~ piercing** *n., no pl.* Piercing, *das;* **~ scanner** *n.* (Med.) [Ganz]körperscanner, *der;* **~ search** *n.* Leibesvisitation, *die;* **~snatcher** *n.* Leichenräuber, *der;* **~ stocking** *n.* Bodystocking, *der;* **~suit** *n.* Body[suit], *der;* **~ surfing** *n., no pl.* Bodysurfing, *das;* **~ weight** *n.* Körpergewicht, *das;* **~work** *n., no pl.* (Motor Veh.) Karosserie, *die*

Boer /ˈbəʊə(r), bʊə(r)/
A *n.* Bure, *der*/Burin, *die*
B *adj.* **the ~ War** der Burenkrieg

boffin /ˈbɒfɪn/ *n.* (Brit. coll.) Eierkopf, *der* (salopp)

bog /bɒg/
A *n.* [1] Moor, *das;* (marsh, swamp) Sumpf, *der* [2] (Brit. sl.: lavatory) Lokus, *der* (salopp)
B *v.t.,* **-gg-: be ~ged down** festsitzen (fig.); nicht weiterkommen; **get ~ged down in details** (fig.) sich in Details verzetteln

b

ℹ The body

German uses the definite article for parts of the body where English uses the possessive adjective, as long as it is clear whose body part it is (which usually means that it belongs to the person who is the subject of the sentence):

He raised his hand
= Er hob die Hand

She closed her eyes
= Sie schloss die Augen

But

She closed his eyes
= Sie schloss ihm die Augen

She passed her hand over my forehead
= Sie fuhr mir mit der Hand über die Stirn

From the last two examples it can be seen that where the owner of the part of the body is not the subject, i.e. not doing the action, German uses the dative of the personal pronoun plus the definite article. This also applies when the owner of the body part is responsible for the action (often an injury), but in this case the pronoun is reflexive (which only makes a difference in the third person):

I've broken my leg
= Ich habe mir das Bein gebrochen

He dislocated his arm
= Er hat sich (*Dat.*) den Arm ausgerenkt

You nearly dislocated his arm
= Du hast ihm fast den Arm ausgerenkt

She hit her head on the beam
= Sie hat sich den Kopf am Balken angestoßen *or* ist mit dem Kopf gegen den Balken gestoßen

Can you put some cream on my back (for me)?
= Kannst du mir den Rücken mit Creme einreiben?

Note the same construction with a noun:

She massaged her son's back
= Sie massierte ihrem Sohn den Rücken

Note also the following impersonal construction:

My head is spinning
= Mir dreht sich *or* schwirrt der Kopf

My feet were tingling
= Es kribbelte mir *or* mich in den Füßen

See also □ **Illnesses.**

Body features

There are many adjectives in German ending in **-ig** describing features corresponding to English adjectives ending in *-ed:*

blue-eyed
= blauäugig

dark-haired
= dunkelhaarig

long-legged
= langbeinig

These are usually used attributively, i.e. before the noun, not separately:

a long-legged blonde
= eine langbeinige Blondine

but

He is blue-eyed
= Er hat blaue Augen

She is dark-haired
= Sie hat dunkle Haare

See also □ **Height, Weight.**

bogey /ˈbəʊgɪ/ *n.* 1 (Golf: one stroke over par) Bogey, *das* 2 ▸ **bogy**

boggle /ˈbɒgl/ *v.i.* 1 (be startled) sprachlos sein; **the imagination ~s at the thought** der Gedanke übersteigt die Vorstellungskraft; **the mind ~s [at the thought]** bei dem Gedanken wird einem schwindlig 2 (hesitate, demur) **~ at** *or* **about sth.** etw. höchst ungern tun

boggy /ˈbɒgɪ/ *adj.* sumpfig; morastig

bog ˈoak *n.* Mooreiche, *die*

ˈbog-standard *adj.* (coll.) stinknormal (salopp)

bogus /ˈbəʊgəs/ *adj.* falsch; gefälscht ‹*Geld, Schmuck, Dokument*›; **~ firm** Schwindelfirma, *die;* **the claim/deal was ~:** die Behauptung/das Geschäft war reiner Schwindel

bogy /ˈbəʊgɪ/ *n.* 1 **B~** (the Devil) der Gottseibeiuns 2 (evil spirit) Gespenst, *das;* **~man** Schreckgestalt, *die* 3 (bugbear) Schreckgespenst, *das* 4 (Brit. coll.: piece of dried mucus) Popel, *der* (ugs.)

Bohemia /bəʊˈhiːmɪə/ *pr. n.* Böhmen (*das*)

Bohemian /bəʊˈhiːmɪən/
A *adj.* 1 (socially unconventional) unkonventionell; unbürgerlich; **a ~ person** ein Bohemien 2 (Geog.) böhmisch; **he/she is ~:** er ist Böhme/sie ist Böhmin
B *n.* 1 (socially unconventional person) Bohemien, *der* 2 (native of Bohemia) Böhme, *der*/Böhmin, *die*

bohemianism /bəʊˈhiːmɪənɪzm/ *n., no pl.* unkonventioneller Lebensstil

boil[1] /bɔɪl/
A *v.i.* 1 kochen; (Phys.) sieden; **the kettle's ~ing** das Wasser im Kessel kocht; **keep the pot ~ing** (fig.) dafür sorgen, dass es weitergeht 2 (fig.) ‹*Wasser, Wellen:*› schäumen, brodeln 3 (fig.: be angry) kochen, schäumen (**with** vor + *Dat.*) 4 (fig. coll.: be hot) sehr heiß sein; **I'm ~ing** mir ist heiß; **be ~ing [hot]** sehr heiß sein; ‹*Wasser:*› kochend heiß sein; **a ~ing hot August day** ein glühend heißer Augusttag
B *v.t.* 1 kochen; **~ sth. dry** etw. verkochen; **it is necessary to ~ the water** man muss das Wasser abkochen; **~ed potatoes** Salzkartoffeln; **~ the kettle** das Wasser heiß machen; **~ed shirt** (dated) gestärktes Frackhemd; **go and ~ your head** (fig. coll.) du kannst mir den Buckel herunterrutschen (salopp) 2 (make by ~ing) kochen ‹*Seife*›; **~ed sweet** (Brit.) hartes [Frucht]bonbon; Hartkaramelle, *die* (fachspr.)
C *n.* Kochen, *das;* **come to/go off the ~:** zu kochen anfangen/aufhören; (fig.) sich zuspitzen/sich wieder beruhigen; **bring to the ~:** zum Kochen bringen; (fig.) auf die Spitze treiben

(Phrasal verbs)
- **~ aˈway** *v.i.* 1 (continue boiling) weiterkochen 2 (evaporate completely) verkochen
- **~ ˈdown**
A *v.i.* einkochen; **~ down to sth.** (fig.) auf etw. (*Akk.*) hinauslaufen
B *v.t.* einkochen; (fig.) kurz zusammenfassen
- **~ ˈover** *v.i.* überkochen
- **~ ˈup**
A *v.t.* kochen
B *v.i.* kochen; (fig.) sich zuspitzen

boil[2] *n.* (Med.) Furunkel, *der*

boiler /ˈbɔɪlə(r)/ *n.* 1 Kessel, *der* 2 (hot-water tank) Boiler, *der* 3 (dated: for laundry) [Wasch]kessel, *der*

boiler: ~house *n.* Kesselhaus, *das;* **~maker** *n.* ▸ℹ **p. 1260** Kesselschmied, *der;* **~ room** *n.* Kesselraum, *der;* **~ suit** *n.* Overall, *der*

boiling: ~ point *n.* ▸ℹ **p. 1620** Siedepunkt, *der;* **be at/reach ~ point** (fig.) auf dem Siedepunkt sein/den Siedepunkt erreichen; **~ ring** *n.* Kochspirale, *die*

boil-in-the-ˈbag *adj.* im Kochbeutel *nachgestellt;* **~ rice** Kochbeutelreis, *der*

boisterous /ˈbɔɪstərəs/ *adj.* 1 (noisily cheerful) ausgelassen 2 (rough) wild; rau ‹*Wind, See, Witterung*›

boisterously /ˈbɔɪstərəslɪ/ *adv.* ▸ **boisterous:** ausgelassen; wild

bold /bəʊld/ *adj.* 1 (courageous) mutig; (daring) kühn 2 (forward) keck; kühn ‹*Worte*›; **make so ~ [as to ...]** so kühn sein[, zu ...]; *see also* **brass A 1** 3 (striking) auffallend, kühn ‹*Farbe, Muster*›; kräftig ‹*Konturen*›; fett ‹*Schlagzeile*›; **bring out in ~ relief** deutlich hervortreten lassen 4 (vigorous) kühn; ausdrucksvoll ‹*Stil, Beschreibung*› 5 (Printing) fett; (secondary ~) halbfett; **in ~ [type]** im Fettdruck

bold: ~-face, ~-faced ▸ **bold 5**

boldly /ˈbəʊldlɪ/ *adv.* 1 (courageously) mutig; (daringly) kühn 2 (forwardly) dreist 3 (strikingly) kräftig ‹*hervortreten*›; mit kühnem Schwung ‹*signieren, malen*›; auffällig ‹*mustern*›

boldness /ˈbəʊldnɪs/ *n., no pl.* 1 (courage, daring) Kühnheit, *die* 2 (forwardness) Dreistigkeit, *die* 3 (strikingness) Kühnheit, *die;* (of description, style) Ausdruckskraft, *die;* (of an outline, of lettering) Deutlichkeit, *die;* (of pattern) Auffälligkeit, *die*

bole /bəʊl/ *n.* (trunk) [Baum]stamm, *der*

bolero /bəˈleərəʊ/ *n., pl.* **~s** Bolero, *der*

Bolivia /bəˈlɪvɪə/ *pr. n.* Bolivien (*das*)

Bolivian /bəˈlɪvɪən/ ▸ℹ **p. 1345**
A *adj.* bolivianisch; **sb. is ~:** jmd. ist Bolivianer/Bolivianerin
B *n.* Bolivianer, *der*/Bolivianerin, *die*

boll /bəʊl/ *n.* Samenkapsel, *die*

bollard /ˈbɒləd/ *n.* (Brit.) Poller, *der*

bollocks /ˈbɒləks/ (coarse)
A *n. pl.* Eier (derb)
B *int.* Scheiße

ˈboll weevil *n.* Baumwollkapselkäfer, *der*

bologna /bəˈləʊnjə/ *n.* (Amer.) **~ [sausage]** ≈ Mortadella, *die*

boloney /bəˈləʊnɪ/ *n.* 1 (coll.) Quatsch, *der* (ugs.) 2 (Amer.: sausage) ▸ **bologna**

Bolshevik /ˈbɒlʃəvɪk/ *n.* 1 (Hist.) Bolschewik, *der* 2 (derog.: revolutionary) Bolschewist, *der*/Bolschewistin, *die* (ugs.)

Bolshevism /ˈbɒlʃəvɪzm/ *n., no pl.* (Hist.) Bolschewismus, *der*

Bolshevist /ˈbɒlʃəvɪst/ (Hist., also derog.: revolutionary)
A *n.* Bolschewist, *der*/Bolschewistin, *die*
B *adj.* bolschewistisch

bolshie, bolshy /ˈbɒlʃɪ/ *adj.* (coll.: uncooperative) aufsässig; rotzig (salopp)

bolster /ˈbəʊlstə(r)/
A *n.* (pillow) Nackenrolle, *die;* (wedge-shaped) Keilkissen, *das*
B *v.t.* (fig.) stärken; **~ sb. up** jmdm. Mut machen; **~ sth. up** etw. stärken; **~ up a regime/one's status** ein Regime stützen/seinen Status aufpolieren (ugs.)

bolt[1] /bəʊlt/
A *n.* 1 (on door or window) Riegel, *der;* (on gun) Kammerverschluss, *der* 2 (metal pin) Schraube, *die;* (without thread) Bolzen, *der* 3 (of crossbow) Bolzen, *der;* **shoot one's ~** (fig.) sein Pulver verschießen 4 **~ [of lightning]** Blitz[strahl], *der;* **[like] a ~ from the blue** (fig.) wie ein Blitz aus heiterem Himmel 5 (sudden dash) **make a ~ for freedom** einen Fluchtversuch machen; **make a ~ for it** das Weite suchen
B *v.i.* 1 davonlaufen; ‹*Pferd:*› durchgehen; ‹*Fuchs, Kaninchen:*› [mit einem Satz] flüchten; **~ out of the shop** aus dem Laden rennen 2 (Hort., Agric.) vorzeitig Samen bilden; ‹*Salat, Kohl:*› schießen
C *v.t.* 1 (fasten with ~) verriegeln; **~ sb. in/out** jmdn. einsperren/aussperren 2 (fasten with ~s with/without thread) verschrauben/mit Bolzen verbinden; **~ sth. to sth.** etw. an etw. (*Akk.*) schrauben/mit Bolzen befestigen 3 (gulp down) **~ [down]** hinunterschlingen ‹*Essen*›; hinunterstürzen ‹*Getränk*› 4 aufjagen ‹*Fuchs, Kaninchen usw.*›
D *adv.* **~ upright** kerzengerade

bolt[2] *v.t.* (sift) sieben

bolt: ~-hole *n.* (lit. or fig.) Schlupfloch, *das;* **~-on** *adj.* aufschraubbar

Bolzano /bɒlˈzɑːnəʊ/ *pr. n.* Bozen (*das*)

bomb /bɒm/
A *n.* 1 Bombe, *die;* **go like a ~** (fig. coll.) ein Bombenerfolg sein; **my new car goes like a ~:** mein neues Auto ist die reinste Rakete; **go**

b

down a ~ with (fig. coll.) ein Bombenerfolg sein bei **2** (coll.: large sum of money) **a ~:** 'ne Masse Geld (ugs.) **3** (coll.: failure) Reinfall, *der* (ugs.)
B *v.t.* bombardieren; **~ a pub** einen Bombenanschlag auf eine Kneipe verüben
C *v.i.* **1** Bomben werfen; **~ing raid** Bombenangriff, *der* **2** (coll.: fail) durchfallen **3** (coll.: travel fast) rasen

Phrasal verb

- **~ 'out** *v.t.* ausbomben

'bomb alert *n.* Bombenalarm, *der*

bombard /bɒm'bɑːd/ *v.t.* (Mil.) beschießen; bombardieren (veralt.); (fig.) bombardieren

bombardier /bɒmbə'dɪə(r)/ *n.* (Brit. Mil.) Unteroffizier [bei der Artillerie]

bombardment /bɒm'bɑːdmənt/ *n.* Beschuss, *der;* Bombardierung, *die* (veralt.); (fig.) Bombardierung, *die*

bombast /'bɒmbæst/ *n., no pl.* Schwulst, *der;* Bombast, *der*

bombastic /bɒm'bæstɪk/ *adj.* bombastisch; schwülstig

bomb: ~ attack *n.* Bombenangriff, *der;* (act of terror) Bombenattentat, *das;* Bombenanschlag, *der;* **suicide ~ attacks** Selbstmordanschläge; Bombenanschläge von Selbstmordattentätern; **~ bay** *n.* Bombenschacht, *der;* **~ blast** *n.* (blast wave) Druckwelle, *die;* (explosion) Bombenexplosion, *die;* **~ disposal** *n.* Räumung von Bomben; *attrib.* **~ disposal expert** Experte für die Räumung von Bomben; **~ disposal squad** Bombenräumkommando, *das*

bombe /bɔ̃b/ *n.* (Gastr.) Eisbombe, *die*

bomber /'bɒmə(r)/ *n.* **1** (Air Force) Bomber, *der* (ugs.) **2** (terrorist) Bombenattentäter, *der/*-attentäterin, *die;* Bombenleger, *der/*-legerin, *die* (ugs.)

'bomber jacket *n.* Bomberjacke, *die*

bombing /'bɒmɪŋ/ *n.* Bombardierung, *die*

bombing: ~ raid *n.* Bombenangriff, *der;* **~ run** *n.* ▸ **bomb run**

bomblet /'bɒmlɪt/ *n.* Bomblette, *die;* Bomblet, *das*

bomb: ~load *n.* Bombenlast, *die;* **~proof** *adj.* bombenfest; **~ run** *n.* Bomben[ziel]anflug, *der;* **~ scare** *n.* Bombendrohung, *die;* **~shell** *n.* Bombe, *die;* (fig.) Sensation, *die;* **come as a** *or* **be something of a ~shell** wie eine Bombe einschlagen; **a blonde ~shell** eine Superblondine; **~ shelter** *n.* Luftschutzraum, *der;* Luftschutzbunker, *der;* **~ site** *n.* Trümmergrundstück, *das;* (larger area) Trümmerfeld, *das*

bona fide /bəʊnə 'faɪdɪ/
A *adj.* (genuine) echt; (sincere) ehrlich; redlich; **~ contract** in gutem Glauben abgeschlossener Vertrag; **~ purchaser** gutgläubiger Erwerber
B *adv.* (genuinely) wahrhaftig; (sincerely) ehrlich; redlich; (in good faith) in gutem Glauben; bona fide (geh.)

bonanza /bə'nænzə/
A *n.* **1** (unexpected success) Goldgrube, *die* (fig.) **2** (large output) reiche Ausbeute
B *adj.* äußerst ertragreich ‹*Farm, Geschäftsjahr*›

bon-bon /'bɒnbɒn/ *n.* Praline, *das*

bonce /bɒns/ *n.* (Brit. coll.: head) Birne, *die* (salopp)

bond /bɒnd/
A *n.* **1** Band, *das* **2** *in pl.* (shackles, lit. or fig.) Fesseln; Bande (dichter. veralt.) **3** (uniting force) Band, *das* **4** (adhesion) **the ~ will be instantaneous/unbreakable** die Haftwirkung wird sofort eintreten/die Teile werden absolut fest aneinander kleben **5** (Commerc.) (debenture) Anleihe, *die;* Schuldverschreibung, *die;* (deed) Schuldschein, *der;* **goods in ~:** Waren unter Zollverschluss **6** (agreement) Übereinkommen, *das;* (covenant) Bund, *der;* **my word is [as good as] my ~:** was ich verspreche, das halte ich auch **7** (Insurance) ≈ Vertrauensschadenversicherung, *die* **8** (Building) [Mauer]verband, *der;* **English ~:** Blockverband, *der* **9** (Chem.) Bindung, *die*
B *v.t.* **1** (join securely) zusammenfügen (**to** mit) **2** (Building) im Verband legen **3** (Commerc.) unter Zollverschluss nehmen; *see also* **bonded 1**

bondage /'bɒndɪdʒ/ *n., no pl.* Sklaverei, *die* (auch fig.); (sexual perversion) Bondage, *das;* Fesseln, *das;* **in ~ to sb.** als jmds. Sklave/Sklavin (auch fig.)

bonded /'bɒndɪd/ *adj.* **1** (Commerc.) unter Zollverschluss; **~ goods** Zolllagergut, *das;* **~ warehouse** Zolllager, *das;* **~ debt** fundierte Schuld (Finanzw.) **2** (cemented, reinforced) verstärkt

'bond: ~ paper *n.* Dokumentenpapier, *das;* (for general use) feines Schreibpapier; **~stone** *n.* (Building) Binder, *der;* **~-washing** *n.* (Finance) *Umwandlung von zu versteuernden Dividendengewinnen in steuerfreie Kapitalerträge*

bone /bəʊn/
A *n.* **1** ▸ℹ **p. 951** Knochen, *der;* (of fish) Gräte, *die;* **~s** (fig.: remains) Gebeine *Pl.* (geh.); **be chilled to the ~** (fig.) völlig durchgefroren sein; **cut prices to the ~:** die Preise äußerst scharf kalkulieren; **pare expenditure to the ~:** sich radikal einschränken; **work one's fingers to the ~** (fig.) bis zum Umfallen arbeiten; **I feel it in my ~s** (fig.) ich habe es im Gefühl; **make old ~s** (fig.) alt werden; **the bare ~s** (fig.) die wesentlichen Punkte; (of a story) die Grundzüge; **close to the** *or* **near the ~** (fig.) (indecent) gewagt; (destitute) am Rande des Existenzminimums; **come** *or* **get close to** *or* **near the ~** (fig.) [ziemlich] gewagt sein; *see also* **dry A 1 2** (material) Knochen, *der;* (ivory) Elfenbein, *das* **3** (stiffener) (in collar) Kragenstäbchen, *das;* (in corset) Korsettstange, *die* **4** (subject of dispute) **have/find a ~ to pick with sb.** mit jmdm. ein Hühnchen zu rupfen haben (ugs.)/einen Grund finden, mit jmdm. Streit anzufangen; **~ of contention** Zankapfel, *der;* **make no ~s about sth./doing sth.** keinen Hehl aus etw. machen/sich nicht scheuen, etw. zu tun
B *v.t.* den/die Knochen herauslösen aus, ausbeinen ‹*Fleisch, Geflügel*›; entgräten ‹*Fisch*›
C *v.i.* **~ up on sth.** (coll.) etw. büffeln (ugs.)

bone: ~ 'china *n.* Knochenporzellan, *das;* **~ 'dry** *adj.* knochentrocken (ugs.); **~fish** *n.* (Amer.) Grätenfisch, *der;* **~head** *n.* (coll.) Holzkopf, *der* (salopp abwertend); **~-headed** *adj.* (coll.) blöd (ugs. abwertend); **~ 'idle, ~ 'lazy** *adjs.* stinkfaul (salopp); **~ marrow** *n.* (Anat.) Knochenmark, *das; attrib.* **~ marrow transplant** Knochenmarktransplantation, *die;* **~meal** *n.* Knochenmehl, *das*

boner /'bəʊnə(r)/ *n.* (coll.) grober Schnitzer; **pull a ~:** sich (*Dat.*) einen groben Schnitzer leisten

bone: ~-shaker *n.* Klapperkiste, *die* (salopp); **~-'weary** *adj.* völlig erschöpft

bonfire /'bɒnfaɪə(r)/ *n.* **1** (at celebration) Freudenfeuer, *das* **2** (for burning rubbish) Feuer, *das;* **make a ~ of sth.** (lit. or fig.) etw. verbrennen

Bonfire Night

In Großbritannien feiert man am 5. November den Jahrestag des Sprengstoffanschlags auf das Parlament von 1605, der von einer Gruppe von Katholiken geplant worden war. Die Verschwörung wurde aufgedeckt, als Guy Fawkes, einer der Beteiligten, mit Schießpulver ertappt wurde. Die Verschwörer wurden hingerichtet. Zum Andenken an sie finden jährlich am 5. November große Feuerwerke statt. Viele Leute entzünden an dem Abend ein Freudenfeuer, auf dem sie eine Nachbildung des Guy Fawkes, kurz *a guy* genannt, verbrennen. Manchmal sammeln Kinder schon vorher Geld für das Feuerwerk, indem sie sich mit einer selbst gebastelten Guy-Puppe auf die Straße stellen und Passanten mit den Worten "*penny for the guy*" um Geldgaben bitten. *Bonfire Night* heißt auch *Guy Fawkes Night.*

bongo /'bɒŋgəʊ/ *n., pl.* **~s** *or* **~es** (drum) Bongo, *das od. die*

bonhomie /'bɒnəmiː/ *n., no pl.* Bonhomie, *die* (geh.); Jovialität, *die*

bonk /bɒŋk/ (Brit.)
A *v.t.* **1** (coll.: hit) hauen **2** (sl.: copulate with) bumsen (salopp)
B *v.i.* (sl.: copulate) bumsen (salopp)

bonkers /'bɒŋkəz/ *adj.* (coll.) verrückt (salopp); wahnsinnig (ugs.); **go ~:** überschnappen (ugs.); **be ~:** spinnen (ugs. abwertend)

bon mot /bɔ̃ 'məʊ, bɒn 'məʊ/ *n., pl.* **bons mots** /bɔ̃ 'məʊ, bɒn 'məʊ/ Bonmot, *das*

bonnet /'bɒnɪt/ *n.* **1** (woman's) Haube, *die;* Bonnet, *das* (hist.); (child's) Häubchen, *das;* (Scotch cap) [Schotten]mütze, *die; see also* **bee 1** **2** (Brit. Motor Veh.) Motor- *od.* Kühlerhaube, *die*

bonny /'bɒnɪ/ *adj.* **1** (Scot. and N. Engl.) (beautiful) schön; hübsch; (fine) prächtig ‹*Bursche, Schiff*›; herrlich ‹*Land, Stadt, Anblick*› **2** (healthy-looking) prächtig ‹*Baby*›; gesund ‹*Gesicht*›

bonsai /'bɒnsaɪ/ *n.* **1** (tree) Bonsai[baum], *der* **2** *no pl., no art.* (method) Bonsai, *das*

bonus /'bəʊnəs/ *n.* **1** zusätzliche Leistung **2** (to shareholders, insurance-policy holder) Bonus, *der;* (to employee) **Christmas ~:** Weihnachtsgratifikation, *die;* **cost-of-living ~:** Teuerungszulage, *die;* **production ~:** Leistungsprämie, *die* **3** (advantage) Pluspunkt, *der*

'bonus point *n.* Bonuspunkt, *der;* (in sports) Extrapunkt, *der;* (fig.) Pluspunkt, *der;* Extrapunkt, *der*

bon vivant /bɔ̃ viː'vɑ̃/ *n., pl.* **~s** *or* **bons vivants** /bɔ̃ viː'vɑ̃/ Gourmet, *der;* Feinschmecker, *der*

bon voyage /bɔ̃ vwɑː'jɑːʒ/ *int.* glückliche Reise

bony /'bəʊnɪ/ *adj.* **1** (of bone) beinern; knöchern; Knochen-; (like bone) knochenartig **2** (big-boned) grobknochig **3** (skinny) knochendürr (ugs.); spindeldürr **4** (full of bones) grätig ‹*Fisch*›; ‹*Fleisch*› mit viel Knochen; **be ~:** viele Gräten/Knochen haben

boo /buː/
A *int.* (*to surprise sb.*) huh; (*expr. disapproval, contempt*) buh; **he wouldn't say '~' to a goose** er ist sehr schüchtern; **cries of '~'** Buhrufe
B *n.* Buh, *das* (ugs.)
C *v.t.* ausbuhen (ugs.); **he was ~ed off the stage** er wurde so ausgebuht, dass er die Bühne verließ (ugs.)
D *v.i.* buhen (ugs.)

boob /buːb/ (Brit. coll.)
A *n.* **1** (mistake) Fehler, *der;* Schnitzer, *der* (ugs.) **2** (simpleton) Dussel, *der* (salopp); Blödian, *der* (ugs. abwertend) **3** (breast) Titte, *die* (derb)
B *v.i.* einen Schnitzer machen (ugs.)

booboo /'buːbuː/ (coll.) ▸ **boob A 1**

booby /'buːbɪ/ *n.* **1** Trottel, *der* (ugs. abwertend) **2** (Ornith.) Tölpel, *der*

booby: ~hatch *n.* (Amer. sl.) Klapsmühle, *die* (salopp); **~ prize** *n. Preis für den schlechtesten Teilnehmer an einem Wettbewerb;* **~ trap** *n.* **1** *Falle, mit der man jmdm. einen Streich spielen will;* **2** (Mil.) versteckte Sprengladung; **~-trap** *v.t.* **1** [für einen Streich] präparieren; **2** (Mil.) **the bomb/the door had been ~-trapped** die Bombe war präpariert worden/an der Tür war eine versteckte Sprengladung angebracht worden

boodle /'buːdl/ *n., no pl.* (coll.) Zaster, *der* (salopp); (for bribery) Schmiergeld, *das* (ugs.)

boogie /'buːgɪ/
A *n.* **1** (Mus.) Boogie, *der* **2** (coll.: dance) Boogie, *der*
B *v.i.* (coll: dance) Boogie tanzen

boogie-woogie /buːgɪ'wuːgɪ/ *n., no pl.* Boogie-Woogie, *der*

book /bʊk/
A *n.* **1** Buch, *das;* **in ~ form** in Buchform; als Buch; **be a closed ~ [to sb.]** (fig.) [jmdm. *od.* für jmdn.] ein Buch mit sieben Siegeln sein; **the ~ of Job** das Buch Hiob; **the ~ of fate** (fig.) das Schicksal; **the ~ of life** (fig.) das Buch des Lebens (Rel.); das Lebensbuch (Rel.); **the [Good] B~:** das Buch der Bücher; die Bibel; **throw the ~ at sb.** (fig.) jmdn. kräftig zusammenstauchen (ugs.); **bring to ~** (fig.) zur Rechenschaft ziehen; **in my ~** (fig.) meiner Ansicht *od.* Meinung nach; **it won't suit my ~** (fig.) es passt mir nicht; **be in sb.'s good/bad ~s** (fig.) bei jmdm. gut/schlecht angeschrieben sein; **I can read you like a ~** (fig.) ich kann in dir lesen wie in einem Buch; **do sth.** *or* **play it/speak by the ~** (fig.) sich an die Regeln

halten/ganz korrekte Angaben machen; **speak** *or* **talk like a ~** (fig.) sich geschraubt ausdrücken (ugs. abwertend); **take a leaf out of sb.'s ~** (fig.) sich (*Dat.*) jmdn. zum Vorbild nehmen; **you could take a leaf out of his ~:** du könntest dir von ihm eine Scheibe abschneiden (ugs.); *see also* **black books; open A 11** 2) (for accounts) Konto- *od.* Rechnungsbuch, *das;* (for notes) [Notiz]buch, *das;* (for exercises) [Schreib]heft, *das* 3) (telephone directory) Telefonbuch, *das;* **be in the ~:** im Telefonbuch stehen 4) (coll.: magazine) Magazin, *das;* Illustrierte, *die* 5) *in pl.* (records, accounts) Bücher; **do the ~s** die Abrechnung machen; **balance the ~s** die Bilanz machen *od.* ziehen; *see also* **keep A 8** 6) *in pl.* (list of members) **be on the ~s** auf der [Mitglieds]liste *od.* im Mitgliederverzeichnis stehen 7) (record of bets) Wettbuch, *das;* **make** *or* **keep a ~ on sth.** Wetten auf etw. (*Akk.*) annehmen 8) **~ of tickets** Fahrscheinheft, *das;* **~ of stamps/matches** Briefmarkenheft/Streichholzbriefchen, *das;* **~ of samples** Musterbuch, *das* 9) (libretto) Textbuch, *das;* (playscript) Textvorlage, *die;* **~ of words** Textbuch, *das;* (fig.) Arbeitsanweisungen *Pl.*

B *v.t.* 1) (engage in advance) buchen ‹*Reise, Flug, Platz [im Flugzeug]*›; [vor]bestellen ‹*Eintrittskarte, Tisch, Zimmer, Platz [im Theater]*›; anmelden ‹*Telefongespräch*›; engagieren, verpflichten ‹*Künstler, Orchester*›; **be fully ~ed** ‹*Vorstellung:*› ausverkauft sein; ‹*Flug[zeug]:*› ausgebucht sein; ‹*Hotel:*› voll belegt *od.* ausgebucht sein 2) (enter in ~) eintragen; (for offence) aufschreiben (ugs.) (**for** wegen) 3) (issue ticket to) **we are ~ed on a flight to Athens** man hat für uns einen Flug nach Athen gebucht

C *v.i.* buchen; (for travel, performance) vorbestellen

Phrasal verbs

• **~ 'in**

A *v.i.* sich eintragen; **we ~ed in at the Ritz** wir sind im Ritz abgestiegen

B *v.t.* 1) (make reservation for) Zimmer/ein Zimmer vorbestellen *od.* reservieren für; **we're ~ed in at the Dorchester** unsere Zimmer sind im Dorchester reserviert 2) (register) eintragen

• **~ 'up**

A *v.i.* buchen

B *v.t.* buchen; **the guest house is ~ed up** die Pension ist ausgebucht *od.* voll belegt

bookable /'bʊkəbl/ *adj.* **be ~:** vorbestellt werden können; ‹*Flug, Urlaub:*› gebucht werden können

book: ~binder *n.* ▶ p. 1260 Buchbinder, *der*/-binderin, *die;* **~binding** *n., no pl.* Buchbinderei, *die;* **~case** *n.* Bücherschrank, *der;* **~ club** *n.* Buchklub, *der;* Buchgemeinschaft, *die;* **~ends** *n. pl.* Buchstützen

Booker Prize (Man Booker Prize)

Der Booker-Preis ist ein britischer Literaturpreis, der seit 1969 jeden Herbst für den besten Roman des Jahres vergeben wird. Der Roman in englischer Sprache, von einem Autor des Commonwealth, Irlands oder Südafrikas verfasst, muss in dem jeweiligen Jahr erstmals von einem britischen Verleger veröffentlicht worden sein. Der Preis wurde ursprünglich von dem Industriekonzern Booker McConnell gestiftet. Seit 2002 wird der Preis für zunächst fünf Jahre von der Man-Gruppe gesponsert. Während dieser Zeit heißt er „Man-Booker-Preis". Die Wahl und Beurteilung der Bücher obliegt dem *Booker Prize Committee*.

bookie /'bʊkɪ/ *n.* ▶ p. 1260 (coll.) Buchmacher, *der*

booking /'bʊkɪŋ/ *n.* 1) Buchung, *die;* (of ticket) Bestellung, *die;* (of table, room, seat) Vorbestellung, *die;* **~ for the concert opens today** der Vorverkauf für das Konzert beginnt heute; **make/cancel a ~:** buchen/eine Buchung rückgängig machen; (for tickets) bestellen/abbestellen; **change one's ~:** umbuchen; (for tickets) umbestellen 2) (of performer) Engagement, *das*

booking: ~ clerk *n.* ▶ p. 1260 Schalterbeamte, *der*/-beamtin, *die;* Fahrkartenverkäufer, *der*/-verkäuferin, *die;* **~ fee** *n.* Buchungsgebühr, *die;* **~ form** *n.* Buchungsformular, *das;* **~ hall** *n.* Schalterhalle, *die;* **~ office** *n.* (in station) [Fahrkarten]schalter, *der;* (in theatre) [Theater]kasse, *die;* (selling tickets in advance) Vorverkaufsstelle, *die*

bookish /'bʊkɪʃ/ *adj.* 1) (studious) gelehrt; (addicted to reading) **be ~:** ein Bücherwurm sein 2) (as in books) schriftsprachlich; papieren (abwertend)

book: ~ jacket *n.* Schutzumschlag, *der;* **~keeper** *n.* ▶ p. 1260 Buchhalter, *der*/Buchhalterin, *die;* **~keeping** *n., no pl.* Buchführung, *die;* Buchhaltung, *die*

booklet /'bʊklɪt/ *n.* Broschüre, *die*

book: ~-lover *n.* Bücherfreund, *der;* **~maker** *n.* ▶ p. 1260 (in betting) Buchmacher, *der*/-macherin, *die;* **~making** *n., no pl.* 1) (in betting) Buchmacherei, *die;* 2) (compiling books) Kompilation, *die;* **~man** *n.* Literat, *der;* **~mark A** *n.* 1) Lesezeichen, *das;* Buchzeichen, *das;* 2) (Computing) Lesezeichen, *das;* **B** *v.t.* (Computing) mit einem Lesezeichen versehen; **~marker** *n.* Lesezeichen, *das;* Buchzeichen, *das;* **~mobile** /'bʊkməbɪ:l/ *n.* (Amer.) Fahrbücherei, *die;* **~ page** *n.* 1) (in newspaper) *Seite mit Buchrezensionen;* ≈ Literaturseite, *die;* 2) (page of ~) Buchseite, *die;* **~plate** *n.* Exlibris, *das;* **~ post** *n., no pl.* Büchersendung, *die;* **~rest** *n.: Halter für das aufgeschlagene Buch;* **~ review** *n.* Buchbesprechung, *die;* **~seller** *n.* ▶ p. 1260 Buchhändler, *der*/-händlerin, *die;* **~shelf** *n.* Bücherbord, *das;* **on my ~shelves** in meinen Bücherregalen; **~shop** *n.* Buchhandlung, *die;* Buchladen, *der;* **~stall** *n.* Bücherstand, *der;* **~store** (Amer.) ▸ **shop**

booksy /'bʊksɪ/ *adj.* (Brit. coll.) hochgestochen (ugs. abwertend) ‹*Stil, Ausdruck, Konversation*›; hochgelahrt (scherzh.) ‹*Person*›

book: ~ token *n.* Büchergutschein, *der;* **~ trough** *n.* Bücherständer, *der;* **~ value** *n.* (Bookk.) Buchwert, *der;* **~work** *n.* Bücherstudium, *das;* **~worm** *n.* (lit. or fig.) Bücherwurm, *der*

Boolean /'bu:lɪən/ *adj.* (Math., Computing) boolesch; Boolesch

boom[1] /bu:m/ *n.* 1) (for camera or microphone) Ausleger, *der* 2) (Naut.) Baum, *der* 3) (floating barrier) [schwimmende] Absperrung

boom[2]

A *v.i.* 1) dröhnen; ‹*Kanone, Wellen, Brandung:*› dröhnen, donnern; ‹*Vogel:*› [dumpf] rufen 2) ‹*Geschäft, Verkauf, Stadt, Gebiet:*› sich sprunghaft entwickeln; ‹*Preise, Aktien:*› rapide steigen; **business is ~ing** das Geschäft boomt *od.* erlebt einen Boom; die Geschäfte florieren

B *n.* 1) (of person) Gebrüll, *das;* (of gun, waves) Dröhnen, *das;* Donnern, *das;* (of bird) [dumpfes] Rufen; [dumpfer] Ruf 2) (in business) [sprunghafter] Aufschwung; Boom, *der;* (in prices) [rapider] Anstieg; *attrib.* **a ~ area** ein Gebiet, das sich sprunghaft entwickelt; **a ~ year** ein Boomjahr 3) (period of economic expansion) Hochkonjunktur, *die;* Boom, *der; attrib.* **the ~ years** die Jahre der Hochkonjunktur

Phrasal verb

• **~ 'out**

A *v.i.* ‹*Stimme:*› dröhnen; ‹*Kanone:*› donnern, dröhnen

B *v.t.* brüllen ‹*Kommando, Befehl*›

boom-and-'bust, boom-'bust *adjs.* konjunkturanfällig; **~ market** Markt mit extremen Konjunkturschwankungen; **~ cycle** Boom-Bust-Zyklus, *der*

boomerang /'bu:məræŋ/

A *n.* (lit. or fig.) Bumerang, *der*

B *v.i.* (fig.) sich als Bumerang erweisen

booming /'bu:mɪŋ/ *adj.* 1) (deep, resonant) donnernd ‹*Stimme*›; schallend ‹*Lachen*›; dröhnend ‹*Klang*› 2) (Econ.) boomend (ugs.) ‹*Wirtschaft, Konjunktur, Tourismus*›

'boom town *n. Stadt in sprunghaftem Aufschwung*

boon /bu:n/ *n.* 1) (blessing) Segen, *der;* Wohltat, *die;* **be a tremendous ~** *or* **a ~ and a blessing to sb.** ein wahrer Segen für jmdn. sein 2) (request, favour) Gunst, *die* (geh.)

'boon companion *n.* Kumpan, *der*

boondoggle /'bu:ndɒgl/ (Amer.)

A *n.* sinnlose Arbeit

B *v.i.* sinnlos arbeiten

boor /bʊə(r)/ *n.* Rüpel, *der* (abwertend)

boorish /'bʊərɪʃ/ *adj.*, **boorishly** /'bʊərɪʃlɪ/ *adv.* flegelhaft (abwertend); rüpelhaft (abwertend)

boorishness /'bʊərɪʃnɪs/ *n., no pl.* Flegelei, *die* (abwertend); Rüpelei, *die* (abwertend)

boost /bu:st/

A *v.t.* 1) steigern; ankurbeln ‹*Wirtschaft*›; in die Höhe treiben ‹*Preis, Wert, Aktienkurs*›; stärken, heben ‹*Selbstvertrauen, Moral*›; (increase reputation of) aufbauen; (recommend vigorously) anpreisen 2) (coll.: push from below) hochschieben; hochheben 3) (Electr.) erhöhen ‹*Spannung*› 4) (Radio) verstärken ‹*Signal*›

B *n.* Auftrieb, *der;* (increase) Zunahme, *die;* **give sb./sth. a ~:** jmdn./einer Sache Auftrieb geben; **be given a ~:** Auftrieb erhalten; **give sales/production a ~:** den Verkauf/die Produktion ankurbeln

booster /'bu:stə(r)/ *n.* 1) (Med.) **~ [shot** *or* **injection]** Auffrischimpfung, *die* 2) (Astronaut.) **~ [rocket/motor]** Starthilfsrakete, *die*/Starthilfstriebwerk, *das*

'booster cushion, 'booster seat *ns.* Sitzerhöhung, *die*

boot[1] /bu:t/

A *n.* 1) Stiefel, *der;* **get the ~** (fig. coll.) rausgeschmissen werden (ugs.); **give sb. the ~** (fig. coll.) jmdn. rausschmeißen (ugs.); **give sb. a ~ up the backside** (fig. coll.) jmdm. den Marsch blasen (salopp); **as tough as old ~s** (fig. coll.) zäh wie Leder; **put the ~ in** (coll.) ihn/sie *usw.* [brutal] treten; **put the ~ in!** (coll.) tritt ihn/sie *usw.* zusammen! (ugs.); **the ~ is on the other foot** (fig.) es ist genau umgekehrt; **you can bet your ~s that ...** (fig. coll.) ..., darauf kannst du Gift nehmen (ugs.); *see also* **big A 7; die**[1] **A 1; heart A 3** 2) (Brit.: of car) Kofferraum, *der* 3) (Brit. coll. derog.: woman) Schreckschraube, *die* (ugs.)

B *v.t.* 1) (coll.) treten; kicken (ugs.) ‹*Ball*›; **~ sb. out** (fig. coll.) jmdn. rausschmeißen (ugs.) 2) (Computing) **~ [up]** booten

boot[2] *n.* **to ~:** noch dazu; obendrein

bootable /'bu:təbl/ *adj.* (Computing) bootfähig; **~ disk** Bootdiskette, *die*

boot: ~black (Amer.) ▸ **shoeblack; ~ device** *n.* (Computing) Bootgerät, *das;* **~ disk** *n.* (Computing) Bootdiskette, *die;* Bootplatte, *die*

booted /'bu:tɪd/ *adj.* gestiefelt

bootee /bu:'ti:/ *n.* (infant's) Babyschuh, *der;* (woman's) Stiefelette, *die*

booth /bu:ð/ *n.* 1) Bude, *die* 2) (telephone ~) Telefonzelle, *die* 3) (polling ~) Wahlkabine, *die*

'bootleg

A *v.t.* schmuggeln; (sell/make) schwarz (ugs.) *od.* illegal verkaufen/brennen

B *adj.* geschmuggelt; (sold/made) schwarz (ugs.) *od.* illegal verkauft/gebrannt

bootlegger /'bu:tlegə(r)/ *n.* ▸ **bootleg A:** Schmuggler, *der;* Schwarzhändler *der;* Schwarzbrenner, *der*

'bootlicker *n.* (derog.) Speichellecker, *der* (abwertend)

boot: ~ sale *n.* (Brit.) *eine Art Flohmarkt, bei dem die Verkaufsgegenstände im Kofferraum des Autos ausgelegt werden;* **~strap** *n.* (Computing) Bootstrapping, *das;* **~straps** *n. pl.* **pull oneself up** *or* **raise oneself by one's own ~straps** (fig.) sich aus eigener Kraft hocharbeiten

booty /'bu:tɪ/ *n., no pl.* Beute, *die*

booze /bu:z/ (coll.)

A *v.i.* saufen (salopp)

B *n., no pl.* 1) (drink) Alkohol, *der* 2) (drinking bout) Besäufnis, *das* (salopp); **go/be on the ~:** [einen] saufen gehen/saufen (salopp)

'booze cruise *n.* 1) (coll.: drunken cruise) Sauftour, *die* (*auf Fähren*) 2) (Brit. coll.: to buy cheap alcohol) *Fahrt mit der Fähre, um billig Alkohol zu kaufen*

boozer /'bu:zə(r)/ *n.* (coll.) 1) (one who boozes) Säufer, *der*/Säuferin, *die* (derb) 2) (Brit. public house) Kneipe, *die* (ugs.)

'booze-up *n.* (coll.) Besäufnis, *das* (salopp); **have a ~:** saufen gehen (salopp)

boozy /'bu:zɪ/ *adj.* (coll.) betrunken; blau *nicht attr.* (ugs.); (addicted to drink) versoffen (salopp)

b

bop /bɒp/ (coll.)
A v.i. (zur Popmusik) tanzen
B n. Tanz, der (zur Popmusik); **have a ~:** tanzen; **put on a ~:** eine Tanzfete (ugs.) veranstalten

bopper /ˈbɒpə(r)/ n. (coll.) jmd., der zur Popmusik tanzt

borage /ˈbɒrɪdʒ/ n. (Bot.) Borretsch, der

borax /ˈbɔːræks/ n. (Chem.) Borax, der

Bordeaux /bɔːˈdəʊ/ n., pl. same /bɔːˈdəʊz/ Bordeaux[wein], der

bordello /bɔːˈdeləʊ/ n., pl. **~s** (esp. Amer.) Bordell, das

border /ˈbɔːdə(r)/
A n. **1** Rand, der; (of tablecloth, handkerchief, dress) Bordüre, die **2** (of country) Grenze, die; **the B~[s]** die Grenze; **north of the B~** (in Scotland) in Schottland **3** (flower bed) Rabatte, die; see also **herbaceous**
B attrib. adj. Grenz‹stadt, -gebiet, -streit›
C v.t. **1** (adjoin) [an]grenzen an (+ Akk.); **be ~ed by** [an]grenzen an (+ Akk.) **2** (put a ~ to, act as ~ to) umranden; einfassen **3** (resemble closely) grenzen an (+ Akk.)
D v.i. **~ on** ▸ **C 1, 3**

border: ~ crossing n. Grenzübergang, der; **~ dispute** n. Grenzstreitigkeit, die

borderer /ˈbɔːdərə(r)/ n. Grenzbewohner, der/-bewohnerin, die

border: ~ incident n. Grenzzwischenfall, der; **~land** Grenzgebiet, das; (fig.) Grenzbereich, der; **~line A** n. Grenzlinie, die; (fig.) Grenze, die; **B** adj. **sb./sth. is ~line** (fig.) jmd. ist/etw. liegt auf der Grenze; **a ~line case/candidate/type** (fig.) ein Grenzfall; **~ post** n. Grenzposten, der; **B~ terrier** n. Borderterrier, der

bore[1] /bɔː(r)/
A v.t. (make hole in) bohren; **~ the rock/the wood** ein Loch in das Gestein/das Holz bohren; **~ rock/wood** Gestein/Holz bohren; **~ one's way through sth.** sich durch etw. hindurchbohren
B v.i. (drill) bohren (**for** nach)
C n. **1** (of firearm, engine cylinder) Bohrung, die (Technik); (of tube, pipe) Innendurchmesser, der **2** (calibre) Kaliber, das **3** ▸ **borehole**

bore[2]
A n. **1** (nuisance) **it's a real ~:** es ist wirklich ärgerlich; **what a ~!** wie ärgerlich!; **she is a real ~:** sie kann einem wirklich auf die Nerven gehen **2** (dull person) Langweiler, der/Langweilerin, die (ugs. abwertend)
B v.t. (weary) langweilen; **sb. is ~d with sth.** etw. langweilt jmdn.; **sb. is ~d with life** jmdn. ödet alles an (ugs.); **I'm ~d** ich langweile mich; ich habe Langeweile; **~ sb. to death** or **to tears** (coll.) jmdn. zu Tode langweilen

bore[3] n. (tidewave) Flutbrandung, die; Bore, die

bore[4] ▸ **bear[2]**

boreal /ˈbɔːrɪəl/ adj. (Ecol.) boreal

boredom /ˈbɔːdəm/ n., no pl. Langeweile, die; **with a look of utter ~ on one's face** mit einem völlig gelangweilten Gesichtsausdruck

ˈborehole n. Bohrloch, das

borer /ˈbɔːrə(r)/ n. (tool) Bohrer, der

boring /ˈbɔːrɪŋ/ adj. langweilig

born /bɔːn/
A be ~: geboren werden; **I was ~ in England** ich bin od. wurde in England geboren; **he was ~ of rich parents** or **~ rich** er war das Kind reicher Eltern; **he was ~ into a rich family** er wurde in eine reiche Familie hineingeboren; **a new era was ~:** eine neue Ära brach an; **be ~ again** (fig.) wieder geboren werden; **I wasn't ~ yesterday** (fig.) ich bin nicht von gestern (ugs.); **there's one ~ every minute** (coll.) die Dummen werden nicht alle; **be ~ of sth.** (fig.) aus etw. entstehen; **be ~ blind/lucky** blind von Geburt sein/ein Glückskind sein; **be ~ a poet** zum Dichter geboren sein; **be ~ to sth.** (fig.) zu etw. geboren od. bestimmt sein; **be ~ to command** zum Befehlen geboren sein
B adj. **1** geboren; **you don't know you are ~** (coll.) du kannst dich nicht beklagen; **~ again** (fig.) wieder geboren; **in all my ~ days** (fig. coll.) in meinem ganzen Leben; mein Lebtag (ugs. veralt.); see also **breed A 3** **2** (destined to be) **be a ~ orator** or **an orator ~:** der geborene Redner od. zum Redner geboren sein

ˈborn-again
A adj. **1** (Relig.) wiedergeboren **2** (fig.: enthusiastic) enthusiastisch
B n. (esp. Amer.: ~ Christian) Wiedergeborene, der/die

borne ▸ **bear[2]**

boron /ˈbɔːrɒn/ n. (Chem.) Bor, das

borough /ˈbʌrə/ n. **1** (Brit. Hist.: town with corporation) Borough, das; Stadt mit Selbstverwaltung; **the ~ of Brighton** ≈ die Stadt Brighton **2** (Brit.: town sending members to Parliament) Borough, das; Stadt[bezirk] mit Vertretung im Parlament **3** (Amer.) **the ~ of ...** (town) die Stadt ...; (village) die Gemeinde ...

borrow /ˈbɒrəʊ/
A v.t. **1** [sich (Dat.)] ausleihen; [sich (Dat.)] borgen; entleihen, ausleihen ‹Buch, Schallplatte usw. aus der Leihbücherei›; [sich (Dat.)] leihen ‹Geld von der Bank›; [sich (Dat.)] leihen, [sich (Dat.)] borgen ‹Geld›; **~ sth. from sb.** [sich (Dat.)] etw. von od. bei jmdm. borgen od. [aus]leihen **2** (fig.) übernehmen ‹Idee, Methode, Meinung›; entlehnen ‹Wort, Ausdruck aus einer anderen Sprache›; **sb. is living on ~ed time** jmds. Uhr ist abgelaufen
B v.i. borgen; (from bank) Kredit aufnehmen (**from** bei)

borrower /ˈbɒrəʊə(r)/ n. (from bank) Kreditnehmer, der; (from library) Entleiher, der

borrowing /ˈbɒrəʊɪŋ/ n. (from bank) Kreditaufnahme, die (**from** bei); (from library) Entleihen, das; Ausleihen, das; (fig.) Übernahme, die; **'haute couture' is a ~ from French** „Haute couture" ist eine Entlehnung aus dem Französischen

borsch /bɔːʃ/ n. Borschtsch, der

Borstal /ˈbɔːstl/ n. (Brit. Hist.) Erziehungsheim, das; Besserungsanstalt für jugendliche Straftäter

bortsch /bɔːtʃ/ ▸ **borsch**

borzoi /ˈbɔːzɔɪ/ n. Barsoi, der

bosh /bɒʃ/ n., no pl., no indef. art. (coll.) Quatsch, der (ugs. abwertend)

bos'n /ˈbəʊsn/ ▸ **boatswain**

Bosnia /ˈbɒznɪə/ n. Bosnien (das)

Bosnia-Herzegovina /bɒznɪəhɜːtsəgəˈviːnə/ pr. n. Bosnia und Herzegovina (das)

Bosnian /ˈbɒznɪən/ ▸ⓘ **p. 1345**
A adj. bosnisch; **sb. is ~:** jmd. ist Bosnier/Bosnierin
B n. Bosnier, der/Bosnierin, die

bosom /ˈbʊzəm/ n. **1** (woman's chest or breasts) Busen, der **2** (of dress) ≈ Vorderseite des Oberteils; (of blouse) ≈ Vorderteil, das **3** (fig.: loving care and affection) Schoß, der; **in the ~ of one's family** im Schoße der Familie; attrib. **a ~ friend** ein guter Freund; ein Busenfreund **4** (fig.: seat of thoughts or emotions) Brust, die; **lay bare one's ~ to sb.** jmdm. sein Herz ausschütten

bosomy /ˈbʊzəmɪ/ adj. vollbusig

Bosphorus /ˈbɒsfərəs/ pr. n. Bosporus, der

boss[1] (coll.)
A n. **1** (master) Boss, der (ugs.); Chef, der; **OK, you're the ~:** du bist der Boss; **who's the ~ in your household?** wer bestimmt bei euch zu Hause? **2** (Amer. Polit.) [Partei]boss, der (ugs.)
B v.t. **~ sb. [about** or **around]** jmdn. herumkommandieren (ugs.)

boss[2] /bɒs/ n. **1** (metal knob, stud) Bosse, die (Kunstwiss.); (on shield) Schildbuckel, der od. die **2** (Archit.) Schlussstein, der

ˈboss-eyed adj. (coll.) schielend; **be ~:** schielen

bossiness /ˈbɒsɪnɪs/ n., no pl. herrische Art

bossy /ˈbɒsɪ/ adj. (coll.) herrisch; **don't be so ~:** hör auf herumzukommandieren (ugs.)

bosun, bo'sun /ˈbəʊsn/ ▸ **boatswain**

botanic /bəˈtænɪk/ adj. **~ garden[s]** botanischer Garten

botanical /bəˈtænɪkl/ adj. botanisch; **~ garden[s]** botanischer Garten

botanist /ˈbɒtənɪst/ n. ▸ⓘ **p. 1260** Botaniker, der/Botanikerin, die

botany /ˈbɒtənɪ/ n., no pl. Botanik, die; Pflanzenkunde, die

botch /bɒtʃ/
A n. (bungled work) ▸ **B 1:** Pfuscherei, die (ugs. abwertend); Patzer, der (ugs.); **make a ~ of sth.** bei etw. pfuschen (ugs. abwertend)
B v.t. **1** (bungle) pfuschen bei (ugs. abwertend) ‹Reparatur, Arbeit›; patzen bei (ugs.) ‹Vortrag, Stabwechsel›; **a ~ed job** eine gepfuschte Arbeit (ugs. abwertend) **2** (repair badly) [notdürftig] flicken
C v.i. ▸ **B 1:** pfuschen (ugs. abwertend); patzen (ugs.)

Phrasal verb
• **~ ˈup** v.t. **1** (bungle) verpfuschen (ugs. abwertend) **2** (repair badly) [notdürftig] flicken

both /bəʊθ/
A adj. beide; **we ~ like cooking** wir kochen beide gern; **~ these books are expensive** die[se] Bücher sind beide teuer; **~ [the] brothers** beide Brüder; **~ our brothers** unsere beiden Brüder; **~ ways** (Brit. Racing) = **each way** ▸ **each A**; **you can't have it ~ ways** beides [zugleich] geht nicht; see also **cut B 1**
B pron. beide; **~ [of them] are dead** beide sind tot; **they are ~ dead** sie sind beide tot; **~ of you/them are ...:** ihr seid/sie sind beide ...; **for them ~:** für sie beide; **Love or hate? — B~:** Liebe oder Hass? — Beides; **go along to bed, ~ of you** ihr geht jetzt ins Bett, alle beide
C adv. **~ A and B, A and B ~:** sowohl A als [auch] B; **~ brother and sister are dead** sowohl der Bruder als auch die Schwester sind tot; **~ you and I** wir beide; **he and I were ~ there** er und ich waren beide da; **she was ~ singing and playing** sie hat gesungen und zugleich gespielt

bother /ˈbɒðə(r)/
A v.t. **1** in pass. (take trouble) **I can't be ~ed [to do it]** ich habe keine Lust[, es zu machen]; **I can't be ~ed with details like that** ich kann mich nicht mit solchen Kleinigkeiten abgeben od. befassen; **can't you even be ~ed to dress properly?** kannst du dich nicht einmal richtig anziehen?; **I can't be ~ed with people who ...:** ich habe nichts übrig für Leute, die ... **2** (annoy) lästig sein od. fallen (+ Dat.); ‹Lärm, Licht:› stören; ‹Schmerz, Wunde, Zahn, Rücken:› zu schaffen machen (+ Dat.); **I'm sorry to ~ you, but ...:** es tut mir Leid, wenn ich Sie störe, aber ...; **don't ~ me now** lass mich jetzt in Ruhe! **3** (worry) Sorgen machen (+ Dat.); ‹Problem, Frage:› beschäftigen; **I'm not ~ed about him/the money** seinetwegen/wegen des Geldes mache ich mir keine Gedanken; **what's ~ing you/is something ~ing you?** was hast du denn/hast du etwas?; **~ oneself** or **one's head about sth.** sich (Dat.) über etw. (Akk.) den Kopf zerbrechen (ugs.); see also **hot A 6** **4** (coll.: confound) **~ it!** wie ärgerlich!; **~ him/her/you/this car!** zum Kuckuck mit ihm/ihr/dir/diesem Auto!
B v.i. (trouble oneself) **~ to do that** sich damit aufhalten, das zu tun; **don't ~ to do sth.** Sie brauchen etw. nicht zu tun; **she didn't even ~ to ask** sie hielt es nicht mal für nötig, zu fragen; **you needn't have ~ed to come** Sie hätten wirklich nicht zu kommen brauchen; **you needn't/shouldn't have ~ed** das wäre nicht nötig gewesen; **don't ~!** nicht nötig!; **~ with sth./sb.** sich mit etw./jmdm. aufhalten; **~ about sth./sb.** sich (Dat.) über etw./jmdn. Gedanken machen
C n. **1** (nuisance) **what a ~!** wie ärgerlich!; **it's a real/such a ~:** es ist wirklich lästig **2** (trouble) Ärger, der; **it's no ~ [for me]** es macht mir gar nichts aus; **the children were no ~ at all** wir hatten mit den Kindern überhaupt keine Schwierigkeiten; **have a spot of ~ with sth.** Schwierigkeiten mit etw. haben; **without any ~ at all** ohne irgendwelche Schwierigkeiten; **it's not worth the ~:** es lohnt nicht; **I'm sorry to have put you to all this ~:** es tut mir leid, Ihnen soviel Umstände gemacht zu haben; **if it isn't too much ~:** wenn es nicht zu viel Mühe macht; **go to the ~ of doing sth.** sich (Dat.) die Mühe machen, etw. zu tun
D int. (coll.) wie ärgerlich!

botheration /bɒðəˈreɪʃn/ int. ▸ **bother D**

bothersome /ˈbɒðəsəm/ *adj.* lästig; unleidlich ‹*Kind*›

bottle /ˈbɒtl/

A *n.* **1** Flasche, *die;* **a beer ~:** eine Bierflasche; **a ~ of beer** eine Flasche Bier **2** (fig. coll.: alcoholic drink) **be too fond of the ~:** dem Alkohol zu sehr zugetan sein; **be on the ~:** trinken; *see also* **hit A 11** **3** (gas cylinder) **a ~ of gas** eine Gasflasche **4** (Brit. coll.: courage, confidence) Mumm, *der* (ugs.); **lose one's ~:** sich (*Dat.*) den Schneid abkaufen lassen (ugs.)

B *v.t.* **1** (put into ~s) in Flaschen [ab]füllen **2** (store in ~s) in Flaschen lagern *od.* aufheben; **~d beer** Flaschenbier, *das;* **~d gas** Flaschengas, *das* **3** (preserve in jars) einmachen

Phrasal verb

• **~ ˈup** *v.t.* **1** (conceal) in sich (*Dat.*) aufstauen **2** (entrap) einschließen

bottle: ~ bank *n.* Altglasbehälter, *der;* **~-fed** *adj.* mit der Flasche gefüttert; **~-fed babies** Flaschenkinder

bottleful /ˈbɒtlfʊl/ *n.* **a ~ of shampoo** eine Flasche Schampon

bottle: ~ glass *n.* Flaschenglas, *das;* **~-green A** *n.* Flaschengrün, *das;* **B** *adj.* flaschengrün; **~neck** *n.* (fig.) Flaschenhals, *der* (ugs.); (in production process also) Engpass, *der;* **~ opener** *n.* Flaschenöffner, *der;* **~ party** *n.* Bottleparty, *die;* **~ top** *n.* Flaschenverschluss, *der*

bottom /ˈbɒtəm/

A *n.* **1** (lowest part) unteres Ende; (of cup, glass, box, chest) Boden, *der;* (of valley, canyon, crevasse, well, shaft) Sohle, *die;* (of canyon, crevasse, well also) Grund, *der;* (of hill, slope, cliff, stairs) Fuß, *der;* **the ~ of the valley** die Talsohle; **[be] at the ~ of the page/list** unten auf der Seite/Liste [sein]; **[be] in the ~ of the box/glass** am Boden des Kastens/Glases [sein]; unten im Kasten/Glas [sein]; **the ~ of my coat/dress is all muddy** mein Mantel/Kleid ist unten ganz schmutzig; **the book right at the ~ of the pile** das Buch ganz unten im Stapel; **~ up** auf dem Kopf; verkehrt herum; **~s up!** (coll.) hoch die Tassen!; **the ~ fell** *or* **dropped out of her world/the market** (fig.) für sie brach eine Welt zusammen/der Markt brach zusammen; **knock the ~ out of sth.** (fig.) etw. zusammenbrechen lassen; *see also* **false bottom** **2** ▸ⓘ **p. 951** (buttocks) Hinterteil, *das* (ugs.); Po[dex], *der* (fam.) **3** (of chair) Sitz, *der;* Sitzfläche, *die* **4** (of sea, lake) Grund, *der;* **on the ~:** auf dem Grund; **go to the ~:** [ver]sinken; **send a ship to the ~:** ein Schiff in den Grund bohren *od.* versenken; **touch ~:** Grund haben; (fig.) den Tiefpunkt erreichen **5** (farthest point) **at the ~ of the garden/street** hinten im Garten/am Ende der Straße; *see also* **heart A 2** **6** (underside) Unterseite, *die* **7** (fig.) **start at the ~:** ganz unten anfangen; **be ~ of the class/ league** der/die Letzte in der Klasse sein/Tabellenletzte[r] sein **8** *usu. in pl.* **~[s]** (of track suit, pyjamas) Hose, *die* **9** (fig.: basis, origin) **be at the ~ of sth.** hinter etw. (*Dat.*) stecken (ugs.); einer Sache (*Dat.*) zugrunde liegen; **get to the ~ of sth.** einer Sache (*Dat.*) auf den Grund kommen; **at ~:** im Grunde genommen **10** (Naut.) Schiffsboden, *der;* **~ up** kieloben **11** (Brit. Motor Veh.) **in ~:** im ersten Gang

B *adj.* **1** (lowest) unterst...; (lower) unter... **2** (fig.: last) letzt...; **be ~:** der/die/das Letzte sein; **you can bet your/I'd [be willing to] bet my ~ dollar** (fig. coll.) jede Wette (ugs.)

C *v.i.* **~ [out]** ‹*Preise:*› den tiefsten Stand erreichen; ‹*Rezession, Rückgang:*› den tiefsten Punkt erreichen

bottom: ~ ˈdog ▸ **underdog**; **~ ˈdrawer** *n.* (fig.) Aussteuer, *die;* **put sth. [away] in one's ~ drawer** etw. für die Aussteuer beiseite legen; **~ feeder** *n.* **1** (Zool.) Grundbewohner, *der;* **2** (Amer. coll.) (person of low status) Unterhund, *der;* (pauper) Habenichts, *der*

bottomless /ˈbɒtəmlɪs/ *adj.* bodenlos; unendlich tief ‹*Meer, Ozean*›; (fig.: inexhaustible) unerschöpflich

bottom ˈline *n.* (fig. coll.) **the ~:** das Fazit

ˈbotulism /ˈbɒtjʊlɪzm/ *n., no pl., no art.* ▸ⓘ **p. 1231** (Med.) Botulismus, *der*

boudoir /ˈbuːdwɑː(r)/ *n.* Boudoir, *das* (veralt.); Damenzimmer, *das* (veralt.)

bouffant /ˈbuːfɑ̃/ *adj.* voll und duftig, füllig ‹*Haar, Frisur*›; bauschig ‹*Kleidung*›

bough /baʊ/ *n.* Ast, *der*

bought ▸ **buy A**

bouillabaisse /buːjəˈbeɪs/ *n.* (Gastr.) Bouillabaisse, *die*

bouillon /ˈbuːjɔ̃/ *n.* (Cookery) Bouillon, *die;* **~ cube** Brühwürfel, *der*

boulder /ˈbəʊldə(r)/ *n.* Felsbrocken, *der*

ˈboulder clay *n.* (Geol.) Geschiebelehm, *der;* (with many boulders) Blocklehm, *der*

boulevard /ˈbuːləvɑːd/ *n.* Boulevard, *der*

boult ▸ **bolt²**

bounce /baʊns/

A *v.i.* **1** springen; (on bumpy road) ‹*Auto:*› holpern; **the ball ~d twice** der Ball sprang zweimal auf; **~ up and down on sth.** auf etw. (*Dat.*) herumspringen **2** (coll.: be rejected by bank) ‹*Scheck:*› platzen (ugs.); **it won't ~:** er ist gedeckt **3** (rush) **~ about** herumspringen *od.* -hüpfen; **~ into/out of the room** ins/aus dem Zimmer stürmen; **~ in/out** hereinplatzen/hinausstürzen

B *v.t.* **1** aufspringen lassen ‹*Ball*›; **he ~d the baby on his knee** er ließ das Kind auf den Knien reiten **2** (Amer. coll.: dismiss) rausschmeißen (ugs.); an die Luft setzen (ugs.)

C *n.* **1** (rebound) Aufprall, *der;* **on the ~:** beim Aufprall **2** (rebounding power) ≈ Elastizität, *die;* (fig.: energy) Schwung, *der;* **there's plenty of/not much ~ in the ball** der Ball springt sehr gut/nicht besonders gut

Phrasal verbs

• **~ ˈback** *v.i.* zurückprallen; (fig.) ‹*Person:*› [plötzlich] wieder da sein

• **~ ˈoff**

A *v.i.* abprallen

B *v.t.* **~ sth. off sth.** etw. von etw. abprallen lassen; **~ off sth.** von etw. abprallen; ‹*Signal:*› von etw. reflektiert werden

bouncer /ˈbaʊnsə(r)/ *n.* (coll.) **1** Rausschmeißer, *der* (ugs.) **2** (Cricket) hoch aufspringender Ball

bouncing /ˈbaʊnsɪŋ/ *adj.* kräftig; stramm

bouncy /ˈbaʊnsɪ/ *adj.* **1** gut springend ‹*Ball*›; federnd ‹*Matratze, Bett*› **2** (fig.: lively) munter

bouncy ˈcastle *n.* Hüpfburg, *die*

bound¹ /baʊnd/

A *n.* **1** *usu. in pl.* (limit) Grenze, *die;* **within the ~s of possibility** *or* **the possible** im Bereich des Möglichen; **keep sth. within ~s** etw. in Grenzen halten; **increase beyond all ~s** über alle Maßen ansteigen; **the ball is out of ~s** der Ball hat die Spielbahn verlassen; **go beyond the ~s of decency** die Grenzen des Anstands verletzen; **sth. is out of ~s [to sb.]** der Zutritt zu etw. ist [für jmdn.] verboten; **the pub is out of ~s** das Betreten des Lokals ist verboten; **beyond the ~s of human knowledge** jenseits der menschlichen Erkenntnisfähigkeit; **there are no ~s to his ambition** sein Ehrgeiz kennt keine Grenzen; **know no ~s** (fig.) keine Grenzen kennen; **keep within the ~s of reason/propriety** vernünftig/im Rahmen bleiben **2** (of territory) Grenze, *die; see also* **beat A 1**

B *v.t., usu. in pass.* begrenzen; **be ~ed by sth.** durch etw. begrenzt werden; **sth. is ~ed by sth.** (fig.) einer Sache (*Dat.*) sind durch etw. Grenzen gesetzt

bound²

A *v.i.* (spring) hüpfen; springen; **~ with joy** vor Freude hüpfen; **~ into the room** ins Zimmer stürzen; **the dog came ~ing up** der Hund kam angesprungen

B *n.* (spring) Satz, *der;* **at** *or* **with one ~:** mit einem Satz; *see also* **leap C**

bound³ *pred. adj.* ▸ⓘ **p. 1013** **be ~ for home/Frankfurt** auf dem Heimweg/nach Frankfurt unterwegs sein; **homeward ~:** auf dem Weg nach Hause; **where are you ~ for?** wohin geht die Reise?; **all passengers ~ for Zürich** alle Passagiere nach Zürich

bound⁴ ▸ **bind A, B**

boundary /ˈbaʊndərɪ/ *n.* Grenze, *die*

boundary ˈwall *n.* Grenzmauer, *die;* (around sth.) Umfassungsmauer, *die*

bounden /ˈbaʊndn/ *attrib. adj.* **~ duty** Pflicht und Schuldigkeit

bounder /ˈbaʊndə(r)/ *n.* (dated coll.) Lump, *der* (abwertend)

boundless /ˈbaʊndlɪs/ *adj.* grenzenlos

bounteous /ˈbaʊntɪəs/ *adj.* (rhet.) ▸ **bountiful**

bountiful /ˈbaʊntɪfl/ *adj.* (generous) großzügig; gütig ‹*Gott*›; (plentiful) reichlich ‹*Ernte, Gaben, Ertrag*›; **Lady B~:** gute Fee

bountifully /ˈbaʊntɪfəlɪ/ *adv.* (generously) großzügig; (plentifully) reichlich

bounty /ˈbaʊntɪ/ *n.* **1** (reward) Kopfgeld, *das;* (for capturing animal) Fangprämie, *die;* (for shooting animal) Abschussprämie, *die* **2** (literary: generosity) Freigebigkeit, *die* **3** (generous amount) Fülle, *die*

bouquet /bʊˈkeɪ, bəʊˈkeɪ, ˈbuːkeɪ/ *n.* **1** (bunch of flowers) Bukett, *das;* [Blumen]strauß, *der;* **bride's ~:** Brautstrauß, *der;* Brautbukett, *das* **2** (fig.: praise) **get a ~:** gelobt werden; **he gets all the ~s** ihm gilt alles Lob; **be meant as a ~:** als Kompliment gemeint sein **3** (perfume of wine) Bukett, *das;* Blume, *die*

bouquet garni /bʊkeɪ gɑːˈniː/ *n., pl.* **bouquets garnis** /bʊkeɪ gɑːˈniː/ (Cookery) Kräutersträußchen, *das;* Bouquet garni, *das* (fachspr.)

bourbon /ˈbɜːbən, ˈbʊəbən/ *n.* (Amer.) **~ [whiskey]** Bourbon, *der*

bourgeois /ˈbʊəʒwɑː/

A *n., pl. same* **1** (middle-class person) Bürger, *der*/Bürgerin, *die;* **the ~** *pl.* die bürgerliche Mittelklasse **2** (person with conventional ideas, selfish materialist) Spießbürger, *der* (abwertend); Spießer, *der*/Spießerin, *die* (abwertend) **3** (capitalist) Bourgeois, *der* (marx.)

B *adj.* **1** (middle-class) bürgerlich **2** (conventional, selfishly materialist) spießbürgerlich (abwertend) **3** (capitalistic) bourgeois (marx.)

bourgeoisie /bʊəʒwɑːˈziː/ *n.* **1** Bürgertum, *das* **2** (capitalist class) Bourgeoisie, *die* (marx.)

bout /baʊt/ *n.* **1** (spell) Periode, *die* **2** (contest) Wettkampf, *der* **3** (fit) Anfall, *der;* **~ of temper** Wutanfall, *der;* **he's out on one of his drinking ~s again** er ist mal wieder auf einer seiner Zechtouren (ugs.)

boutique /buːˈtiːk/ *n.* Boutique, *die*

bovine /ˈbəʊvaɪn/ *adj.* **1** (of cattle) Rinder- **2** (fig.) (heavy) grob; (stupid) erzdumm; (sluggish) träge

bovine spongiform encephalopathy /bəʊvaɪn spʌndʒɪfɔːm ensefəˈlɒpəθɪ/ *n, no pl.* bovine spongiforme Enzephalopathie

bovver /ˈbɒvə(r)/ *n.* (coll.) Zoff, *der* (ugs.)

bow¹ /bəʊ/

A *n.* **1** (curve) Bogen, *der* **2** (weapon) Bogen, *der;* **have two strings to one's ~:** eine Alternative haben; *see also* **longbow** **3** ▸ **saddle bow** **4** (Mus.) Bogen, *der;* (stroke) [Bogen]strich, *der;* **up/down ~:** Auf-/Abstrich, *der* **5** (tied knot or ribbon) Schleife, *die;* **tie the shoelace in a ~:** den Schnürsenkel zu einer Schleife binden **6** (Amer.: of spectacle frame) Bügel, *der*

B *v.t.* streichen ‹*Violine, Viola usw.*›

C *v.i.* den Bogen führen

bow² /baʊ/

A *v.i.* **1** (submit) sich beugen (**to** *Dat.*) **2** **~ [down to** *or* **before sb./sth.]** (bend) sich [vor jmdm./etw.] verbeugen *od.* verneigen **3** (incline head) **~ [to sb.]** sich [vor jmdm.] verbeugen; **~ out** sich formell verabschieden; **~ out of sth.** sich von etw. zurückziehen; *see also* **scrape B 5**

B *v.t.* **1** (cause to bend) beugen; **~ed down by** *or* **with care/responsibilities/age** (fig.) von Sorgen/Verpflichtungen niedergedrückt/vom Alter gebeugt; *see also* **knee 1** **2** (show by ~ing) **he ~ed his acknowledgement of the applause** er verbeugte sich zum Dank für den Applaus; **~ sb. in/out** jmdn. unter Verbeugungen hinein-/hinausgeleiten

C *n.* Verbeugung, *die;* **make one's ~** (make entrance) sich vorstellen; (make exit) sich [formell] verabschieden; **take a ~:** sich [unter Applaus] verbeugen; **they ought to** *or* **can take a ~** (fig.) sie verdienen Hochachtung

b

bow[3] /baʊ/ *n.* (Naut.) 1 *usu. in pl.* Bug, *der;* **in the ~s** im Bug; **on the ~:** am Bug; **shot across the ~s** (fig.) Schuss vor den Bug (ugs.) 2 (rower) Bugmann, *der*

bowdlerize /'baʊdləraɪz/ *v.t.* zensieren; **a ~d version** eine „gereinigte" Fassung

bowel /'baʊəl/ *n.* 1 ▸ⓘ **p. 951** (Anat.) **~s** *pl.*, (Med.) **~:** Darm, *der* 2 *in pl.* (interior) Innere, *das;* **in the ~s of the library/the earth** in den Katakomben der Bibliothek/im Inneren der Erde

bower /baʊə(r)/ *n.* 1 (enclosed by foliage) Laube, *die;* (summer house) Sommerhaus, *das* 2 (poet.) (inner room) Gemach, *das* (geh.); (boudoir) Boudoir, *das*

'bowerbird *n.* Laubenvogel, *der*

bowl[1] /bəʊl/ *n.* 1 (basin) Schüssel, *die;* (shallower) Schale, *die;* **mixing/washing-up ~:** Rühr-/Abwaschschüssel, *die;* **soup ~:** Suppentasse, *die;* **sugar ~:** Zuckerdose, *die;* **a ~ of water** eine Schüssel/Schale Wasser; **a ~ of soup** eine Tasse Suppe 2 (~-shaped part) *schalenförmiger Teil;* (of WC) Schüssel, *die;* (of spoon) Schöpfteil, *der;* (of pipe) [Pfeifen]kopf, *der* 3 (amphitheatre) Freilufttheater, *das;* (Sport) Stadion, *das* 4 (Geog.) Senke, *die*

bowl[2]

A *n.* 1 (ball) Kugel, *die;* (in skittles) [Kegel]kugel, *die;* (in tenpin bowling) [Bowling]kugel, *die* 2 *in pl.* (game) Bowlsspiel, *das;* Bowls, *das*

B *v.i.* 1 (play ~s) Bowls spielen; (play skittles) kegeln; (play tenpin bowling) bowlen 2 (go along) rollen; **~ along** dahinrollen 3 (Cricket) werfen

C *v.t.* 1 (roll) rollen lassen; **~ sb./sth. over** jmdn./etw. umwerfen; **~ sb. over** (fig.) jmdn. überwältigen *od.* (ugs.) umhauen 2 (Cricket etc.) werfen; **~ [down] the wicket** das Tor einwerfen; **~ the batsman [out]/side out** den Schlagmann/die Mannschaft ausschlagen

bow /bəʊ/: **~-'legged** *adj.* krummbeinig; o-beinig (ugs.); **be ~-legged** krumme Beine *od.* (ugs.) O-Beine haben; **~ 'legs** *n. pl.* krumme Beine; O-Beine *Pl.* (ugs.)

bowler[1] /'bəʊlə(r)/ *n.* 1 (Cricket etc.) Werfer, *der* 2 (at bowls) Bowlsspieler, *der*/Bowlsspielerin, *die;* (at bowling) Bowlingspieler, *der*/Bowlingspielerin, *die*

bowler[2] *n.* **~ [hat]** Bowler, *der;* Melone, *die* (ugs. scherzh.)

'bowl fire *n.* Heizsonne, *die*

bowline /'bəʊlɪn/ *n.* 1 **~ [knot]** Palstek, *der* 2 (Naut.: rope) Buline, *die* (Seemannsspr.)

bowling /'bəʊlɪŋ/ *n.* **[tenpin] ~:** Bowling, *das;* **go ~:** bowlen gehen

bowling: ~ alley *n.* (for tenpin ~) Bowlingbahn, *die;* (for skittles) Kegelbahn, *die;* **~ average** ▸ **average A 2**; **~ crease** *n.* (Cricket) Wurflinie, *die;* **~ green** *n.: Rasenfläche für Bowls*

bowman /'bəʊmən/ *n., pl.* **bowmen** /'bəʊmən/ (archer) Bogenschütze, *der*

bowser /'baʊzə(r)/ *n.* (tanker) Tankwagen, *der*

bow: ~sprit /'baʊsprɪt/ *n.* (Naut.) Bugspriet, *der od. das;* **~string** /'baʊstrɪŋ/ *n.* Bogensehne, *die;* **~ tie** /bəʊ'taɪ/ *n.* Fliege, *die;* [Smoking-/Frack]schleife, *die;* **~ window** /bəʊ 'wɪndəʊ/ *n.* Erkerfenster, *das*

bow-wow /'baʊwaʊ/

A *n.* 1 (dog's bark) Gebell, *das* 2 (child lang.: dog) Wauwau, *der* (Kinderspr.)

B *int.* wauwau

box[1] /bɒks/ *n.* (Bot.) 1 (tree) Buchsbaum, *der* 2 (wood) Buchsbaumholz, *das*

box[2] *n.*

A 1 (container) Kasten, *der;* (bigger) Kiste, *die;* (made of cardboard, thin wood, etc.) Schachtel, *die;* **a ~ of cigars** eine Schachtel Zigarren; **pencil ~:** Federkasten, *der;* **cigar ~:** Zigarrenkiste, *die;* **cardboard ~:** [Papp]karton, *der;* (smaller) [Papp-]schachtel, *die;* **~ of matches** Streichholzschachtel, *die* 2 (~ful) **she emptied the whole ~ of beads on to the floor** sie hat die ganze Schachtel [mit] Perlen auf die Erde geschüttet 3 **the ~** (coll.: television) der Kasten (ugs. abwertend); die Flimmerkiste (scherzh.) 4 (facility at newspaper office) ≈ Chiffre, *die* 5 (in theatre etc.) Loge, *die* 6 (casing) Kasten, *der;* (cricketer's etc. shield) ≈ Suspensorium, *das* 7 (confined area) Viereck, *das;* (enclosed by printed lines) Kasten, *der* 8 (Footb. coll.: penalty area) Strafraum, *der* 9 (Baseball) Box, *die* 10 (Brit.: country house) Hütte, *die* 11 (Hist.: coachman's seat) [Kutsch]bock, *der*

B *v.t.* ▸ **A 1**: [in eine Schachtel/in Schachteln *usw.*] verpacken; **~ the compass** (Naut.) alle Kompasspunkte der Reihe nach aufzählen

Phrasal verbs

- **~ 'in** *v.t.* 1 (enclose in ~) in einem Gehäuse unterbringen 2 (enclose tightly) einklemmen; **feel ~ed in** sich eingeengt fühlen
- **~ 'up** *v.t.* 1 (enclose in ~) ▸ **~ A 1**: [in eine Schachtel/in Schachteln *usw.*] verpacken 2 (confine) einzwängen; **I'd hate to be ~ed up anywhere with him** ich wäre nur äußerst ungern irgendwo mit ihm eingesperrt

box[3]

A *n.* (slap, punch) Schlag, *der;* **he gave him a ~ on the ear[s]** er gab ihm eine Ohrfeige

B *v.t.* 1 (slap, punch) schlagen; **he ~ed his ears** *or* **him round the ears** er ohrfeigte ihn; **get one's ears ~ed** eine Ohrfeige bekommen 2 (fight with fists) **~ sb.** gegen jmdn. boxen

C *v.i.* boxen **(with, against** gegen); **~ clever** (Brit. coll.) Grips zeigen (ugs.); sich pfiffig *od.* gewitzt anstellen

Box and Cox /bɒks ənd 'kɒks/ *n.* (two persons who take turns) **like ~:** im ständigen Wechsel; **be like ~:** sich ständig abwechseln

box: ~ camera *n.* Box, *die;* **~car** *n.* (Amer. Railw.) gedeckter [Güter]wagen

boxer /'bɒksə(r)/ *n.* 1 ▸ⓘ **p. 1260** Boxer, *der* 2 (dog) Boxer, *der*

'boxer shorts *n. pl.* Boxershorts *Pl.*

'box file *n.* Aktenkasten, *der*

boxful /'bɒksfʊl/ *n.* **a ~ of chocolates** *etc.* eine [ganze] Schachtel Pralinen *usw.*

'box girder *n.* Kastenträger, *der* (Technik)

boxing /'bɒksɪŋ/ *n., no pl.* Boxen, *das;* **professional/amateur ~:** Berufs-/Amateurboxen, *das*

boxing: B~ Day *n.* (Brit.) zweiter Weihnachtsfeiertag; **~ glove** *n.* Boxhandschuh, *der;* **~ match** *n.* Boxkampf, *der;* **~ ring** *n.* Boxring, *der*

box: ~ junction *n.* (Brit.) *gelb markierter Kreuzungsbereich, in den man bei Stau nicht einfahren darf;* **~-kite** *n.* Kastendrachen, *der;* **~ number** *n.* (at newspaper office) Chiffre, *die;* (at post office) Postfach, *das;* **my post office ~ number is ...:** meine Postfachnummer ist ...; **~ office** *n.* Kasse, *die;* (fig.) **be a ~ office success** ein Kassenerfolg sein; **be good/bad ~ office** gut/schlecht ankommen **(among** bei); **~ pew** *n.* geschlossener Chorstuhl; **~-pleat** *n.* Quetschfalte, *die;* **~room** *n.* (Brit.) Abstellraum, *der;* **~ score** *n.* (Amer.) [tabellarischer] Spielbericht; ≈ Spielbogen, *der;* **~-spanner** *n.* (Brit.) Steckschlüssel, *der;* **~-spring** *n.* Sprungfeder, *die;* **~wood** ▸ **box**[1] **2**

boy /bɔɪ/

A *n.* Junge, *der;* **baby ~:** kleiner Junge; **~s' school** Jungenschule, *die;* **a ~'s name** ein Jungenname; **a little Italian ~:** ein kleiner Italiener; **[my] ~** (as address) [mein] Junge; **here/sit/come on ~!** (to dog) hier!/sitz!/komm!; **good ~!** (to dog) guter Hund!; **the ~s** (male friends) die Kumpels (salopp); **come on, ~s!** los, Jungs!; **~s will be ~s** so sind Jungs/Männer nun mal; **jobs for the ~s** Vetternwirtschaft, *die* (abwertend); **the Smith ~s** die Jungen von Smiths; *see also* **old boy**

B *int.* **[oh] ~:** Junge, Junge! (ugs.)

boy-and-'girl *adj.* teenagerhaft; Teenager‹*romanze, -liebe*›

'boy band *n.* Boyband, *die*

boycott /'bɔɪkɒt/

A *v.t.* boykottieren

B *n.* Boykott, *der*

'boyfriend *n.* Freund, *der*

boyhood /'bɔɪhʊd/ *n.* Kindheit, *die*

boyish /'bɔɪɪʃ/ *adj.* jungenhaft; **she had a ~ haircut/figure** sie hatte einen Knabenhaarschnitt/eine knabenhafte Figur

Boyle's Law /'bɔɪlz lɔː/ *n.* (Phys.) Boyle-Mariotte-Gesetz, *das*

boy: ~-meets-'girl *attrib. adj.* Liebes‹*geschichte, -film*›; **~ 'racer** *n.* (coll.) jugendlicher Raser; **~ 'scout** ▸ **scout**[1] **A 1**

bozo /'bəʊzəʊ/ *n.* (esp. Amer. coll.) Trottel, *der* (ugs. abwertend)

Bp. *abbr.* = **bishop** Bf.

BP *abbr.* 1 = **boiling point** SP 2 = **British Petroleum** BP 3 (Med.) = **British Pharmacopoeia** *amtliches britisches Arzneimittelverzeichnis*

BPR *abbr.* = **business process re-engineering**

bps *abbr.* (Computing) = **bits per second** bps

Br. *abbr.* 1 = **British** brit. 2 = **Brother** Br.

BR *abbr.* (Hist.) = **British Rail[ways]** *britische Eisenbahngesellschaft*

bra /brɑː/ *n.* BH, *der* (ugs.); *attrib.* **~ strap** BH-Träger, *der*

brace /breɪs/

A *n.* 1 (Building: strengthening piece) Strebe *die* 2 *in pl.* (Brit.: trouser straps) Hosenträger 3 (Dent.) [Zahn]spange, *die;* [Zahn]klammer, *die* 4 *pl. same* (pair) **a/two ~ of** zwei/vier 5 (Printing, Mus.) geschweifte Klammer; Akkolade, *die* 6 (Naut.) Brasse, *die. See also* **brace and bit**

B *v.t.* (support, also Building) stützen

C *v. refl.* **~ oneself** (lit. & fig.) sich zusammennehmen; **~ oneself for sth.** (fig.) sich auf etw. (*Akk.*) [innerlich] vorbereiten

brace and 'bit *n.* Bohrwinde, *die*

bracelet /'breɪslɪt/ *n.* 1 (band) Armband, *das;* (chain) Kettchen, *das;* (bangle) Armreif, *der* 2 *in pl.* (coll.: handcuffs) Brasselett, *das* (Gaunerspr.)

bracer /'breɪsə(r)/ (coll.) Muntermacher, *der* (ugs. scherzh.)

brachial /'breɪkɪəl/ *adj.* (Anat.) brachial

bracing /'breɪsɪŋ/ *adj.* belebend

bracken /'brækn/ *n.* [Adler]farn, *der*

bracket /'brækɪt/

A *n.* 1 (support, projection) Konsole, *die;* (of iron) Krageisen, *das;* (lamp support) Lampenhalter, *der* 2 (mark) Klammer, *die;* **open/close ~s** Klammer auf/zu 3 (group, category) Gruppe, *die;* **social ~:** Gesellschaftsschicht, *die*

B *v.t.* 1 (enclose in ~s) einklammern 2 (couple with brace) mit einer Klammer verbinden; (fig.) in Verbindung bringen

brackish /'brækɪʃ/ *adj.* brackig

bract /brækt/ *n.* (Bot.) Braktee, *die*

brad /bræd/ *n.* [flacher] Drahtstift

bradawl /'brædɔːl/ *n.* [flache] Ahle

brae /breɪ/ *n.* (Scot.) (bank) [Ufer]böschung, *die;* (hillside) Hang, *der*

brag /bræg/

A *v.i.*, **-gg-** prahlen **(about** mit)

B *v.t.*, **-gg-** prahlen; **he ~s that he has a Rolls Royce** er prahlt damit, dass er einen Rolls-Royce hat

C *n.* (boast, boasting) Prahlerei, *die;* **his ~ is that ...:** er prahlt damit, dass ...

braggart /'brægət/

A *n.* Prahler, *der*/Prahlerin, *die*

B *adj.* prahlerisch

Brahmin /'brɑːmɪn/ *n.* Brahmane, *der*

Brahminism /'brɑːmɪnɪzm/ *n., no pl.* Brahmanismus, *der*

braid /breɪd/

A *n.* 1 (plait) Flechte, *die* (geh.); Zopf, *der;* (band entwined with hair) Haarband, *das;* Flechtband, *das* (veralt.) 2 (decorative woven band) Borte, *die* 3 (on uniform) Litze, *die;* (with metal threads) Tresse, *die*

B *v.t.* 1 (plait; arrange in ~s) flechten 2 zusammenbinden ‹*Haare*› 3 (trim with ~) mit Borten/Litzen/Tressen besetzen

braiding /'breɪdɪŋ/ *n.* (bands) Bänder; (decorative woven bands) Borten

Braille /breɪl/ *n.* Blindenschrift, *die*

brain /breɪn/

A *n.* 1 ▸ⓘ **p. 951** Gehirn, *das;* **have [got] sex/food/money on the ~:** nur Sex/Essen/Geld im Kopf haben; **he's got her on the ~:** sie geht ihm nicht aus dem Kopf; **use your ~[s]** gebrauch deinen Verstand; **he's got a good ~:** er ist ein kluger Kopf; **you need ~s for that**

dafür braucht man Verstand; **he didn't have the ~s to do it** er war zu dumm, es zu tun; **~ versus brawn** Köpfchen gegen Muskelkraft; **get your ~ in gear before opening your mouth!** (coll.) schalt erst mal dein Gehirn ein, bevor du den Mund aufmachst!; **I need a cup of strong coffee in the morning to help me get my ~ in gear** (coll.) ich brauche morgens eine Tasse starken Kaffee, um wach zu werden; *see also* **rack**[1] **B 3** **2** *in pl.* (Gastr.) Hirn, *das* **3** (coll.: clever person) **she's the ~[s] of the class** sie ist die Intelligenteste in der Klasse; **he's a terrific ~:** er ist wahnsinnig intelligent (ugs.); **the ~ behind the business** der Kopf des Unternehmens
B *v.t.* den Schädel einschlagen (+ *Dat.*); **I'll ~ you!** (coll.) du kriegst gleich eins auf die Rübe! (ugs.)

brain: ~child *n.* (coll.) Geistesprodukt, *das;* **that system was my own ~child** ich war der geistige Vater dieses Systems; **~-dead** *adj.* **1** (Med.) hirntot; **2** (coll. derog.) hirnlos (abwertend) ‹*Person*›; hirnverbrannt (abwertend), hirnrissig (abwertend) ‹*Ansicht, Idee*›; **~ death** *n., no pl.* Hirntod, *der;* **~ drain** *n.* (coll.) Abwanderung [von Wissenschaftlern]; Braindrain, *der*

brainless /ˈbremlɪs/ *adj.* (stupid) hirnlos

brain: ~ power *n.* geistige Leistung; **his ~ power will get him far** mit seiner Intelligenz wird er es weit bringen; **~ scan** *n.* (Med.) Gehirnscan, *der;* **~ scanner** *n.* (Med.) Gehirnscanner, *der;* **~stem** *n.* ▸ⓘ **p. 951** (Anat.) Hirnstamm, *der;* **~storm** *n.* **1** (Brit. coll.) Anfall geistiger Umnachtung; **2** (Amer. coll.) ▸ **~wave 2**; **~storming** *n.* Brainstorming, *das;* **~s trust** *n.* Expertengremium, *das;* **~ surgeon** *n.* Gehirnchirurg, *der;* **~-teaser** *n.* Denk[sport]aufgabe, *die;* **~ trust** *n.* (Amer.) [beratendes] Expertengremium; Braintrust, *der;* **~ tumour** *n.* Gehirntumor, *der;* **~-twister** ▸ **~-teaser**; **~wash** *v.t.* einer Gehirnwäsche unterziehen; **~wash sb. into doing sth.** jmdm. [ständig] einreden, etw. zu tun; **~washing** *n., no pl.* Gehirnwäsche, *die;* **~wave** *n.* **1** (Physiol.) Hirnstromwelle, *die;* **2** (coll.: inspiration) genialer Einfall; **~work** *n., no pl.* Kopfarbeit, *die*

brainy /ˈbremɪ/ *adj.* intelligent

braise /breɪz/ *v.t.* (Cookery) schmoren

brake[1] /breɪk/
A *n.* (apparatus; coll.: pedal etc.) Bremse, *die;* **sth. acts as a ~ on sth.** etw. bremst etw.; **apply** *or* **put on the ~s** die Bremse betätigen; (fig.) zurückstecken; **put the ~[s] on sth.** (fig.) etw. bremsen; **put the ~[s] on spending** die Ausgaben einschränken
B *v.t. & i.* bremsen; **~ hard** scharf bremsen

brake[2] *n.* (Bot.) Adlerfarn, *der*

brake[3] *n.* (thicket) Dickicht, *das*

brake[4] *n.* (Hist.: open carriage) Break, *der od. das*

brake: ~ block *n.* Bremsklotz, *der;* **~ cable** *n.* Bremszug, *der;* Bremsseil, *das;* **~ drum** *n.* Bremstrommel, *die;* **~ fluid** *n.* Bremsflüssigkeit, *die;* **~ horsepower** *n.* Bremsleistung, *die;* Nutzleistung, *die;* **~ lever** *n.* Bremshebel, *der;* **~ light** *n.* Bremslicht, *das;* **~ lining** *n.* Bremsbelag, *der;* **~ pad** *n.* Bremsbelag, *der;* **~ shoe** *n.* Bremsbacke, *die;* **~ van** *n.* (Railw.) Bremswagen, *der*

braking /ˈbreɪkɪŋ/ *n., no pl.* Bremsen, *das*

ˈbraking distance *n.* Bremsweg, *der*

bramble /ˈbræmbl/ *n.* **1** (shrub) Dornenstrauch, *der;* (blackberry bush) Brombeerstrauch, *der* **2** (fruit) Brombeere, *die*

Bramley /ˈbræmlɪ/ *n. englischer Kochapfel*

bran /bræn/ *n.* Kleie, *die*

branch /brɑːnʃ/
A *n.* **1** (bough) Ast, *der;* (twig) Zweig, *der* **2** (of nerve, artery, antlers) Ast, *der;* (of river) [Neben]arm, *der;* (of road, pipe, circuit) Abzweigung, *die;* (of railway) Nebenstrecke, *die;* (of family [of languages], subject) Zweig, *der;* (local establishment) Zweigstelle, *die;* (shop) Filiale, *die*
B *v.i.* **1** sich verzweigen **2** (tend) **~ away from sth.** sich von etw. wegentwickeln **3** (diverge) **~ into sth.** sich in etw. (*Akk.*) aufspalten

Phrasal verbs
- **~ ˈforth** ▸ **~ B 1**
- **~ ˈoff** *v.i.* abzweigen; (fig.) sich abspalten
- **~ ˈout** *v.i.* **1** abzweigen; ▸ **~ B 1** **2** (**~ off**) abzweigen (**from** von) **3** (fig.) **~ out into sth.** sich auch mit etw. befassen; **~ out on one's own** sich selbstständig machen

branch: ~ line *n.* (Railw.) Nebenstrecke, *die;* **~ manager** *n.* ▸ⓘ **p. 1260** Filialleiter, *der*/-leiterin, *die;* **~ office** *n.* Zweigstelle, *die*

brand /brænd/
A *n.* **1** (trade mark) Markenzeichen, *das;* (goods of particular make) Marke, *die;* (fig.: type) Art, *die;* **~ of washing powder/soap** Waschpulvermarke, *die*/Seifenmarke, *die* **2** (permanent mark, stigma) Brandmal, *das;* (on sheep, cattle) Brandzeichen, *das;* (on cigar box, crate) eingebranntes Zeichen; **~ of Cain** Kainsmal, *das* **3** (burning log etc.) [Feuer]brand, *der* (veralt.); (charred log etc.) verkohltes Holzscheit; (poet.: torch) Brand, *der* (geh.)
B *v.t.* **1** (burn) mit einem Brandzeichen markieren ‹*Tier*› **2** (stigmatize [as]) **~ [as]** brandmarken als ‹*Verräter, Verbrecher usw.*› **3** (Brit.: label with trade mark) mit einem Markenzeichen versehen; **~ed goods** Markenware, *die;* **~ed product** Markenprodukt, *das* **4** (impress) einbrennen (**upon** *Dat. od.* in + *Akk.*)

brand: ~-aware *adj.* markenbewusst; **~ awareness** *n., no pl.* Markenbewusstsein, *das;* **~ image** *n.* Markenimage, *das*

branding /ˈbrændɪŋ/ *n.* (Commerc.) Branding, *das*

ˈbranding iron *n.* Brandeisen, *das*

brandish /ˈbrændɪʃ/ *v.t.* schwenken; schwingen ‹*Waffe*›

brand: ~ leader *n.* (product) marktführendes Produkt; (company) Markenführer, *der;* (brand) führende Marke; **~ loyalty** *n.* Markentreue, *die;* **~ management** *n., no pl.* Markenmanagement, *das;* **~ name** *n.* Markenname, *der;* **~-ˈnew** *adj.* nagelneu (ugs.); brandneu (ugs.); **is the car ~-new?** ist der Wagen [fabrik-]neu?; **~ piracy** *n., no pl.* Markenpiraterie, *die*

brandy /ˈbrændɪ/ *n.* Weinbrand, *der;* Kognak, *der*

brandy: ~ ball *n.* (Brit.) Weinbrandtrüffel, *die;* **~ butter** *n.* ≈ Kognakbutter, *die; Creme aus Butter, Zucker und Brandy;* **~ snap** *n.: mit Schlagsahne gefülltes knuspriges Röllchen mit Ingwergeschmack*

brant /brænt/ (Amer.) ▸ **brent**

ˈbran tub *n.: mit Kleie o. ä. gefüllte Kiste, aus der man Geschenke herausfischen kann*

brash[1] /bræʃ/ *adj.* (self-assertive) dreist; (garish) auffällig ‹*Kleidung*›; knallig ‹*Farbe*›

brash[2] *n.* **1** (loose rock) **[stone] ~:** Trümmergestein, *das* **2** (loose ice) Eistrümmer *Pl.*

brash[3] *n.* (Med.) saures Aufstoßen

brashly /ˈbræʃlɪ/ *adv.* ▸ **brash**[1]: dreist; auffällig

brashness /ˈbræʃnɪs/ *n., no pl.* ▸ **brash**[1]: Dreistigkeit, *die*

brass /brɑːs/
A *n.* **1** Messing, *das;* **do sth. as bold as ~:** die Unverfrorenheit haben, etw. zu tun **2** (inscribed tablet) Grabplatte aus Messing **3** **[horse] ~es** Messinggeschirr, *das* **4** **the ~** (Mus.) das Blech (fachspr.); die Blechbläser **5** ▸ **brassware** **6** *no pl., no indef. art.* (Brit. coll.: money) Kies, *der* (salopp) **7** **[top] ~** (coll.: officers, leaders of industry etc.) hohe Tiere (ugs.)
B *attrib. adj.* Messing-; **~ player** (Mus.) Blechbläser, *der*
C *v.t.* **be ~ed off [doing sth.]** (coll.) es satt haben[, etw. zu tun] (ugs.); **be ~ed off with** *or* **about sb./sth.** (coll.) jmdn./etw. satt haben (ugs.)

brass ˈband *n.* Blaskapelle, *die*

brasserie /ˈbræsərɪ/ *n.* Brasserie, *die*

brass: ~ ˈfarthing *n.* **not a ~ farthing** kein rote Heller (ugs.); **he doesn't care a ~ farthing about it** es interessiert ihn nicht für fünf Pfennig (ugs.); **~ hat** *n.* (coll.) hohes Tier (ugs.)

brassica /ˈbræsɪkə/ *n.* (Bot.) Kohlpflanze, *die;* Brassica, *die* (Bot.)

brassiere /ˈbræzɪə(r)/ *n.* (formal) Büstenhalter, *der*

brass: ~ ˈplate *n.* Messingschild, *das;* **~ rubbing** *n.* **1** *no pl., no indef. art.* Frottage, *die* (*von Messingtafeln*); **2** (impression) Frottage, *die* (*einer Messingtafel*); **~ ˈtacks** *n. pl.* **get** *or* **come down to ~ tacks** (coll.) zur Sache kommen; **~ware** *n., no pl.* Messingteile; (utensils, candlesticks, etc.) Messinggerät, *das*

brassy /ˈbrɑːsɪ/ *adj.* **1** (in colour) messing-; (in sound) blechern **2** (loud and showy) auffällig

brat /bræt/ *n.* (derog.: child) Balg, *das od. der* (ugs., meist abwertend); (young rascal) Flegel, *der*

brattish /ˈbrætɪʃ/ *adj.* ungezogen

bravado /brəˈvɑːdəʊ/ *n., pl.* **~es** *or* **~s** Mut, *der;* **be full of ~:** sehr mutig tun; **do sth. out of ~:** so waghalsig sein, etw. zu tun; (as pretence) den starken Mann markieren wollen und etw. tun (ugs.)

brave /breɪv/
A *adj.* **1** mutig; (able to endure sth.) tapfer; **be ~!** nur Mut!/sei tapfer! **2** (literary: splendid) stattlich; prachtvoll; **make a ~ show** einen prächtigen Anblick bieten; **a ~ new world** eine schöne neue Welt
B *n.* [indianischer] Krieger
C *v.t.* trotzen (+ *Dat.*); mutig gegenübertreten (+ *Dat.*) ‹*Kritiker, Interviewer*›; **~ it out** sich durch nichts einschüchtern lassen

bravely /ˈbreɪvlɪ/ *adv.* **1** mutig; (showing endurance) tapfer **2** (literary: splendidly) stattlich; prachtvoll

bravery /ˈbreɪvərɪ/ *n., no pl.* Mut, *der;* (endurance) Tapferkeit, *die*

ˈbravery award *n.* Tapferkeitsauszeichnung, *die*

bravo /brɑːˈvəʊ/ *int.* bravo; **shouts of '~'** Bravorufe

bravura /brəˈvʊərə/ *n.* Bravour, *die;* **~ piece/passage** (Mus.) Bravourstück, *das*

braw /brɔː/ *adj.* (Scot.) schön

brawl /brɔːl/
A *v.i.* **1** sich schlagen **2** ‹*Bach:*› rauschen
B *n.* Schlägerei, *die*

brawn /brɔːn/ *n.* **1** (muscle) Muskel, *der;* (muscularity) Muskeln; **he's got some ~:** er hat ganz schön starke Muskeln; **you need a bit of ~ for that** dafür brauchst du schon ein paar Muskeln; *see also* **brain A 1** **2** (chopped pig's head) ≈ Presskopf, *der;* (in aspic jelly) Schweinskopfsülze, *die*

brawny /ˈbrɔːnɪ/ *adj.* muskulös

bray /breɪ/
A *n.* (of donkey) Iah, *das*
B *v.i.* ‹*Esel:*› iahen, schreien; ‹*Person:*› wiehern

braze /breɪz/
A *v.t.* [hart]löten
B *n.* [Hart]lötung, *die*

brazen /ˈbreɪzn/
A *adj.* **1** dreist; (shameless) schamlos **2** (arch./literary: of brass) Messing-; aus Messing *nachgestellt;* messingen (seltener)
B *v.t.* **~ [out]** trotzen (+ *Dat.*); **~ it out** (deny guilt) es abstreiten; (not admit guilt) es nicht zugeben

ˈbrazen-faced ▸ **brazen A 1**

brazenly /ˈbreɪznlɪ/ *adv.* dreist; (shamelessly) schamlos

brazenness /ˈbreɪznnɪs/ *n., no pl.* Dreistigkeit, *die;* (shamelessness) Schamlosigkeit, *die*

brazier /ˈbreɪzɪə(r), ˈbreɪʒə(r)/ *n.* Kohlenbecken, *das*

Brazil /brəˈzɪl/ *n.* **1** *pr. n.* Brasilien (*das*) **2** ▸ **Brazil nut**

Brazilian /brəˈzɪlɪən/ ▸ⓘ **p. 1345**
A *adj.* brasilianisch; **sb. is ~:** jmd. ist Brasilianer/Brasilianerin
B *n.* Brasilianer, *der*/Brasilianerin, *die*

Braˈzil nut *n.* Paranuss, *die*

breach /briːtʃ/
A *n.* **1** (violation) Verstoß, *der* (**of** gegen); **~ of faith/duty** Vertrauensbruch, *der*/Pflichtverletzung, *die;* **~ of the peace** Störung von Ruhe und Ordnung; (by noise only)

b

ruhestörender Lärm; **~ of contract** Vertragsbruch, *der;* **~ of promise** Wortbruch, *der;* (Law Hist.: breaking off an engagement to marry) Bruch des Eheversprechens; **be in ~ of the regulations** gegen die Verordnungen verstoßen **2** (of relations) Bruch, *der;* **~ of diplomatic relations** Abbruch der diplomatischen Beziehungen
3 (gap) Bresche, *die;* (fig.) Riss, *der;* **stand in the ~** (fig.) in der Schusslinie stehen; **step into the ~** (fig.) in die Bresche treten *od.* springen
B *v.t.* eine Bresche schlagen in (+ *Akk.*); **the wall/dyke was ~ed** in die Mauer wurde eine Bresche geschlagen/der Deich wurde durchbrochen

bread /bred/
A *n.* **1** Brot, *das;* **a piece of ~ and butter** ein Butterbrot; **[some] ~ and butter** [ein paar] Butterbrote; **~ and butter** (fig.) tägliches Brot; **quarrel with one's ~ and butter** (fig.) an dem Ast sägen, auf dem man sitzt; **~ and circuses** Brot und Spiele; **~ and milk** heiße Milch mit eingebrocktem Brot; **~ and water** (lit. or fig.) Wasser und Brot; **have one's ~ buttered on both sides** es in jeder Hinsicht gut getroffen haben; **know which side one's ~ is buttered** wissen, wo etwas zu holen ist; *see also* **water A 2** **2** (necessary food) **[daily] ~:** [tägliches] Brot; **break ~ [with sb.]** (arch.) das Brot [mit jmdm.] brechen; **take the ~ out of sb.'s mouth** (fig.) jmdn. seiner Existenzgrundlage berauben
3 (coll.: money) Kies, *der* (salopp)
B *v.t.* panieren

bread: ~-and-butter 'pudding *n.* Brot-und-Butter-Pudding, *der; Auflauf aus Brot, Butter, Zucker, Rosinen usw.;* **~ bin** *n.* Brotkasten, *der;* **~board** *n.* [Brot]brett, *das;* **~crumb** *n.* Brotkrume, *die;* **~crumbs** (for coating e.g. fish) Paniermehl, *das;* **~fruit** *n.* Brotfrucht, *die;* **~ knife** *n.* Brotmesser, *das;* **~line** *n.* (Amer.) *Warteschlange bei der Ausgabe kostenloser Nahrungsmittel an Bedürftige;* **live on/below the ~line** (fig.) gerade noch/nicht einmal mehr das Notwendigste zum Leben haben; **~ 'roll** *n.* Brötchen, *das;* **~ 'sauce** *n.* (Gastr.) [englische] Brotsauce (Kochk.); **~stick** *n.: stangenförmiges Gebäck aus Brotteig*

breadth /bredθ/ *n.* **1** ▸❶ **p. 1286** (broadness) Breite, *die;* **what is the ~ of ...?** wie breit ist ...?; **be 20 metres in ~:** 20 Meter breit sein **2** (extent) Weite, *die;* (range) **with his ~ of experience/knowledge** bei seiner großen Erfahrung/bei seiner umfassenden Kenntnis; **~ of mind/vision** *etc.* (fig.) große Aufgeschlossenheit/Einbildungskraft *usw.*

bread: ~ tin Brotbüchse, *die;* **~winner** *n.* Ernährer, *der*/Ernährerin *die*

break¹ /breɪk/
A *v.t.*, **broke** /brəʊk/, **broken** /'brəʊkn/ **1** brechen; (so as to damage) zerbrechen; kaputtmachen (ugs.); aufschlagen ‹*Ei zum Kochen*›; zerstören ‹*Ufer*›; zerreißen ‹*Seil*›; (fig.: interrupt) unterbrechen; brechen ‹*Bann, Zauber, Schweigen*›; **~ sth. in two/in pieces** etw. in zwei Teile/in Stücke brechen; **~ the set** Teile des Satzes einzeln abgeben; **the TV/my watch is broken** der Fernseher/meine Uhr ist kaputt (ugs.)
2 (crack) zerbrechen; zertrümmern ‹*Fundament, Schiffsrumpf*›
3 (fracture) sich (*Dat.*) brechen; (pierce) verletzen ‹*Haut*›; **he broke his leg** er hat sich (*Dat.*) das Bein gebrochen; **no bones broken** (fig.) es ist nichts passiert; **~ one's/sb.'s back** (fig.) sich/jmdn. kaputtmachen (ugs.); **~ one's back** (fig.) sich abstrampeln (ugs.); **~ the back of sth.** (fig.) bei etw. das Schwerste hinter sich bringen; **~ a tooth** sich (*Dat.*) ein Stück vom Zahn abbrechen; **~ open** aufbrechen
4 (violate) brechen ‹*Vertrag, Versprechen*›; verletzen, verstoßen gegen ‹*Regel, Tradition*›; nicht einhalten ‹*Verabredung*›; überschreiten ‹*Grenze*›; **~ the law** gegen das Gesetz verstoßen
5 (destroy) zerstören, ruinieren ‹*Freundschaft, Ehe*›
6 (surpass) brechen ‹*Rekord*›
7 (abscond from) **~ jail** [aus dem Gefängnis] ausbrechen; **~ the bounds** ausreißen; **~ ship** sich beim Landgang absetzen (ugs.); *see also* **cover A 10**
8 (weaken) brechen, beugen ‹*Stolz*›; (quash) niederschlagen ‹*Rebellion, Aufstand*›; zusammenbrechen lassen ‹*Streik*›; **~ sb.'s spirit** jmds. Lebensmut brechen; **~ sb.'s heart** jmdm. das Herz brechen; **it broke my heart** es brach mir das Herz; **~ sb.** (crush) jmdn. fertig machen (ugs.); **~ a horse [to the rein]** ein Pferd zureiten; **~ the habit** es sich (*Dat.*) abgewöhnen; **~ the smoking/drinking habit** sich (*Dat.*) das Rauchen/Trinken abgewöhnen; **~ sb. of the smoking habit** jmdm. das Rauchen abgewöhnen; *see also* **make A 16**
9 (cushion) auffangen ‹*Schlag, jmds. Fall*›; abschwächen ‹*Wind*›
10 (make bankrupt) ruinieren; **~ the bank** die Bank sprengen; **you mustn't ~ the bank** (fig. coll.) (spend a lot) du darfst dich nicht in Unkosten stürzen; (ruin yourself) du darfst dich nicht finanziell ruinieren; **it won't ~ the bank** (fig. coll.) es kostet kein Vermögen
11 (reveal) **~ the news that ...:** melden, dass ...; **~ the glad/bad news to sb. that ...:** jmdm. die frohe Nachricht mitteilen/jmdm. die schlechte Nachricht beibringen, dass ...; **I don't know how to ~ this news to you, but ...:** ich weiß nicht, wie ich dir das sagen soll, aber ...
12 (use part of) anbrechen ‹*Banknote*›
13 (unfurl) entfalten ‹*Fahne*›
14 (solve) entschlüsseln, entziffern ‹*Kode, Geheimschrift*›
15 (disprove) entkräften ‹*Alibi*›
16 (Tennis) **~ service/sb.'s service** den Aufschlag des Gegners/jmds. Aufschlag durchbrechen. *See also* **broken B**; **wind¹ A 5**
B *v.i.*, **broke, broken** **1** kaputtgehen (ugs.); entzweigehen; ‹*Faden, Seil:*› [zer]reißen; ‹*Glas, Tasse, Teller:*› zerbrechen; ‹*Eis:*› brechen; (fig.: be interrupted) unterbrochen werden; **sb.'s heart is ~ing** jmdm. bricht das Herz; **~ in two/in pieces** entzweibrechen; **the chocolate ~s easily** die Schokolade bricht sich leicht
2 (crack) ‹*Fenster-, Glasscheibe:*› zerspringen; **the bows of the ship broke against** *or* **on the rocks** der Bug des Schiffes zerschellte an den Felsen; **my back was nearly ~ing** ich brach mir fast das Kreuz
3 (be destroyed) ‹*Freundschaft, Ehe, Bündnis:*› zerbrechen; ‹*Familienbande:*› zerreißen
4 (sever links) **~ with sb./sth.** mit jmdm./etw. brechen
5 (weaken) gebrochen werden; **until he/his will ~s** bis er zusammenbricht/sein Wille gebrochen ist
6 **~ into** einbrechen in (+ *Akk.*) ‹*Haus*›; aufbrechen ‹*Safe*›; **~ into laughter/tears** in Gelächter/Tränen ausbrechen; **he broke into a sweat** ihm brach der Schweiß aus; **~ into a trot/run** *etc.* zu traben/laufen *usw.* anfangen; **sb. ~s into acting/industry** (coll.) jmdm. gelingt der Durchbruch in der Schauspielerei/in der Industrie; **~ into one's capital** sein Kapital angreifen; **~ into a banknote** eine Banknote anbrechen; **~ out of prison** *etc.* aus dem Gefängnis *usw.* ausbrechen
7 (escape) **~ free** *or* **loose [from sb./sb.'s grip]** sich [von jmdm./aus jmds. Griff] losreißen; **~ free from prison** aus dem Gefängnis ausbrechen; **some planks had broken loose** einige Planken waren losgebrochen
8 ‹*Welle:*› sich brechen (**on/against** an + *Dat.*), branden (**on/against** an + *Akk.*/gegen)
9 ‹*Wolkendecke:*› aufreißen; ‹*Sturm:*› losbrechen; ‹*Wetter:*› umschlagen; ‹*Tag:*› anbrechen
10 (change tone) **sb.'s voice ~s** jmd. kommt in den Stimmbruch; (with emotion) jmdm. bricht die Stimme
11 (Boxing) sich aus dem Clinch lösen; **~!** break!
12 (have interval) **~ for coffee/lunch** [eine] Kaffee-/Mittagspause machen; **we'll ~ for five minutes** wir machen fünf Minuten Pause
13 (become public) bekannt werden
C *n.* **1** Bruch, *der;* (of rope) Reißen, *das;* **~ [of service]** (Tennis) Break, *der od. das;* **a ~ in the weather** ein Wetterumschlag; **a ~ with sb./sth.** ein Bruch mit jmdm./etw.; **~ of day** Tagesanbruch, *der;* **at ~ of day** bei Tagesanbruch
2 (gap) Lücke, *die;* (Electr.: in circuit) Unterbrechung, *die;* (broken place) Sprung, *der*
3 (escape from prison) Ausbruch, *der;* (sudden dash) **they made a sudden ~:** sie stürmten plötzlich davon; **they made a ~ for the gateway** sie stürzten zum Tor
4 (interruption) Unterbrechung, *die*
5 (pause, holiday) Pause, *die;* **take** *or* **have a ~:** [eine] Pause machen; **work without a ~:** ohne Pause arbeiten; **go away for a weekend ~:** übers Wochenende verreisen
6 (coll.: fair chance, piece of luck) Chance, *die;* **lucky ~:** große Chance; **that was a bad ~ for him** das war Pech für ihn
7 **[bad] ~** (coll.) (unfortunate remark) ungeschickte Bemerkung; (ill-judged action) Dummheit, *die*
8 (Electr.) Unterbrechen, *das* (**in** *Gen.*)
9 (Billiards etc.) Serie, *die*
10 (Jazz) Break, *der od. das*

(Phrasal verbs)

• **~ a'way**
A *v.t.* **~ sth. away [from sth.]** etw. [von etw.] losbrechen *od.* abbrechen
B *v.i.* **1** **~ away [from sth.]** [von etw.] losbrechen *od.* abbrechen; (separate itself/oneself) sich [von etw.] lösen; (escape) [aus etw.] entkommen; **he broke away from them** er distanzierte sich von ihnen; (escaped) er entkam ihnen **2** (in race) ausreißen; (Footb.) sich freilaufen **3** (get out of control) ‹*Auto:*› ausbrechen. *See also* **breakaway**

• **~ 'down**
A *v.i.* **1** (fail) zusammenbrechen; ‹*Verhandlungen:*› scheitern **2** (cease to function) ‹*Auto:*› eine Panne haben; ‹*Telefonnetz:*› zusammenbrechen; **the machine has broken down** die Maschine funktioniert nicht mehr **3** (be overcome by emotion) zusammenbrechen **4** (Chem.) aufspalten
B *v.t.* **1** (demolish) aufbrechen ‹*Tür*›; zum Einsturz bringen ‹*Mauer*› **2** (suppress) brechen ‹*Widerstand*›; niederreißen ‹*Barriere, Schranke*› **3** (analyse) aufgliedern. *See also* **breakdown**; **broken-down**

• **~ 'in**
A *v.i.* **1** (intrude forcibly) einbrechen; *see also* **break-in** **2** (interrupt) **~ in [on sb./sth.]** [jmdn./etw.] unterbrechen
B *v.t.* **1** (familiarize) eingewöhnen; einarbeiten ‹*Lehrling etc.*›; zureiten ‹*Pferd*› **2** (wear etc. until comfortable) einlaufen ‹*Schuhe*›; sich gewöhnen an (+ *Akk.*) ‹*Brille, Gebiss*› **3** **~ the door in** die Tür aufbrechen

• **~ into** ▸ **~ B 6**

• **~ 'off**
A *v.t.* abbrechen; abreißen ‹*Faden*›; auflösen ‹*Verlobung*›; **~ it off [with sb.]** sich von jmdm. trennen
B *v.i.* **1** abbrechen **2** (cease) aufhören; ‹*Gespräch, Gesang:*› abbrechen; ‹*Diskussion, Verfahren:*› abgebrochen werden

• **~ 'out** *v.i.* (escape, appear) ausbrechen; ‹*Flecken, Pusteln, Schweißtropfen:*› sich bilden; **~ out in spots/a rash** *etc.* Pickel/einen Ausschlag *usw.* bekommen; **he broke out in a cold sweat** ihm brach der kalte Schweiß aus

• **~ out of** ▸ **~ B 6**

• **~ 'through** *v.t. & i.* durchbrechen; *see also* **breakthrough**

• **~ 'up**
A *v.t.* **1** (**~** into pieces) zerkleinern; ausschlachten ‹*Auto*›; abwracken ‹*Schiff*›; aufbrechen ‹*Erde*›; zerbrechen ‹*Stuhl*› **2** (disband) auflösen; auseinander reißen ‹*Familie*›; zerstreuen ‹*Menge*›; **~ it up!** (coll.) auseinander! **3** (disconcert) aus der Fassung bringen **4** (end) zerstören ‹*Freundschaft, Ehe*›
B *v.i.* **1** (**~** into pieces, lit. or fig.) zerbrechen; ‹*Erde, Straßenoberfläche:*› aufbrechen; ‹*Eis:*› brechen **2** (disband) sich auflösen; ‹*Schule:*› schließen; ‹*Schüler, Lehrer:*› in die Ferien gehen **3** (be convulsed) **~ up [with laughter]** in Gelächter ausbrechen **4** (cease) abgebrochen werden; (end relationship) **~ up [with sb.]** sich [von jmdm.] trennen; **they broke up last year** sie trennten sich letztes Jahr **5** ▸ **~ B 9** **6** (mentally) zusammenbrechen. *See also* **break-up**

break² ▸ **brake⁴**

breakable /'breɪkəbl/
A *adj.* zerbrechlich
B *n. in pl.* zerbrechliche Dinge

breakage /ˈbreɪkɪdʒ/ *n.* **1** (breaking) Zerbrechen, *das* **2** (result of breaking) Bruchschaden, *der;* **~s must be paid for** zerbrochene Ware muss bezahlt werden

break: ~away **A** *n.* **1** Ausbrechen, *das;* **a ~away from tradition** ein Bruch mit der Tradition; **2** (Sport: false start) Fehlstart, *der;* **3** (Rugby) [*schnelles*] *Lösen aus dem Gedränge.* **B** *adj.* (Brit.) abtrünnig; *attrib.* **~away group** Splittergruppe, *die;* **~-dancing** *n., no pl.* Breakdancetanzen, *das;* **~down** *n.* **1** (fig.: collapse) **a ~down in the system** (fig.) ein Zusammenbruch des Systems; **2** (mechanical failure) Panne, *die;* (in machine) Störung, *die; attrib.* **~down service** Pannendienst, *der;* **~down truck/van** Abschleppwagen, *der;* **3** (health or mental failure) Zusammenbruch, *der;* **a ~down in health** ein gesundheitlicher Zusammenbruch; **4** (analysis) Aufschlüsselung, *die;* **5** (Chem.) Aufspaltung, *die; attrib.* **~down product** Spaltprodukt, *das* (Chemie)

breaker /ˈbreɪkə(r)/ *n.* **1** (wave) Brecher, *der* **2** **[car] ~:** *jmd., der Autos ausschlachtet;* **~'s [yard]** Autoverwertung, *die*

break ˈeven *v.i.* die Kosten decken; *attrib.* **~ point** Rentabilitätsschwelle, *die*

breakfast /ˈbrekfəst/

A *n.* Frühstück, *das;* **for ~:** zum Frühstück; **have sth. for ~:** etw. zum Frühstück essen/trinken; **eat** *or* **have [one's] ~:** frühstücken; **have a cooked ~:** zum Frühstück etwas Warmes essen; *see also* **wedding breakfast**

B *v.i.* frühstücken; **we ~ed on bacon and eggs** wir aßen Eier mit Speck zum Frühstück

breakfast: ~ cereal *n.* ≈ Frühstücksflocken *Pl.;* **~ room** *n.* Frühstücksraum, *der;* **~ ˈtelevision** *n.* Frühstücksfernsehen, *das;* **~ time** *n.* Frühstückszeit, *die;* **~ TˈV** *n.* ▸ **breakfast television**

ˈbreak-in *n.* Einbruch, *der;* **there has been a ~ at the bank** in der *od.* die Bank ist eingebrochen worden

ˈbreaking *n.* **~ and entering** (Law) Einbruch, *der*

breaking: ~ point *n.* Belastungsgrenze, *die;* **be at ~ point** (mentally) die Grenze der Belastbarkeit erreicht haben; **~ strength** *n.* Belastbarkeit, *die*

break: ~neck *adj.* halsbrecherisch; **~ ˈpoint** *n.* (in Tennis) Breakpunkt, *der;* **~point** *n.* (Computing) Programmstopp, *der;* Haltepunkt, *der;* **~out** *n.* Ausbruch, *der;* **~through** *n.* Durchbruch, *der;* **~-up** *n.* **1** (disintegration) (of earth, soil, road surface) Aufbrechen, *das;* (fig.) Zusammenbruch, *der;* (of weather) Umschlag, *der;* (of old structure) Zerfall, *der;* **2** (disbanding, dispersal) Auflösung, *die;* **3** (ceasing) Ende, *das;* (ending of relationship) Bruch, *der;* **~water** *n.* Wellenbrecher, *der*

bream /briːm/ *n., pl. same* (Zool.) **1** Brachsen, *der* **2** **[sea] ~** (Sparidae) Meerbrassen, *der* **3** (Amer.: sunfish) Sonnenbarsch, *der*

breast /brest/

A *n.* (lit. or fig.) Brust, *die;* **make a clean ~ [of sth.]** (fig.) [etw.] offen bekennen

B *v.t.* (Brit.: climb) übersteigen ‹*Mauer, Hindernis*›; besteigen ‹*Berg*›; **~ the waves** gegen die Wellen ankämpfen; *see also* **tape A 2**

breast: ~bone *n.* ▸**❶ p. 951** Brustbein, *das;* **~ cancer** *n.* ▸**❶ p. 1231** Brustkrebs, *der;* **~fed** *adj.* **be ~fed** gestillt werden; **~feed** *v.t. & i.* stillen; **~feeding** *n., no pl.* das Stillen; **~ milk** *n., no pl.* Muttermilch, *die;* **~plate** *n.* (armour) Brustharnisch, *der;* **~ ˈpocket** *n.* Brusttasche, *die;* **~stroke** *n.* (Swimming) Brustschwimmen, *das;* **do** *or* **swim [the] ~stroke** brustschwimmen

breath /breθ/ *n.* **1** Atem, *der;* **have bad ~:** Mundgeruch haben; **say sth. below** *or* **under one's ~:** etw. vor sich (*Akk.*) hin murmeln; **draw ~:** Atem holen; **as long as I draw ~:** solange ich atme; **a ~ of fresh air** ein wenig frische Luft; **go out for a ~ of fresh air** frische Luft schnappen gehen; **be a ~ of fresh air in sb.'s life** etwas Abwechslung in jmds. Leben bringen; **waste one's ~:** seine Worte verschwenden; **sth. is the ~ of life to sb.** jmd. kann ohne etw. nicht leben; **she caught her ~:** ihr stockte der Atem; **hold one's ~:** den Atem anhalten; **get one's ~ back** wieder zu Atem kommen; **be out of/short of ~:** außer Atem *od.* atemlos sein/kurzatmig sein; **take ~:** [sich] verschnaufen; **pause for ~:** eine Verschnaufpause machen; **take sb.'s ~ away** (fig.) jmdm. den Atem verschlagen; *see also* **save A 5** **2** (one respiration) Atemzug, *der;* **take** *or* **draw a [deep] ~:** [tief] einatmen; **in the same ~:** im selben Atemzug **3** (air movement, whiff) Hauch, *der;* **there wasn't a ~ of air** es regte sich kein Lüftchen; **a ~ of wind** ein Windhauch; **not a ~ of suspicion/rumour** nicht die Spur eines Verdachts/nicht die leiseste Andeutung eines Gerüchts

breathable /ˈbriːðəbl/ *adj.* **1** atembar ‹*Luft, Atmosphäre*› **2** atmungsaktiv ‹*Gewebe, Kleidung*›

breathalyse /ˈbreθəlaɪz/ *v.t.* ins Röhrchen *od.* in die Tüte blasen lassen (ugs.)

breathalyser ® (*Amer.:* **breathalyzer**) /ˈbreθəlaɪzə(r)/ *n.* Alcotest-Röhrchen (Wz) *das; attrib.* **~ test** Alcotest (Wz), *der;* **blow/breathe into a ~:** ins Röhrchen *od.* in die Tüte blasen (ugs.)

breathe /briːð/

A *v.i.* **1** (lit. or fig.) atmen; **~ in** einatmen; **~ out** ausatmen; **~ into sth.** [sanft] in etw. (*Akk.*) [hinein]blasen; *see also* **neck A 1** **2** (take breath) **stop to ~:** eine Verschnaufpause machen; **give me a chance to ~!** lass mich erst wieder zur Besinnung kommen! **3** (blow) [sanft] wehen

B *v.t.* **1** **~ a breath** einen Atemzug tun; **~ one's last** seinen letzten Atemzug tun; **~ fire** Feuer speien; (fig.) Gift und Galle spucken; **~ [in/out]** ein-/ausatmen; **~ new life into sth.** (fig.) etw. mit neuem Leben erfüllen **2** (utter) hauchen; **~ a sigh [of relief]/a sigh of regret** [erleichtert] aufatmen/aufseufzen; **don't ~ a word about** *or* **of this to anyone** sag kein Sterbenswörtchen darüber zu irgendjemandem **3** (show evidence of) atmen (geh.); ausstrahlen

breather /ˈbriːðə(r)/ *n.* **1** (brief pause) Verschnaufpause, *die;* (brief holiday etc.) Erholungspause, *die;* **take** *or* **have a ~:** eine Verschnaufpause/Erholungspause einlegen; **go out for a ~:** ein wenig frische Luft schöpfen **2** (Motor Veh.) Entlüfter, *der*

ˈbreath freshener *n.* Atemerfrischer, *der*

breathing /ˈbriːðɪŋ/ *n., no pl.* Atmen, *das*

breathing: ~ apparatus *n.* **1** (Med.) Beatmungsgerät, *das;* **2** (of fireman etc.) Atemschutzgerät, *das;* **~ space** *n.* (time to breathe) Zeit zum Luftholen; (pause) Atempause, *die;* **~ tube** *n.* Atemschlauch, *der*

breathless /ˈbreθlɪs/ *adj.* atemlos (**with** vor + *Dat.*); **leave sb. ~** (lit. or fig.) jmdm. den Atem nehmen; **we stood ~ while ...:** uns (*Dat.*) stockte der Atem, während ...; **we were ~ with amazement** uns (*Dat.*) blieb vor Staunen die Luft weg (ugs.)

breathlessly /ˈbreθlɪslɪ/ *adv.* atemlos

breathlessness /ˈbreθlɪsnɪs/ *n., no pl.* Atemlosigkeit, *die;* (caused by smoking or illness) Kurzatmigkeit, *die*

breath: ~taking *adj.* atemberaubend; **~ test** *n.* Alcotest (Wz), *der*

breathy /ˈbreθɪ/ *adj.* hauchig ‹*Stimme*›

Brechtian /ˈbrektɪən/ *adj.* (Theatre) brechtsch

bred ▸ **breed A, B**

breech /briːtʃ/ *n.* [Geschütz]verschluss, *der*

breech: ~ birth *n.* (Med.) Steißgeburt, *die;* **~block** *n.* Verschlussblock, *der*

breeches /ˈbrɪtʃɪz/ *n. pl.* **1** (short trousers) **[pair of] ~:** [Knie]bundhose, *die;* **[riding] ~:** Reithose, *die;* Breeches *Pl.* **2** (trousers) Hose, *die;* (knickerbockers) Knickerbocker *Pl.; see also* **big A 7**

ˈbreeches buoy *n.* (Naut.) Hosenboje, *die*

breech: ~-loader *n.* Hinterlader, *der;* **~-loading** *adj.* Hinterlader-

breed /briːd/

A *v.t.,* **bred** /bred/ **1** (be the cause of) erzeugen; hervorrufen **2** (raise) züchten ‹*Tiere, Pflanzen*› **3** (bring up) erziehen; **born and bred sth.** etw. durch und durch sein; **he was born and bred in London** er ist in London geboren und aufgewachsen **4** (bear) gebären ‹*Nachkommen*›; (generate) hervorbringen ‹*Rasse*›

B *v.i.,* **bred** **1** sich vermehren; ‹*Vogel:*› brüten; ‹*Tier:*› Junge haben; **they ~ like flies** *or* **rabbits** sie vermehren sich wie die Kaninchen **2** (arise) entstehen; (spread) sich ausbreiten

C *n.* **1** Art, *die;* (of animals) Rasse, *die;* **~s of cattle** Rinderrassen; **the Jersey ~ [of cattle]** das Jerseyrind; **what ~ of dog is that?** zu welcher Rasse gehört dieser Hund? **2** (lineage) Rasse, *die;* **a noble ~ of men** ein vornehmer Menschenschlag **3** (sort) Art, *die*

breeder /ˈbriːdə(r)/ *n.* ▸**❶ p. 1260** Züchter, *der;* **be a ~ of sth.** etw. züchten; **dog/horse ~:** Hunde-/Pferdezüchter, *der*

ˈbreeder reactor *n.* (Nucl. Engin.) Brutreaktor, *der;* Brüter, *der*

breeding /ˈbriːdɪŋ/ *n.* Erziehung, *die;* **[good] ~:** gute Erziehung; **have ~:** eine gute Erziehung genossen haben

breeding: ~ ground *n.* (lit. or fig.) Brutstätte, *die;* **~ season** *n.* Brutzeit, *die;* **~ site** *n.* Brutplatz, *der*

breeze¹ /briːz/

A *n.* **1** (gentle wind) Brise, *die;* **there is a ~:** es weht eine Brise; **night ~:** nächtliche Brise; **sea ~:** Seebrise, *die* **2** (coll.: easy thing) **be a ~:** ein Kinderspiel sein

B *v.i.* (coll.) **~ along** dahinrollen; (on foot) dahinschlendern; **~ in** hereingeschneit kommen (ugs.)

breeze² *n.* (cinders) Lösche, *die*

breeze: ~ block *n.* (Building) ≈ Leichtstein, *der;* **~way** *n.* (Amer.) überdachter Übergang

breezily /ˈbriːzɪlɪ/ *adv.* (coll.) [frisch und] unbekümmert; (carelessly) leichthin; unbekümmert

breeziness /ˈbriːzɪnɪs/ *n., no pl.* (coll.) (carefree nature) [frische und] unbekümmerte Art; (carelessness) Unbekümmertheit, *die*

breezy /ˈbriːzɪ/ *adj.* **1** (windy) windig **2** (coll.) (brisk and carefree) [frisch und] unbekümmert; (careless) unbekümmert

brekkie, brekky /ˈbrekɪ/ *n.* (coll.) Frühstück, *das*

brent goose /ˈbrent guːs/ *n.* Ringelgans, *die*

brethren ▸ **brother 4**

Breton /ˈbretn/ ▸**❶ p. 1277**

A *adj.* bretonisch; *see also* **English A**

B *n.* **1** (language) Bretonisch, *das; see also* **English B 1** **2** (person) Bretone, *der*/Bretonin, *die*

breve /briːv/ *n.* **1** (Mus.) Brevis, *die* (veralt.); Doppelganze, *die* **2** (of short/unstressed vowel) Halbkreis, *der* (*zur Kennzeichnung kurzer/unbetonter Vokale*)

breviary /ˈbriːvɪərɪ/ *n.* (Eccl.) Brevier, *das*

brevity /ˈbrevɪtɪ/ *n., no pl.* Kürze, *die*

brew /bruː/

A *v.t.* **1** brauen ‹*Bier*›; keltern ‹*Apfelwein*›; **~ [up]** kochen ‹*Kaffee, Tee, Kakao usw.*›; aufbrühen ‹*Tee, Kaffee*›; **~ up** *abs.* Tee kochen; [sich (*Dat.*)] einen Tee kochen *od.* aufbrühen **2** (fig.: put together) **~ [up]** [zusammen]brauen (ugs.) ‹*Mischung*›; (generate) hervorrufen ‹*Empfindungen*›; (formulate) ausbrüten (ugs.) ‹*Plan usw.*›

B *v.i.* **1** ‹*Bier, Apfelwein:*› gären; ‹*Kaffee, Tee:*› ziehen **2** (fig.: gather) ‹*Unwetter:*› sich zusammenbrauen; ‹*Rebellion, Krieg:*› drohen

C *n.* **1** Gebräu, *das* (abwertend); (brewed beer/tea) Bier, *das*/Tee, *der;* **~ [of tea/coffee]** Tee, *der*/Kaffee, *der* **2** (amount brewed) ≈ Abfüllung, *die;* (of tea etc.) **we'll have to make another ~:** wir müssen noch einmal aufbrühen

brewer /ˈbruːə(r)/ *n.* **1** ▸**❶ p. 1260** (person) Brauer, *der* **2** (firm) Brauerei, *die*

brewery /ˈbruːərɪ/ *n.* Brauerei, *die*

brew: ~house *n.* Brauhaus, *das;* **~pub** *n.* (Amer.) Braukneipe, *die;* (including restaurant) Braulokal, *das*

briar ▸ **brier¹, ²**

bribe /braɪb/

A *n.* Bestechung, *die;* **a ~ [of £100]** ein Bestechungsgeld [in Höhe von 100 Pfund]; **take a ~/~s** sich bestechen lassen; **he won't accept ~s** er ist unbestechlich; **offer sb. a ~:** jmdn. bestechen wollen

B *v.t.* bestechen; **he won't be ~d** er ist unbestechlich; ~ **sb. to do/into doing sth.** jmdn. bestechen, damit er etw. tut

bribery /ˈbraɪbərɪ/ *n., no pl.* Bestechung, *die;* **open to** ~: bestechlich; käuflich; **be involved in** ~: in einen Bestechungsfall verwickelt sein

bric-a-brac /ˈbrɪkəbræk/ *n.* Antiquarisches; (smaller things) Nippsachen *Pl.;* ~ **collector** ≈ Antiquitätensammler, *der*

brick /brɪk/

A *n.* **1** (block) Ziegelstein, *der;* Backstein, *der;* (clay) Lehmziegel, *der;* ~**s and mortar** (buildings) Gebäude; (as investment) Immobilien *Pl.;* **drop a** ~ (fig. coll.) ins Fettnäpfchen treten (ugs. scherzh.); **be** *or* **come down on sb. like a load** *or* **ton of** ~**s** (coll.) jmdn. unheimlich fertig machen *od.* zusammenstauchen (ugs.) **2** (toy) Bauklötzchen, *das* **3** (of ice cream) Packung, *die* **4** (coll.: person) feiner Kerl; **you've been a real** ~: du warst ein prima Kumpel (ugs.)

B *adj.* **1** Ziegelstein-; Backstein- **2** (red) ziegelrot

C *v.t.* ~ **up/in** zu-/einmauern

brick: ~**bat** *n.* **1** Backsteinbrocken, *der;* **2** (fig.: uncomplimentary remark) schlechte Kritik; **greet sb. with** ~**bats** jmdn. attackieren; ~**-built** *adj.* backsteinern; Backstein ‹*haus, -mauer*›; **it is** ~**-built** es ist aus Backstein

brickie /ˈbrɪkɪ/ *n.* (Brit. coll.) Maurer, *der*

brick: ~**-kiln** *n.* Ziegelofen, *der;* ~**layer** *n.* ▸ **p. 1260** Maurer, *der;* ~**laying** *n., no pl.* ▸ **p. 1260** Mauern, *das;* ~**-red** *adj.* ziegelrot; ~ ˈ**wall** *n.* Backsteinmauer, *die;* **bang one's head against a** ~ **wall** (fig.) mit dem Kopf gegen die Wand rennen (fig.); **come up against a** ~ **wall** (fig.) plötzlich vor einer Mauer stehen (fig.); ~**work** *n.* **1** (~laying) Mauern, *das;* **2** (structure) [Backstein]mauerwerk, *das;* ~**yard** *n.* Ziegelei, *die*

bridal /ˈbraɪdl/ *adj.* (of bride) Braut-; (of wedding) Hochzeits-; ~ **couple/suite** Brautpaar, *das*/Hochzeitssuite, *die*

ˈ**bridal registry** *n.* Geschenkliste, *die* (*eines Brautpaares*)

bride /braɪd/ *n.* Braut, *die*

ˈ**bridegroom** *n.* Bräutigam, *der*

bridesmaid /ˈbraɪdzmeɪd/ *n.* Brautjungfer, *die;* **chief** ~: erste Brautjungfer

bridge[1] /brɪdʒ/

A *n.* **1** (lit. or fig.) Brücke, *die;* **cross that** ~ **when you come to it** (fig.) alles zu seiner Zeit; *see also* **burn**[1] **B 1** **2** (Naut.) [Kommando]brücke, *die* **3** (of nose) Nasenbein, *das;* Sattel, *der* **4** (of violin, spectacles) Steg, *der* **5** (Dent.) [Zahn]brücke, *die*

B *v.t.* eine Brücke bauen *od.* errichten *od.* schlagen über (+ *Akk.*); ~ **the gap** (fig.) die Kluft überbrücken

bridge[2] *n.* (Cards) Bridge, *das*

ˈ**bridgehead** *n.* Brückenkopf, *der*

ˈ**bridging loan** *n.* (Commerc.) Überbrückungskredit, *der*

bridle /ˈbraɪdl/

A *n.* Zaumzeug, *das;* Zaum, *der*

B *v.t.* **1** aufzäumen ‹*Pferd*› **2** (fig.: restrain) zügeln ‹*Zunge*›; im Zaum halten ‹*Leidenschaft*›

C *v.i.* ~ **at sth.** sich gegen etw. sträuben *od.* (geh.) stemmen

ˈ**bridle path,** ˈ**bridle road,** ˈ**bridleway** *ns.* Reitweg, *der*

Brie /briː/ *n.* Brie[käse], *der*

brief[1] /briːf/ *adj.* **1** (of short duration) kurz; gering, geringfügig ‹*Verspätung*›; **after a** ~ **discussion/the** ~**est of discussions** nach kurzer/ganz kurzer Diskussion **2** (concise) knapp; **in** ~, **to be** ~: kurz gesagt; **make** *or* **keep it** ~: es kurz machen; **be** ~: sich kurz fassen; **the news in** ~: die Nachrichten im Überblick

brief[2]

A *n.* **1** (Law: summary of facts) Schriftsatz, *der;* **hold a** ~ **for sb.** jmdn. als Anwalt [vor Gericht] vertreten; **hold no** ~ **for sb.** (fig.) nicht auf jmds. Seite (*Dat.*) stehen; nicht für jmdn. plädieren *od.* eintreten **2** (Brit. Law: piece of work) Mandat, *das* **3** (Amer. Law: statement of arguments) Darlegung der Beweisgründe **4** (instructions) Instruktionen *Pl.;* Anweisungen *Pl.*

B *v.t.* **1** (Brit. Law) mit der Vertretung eines Falles betrauen **2** (Mil.: instruct) Anweisungen *od.* Instruktionen geben (+ *Dat.*); instruieren; unterweisen **3** (inform, instruct) unterrichten; informieren

ˈ**briefcase** *n.* Aktentasche, *die*

briefing /ˈbriːfɪŋ/ *n.* **1** Briefing, *das;* (of reporters or press) Unterrichtung, *die;* (before raid etc.) Einsatzbesprechung, *die* **2** (instructions) Instruktionen *Pl.;* Anweisungen *Pl.;* (information) Informationen *Pl.*

briefly /ˈbriːflɪ/ *adv.* **1** (for a short time) kurz **2** (concisely) knapp; kurz; **[to put it]** ~, **...:** kurz gesagt ...

briefness /ˈbriːfnɪs/ *n., no pl.* **1** (shortness) Kürze, *die* **2** (conciseness) Knappheit, *die*

briefs /briːfs/ *n. pl.* **[pair of]** ~: Slip, *der*

brier[1] /ˈbraɪə(r)/ *n.* (Bot.: rose) Wilde Rose

brier[2] *n.* **1** (pipe) Bruyèrepfeife, *die* **2** (Bot.: heath) Baumheide, *die*

ˈ**brier rose** *n.* Hundsrose, *die*

brig /brɪg/ *n.* **1** (Naut.) Brigg, *die* **2** (coll.: prison) Bau, *der* (salopp); Bunker, *der* (salopp)

Brig. *abbr.* ▸ **p. 1634 = brigadier** Brig.

brigade /brɪˈgeɪd/ *n.* **1** (Mil.) Brigade, *die;* **the old** ~ (fig.) die alte Garde **2** (organized or uniformed body) Einheit, *die*

brigadier [general] /brɪgəˈdɪə(r) (ˈdʒenrl)/ *n.* ▸ **p. 1634** (Mil.) Brigadegeneral, *der;* Brigadier, *der*

brigand /ˈbrɪgənd/ *n.* Bandit, *der;* Brigant, *der* (geh.)

bright /braɪt/

A *adj.* **1** hell ‹*Licht, Stern, Fleck*›; grell ‹*Scheinwerfer[licht], Sonnenlicht*›; strahlend ‹*Sonnenschein, Stern, Augen*›; glänzend ‹*Metall, Augen*›; leuchtend, lebhaft ‹*Farbe, Blume*›; ~ **reflection** starke Reflexion *od.* Spiegelung; ~ **blue** *etc.* leuchtend blau *usw.;* ~ **yellow/red** leuchtend gelb/rot; knallgelb/-rot (ugs.); **a** ~ **day** ein heiterer *od.* strahlender Tag; ~ **intervals/periods** Aufheiterungen; **the one** ~ **spot** (fig.) der Lichtblick; **the** ~ **lights of the city** (fig.) der Glanz der Großstadt; **look on the** ~ **side** (fig.) die Sache positiv sehen; ~**-eyed and bushy-tailed** (joc.) fidel und munter **2** (cheerful) fröhlich, heiter ‹*Person, Charakter, Stimmung*›; strahlend ‹*Lächeln*›; freundlich ‹*Zimmer, Farbe*› **3** (clever) intelligent; **that wasn't very** ~ **[of you], was it?** das war nicht gerade intelligent [von dir]!; **he is a** ~ **boy** er ist ein heller *od.* aufgeweckter Junge **4** (hopeful) viel versprechend ‹*Zukunft*›; glänzend ‹*Aussichten*›

B *adv.* **1** hell **2** ~ **and early** in aller Frühe

brighten /ˈbraɪtn/

A *v.t.* ~ **[up]** **1** aufhellen ‹*Farbe*›; aufpolieren, zum Glänzen bringen ‹*Metall*› **2** (make more cheerful) aufhellen, aufheitern ‹*Zimmer*›

B *v.i.* ~ **[up]** **1** ‹*Himmel:*› sich aufhellen; **the weather** *or* **it is** ~**ing [up]** es klärt sich auf; es klart auf (Met.) **2** (become more cheerful) ‹*Person:*› vergnügter werden; ‹*Augen:*› [auf]leuchten; ‹*Gesicht:*› sich aufhellen; ‹*Aussichten:*› sich verbessern

brightly /ˈbraɪtlɪ/ *adv.* **1** hell ‹*scheinen, glänzen*›; glänzend ‹*poliert*›; ~ **lit** hell erleuchtet; ~ **coloured** leuchtend bunt **2** (cheerfully) gut gelaunt; strahlend

brightness /ˈbraɪtnɪs/ *n., no pl.* **1** (of light, star, spot) Helligkeit, *die;* (of sunlight) Grelle, *die;* Grellheit, *die;* (of sun, eyes, star) Strahlen, *das;* (of metal, eyes) Glanz, *der;* (of colours) Leuchtkraft, *die;* (of eyes) Leuchten, *das;* **the** ~ **of the reflection** die Stärke der Reflexion **2** (cheerfulness) Fröhlichkeit, *die;* Heiterkeit, *die* **3** (cleverness) Intelligenz, *die;* **the** ~ **of his ideas** seine glänzenden Ideen

ˈ**brightness control** *n.* Helligkeitsregler, *der; attrib.* ~ **switch/button** Helligkeitsregler, *der*

brill[1] /brɪl/ *n., pl. same* (Zool.) Glattbutt, *der*

brill[2] *adj.* (Brit. coll.) super (ugs.)

brilliance /ˈbrɪljəns/, **brilliancy** /ˈbrɪljənsɪ/ *n., no pl.* **1** (brightness) (of light) Helligkeit, *die;* (of star, diamond) Funkeln, *das;* (of flash) Grelle, *die;* Grellheit, *die;* (of colours) Leuchten, *das* **2** (of person, invention, idea, move, achievement) Genialität, *die;* **the** ~ **of his mind** sein genialer Geist **3** (illustriousness) Glanz, *der*

brilliant /ˈbrɪljənt/

A *adj.* **1** (bright) hell ‹*Licht*›; strahlend ‹*Sonne*›; funkelnd ‹*Diamant, Stern*›; leuchtend ‹*Farbe*› **2** (highly talented) genial ‹*Person, Erfindung, Gedanke, Schachzug, Leistung*›; glänzend ‹*Verstand*›; brillant, glänzend ‹*Aufführung, Vorstellung, Idee*›; bestechend ‹*Theorie, Argument*›; **that was** ~ (iron.) das war gekonnt *od.* intelligent (iron.) **3** (illustrious) glänzend ‹*Karriere, Erfolg, Sieg*›; großartig ‹*[Helden]tat*›; **a** ~ **achievement** eine Glanzleistung

B *n.* Brillant, *der*

brilliantine /ˈbrɪljəntiːn/ *n.* Brillantine, *die;* Haarpomade, *die*

brilliantly /ˈbrɪljəntlɪ/ *adv.* **1** hell ‹*scheinen, funkeln, schimmern*›; **it was a** ~ **sunny day** es war ein strahlender Sonnentag; ~ **lit** hell erleuchtet **2** (with great talent) brillant; **a** ~ **thought-out scheme** ein genial ausgedachter Plan **3** (illustriously) glänzend ‹*erfolgreich sein, triumphieren*›

brim /brɪm/

A *n.* **1** (of cup, bowl, hollow) Rand, *der;* **full to the** ~: randvoll **2** (of hat) [Hut]krempe, *die*

B *v.i.*, **-mm-:** **be** ~**ming with sth.** randvoll mit etw. sein; (fig.) strotzen vor etw. (*Dat.*); **be** ~**ming with tears** (fig.) ‹*Augen:*› voller Tränen stehen

Phrasal verb

• ~ ˈ**over** *v.i.* **1** übervoll sein **2** (fig.) **he was** ~**ming over with confidence** er strotzte vor Zuversicht

brim-ˈfull *adj.* **be** ~ **with sth.** randvoll mit etw. sein; **be** ~ **of energy/curiosity** (fig.) vor Energie (*Dat.*) sprühen/vor Neugierde (*Dat.*) platzen; **be** ~ **of new ideas** (fig.) von neuen Ideen übersprudeln

brimless /ˈbrɪmlɪs/ *adj.* ‹*Hut*› ohne Krempe

brimstone /ˈbrɪmstən, -stəʊn/ *n.* **1** *no pl.* (arch.: sulphur) Schwefel, *der;* **fire and** ~: Feuer und Schwefel; **fire-and-**~ **sermon** Feuer-und-Schwefel-Predigt, *die* **2** (butterfly) ~ **[butterfly]** Zitronenfalter, *der*

brindle /ˈbrɪndl/, **brindled** /ˈbrɪndld/ *adjs.* gestreift ‹*Katze*›; gestromt ‹*Kuh, Hund*›

brine /braɪn/ *n.* (salt water) Salzwasser, *das;* Sole, *die;* (for preserving) Pökellake, *die;* [Salz]lake, *die*

bring /brɪŋ/ *v.t.*, **brought** /brɔːt/ **1** bringen; (as a present or favour) mitbringen; ~ **sth. with one** etw. mitbringen; **I haven't brought my towel** ich habe mein Handtuch nicht mitgebracht *od.* dabei; **he brought the chair nearer** er zog den Stuhl näher heran; ~ **sb. before sb.** jmdn. vor jmdn. führen; **what** ~**s you here?** was führt dich hierher?; **who brought you here?** wer hat Sie hergebracht?; **he brought the car to the front door** er fuhr mit dem Wagen vor; **April brought a change in the weather** der April brachte einen Wetterumschwung mit sich; ~ **sb. low** jmdn. erniedrigen; ~ **sth. [up]on oneself/sb.** sich selbst/jmdm. etw. einbrocken; ~ **a business/country through a crisis** ein Unternehmen/ein Land durch eine Krise führen

2 (result in) [mit sich] bringen; **the television appeal brought thousands of replies** auf den Aufruf im Fernsehen meldeten sich Tausende; **the distress call brought help within a matter of minutes** auf den Notruf kam Hilfe in Minutenschnelle; **this will** ~ **shame on you** das wird dir Schande bringen; ~ **honour to sb.** jmdm. Ehre machen; ~ **tears to sb.'s eyes** jmdm. Tränen in die Augen treiben

3 (persuade) ~ **sb. to do sth.** jmdn. dazu bringen *od.* bewegen, etw. zu tun; **I could not** ~ **myself to do it** ich konnte es nicht über mich bringen, es zu tun

4 (initiate, put forward) ~ **a charge/legal action against sb.** gegen jmdn. [An]klage erheben/einen Prozess anstrengen; ~ **a case/matter before a court** einen Fall/eine Sache vor Gericht bringen; ~ **a complaint** eine

Beschwerde vorbringen 5 (be sold for, earn) [ein]bringen ‹*Geldsumme*› 6 (adduce) vorbringen ‹*Argument*›

Phrasal verbs

- **~ a'bout** *v.t.* 1 (cause to happen) verursachen; herbeiführen; **~ it about that ...:** es zustande bringen, dass ... 2 (Naut.) **~ the ship about** das Schiff auf Gegenkurs bringen
- **~ a'long** *v.t.* 1 mitbringen 2 ▸ **~ on 2**
- **~ 'back** *v.t.* 1 (return) zurückbringen; (from a journey) mitbringen 2 (recall) in Erinnerung bringen *od.* rufen; **~ sth. back to sb.** ‹*Musik, Foto usw.:*› jmdn. an etw. (*Akk.*) erinnern; **~ back memories** Erinnerungen wachrufen *od.* wecken 3 (restore, reintroduce) wieder einführen ‹*Sitten, Todesstrafe*›; **~ back the Socialists!** wir wollen die Sozialisten wieder haben; **be brought back to power** wieder an die Macht kommen; **~ sb. back to health** jmdn. wieder gesund machen; **~ sb. back to life** jmdn. wieder beleben; **nothing will ~ him back to life** nichts kann ihn wieder lebendig machen
- **~ 'down** *v.t.* 1 herunterbringen 2 (shoot down out of the air) abschießen; herunterholen (ugs.) 3 (land) herunterbringen ‹*Flugzeug, Drachen*› 4 (kill, wound) zur Strecke bringen ‹*Person, Tier*›; erlegen ‹*Tier*› 5 (reduce) senken ‹*Preise, Inflationsrate, Fieber*›; **~ sb. down to one's own level** jmdn. zu sich *od.* auf sein [eigenes] Niveau herunterziehen 6 (attract) **that'll ~ the boss's wrath down on you[r head]** damit werden Sie sich (*Dat.*) den Zorn des Chefs zuziehen 7 (cause to fall) zu Fall bringen ‹*Gegner, Fußballer*›; einstürzen lassen ‹*Haus, Mauer*›; (fig.) stürzen, zu Fall bringen ‹*Regierung*›; *see also* **house A 9**
- **~ 'forth** *v.t.* 1 (produce) hervorbringen ‹*Frucht*›; zur Welt bringen ‹*Kinder, Junge*› 2 (fig.) vorbringen ‹*Vorschlag, Idee*›; auslösen ‹*Protest, Kritik*›
- **~ 'forward** *v.t.* 1 nach vorne bringen; **~ your chairs forward** rücken Sie nach vorn 2 (draw attention to) vorlegen ‹*Beweise*›; vorbringen ‹*Argument, Beschwerde*›; zur Sprache bringen ‹*Fall, Angelegenheit, Frage*› 3 (move to earlier time) vorverlegen ‹*Termin*› (**to** auf + *Akk.*) 4 (Bookk.) übertragen; **the amount brought forward** der Übertrag
- **~ 'in** *v.t.* 1 hereinbringen; auftragen ‹*Essen*›; einbringen ‹*Ernte*› 2 (introduce) anschneiden ‹*Thema*›; einführen ‹*Mode*›; einbringen ‹*Gesetzesvorlage*›; **why ~ all that in?** das gehört hier nicht hin 3 (yield) einbringen ‹*Verdienst, Summe*›; bringen ‹*Zinsen*› 4 (Law) **~ in a verdict of guilty/not guilty** einen Schuldspruch fällen/auf Freispruch erkennen 5 (call in) hinzuziehen, einschalten ‹*Experten*›
- **~ 'off** *v.t.* 1 (rescue) retten; in Sicherheit bringen 2 (conduct successfully) zustande *od.* zuwege bringen; **~ off a coup** einen Coup landen; **we didn't ~ it off** wir haben es nicht geschafft
- **~ 'on** *v.t.* 1 (cause) verursachen; **brought on by ...** ‹*Krankheit*› infolge von ... 2 (advance progress of) wachsen *od.* sprießen lassen ‹*Blumen, Getreide*›; weiterbringen, fördern ‹*Schüler, Sportler*› 3 (on stage etc.) auftreten lassen 4 (Sport) bringen (ugs.); einsetzen
- **~ 'out** *v.t.* 1 herausbringen; **he put his hand in his pocket and brought out a knife** er griff in die Tasche und zog ein Messer heraus 2 (show clearly) hervorheben, betonen ‹*Unterschied*›; verdeutlichen ‹*Bedeutung*›; herausbringen ‹*Farbe*› 3 (cause to appear) herausbringen ‹*Pflanzen, Blüte*›; **the crisis brought out the best in him** die Krise brachte seine besten Seiten zum Vorschein *od.* ans Licht; **~ sb. out in a rash** bei jmdm. einen Ausschlag verursachen 4 (begin to sell) einführen ‹*Produkt*›; herausbringen ‹*Buch, Zeitschrift*›
- **~ 'over** *v.t.* 1 herüberbringen 2 (convert) **~ sb. over to sth.** jmdn. von etw. überzeugen; **~ sb. over to a cause** jmdn. für eine Sache gewinnen
- **~ 'round** *v.t.* 1 mitbringen ‹*Bekannte, Freunde usw.*›; vorbeibringen ‹*Gegenstände*› 2 (restore to consciousness) wieder zu sich bringen ‹*Ohnmächtigen*› 3 (win over) überreden; herumkriegen (ugs.); **~ sb. round to one's way of thinking** jmdn. von seiner Meinung überzeugen 4 (direct) **~ a conversation round to sth.** ein Gespräch auf etw. (*Akk.*) bringen *od.* lenken
- **~ 'through** *v.t.* durchbringen ‹*Kranken*›
- **~ 'to** *v.t.* 1 (restore to consciousness) wieder zu sich bringen 2 (Naut.) beidrehen
- **~ to'gether** *v.t.* zusammenbringen
- **~ 'up** *v.t.* 1 heraufbringen 2 (educate) erziehen; **~ sb. up to be economical** jmdn. zur Sparsamkeit erziehen; **I was brought up to believe that ...:** ich wurde in dem Glauben erzogen, dass ... 3 (rear) aufziehen; großziehen 4 (call attention to) zur Sprache bringen ‹*Angelegenheit, Thema, Problem*›; **did you have to ~ that up?** mussten Sie davon anfangen?; **~ up the past** die Vergangenheit aufrühren 5 (vomit) erbrechen; wieder von sich geben 6 (Law) **~ sb. up [before a judge]** jmdn. [einem Richter] vorführen 7 (Mil.) an die Front bringen ‹*Truppen, Panzer*› 8 (cause to stop) **~ sb. up short** jmdn. innehalten lassen. *See also* **rear[1] A 2**

bring-and-'buy [sale] *n.* [Wohltätigkeits-]basar, *der*

brink /brɪŋk/ *n.* (lit. or fig.) Rand, *der;* **shiver on the ~** (fig.) mit sich ringen; **be on the ~ of doing sth.** nahe daran sein, etw. zu tun; **be on the ~ of ruin/success** am Rand des Ruins sein *od.* stehen/dem Erfolg greifbar nahe sein; **they were on the ~ of starvation** sie waren kurz vor dem *od.* nahe am Verhungern

brinkmanship /ˈbrɪŋkmənʃɪp/ *n., no pl.* gefährlicher Poker; **be playing a game of ~:** sich auf einen gefährlichen Poker eingelassen haben

briny /ˈbraɪnɪ/
A salzig
B *n.* (Brit. coll.) **the ~:** das Meer

briquette (briquet) /brɪˈket/ *n.* Brikett, *das*

brisk /brɪsk/ *adj.* flott ‹*Gang, Bedienung*›; forsch ‹*Person, Art*›; frisch ‹*Wind*›; (fig.) rege ‹*Handel, Nachfrage*›; lebhaft ‹*Geschäft*›; **we set off at a ~ pace** wir marschierten in flottem Tempo los; **we went for a ~ walk** wir machten einen zünftigen Spaziergang; **business was ~:** das Geschäft florierte; **bidding for the lots was ~:** auf die Auktionsstücke wurde eifrig geboten

brisket /ˈbrɪskɪt/ *n.* (Gastr.) Bruststück, *das;* Brust, *die;* **~ of beef** Rinderbrust, *die;*

briskly /ˈbrɪsklɪ/ *adv.* flott; **the wind blew ~:** es wehte ein frischer Wind; **sell ~:** sich gut verkaufen

briskness /ˈbrɪsknɪs/ *n., no pl.* ▸ **brisk:** Flottheit, *die;* Forschheit, *die;* Frische, *die;* (fig.) Lebhaftigkeit, *die;* **the ~ of trade/demand** der rege Handel/die rege Nachfrage

bristle /ˈbrɪsl/
A *n.* 1 Borste, *die;* **be made of ~:** aus Borsten bestehen 2 **~s** (of beard) [Bart]stoppeln
B *v.i.* 1 **~ [up]** ‹*Haare:*› sich sträuben; **the dog's hair ~d [up], the dog ~d** dem Hund sträubte sich (*Dat.*) das Fell 2 **~ with** (fig.: have many) strotzen *od.* starren vor (+ *Dat.*); **~ with difficulties/obstacles** mit Schwierigkeiten/Hindernissen gespickt sein 3 **~ [up]** (fig.: become angry) ‹*Person:*› ungehalten reagieren

bristly /ˈbrɪslɪ/ *adj.* borstig; stopp[e]lig ‹*Kinn*›; **~ beard** Stoppelbart, *der*

Brit /brɪt/ *n.* (coll.) Brite, *der*/Britin, *die;* Engländer, *der*/Engländerin, *die* (ugs.)

Brit. *abbr.* 1 **= Britain** Gr.-Brit.; Gr.-Br. 2 **= British** brit.

Britain /ˈbrɪtn/ *pr. n.* Großbritannien (*das*); Britannien *das* (hist.; auch Zeitungsjargon)

Britannia /brɪˈtænjə/ *pr. n.* (literary) Britannia, *die* (dichter.)

Briticism /ˈbrɪtɪsɪzm/ *n.* Britizismus, *der*

British /ˈbrɪtɪʃ/ ▸ⓘ **p. 1345**
A *adj.* britisch; **he/she is ~:** er ist Brite/sie ist Britin; **sth. is ~:** etw. ist aus Großbritannien; **the best of ~ [luck]** (coll.) na, [dann mal] viel Glück!; *see also* **English A**
B *n. pl.* **the ~:** die Briten

British: ~ Columbia /brɪtɪʃ kəˈlʌmbɪə/ *pr. n.* Britisch-Kolumbien (*das*); **~ 'Council** *n. britisches Kulturinstitut im Ausland*

> **British Council**
>
> Der *British Council* ist die mit britischen Regierungsmitteln geförderte Organisation für britische Kulturarbeit im Ausland. Die Organisation wurde 1934 gegründet mit dem Ziel eines dauerhaften Verständnisses und einer dauerhaften Wertschätzung Großbritanniens in anderen Ländern durch kulturelle, bildungsmäßige und technische Zusammenarbeit. Er hat Bibliotheken und Außenstellen in vielen Ländern und veranstaltet ein Kulturprogramm mit Vorträgen, Seminaren, Austellungen und Sprachkursen.

Britisher /ˈbrɪtɪʃə(r)/ *n.* Brite, *der*/Britin, *die*

British 'Isles *pr. n. pl.* Britische Inseln

Britishism /ˈbrɪtɪʃɪzm/ ▸ **Briticism**

Briton /ˈbrɪtn/ *n.* Brite, *der*/Britin, *die*

Britpop /ˈbrɪtpɒp/ *n., no pl., no art.* Britpop, *der*

Brittany /ˈbrɪtənɪ/ *pr. n.* Bretagne, *die*

brittle /ˈbrɪtl/ *adj.* 1 spröde ‹*Material*›; zerbrechlich ‹*Glas*›; schwach ‹*Knochen*›; brüchig ‹*Gestein*› 2 (fig.: insecure) empfindlich ‹*Person*›; schwach ‹*Nerven*›

brittle 'bone disease *n.* Glasknochenkrankheit, *die*

brittleness /ˈbrɪtlnɪs/ *n., no pl.* ▸ **brittle:** 1 Sprödigkeit, *die;* Zerbrechlichkeit, *die;* Schwäche, *die;* Brüchigkeit, *die* 2 (fig.) Empfindlichkeit, *die;* Schwäche, *die*

bro. *abbr.* **= brother** Br.

broach /brəʊtʃ/ *v.t.* 1 anzapfen; anstechen ‹*Fass*›; anbrechen ‹*Vorräte*› 2 (fig.) zur Sprache bringen ‹*Vorschlag, Idee*›; anschneiden ‹*Thema*›

broad /brɔːd/
A *adj.* 1 breit; (extensive) weit ‹*Ebene, Meer, Land, Felder*›; ausgedehnt ‹*Fläche*›; **a river sixty feet ~:** ein sechzig Fuß breiter Fluss; **grow ~er** breiter werden; sich verbreitern; **make sth. ~er** etw. verbreitern; **it's as ~ as it is long** (fig.) es ist gehupft wie gesprungen (ugs.) 2 (explicit) deutlich, klar ‹*Hinweis*›; breit ‹*Lächeln*›; **a ~ hint** ein Wink mit dem Zaunpfahl (scherzh.) 3 (clear, main) grob; wesentlich ‹*Fakten*›; **in ~ outline** in groben *od.* großen Zügen; **give the ~ outlines of a plan** einen Plan in groben Zügen erläutern; **draw a ~ distinction between ...:** grob unterscheiden zwischen (+ *Dat.*) ...; *see also* **daylight 1** 4 (generalized) allgemein; (wide-ranging) vielseitig ‹*Interessen*›; **in the ~est sense** im weitesten Sinne; **as a ~ rule/indication** als Faustregel 5 (strongly regional) stark ‹*Akzent*›; breit ‹*Aussprache*›; **he speaks ~ Scots** er spricht breites Schottisch *od.* einen starken schottischen Dialekt 6 (coarse) derb ‹*Humor, Geschichte*› 7 (tolerant) großzügig; liberal; **B~ Church** *liberale Richtung in der Kirche von England;* Broad Church (fachspr.)
B *n.* 1 (broad part) breiter Teil; **the ~ of the back** die Schultergegend 2 (Amer. coll.: woman) Weib, *das* (abwertend); Weibsstück, *das* (salopp abwertend)

broad: ~band *n.* (Computing) Breitband, *das; attrib.* Breitband-; **~ 'bean** *n.* Saubohne, *die;* dicke Bohne; **~-brimmed** /ˈbrɔːdbrɪmd/ *adj.* breitkrempig; **~-brush** *adj.* mehr in die Breite [als in die Tiefe] gehend; pauschal ‹*Beschuldigung, Angriff*›

broadcast /ˈbrɔːdkɑːst/
A *n.* (Radio, Telev.) Sendung, *die;* (live) Übertragung, *die*
B *v.t.*, **~** *or* **~ed, ~** 1 (Radio, Telev.) senden; ausstrahlen; übertragen ‹*Livesendung, Sportveranstaltung*› 2 (spread) aussäen ‹*Samen*›; (fig.) verbreiten ‹*Gerücht, Nachricht*›; ausposaunen (ugs.) ‹*Neuigkeit*›
C *v.i.*, **~** *or* **~ed** ‹*Rundfunk-, Fernsehstation:*› senden; ‹*Redakteur usw.:*› [im Rundfunk/Fernsehen] sprechen
D *adj.* (Radio, Telev.) im Rundfunk/Fernsehen gesendet; Rundfunk-/Fernseh-; **a ~ appeal** ein Aufruf im Rundfunk/Fernsehen

broadcaster /ˈbrɔːdkɑːstə(r)/ *n.* ▸ⓘ **p. 1260** (Radio, Telev.) *jmd., der durch häufige Auftritte im Rundfunk und Fernsehen, besonders als Interviewpartner, Diskussionsteilnehmer od. Kommentator, bekannt ist*

broadcasting /ˈbrɔːdkɑːstɪŋ/ *n., no pl.* (Radio, Telev.) Senden, *das;* (of live programmes) Übertragen, *das;* **written for ~:** für den Rundfunk/das Fernsehen geschrieben; **the early days of ~:** die Anfänge des Rundfunks; **work in ~:** beim Funk arbeiten

broadcast 'media *n.* Rundfunkmedien *Pl.*

broaden /ˈbrɔːdn/

A *v.t.* **1** verbreitern **2** (fig.) ausweiten ‹*Diskussion*›; **~ one's mind** seinen Horizont erweitern; **travel ~s the mind** Reisen bildet

B *v.i.* breiter werden; sich verbreitern; (fig.) sich erweitern; **her smile ~ed into a grin** ihr Lächeln verzog sich zu einem breiten Grinsen

broad: ~ jump *n.* (Amer. Sport) Weitsprung, *der;* **~leaf A** *adj.* ▸ **~leaved; B** *n.* breitblättriges Gewächs; (tree) Laubbaum *der;* **~leaved** *adj.* breitblättrig; Laub‹*baum, -wald*›

broadly /ˈbrɔːdlɪ/ *adv.* **1** deutlich ‹*hinweisen*›; breit ‹*grinsen, lächeln*› **2** (in general) allgemein ‹*beschreiben*›; **~ speaking** allgemein gesprochen; **~ based** auf breiter Grundlage *nachgestellt*

broad: ~-'minded *adj.* tolerant; **have very ~-minded views about sth.** sehr freie Ansichten über etw. (*Akk.*) haben; **~mindedness** /brɔːdˈmaɪndɪdnɪs/ *n., no pl.* Toleranz, *die*

broadness /ˈbrɔːdnɪs/ ▸ **breadth**

broad: ~sheet *n.* **1** (newpaper) großformatige Zeitung; **2** (pamphlet) Flugblatt, *das;* **~-'shouldered** *adj.* breitschultrig; **~side** *n.* **1** (Naut.; also fig.) Breitseite, *die;* **~side on [to sth.]** mit der Breitseite [nach etw.]; **fire [off] a ~side** (lit. or fig.) eine Breitseite abfeuern; **2** ▸ **~sheet2; ~-spectrum** *adj.* Breitspektrum- *od.* Breitband‹*antibiotikum, -präparat*›; mit Breitbandwirkung *nachgestellt;* **~sword** *n.* breites Schwert; Pallasch, *der;* **~way** *n.* Hauptstraße, *die;* **B~way** (Amer.) der Broadway

> **broadsheet**
>
> Ein Zeitung in Großbritannien, die auf großen Zeitungsbögen gedruckt wird, im Gegensatz zu den **tabloids**, der Boulevardpresse, die auf halb so großen Bögen hergestellt werden. Das *broadsheet*-Format wird normalerweise mit der *quality press* (seriösen Presse) assoziiert, mit Zeitungen wie z.B. **The Guardian, The Independent,** und **The Times,** während die meisten Zeitungen der *popular press* (Boulevardpresse), wie z.B. **The Mirror** und **The Sun** das *tabloid*-Format benutzen. **The Independent** bringt allerdings neben ihrer *broadsheet*-Ausgabe auch eine *tabloid*-Version heraus. Und *The Times*, von der es eine Zeit lang ebenfalls zwei Ausgaben gab, erscheint nur noch im *tabloid*-Format.

brocade /brəˈkeɪd/ *n.* Brokat, *der*

broccoli /ˈbrɒkəlɪ/ *n.* **1** (heading ~) Brokkoli, *der;* Spargelkohl, *der* **2** (sprouting ~) Schößlinge des Spargelkohls

brochure /ˈbrəʊʃə(r), brəʊˈʃʊə(r)/ *n.* Broschüre, *die;* Prospekt, *der*

broderie anglaise /ˈbrəʊdrɪ ɑ̃ˈgleɪz/ *n., no pl.* Lochstickerei, *die*

brogue[1] /brəʊg/ *n.* (decorated outdoor shoe) Budapester, *der*

brogue[2] *n.* (accent) irischer Akzent

broil /brɔɪl/ *v.t.* braten; (on gridiron) grillen; **~ing sun** (fig.) brennende Sonne

broiler /ˈbrɔɪlə(r)/ *n.* **1** (chicken) Brathähnchen, *das;* [Gold]broiler, *der* (DDR) **2** (utensil) Grill, *der;* Bratrost, *der*

'broiler house *n.* Hähnchenmästerei, *die*

broke /brəʊk/

A ▸ **break A, B**

B *pred. adj.* (coll.) pleite (ugs.); **go ~:** pleite gehen; **go for ~** (coll.) alles auf eine Karte setzen; alles riskieren

broken /ˈbrəʊkn/

A ▸ **break A, B**

B *adj.* **1** zerbrochen; gebrochen ‹*Bein, Hals*›; verletzt ‹*Haut*›; abgebrochen ‹*Zahn*›; gerissen ‹*Seil*›; kaputt (ugs.) ‹*Uhr, Fernsehen, Fenster*›; **~ glass** Glasscherben; **get ~:** zerbrechen/brechen/reißen/kaputtgehen; **he got a ~ arm** er hat sich (*Dat.*) den Arm gebrochen **2** (uneven) uneben ‹*Fläche*›; bewegt ‹*See, Wasser*› **3** (imperfect) gebrochen; **in ~ English** in gebrochenem Englisch **4** (fig.) ruiniert ‹*Ehe*›; gebrochen ‹*Person, Herz, Stimme*›; unruhig, gestört ‹*Schlaf*›; **come from a ~ home** aus zerrütteten Familienverhältnissen kommen; **in a ~ voice** mit gebrochener Stimme

broken: ~-down *adj.* baufällig ‹*Gebäude*›; kaputt (ugs.) ‹*Wagen, Maschine*›; **~-hearted** /brəʊknˈhɑːtɪd/ *adj.* untröstlich; **~ 'line** *n.* gestrichelte Linie

brokenly /ˈbrəʊknlɪ/ *adv.* gebrochen

broker /ˈbrəʊkə(r)/ *n.* ▸**i** **p. 1260** **1** (Commerc.: middleman) Händler, *der;* Kommissionär, *der;* (of real estate) [Immobilien]makler, *der;* (stock~) [Börsen]makler, *der* **2** ▸ **pawn~** **3** (intermediary) Vermittler, *der;* Unterhändler, *der; see also* **honest 1**

brokerage /ˈbrəʊkərɪdʒ/ *n.* (Commerc.) **1** *no pl.* (activity) Vermittlung, *die* **2** *no pl.* (commission) Vermittlungsgebühr, *die* **3** (firm) Vermittlungsfirma, *die*

brolly /ˈbrɒlɪ/ *n.* (Brit. coll.) [Regen]schirm, *der*

bromide /ˈbrəʊmaɪd/ *n.* **1** (Chem.) Bromsalz, *das* **2** (fig.) (person) Langweiler, *der;* (remark) [Allgemeinplatz, *der;* Plattitüde, *die* (abwertend)

bromine /ˈbrəʊmiːn/ *n.* (Chem.) Brom, *das*

bronchial /ˈbrɒŋkɪəl/ *adj.* ▸**i** **p. 1231** (Anat., Med.) bronchial; Bronchial-; **~ tubes** Bronchien; **~ pneumonia** Bronchopneumonie, *die*

bronchitis /brɒŋˈkaɪtɪs/ *n., no pl.* ▸**i** **p. 1231** (Med.) Bronchitis, *die*

bronco /ˈbrɒŋkəʊ/ *n., pl.* **~s** **1** *wildes od. halbwildes Pferd im Westen der USA* **2** (any horse) Gaul, *der* (ugs.)

brontosaurus /brɒntəˈsɔːrəs/ *n.* Brontosaurus, *der*

Bronx cheer /brɒŋks ˈtʃɪə(r)/ *n.* (Amer.) verächtliches Prusten; **give sb./sth the ~:** jmdn./etw. verächtlich anprusten

bronze /brɒnz/

A *n.* **1** Bronze, *die;* **the B~ Age** die Bronzezeit; **a statuette in ~:** eine Bronzestatuette **2** (colour) Bronze[farbe], *die* **3** (work of art) Bronze, *die* **4** (medal) Bronze, *die*

B *attrib. adj.* Bronze-; (coloured like ~) bronzefarben; bronzen; **~ medal** Bronzemedaille, *die*

C *v.t.* bräunen ‹*Gesicht, Haut*›

D *v.i.* braun werden

bronzed /brɒnzd/ *adj.* [sonnen]gebräunt; braun [gebrannt]

brooch /brəʊtʃ/ *n.* Brosche, *die*

brood /bruːd/

A *n.* **1** Brut, *die;* (of hen) Küken *Pl.;* Küchlein *Pl.* (veralt.) **2** (joc./derog.: human family) Sippe, *die;* Sippschaft, *die;* (children only) Brut, *die*

B *v.i.* **1** (think) [vor sich (*Akk.*) hin] brüten; **~ over** *or* **upon sth.** über etw. (*Akk.*) [nach]grübeln; über etw. (*Dat.*) brüten **2** (sit) ‹*Vogel:*› brüten **3** (fig.: hang close) **thunder clouds ~ed over the valley** Gewitterwolken hingen über dem Tal

'brood mare *n.* Zuchtstute, *die*

broody /ˈbruːdɪ/ *adj.* **1** brütig; **~ hen** Glucke, *die* **2** (fig. coll.) **she is getting** *or* **feeling ~:** in ihr werden Muttergefühle wach **3** (fig.: depressed) grüblerisch; schwermütig

brook[1] /brʊk/ *n.* Bach, *der*

brook[2] *v.t.* dulden; **~ no nonsense/delay** keinen Unfug/Aufschub dulden

broom /bruːm/ *n.* **1** Besen, *der;* **a new ~** (fig.) ein neuer Besen; **a new ~ sweeps clean** (prov.) neue Besen kehren gut **2** (Bot.) (Genista) Ginster, *der;* (Cytisus scoparius) Besenginster, *der*

broom: ~ cupboard *n.* Besenschrank, *der;* **~stick** *n.* Besenstiel, *der*

Bros. *abbr.* **= Brothers** Gebr.

broth /brɒθ/ *n.* **1** (unclarified stock) Brühe, *die* **2** (thin soup) Bouillon, *die;* [Fleisch]brühe, *die*

brothel /ˈbrɒθl/ *n.* Bordell, *das*

brother /ˈbrʌðə(r)/ *n.* **1** Bruder, *der;* **they are ~ and sister** sie sind Geschwister *od.* Bruder und Schwester; **the ~s Robinson** *or* **Robinson ~s** die Brüder Robinson; **the Marx B~s** die Marx Brothers **2** (friend, associate, fellow member) Bruder, *der;* (in trade union) Kollege, *der;* **oh ~!** (coll.) Junge, Junge!; **be ~s in arms** Kameraden sein; *attrib.* **his ~ doctors/officers** seine Ärztekollegen/Offizierskameraden **3** *pl.* (Commerc.) **Hedges B~s** Gebrüder Hedges **4** *pl.* **brethren** /ˈbreðrɪn/ (Eccl.) Bruder, *der*

brotherhood /ˈbrʌðəhʊd/ *n.* **1** *no pl.* Brüderschaft, *die;* brüderliches Verhältnis; **the ~ of all men** (fig.) die Gemeinschaft aller Menschen **2** (association) Bruderschaft, *die;* (Amer.: trade union) Gewerkschaft, *die*

'brother-in-law *n., pl.* **brothers-in-law** Schwager, *der*

brotherly /ˈbrʌðəlɪ/ *adj.* brüderlich; **~ love** Bruderliebe, *die*

brought ▸ **bring**

brouhaha /ˈbruːhɑːhɑː/ *n.* (coll.) (noise) Spektakel, *der* (ugs.); (fuss) Getue, *das*

brow /braʊ/ *n.* **1** (eye~) Braue, *die* **2** (forehead) Stirn, *die* **3** (of hill) [Berg]kuppe, *die*

'browbeat *v.t., forms as* **beat A** unter Druck setzen; einschüchtern; **~ sb. into doing sth.** jmdn. so unter Druck setzen, dass er etw. tut; **I refuse to be ~en** ich lasse mich nicht unter Druck setzen

brown /braʊn/

A *adj.* braun; **as ~ as berries/a berry** schokoladenbraun

B *n.* **1** Braun, *das* **2** (Snooker) braune Kugel **3** (~ clothes) **dressed in ~:** braun gekleidet

C *v.t.* **1** bräunen ‹*Haut, Körper*› **2** (Cookery) [an]bräunen; anbraten ‹*Fleisch*› **3** (Brit. coll.) **be ~ed off with sth./sb.** etw./jmdn. satt haben (ugs.); **be ~ed off with doing sth.** es satt haben, etw. zu tun (ugs.)

D *v.i.* **1** ‹*Haut:*› bräunen; **I don't ~ easily** ich werde nicht leicht braun **2** (Cookery) ‹*Fleisch:*› braun werden

brown: ~ 'ale *n.* dunkles Bier; **~ 'bear** *n.* Braunbär, *der;* **~ 'bread** *n.* ≈ Mischbrot, *das;* (made with wholemeal flour) Vollkornbrot, *das;* **~ 'coal** *n.* Braunkohle, *die;* **~ 'dwarf** *n.* (Astron.) brauner Zwerg; **~-eyed** *adj.* braunäugig; **be ~-eyed** braune Augen haben

'brownfield site *n.* Industriebrache, *die*

'brown goods *n. pl.* braune Ware

brownie /ˈbraʊnɪ/ *n.* **1** **the B~s** die Wichtel (Pfadfinderinnen von 7-11 Jahren); **get ~ points** (fig. coll.) Pluspunkte sammeln **2** (elf) Heinzelmännchen, *das;* Kobold, *der;* Wichtel, *der* **3** (Amer.: cake) *kleiner Schokoladenkuchen, oft mit Nüssen*

browning /ˈbraʊnɪŋ/ *n.* (Cookery) (sugar) brauner Zucker; (flour) braunes Mehl

brownish /ˈbraʊnɪʃ/ *adj.* bräunlich

brown: ~-nose *v.i.* (coll.) hinten reinkriechen (derb); **~ 'paper** *n.* Packpapier, *das;* **~ 'rice** *n.* Naturreis, *der;* **B~shirt** *n.* (Hist.) Braunhemd, *das;* **~stone** *n.* (Amer.) **1** rotbrauner Sandstein; **2** (house) Sandsteinhaus, *das;* **~ 'study** *n.* **be in a ~ study** geistesabwesend *od.* in Gedanken verloren sein; **~ 'sugar** *n.* brauner Zucker

browse /braʊz/

A *v.t.* **1** abgrasen ‹*Weide*›; abfressen ‹*Blätter*› **2** (Computing) **~ sth** in etw. (*Dat.*) suchen

B *v.i.* **1** ‹*Vieh:*› weiden; ‹*Wild:*› äsen; **~ on sth.** etw. fressen **2** (fig.) **~ through a book/a magazine** in einem Buch schmökern/in einer Zeitschrift blättern; **I'm just browsing** (in shop) ich sehe mich nur mal um. **3** (Computing) suchen; **~ through sth.** etw. durchsuchen

C *n.* (fig.) **have a ~:** sich umsehen; **it's worth a ~:** es ist das Reinschauen wert

browser /ˈbraʊzə(r)/ *n.* (Computing) Browser, *der*

Bruges /bruːʒ/ *pr. n.* ▸**i** **p. 1643** Brügge (*das*)

bruise /bruːz/

A *n.* **1** (Med.) blauer Fleck **2** (on fruit) Druckstelle, *die*

B *v.t.* **1** quetschen ‹*Obst, Pflanzen*›; **~ oneself/one's leg** sich stoßen/sich am Bein stoßen; **he was badly ~d when he fell off his bike** er hat sich (*Dat.*) starke Prellungen zugezogen, als er vom Rad fiel; **the peaches are**

~d/easily ~d die Pfirsiche haben Druckstellen/bekommen leicht Druckstellen **2** (fig.) mitnehmen
C *v.i.* ‹*Person:*› blaue Flecken bekommen; ‹*Obst:*› Druckstellen bekommen

bruiser /ˈbruːzə(r)/ *n.* (coll.) Schläger, *der* (abwertend)

brunch /brʌntʃ/ *n.* (coll.) Brunch, *der;* ausgedehntes, spätes Frühstück

brunette /bruːˈnet/
A *n.* Brünette, *die*
B *adj.* brünett

Brunswick /ˈbrʌnzwɪk/ ▸**i** **p. 1643**
A *pr. n.* Braunschweig (*das*)
B *attrib. adj.* Braunschweiger

brunt /brʌnt/ *n.* Hauptlast, *die;* **the main** *or* **full ~ of the attack fell on the French** die Franzosen waren der vollen Wucht des Angriffs ausgesetzt; **the ~ of the financial cuts** die Hauptlast der Einsparungen; **bear the ~:** das meiste abkriegen

brush /brʌʃ/
A *n.* **1** Bürste, *die;* (for sweeping) Hand-, Kehrbesen, *der;* (with short handle) Handfeger, *der;* (for scrubbing) [Scheuer]bürste, *die;* (for painting or writing) Pinsel, *der;* **flat ~:** Flachpinsel, *der* **2** (quarrel, skirmish) Zusammenstoß, *der;* **his first ~ with the law came at an early age** er kam schon früh mit dem Gesetz in Konflikt **3** (light touch) flüchtige Berührung **4** (tail) (of squirrel) Rute, *die;* (of fox) Lunte, *die* **5** **give your hair/teeth a ~:** bürste dir die Haare/putz dir die Zähne; **give your shoes/clothes a ~:** bürste deine Schuhe/Kleider ab **6** (Amer., Austral.: undergrowth) Unterholz, *das* **7** (land covered with undergrowth) Buschland, *das*
B *v.t.* **1** (sweep) kehren; fegen; abbürsten ‹*Kleidung*›; **~ one's teeth/hair** sich (*Dat.*) die Zähne putzen/die Haare bürsten; **~ the dust from one's coat/the shelf** den Staub vom Mantel bürsten/vom Regal wischen **2** (treat) bepinseln, bestreichen ‹*Teigwaren, Gebäck*›; **~ed aluminium/fabric** aufgerautes Aluminium/aufgerauter Stoff **3** (touch in passing) flüchtig berühren; streifen; **~ one's hand over one's hair/brow** sich (*Dat.*) mit der Hand über das Haar/die Stirn fahren
C *v.i.* **~ by** *or* **against** *or* **past sb./sth.** jmdn./etw. streifen

(Phrasal verbs)
- **~ aˈside** *v.t.* beiseite schieben ‹*Personen, Hindernis*›; abtun, vom Tisch wischen ‹*Einwand, Zweifel, Beschwerde*›
- **~ aˈway** *v.t.* abwischen, wegwischen ‹*Staub, Schmutz*›; verscheuchen ‹*Insekt*›
- **~ ˈdown** *v.t.* abbürsten ‹*Kleidungsstück*›; **~ oneself down** sich abbürsten; (with hand) sich abklopfen
- **~ ˈoff** *v.t.* **1** abbürsten ‹*Schmutz usw.*›; (with hand or cloth) abwischen; wegwischen; verscheuchen ‹*Insekt*› **2** (fig.: rebuff) abblitzen lassen (ugs.); **she ~ed me off** sie gab mir einen Korb; *see also* **brush-off**
- **~ ˈup**

A *v.t.* **1** zusammenfegen ‹*Krümel*› **2** auffrischen ‹*Sprache, Kenntnisse*›
B *v.i.* **~ up on** auffrischen. *See also* **brush-up**

ˈbrushfire *n.* Buschfeuer, *das.*

brushless /ˈbrʌʃlɪs/ *adj.* schaumlos ‹*Rasiercreme*›

brush: ~-off *n.* Abfuhr, *die;* **give sb. the ~-off** jmdm. einen Korb geben (ugs.); jmdn. abblitzen lassen (ugs.); **~ stroke** *n.* Pinselstrich, *der;* **~-up** *n.* **1** **I'll have to give my English a ~-up** ich muss meine Englischkenntnisse auffrischen; **2** **have a wash and ~-up** sich frisch machen; **~wood** *n.* **1** Reisig, *das;* **2** (thicket) Dickicht, *das;* Unterholz, *das;* **~work** *n.* Pinselführung, *die*

brusque /brʊsk, brʌsk/ *adj.*, **brusquely** /ˈbrʊsklɪ, ˈbrʌsklɪ/ *adv.* schroff

brusqueness /ˈbrʊsknɪs, ˈbrʌsknɪs/ *n., no pl.* Schroffheit, *die*

Brussels /ˈbrʌslz/ *pr. n.* ▸**i** **p. 1643** Brüssel (*das*)

Brussels: ~ ˈcarpet *n.* Brüsseler Teppich; **~ ˈlace** *n.* Brüsseler Spitze[n]; **~ ˈsprouts** *n. pl.* Rosenkohl, *der;* Kohlsprossen (österr.)

brutal /ˈbruːtl/ *adj.* brutal; (fig.) brutal, schonungslos ‹*Offenheit*›; bitter ‹*Wahrheit*›

brutalism /ˈbruːtəlɪzm/ *n., no pl.* **1** Brutalität, *die* **2** (Art, Archit.) Brutalismus, *der*

brutality /bruːˈtælɪtɪ/ *n.* Brutalität, *die*

brutalization /bruːtəlaɪˈzeɪʃn/ *n.* (treating brutally) brutale Behandlung; (becoming brutalized) Verrohung, *die*

brutalize /ˈbruːtəlaɪz/
A *v.t.* **1** verrohen lassen; brutalisieren **2** (treat brutally) brutal behandeln
B *v.i.* verrohen

brutally /ˈbruːtəlɪ/ *adv.* brutal; **be ~ frank with sb.** (fig.) mit jmdm. schonungslos offen sein

brute /bruːt/
A *n.* **1** (animal) Bestie, *die* **2** (brutal person) Rohling, *der;* brutaler Kerl (ugs.); (thing) höllische Sache; **a ~ of a problem** (fig.) ein höllisches Problem; **a drunken ~:** ein brutaler Trunkenbold; **an unfeeling ~ of a man** eine gefühllose Bestie;
B *attrib. adj.* (without capacity to reason) vernunftlos; irrational; (merely material) roh ‹*Gewalt*›; nackt ‹*Tatsachen*›; bitter ‹*Notwendigkeit*›; **by ~ force** mit roher Gewalt

brutish /ˈbruːtɪʃ/ *adj.* brutal ‹*Flegel*›; tierisch ‹*Leidenschaften, Gelüste*›; **lead a ~ existence** das Leben eines Tieres führen

bryony /ˈbraɪənɪ/ *n.* (Bot.) Zaunrübe, *die*

BS *abbr.* **1** **= British Standard** Britische Norm **2** **= Bachelor of Surgery** „Bachelor" der Chirurgie; *see also* **BSc** **3** (Amer.) **= Bachelor of Science;** *see also* **BSc**

BSc /biːesˈsiː/ *abbr.* **= Bachelor of Science** Bakkalaureus der Naturwissenschaften; **John Clarke ~:** John Clarke, Bakkalaureus der Naturwissenschaften; **he is a** *or* **has a ~** ≈ er hat ein Diplom in Naturwissenschaften; **[study for] one's** *or* **a ~ in physics/chemistry** ≈ ein Diplom in Physik/Chemie [machen wollen]

BSE *abbr.* **= bovine spongiform encephalopathy** BSE

BSI *abbr.* **= British Standards Institution** Britischer Normenausschuss

BST *abbr.* **= British Summer Time** Britische Sommerzeit

Bt. *abbr.* **= baronet**

bubble /ˈbʌbl/
A *n.* **1** Blase, *die;* (small) Perle, *die;* (fig.) Seifenblase, *die;* **blow ~s** [Seifen]blasen machen; **the/his ~ has burst** (fig.) alles ist wie eine Seifenblase zerplatzt **2** (domed canopy) [Glas-]kuppel, *die*
B *v.i.* **1** (form ~s) ‹*Wasser, Schlamm, Lava:*› Blasen bilden; ‹*Suppe, Flüssigkeiten:*› brodeln; (make sound of ~s) ‹*Bach, Quelle:*› plätschern; ‹*Schlamm:*› blubbern **2** (fig.) **~ with sth.** vor etw. (*Dat.*) übersprudeln

(Phrasal verbs)
- **~ ˈover** *v.i.* überschäumen; **~ over with excitement/laughter/joy** (fig.) vor Aufregung/Lachen übersprudeln/vor Freude überquellen
- **~ ˈup** *v.i.* ‹*Gas:*› in Blasen aufsteigen; ‹*Wasser:*› aufsprudeln

bubble: ~ and ˈsqueak *n.* Pfannengericht aus Gemüse und Kartoffeln [mit Fleischresten]; **~ bath** *n.* Schaumbad, *das;* **~ car** *n.* Kabinenroller, *der;* **~ gum** *n.* Bubble-Gum, *der;* Ballonkaugummi, *der;* **~-jet ˈprinter** *n.* Bubble-Jet-Drucker, *der;* **~ pack** *n.* Klarsichtpackung, *die;* **~-wrapped** *adj.* in Luftpolsterfolie verpackt

bubbly /ˈbʌblɪ/
A *adj.* **1** sprudelnd; schäumend ‹*Bade-, Spülwasser*› **2** (fig. coll.) quirlig (ugs.) ‹*Person*›
B *n.* (Brit. coll.) Schampus, *der* (ugs.)

bubonic plague /bjuːbɒnɪk ˈpleɪg/ *n.* ▸**i** **p. 1231** (Med.) Beulenpest, *die*

buccaneer /bʌkəˈnɪə(r)/ *n.* Seeräuber, *der;* Freibeuter, *der* (auch fig.)

Bucharest /bjuːkəˈrest/ *pr. n.* ▸**i** **p. 1643** Bukarest (*das*)

buck[1] /bʌk/
A *n.* **1** (male) männliches Tier; Männchen, *das;* (deer, chamois) Bock, *der;* (rabbit, hare) Rammler, *der* **2** (arch.: dandy) Geck, *der* (abwertend); Stutzer, *der* (abwertend) **3** *attrib.* **~ private** (Amer. Mil. sl.) Schütze Arsch (derb)
B *v.i.* ‹*Pferd:*› bocken
C *v.t.* **1** **~ [off]** ‹*Pferd:*› abwerfen **2** (resist) sich widersetzen (+ *Dat.*)

buck[2] *n.* (coll.) **pass the ~ to sb.** (fig.) jmdm. den Schwarzen Peter zuschieben; jmdm. die Verantwortung aufhalsen; **the ~ stops here** (fig.) die Verantwortung liegt letzten Endes bei mir

buck[3] (coll.)
A *v.i.* **~ ˈup** **1** (make haste) sich ranhalten (ugs.); **~ up!** los, schnell!; auf, los! **2** (cheer up) ein fröhliches Gesicht machen; **~ up!** Kopf hoch!
B *v.t.* **~ ˈup** **1** (cheer up) aufmuntern; **we were ~ed up by the good news** die gute Nachricht hat uns aufgemuntert **2** **~ one's ideas up** (coll.) sich zusammenreißen

buck[4] *n.* ▸**i** **p. 1332** (Amer. and Austral. coll.: dollar) Dollar, *der;* **make a fast ~:** einen schnellen Euro machen (ugs.)

bucked /bʌkt/ *adj.* (coll.) aufgemuntert; **I was** *or* **felt ~ by it** es hat mich aufgemuntert

bucket /ˈbʌkɪt/
A *n.* **1** Eimer, *der;* **a ~ of water** ein Eimer [voll] Wasser; **the rain fell in ~s** (fig.) es goss wie aus Kübeln (ugs.); es schüttete (ugs.); **kick the ~** (fig. coll.) abkratzen (derb); ins Gras beißen (salopp) **2** (of waterwheel) Schaufelkammer, *die*
B *v.i.* **1** (pour down) **the rain is ~ing down** es gießt wie aus Kübeln (ugs.); es schüttet (ugs.) **2** (move jerkily) ‹*Fahrzeug:*› holpern; ‹*Boot:*› schaukeln

bucketful /ˈbʌkɪtfʊl/ *n.* Eimer [voll]; **two ~s of water** zwei Eimer [voll] Wasser

bucket: ~ seat *n.* Schalensitz, *der;* **~ shop** *n.* [nicht ganz seriöses] Maklerbüro; (for air tickets) Reisebüro (*das vor allem Billigflüge vermittelt*)

buckle /ˈbʌkl/
A *n.* Schnalle, *die*
B *v.t.* **1** zuschnallen; **~ sth. on** etw. anschnallen; **~ sth. up** etw. festschnallen *od.* zuschnallen **2** (crumple) verbiegen ‹*Stoßstange, Rad*›
C *v.i.* ‹*Rad, Metallplatte:*› sich verbiegen; **~ under the weight** unter dem Gewicht nachgeben

(Phrasal verb)
- **~ to**

A /ˈ---/ *v.t.* **~ [down] to a task/to work** sich hinter eine Aufgabe klemmen/sich an die Arbeit machen
B /--ˈ-/ *v.i.* sich zusammenreißen (ugs.); sich am Riemen reißen (ugs.)

buckler /ˈbʌklə(r)/ *n.* (Hist.) Rundschild, *der*

buckram /ˈbʌkrəm/ *n.* (Textiles) Buckram, *der*

buck ˈrarebit *n. überbackene Käseschnitte mit pochiertem Ei*

Buck's Fizz /bʌks ˈfɪz/ *n.* Sekt mit Orangensaft

buckshee /ˈbʌkʃiː/ (Brit. coll.)
A *adj.* Gratis-; **a ~ trip** eine Reise zum Nulltarif; eine Gratisreise
B *adv.* gratis, umsonst ‹*bekommen, reisen*›; zum Nulltarif ‹*reisen*›

buck: ~shot *n.* grober Schrot; Rehposten, *der;* **~thorn** *n.* (Bot.) Kreuzdorn, *der;* **~ tooth** *n.* vorstehender Zahn; Raffzahn, *der* (ugs.); **~wheat** *n.* (Agric.) Buchweizen, *der*

bucolic /bjuːˈkɒlɪk/ *adj.* bukolisch

bud /bʌd/
A *n.* Knospe, *die;* **come into ~/be in ~:** knospen; Knospen treiben; **the trees are in ~:** die Bäume schlagen aus; **nip sth. in the ~** (fig.) etw. im Keim ersticken
B *v.i.*, **-dd-** knospen; Knospen treiben; ‹*Baum:*› ausschlagen; **a ~ding painter/actor** (fig.) ein angehender Maler/Schauspieler

Buddha /ˈbʊdə/ *n.* Buddha, *der*

Buddhism /ˈbʊdɪzm/ *n., no pl.* Buddhismus, *der*

Buddhist /ˈbʊdɪst/
A *n.* Buddhist, *der*/Buddhistin, *die*
B *adj.* buddhistisch

buddleia /ˈbʌdlɪə/ *n.* (Bot.) Schmetterlingsstrauch, *der;* Buddleia, *die* (fachspr.)

buddy /ˈbʌdɪ/ (coll.)
A n. Kumpel, *der* (ugs.)
B v.i. ~ **up [with sb.]** sich [mit jmdm.] anfreunden

buddy: ~ **movie** n. (Amer. coll.) Kumpelfilm, *der;* ~ **system** n. (Amer. coll.) Buddysystem, *das*

budge /bʌdʒ/
A v.i. ‹Person, Tier:› sich [von der Stelle] rühren; ‹Gegenstand:› sich bewegen, nachgeben; (fig.: change opinion) nachgeben
B v.t. 1 bewegen; **I can't ~ this screw** ich kriege diese Schraube nicht los 2 (fig.: change opinion) abbringen; **he refuses to be ~d** er lässt sich nicht umstimmen

budgerigar /ˈbʌdʒərɪgɑ:(r)/ n. Wellensittich, *der*

budget /ˈbʌdʒɪt/
A n. Budget, *das;* Etat, *der;* Haushalt[splan], *der;* **keep within ~:** seinen Etat nicht überschreiten; **be on a ~:** haushalten *od.* wirtschaften müssen; *attrib.* ~ **meal/holiday** preisgünstige Mahlzeit/Ferien
B v.i. planen; ~ **for sth.** etw. [im Etat] einplanen
C v.t. [im Etat] einplanen

ˈbudget: ~ **account** n. Konto für laufende Zahlungen; ~ **airline** n. Billigfluglinie, *die*

budgetary /ˈbʌdʒɪtərɪ/ adj. budgetär; Budget‹beratung, -betrag, -entwurf, -vorlage›

ˈbudget: ~ **day** n. Haushaltsdebattentermin, *der;* ~ **speech** n. Etatrede, *die*

budgie /ˈbʌdʒɪ/ n. (coll.) Wellensittich, *der*

budo /ˈbu:dəʊ/ n. Budo, *das*

buff /bʌf/
A adj. gelbbraun
B n. 1 (coll.: enthusiast) Fan, *der* (ugs.) 2 **in the ~:** nackt; im Adams-/Evaskostüm (scherzh.); **strip down to the ~:** sich bis auf die Haut ausziehen 3 (colour) Gelbbraun, *das*
C v.t. 1 (polish) polieren, [blank] putzen ‹Metall, Schuhe usw.› 2 aufrauen ‹Leder›

buffalo /ˈbʌfələʊ/ n., pl. ~**es** *or same* (Zool.) Büffel, *der*

buffer[1] /ˈbʌfə(r)/
A n. 1 (Railw.) Prellbock, *der;* (on vehicle; also Chem., fig.) Puffer, *der* 2 (Computing) Pufferspeicher, *der*
B v.t. dämpfen

buffer[2] n. (Brit. coll.) **old ~:** alter Zausel (ugs.)

buffer: ~ **state** n. Pufferstaat, *der;* ~ **store** n. (Computing) Pufferspeicher, *der;* ~ **zone** n. Pufferzone, *die*

buffet[1] /ˈbʌfɪt/
A n. (blow, lit. or fig.) Schlag, *der;* ~**s of fate** Schicksalsschläge
B v.t. schlagen; ~**ed by the wind/waves** vom Wind geschüttelt/von den Wellen hin und her geworfen

buffet[2] /ˈbʊfeɪ/ n. 1 (Brit.: place) Büfett, *das;* ~ **car** (Railw.) Büfettwagen, *der* 2 (Brit.: meal) Imbiss, *der;* **a cold ~:** ein kaltes Büfett; *attrib.* ~ **lunch/supper/meal** Büfettessen, *das* 3 (cupboard) Büfett, *das;* Geschirrschrank, *der;* (sideboard) Anrichte, *die*

buffeting /ˈbʌfɪtɪŋ/ n. Schütteln, *das;* (fig.) Schläge; ~**s of fate** Schicksalsschläge

buffoon /bəˈfu:n/
A n. Kasper, *der;* Clown, *der*
B v.i. den Clown *od.* Kasper spielen

buffoonery /bəˈfu:nərɪ/ n. Clownerie, *die;* Possenreißerei, *die*

bug /bʌg/
A n. 1 Wanze, *die* 2 (esp. Amer.: small insect) Insekt, *das;* Käfer, *der* 3 (coll.: virus) Bazillus, *der;* **don't you breathe your ~s over me** steck mich nicht an 4 (coll.: disease) Infektion, *die;* Krankheit, *die;* **catch a ~:** sich (*Dat.*) eine Krankheit *od.* (ugs.) was holen; **I don't want to catch that ~ of yours** ich will mich nicht bei dir anstecken 5 (coll.: concealed microphone) Wanze, *die* (ugs.) 6 (coll.: defect) Macke, *die* (salopp); **we have got all the ~s out of the system** wir haben alle Fehler im System beseitigt 7 (coll.: obsession) Tick, *der* (ugs.); **he has a ~ about neatness** er hat einen Ordnungsfimmel (ugs.); **then I got the ~:** dann packte es mich 8 (coll.: enthusiast) Fan, *der* (ugs.)
B v.t., **-gg-:** 1 (coll.: install microphone in) verwanzen ‹Zimmer› (ugs.); abhören ‹Telefon, Konferenz›; ~**ging device** Abhöreinrichtung, *die;* Wanze, *die* (ugs.) 2 (coll.) (annoy) nerven (salopp); den Nerv töten (+ *Dat.*) (ugs.); (bother) beunruhigen; **what's ~ging you?** was ist los mit dir?

bugbear /ˈbʌgbeə(r)/ n. 1 (annoyance, problem) Problem, *das;* Sorge, *die* 2 (object of fear) Schreckgespenst, *das*

bugger /ˈbʌgə(r)/
A n. 1 (sodomite) Analverkehr Ausübender; Sodomit, *der* 2 (coarse) (fellow) Bursche, *der* (ugs.); Macker, *der* (salopp); *as insult* Scheißkerl, *der* (derb); Arschloch, *das* (salopp); **you lucky ~:** du hast vielleicht ein Schwein *od.* Dusel (ugs.); **you poor ~:** du kannst einem Leid tun; **play silly ~s** Scheiß machen (derb) 3 (coarse: thing) Scheißding, *das* (derb); **that door is a ~ to open** diese Scheißtür geht immer so schwer auf (derb) 4 (coarse: damn) **~!** Scheiße! (derb); **I don't give a ~ what you think** ich gebe einen Scheiß drauf, was du denkst (derb)
B v.t. 1 anal verkehren mit 2 (coarse: damn) ~ **you/him** (dismissive) du kannst/der kann mich mal (derb); ~ **this car/him!** (angry) dieses Scheißauto/dieser Scheißkerl! (derb); ~ **it!** ach du Scheiße (derb); (in surprise) **well, ~ me** *or* **I'll be ~ed!** ach du Scheiße *od.* meine Fresse! (derb) 3 (coarse: tire) **be [completely] ~ed** [total] fertig sein (ugs.)

Phrasal verbs
- ~ **aˈbout,** ~ **aˈround** (coarse)
A v.i. Scheiß machen (derb); rumblödeln (ugs.); ~ **about with sth.** mit etw. rumfummeln (ugs.)
B v.t. verarschen (derb)
- ~ **ˈoff** v.i. (coarse) abhauen (ugs.); ~ **off!** hau ab! (ugs.); verdufte! (ugs.); verpiss dich! (salopp)
- ~ **ˈup** v.t. (coarse) verkorksen (ugs.)

bugger-ˈall n. (coarse) rein gar nichts; Null Komma nichts; **be worth ~:** keinen Pfifferling wert sein (ugs.); zum Wischen sein (salopp)

buggery /ˈbʌgərɪ/ n., no pl. Analverkehr, *der*

Buggins's turn /ˈbʌgɪnzɪz tɜ:n/ n. (Brit.) Ernennung aufgrund von Dienstjahren

buggy /ˈbʌgɪ/ n. 1 (horse-drawn or motor vehicle) Buggy, *der* 2 (pushchair) Sportwagen, *der* 3 (Amer.) ▸ **baby buggy**

bugle[-horn] /ˈbju:gl(hɔ:n)/ n. Bügelhorn, *das*

bugler /ˈbju:glə(r)/ n. Hornist, *der*

build /bɪld/
A v.t., **built** /bɪlt/ 1 bauen; errichten ‹Gebäude, Damm›; mauern ‹Schornstein, Kamin›; zusammenbauen *od.* -setzen ‹Fahrzeug›; **the house is still being built** das Haus ist noch im Bau; **the house took three years to ~:** der Bau des Hauses dauerte drei Jahre; **he was the man who built the bridge** er war der Erbauer der Brücke; **the house is solidly built** das Haus ist sehr solide; ~ **a fire** [ein] Feuer machen; ~ **sth. from** *or* **out of sth.** etw. aus etw. machen *od.* bauen; **the dinghy was built from a kit** das Dingi entstand aus einem Bausatz; **be sturdily/strongly built** (fig.) ‹Sache:› solide gebaut sein; ‹Person:› stämmig/kräftig gebaut sein 2 (fig.) aufbauen ‹System, Gesellschaft, Reich, Zukunft›; schaffen ‹bessere Zukunft, Bedingungen, Beziehung›; begründen ‹Ruf›; ~ **one's hopes upon sb./sth.** seine Hoffnungen auf jmdn./etw. setzen; ~ **a new career for oneself** sich (*Dat.*) eine neue Existenz aufbauen
B v.i., **built** 1 bauen 2 (fig.) ‹Drama, Musik:› sich steigern (**to** zu); ~ **on one's successes** auf seinen Erfolgen aufbauen
C n. Bauweise, *die;* (of person) Körperbau, *der*

Phrasal verbs
- ~ **ˈin** v.t. einbauen; *see also* **built-in**
- ~ **into** v.t. ~ **sth. into sth.** (to form part) etw. in etw. (*Akk.*) einbauen; (fig.) ~ **a clause into a contract** eine Klausel in einen Vertrag aufnehmen
- ~ **on** v.t. 1 aufbauen auf (+ *Dat.*); bebauen ‹Gelände› 2 (attach) ~ **sth. on to sth.** etw. an etw. (*Akk.*) anbauen
- ~ **ˈup**
A v.t. 1 bebauen ‹Land, Gebiet› 2 (accumulate) aufhäufen ‹Reserven, Mittel, Kapital›; ~ **up a reputation** sich (*Dat.*) einen Namen machen; ~ **up a fine reputation as a speaker** sich (*Dat.*) einen ausgezeichneten Ruf als Redner erwerben 3 (strengthen) stärken ‹Gesundheit, Widerstandskraft›; widerstandsfähig machen, kräftigen ‹Person, Körper› 4 (increase) erhöhen, steigern ‹Produktion, Kapazität›; verstärken ‹Truppen›; stärken ‹[Selbst]vertrauen›; ~ **up sb.'s hopes [unduly]** jmdm. [falsche] Hoffnung machen 5 (develop) aufbauen ‹Firma, Geschäft›; (expand) ausbauen; ~ **sth. up from nothing** etw. aus dem Nichts aufbauen; ~ **up one's strength** sich kräftigen; ‹Athlet:› seine Muskelkraft trainieren 6 (praise, boost) aufbauen ‹Star, Schauspieler›; **the film was built up to be something marvellous** der Film wurde großartig herausgebracht *od.* angekündigt; **he wasn't half the performer he was built up to be** seine Vorstellung war nicht mal halb so gut wie angekündigt
B v.i. 1 ‹Spannung, Druck:› zunehmen, ansteigen; ‹Musik:› anschwellen; ‹Lärm:› sich steigern (**to** in + *Akk.*); ~ **up to a crescendo** sich zu einem Crescendo steigern 2 ‹Schlange, Rückstau:› sich bilden; ‹Verkehr:› sich verdichten, sich stauen. *See also* **build-up; built-up**

builder /ˈbɪldə(r)/ n. ▸❶ p. 1260 1 Erbauer, *der* 2 (contractor) Bauunternehmer, *der;* ~**'s labourer** Bauarbeiter, *der;* ~**'s merchant** (person) Baustoffhändler, *der;* (firm) Baustoffhandlung, *die*

building /ˈbɪldɪŋ/ n. 1 *no pl.* Bau, *der;* (of vehicle) Zusammenbauen/-setzen, *das;* ~ **commenced three years ago** mit dem Bau wurde vor drei Jahren begonnen; *attrib.* ~ **land** Bauland, *das;* ~ **materials** Baumaterialien; ~ **operations** Baumaßnahmen 2 (structure) Gebäude, *das;* (for living in) Haus, *das*

building: ~ **contractor** n. ▸❶ p. 1260 Bauunternehmer, *der;* ~ **industry** n., *no pl.* Bauindustrie, *die;* Baugewerbe, *das;* ~ **land** n., *no pl.* Bauland, *das;* ~ **line** n. (Archit.) Bauflucht[linie], *die;* ~ **site** n. Baustelle, *die;* ~ **society** n. (Brit.) Bausparkasse, *die;* ~ **trade** n. Baugewerbe, *das;* ~ **works** n. pl. 1 (construction of buildings) Bauarbeiten *Pl.;* 2 (buildings) Bauten *Pl.;* Bauwerke *Pl.*

ˈbuild quality n. Verarbeitungsqualität, *die;* **a car with superb ~:** ein Auto in erstklassiger Verarbeitung

ˈbuild-up n. 1 (publicity) Reklame[rummel], *der;* Werbung, *die;* **give sb./sth. a good ~:** jmdn./etw. groß ankündigen; **give a film a massive ~:** für einen Film kräftig die Werbetrommel rühren 2 (approach to climax) Vorbereitungen *Pl.* (**to** für) 3 (increase) Zunahme, *die;* (of forces) Verstärkung, *die;* **a ~ of traffic** ein [Verkehrs-]stau *od.* eine Stauung

built ▸ **build A, B**

built: ~ **enˈvironment** n. gebaute Umwelt; ~**-in** adj. 1 eingebaut; **a ~-in cupboard/bookcase/kitchen** ein Einbauschrank/-regal/eine Einbauküche; 2 (fig.: instinctive) angeboren; **the system has ~-in safeguards against accidents** (fig.) das System hat eine Art eingebauten Schutz gegen Unfälle; *see also* **obsolescence;** ~**-up** adj. 1 bebaut; **a ~-up area** ein Wohngebiet; **the speed limit applies in all ~-up areas** die Geschwindigkeitsbegrenzung gilt für alle geschlossenen Ortschaften; 2 (prefabricated) vorgefertigt; 3 ~**-up shoulders** [aus]wattierte *od.* gepolsterte Schultern; **a ~-up shoe** ein Schuh mit dickerer Sohle

bulb /bʌlb/ n. 1 (Bot., Hort.) Zwiebel, *die* 2 (of lamp) [Glüh]birne, *die* 3 (of thermometer, chemical apparatus) [Glas]kolben, *der* 4 (of syringe, dropper, horn) Gummiballon, *der*

bulbous /ˈbʌlbəs/ adj. 1 bauchig ‹Form›; bulbös, bulboid ‹Schwellung›; ~ **fingers/nose** Wurstfinger/Knollennase, *die* 2 (Bot.) Zwiebel-; zwiebelartig

Bulgaria /bʌlˈgeərɪə/ pr. n. Bulgarien (*das*)

Bulgarian /bʌlˈgeərɪən/ ▸❶ p. 1277, ▸❶ p. 1345
A adj. bulgarisch; **he/she is ~:** er ist Bulgare/sie ist Bulgarin; *see also* **English A**
B n. 1 (person) Bulgare, *der*/Bulgarin, *die* 2 (lan-

guage) Bulgarisch, *das; see also* **English B 1**

bulge /bʌldʒ/

A *n.* 1 Ausbeulung, *die;* ausgebeulte Stelle; (in line) Bogen, *der;* (in tyre) Wulst, *der od. die* 2 (coll.: increase) Anstieg, *der* (**in** *Gen.*) 3 (Mil.) Frontausbuchtung, *die*

B *v.i.* 1 (swell outwards) sich wölben; **her eyes ~d out of her head** (fig. coll.) die Augen traten ihr [fast] aus dem Kopf; sie bekam Stielaugen (ugs.) 2 (be full) voll gestopft sein (**with** mit)

bulging /ˈbʌldʒɪŋ/ *adj.* prall gefüllt ‹*Einkaufstasche usw.*›; voll gestopft ‹*Hosentasche, Kiste*›; rund ‹*Bauch*›; **~ eyes** hervortretende Augen; (in surprise) staunende Augen

bulimia (nervosa) /bʊˈliːmɪə(nɜːˈvəʊsə)/ *n., no pl.* Bulimie, *die;* Bulimia nervosa, *die* (fachspr.)

bulimic /bʊˈlɪmɪk/

A *n.* Bulimiker, *der*/Bulimikerin, *die*

B *adj.* bulimisch

bulk /bʌlk/

A *n.* 1 (large quantity) **in ~:** in großen Mengen 2 (large shape) massige Gestalt 3 (size) Größe, *die;* **be of great ~:** [sehr] massig sein 4 (volume) Menge, *die;* Umfang, *der;* **sea water is heavier, ~ for ~, than fresh water** Seewasser ist, Quantum für Quantum, schwerer als Süßwasser 5 (greater part) **the ~ of the money/goods** der Groß- *od.* Hauptteil des Geldes/der Waren; **the ~ of the population/votes** die Mehrheit der Bevölkerung/Stimmen 6 (Commerc.) **in ~** (loose) lose; unabgefüllt ‹*Wein*›; (wholesale) en gros; *attrib.* **~ transport** Massentransport, *der;* **~ sales** Großverkauf, *der*

B *v.i.* **~ large** eine wichtige Rolle spielen

C *v.t.* 1 (combine) zu einer Sendung zusammenstellen 2 (make thicker) anschwellen lassen; an Umfang zunehmen lassen

bulk: ~ ˈbuyer *n.* Großabnehmer, *der;* **~ ˈbuying** *n., no pl.* Großeinkauf, *der;* **~ ˈcarrier** *n.* Bulkfrachter, *der;* **~ goods** *n. pl.* Schüttgut, *das;* **~head** *n.* Schott, *das*

bulkiness /ˈbʌlkɪnɪs/ *n., no pl.* (unwieldiness) Unhandlichkeit, *die*

bulk: ~ mail *n., no pl.* (Amer.) Massendrucksachen *Pl.;* Postwurfsendungen *Pl.;* **~ purchase** *n.* Großeinkauf, *der*

bulky /ˈbʌlkɪ/ *adj.* sperrig ‹*Gegenstand*›; beleibt ‹*Person*›; massig, wuchtig ‹*Gestalt, Körper*›; unförmig ‹*Kleidungsstück*›; (unwieldy) unhandlich ‹*Gegenstand, Paket*›; **~ goods** Sperrgut, *das;* **a ~ book** ein dickes Buch

bull¹ /bʊl/

A *n.* 1 Bulle, *der;* (for ~fight) Stier, *der;* **like a ~ in a china shop** (fig.) wie ein Elefant im Porzellanladen; **like a ~ at a gate** wie ein Wilder; **take the ~ by the horns** (fig.) den Stier bei den Hörnern fassen *od.* packen 2 (Astrol.) **the B~:** der Stier; *see also* **archer 2** 3 (whale, elephant) Bulle, *der* 4 (Brit.) ▸ **bullseye 1** 5 (St. Exch.) Haussier, *der*

B *adj.* bullig

bull² *n.* (RC Ch.) Bulle, *die*

bull³ *n.* (coll.) 1 (routine) [lästige] Routine; (Mil.: discipline) Drill, *der* 2 (nonsense) Geschwafel, *das* (ugs. abwertend); Gesülze, *das* (salopp abwertend) 3 (Amer.: blunder) grober Schnitzer

bull: ~-at-a-gate *adj., adv.* wild; rücksichtslos; **~ bar** *n.* Rammschutz, *der;* Rammbügel, *der;* **~ calf** *n.* Bullenkalb, *das;* **~dog** *n.* 1 Bulldogge, *die; attrib.* **he's one of the ~dog breed** (fig.) er ist hartnäckig und fürchtet sich vor nichts; **~dog clip** Flügelklammer, *die;* 2 (Brit. Univ.) Helfer des Proktors; **~doze** *v.t.* 1 planieren ‹*Boden*›; mit der Planierraupe wegräumen ‹*Gebäude*›; **~doze a path** mit der Planierraupe einen Weg bahnen; 2 (fig.: force) **~doze sb. into doing sth.** jmdn. dazu zwingen, etw. zu tun; **the Bill was ~dozed through Parliament by the government** (fig.) das Gesetz wurde von der Regierung im Parlament durchgeboxt; **~dozer** /ˈbʊldəʊzə(r)/ *n.* Planierraupe, *die;* Bulldozer, *der*

bullet /ˈbʊlɪt/ *n.* [Gewehr-, Pistolen]kugel, *die; see also* **bite B 4**

bullet: ~ head *n.* [kugel]runder Kopf; Rundkopf, *der;* **~ hole** *n.* Einschuss, *der;* Einschussloch, *das;* **be riddled with ~ holes** von Kugeln durchsiebt sein

bulletin /ˈbʊlɪtɪn/ *n.* Bulletin, *das;* **we will bring you further ~s to keep you informed** wir bringen Ihnen weitere Meldungen, um Sie auf dem Laufenden zu halten

ˈbulletin board *n.* 1 (Amer.) Anschlagtafel, *die;* (Sch., Univ.) Schwarzes Brett 2 (Computing) Schwarzes Brett; *attrib.* **~ system** Schwarzes-Brett-System, *das*

bullet: ~proof *adj.* kugelsicher; **~proof glass** Panzerglas, *das;* **~ train** *n.* Bullet-Zug, *der;* **~ wound** *n.* Schusswunde, *die*

bull: ~fight *n.* Stierkampf, *der;* **~fighter** *n.* ▸ **i p. 1260** Stierkämpfer, *der;* **~fighting** *n., no pl.* Stierkämpfe; **~finch** *n.* (Ornith.) Gimpel, *der;* **~frog** *n.* Ochsenfrosch, *der;* **~horn** *n.* Megaphon, *das;* Flüstertüte, *die* (ugs. scherzh.)

bullion /ˈbʊljən/ *n., no pl., no indef. art.* Bullion, *das* (fachspr.); **gold/silver ~:** ungemünztes Gold/Silber; (ingots) Gold-/Silberbarren *Pl.*

bullish /ˈbʊlɪʃ/ *adj.* (St. Exch.) haussierend; auf Hausse spekulierend ‹*Kapitalanleger*›; **feel ~:** in Haussestimmung sein; (fig.) in optimistischer Stimmung sein

bull: ~ market *n.* (St. Exch.) Haussemarkt, *der;* **~ neck** *n.* Stiernacken, *der;* **~-necked** *adj.* stiernackig; **~-nose[d]** /ˈbʊlnəʊz(d)/ *adj.* abgerundet

bullock /ˈbʊlək/ *n.* Ochse, *der*

bull: ~ point *n.* (coll.) Vorteil, *der;* **~ring** *n.* Stierkampfarena, *die;* **~ session** *n.* (esp. Amer.) zwanglose Diskussionsrunde; (men only) Männerrunde, *die* (ugs.); **~seye** *n.* 1 (of target) Schwarze, *das;* **score a ~seye** (lit. or fig.) ins Schwarze treffen; 2 (boss of glass) Butzen, *der;* (Naut.) Bullauge, *das;* (Archit.) Ochsenauge, *das;* 3 (boiled sweet) rundes, schwarz-weißes Pfefferminzbonbon; **~shit** (coarse) *n., no pl.* Scheiße, *die* (salopp abwertend); **~ terrier** *n.* Bullterrier, *der*

bully¹ /ˈbʊlɪ/

A *n.* 1 *jmd., der gern Schwächere schikaniert bzw. tyrannisiert;* (esp. schoolboy etc.) ≈ Rabauke, *der* (abwertend); (boss) Tyrann, der 2 (hired ruffian) ▸ **bully boy**

B *v.t.* (persecute) schikanieren; (frighten) einschüchtern; **~ sb. into/out of doing sth.** jmdn. so sehr einschüchtern, dass er etw. tut/lässt

bully² (coll.)

A *adj.* toll (ugs.); prima (ugs.)

B *int.* **~ for you** (also iron.) gratuliere!; **~ for him!** (also iron.) da muss man ihm gratulieren!

bully³ (Hockey)

A *n.* Bully, *das*

B *v.i.* **~ off** das Bully ausführen (fachspr.)

bully: ~ beef *n.* Cornedbeef, *das;* **~ boy** *n.* [angeheuerter] Schläger; **a gang of ~ boys** ein Schlägertrupp

bullying /ˈbʊlɪɪŋ/

A *n., no pl.* Schikanieren, *das*

B *adj.* tyrannisch

ˈbully-off *n.* (Hockey) Bully, *das* (fachspr.)

bulrush /ˈbʊlrʌʃ/ *n.* 1 (Bot.) Teichsimse, *die* 2 (Bibl.) Rohr, *das*

bulwark /ˈbʊlwək/ *n.* 1 (rampart) Wall, *der;* Bollwerk, *das* (auch fig.) 2 (breakwater) Mole, *die* 3 *usu. in pl.* (Naut.) Schanzkleid, *das*

bum¹ /bʌm/ *n.* (Brit. coll.) Hintern, *der* (ugs.); Arsch, *der* (derb)

bum² (coll.)

A *n.* (Amer.) 1 (tramp) Penner, *der* (salopp abwertend); Berber, *der* (salopp) 2 (lazy dissolute person) Penner, *der* (salopp abwertend); Gammler, *der* (ugs. abwertend) 3 **be on the ~** (be a vagrant) rumgammeln (ugs.); als Berber leben (salopp); (cadge) schnorren (ugs.)

B *v.i.,* **-mm-: ~ [about** *or* **around]** rumgammeln (ugs.)

C *v.t.,* **-mm-** schnorren (ugs.) ‹*Zigaretten usw.*› (**off** bei); **~ one's way through France** durch Frankreich gammeln (ugs.)

bumble /ˈbʌmbl/ *v.i.* zockeln (ugs.); **~ about** herumwursteln (ugs.)

ˈbumble-bee *n.* Hummel, *die*

bumbling /ˈbʌmblɪŋ/ *adj.* stümperhaft

bumf /bʌmf/ *n.* (Brit. coll.) 1 (derog.: papers) Papierkram, *der* (ugs.) 2 (dated: toilet paper) Klopapier, *das* (ugs.)

bummer /ˈbʌmə(r)/ *n.* (coll.) (disappointment) Frust, *der* (ugs.); (setback, blow) Schlag ins Kontor (ugs.)

bump /bʌmp/

A *n.* 1 (sound) Bums, *der;* (impact) Stoß, *der;* **this car has had a few ~s** der Wagen hat schon einige Dellen abgekriegt 2 (swelling) Beule, *die* 3 (hump) Buckel, *der* (ugs.); Hubbel, *der* (ugs.) 4 (on skull) Höcker, *der* 5 (coll.: dancer's forward thrust of abdomen) Stoß, *der* [mit dem Bauch]; **~s and grinds** erotische Zuckungen

B *adv.* bums; rums, bums; **the car went ~ into the vehicle in front** das Auto bumste gegen das Fahrzeug vor ihm; **be afraid of things that go ~ in the night** Angst vor komischen Geräuschen in der Nacht haben

C *v.t.* 1 anstoßen; **I ~ed the chair against the wall** ich stieß mit dem Stuhl an die Wand 2 (hurt) **~ one's head/knee** sich am Kopf/Knie stoßen

D *v.i.* 1 **~ against sth.** an etw. (*Akk.*) *od.* gegen etw. stoßen; **~ against sb.** jmdn. anstoßen 2 (move with jolts) rumpeln; **~ down the stairs** die Treppe runterpurzeln (ugs.)

Phrasal verbs

- **~ into** *v.t.* 1 stoßen an (+ *Akk.*) *od.* gegen; (with car, shopping trolley, etc.) fahren gegen ‹*Mauer, Baum*›; **~ into sb.** jmdn. anstoßen; (with vehicle) jmdn. anfahren; **I ~ed into the back of another car** ich hatte einen Auffahrunfall 2 (meet by chance) zufällig [wieder]treffen; **if you ~ into Tom, tell him ...:** wenn dir Tom über den Weg läuft, sag ihm, …
- **~ ˈoff** *v.t.* (coll.) kaltmachen (salopp); umlegen (salopp)
- **~ up** *v.t.* (coll.) aufschlagen ‹*Preise*›; aufbessern ‹*Gehalt*›

bumper /ˈbʌmpə(r)/

A *n.* 1 (Motor Veh.) Stoßstange, *die* 2 (Amer. Railw.) Puffer, *der* 3 (Cricket) Schmetterball, *der*

B *adj.* Rekord‹*ernte, -jahr*›; **~ edition** [besonders umfangreiche] Extra- *od.* Sonderausgabe

bumper: ~ car *n.* [Auto]skooter, *der;* **~-to-~ A** *adj.* **a ~-to-~ traffic jam** ein Stau, bei dem nichts mehr geht/ging; **B** *adv.* Stoßstange an Stoßstange

bumpkin /ˈbʌmpkɪn/ *n.* **[country] ~:** [Bauern]tölpel, *der* (abwertend)

bumptious /ˈbʌmpʃəs/ *adj.,* **bumptiously** /ˈbʌmpʃəslɪ/ *adv.* wichtigtuerisch

bumptiousness /ˈbʌmpʃəsnɪs/ *n., no pl.* Wichtigtuerei, *die*

bumpy /ˈbʌmpɪ/ *adj.* holp[e]rig ‹*Straße, Fahrt, Fahrzeug*›; uneben ‹*Fläche*›; unruhig ‹*Flug*›

bum: ~ ˈrap *n.* (Amer. coll.) Verurteilung unter falscher Anklage; **~'s ˈrush** *n.* (Amer. coll.) Rausschmiss, *der* (ugs.); **give sb. the ~'s rush** jmdn. rausschmeißen (ugs.); **~ ˈsteer** *n.* (Amer. sl.) **give sb. a ~ steer** jmdn. in die falsche Richtung lenken

bun /bʌn/ *n.* 1 süßes Brötchen; (currant ~) Korinthenbrötchen, *das* 2 (hair) [Haar]knoten, *der. See also* **oven**

bunch /bʌntʃ/

A *n.* 1 (of flowers) Strauß, *der;* (of grapes, bananas) Traube, *die;* (of parsley, radishes) Bund, *das;* **~ of flowers/grapes** Blumenstrauß, *der*/Traube, *die;* **a ~ of roses/parsley** ein Strauß Rosen/Bund Petersilie; **a ~ of keys** ein Schlüsselbund 2 (lot) Anzahl, *die;* **a whole ~ of ...:** ein ganzer Haufen … (ugs.); **the best** *or* **pick of the ~:** der/die/das Beste [von allen] 3 (coll.: gang) Bande, *die* (ugs.); (group) Haufen, *der* (ugs.); **look a real ~ of idiots** wie ein Haufen [von] Idioten dastehen (ugs.)

B *v.t.* 1 zu einem Strauß/zu Sträußen binden ‹*Blumen*›; bündeln ‹*Radieschen, Spargel*›; zusammendrängen ‹*Personen*›; **the runners were tightly ~ed as they came round the final bend** die Läufer lagen alle dicht beieinander, als sie in die Zielgerade einbogen 2 (gather into folds) [zusammen]raffen ‹*Kleid*›

(Phrasal verb)
• ~ 'up
A v.i. ‹Personen:› zusammenrücken; ‹Kleid, Stoff:› sich zusammenknüllen
B v.t. zusammenraffen ‹Kleid›

bundle /'bʌndl/
A n. 1 Bündel, das; (of papers) Packen, der; (of hay) Bund, das; (of books) Stapel, der; (of fibres, nerves) Strang, der; **tie sth. up in a ~:** etw. zu einem Bündel zusammenbinden; **in ~s** bündelweise; **she's a ~ of mischief/energy/misery** (fig.) sie hat nichts als Unfug im Kopf/ist ein Energiebündel/ist ein Häufchen Unglück od. Elend 2 (coll.: large amount of money) Vermögen, das; [schöne] Stange Geld (ugs.) 3 (coll.) **go a ~ on sb./sth.** von jmdm./etw. begeistert sein. See also **nerve A 2** 4 (Computing) Paket, das
B v.t. 1 bündeln 2 (throw hastily) **~ sth. into the suitcase/back of the car** etw. in den Koffer stopfen/hinten ins Auto werfen 3 (put hastily) **~ sb. into the car** jmdn. ins Auto verfrachten od. packen 4 (Computing) in einem od. als Paket verkaufen.

(Phrasal verbs)
• ~ **'off** v.t. [eilig] schaffen; schicken
• ~ **'up** v.t. 1 (put in ~s) bündeln 2 (dress warmly) einmummeln (fam.)

'bunfight n. (Brit. coll. joc.) Teegesellschaft, die

bung /bʌŋ/
A n. 1 Spund[zapfen], der 2 (Brit. coll.: bribe) Bestechungsgeld, das; Schmiergeld, das (ugs. abwertend)
B v.t. 1 verspunden; spunden 2 (coll.: throw) schmeißen (ugs.)

(Phrasal verb)
• ~ **'up** v.t. **be/get ~ed up** verstopft sein/verstopfen

bungalow /'bʌŋgələʊ/ n. Bungalow, der

bungee /'bʌndʒɪ/: ~ **cord** n. 1 (rubber strap) Expander, der; 2 (for jumping) Bungeeseil, das; ~ **jump** n. Bungeesprung, der; **~-jump** v.i. Bungee springen; **he ~-jumped 100 metres from a bridge** er sprang am Bungeeseil von einer Brücke 100 Meter in die Tiefe; **~-jumping** n., no pl. Bungeespringen, das

'bunghole n. Spundloch, das

bungle /'bʌŋgl/
A v.t. stümpern bei; ~ **it/the job** alles vermasseln
B n. Stümperei, die (ugs.)

bungler /'bʌŋglə(r)/ n. Stümper, der (abwertend)

bungling /'bʌŋglɪŋ/
A adj. stümperhaft ‹Versuch›; ~ **person** Stümper, der; **you ~ idiot!** du Trottel!
B n. Stümperei, die

bunion /'bʌnjən/ n. ▸ⓘ **p. 1231** (Med.) chronische Bursitis bei Hallux valgus (fachspr.); ≈ entzündeter Ballen

bunk¹ /bʌŋk/ n. (in ship, aircraft, lorry) Koje, die; (in room, sleeping car) Bett, das; (~ bed) Etagenbett, das

bunk² n. (coll.: nonsense) Quatsch, der (salopp); Mist, der (salopp)

bunk³ n. (Brit. coll.) **do a ~:** türmen (salopp); **the cashier did a ~ with the money** der Kassierer brannte mit dem Geld durch (ugs.)

'bunk bed n. Etagenbett, das

bunker /'bʌŋkə(r)/
A n. (fuel ~ also Mil., Golf) Bunker, der
B v.t. (Golf) **be ~ed** im Bunker od. Sand liegen

bunkum /'bʌŋkəm/ n., no pl. Unsinn, der

bunny /'bʌnɪ/ n. Häschen, das

Bunsen burner /bʌnsn 'bɜːnə(r)/ n. Bunsenbrenner, der

bunting¹ /'bʌntɪŋ/ n. (Ornith.) Ammer, die

bunting² n., no pl. 1 (fabric) Fahnentuch, das 2 (flags, decoration) [bunte] Fähnchen; Wimpel Pl.

buoy /bɔɪ/
A n. 1 Boje, die; (buoyant part) Schwimmkörper, der 2 (life~) Rettungsring, der
B v.t. ~ **[up]** über Wasser halten; (fig.: support, sustain) aufrechterhalten; **I was ~ed [up] by the thought that ...:** der Gedanke, dass ..., hielt mich aufrecht od. ließ mich durchhalten

buoyancy /'bɔɪənsɪ/ n. 1 (of body) Auftrieb, der 2 (fig.) (of stock market prices) Aufwärtstendenz, die; (of person) Schwung, der; Elan, der

'buoyancy tank n. (Naut.) Trimmtank, der

buoyant /'bɔɪənt/ adj. 1 Auftrieb habend; schwimmend; **be [more] ~:** [einen größeren] Auftrieb haben; [besser] schwimmen 2 (fig.) rege, lebhaft ‹Markt›; heiter, munter ‹Person›; federnd ‹Schritt›; **share prices were ~ today** die Kurse sind heute gestiegen od. hochgegangen; **in ~ spirits** in Hochstimmung

bur /bɜː(r)/ n. ▸ **burr**

burble /'bɜːbl/ v.i. 1 (speak lengthily) ~ **[on] about sth.** von etw. ständig quasseln (ugs.); ~ **[on] incessantly to sb.** jmdm. die Ohren voll schwatzen (ugs.) 2 (make a murmuring sound) brummeln (ugs.); ‹Baby:› plappern; ‹Bach:› murmeln

burbot /'bɜːbət/ n. (Zool.) Aalquappe, die

burden /'bɜːdn/
A n. 1 (load) Last, die; (fig.) Last, die; Bürde, die (geh.); **beast of ~:** Lasttier, das; **become a ~:** zur Last werden; **be a ~ to sb.** für jmdn. eine Belastung sein; (less serious) jmdm. zur Last fallen; **put a fresh ~ upon sb.** ‹Person:› jmdm. eine zusätzliche Last aufladen; ‹Sache:› für jmdn. eine zusätzliche Belastung darstellen; **put too much of a ~ upon sb.** jmdn. überlasten; **the ~ of proof rests with** or **on you** Sie tragen die Beweislast; **tax ~:** steuerliche Belastung; Steuerlast, die 2 (chief theme) Schwerpunkt, der; Kern, der 3 (of song) Refrain, der 4 (Naut.: tonnage) Tonnage, die; Tragfähigkeit, die
B v.t. belasten; **they were heavily ~ed** sie hatten schwer od. eine schwere Last zu tragen; (fig.) ~ **sb./oneself with sth.** jmdn./sich mit etw. belasten; ~ **sb./oneself with too many responsibilities** jmdm./sich zu viel Verantwortung aufladen

burdensome /'bɜːdnsəm/ adj. schwer ‹Last›; (fig.) lästig ‹Person, Pflicht, Verantwortung›; **become/be ~ to sb.** jmdm. zur Last werden/fallen

burdock /'bɜːdɒk/ n. (Bot.) Klette, die

bureau /'bjʊərəʊ, bjʊə'rəʊ/ n., pl. **~x** /'bjʊərəʊz, bjʊə'rəʊz/ or **~s** 1 (Brit.: writing desk) Schreibschrank, der; Sekretär, der; (Amer.: chest of drawers) Kommode, die 2 (office) Büro, das; (department) Abteilung, die; (Amer.: government department) Dienststelle, die; Amt, das

bureaucracy /bjʊə'rɒkrəsɪ/ n. 1 Bürokratie, die 2 (officials) Beamte Pl.; Bürokraten Pl. (abwertend)

bureaucrat /'bjʊərəkræt/ n. Bürokrat, der/Bürokratin, die (abwertend)

bureaucratic /bjʊərə'krætɪk/ adj. bürokratisch; ~ **mentality** Beamtenmentalität, die

bureaucratically /bjʊərə'krætɪkəlɪ/ adv. bürokratisch

bureau de change /bjʊərəʊ də ʃɑ̃ʒ/ n. Wechselstube, die

burette (Amer.: **buret**) /bjʊə'ret/ n. (Chem.) Bürette, die

burg /bɜːg/ n. (Amer. coll.) Ort, der

burgee /bɜː'dʒiː/ n. (Naut.) [gezackter] Stander; (triangular) Wimpel, der

burgeon /'bɜːdʒən/ v.i. 1 (begin to grow rapidly) blühen; **the arts and sciences ~ed** die Künste und Wissenschaften erlebten eine Blütezeit 2 (bud) ‹Pflanze:› sprießen; ‹Baum:› Knospen treiben, ausschlagen

burger /'bɜːgə(r)/ n. (coll.) Hamburger, der

'burger bar n. (coll.) Hamburgerlokal, das

burgess /'bɜːdʒɪs/ n. 1 (Amer.) Stadtverordnete, der/die 2 (arch.) Bürger, der/Bürgerin, die;

burgh /'bʌrə/ n. (Scot. Hist.) Stadt mit Stadtrechten; freie Stadt

burgher /'bɜːgə(r)/ n. (arch./joc.) Bürger, der/Bürgerin, die

burglar /'bɜːglə(r)/ n. Einbrecher, der

'burglar alarm n. Alarmanlage, die

burglarize /'bɜːgləraɪz/ (Amer.) ▸ **burgle A**

'burglar-proof adj. einbruch[s]sicher

burglary /'bɜːglərɪ/ n. Einbruch, der; (offence) [Einbruchs]diebstahl, der

burgle /'bɜːgl/
A v.t. einbrechen in (+ Akk.); **the shop/he was ~d** in dem Laden/bei ihm wurde eingebrochen
B v.i. einen Einbruch begehen

burgomaster /'bɜːgəmɑːstə(r)/ n. Bürgermeister, der (einer holländ. od. fläm. Stadt)

burgundy n. 1 (wine) Burgunder[wein], der 2 (colour) Burgunderrot, das

Burgundy /'bɜːgəndɪ/ pr. n. Burgund (das)

burial /'berɪəl/ n. Bestattung, die; Begräbnis, das; (funeral) Beerdigung, die; Beisetzung, die (geh.); **Christian ~:** christliches Begräbnis; ~ **at sea** Seebestattung, die

burial: ~ **ground** n. Begräbnisstätte, die; ~ **mound** n. Grabhügel, der; ~ **service** n. Trauerfeier, die

burin /'bjʊərɪn/ n. 1 Stichel, der; Punze, die 2 (Archaeol.) Meißel, der

burka /'bɜːkə/ n. Burka, die

burlap /'bɜːlæp/ n. Sackleinen, das

burlesque /bɜː'lesk/
A adj. burlesk, possenhaft ‹Theaterstück›; parodistisch ‹Literatur, Rede›; ~ **show** Varieteevorstellung, die
B n. 1 Kabarett, das; Varietee, das 2 (book, play) Burleske, die; (parody) Parodie, die 3 (Amer.: variety show) Varietee, das; Tingeltangel, das (abwertend)
C v.t. parodieren

burly /'bɜːlɪ/ adj. kräftig; stämmig; stramm ‹Soldat›

Burma /'bɜːmə/ pr. n. Birma (das)

Burmese /bɜː'miːz/ ▸ⓘ **p. 1277**, ▸ⓘ **p. 1345**
A adj. birmanisch; **sb. is ~:** jmd. ist Birmane/Birmanin; see also **English A**
B n., pl. same 1 (person) Birmane, der/Birmanin, die 2 (language) Birmanisch, das; see also **English B 1**

burn¹ /bɜːn/
A n. ▸ⓘ **p. 1231** (on the skin) Verbrennung, die; (on material) Brandfleck, der; (hole) Brandloch, das; **second-degree ~s** Verbrennungen zweiten Grades
B v.t., **~t** /bɜːnt/ or **~ed** 1 verbrennen; ~ **a hole in sth.** ein Loch in etw. (Akk.) brennen; **money ~s a hole in his pocket** (fig.) das Geld rinnt ihm nur so durch die Finger; ~ **one's boats** or **bridges** (fig.) alle Brücken hinter sich (Dat.) abbrechen
2 (use as fuel) als Brennstoff verwenden ‹Gas, Öl usw.›; heizen mit ‹Kohle, Holz, Torf›; verbrauchen ‹Strom›; (use up) verbrauchen ‹Treibstoff›; verfeuern ‹Holz, Kohle›; ~ **coal in the stove** den Ofen mit Kohle feuern; **this lamp ~s oil** das ist eine Öllampe; **have money to ~** (fig.) Geld wie Heu haben; **I haven't got money to ~:** ich bin doch kein Krösus (ugs.)
3 ▸ⓘ **p. 1231** (injure) verbrennen; ~ **oneself/one's hand** sich verbrennen/sich (Dat.) die Hand verbrennen; **he was severely ~t in the fire** er erlitt schwere Brandverletzungen; ~ **one's fingers, get one's fingers ~t** (fig.) sich (Dat.) die Finger verbrennen (fig.)
4 (spoil) anbrennen lassen ‹Fleisch, Kuchen›; **be ~t** angebrannt sein; **~t toast** verbrannter od. schwarzer Toast
5 (cause burning sensation to) verbrennen; **this curry is ~ing my throat** das Curry verbrennt mir den Hals od. brennt mir im Hals
6 (Computing) brennen ‹CD, CD-ROM›
7 (put to death) ~ **sb. [at the stake/alive]** jmdn. [auf dem Scheiterhaufen/bei lebendigem Leibe] verbrennen
8 (fire, harden) brennen; ~ **wood to make** or **for charcoal** Holz zu Holzkohle verbrennen
9 (corrode) ätzen; verätzen ‹Haut›
10 (parch) **the earth was ~ed brown/dry** die Erde war ganz versengt/ausgedörrt
C v.i., **~t** or **~ed** 1 brennen; ~ **to death** verbrennen; **five people ~ed to death in the fire** fünf Menschen kamen in den Flammen um; **may you ~ in hell** in der Hölle sollst du schmoren (ugs.)
2 (blaze) ‹Feuer:› brennen; ‹Gebäude:› in Flammen stehen, brennen

3 (give light) ‹*Lampe, Kerze, Licht:*› brennen; ~ **lower** ‹*Kerze:*› herunterbrennen; ‹*Lampe:*› schwach brennen
4 ▸ℹ **p. 1231** (be injured) sich verbrennen; **she/her skin ~s easily** sie bekommt leicht einen Sonnenbrand
5 (be spoiled) ‹*Kuchen, Milch, Essen:*› anbrennen
6 (feel hot) brennen; glühen; (fig.) [glut]rot sein (**with** vor + *Dat.*); **her cheeks were ~ing with embarrassment** sie lief vor Verlegenheit rot an; **I was ~ing with shame** ich wurde rot vor Scham; **his ears were ~ing** (fig.) ihm klangen die Ohren
7 (fig.: be passionate) ~ **with rage/anger** vor Wut/Ärger kochen; ~ **with desire/longing [for sb.]** sich vor Verlangen/Sehnsucht [nach jmdm.] verzehren; **be ~ing with curiosity** vor Neugierde sterben; **be ~ing to do sth.** darauf brennen, etw. zu tun
8 (be corrosive) ätzen; ätzend sein

(Phrasal verbs)

• ~ **a'way**
A *v.t.* verbrennen; (by laser etc.) wegbrennen
B *v.i.* **1** (continue to ~) weiterbrennen; vor sich (*Dat.*) hin brennen **2** (diminish, be destroyed) verbrennen; ‹*Kerze, Docht:*› herunterbrennen

• ~ **'down**
A *v.t.* niederbrennen
B *v.i.* ‹*Gebäude:*› niederbrennen, abbrennen; (less brightly) ‹*Feuer, Kerze:*› herunterbrennen

• ~ **'in** *v.t.* (lit. or fig.) einbrennen

• ~ **into** *v.t.* einbrennen in (+ *Akk.*); **the events were ~t into her memory** (fig.) die Ereignisse hatten sich ihrem Gedächtnis *od.* in ihr Gedächtnis eingebrannt

• ~ **'out**
A *v.t.* **1** ausbrennen; **the fire ~ed itself out** das Feuer brannte aus *od.* nieder **2** (fig.) **feel ~ed out** sich erschöpft fühlen; total kaputt sein (ugs.); ~ **oneself out** sich völlig verausgaben *od.* (ugs.) kaputtmachen **3** **the family was ~ed out of house and home** Haus und Hof der Familie waren abgebrannt **4** (Electr.) durchbrennen lassen ‹*Sicherung*›; ausbrennen lassen ‹*Motor*›
B *v.i.* **1** ‹*Kerze, Feuer:*› erlöschen, ausgehen; ‹*Rakete, Raketenstufe:*› ausbrennen **2** (Electr.) durchbrennen

• ~ **'up**
A *v.t.* **1** verbrennen; verbrauchen ‹*Energie*›; ~ **up the road** (fig. coll.) die Straße entlangrasen **2** (Amer.: make furious) in Wut versetzen; zur Weißglut bringen (fig.); fuchsteufelswild machen (ugs.)
B *v.i.* **1** (begin to blaze) auflodern **2** (be destroyed) ‹*Rakete, Meteor, Satellit:*› verglühen

burn² *n.* (Scot.) Bach, *der*

'burned-out *adj.* (lit. or fig.) ausgebrannt

burner /'bɜ:nə(r)/ *n.* Brenner, *der*; *see also* **back burner**; **Bunsen burner**

burning /'bɜ:nɪŋ/
A *adj.* **1** brennend **2** (fig.) glühend ‹*Leidenschaft, Hass, Wunsch*›; brennend ‹*Wunsch, Frage, Problem, Ehrgeiz*›; **sth. is a ~ shame** etw. ist eine wahre Schande *od.* schreit zum Himmel
B *n.* Brennen, *das*; **a smell of ~:** ein Brandgeruch

'burning glass *n.* Brennglas, *das*

burnish /'bɜ:nɪʃ/ *v.t.* polieren

'burn-out *n.* Burn-out, *das* (Med.); totale Erschöpfung *od.* Entkräftung; **risk ~:** Gefahr laufen, sich zu übernehmen

Burns Night

Der Geburtstag des schottischen Dichters Robert Burns (1759-96) wird jedes Jahr am 25. Januar in Schottland gefeiert. Schotten in aller Welt verbringen den Abend mit Tanz, Musik und Gedichten. Sie trinken Whisky, essen typisch schottische Spezialitäten wie *haggis* (gefüllter Schafsmagen) und spielen Dudelsack zu Burns' Gedichten. Die meisten Gedichte und Lieder sind in heimischer Mundart und behandeln volkstümliche, vielfach durch alte schottische Volkslieder angeregte Themen.

burnt ▸ **burn¹ B, C**

burnt: ~ **'offering** *n.* Brandopfer, *das*; (fig. joc.: burnt food) angebranntes Essen; **~-out** ▸ **burned-out**

burp /bɜ:p/ (coll.)
A *n.* Rülpser, *der* (ugs.); (of baby) Bäuerchen, *das* (fam.); **emit a loud ~/a series of ~s** laut/mehrmals rülpsen
B *v.i.* rülpsen (ugs.); aufstoßen
C *v.t.* ein Bäuerchen machen lassen (fam.) ‹*Baby*›

burr /bɜ:(r)/ *n.* **1** (rough edge) Grat, *der* **2** (drill) Bohrer, *der* **3** (Bot.; also fig.) Klette, *die*

burrow /'bʌrəʊ/
A *n.* Bau, *der*
B *v.t.* graben, (ugs.) buddeln ‹*Loch, Höhle, Tunnel*›; ~ **one's way under/through sth.** einen Weg *od.* Gang unter etw. (*Dat.*) durch/durch etw. graben
C *v.i.* [sich (*Dat.*)] einen Gang graben; sich durchbuddeln (ugs.); ~ **into sth.** (fig.) sich in etw. (*Akk.*) einarbeiten; ~ **through sth.** (fig.) sich durch etw. hindurchwühlen

bursar /'bɜ:sə(r)/ *n.* ▸ℹ **p. 1260** *Verwalter der geschäftlichen Angelegenheiten einer Schule/Universität*

bursary /'bɜ:sərɪ/ *n.* Kasse, *die*; (scholarship) Stipendium, *das*

burst /bɜ:st/
A *n.* **1** (split) Bruch, *der*; **a ~ in a pipe** ein Rohrbruch **2** (of flame) Auflodern, *das*; **a sudden ~ of flame** eine Stichflamme **3** (outbreak of firing) Feuerstoß, *der*; Salve, *die* **4** (fig.) **a ~ of applause/cheering** ein Beifallsausbruch/Beifallsrufe *Pl.*; **there was a ~ of laughter** man brach in Lachen aus; ~ **of rage** Wutausbruch, *der*; ~ **of enthusiasm** Begeisterungsausbruch, *der*; **a ~ of speed** ein Spurt **5** (explosion) Explosion, *die*; **a bomb ~:** eine Bombenexplosion
B *v.t.*, ~ zum Platzen bringen; platzen lassen ‹*Luftballon*›; platzen ‹*Reifen*›; sprengen ‹*Kessel*›; ~ **pipe** Rohrbruch, *der*; **the river ~ its banks** der Fluss trat über die Ufer; **he ~ a blood vessel** ihm ist eine Ader geplatzt; **he [almost] ~ a blood vessel** (fig.) ihn traf [fast] der Schlag; ~ **the door open** die Tür aufbrechen *od.* aufsprengen; ~ **one's sides with laughing** (fig.) vor Lachen beinahe platzen
C *v.i.*, ~ **1** platzen; ‹*Granate, Bombe, Kessel:*› explodieren; ‹*Damm:*› brechen; ‹*Flussufer:*› überschwemmt werden; ‹*Furunkel, Geschwür:*› aufgehen, aufplatzen; ‹*Knospe:*› aufbrechen; ~ **open** ‹*Tür, Deckel, Kiste, Koffer:*› aufspringen **2** (be full to overflowing) **be ~ing with sth.** zum Bersten voll sein mit etw.; **be full to ~ing[-point]** proppenvoll sein (ugs.); **be ~ing with pride/impatience** (fig.) vor Stolz/Ungeduld platzen; **be ~ing with health** (fig.) vor Gesundheit strotzen; **be ~ing with happiness/excitement** (fig.) vor Freude/Aufregung außer sich sein; **I can't eat any more. I'm ~ing** (fig.) Ich kann nichts mehr essen. Ich platze [gleich] (ugs.); **be ~ing to say/do sth.** (fig.) es kaum abwarten können, etw. zu sagen/tun **3** (appear, come suddenly) ~ **from sb.'s lips** ‹*Schrei:*› jmds. Lippen entfahren; ~ **through sth.** etw. durchbrechen; **the Beatles ~ upon the pop scene in the early sixties** die Beatles wurden Anfang der 60er-Jahre in die Popszene katapultiert; **the sun ~ through the clouds** die Sonne brach durch die Wolken

(Phrasal verbs)

• ~ **'in** *v.i.* hereinplatzen; hereinstürzen; ~ **in [up]on sb./sth.** bei jmdm./etw. hereinplatzen

• ~ **into** *v.t.* **1** eindringen in; **we ~ into the room** wir stürzten ins Zimmer **2** (suddenly begin) ~ **into tears/laughter** in Tränen/Gelächter ausbrechen; ~ **into flower** [plötzlich] aufblühen; ~ **into song** ein Lied anstimmen; ~ **into flames** in Brand geraten

• ~ **'out** *v.i.* **1** herausstürzen; ~ **out of a room** aus einem Raum [hinaus]stürmen *od.* stürzen **2** (exclaim) losplatzen **3** (suddenly begin) ~ **out laughing/crying** in Lachen/Tränen ausbrechen

burton /'bɜ:tn/ *n.* (Brit. coll.) **go for a ~** (be destroyed) kaputtgehen (ugs.); futsch gehen (salopp); (be lost) hopsgehen (salopp); flötengehen (salopp); (be killed) dran glauben müssen (salopp)

bury /'berɪ/ *v.t.* **1** begraben; beisetzen (geh.) ‹*Toten*›; ~ **sb. at sea** jmdn. auf See bestatten; **be dead and buried** (lit. or fig.) tot und begraben sein; schon lange tot sein; **where is Marx buried?** wo ist *od.* liegt Marx begraben?; ~ **sb. alive** jmdn. lebendig begraben **2** (hide) vergraben; verbuddeln (ugs.); (fig.) begraben; ~ **one's differences** (fig.) seinen Streit begraben; ~ **the hatchet** *or* (Amer.) **tomahawk** (fig.) das Kriegsbeil begraben; ~ **one's face in one's hands** das Gesicht in den Händen vergraben **3** (bring underground) eingraben; abdecken ‹*Wurzeln*›; **buried cable** (Electr.) Erdkabel; **the houses were buried by a landslide** die Häuser wurden durch einen Erdrutsch verschüttet **4** (plunge) ~ **one's teeth in sth.** seine Zähne in etw. (*Akk.*) graben *od.* schlagen; ~ **one's hands in one's pockets** seine Hände in den Taschen vergraben; **sth. buries itself in sth.** etw. bohrt sich in etw. (*Akk.*) **5** (involve deeply) ~ **oneself in one's studies/books** sich in seine Studien vertiefen/in seinen Büchern vergraben

burying /'berɪɪŋ/: ~ **beetle** *n.* Totengräber, *der*; **~-ground**, **~-place** *ns.* Friedhof, *der*; Begräbnisstätte, *die*

bus /bʌs/
A *n.*, *pl.* **~es** ((Amer.:) **~ses**) **1** [Auto-, Omni-]bus, *der*; **go by ~:** mit dem Bus fahren **2** (coll.: car, aircraft) Kiste, *die* (ugs.). *See also* **miss B 4**
B *v.i.*, *also* **-ss-** mit dem Bus fahren
C *v.t.*, *also* **-ss-** mit dem Bus befördern

bus: **~bar** *n.* (Electr.) Stromschiene, *die*; **~boy** *n.* (Amer.) Bedienungshilfe, *die*; Abräumer, *der*

busby /'bʌzbɪ/ *n.* (Brit.) Kalpak, *der*; (worn by guardsmen) Bärenfellmütze, *die*

bus: ~ **company** *n.* ≈ Verkehrsbetrieb, *der*; ~ **conductor** *n.* ▸ℹ **p. 1260** Busschaffner, *der*; ~ **depot** ▸ ~ **garage**; ~ **driver** *n.* ▸ℹ **p. 1260** Busfahrer, *der*; ~ **fare** *n.* [Bus]fahrpreis, *der*; **how much is the ~ fare from A to B?** wieviel kostet die [Bus]fahrt von A nach B?; ~ **garage** *n.* Busdepot, *das*

bush¹ /bʊʃ/ *n.* **1** (shrub) Strauch, *der*; Busch, *der*; (collect.: shrubs) Gebüsch, *das*; Gestrüpp, *das*; *see also* **beat B 3** **2** (woodland) Busch, *der*; **go ~** (Austral.) (leave usual surroundings) abhauen (ugs.); verschwinden (ugs.); (run wild) verwildern; (go berserk) durchdrehen (salopp) **3** ~ **[of hair]** [Haar]schopf, *der*

bush² *n.* **1** (threaded socket) Gewindeanschluss, *der* **2** (metal lining) Buchse, *die* **3** (Electr.) Durchführung, *die*

'bushbaby *n.* (Zool.) Galago, *der*; Buschbaby, *das*

bushed /bʊʃt/ *adj.* (Amer. coll.) erledigt (ugs.); groggy (ugs.)

bushel /'bʊʃl/ *n.* Bushel, *der*; ≈ Scheffel, *der*; **hide one's light under a ~** (fig.) sein Licht unter den Scheffel stellen (Spr.)

bushing /'bʊʃɪŋ/ ▸ **bush²**

bush: ~ **jacket** *n.* Safarijacke, *die*; ~ **league** *n.* (Amer.) Provinzliga, *die* (abwertend); **B~man** *n.* **1** (native) Buschmann, *der*; **2** (language) Buschmännisch, *das*; **~-ranger** *n.* (Austral. Hist.) Strauchdieb, *der* (veralt.); Buschklepper, *der* (veralt.); ~ **'telegraph** *n.* (fig.) Informationssystem, *das*; **the news spread via the ~ telegraph** die Nachricht sprach sich herum; **~whacker** *n.* (Amer., Austral., NZ: backwoodsman) Waldsiedler, *der*

bushy /'bʊʃɪ/ *adj.* (covered with bushes) buschbewachsen; (growing luxuriantly) buschig

busily /'bɪzɪlɪ/ *adv.* eifrig

business /'bɪznɪs/ *n.* **1** (trading operation) Geschäft, *das*; (company, firm) Betrieb, *der*; (large) Unternehmen, *das* **2** *no pl.* (buying and selling) Geschäfte *Pl.*; **on ~:** geschäftlich; **he's in the wool ~:** er ist in der Wollbranche; ~ **is brisk** die Geschäfte florieren; **how's ~ with you?** (lit. or fig.) was machen die Geschäfte [bei Ihnen]?; **~ is ~** (fig.) Geschäft ist Geschäft; **in my ~:** in meiner Branche; **set up in ~:** ein Geschäft *od.* eine Firma gründen; **he's in ~ for himself** er ist selbstständig; **go out of ~:** pleite gehen (ugs.); **go into ~:** Geschäftsmann/-frau werden;

do ~ [with sb.] [mit jmdm.] Geschäfte machen; **I'm glad we were able to do ~:** ich bin froh, dass wir ins Geschäft gekommen sind; **be in ~:** Geschäftsmann/-frau sein; **we're in ~ [again]** (fig.) es kann [wieder] losgehen; **it was ~ as usual** die Geschäfte gingen ihren normalen Gang; **'B~ as usual during alterations'** „Während des Umbaus geht der Verkauf/Betrieb weiter"; **do you want to go into ~ or become a lawyer?** wollen Sie in die Wirtschaft gehen oder Anwalt werden?; **go about one's ~:** seinen Geschäften nachgehen **3▸** (task, duty, province) Aufgabe, *die;* Pflicht, *die;* **that is 'my ~/none of 'your ~:** das ist meine Angelegenheit/nicht deine Sache; **that is 'your ~:** das ist deine Sache; **what ~ is it of yours?** was geht Sie das an?; **send sb. about his ~:** jmdn. abblitzen lassen (ugs.); jmdm. eine Abfuhr erteilen; **mind your own ~:** kümmere dich um deine [eigenen] Angelegenheiten!; **he has no ~ to do that** er hat kein Recht, das zu tun; **make it one's ~ to do sth.** es sich (*Dat.*) angelegen sein lassen, etw. zu tun (geh.); (with more effort) es sich (*Dat.*) zur Aufgabe machen, etw. zu tun; **like nobody's ~** (coll.) wie verrückt (ugs.) **4▸** (matter to be considered) Angelegenheit, *die;* **'any other ~'** „Sonstiges"; **the [main] ~ of the day** das [Haupt]anliegen des Tages; **get on with the ~ in hand** zur Sache kommen **5▸** (difficult matter) Problem, *das;* **a lengthy ~:** eine langwierige Angelegenheit; **it's going to be a ~ getting the piano down the stairs** das wird noch ein Problem geben, das Klavier die Treppe hinunterzukriegen; **what a ~ [this is]!** was für ein Theater!; **make a [great] ~ of sth.** ein [großes] Problem aus etw. machen; (make a fuss) einen [Riesen]wirbel um etw. machen **6▸** (serious work) **get down to [serious] ~:** [ernsthaft] zur Sache kommen; (Commerc.) an die Arbeit gehen; **mean ~:** es ernst meinen; **~ before pleasure** erst die Arbeit, dann das Vergnügen; **combine ~ and pleasure** das Angenehme mit dem Nützlichen verbinden **7▸** (derog.: affair) Sache, *die;* Geschichte, *die* (ugs.) **8▸** *no pl.* (Theatre) Gestik und Mimik, *die*

business: ~ address *n.* Geschäftsadresse, *die;* **~ analyst** *n.* Businessanalyst, *der*/-analystin, *die;* **~ card** *n.* Geschäftskarte, *die;* **~ class** **A** *n., no pl.* Businessklasse, *die; attrib.* Businessklasse-; **B** *adv.* **fly/travel ~ class** in der Businessklasse fliegen/reisen; **~ consultant** *n.* Unternehmensberater, *der*-beraterin, *die;* **~ correspondence** *n.* Geschäftskorrespondenz, *die;* **~ cycle** *n.* Konjunkturzyklus, *der;* **~ deal** *n.* Geschäft, *das;* **~ end** *n.* (coll.) (of tool) vorderes Ende; (of hammer etc.) Kopf, *der;* (of rifle etc.) Lauf, *der;* **~ ethics** *n., usu. constr. as pl.* Wirtschaftsethik, *die;* **~ expenses** *n. pl.* Geschäftskosten *Pl.;* **~ hours** *n. pl.* Geschäftszeit, *die;* (in office) Dienstzeit, *die;* **~ language** *n.* Wirtschaftsprache, *die;* (used in business between countries) Geschäftssprache, *die;* **English ~ language** Wirtschaftsenglisch, *das;* **~ letter** *n.* Geschäftsbrief, *der;* **~like** *adj.* geschäftsmäßig ‹*Art*›; sachlich, nüchtern ‹*Untersuchung*›; geschäftstüchtig ‹*Person*›; **~ lunch** *n.* Arbeitsessen, *das;* **~ machine** *n.* Büromaschine, *die;* **~man** *n.* ▸❶ **p. 1260** Geschäftsmann, *der;* **~ model** *n.* Geschäftsmodell, *das;* **~ park** *n.* Gewerbepark, *der;* **~ plan** *n.* Geschäftsplan, *der;* **~ premises** *n. pl.* Geschäftsräume; **~ process re-engi'neering** *n., no pl.* Ablaufoptimierung, *die;* **~ re'ply envelope** *n.* voradressierter Freiumschlag; **~ re'ply service** *n.* Geschäftskorrespondenzservice, *der;* **~ school** *n.* kaufmännische Fachschule; **~ software** *n., no pl.* (Computing) Business-Software, *die* (fachspr.); Firmensoftware, *die;* **~ studies** *n. pl.* Wirtschaftslehre, *die;* **~ suit** *n.* Straßenanzug, *der;* **~-to-'business** *n.* Business-to-Business; *attrib.* Business-to-Business ‹*Markt, Platform, Lösung usw.*›; **~ tourism** *n., no pl., no indef. art.* Geschäftstourismus, *der;* **~ trip** *n.* Geschäftsreise, *die;* **on a ~ trip** auf Geschäftsreise; **~ unit** *n.* **1▸** (organization within a company) Geschäftseinheit, *die;* **2▸** (premises) Gewerberäume *Pl.;* **~woman** *n.* ▸❶ **p. 1260** Geschäftsfrau, *die*

busk /bʌsk/ *v.i.* Straßenmusik machen

busker /'bʌskə(r)/ *n.* Straßenmusikant, *der*

busking /'bʌskɪŋ/ *n., no pl.* Musizieren auf Straßen und Plätzen

> **busking**
>
> Dies ist der informelle britische Ausdruck für das Musizieren an öffentlichen Plätzen, mit dem Zweck Geld einzunehmen. In den großen britischen Städten gibt es viele *buskers* (Straßenmusikanten), oft auf hohem Niveau. An einigen Orten ist es verboten, Straßenmusik zu machen, z.B. in der Londoner U-Bahn.

bus: ~ lane *n.* (Brit.) Busspur, *die;* **~load** *n.* Busladung, *die;* **~man** /'bʌsmən/ *n.* **a ~man's holiday** (fig.) praktisch gar keine Ferien (weil man dasselbe wie im Berufsalltag tut); **~ pass** *n.* Buskarte, *die;* **~ ride** *n.* Busfahrt, *die;* **B. is only an hour's ~ ride away** B. ist nur eine Busstunde entfernt; **~ route** *n.* Buslinie, *die;* **~ service** *n.* Omnibusverkehr, *der;* (specific service) Busverbindung, *die;* **~ shelter** *n.* Wartehäuschen, *das*

bussing /'bʌsɪŋ/ *n., no pl.* (*Amer.*) *Busbeförderung von Schulkindern in andere Bezirke zur Förderung der Rassenintegration*

bus: ~ station *n.* Omnibusbahnhof, *der;* **~ stop** *n.* Bushaltestelle, *die*

bust¹ /bʌst/ *n.* **1▸** (sculpture) Büste, *die* **2▸** (upper front of body) Brust, *die;* (woman's bosom) Busen, *der;* **what ~ are you?, what is your ~ [measurement]?** welche Oberweite haben Sie?

bust² (coll.)

A *n.* **1▸** (collapse of trade) Pleite, *die* (ugs.); (general) Zusammenbruch, *der* **2▸** (police raid) Razzia, *die*

B *adj.* **1▸** (broken) kaputt (ugs.) **2▸** (bankrupt) bankrott; pleite (ugs.); **go ~:** pleite gehen

C *v.t.,* **~** *or* **~ed** **1▸** (burst) aufplatzen lassen ‹*Koffer usw.*›; (break) kaputtmachen (ugs.); **~ sth. open** etw. aufbrechen **2▸** (esp. Amer.: break up) auffliegen lassen ‹*Verbrecherring*›; (arrest) schnappen (ugs.) **3▸** (coll.: punch) schlagen; hauen (ugs.); **~ sb. on the chin/jaw** jmdm. einen Kinnhaken geben *od.* verabreichen

D *v.i.,* **~** *or* **~ed** kaputtgehen (ugs.); ‹*Lineal usw.:*› zerbrechen; ‹*Bleistiftspitze:*› abbrechen; **be laughing fit to ~:** sich halb tot lachen; **~ in half** auseinander brechen

Phrasal verb

• **~ 'up** *v.t.* kaputtmachen (ugs.) ‹*Ehe, Partnerschaft*›; **~ a place up** in einem Laden Kleinholz machen (salopp)

bustard /'bʌstəd/ *n.* (Ornith.) Trappe, *die*

buster /'bʌstə(r)/ *n.* (sl.) (as address) Meister (*der*) (salopp); (threatening) Freundchen (*das*) (salopp)

bus: ~ terminal *n.* Busbahnhof, *der;* **~ ticket** *n.* Busfahrkarte, *die;* Busfahrschein, *der*

bustier /'bʌstɪeɪ/ *n.* Bustier, *das*

bustle¹ /'bʌsl/

A *v.i.* eilig umherlaufen; **~ in/out/about** geschäftig hinein- *od.* herein-/hinaus- *od.* herauseilen/geschäftig hin und her eilen; **the town centre was bustling with activity** im Stadtzentrum herrschte großer Betrieb *od.* ein reges Treiben

B *v.t.* jagen (ugs.); treiben (ugs.)

C *n.* (activity) Betrieb, *der;* (of fair, streets also) geschäftiges *od.* reges Treiben (**of** auf, in + *Dat.*)

bustle² *n.* (Fashion Hist.) Turnüre, *die*

bustling /'bʌslɪŋ/ *adj.* belebt ‹*Straße, Stadt, Markt usw.*›; emsig, geschäftig ‹*Person, Art*›; rege ‹*Tätigkeit*›

'bust-up *n.* (coll.) Krach, *der* (ugs.); **have a ~:** Krach haben (ugs.); sich verkrachen (ugs.); **there's going to be a ~:** es wird Krach geben

busty /'bʌstɪ/ *adj.* vollbusig

busy /'bɪzɪ/

A *adj.* **1▸** (occupied) beschäftigt; **I'm ~ now** ich habe jetzt zu tun; **keep oneself ~:** sich [selbst] beschäftigen; **keep sb. ~:** jmdn. auf Trab halten; **be ~ at** *or* **with sth.** mit etw. beschäftigt sein; **be ~ in the kitchen** in der Küche zu tun haben; **he was ~ packing** er war mit Packen beschäftigt *od.* war gerade beim Packen; **get ~:** sich an die Arbeit machen; **as ~ as a bee** (fig.) bienenfleißig **2▸** (full of activity) arbeitsreich ‹*Leben*›; ziemlich hektisch ‹*Zeit*›; belebt ‹*Stadt*›; ausgelastet ‹*Person*›; fleißig ‹*Hände*›; rege ‹*Verkehr*›; **a ~ road** eine verkehrsreiche *od.* viel befahrene Straße; **the office was ~ all day** im Büro war den ganzen Tag viel los; **I'm/he's a ~ man** ich habe/er hat viel zu tun; **he leads a very ~ life** er ist immer beschäftigt; **it has been a ~ day/week** heute/diese Woche war viel los; **I had a ~ day/week** ich hatte heute/diese Woche viel zu tun **3▸** (Amer. Teleph.) besetzt

B *v. refl.* **~ oneself with sth.** sich mit etw. beschäftigen; **~ oneself [in] doing sth.** sich damit beschäftigen, etw. zu tun

busy: ~body *n.* G[e]schaftlhuber, *der* (südd., österr.); Wichtigtuer, *der;* **don't be such a ~body** misch dich nicht überall ein; **~ Lizzie** /bɪzɪ 'lɪzɪ/ *n.* (Bot.) Fleißiges Lieschen; **~ signal** *n.* (Amer. Teleph.) Besetztzeichen, *das*

but

A /bət, *stressed* bʌt/ *conj.* **1▸** *coordinating* aber; **Sue wasn't there, ~ her sister was** Sue war nicht da, dafür aber ihre Schwester; **I can't come today ~ I can come tomorrow** heute kann ich [zwar] nicht kommen, aber [ich kann dafür] morgen [kommen]; **he might have been able to help, ~ then he isn't here** er hätte vielleicht helfen können, aber er ist ja nicht hier; **we tried to do it ~ couldn't** wir haben es versucht, aber nicht gekonnt; **~ surely you must have noticed ...:** aber du hast doch sicherlich bemerkt, ...; **~ I 'did!** hab ich doch!; **~ then what if the plane is delayed?** aber was ist, wenn das Flugzeug Verspätung hat? **2▸** *correcting after a negative* sondern; **not that book ~ this one** nicht das Buch, sondern dieses; **not only ... ~ also** nicht nur ..., sondern auch; **I can't change the way my son acts, not ~ what I've tried** ich kann das Verhalten meines Sohnes nicht ändern, obwohl ich es schon versucht habe; **I don't doubt ~ that it's true** ich bezweifle nicht, dass es wahr ist; **I don't deny ~ that ...:** ich leugne nicht ab, dass ... **3▸** *subordinating* ohne dass; **never a week passes ~ he phones** keine Woche vergeht, ohne dass er anruft

B *prep.* außer (+ *Dat.*); **all ~ him** alle außer ihm; **no one ~ you** niemand außer dir; nur du; **anyone ~ Jim** alle mit Ausnahme von *od.* alle außer Jim; **all ~ three** alle außer dreien; **the next ~ one/two** der/die/das über-/überübernächste; **the last ~ one/two** der/die/das vor-/vorvorletzte; **nobody, ~ nobody, may leave the room** niemand, aber auch wirklich niemand darf das Zimmer verlassen; *see also* **all C**; **anything A 3**; **nothing A 1**

C /bət/ *adv.* nur; bloß; **they are ~ children** sie sind doch noch Kinder; **if I could ~ talk to her ...:** wenn ich [doch] nur mit ihr sprechen könnte ...; **we can ~ try** wir können es immerhin versuchen

D *rel. pron.* der/die/das nicht; **there is no one ~ knows that ...:** es gibt niemanden, der nicht weiß, dass ...

E /bʌt/ *n.* Aber, *das;* **no ~s [about it]!** kein Aber!; **there are no ~s about it** da gibt es kein Wenn und kein Aber; *see also* **if B**

butane /'bju:teɪn/ *n.* (Chem.) Butan, *das*

butch /bʊtʃ/ (coll.)

A *adj.* betont männlich ‹*Frau, Kleidung, Frisur*›; betont maskulin, (salopp) macho ‹*Mann*›; **~ haircut** (Amer.) Bürstenschnitt, *der*

B *n.* (woman) kesser Vater (salopp); (man) betont maskuliner Typ; Macho, *der* (salopp)

butcher /'bʊtʃə(r)/

A *n.* **1▸** ▸❶ **p. 1260** Fleischer, *der;* Metzger, *der* (bes. westmd., südd.); Schlachter, *der* (nordd.); **~'s [shop]** Fleischerei, *die;* Metzgerei, *die* (bes. westmd., südd.); **~'s meat** Rind-, Schweine- und Hammelfleisch (*im Gegensatz zu Geflügel, Wild und Speck*); **the ~, the baker, the candlestick-maker** (fig.) ehrbare Bürger; **have** *or* **take a ~'s [hook] at sb./sth.** (coll.) [sich (*Dat.*)] jmdn./etw. angucken (ugs.); *see also* **baker 2▸** (fig.: murderer)

[Menschen]schlächter, *der* **3** (Amer. coll.: vendor) Verkäufer in Eisenbahnzügen
B *v.t.* schlachten; (fig.: murder) niedermetzeln; abschlachten; (fig.: ruin) verhunzen (ugs.), verunstalten ‹*Text usw.*›

butchery /ˈbʊtʃərɪ/ *n.* **1** *no pl.* ~ **[trade** *or* **business]** Fleischerhandwerk, *das* **2** *no pl.* (fig.: needless slaughter) Metzelei, *die;* Gemetzel, *das;* **it's sheer ~!** das ist [ja] das reinste Gemetzel! **3** (slaughterhouse) Schlachthaus, *das*

butler /ˈbʌtlə(r)/ *n.* ▸ⓘ **p. 1260** Butler, *der;* erster Diener

butt¹ /bʌt/ *n.* (vessel) Fass, *das;* (for rainwater) Tonne, *die*

butt² *n.* **1** (end) dickes Ende; (of rifle) Kolben, *der;* (of spear, fishing rod, etc.) Schaft, *der* **2** (of cigarette, cigar) Stummel, *der;* **cigarette ~:** Zigarettenstummel, *der;* Kippe, *die* (ugs.) **3** (Amer. coll.: buttocks) Hintern, *der* (ugs.)

butt³ *n.* **1** (object of teasing or ridicule) Zielscheibe, *die;* Gegenstand, *der;* **be the ~ of ridicule** Zielscheibe des Spottes sein; **make a ~ of sb.** sich über jmdn. lustig machen **2** *in pl.* (shooting range) Schießstand, *der;* Waffenjustierstand, *der* **3** (target) Schießscheibe, *die* **4** (grouse-shooter's stand) Schießstand (*beim Moorhuhnschießen*)

butt⁴
A *n.* (push) (by person) [Kopf]stoß, *der;* (by animal) Stoß [mit den Hörnern], *der;* **give sb. a ~ in the stomach** jmdm. mit dem Kopf in den Bauch stoßen
B *v.i.* **1** (push with head) ‹*Person:*› [mit dem Kopf] stoßen; ‹*Stier, Widder, Ziege:*› [mit den Hörnern] stoßen **2** (meet end to end) ~ **against sth.** an etw. (*Akk.*) stoßen
C *v.t.* **1** (push with head) ‹*Person:*› mit dem Kopf stoßen; ‹*Widder, Ziege:*› mit den Hörnern stoßen; ~ **sb. in the stomach** jmdm. mit dem Kopf in den Bauch stoßen **2** aneinander fügen; zusammenstoßen lassen; ~ **sth. against sth.** etw. mit etw. zusammenstoßen lassen *od.* auf etw. (*Akk.*) stoßen lassen

(Phrasal verb)
• ~ **ˈin** *v.i.* (fig. coll.) dazwischenreden; (meddle) sich [ungefragt] einmischen; **may I ~ in?** darf ich mal kurz stören?

butte /bjuːt/ *n.* (Amer. Geog.) Restberg, *der*

ˈbutt-end ▸ **butt² 1, 2**

butter /ˈbʌtə(r)/
A *n.* Butter, *die;* **he looks as if ~ wouldn't melt in his mouth** (fig.) er sieht aus, als ob er kein Wässerchen trüben könnte; **melted ~:** zerlassene Butter
B *v.t.* buttern; mit Butter bestreichen; **fine words ~ no parsnips** (prov.) Worte allein genügen nicht

(Phrasal verb)
• ~ **ˈup** *v.t.* ~ **sb. up** jmdm. Honig um den Mund *od.* Bart schmieren (fig.)

butter: ~ **bean** *n.* Gartenbohne, *die;* (lima bean) Mondbohne, *die;* Limabohne, *die;* ~ **cream** *n.* Buttercreme, *die;* **~cup** *n.* (Bot.) Butterblume, *die;* ~ **dish** *n.* Butterdose, *die;* **~fingers** *n. sing.* (coll.) Tollpatsch, *der* (*beim Fangen usw.*)

butterfly /ˈbʌtəflaɪ/ *n.* **1** Schmetterling, *der;* **break a ~ on the wheel** (fig.) mit Kanonen nach Spatzen schießen; **have butterflies [in one's stomach]** (fig. coll.) ein flaues Gefühl im Magen haben **2** ▸ **butterfly stroke**

butterfly: ~ **effect** *n., no pl.* Schmetterlingseffekt, *der;* ~ **nut** *n.* Flügelmutter, *die;* ~ **stroke** *n.* (Swimming) Delphinstil, *der;* Delphin (*das*); **do** *or* **swim the ~ stroke** delphinschwimmen; ~ **valve** *n.* Drosselklappe, *die*

butter: ~ **knife** *n.* Buttermesser, *das;* **~milk** *n.* Buttermilch, *die;* **~scotch** *n.* Buttertoffee, *das*

buttery /ˈbʌtərɪ/ *n.* (Univ.) ≈ Cafeteria, *die*

buttock /ˈbʌtək/ *n.* ▸ⓘ **p. 951** (of person) Hinterbacke, *die;* Gesäßhälfte, *die;* (of animal) Hinterbacke, *die;* **~s** Gesäß, *das*

button /ˈbʌtn/
A *n.* **1** (of garment) Knopf, *der;* **as bright as a ~:** putzmunter (ugs.) **2** (of electric bell etc., on fencing foil) Knopf, *der;* **press** *or* **push the ~:** auf den Knopf drücken **3** (Computing) Symbol, *das*
B *v.t.* (fasten) zuknöpfen; einknöpfen ‹*Futter*›; ~ **one's lip** (Amer. sl.) die Klappe halten (salopp)
C *v.i.* [zu]geknöpft werden; **this dress ~s down the back** dieses Kleid wird hinten geknöpft

(Phrasal verb)
• ~ **ˈup**
A *v.t.* zuknöpfen; (fig.) erledigen ‹*Job*›; **have the deal [all] ~ed up** das Geschäft unter Dach und Fach haben (ugs.); **~ed up** (fig.: taciturn) zugeknöpft (ugs.); reserviert
B *v.i.* [zu]geknöpft werden

button: ~ **bar** *n.* (Computing) Symbolleiste, *die;* ~ **battery** *n.* Knopfzelle, *die;* Knopfbatterie, *die;* **~-down** *adj.* Buttondown‹*kragen*›; **~hole A** *n.* **1** Knopfloch, *das; attrib.* **~hole stitch** Knopflochstich, *der;* **2** (Brit.: flowers worn in coat lapel) Knopflochsträußchen, *das;* (single flower) Knopflochblume, *die;* Blume im Knopfloch. **B** *v.t.* (detain) zu fassen kriegen (ugs.); **he was ~holed by X** X hat sich (*Dat.*) ihn geschnappt (ugs.); ~ **mushroom** *n.* Champignon, *der;* **~-through** *adj.* durchgeknöpft ‹*Kleid*›

buttress /ˈbʌtrɪs/
A *n.* **1** (Archit.) Mauerstrebe, *die;* Mauerstütze, *die;* (not built-on) Strebepfeiler, *der;* **~es** Strebewerk, *das* **2** (support) Pfeiler, *der* **3** (fig.) Stütze, *die;* [Eck]pfeiler, *der*
B *v.t.* ~ **[up]** [durch Strebepfeiler] stützen; (fig.) [unter]stützen; stärken; untermauern ‹*Argument*›

ˈbutt weld *n.* Stumpfschweißnaht, *die*

butty /ˈbʌtɪ/ *n.* (coll.) Butterbrot, *das;* Stulle, *die* (nordd.)

butyl /ˈbjuːtɪl/ *n.* **1** (Chem.) Butyl, *das* **2** ~ **[rubber]** Butyl[gummi], *das*

buxom /ˈbʌksəm/ *adj.* drall

buy /baɪ/
A *v.t.*, **bought** /bɔːt/ **1** kaufen; lösen ‹*Fahrkarte*›; ~ **sb./oneself sth.** jmdm./sich etw. kaufen; ~ **and sell goods** Waren an- und verkaufen; **the pound ~s less than it used to** für ein Pfund bekommt man heute weniger als früher; ~ **[oneself]/sb. a pint** sich (*Dat.*) einen Halben genehmigen/jmdm. einen Halben ausgeben; **he bought them a round** er spendierte ihnen eine Runde; **money cannot ~ happiness** Glück kann man nicht kaufen **2** (fig.) erkaufen ‹*Sieg, Ruhm, Frieden*›; einsparen, gewinnen ‹*Zeit*› **3** (bribe) bestechen; kaufen (ugs.); erkaufen ‹*Zustimmung*› **4** (coll.) (believe) schlucken (ugs.); glauben; (accept) akzeptieren; einverstanden sein mit; **I'll ~ that** (believe) das nehm' ich dir ab (ugs.); (agree) ja, das glaube ich **5** ~ **it** (sl.: be killed): **we nearly bought it that time** da hätte es uns beinahe erwischt
B *n.* [Ein]kauf, *der;* **be a good ~:** preiswert sein; **plenty of good ~s** viele preiswerte Artikel; **the best ~:** der/die/das Preiswerteste; der preiswerteste Artikel; **this week's best ~ is ...** der Preisschlager der Woche ist ...

(Phrasal verbs)
• ~ **ˈin** *v.t.* **1** einkaufen, sich eindecken mit ‹*Vorräte, Fleisch usw.*› **2** (at auction) [durch höheres Gebot] zurückkaufen
• ~ **into** *v.t.* **1** ~ **into a business** sich in ein Geschäft einkaufen **2** (accept, embrace) sich einlassen auf (+ *Akk.*)
• ~ **ˈoff** *v.t.* auszahlen ‹*Forderung*›; abfinden ‹*Anspruchserhebenden*›; (bribe) bestechen; kaufen (ugs.)
• ~ **ˈout** *v.t.* auszahlen ‹*Aktionär, Partner*›; aufkaufen ‹*Firma*›
• ~ **ˈup** *v.t.* aufkaufen

buyer /ˈbaɪə(r)/ *n.* **1** Käufer, *der*/Käuferin, *die;* **potential ~:** Kaufinteressent, *der* **2** ▸ⓘ **p. 1260** (Commerc.) Einkäufer, *der*/Einkäuferin, *die* **3** **a ~'s** *or* **~s' market** ein Käufermarkt

buying /ˈbaɪɪŋ/ *n., no pl.* Kaufen, *das*

ˈbuying power /ˈbaɪɪŋ/ *n.* Kaufkraft, *die*

ˈbuyout *n.* Aufkauf, *der;* Management-Buy-Out, *das* (Wirtsch.)

buzz /bʌz/
A *n.* **1** (of insect) Summen, *das;* (of large insect) Brummen, *das;* (of smaller or agitated insect) Schwirren, *das* **2** (sound of buzzer) Summen, *das;* **give one's secretary a ~:** über den Summer seine Sekretärin rufen **3** (of conversation, movement) Gemurmel, *das* **4** (coll.: telephone call) [Telefon]anruf, *der;* **give sb. a ~:** jmdn. anrufen **5** (coll.: thrill) Nervenkitzel, *der* (ugs.)
B *v.i.* **1** ▸ **A 1:** ‹*Insekt:*› summen/brummen/schwirren **2** (signal with buzzer) [mit dem Summer] rufen **3** (sound confusedly) **the courtroom ~ed as ...:** im Gerichtssaal erhob sich *od.* hörte man ein Raunen, als ...; ~ **with excitement** in heller Aufregung sein; **the rumour set the office ~ing** das Gerücht versetzte das Büro in helle Aufregung; **my ears are ~ing** mir sausen die Ohren
C *v.t.* (Aeronaut.) dicht vorbeifliegen *od.* (ugs.) vorbeizischen an (+ *Dat.*)

(Phrasal verbs)
• ~ **aˈbout**, ~ **aˈround**
A *v.i.* herumschwirren; herumsurren; (fig.) ‹*Person:*› herumsausen, herumschwirren
B *v.t.* ~ **around sth.** um etw. [herum]schwirren; ~ **around the room** im Zimmer herumschwirren *od.* umherschwirren
• ~ **ˈoff** *v.i.* (coll.) abhauen (salopp); abzischen (salopp)

buzzard /ˈbʌzəd/ *n.* (Ornith.) **1** (Brit.) Bussard, *der* **2** (Amer.: turkey ~) Amerikanischer Truthahngeier

buzzer /ˈbʌzə(r)/ *n.* Summer, *der*

buzz: **~-saw** *n.* (Amer.) Kreissäge, *die;* **~word** *n.* Schlagwort, *das*

by¹ /baɪ/
A *prep.* **1** (near, beside) an (+ *Dat.*); bei; (next to) neben; **by the window/river** am Fenster/Fluss; **the bus stop by the school** die Haltestelle an der Schule; **she sat by me** sie saß neben mir; **come and sit by me** komm, setz dich zu mir!
2 (to position beside) zu; **go over by the table/wall** geh zum Tisch/zur Wand!; **come by the fire** komm ans Feuer!
3 **by herself** *etc.* ▸ **herself 1**
4 (along) entlang; **by the river** am *od.* den Fluss entlang
5 (via) über (+ *Akk.*); **to Paris by Dover** nach Paris über Dover; **leave by the door/window** zur Tür hinausgehen/zum Fenster hinaussteigen; **they escaped by the back door/a stairway/a ladder** sie flüchteten durch die Hintertür/über eine Treppe/mit[tels] einer Leiter; **we came by the quickest/shortest route** wir sind die schnellste/kürzeste Strecke gefahren
6 (passing) vorbei an (+ *Dat.*); **run/drive by sb./sth.** an jmdm./etw. vorbeilaufen/vorbeifahren
7 (during) bei; **by day/night** bei Tag/Nacht; tagsüber/nachts; **by the light of the moon** im Mondschein
8 (through the agency of) von; **written by ...:** geschrieben von ...; **by sheer good fortune** durch reines Glück
9 (through the means of) durch; **he was killed by lightning/a falling chimney** er ist vom Blitz/von einem umstürzenden Schornstein erschlagen worden; **heated by gas/oil** mit Gas/Öl geheizt; gas-/ölbeheizt; **begin/end by doing sth.** damit beginnen/aufhören, etw. zu tun; **by turning the knob** durch Drehen des Griffs; **grab sb. by the collar** jmdn. am Kragen packen; **I knew him by his voice** ich erkannte ihn an seiner Stimme; **I could tell by his face that ...:** ich erkannte an seinem Gesicht, dass ...; **by bus/ship** *etc.* mit dem Bus/Schiff *usw.;* **by air/sea** mit dem Flugzeug/Schiff; **make a living by sth.** sich (*Dat.*) seinen Lebensunterhalt mit *od.* durch etw. verdienen; **have children by sb.** Kinder von jmdm. haben
10 ▸ⓘ **p. 1047** (not later than) bis; **by now/this time** inzwischen; **by next week she will be in China** nächste Woche ist sie schon in China; **by the time this letter reaches you** bis dich dieser Brief erreicht; **but by that time all the tickets had been sold** aber bis dahin waren schon alle Karten verkauft; **but by that time it was too late** aber da war es schon zu spät; **by the 20th of the month** bis zum 20. des Monats
11 *indicating unit of time* pro; *indicating unit of*

b

length, weight, etc. -weise; **by the second/minute/hour** pro Sekunde/Minute/Stunde; **rent a house by the year** ein Haus für jeweils ein Jahr mieten; **you can hire a car by the day or by the week** man kann sich (*Dat.*) ein Auto tageweise oder wochenweise mieten; **pay sb. by the month** jmdn. monatlich bezahlen; **day by day/month by month, by the day/month** (as each day etc. passes) Tag für Tag/Monat für Monat; **cloth by the metre** Stoff am Meter; **sell sth. by the packet/ton/dozen** etw. paket-/tonnenweise/im Dutzend verkaufen; **10 ft by 20 ft** 10 [Fuß] mal 20 Fuß
12▸ *indicating amount* **by the thousands** zu Tausenden; **one by one** einzeln; **two by two/three by three/four by four** zu zweit/dritt/viert; **little by little** nach und nach
13▸ *indicating factor* durch; **8 divided by 2 is 4** 8 geteilt durch 2 ist 4
14▸ *indicating extent* um; **wider by a foot** um einen Fuß breiter; **win by ten metres** mit zehn Metern Vorsprung gewinnen; **passed by nine votes to two** mit neun zu zwei Stimmen angenommen
15▸ (according to) nach; **by my watch** nach meiner Uhr; **by the left, quick march!** (Mil.) im Geschwindschritt — marsch! [Links, zwo, drei, vier!]
16▸ (slightly inclining to) auf (+ *Dat.*); **north-east by east** Nordost auf Ost
17▸ (about, in the possession of) bei; **have sth. by one** etw. bei sich haben
18▸ (in oaths) bei; **by [Almighty] God** bei Gott[, dem Allmächtigen]

B *adv.* 1▸ (past) vorbei; **march/drive/run/flow by** vorbeimarschieren/-fahren/-laufen/-fließen
2▸ (near) **close/near by** in der Nähe
3▸ (aside, in reserve) auf die Seite; *see also* **put by**
4▸ **by and large** im Großen und Ganzen; **by and by** nach und nach; (in past) nach einer Weile

by² ▸ **bye²**

'by-catch *n.* (Fishing) Beifang, *der*

bye¹ /baɪ/ *int.* (coll.) tschüs (ugs.); ~ **[for] now!** bis später!; tschüs! (ugs.)

bye² *n.* 1▸ (Sport) **draw a ~ in the first round** spielfrei in die zweite Runde kommen 2▸ **by the ~:** = **by the way** ▸ **way A 7** 3▸ (Cricket) *Lauf bei einem Ball, der vom Schlagmann nicht getroffen wurde*

bye-bye¹ /baɪ'baɪ/ *int.* (coll.) Wiedersehen (ugs.); ~ **[for] now!** [also] tschüs! (ugs.)

bye-bye² /'baɪbaɪ/, **bye-byes** /'baɪbaɪz/ *n.* (child lang.) **go [to] ~:** in die Heia gehen (Kinderspr.)

bye-law ▸ **by-law**

'by-election *n.* Nachwahl, *die*

'bygone
A *n.* **let ~s be ~s** die Vergangenheit ruhen lassen
B *adj.* **[in] ~ days** [in] vergangene[n] Tage[n]

'by-law *n.* 1▸ (esp. Brit.) Verordnung, *die;* **the park ~s** die Parkordnung 2▸ (of company etc.) Punkt der Richtlinien; *in pl.* Richtlinien *Pl.*

byline *n.* 1▸ (in newspaper) *Zeile mit dem Namen des Verfassers* 2▸ (Footb.) Tor[aus]linie, *die*

BYOB *abbr.* = **bring your own bottle** Getränke bitte mitbringen

'bypass
A *n.* (road) Umgehungsstraße, *die;* (channel; also Electr.) Nebenleitung, *die;* (Med.) Bypass, *der;* ~ **surgery** (Med.) eine Bypassoperation/Bypassoperationen
B *v.t.* 1▸ umleiten ‹*Flüssigkeit, Gas*› 2▸ **the road ~es the town** die Straße führt um die Stadt herum 3▸ (avoid) aus dem Wege gehen (+ *Dat.*); (fig.: ignore) übergehen

byplay *n., no pl., no indef. art.* (Theatre) Nebenhandlung, *die*

'by-product *n.* Nebenprodukt, *das*

byre /'baɪə(r)/ *n.* (Brit.) Kuhstall, *der*

'byroad *n.* Nebenstraße, *die;* Seitenstraße, *die*

bystander /'baɪstændə(r)/ *n.* Zuschauer, *der*/Zuschauerin, *die*

byte /baɪt/ *n.* (Computing) Byte, *das*

'byway *n.* Seitenweg, *der*

'byword *n.* (proverb) Spruch, *der;* [Sprich]wort, *das;* (person or thing taken as typical or notable example) Inbegriff, *der* (**for** *Gen.*)

Byzantine /bɪ'zæntaɪn, baɪ'zæntaɪn/ *adj.* 1▸ byzantinisch 2▸ (complicated) undurchschaubar

Byzantium /bɪ'zæntɪəm, baɪ'zæntɪəm/ *pr. n.* Byzanz (*das*)

C, c /siː/ *n., pl.* **Cs** *or* **C's** 1▸ (letter) C, c, *das* 2▸ **C** (Mus.) C, c, *das;* **middle C** das eingestrichene c; **C sharp** cis, Cis, *das* 3▸ (Roman numeral) C 4▸ (example) C, c (ohne Artikel) 5▸ **C** (Sch., Univ.: mark) Drei, *die;* **he got a C** er bekam „befriedigend“ *od.* eine Drei

c. *abbr.* 1▸ **= circa** ca. 2▸ ▸❶ **p. 1332 = cent[s]** c 3▸ **= century** Jh. 4▸ **= chapter** Kap. 5▸ **= cubic** Kubik-

C. *abbr.* 1▸ ▸❶ **p. 1620 = Celsius** C 2▸ ▸❶ **p. 1620 = Centigrade** C 3▸ (Geogr.) **= Cape** 4▸ (Pol.) **= Conservative**

© *symb.* **= copyright** ©

ca. *abbr.* **= circa** ca.

CA *abbr.* **= chartered accountant**

cab /kæb/ *n.* 1▸ (taxi) Taxi, *das;* Taxe, *die* (ugs.) 2▸ (Hist.: hackney carriage) [Pferde]droschke, *die* 3▸ (of lorry, truck) Fahrerhaus, *das;* (of crane) Fahrerkabine, *die;* (of train) Führerstand, *der*

CAB *abbr.* **= Citizens' Advice Bureau** ≈ Bürgerbüro, *das*

cabal /kəˈbæl/ *n.* 1▸ (intrigue) Intrige, *die;* Kabale, *die* (veralt.) 2▸ (clique, faction) Clique, *die* (abwertend)

cabaret /ˈkæbəreɪ/ *n.* Varietee, *das;* Cabaret, *das;* (more sophisticated) Kabarett, *das*

cabbage /ˈkæbɪdʒ/ *n.* 1▸ Kohl, *der;* **red/white ~:** Rot-/Weißkohl, *der;* **a [head of] ~:** ein Kopf Kohl; ein Kohlkopf; **as big as ~s** riesengroß ‹*Rosen usw.*› 2▸ (coll.: person) stumpfsinniger Mensch; Trottel, *der* (ugs. abwertend); **become a ~:** stumpfsinnig werden; vertrotteln (ugs. abwertend); **after his accident he became a complete ~:** nach seinem Unfall vegetierte er nur noch dahin

cabbage: ~ lettuce *n.* Kopfsalat, *der;* **~ 'white** *n.* (Zool.) Kohlweißling, *der*

cabbalistic /kæbəˈlɪstɪk/ *adj.* kabbalistisch

cabby /ˈkæbɪ/ (coll.), **'cab-driver** *ns.* Taxifahrer, *der;* (of horse-drawn vehicle) Kutscher, *der*

caber /ˈkeɪbə(r)/ *n.* Pfahl, *der;* Stamm, *der;* **tossing the ~:** Baumstammwerfen, *das*

cabin /ˈkæbɪn/ *n.* 1▸ (in ship) (for passengers) Kabine, *die;* (for crew) Kajüte, *die;* (in aircraft) Kabine, *die* 2▸ (simple dwelling) Hütte, *die* 3▸ (driver's) ▸**cab 3**

cabin: ~ boy *n.* (Naut.) Kabinensteward, *der;* **~ class** *n.* zweite Klasse; **they travelled ~ class** sie reisten zweiter Klasse; **~ cruiser** *n.* Kajütboot, *das*

cabinet /ˈkæbɪnɪt/ *n.* 1▸ Schrank, *der;* (in bathroom, for medicines) Schränkchen, *das;* (display ~) Vitrine, *die;* (for radio, TV, etc.) Gehäuse, *das* 2▸ *also:* **C~** (Polit.) Kabinett, *das; attrib.* **~ meeting** Kabinettssitzung, *die;* **~ reshuffle** Kabinettsumbildung, *die;* Regierungsumbildung, *die*

> **Cabinet**
>
> Das britische Kabinett ist ein Komitee von etwa 20 *Ministers* (Ministern), die vom **Prime Minister** (Premierminister) berufen werden. Jedes Mitglied ist für ein bestimmtes politisches Ressort verantwortlich und das Kabinett als Ganzes entscheidet über die Regierungspolitik. Das *Shadow Cabinet* (Schattenkabinett) wird vom Oppositionsführer berufen, sodass es im Fall eines Regierungswechsels, wie z.B. nach einer *general election* (Parlamentswahl), die Regierungsgeschäfte übernehmen kann.

cabinet: ~maker *n.* ▸❶ **p. 1260** Möbeltischler, *der;* **C~ 'Minister** *n.* Minister, *der;* Mitglied des Kabinetts

cable /ˈkeɪbl/

A *n.* 1▸ (rope) Kabel, *das;* Trosse, *die* (Naut.); (of mountain railway) Seil, *das* 2▸ (Electr., Teleph.) Kabel, *das* 3▸ (cablegram) Kabel, *das;* Überseetelegramm, *das* 4▸ (Naut.) (chain of anchor) Ankerkette, *die;* (measure) Kabellänge, *die*

B *v.t.* (transmit) telegraphisch durchgeben, kabeln ‹*Mitteilung, Nachricht*›; (inform) **~ sb.** jmdm. kabeln

cable: ~-access *adj.* **~-access programme/TV station** lokales Kabelprogramm/lokaler Kabelsender; **~ car** *n.* Drahtseilbahn, *die;* (in street) gezogene Straßenbahn; **~ channel** *n.* Kabelsender, *der;* **music ~ channel** Musikkabelsender, *der;* **~ company** *n.* Kabelgesellschaft, *die;* **~gram** *n.* Kabel, *das;* Überseetelegramm, *das;* **~-knit** *adj.* **~-knit sweater/cardigan** Pullover/Strickjacke mit Zopfmuster; **~ network** *n.* Kabelnetz, *das;* **~ 'railway** *n.* Standseilbahn, *die;* **~-ready** *attrib. adj.* kabeltauglich; **~ stitch** *n.* Zopfmuster, *das;* **~ television, ~ TV** *ns.* Kabelfernsehen, *das;* **~way** *n.* (double-~ ropeway) Seilschwebebahn, *die;* (gondola type) Kleinkabinenbahn, *die*

cabling /ˈkeɪblɪŋ/ *n., no pl.* 1▸ (cables) Kabel *Pl.;* Kabelleitungen *Pl.* 2▸ (installation of cables) Verkabelung, *die; attrib.* **~ system** Kabelsystem, *das*

caboodle /kəˈbuːdl/ *n., no pl.* (coll.) **the whole ~** (things) der ganze Kram (ugs.); das ganze Gelumpe (ugs.); (people) die ganze Bande (salopp) *od.* Sippschaft (ugs.)

caboose /kəˈbuːs/ *n.* 1▸ (on ship) Kombüse, *die* 2▸ (Amer.: on train) Dienstwagen, *der*

cabover /ˈkæbəʊvə(r)/ *n.* (Amer.) Cabover[-Truck], *der*

'cab rank *n.* (Brit.) Taxistand, *der;* Droschken[halte]platz, *der* (Amtsspr.)

cabriolet /kæbrɪəˈleɪ/ *n.* (Hist.) 1▸ (carriage) Kabriolett, *das* 2▸ (car) Kabriolett, *das;* Kabrio, *das* (ugs.)

cacao /kəˈkɑːəʊ, kəˈkeɪəʊ/ *n., pl.* **~s** 1▸ (seed) Kakaobohne, *die* 2▸ (tree) **~ [tree]** Kakaobaum, *der*

cache /kæʃ/

A *n.* 1▸ (hiding place) geheimes [Waffen-/Proviant-]lager; Versteck, *das* 2▸ (things hidden) Lager, *das;* **make a ~ of sth.** etw. verstecken *od.* in Sicherheit bringen 3▸ (Computing) Cache, *der; attrib.* **~ memory** Cache[speicher], *der;* Zwischenspeicher, *der*

B *v.t.* 1▸ verstecken 2▸ (Computing) zwischenspeichern ‹*Daten*›

cachet /ˈkæʃeɪ/ *n.* 1▸ (mark) Siegel, *das* (fig.); Stempel, *der* (fig.) 2▸ (prestige) Ansehen, *das;* Distinktion, *die* (geh.)

cack-handed /kækˈhændɪd/ *adj.* (coll.) 1▸ (left-handed) linkshändig 2▸ (clumsy) tollpatschig (ugs.)

cackle /ˈkækl/

A *n.* 1▸ (clucking of hen) Gackern, *das;* Gegacker, *das* 2▸ (laughter) [meckerndes] Gelächter; (of woman) Gegacker, *das* (abwertend); (laugh) **he gave a loud ~:** er prustete los (ugs.) 3▸ (talk) Geschwätz, *das* (abwertend); **cut the ~!** (coll.) genug geredet!; Schluss mit dem Geschwätz! (ugs.)

B *v.i.* 1▸ ‹*Henne:*› gackern 2▸ (laugh) meckernd lachen; ‹*Frau auch:*› gackern (ugs.)

cacophonous /kəˈkɒfənəs/ *adj.* kakophon (geh.); misstönend (geh.)

cacophony /kəˈkɒfənɪ/ *n.* Kakophonie, *die* (geh.); Missklang, *der* (geh.)

cactus /ˈkæktəs/ *n., pl.* **cacti** /ˈkæktaɪ/ *or* **~es** Kaktus, *der*

cad /kæd/ *n.* (dated derog.) Schuft, *der;* Schurke, *der* (veralt.)

CAD *abbr.* **= computer-aided design** CAD

cadaver /kəˈdɑːvə(r)/ *n.* (of animal) Kadaver, *der;* (of human) Leiche, *die*

cadaverous /kəˈdævərəs/ *adj.* 1▸ (corpse-like) Kadaver-, Leichen- 2▸ (deathly pale) leichenfahl; totenblass 3▸ (gaunt) dürr

CADCAM /ˈkædkæm/ *abbr.* **= computer-aided design; = computer-aided manufacture**

caddie /ˈkædɪ/ (Golf)

A *n.* Caddie, *der*

B *v.i.* **~ for sb.** jmds. Caddie sein; für jmdn. Caddie spielen (ugs.)

caddis/ˈkædɪs/: **~ fly** *n.* Köcherfliege, *die;* Frühlingsfliege, *die;* **~ worm** *n.* Köcherlarve, *die*

caddy[1] /ˈkædɪ/ *n.* Behälter, *der;* (tin) Büchse, *die;* Dose, *die*

caddy[2] ▸**caddie**

cadence /ˈkeɪdəns/ *n.* 1▸ (rhythm) Rhythmus, *der;* **marching/dancing ~:** Marsch-/Tanzrhythmus, *der;* **speech ~:** Sprachmelodie, *die* 2▸ (close of musical phrase, fall of voice) Kadenz, *die*

cadence 'braking *n., no pl.* Stotterbremstechnik, *die*

cadenza /kəˈdenzə/ *n.* (Mus.) [Konzert]kadenz, *die*

cadet /kəˈdet/ *n.* 1▸ (Mil. etc.) Offiziersschüler, *der;* Kadett, *der* (veralt.); **naval/police ~:** Marinekadett/Anwärter für den Polizeidienst; **~ corps** Kadettenkorps 2▸ (younger brother/son) jüngerer Bruder/Sohn

cadge /kædʒ/

A *v.t.* schnorren (ugs.); [sich (*Dat.*)] erbetteln; **could I ~ a lift with you?** können Sie mich vielleicht [ein Stück] mitnehmen?

B *v.i.* schnorren (ugs.)

cadger /ˈkædʒə(r)/ *n.* Schnorrer, *der* (ugs.)

cadmium /ˈkædmɪəm/ *n.* Kadmium, *das*

cadre /ˈkɑːdə(r), kɑːdr/ (Mil., Polit.) Kader, *der*

CAE *abbr.* **= computer-aided engineering** CAE

caecum /ˈsiːkəm/ *n., pl.* **caeca** /ˈsiːkə/ (Anat.) Blinddarm, *der*

Caesar /ˈsiːzə(r)/ *n.* 1▸ Cäsar, Caesar (*der*); (fig.) Alleinherrscher, *der* 2▸ (Med. coll.) Kaiserschnitt, *der*

Caesarean, Caesarian /sɪˈzeərɪən/ *adj. & n.* **~ [birth** *or* **operation** *or* **section]** Kaiserschnitt, *der*

caesium /ˈsiːzɪəm/ *n.* (Chem.) Caesium, *das* (fachspr.); Zäsium, *das; attrib.* **~ clock** Zäsiumuhr, *die*

caesura /sɪˈzjʊːrə/ *n.* (Pros.) Zäsur, *die*

café, cafe /ˈkæfɪ, ˈkæfeɪ/ *n.* 1▸ Lokal, *das;* (tearoom) Café, *das* 2▸ (Amer.: bar) Bar, *die*

café: ~ au lait /kæfeɪ əʊ 'leɪ/ *n., no pl.* Kaffee mit Sahne/Milch; Café crème (schweiz.); Brauner (österr.); **~ society** *n., no pl.* Schickeria, *die*

cafeteria /kæfɪ'tɪərɪə/ *n.* Selbstbedienungsrestaurant, *das;* Cafeteria, *die*

cafetière /kæfə'tjeə/ *n.* Kaffeebereiter, *der*

caff /kæf/ *n.* (Brit. coll.) Café, *das;* **transport ~:** Fernfahrerimbiss, *der*

caffeinated /'kæfɪneɪtɪd/ *adj.* koffeinhaltig

caffeine /'kæfi:n/ *n.* Koffein, *das;* (in tea) T[h]ein, *das*

caftan /'kæftæn/ *n.* Kaftan, *der*

cage /keɪdʒ/
A *n.* **1** Käfig, *der;* (for small birds) Bauer, *das* **2** (Mining) Förderkorb, *der* **3** (of lift) Fahrkabine, *die*
B *v.t.* einsperren; käfigen (fachspr.) ‹*Vögel*›

'cage bird *n.* Käfigvogel, *der*

cagey /'keɪdʒɪ/ *adj.* (coll.) **1** (wary) vorsichtig; **be ~ about sth.** vorsichtig bei etw. sein; sich mit etw. [sehr] zurückhalten; **a ~ buyer** ein wachsamer *od.* misstrauischer Käufer **2** (secretive, uncommunicative) zugeknöpft (ugs.); **be ~ about saying sth.** mit etw. hinterm Berg halten (ugs.)

cagily /'keɪdʒɪlɪ/ *adv.* (coll.) vorsichtig; (shrewdly) clever (ugs.); geschickt

caginess /'keɪdʒɪnɪs/ *n., no pl.* (caution) Vorsicht, *die;* (secretiveness) Zugeknöpftheit, *die*

cagoule /kə'gu:l/ *n.* [leichter, knielanger] Anorak

cagy ▸ **cagey**

cahoots /kə'hu:ts/ *n. pl.* (coll.) **1** (company, partnership) **be in ~ with the devil** mit dem Teufel im Bunde stehen; **go into ~ with sb.** sich mit jmdm. verbünden **2** (collusion) **be in ~ with sb.** mit jmdm. unter einer Decke stecken (ugs.)

CAI *abbr.* **= computer-aided** *or* **computer-assisted instruction**

caiman ▸ **cayman**

Cain /keɪn/ *pr. n.* Kain (*der*); **raise ~** (coll.) Krach schlagen (ugs.)

cairn /keən/ *n.* **1** (pyramid of stones) Steinpyramide, *die;* Cairn, *der* (fachspr.); **a ~ of stones** ein Steinhaufen **2** (dog) **~ [terrier]** Cairn-Terrier, *der; schottischer Zwergterrier*

Cairo /'kaɪərəʊ/ *pr. n.* ▸ **i p. 1643** Kairo (*das*)

caisson /'keɪsən, kə'su:n/ *n.* **1** (watertight chamber) Senkkasten, *der;* Caisson, *der* **2** (floating vessel) Docktor, *das;* Dockponton, *der*

'caisson disease *n.* Druckluftkrankheit, *die;* Caissonkrankheit, *die*

cajole /kə'dʒəʊl/ *v.t.* **~ sb. into sth./into doing sth.** jmdm. etw. einreden/jmdm. einreden, etw. zu tun; **~ sb. out of doing sth.** jmdm. ausreden, etw. zu tun; **~ sth. out of a person** jmdm. etw. entlocken

cajolery /kə'dʒəʊlərɪ/ *n.* Überredungskunst, *die*

Cajun /'keɪdʒən/
A *n.* Cajun, *der*
B *adj.* cajunisch

cake /keɪk/
A *n.* **1** Kuchen, *der;* **a piece of ~:** ein Stück Kuchen/Torte; **a slice of ~:** eine Scheibe Kuchen **2** (fig.) **get a slice of the ~:** sein Teil abbekommen; **go** *or* **sell like hot ~s** weggehen wie warme Semmeln (ugs.); **a piece of ~** (coll.) ein Kinderspiel (ugs.); **you cannot have your ~ and eat it [too]** beides auf einmal geht nicht; **~s and ale** (fig.) reinste Vergnügungen; *see also* **take A 3** **3** (block) **a ~ of soap** ein Riegel *od.* Stück Seife; **a ~ of wax** ein Riegel Wachs; **a ~ of tobacco** ein Plättchen Tabak
B *v.t.* **1** (cover) verkrusten; **~d with dirt/blood** schmutz-/blutverkrustet; **his suit was ~d with mud** sein Anzug war voll Schlamm **2** (form into mass) **rain ~d the soil** Regen machte die Erde klumpig
C *v.i.* (form a mass) verklumpen

cake: ~ shop *n.* Konditorei, *die;* **~ slice** *n.* Tortenheber, *der;* **~ stand** *n.* Etagere, *die;* **~ tin** *n.* Kuchenform, *die;* **~walk** *n.* (dance) Cakewalk, *der;* (easy task) Kinderspiel, *das* (ugs.)

cal. *abbr.* **= calorie[s]** cal.

CAL /kæl/ *abbr.* **= computer-aided** *or* **= computer-assisted learning** computergestütztes Lernen

calabash /'kæləbæʃ/ *n.* **1** (gourd) Flaschenkürbis, *der* **2** (pipe, container) Kalebasse, *die*

calaboose /kælə'bu:s/ *n.* (Amer.) Gefängnis, *das;* Kittchen, *das* (ugs.)

calabrese /kælə'breɪsɪ, 'kæləbri:s/ *n.* Broccoli, *der* (*der Sorte Calabrese*)

calamine /'kæləmaɪn/ *n., no pl.* Kalamin, *das; attrib.* **~ lotion** Kalaminlotion, *die*

calamitous /kə'læmɪtəs/ *adj.* verhängnisvoll

calamity /kə'læmɪtɪ/ *n.* **1** Unheil, *das;* Unglück, *das;* **calamities of nature** Naturkatastrophen **2** (adversity) Schicksalsschlag, *der* **3** (distress) Not, *die;* Elend, *das;* **a ~:** ein Unglück

Calamity 'Jane *n.* Schwarzseherin, *die*

calcification /kælsɪfɪ'keɪʃn/ *n., no pl.* Verkalkung, *die*

calcify /'kælsɪfaɪ/
A *v.i.* verkalken
B *v.t.* verkalken lassen

calcine /'kælsaɪn, 'kælsɪn/
A *v.t.* kalzinieren
B *v.i.* kalziniert werden

calcite /'kælsaɪt/ *n.* (Min.) Kalzit, *der*

calcium /'kælsɪəm/ *n.* Kalzium, *das;* Calcium, *das* (fachspr.)

calcium: ~ 'carbide *n.* Kalziumkarbid, *das;* **~ 'carbonate** *n.* Kalziumkarbonat, *das;* kohlensaures Kalzium

calculable /'kælkjʊləbl/ *adj.* berechenbar; kalkulierbar ‹*Risiko*›

calculate /'kælkjʊleɪt/
A *v.t.* **1** (ascertain) berechnen; (by estimating) ausrechnen; errechnen **2** (plan) **be ~d to do sth.** darauf abzielen, etw. zu tun **3** (Amer. coll.: suppose, believe) meinen; schätzen (ugs.)
B *v.i.* **1** (Math.) rechnen **2** **~ on doing sth.** damit rechnen, etw. zu tun

calculated /'kælkjʊleɪtɪd/ *adj.* (deliberate) vorsätzlich ‹*Handlung, Straftat*›; bewusst ‹*Zurückhaltung, Affront*›; kalkuliert ‹*Risiko*›; (apt, suitable) geeignet

calculating /'kælkjʊleɪtɪŋ/ *adj.* berechnend; **with a ~ eye** mit berechnendem Blick

calculation /kælkjʊ'leɪʃn/ *n.* **1** (result) Rechnung, *die;* **he is out in his ~s** er hat sich verrechnet **2** (calculating) Berechnung, *die* **3** (forecast) Schätzung, *die;* **by my ~s** nach meiner Schätzung

calculator /'kælkjʊleɪtə(r)/ *n.* **1** (person, machine) Rechner, *der* **2** (set of tables) Rechentabelle, *die*

calculus /'kælkjʊləs/ *n., pl.* **calculi** /'kælkjʊlaɪ/ *or* **~es** **1** (Math. etc.) -rechnung, *die;* (infinitesimal ~) Infinitesimalrechnung, *die;* **[the] differential/infinitesimal/integral ~:** [die] Differenzial-/Infinitesimal-/Integralrechnung **2** (Med.) Stein, *der*

Calcutta /kæl'kʌtə/ *pr. n.* ▸ **i p. 1643** Kalkutta (*das*)

caldron (esp. Amer.) ▸ **cauldron**

Caledonia /kælɪ'dəʊnɪə/ *pr. n.* (Hist./poet.) Kaledonien (*das*)

Caledonian /kælɪ'dəʊnɪən/
A *adj.* kaledonisch
B *n.* (joc./Hist.) Kaledonier, *der*/Kaledonierin, *die*

calendar /'kælɪndə(r)/ *n.* **1** Kalender, *der; attrib.* Kalender ‹*woche, -monat, -jahr*›; **[church] ~:** Kirchenkalender, *der* **2** (register, list) Verzeichnis, *das;* (list of canonized saints) Heiligenkalender, *der;* (list of cases for trial) Prozessregister, *das;* (Amer.: list of matters for debate) Tagesordnung, *die*

calender /'kælɪndə(r)/
A *n.* Kalander, *der* (Technik)
B *v.t.* kalandern, kalandrieren (Technik)

calendula /kə'lendjʊlə/ *n.* (Bot.) Ringelblume, *die*

calf[1] /kɑ:f/ *n., pl.* **calves** /kɑ:vz/ **1** (young of bovine animal) Kalb, *das;* (leather) **~[skin]** Kalbsleder, *das;* **a cow in** *or* **with ~:** eine trächtige Kuh **2** (of deer) Kalb, *das;* (of elephant, whale, rhinoceros) Junge, *das. See also* **fat C**; **golden calf**

calf[2] *n., pl.* **calves** ▸ **i p. 951** (Anat.) Wade, *die*

calf: ~ love *n.* [Jugend]schwärmerei, *die;* **~skin** *n.* Kalbfell, *das;* (leather) Kalbsleder, *das*

caliber (Amer.) ▸ **calibre**

calibrate /'kælɪbreɪt/ *v.t.* kalibrieren; eichen, kalibrieren ‹*Messgerät*›

calibration /kælɪ'breɪʃn/ *n.* Kalibrierung, *die;* (of gauge) Eichung, *die;* Kalibrierung, *die*

calibre /'kælɪbə(r)/ *n.* (Brit.) **1** (diameter) Kaliber, *das* **2** (fig.) Format, *das;* Kaliber, *das;* **a man of your ~:** ein Mann Ihres Kalibers *od.* von Ihrem Format

calico /'kælɪkəʊ/
A *n., pl.* **~es** *or* (Amer.) **~s** **1** Kattun, *der* **2** (Amer.: printed cotton fabric) Druckkattun, *der*
B *adj.* **1** Kattun-; kattunen (geh.) **2** (Amer.: multicoloured) bunt

California /kælɪ'fɔ:nɪə/ *pr. n.* Kalifornien (*das*)

Californian /kælɪ'fɔ:nɪən/
A *adj.* kalifornisch
B *n.* Kalifornier, *der*/Kalifornierin, *die*

caliper ▸ **calliper**

caliph /'kælɪf, 'keɪlɪf/ *n.* (Hist.) Kalif, *der*

calisthenics ▸ **callisthenics**

calk ▸ **caulk**

call /kɔ:l/
A *v.i.* **1** (shout) rufen; **~ to sb.** jmdm. zurufen; **~ [out] for help** um Hilfe rufen; **~ [out] for sb.** nach jmdm. rufen; **~ [out] for food/drink** nach Essen/zu trinken verlangen; **~ after sb.** jmdm. hinterherrufen; hinter jmdm. herrufen
2 (pay brief visit) [kurz] besuchen (**at** *Akk.*); vorbeikommen (ugs.) (**at** bei); ‹*Zug:*› halten (**at** in + *Dat.*); **~ at a port/station** einen Hafen anlaufen/an einem Bahnhof halten; **~ on sb.** jmdn. besuchen; bei jmdm. vorbeigehen (ugs.); **the postman ~ed to deliver a parcel** der Postbote war da und brachte ein Päckchen; **a man has ~ed to read the meter** ein Mann ist da, um den Zähler abzulesen; **~ round** vorbeikommen (ugs.)
3 (communicate by telephone) **who is ~ing, please?** wer spricht da, bitte?; **thank you for ~ing** vielen Dank für Ihren Anruf!; (communicate by radio) **this is London ~ing** hier spricht *od.* ist London
B *v.t.* **1** (cry out) rufen; aufrufen ‹*Namen, Nummer*›
2 (cry to) rufen ‹*Person*›
3 (summon) rufen; (into the army) einberufen; (to a duty, to do sth.) aufrufen; **~ him into the room** rufen Sie ihn herein!; **be ~ed home/to arms** nach Hause/zu den Waffen gerufen werden; **he was ~ed to his maker** (literary) er ist in die Ewigkeit abberufen worden (geh. verhüllend); **~ sth. into being** etw. ins Leben rufen; **~ sb.'s bluff** es darauf ankommen lassen (ugs.); **that was ~ed in question** das wurde infrage gestellt *od.* in Zweifel gezogen; **please ~ me a taxi** *or* **~ a taxi for me** bitte rufen Sie mir ein Taxi
4 (communicate with by radio/telephone) rufen/anrufen; (initially) Kontakt aufnehmen mit; **don't ~ us, we'll ~ you** wir sagen Ihnen Bescheid
5 (name) nennen; **he is ~ed Bob** er heißt Bob; **he doesn't mind if you simply ~ him Bob** er hat nichts dagegen, wenn du ihn einfach Bob nennst *od.* einfach Bob zu ihm sagst; **you can ~ him by his first name** ihr könnt ihn mit Vornamen anreden; **what is it ~ed in English?** wie heißt das auf Englisch?; **~ it what you will** wie immer man es auch nennen will; **~ sb. names** jmdn. beschimpfen
6 (rouse) wecken
7 (announce) einberufen ‹*Konferenz*›; ausrufen ‹*Streik*›; anberaumen ‹*Gerichtstermin*›; **~ a halt to sth.** mit etw. Schluss machen; **time was ~ed by the bartender** der Barmann rief „Feierabend“ *od.* (veralt., geh.) bot Feierabend
8 (urge) **duty ~s** die Pflicht ruft; **he was ~ed to preach the Gospel by God** er war von Gott

zur Verkündigung des Evangeliums auserwählt; *see also* **attention A 1**

[9] (nominate) **he was ∼ed to the presidency of the university** er wurde zum Präsidenten der Universität berufen; **be ∼ed to witness sth.** als Zeuge bei etw. aufgerufen werden

[10] (consider) nennen; **I ∼ that selfish** das nenne ich egoistisch; **£1.03 — let's ∼ it one pound** ein Pfund drei Pence — sagen wir ein Pfund (ugs.); **shall we ∼ it ten dollars/even?** sagen wir zehn Dollar/, wir sind quitt? (ugs.); **∼ sth. one's own** etw. sein Eigen nennen

[11] (Cards etc.) ansagen; (in coin-tossing) sagen; **he ∼ed heads and lost** er setzte auf Kopf und verlor. *See also* **account C 3**; **bar[1] A 9**; **day 1**; **spade 1**; **tune A 1**

C *n.* [1] (shout, cry) Ruf, *der;* **a ∼ for help** ein Hilferuf; **he came at my ∼:** er kam, als ich rief; **can you give me a ∼ at 6 o'clock?** können Sie mich um 6 Uhr wecken?; **remain/be within ∼:** in Rufweite bleiben/sein; **on** *or* **at ∼:** dienstbereit

[2] (visit) Besuch, *der;* **make** *or* **pay a ∼ on sb., make** *or* **pay sb. a ∼:** jmdn. besuchen; jmdm. einen Besuch abstatten (geh.); **have to pay a ∼** (coll.: need lavatory) mal [verschwinden] müssen (ugs.)

[3] (telephone ∼) Anruf, *der;* Gespräch, *das;* **give sb. a ∼:** jmdn. anrufen; **make a ∼:** ein Telefongespräch führen; **receive a ∼:** einen Anruf erhalten

[4] (invitation, summons) Aufruf, *der;* (by God) Berufung, *die;* (Theatre) Aufruf, *der;* (by audience) Hervorruf, *der;* **the ∼ of the sea/the wild** der Ruf des Meeres/der Wildnis; **∼ of nature** natürlicher Drang; **answer the ∼ of duty** der Pflicht gehorchen; **a ∼ for unity** ein Aufruf zur Einheit; **a worldwide ∼ for disarmament** ein weltweiter Ruf nach Abrüstung

[5] (need, occasion) Anlass, *der;* Veranlassung, *die;* **what ∼ is there for you to worry?** aus welchem Anlass *od.* Grund sorgen Sie sich?

[6] (of bugle, whistle) Signal, *das;* (of drum) Schlag, *der*

[7] (instrument) Lockinstrument, *das;* Locke, *die* (Jägerspr.)

[8] (esp. Commerc.: demand) Abruf, *der;* (demand made) Inanspruchnahme, *die;* **a ∼ for capital/money** Abruf von Kapital/Geldern; **have many ∼s on one's purse/time** finanziell/zeitlich sehr in Anspruch genommen sein

[9] (Cards etc.) Ansage, *die;* **it is your ∼ now** du musst ansagen; **was your ∼ heads or tails?** hatten Sie Kopf oder Zahl?

[10] (St. Exch.) Kaufoption, *die*

(Phrasal verbs)

- **∼ a'side** *v.t.* beiseite rufen ‹*Person*›
- **∼ a'way** *v.t.* wegrufen; abrufen
- **∼ 'back**

A *v.t.* zurückrufen

B *v.i.* [1] zurückrufen [2] (come back) zurückkommen; noch einmal vorbeikommen (ugs.)

- **∼ 'down** *v.t.* [1] (invoke) herabflehen (geh.) ‹*Segen*›; herausfordern ‹*Unwillen, Tadel*›; **∼ down curses on sb.'s head** jmdn. verfluchen [2] (reprimand) ausschimpfen
- **∼ for** *v.t.* [1] (send for, order) [sich (*Dat.*)] kommen lassen, bestellen ‹*Taxi, Essen, Getränke, Person*› [2] (collect) abholen ‹*Person, Gepäck, Güter*›; **'to be ∼ed for'** „wird abgeholt" [3] (require, demand) erfordern; verlangen; **that remark was not ∼ed for** die Bemerkung war unangebracht; **this ∼s for a celebration** das muss gefeiert werden
- **∼ 'forth** *v.t.* hervorrufen ‹*Protest, Kritik*›; zusammennehmen ‹*Mut, Energie*›; beschwören, lebendig werden lassen ‹*Eindrücke, Erinnerungen, Erlebnisse*›
- **∼ 'in**

A *v.i.* vorbeikommen (ugs.); **I'll ∼ in on you** ich komme bei dir vorbei (ugs.); **I'll ∼ in at your office** ich komme bei dir im Büro vorbei (ugs.)

B *v.t.* [1] aus dem Verkehr ziehen ‹*Waren, Münzen*›; zurückfordern ‹*Bücher*› [2] **∼ in a specialist** einen Fachmann/Facharzt zurate ziehen

- **∼ 'off** *v.t.* (cancel) absagen ‹*Treffen, Verabredung*›; rückgängig machen ‹*Geschäft*›; lösen ‹*Verlobung*›; (stop, end) abbrechen, (ugs.) abblasen ‹*Streik*›; **∼ off your dogs!** rufen Sie Ihre Hunde zurück!
- **∼ on** ▸ **∼ [up]on**
- **∼ 'out**

A *v.t.* alarmieren ‹*Truppen*›; rufen ‹*Wache*›; zum Streik aufrufen ‹*Arbeitnehmer*›

B *v.i.* ▸ **∼ A 1**; **∼ out to warn sb.** jmdm. zurufen, um ihn zu warnen

- **∼ 'up** *v.t.* [1] (imagine, recollect) wachrufen ‹*Erinnerungen, Bilder*›; [herauf]beschwören, erwecken ‹*böse Erinnerungen, Fantasien*› [2] (summon) anrufen, beschwören ‹*Teufel, Geister*› [3] (by telephone) anrufen; **I'll ∼ you up again** ich rufe Sie wieder an [4] (Mil.) einberufen; **they were ∼ed up to go to Iraq** sie wurden nach Irak einberufen; *see also* **call-up**
- **∼ [up]on** *v.t.* **∼ upon God** Gott anrufen; **∼ upon sb.'s generosity/sense of justice** an jmds. Großzügigkeit/Gerechtigkeitssinn (*Akk.*) appellieren; **∼ [up]on sb. to do sth.** jmdn. auffordern, etw. zu tun

call: ∼back *n.* [1] (Amer.: invitation) Einladung zu einer erneuten Audition; (audition) erneute Audition; **receive a ∼back** zu einer erneuten Audition eingeladen werden; [2] (return phone call) Rückruf, *der; attrib.* **∼back system** Callback-System, *das* (fachspr.); [3] (Computing) Callback, *der* (fachspr.); *attrib.* **∼back system/security feature** Callback-Verfahren, *das*/-Sicherheitsfeature, *das;* **∼ barring** *n.*, *no pl.* Anrufersperre, *die;* **∼ box** *n.* Telefonzelle, *die;* **∼ boy** *n.* [1] (in theatre) Gehilfe des Inspizienten/Souffleurs; [2] (in hotel) [Hotel]boy, *der;* **∼ button** *n.* Ruftaste, *die;* **∼ centre** *n.* Callcenter, *das;* **∼ charges** *pl. n.* (Teleph.) Gesprächsgebühren *Pl.;* **∼ diversion** *n.* Rufumleitung, *die*

caller /'kɔːlə(r)/ *n.* [1] Rufende, *der/die;* (visitor) Besucher, *der*/Besucherin, *die;* (on telephone) Anrufer, *der*/Anruferin, *die* [2] (in bingo, square dance) Ansager, *der*/Ansagerin, *die*

'caller display *n.* Rufnummernanzeige, *die*

call: ∼-forwarding *n.*, *no pl.* Anrufweiterschaltung, *die;* **∼ girl** *n.* Callgirl, *das*

calligrapher /kə'lɪgrəfə(r)/ *n.* ▸**❶ p. 1260** Schönschreiber, *der*/Schönschreiberin, *die;* (professional) Kalligraph, *der*/Kalligraphin, *die*

calligraphy /kə'lɪgrəfɪ/ *n.* [1] (beautiful handwriting) Schönschrift, *die;* Kalligraphie, *die;* (as an art) Kalligraphie, *die;* Schönschreiben, *das* [2] (handwriting) Handschrift, *die;* Hand, *die* (geh.)

calling /'kɔːlɪŋ/ *n.* [1] (occupation, profession) Beruf, *der* [2] (divine summons) Berufung, *die*

'calling card *n.* (Amer.) Visitenkarte, *die*

calliper /'kælɪpə(r)/ *n.* [1] *in pl.* **[pair of] ∼s** Greifzirkel, *der;* Tasterzirkel, *der;* Taster, *der* [2] **∼ [splint]** (Med.) Beinschiene, *die* [3] **[brake] ∼:** Bremssattel, *der*

callisthenics /kælɪs'θenɪks/ *n. pl.* Kallisthenie, *die;* leichte Gymnastik

call: ∼ letters *n. pl.* (Amer. Radio/TV) Kennbuchstaben *Pl.;* **∼ meter** *n.* (Teleph.) Gebührenzähler, *der*

callosity /kə'lɒsɪtɪ/ *n.* [1] *no pl.* Schwieligkeit, *die* [2] (lump) Schwiele, *die*

callous /'kæləs/

A *adj.* (unfeeling, insensitive) gefühllos; herzlos ‹*Handlung, Verhalten*›; lieblos ‹*Leben, Welt*›

B *n.* ▸ **callus**

callously /'kæləslɪ/ *adv.* herzlos

callousness /'kæləsnɪs/ *n.*, *no pl.* (want of feeling) Gefühllosigkeit, *die;* (of act, behaviour) Herzlosigkeit, *die;* **his ∼ towards [the feelings of] other people** seine Gleichgültigkeit den Gefühlen anderer gegenüber

'call-out *n.* Einsatz, *der;* **the ∼ could come at any time** es kann jederzeit eine Einsatzanforderung kommen; *attrib.* **call-out fee/charge** Anfahrtskosten *Pl.*

'call-over *n.* Namensruf, *der;* (of betting prices) Verlesen, *das*

callow /'kæləʊ/ *adj.* unreif ‹*Junge, Student*›; grün (ugs.) ‹*Jüngling*›; **in my ∼ youth** als ich noch jung und unreif war

call: ∼ return *n.*, *no pl.: Möglichkeit, die Nummer des letzten Anrufers festzustellen [und mit einem Tastendruck zu wählen]*; **∼ screening** *n.*, *no pl.* [1] (for identifying callers) Call-Screening, *das;* [2] (call barring) Anrufersperre, *die;* **∼ sign**, **∼ signal** *ns.* Rufzeichen, *das;* **∼-up** *n.* (Mil.) Einberufung, *die*

callus /'kæləs/ *n.* [1] (Physiol.) Schwiele, *die;* Kallus, *der* (fachspr.) [2] (Med.) Knochennarbe, *die;* Kallus, *der* (fachspr.) [3] (Bot.) Wundgewebe, *das;* Kallus, *der* (fachspr.)

'call waiting *n.*, *no pl.* (Teleph.) Anklopfen, *das*

calm /kɑːm/

A *n.* [1] (stillness) Stille, *die;* (serenity) Ruhe, *die;* **the peaceful ∼ of the night** die friedliche Stille der Nacht [2] (windless period) Windstille, *die;* Kalme, *die* (Met.); **a dead ∼:** totale Windstille; **the ∼ before the storm** (lit. or fig.) die Ruhe vor dem Sturm

B *adj.* [1] (tranquil, quiet, windless) ruhig; **keep ∼:** ruhig bleiben; Ruhe bewahren; **keep one's voice ∼:** ruhig sprechen [2] (coll.: self-confident) lässig (ugs.); gelassen

C *v.t.* beruhigen ‹*Person*›; besänftigen ‹*Leidenschaften, Zorn*›; **∼ sb. down** jmdn. beruhigen

D *v.i.* **∼ [down]** sich beruhigen; ‹*Sturm:*› abflauen

calmly /'kɑːmlɪ/ *adv.* ruhig; gelassen

calmness /'kɑːmnɪs/ *n.*, *no pl.* Ruhe, *die;* (of water, sea) Stille, *die*

Calor gas ® /'kælə gæs/ *n.* Butangas, *das*

calorie /'kælərɪ/ *n.* Kalorie, *die*

calorific /kælə'rɪfɪk/ *adj.* wärmeerzeugend; **∼ value** Heizwert, *der*

calorimeter /kælə'rɪmɪtə(r)/ *n.* Kalorimeter, *das*

calumniate /kə'lʌmnɪeɪt/ *v.t.* (formal) verleumden

calumny /'kæləmnɪ/

A *n.* Verleumdung, *die*

B *v.t.* verleumden

calvados /'kælvədɒs/ *n.* Calvados, *der*

Calvary /'kælvərɪ/ *n.* (place) Golgatha (*das*); (representation) Kalvarienberg, *der*

calve /kɑːv/ *v.i.* kalben; abkalben (fachspr.)

calves *pl. of* **calf[1,2]**

Calvinism /'kælvɪnɪzm/ *n.*, *no pl.* Kalvinismus, *der*

Calvinist /'kælvɪnɪst/ *n.* Kalvinist, *der*/Kalvinistin, *die*

Calvinistic /kælvɪ'nɪstɪk/, **Calvinistical** /kælvɪ'nɪstɪkl/ *adj.* kalvinistisch

calypso /kə'lɪpsəʊ/ *n.*, *pl.* **∼s** Calypso, *der*

calyx /'keɪlɪks, 'kælɪks/ *n.*, *pl.* **calyces** /'keɪlɪsiːz, 'kælɪsiːz/ *or* **-es** [1] (Bot.) Kelch, *der;* Kalyx, *der* (fachspr.) [2] (Anat.) Kelch, *der*

cam /kæm/ *n.* Nocken, *der*

CAM *abbr.* **= computer-aided** *or* **computer-assisted manufacturing**

camaraderie /kæmə'rɑːdərɪ/ *n.*, *no pl.* Kameradschaft, *die*

camber /'kæmbə(r)/

A *n.* [1] (convexity) Wölbung, *die* [2] (Motor Veh.) Achssturz, *der;* Radsturz, *der*

B *v.t.* wölben; **a ∼ed road** eine gewölbte Straße

Cambodia /kæm'bəʊdɪə/ *pr. n.* (Hist.) Kambodscha (*das*)

Cambodian /kæm'bəʊdɪən/ ▸**❶ p. 1345** (Hist.)

A *adj.* kambodschanisch

B *n.* Kambodschaner, *der*/Kambodschanerin, *die*

Cambrian /'kæmbrɪən/

A *adj.* [1] (Welsh) walisisch; Waliser [2] (Geol.) kambrisch

B *n.* (Geol.) Kambrium, *das*

cambric /'kæmbrɪk/ *n.* Kambrik[batist], *der*

Cambridge /'keɪmbrɪdʒ/: ~ **blue** *n.* Blassblau, *das;* Cambridgeblau, *das*

> **Cambridge Certificate**
>
> Ein Sprachzertifikat über das Leistungsniveau von Lernenden, die Englisch als Fremdsprache studieren. Die Examen werden von der Universität Cambridge auf drei verschiedenen Niveaus abgenommen. Auf dem niedrigsten Niveau führt das Examen zum *First Certificate in English*, auf dem mittleren Niveau zum *Advanced Certificate in English*, und auf dem fortgeschrittenen Niveau führt es zum *Certificate of Proficiency in English*. Viele Sprachschulen innerhalb und außerhalb Großbritanniens bereiten Studierende auf diese Examen vor.

camcorder /'kæmkɔ:də(r)/ *n.* Camcorder, *der;* Kamerarecorder, *der*

came ▸ **come A**

camel /'kæml/ *n.* (Zool.) Kamel, *das*

camellia /kə'mi:lɪə, kə'melɪə/ *n.* (Bot.) Kamelie, *die*

'**camel['s] hair** *n.* Kamelhaar, *das; attrib.* ~ **brush** Haarpinsel, *der;* ~ **coat** Kamelhaarmantel, *der*

cameo /'kæmɪəʊ/ *n., pl.* ~**s** 1 (carving) Kamee, *die* 2 (short sketch) Sketch, *der;* (minor role) Cameorolle, *die; attrib.* ~ **appearance** Cameoauftritt, *der;* **make a** ~ **appearance** in einer Cameorolle auftreten

camera /'kæmərə/ *n.* 1 Kamera, *die;* (for still pictures) Fotoapparat, *der;* Kamera, *die;* **be/go on** ~: vor der Kamera sein/vor die Kamera treten 2 (Law) **in** ~: unter Ausschluss der Öffentlichkeit; (fig.) hinter verschlossenen Türen

camera: ~ **angle** *n.* Kamerawinkel, *der;* ~ **case** *n.* Kameratasche, *die;* ~**man** *n.* ▸❶ **p. 1260** Kameramann, *der;* ~ **phone** *n.* Fotohandy, *das;* ~ **range** *n.* Kamerareichweite, *die;* **in/out of** ~ **range** in/außer Reichweite der Kamera; **go out of** ~ **range** sich aus der Reichweite der Kamera bewegen; ~**-ready** *adj.* belichtungsfertig; ~**-ready copy** belichtungsfertige Druckvorlagen; ~ **shake** *n., no pl.* Verwackeln [der Kamera]; **the photograph suffered from** ~ **shake** das Foto war verwackelt; ~**-shy** *adj.* kamerascheu; ~**work** *n., no pl., no indef. art.* Kameraführung, *die*

Cameroon /'kæməru:n/ *pr. n.* Kamerun *(das)*

camiknickers /'kæmɪnɪkəz/ *n. pl.* (Brit.) Spitzenhemdhöschen, *das*

camisole /'kæmɪsəʊl/ *n.* (arch.) Leibchen, *das;* Mieder, *das;* Kamisol, *das* (veralt.)

camomile /'kæməmaɪl/ *n.* (Bot.) Kamille, *die; attrib.* ~ **tea** Kamillentee, *der*

camouflage /'kæməflɑ:ʒ/

A *n.* (lit. or fig.) Tarnung, *die;* Camouflage, *die* (Milit. veralt./fig. geh.)

B *v.t.* (lit. or fig.) tarnen; camouflieren (veralt./geh.)

camp¹ /kæmp/

A *n.* Lager, *das;* (Mil.) Feldlager, *das;* **the world is divided into two opposing** ~**s** (fig.) die Welt teilt sich in zwei entgegengesetzte Lager; *see also* **foot A 1**

B *v.i.* ~ **[out]** campen; (in tent) zelten; **go** ~**ing** Campen/Zelten fahren/gehen

Phrasal verb

• ~ **'on** *v.i.* (Teleph.) anklopfen

camp²

A *adj.* 1 (affected) affektiert, geziert ‹*Person, Art, Benehmen*› 2 (exaggerated) übertrieben, theatralisch ‹*Gestik, Ausdrucksform*› 3 (homosexual) schwul (ugs.); (effeminate) tuntenhaft (ugs.)

B *n.* Manieriertheit, *die*

C *v.t.* ~ **it up** zu dick auftragen (ugs.); ~ **up a part** bei einer Rolle zu dick auftragen (ugs.)

campaign /kæm'peɪn/

A *n.* 1 (Mil.) Feldzug, *der;* Kampagne, *die* (veralt.); **be on** ~: im Felde stehen (veralt.) 2 (organized course of action) Kampagne, *die;* Feldzug, *der;* **publicity** ~: Werbekampagne, *die; see also* **presidential**

B *v.i.* ~ **for sth.** sich für etw. einsetzen; ~ **against sth.** gegen etw. etwas unternehmen; **be** ~**ing** (for election) ‹*Politiker:*› im Wahlkampf stehen; ~ **hard** einen intensiven Wahlkampf führen

campaigner /kæm'peɪnə(r)/ *n.* 1 Vorkämpfer, *der*/Vorkämpferin, *die* 2 (veteran) Veteran, *der;* alter Kämpfer; **an old** ~: ein alter Kämpfer *od.* (veralt.) Kämpe 3 ~ **for ...:** Anhänger, *der*/Anhängerin, *die* (+ *Gen.*); ~ **against ...:** Gegner, *der*/Gegnerin, *die* (+ *Gen.*)

campaign: ~ **literature** *n.* Werbematerial, *das;* (for election campaign) Wahlwerbung, *die;* ~ **trail** *n.* Wahlkampfreise, *die;* **on the** ~ **trail** im Wahlkampf

campanology /kæmpə'nɒlədʒɪ/ *n., no pl.* Kunst des Glockenläutens

campanula /kæm'pænjʊlə/ *n.* Glockenblume, *die;* Campanula, *die* (fachspr.)

camp: ~ **bed** *n.* Campingliege, *die;* ~**craft** *n., no pl.* Praxis des Lebens im Zelt und im Freien

camper /'kæmpə(r)/ *n.* 1 Camper, *der*/Camperin, *die* 2 (vehicle) ~ **[van]** Wohnmobil, *das*

camp: ~**fire** *n.* Lagerfeuer, *das;* ~ **follower** *n.* Marketender, *der*/Marketenderin, *die;* (fig.: disciple, follower) Mitläufer, *der*/Mitläuferin, *die*

camphor /'kæmfə(r)/ *n.* Kampfer, *der*

camping /'kæmpɪŋ/ *n.* Camping, *das;* (in tent) Zelten, *das*

camping: ~ **ground** (Amer.) ▸ ~ **site;** ~ **holiday** *n.* Campingurlaub, *der;* ~ **site** *n.* Campingplatz, *der;* ~ **stool** ▸ **camp stool;** ~ **stove** *n.* Campingherd, *der;* Campingkocher, *der*

camp: ~ **meeting** *n.* (Amer.) (in the open air) Freilichtgottesdienst, *der;* (in a tent) Zeltgottesdienst, *der;* ~**site** *n.* Campingplatz, *der;* ~ **stool** *n.* Campinghocker, *der*

campus /'kæmpəs/ *n.* 1 (grounds of university) Campus, *der;* Hochschulgelände, *das* 2 (university) Hochschule, *die*

'**campus university** *n.* Campusuniversität, *die*

CAMRA /'kæmrə/ *abbr.* = **Campaign for Real Ale**

'**camshaft** *n.* Nockenwelle, *die*

can¹ /kæn/

A *n.* 1 (milk ~, watering ~) Kanne, *die;* (for oil, petrol) Kanister, *der;* (Amer.: for refuse) Eimer, *der;* Tonne, *die;* **a** ~ **of paint** eine Büchse Farbe; (with handle) ein Eimer Farbe; **carry** *or* **take the** ~ **[back]** (Brit. fig. coll.) die Sache ausbaden (ugs.) 2 (container for preserving) [Konserven]dose, *die;* [Konserven]büchse, *die;* **a** ~ **of tomatoes/sausages** eine Dose *od.* Büchse Tomaten/Würstchen; ~**s of food** Lebensmittelkonserven; **a** ~ **of beer** eine Dose Bier; **a** ~ **of worms** (fig.) eine verzwickte Angelegenheit (ugs.) 3 (Amer. sl.: lavatory) Lokus, *der* (ugs.) 4 (sl.: prison) Knast, *der* (salopp)

B *v.t.,* **-nn-** 1 (preserve) konservieren 2 (put into ~) eindosen; einmachen ‹*Obst*›

can² *v. aux., only in pres.* ~, *neg.* ~**not** /'kænət/, (coll.) ~**'t** /kɑ:nt/, *past* **could** /kʊd/, *neg.* (coll.) **couldn't** /'kʊdnt/ können; (have right, be permitted) dürfen; können; **as much as one** ~: so viel man kann; **as ... as** '~ **be** wirklich sehr ...; ~ **do** (coll.) kein Problem; **he** ~**'t be more than 40** er kann nicht über 40 sein; **you** ~**'t smoke in this compartment** in diesem Abteil dürfen Sie nicht rauchen; **what you say** ~**not be true** was du sagst, kann nicht stimmen; **come nearer, I** ~**'t hear what you're saying** kommen Sie näher, ich kann Sie nicht verstehen; **could you ring me tomorrow?** könnten Sie mich morgen anrufen?; **how [ever] could you do this to me?** wie konnten Sie mir das bloß antun?; **I could have killed him** ich hätte ihn umbringen können; **[that] could be [so]** das könnte *od.* kann sein

Canada /'kænədə/ *pr. n.* Kanada *(das)*

'**Canada goose** *n.* Kanadagans, *die*

Canadian /kə'neɪdɪən/ ▸❶ **p. 1345**

A *adj.* kanadisch; **sb. is** ~: jmd. ist Kanadier/Kanadierin

B *n.* Kanadier, *der*/Kanadierin, *die;* **the French/English** ~**s** die Franko-/Anglokanadier

canaille /kə'nɑ:i:/ *n.* (formal derog.) Pöbel, *der* (abwertend)

canal /kə'næl/ *n.* 1 (watercourse, marking on Mars) Kanal, *der;* **the Panama C**~: der Panamakanal 2 (Zool., Bot.) Gang, *der;* (alimentary ~) [Verdauungs]kanal, *der*

canal: ~ **boat** *n.: langes, schmales Boot zum Befahren der Kanäle;* (Hist.: towed barge) Schleppkahn, *der;* ~ **holiday** *n.* Kanalurlaub, *der;* Kanalferien *Pl.*

canalization /kænəlaɪ'zeɪʃn/ *n., no pl.* Kanalisierung, *die*

canalize /'kænəlaɪz/ *v.t.* kanalisieren ‹*Fluss*›

ca'nalside

A *adj.* am Kanalufer *nachgestellt;* **a** ~ **walk** ein Spaziergang am Kanal

B *adv.* am Kanal[ufer]

C *n.* Kanalufer, *das*

canapé /'kænəpeɪ/ *n.* (food) Cocktailhappen, *der;* Kanapee, *das*

canard /kə'nɑ:d, 'kænɑ:d/ *n.* (false report) Ente, *die* (ugs.)

Canaries /kə'neərɪz/ *pr. n. pl.* Kanarische Inseln *Pl.;* Kanaren *Pl.*

canary /kə'neərɪ/ *n.* Kanarienvogel, *der*

canary: C~ **'Islands** *pr. n. pl.* Kanarische Inseln *Pl.;* ~**-seed** *n.* Kanariensamen, *der;* ~ **'yellow** *n.* Kanariengelb, *das;* ~**-yellow** *adj.* kanariengelb

canasta /kə'næstə/ *n.* (Cards) Canasta, *das*

cancan /'kænkæn/ *n.* Cancan, *der*

cancel /'kænsl/

A *v.t.,* (Brit.) **-ll-** 1 (cross out) streichen ‹*Wort, Satz, Absatz*› 2 (call off) absagen ‹*Besuch, Urlaub, Reise, Sportveranstaltung*›; ausfallen lassen ‹*Veranstaltung, Vorlesung, Zug, Bus*›; fallen lassen ‹*Pläne*›; (annul, revoke) rückgängig machen ‹*Einladung, Vertrag*›; zurücknehmen ‹*Befehl*›; stornieren ‹*Bestellung, Auftrag*›; streichen ‹*Schuld[en]*›; kündigen ‹*Abonnement*›; abbestellen ‹*Zeitung*›; aufheben ‹*Klausel, Gesetz, Recht*›; **the match had to be** ~**led** das Spiel musste ausfallen *od.* abgesagt werden; **the boat to Dublin has been** ~**led** die Fähre nach Dublin fährt *od.* verkehrt nicht; **the lecture has been** ~**led** die Vorlesung fällt aus 3 (balance, neutralize) aufheben; **the arguments** ~ **each other out** die Argumente heben sich gegenseitig auf 4 (deface) entwerten ‹*Briefmarke, Fahrkarte*›; ungültig machen ‹*Scheck*› 5 (Math.) aufheben; wegkürzen (ugs.) 6 (Amer. Mus.) auflösen 7 (Computing) abbrechen ‹*Vorgang*›; zurücknehmen ‹*Befehl*›

B *v.i.,* (Brit.) **-ll-:** ~ **[out]** sich [gegenseitig] aufheben

cancellation /kænsə'leɪʃn/ *n.* ▸ **cancel A:** 1 Streichung, *die* 2 Absage, *die;* Ausfall, *der;* Ausfallen, *das;* Fallenlassen, *das;* Aufgabe, *die;* Rückgängigmachen, *das;* [Zu]rücknahme, *die;* Stornierung, *die;* Streichung, *die;* Kündigung, *die;* Abbestellung, *die;* Aufhebung, *die* 3 Aufhebung, *die* 4 Entwertung, *die;* Ungültigmachen, *das* 5 Aufhebung, *die;* Wegkürzen, *das* (ugs.) 6 Auflösung, *die*

cancel'lation fee *n.* Stornogebühr, *die*

cancer /'kænsə(r)/ *n.* 1 ▸❶ **p. 1231** (Med.) Krebs, *der;* (fig.) Krebsgeschwür, *das;* ~ **of the liver** Leberkrebs, *der* 2 **C**~ (Astrol., Astron.) der Krebs; der Cancer; *see also* **Aries; tropic**

Cancerian /kæn'sɪərɪən/ *n.* (Astrol.) Krebs, *der*

cancerous /'kænsərəs/ *adj.* Krebs‹*geschwulst, -geschwür*›; krebsartig ‹*Wucherung, Wachstum*›; kanzerös (fachspr.); (fig.) bösartig ‹*Hass, Einfluss*›; ~ **growth** krebsartige Wucherung

cancer: ~ **research** *n., no pl.* Krebsforschung, *die;* ~ **stick** *n.* (coll. hum.) Sargnagel, *der* (ugs.)

candela /kæn'delə, -'di:lə/ *n.* (Phys.) Candela, *die*

candelabra /kændɪ'lɑ:brə/ *n.,* **candelabrum** /kændɪ'læbrəm, kændɪ'lɑ:brəm/ *n., pl.* ~ *or* (Amer.) **candelabrums** Leuchter, *der;* (large) Kandelaber, *der*

candid /'kændɪd/ *adj.* offen; ehrlich ‹*Ansicht, Bericht*›; **let me be** ~ **with you** ich will ganz offen mit Ihnen sein

candidacy /'kændɪdəsɪ/ *n.* Kandidatur, *die*

candidate /ˈkændɪdət, ˈkændɪdeɪt/ *n.* 1 Kandidat, *der*/Kandidatin, *die;* Anwärter, *der*/Anwärterin, *die;* **a ~ for Mayor** ein Bürgermeisterkandidat/-kandidatin; **he offered himself as a ~ for the position** er bot sich als Kandidat für den Posten an; **~s for a club/for membership** Anwärter für einen Klub/auf Mitgliedschaft; *attrib.* **~ country** (EU) Kandidatenland, *das* 2 (examinee) Kandidat, *der*/Kandidatin, *die;* **a PhD~:** ein Promotionskandidat *od.* Promovend; **a ~ for a degree** ein Prüfling *od.* Examinand

candidature /ˈkændɪdətʃə(r)/ *n.* (esp. Brit.) Kandidatur, *die*

candid ˈcamera *n.* versteckte Kamera

candidly /ˈkændɪdlɪ/ *adv.* offen; ehrlich; **~, I dislike the whole idea** offen gesagt, gefällt mir die Idee gar nicht

candle /kændl/

A *n.* 1 Kerze, *die;* **burn the ~ at both ends** (fig.) sich übernehmen; sich (*Dat.*) zu viel aufladen; **she can't** *or* **is not fit to hold a ~ to him** (fig.) sie kann ihm nicht das Wasser reichen; **the game is not worth the ~** (fig.) die Sache lohnt sich nicht *od.* ist nicht der Mühe (*Gen.*) wert 2 (unit) **~[power]** Kerze, *die* (veralt.); Candela, *die. See also* **Roman candle**

B *v.t.* gegen das Licht halten, durchleuchten ‹*Eier*›

candle: ~light *n.* Kerzenlicht, *das;* **by ~light** bei Kerzenlicht ‹*lesen*›; im Kerzenschein (geh.) ‹*feiern, speisen*›; **~power** ▸**candle A 2**; **~stick** *n.* Kerzenhalter, *der;* (elaborate) Leuchter, *der;* **~wick** *n.* 1 (of candle) Kerzendocht, *der;* 2 (material) Frottierplüsch, *der*

candour (*Brit.; Amer.:* **candor**) /ˈkændə(r)/ *n.* (frankness) Offenheit, *die;* (honesty) Ehrlichkeit, *die*

candy /ˈkændɪ/

A *n.* 1 Kandis[zucker], *der;* **a ~:** ein Stück Kandis[zucker] 2 (Amer.) (sweets) Süßigkeiten *Pl.;* (sweet) Bonbon, *das od. der*

B *v.t.* kandieren ‹*Früchte*›; **candied lemon/orange peel** Zitronat/Orangeat, *das*

candy: ~-ass *n.* (Amer. coll.) Weichei, *das* (ugs.); Memme, *die* (veraltend, abwertend); *attrib.* feige; **~-assed** /ˈkændɪæst/ *adj.* (Amer. coll.) (cowardly) feige; (despicable) mies; elend; **~floss** *n.* Zuckerwatte, *die;* **~ store** *n.* (Amer.) Süßwarengeschäft, *das;* Bonbonladen, *der* (ugs.); **~-stripe** *n.* Muster mit bunten Streifen [auf weißem Hintergrund]; **~-striped** *adj.* bunt gestreift; **~tuft** *n.* (Bot.) Schleifenblume, *die*

ˈcandytuft (Bot.) *n.* Schleifenblume, *die*

cane /keɪn/

A *n.* 1 (stem of bamboo, rattan, etc.) Rohr, *das;* (of raspberry, blackberry) Spross, *der; see also* **sugar cane** 2 (material) Rohr, *das* 3 (stick) [Rohr]stock, *der;* **get the ~:** eine Tracht Prügel bekommen 4 (esp. Brit.: walking stick) Spazierstock, *der*

B *v.t.* 1 (beat) [mit dem Stock] schlagen 2 (weave) flechten

cane: ~ chair *n.* Rohrstuhl, *der;* **~ sugar** *n.* Rohrzucker, *der*

canine /ˈkeɪnaɪn, ˈkænaɪn/

A *adj.* 1 (of dog[s]) Hunde‹*rasse, -gebell, -natur*› 2 **~ tooth** Eck- *od.* Augenzahn, *der*

B *n.* Eckzahn, *der;* Augenzahn, *der*

caning /ˈkeɪnɪŋ/ *n.* [Ver]prügeln, *das od.* [Ver]hauen, *das* [mit dem Stock]; **he got a ~:** er kriegte eine Tracht Prügel (ugs.) [mit dem Stock]

canister /ˈkænɪstə(r)/ *n.* Büchse, *die;* Dose, *die;* (for petrol, oil etc.) Kanister, *der*

canker /ˈkæŋkə(r)/

A *n.* 1 (disease) (of dogs, cats, rabbits, etc.) Ohrräude, *die;* (of horses) Strahlfäule, *die* 2 (fig.: corrupting influence) [Krebs]geschwür, *das*

B *v.t.* 1 (consume with ~) verrotten 2 (fig.: infect, corrupt) vergiften ‹*Gemüt, Gefühl*›

cannabis /ˈkænəbɪs/ *n.* (Bot.) Kannabis, *der;* Hanf, *der;* (drug) Haschisch, *das;* Marihuana, *das*

cannabis ˈresin *n.* Haschisch, *das;* Cannabisharz, *das* (fachspr.)

canned /kænd/ *adj.* 1 Dosen-; in Dosen *nachgestellt;* **~ fish/meat/fruit** Fisch-/Fleisch-/Obstkonserven *Pl.;* Fisch/Fleisch/Obst in Dosen; **~ beer** Dosenbier; **~ food** [Lebensmittel]konserven *Pl.* 2 (sl.: drunk) abgefüllt (ugs.) 3 (recorded) aufgezeichnet; **~ music/entertainment** Musikkonserve, *die*/Unterhaltungskonserve, *die*

canner /ˈkænə(r)/ *n.* Konservenfabrikant, *der;* (worker) Arbeiter/Arbeiterin in einer Konservenfabrik

cannery /ˈkænərɪ/ *n.* Konservenfabrik, *die*

cannibal /ˈkænɪbl/ *n.* Kannibale, *der*/Kannibalin, *die;* Menschenfresser, *der*/-fresserin, *die* (ugs.); **these animals are ~s** diese Tiere fressen ihre Artgenossen auf

cannibalise ▸**cannibalize**

cannibalism /ˈkænɪbəlɪzm/ *n.* Kannibalismus, *der;* Menschenfresserei, *die* (ugs.); (fig.) Blutdurst, *der*

cannibalistic /kænɪbəˈlɪstɪk/ *adj.* kannibalisch

cannibalize /ˈkænɪbəlaɪz/ *v.t.* ausschlachten ‹*Auto, Flugzeug, Maschine usw.*›

cannily /ˈkænɪlɪ/ *adv.* (cautiously) vorsichtig; (shrewdly) schlau

cannon /ˈkænən/

A *n.* 1 (gun) Kanone, *die* 2 (Brit. Billiards etc.) Karambolage, *die*

B *v.i.* (Brit.) 1 **~ against sth.** gegen etw. prallen; **~ into sb./sth.** mit etw./jmdm. zusammenprallen 2 (Billiards) karambolieren

cannonade /kænəˈneɪd/ (arch.)

A *n.* Kanonade, *die* (veralt.)

B *v.t.* kanonieren (veralt.)

cannon: ~ ball *n.* (Hist.) Kanonenkugel, *die;* **~ fodder** *n.* Kanonenfutter, *das* (salopp abwertend)

cannot ▸**can²**

cannula /ˈkænjʊlə/ *n., pl.* **~e** /ˈkænjʊliː/ *or* **~s** (Med.) Kanüle, *die*

canny /ˈkænɪ/ *adj.* 1 (shrewd) schlau; bauernschlau (ugs.); (thrifty) sparsam 2 (cautious, wary) vorsichtig; umsichtig 3 trocken ‹*Humor*›

canoe /kəˈnuː/

A *n.* Paddelboot, *das;* (Indian ~, Sport) Kanu, *das; see also* **paddle¹ B**

B *v.i.* paddeln; (in Indian ~, Sport) Kanu fahren; **~ down the river** flussabwärts paddeln/im Kanu flussabwärts fahren

canoeing /kəˈnuːɪŋ/ *n., no pl.* Paddeln, *das;* (Sport) Kanufahren, *das;* Kanusport, *der*

canoeist /kəˈnuːɪst/ *n.* Paddelbootfahrer, *der*/-fahrerin, *die;* (Sport) Kanute, *der*/Kanutin, *die;* Kanufahrer, *der*/-fahrerin, *die*

canon /ˈkænən/ *n.* 1 (general law, criterion) Grundregel, *die;* Grundprinzip, *das;* **the ~s of conduct** die Grundregeln des Verhaltens; der Verhaltenskodex 2 ▸**❶ p. 1634** (member of cathedral chapter) Kanoniker, *der;* Kanonikus, *der* 3 (church decree) Kirchengebot, *das* 4 (list of sacred books) Kanon, *der;* (fig.) **the Shakespearean ~:** das Gesamtwerk Shakespeares 5 (Mus.) Kanon, *der*

canonical /kəˈnɒnɪkl/

A *adj.* 1 kanonisch ‹*Gehorsam, Gelübde, Bücher, Schriften*›; **~ dress** Priestertracht *od.* -kleidung, *die;* **~ hours** Gebetszeiten *Pl.;* (Brit.: for weddings) Trauzeiten *Pl.* 2 (authoritative, standard) verbindlich, kanonisch ‹*Urteil, Werte, Vorschriften*›; maßgeblich ‹*Person*› 3 (Mus.) Kanon‹*form, -komposition*›; ‹*Musikstück*› in Kanonform 4 (of cathedral chapter or member of it) Kanoniker-; Chorherren-

B *n. in pl.* Priesterkleidung, *die*

canonisation, canonise ▸**canoniz-**

canonization /kænənaɪˈzeɪʃn/ *n.* Kanonisation, *die;* **~ of saints** Heiligsprechungen

canonize /ˈkænənaɪz/ *v.t.* 1 kanonisieren ‹*Heiligen*›; heilig sprechen ‹*Märtyrer*›; **he was ~d [a saint]** er wurde heilig gesprochen 2 (regard as saint) wie einen Heiligen/eine Heilige/Heilige *Pl.* verehren

canon: ~ law *n.* kanonisches Recht; **~ ˈregular** *n.* regulierter Chorherr

canoodle /kəˈnuːdl/ (coll.)

A *v.i.* [rum]knutschen (salopp)

B *v.t.* abknutschen (salopp)

ˈcan-opener *n.* Dosen-, Büchsenöffner, *der*

canopy /ˈkænəpɪ/

A *n.* 1 Baldachin, *der* (auch fig.); (over entrance) Vordach, *das;* **the ~ of the heavens, the celestial ~:** das Himmelszelt *od.* himmlische Zelt (dichter.); **a ~ of leaves** ein Blätterdach 2 (of parachute) [Fall]schirmkappe, *die* 3 (of aircraft) [Kanzel]haube, *die*

B *v.t.* überwölben

cant¹ /kænt/

A *v.t.* kippen; ankippen, kanten ‹*Fass*›; **~ off** abschrägen; **~ over** umdrehen; umkippen

B *v.i.* (take inclined position, lie aslant) sich neigen

C *n.* (movement) Ruck, *der;* (tilted position) Schräglage, *die;* (bevel) Schräge, *die*

cant²

A *n., no pl.* 1 (derog.: language of class, sect, etc.) Zunftsprache, *die;* Jargon, *der;* **thieves'/beggars' ~:** Rotwelsch, *das;* Gaunersprache, *die* 2 (insincere use of words) Scheinheiligkeit, *die;* (talk) scheinheiliges Gerede 3 (ephemeral catchwords) Phrase, *die* (abwertend); *attrib.* **~ phrases/terms/words** [leere] Phrasen

B *v.i.* 1 ▸**A 1:** (use, speak in ~) Jargon/Rotwelsch reden 2 (talk with affectation of piety) [scheinheilig] schwafeln (abwertend)

can't /kɑːnt/ (coll.) **= cannot;** ▸**can²**

Cantab. /ˈkæntæb/ *abbr.* **= of Cambridge University** der Universität Cambridge

cantabile /kænˈtɑːbɪlɪ/ (Mus.)

A *adv.* cantabile

B *adj.* Kantabile‹*satz, -stil, -ton*›; sangbar ‹*Stück, Musik*›

C *n.* Kantabile, *das*

cantaloup[e] /ˈkæntəluːp/ *n.* Zucker-, Gartenmelone, *die*

cantankerous /kænˈtæŋkərəs/ *adj.* streitsüchtig; knurrig (ugs.) ‹*müde od. launische Person*›; störrisch ‹*Esel, altes Auto usw.*›; **don't be so ~ on Monday mornings** sei doch nicht immer so eklig *od.* mufflig am Montagmorgen! (ugs.)

cantankerously /kænˈtæŋkərəslɪ/ *adv.* ▸**cantankerous: behave** *or* **act ~:** streitsüchtig/knurrig (ugs.)/störrisch/mufflig *od.* eklig (ugs.) sein

cantankerousness /kænˈtæŋkərəsnɪs/ *n., no pl.* ▸**cantankerous:** Streitsucht, *die;* Knurrigkeit, *die* (ugs.); störrisches Benehmen

cantata /kænˈtɑːtə/ *n.* (Mus.) Kantate, *die*

canteen /kænˈtiːn/ *n.* 1 Kantine, *die* 2 (case of cutlery) Besteckkasten, *der*

canter /ˈkæntə(r)/

A *n.* Handgalopp, *der;* Kanter, Canter, *der* (fachspr.); **the horse broke into an easy ~:** das Pferd begann leicht zu galoppieren; **win in a ~** (fig.) spielend gewinnen

B *v.i.* leicht galoppieren; kantern (fachspr.)

C *v.t.* in Handgalopp *od.* Kanter gehen lassen ‹*Pferd*›

ˈCanterbury bell /ˈkæntəbərɪ bel/ *n.* (Bot.) Glockenblume, *die*

canticle /ˈkæntɪkl/ *n.* 1 Lobgesang, *der;* Canticum, *das* (Theol.); (hymn) Preislied, Hohelied, *das* 2 **the C~ of Solomon** *or* **C~s** das Hohe Lied *od.* Hohelied; das Lied der Lieder

cantilever /ˈkæntɪliːvə/ *n.* 1 (bracket) Konsole, *die;* Kragplatte, *die* 2 (beam, girder) Träger, *der*

ˈcantilever: ~ brake *n.* Cantileverbremse, *die;* **~ bridge** *n.* Auslegerbrücke, *die*

canto /ˈkæntəʊ/ *n., pl.* **~s** Gesang, *der;* Canto, *der* (fachspr.)

canton /ˈkæntɒn/ *n.* Kanton, *der*

cantonal /ˈkæntənl/ *adj.* kantonal; Kantons-

Cantonese /kæntəˈniːz/ ▸**❶ p. 1277**, ▸**❶ p. 1345**

A *adj.* kantonesisch; **sb. is ~:** jmd. ist Kantonese/Kantonesin

B *n., pl. same* 1 (person) Kantonese, *der*/Kantonesin, *die* 2 (language) Kantonesisch (*das*)

cantor /ˈkæntə(r)/ *n.* Kantor, *der*

canvas /ˈkænvəs/ *n.* 1 (cloth) Leinwand, *die;* (for tents, tarpaulins, etc.) Segeltuch, *das;* **under ~:** im Zelt; (Naut.) unter Segel; **under full ~:** mit vollen Segeln 2 (Art) Leinwand, *die;* (painting)

Gemälde, *das;* (for tapestry and embroidery) Kanevas, *der;* Gitterleinwand, *die* 3 (of racing boat) Segeltuchbezug, *der;* **win by a ~:** mit einer Nasenlänge gewinnen

canvass /ˈkænvəs/
A *v.t.* 1 (solicit votes in or from) Wahlwerbung treiben in ‹*einem Wahlkreis, Gebiet*›; Wahlwerbung treiben bei ‹*Wählern, Bürgern*›; **~ customers** Kunden werben; **they were ~ed on their political views** man versuchte, ihre politischen Ansichten herauszufinden 2 (Brit.: propose) vorschlagen ‹*Plan, Idee, Handel*› 3 (Amer.: check validity of) auszählen ‹*Stimmen*›
B *v.i.* werben (**on behalf of** für); **~ for votes** um Stimmen werben; **~ for a seat in Parliament** sich um einen Parlamentssitz bewerben; **~ for an applicant** sich für einen Bewerber einsetzen
C *n.* [Wahl]kampagne, *die;* (Amer.: scrutiny of votes) Auszählung, *die*

canvasser /ˈkænvəsə(r)/ *n.* 1 (for votes) Wahlhelfer, *der*/Wahlhelferin, *die* 2 (salesperson) Vertreter, *der*/Vertreterin, *die* 3 (Amer.: checker of votes) Auszähler, *der*/Auszählerin, *die*

canvassing /ˈkænvəsɪŋ/ *n., no pl.* (for votes) Wahlwerbung, *die;* (Commerc.) Kundenwerbung, *die;* (opinion polling) Meinungsforschung, *die*

canyon /ˈkænjən/ *n.* Cañon, *der*

cap /kæp/
A *n.* 1 Mütze, *die;* (nurse's, servant's) Haube, *die;* (bathing ~) Badekappe, *die;* (with peak) Schirmmütze, *die;* (skull~) Kappe, *die;* Käppchen, *das;* **college ~:** *viereckige akademische Kopfbedeckung;* ≈ Barett, *das;* **in ~ and gown** mit Barett und Talar; **if the ~ fits, [he** *etc.* **should] wear it** (fig.) wem die Jacke passt, der soll sie sich (*Dat.*) anziehen; **with ~ in hand** (fig.) demütig; **she set her ~ at him** (fig. dated) sie hatte es auf ihn abgesehen; **~ and bells** Narren- *od.* Schellenkappe, *die; see also* **feather A 1** 2 (of mushroom) Hut, *der;* (of honeycomb) Deckel, *der* 3 (device to seal or close) [Verschluss]kappe, *die;* (petrol ~, radiator-~) Verschluss, *der;* (on milk bottle) Deckel, *der;* (of shoe) Kappe, *die* 4 (Brit. Sport) *Ziermütze als Zeichen der Aufstellung für die [National]mannschaft;* (player) Nationalspieler, *der*/-spielerin, *die;* **get one's ~:** für die [National]mannschaft aufgestellt werden 5 (contraceptive) Pessar, *das* 6 (explosive) Zündhütchen, *das;* (for toy gun) Zündplättchen, *das*
B *v.t.*, **-pp-** 1 verschließen ‹*Flasche*›; zu-, abdecken ‹*Brunnen, Bohrloch*›; mit einer Schutzkappe versehen ‹*Zahn*› 2 (Brit. Sport: award ~ to) aufstellen; **he was ~ped ten times for England** er ist zehnmal für die englische Nationalmannschaft aufgestellt worden 3 (crown) (with clouds, snow, mist) bedecken; (fig.) krönen (**by** durch); **~ped with snow** schneebedeckt 4 (follow with sth. even more noteworthy) überbieten ‹*Geschichte, Witz usw.*›; **to ~ it all** obendrein; **that ~s the lot!** das ist die Höhe!

cap. /kæp/ *abbr.* 1 (Printing etc.) **= capital** Vers. 2 **= chapter** Kap.

CAP *abbr.* (EU) **= Common Agricultural Policy** GAP

capability /keɪpəˈbɪlɪtɪ/ *n.* Fähigkeit, *die;* Vermögen, *das* (geh.); **his ~ of understanding difficult texts** sein Verständnis[-vermögen] für schwierige Texte; **this plot of land has the ~ for further development** dieses Grundstück lässt sich noch weiter erschließen; **~ for growth** Wachstumschancen *Pl.; see also* **nuclear capability**

capable /ˈkeɪpəbl/ *adj.* 1 **be ~ of sth.** ‹*Person:*› zu etw. imstande sein; **show him what you are ~ of** zeig ihm, wozu du imstande bist *od.* wessen du fähig bist; **he is ~ of any crime** er ist zu jedem Verbrechen fähig; **she is quite ~ of neglecting her duties** sie bringt es durchaus fertig, ihre Pflichten zu vernachlässigen; **be ~ of improvement** verbesserungsfähig sein; **be ~ of misinterpretation** sich leicht falsch interpretieren lassen; leicht falsch interpretiert werden; **it is not ~ of being expressed in a few words** es lässt sich nicht in ein paar Worten ausdrücken 2 (gifted, able) fähig ‹*Person, Lehrer usw.*›; **~ fingers** geschickte Finger

capably /ˈkeɪpəblɪ/ *adv.* gekonnt, kompetent ‹*leiten, führen*›

capacious /kəˈpeɪʃəs/ *adj.* geräumig; groß ‹*Gedächtnis, Verstand, Appetit*›; weit, groß ‹*Schuhe, Taschen*›

capaciousness /kəˈpeɪʃəsnɪs/ *n., no pl.* (of room, hall) Geräumigkeit, *die;* (of receptacle) Größe, *die*

capacitance /kəˈpæsɪtəns/ *n.* (Electr.) Kapazitanz, *die*

capacitor /kəˈpæsɪtə(r)/ *n.* (Electr.) Kondensator, *der*

capacity /kəˈpæsɪtɪ/ *n.* 1 (power) Aufnahmefähigkeit, *die;* (to do things) Leistungsfähigkeit, *die;* **this book is within the ~ of young readers** junge Leser sind mit diesem Buch nicht überfordert; **some have more ~ for happiness than others** manche sind zu größeren Glücksempfindungen fähig als andere 2 *no pl.* (maximum amount) Fassungsvermögen, *das;* **the machine is working to ~:** die Maschine ist voll ausgelastet; **a seating ~ of 300** 300 Sitzplätze; **filled to ~** ‹*Saal, Theater*› bis auf den letzten Platz besetzt; **the film drew ~ houses for ten weeks** zehn Wochen lang waren alle Vorstellungen dieses Films ausverkauft; **the star was cheered by a ~ audience** ein volles Haus jubelte dem Star zu 3 ▸ⓘ **p. 1690** (measure) Rauminhalt, *der;* Volumen, *das;* **measure of ~:** Hohlmaß, *das* 4 (position) Eigenschaft, *die;* Funktion, *die;* **in his ~ as critic/lawyer** *etc.* in seiner Eigenschaft als Kritiker/Anwalt *usw.*; **in a civil ~:** als Zivilist 5 (mental power) **he has a mind of great ~:** er ist ein äußerst fähiger Kopf; **have a ~ for genuine love** echter Liebe (*Gen.*) fähig sein 6 (legal competence) Geschäftsfähigkeit, *die;* **he does not have any legal ~:** er ist nicht geschäftsfähig 7 (Electr.) Kapazität, *die*

capacity: ~ audience *n.* saalfüllendes Publikum; **play to/in front of a ~ audience** vor vollem Saal spielen; **~ crowd** *n.* dicht gedrängtes Publikum

caparison /kəˈpærɪsən/ *n., usu. in pl.* (horse's trappings) Schabracke, *die*

cape¹ /keɪp/ *n.* (garment) Umhang, *der;* Cape, *das;* (part of coat) Pelerine, *die*

cape² *n.* (Geog.) Kap, *das;* **the C~ [of Good Hope]** das Kap der guten Hoffnung; **C~ Horn** Kap Hoorn (*das*); **C~ Town** Kapstadt (*das*); **C~ Verde Islands** Kapverdische Inseln *Pl.*

caper¹ /ˈkeɪpə(r)/
A *n.* 1 (frisky movement) Luftsprung, *der;* **cut a ~/~s** einen Luftsprung/Luftsprünge machen 2 (wild behaviour) Kapriole, *die* 3 (coll.: activity, occupation) Masche, *die* (salopp)
B *v.i.* **~ [about]** [herum]tollen; [umher]tollen

caper² *n.* 1 (shrub) Kapernstrauch, *der* 2 *in pl.* (pickled buds) Kapern *Pl.*

capercaillie /kæpəˈkeɪljɪ/, **capercailzie** /kæpəˈkeɪlzɪ/ *ns.* (Ornith.) Auerhahn, *der*

capful /ˈkæpfʊl/ *n.* **one ~:** der Inhalt einer Verschlusskappe

capillary /kəˈpɪlərɪ/
A *adj.* (of hairlike diameter) haardünn; haarfein; Kapillar‹*gefäß*›; (of hair) Haar-; **~ action** Kapillarwirkung, *die;* **~ tube** Kapillare, *die* (fachspr.)
B *n.* Kapillare, *die* (fachspr.)

capital¹ /ˈkæpɪtl/
A *adj.* 1 Todes‹*strafe, -urteil*›; Kapital‹*verbrechen*›; tödlich ‹*Irrtum, Fehler, Laster, Torheit*› 2 *attrib.* groß, Groß-, (fachspr.) Versal‹*buchstabe*›; **~ letters** Großbuchstaben; Versalien (fachspr.); **'I' is written with a ~ letter** „I" wird groß geschrieben *od.* mit großem I geschrieben; **with a ~ A** *etc.* mit großem A *usw. od.* (fachspr.) mit Versal-A *usw.*; (fig.) im wahrsten Sinne des Wortes 3 *attrib.* (principal) Haupt‹*stadt*›; **London is the ~ city of England** London ist die Hauptstadt *od.* (geh.) Kapitale Englands 4 (important, leading) einmalig ‹*Vorteil, Person, Buch, Vorstellung*›; (dated coll.: excellent, first-rate) einmalig; famos (veralt.) ‹*Idee*›; **~!** tadellos!; famos! (veralt.) 5 (Commerc.) **~ funds/stock** Grundkapital, *das;* **~ sum/expenditure/investment** Kapitalbetrag, *der*/-aufwendungen *Pl.*/-anlage, *die*
B *n.* 1 (letter) Großbuchstabe, *der;* **[large] ~s** Großbuchstaben; Versalien (fachspr.); **small ~s** Kapitälchen (fachspr.); **write one's name in [block] ~s** seinen Namen in Blockbuchstaben schreiben 2 (city, town) Hauptstadt, *die;* Kapitale, *die* (geh.) 3 (stock, accumulated wealth, its holders) Kapital, *das;* **personal** *or* **private ~:** Eigenkapital, *das;* **~ and labour** Kapital und Arbeit; (in non-socialist terminology) Arbeitgeber und Arbeitnehmer; **make ~ out of sth.** (fig.) aus etw. Kapital schlagen

capital² *n.* (Archit.) Kapitell, *das;* Kapitäl, *das*

capital: ~ 'gain *n.* Kapitalgewinn, *der;* Kapitalertrag, *der;* **~ 'gains tax** *n.* (Brit.) Steuer auf Kapitalgewinn, *die;* **~ goods** *n. pl.* Investitionsgüter *Pl.*

capitalise ▸ **capitalize**

capitalism /ˈkæpɪtəlɪzm/ *n., no pl.* Kapitalismus, *der;* (possession of capital) Kapitalbesitz, *der;* **~ is ...:** der Kapitalismus ist ...

capitalist /ˈkæpɪtəlɪst/
A *n.* Kapitalist, *der*/Kapitalistin, *die*
B *adj.* kapitalistisch; **the ~ class** die Kapitalistenklasse

capitalistic /kæpɪtəˈlɪstɪk/ *adj.* kapitalistisch

capitalization /kæpɪtəlaɪˈzeɪʃn/ *n.* 1 (Finance) Kapitalisierung, *die* 2 (of letters) Großschreibung, *die*

capitalize /ˈkæpɪtəlaɪz/
A *v.t.* 1 großschreiben ‹*Buchstabe, Wort*› 2 (convert, compute) kapitalisieren ‹*Rente, Reserven*›
B *v.i.* (fig.) **~ on sth.** von etw. profitieren; aus etw. Kapital schlagen (ugs.)

capital: ~ 'levy *n.* Vermögensabgabe, *die;* Kapitalabgabe, *die;* **~ ship** *n.* Großkampfschiff, *das;* **~ territory** *n.* Gebiet der/einer Hauptstadt

capitation /kæpɪˈteɪʃn/ *n.* Kopfsteuer, *die*

capi'tation grant *n.* Zuschuss pro Kopf

Capitol /ˈkæpɪtl/ *n.* Kapitol, *das*

> **Capitol**
>
> Der Sitz des amerikanischen **Congress** auf dem Capitol Hill in Washington D.C.

capitulate /kəˈpɪtjʊleɪt/ *v.i.* kapitulieren

capitulation /kəpɪtjʊˈleɪʃn/ *n.* Kapitulation, *die*

capo /ˈkæpəʊ/ *n., pl.* **~s** (Mus.) Kapodaster, *der*

capon /ˈkeɪpən/ *n.* Kapaun, *der*

'cap pistol *n.* Zündplättchenpistole, *die;* Zündblättchenpistole, *die*

cappuccino /kɑːpʊˈtʃiːnəʊ/ *n., pl.* **~s** Cappuccino, *der*

Capri /kəˈpriː/ *pr. n.* Capri (*das*); **~ pants, ~s** Caprihosen *Pl.*

caprice /kəˈpriːs/ *n.* 1 (change of mind or conduct) Laune, *die;* Kaprice, *die* (geh.); (inclination) Willkür, *die;* **out of sheer ~:** aus einer Laune heraus; **the ~s of English weather** die Launen[haftigkeit] des englischen Wetters 2 (work of art) Capriccio, *das;* Caprice, *die* (geh.)

capricious /kəˈprɪʃəs/ *adj.* launisch; kapriziös (geh.); (irregular, unpredictable) wechselhaft, launisch ‹*Wetter*›; unberechenbar, schwankend ‹*System, Markt*›

capriciously /kəˈprɪʃəslɪ/ *adv.* willkürlich

capriciousness /kəˈprɪʃəsnɪs/ *n., no pl.* Launenhaftigkeit, *die;* (of actions) Willkür, *die;* (of weather) Wechselhaftigkeit, *die;* Launenhaftigkeit, *die*

Capricorn /ˈkæprɪkɔːn/ *n.* (Astrol., Astron.) der Steinbock; der Capricornus; *see also* **Aries; tropic**

Capricornian /kæprɪˈkɔːnɪən/ *n.* (Astrol.) Steinbock, *der*

caps. /kæps/ *abbr.* **= capital letters** Vers.

capsicum /ˈkæpsɪkəm/ *n.* 1 (pod) Pfefferschote, *die* 2 (plant) Paprika, *der*

capsize /kæpˈsaɪz/
A *v.t.* zum Kentern bringen
B *v.i.* kentern

'caps lock *n.* Feststelltaste, *die*

capstan /ˈkæpstən/ *n.* 1 (barrel for cable) Winde, *die;* Spill, *das* (Seemannsspr.) 2 (in tape recorder) Tonwelle, *die;* Tonrolle, *die*

'capstan lathe *n.* Sattelrevolverdrehmaschine, *die*

'cap stone *n.* (top stone) Deckstein, *der;* (coping) Mauerkrone, *die*

capsule /'kæpsjʊl/ *n.* (Med., Physiol., Bot., of rocket) Kapsel, *die*

Capt. *abbr.* **= Captain** Kapt.; Hptm.

captain /'kæptɪn/
A *n.* 1 ▸ⓘ **p. 1634** Kapitän, *der;* (in army) Hauptmann, *der;* (in navy) Kapitän [zur See]; **~ of a ship** Schiffskapitän, *der;* **~ of industry** (fig.) Industriekapitän, *der* (ugs.) 2 (head boy/girl at school) Schulsprecher, *der/*-sprecherin, *die;* **form ~:** Klassensprecher, *der*/-sprecherin, *die* 3 (Sport) Kapitän, *der;* Spielführer, *der/*-führerin, *die* 4 (Amer.: police rank) ≈ Polizeidirektor, *der*
B *v.t.* befehligen ‹*Soldaten, Armee*›; **~ a team** Mannschaftskapitän sein; Kapitän einer Mannschaft sein

captaincy /'kæptɪnsɪ/ *n.* (Sport) Führung, *die*

caption /'kæpʃn/
A *n.* 1 (heading) Überschrift, *die* 2 (wording under photograph/drawing) Bildunterschrift, *die;* (Cinemat., Telev.) Untertitel, *der*
B *v.t.* betiteln; mit Bildunterschrift[en] versehen ‹*Foto, Illustration*›; mit Untertiteln versehen ‹*Film*›

captious /'kæpʃəs/ *adj.* überkritisch

captivate /'kæptɪveɪt/ *v.t.* fesseln (fig.); gefangen nehmen (fig.); **she was ~d by his charm/by Tom** sie war von seinem Charme gefesselt/von Tom fasziniert

captivating /'kæptɪveɪtɪŋ/ *adj.* bezaubernd; einnehmend ‹*Lächeln*›

captivation /kæptɪ'veɪʃn/ *n.* Fesselung, *die* (fig.); Verzauberung, *die*

captive /'kæptɪv/
A *adj.* (taken prisoner) gefangen; ‹*Zustand, Stunden, Ketten*› der Gefangenschaft; **a ~ animal** ein Tier in Gefangenschaft; **be taken ~:** gefangen genommen werden; **hold sb. ~:** jmdn. gefangen halten; **lead/bring sb. ~ somewhere** jmdn. als Gefangenen irgendwohin führen/bringen
B *n.* Gefangener, *der*/Gefangene, *die*

captive: ~ 'audience *n.* unfreiwilliges Publikum; **~ bal'loon** *n.* Fesselballon, *der*

captivity /kæp'tɪvɪtɪ/ *n.* Gefangenschaft, *die;* **in [a state of] ~:** in [der] Gefangenschaft; **be held in ~:** gefangen gehalten werden

captor /'kæptə(r)/ *n.* (of city, country) Eroberer, *der;* (Hist.: of ship) Kaperer, *der;* **his ~:** der/die ihn gefangen nahm

capture /'kæptʃə(r)/
A *n.* 1 (seizing) (of thief etc.) Festnahme, *die;* (of town) Einnahme, *die* 2 (thing or person captured) Fang, *der* 3 (Chess etc.) Schlagen, *das*
B *v.t.* 1 ergreifen, festnehmen ‹*Person*›; [ein]fangen ‹*Tier*›; einnehmen ‹*Stadt*›; holen, ergattern ‹*Preis*›; gefangen nehmen ‹*Fantasie*›; erregen ‹*Aufmerksamkeit*›; (Hist.) kapern ‹*Schiff*›; **~ sb.'s heart** jmds. Herz gewinnen; **they ~d the city from the Romans** sie nahmen den Römern die Stadt ab 2 (put in permanent form) einfangen ‹*Augenblick, Eindruck*› 3 (Chess etc.) schlagen ‹*Figur*› 4 (Computing) erfassen ‹*Daten*›

Capuchin /'kæpjʊtʃɪn/ *n.* (Franciscan friar) Kapuziner[mönch], *der*

'capuchin monkey *n.* Kapuzineraffe, *der;*

capybara /kæpɪ'bɑːrə/ *n.* (Zool.) Capybara, *das;* Wasserschwein, *das*

car /kɑː(r)/ *n.* 1 (motor ~) Auto, *das;* Wagen, *der;* (official) Dienstwagen, *der;* **by ~:** mit dem Auto *od.* Wagen 2 (railway carriage etc.) Wagen, *der* 3 (Amer.: lift cage) Fahrkabine, *die* 4 (of balloon, airship, etc.) Gondel, *die*

'car accident *n.* Autounfall, *der*

carafe /kə'ræf, kə'rɑːf/ *n.* Karaffe, *die*

'car alarm *n.* Autoalarmanlage, *die*

caramel /'kærəmel/ *n.* 1 (toffee) Karamelle, *die;* Karamellbonbon, *das* 2 (burnt sugar or syrup) Karamell, *der* 3 (colour) Karamellfarbe, *die;* bräunliches Gelb

caramelize /'kærəməlaɪz/ *v.t. & i.* karamellisieren

carapace /'kærəpeɪs/ *n.* (of turtle, tortoise) Rückenschild, *der;* (of other crustacean) Schale, *die*

carat /'kærət/ *n.* Karat, *das;* **a 22-~ gold ring, a gold ring of 22 ~s** ein 22-karätiger Goldring

caravan /'kærəvæn/
A *n.* 1 (Brit.) Wohnwagen, *der;* (used for camping) Wohnwagen, *der;* Caravan, *der* 2 (company of merchants, pilgrims, etc.) Karawane, *die*
B *v.i.,* (Brit.) **-nn-: go ~ning** Urlaub im Wohnwagen *od.* Caravan machen

caravanner /'kærəvænə(r)/ *n.* Caravaner, *der*/Caravanerin, *die*

caravanning /'kærəvænɪŋ/ *n., no pl.* Caravaning, *das*

caravan: ~ park, ~ site *ns.* Campingplatz für Wohnwagen

caravel /'kærəvel/ *n.* (Hist.) Karavelle, *die*

caraway /'kærəweɪ/ *n.* Kümmel, *der*

'caraway seed *n.* Kümmelkorn, *das; in pl.* Kümmel, *der*

'car badge *n.* Autoemblem, *das*

carbide /'kɑːbaɪd/ *n.* Karbid, *das;* Carbid, *das* (fachspr.)

carbine /'kɑːbaɪn/ *n.* Karabiner, *der*

carbohydrate /kɑːbə'haɪdreɪt/ *n.* (Chem.) Kohle[n]hydrat, *das*

carbolic /kɑː'bɒlɪk/ *adj.* Karbol‹*säure*›; **~ soap** Karbolseife, *die*

'car bomb *n.* Autobombe, *die*

carbon /'kɑːbən/ *n.* 1 Kohlenstoff, *der* 2 (copy) Durchschlag, *der;* (paper) Kohlepapier, *das* 3 (Electr.) Kohle, *die;* Kohlestift, *der*

carbonade /kɑːbə'neɪd/ *n.* **[beef] ~** (*mit Bier abgeschmeckter*) Rindfleischeintopf

carbonate /'kɑːbəneɪt/
A *n.* Karbonat, (fachspr.) Carbonat, *das*
B *v.t.* mit Kohlensäure versetzen ‹*Getränke*›; **a ~d beverage** ein kohlensäurehaltiges Getränk

carbon: ~ 'copy *n.* Durchschlag, *der;* (fig.) (imitation) Nachahmung, *die;* Abklatsch, *der* (abwertend); (identical counterpart) Ebenbild, *das;* **~ cycle** *n.* Kohlenstoffkreislauf, *der;* **~ 'dating** *n.* Radiokarbonmethode, *die;* Radiokohlenstoffmethode, *die;* **~ di'oxide** *n.* (Chem.) Kohlendioxid, *das;* Kohlendyoxid, *das*

carboniferous /kɑːbə'nɪfərəs/
A *adj.* 1 (producing coal) kohlehaltig 2 (Geol.) Karbon-, Steinkohlen-; **C~ period** Karbon- *od.* Steinkohlenformation, *die*
B *n.* (Geol.) **the C~:** das Karbon

carbonize (**carbonise**) /'kɑːbənaɪz/ *v.t.* karbonisieren ‹*Diamanten, Graphit*›; verkohlen ‹*Kohle*›; (to obtain gas) verkoken ‹*Kohle*›; verschwelen ‹*Torf, Lignit*›; [mit der/einer Färbemasse] beschichten ‹*Papier, Formulare*›

carbon: ~ mo'noxide *n.* (Chem.) Kohlenmonoxid, *das;* Kohlenmonoxyd, *das;* **~ paper** *n.* Kohlepapier, *das;* **~ 'steel** *n.* Kohlenstoffstahl, *der;* **~ tax** *n.* CO_2-Steuer, *die;* **~ tetra'chloride** *n.* (Chem.) Tetrachlorkohlenstoff, *der*

car 'boot sale *n.: Trödelmarkt, bei dem die Händler ihre Waren aus dem Kofferraum ihrer Autos heraus verkaufen*

carborundum /kɑːbə'rʌndəm/ *n.* Karborund, *das*

carboy /'kɑːbɔɪ/ *n.* Korbflasche, *die*

carbuncle /'kɑːbʌŋkl/ *n.* 1 (stone) Karfunkel[stein], *der* 2 (abscess) Karbunkel, *der*

carburettor (*Amer.:* **carburetor**) /kɑːbə'retə(r)/ *n.* Vergaser, *der*

carcass (*Brit. also:* **carcase**) /'kɑːkəs/ *n.* 1 (dead body; joc.: live human body) Kadaver, *der;* (at butcher's) Rumpf, *der;* **~ meat** Frischfleisch, *das* 2 (remains) Überreste *Pl.;* **~es of old cars/bikes** Schrottautos/-räder *Pl.* 3 (of ship, fortification, etc.) Skelett, *das;* (of new building) Rohbau, *der* 4 (of tyre) Karkasse, *die*

'car chase *n.* Autojagd, *die;* Verfolgungsjagd, *die* [im Auto]

carcinogen /kɑː'sɪnədʒən/ *n.* (Med.) Karzinogen, *das* (fachspr.); Krebserreger, *der*

carcinogenic /kɑːsɪnə'dʒenɪk/ *adj.* (Med.) karzinogen (fachspr.); Krebs erregend

carcinoma /kɑːsɪ'nəʊmə/ *n., pl.* **~ta** /kɑːsɪ'nəʊmətə/ *or* **~s** (Med.) Karzinom, *das*

car: ~ coat *n.* Autocoat, *der;* **~ crash** *n.* Autounfall, *der*

card[1] /kɑːd/ *n.* 1 (playing ~) Karte, *die;* **read the ~s** Karten lesen; **be on the ~s** (fig.) zu erwarten sein; **put [all] one's ~s on the table** (fig.) [alle] seine Karten auf den Tisch legen; **have [yet] another ~ up one's sleeve** (fig.) noch einen Trumpf in der Hand haben; noch etwas in petto haben (ugs) 2 *in pl.* (game) Karten *Pl.;* **play ~s** Karten spielen; **lose money at ~s** beim Kartenspiel[en] Geld verlieren 3 (post~, visiting ~, greeting ~, ticket, invitation) Karte, *die;* **let me give you my ~:** ich gebe Ihnen meine Karte 4 (programme at races etc.) Programm, *das* 5 *in pl.* (coll.: employee's documents) Papiere *Pl.;* **ask for/get one's ~s** sich (*Dat.*) seine Papiere geben lassen/seine Papiere kriegen (ugs.) 6 (person) Type, *die* (ugs.); **an odd ~:** eine komische Type 7 (coll.: eccentric person) komischer Vogel (ugs.) 8 (Computing) [Steck-]karte, *die*

card[2] (Textiles)
A *n.* (instrument) Karde, *die;* Kratze, *die*
B *v.t.* karden

cardamom, cardamum /'kɑːdəməm/ *n.* Kardamom, *das od. der*

card: ~board *n.* Pappe, *die;* Pappkarton, *der;* (fig. attrib.) klischeehaft ‹*Figur*›; **~board box** [Papp]arton, *der;* (smaller) [Papp]schachtel, *die;* **~board 'city** *n.: Platz, an dem Obdachlose (oft in Pappkartons) unter freiem Himmel schlafen;* **~board 'cut-out** *n.* 1 (shape) Pappfigur, *die;* Pappkamerad, *der* (ugs.); 2 (fig. derog.: person) Hampelmann, *der* (ugs. abwertend); **~-carrying** *adj.* **a ~-carrying member** ein eingetragenes Mitglied

'car deck *n.* Parkdeck, *das;* Autodeck, *das*

card: ~ file *n.* Kartei, *die;* (large) Kartothek, *die;* **~ game** *n.* Kartenspiel, *das;* **~holder** *n.* Karteninhaber, *der*/-inhaberin, *die*

cardiac /'kɑːdɪæk/ *adj.* (of heart) Herz-; (of stomach) Magen-

cardiac: ~ ar'rest *n.* Herzstillstand, *der;* **~ failure** *n.* Herzversagen, *das*

cardie /'kɑːdɪ/ *n.* (coll.) Strickjacke, *die*

cardigan /'kɑːdɪgən/ *n.* Strickjacke, *die*

cardinal /'kɑːdɪnl/
A *adj.* 1 (fundamental) grundlegend ‹*Frage, Doktrin, Pflicht*›; Kardinal‹*fehler, -problem*›; (chief) hauptsächlich, Haupt‹*argument, -punkt, -merkmal*› 2 (of deep scarlet) scharlachfarben; scharlachrot ‹*Farbe*›; **~ red** scharlachrot
B *n.* 1 ▸ⓘ **p. 1634** (Eccl.) Kardinal, *der* 2 ▸**cardinal number** 3 (songbird) Kardinal, *der*

cardinal: ~ number *n.* ▸ⓘ **p. 1358** Grund-, Kardinalzahl, *die;* **~ points** *n. pl.* Himmelsrichtungen *Pl.;* **~ 'sin** *n.* Todsünde, *die;* **~ 'virtues** *n. pl.* Kardinaltugenden *Pl.;* **~ 'vowel** *n.* (Phonet.) Kardinalvokal, *der*

card: ~ 'index *n.* Kartei, *die;* **~-'index** *v.t.* karteimäßig erfassen *od.* ordnen

carding machine /'kɑːdɪŋməʃiːn/ *n.* Karde, *die*

cardio- /kɑːdɪəʊ/ *in comb.* (Med.) kardio-/Kardio-

'cardiogram *n.* Kardiogramm, *das* (Med.)

'cardiograph *n.* Kardiograph, *der* (Med.)

cardiologist /kɑːdɪ'ɒlɪgɪst/ *n.* ▸ⓘ **p. 1260** Kardiologe, *der*/Kardiologin, *die*

cardiology /kɑːdɪ'ɒlədʒɪ/ *n., no pl.* Kardiologie, *die*

cardio'vascular *adj.* (Med.) kardiovaskulär (fachspr.); Herz-Kreislauf-

card: ~ key *n.* Schlüsselkarte, *die;* **~phone** *n.* Kartentelefon, *das;* **~ playing** *n., no pl.* Kartenspielen, *das;* **all forms of ~ playing** alle Formen des Kartenspiels; **~ room** *n.* Spielzimmer, *das;* **~-sharp, ~ sharper** *ns.* Falschspieler, *der;* **~ swipe** *n.* [Magnet]kartenleser, *der; attrib.* **~ swipe phone** [Magnet]kartentelefon, *das;* **~ table** *n.* Kartentisch, *der;* **~ trick** *n.* Kartentrick, *der;* **~ vote** *n.* Abstimmung durch Wahlmänner (in Gewerkschaften)

cardy ▸ **cardie**

C

C

care /keə(r)/

A *n.* [1] (anxiety) Sorge, *die;* **a life full of ~:** ein Leben voller Sorgen; **cast ~ aside** (arch./literary) seine Sorgen vergessen; **she hasn't got a ~ in the world** sie hat keinerlei Sorgen [2] (pains) Sorgfalt, *die;* **take ~:** sich bemühen; **he takes great ~ over his work** er gibt sich (*Dat.*) große Mühe mit seiner Arbeit [3] (caution) Vorsicht, *die;* **take ~, have a ~:** aufpassen; **take ~** *or* **have a ~ to do sth.** darauf achten, etw. zu tun; **take more ~!** paß [doch] besser auf!; **take ~ to lock the door** vergiss ja *od.* nur nicht, die Tür abzuschließen [4] (attention) **medical ~:** ärztliche Betreuung; **old people need special ~:** alte Menschen brauchen besondere Fürsorge [5] (concern) **~ for sb./sth.** die Sorge um jmdn./etw. [6] ▸ⓘ **p. 1189** (charge) Obhut, *die* (geh.); **~ of,** (Amer.) **in ~ of** (on letter) per Adresse; bei; **be in ~:** in Pflege sein; **put sb. in ~/take sb. into ~:** jmdn. in Pflege geben/nehmen; **take ~ of sb./sth.** (ensure safety of) auf jmdn./etw. aufpassen; (attend to, dispose of) sich um jmdn./etw. kümmern; **take ~ of one's appearance** auf sein Äußeres achten; **take ~ of oneself** für sich selbst sorgen; (as to health) sich schonen; **take ~ [of yourself]!** machs gut! (ugs.); **that will take ~ of itself** das erledigt sich von selbst

B *v.i.* [1] **~ for** *or* **about sb./sth.** (heed) sich um jmdn./etw. kümmern; (feel interest) sich für jmdn./etw. interessieren; **he ~s only for his own interests** er hat nur seine eigenen Interessen im Sinn [2] **~ for** *or* **about sb./sth.** (like) jmdn./etw. mögen; **someone he really ~s for** *or* **about** jemand, der ihm wirklich etwas bedeutet; **he never shows how much he ~s** er zeigt nie die Stärke seiner Zuneigung; **I don't ~ about him** er ist mir völlig gleichgültig; **would you ~ for a drink?** möchten Sie etwas trinken? [3] (feel concern) **I don't ~ [whether/how/what** *etc.***]** es ist mir gleich[, ob/wie/was *usw.*]; **do you ~ if ...:** macht es Ihnen etwas aus, wenn ...; **people who ~:** Leute, die nicht nur an sich selbst denken; **she doesn't appear to ~ [how she dresses]** es scheint ihr gleich zu sein[, wie sie angezogen ist]; **don't you ~?** ist es dir [denn] gleichgültig?; **for all I ~** (coll.) von mir aus (ugs.); **I couldn't ~ less** (coll.) es ist mir völlig einerlei *od.* (ugs.) egal; **I couldn't ~ less about money** (coll.) Geld ist mir völlig gleichgültig; **I couldn't/don't ~ a tinker's cuss** *or* **a hoot** *or* **two hoots** *or* **tuppence about him/it** *etc.* (coll.) er/es *usw.* ist mir piepegal *od.* schnuppe (ugs.); **what do I ~?** (coll.) mir ist es egal (ugs.); **not that I ~** (coll.) obwohl es mir egal ist (ugs.); **who ~s?** (coll.) was solls (ugs.); *see also* **damn B 2** [4] (wish) **~ to do sth.** etw. tun mögen; **would you ~ to try some cake?** darf ich Ihnen ein Stückchen Kuchen anbieten? [5] **~ for sb./sth.** (look after) sich um jmdn./etw. kümmern; **well ~d for** gepflegt; gut versorgt ‹*Person*›; gut erhalten ‹*Auto*›

'care assistant *n.* Pflegehilfskraft, *die*

careen /kə'ri:n/

A *v.t.* (Naut.) kielholen

B *v.i.* [1] (Naut.: be turned over) gekielholt werden; krängen; (fig.) schwanken; torkeln [2] (Amer.: career) rasen

career /kə'rɪə(r)/

A *n.* [1] (way of livelihood) Beruf, *der;* **a teaching ~:** der Beruf des Lehrers; **take up a ~ in journalism** *or* **as a journalist** den Beruf des Journalisten ergreifen; **her modelling ~ was finished** sie musste ihren Beruf als Modell aufgeben; **she's not interested in [having] a ~:** sie interessiert sich nicht für eine Berufslaufbahn [2] (progress in life) [berufliche] Laufbahn; (very successful) Karriere, *die* [3] (swift course) Rasen, *das;* **in our ~ down the slope** als wir den Abhang hinuntersausten; **in full ~:** in rasendem Lauf; ‹*Wagen, Rennboot*› in voller Fahrt; ‹*Pferd*› in gestrecktem Galopp

B *v.i.* rasen; ‹*Pferd, Reiter:*› galoppieren; **go ~ing down the hill** den Hügel hinunterrasen

career: ~ break *n.* [1] (time not in paid work) [berufliche] Auszeit; [2] (change of occupation) [berufliche] Veränderung; **~ change** *n.* Berufswechsel, *der;* **go through a ~ change** sich beruflich umorientieren; **~ de'velopment** *n.* berufliche [Weiter]entwicklung; berufliches Fortkommen; **opportunities for ~ development, ~ development opportunities** Karrierechancen; berufliche Aufstiegsmöglichkeiten; **~ development consultant** Karriereberater, *der/*-beraterin, *die;* **~ 'diplomat** *n.* ▸ⓘ **p. 1260** Berufsdiplomat, *der;* **~ girl** *n.* Karrierefrau, *die*

careerist /kə'rɪərɪst/ *n.* Karrieremacher, *der* (abwertend)

career: ~ ladder *n.* Karriereleiter, *die;* **progress to the top of the ~ ladder** die oberste Stufe der Karriereleiter erklimmen; **~ move** *n.* Karriereschritt, *der;* **make a ~ move from marketing to editorial** vom Marketing in die Redaktion wechseln; **~ prospects** *n. pl.* Berufsaussichten *Pl.;* berufliche Aussichten; **~s adviser** *n.* ▸ⓘ **p. 1260** Berufsberater, *der/*-beraterin, *die;* **~s [advisory] service** *n.* Berufsberatung, *die;* **~s master/~s mistress:** *n.: Lehrer, der/Lehrerin, die die Schüler bei der Wahl des Berufs berät;* **~s office** *n.* Berufsberatung[sstelle], *die;* **~s officer** ▸ **~s adviser; ~ structure** *n.* (Brit.) Laufbahnstruktur, *die;* Karrieremuster, *das;* **~ woman** *n.* Karrierefrau, *die*

'care facility *n.* Pflegeeinrichtung, *die*

'carefree *adj.* sorgenfrei

careful /'keəfl/ *adj.* [1] (thorough) sorgfältig; (watchful, cautious) vorsichtig; **[be] ~!** Vorsicht!; **be ~ to do sth.** darauf achten, etw. zu tun; **he was ~ not to mention the subject** er war darum bemüht, das Thema nicht zu erwähnen; **be ~ that ...:** darauf achten, dass ...; **be ~ for sb./sth.** auf jmdn./etw. achten; **he is ~ for his own interests** er achtet darauf, seine eigenen Interessen zu wahren; **be ~ of sb./sth.** (take care of) mit jmdm./etw. vorsichtig sein; (be cautious of) sich vor jmdm./etw. in Acht nehmen; **be ~ of the roads!** pass auf, wenn du über die Straße gehst!; **be ~ how you word the letter** sei vorsichtig bei der Formulierung des Briefes; **be ~ [about] how/what/where** *etc.* darauf achten, wie/was/wo *usw.;* **be ~ about sth.** auf etw. (*Akk.*) achten; **be ~ about sb.** auf jmdn. aufpassen *od.* achten; **they're so ~ about the baby** sie kümmern sich sehr um das Baby; **be ~ about saying too much** darauf achten, nicht zu viel zu sagen; **do be ~ about drinking and driving** bitte sei vorsichtig mit dem Alkohol, wenn du noch fahren musst; **be ~ with sb./sth.** vorsichtig mit jmdm./etw. umgehen; **he's very ~ with his words** er wählt seine Worte sehr genau [2] (showing care) sorgfältig; **a ~ piece of work** ein sorgfältig gearbeitetes Stück; **after ~ consideration** nach reiflicher Überlegung; **pay ~ attention to what he says** achte genau auf das, was er sagt

carefully /'keəfəlɪ/ *adv.* (thoroughly) sorgfältig; gewissenhaft; (attentively) aufmerksam; (cautiously) vorsichtig; **watch ~:** gut aufpassen

carefulness /'keəflnɪs/ *n., no pl.* Sorgfalt, *die;* (caution) Vorsicht, *die*

'care home *n.* Pflegeheim, *das*

careless /'keəlɪs/ *adj.* [1] (inattentive) unaufmerksam; (thoughtless) gedankenlos; unvorsichtig, leichtsinnig ‹*Fahrer*›; nachlässig ‹*Arbeiter*›; **be ~ about** *or* **of sb./sth.** wenig auf jmdn./etw. achten; **you oughtn't to be so ~ about drinking and driving** du solltest mehr auf deinen Alkoholkonsum achten, wenn du noch fahren musst; **~ of sb./sth.** (unconcerned about) unbekümmert um jmdn./etw.; **~ with sb./sth.** unvorsichtig mit jmdm./etw.; **be ~ [about** *or* **of] how/what/where** *etc.* wenig darauf achten, wie/was/wo *usw.* [2] (showing lack of care) unordentlich, nachlässig ‹*Arbeit*›; gedankenlos ‹*Bemerkung, Handlung*›; unachtsam ‹*Fahren*›; **a [very] ~ mistake** ein [grober] Flüchtigkeitsfehler [3] (nonchalant) ungezwungen; lässig ‹*Aussehen, Geste*›

carelessly /'keəlɪslɪ/ *adv.* [1] (without care) nachlässig; (thoughtlessly) gedankenlos; unvorsichtig, leichtsinnig ‹*fahren*› [2] (nonchalantly) lässig

carelessness /'keəlɪsnɪs/ *n., no pl.* (lack of care) Nachlässigkeit, *die;* (thoughtlessness) Gedankenlosigkeit, *die*

care: ~ manager *n.* ▸ⓘ **p. 1260** Betreuer, *der/*Betreuerin, *die;* **~ order** *n.* (Brit.) Anordnung einer Vormundschaft oder Pflegschaft

carer /'keərə(r)/ *n.* ▸ⓘ **p. 1260** Betreuer, *der/*Betreuerin, *die;* (for sick person also) Pfleger, *der/*Pflegerin, *die;* **be a ~ for** *or* **of sb.** jmdn. versorgen *od.* betreuen; sich um jmdn. kümmern; (for sick person) jmdn. pflegen

caress /kə'res/

A *n.* Liebkosung, *die*

B *v.t.* liebkosen; **~ [each other]** sich *od.* einander liebkosen

caret /'kæret/ *n.: Korrekturzeichen für fehlende Buchstaben od. Wörter in einem Text*

care: ~taker *n.* [1] ▸ⓘ **p. 1260** Hausmeister, *der/*-meisterin, *die;* (in private house) Hausverwalter, *der/*-verwalterin, *die;* [2] *attrib.* **~taker government** Übergangsregierung, *die;* **~taker manager** Interimstrainer, *der/*-trainerin, *die;* **~ worker** *n.* ▸ⓘ **p. 1260** in einem Hilfsberuf Tätige, *der/die;* **~worn** *adj.* von Sorgen gezeichnet; **he looked ~worn** sein Gesicht war von Sorgen gezeichnet

car: ~fare *n.* (Amer.) Fahrgeld, *das;* **~ ferry** *n.* Autofähre, *die;* **~-free** *adj.* autofrei ‹*Zone*›; autolos ‹*Wohnen, Leben*›

cargo /'kɑ:gəʊ/ *n., pl.* **~es** *or* (Amer.) **~s** Fracht, *die;* Ladung, *die;* **a ~ of spices** eine Ladung Gewürze

cargo: ~ boat, ~ ship *ns.* Frachter, *der;* Frachtschiff, *das;* **~ plane** *n.* Frachtflugzeug, *das;* **~ vessel** *n.* Frachter, *der;* Frachtschiff, *das*

car: ~ hire *n.* Autovermietung, *die; attrib.* **~ hire firm** Autovermietung, *die;* **~hop** *n.* (Amer. coll. dated) *Kellner/Kellnerin in einem Drive-in-Restaurant*

Caribbean /kærɪ'bi:ən/

A *n.* **the ~:** die Karibik

B *adj.* karibisch; **the ~ Sea** das Karibische Meer; **~ holiday** Urlaub in der Karibik

caribou /'kærɪbu:/ *n., pl. same* (Zool.) Karibu, *der od. das*

caricature /'kærɪkətjʊə(r)/

A *n.* Karikatur, *die;* (in mime) Parodie, *die;* **do a ~ of sb.** jmdn. karikieren/parodieren

B *v.t.* karikieren; (in mime) parodieren

caricaturist /'kærɪkətjʊərɪst/ *n.* ▸ⓘ **p. 1260** Karikaturist, *der/*Karikaturistin, *die;* (in mime) Parodist, *der/*Parodistin, *die*

caries /'keəri:z/ *n., pl. same* (Med., Dent.) Karies, *die*

carillon /kə'rɪljən, 'kærɪljən/ *n.* Glockenspiel, *das*

'car industry *n.* Auto[mobil]industrie, *die;* Auto[mobil]branche, *die*

caring /'keərɪŋ/ *adj.* sozial ‹*Gesellschaft*›; fürsorglich ‹*Person*›

'car insurance *n.* Autoversicherung, *die;* Kfz-Versicherung, *die*

Carinthia /kə'rɪnθɪə/ *pr. n.* Kärnten (*das*)

Carinthian /kə'rɪnθɪən/

A *n.* Kärntner, *der/*Kärntnerin, *die*

B *adj.* kärntnerisch; **the ~ Lakes** die Kärntner Seen

car: ~jacker /'kɑ:dʒækə(r)/ *n.* Carjacker, *der;* **~jacking** /'kɑ:dʒækɪŋ/ *n.* Carjacking, *das;* **~ journey** *n.* Autofahrt, *die;* **~ key** *n.* Autoschlüssel, *der;* **~ licence** *n.* Fahrzeugschein, *der;* Zulassung, *die* (ugs.); **'~load** *n.* [1] Wagenladung, *die;* **people were arriving by the ~load** es trafen ganze Wagenladungen von Menschen ein; [2] (Amer.) *Mindestladung für ermäßigten Frachtbrief;* **~man** /'kɑ:mən/ *n., pl.* **carmen** /'kɑ:mən/ [Berufskraft]fahrer, *der;* **~ mat** *n.* Fußmatte, *die* (*im Auto*)

Carmelite /'kɑ:mɪlaɪt/

A *n.* (friar) Karmelit[er], *der;* (nun) Karmelit[er]in, *die*

B *adj.* Karmeliter-

carmine /'kɑ:maɪn, 'kɑ:mɪn/

A *n.* Karmin[rot], *das*

B *adj.* karminrot

carnage /ˈkɑːnɪdʒ/ *n.* Gemetzel, *das;* **a scene of ~:** ein Schlachtfeld (fig.); **the dreadful annual ~ on the roads** das alljährliche schreckliche Blutvergießen auf den Straßen

carnal /ˈkɑːnl/ *adj.* **1** (sensual) körperlich; sinnlich; fleischlich (geh.); **~ desires/sins** sinnliche Begierden/Sünden des Fleisches (geh.); **~ lust** Fleischeslust, *die* (geh.) **2** (worldly) profan

carnal ˈknowledge *n.* (Law) **have ~ of sb.** mit jmdm. Geschlechtsverkehr haben

carnation¹ /kɑːˈneɪʃn/ *n.* (Bot.) [Garten]nelke, *die*

carnation²
A *n.* Rosarot, *das*
B *adj.* **~ [pink]** [zart]rosa

carnet /ˈkɑːneɪ/ *n.* (of motorist) Triptyk, *das;* (of camper) Ausweis für Camper

carnival /ˈkɑːnɪvl/ *n.* **1** (festival) Volksfest, *das; attrib.* **~ procession** Festzug, *der* **2** (pre-Lent festivities) Karneval, *der;* Fastnacht, *die;* Fasching, *der* (bes. südd., österr.); (fig.: revelry) ausgelassenes Fest; *attrib.* **~ procession** Karnevals[um]zug, *der* **3** (Amer.) (circus) Zirkus, *der;* (funfair) Jahrmarkt, *der*

carnivore /ˈkɑːnɪvɔː(r)/ *n.* (animal) Fleischfresser, *der;* Karnivore, *der* (Zool.); (plant) Fleisch fressende Pflanze; Karnivore, *die* (Bot.)

carnivorous /kɑːˈnɪvərəs/ *adj.* Fleisch fressend; karnivor (Zool., Bot.)

carob /ˈkærəb/ *n.* **1** (pod) Johannisbrot, *das* **2** (tree) Johannisbrotbaum, *der*

carol /ˈkærl/
A *n.* **1** **[Christmas] ~:** Weihnachtslied, *das;* **~ concert, ~ singing** weihnachtliches Liedersingen; **~ singers** *Leute, die von Haus zu Haus gehen und Weihnachtslieder vortragen;* ≈ Weihnachtssänger *Pl.* **2** (joyous song) fröhliches Lied
B *v.t.,* (Brit.) **-ll-:** **1** (sing as ~) singen ‹*Weihnachtslied*› **2** (sing joyfully) [fröhlich] singen
C *v.i.,* (Brit.) **-ll-:** **1** Weihnachtslieder singen **2** (sing joyfully) [fröhlich] singen

carom /ˈkærəm/ (Amer.)
A *n.* Karambolage, *die; attrib.* **~ billiards** Karambolagebillard, *das*
B *v.i.* (Billiards) karambolieren

carotene /ˈkærətiːn/ *n., no pl.* (Chem.) Karotin, *das*

carotid /kəˈrɒtɪd/ (Anat.)
A *adj.* Karotis-; **~ artery** ▸ **B**
B *n.* Halsschlagader, *die;* Karotis, *die* (fachspr.)

carousal /kəˈraʊzl/ *n.* Zechgelage, *das*

carouse /kəˈraʊz/
A *v.i.* zechen (veralt., noch scherzh.)
B *n.* ▸ **carousal**

carousel /kærʊˈsel, kærʊˈzel/ *n.* **1** (conveyor system) Ausgabeband, *das* **2** (Amer.: roundabout) Karussell, *das*

ˈcar owner *n.* Autobesitzer, *der*

carp¹ /kɑːp/ *n., pl. same* (Zool.) Karpfen, *der*

carp² *v.i.* nörgeln; **~ [on and on] at sb./sth.** an jmdm./etw. [dauernd] herumnörgeln (ugs.)

ˈcar park *n.* Parkplatz, *der;* (underground) Tiefgarage, *die;* (multi-storey) Parkhaus, *das*

ˈcar parking *n., no pl.* Parken, *das; attrib.* **~ facilities are available** Parkplätze [sind] vorhanden

Carpathians /kɑːˈpeiθjənz, kɑːˈpeɪðjənz/ *pr. n. pl.* Karpaten *Pl.*

carpel /ˈkɑːpl/ *n.* (Bot.) Fruchtblatt, *das;* Karpell, *das* (fachspr.)

carpenter /ˈkɑːpɪntə(r)/
A *n.* ▸ **ⓘ p. 1260** Zimmermann, *der;* (for furniture) Tischler, *der*/Tischlerin, *die;* (ship's ~) Schiffszimmermann, *der*
B *v.t.* zimmern; tischlern ‹*Regale*›

carpentry /ˈkɑːpɪntrɪ/ *n., no pl.* **1** (trade) Zimmerhandwerk, *das;* (in furniture) Tischlerhandwerk, *das* **2** (woodwork) **[piece of] ~:** Tischlerarbeit, *die;* (structure) [Holz]konstruktion, *die*

carpet /ˈkɑːpɪt/
A *n.* **1** (covering) Teppich, *der;* **[fitted] ~:** Teppichboden, *der;* **stair ~:** [Treppen]läufer, *der;* **be on the ~** (coll.: be reprimanded) zusammengestaucht werden (ugs.); (be under discussion) zur Debatte stehen; **have sb. on the ~** (coll.: reprimand sb.) jmdn. zusammenstauchen (ugs.); **sweep sth. under the ~** (fig.) etw. unter den Teppich kehren (ugs.); *see also* **red carpet** **2** (expanse) **~ of flowers** Blumenteppich, *der;* **~ of grass/snow/leaves** Gras-/Schnee-/Laubdecke, *die*
B *v.t.* **1** (cover) [mit Teppich(boden)] auslegen; (fig.) bedecken; **snow ~ed the village in [a layer of] white** Schnee bedeckte das Dorf mit einem weißen Teppich **2** (coll.: reprimand) **be ~ed for sth.** wegen etw. zusammengestaucht werden (ugs.)

carpet: ~ bag *n.* Reisetasche, *die;* **~bagger** /ˈkɑːpɪtbægə(r)/ *n.* **1** politischer Karrieremacher; **2** (Hist.) *Politiker aus dem Norden der USA, der in den Südstaaten nach dem Sezessionskrieg rasch Karriere machen wollte;* **~ beater** *n.* Teppichklopfer, *der;* **~ bombing** *n.* Flächenbombardement, *das*

carpeting /ˈkɑːpɪtɪŋ/ *n.* **1** Teppich[boden], *der;* **some ~:** ein Stück Teppichboden; **wall-to-wall ~:** Teppichboden, *der* **2** (fig.) ▸ **carpet A 2**

carpet: ~ layer *n.* ▸ **ⓘ p. 1260** Teppich[ver]leger, *der*/-[ver]legerin, *die* **~ slipper** *n.* Hausschuh, *der;* **~ square** *n.* Teppichplatte, *die;* **~ sweeper** *n.* Teppichkehrer, *der;* Teppichkehrmaschine, *die;* **~ tile** *n.* Teppichfliese, *die*

car: ~ phone *n.* Autotelefon, *das;* **~ pool** *n.* Fahrgemeinschaft, *die;* (of a firm etc.) Fahrzeugpark, *der;* **~port** *n.* Einstellplatz, *der;* **~ radio** *n.* Autoradio, *das*

carrel /ˈkærl/ *n.* [abgeteilter] Arbeitsplatz (*in einer Bibliothek*/(hist.) *in einem Kloster*)

car rental ▸ **car hire**

carriage /ˈkærɪdʒ/ *n.* **1** (horse-drawn vehicle) Kutsche, *die;* **~ and pair/four/six** *etc.* Zwei-/Vier-/Sechsspänner *usw., der; see also* **drive B 1** **2** (Railw.) [Eisenbahn]wagen, *der* **3** (Mech.) Schlitten, *der;* (of typewriter) Schlitten, *der;* Wagen, *der* **4** *no pl.* (conveying, being conveyed) Transport, *der;* **use for ~:** für den Transport benutzen **5** (cost of conveying) Frachtkosten *Pl.;* **~ forward** Fracht[kosten] zulasten des Empfängers; **~ paid** frachtfrei **6** (bearing) Haltung, *die. See also* **gun carriage; invalid carriage**

carriage: ~ bolt *n.* Schlossschraube, *die;* **~ clock** *n.* Reiseuhr, *die;* **~ return** *n.* **~ return [key]** (on typewriter) Wagenrücklauftaste, *die;* (on computer keyboard) Returntaste, *die;* **~way** *n.* Fahrbahn, *die*

ˈcar ride *n.* Autofahrt, *die*

carrier /ˈkærɪə(r)/ *n.* **1** (bearer) Träger, *der;* **~ of good news** Überbringer guter Nachrichten **2** (conductor) **be the ~ of sth.** etw. transportieren *od.* leiten **3** (hired conveyor of goods or passengers) Transportunternehmen, *das;* (person) Transportunternehmer, *der;* **firm of ~s** Transportunternehmen, *das* **4** (on bicycle etc.) Gepäckträger, *der;* (for child passenger) Kindersitz, *der* **5** ▸ **carrier bag** **6** ▸ **carrier wave** **7** ▸ **aircraft carrier** **8** (Med.: of disease) Ausscheider, *der;* (Genetics: of characteristic) Konduktor, *der*

carrier: ~ bag *n.* Tragetasche, *die;* Tragetüte, *die;* **~ pigeon** *n.* Brieftaube, *die;* **by ~ pigeon** mit der Taubenpost; **~ wave** *n.* (Phys.) Trägerwelle, *die*

carrion /ˈkærɪən/ *n.* **1** (flesh) Aas, *das* **2** (fig.: garbage) Unflat, *der;* Schmutz, *der*

ˈcarrion crow *n.* Rabenkrähe, *die;* (Corvus corone) Aaskrähe, *die*

carrot /ˈkærət/ *n.* **1** Möhre, *die;* Karotte, *die;* **grated ~[s]** geraspelte Möhren *od.* Karotten **2** (fig.) Köder, *der;* **dangle a ~ in front of sb.'s nose** jmdm. einen Köder vor die Nase halten; **with ~ and stick** mit Zuckerbrot und Peitsche

ˈcarrot cake *n.* Karottenkuchen, *der*

carroty /ˈkærətɪ/ *adj.* rotblond ‹*Haare*›

carrousel (Amer.) ▸ **carousel**

carry /ˈkærɪ/
A *v.t.* **1** (transport) tragen; (with emphasis on destination) bringen; überbringen ‹*Nachrichten*›; ‹*Tornado:*› fegen; ‹*Strom:*› spülen; ‹*Verkehrsmittel:*› befördern; **~ sth. with one in a bag** etw. in einer Tasche bei sich haben *od.* tragen; **where do you ~ your purse?** wo hast *od.* trägst du dein Portemonnaie?; **~ sth. in one's head** etw. im Kopf haben; **~ sth. round with one** (lit. or fig.) etw. mit sich herumtragen (ugs.); (fig.) etw. nicht vergessen können; **~ all before one** (fig.) nicht aufzuhalten sein
2 (conduct) leiten; **~ sth. into effect** etw. in die Tat umsetzen
3 (support) tragen; (contain) fassen; **~ responsibility** Verantwortung tragen
4 (have with one) **~ [with one]** bei sich haben *od.* tragen; tragen ‹*Waffe, Kennzeichen*›; ‹*Schiff:*› führen ‹*Lichter, Segel*›
5 (possess) besitzen ‹*Autorität, Gewicht*›; *see also* **conviction 2**
6 (hold) **he carries his head in a proud way** er trägt den Kopf hoch; **she carries herself well** sie hat eine gute Haltung; **he carries himself very erect** er hält sich sehr aufrecht
7 (prolong) **~ sth. to a close** *or* **an end** etw. zu Ende führen *od.* bringen; **such plans must be carried to their natural conclusions** solche Pläne müssen [bis zum Ende] durchgezogen werden (ugs.); **~ modesty/altruism** *etc.* **to excess** die Bescheidenheit/den Altruismus *usw.* bis zum Exzess treiben; **~ things to extremes** die Dinge auf die Spitze treiben; *see also* **far A 4**
8 (be infected with) in sich tragen ‹*Krankheit*›
9 (Math.: transfer) im Sinn behalten; **~ one** eins im Sinn
10 (be pregnant with) erwarten ‹*Kind*›; **she was ~ing his child** sie erwartete ein Kind von ihm
11 (win) erringen ‹*Sieg*›; durchbringen ‹*Antrag, Gesetzentwurf, Vorschlag*›; **the motion is carried** der Antrag ist angenommen; **~ one's point [with sb.]** seine Sache [bei jmdm.] durchsetzen; **~ one's hearers/audience with one** die Zuhörer/das Publikum überzeugen; **~ the day** den Sieg davontragen
12 (involve) [mit sich] bringen; bringen ‹*Gewinn, Zinsen*›; **discipline carries both advantages and disadvantages** Disziplin hat ihre Vor- und Nachteile
13 (stock) führen
14 (publish, broadcast) bringen
B *v.i.* ‹*Stimme, Laut:*› zu hören sein; ‹*Geruch:*› zu riechen sein; ‹*Geschoss, Ball:*› [weit] fliegen

(Phrasal verbs)

- **~ aˈway** *v.t.* forttragen; (by force) fortreißen; (fig.) **be** *or* **get carried away** (be inspired) hingerissen sein (**by** von); (lose self-control) sich hinreißen lassen; **don't get carried away!** übertreibs nicht!
- **~ ˈback** *v.t.* **1** (return) zurückbringen **2** ▸ **take back 2**
- **~ ˈforward** *v.t.* (Bookk.) vortragen
- **~ ˈoff** *v.t.* **1** (from place) davontragen; (as owner or possessor) mit sich nehmen; (cause to die) dahinraffen (geh.) **2** (abduct) entführen ‹*Person*› **3** (win) gewinnen ‹*Preis, Medaille*›; erringen ‹*Sieg*› **4** (succeed in doing) durchführen; (cope with) fertig werden mit; **~ it/sth. off [well]** es/etw. [gut] zustande bringen
- **~ ˈon**

A *v.t.* (continue) fortführen ‹*Tradition, Diskussion, Arbeit*›; **~ on the firm** die Firma übernehmen; **~ on [doing sth.]** weiterhin etw. tun; **they carried on talking** sie fuhren fort, sich zu unterhalten
B *v.i.* **1** (continue) weitermachen; **~ on with a plan/project** einen Plan/ein Projekt weiterverfolgen **2** (coll.: behave in unseemly manner) sich danebenbenehmen (ugs.); (make a fuss) Theater machen (ugs.) **3** **~ on with sb.** (flirt) mit jmdm. flirten; (have affair) mit jmdm. ein Verhältnis haben. *See also* **carry-on**

- **~ ˈout** *v.t.* (put into practice) durchführen ‹*Plan, Programm, Versuch*›; in die Tat umsetzen ‹*Plan, Vorschlag, Absicht, Vorstellung*›; ausführen ‹*Anweisung, Auftrag*›; halten ‹*Versprechen*›; vornehmen ‹*Verbesserungen*›; wahr machen ‹*Drohung*›
- **~ ˈover** *v.t.* **1** (postpone) vertagen (**to** auf + *Akk.*) **2** (St. Exch.) prolongieren **3** ▸ **~ forward**. *See also* **~-over**

C

- ~ **'through** v.t. 1 (bring safely through) **~ sb. through** jmdm. durchhelfen 2 (complete) durchführen

'carrycot n. Babytragetasche, die

carryings-on /kærɪŋz'ɒn/ n. pl. (coll.) 1 (questionable behaviour) seltsames Treiben; **there are strange ~ in that house** in diesem Haus geht Seltsames vor 2 (love affairs) Affären

carry: ~-on n. (coll.) 1 Theater, das (ugs.); 2 (flirtation) Flirt, der; (love affair) [Liebes]affäre, die; **~-out** n. **~-out [meal]** Essen od. Mahlzeit zum Mitnehmen; **~-out [restaurant]** Restaurant mit Straßenverkauf; **get a ~-out** sich (Dat.) in einem Restaurant was zu essen holen; (to drink) sich (Dat.) was zu trinken holen; **~-over** n. (St. Exch.) Prolongation, die

car: ~sick adj. **children are often ~:** Kindern wird beim Autofahren oft schlecht; **~ stereo** n. Autostereoanlage, die

cart /kɑːt/

A n. Karren, der; Wagen, der; **horse and ~:** Pferdewagen, der; **be in the ~** (Brit. coll.) in der Tinte sitzen (ugs.); **put the ~ before the horse** (fig.) das Pferd beim Schwanz aufzäumen

B v.t. 1 (carry [as] in ~) karren 2 (fig. coll.: carry with effort) schleppen; **~ sth. around with one** etw. mit sich herumschleppen

Phrasal verb

- ~ **'off** v.t. (coll.) abtransportieren

carte blanche /kɑːt 'blɑ̃ʃ/ n. Carte blanche, die; unbeschränkte Vollmacht

cartel /kɑː'tel/ n. Kartell, das

carter /'kɑːtə(r)/ n. ▸ⓘ p. 1260 Fuhrmann, der

Cartesian /kɑː'tiːzjən/ adj. **~ coordinates** (Math.) kartesische Koordinaten

Carthage /'kɑːθɪdʒ/ pr. n. ▸ⓘ p. 1643 Karthago (das)

'car thief n. Autodieb, der/-diebin, die

'carthorse n. Arbeitspferd, das

Carthusian /kɑː'θjuːzjən/

A adj. Kartäuser-

B n. Kartäuser, der

cartilage /'kɑːtɪlɪdʒ/ n. Knorpel, der

cartilaginous /kɑːtɪ'lædʒɪnəs/ adj. knorpelig

'cartload n. 1 Wagenladung, die; Fuhre, die; **by the ~:** fuhrenweise 2 (fig.: large quantity) **a ~ of books** ein Berg von Büchern; **~s of food** Essen in Hülle und Fülle

cartographer /kɑː'tɒgrəfə(r)/ n. ▸ⓘ p. 1260 Kartograph, der/Kartographin, die

cartographic /kɑːtə'græfɪk/, **cartographical** /kɑːtə'græfɪkl/ adjs. kartographisch

cartography /kɑː'tɒgrəfɪ/ n., no pl. Kartographie, die

carton /'kɑːtn/ n. [Papp]karton, der; **a ~ of milk** eine Tüte Milch; **a ~ of detergent** ein Paket Waschpulver; **a ~ of cigarettes** eine Stange Zigaretten; **a ~ of yoghurt** ein Becher Joghurt

cartoon /kɑː'tuːn/

A n. 1 (amusing drawing) humoristische Zeichnung; Cartoon, der; (satirical illustration) Karikatur, die; (sequence of drawings) [humoristische] Bilderserie; Cartoon, der 2 (film) Zeichentrickfilm, der 3 (Art) Entwurf, der; Karton, der (Kunstwiss.)

B v.t. (draw amusingly) karikieren

cartoonist /kɑː'tuːnɪst/ n. ▸ⓘ p. 1260 Cartoonist, der/Cartoonistin, die; (satirical ~) Karikaturist, der/Karikaturistin, die

car'toon strip n. Comic, der

'car transporter n. Autotransporter, der

cartridge /'kɑːtrɪdʒ/ n. 1 (case for explosive) Patrone, die 2 (spool of film, cassette) Kassette, die 3 (for pickup head) Tonabnehmer, der 4 (ink container) Patrone, die

cartridge: ~ belt n. Patronengurt, der; **~ case** n. Patronenhülse, die; **~ paper** n. (for drawing) Zeichenpapier, das; (for envelopes, gun cartridges) festes, haltbares Papier

cart: ~ road, ~ track ns. ≈ Feldweg, der; **~wheel** n. 1 Wagenrad, das; 2 (Gymnastics) Rad, das; **turn** or **do ~wheels** Rad schlagen; **~wright** /'kɑːtraɪt/ n. ▸ⓘ p. 1260 Stellmacher, der

'car valeting n., no pl. Autoreinigung, die

carve /kɑːv/

A v.t. 1 (cut up) tranchieren, aufschneiden ‹Fleisch, Braten›; tranchieren ‹Hähnchen› 2 (produce by cutting) (from wood) schnitzen; (from stone) meißeln; **~ sth. out of wood/stone** etw. aus Holz schnitzen/aus Stein meißeln; **~ sth. in/into/on sth.** etw. in etw. (Akk.) [ein]ritzen; **~ a tunnel in the rock** einen Tunnel in den Fels hauen; **~ one's way** sich (Dat.) seinen Weg hauen 3 (change by cutting) **he ~d a block of wood/stone into a madonna** er schnitzte aus einem Holzblock/meißelte aus einem Steinblock eine Madonna 4 (adorn by cutting) **the frame was ~d with leaves** der Rahmen war mit geschnitzten/in Stein gehauenen Blättern verziert

B v.i. 1 tranchieren 2 **~ in wood/ivory/stone** in Holz/Elfenbein schnitzen/in Stein meißeln; **~ through sth.** sich (Dat.) einen Weg durch etw. hauen

Phrasal verbs

- ~ **out** v.t. heraushauen; **~ out a tunnel in the rock** einen Tunnel in den Fels hauen od. treiben; **~ out an existence** (fig.) sich (Dat.) eine Existenz aufbauen
- ~ **up** v.t. aufschneiden ‹Fleisch›; aufteilen ‹Erbe, Land›; zerstückeln ‹Leiche›

carver /'kɑːvə(r)/ n. 1 (in wood) [Holz]schnitzer, der; (in stone) Bildhauer, der; (of meat) Trancheur, der 2 (knife) ▸**carving knife** 3 in pl. (knife and fork) Tranchierbesteck, das

carvery /'kɑːvərɪ/ n. (Brit.) Büffet, das; (restaurant) Büffetrestaurant, das

carving /'kɑːvɪŋ/ n. 1 (in or from wood, ivory) Schnitzerei, die; **a ~ of a madonna in wood** eine holzgeschnitzte Madonna; **an ivory ~ of an elephant** ein aus Elfenbein geschnitzter Elefant 2 (in or from stone) Skulptur, die; (on stone) eingeritztes Bild; (ornament) eingeritztes Muster

'carving: ~ fork n. Tranchiergabel, die; **~ knife** n. Tranchiermesser, das

car: ~ wash n. Waschanlage, die; **~ worker** n. ▸ⓘ p. 1260 Automobilarbeiter, der/-arbeiterin, die

caryatid /kærɪ'ætɪd/ n., pl. **~s** or **~es** /kærɪ'ætɪdiːz/ (Archit.) Karyatide, die

Casanova /kæzə'nəʊvə, kæsə'nəʊvə/ n. Casanova, der

cascade /kæs'keɪd/

A (lit. or fig.) Kaskade, die

B v.i. [in Kaskaden] herabstürzen; **her hair ~d down her back** (fig.) ihr Haar fiel in Kaskaden über ihren Rücken hinab

cas'cade effect n. Kaskadeneffekt, der

case[1] /keɪs/ n. 1 (instance, matter) Fall, der; **if there is another ~ of this happening** wenn das noch einmal vorkommt; **if it's a ~ of your not being able to get here** wenn es nur daran liegt, dass du nicht herkommen kannst; **it's just a ~ of concentrating** es ist nur eine Sache der Konzentration; **then that's a different ~:** dann ist das was anderes; **if that's the ~:** wenn das so ist; **it is [not] the ~ that ...:** es trifft [nicht] zu od. stimmt [nicht], dass ...; **it seems to be the ~ that they have ...:** sie scheinen tatsächlich ... zu haben; **as is generally the ~ with ...:** wie das normalerweise bei ... der Fall ist; **such being the ~:** deshalb; **as the ~ may be** je nachdem; **in ~ ...:** falls ...; für den Fall, dass ... (geh.); **[just] in ~** (to allow for all possibilities) für alle Fälle; **in ~ of fire/complaints/burst pipes/danger** bei Feuer/Reklamationen/Rohrbrüchen/Gefahr; **in ~ of emergency** im Notfall; **in ~ of the hostages' being released** falls die Geiseln freigelassen werden; **in the ~ of** bei; **in the ~ of New College** was das New College anbelangt; **in any ~** (regardless of anything else) jedenfalls; **I don't need it in any ~:** ich brauche es sowieso nicht; **we don't want to go to the party and in any ~ it's raining** wir haben keine Lust, auf die Party zu gehen, und außerdem regnet es ja; **in no ~** (certainly not) unter keinen Umständen; auf keinen Fall; **in that ~:** in diesem Fall; **in which ~ he would ...:** in diesem Fall od. dann würde er ... 2 (Med., Police, Soc. Serv., etc., or coll.: person afflicted) Fall, der; **a murder ~:** ein Mordfall; **he is a mental/psychiatric ~:** er ist ein Fall für den Psychiater; **this man is a dangerous ~:** dieser Mann ist gefährlich; **her son is a problem ~:** ihr Sohn ist ein Problemkind 3 (Law) Fall, der; (action) Verfahren, das; **which was that ~ five years ago?** welcher Fall war das vor fünf Jahren?; **the Dreyfus ~:** der Fall Dreyfus; die Dreyfusaffäre (hist.); **the ~ for the prosecution/defence** die Anklage/Verteidigung; **put one's ~:** seinen Fall darlegen; **and that is our ~:** und damit beende ich meine Ausführungen 4 (fig.: set of arguments) Fall, der; (valid set of arguments) **you have no ~ there** das ist kein Argument; **there's a ~ for doing sth.** es gibt Gründe, die dafür sprechen, dass man etw. tut; **have a [good] ~ for doing sth./for sth.** gute Gründe haben, etw. zu tun/für etw. haben; **make out a ~ for sth.** Argumente für etw. anführen 5 (Ling.) Fall, der; Kasus, der (fachspr.) 6 (fig. coll.) (comical person) ulkiger Typ (ugs.); (comical woman) ulkige Nudel (ugs.)

case[2]

A n. 1 Koffer, der; (small) Handkoffer, der; (brief~) [Akten]tasche, die; (for musical instrument) Kasten, der; **violin ~:** Geigenkasten, der; **doctor's ~:** Arzttasche, die; **pen and pencil ~:** Federmäppchen, das 2 (sheath) Hülle, die; (for spectacles, cigarettes) Etui, das; (for jewellery) Schmuckkassette, die; Schmuckkästchen, das 3 (crate) Kiste, die; **~ of oranges** Kiste [mit] Apfelsinen 4 (glass box) Vitrine, die; **[display] ~:** Schaukasten, der 5 (cover) Gehäuse, das; (seed vessel) Hülle, die; (of sausage) Haut, die; (of book) Buchdeckel, der 6 (Printing) Schriftkasten, der; see also **lower case**; **upper case**

B v.t. 1 (box) verpacken 2 (sl.: examine) **~ the joint** sich (Dat.) den Laden mal ansehen (ugs.)

case: ~book n. 1 (Law) Sammlung von Rechtsfällen; 2 (Med.) Sammlung von Krankheitsfällen; 3 (of social worker etc.; also fig.) Fallsammlung, die; **~-bound** adj. mit festem Einband nachgestellt; **be ~-bound** einen festen Einband haben; **~ ending** n. (Ling.) Beugungsendung, die; Kasusendung, die (fachspr.); **~ file** n. Fallakte, die; **~-harden** v.t. härten ‹Metall›; **~-hardened** (fig.) abgebrüht; **~ history** n. 1 (record) [Vor]geschichte, die; 2 (Med.) Krankengeschichte, die; **~ knife** n. Fahrtenmesser, das; **~ law** n. (Law) Fallrecht, das; **~load** n. Fälle Pl.; **he has a heavy ~load, his ~load is heavy** er hat sehr viele Fälle zu bearbeiten; **the [doctor's] ~load** die Anzahl der Patienten; **share the [doctor's] ~load** einen Teil der Patienten übernehmen; **~ 'management** n., no pl. Fallmanagement, das

casement /'keɪsmənt/ n. 1 (part of window) [Fenster]flügel, der; **~ [window]** Flügelfenster, das 2 (poet.: window) Fenster, das

case: ~ notes n. pl. Fallnotizen Pl.; Fallaufzeichnungun Pl.; **~-sensitive** adj. (Computing) zwischen Groß- und Kleinbuchstaben unterscheidend; **commands are ~-sensitive** bei der Eingabe von Befehlen ist die Groß- und Kleinschreibung zu beachten; **~ study** n. Fallstudie, die; **~work** n., no pl., no indef. art. [auf den Einzelfall bezogene] Sozialarbeit; Casework, das (Psychol., Soziol.); **~worker** n. ▸ⓘ p. 1260 [Einzelfälle betreuender] Sozialarbeiter

cash /kæʃ/

A n., no pl., no indef. art. ▸ⓘ p. 1332 1 Bargeld, das; **payment in ~ only** nur Barzahlung; **pay [in] ~, pay ~ down** bar zahlen; **we haven't got the ~:** wir haben [dafür] kein Geld; **be short of ~:** knapp bei Kasse sein (ugs.); **~ on delivery** per Nachnahme 2 (Banking etc.) Geld, das; **can I get ~ for these cheques?** kann ich diese Schecks einlösen?; **you may withdraw £50 in ~:** Sie können 50 Pfund in bar abheben; see also **discount A**

B v.t. 1 einlösen ‹Scheck› 2 (Bridge) ausspielen [und den Stich machen]

(Phrasal verb)

- **~ in**

A /'--/ v.t. sich (Dat.) gutschreiben lassen ‹Scheck›; auf die Bank bringen ‹Geld, Einnahmen›; **~ in one's chips** (fig. coll.) abkratzen (salopp)
B /-'-/ v.i. **~ in on sth.** (lit. or fig.) von etw. profitieren

cash: ~ account n. Kassekonto, das (Buchf.); **~ ad'vance** n. Barvorschuss, der; (payment in advance) Vorauszahlung, die; (from credit card) Barauszahlung, die; **~ and 'carry** n.: Verkaufssystem, bei dem der Kunde bar bezahlt und die Ware selbst nach Hause transportiert; attrib. **~-and-carry store** Cash-and-carry-Laden, der; **~back** n., no pl., no art.: Barauszahlung eines Differenzbetrages bei Kauf mit Geldkarte; **~ book** n. Kassenbuch, das; **~ box** n. Geldkassette, die; **~ call** n. (Finance) Aufforderung zur Kapitalerhöhung; **~ card** n. (prepaid) Geldkarte, die; (ATM card) Geldautomatenkarte, die; **~ 'cow** n. (coll.) Cashcow, die; **~ crop** n.: zum Verkauf bestimmtes landwirtschaftliches Erzeugnis; **~ desk** n. (Brit.) Kasse, die; **~ 'discount** n. Skonto, der od. das; Barzahlungsrabatt, der; **~ dispenser** n. Geldautomat, der

cashew /'kæʃuː/ n. **1** (nut) ▸**cashew nut** **2** (tree) Nierenbaum, der (Bot.); Cashewbaum, der (Bot.)

'cashew nut n. Cashewnuss, die

'cash flow n. (Econ.) Cashflow, der

cashier¹ /kæ'ʃɪə(r)/ n. ▸ℹ p. 1260 Kassierer, der/Kassiererin, die; **~'s office** Kasse, die

cashier² v.t. entlassen; des Amtes entheben (geh.); (Mil.) [unehrenhaft] entlassen; kassieren (veralt.)

'cash-in n. **1** (realization of cash) Flüssigmachung, die; attrib. **~ value** Rückkauf[s]wert, der **2** (case of exploitation) Geldmacherei, die (ugs abwertend)

'cashless adj. bargeldlos; **the ~ society** die bargeldlose Gesellschaft

'cash machine n. Geldautomat, der

cashmere /'kæʃmɪə(r)/ n. Kaschmir, der; **~ wool/sweater** Kaschmirwolle, die/Kaschmirpullover, der

cash: ~ payment n. Barzahlung, die; **make a ~ payment** bar bezahlen; **~point** n. Geldautomat, der; **~point card** n. Bankkarte, die; **~ price** n. Barzahlungspreis, der; **~ register** n. [Registrier]kasse, die; (in shop also) [Laden]kasse, die; **~-rich** adj. ‹Firma, Organisation› mit großen Bar[geld]reserven; ‹Person› mit großem Barvermögen; **~ sale** n. Bargeschäft, das; **~-strapped** /'kæʃstræpt/ adj. (coll.) klamm (ugs.); **~ value** n. Barwert, der; (Insurance) Rückkauf[s]wert, der

casing /'keɪsɪŋ/ n. Gehäuse, das; (of projectile, cable, tyre) Mantel, der

casino /kə'siːnəʊ/ n., pl. **~s** Kasino, das; (for gambling also) Spielkasino, das; [Spiel]bank, die

cask /kɑːsk/ n. Fass, das

'cask-conditioned adj. im Fass vergoren und naturbelassen

casket /'kɑːskɪt/ n. **1** (box) Schatulle, die (veralt.); Kästchen, das **2** (Amer.: coffin) Sarg, der

Caspian Sea /kæspɪən 'siː/ pr. n. Kaspische Meer, das; Kaspisee, der

Cassandra /kə'sændrə/ n. Kassandra, die

cassata /kæ'sɑːtə/ n. Cassata, die od. das

cassava /kə'sɑːvə/ n. **1** (plant) Maniok, der **2** (flour) Tapioka, die

casserole /'kæsərəʊl/

A n. **1** (vessel) Schmortopf, der; (oval also) Bräter, der; (with long handle) Kasserolle, die **2** (food) Schmortopf, der
B v.t. schmoren

cassette /kə'set, kæ'set/ n. Kassette, die; **miniature film ~**: Kleinbildkassette, die

cassette: ~ deck n. Kassettendeck, das; **~ player** n. Kassettengerät, das; **~ recorder** n. Kassettenrecorder, der; **~ tape** n. Kassette, die

cassock /'kæsək/ n. (Eccl.) Soutane, die

cast /kɑːst/

A v.t., **~** **1** (throw) werfen; **~ sth. adrift** etw. abtreiben lassen; **~ loose** losmachen; **~ sth. ashore** etw. an Land spülen; **~ an** or **one's eye over sth.** einen Blick auf etw. (Akk.) werfen; **~ one's eyes round a room** seine Augen od. Blicke durch ein Zimmer schweifen lassen; **~ light on sth.** Licht in etw. (Akk.) werfen; (fig.) Licht in etw. (Akk.) bringen; **~ the line/net** die Angel[schnur]/das Netz auswerfen; **~ a shadow [on/over sth.]** (lit. or fig.) einen Schatten [auf etw. (Akk.)] werfen; **~ a spell on sb./sth.** jmdn./etw. verzaubern; **~ one's vote** seine Stimme abgeben; **~ one's mind back to sth.** an etw. (Akk.) zurückdenken; sich an etw. (Akk.) erinnern; **~ sth. to the winds** (fig.) etw. über Bord werfen (fig.); see also **aspersion**; **lot 7** **2** (shed) verlieren ‹Haare, Winterfell›; abwerfen ‹Gehörn, Blätter, Hülle›; **the snake ~s its skin** die Schlange häutet sich; **the horse ~ a shoe** das Pferd verlor ein Hufeisen; **~ aside** (fig.) beiseite schieben ‹Vorschlag›; ablegen ‹Vorurteile, Gewohnheiten›; vergessen ‹Sorgen, Vorstellungen›; fallen lassen ‹Freunde, Hemmungen›; sich (Dat.) entgehen lassen ‹günstige Gelegenheit›; **she ~ aside her books and the academic life** sie kehrte den Büchern und dem akademischen Leben den Rücken **3** (shape, form) gießen **4** (calculate) stellen ‹Horoskop› **5** (assign role[s] of) besetzen; **~ Joe as sb./in the role of sb.** jmdn./jmds. Rolle mit Joe besetzen; **~ a play/film** die Rollen [in einem Stück/Film] besetzen
B n. **1** (Med.) Gipsverband, der **2** (set of actors) Besetzung, die **3** (model) Abdruck, der **4** (throwing of missile etc., throw of dice) Wurf, der **5** (Fishing) (throw of net) Auswerfen, das; (throw of line) Wurf, der **6** (twist) **develop a ~**: sich verbiegen; **have a ~ in the** or **one's eye** [leicht] schielen **7** (tinge) Schimmer, der **8** (quality) Zuschnitt, der; **~ of mind** Gesinnung, die; **~ of features** Gesichtsschnitt, der

(Phrasal verbs)

- **~ a'bout** v.i. **~ about [to find** or **for sth.]** sich [nach etw.] umsehen
- **~ a'round** ▸**~ about**
- **~ a'way** v.t. **1** wegwerfen **2** **be ~ away on an island** auf einer Insel stranden
- **~ 'down** v.t. **be ~ down [by sth.]** [wegen etw.] niedergeschlagen sein
- **~ in** v.i. **~ in one's lot with sb.** sich mit jmdm. zusammentun
- **~ 'off**

A v.t. **1** (abandon) verlassen ‹Kind›; aufgeben ‹früheres Leben›; ablegen ‹alte Kleider›; (reject) den Laufpass geben (+ Dat.) (ugs.) **2** (Naut.) losmachen **3** (Knitting) abketten **4** (Printing) **~ off [the manuscript]** den Umfang [des Manuskripts] berechnen
B v.i. **1** (Knitting) abketten **2** (Naut.) ablegen. See also **~-off**

- **~ 'on** v.t. & i. (Knitting) anschlagen
- **~ 'up** v.t. **1** (add) zusammenzählen **2** (wash up) an Land spülen

castanet /kæstə'net/ n., usu. in pl. (Mus.) Kastagnette, die

castaway /'kɑːstəweɪ/ n. Schiffbrüchige, der/die

caste /kɑːst/ n. **1** (lit. or fig.) Kaste, die **2** no pl., no art. (class system) Kastenwesen, das; (social position) soziale Stellung; **lose ~**: gesellschaftliches Ansehen einbüßen

castellated /'kæstəleɪtɪd/ adj. (battlemented) mit Zinnen bewehrt

'caste mark n. Kastenzeichen, das

caster /'kɑːstə(r)/ n. **1** ▸**castor** **2** (Printing) [Schrift]gießmaschine, die

castigate /'kæstɪgeɪt/ v.t. (punish) züchtigen (geh.); (criticize) geißeln (geh.)

castigation /kæstɪ'geɪʃn/ n. (punishment) Züchtigung, die (geh.); (criticism) Geißelung, die (geh.)

Castilian /kə'stɪlɪən/

A adj. kastilisch; see also **English A**
B n. **1** (person) Kastilier, der/Kastilierin, die **2** (language) Kastilisch, das; see also **English B 1**

casting /'kɑːstɪŋ/ n. **1** (Metallurgy: product) Gussstück, das; (Art) Abguss, der **2** (Theatre, Cinemat.) Rollenbesetzung, die

casting: ~ couch n. Besetzungscouch, die; **~ 'vote** n. ausschlaggebende Stimme (des Vorsitzenden bei Stimmengleichheit); **the ~ vote rests with the manager** die [letzte] Entscheidung hat der Geschäftsführer

cast: ~ 'iron n. Gusseisen, das; **~-iron** adj. gusseisern; (fig.) eisern ‹Wille, Konstitution, Magen›; handfest, triftig ‹Grund, Entschuldigung›; hieb- und stichfest ‹Alibi, Beweis›; hundertprozentig ‹Garantie›

castle /'kɑːsl/

A n. **1** (stronghold) Burg, die; (mansion) Schloss, das; **Windsor C~**: Schloss Windsor; **an Englishman's home is his ~**: für den Engländer ist sein Haus wie eine Burg; **~s in the air** or **in Spain** Luftschlösser **2** (Chess) Turm, der
B v.i. (Chess) rochieren

'cast-off

A adj. abgelegt
B n. in pl. abgelegte Sachen; **she didn't want her friend's ~s** (fig. joc.) sie wollte nicht die abgelegten Liebhaber ihrer Freundin haben (ugs.)

castor /'kɑːstə(r)/ n. **1** (sprinkler) Streuer, der **2** (wheel) Rolle, die; Laufrolle, die (Technik)

castor: ~ 'oil n. Rizinusöl, das; Kastoröl, das (Kaufmannsspr.); **~ sugar** n. (Brit.) Raffinade, die; Kastorzucker, der (selten)

castrate /kæ'streɪt/ v.t. **1** kastrieren; (fig.) beschneiden ‹Macht› **2** (expurgate) verstümmeln; kastrieren (ugs. scherzh.)

castration /kæ'streɪʃn/ n. **1** Kastration, die; (fig.) Beschneidung, die **2** (expurgation) Verstümmelung, die

castrato /kæ'strɑːtəʊ/, n., pl. **castrati** /kæ'strɑːtiː/ (Mus. Hist.) Kastrat, der

casual /'kæʒjʊəl, 'kæzjʊəl/

A adj. **1** ungezwungen; zwanglos; leger ‹Kleidung›; beiläufig ‹Bemerkung›; flüchtig ‹Bekannter, Bekanntschaft, Blick›; unbekümmert, unbeschwert ‹Haltung, Einstellung›; salopp ‹Ausdrucksweise›; lässig ‹Auftreten›; gemächlich ‹Schritt, Spaziergang›; **I'm just here on a ~ visit** ich habe nur mal vorbeigeschaut (ugs.); **be ~ about sth.** etw. auf die leichte Schulter nehmen; **you can't be so ~ about timekeeping** du musst es mit der Pünktlichkeit schon etwas genauer nehmen; **he's so ~ about his work** er nimmt seine Arbeit einfach nicht richtig ernst; **~ sex** Sex ohne feste Bindung **2** (accidental) zufällig; **by some ~ coincidence** durch Zufall
B n. **1** in pl. (clothes) Freizeitkleidung, die **2** ▸**casual labourer** **3** ▸**casual shoe**

casual: ~ 'contract n. ≈ Aushilfsvertrag, der; **~ 'earnings** n. pl. Nebeneinkünfte Pl.; **~ 'labour** n., no pl. Gelegenheitsarbeit, die; **~ 'labourer** n. ▸ℹ p. 1260 Gelegenheitsarbeiter, der

casually /'kæʒjʊəlɪ, 'kæzjʊəlɪ/ adv. **1** ungezwungen; zwanglos; beiläufig ‹bemerken›; flüchtig ‹anschauen›; gemächlich ‹wandern, spazieren gehen›; lustlos ‹Problem anpacken›; salopp ‹sich ausdrücken›; leger ‹sich kleiden›; **I glanced ~ at the headlines** ich überflog die Schlagzeilen; **I was ~ reading a book** ich blätterte in einem Buch; **he treats/approaches his work too ~**: er nimmt seine Arbeit zu wenig ernst **2** (accidentally) zufällig

casualness /'kæʒjʊəlnɪs, 'kæzjʊəlnɪs/ n., no pl. Ungezwungenheit, die; Zwanglosigkeit, die; (of remark) Beiläufigkeit, die

casual 'shoe n. Freizeitschuh, der

casualty /'kæʒjʊəltɪ, 'kæzjʊəltɪ/ n. **1** (injured person) Verletzte, der/die; (in battle) Verwundete, der/die; (dead person) Tote, der/die **2** (fig.) Opfer, das; (failure) Versager, der **3** no art. (hospital department) Unfallstation, die; **work in ~**: in der Unfallstation arbeiten

casualty: ~ department n. Unfallstation, die; **~ list** n. Verletztenliste, die; Liste der Getöteten/Gefallenen; **~ ward** n. Unfallstation, die

'casualwear n., no pl. Freizeitkleidung, die

casuist /'kæʒjʊɪst, 'kæzjuːɪst/ n. Kasuist, der (Philos.)

casuistry /'kæʒjʊɪstrɪ, 'kæzjuːɪstrɪ/ n., no pl. Kasuistik, die (Philos.)

cat /kæt/ n. **1** Katze, die; **play ~ and mouse with sb.** Katz und Maus mit jmdm. spielen (ugs.); **when the ~'s away [the mice will play]**

C

(prov.) wenn die Katze aus dem Haus ist, tanzen die Mäuse [auf dem Tisch]; **let the ~ out of the bag** (fig.) die Katze aus dem Sack lassen; **be like a ~ on hot bricks** wie auf glühenden Kohlen sitzen; **look like something the ~ brought in** (fig.) aussehen wie unter die Räuber gefallen; **curiosity killed the ~** (fig.) sei nicht so neugierig; **[fight] like ~ and dog** wie Hund und Katze [sein]; **not a ~ in hell's chance** nicht die geringste Chance; **we'll wait and see which way the ~ jumps** (fig.) wir warten ab, bis wir sehen, wie der Hase läuft (ugs.); **a ~ may look at a king** (prov.) das ist doch auch nur ein Mensch; **enough to make a ~ laugh** zum Schreien [komisch] (ugs.); **put the ~ among the pigeons** (fig.) für Aufregung sorgen; **it would be putting the ~ among the pigeons** es würde einigen Aufruhr verursachen; **rain ~s and dogs** in Strömen regnen; **no room to swing a ~** (fig.) kaum Platz zum Umdrehen; **has the ~ got your tongue?** hast du die Sprache verloren? **2** (coll. derog.: malicious woman) Biest, *das;* (coll.: person) Typ, *der;* (coll.: jazz enthusiast) Jazzfan, *der* **3** (Zool.: member of genus Felis) Katze, *die;* **the [great] Cats** die Großkatzen; **the ~ family** die Familie der Katzen **4** ▸ **cat-o'-nine-tails**

CAT *abbr.* = **computer-aided** *or* **-assisted testing**

cataclysm /ˈkætəklɪzm/ *n.* [Natur]katastrophe, *die;* Kataklysmus, *der* (Geol.); (fig.: upheaval) Umwälzung, *die*

cataclysmic /kætəˈklɪzmɪk/ *adj.* katastrophal; verheerend; (fig.) umwälzend; dramatisch ‹*Umwälzung*›

catacomb /ˈkætəkuːm, ˈkætəkəʊm/ *n.* **1** Katakombe, *die* **2** (cellar) Keller[raum], *der*

catafalque /ˈkætəfælk/ *n.* Katafalk, *der;* (movable) Leichenwagen, *der*

Catalan /ˈkætəlæn/ ▸ⓘ **p. 1277,** ▸ⓘ **p. 1345**
A *adj.* katalanisch; *see also* **English A**
B *n.* **1** (person) Katalane, *der*/Katalanin, *die* **2** (language) Katalanisch, *das; see also* **English B 1**

catalog, cataloger (Amer.) ▸ **catalogue, cataloguer**

catalogue /ˈkætəlɒg/
A *n.* Katalog, *der;* **subject ~:** Sachkatalog, *der* (Buchw.)
B *v.t.* katalogisieren

cataloguer /ˈkætəlɒgə(r)/ *n.* Bearbeiter/Bearbeiterin des Katalogs

Catalonia /kætəˈləʊnɪə/ *pr. n.* Katalonien (*das*)

catalyse /ˈkætəlaɪz/ *v.t.* (Chem.; also fig.) katalysieren

catalysis /kəˈtælɪsɪs/ *n., pl.* **catalyses** /kəˈtælɪsiːz/ (Chem.) Katalyse, *die*

catalyst /ˈkætəlɪst/ *n.* (Chem.; also fig.) Katalysator, *der;* **act as a ~:** als Katalysator wirken (**to** bei)

catalytic /kætəˈlɪtɪk/ *adj.* (Chem.; also fig.) katalytisch

catalytic conˈverter *n.* (Motor Veh.) Katalysator, *der*

catalyze (Amer.) ▸ **catalyse**

catamaran /kætəməˈræn/ *n.* (Naut.) Katamaran, *der*

cat-and-ˈdog *adj.* **lead a ~ life** wie Hund und Katze leben

catapult /ˈkætəpʌlt/
A *n.* Katapult, *das*
B *v.t.* **1** (fling) katapultieren; **they were ~ed into action** (fig.) sie wurden [plötzlich] zum Handeln gezwungen; **the tragedy ~ed us into the depths of despair** die Tragödie stürzte uns in tiefste Verzweiflung **2** (launch) katapultieren
C *v.i.* (be flung) katapultiert werden

cataract /ˈkætərækt/ *n.* **1** Katarakt, *der;* Wasserfall, *der;* (fig.) Katarakt, *der* **2** (Med.) grauer Star; Katarakt[a], *die* (fachspr.)

catarrh /kəˈtɑː(r)/ *n.* ▸ⓘ **p. 1231** **1** (discharge) Schleimabsonderung, *die* **2** (inflammation) Katarrh, *der* (Med.)

catastrophe /kəˈtæstrəfɪ/ *n.* Katastrophe, *die;* **end in ~:** in einer Katastrophe enden; **mean ~:** eine Katastrophe bedeuten

catastrophic /kætəˈstrɒfɪk/ *adj.,* **catastrophically** /kætəˈstrɒfɪkəlɪ/ *adv.* katastrophal

catatonia /kætəˈtəʊnɪə/ *n., no pl.* (Psych.) Katatonie, *die*

catatonic /kætəˈtɒnɪk/ *adj.* (Psych.) katatonisch

cat: ~ burglar *n.* Fassadenkletterer, *der*/Fassadenkletterin, *die;* **~call** **A** *n.* ≈ Pfiff, *der;* **B** *v.i.* ≈ pfeifen

catch /kætʃ/
A *v.t.,* **caught** /kɔːt/ **1** (capture) fangen; (lay hold of) fassen; packen; **~ sb. by the arm** jmdn. am Arm packen *od.* fassen; **~ hold of sb./sth.** jmdn./etw. festhalten; (to stop oneself falling) sich an jmdm./etw. festhalten; **he caught hold of me by the throat** er packte mich an der Kehle
2 (intercept motion of) auffangen; fangen ‹*Ball*›; **he caught the door before it slammed** er hielt die Tür fest, bevor sie zuschlagen konnte; **the brambles kept ~ing our clothes** die Dornenranken verfingen sich immer wieder in unseren Kleidern; **~ a thread** einen Faden vernähen; **get sth. caught** *or* **~ sth. on/in sth.** mit etw. an/in etw. (*Dat.*) hängen bleiben; **I got my finger caught** *or* **caught my finger in the door** ich habe mir den Finger in der Tür eingeklemmt; **get caught on/in sth.** an/in etw. (*Dat.*) hängen bleiben; *see also* **breath 1**
3 (travel by) nehmen; (manage to see) sehen; (manage to hear) bekommen ‹*Sender, Sendung*›; (be in time for) [noch] erreichen; [noch] kriegen (ugs.) ‹*Bus, Zug*›; [noch] erwischen (ugs.) ‹*Person*›; **did you ~ her in?** hast du sie zu Hause erwischt? (ugs.); **did you ~ the post?** bist du noch rechtzeitig zum Briefkasten gekommen?
4 (surprise) **~ sb. at/doing sth.** jmdn. bei etw. erwischen (ugs.)/[dabei] erwischen, wie er etw. tut (ugs.); **~ sb. unawares** jmdn. überraschen; **caught by a sudden fall of the dollar** vom plötzlichen Sturz des Dollars überrascht; **caught in a mist/thunderstorm** vom Nebel/Sturm überrascht; **I caught myself thinking how old she looked** ich ertappte mich bei dem Gedanken, wie alt sie doch aussah; **~ sb. in sth./somewhere** jmdn. in etw. (*Dat.*)/irgendwo antreffen; **you'll never ~ me in this pub again** in diesem Lokal siehst du mich nicht mehr; **~ me!/him!** das wirst du nicht erleben!; *see also* **act A 2; bend[1] C 2; hop[2] C 3**
5 ▸ⓘ **p. 1231** (become infected with, receive) sich (*Dat.*) zuziehen *od.* (ugs.) holen; **~ sth. from sb.** sich bei jmdm. mit etw. anstecken; **~ [a] cold** sich erkälten/sich (*Dat.*) einen Schnupfen holen; (fig.) übel dran sein; **he caught this habit from his wife** (fig.) diese Angewohnheit hat er von seiner Frau geerbt (ugs.); **he caught that trick from his brother** (fig.) diesen Trick hat er von seinem Bruder; **you'll ~ a terrible scolding/beating** *etc.* **from your father** dein Vater wird dich furchtbar ausschimpfen/verprügeln *usw.;* **~ it** (fig. coll.) etwas kriegen (ugs.); **you'll ~ it from me** du kannst von mir was erleben (ugs.); *see also* **death 1**
6 (arrest) **~ sb.'s gaze** jmds. Aufmerksamkeit erregen; **~ sb.'s attention/interest** jmds. Aufmerksamkeit erregen/jmds. Interesse wecken; **~ sb.'s fancy** jmdm. gefallen; jmdn. ansprechen; **~ the Speaker's eye** (Parl.) das Wort erhalten; **~ sb.'s eye** jmdm. auffallen; jmdn. auf sich (*Akk.*) aufmerksam machen; ‹*Gegenstand:*› jmdm. ins Auge fallen; (be impossible to overlook) jmdm. ins Auge springen
7 (hit) **~ sb. on/in sth.** jmdn. auf/in etw. (*Akk.*) treffen; **~ sb. a blow [on/in sth.]** jmdm. einen Schlag [auf/in etw. (*Akk.*)] versetzen
8 (grasp in thought) verstehen; mitbekommen; **did you ~ his meaning?** hast du verstanden *od.* mitbekommen, was er meint?; **~ the mood** die Stimmung einfangen; **~ sb.'s likeness** jmdn. treffen
9 ▸ **~ out a**
B *v.i.,* **caught** **1** (begin to burn) [anfangen zu] brennen
2 (become fixed) hängenbleiben; ‹*Haar, Faden:*› sich verfangen; **my coat caught on a nail** ich blieb mit meinem Mantel an einem Nagel hängen
3 **~ at sb.'s sleeve** jmdn. am Ärmel zupfen
C *n.* **1** (of ball) **make [several] good ~es** [mehrmals] gut fangen; **make a ~ with one hand** mit einer Hand fangen
2 (amount caught, lit. or fig.) Fang, *der*
3 (trick, unexpected difficulty) Haken, *der* (**in** an + *Dat.*); **there must be a ~ in it somewhere** da muss irgendwo ein Haken sein; **the ~ is that ...:** der Haken an der Sache ist, dass ...; **~-22** (coll.) Dilemma, *das;* **it's ~-22** (coll.) es ist ein Teufelskreis
4 (fastener) Verschluss, *der;* (of door) Schnapper, *der*
5 (Cricket etc.) ≈ Fang, *der* (*Schlagball*); *Abfangen des Balles, das den Schlagmann aus dem Spiel bringt;* **miss a ~:** einen Ball nicht abfangen; **he is a good ~:** er kann gut fangen

Phrasal verbs

- **~ ˈon** *v.i.* (coll.) **1** (become popular) [gut] ankommen (ugs.); sich durchsetzen **2** (understand) begreifen; kapieren (ugs.)
- **~ ˈout** *v.t.* **1** (Cricket etc.) *durch Abfangen des Balles aus dem Spiel bringen* **2** (detect in mistake etc.) [bei einem Fehler] ertappen; **it's not easy to ~ him out** man kann ihm nicht leicht etwas am Zeug flicken (ugs.); **he was caught out on a point of form** er stolperte über eine Formsache **3** (take unawares) erwischen (ugs.)
- **~ ˈup**

A *v.t.* **1** (reach) **~ sb. up** jmdn. einholen; (in quality, skill) mit jmdm. mitkommen **2** (absorb) **be caught up in sth.** in etw. (*Dat.*) [völlig] aufgehen; **they were completely caught up in each other** sie waren nur mit sich [selbst] beschäftigt **3** (snatch) packen; **sth. gets caught up in sth.** etw. verfängt sich in etw. (*Dat.*)
B *v.i.* (get level) **~ up** einholen; **~ up with sb.** (in quality, skill) mit jmdm. mitkommen; **~ up on sth.** etw. nachholen; **I'm longing to ~ up on your news** ich bin gespannt, was für Neuigkeiten du hast

catch: ~-all *n.* Sammelplatz, *der;* (fig.) Auffangbecken, *das;* **~-all term** Allerweltswort, *das;* **~-as-~-ˈcan** *n.* Catch-as-catch-can, *das;* **play ~-as-~-can** keine Rücksicht nehmen; **~ crop** *n.* (Agric.) Zwischenfrucht, *die*

catcher /ˈkætʃə(r)/ *n.* **1** Fänger, *der*/Fängerin, *die* **2** (Baseball) Fänger, *der*

catching /ˈkætʃɪŋ/ *adj.* ansteckend

ˈcatchline *n.* (Brit.) **1** (Printing) Schlagzeile, *die;* Aufmacher, *der* **2** (in advertising) Werbeslogan, *der;* Werbespruch, *der*

catchment area /ˈkætʃmənt eərɪə/ *n.* (lit. or fig.) Einzugsgebiet, *das*

catch: ~penny *adj.* **~penny goods** Ramsch, *der* (ugs.); Tinnef, *der* (ugs.); **~phrase** *n.* Slogan, *der;* **~ points** *n. pl.* (Railw.) Entgleisungsvorrichtung, *die;* **~ question** *n.* Fangfrage, *die;* **~-up** *n.* **play ~-up** (Amer. coll.) versuchen gleichzuziehen; **~word** *n.* **1** (headword) Kolumnentitel, *der;* (rhyme-word) Reimwort, *das;* (cue) Stichwort, *das;* (slogan) Schlagwort, *das;* **2** (at foot of page) Kustos, *der*

catchy /ˈkætʃɪ/ *adj.* **1** eingängig; **a ~ song** ein Ohrwurm (ugs.) **2** (attractive) reizvoll; ansprechend ‹*Farbe, Kleidung*›

ˈcat door *n.* Katzentür, *die*

catechise ▸ **catechize**

catechism /ˈkætɪkɪzm/ *n.* (Relig.) **1** (book) Katechismus, *der;* **Church C~:** Katechismus der Anglikanischen Kirche **2** (instruction) [Unterweisung im] Katechismus

catechize /ˈkætɪkaɪz/ *v.t.* (Relig.) (instruct) katechisieren; (fig.: question) befragen

categorial /kætɪˈgɔːrɪəl/ *adj.* kategorial (geh.)

categorical /kætɪˈgɒrɪkl/ *adj.* kategorisch; **he was quite ~ about it** er vertrat in dieser Angelegenheit eine recht entschiedene Haltung; **~ imperative** (Philos.) kategorischer Imperativ

categorically /kætɪˈgɒrɪkəlɪ/ *adv.* kategorisch

categorization /kætɪgəraɪˈzeɪʃn/ *n.* Kategorisierung, *die*

categorize (**categorise**) /ˈkætɪgəraɪz/ *v.t.* kategorisieren

C

category /ˈkætɪgərɪ/ *n.* (also Philos.) Kategorie, *die*

cater /ˈkeɪtə(r)/ *v.i.* 1 (provide or supply food) ~ **[for sb./sth.]** [für jmdn./etw.] [die] Speisen und Getränke liefern; ~ **for weddings** Hochzeiten ausrichten 2 (provide requisites etc.) ~ **for sb./sth.** auf jmdn./etw. eingestellt sein; ~ **for the needs of the individual** den Bedürfnissen des Einzelnen gerecht werden; ~ **for all ages** jeder Altersgruppe etwas bieten 3 ~ **to** (pander) nachgeben (+ *Dat.*); entgegenkommen (+ *Dat.*)

catercorner /ˈkætəkɔːnə(r)/, **cater-cornered** /ˈkætəkɔːnəd/ (Amer.) *adv.*, *adj.* diagonal

caterer /ˈkeɪtərə(r)/ *n.* ▸ⓘ **p. 1260** Lieferant von Speisen und Getränken; Caterer, *der* (fachspr.); (for party) Partyservice, *der*

catering /ˈkeɪtərɪŋ/ *n.*, *no pl.* 1 (trade) ~ **[business]** Gastronomie, *die*; **he is interested in ~ as a career** er interessiert sich beruflich für die Gastronomie 2 (service) Lieferung von Speisen und Getränken; Catering, *das* (fachspr.); **who's responsible for the ~ in this hotel?** wer hat in diesem Hotel die Küche unter sich (*Dat.*)?; **do the ~:** für Speisen und Getränke sorgen; ~ **firm/service** ▸**caterer**

caterpillar /ˈkætəpɪlə(r)/ *n.* 1 (Zool.) Raupe, *die* 2 **C~ [tractor]** ® (Mech.) Raupenfahrzeug, *das*

caterpillar: ~ **'track**, ~ **'tread** *ns.* Raupen-, Gleiskette, *die*

caterwaul /ˈkætəwɔːl/

A *v.i.* ‹*Katze:*› schreien, [laut] miauen; ‹*Sänger:*› jaulen (abwertend)

B *n.* Katzengeschrei, *das*; (of singer) Gejaule, *das* (abwertend); ≈ Katzenmusik, *die* (ugs.)

cat: ~**fish** *n.* Wels, *der*; ~ **flap** ▸**cat door**; ~ **food** *n.* Katzenfutter, *das*; ~**gut** *n.* Darm, *der*; (Med.) Katgut, *das*

catharsis /kəˈθɑːsɪs/ *n.*, *pl.* **catharses** /kəˈθɑːsiːz/ (emotional outlet; also Psych.) Katharsis, *die*

cathartic /kəˈθɑːtɪk/

A *adj.* 1 (Med.) abführend; ~ **medicine** Abführmittel, *das* 2 (effecting catharsis; also Psych.) kathartisch

B *n.* (Med.) Abführmittel, *das*

Cathay /kəˈθeɪ/ *pr. n.* (arch./poet.) China; das Reich der Mitte (dichter.)

cathedral /kəˈθiːdrl/ *n.* ~ **[church]** Dom, *der*; Kathedrale, *die* (bes. in England, Frankreich u. Spanien); **Cologne C~:** der Kölner Dom; **Rheims C~:** die Kathedrale von Reims

ca'thedral city *n.* Domstadt, *die*

Catherine /ˈkæθərɪn/ *pr. n.* (Hist., as name of ruler etc.) Katharina (*die*)

'Catherine wheel *n.* 1 (firework) Feuerrad, *das* 2 ▸**cartwheel 2** 3 (Archit.) Radfenster, *das*; Katharinenfenster, *das* (selten)

catheter /ˈkæθɪtə(r)/ *n.* (Med.) Katheter, *der*

catheterize /ˈkæθɪtəraɪz/ *v.t.* (Med.) katheterisieren

cathode /ˈkæθəʊd/ *n.* (Electr.) Kathode, *die*

'cathode ray *n.* Kathodenstrahl, *der*; *attrib.* **cathode-ray tube** Kathodenstrahlröhre, *die*; Braunsche Röhre

catholic /ˈkæθəlɪk, ˈkæθlɪk/

A *adj.* 1 (all-embracing) umfassend; vielseitig ‹*Interessen*›; (universal, universally applicable) allgemein; universell ‹*Lehren*› 2 **C~** (Relig.) katholisch

B *n.* **C~:** Katholik, *der*/Katholikin, *die*

Catholicism /kəˈθɒlɪsɪzm/ *n.*, *no pl.* (Relig.) Katholizismus, *der*

cation /ˈkætaɪən/ *n.* (Phys.) Kation, *das*

catkin /ˈkætkɪn/ *n.* (Bot.) Kätzchen, *das*

cat: ~**lick** *n.* Katzenwäsche, *die*; **give oneself a ~lick** Katzenwäsche machen; ~**like** *adj.* katzenartig; katzenhaft ‹*Art, Bewegung*›; ~ **litter** *n.*, *no pl.* Katzenstreu, *die*; ~ **lover** *n.* Katzenfreund, *der*/-freundin, *die*; ~**mint** *n.* (Bot.) Katzenminze, *die*; ~**nap** *n.* Nickerchen, *das* (ugs.); kurzes Schläfchen; **have** *or* **take a ~nap** ein Nickerchen machen (ugs.); ~**-nip** *n.* (Bot.) Katzenminze, *die*; ~**-o'-'nine-tails** *n.* neunschwänzige Katze; ~**'s-'cradle** *n.* 1 (game) Fadenspiel, *das*; 2 (string pattern) *Figur beim Fadenspiel*; Fadenspannbild, *das*; ~**'s-eye** *n.* 1 (stone) Katzenauge, *das*; 2 (Brit.: reflector) Bodenrückstrahler, *der* (Verkehrsw.); ~**'s-paw** *n.* (person) Handlanger, *der*; Werkzeug, *das* (fig.); ~**'s pyjamas** ▸~**'s whiskers**; ~**'s-tail** *n.* (Bot.) Rohrkolben, *der*; ~**suit** *n.* (woman's) hautenger einteiliger Hosenanzug; (infant's) Overall, *der*; ~**'s 'whiskers** *n. pl.* (coll.: the best) **sb. is the ~'s whiskers** jmd. ist der/die Größte (ugs.); **sth. is the ~'s whiskers** etw. ist spitze (ugs.)

cattery /ˈkætərɪ/ *n.* Katzenpension, *die*

cattily /ˈkætɪlɪ/ *adv.* gehässig

cattish /ˈkætɪʃ/ ▸**catty**

cattle /ˈkætl/ *n. pl.* Vieh, *das*; Rinder *Pl.*; **sheep and ~:** Schafe und Rinder; **700 head of ~:** 700 Rinder *od.* Stück Vieh

cattle: ~ **breeding** *n.*, *no pl.* Rinderzucht, *die*; Viehzucht, *die*; ~ **cake** *n.* (Brit. Agric.) *konzentriertes, gepresstes Viehfutter*; ≈ Presskuchen, *der*; ~ **grid** *n.* (Brit.), ~ **guard** *n.* (Amer.) *mit einem Gitterrost bedeckte Grube als Durchlass bei Weiden od. Gehegen*; ~**man** *n.* ▸ⓘ **p. 1260** 1 (tender) Viehhüter, *der*; 2 (breeder) Viehzüchter, *der*; ~ **market** *n.* Viehmarkt, *der*; (fig.) Fleischbeschau, *die* (ugs. scherzh.); ~ **plague** *n.* Rinderpest, *die*; ~ **prod** *n.* Viehstock, *der*; ~ **ranch** *n.* Rinderranch, *die*; Rinderfarm, *die*; ~ **rustler** *n.* (esp. Amer.) Viehdieb, *der*; ~ **truck** *n.* Viehtransporter, *der*; (Railw.) Viehwagen, *der*

catty /ˈkætɪ/ *adj.* gehässig; **they're so ~ about their colleague** sie sprechen so gehässig über ihre Kollegin

'catwalk *n.* Laufsteg, *der*

Caucasia /kɔːˈkeɪzɪə, kɔːˈkeɪʒə/ *pr. n.* Kaukasien (*das*)

Caucasian /kɔːˈkeɪzɪən, kɔːˈkeɪʒn/

A *adj.* kaukasisch

B *n.* Kaukasier, *der*/Kaukasierin, *die*

Caucasus /ˈkɔːkəsəs/ *pr. n.* Kaukasus, *der*

caucus /ˈkɔːkəs/ *n.* (Brit. derog., Amer.) 1 (committee) *den Wahlkampf und die Richtlinien der Politik bestimmendes regionales Gremium einer Partei* 2 (party meeting) *den Wahlkampf und die Richtlinien der Politik bestimmende Sitzung der regionalen Parteiführung*

caudal /ˈkɔːdl/ *adj.* (Zool.) 1 (of tail) Schwanz-; (at tail) kaudal 2 (of posterior of body) Kaudal-

caught ▸**catch A, B**

cauldron /ˈkɔːldrən, ˈkɒldrən/ *n.* Kessel, *der*

cauliflower /ˈkɒlɪflaʊə(r)/ *n.* Blumenkohl, *der*

cauliflower: ~ **'cheese** *n.* (mit Käse) überbackener Blumenkohl; ~ **'ear** *n.* Blumenkohlohr, *das* (Boxerjargon)

caulk /kɔːk/ *v.t.* kalfatern (Seemannsspr.); abdichten

causal /ˈkɔːzl/ *adj.* kausal; ~ **connection** Kausalzusammenhang, *der*; ~ **sentence** Kausalsatz, *der*

causality /kɔːˈzælɪtɪ/ *n.*, *no pl.* (esp. Ling., Philos.) Kausalität, *die*; **the law[s] of ~:** das Kausalitätsgesetz

causally /ˈkɔːzəlɪ/ *adv.* kausal

causation /kɔːˈzeɪʃn/ *n.* 1 (causing) Verursachung, *die* 2 (relation of cause and effect) Kausalität, *die*

causative /ˈkɔːzətɪv/ *adj.* 1 verursachend 2 (Ling.) kausativ

cause /kɔːz/

A *n.* 1 (what produces effect) Ursache, *die* (**of** für *od.* *Gen.*); (person) Verursacher, *der*/Verursacherin, *die*; **be the ~ of sth.** etw. verursachen 2 (Philos.) Ursache, *die* 3 (reason) Grund, *der*; Anlass, *der*; ~ **for/to do sth.** Grund *od.* Anlass zu etw./, etw. zu tun; **no ~ for concern** kein Grund zur Beunruhigung; **where he saw ~ to do so** wo er es für nötig hielt; **show ~ why ...:** Gründe vorbringen, weshalb ...; **without good ~:** ohne triftigen Grund 4 (object of support) Sache, *die*; **he died in the ~ of peace** er starb für die Sache des Friedens *od.* für den Frieden; **take up sb.'s ~:** sich für jmds. Sache einsetzen; **freedom is our common ~:** Freiheit ist unser gemeinsames Anliegen *od.* Ziel; **be a lost ~:** aussichtslos sein; verlorene Liebesmühe sein (ugs.); **make common ~ with sb.** mit jmdm. gemeinsame Sache machen; **[in] a good ~:** [für] eine gute Sache 5 (Law) (matter) Sache, *die*; (case) Fall, *der*;

B *v.t.* 1 (produce) verursachen; erregen ‹*Aufsehen, Ärgernis*›; hervorrufen ‹*Verstimmung, Unruhe, Verwirrung*› 2 (give) ~ **sb. worry/pain** *etc.* jmdm. Sorge/Schmerzen *usw.* bereiten; ~ **sb. expense** jmdm. Ausgaben verursachen; ~ **sb. trouble/bother** jmdm. Umstände machen 3 (induce) ~ **sb. to do sth.** jmdn. veranlassen, etw. zu tun; ~ **the alarm to go off** den Alarm auslösen; ~ **sb. to lose concentration** jmdm. die Konzentration nehmen; ~ **sb. to be miserable** bewirken, dass sich jemand elend fühlt; ~ **sth. to be done** dazu führen, dass etw. getan wird

cause célèbre /kɔːz seɪˈlebr/ *n.*, *pl.* **causes célèbres** /kɔːz seɪˈlebr/ Cause célèbre, *die* (geh.); aufsehenerregender Fall

causeless /ˈkɔːzlɪs/ *adj.* grundlos

causeway /ˈkɔːzweɪ/ *n.* Damm, *der*

caustic /ˈkɔːstɪk/

A *adj.* 1 (sarcastic) kaustisch (geh.); beißend ‹*Spott*›; bissig ‹*Bemerkung, Worte*›; spitz, scharf ‹*Zunge*› 2 (burning) ätzend; (Chem.) kaustisch; ~ **potash/soda** Ätzkali, *das*/Ätznatron, *das*

B *n.* (substance) Ätzmittel, *das*; Kaustikum, *das* (Med.)

caustically /ˈkɔːstɪkəlɪ/ *adv.* (sarcastically) bissig

cauterisation, cauterise ▸**cauteriz-**

cauterization /kɔːtəraɪˈzeɪʃn/ *n.* (Med.) Kauterisation, *die*

cauterize /ˈkɔːtəraɪz/ *v.t.* (Med.) kauterisieren; (fig.) abstumpfen

caution /ˈkɔːʃn/

A *n.* 1 Vorsicht, *die*; **use ~:** vorsichtig sein 2 (warning) Warnung, *die*; (warning and reprimand) Verwarnung, *die*; **by way of a ~:** als Warnung; **act as a ~ to sb.** jmdm. eine Warnung sein; **just a word of ~:** noch ein guter Rat 3 (dated coll.: sb. comical) **be a ~:** ein Kasper sein (ugs.)

B *v.t.* (warn) warnen; (warn and reprove) verwarnen (**for** wegen); ~ **sb. against sth./doing sth.** jmdn. vor etw. (*Dat.*) warnen/davor warnen, etw. zu tun; ~ **sb. to/not to do sth.** jmdn. ermahnen, etw. zu tun/nicht zu tun

cautionary /ˈkɔːʃənərɪ/ *adj.* [er]mahnend; warnend ‹*Beispiel*›

'caution money *n.* Kaution, *die*; **demand/pay ~:** eine Kaution verlangen/zahlen

cautious /ˈkɔːʃəs/ *adj.* vorsichtig; (circumspect) umsichtig

cautiously /ˈkɔːʃəslɪ/ *adv.* vorsichtig; (circumspectly) umsichtig

cavalcade /kævəlˈkeɪd/ *n.* Kavalkade, *die* (veralt., auch fig.); (convoy of cars) Konvoi, *der*; (procession of cars) Korso, *der*

cavalier /kævəˈlɪə(r)/

A *n.* 1 Kavalier, *der* 2 (Hist.: Royalist) Kavalier, *der* (*Anhänger König Karls I.*) 3 (arch.: horseman) Ritter, *der*

B *adj.* (offhand) keck; (arrogant) anmaßend

cavalry /ˈkævəlrɪ/ *n. constr. as sing. or pl.* Kavallerie, *die*; (soldiers in vehicles) motorisierte Streitkräfte

cavalry: ~**man** /ˈkævəlrɪmən/ *n.*, *pl.* ~**men** /ˈkævəlrɪmən/ Kavallerist, *der*; ~ **officer** *n.* Kavallerieoffizier, *der*; ~ **regiment** *n.* Reiterregiment, *das*; ~ **sword** *n.* Säbel, *der*; ~ **twill** *n.* Kavallerietwill, *der*

cave[1] /keɪv/

A *n.* Höhle, *die*

B *v.t.* aushöhlen

C *v.i.* Höhlen erforschen

Phrasal verb

• ~ **'in** *v.i.* einbrechen; (fig.) (collapse) zusammenbrechen; (submit) nachgeben. *See also* **cave-in**

cave[2] /ˈkeɪvɪ/ *int.* (Brit. dated sl.: look out!) Achtung!; **keep ~:** Schmiere stehen (salopp)

caveat /ˈkævɪæt/ *n.* (warning) Warnung, *die*; (against repetition) Mahnung, *die*; ~ **emptor** /kævɪæt ˈemptɔː(r)/ Ausschluss der Gewährleistung

C

cave: ~ **bear** *n.* (Zool.) Höhlenbär, *der;* ~ **dweller** *n.* Höhlenbewohner, *der;* (fig.) Wilde, *der;* ~**-in** *n.* Einsturz, *der;* ~**man** ▸ ~ **dweller**; ~ **painting** *n.* Höhlenmalerei, *die*

caver /ˈkeɪvə(r)/ *n.* Höhlenforscher, *der*

cavern /ˈkævən/ *n.* (cave, lit. or fig.) Höhle, *die;* (artificial) Kaverne, *die*

cavernous /ˈkævənəs/ *adj.* (like a cavern) höhlenartig; herzhaft ‹*Gähnen*›; (full of caverns) reich an Höhlen

caviare (**caviar**) /ˈkævɪɑː(r), kævɪˈɑː(r)/ *n.* Kaviar, *der;* **it is ~ to the general** (fig.) das ist Perlen vor die Säue geworfen (ugs.)

cavil /ˈkævɪl/
A *v.i.*, (Brit.) **-ll-** kritteln (abwertend); ~ **at/about sth.** etw. bekritteln (abwertend)
B *n.* unsachlicher Anwurf

caving /ˈkeɪvɪŋ/ *n.* Höhlenforschung, *die*

cavity /ˈkævɪtɪ/ *n.* Hohlraum, *der;* (in tooth) Loch, *das;* **nasal/oral/uterine** ~: Nasen-/Mund-/Gebärmutterhöhle, *die*

ˈ**cavity wall** *n.* Hohlmauer, *die; attrib.* ~ **wall insulation** Hohlwandisolierung, *die*

cavort /kəˈvɔːt/ *v.i.* (coll.) ~ **[about** *or* **around]** herumtollen (ugs.)

cavy /ˈkeɪvɪ/ *n.* (*pl.* **-vies**) Meerschweinchen, *das*

caw /kɔː/
A *n.* Krächzen, *das*
B *v.i.* krächzen

cay /keɪ/ *n.* Riff, *das*

cayenne /keɪˈen/ *n.* ~ ˈ**pepper** Cayennepfeffer, *der*

cayman /ˈkeɪmən/ *n.* (Zool.) Kaiman, *der*

CB *abbr.* **1** = **Companion [of the Order] of the Bath** *Mitglied der 3. Klasse des Bathordens* **2** = **citizens' band** CB

CBE *abbr.* = **Commander [of the Order] of the British Empire** *Träger des Ordens des British Empire 3. Klasse*

CBI *abbr.* = **Confederation of British Industry** *britischer Unternehmerverband*

CBS — Columbia Broadcasting System

Neben **ABC** und **NBC** eine der drei ersten amerikanischen nationalen Rundfunkgesellschaften.

cc /siːˈsiː/ *abbr.* ▸ⓘ **p. 1690** = **cubic centimetre(s)** cm³

CCD *abbr.* = **charge-coupled device**

CCTV *abbr.* = **closed-circuit television** CCTV

CD *abbr.* **1** = **civil defence** **2** = **Corps Diplomatique** CD **3** = **compact disc** CD; *attrib.* **CD burner** CD-Brenner, *der;* **CD player** CD-Spieler, *der;* **CD writer** CD-Brenner, *der;* **CD-R** CD-R, *die;* **CD-RW** CD-RW, *die*

CD-I *abbr.* (Computing) = **compact disc (interactive)**

Cdr. *abbr.* = **commander b** Kdt

CD-ROM /siːdiːˈrɒm/ *n.* CD-ROM, *die; attrib.* ~ **drive** CD-ROM-Laufwerk, *das*

CE *abbr.* **1** = **Church of England** **2** = **civil engineer** **3** = **Common Era**

cease /siːs/
A *v.i.* aufhören; **he never ~d in his efforts** er gab seine Bemühungen nie auf; **when the storm ~d** als der Sturm sich legte; ~ **from sth./from doing sth.** mit etw. aufhören/aufhören, etw. zu tun; **without ceasing** ununterbrochen
B *v.t.* **1** (stop) aufhören; ~ **doing** *or* **to do sth.** aufhören, etw. zu tun; ~ **to understand** nicht mehr verstehen; **sth. has ~d to exist** etw. existiert *od.* besteht nicht mehr; **we have ~d manufacturing tyres** wir stellen keine Reifen mehr her; **it never ~s to amaze me** ich kann nur immer darüber staunen **2** (end) aufhören mit; einstellen ‹*Bemühungen, Versuche*›; ~ ˈ**fire** (Mil.) das Feuer einstellen
C *n.* **without** ~: ununterbrochen; ohne Unterbrechung

ˈ**ceasefire** *n.* Waffenruhe, *die;* (signal) Befehl zur Feuereinstellung

ceaseless /ˈsiːslɪs/ *adj.* endlos; unaufhörlich ‹*Anstrengung*›; ständig ‹*Wind, Regen, Lärm*›

ceaselessly /ˈsiːslɪslɪ/ *adv.* unaufhörlich; endlos ‹*streiten*›

cedar /ˈsiːdə(r)/ *n.* **1** Zeder, *die;* ~ **of Lebanon** Libanonzeder, *die* **2** ▸ **cedarwood**

ˈ**cedarwood** *n.* Zedernholz, *das*

cede /siːd/ *v.t.* (surrender) abtreten ‹*Land, Rechte*› (**to** *Dat.*, an + *Akk.*); einräumen ‹*Privilegien*› (**to** *Dat.*); (grant) überlassen ‹*Land*› (**to** *Dat.*); zugestehen ‹*Rechte*› (**to** *Dat.*)

cedilla /sɪˈdɪlə/ *n.* (Ling.) Cedille, *die*

Ceefax ® /ˈsiːfæks/ *n.* (Brit.) Bildschirmtextdienst der BBC

Ceefax

Ein Informationsservice, der in Großbritannien von der **BBC** angeboten wird und eine große Bandbreite abdeckt, von Wetterberichten bis zu Aktienkursen. Die Informationen können über den Fernseher abgerufen werden und erscheinen auf dem Bildschirm.

ceilidh /ˈkeɪlɪ/ *n.* (Scot., Ir.) *zwangloses Beisammensein zum Musizieren, Tanzen, Singen und Geschichtenerzählen*

ceiling /ˈsiːlɪŋ/ *n.* **1** Decke, *die; see also* **hit A 2** **2** (upper limit) Maximum, *das; attrib.* ~ **temperature** maximale Temperatur; *see also* **glass ceiling** **3** (Aeronaut.) Gipfelhöhe, *die* **4** (Meteorol.) **[cloud]** ~: Wolkenuntergrenze, *die;* (height) Wolkenhöhe, *die*

ˈ**ceiling rose** *n.* Deckenrosette, *die*

celandine /ˈseləndaɪn/ *n.* (Bot.) **1** **[greater]** ~: [Großes] Schöllkraut **2** **[lesser]** ~: Scharbockskraut, *das*

celebrant /ˈselɪbrənt/ *n.* (Eccl.) Zelebrant, *der*

celebrate /ˈselɪbreɪt/
A *v.t.* **1** (observe) feiern **2** (Eccl.) zelebrieren, lesen ‹*Messe*›; **the wedding was ~d in St Paul's** die Hochzeit fand in St Paul's statt **3** (extol) verherrlichen
B *v.i.* **1** feiern **2** (officiate at Eucharist) die Eucharistie *od.* das Abendmahl feiern

celebrated /ˈselɪbreɪtɪd/ *adj.* gefeiert, berühmt ‹*Person*›; berühmt ‹*Gebäude, Werk usw.*›

celebration /selɪˈbreɪʃn/ *n.* **1** (observing) Feiern, *das;* (party etc.) Feier, *die;* **in ~ of** aus Anlass (+ *Gen.*); (with festivities) zur Feier (+ *Gen.*); **the ~ of Easter** *etc.* das Feiern *od.* Begehen des Osterfestes *usw.*; **the ~ on her birthday** ihre Geburtstagsfeier; **the Coronation ~s** die Feierlichkeiten anlässlich der Krönung; **this calls for a ~!** das muss gefeiert werden! **2** (performing) **the ~ of the wedding/christening** die Trauung[szeremonie]/Taufe; **the ~ of Communion** die Feier der Kommunion **3** (extolling) Verherrlichung, *die*

celebratory /ˈselɪbreɪtərɪ/ *adj.* feierlich; Fest‹*programm, -essen, -trunk*›

celebrity /sɪˈlebrɪtɪ/ *n.* **1** *no pl.* (fame) Berühmtheit, *die* **2** (person) Berühmtheit, *die;* **that ~ of stage and cinema** der Star von Bühne und Leinwand

celeriac /sɪˈlerɪæk/ *n.* [Wurzel-, Knollen]sellerie, *der od. die*

celerity /sɪˈlerɪtɪ/ *n.* (literary) Schnelligkeit, *die*

celery /ˈselərɪ/ *n.* [Bleich-, Stangen]sellerie, *der od. die*

celesta /sɪˈlestə/ *n.* (Mus.) Celesta, *die*

celestial /sɪˈlestɪəl/ *adj.* **1** (heavenly) himmlisch; ~ **realm** Himmelreich, *das* **2** (of the sky) Himmels-

celibacy /ˈselɪbəsɪ/ *n., no art.* Zölibat, *das od. der* (Rel.); Ehelosigkeit, *die*

celibate /ˈselɪbət/
A *adj.* zölibatär (Rel.); ehelos; **remain** ~: im Zölibat leben (Rel.); ehelos bleiben
B *n.* Zölibatär, *der* (Rel.)

cell /sel/ *n.* **1** (also Biol., Electr.) Zelle, *die* **2** (enclosed cavity) Pore, *die;* (fig.: compartment of brain) Gehirnzelle, *die*

cellar /ˈselə(r)/ *n.* Keller, *der;* (wine storage place, stock of wine) [Wein]keller, *der;* **they keep a good** ~: sie haben einen guten Weinkeller

cell: ~ **biology** *n., no pl.* Zellbiologie, *die;* ~ **culture** *n.* (Biol., Med.) Zellkultur, *die;* ~ **division** *n.* (Biol.) Zellteilung, *die*

cellist /ˈtʃelɪst/ *n.* ▸ⓘ **p. 1260** (Mus.) Cellist, *der*/Cellistin, *die*

ˈ**cellmate** *n.* Zellengenosse, *der*/-genossin, *die*

cello /ˈtʃeləʊ/ *n., pl.* ~**s** (Mus.) Cello, *das*

Cellophane, cellophane ® /ˈseləfeɪn/ *n.* Cellophan Ⓦⓩ, *das*

ˈ**cellphone** *n.* (esp. Amer.) Mobiltelefon, *das;* Handy, *das*

cellular /ˈseljʊlə(r)/ *adj.* **1** porös ‹*Mineral, Gestein, Substanz*›; (Biol.: of cells) zellular; Zell-; ~ **plant** Lagerpflanze, *die;* Zellenpflanze, *die* (veralt.) **2** (with open texture) luftdurchlässig; atmungsaktiv (Werbespr.)

cellular: ~ ˈ**phone** *n.* (esp. Amer.) Mobiltelefon, *das;* ~ ˈ**radio** *n.* Mobilfunk, *der*

cellule /ˈseljuːl/ *n.* (Anat.) kleine Zelle; Cellula, *die* (fachspr.)

cellulite /ˈseljʊlaɪt/ *n., no pl., no indef. art.*: *überschüssige Fettdepots an Oberschenkeln und Hüften*

cellulitis /seljʊˈlaɪtɪs/ *n.* ▸ⓘ **p. 1231** (Med.) Zellulitis, *die;* Zellgewebsentzündung, *die*

celluloid /ˈseljʊlɔɪd/ *n.* **1** Zelluloid, *das* **2** (cinema films) Kino, *das;* ~ **hero** Leinwandheld, *der*

cellulose /ˈseljʊləʊs, ˈseljʊləʊz/ *n.* **1** (Chem.) Zellulose, *die* **2** *in popular use* ~ **[lacquer]** Lack, *der;* ~ **finish** Lackierung, *die*

Celsius /ˈselsɪəs/ *adj.* ▸ⓘ **p. 1620** Celsius; ~ **scale** Celsiusskala, *die*

celt /selt/ *n.* (Archaeol.) Kelt, *der*

Celt /kelt, selt/ *n.* Kelte, *der*/Keltin, *die*

Celtic /ˈkeltɪk, ˈseltɪk/
A *adj.* keltisch
B *n.* Keltisch, *das*

Celtic: ~ ˈ**cross** *n.* Radkreuz, *das;* ~ ˈ**fringe** *n.*: *keltische Randgebiete [Großbritanniens]*

cement /sɪˈment/
A *n.* **1** (Building) Zement, *der;* (mortar) [Zement]mörtel, *der* **2** (sticking substance) Klebstoff, *der;* (for mending broken vases etc. also) Kitt, *der;* (fig.) Band, *das;* Kitt, *der*
B *v.t.* **1** (unite with binder) mit Zement/Mörtel zusammenfügen; (stick together) zusammenkleben; (fig.) zusammenkitten; zementieren ‹*Freundschaft, Beziehung*› **2** (apply ~ to) zementieren/mörteln

cemetery /ˈsemɪtərɪ/ *n.* Friedhof, *der*

C. Eng. *abbr.* = **chartered engineer**

cenotaph /ˈsenətɑːf, ˈsenətæf/ *n.* Kenotaph, *das;* Zenotaph, *das;* **the C~** (Brit.) *Mahnmal in London für die Gefallenen der beiden Weltkriege*

censer /ˈsensə(r)/ *n.* Rauchfass, *das*

censor /ˈsensə(r)/
A *n.* **1** (also Roman Hist.) Zensor, *der;* **get past the ~s** durch die Zensur kommen **2** (judge) Kritiker, *der* **3** (Psych.) Zensur, *die*
B *v.t.* **1** zensieren **2** (make changes in) abändern

censorious /senˈsɔːrɪəs/ *adj.* [übertrieben] kritisch; [übertrieben] scharf ‹*Kritik, Kritiker*›; **be ~ of sb./sth.** jmdn./etw. scharf kritisieren

censorship /ˈsensəʃɪp/ *n.* Zensur, *die*

censorware /ˈsensəweə(r)/ *n., no pl.* (Computing) Censorware, *die* (fachspr.); Zensursoftware, *die*

censure /ˈsenʃə(r)/
A *n.* Tadel, *der;* ~ **of sth.** Tadel für etw.; **propose a vote of** ~: einen Tadelsantrag stellen
B *v.t.* tadeln

census /ˈsensəs/ *n.* Zählung, *die;* **[national]** ~: Volkszählung, *die;* Zensus, *der*

cent /sent/ *n.* ▸ⓘ **p. 1332** Cent, *der;* **I don't** *or* **couldn't care a ~ about that** (coll.) das ist mir völlig egal (ugs.); **it costs 20 ~s** es kostet 20 Cent

cent. *abbr.* = **century** Jh.

centaur /ˈsentɔː(r)/ *n.* (Mythol.) Zentaur, *der;* Kentaur, *der*

centenarian /sentɪˈneərɪən/
A *adj.* hundertjährig; (over 100 years old) mehr als hundert Jahre alt
B *n.* Hundertjährige, *der/die;* (over 100 years old) über Hundertjährige, *der/die;* **he/she lived to be a ~**: er/sie wurde hundert Jahre alt/über hundert Jahre alt

centenary /sen'ti:nərɪ, sen'tenərɪ/
A *adj.* **~ celebrations/festival** Hundertjahrfeier, *die*
B *n.* Hundertjahrfeier, *die;* (birthday) 100. Geburtstag

centennial /sen'tenɪəl/
A *adj.* (100th) hundertst...; (lasting 100 years) hundertjährig; (occurring every 100 years) Jahrhundert-
B *n.* ▸**centenary B**

center (Amer.) ▸**centre**

centering /'sentərɪŋ/ (Amer.) ▸**centring**

centi- /'sentɪ/ *pref.* **1▸** (one-hundredth) Zenti- **2▸** (one hundred) Hundert-/hundert-

centigrade /'sentɪgreɪd/ ▸ⓘ **p. 1620** ▸**Celsius**

centime /'sɑ̃ti:m/ *n.* ▸ⓘ **p. 1332** Centime, *der*

centimetre (*Brit.; Amer.:* **centimeter**) /'sentɪmi:tə(r)/ *n.* ▸ⓘ **p. 911**, ▸ⓘ **p. 1208**, ▸ⓘ **p. 1286**, ▸ⓘ **p. 1690** Zentimeter, *der*

centipede /'sentɪpi:d/ *n.* Hundertfüßer, *der* (Zool.); ≈ Tausendfüßler, *der*

central /'sentrl/
A *adj.* zentral; **be ~ to sth.** von zentraler Bedeutung für etw. sein; **in ~ London** im Zentrum von London; **in a ~ situation** in zentraler Lage; **the ~ part** *or* **portion of the apple/the earth** das Innere des Apfels/der Erde; **the ~ part of the town** das Zentrum der Stadt
B *n., no art.* (Amer.) Vermittlung, *die;* **call ~:** die Vermittlung anrufen

Central: ~ African Re'public *pr. n.* Zentralafrikanische Republik; **~ A'merica** *pr. n.* Mittelamerika (*das*); **~ A'merican A** *adj.* mittelamerikanisch; **B** *n.* Mittelamerikaner, *der*/-amerikanerin, *die;* **~ 'bank** *n.* Zentralbank, *die;* **~ 'Europe** *pr. n.* Mitteleuropa (*das*); **~ Euro'pean A** *adj.* mitteleuropäisch; **B** *n.* Mitteleuropäer, *der*/-europäerin, *die;* **~ 'government** *n.* Zentralregierung, *die;* **c~ 'heating** *n.* Zentralheizung, *die*

centralisation, centralise ▸**centraliz-**

centralism /'sentrəlɪzm/ *n., no pl.* Zentralismus, *der*

centralization /sentrəlaɪ'zeɪʃn/ *n.* Zentralisierung, *die*

centralize /'sentrəlaɪz/ *v.t.* zentralisieren; **~ records** Unterlagen zentral erfassen

central 'locking *n.* (Motor Veh.) Zentralverriegelung, *die*

centrally /'sentrəlɪ/ *adv.* **1▸** (in centre) zentral **2▸** (in leading place) an zentraler Stelle

central: ~ 'nervous system *n.* (Anat., Zool.) Zentralnervensystem, *das;* **~ 'office** *n.* Zentrale, *die;* **~ 'processing unit** *n.* (Computing) Zentraleinheit, *die;* **~ reser'vation** *n.* Mittelstreifen, *der;* **~ 'station** *n.* (Railw.) Hauptbahnhof, *der*

centre /'sentə(r)/ (Brit.)
A *n.* **1▸** Mitte, *die;* (of circle, globe) Mitte, *die;* Zentrum, *das;* Mittelpunkt, *der;* **be the ~ of attention** im Mittelpunkt des Interesses stehen; **be in the ~ of things** im Brennpunkt des Geschehens sein **2▸** (town ~) Innenstadt, *die;* Stadtzentrum, *das* **3▸** (of rotation) Drehpunkt, *der;* (in lathe etc.) Spitzdocke, *die* (Technik) **4▸** (nucleus) Zentrum, *das* **5▸** (serving an area) Zentrum, *das;* **university careers ~:** Studienberatung, *die* **6▸** (filling of chocolate) Füllung, *die* **7▸** (Polit.) Mitte, *die;* **left of ~:** links von der Mitte **8▸** (Sport: player) Mittelfeldspieler, *der*/-spielerin, *die;* (Basketball) Center, *der;* (Football, Hockey: kick or hit) Flanke, *die;* **he kicked/hit a ~:** er schlug eine Flanke [nach innen] **9▸** **~ of attraction** (Phys.) Zentrum der Anziehungskraft; **she likes to be the ~ of attraction** (fig.) sie steht gern im Mittelpunkt [des Interesses]; **sth. is a [great] ~ of attraction** (fig.) etw. ist eine [große] Attraktion; *see also* **gravity 4**; **mass² A 6** **10▸** ▸**centring**
B *adj.* mittler...; **~ party** (Polit.) Partei der Mitte; **the ~ point of the circle/triangle** der Mittelpunkt des Kreises/Dreiecks
C *v.i.* **~ in sth.** seinen Mittelpunkt in etw. (*Dat.*) haben; **~ on sth.** sich auf etw. (*Akk.*) konzentrieren; **the novel ~s on Prague** Prag steht im Mittelpunkt des Romans; **the discussion ~d on pollution** im Mittelpunkt der Diskussion stand die Umweltverschmutzung; **~ [a]round sth.** um etw. kreisen; sich um etw. drehen
D *v.t.* **1▸** (place in ~) in der Mitte anbringen; in der Mitte aufhängen ‹*Bild, Lampe*›; zentrieren ‹*Überschrift*› **2▸** (concentrate) **be ~d/~ sth. in a place** einen Ort zum Mittelpunkt haben/von etw. machen; **~ sth. on sth.** etw. auf etw. (*Akk.*) konzentrieren; **~ a novel [a]round sth.** etw. in den Mittelpunkt eines Romans stellen; **be ~d [a]round sth.** etw. zum Mittelpunkt haben **3▸** (Football, Hockey) [nach innen] flanken

centre: ~ bit *n.* Zentrumbohrer, *der* (Technik); **~board** *n.* (Naut.) Schwert, *das;* **~ circle** *n.* (Football, Basketball, Ice Hockey) Mittelkreis, *der;* **~ console** *n.* (of boat, car) Mittelkonsole, *die;* **~fold** *n.* Faltblatt in der Mitte; **~ 'forward** *n.* (Sport) Mittelstürmer, *der*/-stürmerin, *die;* **~ 'half** *n.* (Sport) Mittelläufer, *der*/-läuferin, *die;* (Football also) Vorstopper, *der*/-stopperin, *die;* **~piece** *n.* (ornament) ≈ Tafelschmuck, *der* (in der Mitte der Tafel); (principal item) Kernstück, *das;* **~ punch** *n.* Körner, *der;* **~ 'spread** *n.* Doppelseite in der Mitte; **~ three-'quarter** *n.* (Rugby) Innendreiviertel[spieler], *der*

centrifugal /sen'trɪfjʊgl/ *adj.* zentrifugal; **~ force** Zentrifugalkraft, *die;* Fliehkraft, *die*

centrifuge /'sentrɪfju:dʒ/
A *n.* Zentrifuge, *die*
B *v.t.* zentrifugieren

centring /'sentrɪŋ/ *n.* (Building) Lehrgerüst, *das*

centripetal /sen'trɪpɪtl/ *adj.* zentripetal; **~ force** Zentripetalkraft, *die*

centrism /'sentrɪzm/ *n.* (Polit. etc.) gemäßigter Kurs; Zentrismus, *der* (abwertend)

centrist /'sentrɪst/ *n.* (Polit. etc.) Vertreter/Vertreterin eines gemäßigten Kurses; Zentrist, *der*/Zentristin, *die* (abwertend)

centurion /sen'tjʊərɪən/ *n.* (Roman Hist.) Zenturio, *der*

century /'sentʃərɪ/ *n.* **1▸** ▸ⓘ **p. 1047** (hundred-year period from a year ..00) Jahrhundert, *das;* (hundred years) hundert Jahre; **~-old** hundertjährig; **centuries-old** jahrhundertealt; seit Jahrhunderten bestehend ‹*Gebäude usw.*› **2▸** (Cricket) hundert Läufe; (more than a hundred) über hundert Läufe **3▸** (hundred) Hundert, *das;* **a ~ of** hundert **4▸** (Roman Hist.) Zenturie, *die*

CEO *abbr.* **= chief executive officer**

cephalopod /'sefələpɒd/ *n.* (Zool.) Kopffüßer, *der*

ceramic /sɪ'ræmɪk/
A *adj.* keramisch; Keramik‹*vase, -kacheln*›
B *n.* Keramik, *die*

ceramic 'hob *n.* [Glas]keramikkochfeld, *das*

ceramics /sɪ'ræmɪks/ *n., no pl.* Keramik, *die*

Cerberus /'sɜ:bərəs/ *n.* Zerberus, *der*

cereal /'sɪərɪəl/
A *n.* **1▸** (kind of grain) Getreide, *das* **2▸** (breakfast dish) Getreideflocken *Pl*
B *adj.* Getreide-; **~ grasses** Getreidepflanzen

cerebellum /serɪ'beləm/ *n.* (Anat.) Kleinhirn, *das;* Cerebellum, *das* (fachspr.)

cerebral /'serɪbrl/ *adj.* **1▸** ▸ⓘ **p. 1231** (of the brain) Gehirn‹*tumor, -blutung, -schädigung*›; zerebral (Anat.) **2▸** (appealing to intellect, intellectual) intellektuell

cerebral 'palsy *n.* ▸ⓘ **p. 1231** (Med.) Zerebralparese, *die;* zerebrale Kinderlähmung

cerebrate /'serɪbreɪt/ *v.i.* (literary) nachdenken

cerebration /serɪ'breɪʃn/ *n.* Gehirntätigkeit, *die*

cerebrum /'serɪbrəm/ *n.* (Anat.) Großhirn, *das;* Cerebrum, *das* (Anat.)

ceremonial /serɪ'məʊnɪəl/
A *adj.* feierlich; (prescribed for ceremony) zeremoniell; **~ clothing** Festkleidung, *die*
B *n.* Zeremoniell, *das*

ceremonially /serɪ'məʊnɪəlɪ/ *adv.* feierlich; festlich ‹*gekleidet*›

ceremonious /serɪ'məʊnɪəs/ *adj.* formell; förmlich ‹*Höflichkeit*›; (according to prescribed ceremony) zeremoniell

ceremoniously /serɪ'məʊnɪəslɪ/ *adv.* formell; förmlich; **he bowed ~:** er verbeugte sich mit aller Förmlichkeit

ceremoniousness /serɪ'məʊnɪəsnɪs/ *n., no pl.* Förmlichkeit, *die*

ceremony /'serɪmənɪ/ *n.* **1▸** Feier, *die;* (formal act) Zeremonie, *die;* **opening/prize-giving ~:** Eröffnungsfeier, *die*/Preisverleihung, *die;* **Christmas ~:** Weihnachtsfeier, *die* **2▸** *no pl., no art.* (formalities) Zeremoniell, *das;* **stand on ~:** Wert auf Förmlichkeiten legen; **without [great] ~:** ohne große Förmlichkeit. *See also* **master A 6**

cerise /sə'ri:z, sə'ri:s/
A *adj.* kirschrot; cerise (fachspr.)
B *n.* Kirschrot, *das;* Cerise, *das* (fachspr.)

cerium /'sɪərɪəm/ *n.* (Chem.) Cer, *das;* Zer, *das*

cert /sɜ:t/ *n.* (Brit. coll.) **1▸** **that's a ~:** das steht fest **2▸** (as winner) todsicherer Tipp (ugs.); **be tipped as a/look [like] a ~:** als todsicherer Tipp gelten **3▸** (for appointment) **be a ~ for the job/as the next party leader** die Stelle mit Sicherheit kriegen/mit Sicherheit der nächste Parteiführer werden; **his record makes him a ~ for the team** durch seine Leistung kommt er bestimmt in die Mannschaft

cert. /sɜ:t/ *abbr.* **= certificate**

certain /'sɜ:tn, 'sɜ:tɪn/ *adj.* **1▸** (settled) bestimmt ‹*Zeitpunkt*› **2▸** (unerring) sicher; (sure to happen) unvermeidlich; sicher ‹*Tod*›; **the course of the tragedy is ~:** der Verlauf der Tragödie steht fest; **for ~:** bestimmt; **I [don't] know for ~ when ...:** ich weiß [nicht] genau, wann ...; **I can't say for ~ that ...:** ich kann nicht mit Bestimmtheit sagen, dass ...; **make ~ of sth.** (ensure) für etw. sorgen; (examine and establish) sich einer Sache (*Gen.*) vergewissern; **we made ~ of a seat on the train** wir sicherten uns einen Sitzplatz im Zug; **we made ~ of a timely arrival** wir sorgten dafür, dass wir rechtzeitig ankamen; **the doctor had to make absolutely ~ of his diagnosis** der Arzt musste in seiner Diagnose absolut sichergehen **3▸** (indisputable) unbestreitbar **4▸** (confident) sicher; **I'm not ~ of** *or* **about the colour** was die Farbe betrifft, da bin ich mir nicht sicher; **of that I'm quite ~:** dessen bin ich [mir] ganz sicher; **we're not ~ about emigrating** wir wissen nicht [recht], ob wir auswandern sollen/können; **are you ~ of the facts?** sind Sie Ihrer Sache sicher?; **she wasn't ~ about** *or* **of her love for him** sie war [sich (*Dat.*)] nicht sicher, ob sie ihn liebte; **be ~ that ...:** sicher sein, dass ... **5▸** **be ~ to do sth.** etw. bestimmt tun; **people were ~ to notice that she'd been crying** die Leute würden bestimmt merken, dass sie geweint hatte **6▸** (particular but as yet unspecified) bestimmt **7▸** (slight; existing but probably not already known) gewiss; **to a ~ extent** in gewisser Weise; **a ~ Mr Smith** ein gewisser Herr Smith

certainly /'sɜ:tnlɪ, 'sɜ:tɪnlɪ/ *adv.* **1▸** (admittedly) sicher[lich]; (definitely) bestimmt; (clearly) offensichtlich **2▸** (in answer) [aber] gewiss; [aber] sicher; **[most] ~ 'not!** auf [gar] keinen Fall!

certainty /'sɜ:tntɪ, 'sɜ:tɪntɪ/ *n.* **1▸** **be a ~:** sicher sein; feststehen; **regard sth. as a ~:** etw. für sicher halten; **it isn't as much of a ~ now as it was** es ist jetzt nicht mehr ganz so sicher **2▸** (absolute conviction, sure fact, assurance) Gewissheit, *die;* **~ of** *or* **about sth./sb.** Gewissheit über etw./jmdn.; **~ that ...:** Gewissheit [darüber], dass ...; **with some ~:** mit einiger Sicherheit; **with ~, for a ~:** mit Sicherheit *od.* Bestimmtheit; **have the ~ of accommodation/sunshine** die Gewissheit haben, eine Unterkunft zu bekommen/dass die Sonne scheint

Cert. Ed. /sɜ:t 'ed/ *abbr.* (Brit.) **= Certificate in Education** ≈ *Berechtigung, an Grund- bzw. Hauptschulen zu unterrichten*

certifiable /'sɜ:tɪfaɪəbl/ *adj.* **1▸** nachweislich; überprüfbar ‹*Ergebnis*›; **what makes a person ~ as dead?** wann kann jemand für tot erklärt werden? **2▸** (as insane) unzurechnungsfähig ‹*Person*›; **~ insanity** Unzurechnungsfähigkeit, *die*

certifiably /'sɜ:tɪfaɪəblɪ/ *adv.* **~ [in]sane** [un]zurechnungsfähig

C

C

certificate
A /sə'tɪfɪkət/ *n.* Urkunde, *die;* (of action performed) Schein, *der;* (*Cinemat.*) *Einblendung zu Beginn eines Films, die angibt, für welches Publikum der Film freigegeben ist;* **doctor's ~:** ärztliches Attest; **teaching ~:** *Zeugnis über eine Ausbildung als Lehrer;* **~ of satisfactory performance** Zeugnis über zufriedenstellende Leistungen; **he gained a ~ of merit in his exam** er bestand die Prüfung mit Auszeichnung
B /sə'tɪfɪkeɪt/ *v.t.* zulassen

Certificate of Secondary Edu'cation *n.* (Brit. Hist.) ≈ Volksschulabschluss, *der*

certification /sɜːtɪfɪ'keɪʃn/ *n.* Bestätigung, *die;* (as teacher etc.) Zulassung, *die;* (as insane) Bescheinigung der Unzurechnungsfähigkeit; (certificate) Bescheinigung, *die*

certified /'sɜːtɪfaɪd/ *adj.* **1** zugelassen; **~ as unfit for human habitation** für unbewohnbar erklärt; **she's a ~ driving instructor** sie ist als Fahrlehrerin zugelassen; **state-~:** staatlich anerkannt; **this film is ~ as unsuitable for children** dieser Film ist als nicht jugendfrei eingestuft worden **2** (declared insane) unzurechnungsfähig

certified: ~ 'cheque *n.* (Finance) bestätigter Scheck; **~ 'mail** *n.* (Amer.) **send sth. by ~ mail** etw. per Einschreiben schicken; **an item of ~ mail** eine Einschreibesendung; **~ public ac'countant** *n.* (Amer.) Wirtschaftsprüfer, *der*/-prüferin, *die*

certify /'sɜːtɪfaɪ/ *v.t.* **1** bescheinigen; bestätigen; (declare by certificate) berechtigen; **~ sb. as competent** jmds. Befähigung bescheinigen *od.* bestätigen; **this is to ~ that ...:** hiermit wird bescheinigt *od.* bestätigt, dass ...; **this building has been certified [as] Crown property** dieses Gebäude ist zum Eigentum der Krone erklärt worden; **certified as a true copy** beglaubigt **2** (declare insane) für unzurechnungsfähig erklären; **you ought to be certified** (coll.) du bist wohl verrückt (salopp)

certitude /'sɜːtɪtjuːd/ *n.* Gewissheit, *die*

cervical /'sɜːvɪkl, sɜː'vaɪkl/ *adj.* (Anat.) **1** (of neck) Hals-; zervikal (Anat.) **2** (of cervix) Gebärmutterhals-; zervikal (Anat.); **~ cancer** Gebärmutterhalskrebs, *der;* **~ smear [test]** [Gebärmutterhals]abstrich, *der*

cervix /'sɜːvɪks/ *n., pl.* **cervices** /'sɜːvɪsiːz/ (Anat.: of uterus) Gebärmutterhals, *der*

Cesarean, Cesarian (Amer.) ▸ **Caesarean**

CESDP *abbr.* (EU) = **Common European Security and Defence Policy** GESVP

cesium (Amer.) ▸ **caesium**

cessation /se'seɪʃn/ *n.* Ende, *das;* (interval) Nachlassen, *das*

cession /'seʃn/ *n.* Abtretung, *die*

cesspit /'sespɪt/ *n.* **1** (refuse pit) Abfallgrube, *die* **2** ▸ **cesspool**

cesspool /'sespuːl/ *n.* Senk- *od.* Jauchegrube, *die;* (fig.) Sumpf, *der;* **~ of iniquity** Sündenpfuhl, *der*

cetacean /sɪ'teɪʃn/ *n.* (Zool.) Waltier, *das*

Ceylon /sɪ'lɒn/ *pr. n.* (Hist.) Ceylon *(das)*

cf. *abbr.* = **compare** vgl.

c.f. *abbr.* = **carried forward** Vortrag (Buchf.)

CFC *abbr.* (Chem., Ecol.) = **chlorofluorocarbon** FCKW, *das*

CFE *n.* (Brit.) = **College of Further Education**

CFI *abbr.* (EU) = **Court of First Instance** GEI

CFSP *abbr.* (EU) = **Common Foreign and Security Policy** GASP

ch. *abbr.* **1** = **chapter** Kap. **2** = **church** K.

cha /tʃɑː/ ▸ **char³**

cha-cha /'tʃɑːtʃɑː/
A *n.* Cha-Cha-Cha, *der*
B *v.i.* Cha-Cha-Cha tanzen

chad /tʃæd/ *n.* (Computing) Stanzabfall, *der*

Chad /tʃæd/ *pr. n.* Tschad, *der*

chafe /tʃeɪf/
A *v.t.* (make sore) aufscheuern; wund scheuern; (rub) reiben; (fig.) reizen; ärgern
B *v.i.* ‹*Person, Tier:*› sich scheuern; ‹*Gegenstand:*› scheuern (**[up]on, against** an + *Dat.*); **my skin ~s easily** meine Haut wird leicht wund; **~ at** *or* **under sth.** (fig.) sich über etw. (*Akk.*) ärgern

chafer /'tʃeɪfə(r)/ *n.* (Zool.) [Mai]käfer, *der*

chaff /tʃɑːf/
A *v.t.* **~ sb. about sth.** jmdn. wegen etw. necken *od.* (ugs.) mit etw. aufziehen
B *v.i.* scherzen; flachsen (ugs.)
C *n.* **1** (banter) Neckerei, *die;* Flachserei, *die* (ugs.); **enough of the ~!** genug geflachst! (ugs.) **2** (husks of corn, etc.) Spreu, *die; see also* **wheat** **3** (cattle food) Häcksel, *das*

chaffinch /'tʃæfɪnʃ/ *n.* (Ornith.) Buchfink, *der*

chagrin /'ʃægrɪn/
A *n.* Kummer, *der;* (annoyance) Verdruss, *der;* **much to sb.'s ~:** zu jmds. großen Kummer *od.* Verdruss
B *v.t.* bekümmern; **be** *or* **feel ~ed at** *or* **by sth.** niedergeschlagen *od.* bekümmert sein wegen etw.

chain /tʃeɪn/
A *n.* **1** Kette, *die;* (fig.) Fessel, *die;* (of flowers) Kranz, der; (to stop skidding) Schneekette, *die;* (jewellery) [Hals]kette, *die;* (barrier) Sperrkette, *die;* **~ of office** Amtskette, *die;* **be in ~s** in Ketten sein; **be/put on a ~:** an der Kette sein/an die Kette legen; **door ~:** Tür- *od.* Sicherungskette, *die* **2** (series) Kette, *die;* Reihe, *die;* **~ of events** Reihe *od.* Kette von Ereignissen; **~ of ideas** Gedankenkette, *die;* **~ of mountains** Gebirgskette, *die;* **~ of islands/lakes** Insel-/Seenkette, *die;* **~ of shops/hotels** Laden-/Hotelkette, *die* **3** (measurement) Chain, *das* (≈ 20 m)
B *v.t.* (lit. or fig.) **~ sb./sth. to sth.** jmdn./etw. an etw. (*Akk.*) [an]ketten; **the dog must be kept ~ed up** der Hund muss an der Kette bleiben

chain: ~ armour *n.* Kettenpanzer, *der;* **~ gang** *n.* Trupp aneinander geketteter Sträflinge; **~ guard** *n.* Kettenschutz, *der;* (closed) Kettenkasten, *der;* **~ letter** *n.* Kettenbrief, *der;* **~-link fencing** *n.* Maschendraht, *der;* **~ mail** *n.* Kettenpanzer, *der;* **~ re'action** *n.* (Chem., Phys.; also fig.) Kettenreaktion, *die;* **~saw** *n.* Kettensäge, *die;* **~-smoke** *v.t. & i.* Kette rauchen (ugs.); **~-smoker** *n.* Kettenraucher, *der*/-raucherin, *die;* **~-smoking** *n., no pl.* Kettenrauchen, *das;* **~ stitch** *n.* Kettenstich, *der;* **~ store** *n.* Kettenladen, *der* (Wirtsch.); **~ wheel** *n.* Kettenblatt, *das*

chair /tʃeə(r)/
A *n.* **1** Stuhl, *der;* (armchair, easy ~) Sessel, *der;* **take a ~ [please]** bitte nehmen Sie Platz; **hairdresser's ~:** Frisierstuhl, *der* **2** (professorship) Lehrstuhl, *der;* (of authority) [Thron]sessel, *der* **3** (at meeting) Vorsitz, *der;* (~man) Vorsitzende, *der/die;* **be** *or* **preside in/take the ~:** den Vorsitz haben *od.* führen/übernehmen; **leave** *or* **vacate the ~:** den Vorsitz abgeben; **address the ~:** den Vorsitzenden ansprechen
B *v.t.* **1** (preside over) den Vorsitz haben *od.* führen bei; **~ a meeting** den Vorsitz bei einer Versammlung haben *od.* führen; **the meeting was ~ed by ...:** den Vorsitz bei der Versammlung hatte *od.* führte... **2** (Brit.: carry as victor) *im Triumph tragen*

chair: ~ back *n.* Rückenlehne, *die;* **~lift** *n.* Sessellift, *der*

chairman /'tʃeəmən/ *n., pl.* **chairmen** /'tʃeəmən/ **1** ▸ **i** **p. 1260**, ▸ **i** **p. 1634** Vorsitzende, *der/die;* Präsident, *der*/Präsidentin, *die;* **Mr/Madam C~:** Herr Vorsitzender/Frau Vorsitzende; **~ of the firm** Firmenleiter, *der;* **~'s report** Geschäftsbericht, *der; see also* **board A 10** **2** (master of ceremonies) Conferencier, *der*

chairmanship /'tʃeəmənʃɪp/ *n.* Vorsitz, *der*

chair: ~person *n.* Vorsitzende, *der/die;* **~woman** *n.* Vorsitzende, *die*

chaise /ʃeɪz/ *n.* (esp. Hist.) Cab, *das;* **closed** *or* **covered ~:** Chaise, *die*

chaise longue /ʃeɪz 'lɒŋ/ *n.* Chaiselongue, *die*

chalcedony /kæl'sedənɪ/ *n.* (Min.) Chalzedon, *der*

chalet /'ʃæleɪ/ *n.* Chalet, *das*

chalet 'bungalow *n.: einem Chalet ähnliches, aber kleineres Haus mit tief heruntergezogenem Satteldach*

chalice /'tʃælɪs/ *n.* (poet./Eccl.) Kelch, *der*

chalk /tʃɔːk/
A *n.* Kreide, *die;* (Geol.) Oberkreide, *die;* **a drawing in ~/~s** eine Kreidezeichnung; **as white as ~:** kreidebleich; **by a long ~** (Brit. coll.) bei weitem; mit Abstand; **not by a long ~** (Brit. coll.) bei weitem nicht; **as different as ~ and cheese** so verschieden wie Tag und Nacht; **~ and talk** Tafelunterricht, *der*
B *v.t.* mit Kreide schreiben/malen/zeichnen *usw.*

Phrasal verbs
• **~ 'out** *v.t.* [mit Kreide] zeichnen; **she had her future career ~ed out** (fig.) ihr künftiger Lebensweg war vorgezeichnet
• **~ 'up** *v.t.* **1** [mit Kreide] an- *od.* aufschreiben **2** (fig.: register) zu verzeichnen haben, für sich verbuchen können ‹*Erfolg:*› **3** **~ it up** (fig.) es auf die Rechnung setzen; **~ it up to sb.'s account** (fig.) es auf jmds. Rechnung setzen

chalk: ~face *n.* (Brit.) **at the ~face** im Unterricht *od.* Klassenzimmer; **those at the ~face** die Schulpraktiker; **~-pit** *n.* Kalksteinbruch, *der;* **~-stripe** *n.* (Textiles) Kreidestreifen, *der*

chalky /'tʃɔːkɪ/ *adj.* kalkig

challenge /'tʃælɪndʒ/
A *n.* **1** (to contest or duel; also Sport) Herausforderung, *die* (**to** *Gen.*); **issue a ~ to sb.** jmdn. herausfordern **2** (call for a response) Herausforderung, *die* (**to** an + *Akk.*); **the main ~ facing us today** die größte Herausforderung *od.* Aufgabe für uns heute; **rise to a ~:** sich einer Herausforderung gewachsen zeigen; **pose a ~ to sb.** für jmdn. eine Herausforderung bedeuten **3** (of sentry) Aufforderung, *die;* (call for password) Anruf, *der* **4** (person, task) Herausforderung, *die;* **accept a ~:** sich einer Herausforderung (*Dat.*) stellen; **hold a ~ for sb.** einen Reiz für jmdn. haben **5** (Law: exception taken) Ablehnung, *die;* (Amer.: to a vote) Anfechtung, *die*
B *v.t.* **1** (to contest etc.) herausfordern; **~ sb. to a duel** jmdn. zum Duell [heraus]fordern; **~ sb. to a match/fight/debate** jmdn. zu einem Wettkampf/zum Kampf/zu einem Streitgespräch herausfordern; **~ the world record** versuchen, einen neuen Weltrekord aufzustellen **2** (fig.) auffordern; **~ sb.'s authority** jmds. Autorität *od.* Befugnis infrage stellen **3** (demand password etc. from) ‹*Wachposten:*› anrufen **4** (Law) **~ a juryman** einen Geschworenen ablehnen; **~ [the] evidence [of a witness]** gegen die Aussage [eines Zeugen] Einspruch erheben **5** (question) infrage stellen; anzweifeln; **~ sb.'s right to do sth.** jmds. Recht anzweifeln, etw. zu tun; **~ a belief/principle** eine Glaubenslehre/ein Prinzip infrage stellen; **~ a verdict** ein Urteil kritisieren; **~ an opinion** einer Ansicht widersprechen **6** (stimulate) erregen

'challenge cup *n.* Wanderpokal, *der*

challenged /'tʃælɪndʒd/ *adj.* (euphem. or joc.) behindert; **physically/vertically ~:** körperbehindert/kleinwüchsig; **mentally ~:** geistig behindert

challenger /'tʃælɪndʒə(r)/ *n.* Herausforderer, *der*/Herausforderin, *die*

challenging /'tʃælɪndʒɪŋ/ *adj.* herausfordernd; fesselnd, faszinierend ‹*Problem*›; anspruchsvoll ‹*Arbeit*›

chamber /'tʃeɪmbə(r)/ *n.* **1** (poet./arch.: room) Gemach, *das* (geh.); (bedroom) [Schlaf]gemach, *das* (geh.) **2** *in pl.* (Brit.) (set of rooms) Geschäftsräume *Pl.;* (lawyer's rooms) ≈ Praxisräume *Pl.;* (judge's room) ≈ Amtszimmer, *das;* **in ~s** ≈ im Amtszimmer **3** (of deliberative or judicial body) Sitzungszimmer, *das;* Sitzungssaal, *der;* **Upper/Lower C~** (Parl.) Ober-/Unterhaus, *das* **4** (Anat.; in machinery, esp. of gun; artificial compartment) Kammer, *die;* **~ of the heart/eye** Herz-/Augenkammer, *die. See also* **cloud chamber**, **horror A 3**

'chamber concert *n.* Kammerkonzert, *das*

chamberlain /'tʃeɪmbəlɪn/ *n.* Kammerherr, *der;* (of corporation etc.) [Stadt]kämmerer, *der;* **Lord Great C~ [of England]** (Brit.) *Hofbeamter mit bestimmten zeremoniellen Aufgaben;* **Lord C~ [of the Household]** (Brit.) *Vorsteher des königlichen Hofstaates*

chamber: ~maid *n.* ▸ⓘ **p. 1260** Zimmermädchen, *das;* **~ music** *n.* Kammermusik, *die;* **C~ of 'Commerce** *n.* Industrie- und Handelskammer, *die;* **~ orchestra** *n.* Kammerorchester, *das;* **~ pot** *n.* Nachttopf, *der*

chameleon /kəˈmiːlɪən/ *n.* (Zool.; also fig.) Chamäleon, *das*

chamfer /ˈtʃæmfə(r)/
A *v.t.* abfasen (Technik)
B *n.* Fase, *die* (Technik)

chamois /ˈʃæmwɑː/ *n., pl. same* /ˈʃæmwɑːz/ [1] (Zool.) Gämse, *die* [2] (leather) Chamois[leder], *das;* **~ leather** /ˈʃæmwɑː-, ˈʃæmɪ-/ Chamoisleder, *das*

chamomile ▸**camomile**

champ¹ /tʃæmp/
A *v.t.* ‹*Pferd:*› [geräuschvoll] kauen ‹*Futter*›; ‹*Pferd:*› [geräuschvoll] kauen auf (+ *Dat.*) ‹*Gebiss*›; ‹*Person:*› [geräuschvoll] kauen
B *v.i.* [geräuschvoll] kauen (**on, at** an, auf + *Dat.*); **be ~ing [at the bit] to do sth.** (fig.) voll Ungeduld darauf brennen, etw. zu tun

champ² (coll.) ▸**champion A 2, 3**

champagne /ʃæmˈpeɪn/ *n.* Sekt, *der;* (from C~) Champagner, *der*

champagne: ~-coloured *adj.* champagnerfarben; **~ glass** *n.* Sektglas, *das*

champers /ˈʃæmpəz/ *n.* (Brit. coll.) Schampus, *der* (ugs.)

champion /ˈtʃæmpɪən/
A *n.* [1] (defender) Verfechter, *der*/Verfechterin, *die;* **he is a ~ of the poor** er ist ein Anwalt der Armen [2] (Sport) Meister, *der*/Meisterin, *die;* Champion, *der;* **the ice skating/discus ~:** der Meister/die Meisterin im Eiskunstlauf/Diskuswurf; **world ~:** Weltmeister, *der*/-meisterin, *die;* **the world lightweight ~:** der Weltmeister im Leichtgewicht [3] (animal or plant best in contest) Sieger, *der;* **be a ~:** prämiert *od.* preisgekrönt sein [4] *attrib.* **~ dog** preisgekrönter Hund; **~ boxer** Champion im Boxen
B *v.t.* verfechten ‹*Sache*›; **~ a person** sich für eine Person einsetzen
C *adj., adv.* (N. Engl. coll.) klasse (ugs.)

championship /ˈtʃæmpɪənʃɪp/ *n.* [1] (Sport) Meisterschaft, *die;* **defend the ~:** den Titel *od.* die Meisterschaft verteidigen; **the world figure skating ~s** die Weltmeisterschaften im Eiskunstlauf; *attrib.* **~ title/match** Titel, *der*/Titelkampf, *der;* **compete for the ~ title** um den Titel kämpfen [2] (advocacy) **~ of a cause** Engagement für eine Sache

chance /tʃɑːns/
A *n.* [1] *no art.* (fortune) Zufall, *der; attrib.* Zufalls-; zufällig; **~ encounter** Zufallsbegegnung, *die;* **as ~ would have it** wie der Zufall *od.* das Schicksal es wollte; **leave sth. to ~, let ~ decide** es dem Zufall *od.* Schicksal überlassen; **trust to ~:** auf den Zufall *od.* sein Glück vertrauen; **game of ~:** Glücksspiel, *das;* **the result of ~:** [reiner] Zufall; **pure ~:** reiner Zufall; **by ~:** zufällig; durch Zufall; **it's not just ~:** es ist kein Zufall
[2] (trick of fate) Zufall, *der;* **by [any] ~, by some ~ or other** zufällig; **could you by any ~ give me a lift?** könntest du mich vielleicht mitnehmen?
[3] (opportunity) Chance, *die;* Gelegenheit, *die;* (possibility) Chance, *die;* Möglichkeit, *die;* **give sb. a ~:** jmdm. eine Chance geben; **give sb. half a ~:** jmdm. nur die [geringste] Chance geben; **given the ~:** wenn ich *usw.* die Gelegenheit dazu hätte; **give sth. a ~ to do sth.** einer Sache (*Dat.*) Gelegenheit geben, etw. zu tun; **offer sb. the ~ of doing sth.** jmdm. die Möglichkeit *od.* Gelegenheit bieten, etw. zu tun; **get a/the ~ to do sth.** eine/die Gelegenheit haben, etw. zu tun; **~ would be a fine thing!** (coll.) keine Chance! (ugs.); **have a ~ to do sth., have the ~ of doing sth.** die Gelegenheit *od.* Möglichkeit haben, etw. zu tun; **this is my big ~:** das ist die Chance für mich; **now's your ~!** das ist deine Chance!; **have no ~ of doing** *or* **to do sth.** keine Gelegenheit haben, etw. zu tun; **not have much ~ of doing** *or* **to do sth.** kaum eine Gelegenheit haben, etw. zu tun; **on the [off] ~ of doing sth./that ...:** in der vagen Hoffnung, etw. zu tun/dass ...; **be in with a ~ of doing sth.** [gute] Aussichten haben, etw. zu tun; **stand a ~ of doing sth.** die Chance haben, etw. zu tun; **no ~!** (coll.) unmöglich!; ist nicht drin! (ugs.)
[4] *in sing. or pl.* (probability) **have a good/fair ~ of doing sth.** gute Aussichten haben, etw. zu tun; **[is there] any ~ of your attending?** besteht eine Chance, dass Sie kommen können?; **what ~ [of a breakthrough] is there?** wie stehen die Chancen [für einen Durchbruch]? **there is every/not the slightest ~ that...** es ist sehr gut möglich/es besteht keine Möglichkeit, dass ...; **there's a good/fair ~ of its working out** es besteht eine gute Chance, dass es gelingt; **there's little ~ of its being a success** es wird wohl kaum ein Erfolg werden; **the ~s are that ...** es ist wahrscheinlich, dass ...; **the ~s are against it** es ist unwahrscheinlich; **the ~s against its happening are slight** die Chancen, dass es nicht geschieht, sind gering; **the ~s are ten to one against its being a success** die Chancen, dass es ein Erfolg sein wird, stehen [nur] 1 zu 10; **sb.'s ~s are slim** jmds. Aussichten sind gering
[5] (risk) **take one's ~:** es darauf ankommen lassen; **take a ~/~s** ein Risiko/Risiken eingehen; es riskieren; **take a ~ on sth.** es bei etw. auf einen Versuch ankommen lassen
B *v.i.* zufällig geschehen *od.* sich ereignen; **it ~d that ...:** es traf *od.* fügte sich, dass ...; **~ to do sth.** zufällig etw. tun; **she ~d to be sitting there** zufällig saß sie gerade da; **~ [up]on sth./sb.** zufällig auf etw./jmdn. stoßen
C *v.t.* riskieren; **~ it** es riskieren *od.* darauf ankommen lassen; **we'll have to ~ that happening** wir müssen es riskieren; **~ one's arm** (Brit. coll.) es riskieren; **~ one's luck** sein Glück versuchen

chancel /ˈtʃɑːnsl/ *n.* (Eccl.) Altarraum, *der;* (choir) Chor, *der*

chancellery /ˈtʃɑːnsələrɪ/ *n.* (office) ≈ Botschaft, *die;* (of consul) Konsulat, *das*

chancellor /ˈtʃɑːnsələ(r)/ *n.* [1] (Polit., Law, Univ.) Kanzler, *der;* **C~ of the Exchequer** (Brit.) Schatzkanzler, *der;* **Lord [High] C~** (Brit.) Lordkanzler, *der* [2] (chief minister of State) Kanzler, *der;* **Federal C~:** Bundeskanzler, *der*

chancery /ˈtʃɑːnsərɪ/ *n.* [1] **C~** (Brit. Law) Gerichtshof des Lordkanzlers; **Court of C~** (Hist.) Kanzleigericht, *das* (veralt.) [2] (Brit. Diplom.) ≈ Botschaft, *die*/Gesandtschaft, *die* [3] (public records office) Archiv, *das*

chancy /ˈtʃɑːnsɪ/ *adj.* riskant; gewagt

chandelier /ʃændəˈlɪə(r)/ *n.* Kronleuchter, *der*

chandler /ˈtʃɑːndlə(r)/ *n.* ▸ⓘ **p. 1260** (arch.) Krämer, *der; see also* **ship's chandler**

change /tʃeɪndʒ/
A *n.* [1] (of name, address, lifestyle, outlook, condition, etc.) Änderung, *die;* (of job, surroundings, government, etc.) Wechsel, *der;* **there has been a ~ of plan** der Plan ist geändert worden; **sth. undergoes a ~:** etw. ändert sich; (more profoundly) etw. verändert sich; **How is she, doctor? — No ~:** Wie geht es ihr, Doktor? — Unverändert; **see a ~ in sb.** eine Veränderung an jmdm. bemerken; **this last year has seen many ~s** das vergangene Jahr hat viele Veränderungen [mit sich] gebracht; **there has been a ~ in sb./sth.** eine Veränderung ist in jmdm. vorgegangen/es hat bei etw. eine Änderung gegeben; **make ~s/a ~:** einiges ändern/etwas verändern (**to, in** an + *Dat.*); **make a ~ [of trains/buses]** umsteigen; **a ~ in the weather** ein Wetterungs- *od.* Wetterumschlag; **a ~ for the better/worse** eine Verbesserung/Verschlechterung; **a ~ of air would do her good** eine Luftveränderung täte ihr gut; **a ~ of scene/environment** ein positiver Ortswechsel; **the ~ [of life]** die Wechseljahre; **a ~ of drivers every four hours** ein Fahrerwechsel alle vier Stunden; **a ~ of heart** ein Sinneswandel
[2] *no pl., no art.* (process of changing) Veränderung, *die;* **be for/against ~:** für/gegen eine Veränderung sein; **~ came slowly** nur allmählich zeigte sich eine Veränderung
[3] (for the sake of variety) Abwechslung, *die;* **[just] for a ~:** [nur so] zur Abwechslung; (iron.) zur Abwechslung mal; **make a ~** (be different) mal etwas anderes sein (**from** als); **that makes a ~** (iron.) das ist ja [et]was ganz Neues!; **a ~ is as good as a rest** (prov.) Abwechslung wirkt Wunder
[4] ▸ⓘ **p. 1332** *no pl., no indef. art.* (money) Wechselgeld, *das;* **[loose** *or* **small] ~:** Kleingeld, *das;* **give ~,** (Amer.) **make ~:** herausgeben; **give sb. his/her ~:** jmdm. das Wechselgeld [heraus]geben; **give sb. 40p in ~:** jmdm. 40p [Wechselgeld] herausgeben; **can you give me ~ for 50p?** können Sie mir 50p wechseln?; **[here is] 15 euros ~:** 15 Euro zurück; **I haven't got ~ for a pound** ich kann auf ein Pfund nicht herausgeben; **[you can] keep the ~:** behalten Sie den Rest; [es] stimmt so; **get no ~ out of sb.** (fig. coll.) nichts aus jmdm. rauskriegen (ugs.)
[5] **a ~ [of clothes]** (fresh clothes) Kleidung zum Wechseln
[6] (of moon) Mondwechsel, *der*
[7] *usu. in pl.* (Bell-ringing) Schlagtonfolge, *die* (Musik); **ring the ~s** (fig.) für Abwechslung sorgen
B *v.t.* [1] (switch) wechseln; auswechseln ‹*Glühbirne, Batterie, Zündkerzen*›; **~ one's clothes** seine Kleider *od.* Kleidung wechseln; sich umziehen; **~ one's address/name** seine Anschrift/seinen Namen ändern; **~ trains/buses** umsteigen; **~ schools/one's doctor** die Schule/den Arzt wechseln; **he's always changing jobs** er wechselt ständig den Job; **~ seats** sich woanders hinsetzen *od.* auf einen anderen Platz setzen (*see also* **3**); **~ the record** eine andere Platte auflegen; **~ the bed** das Bett frisch beziehen; die Bettwäsche wechseln; **~ the baby** das Baby [frisch] wickeln *od.* trockenlegen; **~ ownership** den Besitzer wechseln; *see also* **gear A 1; hand A 1, 3; horse A 1; side A 9**
[2] (transform) verwandeln; (alter) ändern; **~ sth./sb. into sth./sb.** etw./jmdn. in etw./jmdn. verwandeln; **she ~d him from a prince into a frog** sie verwandelte den Prinzen in einen Frosch; **marriage ~d his way of life** die Ehe veränderte sein Leben; **you won't be able to ~ him** du kannst ihn nicht ändern; **~ direction** die Richtung ändern; *see also* **colour A 3; mind A 2; step A 5; tune A 1**
[3] (exchange) eintauschen; **~ seats** die Plätze tauschen (*see also* **1**); **~ seats with sb.** mit jmdm. den Platz tauschen; **~ sth./sb. for sth./sb.** etw./jmdn. für etw./jmdn. eintauschen; **take sth. back to the shop and ~ it for sth.** etw. [zum Laden zurückbringen und] gegen etw. umtauschen; *see also* **place A 6**
[4] ▸ⓘ **p. 1332** (in currency or denomination) wechseln ‹*Geld*›; **~ one's money into euros** sein Geld in Euro umtauschen
C *v.i.* [1] (alter) sich ändern; ‹*Person, Land:*› sich verändern; ‹*Wetter:*› umschlagen, sich ändern; **has she ~d?** hat sie sich verändert?; (for the better also) hat sie sich geändert?; **she'll never ~!** sie wird sich nie ändern!; **wait for the lights to ~:** warten, dass es grün/rot wird; **~ for the better** sich verbessern; **conditions ~d for the worse** die Lage verschlechterte sich
[2] (into something else) sich verwandeln; **he ~d from a prince into a frog** aus dem Prinzen wurde ein Frosch; **the wind ~s from east to west** der Wind dreht von Ost nach West; **Britain ~d to the metric system** Großbritannien führte das metrische System ein; **almost overnight it seemed to ~ from winter to spring** fast über Nacht schien sich der Winter in den Frühling verwandelt zu haben
[3] (exchange) tauschen; **~ with sb.** mit jmdm. tauschen
[4] (put on other clothes) sich umziehen; **~ out of/into sth.** etw. ausziehen/anziehen
[5] (take different train or bus) umsteigen; **where do I ~?** wo muss ich umsteigen?; **all ~!** Endstation! Alles aussteigen!; **~ at Bristol** in Bristol umsteigen

Phrasal verbs

- **~ 'down** *v.i.* (Motor Veh.) herunterschalten
- **~ 'over** *v.i.* [1] (to something else) **~ over from sth. to sth.** von etw. zu etw. übergehen; **the student ~d over to medicine** der Student wechselte zum Fach Medizin über; **they ~d over from one system to another** sie stellten

das System auf ein anderes um 2 (exchange places) die Plätze wechseln; (Sport) [die Seiten] wechseln. *see also* **~over**
• **~ 'round**
A *v.i.* wechseln; (Sport) [die Seiten] wechseln
B *v.t.* umstellen ‹*Möbel, Tagesordnung[spunkte]*›; umräumen ‹*Zimmer*›
• **~ 'up** *v.i.* (Motor Veh.) hochschalten

C

changeability /tʃeɪndʒəˈbɪlɪtɪ/ ▸**changeableness**

changeable /ˈtʃeɪndʒəbl/ *adj.* veränderlich; (irregular, inconstant) unbeständig ‹*Charakter, Wetter*›; wankelmütig ‹*Person*›; wechselhaft, veränderlich ‹*Wetter*›; wechselnd ‹*Wind, Stimmung*›

changeableness /ˈtʃeɪndʒəblnɪs/ *n., no pl.* Veränderlichkeit, *die;* (inconstancy) Unbeständigkeit, *die;* (of person) Wankelmütigkeit, *die*

'change[-giving] machine *n.* Geldwechsler, *der*

changeless /ˈtʃeɪndʒlɪs/ *adj.* unveränderlich

changeling /ˈtʃeɪndʒlɪŋ/ *n.* Wechselbalg, *der*

change: ~ management *n., no pl.* 1 (management of change) Veränderungsmanagement, *das;* 2 (Computing) Changemanagement, *das;* **~over** *n.* 1 Wechsel, *der;* **~over from sth. to sth.** Umstellung von etw. auf etw. (*Akk.*); **the ~over from one government to the next** der Wechsel von einer Regierung zur nächsten; **the sudden ~over in public opinion** der plötzliche Umschwung der öffentlichen Meinung; 2 (Sport: of baton in relay race) Stabwechsel, *der;* (of teams changing ends) Seitenwechsel, *der;* **~-ringing** *n., no pl.* Wechselläuten, *das*

changing /ˈtʃeɪndʒɪŋ/
A *adj.* wechselnd; sich ändernd
B *n.* **the C~ of the Guard** die Wachablösung (der brit. Hofwache)

changing: ~ cubicle *n.* Umkleidekabine, *die;* **~ mat** *n.* Wickelunterlage, *die;* **~ room** *n.* (Brit.) 1 (Sport) Umkleideraum, *der;* 2 (in shop) Umkleidekabine, *die*

channel /ˈtʃænl/
A *n.* 1 Kanal, *der;* (gutter) Rinnstein, *der;* (navigable part of waterway) Fahrrinne, *die;* **the C~** (Brit.) der [Ärmel]kanal; **~ of a/the river** Flussbett, *das* 2 (fig.) Kanal, *der;* **your application will go through the usual ~s** Ihre Bewerbung wird auf dem üblichen Weg weitergeleitet; **you must apply through the official ~s** Sie müssen mit Ihrer Bewerbung den Dienstweg einhalten; **direct sb.'s talents into the right ~:** jmds. Talente in die richtige Bahn lenken 3 (Telev., Radio) Kanal, *der* 4 (on recording tape etc.) Spur, *die* 5 (groove) Rille, *die;* (flute) Kannelüre, *die*
B *v.t.*, (Brit.) **-ll-** (convey) übermitteln; (fig.: guide, direct) lenken, richten (**into** auf + *Akk.*)

Channel: ~-changer *n.* Fernbedienung, *die;* **~ 'ferry** (*also* **C~ ferry**) *n.* Kanalfähre, *die;* **~-hop** *v.i.* (coll.) 1 (Telev.) zappen (ugs.); 2 (cross the English Channel) kurz mal über den Kanal fahren; **~-hopping** *n., no pl.* (coll.) 1 (Telev.) Zappen, *das;* 2 *also:* **C~-hopping** (across the English Channel) Kanalhopping, *das;* **~ Islands** *pr. n. pl.* Kanalinseln *Pl.;* **~ selector** *n.* Kanalwähler, *der;* (for TV) Fernbedienung, *die;* **~-surfing** *n., no pl.* Zappen, *das;* **C~ 'Tunnel** *n.* [Ärmel]kanaltunnel, *der; attrib.* **~ Tunnel rail link** *schnelle Bahnverbindung zwischen London und dem Kanaltunnel*

Channel Five

Ein britischer privater Fernsehsender, der populäre leichte Unterhaltung ausstrahlt.

Channel Four

Ein britischer privater Fernsehsender mit einem umfangreichen sozialen und kulturellen Programm. Er hat ein Renommee für exzellente Dokumentationen und für die Berichterstattung über kulturelle und künstlerische Ereignisse.

chant /tʃɑːnt/
A *v.t.* 1 (Eccl.) singen 2 (utter rhythmically) skandieren
B *v.i.* 1 (Eccl.) singen 2 (utter slogans etc.) Sprechchöre anstimmen
C *n.* 1 (Eccl., Mus.) Gesang, *der* 2 (sing-song) Singsang, *der;* (slogans) Sprechchor, *der*

chanterelle /ʃɑːntəˈrel/ *n.* (Bot.) Pfifferling, *der*

chaos /ˈkeɪɒs/ *n., no indef. art.* Chaos, *das;* **be in [a state of] [complete] ~:** ein [einziges] Chaos sein; **it's absolute ~:** es herrscht ein totales Chaos; **cause ~:** zu einem Chaos führen

'chaos theory *n.* (Phys.) Chaostheorie, *die*

chaotic /keɪˈɒtɪk/ *adj.*, **chaotically** /keɪˈɒtɪkəlɪ/ *adv.* chaotisch

chap[1] /tʃæp/ *n.* (Brit. coll.) Bursche, *der;* Kerl, *der;* **old ~:** alter Knabe (ugs.); **my dear ~:** mein lieber Mann (ugs.); **would you ~s lend a hand?** könntet ihr mal helfen, Jungs?; **hello, old ~!** hallo, alter Junge!

chap[2]
A *v.t.*, **-pp-** aufplatzen lassen; **my hands are ~ped** meine Hände sind [ganz] aufgesprungen; **~ped skin** aufgesprungene *od.* rissige Haut
B *n. usu. in pl.* Riss, *der*

chap[3] *n.* (jaw) Kinnbacke, *die;* (Gastr.: of pig) Schweinebacke, *die*

chap. *abbr.* = **chapter** Kap.

chaparral /ʃæpəˈræl/ *n.* (Amer.) Chaparral, *das*

chapat[t]i /tʃəˈpætɪ/ *n.* [indisches] Fladenbrot

'chap-book *n.* (Hist.) Volksbuch, *das*

chapel /ˈtʃæpl/ *n.* 1 Kapelle, *die;* **~ of rest** (Brit.) *Raum in einem Bestattungsinstitut, in dem Tote bis zur Beerdigung aufgebahrt werden;* ≈ Kapelle, *die* 2 (Brit.: of Nonconformists) Kirche, *die* 3 (subordinate to parish church) ≈ Filialkirche, *die*

chaperone /ˈʃæpərəʊn/ (**chaperon** /ˈʃæpərɒn/)
A *n.* Anstandsdame, *die;* (joc.) Anstandswauwau, *der* (ugs. scherzh.)
B *v.t.* beaufsichtigen; (escort) begleiten

chaplain /ˈtʃæplɪn/ *n.* Kaplan, *der*

chaplaincy /ˈtʃæplɪnsɪ/ *n.* 1 Amt eines Kaplans 2 (building) Haus des/eines Kaplans

chaplet /ˈtʃæplɪt/ *n.* 1 (Hist.: wreath) Schappel, *das;* Kranz, *der* 2 (string of beads) (RC Ch.) Rosenkranz, *der;* (as necklace) Perlenkette, *die*

chappie, chappy /ˈtʃæpɪ/ *n.* (coll.) **a nice ~:** ein liebes Kerlchen; **the Czech ~s** die tschechischen Jungs

chaps /tʃæps/ *n. pl.* (Amer.: overalls) lederne Beinschützer

chapter /ˈtʃæptə(r)/ *n.* 1 (of book) Kapitel, *das;* **[quote sth.] ~ and verse** [etw.] mit genauer Quellenangabe [zitieren]; **give ~ and verse for sth.** etw. hieb- und stichfest belegen 2 (fig.) **~ in *or* of sb.'s life** Abschnitt in jmds. Leben; **~ of history** Kapitel [in] der Geschichte; *see also* **accident 4** 3 (Eccl.) Kapitel, *das* 4 (Amer.: branch of a society) Sektion, *die*

chapter: ~ heading *n.* [Kapitel]überschrift, *die;* **~ house** *n.* 1 Kapitelsaal, *der;* 2 (Amer.: for student meetings) ≈ Klubhaus, *das*

char[1] /tʃɑː(r)/ *v.t. & i.*, **-rr-** (burn) verkohlen

char[2] ▸❶ **p. 1260**
A *n.* (Brit.: cleaner) Putzfrau, *die*
B *v.i.*, **-rr-** (be cleaner) als Putzfrau arbeiten; putzen; **~ for sb.** bei jmdm. putzen *od.* als Putzfrau arbeiten

char[3] *n.* (Brit. coll.: tea) Tee, *der;* **a cup of ~:** eine Tasse Tee

charabanc /ˈʃærəbæŋ/ *n.* (Brit. dated) [*offener*] *Bus für Ausflugsfahrten usw.*

character /ˈkærɪktə(r)/ *n.* 1 (mental or moral qualities, integrity) Charakter, *der;* (description of qualities) Charakterbild, *das;* **be of good ~:** ein guter Mensch sein; einen guten Charakter haben; **a woman of ~:** eine Frau mit Charakter; **strength of ~:** Charakterstärke, *die* 2 (reputation) Ruf, *der;* (testimonial) Zeugnis, *das* 3 *no pl.* (individuality, style) Charakter, *der;* (characteristic, esp. Biol.) Charakteristikum, *das;* **the town has a ~ all of its own** die Stadt hat einen ganz eigenen Charakter; **have no ~:** charakterlos *od.* ohne Charakter sein; **his face has ~:** er hat ein charakter- *od.* ausdrucksvolles Gesicht 4 (in novel etc.) Charakter, *der;* (part played by sb.) Rolle, *die;* **be in/out of ~** (fig.) typisch/untypisch sein; **his behaviour was quite out of ~** (fig.) sein Betragen war ganz und gar untypisch für ihn; **act in/out of ~** (fig.) sich typisch/untypisch verhalten 5 (coll.: extraordinary person) Original, *das;* **be [quite] a ~/a real ~:** ein [echtes/richtiges] Original sein; **what a ~!** was für ein Mann/eine Frau! 6 (personage) Persönlichkeit, *die;* Gestalt, *die;* (coll.: individual) Mensch, *der;* (derog.) Individuum, *das;* **a public ~:** eine Persönlichkeit des öffentlichen Lebens 7 (graphic symbol; Computing) Zeichen, *das;* (set of letters) Schrift, *die*

character: ~ actor *n.* Chargenspieler, *der;* **~ actress** *n.* Chargenspielerin, *die;* **~ assassination** *n.* Rufmord, *der;* **~-building** A *n.* Charakterbildung, *die;* B *adj.* charakterbildend; **~ code** *n.* (Computing) Zeichencode, *der;* **~-forming** *adj.* charakterbildend; **be ~-forming** den Charakter bilden *od.* formen

characterisation, characterise ▸**characteriz-**

characteristic /kærɪktəˈrɪstɪk/
A *adj.* charakteristisch (**of** für)
B *n.* 1 charakteristisches Merkmal; Charakteristikum, *das;* **one of the main ~s** eines der charakteristischsten Merkmale 2 ▸**characteristic curve**

characteristically /kærɪktəˈrɪstɪkəlɪ/ *adv.* in charakteristischer Weise; **~ American** typisch amerikanisch; **~ enough for him, he ...:** es ist/war typisch *od.* bezeichnend für ihn, dass er ...

characteristic 'curve *n.* Kennlinie, *die*

characterization /kærɪktəraɪˈzeɪʃn/ *n.* Charakterisierung, *die*

characterize /ˈkærɪktəraɪz/ *v.t.* charakterisieren

characterless /ˈkærɪktəlɪs/ *adj.* nichts sagend; charakterlos

character: ~ part *n.* (Theatre) Charge, *die;* **~ recognition** *n., no pl.* (Computing) Zeichenerkennung, *die;* **~ set** *n.* (Computing) Zeichensatz, *der;* **~ sketch** *n.* Charakterskizze, *die;* **~ study** *n.* Charakterstudie, *die;* **~ witness** *n.* Leumundszeuge, *der*/-zeugin, *die*

charade /ʃəˈrɑːd/ *n.* Scharade, *die;* (fig.) Farce, *die;* **play [a game of] ~s** Scharade spielen; **be an absolute ~** (fig.) die reinste Farce sein

charbroil /ˈtʃɑːbrɔɪl/ *v.t.* (Amer.) [auf dem Holzkohlengrill] grillen

charbroiled /ˈtʃɑːbrɔɪld/ *adj.* (Amer.) [auf dem Holzkohlengrill] gegrillt; vom Holzkohlengrill *nachgestellt*

charcoal /ˈtʃɑːkəʊl/ *n.* 1 Holzkohle, *die;* (for drawing) Kohle, *die* 2 ▸**charcoal grey**

charcoal: ~ biscuit *n.: Keks mit Holzkohle zur Förderung der Verdauung;* **~-burner** *n.* Köhler, *der;* **~ drawing** *n.* Kohlezeichnung, *die;* **~ 'grey** *n.* [Kohlen]grau, *das;* **~ pencil** *n.* Kohlestift, *der*

chard /tʃɑːd/ *n.* (Bot.) Mangold, *der*

charge /tʃɑːdʒ/
A *n.* 1 ▸❶ **p. 1332** (price) Preis, *der;* (payable to telephone company, bank, authorities, etc., for services) Gebühr, *die;* **what's your ~?** wie viel verlangen *od.* berechnen Sie?; **what would the ~ be for doing that?** was würde es kosten, das zu tun?; **is there a ~ for it?** kostet das etwas?; **make a ~ of £1/no ~ for sth.** ein Pfund/nichts für etw. berechnen; **at no extra ~:** ohne Extrakosten; **incidental ~s** Nebenkosten
2 (care) Verantwortung, *die;* (task) Auftrag, *der;* (person entrusted) Schützling, *der;* **be in ~ of a child** ein Kind betreuen; **the boy was placed in his ~:** der Junge wurde in seine Obhut gegeben; der Junge wurde ihm anvertraut; **the patients in *or* under her ~:** die ihr anvertrauten Patienten; **be under sb.'s ~:** unter jmds. Obhut stehen; sich in jmds. Obhut befinden; **leave sb. in [full] ~ of sth.** jmdm. die [volle]

Verantwortung für etw. übertragen; **the officer/teacher in ~:** der Dienst habende Offizier/der verantwortliche Lehrer; **be in ~:** die Verantwortung haben; **be in ~ of sth.** für etw. die Verantwortung haben; (be the leader) etw. leiten; **put sb. in ~ of sth.** jmdn. mit der Verantwortung für etw. betrauen; (make leader) jmdm. die Leitung einer Sache (*Gen.*) übertragen; **take ~:** die Verantwortung übernehmen; (fig. coll.: get out of control) außer Kontrolle geraten; **take ~ of sth.** (become responsible for) etw. übernehmen; (as deputy) sich um etw. kümmern; (for safe keeping) etw. in Verwahrung nehmen; **the police took ~ of the evidence** die Polizei stellte das Beweisstück sicher; **give sb. in ~** (Brit.) jmdn. der Polizei übergeben **3** (Law: accusation) Anklage, *die;* **make a ~ against sb.** jmdn. beschuldigen; **bring a ~ of sth. against sb.** jmdn. wegen etw. beschuldigen/verklagen; ‹*Staatsanwalt:*› jmdn. wegen etw. anklagen; **press ~s** Anzeige erstatten; **face a ~ [of sth.]** sich [wegen etw.] vor Gericht zu verantworten haben; **on a ~ of** wegen; **[stand] convicted on all six ~s** in allen sechs Anklagepunkten für schuldig befunden [werden]; **what's the ~?** wie lautet die Anklage?; was liegt gegen mich/ihn *usw.* vor?; **lay to sb.'s ~:** jmdm. zur Last legen **4** (allegation) Beschuldigung, *die* **5** (attack) Angriff, *der;* Attacke, *die;* **return to the ~** (fig.) es erneut versuchen **6** (of explosives etc.) Ladung, *die;* (in blast furnace etc.) Gicht, *die* **7** (of electricity) Ladung, *die;* **put the battery on ~:** die Batterie an das Ladegerät anschließen; **poetry/person with an emotional ~** (fig.) von [tiefen] Gefühlen geprägte Dichtung/geprägter Mensch **8** (directions) Anweisung, *die;* (of judge to jury) Rechtsbelehrung, *die* **9** (Her.) Wappenbild, *das*

B *v.t.* **1** ▸ⓘ **p. 1332** (demand payment of or from) **~ sb. sth., ~ sth. to sb.** jmdm. etw. berechnen; etw. von jmdm. verlangen (ugs.); **be ~d** bezahlen müssen; **I wasn't ~d for it** ich musste nichts dafür bezahlen; mir wurde nichts dafür berechnet; **~ sb. £1 for sth.** jmdm. ein Pfund für etw. berechnen; **customers are ~d for breakages** Kunden haften für Bruchschäden; **~ sth. [up] to sb.'s account** jmds. Konto mit etw. belasten; jmdm. etw. in Rechnung stellen; **to whom is the dress to be ~d?** auf wessen Rechnung geht das Kleid?; **~ it [up] to the firm** stellen Sie das der Firma in Rechnung; **I'd like to ~ this dress** ich möchte dieses Kleid über mein Kreditkonto bezahlen **2** (Law: accuse) anklagen; **~ sb. with sth.** jmdn. wegen etw. anklagen **3** (blame) beschuldigen; bezichtigen; **~ sb. with doing sth.** jmdn. beschuldigen, etw. getan zu haben; **~ sb. with being lazy** jmdm. vorwerfen, er/sie sei faul **4** (formal: entrust) **~ sb. with sth.** jmdn. mit etw. betrauen; **~ oneself with sth.** etw. übernehmen **5** (load) laden ‹*Gewehr*›; beschicken ‹*Hochofen*› **6** (Electr.) laden; [auf]laden ‹*Batterie*›; **~d with emotion** (fig.) voller Gefühl; gefühlsgeladen **7** (rush at) angreifen **8** (formal: command) befehlen; **~ sb. to do sth.** jmdm. befehlen, etw. zu tun; **the judge ~d the jury** der Richter erteilte den Geschworenen Rechtsbelehrung

C *v.i.* **1** (attack) angreifen; **~!** Angriff!; Attacke!; **~ at sb./sth.** jmdn./etw. angreifen; **he ~d into a wall** (fig.) er krachte gegen eine Mauer **2** (coll.: hurry) sausen

chargeable /'tʃɑːdʒəbl/ *adj.* **1** **be ~ to sb.** auf jmds. Kosten gehen **2** (Law) **be ~ with sth.** wegen einer Sache belangt werden können

charge: ~ account *n.* (Amer.) Kreditkonto, *das;* **~ card** *n.* Kreditkarte, *die;* **~-coupled** *adj.* ladungsgekoppelt; **~-coupled device** ladungsgekoppeltes Bauelement; CCD, *das*

chargé d'affaires /ʃɑːʒeɪ dæ'feə(r)/ *n., pl.* **chargés d'affaires** /ʃɑːʒeɪ dæ'feə(r)/ ▸ⓘ **p. 1260** Chargé d'affaires, *der;* [diplomatischer] Geschäftsträger

charge: ~-hand *n.* (Brit.) Vorarbeiter, *der*/Vorarbeiterin, *die;* **~-nurse** *n.* (Brit.) Stationsschwester, *die*

charger /'tʃɑːdʒə(r)/ *n.* **1** (Mil.: cavalry horse) [Kavallerie]pferd, *das;* (of knight) Schlachtross, *das* (veralt.) **2** (poet.: horse) Ross, *das* (dichter.) **3** (arch.: dish) Platte, *die* **4** (Electr.) [Batterie]ladegerät, *das*

'charge sheet *n.* **1** *Buch, in dem auf einem Polizeirevier Festnahmen und Beschuldigungen registriert werden* **2** (Mil.) Anklageschrift, *die*

'chargrill *v.t.* grillen

charily /'tʃeərɪlɪ/ *adv.* vorsichtig

chariot /'tʃærɪət/ *n.* (Hist.) (for fighting or racing) [zweirädriger] Streitwagen; (carriage) [leichter, vierrädriger] Wagen

charioteer /tʃærɪə'tɪə(r)/ *n.* Wagenlenker, *der*

charisma /kə'rɪzmə/ *n., pl.* **~ta** /kə'rɪzmətə/ Charisma, *das*

charismatic /kærɪz'mætɪk/ *adj.* charismatisch

charitable /'tʃærɪtəbl/ *adj.* **1** (generous) großzügig **2** (lenient) nachsichtig; großzügig **3** (of or for charity) karitativ; wohltätig, karitativ ‹*Organisation, Werke*›

charity /'tʃærɪtɪ/ *n.* **1** (leniency) Nachsicht, *die* **2** (Christian love) Nächstenliebe, *die;* **faith, hope, and ~:** Glaube, Hoffnung, Liebe **3** (kindness) Güte, *die* **4** (beneficence) Wohltätigkeit, *die;* **live on ~/accept ~:** von Almosen leben/Almosen annehmen; **~ begins at home** (prov.) das Hemd ist einem näher als der Rock; **give money to ~:** Geld für wohltätige Zwecke spenden; **collect for ~:** für wohltätige Zwecke sammeln; **be in aid of ~:** für einen wohltätigen Zweck sein **5** (institution) wohltätige Organisation **6** (educational trust) gemeinnützige Bildungseinrichtung

'charity: ~ concert *n.* Benefizkonzert, *das;* **~ match** *n.* Benefizspiel, *das;* **~ performance** *n.* Benefizvorstellung, *die;* Wohltätigkeitsvorstellung, *die;* **~ shop** *n.*: *Secondhandladen, dessen Erlöse einem wohltätigen Zweck dienen*

charlady /'tʃɑːleɪdɪ/ *n.* (Brit.) ▸**char² A**

charlatan /'ʃɑːlətən/ *n.* Scharlatan, *der*

Charlemagne /'ʃɑːləmeɪn/ *pr. n.* Karl der Große

Charles /tʃɑːlz/ *pr. n.* (Hist., as name of ruler etc.) Karl (*der*)

charleston /'tʃɑːlstən/ *n.* Charleston, *der*

charley horse /'tʃɑːlɪ hɔːs/ *n.* (Amer. coll.) Muskelkater, *der*

charlie /'tʃɑːlɪ/ *n.* **be/look a right ~** (coll.) dämlich sein/aussehen (ugs.); **feel a proper ~** (coll.) sich (*Dat.*) richtig blöd *od.* dämlich vorkommen (ugs.)

charm /tʃɑːm/

A *n.* **1** (act) Zauber, *der;* (thing) Zaubermittel, *das;* (words) Zauberspruch, *der;* Zauberformel, *die;* **lucky ~:** Glücksbringer, *der;* **work like a ~:** Wunder wirken **2** (talisman) Talisman, *der* **3** (trinket) Anhänger, *der;* Berlocke, *die* (veralt.) **4** (attractiveness) Reiz, *der;* (of person) Charme, *der;* **have ~** ‹*Person:*› Charme haben; ‹*Schloss, Buch:*› seinen eigenen Reiz haben; **place of great ~:** reizvoller Ort; **person of great ~:** sehr charmanter Mensch; **turn on the ~** (coll.) auf charmant machen (ugs.)

B *v.t.* **1** (captivate) bezaubern ; **be ~ed with sth.** von etw. bezaubert *od.* begeistert sein; **she can ~ the birds out of the trees** sie kann mit ihrem Charme alles erreichen; **~ed, I'm sure** (coll. iron.) [wie] charmant (iron.) **2** (by magic) verzaubern; beschwören ‹*Schlange*›; **~ sth. out of sb.** jmdm. etw. [durch Zauberei] entlocken; **bear** *or* **lead a ~ed life** unter einem Glücksstern geboren sein; ein Glückskind sein

charmer /'tʃɑːmə(r)/ *n.* (man) Charmeur, *der;* (woman) bezauberndes Geschöpf

charming /'tʃɑːmɪŋ/ *adj.* bezaubernd; charmant, bezaubernd ‹*Person, Lächeln*›; **~!** (iron.) [wie] charmant! (iron.)

charmingly /'tʃɑːmɪŋlɪ/ *adv.* bezaubernd; charmant ‹*lächeln*›

'charm offensive *n.* Charmeoffensive, *die;* **launch a ~:** eine Charmeoffensive starten

charnel house /'tʃɑːnlhaʊs/ *n.* Leichenhalle, *die;* (for bones) Beinhaus, *das*

chart /tʃɑːt/

A *n.* **1** (map) Karte, *die;* **naval ~:** Seekarte, *die;* **weather ~:** Wetterkarte, *die* **2** (graph etc.) Schaubild, *das;* (diagram) Diagramm, *das* **3** (tabulated information) Tabelle, *die;* **the ~s** (of pop records) die Hitliste

B *v.t.* grafisch darstellen; (map) kartographisch erfassen; kartographieren; (fig.: describe) schildern ‹*Werdegang, Leben*›

'chart-buster *n.* Hit, *der*

charter /'tʃɑːtə(r)/

A *n.* **1** Charta, *die;* (of foundation also) Gründungs- *od.* Stiftungsurkunde, *die;* (fig.) Freibrief, *der;* **grant a ~ to a city** einem Ort das Stadtrecht verleihen; **the Great C~** (Hist.) die Magna Charta; **C~ of Fundamental Rights** (EU) Charta der Grundrechte **2** (deed conveying land) ≈ [Besitz]urkunde, *die* **3** (privilege, admitted right) Privileg, *das;* Vorrecht, *das* **4** (Transport) **be on ~:** gechartert sein

B *v.t.* (Transport) chartern ‹*Schiff, Flugzeug*›; mieten ‹*Bus*›

chartered/'tʃɑːtəd/: **~ ac'countant** *n.* ▸ⓘ **p. 1260** (Brit.) Wirtschaftsprüfer, *der*/-prüferin, *die;* **~ 'aircraft** *n.* Charterflugzeug, *das;* Chartermaschine, *die;* **~ engi'neer** *n.* ▸ⓘ **p. 1260** (Brit.) Ingenieur, *der*/Ingenieurin, *die* (der/die Mitglied eines Verbands ist); **~ li'brarian** *n.* ▸ⓘ **p. 1260** (Brit.) Bibliothekar, *der*/Bibliothekarin, *die* (der/die Mitglied eines Verbands ist); **~ sur'veyor** *n.* ▸ⓘ **p. 1260** (Brit.) Vermessungsingenieur, *der*/-ingenieurin, *die* (der/die Mitglied eines Verbands ist)

charter: ~ flight *n.* Charterflug, *der;* **C~ Mark** *n.* (Brit.) *Auszeichnung für besondere Bürgerfreundlichkeit;* **~ party** *n.* (Transport) Charterpartie, *die;* **~ plane** ▸**chartered aircraft**

chart: ~ plotter *n.* Kartenplotter, *der;* **~ recorder** *n.* Linienschreiber, *der;* **~ table** *n.* Kartentisch, *der;* **~-topper** *n.* Spitzenreiter, *der;* **be [a/the] ~-topper** die Charts anführen

charwoman /'tʃɑːwʊmən/ ▸**char² A**

chary /'tʃeərɪ/ *adj.* **1** (sparing, ungenerous) zurückhaltend (**of** mit); **be ~ of doing sth.** zurückhaltend damit sein, etw. zu tun **2** (cautious) vorsichtig; **be ~ of doing sth.** darauf bedacht sein, etw. nicht zu tun

chase¹ /tʃeɪs/

A *n.* **1** Verfolgungsjagd, *die;* **car ~:** Verfolgungsjagd im Auto; **give ~ [to the thief]** [dem Dieb] hinterherjagen **2** (Hunting) Jagd, *die;* (steeple~) Jagdrennen, *das;* Steeplechase, *die*

B *v.t.* (pursue) jagen; **~ sth.** (fig.) einer Sache (*Dat.*) nachjagen; hinter etw. (*Dat.*) her sein (ugs.); **~ yourself** *imper.* (fig. coll.) verschwinde (ugs.)

C *v.i.* **~ after sb./sth.** hinter jmdm./etw. herjagen; **I've been chasing about all over the place** (coll.) ich bin überall herumgerast (ugs.)

Phrasal verbs

- **~ around**

A /--'-/ *v.i.* **~ around after sb.** jmdm. hinterherrennen

B /'---/ *v.t.* **~ around town** in der Stadt herumrennen (ugs.)

- **~ a'way** *v.t.* wegjagen
- **~ 'off** *v.i.* davonjagen
- **~ round** ▸**~ around**
- **~ 'up** *v.t.* (coll.) ausfindig machen

chase² *v.t.* (Metalw.) ziselieren

chaser /'tʃeɪsə(r)/ *n.* **1** (horse) Steepler, *der* (Reitsport) **2** **drink sth. as a ~** (coll.) etw. zum Nachspülen trinken (ugs.); **drink beer with vodka ~s** Bier trinken und mit Wodka nachspülen

chasm /'kæzm/ *n.* (lit. or fig.) Kluft, *die*

chassis /'ʃæsɪ/ *n., pl. same* /'ʃæsɪz/ (Motor Veh.) Chassis, *das;* Fahrgestell, *das*

'chassis number *n.* Fahr[zeug]gestellnummer, *die*

chaste /tʃeɪst/ *adj.* 1 keusch 2 (decent) gesittet ‹*Worte, Ausdruck, Antwort*› 3 (restrained) schlicht ‹*Erscheinung, Kleidung*›

chastely /ˈtʃeɪstlɪ/ *adv.* ▸**chaste**: keusch; gesittet; schlicht

chasten /ˈtʃeɪsn/ *v.t.* 1 züchtigen (geh.); strafen 2 (fig.) dämpfen ‹*Stimmung*›; demütigen ‹*Person*›

chastening /ˈtʃeɪsənɪŋ/ *adj.* ernüchternd

chastise /tʃæˈstaɪz/ *v.t.* 1 (punish) züchtigen (geh.); bestrafen 2 (thrash) züchtigen (geh.)

chastisement /tʃæˈstaɪzmənt/ *n.* Züchtigung, *die* (geh.); Strafe, *die*

chastity /ˈtʃæstɪtɪ/ *n., no pl.* Keuschheit, *die*; **vow of ~:** Keuschheitsgelübde, *das*

ˈchastity belt *n.* Keuschheitsgürtel, *der*

chasuble /ˈtʃæzjʊbl/ *n.* (Eccl.) Messgewand, *das*; Kasel, *die*

chat /tʃæt/

A *n.* 1 Schwätzchen, *das*; Plausch, *der* (bes. südd., österr.); **have a ~ about sth.** sich über etw. (*Akk.*) unterhalten 2 *no pl., no indef. art.* (~ting) Geplauder, *das* 3 (Computing) Chat, *der*; *attrib.* Chat-

B *v.i.*, **-tt-:** 1 plaudern; **~ with** *or* **to sb. about sth.** mit jmdm. von etw. plaudern; sich mit jmdm. über etw. (*Akk.*) unterhalten 2 (Computing) chatten

Phrasal verb

• **~ ˈup** *v.t.* (Brit. coll.) sich heranmachen an (+ *Akk.*) (ugs.); (amorously) anmachen (ugs.)

chateau, château /ˈʃætəʊ/ *n., pl.* **~x** /ˈʃætəʊz/ Château, *das*; **~-bottled wine** Schlossabzug, *der*

chat: **~ line** *n.* Chatline, *die*; **~ room** *n.* (Computing) Chat-room *der*; **~ show** *n.* Talk-Show, *die*

chattel /ˈtʃætl/ *n., usu. in pl.* **~[s]** bewegliche Habe (geh.); *see also* **good C 7**

chatter /ˈtʃætə(r)/

A *v.i.* 1 schwatzen; ‹*Kind:*› schwatzen, plappern; ‹*Affe:*› schnattern 2 (rattle) ‹*Zähne:*› klappern; **his teeth ~ed** er klapperte mit den Zähnen

B *n.* 1 Schwatzen, *das*; (of child) Plappern, *das*; Schwatzen, *das*; (of monkey) Schnattern, *das* 2 (of teeth) Klappern, *das*

chatterbox /ˈtʃætəbɒks/ *n.* Quasselstrippe, *die* (ugs.); (child) Plappermäulchen, *das*

chattily /ˈtʃætɪlɪ/ *adv.* im Plauderton

chattiness /ˈtʃætɪnɪs/ *n., no pl.* Gesprächigkeit, *die*; Schwatzhaftigkeit, *die* (abwertend)

chatty /ˈtʃætɪ/ *adj.* gesprächig; schwatzhaft (abwertend)

chauffeur /ˈʃəʊfə(r), ʃəʊˈfɜː(r)/ ▸❶ **p. 1260**

A *n.* Fahrer, *der*; Chauffeur, *der*; **~-driven car** Wagen mit Chauffeur

B *v.t.* fahren; chauffieren (veralt.)

chauvinism /ˈʃəʊvɪnɪzm/ *n., no pl.* Chauvinismus, *der*; **male ~:** männlicher Chauvinismus

chauvinist /ˈʃəʊvɪnɪst/ *n.* Chauvinist, *der*/Chauvinistin, *die*; **male ~/[male] ~ pig** Chauvinist, *der*/Chauvinistenschwein, *das*

chauvinistic /ʃəʊvɪˈnɪstɪk/ *adj.* chauvinistisch

cheap /tʃiːp/

A *adj.* 1 (inexpensive) billig; **~ ticket** (at reduced rate) verbilligte Fahrkarte; **be ~ and nasty** billiger Ramsch sein; **be ~ at the price** sehr preiswert sein; (fig.) es wert sein; **on the ~** (coll.) billig; **do it on the ~** (coll.) es billig machen (ugs.) 2 (easily got or made) billig 3 (worthless) billig ‹*Aussehen*›; gemein ‹*Lügner*›; schäbig ‹*Verhalten, Betragen*›; **feel ~:** sich (*Dat.*) schäbig vorkommen; **hold ~:** gering schätzen; **make oneself ~:** sich [selbst] herabsetzen 4 (Finance) billig ‹*Geld*›

B *adv.* billig; **I got it ~:** ich habs billig gekriegt (ugs.); **be going ~:** besonders günstig sein (ugs.)

cheapen /ˈtʃiːpn/

A *v.t.* verbilligen; verringern ‹*Kosten*›; (fig.) herabsetzen; **~ oneself** sich [selbst] herabsetzen; **feel ~ed** sich gedemütigt fühlen

B *v.i.* billiger werden

ˈcheapjack

A *n.* Straßenhändler, *der*; billiger Jakob (ugs.)

B *adj.* Billig-

cheaply /ˈtʃiːplɪ/ *adv.* ▸**cheap A**: billig; gemein; schäbig

cheapness /ˈtʃiːpnɪs/ *n., no pl.* niedriger Preis; (fig.) Gewöhnlichkeit, *die*

ˈcheapskate *n.* (coll.) Geizkragen, *der* (ugs. abwertend)

cheat /tʃiːt/

A *n.* 1 (person) Schwindler, *der*/Schwindlerin, *die* 2 (act) Schwindel, *der*; **that's a ~!** das ist Betrug!

B *v.t.* 1 hintergehen; betrügen; **~ sb./sth. [out] of sth.** jmdn./etw. um etw. betrügen; **~ sb. into doing sth.** jmdn. durch Täuschung dazu bringen, etw. zu tun 2 (escape) **~ sb.** jmdm. entgehen; **~ death** dem Tod entkommen

C *v.i.* betrügen; (Sch.) täuschen; **~ at cards** beim Kartenspielen mogeln

ˈcheat sheet *n.* (Amer. coll.) Mogelzettel, *der* (abwertend); Spickzettel, *der* (ugs.)

Chechen /ˈtʃetʃn/

A *adj.* tschetschenisch; **he/she is ~:** er ist Tschetschene/sie ist Tschetschenin

B *n.* 1 (Person) Tschetschene, *der*/Tschetschenin, *die* 2 (language) Tschetschenisch, *das*

Chechenia, Chechnya /tʃeʃˈnɪɑː/ *pr. ns.* Tschetschenien (*das*)

Chechen Reˈpublic /tʃetʃn rɪˈpʌblɪk/ *n.* Tschetschenische Republik

check[1] /tʃek/

A *n.* 1 (stoppage, thing that restrains) Hindernis, *das*; (restraint) Kontrolle, *die*; **[hold** *or* **keep sth.] in ~:** [etw.] unter Kontrolle [halten]; **hold** *or* **keep one's temper in ~:** sich beherrschen; **act as a ~ upon sth.** etw. unter Kontrolle halten; **a ~ must be put on sth.** etw. muss unter Kontrolle gebracht werden; **~s and balances** Kontrollmechanismen *Pl.*; **[a system of] ~s and balances** System gegenseitiger Kontrolle 2 (for accuracy) Kontrolle, *die*; **make a ~ on sth./sb.** etw./jmdn. überprüfen *od.* kontrollieren; **give sth. a ~:** etw. überprüfen *od.* kontrollieren; **keep a ~ on** überprüfen; kontrollieren; überwachen ‹*Verdächtigen*› 3 (token) (for left luggage) Gepäckaufbewahrungsschein, *der*; (Amer.: in theatre) Garderobenmarke, *die*; (for seat-holder) Platzkarte, *die*; (of verification) Kontrollzeichen, *das*; (Amer.: bill in restaurant etc.) Rechnung, *die* 4 (rebuff; also Mil.) Widerstand, *der* 5 (Chess) Schach, *das*; **be in ~:** im Schach stehen; **put sb. in ~:** jmdm. Schach bieten 6 (Hunting) Stocken [beim Verlieren der Fährte] 7 (Amer.: counter at cards) Spielmarke, *die*; *see also* **cash in A** 8 (Amer.) ▸**cheque**

B *v.t.* 1 (restrain) unter Kontrolle halten; unterdrücken ‹*Ärger, Lachen*›; **~ oneself** sich beherrschen 2 (examine accuracy of) nachprüfen; nachsehen ‹*Hausaufgaben*›; kontrollieren ‹*Fahrkarte*›; (Amer.: mark with tick) abhaken; (Amer.: deposit) aufgeben ‹*Gepäck*› 3 (stop; also Mil.) aufhalten 4 (Chess) Schach bieten (+ *Dat.*)

C *v.i.* 1 (test) **~ on sth.** etw. überprüfen; **~ with sb.** bei jmdm. nachfragen; **just ~ing** (coll. joc.) wollte mich nur vergewissern 2 (Amer.: agree) übereinstimmen 3 (Hunting) stocken

D *int.* 1 (Chess) Schach 2 (Amer.) einverstanden

Phrasal verbs

• **~ ˈback** *v.i.* nachsehen

• **~ ˈin**

A *v.t.* eintragen; (at airport) **~ in one's luggage** sein Gepäck abfertigen lassen *od.* einchecken

B *v.i.* (arrive at hotel) ankommen; (sign the register) sich eintragen; (report one's arrival) sich melden; (at airport) einchecken. *See also* **check-in**

• **~ ˈoff** *v.t.* abhaken

• **~ ˈout**

A *v.t.* überprüfen

B *v.i.* abreisen; **~ out [of one's hotel]** abreisen; (pay) seine Hotelrechnung bezahlen; **~ out of the supermarket** im Supermarkt bezahlen. *See also* **checkout**

• **~ ˈover** *v.t.* durchsehen

• **~ ˈthrough** *v.t.* kontrollieren; durchsehen ‹*Brief, Rechnung*›

• **~ ˈup** *v.i.* überprüfen; **~ up on sb./sth.** jmdn./etw. überprüfen *od.* kontrollieren; **the police will ~ up on you** die Polizei wird Nachforschungen über dich anstellen. *See also* **check-up**

check[2] *n.* (pattern) Karo, *das*; **a shirt of red and white ~:** ein rotweiß kariertes Hemd

checked /tʃekt/ *adj.* (patterned) kariert

checker /ˈtʃekə(r)/ *n.* Prüfer, *der*/Prüferin, *die*; Kontrolleur, *der*

ˈcheckerboard *n.* (Amer.) Schachbrett, *das*

checkers /ˈtʃekəz/ *n., no pl.* (*Amer.*) ▸**draughts**

ˈcheck-in *n.* Abfertigung, *die*; *attrib.* Abfertigungs-

ˈchecking account *n.* (Amer.) Girokonto, *das*

check: **~list** *n.* Verzeichnis, *das*; Checkliste, *die* (Technik, Flugw.); **~ mark** *n.* (Amer.) Häkchen, *das*; **~mate** /ˈtʃekmeɪt/ **A** *n.* [Schach]matt, *das*; **B** *int.* [schach]matt; **C** *v.t.* 1 matt setzen; 2 (fig.) zunichte machen; **~out** *n.* Abreise, *die*; (desk) Kasse, *die*; *attrib.* **~out assistant** Kassierer, *der*/Kassiererin, *die*; **~out desk** *or* **point** *or* **counter** Kasse, *die*; **~point** *n.* Kontrollpunkt, *der*; **~room** *n.* (Amer.) 1 (cloakroom) Garderobe, *die*; 2 (for left luggage) Gepäckaufbewahrung, *die*; **~-up** *n.* (Med.) Untersuchung, *die*; **get/have a ~-up** untersucht werden; **go to the doctor for a ~-up** sich beim Arzt untersuchen lassen

Cheddar /ˈtʃedə(r)/ *n.* Cheddar[käse], *der*

cheek /tʃiːk/

A *n.* 1 ▸❶ **p. 951** Backe, *die*; Wange, *die* (geh.); **~ by jowl** Seite an Seite; dicht nebeneinander ‹*stehen, wohnen*›; **dance ~ to ~:** Wange an Wange tanzen; **turn the other ~** (fig.) die andere Wange darbieten 2 (impertinence) Frechheit, *die*; **have the ~ to do sth.** die Frechheit *od.* Stirn besitzen, etw. zu tun; **I like your ~** (iron.) du hast vielleicht Nerven! (ugs.); **none of your ~:** sei nicht so frech; **have plenty of ~:** ziemlich unverschämt sein 3 ▸❶ **p. 951** *in pl.* (coll.: buttocks) Hinterbacken (ugs.)

B *v.t.* **~ sb.** zu jmdm. frech sein

ˈcheekbone *n.* Backenknochen, *der*

cheekily /ˈtʃiːkɪlɪ/ *adv.* frech; **behave ~:** frech sein

cheekiness /ˈtʃiːkɪnɪs/ *n., no pl.* Frechheit, *die*

ˈcheek pouch *n.* (Zool.) Backentasche, *die*

cheeky /ˈtʃiːkɪ/ *adj.* frech; **~ girl** freches Ding (ugs.); **~ boy** frecher Bengel; **~ devil/monkey** (coll.) Frechdachs, *der* (ugs.)

cheep /tʃiːp/

A *v.i.* piep[s]en

B *n.* Piep[s]en, *das*; **not a ~ [out of sb.]** (fig. coll.) kein Pieps [von jmdm.] (ugs.)

cheer /tʃɪə(r)/

A *n.* 1 (applause) Beifallsruf, *der*; **give sb. a [big] ~:** jmdm. zujubeln; **give three ~s for sb.** jmdn. [dreimal] hochleben lassen; **two ~s** (iron.) ist ja großartig (iron.) 2 *in pl.* (Brit. coll.: as a toast) prost 3 *in pl.* (Brit. coll.: thank you) danke 4 *in pl.* (Brit. coll.: goodbye) tschüs (ugs.) 5 (arch.: frame of mind) **be of good ~:** sei/seid guten Mutes (geh.)

B *v.t.* 1 (applaud) **~ sth./sb.** etw. bejubeln/jmdm. zujubeln 2 (gladden) aufmuntern; aufheitern

C *v.i.* jubeln

Phrasal verbs

• **~ ˈon** *v.t.* anfeuern ‹*Sportler, Wettkämpfer*›

• **~ ˈup**

A *v.t.* aufheitern

B *v.i.* bessere Laune bekommen; **~ up!** Kopf hoch!

cheerful /ˈtʃɪəfl/ *adj.* (in good spirits) fröhlich; gut gelaunt; (bright, pleasant) heiter; erfreulich ‹*Aussichten*›; lustig ‹*Feuer*›; (willing) bereitwillig; **make sb. ~:** jmdn. heiter stimmen

cheerfully /ˈtʃɪəfəlɪ/ *adv.* vergnügt; **the fire blazed ~:** das Feuer brannte lustig; **~ assuming that …** (iron.) in der unbekümmerten Annahme, dass …

cheerily /ˈtʃɪərɪlɪ/ *adv.* fröhlich

cheering /'tʃɪərɪŋ/
A *adj.* 1 (gladdening) fröhlich stimmend 2 (applauding) jubelnd
B *n.* Jubeln, *das*

cheerio /tʃɪərɪ'əʊ/ *int.* 1 (Brit. coll.: goodbye) tschüs (ugs.) 2 (dated: as a toast) zum Wohl

'cheerleader *n.: jmd., der andere zu Beifall, Hochrufen usw. anfeuert*

cheerless /'tʃɪəlɪs/ *adj.* freudlos; düster ‹*Aussichten*›

cheery /'tʃɪərɪ/ *adj.* fröhlich

cheese /tʃi:z/ *n.* 1 (food) Käse, *der;* **~s** Käsesorten 2 (whole) Käselaib, *der;* (piece) Stück Käse 3 **say ~!** (Photog.) bitte recht freundlich!; **hard ~!** (dated coll.) Pech gehabt! (ugs.). *See also* **lemon cheese**

cheese: ~board *n.* Käseplatte, *die;* **~cake** *n.* 1 Käsetorte, *die;* 2 *no pl., no indef. art.* (coll.) Pin-up-Girls *Pl.;* **~cloth** *n.* [indischer] Baumwollstoff; **~-cutter** *n. Draht zum Schneiden von Käse;* **~ dish** *n.* ≈ Käseglocke, *die*

cheesed off /tʃi:zd 'ɒf/ *adj.* (Brit. coll.) angeödet; **I am ~ with school** die Schule ödet mich an (ugs.) *od.* stinkt mir (salopp); **I'm ~:** mir stinkts! (salopp)

cheese: ~-grater *n.* Käseraspel, *die;* **~-paring** **A** *adj.* knauserig; **B** *n.* Knauserei, *die;* **~ 'spread** *n.* Streichkäse, *der;* **~ 'straw** *n.* Käsestange, *die;* **~ wire** *n., no pl.* Käseschneidedraht, *der;* Käsedraht, *der*

cheesy /'tʃi:zɪ/ *adj.* 1 (like cheese) käsig; Käse‹*geschmack, -geruch, -keks, -soße*› 2 (coll.) (cheap, second-rate) schrottig (ugs. abwertend); (sentimental) schnulzig (ugs. abwertend); (insincere) verlogen

cheetah /'tʃi:tə/ *n.* (Zool.) Gepard, *der*

chef /ʃef/ *n.* ▸**i** **p. 1260** Küchenchef, *der;* (as profession) Koch, *der*

Chelsea/'tʃelsɪ/: **~ 'bun** *n.* ≈ Rosinenbrötchen, *das;* **~ 'pensioner** *n.: Insasse des Chelsea Royal Hospital für alte und kriegsversehrte Soldaten*

chemical /'kemɪkl/
A *adj.* chemisch
B *n.* Chemikalie, *die*

chemical: ~ 'agent *n.* chemischer Wirkstoff; (Mil.) chemischer Kampfstoff; **~ engi'neer** *n.* ▸**i** **p. 1260** Chemieingenieur, *der/-ingenieurin, die;* **~ engi'neering** *n., no pl.* Chemotechnik, *die;* **~ firm** *n.* Chemiebetrieb, *der*

chemically /'kemɪkəlɪ/ *adv.* chemisch

chemical: ~ 'toilet *n.* chemische Toilette; Chemietoilette, *die;* **~ 'warfare** *n., no pl.* chemische Krieg[s]führung; **~ 'weapon** *n.* chemische Waffe; Chemiewaffe, *die;* **~ worker** *n.* ▸**i** **p. 1260** Chemiearbeiter, *der/-arbeiterin, die*

chemise /ʃə'mi:z/ *n.* Unterkleid, *das*

chemist /'kemɪst/ *n.* ▸**i** **p. 1260** 1 (person skilled in chemistry) Chemiker, *der/*Chemikerin, *die* 2 (Brit.: pharmacist) Drogist, *der/*Drogistin, *die;* **~'s [shop]** Drogerie, *die;* (dispensary) Apotheke, *die; see also* **baker**

chemistry /'kemɪstrɪ/ *n., no pl.* 1 *no indef. art.* Chemie, *die;* **the ~ of iron** die chemischen Eigenschaften des Eisens 2 (fig.) unerklärliche Wirkungskraft

chemistry: ~ laboratory *n.* Chemiesaal, *der;* **~ set** *n.* Chemiebaukasten, *der*

chemoreceptor /'ki:məʊrɪseptə(r)/ *n.* (Biol.) Chemorezeptor, *der*

chemotherapy /ki:mə(ʊ)'θerəpɪ/ *n.* Chemotherapie, *die*

chenille /ʃə'ni:l/ *n.* Chenille, *die*

cheque /tʃek/ *n.* ▸**i** **p. 1332** Scheck, *der;* **write a ~:** einen Scheck ausfüllen; **will you take a ~?** kann ich mit Scheck bezahlen?; **pay by ~:** mit [einem] Scheck bezahlen

cheque: ~book *n.* Scheckbuch, *das;* **~book journalism** *n.* Scheckbuchjournalismus, *der;* **~ card** *n.* Scheckkarte, *die*

chequer /'tʃekə(r)/
A *n.* Karomuster, *das*
B *v.t.* karieren

'chequerboard *n.* Schachbrett, *das*

chequered /'tʃekəd/ *adj.* 1 kariert; **a lawn ~ with sunlight and shade** ein von Licht und Schatten gefleckter Rasen 2 (fig.) bewegt ‹*Geschichte, Leben, Laufbahn*›

cherish /'tʃerɪʃ/ *v.t.* 1 (value and keep) hegen ‹*Hoffnung, Gefühl*›; in Ehren halten ‹[*Erinnerungs*]*gegenstand*›; **~ an illusion** sich einer Illusion (*Dat.*) hingeben; **~ sb.'s memory** jmds. Andenken in Ehren bewahren 2 (foster) **~ sb.** [liebevoll] für jmdn. sorgen; **to love and to ~, till death us do part** (in marriage ceremony) zu lieben und zu ehren, bis dass der Tod uns scheidet

cheroot /ʃə'ru:t/ *n.* Stumpen, *der*

cherry /'tʃerɪ/
A *n.* 1 (fruit) Kirsche, *die;* **it's no use having two bites at a ~** (fig.) es hat keinen Sinn, das Ganze zweimal durchzuführen; **we may get two bites at the ~** (fig.) wir werden vielleicht eine zweite Chance haben 2 (tree) Kirschbaum, *der*
B *adj.* kirschrot; **a bright ~ red** ein helles Kirschrot

cherry: ~ blossom *n.* Kirschblüte, *die;* **~ 'brandy** *n.* Cherry Brandy, *der;* ≈ Kirschlikör, *der;* **~-pick** **A** *v.t.* sich (*Dat.*) [her]aussuchen (**from** aus); **B** *v.i.* sich (*Dat.*) die Rosinen herauspicken; **~ 'pie** *n.* 1 Kirschkuchen, *der;* 2 (Brit.: flower) Vanillestrauch, *der;* **~ stone** *n.* Kirschkern, *der*

cherub /'tʃerəb/ *n.* 1 *pl.* **~im** /'tʃerəbɪm/ (Theol., of celestial order) Cherub, *der* 2 *pl.* **~s** (Art) Putte, *die;* Putto, *der;* (child) Engelchen, *das*

cherubic /tʃɪ'ru:bɪk/ *adj.* cherubinisch; engelhaft; **~ face** Engelsgesicht, *das*

chervil /'tʃɜ:vɪl/ *n.* (Bot.) Kerbel, *der*

Cheshire/'tʃeʃə(r), 'tʃeʃɪə(r)/: **~ 'cat** *n.* **grin like a ~ cat** übers ganze Gesicht grinsen; **~ 'cheese** *n.* Cheshirekäse, *der*

chess /tʃes/ *n., no pl., no indef. art.* das Schach[spiel]; **play ~:** Schach spielen; **be good at ~:** gut Schach spielen

chess: ~board *n.* Schachbrett, *das;* **~man** *n.* Schachfigur, *die;* **~ player** *n.* Schachspieler, *der/-spielerin, die*

chest /tʃest/ *n.* 1 Kiste, *die;* (for clothes or money) Truhe, *die;* (treasury; also fig.) Kasse, *die* 2 ▸**i** **p. 951,** ▸**i** **p. 1231** (part of body) Brust, *die;* (Anat.) Brustkorb, *der;* Brustkasten, *der* (ugs.); **cold on the ~:** Bronchitis, *die;* **get sth. off one's ~** (fig. coll.) sich (*Dat.*) etw. von der Seele reden; **play sth. close to one's ~** (fig. coll.) so wenig wie möglich über etw. (*Akk.*) erwähnen

-chested /tʃestɪd/ *adj. in comb.* -brüstig; **a broad-~ man** ein Mann mit einem breiten Brustkorb

chesterfield /'tʃestəfi:ld/ *n.* gepolstertes Sofa (*mit hohen Armlehnen*)

chest: ~ expander *n.* Expander, *der;* **~ freezer** *n.* Gefriertruhe, *die;* **~ infection** *n.* Brustkorbinfektion, *die;* **~ measurement** *n.* Brustumfang, *der;* Brustweite, *die*

chestnut /'tʃesnʌt/
A *n.* 1 (tree) Kastanie, *die;* **Spanish** *or* **sweet ~:** Edelkastanie, *die; see also* **horse chestnut** 2 (fruit) Kastanie, *die;* **pull the ~s out of the fire** (fig.) die Kastanien aus dem Feuer holen (ugs.) 3 (colour) Kastanienbraun, *das* 4 ▸**chestnut wood** 5 (stale story or topic) **[old] ~:** alte *od.* olle Kamelle (ugs.) 6 (horse) Fuchs, *der*
B *adj.* (colour) **~[-brown]** kastanienbraun

chestnut: ~ tree ▸**chestnut A 1;** **~ wood** *n.* Kastanienholz, *das*

chest of 'drawers Kommode, *die*

chesty /'tʃestɪ/ *adj.* (coll.) anfällig (*für Erkältungen*); tief sitzend ‹*Husten*›; **be ~:** es auf der Brust haben (ugs.); **you sound rather ~ today** du klingst heute ziemlich erkältet

chevron /'ʃevrən/ *n.* 1 (badge) Winkel, *der* 2 (Her.) Sparren, *der;* Chevron, *der* 3 (traffic sign) Winkel (*auf Richtungstafeln o. Ä.*)

chew /tʃu:/
A *v.t.* kauen; **~ one's fingernails** an den [Finger]nägeln kauen; **~ the rag** *or* **the fat [about sth.]** (fig.) [über etw. (*Akk.*)] meckern (ugs.); *see also* **bite off**; **cud**
B *v.i.* kauen (**on** auf + *Dat.*); **~ on** *or* **over sth.** (fig.) sich (*Dat.*) etw. durch den Kopf gehen lassen
C *n.* Kauen, *das*

Phrasal verb
• **~ 'out** *v.t.* (Amer. coll.) zusammenstauchen (ugs.)

chewing gum /'tʃu:ɪŋgʌm/ *n.* Kaugummi, *der od. das*

chewy /'tʃu:ɪ/ *adj.* zäh ‹*Fleisch, Bonbon*›

Chianti /kɪ'æntɪ/ *n.* Chianti[wein], *der*

chiaroscuro /kjɑ:rə'skʊərəʊ/ *n., pl.* **~s** (in painting) Clair-obscur, *das;* (fig. also) Helldunkel, *das*

chic /ʃi:k/
A *adj.* schick; elegant
B *n.* Schick, *der*

chicane /ʃɪ'keɪn/ *n.* (Sport) Schikane, *die*

chicanery /ʃɪ'keɪnərɪ/ *n.* 1 *no pl.* (deception) Täuschungsmanöver, *das;* (legal trickery) Rechtsverdrehung, *die* 2 (sophistry) Winkelzug, *der;* Trick, *der*

chichi /'ʃi:ʃi:/
A *adj.* überspannt, affektiert ‹*Person, Verhalten*›; extravagant ‹*Gegenstand*›
B *n.* Chichi, *das*

chick /tʃɪk/ *n.* 1 Küken, *das* 2 (coll.: child) Kleine, *das* 3 (sl.: young woman) Biene, *die* (ugs.)

chickadee /'tʃɪkədi:/ *n.* (Ornith.) Chickadee-Meise, *die*

chicken /'tʃɪkɪn/
A *n.* 1 Huhn, *das;* (grilled, roasted) Hähnchen, *das;* **don't count your ~s [before they are hatched]** (prov.) man soll den Pelz nicht verkaufen, ehe man den Bären erlegt hat 2 (coll.: youthful person) Küken, *das;* **she's no ~** (is no longer young) sie ist nicht mehr die Jüngste; (is experienced) sie ist kein [kleines] Kind mehr 3 (coll.: game) **play ~:** eine Mutprobe ablegen 4 (coll.: coward) Angsthase, *der*
B *adj.* (coll.) feig[e]
C *v.i.* **~ out** (coll.) kneifen; **~ out of sth.** sich vor etw. (*Dat.*) drücken; vor etw. (*Dat.*) kneifen

chicken: ~-and-'egg *adj.* Huhn-Ei- ‹*Frage*›; **~-breasted** *adj.* hühnerbrüstig; flachbrüstig; **~ feed** *n.* 1 Hühnerfutter, *das;* 2 (fig. coll.) eine lächerliche Summe; **the firm pays them ~ feed** die Firma zahlt ihnen einen Hungerlohn; **~-hearted** *adj.* feige; hasenfüßig; **~ 'pie** *n.* Hühnerpastete, *die;* **~pox** *n.* ▸**i** **p. 1231** (Med.) Windpocken *Pl.;* **~ run** *n.* Auslauf, *der* (Landw.); **~ 'salad** *n.* Geflügelsalat, *der;* **~ 'soup** *n.* Hühnersuppe, *die;* **~ wire** *n.* Maschendraht, *der*

chick: ~pea *n.* Kichererbse, *die;* **~weed** *n.* (Bot.) Vogelmiere, *die;* Hühnerdarm, *der*

chicory /'tʃɪkərɪ/ *n.* 1 (plant) Chicorée, *der od. die;* (for coffee) Zichorie, *die;* (flower) Wegwarte, *die* 2 (Amer.: endive) Endivie, *die*

chide /tʃaɪd/, **~d** *or* **chid** /tʃɪd/, **~d** *or* **chid** *or* (arch./literary) **chidden** /'tʃɪdn/
A *v.t.* schelten (geh.) (**for** wegen)
B *v.i.* schelten (geh.)

chief /tʃi:f/
A *n.* 1 (of state, town, clan) Oberhaupt, *das;* (of party) Vorsitzende, *der;* (of tribe) Häuptling, *der;* **~ of state** Staatschef, *der* 2 (of department) Leiter, *der;* (coll.: one's superior, boss) Chef, *der;* Boss, *der;* **~ of police** Polizeipräsident, *der;* **~ of staff** (of a service) Generalstabschef, *der;* (commander) Stabschef, *der* 3 **in ~** *postpos.* hauptsächlich; **Colonel-in-C~:** Regimentskommandeur, *der* 4 (Her.) Schildhaupt, *das*
B *adj., usu. attrib.* 1 Ober-; **~ priest** Oberpriester, *der;* **~ clerk** Bürochef, *der;* **~ engineer** erster Maschinist (Seew.); **[Lord] C~ Justice** (Brit.) [Lord] Oberrichter, *der* 2 (first in importance, influence, etc.) Haupt-; **~ reason/aim** Hauptgrund, *der/*-ziel, *das;* **his ~ crime** das Schlimmste, was er sich (*Dat.*) geleistet hat; **his ~ hope** seine größte Hoffnung 3 (prominent, leading) führend; **~ culprit** Hauptschuldige, *der/die;* **~ offender** Haupttäter, *der/*-täterin, *die*

chief ex'ecutive [officer] *n.* Hauptgeschäftsführer, *der/*-führerin, *die;* **the chairman**

C

C

and ~ (person holding both positions) der Präsident *od.* Vorsitzende und geschäftsführende Direktor/die Präsidentin *od.* Vorsitzende und geschäftsführende Direktorin

chiefly /ˈtʃiːflɪ/ *adv.* hauptsächlich; vor allem

chieftain /ˈtʃiːftən/ *n.* (of Highland clan) Oberhaupt, *das;* (of tribe) Stammesführer, *der;* (of band of robbers) Hauptmann, *der* (hist.)

chiff-chaff /ˈtʃɪftʃæf/ *n.* (Ornith.) Zilpzalp, *der*

chiffon /ˈʃɪfɒn/
A *n.* (Textiles) Chiffon, *der*
B *adj.* Chiffon-

chignon /ˈʃiːnjɔ̃/ *n.* Chignon, *der;* [Haar]knoten, *der*

chihuahua /tʃɪˈwɑːwə/ *n.* Chihuahua, *der*

chilblain /ˈtʃɪlbleɪn/ *n.* Frostbeule, *die*

child /tʃaɪld/ *n., pl.* **~ren** /ˈtʃɪldrən/ Kind, *das;* **when I was a ~:** als ich klein war; **a ~'s guide to ...** (fig.) ...für Kinder; **[be] with ~** (dated) schwanger [sein]; **the ~ is the father of the man** (prov.) *Einflüsse und Erfahrungen der Kindheit bestimmen den Charakter des Erwachsenen*

child: ~ abuse *n., no pl.* (sexual) sexueller Missbrauch von Kindern; (physical) Kindesmisshandlung, *die;* **~ abuser** *n.* (sexually) Kinderschänder, *der*/-schänderin, *die;* Kindesmissbraucher, *der*/-missbraucherin, *die;* (physically) Kindesmisshandler, *der*/-misshandlerin, *die;* **~bearing** A *n.* Schwangerschaften *Pl.;* B *adj.* **~bearing age** Gebäralter, *das;* **of ~bearing age** im gebärfähigen Alter; **~ 'benefit** *n.* (Brit.) Kindergeld, *das;* **~birth** *n.* Geburt, *die;* **die in ~birth** bei der Geburt *od.* im Wochenbett sterben; **~ bride** *n.* Kinderbraut, *die;* **~ care** *n.* 1 Betreuung von Kindern; 2 (social services department) Kinderfürsorge, *die;* **~ 'guidance** *n.* Erziehungsberatung, *die*

childhood /ˈtʃaɪldhʊd/ *n.* Kindheit, *die;* **in ~:** als Kind; **from** *or* **since ~:** schon als Kind; **be in one's second ~:** an Altersschwachsinn leiden

childish /ˈtʃaɪldɪʃ/ *adj.*, **childishly** /ˈtʃaɪldɪʃlɪ/ *adv.* kindlich; (derog.) kindisch

childishness /ˈtʃaɪldɪʃnɪs/ *n., no pl.* Kindlichkeit, *die;* (derog.) kindisches Wesen; (behaviour) kindisches Benehmen

'child language *n., no pl.* Kindersprache, *die*

childless /ˈtʃaɪldlɪs/ *adj.* kinderlos

childlike /ˈtʃaɪldlaɪk/ *adj.* kindlich

child: ~ lock *n.* (in car, on TV/computer) Kindersicherung, *die;* **~minder** *n.* ▸ℹ **p. 1260** (Brit.) Tagesmutter, *die;* **~ por'nography** *n., no pl.* Kinderpornographie, *die;* **~ 'prodigy** *n.* Wunderkind, *das;* **~proof** *adj.* kindersicher; **~proof (door) lock** (in car) Kindersicherung, *die;* **~ psy'chiatrist** *n.* ▸ℹ **p. 1260** Kinderpsychiater, *der*/-psychiaterin, *die;* **~ psy'chiatry** *n., no pl.* Kinderpsychiatrie, *die;* **~ psy'chologist** *n.* ▸ℹ **p. 1260** Kinderpsychologe, *der*/-psychologin, *die;* **~ psy'chology** *n., no pl.* Kinderpsychologie, *die*

children *pl. of* **child**

child: ~ seat *n.* Kindersitz, *der;* **~'s play** *n., no pl.* (fig.) Kinderspiel, *das;* **it's ~'s play!** es ist ein Kinderspiel!; **C~ Sup'port Agency** *n.* (Brit.) *staatliche Einrichtung zur Durchsetzung von Unterhaltsansprüche für Kinder;* **~ 'welfare** *n.* Kinderfürsorge, *die*

Chile /ˈtʃɪlɪ/ *pr. n.* Chile *(das)*

Chilean /ˈtʃɪlɪən/ ▸ℹ **p. 1345**
A *adj.* chilenisch; **sb. is ~:** jmd. ist Chilene/Chilenin
B *n.* Chilene, *der*/Chilenin, *die; see also* **English A**

Chile: ~ 'pine *n.* (Bot.) Chilefichte, *die;* **~ saltpetre** *n.* Chilesalpeter, *der*

chili ▸**chilli**

chill /tʃɪl/
A *n.* 1 (cold sensation) Frösteln, *das;* (feverish shivering) Schüttelfrost, *der;* (illness) Erkältung, *die;* **catch a ~:** sich verkühlen *od.* erkälten 2 (unpleasant coldness) Kühle, *die;* (fig.) Abkühlung, *die;* **take the ~ off [sth.]** etw. leicht erwärmen; **there's a ~ in the air** es ist ziemlich kühl [draußen] 3 (depressing influence) Ernüchterung, *die;* **her presence at the party cast** *or* **spread a ~ over things** durch ihre Anwesenheit bei der Party entstand eine frostige Atmosphäre 4 (of manner) Frostigkeit, *die*
B *v.t.* 1 (make cold, preserve) kühlen; **I was ~ed to the marrow** ich war ganz durchgefroren 2 (Metallurgy) abschrecken
C *v.i.* 1 abkühlen 2 ▸ **~ out**
D *adj.* (literary; lit. or fig.) kühl

Phrasal verb
• **~ out** *v.i.* (coll.) (relax) sich entspannen; (calm down) sich abregen (ugs.)

chiller /ˈtʃɪlə/ *n* 1 (refrigerator) Kühlgerät, *das* 2 (coll.: film) Schocker, *der* (ugs.); **political/psychological ~:** Polit-/Psychothriller, *der*

'chill factor ▸**wind chill factor**

chilli /ˈtʃɪlɪ/ *n., pl.* **~es** Chili, *der;* **~ con carne** /tʃɪlɪ kɒn ˈkɑːnɪ/ (Gastr.) Chili con carne

chilliness /ˈtʃɪlɪnɪs/ *n., no pl.* (lit. or fig.) Kühle, *die*

chilling /ˈtʃɪlɪŋ/ *adj.* (fig.) ernüchternd; frostig ‹*Art, Worte, Blick*›

chilly /ˈtʃɪlɪ/ *adj.* 1 (lit. or fig.) kühl 2 (feeling somewhat cold) **I am rather ~:** mir ist ziemlich kühl; (sensitive to cold) **I'm rather a ~ person** ich friere ziemlich leicht

Chiltern Hundreds /tʃɪltən ˈhʌndrədz/ *n.* (Brit. Polit.) *Kronamt, dessen Übernahme Parlamentariern die Aufgabe ihres Parlamentssitzes ermöglicht;* **apply for the ~:** seinen Unterhaussitz aufgeben

chimaera ▸**chimera**

chime /tʃaɪm/
A *n.* 1 Geläute, *das;* **ring the ~s** die Glocken läuten 2 (set of bells) Glockenspiel, *das*
B *v.i.* läuten; ‹*Turmuhr:*› schlagen; **chiming clock** Schlaguhr, *die*
C *v.t.* erklingen lassen ‹*Melodie*›; schlagen ‹*Stunde, Mitternacht*›

Phrasal verb
• **~ 'in** *v.i.* 1 (Mus.) einstimmen; (fig.) übereinstimmen (**with** mit) 2 (interject remark) sich [in die Unterhaltung] einmischen

chimera /kaɪˈmɪərə, kɪˈmɪərə/ *n.* 1 (hybrid) [bunte, fantastische] Mischung; (fanciful conception) Schimäre, *die* 2 (bogy) Schimäre, *die;* Schreckgespenst, *das* 3 (Biol.) Chimäre, *die*

chimerical /kaɪˈmerɪkl, kɪˈmerɪkl/ *adj.* schimärisch (geh.); trügerisch

chimney /ˈtʃɪmnɪ/ *n.* 1 (of house, factory, etc.) Schornstein, *der;* (of house also) Kamin, *der* (bes. südd.); (of factory or ship also) Schlot, *der;* (above open fire) Rauchfang, *der;* **the smoke goes up the ~:** der Rauch zieht durch den Kaminschacht ab; **come down the ~:** durch den Schornstein kommen; **smoke like a ~** (fig.) wie ein Schlot rauchen 2 (of lamp) [Lampen]zylinder, *der* 3 (vent of volcano etc.) Schlot, *der* 4 (Mountaineering) Kamin, *der*

chimney: ~ breast *n.* Kaminmantel, *der;* **~ corner, ~ nook** *ns.* Sitzecke am Kamin; **~ piece** *n.* Kaminsims, *der;* **~ pot** *n.* ≈ Schornsteinkopf, *der;* **~ stack** ▸**stack A 4;** **~ sweep** *n.* ▸ℹ **p. 1260** Schornsteinfeger, *der*

chimp /tʃɪmp/ (coll.), **chimpanzee** /tʃɪmpənˈziː/ *ns.* Schimpanse, *der*

chin /tʃɪn/ *n.* ▸ℹ **p. 951** Kinn, *das;* **keep one's ~ up** (fig.) den Kopf nicht hängen lassen; **~ up!** Kopf hoch!; **take it on the ~** (suffer severe blow) einen harten Schlag einstecken müssen; (endure sth. courageously) es mit Fassung tragen; *see also* **stick out A 1**

china *n.* Porzellan, *das;* (crockery) Geschirr, *das;* **broken ~:** Scherben *Pl.*

China /ˈtʃaɪnə/ *pr. n.* China *(das)*

china: ~ cabinet *n.* Vitrine, *die;* **~ 'clay** *n.* Porzellanerde, *die;* **~ cupboard** *n.* Geschirrschrank, *der*

China: ~man /ˈtʃaɪnəmən/ *n., pl.* **~men** /ˈtʃaɪnəmən/ (derog.) Chinese, *der;* **c~ shop** ▸**bull A 1;** **~ 'tea** *n.* Chinatee, *der;* **~town** *n.* Chinesenviertel, *das;* **c~ware** *n., no pl.* Porzellan, *das*

chinch [bug] /ˈtʃɪntʃ(bʌg)/ *n.* (Amer.) 1 Bettwanze, *die* 2 (destroying grain) Getreidewanze, *die*

chinchilla /tʃɪnˈtʃɪlə/ *n.* 1 (Zool.) Chinchilla, *die* 2 (fur) Chinchilla[pelz], *der* 3 (cat) Chinchillaperser, *der;* (rabbit) Chinchilla, *das*

chin-chin /tʃɪnˈtʃɪn/ *int.* (Brit.) (greeting) hallo! (ugs.); (farewell) tschüs! (ugs.); cheerio!; (as a toast) prost!

chine[1] /tʃaɪn/ *n.* (Brit. Geog.: ravine) ≈ Klamm, *die*

chine[2] *n.* 1 (backbone) Rückgrat, *das;* (Cookery: joint of meat) Rückenstück, *das* 2 (Geog.: ridge) Kamm, *der*

Chinese /tʃaɪˈniːz/ ▸ℹ **p. 1277,** ▸ℹ **p. 1345**
A *adj.* chinesisch; **sb. is ~:** jmd. ist Chinese/Chinesin; *see also* **English A**
B *n.* 1 *pl. same* (person) Chinese, *der*/Chinesin, *die* 2 (language) Chinesisch, *das; see also* **English B 1**

Chinese: ~ 'boxes *n. pl.* Satz ineinander passender Schachteln; **~ 'burn** *n.* tausend Stecknadeln; **give sb. a ~ burn** bei jmdm. tausend Stecknadeln machen; **~ 'goose** *n.* Höckergans, *die;* **~ 'lantern** *n.* 1 (of paper) Lampion, *der;* 2 (Bot.) Judenkirsche, *die;* **~ 'puzzle** *n.* chinesisches Geduldsspiel; **~ 'wall** *n.* (fig.) chinesische Mauer; **~ 'white** *n.* Zinkweiß, *das*

chink[1] *n.* 1 Spalt, *der;* **a ~ in sb.'s armour** (fig.) jmds. schwache Stelle 2 **a ~ of light** ein Lichtspalt

chink[2]
A *n.* (sound) ▸**clink[1] A**
B *v.i. & t.* ▸**clink[1] B, C**

Chink /tʃɪŋk/ *n.* (sl. derog.) Schlitzauge, *das* (abwertend)

chinless /ˈtʃɪnlɪs/ *adj.* 1 mit fliehendem Kinn *nachgestellt;* **be ~:** ein fliehendes Kinn haben 2 (fig.) **~ wonder** (Brit. joc.) *bornierter Vertreter der Oberschicht*

chinoiserie /ʃɪnˈwɑːzərɪ/ *n.* Chinoiserie, *die*

chin: ~ rest *n.* Kinnstütze, *die;* **~strap** *n.* (of helmet) Kinnriemen, *der;* (of bonnet) Kinnband, *das*

chintz /tʃɪnts/ *n.* Chintz, *der*

chintzy /ˈtʃɪntsɪ/ *adj.* auffällig bunt und billig

'chin-up *n.* (esp. Amer.) Klimmzug, *der*

'chinwag (coll.)
A *n.* Schwatz, *der*
B *v.i.* schwatzen

chip /tʃɪp/
A *n.* 1 Splitter, *der;* **have a ~ on one's shoulder** (fig.) einen Komplex haben; *see also* **block A 3** 2 (of potato) [Kartoffel]stäbchen, *das* 3 *in pl.* (Brit.: fried) Pommes frites *Pl.;* (Amer.: crisps) Kartoffelchips *Pl.* 4 **there is a ~ on this cup/paintwork** diese Tasse ist angeschlagen/etwas Farbe ist abgeplatzt 5 (Gambling) Chip, *der;* Jeton, *der;* **have had one's ~s** (Brit. fig. coll.) erledigt sein (ugs.); **when the ~s are down** (fig. coll.) wenns ernst wird; *see also* **cash in A** 6 (Electronics) Chip, *der* 7 (for making baskets) Span, *der;* **~ [basket]** (Brit.) Spankorb, *der* 8 ▸**chip shot**
B *v.t.,* **-pp-:** 1 anschlagen ‹*Geschirr*›; Späne abschlagen von ‹*Holz*›; **~ [off]** abschlagen; **the paint is ~ped** der Lack ist abgesprungen 2 (cut into **~s**) **~ped potatoes** Kartoffelstäbchen 3 **~ the ball** (Golf) den Ball mit einem kurzen Annäherungsschlag auf das Grün bringen; (Football) den Ball anheben
C *v.i.,* **-pp-: this china ~s easily** von diesem Porzellan platzt leicht etwas ab

Phrasal verb
• **~ 'in** (coll.)
A *v.i.* 1 (interrupt) sich einmischen; **who asked you to ~ in with your opinion?** wer hat dich nach deiner Meinung gefragt? 2 (contribute money) etwas beisteuern; **~ in with £5** sich mit 5 Pfund beteiligen
B *v.t.* (contribute) beisteuern

chip: ~ and 'pin *n.* Chip und Pin; **~-based** *adj.* chipbasiert; **~ technology** Chiptechnologie, *die;* **~-based card** *n.* Chipkarte, *die;* **~board** *n.* Spanplatte, *die*

chipmunk /ˈtʃɪpmʌŋk/ *n.* (Zool.) Chipmunk, *das*

chipolata /tʃɪpəˈlɑːtə/ *n.*: *kleine, scharf gewürzte Wurst;* Chipolata, *die*

ˈ**chip pan** *n.* Fritteuse, *die*

chipper /ˈtʃɪpə(r)/ *adj.* fröhlich

chipping /ˈtʃɪpɪŋ/ *n.* Splitter, *der;* (stone also) Steinchen, *das;* **~s** (Road Constr.) Splitt, *der;* **'loose ~s'** „Rollsplitt"

chippy /ˈtʃɪpɪ/ *n.* (Brit. coll.) Pommes-frites-Bude, *die;* Frittenbude, *die* (ugs.)

chip: ~set *n.* (Computing) Chipsatz, *der;* **~ shop** *n.* (Brit.) ▸**chippy**; **~ shot** *n.* (Golf) kurzer Annäherungsschlag; (Footb.) kurzer Heber

chiropodist /kɪˈrɒpədɪst, ʃɪˈrɒpədɪst/ *n.* ▸❶ **p. 1260** Fußpfleger, *der*/-pflegerin, *die*

chiropody /kɪˈrɒpədɪ, ʃɪˈrɒpədɪ/ *n.* Fußpflege, *die*

chiropractor /kaɪərəˈpræktə(r)/ *n.* ▸❶ **p. 1260** (Med.) Chiropraktiker, *der*/-praktikerin, *die*

chirp /tʃɜːp/

A *v.i.* zwitschern; ‹*Sperling:*› tschilpen; ‹*Grille:*› zirpen; (talk merrily) jubilieren

B *n.* Zwitschern, *das;* (of sparrow) Tschilpen, *das;* (of grasshopper) Zirpen, *das*

Phrasal verb

• **~ ˈup** *v.i.* munter werden

chirpily /ˈtʃɜːpɪlɪ/ *adv.*, **chirpy** /ˈtʃɜːpɪ/ *adj.* (coll.) vergnügt

chirrup /ˈtʃɪrəp/

A *v.i.* zwitschern; ‹*Sperling:*› tschilpen

B *n.* Zwitschern, *das;* (of sparrow) Tschilpen, *das*

chisel /ˈtʃɪzl/

A *n.* Meißel, *der;* (for wood) Stemmeisen, *das;* Beitel, *der; see also* **cold chisel**

B *v.t.*, (Brit.) **-ll-** **1** meißeln; (in wood) hauen; stemmen; **finely ~led features** fein gemeißelte [Gesichts]züge (geh.) **2** (coll.: defraud) hereinlegen (ugs.); **~ sb. out of sth.** jmdn. um etw. bringen

chiseller (*Amer.:* **chiseler**) /ˈtʃɪzələ(r)/ *n.* (coll.: swindler) Betrüger, *der*/Betrügerin, *die*

chit¹ /tʃɪt/ *n.* **1** (young child) Balg, *das od. der* (bes. südd.); Gör, *das* (nordd.); **be a mere ~ of a child** nur ein Kind sein **2** (usu. derog.: woman) junges Ding; **only a ~ of a girl** noch ein halbes Kind

chit² *n.* (note) Notiz, *die;* (certificate) Zeugnis, *das;* (bill) Rechnung, *die;* (receipt) Quittung, *die;* (from doctor) Krankmeldung, *die*

chit-chat /ˈtʃɪttʃæt/

A *n.* Plauderei, *die*

B *v.i.*, **-tt-** plaudern

chitterling /ˈtʃɪtəlɪŋ/ *n.*, *usu. in pl.* Schweinsdarm, *der*

chivalric /ˈʃɪvlrɪk/ *adj.* (of chivalry) **the ~ ages** die Ritterzeit

chivalrous /ˈʃɪvlrəs/ *adj.* ritterlich; **~ age** Ritterzeit, *die;* **~ deed** ritterliche Tat

chivalrously /ˈʃɪvlrəslɪ/ *adv.* ritterlich

chivalry /ˈʃɪvlrɪ/ *n.*, *no pl.* **1** Ritterlichkeit, *die* **2** (medieval knightly system) Rittertum, *das;* **Age of C~:** Ritterzeit, *die;* **the Age of C~ is not dead** es gibt noch richtige Kavaliere

chives /tʃaɪvz/ *n. pl.* Schnittlauch, *der*

chiv[v]y /ˈtʃɪvɪ/ *v.t.* hetzen; (harass) schikanieren; **~ sb. into doing sth.** jmdn. drängen, etw. zu tun; **~ sb. about sth.** jmdn. wegen etw. drängen

Phrasal verb

• **~ aˈlong** *v.t.* antreiben

chloride /ˈklɔːraɪd/ *n.* (Chem.) Chlorid, *das;* (bleaching agent) chloridhaltiges Bleichmittel

chlorinate /ˈklɔːrɪneɪt/ *v.t.* chloren

chlorination /klɔːrɪˈneɪʃn/ *n.* Chlorung, *die*

chlorine /ˈklɔːriːn/ *n.* Chlor, *das*

chlorofluorocarbon /klɔːrəʊflʊərəʊˈkɑːbən/ *n.* Chlorfluorkohlenstoff, *der*

chloroform /ˈklɒrəfɔːm/

A *n.* Chloroform, *das*

B *v.t.* chloroformieren

chlorophyll /ˈklɒrəfɪl/ *n.* (Bot.) Chlorophyll, *das*

choc /tʃɒk/ *n.* (Brit. coll.) Schokopraline, *die*

chocaholic /tʃɒkəˈhɒlɪk/ ▸ **chocoholic**

ˈ**choc ice** *n.* Eis mit Schokoladenüberzug

chock /tʃɒk/

A *n.* Bremsklotz, *der;* (on rail) Bremsschuh, *der*

B *v.t.* blockieren

ˈ**chock-a-block** *pred. adj.* (esp. Brit. coll.) voll gepfropft

chocker /ˈtʃɒkə(r)/ *adj.* (Brit. sl.) sauer (salopp); **be ~ with** *or* **of sth.** von etw. die Nase gestrichen voll haben (salopp)

ˈ**chock-full** *pred. adj.* (coll.) gestopft voll (ugs.); **~ with sth.** mit etw. voll gepfropft

chockie /ˈtʃɒkɪ/ ▸**choc**

chocoholic /tʃɒkəˈhɒlɪk/ *n.* (coll.) [absoluter] Schokofan (ugs.); (addict) Schokoladensüchtige, *der/die*

chocolate /ˈtʃɒkələt, ˈtʃɒklət/

A *n.* **1** Schokolade, *die;* (sweetmeat) Praline, *die;* **drinking ~:** Trinkschokolade, *die* **2** (colour) Schokoladenbraun, *das*

B *adj.* **1** (with flavour of ~) Schokoladen- **2** (with colour of ~) **~[-brown]** schokoladenbraun

chocolate: ~ ˈbiscuit *n.* Schokoladenkeks, *der;* **~ box** **A** *n.* Pralinenschachtel, *die;* Bonbonniere, *die;* **B** *adj.* (fig.) kitschig; **~-coated** *adj.* mit Schokoladeüberzug *nachgestellt;* **~ drop** *n.* Schokodrops, *der od. das;* **~ éˈclair** *n.* Schokoladenéclair, *das*

chocolatey /ˈtʃɒklətɪ/ *adj.* schokoladig

choice /tʃɔɪs/

A *n.* **1** Wahl, *die;* **if the ~ were mine, if I had the ~:** wenn ich die Wahl hätte; **by** *or* **for ~:** am liebsten; **of my/his** *etc.* **~:** meiner/seiner *usw.* Wahl; **take your ~:** suchen Sie sich (*Dat.*) eine/einen/eins aus; wählen Sie; (truculently) entscheiden Sie sich; **take one's ~ of sth. from sth.** etw. aus etw. auswählen; **make a [good] ~:** eine [gute] Wahl treffen; **make a careful ~:** sorgfältig [aus]wählen; **give sb. the ~:** jmdm. die Wahl lassen; **the ~ is yours** Sie haben die Wahl; **you have a free ~:** Sie können frei wählen; **do sth. from ~:** etw. freiwillig tun; **if I were given the ~:** wenn man mir die Wahl ließe; **have no ~ but to do sth.** keine andere Wahl haben, als etw. zu tun; **leave sb. no ~:** jmdm. keine [andere] Wahl lassen; **you have several ~s** Sie haben mehrere Möglichkeiten **2** (thing chosen) **his ~ of wallpaper was ...:** die Tapete, die er sich ausgesucht hatte, war ...; **the curtains were your ~:** die Vorhänge hast du ausgesucht; **this is my ~:** ich habe mich dafür entschieden; *see also* **Hobson's choice** **3** (variety) Auswahl, *die;* **there is a ~ of three** es gibt drei zur Auswahl; **be spoilt for ~:** die Qual der Wahl haben; **have a ~:** die Auswahl haben

B *adj.* ausgewählt; auserlesen (geh.); **~ wine** erlesener Wein (geh.); **~ tomatoes/fruit** Tomaten/Obst erster Wahl

choir /ˈkwaɪə(r)/ *n.* (also Archit.) Chor, *der*

choir: ~boy *n.* Chorknabe, *der;* **~master** *n.* Chorleiter, *der;* **~ practice** *n.* Chorprobe, *die;* **~ school** *n.* [*Konfessions*]*schule für Chorknaben;* **~-screen** *n.* Chorschranke, *die;* **~-stall** ▸**stall¹ A 3**

choke /tʃəʊk/

A *v.t.* **1** (lit. or fig.) ersticken; **a fish bone was choking him** er drohte an einer Fischgräte zu ersticken; **you'll ~ yourself** du wirst ersticken; **in a voice ~d with emotion** (fig.) mit vor Erregung versagender Stimme; **be/get ~d up about sth.** (fig. coll.) sich (*Dat.*) etw. sehr zu Herzen nehmen **2** (strangle) erdrosseln; **~ to death** erdrosseln; **the collar was choking him** der Kragen würgte ihn **3** (fill completely) voll stopfen; (block up) verstopfen

B *v.i.* **1** (temporarily) keine Luft [mehr] bekommen; (permanently) ersticken (**on** an + *Dat.*) **2** (from emotion) **he almost ~d with rage** er brachte vor Wut fast keinen Ton heraus

C *n.* **1** (Motor Veh.) Choke, *der* **2** (Electr.) Drosselspule, *die*

Phrasal verbs

• **~ ˈback** *v.t.* unterdrücken ‹*Wut*›; zurückhalten ‹*Tränen*›; hinunterschlucken (ugs.) ‹*Wut, Worte*›

• **~ ˈdown** *v.t.* unterdrücken

• **~ ˈoff** *v.t.* (fig. coll.) abwimmeln (ugs.); (tell off) einen Rüffel verpassen (+ *Dat.*)

choked /tʃəʊkt/ *adj.* (coll.: disgusted) sauer (salopp)

ˈ**choke point** *n.* (Amer.) Nadelöhr, *das*

choker /ˈtʃəʊkə(r)/ *n.* (high collar) Stehkragen, *der;* (necklace) Halsband, *das*

choler /ˈkɒlə(r)/ *n.* **1** (Hist.) Galle, *die* **2** (poet./arch.: anger) **in ~:** wutentbrannt; **fit of ~:** Zornesausbruch, *der* (geh.)

cholera /ˈkɒlərə/ *n.* ▸❶ **p. 1231** (Med.) Cholera, *die*

choleric /ˈkɒlərɪk/ *adj.* cholerisch

cholesterol /kəˈlestərɒl/ *n.* (Med.) Cholesterin, *das*

chomp /tʃɒmp/ ▸**champ¹**

choo-choo /ˈtʃuːtʃuː/ *n.* (child lang./coll.) Puffpuff, *die* (Kinderspr.)

choose /tʃuːz/

A *v.t.*, **chose** /tʃəʊz/, **chosen** /ˈtʃəʊzn/ **1** (select) wählen; (from a group) auswählen; **~ a career** einen Beruf wählen; **~ sb. as** *or* **to be** *or* **for leader** jmdn. zum Anführer wählen; **~ sb. from among ...:** jmdn. unter (+ *Dat.*) *od.* aus ... auswählen; **carefully chosen words** sorgfältig gewählte Worte; **the chosen [few]** (Theol.) die [wenigen] Auserwählten; **the chosen people** *or* **race** (Theol.) das auserwählte Volk **2** (decide) **~/~ not to do sth.** sich dafür/dagegen entscheiden, etw. zu tun; **he chose rather to study** er zog es vor zu lernen; **she did not ~ to wear ˈblack** sie zog es vor, nicht Schwarz zu tragen; **she did not ˈ~ to wear black** sie hat nicht freiwillig Schwarz getragen; **there's nothing/not much/little to ~ between them** sie unterscheiden sich in nichts/nicht sehr/nur wenig voneinander

B *v.i.*, **chose, chosen** wählen; **when I ~:** wenn es mir passt; **do just as you ~:** machen Sie es so, wie Sie möchten; **~ between ...:** zwischen ... wählen; **~ from sth.** aus etw./(from several) unter etw. (*Dat.*) [aus]wählen; **there are several to ~ from** es stehen mehrere zur Auswahl; **he cannot ~ but submit** er hat keine andere Wahl, als nachzugeben; **if you/we** *etc.* **so ~:** wenn Sie/wir *usw.* [es] möchten *od.* wollen; **as you ~:** wie Sie möchten

chooser /ˈtʃuːzə(r)/ ▸**beggar A 1**

choos[e]y /ˈtʃuːzɪ/ *adj.* (coll.) wählerisch

chop¹ /tʃɒp/

A *n.* **1** Hieb, *der* **2** (of meat) Kotelett, *das* **3** (coll.) **get the ~** (be killed) abgemurkst werden (salopp); (be dismissed) rausgeworfen werden (ugs.); **sth. gets the ~:** etw. wird abgeschafft; **give sb. the ~** (dismiss) jmdn. rauswerfen (ugs.); (kill) jmdn. abmurksen (salopp); **be due for the ~:** die längste Zeit existiert haben (ugs.). *See also* **karate chop**

B *v.t.*, **-pp-** **1** hacken ‹*Holz*›; klein schneiden ‹*Fleisch, Obst, Gemüse*›; **they ~ped a way through the undergrowth** sie schlugen einen Weg durch das Unterholz; **~ped herbs** gehackte Kräuter **2** (Sport) schneiden ‹*Ball*›

C *v.i.*, **-pp-:** **~ [away] at sth.** auf etw. (*Akk.*) einhacken; **~ through the bone** den Knochen durchhacken

Phrasal verbs

• **~ ˈdown** *v.t.* fällen ‹*Baum*›; umhauen ‹*Busch, Pfosten*›

• **~ ˈoff** *v.t.* abhacken

• **~ ˈup** *v.t.* klein schneiden ‹*Fleisch, Obst, Gemüse*›; zerhacken ‹*Möbel*›; zerkleinern ‹*Holz*›; **~ped-up parsley** [klein]gehackte Petersilie

chop² *n.* **1** (jaw) Kiefer, *der* **2** *in pl.* Maul, *das;* (coll.: person's mouth) Klappe, *die* (*salopp*); *see also* **lick A 1**

chop³ *v.i.*, **-pp-:** **she's always ~ping and changing** sie überlegt es sich (*Dat.*) dauernd anders; **keep ~ping and changing** ‹*Wetter:*› [sich] dauernd ändern

Phrasal verb

• **~ aˈbout** *v.i.* (coll.) sprunghaft sein; ‹*Wind:*› umspringen

ˈ**chophouse** *n.* (coll.) Gaststätte, *die*

chopper /ˈtʃɒpə(r)/ *n.* **1** (axe) Beil, *das;* (cleaver) Hackbeil, *das* **2** (coll.: helicopter) Hubschrauber, *der* **3** *in pl.* (coll.: teeth) Beißerchen (ugs.)

C

chopping: ~ board *n.* Hackbrett, *das;* **~ knife** *n.* Hackmesser, *das;* (with curved blade) Wiegemesser, *das*

choppy /ˈtʃɒpɪ/ *adj.* bewegt; kabbelig (Seemannsspr.)

ˈchopstick *n.* [Ess]stäbchen, *das*

chop suey /tʃɒpˈsuːɪ, tʃɒpˈsjuːɪ/ *n.* (Gastr.) Chopsuey, *das*

choral¹ /ˈkɔːrl/ *adj.* Chor-; chorisch; **~ piece** Komposition für Chor

chorale (**choral²**) /kɔːˈrɑːl/ *n.* **1** Choral, *der* **2** (group) Chor, *der*

choral/ˈkɔːrl/: **~ service** *n.* Gottesdienst mit Chorgesang; **~ society** *n.* Gesangverein, *der*

chord¹ /kɔːd/ *n.* **1** (string of harp etc.; also fig.) Saite, *die;* **strike a [familiar/responsive] ~ with sb.** (fig.) bei jmdm. eine Saite zum Erklingen bringen/bei jmdm. Echo finden; **touch the right ~** (fig.) den richtigen Ton anschlagen *od.* treffen **2** (Math.) Sehne, *die;* (Aeron.: of wing) Flügeltiefe, *die*

chord² *n.* (Mus.) Akkord, *der;* **common ~:** Dreiklang [mit reiner Quinte]

chore /tʃɔː(r)/ *n.* [lästige] Routinearbeit; **do the [general] household ~s** die üblichen Hausarbeiten erledigen; **writing letters is a ~:** Briefe zu schreiben ist eine lästige Pflicht

chorea /kəˈriːə/ *n.* (Med.) Chorea, *die* (fachspr.); Veitstanz, *der*

choreograph /ˈkɒrɪəgrɑːf/ *v.t. & i.* choreographieren

choreographer /kɒrɪˈɒgrəfə(r)/ *n.* ▸ **i** **p. 1260** Choreograph, *der*/Choreographin, *die*

choreographic /kɒrɪəˈgræfɪk/ *adj.* choreographisch

choreography /kɒrɪˈɒgrəfɪ/ *n.* Choreographie, *die*

chorister /ˈkɒrɪstə(r)/ *n.* **1** (choirboy) Chorknabe, *der* **2** (Amer.: leader of choir) Chorleiter, *der*

chortle /ˈtʃɔːtl/

A *v.i.* vor Lachen glucksen; (contemptuously) [hämisch] kichern

B *n.* Glucksen, *das;* **reply/say with a ~:** glucksend erwidern/sagen

chorus /ˈkɔːrəs/

A *n.* **1** (utterance) Chor, *der;* **they broke [out] into a ~ of ...:** sie fingen an, im Chor ... zu singen/rufen; **say sth. in ~:** etw. im Chor sagen; **the football fans kept up a ~ of 'Scotland'** die Fußballfans hörten nicht auf, im Chor „Scotland" zu rufen **2** (of singers) Chor, *der;* (of dancers) Ballett, *das;* **be in the ~:** zum Chor/zum Ballett gehören **3** (of popular song) Refrain, *der* **4** (Mus.: composition) Chor, *der*

B *v.t.* im Chor singen/sprechen

chorus: ~ girl *n.* Chorsängerin, *die;* (dancer) [Revue]girl, *das;* **~ line** *n.* Ballett, *das;* **~-master** *n.* Chorleiter, *der*

chose, chosen ▸ **choose**

chough /tʃʌf/ *n.* (Ornith.) **[Cornish] ~:** Alpenkrähe, *die;* **[alpine] ~:** Alpendohle, *die*

choux /ʃuː/ *n.* **~ [pastry]** Brandteig, *der*

chow /tʃaʊ/ *n.* **1** (dog) Chow-Chow, *der* **2** (Amer. sl.: food) Futterage, *die* (ugs.); Futter, *das* (salopp)

chowder /ˈtʃaʊdə(r)/ *n.* (Amer.) *Suppe od. Eintopf mit Fisch od. Muscheln, Pökelfleisch od. Schinken, Milch, Kartoffeln u. Gemüse*

Christ /kraɪst/

A *n.* Christus (*der*); *see also* **before B 1**

B *int.* (sl.) **[oh] ~!, ~ almighty!** Herrgott noch mal! (ugs.)

Christadelphian /krɪstəˈdelfɪən/ *n.* Christadelphian, *der* (*Mitglied einer chiliastischen Sekte*)

ˈChrist child *n.* Christkind, *das*

christen /ˈkrɪsn/ *v.t.* **1** taufen; **she was ~ed Martha** sie wurde [auf den Namen] Martha getauft **2** (coll.: use for first time) einweihen (ugs. scherzh.)

Christendom /ˈkrɪsndəm/ *n., no pl., no art.* die christliche Welt; (Christians) die Christenheit; die Christen

christening /ˈkrɪsənɪŋ/ *n.* Taufe, *die;* **her ~ will be next Sunday** sie wird nächsten Sonntag getauft

Christian /ˈkrɪstjən/

A *adj.* christlich

B *n.* Christ, *der*/Christin, *die*

Christian: ~ ˈDemocrat *n.* Christdemokrat, *der*/-demokratin, *die;* **~ Demoˈcratic** *adj.* christdemokratisch; **~ Democratic Party** Christlich-Demokratische Partei; **~ ˈera** *n.* **in the first centuries of the ~:** in den ersten Jahrhunderten christlicher Zeitrechnung

Christianity /krɪstɪˈænɪtɪ/ *n., no pl., no art.* das Christentum

Christian: ~ name *n.* Vorname, *der;* **~ ˈScience** *n.* Christian Science, *die;* Christliche Wissenschaft; **~ ˈScientist** *n.* Christian Scientist, *der;* Christlicher Wissenschaftler

Christlike /ˈkraɪstlaɪk/ *adj.* christusgleich

Christmas /ˈkrɪsməs/ *n.* ▸ **i** **p. 1189** Weihnachten, *das od. Pl.;* **merry** *or* **happy ~:** frohe *od.* fröhliche Weihnachten; **what did you get for ~?** was hast du zu Weihnachten bekommen?; **at ~:** [zu *od.* an] Weihnachten

Christmas

In England und Amerika sind keine bestimmten Bräuche mit Heiligabend verbunden. Allerdings gehen manche Leute zur Mitternachtsmesse. Die meisten Kinder hängen einen Strumpf am Ende ihres Bettes oder am Kamin auf, den der Tradition zufolge *Father Christmas*, auch *Santa Claus* oder kurz *Santa* genannt, in der Nacht vom 24. zum 25. füllt. Oft stellen die Kinder noch einen Teller mit Weihnachtsgebäck für Santa bereit, damit er bei der Geschenkausgabe etwas zum Knabbern hat. Dann gehen sie in Vorfreude auf den 25. früh ins Bett. Wenn die Kinder schlafen, füllen die Eltern heimlich den Strumpf mit Süßigkeiten und kleinen Geschenken. Am 25. findet morgens die Bescherung unter dem Weihnachtsbaum statt. Mittags versammelt sich die ganze Familie zum traditionellen Weihnachtsessen — meist gibt es Truthahn. *Christmas pudding*, *mince pies* (gefüllte süße Pasteten) und *Christmas cake* (mit Marzipan und Zuckerguss verzierter, reichhaltiger Gewürzkuchen) gehören zum typischen britischen Weihnachtsgebäck.

Christmas: ~ box *n.* (Brit.) *Geschenk/Trinkgeld zu Weihnachten für den Postboten, Zeitungsjungen usw.;* **~ cake** *n.* Weihnachtskuchen, *der; mit Marzipan und Zuckerguss verzierter, reichhaltiger Gewürzkuchen;* **~ card** *n.* Weihnachtskarte, *die;* **~ ˈcarol** *n.* Weihnachtslied, *das;* **~ ˈDay** *n.* erster Weihnachtsfeiertag; **~ ˈEve** *n.* Heiligabend, *der;* **~ ˈholiday** *n.* Weihnachtsurlaub, *der;* **the ~ holidays** die Weihnachtsferien; **~ present** *n.* Weihnachtsgeschenk, *das;* **~ ˈpudding** *n.* Plumpudding, *der;* **~ ˈrose** *n.* Christrose, *die;* **~ ˈstocking** *n.: von den Kindern am Heiligabend aufgehängter Strumpf, den der Weihnachtsmann mit Geschenken füllen soll*

Christmassy /ˈkrɪsməsɪ/ *adj.* weihnachtlich; **it doesn't feel very ~:** es herrscht keine rechte Weihnachtsstimmung

Christmas: ~-tide, ~ time *ns.* Weihnachtszeit, *die;* **at ~-tide** *or* **~ time** in der *od.* zur Weihnachtszeit; **~ tree** *n.* Weihnachtsbaum, *der*

chromatic /krəˈmætɪk/ *adj.* chromatisch

chromatic ˈscale *n.* (Mus.) chromatische Tonleiter

chromatography /krəʊməˈtɒgrəfɪ/ *n.* (Chem.) Chromatographie, *die*

chrome /krəʊm/ *n.* **1** (chromium-plate) Chrom, *das* **2** (colour) Chromgelb, *das*

chrome: ~ ˈsteel *n.* Chromstahl, *der;* **~ ˈyellow** ▸ **chrome 1**

chromium /ˈkrəʊmɪəm/ *n.* Chrom, *das*

chromium: ~-plate **A** *n.* Chrom, *das;* **B** *v.t.* verchromen; **~-plated** *adj.* verchromt; **~-ˈplating** *n.* Verchromung, *die*

chromosome /ˈkrəʊməsəʊm/ *n.* (Biol.) Chromosom, *das*

ˈchromosome map *n.* (Biol.) Chromosomenkarte, *die*

chronic /ˈkrɒnɪk/ *adj.* **1** chronisch; **~ sufferers from arthritis** Personen, die an chronischer Arthritis leiden; **~ fatigue syndrome** chronisches Müdigkeitssyndrom; **he had been plagued by ~ doubts** ihn hatten ständig Zweifel geplagt **2** (Brit. coll.: bad, intense) katastrophal (ugs.); **be ~:** eine [einzige] Katastrophe sein (ugs.); **it hurt something ~:** es hat wahnsinnig weh getan (ugs.)

chronically /ˈkrɒnɪkəlɪ/ *adv.* chronisch; **she was ~ afraid of ...:** sie hatte [eine] chronische Angst vor ...

chronicle /ˈkrɒnɪkl/

A *n.* **1** Chronik, *die* **2** (account) Schilderung, *die* **3** (Bibl.) **C~s** Chronik, *die*

B *v.t.* [chronologisch] aufzeichnen; **he ~d these events** er verfasste eine Chronik dieser Ereignisse

chronicler /ˈkrɒnɪklə(r)/ *n.* ▸ **i** **p. 1260** Chronist, *der*

chronological /krɒnəˈlɒdʒɪkl/ *adj.*, **chronologically** /krɒnəˈlɒdʒɪkəlɪ/ *adv.* chronologisch

chronology /krəˈnɒlədʒɪ/ *n.* Chronologie, *die;* (table) Zeittafel, *die*

chronometer /krəˈnɒmɪtə(r)/ *n.* Chronometer, *das*

chrysalis /ˈkrɪsəlɪs/ *n., pl.* **~es** *or* **chrysalides** /krɪˈsælɪdiːz/ (Zool.) **1** (pupa) Chrysalide, *die* (Zool.); Puppe, *die* **2** (case enclosing pupa) Puppenhülle, *die*

chrysanth /krɪˈsænθ/ *n.* (coll.) ▸ **chrysanthemum**

chrysanthemum /krɪˈsænθɪməm/ *n.* (Bot.) **1** (flower) Chrysantheme, *die* **2** (plant) Chrysanthemum, *das;* Wucherblume, *die*

chub /tʃʌb/ *n., pl. same* (Zool.) Döbel, *der*

chubby /ˈtʃʌbɪ/ *adj.* **1** (plump) pummelig; rundlich ‹*Gesicht*›; **~ cheeks** Pausbacken (fam.) **2** (plump-faced) pausbäckig

chuck¹ /tʃʌk/

A *v.t.* **1** (coll.: throw) schmeißen (ugs.) **2** **~ sb. under the chin** jmdm. einen Stups unters Kinn geben **3** (coll.: throw out) wegschmeißen (ugs.); **~ it!** (coll.) hör schon auf [damit]!; **~ the whole thing** alles hinschmeißen

B *n.* **1** **give sb. a ~ under the chin** jmdm. einen Stups unters Kinn geben **2** (coll.: dismissal) **give sb. the ~ [from his/her job]** jmdn. [aus der Firma *usw.*] rausschmeißen (ugs.); **get the ~:** rausfliegen (ugs.)

Phrasal verbs

- **~ aˈway** *v.t.* (coll.) wegschmeißen (ugs.); (fig.: waste) zum Fenster rauswerfen (ugs.) ‹*Geld*› (**on** für); vertun ‹*Chance, Gelegenheit*›
- **~ ˈout** *v.t.* (coll.) wegschmeißen (ugs.); (fig.: eject) rausschmeißen (ugs.)

chuck² *n.* (of drill, lathe) Futter, *das*

chuck³ *n.* (Amer. coll.: food) Futter, *das* (salopp)

chucker-out /tʃʌkəˈraʊt/ *n.* (coll.) Rausschmeißer, *der* (ugs.)

chuckle /ˈtʃʌkl/

A *v.i.* **1** leise [vor sich hin] lachen (**at** über + *Akk.*) **2** (exult) sich (*Dat.*) eins lachen

B *n.* leises, glucksendes Lachen; **have a ~ [to oneself] about sth.** leise über etw. (*Akk.*) vor sich hin lachen

chuckle: ~-head *n.* Schwachkopf, *der* (abwertend); **~-headed** *adj.* schwachköpfig (abwertend)

ˈchuck wagon *n.* (Amer. coll.) *Proviantwagen mit Kochvorrichtung (auf einer Ranch usw.)*

chuff /tʃʌf/ *v.i.* puffen (ugs.)

chuffed /tʃʌft/ *pred. adj.* (Brit. coll.) zufrieden (**about, at, with** über + *Akk.*); **be ~:** sich freuen

chug /tʃʌg/

A *v.i.*, **-gg-** ‹*Motor:*› tuckern

B *n.* Tuckern, *das*

chum /tʃʌm/ *n.* (coll.) **1** Kumpel, *der* (salopp); **be great ~s** dicke Freunde sein (ugs.) **2** (Austral., NZ) **new ~:** Neuling, *der*

Phrasal verb

- ~ **'up** *v.i.* (coll.) ~ **up [with sb.]** sich [mit jmdm.] anfreunden

chummy /'tʃʌmɪ/ *adj.* (coll.) freundlich; **be ~ with sb.** mit jmdm. dick befreundet sein (ugs.)

chump /tʃʌmp/ *n.* **1** (coll.: foolish person) Trottel, *der* (ugs.) **2** **be off one's ~** (Brit. coll.) nicht bei Trost sein (ugs.)

chump 'chop *n.* ≈ Lammkotelett, *das*

chunder /'tʃʌndə(r)/ (coll.)
A *v.i.* kotzen (ugs.)
B *n., no pl.* Kotze, *die* (ugs.)

chunk /tʃʌŋk/ *n.* dickes Stück; (broken off) Brocken, *der;* (large amount) guter Brocken; **~ of wood** Holzklotz, *der*

chunky /'tʃʌŋkɪ/ *adj.* **1** (containing chunks) ‹*Orangenmarmelade, Hundefutter*› mit ganzen Stücken **2** (small and sturdy, short and thick) stämmig; **~ fingers** kurze, dicke Finger; **~ book** kleines, dickes Buch **3** (made of thick, bulky material) dick ‹*Pullover, Strickjacke*›

Chunnel /'tʃʌnl/ *n.* (Brit. coll.) [Ärmel]kanaltunnel, *der*

chunter /'tʃʌntə(r)/ *v.i.* (coll.) **1** (murmur) brummeln; brabbeln **2** (grumble) murren

chupatty ▸ **chapat[t]i**

church /tʃɜːtʃ/ *n.* **1** Kirche, *die;* **in** *or* **at ~:** in der Kirche; **after ~:** nach der Kirche; **go to ~:** in die *od.* zur Kirche gehen **2** **C~** (body) die Kirche; **go into the C~:** Geistlicher werden; **the C~ of England** die Kirche von England; **the C~ militant/triumphant** Ecclesia militans/triumphans, *die* (Rel.)

church: ~goer *n.* Kirchgänger, *der*/-gängerin, *die;* **~going** **A** *n., no pl.* Kirchenbesuch, *der;* **B** *attrib. adj.* regelmäßig den Gottesdienst besuchend; **~ 'hall** *n.* (room) Gemeindesaal, *der;* (building) Gemeindehaus, *das;* **~man** /'tʃɜːtʃmən/ *n., pl.* **~men** /-mən/ **1** (member of clergy) Geistliche, *der;* **2** (member of church) Mitglied der Kirche; **~ 'mouse** *n.* **as poor as a ~ mouse** arm wie eine Kirchenmaus (ugs. scherzh.); **~ parade** *n.* gemeinsamer Kirchgang (*von Soldaten, Pfadfindern usw.*); **~warden** *n.* **1** Kirchenvorsteher, *der*/-vorsteherin, *die;* **2** (Amer.: **~** administrator) [*für die Finanzen zuständiger*] *Beauftragter der Protestantischen Episkopalkirche;* **~woman** *n.* [weibliches] Mitglied der Kirche

> **Church of England**
>
> Die anglikanische Kirche ist die englische Staatskirche. Ihr Oberhaupt ist der regierende Monarch. Die Bischöfe, an deren Spitze der Erzbischof von Canterbury steht, werden im Namen des Königs oder der Königin vom Premierminister ernannt. Die Trennung von der römisch-katholischen Kirche erfolgte im 16. Jahrhundert durch die Lossagung Heinrichs VIII. vom Papst. Er ließ sich im **Act of Supremacy** zum Oberhaupt der Kirche erklären, um eine Scheidung von Katharina von Aragonien zu ermöglichen. Die Hauptrichtung innerhalb der anglikanischen Kirche ist die *High Church*; hochkirchlich und liturgiebetont, steht sie der katholischen Kirche am nächsten. Die vom Methodismus beeinflusste *Low Church* bezieht sich unter Verzicht auf strenge liturgische Ordnung auf die Bibel.

> **Church of Scotland**
>
> Die Staatskirche von Schottland baut auf der Presbyterialverfassung auf. Durch das „Revolution Settlement" von 1690 wurde die reformierte presbyterianische Kirche zur Nationalkirche Schottlands. Im Gegensatz zur **Church of England** nennen sich die Geistlichen Pfarrer und nicht Priester. Eine Vollversammlung aus Pfarrern und leitenden Ältesten tritt jährlich zur Wahl des für ein Jahr amtierenden Moderators zusammen.

churchy /'tʃɜːtʃɪ/ *adj.* streng kirchlich; kirchenfromm (abwertend)

'churchyard *n.* Kirchhof, *der* (veralt.); Friedhof, *der* (*bei einer Kirche*)

churl /tʃɜːl/ *n.* **1** (derog.) (ill-bred person) ungehobelter Kerl (ugs. abwertend); (surly person) Griesgram, *der* (abwertend) **2** (arch.) (peasant) Bauer, *der;* (person of low birth) einfacher *od.* gemeiner Mann

churlish /'tʃɜːlɪʃ/ *adj.* (derog.) (ill-bred) ungehobelt (abwertend); (surly) griesgrämig (abwertend)

churlishly /'tʃɜːlɪʃlɪ/ *adv.* (derog.) ▸ **churlish**: ungehobelt; griesgrämig

churlishness /'tʃɜːlɪʃnɪs/ *n., no pl.* (*derog.*) ▸ **churlish**: Ungehobeltheit, *die;* Griesgrämigkeit, *die*

churn /tʃɜːn/
A *n.* (Brit.) **1** (for making butter) Butterfass, *das* **2** (milk can) Milchkanne, *die*
B *v.t.* **1** verbuttern; **~ butter** buttern **2** aufwühlen ‹*Wasser, Schlamm*›
C *v.i.* ‹*Meer:*› wallen (geh.); ‹*Schiffsschraube:*› wirbeln; ‹*Räder:*› durchdrehen; **my stomach was ~ing** mir drehte sich der Magen um

Phrasal verbs

- ~ **'out** *v.t.* massenweise produzieren (ugs.); **he's been ~ing out three books a year** er hat pro Jahr drei Bücher produziert
- ~ **'up** *v.t.* aufwühlen

'churn rate *n.* (Commerc.) Kündigungsrate, *die;* Kündigungsquote, *die*

chute /ʃuːt/ *n.* **1** Schütte, *die;* (for persons) Rutsche, *die;* **escape ~** (in aircraft) Notrutsche, *die* **2** (coll.: parachute) [Fall]schirm, *der*

chutney /'tʃʌtnɪ/ *n.* Chutney, *das*

chutzpah /'hʊtspə/ *n.* (coll.) Chuzpe, *die* (salopp abwertend)

CI *abbr.* (Brit.) = **Channel Islands**

CIA *abbr.* (Amer.) = **Central Intelligence Agency** CIA, *der od. die*

ciborium /sɪ'bɔːrɪəm/ *n., pl.* **ciboria** /sɪ'bɔːrɪə/ (Archit., Eccl.) Ziborium, *das*

cicada /sɪ'kɑːdə/ *n.* (Zool.) Zikade, die

CID *abbr.* (Brit.) = **Criminal Investigation Department** C. I. D.; **the ~:** die Kripo

cider /'saɪdə(r)/ *n.* ≈ Apfelwein, *der;* (from France) Cidre, *der*

cider: ~ apple *n.* Mostapfel, *der;* **~ press** *n.* Mostpresse, *die*

cig /sɪg/ *n.* (coll.) Glimmstängel, *der* (ugs.)

cigar /sɪ'gɑː(r)/ *n.* Zigarre, *die;* **close, but no ~** (Amer. coll.) knapp daneben ist auch vorbei

cigarette /sɪgə'ret/ *n.* Zigarette, *die*

cigarette: ~ ash *n., no pl.* Zigarettenasche, *die;* **~ card** *n.* Zigarettenbild, *das;* **~ case** *n.* Zigarettenetui, *das;* **~ end** *n.* Zigarettenstummel, *der;* **~ holder** *n.* Zigarettenspitze, *die;* **~ lighter** *n.* Feuerzeug, *das;* (in car) Zigarettenanzünder, *der;* **~ machine** *n.* Zigarettenautomat, *der;* **~ packet** *n.* Zigarettenschachtel, *die;* **~ paper** *n.* Zigarettenpapier, *das*

cigar: ~ lighter ▸ **cigarette lighter**; **~-shaped** *adj.* zigarrenförmig

cilium /'sɪlɪəm/ *n., pl.* **cilia** /'sɪlɪə/ (Biol., Anat.) Wimper, *die;* Zilie, *die* (fachspr.)

C.-in-C. *abbr.* (Mil.) = **Commander-in-Chief**

cinch /sɪntʃ/
A *n.* **1** (coll.) (easy thing) Klacks, *der* (ugs.); Kinderspiel, *das;* (Amer.: sure thing) todsichere Sache (ugs.); **that's a ~:** [das ist] ganz klar! (ugs.); klarer Fall! (ugs.) **2** (Amer.: saddle girth) Sattelgurt, *der*
B *v.t.* (Amer.) **1** (coll.: make certain of) **~ sth. for sb.** jmdm. etw. sichern **2** (put girth on) **~ a horse** den Sattelgurt eines Pferdes schnallen

cinchona /sɪŋ'kəʊnə/ *n.* **1** (Med.) Chinarinde, *die* **2** (Bot.) Chinarindenbaum, *der*

cinder /'sɪndə(r)/ *n.* **1** Zinder, *der;* ausgeglühtes Stück Holz/Kohle; **~s** Asche, *die;* **burnt to a ~:** völlig verkohlt **2** (glowing ember) glühendes Stück Holz/Kohle **3** (slag) Schlacke, *die*

Cinderella /sɪndə'relə/ *n.* **1** (person) Aschenbrödel, *das;* Aschenputtel, *das* **2** (fig.: thing) Stiefkind, *das*

cinder: ~-path *n.* Schlackenweg, *der* (Bauw.); **~-track** *n.* Aschenbahn, *die*

cine /'sɪnɪ/ *adj.* Schmalfilm-

cine: ~ camera *n.* Filmkamera, *die;* **~ film** *n.* Schmalfilm, *der*

cinema /'sɪnɪmə/ *n.* **1** (Brit.: building) Kino, *das;* **go to the ~:** ins Kino gehen; **what's on at the ~?** was gibts im Kino? **2** *no pl., no art.* (cinematography) Kinematographie, *die* **3** (films, film production) Film, *der;* Kino, *das* (seltener)

cinema: ~ complex *n.* Kinozentrum, *das;* **~-goer** *n.* (Brit.) Kinogänger, *der*/-gängerin, *die*

cinematic /sɪnɪ'mætɪk/ *adj.* filmisch; **~ art** Filmkunst, *die*

cinematographic /sɪnɪmætə'græfɪk/ *adj.* kinematographisch

cinematography /sɪnɪmə'tɒgrəfɪ/ *n., no pl.* Kinematographie, *die*

cineplex ® /'sɪnɪpleks/ *n.* (Amer.) Multiplex, *das*

cineraria /sɪnə'reərɪə/ *n.* (Bot.) Zinerarie, *die;* Aschenpflanze, *die*

cinnabar /'sɪnəbɑː(r)/ *n.* Zinnober, *der*

cinnamon /'sɪnəmən/ *n.* Zimt, *der;* (plant) Zimtbaum, *der*

cinquefoil /'sɪŋkfɔɪl/ *n.* **1** (Bot.) Fingerkraut, *das* **2** (Archit.) Fünfpass, *der*

Cinque Ports /sɪŋk 'pɔːts/ *n. pl.* Cinque Ports *Pl.* (hist.; südenglischer Städtebund)

cipher /'saɪfə(r)/
A *n.* **1** (code, secret writing) Chiffre, *die;* Geheimschrift, *die;* (key) Kode, *der;* (method) Chiffrierung, *die;* Kodierung, *die;* **in ~:** chiffriert **2** (symbol for zero) [Ziffer] Null, *die* **3** (fig.: nonentity) Nummer, *die* **4** (monogram) Monogramm, *das*
B *v.t.* (put into code) chiffrieren

circa /'sɜːkə/ *prep.* zirka

circadian /sɜː'keɪdɪən/ *adj.* (Physiol.) zirkadian

circle /'sɜːkl/
A *n.* **1** (also Geom.) Kreis, *der;* **great/small ~** (Geom., Naut., Aeronaut., Astron.) Groß-/Kleinkreis, *der;* **fly/stand in a ~:** im Kreis fliegen/stehen; (inside a **~**) in einem Kreis fliegen/stehen; **run round in ~s** (fig. coll.) hektisch herumlaufen (ugs.); **go round in ~s** im Kreis laufen; (fig.) sich im Kreis drehen; **~ of friends** Freundeskreis, *der;* **come full ~** (fig.) zum Ausgangspunkt zurückkehren; **things have now come full ~:** der Kreis schließt sich *od.* hat sich geschlossen **2** ▸ **vicious circle** **3** (seats in theatre or cinema) Rang, *der* **4** (Archaeol.) [Stein]kreis, *der* **5** (Hockey) Schusskreis, *der*
B *v.i.* kreisen; (walk in a **~**) im Kreis gehen
C *v.t.* **1** (move in a **~** round) umkreisen; **the aircraft ~d the airport** das Flugzeug kreiste über dem Flughafen **2** (draw **~** round) einkreisen

Phrasal verbs

- ~ **'back** *v.i.* auf einem Umweg zurückkehren
- ~ **'round** *v.i.* kreisen

circlet /'sɜːklɪt/ *n.* (of gold etc.) Reif, *der;* (of flowers) Kranz, *der*

circuit /'sɜːkɪt/ *n.* **1** (Electr.) Schaltung, *die;* (path of current) Stromkreis, *der* **2** (Motor racing) Rundkurs, *der* **3** (journey round) Runde, *die;* (by car etc.) Rundfahrt, *die;* **we made a ~ of the lake** wir machten einen Rundgang/eine Rundfahrt um den See **4** (judge's itinerary) *dienstliche Rundreise* (*eines Richters, der in Städten in England und Wales in Zivil- u. Strafsachen Gerichtssitzungen abhält*); (district visited) Gerichtsbezirk, *der;* **go on ~:** den Gerichtsbezirk bereisen **5** (sequence of sporting events) **on the professional tennis/golf ~:** bei den Turnieren der professionellen Tennis-/Golfspieler

circuit: ~ board *n.* (Computing) Schaltbrett, *das;* **~-breaker** *n.* (Electr.) Leistungsschalter, *der;* (as protection) Leistungsschutzschalter, *der;* **~ diagram** *n.* (Electr.) Schaltplan, *der*

circuitous /sə'kjuːɪtəs/ *adj.* umständlich; **the path followed a ~ route** der Pfad machte einen weiten Bogen; **reach sb. by a ~ route** jmdn. auf Umwegen erreichen

circuitry /'sɜːkɪtrɪ/ *n.* (Electr.) Schaltungen *Pl.*

circular /'sɜːkjʊlə(r)/
A *adj.* **1** (round) kreisförmig; **~ form** Kreisform, *die* **2** (moving in circle) Kreis‹*bahn, -bewegung*› **3** (Logic) **that argument is ~:** das ist ein Zirkelschluss *od.* -beweis

B n. (letter, notice) Rundbrief, *der;* Rundschreiben, *das;* (advertisement) Werbeprospekt, *der*

circular 'breathing n., *no pl.* zirkuläres Atmen; (technique used by wind players) Zirkuläratmung, *die*

circularize (circularise) /'sɜ:kjʊləraɪz/ *v.t.* **every household was ~d** jeder Haushalt erhielt ein Rundschreiben/einen Werbeprospekt

circular: ~ 'letter n. ▸**circular B; ~ 'saw** n. Kreissäge, *die;* **~ 'tour** n. (Brit.) Rundfahrt, *die* (**of** durch)

circulate /'sɜ:kjʊleɪt/

A *v.i.* ‹*Blut, Flüssigkeit:*› zirkulieren; ‹*Geld, Gerüchte:*› zirkulieren, in Umlauf sein, kursieren; ‹*Nachrichten:*› sich herumsprechen; ‹*Verkehr:*› fließen; ‹*Personen, Wein usw.:*› herumgehen (ugs.), die Runde machen (ugs.)

B *v.t.* in Umlauf setzen ‹*Gerücht*›; in Verkehr bringen ‹*Falschgeld*›; verbreiten ‹*Nachricht, Information*›; zirkulieren lassen ‹*Aktennotiz, Rundschreiben*›; herumgehen lassen ‹*Buch, Bericht*› (**around** in + *Dat.*)

circulation /sɜ:kjʊ'leɪʃn/ *n.* **1** (Physiol.) Kreislauf, *der;* Zirkulation, *die* (Med.); (of sap, water, atmosphere) Zirkulation, *die;* **~ trouble, poor ~:** schlechte Durchblutung; Kreislaufstörungen *Pl.* **2** (of news, rumour, publication) Verbreitung, *die;* **have a wide ~:** große Verbreitung finden; **that document was not intended for public ~:** das Dokument war nicht für die Öffentlichkeit bestimmt **3** (of notes, coins) Umlauf, *der;* **withdraw from ~:** aus dem Umlauf ziehen; **put/come into ~:** in Umlauf bringen/kommen **4** (fig.) **be back in ~** (after illness etc.) wieder auf dem Posten sein; (after emotional crisis) wieder am normalen Leben teilnehmen; **be out of ~:** aus dem Verkehr gezogen sein (ugs. scherzh.) **5** (number of copies sold) verkaufte Auflage

circu'lation figures n. pl. Verkaufsauflage, *die*

circulatory /sɜ:kjʊ'leɪtərɪ, 'sɜ:kjʊlətərɪ/ *adj.* (Physiol., Bot.) Kreislauf-; **~ system** Kreislauf, *der*

circumcise /'sɜ:kəmsaɪz/ *v.t.* beschneiden

circumcision /sɜ:kəm'sɪʒn/ *n.* **1** Beschneidung, *die* **2** **C~** (Eccl.) Beschneidung Christi

circumference /sə'kʌmfərəns/ *n.* Umfang, *der;* (periphery) Kreislinie, *die;* **be ... in ~:** einen Umfang von ... haben

circumflex /'sɜ:kəmfleks/

A *adj.* **~ accent** Zirkumflex, *der*

B *n.* Zirkumflex, *der*

circumlocution /sɜ:kəmlə'kju:ʃn/ *n.* **1** *no pl.* (use of many words) Weitschweifigkeit, *die;* (evasive talk) Drumherumreden, *das* (ugs.); **without ~:** ohne Umschweife **2** (roundabout expression) umständliche Formulierung

circumnavigate /sɜ:kəm'nævɪgeɪt/ *v.t.* umfahren; (by sailing boat) umsegeln

circumnavigation /sɜ:kəmnævɪ'geɪʃn/ *n.* Umfahrung, *die;* (by sailing boat) Umseglung, *die*

circumscribe /'sɜ:kəmskraɪb/ *v.t.* (lay down limits of) eingrenzen; einschränken ‹*Macht, Handlungsfreiheit usw.*›; **our choice was ~d** unsere Auswahl war begrenzt

circumspect /'sɜ:kəmspekt/ *adj.* umsichtig; **we must be ~ about making new investments** neue Investitionen wollen [von uns] genau überlegt sein

circumspection /sɜ:kəm'spekʃn/ *n., no pl.* Umsicht, *die*

circumspectly /'sɜ:kəmspektlɪ/ *adv.* umsichtig; vorsichtig ‹*sich nähern*›

circumstance /'sɜ:kəmstəns/ *n.* **1** *usu. in pl.* Umstand *der;* **by force of ~[s]** durch den Zwang der Umstände; **in *or* under the ~s** unter den gegebenen *od.* diesen Umständen; **in certain ~s** unter [gewissen] Umständen; **under no ~s** unter [gar] keinen Umständen **2** *in pl.* (financial state) Verhältnisse **3** *no pl.* (full detail in narrative) Detailschilderung, *die* **4** *no pl.* (ceremony) Prachtentfaltung, *die;* Gepränge, *das* (geh.) **5** (incident, occurrence, fact) Umstand, *der.* *See also* **creature 3**

circumstantial /sɜ:kəm'stænʃl/ *adj.* **1** **~ evidence** Indizienbeweise *Pl.;* **the evidence was purely ~:** der Beweis war nur auf Indizien gegründet **2** (detailed) detailliert; ins Einzelne gehend

circumvent /sɜ:kəm'vent/ *v.t.* umgehen; hinters Licht führen ‹*Gegner, Feind*›

circumvention /sɜ:kəm'venʃn/ *n.* Umgehung, *die*

circus /'sɜ:kəs/ *n.* **1** Zirkus, *der;* (arena) Arena, *die* **2** (Brit.: in town) [runder] Platz

cirque /sɜ:k/ *n.* (Geog.) Kar, *das*

cirrhosis /sɪ'rəʊsɪs/ *n., pl.* **cirrhoses** /sɪ'rəʊsi:z/ ▸**❶ p. 1231** (Med.) Zirrhose, *die;* **~ of the liver** Leberzirrhose, *die*

cirrus /'sɪrəs/ *n., pl.* **cirri** /'sɪraɪ/ (Meteorol.) Zirrus, *der*

CIS *abbr.* = **Commonwealth of Independent States**

cissy /'sɪsɪ/ ▸**sissy**

cist /sɪst/ *n.* (Archaeol.) (coffin) [Stein]kistengrab, *das;* (burial chamber) Kammergrab, *das*

Cistercian /sɪ'stɜ:ʃn/

A *n.* Zisterzienser, *der*/Zisterzienserin, *die*

B *adj.* Zisterzienser-

cistern /'sɪstən/ *n.* Wasserkasten, *der;* (in roof) Wasserbehälter, *der*

citadel /'sɪtədəl/ *n.* (fortress) Zitadelle, *die*

citation /saɪ'teɪʃn/ *n.* **1** *no pl.* (citing) Zitieren, *das* **2** (quotation) Zitat, *das* **3** (announcement accompanying award) Text der Verleihungsurkunde **4** (Mil.: mention in dispatch) lobende Erwähnung

cite /saɪt/ *v.t.* **1** (quote) zitieren; anführen ‹*Beispiel*› **2** (Mil.: mention in dispatch) lobend erwähnen (**for** wegen) **3** (Law) vorladen ‹*Person*›

citizen /'sɪtɪzən/ *n.* **1** (of town, city) Bürger, *der*/Bürgerin, *die* **2** (of state) [Staats]bürger, *der*/-bürgerin, *die;* **he is a British ~:** er ist britischer Staatsbürger *od.* Brite; **~ of the world** (fig.) Weltbürger, *der*/-bürgerin, *die;* **C~s' Advice Bureau** (Brit.) Bürgerberatungsstelle, *die;* **~'s arrest** Festnahme durch eine Zivilperson; **~s' band radio** CB-Funk, *der;* (radio set) CB-Funkgerät, *das* **3** (Amer.: civilian) Zivilist, *der*

citizenry /'sɪtɪzənrɪ/ *n.* Bürgerschaft, *die*

citizenship /'sɪtɪzənʃɪp/ *n.* Staatsbürgerschaft, *die*

citric acid /sɪtrɪk 'æsɪd/ *n.* (Chem.) Zitronensäure, *die*

citron /'sɪtrən/ *n.* **1** (fruit) Zitrone, *die* **2** (tree) Zitronenbaum, *der*

citrus /'sɪtrəs/ *n.* **1** **~ [fruit]** Zitrusfrucht, *die* **2** (tree) Zitrusgewächs, *das*

city /'sɪtɪ/ *n.* ▸**❶ p. 1643** **1** [Groß]stadt, *die;* **the ~ of Birmingham** die Stadt Birmingham; **the C~:** die [Londoner] City; das Londoner Banken- und Börsenviertel; **Heavenly C~, C~ of God** Himmelreich, *das* **2** (Brit.: town created ~ by charter) Stadt, *die* (*Ehrentitel für bestimmte Städte, meist Bischofssitze*) **3** (Amer.: municipal corporation) ≈ Stadtgemeinde, *die* **4** *attrib.* [Groß]stadt‹*leben, -verkehr*›; **~ lights** Lichter der Großstadt; **~ wall** Stadtmauer, *die;* **~ workers** Leute, die in der Stadt arbeiten

> **City**
>
> *The City of London* ist das Gebiet innerhalb der alten Stadtgrenzen von London. Heute ist es das Geschäfts- und Finanzzentrum Londons und viele Banken und andere Geldinstitute haben dort ihre Hauptstellen. Wenn Leute über die *City* sprechen, beziehen sie sich oft auf diese Institutionen und nicht auf den Ort.

city: ~ 'centre *n.* Stadtzentrum, *das;* Innenstadt, *die;* **~ desk** *n.* (Amer.) Lokalredaktion, *die;* **C~ editor** *n.* (Brit.) Wirtschaftsredakteur, *der;* **~ editor** *n.* (Amer.) Lokalredakteur, *der;* **~ 'fathers** *n. pl.* Stadtväter *Pl.* (ugs. scherzh.); **~ 'hall** *n.* (Amer.) **1** Rathaus, *das;* **2** *no pl., no art.* (municipal officers) die Stadtverwaltung; **~ limits** *n. pl.* (Amer.) Stadtgrenze, *die;* Stadtgrenzen *Pl.;* **outside Orlando ~ limits** außerhalb des Stadtgebiets von Orlando; **C~ page** *n.* (Brit.) Wirtschaftsseite, *die;* **C~ pages** Wirtschaftsteil, *der;* **~ 'slicker** *n.* **1** (derog.: plausible rogue) raffinierter Großstadttyp (ugs.); **2** (sophisticated ~-dweller) eleganter Großstädter; **~-state** *n.* (Hist.) Stadtstaat, *der*

> **City Technology College (CTC)**
>
> Eine Form der *secondary school* in Großbritannien, die gemeinsam von der Regierung und privaten Unternehmen eingerichtet wurde. Diese Colleges liegen in den Stadtzentren und legen besonderen Wert auf die Vermittlung von Mathematik, Naturwissenschaften und Technologie.

civet /'sɪvɪt/ *n.* **~[cat]** Zibetkatze, *die;*

civic /'sɪvɪk/ *adj.* **1** (of citizens, citizenship) [Staats-]bürger-; [staats]bürgerlich; **my ~ responsibility** meine Verantwortung als Staatsbürger **2** (of city) Stadt-; städtisch; **~ authorities** Stadtverwaltung, *die;* **~ centre** Verwaltungszentrum der Stadt

civics /'sɪvɪks/ *n., no pl.* Gemeinschaftskunde, *die;* Staatsbürgerkunde, *die* (DDR)

civies ▸**civvies**

civil /'sɪvɪl, 'sɪvl/ *adj.* **1** (not military) zivil; **in ~ life** im Zivilleben; **the ~ authorities** die Zivilbehörden **2** (polite, obliging) höflich **3** (Law) Zivil‹*gerichtsbarkeit, -prozess, -verfahren*›; zivilrechtlich **4** (of citizens) bürgerlich; Bürger‹*krieg, -recht, -pflicht*› **5** (defined by enactment) bürgerlich ‹*Jahr, Zeit*› **6** (not ecclesiastical) weltlich

civil: ~ avi'ation *n.* Zivilluftfahrt, *die;* **~ de'fence** *n.* Zivilschutz, *der;* **~ diso'bedience** *n.* ziviler Ungehorsam; **~ engi'neer** *n.* ▸**❶ p. 1260** Bauingenieur, *der*/-ingenieurin, *die;* **~ engi'neering** *n.* Hoch- und Tiefbau, *der*

civilian /sɪ'vɪljən/

A *n.* Zivilist, *der*

B *adj.* Zivil-; **wear ~ clothes** Zivil[kleidung] tragen

civilisation, civilise ▸**civiliz-**

civility /sɪ'vɪlɪtɪ/ *n.* **1** *no pl.* Höflichkeit, *die* **2** *in pl.* Höflichkeiten; (remarks also) Höflichkeitsfloskeln

civilization /sɪvɪlaɪ'zeɪʃn/ *n.* Zivilisation, *die*

civilize /'sɪvɪlaɪz/ *v.t.* **1** zivilisieren **2** (refine) **~ sb.** jmdm. Manieren beibringen

civilized /'sɪvɪlaɪzd/ *adj.* zivilisiert; (refined) kultiviert

civil: ~ 'law *n.* Zivilrecht, *das;* **~ 'liberty** *n., usu. in pl.* bürgerliche Freiheit; **~ list** *n.* (Brit.) Zivilliste, *die*

civilly /'sɪvɪlɪ, 'sɪvəlɪ/ *adv.* höflich

civil: ~ 'marriage *n.* Ziviltrauung, *die;* standesamtliche Trauung; **~ 'rights** *n. pl.* Bürgerrechte; **~ rights movement** Bürgerrechtsbewegung, *die;* **~ 'servant** *n.* ▸**❶ p. 1260** ≈ [Staats]beamte, *der*/-beamtin, *die;* **C~ 'Service** *n.* öffentlicher Dienst; **~ 'war** *n.* Bürgerkrieg, *der*

civvies /'sɪvɪz/ *n. pl.* (Brit. sl.) Zivil, *das;* Zivilklamotten *Pl.* (ugs.)

Civvy Street /'sɪvɪ stri:t/ *n., no pl., no art.* (Brit. coll.) das Zivilleben; **get back to ~:** ins Zivilleben zurückkehren

CJD *abbr.* ▸**❶ p. 1231** = **Creutzfeldt-Jakob disease**

cl. *abbr.* = **class** Kl.

clad[1] /klæd/ *adj.* (arch./literary/joc.) gekleidet; **walls ~ in ivy** mit Efeu bewachsene Mauern; *see also* **ironclad; ivy-clad**

clad[2] *v.t.*, **-dd-** verkleiden

cladding /'klædɪŋ/ *n.* Verkleidung, *die*

claim /kleɪm/

A *v.t.* **1** (demand as one's due property) Anspruch erheben auf (+ *Akk.*), beanspruchen ‹*Thron, Gebiete*›; fordern ‹*Lohnerhöhung, Schadensersatz*›; beantragen ‹*Arbeitslosenunterstützung, Sozialhilfe usw.*›; abholen ‹*Fundsache*›; **~ one's luggage** sein Gepäck [ab]holen **2** (represent oneself as having) für sich beanspruchen, in Anspruch nehmen ‹*Sieg*› **3** (profess, contend) behaupten; **the new system is ~ed to have many advantages** das neue System soll viele Vorteile bieten **4** (need, deserve) in Anspruch nehmen ‹*Interesse, Aufmerksamkeit*› **5** (result in loss of) fordern ‹*Opfer, Menschenleben*›

B *v.i.* **1** (Insurance) Ansprüche geltend machen **2** (for costs) **~ for damages/expenses** Schadenersatz fordern/sich (*Dat.*) Auslagen rückerstatten lassen

C *n.* **1** Anspruch, *der* (**to** auf + *Akk.*); **lay ~ to sth.** auf etw. (*Akk.*) Anspruch erheben; **make too many ~s on sth.** etw. zu sehr in Anspruch nehmen **2** (assertion) **make ~s about sth.** Behauptungen über etw. (*Akk.*) aufstellen **3** (pay ~) Forderung, *die* (**for** nach); **put in a ~ for a pay rise** eine Lohnerhöhung fordern **4** **~ [for expenses]** Spesenabrechnung, *die* (**for** über + *Akk.*); **~ for damages** Schadenersatzforderung, *die* **5** (Mining) Claim, *das;* **stake a ~:** ein Claim abstecken; **stake a ~ to sth.** (fig.) ein Anrecht auf etw. (*Akk.*) anmelden; **I staked my ~ to the seat** ich habe mir den Platz gesichert **6** (Insurance) [Versicherungs]anspruch, *der* **7** (in patent) [Patent]anspruch, *der*

Phrasal verb

- **~ 'back** *v.t.* zurückfordern; **~ tax/expenses** *etc.* **back** sich (*Dat.*) Steuern/Spesen *usw.* rückerstatten lassen (**from** von)

claimant /'kleɪmənt/ *n.* (for rent rebate, social security benefit) Antragsteller, *der*/-stellerin, *die;* (for inheritance) Erbberechtigte, *der/die;* **~ to a title** Titelanwärter, *der*/-anwärterin, *die;* **~ to the throne** Thronanwärter, *der*/-anwärterin, *die*

'claim form *n.* **1** (Insurance) Antragsformular, *das* **2** (for expenses) Spesenabrechnungsformular, *das*

'claims department *n.* (Insurance) Schadensabteilung, *die*

clairvoyance /kleə'vɔɪəns/ *n., no pl.* Hellsehen, *das*

clairvoyant /kleə'vɔɪənt/

A *n.* Hellseher, *der*/Hellseherin, *die*

B *adj.* hellseherisch

clam /klæm/

A *n.* Klaffmuschel, *die;* (Mercenaria mercenaria) Quahogmuschel, *die;* **shut up like a ~** (fig.) ausgesprochen wortkarg werden

B *v.i.*, **-mm-:** **~ up** (coll.) den Mund nicht [mehr] aufmachen

'clambake *n.* (Amer.) Picknick, *das* (*bes. am Strand, bei dem Muscheln und Fisch auf heißen Steinen gebacken werden*)

clamber /'klæmbə(r)/

A *v.i.* klettern; kraxeln (ugs., bes. südd., österr.); ‹*Baby:*› krabbeln; **~ up a wall** auf eine Mauer klettern; eine Mauer hochklettern

B *n.* Kletterei, *die;* Kraxelei, *die* (ugs., bes. südd., österr.)

clamminess /'klæmɪnɪs/ *n., no pl.* ▸ **clammy**: Feuchtigkeit, *die;* Klammheit, *die*

clammy /'klæmɪ/ *adj.* feucht; kalt und schweißig ‹*Hände, Gesicht, Haut*›; klamm ‹*Kleidung usw.*›; nasskalt ‹*Luft usw.*›; **~ with sweat** klebrig von Schweiß

clamor (Amer.) ▸ **clamour**

clamorous /'klæmərəs/ *adj.* lärmend ‹*Menge*›; lautstark ‹*Protest, Forderung*›

clamour /'klæmə(r)/ (Brit.)

A *n.* **1** (noise, shouting) Lärm, *der;* lautes Geschrei **2** (protest) [lautstarker] Protest; (appeal, demand) [lautstarke] Forderung (**for** nach)

B *v.i.* **1** (shout) schreien **2** (protest, demand) **~ against sth.** gegen etw. [lautstark] protestieren; **~ for sth.** nach etw. schreien; **~ to be let out** lautstark fordern, herausgelassen zu werden

clamp /klæmp/

A *n.* Klammer, *die;* (Woodw.) Schraubzwinge, *die; see also* **wheel clamp**

B *v.t.* **1** klemmen; einspannen ‹*Werkstück*›; (Med.) klammern; **~ two pieces of wood together** zwei Holzstücke miteinander verklammern **2** **~ a vehicle** eine Parkkralle an ein Fahrzeug anbringen

C *v.i.* (fig.) **~ down on sb./sth.** gegen jmdn./etw. rigoros vorgehen; **~ down on expenses** die Ausgaben radikal drosseln

'clampdown *n.* rigoroses Vorgehen (**on** gegen); **the credit ~, the ~ on credit** das Anziehen der Kreditbremse

'clamshell phone *n.* Klapphandy, *das*

clan /klæn/ *n.* **1** Sippe, *die;* (of Scottish Highlanders) Clan, *der* **2** (derog.: group, set) Clan, *der;* Sippschaft, *die* (abwertend)

clandestine /klæn'destɪn/ *adj.*, **clandestinely** /klæn'destɪnlɪ/ *adv.* heimlich

clang /klæŋ/

A *n.* (of bell) Läuten, *das;* (of hammer) Klingen, *das;* (of sword) Klirren, *das*

B *v.i.* ‹*Glocke:*› läuten; ‹*Hammer:*› klingen; ‹*Schwert:*› klirren

clanger /'klæŋə(r)/ *n.* (Brit. coll.) Schnitzer, *der* (ugs.); **drop a ~:** sich (*Dat.*) einen Schnitzer leisten (ugs.)

clangor (Amer.) ▸ **clangour**

clangorous /'klæŋgərəs/ *adj.* [laut] schallend

clangour /'klæŋgə(r)/ *n.* (Brit.) [lauter] Schall

clank /klæŋk/

A *n.* Klappern, *das;* (of sword, chain) Klirren, *das*

B *v.i.* klappern; ‹*Schwert, Kette:*› klirren; ‹*Kette:*› rasseln

C *v.t.* klirren mit ‹*Schwert, Kette*›

clannish /'klænɪʃ/ *adj.* (derog.) cliquenbewusst; klüngelnd (ugs.)

clap¹ /klæp/

A *n.* **1** Klatschen, *das;* **give sb. a ~:** jmdm. applaudieren *od.* Beifall klatschen **2** (slap) Klaps, *der* (ugs.); **give sb. a congratulatory ~ on the back** jmdm. anerkennend auf die Schulter klopfen **3** **~ of thunder** Donnerschlag, *der*

B *v.i.*, **-pp-** klatschen

C *v.t.*, **-pp-** **1** **~ one's hands** in die Hände klatschen; **~ sth.** etw. beklatschen; **~ sb.** jmdm. Beifall klatschen **2** (slap) **~ sb. on the back** jmdm. auf die Schulter klopfen **3** (place) **~ sb. in prison** jmdn. ins Gefängnis werfen *od.* (ugs.) stecken; **the prisoner was ~ped in irons** der Gefangene wurde in Ketten gelegt; **~ one's hand over sb.'s mouth** jmdm. den Mund zuhalten; **~ eyes on sb./sth.** jmdn./etw. zu Gesicht bekommen **4** **~ped out** (coll.) schrottreif (ugs.) ‹*Auto, Flugzeug*›; kaputt (ugs.) ‹*Person, Idee*›

Phrasal verb

- **~ on** *v.t.* **1** draufschlagen ‹*Steuern usw.*›; **the airlines ~ped 25% on the fare** die Fluggesellschaften haben auf den Flugpreis 25% aufgeschlagen; **a preservation order has been ~ped on my house** die haben mein Haus einfach unter Denkmalschutz gestellt (ugs.) **2** (Naut.) **~ on sail** mehr Segel setzen (Seemannsspr.) **3** (put on hastily) aufstülpen ‹*Hut*›; **~ handcuffs on sb.** jmdm. Handschellen anlegen

clap² *n.* (coarse) Tripper, *der;* **pick up a dose of the ~:** sich (*Dat.*) einen Tripper holen

clapboard /'klæpbɔːd, 'klæbəd/ *n.* (Amer.) Schindel, *die*

Clapham /'klæpəm/ *n.* **the man on the ~ omnibus** (Brit.) der kleine Mann; der Durchschnittsbürger

clapper /'klæpə(r)/ *n.* **1** (of bell) Klöppel, *der;* Schwengel, *der* **2** **like the ~s** (Brit. coll.) mit einem Affenzahn *od.* Affentempo (salopp)

'clapperboard *n.* (Cinemat.) Synchronklappe, *die*

clapping /'klæpɪŋ/ *n., no pl.* Beifall, *der;* Applaus, *der*

claptrap /'klæptræp/ *n., no pl.* **1** (pretentious assertions) [leere] Phrasen **2** (coll.: nonsense) Geschwafel, *das* (ugs. abwertend); Geschwätz, *das* (ugs. abwertend)

claque /klɑːk, klæk/ *n.* Claque, *die*

claret /'klærət/

A *n.* roter Bordeauxwein; Claret, *der*

B *adj.* weinrot

clarification /klærɪfɪ'keɪʃn/ *n.* **1** Klärung, *die;* (explanation) Klarstellung, *die;* **I should like more ~ on several points** zu einigen Punkten hätte ich gern nähere Erläuterungen **2** (of liquid) Klärung, *die;* Klären, *das*

clarify /'klærɪfaɪ/ *v.t.* **1** (make clear) klären ‹*Situation, Problem usw.*›; (by explanation) klarstellen; erläutern ‹*Bedeutung, Gedanken, Aussage, Bemerkung*›; **the discussion helped me to ~ my thoughts about the matter** die Diskussion half mir, mir über die Sache klarzuwerden **2** (purify, make transparent) reinigen; klären ‹*Abwasser, Flüssigkeit*›

clarinet /klærɪ'net/ *n.* (Mus.) Klarinette, *die*

clarinettist (*Amer.:* **clarinetist**) /klærɪ'netɪst/ *n.* ▸ **i** **p. 1260** (Mus.) Klarinettist, *der*/Klarinettistin, *die*

clarion /'klærɪən/ *attrib. adj.* hell klingend; **like a ~ call** wie ein Fanfarenstoß

clarity /'klærɪtɪ/ *n., no pl.* Klarheit, *die*

clash /klæʃ/

A *v.i.* **1** scheppern (ugs.); ‹*Gangschaltung:*› krachen; ‹*Becken:*› dröhnen; ‹*Schwerter:*› aneinander schlagen **2** (meet in conflict) zusammenstoßen; aufeinander stoßen; **~ with sb.** mit jmdm. zusammenstoßen **3** (disagree) sich streiten; **~ with sb.** mit jmdm. eine Auseinandersetzung haben **4** (be incompatible) aufeinander prallen; ‹*Interesse, Ereignis:*› kollidieren (**with** mit); ‹*Persönlichkeit, Stil:*› nicht zusammenpassen (**with** mit); ‹*Farbe:*› sich beißen (ugs.) (**with** mit)

B *v.t.* gegeneinander schlagen

C *n.* **1** (of cymbals) Dröhnen, *das;* (of swords) Aneinanderschlagen, *das;* (of gears) Krachen, *das* **2** (meeting in conflict) Zusammenstoß, *der* **3** (disagreement) Auseinandersetzung, *die* **4** (incompatibility) Unvereinbarkeit, *die;* (of personalities, styles, colours) Unverträglichkeit, *die;* (of events) Überschneidung, *die;* **~ of interests** Interessenkonflikt, *der*

clasp /klɑːsp/

A *n.* **1** Verschluss, *der;* Schließe, *die;* (of belt) Schnalle, *die* **2** (embrace) Umarmung, *die* **3** (grasp) Griff, *der* **4** (on medal ribbon) Ordensspange, *die*

B *v.t.* **1** (embrace) drücken (**to** an + *Akk.*); **the lovers lay ~ed in each other's arms** die Liebenden lagen eng umschlungen **2** (grasp) umklammern; **~ hands** sich [gegenseitig] bei den Händen fassen; **~ sth. in one's hand** etw. mit der Hand umklammern; **~ one's hands** die Hände falten; **he stood with his hands ~ed behind his back** er stand da, die Hände auf dem Rücken verschränkt

'clasp knife *n.* Klappmesser, *das*

class /klɑːs/

A *n.* **1** (in society) Gesellschaftsschicht, *die;* Klasse, *die* (Soziol.); (system) Klassensystem, *das* **2** (Educ.) Klasse, *die;* (Sch.: lesson) Stunde, *die;* (Univ.: seminar etc.) Übung, *die;* **teach a ~** (Univ.) eine Übung abhalten; **in ~:** im Unterricht; während des Unterrichts; **a French ~:** eine Französischstunde; **the ~ of 1970** (Amer.) der Jahrgang 1970 **3** (division according to quality) Klasse, *die;* (of hotel) [Hotel]kategorie, *die;* **be in a ~ by itself** *or* **on its own/of one's own** *or* **by oneself** eine Klasse für sich sein; **he's not in the same ~ as ...:** er hat nicht die Klasse von ... **4** (coll.: quality) Klasse, *die* (ugs.); **there's not much ~ about her** sie hat keine Klasse; **have [no] ~:** [keine] Klasse haben; *attrib.* **a ~ football player** ein klasse Fußballer (ugs.) **5** (group, set; also Biol.) Klasse, *die* **6** (Univ.: of degree) Prädikat, *das* **7** (Mil.) Rekrutenjahrgang, *der;* Jahrgang, *der*

B *v.t.* einordnen; **~ sth. as sth.** etw. als etw. einstufen

class: ~ action *n.* (Amer. Law) Sammelklage, *die;* **~-conscious** *adj.* klassenbewusst; **~ consciousness** *n.* Klassenbewusstsein, *das;* **~ distinction** *n.* Klassenunterschied, *der*

classic /'klæsɪk/

A *adj.* klassisch

B *n.* **1** *in pl.* (classical studies) Altphilologie, *die* **2** (writer; follower of ~ models) Klassiker, *der* **3** (garment) klassisch-zeitlose Kleidung **4** (book, play, film) Klassiker, *der* **5** (Brit.: horse race) Klassiker [unter den Pferderennen]

classical /'klæsɪkl/ *adj.* klassisch; **~ scholar/studies** Altphilologe, *der*/Altphilologie, *die;* **the ~ period** die Klassik; **the ~ world** die

Antike; ~ **education** humanistische [Schul]bildung
classically /ˈklæsɪkəlɪ/ *adv.* klassisch
classicism /ˈklæsɪsɪzm/ *n.* Klassizismus, *der*
classicist /ˈklæsɪsɪst/ *n.* Anhänger des Klassizismus; (classics scholar) Altphilologe, *der/*-philologin, *die*
classifiable /ˈklæsɪfaɪəbl/ *adj.* klassifizierbar; **be ~ into five main types** sich in fünf Hauptgruppen einteilen lassen
classification /klæsɪfɪˈkeɪʃn/ *n.* Klassifikation, *die*
classified /ˈklæsɪfaɪd/ *adj.* 1 (arranged in classes) gegliedert; unterteilt; ~ **advertisement** Kleinanzeige, *die;* ~ **directory** Branchenverzeichnis, *das;* ~ **results** Sportergebnisse 2 (officially secret) geheim
classifieds /ˈklæsɪfaɪdz/ *n. pl.* Kleinanzeigen *Pl.*
classify /ˈklæsɪfaɪ/ *v.t.* 1 klassifizieren; ~ **books by subjects** Bücher nach Fachgebieten [ein]ordnen 2 (designate as secret) für geheim erklären
classless /ˈklɑːslɪs/ *adj.* klassenlos ‹*Gesellschaft*›
class: ~ **list** *n.* (Univ.) Liste der Prüfungsergebnisse; **~mate** *n.* Klassenkamerad, *der/*-kameradin, *die;* **~room** *n.* (Sch.) Klassenzimmer, *das;* Klasse, *die; attrib.* **~room assistant** Unterrichtsassistent, *der/*-assistentin, *die;* ~ **'struggle** *n.* Klassenkampf, *der;* ~ **system** *n.* Klassensystem, *das;* ~ **'teacher** *n.* Klassenlehrer, *der/*-lehrerin, *die;* ~ **'trip** *n.* Klassenausflug, *der;* (lasting several days) Klassenfahrt, *die;* Klassenreise, *die;* ~ **'war** *n.* Klassenkampf, *der;* **~work** *n.* Arbeit am Studienplatz
classy /ˈklɑːsɪ/ *adj.* (coll.) klasse (ugs.); nobel ‹*Vorort, Hotel*›
clatter /ˈklætə(r)/
A *n.* Klappern, *das;* **the kettle fell with a ~ to the ground** der Kessel fiel scheppernd zu Boden
B *v.i.* 1 klappern 2 (move or fall with a ~) poltern
C *v.t.* klappern mit
clause /klɔːz/ *n.* 1 Klausel, *die* 2 (Ling.) Teilsatz, *der;* **[subordinate]** ~: Nebensatz, *der;* Gliedsatz, *der*
claustrophobia /klɔːstrəˈfəʊbɪə/ *n., no pl.* (Psych.) Klaustrophobie, *die*
claustrophobic /klɔːstrəˈfəʊbɪk/ *adj.* beengend ‹*Ort, Atmosphäre*›; an Klaustrophobie leidend ‹*Person*›
clavicle /ˈklævɪkl/ *n.* (Anat.) Schlüsselbein, *das;* Clavicula, *die* (fachspr.)
claw /klɔː/
A *n.* 1 (of bird, animal) Kralle, *die;* (of crab, lobster, etc.) Schere, *die;* (foot with ~) Klaue, *die;* **the cat bared its ~s** die Katze zeigte die Krallen; **get one's ~s into sb.** (fig. coll.) auf jmdm. herumhacken (ugs.) 2 (of hammer) Klaue, *die;* (of cine camera, projector) Greifer, *der*
B *v.t.* kratzen; **the two women ~ed each other** die beiden Frauen gingen mit den Fingernägeln aufeinander los; ~ **one's way to the top** sich zum Gipfel durchkämpfen; (fig.) sich nach oben durchboxen (ugs.)
C *v.i.* ~ **at sth.** sich an etw. (*Akk.*) krallen; **she ~ed desperately for the door handle** sie versuchte verzweifelt, die Türklinke zu fassen
(Phrasal verb)
• ~ **'back** *v.t.* wieder eintreiben ‹*Geld, Unterstützung*›; wieder an sich reißen ‹*Kontrolle*›; wettmachen ‹*Defizit*›
'clawback *n.* Wiedereintreiben, *das*
clay /kleɪ/ *n.* Lehm, *der;* (for pottery) Ton, *der*
clayey /ˈkleɪɪ/ *adj.* lehmig
clay: ~ **'pigeon** *n.* (Sport) Tontaube, *die;* ~ **'pigeon shooting** *n.* Tontaubenschießen, *das;* ~ **'pipe** *n.* Tonpfeife, *die*
clean /kliːn/
A *adj.* 1 sauber; frisch ‹*Wäsche, Hemd*› 2 (unused, fresh) sauber; (free of defects) einwandfrei; sauber; **start with/have a ~ sheet** (fig.) ganz neu beginnen/eine reine Weste haben (ugs.); **he has a ~ record** gegen ihn liegt nichts vor; **make a ~ start** noch einmal neu anfangen; **come ~** (coll.) (confess) auspacken (ugs.); (tell the truth) mit der Wahrheit [he]rausrücken (ugs.); **have ~ hands** *or* **fingers** (fig.) eine reine Weste haben (ugs.) 3 (well-formed, shapely) makellos ‹*Glieder, Taille*›; **a ship/car with ~ lines** ein Schiff/Auto mit klarer Linienführung 4 (regular, complete) glatt ‹*Bruch*›; glatt, sauber ‹*Schnitt*›; **make a ~ break [with** *or* **from sth.]** (fig.) einen Schlussstrich [unter etw. (*Akk.*)] ziehen; **make a ~ break with sb.** sich endgültig von jmdm. trennen; **make a ~ job of sth.** (fig. coll.) etw. vernünftig machen; etw. sauber hinkriegen (ugs., auch iron.) 5 (cleanly) sauber; (house-trained) stubenrein, sauber 6 (free from disease) gesund; (Relig.: not prohibited) rein 7 (deft) sauber 8 (not obscene or indecent) sauber; stubenrein (scherzh.) ‹*Witz*›; **be good ~ fun** völlig harmlos sein; **keep the jokes ~!** bitte nur stubenreine Witze! (scherzh.) 9 (sportsmanlike, fair) sauber 10 (free from knots) astrein ‹*Holz*›
B *adv.* 1 (completely, outright, simply) glatt; einfach ‹*vergessen*›; **we're ~ out of whisky** wir haben überhaupt keinen Whisky mehr; **the fox got ~ away** der Fuchs ist uns/ihnen *usw.* glatt entwischt 2 (fairly) sauber ‹*spielen, kämpfen*›
C *v.t.* sauber machen; putzen ‹*Zimmer, Haus, Fenster, Schuh*›; reinigen ‹*Teppich, Möbel, Käfig, Kleidung, Wunde*›; fegen, kehren ‹*Kamin*›; ausnehmen ‹*Fisch*›; (with cloth) aufwischen ‹*Fußboden*›; ~ **that dirt off your face** wisch dir den Schmutz aus dem Gesicht!; ~ **the house from top to bottom** großen Hausputz halten; ~ **one's hands/teeth** sich (*Dat.*) die Hände waschen/sich (*Dat.*) die Zähne putzen; ~ **one's plate** (eat everything) seinen Teller leer essen
D *v.i.* sich reinigen lassen
E *n.* **this carpet needs/your teeth need a good ~:** dieser Teppich muss gründlich gereinigt werden/du musst dir gründlich die Zähne putzen; **give your shoes/face/jacket a ~:** putz deine Schuhe/wasch dir das Gesicht/mach deine Jacke sauber
(Phrasal verbs)
• ~ **'down** *v.t.* waschen ‹*Auto*›; abwaschen ‹*Tür, Wand*›
• ~ **'out** *v.t.* 1 (remove dirt from) sauber machen; ausmisten ‹*Stall*›; (remove rubbish from) entrümpeln 2 (coll.) ~ **sb. out** (take all sb.'s money) jmdn. total schröpfen (ugs.); **I'm completely ~ed out** ich bin total blank (ugs.); **the tobacconist was ~ed out of cigarettes** beim Tabakhändler war alles an Zigaretten aufgekauft worden; **sb. is ~ed out of sherry** jmdm. ist der Sherry ausgegangen. *See also* **clean-out**
• ~ **'up**
A *v.t.* 1 aufräumen ‹*Zimmer, Schreibtisch*›; beseitigen ‹*Trümmer, Unordnung*› 2 ~ **oneself up** sich sauber machen; (get washed) sich waschen 3 (coll.: acquire) absahnen (ugs.) ‹*Geld*›; ~ **up a fortune** ein Vermögen machen 4 (Mil.) ausheben ‹*Schlupfwinkel des Feindes*› 5 (fig.) säubern ‹*Stadt*›; aufräumen mit ‹*Korruption, Laster, Drogenhandel*›
B *v.i.* 1 aufräumen 2 ▸**A 2** 3 (coll.: make money) absahnen (ugs.). *See also* **~-up**
'clean-cut *adj.* klar [umrissen]; **his ~ features** seine klar geschnittenen Gesichtszüge
cleaner /ˈkliːnə(r)/ *n.* 1 ▸**ⓘ p. 1260** (person) Raumpfleger, *der/*-pflegerin, *die;* (woman also) Putzfrau, *die;* Rein[e]machefrau, *die* 2 (vacuum ~) Staubsauger, *der;* (substance) Reinigungsmittel, *das;* Reiniger, *der* 3 *usu. in pl.* (dry-~) Reinigung, *die;* **take sth. to the ~s** etw. in die Reinigung bringen; **take sb. to the ~s** (coll.) jmdn. bis aufs Hemd ausziehen (ugs.)
'clean fuel *n.* sauberer Brennstoff; (for vehicle) sauberer Kraftstoff
cleaning /ˈkliːnɪŋ/: **~-rag** *n.* Putzlappen, *der;* **~-woman** *n.* ▸**ⓘ p. 1260** Putzfrau, *die*
clean-limbed /ˈkliːnlɪmd/ *adj.* wohlproportioniert; wohlgeformt
cleanliness /ˈklenlɪnɪs/ *n., no pl.* Reinlichkeit, *die;* Sauberkeit, *die;* ~ **is next to godliness** (prov.) Reinlichkeit ist die erste Tugend nach Gottseligkeit (veralt.)
'clean-living *adj.* von untadeligem Lebenswandel *nachgestellt*
cleanly[1] /ˈkliːnlɪ/ *adv.* sauber; **the bone broke ~:** der Knochen ist glatt gebrochen
cleanly[2] /ˈklenlɪ/ *adj.* sauber
cleanness /ˈkliːnnɪs/ *n., no pl.* 1 Sauberkeit, *die* 2 (freshness) Sauberkeit, *die;* (freedom from defects) Makellosigkeit, *die* 3 (shapeliness) Wohlgeformtheit, *die;* **the ~ of the ship's lines** die klare Linienführung des Schiffes 4 (regularity of cut or break) Glätte, *die* 5 (cleanliness) Sauberkeit, *die;* **the ~ of her habits** ihre Sauberkeit 6 (deftness) Sauberkeit, *die* 7 (of joke, entertainment, etc.) Harmlosigkeit, *die* 8 (of fight, contest, etc.) Sauberkeit, *die*
clean: **~-out** *n.* **give sth. a ~-out:** etw. sauber machen; **sth. needs a [good] ~-out** etw. muss [gründlich] sauber gemacht werden; ~ **room** *n.* Rein[st]raum, *der*
cleanse /klenz/ *v.t.* 1 (spiritually purify) läutern; **~d of** *or* **from sin** von der Sünde befreit 2 (clean) [gründlich] reinigen 3 (Bibl.) heilen ‹*Aussatz, Aussätzige*›
cleanser /ˈklenzə(r)/ *n.* 1 Reinigungsmittel, *das;* Reiniger, *der* 2 (for skin) Reinigungscreme, *die;* (fluid) Reinigungsmilch, *die*
'clean-shaven *adj.* glatt rasiert
cleansing/ˈklenzɪŋ/: ~ **cream** *n.* Reinigungscreme, *die;* ~ **department** *n.* Stadtreinigung, *die;* ~ **tissue** *n.* Papiertuch, *das*
'clean-up *n.* 1 **give sth./oneself a ~:** etw./sich sauber machen; **sth. needs a ~:** etw. muss sauber gemacht werden 2 (reducing crime or corruption) Säuberungsaktion, *die*
clear /klɪə(r)/
A *adj.* 1 klar; rein ‹*Haut, Teint*›; **as ~ as a bell** glockenhell
2 (distinct) scharf ‹*Bild, Foto, Umriss*›; deutlich ‹*Abbild*›; klar ‹*Ton*›; klar verständlich ‹*Wort*›
3 (obvious, unambiguous) klar ‹*Aussage, Vorteil, Vorsprung, Mehrheit, Sieg, Fall*›; **you have a ~ duty to report these thefts** es ist eindeutig Ihre Pflicht, diese Diebstähle zu melden; **make oneself ~:** sich deutlich *od.* klar [genug] ausdrücken; **make sth. ~:** etw. deutlich zum Ausdruck bringen; **make it ~ [to sb.] that …:** [jmdm.] klar und deutlich sagen, dass …; **let's get this/one thing ~:** lass uns das klarstellen/eins wollen wir klarstellen; **in ~:** im Klartext
4 (free) frei; (Horse riding) fehlerfrei ‹*Runde*›; **[be] ~ of a place** aus einem Ort heraus[sein]; ~ **of debt** schuldenfrei; frei von Schulden; **he is ~ of blame** ihm kann man keinen Vorwurf machen; **be ~ of suspicion** nicht unter Verdacht stehen; **we're in the ~** (free of suspicion) auf uns fällt kein Verdacht; (free of trouble) wir haben es geschafft; **be three points ~:** drei Punkte Vorsprung haben
5 (complete) **a ~ six inches** volle sechs Zoll; **three ~ days/lines** drei volle *od.* volle drei Tage/Zeilen
6 (open, unobstructed) frei; **keep sth. ~** (not block) etw. freihalten; ~ **of snow** schneefrei; frei von Schnee; **have a ~ run** freie Fahrt haben; **all ~** (one will not be detected) die Luft ist rein (ugs.); **the way is [now] ~ [for sb.] to do sth.** (fig.) es steht [jmdm.] nichts [mehr] im Wege, etw. zu tun; *see also* **all-~**
7 (discerning) klar; **keep a ~ head** einen klaren *od.* kühlen Kopf bewahren; **a ~ thinker** jmd., der klar denken kann
8 (certain, confident) **be ~ [on or about sth.]** sich (*Dat.*) [über etw. (*Akk.*)] im Klaren sein; **are you ~ in your own mind that …?** sind Sie ganz sicher, dass …?
9 (without deduction, net) ~ **profit** Reingewinn, *der. See also* **coast A 1; conscience**
B *adv.* 1 (apart, at a distance) **keep ~ of sth./sb.** etw./jmdn. meiden; **'keep ~'** (don't approach) „Vorsicht [Zug *usw.*]"; **please stand** *or* **keep ~ of the door** bitte von der Tür zurücktreten; **move sth. ~ of sth.** etw. von etw. wegräumen; **the driver was pulled ~ of the wreckage** man zog den Fahrer aus dem Wrack seines Wagens; **the driver leaped ~ just before the crash** der Fahrer konnte im Moment vor dem Zusammenstoß noch abspringen

2 (distinctly) deutlich ‹*sprechen, sehen, hören*›
3 (completely) **the prisoners had got ~ away** die Häftlinge waren auf und davon (ugs.)
4 (Amer.: all the way) ganz; **~ through to Boston** direkt bis Boston
C *v.t.* **1** (make ~) klären ‹*Flüssigkeit*›; reinigen ‹*Blut*›; **~ the air** lüften; (fig.) die Atmosphäre reinigen; **~ one's mind of doubts/anxieties** (fig.) seine Zweifel/Ängste loswerden; **he tried to ~ his head** (fig.) er versuchte, einen klaren Kopf zu bekommen; **~ one's conscience** sein Gewissen erleichtern
2 (free from obstruction) räumen ‹*Straße*›; abräumen ‹*Regal, Schreibtisch*›; reinigen ‹*Pfeife*›; freimachen ‹*Abfluss, Kanal*›; **~ the streets of snow** den Schnee von den Straßen räumen; **~ a space for sb./sth.** für jmdn./etw. Platz machen; **~ one's throat** sich räuspern; **~ the ground** (fig.) die Bahn frei machen; **~ land [for cultivation]** Land roden [um es urbar zu machen]; *see also* **deck A 1; way A 6**
3 (make empty) räumen; leeren ‹*Briefkasten*›; **~ the room** das Zimmer räumen; **~ the table** den Tisch abräumen; **~ one's desk** seinen Schreibtisch ausräumen; **~ a country of bandits** ein Land von Banditen befreien; **~ the court** den Saal räumen; **~ one's plate** seinen Teller leer essen
4 (remove) wegräumen; beheben ‹*Verstopfung*›; **~ sth. out of the way** etw. aus dem Weg räumen
5 (pass over without touching) nehmen ‹*Hindernis*›; überspringen ‹*Latte*›; (pass by) vorbeikommen
6 (show to be innocent) freisprechen; **~ oneself** seine Unschuld beweisen; **~ sb. of sth.** jmdn. von etw. freisprechen; **seek to ~ oneself of a charge** versuchen, eine Anschuldigung zu widerlegen; **~ one's name** seine Unschuld beweisen
7 (declare fit to have secret information) für unbedenklich erklären
8 (get permission for) **~ sth. with sb.** etw. von jmdm. genehmigen lassen; (give permission for) **~ a plane for take-off/landing** einem Flugzeug Start-/Landeerlaubnis erteilen
9 (at customs) **~ customs** vom Zoll abgefertigt werden; **~ sth. through customs** etw. [zollamtlich] abfertigen
10 (make as gain) verdienen ‹*Geld*›; **~ one's expenses** seine Ausgaben wieder hereinbekommen
11 (pay off) begleichen ‹*Schuld*›
12 (pass through bank) **~ a cheque** einen Scheck verrechnen
13 (get rid of) **~ [old] stock** Lagerbestände räumen; **'reduced to ~'** „reduziertes Einzelstück"
14 (Sport: move away) klären; **the ball was ~ed upfield** der Ball wurde ins Feld hinausgeschlagen
D *v.i.* **1** (become ~) klar werden; sich klären; ‹*Wetter, Himmel:*› aufklaren (Met.), sich aufheitern; (fig.) ‹*Gesicht:*› sich aufhellen
2 (disperse) sich verziehen; ‹*Nebel:*› sich auflösen, sich verziehen
3 (Sport) klären

Phrasal verbs

• **~ a'way**
A *v.t.* wegschaffen; (from the table) abräumen ‹*Geschirr, Besteck*›
B *v.i.* **1** abräumen **2** (disperse) ‹*Nebel:*› sich auflösen, sich verziehen
• **~ 'off**
A *v.t.* begleichen ‹*Schulden*›; abzahlen, abtragen ‹*Hypothek*›; aufarbeiten ‹*Rückstand*›
B *v.i.* (coll.) abhauen (salopp)
• **~ 'out**
A *v.t.* ausräumen
B *v.i.* (coll.) verschwinden. *See also* **~-out**
• **~ 'up**
A *v.t.* **1** beseitigen ‹*Unordnung*›; wegräumen ‹*Abfall*›; aufräumen ‹*Platz, Sachen*› **2** (explain, solve) klären
B *v.i.* **1** aufräumen; Ordnung machen **2** (become ~) ‹*Wetter:*› aufklaren (Met.), sich aufhellen **3** (disappear) ‹*Symptome, Ausschlag:*› zurückgehen. *See also* **~-up**

clearance /ˈklɪərəns/ *n.* **1** (of obstruction) Beseitigung, *die;* (of old building) Abriss, *der;* (of forest) Abholzung, *die;* **make a ~:** gründlich aufräumen **2** (of people) Räumung, *die* **3** (of cheque) Verrechnung, *die;* Clearing, *das* (Finanzw.) **4** (of ship at customs) Klarierung, *die* (Seemannsspr.); (certificate) [Zoll]papiere *Pl.* **5** (for aircraft to land/take off) Lande-/Starterlaubnis, *die* **6** (security ~) *Einstufung als unbedenklich [im Sinne der Sicherheitsbestimmungen];* (document) ≈ Sonderausweis, *der* **7** (clear space) Spielraum, *der;* (headroom) lichte Höhe **8** (Sport) Abwehr, *die;* **make a poor ~:** schlecht abwehren

clearance: ~ order *n.* Räumungsbefehl, *der;* **~ sale** *n.* Räumungsverkauf, *der*

clear: ~-cut *adj.* klar umrissen; klar ‹*Sieg, Abgrenzung, Ergebnis, Entscheidung*›; [gestochen] scharf ‹*Umriss, Raster*›; **~felling** /ˈklɪəfelɪŋ/ *n., no pl.* Kahlschlag, *der;* Kahlhieb, *der;* **after ~felling** nach dem Abholzen; **~-headed** *adj.* besonnen; **remain ~-headed** einen kühlen *od.* klaren Kopf bewahren

clearing /ˈklɪərɪŋ/ *n.* (land) Lichtung, *die*

clearing: ~ bank *n.* (Commerc.) Clearingbank, *die;* **~ house** *n.* (Commerc.) Abrechnungsstelle, *die;* Clearingstelle, *die;* (fig.) Zentrale, *die*

clearly /ˈklɪəlɪ/ *adv.* **1** (distinctly) klar; deutlich ‹*sprechen*› **2** (obviously, unambiguously) eindeutig; klar ‹*denken*›; **please explain yourself more ~:** bitte erklären Sie sich deutlicher; **~, immediate action is called for** ohne Frage ist sofortiges Handeln vonnöten

clearness /ˈklɪənɪs/ *n., no pl.* **1** Klarheit, *die;* (of skin, complexion) Reinheit, *die* **2** (distinctness) (of photograph, outline) Schärfe, *die;* (of articulation, words, reflection) Deutlichkeit, *die;* (of note, sound, image) Klarheit, *die* **3** (obviousness, unambiguousness) Eindeutigkeit, *die;* Klarheit, *die;* (of argument also) Schärfe, *die*

clear: ~-out *n.* Entrümpelung, *die;* **have a ~-out** eine Aufräum- *od.* Entrümpelungsaktion starten; **sth. needs a good ~-out** etw. muss einmal gründlich entrümpelt werden; **~-sighted** *adj.* weitsichtig; vorausschauend; **~ 'soup** *n.* klare Brühe

clearstory (Amer.) ▸ **clerestory**

clear: ~-thinking *adj.* klar denkend; **~-up** *n.* Aufräumen, *das;* **have a [good] ~-up** [gründlich] aufräumen; **~way** *n.* (Brit.) Straße mit Halteverbot

cleat /kliːt/ *n.* **1** (to give footing on gangway) Querleiste, *die;* (to prevent rope from slipping) Klampe, *die* (Seemannsspr.) **2** (wedge) Keil, *der* **3** (to strengthen woodwork) Leiste, *die* **4** (on boot, shoe) Stollen, *der*

cleavage /ˈkliːvɪdʒ/ *n.* **1** (act of splitting) Spaltung, *die;* (tendency) Spaltbarkeit, *die;* (fig.) Kluft, *die;* **the sharp ~ of opinions/interests** das deutliche Auseinandergehen der Meinungen/Interessen **2** (between breasts) Dekolleté, *das* **3** (Biol.) Spaltung, *die*

cleave[1] /kliːv/ *v.t.*, **~d** *or* **clove** /kləʊv/ *or* **cleft** /kleft/, **~d** *or* **cloven** /ˈkləʊvn/ *or* **cleft** (literary) **1** (split) spalten **2** (make way through) durchpflügen ‹*Wellen, Wasser*›; **~ one's way through sth.** sich [mühsam] einen Weg durch etw. bahnen. *See also* **cleft**[2] **B; cloven B**

cleave[2] *v.i.* (literary: adhere) kleben (**to** an + *Dat.*); **~ to sb./sth.** (fig.) jmdm./einer Sache treu bleiben

cleaver /ˈkliːvə(r)/ *n.* Hackbeil, *das*

clef /klef/ *n.* (Mus.) Notenschlüssel, *der*

cleft[1] /kleft/ *n.* Spalte, *die;* (fig.) Kluft, *die*

cleft[2]
A ▸ **cleave**[1]
B *adj.* gespalten; **~ palate** Gaumenspalte, *die;* **be [caught] in a ~ stick** (fig.) in der Klemme sitzen (ugs.)

clematis /ˈklemətɪs, kləˈmeɪtɪs/ *n.* (Bot.) Klematis, *die*

clemency /ˈklemənsɪ/ *n., no pl.* **1** (mercy) Milde, *die;* Nachsicht, *die;* **show ~ to sb.** jmdm. gegenüber Milde *od.* Nachsicht walten lassen **2** (of weather, climate) Milde, *die*

clementine /ˈklemәntiːn, ˈklemәntaɪn/ *n.* Klementine, *die*

clench /klentʃ/ *v.t.* **1** (close tightly) zusammenpressen; **~ one's fist** *or* **fingers** die Faust ballen; **with one's fist ~ed** *or* **[one's] ~ed fist** mit geballter Faust; **they gave the ~ed-fist salute** sie hoben die geballte Faust zum Gruß; **~ one's teeth** die Zähne zusammenbeißen; **through ~ed teeth** durch die zusammengebissenen Zähne **2** (grasp firmly) umklammern; **~ sth. between one's teeth** etw. zwischen die Zähne klemmen **3** (secure by bending) umschlagen (Nagel)

clerestory /ˈklɪəstɔːrɪ/ *n.* **1** (Archit.) Lichtgaden, *der* **2** (Amer. Railw.) *erhöhter Teil des Daches eines Eisenbahnwagens mit Fenstern od. Luftsaugern*

clergy /ˈklɜːdʒɪ/ *n. pl.* Geistlichkeit, *die;* Klerus, *der;* **thirty ~:** dreißig Geistliche

clergyman /ˈklɜːdʒɪmən/ *n., pl.* **clergymen** /ˈklɜːdʒɪmən/ ▸ ❶ **p. 1260** Geistliche, *der*

cleric /ˈklerɪk/ *n.* Kleriker, *der*

clerical /ˈklerɪkl/ *adj.* **1** (of clergy) klerikal; geistlich; **~ collar** Kollar, *das* **2** (of or by clerk) **~ duties/task/occupation/work** Büroarbeit, *die;* **~ error** Schreibfehler, *der;* **~ staff** Büropersonal, *das;* **~ worker** ▸ ❶ **p. 1260** Büroangestellte, *der/die;* Bürokraft, *die*

clerihew /ˈklerɪhjuː/ *n.* (Lit.) Clerihew, *das*

clerk /klɑːk/ *n.* ▸ ❶ **p. 1260** **1** Angestellte, *der/die;* (in bank) Bankangestellte, *der/die;* (in office) Büroangestellte, *der/die;* (in shop, firm) kaufmännischer Angestellter/kaufmännische Angestellte **2** (in charge of records) Schriftführer, *der*/Schriftführerin, *die* **3** **~ of the course** (Horseracing) Assistent der Rennleitung; **~ of [the] works** (Building) Bauleiter, *der* **4** (Eccl.: lay officer) Küster, *der;* Kirchendiener, *der;* (arch./Law: clergyman) **~ [in holy orders]** Geistliche, *der* **5** (Brit. Parl.) Parlamentssekretär, *der* **6** (Amer.: assistant in shop) Verkäufer, *der*/Verkäuferin, *die;* (in hotel) Hotelangestellte, *der/die*

clever /ˈklevə(r)/ *adj.*, **~er** /ˈklevərə(r)/, **~est** /ˈklevərɪst/ **1** gescheit; klug; **be ~ at mathematics/thinking up excuses** gut in Mathematik/findig im Ausdenken von Entschuldigungen sein **2** (skilful, dextrous) geschickt; **be ~ with one's hands** geschickte Hände haben **3** (ingenious) brillant, geistreich ‹*Idee, Argument, Rede, Roman, Gedicht*›; geschickt ‹*Verkleidung, Täuschung, Vorgehen*›; glänzend (ugs.) ‹*Idee, Erfindung, Mittel*› **4** (smart, cunning) clever; raffiniert ‹*Schritt, Taktik, Täuschung*›; schlau, gewitzt, raffiniert ‹*Person*›

clever: ~-~ *adj.* (derog.) superklug (iron.); **~-clogs** *n. sing., pl. same:* ▸ **~-sticks**; **~ Dick** *n.* (coll. derog.) Schlaumeier, *der* (ugs.); **all right, ~ Dick!** schon gut, du Schlaumeier! (ugs.)

cleverly /ˈklevəlɪ/ *adv.* **1** klug **2** (skilfully, dextrously) geschickt

cleverness /ˈklevənɪs/ *n., no pl.* **1** Klugheit, *die;* (talent) Begabung, *die* (**at** für) **2** (skilfulness, dexterity) Geschicklichkeit, *die;* **his ~ with his hands** seine handwerkliche Begabung **3** (ingenuity) Brillanz, *die* **4** (smartness) Cleverness, *die;* Raffiniertheit, *die;* (of person also) Schläue, *die*

'clever-sticks *n. sing., pl. same* (coll. derog.) Superschlaue, *der/die* (iron.)

clew /kluː/ (Naut.)
A *n.* (of hammock) Schlaufe, *die;* (of sail) [Schot]horn, *das* (Seemannsspr.)
B *v.t.* **~ up** aufgeien (Seemannsspr.)

cliché /ˈkliːʃeɪ/ *n.* (also Printing) Klischee, *das*

click /klɪk/
A *n.* **1** Klicken, *das* **2** (Ling.) Schnalzlaut, *der*
B *v.t.* **1** zuschnappen lassen ‹*Schloss, Tür*›; **~ the shutter of a camera** den Verschluss einer Kamera auslösen; **~ one's heels/tongue** die Hacken zusammenschlagen/mit der Zunge schnalzen; **~ finger and thumb** mit Daumen und Finger schnalzen **2** (Computing) anklicken; drücken ‹*Maustaste*›
C *v.i.* **1** klicken; ‹*Absätze, Stricknadeln:*› klappern **2** (coll.: agree) **~ with sth.** mit etw. übereinstimmen **3** (be successful) [gut] ankommen (ugs.); (coll.: fall into context) **it's just ~ed** ich hab's (ugs.); **the name ~ed** ich konnte mit dem Namen etwas anfangen; **~ with sb.** (coll.) mit jmdm. gleich prima auskommen (ugs.); **they ~ed immediately** sie kamen gleich prima miteinander aus (ugs.)

C

C

Phrasal verb

- ~ **on** *v.t.* (Computing) anklicken; ~ **on sth.** etw. *(Akk.)* anklicken

clickable /ˈklɪkəbl/ *adj.* (Computing) anklickbar ‹*Text, Bild*›

ˈclick beetle *n.* Schnellkäfer, *der*

ˈclickthrough *n.* (Computing) Clickthrough, *der*

client /ˈklaɪənt/ *n.* **1** (of lawyer, solicitor, barrister, social worker) Klient, *der*/Klientin, *die;* (esp. of barrister) Mandant, *der*/Mandantin, *die;* (of architect) Auftraggeber, *der*/-geberin, *die* **2** (customer) Kunde, *der*/Kundin, *die* **3** (Computing) Client, *der*

clientele /kliːɒnˈtel/ *n.* (of shop) Kundenkreis, *der;* Kundschaft, *die;* (of theatre) Publikum, *das;* (of lawyer) Klientel, *die*

client-ˈserver *adj.* (Computing) Client-Server-‹*Netzwerk, Applikation, Architektur, Lösung*›

cliff /klɪf/ *n.* (on coast) Kliff, *das;* (inland) Felswand, *die*

cliff: ~ **face** *n.* Felswand, *die;* Klippenwand, *die;* ~**hanger** *n.* Thriller, *der;* ~**-hanging** *adj.* äußerst spannend; atemberaubend; ~**top** *n.* Kliffspitze, *die;* (inland) Felsenspitze, *die;* **on the ~top** auf dem Kliff/Felsen

climacteric /klaɪˈmæktərɪk, klaɪmækˈterɪk/

A *adj.* **1** (critical) entscheidend **2** (Med.) klimakterisch

B *n.* (Med.) Klimakterium, *das* (fachspr.); Wechseljahre *Pl.;* (fig.) Wendepunkt, *der*

climactic /klaɪˈmæktɪk/ *adj.* ~ **scene/event** Höhepunkt, *der*

climate /ˈklaɪmət/ *n.* Klima, *das;* **the ~ of opinion** (fig.) die allgemeine Meinung

climate: ~ **change** *n.* Klimawechsel, *der;* ~ **control** *n.* Klimatisierung, *die;* **automatic ~ control** Klimaautomatik, *die;* ~**-controlled** *adj.* klimatisiert ‹*Gebäude, Büro usw.*›

climatic /klaɪˈmætɪk/ *adj.* klimatisch

climatology /klaɪməˈtɒlədʒɪ/ *n.*, *no pl.* Klimatologie, *die;* Klimakunde, *die*

climax /ˈklaɪmæks/

A *n.* **1** Höhepunkt, *der* **2** (orgasm) Höhepunkt, *der;* Orgasmus, *der*

B *v.i.* seinen Höhepunkt erreichen; ~ **in sth.** mit etw. seinen Höhepunkt erreichen

climb /klaɪm/

A *v.t.* hinaufsteigen ‹*Treppe, Leiter, Hügel, Berg*›; hinaufklettern ‹*Mauer, Seil, Mast*›; klettern auf ‹*Baum*›; ‹*Auto:*› hinaufkommen ‹*Hügel*›; **this mountain had never been ~ed before** dieser Berg war noch nie zuvor bestiegen worden; **the prisoners escaped by ~ing the wall** die Gefangenen entkamen, indem sie über die Mauer kletterten

B *v.i.* **1** klettern (**up** auf + *Akk.*); ~ **into/out of** steigen in (+ *Akk.*)/aus ‹*Auto, Bett*›; ~ **aboard** einsteigen; ~**ing plants/roses** Kletterpflanzen/-rosen **2** ‹*Flugzeug, Sonne:*› aufsteigen **3** (slope upwards) ansteigen **4** (in social rank) aufsteigen

C *n.* (ascent) Aufstieg, *der;* (of road) Steigung, *die;* (of aeroplane) Steigflug, *der;* **the pilot put the plane into a steep ~:** der Pilot zog die Maschine steil nach oben; **the first ~ of Everest** die erste Besteigung des Everest

Phrasal verb

- ~ **ˈdown** *v.i.* **1** hinunterklettern; (from horse) absteigen **2** (fig.: retreat, give in) nachgeben; einlenken; ~ **down over an issue** in einer Frage nachgeben; *see also* **climbdown**

climbable /ˈklaɪməbl/ *adj.* besteigbar

ˈclimbdown *n.* Rückzieher, *der* (ugs.)

climber /ˈklaɪmə(r)/ *n.* **1** (mountaineer) Bergsteiger, *der;* (of cliff, rock face) Kletterer, *der* **2** (plant) Kletterpflanze, *die*

climbing: ~ **boot** *n.* Kletterschuh, *der;* ~ **frame** *n.* Klettergerüst, *das;* ~ **iron** *n.* Steigeisen, *das;* ~ **speed** *n.* (Aeronaut.) Steiggeschwindigkeit, *die;* ~ **wall** *n.* Kletterwand, *die*

clime /klaɪm/ *n.* (literary) **1** *in sing. or pl.* (region) Gefilde, *das* (geh.) **2** (climate) Klima, *das*

clinch /klɪntʃ/

A *v.t.* **1** (confirm or settle conclusively) zum Abschluss bringen ‹*Angelegenheit, Meinungsverschiedenheit*›; perfekt machen (ugs.) ‹*Geschäft, Handel*›; **that ~es it** damit ist der Fall klar **2** ▸ **clench 3**

B *n.* **1** (Boxing) Clinch, *der* **2** (coll.: embrace) Umschlingung, *die;* Clinch, *der* (ugs. scherzh.); **go into a ~:** sich eng umschlingen; in den Clinch gehen (ugs. scherzh.)

clincher /ˈklɪntʃə(r)/ *n.* entscheidender Faktor; **be the ~:** den Ausschlag geben

cling /klɪŋ/ *v.i.*, **clung** /klʌŋ/ **1** ~ **to sth./sb.** sich an etw./jmdn. klammern; ‹*Schmutz:*› einer Sache/jmdm. anhaften; ‹*Staub:*› sich auf etw./jmdn. setzen; ‹*Klette:*› an etw./jmdm. hängen; ‹*Schlamm usw.:*› an etw./jmdm. haften bleiben; **the lovers clung to each other** die Liebenden hielten sich umschlungen; **his sweat-soaked shirt clung to his back** das durchgeschwitzte Hemd klebte ihm am Rücken; **her perfume still ~s to the scarf** der Duft ihres Parfüms haftet noch immer an dem Schal; ~ **together** aneinander haften; (Personen:) sich aneinander klammern; **a ~ing dress** ein eng anliegendes Kleid **2** (remain stubbornly faithful) ~ **to sb./sth.** sich an jmdn./etw. klammern

cling: ~ **film** *n.* Klarsichtfolie, *die;* ~**[stone] peach** *n.* (Bot.) Härtling, *der;* ~ **wrap** *n.* [Frischhalte]folie, *die*

clingy /ˈklɪŋɪ/ *adj.* (coll.) **1** eng anliegend *od.* sitzend; hauteng ‹*Kleid, Top*› **2** (emotionally dependant) anhänglich; anlehnungsbedürftig ‹*Person, Kind*›; **her boyfriend is so ~:** ihr Freund klammert zu sehr (ugs.)

clinic /ˈklɪnɪk/ *n.* **1** (place) [Abteilung einer] Klinik; (occasion) Sprechstunde, *die* **2** (private hospital) Privatklinik, *die;* (specified hospital) Klinik, *die;* **dental ~:** Zahnklinik, *die* **3** (medical teaching at bedside) Klinik, *die;* Klinikum, *das* **4** (Amer.: conference, short course) Seminar, *das*

clinical /ˈklɪnɪkl/ *adj.* **1** (Med.) klinisch ‹*Medizin, Tod*›; ~ **thermometer** Fieberthermometer, *das* **2** (objective, dispassionate) nüchtern; (coldly detached) kühl; distanziert ‹*Haltung*›; klinisch ‹*Interesse*› **3** (bare, functional) steril

clinically /ˈklɪnɪkəlɪ/ *adv.* **1** (Med.) klinisch **2** (dispassionately) nüchtern

clinical: ~ **psyˈchologist** *n.* ▸ **i** **p. 1260** klinischer Psychologe/klinische Psychologin; ~ **psyˈchology** *n.*, *no pl.* klinische Psychologie; ~ **ˈtrial** *n.* klinischer Versuch *od.* Test

clink[1] /klɪŋk/

A *n.* (of glasses, bottles) Klirren, *das;* (of coins, keys) Klimpern, *das*

B *v.i.* ‹*Flaschen, Gläser:*› klirren; ‹*Münzen, Schlüssel:*› klimpern

C *v.t.* klirren mit ‹*Glas*›; klimpern mit ‹*Kleingeld, Schlüssel*›

clink[2] *n.* (sl.: prison) Knast, *der* (salopp); **be in ~:** im Knast sitzen (salopp); **be put in ~:** in den Knast kommen (salopp)

clinker /ˈklɪŋkə(r)/ *n.* Schlacke, *die*

ˈclinker-built *adj.* in Klinkerbauweise [gebaut]; **a ~ boat** ein klinkergebautes Boot *od.* Klinkerboot

clip[1] /klɪp/

A *n.* **1** Klammer, *die;* (for paper) Büroklammer, *die;* (of pen) Klipp, *der;* (hose ~) Schelle, *die;* (for wires) Klemme, *die* **2** (piece of jewellery) Klipp, *der;* Clip, *der* **3** (set of cartridges) Ladestreifen, *der*

B *v.t.*, **-pp-:** ~ **sth. [on] to sth.** etw. an etw. (*Akk.*) klammern; ~ **papers together** Schriftstücke zusammenklammern; ~ **the leads to the battery terminals** die Kabel an die Batteriepole klemmen

Phrasal verb

- ~ **ˈon**

A *v.i.* angeklemmt *od.* angesteckt werden; ‹*Sonnenbrille*›; aufgesteckt werden

B *v.t.* anlegen ‹*Ohrring*›; anstecken ‹*Brosche, Mikrofon*›; aufstecken ‹*Sonnenbrille*›. *see also* **clip-on**

clip[2]

A *v.t.*, **-pp-** **1** (cut) schneiden ‹*Fingernägel, Haar, Hecke*›; scheren ‹*Wolle*›; stutzen ‹*Flügel*›; ~ **sb.'s wings** (fig.) jmdm. die Flügel stutzen; ~ **a second off the record** einen Rekord um eine Sekunde unterbieten **2** scheren ‹*Schaf*›; trimmen ‹*Hund*› **3** lochen, entwerten ‹*Fahrkarte*› **4** (coll.: hit) ~ **sb.'s ear** jmdm. eins *od.* ein paar hinter die Ohren geben (ugs.); ~ **sb. on the jaw** jmdm. einen Kinnhaken verpassen (ugs.); ~ **the crash barrier** die Leitplanke streifen **5** ~ **one's words/letters** abgehackt sprechen **6** (Amer.: cut from newspaper) ausschneiden

B *n.* **1** (of fingernails, hedge) Schneiden, *das;* (of dog) Trimmen, *das;* (of sheep) Schur, *die;* **give the hedge a ~:** die Hecke schneiden **2** (extract from film) [Film]ausschnitt, *der* **3** (blow with hand) Schlag, *der;* ~ **round** *or* **on** *or* **over the ear** Ohrfeige, *die;* ~ **on the jaw** Kinnhaken, *der* **4** **be going at a good** *or* **fast ~** (coll.) einen ziemlichen Zahn draufhaben (ugs.) **5** (quantity of wool) Schur, *die*

clip: ~ **art** *n.* (Computing) Clipart, *die;* ~**board** **1** *n.* Klemmbrett, *das;* **2** (Computing) Zwischenablage, *die;* ~**-clop** /ˈklɪpklɒp/ **A** *n.* Klappern, *das;* Klippklapp, *das;* **B** *v.i.*, **-pp-** klappern; ~ **frame** *n.* [rahmenloser] Bilderhalter; ~ **joint** *n.* (coll. derog.) Nepplokal, *das* (ugs. abwertend); ~**-on** *adj.* **a ~-on accessory** ein Accessoire zum Anstecken; **~-on sunglasses** eine Sonnenbrille zum Aufstecken; **a ~-on handle** ein Griff zum Feststecken

clipped /klɪpt/ *adj.* abgehackt ‹*Wörter*›

clipper /ˈklɪpə(r)/ *n.* **1** *in pl.* (for hair) Haarschneidemaschine, *die* **2** (Naut.) Klipper, *der*

clipping /ˈklɪpɪŋ/ *n.* **1** (piece clipped off) Schnipsel, *der od. das* **2** (newspaper cutting) Ausschnitt, *der*

clique /kliːk/ *n.* Clique, *die*

cliquey /ˈkliːkɪ/, **cliquish** /ˈkliːkɪʃ/ *adjs.* (derog.) **be ~:** zur Cliquenbildung neigen; **a ~ attitude** eine Neigung zur Cliquenbildung

clitoris /ˈklɪtərɪs/ *n.* (Anat.) Kitzler, *der;* Klitoris, *die* (fachspr.)

cloak /kləʊk/

A *n.* **1** Umhang, *der;* Mantel, *der* (hist.); (fig.) ~ **of snow** Schneedecke, *die;* **under the ~ of darkness** im Schutz der Dunkelheit; **use sth. as a ~ for sth.** etw. als Deckmantel für etw. benutzen; **a ~ of secrecy** ein Mantel des Schweigens **2** *in pl.* (Brit. euphem.: lavatory) Toilette, *die*

B *v.t.* **1** [ein]hüllen **2** (fig.) ~**ed in mist/darkness** in Nebel/Dunkel gehüllt; **sth. is ~ed in secrecy** über etw. (*Akk.*) wird der Mantel des Schweigens gebreitet

cloak: ~**-and-ˈdagger** *adj.* mysteriös; Spionage‹*stück, -tätigkeit*›; ~**room** *n.* Garderobe, *die;* (Brit. euphem.: lavatory) Toilette, *die;* ~**room attendant** ▸ **i** **p. 1260** Garderobier, *der*/Garderobiere, *die*/Toilettenmann, *der*/-frau, *die*

clobber[1] /ˈklɒbə(r)/ *n.* (Brit. coll.) Klamotten *Pl.* (salopp)

clobber[2] *v.t.* (coll.) **1** (hit) zusammenschlagen; (fig.: financially) zur Ader lassen (ugs. scherzh.); schröpfen (ugs.) **2** (defeat, criticize) in die Pfanne hauen (salopp)

cloche /klɒʃ/ *n.* **1** (Agric., Hort.) [Frühbeet]abdeckung, *die;* (polythene) Folientunnel,*der* **2** ~ **['hat]** Glocke, *die;* Glockenhut, *der*

clock /klɒk/

A *n.* **1** ▸ **i** **p. 1001** Uhr, *die;* **[work] against the ~:** gegen die Zeit [arbeiten]; **beat the ~ [by ten minutes]** [10 Minuten] früher fertig werden; **put** *or* **turn the ~ back** (fig.) die Zeit zurückdrehen; **round the ~:** rund um die Uhr; **hold the ~ on sb.** jmds. Zeit stoppen; **watch the ~** (fig.) [dauernd] auf die Uhr sehen (weil man ungeduldig auf den Arbeitsschluss wartet) **2** (coll.) (speedometer) Tacho, *der* (ugs.); (milometer) ≈ Kilometerzähler, *der;* (taximeter) Taxameter, *das* **3** (coll.: stopwatch) Uhr, *die* **4** (Bot.: seedhead) Haarkelch, *der* (Bot.) **5** (Brit. sl.: face) Visage, *die* (salopp abwertend). *See also* **o'clock**

B *v.t.* **1** ~ **[up]** zu verzeichnen haben ‹*Sieg, Zeit, Erfolg*›; erreichen ‹*Geschwindigkeit*›; zurücklegen ‹*Entfernung, Kilometer*›; ~ **3.43.7/a personal best** ‹*Läufer:*› 3:43,7/eine persönliche Bestzeit laufen **2** (coll.: time) stoppen (**at** mit) **3** (coll.: hit) ~ **sb. [one]** jmdm. eins überbraten (ugs.)

Phrasal verbs

- ~ **ˈin**, ~ **ˈon** *v.i.* [bei Arbeitsantritt] stechen *od.* stempeln; **the night shift ~s in** *or* **on at 8 p.m.** die Nachtschicht beginnt abends um acht

ℹ The clock

What time is it?
= Wie viel Uhr ist es?, Wie spät ist es?
Could you tell me the time?
= Könnten Sie mir sagen, wie spät es ist?
What time do you make it?
= Wie viel Uhr hast du?
By my watch it's five to/ten past nine
= Nach meiner Uhr ist es fünf vor/zehn nach neun
My watch is fast/slow
= Meine Uhr geht vor/nach
It's just after* or *just gone ten
= Es ist etwas nach zehn
It's gone eleven
= Es ist elf Uhr vorbei
It's coming up to seven
= Es ist gleich sieben

Unlike English, German uses the twenty-four hour clock most of the time, even sometimes in conversation, and it is certainly the only possibility when quoting times in print or on radio and television. Note that when such times are spoken, the word **Uhr** is never omitted, and it is immediately followed by the number of minutes – these cannot come before with **vor** or **nach,** nor can **Viertel** be used for "quarter" or **halb** for "half". However the twelve hour clock is also used in conversation and letters, followed by **nachmittags, abends** ("in the afternoon", "in the evening"), etc. if it is necessary to make this clear.

WRITTEN	SPOKEN
1.00 a.m./0100 = 1 Uhr	***one [a.m. or in the morning]/one hundred hours*** eins, ein Uhr [nachts *or* morgens]/ein Uhr
1.00 p.m./1300 = 13 Uhr	***one [p.m. or in the afternoon]/thirteen hundred hours*** eins, ein Uhr [mittags]/dreizehn Uhr
2.05 a.m./0205 = 2.05 Uhr	***five past two (in the morning)/[o] two o five*** fünf [Minuten] nach zwei [Uhr nachts *or* morgens]/zwei Uhr fünf
2.05 p.m./1405 = 14.05 Uhr	***five past two [in the afternoon]/fourteen o five*** fünf [Minuten] nach zwei [Uhr nachmittags]/vierzehn Uhr fünf
4.15 a.m./0415 = 4.15 Uhr	***four fifteen [a.m.], a quarter past four [in the morning]/[o] four fifteen*** Viertel nach vier [morgens]/vier Uhr fünfzehn
4.15 p.m./1615 = 16.15 Uhr	***four fifteen [p.m.], a quarter past four [in the afternoon]*** Viertel nach vier [nachmittags]/sechzehn Uhr fünfzehn
5.30 a.m./0530 = 5.30 Uhr	***five thirty [a.m.], half past five [in the morning]/[o] five thirty*** halb sechs [morgens]/fünf Uhr dreißig
5.30 p.m./1730 = 17.30 Uhr	***five thirty [p.m.], half past five [in the afternoon]/seventeen thirty*** halb sechs [abends]/siebzehn Uhr dreißig
7.45 a.m./0745 = 7.45 Uhr	***seven forty-five [a.m.], a quarter to eight [in the morning]/[o] seven forty-five*** Viertel vor acht [morgens]/sieben Uhr fünfundvierzig
7.45 p.m./1945 = 19.45 Uhr	***seven forty-five p.m., a quarter to eight [in the evening]/nineteen forty-five*** Viertel vor acht [abends]/neunzehn Uhr fünfundvierzig
12.00 [midnight]/, 0000, 2400 = 0 Uhr, 24 Uhr	***twelve [o'clock], [twelve] midnight/oo double o, twenty-four hundred hours*** zwölf, zwölf Uhr [nachts]/null Uhr, vierundzwanzig Uhr
12 [noon]/1200 = 12 Uhr	***twelve [o'clock], [twelve] noon/twelve hundred hours*** zwölf, zwölf Uhr [mittags]/zwölf Uhr

N.B. When using the twenty-four hour clock, 0000 = null Uhr indicates the beginning of the day, 2400 = vierundzwanzig Uhr the end of the day.

When?

at with a time is **um:**

He came at eight o'clock
= Er kam um acht Uhr
[At] what time do you want breakfast?
= Um wie viel Uhr wollen Sie frühstücken?
at half past
= um halb
at half past eight, at half eight
= um halb neun
at six exactly, on the dot of six
= genau um sechs, [um] Punkt sechs
at about ten
= gegen zehn
at twelve at the latest
= spätestens um zwölf
It must be ready by eleven
= Es muss bis elf fertig sein
I won't be there until six
= Ich bin erst um sechs dort
closed from 1 to 2 p m.
= von 13 bis 14 Uhr geschlossen
every hour on the hour
= stündlich zur vollen Stunde

- **~ 'off, ~ 'out** *v.i.* [bei Arbeitsschluss] stechen *od.* stempeln; **we ~ off** *or* **out earlier than usual on a Friday** freitags machen wir früher Feierabend

clock: ~-face *n.* Zifferblatt, *das;* **~ golf** *n.* Uhrengolf, *das;* **~maker** *n.* ▸ℹ **p. 1260** Uhrmacher, *der*/-macherin, *die;* **~ 'radio** *n.* Radiowecker, *der;* **~ tower** *n.* Uhr[en]turm, *der;* **~-watcher** *n. jmd., der keine Sekunde länger als vorgeschrieben am Arbeitsplatz bleibt;* **~-watching** *n.* ständiges Auf-die-Uhr-Sehen (*weil man ungeduldig auf den Arbeitsschluss wartet*)

'clockwise
A *adv.* im Uhrzeigersinn
B *adj.* im Uhrzeigersinn *nachgestellt;* rechtsläufig (Technik); **in a ~ direction** im Uhrzeigersinn

'clockwork *n.* Uhrwerk, *das;* **~ [mechanism]** Aufziehmechanismus, *der;* Uhrwerk, *das* (veralt.); **a ~ car** ein Aufziehauto; **as regular as ~** (fig.) absolut regelmäßig; **with ~ precision/regularity** (fig.) absolut genau/regelmäßig; **go like ~** (fig.) klappen wie am Schnürchen (ugs.)

clockwork 'radio *n.* Aufziehradio, *das*

clod /klɒd/ *n.* **1** (lump) Klumpen, *der;* (of earth) Scholle, *die* **2** (derog.: dolt) Tölpel, *der* (abwertend)

'clodhopper *n.* **1** ▸**clod 2** **2** (coll.: shoe) Elbkahn, der (ugs. scherzh.); Quadratlatschen, *der* (salopp scherzh.)

clog /klɒg/
A *n.* Holzschuh, *der;* ([fashionable] wooden-soled shoe) Clog, *der;* **pop one's ~s** (Brit. coll.) den Löffel abgeben (ugs.)
B *v.t.,* **-gg-** **1** **~ [up]** verstopfen ⟨*Rohr, Poren*⟩; blockieren ⟨*Rad, Maschinerie*⟩; **be ~ged [up] with sth.** mit etw. verstopft/durch etw. blockiert sein **2** (impede) hemmen; (obstruct) blockieren **3** **~ [up]** (encumber) belasten

'clog dance *n.* Holzschuhtanz, *der*

cloister /ˈklɔɪstə(r)/
A *n.* **1** (covered walk) Kreuzgang, *der* **2** (convent, monastery; monastic life) Kloster, *das*
B *v. refl.* **~ oneself in one's study** (fig.) sich in sein Studierzimmer einschließen

cloistered /ˈklɔɪstəd/ *adj.* in einem Kloster lebend; (fig.) klösterlich ⟨*Abgeschiedenheit, Dasein*⟩

clomp /klɒmp/
A *v.i.* stapfen
B *n.* stapfendes Geräusch

clone /kləʊn/ (Biol.)
A *n.* Klon, *der;* (fig.: copy) [schlechte] Kopie
B *v.t.* klonen

clonk /klɒŋk/ *n.* (coll.) **1** (sound) harter Schlag **2** **get a ~ on the head** eins gegen die Birne kriegen (ugs.)

close
A /kləʊs/ *adj.* **1** (near in space) dicht; nahe; **be ~ to sth.** nahe bei *od.* an etw. (*Dat.*) sein; **how ~ is London to the South coast?** wie weit ist London von der Südküste entfernt?; **you're too ~ to the fire** du bist zu dicht *od.* nah am Feuer; **fly ~ to the ground** dicht über dem Boden fliegen; **I wish we lived ~r to your parents** ich wünschte, wir würden näher bei deinen Eltern wohnen; **be ~ to tears/breaking point** den Tränen/einem Zusammenbruch nahe sein; **be ~ to exhaustion** vor Erschöpfung fast umfallen; **at ~ quarters, the building looked less impressive** aus der Nähe betrachtet, wirkte das Gebäude weniger imposant; **fighting at ~ quarters** der Kampf Mann gegen Mann; **at ~ range** aus kurzer Entfernung
2 (near in time) nahe (**to** an + *Dat.*); **war is ~:** ein Krieg steht unmittelbar bevor
3 (in near or intimate relation) eng ‹*Freund, Freundschaft, Beziehung, Zusammenarbeit, Verbindung*›; nahe ‹*Verwandte, Angehörige, Bekanntschaft*›; **be/become ~ to sb.** jmdm. nahe stehen/nahe kommen
4 (rigorous, painstaking) eingehend, genau ‹*Untersuchung, Prüfung, Befragung usw.*›; streng, verschärft ‹*Haft, Arrest*›; **pay ~ attention** genau aufpassen
5 (stifling) stickig ‹*Luft, Raum*›; drückend, schwül ‹*Wetter*›
6 (nearly equal) hart ‹[*Wett*]*kampf, Spiel*›; knapp ‹*Ergebnis*›; **a ~ race** ein Kopf-an-Kopf-Rennen; **that was too ~ for comfort** das ging gerade noch gut; **I had a ~ call** *or* **shave** *or* **thing** (coll.) ich bin gerade noch davongekommen; **that was a ~ call** *or* **shave** *or* **thing** (coll.) das war knapp!
7 (fitting exactly) genau passend ‹*Kleidungsstück*›; (nearly matching) wortgetreu ‹*Übersetzung*›; getreu, genau ‹*Imitation, Kopie*›; groß ‹*Ähnlichkeit*›; **be the ~st equivalent to sth.** einer Sache (*Dat.*) am ehesten entsprechen; **bear a ~ resemblance to sb.** jmdm. sehr ähnlich sehen; große Ähnlichkeit mit jmdm. haben
8 (narrow, confined) eng ‹*Raum*›
9 (dense) dicht, fest (Gewebe); dicht, undurchdringlich ‹*Dickicht, Gestrüpp*›; eng ‹*Schrift*›; (fig.) lückenlos, stichhaltig ‹*Beweisführung, Argument*›
10 (concealed) verborgen; **keep** *or* **lie ~:** sich verborgen *od.* versteckt halten; (secret) **keep sth. ~:** etw. geheim halten; (secretive) **be ~ about sth.** in Bezug auf etw. (*Akk.*) verschwiegen sein
11 (niggardly) knauserig (ugs. abwertend)
12 (Phonet.) geschlossen ‹*Vokal*›
B /kləʊs/ *adv.* **1** (near) nah[e]; **come ~ to the truth** der Wahrheit nahe kommen; **that's the ~st I've ever come to being involved in an accident** so knapp *od.* (ugs.) haarscharf bin ich noch nie einem Unfall entgangen; **be ~ at hand** in Reichweite sein; ‹*Ereignis:*› nahe bevorstehen; **~ by** in der Nähe; **~ by the river** in der Nähe des Flusses; nahe am Fluss; **the lamb stayed ~ by its mother's side** das Lamm blieb dicht an der Seite seiner Mutter; **~ on 60 years** fast 60 Jahre; **~ on 2 o'clock** kurz vor 2 [Uhr]; **~ to sb./sth.** nahe bei jmdm./etw.; **don't stand so ~ to the edge of the cliff** stell dich nicht so nah *od.* dicht an den Rand des Kliffs; **come ~ to tears** den Tränen nahe sein; **she came ~ to being the best/the winner** sie wäre fast *od.* beinah[e] die Beste geworden/sie hätte fast *od.* beinah[e] gewonnen; **~ together** dicht beieinander; **can't you stand ~r together?** könnt ihr nicht etwas mehr zusammenrücken?; **try not to come too ~ together** versucht, einander nicht zu nahe zu kommen; **these deadlines come too ~ together** diese Termine liegen zu nahe zusammen; **it brought them ~r together** (fig.) es brachte sie einander näher; **~ behind** dicht dahinter; **leave sth./stand ~ behind sb./sth.** etw. dicht hinter jmdm./etw. lassen/dicht hinter jmdm./etw. stehen; **see sth. [from] ~ 'to** *or* **'up** etw. aus der Nähe sehen; **go ~:** es beinahe schaffen
2 (in ~ manner) fest ‹*schließen*›; genau ‹*hinsehen*›; **on looking ~r** bei genauerem Hinsehen
C /kləʊz/ *v.t.* **1** (shut) schließen, (ugs.) zumachen ‹*Augen, Tür, Fenster, Geschäft*›; zuziehen ‹*Vorhang*›; (declare shut) schließen ‹*Laden, Geschäft, Fabrik, Betrieb, Werk, Zeche*›; stillegen ‹*Betrieb, Werk, Zeche, Bahnlinie*›; sperren ‹*Straße, Brücke*›; **behind ~d doors** hinter verschlossenen Türen; **~ one's eyes to sth.** (fig.) die Augen vor etw. (*Dat.*) verschließen
2 (conclude) schließen, beenden ‹*Besprechung, Rede, Diskussion*›; schließen ‹*Versammlung, Sitzung*›; abschließen ‹*Handel, Geschäft*›; **~ an account** ein Konto auflösen; **the matter is ~d** der Fall *od.* die Sache ist abgeschlossen
3 (make smaller) schließen (auch fig.) ‹*Lücke*›; zustopfen ‹*Riss*›; **~ the gap between rich and poor** die Kluft zwischen Arm und Reich überwinden
4 (Electr.) schließen ‹*Stromkreis*›
D /kləʊz/ *v.i.* **1** (shut) sich schließen; ‹*Tür:*› zugehen (ugs.), sich schließen; **the door/lid doesn't ~ properly** die Tür/der Deckel schließt nicht richtig; **the valve won't ~:** das Ventil schließt nicht
2 ‹*Laden, Geschäft, Fabrik:*› schließen, (ugs.) zumachen; (permanently) ‹*Betrieb, Werk, Zeche:*› geschlossen *od.* stillgelegt werden; ‹*Geschäft:*› geschlossen werden, (ugs.) zumachen; ‹*Theaterstück:*› abgesetzt werden
3 (come to an end) zu Ende gehen; enden; (finish speaking) schließen; **in closing** abschließend
4 (come closer, within striking distance) sich nähern; aufschließen (bes. Sport); (join battle) aufeinander treffen; aneinander geraten; **I ~d with him in hand-to-hand fighting** ich fing ein Handgemenge mit ihm an
E *n.* **1** /kləʊz/ *no pl.* Ende, *das;* Schluss, *der;* **come** *or* **draw to a ~:** zu Ende gehen; **bring** *or* **draw sth. to a ~:** einer Sache (*Dat.*) ein Ende bereiten; etw. zu Ende bringen; **at ~ of business** bei Geschäftsschluss; **~ of play** (Cricket) Ende des Spieltages
2 /kləʊz/ (Mus.) Kadenz, *die*
3 /kləʊs/ (Brit.: precinct of cathedral) Domhof, *der;* (cul-de-sac) Sackgasse, *die;* (enclosed place) Hof, *der*

Phrasal verbs
• **~ 'down** /kləʊz/
A *v.t.* schließen; zumachen (ugs.); stilllegen ‹*Werk, Zeche*›; einstellen ‹*Betrieb, Arbeit*›
B *v.i.* geschlossen werden, zugemacht werden (ugs.); ‹*Werk, Zeche:*› stillgelegt werden; (Brit.) ‹*Rundfunkstation:*› Sendeschluss haben
• **~ 'in** *v.i.* ‹*Nacht, Dunkelheit:*› hereinbrechen; ‹*Tage:*› kürzer werden; **~ in [up]on sb./sth.** (draw nearer) sich jmdm./etw. nähern; (draw around) jmdn./etw. umzingeln
• **~ 'off** *v.t.* [ab]sperren; abriegeln
• **~ 'out** *v.t.* (Amer.) absetzen, abstoßen ‹*Waren*›; auflösen ‹*Betrieb*›
• **~ 'up**
A *v.i.* **1** aufrücken **2** ‹*Blume:*› sich schließen **3** (lock up) abschließen
B *v.t.* abschließen. *See also* **close-up**

close-cropped /ˈkləʊskrɒpt/ *adj.* kurz geschoren

closed /kləʊzd/ *adj.* **1** (no longer open) geschlossen ‹*Laden, Geschäft, Fabrik*›; **we're ~:** wir haben geschlossen; **'~'** „Geschlossen"; **the subject is ~:** das Thema ist [für mich] erledigt **2** (restricted) [der Öffentlichkeit] nicht frei zugänglich; (Sport) nur für Teilnehmer einer bestimmten Gruppe/Klasse offen ‹*Wettbewerb etc.*›; **a women's ~ golf tournament** ein Golfturnier für Damen; *see also* **scholarship 1** **3** (Phonet.) geschlossen ‹*Silbe*›. *See also* **book A 1**

closed: ~-circuit *adj.* **~-circuit television** interne Fernsehanlage; (for supervision) Videoüberwachungsanlage, *die*

close-down /ˈkləʊzdaʊn/ *n.* **1** (closing) Schließung, *die;* (of works, railway, mine) Stillegung, *die;* (of project, operation) Einstellung, *die* **2** (Radio, Telev.) Sendeschluss, *der*

closed: ~ season (Amer.) ▸ **close season**; **~ 'shop** *n.* Closed Shop, *der;* **we have** *or* **operate a ~ shop in this factory** in unserer Fabrik besteht Gewerkschaftszwang

close /kləʊs/: **~-fisted** *adj.* geizig; knauserig (ugs. abwertend); **~-fitting** *adj.* eng anliegend; knapp sitzend ‹*Anzug*›; **~-grained** *adj.* fest ‹*Gewebe*›; fein gemasert ‹*Holz*›; feinnarbig ‹*Leder*›; **~ 'harmony** *n.* (Mus.) enge Lage; **~-hauled** *adj.* (Naut.) hart am Wind segelnd ‹*Schiff*›; **~-knit** *adj.* fest zusammengewachsen

closely /ˈkləʊslɪ/ *adv.* **1** dicht; **follow me ~:** bleib *od.* geh dicht hinter mir!; **look ~ at** genau betrachten; **look ~ into** (fig.) näher untersuchen; **the first explosion was ~ followed by two more** unmittelbar auf die [erste] Explosion folgten zwei weitere **2** (intimately) eng; **we're not ~ related** wir sind nicht nah miteinander verwandt **3** (rigorously, painstakingly) genau; genau, eingehend ‹*befragen, prüfen*›; streng, scharf ‹*bewachen*›; **a ~ guarded secret** ein streng *od.* sorgsam gehütetes Geheimnis **4** (nearly equally) **~ fought/contested** hart umkämpft; **the contest was ~ fought** man kämpfte hart um den Sieg **5** (exactly) genau; **~ resemble sb.** jmdm. sehr ähneln **6** (densely) dicht; **~ printed/written** eng bedruckt/beschrieben; **~ reasoned** (fig.) schlüssig

closeness /ˈkləʊsnɪs/ *n., no pl.* **1** (nearness in space or time) Nähe, *die* **2** (intimacy) Enge, *die;* **the ~ of their friendship** die Tiefe ihrer Freundschaft **3** (rigorousness) Genauigkeit, *die;* (of questioning) Nachdrücklichkeit, *die;* (of guard, watch) Strenge, *die* **4** (of atmosphere, air) Schwüle, *die* **5** (of contest, election, etc.) knapper Ausgang **6** (exactness) **the ~ of the fit** der genaue Sitz; **the ~ of a translation** die Worttreue einer Übersetzung; **the ~ of the resemblance** die große Ähnlichkeit

close /kləʊs/: **~-range** *adj.* ‹*Sicht, Betrachtung*› aus nächster Nähe; **~-range weapon** Nahkampfwaffe, *die;* **~-range shots** (Photog.) Nahaufnahmen; **~ season** *n.* Schonzeit, *die;* **~-set** *adj.* dicht beieinander liegend ‹*Augen*›; dicht ‹*Hecke*›

closet /ˈklɒzɪt/ *n.* **1** (Amer.: cupboard) Schrank, *der;* **come out of the ~** (fig.) sich nicht länger verstecken **2** (water ~) Klosett, *das*

closeted /ˈklɒzɪtɪd/ *adj.* **be ~ together/with sb.** eine Besprechung/mit jmdm. eine Besprechung hinter verschlossenen Türen haben

close-up /ˈkləʊsʌp/ *n.* (Cinemat., Telev.) **~ [picture/shot]** Nahaufnahme *die;* (of face etc.) Großaufnahme, *die;* **in ~:** in Nahaufnahme/Großaufnahme

closing /ˈkləʊzɪŋ/: **~ date** *n.* (for competition) Einsendeschluss, *der;* (to take part) Meldefrist, *die;* **the ~ date for applications for the job is ...:** Bewerbungen bitte bis zum ... einreichen; **~-down sale** *n.* [Total]ausverkauf, *der;* **~ entry** *n.* (Bookk.) Schlusseintrag, *der;* **~ time** *n.* (of public house) Polizeistunde, *die;* (of shop) Ladenschlusszeit, *die;* **it's nearly ~ time** es wird gleich geschlossen

closure /ˈkləʊʒə(r)/ *n.* **1** (closing) Schließung, *die;* (of factory, pit also) Stilllegung, *die;* (of road, bridge) Sperrung, *die;* **a two-year ~** eine zweijährige Stilllegung **2** (Parl.) Schluss der Debatte **3** (cap, stopper) [Flaschen]verschluss, *der*

clot /klɒt/
A *n.* **1** Klumpen, *der;* **a ~ [of blood] had formed over the wound/in the artery** geronnenes Blut hatte die Wunde verschlossen/ein Blutgerinnsel hatte sich in der Arterie gebildet **2** (Brit. coll.: stupid person) Trottel, *der* (ugs. abwertend)
B *v.i.*, **-tt-** ‹*Blut:*› gerinnen; ‹*Sahne:*› klumpen

cloth /klɒθ/ *n., pl.* **~s** /klɒθs/ **1** Stoff, *der;* Tuch, *das;* **~ of gold/silver** gold-/silberdurchwirkter Stoff; **bound in ~:** mit Leineneinband *nachgestellt;* **cut one's coat according to one's ~** (fig.) sich nach der Decke strecken (ugs.) **2** (piece of ~) Tuch, *das;* (dish~) Spültuch, *das;* (table~) Tischtuch, *das;* [Tisch]decke, *die;* (duster)

Staubtuch, *das* **3** *no pl.* (clerical profession) **a gentleman of the ~:** ein Geistlicher; **the ~** (clergy) die Geistlichkeit

cloth: ~ binding *n.* Leineneinband, *der;* **~-bound** *adj.* mit Leineneinband *nachgestellt;* **~-cap** *adj.* **he tried to project a ~-cap image** er versuchte, das Image des [typischen] Arbeiters zu vermitteln; **a ~-cap comedian/entertainer** ein Komiker/Entertainer für die Arbeiterklasse

clothe /kləʊð/ *v.t.* kleiden; (fig.) **~ one's sentiments/ideas in words** seine Gefühle/Gedanken in Worte kleiden; **the cherry trees were ~d in blossom** die Kirschbäume standen in voller Blüte; **the hills were ~d in snow** die Hügel waren mit Schnee bedeckt

'cloth-eared *adj.* (coll. derog.) schwerhörig

clothes /kləʊðz/ *n. pl.* Kleider *Pl.*; (collectively) Kleidung, *die;* **with one's ~ on** angezogen; **put one's ~ on** sich anziehen; **without any ~ on** völlig unbekleidet; **take one's ~ off** sich ausziehen

clothes: ~ basket *n.* Wäschekorb, *der;* **~ brush** *n.* Kleiderbürste, *die;* **~-drier, ~-dryer** *ns.* Wäscheständer, *der;* (rotary drier) Wäschespinne, *die;* **~ hanger** *n.* Kleiderbügel, *der;* **~ horse** *n.* Wäscheständer, *der;* **~ line** *n.* Wäscheleine, *die;* **~ moth** *n.* Motte, *die;* **~ peg** (Brit.), **~pin** (Amer.) *ns.* Wäscheklammer, *die*

clothier /'kləʊðɪə(r)/ *n.* ▸❶ **p. 1260** (formal) Herrenausstatter, *der*

clothing /'kləʊðɪŋ/ *n., no pl.* Kleidung, *die;* **article of ~:** Kleidungsstück, *das;* **bloodstained ~ was found** blutbefleckte Kleidungsstücke wurden gefunden

'clothing allowance *n.* Kleidergeld, *das*

clotted cream /klɒtɪd 'kri:m/ *n.: sehr fetter Rahm;* Dickrahm, *der*

cloture /'kləʊtʃə(r)/ (Amer.) ▸**closure 2**

cloud /klaʊd/

A *n.* **1** Wolke, *die;* (collective) Bewölkung, *die;* **be** *or* **live in the ~s** (fig.) auf Wolken *od.* in den Wolken schweben; **walk** *or* **go round with one's head** *or* **have one's head in the ~s** (fig.) (be unrealistic) in den Wolken schweben; (be absent-minded) mit seinen Gedanken ganz woanders sein; **[be] on ~ seven** *or* **nine** (fig. coll.) im sieb[en]ten Himmel [sein] (ugs.); **every ~ has a silver lining** (prov.) es hat alles sein Gutes; **there wasn't a ~ in the sky** (lit. or fig.) es zeigte sich [noch] kein Wölkchen am Himmel; **a ~ on the horizon** (fig.) ein Wölkchen am Horizont **2** **~ of dust/smoke** Staub-/Rauchwolke, *die* **3** (fig.: cause of gloom or suspicion) dunkle Wolke; **the ~ of suspicion hangs over him** der Schatten des Verdachts liegt auf ihm; **he left under a ~:** unter zweifelhaften Umständen schied er aus dem Dienst

B *v.t.* **1** verdunkeln ‹*Himmel*›; blind machen ‹*Fenster[scheibe], Spiegel*› **2** (fig.: cast gloom or trouble on) trüben ‹*Glück, Freude, Aussicht*›; umwölken ‹*Gesicht, Stirn*›; überschatten ‹*Zukunft*›; (make unclear) trüben ‹*Urteilsvermögen, Verstand, Bewusstsein*›; verunklaren ‹*Problem*›

Phrasal verb

• **~ 'over** *v.i.* sich bewölken; ‹*Spiegel:*› beschlagen; **her face ~ed over** ihr Gesicht verdüsterte sich (geh.)

cloud: ~ bank *n.* Wolkenbank, *die;* **~ base** *n.* Wolkenuntergrenze, *die;* **~berry** *n.* Moltebeere, *die;* **~burst** *n.* Wolkenbruch, *der;* **~-capped** *adj.* wolkenverhangen ‹*Gipfel*›; **~ chamber** *n.* (Phys.) Nebelkammer, *die;* **~ cover** *n.* Wolkendecke, *die;* **~ 'cuckoo land** *n.* Wolkenkuckucksheim, *das* (geh.)

cloudiness /'klaʊdɪnɪs/ *n.* **1** (of liquid) Trübheit, *die* **2** (of sky) Bewölkung, *die*

cloudless /'klaʊdlɪs/ *adj.* wolkenlos

cloudy /'klaʊdɪ/ *adj.* bewölkt, bedeckt, wolkig ‹*Himmel*›; trübe ‹*Wetter, Flüssigkeit, Glas*›; wolkig ‹*Edelstein, Mineral*›; **it is getting ~:** der Himmel bewölkt sich

clout /klaʊt/

A *n.* **1** (coll.: hit) Schlag, *der;* **get a ~ round the ears** eins hinter die Ohren kriegen (ugs.) **2** (coll.: power, influence) Schlagkraft, *die* **3** **~ [nail]** Pappnagel, *der*

B *v.t.* (coll.) hauen (ugs.); **~ sb. round the ear/on the head** jmdm. eins hinter die Ohren/auf den Deckel geben (ugs.); **~ sb. [one]** jmdm. eine runterhauen (salopp)

clove¹ /kləʊv/ *n.* Brutzwiebel, *die;* (of garlic) [Knoblauch]zehe, *die*

clove² *n.* **1** (spice) [Gewürz]nelke, *die;* (plant) Gewürznelkenbaum, *der;* **oil of ~s** Nelkenöl, *das* **2** **~ [gillyflower]** Gartennelke, *die*

clove³ ▸**cleave¹**

'clove hitch *n.* Webeleinenstek, *der*

cloven /'kləʊvn/

A ▸**cleave¹**

B *adj.* **~ foot/hoof** Spaltfuß, *der* (*veralt.*)/ Spalthuf, *der* (veralt.); (of devil) Pferdefuß, *der*

clover /'kləʊvə(r)/ *n.* Klee, *der;* **be/live in ~** (fig.) wie Gott in Frankreich leben

'cloverleaf *n.* (also Amer. Road Constr.) Kleeblatt, *das*

clown /klaʊn/

A *n.* **1** Clown, *der;* **act** *or* **play the ~:** den Clown spielen **2** (ignorant person) Dummkopf, *der* (ugs.); (ill-bred person) ungehobelter Klotz

B *v.i.* **~ [about** *or* **around]** den Clown spielen (abwertend)

clownish /'klaʊnɪʃ/ *adj.* (derog.) albern (abwertend)

cloy /klɔɪ/

A *v.t.* übersättigen; überfüttern; **~ the appetite** sich (*Dat.*) den Appetit verderben

B *v.i.* seinen Reiz verlieren; an Reiz verlieren

cloying /'klɔɪɪŋ/ *adj.* (lit. or fig.) süßlich

cloze /kləʊz/ *n.* **~ test** (Educ.) Ergänzungstest, *der*

club /klʌb/

A *n.* **1** (weapon) Keule, *die;* (Indian ~) [Gymnastik]keule, *die;* (golf ~) Golfschläger, *der* **2** (association) Klub, *der;* Club, *der;* Verein, *der;* **social ~:** ≈ Vereinsgaststätte, *die;* (of firm) ≈ Gemeinschaftsräume *Pl.;* **Conservative ~:** Club der Konservativen; **join the ~** (fig.) mitmachen; **join the** *or* **welcome to the ~!** (fig.) du also auch!; **be in the ~** (Brit. fig. coll.) ein Kind kriegen (ugs.); **put sb. in the ~** (Brit. fig. coll.) jmdm. ein Kind machen (ugs.) **3** (premises) Klub, *der;* (buildings/grounds) Klubhaus/-gelände, *das* **4** (Cards) Kreuz, *das;* Treff, *das;* **the ace/seven of ~s** das Kreuzas/die Kreuzsieben; **~s are trumps** Kreuz ist Trumpf

B *v.t.*, **-bb-** **1** (beat) prügeln; (with ~) knüppeln **2** (contribute) **~ [together]** zusammenlegen ‹*Geld, Ersparnisse*›

C *v.i.*, **-bb-:** **~ together** sich zusammentun; (in order to buy something) zusammenlegen

clubbable /'klʌbəbl/ *adj.* gesellig

clubber /'klʌbə(r)/ *n.* Nachtklubgänger, *der*/-gängerin, *die;* (disco-goer) Discogänger, *der*/-gängerin, *die*

clubbing /'klʌbɪŋ/ *n., no pl.* Besuch von Nachtlokalen/Discos; **go ~:** Nachtlokale/Discos aufsuchen

club: ~ car *n.* (Amer.) Salonwagen, *der;* **~ chair** *n.* Klubsessel, *der;* **~ class** *n.* (Brit.) Clubklasse, *die;* **~ foot** *n.* Klumpfuß, *der;* **~house** *n.* Klubhaus, *das;* **~land** *n.* (Brit.) **1** (neighbourhood) Nachtklubviertel, *das;* **2** (world of nightclubs) Nachtleben, *das;* **~man** *n.* Klubmensch, *der* (jmd., der in seinem Klub/in Klubs zu Hause ist); Vereinsmeier, *der* (abwertend); **~moss** *n.* (Bot.) Bärlapp, *der;* (Selaginella) Moosfarn, *der;* **~room** *n.* Klubraum, *der;* **~root** *n.* (Bot.) Kohlhernie, *die;* Knotensucht, *die;* **~ 'sandwich** *n.* (Amer.) Club-Sandwich, *das;* Doppeldecker, *der* (ugs.)

cluck /klʌk/

A *n.* Gackern, *das;* (to call chicks) Glucken, *das*

B *v.i.* gackern; (to call chicks) glucken

clue /klu:/

A *n.* **1** (fact, principle) Anhaltspunkt, *der;* (in criminal investigation) Spur, *die;* **find a ~ to a mystery/problem** einen Zugang zu einem Geheimnis/einem Problem finden; **the fingerprints are a ~ as to who murdered the man** die Fingerabdrücke können auf die Spur des Mörders führen **2** (fig. coll.) **give sb. a ~:** jmdm. einen Tipp geben; **not have a ~:** keine Ahnung haben (ugs.); **he never seems to have a ~ about anything** er hat offenbar nie die geringste Ahnung **3** (in crossword) Frage, *die*

B *v.t.* (coll.: inform) **~ sb. up** jmdm. Bescheid sagen; **be ~d up about** *or* **on sth., be ~d in on sth.** über etw. (*Akk.*) Bescheid wissen; **keep sb. ~d up** jmdn. auf dem Laufenden halten

clueless /'klu:lɪs/ *adj.* (coll. derog.) unbedarft (ugs.) ‹*Person*›; **he's completely ~:** er hat absolut keine Ahnung

clump /klʌmp/

A *n.* (of trees, bushes, flowers) Gruppe, *die;* (of grass) Büschel, *das;* **a ~ of shrubs** ein Gebüsch

B *v.i.* **1** (tread) stapfen **2** (form ~) klumpen

C *v.t.* **1** (heap, plant together) zusammengruppieren; in Gruppen anordnen **2** (coll.: hit) hauen (ugs.)

clumsily /'klʌmzɪlɪ/ *adv.* ▸**clumsy**: schwerfällig; unbeholfen; plump

clumsiness /'klʌmzɪnɪs/ *n., no pl.* ▸**clumsy**: Schwerfälligkeit, *die;* Plumpheit, *die*

clumsy /'klʌmzɪ/ *adj.* **1** (awkward) schwerfällig, unbeholfen ‹*Person, Bewegungen*›; ungeschickt ‹*Hände*›; plump ‹*Form, Figur*›; tollpatschig ‹*Heranwachsender*› **2** (ill-contrived) plump ‹*Verse, Nachahmung*›; unbeholfen ‹*Worte*›; primitiv ‹*Vorrichtung, Maschine, Erfindung*› **3** (tactless) plump

clung ▸**cling**

clunky /'klʌŋkɪ/ *adj.* **1** (old-fashioned, awkward to use) klobig und altmodisch; (fig.) schwerfällig **2** (clumpy, clumsy) plump ‹*Schuhe, Stiefel*› **3** (making a clunking sound) klackend

cluster /'klʌstə(r)/

A *n.* **1** (of grapes, berries) Traube, *die;* (of fruit, flowers, curls) Büschel, *das;* (of eggs) Gelege, *das;* (of trees, shrubs) Gruppe, *die* **2** (of stars, cells) Haufen, *der;* (of houses, huts, etc.) Gruppe, *die;* Haufen, *der;* (of coral animals, bees, spectators) Traube, *die;* (of islands) Gruppe, *die;* (of diamonds on brooch) Kranz, *der;* Besatz, *der* **3** (Ling.) Cluster, *der*

B *v.t.* **be ~ed with sth.** dicht mit etw. bestanden sein

C *v.i.* **~ [a]round sb./sth.** sich um jmdn./etw. scharen *od.* drängen

'cluster bomb *n.* Streubombe, *die*

clutch¹ /klʌtʃ/

A *v.t.* umklammern; **the mother ~ed the child to her breast** die Mutter drückte das Kind fest an ihre Brust

B *v.i.* **~ at sth.** nach etw. greifen; (fig.) sich an etw. (*Akk.*) klammern; *see also* **straw 2**

C *n.* **1** (tight grasp) Umklammerung, *die* **2** *in pl.* (fig.: control) Klauen; **fall into sb.'s ~es** jmdm. in die Klauen fallen; in jmds. Klauen (*Akk.*) fallen; **get out of sb.'s ~es** sich aus jmds. Klauen befreien **3** (grasping) **make a ~ at sth./sb.** nach etw./jmdm. greifen **4** (Motor Veh., Mech.) Kupplung, *die;* **let in the ~, put the ~ in** einkuppeln; **disengage the ~, let the ~ out** auskuppeln; **~ pedal** Kupplungspedal, *das*

clutch² *n.* (of eggs) Gelege, *das;* (of chicks) Brut, *die*

'clutch bag *n.* Unterarmtasche, *die*

clutter /'klʌtə(r)/

A *n.* **1** Durcheinander, *das;* **in a ~:** in einem Durcheinander; völlig verkramt (ugs.); **he pushed the ~ into a corner** er schob den ganzen Kram in eine Ecke **2** (on radar screen) Störflecke *Pl.*

B *v.t.* **~ [up] the table/room** überall auf dem Tisch/im Zimmer herumliegen; **be ~ed [up] with sth.** ‹*Zimmer:*› mit etw. voll gestopft sein; ‹*Tisch:*› mit etw. übersät sein; **be ~ed [up] with holidaymakers/cabs** von Urlaubern/Taxis wimmeln; **a ~ed room** ein total voll gestopftes Zimmer

cm. *abbr.* ▸❶ **p. 911**, ▸❶ **p. 1208**, ▸❶ **p. 1286** **= centimetre[s]** cm

CND *abbr.* (Brit.) **= Campaign for Nuclear Disarmament** Kampagne für atomare Abrüstung

CNN *n.* **= Cable News Network**

CNN — Cable News Network

Eine amerikanische Fernsehgesellschaft, die 24 Stunden am Tag über Satellit Nachrichten und Informationsprogramme überträgt.

C

c/o *abbr.* ▸❶ p. 1287 = care of bei; c/o

Co. *abbr.* 1 = company Co.; = and Co. /ənd kəʊ/ (coll.) und Co. (ugs.) 2 = county

CO *abbr.* 1 = Commanding Officer 2 = conscientious objector KDV

coach /kəʊtʃ/

A *n.* 1 (road vehicle) Kutsche, *die;* (state ~) [Staats-]karosse, *die;* ~ **and four/six** Vier-/Sechsspänner, *der; see also* **drive B 1** 2 (railway carriage) Wagen, *der* 3 (bus) [Reise]bus, *der;* **by ~:** mit dem Bus 4 (tutor) Privat- *od.* Nachhilfelehrer, *der/*-lehrerin, *die;* (sport instructor) Trainer, *der/*Trainerin, *die;* (baseball ~) Coach, *der*

B *v.t.* trainieren; ~ **a pupil for an examination** einen Schüler auf eine Prüfung vorbereiten

coach: ~ **bolt** *n.* (Brit.) Schlossschraube, *die;* ~**builder** *n.* ▸❶ p. 1260 Karosseriebauer, *der;* ~ **driver** *n.* ▸❶ p. 1260 Busfahrer, *der/*-fahrerin, *die;* ~ **house** *n.* Remise, *die*

coaching /ˈkəʊtʃɪŋ/ *n., no pl.* 1 (teaching) Privatunterricht, *der* 2 (Sport) Training, *das* 3 (travelling) ~ **days** Postkutschenzeit, *die;* ~ **inn** Herberge einer Poststation (hist.)

coach: ~**load** *n.* **a ~load of football supporters** ein Bus voll Fußballanhänger; ~**man** /ˈkəʊtʃmən/ *n., pl.* ~**men** /ˈkəʊtʃmən/ Kutscher, *der;* ~ **operator** *n.* Busunternehmer, *der/*-unternehmerin, *die;* (company) Busunternehmen, *das;* ~ **park** *n.* Busparkplatz, *der;* ~ **party** *n.* Reisegesellschaft, *die;* ~ **station** *n.* Busbahnhof, *der;* ~ **tour** *n.* Rundreise [im Omnibus], *die;* Omnibusreise, *die;* ~**work** *n.* Karosserie, *die*

coagulant /kəʊˈægjʊlənt/ *n.* (Med.) blutgerinnungsförderndes Mittel; Koagulans, *das* (fachspr.)

coagulate /kəʊˈægjʊleɪt/

A *v.t.* gerinnen lassen; koagulieren (fachspr.)

B *v.i.* gerinnen; koagulieren (fachspr.)

coagulation /kəʊægjʊˈleɪʃn/ *n.* 1 (process) Gerinnung, *die;* Koagulation, *die* (fachspr.) 2 (mass) Gerinnsel, *das;* Koagulat, *das* (fachspr.)

coal /kəʊl/ *n.* 1 Kohle, *die;* (hard ~) Steinkohle, *die* 2 (piece of ~) Stück Kohle; **live ~s** Glut, *die;* **heap ~s of fire on sb.'s head** (fig.) feurige Kohlen auf jmds. Haupt (*Akk.*) sammeln (fig.); **haul** *or* **call sb. over the ~s** (fig.) jmdm. die Leviten lesen (ugs.); **carry ~s to Newcastle** (fig.) Eulen nach Athen tragen (fig.)

coal: ~**bed** *n.* Kohlenflöz, *der;* ~**-black** *adj.* kohlrabenschwarz; ~ **box** *n.* Kohlenkasten, *der;* ~ **bunker** *n.* Kohlenbunker, *der;* ~**-burning** *adj.* kohlebefeuert; Kohle‹*herd, -heizung, kraftwerk*›; ~ **cellar** *n.* Kohlenkeller, *der;* ~ **dust** *n.* Kohlenstaub, *der*

coalesce /kəʊəˈles/ *v.i.* 1 sich verbinden; eine Verbindung eingehen 2 (unite) sich vereinigen

coalescence /kəʊəˈlesəns/ *n.* Verbindung, *die;* (fig.) Vereinigung, *die*

coal: ~**face** *n.* Streb, *der;* **at the ~face** im Streb *od.* vor Ort; ~**field** *n.* Kohlenrevier, *das;* ~ **fire** *n.* Kohlenfeuer, *das;* ~**-fired** *adj.* mit Kohle beheizt; kohlebeheizt; ~**-fired power station** Kohlekraftwerk, *das;* ~ **gas** *n.* Leuchtgas, *das;* Stadtgas, *das;* ~**-hole** *n.* (Brit.) 1 Kohlenbunker, *der;* 2 (cellar) Kohlenkeller, *der;* ~**house** *n.* Kohlenschuppen, *der*

coalition /kəʊəˈlɪʃn/ *n.* (Polit.) Koalition, *die;* (union, fusion) Zusammenschluss, *der* (*von Gruppen, Firmen*); **a ~ of plans/projects** eine Planungsgemeinschaft; **a ~ of interests** eine Interessenkoalition

coaˈlition government *n.* Koalitionsregierung, *die*

coal: ~**man** *n.* ▸❶ p. 1260 Kohlenmann, *der* (ugs.); ~ **measures** *n. pl.* (Geol.) Kohlevorkommen, *das;* ~ **merchant** *n.* ▸❶ p. 1260 Kohlenhändler, *der;* ~ **mine** *n.* [Kohlen]bergwerk, *das;* ~ **miner** *n.* ▸❶ p. 1260 [im Kohlenbergbau tätiger] Grubenarbeiter; ~ **mining** *n.* Kohlenbergbau, *der;* ~ **oil** *n.* (Amer.) Paraffin, *das;* ~ **scuttle** *n.* Kohleneimer, *der;* Kohlenschütte, *die;* ~**-seam** *n.* Kohlenflöz, *der;* ~ **shed** ▸ ~**house;** ~ **shovel** *n.* Kohlenschaufel, *die;* ~ **tar** *n.* Steinkohlenteer, *der;* ~ **tit** *n.* (Ornith.) Tannenmeise, *die*

coaming /ˈkəʊmɪŋ/ *n.* (Naut.) Süllrand, *der*

coarse /kɔːs/ *adj.* 1 (inferior) derb, einfach ‹*Essen*› 2 (in texture) grob; rau, grob ‹*Haut, Teint*› 3 (unrefined, rude, obscene) derb; roh ‹*Geschmack, Kraft*›; primitiv ‹*Person, Geist*›; ungehobelt ‹*Manieren, Person*›; gemein ‹*Lachen, Witz, Geräusch*›

coarse: ~ **ˈfish** *n.* (esp. Brit.) Süßwasserfisch, *der* (außer Lachs und Forelle); ~**-grained** *adj.* grob gekörnt ‹*Sand, Salz, Papier*›; grob genarbt ‹*Leder*›; grob gemasert ‹*Holz*›

coarsely /ˈkɔːslɪ/ *adv.* ▸ **coarse:** 1 derb; einfach 2 grob; rau 3 derb; roh; primitiv; ungehobelt; gemein

coarsen /ˈkɔːsn/

A *v.t.* vergröbern

B *v.i.* sich vergröbern

coarseness /ˈkɔːsnɪs/ *n., no pl.* ▸ **coarse:** 1 Derbheit, *die;* Einfachheit, *die* 2 Grobheit, *die;* Rauheit, *die* 3 Derbheit, *die;* Rohheit, *die;* Primitivität, *die;* Ungehobeltheit, *die;* Gemeinheit, *die*

coast /kəʊst/

A *n.* 1 Küste, *die;* **on the ~:** an der Küste; **off the ~:** vor der Küste; **the ~ is clear** (fig.: there is no danger) die Luft ist rein (fig.) 2 (Amer.) **the C~:** die Pazifik- *od.* Westküste [der USA] 3 (Amer.: slide) Rodelbahn, *die;* **go for a ~:** rodeln gehen

B *v.i.* 1 (ride) im Freilauf fahren 2 (fig.: progress) **they are just ~ing along in their work** sie tun bei der Arbeit nur das Nötigste; sie arbeiten nur im Schongang (ugs.); **he ~s through every examination** er schafft jede Prüfung spielend 3 (sail) die Küste entlang fahren 4 (Amer.: toboggan) hinunterfahren

coastal /ˈkəʊstl/ *adj.* Küsten-; ~ **traffic** Küstenschifffahrt, *die*

coaster /ˈkəʊstə(r)/ *n.* 1 (mat) Untersetzer, *der* 2 (tray) Tablett, *das* 3 (ship) Küstenmotorschiff, *das;* Kümo, *das* 4 (Amer.: sledge) Rodelschlitten, *der*

coast: ~**guard** *n.* 1 ▸❶ p. 1260 (person) Angehörige[r] der Küstenwacht; 2 (organization) Küstenwache, -wacht, *die;* ~**guard station** *n.* Küstenwache, *die;* Küstenwacht, *die;* ~**guard vessel** *n.* Küstenwachtboot, *das;* ~**line** *n.* Küste, *die;* ~ **road** *n.* Küstenstraße, *die*

coat /kəʊt/

A *n.* 1 Mantel, *der;* (man's jacket) Jackett, *das;* Rock, *der* (veralt.); **turn one's ~** (fig.) sein Mäntelchen nach dem Winde hängen (ugs. abwertend); *see also* **cloth 1** 2 (layer) Schicht, *die* 3 (animal's hair, fur, etc.) Fell, *das;* (of bird) Federkleid, *das* 4 ▸ **coating** 5 (skin, rind, husk) Schale, *die* 6 (Anat.) Haut, *die*

B *v.t.* überziehen; (with paint) streichen

ˈcoat dress *n.* Mantelkleid, *das*

coated /ˈkəʊtɪd/ *adj.* gestrichen ‹*Papier*›; belegt ‹*Zunge*›; imprägniert ‹*Stoff*›; getönt ‹*Glas, Linsen*›; ~ **with dust/sugar** staubbedeckt/mit Zucker überzogen

coat: ~ **hanger** *n.* Kleiderbügel, *der;* ~ **hook** *n.* Kleiderhaken, *der*

coating /ˈkəʊtɪŋ/ *n.* (of paint) Anstrich, *der;* (of dust, snow, wax, polish, varnish) Schicht, *die;* (for ceramic glazes) Überzug, *der*

coat: ~ **of ˈarms** *n.* Wappen, *das;* ~**-tails** *n. pl.* Frackschöße

co-author /kəʊˈɔːθə(r)/

A *n.* Mitautor, *der/*-autorin, *die;* **they were ~s of the book** sie haben das Buch gemeinsam verfasst

B *v.t.* gemeinsam verfassen ‹*Buch, Dokument*›

coax /kəʊks/ *v.t.* überreden; ~ **sb. to do sth.** jmdn. überreden *od.* dazu bringen, etw. zu tun; ~ **sb. into doing sth.** jmdn. herumkriegen (ugs.), etw. zu tun; ~ **a fire to burn/an engine into life** ein Feuer/einen Motor in Gang bringen; ~ **a smile/some money out of sb.** jmdm. ein Lächeln/etw. Geld entlocken; ~ **sb. out of doing sth.** jmdm. ausreden, etw. zu tun

coaxial /kəʊˈæksɪəl/ *adj.* koaxial

coaxing /ˈkəʊksɪŋ/ *n.* Überredung, *die;* Zureden, *das*

cob /kɒb/ *n.* 1 (nut) Haselnuss, *die* 2 (swan) männlicher Schwan 3 (horse) Cob, *die; kleines, stämmiges Pferd* 4 ▸ **corn cob** 5 (loaf) rundes Brot

cobalt /ˈkəʊbɔːlt, ˈkəʊbɒlt/ *n.* 1 (element) Kobalt, *das* 2 (pigment, colour) Kobaltblau, *das*

cobber /ˈkɒbə(r)/ *n.* (Austral. and NZ coll.) Kumpel, *der* (ugs.)

cobble[1] /ˈkɒbl/

A *n.* (stone) Pflaster-, Kopfstein, *der;* Katzenkopf, *der;* **rumble over the ~s** über das Kopfsteinpflaster rumpeln

B *v.t.* pflastern ‹*Straße*›; ~**d streets** Straßen mit Kopfsteinpflaster

cobble[2] *v.t.* (put together, mend) flicken; ~ **up plans/verses** [sich (*Dat.*)] Pläne zusammenbasteln (ugs.) *od.* zusammenreimen/[sich (*Dat.*)] Gedichte zusammenstoppeln (ugs.); ~ **together** zusammenbasteln; zusammenmischen ‹*Essen, Mannschaft*›

cobbler /ˈkɒblə(r)/ *n.* 1 ▸❶ p. 1260 Schuster, *der;* Flickschuster, *der* (veralt.) 2 *in pl.* (Brit. sl.: nonsense) Scheiße, *die* (derb); Mist, *der* (salopp); **a load of ~s** totaler Mist (salopp)

ˈcobblestone ▸ **cobble**[1] **A**

Coblenz /kəʊˈblents/ *pr. n.* Koblenz (*das*)

ˈcobnut ▸ **cob 1**

cobra /ˈkɒbrə/ *n.* (Zool.) Kobra, *die*

cobweb /ˈkɒbweb/ *n.* 1 (network) Spinnengewebe, *das;* Spinnennetz, *das;* (material) Spinn[en]weben *Pl.;* Spinn[en]fäden *Pl.* 2 *in pl.* (rubbish) Hirngespinste *Pl.;* **blow away the ~s** (fig.) für einen klaren Kopf sorgen

Coca-Cola ® *n.* /kəʊkəˈkəʊlə/ Coca-Cola (Wz), *das od. die*

cocaine /kəˈkeɪn/ *n.* Kokain, *das*

coccyx /ˈkɒksɪks/ *n.* (Zool.) Steiß, *der;* (Anat.) Steißbein, *das*

cochineal /kɒtʃɪˈniːl/ *n.* Koschenille, *die*

cochlea /ˈkɒklɪə/ *n. pl.* ~**e** /ˈkɒklɪiː/ (Anat.) Schnecke, *die;* Cochlea, *die* (fachspr.)

cock[1] /kɒk/

A *n.* 1 (bird, lobster, crab, salmon) Männchen, *das;* (domestic fowl) Hahn, *der;* (wood~) Waldschnepfe, *die;* **that ~ won't fight** (fig.) das hat keinen Zweck 2 (sl.: man) Bengel, *der* (ugs.); Bursche, *der* (ugs.); **old ~:** alter Junge (ugs.) 3 (spout, tap, etc.) Hahn, *der* 4 (coarse: penis) Schwanz, *der* (salopp); Pimmel, *der* (salopp) 5 (in gun) Hahn, *der;* **be/start/go off at half ~** (fig.) danebengehen (ugs.); ein Reinfall sein (ugs.)

B *v.t.* 1 (erect, stand up) aufstellen, (fig.) spitzen ‹*Ohren*›; ~ **one's eye at sb.** zu jmdm. hinblicken; (wink) jmdm. zublinzeln 2 (bend) anwinkeln ‹*Knie-, Handgelenk*›; **the parrot ~ed its head [to one side]** der Papagei legte den Kopf auf die Seite 3 (put on slanting) schief *od.* schräg aufsetzen ‹*Hut*›; (turn up brim of) hochstülpen ‹*Hut*›; **a ~ed hat** ein Hut mit hoher Krempe; (triangular hat) ein Dreispitz; **knock sb./sth. into a ~ed hat** (fig.) (destroy) jmdn./etw. zerschmettern (fig.); (surpass) jmdn./etw. weit übertreffen; jmdn./etw. in den Sack stecken (ugs. fig.) 4 ~ **a/the gun** den Hahn spannen

Phrasal verb

- ~ **ˈup** *v.t.* (Brit. sl.) versauen (salopp); *see also* **cock-up**

cock[2] *n.* (dated: pile of hay, straw, etc.) Haufen, *der*

cockade /kəˈkeɪd/ *n.* Kokarde, *die*

cock-a-doodle-doo /kɒkəduːdlˈduː/ *n.* (crowing) Kikeriki, *das;* (child lang.: cock) Kikeriki, *der*

cock-a-hoop /kɒkəˈhuːp/

A *adj.* überschwänglich; (boastful) triumphierend; **be ~:** triumphieren

B *adv.* überschwänglich; (boastfully) triumphierend

cock and ˈbull story *n.* Lügengeschichte, *die*

cockatoo /kɒkəˈtuː/ *n.* (parrot) Kakadu, *der*

cockchafer /ˈkɒktʃeɪfə(r)/ *n.* Maikäfer, *der*

ˈcockcrow *n.* **at ~:** beim ersten Hahnenschrei

cockerel /ˈkɒkərəl/ *n.* junger Hahn

cocker [spaniel] /ˈkɒkə(ˈspænjəl)/ *n.* Cockerspaniel, *der*

cock-eyed /ˈkɒkaɪd/ *adj.* 1 (crooked) schief 2 (absurd) verrückt 3 (coll.: squinting) schielend ‹*Blick*›; **be ~:** schielen

ˈ**cockfighting** *n.* Hahnenkampf, *der*

cockily /ˈkɒkɪlɪ/ *adv.* anmaßend; frech

cockiness /ˈkɒkɪnɪs/ *n., no pl.* Anmaßung, *die;* Frechheit, *die*

cockle /kɒkl/ *n.* 1 (bivalve, shell) Herzmuschel, *die* 2 **warm the ~s of sb.'s heart** es jmdm. warm ums Herz werden lassen

cockney /ˈkɒknɪ/
A *adj.* Cockney-
B *n.* 1 (person) waschechter Londoner/waschechte Londonerin; Cockney, *der* 2 (dialect) Cockney, *das*

cockney

Das *cockney* ist ein englischer Dialekt, der von Londonern, vor allem Bewohnern des *East End* – im Londoner Osten – gesprochen wird. Ein waschechter Cockney war früher jemand aus der Arbeiterklasse, der in Hörweite der Glocken der Kirche Saint Mary-le-Bow geboren war; heute kann man *cockney* in allen Stadtteilen Londons hören. Charakteristisch ist die Veränderung der Vokale und das Weglassen des h am Anfang eines Wortes. Eine weitere sprachliche Eigenart der Cockneymundart ist der *rhyming slang*. Bei diesem Slang wird das eigentliche Wort durch eine sich darauf reimende Phrase ersetzt (z. B. *apples and pears = stairs*).

cock: ~ of the ˈwalk *n.* (fig.) **be the ~ of the walk** die Szene beherrschen; (domineer) den Ton angeben; **~ of the ˈwood** *n.* 1 (capercaillie) Auerhahn, *der;* 2 (Amer.: woodpecker) Haubenschwarzspecht, *der;* **~pit** *n.* 1 (Aeronaut.) Cockpit, *das;* [Piloten]kanzel, *die;* 2 (in racing car) Cockpit, *das;* (in boat) Plicht, *die;* Cockpit, *das;* 3 (for ~fighting) Hahnenkampfplatz, *der*

cockroach /ˈkɒkrəʊtʃ/ *n.* [Küchen-, Haus-]schabe, *die;* Kakerlak, *der*

cockscomb /ˈkɒkskəʊm/ *n.* (Ornith., Bot.) Hahnenkamm, *der*

cocksure /kɒkˈʃʊə(r)/ *adj.* 1 (convinced) todsicher 2 (self-confident) selbstsicher; (dogmatic) selbstgerecht; **be ~ of oneself** sich (*Dat.*) seiner Sache (*Gen.*) [unberechtigterweise] völlig sicher sein

cocktail /ˈkɒkteɪl/ *n.* Cocktail, *der; see also* **fruit cocktail**

cocktail: ~ cabinet *n.* Hausbar, *die;* **~ dress** *n.* Cocktailkleid, *das;* **~ glass** *n.* Cocktailglas, *das;* **~ party** *n.* Cocktailparty, *die;* **~ sausage** *n.* Cocktailwürstchen, *das;* **~ shaker** *n.* Mixbecher, *der;* **~ stick** *n.* Partystick, *der od. das*

ˈ**cock-up** *n.* (Brit. sl.) Schlamassel, *der* (ugs.); **make a ~ of sth.** bei etw. Scheiße bauen (derb)

cocky /ˈkɒkɪ/ *adj.* anmaßend

coco /ˈkəʊkəʊ/ ▸**coconut 1**

cocoa /ˈkəʊkəʊ/ *n.* Kakao, *der*

ˈ**cocoa bean** *n.* Kakaobohne, *die*

coconut /ˈkəʊkənʌt/ *n.* 1 (tree) Kokospalme, *die* 2 (nut) Kokosnuss, *die* 3 (coll.: head) Rübe, *die* (derb)

coconut: ~ ˈbutter *n.* Kokosfett, *das;* **~ ˈmatting** *n.* Kokosmatten *Pl.;* **~ milk** *n.* Kokosmilch, *die;* **~ palm** ▸**coconut 1;** **~ shy** *n.* Wurfbude, *die*

cocoon /kəˈku:n/
A *n.* 1 (Zool.) Kokon, *der* 2 (covering) Hülle, *die*
B *v.t.* (wrap as in ~) einmummen

cod¹ /kɒd/ *n., pl. same* Kabeljau, *der;* (in Baltic) Dorsch, *der*

cod² (dated coll.)
A *v.t.*, **-dd-** 1 (fool) vergackeiern (salopp); verscheißern (derb) 2 (parody) verulken (ugs.)
B *v.i.*, **-dd-** rumblödeln (ugs.); flachsen (ugs.)

COD *abbr.* **= cash on delivery; collect on delivery** (Amer.) p. Nachn.

coda /ˈkəʊdə/ *n.* (Mus.) Koda, *die*

coddle /ˈkɒdl/ *v.t.* 1 [ver]hätscheln ‹*Kind*›; verwöhnen ‹*Kranken*› 2 (Cookery) schwach pochieren ‹*Eier*›

code /kəʊd/
A *n.* 1 (collection of statutes etc.) Kodex, *der;* Gesetzbuch, *das;* **a ~ of laws** ein Gesetzbuch; eine Gesetzessammlung; **~ of religion/literature/society** religiöse/literarische/gesellschaftliche Normen; **~ of honour** Ehrenkodex, *der;* **~s of behaviour** Verhaltensnormen; Verhaltenskodizes (geh.) 2 (system of signals) Kode, Code, *der;* (coded word, etc.) Chiffre, *die;* **be in ~:** verschlüsselt sein; **put sth. into ~:** etw. verschlüsseln; *see also* **genetic 1**
B *v.t.* chiffrieren, verschlüsseln ‹*Nachricht*›

code: ~ book *n.* Signalbuch, *das;* **~ name** *n.* Deckname, *der;* **~ number** *n.* Kenn-, Tarnzahl, *die;* **~ word** *n.* Kennwort, *das*

codeine /ˈkəʊdi:n/ *n., no pl.* (Med.) Kodein, *das*

codex /ˈkəʊdeks/ *n., pl.* **codices** /ˈkəʊdɪsi:z/ 1 (manuscript volume) Kodex, *der* 2 (of drugs etc.) *pharmazeutisches Nachschlagewerk*

ˈ**codfish** ▸**cod¹**

codger /ˈkɒdʒə(r)/ *n.* (coll. derog.) Knacker, *der* (salopp)

codicil /ˈkəʊdɪsɪl/ *n.* Kodizill, *das*

codification /kəʊdɪfɪˈkeɪʃn/ *n.* Kodifizierung, *die;* Kodifikation, *die*

codify /ˈkəʊdɪfaɪ/ *v.t.* kodifizieren ‹*Gesetze, Rechtsnormen*›; festlegen, kodifizieren ‹*Rechtschreibung, Grammatik*›

coding /ˈkəʊdɪŋ/ *n.* 1 (action) Chiffrieren, *das* 2 (result) verschlüsselte Informationen

ˈ**co-director** *n.* (of film, show, play) Koregisseur, *der*/Koregisseurin, *die;* (of company, institute) Mitdirektor, *der*/-direktorin, *die*

codling *n.* (fish) Dorsch, *der*

cod-liver ˈoil *n.* Lebertran, *der*

codpiece /ˈkɒdpi:s/ *n.* (Hist.) Hosenlatz, *der*

co-driver /ˈkəʊdraɪvə(r)/ *n.* Beifahrer, *der*/-fahrerin, *die*

cods /kɒdz/, **codswallop** /ˈkɒdzwɒləp/ *ns.* (Brit. coll.) Stuss, *der* (ugs.); **this is a load of ~:** das ist großer Stuss

coed /ˈkəʊed/ (esp. Amer. coll.)
A *n.* Studentin, *die*
B *adj.* koedukativ; Koedukations-; **~ school** gemischte Schule

co-edition /kəʊɪˈdɪʃn/ *n.* gemeinsame Ausgabe

ˈ**co-editor** *n.* Mitherausgeber, *der*/-herausgeberin, *die*

coeducation /kəʊedjʊˈkeɪʃn/ *n.* Koedukation, *die*

coeducational /kəʊedjʊˈkeɪʃənl/ *adj.* koedukativ; Koedukations-

coefficient /kəʊɪˈfɪʃənt/ *n.* (Math., Phys.) Koeffizient, *der*

coelacanth /ˈsi:ləkænθ/ *n.* (Zool.) Coelacanthus, *der*

coequal /kəʊˈi:kwəl/ *adj.* ebenbürtig (geh.)

coerce /kəʊˈɜ:s/ *v.t.* zwingen; **~ sb. into sth.** jmdn. zu etw. zwingen; **~ sb. into doing sth.** jmdn. dazu zwingen, etw. zu tun

coercion /kəʊˈɜ:ʃn/ *n.* Zwang, *der*

coercive /kəʊˈɜ:sɪv/ *adj.* Zwangs‹*gewalt, -herrschaft, -gesetz, -maßnahmen*›

coexist /kəʊɪgˈzɪst/ *v.i.* ‹*Ideen, Überzeugungen:*› nebeneinander bestehen, koexistieren; **~ [together] with sb./sth.** neben jmdm./etw. bestehen; mit jmdm./etw. koexistieren

coexistence /kəʊɪgˈzɪstəns/ *n.* Koexistenz, *die;* **peaceful ~:** friedliche Koexistenz

coexistent /kəʊɪgˈzɪstənt/ *adj.* (formal) nebeneinander bestehend ‹*Systeme, Regierungen*›

coextensive /kəʊɪkˈstensɪv/ *adj.* (formal) **be ~:** übereinstimmen; sich decken

C. of E. /si:əvˈi:/ *abbr.* **= Church of England**

coffee /ˈkɒfɪ/ *n.* 1 Kaffee, *der;* **drink** *or* **have a cup of ~:** eine Tasse Kaffee trinken; **three black/white ~s** drei [Tassen] Kaffee ohne/mit Milch; **I was invited to ~:** ich bin zum Kaffee[trinken] eingeladen worden; **wake up and smell the ~!** (esp. Amer. coll.) sieh den Tatsachen ins Auge! 2 (colour) Kaffeebraun, *das*

coffee: ~ bar *n.* Café, *das;* (in department store, university, etc.) Erfrischungsraum, *der;* **~ bean** *n.* Kaffeebohne, *die;* **~ break** *n.* Kaffeepause, *die;* **~ cup** *n.* Kaffeetasse, *die;* **~ ˈessence** *n.* Kaffee-Extrakt, *der;* **~ filter** *n.* Kaffeefilter, *der;* **~ grinder** *n.* Kaffeemühle, *die;* **~ grounds** *n. pl.* Kaffeesatz, *der;* **~ house** *n.* Café, *das;* (Hist.) Kaffeehaus, *das;* **~ machine, ~ maker** *ns.* Kaffeeautomat, *der;* **~ mill** *n.* Kaffeemühle, *die;* **~ morning** *n.* Morgenkaffee, *der* (*als Wohltätigkeitsveranstaltung*); **~ percolator** *n.* Kaffeemaschine, *die;* **~ pot** *n.* Kaffeekanne, *die;* **~ shop** *n.* Kaffeestube, *die;* Café, *das;* (selling ~ beans etc.) Kaffeegeschäft, *das;* **~ stall** *n.* Kaffeebar, *die;* (serving other light refreshments also) Erfrischungsstand, *der;* **~ table** *n.* Couchtisch, *der; attrib.* **~ table book** Bildband [in Luxusausstattung]; **~ whitener** *n.* Kaffeeweißer, *der*

coffer /ˈkɒfə(r)/ *n.* 1 (box) Truhe, *die* 2 *in pl.* (treasure, funds) **the household ~s** die Privatschatulle; **the ~s of the government** der Staatssäckel (scherzh.) 3 (Archit.) Kassette, *die* 4 (Constr.) **~[dam]** Caisson, *der*

coffin /ˈkɒfɪn/ *n.* Sarg, *der; see also* **nail A 2**

cog /kɒg/ *n.* (Mech.) Zahn, *der;* **be just a ~ [in the wheel/machine]** (fig.) bloß ein Rädchen im Getriebe sein

cogency /ˈkəʊdʒənsɪ/ *n.* (of argument, reason) Stichhaltigkeit, *die;* (of narration, description, slogan) Überzeugungskraft, *die*

cogent /ˈkəʊdʒənt/ *adj.* (convincing) überzeugend ‹*Argument, Grund*›; zwingend ‹*Grund*›; (valid) stichhaltig ‹*Kritik, Analyse*›

cogently /ˈkəʊdʒəntlɪ/ *adv.* ▸**cogent**: überzeugend; zwingend; stichhaltig

cogitate /ˈkɒdʒɪteɪt/ (formal/joc.)
A *v.i.* nachsinnen, nachdenken (**on** über + *Akk.*)
B *v.t.* nachsinnen, nachdenken über (+ *Akk.*)

cogitation /kɒdʒɪˈteɪʃn/ *n.* (formal/joc.) Nachdenken, *das;* Nachsinnen, *das;* **after much ~:** nach langem Grübeln

cognac /ˈkɒnjæk/ *n.* Cognac, *der* (Wz)

cognate /ˈkɒgneɪt/ *adj.* (Ling.) verwandt

cognisance, cognisant ▸**cogniz-**

cognition /kɒgˈnɪʃn/ *n.* Erkenntnis, *die*

cognitive /ˈkɒgnɪtɪv/ *adj.* kognitiv ‹*Fähigkeiten*›; Erkenntnis‹*gehalt, -kräfte*›

cognizance /ˈkɒgnɪzəns/ *n.* (formal) 1 *no pl.* (awareness) Kenntnis, *die;* **have ~ of sth.** von etw. Kenntnis haben; **take ~ of sb./sth.** jmdn./etw. zur Kenntnis nehmen 2 *no pl.* ([right of] dealing with a matter legally) Zuständigkeit, *die* (**of** in + *Dat.*)

cognizant /ˈkɒgnɪzənt/ *adj.* (formal) 1 (having knowledge) in Kenntnis (**of** *Gen.*) 2 (having jurisdiction) zuständig (**of** für)

cognoscenti /kɒnjəˈʃenti:, kɒnjəˈʃentɪ/ *n. pl.* Kenner

cog: ~ railway *n.* (esp. Amer.) Zahnradbahn, *die;* **~wheel** *n.* Zahnrad, *das*

cohabit /kəʊˈhæbɪt/ *v.i.* zusammenleben; in eheähnlicher Gemeinschaft leben (Rechtsspr.)

cohabitation /kəʊhæbɪˈteɪʃn/ *n.* Zusammenleben, *das;* eheähnliche Gemeinschaft (Rechtsspr.)

cohere /kəʊˈhɪə(r)/ *v.i.* 1 ‹*Teile, Ganzes, Gruppe:*› zusammenhalten 2 ‹*Argumentation, Komposition, Aufsatz:*› in sich (*Dat.*) geschlossen sein

coherence /kəʊˈhɪərəns/ *n.* 1 Zusammenhang, *der;* Kohärenz, *die* (geh.); (in work, system, form) Geschlossenheit, *die* 2 (Phys.) Kohärenz, *die*

coherent /kəʊˈhɪərənt/ *adj.* 1 (cohering) zusammenhängend 2 (fig.) zusammenhängend; kohärent (geh.); in sich (*Dat.*) geschlossen ‹*System, Ganzes, Werk, Aufsatz, Form*›; **a ~ presentation of the facts** eine [in sich (*Dat.*)] stimmige Darlegung der Fakten 3 (Phys.) kohärent

coherently /kəʊˈhɪərəntlɪ/ *adv.* zusammenhängend; im Zusammenhang

cohesion /kəʊˈhi:ʒn/ *n.* 1 (sticking together) Zusammenhängen, *das;* (of substances) Haften, *das* 2 (fig.) (of group, state, community) Zusammenhalt, *der;* Kohäsion, *die* (geh.) 3 (Phys.) Kohäsion, *die*

Co'hesion Fund *n.* (EU) Kohäsionsfonds, *der*

cohesive /kəʊ'hi:sɪv/ *adj.* geschlossen, in sich (*Dat.*) ruhend ‹*Ganzes, Einheit, Form*›; stimmig ‹*Stil, Argument*›; kohäsiv ‹*Masse, Mischung*›

cohort /'kəʊhɔ:t/ *n.* 1 (division of Roman army, band of warriors) Kohorte, *die* 2 (group) Gruppe, *die* 3 (Amer.: assistant, colleague) Helfer, *der*/Helferin, *die*

coiffure /kwɑ:'fjʊə(r)/ *n.* Frisur, *die;* Coiffure, *die* (veralt., geh.)

coil /kɔɪl/

A *v.t.* 1 (arrange) aufwickeln; **the snake ~ed itself round a branch** die Schlange wand sich um einen Ast 2 (twist) aufdrehen; **the snake ~ed itself up** die Schlange rollte sich auf

B *v.i.* 1 (twist) **~ round sth.** etw. umschlingen 2 (move sinuously) sich winden; ‹*Rauch:*› sich ringeln

C *n.* 1 **~s of rope/wire/piping** aufgerollte Seile *Pl.*/aufgerollter Draht/aufgerollte Leitungen *Pl.* 2 (single turn of ~ed thing) Windung, *die* 3 (length of ~ed rope etc.) Stück, *das* 4 (lock of hair) Locke, *die* 5 (contraceptive device) Spirale, *die* 6 (Electr.) Spule, *die*

'coil spring *n.* Spiralfeder, *die*

coin /kɔɪn/

A ▸ ❶ p. 1332 *n.* Münze, *die;* (metal money) Münzen *Pl.;* Münzgeld, *das;* **in ~:** in Münzen; **the other side of the ~** (fig.) die Kehrseite der Medaille; **pay sb. in his own ~** (fig.) jmdm. in *od.* mit gleicher Münze heimzahlen

B *v.t.* 1 (invent) prägen ‹*Wort, Redewendung*›; **…, to ~ a phrase** (iron.) …, um mich ganz originell auszudrücken 2 (make) prägen ‹*Geld*›; **~ money** (fig.) Geld scheffeln 3 (make into money) münzen (Gold, Silber usw.)

coinage /'kɔɪnɪdʒ/ *n.* 1 (system) Währung, *die* 2 (coins) Münzen *Pl.;* Hartgeld, *das* 3 (coining) Prägung, *die;* Prägen, *das* 4 (invention) Prägung, *die;* **'e-book' and 'bioterrorism' are modern ~s** „E-Book" und „Bioterrorismus" sind Neuprägungen

'coin-box telephone *n.* Münzfernsprecher, *der*

coincide /kəʊɪn'saɪd/ *v.i.* 1 (in space) sich decken; **~ with one another** sich decken 2 (in time) ‹*Ereignisse, Veranstaltungen:*› zusammenfallen 3 (agree together, concur in opinion) übereinstimmen (**with** mit); **~ in sth.** in etw. (*Dat.*) übereinstimmen

coincidence /kəʊ'ɪnsɪdəns/ *n.* 1 (being coincident) Deckungsgleichheit, *die;* (of two points) Zusammenfall, *der* 2 (instance) Zufall, *der;* **by pure** *or* **sheer ~:** rein zufällig; **it was a happy ~:** es traf sich gut; **by a curious ~:** durch einen merkwürdigen Zufall 3 (of events) Duplizität der Ereignisse; Koinzidenz, *die*

coincident /kəʊ'ɪnsɪdənt/ *adj.* (formal) (in space) deckungsgleich ‹*Figuren*›; (in time or place) zusammenfallend; (agreeing) übereinstimmend; **be ~ with sth.** mit etw. deckungsgleich sein/zusammenfallen/übereinstimmen

coincidental /kəʊɪnsɪ'dentl/ *adj.* zufällig; **be ~ with sth.** mit etw. zufällig zusammentreffen

coincidentally /kəʊɪnsɪ'dentəlɪ/ *adv.* gleichzeitig; (by coincidence) zufälligerweise

coiner /'kɔɪnə(r)/ *n.* (esp. Brit.) Falschmünzer, *der*

'coin-operated *adj.* Münz-

coir /'kɔɪə(r)/ *n.* Coir, *das od. die;* Kokosfaser, *die*

coition /kəʊ'ɪʃn/, **coitus** /'kəʊɪtəs/ *ns.* (Med.) Koitus, *der;* Beischlaf, *der*

coitus interruptus /kəʊɪtəs ɪntə'rʌptəs/ *n.* Coitus interruptus, *der*

coke[1] /kəʊk/

A *n.* Koks, *der*

B *v.t.* verkoken

coke[2] *n.* (coll.: cocaine) Koks, *der* (salopp)

Coke ® /kəʊk/ *n.* (drink) Coke, *das* (Wz)

col /kɒl/ *n.* [Berg]sattel, *der*

col. *abbr.* **= column** Sp.

Col. *abbr.* **= Colonel** Obst.

cola /'kəʊlə/ *n.* Cola, *das od. die* (ugs.)

colander /'kʌləndə(r)/ *n.* Sieb, *das;* Durchschlag, *der*

cold /kəʊld/

A *adj.* 1 kalt; **I feel ~:** ich friere; mir ist kalt; **her hands/feet were ~:** sie hatte kalte Hände/Füße 2 (without ardour etc.) kalt ‹*Intellekt, Herz*›; [betont] kühl ‹*Person, Ansprache, Aufnahme, Begrüßung*›; eiskalt ‹*Handlung*›; unterdrückt ‹*Wut*›; **go ~ on sth.** das Interesse an etw. (*Dat.*) verlieren; **leave sb. ~:** jmdn. kalt lassen (ugs.) 3 (dead) kalt 4 (coll.: unconscious) bewusstlos; k.o. (ugs.); **he laid him out ~:** er schlug ihn k.o.; **the punch knocked him out ~:** durch den Schlag ging er bewusstlos zu Boden 5 (coll.: at one's mercy) **have sb. ~:** jmdn. am Kragen haben (ugs.) 6 (sexually frigid) [gefühls-]kalt 7 (slow to warm) kalt ‹*Boden*› 8 (unrehearsed) ohne Vorbereitung *nachgestellt* 9 (chilling, depressing) kalt ‹*Farbe*›; nackt ‹*Tatsache, Statistik*› 10 (uninteresting) fade ‹*Geschichte*›; **the news is already ~:** für die Sache interessiert sich niemand mehr 11 (Hunting) kalt ‹*Fährte*›; (in children's games) **you're ~ and getting ~er** kalt, noch kälter

B *adv.* 1 (in ~ state) kalt; (without preparation) ohne Vorbereitung ‹*tun*› 2 (Amer. coll.: completely) voll (salopp)

C *n.* 1 Kälte, *die;* **shiver with ~:** vor Kälte (*Dat.*) zittern; **be left out in the ~** (fig.) links liegen gelassen werden 2 ▸ ❶ p. 1231 (illness) Erkältung, *die;* **~ [in the head]** Schnupfen, *der.* See *also* **blood A 1, 4; catch A 5; cold turkey; fish A 3; snap C 5; water**

cold: ~-blooded /'kəʊldblʌdɪd/ *adj.* 1 wechselwarm ‹*Tier*›; kaltblütig (selten); **~-blooded animals** Kaltblüter *Pl.;* wechselwarme Tiere; 2 (callous) kaltblütig ‹*Person, Mord*›; **~-call** A *v.t.* unangemeldet besuchen; (phone) kalt anrufen; B *n.* unangemeldeter Besuch; (phone call) Kaltanruf, *der;* **~-calling** *n., no pl.* unangemeldete Besuche; (by phone) Kaltanrufe *Pl.;* **~ chisel** *n.* (Metalw.) Kaltmeißel, *der;* **~ 'comfort** *n.* ein schwacher Trost; **~ cream** *n.* Coldcream, *die od. das;* **~ cuts** *n. pl.* Aufschnitt, *der;* **~ frame** *n.* Frühbeet, *das;* **~ 'front** *n.* (Meteorol.) Kaltfront, *die;* **~ 'fusion** *n., no pl.* (Phys.) kalte Fusion; **~-hearted** *adj.* kaltherzig

coldly /'kəʊldlɪ/ *adv.* [betont] kühl; [eis]kalt ‹*handeln*›

cold 'meat *n.* 1 kaltes Fleisch; **~s** Aufschnitt, *der* 2 (sl.: corpse) Kadaver, *der* (salopp)

coldness /'kəʊldnɪs/ *n., no pl.* 1 Kälte, *die;* **the ~ of the weather** die Kälte; das kalte Wetter 2 (feeling cold) Frieren, *das;* (of hands, feet) Kälte, *die* 3 (lack of ardour etc.) (of heart, intellect) Kälte, *die;* (of person, attitude, manner, look) betonte Kühle 4 (of dead body, colour) Kälte, *die*

cold: ~-pressed *adj.* kaltgepresst; **~-'shoulder** *v.t.* schneiden (fig.); **~ sore** *n.* Erkältungsbläschen, *das;* **~ 'steel** *n.* kalter Stahl (dichter.); Hieb- und Stichwaffen *Pl.;* **~ 'storage** *n.* Kühllagerung, *die;* **put sth. in ~ storage** (fig.) etw. auf Eis legen (fig.); **~store** *n.* Kühlhaus, *das;* **~ 'sweat** *n.* kalter Schweiß; **break out in a ~ sweat** in kalten Schweiß ausbrechen; **~ 'turkey** *n.* (Amer. sl.) Totalentzug, *der;* Cold turkey, *der* (Drogenjargon); *attrib.* **the ~ turkey cure/treatment** Totalentzugstherapie, *die;* **~ 'war** *n.* kalter Krieg; **~ wave** *n.* Kältewelle, *die;* **~-work** *v.t.* kaltformen ‹*Metall*›

coleslaw /'kəʊlslɔ:/ *n.* Kohl-, Krautsalat, *der*

coleus /'kəʊlɪəs/ *n.* (Bot.) Buntnessel, *die*

colic /'kɒlɪk/ *n.* Kolik, *die*

coliseum /kɒlɪ'si:əm/ *n.* (Amer.) Stadion, *das*

colitis /kə'laɪtɪs/ *n.* ▸ ❶ p. 1231 (Med.) Entzündung des Dickdarms; Kolitis, *die* (fachspr.)

collaborate /kə'læbəreɪt/ *v.i.* 1 (work jointly) zusammenarbeiten; **~ [with sb.] on sth.** zusammen [mit jmdm.] an etw. (*Dat.*) arbeiten; **~ [with sb.] on** *or* **in doing sth.** mit jmdm. bei etw. zusammenarbeiten 2 (cooperate with enemy) kollaborieren (abwertend); zusammenarbeiten

collaboration /kəlæbə'reɪʃn/ *n.* Zusammenarbeit, *die;* (with enemy) Kollaboration, *die* (abwertend); **work in ~ with sb.** mit jmdm. zusammenarbeiten

collaborative /kə'læbərətɪv/ *adj.* kooperativ

collaborator /kə'læbəreɪtə(r)/ *n.* Mitarbeiter, *der*/-arbeiterin, *die;* (with enemy) Kollaborateur, *der*/Kollaborateurin, *die* (abwertend); **they were ~s on this book** sie haben zusammen an diesem Buch gearbeitet

collage /'kɒlɑ:ʒ/ *n.* Collage, *die*

collagen /'kɒlədʒən/ *n., no pl.* (Biochem.) Kollagen, *das*

collapse /kə'læps/

A *n.* 1 (of person) (physical, mental breakdown) Zusammenbruch, *der;* (heart attack; of lung, blood vessel, circulation) Kollaps, *der;* (cerebral haemorrhage) Gehirnschlag, *der* 2 (of tower, bridge, structure, wall, roof) Einsturz, *der;* (of tent) Zusammenfallen, *das;* (of table, chair) Zusammenbruch, *der* 3 (fig.: failure) Zusammenbruch, *der;* (of negotiations, plans, hopes) Scheitern, *das;* (of civilization, empire, society, system) Zerfall, *der;* (of prices, currency) Sturz, *der*

B *v.i.* 1 ‹*Person:*› zusammenbrechen, (Med.) kollabieren; ‹*Lunge, Gefäß, Kreislauf:*› kollabieren; **his circulation ~d** er erlitt einen Kreislaufkollaps; **~ into tears** weinend zusammenbrechen; **~ with laughter** (fig.) sich vor Lachen kugeln 2 ‹*Zelt:*› in sich zusammenfallen; ‹*Tisch, Stuhl:*› zusammenbrechen; ‹*Turm, Brücke, Gebäude, Mauer, Dach:*› einstürzen 3 (fig.: fail) ‹*Verhandlungen, Pläne, Hoffnungen:*› scheitern; ‹*Zivilisation, Reich, Gesellschaft, System:*› zerfallen; ‹*Geschäft, Unternehmen usw.:*› zusammenbrechen, zugrunde gehen; ‹*Traum:*› zerbrechen; ‹*Preise, Währung:*› [zusammen]stürzen 4 (fold down) ‹*Fernrohr, Spazierstock:*› sich zusammenschieben lassen; ‹*Regenschirm, Fahrrad, Tisch:*› sich zusammenklappen lassen

C *v.t.* zusammenklappen ‹*Regenschirm, Fahrrad, Tisch*›; zusammenschieben ‹*Fernrohr*›

collapsible /kə'læpsɪbl/ *adj.* Klapp-, zusammenklappbar ‹*Stuhl, Tisch, Fahrrad*›; Falt-, faltbar ‹*Boot*›; zusammenschiebbar ‹*Fernrohr*›; **it is ~:** es lässt sich zusammenklappen/falten/zusammenschieben

collar /'kɒlə(r)/

A *n.* 1 Kragen, *der;* **with ~ and tie** mit Krawatte; **[surgical] ~:** Halsmanschette, *die;* **hot under the ~** (fig.) (embarrassed) verlegen; (angry) wütend 2 (for dog) [Hunde]halsband, *das;* Halsung, *die* (Jagdw.) 3 (for horse) Kumt, *das;* Kummet, *das* 4 (on bolt, pipe, etc.) Bund, *der*

B *v.t.* 1 (seize) am Kragen kriegen (ugs.); schnappen (ugs.) 2 (coll.: appropriate) sich (*Dat.*) unter den Nagel reißen (salopp); klemmen (salopp)

collar: ~bone *n.* (Anat.) Schlüsselbein, *das;* **~ button** *n.* 1 (Brit.) Hemd[en]knopf, *der;* 2 (Amer.: stud) Kragenknopf, *der;* **~ stud** *n.* (esp. Brit.) Kragenknopf, *der*

collate /kə'leɪt/ *v.t.* 1 (Bibliog.: compare) kollationieren (Buchw.) ‹*Manuskripte, Druckbögen*›; **~ a copy with the original** eine Abschrift mit dem Original vergleichen 2 (put together) zusammenstellen ‹*Daten, Beweismaterial*›

collateral /kə'lætərl/

A *adj.* 1 (subordinate) nebensächlich ‹*Dinge, Themen*›; (contributory) **~ evidence** zusätzliches Beweismaterial 2 **~ relatives** Verwandte einer Seitenlinie

B *n.* 1 (person) Kollateralverwandte, *der/die* (veralt.) 2 (property pledged as guarantee) **~ [security]** Sicherheiten *Pl.*

col'lateral damage *n., no pl.* Kollateralschäden *Pl.*

collation /kə'leɪʃn/ *n.* 1 Textvergleich, *der;* (of book or set of sheets) Kollationierung, *die* (Buchw.) 2 (light meal) Imbiss, *der;* Kollation, *die* (veralt., landsch.); (in RC Ch.) Kollation, *die;* **cold ~:** kaltes Büfett

collator /kə'leɪtə(r)/ *n.* (Computing) Mischer, *der*

colleague /'kɒli:g/ *n.* Kollege, *der*/Kollegin, *die*

collect[1] /kə'lekt/

A *v.i.* 1 (assemble) sichversammeln 2 (accumulate) ‹*Staub, Müll usw.:*› sich ansammeln

B *v.t.* 1 (assemble) sammeln; aufsammeln ‹*Müll,*

leere Flaschen usw.›; ~ **volunteers** Freiwillige zusammenbringen; ~ **[up] one's belongings** seine Siebensachen (ugs.) zusammensuchen; **she ~ed a lot of praise/good marks** sie hat viel Lob/viele gute Noten eingeheimst (ugs.); ~ **dust** Staub anziehen **2** (fetch, pick up) abholen ‹*Menschen, Dinge*›; ~ **a parcel from the post office** ein Paket bei *od.* auf der Post abholen; ~ **sb. from the station** jmdn. am Bahnhof *od.* von der Bahn abholen **3** (get from others) eintreiben ‹*Steuern, Zinsen, Schulden*›; [wohltätig] sammeln ‹*Geld, Altkleider*›; kassieren ‹*Miete, Fahrgeld*›; beziehen ‹*Zahlungen, Sozialhilfe*›; einsammeln ‹*Fahrkarten*›; ~ **on delivery** (Amer.) per Nachnahme **4** (as hobby) sammeln ‹*Münzen, Bücher, Briefmarken, Gemälde usw.*› **5** (regain control of) ~ **one's wits/thoughts** seine Gedanken sammeln **6** (coll. abs.: receive money) abkassieren (ugs.) (**on** bei)

C *adj.* (Amer.) **a ~ telephone call** ein R-Gespräch; **a ~ telegram** ein Nachnahmetelegramm

D *adv.* (Amer.) **send a message ~:** eine vom Empfänger zu bezahlende Nachricht senden; **pay for the goods ~:** die Ware bei Lieferung bezahlen; **he called New York ~:** er führte ein R-Gespräch nach New York

collect² /ˈkɒlekt/ *n.* (Eccl.) Altargebet, *das;* Kollekte, *die* (veralt.)

collectable /kəˈlektəbl/

A *adj.* (worth collecting) als Sammelobjekt geeignet

B *n.* Sammelobjekt, *das*

collected /kəˈlektɪd/ *adj.* **1** (gathered) gesammelt **2** (calm) gesammelt; gelassen

collectedly /kəˈlektɪdlɪ/ *adv.* gesammelt; gelassen

collection /kəˈlekʃn/ *n.* **1** (collecting) Sammeln, *das;* (of rent, fares) Kassieren, *das;* (of taxes, interest, debts) Eintreiben, *das;* (of goods, persons) Abholen, *das;* **make** *or* **hold a ~ of old clothes** eine Altkleidersammlung durchführen **2** (amount of money collected) Sammlung, *die;* (in church) Kollekte, *die;* **take the ~:** einsammeln **3** (of mail) Abholung, *die;* (from postbox) Leerung, *die* **4** (group collected) (of coins, books, stamps, paintings, etc.) Sammlung, *die;* (of fashionable clothes) Kollektion, *die;* (of people) Ansammlung, *die* **5** (accumulated quantity) Ansammlung, *die*

collective /kəˈlektɪv/

A *adj.* kollektiv; gesamt; ~ **interests** gemeinsame Interessen; Gesamt- *od.* Kollektivinteressen; ~ **leadership/responsibility** kollektive Führung/Verantwortung; ~ **guilt** Kollektivschuld, *die;* ~ **agreement** Tarifvertrag, *der*

B *n.* **1** Genossenschaftsbetrieb, *der* **2** ▸**collective noun**

collective: ~ **ˈbargaining** *n.* Tarifverhandlungen *Pl.;* ~ **ˈfarm** *n.* landwirtschaftliche Produktionsgenossenschaft, LPG, *die* (bes. DDR); Kolchose, *die*

collectively /kəˈlektɪvlɪ/ *adj.* gemeinsam; **work/act** ~: gemeinsam arbeiten/handeln

collective: ~ **ˈnoun** *n.* (Ling.) Kollektivum, *das;* Sammelbegriff, *der;* ~ **ˈownership** *n.* Kollektiveigentum, *das* (**of** an + *Dat.*); Gemeineigentum, *das* (**of** an + *Dat.*); ~ **seˈcurity** *n.* kollektive Sicherheit

collectivism /kəˈlektɪvɪzm/ *n.* Kollektivwirtschaft, *die;* (doctrine) Kollektivismus, *der*

collectivization /kəlektɪvaɪˈzeɪʃn/ *n., no pl.* Kollektivierung, *die*

collector /kəˈlektə(r)/ *n.* **1** (of stamps, coins, etc.) Sammler, *der*/Sammlerin, *die;* (of taxes) Einnehmer, *der*/Einnehmerin, *die;* (of rent, cash) Kassierer, *der*/Kassiererin, *die;* (of jumble) Abholer, *der*/Abholerin, *die; see also* **ticket collector** **2** (of electric train) Stromabnehmer, *der*

collector: **~'s item, ~'s piece** *ns.* Liebhaberstück, *das;* Sammlerstück, *das*

colleen /kɒˈliːn/ *n.* (Ir.) [junges] Mädel

college /ˈkɒlɪdʒ/ *n.* **1** (esp. Brit.: independent corporation in university) College, *das* **2** (small university) [private] Hochschule **3** (place of further education) Fach[hoch]schule, *die;* **military/naval ~:** Militär-/Marineakademie; **go to ~** (esp. Amer.) studieren; **start ~** (esp. Amer.) sein Studium aufnehmen **4** (esp. Brit.: school) Internatsschule, *die;* Kolleg, *das* **5** (of physicians, surgeons) [Ärzte]kammer, *die;* (of cardinals) Kollegium, *das*

College: ~ **of ˈArms** *n.* (esp. Brit.) Heroldsamt, *das;* ~ **of Eduˈcation** Pädagogische Hochschule; (for graduates) Studienseminar, *das*

> **college of further education (CFE)**
>
> Ein Collegetyp in Großbritannien, der Personen über 16 Jahren Voll- und Teilzeitkurse anbietet. Dazu gehören Vorbereitungskurse für **GCSE** und **A levels** sowie Tages- und Abendkurse in diversen Fächern wie Fremdsprachen und Informatik bis hin zu Töpferei und Autowartung.

collegiate /kəˈliːdʒət/ *adj.* College‹*leben, -system usw.*›; **Oxford has a ~ structure/is a ~ university** die Universität von Oxford ist nach dem Collegesystem organisiert

collide /kəˈlaɪd/ *v.i.* **1** (come into collision) zusammenstoßen (**with** mit); ‹*Schiff:*› kollidieren **2** (be in conflict) zusammenprallen; kollidieren

collie /ˈkɒlɪ/ *n.* Collie, *der*

collier /ˈkɒlɪə(r)/ *n.* **1** ▸ⓘ **p. 1260** ▸**coal miner** **2** (ship) Kohlenschiff, *das*

colliery /ˈkɒljərɪ/ *n.* Kohlengrube, *die*

collision /kəˈlɪʒn/ *n.* **1** (colliding) Zusammenstoß, *der;* (between ships) Kollision, *die;* **come into ~:** zusammenstoßen; ‹*Schiffe:*› in Kollision geraten, kollidieren; **a head-on ~ of a car with a bus** *or* **between a car and a bus** ein Frontalzusammenstoß eines PKW mit einem Bus **2** (fig.) Konflikt, *der;* Kollision, *die;* **come into ~ with the law** in Konflikt mit dem Gesetz geraten

colˈlision course *n.* (lit. or fig.) Kollisionskurs, *der;* **on a ~:** auf Kollisionskurs

colˈlision damage waiver *n.* CDW-Versicherung, *die*

collocate /ˈkɒləkeɪt/

A *v.t.* **1** (place together) zusammenstellen **2** (arrange) [an]ordnen **3** (put in a place) aufführen **4** (Ling.) kombinieren, (fachspr.) kollokieren ‹*Wörter*›

B *v.i.* (Ling.) kollokieren

collocation /kɒləˈkeɪʃn/ *n.* Zusammenstellung, *die;* (arrangement) Anordnung, *die;* (Ling.: of words) Kollokation, *die*

collocator /ˈkɒləkeɪtə(r)/ *n.* (Ling.) Kollokator, *der*

colloid /ˈkɒlɔɪd/ *n.* (Chem.) Kolloid, *das*

colloidal /kəˈlɔɪdl/ *adj.* (Chem.) kolloid[al]

colloquial /kəˈləʊkwɪəl/ *adj.* umgangssprachlich; ~ **language** Umgangssprache, *die*

colloquialism /kəˈləʊkwɪəlɪzm/ *n.* **1** (style) Umgangssprache, *die* **2** (a form) umgangssprachlicher Ausdruck

colloquially /kəˈləʊkwɪəlɪ/ *adv.* umgangssprachlich

colloquium /kəˈləʊkwɪəm/ *n., pl.* **colloquia** /kəˈləʊkwɪə/ Kolloquium, *das*

colloquy /ˈkɒləkwɪ/ *n.* (formal) **1** *no pl.* (act of conversing) Konversation, *die* **2** (a conversation) Unterhaltung, *die*

collude /kəˈluːd/ *v.i.* konspirieren; ~ **in sth./in doing sth.** heimlich etw. vereinbaren/heimlich übereinkommen, etw. zu tun

collusion /kəˈljuːʒn, kəˈluːʒn/ *n.* geheime Absprache; **act in ~ with sb.** mit jmdm. gemeinsame Sache machen

collywobbles /ˈkɒlɪwɒblz/ *n. pl.* (coll.) (feeling of apprehension) flaues Gefühl (ugs.) [im Magen]; (stomach ache) Bauchschmerzen *Pl.*

cologne ▸**eau de Cologne**

Cologne /kəˈləʊn/ ▸ⓘ **p. 1643**

A *pr. n.* Köln (*das*)

B *attrib. adj.* Kölner

Colombia /kəˈlɒmbɪə/ *pr. n.* Kolumbien (*das*)

Colombian /kəˈlɒmbɪən/ ▸ⓘ **p. 1345**

A *adj.* kolumbianisch

B *n.* Kolumbianer, *der*/Kolumbianerin, *die*

colon¹ /ˈkəʊlən/ *n.* Doppelpunkt, *der;* Kolon, *das* (veralt.)

colon² /ˈkəʊlən, ˈkəʊlɒn/ *n.* ▸ⓘ **p. 951** (Anat.) Grimmdarm, *der*

colonel /kɜːnl/ *n.* ▸ⓘ **p. 1634** **1** (highest regimental officer) Oberst, *der* **2** (member of military junta) Obrist, *der* (*abwertend*). *See also* **blimp 1**; **chief A 3**

colonial /kəˈləʊnɪəl/ *adj.* **1** (of colony) Kolonial-; kolonial; ~ **empire** Kolonialreich, *das;* **C~ Office** (Hist.) Kolonialministerium, *das* **2** (Amer.: of period of British colonies) kolonial; Kolonial-; ~ **architecture** Kolonialstil, *der*

colonialism /kəˈləʊnɪəlɪzm/ *n.* Kolonialismus, *der*

colonialist /kəˈləʊnɪəlɪst/ *n.* Kolonialist, *der*/Kolonialistin, *die; attrib.* kolonialistisch

colonic /kəʊˈlɒnɪk/ *adj.* (Med.) Kolon-; des Grimmdarms *nachgestellt*

colonic irˈrigation *n.* (Med.) Dickdarmspülung, *die*

colonisation, colonise ▸**coloniz-**

colonist /ˈkɒlənɪst/ *n.* Siedler, *der*/Siedlerin, *die;* Kolonist, *der*/Kolonistin, *die*

colonization /kɒlənaɪˈzeɪʃn/ *n.* Kolonisation, *die;* Kolonisierung, *die*

colonize /ˈkɒlənaɪz/ *v.t.* kolonisieren; besiedeln ‹*unbewohntes Gebiet*›

colonnade /kɒləˈneɪd/ *n.* (Archit.) Säulengang, *der;* Kolonnade, *die*

colony /ˈkɒlənɪ/ *n.* Kolonie, *die;* **a ~ of artists/ants** eine Künstlerkolonie/ein Ameisenstaat

colophon /ˈkɒləfən/ *n.* **1** (tailpiece) Kolophon, *der* **2** (on title page) Signet, *das*

color (Amer.) ▸**colour**

Colorado beetle /kɒləˈrɑːdəʊ biːtl/ *n.* Kartoffelkäfer, *der;* Coloradokäfer, *der* (fachspr.)

coloration /kʌləˈreɪʃn/ *n.* **1** (colouring) Kolorierung, *die* **2** (colour) Färbung, *die*

coloratura /kɒlərɑˈtʊrə, kɒlərəˈtjʊrə/ *n.* (Mus.) Koloratur, *die;* ~ **soprano** Koloratursopran, *der*

colored (Amer.) ▸**coloured**

colossal /kəˈlɒsl/ *adj.* **1** (gigantic, huge) ungeheuer; gewaltig ‹*Bauwerk*› **2** (of or like a colossus) riesenhaft, kolossal ‹*Mann, Statue*› **3** (coll.: remarkable, splendid) ungeheuer, (veralt.) kolossal ‹*Irrtum, Glücksfall*›

colossus /kəˈlɒsəs/ *n., pl.* **colossi** /kəˈlɒsaɪ/ *or* **~es** Koloß, *der*

colostomy /kəˈlɒstəmɪ/ *n.* (Med.) Kolostomie, *die*

colour /ˈkʌlə(r)/ (Brit.)

A *n.* **1** Farbe, *die;* **primary ~s** Grundfarben *Pl.;* Primärfarben *Pl.* (fachspr.); **secondary ~s** Mischfarben *Pl.;* **what ~ is it?** welche Farbe hat es?; **see the ~ of sb.'s money** (fig.) Geld sehen (ugs.) **2** (Art, Her.) Farbe, *die;* (Art: colouring) Farbe, *die;* Farbgebung, *die;* **a box of ~s** ein Mal- *od.* Tuschkasten **3** (complexion) [Gesichts]farbe, *die;* **change ~:** die Farbe ändern; (go red/pale) rot/blass werden; **lose/gain ~:** Farbe verlieren/wieder Farbe bekommen; **get one's ~ back** wieder etwas Farbe kriegen; **bring the ~ back to sb.'s cheeks** jmdm. wieder Farbe geben; **he is/feels/looks a bit off ~ today** ihm ist heute nicht besonders gut/er fühlt sich heute nicht besonders gut/er sieht heute nicht besonders gut aus; **have a high ~:** rot im Gesicht sein; ein rotes Gesicht haben **4** (racial) Hautfarbe, *die* **5** *usu. in pl.* (appearance, aspect) Farben *Pl.;* **appear in its true ~s** sich so zeigen, wie es wirklich ist; **see sth. in its true ~s** etw. so sehen, wie es wirklich ist **6** (appearance of reasonableness) **give** *or* **lend ~ to sth.** etw. glaubhaft *od.* glaubwürdig erscheinen lassen **7** (character, tone, quality, etc.) Charakter, *der;* Gepräge, *das;* (aspect, appearance) Anstrich, *der;* **add ~ to a story** einer Erzählung Farbe *od.* Kolorit geben; **local ~:** Lokalkolorit, *das* **8** *in pl.* (ribbon, dress, etc., worn as symbol of party, club, etc.) Farben *Pl.;* **get** *or* **win one's ~s** (Brit. Sport) als Vollmitglied aufgenommen werden; **give sb. his ~s** (Brit. Sport) jmdn. als Vollmitglied aufnehmen; **show one's [true] ~s** *or* **oneself in one's true ~s** (fig.) sein wahres Gesicht zeigen **9** *in pl.* (national flag) Farben *Pl.* **10** (flag) Fahne, *die;* (of ship) Flagge, *die;* **Queen's/King's/regimental ~:** Regimentsfahne, *die;* **serve with the ~s** (Hist.) der Fahne dienen (veralt.); **join the ~s** (Hist.) den bunten Rock anziehen (veralt.); **come off/pass with flying ~s** (fig.) glänzend abschneiden; **nail one's ~s to the mast** (fig.) Farbe bekennen; sich zu seiner Überzeugung bekennen;

C

lower one's ~ (fig.) zurückstecken [11] (Mus.) (timbre, quality) Klangfarbe, *die. See also* **troop** C
B *v.t.* [1] (give ~ to) Farbe geben (+ *Dat.*) [2] (paint) malen; **~ in** ausmalen ‹*Bild, Figur*›; **~ a wall red** eine Wand rot anmalen [3] (stain, dye) färben ‹*Material, Stoff*› [4] (disguise) verstecken [5] (misrepresent) [schön]färben ‹*Nachrichten, Bericht*› [6] (fig.: influence) beeinflussen
C *v.i.* [1] ‹*Blätter, Trauben:*› sich verfärben [2] (blush) **~ [up]** erröten; rot werden

colouration (Brit.) ▸ **coloration**

colour: ~ bar *n.* Rassenschranke, *die;* **~-blind** *adj.* farbenblind; **a ~-blind person** ein Farbenblinder/eine Farbenblinde; **~-blindness** *n.* Farbenblindheit, *die;* **~ code** *n.* Farbkennzeichnung, *die;* **~-coded** *adj.* mit Farbkennzeichnung *nachgestellt*

coloured /ˈkʌləd/ (Brit.)
A *adj.* [1] farbig; **yellow-/green-~:** gelb/grün; **~ paper** (for printing or wrapping) farbiges Papier; (for making designs) Buntpapier, *das;* **~ pencil** Farbstift, *der* [2] (of non-white descent) farbig; **~ people** Farbige *Pl.* [3] (S. Afr.: of mixed descent) gemischtrassig; gemischtrassisch; **~ people** Mischlinge *Pl.*
B *n.* [1] Farbige, *der/die* [2] (S. Afr.: person of mixed descent) Mischling, *der*

colour: ~-fast *adj.* farbecht; **~ film** *n.* Farbfilm, *der;* **~ filter** *n.* Farbfilter, *der*

colourful /ˈkʌləfl/ *adj.* (Brit.) bunt; farbenfroh, bunt ‹*Bild, Schauspiel*›; farbig, anschaulich ‹*Sprache, Stil, Bericht*›; buntbewegt ‹*Zeitepoche, Leben*›

colourfully /ˈkʌləfəlɪ/ *adv.* (Brit.) bunt; **~ dressed/striped/painted** bunt gekleidet/-gestreift/-bemalt *attr.*

colouring /ˈkʌlərɪŋ/ *n.* (Brit.) [1] (action) Malen, *das;* **~ 'in** Ausmalen, *das* [2] (colours) Farben *Pl.* [3] (facial complexion) Teint, *der* [4] **~ [matter]** (in food etc.) Farbstoff, *der*

colouring book *n.* Malbuch, *das*

colourless /ˈkʌləlɪs/ *adj.* (Brit.) [1] (without colour) farblos ‹*Flüssigkeit, Gas*›; (pale) blass ‹*Teint*›; (dull-hued) grau, düster ‹*Bild, Stoff, Himmel, Meer*› [2] (fig.) farblos, langweilig ‹*Geschichte, Schilderung, Stil*›; unauffällig ‹*Person*›

colour: ~ magazine ▸ **~ supplement; ~ photograph** *n.* Farbfotografie, -aufnahme, *die;* **~ photography** *n.* Farbfotografie, *die;* **~ printer** *n.* Farbdrucker, *der;* **~ printing** *n.* Farbdruck, *der;* **~ scheme** *n.* Farb[en]zusammenstellung, *die;* **~-sergeant** *n.* (Mil.) ≈ Hauptfeldwebel, *der;* **~ supplement** *n.* Farbbeilage, *die;* **~ television** *n.* Farbfernsehen, *das;* (set) Farbfernsehgerät, *das;* **~ transparency** *n.* Farbdia, *das;* **~way** *n.* farbliche Ausführung; **our sweater comes in two ~ways** unser Pullover ist in zwei Farbstellungen lieferbar

colt /kəʊlt/ *n.* [1] [Hengst]fohlen, *das;* (player in junior team) Fohlen, *das* [2] (inexperienced person) (girl) Küken, *das* (ugs.); (boy) junger Dachs (ugs.) *od.* Springer (ugs.)

coltsfoot /ˈkəʊltsfʊt/ *n., pl.* **~s** (Bot.) Huflattich, *der*

columbine /ˈkɒləmbaɪn/ *n.* (Bot.) Akelei, *die*

Columbus /kəˈlʌmbəs/ *pr. n.* Kolumbus (*der*)

column /ˈkɒləm/ *n.* [1] Säule, *die* [2] (in machine) Ständer, *der;* (of tripod) Säule, *die* [3] (of liquid, vapour, etc.) Säule, *die;* **~ of mercury/smoke** Quecksilber-/Rauchsäule, *die* [4] (division of page, table, etc.) Spalte, *die;* Kolumne, *die;* **a ~ of figures** eine Zahlenkolonne; **in two ~s** zweispaltig [5] (in newspaper) Spalte, *die;* Kolumne, *die;* **the sports ~:** der Sportteil; **the gossip ~:** die Klatschspalte (ugs. abwertend) [6] (of troops, vehicles, ships) Kolonne, *die;* **dodge the ~** (fig. coll.) sich drücken (ugs.) [7] (Amer.: party, faction) Lager, *das*

columnar /kəˈlʌmnə(r)/ *adj.* säulenförmig

ˈcolumn inch *n.* **advertisement of two ~es** ≈ Anzeige von 50 Millimeterzeilen

columnist /ˈkɒləmɪst/ *n.* Kolumnist, *der*/Kolumnistin, *die;* **TV ~:** Fernsehkommentator, *der*/-kommentatorin, *die*

coma /ˈkəʊmə/ *n.* [1] (Med.) Koma, *das;* **be in a ~:** im Koma liegen; **go into a ~:** ins Koma fallen [2] (fig.: torpor) Dämmerzustand, *der*

comatose /ˈkəʊmətəʊs/ *adj.* [1] (Med.) komatös; **be ~:** im Koma liegen [2] (joc.: through drink, drugs) wie im Koma *präd.*

comb /kəʊm/
A *n.* [1] (also as tech. term) Kamm, *der;* (curry-~) Striegel, *der* [2] (action) **give one's hair a ~:** sich (*Dat.*) die Haare kämmen [3] (honey~) Wabe, *die*
B *v.t.* [1] kämmen ‹*Haare, Flachs, Wolle*›; **~ sb.'s/one's hair** jmdm./sich die Haare kämmen; jmdn./sich kämmen; **~ sth. out of sb.'s hair** jmdm. etw. aus den Haaren kämmen [2] (curry) striegeln ‹*Pferd*› [3] (search) durchkämmen ‹*Gelände, Wald*›

Phrasal verb

• **~ 'out** *v.t.* [1] auskämmen ‹*Haare*› [2] (separate for removal) aussortieren [3] (search) durchkämmen; durchforsten

combat /ˈkɒmbæt/
A *n.* Kampf, *der;* **single ~:** Einzelkampf, *der;* (duel) Zweikampf, *der*
B *v.t.* (fig.: strive against) bekämpfen
C *v.i.* (engage in battle or contest) kämpfen

ˈcombat aircraft *n.* Kampfflugzeug, *das*

combatant /ˈkɒmbətənt/
A *adj.* zur Kampftruppe gehörend
B *n.* (in war) Kombattant, *der;* (in duel) Kämpfer, *der*

combat: ~ dress *n.* Kampfanzug, *der;* **~ fatigue** *n.* Frontneurose, *die*

combative /ˈkɒmbətɪv/ *adj.,* **combatively** /ˈkɒmbətɪvlɪ/ *adv.* streitlustig

combativeness /ˈkɒmbətɪvnɪs/ *n., no pl.* Streitlust, *die*

ˈcombat mission *n.* Kampfeinsatz, *der*

combe (Brit.) ▸ **coomb**

combed /kəʊmd/ *adj.* gekämmt

comber /ˈkəʊmə(r)/ *n.* (wave, breaker) Sturzwelle, *die*

combination /kɒmbɪˈneɪʃn/ *n.* [1] Kombination, *die;* **in ~:** zusammen [2] (Chem.) Verbindung, *die* [3] (Brit. Motor Veh.) Motorrad mit Beiwagen [4] *in pl.* (dated Brit.: undergarment) Kombination, *die* (veralt.); Hemdhose, *die* (veralt.)

combiˈnation lock *n.* Kombinationsschloss, *das*

combine
A /kəmˈbaɪn/ *v.t.* [1] (join together) kombinieren; zusammenfügen (**into** zu); vereinigen ‹*Städte*› [2] (possess together) vereinigen; in sich (*Dat.*) vereinigen ‹*Eigenschaften*› [3] (cause to coalesce) verbinden ‹*Substanzen*›
B *v.i.* [1] (join together, coalesce) ‹*Stoffe:*› sich verbinden [2] (cooperate) zusammenwirken; ‹*Parteien:*› sich zusammentun
C /ˈkɒmbaɪn/ *n.* [1] Konzern, *der;* (in socialist economy) Kombinat, *das* [2] (machine) **~ [harvester]** Mähdrescher, *der;* Kombine, *die*

combined /kəmˈbaɪnd/ *adj.* vereint; **a ~ operation** eine gemeinsame Operation

combined: ~-cycle *adj.* Kombizyklus-; Kombi‹*kraftwerk*›; **~ drug therapy** *n.* (Med.) Kombinationstherapie, *die*

combings /ˈkəʊmɪŋz/ *n. pl.* ausgekämmte Haare

combining form /kəmˈbaɪnɪŋ fɔːm/ *n.* (Ling.) Wortbildungselement, *das*

combo /ˈkɒmbəʊ/ *n., pl.* **~s** Combo, *die*

combust /kəmˈbʌst/ *v.t.* verbrennen

combustible /kəmˈbʌstɪbl/ *adj.* [1] brennbar [2] (fig.) entflammbar; erregbar

combustion /kəmˈbʌstʃn/ *n.* Verbrennung, *die;* **~ chamber** (Mech. Engin.) (of jet engine) Brennkammer, *die;* (of internal-~ engine) Verbrennungsraum, *der*

come /kʌm/
A *v.i.,* **came** /keɪm/, **come** [1] (start or move towards or to sth. or sb.) kommen; **~ here!** komm [mal] her!; **[I'm] coming!** [ich] komme schon!; **~ running** angelaufen kommen; **~ running into the room** ins Zimmer gerannt kommen; **~ laughing into the room** lachend ins Zimmer kommen; **not know whether** *or* **if one is coming or going** nicht wissen, wo einem der Kopf steht; **~, ~!** aber ich bitte dich!; **~ [now]!** (fig.) (encouraging) komm!; (don't be hasty) [also] komm! (ugs.)
[2] (arrive at a place) kommen; **they came to a house/town** sie kamen zu einem Haus/in eine Stadt; **he has just ~ from school/America** er ist gerade aus der Schule/aus Amerika gekommen; **let 'em all ~!, ~ one ~ all** (coll.) sollen sie doch alle kommen!; **~ and see me soon** besuchen Sie mich bald einmal!; **the news came as a surprise** die Nachricht kam überraschend; **Christmas/Easter is coming** bald ist Weihnachten/Ostern
[3] (traverse) kommen; **he has ~ a long way** er kommt von weit her; **the project has ~ a long way** (fig.) das Projekt ist schon weit gediehen
[4] (be brought) kommen; **~ to sb.'s notice** *or* **attention/knowledge** jmdm. auffallen/zu Ohren kommen
[5] (enter) kommen; **the train came into the station** der Zug fuhr in den Bahnhof ein
[6] (occur) kommen; (in list etc.) stehen; **the adjective ~s before the noun** das Adjektiv steht vor dem Substantiv
[7] (be~, be) **the shoelaces have ~ undone** die Schnürsenkel sind aufgegangen; **the handle has ~ loose** der Griff ist lose; **it ~s cheaper to buy things in bulk** es ist *od.* (ugs.) kommt billiger, en gros einzukaufen; **it all came right in the end** es ging alles gut aus; **it will all ~ right in the end** es wird schon alles gut gehen; **it ~s easily/naturally to him** das fällt ihm leicht; **what you say ~s to this: ...:** was du sagst, läuft auf Folgendes hinaus: ...; **when it ~s to cooking** wenn es ums Kochen geht; **~ to that, if it ~s to that** wenn es darum geht; **~ to oneself** zu sich selbst kommen; **have ~ to believe/realize that ...:** zu der Überzeugung/Einsicht gelangt sein, dass ...; **we came to know him better** wir lernten ihn allmählich *od.* nach und nach besser kennen
[8] (become present) kommen; **in the coming week/month** kommende Woche/kommenden Monat; **be a coming man** der kommende Mann sein; **this coming Christmas** Weihnachten dieses Jahr; **she had it coming to her** das hat sie sich (*Dat.*) selbst zu verdanken (iron.); **you've got it coming to you if you go on behaving like that** du kannst dich auf was gefasst machen, wenn du so weitermachst (ugs.)
[9] **to ~** (future) künftig; **in years to ~:** in künftigen Jahren; **for some time to ~:** [noch] für einige Zeit
[10] (be left or willed) **he has a lot of money coming to him** er erbt einmal viel Geld; **the farm came to him on his father's death** beim Tod seines Vaters bekam er den Hof
[11] (be result) kommen; **that's what ~s of grumbling** das kommt vom Schimpfen; **nothing came of it** es ist nichts daraus geworden; **~ of noble parents** aus adligem Elternhaus stammen; **the suggestion came from him** der Vorschlag war *od.* stammte von ihm
[12] (reach, extend) **the motorway ~s within 10 miles of us** die Autobahn ist nur zehn Meilen von uns entfernt
[13] (happen) **how ~s it that you ...?** wie kommt es, dass du ...?; **how did you ~ to break your leg?** wie hast du dir denn das Bein gebrochen?; **how ~?** (coll.) wieso?; weshalb?; **~ what may** komme, was wolle (geh.); ganz gleich, was kommt
[14] (be available) ‹*Waren:*› erhältlich sein; **this dress ~s in three sizes** dieses Kleid gibt es in drei Größen *od.* ist in drei Größen erhältlich; **as tough/clever/stupid as they ~:** zäh/schlau/dumm wie sonst was (ugs.)
[15] (coll.: play a part) **~ the bully with sb.** bei jmdm. den starken Mann markieren (salopp); **don't ~ the innocent with me** spiel mir nicht den Unschuldsengel vor! (ugs.); **don't ~ that game with me** komm mir bloß nicht mit dieser Tour *od.* Masche! (salopp); **~ it strong** [es] übertreiben; **~ it too strong** zu dick auftragen (ugs.)
[16] **~ [next] Friday/next week** [nächsten] Freitag/nächste Woche; **it's two years ~**

Christmas since we were divorced Weihnachten sind wir zwei Jahre geschieden [17] (sl.: have orgasm) kommen (salopp)
B *n.* (sl.: semen) Soße, *die* (derb)

Phrasal verbs

- **~ a'bout** *v.i.* [1] passieren; **how did it ~ about that ...?** wie kam es, dass ...? [2] (Naut.) wenden
- **~ across**

A /--'-/ *v.i.* [1] (be understood) ‹*Bedeutung:*› verstanden werden; ‹*Mitteilung, Rede:*› ankommen (ugs.), rüberkommen (salopp) [2] (coll.: make an impression) wirken (**as** wie); **he always wants to ~ across as a tough guy** er will immer den harten Burschen mimen (ugs.) [3] **~ across with** (coll.: give, hand over) rausrücken (ugs.) ‹*Geld, Schlüssel*›; rausrücken mit (ugs.) ‹*Informationen*›
B /'---/ *v.t.* **~ across sb./sth.** jmdm./einer Sache begegnen; **have you ~ across my watch?** ist dir meine Uhr begegnet? (ugs.)

- **~ a'long** *v.i.* (coll.) [1] (hurry up) **~ along!** komm/kommt!; nun mach/macht schon! (ugs.) [2] (try harder) **~ along, now!** nun überleg aber mal! [3] (make progress) **~ along nicely** gute Fortschritte machen; **her maths is coming along nicely** in Mathematik macht sie recht gute Fortschritte *od.* kommt sie recht gut voran [4] (arrive, present oneself/itself) ‹*Person:*› ankommen; ‹*Gelegenheit, Stelle:*› sich bieten; **he'll take any job that ~s along** er nimmt jeden Job, der sich ihm bietet [5] (to place) mitkommen (**with** mit)
- **~ at** *v.t.* [1] herausfinden ‹*Tatsachen, Wahrheit*› [2] (attack) losgehen auf (+ *Akk.*); **he came at me with a knife** er ging mit einem Messer auf mich los
- **~ a'way** *v.i.* [1] weggehen [2] (become detached) sich lösen (**from** von); abgehen (ugs.) (**from** von) [3] (be left) **~ away with the impression/feeling that ...:** mit dem Eindruck/Gefühl gehen, dass ...
- **~ 'back** *v.i.* [1] (return) zurückkommen; ‹*Gedächtnis, Vergangenes:*› wiederkehren [2] (return to memory) **it will ~ back [to me]** es wird mir wieder einfallen [3] **~ back [into fashion]** wiederkommen; wieder in Mode kommen [4] (retort) **~ back at sb. with sth.** jmdm. etw. entgegnen; **the team came back strongly** die Mannschaft spielte glänzend auf. *see also* **~back**
- **~ between** *v.t.* treten zwischen (+ *Akk.*)
- **~ by**

A /'--/ *v.t.* (obtain, receive) kriegen (ugs.); bekommen; **was the money honestly ~ by?** ist das Geld auf ehrliche Weise erworben worden?
B /-'-/ *v.i.* vorbeikommen

- **~ 'down** *v.i.* [1] (collapse) herunterfallen; runterfallen (ugs.); (fall) ‹*Schnee, Regen, Preis:*› fallen; **the beams came down on my head** die Balken fielen mir auf den Kopf [2] (~ to place regarded as lower) herunterkommen; runterkommen (ugs.); (~ southwards) runterkommen (ugs.) [3] (Brit.: leave university) **~ down [from Oxford]** sein Studium [in Oxford] abschließen; **when he came down [from Oxford] he got married** als er sein Studium [in Oxford] abgeschlossen hatte, heiratete er [4] (land) [not]landen; (crash) abstürzen; **~ down in a field** auf einem Acker [not]landen/auf einen Acker stürzen [5] (be transmitted) ‹*Sage, Brauch:*› überliefert werden [6] **~ down to** (reach) reichen bis [7] **~ down to** (be reduced to) hinauslaufen auf (+ *Akk.*) [8] **~ down to** (be a question of) ankommen (**to** auf + *Akk.*) [9] (be reduced; suffer change for the worse) angewiesen sein (**to** auf + *Akk.*); **she has ~ down in the world** sie hat einen Abstieg erlebt [10] (make a decision) **~ down in favour of sb./sth.** sich zu gunsten jmds./einer Sache entscheiden; **~ down on the side of sb./sth.** sich für jmdn./etw. einsetzen [11] **~ down on** (rebuke, pounce on) fertig machen (ugs.); **~ down on sb. for sth.** jmdn. wegen etw. rankriegen (ugs.) [12] **~ down with** bekommen ‹*Krankheit*›. *See also* **~down**; **earth A 1**
- **~ 'forth** *v.i.* herauskommen
- **~ 'in** *v.i.* [1] (enter) hereinkommen; reinkommen (ugs.); **~ in!** herein!; **this is where we came in** (fig.) wie gehabt [2] ‹*Flut:*› kommen [3] (be received) ‹*Nachrichten, Bericht:*› hereinkommen [4] (in radio communication) melden; **Come in, Tom, ~ in, Tom. Over** Tom melden, Tom melden. Ende [5] (make next contribution to discussion etc.) sich einschalten; **would you like to ~ in here, Mr Brown?** würden Sie bitte an dieser Stelle fortfahren, Mr. Brown? [6] (become fashionable) in Mode kommen; aufkommen [7] (become seasonable or available) reinkommen (ugs.); *see also* **handy 2** [8] (gain power, be elected) an die Regierung kommen; ans Ruder kommen (ugs.); rankommen (ugs.) [9] (in race) einlaufen als *od.* durchs Ziel gehen als ‹*Erster usw.*› [10] (as income) ‹*Geld:*› hereinkommen; reinkommen (ugs.) [11] (find a place; have a part to play) **where do I ~ in?** welche Rolle soll ich spielen?; **~ in on sth.** sich an etw. (*Dat.*) beteiligen [12] **~ in for** erregen ‹*Bewunderung, Aufmerksamkeit*›; auf sich (*Akk.*) ziehen, hervorrufen ‹*Kritik*›
- **~ into** *v.t.* [1] (enter) hereinkommen in (+ *Akk.*); ‹*Zug:*› einfahren in ‹*Bahnhof*›; ‹*Schiff:*› einlaufen in ‹*Hafen*› [2] (inherit) erben ‹*Vermögen*› [3] (play a part) **wealth does not ~ into it** Reichtum spielt dabei keine Rolle; **where do I ~ into it?** welche Rolle soll ich [dabei] spielen?
- **~ near** *v.t.* **~ near [to] doing sth.** drauf und dran sein, etw. zu tun (ugs.); **he came near [to] committing suicide** er war kurz davor, sich das Leben zu nehmen
- **~ off**

A /-'-/ *v.i.* [1] (become detached) ‹*Griff, Knopf:*› abgehen; (be removable) sich abnehmen lassen; ‹*Fleck:*› weg-, rausgehen (ugs.) [2] (fall from sth.) runterfallen [3] (emerge from contest etc.) abschneiden [4] (succeed) ‹*Pläne, Versuche:*› Erfolg haben, (ugs.) klappen; **the play/experiment/wedding/holiday didn't ~ off** das Stück war kein Erfolg/das Experiment war erfolglos/die Ehe/der Urlaub war ein Reinfall (ugs.) [5] (take place) stattfinden; **their marriage/holiday did not ~ off** aus ihrer Hochzeit/ihrem Urlaub wurde nichts [6] (coll.: have orgasm) kommen (salopp)
B *v.t.* **~ off a horse/bike** vom Pferd/Fahrrad fallen; **~ 'off it!** (coll.) nun mach mal halblang! (ugs.)

- **~ on**

A /-'-/ *v.i.* [1] (continue coming, follow) kommen; **~ on!** komm, komm/kommt, kommt!; (encouraging) na, komm; (impatient) na, komm schon; (incredulous) ach komm!; **I'll ~ on later** ich komme später nach [2] (make progress) **my work is coming on very well** meine Arbeit macht gute Fortschritte; mit meiner Arbeit geht es gut voran [3] (begin to arrive) ‹*Nacht, Dunkelheit, Winter:*› anbrechen; **the rain came on, it came on to rain** es begann zu regnen; **he thought he had a cold coming on** er glaubte, eine Erkältung zu kriegen [4] (be heard or seen on television etc.) gegeben werden; **the film/opera** *etc.* **doesn't ~ on till 8 o'clock** der Film/die Oper *usw.* ist erst um 8 Uhr [5] (appear on stage or scene) auftreten. *See also* **come-on**
B /'--/ *v.t.* ▸ **~ upon**

- **~ 'out** *v.i.* [1] herauskommen; **~ out [on strike]** in den Streik treten [2] (emerge from examination etc.) **~ out top/second/bottom** am besten/zweitbesten/schlechtesten abschneiden [3] (appear, become visible) ‹*Sonne, Knospen, Blumen:*› herauskommen, (ugs.) rauskommen; ‹*Sterne:*› zu sehen sein [4] (be revealed) ‹*Wahrheit, Nachrichten:*› herauskommen, (ugs.) rauskommen; **the results came out negative** die Resultate waren negativ; **the answer came out wrong** das Ergebnis war falsch [5] (be published, declared, etc.) herauskommen; rauskommen (ugs.); ‹*Ergebnisse, Zensuren:*› bekannt gegeben werden [6] (be solved) ‹*Aufgabe, Rätsel:*› sich lösen lassen [7] (make debut) debütieren [8] (be released from prison) rauskommen (ugs.); herauskommen [9] (declare oneself) **~ out for** *or* **in favour of sth.** sich für etw. aussprechen; etw. befürworten; **~ out against sth.** sich gegen etw. aussprechen [10] ‹*Homosexuelle[r]:*› sich öffentlich zu seiner Homosexualität bekennen [11] (be satisfactorily visible) herauskommen; **you have ~ out very well in all of these photos** du bist auf allen Fotos gut getroffen; **the photo has not ~ out** das Foto ist nichts geworden [12] (be covered) **his face came out in pimples** er bekam im ganzen Gesicht Pickel; **she came out in a rash** sie bekam einen Ausschlag [13] (be removed) ‹*Fleck, Schmutz:*› rausgehen (ugs.) [14] **~ out with** herausrücken mit (ugs.) ‹*Wahrheit, Fakten*›; loslassen (ugs.) ‹*Flüche, Bemerkungen*›
- **~ 'over**

A *v.i.* [1] (~ from some distance) herüberkommen [2] (change sides or opinions) **~ over to sb./sth.** sich jmdm./einer Sache anschließen [3] ▸ **~ across A 2** [4] **she came over funny/dizzy** ihr wurde auf einmal ganz komisch/schwindlig (ugs.); **he came over faint** ihm wurde plötzlich schwarz vor [den] Augen
B *v.t.* kommen über (+ *Akk.*); **what has ~ 'over him?** was ist über ihn gekommen?

- **~ 'round** *v.i.* [1] (make informal visit) vorbeischauen [2] (recover) wieder zu sich kommen [3] (be converted) es sich [anders] (*Dat.*) überlegen; **he came round to my way of thinking** er hat sich meiner Auffassung (*Dat.*) angeschlossen [4] (recur) **Christmas ~s round again** wir haben wieder Weihnachten
- **~ 'through**

A *v.i.* durchkommen
B *v.t.* (survive) überleben

- **~ to**

A /'--/ *v.t.* [1] (amount to) ‹*Rechnung, Gehalt, Kosten:*› sich belaufen auf (+ *Akk.*); **his plans came to nothing** aus seinen Plänen wurde nichts; **he/it will never ~ to much** aus ihm wird nichts Besonderes werden/daraus wird nicht viel [2] (inherit) erben ‹*Vermögen*›; **~ to oneself** ▸ **B** [3] (arrive at) **what is the world coming to?** wohin ist es mit der Welt gekommen?; **this is what he has ~ to** so weit ist es also mit ihm gekommen
B /-'-/ *v.i.* wieder zu sich kommen

- **~ to'gether** *v.i.* ‹*Personen:*› zusammenkommen; ‹*Ereignisse:*› zusammenfallen
- **~ under** *v.t.* [1] (be classed as or among) kommen unter (+ *Akk.*) [2] (be subject to) geraten *od.* kommen unter (+ *Akk.*); **these shops have ~ under new management** diese Läden stehen unter neuer Leitung
- **~ 'up** *v.i.* [1] (~ to place regarded as higher) hochkommen; heraufkommen; (~ northwards) raufkommen (ugs.); **he ~s up to London every other weekend** er kommt jedes zweite Wochenende nach London [2] (Brit.: join university) **~ up [to Cambridge]** sein Studium [in Cambridge] beginnen [3] **~ up to sb.** (approach for talk) auf jmdn. zukommen [4] **~ up with sb.** (get abreast) jmdn. einholen [5] (arise out of ground) herauskommen; rauskommen (ugs.) [6] (be discussed) ‹*Frage, Thema:*› angeschnitten werden, aufkommen; ‹*Name:*› genannt werden; ‹*Fall:*› verhandelt werden [7] (present itself) sich ergeben; **~ up for sale/renewal** zum Kauf angeboten werden/erneuert werden müssen; **coming up** (coll.: sth. is nearly ready) kommt gleich [8] **~ up to** (reach) reichen bis an (+ *Akk.*); (be equal to) entsprechen (+ *Dat.*) ‹*Erwartungen, Anforderungen*› [9] **~ up against sth.** (fig.) auf etw. (*Akk.*) stoßen [10] **~ up with** vorbringen ‹*Vorschlag*›; wissen ‹*Lösung, Antwort*›; haben ‹*Erklärung, Idee*›; geben, liefern ‹*Informationen*›
- **~ upon** *v.t.* [1] (attack) kommen über (+ *Akk.*); **disaster/war came upon them** Unheil/Krieg kam über sie (geh.) *od.* brach über sie herein (geh.) [2] (meet by chance) begegnen (+ *Dat.*)
- **~ with** *v.t.* (be supplied together with) **this model ~s with ...:** zu diesem Modell gehört ...

'comeback *n.* [1] (return to profession etc.) Comeback, *das* [2] (coll.: retort) Reaktion, *die*; **I got an immediate ~ from him that ...:** er entgegnete mir darauf sofort, dass ... [3] (means of redress) **have no ~:** [etw.] nicht beanstanden können

comedian /kə'mi:dɪən/ *n.* ▸ ❶ **p. 1260** Komiker, *der*

comedienne /kəmi:dɪ'en, kəmedɪ'en/ *n.* ▸ ❶ **p. 1260** Komikerin, *die*

'comedown *n.* (loss of prestige etc.) Abstieg, *der*

comedy /'kɒmɪdɪ/ *n.* [1] (Theatre) Lustspiel, *das*; Komödie, *die* [2] (humorous incident in life) komischer Vorfall; **a ~ of errors** eine einzige Kette

C

komischer Irrtümer **3▸** (humour) Witz, *der;* Witzigkeit, *die*

'comedy club *n.* Comedyklub, *der*

come-'hither *attrib. adj.* einladend

comeliness /'kʌmlɪnɪs/ *n., no pl.* Ansehnlichkeit, *die*

comely /'kʌmlɪ/ *adj.* gut aussehend; ansehnlich

'come-on *n.* (coll.) (lure) **give sb. the ~:** jmdn. anmachen (salopp)

comer /'kʌmə(r)/ *n.* **the competition is open to all ~s** an dem Wettbewerb kann sich jeder beteiligen; **the first ~:** derjenige, der zuerst kommt

comestible /kə'mestɪbl/ *n. usu. in pl.* Nahrungsmittel, *das*

comet /'kɒmɪt/ *n.* (Astron.) Komet, *der*

comeuppance /kʌm'ʌpəns/ *n.* **get one's ~:** die Quittung kriegen (fig.)

comfort /'kʌmfət/

A *n.* **1▸** (consolation) Trost, *der;* **it is a ~/no ~ to know that ...:** es ist tröstlich/alles andere als tröstlich zu wissen, dass ...; **he takes ~ from the fact that ...:** er tröstet sich mit der Tatsache, dass ... **2▸** (physical well-being) Behaglichkeit, *die;* **live in great ~:** sehr behaglich *od.* bequem leben **3▸** (person) Trost, *der;* **be a ~ to sb.** jmdm. *od.* für jmdn. ein Trost sein **4▸** (cause of satisfaction) Tröstung, *die* **5▸** *usu. in pl.* (things that make life easy) Komfort, *der o. Pl.;* **with every modern ~** *or* **all modern ~s** mit allem modernen Komfort; **he likes his ~s** er schätzt den Komfort; **creature ~s** leibliches Wohl. *See also* **cold comfort**

B *v.t.* trösten; (give help to) sich annehmen (+ *Gen.*)

comfortable /'kʌmfətəbl/

A *adj.* **1▸** (giving, having, providing comfort) bequem ‹*Bett, Sessel, Schuhe, Leben*›; komfortabel ‹*Haus, Hotel, Zimmer*›; (fig.) ausreichend ‹*Einkommen, Rente*›; **a ~ victory** ein leichter Sieg; **a ~ majority** eine gute Mehrheit **2▸** (at ease) **be/feel ~:** sich wohl fühlen; **make yourself ~:** machen Sie es sich (*Dat.*) bequem; **the patient/his condition is ~:** der Patient/er ist schmerzfrei **3▸** (having an easy conscience) **she didn't feel very ~ about it** ihr war nicht ganz wohl bei der Sache

B *n.* (Amer.) Deckbett, *das*

comfortably /'kʌmfətəblɪ/ *adv.* bequem; komfortabel ‹*eingerichtet*›; gut, leicht ‹*gewinnen*›; **they are ~ off** es geht ihnen gut

comforter /'kʌmfətə(r)/ *n.* **1▸** (person) Tröster, *der*/Trösterin, *die* **2▸** (esp. Brit.: baby's dummy) Schnuller, *der* **3▸** (esp. Brit.: woollen scarf) Schal, *der* **4▸** (Amer.: warm quilt) Deckbett, *das*

'comfort food *n.* Trostfutter, *das* (ugs.)

comforting /'kʌmfətɪŋ/ *adj.* beruhigend ‹*Gedanke*›; tröstend ‹*Worte*›; wohlig ‹*Wärme*›; **we gave her a ~ cup of tea** wir gaben ihr zur Beruhigung eine Tasse Tee

comfortless /'kʌmfətlɪs/ *adj.* unbequem; ‹*Hotel, Zimmer*› ohne Komfort; ungemütlich ‹*Person, Leben*›; unangenehm ‹*Gedanke*›; unwirtlich ‹*Landschaft, Welt*›

comfort: ~ station *n.* (Amer.) öffentliche Toilette; Bedürfnisanstalt, *die* (veralt.); **~ zone** *n.* Kuschelecke, *die*

comfrey /'kʌmfrɪ/ *n.* (Bot.) Beinwell, *der;* Schwarzwurz, *die*

comfy /'kʌmfɪ/ *adj.* (coll.) bequem; gemütlich ‹*Hotel, Zimmer*›; **make yourself ~:** machs dir gemütlich; **are you ~?** sitzt/liegst *usw.* du bequem?

comic /'kɒmɪk/

A *adj.* **1▸** (burlesque, funny) komisch; belustigend **2▸** (of or in the style of comedy) humoristisch ‹*Dichtung, Dichter*›; **~ relief** befreiende Komik

B *n.* **1▸** ▸ℹ **p. 1260** (comedian) Komiker, *der*/Komikerin, *die* **2▸** (periodical) Comicheft, *das* **3▸** (amusing person) Witzbold, *der;* ulkiger Vogel (ugs.)

comical /'kɒmɪkl/ *adj.* ulkig; komisch

comically /'kɒmɪkəlɪ/ *adv.* ulkig; komisch

comic: ~ 'opera *n.* (lit. or fig.) komische Oper; **~ strip** *n.* Comic, *der;* **~ strips** Comicstrips; Comics

coming /'kʌmɪŋ/

A *adj.* ▸**come**

B *n.* (of person) Ankunft, *die;* (of time) Beginn, *der;* (of institution) Einführung, *die;* **~s and goings** das Kommen und Gehen

comma /'kɒmə/ *n.* Komma, *das*

command /kə'mɑ:nd/

A *v.t.* **1▸** (order, bid) befehlen (**sb.** jmdm.); **he ~ed that the work should be done immediately** er befahl, die Arbeit sofort auszuführen **2▸** (be in ~ of) befehligen ‹*Schiff, Armee, Streitkräfte*›; (have authority over or control of) gebieten über (+ *Akk.*) (geh.); beherrschen **3▸** (have at one's disposal) verfügen über (+ *Akk.*) ‹*Gelder, Ressourcen, Wortschatz*› **4▸** (restrain) **~ oneself/one's temper** sich beherrschen **5▸** (deserve and get) verdient haben ‹*Achtung, Respekt*›; **he ~s a high fee** er kann ein hohes Honorar verlangen **6▸** überragen ‹*Küste, Stadt, Bucht, Hafen*›; **the hill ~s a fine view [of ...]** der Berg bietet eine schöne Aussicht auf (+ *Akk.*)

B *v.i.* **1▸** (be supreme) befehlen; Befehle geben **2▸** (be in ~) das Kommando *od.* die Befehlsgewalt haben

C *n.* **1▸** Kommando, *das;* (in writing) Befehl, *der;* **at** *or* **by sb.'s ~:** auf jmds. Befehl (*Akk.*) [hin]; **at the ~ 'halt'** auf das Kommando „stehen bleiben" [hin]; **word of ~:** Befehl, *der;* Kommando, *das* **2▸** (exercise or tenure) Kommando, *das;* Befehlsgewalt, *die;* **be in ~ of an army/ship** eine Armee/ein Schiff befehligen; **the army is under the ~ of General X** die Armee steht unter dem Befehl von General X; **have/take ~ of ...:** das Kommando über (+ *Akk.*) ... haben-/übernehmen; **officer in ~:** befehlshabender Offizier **3▸** (control, mastery, possession) Beherrschung, *die;* **have a good ~ of French** das Französische gut beherrschen; **all the money at his ~:** das gesamte ihm zur Verfügung stehende Geld **4▸** (body of troops) Kommando, *das;* (district under ~) Abschnitt, *der;* Befehlsbereich, *der;* (ship) Schiff, *das* **5▸** (Computing) Befehl, *der*

commandant /kɒmən'dænt/ *n.* Kommandant, *der;* **C~-in-Chief** Oberbefehlshaber, *der*

commandeer /kɒmən'dɪə(r)/ *v.t.* **1▸** (take arbitrary possession of) sich (*Dat.*) aneignen; requirieren (scherzh.) **2▸** (seize for military service) einziehen ‹*Männer*›; beschlagnahmen, requirieren ‹*Pferde, Vorräte, Gebäude*›

commander /kə'mɑ:ndə(r)/ *n.* ▸ℹ **p. 1634** **1▸** (one who commands) Führer, *der;* Leiter, *der* **2▸** (naval officer below captain) Fregattenkapitän, *der* **3▸** (Police) Abschnittsleiter, *der* **4▸** **C~-in-Chief** Oberbefehlshaber, *der. See also* **wing commander**

commanding /kə'mɑ:ndɪŋ/ *adj.* **1▸** gebieterisch ‹*Persönlichkeit, Erscheinung, Stimme*›; imposant, eindrucksvoll ‹*Statur, Gestalt*›; **be in a ~ position** Befehlsbefugnis haben; (Sport) stark in Führung liegen **2▸** beherrschend ‹*Ausblick, Lage*›; **~ heights** (fig.) Kommandohöhen *Pl.*

commanding 'officer *n.* Befehlshaber, *der*/Befehlshaberin, *die*

command: ~ key *n.* (Computing) Befehlstaste, *die;* **~ line** *n.* (Computing) Befehlszeile, *die;* Kommandozeile, *die*

commandment /kə'mɑ:ndmənt/ *n.* Gebot, *das;* **the Ten C~s** die Zehn Gebote

commando /kə'mɑ:ndəʊ/ *n., pl.* **~s** **1▸** (unit) Kommando, *das;* Kommandotrupp, *der* **2▸** (member of ~) Angehöriger eines Kommando[trupp]s

command: C~ Paper *n.* (Brit.) königliche Parlamentsvorlage; **~ performance** *n.* königliche Galavorstellung; **~ post** *n.* Kommandozentrale, *die*

commemorate /kə'meməreɪt/ *v.t.* gedenken (+ *Gen.*); **Easter ~s the resurrection of Christ** zu Ostern wird die Wiederauferstehung Christi gefeiert; **in order to ~ the victory** zum Gedenken an den Sieg

commemoration /kəmemə'reɪʃn/ *n.* **1▸** (act) Gedenken, *das;* **in ~ of** zum Gedenken an (+ *Akk.*); **the ~ of sb.'s death** das Gedenken an jmds. Tod (*Akk.*) **2▸** (church service) Gedenkgottesdienst, *der*

commemorative /kə'memərətɪv/ *adj.* Gedenk-; **~ of** zum Gedenken an (+ *Akk.*)

commence /kə'mens/ *v.t. & i.* beginnen; **building ~d** mit dem Bau wurde begonnen; **~ to do** *or* **~ doing sth.** beginnen, etw. zu tun

commencement /kə'mensmənt/ *n.* Beginn, *der*

commend /kə'mend/ *v.t.* **1▸** (praise) loben; **~ sb. [up]on sth.** jmdn. wegen etw. loben; **~ sb./sth. to sb.** jmdm. jmdn./etw. empfehlen; **be highly ~ed** eine sehr gute Beurteilung bekommen **2▸** (entrust or commit to person's care) anvertrauen

commendable /kə'mendəbl/ *adj.* lobenswert; löblich

commendably /kə'mendəblɪ/ *adv.* lobenswert

commendation /kɒmen'deɪʃn/ *n.* **1▸** (praise) Lob, *das;* (official) Belobigung, *die;* (award) Auszeichnung, *die* **2▸** (act of commending) Empfehlung, *die*

commendatory /kə'mendətərɪ/ *adj.* lobend

commensurable /kə'menʃərəbl, kə'mensjərəbl/ *adj.* **1▸** vergleichbar (**with, to** mit) **2▸** (proportionate) **be ~ with sth.** einer Sache (*Dat.*) entsprechen

commensurate /kə'menʃərət, kə'mensjərət/ *adj.* **~ to** *or* **with** entsprechend (+ *Dat.*); **be ~ to** *or* **with sth.** einer Sache (*Dat.*) entsprechen

comment /'kɒment/

A *n.* **1▸** (explanatory note, remark) Bemerkung, *die* (**on** über + *Akk.*); (marginal note) Anmerkung, *die* (**on** über + *Akk.*); **no ~!** (coll.) kein Kommentar! **2▸** (criticism) Rederei, *die* (ugs.) **3▸** *no pl.* (gossip) Gerede, *das* **4▸** (illustration) Deutung, *die;* Beschreibung, *die*

B *v.i.* **1▸** (make remarks) **~ on sth.** über etw. (*Akk.*) Bemerkungen machen; **he ~ed that ...:** er bemerkte, dass ... **2▸** (write explanatory notes) **~ on a text/manuscript** einen Text/ein Manuskript kommentieren

commentary /'kɒməntərɪ/ *n.* **1▸** (series of comments, expository treatise) Kommentar, *der* (**on** zu) **2▸** (comment) Erläuterung, *die* (**on** zu); **the sombre factories are a sad ~ upon our civilization** die düsteren Fabriken sind traurige Zeugnisse unserer Kultur **3▸** (Radio, Telev.) **[live** *or* **running] ~:** Livereportage, *die*

commentate /'kɒmənteɪt/ *v.i.* **~ on sth.** etw. kommentieren

commentator /'kɒmənteɪtə(r)/ *n.* ▸ℹ **p. 1260** Kommentator, *der*/Kommentatorin, *die;* (Sport) Reporter, *der*/Reporterin, *die*

'comment card *n.* Feedbackkarte, *die*

commerce /'kɒmɜ:s/ *n.* Handel, *der;* (between countries) Handel[sverkehr], *der;* **the world of ~:** die Geschäftswelt

commercial /kə'mɜ:ʃl/

A *adj.* **1▸** Handels-; kaufmännisch ‹*Ausbildung*›; **the ~ world** die Geschäftswelt **2▸** (interested in financial return) kommerziell **3▸** (impure) handelsüblich

B *n.* Werbespot, *der;* **during the ~s on TV** während der Fernsehwerbung

commercial: ~ 'art *n.* Gebrauchs-, Werbegrafik, *die;* **~ 'bank** *n.* private Geschäftsbank; **~ 'break** *n.* Werbepause, *die;* **~ 'broadcasting** *n.* Werbefunk und -fernsehen; **~ college** *n.* Fach[hoch]schule für kaufmännische Berufe; [höhere] Handelsschule; **~ correspondence** *n.* Handelskorrespondenz, *die*

commercialise ▸**commercialize**

commercialism /kə'mɜ:ʃəlɪzm/ *n.* Kommerzialismus, *der*

commercialize /kə'mɜ:ʃəlaɪz/ *v.t.* kommerzialisieren; vermarkten

commercial 'law *n., no pl.* Handelsrecht, *das*

commercially /kə'mɜ:ʃəlɪ/ *adv.* kommerziell

commercial: ~ 'radio *n.* Werbefunk, *der;* **~ 'television** *n.* kommerzielles Fernsehen; Werbefernsehen, *das;* **~ 'traveller** *n.* ▸ℹ **p. 1260** Handelsvertreter, *der*/-vertreterin, *die;* **~ 'value** *n.* Handelswert, *der;* Marktwert, *der;* **~ 'vehicle** *n.* Nutzfahrzeug, *das*

Commie /ˈkɒmɪ/ *n.* (coll. derog.) Rote, *der/die* (abwertend)

commingle /kəˈmɪŋgl/ (formal)
A *v.t.* vermischen
B *v.i.* sich vermischen

comminuted /ˈkɒmɪnju:tɪd/ *adj.* (Med.) ~ **fracture** Trümmerbruch, *der*

commis /ˈkɒmɪ, ˈkɒmɪs/ *adj.* ~ **chef** Assistenzkoch, *der*

commiserate /kəˈmɪzəreɪt/ *v.i.* ~ **with sb.** mit jmdm. mitfühlen; (express one's commiseration) jmdm. sein Mitgefühl aussprechen (**on** zu)

commiseration /kəmɪzəˈreɪʃn/ *n.* **1** Mitgefühl, *das* **2** *in sing. or pl.* (condolence) Teilnahme, *die;* Beileid, *das*

commissar /ˈkɒmɪsɑ:(r)/ *n.* (Hist.) Kommissar, *der*

commissariat /kɒmɪˈseərɪət/ *n.* Intendantur, *die*

commissary /ˈkɒmɪsərɪ, kəˈmɪsərɪ/ *n.* **1** (Mil.) Verpflegungsoffizier, *der* **2** (Amer.: store for supply of food etc.) Laden, *der* (*auf Baustellen, in Lagern, Bergwerken usw.*)

commission /kəˈmɪʃn/
A *n.* **1** (authority) Vollmacht, *die* **2** (body of persons having authority, department of Commissioner) Kommission, *die* **3** (instruction, piece of work) Auftrag, *der* **4** **Royal C~** (Brit.) Königliche [Untersuchungs]kommission **5** (warrant conferring authority) Ernennung, *die;* Bestellung, *die;* (in armed services) Ernennungsurkunde, *die;* Offizierspatent, *das* (veralt.); **get one's ~:** zum Offizier ernanntwerden; **resign one's ~:** aus dem Offiziersdienst ausscheiden; den Dienst quittieren (veralt.) **6** (pay of agent) Provision, *die;* **sell goods on ~:** Waren auf Provisionsbasis verkaufen **7** (act of committing crime etc.) Begehen, *das;* Begehung, *die* **8** **in/out of ~** ‹*Kriegsschiff*› in/außer Dienst; ‹*Auto, Maschine, Lift usw.*› in/außer Betrieb
B *v.t.* **1** beauftragen ‹*Künstler*›; in Auftrag geben ‹*Gemälde usw.*› **2** (empower by ~) bevollmächtigen; **~ed officer** Offizier, *der* **3** (give command of ship to) zum Kapitän ernennen **4** (prepare for service) in Dienst stellen ‹*Schiff*› **5** (bring into operation) in Betrieb setzen ‹*Kraftwerk, Fabrik*›

commissionaire /kəmɪʃəˈneə(r)/ *n.* ▸ℹ **p. 1260** (esp. Brit.) Portier, *der*

commissioner /kəˈmɪʃənə(r)/ *n.* **1** (person appointed by commission) Beauftragte, *der/die;* (of police) Präsident, *der* **2** (member of commission) Kommissions-, Ausschussmitglied, *das* **3** (representative of supreme authority, also EU) Kommissar, *der;* **High C~:** Hochkommissar, *der* **4** **C~ for Oaths** Notar, *der*/Notarin, *die*

commissioning 'editor *n.* [Verlags]lektor, *der*/-lektorin, *die*

commit /kəˈmɪt/ *v.t.*, **-tt-** **1** (perpetrate) begehen, verüben ‹*Mord, Selbstmord, Verbrechen, Raub*›; begehen ‹*Dummheit, Bigamie, Fehler, Ehebruch*›; **thou shalt not ~ adultery** (Bibl.) du sollst nicht ehebrechen **2** (pledge, bind) **~ oneself/sb. to doing sth.** sich/jmdn. verpflichten, etw. zu tun; **~ oneself to a course of action** sich auf eine Vorgehensweise festlegen **3** (entrust) anvertrauen (**to** *Dat.*); **~ sth. to a person/a person's care** jmdm. etw. anvertrauen/etw. jmds. Obhut (*Dat.*) anvertrauen; **~ sth. to the flames/waves** etw. den Flammen/Wellen übergeben (geh.); **~ sth. to writing/paper** etw. zu Papier bringen; *see also* **memory 1** **4** (consign to custody) **~ sb. for trial** jmdn. dem Gericht überstellen; **~ sb. to prison** jmdn. ins Gefängnis einliefern

commitment /kəˈmɪtmənt/ *n.;* **1** (to course of action or opinion) Verpflichtung, *die* (**to** gegenüber); (by conviction) Engagement, *das* (**to** für) **2** ▸**committal 1**

committal /kəˈmɪtl/ *n.* **1** (to prison) Einlieferung, *die;* (to hospital) Einweisung, *die* **2** (to grave) Bestattung, *die;* **~ service** Bestattungsgottesdienst, *der*

committed /kəˈmɪtɪd/ *adj.* **1** verpflichtet (**to** zu); festgelegt (**to** auf + *Akk.*) **2** (morally dedicated) engagiert

committee /kəˈmɪtɪ/ *n.* Ausschuss, *der* (auch Parl.); Komitee, *das*

com'mittee man, com'mittee woman *ns.* Ausschussmitglied, *das*

commode /kəˈməʊd/ *n.* **1** (chest of drawers) Kommode, *die* **2** (chamber pot) **[night] ~:** Nachtstuhl, *der*

commodious /kəˈməʊdɪəs/ *adj.* geräumig

commodity /kəˈmɒdɪtɪ/ *n.* **1** (utility item) Gebrauchsgegenstand, *der;* (not luxury) Gebrauchsartikel, *der;* **household ~:** Haushaltsartikel, *der;* **a rare/precious ~** (fig.) etwas Seltenes/Kostbares **2** (St. Exch.) [vertretbare] Ware; (raw material) Rohstoff, *der*

commodore /ˈkɒmədɔ:(r)/ *n.* **1** (naval officer) Flottillenadmiral, *der* **2** (of squadron) Kommodore, *der* **3** (of yacht club) Präsident, *der*/Präsidentin, *die* **4** (senior captain of shipping line) Kommodore, *der*

common /ˈkɒmən/
A *adj.*, **~er** /ˈkɒmənə(r)/, **~est** /ˈkɒmənɪst/ **1** (belonging equally to all) gemeinsam ‹*Ziel, Interesse, Sache, Unternehmung, Vorteil, Merkmal, Sprache*›; **~ to all birds** allen Vögeln gemeinsam; **~ Foreign and Security Policy** (EU) gemeinsame Außen- und Sicherheitpolitik; *see also* **cause A 4; consent B 1** **2** (belonging to the public) öffentlich; **the ~ good** das Gemeinwohl; **a ~ belief** [ein] allgemeiner Glaube; **a ~ prostitute** *or* **harlot** (arch.) eine Straßendirne (veralt.); **a ~ criminal** ein gewöhnlicher *od.* gemeiner Verbrecher; **have the ~ touch** volkstümlich sein **3** (usual) gewöhnlich, normal; (frequent) häufig ‹*Vorgang, Erscheinung, Ereignis, Erlebnis*›; allgemein verbreitet ‹*Sitte, Wort, Redensart*›; allgemein bekannt ‹*Marke, Produkt*›; (Bot., Zool.: of the most familiar type) gemein ‹*Farnkraut, Sperling usw.*›; **a ~ sight** ein ganz gewöhnlicher *od.* alltäglicher Anblick; **such a thing is ~ nowadays** so etwas ist heutzutage ganz normal; (is frequent) kommt heutzutage häufig vor; **a word in ~ usage** ein Wort des allgemeinen Sprachgebrauchs; **drugs are in ~ use today** die Einnahme von Drogen ist heute weit verbreitet; **~ honesty/courtesy** [ganz] normale Ehrlichkeit/Höflichkeit; **~ or garden** (coll.) ganz gewöhnlich *od.* normal; **a ~ or garden subject/programme** ein Feld-Wald-und-Wiesen-Thema/-Programm (ugs.); **a hotel out of the ~ run** ein Hotel, das über dem Durchschnitt liegt; **no ~ mind** ein außergewöhnlicher Kopf (fig.) **4** (without rank or position) einfach; gemein (veralt.); *see also* **herd A 2** **5** (vulgar) gemein; gewöhnlich (abwertend), ordinär (ugs. abwertend) ‹*Ausdrucksweise, Mundart, Aussehen, Benehmen*›; **be as ~ as muck** schrecklich ordinär *od.* gewöhnlich sein **6** (Math.) gemeinsam **7** (Ling.) **~ noun** Gattungsbegriff, *der;* **~ gender** doppeltes Geschlecht
B *n.* **1** (land) Gemeindeland, *das;* Allmende, *die* **2** **have sth./nothing/a lot in ~ [with sb.]** etw./nichts/viel [mit jmdm.] gemein[sam] haben; **in ~ with most of his friends he wanted ...:** ebenso wie die meisten seiner Freunde wollte er ... **3** (coll.: ~ sense) Grips, *der* (ugs.); **use your ~!** denk doch mal ein bisschen nach! (ugs.)

common: C~ Agri'cultural Policy *n.* (EU) gemeinsame Agrarpolitik; **~ 'carrier** *n.* **1** (in transportation) (person) Transportunternehmer, *der*/-unternehmerin, *die;* (company) Transportunternehmen, *das;* Verkehrsträger, *der;* **2** (Amer.: Telecommunications) Netzbetreiber, *der;* **~ 'cold** *n.* ▸ℹ **p. 1231** Erkältung, *die;* **~ de'nominator** *n.* (Math.) gemeinsame Nenner, *der;* **the least** *or* **lowest ~ denominator** (lit. or fig.) der kleinste gemeinsame Nenner; **~ 'entrance** *n.* (Brit.) *Aufnahmeprüfung für eine Privatschule*

commoner /ˈkɒmənə(r)/ *n.* **1** (one of the people) Bürgerliche, *der/die* **2** (student) *Student, der kein Stipendium erhält*

common: ~ 'factor *n.* (Math.) gemeinsamer Teiler; **~ 'ground** *n.* gemeinsame Basis; **~ 'knowledge** *n.* **it's [a matter of] ~ knowledge that ...** es ist allgemein bekannt, dass ...; **~ land** *n.* Gemeindeland, *das;* **~ 'law** *n.* Common Law, *das;* **~ law** *adj.* **~ law marriage** eheähnliche Gemeinschaft; **she's his ~ law wife/he's her ~ law husband** sie lebt mit ihm/er lebt mit ihr in eheähnlicher Gemeinschaft

commonly /ˈkɒmənlɪ/ *adv.* **1** (generally) im Allgemeinen; gemeinhin **2** (vulgarly) gewöhnlich (abwertend)

common: C~ 'Market *n.* Gemeinsamer Markt; **~ 'multiple** *n.* (Math.) gemeinsames Vielfaches; **the least** *or* **lowest ~ multiple** das kleinste gemeinsame Vielfache

commonness /ˈkɒmənnɪs/ *n.*, *no pl.* **1** (usualness) Gewöhnlichkeit, *die;* Normalität, *die;* (frequency) Häufigkeit, *die* **2** (vulgarity) Gewöhnlichkeit, *die* (abwertend)

commonplace /ˈkɒmənpleɪs/
A *n.* (platitude) Gemeinplatz, *der;* (anything usual or trite) Alltäglichkeit, *die*
B *adj.* nichts sagend, banal ‹*Person, Bemerkung, Buch*›; alltäglich ‹*Angelegenheit, Ereignis*›

common: C~ 'Prayer *n.* Liturgie, *die* (der Kirche von England); **the Book of C~ Prayer** *liturgisches Buch der Kirche von England;* **~ room** *n.* (Brit.) Gemeinschaftsraum, *der;* (for lecturers) Dozentenzimmer, *das*

commons /ˈkɒmənz/ *n. pl.* **1** **the [House of] C~:** das Unterhaus **2** (Brit.: common people) einfache Volk, *das*

> **House of Commons**
>
> Eines der zwei Häuser der britischen **Houses of Parliament**, das Unterhaus des britischen Parlaments. Die gewählten **Members of Parliament** treten hier zusammen, um innen- und außenpolitische Themen zu debattieren und über Gesetzesvorschläge abzustimmen.

common: ~ 'sense *n.* gesunder Menschenverstand; **~ sense** *adj.* vernünftig; gesund ‹*Ansicht, Standpunkt*›; **~ stock** *n.* (Amer. Finance) Stammaktien; **~ time** *n.* (Mus.) Viervierteltakt, *der*

commonwealth /ˈkɒmənwelθ/ *n.* **1** **the [British] C~ [of Nations]** das Commonwealth; **C~ Day** Commonwealthtag, *der* **2** (independent state) Staat, *der;* Gemeinwesen, *das;* (republic or democratic state) Republik, *die;* **C~ of Australia** Australischer Bund **3** **the C~** (Brit. Hist.) *die Republik unter Cromwell*

> **Commonwealth**
>
> *Commonwealth* hat zwei Bedeutungen. Geschichtlich bezeichnet man damit die Zeit von 1649 bis 1660, als England nicht von einem König oder einer Königin regiert wurde. In den Jahren nach dem Tod Karls I. übernahm das Unterhaus vier Jahre lang die Regierung. Ab 1653 war Oliver Cromwell (1599-1658) Lordprotektor mit diktatorischen Vollmachten. Das Ende des Commonwealth kam mit der Restauration Karls II. Daneben bezeichnet „Commonwealth" die Gemeinschaft der 54 unabhängigen Staaten, die noch lose mit Großbritannien verbunden sind. Die meisten Mitgliedsstaaten waren früher Länder des *British Empire*, des ehemaligen britischen Weltreichs. Die Umwandlung des British Empire zum *British Commonwealth of Nations* erfolgte 1931 durch ein Westminsterstatut. Seit 1949 gilt die Kurzbezeichnung *Commonwealth*.

Commonwealth of Independent 'States *n.* Gemeinschaft Unabhängiger Staaten

commotion /kəˈməʊʃn/ *n.* (noisy confusion) Tumult, *der;* (insurrection) Aufruhr, *der;* **make a ~:** einen Tumult *od.* einen großen Spektakel veranstalten

communal /ˈkɒmjʊnl/ *adj.* **1** (of or for the community) gemeindlich; Gemeinde-, kommunal ‹*Verwaltung*›; **~ living/life** Gemeinschaftsleben, *das* **2** (for the common use) gemeinsam; Gemeinschafts‹*küche, -schüssel, -bad, -grab, -zelle, -ehe*›

communally /ˈkɒmjʊnəlɪ/ *adv.* gemeinsam; gemeinschaftlich; **be ~ owned** Gemeinschaftsbesitz sein

commune[1] /ˈkɒmju:n/ *n.* **1** Kommune, *die* **2** (territorial division) Gemeinde, *die;* Kommune, *die*

commune[2] /kəˈmju:n/ *v.i.* **1** **~ with sb./sth.** mit jmdm./etw. Zwiesprache halten (geh.); ~

together miteinander Zwiesprache halten (geh.) 2 (Amer. Eccl.) das Abendmahl empfangen; (RC Ch.) kommunizieren

communicable /kəˈmjuːnɪkəbl/ *adj.* übertragbar ‹*Krankheit*›; vermittelbar, kommunizierbar ‹*Ideen, Informationen*›

communicant /kəˈmjuːnɪkənt/ *n.* (RC Ch.) Kommunizierende, *der/die;* (Protestant Ch.) Empfänger/Empfängerin des Abendmahls

communicate /kəˈmjuːnɪkeɪt/

A *v.t.* (impart, transmit) übertragen ‹*Wärme, Bewegung, Krankheit*›; übermitteln ‹*Nachrichten, Informationen*›; vermitteln ‹*Gefühle, Ideen*›; **he ~d the plan to his friends** er teilte seinen Freunden den Plan mit

B *v.i.* 1 (have common door) verbunden sein; **communicating rooms** Zimmer mit einer Verbindungstür 2 **~ with sb.** mit jmdm. kommunizieren; **she has difficulty in communicating** sie hat Kommunikationsschwierigkeiten 3 (RC Ch.) kommunizieren; (Protestant Ch.) das Abendmahl empfangen

communication /kəmjuːnɪˈkeɪʃn/ *n.* 1 (imparting of news, information) Übermittlung, *die;* (imparting of ideas) Vermittlung, *die;* (imparting of disease, motion, heat, etc.) Übertragung, *die;* **~ with the spacecraft/the mainland** die Verbindung zum Raumschiff/Festland; **~ among the deaf and dumb** die Verständigung unter Taubstummen 2 (information given) Mitteilung, *die* (**to** an + *Akk.*) 3 (interaction with sb.) Verbindung, *die;* **lines of ~:** Verbindungslinien; **means/systems of ~:** Kommunikationsmittel/-systeme; **be in ~ with sb.** mit jmdm. in Verbindung stehen; **breakdown in ~, ~ breakdown** Zusammenbruch der Kommunikation 4 *in pl.* (conveying information) Kommunikation, *die;* (science, practice) Kommunikationswesen, *das;* (Mil.) Nachschublinien *Pl.*

communication: ~ cord *n.* Notbremse, *die;* **~ gap** *n.* Kommunikationslücke, *die;* **~ link** *n.* Nachrichtenverbindung, *die;* **~ problem** *n.* Kommunikationsproblem, *das;* **~s centre** *n.* Kommunikationszentrale, *die;* (during a disaster relief effort or major accident response) Nachrichtenzentrale, *die;* (for military information) Fernmeldestelle, *die;* Fernmeldezentrale, *die;* **~s network** *n.* Kommunikationsnetz[werk], *das;* **~s satellite** *n.* Nachrichten- *od.* Kommunikationssatellit, *der;* **~s software** *n.* Kommunikationssoftware, *die;* **~ theory** *n.* Kommunikationstheorie, *die*

communicative /kəˈmjuːnɪkətɪv/ *adj.* gesprächig; mitteilsam

communicator /kəˈmjuːnɪkeɪtə(r)/ *n.* Kommunikator, *der*/Kommunikatorin, *die*

communion /kəˈmjuːnɪən/ *n.* 1 **[Holy] C~** (Protestant Ch.) das [heilige] Abendmahl; (RC Ch.) die [heilige] Kommunion; **receive** *or* **take [Holy] C~:** das [heilige] Abendmahl/die [heilige] Kommunion empfangen 2 (fellowship) Gemeinschaft, *die;* **the ~ of saints** die Gemeinschaft der Heiligen; **~ with nature/God** Zwiesprache mit der Natur/mit Gott

communion: ~ cup *n.* Abendmahlskelch, *der;* **~ rail** *n.* Kommunionbank, *die;* **~ service** *n.* Abendmahlsgottesdienst, *der*

communiqué /kəˈmjuːnɪkeɪ/ *n.* Kommuniqué, *das*

communism /ˈkɒmjʊnɪzm/ *n.* Kommunismus, *der;* **C~:** der Kommunismus

communist, Communist /ˈkɒmjʊnɪst/

A *n.* Kommunist, *der*/Kommunistin, *die*

B *adj.* kommunistisch; **the C~ Party/Manifesto** die Kommunistische Partei/das Kommunistische Manifest; **~-led/-dominated** von Kommunisten angeführt/beherrscht

communistic /kɒmjʊˈnɪstɪk/ *adj.* kommunistisch

community /kəˈmjuːnɪtɪ/ *n.* 1 (organized body) Gemeinwesen, *das* 2 (persons living in same place, having common religion, etc.) **the Jewish ~:** die jüdische Gemeinde; **a ~ of monks** eine Mönchsgemeinde 3 *no pl.* (public) Öffentlichkeit, *die;* **the ~ at large** die breite Öffentlichkeit 4 (body of nations) Gemeinschaft, *die;* **the ~ of nations** die Völkergemeinschaft 5 *no pl.* (sharedness) Gemeinschaft, *die;* **a sense of ~:** ein Gemeinschaftsgefühl

community: ~ ˈcare *n., no pl.* ≈ ambulante Betreuung; **~ centre** *n.* Gemeindezentrum, *das;* Kulturhaus, *das;* **~ ˈcharge** *n.* (Brit. Hist.) Gemeindesteuer, *die;* **~ chest** *n.* (Amer.) Sozialfonds, *der* (*einer Gemeinde*); **~ council** *n.* (Brit.) Gemeinderat, *der;* **~ home** *n.* (Brit.) Jugendhof, *der;* **~ ˈhospital** *n.* Kreiskrankenhaus, *das;* (in a region) Bezirkskrankenhaus, *das;* **~ ˈmedicine** *n.* Sozialhygiene, *die;* **~ reˈlations** *n. pl.* Verhältnis zwischen den Bevölkerungsgruppen; **~ ˈservice** *n.* [*freiwilliger od. als Strafe auferlegter*] *sozialer Dienst;* **~ singing** *n.* gemeinsames Singen; **~ spirit** *n.* Gemeinschaftsgeist, *der;* **~ worker** *n.* ▸ⓘ **p. 1260** Sozialarbeiter, *der*/-arbeiterin, *die;* Sozialpfleger, *der*/-pflegerin, *die*

> **community college**
>
> Ein Collegetyp in den Vereinigten Staaten, der als berufsbildende Einrichtung eine Vielzahl von praktischen Kursen für die Allgemeinheit anbietet. Die meisten *community colleges* befinden sich in städtischen Zentren und werden von einem Kuratorium, in dem Wirtschaftsvertreter der Region vertreten sind, betreut. Die Abschlüsse entsprechen denen an einer **high school** oder an einem College mit 2-jähriger Unterrichtszeit.

> **community service**
>
> In Großbritannien gibt es auf kommunaler Ebene ehrenamtliche Helfer, die z.B. Senioren oder Behinderte pflegen oder Reparaturen an Gemeindezentren und anderen Einrichtungen ausführen. Diese Art von Sozialdienst wird manchmal auch Straftätern auferlegt, als Alternative zu einer Haftstrafe.

commutable /kəˈmjuːtəbl/ *adj.* 1 (interchangeable) austauschbar 2 (convertible) umwandelbar

commutation /kɒmjʊˈteɪʃn/ *n.* 1 (of punishment) Umwandlung, *die* 2 (Electr.) Kommutierung, *die*

commuˈtation ticket *n.* (Amer.) Zeitkarte, *die*

commutator /ˈkɒmjʊteɪtə(r)/ *n.* (Electr.) Kommutator, *der;* Stromwender, *der*

commute /kəˈmjuːt/

A *v.t.* 1 (change to sth. milder) umwandeln ‹*Strafe*› (**to** in + *Akk.*) 2 (change to sth. different) umwandeln 3 (interchange) austauschen ‹*Dinge, Begriffe*› 4 (make payment) ablösen ‹*Verpflichtung, Schulden*› (**for, into** durch)

B *v.i.* 1 (travel daily) pendeln 2 (Amer.: hold season ticket) eine Zeitkarte haben

commuter /kəˈmjuːtə(r)/ *n.* Pendler, *der*/Pendlerin, *die*

comˈmuter: ~ belt *n.* großstädtischer Einzugsbereich; **~ traffic** *n.* Pendlerverkehr, *der;* **~ train** *n.* Pendlerzug, *der*

compact[1] /kəmˈpækt/

A *adj.* kompakt; komprimiert ‹*Stil, Sprache*›

B *v.t.* 1 (put firmly together) zusammenpressen 2 (fig.: condense) zusammenfügen (**into** zu)

compact[2] /ˈkɒmpækt/ *n.* 1 Puderdose [mit Puder(stein)] 2 (Amer.: car) Kompaktauto, *das;* Kompaktwagen, *der*

compact[3] *n.* (agreement) Vertrag, *der;* **a ~ with the devil** ein Pakt mit dem Teufel

compact: ~ camera *n.* Kompaktkamera, *die;* **~ ˈdisc** *n.* Compactdisc, *die;* Kompaktschallplatte, *die; attrib.* **~ ˈdisc player** CD-Spieler, *der;* **~ disc interˈactive** *n.* CD-interaktiv, *die*

compactly /kəmˈpæktlɪ/ *adv.* kompakt; komprimiert ‹*ausgedrückt*›

compactness /kəmˈpæktnɪs/ *n., no pl.* Kompaktheit, *die*

companion[1] /kəmˈpænjən/ *n.* 1 (one accompanying) Begleiter, *der*/Begleiterin, *die;* **my travelling ~s** meine Reisebegleiter 2 (associate) Kamerad, *der*/Kameradin, *die;* Gefährte, *der*/Gefährtin, *die* (geh.); Genosse, *der*/Genossin, *die* (veralt.); **the ~s of his youth** seine Jugendgefährten; **his drinking ~s** seine Zechgenossen (veralt.) *od.* (ugs.) -brüder; **~ in arms** Kampfgefährte, *der* 3 (Brit.: of [knightly] order) *unterste Stufe verschiedener* [*Ritter*]*orden, z. B.* **C~ of the Bath,** (nicht ritterlich) **C~ of Honour/Literature** 4 (woman living with another) Gesellschafterin, *die* 5 (handbook) Ratgeber, *der;* **Gardener's C~:** Ratgeber für den Gartenfreund; **C~ to Music/the Theatre** Musik-/Theaterführer, *der* 6 (matching thing) Gegenstück, *das;* Pendant, *das; attrib.;* **the ~ volume to ...:** der Begleitband zu ... 7 (Astron.) Begleiter, *der*

companion[2] *n.* (Naut.) 1 Kajütskappe, *die* 2 (stairs) ▸ **companionway**

companionable /kəmˈpænjənəbl/ *adj.* freundlich

companion: ~ hatch *n.* (Naut.) Luke, *die;* Luk, *das* (fachspr.); **~ ladder** *n.* (Naut.) Niedergang, *der;* **~ set** *n.* Kaminbesteck, *das*

companionship /kəmˈpænjənʃɪp/ *n.* Gesellschaft, *die;* (fellowship) Kameradschaft, *die;* Freundschaft, *die*

comˈpanionway *n.* (Naut.) Niedergang, *der*

company /ˈkʌmpənɪ/ *n.* 1 (persons assembled, companionship) Gesellschaft, *die;* **expect/receive ~:** Besuch *od.* Gäste *Pl.* erwarten/empfangen; **for ~:** zur Gesellschaft; **two is ~, three is a crowd** zu zweit ist es gemütlich, ein Dritter stört; **keep one's own ~:** für sich bleiben; **he likes his own ~:** er ist gern für sich; **in ~ with sb.** in jmds. Gesellschaft (*Dat.*); **be in ~:** in Gesellschaft sein; **bear** *or* **keep sb. ~:** jmdm. Gesellschaft leisten; **keep ~ with sb.** mit jmdm. verkehren; **part ~ with sb./sth.** sich von jmdm./etw. trennen 2 (companion[s]) **low ~:** schlechte Gesellschaft; **the ~ he keeps** sein Umgang; seine Gesellschaft; **be good/bad** *etc.* **~:** ein guter/schlechter Gesellschafter sein 3 (firm) Gesellschaft, *die;* Firma, *die; attrib.* **~ car** Firmenwagen, *der;* **~ policy** Unternehmenspolitik, *die;* Firmenpolitik, *die* 4 (Commerc.) **Jones and C~:** Jones & Co. 5 (of actors) Truppe, *die;* Ensemble, *das* 6 (of Guides) Trupp, *der* 7 (Mil.) Kompanie, *die; attrib.* **~ sergeant major** Kompaniefeldwebel, *der* 8 (Navy) **ship's ~:** Besatzung, *die*

company: ~ director *n.* Direktor, *der*/Direktorin, *die;* **~ law** *n.* Gesellschaftsrecht, *das;* **~ ˈpension scheme** *n.* betriebliche Altersversorgung *od.* Rentenversicherung; **~ time** *n.* Arbeitszeit, *die*

comparability /kɒmpərəˈbɪlɪtɪ/ *n., no pl.* Vergleichbarkeit, *die*

comparable /ˈkɒmpərəbl/ *adj.* vergleichbar (**to, with** mit)

comparably /ˈkɒmpərəblɪ/ *adv.* in vergleichbarer Weise; vergleichbar

comparative /kəmˈpærətɪv/

A *adj.* 1 vergleichend ‹*Anatomie, Sprachwissenschaft usw.*›; **~ religion** vergleichende Religionswissenschaft 2 (estimated by comparison) **the ~ merits/advantages of the proposals** die Vorzüge/Vorteile der Vorschläge im Vergleich 3 (relative) relativ; **in ~ comfort** relativ *od.* verhältnismäßig komfortabel; **with ~ ease** relativ *od.* verhältnismäßig leicht 4 (Ling.) komparativ (fachspr.); **the ~ degree** der Komparativ; die erste Steigerungsstufe; **a ~ adjective/adverb** ein Adjektiv/Adverb im Komparativ; ≈ ein gesteigertes Adjektiv/Adverb

B *n.* (Ling.) Komparativ, *der;* erste Steigerungsstufe

comparative ˈliterature *n., no pl.* vergleichende Literaturwissenschaft; Komparatistik, *die*

comparatively /kəmˈpærətɪvlɪ/ *adv.* 1 (by means of comparison) vergleichend; im Vergleich 2 (relatively) relativ; verhältnismäßig

compare /kəmˈpeə(r)/

A *v.t.* 1 vergleichen (**to, with** mit); **~ two/three** *etc.* **things** zwei/drei *usw.* Dinge [miteinander]

Points of the compass

	COMPASS POINT	DIRECTION, AREA	ABBR	ADJECTIVE, ADVERB, PREPOSITION
north	Nord	Norden	N	nördlich
south	Süd	Süden	S	südlich
east	Ost	Osten	O	östlich
west	West	Westen	W	westlich
north-east	Nordost	Nordosten	NO	nordöstlich
north-west	Nordwest	Nordwesten	NW	nordwestlich
south-east	Südost	Südosten	SO	südöstlich
south-west	Südwest	Südwesten	SW	südwestlich
north-north-east	Nordnordost	Nordnordosten	NNO	nordnordöstlich
north-north-west	Nordnordwest	Nordnordwesten	NNW	nordnordwestlich
south-south-east	Südsüdost	Südsüdosten	SSO	südsüdöstlich
south-south-west	Südsüdwest	Südsüdwesten	SSW	südsüdwestlich
east-north-east	Ostnordost	Ostnordosten	ONO	ostnordöstlich
west-north-west	Westnordwest	Westnordwesten	WNW	westnordwestlich
east-south-east	Ostsüdost	Ostsüdosten	OSO	ostsüdöstlich
west-south-west	Westsüdwest	Westsüdwesten	WSW	westsüdwestlich

The forms **Nord, Süd, Ost** and **West** and their derivatives have no gender (except in the nautical sense of a wind) and exist mainly as labels for the points of the compass. They are also used in nautical and meteorological contexts, without an article. The more commonly used forms are **Norden, Süden, Osten** and **Westen** and their combinations, which are masculine and can be used with the article, indicating either a direction or an area.

Directions

The wind is from the north/the north-east
= Der Wind kommt von Norden/Nordosten *or* (*Meteorol., Naut.*) von Nord/Nordost

We are going north tomorrow
= Wir fahren morgen nach Norden

They were travelling westwards **or** ***in a westerly direction***
= Sie fuhren in Richtung Westen *or* in westliche Richtung

The road runs due north
= Die Straße führt genau nach Norden

the northbound train
= der Zug in Richtung Norden

The aircraft/ship is southward bound
= Das Flugzeug fliegt/Das Schiff fährt nach Süden

The sitting room faces north
= Das Wohnzimmer geht nach Norden

Locations

the South of England
= der Süden Englands *or* von England, Südengland

the Deep South
= der tiefe Süden

the far North
= der hohe Norden

the Middle/Far East
= der Nahe/Ferne Osten

They live in the South-West
= Sie wohnen im Südwesten

She comes from the North-East
= Sie stammt aus dem Nordosten

It's a few miles to the west
= Es liegt ein paar Meilen westlich *or* nach Westen

further [to the] east
= weiter östlich *or* nach Osten

25 miles [to the] north of London
= 40 Kilometer nördlich von London

just to the south of the island/of Crete
= etwas südlich der Insel/von Kreta

The terms **nördlich, südlich** etc. operate in combination with **von** + dative or as prepositions with the genitive in the sense [*to the*] *north of, south of* etc. The use with the genitive is more common where there is an article, that is, with nouns rather than place names.

Adjectives

The English adjectives *north/northern, south/southern* etc. are frequently translated by the combining forms **Nord-, Süd-** etc. rather than the adjectives **nördlich, südlich** etc. This is especially the case with countries and other geographical names:

Northern/Southern Italy
= Norditalien/Süditalien

the West Coast
= die Westküste

North/South America
= Nordamerika /Südamerika

the north face of the Eiger
= die Eigernordwand

West/East Africa
= Westafrika/Ostafrika

the south side
= die Südseite

the Southern States
= die Südstaaten

nördlich, südlich etc. are generally used for less specific terms, as is illustrated by the difference between

South Africa
= Südafrika

southern Africa
= das südliche Afrika

the north wind
= der Nordwind

northerly winds
= nördliche Winde, Winde aus nördlichen Richtungen

However it would be a mistake to think that the German adjectives are straightforward equivalents for the English *northern, southern* etc. Consider for instance:

East **or** ***Eastern Germany***
= Ostdeutschland

West **or** ***Western Germany***
= Westdeutschland

Cf. also:

a southern climate
= ein südliches Klima

the easternmost or most easterly point
= der östlichste Punkt

Western journalists
= westliche Journalisten

the Western countries
= die westlichen Länder

But:

the Western Powers
= die Westmächte

the Eastern Bloc
= der Ostblock

vergleichen; **~d with** *or* **to sb./sth.** verglichen mit *od.* im Vergleich zu jmdm./etw.; **X is not to be ~d to Y** X lässt sich nicht mit Y vergleichen; **~ notes about sth.** Erfahrungen über etw. (*Akk.*) austauschen **2▸** (Ling.) steigern; komparieren (fachspr.)
B *v.i.* sich vergleichen lassen
C *n.* (literary) **beyond** *or* **without ~:** unvergleichlich; **lovely beyond ~:** unvergleichlich *od.* einmalig reizvoll

comparison /kəmˈpærɪsn/ *n.* **1▸** (act of comparing, simile) Vergleich, *der;* **the ~ of X and** *or* **with Y** ein Vergleich von *od.* zwischen X und Y; **in** *or* **by ~ [with sb./sth.]** im Vergleich [zu jmdm./etw.]; **this one is cheaper in** *or* **by ~:** dieser ist vergleichsweise billiger; **beyond [all] ~:** über jeden Vergleich erhaben; **there's no ~ between them** man kann sie einfach nicht vergleichen; **bear** *or* **stand ~:** einem Vergleich standhalten; **~s are odious** Vergleiche sind immer ungerecht **2▸** (Ling.) Steigerung, *die;* **degrees of ~:** Steigerungsstufen

comˈparison site *n.* (on Internet) Vergleichsseite, *die*

compartment /kəmˈpɑːtmənt/ *n.* (in drawer, desk, etc.) Fach, *das;* (fig.) Schubfach, *das;* (of railway carriage) Abteil, *das;* (Naut.) Abteilung, *die*

compartmentalize /kɒmpɑːtˈmentəlaɪz/ *v.t.* aufgliedern; (excessively) aufsplittern

compass /ˈkʌmpəs/
A *n.* **1▸** *in pl.* **[a pair of] ~es** ein Zirkel **2▸** ▸ⓘ **p. 1013** (for navigating) Kompass, *der;* **mariner's ~:** Magnetkompass, *der;* **the four points of the ~:** die vier Himmelsrichtungen **3▸** (boundary) Umkreis, *der* **4▸** (extent) Gebiet, *das;* (fig.: scope) Rahmen, *der;* **beyond the ~ of the human mind** jenseits des menschlichen Fassungsvermögens; **in a small ~:** im kleinen Rahmen **5▸** (Mus.) (of instrument) Tonraum, *der;* (of voice) Umfang, *der*
B *v.t.* (grasp mentally) erfassen

compass: ~ bearing *n.* Kompasspeilung, *die;* **take a ~ bearing** eine [Kompass]peilung vornehmen; **~ card** *n.* Kompass-, Windrose, *die*

compassion /kəmˈpæʃn/ *n., no pl.* Mitgefühl, *das* (**for, on** mit)

compassionate /kəmˈpæʃənət/ *adj.* mitfühlend; **on ~ grounds** aus persönlichen Gründen; (for family reasons) aus familiären Gründen

compassionate ˈleave *n.* (Brit.) Sonderurlaub aus familiären Gründen

comˈpassion fatigue *n., no pl.* Spendenmüdigkeit, *die*

compatibility /kəmpætɪˈbɪlɪtɪ/ *n., no pl.* (consistency, mutual tolerance) Vereinbarkeit, *die;* (of people) Zueinanderpassen, *das;* (of equipment etc.) Aufeinander-Abgestimmtsein, *das;* Zueinanderpassen, *das;* (Computing) Kompatibilität, *die;* (of drugs) Verträglichkeit, *die*

compatible /kəmˈpætɪbl/ *adj.* (consistent, mutually tolerant) vereinbar; zueinander passend ‹*Personen*›; aufeinander abgestimmt, zueinander

C

passend, (Computing) kompatibel ‹*Geräte, Maschinen*›; verträglich ‹*Medikamente*›

compatriot /kəmˈpætrɪət, kəmˈpeɪtrɪət/ *n.* Landsmann, *der*/-männin, *die*

compel /kəmˈpel/ *v.t.*, **-ll-** zwingen; **~ sb. to do sth.** jmdn. [dazu] zwingen, etw. zu tun; **~ sb.'s admiration/respect** jmdm. Bewunderung/Achtung abnötigen; **he felt ~led to tell her** er sah sich gezwungen *od.* genötigt, es ihr zu sagen

compelling /kəmˈpelɪŋ/ *adj.* bezwingend

compellingly /kəmˈpelɪŋlɪ/ *adv.* mit bezwingender Überzeugungskraft/Logik

compendious /kəmˈpendɪəs/ *adj.* kompendiarisch (veralt.); kurz gefasst, knapp ‹*Buch, Aufzeichnungen*›

compendium /kəmˈpendɪəm/ *n.*, *pl.* **~s** *or* **compendia** /kəmˈpendɪə/ Abriss, *der;* Kurzfassung, *die;* (summary) Kompendium, *das;* **~ of games** Spielemagazin, *das*

compensate /ˈkɒmpenseɪt/

A *v.i.* **1** (make amends for) **~ for sth.** etw. ersetzen; **~ for injury** *etc.* für Verletzung *usw.* Schaden[s]ersatz leisten **2** (Psych.) **~ for sth.** etw. kompensieren

B *v.t.* **1** **~ sb. for sth.** jmdn. für etw. entschädigen **2** (Mech.) ausgleichen ‹*Pendel*›

compensation /kɒmpenˈseɪʃn/ *n.* **1** Ersatz, *der;* (for damages, injuries, etc.) Schaden[s]ersatz, *der;* (for requisitioned property) Entschädigung, *die;* Ausgleichszahlung, *die;* **£100 in ~** *or* **by way of ~:** 100 Pfund Schaden[s]ersatz; **but he had the ~ of knowing that ...:** aber er hatte die Genugtuung zu wissen, dass ...; **growing old has its ~s** das Altwerden hat auch seine guten Seiten **2** (Psych.) Kompensation, *die*

compère /ˈkɒmpeə(r)/ (Brit.)

A *n.* Conférencier, *der;* Showmaster, *der*

B *v.t.* konferieren ‹*Show*›

compete /kəmˈpiːt/ *v.i.* konkurrieren (**for** um); (Sport) kämpfen; **~ with sb./sth.** mit jmdm./etw. konkurrieren; **he ~d against** *or* **with his rivals for the title** er kämpfte gegen seine *od.* mit seinen Rivalen um den Titel; **~ in a race** an einem Rennen teilnehmen; **be [un]able to ~:** [nicht] konkurrenzfähig sein; **~ with one another** miteinander wetteifern

competence /ˈkɒmpɪtəns/, **competency** /ˈkɒmpɪtənsɪ/ *ns.* **1** (ability) Fähigkeiten *Pl.*; **a high degree of ~ in French** sehr gute Französischkenntnisse; (of native speaker) hohe Sprachkompetenz im Französischen **2** (Law) Zuständigkeit, *die* **3** (Ling.) Kompetenz, *die*

competent /ˈkɒmpɪtənt/ *adj.* **1** (qualified) fähig; befähigt; **not ~ to do sth.** nicht kompetent, etw. zu tun **2** (effective) angemessen, adäquat ‹*Antwort, Kenntnisse*› **3** (appropriate) angemessen; geboten **4** (Law) zuständig ‹*Richter, Gericht*›; zugelassen ‹*Zeuge*›; zulässig ‹*Beweismaterial*›

competently /ˈkɒmpɪtəntlɪ/ *adv.* sachkundig; kompetent

competition /kɒmpɪˈtɪʃn/ *n.* **1** (contest) Wettbewerb, *der;* (in magazine etc.) Preisausschreiben, *das* **2** (those competing) Konkurrenz, *die;* (Sport) Gegner *Pl.* **3** (act of competing) Konkurrenz, *die;* **spirit of ~:** Konkurrenz- *od.* Wettbewerbsdenken, *das;* **be in ~ with sb.** mit jmdm. konkurrieren *od.* im Wettbewerb stehen

compeˈtition: ~ commissioner *n.* (EU) Wettbewerbskommisar, *der*/-kommissarin, *die;* **~ law** *n.* Wettbewerbsgesetz, *das*

competitive /kəmˈpetɪtɪv/ *adj.* **1** leistungswillig ‹*person*›; **~ sports** Wettkampf- *od.* Leistungssport, *der;* **~ spirit** Konkurrenz- *od.* Wettbewerbsdenken, *das;* **a ~ examination** eine Auswahlprüfung; **on a ~ basis** nach Leistung; **~ advantage/disadvantage** Wettbewerbsvorteil, *der*/-nachteil, *der* **2** (comparable with rivals) leistungs-, wettbewerbsfähig ‹*Preis, Unternehmen*›; **a very ~ market** ein Markt mit starker Konkurrenz

competitively /kəmˈpetɪtɪvlɪ/ *adv.* **they were bidding ~:** sie boten um die Wette (ugs.); **these models are ~ priced** der Preis dieser Modelle ist wettbewerbs- *od.* konkurrenzfähig

competitiveness /kəmˈpetɪtɪvnɪs/ *n.*, *no pl.* **1** (of company, product) Wettbewerbsfähigkeit, *die;* **2** (of person) Leistungswille, *der*

competitive ˈtendering *n.*, *no pl.* Ausschreibungsverfahren, *das;* Ausschreibung, *die*

competitor /kəmˈpetɪtə(r)/ *n.* Konkurrent, *der*/Konkurrentin, *die;* Mitbewerber, *der*/-bewerberin *die* (fachspr.); (in contest, race) Teilnehmer, *der*/-nehmerin, *die;* (for job) Mitbewerber, *der*/-bewerberin, *die;* **our ~s** unsere Konkurrenz

compilation /kɒmpɪˈleɪʃn/ *n.* Zusammenstellung, *die;* Kompilation, *die* (geh.); (of dictionary, guidebook) Verfassen, *das*

compile /kəmˈpaɪl/ *v.t.* **1** (put together) zusammenstellen; kompilieren (geh.); verfassen ‹*Wörterbuch, Reiseführer*› **2** (accumulate) sammeln ‹*Punkte*›

compiler /kəmˈpaɪlə(r)/ *n.* **1** Verfasser, *der*/Verfasserin, *die;* Kompilator, *der*/Kompilatorin, *die* (geh.) **2** (Computing) Compiler, *der*

complacency /kəmˈpleɪsənsɪ/ *n.*, *no pl.* Selbstzufriedenheit, Selbstgefälligkeit, *die*

complacent /kəmˈpleɪsənt/ *adj.* selbstzufrieden; selbstgefällig

complacently /kəmˈpleɪsəntlɪ/ *adv.* selbstzufrieden; selbstgefällig

complain /kəmˈpleɪn/ *v.i.* (express dissatisfaction) sich beklagen *od.* beschweren (**about, at** über + *Akk.*); **~ of sth.** über etw. (*Akk.*) klagen; **his continual ~ing** sein ständiges Klagen; **she ~s of [having] toothache** sie klagt über Zahnschmerzen; **I have nothing to ~ about/of** ich habe keine Beanstandungen/ich kann nicht klagen

complaint /kəmˈpleɪnt/ *n.* **1** (utterance of grievance) Beanstandung, *die;* Beschwerde, *die;* Klage, *die;* (formal accusation, expression of grief) Klage, *die;* **have/cause grounds for ~:** Grund zur Klage haben/Anlass zu Beschwerden geben **2** ▸ **p. 1231** (bodily ailment) Leiden, *das;* **a heart ~:** ein Herzleiden

comˈplaints department *n.* Reklamationsabteilung, *die;* (of an organization) Beschwerdestelle, *die*

complaisance /kəmˈpleɪzəns/ *n.*, *no pl.* (formal) Entgegenkommen, *das;* (deference) Respekt, *der*

complaisant /kəmˈpleɪzənt/ *adj.* (formal) entgegenkommend

complement

A /ˈkɒmplɪmənt/ *n.* **1** (what completes) Vervollständigung, *die;* Komplement, *das* (geh.) **2** (full number) **a [full] ~:** die volle Zahl; (of people) die volle Stärke; **the ship's ~:** die volle Schiffsbesatzung **3** (Ling.) Ergänzung, *die*

B /ˈkɒmplɪment/ *v.t.* ergänzen

complementary /kɒmplɪˈmentərɪ/ **1** (completing) ergänzend **2** (completing each other) einander ergänzend; **they are ~ to one another** sie ergänzen einander

complementary: ~ ˈcolour *n.* Komplementärfarbe, *die;* **~ ˈmedicine** *n.* Komplementärmedizin, *die*

complete /kəmˈpliːt/

A *adj.* **1** vollständig; (in number) vollzählig; komplett; **a ~ edition** eine Gesamtausgabe; **the ~ works of Schiller** Schillers sämtliche Werke; **make a ~ confession** ein umfassendes Geständnis ablegen; **a house ~ with contents** ein Haus mit allem Inventar **2** (finished) fertig; abgeschlossen ‹*Arbeit*›; fertig gestellt ‹*Gebäude, Bauwerk*› **3** (absolute) völlig; total, komplett ‹*Idiot, Reinfall, Ignoranz*›; absolut ‹*Chaos, Katastrophe*›; vollkommen ‹*Ruhe*›; total, (ugs.) blutig ‹*Anfänger, Amateur*›; **a ~ stranger** ein völlig Fremder; **meet with ~ approval** uneingeschränkte Zustimmung finden **4** (accomplished) perfekt ‹*Sportler, Reiter, Gentleman usw.*›

B *v.t.* **1** (finish) beenden; fertig stellen ‹*Gebäude, Arbeit*›; abschließen ‹*Vertrag*› **2** (make whole) vervollkommnen, vollkommen machen ‹*Glück*›; vervollständigen, (geh.) komplettieren ‹*Sammlung*› **3** (make whole amountof) vollzählig machen; voll machen (ugs.) **4** ausfüllen ‹*Fragebogen, Formular*›

completely /kəmˈpliːtlɪ/ *adv.* völlig; absolut ‹*erfolgreich*›

completeness /kəmˈpliːtnɪs/ *n.*, *no pl.* Vollständigkeit, *die;* (in numbers) Vollzähligkeit, *die*

completion /kəmˈpliːʃn/ *n.* Beendigung, *die;* (of building, work) Fertigstellung, *die;* (of contract) Abschluss, *der;* (of questionnaire, form) Ausfüllen, *das;* **on ~ of the course** nach Abschluss des Kurses; **on ~ of all the formalities** nach Erledigung aller Formalitäten; **on ~ of the sale** bei Kaufabschluss

comˈpletion date *n.* Datum der Fertigstellung/des Vertragsabschlusses

complex /ˈkɒmpleks/

A *adj.* **1** (complicated) kompliziert **2** (composite) komplex **3** (Ling.) **a ~ sentence** ein Satzgefüge **4** (Chem., Math.) komplex

B *n.* (also Psych.) Komplex, *der;* **a [building] ~:** ein Gebäudekomplex; **have a ~ about sth.** (coll.) Komplexe wegen etw. haben

complexion /kəmˈplekʃn/ *n.* Gesichtsfarbe, *die;* Teint, *der;* (fig.) Gesicht, *das;* **of various political ~s** verschiedener politischer Richtungen; **that puts a different ~ on the matter** dadurch sieht die Sache schon anders aus

-complexioned /kəmˈplekʃnd/ *adj. in comb.* **sallow-/fair-~:** mit gelblichem Teint/mit hellem Teint

complexity /kəmˈpleksɪtɪ/ *n.* ▸ **complex A**: Komplexität, *die;* Kompliziertheit, *die*

compliance /kəmˈplaɪəns/ *n.* **1** (action) Zustimmung, *die* (**with** zu); **act in ~ with sth.** gemäß etw. handeln **2** (unworthy submission) Unterwürfigkeit, *die;* Willfährigkeit, *die* (geh.)

compliant /kəmˈplaɪənt/ *adj.* unterwürfig; willfährig (geh.)

complicate /ˈkɒmplɪkeɪt/ *v.t.* komplizieren; verkomplizieren

complicated /ˈkɒmplɪkeɪtɪd/ *adj.* kompliziert

complication /kɒmplɪˈkeɪʃn/ *n.* **1** Kompliziertheit, *die* **2** (circumstance; also Med.) Komplikation, *die*

complicit /kəmˈplɪsɪt/ *adj.* **be ~ in sth.** in etw. (*Akk.*) verwickelt *od.* verstrickt sein; (deliberately) an etw. (*Dat.*) beteiligt sein

complicity /kəmˈplɪsɪtɪ/ *n.* Mittäterschaft, *die;* Komplizenschaft, *die* (**in** bei)

compliment

A /ˈkɒmplɪmənt/ *n.* **1** (polite words) Kompliment, *das;* **pay sb. a ~ [on sth.]** jmdm. [wegen etw.] ein Kompliment machen; **return the ~:** das Kompliment erwidern; (fig.) zurückschlagen; **my ~s to the chef** mein Kompliment dem Küchenchef **2** *in pl.* (formal greetings) Grüße *Pl.;* Empfehlung, *die;* **my ~s to your parents** eine Empfehlung an Ihre Eltern (geh.); **give them my ~s** bitte empfehlen Sie mich ihnen (geh.); bitte grüßen Sie sie von mir; **the ~s of the season** Grüße zum Fest; **with the ~s of the management/author** mit den besten Empfehlungen, die Geschäftsleitung/der Verfasser

B /ˈkɒmplɪment/ *v.t.* (say polite words to) **~ sb. on sth.** jmdm. Komplimente wegen etw. machen

complimentary /kɒmplɪˈmentərɪ/ *adj.* **1** (expressing compliment) schmeichelhaft **2** (given free as compliment) Frei-; **a ~ ticket/copy** eine Freikarte/ein Freiexemplar

compline /ˈkɒmplɪn, ˈkɒmplaɪn/ *n.* (Eccl.) Komplet, *die*

comply /kəmˈplaɪ/ *v.i.* **~ with sth.** sich nach etw. richten; **~ with a treaty/conditions** einen Vertrag/Bedingungen erfüllen; **he refused to ~:** er wollte sich nicht danach richten

component /kəmˈpəʊnənt/

A *n.* **1** Bestandteil, *der;* (of machine) [Einzel]teil, *das;* (in manufacturing) Teilfabrikat, *das* **2** (Math.) Komponente, *die*

B *adj.* **a ~ part** ein Bestandteil; **the ~ parts of a car** die [Einzel]teile eines Wagens

comport /kəmˈpɔːt/ *v. refl.* (formal) sich verhalten

compose /kəmˈpəʊz/ *v.t.* **1** (make up) bilden; **be ~d of** sich zusammensetzen aus **2** (construct) verfassen ‹*Rede, Gedicht, Liedertext, Libretto*›; abfassen, aufsetzen ‹*Brief*› **3** (Mus.)

komponieren 4) (Printing) setzen 5) (arrange) in Ordnung bringen ‹*Aussehen, Kleider usw.*›; ~ **oneself to** *or* **for an action** sich auf eine Handlung konzentrieren; ~ **one's thoughts** Ordnung in seine Gedanken bringen 6) (calm) ~ **oneself** sich zusammennehmen 7) (put together) anordnen, arrangieren ‹*Blumen, Sträucher usw.*›

composed /kəm'pəʊzd/ *adj.* (calm) gefasst

composer /kəm'pəʊzə(r)/ *n.* 1) ▸ⓘ **p. 1260** (of music) Komponist, *der*/Komponistin, *die* 2) (of poem etc.) Verfasser, *der*/Verfasserin, *die*

composite /'kɒmpəzɪt/

A *adj.* 1) zusammengesetzt; **a ~ illustration/photograph** eine Bild-/Fotomontage 2) (Bot.) ~ **flower/plant** Korbblütler, *der;* Komposite, *die* (fachspr.)

B *n.* 1) Gemisch, *das;* Komposition, *die* (geh.) 2) (Bot.) Korbblütler, *der;* Komposite, *die* (fachspr.)

composition /kɒmpə'zɪʃn/ *n.* 1) (act) Zusammenstellung, *die;* (construction) Herstellung, *die;* (formation of words) Wortbildung, *die;* Komposition, *die* (fachspr.) 2) (constitution) (of soil, etc.) Zusammensetzung, *die;* (mental constitution) Wesen, *das;* (of picture) Aufbau, *der* 3) (composed thing) (mixture) Gemisch, *das;* (piece of writing) Darstellung, *die;* (essay) Aufsatz, *der;* (piece of music) Komposition, *die* 4) (construction in writing) (of sentences) Konstruktion, *die;* (of prose, verse) Verfassen, *das;* (literary production) Schreiben, *das;* (Mus.) Komposition, *die;* Komponieren, *das;* (art of ~) Komposition, *die;* Kompositionslehre, *die* 5) (Printing) Setzen, *das;* Satz, *der* 6) (formal: compromise) Abmachung, *die;* (with creditors etc.) Vergleich, *der;* Akkord, *der;* (sum paid to creditors) Vergleichssumme, *die* 7) (formal: of disagreement) Beilegung, *die*

compositor /kəm'pɒzɪtə(r)/ *n.* ▸ⓘ **p. 1260** (Printing) Schriftsetzer, *der*/-setzerin, *die*

compos mentis /kɒmpɒs 'mentɪs/ *adj.* zurechnungsfähig; bei Trost (ugs.)

compost /'kɒmpɒst/

A *n.* Kompost, *der;* (fig.) Nährboden, *der*

B *v.t.* kompostieren

compostable /kɒm'pɒstəbl/ *adj.* kompostierbar; **be ~:** kompostiert werden können

compost: ~ bin *n.* Kompostbehälter, *der;* Komposttonne, *die;* ~ **heap, ~ pile** *ns.* Komposthaufen, *der*

composure /kəm'pəʊʒə(r)/ *n.* Gleichmut, *der;* **lose/regain one's ~:** die Fassung verlieren/wieder finden; **upset sb.'s ~:** jmdn. aus der Fassung bringen

compote /'kɒmpəʊt/ *n.* Kompott, *das*

compound[1]

A /'kɒmpaʊnd/ *adj.* 1) (of several ingredients) zusammengesetzt; **a ~ substance** eine Verbindung 2) (of several parts) kombiniert; **a ~ word** ein zusammengesetztes Wort; eine Zusammensetzung 3) (Zool.) ~ **eye** Facettenauge, *das* 4) (Bot.) zusammengesetzt 5) (Med.) ~ **fracture** komplizierter Bruch 6) (Ling.) zusammengesetzt ‹*Zeit*›; ~ **sentence** Satzreihe, *die*

B *n.* 1) (mixture) Mischung, *die* 2) (Ling.)Kompositum, *das;* Zusammensetzung, *die* 3) (Chem.) Verbindung, *die*

C /kəm'paʊnd/ *v.t.* 1) (mix) mischen ‹*Bestandteile*›; (fig.) vereinigen; (combine) zusammensetzen ‹*Wort*›; (make up) herstellen ‹*Präparat*›; **be ~ed of ...:** sich aus ... zusammensetzen 2) (increase, complicate) verschlimmern ‹*Schwierigkeiten, Verletzung usw.*› 3) (formal: settle) beilegen ‹*Affäre, Meinungsverschiedenheit*›; begleichen ‹*Schulden*›

D *v.i.* (formal) ~ **with sb. for sth.** sich mit jmdm. auf etw. (*Akk.*) einigen

compound[2] /'kɒmpaʊnd/ *n.* 1) (enclosed space) umzäuntes Gebiet *od.* Gelände; **prison ~:** Gefängnishof, *der* 2) (enclosure round building) Grundstück, *das;* **embassy ~:** Botschaftsgelände, *das*

compound interest /kɒmpaʊnd 'ɪntrɪst/ *n.* (Finance) Zinseszinsen *Pl.;* Zinseszins, *der*

comprehend /kɒmprɪ'hend/ *v.t.* 1) (understand) begreifen; verstehen 2) (include, embrace) umfassen

comprehensibility /kɒmprɪhensɪ'bɪlɪtɪ/ *n., no pl.* Fasslichkeit, *die;* Verständlichkeit, *die*

comprehensible /kɒmprɪ'hensɪbl/ *adj.* fassbar; verständlich; ~ **only to specialists** nur Fachleuten *od.* für Fachleute verständlich

comprehensibly /kɒmprɪ'hensɪblɪ/ *adv.* verständlich

comprehension /kɒmprɪ'henʃn/ *n.* 1) (understanding) Verständnis, *das;* **her behaviour is beyond my ~:** für ihr Benehmen habe ich kein Verständnis 2) ~ **[exercise/test]** Übung zum Textverständnis

comprehensive /kɒmprɪ'hensɪv/

A *adj.* 1) (inclusive) umfassend; universal ‹*Verstand*›; allseitig, universal ‹*Begriffsvermögen*› 2) (Sch.) ~ **school** Gesamtschule, *die;* **go ~** ‹*Schule:*› zur Gesamtschule [gemacht] werden; ‹*Stadt:*› die Gesamtschule einführen 3) (Insurance) Vollkasko-; ~ **policy** Vollkaskoversicherung, *die;* **have you ~ insurance?** sind Sie vollkaskoversichert?

B *n.* (Sch.) Gesamtschule, *die*

> **comprehensive school**
>
> Einer Gesamtschule entsprechende große staatliche weiterführende Schule in Großbritannien für Kinder aller Leistungsstufen im Alter von 11 bis 18 Jahren. *Comprehensive schools* wurden in den 1960er Jahren in Großbritannien eingeführt, um die akademische **grammar school** und die weniger akademische *secondary modern school* (eine inzwischen abgeschaffte Hauptschule) in einer organisatorischen Einheit zu integrieren und so eine Schulart zu schaffen, die allen Kindern die gleichen Chancen geben sollte.

comprehensively /kɒmprɪ'hensɪvlɪ/ *adv.* umfassend; ~ **beaten** deutlich geschlagen

comprehensiveness /kɒmprɪ'hensɪvnɪs/ *n., no pl.* Allseitigkeit, *die;* **the ~ of the book is surprising** das Buch ist überraschend umfassend

compress

A /kəm'pres/ *v.t.* 1) (squeeze) zusammenpressen (**into** zu) 2) komprimieren ‹*Luft, Gas, Bericht*› 3) (Computing) komprimieren

B /'kɒmpres/ *n.* (Med.) Kompresse, *die*

compressed air /kəmprest 'eə(r)/ *adj.* Druck-, Pressluft, *die*

compressible /kəm'presɪbl/ *adj.* zusammendrückbar; (Phys.) kompressibel

compression /kəm'preʃn/ *n.* Kompression, *die;* Verdichtung, *die*

compressor /kəm'presə(r)/ *n.* Kompressor, *der;* Verdichter, *der*

comprise /kəm'praɪz/ *v.t.* (include) umfassen; (not exclude) einschließen; (consist of) bestehen aus; (compose, make up) bilden

compromise /'kɒmprəmaɪz/

A *n.* Kompromiss, *der; attrib.* ~ **decision/agreement** Kompromissentscheidung/-vereinbarung, *die*

B *v.i.* Kompromisse/einen Kompromiss schließen; ~ **with sb. over sth.** mit jmdm. einen Kompromiss in etw. (*Dat.*) schließen; **agree to ~:** einem Kompromiss zustimmen

C *v.t.* (bring under suspicion) kompromittieren; (bring into danger) schaden (+ *Dat.*); ~ **oneself** sich kompromittieren; ~ **one's reputation** seinem Ruf schaden

compromising /'kɒmprəmaɪzɪŋ/ *adj.* kompromittierend

comptroller /kən'trəʊlə(r)/ *n.* ▸ⓘ **p. 1260** Controller, *der;* *Mitarbeiter des betriebswirtschaftlichen Rechnungswesens;* **C~ General** ≈ Präsident des Rechnungshofes

compulsion /kəm'pʌlʃn/ *n.* (also Psych.) Zwang, *der;* **be under no ~ to do sth.** keineswegs etw. tun müssen

compulsive /kəm'pʌlsɪv/ *adj.* 1) (also Psych.) zwanghaft; pathologisch ‹*Lügner*›; **he is a ~ eater/gambler** er leidet unter Esszwang/er ist dem Spiel verfallen 2) (irresistible) **this book is ~ reading/this TV programme is ~ viewing** von diesem Buch/dieser Fernsehsendung kann man sich nicht losreißen

compulsively /kəm'pʌlsɪvlɪ/ *adv.* **do sth. ~:** etw. wie unter einem [inneren] Zwang tun

compulsorily /kəm'pʌlsərɪlɪ/ *adv.* zwangsweise

compulsory /kəm'pʌlsərɪ/ *adj.* obligatorisch; **be ~:** obligatorisch *od.* Pflicht sein; **a ~ subject** ein Pflichtfach; ~ **purchase** Enteignung, *die*

compunction /kəm'pʌŋkʃn/ *n.* Schuldgefühle; Gewissensbisse *Pl.*

computation /kɒmpjʊ'teɪʃn/ *n.* Berechnung, *die;* **form of ~:** Rechenart, *die*

computational /kɒmpjʊ'teɪʃənl/ *adj.* Computer-; Rechen‹*leistung, -fähigkeit, -zeit*›

computational lin'guistics *n., no pl.* Computerlinguistik, *die*

compute /kəm'pju:t/

A *v.t.* berechnen (**at** auf + *Akk.*)

B *v.i.* 1) (make reckoning) rechnen 2) (use computer) Computer/einen Computer benutzen

computer /kəm'pju:tə(r)/ *n.* Computer, *der*

computer: ~-aided *adj.* computergestützt; **~-aided design** computergestütztes Entwerfen; **~-aided engineering** computergestütztes Konstruieren; ~ **ani'mation** *n.* Computeranimation, *die;* ~ **'architecture** *n.* Rechnerarchitektur, *die;* ~ **assisted** *adj.* ▸ **~-aided**; ~ **chip** *n.* Computerchip, *der;* Mikrochip, *der;* **~-controlled** *adj.* computergesteuert ‹*Kamera, Maschine, Prozess*›; ~ **crime** *n.* 1) *no pl.* Computerkriminalität, *die;* 2) (individual crime) Computerdelikt, *das;* ~ **'dating** *n., no pl.* Partnervermittlung per Computer; *attrib.* ~ **dating agency/service** Computer-Partnervermittlung[sagentur], *die;* ~ **fraud** *n.* Computerbetrug, *der;* Computerbetrügerei, *die;* ~ **game** *n.* Computerspiel, *das;* ~ **'graphics** *n. pl.* Computergrafik, *die*

computerisation, computerise, computerised ▸ **computeriz-**

computerization /kəmpju:təraɪ'zeɪʃn/ *n.* Computerisierung, *die*

computerize /kəm'pju:təraɪz/ *v.t.* computerisieren; auf Computer umstellen ‹*Buchhaltung*›

computerized /kəm'pju:təraɪzd/ *adj.* computerisiert

computerized to'mography /tə'mɒgrəfɪ/ *n.* (Med.) Computertomographie, *die*

computer: ~ 'literacy *n., no pl.* Computerverständnis, *das;* Computerkenntnisse *Pl.;* Computerfähigkeiten *Pl.;* **~-'literate** *adj.* mit Computern vertraut; **~-'operated** *adj.* computergesteuert; rechnergesteuert; ~ **'processing** *n.* elektronische Datenverarbeitung; ~ **'program** *n.* Programm, *das;* ~ **'programmer** *n.* ▸ⓘ **p. 1260** Programmierer, *der*/Programmiererin, *die;* ~ **'programming** *n., no pl.* Programmieren, *das;* ~ **room** *n.* Computerraum, *der;* ~ **'science** *n.* Computerwissenschaft, *die;* ~ **'scientist** *n.* ▸ⓘ **p. 1260** Computerwissenschaftler, *der*/-wissenschaftlerin, *die;* Informatiker, *der*/Informatikerin, *die;* ~ **terminal** *n.* Terminal, *das;* ~ **'typesetting** *n.* Computersatz, *der;* ~ **virus** *n.* [Computer]virus, *das od. der*

computing /kəm'pju:tɪŋ/*n.* 1) EDV, *die;* elektronische Datenverarbeitung; **personal ~:** PC-Nutzung, *die* 2) *attrib.* Computer-; ~ **skills** Computerkenntnisse *Pl.;* ~ **time** Rechenzeit, *die*

comrade /'kɒmreɪd/ *n.* 1) Kamerad, *der*/Kameradin, *die;* **~-in-arms** Kampfgefährte, *der;* Waffenbruder, *der* (geh.) 2) (Polit.) Genosse, *der*/Genossin, *die*

comradely /'kɒmreɪdlɪ, 'kɒmrɪdlɪ/ *adj.* kameradschaftlich

comradeship /'kɒmreɪdʃɪp, 'kɒmrɪdʃɪp/ *n., no pl.* Kameradschaft, *die;* **a spirit of ~:** Kameradschaftsgeist

con[1] /kɒn/ (coll.)

A *n.* Schwindel, *der*

B *v.t.,* **-nn-** 1) (swindle) reinlegen (ugs.); ~ **sb. out of sth.** jmdm. etw. abschwindeln *od.* (ugs.) abgaunern 2) (persuade) beschwatzen (ugs.); ~ **sb. into sth.** jmdm. etw. aufschwatzen (ugs.);

C

~ **sb. into believing sth.** jmdm. etw. einreden

con² *n., adv., prep.* ▸**pro¹**

con³ *n.* (coll.: convict) Knacki, *der* (salopp)

concatenation /kɒnkætɪˈneɪʃn/ *n.* (lit. or fig.) Verkettung, *die*

concave /ˈkɒnkeɪv/ *adj.* konkav; ~ **mirror/lens** Konkav- *od.* Hohlspiegel, *der*/Konkavlinse, *die*

concavity /kənˈkævɪtɪ/ *n.* Konkavität, *die*

conceal /kənˈsiːl/ *v.t.* verbergen (**from** vor + *Dat.*); ~ **the true state of affairs from sb.** jmdm. den wirklichen Sachverhalt verheimlichen; ~ **vital facts** entscheidende Tatsachen unterschlagen

concealed /kənˈsiːld/ *adj.* verdeckt; ~ **lighting** indirekte Beleuchtung

concealment /kənˈsiːlmənt/ *n.* ▸**conceal**: Verbergen, *das;* Verheimlichung, *die;* Unterschlagung, *die;* **stay in** ~: sich versteckt halten

concede /kənˈsiːd/ *v.t.* (admit, allow) zugeben; (grant) zugestehen, einräumen ‹*Recht, Privileg*›; (Sport) abgeben ‹*Punkte, Spiel*› (**to** an + *Akk.*); zulassen ‹*Tor*›; in Kauf nehmen ‹*Elfmeter*›; ~ **[defeat]** (in election etc.) seine Niederlage eingestehen

conceit /kənˈsiːt/ *n.* **1** *no pl.* (vanity) Einbildung, *die* **2** *in pl.* (Lit.) Konzetti *Pl.*

conceited /kənˈsiːtɪd/ *adj.* eingebildet

conceitedly /kənˈsiːtɪdlɪ/ *adv.* eingebildet

conceitedness /kənˈsiːtɪdnɪs/ *n.* Einbildung, *die*

conceivable /kənˈsiːvəbl/ *adj.* vorstellbar; **it's scarcely ~ that ...:** man kann sich (*Dat.*) kaum vorstellen, dass ...

conceivably /kənˈsiːvəblɪ/ *adv.* möglicherweise; **he cannot ~ have done it** er kann es unmöglich getan haben

conceive /kənˈsiːv/

A *v.t.* **1** empfangen ‹*Kind*› **2** (form in mind) sich (*Dat.*) vorstellen *od.* denken; haben, kommen auf (+ *Akk.*) ‹*Idee, Plan*›; ~ **a dislike for sb./sth.** eine Abneigung gegen jmdn./etw. entwickeln; ~ **a liking for sb./sth.** Zuneigung zu jmdm./etw. fassen; **when the idea was first ~d** als man erstmals auf die Idee kam **3** (think) meinen; glauben **4** (express) fassen; ausdrücken

B *v.i.* **1** (become pregnant) empfangen **2** ~ **of sth.** sich (*Dat.*) etw. vorstellen

concentrate /ˈkɒnsəntreɪt/

A *v.t.* konzentrieren, zusammenziehen ‹*Truppen, Flotte*›; zusammendrängen ‹*Wissen, Informationen*›; ~ **one's efforts/energies [up]on sth.** seine Bemühungen/Energien auf etw. (*Akk.*) konzentrieren; ~ **one's mind on sth.** sich auf etw. (*Akk.*) konzentrieren; ~ **the mind** jmds. Gedanken ausschließlich beschäftigen

B *v.i.* sich konzentrieren (**on** auf + *Akk.*); ~ **on doing sth.** sich darauf konzentrieren, etw. zu tun

C *n.* Konzentrat, *das;* (animal food) Kraftfutter, *das*

concentrated /ˈkɒnsəntreɪtɪd/ *adj.* konzentriert; geballt ‹*Hass, Eifersucht*›

concentration /kɒnsənˈtreɪʃn/ *n.* **1** (also Chem.) Konzentration, *die;* **power[s] of ~:** Konzentrationsfähigkeit, *die;* Konzentrationsvermögen, *das;* **lose one's ~:** sich nicht mehr konzentrieren können **2** (people brought together) Ansammlung, *die;* (of troops etc.) Konzentration, *die*

concenˈtration camp *n.* Konzentrationslager, *das;* KZ, *das*

concentric /kənˈsentrɪk/ *adj.* konzentrisch; **the circles were ~ with each other** die Kreise hatten einen gemeinsamen Mittelpunkt

concept /ˈkɒnsept/ *n.* **1** (notion) Begriff, *der;* (idea) Vorstellung, *die* **2** (invention) Idee, *die;* Konzept, *das;* **a new ~ in make-up** eine neue Make-up-Idee; ein neues Make-up-Konzept

ˈconcept car *n.* Konzeptauto, *das*

conception /kənˈsepʃn/ **1** (idea) Vorstellung, *die* (**of** von); **I had no ~ of how ...:** ich hatte keine Vorstellung, wie ...; **the original ~ of a picture** die ursprüngliche Konzeption eines Bildes **2** (conceiving) **great powers of ~:** ein großes Vorstellungsvermögen **3** (of child) Empfängnis, *die*

conceptual /kənˈseptjʊəl/ *adj.* begrifflich

conceptual: ~ **ˈart** *n., no pl.* Konzeptkunst, *die;* ~ **ˈartist** *n.* Konzeptkünstler, *der*/-künstlerin, *die*

conceptualize /kənˈseptjʊəlaɪz/ *v.t.* begrifflich fassen

conceptually /kənˈseptjʊəlɪ/ *adv.* begrifflich; **the plan is ~ good** in der Vorstellung *od.* als Idee ist der Plan gut

concern /kənˈsɜːn/

A *v.t.* **1** (affect) betreffen; **as ~s ..., so far as ... is ~ed** was ... betrifft; **all that ~s us is whether ...:** uns hat nur zu interessieren, ob ...; **'to whom it may ~'** ≈ „Bestätigung"; (on certificate, testimonial) ≈ „Zeugnis" **2** (interest) ~ **oneself with** *or* **about sth.** sich mit etw. befassen; **she does not ~ herself with politics** sie kümmert sich nicht um Politik **3** (trouble) **the news/her health greatly ~s me** ich bin über diese Nachricht tief beunruhigt/ihre Gesundheit bereitet mir große Sorgen

B *n.* **1** (relation) **have no ~ with sth.** mit etw. nichts zu tun haben; **have a ~ in sth.** an etw. (*Dat.*) beteiligt sein *od.* einen Anteil haben **2** (anxiety) Besorgnis, *die;* (interest) Interesse, *das;* **a matter of general ~:** eine Sache, die alle beunruhigt/eine Sache von allgemeinem Interesse; **an expression of ~ on one's face** ein besorgter Gesichtsausdruck; **express ~:** Sorge ausdrücken **3** (matter) Angelegenheit, *die;* **that's no ~ of mine** das geht mich nichts an; **it's his ~:** das ist seine Sache *od.* seine Angelegenheit **4** (firm) Unternehmen, *das; see also* **going B 5**

concerned /kənˈsɜːnd/ *adj.* **1** (involved) betroffen; (interested) interessiert; **the people ~:** die Betroffenen; **the firms/countries ~:** die betroffenen Firmen/Länder; **we are not ~ with it** damit haben wir nichts zu tun; **where work/health** *etc.* **is ~:** wenn es um die Arbeit/die Gesundheit *usw.* geht; **as** *or* **so far as I'm ~:** was mich betrifft *od.* anbelangt; **not as far as I'm ~:** von mir aus nicht **2** (implicated) verwickelt (**in** in + *Akk.*) **3** (troubled) besorgt; **I am ~ to hear/learn that ...:** ich höre/erfahre mit Sorge, dass ...; **I was ~ at the news** die Nachricht beunruhigte mich; **I am very ~ for** *or* **about him/his health** er/seine Gesundheit macht mir Sorgen

concerning /kənˈsɜːnɪŋ/ *prep.* bezüglich

concernment /kənˈsɜːnmənt/ *n.* (formal) **1** Beteiligung, *die* **2** (anxiety) Sorge, *die*

concert

A /ˈkɒnsət/ *n.* **1** (of music) Konzert, *das* **2** (agreement, union) Übereinkunft, *die;* **work in ~ with sb.** mit jmdm. zusammenarbeiten **3** (combined sounds) Chor, *der;* Konzert, *das;* **in ~:** im Chor

B /kənˈsɜːt/ *v.t.* abstimmen ‹*Maßnahmen, Pläne*›

concerted /kənˈsɜːtɪd/ *adj.* vereint; gemeinsam; ~ **action** eine konzertierte Aktion; **make a ~ effort** mit vereinten Kräften vorgehen

concert: ~**-goer** *n.* Konzertbesucher, *der*/-besucherin, *die;* ~ **ˈgrand** *n.* Konzertflügel, *der;* ~ **hall** *n.* Konzertsaal, *der;* (building) Konzerthalle, *die*

concertina /kɒnsəˈtiːnə/

A *n.* (Mus.) Konzertina, *die*

B *v.i.* [wie eine Ziehharmonika] zusammengeschoben werden

ˈconcertmaster *n.* (esp. Amer.) Konzertmeister, *der*

concerto /kənˈtʃɜːtəʊ, kənˈtʃeətəʊ/ *n., pl.* ~**s** *or* **concerti** /kənˈtʃeətiː/ (Mus.) Konzert, *das*

concert: ~ **overture** *n.* (Mus.) Konzertouvertüre, *die;* ~ **pianist** *n.* Konzertpianist, *der*/-pianistin, *die;* ~ **pitch** *n.* Kammerton, *der*

concession /kənˈseʃn/ *n.* Konzession, *die;* (act of conceding, yielding) Zugeständnis, *das*

concessionaire /kənseʃəˈneə(r)/ *n.* Konzessionär, *der*/Konzessionärin, *die*

concessionary /kənˈseʃənərɪ/ *adj.* Konzessions-; ~ **rate/fare** ermäßigter Tarif

concessionnaire ▸**concessionaire**

concessive /kənˈsesɪv/ *adj.* (Ling.) konzessiv; einräumend; **a ~ clause** ein Konzessiv- *od.* Einräumungssatz

conch /kɒntʃ, kɒŋk/ *n.* (Zool.) Meeresschnecke, *die;* (shell) Gehäuse einer Meeresschnecke

concierge /ˈkɔːnsɪeəʒ, ˈkɒnsɪeəʒ/ *n.* Concierge, *der/die;* (in hotel) Empfangschef, *der*

conciliate /kənˈsɪlɪeɪt/

A *v.t.* **1** (reconcile) in Einklang bringen ‹*Gegensätze, Theorien*› **2** (pacify) besänftigen; beschwichtigen

B *v.i.* vermitteln; (in industrial dispute) schlichten

conciliation /kənsɪlɪˈeɪʃn/ *n.* **1** (reconcilement) Versöhnung, *die* **2** (pacification) Besänftigung, *die;* Beschwichtigung, *die* **3** (in industrial relations) Schlichtung, *die;* ~ **board** Schlichtungsausschuss, *der*

conciliator /kənˈsɪlɪeɪtə(r)/ *n.* Schlichter, *der*/Schlichterin, *die*

conciliatory /kənˈsɪljətərɪ/ *adj.* versöhnlich; (pacifying) beschwichtigend; besänftigend

concise /kənˈsaɪs/ *adj.* kurz und prägnant; knapp, konzis ‹*Stil*›; **be ~** ‹*Person:*› sich knapp fassen; **a ~ dictionary** ein Handwörterbuch

concisely /kənˈsaɪslɪ/ *adv.* kurz und prägnant; knapp, konzis ‹*schreiben*›

conciseness /kənˈsaɪsnɪs/, **concision** /kənˈsɪʒn/ *ns., no pl.* Kürze, *die;* Prägnanz, *die*

conclave /ˈkɒnkleɪv/ *n.* **1** (RC Ch.) Konklave, *das* **2** (private meeting) Klausurtagung, *die*

conclude /kənˈkluːd/

A *v.t.* **1** (end) beschließen; beenden **2** (infer) schließen; folgern **3** (reach decision) beschließen; ~ **from the evidence that ...:** aufgrund des Beweismaterials zu dem Schluss kommen, dass ... **4** (agree on) schließen ‹*Bündnis, Vertrag*›

B *v.i.* (end) schließen

concluding /kənˈkluːdɪŋ/ *attrib. adj.* abschließend

conclusion /kənˈkluːʒn/ *n.* **1** (end) Abschluss, *der;* **in ~:** zum Abschluss **2** (result) Ausgang, *der* **3** (decision reached) Beschluss, *der;* **come to a ~:** einen Beschluss fassen **4** (inference) Schluss, *der;* **draw** *or* **reach a ~:** zu einem Schluss kommen **5** (Logic) [Schluss]folgerung, *die;* Konklusion, *die* (fachspr.) **6** (agreement) Abschluss, *der*

conclusive /kənˈkluːsɪv/ *adj.* schlüssig

conclusively /kənˈkluːsɪvlɪ/ *adv.* abschließend ‹*regeln*›; schlüssig ‹*beweisen, belegen*›; eindeutig ‹*klären*›

conclusiveness /kənˈkluːsɪvnɪs/ *n., no pl.* Schlüssigkeit, *die*

concoct /kənˈkɒkt/ *v.t.* zubereiten; zusammenbrauen ‹*Trank*›; (fig.) sich (*Dat.*) ausdenken ‹*Geschichte*›; aushecken ‹*Komplott, Intrige usw.*›; sich (*Dat.*) zurechtlegen ‹*Ausrede, Alibi*›

concoction /kənˈkɒkʃn/ *n.* **1** (preparing) Zubereitung, *die* **2** (drink) Gebräu, *das;* (meal) Fraß, *der* (ugs.)

concomitant /kənˈkɒmɪtənt/ (formal)

A *adj.* begleitend; (simultaneous) gleichzeitig; ~ **circumstances** Begleitumstände

B *n.* Begleiterscheinung, *die*

concord /ˈkɒŋkɔːd, ˈkɒnkɔːd/ *n.* **1** (agreement) Eintracht, *die* **2** (treaty) Freundschaftsvertrag, *der* **3** (Mus.) Harmonie, *die* **4** (Ling.) Kongruenz, *die*

concordance /kənˈkɔːdəns/ *n.* **1** (formal: agreement) Übereinstimmung, *die* **2** (index) Konkordanz, *die*

concordant /kənˈkɔːdənt/ *adj.* (formal) übereinstimmend; **be ~ with sth.** mit etw. übereinstimmen

concordat /kənˈkɔːdæt/ *n.* Konkordat, *das*

concourse /ˈkɒŋkɔːs, ˈkɒnkɔːs/ *n.* (of public building) Halle, *die;* **station ~:** Bahnhofshalle, *die*

concrete /ˈkɒnkriːt/

A *adj.* (specific) konkret; ~ **noun** (Ling.) Konkretum, *das*

B *n.* Beton, *der; attrib.* Beton-; aus Beton *präd.*

C *v.t.* betonieren; (embed in ~) ~ **[in]** einbetonieren

concretely /ˈkɒnkriːtlɪ/ *adv.* konkret

concrete/ˈkɒnkriːt/: ~ **mixer** *n.* Betonmischer, *der;* Betonmischmaschine, *die;* ~ ˈ**poetry** *n.* konkrete Poesie

concretion /kənˈkriːʃn/ *n.* 1 *no pl.* (coalescence) Verwachsung, *die;* Zusammenwachsen, *das* 2 (Med.) Konkrement, *das* 3 (Geol.) Konkretion, *die*

concubine /ˈkɒŋkjʊbaɪn/ *n.* 1 (formal: cohabiting mistress) Konkubine, *die* 2 (secondary wife) Nebenfrau, *die*

concur /kənˈkɜː(r)/ *v.i.*, **-rr-** 1 (agree) ~ **[with sb.] [in sth.]** [jmdm.] [in etw. (*Dat.*)] zustimmen *od.* beipflichten 2 (coincide, combine) zusammenkommen

concurrence /kənˈkʌrəns/ *n., no pl.* 1 (general agreement) Übereinstimmung, *die* 2 (coincidence) Zusammentreffen, *das*

concurrent /kənˈkʌrənt/ *adj.* 1 gleichzeitig; **be ~ with sth.** gleichzeitig mit etw. stattfinden; ~ **sentences** zu einer Gesamtstrafe zusammengefasste Einzelstrafen 2 (agreeing) übereinstimmend; **be ~ with sth.** mit etw. übereinstimmen

concurrently /kənˈkʌrəntlɪ/ *adv.* 1 (simultaneously) gleichzeitig 2 (Law) **run** ~ ‹*Gefängnisstrafen:*› zu einer Gesamtstrafe zusammengefasst sein/werden

concuss /kənˈkʌs/ *v.t.* **be ~ed** eine Gehirnerschütterung haben

concussion /kənˈkʌʃn/ *n.* (Med.) Gehirnerschütterung, *die;* Konkussion, *die* (fachspr.)

condemn /kənˈdem/ *v.t.* 1 (censure) verdammen 2 (Law: sentence) verurteilen; (fig.) verdammen; ~ **sb. to death/to life imprisonment** jmdn. zum Tode/zu lebenslanger Haft verurteilen; **be ~ed to do sth.** (fig.) dazu verdammt sein, etw. zu tun 3 (give judgement against) aburteilen 4 (show to be guilty) überführen 5 (declare unfit) für unbewohnbar erklären ‹*Gebäude*›; für ungenießbar erklären ‹*Fleisch*›

condemnation /kɒndemˈneɪʃn/ *n.* 1 (censure) Verdammung, *die* 2 (Law: conviction) Verurteilung, *die*

condemnatory /kənˈdemnətərɪ/ *adj.* verdammend; scharf missbilligend ‹*Blick*›

condemned /kənˈdemd/ *adj.* 1 verurteilt; **a ~ man** ein zum Tode Verurteilter; ein Todeskandidat 2 **a ~ house** ein Haus, das auf der Abrissliste steht 3 ~ **cell** Todeszelle, *die*

condensate /kənˈdenseɪt, ˈkɒndənseɪt/ *n.* Kondensat, *das*

condensation /kɒndenˈseɪʃn/ *n.* 1 *no pl.* (condensing) Kondensation, *die* 2 (what is condensed) Kondensat, *das;* (water) Kondenswasser, *das* 3 (abridgement) [Ver]kürzung, *die;* (abridged form) Kurzfassung, *die*

condenˈsation trail *n.* (Aeronaut.) Kondensstreifen, *der*

condense /kənˈdens/

A *v.t.* 1 komprimieren; **~d milk** Kondensmilch, *die* 2 (Phys., Chem.) kondensieren 3 (make concise) zusammenfassen; **in a ~d form** in verkürzter Form

B *v.i.* kondensieren

condenser /kənˈdensə(r)/ *n.* 1 (of steam engine) Kondensator, *der* 2 (Electr.) ▸**capacitor** 3 (Chem.) Kühler, *der*

condescend /kɒndɪˈsend/ *v.i.* ~ **to do sth.** geruhen (geh.), etw. zu tun; sich dazu herablassen, etw. zu tun; ~ **to sb.** jmdn. von oben herab behandeln

condescending /kɒndɪˈsendɪŋ/ *adj.* (derog.) herablassend

condescendingly /kɒndɪˈsendɪŋlɪ/ *adv.* (derog.) herablassend; von oben herab

condescension /kɒndɪˈsenʃn/ *n.* (derog.: patronizing manner) Herablassung, *die;* **his air of ~:** sein herablassendes Gebaren

condiment /ˈkɒndɪmənt/ *n.* Gewürz, *das*

condition /kənˈdɪʃn/

A *n.* 1 (stipulation) [Vor]bedingung, *die;* Voraussetzung, *die;* **make it a ~ that ...:** es zur Bedingung machen, dass ...; **on [the] ~ that ...:** unter der Voraussetzung *od.* Bedingung, dass ... 2 (in pl.: circumstances) Umstände *Pl.;* **weather/light ~s** Witterungsverhältnisse/Lichtverhältnisse; **under** *or* **in present ~s** unter den gegenwärtigen Umständen *od.* Bedingungen; **living/working ~s** Unterkunfts-/Arbeitsbedingungen 3 (state of being) (of athlete, etc.) Kondition, *die;* Form, *die;* (of thing) Zustand, *der;* (of invalid, patient, etc.) Verfassung, *die;* **keep sth. in good ~:** etw. in gutem Zustand erhalten; **be out of ~/in [good] ~** ‹*Person:*› schlecht/gut in Form sein; **sb. is in no ~ to do sth.** jmds. Gesundheitszustand erlaubt ihm nicht, etw. zu tun; **she's in no ~ to travel/drive** sie ist nicht reisefähig/fahrtüchtig; **get into ~** (Sport) sich in Form *od.* Kondition bringen 4 ▸❶ **p. 1231** (Med.) Leiden, *das;* **have a heart/lung** *etc.* **~:** ein Herz-/Lungenleiden *usw.* haben; herz-/lungenleidend sein

B *v.t.* 1 (determine) bestimmen 2 (make suitable or fit) in Form bringen ‹*Sportler, Tier, Haar*› 3 (accustom) dressieren ‹*Pferd, Hund*›; ~ **sb. to sth.** jmdn. an etw. (*Akk.*) gewöhnen; **be ~ed to do sth.** gewöhnt sein, etw. zu tun; **be ~ed to respond to a stimulus** konditioniert sein, auf einen Reiz zu reagieren; *see also* **reflex A**

conditional /kənˈdɪʃənl/

A *adj.* 1 bedingt; **be ~ [up]on sth.** von etw. abhängen 2 (Ling.) konditional; bedingend; ~ **clause** Konditional- *od.* Bedingungssatz, *der;* ~ **mood/tense** Konditional[is], *der*

B *n.* (Ling.) Konditional[is], *der*

conditionally /kənˈdɪʃənəlɪ/ *adv.* mit *od.* unter Vorbehalt

conditioner /kənˈdɪʃənə(r)/ *n.* 1 ▸**air conditioner** 2 ▸**hair conditioner**

condo /ˈkɒndəʊ/ *n.* (Amer. coll.) ▸**condominium 2**

condole /kənˈdəʊl/ *v.i.* (formal) ~ **with sb. [up]on sth.** jmdm. zu etw. seine Anteilnahme *od.* sein Mitgefühl aussprechen; ~ **with sb. on the death of his mother** jmdm. zum Tode seiner Mutter kondolieren

condolence /kənˈdəʊləns/ *n.* Anteilnahme, *die;* Mitgefühl, *das;* (on death) Beileid, *das;* **offer sb. one's ~s** jmdm. sein Mitgefühl/sein Beileid *od.* seine Teilnahme aussprechen; **letter of ~:** Beileidsbrief, *der;* Kondolenzbrief, *der;* **please accept my ~s** darf ich Ihnen mein Beileid *od.* meine [An]teilnahme aussprechen?

condom /ˈkɒndəm/ *n.* Kondom, *das od. der;* Präservativ, *das*

condominium /kɒndəˈmɪnɪəm/ *n.* 1 (Polit.) Kondominium, *das* 2 (Amer.: property) Appartementhaus [mit Eigentumswohnungen]; (single dwelling) Eigentumswohnung, *die*

condone /kənˈdəʊn/ *v.t.* 1 hinwegsehen über (+ *Akk.*); (approve) billigen 2 (Law) in Kauf nehmen; stillschweigend billigen

condor /ˈkɒndə(r)/ *n.* (Ornith.) Kondor, *der*

conduce /kənˈdjuːs/ *v.i.* (formal) ~ **to** förderlich sein (+ *Dat.*); beitragen zu

conducive /kənˈdjuːsɪv/ *adj.* **be ~ to sth.** einer Sache (*Dat.*) förderlich sein; zu etw. beitragen

conduct

A /ˈkɒndʌkt/ *n.* 1 (behaviour) Verhalten, *das;* **good ~:** gute Führung; **rules of ~:** Verhaltensregeln 2 (way of ~ing) Führung, *die;* (of conference, inquiry, operation) Leitung, *die;* Durchführung, *die;* **his ~ of the war** seine Kriegsführung; **their ~ of the negotiations** ihre Verhandlungsführung 3 (leading, guidance) Geleit, *das; see also* **safe conduct**

B /kənˈdʌkt/ *v.t.* 1 (Mus.) dirigieren 2 (direct) führen ‹*Geschäfte, Krieg, Gespräch*›; durchführen ‹*Operation, Untersuchung*›; leiten ‹*Konferenz*›; ~ **one's affairs** seine Geschäfte führen 3 (Phys.) leiten ‹*Wärme, Elektrizität*› 4 ~ **oneself** sich verhalten 5 (guide) führen; ~ **sb. away [from]** jmdn. wegführen [von]; **a ~ed tour [of a museum/factory]** eine [Museums-/Werks-]führung

conduction /kənˈdʌkʃn/ *n.* (Phys.) Leitung, *die*

conductive /kənˈdʌktɪv/ *adj.* leitend; **thermally ~:** wärmeleitend

conductivity /kɒndʌkˈtɪvɪtɪ/ *n.* (Phys.) Leitfähigkeit, *die;* Konduktivität, *die* (fachspr.)

conductor /kənˈdʌktə(r)/ *n.* 1 ▸❶ **p. 1260** (Mus.) Dirigent, *der*/Dirigentin, *die* 2 ▸❶ **p. 1260** (of bus, tram) Schaffner, *der;* (Amer.: of train) Zugführer, *der;* Schaffner, *der* (ugs.) 3 (Phys.) Leiter, *der;* Konduktor, *der* (fachspr.); ~ **rail** Strom-, Sammelschiene, *die*

conductress /kənˈdʌktrɪs/ *n.* ▸❶ **p. 1260** Schaffnerin, *die*

conduit /ˈkɒndɪt, ˈkɒndjʊɪt/ *n.* 1 Leitung, *die;* Kanal, *der* (auch fig.) 2 (Electr.) Isolierrohr, *das*

cone /kəʊn/

A *n.* 1 Kegel, *der;* Konus, *der* (fachspr.); (traffic ~) Leitkegel, *der;* Pylon, *der* (fachspr.); Pylone, *die* (fachspr.) 2 (Bot.) Zapfen, *der* 3 **ice cream ~:** Eistüte, *die* 4 (Anat.) Zapfen, *der*

B *v.t.* ~ **off** [mit Leitkegeln *od.* Pylonen] absperren ‹*Straße, Fahrbahn*›

coney /ˈkəʊnɪ/ *n.* 1 (rabbit) Kaninchen, *das* 2 (fur) Kaninchenfell, *das;* Kanin, *das* (Kürschnerei, Mode)

confab /ˈkɒnfæb/ *n.* (coll.) Unterhaltung, *die;* Schwätzchen, *das* (ugs.); (discussion) Besprechung, *die*

confection /kənˈfekʃn/ *n.* 1 Konfekt, *das* 2 (mixing, compounding) Anfertigung, *die* 3 (article of dress) [Damen]modeartikel, *der*

confectioner /kənˈfekʃənə(r)/ *n.* ▸❶ **p. 1260** (maker) Hersteller von Süßigkeiten; (retailer) Süßwarenhändler, *der;* (cake decorator) Konditor, *der;* Zuckerbäcker, *der* (veralt., südd., österr.); **~'s [shop]** Süßwarengeschäft, *das;* **~s' sugar** (Amer.) Puderzucker, *der*

confectionery /kənˈfekʃənərɪ/ *n.* 1 Süßwaren *Pl.;* (cakes etc.) Konditoreiwaren *Pl.* 2 (shop) Süßwarengeschäft, *das* 3 (confectioner's art) Konditorei, *die;* Zuckerbäckerei, *die* (veralt., südd., österr.)

confederacy /kənˈfedərəsɪ/ *n.* 1 (league, alliance) Bündnis, *das* 2 (conspiracy) Verschwörung, *die* 3 (body) Konföderation, *die;* **the [Southern] C~** (Amer. Hist.) die Konföderierten [Staaten]

confederate

A /kənˈfedərət/ *adj.* 1 (allied) verbündet 2 (Polit.) konföderiert; **the C~ States** (Amer. Hist.) die Konföderierten Staaten von Amerika

B *n.* Verbündete, *der/die;* (accomplice) Komplize, *der*/Komplizin, *die;* **C~** (Amer. Hist.) Konföderierte, *der*

C /kənˈfedəreɪt/ *v.t.* vereinigen

D *v.i.* sich verbünden *od.* zusammenschließen

confederation /kənfedəˈreɪʃn/ *n.* 1 (Polit.) [Staaten]bund, *der;* **the Swiss C~:** die Schweizerische Eidgenossenschaft 2 (alliance) Bund, *der;* **C~ of British Industry** *britischer Unternehmerverband*

confer /kənˈfɜː(r)/

A *v.t.*, **-rr-:** ~ **a title/degree/knighthood [up]on sb.** jmdm. einen Titel/Grad verleihen/jmdn. zum Ritter schlagen; ~ **a quality [up]on sth.** einer Sache (*Dat.*) eine Eigenschaft verleihen

B *v.i.*, **-rr-:** ~ **with sb.** sich mit jmdm. beraten

conference /ˈkɒnfərəns/ *n.* 1 (meeting) Konferenz, *die;* Tagung, *die* 2 (consultation) Beratung, *die;* (business discussion) Besprechung, *die;* **be in ~:** in einer Besprechung sein

conference: ~ **call** *n.* Konferenzgespräch, *das;* ~ **centre** *n.* Konferenzzentrum, *das;* Tagungszentrum, *das;* ~ **hall** *n.* Konferenzhalle, *die;* Konferenzsaal, *der;* ~ **room** *n.* Konferenzraum, *der;* (smaller) Besprechungszimmer, *das;* ~ **table** *n.* Konferenztisch, *der;* **get round the ~ table** (fig.) sich an den Verhandlungstisch setzen

conferment /kənˈfɜːmənt/ *n.* Verleihung, *die*

confess /kənˈfes/

A *v.t.* 1 zugeben; gestehen; **he ~ed himself to be the culprit** er gestand, der Schuldige zu sein; **I ~ myself a traditionalist** ich bekenne mich als Traditionalist 2 (Eccl.) beichten; ~ **one's sins to a priest** einem Priester seine Sünden beichten *od.* bekennen 3 (Eccl.) **the priest ~ed the penitent** der Priester nahm dem reuigen Sünder die Beichte ab

B *v.i.* 1 ~ **to sth.** etw. gestehen; ~ **to being unable to do sth.** gestehen *od.* zugeben, dass

C

man etw. nicht kann [2] (Eccl.) beichten (**to sb.** jmdm.); ‹*Priester:*› die Beichte abnehmen

confessed /kən'fest/ *adj.* geständig ‹*Verbrecher*›; **a ~ homosexual** jemand, der sich dazu bekennt, homosexuell zu sein

confessedly /kən'fesɪdlɪ/ *adv.* zugegebenermaßen; (avowedly) eingestandenermaßen

confession /kən'feʃn/ *n.* [1] (of offence etc.) Geständnis, *das;* **on** *or* **by one's own ~:** nach eigenem Geständnis; **I have a ~ to make** ich muss ein Geständnis ablegen [2] (Eccl.: of sins etc.) Beichte, *die;* **~ of sins** Sündenbekenntnis, *das;* **hear sb.'s ~:** jmdm. die Beichte abnehmen; **make one's ~:** seine Sünden bekennen [3] (thing confessed) Geständnis, *das* [4] (Relig.: denomination) Konfession, *die;* **what ~ is he?** welcher Konfession ist er?; **Roman Catholic** *etc.* **by ~:** römisch-katholischer *usw.* Konfession [5] (Eccl.: confessing) Bekenntnis, *das;* **~ of faith** Glaubensbekenntnis, *das*

confessional /kən'feʃənl/ (Eccl.)

[A] *adj.* (of confession) bekennend; (denominational) konfessionell; **~ schools** Konfessionsschulen

[B] *n.* [1] (stall) Beichtstuhl, *der* [2] (act) Beichte, *die*

confessor /kən'fesə(r)/ *n.* (Eccl.) Beichtvater, *der*

confetti /kən'fetɪ/ *n.* Konfetti, *das*

confidant /'kɒnfɪdænt, kɒnfɪ'dænt/ *n.* Vertraute, *der*

confidante /'kɒnfɪdænt, kɒnfɪ'dænt/ *n.* Vertraute, *die*

confide /kən'faɪd/

[A] *v.i.* **~ in sb.** sich jmdm. anvertrauen; **~ to sb. about sth.** jmdm. etw. anvertrauen

[B] *v.t.* **~ sth. to sb.** jmdm. etw. anvertrauen; **he ~d that he ...:** er gestand, dass er ...

confidence /'kɒnfɪdəns/ *n.* [1] (firm trust) Vertrauen, *das;* **have [complete** *or* **every/no] ~ in sb./sth.** [volles/kein] Vertrauen zu jmdm./etw. haben; **have [absolute] ~ that ...:** [absolut] sicher sein, dass ...; **place** *or* **put one's ~ in sb./sth.** sein Vertrauen in jmdn./etw. setzen; auf jmdn./etw. bauen [2] (assured expectation) Gewissheit, *die;* Sicherheit, *die;* **in full ~ of success** voller Erfolgsgewissheit [3] (self-reliance) Selbstvertrauen, *das* [4] (boldness) Dreistigkeit, *die* [5] (telling of private matters) Vertraulichkeit, *die;* **in ~:** im Vertrauen; **this is in [strict] ~:** das ist [streng] vertraulich; **take sb. into one's ~:** jmdn. ins Vertrauen ziehen; **be in sb.'s ~:** jmds. Vertrauen genießen [6] (thing told in ~) Vertraulichkeit, *die*

confidence: ~ game (Amer.) ▸ **~ trick; ~ man** *n.* Trickbetrüger, *der;* Bauernfänger, *der* (ugs.); **~ trick** *n.* (Brit.) Trickbetrug, *der;* Bauernfängerei, *die* (ugs.); **~ trickster** (Brit.) ▸ **~ man**

confident /'kɒnfɪdənt/ *adj.* [1] (trusting, fully assured) zuversichtlich (**about** in Bezug auf + *Akk.*); **be ~ that [sth. will happen]** sicher sein, dass [etw. geschieht]; **be ~ of sth.** auf etw. (*Akk.*) vertrauen [2] (bold) dreist [3] (self-assured) selbstbewusst

confidential /kɒnfɪ'denʃl/ *adj.* [1] (uttered in confidence) vertraulich [2] (entrusted with secrets) persönlich; privat; **~ secretary** Privatsekretär, *der*/-sekretärin, *die*

confidentiality /kɒnfɪdenʃɪ'ælɪtɪ/ *n., no pl.* Vertraulichkeit, *die*

confidentially /kɒnfɪ'denʃəlɪ/ *adv.* vertraulich

confidently /'kɒnfɪdəntlɪ/ *adv.* zuversichtlich

confiding /kən'faɪdɪŋ/ *adj.*, **confidingly** /kən'faɪdɪŋlɪ/ *adv.* vertrauensvoll

configuration /kənfɪgjʊ'reɪʃn/ *n.* [1] (arrangement, outline) Gestaltung, *die* [2] (Astron., Computing) Konfiguration, *die*

configure /kən'fɪgə(r)/ *v.t.* (esp. Computing) konfigurieren

confine /kən'faɪn/ *v.t.* [1] einsperren; eindämmen ‹*Flut, Feuer usw.*›; **be ~d to bed/the house** ans Bett/Haus gefesselt sein; **be ~d to barracks** keinen Ausgang bekommen; **be ~d to a small area** auf ein kleines Gebiet begrenzt sein [2] (fig.) **~ sb./sth. to sth.** jmdn./etw. auf etw. (*Akk.*) beschränken; **~ oneself to sth./doing sth.** sich auf etw. (*Akk.*) beschränken/sich darauf beschränken, etw. zu tun [3] (imprison) einsperren;

confined /kən'faɪnd/ *adj.* begrenzt

confinement /kən'faɪnmənt/ *n.* [1] (imprisonment) Einsperrung, *die;* (in asylum) Einweisung, *die* [2] (being confined) **put/keep sb. in ~:** jmdn. in Haft nehmen/halten; **~ in hospital** ein Krankenhausaufenthalt; **animals kept in ~:** gefangen gehaltene Tiere [3] (childbirth) Niederkunft, *die* [4] (limitation) Beschränkung, *die* (**to** auf + *Akk.*)

confines /'kɒnfaɪnz/ *n. pl.* Grenzen

confirm /kən'fɜ:m/ *v.t.* [1] bestätigen; **be ~ed in one's suspicions** sich in seinem Verdacht bestätigt sehen [2] (Protestant Ch.) konfirmieren; einsegnen; (RC Ch.) firmen

confirmation /kɒnfə'meɪʃn/ *n.* [1] Bestätigung, *die* [2] (Protestant Ch.) Konfirmation, *die;* Einsegnung, *die;* (RC Ch.) Firmung, *die;* **~ class[es]** Konfirmanden-/Firmunterricht, *der* [3] (of Jewish faith) Konfirmation, *die*

confirmatory /kən'fɜ:mətərɪ/ *adj.* bestätigend

confirmed /kən'fɜ:md/ *adj.* [1] (unlikely to change) eingefleischt ‹*Junggeselle*›; überzeugt ‹*Atheist, Vegetarier*›; unheilbar ‹*Trinker, Kranker*› [2] (Protestant Ch.) konfirmiert; (RC Ch.) gefirmt

confiscate /'kɒnfɪskeɪt/ *v.t.* beschlagnahmen; konfiszieren; **~ sth. from sb.** jmdm. etw. wegnehmen

confiscation /kɒnfɪs'keɪʃn/ *n.* Beschlagnahme, *die;* Konfiskation, *die*

conflagration /kɒnflə'greɪʃn/ *n.* Feuersbrunst, *die* (geh.); Großbrand, *der*

conflate /kən'fleɪt/ *v.t.* verschmelzen

conflation /kən'fleɪʃn/ *n.* Verschmelzung, *die*

conflict

[A] /'kɒnflɪkt/ *n.* [1] (fight) Kampf, *der;* (prolonged) Krieg, *der;* **come into ~ with sb./sth.** mit jmdm./etw. in Konflikt geraten; **be in ~ with sb./sth.** (fig.) mit jmdm./etw. im Kampf liegen [2] (clashing) Konflikt, *der;* **a ~ of views/interests** ein Meinungs-/Interessenkonflikt [3] (Psych.) Konflikt, *der*

[B] /kən'flɪkt/ *v.i.* (be incompatible) sich (*Dat.*) widersprechen; **~ with sth.** einer Sache (*Dat.*) widersprechen; zu einer Sache im Widerspruch stehen

conflicting /kən'flɪktɪŋ/ *adj.* widersprüchlich

confluence /'kɒnflʊəns/ *n.* Zusammenfluss, *der*

conform /kən'fɔ:m/

[A] *v.i.* [1] entsprechen (**to** *Dat.*); **~ to a pattern** sich mit einem Muster decken; (fig.) einem Muster entsprechen; **those who do not ~ will be asked to leave the club** wer sich nicht einfügt, wird aufgefordert, den Klub zu verlassen [2] (comply) **~ to** *or* **with sth./with sb.** sich nach etw./jmdm. richten

[B] *v.t.* **~ sth. to sth.** etw. an etw. (*Akk.*) anpassen; etw. auf etw. (*Akk.*) abstimmen (fig.)

conformation /kɒnfɔ'meɪʃn/ *n.* [1] (structure) Gestalt, *die* [2] (adaptation) Anpassung, *die* (**to** an + *Akk.*)

conformism /kən'fɔ:mɪzm/ *n.* Konformismus, *der*

conformist /kən'fɔ:mɪst/ *n.* Konformist, *der*/Konformistin, *die*

conformity /kən'fɔ:mɪtɪ/ *n.* Übereinstimmung, *die* (**with, to** mit)

confound /kən'faʊnd/ *v.t.* [1] **~ it!** verflixt noch mal! (ugs.); **~ him** *or* **the man!** der verflixte Kerl! (ugs.) [2] (defeat) vereiteln ‹*Plan, Hoffnung*› [3] (confuse) verwirren [4] (discomfit) ins Unrecht setzen [5] (make indistinguishable) durcheinander bringen; verwischen ‹*Unterschied*› [6] (mix up mentally) verwechseln [7] (throw into disorder) durcheinander werfen

confounded /kən'faʊndɪd/ *adj.*, **confoundedly** /kən'faʊndɪdlɪ/ *adv.* (coll. derog.) verdammt

confront /kən'frʌnt/ *v.t.* [1] gegenüberstellen; konfrontieren; **~ sb. with sth./sb.** jmdn. mit etw./[mit] jmdm. konfrontieren; **he was ~ed with** *or* **by an angry mob** er sah sich [mit] einer wütenden Menge konfrontiert [2] (stand facing) gegenüberstehen (+ *Dat.*); **enemies ~ing one another** einander gegenüberstehende Feinde; **find oneself ~ed by** *or* **with a problem** sich [mit] einem Problem konfrontiert sehen [3] (face in defiance) ins Auge sehen (+ *Dat.*) [4] (oppose) widersprechen (+ *Dat.*); (make comparison) gegenüberstellen

confrontation /kɒnfrən'teɪʃn/ *n.* Konfrontation, *die;* (with witnesses) Gegenüberstellung, *die*

confrontational /kɒnfrən'teɪʃənl/ *adj.* auf Konfrontation ausgerichtet

Confucianism /kən'fju:ʃənɪzm/ *n., no pl.* Konfuzianismus, *der*

confuse /kən'fju:z/ *v.t.* [1] (disorder) durcheinander bringen; verwirren; (blur) verwischen; **~ the issue** den Sachverhalt unklar machen; **it simply ~s matters** das verwirrt die Sache nur [2] (mix up mentally) verwechseln; **~ two things** zwei Dinge [miteinander] verwechseln [3] (perplex) konfus machen; verwirren

confused /kən'fju:zd/ *adj.* konfus; wirr ‹*Gedanken, Gerüchte*›; verworren ‹*Lage, Situation*›; (embarrassed) verlegen

confusing /kən'fju:zɪŋ/ *adj.* verwirrend

confusion /kən'fju:ʒn/ *n.* [1] (disordering) Verwirrung, *die;* (mixing up) Verwechslung, *die;* **~ of tongues** Sprachverwirrung, *die* [2] (state) Verwirrung, *die;* (embarrassment) Verlegenheit, *die;* **throw sb./sth. into ~:** jmdn./etw. [völlig] durcheinander bringen; **reply/blush in ~:** verlegen antworten/erröten; **in [total] ~:** in völligem Durcheinander ‹*fliehen*›; [völlig *od.* wild] durcheinander ‹*daliegen*›; **a scene of total ~:** ein totales Chaos

confutation /kɒnfjʊ'teɪʃn/ *n.* Widerlegung, *die*

confute /kən'fju:t/ *v.t.* widerlegen

conga /'kɒŋgə/ *n.* Conga, *die*

congeal /kən'dʒi:l/

[A] *v.i.* [1] (coagulate) gerinnen; **~ into sth.** (fig.) zu etw. erstarren [2] (freeze) gefrieren

[B] *v.t.* [1] (coagulate) gerinnen lassen; koagulieren [2] (solidify by cooling) gefrieren lassen

congenial /kən'dʒi:nɪəl/ *adj.* [1] (kindred) geistesverwandt; **~ spirits** kongeniale Geister [2] (agreeable) angenehm

congeniality /kəndʒi:nɪ'ælɪtɪ/ *n., no pl.* Geistesverwandtschaft, *die*

congenital /kən'dʒenɪtl/ *adj.* angeboren; kongenital (fachspr.); **a ~ idiot** ein von Geburt an Schwachsinniger; **a ~ defect** ein Geburtsfehler

congenitally /kən'dʒenɪtəlɪ/ *adv.* von Geburt an

conger /'kɒŋgə(r)/ *n.* (Zool.) **~ [eel]** Meer- *od.* Seeaal, *der*

congest /kən'dʒest/ *v.t.* verstopfen

congested /kən'dʒestɪd/ *adj.* überfüllt, verstopft ‹*Straße*›; übervölkert ‹*Stadtviertel*›; **my nose is ~:** ich habe eine verstopfte Nase

congestion /kən'dʒestʃn/ *n.* (of traffic etc.) Stauung, *die;* (overpopulation) Übervölkerung, *die;* **~ of the lungs** (Med.) Lungenstauung, *die;* **nasal ~:** verstopfte Nase

con'gestion charge *n.* Staugebühr, *die*

conglomerate

[A] /kən'glɒməreɪt/ *v.t.* (lit. or fig.) verschmelzen

[B] *v.i.* sich zusammenballen; (fig.) sich versammeln

[C] /kən'glɒmərət/ *n.* [1] (Commerc.) Großkonzern, *der* [2] (Geol.) Konglomerat, *das*

conglomeration /kənglɒmə'reɪʃn/ *n.* Konglomerat, *das;* (collection) Ansammlung, *die*

Congo /'kɒŋgəʊ/ *pr. n.* ▸ⓘ **p. 1491** (Geog.: river, country) Kongo, *der*

Congolese /kɒŋgə'li:z/ ▸ⓘ **p. 1345**

[A] *adj.* kongolesisch

[B] *n.* Kongolese, *der*/Kongolesin, *die*

congratulate /kən'grætjʊleɪt/ *v.t.* gratulieren (+ *Dat.*); **~ sb./oneself [up]on sth.** jmdm./sich zu etw. gratulieren

congratulation /kəngrætjʊ'leɪʃn/

[A] *int.* **~s!** herzlichen Glückwunsch! (**on** zu); (on passing exam etc.) ich gratuliere!

[B] *n.* [1] *in pl.* Glückwünsche *Pl.;* **offer sb. one's**

~**s** jmdm. gratulieren; jmdn. beglückwünschen 2 (action) Gratulation, *die*

congratulatory /kən'grætjʊlətərɪ/ *adj.* beglückwünschend; ~ **note/letter** Glückwunschschreiben, *das*/-brief, *der*

congregate /'kɒŋgrɪgeɪt/
A *v.i.* sich versammeln; zusammenkommen
B *v.t.* versammeln

congregation /kɒŋgrɪ'geɪʃn/ *n.* 1 (Eccl.) Gemeinde, *die* 2 (Brit. Univ.) ≈ Konzil, *das*

congress /'kɒŋgres/ *n.* 1 (meeting of heads of state etc.) Kongress, *der;* **the C~ of Vienna** der Wiener Kongress; **a party ~:** ein Parteitag 2 (association) Verband, *der* 3 **C~** (Amer.: legislature) der Kongress

> **Congress**
>
> Die nationale gesetzgebende Versammlung in den Vereinigten Staaten. Der Kongress tritt im **Capitol** zusammen und besteht aus zwei Kammern, **Senate** (Senat) und **House of Representatives** (Repräsentantenhaus). Die Funktion des Kongresses ist es, Gesetze zu erlassen. Jedes Gesetz muss von beiden Kammern angenommen und anschließend vom **President** (Präsident) verabschiedet werden.

congressional /kən'greʃənl/ *adj.* Kongress-; ‹*Erlaubnis*› des Kongresses; ~ **district** Kongresswahlbezirk, *der*

Congress: ~**man** /'kɒŋgresmən/ *n., pl.* ~**men** /'kɒŋgresmən/ (Amer.) Kongressabgeordnete, *der;* ~**woman** *n.* (Amer.) Kongressabgeordnete, *die*

congruence /'kɒŋgrʊəns/, **congruency** /'kɒŋgrʊənsɪ/ *n.* 1 Übereinstimmung, *die* 2 (Geom.) Kongruenz, *die;* Deckungsgleichheit, *die*

congruent /'kɒŋgrʊənt/ *adj.* 1 (formal) übereinstimmend 2 (Geom.) kongruent; deckungsgleich

congruity /kɒŋ'gru:ɪtɪ/ *n.* Übereinstimmung, *die;* Kongruenz, *die* (geh.)

conic /'kɒnɪk/ *adj.* Kegel-; ~ **section** Kegelschnitt, *der*

conical /'kɒnɪkl/ *adj.* konisch; kegelförmig; *see also* **projection 9**

conifer /'kɒnɪfə(r), 'kəʊnɪfə(r)/ *n.* Nadelbaum, *der;* Konifere, *die;* ~**s** Nadelhölzer

coniferous /kə'nɪfərəs/ *adj.* Nadel-; ~ **tree** Nadelbaum, *der;* Konifere, *die;* ~ **forest** Nadelwald, *der*

conjectural /kən'dʒektʃərl/ *adj.* auf Mutmaßungen (geh.) *od.* Vermutungen beruhend; konjektural (Literaturw.); **all this is ~:** all das ist Vermutung; **a ~ emendation of a text** eine Konjektur (Literaturw.)

conjecturally /kən'dʒektʃərəlɪ/ *adv.* aufgrund von Mutmaßungen (geh.) *od.* Vermutungen

conjecture /kən'dʒektʃə(r)/
A *n.* 1 Mutmaßung, *die* (geh.); Vermutung, *die;* **rely on ~:** sich auf Mutmaßungen (*Akk.*) stützen 2 (Lit.) Konjektur, *die*
B *v.t.* mutmaßen (geh.); vermuten
C *v.i.* (guess) Mutmaßungen (geh.) *od.* Vermutungen anstellen

conjoin /kən'dʒɔɪn/
A *v.t.* verbinden
B *v.i.* sich verbinden

conjoint /kən'dʒɔɪnt/ *adj.* (formal) 1 (united) gemeinsam 2 (associated) Mit-

conjointly /kən'dʒɔɪntlɪ/ *adv.* gemeinsam

conjugal /'kɒndʒʊgl/ *adj.* ehelich; **the ~ state** der Stand der Ehe; ~ **bliss/worries** Eheglück, *das*/Ehesorgen

conjugate
A /'kɒndʒʊgeɪt/ *v.t.* (Ling.) konjugieren
B *v.i.* 1 (Ling.) konjugiert werden 2 (Biol.) sich paaren *od.* vereinigen
C /'kɒndʒʊgət/ *adj.* 1 gepaart 2 (Ling.) wurzelverwandt 3 (Math.) konjugiert
D *n.* (Ling.) wurzelverwandtes Wort

conjugation /kɒndʒʊ'geɪʃn/ *n.* 1 (joining together) Vereinigung, *die* 2 (Ling., Biol.) Konjugation, *die*

conjunction /kən'dʒʌŋkʃn/ *n.* 1 Verbindung, *die;* **in ~ with sb./sth.** in Verbindung mit jmdm./etw. 2 (formal: of events) Zusammentreffen, *das* 3 (Ling.) Konjunktion, *die;* Bindewort, *das* 4 (Astrol., Astron.) Konjunktion, *die*

conjunctivitis /kəndʒʌŋktɪ'vaɪtɪs/ *n.* ▸ℹ **p. 1231** (Med.) Bindehautentzündung, *die;* Konjunktivitis, *die* (fachspr.)

conjure
A *v.t.* 1 /kən'dʒʊə(r)/ (formal: beseech) beschwören; anflehen 2 /'kʌndʒə(r)/ (by magic) beschwören ‹*Geister*›
B /'kʌndʒə(r)/ *v.i.* zaubern; **conjuring trick** Zaubertrick, *der;* Zauberkunststück, *das;* **a name to ~ with** ein exotischer *od.* geheimnisvoller Name; (because of great importance) ein klangvoller Name

Phrasal verbs
- ~ **'away** *v.t.* wegzaubern
- ~ **'up** *v.t.* beschwören ‹*Geister, Teufel*›; (fig.) heraufbeschwören

conjuror (**conjurer**)/'kʌndʒərə(r)/ *n.* Zauberkünstler, *der*/-künstlerin, *die;* Zauberer, *der*/Zauberin, *die*

conk[1] /kɒŋk/ *v.i.* ~ **'out** (coll.) schlappmachen (ugs.); ‹*Maschine, Auto usw.:*› den Geist aufgeben (scherzh.), kaputtgehen (ugs.)

conk[2] *n.* (coll.) 1 (nose) Zinken, *der* (ugs.); Rüssel, *der* (salopp) 2 (head) Rübe, *die* (salopp); Birne, *die* (salopp)

conker /'kɒŋkə(r)/ *n.* (horse chestnut) [Ross]kastanie, *die;* **play ~s** ein Wettspiel mit Kastanien machen

'conman (coll.) ▸ **confidence man**

connect /kə'nekt/
A *v.t.* 1 (join together) verbinden (**to, with** mit); (Electr.) anschließen (**to, with** an + *Akk.*) 2 (join in sequence) verbinden; verknüpfen 3 (associate) verbinden; ~ **sth. with sth.** etw. mit etw. verbinden *od.* in Verbindung bringen; **be ~ed with sb./sth.** mit jmdm./etw. in Verbindung stehen
B *v.i.* 1 (join) ~ **with sth.** mit etw. zusammenhängen *od.* verbunden sein; ‹*Zug, Schiff usw.:*› Anschluss haben an etw. (*Akk.*) 2 (form logical sequence) einen Zusammenhang/Zusammenhänge darstellen 3 (coll.: hit) einen Haken *usw.* landen (**with** auf, an + *Dat.*)

Phrasal verb
- ~ **'up** *v.t.* anschließen

connected /kə'nektɪd/ *adj.* 1 (logically joined) zusammenhängend; **sth. is ~ with sth.** etw. hängt mit etw. zusammen; etw. hat mit etw. zu tun 2 (related) verwandt; **he is well ~:** er hat einflussreiche Verwandte

connecting/kə'nektɪŋ/: ~ **door** *n.* Verbindungstür, *die;* ~ **rod** *n.* (Mech. Engin.) Pleuelstange, *die*

connection /kə'nekʃn/ *n.* 1 (act, state) Verbindung, *die;* (Electr.; of telephone) Anschluss, *der;* **cut the ~:** die Verbindung abbrechen; **the Italian ~:** die Beziehungen zu Italien; **run in ~ with sth.** ‹*Zug usw.:*› Anschluss haben an etw. (*Akk.*) 2 (fig.: of ideas) Zusammenhang, *der;* **in this ~:** in diesem Zusammenhang; **in ~ with sth.** im Zusammenhang mit etw.: 3 (part) Verbindung, *die;* Verbindungsstück, *das* 4 (train, boat, etc.) Anschluss, *der;* **miss a ~:** einen Anschluss verpassen; **catch** *or* **make a ~:** einen Anschluss erreichen *od.* (ugs.) kriegen 5 (family relationship) Verwandtschaft, *die* 6 (person) (relative) Verwandte, *der/die;* **business ~s** Geschäftsbeziehungen; **have ~s** Beziehungen haben 7 (personal dealings) **he has no ~ with the firm of this name** er hat keinerlei Verbindung zu dem gleichnamigen Unternehmen 8 (sl.: supplier of narcotics) Dealer, *der* (Jargon)

connective /kə'nektɪv/ *adj.* 1 verbindend 2 (Anat.) ~ **tissue** Bindegewebe, *das*

connector /kə'nektə(r)/ *n.* Verbinder, *der*

connexion (Brit.) ▸ **connection**

conning tower /'kɒnɪŋtaʊə(r)/ *n.* (Naut.) Kommandoturm, *der*

connivance /kə'naɪvəns/ *n.* stillschweigende Duldung

connive /kə'naɪv/ *v.i.* 1 ~ **at sth.** (disregard) über etw. (*Akk.*) hinwegsehen; etw. stillschweigend dulden 2 (conspire) ~ **with sb.** mit jmdm. gemeinsame Sache machen (**in** bei)

connoisseur /kɒnə'sɜ:(r)/ *n.* Kenner, *der;* **a ~ of wine** ein Weinkenner

connotation /kɒnə'teɪʃn/ *n.* Assoziation, *die;* Konnotation, *die* (Sprachw.)

connote /kə'nəʊt/ *v.t.* (formal) 1 (suggest) suggerieren 2 (signify) bezeichnen

connubial /kə'nju:bɪəl/ *adj.* ehelich; Ehe-

conquer /'kɒŋkə(r)/ *v.t.* besiegen ‹*Gegner, Leidenschaft, Gewohnheit*›; erobern ‹*Land*›; bezwingen ‹*Berg, Gegner*›; **I came, I saw, I ~ed** ich kam, ich sah, ich siegte

conqueror /'kɒŋkərə(r)/ *n.* Sieger, *der*/Siegerin, *die* (**of** über + *Akk.*); (of a mountain) Bezwinger, *der;* (of a country) Eroberer, *der;* **[William] the C~:** Wilhelm der Eroberer

conquest /'kɒŋkwest/ *n.* 1 Eroberung, *die;* **the [Norman] C~:** die Eroberung Englands durch die Normannen 2 (territory) Eroberung, *die;* erobertes Gebiet 3 (fig.: of mountain) Bezwingung, *die;* Sieg, *der* (**of** über + *Akk.*)

'con rod *n.* (Motor Veh. coll.) Pleuelstange, *die*

conscience /'kɒnʃəns/ *n.* Gewissen, *das;* **have a good** *or* **clear/bad** *or* **guilty ~:** ein gutes/schlechtes Gewissen haben; **have no ~:** gewissenlos sein; **with a clear** *or* **easy ~:** mit gutem Gewissen; guten Gewissens (geh.); **have sth. on one's ~:** wegen etw. ein schlechtes Gewissen haben; **that is still on my ~:** das liegt mir immer noch auf der Seele; **in all ~:** ehrlicherweise; (without doubt) zweifellos; **freedom** *or* **liberty of ~:** Gewissensfreiheit, *die;* Freiheit des Gewissens; **a matter of ~:** eine Gewissensfrage

conscience: ~ **clause** *n.* (Law) Gewissensklausel, *die;* ~ **money** *n.* freiwillige Geldbuße; ~**-smitten**, ~**-stricken**, ~**-struck** *adjs.* schuldbewusst

conscientious /kɒnʃɪ'enʃəs/ *adj.* pflichtbewusst; (meticulous) gewissenhaft; ~ **objector** Wehrdienstverweigerer [aus Gewissensgründen]

conscientiously /kɒnʃɪ'enʃəslɪ/ *adv.* pflichtbewusst; (meticulously) gewissenhaft

conscientiousness /kɒnʃɪ'enʃəsnɪs/ *n., no pl.* Pflichtbewusstsein, *das;* (meticulousness) Gewissenhaftigkeit, *die*

conscious /'kɒnʃəs/
A *adj.* 1 **be ~ of sth.** sich (*Dat.*) einer Sache (*Gen.*) bewusst sein; **I was ~ that ...:** mir war bewusst, dass ...; **but he is not ~ of it** aber es ist ihm nicht bewusst; **I suddenly became ~ that ...:** mir wurde plötzlich bewusst, dass ... 2 *pred.* (awake) bei Bewusstsein *präd.;* **become ~:** wach werden; **become ~ again** wieder zu sich kommen 3 (realized by doer) bewusst ‹*Handeln, Versuch, Bemühung*› 4 (self-~) gewollt ‹*Auftreten, Gehabe*›
B *n.* Bewusste, *das* (Psych.)

consciously /'kɒnʃəslɪ/ *adv.* bewusst; **be ~ superior** sich (*Dat.*) seiner Überlegenheit (*Gen.*) bewusst sein

consciousness /'kɒnʃəsnɪs/ *n., no pl.* 1 Bewusstsein, *das;* **lose/recover** *or* **regain ~:** das Bewusstsein verlieren/wiedererlangen; bewusstlos werden/wieder zu sich kommen 2 (totality of thought) Bewusstsein, *das* 3 (perception) Bewusstsein, *das;* Bewusstheit, *die*

conscript
A /kən'skrɪpt/ *v.t.* einberufen ‹*Soldaten*›; ausheben ‹*Armee*›; **be ~ed into the army** zum Wehrdienst einberufen werden
B /'kɒnskrɪpt/ *n.* Einberufene, *der/die;* **an army of ~s** eine Armee von Wehrpflichtigen

conscription /kən'skrɪpʃn/ *n.* (action) Einberufung, *die;* (compulsory military service) Wehrpflicht, *die*

consecrate /'kɒnsɪkreɪt/ *v.t.* (Eccl.; also fig.) weihen; konsekrieren; ~ **sb. a bishop** jmdn. zum Bischof weihen

consecration /kɒnsɪ'kreɪʃn/ *n.* (Eccl.; also fig.) Weihe, *die;* Konsekration, *die*

consecutive /kən'sekjʊtɪv/ *adj.* 1 (following continuously) aufeinander folgend ‹*Monate,*

Jahre›; fortlaufend ‹*Zahlen*›; **this is the fifth ~ day that ...:** heute ist schon der fünfte Tag, an dem ... **2** (in logical sequence) folgerichtig **3** (Ling.) konsekutiv; Konsekutiv-; **~ clause** Konsekutiv-/Folgesatz, *der*

consecutive interpre'tation *n.* Konsekutivdolmetschen, *das*

consecutively /kən'sekjʊtɪvlɪ/ *adv.* hintereinander; fortlaufend ‹*nummeriert*›

consensual /kən'sensjʊəl/ *adj.* konsensorientiert; einvernehmlich ‹*Sex*›

consensus /kən'sensəs/ *n.* Einigkeit, *die;* Konsens[us], *der* (*geh.*); *attrib.* ‹*Politik, Regierungsstil usw.*› des Miteinander *od.* der Gemeinsamkeit; **the general ~ is that ...:** es besteht allgemeiner Konsens (geh.) *od.* allgemeine Einigkeit darüber, dass ...; **the ~ of opinion is in favour of the amendment** die allgemeine Mehrheit *od.* die Mehrheitsmeinung ist für den Änderungsantrag

consent /kən'sent/

A *v.i.* zustimmen; **~ to sth.** einer Sache (*Dat.*) zustimmen; in eine Sache einwilligen; **~ to do sth.** einwilligen, etw. zu tun; **~ing adults** zum Geschlechtsverkehr bereite Erwachsene

B *n.* **1** (agreement) Zustimmung, *die* (**to** zu); Einwilligung, *die* (**to** in + *Akk.*); **by common** *or* **general ~:** nach allgemeiner Auffassung; (as wished by all) auf allgemeinen Wunsch; **age of ~** *Alter, in dem man hinsichtlich Heirat und Geschlechtsleben nicht mehr als minderjährig gilt;* ≈ Ehemündigkeitsalter, *das* **2** (permission) Zustimmung, *die;* Erlaubnis, *die;* **give/refuse [sb.] one's ~:** [jmdm.] seine Zustimmung geben/verweigern

con'sent form *n.* Einverständniserklärung, *die*

consequence /'kɒnsɪkwəns/ *n.* **1** (result) Folge, *die;* **in ~:** folglich; infolgedessen; **in ~ of** als Folge (+ *Gen.*); **as a ~:** infolgedessen; **as a ~ of** infolge (+ *Gen.*); **with the ~ that ...:** mit dem Ergebnis, dass ...; **accept** *or* **take the ~s** die Folgen tragen **2** (importance) Bedeutung, *die;* **be of no ~:** unerheblich *od.* ohne Bedeutung sein; **nothing of ~:** nichts von Bedeutung; nichts Erhebliches; **persons of [no] ~** (significant) [un]bedeutende/(influential, high-ranking) [un]wichtige Leute; **he's of no ~:** er ist unbedeutend *od.* unwichtig

consequent /'kɒnsɪkwənt/ *adj.* **1** (resultant) daraus folgend; sich daraus ergebend; (following in time) darauf folgend; **be ~ [up]on sth.** (formal) die Folge einer Sache (*Gen.*) sein **2** (logically consistent) folgerichtig

consequential /kɒnsɪ'kwenʃl/ *adj.* **1** (resulting) daraus folgend; sich daraus ergebend; (following in time) darauf folgend **2** (indirectly following) indirekt; sich indirekt ergebend; **~ damage[s]** Folgeschäden *Pl.* **3** (self-important) überheblich ‹*Lächeln, Stimme, Person*›

consequentially /kɒnsɪ'kwenʃəlɪ/ *adv.* **1** (indirectly) indirekt **2** (self-importantly) überheblich

consequently /'kɒnsɪkwəntlɪ/ *adv.* infolgedessen; folglich

conservancy /kən'sɜːvənsɪ/ *n.* **1** (Brit.: conserving body) *Behörde, der der Natur-/Gewässerschutz usw. untersteht;* **the Nature C~:** die Naturschutzbehörde **2** (preservation) Naturschutz, *der*

conservation /kɒnsə'veɪʃn/ *n.* **1** (preservation) Schutz, *der;* Erhaltung, *die;* (wise utilization) sparsamer Umgang (**of** mit); **wildlife ~:** Schutz wild lebender Tierarten **2** (Phys.) **~ of energy/momentum** Erhaltung der Energie/des Impulses

conser'vation area *n.* (Brit.) (rural) Landschaftsschutzgebiet, *das;* (urban) unter Denkmalschutz stehendes Gebiet

conservationist /kɒnsə'veɪʃənɪst/ *n.* Naturschützer, *der*/-schützerin, *die*

conservatism /kən'sɜːvətɪzm/ *n.* Konservati[vi]smus, *der*

conservative /kən'sɜːvətɪv/

A *adj.* **1** (conserving) erhaltend; konservierend; **~ surgery** konservative Chirurgie **2** (averse to change) konservativ **3** (not too high) vorsichtig, eher zu niedrig ‹*Zahlen, Schätzung*›; **at a ~ estimate** nach vorsichtiger *od.* (Jargon) konservativer Schätzung **4** (avoiding extremes) konservativ ‹*Geschmack, Ansichten, Baustil*› **5** (Brit. Polit.) konservativ; **the C~ Party** die Konservative Partei

B *n.* **1** **C~** (Brit. Polit.) Konservative, *der/die* **2** (~ person) Konservative, *der/die*

> **Conservative Party**
>
> Eine der Volksparteien Großbritanniens. Sie ist eine Partei der politischen Rechten, die für Kapitalismus, freie Marktwirtschaft und private Industrie und Dienstleistung eintritt. Sie entwickelte sich etwa 1830 aus der alten *Tory Party* und wird auch heute noch häufig so genannt. Die Farbe der Partei ist Blau.

conservatively /kən'sɜːvətɪvlɪ/ *adv.* vorsichtig, eher zu niedrig ‹*geschätzt*›

conservatoire /kən'sɜːvətwɑː(r)/ *n.* (school of music) Konservatorium, *das;* (school of other arts) Kunsthochschule, *die*

conservatory /kən'sɜːvətərɪ/ *n.* **1** (greenhouse) Wintergarten, *der* **2** (Amer.) ▸**conservatoire**

conserve /kən'sɜːv/

A *v.t.* **1** erhalten ‹*Gebäude, Kunstwerk, Wälder*›; bewahren ‹*Ideale, Prinzipien*›; schonen ‹*Gesundheit, Kräfte*› **2** *esp. in p. p.* (Phys.) erhalten ‹*Energie, Impuls*›

B *n. often in pl.* Eingemachte, *das;* **~s** Eingemachtes

consider /kən'sɪdə(r)/ *v.t.* **1** (look at) betrachten; (think about) **~ sth.** an etw. (*Akk.*) denken **2** (weigh merits of) denken an (+ *Akk.*); **he's ~ing emigrating** er denkt daran *od.* trägt sich mit dem Gedanken, auszuwandern; **five candidates are being ~ed** fünf Kandidaten sind in der engeren Wahl **3** (reflect) sich (*Dat.*) überlegen; bedenken; **you must ~ that you/whether or not you ...:** du musst bedenken *od.* dir überlegen, dass du/ob du ... oder nicht; **just ~!** (abs.) überleg [dir das] doch mal! **4** (have opinion) annehmen; finden; **we ~ that you are not to blame** wir sind der Ansicht *od.* finden, dass Sie nicht schuld sind **5** (regard as) halten für; **I ~ him [to be** *or* **as] a swindler** ich halte ihn für einen Betrüger; **do you ~ yourself educated?** hältst du dich für gebildet?; **~ yourself under arrest** betrachten Sie sich als verhaftet; **she is ~ed a great beauty** sie gilt als große Schönheit **6** (allow for) berücksichtigen; **~ other people's feelings** auf die Gefühle anderer Rücksicht nehmen; **all things ~ed** alles in allem

considerable /kən'sɪdərəbl/ *adj.* **1** (no little) beträchtlich; erheblich ‹*Schwierigkeiten, Ärger*›; groß ‹*Freude, Charakterstärke*›; eingehend ‹*Überlegung*›; (imposing) ansehnlich ‹*Gebäude, Edelstein*› **2** (important) bedeutend ‹*Person, Künstler*›

considerably /kən'sɪdərəblɪ/ *adv.* erheblich; (in amount) beträchtlich

considerate /kən'sɪdərət/ *adj.* rücksichtsvoll; (thoughtfully kind) entgegenkommend; **be ~ to[wards] sb.** rücksichtsvoll gegenüber jmdm. sein; auf jmdn. Rücksicht nehmen

considerately /kən'sɪdərətlɪ/ *adv.* rücksichtsvoll; (obligingly) entgegenkommend

considerateness /kən'sɪdərətnɪs/ *n.* Rücksichtnahme, *die* (**for** auf + *Akk.*); (obligingness) Entgegenkommen, *das*

consideration /kənsɪdə'reɪʃn/ *n.* **1** Überlegung, *die;* (meditation) Betrachtung, *die;* **take sth. into ~:** etw. berücksichtigen *od.* bedenken; **give sth. one's ~:** etw. in Erwägung ziehen; **the matter is under ~:** die Angelegenheit wird geprüft; **in ~ of** unter Berücksichtigung (+ *Gen.*); **leave sth. out of ~:** etw. unberücksichtigt lassen; etw. außer Betracht lassen **2** (thoughtfulness) Rücksichtnahme, *die* (**for** auf + *Akk.*); **show ~ for sb.** Rücksicht auf jmdn. nehmen **3** (sth. as reason) Umstand, *der;* **an important ~:** ein wichtiger Faktor **4** (payment) Bezahlung, *die;* **for a ~:** gegen Entgelt **5** (Law) Ausgleich, *der;* Ersatz, *der*

considered /kən'sɪdəd/ *adj.* **1** **~ opinion** feste *od.* ernsthafte Überzeugung **2** **be highly ~ [by others]** [bei anderen] in hohem Ansehen stehen

considering /kən'sɪdərɪŋ/ *prep.* **~ sth.** wenn man etw. bedenkt; **~ [that] ...:** wenn man bedenkt, dass ...; **that's not so bad, ~** (coll.) das ist eigentlich gar nicht mal so schlecht (ugs.)

consign /kən'saɪn/ *v.t.* **1** anvertrauen (**to** *Dat.*); **~ a child to its uncle's care** ein Kind in die Obhut seines Onkels geben; **~ sth. to the scrap heap** (lit. or fig.) etw. auf den Schrotthaufen werfen; **~ a letter to the flames** einen Brief dem Feuer übergeben (geh.) **2** (Commerc.) übersenden, (fachspr.) konsignieren ‹*Güter*› (**to** an + *Akk.*); senden ‹*Brief, Paket*› (**to** an + *Akk.*)

consignment /kən'saɪnmənt/ *n.* (Commerc.) **1** (consigning) Übersendung, *die* (**to** an + *Akk.*); Konsignation, *die* (fachspr.) (**to** an + *Akk.*); **~ note** Frachtbrief, *der* **2** (goods) Sendung, *die;* (large) Ladung, *die*

consist /kən'sɪst/ *v.i.* **1** **~ of** bestehen aus **2** **~ in** bestehen in (+ *Dat.*)

consistence /kən'sɪstəns/, **consistency** /kən'sɪstənsɪ/ *ns.* **1** (density) Konsistenz, *die;* **mixtures of various consistencies** Mischungen verschiedener Konsistenz **2** (being consistent) Konsequenz, *die;* **~ of style** stilistische Konsistenz

consistent /kən'sɪstənt/ *adj.* **1** (compatible) [miteinander] vereinbar; **be ~ with sth.** mit etw. übereinstimmen; mit etw. vereinbar sein **2** (uniform) beständig; gleich bleibend ‹*Qualität*›; einheitlich ‹*Verfahren, Vorgehen, Darstellung*› **3** (adhering to principles) konsequent

consistently /kən'sɪstəntlɪ/ *adv.* (compatibly, in harmony) in Übereinstimmung ‹*handeln*›; (uniformly) einheitlich ‹*gestalten*›; konsistent ‹*denken*›; (persistently) konsequent ‹*behaupten, verfolgen, handeln*›

consistory /kən'sɪstərɪ, 'kɒnsɪstərɪ/ *n.* (RC Ch.) Konsistorium, *das*

consolation /kɒnsə'leɪʃn/ *n.* **1** (act) Tröstung, *die;* Trost, *der;* **words of ~:** Worte des Trostes; tröstende Worte; **a letter of ~:** ein trostvoller Brief **2** (consoling circumstance) Trost, *der;* **that's one ~!** das ist tröstlich *od.* ein Trost!

conso'lation prize *n.* Trostpreis, *der*

consolatory /kən'sɒlətərɪ, kən'səʊlətərɪ/ *adj.* tröstend, trostvoll (**to** für)

console[1] /kən'səʊl/ *v.t.* trösten; **~ sb. for a loss** jmdn. über einen Verlust hinwegtrösten

console[2] /'kɒnsəʊl/ *n.* **1** (Mus.) Spieltisch, *der* **2** (panel) [Schalt]pult, *das;* (of car, games ~) Konsole, *die;* **3** (cabinet) Truhe, *die*

consolidate /kən'sɒlɪdeɪt/

A *v.t.* **1** (strengthen) festigen ‹*Macht, Stellung*›; (fig.) konsolidieren ‹*Stellung, Einfluss, Macht*› **2** (combine) zusammenlegen ‹*Territorien, Grundstücke, Firmen*›; konsolidieren ‹*Schulden, Anleihen*›

B *v.i.* **1** (become solid) hart werden **2** (merge) ‹*Firmen:*› fusionieren

consolidation /kənsɒlɪ'deɪʃn/ *n., no pl.* **1** (strengthening) Festigung, *die;* (fig.) Konsolidierung, *die* **2** (combining) Zusammenlegung, *die;* (of debts, loans) Konsolidation, *die*

consoling /kən'səʊlɪŋ/ *adj.* tröstlich

consommé /kən'sɒmeɪ/ *n.* (Gastr.) Kraftbrühe, *die;* Consommé, *die* (fachspr.)

consonance /'kɒnsənəns/ *n.* **1** (Mus.) Harmonie, *die;* (of two notes) Konsonanz, *die* **2** (fig. formal) Übereinstimmung, *die* **3** (Phonet.) Konsonanz, *die*

consonant /'kɒnsənənt/

A *n.* Konsonant, *der;* Mitlaut, *der;* **~ shift** Lautverschiebung, *die*

B *adj.* **1** (formal) **be ~ with** *or* **to sth.** im Einklang mit etw. stehen **2** (Mus.) konsonant **3** (Phonet.) gleichklingend

consonantal /kɒnsə'næntl/ *adj.* (Phonet.) konsonantisch

consort[1] /'kɒnsɔːt/ *n.* Gemahl, *der*/Gemahlin, *die;* **queen ~:** Gemahlin des Königs; Königin, *die* (volkst.)

consort[2] /kən'sɔːt/ *v.i.* **1** (keep company) verkehren (**with** mit) **2** (arch.: agree) übereinstimmen (**with, to** mit)

consort[3] /'kɒnsɔ:t/ *n.* (Mus.) Consort, *das*

consortium /kən'sɔ:tɪəm/ *n., pl.* **consortia** /kən'sɔ:tɪə/ (association) Konsortium, *das*

conspectus /kən'spektəs/ *n.* Übersicht, *die*

conspicuous /kən'spɪkjʊəs/ *adj.* [1] (clearly visible) unübersehbar; **make oneself ~:** dafür sorgen, dass man deutlich sichtbar ist; **leave sth. in a ~ position** etw. sichtbar liegen lassen [2] (noticeable) auffallend; **be ~:** sehr auffallen; **make oneself ~ by one's absence** durch Abwesenheit auffallen *od.* (iron.) glänzen; **~ expenditure/consumption** Prestigeausgaben/demonstrativer Konsum [3] (obvious, noteworthy) auffallend ‹*Schönheit*›; herausragend ‹*Tapferkeit*›; **~ for their loyalty** bekannt für ihre Loyalität; **the most ~ example** das augenfälligste Beispiel; das Paradebeispiel

conspicuously /kən'spɪkjʊəslɪ/ *adv.* [1] (very visibly) unübersehbar [2] (obviously) auffallend

conspicuousness /kən'spɪkjʊəsnɪs/ *n., no pl.* [1] (being clearly visible) Unübersehbarkeit, *die* [2] (obviousness) Auffälligkeit, *die*

conspiracy /kən'spɪrəsɪ/ *n.* [1] (conspiring) Verschwörung, *die;* **be in ~ against sb.** sich gegen jmdn. verschworen haben [2] (plot) Komplott, *das;* **form a ~:** ein Komplott schmieden; **~ of silence** verabredetes Stillschweigen [3] (Law) Verabredung zu einer Straftat; **~ to murder** Mordkomplott, *das*

con'spiracy theory *n.* Verschwörungstheorie, *die*

conspirator /kən'spɪrətə(r)/ *n.* Verschwörer, *der*/Verschwörerin, *die*

conspiratorial /kənspɪrə'tɔ:rɪəl/ *adj.* verschwörerisch

conspire /kən'spaɪə(r)/ *v.i.* (lit. or fig.) sich verschwören

constable /'kʌnstəbl, 'kɒnstəbl/ *n.* ►❶ p. 1260, ►❶ p. 1634 [1] (Brit.) ►**police constable** [2] (Brit.) **Chief C~:** ≈ Polizeipräsident, *der*/-präsidentin, *die*

constabulary /kən'stæbjʊlərɪ/
[A] *n.* Polizei, *die;* (unit) Polizeieinheit, *die*
[B] *adj.* Polizei-

Constance /'kɒnstəns/ *pr. n.* (Geog.) Konstanz (*das*); **Lake ~:** der Bodensee

constancy /'kɒnstənsɪ/ *n.* [1] (steadfastness) Standhaftigkeit, *die* [2] (faithfulness) Treue, *die* [3] (unchangingness) Beständigkeit, *die;* (uniformity) Gleichmäßigkeit, *die*

constant /'kɒnstənt/
[A] *adj.* [1] (unceasing) ständig; anhaltend ‹*Regen*›; **it's ~ laughter when they're around** es wird ununterbrochen gelacht, wenn sie da sind; **be a ~ reminder of sth./sb.** ständig an etw./ jmdn. erinnern; **we had ~ rain** es hat dauernd geregnet; **there was a ~ stream of traffic** der Verkehr floss ununterbrochen [2] (unchanging) gleich bleibend; konstant [3] (steadfast) standhaft; **be ~ in one's determination** stets an seinem Entschluss festhalten [4] (faithful) treu; **be ~ [to sb.]** [jmdm.] treu sein
[B] *n.* (Phys., Math.; also fig.) Konstante, *die*

constantly /'kɒnstəntlɪ/ *adv.* [1] (unceasingly) ständig [2] (unchangingly) konstant [3] (steadfastly) standhaft [4] (faithfully) treu

constellation /kɒnstə'leɪʃn/ *n.* Sternbild, *das;* Konstellation, *die* (Astron.)

consternation /kɒnstə'neɪʃn/ *n.* Bestürzung, *die;* (confusion) Aufregung, *die;* **in ~:** bestürzt/aufgeregt; **be filled with ~:** sehr bestürzt/aufgeregt sein

constipate /'kɒnstɪpeɪt/ *v.t.* zu Verstopfung führen bei; **be ~d** an Verstopfung leiden

constipation /kɒnstɪ'peɪʃn/ *n.* ►❶ p. 1231 Verstopfung, *die;* Konstipation, *die* (Med.)

constituency /kən'stɪtjʊənsɪ/ *n.* (voters) Wählerschaft, *die* (*eines Wahlkreises*); (area) Wahlkreis, *der*

constituent /kən'stɪtjʊənt/
[A] *adj.* (composing a whole) **~ part** Bestandteil, *der;* **~ member** Mitglied, *das;* **the ~ gases in air/~ parts of water** die Gase, aus denen Luft/die Teile, aus denen Wasser besteht
[B] *n.* [1] (component part) Bestandteil, *der* [2] (member of constituency) Wähler, *der* /Wählerin, *die* (*eines Wahlkreises*)

constitute /'kɒnstɪtju:t/ *v.t.* [1] (form) sein; **~ a threat to** eine Gefahr sein für [2] (make up) bilden; begründen ‹*Anspruch*›; **be ~d of bricks and mortar** aus Ziegelsteinen und Mörtel bestehen [3] (give legal form to) gründen ‹*Partei, Organisation*›; konstituieren ‹*Versammlung*›

constitution /kɒnstɪ'tju:ʃn/ *n.* [1] (of person) Konstitution, *die* [2] (mode of State organization) Staatsform, *die* [3] (body of laws and principles) Verfassung, *die;* **written ~:** schriftlich festgelegte Verfassung [4] (giving legal form) Gründung, *die*

constitutional /kɒnstɪ'tju:ʃənl/
[A] *adj.* [1] (of bodily or mental constitution) konstitutionell [2] (Polit.) (of constitution) der Verfassung *nachgestellt;* (authorized by or in harmony with constitution) verfassungsmäßig; konstitutionell ‹*Monarchie*›; **~ law** Verfassungsrecht, *das* [3] (essential) wesentlich; grundsätzlich ‹*Fähigkeit*›
[B] *n.* Spaziergang, *der*

constitutionality /kɒnstɪtju:ʃə'nælɪtɪ/ *n., no pl.* Verfassungskonformität, *die*

constitutionally /kɒnstɪ'tju:ʃənəlɪ/ *adv.* [1] (in bodily or mental constitution) konstitutionell [2] (Polit.) verfassungsmäßig [3] (essentially) wesentlich

constrain /kən'streɪn/ *v.t.* [1] zwingen [2] (confine) [auf]halten; (fig.) zügeln

constrained /kən'streɪnd/ *adj.* gequält; gezwungen ‹*Pose*›; steif ‹*Bewegung, Pose*›

constraint /kən'streɪnt/ *n.* [1] Zwang, *der;* **he felt himself under some ~ to speak** er fühlte sich gezwungen zu sprechen [2] (confinement) Enge, *die;* (limitation) Einschränkung, *die* [3] (restraint) Gezwungenheit, *die;* **the atmosphere was one of ~:** die Atmosphäre war gezwungen *od.* steif

constrict /kən'strɪkt/ *v.t.* (make narrow) verengen; **roadworks are ~ing the flow of traffic** Straßenarbeiten behindern den Verkehrsfluss

constriction /kən'strɪkʃn/ *n.* (narrowing) Verengung, *die;* **~ of the neck/throat** Einschnürung des Halses/der Kehle

construct
[A] /kən'strʌkt/ *v.t.* [1] (build) bauen; (fig.) aufbauen; erstellen ‹*Plan*›; entwickeln ‹*Idee*› [2] (Ling.; Geom.: draw) konstruieren
[B] /'kɒnstrʌkt/ *n.* [1] Konstrukt, *das* [2] (Ling.) Konstruktion, *die*

construction /kən'strʌkʃn/ *n.* [1] (constructing) Bau, *der;* (of sentence) Konstruktion, *die;* (fig.) (of empire, kingdom) Errichtung, *die;* Aufbau, *der;* (of plan, syllabus) Erstellung, *die;* (of idea) Entwicklung, *die;* **~ work** Bauarbeiten *Pl.;* **~ worker** ►❶ p. 1260 Bauarbeiter, *der;* **of wooden ~:** aus Holz gebaut; **be under ~:** im Bau sein [2] (thing constructed) Bauwerk, *das;* (fig.) Gebilde, *das;* **a wooden ~:** eine Holzkonstruktion [3] (Ling.; Geom.: drawing) Konstruktion, *die* [4] (interpretation) Deutung, *die;* **what ~ would you put upon ...?** wie würden Sie ... interpretieren *od.* auslegen?

constructional /kən'strʌkʃənl/ *adj.* Bau‹*vorhaben, -plan, -weise*›; Konstruktions‹*element, -teil, -basis*›; **~ kit** Bausatz, *der;* **~ toy** Spielzeug zum Aufbauen

construction: ~ company *n.* Bauunternehmen, *das;* Baufirma, *die;* **~ industry** *n.* Bauindustrie, *die;* Baugewerbe, *das*

constructive /kən'strʌktɪv/ *adj.* [1] (of construction; of structure of building) konstruktiv; Bau‹*arbeiter, -material, -element, -plan*› [2] (tending to construct) konstruktiv ‹*Philosophie, Methode*›; schöpferisch ‹*Talent, Intelligenz*› [3] (helpful) konstruktiv [4] (inferred) indirekt

constructively /kən'strʌktɪvlɪ/ *adv.* [1] (in construction) bautechnisch gesehen [2] (helpfully) konstruktiv

construe /kən'stru:/ *v.t.* [1] (Ling.) (combine) konstruieren; (analyse) zerlegen; (translate) übersetzen [2] (interpret) auslegen; auffassen; **I ~d his words as meaning that ...:** ich habe ihn so verstanden, dass ...

consul /'kɒnsl/ *n.* Konsul, *der*

consular /'kɒnsjʊlə(r)/ *adj.* (of State agent) konsularisch; **~ rank** Rang eines Konsuls

consulate /'kɒnsjʊlət/ *n.* [1] (period) Amtszeit [als Konsul] [2] (establishment) Konsulat, *das* [3] (Roman & French Hist.) Konsulat, *das*

consulship /'kɒnslʃɪp/ ►**consulate 1, 3**

consult /kən'sʌlt/
[A] *v.i.* sich beraten (**with** mit); **~ together** sich miteinander beraten
[B] *v.t.* [1] (seek information from) konsultieren; befragen ‹*Orakel*›; fragen, konsultieren, zu Rate ziehen ‹*Arzt, Fachmann*›; **~ a list/book** in einer Liste/einem Buch nachsehen; **~ one's watch** auf die Uhr sehen; **~ a dictionary** in einem Wörterbuch nachschlagen [2] (consider) berücksichtigen; bedenken

consultancy /kən'sʌltənsɪ/ *n.* [1] (of adviser) Beraterstelle, *die;* **~ fee** Beratungsgebühr, *die* [2] (of physician) ≈ Chefarztstelle, *die*

consultant /kən'sʌltənt/
[A] *n.* ►❶ p. 1260 [1] (adviser) Berater, *der* /Beraterin, *die* [2] (physician) ≈ Chefarzt, *der*/-ärztin, *die*
[B] *attrib. adj.* ►**consulting**

consultation /kɒnsʌl'teɪʃn/ *n.* Beratung, *die* (**on** über + *Akk.*); **have a ~ with sb.** sich mit jmdm. beraten; **by ~ of a dictionary/of an expert** durch Konsultation eines Wörterbuchs/Experten; **they are in ~ with the management about wages** sie stehen mit der Betriebsleitung in Lohnverhandlungen; **act in ~ with sb.** in Absprache mit jmdm. handeln

consultative /kən'sʌltətɪv/ *adj.* beratend; konsultativ; **work on a ~ basis** *or* **in a ~ capacity for sb.** als Berater für jmdn. arbeiten; **~ document** ≈ Entwurf als Diskussionsgrundlage; (governmental) Regierungsentwurf, *der*

consulting /kən'sʌltɪŋ/ *attrib. adj.* beratend ‹*Architekt, Chemiker, Ingenieur*›; **~ physician** Konsiliararzt, *der*/-ärztin, *die*

con'sulting room *n.* Sprechzimmer, *das*

consumable /kən'sju:məbl/ *adj.* [1] (exhaustible) kurzlebig ‹*Konsumgüter*› [2] (edible, drinkable) genießbar

consume /kən'sju:m/ *v.t.* [1] (use up) verbrauchen; ‹*Person:*› aufwenden, ‹*Sache:*› kosten ‹*Zeit, Energie*› [2] (destroy) vernichten; (eat, drink) konsumieren; verkonsumieren (ugs.); **'nothing is to be ~d on these premises'** „Verzehr von Speisen und Getränken nicht gestattet" [3] (fig.) **be ~d with love/passion** sich in Liebe/Leidenschaft verzehren; **be ~d with fear/jealousy/envy/longing** sich vor Angst/ Eifersucht/Neid/Sehnsucht verzehren (geh.)

consumer /kən'sju:mə(r)/ *n.* (Econ.) Verbraucher, *der*/Verbraucherin, *die;* Konsument, *der*/Konsumentin, *die; see also* **durable B**

consumer: ~ ad'vice *n., no pl.* Verbraucherberatung, *die; attrib.* **~ advice centre** Verbraucherberatung[sstelle], *die;* **~ 'choice** *n.* Verbraucherwahl, *die;* **~ 'confidence** *n., no pl.* Verbrauchervertrauen, *das;* **~ confidence in digital TV** das Vertrauen der Verbraucher ins Digitalfernsehen; **~ 'credit** *n.* (Econ.) Verbraucherkredit, *der;* **~ goods** *n. pl.* Konsumgüter

consumerism /kən'sju:mərɪzm/ *n., no pl., no art.* Konsumerismus, *der*

consumerist /kən'sju:mərɪst/
[A] *n.* Verbraucherschützer, *der*/-schützerin, *die*
[B] *adj.* konsumorientiert; Konsum‹*gesellschaft*›

consumer: ~ pro'tection *n., no pl.* Verbraucherschutz, *der;* **~ 'research** *n., no pl.* Verbrauchsforschung, *die;* Konsumforschung, *die;* **~ re'sistance** ►**sales resistance;** **~ 'spending** *n., no pl.* Verbraucherausgaben *Pl.;* Konsumausgaben *Pl.;* **a boom in ~ spending/a ~ spending boom** ein Konsumboom; **~ survey** *n.* Verbraucherbefragung, *die;* Verbraucherumfrage, *die*

consuming /kən'sju:mɪŋ/ *adj.* ganz in Anspruch nehmend, verzehrend (geh.) ‹*Sehnsucht, Ehrgeiz*›; **stamp-collecting is a ~ interest of his** sein Interesse am Briefmarkensammeln nimmt ihn ganz in Anspruch

consummate
[A] /kən'sʌmət/ *adj.* [1] (perfect) vollkommen; **with ~ ease** mühelos [2] (accomplished) perfekt; **a ~ artist** ein vollendeter Künstler

C

B /ˈkɒnsəmeɪt, ˈkɒnsjʊmeɪt/ *v.t.* vollenden, zum Abschluss bringen ‹*Diskussion, Geschäftsverhandlungen*›; vollziehen ‹*Ehe*›

consummately /kənˈsʌmətlɪ/ *adj.* (highly) höchst; (perfectly) vollendet; (completely) völlig

consummation /kɒnsəˈmeɪʃn/ *n.* **1** (completion) Vollendung, *die;* (of discussion, business) Abschluss, *der;* (of marriage) Vollzug, *der* **2** (goal) Erfüllung, *die;* (perfection, perfected thing) Vollendung, *die*

consumption /kənˈsʌmpʃn/ *n.* **1** (using up, eating, drinking) Verbrauch, *der* (**of** an + *Dat.*); (act of eating or drinking) Verzehr, *der* (**of** von); **∼ of electricity/fuel/sugar** Strom-/Kraftstoff-/Zuckerverbrauch, *der;* **∼ of alcohol** Alkoholkonsum, *der;* **what is our milk ∼?** wieviel Milch verbrauchen wir? **2** (destruction) Vernichtung, *die;* (waste) Vergeudung, *die* **3** (Econ.) Verbrauch, *der;* Konsum, *der* **4** ▸**❶ p. 1231** (Med. dated) Schwindsucht, *die* (veralt.)

consumptive /kənˈsʌmptɪv/

A *adj.* (Med. dated) schwindsüchtig (veralt.)

B *n.* Tuberkulosekranke, *der/die;* Schwindsüchtige, *der/die* (veralt.)

cont. *abbr.* **= continued** Forts.

contact

A /ˈkɒntækt/ *n.* **1** (state of touching) Berührung, *die;* Kontakt, *der;* (fig.) Verbindung, *die;* Kontakt, *der;* **point of ∼:** Berührungspunkt, *der;* **be in ∼ with sth.** etw. berühren; **be in ∼ with sb.** (fig.) mit jmdm. in Verbindung stehen *od.* Kontakt haben; **come in** *or* **into ∼ [with sth.]** [mit etw.] in Berührung kommen; **come into ∼ with sb./sth.** (fig.) mit jmdm./etw. etwas zu tun haben; **make ∼ with sth.** etw. berühren; **make ∼ with sb.** (fig.) sich mit jmdm. in Verbindung setzen; mit jmdm. Kontakt aufnehmen; **lose ∼ with sb.** (fig.) den Kontakt mit jmdm. verlieren; **renew ∼ [with sb.]** (fig.) den Kontakt [mit *od.* zu jmdm.] wieder aufnehmen **2** (Electr.) (connection) Kontakt, *der;* **make/break a/the ∼:** einen/den Kontakt herstellen/unterbrechen; **when the two wires make ∼:** wenn die beiden Drähte sich berühren **3** (Med.: person) Kontaktperson, *die* **4** (adviser etc.) Verbindung, *die;* Kontakt, *der*

B /ˈkɒntækt, kənˈtækt/ *v.t.* **1** (get into touch with) sich in Verbindung setzen mit; **can I ∼ you by telephone?** sind Sie telefonisch zu erreichen?; **try to ∼ sb.** jmdn. zu erreichen versuchen; **∼ your bank manager about the loan** wenden Sie sich bezüglich des Darlehens an den Direktor Ihrer Bank; **∼ sb. by letter** sich schriftlich mit jmdm. in Verbindung setzen **2** (begin dealings with) Kontakt aufnehmen mit

contact: ∼ lens *n.* Kontaktlinse, *die;* **∼ man** *n.* Kontaktmann, *der;* Mittelsmann, *der;* **∼ print** *n.* (Photog.) Kontaktabzug, *der*

contagion /kənˈteɪdʒn/ *n.* **1** (communication of disease) Ansteckung, *die* **2** (contagious disease) ansteckende Krankheit **3** (moral corruption) Seuche, *die* (fig.)

contagious /kənˈteɪdʒəs/ *adj.* (lit. or fig.) ansteckend; **∼ area/water** verseuchtes Gebiet/Wasser; **he is ∼/is no longer ∼:** er hat eine ansteckende Krankheit/er steckt niemanden mehr an

contain /kənˈteɪn/ *v.t.* **1** (hold as contents, include) enthalten; (comprise) umfassen; **be ∼ed within a space/between limits** sich in einem Gebiet/zwischen Grenzen befinden **2** (prevent from moving) halten; (prevent from spreading; also Mil.) aufhalten; eindämmen ‹*Krankheit*›; (restrain) unterdrücken; **he could hardly ∼ himself for joy** er konnte vor Freude kaum an sich (*Akk.*) halten

container /kənˈteɪnə(r)/ *n.* Behälter, *der;* (cargo ∼) Container, *der;* **cardboard/wooden ∼:** Pappkarton, *der*/Holzkiste, *die;* **in cylindrical/circular plastic ∼s** in Plastiktrommeln/in [runden] Plastikbehältern

container: ∼ gardening *n., no pl.* Haltung von Kübelpflanzen; **∼-grown** *adj.* im Container gezogen ‹*Pflanze, Gemüse usw.*›; Kübel‹*pflanze*›

containerize /kənˈteɪnəraɪz/ *v.t.* in Container verpacken; auf Containertransport umstellen ‹*Handelsweg, Verfahren*›

container: ∼ lorry *n.* Containerlastzug, *der;* Containerlaster, *der;* **∼ ship** *n.* Containerschiff, *das;* **∼ transport** *n., no pl.* Containertransport, *der*

containment /kənˈteɪnmənt/ *n.* Eindämmung, *die;* (Mil.) Aufhalten, *das*

contaminant /kənˈtæmɪnənt/ *n.* verunreinigende Substanz

contaminate /kənˈtæmɪneɪt/ *v.t.* **1** (pollute) verunreinigen; (with radioactivity) verseuchen **2** (infect, lit. or fig.) infizieren; (fig.: spoil) verseuchen

contamination /kəntæmɪˈneɪʃn/ *n.* ▸**contaminate**: Verunreinigung, *die;* Verseuchung, *die;* Infizierung, *die*

contango /kənˈtæŋgəʊ/ *n., pl.* **∼s** (Brit. Finance) Report, *der* (Bankw.)

contemplate /ˈkɒntəmpleɪt/

A *v.t.* **1** betrachten; (mentally) nachdenken über (+ *Akk.*); *see also* **navel** **2** (expect) rechnen mit; (consider) in Betracht ziehen; **∼ sth./doing sth.** an etw. (*Akk.*) denken/daran denken, etw. zu tun; **I wouldn't even ∼ the idea** das käme für mich überhaupt nicht in Betracht

B *v.i.* nachdenken

contemplation /kɒntəmˈpleɪʃn/ *n.* **1** Betrachtung, *die;* (mental) Nachdenken, *das* (**of** über + *Akk.*) **2** (expectation) Erwartung, *die;* (consideration) Erwägung, *die;* **be in ∼:** erwogen werden **3** (meditation) Kontemplation, *die*

contemplative /kənˈtemplətɪv, ˈkɒntəmpleɪtɪv/ *adj.* besinnlich; kontemplativ (geh.)

contemporaneous /kəntempəˈreɪnɪəs/ *adj.* (formal) gleichzeitig; (of the same period) aus derselben Zeit *nachgestellt*

contemporary /kənˈtempərərɪ/

A *adj.* **1** zeitgenössisch; (present-day) heutig; zeitgenössisch; **A is ∼ with B** A und B finden zur gleichen Zeit statt; **the design is highly/very ∼:** das Design ist hochmodern **2** (equal in age) gleichaltrig; **A is ∼ with B** A und B sind gleichaltrig

B *n.* **1** (person belonging to same time) Zeitgenosse, *der/*-genossin, *die* (**to** von); **we were contemporaries** *or* **he was a ∼ of mine at university/school** er war ein Studienkollege *od.* Kommilitone/Schulkamerad von mir **2** (person of same age) Altersgenosse, *der/*-genossin, *die;* **they are contemporaries** sie sind gleichaltrig *od.* Altersgenossen; **he is a ∼ of hers** er ist [genau]so alt wie sie

contempt /kənˈtempt/ *n.* **1** Verachtung, *die* (**of, for** für); *see also* **familiarity 3** **2** (disregard) Missachtung, *die;* **in ∼ of all rules** unter Missachtung aller Regeln **3** (being despised) **have** *or* **hold sb. in ∼:** jmdn. verachten; **bring sb. into ∼:** jmdn. in Verruf bringen; **fall into ∼:** in Verruf kommen; *see also* **beneath A 1** **4** (Law) Ungehorsam, *der;* **∼ of court** *Ungehorsam od. Missachtung gegenüber der Justiz;* (in face of court) ≈ Ungebühr vor Gericht

contemptible /kənˈtemptɪbl/ *adj.* verachtenswert; **Old C∼s** (coll.) *1914 nach Frankreich geschicktes britisches Expeditionskorps*

contemptibly /kənˈtemptɪblɪ/ *adv.* verachtenswert

contemptuous /kənˈtemptjʊəs/ *adj.* verächtlich; überheblich ‹*Person*›; **be ∼ of sth./sb.** etw./jmdn. verachten; **∼ of danger/warning** die Gefahr verachtend/alle Warnungen missachtend; **with** *or* **in ∼ disdain** voller Verachtung

contemptuously /kənˈtemptjʊəslɪ/ *adv.* verächtlich

contend /kənˈtend/

A *v.i.* **1** (strive) **∼ [with sb. for sth.]** [mit jmdm. um etw.] kämpfen **2** (struggle) **be able/have to ∼ with** fertig werden können/müssen mit; bewältigen können/müssen ‹*Post, Hindernis*›; ins Reine kommen können/müssen mit ‹*Gewissen*›; **I've got enough to ∼ with at the moment** ich habe schon so genug um die Ohren (ugs.); **∼ with/against the waves** mit den Wellen kämpfen/gegen die Wellen ankämpfen **3** (arch.: argue) **∼ with sb. about sth.** mit jmdm. über etw. streiten

B *v.t.* **∼ that …** behaupten, dass …

contender /kənˈtendə(r)/ *n.* Bewerber, *der*/Bewerberin, *die*

content¹ /ˈkɒntent/ *n.* **1** *in pl.* Inhalt, *der;* **the ∼s of the room had all been damaged** alles im Zimmer war beschädigt worden; **the ∼s of this medicine are listed on the packet** die Zusammensetzung dieses Medikaments ist auf der Packung angegeben; **[table of] ∼s** Inhaltsverzeichnis, *das;* **something in the ∼s of the letter has made her very upset** etwas, was in dem Brief steht, hat sie ganz aus der Fassung gebracht **2** (amount contained) Gehalt, *der* (**of** an + *Dat.*) **3** (capacity) Fassungsvermögen, *das;* (volume) Volumen, *das* **4** (constituent elements, substance) Gehalt, *der*

content² /kənˈtent/

A *pred. adj.* zufrieden (**with** mit); **not rest ∼ until** nicht zufrieden sein, bis; **not ∼ with being late every morning, he also wants a pay rise** nicht genug [damit], dass er jeden Morgen zu spät kommt, er will auch noch eine Gehaltserhöhung; **be ∼ to do sth.** bereit sein, etw. zu tun; (pleased) etw. gern tun; **I should be well ∼ to do so** das würde ich recht gern tun

B *n.* **to one's heart's ∼:** nach Herzenslust

C *v.t.* zufriedenstellen; befriedigen; **∼ oneself with sth./sb.** sich mit etw./jmdm. zufrieden geben

contented /kənˈtentɪd/ *adj.* zufrieden (**with** mit); glücklich ‹*Kindheit, Ehe, Leben*›; **be ∼ to do sth.** sich damit abfinden, etw. zu tun

contentedly /kənˈtentɪdlɪ/ *adv.* zufrieden

contentedness /kənˈtentɪdnɪs/ *n., no pl.* Zufriedenheit, *die*

contention /kənˈtenʃn/ *n.* **1** (dispute) Streit, *der;* Auseinandersetzung, *die;* (rivalry) Kampf, *der;* **the matter in ∼:** die Streitfrage; **sth. is the subject of much ∼:** etw. wird heftig diskutiert *od.* ist eine sehr strittige Frage; **be in/out of ∼:** im/aus dem Rennen sein; **put sb. in/out of ∼:** jmdn. ins Rennen bringen/aus dem Rennen werfen; **be in ∼ with sb.** sich mit jmdm. streiten **2** (point asserted) Behauptung, *die; see also* **put¹ A 6**

contentious /kənˈtenʃəs/ *adj.* **1** (quarrelsome) streitsüchtig; streitlustig **2** (involving contention) strittig ‹*Punkt, Frage, Thema*›; umstritten ‹*Verhalten, Argument, Angelegenheit*›

contentiously /kənˈtenʃəslɪ/ *adv.* provozierend; **a ∼ worded question** eine kontrovers formulierte Frage

contentment /kənˈtentmənt/ *n.* Zufriedenheit, *die;* **smile with ∼:** zufrieden lächeln

ˈcontent provider *n.* (on Internet) Content-provider, *der*

contest

A /ˈkɒntest/ *n.* (competition) Wettbewerb, *der;* (Sport) Wettkampf, *der*

B /kənˈtest/ *v.t.* **1** (dispute) bestreiten; anfechten ‹*Anspruch, Recht*›; infrage stellen ‹*Behauptung, These*› **2** (fight for) kämpfen um **3** (compete in) kandidieren bei; (compete for) kandidieren für

C *v.i.* **∼ with** *or* **against sb./sth.** sich mit jmdm./etw. auseinander setzen

contestable /kənˈtestəbl/ *adj.* anfechtbar

contestant /kənˈtestənt/ *n.* (competitor) Teilnehmer, *der*/Teilnehmerin, *die* (**in** an + *Dat.*, bei); (in election) Bewerber, *der*/Bewerberin, *die* (**for** um, für); (in fight) Gegner, *der*/Gegnerin, *die*

contestation /kɒntesˈteɪʃn/ *n.* **1** (contesting) Bestreiten, *das;* (of claim, right) Anfechtung, *die* **2** (disputation) Streit, *der* **3** (assertion) Behauptung, *die*

context /ˈkɒntekst/ *n.* **1** Kontext, *der;* **in/out of ∼:** im/ohne Kontext; **this sentence is quoted out of [its proper] ∼:** dieser Satz ist aus dem Zusammenhang gerissen; **in this ∼:** in diesem Zusammenhang **2** (fig.: ambient conditions) Umgebung, *die;* **in the ∼ of** im Rahmen (+ *Gen.*)

ˈcontext-sensitive *adj.* **1** (Ling.) contextsensitiv (fachspr.); kontextabhängig **2** (Computing) **∼ help** kontextabhängige Hilfe; **∼ menu** Kontextmenü, *das*

contextual /kənˈtekstjʊəl/ *adj.* kontextuell

contextualize /kənˈtekstjʊəlaɪz/ *v.t.* (place in context) in einen Kontext einordnen

contiguity /kɒntɪ'gju:ɪtɪ/ *n., no pl.* (formal) **1** (contact) Berührung, *die* **2** (proximity) [unmittelbare] Nähe

contiguous /kən'tɪgjʊəs/ *adj.* (formal) (touching) sich berührend; (adjoining, neighbouring) aneinander grenzend; **be ~:** sich berühren/aneinandergrenzen/aufeinanderfolgen; **be ~ to sth.** etw. berühren/an etw. (*Akk.*) grenzen

continence /'kɒntɪnəns/ *n.* **1** (temperance) Mäßigkeit, *die;* (chastity) [sexuelle] Enthaltsamkeit **2** (Med.) Kontinenz, *die*

continent¹ /'kɒntɪnənt/ *n.* Kontinent, *der;* Erdteil, *der;* **the ~s of Europe, Asia, Africa** die Erdteile Europa, Asien, Afrika; **the C~:** das europäische Festland; der Kontinent

continent² *adj.* **1** (temperate) maßvoll; (chaste) [sexuell] enthaltsam **2** (Med.) **be ~:** Harn und Stuhl zurückhalten können

continental /kɒntɪ'nentl/

A *adj.* **1** kontinental; **~ Europe** Kontinentaleuropa (*das*) **2** **C~** (mainland European) kontinental[europäisch]

B *n.* **C~:** Kontinentaleuropäer, *der*/-europäerin, *die*

continental: ~ 'breakfast *n.* kontinentales Frühstück (*im Unterschied zum englischen Frühstück*); **~ climate** *n.* (Geog.) Kontinentalklima, *das;* **~ 'drift** *n., no pl.* (Geol.) Kontinentalverschiebung, *die;* Kontinentaldrift, *die;* **~ quilt** (Brit.) *n.* [Stepp]federbett, *das;* **~ 'shelf** *n.* (Geog.) Festland[s]sockel, *der*

contingency /kən'tɪndʒənsɪ/ *n.* **1** (chance event) Eventualität, *die;* (possible event) Eventualfall, *der* **2** (incidental event) unvorhergesehenes Ereignis; (incidental expense) unvorhergesehene Ausgabe

contingency: ~ fund *n.* Fonds für unvorhergesehene Ausgaben; **~ plan** *n.* Alternativplan, *der*

contingent /kən'tɪndʒənt/

A *adj.* **1** (fortuitous) zufällig **2** (incidental) unvorhergesehen **3** (Philos.) kontingent **4** (conditional) abhängig (**[up]on** von)

B *n.* (Mil.; also fig.) Kontingent, *das*

continual /kən'tɪnjʊəl/ *adj.* (frequently happening) ständig; (without cessation) unaufhörlich; **there have been ~ quarrels** es gab ständig *od.* dauernd Streit; **she's a ~ chatterbox** ihr Mundwerk steht nie still (ugs.)

continually /kən'tɪnjʊəlɪ/ *adv.* (frequently) ständig; immer wieder; (without cessation) unaufhörlich; **~ tired** immer müde

continuance /kən'tɪnjʊəns/ *n.* **1** (continuing) Fortbestand, *der;* (of happiness, noise, rain) Fortdauer, *die;* (remaining) Verbleiben, *das* **2** (Amer. Law: adjournment) Vertagung, *die* (**until** auf + *Akk.*)

continuation /kəntɪnjʊ'eɪʃn/ *n.* **1** Fortsetzung, *die;* **a ~ of these good relations** eine Fortdauer dieser guten Beziehungen **2** (St. Exch.) Reportgeschäft, *das*

continue /kən'tɪnju:/

A *v.t.* **1** fortsetzen; **'to be ~d'** „Fortsetzung folgt"; **'~d on page 2'** „Fortsetzung auf S. 2"; **~ doing** *or* **to do sth.** etw. weiter tun; **it ~d to rain** es regnete weiter; **it ~s to be a problem** es ist weiterhin ein Problem; **'...', he ~d** „...", fuhr er fort; **do ~ what you were saying** sprechen Sie nur weiter!; **I'll ~ the story where I left off** ich werde die Geschichte von da an weitererzählen, wo ich aufgehört habe **2** (Amer. Law: adjourn) vertagen (**until** auf + *Akk.*)

B *v.i.* **1** (persist) ‹*Wetter, Zustand, Krise usw.:*› andauern; (persist in doing sth.) weitermachen (ugs.); nicht aufhören; (last) dauern; **this tradition still ~s** diesen Brauch gibt es immer noch; dieser Brauch lebt weiter; **if the rain ~s** wenn der Regen anhält; **if you ~ like this/in this manner** wenn Sie so weitermachen (ugs.); **how long is his speech likely to ~?** wie lange dauert seine Rede wohl noch?; **~ with sth.** mit etw. fortfahren; **we ~d with the work until midnight** wir arbeiteten weiter bis Mitternacht; **~ with a plan** einen Plan weiterverfolgen; **~ on one's way** seinen Weg fortsetzen **2** (stay) bleiben; **~ in power** an der Macht bleiben; **~ in control** die Kontrolle behalten; **she ~d in mourning for him all her life** sie trauerte ihr ganzes Leben lang um ihn **3** (not become other than) weiterhin sein; **he ~s feverish** er hat immer noch Fieber

continued /kən'tɪnju:d/ *adj.* fortgesetzt ‹*Bemühungen*›; **~ existence** Weiterbestehen, *das*

continuity /kɒntɪ'nju:ɪtɪ/ *n., no pl.* **1** (of path, frontier) ununterbrochener Verlauf; (unbroken succession, logical sequence, consistency) Kontinuität, *die* **2** (Cinemat., Telev., Radio) (scenario) Szenario, *das;* (script) Skript, *das;* (linking announcements) Zwischentext, *der*

conti'nuity girl *n.* ▸ⓘ **p. 1260** (dated) Skriptgirl, *das*

continuo /kən'tɪnjʊəʊ/ *n., pl.* **~s** (Mus.) **1** (accompaniment) Generalbass, *der;* Basso continuo, *der* **2** (instruments) Generalbassinstrumente

continuous /kən'tɪnjʊəs/ *adj.* **1** ununterbrochen; anhaltend ‹*Regen, Sonnenschein, Anstieg*›; ständig ‹*Kritik, Streit, Änderung*›; fortlaufend ‹*Mauer*›; durchgezogen ‹*Linie*› **2** (Ling.) **~ [form]** Verlaufsform, *die;* **present ~** *or* **~ present/past ~** *or* **~ past** Verlaufsform des Präsens/Präteritums

continuous as'sessment *n., no pl.* (Brit. Educ.) ständige Leistungskontrolle

continuously /kən'tɪnjʊəslɪ/ *adv.* (in space) durchgehend; nahtlos ‹*aneinander fügen*›; (in time or sequence) ununterbrochen; unablässig, anhaltend ‹*ansteigen*›; ständig ‹*sich ändern*›

continuous 'stationery *n.* Endlosdruck, *der* (Druckw.)

continuum /kən'tɪnjʊəm/ *n., pl.* **continua** /kən'tɪnjʊə/ Kontinuum, *das*

contort /kən'tɔ:t/ *v.t.* verdrehen (auch fig.); verzerren ‹*Gesicht, Gesichtszüge*›; verrenken, verdrehen ‹*Körper*›; **his face was ~ed with anger** sein Gesicht war wutverzerrt

contortion /kən'tɔ:ʃn/ *n.* Verzerrung, *die;* (of body) Verdrehung, *die;* Verrenkung, *die*

contortionist /kən'tɔ:ʃənɪst/ *n.* Schlangenmensch, *der*

contour /'kɒntʊə(r)/ *n.* **1** (outline) Kontur, *die* **2** ▸**contour line**

contour: ~ line *n.* (Geog., Surv.) Höhen[schicht]linie, *die;* **~ map** *n.* Höhenlinienkarte, *die;* **~ ploughing** *n.* (Agric.) Konturpflügen, *das*

contra /'kɒntrə/

A *prep. & adv.* **pro and ~:** pro und kontra

B *n.* **the pros and ~s** das Pro und Kontra

contraband /'kɒntrəbænd/

A *n.* (smuggled goods) Schmuggelware, *die;* **~ of war** Konterbande, *die* (Völkerrecht)

B *adj.* geschmuggelt; **~ goods** Schmuggelware, *die*

contrabassoon /'kɒntrəbəsu:n/ *n.* Kontrafagott, *das*

contraception /kɒntrə'sepʃn/ *n.* Empfängnisverhütung, *die*

contraceptive /kɒntrə'septɪv/

A *adj.* empfängnisverhütend; kontrazeptiv (Med.); **~ device/method** Verhütungsmittel, *das*/-methode, *die*

B *n.* Verhütungsmittel, *das*

contract

A /'kɒntrækt/ *n.* **1** Vertrag, *der;* **~ of employment** Arbeitsvertrag, *der;* **be under ~ to do sth.** vertraglich verpflichtet sein, etw. zu tun; **exchange ~s** (Law) die Vertragsurkunden austauschen; **marriage ~:** Ehevertrag, *der* **2** (Bridge etc.) Kontrakt, *der* **3** ▸**contract bridge**

B /kən'trækt/ *v.t.* **1** (cause to shrink, make smaller) schrumpfen lassen; (draw together) zusammenziehen; verengen ‹*Pupillen*› **2** (form) **~ marriage** die Ehe eingehen *od.* schließen; **~ a habit** eine Angewohnheit annehmen **3** (become infected with) sich (*Dat.*) zuziehen; **~ sth. from sb.** sich mit etw. bei jmdm. anstecken; **~ sth. from ...:** an etw. (*Dat.*) durch ... erkranken **4** (incur) machen ‹*Schulden*› **5** (Ling.) zusammenziehen ‹*Wort, Silbe*›

C *v.i.* **1** (enter into agreement) Verträge/einen Vertrag schließen; **~ for sth.** etw. vertraglich zusichern; **~ to do sth.** *or* **that one will do sth.** sich vertraglich verpflichten, etw. zu tun **2** (shrink, become smaller, be drawn together) sich zusammenziehen; ‹*Pupillen:*› sich verengen

(Phrasal verb)

• **~ 'out**

A *v.i.* **~ out [of sth.]** sich [an etw. (*Dat.*)] nicht beteiligen; (withdraw) [aus etw.] aussteigen (ugs.)

B *v.t.* **~ work out [to another firm]** Arbeit [an eine andere Firma] vergeben

contract bridge /kɒntrækt 'brɪdʒ/ *n.* Kontraktbridge, *das*

contractile /kən'træktaɪl/ *adj.* (Anat.: capable of contracting) kontraktil

contraction /kən'trækʃn/ *n.* **1** (shrinking) Kontraktion, *die* (Physik); (of eye pupils) Verengung, *die* **2** (Physiol.: of muscle) Zusammenziehung, *die;* Kontraktion, *die* (Med.) **3** (Ling.) Kontraktion, *die* **4** (catching) Ansteckung, *die* (**of** mit) **5** (forming) Annahme, *die;* (of marriage) Schließen, *das;* **~ of debts** Schuldenmachen, *das*

contract: ~ 'killer *n.* Auftragskiller, *der* /-killerin, *die;* **~ 'killing** *n.* Auftragsmord, *der*

contractor /kən'træktə(r)/ *n.* ▸ⓘ **p. 1260** Auftragnehmer, *der*/-nehmerin, *die; see also* **building contractor**

contractual /kən'træktjʊəl/ *adj.*, **contractually** /kən'træktjʊəlɪ/ *adv.* vertraglich

'contract work *n., no pl.* Auftragsarbeit, *die;* **do ~:** Auftragsarbeiten übernehmen

contradict /kɒntrə'dɪkt/ *v.t.* widersprechen (+ *Dat.*)

contradiction /kɒntrə'dɪkʃn/ *n.* Widerspruch, *der* (**of** gegen); **in ~ to sth./sb.** im Widerspruch *od.* Gegensatz zu etw./jmdm.; **be a ~ to** *or* **of sth.** im Widerspruch zu etw. stehen; **a ~ in terms** ein Widerspruch in sich selbst; eine Contradictio in adjecto (Rhet.)

contradictory /kɒntrə'dɪktərɪ/ *adj.* **1** widersprechend; (mutually opposed) widersprüchlich; **that is ~ to what was said last week** das widerspricht dem, was letzte Woche gesagt wurde **2** (inclined to contradict) widersetzlich; (inconsistent) widersprüchlich

contradistinction /kɒntrədɪ'stɪŋkʃn/ *n.* Unterscheidung, *die;* **in ~ to sth.** im Unterschied zu etw.

'contraflow *n.* Gegenverkehr auf einem Fahrstreifen; **~ system** Verkehrsführung mit Gegenverkehr

contralto /kən'træltəʊ/ *n., pl.* **~s** (Mus.) **1** (voice) Alt, *der;* (very low) Kontraalt, *der* **2** (singer) Altistin, *die;* Alt, *der* (selten); (with very low voice) Kontraalt, *der* **3** (part) Alt, *der;* (for very low voice) zweiter Alt; Alt II

contraption /kən'træpʃn/ *n.* (coll.) (strange machine) Apparat, *der* (ugs.); (vehicle) Vehikel, *das;* (device) [komisches] Gerät

contrapuntal /kɒntrə'pʌntl/ *adj.* (Mus.) kontrapunktisch

contrarily /kən'treərɪlɪ/ *adv.* widerspenstig; widerborstig

contrariness /kən'treərɪnɪs/ *n., no pl.* Widerspenstigkeit, *die;* Widerborstigkeit, *die*

contrariwise /kən'treərɪwaɪz/ *adv.* **1** (on the other hand) andererseits **2** (in the opposite way) umgekehrt

contrary

A *adj.* **1** /'kɒntrərɪ/ entgegengesetzt; **be ~ to sth.** im Gegensatz zu etw. stehen; **the result was ~ to expectation** das Ergebnis entsprach nicht den Erwartungen **2** (opposite) entgegengesetzt; (adverse) widrig ‹*Wind*› **3** /kən'treərɪ/ (perverse) widerspenstig; widerborstig; **he's ~ by nature** er ist von Natur aus voller Widerspruchsgeist

B /'kɒntrərɪ/ *n.* **the ~:** das Gegenteil; **be/do completely the ~:** das genaue Gegenteil sein/tun; **go by contraries** anders als erwartet verlaufen; ‹*Traum:*› das Gegenteil bedeuten; ‹*Stimmung:*› [grundsätzlich] konträr sein; **on the ~:** im Gegenteil; **appearances to the ~, ...:** dem äußeren Anschein zum Trotz, ...; **quite the ~:** ganz im Gegenteil

C *adv.* **~ to sth.** entgegen einer Sache; **~ to expectation** wider Erwarten

contrast
A /kən'trɑːst/ *v.t.* gegenüberstellen; kontrastieren lassen, [deutlich] voneinander abheben ‹*Farben*›; **~ sth. with sth.** etw. von etw. [deutlich] abheben; **be ~ed with sth.** sich [deutlich] von etw. abheben
B *v.i.* **~ with sth.** mit etw. kontrastieren; sich von etw. abheben
C /'kɒntrɑːst/ *n.* **1** (juxtaposition) Kontrast, *der* (**with** zu); **what a ~!** welch ein Gegensatz!; **in ~, ...:** im Gegensatz dazu, ...; **[be] in ~ with sth.** im Gegensatz *od.* Kontrast zu etw. [stehen]; **by way of ~:** als Kontrast **2** (thing) **a ~ to sth.** ein Gegensatz zu etw.; (person) **be a ~ to sb.** [ganz] anders sein als jmd. **3** (Photog., Telev., Psych.) Kontrast, *der* **4** **~ medium** (Med.) Kontrastmittel, *das*

contrasting /kən'trɑːstɪŋ/ *adj.* gegensätzlich; kontrastierend ‹*Farbe*›; (very different) sehr unterschiedlich

contravene /kɒntrə'viːn/ *v.t.* (infringe) verstoßen gegen ‹*Recht, Gesetz*›; zuwiderhandeln (+ *Dat.*) ‹*Beschluss, Rat, Empfehlung*›; (conflict with) widersprechen (+ *Dat.*)

contravention /kɒntrə'venʃn/ *n.* **~ of the law/rules/moral standards** Verstoß gegen das Gesetz/die Regeln/die Moral; **be in ~ of sth.** im Widerspruch zu etw. stehen; **act in ~ of sth.** einer Sache (*Dat.*) zuwiderhandeln

contretemps /'kɔ̃trətɑ̃/ *n., pl. same* /'kɔ̃trətɑ̃z/ Missgeschick, *das;* Malheur, *das* (ugs.)

contribute /kən'trɪbjuːt/
A *v.t.* **~ sth. [to** *or* **towards sth.]** etw. [zu etw.] beitragen/(cooperatively) beisteuern; **~ money towards sth.** für etw. Geld beisteuern/(for charity) spenden; **he regularly ~s articles to the 'Guardian'** er schreibt regelmäßig für den „Guardian"
B *v.i.* **~ to** *or* **towards a jumble sale** etwas zu einem Trödelmarkt beisteuern; **if only the child would ~ more in class** wenn das Kind nur mehr zum Unterricht beitragen würde; **everyone ~d towards the production** jeder trug etwas zur Aufführung bei; **~ to charity** für karitative Zwecke spenden; **~ to sb.'s misery/disappointment** jmds. Kummer/Enttäuschung vergrößern; **~ to a newspaper** für eine Zeitung schreiben; **he ~d to the 'Encyclopaedia Britannica'** er hat an der „Encyclopaedia Britannica" mitgearbeitet; **~ to the success of sth.** zum Erfolg einer Sache (*Gen.*) beitragen

contribution /kɒntrɪ'bjuːʃn/ *n.* **1** (act of contributing) **make a ~ to a fund** etw. für einen Fonds spenden; **the ~ of clothing and money to sth.** das Spenden von Kleidern und Geld für etw. **2** (thing contributed) Beitrag, *der;* (for charity) Spende, *die* (**to** für); **~s of clothing and money** Kleider- und Geldspenden; **make a ~ to sth.** einen Beitrag zu etw. leisten

contributor /kən'trɪbjʊtə(r)/ *n.* **1** (giver) Spender, *der*/Spenderin, *die* **2** (to encyclopedia, dictionary, etc.) Mitarbeiter, *der*/Mitarbeiterin, *die* (**to** *Gen.*); **he is a regular ~ [of articles] to the 'Guardian'** er schreibt regelmäßig [Artikel] für den „Guardian"

contributory /kən'trɪbjʊtərɪ/ *adj.* **1** (that contributes) **a ~ factor to his state of mind/in the poor state of the economy** ein Faktor, der bei seiner Verfassung/bei der schlechten Wirtschaftslage eine Rolle spielt; **~ funds** Hilfsfonds; **~ negligence** (Law) Mitverschulden, *das* **2** (operated by contributions) **be run on a ~ basis** mit Beiträgen *od.* Spenden finanziert werden; **~ insurance payments** Versicherungspflichtbeiträge

'con trick (coll.) ▸ **confidence trick**

contrite /'kɒntraɪt/ *adj.* zerknirscht; (showing contrition) reuevoll; **~ sigh/tears/words** Seufzer/Tränen/Worte der Reue; **~ apology** zerknirschte Entschuldigung

contritely /'kɒntraɪtlɪ/ *adv.* zerknirscht

contrition /kən'trɪʃn/ *n.* Reue, *die;* **~ leads to absolution** Kontrition ist die Voraussetzung für die Absolution (kath. Theol.); **hang one's head in ~:** den Kopf reumütig senken

contrivance /kən'traɪvəns/ *n.* **1** (contriving) Plan, *der;* **deceitful ~s** faule Tricks (ugs. abwertend) **2** (invention) Ersinnen, *das;* (inventive capacity) Erfindungsgabe, *die* **3** (device) Gerät, *das*

contrive /kən'traɪv/ *v.t.* **1** (manage) **~ to do sth.** es fertig bringen *od.* zuwege bringen, etw. zu tun; **can you ~ to be here by 6 a.m.?** können Sie es einrichten, bis 6 Uhr morgens hier zu sein?; **they ~d to meet** es gelang ihnen, sich zu treffen **2** (devise) sich (*Dat.*) ausdenken; ersinnen (geh.); **~ ways and means of doing sth.** Mittel und Wege finden, etw. zu tun

contrived /kən'traɪvd/ *adj.* künstlich

control /kən'trəʊl/
A *n.* **1** (power of directing, restraint) Kontrolle, *die* (**of** über + *Akk.*); (management) Leitung, *die;* **~ of the economy** Wirtschaftslenkung, *die;* **board of ~:** Aufsichtsbehörde, *die;* **~ over ecclesiastical matters** höchste Gewalt in kirchlichen Dingen; **governmental ~:** Regierungsgewalt, *die;* **~ of the vehicle/machine is totally automatic** das Fahrzeug/die Maschine hat vollautomatische Steuerung; **have ~ of sth.** die Kontrolle über etw. (*Akk.*) haben; etw. kontrollieren; (take decisions) für etw. zuständig sein; **take ~ of** die Kontrolle übernehmen über (+ *Akk.*); **keep ~ of sth.** etw. unter Kontrolle halten; **be in ~ [of sth.]** die Kontrolle [über etw. (*Akk.*)] haben; **be in ~ of the situation** die Situation unter Kontrolle haben; **who's in ~ here?** wer hat hier zu bestimmen?; **be in ~ of education** für das Erziehungswesen zuständig sein; **[go** *or* **get] out of ~** *or* **beyond [sb.'s] ~:** außer Kontrolle [geraten]; **circumstances beyond sb.'s ~:** unvorhersehbare, nicht in jmds. Hand liegende Umstände; **[get sth.] under ~:** [etw.] unter Kontrolle [bringen]; **keep oneself/sth. under ~:** sich/etw. in der Gewalt haben; **everything's under ~** (fig.) alles in Ordnung; **lose ~ [of sth.]** die Kontrolle [über etw. (*Akk.*)] verlieren; **lose ~ of the situation** die Situation nicht mehr unter Kontrolle haben; **gain ~ of sth.** etw. unter Kontrolle bekommen; **lose/regain ~ of oneself** die Beherrschung verlieren/wiedergewinnen; **have some/complete/no ~ over sth.** eine gewisse/die absolute/keine Kontrolle über etw. (*Akk.*) haben; **have ~ over oneself** sich in der Gewalt haben; **he has no ~ over himself** er hat sich nicht in der Gewalt; *see also* **flight control**
2 (standard of comparison) Kontrollobjekt, *das;* (person) Kontrollperson, *die;* **~ experiment** Kontrollversuch, *der*
3 (device) Regler, *der;* **~s** (as a group) Schalttafel, *die;* (of TV, stereo system) Bedienungstafel, *die;* **at the ~s** an der Schalttafel; **be at the ~s** an der Schalttafel sitzen; ‹*Fahrer, Pilot:*› am Steuer sitzen; (fig.) das Steuer in der Hand haben
4 *in pl.* (means of regulating) Beschränkung, *die;* Kontrolle, *die;* **impose ~s on imports** Importbeschränkungen einführen
5 (Spiritualism) Kontrolle, *die* (Parapsych.); Kontrollgeist, *der* (Parapsych.)
6 (checkpoint for rally cars) Kontrollpunkt, *der*
B *v.t.*, **-ll-** **1** (have ~ of) kontrollieren; steuern, lenken ‹*Auto*›; leiten ‹*Firma*›; **you must ~ your dog** Sie müssen Ihren Hund unter Kontrolle halten; **he ~s the financial side of things** er ist für die Finanzen zuständig *od.* hat die Finanzen unter sich; **~ a class** eine Klasse fest im Griff haben; **~ling company** (Econ.) Kontrollgesellschaft, *die;* **~ling interest** Mehrheitsbeteiligung, *die* (Wirtsch.)
2 (hold in check) beherrschen; zügeln ‹*Zorn, Ungeduld, Temperament*›; im Zaum halten ‹*Zunge*›; (regulate) kontrollieren; regulieren ‹*Geschwindigkeit, Temperatur*›; einschränken ‹*Export, Ausgaben*›; regeln ‹*Verkehr*›; unterdrücken ‹*Gefühlsäußerung*›; **~ yourselves, children!** nehmt euch zusammen, Kinder!
3 (check, verify) [über]prüfen

control: ~ centre *n.* Kontrollzentrum, *das;* **~ character** *n.* (Computing) Steuer[ungs]zeichen, *das;* **~ desk** *n.* Schaltpult, *das;* **~ freak** *n.* (coll.) Kontrollfreak, *der;* **~ group** *n.* Kontrollgruppe, *die*

controlled 'substance *n.* verbotene Substanz

controller /kən'trəʊlə(r)/ *n.* **1** (director) Leiter, *der*/Leiterin, *die;* Chef, *der*/Chefin, *die* (ugs.) **2** ▸ **comptroller**

control: ~ panel *n.* Schalttafel, *die;* **~ rod** *n.* Steuerstab, *der;* Regelstab, *der;* **~ room** *n.* Kontrollraum, *der;* (in theatre) Stellwarte, *die;* (Radio, Telev.) Regieraum, *der;* (in power station) Schaltwarte, *die;* **~ tower** *n.* Kontrollturm, *der;* Tower, *der*

controversial /kɒntrə'vɜːʃl/ *adj.* (causing controversy) umstritten ‹*Mode, Kunstwerk, Gesetz, Idee*›; strittig ‹*Frage, Punkt, Angelegenheit*›; (given to controversy) streitsüchtig; (lacking neutrality) polemisch

controversy /'kɒntrəvɜːsɪ, kən'trɒvəsɪ/ *n.* Kontroverse, *die;* Auseinandersetzung, *die;* **much ~:** eine längere Kontroverse *od.* Auseinandersetzung; **sth. is beyond ~:** etw. ist unumstritten

controvert /'kɒntrəvɜːt, kɒntrə'vɜːt/ *v.t.* (formal) bestreiten; ‹*Argument, Theorie:*› widersprechen (+ *Dat.*)

contuse /kən'tjuːz/ *v.t.* prellen

contusion /kən'tjuːʒn/ *n.* Prellung, *die*

conundrum /kə'nʌndrəm/ *n.* (riddle) (*auf einem Wortspiel beruhendes*) Rätsel; (hard question) Problem, *das;* **pose ~s** Rätsel aufgeben

conurbation /kɒnɜː'beɪʃn/ *n.* Konurbation, *die* (Soziol.); ≈ Stadtregion, *die*

convalesce /kɒnvə'les/ *v.i.* genesen; rekonvaleszieren (Med.)

convalescence /kɒnvə'lesəns/ *n.* Genesung, *die;* Rekonvaleszenz, *die* (Med.)

convalescent /kɒnvə'lesənt/
A *adj.* rekonvaleszent (Med.); **you'll be ~ for a few weeks** Ihre Genesung wird ein paar Wochen dauern; **~ patient** Rekonvaleszent, *der*/Rekonvaleszentin, *die* (Med.)
B *n.* Rekonvaleszent, *der*/Rekonvaleszentin, *die* (Med.); Genesende, *der/die*

convalescent: ~ home, ~ hospital *ns.* Genesungsheim, *das*

convection /kən'vekʃn/ *n.* (Phys., Meteorol.) Konvektion, *die;* **~ current** Konvektionsstrom, *der*

convective /kən'vektɪv/ *adj.* (Phys., Meteorol.) konvektiv

convector /kən'vektə(r)/ *n.* Konvektor, *der*

convene /kən'viːn/
A *v.t.* einberufen
B *v.i.* zusammenkommen; ‹*Gericht, gewählte Vertreter:*› zusammentreten; ‹*Konferenz, Versammlung:*› beginnen

convener /kən'viːnə(r)/ *n.* (Brit.) *jmd., der eine Versammlung einberuft/leitet*

convenience /kən'viːnɪəns/ *n.* **1** *no pl.* (suitableness, advantageousness) Annehmlichkeit, *die;* **its ~ to** *or* **for the city centre** seine günstige Lage zum Stadtzentrum; **marriage of ~:** Vernunftehe, *die; see also* **flag[1] A 2** (personal satisfaction) Bequemlichkeit, *die;* Wohlbefinden, *das;* **for sb.'s ~, for ~'s sake** zu jmds. Bequemlichkeit; **is it to your ~?** passt es Ihnen?; **at your ~:** wann es Ihnen passt; **at your earliest ~:** möglichst bald; baldmöglichst (Papierdt.) **3** (advantage) **be a ~ to sb.** angenehm *od.* praktisch für jmdn. sein; **having a car is such a ~:** ein Auto zu haben ist so angenehm *od.* praktisch; **make a ~ of sb.** jmdn. ausnutzen **4** (advantageous thing) Annehmlichkeit, *die;* **a car is a [great] ~ to have** es ist [sehr] angenehm *od.* praktisch, ein Auto zu haben **5** (esp. Admin.: toilet) Toilette, *die;* **public ~:** öffentliche Toilette *od.* (Amtsspr.) Bedürfnisanstalt

convenience: ~ food *n.* Fertignahrung, *die;* **~ store** *n.* (esp. Amer.) Convenience-Store, *der;* Convenience-Shop, *der*

convenient /kən'viːnɪənt/ *adj.* **1** (suitable, not troublesome) günstig; (useful) praktisch; angenehm; **be ~ to** *or* **for sb.** günstig für jmdn. sein; **would it be ~ to you?** würde es Ihnen passen?; wäre es Ihnen recht?; **it's not very ~ at the moment** es passt im Augenblick nicht gut; **if it is not ~ to have us to stay** wenn es ungelegen kommt, dass wir bleiben 2 (of easy access) **be ~ to** *or* **for sth.** günstig zu etw. liegen; **our house is very ~ to** *or* **for the city centre** wir haben es nicht weit zum Stadtzentrum 3 (opportunely available or occurring) **a ~ taxi** ein Taxi, das gerade da steht/angefahren kommt

conveniently /kən'vi:nıəntlı/ *adv.* 1 (suitably, without difficulty, accessibly) günstig ‹*gelegen, angebracht*›; leicht ‹*gesehen werden*›; angenehm ‹*ruhig*›; **when can you ~ drop round?** wann passt es dir *od.* wann kannst du es einrichten, mal vorbeizukommen?; **we're ~ situated for the shops** wir haben es nicht weit zu den Geschäften 2 (opportunely) angenehmerweise; **very ~, we were only a mile from a garage** glücklicherweise waren wir nur eine Meile von einer Werkstatt entfernt

convenor ► **convener**

convent /'kɒnvənt/ *n.* Kloster, *das;* **~ of nuns** Nonnenkloster, *das;* **enter a ~:** ins Kloster gehen

convention /kən'venʃn/ *n.* 1 (a practice) Brauch, *der;* **it is the ~ to do sth.** es ist Brauch, etw. zu tun; **~s of spelling** Rechtschreibregeln 2 *no art.* (established customs) Konvention, *die;* **break with ~:** sich über die Konventionen hinwegsetzen 3 (formal assembly) Konferenz, *die* 4 (agreement between parties) Abkommen, *das;* Übereinkunft, *die;* (agreement between States) Konvention, *die* (bes. Völkerrecht)

conventional /kən'venʃənl/ *adj.* konventionell; (not spontaneous) formell; **it is ~ wisdom that ...:** man glaubt allgemein, dass ...; **it is ~ to send flowers** es ist üblich, Blumen zu schicken; **~ weapons** konventionelle Waffen

conventionally /kən'venʃənəlı/ *adv.* konventionell

conventioneer /kənvenʃə'nıə(r)/ *n.* (Amer.) Konferenzteilnehmer, *der*/-teilnehmerin, *die*

'convent school *n.* Klosterschule, *die*

converge /kən'vɜ:dʒ/ *v.i.* **~ [on each other]** aufeinander zulaufen; ‹*Gedanken, Meinungen, Ansichten:*› sich [einander] annähern, (geh.) konvergieren; **~ on sb.** auf jmdn. zulaufen; **they ~d on the scene of the accident** sie liefen am Unfallort zusammen

convergence /kən'vɜ:dʒəns/ *n.* 1 Annäherung, *die;* Konvergenz, *die* (geh.); (of roads, rivers) Zusammentreffen, *das;* **at the ~ of the roads** an der Stelle, wo die Straßen zusammentreffen 2 (Math., Biol., Psych.) Konvergenz, *die* 3 (EU) Konvergenz, *die; attrib.* **~ criteria** Konvergenzkriterien

convergent /kən'vɜ:dʒənt/ *adj.* 1 aufeinander zulaufend; konvergierend (geh.), sich einander annähernd ‹*Meinungen, Gedanken, Ansichten*› 2 (Math., Biol., Psych.) konvergent; **~ lens** (Optics) Sammellinse, *die*

conversant /kən'vɜ:sənt/ *pred. adj.* vertraut (**with** mit)

conversation /kɒnvə'seıʃn/ *n.* Unterhaltung, *die;* Gespräch, *das;* Konversation, *die* (geh.); (in language-teaching) Konversation, *die;* **be in ~ [with sb.]** sich [mit jmdm.] unterhalten; **be deep in ~:** in ein Gespräch vertieft sein; **enter into ~ with sb.** mit jmdm. ein Gespräch anfangen *od.* anknüpfen; **make [polite] ~ with sb.** mit jmdm. Konversation machen; **in the course of ~:** im Verlauf des Gesprächs; **come up in ~:** gesprächsweise erwähnt werden; **he hasn't much ~:** man kann sich kaum mit ihm unterhalten; **have a ~ with sb.** mit jmdm. ein Gespräch führen

conversational /kɒnvə'seıʃənl/ *adj.* gesprächig ‹*Person*›; ungezwungen ‹*Art*›; **talk in ~ tones/in a ~ manner** im Plauderton/ungezwungen sprechen; **~ English** gesprochenes Englisch; **the discussion remained on a casual, ~ level** die Diskussion blieb auf der Ebene einer zwanglosen Unterhaltung

conversationalist /kɒnvə'seıʃənəlıst/ *n.* Unterhalter, *der*/Unterhalterin, *die;* **be a/no great ~:** gut/nicht gut Konversation machen können

conversationally /kɒnvə'seıʃənəlı/ *adv.* **'Nice day today', he remarked ~:** „Schöner Tag heute", stellte er fest, um ein Gespräch zu beginnen

conver'sation piece *n.* (topic of conversation) Gesprächsthema, *das*

converse¹ /kən'vɜ:s/ *v.i.* (formal) **~ [with sb.] [about** *or* **on sth.]** sich [mit jmdm.] [über etw. (*Akk.*)] unterhalten

converse² /'kɒnvɜ:s/

A *adj.* entgegengesetzt; umgekehrt ‹*Fall, Situation*›

B *n.* 1 (opposite) Gegenteil, *das* 2 (Math.) Kehrsatz, *der* 3 (Logic) Konversion, *die*

conversely /kən'vɜ:slı/ *adv.* umgekehrt

conversion /kən'vɜ:ʃn/ *n.* 1 (transforming) Umwandlung, *die* (**into** in + *Akk.*) 2 (adaptation, adapted building) Umbau, *der;* **do a ~ on sth.** etw. umbauen 3 (of person) Bekehrung, *die* (**to** zu); Konversion, *die* (Rel.) 4 (to different units or expression) Übertragung, *die* (**into** in + *Akk.*) 5 (Finance, Logic, Theol., Psych., Phys.) Konversion, *die;* (calculation) Umrechnung, *die;* (Rugby, Amer. Footb.) Erhöhung, *die*

con'version table *n.* Umrechnungstabelle, *die*

convert

A /kən'vɜ:t/ *v.t.* 1 (transform, change in function) umwandeln (**into** in + *Akk.*) 2 (adapt) **~ sth. [into sth.]** etw. [zu etw.] umbauen 3 (bring over) **~ sb. [to sth.]** (lit. or fig.) jmdn. [zu etw.] bekehren 4 (to different units or expressions) übertragen (**into** in + *Akk.*) 5 (Finance) konvertieren; (calculate) umrechnen (**into** in + *Akk.*) 6 (Rugby, Amer. Footb.) erhöhen 7 **~ to one's own use** sich (*Dat.*) aneignen

B *v.i.* 1 (be transformable, be changeable in function) **~ into sth.** sich in etw. (*Akk.*) umwandeln lassen 2 (be adaptable) sich umbauen lassen 3 (to new method etc.) umstellen (**to** auf + *Akk.*)

C /'kɒnvɜ:t/ *n.* 1 (Relig.) Konvertit, *der*/Konvertitin, *die* 2 (fig.) **the new ~s to the Party** die neuen Anhänger der Partei; **he became a ~ to Asian philosophy** er wurde ein Anhänger der asiatischen Philosophie

converter /kən'vɜ:tə(r)/ *n.* 1 (Metall.) Konverter, *der* 2 (Electr.) Umformer, *der*

convertibility /kənvɜ:tı'bılıtı/ *n., no pl.* 1 Umwandelbarkeit, *die* 2 (Finance) Konvertierbarkeit, *die*

convertible /kən'vɜ:tıbl/

A *adj.* 1 **be ~ into sth.** sich in etw. (*Akk.*) umwandeln lassen; **~ sofa** Ausziehcouch, *die* 2 (able to be altered) **be ~ [into sth.]** sich zu etw. umbauen lassen 3 (Finance) **be ~ into sth.** in etw. (*Akk.*) konvertierbar sein

B *n.* (car) Kabrio, *das;* Cabrio, *das*

convex /'kɒnveks/ *adj.* konvex; *attrib.* Konvex‹*linse, -spiegel*›

convexity /kən'veksıtı/ *n.* Wölbung, *die;* Konvexität, *die* (Optik)

convey /kən'veı/ *v.t.* 1 (transport) befördern; (transmit) übermitteln ‹*Nachricht, Grüße*›; **the TV pictures are ~ed by satellite** die Fernsehbilder werden per Satellit übertragen 2 (impart) vermitteln; **words cannot ~ it** Worte können es nicht wiedergeben; **the message ~ed nothing whatever to me** die Nachricht sagte mir überhaupt nichts; **~ one's meaning to sb.** jmdm. deutlich machen, was man meint 3 (Law) **~ property [to sb.]** [jmdm.] Eigentum übertragen *od.* überschreiben

conveyance /kən'veıəns/ *n.* 1 (transportation) Beförderung, *die;* (of sound, picture, heat, light) Übertragung, *die;* (of message, greetings) Übermittlung, *die* 2 (formal: vehicle) Beförderungsmittel, *das* 3 (Law) Übertragung, *die;* Überschreibung, *die;* **[deed of] ~:** Übertragungsurkunde, *die*

conveyancing /kən'veıənsıŋ/ *n.* (Law) **~ [of property]** [Eigentums]übertragung, *die*

conveyer, conveyor /kən'veıə(r)/ *n.* Förderer, *der* (Technik); **[bucket] ~:** Becherwerk, *das;* **[chain] ~:** Kettenförderer, *der;* **~ [belt]** (Industry) Förderband, *das;* (in manufacture also) Fließband, *das*

convict

A /'kɒnvıkt/ *n.* Strafgefangene, *der/die*

B /kən'vıkt/ *v.t.* 1 (declare guilty) für schuldig befinden; verurteilen; **be ~ed** verurteilt werden 2 (prove guilty) **~ sb. of sth.** jmdn. einer Sache (*Gen.*) überführen

conviction /kən'vıkʃn/ *n.* 1 (Law) Verurteilung, *die* (**for** wegen); **have you [had] any previous ~s?** sind Sie vorbestraft?; **he has no criminal ~s at all** er hat keinerlei Vorstrafen 2 (settled belief) Überzeugung, *die;* **a vegetarian by ~:** ein überzeugter Vegetarier; **it is their ~ that ...:** sie sind der Überzeugung, dass ...; **her ~ of the existence of God/of his innocence** ihr fester Glaube an die Existenz Gottes/an seine Unschuld; **what are his political ~s?** wie sind seine politischen Anschauungen?; **carry ~:** überzeugend sein; ‹*Stimme:*› überzeugend klingen

con'viction politics *n., no pl.* Gesinnungspolitik, *die*

convince /kən'vıns/ *v.t.* überzeugen; **~ sb. that ...:** jmdn. davon überzeugen, dass ...; **be ~d that ...:** davon überzeugt sein, dass ...; **manage to ~ oneself that ...:** sich (*Dat.*) einreden, dass ...; **~ sb. of sth.** jmdn. von etw. überzeugen

convincing /kən'vınsıŋ/ *adj.* überzeugend; täuschend ‹*Ähnlichkeit*›

convincingly /kən'vınsıŋlı/ *adv.* überzeugend

convivial /kən'vıvıəl/ *n.* fröhlich

conviviality /kənvıvı'ælıtı/ *n., no pl.* Fröhlichkeit, *die*

convivially /kən'vıvıəlı/ *adv.* fröhlich

convocation /kɒnvə'keıʃn/ *n.* 1 (calling together) Zusammenrufen, *das;* (of council, synod) Einberufung, *die* 2 (assembly) Versammlung, *die* 3 (Brit. Eccl.) Provinzialsynode, *die* 4 (Brit. Univ.) *universitäre gesetzgebende Versammlung;* ≈ Vollversammlung, *die*

convoke /kən'vəʊk/ *v.t.* zusammenrufen; einberufen ‹*Versammlung, Synode, Rat*›

convoluted /'kɒnvəlu:tıd/ *adj.* 1 (twisted) verschlungen; verdreht ‹*Körperhaltung*› 2 (complex) kompliziert

convolution /kɒnvə'lu:ʃn/ *n.* Windung, *die;* **the ~s of the winding road** die Biegungen der kurvenreichen Straße

convolvulus /kən'vɒlvjʊləs/ *n.* (Bot.) Winde, *die*

convoy /'kɒnvɔı/

A *n.* Konvoi, *der;* **in ~:** im Konvoi

B *v.t.* Geleitschutz geben (+ *Dat.*)

convulse /kən'vʌls/ *v.t.* 1 **be ~d** von Krämpfen geschüttelt werden; (fig.) **be ~d with laughter** sich vor Lachen biegen (ugs.); **be ~d with rage/fury** sich vor Wut krümmen 2 (shake, lit. or fig.) erschüttern

convulsion /kən'vʌlʃn/ *n.* 1 *in pl.* Schüttelkrampf, *der* (Med.); Krämpfe; (fig.) **~s of laughter** Lachkrampf, *der;* **we were in absolute ~s** wir bogen uns förmlich vor Lachen (ugs.) 2 (shaking, lit. or fig.) Erschütterung, *die*

convulsive /kən'vʌlsıv/ *adj.*, **convulsively** /kən'vʌlsıvlı/ *adv.* konvulsivisch

cony ► **coney**

coo /ku:/

A *int.* (of person) oh; (of dove) ruckedigu

B *n.* (of dove) **the ~[s]** das Gurren

C *v.i.* gurren; ‹*Baby:*› gurren (fig.)

D *v.t.* & *i.* gurren (auch fig.)

cooee /'ku:i:/

A *int.* huhu (ugs.)

B *v.i.* **they ~d to us** sie riefen uns „huhu" zu

cook /kʊk/

A *n.* ► **p. 1260** Koch, *der*/Köchin, *die;* **too many ~s spoil the broth** (prov.) viele Köche verderben den Brei (Spr.)

B *v.t.* 1 garen; zubereiten, kochen ‹*Mahlzeit*›; (fry, roast) braten; (boil) kochen; **how would you ~ this piece of meat?** wie würden Sie dieses Stück Fleisch zubereiten?; **~ed in the oven** im Backofen zubereitet *od.* (Kochk.) gegart; **~ed meal** warme Mahlzeit; **how long should one ~ this joint?** wie lange sollte man diesen Braten garen lassen? (Kochk.); *abs.* **do you ~ with gas or electricity?** kochen Sie mit Gas oder mit Strom?; **she knows how to ~:** sie kann gut kochen *od.* kocht gut; **~ sb.'s goose [for him]** (fig.) jmdm. alles verderben; **he ~ed**

his own goose er hat sich (*Dat.*) alles verdorben *od.* (ugs.) vermasselt 2 (fig. coll.: falsify) frisieren (ugs.) 3 (Brit. coll.: fatigue) **be ~ed** fix und fertig sein (ugs.)

C *v.i.* kochen; garen (Kochk.); **the meat was ~ing slowly** das Fleisch garte langsam; **what's ~ing?** (fig. coll.) was liegt an? (ugs.)

Phrasal verb

• **~ 'up** *v.t.* sich (*Dat.*) ausbrüten, (ugs.) aushecken ‹*Plan*›; erfinden ‹*Geschichte*›

cook: ~book ▸**cookery book**; **~-chill 'food** *n.*: *durch rasche Abkühlung haltbar gemachte Fertiggerichte*

cooker /ˈkʊkə(r)/ *n.* 1 (Brit.: appliance) Herd, *der;* **electric/gas ~:** Elektroherd/Gasherd, *der* 2 (vessel) Kochgefäß, *das* 3 (fruit) **are those apples eaters or ~s?** sind diese Äpfel zum Essen oder zum Kochen?

'cooker hood *n.* Dunstabzugshaube, *die*

cookery /ˈkʊkərɪ/ *n.* 1 Kochen, *das* 2 (Amer.: place) Küche, *die*

cookery: ~ book *n.* (Brit.) Kochbuch, *das;* **~ course** *n.* Kochkurs, *der*

cookhouse /ˈkʊkhaʊs/ *n.* (Mil.) Feldküche, *die*

cookie /ˈkʊkɪ/ *n.* 1 (Scot.) Plätzchen, *das* 2 (Amer.: biscuit) Keks, *der;* **that's the way the ~ crumbles** (fig. coll.) es kommt, wie es kommen muss 3 (coll.: person) (woman) Person, *die;* (attractive woman) Klasseweib, *das* (ugs.); (man) Typ, *der* (ugs.) 4 (Computing) Cookie, *das*

cooking /ˈkʊkɪŋ/ *n.* Kochen, *das;* **German ~:** die deutsche Küche; **your ~ is marvellous** du kochst wunderbar; **do one's own ~:** für sich selbst kochen; **do the ~:** kochen

cooking: ~ apple *n.* Kochapfel, *der;* **~ fat** *n.* Bratfett, *das;* **~ salt** *n.* Speisesalz, *das;* **~ sherry** *n. Sherry zum Kochen;* **~ utensil** *n.* Küchengerät, *das;* **~ vessel** *n.* Kochgefäß, *das*

cook: ~out *n.* (Amer.) ≈ Grillparty, *die;* **have a ~out** im Freien kochen; **~ stove** *n.* (Amer.) [Koch]herd, *der;* **~top** *n.* (Amer.) Kochfeld, *das*

cool /kuːl/

A *adj.* 1 kühl; luftig ‹*Kleidung*›; **I wait until my tea is ~ enough to drink** ich warte, bis mein Tee so weit abgekühlt ist, dass ich ihn trinken kann; **I am/feel ~:** mir ist kühl; **'store in a ~ place'** „kühl aufbewahren"; **bake in a ~ oven** bei schwacher Hitze backen 2 (unexcited) **he kept** *or* **stayed ~:** er blieb ruhig *od.* bewahrte die Ruhe; **play it ~** (coll.) ruhig bleiben; cool vorgehen (salopp); **she's always so ~ about things** sie ist immer so ruhig und besonnen; **he was ~, calm, and collected** er war ruhig und gelassen; **a ~ customer** ein kühler Kopf; **keep a ~ head** einen kühlen Kopf bewahren; *see also* **cucumber** 3 (unemotional, unfriendly) kühl; (calmly audacious) kaltblütig; unverfroren ‹*Forderung*›; **be a ~ customer** (fig.) ganz schön unverschämt sein; **a ~ £3,000/thousand** (coll.) glatt 3 000 Pfund/ein glatter Tausender (ugs.) 4 (Jazz) *in der Art des Cooljazz;* **~ jazz** Cooljazz, *der* 5 (coll.: excellent) cool (salopp); geil (ugs.)

B *n.* 1 (coolness) Kühle, *die* 2 (~ air, place) **sit in the ~:** im Kühlen sitzen; **store sth. in the ~:** etw. kühl aufbewahren 3 (coll.: composure) **keep/lose one's ~:** die Ruhe bewahren/verlieren

C *v.i.* abkühlen; **the weather has ~ed** es ist kühler geworden; **wait until your milk ~s a bit** lass deine Milch etwas abkühlen; (fig.) **our relationship has ~ed** unsere Beziehung ist kühler geworden; **the first heat of passion had ~ed** die erste Leidenschaft war verflogen; **~ towards sb./sth.** an jmdm./etw. das Interesse verlieren

D *v.t.* kühlen; (from high temperature) abkühlen; (fig.) abkühlen ‹*Leidenschaft, Raserei, Liebe*›; **[have to] ~ one's heels** lange warten [müssen]; **~ it!** (coll.) reg dich ab! (ugs.)

Phrasal verbs

• **~ 'down**

A *v.i.* 1 ‹*Tee:*› abkühlen; ‹*Luft:*› sich abkühlen 2 (fig.) sich beruhigen; **his anger has ~ed down** sein Zorn hat sich gelegt

B *v.t.* abkühlen; (fig.) besänftigen; (disillusion) ernüchtern

• **~ 'off**

A *v.i.* 1 abkühlen; **the weather has ~ed off** es ist kühler geworden; **we need a few minutes to ~ off** wir brauchen ein paar Minuten, um uns abzukühlen 2 (fig.) sich beruhigen; ‹*Zorn, Begeisterung, Interesse, Leidenschaft:*› sich legen, nachlassen; ‹*Freundschaft:*› sich abkühlen

B *v.t.* abkühlen; (fig.) beruhigen; besänftigen; abkühlen ‹*Leidenschaft, Begeisterung*›

coolant /ˈkuːlənt/ *n.* Kühlmittel, *das;* (for cutting-tool) Schneidflüssigkeit, *die* (Technik); (for internal-combustion engine) Kühlwasser, *das*

'cool box *n.* Kühlbox, *die*

cooler /ˈkuːlə(r)/ *n.* 1 (vessel) Kühler, *der* 2 (Amer.: refrigerator) Kühlschrank, *der* 3 (coll.: prison) Knast, *der* (ugs.)

'cool-headed *adj.* kühl; nüchtern

coolie /ˈkuːlɪ/ *n.* Kuli, *der*

'coolie hat *flacher Hut [der chinesischen Kulis];* Chinesenhut, *der*

cooling /ˈkuːlɪŋ/: **~ fan** *n.* Kühlgebläse, *das* (Technik); **~-'off period** *n.* Rücktrittsfrist, *die;* **~ tower** *n.* Kühlturm, *der*

coolly /ˈkuːllɪ/ *adv.* 1 kühl 2 (fig.) (calmly) ruhig; (unemotionally, in unfriendly manner) kühl; (impudently) kaltblütig; unverfroren ‹*verlangen, fordern*›

coolness /ˈkuːlnɪs/ *n., no pl.* Kühle, *die;* (fig.) (calmness) Ruhe, *die;* (unemotional nature, unfriendliness) Kühle, *die;* (impudence) Kaltblütigkeit, *die;* (insolence) Unverfrorenheit, *die*

coomb /kuːm/ *n.* (Brit.) (on hill flank) *Taleinschnitt an der Seite eines Berges;* (short valley) Schlucht, *die*

coon /kuːn/ *n.* 1 (Amer.: racoon) Waschbär, *der* 2 (sl. derog.) (black person) Nigger, *der* (abwertend); (black woman) Niggerweib, *das* (abwertend)

'coonskin *n.* (Amer.) Waschbärfell, *das;* Waschbär[pelz], *der;* (cap) Waschbärmütze, *die;* (jacket) Waschbärjacke, *die*

coop /kuːp/

A *n.* (cage) Geflügelkäfig, *der;* (for poultry) Hühnerstall, *der;* (fowl-run) Auslauf, *der*

B *v.t.* **~ in** *or* **up** einpferchen

co-op /ˈkəʊɒp/ *n.* (coll.) 1 (Brit.) (society) Genossenschaft, *die;* (shop) Konsum[laden], *der* 2 (Amer.) ▸**cooperative B 2**

cooper /ˈkuːpə(r)/ *n.* Böttcher, *der*/Böttcherin, *die*

cooperate /kəʊˈɒpəreɪt/ *v.i.* mitarbeiten (**in** bei); (with each other) zusammenarbeiten (**in** bei); (not obstruct) mitmachen (ugs.); ‹*Dinge, Ereignisse:*› zusammenwirken; (Polit., Econ. also) kooperieren (**in** bei); **~ with sb.** mit jmdm. zusammenarbeiten/kooperieren; **the patient refused to ~:** der Patient verweigerte die Mitarbeit *od.* war nicht kooperativ; **~ with the police** die Polizei unterstützen

cooperation /kəʊɒpəˈreɪʃn/ *n.* 1 ▸**cooperate:** Mitarbeit, *die;* Zusammenarbeit, *die;* Kooperation, *die;* **with the ~ of** unter Mitarbeit von; **in ~ with** in Zusammenarbeit mit 2 (Econ.) Genossenschaft, *die;* **the principle of ~:** das genossenschaftliche Prinzip

cooperative /kəʊˈɒpərətɪv/

A *adj.* 1 (offering cooperation) kooperativ; (helpful) hilfsbereit 2 (Econ.) genossenschaftlich

B *n.* 1 Genossenschaft, *die;* Kooperative, *die* (DDR); (shop) Genossenschaftsladen, *der;* **workers' ~:** Produktivgenossenschaft, *die* 2 (Amer.: dwelling) *gemeinschaftlich gemieteter/gekaufter Wohnraum*

cooperative: ~ shop *n.* ▸**~ store; ~ society** *n.* Genossenschaft, *die;* **~ store** *n.* Genossenschaftsladen, *der*

co-opt /kəʊˈɒpt/ *v.t.* kooptieren; hinzuwählen; **be ~ed [on] to a committee** von einem Komitee kooptiert werden

co-option /kəʊˈɒpʃn/ *n.* Koop[ta]tion, *die*

coordinate

A /kəʊˈɔːdɪnət/ *adj.* 1 (equal in rank) gleichrangig 2 (Ling.) nebengeordnet

B *n.* 1 (Math.) Koordinate, *die* 2 *in pl.* (clothes) Kombination, *die*

C /kəʊˈɔːdɪmeɪt/ *v.t.* 1 koordinieren; **~ one's thoughts** seine Gedanken sammeln *od.* ordnen 2 (Ling.) **coordinating conjunction** koordinierende *od.* nebenordnende Konjunktion

coordination /kəʊɔːdɪˈneɪʃn/ *n.* Koordination, *die;* **he lacks ~:** er hat Koordinationsschwierigkeiten

coordinator /kəʊˈɔːdɪneɪtə(r)/ *n.* Koordinator, *der*/Koordinatorin, *die*

coot /kuːt/ *n.* 1 (Ornith.) **[bald] ~:** Blässhuhn, *das;* **be [as] bald as a ~:** völlig kahl sein 2 (coll.: stupid person) **[silly] ~:** dummes Huhn

co-owner /kəʊˈəʊnə(r)/ *n.* Miteigentümer, *der*/-eigentümerin, *die;* (of business) Mitinhaber, *der*/-inhaberin, *die*

cop¹ /kɒp/ *n.* (coll.: police officer) Bulle, *der* (salopp); Polyp, *der* (salopp); **she's a ~:** sie ist von der Polente (salopp); **~s and robbers** Räuber und Gendarm

cop² (coll.)

A *v.t.*, **-pp-:** 1 **when …, you'll ~ it** (be punished) wenn …, dann kannst du was erleben 2 **they ~ped it** (were killed) sie mussten dran glauben (salopp)

B *n.* **it's a fair ~!** guter Fang!; **no ~, not much ~:** nichts Besonderes

Phrasal verb

• **~ 'out** *v.i.* (coll.) 1 (escape) abhauen (salopp); **~ out of society** [aus der Gesellschaft] aussteigen (ugs.) 2 (give up) alles hinwerfen (ugs.) 3 (go back on one's promise) **you can't ~ out like that** du kannst mich/ihn *usw.* doch nicht so hängen lassen (ugs.). *See also* **cop-out**

copartner /kəʊˈpɑːtnə(r)/ *n.* Partner, *der*/Partnerin, *die;* Teilhaber, *der*/-haberin, *die*

copartnership /kəʊˈpɑːtnəʃɪp/ *n.* (relationship) Partnerschaft, *die;* Teilhaberschaft, *die;* (company) Sozietät, *die*

cope¹ /kəʊp/ *v.i.* 1 (be able to contend) **~ with sb./sth.** mit jmdm./etw. fertig werden; **~ with a handicapped child** mit einem behinderten Kind zurechtkommen 2 (deal with sth.) klarkommen (ugs.); **we must find someone who will ~:** wir brauchen jemanden, der die Sache in die Hand nimmt

cope² *n.* (Eccl.) Pluviale, *das* (kath. Kirche)

Copenhagen /kəʊpnˈheɪgn/ *pr. n.* ▸❶ **p. 1643** Kopenhagen (*das*)

Copernican /kəˈpɜːnɪkn/ *adj.* kopernikanisch

copier /ˈkɒpɪə(r)/ *n.* (machine) Kopiergerät, *das;* Kopierer, *der* (ugs.)

co-pilot /ˈkəʊpaɪlət/ *n.* Kopilot, *der*/Kopilotin, *die*

coping /ˈkəʊpɪŋ/ *n.* Mauerabdeckung, *die*

'coping stone *n.* Abdeckplatte, *die*

copious /ˈkəʊpɪəs/ *adj.* (plentiful) reichhaltig; voll ‹*Haar*›; (informative) umfassend

copiously /ˈkəʊpɪəslɪ/ *adv.* (plentifully) reichlich; (informatively) umfassend

copiousness /ˈkəʊpɪəsnɪs/ *n., no pl.* (plentifulness) Fülle, *die*

'cop-out *n.* (coll.) Drückebergerei, *die* (ugs. abwertend); **that's a ~:** das ist Drückebergerei (ugs. abwertend)

copper¹ /ˈkɒpə(r)/

A *n.* 1 Kupfer, *das* 2 (coin) Kupfermünze, *die;* **a few ~s** etwas Kupfergeld; **it only costs a few ~s** es kostet nur ein paar Cent 3 (boiler) [Kupfer]kessel, *der;* (for laundry) Waschkessel, *der*

B *attrib. adj.* 1 (made of ~) kupfern; Kupfer‹*münze, -kessel, -rohr*› 2 (coloured like ~) kupferfarben; kupfern

copper² (Brit. coll.) ▸**cop¹**

copper: ~ 'beech *n.* Blutbuche, *die;* **~-bottomed** *adj.* gekupfert (Seew.) ‹*Schiff*›; ‹*Pfanne*› mit Kupferboden; (fig.) (authentic) waschecht; (financially reliable) todsicher (ugs.); **~-coloured** *adj.* kupferfarben; **~plate** **A** *n.* 1 (metal plate) Kupferplatte, *die;* 2 (print) Kupferstich, *der;* **B** *adj.* **~plate writing** ≈ Schönschrift, *die; Schreib- und Druckschrift mit dickem Ab- und dünnem Aufstrich*

coppery /ˈkɒpərɪ/ *adj.* kupferfarben; kupfern

coppice /ˈkɒpɪs/ *n.* Wäldchen, *das;* Niederwald, *der* (Forstw.)

'coppice wood *n.* Unterholz, *das*

copra /ˈkɒprə/ *n.* Kopra, *die*

copse /kɒps/ ▸**coppice**
'cop shop *n.* (Brit. coll.) Wache, *die;* Revier, *das*
Copt /kɒpt/ *n.* Kopte, *der*/Koptin, *die*
Coptic /'kɒptɪk/
A *adj.* koptisch
B *n.* (language) Koptisch, *das*
copula /'kɒpjʊlə/ *n.* (Ling.) Kopula, *die*
copulate /'kɒpjʊleɪt/ *v.i.* kopulieren
copulation /kɒpjʊ'leɪʃn/ *n.* Kopulation, *die*
copy /'kɒpɪ/
A *n.* **1** (reproduction) Kopie, *die;* (imitation) Nachahmung, *die;* (with carbon paper etc.) (typed) Durchschlag, *der;* (written) Durchschrift, *die;* **write a ~:** eine Abschrift machen; *see also* **fair² A 8; rough ~ 2** (specimen) Exemplar, *das;* **have you a ~ of today's 'Times'?** haben Sie die „Times" von heute?; **send three copies of the application** die Bewerbung in dreifacher Ausfertigung schicken; **top ~:** Original, *das* **3** (manuscript etc. for printing) Druckvorlage, *die;* **supply ~:** die Druckvorlage liefern; **make good ~** (Journ. coll.: news) ein klasse Stoff sein (ugs.); **[advertising] ~:** Werbetext, *der*
B *v.t.* **1** (make ~ of) kopieren; (by photocopier) [foto-]kopieren; (transcribe) abschreiben **2** (imitate) nachahmen
C *v.i.* **1** kopieren; **~ from sb./sth.** jmdn./etw. kopieren **2** (in exam etc.) abschreiben; **~ from** *or* **off sb./sth.** bei jmdm./aus etw. abschreiben
Phrasal verb
• **~ 'out** *v.t.* abschreiben
copy: ~book *n. attrib.* wie im Bilderbuch *nachgestellt;* Bilderbuch‹*landschaft, -wetter*›; *see also* **blot B 2; ~cat** *n.* (coll.) **you're such a ~cat!** du musst immer alles nachmachen!; **~desk** *n.* (Amer.) Redaktionstisch, *der;* **~editor** *n.* Redakteur, *der*/Redakteurin, *die* (*für formale Manuskriptbearbeitung und redaktionelles Korrekturlesen*)
copyist /'kɒpɪɪst/ *n.* Kopist, *der*
copy: ~-protected *adj.* (Computing) kopiergeschützt; **~ protection** *n.* (Computing) Kopierschutz, *der;* **~right A** *n.* Copyright, *das;* Urheberrecht, *das;* **be out of ~right** gemeinfrei [geworden] sein; **protected by ~right** urheberrechtlich geschützt; **B** *adj.* urheberrechtlich geschützt; *attrib.* **~right library** (Brit.) *Bibliothek, die Anspruch auf ein Freiexemplar jedes in Großbritannien veröffentlichten Buches hat;* **C** *v.t.* urheberrechtlich schützen; **~ typist** *n.* ▸ℹ **p. 1260** Schreibkraft (*die nur nach schriftlichen Vorlagen arbeitet*); **~writer** *n.* ▸ℹ **p. 1260** [Werbe]texter, *der*/-texterin, *die*
coquetry /'kɒkɪtrɪ, 'kəʊkɪtrɪ/ *n.* Koketterie, *die;* (fig.) Kokettieren, *das*
coquette /kə'ket/
A *n.* Kokette, *die*
B *v.i.* kokettieren
coquettish /kə'ketɪʃ/ *adj.* kokett
cor /kɔ:(r)/ *int.* (Brit. sl.) Mensch! (salopp)
coracle /'kɒrəkl/ *n.* (Brit.) Coracle, *das* (Fischerboot aus lederüberzogenem Flechtwerk)
coral /'kɒrl/
A *n.* Koralle, *die*
B *attrib. adj.* korallen; Korallen‹*insel, -riff, -rot*›
cor anglais /kɔ:r 'ãgleɪ, kɔ:r 'ɒŋgleɪ/ *n.* (Mus.) **1** (instrument) Englischhorn, *das;* Englisch Horn, *das* (fachspr.) **2** (organ stop) Englisch Horn, *das*
corbel /kɔ:bl/ *n.* (Archit.) (of stone) Kragstein, *der;* (of timber) Sattelholz, *das*
'corbel table *n.* (Archit.) Bogenfries, *der*
cord /kɔ:d/ *n.* **1** Kordel, *die;* (strong string) Schnur, *die* **2** (Anat.) ▸**spermatic cord; spinal cord; umbilical cord; vocal cords** **3** (rib) Rippe, *die;* (cloth) Cord, *der* **4** *in pl.* (trousers) **[pair of] ~s** Cordhose, *die* **5** (Amer. Electr.: flex) Kabel, *das*
cordage /'kɔ:dɪdʒ/ *n.* (Naut.) Tauwerk, *das*
cordate /'kɔ:deɪt/ *adj.* (Biol.) herzförmig
cordial /'kɔ:dɪəl/
A *adj.* herzlich; **a ~ dislike for sb.** eine tief empfundene Abneigung gegenüber jmdm
B *n.* (drink) Sirup, *der*
cordiality /kɔ:dɪ'ælɪtɪ/ *n., no pl.* Herzlichkeit, *die*
cordially /'kɔ:dɪəlɪ/ *adv.* herzlich; **~ dislike sb.** eine tief empfundene Abneigung gegenüber jmdm. haben; **~ yours** mit herzlichen Grüßen
cordillera /kɔ:dɪ'ljeərə/ *n.* (Geog.) Kettengebirge, *das*
cordite /'kɔ:daɪt/ *n.* Kordit, *der*
cordless /'kɔ:dlɪs/ *adj.* **1** (without cord) ohne Kordel *nachgestellt* **2** (without flex) ohne Kabel *nachgestellt*
cordless 'phone *n.* Schnurlostelefon, *das*
cordon /'kɔ:dn/
A *n.* **1** (line of police; also Mil.) Kordon, *der;* **a ~ of policemen** ein Polizeikordon; *see also* **throw around 2** **2** (fruit tree) Schnurbaum, *der;* Kordon, *der*
B *v.t.* **~ [off]** absperren; abriegeln
cordon bleu /kɔ:dɔ̃ 'blɜ:/ *n.* Meisterkoch, *der*/-köchin, *die;* **~ cookery** feine Küche
corduroy /'kɔ:dərɔɪ, 'kɔ:djʊrɔɪ/ *n.* **1** (material) Cordsamt, *der* **2** *in pl.* (trousers) Cordsamthose, *die*
core /kɔ:(r)/
A *n.* **1** (of fruit) Kerngehäuse, *das* **2** (Geol.) (rock sample) [Bohr]kern, *der;* (of earth) [Erd]kern, *der* **3** (Electr.: of soft iron) [Eisen]kern, *der* **4** (fig.: innermost part) **get to the ~ of the matter** zum Kern der Sache kommen; **rotten to the ~:** verdorben bis ins Mark; **English to the ~:** durch und durch englisch; **shake sb. to the ~:** jmdn. zutiefst erschüttern **5** (Industry: internal mould) Kern, *der* **6** (Nucl. Engin.) Core, *das;* Reaktorkern, *der* **7** (Computing) Magnetkern, *der* **8** (of rope, electrical cable) Seele, *die*
B *v.t.* entkernen ‹*Apfel, Birne*›
Coreper /'kəʊrepeə(r)/ *n.* (EU) AStV, *der*
corer /'kɔ:rə(r)/ *n.* Entkerner, *der*
co-respondent /kəʊrɪ'spɒndənt/ *n.* Mitbeklagte, *der/die* (*im Scheidungsprozess*)
core: ~ subject *n.* Kernfach, *das;* **~ time** *n.* (Brit.) Kernzeit, *die*
Corfu /kɔ:'fu:/ *pr. n.* Korfu (*das*)
corgi /'kɔ:gɪ/ *n.* **[Welsh] ~:** Welsh Corgi, *der*
coriander /kɒrɪ'ændə(r)/ *n.* Koriander, *der*
cori'ander seed *n.* Koriander, *der*
Corinth /'kɒrɪnθ/ *pr. n.* ▸ℹ **p. 1643** Korinth (*das*)
cork /kɔ:k/
A *n.* **1** (bark) Kork, *der* **2** (bottle stopper) Korken, *der* **3** (fishing float) Schwimmer, *der* **4** *attrib.* Kork-
B *v.t.* zukorken; verkorken
Phrasal verb
• **~ 'up** *v.t.* zukorken; verkorken; **~ up one's emotions** seine Gefühle unterdrücken
corkage /'kɔ:kɪdʒ/ *n., no pl.* Korkengeld, *das*
corked /kɔ:kt/ *adj.* **1** (stopped with cork) verkorkt **2** (impaired) korkig ‹*Wein*›
corker /'kɔ:kə(r)/ *n.* (coll.) (thing) **that joke was a real ~, that was a ~ of a joke** der Witz war echt Spitze (ugs.); (person) **she's/he's a real ~:** sie/er ist einsame Spitze (ugs.)
corking /'kɔ:kɪŋ/ *adj.* (coll.) (large) Riesen-; (excellent) klasse (ugs.)
cork: ~screw A *n.* (bottle opener) Korkenzieher, *der;* (spiral) Spirale, *die;* **B** *v.i.* ‹*Flugzeug:*› trudeln; **~ 'tile** *n.* Korkplatte, *die;* **~-tipped** *adj.* (Brit.) ‹*Zigarette*› mit Korkmundstück; **~wood** *n.* **1** (wood) Korkholz, *das;* **2** (tree) Korkholzbaum, *der*
corky /'kɔ:kɪ/ *adj.* korkig
corm /kɔ:m/ *n.* (Bot.) Knolle, *die*
cormorant /'kɔ:mərənt/ *n.* (Ornith.) Kormoran, *der*
corn¹ /kɔ:n/ *n.* **1** (cereal) Getreide, *das;* (esp. rye, wheat also) Korn, *das;* **[sweet]~** (maize) Mais, *der;* **~ on the cob** [gekochter/gerösteter] Maiskolben **2** (seed) Korn, *das*
corn² *n.* (on foot) Hühnerauge, *das;* **tread on sb.'s ~s** (fig.) jmdn. auf die Hühneraugen treten (ugs.)
corn cob *n.* Maiskolben, *der*
corncrake /'kɔ:nkreɪk/ *n.* (Ornith.) Wachtelkönig, *der*
corn: ~ dog *n.* (Amer.) Mais-Hotdog, *der;* **~ dolly** *n.* Strohpuppe, *die*
cornea /'kɔ:nɪə/ *n.* (Anat.) Hornhaut, *die;* Cornea, *die* (fachspr.)
corneal /'kɔ:nɪəl/ *adj.* (Anat.) Korneal- (fachspr.); Hornhaut-
corned beef /kɔ:nd 'bi:f/ *n.* Cornedbeef, *das*
cornelian 'cherry *n.* Kornelkirsche, *die*
corner /'kɔ:nə(r)/
A *n.* **1** Ecke, *die;* (curve) Kurve, *die;* **on the ~:** an der Ecke/in der Kurve; **at the ~:** an der Ecke; **~ of the street** Straßenecke, *die;* **sharp ~:** scharfe *od.* enge Kurve; **cut [off] a/the ~:** eine/die Kurve schneiden; **cut ~s** (fig.) auf die Schnelle arbeiten (ugs.); **cut ~s with sth.** (fig.) bei etw. pfuschen (ugs.); **[sth. is] just [a]round the ~:** [etw. ist] gleich um die Ecke; **Christmas is just round the ~** (fig. coll.) Weihnachten steht vor der Tür; **turn the ~:** um die Ecke biegen; **he has turned the ~ now** (fig.) er ist jetzt über den Berg (ugs.) **2** (hollow angle between walls) Ecke, *die;* (of mouth, eye) Winkel, *der;* **~ of the mouth/eye** Mund-/Augenwinkel, *der;* **drive sb. into a ~:** jmdn. in die Enge treiben; *see also* **paint B 1; tight A 9** **3** (Boxing, Wrestling) Ecke, *die* **4** (secluded place) Eckchen, *das;* Plätzchen, *das;* (remote region) Winkel, *der;* **from the four ~s of the earth** aus aller Welt **5** (Hockey/Footb.) Ecke, *die;* **score from a ~:** eine Ecke verwandeln; **take a ~:** eine Ecke schlagen/treten **6** (Commerc.) Corner, *der;* Schwänze, *die*
B *v.t.* **1** (drive into ~) in eine Ecke treiben; (fig.) in die Enge treiben; **have [got] sb. ~ed** jmdn. in der Falle haben **2** (Commerc.) **~ the market in coffee** die Kaffeevorräte aufkaufen; den Kaffeemarkt aufschwänzen (fachspr.)
C *v.i.* die Kurven nehmen; **~ well/badly** eine gute/schlechte Kurvenlage haben; **when ~ing** beim Kurvenfahren
corner: ~ cupboard *n.* Eckschrank, *der;* **~ flag** *n.* (Sport) Eckfahne, *die;* **~ hit** *n.* (Hockey) Eckball, *der;* Eckschlag, *der;* **score [a goal] from a ~ hit** einen Eckball verwandeln; **take a ~ hit** eine Ecke schlagen; **~ kick** *n.* (Footb.) Eckball, *der;* Eckstoß, *der;* **score from a ~ kick** einen Eckstoß verwandeln; **take a ~ kick** eine Ecke treten; **~ seat** *n.* Ecksitz, *der;* **~ shop** *n.* Tante-Emma-Laden, *der* (ugs.); **~stone** *n.* Eckstein, *der;* (fig.) Eckpfeiler, *der*
cornet /'kɔ:nɪt/ *n.* **1** (Brit.: wafer) [Eis]tüte, *die;* Eishörnchen, *das* **2** (Mus.) (instrument) Kornett, *das*
corn: ~ exchange *n.* Getreidebörse, *die;* **~field** *n.* Kornfeld, *das;* (Amer.) Maisfeld, *das;* **~flakes** *n. pl.* Cornflakes *Pl.;* **~flour** *n.* **1** (Brit.: ground maize) Maismehl, *das;* **2** (flour of rice etc.) Stärkemehl, *das;* **~flower** *n.* Kornblume, *die*
cornice /'kɔ:nɪs/ *n.* **1** (Archit.) Kranzgesims, *das* **2** (moulding) Fries, *der* (*an der Wand unmittelbar unter der Decke*) **3** (Mount.) [Schnee-]wächte, *die*
Cornish /'kɔ:nɪʃ/
A *adj.* kornisch
B *n.* Kornisch, *das*
Cornish: ~ 'cream ▸**Devonshire cream; ~ pasty** /kɔ:nɪʃ 'pæstɪ/ *n.: mit Fleisch, Kartoffeln und Zwiebeln gefülltes Blätterteiggebäck*
corn: ~ marigold *n.* Saatwucherblume, *die;* **~starch** (Amer.) ▸**~flour 1**
cornucopia /kɔ:njʊ'kəʊpɪə/ *n.* Füllhorn, *das;* **a ~ of information** (fig.) Information in Hülle und Fülle
corny /'kɔ:nɪ/ *adj.* (coll.) (old-fashioned) altmodisch ‹*Witz usw.*›; (trite) abgedroschen (ugs.); (sentimental) schmalzig (abwertend)
corolla /kə'rɒlə/ *n.* (Bot.) Krone, *die;* Korolla, *die*
corollary /kə'rɒlərɪ/ *n.* (proposition) Korollar[ium], *das* (Logik); (inference) Schluss, *der;* Folgerung, *die;* (consequence) [logische *od.* natürliche] Folge

corona /kə'rəʊnə/ n., pl. **~e** /kə'rəʊniː/ or **~s** 1) (circle of light round sun or moon) Hof, der; (gaseous envelope of sun) Korona, die 2) (Anat.) Corona, die

coronary /'kɒrənərɪ/
A adj. (Anat.) koronar
B n. (Med.) ▸**coronary thrombosis**

coronary: ~ 'artery n. (Anat.) Herzkranzarterie, die; Koronararterie, die (fachspr.); **~ throm'bosis** n. ▸ⓘ p. 1231 (Med.) Koronarthrombose, die

coronation /kɒrə'neɪʃn/ n. Krönung, die

coroner /'kɒrənə(r)/ n. Coroner, der; Beamter, der gewaltsame od. unnatürliche Todesfälle untersucht

coronet /'kɒrənet/ n. Krone, die

Corp. abbr. 1) (Mil.) = **corporal** ≈ Uffz. 2) (Amer.) = **corporation**

corpora pl. of **corpus**

corporal[1] /'kɔːpərl/ adj. körperlich; **~ punishment** Körperstrafen Pl.

corporal[2] n. ▸ⓘ p. 1634 (Mil.) Korporal, der (hist., österr.); ≈ Hauptgefreite, der; ≈ Stabsgefreite, der (DDR)

corporate /'kɔːpərət/ adj. 1) (forming corporation) körperschaftlich; **~ body, body ~**: Körperschaft, die; juristische Person 2) (of corporation) körperschaftlich; korporativ

corporate hospi'tality n., no pl. Kundenbewirtung, die

corporately /'kɔːpərətlɪ/ adv. körperschaftlich; korporativ

corporate 'raider n. Firmenaufkäufer, der/-aufkäuferin, die

corporation /kɔːpə'reɪʃn/ n. 1) (civic authority) **[municipal] ~**: Gemeindeverwaltung, die; (of borough, city) Stadtverwaltung, die 2) (united body) Körperschaft, die; Korporation, die; (artificial person) juristische Person; attrib. **~ tax** Körperschaft[s]steuer, die 3) (coll.: belly) Schmerbauch, der (ugs.); Wampe, die (ugs. abwertend)

corporative /'kɔːpərətɪv/ adj. 1) (of civic authorities) behördlich; (of united body) korporativ; (of artificial body) körperschaftlich 2) (organized in corporations) berufsständisch organisiert; korporativ ‹Organisation›; (governed by corporations) **~ state** Ständestaat, der

corporeal /kɔː'pɔːrɪəl/ adj. 1) (bodily) körperlich 2) (material) materiell; stofflich

corps /kɔː(r)/ n., pl. same /kɔːz/ Korps, das; see also **diplomatic corps**

corps: ~ de ballet /kɔː də 'bæleɪ/ n. Corps de ballet, das; Ballettkorps, das; **~ diplomatique** /kɔː dɪpləmæ'tiːk/ Corps diplomatique, das; diplomatisches Korps

corpse /kɔːps/ n. Leiche, die; Leichnam, der (geh.)

corpulence /'kɔːpjʊləns/, **corpulency** /'kɔːpjʊlənsɪ/ n. Korpulenz, die

corpulent /'kɔːpjʊlənt/ adj. korpulent

corpus /'kɔːpəs/ n., pl. **corpora** /'kɔːpərə/ (texts) Sammlung, die; Korpus, das

Corpus Christi /kɔːpəs 'krɪstɪ/ n. (Eccl.) Fronleichnam (der); Fronleichnamsfest, das

corpuscle /'kɔːpəsl/ n. 1) (Phys.) Korpuskel, das od. die 2) (Anat.) Corpusculum, das; **[blood] ~s** Blutkörperchen

corral /kə'rɑːl/
A n. 1) (Amer.: pen) Pferch, der 2) (Hist.: defensive enclosure) Wagenburg, die 3) (for wild animals) Korral, der
B v.t., **-ll-** 1) (Hist.: form into ~) zu einer Wagenburg formieren 2) (confine in ~) einpferchen 3) (Amer. coll.: acquire) einsacken (ugs.); mit Beschlag belegen ‹Person›

correct /kə'rekt/
A v.t. 1) (amend) korrigieren; verbessern, korrigieren ‹Fehler, Formulierung, jmds. Englisch/Deutsch›; **~ a few points** einige Punkte richtig stellen; **~ed for spelling mistakes** auf Rechtschreibfehler hin korrigiert; **these glasses should ~ your eyesight/vision** mit dieser Brille müssten Sie richtig sehen können; **~ the focus** die Bildschärfe richtig einstellen; **~ me if I'm wrong** ich könnte mich natürlich irren; **I stand ~ed** ich nehme das zurück 2) (counteract) ausgleichen ‹etw. Schädliches› 3) (admonish) zurechtweisen (**for** wegen) 4) (punish) bestrafen 5) (bring to standard) korrigieren (**for** hinsichtlich) 6) (eliminate aberration from) korrigieren (Optik)
B adj. richtig; korrekt; (precise) korrekt; akkurat; **that is ~**: das stimmt; **have you the ~ time?** haben Sie die genaue Uhrzeit?; **is that clock ~?** geht die Uhr richtig?; **am I ~ in assuming that ...?** gehe ich recht in der Annahme, dass ...?; **the ~ thing for you to do is to speak to the manager** darüber sollten Sie mit dem Abteilungsleiter sprechen; **what is the ~ thing to do in such a situation?** was soll man in so einer Situation korrekterweise tun?; **~ to five decimal places** auf fünf Dezimalstellen genau

correcting fluid /kə'rektɪŋ fluːɪd/ n. Korrekturflüssigkeit, die

correction /kə'rekʃn/ n. 1) (correcting) Korrektur, die; **I speak under ~**: ich sage das mit od. unter Vorbehalt; **I'm open to ~**: ich lasse mich korrigieren 2) (corrected version) **~s to the manuscript** Manuskriptkorrekturen; **the pupils had to write out** or **do their ~s** die Schüler mussten die Verbesserung od. Berichtigung schreiben 3) (punishment) Bestrafung, die; **house of ~** (arch.) Erziehungsheim, das; Besserungsanstalt, die (veralt.)

corrective /kə'rektɪv/ adj. korrigierend; **take ~ action** korrigierend eingreifen

correctly /kə'rektlɪ/ adv. richtig; korrekt; (precisely) korrekt; akkurat; **behave very ~**: sich sehr korrekt benehmen

correctness /kə'rektnɪs/ n., no pl. ▸**correct** B: Richtigkeit, die; Korrektheit, die; Akkuratesse, die

corrector /kə'rektə(r)/ n. Korrektor, der/Korrektorin, die

correlate /'kɒrɪleɪt/
A v.i. einander entsprechen; **~ with** or **to sth.** einer Sache (Dat.) entsprechen
B v.t. **~ sth. with sth.** etw. zu etw. in Beziehung setzen
C n. Korrelat, das

correlation /kɒrɪ'leɪʃn/ n. [Wechsel]beziehung, die; Korrelation, die (bes. Math., Naturw.); (connection) Zusammenhang, der

correlative /kə'relətɪv/ adj. 1) (having correlation) **~ [with** or **to sth.]** [mit etw.] korrelierend; **be ~ with** or **to sth.** mit etw. korrelieren 2) (Ling.) korrelativ

correspond /kɒrɪ'spɒnd/ v.i. 1) (be analogous, agree in amount) **~ [to each other]** einander entsprechen; **~ to sth.** einer Sache (Dat.) entsprechen; **do the classes ~ in number?** sind die Klassen gleich stark? 2) (agree in position) **~ [to sth.]** [mit etw.] übereinstimmen; (be in harmony) **~ [with** or **to sth.]** [mit etw.] zusammenpassen od. (geh.) korrespondieren 3) (communicate) **~ with sb.** mit jmdm. korrespondieren; **do you still ~ with your old school friends?** hast du noch Briefkontakt mit deinen alten Schulfreunden?

correspondence /kɒrɪ'spɒndəns/ n. 1) Übereinstimmung (**with, to** mit, **between** zwischen); **the ~ of form with** or **to** or **and content** die Übereinstimmung von Form und Inhalt 2) (communication, letters) Briefwechsel, der; Korrespondenz, die; **be in ~ with sb.** mit jmdm. im Briefwechsel od. in Korrespondenz stehen

correspondence: ~ college n. Fernschule, die; **~ column** n. Rubrik „Leserbriefe“; **~ course** n. Fernkurs, der; **~ school** ▸**~ college**

correspondent /kɒrɪ'spɒndənt/ n. 1) Briefschreiber, der/-schreiberin, die; (penfriend) Brieffreund, der/-freundin, die; (to newspaper) Leserbriefschreiber, der/-schreiberin, die; **be a good/bad ~**: ein fleißiger/fauler Briefschreiber sein 2) ▸ⓘ p. 1260 (Radio, Telev., Journ., etc.) Berichterstatter, der/-erstatterin, die; Korrespondent, der/Korrespondentin, die 3) (business ~) Geschäftspartner, der/-partnerin, die; Korrespondent, der/Korrespondentin, die (Kaufmannsspr.)

corresponding /kɒrɪ'spɒndɪŋ/ adj. 1) entsprechend (**to** Dat.); **the number of calories ~ to the amount of energy** die Anzahl der Kalorien, die der Energiemenge entspricht 2) **~ member** korrespondierendes Mitglied

correspondingly /kɒrɪ'spɒndɪŋlɪ/ adv. entsprechend

corrida /kɒ'riːdə/ n. Stierkampf, der; Corrida, die

corridor /'kɒrɪdɔː(r)/ n. 1) (inside passage) Flur, der; Gang, der; Korridor, der; (outside passage) Galerie, die; **in the ~s of power** (fig.) in den politischen Schaltstellen 2) (Railw.) [Seiten]gang, der

corridor: ~ coach n. (Railw.) Durchgangswagen, der; **~ train** n. Zug mit Durchgangswagen

corrie /'kɒrɪ/ n. (esp. Scot.) Kar, das (Geol.)

corrigenda /kɒrɪ'dʒendə/ n. pl. zu verbessernde Fehler; (in book) Korrigenda Pl.

corroborate /kə'rɒbəreɪt/ v.t. bestätigen; bekräftigen ‹Anspruch, Überzeugung›; (formally) [offiziell] bestätigen

corroboration /kərɒbə'reɪʃn/ n. ▸**corroborate**: Bestätigung, die; Bekräftigung, die; **in ~ of sth.** als od. zur Bestätigung od. Bekräftigung einer Sache (Gen.)

corroborative /kə'rɒbərətɪv/ adj. bekräftigend; bestätigend ‹Aussage›; erhärtend ‹Beweis›

corrode /kə'rəʊd/
A v.t. zerfressen; korrodieren, zerfressen ‹Metall, Gestein›; (fig.) aushöhlen
B v.i. zerfressen werden; ‹Gestein, Metall:› korrodieren, zerfressen werden; (fig.) ausgehöhlt werden

corrosion /kə'rəʊʒn/ n. Zerfall, der; (of metal, stone) Korrosion, die; (fig.) Aushöhlung, die

cor'rosion-resistant adj. korrosionsbeständig

corrosive /kə'rəʊsɪv/
A adj. zerstörend; korrosiv (bes. Chemie, Geol.); ätzend ‹Chemikalien›; (fig.) zerstörerisch
B n. Korrosion verursachender Stoff; (fig.) zerstörerische Kraft

corrosiveness /kə'rəʊsɪvnɪs/ n., no pl. zerstörende Wirkung; (of chemicals) ätzende Wirkung; (fig.) zersetzende Wirkung

corrugate /'kɒrʊgeɪt/ v.t. zerfurchen; (bend into ridges) wellen; **~d cardboard/paper** Wellpappe, die; **~d iron** Wellblech, das

corrugation /kɒrʊ'geɪʃn/ n. 1) Zerfurchung, die 2) (wrinkle, ridge mark) Furche, die; (ridge made by bending) Rille, die

corrupt /kə'rʌpt/
A adj. 1) (rotten) verunreinigt; schlecht; verfault ‹Körper› 2) (depraved) verkommen; verdorben (geh.); (influenced by bribery) korrupt; **~ practices** Korruption, die 3) (impure) verdorben, korrumpiert ‹Sprache›; (vitiated) verfälscht ‹Text, Buch›
B v.t. 1) (taint) verderben; verschmutzen ‹Luft, Wasser›; (fig.) zerstören 2) (deprave) korrumpieren; (bribe) bestechen 3) (destroy purity of) verderben; korrumpieren; (vitiate) verfälschen

corruption /kə'rʌpʃn/ n. 1) (decomposition) Fäulnis, die; Verwesung, die 2) (moral deterioration) Verdorbenheit, die (geh.) 3) (use of corrupt practices) Korruption, die 4) (perversion) Korrumpierung, die; Entstellung, die; (vitiation) Verfälschung, die

corruptness /kə'rʌptnɪs/ n., no pl. ▸**corrupt** A: Verunreinigung, die; Verfaultheit, die; Verkommenheit, die; Verdorbenheit, die (geh.); Korruptheit, die; Korrumpiertheit, die; Verfälschung, die

corsage /kɔː'sɑːʒ/ n. 1) (bodice) Korsage, die; Mieder, das 2) (bouquet) [Ansteck]sträußchen, das

corsair /'kɔːseə(r)/ n. (Hist.) Korsar, der

corselette /'kɔːsəlet/ n. Korselett, das

corset /'kɔːsɪt/
A n. 1) in sing. or pl. (woman's undergarment) Korsett, das 2) (garment worn for injury etc.) [Stütz]korsett, das
B v. refl. sich schnüren
C v.t. (fig.) einengen

Corsica /'kɔːsɪkə/ pr. n. Korsika (das)

Corsican /ˈkɔːsɪkən/ ▸❶ p. 1277, ▸❶ p. 1345
A adj. korsisch; **sb. is ~:** jmd. ist Korse/Korsin
B n. 1 (person) Korse, der/Korsin, die 2 (dialect) Korsisch, das

cortège /kɔːˈteɪʒ/ n. (funeral procession) Trauerzug, der

cortex /ˈkɔːteks/ n., pl. **cortices** /ˈkɔːtɪsiːz/ (Bot., Anat., Zool.) Rinde, die; Kortex, der (fachspr.)

cortical /ˈkɔːtɪkl/ adj. (Bot., Anat., Zool.) Rinden-; kortikal (fachspr.)

cortisone /ˈkɔːtɪzəʊn/ n. Kortison, das (Med.); Cortison, das (fachspr.)

corundum /kəˈrʌndəm/ n. Korund, der

coruscate /ˈkɒrəskeɪt/ v.i. funkeln; [auf]blitzen; (fig.) glänzen; brillieren

corvette /kɔːˈvet/ n. (Naut.) Korvette, die

cos¹ /kɒs/ n. Römischer Salat; Sommerendivie, die

cos², 'cos /kɒz/ (coll.) ▸**because**

cos³ /kɒs, kɒz/ abbr. (Math.) = **cosine** cos

cosecant /kəʊˈsiːkənt/ n. (Math.) Kosekans, der

cosh /kɒʃ/ (Brit. coll.)
A n. Totschläger, der; Knüppel, der
B v.t. niederknüppeln

co-signatory /kəʊˈsɪgnətərɪ/
A adj. mitunterzeichnend
B n. Mitunterzeichner, der/-unterzeichnerin, die

cosily /ˈkəʊzɪlɪ/ adv. bequem; gemütlich, behaglich ‹plaudern, wohnen›

cosine /ˈkəʊsaɪn/ n. (Math.) Kosinus, der

cosiness /ˈkəʊzɪnɪs/ n., no pl. ▸**cosy A 1**: Gemütlichkeit, die; Behaglichkeit, die

cosmetic /kɒzˈmetɪk/
A adj. (lit. or fig.) kosmetisch; **~ surgery** Schönheitschirurgie, die
B n. Kosmetikum, das

cosmetician /kɒzmeˈtɪʃn/ n. ▸❶ p. 1260 (Amer.) Kosmetiker, der/Kosmetikerin, die

cosmic /ˈkɒzmɪk/ adj. (lit. or fig.) kosmisch; **~ radiation** or **rays** kosmische Strahlung; Höhenstrahlung, die

cosmological /kɒzməˈlɒdʒɪkl/ adj. (Astron., Philos.) kosmologisch

cosmologist /kɒzˈmɒlədʒɪst/ n. (Astron.) Kosmologe, der/Kosmologin, die

cosmology /kɒzˈmɒlədʒɪ/ n. (Astron., Philos.) Kosmologie, die (fachspr.)

cosmonaut /ˈkɒzmənɔːt/ n. ▸❶ p. 1260 Kosmonaut, der/Kosmonautin, die

cosmopolitan /kɒzməˈpɒlɪtən/
A adj. kosmopolitisch; weltbürgerlich
B n. Kosmopolit, der/Kosmopolitin, die (geh.); Weltbürger, der/-bürgerin, die

cosmos /ˈkɒzmɒs/ n. 1 Kosmos, der; Weltall, das 2 (fig.: system) Kosmos, der

Cossack /ˈkɒsæk/ n. Kosak, der/Kosakin, die; **~ hat** Kosakenmütze, die; **~ trousers** Stiefelhose, die

cosset /ˈkɒsɪt/ v.t. [ver]hätscheln

cost /kɒst/
A n. 1 ▸❶ p. 1332 Kosten Pl.; **the ~ of bread/gas/oil** der Brot-/Gas-/Ölpreis; **the ~ of heating a house** die Heizkosten für ein Haus; **the ~ of travelling by public transport** die Kosten für die Benutzung der öffentlichen Verkehrsmittel; **regardless of ~, whatever the ~:** ganz gleich, was es kostet; **bear the ~ of sth.** die Kosten für etw. tragen; **do sth. at great/little ~ to sb./sth.** etw. unter großer/geringer finanzieller Belastung für jmdn./etw. tun; **[sell sth.] at ~:** [etw.] zum Selbstkostenpreis [verkaufen] 2 (fig.) Preis, der; **at all ~s, at any ~:** um jeden Preis; **at the ~ of sth.** auf Kosten einer Sache (Gen.); **at great ~ in human lives** um den Preis vieler Menschenleben; **whatever the ~:** koste es, was es wolle; **to my/his** etc. **~:** zu meinem/seinem usw. Nachteil; **as I know to my ~:** wie ich aus bitterer Erfahrung weiß; see also **count¹ B 1** 3 in pl. (Law) [Gerichts]kosten Pl.; **which party was ordered to pay ~s?** welche Seite hatte die [Gerichts]kosten zu tragen? **in the case A v. B, A was awarded ~s** in der Sache A gegen B wurden A die Kosten erstattet
B v.t. 1 ▸❶ p. 1332 p.t., p.p. **~** (lit. or fig.) kosten; **how much does it ~?** was kostet es?; **~ money** Geld kosten; **~ what it may, whatever it may ~:** koste es, was es wolle; **~ sb. sth.** jmdn. etw. kosten; **it'll ~ you** (coll.) das wird ein teures Vergnügen; **~ sb. dear[ly]** jmdm. od. jmdn. teuer zu stehen kommen; see also **arm¹ 1; earth A 6** 2 p.t., p.p. **~ed** (Commerc.: fix price of) **~ sth.** den Preis für etw. kalkulieren

cost accountant n. ▸❶ p. 1260 (Commerc.) Betriebskalkulator, der

co-star /ˈkəʊstɑː(r)/ (Cinemat., Theatre)
A n. **be a/the ~:** eine der Hauptrollen/die zweite Hauptrolle spielen; **Bogart and Bacall were ~s** Bogart und Bacall spielten die Hauptrollen
B v.i., **-rr-** eine der Hauptrollen spielen
C v.t., **-rr-: the film ~red Robert Redford** der Film zeigte Robert Redford in einer der Hauptrollen

Costa Rican /kɒstə ˈriːkən/ ▸❶ p. 1345
A adj. costa-ricanisch
B n. Costa-Ricaner, der/Costa-Ricanerin, die

cost: ~-'benefit adj. Kosten-Nutzen-; **~ centre** n. (Bookk.) Kostenstelle, die; **~ cutting** n. Kostensenkung, die; Kostendampfung, die; attrib. **~-cutting measures/programme** Sparmaßnahmen/Sparprogramm, das; **~-effective** adj. rentabel

coster[monger] /ˈkɒstə(mʌŋgə(r))/ n. (Brit.) Straßenhändler, der/-händlerin, die

costing /ˈkɒstɪŋ/ n. 1 (estimation of costs) Kostenberechnung, die 2 (costs) Kosten Pl.

costly /ˈkɒstlɪ/ adj. 1 teuer; kostspielig 2 (fig.) **a ~ victory** ein teuer erkaufter Sieg; **a ~ error** ein folgenschwerer Irrtum

cost: ~ of 'living n. Lebenshaltungskosten Pl; **~-of-living allowance** Ausgleichszulage, die; **~-of-living bonus** Teuerungszulage, die; **~-of-living index** Lebenshaltungsindex, der; **~ price** n. Selbstkostenpreis, der

costume /ˈkɒstjuːm/
A n. 1 Kleidermode, die; (theatrical ~) Kostüm, das; **the ~ of the nation** die Nationaltracht; **historical ~s** historische Kostüme; **Highland ~:** schottische Tracht 2 (dated: jacket and skirt) Kostüm, das
B v.t. ausstatten

costume: ~ ball n. Kostümfest, das; Kostümball, der; **~ designer** n. Kostümbildner, der/-bildnerin, die; **~ 'jewellery** n. Modeschmuck, der; **~ piece, ~ play** ns. Kostümstück, das

costumier /kɒˈstjuːmɪə(r)/ (**costumer** /ˈkɒstjʊmə(r)/) ns. ▸❶ p. 1260 Kostümschneider, der/-schneiderin, die; (hirer of costumes) Kostümverleiher, der/-verleiherin, die

cosy /ˈkəʊzɪ/
A adj. 1 gemütlich; behaglich ‹Atmosphäre›; bequem ‹Sessel›; **feel ~:** sich wohl od. behaglich fühlen; **be ~:** es gemütlich haben; **a ~ feeling** ein Gefühl der Behaglichkeit 2 (derog.: complacent, convenient) bequem; **they have a very ~ relationship** sie passen zueinander wie ein altes Paar Filzpantoffeln
B n. ▸**egg cosy; tea cosy**

Phrasal verb

• **~ 'up to** v.i. (coll.) **~ up to the fireplace** es sich (Dat.) am Kamin gemütlich machen; **~ up to sb.** mit jmdm. vertraulich werden; (ingratiate oneself with sb.) sich bei jmdm. einschmeicheln

cot /kɒt/ n. (Brit.: child's bed) Kinderbett, das; **the baby cried in his ~:** das Baby schrie in seinem Bettchen

cotangent /kəʊˈtændʒənt/ n. (Math.) Kotangens, der

'cot death n. (Brit.) plötzlicher Kindstod; Cotdeath, der (Med.)

cote /kəʊt/ n. Stall, der; see also **dovecote**

coterie /ˈkəʊtərɪ/ n. Zirkel, der; **artistic ~:** Künstlerkreis, der

cotoneaster /kətəʊnɪˈæstə(r)/ n. (Bot.) Zwergmispel, die

cottage /ˈkɒtɪdʒ/ n. Cottage, das; Häuschen, das

cottage: ~ 'cheese n. Hüttenkäse, der; **~ 'hospital** n.: kleines [Land]krankenhaus ohne ständige ärztliche Betreuung; **~ industry** n. Heimarbeit, die; **~ loaf** n.: eine Art rundes Weißbrot; **~ 'pie** n.: mit Kartoffelbrei überbackenes Hackfleisch

cottager /ˈkɒtɪdʒə(r)/ n. Cottagebewohner, der/-bewohnerin, die

cotter /ˈkɒtə(r)/ n. **~ [pin]** Splint, der

cotton /ˈkɒtn/
A n. (substance, plant) Baumwolle, die; (thread) Baumwollgarn, das; (cloth) Baumwollstoff, der
B attrib. adj. Baumwoll-
C v.i. **~ 'on** (coll.) kapieren (ugs.); **~ 'on to** (coll.) (catch on to) spitzkriegen (ugs.); (understand) kapieren (ugs.); **~ to sb.** (Amer.) sich mit jmdm. anfreunden

cotton: ~ belt n. (Geog.) Baumwollgürtel, der; **~ candy** n. (Amer.) Zuckerwatte, die; **~ gin** n. (machine) Egreniermaschine, die (fachspr.); **~ mill** n. Baumwollspinnerei, die; **~-picking** adj. (Amer. coll.) verdammt; verflucht; **~ plant** n. Baumwollpflanze, die; **~ 'print** n. bedruckter Baumwollstoff; **~ reel** n. [Näh]garnrolle, die; **~ spinner** n. Baumwollspinner, der/-spinnerin, die; **~ spinning** n. Baumwollspinnerei, die; **~tail** n. (Amer. Zool.) Waldkaninchen, das; Baumwollschwanzkaninchen, das; **~ 'waste** n. Putzwolle, die; **~ 'wool** n. 1 Watte, die; **~-wool ball** Wattebausch, der; **wrap sb. up** or **keep sb. in ~ wool** (fig.) jmdn. in Watte packen; 2 (Amer.: raw ~) Rohbaumwolle, die

cottony /ˈkɒtənɪ/ adj. baumwollartig ‹Substanz›; flaumig, behaart ‹Blatt›

cotyledon /kɒtɪˈliːdən/ n. (Bot.) Keimblatt, das

couch¹ /kaʊtʃ/
A n. 1 (sofa) Couch, die 2 **doctor's ~:** [Untersuchungs]liege, die; **psychiatrist's ~:** Couch [des Psychiaters] 3 (arch./literary: bed) Lager, das
B v.t. formulieren; **~ed in modest terms** in bescheidener Sprache abgefasst

couch² /kuːtʃ, kaʊtʃ/ n. **~[grass]** (Bot.) Quecke, die

couchette /kuːˈʃet/ n. (Railw.) Liegewagen, der; (berth) Liegewagenplatz, der

couch po'tato n. (coll.) Couchpotato[e], der

cougar /ˈkuːgə(r)/ n. (Amer. Zool.) Puma, der

cough /kɒf/
A n. (act of coughing, condition) Husten, der; **give a ~:** husten; **have a [bad] ~:** [einen schlimmen] Husten haben
B v.i. 1 husten 2 ‹Motor:› stottern
C v.t. **~ out** [her]aushusten; (say with ~) husten; **~ up** [her]aushusten; (coll.: pay) ausspucken (ugs.); **come on, ~ up!** na los, spuck's aus!

'cough drop ▸**cough sweet**

coughing /ˈkɒfɪŋ/ n. Husten, das; Gehuste, das; **there was a lot of ~:** es wurde ständig gehustet; **a bout of ~:** ein Hustenanfall

cough: ~ medicine n. Hustenmittel, das; **~ mixture** n. Hustensaft, der; **~ sweet** n. Hustenbonbon, das od. der

could ▸**can²**

couldn't /ˈkʊdnt/ (coll.) = **could not;** ▸**can²**

coulomb /ˈkuːlɒm/ n. (Electr.) Coulomb, das; Amperesekunde, die

council /ˈkaʊnsl/ n. 1 Ratsversammlung, die; **family ~:** Familienrat, der 2 (administrative/advisory body) Rat, der; **local ~:** Gemeinderat, der; **city/town ~:** Stadtrat, der; **C~ of Europe** Europarat, der; **C~ of Ministers** (EU) Ministerrat, der 3 (Eccl.) Konzil, das; **diocesan ~:** Diözesanrat, der

> **council**
>
> Gewählte Versammlung, die für die Verwaltung eines bestimmten Gebietes in Großbritannien zuständig ist. Dieses Gebiet kann eine **county** (Grafschaft) sein, Teil eines Landkreises, eine Stadt oder ein Teil einer größeren Stadt. Der *council* ist dafür verantwortlich, die Straßen und Gemeinschaftseinrichtungen instand zu halten, und stellt eine breite Palette öffentlicher Dienstleistungen bereit.

council: ~ chamber n. Sitzungssaal [des Rats]; **~ estate** n. Wohnviertel mit Sozialwohnungen; **~ flat** n. (esp. Brit.) Sozialwohnung, die; **~ house** n. Haus des sozialen

Wohnungsbaus; ~ **housing** *n.* sozialer Wohnungsbau

council house

Ein Haus in Großbritannien, das vom lokalen **council** zu einem vergleichsweise niedrigen Preis vermietet wird. Diese Häuser und *council flats* (Sozialwohnungen) sind Eigentum des *councils*. Allerdings wurden ab 1980 viele dieser Wohnungen an ihre Bewohner verkauft.

councillor /ˈkaʊnsələ(r)/ *n.* ▸❶ **p. 1260**, ▸❶ **p. 1634** Ratsmitglied, *das;* **town** ~: Stadtrat, *der*/-rätin, *die*

council: ~ **man** /ˈkaʊnslmən/ *n., pl.* ~**men** /ˈkaʊnslmən/ (esp. Amer.) [Gemeinde-/Stadt]ratsmitglied, *das;* ~ **meeting** *n.* Ratssitzung, *die;* ~ **of ˈwar** *n.* (lit. or fig.) Kriegsrat, *der;* ~ **tax** *n., no pl.* (Brit.) Wohnsteuer, *die;* ~ **tenant** *n.* Sozialmieter, *der*/-mieterin, *die*

council tax

Eine Steuer, die jeder Haushalt in Großbritannien an die lokale oder kommunale Verwaltung entrichten muss. Die Höhe der *council tax* berechnet sich aus dem Schätzwert des Hauses bzw. der Wohnung sowie aus der Anzahl der Personen im Haushalt.

counsel /ˈkaʊnsl/
A *n.* **1** (consultation) Beratung, *die;* **take/hold** ~ **with sb. [about sth.]** sich mit jmdm. [über etw. (*Akk.*)] beraten **2** Rat[schlag], *der;* ~ **of perfection** Vollkommenheitsforderung, *die* (Rel.); (fig.) ideale Forderung; **keep one's own** ~: seine Meinung für sich behalten **3** *pl. same* (Law) Rechtsanwalt, *der*/-anwältin, *die;* ~ **for the defence** Verteidiger, *der*/Verteidigerin, *die;* ~ **for the prosecution** Anklagevertreter, *der*/-vertreterin, *die;* Staatsanwalt, *der*/-anwältin, *die;* **Queen's/King's C~**: Anwalt/Anwältin der Krone; Kronanwalt, *der*/-anwältin, *die*
B *v.t.*, (Brit.) **-ll-**: **1** (advise) beraten; ~ **sb. to do sth.** jmdm. raten *od.* den Rat geben, etw. zu tun **2** (suggest) ~ **forbearance** *etc.* zur Nachsicht *usw.* raten

counselling (*Amer.:* **counseling**) /ˈkaʊnsəlɪŋ/ *n.* Beratung, *die;* **marriage** ~: Eheberatung, *die*

counsellor, (Amer.) **counselor** /ˈkaʊnsələ(r)/ *n.* ▸❶ **p. 1260** **1** Berater, *der*/Beraterin, *die;* **marriage-guidance** ~: Eheberater, *der*/-beraterin, *die;* **[student]** ~: Studienberater, *der*/-beraterin, *die* **2** (Diplom.) Botschaftsrat, *der*/-rätin, *die* **3** (Law) ~ **[-at-law]** (Amer.: barrister) Rechtsanwalt, *der*/-anwältin, *die* **4** (Brit.) **C~ of State** Stellvertreter des Königs/der Königin

count¹ /kaʊnt/
A *n.* **1** Zählen, *das;* Zählung, *die* ; **keep** ~ **[of sth.]** [etw.] zählen; **I'm going to keep** ~ **of the number of times he says 'incredible'** ich werde mitzählen, wie oft er „unglaublich" sagt; **lose** ~: beim Zählen durcheinander geraten; **lose** ~ **of sth.** etw. gar nicht mehr zählen können; **have/take/make a** ~: zählen; **on the** ~ **of three** bei „drei" **2** (sum total) Ergebnis, *das* **3** (Law) Anklagepunkt, *der;* **on all** ~**s** in allen [Anklage]punkten; **on that** ~ (fig.) in diesem Punkt **4** (Boxing) Auszählen, *das;* **be out for the** ~: ausgezählt werden; (fig.) hinüber sein (ugs.) **5** (Phys.) (event) Impuls, *der;* (total number) Impulszahl, *die*
B *v.t.* **1** zählen; ~ **ten** bis zehn zählen; ~ **the votes** die Stimmen [aus]zählen; ~ **again** nachzählen; ~ **the pennies** (fig.) jeden Cent umdrehen; sparsam sein; ~ **the cost** (fig.) unter den Folgen zu leiden haben **2** (include) mitzählen; **be** ~**ed against sb.** gegen jmdn. sprechen; **not** ~**ing** abgesehen von **3** (consider) halten für; ~ **oneself lucky** sich glücklich schätzen können; ~ **sb. as one of us/a friend** jmdn. als einen von uns/als Freund betrachten; **I** ~ **him [as] one of the family** er gehört für mich zur Familie; ~ **sb. among one's friends/clients** jmdn. zu seinen Freunden/Kunden zählen
C *v.i.* **1** zählen; ~ **from one to ten** von eins bis zehn zählen; ~ **[up] to ten** bis zehn zählen **2** (be included) zählen; **every moment** ~**s** jede Sekunde zählt; ~ **against sb.** gegen jmdn. sprechen; **money** ~**s/looks** ~: Geld/Aussehen ist wichtig; **money is what** ~**s** Geld ist das, was zählt; ~ **for much/little** viel/wenig zählen; **appearances** ~ **for a great deal** *or* **a lot** der äußere Schein macht viel aus **3** (conduct a reckoning) zählen; ~**ing from now** von jetzt an [gerechnet]; ab jetzt

Phrasal verbs

- ~ **ˈdown**
A *v.i.* rückwärts zählen
B *v.t.* ~ **sth. down** den *od.* das Count-down für etw. durchführen. *See also* **countdown**
- ~ **ˈin** *v.t.* mitrechnen; ~ **sb. in on a venture** jmdn. bei einem Unternehmen einplanen; **shall I** ~ **you in?** machst/kommst du mit? **you can** ~ **me in** ich bin dabei
- ~ **on** *v.t.* ~ **on sb./sth.** sich auf jmdn./etw. verlassen; **you mustn't** ~ **on winning first prize** du darfst nicht damit rechnen, den ersten Preis zu gewinnen
- ~ **ˈout** *v.t.* **1** (one by one) abzählen **2** (exclude) **[you can]** ~ **me out** ich komme/mache nicht mit **3** (Boxing) auszählen **4** (Brit. Parl.) ~ **the House out** die Sitzung wegen Beschlussunfähigkeit vertagen
- ~ **ˈup** *v.t.* zusammenzählen; zusammenrechnen
- ~ **upon** ▸~ **on**

count² *n.* ▸❶ **p. 1634** (nobleman) Graf, *der*

countable /ˈkaʊntəbl/ *adj.* (also Ling.) zählbar

ˈcountdown *n.* Countdown, *der od. das*

countenance /ˈkaʊntɪnəns/
A *n.* **1** (literary: face) Antlitz, *das* (dichter.) **2** (formal: expression) Gesichtsausdruck, *der;* **change** ~: den Gesichtsausdruck verändern; **keep** ~: keine Miene verziehen **3** (dated/formal: composure) Haltung, *die;* **keep sb. in** ~ (arch.) jmdn. ermuntern *od.* aufrichten; **keep one's** ~: Haltung *od.* die Fassung bewahren; **lose** ~: die Fassung verlieren; **put sb. out of** ~: jmdn. aus der Fassung bringen **4** (dated/formal: moral support) Ermutigung, *die;* [moralische] Unterstützung; **give** ~ **to sb./sth.** jmdn./etw. unterstützen
B *v.t.* (formal) (approve) billigen; gutheißen; (support) unterstützen

counter¹ /ˈkaʊntə(r)/ *n.* **1** (in shop) Ladentisch, *der;* (in cafeteria, restaurant, train) Büfett, *das;* (in post office, bank) Schalter, *der;* ~ **clerk** ▸❶ **p. 1260** Schalterbeamte, *der*/-beamtin, *die;* **these medicines/weapons can be bought over the** ~: diese Arzneimittel kann man ohne Rezept kaufen/diese Waffen kann man ohne Waffenschein kaufen; **[buy/sell sth.] under the** ~ (fig.) [etwas] unter dem Ladentisch [kaufen/verkaufen] **2** (small disc for games) Spielmarke, *die;* (token representing coin) Jeton, *der* **3** (apparatus for counting) Zähler, *der*

counter²
A *adj.* entgegengesetzt; Gegen-/gegen-
B *v.t.* **1** (oppose, contradict) begegnen (+ *Dat.*) **2** (meet by ~move) kontern; zurückschlagen
C *v.i.* **1** (make ~move) antworten; kontern **2** (Boxing) kontern
D *adv.* **1** (in the opposite direction) in entgegengesetzter Richtung; **go/run** ~: in die falsche Richtung gehen/laufen **2** (contrary) **act** ~ **to** zuwiderhandeln (+ *Dat.*); **go** ~ **to** zuwiderlaufen (+ *Dat.*); **run** ~ **to** im Widerspruch stehen zu
E *n.* **1** (Boxing) Konter, *der* **2** (~move) Antwort, *die* (**to** auf + *Akk.*)

counter³ *n.* (Naut.) Gilling, *die*

counter: ~**ˈact** *v.t.* entgegenwirken (+ *Dat.*); ~**ˈaction** *n.* Gegenwirkung, *die;* ~**argument** *n.* Gegenargument, *das;* ~**-attack** (lit. or fig.) **A** *n.* Gegenangriff, *der;* **B** *v.t.* ~**-attack sb.** gegen jmdn. einen Gegenangriff richten; **C** *v.i.* zurückschlagen; ~**-attraction** *n.* **1** (rival) Konkurrenz, *die;* **2** (of contrary tendency) entgegengesetzte Anziehungskraft; ~**balance** **A** *v.t.* ein Gegengewicht bilden zu; (fig.: neutralize) ausgleichen; **B** *n.* (lit. or fig.) Gegengewicht, *das;* ~**blast** *n.* Gegenschlag, *der;* ~**charge** *n.* Gegenbeschuldigung, *die;* Gegenklage, *die* (Rechtsspr.); ~**check** *n.* **1** (double check) Gegenkontrolle, *die;* **2** (check that opposes a thing) Gegenkraft, *die;* ~**claim** (Law) **A** *n.* Gegenforderung, *die;* **B** *v.t.* eine Gegenforderung erheben auf (+ *Akk.*); ~**ˈclockwise** ▸**anticlockwise**; ~**culture** *n.* Gegenkultur, *die;* ~**-ˈespionage** *n.* Spionageabwehr, *die;* Gegenspionage, *die*

counterfeit /ˈkaʊntəfɪt, ˈkaʊntəfiːt/
A *adj.* falsch, unecht ‹*Schmuck*›; falsch, gefälscht ‹*Unterschrift, Münze, Banknote*›; (fig. literary) vorgetäuscht ‹*Emotionen*›; ~ **money** Falschgeld, *das*
B *v.t.* **1** (forge) fälschen **2** (fig.: simulate) vortäuschen

counterfeiter /ˈkaʊntəfɪtə(r)/ *n.* (forger) Fälscher, *der*/Fälscherin, *die*

counter: ~**foil** *n.* Kontrollabschnitt, *der;* ~**insurgency** /kaʊntərɪnˈsɜːdʒənsɪ/ *n., no pl.* Aufstandsbekämpfung, *die; attrib.* ~**insurgency forces** Antiguerillatruppen; ~**-inˈtelligence** *n.* ▸~**-espionage**; ~**-inˈtuitive** *adj.* überraschend ‹*Ergebnis, Wirkung*›; abwegig [erscheinend] ‹*Idee, Argument, Behauptung*›; ~**ˈirritant** *n.* (Med.) Hautreizmittel, *das*

countermand /kaʊntəˈmɑːnd/ *v.t.* **1** (revoke) widerrufen **2** (cancel order for) abstellen ‹*Waren*›; ~ **an action/payment** die Anweisung für eine Handlung/Zahlung zurücknehmen **3** (recall) zurückrufen

counter: ~**measure** *n.* Gegenmaßnahme, *die;* ~**move** *n.* Gegenzug, *der;* ~**offensive** *n.* (Mil.) Gegenoffensive, *die;* ~**-offer** *n.* Gegenangebot, *das*

counterpane /ˈkaʊntəpeɪn/ *n.* (dated) Tagesdecke, *die*

counter: ~**part** *n.* Gegenstück, *das* (**of** zu); Pendant, *das* (geh.) (**of** zu); ~**point** *n.* (Mus.) Kontrapunkt, *der;* ~**poise** *n.* Gegengewicht, *das;* ~**proˈductive** *adj.* das Gegenteil des Gewünschten bewirkend; **sth. is** ~**productive** etw. bewirkt das Gegenteil des Gewünschten; ~**-proposal** *n.* Gegenvorschlag, *der;* **C~-Reformation** *n.* (Hist.) Gegenreformation, *die;* ~**-revolution** *n.* Gegenrevolution, *die;* Konterrevolution, *die* (bes. marx.); ~**-revolutionary** **A** *adj.* gegenrevolutionär; konterrevolutionär (bes. marx.); **B** *n.* Konterrevolutionär, *der*/-revolutionärin, *die;* ~**shaft** *n.* (Mech. Engin.) Transmissionswelle, *die;* (Amer.: layshaft) Vorgelegewelle, *die;* ~**sign** **A** *v.t.* **1** (add signature to) gegenzeichnen; **2** (ratify) bestätigen; **B** *n.* (Mil.: password) Parole, *die;* ~**ˈsignature** *n.* Gegenunterschrift, *die;* ~**sink** *v.t.*, ~**sunk** /ˈkaʊntəsʌŋk/ (Woodw., Metalw.) **1** (bevel off) senken ‹*Loch*›; **2** (sink) versenken ‹*Schraube*›; ~**stroke** *n.* Gegenschlag, *der;* ~**-ˈtenor** *n.* (Mus.) Contratenor, *der;* ~**ˈterrorism** *n., no pl.* Terrorbekämpfung, *die;* ~**weight** *n.* Gegengewicht, *das*

countess /ˈkaʊntɪs/ *n.* ▸❶ **p. 1634** Gräfin, *die*

counting house /ˈkaʊntɪŋhaʊs/ *n.* (dated) Kontor, *das* (veralt.)

countless /ˈkaʊntlɪs/ *adj.* zahllos; ~ **numbers of** eine zahllose Menge von

ˈcount noun *n.* (Ling.) zählbares Substantiv; Individualsubstantiv, *das*

countrified /ˈkʌntrɪfaɪd/ *adj.* ländlich

country /ˈkʌntrɪ/ *n.* **1** Land, *das;* (fatherland) Heimat, *die;* **sb.'s [home]** ~: jmds. Heimat; **fight/die for one's** ~: für sein [Vater]land kämpfen/sterben; **farming** ~: Ackerland, *das;* **this is excellent bird-watching** ~: das ist eine Gegend, in der man hervorragend Vögel beobachten kann; **densely wooded** ~: dicht bewaldetes Gebiet; **this is unknown** ~ **to me** (fig.) das ist Neuland *od.* unbekanntes Gelände für mich; **[the] Hardy** ~: das Land Hardys **2** (rural district) Land, *das;* (~side) Landschaft, *die;* ~ **road/air** Landstraße, *die*/Landluft, *die;* ~ **inn** [ländlicher] Gasthof; **[be/live** *etc.***] in the** ~: auf dem Land [sein/leben *usw.*]; **to the** ~: aufs Land; **[go/travel** *etc.***] across** ~: über Land [fahren/reisen *usw.*]; **up** ~ (Richtung) ins Landesinnere; (Lage) im Landesinneren; **in the** ~ (Cricket coll.) weit draußen **3** (Brit.: population) Volk, *das;* **appeal** *or* **go to the** ~: den Wähler entscheiden lassen

country: ~**-and-ˈwestern** *adj.* Country-und-Western-; ~ **club** *n.* Country Club, *der;* ~ **ˈcousin** *n.* Landei, *das* (ugs. abwertend);

(woman also) Landpomeranze, *die* (ugs. abwertend); ~ **'dance** *n.* Kontertanz, *der;* ~ **'dancing** *n.* Kontertanz, *der*

countryfied ▸**countrified**

country: ~ **folk** *n.* Landbewohner *Pl.;* ~ **'gentleman** *n.* Landbesitzer, *der;* ~ **'house** *n.* Landhaus, *das;* ~ **life** *n.* Landleben, *das;* **~man** /'kʌntrɪmən/ *n., pl.* **~men** /'kʌntrɪmən/ **1** (national) Landsmann, *der;* **[my/her** *etc.***] fellow ~man** [mein/ihr *usw.*] Landsmann; **2** (rural) Landbewohner, *der;* ~ **music** *n.* Countrymusic, *die;* ~ **'park** *n.* Naturpark, *der;* ~ **people** *n. pl.* Landbewohner *Pl.;* ~ **'seat** *n.* Landsitz, *der;* **~side** *n.* **1** (rural areas) Land, *das;* **the preservation of the ~side** die Erhaltung der Landschaft; **2** (rural scenery) Landschaft, *die;* **C~side Commission** *n.* (Brit.) Landschaftsschutzkommission, *die;* **~wide** *adj.* landesweit; **~woman** *n.* **1** (national) Landsmännin, *die;* **my fellow ~woman** meine Landsmännin; **2** (rural) Landbewohnerin, *die*

county /'kaʊntɪ/

A *n.* **1** (Brit.) Grafschaft, *die;* (Amer., Commonwealth) Verwaltungsbezirk, *der* **2** (Brit.: gentry) Gentry [der/einer Grafschaft]

B *adj.* (Brit.) *den Lebensstil reicher Grundbesitzer pflegend;* ≈ junkerhaft

> **county**
>
> Ein Verwaltungsbezirk in vielen Teilen Großbritanniens. Die *counties* bilden die Hauptverwaltungseinheiten und viele haben noch die alten Grenzen. Allerdings wurden in den letzten Jahrzehnten viele Grenzen und Namen geändert und die Bezeichnung *county* wird jetzt nicht immer verwendet. In Schottland werden die Hauptverwaltungsbezirke **regions** genannt. In den USA sind die einzelnen Staaten überwiegend in *counties* unterteilt.

county: ~ **'borough** *n.* (Hist./Ir.) *Stadt mit dem Status einer Grafschaft;* ~ **'council** *n.* Grafschaftsrat, *der;* ~ **'court** *n.* (Law) (Brit.) Grafschaftsgericht, *das;* (Amer.) *Zivil- und Strafgericht;* ~ **'cricket** *n.* (Brit.) *Kricketspiele zwischen Grafschaftsauswahlen;* ~ **family** *n.: alteingesessene [Adels]familie;* ~ **school** *n.: von der Grafschaft bezuschusste öffentliche Schule;* ~ **'seat** *n.* (Amer.) ≈ Bezirksstadt, *die;* ~ **'town** *n.* (Brit.) *Verwaltungssitz einer Grafschaft*

coup /ku:/ *n.* **1** Coup, *der;* **pull off** (coll.) *or* **make a ~:** einen Coup landen (ugs.) **2** ▸**coup d'état**

coup: ~ **de grâce** /ku: də 'grɑ:s/ *n.* Todesstoß, *der;* ~ **d'état** /ku: der'tɑ:/ *n.* Staatsstreich, *der;* ~ **de théâtre** /ku: də ter'ɑ:tr/ *n.* Theatercoup, *der*

coupé /'ku:peɪ/ (Amer.: **coupe** [ku:p]) *n.* (car) Coupé, *das*

couple /kʌpl/

A *n.* **1** (pair) Paar, *das;* (married) [Ehe]paar, *das;* (dancing) [Tanz]paar, *das;* **in ~s** paarweise **2** **a ~ [of]** (a few) ein paar; (two) zwei; **a ~ of people/things/days/weeks** *etc.* ein paar/zwei Leute/Dinge/Tage/Wochen *usw.;* **a ~ of times** ein paarmal/zweimal **3** (Mech.) Kräftepaar, *das*

B *v.t.* **1** (associate) verbinden; **be ~d with sth.** mit etw. verbunden sein **2** (fasten together) koppeln

C *v.i.* sich paaren

Phrasal verbs

- ~ **'on** *v.t.* ankoppeln
- ~ **to'gether** *v.t.* ankoppeln; (fig.) miteinander in Verbindung bringen
- ~ **'up** *v.t.* ankoppeln

coupler /'kʌplə(r)/ *n.* (Mus.) Koppel, *die*

couplet /'kʌplɪt/ *n.* (Pros.) Verspaar, *das;* (rhyming) Reimpaar, *das*

coupling /'kʌplɪŋ/ *n.*(Railw., Mech. Engin.) Kupplung, *die*

coupon /'ku:pɒn/ *n.* (detachable ticket) Abschnitt, *der;* (for rationed goods) Marke, *die;* (in advertisement) Gutschein, *der;* Coupon, *der;* (entry form for football pool etc.) Tippschein, *der;* (voucher) Gutschein, *der*

courage /'kʌrɪdʒ/ *n.* Mut, *der;* **have/lack the ~ to do sth.** den Mut haben/nicht den Mut haben, etw. zu tun; **take one's ~ in both hands** sein Herz in beide Hände nehmen; **sb. takes ~ from sth.** etw. macht jmdm. Mut; **take ~!** nur Mut!; **lose ~:** den Mut verlieren; **have the ~ of one's convictions** zu seiner Überzeugung stehen

courageous /kə'reɪdʒəs/ *adj.* mutig

courageously /kə'reɪdʒəslɪ/ *adv.* mutig

courageousness /kə'reɪdʒəsnɪs/ *n., no pl.* Mut, *der*

courgette /kʊə'ʒet/ *n.* (Brit.) Zucchino, *der*

courier /'kʊrɪə(r)/ *n.* ▸**ⓘ p. 1260** **1** (Tourism) Reiseleiter, *der*/-leiterin, *die* **2** (messenger) Kurier, *der*

'courier company *n.* Kurierdienst, *der*

course /kɔ:s/

A *n.* **1** (of ship, plane) Kurs, *der;* **change [one's] ~** (lit. or fig.) den Kurs wechseln; ~ **[of action]** Vorgehensweise, *die;* **what are our possible ~s of action?** welche Möglichkeiten haben wir?; **the most sensible ~ would be to ...:** das Vernünftigste wäre, zu ...; **in the ordinary ~ of things** *or* **events** unter normalen Umständen; **the ~ of nature/history** der Lauf der Dinge/Geschichte; **run** *or* **take its ~:** seinen/ihren Lauf nehmen; **let things take their ~:** den Dingen ihren Lauf lassen; **off/on ~:** vom Kurs abgekommen/auf Kurs; **be on ~ for sth.** (fig.) auf etw. (*Akk.*) zusteuern **2** **of ~:** natürlich; **[do sth.] as a matter of ~:** [etw.] selbstverständlich [tun] **3** (progression) Lauf, *der;* **in due ~:** zu gegebener Zeit; **the road is in ~ of construction** die Straße wird gerade gebaut; **be in the ~ of doing sth.** gerade dabei sein, etw. zu tun; **in the ~ of a few minutes** im Laufe von wenigen Minuten; **in the ~ of the lesson/the day/his life** im Lauf[e] der Stunde/des Tages/seines Lebens; **in the ~ of time/our relationship** im Lauf[e] der Zeit/unserer Beziehung **4** (of river etc.) Lauf, *der* **5** (of meal) Gang, *der* **6** (Sport) Kurs, *der;* (for race) Rennstrecke, *die;* **[golf] ~:** [Golf]platz, *der* **7** (Educ.) Kurs[us], *der;* (for employee also) Lehrgang, *der;* (book) Lehrbuch, *das;* **a ~ of lectures** eine Vorlesungsreihe; **go to** *or* **attend/do a ~ in sth.** einen Kurs in etw. (*Dat.*) besuchen/machen; **be/go on a ~:** auf einem Lehrgang sein/zu einem Lehrgang gehen **8** (Med.) **a ~ of treatment** eine Kur; **a ~ of tablets** eine Tablettenkur **9** (Building) Schicht, *die*

B *v.i.* (rhet.: flow) strömen

course: **~book** *n.* (Brit.) Lehrbuch, *das;* ~ **ma'terial** *n.* Unterrichtsmaterial, *das;* **~work** *n., no pl.* Kursarbeit, *die*

coursing /'kɔ:sɪŋ/ *n.* (Sport) Hetzjagd, *die*

court /kɔ:t/

A *n.* **1** Hof, *der;* (Brit.: quadrangle) [Innen]hof [des/eines Colleges] (in Cambridge); (hall in building) ≈ Halle, *die* **2** (Sport) Spielfeld, *das;* (Tennis, Squash also) Platz, *der* **3** (of sovereign) Hof, *der;* **the C~ of St James's** (Brit.) der englische Königshof; **hold ~** (fig.) Hof halten (scherzh.) **4** (Law) Gericht, *das;* (**~room**) Gerichtssaal, *der;* ~ **of law** *or* **justice** Gerichtshof, *der;* **go to ~ [over sth.]** [wegen *od.* mit etw.] vor Gericht gehen; **take sb. to ~:** jmdn. vor Gericht bringen *od.* verklagen; **appear in ~:** vor Gericht erscheinen; **the case comes up in ~ today** der Fall wird heute verhandelt; **settle sth. in ~:** etw. gerichtlich klären; **out of ~:** außergerichtlich; (fig.) indiskutabel; **rule/laugh sth. out of ~** (fig.) etw. verwerfen/auslachen; **C~ of First Instance** (EU) Gericht erster Instanz **5** (managing body) Rat, *der;* **C~ of Auditors** (EU) Europäischer Rechnungshof **6** *no art.* (dated: attentions) **pay ~ to sb.** jmdn. hofieren (veralt.); **pay ~ to a woman** einer Frau den Hof machen (veralt.)

B *v.t.* **1** (woo) ~ **sb.** jmdn. umwerben; **~ing couple** Liebespärchen, *das;* **are they ~ing?** sind sie ein Pärchen? **2** (Zool., Ornith.) umwerben **3** (fig.) suchen ‹*Gunst, Ruhm, Gefahr*›; **he is ~ing disaster/danger** er wandelt am Rande des Abgrunds (fig. geh.); ~ **death** sein Leben riskieren

court: ~ **card** *n.* Figurenkarte, *die;* ~ **'circular** *n.* (Brit.) Hofnachrichten *Pl.;* ~ **dress** *n.* Hofkleid, *das*

courteous /'kɜ:tɪəs/ *adj.* höflich; ~ **manners** gute Manieren

courteously /'kɜ:tɪəslɪ/ *adv.* höflich; **behave ~:** höflich sein

courtesan /kɔ:tɪ'zæn/ *n.* Kokotte, *die;* Kurtisane, *die* (hist.)

courtesy /'kɜ:təsɪ/ *n.* Höflichkeit, *die;* **drinks were [served] by ~ of sb.** die Getränke gingen auf jmds. Kosten; **by ~ of the museum** mit freundlicher Genehmigung des Museums; **by ~** (with some exaggeration) mit viel Wohlwollen; (as mark of politeness) aus Höflichkeit

courtesy: ~ **bus** *n.* gebührenfreier [Shuttle-]bus; ~ **call** *n.* Höflichkeitsbesuch, *der;* ~ **car** *n.* (supplied by hotel etc.) kostenfreies Shuttle-Fahrzeug; (for use while one's own car is being repaired) kostenloses Ersatzfahrzeug; ~ **light** *n.* (Motor Veh.) Innenbeleuchtung, *die;* ~ **title** *n.: Höflichkeitsanrede mit einem höheren Titel, als die betreffende Person besitzt*

'court house *n.* (Law) Gerichtsgebäude, *das;* (*Amer.*) *Verwaltungsgebäude eines Verwaltungsbezirks [mit Bezirksgefängnis]*

courtier /'kɔ:tɪə(r)/ *n.* Höfling, *der*

courtly /'kɔ:tlɪ/ *adj.* vornehm; ~ **love** (Hist.) Minne, *die*

court: ~ **'martial** *n., pl.* **~s martial** (Mil.) Kriegsgericht, *das;* **be tried by ~ martial** vor das/ein Kriegsgericht kommen; **~-'martial** *v.t.,* (Brit.) **-ll-** vor das/ein Kriegsgericht stellen; **C~ of Ap'peal** *n.* (Brit.) Berufungsgericht, *das;* ~ **'order** *n.* gerichtliche *od.* richterliche Anordnung; **~room** *n.* (Law) Gerichtssaal, *der*

courtship /'kɔ:tʃɪp/ *n.* Werben, *das*

court: ~ **shoe** *n.* Pumps, *der;* **~yard** *n.* Hof, *der*

cousin /'kʌzn/ *n.* **[first] ~:** Cousin, *der*/Cousine, *die;* Vetter, *der*/(veralt.) Base, *die;* **[second] ~:** Cousin/Cousine zweiten Grades; **they are ~s** sie sind Cousins/Cousinen/Cousin und Cousine; **first ~ once removed** (first ~'s child) Kind eines Cousins/einer Cousine; (parent's ~) Cousin/Cousine des Vaters/der Mutter; **sth. is first ~ to sth.** (fig.) etw. ist fast das gleiche wie etw.

couture /ku:'tjʊə(r)/ *n.* Couture, *die; see also* **haute couture**

couturier /ku:'tjʊərjeɪ/ *n.* Couturier, *der;* Modeschöpfer, *der*

couturière /ku:'tjʊərjeə(r)/ *n.* Modeschöpferin, *die*

cove[1] /kəʊv/ *n.* **1** (Geog.) [kleine] Bucht **2** (sheltered recess) Einbuchtung, *die*

cove[2] *n.* (dated Brit. coll.) Kerl, *der*

coven /kʌvn/ *n.* ≈ Hexensabbat, *der; Zusammenkunft von [dreizehn] Hexen*

covenant /'kʌvənənt/

A *n.* **1** formelle Übereinkunft **2** (Law) [besiegelter] Vertrag; **deed of ~:** Vertragsurkunde, *die* **3** (Bibl.) Bund, *der*

B *v.i.* (also Law) ~ **[with sb.] [for sth.]** [mit jmdm.] [etw.] vertraglich festlegen

C *v.t.* (also Law) [vertraglich] vereinbaren

Coventry /'kɒvəntrɪ/ *n.* **send sb. to ~** (fig.) jmdn. [demonstrativ] schneiden

cover /'kʌvə(r)/

A *n.* **1** (piece of cloth) Decke, *die;* (of cushion, bed) Bezug, *der;* (lid) Deckel, *der;* (of hole, engine, typewriter, etc.) Abdeckung, *die;* **put a ~ on** *or* **over** zudecken; abdecken ‹*Loch, Fußboden, Grab, Fahrzeug, Maschine*›; beziehen ‹*Kissen, Bett*› **2** (of book) Einband, *der;* (of magazine) Umschlag, *der;* (of record) [Platten]hülle, *die;* Cover, *das;* **read sth. from ~ to ~:** etw. von vorn bis hinten lesen; **on the [front/back] ~:** auf dem [vorderen/hinteren] Buchdeckel; (of magazine) auf der Titelseite/hinteren Umschlagseite; **a removable paper ~:** ein loser Papierumschlag **3** (Post: envelope) [Brief]umschlag, *der;* **under plain ~:** in neutralem Umschlag; **[send sth.] under separate ~:** [etw.] mit getrennter Post [schicken] **4** *in pl.* (bedclothes) Bettzeug, *das* **5** (of pneumatic tyre) Decke, *die*

6▸ (hiding place, shelter) Schutz, *der;* **take ~ [from sth.]** Schutz [vor etw. (*Dat.*)] suchen; **take ~ from the rain** sich unterstellen; **[be/go] under ~** (from bullets etc.) in Deckung [sein/gehen]; **under ~** (from rain) überdacht ‹*Sitzplatz*›; regengeschützt; **keep sth. under ~:** etw. abgedeckt halten; **under ~ of darkness** im Schutz der Dunkelheit
7▸ (Mil.: supporting force) Deckung, *die;* **fighter ~:** Deckung durch Jagdflugzeuge; *see also* **air cover**
8▸ (protection) Deckung, *die;* **give sb./sth. ~:** jmdm. Deckung geben
9▸ (pretence) Vorwand, *der;* (false identity, screen) Tarnung, *die;* **under ~ of charity** unter dem Deckmantel der Barmherzigkeit; **blow sb.'s ~** (coll.) jmdn. enttarnen
10▸ (Hunting) Deckung, *die;* **break ~:** aus der Deckung herauskommen
11▸ (Insurance) **[insurance] ~:** Versicherung, *die;* **get ~ against sth.** sich gegen etw. versichern; **have adequate ~:** ausreichend versichert sein
12▸ (place laid at table) Gedeck, *das*
13▸ (~ version) Coverversion, *die*
B *v.t.* **1▸** bedecken; **~ a book with leather** ein Buch in Leder binden; **~ your mouth while coughing** halte die Hand vor den Mund, wenn du hustest; **~ the table with a cloth** ein Tischtuch auf den Tisch legen; **~ a roof with shingles** ein Dach mit Schindeln decken; **~ a chair with chintz** einen Stuhl mit Chintz beziehen; **~ a pan with a lid/a car with plastic sheeting** eine Pfanne mit einem Deckel/ein Auto mit einer Plastikplane zudecken; **she ~ed her face with her hands** sie verbarg das Gesicht in den Händen; **~ed with blood** blutüberströmt; **the roses are ~ed with greenfly** die Rosen sind voller Blattläuse; **cats are ~ed with fur** Katzen haben ein Fell; **floodwaters ~ed the town** die Stadt war überflutet; **the children were ~ed in mud** die Kinder waren von oben bis unten voller Schlamm; **the car ~ed us with mud** das Auto bespritzte uns von oben bis unten mit Schlamm; **sb. is ~ed in** *or* **with confusion/shame** (fig.) jmd. ist ganz verlegen/sehr beschämt; *see also* **glory A 2**
2▸ (conceal, lit. or fig.) verbergen; (for protection) abdecken
3▸ (travel) zurücklegen
4▸ *in p.p.* (having roof) überdacht; **~ed market** Markthalle, *die;* **a ~ed wagon** ein Planwagen
5▸ (deal with) behandeln; (include) abdecken; **~ all possible cases** alle möglichen Fälle abdecken; **an examination ~ing last year's work** eine Prüfung über den Stoff des vergangenen Jahres; **this book does not fully ~ the subject** dieses Buch behandelt das Thema nicht vollständig
6▸ (Journ.) berichten über (+ *Akk.*)
7▸ (suffice to defray) decken; **~ expenses** die Kosten decken; **£10 will ~ my needs for the journey** 10 Pfund werden für die Reisekosten reichen
8▸ (shield) decken; **I'll keep you ~ed** ich gebe dir Deckung
9▸ **~ oneself** (fig.) sich absichern; (Insurance) **~ oneself against sth.** sich gegen etw. versichern
10▸ (aim gun at) in Schach halten (ugs.); **I've got you ~ed** ich habe meine Waffe auf dich gerichtet
11▸ (command) kontrollieren ‹*Gelände*›
12▸ ‹*Hengst:*› decken
13▸ (record new version of) covern

(Phrasal verbs)

- **~ for** *v.t.* einspringen für
- **~ 'in** *v.t.* überdachen; (fill in) zuschütten
- **~ 'over** *v.t.* zudecken; (with gold etc.) überziehen
- **~ 'up**

A *v.t.* (conceal) zudecken; (fig.) vertuschen
B *v.i.* (fig.: conceal) es vertuschen; **~ up for sb.** jmdn. decken. *See also* **cover-up**

'cover address *n.* Deckadresse, *die*

coverage /ˈkʌvərɪdʒ/ *n., no pl.* **1▸** (Radio, Telev.: area) Sendebereich, *der;* **provide a greater ~ of the country** den Sendebereich innerhalb des Landes vergrößern **2▸** (Journ., Radio, Telev.: treatment) Berichterstattung, *die* (**of** über + *Akk.*); **newspaper/broadcast ~:** Berichterstattung in der Presse/in Funk und Fernsehen; **give sth. [full/limited] ~:** [ausführlich/kurz] über etw. (*Akk.*) berichten **3▸** (Advertising) Abdeckung des Marktes **4▸** (Insurance) Deckung, *die*

coverall /ˈkʌvərɔːl/ *n. usu. in pl.* (esp. Amer.) Overall, *der;* (for baby) Strampelanzug, *der*

cover: ~ charge *n.* [Preis für das] Gedeck; **~ girl** *n.* Covergirl, *das*

covering /ˈkʌvərɪŋ/ *n.* (material) Decke, *die;* (of billiard table, aircraft wing) Bespannung, *die;* (of chair, bed) Bezug, *der*

covering: ~ letter *n.* Begleitbrief, *der;* **~ note** *n.* [kurzes] Begleitschreiben

coverlet /ˈkʌvəlɪt/ *n.* Tagesdecke, *die*

cover: ~ letter (Amer.) ▸ **covering letter**; **~ note** *n.* (Insurance) Deckungskarte, *die;* **~ story** *n.* **1▸** (Journ.) Titelgeschichte, *die;* **2▸** (espionage) [zur Tarnung erfundene] Geschichte

covert
A /ˈkʌvət/ *adj.* versteckt
B /ˈkʌvət, ˈkʌvə(r)/ *n.* (shelter) Schlupfwinkel, *der;* (thicket) Dickicht, *das*

covertly /ˈkʌvətlɪ/ *adv.* versteckt; **glance ~ at sb./sth.** jmdn./etw. verstohlen anschauen

cover: ~-up *n.* Verschleierung, *die;* **the Watergate ~-up** die Watergate-Affäre; **~ version** *n.* Coverversion, *die*

covet /ˈkʌvɪt/ *v.t.* begehren (geh.)

covetous /ˈkʌvɪtəs/ *adj.* (desirous) begehrlich (geh.); (avaricious) habgierig; **be ~ of sth.** etw. begehren (geh.)

covetously /ˈkʌvɪtəslɪ/ *adv.* begehrlich (geh.)

covetousness /ˈkʌvɪtəsnɪs/ *n., no pl.* Begehrlichkeit, *die*

covey /ˈkʌvɪ/ *n.* (Hunting) Kette, *die* (Jägerspr.)

cow[1] /kaʊ/ *n.* **1▸** Kuh, *die;* **till the ~s come home** (fig. coll.) bis in alle Ewigkeit (ugs.) **2▸** (female elephant, whale, etc.) Kuh, *die;* **~ buffalo/elephant** Büffelkuh, *die*/Elefantenkuh, *die* **3▸** (sl. derog.: woman) Kuh, *die* (salopp abwertend)

cow[2] *v.t.* einschüchtern; **~ sb. into submission** jmdn. so einschüchtern, dass er sich unterordnet; **have a ~ed look/appearance** verschüchtert aussehen

coward /ˈkaʊəd/ *n.* Feigling, *der;* **the ~'s way out** die feige Art, sich aus der Affäre zu ziehen

cowardice /ˈkaʊədɪs/ *n.* Feigheit, *die; see also* **moral cowardice**

cowardly /ˈkaʊədlɪ/ *adj.* feig[e]

cow: ~bell *n.* Kuhglocke, *die;* **~boy** *n.* Cowboy, *der;* (Brit. coll.: unscrupulous businessman, tradesman, etc.) Betrüger, *der;* **play Cowboys and Indians** Cowboy und Indianer spielen; **~catcher** *n.* (Amer. Railw.) Bahnräumer, *der;* Kuhfänger, *der;* **~ dung** *n.* Kuhmist, *der*

cower /ˈkaʊə(r)/ *v.i.* sich ducken; (squat) kauern; **~ in fear** sich ängstlich ducken; **stand ~ing in the corner** geduckt in der Ecke stehen

cow: ~hand *n.* Cowboy, *der;* **~herd** *n.* ▸ **i p. 1260** Kuhhirte, *der;* **~hide** *n.* Rindsleder, *das*

cowl /kaʊl/ *n.* **1▸** (of monk) Kutte, *die;* (hood) Kapuze, *die* **2▸** (of chimney) Schornsteinaufsatz, *der*

'cowlick *n.* [Haar]tolle, *die* (ugs.)

cowling /ˈkaʊlɪŋ/ *n.* (Aeronaut., Motor Veh.) Motorhaube, *die*

'cowman *n.* ▸ **i p. 1260** Stallknecht, *der*

'co-worker *n.* Kollege, *der*/Kollegin, *die*

cow: ~ parsley *n.* (Bot.) Wiesenkerbel, *der;* **~pat** *n.* Kuhfladen, *der;* **~pox** *n.* Kuhpocken *Pl.;* **~puncher** /ˈkaʊpʌnʃə(r)/ *n.* (Amer.) Cowboy, *der*

cowrie, cowry /ˈkaʊrɪ/ *n.* Kaurischnecke, *die;* (shell) Kaurimuschel, *die*

co-write /ˈkəʊraɪt/ *v.t.* mitverfassen

co-writer /ˈkəʊraɪtə(r)/ *n.* Mitverfasser, *der*/-verfasserin, *die;* Koautor, *der*/Koautorin, *die*

cow: ~shed *n.* Kuhstall, *der;* **~slip** *n.* **1▸** Schlüsselblume, *die;* **2▸** (Amer.: marsh marigold) Sumpfdotterblume, *die;* **~'s milk** *n.* Kuhmilch, *die*

cox /kɒks/
A *n.* Steuermann, *der*
B *v.t.* (esp. Rowing) steuern; **~ a crew** Steuermann einer Mannschaft sein; **~ed four** Vierer mit Steuermann
C *v.i.* steuern

coxcomb /ˈkɒkskəʊm/ *n.* (literary/arch.) Stutzer, *der* (veralt.)

coxless /ˈkɒkslɪs/ *adj.* ohne Steuermann

coxswain /ˈkɒksweɪn, ˈkɒksn/ ▸ **cox A**

coy /kɔɪ/ *adj.* gespielt schüchtern; geziert ‹*Benehmen, Ausdruck*›; **play ~:** auf schüchtern machen

coyly /ˈkɔɪlɪ/ *adv.* gespielt schüchtern; geziert ‹*sich benehmen*›

coyness /ˈkɔɪnɪs/ *n., no pl.* Schüchternheit, *die;* (of behaviour) Geziertheit, *die*

coyote /kəˈjəʊtɪ, ˈkɔɪəʊt/ *n.* (Zool.) Kojote, *der*

coypu /ˈkɔɪpuː/ *n.* (Zool.) Biberratte, *die;* Nutria, *die*

cozily, coziness, cozy (Amer.) ▸ **cos-**

cp. *abbr.* **= compare** vgl.

Cpl. *abbr.* **= Corporal** Korp.

c.p.s. *abbr.* **= cycles per second** Hz

CPU *abbr.* (Computing) **= central processing unit** ZE

Cr. *abbr.* **1▸ = creditor** Gl. **2▸ = Councillor** ≈ StR

crab /kræb/
A *n.* **1▸** Krabbe, *die* **2▸** (Astrol.) **the C~:** der Krebs; *see also* **archer 2** **3▸** (Rowing) **catch a ~:** einen Krebs fangen **4▸** (Bot.) ▸ **crab apple**
B *v.i.*, **-bb-** (coll.) **~ about sth.** über etw. (*Akk.*) meckern (ugs.)

'crab apple *n.* Holzapfel, *der*

crabbed /kræbd/ *adj.* **1▸** (perverse) starrköpfig **2▸** (morose) griesgrämig **3▸** (badly formed) unleserlich ‹*Handschrift*›

crabby /ˈkræbɪ/ ▸ **crabbed 1, 2**

crabwise /ˈkræbwaɪz/ *adv.* seitwärts [wie eine Krabbe]

crack /kræk/
A *n.* **1▸** (noise) Krachen, *das;* **a ~ of the whip** ein Peitschenknall; **give sb./have a fair ~ of the whip** (fig.) jmdm. eine Chance geben/eine Chance haben; **the ~ of doom** (fig.) die Posaunen des Jüngsten Gerichts **2▸** (in china, glass, eggshell, ice, etc.) Sprung, *der;* (in rock) Spalte, *die;* (chink) Spalt, *der;* **there's a ~ in the ceiling** die Decke hat einen Riss; *see also* **paper over** **3▸** (blow) Schlag, *der* **4▸** (coll.: try) Versuch, *der;* **have a ~ at sth./at doing sth.** etw. in Angriff nehmen/versuchen, etw. zu tun **5▸** **the/at the ~ of dawn** *or* **day** der/bei Tagesanbruch **6▸** (coll.: wisecrack) [geistreicher] Witz **7▸** (sl.: drug) **~ [cocaine]** Crack, *das*
B *adj.* (coll.) erstklassig
C *v.t.* **1▸** (break, lit. or fig.) knacken ‹*Nuss, Problem*›; knacken (salopp) ‹*Safe, Kode*›; **~ a bottle** (fig.) einer Flasche den Hals brechen (ugs. scherzh.); **~ sth. open** etw. aufbrechen **2▸** (make a ~ in) anschlagen ‹*Porzellan, Glas*›; **~ one's head/skull** sich (*Dat.*) den Kopf/Schädel aufschlagen **3▸** **~ a whip** mit einer Peitsche knallen; **~ the whip** (fig.) Druck machen (ugs.); **~ one's knuckles** mit den Knöcheln knacken **4▸** **~ a joke** einen Witz machen **5▸** (Chem.: decompose) kracken
D *v.i.* **1▸** ‹*Porzellan, Glas:*› einen Sprung/Sprünge bekommen; ‹*Haut:*› aufspringen, rissig werden; ‹*Eis:*› Risse bekommen **2▸** (make sound) ‹*Peitsche:*› knallen; ‹*Gelenk:*› knacken; ‹*Gewehr:*› krachen **3▸** (change) ‹*Stimme:*› brechen (geh.), versagen (**with** vor + *Dat.*); **his voice is ~ing** (at age of puberty) er ist im Stimmbruch **4▸** (yield under torture etc.) zusammenbrechen **5▸** (coll.) **get ~ing!** mach los! (ugs.); **let's get ~ing** fangen wir endlich an; **get ~ing [with sth.]** [mit etw.] loslegen (ugs.)

(Phrasal verbs)

- **~ 'down** *v.i.* (coll.) **~ down [on sb./sth.]** [gegen jmdn./etw.] [hart] vorgehen; *see also* **~-down**

• ~ **'up** (coll.)
A v.i. ‹*Flugzeug:*› auseinander brechen; ‹*Gesellschaft, Person:*› zusammenbrechen; **~ up [laughing]** einen Lachkrampf kriegen
B v.t. **he/it** *etc.* **is not all he/it** *etc.* **is ~ed up to be** so toll ist er/es *usw.* nun auch wieder nicht[, wie er/es dargestellt wird]; **she is ~ed up to be brilliant** sie soll brillant sein (ugs.). *See also* **~-up**

crack: ~ baby *n.* (coll.) Crackbaby, *das;* **~-brained** *adj.* (coll.) bescheuert (salopp abwertend) ‹*Person*›; hirnrissig (abwertend) ‹*Idee usw.*›; **~ co'caine** *n., no pl.* Crack, *das;* **~-down** *n.* (coll.) **there will be a ~-down** man wird hart durchgreifen; **have/order a ~-down on sb./sth.** drastische Maßnahmen gegen jmdn./etw. ergreifen/anordnen

cracked /krækt/ *adj.* **1** gesprungen ‹*Porzellan, Ziegel, Glas*›; rissig, aufgesprungen ‹*Haut, Erdboden*›; rissig ‹*Verputz*›; brüchig ‹*Stimme*› **2** (coll.: crazy) übergeschnappt (ugs.)

cracker /'krækə(r)/ *n.* **1** (paper toy) **[Christmas] ~:** ≈ Knallbonbon, *der od. das* **2** (firework) Knallkörper, *der* **3** (thin dry biscuit) Cracker, *der;* (Amer.: biscuit) Keks, *der* **4** ▸ **crackerjack B** **5** (Computing) Cracker, *der* (fachspr.); Computerknacker, *der*

'crackerjack (Amer. coll.)
A *adj.* fantastisch (ugs.)
B *n.* (person) Ass, *das* (ugs.); (thing) Knüller, *der* (ugs.)

crackers /'krækəz/ *pred. adj.* (Brit. coll.) übergeschnappt (ugs.); **go ~:** überschnappen (ugs.)

'crack house *n.* (coll.) Crackhaus, *das*

crackle /krækl/
A *v.i.* knistern; ‹*Maschinengewehr:*› knattern; ‹*Feuer:*› prasseln; ‹*Blätter:*› rascheln; **the telephone line/the radio ~s** in der Telefonleitung/im Radio knackt es
B *n.* Knistern, *das;* (of leaves) Rascheln, *das;* (of telephone line) Knacken, *das;* (of machine gun) Knattern, *das;* (of fire) Prasseln, *das*

crackling /'kræklɪŋ/ *n., no pl., no indef. art.* (Cookery) Kruste, *die*

crackly /'kræklɪ/ *adj.* knisternd

'crackpot *n.* (coll.) Spinner, *der*/Spinnerin, *die* (ugs.); *attrib.* **~ ideas/schemes** hirnrissige Ideen/Pläne (abwertend)

cracksman /'kræksmən/ *n., pl.* **cracksmen** /'kræksmən/ Einbrecher, *der*

'crack-up *n.* (coll.) Zusammenbruch, *der*

Cracow /'krækaʊ/ *pr. n.* ▸❶ **p. 1643** Krakau *(das)*

cradle /kreɪdl/
A *n.* **1** (cot, lit. or fig.) Wiege, *die;* **from the ~:** von der Wiege an; von Kindesbeinen an; **from the ~ to the grave** von der Wiege bis zur Bahre **2** (Building) Hängebühne, *die;* (to support ship) Stapel, *der* **3** (Teleph.) Gabel, *die*
B *v.t.* wiegen; **~ sb./sth. in one's arms** jmdn. in den Armen halten/etw. im Arm halten

cradle: ~-snatch *v.i.* (coll.) **Your boyfriend/girlfriend is much younger than you. You're ~-snatching** Dein Freund/deine Freundin ist viel jünger als du. Du vergreifst dich ja an kleinen Kindern (ugs. scherzh.); **~-snatcher** *n.* (coll.) *jmd., der mit einer sehr viel jüngeren Person eine Liebesbeziehung eingeht;* **~-snatching** *n., no pl.* **You can't ask her out. That would be ~-snatching** Du kannst sie nicht einladen. Das wäre Verführung einer Minderjährigen (scherzh.); **~ song** *n.* Wiegenlied, *das*

craft /krɑːft/ *n.* **1** (trade) Handwerk, *das;* (art) Kunsthandwerk, *das;* (in school) **~[s]** Werken, *das* **2** *no pl.* (skill) Kunstfertigkeit, *die* **3** *no pl.* (cunning) List, *die;* **be full of ~:** sehr gewitzt sein **4** *pl. same* (boat) Boot, *das;* (air~) Flugzeug, *das;* (space~) Raumfahrzeug, *das*

craft: ~ centre *n.* Kunstgewerbezentrum, *das;* **~ fair** *n.* Kunstgewerbemarkt, *der*

craftily /'krɑːftɪlɪ/ *adv.* listig

craftiness /'krɑːftɪnɪs/ *n., no pl.* Schläue, *die*

craftsman /'krɑːftsmən/ *n., pl.* **craftsmen** /'krɑːftsmən/ Handwerker, *der;* (skilled person) **a real ~:** ein wahrer Künstler

craftsmanship /'krɑːftsmənʃɪp/ *n., no pl.* (skilled workmanship) handwerkliches Können; (performance) **shoddy ~:** schludrige Arbeit

'craftwork *n., no pl.* Kunsthandwerk, *das*

crafty /'krɑːftɪ/ *adj.* listig; **as ~ as a fox** schlau wie ein Fuchs

crag /kræg/ *n.* Felsspitze, *die*

craggy /'krægɪ/ *adj.* (rugged) zerklüftet; zerfurcht ‹*Gesicht*›; (rocky) felsig; (steep) schroff

crake /kreɪk/ *n.* (Ornith.) Ralle, *die*

cram /kræm/
A *v.t.,* **-mm- 1** (overfill) voll stopfen (ugs.); (force) stopfen; **~med with information** voll gepackt mit Informationen; **~ people into a bus** Leute in einen Bus zwängen; **the bus was ~med** der Bus war gerammelt voll (ugs.) *od.* war überfüllt; *see also* **throat 1** **2** (for examination) **~ pupils** mit Schülern pauken (ugs.); **~ up maths** Mathe pauken *od.* büffeln (ugs.) **3** (feed to excess) mästen; **~ poultry** *etc.* Geflügel *usw.* mästen *od.* (bes. südd.) stopfen
B *v.i.,* **-mm-** (for examination) büffeln (ugs.); pauken (ugs.)

Phrasal verb
• **~ 'in**
A *v.i.* [sich] herein-/hineindrängen
B *v.t.* hineinstopfen

'cram-full ▸ **chock-full**

crammer /'kræmə(r)/ *n.* (place) Presse, *die* (ugs. abwertend); (person) [Ein]pauker, *der* (ugs.)

cramp /kræmp/
A *n.* **1** (Med.) Krampf, *der;* **suffer an attack of ~:** einen Krampf bekommen; **have ~ [in one's leg/arm]** einen Krampf [im Bein/Arm] haben; *see also* **writer's cramp** **2** (Woodw.) Schraubzwinge, *die* **3** (Building) **~[-iron]** [Bau]klammer, *die*
B *v.t.* **1** (confine) einengen; **~ [up]** zusammenpferchen; **~ sb.'s style** jmdn. einengen **2** (restrict) lähmen ‹*Willen, Eifer, Fleiß, Handel*›

cramped /kræmpt/ *adj.* eng ‹*Raum*›; gedrängt ‹*Handschrift*›

crampon /'kræmpən/ (*Amer.:* **crampoon** /kræm'puːn/) *n.* **1** (metal hook) Kanthaken, *der* **2** (on boot) Steigeisen, *das*

cranberry /'krænbərɪ/ *n.* Cranberry, *die;* ≈ Preiselbeere, *die;* (Vaccinium oxycoccos) Moosbeere, *die* (Bot.); (Vaccinium macrocarpon) Großfrüchtige Moosbeere (Bot.); **~ sauce** Preiselbeersoße, *die*

crane /kreɪn/
A *n.* **1** (machine) Kran, *der* **2** (Ornith.) Kranich, *der*
B *v.t.* **~ one's neck** den Hals recken
C *v.i.* den Hals recken; **~ forward** den Hals [nach vorn] recken

crane: ~ driver *n.* ▸❶ **p. 1260** Kranführer, *der;* **~ fly** *n.* (Zool.) Schnake, *die;* **~sbill** *n.* (Bot.) Storch[en]schnabel, *der*

crania *pl. of* **cranium**

cranial /'kreɪnɪəl/ *adj.* (Anat.) Schädel-; kranial (fachspr.)

cranium /'kreɪnɪəm/ *n., pl.* **crania** /'kreɪnɪə/ *or* **~s** (Anat.) Schädel, *der;* Kranium, *das* (fachspr.); (bones enclosing the brain) Hirnschädel, *der*

crank[1] /kræŋk/
A *n.* **1** (Mech. Engin.) [Hand]kurbel, *die* **2** (of bicycle) **~ [arm]** Tretkurbel, *die*
B *v.t.* (turn with ~) ankurbeln

Phrasal verb
• **~ 'up** *v.t.* (Motor Veh.) ankurbeln

crank[2] *n.* Irre, *der/die* (salopp); **health ~:** Gesundheitsfanatiker, *der*/-fanatikerin, *die* (ugs.)

crank: ~ arm *n.* (of bicycle) Tretkurbel, *die;* **~case** *n.* (Mech. Engin.) Kurbelwellengehäuse, *das;* **~pin** *n.* (Mech. Engin.) Kurbelzapfen, *der;* **~shaft** *n.* (Mech. Engin.) Kurbelwelle, *die*

cranky /'kræŋkɪ/ *adj.* **1** (eccentric) schrullig; verschroben **2** (esp. Amer.: ill-tempered) griesgrämig

cranny /'krænɪ/ *n.* Ritze, *die; see also* **nook**

crap[1] /kræp/ (coarse)
A *n.* **1** (faeces) Scheiße, *die* (derb); **have a ~:** scheißen (derb) **2** (nonsense) Scheiß, *der* (salopp abwertend); **a load of ~:** ein Haufen Scheiß (salopp abwertend)
B *v.i.,* **-pp-** scheißen (derb)

crap[2] *n.* (Amer.: throw in craps) Fehlwurf, *der;* Crap, *der;* **~ game** Craps, *das*

crape /kreɪp/ *n.* [schwarzer] Krepp; (ribbon) Trauerflor, *der*

crappy /'kræpɪ/ *adj.* (coarse) beschissen (derb); **~ film/café** Scheißfilm, *der*/Scheißcafé, *das* (derb)

craps /kræps/ *n. pl.* (Amer.: dice game) Craps, *das;* **shoot ~:** Craps spielen

crash /kræʃ/
A *n.* **1** (noise) Krachen, *das;* **fall with a ~:** mit einem lauten Krach fallen; **a sudden ~ of thunder** ein plötzlicher Donnerschlag **2** (collision) Zusammenstoß, *der;* **plane/train ~:** Flugzeugunglück, *das*/Eisenbahnunglück, *das;* **have a ~:** einen Unfall haben; **in a [car] ~:** bei einem [Auto]unfall; **be in a [car] ~:** in einen [Auto]unfall verwickelt sein **3** (Finance etc.) Zusammenbruch, *der;* **the great ~ on Wall Street** der große Börsenkrach in der Wall Street **4** *attrib.* (intensive) **~ job** Noteinsatz, *der;* **~ measures** Sofortmaßnahmen *Pl*
B *adv.* krachend; **~, bang, wallop** (coll.) holterdiepolter (ugs.)
C *v.i.* **1** (make a noise) krachen **2** (go noisily) krachen; **~ down** herunterkrachen; **~ about one's ears** (fig.) zusammenbrechen **3** (have a collision) einen Unfall haben; ‹*Flugzeug, Flieger:*› abstürzen; **~ into sth.** gegen etw. krachen **4** (Finance etc., Computing) zusammenbrechen
D *v.t.* **1** (smash) schmettern **2** (cause to have collision) einen Unfall haben mit; **~ a plane** mit dem Flugzeug abstürzen **3** (pass illegally) überfahren; **he ~ed the lights** er fuhr bei Rot über die Ampel **4** ▸ **gatecrash A**

Phrasal verbs
• **~ a'bout** *v.i.* laut herumtollen
• **~ 'out** *v.i.* (coll.) pennen (salopp); (go to sleep) einpennen (salopp)

crash: ~ barrier *n.* Leitplanke, *die;* **~ course** *n.* Intensivkurs, *der;* **~ diet** *n.* radikale Diät; ≈ Nulldiät, *die;* **~-dive** **A** *v.t.* schnell untertauchen lassen ‹*U-Boot*›; abstürzen lassen ‹*Flugzeug*›; **B** *v.i.* ‹*Unterseeboot:*› schnell untertauchen; **~-dive on sth.** im Sturzflug auf etw. (*Akk.*) herabstoßen; **C** *n.* (of submarine) schnelles Untertauchen; (of aircraft) Sturzflug, *der;* **~ helmet** *n.* Sturzhelm, *der*

crashing /'kræʃɪŋ/ *adj.* (coll.) **be a ~ bore** wahnsinnig langweilig sein (ugs.)

crash: ~-land **A** *v.t.* **~-land a plane** mit einem Flugzeug bruchlanden; **B** *v.i.* bruchlanden; **~-landing** *n.* Bruchlandung, *die;* **~ pad** *n.* (coll.) Schlafplatz, *der;* Penne, *die* (salopp); **~ programme** *n.* Sofortprogramm, *das;* **~-test** *v.t.* einem Crashtest unterziehen; **~-test dummy** *n.* Crashtest-dummy, *der* (fachspr.); Crashtestpuppe, *die*

crass /kræs/ *adj.* grob ‹*Benehmen*›; haarsträubend ‹*Dummheit, Unwissenheit*›; (grossly stupid) strohdumm

crassly /'kræslɪ/ *adv.* grob, unfein ‹*sich benehmen*›; grob, krass ‹*fehldeuten*›

crassness /'kræsnɪs/ *n., no pl.* Krassheit, *die;* (of person) Grobheit, *die;* (stupidity) Dummheit, *die*

crate /kreɪt/
A *n.* **1** (case) Kiste, *die;* **a ~ of beer/lemonade** ein Kasten Bier/Limonade **2** (coll.: vehicle) Kiste, *die* (ugs.)
B *v.t.* **~ [up]** in eine Kiste/in Kisten packen

crater /'kreɪtə(r)/ *n.* Krater, *der*

crater 'lake *n.* Kratersee, *der*

cravat /krə'væt/ *n.* Schalkrawatte, *die;* (Hist.: necktie) Krawatte, *die*

crave /kreɪv/
A *v.t.* **1** (beg) erbitten; erflehen ‹*Gnade*› **2** (long for) sich sehnen nach
B *v.i.* **~ for** *or* **after** ▸ **A**

craven /kreɪvn/
A *adj.* feige; **a ~ coward** ein elender *od.* erbärmlicher Feigling
B *n.* Feigling, *der*

cravenly /'kreɪvnlɪ/ *adv.* feige

craving /ˈkreɪvɪŋ/ *n.* Verlangen, *das;* **have a ~ for sth.** ein [dringendes] Verlangen nach etw. haben

craw /krɔː/ *n.* Kropf, *der;* **stick in sb.'s ~** (fig.) jmdm. gegen den Strich gehen

crawfish /ˈkrɔːfɪʃ/ *n., pl. same* Languste, *die*

crawl /krɔːl/

A *v.i.* **1** kriechen; **the baby/insect ~s along the ground** das Baby/Insekt krabbelt über den Boden **2** (coll.: behave abjectly) kriechen (abwertend); **~ to sb.** vor jmdm. buckeln *od.* kriechen; **don't you come ~ing back to me** du brauchst nicht wieder angekrochen zu kommen **3** **be ~ing** (be covered or filled) wimmeln (**with** von) **4** ▸ **creep A 2**

B *n.* **1** Kriechen, *das;* (of insect, baby also) Krabbeln, *das;* (slow speed) Schneckentempo, *das;* **move/go at a ~:** sich im Schneckentempo bewegen/im Schneckentempo fahren **2** (swimming stroke) Kraulen, *das;* **do** *or* **swim the ~:** kraulen

crawler /ˈkrɔːlə(r)/ *n.* **1** *usu. in pl.* (baby's overall) Spielanzug, *der* **2** (coll. derog.: abject person) Kriecher, *der* (abwertend) **3** (Computing) Crawler, *der*

ˈcrawler lane *n.* Kriechspur, *die*

crayfish /ˈkreɪfɪʃ/ *n., pl. same* **1** Flusskrebs, *der* **2** (crawfish) Languste, *die*

crayon /ˈkreɪən/ *n.* **1** (pencil) **[coloured] ~:** Buntstift, *der;* (of wax) Wachsmalstift, *der;* (of chalk) Kreidestift, *der* **2** (drawing) [Kreide]zeichnung, *die*

craze /kreɪz/

A *n.* **1** (temporary enthusiasm) Begeisterung, *die;* Fimmel, *der* (ugs. abwertend); **there's a ~ for doing sth.** es ist gerade große Mode, etw. zu tun **2** (mania) Manie, *die*

B *v.t. usu. in p. p.* (make insane) zum Wahnsinn treiben; **be [half] ~d with pain/grief** *etc.* [halb] wahnsinnig vor Schmerz/Kummer *usw.* sein; **a ~d look/expression [on sb.'s face]** ein vom Wahnsinn verzerrtes Gesicht

crazily /ˈkreɪzɪlɪ/ *adv.* verrückt; (of motion) wie verrückt

craziness /ˈkreɪzɪnɪs/ *n., no pl.* Verrücktheit, *die;* **sheer ~:** heller Wahnsinn

crazy /ˈkreɪzɪ/ *adj.* **1** (mad) verrückt; wahnsinnig; **go ~:** verrückt *od.* wahnsinnig werden; **drive** *or* **send sb. ~:** jmdn. verrückt *od.* wahnsinnig machen (ugs.); **like ~** (coll.) wie verrückt (ugs.) **2** (coll.: enthusiastic) **be ~ about sb./sth.** nach jmdm./etw. verrückt sein (ugs.); **she's ~ about dancing** sie ist ganz wild aufs Tanzen (ugs.); **football/pop music ~:** verrückt nach Fußball/Popmusik (ugs.) **3** (coll.: exciting) irre (salopp) **4** (of irregular pieces) **~ paving** gestückeltes Pflaster; **~ quilt** Flickendecke, *die* **5** **lean [over] at a ~ angle** gefährlich schief stehen

ˈcrazy bone *n.* (Amer.) Musikantenknochen, *der*

CRC *n.* = **camera-ready copy**

creak /kriːk/

A *n.* (of gate, door) Quietschen, *das;* (of floorboard, door, chair) Knarren, *das*

B *v.i.* ‹*Tor, Tür:*› quietschen; ‹*Diele, Tür, Stuhl:*› knarren; ‹*Gelenke:*› knacken; **the old car ~ed to a halt** der alte Wagen kam quietschend zum Stehen

creaky /ˈkriːkɪ/ *adj.* quietschend ‹*Tor, Tür*›; knarrend ‹*Stuhl, Treppe, Stiefel, Tür*›

cream /kriːm/

A *n.* **1** Sahne, *die* **2** (Cookery) (sauce) Sahnesoße, *die;* (dessert) Creme, *die;* (chocolate) gefülltes Bonbon; (biscuit) gefüllter Keks; **~ of mushroom soup** Champignoncremesuppe, *die;* **custard ~s** Kekse mit Vanillecremefüllung **3** (cosmetic preparation) Creme, *die* **4** (fig.: best) Beste, *das;* **the ~ of society** die Creme der Gesellschaft; **the ~ of the applicants** die besten Bewerber **5** (colour) Creme, *das*

B *adj.* **1** **~[-coloured]** creme[farben] **2** (Cookery) **~ soup/sauce** Cremesuppe, *die*/Sahnesoße, *die*

C *v.t.* cremig rühren *od.* schlagen; schaumig rühren ‹*Butter*›; **~ed potatoes** Kartoffelpüree, *das*

(Phrasal verb)

• **~ ˈoff** *v.t.* **~ off the best players** die besten Spieler wegschnappen (ugs.)

cream: ~ ˈbun *n.* ≈ Eclair, *das;* **~ cake** *n.* Cremetorte, *die;* (small) Cremetörtchen, *das;* (with whipped ~) Sahnetorte, *die*/Sahnetörtchen, *das;* **~ ˈcheese** *n.* ≈ Frischkäse, *der;* **~ ˈcracker** *n.* ≈ Cracker, *der*

creamer /ˈkriːmə(r)/ *n.* (Amer.: jug) Sahnekännchen, *das*

creamery /ˈkriːmərɪ/ *n.* (butter factory) Molkerei, *die;* (shop) Milchgeschäft, *das*

cream: ~jug *n.* Sahnekännchen, *das;* **~ of ˈtartar** *n.* Weinstein, *der;* **~ ˈpuff** *n.* Windbeutel, *der;* **~ ˈtea** *n.* Tee mit Marmeladetörtchen und Sahne

creamy /ˈkriːmɪ/ *adj.* **1** (with cream) sahnig; (like cream) cremig **2** **~[-coloured]** creme[farben]

crease /kriːs/

A *n.* **1** (pressed) Bügelfalte, *die;* (accidental; in skin) Falte, *die;* (in fabric) Falte, *die;* Knitter, *der;* (in paper) Kniff, *der;* Knick, *der;* **put a ~ in trousers** Bügelfalten in Hosen bügeln **2** (Cricket) Linie, *die*

B *v.t.* (press) eine Falte/Falten bügeln in (+ *Akk.*); (accidentally) knittern; (extensively) zerknittern

C *v.i.* Falten bekommen; knittern

(Phrasal verb)

• **~ ˈup** *v.i.* (coll.: in amusement) sich [vor Lachen] kringeln (ugs.)

ˈcrease-resistant *adj.* knitterfrei

create /krɪˈeɪt/

A *v.t.* **1** schaffen; erschaffen (geh.); verursachen ‹*Verwirrung*›; machen ‹*Eindruck*›; ‹*Sache:*› mit sich bringen, ‹*Person:*› machen ‹*Schwierigkeiten*›; **~ a scene** eine Szene machen; **~ a sensation** für eine Sensation sorgen **2** (design) schaffen; kreieren ‹*Mode, Stil*› **3** (invest with rank) ernennen; **~ sb. a peer** jmdn. zum Peer erheben *od.* ernennen

B *v.i.* (Brit. coll.: make a fuss) Theater machen (ugs.)

creation /krɪˈeɪʃn/ *n.* **1** *no pl.* (act of creating) Schaffung, *die;* (of the world) Erschaffung, *die;* Schöpfung, *die* (geh.) **2** *no pl.* (all created things) Schöpfung, *die;* **the wonders of C~:** die Wunder der Schöpfung; **all [of] ~, the whole of ~:** alle Kreatur (geh.); alle Geschöpfe **3** *no pl.* (investing with title, rank, etc.) Ernennung, *die* **4** (Fashion) Kreation, *die*

creationism /krɪˈeɪʃənɪzm/ *n.* Kreatianismus, *der*

creationist /krɪˈeɪʃənɪst/ *n.* Anhänger des Kreatianismus

creative /krɪˈeɪtɪv/

A *adj.*, **creatively** /krɪˈeɪtɪvlɪ/ *adv.* schöpferisch; kreativ

B *n.* Kreative, *der/die*

creative: ~ acˈcountancy, ~ acˈcounting *ns., no pl.* (coll.) kreative Buchführung; **~ ˈarts** *n. pl.* kreative Künste

creativeness /krɪˈeɪtɪvnɪs/, **creativity** /kriːeɪˈtɪvɪtɪ/ *ns., no pl.* Kreativität, *die*

creator /krɪˈeɪtə(r)/ *n.* Schöpfer, *der*/Schöpferin, *die;* **the C~:** der Schöpfer

creature /ˈkriːtʃə(r)/ *n.* **1** (created being) Geschöpf, *das;* Kreatur, *die* (geh.); **all living ~s** alle Lebewesen; alle Kreatur (geh.) **2** (human being) Geschöpf, *das;* (derog.) Kerl, *der* (abwertend); (woman) **the ~ with the red hair** die mit den roten Haaren (ugs.); **lovely ~:** reizendes Geschöpf; **wicked/deserving ~:** böser/verdienstvoller Mensch; **~ of habit** Gewohnheitsmensch, *der;* Gewohnheitstier, *das* (scherzh.) **3** (minion, lit. or fig.) Kreatur, *die* (abwertend); **~s of circumstance** Opfer der Umstände. *See also* **comfort A 5**

crèche /kreʃ/ *n.* [Kinder]krippe, *die*

credence /ˈkriːdəns/ *n.* **1** (belief) Glaube, *der;* **give** *or* **attach ~ to sth./sb.** einer Sache (*Dat.*)/jmdm. Glauben schenken; **lend ~ to sth.** etw. glaubwürdig machen *od.* erscheinen lassen; **gain ~:** an Glaubwürdigkeit gewinnen; **worthy of ~:** glaubwürdig **2** (Eccl.) **~ [table]** Kredenz, *die*

credential /krɪˈdenʃl/ *n. usu. in pl.* (testimonial) Zeugnis, *das;* (of ambassador) Beglaubigungsschreiben, *das;* (letter[s of introduction) Referenzen *Pl.;* **present one's ~s** seine Referenzen vorlegen

credibility /kredɪˈbɪlɪtɪ/ *n.* Glaubwürdigkeit, *die;* **~ gap** Mangel an Glaubwürdigkeit

credible /ˈkredɪbl/ *adj.* glaubwürdig ‹*Mensch, Aussage*›; glaubhaft ‹*Aussage*›

credibly /ˈkredɪblɪ/ *adv.* glaubwürdig; glaubhaft

credit /ˈkredɪt/

A *n.* **1** *no pl.* (commendation) Anerkennung, *die;* (honour) Ehre, *die;* (good reputation) Ansehen, *das* (**with** bei); **give sb. [the] ~ for sth.** jmdm. für etw. Anerkennung zollen (geh.); **get [the] ~ for sth.** Anerkennung für etw. finden; **take the ~ for sth.** die Anerkennung für etw. einstecken; **all ~ to her/them for not giving in** alle Achtung, dass sie nicht nachgegeben hat/haben; **[we must give] ~ where ~ is due** Ehre, wem Ehre gebührt; **it is [much** *or* **greatly/little] to sb.'s/sth.'s ~ that ...:** es macht jmdm./einer Sache [große/wenig] Ehre, dass ...; **it is to his ~ that ...:** es ehrt ihn, dass ...; **do ~ to sb./sth., do sb./sth. ~, be a ~ to sb./sth.** jmdm./einer Sache Ehre machen; **reflect [great/little] ~ on sb./sth.** jmdm./einer Sache [große/wenig] Ehre machen **2** *in pl.* (in book) Liste der Mitarbeiter und sonstigen Beteiligten; (in film, play, etc.) Liste der Mitwirkenden und sonstigen Beteiligten; **~s, ~ titles** (at beginning of film) Vorspann, *der;* (at end) Nachspann, *der* **3** *no pl., no art.* (belief) Glaube, *der;* **give ~ to sth.** einer Sache (*Dat.*) Glauben schenken; **gain ~:** an Glaubwürdigkeit gewinnen **4** *no pl.* (Commerc.) Kredit, *der;* **give [sb.] ~:** [jmdm.] Kredit geben; **deal on ~:** Kredit geben; **buy [sth.] on ~:** [etw.] auf Kredit kaufen; **six months' ~:** Kredit mit sechsmonatiger Laufzeit; **their ~ is excellent** sie sind unbedingt kreditwürdig **5** *no pl.* (Finance, Bookk.) Guthaben, *das;* **be in ~** ‹*Konto:*› im Haben sein; ‹*Person:*› mit seinem Konto im Haben sein; **get a ~ line** Kredit bekommen; **she has sth. to her ~:** ihr ist etw. gutzuschreiben; **letter of ~:** Kreditbrief, *der;* Akkreditiv, *das* (Bankw.) **6** (fig.) **have sth. to one's ~:** etw. vorzuweisen haben; **we must give him ~ for being able to finish it by tomorrow** wir dürfen annehmen, dass er es bis morgen erledigen kann; **he's cleverer than I gave him ~ for** er ist klüger, als ich dachte; **I gave you ~ for being a kind man** ich habe dich für einen netten Menschen gehalten; **I gave her ~ for better taste** ich hatte ihr einen besseren Geschmack zugetraut **7** (Amer. Educ.) Schein, *der*

B *v.t.* **1** (believe) glauben **2** (accredit) **~ sb. with sth.** jmdm. etw. zutrauen; **~ sth. with sth.** einer Sache (*Dat.*) etw. zuschreiben **3** (Finance, Bookk.) gutschreiben; **~ £10 to sb./sb.'s account** jmdm./jmds. Konto 10 Pfund gutschreiben; **be ~ed with £10** 10 Pfund gutgeschrieben bekommen

creditable /ˈkredɪtəbl/ *adj.* anerkennenswert

creditably /ˈkredɪtəblɪ/ *adv.* achtbar

credit: ~ account *n.* Kreditkonto, *das;* **~ agency** *n.* [Kredit]auskunftei, *die;* **~ balance** *n.* Guthaben, *das;* **~ card** *n.* ▸ **❶ p. 1332** Kreditkarte, *die;* **~ facilities** *n. pl.* [Kredit]fazilität, *die* (fachspr.); **~ limit** *n.* Kreditlinie, *die;* **~ note** *n.* Gutschein, *der*

creditor /ˈkredɪtə(r)/ *n.* **1** (one to whom debt is owing) Gläubiger, *der*/Gläubigerin, *die* **2** (one who gives credit for money or goods) Kreditgeber, *der*/-geberin, *die*

credit: ~ rating *n.* [Einschätzung der] Kreditwürdigkeit; **have a good/bad ~ rating** als kreditwürdig/kreditunwürdig eingeschätzt werden; **~ sale** *n.* Kreditkauf, *der;* **~ side** *n.* (Finance) Habenseite, *die;* (fig.) **on the ~ side she has experience** für sie spricht ihre Erfahrung; **~ squeeze** *n.* Kreditrestriktion, *die;* **~ standing** *n.* Bonität, *die;* Kreditwürdigkeit, *die;* **~ transfer** *n.* (Finance) Banküberweisung, *die;* **~worthiness** *n.* Kreditwürdigkeit, *die;* **~ worthy** *adj.* kreditwürdig

credo /ˈkriːdəʊ, ˈkreɪdəʊ/ *n., pl.* **~s** Glaubensbekenntnis, *das;* Kredo, *das*

credulity /krɪˈdjuːlɪtɪ/ *n.*, *no pl.* Leichtgläubigkeit, *die*

credulous /ˈkredjʊləs/ *adj.* leichtgläubig; naiv ‹*Erstaunen, Verhalten*›

credulously /ˈkredjʊləslɪ/ *adv.* leichtgläubig; **believe sth. too ~:** etw. allzu arglos glauben

creed /kriːd/ *n.* (lit. or fig.) Glaubensbekenntnis, *das*

creek /kriːk/ *n.* **1** (Brit.) (inlet on sea coast) [kleine] Bucht; (small harbour) [kleiner] Hafen **2** (short arm of river) [kurzer] Flussarm **3** (Amer.: tributary of river) Nebenfluss, *der;* (Austral., NZ: stream) Bach, *der* **4** **be up the ~** (coll.: be in difficulties or trouble) in der Klemme *od.* Tinte sitzen (ugs.); (be wrong) ‹*Antwort usw.:*› völlig falsch sein; ‹*Person:*› auf dem Holzweg sein

creel /kriːl/ *n.* Fischkorb, *der*

creep /kriːp/

A *v.i.*, **crept** /krept/ **1** kriechen; (move timidly, slowly, stealthily) schleichen; **~ and crawl** (fig.) kriechen; **~ing Jesus** (Brit. coll.) Scheinheilige, *der/die;* (fig.: develop gradually) **~ing inflation/sickness** schleichende Inflation/Krankheit; (insinuate oneself/itself unobserved) **~ into sth.** sich in etw. (*Akk.*) einschleichen **2** **make sb.'s flesh ~:** jmdm. eine Gänsehaut über den Rücken jagen; **the thought made my flesh ~:** bei dem Gedanken lief mir eine Gänsehaut über den Rücken

B *n.* **1** *in pl.* (coll.) **give sb. the ~s** jmdm. nicht [ganz] geheuer sein **2** (coll.: person) Fiesling, *der* (salopp abwertend) **3** (Metallurgy) Kriechen, *das*

Phrasal verbs

- **~ 'in** *v.i.* [sich] hinein-/hereinschleichen; (fig.) ‹*Irrtum, Enttäuschung usw.:*› sich einschleichen
- **~ 'on** *v.i.* **time is ~ing on** die Zeit verrinnt [unaufhaltsam]
- **~ 'up** *v.i.* (approach) sich anschleichen; **~ up on sb.** sich an jmdn. anschleichen; (fig.) für jmdn. langsam näher rücken

creeper /ˈkriːpə(r)/ *n.* **1** (Bot.) (growing along ground) Kriechpflanze, *die;* (growing up wall etc.) Kletterpflanze, *die;* Rankengewächs, *das* **2** (Ornith.) [Wald]baumläufer, *der* **3** (coll.: soft-soled shoe) *Schuh mit dicker, weicher Sohle;* Leisetreter, *der* (scherzh.)

creepy /ˈkriːpɪ/ *adj.* unheimlich; gruselig, schaurig ‹*Geschichte, Film*›

creepy-crawly /kriːpɪ ˈkrɔːlɪ/ (coll./child lang.)

A *n.* **she's got a horror of creepy-crawlies** sie hat eine Heidenangst vor allem, was krabbelt; **there's a ~ in the bathtub** da krabbelt was in der Badewanne (ugs.)

B *adj.* krabbelnd ‹*Insekt*›

cremate /krɪˈmeɪt/ *v.t.* einäschern; kremieren (schweiz.)

cremation /krɪˈmeɪʃn/ *n.* Einäscherung, *die;* Kremation, *die*

crematorium /kreməˈtɔːrɪəm/ *n.*, *pl.* **crematoria** /kreməˈtɔːrɪə/ *or* **~s** Krematorium, *das*

crematory /ˈkremətərɪ/ *n.* (Amer.) Krematorium, *das*

crème: ~ de la ~ /kreɪm dlɑːˈkreɪm/ *n.* Crème de la crème, *die* (geh.); **~ de menthe** /kreɪm də ˈmɑ̃θ/ *n.* Pfefferminzlikör, *der*

crenellated /ˈkrenəleɪtɪd/ *adj.* kreneliert (veralt.); mit Zinnen versehen

Creole /ˈkriːəʊl/ ▸ **p. 1277**

A *n.* **1** (person) Kreole, *der/*Kreolin, *die;* (of mixed European and Black African descent) Mulatte, *der/*Mulattin, *die* **2** (language) Kreolisch, *das*

B *adj.* kreolisch

creosote /ˈkriːəsəʊt/

A *n.* Kreosot, *das*

B *v.t.* mit Kreosot behandeln

crêpe /kreɪp/ *n.* **1** Krepp, *der* **2** (~ rubber) Kreppgummi, *der;* **~ soles** Kreppsohlen *Pl.* **3** (pancake) dünner Eierkuchen

crêpe: ~ de Chine /kreɪp də ˈʃiːn/ *n.* Crêpe de Chine, *der;* **~ 'paper** *n.* Krepppapier, *das;* **~ 'rubber** *n.* Kreppgummi, *der;* **~ Suzette** /kreɪp suːˈzet/ *n.* (Cookery) Crêpe Suzette, *die*

crept ▸ **creep A**

crescendo /krɪˈʃendəʊ/ *n.*, *pl.* **~s** (Mus.) Crescendo, *das;* (fig.) Zunahme, *die;* **a ~ of cheers** immer lauter werdende Jubelrufe; **reach a ~** (fig. coll.) einen Höhepunkt erreichen

crescent /ˈkresənt/

A *n.* **1** Mondsichel, *die;* (as emblem) Halbmond, *der;* **~-shaped** halbmondförmig **2** (Brit.: street) [kleinere] halbkreisförmige Straße **3** (~-shaped object) Bogen, *der*

B *adj.* halbmondförmig; **the ~ moon** die Mondsichel

cress /kres/ *n.* Kresse, *die;* **garden ~:** Gartenkresse, *die; see also* **mustard 1**; **watercress**

crest /krest/ *n.* **1** (on bird's or animal's head) Kamm, *der;* (neck of horse) Genick, *das;* (plume of feathers) Federschopf, *der* **2** (top of mountain or wave) Kamm, *der;* (top of roof) Dachfirst, *der;* **[be/ride] on the ~ of a** *or* **the wave** (fig.) ganz oben [sein/schwimmen] **3** (Her.) Helmzier, *die;* (emblem) Emblem, *das*

crested /ˈkrestɪd/ *adj.* **1** ‹*Vogel, Tier*› mit einem Kamm; **~ tit/lark** Haubenmeise/-lerche, *die* **2** ‹*Siegel, Briefpapier usw.*› mit einem Emblem versehen

'crestfallen *adj.* (fig.) niedergeschlagen

Cretaceous /krɪˈteɪʃəs/

A *adj.* (Geol.) Kreide-; kretazeisch (fachspr.); **the ~ period** die Kreidezeit

B *n.* (Geol.) Kreide, *die*

Cretan /ˈkriːtn/

A *adj.* kretisch

B *n.* Kreter, *der/*Kreterin, *die*

Crete /kriːt/ *pr. n.* Kreta (*das*)

cretin /ˈkretɪn/ *n.* **1** (Med.) Kretin, *der* **2** (coll.: fool) Trottel, *der* (ugs. abwertend)

cretinous /ˈkretɪnəs/ *adj.* **1** (Med.) kretinoid **2** (coll.: stupid) schwachsinnig (abwertend)

cretonne /krɪˈtɒn, ˈkretɒn/ *n.* (Textiles) Cretonne, *die od. der*

Creutzfeldt-Jakob disease /ˈkrɔɪtsfelt ˈjækɒb/ *n.* ▸ **p. 1231** (Med.) Creutzfeldt-Jakob-Krankheit, *die*

crevasse /krɪˈvæs/ *n.* Gletscherspalte, *die*

crevice /ˈkrevɪs/ *n.* Spalt, *der;* (of skin) Riss, *der*

crew /kruː/

A *n.* **1** (of ship, aircraft, etc.) Besatzung, *die;* Crew, *die;* (excluding officers) Mannschaft, *die;* Crew, *die;* (of train) Personal, *das;* (Sport) Mannschaft, *die;* Crew, *die* **2** (associated body) Gruppe, *die;* (gang of workers) Kolonne, *die;* (often derog.: set) Haufen, *der;* **a motley ~:** ein bunt zusammengewürfelter Haufen

B *v.i.* die Mannschaft/Mitglied der Mannschaft sein; **he ~s on my boat** er gehört zu meiner Mannschaft

C *v.t.* **~ a boat** Mitglied der Mannschaft eines Bootes sein

crew: ~ cut *n.* Bürstenschnitt, *der;* **~-man** /ˈkruːmən/ *n.*, *pl.* **~-men** /ˈkruːmən/ Besatzungsmitglied, *das;* **~ neck** *n.* enger, runder Halsausschnitt; **a ~-neck pullover** ein Pullover mit engem, rundem Halsausschnitt

crib /krɪb/

A *n.* **1** (cot) Gitterbett, *das* **2** (model of manger scene; manger) Krippe, *die* **3** (coll.) (translation) Klatsche, *die* (Schülerspr.); (plagiarism) **that's a ~:** das ist abgekupfert (salopp)

B *v.t.*, **-bb-** (coll.) (plagiarize) abkupfern (salopp)

cribbage /ˈkrɪbɪdʒ/ *n.* (Cards) Cribbage, *das*

'crib death (Amer.) ▸ **cot death**

crick /krɪk/

A *n.* **a ~ [in one's neck/back]** ein steifer Hals/Rücken

B *v.t.* **~ one's neck/back** einen steifen Hals/Rücken bekommen

cricket[1] /ˈkrɪkɪt/ *n.* (Sport) Kricket, *das;* **it's/that's not ~** (Brit. dated coll.) das ist nicht die feine Art (ugs.)

cricket[2] *n.* (Zool.) Grille, *die;* **as lively as a ~:** putzmunter (ugs.)

cricket: ~ bag *n.* *Tasche für das Schlagholz usw.;* **~ ball** *n.* Kricketball, *der;* **~ bat** Schlagholz, *das*

cricketer /ˈkrɪkɪtə(r)/ *n.* Kricketspieler, *der/*-spielerin, *die*

cricket: ~ match *n.* Kricketspiel, *das;* **~ pitch** *n.* Kricketfeld, *das* (*zwischen den Toren*)

cri de cœur /kriː də ˈkɜː(r)/ *n.*, *pl.* **cris de cœur** /kriː də ˈkɜː(r)/ (complaint) Stoßseufzer, *der;* (appeal) [verzweifelter] Hilferuf

crier /ˈkraɪə(r)/ *n.* (in lawcourt) Gerichtsdiener, *der* (veralt.); (in a town) Ausrufer, *der*

crikey /ˈkraɪkɪ/ *int.* (coll.) Jesses (ugs.)

crime /kraɪm/ *n.* **1** Verbrechen, *das* **2** *collect.*, *no pl.* **a wave of ~:** eine Welle von Straftaten; **juvenile ~ is on the increase** die Jugendkriminalität nimmt zu; **lead a life of ~:** ein Krimineller sein; **~ doesn't pay** Verbrechen lohnen sich nicht **3** (fig. coll.: shameful action) Sünde, *die*

Crimea /kraɪˈmiːə/ *pr. n.* Krim, *die*

Crimean /kraɪˈmiːən/ *adj.* **the ~ War** der Krimkrieg

crime: ~ desk *n.* Verbrechensabteilung, *die;* Kriminalabteilung, *die;* **~ prevention** *n.*, *no pl.* Verbrechensverhütung, *die; attrib.* **C~ Prevention Officer** *Polizeibeamter, dessen/-beamtin, deren Aufgabe aktive, vorbeugende Verbrechensbekämpfung ist;* **~ rate** *n.* Kriminalitätsrate, *die;* **~ sheet** *n.* (Mil.) Strafregister, *das;* **~ story** *n.* Kriminalgeschichte, *die;* **~ wave** *n.* Welle von Straftaten; **~-writer** *n.* Kriminalschriftsteller, *der/*-schriftstellerin, *die*

criminal /ˈkrɪmɪnl/

A *adj.* **1** (illegal) kriminell; strafbar; (concerned with criminals and crime) Straf-; **~ act** *or* **deed/offence** Straftat, *die;* **take ~ proceedings against sb.** strafrechtlich gegen jmdn. vorgehen; **~ judge** Strafrichter, *der* **2** (guilty of crime) kriminell; straffällig; **~ gang** Verbrecherbande, *die* **3** (tending to be guilty of crime) kriminell **4** (fig. coll.) kriminell (ugs.); **it's ~ to do that** es ist eine Schande, das zu tun; **it's a ~ shame** es ist einfach ungeheuerlich; **it's a ~ waste** es ist eine sträfliche Verschwendung

B *n.* Kriminelle, *der/die*

criminal: ~ charge *n.* Anklage, *die;* **face ~ charges [for sth.]** sich [wegen etw.] vor Gericht zu verantworten haben; **there are ~ charges against him** er steht unter Anklage; **~ 'code** *n.* Strafgesetzbuch, *das;* **~ 'court** *n.* Strafgericht, *das;* Kriminalgericht, *das* (veralt.); **C~ Investi'gation Department** *n.* (Brit.) Kriminalpolizei, *die*

criminality /krɪmɪˈnælɪtɪ/ *n.* Kriminalität, *die*

criminalize /ˈkrɪmɪnəlaɪz/ *v.t.* unter Strafe stellen ‹*Tat, Verhalten*›; kriminalisieren ‹*Person*›

criminal: ~ 'law *n.* Strafrecht, *das;* **~ 'lawyer** *n.* Anwalt/Anwältin für Strafsachen; **~ 'libel** *n.* [schriftliche] Verleumdung

criminally /ˈkrɪmɪnəlɪ/ *adv.* kriminell; (according to criminal law) strafrechtlich

criminal 'record *n.* Strafregister, *das;* **have a ~:** vorbestraft sein

criminologist /krɪmɪˈnɒlədʒɪst/ *n.* ▸ **p. 1260** Kriminologe, *der/*Kriminologin, *die*

criminology /krɪmɪˈnɒlədʒɪ/ *n.* Kriminologie, *die*

crimp /krɪmp/ *v.t.* kräuseln; **~ed hair** onduliertes Haar

Crimplene ® /ˈkrɪmpliːn/ *n.* Crimplene, *das* (Wz); *knitterfreier Stoff*

crimson /ˈkrɪmzn/

A *adj.* purpurrot; **turn ~** ‹*Himmel:*› sich blutrot färben; (with anger) ‹*Mensch:*› rot anlaufen; (blush) puterrot werden

B *n.* Purpurrot, *das*

C *v.i.* purpurrot werden

cringe /krɪndʒ/ *v.i.* **1** (cower) zusammenzucken; ‹*Hund:*› sich ducken, kuschen; **~ at sth.** bei etw. zusammenzucken; **~ away** *or* **back [from sb./sth.]** [vor jmdm./etw.] zurückschrecken; **it makes me ~:** es lässt mich zusammenzucken; (in disgust) da wird mir schlecht **2** (behave obsequiously) kriechen (abwertend); kuschen; **~ before sb.** vor jmdm. kriechen *od.* kuschen; **go cringing to sb.** zu jmdm. gekrochen kommen

cringing /ˈkrɪndʒɪŋ/ *adj.* kriecherisch (abwertend); **a ~ person** ein Kriecher (abwertend)

crinkle /krɪŋkl/

A *n.* Knick, *der;* (in fabric) Knitterfalte, *die;* (in hair) Kräusel, *die;* (in skin) Fältchen, *das*

C

B v.t. knicken; zerknittern ‹Stoff, Papier›; kräuseln ‹Haar›
C v.i. ‹Stoff, Papier:› knittern; ‹Haar:› sich kräuseln; ‹Haut:› Fältchen bekommen; ‹Papierrand:› sich wellen
crinkly /ˈkrɪŋklɪ/ adj. zerknittert ‹Stoff, Papier›; gekräuselt ‹Haar›; faltig ‹Haut›
crinoline /ˈkrɪnəlɪn, ˈkrɪnəliːn/ n. (Hist.) Krinoline, die
cripes /kraɪps/ int. (dated coll.) Jesses (ugs.)
cripple /krɪpl/
A n. (lit. or fig.) Krüppel, der
B v.t. zum Krüppel machen; (fig.) lähmen
crippled /krɪpld/ adj. verkrüppelt ‹Arm, Baum, Bettler›; **be ~ with rheumatism** durch Rheuma gelähmt sein; **industry was ~ by the strikes** die Streiks haben die ganze Industrie lahmgelegt; **small firms, ~ by inflation** kleine, durch [die] Inflation geschwächte Firmen; **a ~ ship/plane** ein schwer beschädigtes Schiff/Flugzeug
crippling /ˈkrɪplɪŋ/ adj. zur Verkrüppelung führend ‹Krankheit, Verletzung›; (fig.) erdrückend ‹Preise, Inflationsrate, Steuern, Mieten›; lähmend ‹Streik, Schmerzen›; **deal sb. a ~ blow** (fig.) jmdm. einen vernichtenden Schlag versetzen
crisis /ˈkraɪsɪs/ n., pl. **crises** /ˈkraɪsiːz/ Krise, die; **reach ~ point** einen kritischen Punkt erreichen; **a time of ~:** eine kritische Zeit; **at times of ~:** in Krisenzeiten; **suffer a ~:** eine Krise durchmachen
crisis ˈmanagement n. Krisenmanagement, das
crisp /krɪsp/
A adj. knusprig ‹Brot, Keks, Kruste, Speck›; knackig ‹Apfel, Gemüse›; steif ‹Papier›; trocken ‹Herbstblätter, Zweige›; frisch [gebügelt/gestärkt] ‹Wäsche›; [druck]frisch ‹Banknote›; verharscht ‹Schnee›; (clearly defined) scharf ‹Züge, Umrisse, Kanten›; (bracing) frisch ‹Brise, Seeluft›; (brisk) knapp [und klar] ‹Stil›; frisch [und flott (ugs.)] ‹Auftreten, Erscheinung›; **~ intonation/speech** klare Intonation/Sprache
B n. **1** usu. in pl. (Brit.: potato ~) [Kartoffel]chip, der **2** (sth. overcooked) **be burned to a ~:** verbrannt sein
C v.t. (make ~) **~ [up]** aufbacken ‹Brot›; knusprig backen ‹Speck›; knackig machen ‹Gemüse›
ˈcrispbread n. Knäckebrot, das
crisper /ˈkrɪspə(r)/ n. Gemüsefach, das
crisply /ˈkrɪsplɪ/ adv. knusprig ‹gebacken›; klar ‹sprechen›; frisch ‹gebügelt, gestärkt›
crispness /ˈkrɪspnɪs/ n., no pl. (of bread, biscuit, bacon) Knusprigkeit, die; (of apple, vegetable) Knackigkeit, die; (of style) Knappheit [und Klarheit], die; (of manner) Frische [und Knappheit], die
crispy /ˈkrɪspɪ/ adj. knusprig ‹Brot, Keks, Speck›; knackig ‹Apfel, Gemüse›
crispy ˈnoodles n. pl. gebratene Nudeln
criss-cross /ˈkrɪskrɒs/
A n. Gewirr, das
B adj. **~ pattern** Muster aus gekreuzten Linien
C adv. kreuz und quer
D v.t. (intersect repeatedly) wiederholt schneiden
E v.i. (move crosswise) kreuz und quer laufen/fahren/fliegen usw.; (intersect repeatedly) kreuz und quer verlaufen
criterion /kraɪˈtɪərɪən/ n., pl. **criteria** /kraɪˈtɪərɪə/ Kriterium, das; **by what ~ will the issue be judged?** nach welchen Kriterien wird man die Angelegenheit beurteilen?
critic /ˈkrɪtɪk/ n. ▸**i** **p. 1260** Kritiker, der/Kritikerin, die; **literary ~:** Literaturkritiker, der/-kritikerin, die
critical /ˈkrɪtɪkl/ adj. **1** kritisch; **be ~ of sb./sth.** jmdn./etw. kritisieren; **cast a ~ eye over sth.** etw. mit kritischen Augen betrachten; **the play received ~ acclaim** das Stück fand die Anerkennung der Kritik; **~ skills/ability** Kritikfähigkeit, die; **~ edition** kritische Ausgabe **2** (involving risk, crucial) kritisch ‹Zustand, Punkt, Phase›; entscheidend ‹Faktor, Test›; gefährlich ‹Operation›
critical ˈcare n., no pl. (Med.) Intensivpflege, die; attrib. **~ unit/centre** Intensivstation, die/Intensivpflegezentrum, das; **~ beds/nurse** Intensiv[kranken]betten/Intensiv[krankenschwester, die
critically /ˈkrɪtɪkəlɪ/ adv. kritisch; **be ~ important** von entscheidender Bedeutung sein; **be ~ ill** ernstlich krank sein
critical: ~ ˈmass n. (Phys.) kritische Masse; **~ ˈpath** n. (Managem.) kritischer Pfad od. Weg; **~ path anˈalysis** n., no pl. (Managem.) kritische Pfadanalyse
criticise ▸**criticize**
criticism /ˈkrɪtɪsɪzm/ n. Kritik, die (**of** an + Dat.); **come in for a lot of ~:** heftig kritisiert werden; **be open to ~:** (receptive) für Kritik offen sein; (liable to be criticized) der Kritik ausgesetzt sein; **literary ~:** Literaturkritik, die
criticize /ˈkrɪtɪsaɪz/ v.t. kritisieren (**for** wegen); (review) besprechen; rezensieren; **~ sb. for sth.** jmdn. wegen etw. kritisieren
critique /krɪˈtiːk/ n. Kritik, die
critter /ˈkrɪtə(r)/ n. (coll. joc.) Viech, das (ugs.); (derog.: person) Kerl, der (ugs. abwertend); (female) Person, die (abwertend)
croak /krəʊk/
A n. (of frog) Quaken, das; (of raven, person) Krächzen, das
B v.i. **1** ‹Frosch:› quaken; ‹Rabe, Person:› krächzen **2** (sl.: die) abkratzen (salopp)
C v.t. krächzen
croaky /ˈkrəʊkɪ/ adj. krächzend
Croat /ˈkrəʊæt/ n. **1** (person) Kroate, der/Kroatin, die **2** (language) Kroatisch, das
Croatia /krəʊˈeɪʃə/ pr. n. Kroatien (das)
Croatian /krəʊˈeɪʃən/ ▸**i** **p. 1345**
A adj. kroatisch; **sb. is ~:** jmd. ist Kroate/Kroatin
B n. ▸**Croat**
croc /krɒk/ n. (coll.: crocodile) Krokodil, das
crochet /ˈkrəʊʃeɪ, ˈkrəʊʃɪ/
A n. Häkelarbeit, die; **~ hook** Häkelhaken, der
B v.t., p. t. and p. p. **~ed** /ˈkrəʊʃeɪd, ˈkrəʊʃɪd/ häkeln
crocheting /ˈkrəʊʃeɪɪŋ, ˈkrəʊʃɪɪŋ/ n. Häkeln, das; (product) Häkelarbeit, die
crock[1] /krɒk/ n. **1** (pot) Topf, der (aus Ton); (jar) Krug, der (aus Ton); see also **gold A 2** **2** (broken piece of earthenware) [Ton]scherbe, die
crock[2] (coll.)
A n. (person) Wrack, das (fig.); (vehicle) [Klapper]kiste, die (ugs.)
B v.i. **~ up** zusammenklappen
C v.t. **~ [up]** den Rest geben (+ Dat.) (ugs.)
crockery /ˈkrɒkərɪ/ n. Geschirr, das
crocodile /ˈkrɒkədaɪl/ n. **1** Krokodil, das; (skin) Krokodilleder, das; Kroko, das **2** (Brit. coll.: line of schoolchildren) Schulkinder in Zweierreihen; **walk in a ~:** zwei und zwei [hintereinander] gehen
crocodile: ~ clip n. (Electr.) Krokodilklemme, die; **~ tears** n. pl. Krokodilstränen Pl. (ugs.)
crocus /ˈkrəʊkəs/ n. Krokus, der
Croesus /ˈkriːsəs/ n. Krösus, der; **be as rich as ~:** ein [wahrer] Krösus sein
croft /krɒft/ n. (Brit.) **1** [kleines] Stück Acker-/Weideland **2** (smallholding) [kleines] Pachtgut
crofter /ˈkrɒftə(r)/ n. (Brit.) Pächter, der/Pächterin, die
crofting /ˈkrɒftɪŋ/ n., no pl., no art. (Brit.) Bewirtschaftung kleiner Pachtgüter
croissant /ˈkrwɑːsɑ̃/ n. Hörnchen, das
cromlech /ˈkrɒmlek/ n. **1** ▸**dolmen** **2** (stone circle) Kromlech, der
crone /krəʊn/ n. **a[n old] ~:** ein altes Weib
crony /ˈkrəʊnɪ/ n. Kumpel, der; (female) Freundin, (die;) (drinking companion) Kumpan, der; **they were old cronies** sie waren gute, alte Freunde
cronyism /ˈkrəʊnɪɪzm/ n., no pl. (derog.) Günstlingswirtschaft, die (abwertend); Vetternwirtschaft, die (abwertend)
crook /krʊk/
A n. **1** (coll.: rogue) Gauner, der **2** (staff) Hirtenstab, der; (of bishop) [Krumm]stab, der **3** (hook) Haken, der **4** (of arm) [Arm]beuge, die **5** (curve in river, road, etc.) Biegung, die
B adj. (Austral. and NZ coll.) mies (ugs.); (ill) krank; (bad-tempered) sauer (ugs.); **go ~:** sauer werden (**at, on** + Akk.)
C v.t. biegen; **~ one's finger** seinen Finger krümmen; **she has only to ~ her little finger** (fig.) sie braucht nur mit dem kleinen Finger zu winken
crooked
A /krʊkt/ p.t. and p.p. of **crook C**
B adj. **1** /ˈkrʊkɪd/ krumm; schief ‹Lächeln›; (fig.: dishonest) betrügerisch; **the picture on the wall is ~:** das Bild an der Wand hängt schief; **you've got your hat on ~:** dein Hut sitzt schief; **a ~ person** (fig.) ein Gauner; **~ dealings** krumme Geschäfte **2** /krʊkt/ (having a transverse handle) **a ~ stick** ein Krückstock
crookedly /ˈkrʊkɪdlɪ/ adv. schief; **a tree that has grown ~:** ein krumm gewachsener Baum; (fig.: dishonestly) **deal ~:** krumme Geschäfte machen; **~ acquired** unrechtmäßig erworben
crookedness /ˈkrʊkɪdnɪs/ n., no pl. Verkrümmung, die; (fig.: dishonesty) Unehrlichkeit, die
croon /kruːn/
A v.t. & i. [leise] singen; ‹Popsänger:› schmachtend singen; schnulzen (ugs. abwertend)
B n. [leises] Singen
crooner /ˈkruːnə(r)/ n.: Sänger mit schmachtender Stimme; Schnulzensänger, der (ugs. abwertend)
crop /krɒp/
A n. **1** (Agric.) [Feld]frucht, die; (season's total yield) Ernte, die; (fig.) [An]zahl, die; **cereal ~:** Getreide, das; **get the ~s in** die Ernte einbringen; **arable ~s** Feldfrüchte Pl.; **~ of apples** Apfelernte, die **2** (of bird) Kropf, der **3** (of whip) [Peitschen]stiel, der; **[hunting] ~:** Jagdpeitsche, die **4** (of hair) kurzer Haarschnitt; (style) Kurzhaarfrisur, die
B v.t., **-pp-** **1** (cut off) abschneiden; (cut short) stutzen ‹Bart, Haare, Hecken, Flügel›; kupieren ‹Ohren, Schwanz› (bei Hunden od. Pferden); abschneiden ‹Kante›; ‹Tier:› abweiden ‹Gras›; **have one's hair ~ped** sich (Dat.) das Haar kurz schneiden lassen **2** (reap) ernten
C v.i., **-pp-** tragen
Phrasal verbs
- **~ ˈout** ▸**~ up 2**
- **~ ˈup** v.i. **1** (occur) auftauchen; (be mentioned) erwähnt werden **2** (Geol.) ausbeißen

crop: ~ circle n. Kornkreis, der; **~-dusting** n., no pl. (Agric.) Schädlingsbekämpfung aus der Luft; **~-eared** adj. ‹Tier› mit gestutzten od. kupierten Ohren
cropper /ˈkrɒpə(r)/ n. (coll.: heavy fall) [schwerer] Sturz; **come a ~:** einen Sturz bauen (ugs.); (fig.) auf die Nase fallen (ugs.)
crop: ~ rotation n. (Agric.) Fruchtfolge, die; **~-spraying** n. (Agric.) Schädlingsbekämpfung (mit Sprühmitteln); **~ top** n. bauch- od. nabelfreies Top
croquet /ˈkrəʊkeɪ, ˈkrəʊkɪ/ n. Krocket[spiel], das
croquette /krəˈket/ n. (Cookery) Krokette, die
crosier /ˈkrəʊzɪə(r)/ n. Krummstab, der
cross /krɒs/
A n. **1** Kreuz, das; (monument) [Gedenk]kreuz, das; (sign) Kreuzzeichen, das; **the C~:** das Kreuz [Christi]; **make the sign of the C~:** das Kreuzzeichen machen; ein Kreuz schlagen
2 (~-shaped thing or mark) Kreuz[zeichen], das; **mark with a ~:** ankreuzen
3 (mixture, compromise) Mittelding, das (**between** zwischen + Dat.); Mischung, die (**between** aus)
4 (trial, affliction, cause of trouble) Kreuz, das; Leid, das; **take [up] one's ~:** sein Kreuz auf sich nehmen; **we all have our [little] ~es to bear** wir haben alle unser Kreuz zu tragen
5 (intermixture of breeds) Kreuzung, die
6 (Astron.) **[Southern] C~:** Kreuz des Südens; Südliches Kreuz
7 (decoration) Kreuz, das; **Grand C~:** Großkreuz, das
8 (Footb.) Querpass, der; (Boxing) Cross, der
9 **on the ~:** quer
10 (Dressmaking) **cut on the ~:** schräg [zum Fadenlauf] zugeschnitten

B *v.t.* **1** (place crosswise) [über]kreuzen; **~ one's arms/legs** die Arme verschränken/die Beine übereinander schlagen; **~ one's fingers** *or* **keep one's fingers ~ed [for sb.]** (fig.) [jmdm.] die *od.* den Daumen drücken/halten; **~ swords [with sb.]** (fig.) [mit jmdm.] die Schwerter kreuzen *od.* sich streiten (**on** über + *Akk.*); **I got a ~ed line** (Teleph.) es war jemand in der Leitung; **you've got your** *or* **the lines** *or* **wires ~ed** (fig. coll.) du hast da etwas falsch verstanden; **~ a fortune teller's hand** *or* **palm with silver** einer Wahrsagerin Geld in die Hand drücken
2 (go across) kreuzen; überqueren ‹*Straße, Gewässer, Gebirge*›; durchqueren ‹*Land, Wüste, Zimmer*›; **~ the picket line** die Streikpostenkette durchbrechen; **~ the road** über die Straße gehen; **we can ~** *abs.* die Straße ist frei; wir können gehen/fahren; **'~ now'** „Gehen"; **the bridge ~es the river** die Brücke führt über den Fluss; **the lines ~ each other** die Linien schneiden sich; **a train ~ed the river** ein Zug fuhr über den Fluss; **a plane ~es the desert** ein Flugzeug fliegt über *od.* überfliegt die Wüste; **~ sb.'s mind** (fig.) jmdm. einfallen; **it seems never to have ~ed his mind to do it** es scheint ihm nie in den Sinn gekommen zu sein *od.* es scheint ihm nie der Gedanke gekommen zu sein, es zu tun; **~ sb.'s path** (fig.) jmdm. über den Weg laufen (ugs.); jmdm. begegnen
3 (Brit.) **~ a cheque** einen Scheck zur Verrechnung ausstellen; **a ~ed cheque** ein Verrechnungsscheck
4 (make sign of ~ on) **~ oneself** sich bekreuzigen; **~ my heart** Ehrenwort!
5 (thwart) durchkreuzen ‹*Plan*›; zerstören ‹*Hoffnung*›; vereiteln ‹*Wunsch, Hoffnung*›; **be ~ed in love** Unglück in der Liebe haben; **he ~es me in everything I do** er kommt mir bei allem in die Quere
6 (cause to interbreed) kreuzen; (**~-fertilize**) kreuzbefruchten. *See also* **bridge**[1] **A 1**; **T 1**

C *v.i.* (meet and pass) aneinander vorbeigehen; **~ [in the post]** ‹*Briefe:*› sich kreuzen; **our paths have ~ed several times** (fig.) unsere Wege haben sich öfters gekreuzt

D *adj.* **1** (transverse) Quer-; **~ traffic** kreuzender Verkehr
2 (peevish) verärgert; ärgerlich ‹*Worte*›; **sb. will be ~:** jmd. wird ärgerlich *od.* böse werden; **be ~ with sb.** böse auf jmdn. *od.* mit jmdm. sein; **as ~ as two sticks** (coll.) unleidlich
3 (Cricket) **~ bat** *schräg gehaltenes Schlagholz*

Phrasal verbs
- **~ 'off** *v.t.* streichen; **~ a name off a list** einen Namen von einer Liste streichen
- **~ 'out** *v.t.* ausstreichen
- **~ 'over** *v.t.* überqueren; *abs.* hinübergehen

cross- *in comb.* **1** ▸**cross A 1** Kreuz- **2** ▸**cross D** Quer- **3** **= across** quer durch

cross: ~bar *n.* **1** [Fahrrad]stange, *die;* **2** (Footb.) Querlatte, *die;* **~-beam** *n.* Querbalken, *der;* **~-bench** *n.* (Brit. Parl.) *quergestellte Bank, auf der die „cross-benchers" sitzen;* **~-bencher** *n.* Abgeordnete, *der/die weder der Regierungspartei noch der Opposition angehört;* **~bill** *n.* (Ornith.) Kreuzschnabel, *der;* **~bones** *n. pl.* gekreuzte Knochen *Pl.* (*unter Totenkopf*); **~bow** *n.* Armbrust, *die;* **~-bred** *adj.* gekreuzt; **~-breed A** *n.* Hybride, *die;* (animal) Bastard, *der;* **B** *v.t.* kreuzen; **~-buttock** *n.* (Wrestling) Hüftwurf, *der;* **~-Channel** *adj.* **~-Channel traffic/ferry** Verkehr/Fähre über den Kanal; **~-check A** *n.* Gegenprobe, *die;* **B** *v.t.* [nochmals] nachprüfen; nachkontrollieren; **~-country A** *adj.* Querfeldein-; **~-country running** Crosslauf, *der;* Querfeldeinlauf, *der;* **~-country skiing** Skilanglauf, *der;* **B** *adv.* querfeldein; **~-cultural** *adj.* interkulturell; **~-current** *n.* (lit. or fig.) Gegenströmung, *die;* **~-dressing** *n.* Crossdressing, *das;* **~-examination** *n.* Kreuzverhör, *das;* **undergo** *or* **be under ~-examination** ins Kreuzverhör genommen werden; **~-examine** *v.t.* ins Kreuzverhör nehmen; einem Kreuzverhör unterziehen; **~-eyed** *adj.* [nach innen] schielend; **be ~-eyed** schielen; **~-fertili'zation** *n.* Fremdbestäubung, *die;* Kreuzbefruchtung, *die;* (fig.) gegenseitige Befruchtung; **~-'fertilize** *v.t.* fremdbestäuben; kreuzbefruchten; (fig.) sich gegenseitig befruchten; **~fire** *n.* (lit. or fig.) Kreuzfeuer, *das;* **~-grained** *adj.* (fig.) verquer, vertrackt ‹*Situation, Problem*›; querköpfig ‹*Person*›; **~-head[ing]** *n.* Überschrift, *die*

crossing /ˈkrɒsɪŋ/ *n.* **1** (act of going across) Überquerung, *die;* **a Channel ~:** eine Überfahrt über den Kanal **2** (road or rail intersection) Kreuzung, *die* **3** (pedestrian ~) Überweg, *der;* **[railway] ~:** Bahnübergang, *der* **4** (in church) Vierung, *die*

cross-legged /ˈkrɒslegd/ *adv.* mit gekreuzten Beinen; (with feet across thighs) im Schneidersitz

crossly /ˈkrɒslɪ/ *adv.* verärgert

crossness /ˈkrɒsnɪs, ˈkrɔːsnɪs/ *n., no pl.* Verärgerung, *die*

cross: ~-over *n.* Übergang, *der;* (Railw.) Gleiskreuzung, *die;* **~ ownership** *n., no pl.* Überkreuzbeteiligung, *die;* **~-party** *adj.* parteiübergreifend ‹*Unterstützung, Verhandlungen*›; **committee of ~-party MPs** Ausschuss mit Abgeordneten verschiedener Parteien; **~patch** *n.* Griesgram, *der;* Miesepeter, *der;* **~piece** *n.* Querbalken, *der;* **~-ply tyre** *n.* Diagonalreifen, *der;* **~-'pollinate** *v.t.* kreuzbestäuben; **~ 'purposes** *n. pl.* **talk at ~ purposes** aneinander vorbeireden; **be at ~ purposes [with sb.]** (have different aims) gegensätzliche Vorstellungen haben; (misunderstand) [jmdn.] missverstehen; **~-'question** *v.t.* ins Kreuzverhör nehmen; **~-refer** *v.i.* einen Querverweis machen; **~ 'reference** *n.* Querverweis, *der;* **~-reference** *v.t.* verweisen ‹*Person, Stichwort*› (**to** auf + *Akk.*); mit Querverweisen versehen ‹*Eintrag, Werk*›; **~roads** *n. sing.* Kreuzung, *die;* (fig.) Wendepunkt, *der;* **be at a/the ~roads** (fig.) am Scheideweg stehen; **~ section** *n.* Querschnitt, *der;* (fig.) repräsentative Auswahl; **in ~ section** im Querschnitt; **a ~ section of the population** ein Querschnitt durch die Bevölkerung; **~-stitch** *n.* Kreuzstichstickerei, *die;* (stitch) Kreuzstich, *der;* **~ street** *n.* (Amer.) Querstraße, *die;* **~-subsidy** *n.* Quersubventionierung, *die;* **~talk** *n.* (Communications) Übersprechen, *das;* **~-town A** *adj.* **a ~-town route/road** eine Strecke/Straße, die quer durch die Stadt führt; **a ~-town bus** ein Bus, der quer durch die Stadt fährt; **B** *adv.* (Amer.) quer durch die Stadt ‹*gehen, fahren*›; **~-voting** *n., no pl. Stimmabgabe für eine andere als die eigene Partei;* **~walk** *n.* (Amer.) Fußgängerüberweg, *der*

crossways /ˈkrɒsweɪz/ ▸**crosswise B**

'crosswind *n.* Seitenwind, *der*

crosswise /ˈkrɒswaɪz/
A *adj.* Quer-
B *adv.* kreuzweise; (of one in relation to another) quer

crossword /ˈkrɒswɜːd/ *n.* **~ [puzzle]** Kreuzworträtsel, *das*

crotch /krɒtʃ/ *n.* **1** (of tree) Gabelung, *die* **2** (of trousers, body) Schritt, *der;* **kick sb. in the ~:** jmdn. zwischen die Beine treten

crotchet /ˈkrɒtʃɪt/ *n.* (Brit. Mus.) Viertelnote, *die*

crotchety /ˈkrɒtʃɪtɪ/ *adj.* launisch; quengelig ‹*Kind*›

crotchless /ˈkrɒtʃlɪs/ *adj.* im Schritt offen; **~ panties** Slip ouvert, *der;* Ouvert-Slip, *der*

crouch /kraʊtʃ/ *v.i.* [sich zusammen]kauern; **~ down** sich niederkauern; ‹*Person:*› sich hinhocken

croup[1] /kruːp/ *n.* (of horse) Kruppe, *die*

croup[2] *n.* (Med.) Krupp, *der*

croupier /ˈkruːpɪə(r), ˈkruːpɪeɪ/ *n.* ▸ⓘ **p. 1260** Croupier, *der*

crouton /ˈkruːtɔ̃/ *n.* (Gastr.) Croûton, *der*

crow /krəʊ/
A *n.* **1** (bird) Krähe, *die;* **as the ~ flies** Luftlinie; **eat ~** (Amer. fig.) zu Kreuze kriechen **2** (cry of cock or infant) Krähen, *das* **3** ▸**crowbar**
B *v.i.* **1** ‹*Hahn, Baby:*› krähen **2** (exult) **~ over** [hämisch] frohlocken über (+ *Akk.*)

crow: ~bar *n.* Brechstange, *die;* **~berry** *n.* (Bot.) Krähenbeere, *die*

crowd /kraʊd/
A *n.* **1** (large number of persons) Menschenmenge, *die;* **~[s] of people** Menschenmassen *Pl.*; **he would pass in a ~:** er ist passabel; **stand out from the ~:** aus der Menge herausragen **2** (mass of spectators, audience) Zuschauermenge, *die* **3** (multitude) breite Masse; **follow the ~** (fig.) mit der Herde laufen; **be just one of the ~** (fig.) in der Masse untergehen **4** (coll.: company, set) Clique, *die;* **a strange ~:** ein komischer Haufen **5** (large number of things) Menge, *die;* **a ~ of thoughts/new ideas** eine Menge Gedanken/ein Haufen neuer Ideen
B *v.t.* **1** (collect in a ~) **be ~ed at a place** sich an einem Ort drängen **2** (fill, occupy, cram) füllen; **~ people into a bus/room** Leute in einen Bus/ein Zimmer pferchen; **~ sth. with sth.** etw. mit etw. voll stopfen; **the port was ~ed with ships** im Hafen lagen die Schiffe dicht an dicht; **the streets were ~ed with people** die Straßen waren voll mit Leuten **3** (fig.: fill) ausfüllen; **the year was ~ed with incidents** es war ein sehr ereignisreiches Jahr **4** (come close to) [absichtlich] fast berühren **5** (force) drängen; **~ sb. into doing sth.** jmdn. drängen, etw. zu tun **6** (Amer. coll.: approach) **he's ~ing thirty** er geht auf die Dreißig zu
C *v.i.* **1** (collect) sich sammeln; **~ around sb./sth.** sich um jmdn./etw. drängen *od.* scharen **2** (force itself) strömen; **memories were ~ing in [on him]** Erinnerungen stürmten auf ihn ein; **~ into/through sth.** in (+ *Akk.*)/durch etw. strömen *od.* drängen

Phrasal verb
- **~ 'out** *v.t.* herausdrängen; **be ~ed out by sth.** von etw. verdrängt werden

crowd: ~ control *n.: Ordnungsdienst bei Großveranstaltungen;* **~ control barrier** *n.* [Polizei]absperrung, *die*

crowded /ˈkraʊdɪd/ *adj.* überfüllt; voll ‹*Programm*›; ereignisreich ‹*Tag, Leben, Karriere*›; **~ 'out** (coll.) proppenvoll (ugs.); gerammelt voll (ugs.)

crowd: ~-pleaser /ˈkraʊd pliːzə(r)/ *n.* Publikumsliebling, *der;* (thing) Publikumserfolg, *der;* **~-puller** /ˈkraʊd pʊlə(r)/ *n.* (coll.) Publikumsmagnet, *der;* **~ safety** *n., no pl.* Publikumssicherheit, *die;* Besuchersicherheit, *die;* **~ scene** *n.* Massenszene, *die;* **~ trouble** *n.* [Publikums]ausschreitungen *Pl.*

'crowfoot *n.* (Bot.) Hahnenfuß, *der*

crown /kraʊn/
A *n.* **1** (of monarch; device, ornament) Krone, *die;* **the C~:** die Krone; **succeed to the C~:** die Thronfolge antreten; **be heir to the C~:** Thronfolger/-folgerin sein; **the world heavyweight ~:** der Weltmeisterschaftstitel im Schwergewicht **2** (wreath of flowers etc.) Sieger-, Ehrenkranz, *der* **3** (bird's crest) Kamm, *der* **4** (of head) Scheitel, *der;* (of arched structure) Scheitelpunkt, *der;* (of arch) Kappe, *die;* (of tree, tooth) Krone, *die;* (of hat) Kopfteil, *das;* (thing that forms the summit) Gipfel, *der;* (fig.) Krönung, *die* **5** (coin) Krone, *die*
B *v.t.* **1** krönen; **~ sb. king/queen** jmdn. zum König/zur Königin krönen **2** (surmount) krönen; **the hill was ~ed with trees** die Kuppe des Hügels war mit Bäumen bewachsen **3** (put finishing touch to) krönen; **to ~ [it] all** zur Krönung des Ganzen; (to make things even worse) um das Maß voll zu machen **4** (bring to happy ending) krönen; **success ~ed his efforts** seine Anstrengungen waren von Erfolg gekrönt **5** (coll.: hit on the head) einen überbraten (salopp) (+ *Dat.*) **6** (Draughts) zur Dame machen; eine Dame bekommen mit **7** (Dent.) überkronen; eine Krone machen für

crown: ~ 'cap *n.* Kron[en]korken, *der;* **C~ 'Colony** *n.* Kronkolonie, *die;* **C~ 'Court** *n.* (Brit. Law) Krongericht, *das*

crowned /kraʊnd/ *adj.* **1** (invested with royal crown) gekrönt **2** (provided with a crown) mit einer Krone; *see also* **head A 1**

'crown green *n.: Bowlingrasen, der in der Mitte höher ist als an den Seiten*

crowning /ˈkraʊnɪŋ/
A *n.* Krönung, *die*

B *adj.* krönend; **her ~ glory is her hair** ihr Haar ist ihre größte Zier

crown: ~ 'jewels *n. pl.* Kronjuwelen; **~ land** *n.* Ländereien *Pl.* der Krone; **~ of 'thorns** *n.* (Zool., Relig.) Dornenkrone, *die;* **C~ 'prince** *n.* (lit. or fig.) Kronprinz, *der;* **C~ 'princess** *n.* Kronprinzessin, *die*

crow: ~'s-foot *n., usu. in pl.* Krähenfuß, *der;* **~'s-nest** *n.* (Naut.) Krähennest, *das;* Mastkorb, *der*

C

crozier ▸**crosier**

crucial /ˈkruːʃl/ *adj.* entscheidend (**to** für)

crucially /ˈkruːʃəlɪ/ *adv.* entscheidend; **be ~ important** von entscheidender Wichtigkeit sein

crucible /ˈkruːsɪbl/ *n.* [Schmelz]tiegel, *der*

crucifix /ˈkruːsɪfɪks/ *n.* Kruzifix, *das*

crucifixion /kruːsɪˈfɪkʃn/ *n.* Kreuzigung, *die*

cruciform /ˈkruːsɪfɔːm/ *adj.* kreuzförmig

crucify /ˈkruːsɪfaɪ/ *v.t.* **1** kreuzigen **2** (torment, persecute) peinigen; verfolgen; (severely criticize) verreißen

crud /krʌd/ *n.* (sl.) **1** (impurity etc.) Verunreinigung, *die;* Fremdstoff, *der* **2** (nonsense) Schrott, *der* (salopp); Mist, *der* (ugs.)

crude /kruːd/

A *adj.* **1** (in natural or raw state) roh; Roh-; **~ oil/ore** Rohöl, *das*/Roherz, *das* **2** (fig.: rough, unpolished) primitiv; simpel; grob ‹*Entwurf, Skizze*› **3** (rude, blunt) ungehobelt, ungeschliffen ‹*Person, Benehmen*›; grob, derb ‹*Worte*›; ordinär ‹*Witz*› **4** (not adjusted or corrected) unbereinigt ‹*Statistik*›; roh ‹*Ziffer*›

B *n.* Rohöl, *das;* Erdöl, *das*

crudely /ˈkruːdlɪ/ *adv.* (roughly) grob ‹*skizzieren, schätzen, entwerfen*›; (rudely, bluntly) ungehobelt, ungeschliffen ‹*sich benehmen*›; derb, plump ‹*sagen*›; ordinär ‹*reden*›

crudeness /ˈkruːdnɪs/ *n. no pl.* **1** (roughness) Primitivität, *die;* (of theory, design, plan) Skizzenhaftigkeit, *die* **2** (rudeness, bluntness) (of person, behaviour, manners) Ungeschliffenheit, *die;* (of words) Derbheit, *die;* (of joke) Geschmacklosigkeit, *die*

crudity /ˈkruːdɪtɪ/ *n.* **1** *no pl.* ▸**crudeness** **2** (crude remark) Grobheit, *die*

cruel /ˈkruːəl/ *adj.,* (Brit.) **-ll-** **1** grausam; **be ~ to sb.** grausam zu jmdm. sein; **be ~ to animals** ein Tierquäler sein; **be ~ to one's dog** seinen Hund quälen **2** (causing pain or suffering) grausam; unbarmherzig; **be ~ to be kind** in jmds. Interesse unbarmherzig sein müssen

cruelly /ˈkruːəlɪ/ *adv.* grausam; unbarmherzig ‹*kritisieren*›; **life treated him ~:** das Leben spielte ihm grausam mit

cruelty /ˈkruːəltɪ/ *n.* ▸**cruel**: Grausamkeit, *die;* Unbarmherzigkeit, *die;* **~ to animals** Tierquälerei, *die;* **~ to children** Kindesmisshandlung, *die*

'cruelty-free *adj.* ohne Tierquälerei hergestellt

cruet /ˈkruːɪt/ *n.* **1** Essig-/Ölfläschchen, *das* **2** ▸**cruet stand**

'cruet stand *n.* Menage, *die*

cruise /kruːz/

A *v.i.* **1** (sail for pleasure) eine Kreuzfahrt machen **2** (at random) ‹*Fahrzeug, Fahrer:*› herumfahren **3** (at economical speed) ‹*Fahrzeug:*› mit Dauergeschwindigkeit fahren; ‹*Flugzeug:*› mit Reisegeschwindigkeit fliegen; **cruising speed** Reisegeschwindigkeit, *die;* **we are now cruising at a height/speed of ...:** wir fliegen nun in einer Flughöhe/mit einer Reisegeschwindigkeit von ... **4** (for protection of shipping) kreuzen

B *n.* Kreuzfahrt, *die;* **go on** *or* **for a ~:** eine Kreuzfahrt machen

cruise: ~ control *n.* Tempomat, *der;* **~ missile** *n.* Marschflugkörper, *der*

cruiser /ˈkruːzə(r)/ *n.* Kreuzer, *der*

'cruiserweight *n.* (Boxing etc.) Halbschwergewicht, *das;* (person also) Halbschwergewichtler, *der*

'cruise ship *n.* Kreuzfahrtschiff, *das*

cruising: ~ altitude *n.* Reiseflughöhe, *die;* **~ speed** *n.* Reisegeschwindigkeit, *die*

crumb /krʌm/

A *n.* **1** Krümel, *der;* Brösel, *der;* (fig.) Brocken, *der;* **~s of wisdom** ein bisschen Weisheit; **~s from the rich man's table** (fig.) Brosamen, die von des Reichen Tische fallen; **~[s] of comfort** kleiner Trost **2** (soft part of bread) Krume, *die*

B *v.t.* (cover with ~s) panieren

crumble /ˈkrʌmbl/

A *v.t.* zerbröckeln ‹*Brot*›; zerkrümeln ‹*Keks, Kuchen*›; **~ sth. into/onto sth.** etw. in/auf etw. (*Akk.*) bröckeln *od.* krümeln

B *v.i.* ‹*Brot, Kuchen:*› krümeln; ‹*Gestein:*› [zer]bröckeln; ‹*Mauer:*› zusammenfallen; (fig.) ‹*Hoffnung:*› sich zerschlagen; ‹*Reich, Gesellschaft:*› zerfallen, zugrunde gehen

C *n.* (Cookery) **1** (dish) *mit Streuseln bestreutes und überbackenes* [*Apfel-, Rhabarber- usw.*]*dessert* **2** (substance) Streusel *Pl.*

crumbly /ˈkrʌmblɪ/ *adj.* krümelig ‹*Keks, Kuchen, Brot*›; bröckelig ‹*Gestein, Erde*›

crumbs /krʌmz/ *int.* (Brit. coll.) Mensch (ugs.); verflixt (ugs.)

crummy /ˈkrʌmɪ/ *adj.* (coll.) **1** (dirty, unpleasant) schmuddelig (ugs.); verdreckt (ugs.) **2** (inferior, worthless) mies (ugs.)

crumpet /ˈkrʌmpɪt/ *n.* **1** (cake) *weiches Hefeküchlein zum Toasten* **2** (sl.: women) Weiber *Pl.* (salopp); Miezen *Pl.* (salopp); **a bit/piece of ~:** ein Weib **3** (arch. coll.: head) Birne, *die* (salopp); Rübe, *die* (salopp); **off one's ~:** übergeschnappt

crumple /ˈkrʌmpl/

A *v.t.* **1** (crush) zerdrücken; zerquetschen **2** (ruffle, wrinkle) zerknittern ‹*Kleider, Papier, Stoff*›; **~ [up] a piece of paper** ein Stück Papier zerknüllen

B *v.i.* ‹*Kleider, Stoff, Papier:*› knittern; **~ [up]** (fig.) ‹*Person:*› zusammensinken

'crumple zone *n.* (Motor Veh.) Knautschzone, *die*

crunch /krʌnʃ/

A *v.t.* [geräuschvoll] knabbern ‹*Keks, Zwieback*›; [geräuschvoll] nagen an (+ *Dat.*) ‹*Knochen*›

B *v.i.* **1** **~ away [at sth.]** [an etw. (*Dat.*)] herumknabbern *od.* -nagen **2** ‹*Schnee, Kies:*› knirschen; ‹*Eis:*› [zer]splittern; **the wheels ~ed on the gravel** der Kies knirschte unter den Rädern; **he ~ed through the snow** er ging durch den knirschenden Schnee

C *n.* **1** (crunching noise) Knirschen, *das* **2** (decisive event) **when it comes to the ~, when the ~ comes** wenn es hart auf hart geht

crunchy /ˈkrʌnʃɪ/ *adj.* knusprig ‹*Gebäck, Nüsse*›; knackig ‹*Apfel*›

crupper /ˈkrʌpə(r)/ *n.* **1** (strap) Schweifriemen, *der* **2** (of horse) Kruppe, *die*

crusade /kruːˈseɪd/

A *n.* (Hist.) Kreuzzug, *der;* **a ~ against sth.** (fig.) ein Feldzug *od.* Kreuzzug gegen etw

B *v.i.* einen Kreuzzug unternehmen; (fig.) zu Felde ziehen

crusader /kruːˈseɪdə(r)/ *n.* (Hist.) Kreuzfahrer, *der;* Kreuzritter, *der*

crush /krʌʃ/

A *v.t.* **1** (compress with violence) quetschen; auspressen ‹*Trauben, Obst*›; (kill, destroy) zerquetschen; zermalmen; **~ to death** zu Tode quetschen; **~ed strawberry** (colour) Erdbeerrot, *das* **2** (reduce to powder) zerstampfen; zermahlen; zerstoßen ‹*Gewürze, Tabletten*› **3** (fig.: subdue, overwhelm) niederwerfen, niederschlagen ‹*Aufstand*›; vernichten ‹*Feind*›; zunichte machen ‹*Hoffnungen, Wünsche*›; **her angry look ~ed him** vernichtend traf ihn ihr zorniger Blick **4** (crumple, crease) zerknittern ‹*Kleid, Stoff*›; zerdrücken, verbeulen ‹*Hut*›

B *n.* **1** (crowded mass) Gedränge, *das;* Gewühl, *das* **2** (coll.) (infatuation) Schwärmerei, *die;* (person) Schwarm, *der* (ugs.); **have/get a ~ on sb.** in jmdn. verknallt sein/sich in jmdn. verknallen (ugs.) **3** (drink) Saftgetränk, *das* **4** (coll.: crowded gathering) Rummel, *der* (ugs.)

crush: ~ bar *n.* Bar, *die* (*im Foyer eines Theaters*); **~ barrier** *n.* Absperrgitter, *das*

crushing /ˈkrʌʃɪŋ/ *adj.* niederschmetternd ‹*Antwort*›; vernichtend ‹*Niederlage, Schlag*›

crust /krʌst/ *n.* **1** (of bread) Kruste, *die;* Rinde, *die* **2** (hard surface, coating, deposit) Kruste, *die;* **the earth's ~:** die Erdkruste **3** (of pie) Teigdeckel, *der* **4** (scab) Kruste, *die;* Schorf, *der* **5** (fig.: superficial hardness) Panzer, *der* **6** (in wine bottle) Depot, *das. See also* **last**[1] **A**; **upper A 2**

crustacean /krʌˈsteɪʃn/ *n.* Krusten- *od.* Krebstier, *das;* Krustazee, *die* (fachspr.)

crusted /ˈkrʌstɪd/ *adj.* (having a crust) verkrustet; abgelagert ‹*Wein*›; **~ snow** Harsch, *der*

crusty /ˈkrʌstɪ/ *adj.* **1** (crisp) knusprig **2** (hard) hart **3** (irritable, curt) barsch

crutch /krʌtʃ/ *n.* **1** (lit. or fig.) Krücke, *die;* **go about on ~es** an Krücken gehen **2** ▸**crotch 2**

crux /krʌks/ *n., pl.* **~es** *or* **cruces** /ˈkruːsiːz/ **1** (difficult matter, puzzle) Rätsel, *das;* harte Nuss (ugs.); **the ~ of the matter** der Haken bei der Sache **2** (decisive point) Kern[punkt], *der;* **the ~ of the matter** der springende Punkt bei der Sache

cry /kraɪ/

A *n.* **1** (loud utterance of grief) Schrei, *der;* (loud utterance of words) Schreien, *das;* Geschrei, *das;* (of hounds or wolves) Heulen, *das;* Geheul, *das;* (of birds) Schreien, *das;* Geschrei, *das;* **a ~ of pain/rage/happiness** ein Schmerzens-/Wut-/Freudenschrei; **a far ~ from ...** (fig.) etwas ganz anderes als ...; **be in full ~** ‹*Hundemeute:*› laut bellend hinter der Beute herhetzen; **be in full ~ after sb.** (fig.) jmdn. mit großem Geheul verfolgen **2** (appeal, entreaty) Appell, *der;* **a ~ for freedom/independence/justice** ein Ruf nach Freiheit/Unabhängigkeit/Gerechtigkeit; **a ~ for mercy** eine flehentliche Bitte um Gnade; **a ~ for help** ein Hilferuf **3** (proclamation of goods or business) Ausrufen, *das* **4** (public demand) Ruf, *der* **5** (watchword) Losung, *die;* Parole, *die;* (in battle) Schlachtruf, *der* **6** (fit or spell of weeping) **have a good ~:** sich ausweinen; **it will do her good to have a ~:** es wird ihr gut tun, sich einmal richtig auszuweinen

B *v.t.* **1** rufen; (loudly) schreien **2** (weep) weinen; **~ bitter tears over sth.** bittere Tränen wegen etw. weinen *od.* über etw. (*Akk.*) vergießen; **~ one's eyes out** sich (*Dat.*) die Augen ausweinen *od.* aus dem Kopf weinen; **~ oneself to sleep** sich in den Schlaf weinen **3** **~ one's wares** (lit. or fig.) seine Waren anpreisen

C *v.i.* **1** rufen; (loudly) schreien; **~ [out] for sth./sb.** nach etw./jmdm. rufen *od.* schreien; **~ [out] for mercy** um Gnade flehen; **~ [out] for help** um Hilfe schreien; **~ to sb. [to come]** jmdn. zurufen[, er solle kommen *od.* dass er kommen soll]; **~ with pain** vor Schmerz[en] schreien; **sth. cries out for sth.** (fig.) etw. schreit nach etw.; **[well,] for ~ing out loud** (coll.) das darf doch wohl nicht wahr sein! (ugs.); **what's the matter, for ~ing out loud?** was ist los, um Himmels willen?; **~ for the moon** (fig.) Unmögliches verlangen **2** (weep) weinen (**over** wegen); **~ for sth.** nach etw. weinen; (fig.) einer Sache (*Dat.*) nachweinen; *see also* **milk A 3** ‹*Möwe:*› schreien; ‹*Hund:*› bellen

Phrasal verbs

- **~ 'down** *v.t.* **~ sb./sth.** jmdn./etw. herabsetzen *od.* (ugs.) mies machen
- **~ 'off** *v.i.* absagen; einen Rückzieher machen (ugs.)
- **~ 'out** *v.i.* aufschreien; *see also* **~ C 1**
- **~ 'up** *v.t.* **~ sth./sb. up** etw./jmdn. hochjubeln (ugs.) *od.* in den Himmel heben (ugs.); **it/he wasn't all it/he was cried up to be** so großartig war es/er nun auch wieder nicht

'cry-baby *n.* Heulsuse, *die* (ugs.)

cryer ▸**crier**

crying /ˈkraɪɪŋ/ *adj.* weinend ‹*Kind*›; schreiend ‹*Unrecht*›; dringend ‹*Bedürfnis, Notwendigkeit*›; dringlich ‹*Forderung*›; krass ‹*Missverhältnis*›; **it is a ~ shame** es ist eine wahre Schande

cryo- /kraɪəʊ/ *in comb.* Kryo-/kryo-

cryogenic /kraɪəˈdʒenɪk/ *adj.* **~ laboratory** Tieftemperaturlabor, *das*

cryogenics /kraɪəˈdʒenɪks/ *n., no pl.* **1** (Phys.) Kryogenik, *die* **2** ▸**cryonics**

cryonics /kraɪˈɒnɪks/ *n., no pl.* Kryonik, *die*

cryosurgery /ˈkraɪəʊsɜːdʒərɪ/ *n., no pl.* Kryochirurgie, *die*

crypt /krɪpt/ *n.* Krypta, *die*

cryptic /ˈkrɪptɪk/ *adj.* [1] (secret, mystical) geheimnisvoll [2] (obscure in meaning) undurchschaubar; kryptisch

cryptically /ˈkrɪptɪkəlɪ/ *adv.* ▸**cryptic**: geheimnisvoll; undurchschaubar; kryptisch

crypto- /krɪptəʊ/ *in comb.* Krypto-

cryptogram /ˈkrɪptəgræm/ *n.* verschlüsselter Text; Geheimtext, *der*

cryptographic /krɪptəˈgræfɪk/ *adj.* verschlüsselt; (employing cryptography) Verschlüsselungs-

cryptography /krɪpˈtɒgrəfɪ/ *n.* Kryptographie, *die*

crystal /ˈkrɪstl/
A *n.* [1] (Chem., Min., etc.) Kristall, *der* [2] ▸**crystal glass**
B *adj.* (made of ~ glass) kristallen; ~ **bowl/vase** Kristallschale, *die*/-vase, *die*

crystal: ~ **ˈball** *n.* Kristallkugel, *die;* **I haven't got a ~ ball!** ich bin [doch] kein Hellseher!; ~ **clear** *adj.* kristallklar; kristallen (geh.); (fig.) glasklar; **make sth. ~ clear** (fig.) etw. ganz klar machen; **~-gazing** *n.* Hellseherei, *die;* Kristallomantie, *die* (fachspr.); ~ **ˈglass** *n.* Bleikristall, *das;* Kristallglas, *das*

crystalline /ˈkrɪstəlaɪn/ *adj.* [1] (made of crystal) Kristall-; kristallen [2] (Chem., Min.) kristallin[isch]

crystallisation, crystallise ▸**crystalliz-**

crystallization /krɪstəlaɪˈzeɪʃn/ *n.* Kristallbildung, *die;* Kristallisation, *die;* (fig.) Kristallisierung, *die*

crystallize /ˈkrɪstəlaɪz/
A *v.t.* auskristallisieren ‹*Salze*›; kandieren ‹*Früchte*›; ~ **one's thoughts** (fig.) seinen Gedanken feste Form geben
B *v.i.* kristallisieren; (fig.) feste Form annehmen

crystallographer /krɪstəˈlɒgrəfə(r)/ *n.* Kristallograph, *der*/-graphin, *die*

crystallography /krɪstəˈlɒgrəfɪ/ *n.* Kristallographie, *die*

c/s *abbr.* = **cycle[s] per second** Hz

CSA *abbr.* (Brit.) = **Child Support Agency**

CSCE *abbr.* = **Conference on Security and Cooperation in Europe** KSZE

CSE *abbr.* (Brit. Hist.) = **Certificate of Secondary Education**

CS ˈgas *n.* CS, *das* (fachspr.); ≈ Tränengas, *das*

ct *abbr.* [1] = **carat** Kt. [2] = **cent** ct., Ct.

CT *abbr.* = **computerized tomography** CT

cu. *abbr.* = **cubic** Kubik-

cub /kʌb/ *n.* [1] Junge, *das;* (of wolf, fox, dog) Welpe, *der;* Junge, *das* [2] **Cub** ▸**Cub Scout** [3] (Amer.: apprentice) Lehrling, *der*

Cuba /ˈkjuːbə/ *pr. n.* Kuba (*das*)

Cuban /ˈkjuːbn/ ▸ⓘ **p. 1345**
A *adj.* kubanisch; **sb. is ~:** jmd. ist Kubaner/Kubanerin
B *n.* Kubaner, *der*/Kubanerin, *die*

Cuban ˈheel *n.* Blockabsatz, *der*

cubby[hole] /ˈkʌbɪ(həʊl)/ *n.* Kämmerchen, *das;* (snug place) Kuschelecke, *die*

cube /kjuːb/
A *n.* [1] Würfel, *der;* Kubus, *der* (fachspr.) [2] (Math.) dritte Potenz; Kubus, *der* (fachspr.)
B *v.t.* in die dritte Potenz erheben ‹*Zahl*›; hoch drei nehmen; **2 ~d is 8** 2 hoch 3 ist 8; die dritte Potenz von 2 ist 8

cube: ~ **farm** *n.* (coll.) Großraumbüro mit Trennwänden; ~ **ˈroot** *n.* Kubikwurzel, *die;* **the ~ root of 8 is 2** die dritte Wurzel aus 8 ist 2; ~ **sugar** *n.* Würfelzucker, *der*

cubic /ˈkjuːbɪk/ *adj.* [1] würfelförmig; **have a ~ form** würfelförmig sein; die Form eines Würfels haben [2] ▸ⓘ **p. 1690** (of three dimensions) Kubik-; Raum-; ~ **content** Rauminhalt, *der;* ~ **metre/centimetre/foot/yard** Kubikmeter/-zentimeter/-fuß/-yard, *der* [3] (Math.) kubisch; ~ **equation** Gleichung dritten Grades

cubical /ˈkjuːbɪkl/ ▸**cubic 1**

cubicle /ˈkjuːbɪkl/ *n.* [1] (sleeping compartment) Alkoven, *der* [2] (for dressing, private discussion, etc.) Kabine, *die*

cubism /ˈkjuːbɪzm/ *n.* (Art) Kubismus, *der*

cubist /ˈkjuːbɪst/ *n.* (Art) Kubist, *der*/Kubistin, *die*

cubit /ˈkjuːbɪt/ *n.* (Hist.) Elle, *die*

ˈcub reporter *n.* (coll.) unerfahrener [junger] Reporter/unerfahrene [junge] Reporterin

ˈCub Scout *n.* Wölfling, *der*

cuckold /ˈkʌkəld/ (arch.)
A *n.* Hahnrei, *der* (veralt.); gehörnter Ehemann (scherzh.)
B *v.t.* Hörner aufsetzen (+ *Dat.*) (scherzh.); hörnen (scherzh.)

cuckoo /ˈkʊkuː/
A *n.* [1] Kuckuck, *der;* ~ **in the nest** (fig.) Fremdkörper, *der* [2] (simpleton) Einfaltspinsel, *der* (ugs.); Heini, *der* (ugs.)
B *adj.* (coll.) meschugge *nicht attr.* (salopp); **a ~ notion/idea** eine bekloppte Idee (salopp)

cuckoo: ~ **clock** *n.* Kuckucksuhr, *die;* ~ **flower** *n.* (Bot.) [1] (lady's smock) Wiesenschaumkraut, *das;* [2] (ragged robin) Kuckuckslichtnelke, *die;* **~-pint** /ˈkʊkuːpɪnt/ *n.* (Bot.) Aron[s]stab, *der*

cucumber /ˈkjuːkʌmbə(r)/ *n.* [Salat]gurke, *die;* **be as cool as a ~:** taufrisch sein; (fig.: remain calm) einen kühlen Kopf behalten

cud /kʌd/ *n.* wiedergekäutes Futter; **chew the ~:** wiederkäuen; (fig.) vor sich hin grübeln

cuddle /ˈkʌdl/
A *n.* Liebkosung, *die;* enge Umarmung; **give sb. a ~:** jmdn. drücken *od.* in den Arm nehmen; **have a ~:** schmusen
B *v.t.* schmusen mit; hätscheln ‹*kleines Kind*›
C *v.i.* schmusen; ~ **up** sich zusammenkuscheln; (in bed) sich einmummeln; **he ~d up beside her** er kuschelte sich an ihre Seite

cuddlesome /ˈkʌdlsəm/ *adj.* zum Liebhaben *od.* Schmusen *nachgestellt*

cuddly /ˈkʌdlɪ/ *adj.* [1] (given to cuddling) verschmust [2] ▸**cuddlesome**

cuddly ˈtoy *n.* Plüschtier, *das*

cudgel /ˈkʌdʒl/
A *n.* Knüppel, *der;* **take up the ~s for sb./sth.** (fig.) [energisch] für jmdn./etw. eintreten
B *v.t.*, (Brit.) **-ll-** knüppeln; ~ **one's brains** (fig.) sich (*Dat.*) das [Ge]hirn zermartern

cue¹ /kjuː/ *n.* (Billiards etc.) Queue, *das;* Billardstock, *der*

cue²
A *n.* [1] (Theatre) Stichwort, *das;* (Music) Stichnoten *Pl.;* (Cinemat., Broadcasting) Zeichen zum Aufnahmebeginn; **be/speak/play on ~:** rechtzeitig einsetzen; **enter on ~:** auf das Stichwort hin auftreten [2] (sign when or how to act) Wink, *der;* Zeichen, *das;* **take one's ~ from sb.** (lit. or fig.) sich nach jmdm. richten
B *v.t.* (label) kennzeichnen

cuff¹ /kʌf/ *n.* [1] Manschette, *die;* **off the ~** (fig.) aus dem Stegreif [2] (Amer.: trouser turn-up) [Hosen]aufschlag, *der* [3] *in pl.* (coll.: handcuffs) Handschellen *Pl.*

cuff²
A *v.t.* ~ **sb.'s ears,** ~ **sb. over the ears** jmdm. eins hinter die Ohren geben (ugs.); ~ **sb.** jmdm. einen Klaps geben
B *n.* Klaps, *der;* **give sb. a ~ on the ears** jmdm. eins hinter die Ohren geben (ugs.)

ˈcuff link *n.* Manschettenknopf, *der*

cuirass /kwɪˈræs/ *n.* (armour) Küraß, *der;* Brustharnisch, *der*

cuisine /kwɪˈziːn/ *n.* Küche, *die;* **French/Italian** *etc.* **~:** französische/italienische *usw.* Küche

cul-de-sac /ˈkʌldəsæk/ *n., pl.* **culs-de-sac** /ˈkʌldəsæk/ Sackgasse, *die*

culinary /ˈkʌlɪnərɪ/ *adj.* kulinarisch; **the ~ arts** die Kochkunst; ~ **herbs/plants** *etc.* Küchenkräuter/-gewächse *usw.*

cull /kʌl/
A *v.t.* [1] (select) auswählen [2] (select and kill) erlegen; (shoot) abschießen [3] (literary: pick) pflücken;
B *n.* [1] (act of ~ing) Erlegung, *die;* (shooting) Abschuss, *der;* ~ **of seals** Robbenschlag, *der* [2] (~ed animal) Merztier, *das*

cullet /ˈkʌlɪt/ *n.* (Glass-making) Glasscherben; Glasbruch, *der*

culm /kʌlm/ *n.* (Bot.) Halm, *der*

culminate /ˈkʌlmɪneɪt/ *v.i.* (reach highest point, lit. or fig.) gipfeln; kulminieren; ~ **in sth.** in etw. (*Dat.*) seinen Höchststand erreichen

culmination /kʌlmɪˈneɪʃn/ *n.* Höhepunkt, *der;* Kulmination, *die* (geh.)

culottes /kjuːˈlɒt/ *n. pl.* Hosenrock, *der*

culpable /ˈkʌlpəbl/ *adj.* schuldig ‹*Person*›; strafbar ‹*Handlung*›; **hold sb. ~:** jmdn. für schuldig halten; ~ **negligence** grobe Fahrlässigkeit

culpably /ˈkʌlpəblɪ/ *adv.* sträflich

culprit /ˈkʌlprɪt/ *n.* (guilty of crime) Schuldige, *der/die;* Täter, *der*/Täterin, *die;* (guilty of wrong) Übeltäter, *der*/-täterin, *die;* Missetäter, *der*/-täterin, *die*

cult /kʌlt/ *n.* Kult, *der;* **the ~ of the dead** der Totenkult; *attrib.* Kult‹*film, -figur, -objekt, -status usw.*›

cultivar /ˈkʌltɪvɑː(r)/ *n.* (Bot.) Züchtung, *die;* Zuchtform, *die*

cultivate /ˈkʌltɪveɪt/ *v.t.* [1] (prepare and use for crops) kultivieren; bestellen, bebauen ‹*Feld, Land*›; (prepare with cultivator) mit dem Kultivator bearbeiten [2] (produce by culture) anbauen, züchten ‹*Pflanzen*›; züchten ‹*Tiere*› [3] (fig.) (improve, develop) kultivieren ‹*Stimme, Sprache*›; kultivieren, entwickeln ‹*Geschmack*›; kultivieren, verfeinern ‹*Manieren*›; (pay attention to, cherish) kultivieren ‹*Freundschaft, Gefühl, Gewohnheit*›; pflegen ‹*Freundschaft, Verbindung*›; entwickeln ‹*Kunst, Fertigkeit*›; betreiben ‹*Wissenschaft*›; ~ **sb.** die Verbindung mit jmdm. pflegen; sich (*Dat.*) jmdn. warm halten (ugs.); ~ **one's mind** sich bilden [4] züchten ‹*Bakterien*›

cultivated /ˈkʌltɪveɪtɪd/ *adj.* [1] kultiviert; gezüchtet ‹*Pflanzen*›; bebaut ‹*Land, Feld*›; ~ **plant** Zuchtpflanze, *die* [2] (fig.) kultiviert ‹*Manieren, Sprache, Geschmack*›; kultiviert, gebildet ‹*Person*›

cultivation /kʌltɪˈveɪʃn/ *n.* (lit. or fig.) Kultivierung, *die;* (of a skill) Entwicklung, *die;* ~ **of plants** Anbau von Pflanzen; ~ **of land** Landbau, *der;* Pflanzenbau, *der;* **land that is under ~:** Boden, der landwirtschaftlich genutzt wird; **bring land into ~:** Land urbar machen; (fig.) ~ **of the mind** Bildung, *die*

cultivator /ˈkʌltɪveɪtə(r)/ *n.* [1] (person) Ackerbauer, *der* [2] (implement) Handkultivator, *der;* (machine) Kultivator, *der;* Grubber, *der*

cultural /ˈkʌltʃərl/ *adj.* kulturell ‹*Entwicklung, Ereignis, Interessen, Beziehungen*›; ~ **revolution/anthropology** Kulturrevolution/-anthropologie, *die;* **there are ~ activities** es wird kulturell etwas geboten

culturally /ˈkʌltʃərəlɪ/ *adv.* kulturell

culture /ˈkʌltʃə(r)/
A *n.* [1] Kultur, *die;* **the two ~s** die entgegengesetzten Bereiche Geisteswissenschaft und Naturwissenschaft [2] (intellectual development) [Geistes]bildung, *die;* Kultur, *die* [3] **physical ~:** Fitnesstraining, *das;* **beauty ~:** Schönheitspflege, *die* [4] (Agric.) Kultur, *die;* (tillage of the soil) Landbau, *der;* (rearing, production) Zucht, *die;* **methods of ~:** Anbaumethoden *Pl.* [5] (of bacteria) Kultur, *die*
B *v.t.* züchten ‹*Bakterien*›

cultured /ˈkʌltʃəd/ *adj.* [1] (cultivated, refined) kultiviert; gebildet [2] ~ **pearl** Zuchtperle, *die*

culture: ~ **shock** *n.* Kulturschock, *der;* ~ **vulture** *n.* (joc.) Kulturfanatiker, *der*/-fanatikerin, *die* (ugs.)

culvert /ˈkʌlvət/ *n.* [1] (for water) [unterirdischer] Kanal, *der* [2] (for electric cable) Kabelkanal, *der*

cum /kʌm/ *prep.* [1] (Finance) ~ **dividend** mit Dividende [2] (indicating combined nature or function) **dining-~-sitting room** Wohn- und Speisezimmer, *das;* **dinner-~-cocktail dress** Abend- und Cocktailkleid, *das*

cumbersome /ˈkʌmbəsəm/ *adj.* lästig, hinderlich ‹*Kleider*›; sperrig ‹*Gepäck, Pakete*›; unhandlich ‹*Paket*›; schwerfällig ‹*Bewegung,*

Stil, Arbeitsweise, Ausdruck›; umständlich ‹Methode›

cumin /ˈkʌmɪn/ *n.* (Bot.) Kreuzkümmel, *der*

cummerbund /ˈkʌməbʌnd/ *n.* Kummerbund, *der*

cummin ▸ **cumin**

cumulate /ˈkjuːmjʊleɪt/, **cumulation** /kjuːmjʊˈleɪʃn/ ▸ **accumul-**

cumulative /ˈkjuːmjʊlətɪv/ *adj.* 1▸ (increased by successive additions) kumulativ (geh.); ~ **strength/effect** Gesamtstärke/-wirkung, *die;* ~ **evidence** Häufung von Beweismaterial 2▸ (formed by successive additions) zusätzlich; Zusatz-; kumulierend, kumuliert ‹Bibliographie›

cumulatively /ˈkjuːmjʊlətɪvlɪ/ *adv.* kumulativ

cumulus /ˈkjuːmjʊləs/ *n., pl.* **cumuli** /ˈkjuːmjʊlaɪ/ (Meteorol.) Kumuluswolke, *die*

cuneiform /ˈkjuːnɪfɔːm, ˈkjuːnɪfɔːm/ *adj.* keilförmig; ‹Text, Dokument, Inschrift› in Keilschrift; ~ **writing** Keilschrift, *die*

cunnilingus /kʌnɪˈlɪŋgəs/ *n., no pl., no art.* Cunnilingus, *der*

cunning /ˈkʌnɪŋ/

A *n.* 1▸ Schläue, *die;* Gerissenheit, *die* 2▸ (arch.: skill) Geschicklichkeit, *die;* Geschick, *das*

B *adj.* 1▸ schlau; gerissen 2▸ (arch.: skilful) geschickt 3▸ (Amer.: quaint, small) niedlich

cunningly /ˈkʌnɪŋlɪ/ *adv.* schlau ‹reden, denken›; listig ‹täuschen›; gerissen ‹handeln›; *as sentence-modifier* schlauerweise

cunt /kʌnt/ *n.* (coarse) 1▸ (female genitals) Fotze, *die* (vulg.); Möse, *die* (vulg.) 2▸ (derog.) (woman) Fotze, *die* (vulg.); Schlampe, *die* (derb); (man) Arschloch, *das* (derb)

cup /kʌp/

A *n.* 1▸ (drinking vessel) Tasse, *die;* **there's many a slip between the ~ and the lip** (fig.) da kann immer noch etwas dazwischenkommen; **in one's ~s** (fig.) in angetrunkenem Zustand 2▸ (prize, competition) Pokal, *der* 3▸ (cupful) Tasse, *die;* **a ~ of coffee/tea** eine Tasse Kaffee/Tee; **another ~ of tea** (fig.) etwas ganz anderes; **it's [not] my ~ of tea** (fig. coll.) das ist [nicht] mein Fall (ugs.) 4▸ (flavoured wine etc.) Bowle, *die* 5▸ (Eccl.) Kelch, *der* 6▸ (fig.: fate, experience) **his ~ [of happiness/sorrow] was full** er war überglücklich/das Maß seiner Leiden war voll 7▸ (of brassière) Körbchen, *das;* **A/B** *etc.* ~: A-/B-Körbchen *usw*

B *v.t.*, **-pp-** 1▸ (take or hold as in ~) ~ **one's chin in one's hand** das Kinn in die Hand stützen; ~ **water** Wasser [mit der hohlen Hand] schöpfen 2▸ (make ~-shaped) hohl machen; ~ **one's hand to one's ear** die Hand ans Ohr halten

cupboard /ˈkʌbəd/ *n.* Schrank, *der*

cupboard: ~ **love** *n.* geheuchelte Zuneigung; **it's just ~ love** es ist nur Getue (ugs.); ~ **space** *n., no pl.* Schrankraum, *der;* **take up ~ space** Platz im Schrank wegnehmen

ˈ**cupcake** *n.: kleiner [Rühr]kuchen in einem Förmchen aus Papier*

Cup ˈFinal *n.* (Footb.) Pokalendspiel, *das*

cupful /ˈkʌpfʊl/ *n.* Tasse, *die;* **a ~ of water** eine Tasse Wasser

Cupid /ˈkjuːpɪd/ *n.* (god) Amor, *der;* Cupido, *der;* (representation) Amorette, *die;* **~'s bow** Amors Bogen

cupidity /kjuːˈpɪdɪtɪ/ *n., no pl.* Begierde, *die* (**for** nach); Gier, *die* (**for** nach)

cupola /ˈkjuːpələ/ *n.* Kuppel, *die;* (ceiling of dome) Kuppel, *die;* Kuppelgewölbe, *das*

cuppa /ˈkʌpə/, **cupper** /ˈkʌpə(r)/ *n.* (Brit. coll.) Tasse Tee

ˈ**cup tie** *n.* Pokalspiel, *das*

cur /kɜː(r)/ *n.* (derog.) 1▸ (dog) Köter, *der* (ugs. abwertend) 2▸ (fig.: person) [Schweine]hund, *der* (derb abwertend)

curable /ˈkjʊərəbl/ *adj.* heilbar; **the patient is ~:** der Patient kann geheilt werden; **not ~** (lit. or fig.) unheilbar

curaçao /ˈkjʊərəsəʊ/ *n.* Curaçao, *der*

curare /kjʊəˈrɑːrɪ/ *n.* Curare, *das*

curate /ˈkjʊərət/ *n.* 1▸ (Eccl.) Kurat, *der;* Hilfsgeistliche, *der* 2▸ **sth. is a** *or* **like the ~'s egg** (fig.) etw. hat seine guten und seine schlechten Seiten

curative /ˈkjʊərətɪv/ *adj.* heilend; Heil-; **be ~:** heilend wirken; heilen

curator /kjʊəˈreɪtə(r)/ *n.* ▸❶ **p. 1260** 1▸ (of museum) Direktor, *der*/Direktorin, *die* 2▸ (person in charge) Verwalter, *der*/Verwalterin, *die*

curb /kɜːb/

A *v.t.* (lit. or fig.) zügeln

B *n.* 1▸ (chain or strap for horse) Kandare, *die;* **put a ~ on** (fig.) an die Kandare nehmen ‹Person›; zügeln ‹Gefühle›; einschränken ‹Ausgaben, Einfuhr› 2▸ ▸ **kerb**

ˈ**curb cut** *n.* (Amer.) Bordsteinabsenkung, *die*

ˈ**curd cheese** *n.* ≈ Quark, *der*

curdle /ˈkɜːdl/

A *v.t.* (lit. or fig.) gerinnen lassen; *see also* **blood-curdling**

B *v.i.* (lit. or fig.) gerinnen

curds /kɜːdz/ *n. pl.* ≈ Quark, *der;* ~ **and whey** Quark [mit Molke]

cure /kjʊə(r)/ ▸❶ **p. 1231**

A *n.* 1▸ (thing that ~s) [Heil]mittel, *das* (**for** gegen); (fig.) Mittel, *das* 2▸ (restoration to health) Heilung, *die* 3▸ (treatment) Behandlung, *die;* **take a ~ at a spa** in *od.* zur Kur gehen 4▸ (spiritual charge) ~ **of souls** Seelsorge, *die*

B *v.t.* 1▸ heilen; kurieren; ~ **sb. of a disease** jmdn. von einer Krankheit heilen 2▸ (fig.) kurieren; **he was ~d of his bad habits** er wurde von seinen schlechten Gewohnheiten kuriert; ihm wurden seine schlechten Gewohnheiten ausgetrieben 3▸ (preserve) haltbar machen ‹Nahrungsmittel›; [ein]pökeln ‹Fleisch›; räuchern ‹Fisch›; trocknen ‹Häute, Tabak› 4▸ (harden) aushärten ‹Beton, Kunststoffe›

ˈ**cure-all** *n.* Allheilmittel, *das*

curfew /ˈkɜːfjuː/ *n.* 1▸ Ausgangssperre, *die* 2▸ (Hist.: bell) Abendglocke, *die*

Curia /ˈkjʊərɪə/ *n.* Kurie, *die*

curie /ˈkjʊərɪ/ *n.* (Phys.) Curie, *das*

curio /ˈkjʊərɪəʊ/ *n., pl.* **~s** Kuriosität, *die*

curiosity /kjʊərɪˈɒsɪtɪ/ *n.* 1▸ (desire to know) Neugier[de], *die* (**about** in Bezug auf + *Akk.*); ~ **killed the cat** (fig.) die Neugier ist schon manchem zum Verhängnis geworden 2▸ (strange object, matter) Kuriosität, *die* 3▸ *no pl.* (strangeness) Fremdartigkeit, *die*

curious /ˈkjʊərɪəs/ *adj.* 1▸ (inquisitive) neugierig; (eager to learn) wissbegierig; **be ~ about sth.** (eagerly awaiting) auf etw. (*Akk.*) neugierig sein; **be ~ about sb.** in Bezug auf jmdn. neugierig sein; **be ~ to know sth.** etw. gern wissen wollen; **he was ~ to know what ...:** er wollte zu gerne wissen, was ... 2▸ (strange, odd) merkwürdig; seltsam; **how [very] ~!** [sehr] seltsam!; **~er and ~er** (coll.) es wird immer geheimnisvoller

curiously /ˈkjʊərɪəslɪ/ *adv.* ▸ **curious**: neugierig ‹fragen, gucken›; seltsam, merkwürdig ‹sprechen, sich verhalten›; **it was ~ quiet** es war merkwürdig still; ~ **[enough]** (as sentence-modifier) merkwürdigerweise; seltsamerweise

curiousness /ˈkjʊərɪəsnɪs/ *n., no pl.* (inquisitiveness) Neugier[de], *die;* (oddness) Merkwürdigkeit, *die;* Sonderbarkeit, *die*

curl /kɜːl/

A *n.* 1▸ (of hair) Locke, *die;* **put one's/sb.'s hair in ~s** sich/jmdm. das Haar locken; **hair in ~s** gelocktes Haar; **hair in tight ~s** Kraushaar, *das* 2▸ (sth. spiral or curved inwards) **the ~ of a leaf/wave** ein gekräuseltes Blatt/eine gekräuselte Welle; **a ~ of smoke** ein Rauchkringel 3▸ (act of curling) Kräuseln, *das;* **with a ~ of the lip** mit gekräuselten Lippen

B *v.t.* 1▸ (cause to form coils) locken; (tightly) kräuseln; **she ~ed her hair** sie legte ihr Haar in Locken (*Akk.*) 2▸ (bend, twist) kräuseln ‹Blätter, Lippen›; **the animal ~ed itself into a ball** das Tier rollte sich zu einer Kugel zusammen; **it's enough to ~ your hair** (fig.) da stehen einem ja die Haare zu Berge!

C *v.i.* 1▸ (grow in coils) sich locken; (tightly) sich kräuseln; **her hair ~s naturally** sie hat Naturlocken; (tightly) sie hat eine Naturkrause; **it's enough to make your hair ~** (fig.) da stehen einem ja die Haare zu Berge! 2▸ (move in spiral form) ‹Straße, Fluss:› sich winden, sich schlängeln; **the smoke ~ed upwards** der Rauch stieg in Kringeln hoch

Phrasal verb

• ~ ˈ**up**

A *v.t.* hochbiegen; ~ **oneself up** (roll into shape of ball) sich zusammenrollen; sich einrollen

B *v.i.* (roll into curved shape) sich zusammenrollen; sich einrollen; (fig.: writhe with horror) erschauern; **he ~ed up on the sofa** er machte es sich (*Dat.*) auf dem Sofa bequem *od.* (ugs.) fläzte sich auf das Sofa; **she ~ed up with a book** sie machte es sich (*Dat.*) mit einem Buch gemütlich

curler /ˈkɜːlə(r)/ *n.* Lockenwickler, *der;* **in ~s** mit Lockenwicklern

curlew /ˈkɜːljuː/ *n.* (Ornith.) Brachvogel, *der*

curlicue /ˈkɜːlɪkjuː/ *n.* Schnörkel, *der*

curling /ˈkɜːlɪŋ/ *n.* (game) Curling, *das;* ≈ Eisschießen, *das*

curling: **~-iron** *n.,* (Brit.) **~-tongs** *n. pl.* Brennschere, *die;* (electrical appliance) Lockenstab, *der*

curly /ˈkɜːlɪ/ *adj.* lockig, (tightly) kraus ‹Haar›; kraus ‹Salat›; gewellt, gekräuselt ‹Blatt›; Schnörkel‹schrift, -muster,› verschnörkelt ‹Schrift, Muster›

curly: **~-haired** *adj.* lockenköpfig; mit lockigem Haar; **~-head** *n.* Lockenkopf, *der;* (with tight curls) Krauskopf, *der;* **~-headed** ▸ **~-haired**

curmudgeon /kəˈmʌdʒən/ *n.* Griesgram, *der* (abwertend); Brummbär, *der* (ugs.)

currant /ˈkʌrənt/ *n.* 1▸ (dried fruit) Korinthe, *die* 2▸ (fruit) Johannisbeere, *die;* (plant) Johannisbeerstrauch, *der; see also* **blackcurrant**; **flowering**; **redcurrant**

currency /ˈkʌrənsɪ/ *n.* 1▸ ▸❶ **p. 1332** (money) Währung, *die;* (circulation) Umlauf, *der;* **foreign currencies** Devisen *Pl.;* **withdraw from ~:** aus dem Verkehr ziehen 2▸ (other commodity) [Tausch]ware, *die;* Zahlungsmittel, *das* 3▸ (prevalence) (of word, idea, story, rumour) Verbreitung, *die;* (of expression) Gebräuchlichkeit, *die;* **gain wide ~:** weite Verbreitung finden; **give ~ to a rumour** ein Gerücht in Umlauf bringen

ˈ**currency converter** *n.* Währungs[um]rechner, *der*

current /ˈkʌrənt/

A *adj.* 1▸ (in general circulation or use) kursierend, umlaufend ‹Geld, Geschichte, Gerücht›; verbreitet ‹Meinung›; gebräuchlich ‹Wort›; gängig ‹Redensart›; **these coins are no longer ~:** diese Münzen sind nicht mehr in Umlauf 2▸ laufend ‹Jahr, Monat›; **in the ~ year** in diesem Jahr 3▸ (belonging to the present time) aktuell ‹Ereignis, Mode›; Tages‹politik, -preis›; derzeitig ‹Politik, Preis›; gegenwärtig ‹Krise, Aufregung›; ~ **issue/edition** letzte Ausgabe/neueste Auflage; ~ **affairs** Tagespolitik, *die;* aktuelle Fragen

B *n.* 1▸ ▸❶ **p. 1491** (of water, air) Strömung, *die;* **air/ocean ~:** Luft-/Meeresströmung, *die;* **swim against/with the ~:** gegen den/mit dem Strom schwimmen; **upward/downward ~ of air** (in atmosphere) Aufwind/Abwind, *der* 2▸ (Electr.) Strom, *der;* (intensity) Stromstärke, *die* 3▸ (running stream) Strömung, *die* 4▸ (tendency of events, opinions, etc.) Tendenz, *die;* Trend, *der;* **the ~ of public opinion** der Trend in der öffentlichen Meinung; **go against/with the ~:** gegen den/mit dem Strom schwimmen

ˈ**current account** *n.* Girokonto, *das;* (in balance of payments) Leistungsbilanz, *die*

currently /ˈkʌrəntlɪ/ *adv.* gegenwärtig; momentan; zur Zeit; **he is ~ writing a book** er schreibt gerade *od.* zur Zeit an einem Buch; **it is ~ thought** *or* **believed that ...:** heute glaubt man, dass ...

curricular /kəˈrɪkjʊlə(r)/ *adj.* (Educ.) kurrikular

curriculum /kəˈrɪkjʊləm/ *n., pl.* **curricula** /kəˈrɪkjʊlə/ (Educ.) Lehrplan, *der;* Curriculum, *das;* **be on the ~:** auf dem Lehrplan stehen

curriculum vitae /kərɪkjʊləm ˈviːtaɪ/ *n.* Lebenslauf, *der*

curry[1] /'kʌrɪ/ (Cookery)
A *n.* Curry[gericht], *das*
B *v.t.* mit Curry würzen

curry[2] *v.t.* **1** striegeln ‹*Pferd*› **2** zurichten ‹*Leder*› **3** ~ **favour [with sb.]** sich [bei jmdm.] einschmeicheln *od.* lieb Kind machen (ugs.)

curry: ~-comb *n.* Striegel, *der;* ~ **powder** *n.* Currypulver, *das;* Curry, *das od. der*

curse /kɜːs/
A *n.* **1** Fluch, *der;* **be under a ~:** unter einem Fluch stehen; **put a ~ on sb./sth.** einen Fluch über jmdn./etw. aussprechen; jmdn./etw. mit einem Fluch belegen; **call down ~s [from Heaven] upon sb.** jmdn. verfluchen **2** (profane oath) Fluch, *der,* Verwünschung, *die;* **bawl ~s at sb.** Flüche gegen jmdn. ausstoßen; **a thousand ~s on this old car** (joc.) zum Teufel mit diesem verfluchten alten Auto!; **~s! he's diddled me again** (joc. coll.) verflucht! der Kerl hat mich wieder reingelegt (ugs.) **3** (great evil) Geißel, *die;* Plage, *die* **4** (coll.: menstruation) **the ~:** die Tage (ugs.)
B *v.t.* **1** (utter ~ against) verfluchen **2** (as oath) **~ it/you!** verflucht!; verdammt! **3** (afflict) strafen; **~d with poverty** mit Armut geschlagen *od.* gestraft
C *v.i.* fluchen (**at** über + *Akk.*); **he started cursing and swearing** er fing an, heftig zu fluchen

cursed /'kɜːsɪd/ *adj.* **1** (under a curse) verflucht; verwünscht **2** (damnable) verdammt

cursive /'kɜːsɪv/ *adj.* kursiv; ~ **writing** Schreibschrift, *die*

cursor /'kɜːsə(r)/ *n.* Läufer, *der;* (on screen) Cursor, *der;* Schreibmarke, *die*

cursorily /'kɜːsərɪlɪ/ *adv.* flüchtig ‹*lesen*›; oberflächlich ‹*untersuchen*›

'cursor key *n.* (Computing) Cursortaste, *die*

cursory /'kɜːsərɪ/ *adj.* flüchtig ‹*Blick*›; oberflächlich ‹*Untersuchung, Bericht, Studium*›

curt /kɜːt/ *adj.* (discourteously brief) kurz und schroff ‹*Brief, Mitteilung*›; kurz angebunden ‹*Person, Art*›; **he gave a ~ nod and left** er nickte kurz und ging

curtail /kɜː'teɪl/ *v.t.* kürzen; abkürzen ‹*Urlaub*›; beschneiden ‹*Macht*›

curtailment /kɜː'teɪlmənt/ *n.* Kürzung, *die;* (of power) Beschneidung, *die*

curtain /'kɜːtən/
A *n.* **1** Vorhang, *der;* (with net ~s) Übergardine, *die;* **draw** *or* **pull the ~s** (open) die Vorhänge aufziehen; (close) die Vorhänge zuziehen; **draw** *or* **pull back the ~s** die Vorhänge aufziehen **2** (fig.) **a ~ of fog/mist** ein Nebelschleier; **a ~ of smoke/flames/rain** eine Rauch-/Flammen-/Regenwand **3** (Theatre) Vorhang, *der;* (end of play) Schlussszene, *die;* (rise of ~ at start of play) Aufgehen des Vorhanges; Aktbeginn, *der;* (fall of ~ at end of scene) Fallen des Vorhanges; Aktschluss, *der;* **the ~ rises/falls** der Vorhang hebt sich/fällt **4** ▸**curtain call** **5** ▸**Iron Curtain** **6** *in pl.* (coll.: the end) Ende, *das;* **that's ~s for him** jetzt ist er erledigt (ugs.). *See also* **safety curtain**
B *v.t.* ~ **a window** an einem Fenster Vorhänge/einen Vorhang aufhängen *od.* anbringen; ~ **off** mit einem Vorhang abteilen; durch einen Vorhang abtrennen

curtain: ~ call *n.* Vorhang, *der;* **get/take a ~ call** einen Vorhang bekommen/vor den Vorhang treten; ~ **hook** *n.* Gardinenhaken, *der;* ~ **lecture** *n.* Gardinenpredigt, *die;* ~ **rail** *n.* Gardinenstange, *die;* **~-raiser** *n.* [kurzes] Vorspiel; (fig.) Auftakt, *der;* ~ **ring** *n.* Gardinenring, *der;* ~ **rod** *n.* Gardinenstange, *die;* ~ **runner** *n.* Gardinenröllchen, *das;* ~ **track** Gardinenleiste, *die*

curtly /'kɜːtlɪ/ *adv.* kurz ‹*sprechen*›; knapp ‹*schreiben, antworten*›

curtsy (**curtsey**) /'kɜːtsɪ/
A *n.* Knicks, *der;* **make** *or* **drop a ~ to sb.** vor jmdm. einen Knicks machen
B *v.i.* ~ **to sb.** vor jmdm. knicksen *od.* einen Knicks machen

curvaceous /kɜː'veɪʃəs/ *adj.* kurvenreich (ugs.); **a ~ figure** eine üppige Figur

curvature /'kɜːvətʃə(r)/ *n.* Krümmung, *die;* ~ **of the spine** Rückgratverkrümmung, *die*

curve /kɜːv/
A *v.t.* krümmen
B *v.i.* ‹*Straße, Fluss:*› (once) eine Biegung machen; (repeatedly) sich winden; ‹*Horizont:*› sich krümmen; ‹*Linie:*› einen Bogen machen *od.* beschreiben; **the road ~s round the town** die Straße macht einen Bogen um die Stadt
C *n.* **1** Kurve, *die* **2** (surface; ~d form or thing) (of vase, figure) Rundung, *die;* **there's a ~ in the road/river** die Straße/der Fluss macht einen Bogen *od.* eine Biegung

curved /kɜːvd/ *adj.* krumm; gebogen; gekrümmt ‹*Horizont, Raum, Linie*›

cushion /'kʊʃn/
A *n.* **1** Kissen, *das* **2** (for protection) Kissen, *das;* Polster, *das* **3** (of billiard table) Bande, *die* **4** (of hovercraft) Luftkissen, *das*
B *v.t.* **1** [aus]polstern ‹*Stuhl*›; ~ **sb. against sth.** (fig.) jmdn. gegen etw. schützen; **~ed seats** Polsterstühle **2** (absorb) dämpfen ‹*Aufprall, Stoß*›

cushy /'kʊʃɪ/ *adj.* (coll.) bequem; gemütlich; **a ~ job** *or* **number** ein ruhiger Job

cusp /kʌsp/ *n.* **1** Spitze, *die;* (of tooth) Höcker, *der* **2** (Astrol.) Übergang, *der* **3** (point of transition) Scheidepunkt, *der;* **on the ~ of a golden age** an der Schwelle zu einem goldenen Zeitalter

cuss /kʌs/ (coll.)
A *n.* **1** (curse) Fluch, *der;* Beschimpfung, *die;* **sb. does not give** *or* **care a ~:** jmdm. ist es vollkommen schnuppe (ugs.); **he/it is not worth a tinker's ~:** er/es ist keinen Pfifferling *od.* roten Heller wert (ugs.) **2** (usu. derog.: person) Kerl, *der* (ugs.)
B *v.i.* fluchen; schimpfen
C *v.t.* verfluchen; beschimpfen

cussed /'kʌsɪd/ *adj.* (coll.) **1** (perverse, obstinate) stur (ugs.) **2** (cursed) verdammt (ugs.); verflixt (ugs.)

cussedness /'kʌsɪdnɪs/ *n., no pl.* Sturheit, *die;* **from sheer ~:** aus reiner Sturheit

'cuss word *n.* (coll.) Fluch, *der;* Verwünschung, *die*

custard /'kʌstəd/ *n.* **1** ~ **[pudding]** ≈ Vanillepudding, *der* **2** (sauce) ≈ Vanillesoße, *die*

custard: ~ apple *n.* Zimt-, Rahmapfel, *der;* ~ **'pie** *n.* (pie) *Kuchen mit einer Füllung aus Vanillepudding;* (in comedy) Sahnetorte, *die; attrib.* ~ **pie comedy** Slapstickkomödie, *die;* ~ **powder** *n.* Vanillesoßenpulver, *das;* ~ **'tart** *n.* Puddingtörtchen, *das;* Puddingtorte, *die*

custodial /kʌs'təʊdɪəl/ *adj.* ~ **sentence** Freiheitsstrafe, *die*

custodian /kʌs'təʊdɪən/ *n.* ▸❶ **p. 1260** (of public building, of prisoner) Wärter, *der*/Wärterin, *die;* Aufseher, *der*/Aufseherin, *die;* (of park, museum) Wächter, *der*/Wächterin, *die;* (of valuables, traditions, culture, place) Hüter, *der*/Hüterin, *die;* (of child) Vormund, *der*

custody /'kʌstədɪ/ *n.* **1** (guardianship, care) Obhut, *die;* **be in the ~ of sb.** unter jmds. Obhut (*Dat.*) stehen; **put** *or* **place sb./sth. in sb.'s ~:** jmdn./etw. in jmds. Obhut (*Akk.*) geben; **the child is in the ~ of his uncle** sein Onkel hat die Vormundschaft über *od.* für das Kind; **in safe ~:** in sicherer Obhut; **the mother was given** *or* **awarded [the] ~ of the children** die Kinder wurden der Mutter zugesprochen **2** (imprisonment) **[be] in ~:** in Haft [sein]; **take sb. into ~:** jmdn. verhaften *od.* festnehmen

custom /'kʌstəm/ *n.* **1** Brauch, *der;* Sitte, *die;* **it was his ~ to smoke a cigar after dinner** er pflegte nach dem Essen eine Zigarre zu rauchen; er rauchte gewöhnlich eine Zigarre nach dem Essen **2** *in pl.* (duty on imports) Zoll, *der;* **[the] Customs** (government department) der Zoll; **go through C~s** durch den Zoll gehen (ugs.) **3** (Law) Gewohnheitsrecht, *das* **4** (business patronage, regular dealings) Kundschaft, *die* (veralt.); **I shall withdraw my ~ from that shop** ich werde in dem Laden nichts mehr kaufen; **we should like to have your ~:** wir hätten Sie gern zum/zur *od.* als Kunden/Kundin **5** (regular ~ers) Kundschaft, *die*

customarily /'kʌstəmərɪlɪ/ *adv.* in der Regel; üblicherweise

customary /'kʌstəmərɪ/ *adj.* **1** üblich **2** (Law) gewohnheitsmäßig; Gewohnheits-

custom: ~-built *adj.* spezial[an]gefertigt; **~-built clothes** (Amer.) maßgeschneiderte Kleidung; ~ **clothes** *n. pl.* (Amer.) maßgeschneiderte Kleidung

customer /'kʌstəmə(r)/ *n.* **1** Kunde, *der*/Kundin, *die;* (of restaurant) Gast, *der;* (of theatre) Besucher, *der*/Besucherin, *die;* (of library) Benutzer, *der*/Benutzerin, *die* **2** (coll.: person) Kerl, *der* (ugs.); **a queer/an awkward ~:** ein schwieriger Kunde (ugs.)

customer: ~ 'care *n., no pl.* Kundenbetreuung, *die;* ~ **'careline** *n.* Kundenhotline, *die;* ~ **'service** *n.* Kundendienst, *der;* ~ **'service department** *n.* Kundenservice, *der;* Kundenserviceabteilung, *die*

'custom house *n.* Zollamt, *das*

customize (**customise**) /'kʌstəmaɪz/ *v.t.* speziell anfertigen; (alter) umbauen; den Benutzerwünschen anpassen ‹*Hardware, Software*›

'custom-made *adj.* spezial[an]gefertigt; maßgeschneidert ‹*Kleidung*›

customs: ~ clearance *n.* Zollabfertigung, *die;* **get ~ clearance for sth.** etw. zollamtlich abfertigen lassen; ~ **declaration** *n.* Zollerklärung, *die;* ~ **duty** *n.* Zoll, *der;* ~ **hall** *n.* Zollabfertigungshalle, *die;* ~ **inspection** *n.* Zollkontrolle, *die;* ~ **officer** *n.* ▸❶ **p. 1260** Zollbeamter, *der*/-beamtin, *die;* ~ **union** *n.* Zollunion, *die*

cut /kʌt/
A *v.t.,* **-tt-,** ~**:** **1** (penetrate, wound) schneiden; ~ **one's finger/leg** sich (*Dat. od. Akk.*) in den Finger/ins Bein schneiden; **he ~ himself on broken glass** er hat sich an einer Glasscherbe geschnitten; **he ~ his head open** er schlug sich (*Dat.*) den Kopf auf; **the icy blasts that ~ one to the marrow** (fig.) die eisigen Winde, die einem durch und durch *od.* durch Mark und Bein gehen; **the remark ~ him to the quick** (fig.) die Bemerkung traf ihn ins Mark
2 (divide) (with knife) schneiden; durchschneiden ‹*Seil*›; (with axe) durchhacken; ~ **sth. in half/two/three** etw. halbieren/zweiteilen/dreiteilen; ~ **sth. [in]to pieces** etw. in Stücke schneiden/hacken; ~ **one's ties** *or* **links** alle Verbindungen abbrechen; alle Brücken hinter sich (*Dat.*) abbrechen; ~ **no ice with sb.** (fig. coll.) keinen Eindruck auf jmdn. machen; jmdm. nicht imponieren (ugs.); ~ **the knot** (fig.) das Problem lösen
3 (detach, reduce) schneiden ‹*Haare*›; abschneiden; schneiden, stutzen ‹*Hecke*›; mähen ‹*Getreide, Gras*›; ~ (*p.p.*) **flowers** Schnittblumen; ~ **one's nails** sich (*Dat.*) die Nägel schneiden
4 (shape, fashion) schleifen ‹*Glas, Edelstein, Kristall*›; hauen, schlagen ‹*Stufen*›; treiben ‹*Tunnel*›; einhauen ‹*Inschrift*›; ~ **a key** einen Schlüssel feilen; ~ **figures in wood/stone** Figuren aus Holz schnitzen/aus Stein hauen; ~ **a record** eine Schallplatte schneiden
5 (meet and cross) ‹*Straße, Linie, Kreis:*› schneiden; **the two lines ~ one another at right angles** die beiden Linien schneiden sich im rechten Winkel
6 (fig.: renounce, refuse to recognize) schneiden; ~ **sb. dead** jmdn. wie Luft behandeln
7 (carve) [auf]schneiden ‹*Fleisch, Geflügel*›; abschneiden ‹*Scheibe*›; ~ (*p.p.*) **loaf** (Brit. dated) Schnittbrot, *das*
8 (reduce) senken ‹*Preise*›; verringern, einschränken ‹*Menge, Produktion*›; mindern ‹*Qualität*›; drosseln ‹*Tempo, Produktion*›; kürzen ‹*Ausgaben, Lohn*›; verkürzen ‹*Arbeitszeit, Urlaub*›; (cease, stop) einstellen ‹*Dienstleistungen, Lieferungen*›; abstellen ‹*Strom*›; (coll.) aufhören mit ‹*Tätigkeit*›; **these scenes were ~ by the censor** diese Szenen hat die Zensur herausgeschnitten
9 ▸**figure A 4**
10 (absent oneself from) schwänzen ‹*Schule, Unterricht*›
11 ~ **a loss** der Sache (*Dat.*) ein Ende machen (*ehe der Schaden noch größer wird*); ~ **one's losses** höherem Verlust vorbeugen

12 **~ sth. short** (lit. or fig.: interrupt, terminate) etwas abbrechen; **the war ~ short his career** der Krieg hat seine Karriere vorzeitig beendet; **~ sb. short** jmdn. unterbrechen; (impatiently) jmdm. ins Wort fallen; **to ~ a long story short** der langen Rede kurzer Sinn
13 (Cards) abheben; **~ the pack [of cards]** [die Karten] abheben
14 **~ a tooth** einen Zahn bekommen; **~ one's teeth on sth.** (fig.) sich (*Dat.*) die ersten Sporen an etw. (*Dat.*) od. mit etw. verdienen
15 **be ~ and dried** genau festgelegt *od.* abgesprochen sein; **her opinions are ~ and dried** ihre Ansichten sind unverrückbar
16 (Cricket, Tennis) [an]schneiden ‹*Ball*›
17 (Cinemat.) schneiden; cutten
18 (Computing) **~ and paste** ausschneiden und einfügen
19 **half ~** (coll.) angetrunken. *See also* **cloth 1**; **corner A 1**; **eye tooth**; **fine² A 7**

B *v.i.*, **-tt-**, **~**: **1** ‹*Messer, Schwert usw.*:› schneiden; ‹*Papier, Tuch, Käse*:› sich schneiden lassen; **~ into a cake** einen Kuchen anschneiden; **~ both ways** (fig.) ein zweischneidiges Schwert sein (fig.)
2 (cross, intersect) sich schneiden
3 (pass) **~ through** *or* **across the field/park** [quer] über das Feld/durch den Park gehen; **~ across sth.** (fig.) sich über etw. (*Akk.*) hinwegsetzen
4 (Cinemat.) (stop the cameras) abbrechen; (go quickly to another shot) überblenden (**to** zu); **the film director cried '~!'** der Regisseur rief: „Schnitt!" *od.* „Aus!"
5 (coll.: run) **~ along** sich auf die Socken machen (ugs.); **~ and run** abhauen (ugs.). *See also* **loose A 1**

C *n.* **1** (act of ~ting) Schnitt, *der*
2 (stroke, blow) (with knife) Schnitt, *der;* (with sword, whip) Hieb, *der;* (injury) Schnittwunde, *die;* **the ~ and thrust of politics** (fig.) das Spannungsfeld der Politik; **the ~ and thrust of debate** (fig.) die Hitze der Debatte
3 (reduction) (in wages) Kürzung, *die;* (in expenditure, budget) Kürzung, *die;* Einsparung, *die;* (in prices) Senkung, *die;* (in time, working hours, holiday, etc.) Verkürzung, *die;* (in services) Verringerung, *die;* (in production, output, etc.) Einschränkung, *die;* (in quality) Minderung, *die;* **make the ~** (Sport, esp. Golf) sich für den weiteren Wettkampf qualifizieren
4 (wounding act or utterance) Seitenhieb, *der* (**at** gegen); Affront, *der* (geh.); **the unkindest ~ of all** der schlimmste Schlag
5 (of meat) Stück, *das*
6 ▸**wood~**
7 (coll.: commission, share) Anteil, *der*
8 (way thing is ~) (of gem) Schliff, *der;* (of hair: style) [Haar]schnitt, *der;* Frisur, *die;* (of clothes) Schnitt, *der;* **be a ~ above [the rest]** [den anderen] um einiges überlegen sein
9 (in play, book, etc.) Streichung, *die;* (in film) Schnitt, *der;* **make ~s** Streichungen/Schnitte vornehmen
10 (channel made for river) Rinne, *die;* Einschnitt, *der. See also* **jib¹ 1**; **short cut**

Phrasal verbs

- **~ 'away** ▸**~ off 1**
- **~ 'back**

A *v.t.* **1** (reduce) einschränken ‹*Produktion*›; verringern ‹*Investitionen*› **2** (prune) stutzen
B *v.i.* **1** (reduce) **~ back on sth.** etw. einschränken **2** (Cinemat.) zurückblenden. *See also* **~back**

- **~ 'down**

A *v.t.* **1** (fell) fällen **2** (kill) töten; **~ sb. down with a sword** jmdn. mit dem Schwert erschlagen *od.* (geh.) niederstrecken **3** (reduce) einschränken; **~ an article down** einen Artikel zusammenstreichen *od.* kürzen; **~ sb. down to size** (fig.) jmdn. auf seinen Platz verweisen
B *v.i.* (reduce) **~ down on sth.** etw. einschränken; **~ down on tobacco** den Tabakverbrauch einschränken; **~ down on clothes** die Ausgaben für die Garderobe einschränken

- **~ 'in**

A *v.i.* **1** (come in abruptly, interpose) sich einschalten; unterbrechen; **~ in on sb./sth.** jmdn./etw. unterbrechen **2** (after overtaking) schneiden; **~ in in front of sb.** jmdn. schneiden **3** (take dance partner from another) **~ in [on sb.]** [jmdn.] abklatschen **4** (switch itself on) ‹*Motor usw.*:› sich einschalten
B *v.t.* (give share of profit to) beteiligen ‹*Komplizen*›

- **~ 'off** *v.t.* **1** (remove by cutting) abschneiden; abtrennen; (with axe etc.) abschlagen **2** (interrupt, make unavailable) abschneiden ‹*Zufuhr*›; streichen ‹*Zuschuss*›; abstellen ‹*Strom, Gas, Wasser*›; unterbrechen ‹*Telefongespräch, Sprecher am Telefon*› **3** (isolate) abschneiden; **be ~ off by the snow/tide** durch den Schnee/die Flut [von der Außenwelt] abgeschnitten sein **4** (prevent, block) abschneiden; **their retreat was ~ off** ihnen wurde der Rückzug abgeschnitten **5** (exclude from contact with others) **~ sb. off from friends/the outside world** jmdn. von seinen Freunden trennen/von der Außenwelt abschneiden; **~ oneself off** sich absondern **6** (disinherit) enterben; **~ sb. off with a shilling** jmdn. mit einem Apfel und einem Ei abspeisen (ugs.). *see also* **cut-off**
- **~ 'out**

A *v.t.* **1** (remove by cutting) ausschneiden; **~ sth. out of sth.** etw. aus etw. ausschneiden **2** (omit) [heraus]streichen **3** (stop doing or using) aufhören mit; **~ out cigarettes/alcohol/drugs** aufhören, Zigaretten zu rauchen/Alkohol zu trinken/Drogen zu nehmen; **~ it** *or* **that out** (coll.) hör/hört auf damit!; lass/lasst das sein! **4** (defeat) ausstechen (ugs.) ‹*Rivalen, Konkurrenten, Gegner*› **5** (shape) zuschneiden ‹*Stoff, Kleid, Leder*› **6** (disconnect electrically) ausschalten ‹*Motor, Licht*›; abstellen ‹*Motor*›; abschalten ‹*Strom*› **7** (make suitable) **be ~ out for sth.** für etw. geeignet sein; **he was not ~ out to be a teacher** er war nicht zum Lehrer gemacht; er taugte nicht zum Lehrer; **Peter and Susan seem to be ~ out for each other** Peter und Susan sind füreinander wie geschaffen
B *v.i.* (cease functioning) ‹*Motor*:› aussetzen; ‹*Gerät*:› sich abschalten. *see also* **cut-out**

- **~ 'up**

A *v.t.* **1** (~ in pieces) zerschneiden; in Stücke schneiden ‹*Fleisch, Gemüse*›; (chop) zerhacken **2** (injure) verletzen; (fig.: criticize) zerreißen; **~ up the enemy** den Feind vernichten; **be ~ up about sth.** (fig.) zutiefst betroffen über etw. (*Akk.*) sein
B *v.i.* **~ up rough** Krach schlagen (ugs.); Radau machen (ugs.)

cutaneous /kjuːˈteɪnɪəs/ *adj.* Haut-; kutan (fachspr.)

cut: ~away *adj.* Schnitt-; **~away model** Schnittmodell, *das;* **~back** *n.* (reduction) Kürzung, *die;* (Cinemat.) Rückblende, *die*

cute /kjuːt/ *adj.* (coll.) **1** (attractive) süß, niedlich ‹*Kind, Mädchen*›; entzückend ‹*Stadt, Haus*› **2** (shrewd) schlau; gerissen; (ingenious) raffiniert ‹*Gerät*›; einfallsreich ‹*Person*›; pfiffig ‹*Erklärung*›

cut 'glass *n.* Kristall[glas], *das*

'cut-glass *adj.* Kristall-

cuticle /ˈkjuːtɪkl/ *n.* Epidermis, *die* (fachspr.); Oberhaut, *die;* (of nail) Nagelhaut, *die*

'cuticle remover *n.* Nagelhautentferner, *der*

cutie /ˈkjuːtɪ/ *n.* (coll.) **1** (woman) Süße, *die* **2** (usu. joc.: man) irrer Typ (ugs.)

cutlass /ˈkʌtləs/ *n.* **1** (Hist.) Entersäbel, *der* **2** ▸**machete**

cutler /ˈkʌtlə(r)/ *n.* ▸**i** **p. 1260** Messerschmied, *der*

cutlery /ˈkʌtlərɪ/ *n.* Besteck, *das*

cutlet /ˈkʌtlɪt/ *n.* **1** (of mutton or lamb) Kotelett, *das* **2** **veal ~**: Frikandeau, *das* **3** (minced meat etc. in shape of ~) Hacksteak, *das;* **nut/cheese/potato ~**: *aus Nüssen/Käse/Kartoffeln hergestelltes Gericht in Form eines Schnitzels od. Koteletts*

cut: ~-off *n.* **1** Trennung, *die; attrib.* **~-off point** Trennungslinie, *die;* **2** *as tech. term* Ausschaltmechanismus, *der;* Ausschaltung, *die;* **~-out** *n.* (Electr.) Unterbrecher, *der;* (figure ~ out of material) Ausschneidefigur, *die; attrib.* **~-out box** (Amer.) ▸**fuse box**; **~over** *n.* Umstellung, *die;* (**to** auf + *Akk.*); **~-price** *adj.* herabgesetzt; **~-price goods** Waren zu herabgesetzten Preisen; **~-price offer** Billigangebot, *das;* **~-rate** *adj.* verbilligt; herabgesetzt

cutter /ˈkʌtə(r)/ *n.* **1** (person) (of cloth) Zuschneider, *der*/-schneiderin, *die;* (of stones) Steinmetz, *der;* (of glass, gems) Schleifer, *der*/Schleiferin, *die;* (of films) Cutter, *der*/Cutterin, *die;* Schnittmeister, *der*/-meisterin, *die;* (miner) Hauer, *der* **2** (machine) Schneidmaschine, *die;* Schneidwerkzeug, *das;* (rotary cutting tool) Bohrkrone, *die;* Bohrkopf, *der;* (cutting stylus) Cutter, *der* **3** (Naut.) Kutter, *der*

'cutthroat

A *n.* **1** Strolch, *der;* (murderer) Killer, *der* (ugs.) **2** (Amer.: trout) Purpurforelle, *die*
B *adj.* **1** mörderisch, gnadenlos ‹*Wettbewerb*› **2** **~ razor** Rasiermesser, *das*

cutting /ˈkʌtɪŋ/

A *adj.* beißend ‹*Bemerkung, Antwort*›; schneidend ‹*Wind*›; **~ edge** Schneide, *die;* **~ tool** Schneidewerkzeug, *das*
B *n.* **1** (esp. Brit.: from newspaper) Ausschnitt, *der* **2** (esp. Brit.: excavation for railway, road etc.) Einschnitt, *der* **3** (of plant) Ableger, *der*

cutting: ~ edge *n.* **be at the ~ edge of technology** auf dem Gebiet der Technologie führend sein; die Speerspitze der Technologie sein; **be at the ~ edge of fashion** auf dem Gebiet der Mode führend sein; **~ room** *n.* (Cinemat., Telev.) Schneideraum, *der*

cuttle[fish] /ˈkʌtl(fɪʃ)/ *n.* Tintenfisch, *der;* Sepia, *die* (fachspr.)

'cutwater *n.* (of bridge) Eisbrecher, *der;* (of ship) Bugkante, *die*

c.v. *abbr.* = **curriculum vitae**

c.w.o. *abbr.* = **cash with order** Barzahlung *od.* Kasse bei Auftragserteilung

cwt. *abbr.* = **hundredweight** ≈ Ztr.

cyan /ˈsaɪən/

A *adj.* grünstichig blau
B *n.* Cyanblau, *das*

cyanide /ˈsaɪənaɪd/ *n.* Cyanid, *das*

cyanogen /saɪˈænədʒən/ *n.* (Chem.) Cyan, *das*

cyber: ~art /ˈsaɪbərɑːt/ *n., no pl.* Cyberkunst, *die;* **~café** /ˈsaɪbəkæfeɪ/ *n.* Cybercafé, *das;* Internetcafé, *das;* **~citizen** /ˈsaɪbəsɪtɪzn/ *n.* Cybercitizen, *der* (fachspr.); Internetbürger, *der*/-bürgerin, *die;* **~crime** /ˈsaɪbəkraɪm/ *n.* Internetkriminalität, *die;* (criminal act) Internetverbrechen, *das;* **~criminal** /ˈsaɪbəkrɪmɪnl/ *n.* Internetkriminelle, *der/die*

cybernaut /ˈsaɪbənɔːt/ *n.* **1** (user of virtual reality devices) Cybernaut, *der*/Cybernautin, *die* **2** (Internet user) Internetfreak, *der*

cybernetics /saɪbəˈnetɪks/ *n., no pl.* Kybernetik, *die*

cyber: ~police /ˈsaɪbəpəliːs/ *n., no pl.* Cyberpolizei, *die;* **~sex** /ˈsaɪbəseks/ *n., no pl.* Cybersex, *der;* **~space** /ˈsaɪbəspeɪs/ *n., no pl.* Cyberspace, *der;* **~squatting** /ˈsaɪbəskwɒtɪŋ/ *n., no pl.* (Computing) Cybersquatting, *das;* **~stalker** /ˈsaɪbəstɔːkə(r)/ *n.* Cyberstalker, *der*/-stalkerin, *die;* **~world** /ˈsaɪbəwɜːld/ *n* Cyberwelt, *die;* Internetwelt, *die*

cyborg /ˈsaɪbɔːg/ *n.* Cyborg, *der* (fachspr.); Robotermensch, *der*

cyclamen /ˈsɪkləmən/ *n.* (Bot.) Alpenveilchen, *das;* Zyklamen, *das* (fachspr.)

cycle /ˈsaɪkl/

A *n.* **1** (recurrent period) Zyklus, *der;* (period of completion) Turnus, *der;* **~ of the seasons** Jahreszyklus, *der;* **~ per second** (Phys., Electr.) Schwingung pro Sekunde; Hertz, *das* **2** (recurring series) Kreislauf, *der;* (complete set or series) Zyklus, *der* **3** (bicycle) Rad, *das*
B *v.i.* Rad fahren; mit dem [Fahr]rad fahren

cycle: ~ computer *n.* Fahrradcomputer, *der;* **~ lane** *n.* Fahrradspur, *die;* **~ race** *n.* Radrennen, *das;* **~ ride** *n.* [Fahr]radfahrt, *die;* **go for a ~ ride** eine [Fahr]radtour machen; **it's a 10-minute ~ ride to town** mit dem [Fahr]rad braucht man 10 Minuten bis zur Stadt; **~ shed** *n.* Fahrradstand, *der;* **~ shop** *n.* Fahrradgeschäft, *das;* Fahrradladen, *der;* **~ track**, *n.* Rad[fahr]weg, *der;* (for racing) Radrennbahn, *die;* **~ way** *n.* Rad[fahr]weg, *der*

cyclic /ˈsaɪklɪk/, **cyclical** /ˈsaɪklɪkl/ *adj.*, **cyclically** /ˈsaɪklɪkəlɪ/ *adv.* zyklisch

cycling /ˈsaɪklɪŋ/ *n.* (activity) Radfahren, *das;* (sport) Radsport, *der;* **amateur ~:** Amateur-Radrennsport, *der; attrib.* **~ enthusiast** Radsportfan, *der;* **~ holiday** Fahrradurlaub, *der;* **~ shorts** Radlerhose, *die*

cyclist /ˈsaɪklɪst/ *n.* Radfahrer, *der*/-fahrerin, *die*

cyclo-cross *n.* Querfeldeinrennen, *das*

cyclone /ˈsaɪkləʊn/ *n.* (system of winds) Tiefdruckgebiet, *das;* Zyklon, *die* (fachspr.); (violent hurricane) Zyklon, *der*

cyclonic /saɪˈklɒnɪk/ *adj.* Zyklon‹*wind, -stärke*›; **~ storm** Zyklon, *der*

Cyclops /ˈsaɪklɒps/ *n., pl. same or* **~es** *or* **Cyclopes** /saɪˈkləʊpiːz/ (Mythol.) Zyklop, *der*

cyclotron /ˈsaɪklətrɒn/ *n.* (Phys.) Zyklotron, *das*

cygnet /ˈsɪɡnɪt/ *n.* junger Schwan

cylinder /ˈsɪlɪndə(r)/ *n.* (also Geom., Motor Veh.) Zylinder, *der;* (of revolver, carding machine) Trommel, *die;* (for compressed or liquefied gas) Gasflasche, *die;* (of diving apparatus) [Sauerstoff]flasche, *die;* (of platen press, typewriter, mower) Walze, *die*

cylinder: ~ block *n.* Motorblock, *der;* **~ head** *n.* Zylinderkopf, *der*

cylindrical /sɪˈlɪndrɪkl/ *adj.* zylindrisch; *see also* **projection 9**

cymbal /ˈsɪmbl/ *n.* (Mus.) Beckenteller, *der;* **~s** Becken *Pl.*

cyme /saɪm/ *n.* (Bot.) Trugdolde, *die*

cynic /ˈsɪnɪk/ *n.* **1** Zyniker, *der* **2** **C~** (Greek philosopher) Kyniker, *der*

cynical /ˈsɪnɪkl/ *adj.* zynisch; bissig ‹*Artikel, Bemerkung, Worte*›; **be ~ about sth.** sich zynisch zu etw. äußern

cynically /ˈsɪnɪkəlɪ/ *adv.* zynisch

cynicism /ˈsɪnɪsɪzm/ *n.* Zynismus, *der*

cypher ▸ **cipher**

cypress /ˈsaɪprɪs/ *n.* Zypresse, *die*

Cyprian /ˈsɪprɪən/, **Cypriot** /ˈsɪprɪət/ ▸ⓘ **p. 1345**

A *adjs.* zyprisch; zypriotisch

B *ns.* Zypriot, *der*/Zypriotin, *die;* Zyprer, *der*/Zyprerin, *die*

Cyprus /ˈsaɪprəs/ *pr. n.* Zypern (*das*)

Cyrillic /sɪˈrɪlɪk/ *adj.* kyrillisch

cyst /sɪst/ *n.* ▸ⓘ **p. 1231** (Biol., Med.) Zyste, *die*

cystic fibrosis /sɪstɪk faɪˈbrəʊsɪs/ *n., no pl.* (Med.) Mukoviszidose, *die*

cystitis /sɪsˈtaɪtɪs/ *n.* ▸ⓘ **p. 1231** (Med.) Zystitis, *die* (Med.); Blasenentzündung, *die*

cytology /saɪˈtɒlədʒɪ/ *n.* Zytologie, *die*

cytoplasm /ˈsaɪtəplæzm/ *n.* (Biol.) Zytoplasma, *das*

czar *etc.* ▸ **tsar** *etc.*

Czech /tʃek/ ▸ⓘ **p. 1277**, ▸ⓘ **p. 1345**

A *adj.* tschechisch; **sb. is ~:** jmd. ist Tscheche/Tschechin; *see also* **English A**

B *n.* **1** (language) Tschechisch, *das; see also* **English B 1** **2** (person) Tscheche, *der*/Tschechin, *die*

Czechoslovak /tʃekəʊˈsləʊvæk/ (Hist.) ▸ **Czechoslovakian**

Czechoslovakia /tʃekəʊsləˈvækɪə/ *pr. n.* (Hist.) die Tschechoslowakei

Czechoslovakian /tʃekəʊsləˈvækɪən/ ▸ⓘ **p. 1345** (Hist.)

A *adj.* tschechoslowakisch

B *n.* Tschechoslowake, *der*/Tschechoslowakin, *die*

Czech Republic *n.* Tschechische Republik; Tschechien (*das*)

Dd

d

D, d /diː/ *n., pl.* **Ds** *or* **D's** 1 (letter) D, d, *das* 2 **D** (Mus.) D, d, *das;* **D sharp** dis, Dis, *das;* **D flat** des, Des, *das* 3 (Roman numeral) D 4 **D** (Sch., Univ.: mark) Vier, *die;* **he got a D** er bekam „ausreichend" *od.* eine Vier

d. *abbr.* 1 = **daughter** T. 2 = **deci-** d 3 = **delete** d. 4 = **died** gest. 5 (Brit. Hist.) = **penny/pence** d.

D. *abbr.* 1 (Amer.) = **Democrat** 2 = **dimensional**

'd /d/ (coll.) = **would, had, should**

DA *abbr.* ▸❶ **p. 1260** (Amer.) = **District Attorney**

dab¹ /dæb/

A *n.* 1 Tupfer, *der* 2 (slight blow, tap) Klaps, *der;* (bird's peck) Picken, *das* 3 *in pl.* (Brit. coll.: fingerprints) Fingerabdrücke *Pl.*

B *v.t.,* **-bb-** 1 (press with sponge etc.) abtupfen; (press on surface) **~ sth. on** *or* **against sth.** etw. auf etw. (*Akk.*) tupfen 2 (strike lightly, tap) **~ sb.** jmdm. einen Klaps geben 3 ‹*Vogel:*› picken

C *v.i.,* **-bb-:** **~ at sth.** etw. ab- *od.* betupfen

dab² *n.* (Zool.) Kliesche, *die;* Scharbe, *die*

dab³ (Brit. coll.: expert)

A *n.* Könner, *der;* Ass, *das* (ugs.) (**at** in + *Dat.*)

B *adj.* geschickt; **be a ~ hand at cricket/making omelettes** ein Ass im Kricket/Eierkuchenbacken sein (ugs.)

dabble /ˈdæbl/

A *v.t.* 1 (wet slightly) befeuchten; (move in water) **~ one's feet in the water** mit den Füßen im Wasser planschen 2 (soil, splash) bespritzen

B *v.i.* (engage in) **~ at/in sth.** sich in etw. (*Dat.*) versuchen; in etw. (*Dat.*) dilettieren

dabbler /ˈdæblə(r)/ *n.* Amateur, *der;* Dilettant, *der* (abwertend)

dabchick /ˈdæbtʃɪk/ *n.* (Ornith.) Lappentaucher, *der;* Steißfuß, *der*

dace /deɪs/ *n., pl. same* (Zool.) Hasel, *der;* Häsling, *der*

dacha /ˈdætʃə/ *n.* Datscha, *die;* (bes. DDR:) Datsche, *die*

dachshund /ˈdækshʊnd/ *n.* Dackel, *der;* Dachshund, *der* (fachspr.)

dactyl /ˈdæktɪl/ *n.* (Pros.) Daktylus, *der*

dad /dæd/ *n.* (coll.) Vater, *der*

Dadaism /ˈdɑːdɑːɪzm/ *n.* (Art Hist.) Dadaismus, *der*

daddy /ˈdædɪ/ *n.* (coll.) 1 Vati, *der* (fam.); Papi, *der* (fam.); Papa, *der* (fam.) 2 (man) Alte, *der* (ugs.) 3 (oldest/most important person) König, *der* (ugs.); **the ~ of them all** der/die/das Allergrößte (ugs.)

daddy-'long-legs *n. sing.* (Zool.) 1 (crane fly) Schnake, *die* 2 (Amer.: harvestman) Weberknecht, *der;* Kanker, *der*

dado /ˈdeɪdəʊ/ *n., pl.* **~s** *or* (Amer.) **~es** 1 (of room wall) Sockel, *der; attrib.* **~ rail** Sockel, *der* 2 (of column) Kehle, *die*

daemon /ˈdiːmən/ *n.* Dämon, *der*

daffodil /ˈdæfədɪl/ *n.* Gelbe Narzisse; Osterglocke, *die*

daffy /ˈdæfɪ/ *adj.* (coll.) blöd[e] (ugs.); dämlich (ugs.)

daft /dɑːft/ *adj.* 1 (foolish, wild) doof (ugs.); blöd[e] (ugs.); **what a ~ thing to do!** so was Doofes (ugs.) *od.* Blödes (ugs.)! 2 (crazy) verrückt (ugs.); übergeschnappt (ugs.); **be ~ about sth./sb.** verrückt nach etw./jmdm. sein

dagger /ˈdægə(r)/ *n.* 1 Dolch, *der;* **be at ~s drawn with sb.** (fig.) mit jmdm. auf Kriegsfuß stehen; **look ~s at sb.** jmdn. finster anblicken; jmdm. finstere Blicke zuwerfen 2 (Printing) Kreuz, *das*

dago /ˈdeɪgəʊ/ *n., pl.* **~s** *or* **~es** (sl. derog.) 1 (Spaniard, Portuguese, Italian) Welsche, *der* (veralt. abwertend); Kanake, *der* (derb abwertend) 2 (any foreigner) Kanake, *der* (derb abwertend)

daguerreotype /dəˈgerətaɪp/ *n.* Daguerreotypie, *die*

dahlia /ˈdeɪlɪə/ *n.* Dahlie, *die*

daily /ˈdeɪlɪ/

A *adj.* täglich; **~ [news]paper** Tageszeitung, *die;* **the ~ grind [of life]** der Alltagstrott; **on a ~ basis** tageweise

B *adv.* täglich; jeden Tag; (constantly) Tag für Tag; täglich

C *n.* 1 (newspaper) Tageszeitung, *die* 2 (Brit. coll.: charwoman) Reinemachefrau, *die. See also* **bread A 2; dozen 2**

> **The Daily Telegraph**
>
> Eine britische überregionale Tageszeitung. Der *Sunday Telegraph* wird von demselben Verlagshaus publiziert. Die Zeitung zählt zu den **broadsheet**-Zeitungen und damit zur seriösen Presse. Sie vertritt Ansichten der politischen Rechten und wurde in der Vergangenheit durch die Äußerung von sehr rechten Positionen bekannt. Traditionell vertritt sie die Interessen der **Conservative Party**, äußert jedoch auch oft Kritik an der konservativen Politik.

daintily /ˈdeɪntɪlɪ/ *adv.* zierlich; anmutig ‹*gehen, sich bewegen*›

daintiness /ˈdeɪntɪnɪs/ *n., no pl.* Zierlichkeit, *die;* (of movement, manner, etc.) Anmut, *die*

dainty /ˈdeɪntɪ/

A *adj.* 1 (of delicate beauty) zierlich; anmutig ‹*Bewegung, Person*›; zart, fein ‹*Gesichtszüge*› 2 (choice) delikat, köstlich ‹*Essen*› 3 (having delicate tastes) empfindsam; feinfühlig

B *n.* (lit. or fig.) Delikatesse, *die;* Leckerbissen, *der*

dairy /ˈdeərɪ/ *n.* 1 Molkerei, *die* 2 (shop) Milchladen, *der*

dairy: ~ cattle *n.* Milchvieh, *das;* **~ cream** *n.* [echter] Rahm; [echte] Sahne; **~ farm** *n.* Milchbetrieb, *der;* **~ farmer** *n.* Milchbauer, *der*

dairying /ˈdeərɪɪŋ/ *n.* Milchwirtschaft, *die*

dairy: ~maid *n.* Molkereiangestellte, *die;* **~man** /ˈdeərɪmən/ *n., pl.* **~men** /ˈdeərɪmən/ Milchmann, *der;* **~ produce** *n.,* **~ products** *n. pl.* Molkereiprodukte

dais /ˈdeɪɪs, deɪs/ *n.* Podium, *das*

daisy /ˈdeɪzɪ/ *n.* Gänseblümchen, *das;* (ox-eye) Margerite, *die;* **be pushing up [the] daisies** (fig. coll.) sich (*Dat.*) die Radieschen von unten ansehen (salopp); *see also* **fresh A 5**

daisy: ~ chain *n.* Kranz aus Gänseblümchen; **~ wheel** *n.* Typenrad, *das*

dale /deɪl/ *n.* (literary/N. Engl.) Tal, *das; see also* **up B 1**

dalliance /ˈdælɪəns/ *n.* (literary) Tändelei, *die* (veralt. geh.)

dally /ˈdælɪ/ *v.i.* 1 (amuse oneself, sport) **~ with sb.** mit jmdm. spielen *od.* leichtfertig umgehen; (flirt) mit jmdm. schäkern (ugs.) *od.* flirten; **~ with an idea** mit einem Gedanken spielen 2 (idle, loiter) [herum]trödeln (ugs.); **~ [over sth.]** mit etw. trödeln (ugs.)

Dalmatian /dælˈmeɪʃn/ *n.* Dalmatiner, *der*

dam¹ /dæm/

A *n.* 1 [Stau]damm, *der* 2 (barrier made by beavers) Damm, *der*

B *v.t.,* **-mm-:** 1 (lit. or fig.) **~ [up/back] sth.** etw. abblocken; **~ [up/back] the flow of words** dem Wortschwall Einhalt gebieten; **~ [up/back] one's feelings** seine Gefühle zurückhalten 2 (furnish or confine with ~) eindämmen; aufstauen

dam² *n.* (Zool.) Muttertier, *das*

damage /ˈdæmɪdʒ/

A *n.* 1 *no pl.* Schaden, *der;* **do a lot of ~ to sb./sth.** jmdm./einer Sache großen Schaden zufügen; jmdm. sehr schaden/etw. stark beschädigen; **the ~ is done now** es ist nun einmal passiert 2 *no pl.* (loss of what is desirable) **to sb.'s great ~:** zu jmds. großem Leidwesen 3 *in pl.* (Law) Schaden[s]ersatz, *der* 4 *no pl.* (Brit. coll.: cost) **what's the ~?** was kostet der Spaß? (ugs.)

B *v.t.* 1 beschädigen; **smoking can ~ one's health** Rauchen gefährdet die Gesundheit 2 (detract from) schädigen; **the article ~d his good reputation** der Artikel hat seinem guten Ruf geschadet; **that ~d his chances [of promotion]/his pride** das hat seine [Aufstiegs]chancen geschmälert/seinen Stolz verletzt

'damaged goods *n. pl.* 1 (faulty merchandise) fehlerhafte Ware; Ausschussware, *die* 2 (fig., derog.: person considered second-rate) nutzlos *od.* wertlos gewordener Mensch

'damage limitation exercise *n.* Schadensbegrenzungsversuch, *der;* **be engaged in a ~:** versuchen, zu retten, was [noch] zu retten ist

damaging /ˈdæmɪdʒɪŋ/ *adj.* schädlich (**to** für)

damask /ˈdæməsk/

A *n.* 1 (material) Damast, *der* 2 (twilled table linen) Damastdecke, *die*

B *adj.* damasten

damask 'rose *n.* Damaszenerrose, *die*

dame /deɪm/ *n.* 1 **D~** (Brit.) Dame (*Titel der weiblichen Träger verschiedener Orden im Ritterstand*) 2 **D~** (literary/poet.: title of woman of rank) Dame, *die* 3 (arch./poet./joc./Amer. sl.) Weib, *das* 4 (in pantomime) komische Alte

damfool /ˈdæmfuːl/ (coll.)

A *adj.* idiotisch (ugs.); blöd (ugs.); **~ action/remark** *etc.* Blödsinn, *der* (ugs.); **that was a ~ thing to do!** das war saublöd! (ugs.)

B *n.* Idiot, *der* (ugs.); Blödmann, *der* (salopp)

dammit /ˈdæmɪt/ *int.* (coll.) verdammt noch mal! (ugs.); **as ... as ~:** verdammt ... (ugs.); **as near as ~:** jedenfalls so gut wie (ugs.)

damn /dæm/

A *v.t.* 1 (condemn, censure) verreißen ‹*Buch, Film, Theaterstück*›; **~ with faint praise** durch kühles Lob ablehnen 2 (doom to hell, curse) verdammen 3 (coll.) **~ [it]!, ~ and blast [it]!** verflucht [noch mal]! (ugs.); zum Teufel [noch mal]! (ugs.); **~ it all!** verdammt noch mal! (ugs.); zum Donnerwetter! (ugs.); **~ all** (Brit. coll.) nicht die Bohne (ugs.); **~ you/him!** hol dich/ihn der Teufel! (salopp); **[well,] I'll be** *or* **I'm ~ed** ich werd verrückt (ugs.) *od.* dreh durch (salopp); **[I'll be** *or* **I'm] ~ed if I know** ich habe nicht die leiseste Ahnung; **[I'll be** *or* **I'm] ~ed if I'll go to meet him** ich werde ihn auf gar keinen Fall *od.* garantiert nicht treffen; **I'm ~ed if I can**

find it ich kann es beim besten Willen nicht finden; *see also* **God** 4▸ (be the ruin of) zu Fall bringen

B *n.* 1▸ (curse) Fluch, *der* 2▸ **he didn't give** *or* **care a ~ [about it]** ihm war es völlig Wurscht (ugs.) *od.* scheißegal (salopp); **I don't give a ~ for that girl** das Mädchen ist mir völlig schnuppe *od.* Wurscht (ugs.)

C *adj.* verdammt (ugs.); Scheiß- (salopp)

D *adv.* verdammt

damnable /ˈdæmnəbl/ *adj.* grässlich, scheußlich ‹*Wetter*›; ungeheuerlich ‹*Lüge, Anschuldigung*›; **~ luck** entsetzliches Pech

damnably /ˈdæmnəblɪ/ *adv.* verdammt

damnation /dæmˈneɪʃn/

A *n.* Verdammnis, *die*

B *int.* verdammt [noch mal]! (ugs.)

damned /dæmd/

A *adj.* 1▸ (doomed) verdammt 2▸ (infernal, unwelcome) verdammt (ugs.); **I can't see a ~ thing in this fog** so'n Mist, ich sehe überhaupt nichts [mehr] bei diesem Nebel (ugs.); **I have to walk back in this rain. What a ~ nuisance!** Verdammter Mist! Jetzt muss ich bei dem Regen zurücklaufen! (ugs.) 3▸ **do/try one's ~est** sein Möglichstes tun

B *adv.* verdammt (ugs.); **I should ~ well hope so/think so** das will ich aber [auch] schwer hoffen (ugs.) /stark annehmen

C *n. pl.* **the ~:** die Verdammten

damning /ˈdæmɪŋ/ *adj.* 1▸ (expressing severe criticism) vernichtend ‹*Urteil, Kritik, Worte*› 2▸ (that proves guilt) belastend ‹*Beweise*›

Damocles /ˈdæməkliːz/ *pr. n.* Damokles (*der*); **sword of ~:** Damoklesschwert, *das*

damp /dæmp/

A *adj.* feucht; **a ~ squib** (fig.) ein Reinfall

B *v.t.* 1▸ befeuchten; [ein]sprengen ‹*Wäsche*› 2▸ (stifle, extinguish) dämpfen ‹*Lärm*›; **~ [down] a fire** ein Feuer ersticken 3▸ (Mus., Phys.) dämpfen 4▸ (discourage, depress) dämpfen ‹*Eifer, Begeisterung*›; **~ sb.'s spirits** jmdm. den Mut nehmen

C *n.* (moisture) Feuchtigkeit, *die*

ˈdamp course ▸**damp-proof**

dampen /ˈdæmpn/ ▸**damp B 1, 4**

dampener /ˈdæmpənə(r)/ ▸**damper 1**

damper /ˈdæmpə(r)/ *n.* 1▸ (sth. that checks or depresses) **put a ~ on sth.** einer Sache (*Dat.*) einen Dämpfer aufsetzen; **his presence put a ~ on us** seine Anwesenheit dämpfte unsere Stimmung 2▸ (Mus.) Dämpfer, *der* 3▸ (in vehicle) Stoßdämpfer, *der* 4▸ (in flue) Luftklappe, *die*

dampness /ˈdæmpnɪs/ *n. no pl.* Feuchtigkeit, *die*; **~ in the air** Luftfeuchtigkeit, *die*

ˈdamp-proof *adj.* feuchtigkeitsbeständig; **~ course** Sperrschicht, *die* (*gegen aufsteigende Bodenfeuchtigkeit*)

damsel /ˈdæmzl/ *n.* (arch./literary) Maid, *die* (veralt.); **a ~ in distress** (joc.) eine hilflose junge Dame

ˈdamselfly *n.* Kleinlibelle, *die*

damson /ˈdæmzn/ *n.* 1▸ (fruit) Haferpflaume, *die* 2▸ (tree) Haferpflaumenbaum, *der*

damson ˈplum *n.* große Haferpflaume

dance /dɑːns/

A *v.i.* 1▸ tanzen; **~ to sb.'s tune** (fig.) nach jmds. Pfeife tanzen 2▸ (jump about, skip) herumtanzen; **~ about in agony/with rage** vor Schmerzen/Zorn rasen; **~ for joy** vor Freude an die Decke springen; einen Freudentanz aufführen 3▸ (bob up and down) tanzen; **the boat was dancing on the waves** das Boot tanzte *od.* schaukelte auf den Wellen

B *v.t.* 1▸ tanzen; **~ attendance on sb.** (fig.) jmdn. vorn und hinten bedienen (ugs.); um jmdn. herumscharwenzeln (ugs. abwertend) 2▸ (move up and down, dandle) schaukeln

C *n.* 1▸ Tanz, *der*; **lead sb. a [merry] ~** (fig.) jmdn. [schön] an der Nase herumführen 2▸ (party) Tanzveranstaltung, *die*; (private) Tanzparty, *die* 3▸ (tune in ~ rhythm) Tanz, *der*; **~ music** Tanzmusik, *die* 4▸ ▸ℹ **p. 1231** (Med.) **St. Vitus's ~:** Veitstanz, *der*

dance: ~ band *n.* Tanzkapelle, *die*; **~ floor** *n.* Tanzfläche, *die*; **~ hall** *n.* Tanzsaal, *der*

dancer /ˈdɑːnsə(r)/ *n.* Tänzer, *der*/Tänzerin, *die*

ˈdance step *n.* Tanzschritt, *der*

dancing/ˈdɑːnsɪŋ/: **~ girl** *n.* Tänzerin, *die*; **~ master** *n.* Tanzlehrer, *der*; **~ partner** *n.* Tanzpartner, *der*/-partnerin, *die*; **~ step** *n.* Tanzschritt, *der*

dandelion /ˈdændɪlaɪən/ *n.* Löwenzahn, *der*; (with seedhead) Pusteblume, *die* (Kinderspr.)

dander /ˈdændə(r)/ *n.* (coll.) Rage, *die* (ugs.); **get one's/sb.'s ~ up** in Rage kommen (ugs.)/jmdn. in Rage bringen (ugs.)

dandify /ˈdændɪfaɪ/ *v.t.* herausputzen

dandle /ˈdændl/ *v.t.* schaukeln

dandruff /ˈdændrʌf/ *n.* [Kopf]schuppen *Pl.*

dandy /ˈdændɪ/

A *n.* (person) Dandy, *der* (geh.); Geck, *der* (abwertend); Stutzer, *der* (veralt. abwertend)

B *adj.* (coll.) **[fine and] ~:** prima (ugs.)

Dane /deɪn/ *n.* ▸ℹ **p. 1345** Däne, *der*/Dänin, *die*

danger /ˈdeɪndʒə(r)/ *n.* Gefahr, *die*; **a ~ to sb./sth.** eine Gefahr für jmdn./etw.; **'~!'** „Vorsicht!"; (stronger) „Lebensgefahr!"; **there is [a/the] ~ of war/disease** es besteht Kriegs-/Seuchengefahr; **[a] ~ of invasion** die Gefahr einer Invasion; **in ~:** in Gefahr; **put sb. in ~:** jmdn. in Gefahr bringen; **in ~ of one's life/of death** in Lebensgefahr/Todesgefahr; **be in ~ of doing sth.** ‹*Person:*› Gefahr laufen, etw. zu tun; ‹*Sache:*› drohen, etw. zu tun; **out of ~:** außer Gefahr

danger: ~ area *n.* Gefahrenzone, *die*; **~ level** *n.* Gefahrengrenze, *die*; **~ list** *n.* **be on/off the ~ list** in/außer Lebensgefahr sein; **~ money** *n.* Gefahrenzulage, *die*

dangerous /ˈdeɪndʒərəs/ *adj.* gefährlich; **~ to health** gesundheitsgefährdend

dangerously /ˈdeɪndʒərəslɪ/ *adv.* gefährlich; **he drives ~:** er hat einen gefährlichen Fahrstil; **he's ~ overweight** er hat gefährliches Übergewicht

danger: ~ point *n.* Gefahrenpunkt, *der*; **~ signal** *n.* Warnzeichen, *das*; **~ zone** *n.* Gefahrenzone, *die*

dangle /ˈdæŋgl/

A *v.i.* baumeln (**from** an + *Dat.*)

B *v.t.* baumeln lassen; **~ [the prospect of] sth. in front of sb.** (fig.) jmdm. etw. [als Anreiz] in Aussicht stellen

Danish /ˈdeɪnɪʃ/ ▸ℹ **p. 1277**, ▸ℹ **p. 1345**

A *adj.* dänisch; **sb. is ~:** jmd. ist Däne/Dänin; *see also* **English A**

B *n.* Dänisch, *das*; *see also* **English B 1**

Danish: ~ ˈblue *n.* dänischer Blauschimmelkäse; Danablu Ⓦⓩ, *der*; **~ ˈpastry** *n.* Plunderstück, *das*

dank /dæŋk/ *adj.* feucht

Danube /ˈdænjuːb/ *pr. n.* ▸ℹ **p. 1491** Donau, *die*

daphne /ˈdæfnɪ/ *n.* (Bot.) Seidelbast, *der*

dapper /ˈdæpə(r)/ *adj.* (neat) adrett; schmuck (veralt.); (sprightly) munter

dapple /ˈdæpl/ *v.t.* [be]sprenkeln

dappled /ˈdæpld/ *adj.* gesprenkelt; gefleckt ‹*Pferd, Kuh*›

dapple-ˈgrey

A *adj.* **~ mare** Apfelschimmelstute, *die*

B *n.* Apfelschimmel, *der*

Darby and Joan /dɑːbɪ ən ˈdʒəʊn/ *n., pl.* **Darbies and Joans** *treues, altes Ehepaar*; ≈ Philemon und Baucis (geh.)

Darby and ˈJoan club *n.* (Brit.) Seniorenklub, *der*

dare /deə(r)/

A *v.t., pres.* **he ~** *or* **~s**, *neg.* **~ not**, (coll.) **~n't** /deənt/ 1▸ (venture) [es] wagen; sich (*Akk.*) trauen; **if you ~ [to] give away the secret** wenn du es wagst, das Geheimnis zu verraten; **we didn't ~ [to] go any further** wir wagten [es] nicht *od.* trauten uns nicht, noch weiter zu gehen; **we ~ not/~d not** *or* (coll.) **didn't ~ tell him the truth** wir wagen/wagten [es] nicht *od.* trauen/trauten uns nicht, ihm die Wahrheit zu sagen; **you wouldn't ~:** das wagst du nicht; du traust dich nicht; **just you ~!** untersteh dich!; das versuch mal! (ugs.); **don't you ~!** untersteh dich!; wehe!; **how ~ you [do ...]?** wie kannst du es wagen[, ... zu tun]?; **how ~ you!** was fällt dir ein!; (formal) was erlauben Sie sich!; **I ~ say** (supposing) ich nehme an; (confirming) das glaube ich gern 2▸ (attempt) wagen ‹*Aufstieg, Flucht*›; sich wagen an (+ *Akk.*) ‹*Projekt, Berg*›; (take the risk of) riskieren; herausfordern ‹*Zorn der Götter*› 3▸ (challenge) herausfordern; **~ sb. to do sth.** jmdn. dazu aufstacheln, etw. zu tun; **I ~ you!** trau dich!; **I ~ you to** *or* **I bet you ~n't call the boss by his first name** wetten, dass du dich nicht traust, den Chef beim Vornamen zu rufen?

B *n.* (act of daring) **do sth. for/as a ~:** etw. als Mutprobe tun; (challenge) **Go on! It's a ~!** Los! Sei kein Frosch!

ˈdaredevil *n.* Draufgänger, *der*/-gängerin, *die*

daren't /deənt/ (coll.) = **dare not**

daring /ˈdeərɪŋ/

A *adj.* (bold) kühn; waghalsig ‹*Kunststück, Tat*›; (fearless) wagemutig

B *n.* Kühnheit, *die*

daringly /ˈdeərɪŋlɪ/ *adv.* (boldly) kühn; (fearlessly) wagemutig

dark /dɑːk/

A *adj.* 1▸ (without light) dunkel; dunkel, finster ‹*Nacht, Haus, Straße*›; (gloomy) düster; dunkel, finster ‹*Wolke*› 2▸ dunkel ‹*Farbe*›; (brown-complexioned) dunkelhäutig; (**~-haired**) dunkelhaarig; **~-blue/-brown/-green** *etc.* dunkelblau/-braun/-grün *usw.*; *see also* **blue**[1] **B 5** 3▸ (evil) finster; übel ‹*Zauber, Ruf, Fluch*›; düster ‹*Drohung, Bedeutung*›; furchtbar ‹*Grausamkeiten*› 4▸ (cheerless) finster; düster ‹*Bild*›; (sad) düster ‹*Stimmung, Gedanke*›; (frowning) finster; **don't always look on the ~ side of things** sieh doch nicht immer alles so schwarz *od.* düster 5▸ (obscure) dunkel; schwierig ‹*Frage*›; **he's a ~ one as far as his plans are concerned** er ist so verschwiegen, was seine Pläne anbelangt; **keep sth./it ~:** etw./es geheim halten (**from** vor + *Dat.*); **be in ~est Africa** im tiefsten *od.* finstersten Afrika sein

B *n.* 1▸ (absence of light) Dunkel, *das*; **in the ~:** im Dunkeln 2▸ *no art.* (nightfall) Einbruch der Dunkelheit 3▸ **the ~** (fig.: lack of knowledge) **keep sb./be [kept] in the ~ about/as to sth.** jmdn. über etw. (*Akk.*) im Dunkeln lassen/über etw. (*Akk.*) im Dunkeln gelassen werden; **a leap in the ~:** ein Sprung ins Ungewisse; **it was a shot in the ~:** es war aufs Geratewohl geraten/versucht

ˈDark Ages *n. pl.* [frühes] Mittelalter

darken /ˈdɑːkn/

A *v.t.* 1▸ verdunkeln; **the sun had ~ed her skin** die Sonne hatte ihre Haut gebräunt 2▸ (fig.) verdüstern; verfinstern ‹*Miene*›; **never ~ my door again!** du betrittst mir meine Schwelle nicht mehr!

B *v.i.* 1▸ ‹*Zimmer:*› dunkel werden; ‹*Wolken, Himmel:*› sich verfinstern; **the day ~ed** es wurde dunkel 2▸ (fig.) sich verfinstern

dark: ~ ˈglasses *n. pl.* dunkle Brille; **~-haired** *adj.* dunkelhaarig; **~ ˈhorse** *n.* unbekanntes Pferd; (fig.: little-known yet successful person) [erfolgreicher] Außenseiter; (fig.: secretive person) **be a ~ horse** ein stilles Wasser sein

darkie, darky /ˈdɑːkɪ/ *n.* (offensive coll.) Schwarze, *der*/*die*

darkish /ˈdɑːkɪʃ/ *adj.* ziemlich dunkel

darkly /ˈdɑːklɪ/ *adv.* 1▸ dunkel 2▸ (ominously) finster; (obscurely, dimly) dunkel

ˈdark matter *n., no pl.* (Astron.) Dunkelmaterie, *die*

darkness /ˈdɑːknɪs/ *n., no pl.* 1▸ (dark) Dunkelheit, *die* 2▸ (wickedness, ominousness) Finsterkeit, *die*; **the powers of ~:** die Mächte der Finsternis 3▸ (obscurity) Dunkelheit, *die*

ˈdarkroom *n.* Dunkelkammer, *die*

darky ▸**darkie**

darling /ˈdɑːlɪŋ/

A *n.* Liebling, *der*; **she was his ~:** sie war seine Liebste *od.* sein Schatz; **her little ~s** ihre Lieblinge; **you 'are a ~** (coll.) du bist ein Schatz

B *adj.* geliebt; (coll.: delightful) reizend

darn[1] /dɑːn/

A *v.t.* stopfen

B *n.* gestopfte Stelle

darn[2] (coll.: damn)

A *v.t.* **~ you** *etc.*! zum Kuckuck mit dir *usw.*!

d

(salopp); ~ **[it]!** verflixt [und zugenäht]! (ugs.); ~ **it all!** verflixt noch mal! (ugs.); **I'll be ~ed** ich werd nicht mehr (salopp); **I'm** *or* **I'll be ~ed if I'll help you** ich werde dir auf gar keinen Fall helfen; **I'm** *or* **I'll be ~ed if I know** ich habe nicht die leiseste Ahnung (ugs.)
B *n.* ▸**damn B 2**
C *adj.* verflixt (ugs.)
D *adv.* verflixt (ugs.); ~ **stupid** schrecklich dumm

darned /dɑːnd/ (coll.)
A *adj.* verflixt (ugs.); **you ~ fool!** du verdammter Narr!; *see also* **damned A 2, 3**
B *adv.* verflixt; **don't be so ~ stubborn!** sei nicht so verdammt *od.* furchtbar stur!; *see also* **damned B**

darning /ˈdɑːnɪŋ/ *n.* Stopfen, *das;* **there's a lot of ~ to be done** es sind eine Menge Sachen zu stopfen

ˈ**darning needle** *n.* Stopfnadel, *die*

dart /dɑːt/
A *n.* **1** (missile) Pfeil, *der* **2** (Sport) Wurfpfeil, *der;* **~s** *sing.* (game) Darts, *das* **3** (Zool.) Stachel, *der* **4** (rapid motion) Satz, *der;* **the child made a sudden ~ into the road** das Kind rannte plötzlich auf die Fahrbahn **5** (Dressmaking: tapering tuck) Abnäher, *der*
B *v.t.* ~ **a look at sb.** jmdm. einen Blick zuwerfen; **the toad ~ed its tongue out** die Kröte ließ ihre Zunge herausschnellen
C *v.i.* (start rapidly) sausen; ~ **towards sth.** auf etw. (*Akk.*) zustürzen; **her eyes ~ed towards the staircase** sie warf einen raschen Blick zur Treppe; **the fish ~ed through the water** der Fisch schnellte durch das Wasser

ˈ**dartboard** *n.* Dartsscheibe, *die*

Darwinian /dɑːˈwɪnɪən/
A *adj.* darwinistisch
B *n.* Darwinist, *der*/Darwinistin, *die*

Darwinism /ˈdɑːwɪnɪzm/ *n., no pl.* Darwinismus, *der*

Darwinist /ˈdɑːwɪnɪst/ ▸**Darwinian A, B**

dash /dæʃ/
A *v.i.* (move quickly) sausen; (coll.: hurry) sich eilen; ~ **along behind sb./sth.** hinter jmdm./etw. herrasen; ~ **away from sb./sth.** von jmdm./etw. wegrasen; ~ **down/up [the stairs]** [die Treppe] hinunter-/hinaufstürzen; ~ **up to sb./sth.** auf jmdn./etw. zustürzen; **I must just ~ to the loo** ich muss noch [eben] schnell aufs Klo; ~ **against sth.** ‹*Wellen usw.:*› gegen etw. peitschen *od.* schlagen
B *v.t.* **1** (shatter) ~ **sth. [to pieces]** etw. [in tausend Stücke] zerschlagen *od.* zerschmettern **2** (fling) schleudern; schmettern; (splash) schütten; (bespatter) bespritzen (**with** mit) **3** (frustrate) **sb.'s hopes are ~ed** jmds. Hoffnungen haben sich zerschlagen **4** (coll.) ▸**darn² A**
C *n.* **1** **make a ~ for sth.** zu etw. rasen (ugs.); **make a ~ at sb.** auf jmdn. losstürzen (ugs.); **make a ~ for shelter** rasch Schutz suchen; **make a ~ for freedom** plötzlich versuchen, wegzulaufen **2** (horizontal stroke) Gedankenstrich, *der* **3** (Morse signal) Strich, *der* **4** (slight admixture) Schuss, *der;* **a ~ of salt** eine Prise Salz; **add a ~ of colour to sth.** einer Sache (*Dat.*) etwas Farbe geben; **beige with a ~ of brown** beige mit einem Stich ins Braune **5** (vigorous action) Schwung, *der;* (showy appearance etc.) **cut a ~:** Aufsehen erregen **6** ▸**dashboard**

Phrasal verbs

• ~ **aˈway**
A *v.i.* (rush) davonjagen; (coll: hurry) **they had to ~ away** sie mussten schnell weg; **you're not going to ~ away so soon, surely** du willst doch nicht schon wieder weg
B *v.t.* wegstoßen

• ~ **ˈoff**
A *v.i.* ▸~ **away A**
B *v.t.* rasch schreiben

• ~ **ˈout** *v.t.* ~ **sb.'s brains out** jmdm. den Schädel einschlagen

ˈ**dashboard** *n.* (Motor Veh.) Armaturenbrett, *das*

dashed /dæʃt/ ▸**darned**

dashing /ˈdæʃɪŋ/ *adj.* schneidig

dastardly /ˈdæstədlɪ/ *adj.* feige; (malicious) hinterhältig

data /ˈdeɪtə, ˈdɑːtə/ *n. pl., constr. as pl. or sing.* Daten *Pl.; see also* **datum**

data: ~ **analysis** *n.* Datenanalyse, *die;* ~ **analyst** *n.* Datenanalytiker, *der*/-analytikerin, *die;* **~back** *n.* Datenrückwand, *die;* ~ **bank** *n.* Datenbank, *die;* **~base** *n.* Datenbank, *die; attrib.* **~base management system** Datenbank-Managementsystem, *das;* ~ **capture** *n., no pl.* Datenerfassung, *die;* ~ **collection** *n., no pl.* Datensammlung, *die;* ~ **communications** *n. pl.* (Computing) Datenaustausch, *der;* ~ **encryption** *n., no pl.* Datenverschlüsselung, *die;* ~ **entry** *n., no. pl.* (Computing) Dateneingabe, *die;* ~ **file** *n.* (Computing) Datei, *die;* **~glove** *n.* (Computing) Datenhandschuh, *der;* ~ **handling** ▸~ **processing;** ~ **highway** *n.* (Computing) Datenautobahn, *die;* ~ **input** *n.* (Computing) Dateneingabe, *die;* ~ **link** *n.* (Computing) Datenleitung, *die;* ~ **management** *n., no pl.* (Computing) Datenmanagement, *das;* ~ **mining** *n., no pl.* (Computing) Datamining, *das;* ~ **processing** *n.* (Computing) Datenverarbeitung, *die;* ~ **processor** *n.* (Computing) Datenverarbeitungsanlage, *die;* ~ **proˈtection** *n., no pl.* (Computing) Datenschutz, *der;* **D~ Proˈtection Act** *n.* Datenschutzgesetz, *das;* ~ **recovery** *n., no pl.* (Computing) Datenrückgewinnung, *die;* ~ **retrieval** *n., no pl.* (Computing) Retrieval, *das;* Datenabruf, *der; attrib.* ~ **retrieval system** Retrievalsystem, *das;* ~ **security** *n., no pl.* (Computing) Datensicherung, *die;* ~ **set** *n.* (Computing) Datensatz, *der;* ~ **sheet** *n.* Informationsblatt, *das;* ~ **storage** *n., no pl.* (Computing) Datenspeicherung, *die;* (capacity) Speicherkapazität, *die;* Speicherplatz, *der;* ~ **terminal** *n.* (Computing) Datenterminal, *das;* ~ **transmission** *n., no pl.* (Computing) Datenübertragung, *die;* ~ **warehouse** *n.* (Computing) Datenlager, *das;* ~ **warehousing** *n., no pl.* (Computing) Datenhortung, *die*

date¹ /deɪt/ *n.* (Bot.) **1** (fruit) Dattel, *die* **2** (tree) ▸**date palm**

date²
A *n.* **1** ▸❶ **p. 1047** Datum, *das;* (on coin etc.) Jahreszahl, *die;* ~ **of birth** Geburtsdatum, *das;* **what are his ~s?** von wann bis wann hat er gelebt?; **the last ~ for payment** der letzte Termin für die Zahlung **2** (coll.: appointment) Verabredung, *die;* **have/make a ~ with sb.** mit jmdm. verabredet sein/sich mit jmdm. verabreden; **go [out] on a ~ with sb.** mit jmdm. ausgehen; *see also* **blind ~ 3** (Amer. coll.: person) Freund, *der*/Freundin, *die* **4** (period) [Entstehungs]zeit, *die* **5** **be out of ~:** altmodisch sein; (expired) nicht mehr gültig sein; **to ~:** bis heute; *see also* **up to date; up-to-date**
B *v.t.* **1** (mark with ~, refer to a time) datieren; ~ **sth. to a time** etw. einer Zeit zuordnen **2** (coll: make seem old) alt machen **3** (coll.: make ~ with) ~ **[each other]/sb.** miteinander/mit jmdm. gehen (ugs.)
C *v.i.* **1** ~ **back to/~ from a certain time** aus einer bestimmten Zeit stammen **2** (coll.: become out of ~) aus der Mode kommen

dated /ˈdeɪtɪd/ *adj.* altmodisch; **a ~ fashion** eine Mode von gestern

date: ~ **line** *n.* **1** (Geog.) Datumsgrenze, *die;* **2** (in newspaper etc.) *Zeile, in der das Datum steht;* ≈ Kopf, *der;* ~ **palm** *n.* Dattelpalme, *die;* ~ **rape** *n.: Vergewaltigung der eigenen Freundin oder Vergewaltigung einer Frau während einer Verabredung mit ihr;* ~ **stamp** *n.* Datumsstempel, *der;* **~-stamp** *v.t.* abstempeln; mit einem Datumsstempel versehen

ˈ**dating agency** /ˈdeɪtɪŋ/ *n.* Partnervermittlung, *die*

dative /ˈdeɪtɪv/ (Ling.)
A *adj.* Dativ-; dativisch; ~ **case** Dativ, *der*
B *n.* Dativ, *der*

datum /ˈdeɪtəm, ˈdɑːtəm/ *n., pl.* **data** /ˈdeɪtə, ˈdɑːtə/ **1** (premiss) Datum, *das;* Faktum, *das* **2** (fixed starting point) Nullpunkt, *der*

ˈ**datum line** *n.* (Surv.) Normalnull, *das*

daub /dɔːb/
A *v.t.* **1** (coat) bewerfen; verschmieren ‹*Geflecht*›; (smear, soil) beschmieren **2** (lay crudely) schmieren
B *v.i.* ‹*Künstler:*› die Leinwand voll schmieren (abwertend)
C *n.* **1** (plaster etc.) Bewurf, *der* **2** (crude painting) Kleckserei, *die* (ugs. abwertend); (large) Schinken, *der* (ugs. abwertend) **3** (smear) Fleck, *der;* **covered with great ~s of sth.** reichlich mit etw. beschmiert

daughter /ˈdɔːtə(r)/ *n.* (lit. or fig.) Tochter, *die*

ˈ**daughter-in-law** *n., pl.* **daughters-in-law** Schwiegertochter, *die*

daunt /dɔːnt/ *v.t.* entmutigen; schrecken (geh.); **nothing ~ed** unverzagt

dauntless /ˈdɔːntlɪs/ *adj.* unerschrocken

dauphin /ˈdɔːfɪn/ *n.* (Hist.) Dauphin, *der*

davenport /ˈdævnpɔːt/ *n.* **1** (Brit.: writing desk) Sekretär, *der* **2** (Amer.: sofa) Sofa, *das*

davit /ˈdævɪt/ *n.* [Boots]davit, *der*

Davy [lamp] /ˈdeɪvɪ (læmp)/ *n.* Wetterlampe, *die;* Davy-Lampe, *die*

dawdle /ˈdɔːdl/
A *v.i.* bummeln (ugs.)
B *v.t.* ~ **away** verbummeln (ugs.)
C *n.* (dawdling) Bummelei, *die* (ugs.); (stroll) Bummel, *der* (ugs.)

dawn /dɔːn/
A *v.i.* **1** dämmern; **day[light] ~ed** der Morgen dämmerte; der Tag brach an **2** (fig.) ‹*Zeitalter:*› anbrechen; ‹*Idee:*› aufkommen; ‹*Liebe, Hoffnung:*› erwachen; **until the meaning finally ~ed** bis schließlich der Sinn klar wurde; **sth. ~s on** *or* **upon sb.** etw. dämmert jmdm.; **hasn't it ~ed on you that ...?** ist dir nicht langsam klar geworden, dass ...?; **the idea ~ed on her that ...:** ihr kam die Idee, dass ...
B *n.* **1** [Morgen]dämmerung, *die;* **from ~ to dusk** von früh bis spät; **it is ~:** die Dämmerung bricht an; es wird hell; **at ~:** im Morgengrauen; **[the] ~ breaks** der Tag bricht an; **in the ~:** in der Morgendämmerung; **into the ~:** gen Sonnenaufgang (geh.) **2** (fig.) Morgenröte, *die* (geh.); (of idea, love, hope) Keimen, *das* (geh.); **at the ~ of civilization** in der Morgenröte der Zivilisation (geh.)

dawn ˈchorus *n.* morgendlicher Gesang der Vögel

dawning /ˈdɔːnɪŋ/ *n.* **1** Anbruch, *der;* **at the ~ of the day** bei Tagesanbruch **2** (fig.) Anfänge *Pl.;* **at the ~ of a new era/civilization** bei Anbruch eines neuen Zeitalters/in den Anfängen der Zivilisation

ˈ**dawn raid** *n.* (St. Exch.) *frühzeitiges, heimliches Aufkaufen von Aktien (um überraschend eine Aktienmehrheit zu erlangen)*

day /deɪ/ *n.* **1** ▸❶ **p. 1001,** ▸❶ **p. 1048** Tag, *der;* **on a ~ like today:** an einem Tag wie heute; **all ~ [long]** den ganzen Tag [lang]; **take all ~** (fig.) eine Ewigkeit brauchen; **as happy as the ~ is long** äußerst glücklich; **the ~ of ~s** der Tag der Tage; **all ~ and every ~:** tagaus, tagein; **not for many a long ~:** schon lange nicht mehr; **to this ~, from that ~ to this** bis zum heutigen Tag; **as clear as ~:** augenfällig; **for two ~s** zwei Tage [lang]; **what's the ~** *or* **what ~ is it today?** welcher Tag ist heute?; **twice a ~:** zweimal täglich *od.* am Tag; **in a ~/two ~s** (within) in *od.* an einem Tag/in zwei Tagen; **in a ~['s time]/a few ~s[' time]** in einem Tag/in ein paar Tagen; **in six ~s[' time]** in sechs Tagen; **in eight ~s** in genau acht Tagen; **[on] the ~ after/before** am Tag danach/davor; **[on] the ~ after/before sth.** am Tag nach/vor etw. (*Dat.*); **[on] the ~ after/before we met** am Tag, nach dem/bevor wir uns trafen; **[the] next/[on] the following/[on] the previous ~:** am nächsten/folgenden/vorhergehenden Tag; **the ~ before yesterday/after tomorrow** vorgestern/übermorgen; **the other ~:** neulich; **only the other ~:** erst vor ein paar Tagen; **every other ~:** alle zwei Tage; **from this/that ~ [on]** von heute an/von diesem Tag an; **one ~ he came** eines Tages kam er; **come and see us one ~:** komm irgendwann einmal vorbei; **one ~ ..., the next ...:** heute ..., morgen ...; **one of**

ℹ Dates

Unlike English which has several variations (May 10, 10 May, May 10th, 10th May etc.), dates in German are always written in the same way:

der 10. Mai

The accusative form is used at the head of letters, preceded by the name of the place:

Amstetten, den 25. August 2005

Dates written all in numbers are found in German as in English, particularly in business letters:

Frankfurt a.M., den 15.1.2005

With reference to your letter of the 4.1.2005 **or (Amer.)** ***1.4.2005*** = Bezug nehmend auf Ihr Schreiben vom 4.1.2005 (*spoken*: vom vierten Ersten zweitausend[und]fünf)

Saying dates

What's the date?
= Welches Datum haben wir heute?, Der Wievielte ist heute?

It's May the tenth
= Es ist der zehnte Mai

What date is the wedding?
= Wann ist die Hochzeit?; (*if the month is known)* Am Wievielten ist die Hochzeit?

The wedding is on the 22nd **(*twenty-second*)**
= Die Hochzeit ist am 22. (Zweiundzwanzigsten)

	WRITTEN	SPOKEN
May 1st, May 1	der 1. Mai	der erste Mai
May 21st, May 21	der 21. Mai	der einundzwanzigste Mai
May 30th, May 30	der 30. Mai	der dreißigste Mai
Monday May 3rd 1994	Montag, der 3. Mai 1994	Montag, der dritte Mai neunzehnhundertvierundneunzig
21.5.66 **or (Amer.)** ***5.21.66***	21.5.66	der einundzwanzigste Fünfte sechsundsechzig
1900	1900	neunzehnhundert

the year 2000	das Jahr 2000	das Jahr zweitausend
2006	2006	zweitausend[und]sechs
230 AD	230 n.Chr.	zweihundertdreißig nach Christus
55 BC	55 v.Chr.	fünfundfünfzig vor Christus
the 16th century	das 16. Jahrhundert *or* Jh.	das sechzehnte Jahrhundert

Saying when

on with days and dates is translated by **an** with the definite article, conflated to **am,** whether there is a definite article in English or not:

on Friday
= am Freitag*

on March 6th
= am 6. März (*spoken* am sechsten März)

on Friday March 6th
= am Freitag, den *or* dem 6. März

on the first of next month
= am nächsten Ersten

An exception is not unnaturally:

It happened on a Tuesday
= Es geschah an einem Dienstag

If an adjective follows *a* or *one*, the genitive construction can be used:

on a fine Sunday, one fine Sunday
= eines schönen Sonntags

*With days of the week the **am** can be omitted colloquially:

She's coming on Friday
= Sie kommt Freitag

in with months is **in** plus the definite article, conflated to **im:**

in June
= im Juni

last June
= voriges Jahr im Juni

next June
= im Juni nächsten Jahres

But note:

at the end/beginning of June
= Ende/Anfang Juni

in the middle of July
= Mitte Juli

When giving the year when something happened in German, the year is usually given on its own without any preposition, although "im Jahre" can be added in more formal language or when "v.Chr." or "n.Chr." follow:

He died in 1945
= Er starb 1945

in 55 BC
= im Jahre 55 v.Chr.

in 27 AD
= im Jahre 27 n.Chr.

Other phrases:

from November/November 5th **(*onwards*)**
= ab November/ab dem 5. November, vom November an/vom 5. November an

from next Tuesday
= ab kommendem Dienstag

from the 21st to the 30th
= vom 21. bis zum 30.

It will be ready by Friday/by the 14th
= Es wird bis Freitag/bis zum 14. fertig

It won't be ready until Friday
= Es wird erst [am] Freitag fertig

around May 16th
= um den 16. Mai [herum]

in the sixties or 60s
= in den Sechzigerjahren *or* 60er-Jahren

in the 1880s
= in den Achtzigerjahren des 19. Jahrhunderts, in den 1880er-Jahren

the 1912 uprising
= der Aufstand von 1912

the 19th century novel
= der Roman des 19. Jahrhunderts

a 17th century composer
= ein Komponist des 17. Jahrhunderts

a 14th century building
= ein Gebäude aus dem 14. Jahrhundert

these [fine] ~s eines [schönen] Tages; **two ~s ago** vor zwei Tagen; **some ~:** eines Tages; irgendwann einmal; **for the ~:** für einen Tag; **to the ~:** auf den Tag genau; **~ after ~:** Tag für Tag; **~ by ~, from ~ to ~:** von Tag zu Tag; **from one ~ to the next** von einem Tag zum andern; **~ in ~ out** tagaus, tagein; **it's all in the/a ~'s work** das gehört dazu (ugs.); **call it a ~** (end work) Feierabend machen; (more generally) Schluss machen; (fig.) es gut sein lassen (ugs.); **at the end of the ~** (fig.) letzten Endes; **early in the ~** (fig.) früh; **he's 65 if he's a ~:** er ist mindestens 65; **it's not my ~:** ich habe [heute] einen schlechten Tag; **it's my ~:** ich habe [heute] einen guten Tag; **on his ~:** wenn er seinen guten Tag hat; **that will be the ~** (iron.) das möchte ich sehen/erleben (ugs.); **it's been one of those ~s** das war vielleicht ein Tag (ugs.); **soup/dish of the ~:** Tagessuppe, *die*/Stammessen, *das; see also* **any A 5**; **good A 13**; **late B 5**; **make A 16**; **off A 5**

2 (daylight) **before/at ~:** vor/bei Tagesanbruch

3 *in sing. or pl.* (period) **in the ~s when ...:** zu der Zeit, als ...; **in his/that/Queen Anne's ~:** zu seiner/jener Zeit/zur Zeit der Königin Anne; **in former/earlier ~s** in früheren Zeiten; **these ~s** heutzutage; **in those ~s** damals; zu jener Zeit; **in this ~ and age, at the present ~:** heutzutage; **this ~ and age, the [present] ~:** die heutige Zeit; **have seen/known better ~s** bessere Tage gesehen/gekannt haben; **I have seen the ~ when ...:** zu meiner Zeit ...; **those were the ~s** das waren noch Zeiten; (iron.) schöne Zeiten waren das; *see also* **bad A 1; good A 4**

4 *in sing. or pl.* (lifetime) **in our ~[s]** zu unserer Zeit; **end one's ~s** seine Tage beenden

5 (time of prosperity) **in one's ~:** zu seiner Zeit; (during lifetime) in seinem Leben; **sth.'s ~ is over** die Zeiten einer Sache (*Gen.*) sind vorbei; **every dog has its ~:** jeder hat einmal seine Chance; **it has had its ~:** es hat ausgedient (ugs.)

6 (victory) **win** *or* **carry the ~:** den Sieg davontragen

7 (~ for regular event) **Monday is my ~:** montags bin ich an der Reihe (ugs.); **it's my ~ [for doing** *or* **to do sth.]** ich bin an der Reihe[, etw. zu tun]; **whose ~ is it?** wer ist an der Reihe?

-day *adj. suf.* -tägig; **three-~[s]-old** drei Tage alt; **five-~ week** Fünftagewoche, *die*

day: ~bed *n.* Liegesofa, *das;* **~book** *n.* (Commerc.) Journal, *das;* **~ boy** *n.* (Brit.) externer Schüler; **~break** *n.* Tagesanbruch, *der;* **at ~break** bei Tagesanbruch; **~ care** *n.* Ganztagsbetreuung, *die; attrib.* **~-care centre** Tagesstätte, *die;* (for children) Kindertagesstätte, *die;* [Kinder]krippe, *die;* (for the elderly) Altenzentrum, *das;* Altentagesstätte, *die;* (for the disabled) Tagesbetreuungsstätte, *die;* **~ centre** *n.* Tagesstätte, *die;* **~dream** **A** *n.* Tagtraum, *der;* **lost in a ~dream** traumverloren; **B** *v.i.* träumen; **~dreamer** *n.* Tagträumer, *der*/-träumerin, *die;* **~ girl** *n.* (Brit.) externe Schülerin; **~ job** *n.* Hauptberuf, *der;* **have a ~ job in a cannery** tagsüber in einer Konservenfabrik arbeiten; **don't give up the ~ job** (coll.) bleib bei deinem Leisten; **~light** *n.* **1** (light of ~) Tageslicht, *das;* **by ~light** bei Tageslicht; **go on working while it's still ~light** weiterarbeiten, solange es noch hell ist; **~light comes** es wird hell; der Tag bricht an; **it's [already] ~light** es ist [schon] hell; **during the hours of ~light, in ~light** bei Tag[eslicht]; **in broad ~light** am helllichten Tag[e]; **~light saving [time]** Sommerzeit, *die;* **2** (dawn) **at** *or* **by/before ~light** bei/vor Tagesanbruch; **3** (fig.) **bring sth. into the ~light** etw. ans Tageslicht bringen; **I see ~light** ich denke, die Situation lichtet sich; (understand) mir geht ein Licht auf (ugs.); **scare/beat the [living] ~lights out of sb.** (coll.) jmdn. zu Tode erschrecken/(ugs.) windelweich schlagen; **it's ~light robbery** es ist der reine Wucher; **4** (visible interval) Luft, *die;* **~light hours** *n.*

d

ℹ Days of the week

ENGLISH	GERMAN	ABBREVIATION
Monday	**Montag**	**Mo**
Tuesday	**Dienstag**	**Di**
Wednesday	**Mittwoch**	**Mi**
Thursday	**Donnerstag**	**Do**
Friday	**Freitag**	**Fr**
Saturday	**Samstag***	**Sa**
Sunday	**Sonntag**	**So**

Note that the week is considered as beginning on Monday. The abbreviations given are used mainly in printed matter, such as calendars, diaries, timetables and notices giving opening times, rather than in private or business correspondence. All the days of the week are masculine.

*An alternative for **Samstag** used mainly in North Germany is **Sonnabend**.

Saying when

As with dates, the English *on* is translated by **am:**

I am leaving on Wednesday
= Ich fahre am Mittwoch

Sometimes this is omitted in speech or a letter, especially where there are further details in the sentence:

I am leaving on Wednesday for Cairo
= Ich fahre Mittwoch nach Kairo

One exception to the use of **am** is naturally enough when the indefinite article *a* or *one* is used for a particular occasion:

Her birthday is on a Tuesday
= Ihr Geburtstag ist an einem Dienstag

It happened one wet Sunday
= Es geschah an einem verregneten Sonntag

One Saturday I met him at the zoo
= Eines Samstags traf ich ihn im Zoo

Repeated events are another exception to the use of **am:**

I go home on Fridays/every Friday
= Ich fahre freitags/jeden Freitag nach Hause

Her evening class is on Mondays* or *on a Monday
= Ihr Abendkurs ist montags

Notice that the adverbial forms **montags, dienstags** etc. are written with a small letter.

Some more expressions for less frequent or regular events:

every other Thursday
= jeden zweiten Donnerstag

every third Monday
= jeden dritten Montag

most Saturdays
= fast jeden Samstag

some Wednesdays
= manchmal am Mittwoch

on the occasional* or *odd Friday
= ab und zu am Freitag

Looking backwards and forwards

last Thursday
= letzten Donnerstag

[on] the preceding Thursday
= am vorangehenden Donnerstag

[on] the Thursday before last
= vorletzten Donnerstag

a week ago on Thursday
= Donnerstag vor einer Woche

I shall see her next Monday* or *this [coming] Monday
= Ich werde sie [am] nächsten *or* kommenden Montag sehen

I saw her the next* or *the following Monday
= Ich habe sie am [darauf] folgenden Montag gesehen

the Monday after next
= übernächsten Montag

a week on Monday
= Montag in einer Woche

from Saturday [on]
= ab Samstag, von Samstag an

It has to be ready by Friday
= Es muss bis Freitag fertig sein

Times of day

on Monday morning
= [am] Montagmorgen

on Wednesday afternoon
= [am] Mittwochnachmittag

on Thursday evening
= [am] Donnerstagabend

on Friday night
= (*early*) [am] Freitagabend; (*late*) Freitagnacht

And if it's habitual:

on Monday mornings
= montagmorgens

on Wednesday afternoons
= mittwochnachmittags

on Thursday evenings
= donnerstagabends

on Friday nights
= (*early*) freitagabends; (*late*) freitagnachts

Today

What day is it [today]?
= Welchen Tag haben wir heute?

It's Tuesday [today]
= Heute ist Dienstag

Belonging to a certain day

German has more than one way of expressing this, where in English we have simply the name of the day with or without an apostrophe s; there are adjectives for all the days of the week except Wednesday (**Mittwoch**) which relate to a habitual occurrence, or a compound can be formed, especially for a particular institution:

his [regular] Sunday walk
= sein sonntäglicher Spaziergang

the Sunday papers
= die Sonntagszeitungen

a Sunday driver
= ein Sonntagsfahrer

Monday's trains
= die Züge am Montag

Wednesday's classes
= die Schulstunden am Mittwoch

Tuesday's paper
= die Zeitung von Dienstag

There will be a Saturday [train] service
= Die Züge werden wie an einem Samstag verkehren

Wednesday's sailing is cancelled
= Das Schiff am Mittwoch fällt aus

See also ◻ **Dates**

pl. Tag, *der;* **during/in ~light hours** bei Tag[eslicht]; **~-long** *attrib. adj.* den ganzen Tag dauernd; **~ nursery** *n.* **1** (room) Kinderzimmer, *das;* **2** (school) Kindergarten, *der;* **~ patient** *n.* Tages[klinik]patient, *der*/-patientin, *die;* **~ release** *n.* (Brit.) [tageweise] Freistellung zur Fortbildung; **on ~ release** unter Inanspruchnahme von tageweiser Freistellung; *attrib.* **~-release course** Fortbildungskurs, *der;* Fortbildung, *die;* **~ return** **A** *attrib. adj.* **~ return ticket** ▸**B**; **B** *n.* Tagesrückfahrkarte, *die;* **~ school** *n.* Tagesschule, *die;* **~ shift** *n.* Tagschicht, *die;* **be on [the] ~ shift** Tagschicht haben; **~time** *n.* Tag, *der;* **in** *or* **during the ~time** während des Tages; tagsüber; **~-to-~** *adj.* [tag]täglich; **~-to-~ life** Alltagsleben, *das;* **~ trader** *n.* Tageshändler, *der*/-händlerin, *die;* **~ trip** *n.* Tagesausflug, *der;* **~ tripper** *n.* Tagesausflügler, *der*/-ausflüglerin, *die*

daze /deɪz/
A *v.t.* benommen machen; **be ~d** benommen sein (**at** von)
B *n.* Benommenheit, *die;* **in a [complete/bit of a] ~:** [völlig/ein wenig] benommen

dazzle /ˈdæzl/ *v.t.* (lit., or fig.: delude) blenden; (fig.: confuse, impress) überwältigen

dB *abbr.* **= decibel[s]** dB

DBMS *abbr.* (Computing) **= database management system** DBMS

DC *abbr.* **1** (Electr.) **= direct current** GS **2** (Geog.) **= District of Columbia** Bundesdistrikt Columbia **3** (Mus.) **= da capo** d.c.

DD *abbr.* **= Doctor of Divinity** ≈ Dr. theol.; *see also* **BSc**

D-Day /ˈdiːdeɪ/ *n.* **1** (6 June 1944) *Tag der Landung der Alliierten in der Normandie* **2** (starting day) der Tag X

DDT /diːdiːˈtiː/ *n.* DDT, *das*

deacon /ˈdiːkn/ *n.* Diakon, *der*

deaconess /ˈdiːkənɪs/ *n.* Diakonin, *die*

deactivate /diːˈæktɪveɪt/ *v.t.* entschärfen ‹*Bombe*›; desaktivieren ‹*Chemikalie*›; abschalten ‹*Maschine, Motor*›

dead /ded/
A *adj.* **1** tot; tot, abgestorben ‹*Gewebe, Pflanze*›; **[as] ~ as a doornail/as mutton** mausetot (ugs.); **be ~ from the neck up** (coll.) gehirnamputiert sein (salopp); **I wouldn't be seen ~ doing sth./in that dress** (coll.) ich würde nie im Leben etw. tun/dieses Kleid anziehen (ugs.); **I wouldn't be seen ~ in a place like that** (coll.) keine zehn Pferde würden mich an solch einen Ort bringen (ugs.); **~ men tell no tales** (prov.) Tote reden nicht; *see also* **body A 2**; **bury 1**; **go¹ A 10** **2** (inanimate, extinct) tot ‹*Materie*›; erloschen ‹*Vulkan, Gefühl, Interesse*›; ausgestorben ‹*Spezies*›; (without power) verbraucht, leer ‹*Batterie*›; ausgebrannt ‹*Glühbirne*›; (extinguished) ausgegangen ‹*Zigarette*›; erloschen ‹*Feuer*›; (not glowing) ausgeglüht ‹*Kohle, Asche*›; **the fire is ~:** das Feuer ist aus (ugs.); *see also* **dodo** **3** (dull, lustreless) stumpf ‹*Haar, Farbe*›; (without force) wirkungslos ‹*Gesetz, Politik*›; (without warmth) kalt ‹*Stimme, Ton*›; ausgestorben, tot ‹*Stadt*›; (quiet) [toten]still ‹*Nacht, Wald, Straße*›; unbelebt, tot ‹*Straße*›; (unexciting) öde ‹*Party, Geschmack*›; (flat) schal, abgestanden ‹*Getränk*› **4** (inactive, unproductive) tot ‹*Telefon, Leitung, Saison, Kapital, Ball*›; unfruchtbar ‹*Land, Erde*›; **go ~:** zusammenbrechen; (lose interest) Interesse verlieren (**on** an + *Dat.*); **the phone has gone ~:** die Leitung ist tot; **the motor is ~:** der Motor läuft nicht; **a ~ engine** eine Maschine, die/ein Motor, der nicht läuft **5** *expr. completeness* plötzlich ‹*Halt*›; völlig ‹*Stillstand*›; genau ‹*Mitte*›; (coll.: absolute) absolut; **~ silence** *or* **quiet** Totenstille, *die;* **~ calm** Flaute, *die;* Windstille, *die;* **~ faint** [totenähnliche] Ohnmacht; **~ trouble** große Schwierigkeiten *Pl.*; **a ~ shot** ein unfehlbarer Schütze **6** (benumbed) taub; (sleeping) schlafend;

be ~ to sth. (lit. or fig.) etw. nicht mehr empfinden; **be ~ to shame** gar kein Schamgefühl haben; **be ~ to the world** (unconscious) bewusstlos sein; weggetreten sein (ugs.); (asleep) tief und fest schlafen **7** (exhausted) erschöpft; kaputt (ugs.); **I feel absolutely ~:** ich bin völlig erschöpft

B *adv.* **1** (completely) völlig; **~ silent** totenstill; **~ straight** schnurgerade; **~ tired** todmüde; **~ easy** *or* **simple/slow** kinderleicht/ganz langsam; **'~ slow'** „besonders langsam fahren"; **~ drunk** stockbetrunken (ugs.); **~ level** völlig eben; **~ still** regungslos; (without wind) windstill; **make ~ certain** *or* **sure of sth.** etw. todsicher machen; **be ~ against sth.** absolut gegen etw. sein **2** (exactly) **~ on the target** genau im Ziel; **~ on time** auf die Minute; **~ on two [o'clock]** Punkt zwei [Uhr]

C *n.* **1** **in the ~ of winter/night** mitten im Winter/in der Nacht; **it was the ~ of winter** es war mitten im Winter **2** *pl.* **the ~:** die Toten *Pl.*

dead: ~-[and-]a'live *adj.* langweilig; öde ‹*Ort, Leben*›; **~ beat** /-'-/ *adj.* (exhausted) völlig zerschlagen; (without money) bettelarm; **~beat** /'--/ *n.* (coll.) (sponger) Nassauer, *der* (ugs.); (penniless person) **he is a ~beat** er ist bettelarm; **~ 'duck** *n.* (coll.) **1** (person) Null, *die* (ugs.); **2** (thing) **it is a ~ duck** das kann man vergessen

deaden /'dedn/ *v.t.* dämpfen; abstumpfen ‹*Gefühl*›; betäuben ‹*Nerv, Körperteil, Schmerz*›; **~ sb./sth. to sth.** jmdn./etw. gegen etw. unempfindlich machen

dead: ~ 'end *n.* (closed end) Absperrung, *die;* (street; also fig.) Sackgasse, *die;* **~-end** *attrib. adj.* **1** **~-end street/road** Sackgasse, *die;* **2** (fig.) aussichtslos; **she's in a ~-end job** in ihrem Job hat sie keine Aufstiegschancen; **he is a ~-end kid** er ist in ärmlichen Verhältnissen aufgewachsen; **~eye** *n.* (Naut.) Jungfer, *die;* **~ head** *n.* (flower head) verblühte Blüte; **~ 'heat** *n.* totes Rennen; **finish** *or* **end in a ~ heat** unentschieden ausgehen; **~ 'language** *n.* tote Sprache; **~ 'letter** *n.* **1** (law) Gesetz, das nicht angewendet wird; **be a ~ letter** nur noch auf dem Papier bestehen; **2** (letter) unzustellbarer Brief; **~ 'lift** *n.* Gewaltleistung, *die;* **~light** *n.* (Naut.) [Seeschlag]blende, *die;* **~line** *n.* **1** (line of limit) *Linie um ein Gefängnis o. Ä., die von den Gefangenen nicht überschritten werden darf;* **2** (time limit) [letzter] Termin; **meet the ~line** den Termin einhalten; **set a ~line for sth.** eine Frist für etw. setzen

deadliness /'dedlɪnɪs/ *n., no pl.* (fatal quality) tödliche Wirkung

dead: ~lock **A** *n.* **1** (standstill) völliger Stillstand; **come to a** *or* **reach [a] ~lock/be at ~lock** an einem toten Punkt anlangen/angelangt sein; **the negotiations had reached ~lock** die Verhandlungen waren festgefahren; **2** (lock) einfaches Schloss ohne Feder; **B** *v.t.* blockieren; **~ 'loss** *n.* **1** (complete loss) [totaler] Verlust; **2** (coll.) (worthless thing) totaler Reinfall (ugs.); (person) hoffnungsloser Fall (ugs.)

deadly /'dedlɪ/

A *adj.* **1** tödlich; (fig. coll.: awful) fürchterlich; (very boring) todlangweilig; (very dangerous) lebensgefährlich; **~ enemy** Todfeind, *der;* **~ fear** Todesangst, *die;* **he looked ~** (dangerous) er sah furchterregend aus; **I'm in ~ earnest about this** es ist mir todernst damit **2** (accurate) [absolut] exakt **3** (Theol.) **~ sin** Todsünde, *die*

B *adv.* tod-; (extremely) äußerst; **~ pale** totenblass; **~ dull** todlangweilig

deadly 'nightshade *n.* (Bot.) Tollkirsche, *die*

dead: ~ man's 'handle *n.* (Transport) Sicherheitsfahrschalter, *der;* **~ march** *n.* Trauermarsch, *der;* **~ men** *n. pl.* (coll.: bottles) leere Flaschen; tote Marine (salopp scherzh.)

deadness /'dednɪs/ *n., no pl.* (numbness) Gefühllosigkeit, *die;* (inactivity) Öde, *die;* Trostlosigkeit, *die*

dead: ~ 'on **A** *adj.* [ganz] genau; **he was ~ on with his shot** er hat mit seinem Schuss genau getroffen; **you were ~ on when you said that** du hattest vollkommen Recht, als du das sagtest; **B** *adv.* [ganz] genau; **~pan** *adj.* unbewegt; **he looked ~pan** *or* **had a ~pan expression** er verzog keine Miene; **~ 'reckoning** *n.* (Naut.) Koppeln, *das;* Besteckrechnung, *die;* **~ ringer** /ded 'rɪŋə(r)/ *n.* (coll.) Doppelgänger, *der*/-gängerin, *die;* **a ~ ringer for Trotski** ein Doppelgänger *od.* Double Trotskis; **a ~ ringer for his father** ein Ebenbild seines Vaters; **be a ~ ringer for sb.** jmdm. zum Verwechseln ähnlich sehen; **D~ 'Sea** *pr. n.* **the D~ Sea** das Tote Meer; **D~ Sea Scrolls** *pr. n. pl.* Schriftrollen von Kumran *od.* vom Toten Meer; **~ weight** *n.* **1** (inert mass) Eigengewicht, *das;* Totgewicht, *das* (Technik); (fig.) schwere Bürde; **2** (Naut.: weight of cargo etc.) Tragfähigkeit, *die;* Deadweight, *das;* **~ 'wood** *n.* **1** totes Holz; **2** (fig.) **be just ~ wood** völlig überflüssig sein; **get rid of much of the ~ wood** (persons) viele Nieten loswerden (ugs.); (things) viel Überflüssiges loswerden

deaf /def/

A *adj.* **1** (without hearing) taub; **~ and dumb** taubstumm; **~ in one ear** auf einem Ohr taub; **go** *or* **become ~:** taub werden **2** (insensitive) **musically ~:** unmusikalisch; **be ~ to sth.** kein Ohr für etw. haben; (fig.) taub gegenüber etw. sein; **turn a ~ ear [to sth./sb.]** sich [gegenüber etw./jmdm.] taub stellen; **fall on ~ ears** kein Gehör finden

B *n. pl.* **the ~:** die Gehörlosen *Pl.*

deaf: ~ aid *n.* Hörgerät, *das;* **~-and-'dumb alphabet, ~-and-'dumb language** *ns.* Taubstummensprache, *die;* **~-'blind** *adj.* taubblind

deafen /'defn/ *v.t.* **~ sb.** bei jmdm. zur Taubheit führen; **I was ~ed by the noise** (fig.) ich war von dem Lärm wie betäubt

deafening /'defənɪŋ/ *adj.* ohrenbetäubend ‹*Lärm, Musik, Geschrei*›

deaf 'mute *n.* Taubstumme, *der/die*

deafness /'defnɪs/ *n., no pl.* Taubheit, *die;* **cause ~ in sb.** bei jmdm. zur Taubheit führen

deal[1] /di:l/

A *v.t.,* **dealt** /delt/ **1** (Cards) austeilen; **who ~t the cards?** wer hat gegeben?; **he was ~t four aces** er bekam vier Asse **2** (deliver as share) **~ sb. sth.** jmdm. etw. zuteil werden lassen (geh.) **3** (administer) versetzen; **~ sb. a blow** (lit. or fig.) jmdm. einen Schlag versetzen **4** (distribute) verteilen

B *v.i.,* **dealt** **1** (do business) **~ with sb.** mit jmdm. Geschäfte machen; **~ in sth.** mit etw. handeln **2** (occupy oneself) **~ with sth.** sich mit etw. befassen; (manage) mit etw. fertig werden; **this point must be ~t with** dieser Punkt muss behandelt werden; **I'll ~ with the washing-up** ich kümmere mich um den Abwasch; **the play ~s with the Civil War** das Stück handelt vom Bürgerkrieg **3** (associate) **~ with sb.** mit jmdm. zu tun haben **4** (behave) **~ gently/circumspectly with sb./sth.** mit jmdm./etw. sanft/vorsichtig umgehen **5** (take measures) **~ with sb.** mit jmdm. fertig werden

C *n.* **1** (arrangement, bargain) Geschäft, *das;* **new ~:** neue Bedingungen; (Polit.) Reformprogramm, *das;* **make a ~ with sb.** mit jmdm. ein Geschäft abschließen; **you've got a good ~ there** da hast du ein gutes Geschäft gemacht; **it's a ~!** abgemacht!; **big ~!** (iron.) na und?; **fair ~** (bargain) gutes Geschäft; (treatment) faire *od.* gerechte Behandlung; **raw** *or* **rough ~** (treatment) ungerechte Behandlung; (bad luck) Pech, *das* **2** (agreement) **make** *or* **do a ~ with sb.** mit jmdm. eine Vereinbarung treffen; **let's stick to our ~:** lass uns bei unserer Abmachung bleiben **3** (Cards) **it's your ~:** du gibst

Phrasal verb

- **~ 'out** *v.t.* verteilen; **~ sth. out to sb.** etw. an jmdn. verteilen

deal[2] *n.* **a great** *or* **good ~,** (coll.) **a ~:** viel; (often) ziemlich viel; **a great** *or* **good ~ of,** (coll.) **a ~ of** eine [ganze] Menge, viel; **we resent it a [great/good] ~ that ...** (coll.) es ärgert uns ganz schön, dass ... (ugs.)

deal[3] *n.* (fir/pine timber) [Tannen-/Kiefern]holz, *das*

dealer /'di:lə(r)/ *n.* **1** ▸ⓘ **p. 1260** (trader) Händler, *der;* **he's a ~ in antiques** er ist Antiquitätenhändler *od.* handelt mit Antiquitäten **2** (Cards) Geber, *der;* **he's the ~:** er gibt **3** ▸ⓘ **p. 1260** (Stock Exch.) Börsenmakler, *der*

dealership /'di:ləʃɪp/ *n.* (Commerc.) Vertretung, *die;* **a network of Ford ~s** ein Netz von Fordvertragshändlern

dealing /'di:lɪŋ/ *n.* **have ~s with sb.** mit jmdm. zu tun haben

'dealmaker *n.* Geschäftemacher, *der*/-macherin, *die*

dealt ▸ **deal**[1] **A, B**

dean /di:n/ *n.* **1** (Eccl.) Dechant, *der;* Dekan, *der* **2** (in college, university, etc.) (resident fellow) *Fellow mit Aufsichts- und Beratungsfunktion;* (head of faculty) Dekan, *der*

deanery /'di:nərɪ/ *n.* **1** (office) Dekanat, *das* **2** (house) Dekanei, *die* **3** (Brit.: group of parishes) Dekanat, *das*

dear /dɪə(r)/

A *adj.* **1** (beloved; also iron.) lieb; geliebt; (sweet; also iron.) entzückend; reizend; **my ~ sir/madam** [mein] lieber Herr/[meine] liebe Dame; **my ~ man/woman** guter Mann/gute Frau; **my ~ Jones/child/girl** [mein] lieber Jones/liebes Kind/liebes Mädchen; **sb./sth. is [very] ~ to sb.['s heart]** jmd. liebt jmdn./etw. [über alles]; **sb. holds sb./sth. ~ [to him/to his heart]** jmd./etw. liegt jmdm. [sehr] am Herzen; **run for ~ life** um sein Leben rennen; **my ~est wish** mein innigster *od.* sehnlichster Wunsch; **his ~est ambition** sein höchstes Ziel **2** ▸ⓘ **p. 1287** (beginning letter) **D~ Sir/Madam** Sehr geehrter Herr/Sehr geehrte Frau; **D~ Mr Jones/Mrs Jones** Sehr geehrter Herr Jones/Sehr verehrte Frau Jones; **D~ Malcolm/Emily** Lieber Malcolm/Liebe Emily; **Dearest Auntie Minnie** Liebste Tante Minnie; **My ~ Smith** (Brit.: less formal) Lieber Herr Smith; (between old schoolfellows etc.) Lieber Smith; (more formal) Sehr geehrter Herr Smith **3** (in addressing sb.) lieb; (in exclamation) **~ God!** ach du lieber Gott! *see also* **madam 1**; **sir 2** **4** (expensive) teuer

B *int.* **~, ~!, ~ me!, oh ~!** [ach] du liebe *od.* meine Güte!

C *n.* **1** **you 'are a ~** (coll.) du bist wirklich lieb; **she is a ~:** sie ist ein Schatz **2** **[my] ~** (to wife, husband, younger relative) [mein] Liebling; [mein] Schatz; (to aunt) Tantchen; (to little girl/boy) [meine] Kleine/[mein] Kleiner; (to man/woman) guter Mann/gute Frau; **~est** Liebling (*der*)

D *adv.* teuer; *see also* **cost B 1**

dearie /'dɪərɪ/ *n.* Kleine, *der/die;* **~ me!** [ach] du liebe *od.* meine Güte!

Dear 'John letter *n.* (coll.) Trennungsbrief, *der*

dearly /'dɪəlɪ/ *adv.* **1** (very fondly, earnestly) von ganzem Herzen; **I'd ~ love to do that** ich würde das liebend gern tun **2** (at high price) teuer; **you'll pay ~ for it** (fig.) du wirst teuer dafür bezahlen müssen

dearth /dɜ:θ/ *n.* Mangel, *der* (**of** an + *Dat.*); **there is a ~ of sth.** es besteht *od.* herrscht Mangel an etw. (*Dat.*); **there is no ~ of sth.** es fehlt nicht an etw. (*Dat.*)

death /deθ/ *n.* **1** Tod, *der;* **end in/mean ~:** zum Tod führen; **be afraid of ~:** Angst vor dem Tod haben; **after ~:** nach dem Tod; **[as] sure as ~:** todsicher; **meet one's ~:** den Tod finden (geh.); **catch one's ~ [of cold]** (coll.) sich (*Dat.*) den Tod holen (ugs.); **drink will be the ~ of him** er trinkt sich noch zu Tode; **... to ~:** zu Tode ...; **bleed to ~:** verbluten; **freeze to ~:** erfrieren; **beat sb. to ~:** jmdn. totschlagen; **burn [sb.] to ~:** [jmdn.] verbrennen; **he worked/drank himself to ~:** er hat sich totgearbeitet/totgetrunken (ugs.); **I'm scared to ~** (fig.) mir ist angst und bange (**about** vor + *Dat.*); **be sick** *or* **tired to ~ of sth.** (fig.) etw. gründlich satt haben; **be tickled to ~ by sth.** (fig.) sich über etw. totlachen; **be done to ~:** getötet werden; (fig.) zu Tode geritten werden; **be worked to ~:** zu Tode geschunden werden; (fig.) zu Tode geritten werden; **[fight] to the ~:** auf Leben und Tod [kämpfen]; **be in at the ~** (fig.) das Ende miterleben; **a fate worse than ~** (joc.) das Allerschlimmste;

~ **or glory!** Ruhm oder Untergang!; ~ **to fascism!** Tod dem Faschismus!; **D~** (personified) der Tod; **be at ~'s door** an der Schwelle des Todes stehen; **feel/look like ~ [warmed up]** (coll.) sich wie eine Leiche auf Urlaub fühlen/ wie eine Leiche auf Urlaub aussehen (salopp) **2** (instance) Todesfall, *der;* **how many ~s were there?** wie viele Tote gab es?

death: ~bed *n.* Totenbett, *das;* Sterbebett, *das; attrib.* auf dem Sterbebett *nachgestellt;* **on one's ~bed** auf dem Sterbebett; ~ **blow** *n.* (lit. or fig.) Todesstoß, *der* (**to** für); ~ **cell** *n.* Todeszelle, *die;* ~ **certificate** *n.* (from authorities) Sterbeurkunde, *die;* (from doctor) Totenschein, *der;* **~-dealing** *attrib. adj.* todbringend; **~-defying** *adj.* todesmutig; ~ **duty** *n.* (Brit. Hist.) Erbschaftssteuer, *die;* ~ **knell** *n.* (lit. or fig.) Totengeläut, *das*

deathless /ˈdeθlɪs/ *adj.* (poet./literary) unsterblich; (fig.) unvergänglich; ~ **prose** (iron.) hochgestochene Prosa

deathly /ˈdeθlɪ/

A *adj.* tödlich; ~ **stillness/hush** Totenstille, *die;* ~ **pallor** Totenblässe, *die*

B *adv.* tödlich; ~ **pale** totenblass; ~ **still/quiet** totenstill

death: ~ mask *n.* Totenmaske, *die;* ~ **penalty** *n.* Todesstrafe, *die;* ~ **rate** *n.* Sterblichkeitsziffer, *die;* ~ **rattle** *n.* Todesröcheln, *das;* ~ **ray** *n.* tödlicher Strahl; ~ **roll** *n.* Verlustliste, *die;* (after battle) Gefallenenliste, *die;* ~ **row** /deθ ˈrəʊ/ *n.* [Reihe von] Todeszellen; ~ **sentence** *n.* Todesurteil, *das;* **~'s head** *n.* Totenkopf, *der;* ~ **squad** *n.* Todesschwadron, *die;* Killerkommando, *das;* ~ **tax** (Amer.) Erbschaftssteuer, *die;* ~ **threat** *n.* Morddrohung, *die;* ~ **throes** *n. pl.* Todeskampf, *der;* Agonie, *die* (geh.); **be in one's [last] ~ throes** mit dem Tode[e] ringen; in Agonie liegen (geh.); **be in its [last] ~ throes** ‹*Tier:*› am Verenden sein; (fig.) ‹*politisches System:*› in Agonie liegen (geh.); ~ **toll** *n.* Zahl der Todesopfer; Blutzoll, *der* (geh.); ~ **trap** *n.* lebensgefährliche Sache; **this corner/house/car is a ~ trap** diese Kurve/dieses Haus/Auto ist lebensgefährlich; ~ **warrant** *n.* Exekutionsbefehl, *der;* (fig.) Todesurteil, *das;* **~-watch [beetle]** *n.* (Zool.) Totenuhr, *die;* ~ **wish** *n.* (Psych.) Todeswunsch, *der;* ~ **zone** *n.* Todeszone, *die*

deb /deb/ *n.* (coll.) Debütantin, *die*

débâcle /deɪˈbɑːkl/ *n.* Debakel, *das* (geh.)

debar /dɪˈbɑː(r)/ *v.t.*, **-rr-** ausschließen; ~ **sb. from doing sth.** jmdn. davon ausschließen, etw. zu tun

debase /dɪˈbeɪs/ *v.t.* **1** verschlechtern; herabsetzen, entwürdigen ‹*Person*›; ~ **oneself** sich erniedrigen **2** (Hist.) ~ **the coinage** den Wert der Währung mindern

debatable /dɪˈbeɪtəbl/ *adj.* **1** (questionable) fraglich **2** ~ **ground** umstrittenes Gebiet

debate /dɪˈbeɪt/

A *v.t.* debattieren über (+ *Akk.*); **be ~d** diskutiert *od.* debattiert werden

B *v.i.* ~ **[up]on sth.** etw. debattieren; ~ **about sth.** über etw. (*Akk.*) debattieren *od.* streiten

C *n.* Debatte, *die;* **there was much ~ about whether ...:** es wurde viel darüber debattiert, ob ...

debating /dɪˈbeɪtɪŋ/: ~ **point** *n.* (*für die Sache unerheblicher, nur aus rhetorischen Gründen vorgebrachter*) Diskussionspunkt; ~ **society** *n.* (regelmäßig zusammentretende) Diskussionsrunde

debauch /dɪˈbɔːtʃ/ (literary)

A *v.t.* **1** verderben **2** (seduce) verführen

B *n.* Gelage, *das*

debauched /dɪˈbɔːtʃt/ *adj.* verderbt (geh.)

debauchery /dɪˈbɔːtʃərɪ/ *n.* (literary) Ausschweifung, *die*

debenture /dɪˈbentʃə(r)/ *n.* (Finance) Schuldverschreibung, *die*

debilitate /dɪˈbɪlɪteɪt/ *v.t.* schwächen

debilitating /dɪˈbɪlɪteɪtɪŋ/ *adj.* anstrengend ‹*Klima*›; schwächend ‹*Krankheit*›

debility /dɪˈbɪlɪtɪ/ *n.* Schwäche, *die*

debit /ˈdebɪt/

A *n.* (Bookk.) Soll, *das;* (~ side) Soll, *das;* Debet, *das;* ~ **balance** Lastschrift, *die;* ~ **side** (Finance) Sollseite, *die*

B *v.t.* belasten; ~ **a sum against** *or* **to sb./sb.'s account,** ~ **sb./sb.'s account with a sum** jmdn./jmds. Konto mit einer Summe belasten

ˈ**debit card** Debitkarte, *die*

debonair /debəˈneə(r)/ *adj.* frohgemut

debrief /diːˈbriːf/ *v.t.* (coll.) befragen (*bei Rückkehr von einem Einsatz usw.*)

debriefing /diːˈbriːfɪŋ/ *n.* (coll.) Befragung, *die;* **hold a ~ session** sich Bericht erstatten lassen

debris /ˈdebriː, ˈdeɪbriː/ *n.*, *no pl.* Trümmer *Pl.*

debt /det/ *n.* Schuld, *die;* **owe sb. a ~ of gratitude** *or* **thanks** jmdm. Dank schulden; [tief] in jmds. Schuld stehen; ~ **of honour** Ehrenschuld, *die;* **National D~:** Staatsverschuldung, *die;* **be in ~:** Schulden haben; verschuldet sein; **get** *or* **run into ~:** in Schulden geraten; sich verschulden; **get out of ~:** aus den Schulden herauskommen; **be in sb.'s ~:** in jmds. Schuld stehen

debt: ~ burden *n.* Schuldenlast, *die;* ~ **collector** *n.* Inkassobevollmächtigte, *der/die;* Schuldeneintreiber, *der* (veralt.); ~ **counselling** *n.*, *no pl.* Schuldnerberatung, *die; attrib.* ~ **counselling service** Schuldnerberatung[sstelle], *die;* ~ **financing** *n.*, *no pl.* Schuldenfinanzierung, *die*

debtor /ˈdetə(r)/ *n.* Schuldner, *der/* Schuldnerin, *die*

ˈ**debt relief** *n.*, *no pl.* Schuldenerlass, *der*

debug /diːˈbʌg/ *v.t.*, **-gg-** **1** (Computing) debuggen **2** (fig. coll.) (remove microphones from) von Wanzen befreien

debugger /diːˈbʌgə(r)/ *n.* (Computing) Debugger, *der*

debunk /diːˈbʌŋk/ *v.t.* (coll.) (remove false reputation from) entlarven; (expose falseness of) bloßstellen

debut (*Amer.:* **debut**) /ˈdeɪbjuː, ˈdeɪbuː/ *n.* Debüt, *das;* **make one's ~:** debütieren

debutante /ˈdebjuːtɑːnt/ *n.* Debütantin, *die*

Dec. *abbr.* **= December** Dez.

decade /ˈdekeɪd/ *n.* Jahrzehnt, *das;* Dekade, *die*

decadence /ˈdekədəns/ *n.* Dekadenz, *die*

decadent /ˈdekədənt/ *adj.* dekadent

decaf, decaff /ˈdiːkæf/ *n.* (coll.) *or* ®: koffeinfreier Kaffee; ≈ Kaffee Hag (Wz), *der*

decaffeinated /diːˈkæfɪneɪtɪd/ *adj.* entkoffeiniert; koffeinfrei (veralt.)

decagon /ˈdekəgən/ *n.* Zehneck, *das*

Decalogue /ˈdekəlɒg/ *n.* **the ~:** der Dekalog; die Zehn Gebote

decamp /dɪˈkæmp/ *v.i.* **1** (abscond) verschwinden (ugs.) **2** (leave camp) das Lager abbrechen

decant /dɪˈkænt/ *v.t.* abgießen; dekantieren ‹*Wein*›; (fig.) abladen

decanter /dɪˈkæntə(r)/ *n.* Karaffe, *die*

decapitate /dɪˈkæpɪteɪt/ *v.t.* köpfen ‹*Person, Blume*›; enthaupten (geh.)

decathlete /dɪˈkæθliːt/ *n.* (Sport) Zehnkämpfer, *der*

decathlon /dɪˈkæθlən/ *n.* (Sport) Zehnkampf, *der*

decay /dɪˈkeɪ/

A *v.i.* **1** (become rotten) verrotten; [ver]faulen; ‹*Zahn:*› faul *od.* (fachspr.) kariös werden; ‹*Gebäude, Tuch:*› zerfallen **2** (decline) verfallen **3** (Phys.: decrease) zerfallen

B *n.* **1** (rotting) Verrotten, *das;* (of tooth) Fäule, *die;* (of building) Zerfall, *der;* Verfall, *der* **2** (decline) Verfall, *der;* (of nation) Verfall, *der;* Niedergang, *der* **3** (decayed tissue etc.) Zersetzung, *die;* Fäulnis, *die* **4** (Phys.: decrease) Zerfall, *der*

decease /dɪˈsiːs/ (Law/formal)

A *n.* Ableben, *das* (geh.)

B *v.i.* versterben (geh.); sterben

deceased /dɪˈsiːst/ (Law/formal)

A *adj.* verstorben; **the ~ man** der Tote *od.* Verstorbene; **Jim Fox ~:** der verstorbene Jim Fox

B *n.* Verstorbene, *der/die*

decedent /dɪˈsiːdənt/ *n.* (Amer. Law) Verstorbene, *der/die*

deceit /dɪˈsiːt/ *n.* (misrepresentation) Täuschung, *die;* Betrug, *der;* (trick) Täuschungsmanöver, *das;* Betrügerei, *die;* (being deceitful) Falschheit, *die*

deceitful /dɪˈsiːtfl/ *adj.* falsch ‹*Person, Art, Charakter*›; hinterlistig ‹*Trick*›; **that was a ~ thing to say** es war hinterlistig, das zu sagen

deceitfully /dɪˈsiːtfəlɪ/ *adv.* ▸**deceitful**: falsch; hinterlistig

deceitfulness /dɪˈsiːtflnɪs/ *n.*, *no pl.* ▸**deceitful**: Falschheit, *die;* Hinterlistigkeit, *die*

deceive /dɪˈsiːv/ *v.t.* täuschen; (be unfaithful to) betrügen; **if my eyes/ears do not ~ me** wenn ich richtig sehe/höre; ~ **sb. into doing sth.** jmdn. [durch Täuschung] dazu bringen, etw. zu tun; ~ **oneself** sich täuschen; (delude oneself) sich (*Dat.*) etwas vormachen (ugs.); **[let oneself] be ~d** sich täuschen lassen; **[let oneself] be ~d into doing sth.** sich dazu bringen lassen, etw. zu tun

deceiver /dɪˈsiːvə(r)/ *n.* Betrüger, *der/* Betrügerin, *die*

decelerate /diːˈseləreɪt/

A *v.t.* verlangsamen

B *v.i.* ‹*Fahrzeug, Fahrer:*› die Fahrt verlangsamen

deceleration /diːseləˈreɪʃn/ *n.* Verlangsamung, *die*

December /dɪˈsembə(r)/ *n.* ▸❶ p. 1047 Dezember, *der;* *see also* **August**

decency /ˈdiːsənsɪ/ *n.* **1** (modesty, propriety) Anstand, *der;* (of manners, literature, language) Schicklichkeit, *die* (geh.); (fairness, respectability) Anständigkeit, *die;* **it is [a matter of] common ~:** es ist eine Frage des Anstands; es gehört sich **2** *in pl.* (requirements of propriety) Anstandsregeln *Pl.*

decent /ˈdiːsənt/ *adj.* **1** (seemly) schicklich (geh.); anständig ‹*Person*›; **are you ~?** (coll.) hast du was an? (ugs.) **2** (passable, respectable) annehmbar; anständig ‹*Person, ugs. auch Preis, Gehalt*›; **do the ~ thing** das einzig Richtige tun **3** (Brit.: kind) nett; **that is very ~ of you** das ist sehr liebenswürdig von Ihnen; **be ~ about sth.** auf etw. (*Akk.*) nett reagieren

decently /ˈdiːsəntlɪ/ *adv.* **1** (in seemly manner) anständig; geziemend (geh.); schicklich (geh.) **2** (passably, respectably) annehmbar **3** (Brit.: kindly) netterweise (ugs.); **behave ~:** sich nett verhalten

decentralisation, decentralise ▸**decentraliz-**

decentralization /diːsentrəlaɪˈzeɪʃn/ *n.* Dezentralisierung, *die*

decentralize /diːˈsentrəlaɪz/ *v.t.* dezentralisieren

deception /dɪˈsepʃn/ *n.* **1** (deceiving, trickery) Betrug, *der;* (being deceived) Täuschung, *die;* **use ~:** betrügen **2** (trick) Betrügerei, *die*

deceptive /dɪˈseptɪv/ *adj.* trügerisch

deceptively /dɪˈseptɪvlɪ/ *adv.* täuschend

decibel /ˈdesɪbel/ *n.* Dezibel, *das*

decide /dɪˈsaɪd/

A *v.t.* **1** (settle, judge) entscheiden über (+ *Akk.*); ~ **sth. by tossing a coin** etw. durch Werfen einer Münze entscheiden; ~ **the winner** entscheiden, wer gewonnen hat; ~ **that ...:** entscheiden, dass ... **2** (resolve) **be ~d** sich entschieden haben; ~ **that ...:** beschließen, dass ...; ~ **to do sth.** sich entschließen, etw. zu tun

B *v.i.* sich entscheiden (**between** zwischen + *Dat.*, **in favour of** zugunsten von, **against** gegen, **on** für); ~ **against/on doing sth.** sich dagegen/ dafür entscheiden, etw. zu tun

decided /dɪˈsaɪdɪd/ *adj.* **1** (unquestionable) entschieden; eindeutig; **he made a ~ effort** er hat sich deutlich *od.* entschieden bemüht **2** (not hesitant) bestimmt; entschlossen, entschieden ‹*Haltung, Ansicht*›

decidedly /dɪˈsaɪdɪdlɪ/ *adv.* **1** (unquestionably) entschieden; deutlich **2** (firmly) bestimmt

decider /dɪˈsaɪdə(r)/ *n.* (game) Entscheidungsspiel, *das*

deciduous /dɪˈsɪdjʊəs/ *adj.* (Bot.) ~ **leaves** Blätter, die abgeworfen werden; ~ **tree** laubwerfender Baum; ≈ Laubbaum, *der*

decilitre /ˈdesɪliːtə(r)/ *n.* Deziliter, *der od. das*

decimal /ˈdesɪml/ ▸ℹ p. 1358
A adj. Dezimal-; dezimal; **go ~:** sich auf das Dezimalsystem umstellen
B n. Dezimalbruch, *der*

decimal: ~ 'coinage, ~ 'currency ns. Dezimalwährung, *die;* **~ 'fraction** n. Dezimalbruch, *der*

decimalize (decimalise) /ˈdesɪməlaɪz/ v.t. (express as decimal) als Dezimalzahl schreiben; (convert to decimal system) dezimalisieren

decimal: ~ 'place n. Dezimale, *die;* **calculate sth. to five ~ places** etw. auf fünf Stellen nach dem Komma ausrechnen; **~ 'point** n. Komma, *das;* **~ system** n. Dezimalsystem, *das*

decimate /ˈdesɪmeɪt/ v.t. dezimieren ‹*Bevölkerung, Truppe*›; drastisch verringern ‹*Zahl*›

decimation /desɪˈmeɪʃn/ n., no pl. Dezimierung, *die*

decimetre /ˈdesɪmiːtə(r)/ n. Dezimeter, *der*

decipher /dɪˈsaɪfə(r)/ v.t. entziffern

decipherable /dɪˈsaɪfərəbl/ adj. entzifferbar

decision /dɪˈsɪʒn/ n. **1** (settlement, judgement, conclusion) Entscheidung, *die* (**on** über + *Akk.*); (resolve) Entschluss, *der;* **it's 'your ~:** die Entscheidung liegt ganz bei dir; **come to** *or* **arrive at** *or* **reach a ~:** zu einer Entscheidung kommen; **has there been a ~?** ist eine Entscheidung gefallen?; **make** *or* **take a ~:** eine Entscheidung treffen; **make a firm ~ to do sth.** den festen Entschluss fassen, etw. zu tun; **leave the ~ to sb.** jmdm. die Entscheidung überlassen; **~s, ~s!** immer diese Entscheidungen! **2** *no pl.* (resoluteness) Entschlossenheit, *die*

de'cision-making n. Beschlussfassung, *die*

decisive /dɪˈsaɪsɪv/ adj. **1** (conclusive) entscheidend **2** (decided) entschlussfreudig ‹*Person*›; bestimmt ‹*Charakter, Art*›

decisively /dɪˈsaɪsɪvlɪ/ adv. **1** (conclusively) entscheidend **2** (decidedly) entschlossen

decisiveness /dɪˈsaɪsɪvnɪs/ n., no pl. **1** (conclusiveness) entscheidende Bedeutung **2** (decidedness) Entschlossenheit, *die*

deck /dek/
A n. **1** (of ship) Deck, *das;* **above ~:** auf Deck; **below ~[s]** unter Deck; **clear the ~s [for action** *etc.*] das Schiff klarmachen [zum Gefecht *usw.*]; (fig.) alles startklar machen; **on ~:** an Deck; **all hands on ~!** alle Mann an Deck!; **it was all hands on ~** (fig.) alle packten mit an **2** (of bus etc.) Deck, *das;* **the upper ~:** das Oberdeck **3** (sunbathing platform) ≈ Sonnenterrasse, *die* **4** (tape ~) Tapedeck, *das;* (record ~) Plattenspieler, *der* **5** (coll.: ground) Boden, *der;* **hit the ~:** auf den Boden schlagen **6** (Amer.: pack) **a ~ of cards** ein Spiel Karten; **split/shuffle the ~:** die Karten austeilen/mischen
B v.t. **~ sth. [with sth.]** etw. [mit etw.] schmücken; **they were ~ed in all their finery** sie waren prächtig herausgeputzt

(Phrasal verb)
- **~ 'out** v.t. herausputzen ‹*Person*›; [aus]schmücken ‹*Raum*›

deck: ~chair n. Liegestuhl, *der;* (on ship) Liegeod. Deckstuhl, *der;* **~hand** n. (Naut.) Decksmann, *der*

decking /ˈdekɪŋ/ n., no pl. **1** (of ship) Deck, *das* **2** (material for floors) [Boden]belag, *der*

deckle /ˈdekl/: **~-'edge** n. Büttenrand, *der;* **~-'edged** adj. mit Büttenrand

declaim /dɪˈkleɪm/
A v.i. **1** **~ against sb./sth.** gegen jmdn./etw. eifern *od.* (ugs.) wettern **2** (deliver impassioned speech) eifern; deklamieren (veralt.)
B v.t. deklamieren ‹*Gedicht*›; verkünden (geh.) ‹*Botschaft*›

declamatory /dɪˈklæmətərɪ/ adj. deklamatorisch ‹*Stil, Rede, Art*›; leidenschaftlich ‹*Kritik, Worte*›

declaration /dekləˈreɪʃn/ n. Erklärung, *die;* (at customs) Deklaration, *die;* Zollerklärung, *die;* (of the truth, one's errors) Eingeständnis, *das;* **~ of love** Liebeserklärung, *die;* **income tax ~:** Einkommensteuererklärung, *die;* **~ of the poll** *or* **election results** Bekanntgabe der Wahlergebnisse; **~ of war** Kriegserklärung, *die;* **make a ~:** eine Erklärung abgeben; (of guilt) ein Geständnis ablegen; **D~ of Human Rights** Menschenrechtserklärung, *die*

> **Declaration of Independence**
>
> Die Erklärung, mit der sich die 13 nordamerikanischen Kolonien als Vereinigte Staaten von Amerika von Großbritannien lösten. Die unter Thomas Jefferson (1743-1826) vorbereitete Unabhängigkeitserklärung wurde am 4. Juli 1776 vom *Continental Congress* in Philadelphia angenommen. Sie war von Benjamin Franklin (1706-90), John Adams (1735-1848) und anderen bedeutenden Staatsmännern unterzeichnet. Der 4. Juli — **Independence Day** — ist ein Feiertag zum Gedenken an die Unabhängigkeit der Nation.

declare /dɪˈkleə(r)/
A v.t. **1** (announce) erklären; zugeben ‹*Schuld, Wissen*›; (state explicitly) kundtun (geh.) ‹*Wunsch, Absicht*›; Ausdruck verleihen (+ *Dat.*) (geh.) ‹*Erwartung, Hoffnung*›; (prove) bezeugen; **[well,] I [do] ~!** (dated) das darf [doch] nicht wahr sein! (ugs.) **2** (pronounce) **~ sth./sb. [to be] sth.** etw./jmdn. für etw. erklären; **~ oneself** sich zu erkennen geben **3** (acknowledge) deklarieren; angeben ‹*Einkünfte*›; *see also* **interest A 6**
B v.i. **~ for/against sb./sth.** sich für/gegen jmdn./etw. erklären

declassify /diːˈklæsɪfaɪ/ v.t. freigeben

declension /dɪˈklenʃn/ n. (Ling.) Deklination, *die*

declination /deklɪˈneɪʃn/ n. **1** (downward bend) Neigung, *die* **2** (Amer.: formal refusal) Ablehnung, *die*

decline /dɪˈklaɪn/
A v.i. **1** (fall off) nachlassen; ‹*Moral:*› sinken, nachlassen; ‹*Preis, Anzahl:*› sinken, zurückgehen; ‹*Gesundheitszustand:*› sich verschlechtern; ‹*Reich, Kultur:*› verfallen; **~ in popularity** an Beliebtheit verlieren; **his strength ~d rapidly** seine Kräfte nahmen rasch ab **2** (slope downwards) abfallen; (droop) sich neigen **3** **his declining years** die letzten Jahre seines Lebens **4** (refuse) **~ with thanks** (also iron.) dankend ablehnen
B v.t. **1** (refuse) ablehnen; **~ to do sth.** *or* **doing sth.** [es] ablehnen, etw. zu tun; **they ~d to make any comment** sie lehnten jede Stellungnahme ab **2** (Ling.) deklinieren
C n. Nachlassen, *das* (**in** *Gen.*); **a ~ in prices/numbers** ein Sinken der Preise/Anzahl; **the ~ of the empire** der Verfall des Reiches; **~ and fall** Verfall und Untergang; **a ~ in wealth/poverty/the birth rate** eine Abnahme des Wohlstands/ein Rückgang der Armut/der Geburten; **be on the ~:** nachlassen; **he is on the ~:** er ist auf dem absteigenden Ast (ugs.); **be in ~:** rückläufig sein

declutch /diːˈklʌtʃ/ v.i. (Motor Veh.) auskuppeln; **double-~:** Zwischengas geben

decoction /dɪˈkɒkʃn/ n. (product) Dekokt, *das* (Pharm.); Abkochung, *die*

decode /diːˈkəʊd/ v.t. dekodieren, dechiffrieren ‹*Mitteilung, Signal*›; entschlüsseln ‹*Schrift, Hieroglyphen*›

decoder /diːˈkəʊdə(r)/ n. (Electronics) Decoder, *der*

décolleté /deɪˈkɒlteɪ/
A adj. dekolletiert ‹*Kleid, Dame*›
B n. Dekolleté, *das*

decolonize (decolonise) /diːˈkɒlənaɪz/ v.t. dekolonisieren

decommission /diːkəˈmɪʃən/ v.t. stilllegen; außer Dienst stellen ‹*Schiff*›

decompose /diːkəmˈpəʊz/ v.i. sich zersetzen

decomposition /diːkɒmpəˈzɪʃn/ n. Zersetzung, *die;* (rotting also) Verrottung, *die*

decompress /diːkəmˈpres/ v.t. (also Computing) dekomprimieren

decompression /diːkəmˈpreʃn/ n. (also Computing) Dekompression, *die*

decom'pression: ~ chamber n. Dekompressionskammer, *die;* **~ sickness** n., no pl. Dekompressionskrankheit, *die*

decongestant /diːkənˈdʒestənt/ n. (Med.) Abschwellung bewirkendes Mittel; **bronchial ~:** ≈ Hustensaft, *der;* **nasal ~:** Nasenspray, *das;* (drops) Nasentropfen *Pl.*

decontaminate /diːkənˈtæmɪneɪt/ v.t. dekontaminieren (fachspr.); entseuchen

decontamination /diːkəntæmɪˈneɪʃn/ n. Dekontamination, *die* (fachspr.); Entseuchung, *die*

decontrol /diːkənˈtrəʊl/ v.t., **-ll-** (Admin.) freigeben

decor /ˈdeɪkɔː(r)/ n. Ausstattung, *die;* Dekor, *der od. das*

decorate /ˈdekəreɪt/ v.t. **1** (adorn) schmücken ‹*Raum, Straße, Baum*›; verzieren ‹*Kuchen, Kleid*›; dekorieren ‹*Schaufenster*›; (with wallpaper) tapezieren; (with paint) streichen **2** (invest with order etc.) auszeichnen; dekorieren

decorated /ˈdekəreɪtɪd/ adj. **1** geschmückt ‹*Zimmer*›; verziert ‹*Kuchen*› **2** (Archit.) **D~ style** Decorated style, *der* (fachspr.) (Stil der englischen Hochgotik)

decoration /dekəˈreɪʃn/ n. **1** ▸**decorate 1**: Schmücken, *das;* Verzieren, *das;* Dekoration, *die;* Tapezieren, *das;* Streichen, *das* **2** (adornment) (thing) Schmuck, *der;* (in shop window) Dekoration, *die* **3** (medal etc.) Auszeichnung, *die;* Dekoration, *die;* **D~ Day** (Amer.) *amerikanischer Heldengedenktag* (30. Mai) **4** *in pl.* **Christmas ~s** Weihnachtsschmuck, *der*

decorative /ˈdekərətɪv/ adj. dekorativ

decoratively /ˈdekərətɪvlɪ/ adv. dekorativ

decorator /ˈdekəreɪtə(r)/ n. Maler, *der*/Malerin, *die;* (paperhanger) Tapezierer, *der*/Tapeziererin, *die;* **[firm of] ~s** Malerbetrieb, *der*

decorous /ˈdekərəs/ adj., **decorously** /ˈdekərəslɪ/ adv. schicklich (geh.)

decorousness /ˈdekərəsnɪs/ n., no pl. Schicklichkeit, *die* (geh.)

decorum /dɪˈkɔːrəm/ n. Dekorum, *das* (geh. veralt.); (seemliness also) Schicklichkeit, *die* (geh.); **behave with ~:** sich schicklich benehmen

decoy
A /dɪˈkɔɪ/ v.t. **1** (allure) locken; (ensnare) betören; **~ sb./sth. into sth.** jmdn./etw. in etw. (*Akk.*) locken; **~ sb./sth. into doing sth.** jmdn./etw. dazu verleiten, etw. zu tun **2** (Hunting) locken
B /dɪˈkɔɪ, ˈdiːkɔɪ/ n. **1** (Hunting) Lockvogel, *der* **2** (person) Lockvogel, *der* **3** (bait) Verlockung, *die*

decrease
A /dɪˈkriːs/ v.i. abnehmen; ‹*Anzahl, Einfuhr, Produktivität:*› abnehmen, zurückgehen; ‹*Stärke, Gesundheit:*› nachlassen; **~ in value/size/weight/popularity** an Wert/Größe/Gewicht/Popularität verlieren; **~ in price** im Preis fallen; billiger werden
B v.t. reduzieren; [ver]mindern ‹*Wert, Lärm, Körperkraft*›; schmälern ‹*Popularität, Macht*›; senken ‹*Standard, Kaufkraft*›
C /ˈdiːkriːs/ n. Rückgang, *der;* (in weight, knowledge, stocks) Abnahme, *die;* (in strength, power, energy) Nachlassen, *das;* (in value, noise) Minderung, *die;* (in standards) Senkung, *die;* **a ~ in inflation/strength/speed** ein Rückgang der Inflation/ein Nachlassen der Kräfte/eine Minderung der Geschwindigkeit; **be on the ~** ▸**A**

decreasingly /dɪˈkriːsɪŋlɪ/ adv. immer weniger

decree /dɪˈkriː/
A n. **1** (ordinance) Dekret, *das;* Erlass, *der* **2** (Law) Urteil, *das;* **~ nisi/absolute** vorläufiges/endgültiges Scheidungsurteil
B v.t. (ordain) verfügen

decrepit /dɪˈkrepɪt/ adj. altersschwach; (dilapidated) heruntergekommen ‹*Haus, Stadt*›; schrottreif ‹*Auto, Maschine*›

decrepitude /dɪˈkrepɪtjuːd/ n., no pl. Altersschwäche, *die;* (of house) heruntergekommener Zustand; (of car, machine) schrottreifer Zustand

decriminalize /diːˈkrɪmɪnəlaɪz/ v.t. entkriminalisieren

decry /dɪˈkraɪ/ v.t. verwerfen

decrypt /diːˈkrɪpt/ vt (also Computing) entschlüsseln

d

decryption /diːˈkrɪpʃn/ *n.* (also Computing) Entschlüsselung, *die*

dedicate /ˈdedɪkeɪt/ *v.t.* 1 (with name of honoured person) ~ **sth. to sb.** jmdm. etw. widmen; **a statue ~d to the memory of ...:** eine Statue zum Gedenken an ... 2 (give up) ~ **one's life to sth.** sein Leben einer Sache (*Dat.*) weihen 3 (devote solemnly) weihen

dedicated /ˈdedɪkeɪtɪd/ *adj.* 1 (devoted) **be ~ to sth./sb.** nur für etw./jmdn. leben 2 (devoted to vocation) hingebungsvoll; **a ~ teacher/politician** ein Lehrer/Politiker mit Leib und Seele

dedication /dedɪˈkeɪʃn/ *n.* 1 (act, inscription) Widmung, *die* (**to** *Dat.*); (in book) Widmung, *die;* Zueignung, *die;* (on building, monument) Inschrift, *die* 2 (devotion) Hingabe, *die* 3 (ceremony) Weihe, *die*

deduce /dɪˈdjuːs/ *v.t.* ~ **sth. [from sth.]** etw. [aus etw.] ableiten; auf etw. (*Akk.*) [aus etw.] schließen; ~ **from sth. that ...:** aus etw. schließen, dass ...

deducible /dɪˈdjuːsɪbl/ *adj.* ableitbar, (Philos.) deduzierbar (**from** aus)

deduct /dɪˈdʌkt/ *v.t.* ~ **sth. [from sth.]** etw. [von etw.] abziehen

deductible /dɪˈdʌktɪbl/ *adj.* **be ~:** einbehalten werden [können]

deduction /dɪˈdʌkʃn/ *n.* 1 (deducting) Abzug, *der* 2 (deducing, thing deduced) Ableitung, *die* 3 (amount) Abzüge *Pl.*; **a ~ from the price** ein Preisnachlass

deductive /dɪˈdʌktɪv/ *adj.* deduktiv

deductively /dɪˈdʌktɪvlɪ/ *adv.* deduktiv

deed /diːd/

A *n.* 1 Tat, *die* 2 (Law) [gesiegelte] Urkunde; ~ **of transfer** Übertragungsurkunde, *die; see also* **covenant A 2**

B *v.t.* (Amer.) ~ **sth. to sb.** jmdm. etw. [urkundlich] übertragen

deed: ~ **box** *n.: Kasten zur Aufbewahrung von Urkunden;* ≈ Dokumentenbox, *die;* ~ **poll** /ˈdiːd pəʊl/ *n.* (Law) einseitiges Rechtsgeschäft (Rechtsw.)

deejay /diːˈdʒeɪ/ *n.* (coll.) Diskjockey, *der*

deem /diːm/ *v.t.* erachten für; **[as] I ~ed** wie mir schien; **she is ~ed to be the best singer** sie gilt als die beste Sängerin; **he shall be ~ed to have given his assent** man wird annehmen, dass er seine Zustimmung gegeben hat

deep /diːp/

A *adj.* 1 ▸ⓘ **p. 1208** (extending far down, going far in, lit. or fig.) tief; **water ten feet ~:** drei Meter tiefes Wasser; **take a ~ breath/drink** tief Atem holen/einen tiefen Schluck nehmen 2 (lying far down or back or inwards) tief; **ten feet ~ in water** drei Meter tief unter Wasser; **be ~ in thought/prayer** in Gedanken/im Gebet versunken sein; **be ~ in discussion** mitten in einer Diskussion sein; **be ~ in debt** hoch verschuldet sein; **be standing three ~:** drei hintereinander stehen 3 (profound) tief ‹*Grund*›; ernst ‹*Problem, Sache*›; gründlich ‹*Studium, Forschung*›; tiefgründig ‹*Bemerkung*›; **give sth. ~ thought** über etw. (*Akk.*) gründlich nachdenken; **he's a ~ one** (coll.) er ist ein stilles Wasser (ugs.); **in ~ space** [tief] im Weltraum 4 (heartfelt) tief; aufrichtig ‹*Interesse, Dank*› 5 (low-pitched, intense) tief; (full-toned) volltönend; **the ~-blue sea** das tiefblaue Meer 6 (Cricket) *weit vom Schlagmann entfernt. See also* **end A 6**

B *adv.* tief; **still waters run ~** (prov.) stille Wasser sind tief (Spr.); ~ **down** (fig.) im Innersten

C *n.* 1 (~ part) **~s** Tiefen *Pl.*; **the ~** (poet.) der Ozean 2 (abyss, lit. or fig.) Tiefe, *die* 3 (Cricket) **the ~:** *äußerer Rand des Spielfeldes*

deep 'breathing *n.* tiefes Atmen; ~ **[exercise]** Atemübung, *die*

deepen /ˈdiːpn/

A *v.t.* 1 tiefer machen; vertiefen 2 (make lower) tiefer werden lassen ‹*Stimme*› 3 (increase, intensify) vertiefen; intensivieren ‹*Farbe*›

B *v.i.* 1 tiefer werden 2 (intensify) sich vertiefen

deepening /ˈdiːpənɪŋ/ *n., no pl.* (EU) Vertiefung, *die*

deep: ~-**'freeze** **A** *n.* ((Amer.) ®) Tiefkühltruhe, *die;* (in shop also) Tiefkühlbox, *die;* (upright) Gefrierschrank, *der;* **B** *v.t.* tiefgefrieren; ~-**fried** *adj.* frittiert; ~-**laid** *adj.* ausgeklügelt; ausgetüftelt

deeply /ˈdiːplɪ/ *adv.* 1 (to great depth, lit. or fig.) tief; **drink ~:** einen kräftigen Zug *od.* Schluck nehmen 2 tief ‹*beeindruckt, gerührt, verletzt, getroffen*›; äußerst ‹*interessiert, dankbar, engagiert, selbstbewusst*›; **be ~ in love** sehr verliebt sein; **be ~ indebted to sb.** jmdm. sehr zu Dank verpflichtet sein; **sleep ~:** tief *od.* fest schlafen; **read/study ~:** sehr aufmerksam lesen/studieren

deepness /ˈdiːpnɪs/ *n., no pl.* Tiefe, *die;* (of interest, gratitude) Ausmaß, *das*

deep: ~-**rooted** *adj.* tief ‹*Abneigung*›; tief verwurzelt ‹*Tradition*›; ~-**sea** *adj.* Tiefsee-; ~-**'seated** *adj.* tief sitzend; **D~ 'South** *n.* (Amer.) tiefer Süden (*die Staaten der USA am Golf von Mexiko*); ~ **'space** *n.* [erdferne] Weltraum, *der;* All, *das;* ~-**vein throm'bosis** *n.* (Med.) tiefe Venenthrombose

deer /dɪə(r)/ *n., pl. same* Hirsch, *der;* (roe ~) Reh, *das*

deer: ~ **forest** *n.* Jagdgehege, *das;* ~ **park** *n.* Wildpark, *der;* ~**skin** *n.* Rehleder, *das;* ~**stalker** *n.* 1 (person) Jäger (*auf der Pirsch*); 2 (hat) Mütze (*aus Stoff mit einem Schild vorn und hinten*); ≈ Sherlock-Holmes-Mütze, *die*

de-escalate /diːˈeskəleɪt/ *v.t.* deeskalieren

de-escalation /diːeskəˈleɪʃn/ *n., no pl.* Deeskalation, *die* (geh.); (of a conflict) Entschärfung, *die*

deface /dɪˈfeɪs/ *v.t.* verunstalten; verschandeln ‹*Gebäude*›

defacement /dɪˈfeɪsmənt/ *n.* Verunstaltung, *die;* (of building) Verschandelung, *die*

de facto /diː ˈfæktəʊ, deɪ ˈfæktəʊ/

A *adj.* de facto; **a ~ government** eine De-facto-Regierung

B *adv.* de facto

defamation /defəˈmeɪʃn, diːfəˈmeɪʃn/ *n.* Diffamierung, *die*

defamatory /dɪˈfæmətərɪ/ *adj.* diffamierend; **be ~ about sb.** jmdn. diffamieren

defame /dɪˈfeɪm/ *v.t.* diffamieren; beschmutzen ‹*Name, Ansehen*›

default /dɪˈfɔːlt, dɪˈfɒlt/

A *n.* 1 (lack) Mangel, *der;* **in ~ of** mangels (+ *Gen.*); in Ermangelung (geh.) (+ *Gen.*) 2 (Law) (failure to act) Versäumnis, *das;* (failure to appear) Säumnis, *die od. das;* **judgement by ~:** Versäumnisurteil, *das* 3 (failure to pay) Verzug, *der;* (failure to act or appear) Ausbleiben, *das;* (Sport) Nichterscheinen, *das;* ~ **of payment** Zahlungsverzug, *der;* **lose/go by ~:** durch Abwesenheit verlieren/nicht zur Geltung kommen; **win by ~:** durch Nichterscheinen des Gegners gewinnen 4 (Computing) Standardeinstellung, *die;* Voreinstellung, *die*

B *v.i.* 1 versagen; ~ **on one's payments/debts** seinen Zahlungsverpflichtungen nicht nachkommen 2 (Computing) zur Standardeinstellung *od.* Voreinstellung wechseln

defaulter /dɪˈfɔːltə(r), dɪˈfɒltə(r)/ *n.* 1 (Brit. Mil.) Straffällige, *der* 2 (one who fails to pay) säumiger Schuldner/säumige Schuldnerin

defeat /dɪˈfiːt/

A *v.t.* 1 (overcome) besiegen; (in battle or match also) schlagen; ablehnen, zu Fall bringen ‹*Antrag, Vorschlag*› 2 (baffle) **sth. ~s me** ich kann etw. nicht begreifen; **it ~s me why ...:** ich verstehe einfach nicht, warum ...; (frustrate) **the task has ~ed us** diese Aufgabe hat uns überfordert; ~ **the object/purpose of sth.** etw. völlig sinnlos machen; ~ **one's own object** seine eigenen Pläne durchkreuzen

B *n.* (being defeated) Niederlage, *die;* (defeating) Sieg, *der* (**of** über + *Akk.*); **the ~ of a motion/bill** das Scheitern eines Antrags/Gesetzentwurfs; **admit ~:** seine Niederlage eingestehen

defeatism /dɪˈfiːtɪzm/ *n.* Defätismus, *der*

defeatist /dɪˈfiːtɪst/

A *n.* Defätist, *der*

B *adj.* defätistisch; **you're so ~ about things** du siehst die Dinge immer so schwarz

defecate /ˈdefəkeɪt/ *v.i.* Kot ausscheiden; defäkieren (Med.)

defecation /defəˈkeɪʃn/ *n.* Ausscheidung, *die;* Defäkation, *die* (Med.)

defect

A /ˈdiːfekt, dɪˈfekt/ *n.* 1 (lack) Mangel, *der* 2 (shortcoming) Fehler, *der;* (in construction, body, mind, etc. also) Defekt, *der;* **the ~s in his character, his character ~s** seine Charakterfehler

B /dɪˈfekt/ *v.i.* überlaufen (**to** zu); ~ **from the cause** sich von der Sache lossagen

defection /dɪˈfekʃn/ *n.* Abfall, *der;* (desertion) Flucht, *die;* ~ **from the army** Desertion aus der Armee

defective /dɪˈfektɪv/ *adj.* 1 (faulty) defekt ‹*Maschine*›; gestört ‹*Gehirn*›; fehlerhaft ‹*Sprache, Material, Arbeiten, Methode, Plan*›; mangelhaft, gestört ‹*Verdauung, Kreislauf, Wachstum, Entwicklung*›; **sb./sth. is ~ in sth.** es mangelt jmdm./einer Sache an etw. (*Dat.*); **have a ~ heart** einen Herzfehler haben 2 (mentally deficient) geistig gestört 3 (Ling.) defektiv

defectiveness /dɪˈfektɪvnɪs/ *n., no pl.* Fehlerhaftigkeit, *die*

defector /dɪˈfektə(r)/ *n.* Überläufer, *der*/-läuferin, *die;* (from a cause or party) Abtrünnige, *der/die;* (from army) Deserteur, *der*

defence /dɪˈfens/ *n.* (Brit.) 1 (defending) Verteidigung, *die;* (of body against disease) Schutz, *der;* **in ~ of** zur Verteidigung (+ *Gen.*) 2 (thing that protects, means of resisting attack) Schutz, *der* 3 (justification) Rechtfertigung, *die;* **in sb.'s ~:** zu jmds. Verteidigung; **come to sb.'s ~:** jmdm. zur Seite springen 4 (military resources) Verteidigung, *die* 5 *in pl.* (fortification) Befestigungsanlagen *Pl.*; (fig.) Widerstandskraft, *die;* **sb.'s ~s are down** (fig.) jmds. Widerstandskraft ist erschöpft 6 (Law) Verteidigung, *die;* **the case for the ~:** die Verteidigung; ~ **witness** Zeuge/Zeugin der Verteidigung 7 (Sport) Verteidigung, *die*

de'fence budget *n.* Verteidigungshaushalt, *der*

defenceless /dɪˈfenslɪs/ *adj.* (Brit.) wehrlos; **look ~:** hilflos dreinschauen

de'fence mechanism *n.* (Physiol., Psych.) Abwehrmechanismus, *der*

defend /dɪˈfend/

A *v.t.* 1 (protect) schützen (**from** vor + *Dat.*); (by fighting) verteidigen 2 (uphold by argument, vindicate, speak or write in favour of) verteidigen; verteidigen, rechtfertigen ‹*Politik, Handeln*› 3 (Sport) verteidigen ‹*Titel, Tor*› 4 (Law) verteidigen; ~ **oneself** sich selbst verteidigen

B *v.i.* (Sport) verteidigen

defendant /dɪˈfendənt/ *n.* (Law) (accused) Angeklagte, *der/die;* (sued) Beklagte, *der/die*

defender /dɪˈfendə(r)/ *n.* 1 (one who defends) Verteidiger, *der;* (of principle, method, etc.) Verfechter, *der* 2 (Sport) (of championship) Titelverteidiger, *der*/-verteidigerin, *die;* (of goal) Verteidiger, *der*/Verteidigerin, *die*

defense, defenseless (Amer.) ▸ **defence, defenceless**

defensible /dɪˈfensɪbl/ *adj.* 1 (easily defended) wehrhaft 2 (justifiable) vertretbar

defensive /dɪˈfensɪv/

A *adj.* 1 (protective) defensiv ‹*Strategie, Handlung*›; ~ **player** Defensivspieler, *der;* ~ **wall** Schutzwall, *der;* ~ **fortification** Verteidigungsanlage, *die* 2 (by argument) rechtfertigend 3 (excessively self-justifying) **he's always so ~ when he's criticized** er will sich immer um jeden Preis rechtfertigen, wenn er kritisiert wird

B *n.* Defensive, *die;* **be/act on the ~:** in der Defensive sein; **she's always so much on the ~:** sie geht immer gleich in die Defensive

defensively /dɪˈfensɪvlɪ/ *adv.* **act ~:** sich in übertriebener Weise rechtfertigen

defer[1] /dɪˈfɜː(r)/ *v.t.*, **-rr-** 1 (postpone) aufschieben; ~**red annuity** aufgeschobene Rente; ~**red payment** Ratenzahlung, *die;* ~**red shares/stock** Nachzugsaktien *Pl.* 2 (Amer.: postpone call-up of) zurückstellen

defer[2] *v.i.*, **-rr-:** ~ **[to sb.]** sich [jmdm.] beugen; ~ **to sb.'s wishes** sich jmds. Wünschen fügen

deference /ˈdefərəns/ *n.* Respekt, *der;* Ehrerbietung, *die* (geh.); **in ~ to sb./sth.** aus Achtung vor jmdm./etw.; **in ~ to your wishes** Ihren Wünschen entsprechend

deferential /defəˈrenʃl/ *adj.* respektvoll; groß ‹*Respekt*›; **be ~ to sb./sth.** jmdm./einer Sache mit Respekt begegnen

deferentially /defəˈrenʃəlɪ/ *adv.* respektvoll

deferment /dɪˈfɜːmənt/ *n.* 1 (deferring) Aufschub, *der* 2 (Amer.: postponement of call-up) **have a ~:** zurückgestellt sein

defiance /dɪˈfaɪəns/ *n.* Trotz, *der;* (open disobedience) Missachtung, *die;* **act of ~:** Herausforderung, *die;* **in ~ of sb./sth.** jmdm./einer Sache zum Trotz

defiant /dɪˈfaɪənt/ *adj.* trotzig ‹*Tonfall, Kind, Benehmen*›

defiantly /dɪˈfaɪəntlɪ/ *adv.* aufsässig

defibrillator /diːˈfɪbrɪleɪtə(r)/ *n.* (Med.) Defibrillator, *der*

deficiency /dɪˈfɪʃənsɪ/ *n.* 1 (lack) Mangel, *der* (**of, in** an + *Dat.*); **mental ~:** geistige Behinderung; **nutritional ~:** Ernährungsmangel, *der* 2 (inadequacy) Unzulänglichkeit, *die* 3 (deficit) Defizit, *das*

deˈficiency disease *n.* Mangelkrankheit, *die*

deficient /dɪˈfɪʃənt/ *adj.* 1 (not having enough) **sb./sth. is ~ in sth.** jmdm./einer Sache mangelt es an etw. (*Dat.*); **be [mentally] ~:** geistig behindert sein 2 (not being enough) nicht ausreichend; (in quality also) unzulänglich

deficit /ˈdefɪsɪt/ *n.* Defizit, *das* (**of** an + *Dat.*); **a ~ of manpower** ein Mangel an Arbeitskräften

ˈdeficit spending *n.* (Finance) Defizitfinanzierung, *die*

defile[1]

A /dɪˈfaɪl/ *v.i.* [hintereinander] marschieren; defilieren (geh.)

B /ˈdiːfaɪl/ *n.* 1 (narrow way) Engpass, *der* 2 (gorge) Hohlweg, *der*

defile[2] /dɪˈfaɪl/ *v.t.* 1 (pollute) verpesten ‹*Luft*›; verseuchen ‹*Wasser*› 2 (desecrate) beflecken ‹*Unschuld, Reinheit*›

defilement /dɪˈfaɪlmənt/ *n.* 1 Verschandelung, *die;* (of air) Verpestung, *die* 2 (desecration) Befleckung, *die*

definable /dɪˈfaɪnəbl/ *adj.* (able to be set forth) definierbar; erklärbar; **love is not ~ in words** Liebe kann man nicht mit Worten erklären

define /dɪˈfaɪn/ *v.t.* 1 (mark out limits of, make clear) definieren; festlegen; **be ~d [against sth.]** sich [gegen etw.] abzeichnen; **~ one's position** (fig.) Stellung beziehen (**on** zu) 2 (set forth essence or meaning of) definieren 3 (characterize) charakterisieren

definite /ˈdefɪnɪt/ *adj.* (having exact limits) bestimmt; (precise) eindeutig, definitiv ‹*Antwort, Entscheidung*›; eindeutig ‹*Beschluss, Verbesserung, Standpunkt*›; eindeutig, klar ‹*Vorteil*›; klar *od.* scharf umrissen ‹*Ziel, Plan, Thema*›; klar ‹*Konzept, Linie, Vorstellung*›; deutlich ‹*Konturen, Umrisse*›; genau ‹*Zeitpunkt*›; entschlossen ‹*Schritte, Stimme, Person*›; **..., but that is not yet ~:** ..., aber das ist noch nicht endgültig; **you don't seem to be very ~:** Sie scheinen sich nicht ganz sicher zu sein; **she was so ~ about marrying him** sie war so fest entschlossen, ihn zu heiraten

definitely /ˈdefɪnɪtlɪ/

A *adv.* bestimmt; eindeutig ‹*festlegen, größer sein, verbessert, erklären*›; endgültig ‹*entscheiden, annehmen*›; fest ‹*vereinbaren*›; **she's ~ going to America** sie fährt auf jeden Fall nach Amerika

B *int.* (coll.) na klar (ugs.)

definition /defɪˈnɪʃn/ *n.* 1 Definition, *die;* **by ~:** per definitionem (geh.) 2 (making or being distinct, degree of distinctness) Schärfe, *die;* **improve the ~ on the TV** den Fernseher schärfer einstellen

definitive /dɪˈfɪnɪtɪv/ *adj.* 1 (decisive) endgültig, definitiv ‹*Beschluss, Antwort, Urteil*›; entschieden ‹*Ton, Art*›; entscheidend ‹*Vorsprung*› 2 (most authoritative) maßgeblich 3 (Philat.) **~ stamp** Dauermarke, *die*

definitively /dɪˈfɪnɪtɪvlɪ/ *adv.* endgültig; definitiv; mit Entschiedenheit ‹*beanspruchen, behaupten*›

deflate /dɪˈfleɪt/

A *v.t.* 1 (release air etc. from) **~ a tyre/balloon** die Luft aus einem Reifen/Ballon ablassen 2 (cause to lose conceitedness) ernüchtern; **~ sb.'s opinion of himself** jmds. Selbsteinschätzung (*Dat.*) einen Dämpfer versetzen (ugs.) 3 (Econ.) deflationieren

B *v.i.* 1 ‹*Reifen:*› Luftdruck verlieren 2 (Econ.) deflationieren

deflation /dɪˈfleɪʃn/ *n.* (Econ., Geol.) Deflation, *die*

deflationary /dɪˈfleɪʃənərɪ/ *adj.* (Econ.) deflationär

deflect /dɪˈflekt/

A *v.t.* (bend) umleiten ‹*Fluss*›; brechen, beugen ‹*Licht*›; (cause to deviate) **~ sb./sth. [from sb./sth.]** jmdn./etw. [von jmdm./einer Sache] ablenken

B *v.i.* (bend) einen Bogen machen; (deviate) abbiegen; (fig.) abweichen

deflection ▸ **deflexion**

deflector /dɪˈflektə(r)/ *n.* Deflektor, *der*

deflexion /dɪˈflekʃn/ *n.* (Brit.) 1 (bending) Umleitung, *die;* (deviation) Ablenkung, *die;* (turn) Abweichung, *die;* (fig.) Ablenkung, *die* 2 (Phys.) Ausschlag, *der*

deflower /diːˈflaʊə(r)/ *v.t.* deflorieren

defocus /diːˈfəʊkəs/ *v.t.*, **-s-** *or* **-ss-** unscharf machen; (Phys.) defokussieren ‹*Strahl*›

defoliant /diːˈfəʊlɪənt/ *n.* Entlaubungsmittel, *das*

defoliate /diːˈfəʊlɪeɪt/ *v.t.* entlauben

defoliation /diːfəʊlɪˈeɪʃn/ *n.* Entlaubung, *die*

deforestation /diːfɒrɪˈsteɪʃn/ *n.* Entwaldung, *die;* Abholzung, *die*

deform /dɪˈfɔːm/

A *v.t.* 1 (deface) deformieren; verunstalten 2 (misshape) verformen

B *v.i.* 1 (become disfigured) entstellt werden 2 (Phys.) sich verformen

deformation /diːfɔːˈmeɪʃn/ *n.* 1 (disfigurement) Deformation, *die;* Entstellung, *die* 2 (Phys.) Verformung, *die*

deformed /dɪˈfɔːmd/ *adj.* entstellt ‹*Gesicht*›; verunstaltet ‹*Person, Körperteil*›

deformity /dɪˈfɔːmɪtɪ/ *n.* (being deformed) Missgestalt, *die;* (malformation) Verunstaltung, *die*

DEFRA /ˈdefrə/ *abbr.* (Brit.) = **Department for Environment, Food, and Rural Affairs** Ministerium für Umwelt, Ernährung und ländliche Angelegenheiten

defraud /dɪˈfrɔːd/ *v.t.* **~ sb. [of sth.]** jmdn. [um etw.] betrügen

defray /dɪˈfreɪ/ *v.t.* bestreiten ‹*Kosten*›

defrayal /dɪˈfreɪəl/, **defrayment** /dɪˈfreɪmənt/ *ns.* Bestreitung, *die*

defrock /diːˈfrɒk/ ▸ **unfrock**

defrost /diːˈfrɒst/ *v.t.* auftauen ‹*Speisen*›; abtauen ‹*Kühlschrank*›; enteisen ‹*Windschutzscheibe, Fenster*›

deft /deft/ *adj.* sicher und geschickt

deftly /ˈdeftlɪ/ *adv.* sicher und geschickt

deftness /ˈdeftnɪs/ *n., no pl.* Geschicklichkeit, *die*

defunct /dɪˈfʌŋkt/ *adj.* tot, verstorben ‹*Person*›; (extinct) ausgestorben; (fig.) defekt ‹*Maschine*›; veraltet ‹*Gesetz*›; eingegangen ‹*Zeitung*›; stillgelegt ‹*Betrieb, Bahnlinie*›; überholt, vergessen ‹*Brauch, Idee, Mode*›

defuse /diːˈfjuːz/ *v.t.* (lit. or fig.) entschärfen

defy /dɪˈfaɪ/ *v.t.* 1 auffordern; **~ sb. to do sth.** jmdn. auffordern, etw. zu tun 2 (resist openly) **~ sb.** jmdm. trotzen *od.* Trotz bieten; (refuse to obey) **~ sb./sth.** sich jmdm./einer Sache widersetzen 3 (present insuperable obstacles to) widerstehen; **it defies explanation** das spottet jeder Erklärung

degeneracy /dɪˈdʒenərəsɪ/ *n.* (also Biol.) Degeneration, *die*

degenerate

A /dɪˈdʒenəreɪt/ *v.i.* 1 **~ [into sth.]** [zu etw.] verkommen *od.* degenerieren 2 (Biol.) **~ [into sth.]** [zu etw.] verkümmern *od.* degenerieren

B /dɪˈdʒenərət/ *adj.* (also Biol.) degeneriert; **become ~:** degenerieren

degeneration /dɪdʒenəˈreɪʃn/ *n.* (also Biol., Med.) Degeneration, *die*

degradation /degrəˈdeɪʃn/ *n.* 1 (abasement) Erniedrigung, *die* 2 (demotion; also Geol.) Degradierung, *die* 3 (Biol.) Degeneration, *die* 4 (Chem.) Abbau, *der*

degrade /dɪˈgreɪd/ *v.t.* 1 (abase) erniedrigen; herabsetzen ‹*Ansehen, Maßstab*› 2 (demote) degradieren 3 (Chem.) abbauen 4 (Geol.) zerfallen lassen; erodieren

degrading /dɪˈgreɪdɪŋ/ *adj.* entwürdigend; erniedrigend

degree /dɪˈgriː/ *n.* 1 ▸❶ p. 1620 (Math., Phys.) Grad, *der;* **an angle/a temperature of 45 ~s** ein Winkel/eine Temperatur von 45 Grad 2 (stage in scale or extent) Grad, *der;* **by ~s** allmählich; **a certain ~ of imagination** ein gewisses Maß an Phantasie; **to a high ~:** in hohem Grade *od.* Maße; **to some** *or* **a certain ~:** [bis] zu einem gewissen Grad; **to the last ~:** in höchstem Grade; **obstinate to a ~:** reichlich widerspenstig (ugs.); **to what ~?** [in]wieweit? 3 (relative condition) Art, *die;* **in its ~:** auf seine Art 4 (step in genealogical descent) [Verwandtschafts]grad, *der* 5 **forbidden** *or* **prohibited ~s** *Verwandtschaftsgrade, die eine Heirat ausschließen* 6 (rank) Stand, *der* 7 (academic rank) [akademischer] Grad; **take/receive a ~ in sth.** einen akademischen Grad in etw. (*Dat.*) erwerben/verliehen bekommen; **have a ~ in physics/maths** einen Hochschulabschluss in Physik/Mathematik haben 8 (Ling.) **~s of comparison** Steigerungsstufen *Pl.;* **positive/comparative/superlative ~:** Positiv, *der*/Komparativ, *der*/Superlativ, *der* 9 **give sb. the third ~:** jmdn. schonungslos ins Verhör nehmen

degree: ~ ceremony *n.* Feierstunde zur Verleihung der akademischen Würde; **~ certificate** *n.* Abschlusszeugnis, *das;* Diplom, *das;* **~ course** *n.* Bachelor-Studium, *das;* **~ day** *n.* Tag der Verleihung der akademischen Würde

dehumanize (**dehumanise**) /diːˈhjuːmənaɪz/ *v.t.* entmenschlichen; dehumanisieren

dehumidifier /diːhjuːˈmɪdɪfaɪə(r)/ *n.* [Luft]entfeuchter, *der*

dehumidify /diːhjuːˈmɪdɪfaɪ/ *v.t.* entfeuchten

dehydrate /diˈhaɪdreɪt/ *v.t.* 1 (remove water from) das Wasser entziehen (+ *Dat.*), austrocknen ‹*Körper*›; **~d** dehydratisiert (fachspr.); getrocknet 2 (make dry) austrocknen

dehydration /diːhaɪˈdreɪʃn/ *n.* ▸**dehydrate**: Dehydration, *die* (fachspr.); Austrocknung, *die*

de-ice /diːˈaɪs/ *v.t.* enteisen

de-icer /diːˈaɪsə(r)/ *n.* Defroster, *der*

deification /deɪɪfɪˈkeɪʃn/ *n., no pl.* Vergottung, *die;* Deifikation, *die;* (worship) Vergötterung, *die*

deify /ˈdiːɪfaɪ/ *v.t.* (make a god of) vergotten; deifizieren; (worship) vergöttern

deign /deɪn/ *v.t.* **~ to do sth.** sich [dazu] herablassen, etw. zu tun

deism /ˈdiːɪzm/ *n.* Deismus, *der*

deist /ˈdiːɪst/ *n.* Deist, *der*/Deistin, *die*

deity /ˈdiːɪtɪ/ *n.* 1 (god) Gottheit, *die;* **the D~:** Gott; die Gottheit (geh.) 2 (divine status) Göttlichkeit, *die;* Gottheit, *die* (geh.)

déjà vu /deɪʒɑː ˈvuː/ *n., no pl.*, *no art.* Déjà-vu, *das;* **a sense of ~:** ein Déjà-vu-Gefühl

dejected /dɪˈdʒektɪd/ *adj.* niedergeschlagen

dejection /dɪˈdʒekʃn/ *n.* Niedergeschlagenheit, *die*

delay /dɪˈleɪ/

A *v.t.* 1 (postpone) verschieben; **he ~ed his visit for a few weeks** er verschob seinen Besuch einige Wochen 2 (make late) aufhalten; verzögern ‹*Ankunft, Abfahrt*›; **the train has been seriously ~ed** der Zug hat beträchtliche Verspätung 3 (hinder) aufhalten; (retard) **be ~ed** ‹*Veranstaltung:*› verspätet *od.* später erfolgen

B *v.i.* (wait) warten; (loiter) trödeln (ugs.); **don't ~:** warte nicht damit; **~ in doing sth.** zögern, etw. zu tun

C n. **1** Verzögerung, die (**to** bei); **what's the ~ now?** weshalb geht es jetzt nicht weiter?; **without ~:** unverzüglich; **without further ~:** ohne weitere Verzögerung **2** (Transport) Verspätung, die; **trains are subject to ~:** es ist mit Zugverspätungen zu rechnen

delayed-action /dɪleɪdˈækʃn/ adj. **~ bomb** Bombe mit Zeitzünder; **~ mechanism** (Photog.) Selbstauslöser, der; **~ drug** Medikament mit Depotwirkung

delayering /di:ˈleɪərɪŋ/ n., no pl. (Ind.) Hierarchieabbau, der; Hierarchieverflachung, die

delectable /dɪˈlektəbl/ adj. köstlich; **she looked ~:** sie sah reizend aus

delectation /di:lekˈteɪʃn/ n. Ergötzen, das (geh.); Vergnügen, das

delegate
A /ˈdelɪgət/ n. **1** (elected representative) Delegierte, der/die; (of firm) Beauftragte, der/die **2** (deputy) Vertreter, der/Vertreterin, die **3** (member of deputation) Delegierte, der/die
B /ˈdelɪgeɪt/ v.t. **1** (depute) delegieren **2** (commit) **~ power/responsibility/a task [to sb.]** Macht/Verantwortlichkeit/eine Aufgabe [an jmdn.] delegieren; **he does not know how to ~:** er will alles selbst erledigen

delegation /delɪˈgeɪʃn/ n. **1** (body of delegates) Delegation, die **2** (deputation) Abordnung, die; Delegation, die **3** (entrusting of authority to deputy) Delegation, die (**to** an + Akk.)

delete /dɪˈli:t/ v.t. streichen (**from** in + Dat.); (Computing) löschen; **~ where inapplicable** Nichtzutreffendes streichen

deˈlete key n. (Computing) Löschtaste, die

deleterious /delɪˈtɪərɪəs/ adj. schädlich (**to** für); **~ [to health]** gesundheitsschädlich

deletion /dɪˈli:ʃn/ n. Streichung, die; (Computing) Löschung, die

delft /delft/ n. **~ [pottery]/tiles** etc. Delfter Keramik/Kacheln usw.

deli /ˈdelɪ/ (coll.) ▸**delicatessen**

deliberate
A /dɪˈlɪbərət/ adj. **1** (intentional) absichtlich; bewusst ‹Lüge, Irreführung›; vorsätzlich ‹Verbrechen› **2** (fully considered) wohlerwogen; [sorgfältig] überlegt **3** (cautious) behutsam **4** (unhurried and considered) bedächtig
B /dɪˈlɪbəreɪt/ v.i. **1** (think carefully) **~ on sth.** über etw. (Akk.) [sorgfältig] nachdenken **2** (debate) **~ over** or **on** or **about sth.** über etw. (Akk.) beraten
C v.t. ‹Gruppe:› beraten; ‹Einzelner:› überlegen

deliberately /dɪˈlɪbərətlɪ/ adv. **1** (intentionally) absichtlich; mit Absicht; vorsätzlich ‹ein Verbrechen begehen› **2** (with full consideration) **[very] ~:** [ganz] bewusst **3** (in unhurried manner) bedächtig

deliberation /dɪlɪbəˈreɪʃn/ n. **1** (care) Sorgfalt, die **2** (unhurried nature) Bedächtigkeit, die **3** (careful consideration) Überlegung, die; **after much ~:** nach reiflicher Überlegung **4** (discussion) Beratung, die

deliberative /dɪˈlɪbərətɪv/ adj. beratend

delicacy /ˈdelɪkəsɪ/ n. **1** (tactfulness and care) Feingefühl, das; Delikatesse, die (geh.) **2** (fineness) Zartheit, die; Feinheit, die **3** (weakliness) Zartheit, die **4** (need of discretion etc.) Delikatheit, die **5** (food) Delikatesse, die

delicate /ˈdelɪkət/ adj. **1** (easily injured) empfindlich ‹Organ›; zart ‹Gesundheit, Konstitution›; (sensitive) sensibel, empfindlich ‹Person, Natur›; empfindlich ‹Waage, Instrument, Verfassung› **2** (requiring careful handling) empfindlich; (fig.) delikat, heikel ‹Frage, Angelegenheit, Problem› **3** (fine, of exquisite quality, subdued) zart; fein; delikat; (dainty) delikat **4** (subtle) fein **5** (deft, light) geschickt; zart **6** (tactful) taktvoll; behutsam

delicately /ˈdelɪkətlɪ/ adv. fein; **~ put** taktvoll ausgedrückt

delicatessen /delɪkəˈtesən/ n. Feinkostgeschäft, das; Delikatessengeschäft, das

delicious /dɪˈlɪʃəs/ adj. köstlich, lecker ‹Speise, Geschmack›; köstlich ‹Anblick, Spaß, Humor›

deliciously /dɪˈlɪʃəslɪ/ adv. köstlich; herrlich ‹kühl, lustig›

deliciousness /dɪˈlɪʃəsnɪs/ n., no pl. Köstlichkeit, die

delight /dɪˈlaɪt/
A v.t. erfreuen
B v.i. **sb. ~s in doing sth.** es macht jmdm. Freude, etw. zu tun; **~ to do sth.** etw. gern tun
C n. **1** (great pleasure) Freude, die; **~ at sth./at doing sth.** Freude über etw. (Akk.) /darüber, etw. zu tun; **~ in sth./in doing sth.** Freude an etw. (Dat.) /daran, etw. zu tun; **to my/our ~:** zu meiner/unserer Freude; **sb. takes ~ in doing sth.** es macht jmdm. Freude, etw. zu tun **2** (cause of pleasure) Vergnügen, das; **these cakes are a ~ to eat** diese Kuchen schmecken köstlich

delighted /dɪˈlaɪtɪd/ adj. freudig ‹Schrei›; **be ~** ‹Person:› hocherfreut sein; **be ~ by** or **with sth.** sich über etw. (Akk.) freuen; **be ~ to do sth.** sich freuen, etw. zu tun; **we shall be ~ to accept your invitation** wir werden Ihre Einladung gern annehmen

delightedly /dɪˈlaɪtɪdlɪ/ adv. erfreut

delightful /dɪˈlaɪtfl/ adj. wunderbar; köstlich ‹Geschmack, Klang›; reizend ‹Person, Landschaft›

delightfully /dɪˈlaɪtfəlɪ/ adv. wunderbar; bezaubernd ‹singen, tanzen, hübsch›; angenehm ‹hell, luftig›

delimit /dɪˈlɪmɪt/ v.t. begrenzen ‹Gebiet, Region›; (fig.) eingrenzen

delimitation /dɪlɪmɪˈteɪʃn/ n. Begrenzung, die; (fig.) Eingrenzung, die

delineate /dɪˈlɪnɪeɪt/ v.t. (draw) zeichnen; (describe) darstellen; **sharply ~d** sich scharf abzeichnend

delinquency /dɪˈlɪŋkwənsɪ/ n. **1** no pl. Kriminalität, die **2** (misdeed) Straftat, die

delinquent /dɪˈlɪŋkwənt/
A n. (bes. jugendlicher) Randalierer, der
B adj. **1** (offending) kriminell **2** (Amer.: in arrears) säumig

deliquescent /delɪˈkwesənt/ adj. (Chem.) deliqueszent

delirious /dɪˈlɪrɪəs/ adj. **1** delirant (Med.); **be ~:** im Delirium sein; ≈ fantasieren **2** (wildly excited) **be ~ [with sth.]** außer sich (Dat.) [vor etw. (Dat.)] sein **3** (ecstatic, wild) wahnsinnig; rasend ‹Zorn, Wut›

deliriously /dɪˈlɪrɪəslɪ/ adv. **1** wie im Delirium **2** (ecstatically) wahnsinnig

delirium /dɪˈlɪrɪəm/ n. Delirium, das

delirium tremens /dɪlɪrɪəm ˈtri:menz/ n., no pl. Delirium tremens, das (Med.); Säuferwahn, der (veralt.)

deliver /dɪˈlɪvə(r)/ v.t. **1** (utter) halten ‹Rede, Vorlesung, Predigt›; vorbringen ‹Worte›; vortragen ‹Verse›; (pronounce) verkünden ‹Urteil, Meinung, Botschaft› **2** (launch) werfen ‹Ball›; versetzen ‹Stoß, Schlag, Tritt›; vortragen ‹Angriff› **3** (hand over) bringen; liefern ‹Ware›; zustellen ‹Post, Telegramm›; überbringen ‹Botschaft›; **~ sth. to the door** etw. ins Haus liefern; **~ [the goods]** (fig.) es schaffen (ugs.); (fulfil promise) halten, was man versprochen hat **4** (give up) aushändigen; **stand and ~!** halt, Geld her! **5** (render) erzählen ‹Geschichte›; geben, liefern ‹Bericht, Beschreibung›; stellen ‹Ultimatum›; geben ‹Versprechen›; ablegen ‹Gelübde› **6** (Law) aushändigen ‹Dokument› **7** (assist in giving birth, aid in being born) entbinden; (give birth to) gebären; **be ~ed [of a child]** [von einem Kind] entbunden werden **8** (save) **~ sb./sth. from sb./sth.** jmdn./etw. von jmdm./etw. erlösen; **~ us from evil** (Relig.) erlöse uns von dem Übel od. Bösen (bibl.)

Phrasal verb
• **~ ˈup** v.t. aushändigen; übergeben

deliverable /dɪˈlɪvərəbl/
A adj. lieferfertig ‹Produkt›; erzeugbar ‹Schub›
B n. [lieferfertiges] Produkt

deliverance /dɪˈlɪvərəns/ n. Erlösung, die (**from** von); **~ from captivity** Befreiung aus der Gefangenschaft

delivery /dɪˈlɪvərɪ/ n. **1** (handing over) Lieferung, die; (of letters, parcels) Zustellung, die; **there is no charge for ~:** Lieferung frei Haus; **there are no deliveries on Sunday** sonntags wird keine Post zugestellt od. ausgetragen; **take ~ of sth.** etw. annehmen; **pay on ~:** bei Lieferung bezahlen; (Post) per Nachnahme bezahlen **2** (Sport) Wurf, der; **~ of a blow/punch** Schlag, der **3** (uttering) Vortragen, das; (manner of uttering) Vortragsweise, die; Vortrag, der **4** (childbirth) Entbindung, die

delivery: ~ boy n. Austräger, der; **~ date** n. Liefertermin, der; **~ girl** n. Austrägerin, die; **~ man** n. Lieferant, der; Ausfahrer, der (landsch.); **~ note** n. Lieferschein, der; **~ room** n. (Med.) Kreißsaal, der; **~ service** n. Zustelldienst, der; **~ van** n. Lieferwagen, der

dell /del/ n. [bewaldetes] Tal; Grund, der (veralt.)

delouse /di:ˈlaʊs/ v.t. entlausen

delphinium /delˈfɪnɪəm/ n. (Bot.) Rittersporn, der

delta /ˈdeltə/ n. **1** (of river; Greek letter) Delta, das **2** (Sch., Univ.: mark) Vier, die

delta ˈwing n. Deltaflügel, der; **~ aircraft** Deltaflugzeug, das

delude /dɪˈlju:d, dɪˈlu:d/ v.t. täuschen; **~ sb. into believing that ...:** jmdm. weismachen, dass ...; **stop deluding yourself!** machen Sie sich doch nichts vor!

deluge /ˈdelju:dʒ/
A n. **1** (rain) sintflutartiger Regen **2** (Bibl.) **the D~:** die Sintflut **3** **~ of complaints/letters** Flut von Beschwerden/Briefen
B v.t. (lit. or fig.) überschwemmen; **~ sb. with questions** jmdn. mit Fragen überschütten

delusion /dɪˈlju:ʒn, dɪˈlu:ʒn/ n. Illusion, die; (as symptom or form of madness) Wahnvorstellung, die; **be under a ~:** einer Täuschung unterliegen; **be under the ~ that ...:** sich (Dat.) der Täuschung hingeben, dass ...; **have ~s of grandeur** größenwahnsinnig sein

delusive /dɪˈlju:sɪv, dɪˈlu:sɪv/ adj., **delusively** /dɪˈlju:sɪvlɪ, dɪˈlu:sɪvlɪ/ adv. trügerisch

de luxe /dəˈlʌks, dəˈlu:ks/ adj. Luxus-

delve /delv/ v.i. **1** (arch./poet.: dig) graben (**for** nach) **2** (search) **~ into sth. [for sth.]** tief in etw. (Akk.) greifen[, um etw. herauszuholen] **3** (research) **~ into sth.** sich in etw. (Akk.) vertiefen; **~ into sb.'s past** in jmds. Vergangenheit nachforschen

Dem. abbr. (Amer.) = **Democrat** Dem.

demagogue (Amer.: **demagog**) /ˈdeməgɒg/ n. Demagoge, der/Demagogin, die

demagoguery /ˈdeməgɒgərɪ/, **demagogy** /ˈdeməgɒgɪ/ ns. Demagogie, die

demand /dɪˈmɑ:nd/
A n. **1** (request) Forderung, die (**for** nach); **a ~ for sb. to do sth.** eine Forderung, dass jmd. etw. tun soll; **payable on ~:** zahlbar bei Sicht (Kaufmannsspr.); **final ~:** letzte Mahnung **2** (desire for commodity) Nachfrage, die (**for** nach); **by popular ~:** auf vielfachen Wunsch; **sth./sb. is in [great] ~:** etw. ist [sehr] gefragt/jmd. ist [sehr] begehrt; **~ for teachers/clerks** Bedarf an Lehrern/Büroangestellten **3** (claim) **make ~s on sb.** jmdn. beanspruchen; **make too many ~s on sb.'s patience/time** jmds. Geduld/Zeit zu sehr beanspruchen; **I have many ~s on my time** ich bin zeitlich sehr beansprucht. See also **supply B 1**
B v.t. **1** (ask for, require, need) verlangen (**of, from** von); fordern ‹Recht, Genugtuung›; **~ to know/see sth.** etw. zu wissen/zu sehen verlangen; **he ~ed to be told everything** er wollte unbedingt alles wissen; **~ money with menaces** Geld erpressen **2** (insist on being told) unbedingt wissen wollen; **he ~ed my business** er fragte mich nachdrücklich, was ich wünschte

demanding /dɪˈmɑ:ndɪŋ/ adj. anspruchsvoll; (taxing) anstrengend ‹Kind›; **physically [very] ~:** körperlich [sehr] anstrengend

deˈmand note n. **1** (Brit.: request for payment) Zahlungsaufforderung, die **2** (Amer.: bill payable at sight) Sichtwechsel, der

demanning /di:ˈmænɪŋ/ n., no pl. (Brit. Ind.) Personalabbau, der

demarcate /ˈdi:mɑ:keɪt/ v.t. festlegen ‹Grenze›; demarkieren (geh.); **~ sth. from sth.** etw. von etw. abgrenzen

demarcation /di:mɑ:ˈkeɪʃn/ n. (of frontier) Demarkation, die (geh.); (of topics) Abgrenzung, die; **line of ~** (frontier) Demarkationslinie, die;

(of topics) Trennungslinie, *die*

demar'cation dispute *n.* Streit um die Abgrenzung der Zuständigkeitsbereiche

démarche /'deɪmɑːʃ/ *n.* (Diplom.) Demarche, *die*

demean /dɪ'miːn/ *v. refl.* (lower one's dignity) **~ oneself [to do sth.]** sich [dazu] erniedrigen[, etw. zu tun]; **~ oneself by sth./doing sth.** sich durch etw. erniedrigen/sich dadurch erniedrigen, dass man etw. tut

demeaning /dɪ'miːnɪŋ/ *adj.* erniedrigend

demeanour (*Brit.; Amer.:* **demeanor**) /dɪ'miːnə(r)/ *n.* Benehmen, *das*

demented /dɪ'mentɪd/ *adj.* wahnsinnig; **be ~ with worry** verrückt vor Angst sein (ugs.); **like somebody ~:** wie ein Wahnsinniger/eine Wahnsinnige

dementedly /dɪ'mentɪdlɪ/ *adv.* wie von Sinnen

dementia /dɪ'menʃə/ (Med.) Demenz, *die*

demerara /demə'reərə/ *n.* **~ [sugar]** brauner Zucker; Farin, *der*

demerge /diː'mɜːdʒ/

A *v.t.* (Brit.) abtrennen, ausgliedern ‹*einzelne Unternehmensbereiche*›; **the company ~d its subsidiary** die Firma trennte sich von ihrer Tochtergesellschaft

B *v.i.* sich abspalten (**from** von)

demerger /diː'mɜːdʒə(r)/ *n.* Defusionierung, *die;* Demerger, *der* (fachspr.); *attrib.* **~ plan/project** Demergerplan, *der*/-projekt, *das*

demerit /diː'merɪt/ *n.* 1) Schwäche, *die* 2) (quality deserving blame) [Charakter]fehler, *der;* (action) Fehlverhalten, *das* 3) (Amer.: mark) Strafpunkt, *der*

demesne /dɪ'miːn, dɪ'meɪn/ *n.* (land attached to mansion etc.) Grundstück des Landsitzes

demi- /'demɪ/ *pref.* Halb-

'demigod *n.* Halbgott, *der*

demijohn /'demɪdʒɒn/ *n.* Demijohn, *der* (fachspr.); Korbflasche, *die*

demilitarisation, demilitarise ▸ **demilitariz-**

demilitarization /diːmɪlɪtəraɪ'zeɪʃn/ *n.* Entmilitarisierung, *die*

demilitarize /diː'mɪlɪtəraɪz/ *v.t.* entmilitarisieren

demi-monde /'demɪmɔ̃d/ *n.* Demimonde, *die* (geh.); Halbwelt, *die*

demise /dɪ'maɪz/ *n.* (death) Ableben, *das* (geh.); (fig.) Verschwinden, *das;* (of firm, party, creed, etc.) Untergang, *der*

demisemiquaver /demɪ'semɪkweɪvə(r), 'demɪsemɪkweɪvə(r)/ *n.* (Brit. Mus.) Zweiunddreißigstelnote, *die*

demist /diː'mɪst/ *v.t.* (Brit.) trockenblasen; (with cloth etc.) trockenreiben

demister /diː'mɪstə(r)/ *n.* (Brit.) Defroster, *der;* Gebläse, *das*

demo /'deməʊ/ *n., pl.* **~s** (coll.) Demo, *die* (ugs.)

demob /diː'mɒb/ (Brit. coll.)

A *v.t.*, **-bb-** aus dem Kriegsdienst entlassen

B *n.* Entlassung aus dem Kriegsdienst

demobilisation, demobilise ▸ **demobiliz-**

demobilization /diːməʊbɪlaɪ'zeɪʃn/ *n.* Demobilisation, *die;* (of soldier) Entlassung aus dem Kriegsdienst

demobilize /diː'məʊbɪlaɪz/ *v.t.* demobilisieren ‹*Armee, Kriegsschiff*›; aus dem Kriegsdienst entlassen ‹*Soldat*›

democracy /dɪ'mɒkrəsɪ/ *n.* Demokratie, *die*

democrat /'deməkræt/ *n.* 1) (advocate of democracy) Demokrat, *der*/Demokratin, *die* 2) **D~** (Amer. Polit.) Demokrat, *der*/Demokratin, *die*

democratic /demə'krætɪk/ *adj.* 1) demokratisch 2) (Amer. Polit.) **D~ Party** Demokratische Partei

> **Democratic Party**
>
> Neben der **Republican Party** eine der zwei großen politischen Parteien in den USA. Die demokratische Partei gilt als die liberalere, besonders in Fragen der Gesellschaftspolitik. Aus diesem Grund erhält sie viel Unterstützung aus den Reihen von Minderheitengruppierungen und Gewerkschaften.

democratically /demə'krætɪkəlɪ/ *adv.* demokratisch

democratize /dɪ'mɒkrətaɪz/ *v.t.* demokratisieren

demographic /diːmə'græfɪk, demə'græfɪk/, **demographical** /diːmə'græfɪkl, demə'græfɪkl/ *adj.* demographisch

demography /dɪ'mɒgrəfɪ/ *n., no pl.* Demographie, *die*

demolish /dɪ'mɒlɪʃ/ *v.t.* 1) (pull down) abreißen; (break to pieces) zerstören; demolieren; schleifen, niederreißen ‹*Festungsanlagen*›; **~ by bombing** zerbomben 2) (overthrow) auflösen ‹*Institution*›; abschaffen ‹*System, Privilegien*›; widerlegen, umstoßen ‹*Theorie*›; entkräften ‹*Einwand*›; zerstören ‹*Legende, Mythos*› 3) (joc.: eat up) verschlingen

demolition /demə'lɪʃn, diːmə'lɪʃn/ *n.* 1) ▸ **demolish 1:** Abriss, *der;* Zerstörung, *die;* Demolierung, *die;* Schleifung, *die;* **~ contractors** Abbruchunternehmen, *das;* **due for ~:** abbruchreif; **~ work** Abbrucharbeit, *die* 2) ▸ **demolish 2:** Auflösung, *die;* Abschaffung, *die;* Widerlegung, *die;* Entkräftung, *die;* Zerstörung, *die*

demon /'diːmən/ *n.* 1) Dämon, *der* 2) (person, animal) Teufel, *der;* **~ bowler** (Cricket) sehr schneller Werfer; **he is a ~ for work** er arbeitet wie ein Besessener

demonetize (**demonetise**) /diː'mʌnɪtaɪz/ *v.t.* (Finance) demonetisieren (Bankw.); aus dem Umlauf ziehen

demoniac /dɪ'məʊnɪæk/

A *adj.* dämonisch; (possessed) besessen

B *n.* Besessene, *der/die*

demoniacal /diːmə'naɪəkl, demə'naɪəkl/ *adj.* dämonisch

demonic /diː'mɒnɪk/ ▸ **demoniac A**

demonize /'diːmənaɪz/ *v.t.* dämonisieren

demonstrability /demənstrə'bɪlɪtɪ, dɪmɒnstrə'bɪlɪtɪ/ *n., no pl.* Beweisbarkeit, *die*

demonstrable /'demənstrəbl, dɪ'mɒnstrəbl/ *adj.* beweisbar; nachweislich ‹*Schaden*›; **it is ~ that ...:** man kann beweisen, dass ...; es lässt sich nachweisen, dass ...

demonstrably /'demənstrəblɪ, dɪ'mɒnstrəblɪ/ *adv.* nachweislich

demonstrate /'demənstreɪt/

A *v.t.* 1) (by examples, experiments, etc.) zeigen; demonstrieren; (show, explain) vorführen ‹*Vorrichtung, Gerät*› 2) (be proof of) zeigen; beweisen 3) (logically prove the truth of) beweisen; nachweisen 4) (prove the existence of) zeigen ‹*Gefühl, Bedürfnis, Gutwilligkeit*›

B *v.i.* 1) (make, take part in, a meeting or procession) demonstrieren 2) (give a demonstration) **~ on sth./sb.** etw./jmdn. als Demonstrationsobjekt benutzen

demonstration /demən'streɪʃn/ *n.* 1) (as way of teaching) Demonstration, *die;* praktische Vorführung; **cookery ~s** Anschauungsunterricht im Kochen 2) (showing of appliances etc.) Vorführung, *die;* **give sb. a ~ of sth.** jmdm. etw. vorführen 3) (meeting, procession) Demonstration, *die* 4) (exhibition of feeling etc.) Ausdruck, *der;* **make a ~ of sth.** etw. zeigen 5) (proof) Beweis, *der*

demonstrative /dɪ'mɒnstrətɪv/ *adj.* 1) (with open expression) offen; unverhohlen ‹*Freude*› 2) (serving to point out or to exhibit) anschaulich 3) (logically conclusive) schlüssig ‹*Beweis, Argument*› 4) (Ling.) Demonstrativ-; hinweisend

demonstrator /'demənstreɪtə(r)/ *n.* 1) (in a meeting or procession) Demonstrant, *der*/Demonstrantin, *die* 2) (Commerc.) Vorführer, *der*/Vorführerin, *die*

demoralisation, demoralise ▸ **demoraliz-**

demoralization /dɪmɒrəlaɪ'zeɪʃn/ *n.* Demoralisierung, *die*

demoralize /dɪ'mɒrəlaɪz/ *v.t.* demoralisieren

demote /diː'məʊt/ *v.t.* degradieren (**to** zu); zurückstufen ‹*Schüler*›

demotic /dɪ'mɒtɪk/ *adj.* 1) (popular) volkstümlich 2) **~ Greek** Demotike, *die*

demotion /diː'məʊʃn/ *n.* Degradierung, *die* (**to** zu); (Sch.) Zurückstufung, *die*

demotivate /diː'məʊtɪveɪt/ *v.t.* demotivieren

demur /dɪ'mɜː(r)/ *v.i.*, **-rr-** Einwände erheben; **~ to sth.** gegen etw. Einwände erheben; **~ at doing sth.** Einwände dagegen erheben, etw. zu tun

demure /dɪ'mjʊə(r)/ *adj.* 1) (affectedly quiet and serious) betont zurückhaltend 2) (sober) nüchtern; (grave, composed) ernst; gesetzt ‹*Benehmen*› 3) (decorous) sittsam (veralt.); gesittet ‹*Rede*›

demurely /dɪ'mjʊəlɪ/ *adv.* zurückhaltend; **~ dressed** sittsam (veralt.) gekleidet

demystify /diː'mɪstɪfaɪ/ *v.t.* entmystifizieren

demythologize (**demythologise**) /diːmɪ'θɒlədʒaɪz/ *v.t.* entmythologisieren

den /den/ *n.* 1) (of wild beast) Höhle, *die;* **fox's ~:** Fuchsbau, *der;* **Daniel in the lions' ~** (Bibl.) Daniel in der Löwengrube 2) (resort of criminals etc.) **~ of thieves, thieves' ~:** Diebeshöhle, *die;* Diebesnest, *das;* **~ of vice** *or* **iniquity** Lasterhöhle, *die* (ugs. abwertend); **robbers' ~:** Räuberhöhle, *die* (veralt.) 3) (small room) Bude, *die* (ugs.)

denationalisation, denationalise ▸ **denationaliz-**

denationalization /diːnæʃənəlaɪ'zeɪʃn/ *n., no pl.* Privatisierung, *die*

denationalize /diː'næʃənəlaɪz/ *v.t.* privatisieren

denaturalize (**denaturalise**) /diː'nætʃərəlaɪz/ *v.t.* 1) (make unnatural) denaturieren; (make unfit for drinking etc.) denaturieren (Chemie, Physik); ungenießbar machen; vergällen (Chemie) ‹*Alkohol*›; **~d** denaturiert (Chemie, Physik); ungenießbar 2) (deprive of citizenship) denaturalisieren

denature /diː'neɪtʃə(r)/ *v.t.* denaturieren

denazification /diːnɑːtsɪfɪ'keɪʃn/ *n.* Entnazifizierung, *die*

denazify /diː'nɑːtsɪfaɪ/ *v.t.* entnazifizieren

dendrochronology /dendrəʊkrə'nɒlədʒɪ/ *n.* Dendrochronologie, *die;* Jahresringforschung, *die*

deniable /dɪ'naɪəbl/ *adj.* bestreitbar; (refutable) widerlegbar

denial /dɪ'naɪəl/ *n.* 1) (refusal) Verweigerung, *die;* (of request, wish) Ablehnung, *die* 2) (contradiction) Leugnen, *das;* **an official ~:** ein offizielles Dementi; **~ of [the existence of] God** Gottesleugnung, *die* 3) (disavowal of person) Verleugnung, *die* 4) **be in ~:** die Augen vor der Wahrheit schließen

denial of 'service attack *n.* (Computing) Dienstverweigerungsangriff, *der*

denier /'denjə(r)/ *n.* Denier, *das* (Textilw.); **20 ~ stockings** 20-den-Strümpfe

denigrate /'denɪgreɪt/ *v.t.* verunglimpfen; **~ sb.'s character** jmdn. verunglimpfen *od.* (ugs.) schlecht machen

denigration /denɪ'greɪʃn/ *n.* Verunglimpfung, *die*

denigratory /'denɪgreɪtərɪ/ *adj.* verunglimpfend

denim /'denɪm/ *n.* 1) (fabric) Denim (Wz), *der;* Jeansstoff, *der;* **~ jacket** Jeansjacke, *die* 2) *in pl.* (garment) Bluejeans *Pl.;* (for workman) Arbeitsanzug, *der*/-hose, *die*

denizen /'denɪzən/ *n.* (inhabitant, occupant) Bewohner, *der*/Bewohnerin, *die*

Denmark /'denmɑːk/ *pr. n.* Dänemark (*das*)

denominate /dɪ'nɒmɪneɪt/ *v.t.* bezeichnen

denomination /dɪnɒmɪ'neɪʃn/ *n.* 1) (class of units) Einheit, *die;* **coins/paper money of the smallest ~:** Münzen/Papiergeld mit dem geringsten Nennwert 2) (Relig.) Konfession, *die* 3) (name, designation) Bezeichnung, *die* 4) (class, kind) Art, *die*

denominational /dɪnɒmɪˈneɪʃənl/ *adj.* (Relig.) konfessionell; **~ school** Konfessions- *od.* Bekenntnisschule, *die*

denominator /dɪˈnɒmɪneɪtə(r)/ *n.* (Math.) Nenner, *der; see also* **common denominator**

denotation /di:nəˈteɪʃn/ *n.* **1** (marking) Kennzeichnung, *die* **2** (sign, indication) Zeichen, *das* **3** (designation) Bezeichnung, *die* **4** (meaning) Bedeutung, *die;* (esp. Ling.) Denotation, *die*

denote /dɪˈnəʊt/ *v.t.* **1** (indicate) hindeuten auf (+ *Akk.*); **~ that …:** darauf hindeuten, dass … **2** (designate) bedeuten; (by specified symbol) bezeichnen **3** (signify) symbolisieren; bedeuten

dénouement, denouement /deɪˈnu:mɑ̃/ *n.* Ausgang, *der;* Auflösung, *die*

denounce /dɪˈnaʊns/ *v.t.* **1** (inform against) denunzieren (abwertend); (accuse publicly) beschuldigen; (openly attack) anprangern; **~ sb. to sb.** jmdn. bei jmdm. denunzieren; **~ sb. as a spy** jmdn. beschuldigen, ein Spion zu sein **2** (terminate) [auf]kündigen

denouncement /dɪˈnaʊnsmənt/ ▸ **denunciation**

dense /dens/ *adj.* **1** (compacted in substance) dicht; massiv ‹*Körper*›; (Photog.) undurchlässig ‹*Negativ*› **2** (crowded together) dicht gedrängt; eng ‹*Schrift*›; **the population is very ~:** die Bevölkerungsdichte ist sehr hoch **3** (stupid) dumm; **he's pretty ~:** er ist ziemlich schwer von Begriff

densely /ˈdenslɪ/ *adv.* dicht; **~ packed** dicht gedrängt

denseness /ˈdensnɪs/ *n., no pl.* **1** Dichte, *die* **2** (stupidity) Begriffsstutzigkeit, *die*

density /ˈdensɪtɪ/ *n.* **1** (also Phys.) Dichte, *die;* **population ~:** Bevölkerungsdichte, *die* **2** (Photog.) Schwärzung, *die;* Dichte, *die*

dent /dent/

A *n.* Beule, *die;* Delle, *die* (landsch.); (fig. coll.) Loch, *das;* **make a ~ in production/in sb.'s savings** ein Loch in die Produktion/in jmds. Ersparnisse reißen; **make a bit of a ~ in sb.'s pride** jmds. Stolz leicht anknacksen (ugs.)

B *v.t.* einbeulen; verbeulen; eindellen ‹*Holz, Tisch*› (ugs.); (fig.) anknacksen (ugs.); **he ~ed his car in a collision** sein Auto wurde bei einem Zusammenstoß verbeult *od.* eingebeult

dental /ˈdentl/

A *adj.* **1** Zahn-; **~ care** Zahnpflege, *die;* **~ treatment** zahnärztliche Behandlung; **~ training** Ausbildung in der Zahnheilkunde **2** (Phonet.) Dental-; **~ consonant** ▸ **B**

B *n.* (Phonet.) Dental, *der;* Zahnlaut, *der*

dental: ~ assistant *n.* ▸ℹ **p. 1260** Zahnarzthelfer, *der*/-helferin, *die;* **~ floss** *n.* Zahnseide, *die;* **~ hygienist** *n.* ▸ℹ **p. 1260** Zahnhygieniker, *der*/-hygienikerin, *die;* **~ mechanic** *n.* ▸ℹ **p. 1260** Zahntechniker, *der*/-technikerin, *die;* **~ practice** *n.* Zahnarztpraxis, *die;* **~ practitioner** *n.* ▸ℹ **p. 1260** Zahnarzt, *der*/-ärztin, *die;* **~ receptionist** *n.* ▸ℹ **p. 1260** Sprechstundenhilfe, *die;* **~ surgeon** *n.* ▸ℹ **p. 1260** Zahnarzt, *der*/-ärztin, *die;* **~ technician** *n.* ▸ℹ **p. 1260** Zahntechniker, *der*/-technikerin, *die*

dentate /ˈdenteɪt/ *adj.* (Bot., Zool.) gezähnt

dentine /ˈdenti:n/ (*Amer.:* **dentin** /ˈdentɪn/) *n.* (Med.) Dentin, *das* (fachspr.); Zahnbein, *das*

dentist /ˈdentɪst/ *n.* ▸ℹ **p. 1260** Zahnarzt, *der*/-ärztin, *die;* **at the ~['s]** beim Zahnarzt; **~'s chair** Zahnarztstuhl, *der*

dentistry /ˈdentɪstrɪ/ *n., no pl.* Zahnheilkunde, *die*

denture /ˈdentʃə(r)/ *n.* **~[s]** Zahnprothese, *die;* [künstliches] Gebiss; **partial ~:** Teilprothese, *die*

denuclearize (denuclearise) /di:ˈnju:klɪəraɪz/ *v.t.* atomwaffenfrei machen

denudation /di:nju:ˈdeɪʃn/ *n.* (of valley, slope) Abholzung, *die;* (of tree) Entlaubung, *die;* (fig.) Entzug, *der;* (Geol.) Denudation, *die* (fachspr.); Abtragung, *die*

denude /dɪˈnju:d/ *v.t.* **1** abholzen, kahl schlagen ‹*Tal, Hang*›; **~ a tree [of its leaves]** einen Baum entlauben; **~d of trees** abgeholzt; **~ sb. of sth.** (fig.) jmdm. etw. entziehen **2** (Geol.) erodieren (fachspr.)

denunciation /dɪnʌnsɪˈeɪʃn/ *n.* **1** Denunziation, *die* (abwertend); (public accusation) Beschuldigung, *die;* (act of attacking) Anprangerung, *die* **2** (of treaty etc.) [Auf]kündigung, *die*

deny /dɪˈnaɪ/ *v.t.* **1** (declare untrue) bestreiten; zurückweisen ‹*Beschuldigung*›; **he denied knowing it** er bestritt, es zu wissen; **it cannot be denied** *or* **there is no ~ing the fact that …:** es lässt sich nicht bestreiten *od.* leugnen, dass …; **he denied this to be the case** er bestritt, dass dies der Fall sei; **~ all knowledge of sth.** bestreiten, irgendetwas von etw. zu wissen **2** (refuse) verweigern; **~ sb. sth.** jmdm. etw. verweigern; **he can't ~ her anything** er kann ihr nichts abschlagen; **recognition was denied [to] him** die Anerkennung blieb ihm versagt; **~ sb.'s request** jmdm. seine Bitte abschlagen **3** (disavow, repudiate; refuse access to) verleugnen; ablehnen ‹*Verantwortung*› **4** (Relig.) **~ oneself** *or* **the flesh** sich kasteien

deodorant /di:ˈəʊdərənt/

A *adj.* desodorierend; **~ spray** Deo[dorant]spray, *der od. das*

B *n.* Deodorant, *das*

deodorisation, deodorise ▸ **deodoriz-**

deodorization /di:əʊdəraɪˈzeɪʃn/ *n.* Desodorierung, *die*

deodorize /di:ˈəʊdəraɪz/ *v.t.* desodorieren

deoxygenate /di:ˈɒksɪdʒəneɪt/ *v.t.* de[s]oxygenieren

deoxyribonucleic acid /di:ɒksɪraɪbəʊnju:kleɪɪk ˈæsɪd/ *n., no pl.* Desoxyribonukleinsäure, *die*

dep. *abbr.* **1** **= departs** (Railw.) Abf.; (Aeronaut.) Abfl. **2** **= deputy** stellv.

depart /dɪˈpɑ:t/

A *v.i.* **1** (go away, take one's leave) weggehen; fortgehen; sich entfernen (geh.) **2** (set out, start, leave) abfahren; ‹*Schiff auch:*› auslaufen, ablegen; ‹*Flugzeug:*› abfliegen; (on one's journey) abreisen; **ready to ~:** abfahrbereit **3** (fig.: deviate) **~ from sth.** von etw. abweichen **4** (literary: die) **~ from this life** aus dem Leben *od.* von hinnen scheiden (geh.); **he has ~ed from us** er ist von uns gegangen (verhüll.)

B *v.t.* (literary) **~ this life/world** aus dem Leben/aus dieser Welt scheiden (geh.)

departed /dɪˈpɑ:tɪd/

A *adj.* **1** (bygone) vergangen **2** (deceased) dahingeschieden (geh. verhüll.)

B *n.* **the ~:** der/die Dahingeschiedene; die Dahingeschiedenen (geh. verhüll.)

department /dɪˈpɑ:tmənt/ *n.* **1** (of municipal administration) Amt, *das;* (of State administration) Ministerium, *das;* (of university) Seminar, *das;* (of shop) Abteilung, *die;* **the shipping ~/personnel ~:** die Versand-/Personalabteilung; **D~ of Employment/Education** Arbeits-/Erziehungsministerium, *das;* **D~ for Education and Skills** (Brit.) Ministerium für Bildung und Qualifikationserwerb; **D~ of Trade and Industry** (Brit.) Ministerium für Handel und Industrie; ≈ Wirtschaftsministerium, *das;* **D~ for Work and Pensions** (Brit.) Ministerium für Arbeit und Renten; **English ~:** anglistisches *od.* englisches Seminar; **history ~:** Seminar *od.* Institut für Geschichte; **~ of pathology** Pathologie, *die;* pathologisches Institut; (in hospital) pathologische Abteilung **2** (administrative district in France) Departement, *das* **3** (fig.: area of activity) Ressort, *das;* **it's not my ~:** da kenne ich mich nicht aus; (not my responsibility) dafür bin ich nicht zuständig

departmental /di:pɑ:tˈmentl/ *adj.* **1** ▸ **department 1, 2:** Amts-; Ministerial-; Seminar-; Abteilungs-; Departement- **2** **be ~:** die Abteilung betreffen

departmentally /di:pɑ:tˈmentəlɪ/ *adv.* ▸ **departmental 1:** auf Amts-/Ministerial-/Seminar-/Abteilungsebene

deˈpartment store *n.* Kaufhaus, *das*

departure /dɪˈpɑ:tʃə(r)/ *n.* **1** (going away) Abreise, *die;* **take one's ~:** sich entfernen (geh.); **after sb.'s ~:** nachdem jmd. weggegangen war/ist; **make a hasty ~:** sich rasch entfernen **2** (deviation) **~ from sth.** Abweichen von etw. **3** (of train, bus, ship) Abfahrt, *die;* (of aircraft) Abflug, *der;* **two ~s a day** täglich zwei Abfahrtszeiten **4** (of action or thought) Ansatz, *der;* **point of ~:** Ansatzpunkt, *der;* **this product is a new ~ for us** mit diesem Produkt schlagen wir einen neuen Weg ein

departure: ~ gate *n.* Flugsteig, *der;* **~ lounge** *n.* Abflughalle, *die;* **~ platform** *n.* [Abfahrt]gleis, *das;* **~ time** *n.* (of train, bus) Abfahrtzeit, *die;* (of aircraft) Abflugzeit, *die*

depend /dɪˈpend/ *v.i.* **1** **~ [up]on** abhängen von; **it [all] ~s on whether/what/how …:** das hängt [ganz] davon ab *od.* kommt ganz darauf an, ob/was/wie …; **that ~s** es kommt darauf an; **~ing on how …:** je nachdem, wie … **2** (rely, trust) **~ [up]on** sich verlassen auf (+ *Akk.*); (have to rely on) angewiesen sein auf (+ *Akk.*); **~ on sb. for help** sich auf jmds. Hilfe verlassen/auf jmds. Hilfe angewiesen sein

dependability /dɪpendəˈbɪlɪtɪ/ *n., no pl.* Verlässlichkeit, *die;* Zuverlässigkeit, *die*

dependable /dɪˈpendəbl/ *adj.* verlässlich; zuverlässig

dependably /dɪˈpendəblɪ/ *adv.* zuverlässig

dependant /dɪˈpendənt/ *n.* **1** Abhängige, *der/die;* **~s** (Taxation) abhängige Angehörige **2** (servant) Bedienstete, *der/die*

dependence /dɪˈpendəns/ *n.* **1** Abhängigkeit, *die;* **~ [up]on sb./sth.** Abhängigkeit von jmdm./etw. **2** (reliance) **put** *or* **place ~ [up]on sb.** sich auf jmdn. verlassen

dependency /dɪˈpendənsɪ/ *n.* **1** (country) Territorium, *das* **2** (condition of being dependent) Abhängigkeit, *die* (**on** von); **~ culture** (Sociol.) Kultur der Abhängigkeit [vom Staat]

dependent /dɪˈpendənt/

A *n.* ▸ **dependant**

B *adj.* **1** (also Ling., Math.) abhängig; **be ~ on sth.** von etw. abhängen *od.* abhängig sein **2** **be ~ on** (be unable to do without) angewiesen sein auf (+ *Akk.*); abhängig sein von ‹*Droge, Ursache*›; **be ~ on heroin** heroinabhängig sein

depict /dɪˈpɪkt/ *v.t.* darstellen

depiction /dɪˈpɪkʃn/ *n.* Darstellung, *die*

depilate /ˈdepɪleɪt/ *v.t.* enthaaren; depilieren (Med.)

depilatory /dɪˈpɪlətərɪ/

A *adj.* Enthaarungs-

B *n.* Enthaarungsmittel, *das*

deplete /dɪˈpli:t/ *v.t.* **1** (reduce in number or amount) erheblich verringern; **the audience is ~d** die Zuschauerzahl hat sich deutlich verringert; **our stores are ~d** unser Vorrat ist zusammengeschrumpft; **air ~d of oxygen** Luft mit wenig Sauerstoff **2** (empty) entleeren; (exhaust) erschöpfen

depleted uˈranium *n., no pl.* abgereichertes Uran; *attrib.* **~ weapons** Waffen mit abgereichertem Uran

depletion /dɪˈpli:ʃn/ *n.* **1** Verringerung, *die* **2** (emptying) Entleerung, *die;* (exhausting) Erschöpfung, *die*

deplorable /dɪˈplɔ:rəbl/ *adj.* beklagenswert; erbärmlich ‹*Essen, Leistung*›

deplorably /dɪˈplɔ:rəblɪ/ *adv.* erbärmlich; **~ neglected** schändlich verwahrlost

deplore /dɪˈplɔ:(r)/ *v.t.* **1** (disapprove of) verurteilen **2** (bewail, regret) beklagen; **sth. is to be ~d** etw. ist beklagenswert

deploy /dɪˈplɔɪ/

A *v.t.* **1** (bring into effective action) einsetzen **2** (Mil.) einsetzen; (extend) ausschwärmen lassen

B *v.i.* (Mil.) eingesetzt werden

deployment /dɪˈplɔɪmənt/ *n.* Einsatz, *der*

deponent /dɪˈpəʊnənt/

A *adj.* (Ling.) **~ verb** Deponens, *das*

B *n.* **1** (Law) ≈ Zeuge, *der*/Zeugin, *die* **2** (Ling.) Deponens, *das*

depopulate /di:ˈpɒpjʊleɪt/ *v.t.* entvölkern

depopulation /di:pɒpjʊˈleɪʃn/ *n.* Entvölkerung, *die*

deport /dɪˈpɔ:t/

A *v.t.* deportieren; (from country) ausweisen

B v. refl. sich benehmen

deportation /di:pɔ:ˈteɪʃn/ n. Deportation, *die;* (from country) Ausweisung, *die*

deporˈtation order n. Abschiebungsanordnung, *die*

deportee /di:pɔ:ˈti:/ n. Deportierte, *der/die;* (from country) Ausgewiesene, *der/die*

deportment /dɪˈpɔ:tmənt/ n. Benehmen, *das*

depose /dɪˈpəʊz/

A v.t. absetzen; **~ sb. from an office** jmdn. eines Amtes entheben

B v.i. & t. (Law) [unter Eid] aussagen

deposit /dɪˈpɒzɪt/

A n. **1** (in bank) Depot, *das;* (credit) Guthaben, *das;* (Brit.: at interest) Sparguthaben, *das;* **make a ~:** etwas einzahlen; **have £70 on ~:** ein [Spar]guthaben von 70 Pfund haben **2** (payment as pledge) Kaution, *die;* (first instalment) Anzahlung, *die;* **pay** or **make** or **leave a ~:** eine Kaution zahlen *od.* hinterlegen/eine Anzahlung leisten; **there is a five pence ~ on the bottle** auf der Flasche sind fünf Pence Pfand; **put down a ~ on sth.** eine Anzahlung für etw. leisten; **lose one's ~** (Polit.) die Kaution verlieren **3** (for safe keeping) anvertrautes Gut **4** (natural accumulation) (of sand, mud, lime, etc.; also Med.) Ablagerung, *die;* (of ore, coal, oil) Lagerstätte, *die;* (in glass, bottle) Bodensatz, *der*

B v.t. **1** (lay down in a place) ablegen; abstellen ‹*etw. Senkrechtes, auch Tablett, Teller usw.*›; absetzen ‹*Mitfahrer*› **2** (leave lying) ‹*Wasser usw.:*› ablagern; **be ~ed** sich ablagern; **~ a layer of sand/dust over sth.** etw. mit einer Schicht Sand/Staub überziehen **3** (in bank) deponieren, [auf ein Konto] einzahlen ‹*Geld*›; (Brit.: at interest) [auf ein Sparkonto] einzahlen; **~ money in a bank** Geld bei einer Bank einzahlen **4** (pay as pledge) anzahlen

deˈposit account n. (Brit.) Sparkonto, *das*

deposition /depəˈzɪʃn, di:pəˈzɪʃn/ n. **1** (depositing) (of papers, money, etc.) Hinterlegung, *die* (**with** bei); (of mud, coal, ore, etc.) Ablagerung, *die* **2** (from office) Absetzung, *die* **3** (Law: giving of evidence, allegation) [eidliche Zeugen]aussage

depositor /dɪˈpɒzɪtə(r)/ n. (Banking) Einleger, *der*/Einlegerin, *die*

depository /dɪˈpɒzɪtərɪ/ n. (storehouse) Lagerhaus, *das;* (place for safe keeping) Aufbewahrungsort, *der;* (fig.) Fundgrube, *die*

depot /ˈdepəʊ/ n. **1** Depot, *das* **2** (storehouse) Lager, *das;* **grain ~:** Getreidespeicher, *der* **3** **[bus] ~** (Brit.) Depot, *das;* Omnibusgarage, *die;* (Amer.: bus station) Omnibusbahnhof, *der;* (Amer.: railway station) Bahnhof, *der*

deprave /dɪˈpreɪv/ v.t. verderben

depraved /dɪˈpreɪvd/ adj. verdorben; lasterhaft ‹*Gewohnheit*›

depravity /dɪˈprævɪtɪ/ n. Lasterhaftigkeit, *die;* Verderbtheit, *die* (geh.); Verdorbenheit, *die*

deprecate /ˈdeprɪkeɪt/ v.t. **1** (disapprove of) missbilligen **2** (plead against) abzuwenden suchen

deprecation /deprɪˈkeɪʃn/ n. Missbilligung, *die*

deprecatory /deprɪˈkeɪtərɪ/ adj. **1** (disapproving) missbilligend **2** (apologetic, appeasing) beschwichtigend

depreciate /dɪˈpri:ʃɪeɪt, dɪˈpri:sɪeɪt/

A v.t. **1** (diminish in value) abwerten; herabsetzen; abwerten ‹*Währung*› **2** (disparage) herabsetzen

B v.i. an Wert verlieren

depreciation /dɪpri:ʃɪˈeɪʃn, dɪpri:sɪˈeɪʃn/ n. (of money, currency, property) Wertverlust, *der;* (of person) Herabsetzung, *die;* **allowance for ~:** Abschreibung, *die*

depreciatory /dɪˈpri:ʃətərɪ/ adj. verächtlich; abfällig

depredation /deprɪˈdeɪʃn/ n. **1** Verwüstung, *die* **2** (ravages of disease etc.) verheerende Wirkung

depress /dɪˈpres/ v.t. **1** (deject) deprimieren **2** (push or pull down) herunterdrücken; (cause to move to a lower level) absenken **3** (reduce activity of) unterdrücken; sich nicht entfalten lassen ‹*Handel, Wirtschaftswachstum*›

depressant /dɪˈpresənt/

A adj. (Med.) beruhigend; sedativ (fachspr.)

B n. **1** (influence) Hemmnis, *das* **2** (Med.) Beruhigungsmittel, *das;* Sedativ[um], *das* (fachspr.)

depressed /dɪˈprest/ adj. deprimiert ‹*Person, Stimmung*›; abgesenkt ‹*Gelände, Ebene*›; geschwächt ‹*Industrie*›; **~ area** Notstandsgebiet, *das*

depressing /dɪˈpresɪŋ/ adj. deprimierend

depressingly /dɪˈpresɪŋlɪ/ adv. deprimierend

depression /dɪˈpreʃn/ n. **1** Depression, *die* **2** (sunk place) Vertiefung, *die* **3** (Meteorol.) Tief[druckgebiet], *das;* Depression, *die* (fachspr.) **4** (reduction in vigour, vitality) Schwächung, *die* **5** (Econ.) **the D~:** die Weltwirtschaftskrise; **economic ~:** Wirtschaftskrise, *die;* Depression, *die* **6** (lowering, sinking) Senkung, *die;* (pressing down) Herunterdrücken, *das*

depressive /dɪˈpresɪv/

A adj. **1** (tending to depress) bedrückend; deprimierend **2** (Psych.) depressiv

B n. (Psych.) Depressive, *der/die*

depressurize (**depressurise**) /di:ˈpreʃəraɪz/ v.t. dekomprimieren

deprival /dɪˈpraɪvl/ ▸**deprivation 1**

deprivation /deprɪˈveɪʃn, di:praɪˈveɪʃn/ n. **1** (being deprived) Entzug, *der;* (of one's rights, liberties, or title) Aberkennung, *die* **2** (loss of desired thing) Entbehrung, *die;* **that is a great ~:** das ist ein großer Verlust; **oxygen ~:** Sauerstoffmangel, *der*

deprive /dɪˈpraɪv/ v.t. **1** (strip, bereave) **~ sb. of sth.** jmdm. etw. nehmen; (debar from having) jmdm. etw. vorenthalten; **trees that ~ a house of light** Bäume, die einem Haus das Licht nehmen; **the village was ~d of electricity** das Dorf war ohne Stromversorgung; **he will be ~d of his right to vote** ihm wird das Wahlrecht entzogen werden; **~ sb. of citizenship** jmdm. die Staatsbürgerschaft aberkennen; **~ sb. of his command** jmdm. das Kommando entziehen; **am I depriving you of it?** brauchen Sie das gerade?; **be ~d of one's car/books** auf sein Auto/seine Bücher verzichten müssen; **be ~d of light** nicht genug Licht haben; **~ sb. of a pleasure** jmdm. ein Vergnügen vorenthalten; jmdn. eines Vergnügens berauben (geh.) **2** (depose) absetzen **3** (prevent from having normal life) benachteiligen

deprived /dɪˈpraɪvd/ adj. benachteiligt ‹*Kind, Familie usw.*›

deprogramme (**deprogram**) /di:ˈprəʊgræm/ v.t. entprogrammieren

Dept. abbr. = **Department** Amt/Min./Seminar/Abt.

depth /depθ/ n. **1** ▸ⓘ **p. 1208** (lit. or fig.) Tiefe, *die;* **at a ~ of 3 metres** in einer Tiefe von 3 Metern; **3 feet in ~:** 3 Fuß tief; **what is the ~ of the pond?** wie tief ist der Teich?; **~ of thought/meaning** Gedankentiefe, *die*/Bedeutungsgehalt, *der;* **from/in the ~s of the forest/ocean** aus/in der Tiefe des Waldes/des Ozeans; **from the ~s of his soul** aus tiefster Seele; **sink** or **fall into the ~s of oblivion/despair** völlig in Vergessenheit/in tiefste Verzweiflung geraten; **sink** or **fall to such ~s that ...** (fig.) so tief sinken, dass ...; **in the ~s of winter** im tiefen Winter; **great ~ of feeling** große Gefühls- *od.* Ausdruckstiefe **2** (mental profundity) geistige Tiefe **3** **in ~:** gründlich, intensiv ‹*studieren*›; **an in-~ study/analysis** *etc.* eine gründliche Untersuchung/Analyse *usw.;* **defence in ~:** tief gestaffelte Verteidigung **4** **be out of one's ~:** nicht mehr stehen können; keinen Grund mehr unter den Füßen haben; (fig.) ins Schwimmen kommen (ugs.); überfordert sein; **go/get out of one's ~** (lit. or fig.) den Grund unter den Füßen verlieren; **don't go out of your ~:** geh nicht zu tief hinein

depth: ~ bomb, ~ charge ns. Wasserbombe, *die;* **~-charge** v.t. mit Wasserbomben angreifen; **~ of field** n. (Photog.) Schärfentiefe, *die;* **~ psychology** n. Tiefenpsychologie, *die*

deputation /depjʊˈteɪʃn/ n. Abordnung, *die;* Delegation, *die*

depute

A /dɪˈpju:t/ v.t. **1** (commit task or authority to) **~ sb. to do sth.** jmdn. beauftragen, etw. zu tun; **~ sth. to sb.** etw. auf jmdn. übertragen **2** (appoint as deputy) **~ sb. to do sth.** jmdn. [als Stellvertreter] damit betrauen, etw. zu tun

B /ˈdepju:t/ n. (Scot.: deputy) Stellvertreter, *der*/-vertreterin, *die*

deputize (**deputise**) /ˈdepjʊtaɪz/ v.i. als Stellvertreter einspringen; **~ for sb.** jmdn. vertreten

deputy /ˈdepjʊtɪ/ n. **1** attrib. stellvertretend; **~ sheriff** ▸ⓘ **p. 1260** (Amer.) Hilfssheriff, *der* **2** (person appointed to act for another) [Stell]vertreter, *der*/-vertreterin, *die;* **act as ~ for sb.** jmdn. vertreten **3** (parliamentary representative) Abgeordnete, *der/die;* Deputierte, *der/die;* **Chamber of Deputies** Abgeordnetenkammer, *die* **4** (Brit.: coalmine overseer) Steiger, *der*

derail /dɪˈreɪl, di:ˈreɪl/ v.t. usu. in pass. zum Entgleisen bringen; **be ~ed** entgleisen

derailleur /di:ˈreɪlə(r), di:ˈreɪljə(r)/ n. **~ [gear]** Kettenschaltung, *die*

derailment /dɪˈreɪlmənt, di:ˈreɪlmənt/ n. Entgleisung, *die;* **cause the ~ of sth.** etw. zum Entgleisen bringen

derange /dɪˈreɪndʒ/ v.t. **1** (throw into confusion, put out of order) durcheinander bringen; (make insane) geistig verwirren **2** (disturb, interrupt) stören

deranged /dɪˈreɪndʒd/ adj. **[mentally] ~:** geistesgestört

derangement /dɪˈreɪndʒmənt/ n. **1** Unordnung, *die;* **cause ~ of** durcheinander bringen **2** **[mental] ~:** Geistesgestörtheit, *die*

Derby /ˈdɑ:bɪ/ n. **1** (annual horse race at Epsom) Derby [in Epsom], *das;* (other race or contest) Derby, *das;* **~ Day** Tag des Derbys [in Epsom]; **local ~:** Lokalderby, *das* **2** **d~** (Amer.: bowler hat) Melone, *die*

derecognition /di:rekəgˈnɪʃn/ n., no pl. Entzug der Anerkennung

derecognize /di:ˈrekəgnaɪz/ v.t. die Anerkennung entziehen (+ *Dat.*)

deregulate /di:ˈregjʊleɪt/ v.t. deregulieren (fachspr.); dem freien Wettbewerb überlassen

deregulation /di:regjʊˈleɪʃn/ n. Deregulation, *die* (fachspr.); Deregulierung, *die* (fachspr.)

derelict /ˈderɪlɪkt/

A adj. **1** (abandoned) verlassen und verfallen; aufgegeben ‹*Schiff*› **2** (Amer.: negligent) nachlässig

B n. **1** (abandoned property) herrenloses Gut; (ship) aufgegebenes Schiff; (wreck) [treibendes] Wrack **2** (person) Ausgestoßene, *der/die*

dereliction /derɪˈlɪkʃn/ n. **1** (abandoning) Vernachlässigung, *die;* (state) verkommener Zustand; **the building is in a state of ~:** das Gebäude ist verkommen **2** (neglect) **~ of duty** Pflichtverletzung, *die*

derestrict /di:rɪˈstrɪkt/ v.t. [wieder] freigeben; **~ed road** Straße ohne Geschwindigkeitsbeschränkung

derestriction /di:rɪˈstrɪkʃn/ n. Freigabe, *die*

deride /dɪˈraɪd/ v.t. (treat with scorn) sich lustig machen über (+ *Akk.*); (laugh scornfully at) verlachen

de rigueur /də rɪˈgɜ:(r)/ pred. adj. de rigueur *nicht attr.* (veralt.); unerlässlich

derision /dɪˈrɪʒn/ n. Spott, *der;* **be an object of ~:** Zielscheibe des Spottes sein; **bring sb./sth. into ~:** jmdn./etw. zum Gespött *od.* lächerlich machen

derisive /dɪˈraɪsɪv/ adj. (ironical) spöttisch; (scoffing) verächtlich

derisively /dɪˈraɪsɪvlɪ/ adv. ▸**derisive**: spöttisch; verächtlich

derisory /dɪˈraɪsərɪ, dɪˈraɪzərɪ/ adj. **1** (ridiculously inadequate) lächerlich **2** (scoffing) verächtlich; (ironical) spöttisch

derivation /derɪˈveɪʃn/ n. **1** (obtaining from a source) Herleitung, *die* **2** (extraction, origin) Herkunft, *die;* (descent) Abstammung, *die* **3** (Ling.) Ableitung, *die;* Derivation, *die* (fachspr.); (origin) Ursprung, *der;* Herkunft, *die*

derivative /dɪˈrɪvətɪv/

A adj. abgeleitet; (lacking originality) nachahmend;

epigonal; (secondary) indirekt
B *n.* **1** Abkömmling, *der;* (word) Ableitung, *die;* Derivat[iv], *das* (Sprachw.); (chemical substance) Derivat, *das* **2** (Finance) **~s** Derivate *Pl.*, **~s market** Derivatenmarkt, *der;* **~s trader** Derivatenhändler, *der* **3** (Math.) Ableitung, *die*

derive /dɪˈraɪv/
A *v.t.* **1** (get, obtain, form) **~ sth. from sth.** etw. aus etw. gewinnen; **he ~s much of his earnings from freelance work** er bezieht einen großen Teil seines Einkommens aus freiberuflicher Tätigkeit; **the river ~s its name** *or* **the name of the river is ~d from a Greek god** der Name des Flusses geht auf eine griechische Gottheit zurück; **he ~s pleasure from his studies** er hat Freude an seinem Studium; **~ profit/advantage from sth.** aus etw. Nutzen/seinen Vorteil ziehen **2** (deduce) ableiten; herleiten **3** **~ one's origin/ancestry/pedigree from sth.** aus etw. stammen
B *v.i.* **~ from** beruhen auf (+ *Dat.*); **the word ~s from Latin** das Wort stammt *od.* kommt aus dem Lateinischen

dermatitis /dɜːməˈtaɪtɪs/ *n.* ▸**i** **p. 1231** (Med.) Hautentzündung, *die;* Dermatitis, *die* (fachspr.)

dermatologist /dɜːməˈtɒlədʒɪst/ *n.* ▸**i** **p. 1260** (Med.) Hautarzt, *der*/-ärztin, *die;* Dermatologe, *der*/Dermatologin, *die*

dermatology /dɜːməˈtɒlədʒɪ/ *n.* (Med.) Dermatologie, *die*

derogate /ˈderəgeɪt/ *v.i.* (formal) **~ from sth.** etw. schmälern

derogation /derəˈgeɪʃn/ *n.* (formal) Schmälerung, *die* (**from** *Gen.*)

derogatory /dɪˈrɒgətərɪ/ *adj.* **1** (depreciatory) abfällig; abschätzig; **~ sense [of a word]** abwertende Bedeutung [eines Wortes] **2** (tending to detract) **be ~ to sth.** einer Sache (*Dat.*) abträglich sein; **be regarded as ~:** als etwas Ehrenrühriges angesehen werden

derrick /ˈderɪk/ *n.* **1** (for moving or hoisting) [Derrick]kran, *der* **2** (over oil well) Bohrturm, *der*

derring-do /derɪŋˈduː/ *n.* (literary) Wagemut, *der;* **a deed of ~:** eine wagemutige Tat

derv /dɜːv/ *n.* (Brit. Motor Veh.) Diesel[kraftstoff], *der*

dervish /ˈdɜːvɪʃ/ *n.* Derwisch, *der*

desalination /diːsælɪˈneɪʃn/ *n.* Entsalzung, *die*

descale /diːˈskeɪl/ *v.t.* entkalken

descant
A /ˈdeskænt/ *n.* **1** (Mus.) Diskant, *der* **2** (poet.: melody) Weise, *die;* Melodie, *die*
B /dɪˈskænt/ *v.i.* **1** (formal: talk lengthily) **~ upon sth.** sich über etw. (*Akk.*) verbreiten **2** (sing **~**) Diskant singen

ˈdescant recorder *n.* (Mus.) Sopranflöte, *die*

descend /dɪˈsend/
A *v.i.* **1** (go down) hinuntergehen/-steigen/-klettern/-fahren; (come down) herunterkommen; (sink) niedergehen (**on** auf + *Dat.*); **the lift ~ed** der Aufzug fuhr nach unten; **~ in the lift** mit dem Aufzug nach unten fahren; **~ into hell** zur Hölle hinabsteigen *od.* niederfahren; **~ on sb.** (fig.) über jmdn. hereinbrechen; **night ~ed upon the village** die Nacht senkte sich auf das Dorf herab **2** (slope downwards) abfallen; **the hill ~s into/towards the sea** der Hügel fällt zum Meer hin ab **3** (in quality, thought, etc.) herabsinken; **~ from the general to the particular** vom Allgemeinen zum Besonderen gehen *od.* kommen **4** (in pitch) fallen; sinken; tiefer werden; **~ to a low note** auf einen tiefen Ton hinuntergehen **5** (make sudden attack) **~ on sth.** über etw. (*Akk.*) herfallen; **~ on sb.** (lit., or fig.: arrive unexpectedly) jmdn. überfallen; **~ on a country** in ein Land einfallen **6** (fig.: lower oneself) **~ to sth.** sich zu etw. erniedrigen **7** (pass by inheritance) vererbt werden (**to** an + *Akk.*) **8** (derive) abstammen (**from** von); (have origin) zurückgehen (**from** auf + *Akk.*) **9** (go forward in time) weitergehen
B *v.t.* **1** (go/come down) hinunter- / heruntergehen /-steigen /-klettern /-fahren; hinab-/herabsteigen (geh.) **2** (go along) hinuntergehen/-fahren ‹*Straße*›

descendant /dɪˈsendənt/ *n.* Nachkomme, *der;* **be ~s/a ~ of** abstammen von

descended /dɪˈsendɪd/ *adj.* **be ~ from sb.** von jmdm. abstammen

descent /dɪˈsent/ *n.* **1** (going or coming down) (of person) Abstieg, *der;* (of parachute, plane, bird, avalanche) Niedergehen, *das;* **the ~ of the mountain took us a few hours** für den Abstieg vom Berg brauchten wir einige Stunden; **the D~ from the Cross** die Kreuzabnahme **2** (way) Abstieg, *der;* **the ~ leading to the river** der Weg hinunter zum Fluss **3** (slope) Abfall, *der;* **the road made a sharp ~ into the valley** die Straße fiel zum Tal hin steil ab; **the ~ was very steep** das Gefälle war sehr stark **4** (sudden attack) **the Danes made numerous ~s upon the English coast** die Dänen fielen mehrfach an der englischen Küste ein **5** (decline, fall) Abstieg, *der* **6** (lineage) Abstammung, *die;* Herkunft, *die;* **be of Russian/noble ~:** russischer/adliger Abstammung sein **7** (transmission by inheritance) Herkunft, *die;* **jazz traces its ~ from African music** der Jazz hat seine Ursprünge in afrikanischer Musik

describable /dɪˈskraɪbəbl/ *adj.* beschreibbar; **be ~:** zu beschreiben sein; **it's not ~ in words** es ist unbeschreiblich *od.* nicht mit Worten zu beschreiben

describe /dɪˈskraɪb/ *v.t.* **1** (set forth in words) beschreiben; schildern; (distinguish) bezeichnen; **it can't be ~d in words** es ist unbeschreiblich *od.* nicht mit Worten zu beschreiben; **~ [oneself] as ...:** [sich] als ... bezeichnen; **sth. can hardly be ~d as ...:** etw. ist kaum ... zu nennen **2** (move in, draw) beschreiben ‹*Kreis, Bogen, Kurve*›

description /dɪˈskrɪpʃn/ *n.* **1** (describing, verbal portrait) Beschreibung, *die;* Schilderung, *die;* **she is beautiful beyond ~:** sie ist unbeschreiblich schön; **he answers [to]** *or* **fits the ~:** er entspricht der Beschreibung (*Dat.*) **2** (sort, class) Art, *die;* **cars of every ~:** Autos aller Art **3** (more or less complete definition) Beschreibung, *die;* (designation) Bezeichnung, *die*

descriptive /dɪˈskrɪptɪv/ *adj.* **1** anschaulich; beschreibend ‹*Lyrik*›; deskriptiv ‹*Analyse*›; **a purely ~ report** ein reiner Tatsachenbericht **2** (not expressing feelings or judgements; also Ling.) deskriptiv

descriptively /dɪˈskrɪptɪvlɪ/ *adv.* anschaulich ‹*schreiben, sprechen*›; deskriptiv ‹*analysieren*›

descry /dɪˈskraɪ/ *v.t.* (catch sight of) erblicken; erspähen; (fig.: perceive) erkennen

desecrate /ˈdesɪkreɪt/ *v.t.* entweihen; schänden

desecration /desɪˈkreɪʃn/ *n.* Entweihung, *die;* Schändung, *die*

desegregate /diːˈsegrɪgeɪt/ *v.t.* die Rassentrennung aufheben an (+ *Dat.*)

desegregation /diːsegrɪˈgeɪʃn/ *n.* Aufhebung der Rassentrennung (**of** an + *Dat.*)

deselect /diːsɪˈlekt/ *v.t.* **1** (Brit. Polit.) nicht mehr als Wahlkandidat vorsehen **2** (Computing) deselektieren

deselection /diːsɪˈlekʃn/ *n.*, *no pl.* **1** (Brit. Polit.) Entzug der Kandidatur; Streichung von der Kandidatenliste **2** (Computing) Löschung der Auswahl

desensitize (desensitise) /diːˈsensɪtaɪz/ *v.t.* (Med., Phot., Psych.) desensibilisieren

desert[1] /ˈdezət/
A *n.* Wüste, *die;* (fig.) Einöde, *die;* **the Sahara D~:** die Wüste Sahara; **a cultural ~** (fig.) kulturelles Ödland
B *adj.* öde; Wüsten‹*klima, -stamm*›

desert[2] /dɪˈzɜːt/
A *v.t.* verlassen; im Stich lassen ‹*Frau, Familie usw.*›
B *v.i.* (run away) davonlaufen; ‹*Soldat:*› desertieren; **~ to sb.** zu jmdm. überlaufen

desert[3] /dɪˈzɜːt/ *n.* **1** *in pl.* (what is deserved) Verdienste *Pl.*; **meet with** *or* **get one's [just] ~s** das bekommen, was man verdient hat **2** (deserving) Verdienst, *das*

deserted /dɪˈzɜːtɪd/ *adj.* verlassen; **the streets were ~:** die Straßen waren wie ausgestorben

deserter /dɪˈzɜːtə(r)/ *n.* Deserteur, *der;* Fahnenflüchtige, *der/die*

desertification /dezɜːtɪfɪˈkeɪʃn/ *n.*, *no pl.* Verwüstung, *die;* Desertifikation, *die*

desertion /dɪˈzɜːʃn/ *n.* Verlassen, *das;* (of one's duty) Vernachlässigen, *das;* (Mil.) Desertion, *die;* Fahnenflucht, *die;* **~ to the enemy** Überlaufen zum Feind

desert /ˈdezət/: **~ ˈisland** *n.* einsame Insel; **~ ˈstate** *n.* Wüstenstaat, *der;* **~ wind** *n.* Wüstenwind, *der*

deserve /dɪˈzɜːv/
A *v.t.* verdienen; **he ~s to win** er verdient [es] zu gewinnen; **he ~s to be punished** er verdient [es], bestraft zu werden; er verdient Strafe; **what have I done to ~ this?** womit habe ich das verdient?; **he got what he ~d** er hat es nicht besser verdient
B *v.i.* (formal) **~ well of** sich verdient gemacht haben um

deservedly /dɪˈzɜːvɪdlɪ/ *adv.* verdientermaßen; **and ~ so** und das zu Recht; **be ~ punished** zu Recht bestraft werden

deserving /dɪˈzɜːvɪŋ/ *adj.* **1** (worthy) verdienstvoll; **donate money to a ~ cause** Geld für einen guten Zweck geben; **the ~ poor** die unverschuldet Bedürftigen **2** (meritorious) **be ~ of sth.** etw. verdienen; **people most ~ of help** Leute, die am ehesten Hilfe verdienen

déshabillé /deɪzæˈbiːeɪ/ *n.* Nachlässigkeit in der Kleidung; **in ~:** nachlässig gekleidet; (partly undressed) halb bekleidet

desiccated /ˈdesɪkeɪtɪd/ *adj.* getrocknet; (fig.) vertrocknet ‹*Person*›; **~ fruit** Dörr- *od.* Backobst, *das*

desideratum /dɪzɪdəˈreɪtəm/ *n.*, *pl.* **desiderata** /dɪzɪdəˈreɪtə/ (literary) Desiderat, *das* (geh.); Desideratum, *das* (geh.)

design /dɪˈzaɪn/
A *n.* **1** (preliminary sketch) Entwurf, *der;* **~s of costumes** Kostümentwürfe; **a technical ~:** eine technische Zeichnung **2** (pattern) Muster, *das* **3** *no art.* (art) Design, *das;* Gestaltung, *die* (geh.) **4** (established form of a product) Entwurf, *der;* (of machine, engine, etc.) Bauweise, *die* **5** (general idea, construction from parts) Konstruktion, *die;* **a machine of faulty/good ~:** eine schlecht/gut konstruierte Maschine **6** (mental plan) Planung, *die;* **argument from ~** (Theol.) theologischer Gottesbeweis **7** *in pl.* (scheme of attack) **have ~s on sb./sth.** es auf jmdn./etw. abgesehen haben **8** (purpose) Absicht, *die;* **by ~:** mit Absicht; absichtlich
B *v.t.* **1** (draw plan of) entwerfen; konstruieren, entwerfen ‹*Maschine, Fahrzeug, Flugzeug*› **2** (make preliminary sketch of) entwerfen **3** (contrive, plan) planen; aufstellen ‹*Lehrplan*› **4** (intend) beabsichtigen; **be ~ed to do sth.** ‹*Maschine, Werkzeug, Gerät:*› etw. tun sollen; **the book is ~ed as an aid to beginners** das Buch ist als Hilfe für Anfänger konzipiert **5** (set apart) vorsehen; **be ~ed for sb./sth.** für jmdn./etw. gedacht *od.* vorgesehen sein **6** (destine) bestimmen
C *v.i.* Entwürfe machen

designate
A /ˈdezɪgnət/ *postpos. adj.* designiert
B /ˈdezɪgneɪt/ *v.t.* **1** (serve as name of, describe) bezeichnen; (serve as distinctive mark of) kennzeichnen; **~ sth. A** etw. als A bezeichnen/kennzeichnen **2** (specify, particularize) angeben; aufzeigen ‹*Fehler, Mangel*› **3** (appoint to office) designieren (geh.); **be ~d as sb.'s successor** zu jmds. Nachfolger ernannt werden

designated ˈdriver *n.: Person, die nüchtern bleibt, um (z.B. nach einer Party) andere nach Hause zu fahren;* **I was the ~:** ich sollte [nüchtern bleiben und] fahren

designation /dezɪgˈneɪʃn/ *n.* **1** Bezeichnung, *die* **2** (appointing to office) Designation, *die*

designedly /dɪˈzaɪnɪdlɪ/ *adv.* absichtlich

designer /dɪˈzaɪnə(r)/ *n.* ▸**i** **p. 1260** Designer, *der*/Designerin, *die;* (of machines, buildings) Konstrukteur, *der*/Konstrukteurin, *die;* (of clothes) Modedesigner, *der*/-designerin, *die;* (Theatre: stage **~**) Bühnenbildner, *der*/-bildnerin, *die;* *attrib.* Modell‹*kleidung, -jeans*›

designer: ~ **'baby** *n.* Designerbaby, *das;* ~ **'drug** *n.* Designerdroge, *die*

designing /dɪ'zaɪnɪŋ/ *adj.* (crafty, artful, scheming) ränkevoll; intrigant

de'sign studio *n.* Designerbüro, *das;* Designagentur, *die*

desirability /dɪzaɪərə'bɪlɪtɪ/ *n.*, *no pl.* Wünschbarkeit, *die* (bes. schweiz.); **consider the ~ of sth.** erwägen, ob etw. wünschenswert ist

desirable /dɪ'zaɪərəbl/ *adj.* **1** (worth having or wishing for) wünschenswert; **'knowledge of French ~'** „Französischkenntnisse erwünscht" **2** (causing desire) attraktiv; begehrenswert ‹*Frau*›

desire /dɪ'zaɪə(r)/

A *n.* **1** (wish) Wunsch, *der* (**for** nach); (longing) Sehnsucht, *die* (**for** nach); **~ to do sth.** Wunsch, etw. zu tun; **~ for wealth** Verlangen nach Reichtum; **~ for freedom/peace** Freiheits-/Friedenswille, *der;* **his ~ for adventure** seine Abenteuerlust; **I have no ~ to see him** ich habe nicht den Wunsch, ihn zu sehen; **I have no ~ to cause you any trouble** ich möchte Ihnen keine Unannehmlichkeiten bereiten **2** (request) Wunsch, *der;* **at your ~:** auf Ihren Wunsch **3** (thing desired) **she is my heart's ~:** sie ist die Frau meines Herzens **4** (lust) Verlangen, *das;* **fleshly ~s** fleischliche Begierden

B *v.t.* **1** (wish) sich (*Dat.*) wünschen; (long for) sich sehnen nach; **he only ~d her happiness** er wollte nur ihr Glück **2** (request) wünschen; **as ~d, the door has been painted red** die Tür ist, wie gewünscht, rot gestrichen worden; **the furniture can be arranged as ~d** die Einrichtung kann ganz nach Wunsch gestaltet werden; **what do you ~ me to do?** was habe ich zu tun? **3** (ask for) **leave much to be ~d** viel zu wünschen übrig lassen **4** (sexually) begehren ‹*Mann, Frau*› **5** (arch.: pray, entreat) ersuchen (geh.)

desirous /dɪ'zaɪərəs/ *pred. adj.* (formal) **be ~ to do sth.** den Wunsch haben, etw. zu tun; **be ~ of sth.** etw. wünschen

desist /dɪ'zɪst, dɪ'sɪst/ *v.i.* (literary) einhalten (geh.); **~ from sth.** von etw. ablassen (geh.); **~ in one's efforts to do sth.** von seinen Bemühungen ablassen, etw. zu tun

desk /desk/ *n.* **1** Schreibtisch, *der;* (in school) Tisch, *der;* (teacher's raised ~) Pult, *das;* **~ unit** Schreibplatz, *der;* **~ copy** Arbeitsexemplar, *das;* **~ dictionary** Wörterbuch für den Schreibtisch **2** (compartment) (for cashier) Kasse, *die;* (for receptionist) Rezeption, *die;* **information ~:** Auskunft, *die;* **sales ~:** Verkauf, *der* **3** (music stand) Notenpult, *das* **4** (section of newspaper office) Ressort, *das*

desk: **~-bound** *adj.* an den Schreibtisch gefesselt (fig.); **~ calendar**, **~ diary** *ns.* Tischkalender, *der;* **~ editor** *n.* ▸❶ **p. 1260** Manuskriptbearbeiter, *der*/-bearbeiterin, *die;* Lektor, *der*/Lektorin, *die;* **~ lamp** *n.* Schreibtischlampe, *die;* **~top** **A** *adj.* **~top publishing** Desktoppublishing, *das;* **~top computer** Tischcomputer, *der;* Desktop[computer], *der;* **B** *n.* **1** (**~top computer**) Desktop-PC, *der;* **2** (of computer screen) Desktop, *der*

desolate

A /'desələt/ *adj.* **1** (ruinous, neglected, barren) trostlos ‹*Haus, Ort*›; desolat ‹*Zustand*› **2** (solitary) einsam **3** (uninhabited) öde; verlassen **4** (forlorn, wretched) trostlos ‹*Leben*›; arm ‹*Seele*›; verzweifelt ‹*Schrei*›

B /'desəleɪt/ *v.t.* **1** (depopulate) entvölkern **2** (devastate) verwüsten ‹*Land*› **3** (make wretched) in Verzweiflung stürzen

desolation /desə'leɪʃn/ *n.* **1** (neglected, solitary, or barren state) Öde, *die;* (state of ruin) Verwüstung, *die* **2** (loneliness, being forsaken) Verlassenheit, *die* **3** (grief, wretchedness) Trostlosigkeit, *die*

despair /dɪ'speə(r)/

A *n.* **1** Verzweiflung, *die;* **commit suicide in ~:** aus Verzweiflung Selbstmord begehen; **a cry of ~:** ein Verzweiflungsschrei; **his ~ of ever seeing her again** seine aufgegebene Hoffnung, sie je wiederzusehen **2** (cause) **be the ~ of sb.** jmdn. zur Verzweiflung bringen *od.* verzweifeln lassen

B *v.i.* **1** verzweifeln **2** **~ of doing sth.** die Hoffnung aufgeben, etw. zu tun; **~ of sth.** die Hoffnung auf etw. (*Akk.*) aufgeben

despatch (Brit.) ▸**dispatch**

desperado /despə'rɑːdəʊ/ *n.*, *pl.* **~es** (*Amer.:* **~s**) Desperado, *der*

desperate /'despərət/ *adj.* **1** verzweifelt; (coll.: urgent) dringend; **get** *or* **become ~:** verzweifeln; **feel ~:** verzweifelt sein; **be ~ for sth.** etw. dringend brauchen; **he was ~ for a beer** (coll.) er lechzte nach einem Bier; **be ~ to do sth.** verzweifelt versuchen, etw. zu tun; **don't do anything ~:** tun Sie nur nichts Unüberlegtes! **2** (staking all on a small chance) extrem ‹*Maßnahmen, Lösung*›; **a ~ disease must have a ~ remedy** (fig.) extreme Situationen erfordern extreme Maßnahmen **3** (extremely dangerous or serious) verzweifelt ‹*Lage, Situation*›; **things are getting ~:** die Lage wird immer verzweifelter **4** (extremely bad) schrecklich; **be in ~ need of sth.** etw. äußerst dringend brauchen

desperately /'despərətlɪ/ *adv.* **1** verzweifelt; hoffnungslos ‹*verliebt*›; (urgently) dringend; (recklessly, with extreme energy) verzweifelt; **be ~ ill** *or* **sick** todkrank sein **2** (appallingly, shockingly, extremely) schrecklich (ugs.)

desperation /despə'reɪʃn/ *n.* Verzweiflung, *die;* **out of** *or* **in [sheer] ~:** aus [lauter] Verzweiflung; **be in ~:** verzweifelt sein; **act** *or* **deed of ~:** Verzweiflungstat, *die;* **fight with ~:** verzweifelt kämpfen

despicable /'despɪkəbl/ *adj.*, **despicably** /'despɪkəblɪ/ *adv.* verabscheuungswürdig

despise /dɪ'spaɪz/ *v.t.* verachten; verschmähen (geh.) ‹*Geschenke*›; **this is not to be ~d** das ist nicht zu verachten

despite /dɪ'spaɪt/ *prep.* trotz; **~ what she said** ungeachtet dessen, was sie sagte; **~ his warning** trotz seiner Warnung

despoil /dɪ'spɔɪl/ *v.t.* (literary) berauben (**of** *Gen.*); ausplündern

despoliation /dɪspəʊlɪ'eɪʃn/ *n.* Plünderung, *die*

despond /dɪ'spɒnd/ *n.* (arch.) **Slough of D~** (literary) Pfuhl der Verzweiflung (dichter.)

despondency /dɪ'spɒndənsɪ/ *n.*, *no pl.* Niedergeschlagenheit, *die;* **view a situation with ~:** einer Lage sehr mutlos gegenüberstehen; **fall into ~:** den Mut verlieren; **answer in a tone of ~:** bedrückt antworten

despondent /dɪ'spɒndənt/ *adj.* niedergeschlagen; bedrückt; **be ~ about sth.** wegen etw. *od.* über etw. (*Akk.*) bedrückt sein; **feel ~:** niedergeschlagen sein; **grow** *or* **get ~:** mutlos werden; **don't become ~!** nur Mut!

despondently /dɪ'spɒndəntlɪ/ *adv.* niedergeschlagen

despot /'despɒt/ *n.* Despot, *der*

despotic /dɪ'spɒtɪk/ *adj.*, **despotically** /dɪ'spɒtɪkəlɪ/ *adv.* despotisch

despotism /'despətɪzm/ *n.* (tyranny) Despotie, *die;* Gewaltherrschaft, *die;* (political system) Despotismus, *der;* (fig.: absolute power) Tyrannei, *die*

dessert /dɪ'zɜːt/ *n.* **1** süße Nachspeise **2** (Brit.: after dinner) Dessert, *das;* Nachtisch, *der*

dessert: **~ apple** *n.* Dessertapfel, *der;* **~spoon** *n.* Esslöffel, *der;* **~spoonful** *n.* Esslöffel, *der;* **a ~spoonful** ein Esslöffel; **~ wine** *n.* Dessertwein, *der*

destabilization (**destabilisation**) /diːsteɪbɪlaɪ'zeɪʃn/ *n.*, *no pl.* (Polit.) Destabilisierung, *die*

destabilize (**destabilise**) /diː'steɪbɪlaɪz/ *v.t.* (Polit.) destabilisieren

destination /destɪ'neɪʃn/ *n.* (of person) Reiseziel, *das;* (of goods) Bestimmungsort, *der;* (of train, bus) Zielort, *der;* **arrive at one's ~:** am Ziel ankommen; **place/port of ~:** Bestimmungsort, *der*/-hafen, *der*

destination 'wedding *n.: Hochzeit an einem entfernten Ort*

destine /'destɪn/ *v.t.* bestimmen; **~ sb. for sth.** jmdn. für etw. bestimmen; ‹*Schicksal:*› jmdn. für etw. vorbestimmen; **be ~d to do sth.** dazu ausersehen *od.* bestimmt sein, etw. zu tun; **we were ~d [never] to meet again** wir sollten uns [nie] wieder sehen; **be ~d for sth.** für etw. bestimmt sein; **qualities which ~d him for leadership** Eigenschaften, die ihn für Führungsaufgaben prädestinierten

destiny /'destɪnɪ/ *n.* **1** Schicksal, *das;* Los, *das;* **find one's ~:** seine Bestimmung finden **2** *no art.* (power) das Schicksal

destitute /'destɪtjuːt/ *adj.* **1** (without resources) mittellos; **the ~ [poor]** die Mittellosen **2** (devoid) **be ~ of sth.** (formal) einer Sache (*Gen.*) bar sein (geh.)

destitution /destɪ'tjuːʃn/ *n.*, *no pl.* Armut, *die;* Not, *die*

destock /diː'stɒk/ *v.i.* (Brit.) den [Lager]bestand reduzieren

destocking /diː'stɒkɪŋ/ *n.*, *no pl.* (Brit.) [Lager-]bestandsreduzierung, *die*

destroy /dɪ'strɔɪ/ *v.t.* **1** (demolish) zerstören; kaputtmachen (ugs.) ‹*Tisch, Stuhl, Uhr, Schachtel*›; **the paintings were ~ed by fire** die Gemälde wurden durch einen Brand vernichtet **2** (make useless) vernichten ‹*Ernte, Papiere, Dokumente*› **3** (kill, annihilate) vernichten ‹*Feind, Insekten*›; **the dog will have to be ~ed** der Hund muss eingeschläfert werden **4** (fig.) zunichte machen ‹*Hoffnungen, Chancen*›; ruinieren ‹*Zukunft*›; zerstören ‹*Glück, Freundschaft, Schönheit, Macht*›

destroyer /dɪ'strɔɪə(r)/ *n.* (also Naut.) Zerstörer, *der*

destruct /dɪ'strʌkt/

A *v.t. & i.* zerstören

B *n.* Zerstörung, *die*

destruction /dɪ'strʌkʃn/ *n.* **1** Zerstörung, *die;* (of documents, mankind, a regime, an enemy) Vernichtung, *die;* (of toys, small objects) Kaputtmachen, *das* (ugs.); (of hopes) Zunichtemachen, *das;* **bring about one's own ~:** sich selbst zugrunde richten **2** (cause of ruin) Untergang, *der*

destructive /dɪ'strʌktɪv/ *adj.* **1** (destroying, tending to destroy) zerstörerisch; verheerend ‹*Sturm, Feuer, Krieg*›; zersetzend ‹*Einfluss, Haltung, Tendenz*›; destruktiv ‹*Mensch*›; **~ urge** Destruktionstrieb, *der* (Psych.); Zerstörungswut, *die* **2** (negative) destruktiv ‹*Kritik, Vorstellung, Kommentar, Einfluss, Ziel*›

destructively /dɪ'strʌktɪvlɪ/ *adv.* zerstörerisch; **behave ~:** sich destruktiv aufführen

destructor /dɪ'strʌktə(r)/ *n.* (Brit.) Müllverbrennungsanlage, *die*

desuetude /dɪ'sjuːɪtjuːd, 'deswɪtjuːd/ *n.* (literary) **fall into ~:** in Vergessenheit geraten; ‹*Wort, Sitte:*› außer Gebrauch kommen

desultory /'desəltərɪ/ *adj.* **1** (going from one subject to another, disconnected) sprunghaft; zwanglos, ungezwungen ‹*Gespräch*› **2** (unmethodical) planlos

detach /dɪ'tætʃ/ *v.t.* **1** (unfasten) entfernen; ablösen ‹*Aufgeklebtes*›; abbrechen ‹*Angewachsenes*›; abtrennen ‹*zu Entfernendes*›; abnehmen ‹*wieder zu Befestigendes*›; abhängen ‹*Angekuppeltes*›; herausnehmen ‹*innen Befindliches*›; **a couple of pages of the book have become ~ed** einige Seiten des Buches sind lose; **~ oneself from sb.** sich von jmdm. lösen **2** (Mil., Navy) abkommandieren (**from** aus); detachieren (veralt.)

detachable /dɪ'tætʃəbl/ *adj.* abnehmbar; herausnehmbar ‹*Futter*›

detached /dɪ'tætʃt/ *adj.* **1** (impartial) unvoreingenommen; (unemotional) unbeteiligt; **~ garage** freistehende Garage **2** (separate) **~ house** Einzelhaus, *das;* **~ retina** abgelöste Netzhaut

detachment /dɪ'tætʃmənt/ *n.* **1** (detaching) ▸**detach 1**: Entfernen, *das;* Ablösen, *das;* Abbrechen, *das;* Abtrennen, *das;* Abnehmen, *das;* Abhängen, *das;* Herausnehmen, *das* **2** (Mil., Navy) Abteilung, *die;* Detachement, *das* (veralt.) **3** (being aloof) Abstand, *der;* Distanz, *die* **4** (independence of judgement) Unvoreingenommenheit, *die*

detail /'diːteɪl/

A *n.* **1** (item) Einzelheit, *die;* Detail, *das;* **enter** *or* **go into ~s** ins Detail gehen; auf Einzelheiten eingehen; **a minor ~:** eine Kleinigkeit; **leave the ~s to sb. else** die Kleinarbeit [einem] anderen überlassen; **our correspondent will**

be giving you the ~s unser Korrespondent wird [Ihnen] im Einzelnen darüber berichten; **plan sth. down to the last ~:** etw. bis ins letzte Detail planen; **but that is a ~** (iron.) aber was macht das schon? [2] (dealing with things item by item) **in ~:** Punkt für Punkt; **have too much ~:** zu sehr ins Einzelne *od.* Detail gehen; **we haven't discussed anything in ~ yet** wir haben bisher noch nicht im Einzelnen darüber gesprochen; **in great** *or* **much ~:** in allen Einzelheiten; **in greater ~:** [noch] näher; **in minute ~:** haarklein; **go into ~:** ins Detail gehen; auf Einzelheiten eingehen; **attention to ~:** Sorgfalt in den Details [3] (account) Aufstellung, *die* [4] (in building, picture, etc.) Detail, *das* [5] (part of picture) Ausschnitt, *der* [6] (Mil.) Dienstplan, *der* [7] (body for special duty) Kommando, *das*

d

B *v.t.* [1] (list) einzeln aufführen; **be fully ~ed** (stated, described) im Detail ausgeführt werden [2] (Mil.) abkommandieren

detailed /ˈdiːteɪld/ *adj.* detailliert; eingehend ‹*Studie*›

detain /dɪˈteɪn/ *v.t.* [1] (keep in confinement) festhalten; (take into confinement) verhaften [2] (delay) aufhalten; **do not let me ~ you** lassen Sie sich durch mich nicht aufhalten

detainee /dɪteɪˈniː/ *n.* Verhaftete, *der/die*

detect /dɪˈtekt/ *v.t.* [1] (discover presence of) entdecken; bemerken ‹*Trauer, Verärgerung*›; wahrnehmen ‹*Bewegung*›; aufdecken ‹*Irrtum, Verbrechen*›; durchschauen ‹*Beweggrund*›; feststellen ‹*Strahlung*›; **~ a note of anger in sb.'s voice** eine gewisse Verärgerung aus jmds. Stimme heraushören [2] (reveal guilt of) **~ sb. in doing sth.** jmdn. bei etw. ertappen

detectable /dɪˈtektəbl/ *adj.* feststellbar; wahrnehmbar ‹*Bewegung*›

detection /dɪˈtekʃn/ *n.* [1] ▸**detect 1**: Entdeckung, *die;* Bemerken, *das;* Wahrnehmung, *die;* Aufdeckung, *die;* Durchschauen, *das;* Feststellung, *die;* **in order to escape ~:** um nicht entdeckt zu werden; **try to escape ~:** versuchen, unentdeckt zu bleiben [2] (work of detective) Ermittlungsarbeit, *die*

detective /dɪˈtektɪv/

A *n.* ▸ⓘ **p. 1260** Detektiv, *der;* (policeman) Kriminalbeamte, *der*/Kriminalbeamtin, *die;* **private ~:** Privatdetektiv, *der*

B *attrib. adj.* Kriminal-; **~ novel** Kriminalroman, *der;* **~ work** Ermittlungsarbeit, *die;* **~ story** Detektivgeschichte, *die*

detector /dɪˈtektə(r)/ *n.* [1] (device) Detektor, *der;* (indicator) Anzeiger, *der* [2] (Electr.) [Kristall-]detektor, *der*

détente /deɪˈtɑ̃t/ *n.* (Polit.) Entspannung, *die*

detention /dɪˈtenʃn/ *n.* [1] Festnahme, *die;* (confinement) Haft, *die* [2] (Sch.) Nachsitzen, *das;* (Mil.) Arrest, *der* (veralt.); **give sb. two hours' ~:** jmdn. zwei Stunden nachsitzen lassen [3] (delay) [unfreiwilliger] Aufenthalt

de'tention: ~ camp *n.* (prison camp) [Gefangenen]lager, *das;* (internment camp) [Internierungs]lager, *das;* **~ centre** *n.* (Brit.) Jugendstrafanstalt, *die*

deter /dɪˈtɜː(r)/ *v.t.*, **-rr-** abschrecken; **~ sb. from sth.** jmdn. von etw. abhalten; **~ sb. from doing sth.** jmdn. davon abhalten, etw. zu tun; **the danger did not ~ him** er ließ sich durch die Gefahr nicht abschrecken; die Gefahr schreckte ihn nicht (geh.); **be ~red by sth.** sich durch etw. abschrecken lassen

detergent /dɪˈtɜːdʒənt/

A *adj.* reinigend

B *n.* Reinigungsmittel, *das;* (for washing) Waschmittel, *das;* Detergens, *das* (Chemie)

deteriorate /dɪˈtɪərɪəreɪt/

A *v.t.* verschlechtern; verringern, mindern ‹*Wert*›

B *v.i.* sich verschlechtern; ‹*Haus:*› verfallen, verkommen; ‹*Holz, Leder:*› verrotten; **his condition** *or* **he has ~d** sein Zustand hat sich verschlechtert; **his work has ~d** seine Arbeit hat nachgelassen; **~ in value** an Wert verlieren

deterioration /dɪtɪərɪəˈreɪʃn/ *n.* ▸**deteriorate B**: Verschlechterung, *die;* Verfall, *der;* Verrottung, *die;* **preserve paintings from ~:** Gemälde vor Schädigungen schützen

determinable /dɪˈtɜːmɪnəbl/ *adj.* (capable of being fixed or ascertained) bestimmbar; **sth. is ~:** etw. lässt sich bestimmen

determinate /dɪˈtɜːmɪnət/ *adj.* [1] (limited, finite) begrenzt [2] (distinct) bestimmt [3] (definitive) eindeutig; fest ‹*Begriff*›

determination /dɪtɜːmɪˈneɪʃn/ *n.* [1] (ascertainment, definition) Bestimmung, *die* [2] (resoluteness) Entschlossenheit, *die;* **with [sudden] ~:** [kurz] entschlossen; **he had an air of ~ about him** er wirkte fest entschlossen [3] (intention) [feste] Absicht [4] (Law: ending) Ablauf, *der* [5] (judicial decision) Entscheidung, *die* [6] (fixing beforehand) Festlegung, *die*

determine /dɪˈtɜːmɪn/

A *v.t.* [1] (decide) beschließen; **~ to do sth.** beschließen, etw. zu tun; sich entschließen, etw. zu tun [2] (make decide) veranlassen; **~ sb. to do sth.** jmdn. dazu veranlassen, etw. zu tun [3] (be a decisive factor for) bestimmen; entscheiden über (+ *Akk.*) [4] (ascertain, define) feststellen; bestimmen [5] (fix beforehand) festlegen [6] (Law: end) beenden

B *v.i.* (decide) **~ on doing sth.** beschließen, etw. zu tun; **~ on sth.** sich für etw. entscheiden

determined /dɪˈtɜːmɪnd/ *adj.* [1] (resolved) **be ~ to do** *or* **on doing sth.** etw. unbedingt tun wollen; fest entschlossen sein, etw. zu tun; **sb. is ~ that ...:** es ist für jmdn. beschlossene Sache, dass ...; **I am ~ that he shall win** ich werde alles Mögliche tun, dass er siegt [2] (resolute) entschlossen; resolut ‹*Person*› [3] (fixed) bestimmt

determinedly /dɪˈtɜːmɪndlɪ/ *adv.* entschlossen

determiner /dɪˈtɜːmɪnə(r)/ *n.* (Ling.) Determinator, *der*

determinism /dɪˈtɜːmɪnɪzm/ *n.* Determinismus, *der*

determinist /dɪˈtɜːmɪnɪst/

A *adj.* deterministisch

B *n.* Determinist, *der*/Deterministin, *die*

deterministic /dɪtɜːmɪˈnɪstɪk/ *adj.* deterministisch

deterrence /dɪˈterəns/ *n.* Abschreckung, *die*

deterrent /dɪˈterənt/

A *adj.* abschreckend

B *n.* Abschreckungsmittel, *das* (**to** für); **~ strategy** Strategie der Abschreckung

detest /dɪˈtest/ *v.t.* verabscheuen; **~ doing sth.** es verabscheuen, etw. zu tun

detestable /dɪˈtestəbl/ *adj.* verabscheuenswert; verabscheuungswürdig

detestably /dɪˈtestəblɪ/ *adv.* abscheulich

detestation /diːteˈsteɪʃn/ *n.*, *no pl.* Abscheu, *der* (**of** vor + *Dat.*)

dethrone /diːˈθrəʊn/ *v.t.* (lit. or fig.) entthronen

dethronement /diːˈθrəʊnmənt/ *n.* (lit. or fig.) Entthronung, *die*

detonate /ˈdetəneɪt/

A *v.i.* detonieren

B *v.t.* zur Explosion bringen; zünden

detonation /detəˈneɪʃn/ *n.* [1] (detonating) Detonation, *die* [2] (Motor Veh.) Klopfen, *das*

detonator /ˈdetəneɪtə(r)/ *n.* [1] (part of bomb or shell) Sprengkapsel, *die;* Detonator, *der* [2] (Railw.) Knallkapsel, *die*

detour /ˈdiːtʊə(r)/

A *n.* Umweg, *der;* (in a road, river) Bogen, *der;* Schleife, *die;* (diversion) Umleitung, *die;* **make a ~:** einen Umweg machen

B *v.t.* umleiten

detox (coll.)

A /ˈdiːtɒks/ *n.* Entzug, *der;* **be in ~:** auf Entzug sein

B /diːˈtɒks/ *v.t.* entziehen (ugs.) ‹*Drogensüchtigen, Alkoholiker*›

C /diːˈtɒks/ *v.i.* einen Entzug machen.

detoxification /diːtɒksɪfɪˈkeɪʃn/ *n.*, *no pl.* Entgiftung, *die;* Detoxikation, *die* (fachspr.)

detoxify /diːˈtɒksɪfaɪ/

A *v.t.* entgiften; unschädlich machen ‹*Gift usw.*›

B *v.i* sich entgiften

detract /dɪˈtrækt/ *v.i.* **~ from sth.** etw. beeinträchtigen; **~ from sb.'s merits** jmds. Verdienste schmälern

detraction /dɪˈtrækʃn/ *n.* Beeinträchtigung, *die* (**from** *Gen.*); (defamation) Schmähung, *die*

detractor /dɪˈtræktə(r)/ *n.* Verleumder, *der*/Verleumderin, *die*

detriment /ˈdetrɪmənt/ *n.* Schaden, *der;* **to the ~ of sth.** zum Nachteil *od.* Schaden einer Sache (*Gen.*); **without ~ to** ohne Schaden für; **I know nothing to his ~:** mir ist nichts Nachteiliges über ihn bekannt

detrimental /detrɪˈmentl/ *adj.* schädlich; **be ~ to sth.** einer Sache (*Dat.*) schaden *od.* (geh.) abträglich sein

detrimentally /detrɪˈmentəlɪ/ *adv.* auf schädliche Weise

detritus /dɪˈtraɪtəs/ *n.*, *no pl.* [1] (debris) Überbleibsel, *das* [2] (Geol.) Geröll, *das;* Detritus, *der*

de trop /də ˈtrəʊ/ *pred. adj.* fehl am Platz; überflüssig

deuce¹ /djuːs/ *n.* [1] (on dice; arch. Cards) Zwei, *die* [2] (Tennis) Einstand, *der*

deuce² (coll.) ▸**devil A 3**

deuced /djuːsɪd, djuːst/ *adj.*, *adv.* (arch.) ▸**damned A 2, 3, B**

deus ex machina /deɪəs eks ˈmɑːkɪnə, diːəs eks ˈmɑːkɪnə/ *n.* Deus ex Machina, *der*

deuterium /djuːˈtɪərɪəm/ *n.* Deuterium, *das*

Deuteronomy /djuːtəˈrɒnəmɪ/ *n.* (Bibl.) das fünfte Buch Mose

Deutschmark /ˈdɔɪtʃmɑːk/ *n.* (Hist.) Deutsche Mark

devaluation /diːvæljuːˈeɪʃn/ *n.* [1] Abwertung, *die* [2] (Econ.) Abwertung, *die;* Devalvation, *die*

devalue /diːˈvæljuː/ *v.t.* [1] (reduce value of) abwerten [2] (Econ.) abwerten; devalvieren

devastate /ˈdevəsteɪt/ *v.t.* verwüsten; verheeren; (fig.) niederschmettern

devastating /ˈdevəsteɪtɪŋ/ *adj.* verheerend; niederschmetternd ‹*Nachricht, Analyse*›; vernichtend ‹*Spielweise, Kritik*›

devastation /devəˈsteɪʃn/ *n.*, *no pl.* Verwüstung, *die;* Verheerung, *die*

develop /dɪˈveləp/

A *v.t.* [1] (bring into existence) entwickeln; aufbauen ‹*Handel, Handelszentrum*›; **the girl had ~ed a mature figure** die Figur des Mädchens war voll entwickelt; **the machine was ~ed from their plans** die Maschine wurde nach ihren Plänen entwickelt; **~ a business from scratch** ein Geschäft neu aufziehen [2] (bring to more evident form) entwickeln ‹*Instinkt, Fähigkeiten, Kräfte*›; entfalten ‹*Persönlichkeit, Individualität*›; erschließen ‹*natürliche Ressourcen*› [3] (bring to fuller form) entwickeln; (expand; make more sophisticated) weiterentwickeln; ausbauen ‹*Verkehrsnetz, System, Handel, Verkehr, Position*›; wachsen lassen ‹*Pflanze, Korn*›; **~ sth. further** etw. weiterentwickeln; **~ an essay into a book** einen Essay zu einem Buch ausbauen; **a highly ~ed civilization** eine hoch entwickelte Zivilisation [4] (begin to exhibit, begin to suffer from) annehmen ‹*Gewohnheit*›; bei sich entdecken ‹*Vorliebe*›; bekommen ‹*Krankheit, Fieber, Lust*›; entwickeln ‹*Talent, Stärke*›; erkranken an (+ *Dat.*) ‹*Krebs, Tumor*›; **~ a taste for sth.** Geschmack an etw. (*Akk.*) finden; **the car ~ed a fault** an dem Wagen ist ein Defekt aufgetreten [5] (Photog.) entwickeln [6] (construct buildings etc. on, convert to new use) erschließen; sanieren ‹*Altstadt*›; aufschließen ‹*Schacht*› [7] (Mus.) durchführen ‹*Thema*› [8] (Chess) entwickeln [9] (Amer.: make known) an den Tag bringen

B *v.i.* [1] (come into existence, become evident) sich entwickeln (**from** aus; **into** zu); ‹*Defekt, Symptome, Erkrankungen:*› auftreten [2] (become fuller) sich [weiter]entwickeln (**into** zu) [3] (Amer.: become known) an den Tag kommen; **it ~ed that ...:** es stellte sich heraus, dass ...

developable /dɪˈveləpəbl/ *adj.* entwicklungsfähig; erschließungsfähig ‹*Gebiet*›

developer /dɪˈveləpə(r)/ *n.* [1] (Photog.) (chemical agent) Entwickler, *der* [2] (person who develops real estate) ≈ Bauunternehmer, *der* [3] (person who matures) **late** *or* **slow ~:** Spätentwickler, *der*

developing: ~ country *n.* Entwicklungsland, *das;* **~ world** *n.* Entwicklungsländer *Pl.*

development /dɪ'veləpmənt/ *n.* 1 (bringing into existence) Entwicklung, *die* (**from** aus, **into** zu) 2 (bringing into more evident form) (of individuality) Entfaltung, *die;* (of heat, gas, vapour) Entwicklung, *die;* (of natural resources etc.) Erschließung, *die;* **sth. is in the course of ~:** etw. befindet sich in der Entwicklung 3 (bringing into fuller form) Entwicklung, *die;* (expansion) Ausbau, *der;* Weiterentwicklung, *die;* **be capable of [further] ~:** noch weiter entwicklungsfähig sein 4 (beginning to exhibit) Entwicklung, die; (of a talent also) Entfaltung, *die;* (beginning to suffer from) Beginn, *der* 5 (of land etc.) Erschließung, *die;* **regional ~:** Regionalplanung, *die* 6 (evolution) Entwicklung, *die* 7 (full-grown state) Vollendung, *die* 8 (developed product or form) **a ~ of sth.** eine Fortentwicklung *od.* Weiterentwicklung einer Sache; **at that time tea bags were a new ~:** damals waren Teebeutel eine Neuerung 9 (Photog.) Entwickeln, *das;* Entwicklung, *die* 10 (Mus.) Durchführung, *die* 11 (Chess) Entwicklung, *die* 12 (developed land) **[new] ~:** Neubaugebiet, *das*

developmental /dɪveləp'mentl/ *adj.* Entwicklungs-

de'velopment area *n.* (Brit.) Entwicklungsgebiet, *das;* (in town) Erschließungsgebiet, *das;* (in old town) Sanierungsgebiet, *das*

deviance /'di:vɪəns/, **deviancy** /'di:vɪənsɪ/ *n.* abweichendes Verhalten; Devianz, *die* (Soziol.)

deviant /'di:vɪənt/

A *adj.* [von der Norm] abweichend; deviant (Soziol.)

B *n.* [von der Norm] Abweichende, *der/die/das;* **a sexual ~:** jmd. mit [von der Norm] abweichendem Sexualverhalten; sexuell devianter Mensch (Soziol.)

deviate /'di:vɪeɪt/ *v.i.* (lit. or fig.) abweichen

deviation /di:vɪ'eɪʃn/ *n.* 1 (deviating) Abweichung, *die* 2 (of compass needle) Ablenkung, *die;* Deviation, *die* 3 (Statistics) **[standard] ~:** [Standard]abweichung, *die*

deviationism /di:vɪ'eɪʃənɪzm/ *n.* (Polit.) Abweichlertum, *das*

deviationist /di:vɪ'eɪʃənɪst/ *n.* (Polit.) Abweichler, *der*/Abweichlerin, *die*

device /dɪ'vaɪs/ *n.* 1 (contrivance) Gerät, *das;* (as part of sth.) Vorrichtung, *die;* **nuclear ~:** atomarer Sprengkörper 2 (plan, scheme) List, *die;* **rhetorical ~s** rhetorische Kunstgriffe 3 (drawing, design, figure) Verzierung, *die* 4 (emblematic or heraldic design) Emblem, *das* 5 (motto) Motto, *das;* Devise, *die* 6 *in pl.* (fancy, will) **leave sb. to his own ~s** jmdn. sich (*Dat.*) selbst überlassen; **be left to one's own ~s** sich (*Dat.*) selbst überlassen sein

devil /'devl/

A *n.* 1 (Satan) **the D~:** der Teufel 2 (heathen god) Götze, *der;* (evil spirit, Satan's follower) Teufel, *der;* **the ~ of greed** der Dämon Habgier 3 *or* **D~** (coll.) **who/where/what** *etc.* **the ~?** wer/wo/was *usw.* zum Teufel? (salopp); **the ~ take him!** hol ihn der Teufel! (salopp); **he's got the ~ in him** er hat den Teufel im Leib (ugs.); **the ~!** Teufel auch! (salopp); **the ~ knows** weiß der Teufel (salopp); **there will be the ~ to pay** da ist der Teufel los (ugs.); **go to the ~:** zum Teufel gehen (salopp); sich zum Teufel scheren (salopp); **[you can] go to the ~!** scher dich zum Teufel! (salopp); **work/shout like the ~:** wie ein Besessener arbeiten/schreien; **run/fight like the ~:** wie der Teufel rennen/kämpfen (ugs.); **between the ~ and the deep [blue] sea** in einer Zwickmühle (ugs.); **~ take it!** verdammt noch mal!; **it was ~ take the hindmost** es galt nur noch: Rette sich, wer kann!; **play the ~ with sb./sth.** jmdm./einer Sache übel mitspielen; **better the ~ one knows** lieber das bekannte Übel; **speak** *or* **talk of the ~ [and he will appear]** wenn man vom Teufel spricht[, kommt er]; *see also* **idle A 6; needs** 4 **a** *or* **the ~ of a mess** ein verteufelter Schlamassel (ugs.); **be in a ~ of a mess** im dicksten Schlamassel sitzen (ugs.); **a** *or* **the ~ of a problem** ein verteufelt schwieriges Problem; **have a ~ of a temper** verteufelt jähzornig sein (ugs.); **have the ~ of a time** es verteufelt schwer haben; **be a ~!** sei kein Frosch!; **he is a ~ of a [good] teacher** er ist ein verdammt guter Lehrer (ugs.); **this car is the [very] ~ to start** dieses Auto lässt sich verteufelt schwer starten (ugs.); **the crossword is a real ~:** das Kreuzworträtsel ist verteufelt schwer (ugs.) 5 (wicked or cruel person, vicious animal) Teufel, *der* (fig.); (mischievously energetic or self-willed person) Teufel, *der* (fig. ugs.); Teufelsbraten, *der* (ugs. scherzh.); (able, clever person) Ass, *das* (ugs.); **he's a ~ with the women** er spielt mit den Frauen; **he's a clever ~:** er ist ein schlauer Hund (ugs.); **you ~!** (ugs.) du Schlingel!; **a poor ~:** ein armer Teufel; **lucky ~:** Glückspilz, *der* (ugs.); **unlucky ~:** Unglücksrabe, *der* (ugs.); **cheeky/naughty ~:** Frechdachs, *der* (fam., meist scherzh.); **queer** *or* **odd ~:** komischer Kauz 6 (fighting spirit) Kampfgeist, *der* 7 (Law dated) [*unbezahlter*] *Gehilfe eines Anwalts* 8 (S.Afr.) **[dust] ~:** Sandsturm, *der*

B *v.t.*, (Brit.) **-ll-** 1 (Cookery) *klein geschnitten und scharf gewürzt braten* 2 (Amer. coll.: harass, worry) piesacken (ugs.)

'devilfish *n.* 1 (anglerfish) Seeteufel, *der* 2 (Amer.: ray) Teufelsrochen, *der*

devilish /'devəlɪʃ/

A *adj.* 1 (of the Devil) teuflisch ‹*Künste, Zauberei*›; ‹*Erfindung, Lehre*› des Teufels 2 (damnable) teuflisch

B *adv.* (arch. coll.) verteufelt (ugs.)

devilishly /'devəlɪʃlɪ/ *adv.* (diabolically) teuflisch; (exceedingly) verteufelt (ugs.)

'devil-may-care *adj.* sorglos-unbekümmert

devilment /'devlmənt/ *n.* 1 (mischief) Unfug, *der;* (wild spirits) Übermut, *der;* **be up to some ~:** Unfug treiben *od.* anstellen 2 (devilish phenomenon) Teufelei, *die*

devilry /'devlrɪ/ *n.* 1 (black magic) Teufelskunst, *die* 2 (wickedness, cruelty) teuflische Bosheit; (action) Teufelei, *die* 3 (mischief) Unfug, *der;* (hilarity) Schabernack, *der;* **out of sheer ~:** aus purem Schabernack

devil: ~'s 'advocate *n.* (RC Ch.; also fig.) Advocatus Diaboli, *der;* **~'s 'coach-horse** *n.* (Brit. Zool.) Schwarzer *od.* Stinkender Moderkäfer; **~s-on-'horseback** *n.* (Gastr.) Austern in Röllchen aus Frühstücksspeck; Austern auf englische Art; **~'s 'own** *attrib. adj.* **the ~'s own** ein/eine verteufelt... (ugs.); **[take] the ~'s own time** eine verteufelt lange Zeit [dauern] (ugs.); **he has the ~'s own luck** er hat verteufeltes Glück (ugs.)

devious /'di:vɪəs/ *adj.* 1 (winding) verschlungen; **take a ~ route** einen Umweg fahren 2 (unscrupulous, insincere) verschlagen ‹*Person*›; hinterhältig ‹*Person, Methode, Tat*›

deviously /'di:vɪəslɪ/ *adv.* hinterhältigerweise; **behave ~:** sich hinterhältig verhalten

deviousness /'di:vɪəsnɪs/ *n.*, *no pl.* Hinterhältigkeit, *die;* Verschlagenheit, *die*

devise /dɪ'vaɪz/ *v.t.* (plan) entwerfen; schmieden ‹*Pläne*›; kreieren ‹*Mode, Stil*›; ausarbeiten ‹*Programm*›

devoid /dɪ'vɔɪd/ *adj.* **~ of sth.** (lacking) ohne etw.; bar einer Sache (*Gen.*) (geh.); (free from) frei von etw.

devolution /di:və'lu:ʃn/ *n.* 1 (deputing, delegation) Übertragung, *die;* Delegieren, *das;* (Polit.) Dezentralisierung, *die* 2 (descent of property, power, etc.) Übergang, *der* (**on [to]** auf + *Akk.*) 3 (Biol.) Degeneration, *die* 4 (Brit. Polit.) *Übertragung von administrativer Unabhängigkeit;* Devolution, *die* (fachspr.)

devolve /dɪ'vɒlv/ *v.i.* 1 (be transferred) **~ [up]on sb.** ‹*Pflicht, Verantwortung, Aufgabe:*› jmdm. zufallen 2 (descend) vererbt werden; **~ to sb.** auf jmdn. übergehen

Devonian /dɪ'vəʊnɪən/

A *adj.* (Geol.) devonisch

B *n.* (Geol.) Devon, *das*

Devonshire cream /devnʃɪə 'kri:m/ *n.* ▸ **clotted cream**

devote /dɪ'vəʊt/ *v.t.* (consecrate) widmen; **~ one's thoughts/energy to sth.** sein Denken/seine Energie auf etw. (*Akk.*) verwenden; **~ sums of money to sth.** Geldsummen für etw. bestimmen

devoted /dɪ'vəʊtɪd/ *adj.* treu; ergeben ‹*Diener*›; aufrichtig ‹*Freundschaft, Liebe, Verehrung*›; **he is very ~ to his work/his wife** er geht in seiner Arbeit völlig auf/liebt seine Frau innig

devotedly /dɪ'vəʊtɪdlɪ/ *adv.* [treu] ergeben; innig ‹*lieben*›

devotee /devə'ti:/ *n.* 1 (enthusiast) Anhänger, *der*/Anhängerin, *die;* (of music, art) Liebhaber, *der*/Liebhaberin, *die;* (of a person) Verehrer, *der*/Verehrerin, *die* 2 (pious person) [fanatischer/glühender] Anhänger/[fanatische/glühende] Anhängerin

devotion /dɪ'vəʊʃn/ *n.* 1 (addiction, loyalty, devoutness) **~ to sb./sth.** Hingabe an jmdn./etw.; **~ to music/the arts** Liebe zur Musik/Kunst; **~ to duty** Pflichteifer, *der* 2 (devoting) Weihung, *die* 3 (divine worship) Anbetung, *die* (**to** *Gen.*) 4 *in pl.* (prayers) Gebet, *das;* **be at one's ~s** seine Andacht halten; **book of ~s** Andachtsbuch, *das*

devotional /dɪ'vəʊʃənl/ *adj.* fromm; andächtig ‹*Gebet*›; religiös ‹*Literatur, Lied*›; Andachts- ‹*buch, -übung*›

devour /dɪ'vaʊə(r)/ *v.t.* 1 verschlingen; ‹*Pest:*› dahinraffen (geh.) 2 (absorb the attention of) verzehren; **he was ~ed by anxiety** er verzehrte sich vor Angst

devouring /dɪ'vaʊərɪŋ/ *adj.* verzehrend ‹*Hunger, Leidenschaft, Feuer*›; verschlingend ‹*Fluten*›; Menschen fressend, alles verschlingend ‹*Ungeheuer, Tier*›

devout /dɪ'vaʊt/ *adj.* fromm; sehnlich ‹*Wunsch*›; inständig ‹*Hoffnung*›

devoutly /dɪ'vaʊtlɪ/ *adv.* in [frommer] Andacht ‹*knien, beten, bekennen*›; inständig ‹*hoffen, wünschen*›

dew /dju:/

A *n.* Tau, *der*

B *v.t.* (poet./literary) betauen (geh.)

dew: ~berry *n.* Brombeere, *die;* **~claw** *n.* Afterklaue, *die;* **~drop** *n.* Tautropfen, *der*

Dewey system /'dju:ɪ sɪstəm/ *n.* (Bibliog.) Dezimalklassifikation, *die*

dewlap /'dju:læp/ *n.* (of animal) Wamme, *die;* (of person) Doppelkinn, *das*

dew: ~ point *n.* (Phys.) Taupunkt, *der;* **~ pond** *n.* (Brit.) *flacher, künstlich angelegter Teich, in dem sich Tau- und Regenwasser sammelt*

dewy /'dju:ɪ/ *adj.* taufeucht; tauig (geh.)

'dewy-eyed *adj.* naiv; **go all ~:** ganz feuchte Augen bekommen

dexter /'dekstə(r)/ *adj.* (Her.) recht...; dexter (fachspr.)

dexterity /dek'sterɪtɪ/ *n.*, *no pl.* (skill) Geschicklichkeit, *die;* **~ in argument** Redegewandtheit, *die*

dexterous (**dextrous**) /'dekstrəs/ *adj.* 1 (nimble of hand, skilful, clever) geschickt 2 (using right hand) rechtshändig

dexterous[ly] ▸ **dextr-**

dextrose /'dekstrəʊs/ *n.* (Chem.) Traubenzucker, *der;* Dextrose, *die* (fachspr.)

dextrously /'dekstrəslɪ/ *adv.* geschickt; mit großem Geschick

DfES *abbr.* (Brit.) **= Department for Education and Skills** Ministerium für Bildung und Qualifikationserwerb

dhow /daʊ/ *n.* (Naut.) D[h]au, *die*

DHSS *abbr.* (Brit. Hist.) **= Department of Health and Social Security** *Amt für Gesundheit und Sozialwesen*

dia. *abbr.* **= diameter** D.; Durchm.

diabetes /daɪə'bi:ti:z/ *n.*, *pl. same* ▸ **i p. 1231** (Med.) Zuckerkrankheit, *die;* Diabetes, *der* (fachspr.)

diabetic /daɪə'betɪk, daɪə'bi:tɪk/ (Med.)

A *adj.* 1 (of diabetes) diabetisch 2 (having diabetes) diabetisch (Med.); zuckerkrank 3 (for diabetics) Diabetiker‹*nahrung, -schokolade usw.*›

B *n.* Diabetiker, *der*/Diabetikerin, *die;* Zuckerkranke, *der/die*

d

diabolic /daɪəˈbɒlɪk/, **diabolical** /daɪəˈbɒlɪkl/ *adj.* 1 (cruel, wicked) teuflisch; diabolisch; (coll.: extremely bad) mörderisch (ugs.) ‹*Hitze*›; teuflisch (ugs.) ‹*Kälte, Wetter*›; **this child is a ~ nuisance!** (coll.) dieses Kind kann einen zur Weißglut treiben! (ugs.); **shopping today was ~** (coll.) das Einkaufen heute war die reinste Hölle (ugs.) 2 (of the Devil) diabolisch; teuflisch

diabolically /daɪəˈbɒlɪkəlɪ/ *adv.* (coll.) teuflisch (ugs.) ‹*kalt, grausam*›; mörderisch (ugs.) ‹*heiß*›

diachronic /daɪəˈkrɒnɪk/ *adj.*, **diachronically** /daɪəˈkrɒnɪkəlɪ/ *adv.* (Ling.) diachronisch

diacritic /daɪəˈkrɪtɪk/, **diacritical** /daɪəˈkrɪtɪkl/

A *adj.* 1 (distinctive) distinktiv (geh.) 2 (Ling.) **~ mark** *or* **sign** diakritisches Zeichen

B *n.* (Ling.) diakritisches Zeichen

diadem /ˈdaɪədem/ *n.* Diadem, *das;* (wreath) Kranz, *der*

diaeresis /daɪˈɪərɪsɪs/ *n., pl.* **diaereses** /daɪˈɪrɪsiːz/ Trema, *das*

diagnose /daɪəgˈnəʊz/ ▸ ❶ **p. 1231** *v.t.* diagnostizieren ‹*Krankheit*›; feststellen ‹*Fehler*›

diagnosis /daɪəgˈnəʊsɪs/ *n., pl.* **diagnoses** /daɪəgˈnəʊsiːz/ 1 ▸ ❶ **p. 1231** (of disease) Diagnose, *die;* **make a ~:** eine Diagnose stellen 2 (of difficulty, fault) Feststellung, *die*

diagnostic /daɪəgˈnɒstɪk/

A *adj.* diagnostisch; **~ sign** (Med.) Symptom, *das*

B *n.* (Med.) Symptom, *das*

diagnostics /daɪəgˈnɒstɪks/ *n. sing.* Diagnostik, *die*

diagonal /daɪˈægənl/

A *adj.* diagonal

B *n.* Diagonale, *die*

diagonally /daɪˈægənəlɪ/ *adv.* diagonal

diagram /ˈdaɪəgræm/

A *n.* 1 (sketch) schematische Darstellung; **I'll make a ~ to show you how to get there** ich zeichne Ihnen auf, wie Sie dorthin kommen 2 (graphic or symbolic representation) Diagramm, *das* 3 (Geom.) Diagramm, *das*

B *v.t.,* (Brit.) **-mm-** [in einem Diagramm] grafisch darstellen; (make sketch of) aufzeichnen

diagrammatic /daɪəgrəˈmætɪk/ *adj.*, **diagrammatically** /daɪəgrəˈmætɪkəlɪ/ *adv.* diagrammatisch

dial /ˈdaɪəl/

A *n.* 1 (of clock or watch) Zifferblatt, *das* 2 (of gauge, meter, etc., on radio or television) Skala, *die* 3 **[sun]~:** Sonnenuhr, *die* 4 (Teleph.) Wählscheibe, *die* 5 (Brit. coll.: face) Visage, *die* (salopp abwertend)

B *v.t.,* (Brit.) **-ll-** (Teleph.) wählen; **~ [London] direct** [nach London] durchwählen; **~ a call to somewhere/to sb.** irgendwo/bei jmdm. anrufen

C *v.i.,* (Brit.) **-ll-** (Teleph.) wählen

dialect /ˈdaɪəlekt/ *n.* Dialekt, *der;* Mundart, *die;* (of class) Ausdrucksweise, *die; attrib.* **~ expression** mundartlicher *od.* dialektaler Ausdruck

dialectal /daɪəˈlektl/ *adj.* dialektal; mundartlich

dialectic /daɪəˈlektɪk/

A *n. in sing. or pl. constr. as sing.* Dialektik, *die*

B *adj.* 1 dialektisch 2 (dialectal) dialektal; dialektisch

dialectical /daɪəˈlektɪkl/ *adj.* 1 ▸ **dialectic B 1** 2 **~ materialism** dialektischer Materialismus

ˈdial-in *adj* (Computing) ▸ **dial-up**

dialler, dialer /ˈdaɪələ(r)/ *n.* (Computing, Teleph.) Dialer, *der*

dialling: ~ code *n.* (Brit.) Vorwahl, *die;* Ortsnetzkennzahl, *die;* **~ tone** *n.* (Brit.) Wählton, *der*

dialogue (*Amer.:* **dialog**) /ˈdaɪəlɒg/ *n.* Dialog, *der;* **written in ~ [form]** in der Form eines Dialogs geschrieben

ˈdialogue box *n.* (Computing) Dialogbox, *die;* Dialogfenster, *das*

ˈdial-out *adj.* (Computing) **~ modem/connection/communication** Wählmodem, *das*/-leitung, *die*/-verbindung, *die*

ˈdial tone (Amer.) ▸ **dialling tone**

ˈdial-up *adj.* Einwahl-; **be ~:** per Einwahl erfolgen

dialysis /daɪˈælɪsɪs/ *n., pl.* **dialyses** /daɪˈælɪsiːz/ 1 (Chem.) Dialyse, *die* 2 (Med.) [Hämo]dialyse, *die* (fachspr.); Blutwäsche, *die; attrib.* **~ machine** Dialyseapparat, *der*

diameter /daɪˈæmɪtə(r)/ *n.* 1 Durchmesser, *der;* Diameter, *der* (Geom.) 2 **a magnification of eight ~s** eine achtfache Vergrößerung; **magnify 2,000 ~s** zweitausendfach vergrößern

diametrical /daɪəˈmetrɪkl/ *adj.* diametral; **I hold opinions in ~ opposition to his** meine Ansichten sind seinen diametral entgegengesetzt

diametrically /daɪəˈmetrɪkəlɪ/ *adv.* 1 (in direct opposition) diametral ‹*entgegengesetzt, widersprechen*› 2 (straight through) diametrisch

diamond /ˈdaɪəmənd/

A *n.* 1 Diamant, *der;* **it was [a case of] ~ cut ~** (fig.) da sind die Richtigen aneinander geraten 2 (figure) Raute, *die;* Rhombus, *der* 3 (Cards) Karo, *das; see also* **club A 4** 4 (tool) [Glaser]diamant, *der* 5 (Baseball) (space enclosed by bases) Innenfeld, *das;* (entire field) Spielfeld, *das. See also* **rough diamond**

B *adj.* 1 (made of ~[s]) diamanten; (set with ~[s]) diamantenbesetzt; Diamant‹*ring, -staub, -schmuck*› 2 (rhomb-shaped) rautenförmig

diamond: ~ drill *n.* Diamantbohrer, *der;* **~-field** *n.* Diamantlagerstätte, *die;* **~ ˈjubilee** *n.* 60-jähriges/75-jähriges Jubiläum; **~ merchant** *n.* Diamantenhändler, *der*/-händlerin, *die;* **~ mine** *n.* Diamantenbergwerk, *das;* **~-shaped** *adj.* rautenförmig; **~ ˈwedding** *n.* diamantene Hochzeit

dianthus /daɪˈænθəs/ *n.* (Bot.) Nelke, *die*

diaper /ˈdaɪəpə(r)/ *n.* 1 (Amer.: nappy) Windel, *die* 2 (fabric) *mit kleinen Rauten o. Ä. gemustertes* [*Jacquard*]*gewebe*

diaphanous /daɪˈæfənəs/ *adj.* durchsichtig

diaphragm /ˈdaɪəfræm/ *n.* Diaphragma, *das* (fachspr.); (Anat. also) Zwerchfell, *das;* (Zool., Bot. also) Scheidewand, *die;* (Photog. also) Blende, *die;* (contraceptive also) Pessar, *das;* (Mech., Teleph. also) Membran, *die*

diapositive /daɪəˈpɒzɪtɪv/ *n.* (Photog.) Diapositiv, *das*

diarist /ˈdaɪərɪst/ *n.* Tagebuchautor, *der*/-autorin, *die*

diarrhoea (*Amer.:* **diarrhea**) /daɪəˈriːə/ *n.* Durchfall, *der;* Diarrhö[e], *die* (Med.)

diary /ˈdaɪərɪ/ *n.* 1 Tagebuch, *das;* **keep a ~:** [ein] Tagebuch führen 2 (for appointments) Terminkalender, *der;* **pocket/desk ~:** Taschen-/Tischkalender, *der*

Diaspora /daɪˈæspərə/ *n.* Zerstreuung der Juden; (persons) Diaspora, *die*

diastolic /daɪəˈstɒlɪk/ *adj.* (Physiol.) diastolisch

diatom /ˈdaɪətəm/ *n.* (Biol.) Kieselalge, *die*

diatonic /daɪəˈtɒnɪk/ *adj.* (Mus.) diatonisch

diatribe /ˈdaɪətraɪb/ *n.* (speech) Schmährede, *die;* (piece of writing) Schmähschrift, *die*

dibber /ˈdɪbə(r)/ ▸ **dibble A**

dibble /ˈdɪbl/

A *n.* Pflanzholz, *das*

B *v.t.* [mit dem Pflanzholz] pflanzen

dice /daɪs/

A *n., pl. same* 1 (cube) Würfel, *der;* **throw ~:** würfeln; **throw ~ for sth.** etw. auswürfeln; **no ~!** (fig. coll.) kommt nicht infrage! 2 *in sing.* (game) Würfelspiel, *das;* **play ~:** würfeln 3 *in pl.* (Cookery) Würfel *Pl.;* **cut into ~:** würfeln

B *v.i.* würfeln (**for** um); **~ with death** mit seinem Leben spielen

C *v.t.* (Cookery) würfeln

dicey /ˈdaɪsɪ/ *adj.* (coll.) riskant; (unreliable) unzuverlässig

dichotomy /daɪˈkɒtəmɪ, dɪˈkɒtəmɪ/ *n.* Dichotomie, *die*

dick /dɪk/ *n.* 1 (coll.: detective) Schnüffler, *der* (ugs. abwertend) 2 (coarse: penis) Schwanz, *der* (derb); Riemen, *der* (*derb*). *See also* **clever Dick; tom 1**

dickens /ˈdɪkɪnz/ *n.* (coll.) **what/why/who** *etc.* **the ~ ...:** was/warum/wer *usw.* zum Kuckuck ... (salopp)

Dickensian /dɪˈkenzɪən/

A *n.* Dickensianer

B *adj.* dickenssch; **~ conditions** Zustände, wie man sie aus Dickens' Romanen kennt

ˈdickhead *n.* (coarse) Arsch, *der* (derb)

dicky[1] (**dickey**) /ˈdɪkɪ/ *n.* 1 ▸ **dicky bird** 2 (Brit. Hist.: seat) Klappsitz (*im Fond eines Zweisitzers*) 3 (coll.: shirt front) Vorhemd, *das*

dicky[2] *adj.* (coll.) mies (ugs. abwertend); klapprig (ugs.) ‹*Herz*›

ˈdicky bird *n.* (child lang./coll.) Piepvogel, *der* (Kinderspr.); (coll.: word) **not a ~:** kein Sterbenswörtchen

dicta *pl. of* **dictum**

Dictaphone ® /ˈdɪktəfəʊn/ *n.* Diktaphon, *das* (fachspr.); Diktiergerät, *das*

dictate

A /dɪkˈteɪt/ *v.t. & i.* diktieren; (prescribe) vorschreiben; **~ to** Vorschriften machen (+ *Dat.*); **I will not be ~d to** ich lasse mir keine Vorschriften machen

B /ˈdɪkteɪt/ *n., usu. in pl.* Diktat, *das*

dicˈtating machine *n.* Diktiergerät, *das*

dictation /dɪkˈteɪʃn/ *n.* Diktat, *das;* **take a ~:** ein Diktat aufnehmen

dictator /dɪkˈteɪtə(r)/ *n.* (lit. or fig.) Diktator, *der;* **be a ~** (fig.) diktatorisch sein

dictatorial /dɪktəˈtɔːrɪəl/ *adj.*, **dictatorially** /dɪktəˈtɔːrɪəlɪ/ *adv.* (lit. or fig.) diktatorisch

dictatorship /dɪkˈteɪtəʃɪp/ *n.* (lit. or fig.) Diktatur, *die*

diction /ˈdɪkʃn/ *n.* Diktion, *die* (geh.)

dictionary /ˈdɪkʃən(ə)rɪ/ *n.* Wörterbuch, *das; see also* **walking A**

dictum /ˈdɪktəm/ *n., pl.* **~s** *or* **dicta** /ˈdɪktə/ 1 (pronouncement, maxim) Spruch, *der;* Diktum, *das* (geh.) 2 (Law) richterliche Meinung

did ▸ **do**[1]

didactic /dɪˈdæktɪk, daɪˈdæktɪk/ *adj.* 1 didaktisch 2 (authoritarian) schulmeisterlich (abwertend)

diddle /ˈdɪdl/ *v.t.* (coll.) übers Ohr hauen (ugs.); **~ sb. out of sth.** jmdm. etw. abluchsen (salopp); **~ sb. into doing sth.** jmdn. so verschaukeln, dass er etw. tut (ugs.)

diddums /ˈdidəmz/ *n.* (child lang./coll.) der/die arme Kleine; **[poor little] ~!** armes Kleines!

didgeridoo /dɪdʒərɪˈduː/ *n.* Didgeridoo, *das*

didn't /ˈdɪdnt/ (coll.) **= did not;** ▸ **do**[1]

dido /ˈdaɪdəʊ/ *n., pl.* **~s** *or* **~es** (Amer. coll.) Mätzchen, *das* (ugs.)

die[1] /daɪ/

A *v.i.,* **dying** /ˈdaɪɪŋ/ 1 sterben; ‹*Tier, Pflanze:*› eingehen, (geh.) sterben; ‹*Körperteil:*› absterben; **be dying** sterben; **~ from** *or* **of sth.** an etw. (*Dat.*) sterben; **~ of grief** vor Kummer sterben; **~ of a heart attack/a brain tumour** einem Herzanfall/Hirntumor erliegen; **~ from one's injuries** seinen Verletzungen erliegen; **~ a rich man** als reicher Mann sterben; **~ by one's own hand** (literary) Hand an sich (*Akk.*) legen (geh.); **~ in one's bed** im Bett sterben; **~ in one's boots** (working) in den Sielen sterben; ‹*Soldat:*› im Kampf fallen; **sb. would ~ rather than do sth.** um nichts in der Welt würde jmd. etw. tun; **never say ~** (fig.) nur nicht den Mut verlieren 2 (fig.) **be dying for sth.** etw. unbedingt brauchen; **be dying for a cup of tea** nach einer Tasse Tee lechzen; **be dying to do sth.** darauf brennen, etw. zu tun; **I'm dying to know how she ...:** ich möchte zu gerne wissen, wie sie ...; **be dying of boredom/curiosity** vor Langeweile sterben/vor Neugier platzen; **~ [laughing]** sich totlachen (ugs.); **I [nearly] ~d with** *or* **of embarrassment** es war mir furchtbar peinlich; **~ with** *or* **of shame** sich zu Tode schämen 3 (disappear) in Vergessenheit geraten; ‹*Gefühl, Liebe, Ruhm:*› vergehen; ‹*Ton:*› verklingen; ‹*Flamme:*› verlöschen; ‹*Worte, Lächeln:*› ersterben (geh.); **the secret ~d with them** sie haben das Geheimnis mit ins Grab genommen 4 (coll.: cease to function) ‹*Zeitschrift, Firma:*› eingehen (ugs.); **the engine**

~d on me der Motor ist mir abgestorben
B *v.t.*, **dying:** ~ **a natural/violent death** eines natürlichen/gewaltsamen Todes sterben; **let the matter ~ a natural death** die Sache langsam einschlafen lassen; **sth. ~s the death** (coll.) mit etw. ist nichts mehr (ugs.)

(Phrasal verbs)

- ~ **a'way** *v.i.* ‹*Laut, Geräusch:*› schwächer werden; ‹*Wind, Zorn:*› sich legen
- ~ **'back** *v.i.* absterben
- ~ **'down** *v.i.* ‹*Sturm, Wind, Protest, Aufruhr:*› sich legen; ‹*Flammen:*› kleiner werden; ‹*Feuer:*› herunterbrennen; ‹*Lärm:*› leiser werden; ‹*Kämpfe:*› nachlassen; ‹*Epidemie:*› abklingen
- ~ **'off** *v.i.* ‹*Pflanzen, Tiere:*› [nacheinander] eingehen; ‹*Blätter:*› [nacheinander] absterben; ‹*Menschen:*› [nacheinander] sterben
- ~ **'out** *v.i.* aussterben

die² *n.* **1** *pl.* **dice** /daɪs/ (formal) Würfel, *der;* **the ~ is cast** die Würfel sind gefallen; **as straight** *or* **true as a ~:** schnurgerade ‹*Weg, Linie*›; (fig.) grundehrlich **2** *pl.* **~s** (engraved stamp) Stempel, *der* **3** *pl.* **~s** (Metalw.) Gussform, *die;* (in drop-forging) Gesenk, *das* **4** (for cutting threads) [Gewinde]schneideisen, *das*

die: ~back *n., no pl.* Absterben, *das;* (of trees) Wipfeldürre, *die;* **~-cast A** *adj.* druckgegossen; **B** *v.t.* druckgießen; **~-casting** *n.* **1** *no pl.* (process) [Kokillen]guss, *der;* **2** (product) Gussstück, *das;* **~hard A** *n.* hartnäckiger Typ; (reactionary) Ewiggestrige, *der/die;* **B** *adj.* hartnäckig; (dyed-in-the-wool) eingefleischt; (reactionary) ewiggestrig

diesel /'di:zl/ *n.* ~ **[engine]** Diesel[motor], *der;* ~ **[lorry/car]** Diesel, *der;* ~ **[train]** (Railw.) Dieseltriebwagen, *der;* ~ **[fuel]** Diesel[kraftstoff], *der*

diesel-e'lectric *adj.* dieselelektrisch

'diesel oil *n.* Dieseltreibstoff, *der*

diet¹ /'daɪət/
A *n.* **1** (for slimming) Diät, *die;* Schlankheitskur, *die;* **be/go on a ~:** eine Schlankheitskur *od.* Diät machen **2** (Med.) Diät, *die;* Schonkost, *die* **3** (habitual food) Kost, *die*
B *v.i.* eine Schlankheitskur *od.* Diät machen

diet² *n.* (Polit.) Reichstag, *der*

dietary /'daɪətərɪ/ *adj.* ~ **rules** Diätvorschriften; ~ **habits** Essgewohnheiten; ~ **deficiencies** mangelhafte Ernährung

dietetic /daɪə'tetɪk/ *adj.* Diät-; diätetisch

dietetics /daɪə'tetɪks/ *n., no pl.* Ernährungslehre, *die;* Diätetik, *die* (fachspr.)

dietitian (**dietician**) /daɪə'tɪʃn/ *n.* ▸ⓘ **p. 1260** Diätassistent, *der/*-assistentin, *die*

'diet sheet *n.* Diätplan, *der*

differ /'dɪfə(r)/ *v.i.* **1** (vary, be different) sich unterscheiden; **the two accounts of what happened ~ed greatly** die beiden Berichte von den Ereignissen wichen stark voneinander ab; **opinions/ideas ~:** die Meinungen/Vorstellungen gehen auseinander; **tastes/temperaments ~:** die Geschmäcker (ugs.) / Temperamente sind verschieden; **people ~:** es sind nicht alle Menschen gleich; ~ **from sb./sth. in that ...:** sich von jmdm./etw. dadurch *od.* darin unterscheiden, dass ... **2** (disagree) anderer Meinung sein; ~ **with sb. over** *or* **on sth.** über etw. (*Akk.*) anderer Meinung sein als jmd.; *see also* **agree A 1**; **beg A 2**

difference /'dɪfərəns/ *n.* **1** Unterschied, *der;* ~ **in age** Altersunterschied, *der;* **have a ~ of opinion [with sb.]** eine Meinungsverschiedenheit [mit jmdm.] haben; **there is a ~ in her now** (in appearance) sie sieht jetzt anders aus; (in character) sie hat sich geändert; **it makes a ~:** es ist ein *od.* (ugs.) macht einen Unterschied; **what ~ would it make if ...?** was würde es schon ausmachen, wenn ...?; **the new curtains make a big ~ to the room** mit den neuen Vorhängen sieht das Zimmer schon ganz anders aus; **it makes a ~:** es ist ein *od.* (ugs.) macht einen Unterschied; **as if that made any ~:** als ob das etwas ändern würde; **make all the ~ [in the world]** ungeheuer viel ausmachen; **I could [as well] have stayed at home for all the ~ it made** da hätte ich auch gleich zu Hause bleiben können; **make no ~ [to sb.]** [jmdm.] nichts ausmachen; **a holiday with a ~:** Urlaub — einmal anders; **same ~** (coll.) ein und dasselbe **2** (between amounts) Differenz, *die;* **pay the ~:** den Rest[betrag] bezahlen; **split the ~:** sich (*Dat.*) den Rest[betrag] teilen; (fig.) einen Kompromiss machen **3** (dispute) **have a ~ with sb.** mit jmdm. eine Auseinandersetzung haben; **resolve** *or* **settle one's ~s** seine Differenzen beilegen

different /'dɪfərənt/ *adj.* verschieden; (pred. also) anders; (attrib. also) ander...; **be ~ from** *or* (esp. Brit.) **to** *or* (Amer.) **than ...:** anders sein als ...; **the two sisters are very ~ from each other** die beiden Schwestern sind sehr verschieden; **she was totally ~ from** *or* **to what I'd expected** sie war ganz anders, als ich erwartet hatte; ~ **viewpoints/cultures** unterschiedliche Standpunkte/Kulturen; **how are they ~?** worin *od.* wodurch unterscheiden sie sich?; **I feel a ~ person** ich fühle mich wie neugeboren; **I asked several ~ people** ich habe mehrere *od.* verschiedene Leute gefragt; **wear a ~ dress on every occasion** zu jedem Anlass ein anderes Kleid tragen; **oh, that's ~:** ach so, das ist was anderes; **a holiday that is ~:** Urlaub — einmal anders; **the same, only ~** (coll.) fast der-/die-/dasselbe

differential /dɪfə'renʃl/
A *adj.* **1** unterschiedlich; ungleich ‹*Behandlung*›; gestaffelt ‹*Lohn, Kosten*›; unterscheidend ‹*Merkmal*›; ~ **tariffs/duties** (Commerc.) Differenzialtarife/-zölle **2** (Math.) ~ **calculus** Differenzialrechnung, *die;* ~ **equation** Differenzialgleichung, *die;* ~ **coefficient** ▸**derivative B 2**
B *n.* **1** (Commerc.) **[wage] ~:** [Einkommens]unterschied, *der;* **price ~s** Preisunterschiede **2** (Motor Veh.) Differenzial[getriebe], *das;* Ausgleichsgetriebe, *das*

differentiate /dɪfə'renʃɪeɪt/
A *v.t.* **1** unterscheiden **2** (Biol.) herausbilden **3** (Math.) differenzieren
B *v.i.* **1** (recognize the difference) unterscheiden; differenzieren **2** (treat sth. differently) einen Unterschied machen; differenzieren

differentiation /dɪferenʃɪ'eɪʃn/ *n.* **1** Unterscheidung, *die;* Differenzierung, *die* **2** (Biol., Math.) Differenzierung, *die*

differently /'dɪfərəntlɪ/ *adv.* anders (**from,** *esp. Brit.* **to** als); ~ **[to** *or* **from each other]** verschieden; (with different result, at various times) unterschiedlich; **they reacted ~ to the news** sie reagierten unterschiedlich auf die Nachricht

differing /'dɪfərɪŋ/ *adj.* unterschiedlich

difficult /'dɪfɪkəlt/ *adj.* **1** schwer; schwierig; **a ~ writer** ein schwieriger Schriftsteller; **he finds it ~ to do sth.** ihm fällt es schwer, etw. zu tun; **make things ~ for sb.** es jmdm. nicht leicht machen; **the ~ thing is ...:** die Schwierigkeit ist ... **2** (unaccommodating) schwierig; **he is being ~:** er macht Schwierigkeiten; **he is ~ to get on with** es ist schwer, mit ihm auszukommen

difficulty /'dɪfɪkəltɪ/ *n.* **1** Schwierigkeit, *die;* **with [great] ~:** [sehr] mühsam; **with the greatest ~:** unter größten Schwierigkeiten; **without [great] ~:** ohne große Probleme; mühelos; **have ~ [in] doing sth.** Schwierigkeiten haben, etw. zu tun; **experience** *or* **have [some] ~ in walking** Beschwerden beim Gehen haben **2** *usu. in pl.* (trouble) **be in ~** *or* **difficulties** in Schwierigkeiten sein; **under great difficulties** unter großen Schwierigkeiten; **fall** *or* **get into difficulties** in Schwierigkeiten kommen *od.* geraten

diffidence /'dɪfɪdəns/ *n., no pl.* Zaghaftigkeit, *die;* (modesty) Zurückhaltung, *die*

diffident /'dɪfɪdənt/ *adj.* zaghaft; (modest) zurückhaltend

diffraction /dɪ'frækʃn/ *n.* (Phys.) Beugung, *die;* Diffraktion, *die* (veralt.)

diffuse
A /dɪ'fju:z/ *v.t.* verbreiten; diffundieren (fachspr.); **~d lighting/traces** diffuse Beleuchtung/Spuren
B /dɪ'fju:z/ *v.i.* sich ausbreiten (**through** in + *Dat.*); diffundieren (fachspr.)
C /dɪ'fju:s/ *adj.* **1** (dispersed) diffus **2** (verbose) weitschweifig; diffus (fig.)

diffuser /dɪ'fju:zə(r)/ *n.* Diffusor, *der*

diffusion /dɪ'fju:ʒn/ *n.* **1** (also Anthrop.) Verbreitung, *die* **2** (Phys.) Diffusion, *die*

dig /dɪg/
A *v.i.*, **-gg-, dug** /dʌg/ **1** graben (**for** nach) **2** (Archaeol.: excavate) Ausgrabungen machen; graben; (fig.: search) ~ **for information** versuchen, Informationen zu bekommen **3** ~ **at sb.** eine [spitze] Bemerkung über jmdn. machen
B *v.t.*, **-gg-, dug 1** graben; ~ **a hole [in sth.]** ein Loch [in etw. (*Akk.*)] graben **2** (turn up with spade etc.) umgraben; (obtain by digging) ~ **potatoes/peat** Kartoffeln ernten *od.* (landsch.) ausmachen/Torf stechen **3** (Archaeol.) ausgraben **4** (coll.: appreciate) stark finden (Jugendspr.); (understand) schnallen (salopp)
C *n.* **1** Grabung, *die* **2** (Archaeol. coll.) Ausgrabung, *die;* (site) Ausgrabungsort, *der* **3** (fig.) Anspielung, *die* (**at** auf + *Akk.*); **have** *or* **make a ~ at sb./sth.** eine [spitze] Bemerkung über jmdn./etw. machen **4** ▸**rib A1**

(Phrasal verbs)

- ~ **'in**
  A *v.i.* **1** (Mil.) sich eingraben; (fig.) sich festsetzen **2** (coll.: begin eating, eat) zulangen (ugs.)
  B *v.t.* **1** (Mil.) eingraben; ~ **oneself in** sich eingraben; (fig.) sich etablieren **2** (thrust) **the cat dug its claws in** die Katze krallte sich fest; ~ **one's heels** *or* **toes in** (fig.) sich auf die Hinterbeine stellen (ugs.) **3** (mix with soil) eingraben
- ~ **into** *v.t.* **1** wühlen in (+ *Akk.*) ‹*Tasche*›; eindringen in (+ *Akk.*) ‹*Materie*›; vordringen in (+ *Akk.*) ‹*Vergangenheit, Geschichte*› **2** (coll.: begin eating) zulangen bei (ugs.) **3** (take from) ~ **into one's savings** seine Ersparnisse angreifen; **have to ~ into one's pocket** in die Tasche greifen müssen **4** (mix with) ~ **compost into the soil** Kompost untergraben **5** (embed itself in) sich graben in (+ *Akk.*)
- ~ **'out** *v.t.* (lit. or fig.) ausgraben; ~ **sb. out from underneath the debris/out of the wreckage** jmdn. aus den Trümmern bergen
- ~ **'up** *v.t.* **1** umgraben ‹*Garten, Rasen, Erde*›; ausgraben ‹*Pflanzen, Knochen, Leiche, Schatz*›; aufreißen ‹*Straße*› **2** (fig.: find) ausgraben ‹*Fakten, Informationen*›; (coll. derog.: obtain) aufgabeln (ugs.)

digest
A /dɪ'dʒest, daɪ'dʒest/ *v.t.* **1** (assimilate, lit or fig.) verdauen **2** (consider) durchdenken
B /'daɪdʒest/ *n.* **1** (periodical) Digest, *der od. das* (*Zeitschrift mit Auszügen aus Büchern od. anderen Zeitschriften*) **2** (summary) Zusammenfassung, *die*

digestible /dɪ'dʒestɪbl, daɪ'dʒestɪbl/ *adj.* verdaulich; (fig.) verständlich

digestion /dɪ'dʒestʃn, daɪ'dʒestʃn/ *n.* Verdauung, *die;* Digestion, *die* (Physiol.); (fig.) [geistige] Verarbeitung

digestive /dɪ'dʒestɪv, daɪ'dʒestɪv/
A *adj.* Verdauungs-; ~ **biscuit** (Brit.) ▸**B**
B *n.* (Brit.: biscuit) Keks (*aus Vollkornmehl*)

digestive: ~ **juices** *n. pl.* Verdauungssäfte *Pl.;* ~ **tract** *n.* Verdauungstrakt, *der*

digger /'dɪgə(r)/ *n.* **1** (Archaeol.) Ausgräber, *der/*Ausgräberin, *die;* (miner) Bergmann, *der;* (gold-~) Goldgräber, *der* **2** (Mech.) Bagger, *der;* (garden tool) Grabschaufel, *die;* **trench ~:** Grabenbagger, *der* **3** (fig. coll.) (Australian) Australier, *der/*Australierin, *die;* (New Zealander) Neuseeländer, *der/*Neuseeländerin, *die*

diggings /'dɪgɪŋz/ *n. pl.* **1** (Mining) [Gold]lagerstätte, *die* **2** (Archaeol.) Ausgrabungsort, *der*

digit /'dɪdʒɪt/ *n.* **1** (numeral) Ziffer, *die;* **a six-~ number** eine sechsstellige Zahl **2** (Zool., Anat.) (finger) Finger, *der;* (toe) Zehe, *die*

digital /'dɪdʒɪtl/ *adj.* **1** (numerical) digital; ~ **access lock** digitale Zugriffsperre; ~ **audio tape** Digitaltonband, *das;* ~ **camera** Digitalkamera, *die;* ~ **clock/watch** Digitaluhr, *die;* ~ **computer** Digitalrechner, *der;* ~ **divide** digitale Kluft; ~ **economy** digitalisierte Wirtschaft; Digitalökonomie, *die;* ~ **highway** digitale Datenautobahn; ~ **image** Digitalbild, *das;* digitales Bild; ~ **radio** Digitalradio, *das* ~ **recording** Digitalaufnahme, die; ~ signature digitale Unterschrift; ~ television, ~ TV (TV set) Digitalfernseher, der; (system) Digitalfernsehen, das; ~ video disc DVD, die; Digital Video Disc, die [2] (Zool., Anat.) digital

digitally /ˈdɪdʒɪtəlɪ/ adv. digital; ~ remastered digital aufbereitet ‹Film, Aufnahme›

digitize (**digitise**) /ˈdɪdʒɪtaɪz/ v.t. (Computing) digitalisieren

dignified /ˈdɪgnɪfaɪd/ adj. würdig; (self-respecting, stately) würdevoll

dignify /ˈdɪgnɪfaɪ/ v.t. [1] (make stately) Würde verleihen (+ Dat.) [2] (give distinction to) Glanz verleihen (+ Dat.); auszeichnen ‹Person› [3] (give grand title to) aufwerten (fig.)

dignitary /ˈdɪgnɪtərɪ/ n. Würdenträger, der; **dignitaries** (notabilities) Honoratioren; **church ~**: kirchlicher Würdenträger

dignity /ˈdɪgnɪtɪ/ n. Würde, die; **speak with quiet ~**: ruhig und würdevoll sprechen; **he is not one to stand on his ~**: er hat keine Angst, sich (Dat.) etwas zu vergeben; **be beneath one's ~**: unter seiner Würde sein

digress /daɪˈgres, dɪˈgres/ v.i. abschweifen (**from** von, **on** zu)

digression /daɪˈgreʃn, dɪˈgreʃn/ n. Abschweifung, die; (passage) Exkurs, der

digs /dɪgz/ n. pl. (Brit. coll.) Bude, die (ugs.); **he's in ~**: er hat eine [eigene] Bude (ugs.)

dike ▸ **dyke**

diktat /ˈdɪktæt/ n. [1] (decree) Anordnung, die [2] (severe settlement) Diktat, das

dilapidated /dɪˈlæpɪdeɪtɪd/ adj. verfallen ‹Gebäude›; verwahrlost ‹Äußeres, Erscheinung›

dilapidation /dɪlæpɪˈdeɪʃn/ n., no pl. Verfall, der; **in a state of ~**: in verwahrlostem Zustand

dilatation /daɪləˈteɪʃn, dɪləˈteɪʃn/ n. [1] ▸ **dilation** [2] (Med.) Dilatation, die (fachspr.); Erweiterung, die

dilate /daɪˈleɪt, dɪˈleɪt/
[A] v.i. [1] sich weiten [2] (discourse) ~ **[up]on sth.** sich über etw. (Akk.) verbreiten
[B] v.t. ausdehnen; blähen ‹Nüstern›

dilation /daɪˈleɪʃn, dɪˈleɪʃn/ n. Dilatation, die; (Phys. also) Ausdehnung, die; (Med. also) Erweiterung, die

dilatory /ˈdɪlətərɪ/ adj. langsam; saumselig (geh.); zögernd ‹Antwort, Reaktion›; (causing delay) **be ~ in** sich (Dat.) [viel] Zeit lassen bei

dildo /ˈdɪldəʊ/ n., pl. **~s** Godemiché, der

dilemma /dɪˈlemə, daɪˈlemə/ n. (also Logic) Dilemma, das; **be on the horns of** or **faced with a ~**: vor einem Dilemma stehen

dilettante /dɪlɪˈtæntɪ/
[A] n., pl. **dilettanti** /dɪlɪˈtæntiː/ or **~s** Dilettant, der/Dilettantin, die; Laie, der
[B] adj. dilettantisch; laienhaft ‹Interesse›

diligence /ˈdɪlɪdʒəns/ n. Fleiß, der; (purposefulness) Eifer, der

diligent /ˈdɪlɪdʒənt/ adj. fleißig; (purposeful) eifrig; sorgfältig, gewissenhaft ‹Arbeit, Suche›

diligently /ˈdɪlɪdʒəntlɪ/ adv. fleißig; (purposefully) eifrig; **execute one's duties ~**: seine Pflichten gewissenhaft erfüllen

dill /dɪl/ n. (Bot.) Dill, der

dill: ~ pickle n.: mit Dill eingelegte Gurke usw.; **~-water** n. Dillöl, das (Pharm.)

dilly /ˈdɪlɪ/ n. (coll.) irre Type (ugs.); (thing) irres Ding (ugs.)

dilly-dally /ˈdɪlɪdælɪ/ v.i. (coll.) [1] (dawdle) trödeln [2] (vacillate) ~ **over the choice of sth.** sich nicht für etw. entscheiden können; **stop ~ing!** entscheide dich endlich!

diluent /ˈdɪljʊənt/ n. Verdünnungsmittel, das

dilute
[A] /daɪˈljuːt, ˈdaɪljuːt/ adj. [1] verdünnt [2] (washed out) verwaschen ‹Farbe›; (faded) verblasst, ausgebleicht ‹Farbe› [3] (fig.) blass (geh.)
[B] /daɪˈljuːt/ v.t. [1] verdünnen [2] ausbleichen ‹Farbe› [3] (fig.) abschwächen; entschärfen

dilution /daɪˈljuːʃn, daɪˈluːʃn/ n. [1] (act) Verdünnen, das [2] (state, substance) Verdünnung, die [3] (fig.) Abschwächung, die

dim /dɪm/
[A] adj. [1] schwach, trüb ‹Licht, Flackern›; matt, gedeckt ‹Farbe›; dämmrig, dunkel ‹Zimmer›; undeutlich, verschwommen ‹Gestalt›; **grow ~**: schwächer werden [2] (fig.) blass; verschwommen; **in the ~ and distant past** in ferner Vergangenheit; **have a ~ suspicion that ...**: den leisen Verdacht haben, dass ...; **have only a ~ understanding of sth.** nur eine ungefähre od. vage Vorstellung von etw. haben [3] (indistinct) schwach, getrübt ‹Seh-, Hörvermögen›; **his eyesight/hearing had grown ~**: seine Augen hatten/sein Gehör hatte nachgelassen [4] (coll.) (stupid) beschränkt; (clumsy) ungeschickt [5] **take a ~ view of sth.** (coll.) von etw. nicht erbaut sein
[B] v.i., **-mm-** (lit. or fig.) schwächer werden
[C] v.t., **-mm-** [1] verdunkeln; verdüstern; (fig.) trüben; dämpfen; **~ the lights** (Theatre, Cinemat.) die Lichter langsam verlöschen lassen [2] (Amer. Motor Veh.) abblenden

Phrasal verb

• **~ 'out** v.t. [1] verdunkeln [2] (Theatre) **~ out the lights on stage** die Bühne abblenden. See also **dim-out**

dime /daɪm/ n. (Amer.) Zehncentstück, das; ≈ Groschen, der (ugs.); **be a ~ a dozen** (fig.) Dutzendware sein (fig. abwertend); **it's not worth a ~** (fig.) es ist keinen Pfifferling wert (ugs.); **~ novel** Groschenroman, der (abwertend)

dimension /dɪˈmenʃn, daɪˈmenʃn/
[A] n. (lit. or fig.) Dimension, die; **~s** (measurements) Abmessungen; Maße
[B] v.t. dimensionieren

-dimensional /dɪˈmenʃənl, daɪˈmenʃənl/ adj. in comb. -dimensional

diminish /dɪˈmɪnɪʃ/
[A] v.i. nachlassen; ‹Zahl:› sich verringern; ‹Vorräte, Autorität, Einfluss:› abnehmen; ‹Wert, Bedeutung, Ansehen:› geringer werden; **~ in value/number** an Wert verlieren/an Zahl od. zahlenmäßig abnehmen
[B] v.t. vermindern; verringern; (fig.) herabwürdigen ‹Person›; schmälern ‹Ansehen, Ruf›

diminished /dɪˈmɪnɪʃt/ adj. geringer ‹Wert, Anzahl, Einfluss, Popularität›; vermindert ‹Stärke, Fähigkeit›; verringert ‹Belegschaft›; verkleinert ‹Reich›; **[plead] ~ responsibility** (Law) [auf] verminderte Zurechnungsfähigkeit [plädieren]; **~ interval** (Mus.) vermindertes Intervall

diminishing /dɪˈmɪnɪʃɪŋ/ adj. sinkend; abnehmend ‹Vorräte›; schwindend ‹Kraft, Einfluss, Macht›; **law of ~ returns** (Econ.) Gesetz vom abnehmenden Ertragszuwachs; Ertragsgesetz, das

diminuendo /dɪmɪnjʊˈendəʊ/ (Mus.) n., pl. **~s** Diminuendo, das

diminution /dɪmɪˈnjuːʃn/ n. (of number, supplies) Verringerung, die; (of value) Minderung, die; (of strength, influence) Schwinden, das; (of reputation, fame) Schmälerung, die; (Mus.) Diminution, die

diminutive /dɪˈmɪnjʊtɪv/
[A] adj. [1] winzig [2] (Ling.) diminutiv
[B] n. (Ling.) Diminutiv[um], das

dimly /ˈdɪmlɪ/ adv. schwach; undeutlich ‹sehen›; ungefähr ‹begreifen›; **I ~ remember it** ich erinnere mich noch dunkel daran

dimmer /ˈdɪmə(r)/ n. [1] **~ [switch]** Dimmer, der; Helligkeitsregler, der [2] (Amer. Motor Veh.: switch) Abblendschalter, der

dimness /ˈdɪmnɪs/ n., no pl. [1] Trübheit, die; (almost darkness) Halbdunkel, das [2] (fig.) Undeutlichkeit, die; Unklarheit, die

dimorphic /daɪˈmɔːfɪk/ adj. (Biol., Chem., Min.) dimorph

dimorphism /daɪˈmɔːfɪzm/ n. (Biol., Chem., Min.) Dimorphie, die

'dim-out n. [1] Verdunk[e]lung, die [2] (Theatre) Abblendung, die

dimple /ˈdɪmpl/ n. Grübchen, das; (on golf ball etc.) kleine Vertiefung

dim: ~wit n. (coll.) Dummkopf, der (ugs.); **~-witted** /ˈdɪmwɪtɪd/ adj. (coll.) dusselig (salopp); dämlich (ugs. abwertend)

din /dɪn/
[A] n. Lärm, der
[B] v.t., **-nn-: ~ sth. into sb.** jmdm. etw. einhämmern od. einbläuen

din-din[s] /ˈdɪndɪn(z)/ n. (child lang.) Fresschen, das (ugs.)

dine /daɪn/
[A] v.i. (at midday/in the evening) [zu Mittag/zu Abend] essen od. (geh.) speisen; dinieren (geh.); **~ off/on sth.** etw. [zum Mittag-/Abendessen] verzehren; **~ off sth.** (eat from) von etw. speisen
[B] v.t. bewirten; see also **wine and dine**

Phrasal verb

• **~ 'out** v.i. [1] auswärts [zu Mittag/Abend] essen [2] **~ out on sth.** wegen etw. zum Essen eingeladen werden

diner /ˈdaɪnə(r)/ n. [1] Gast, der (zum Abendessen) [2] (Railw.) Speisewagen, der [3] (Amer.: restaurant) Restaurant, das

ding-a-ling /ˈdɪŋəlɪŋ/ ▸ **ting-a-ling**

ding-dong /ˈdɪŋdɒŋ/
[A] n. [1] Bimbam, das [2] (coll.: argument) Krach, der (ugs.)
[B] adj. hin- und herwogend
[C] adv. mit Feuereifer

dinghy /ˈdɪŋgɪ, ˈdɪŋɪ/ n. Ding[h]i, das; (inflatable) Schlauchboot, das

dingle /ˈdɪŋgl/ n. waldiges kleines Tal

dingo /ˈdɪŋgəʊ/ n., pl. **~es** [1] (dog) Dingo, der [2] (Austral. coll.: rogue) [gemeiner] Hund (salopp)

dingy /ˈdɪndʒɪ/ adj. schmuddelig

dining/ˈdaɪnɪŋ/: **~ area** n. ≈ Essecke, die; **~ car** n. (Railw.) Speisewagen, der; **~ chair** n. Esszimmerstuhl, der; **~ hall** n. Speisesaal, der; **~ room** n. (in private house) Esszimmer, das; (in hotel etc.) Speisesaal, der; **~ table** n. Esstisch, der

dinkum /ˈdɪŋkəm/ (Austral. and NZ coll.) adj. astrein (ugs.); **fair ~**: echt (ugs.); **[the] ~ oil** die Wahrheit

dinky /ˈdɪŋkɪ/ adj. (coll.) [1] (Brit.: small and neat) niedlich [2] (Amer.: trifling) kümmerlich

dinner /ˈdɪnə(r)/ n. Essen, das; (at midday also) Mittagessen, das; (in the evening also) Abendessen, das; (formal event) Diner, das; **have** or **eat [one's] ~**: zu Mittag/Abend essen; **go out to ~**: [abends] essen gehen; (to friends) zum [Abend]essen eingeladen sein; **~'s ready!** [das] Essen ist fertig!; **be at** or **having** or **eating [one's] ~**: gerade beim Essen sein; **have people [in] to** or **for ~**: Gäste zum Essen haben

dinner: ~ dance n.: Abendessen mit anschließendem Tanz; **~ gong** n. Gong, der; **~ hour** n. Mittagspause, die; **~ jacket** n. (Brit.) Dinnerjacket, das; **~ lady** n. ▸ ❶ p. 1260 (Brit.) Serviererin beim Mittagessen in der Schule; **~ money** n., no pl. (Brit.) Essensgeld, das; **~ party** n. Abendeinladung, die (mit Essen); (more formal) Abendgesellschaft, die; **~ plate** n. flacher Teller; Essteller, der; **~ service** n. Essgeschirr, das; **~ table** n. Esstisch, der; **be at** or **seated round the ~ table** bei Tisch sitzen; **~ time** n. Essenszeit, die; **at ~ time** zur Essenszeit; (12-2 p.m.) mittags

dinosaur /ˈdaɪnəsɔː(r)/ n. Dinosaurier, der

dint /dɪnt/ n. [1] **by ~ of** durch; **by ~ of doing sth.** indem jmd. etw. tut [2] ▸ **dent A**

diocesan /daɪˈɒsɪsən/ adj. (Eccl.) diözesan; **~ synod** Diözesansynode, die

diocese /ˈdaɪəsɪs/ n. (Eccl.) Diözese, die

diode /ˈdaɪəʊd/ n. (Electron.) Diode, die

dioxide /daɪˈɒksaɪd/ n. (Chem.) Dioxid, das; Dioxyd, das

dioxin /daɪˈɒksɪn/ n. (Chem.) Dioxin, das

dip /dɪp/
[A] v.t., **-pp-** [1] [ein]tauchen (**in** in + Akk.); **she ~ped her hand into the sack** sie griff in den Sack [2] (dye) in ein Färbemittel tauchen [3] (Agric.) dippen ‹Schaf› [4] (Brit. Motor Veh.) **~ one's [head]lights** abblenden; **[drive with** or **on] ~ped headlights** [mit] Abblendlicht [fahren]
[B] v.i., **-pp-** [1] (go down) sinken; **the sun ~ped below the horizon** die Sonne versank hinter dem Horizont [2] (Aeronaut.) vor dem Steigen plötzlich absacken [3] (incline downwards, lit. or fig.) abfallen; **the magnetic needle ~s** die

Magnetnadel neigt sich **4** (go under water) [ein-]tauchen; **~ under** untertauchen **5** (Brit. Motor Veh.) abblenden

C *n.* **1** (dipping) [kurzes] Eintauchen; **give sb./sth. a ~ in sth.** jmdn./etw. in etw. (*Akk.*) [kurz] eintauchen; *see also* **lucky ~** **2** (bathe) [kurzes] Bad **3** (of stratum) Fallen, *das* (Geol.); (of road) Senke, *die;* (hollow, depression in landscape) Mulde, *die* **4** (Gastr.) Dip, *der* **5** (for sheep) Räudebad, *das* **6** (underworld sl.: pickpocket) Krebs, *der* (Gaunerspr.)

Phrasal verb

• **~ into** *v.t.* **1** greifen in (+ *Akk.*); (put ladle into) den Löffel tauchen in (+ *Akk.*); (fig.) **~ into one's pocket** *or* **purse** tief in die Tasche greifen; **~ into one's reserves/savings** seine Reserven antasten/Ersparnisse angreifen **2** (look cursorily at) einen flüchtigen Blick werfen in (+ *Akk.*); **the book is good for ~ping into** man kann das Buch gut in kurzen Abschnitten lesen

Dip. *abbr.* **= Diploma** Dipl.

DipEd /dɪpˈed/ *abbr.* **= Diploma in Education** Pädagogikdiplom, *das; see also* **BSc**

diphtheria /dɪfˈθɪərɪə/ *n.* ▸❶ **p. 1231** (Med.) Diphtherie, *die*

diphthong /ˈdɪfθɒŋ/ *n.* (Phonet.) Diphthong, *der* (fachspr.); Doppellaut, *der*

diploma /dɪˈpləʊmə/ *n.* **1** (Educ.) Diplom, *das* **2** (conferring honour) [Ehren]urkunde, *die* **3** (charter) Charte, *die*

diplomacy /dɪˈpləʊməsɪ/ *n.* (Polit.; also fig.) Diplomatie, *die;* **use ~** (fig.) diplomatisch vorgehen

diplomat /ˈdɪpləmæt/ *n.* ▸❶ **p. 1260** (Polit.; also fig.) Diplomat, *der*/Diplomatin, *die*

diplomatic /dɪpləˈmætɪk/ *adj.*, **diplomatically** /dɪpləˈmætɪkəlɪ/ *adv.* (Polit.; also fig.) diplomatisch

diplomatic: ~ ˈbag *n.* **~ bags** Kuriergepäck, *das;* **~ corps** *n.* diplomatisches Korps; **~ imˈmunity** *n.* diplomatische Immunität; **~ ˈpassport** *n.* Diplomatenpass, *der;* **~ service** *n.* diplomatischer Dienst

diplomatist /dɪˈpləʊmətɪst/ ▸**diplomat**

dipole /ˈdaɪpəʊl/ *n.* (Electr., Magn., Chem., Radio) Dipol, *der*

dipper /ˈdɪpə(r)/ *n.* **1** (excavating machine) Löffelbagger, *der* **2** (Ornith.) Wasseramsel, *die* **3** (ladle) Schöpfkelle, *die* **4** (Amer. Astron.) **Big/Little D~:** Großer/Kleiner Wagen *od.* Bär **5** ▸**big dipper a**

dippy /ˈdɪpɪ/ *adj.* (coll.) übergeschnappt (ugs.); **go ~:** überschnappen (ugs.); **be ~ about sb./sth.** verrückt nach jmdm./etw. sein

dipsomania /dɪpsəˈmeɪnɪə/ *n.*, *no pl.* Dipsomanie, *die*

dipsomaniac /dɪpsəˈmeɪnɪæk/ *n.* Dipsomane, *der*/Dipsomanin, *die*

dip: ~stick *n.* [Öl-/Benzin]messstab, *der;* **~ switch** *n.* (Brit. Motor Veh.) Abblendschalter, *der*

dire /daɪə(r)/ *adj.* **1** (dreadful) entsetzlich; furchtbar **2** (ominous) unheilvoll **3** (extreme) **~ necessity** dringende Notwendigkeit; **be in ~ need of sth.** etw. dringend benötigen *od.* brauchen; **in cases of ~ emergency** im äußersten Notfall; **be in ~ [financial] straits** in einer ernsten [finanziellen] Notlage sein

direct /dɪˈrekt, daɪˈrekt/

A *v.t.* **1** ▸❶ **p. 1699** (turn) richten (**to[wards]** auf + *Akk.*); **~ one's steps towards sth.** seine Schritte nach etw. lenken; **~ sb.'s attention to sth.** jmds. Aufmerksamkeit auf etw. (*Akk.*) lenken; **the remark/wink was ~ed at you** die Bemerkung/das Zwinkern galt dir; **~ a blow at sb.** nach jmdm. schlagen; **the bomb/missile was ~ed at** die Bombe/das Geschoss galt (+ *Dat.*); **government policy is ~ed at reducing inflation** die Regierungspolitik ist darauf ausgerichtet, die Inflation einzudämmen; **~ sb. to a place** jmdm. den Weg zu einem Ort weisen *od.* sagen; **~ a parcel to sb./an address in L.** ein Paket an jmdn. adressieren/an eine Adresse in L. senden *od.* schicken **2** (control) leiten; beaufsichtigen ⟨*Arbeitskräfte, Arbeitsablauf*⟩; lenken ⟨*Volksmassen*⟩; regeln, dirigieren ⟨*Verkehr*⟩; **does fate ~ our actions?** lenkt das Schicksal unser Tun? **3** (order) anweisen; **~ sb. to do sth.** jmdn. anweisen, etw. zu tun; **~ sth. to be done** *or* **that sth. [should] be done** anordnen, dass etw. zu tun sei; **as ~ed [by the doctor]** wie [vom Arzt] verordnet; nach [ärztlicher] Verordnung **4** (Theatre, Cinemat., Telev., Radio) Regie führen bei; inszenieren; **~ed by Orson Welles** unter der Regie von Orson Welles

B *adj.* **1** (straight, without intermediaries; also Geneal., Logic) direkt; durchgehend ⟨*Zug*⟩; unmittelbar ⟨*Ursache, Gefahr, Auswirkung*⟩; (immediate) unmittelbar, persönlich ⟨*Erfahrung, Verantwortung, Beteiligung*⟩; **be in the ~ line of fire** genau in der Schusslinie stehen; **'keep away from ~ heat'** „nicht unmittelbar der Hitze aussetzen!" **2** (diametrical) genau ⟨*Gegenteil*⟩; direkt ⟨*Widerspruch*⟩; diametral ⟨*Gegensatz*⟩ **3** (frank) direkt; offen; glatt ⟨*Absage*⟩; **he's a very ~ person** er ist immer sehr direkt *od.* geradeheraus; **be ~ with sb.** offen zu jmdm. sein

C *adv.* direkt

direct: ~ ˈaccess *n.*, *no pl.* (Computing) direkter Zugriff; Direktzugriff, *der;* **~ ˈaction** *n.*, *no pl.* direkte Aktion; **~ ˈcurrent** *n.* (Electr.) Gleichstrom, *der;* **~ ˈdebit** *n.* (Brit.) Lastschriftverfahren, *das;* **~ ˈdialling** *n.*, *no pl.* Durchwahl, *die;* **we will soon have ~ dialling** wir werden bald ein Durchwahlsystem haben; **~ eˈlection** *n.* Direktwahl, *die;* **~ ˈflight** *n.* Direktflug, *der;* **~-ˈgrant school** *n.* (Brit. Hist.) *staatlich unterstützte Privatschule;* **~ ˈhit** *n.* Volltreffer, *der*

direction /dɪˈrekʃn, daɪˈrekʃn/ *n.* **1** (guidance) Führung, *die;* (of firm, orchestra) Leitung, *die;* (of play, film, TV or radio programme) Regie, *die;* (of play also) Spielleitung, *die* **2** *usu. in pl.* (order) Anordnung, *die;* (instruction) **~s [for use]** Gebrauchsanweisung, *die;* **~s for use** (of machine) Bedienungsanleitung, *die;* **on** *or* **by sb.'s ~:** auf jmds. Anordnung (*Akk.*) [hin]; **give sb. ~s to the museum/to York** jmdm. den Weg zum Museum/nach York beschreiben **3** ▸❶ **p. 1699** (point moved towards or from, lit. or fig.) Richtung, *die;* **from which ~?** aus welcher Richtung?; **travel in a southerly ~/in the ~ of London** in südliche[r] Richtung/in Richtung London reisen; **go in the ~ of the tower** in Richtung des Turms gehen; **in the ~ of** (fig.) in Richtung auf (+ *Akk.*); **sense of ~:** Orientierungssinn, *der;* (fig.) Orientierung, *die;* **lose all sense of ~** (lit. or fig.) jede Orientierung verlieren; **complaints poured in from all ~s** (fig.) von allen Seiten hagelte es Beschwerden

directional /dɪˈrekʃənl, daɪˈrekʃənl/ *adj.* **1** (spatial) Richtungs-; **~ gyro** Kurskreisel, *der* **2** (directorial) führend ⟨*Rolle*⟩; steuernd ⟨*Kontrolle*⟩ **3** (Communications) Richt-

direction: ~ finder *n.* (Communications) Peilgerät, *das;* **~ indicator** *n.* (Motor Veh.) [Fahrt-]richtungsanzeiger, *der*

directive /dɪˈrektɪv, daɪˈrektɪv/ *n.* Weisung, *die;* Direktive, *die;* (esp. EU) Richtlinie, *die;* Verordnung, *die*

direct ˈlabour *n.* **do the work by ~:** die Arbeit mit eigenen Arbeitskräften ausführen

directly /dɪˈrektlɪ, daɪˈrektlɪ/

A *adv.* **1** (in direct manner) direkt; unmittelbar ⟨*folgen, verantwortlich sein*⟩ **2** (exactly) direkt; genau; wörtlich ⟨*zitieren, abschreiben*⟩ **3** (at once) direkt; umgehend **4** (shortly) gleich; sofort

B *conj.* (Brit. coll.) sowie

direct: ~ ˈmail *n.*, *no pl.* Werbepost, *die;* **~ ˈmarketing** *n.*, *no pl.* Direktmarketing, *das;* Direktvermarktung, *die*

directness /dɪˈrektnɪs, daɪˈrektnɪs/ *n.*, *no pl.* **1** (of route, course) Geradheit, *die;* **~ of aim** Zielgenauigkeit, *die* **2** (fig.) Direktheit, *die;* **he replied with ~ and honesty** er antwortete offen und ehrlich

diˈrect object *n.* (Ling.) direktes Objekt

director /dɪˈrektə(r), daɪˈrektə(r)/ *n.* ▸❶ **p. 1260** **1** (Commerc.) Direktor, *der*/Direktorin, *die;* (of project) Leiter, *der*/Leiterin, *die;* **board of ~s** Aufsichtsrat, *der* **2** (Theatre, Cinemat., Telev., Radio) Regisseur, *der*/Regisseurin, *die;* (Mus., esp. Amer.) Dirigent, *der*/Dirigentin, *die*

directorate /dɪˈrektərət, daɪˈrektərət/ *n.* **1** (position, period of service) Direktorat, *das;* (of project) Leitung, *die* **2** (board of directors) Direktorium, *das*

Directorate-ˈGeneral *n.* (EU) Generaldirektorat, *das*

director ˈgeneral *n.*, *pl.* **directors general** Generaldirektor, *der*/-direktorin, *die;* (Telev., Radio) ≈ Intendant, *der*/Intendantin, *die*

directorial /dɪrekˈtɔːrɪəl, daɪrekˈtɔːrɪəl/ *adj.* **1** direktorial **2** (Theatre, Cinemat., Telev., Radio) als Regisseur/Regisseurin *nachgestellt*

directorship /dɪˈrektəʃɪp, daɪˈrektəʃɪp/ *n.* (Commerc.) Leitung, *die;* **hold two ~s** in zwei Aufsichtsräten sein

directory /dɪˈrektərɪ, daɪˈrektərɪ/ **1** *n.* (of local residents) Adressbuch, *das;* (telephone **~**) Telefonbuch, *das;* Fernsprechbuch, *das* (postamtl.); (of tradesmen etc.) Branchenverzeichnis, *das;* **~ enquiries** (Brit.), **~ information** (Amer.) [Fernsprech]auskunft, *die* **2** (Computing) Verzeichnis, *das*

direct: ~ proˈportion *n.* direkte Proportionalität; **~ question** *n.* (Ling.) direkter Fragesatz; **~ rule** *n.*, *no pl.* Direktregierung, *die;* **impose ~ rule on a country** ein Land unter Direktregierung stellen; **~ ˈselling** *n.*, *no pl.* Direktverkauf, *der;* **~ ˈspeech** *n.*, *no pl.* (Ling.) direkte Rede; **~ tax** *n.* direkte Steuer; **~ taxation** *n.*, *no pl.* direkte Besteuerung

direly /ˈdaɪəlɪ/ *adv.* **be ~ in need of sth.** etw. dringend brauchen

dirge /dɜːdʒ/ *n.* **1** (for the dead) Grabgesang, *der* **2** (mournful song) Klagegesang, *der;* Klage, *die* (dichter.)

dirigible /ˈdɪrɪdʒɪbl, dɪˈrɪdʒɪbl/

A *adj.* lenkbar

B *n.* Luftschiff, *das*

dirk /dɜːk/ *n.* [längerer] Dolch

dirndl /ˈdɜːndl/ *n.* Dirndl[kleid], *das;* **~ [skirt]** Dirndlrock, *der*

dirt /dɜːt/ *n.*, *no pl.* **1** Schmutz, *der;* Dreck, *der* (ugs.); **be covered in ~:** ganz schmutzig sein; (stronger) vor Schmutz starren; **~ cheap** spottbillig; **treat sb. like ~:** jmdn. wie [den letzten] Dreck behandeln (salopp); **do sb. ~** (fig. coll.) jmdm. eins auswischen (ugs.) **2** (soil) Erde, *die* **3** (fig.) (lewdness) Schmutz, *der;* (worthless thing) Dreck, *der* (salopp abwertend); Schund, *der* (ugs.); (person) Abschaum, *der;* **give me the ~ on him** (coll.) sag mir, wo er Dreck am Stecken hat (ugs.)

ˈdirt farmer *n.* (Amer.) [richtiger] Farmer (der selbst sein Land bestellt)

dirtiness /ˈdɜːtɪnɪs/ *n.*, *no pl.* Schmutzigkeit, *die*

dirt: ~ road *n.* (Amer.) unbefestigte Straße; **~ track** *n.* (Sport) Aschenbahn, *die;* (made of earth) ≈ Sandbahn, *die*

dirty /ˈdɜːtɪ/

A *adj.* **1** schmutzig; dreckig (ugs.); **get one's shoes/hands ~:** sich (*Dat.*) die Schuhe/Hände schmutzig machen; **get sth. ~:** etw. schmutzig machen; **~ money** Schmutzzulage, *die* **2** (with dark tinge) schmutzig ⟨*Farbe*⟩; **~ grey colour** schmutzig graue Farbe **3** **~ weather** stürmisches Wetter; Dreckwetter, *das* (ugs. abwertend) **4** (coll.: causing fallout) ⟨*Kernwaffe:*⟩ mit starkem Fallout; schmutzig (fig.) **5** **~ look** (coll.) giftiger Blick; **give sb. a ~ look** jmdn. giftig ansehen **6** (ill-gotten) schmutzig ⟨*Geld*⟩ **7** (fig.: obscene) schmutzig; schlüpfrig; (sexually illicit) **spend a ~ weekend together** ein Liebeswochenende zusammen verbringen; (lascivious) **have a ~ mind** eine schmutzige Fantasie haben; **~ old man** alter Lustmolch (ugs. abwertend); geiler alter Bock (salopp abwertend) **8** (despicable, sordid) schmutzig ⟨*Lüge, Gerücht, Geschäft*⟩; dreckig (salopp abwertend), gemein ⟨*Lügner, Betrüger*⟩; (unsportsmanlike) unfair; **do the ~ on sb.** (coll.) jmdn. [he]reinlegen (ugs.); **~ dog** (fig. coll.) Schwein, *das* (ugs. abwertend); **~ trick** gemeiner Trick; **play sb. a ~ trick** jmdn. ganz gemein übers Ohr hauen (ugs.); **~ work [at the crossroads]** (coll.) schmutziges Geschäft; **do sb.'s/the ~ work** sich (*Dat.*) für

jmdn./sich (*Dat.*) die Finger schmutzig machen; **get the ~ end of the stick** (coll.) der Dumme sein (ugs.)
B *adv.* (coll.) **~ great** riesig (ugs.)
C *v.t.* schmutzig machen; beschmutzen
dirty: ~ 'bomb *n.* schmutzige Bombe; **~ 'war** *n.* schmutziger Krieg; **~ 'word** *n.* unanständiges Wort; (fig.) Schimpfwort, *das*
disability /dɪsə'bɪlɪtɪ/ *n.* **1** Behinderung, *die;* (inability to be gainfully employed) Invalidität, *die;* Erwerbsunfähigkeit, *die;* **suffer from** *or* **have a ~:** behindert/erwerbsunfähig sein **2** (cause of inability) Behinderung, *die*
disability: ~ allowance *n.* Erwerbsunfähigkeitsentschädigung, *die;* **~ pension** *n.* Erwerbsunfähigkeitsrente, *die*
disable /dɪ'seɪbl/ *v.t.* **1** **~ sb. [physically]** jmdn. zum Invaliden machen; **be ~d by sth.** durch etw. behindert sein; **be permanently ~d by sth.** eine bleibende Behinderung bei etw. davontragen; **strikes which ~ the economy** Streiks, die die Wirtschaft lahm legen **2** (make unable to fight) kampfunfähig machen ‹*Feind, Schiff, Panzer, Flugzeug*›; kampfunfähig schlagen ‹*Boxer*›; unbrauchbar machen ‹*Gewehr, Kanone*›
disabled /dɪ'seɪbld/
A *adj.* **1** behindert; **~ access** behindertengerechter Zugang; **~ driver** behinderter Autofahrer; **~ ex-serviceman** Kriegsinvalide, *der;* **physically/mentally ~:** körperbehindert/geistig behindert **2** (unable to fight) kampfunfähig ‹*Schiff, Panzer, Flugzeug, Boxer*›; unbrauchbar ‹*Kanone, Gewehr*›
B *n. pl.* **the [physically/mentally] ~:** die [Körper]behinderten/[geistig] Behinderten
disablement /dɪ'seɪblmənt/ *n., no pl.* Behinderung, *die*
disabuse /dɪsə'bju:z/ *v.t.* **~ sb. of sth.** jmdn. von etw. abbringen
disadvantage /dɪsəd'vɑ:ntɪdʒ/
A *n.* **1** Nachteil, *der;* (state of being disadvantaged) Benachteiligung, *die;* **be at a ~:** im Nachteil sein; benachteiligt sein; **his inexperience put him at a ~:** er war durch seine mangelnde Erfahrung benachteiligt **2** *no pl.* (damage) Schaden, *der;* **be to sb.'s/sth.'s ~:** sich zu jmds. Nachteil/zum Nachteil einer Sache auswirken
B *v.t.* benachteiligen
disadvantaged /dɪsəd'vɑ:ntɪdʒd/ *adj.* benachteiligt
disadvantageous /dɪsædvən'teɪdʒəs/ *adj.* **1** nachteilig; ungünstig ‹*Zeitpunkt*›; **be ~ to sb./sth.** für jmdn./etw. von Nachteil sein **2** (unflattering) unvorteilhaft
disaffected /dɪsə'fektɪd/ *adj.* **1** (disloyal) illoyal (**to** gegenüber) **2** (estranged) entfremdet (**from** *Dat.*)
disaffection /dɪsə'fekʃn/ *n., no pl.* Entfremdung, *die* (**from** von)
disagree /dɪsə'gri:/ *v.i.* **1** anderer Meinung sein; **~ with sb.** mit jmdm. nicht übereinstimmen; anderer Meinung als jmd. sein; **~ with sth.** mit etw. nicht übereinstimmen; **~ [with sb.] about** *or* **over sth.** sich [mit jmdm.] über etw. (*Akk.*) nicht einig sein; *see also* **agree A 1** **2** (quarrel) eine Auseinandersetzung haben **3** (be mutually inconsistent) nicht übereinstimmen **4** **~ with sb.** (have bad effects on) jmdm. nicht bekommen
disagreeable /dɪsə'grɪəbəl/ *adj.* unangenehm; unappetitlich ‹*Nahrungsmittel*›
disagreeably /dɪsə'grɪəblɪ/ *adv.* **1** unangenehm **2** (bad-temperedly) übellaunig
disagreement /dɪsə'gri:mənt/ *n.* **1** (difference of opinion) Uneinigkeit, *die;* (refusal to agree) **be in ~:** geteilter Meinung sein; **be in ~ with sb./sth.** mit jmdm./etw. nicht übereinstimmen **2** (strife, quarrel) Meinungsverschiedenheit, *die* **3** (discrepancy) Diskrepanz, *die*
disallow /dɪsə'laʊ/ *v.t.* nicht gestatten; abweisen ‹*Antrag, Anspruch, Klage*›; (refuse to admit) nicht anerkennen; nicht gelten lassen; (Sport) nicht geben ‹*Tor*›
disambiguate /dɪsæm'bɪgjʊeɪt/ *v.t.* eindeutig machen; disambiguieren (Sprachw.)

disappear /dɪsə'pɪə(r)/ *v.i.* verschwinden; ‹*Brauch, Kunst, Tierart:*› aussterben; ‹*Angst, Ärger, Laune:*› verfliegen; **do a ~ing act** *or* **trick** (fig.) spurlos verschwinden
disappearance /dɪsə'pɪərəns/ *n.* Verschwinden, *das;* (of customs; extinction) Aussterben, *das*
disappoint /dɪsə'pɔɪnt/ *v.t.* enttäuschen; **be ~ed in** *or* **by** *or* **with sb./sth.** von jmdm./etw. enttäuscht sein; **he was ~ed at** *or* **by** *or* **with having failed/the way things had changed** er war enttäuscht [darüber], dass er durchgefallen war/darüber, wie sich die Dinge verändert hatten
disappointed /dɪsə'pɔɪntɪd/ *adj.* enttäuscht
disappointing /dɪsə'pɔɪntɪŋ/ *adj.* enttäuschend; **how ~!** so eine Enttäuschung!
disappointingly /dɪsə'pɔɪntɪŋlɪ/ *adv.* enttäuschend; **~, he only came fourth** enttäuschenderweise wurde er nur Vierter
disappointment /dɪsə'pɔɪntmənt/ *n.* Enttäuschung, *die;* **come as a ~ to sb.** eine Enttäuschung für jmdn. sein
disapprobation /dɪsæprə'beɪʃn/, **disapproval** /dɪsə'pru:vl/ *ns.* Missbilligung, *die;* **show one's/cause disapproval** sein Missfallen zeigen/Missfallen erregen; **with disapproval** missbilligend; mit Missbilligung
disapprove /dɪsə'pru:v/
A *v.i.* dagegen sein; **~ of sb./sth.** jmdn. ablehnen/etw. missbilligen; **~ of sb. doing sth.** es missbilligen, wenn jmd. etw. tut
B *v.t.* missbilligen
disapproving /dɪsə'pru:vɪŋ/ *adj.*, **disapprovingly** /dɪsə'pru:vɪŋlɪ/ *adv.* missbilligend
disarm /dɪs'ɑ:m/
A *v.t.* **1** entwaffnen; entschärfen ‹*Bombe*› **2** (fig.) entwaffnen; verstummen lassen ‹*Kritik*›; abbauen ‹*Feindseligkeit*›
B *v.i.* abrüsten
disarmament /dɪs'ɑ:məmənt/ *n.* Abrüstung, *die;* **~ talks** Abrüstungsgespräche
disarming /dɪs'ɑ:mɪŋ/ *adj.* entwaffnend
disarmingly /dɪs'ɑ:mɪŋlɪ/ *adv.* entwaffnend
disarrange /dɪsə'reɪndʒ/ *v.t.* durcheinander bringen; zerzausen ‹*Haar*›
disarray /dɪsə'reɪ/
A *n.* Unordnung, *die;* (confusion) Wirrwarr, *der;* **fall into ~:** durcheinander geraten; **be in ~:** in Unordnung sein
B *v.t.* in Unordnung bringen
disassemble /dɪsə'sembl/ *v.t.* auseinander nehmen ‹*Maschine*›; abbauen ‹*Gebäude, Anlage*›
disassembly /dɪsə'semblɪ/ *n.* (of machine) Auseinandernehmen, *das;* (of structure) Abbau, *der*
disassociation /dɪsəsəʊsɪ'eɪʃn/ ▸**dissociation 1**
disaster /dɪ'zɑ:stə(r)/ *n.* **1** Katastrophe, *die;* **air ~:** Flugzeugunglück, *das;* (with many deaths also) Flugzeugkatastrophe, *die;* **a railway/mining ~:** ein Eisenbahn-/Grubenunglück; **natural ~:** Naturkatastrophe, *die;* **motorway ~:** schwerer Unfall auf der Autobahn; **end in ~:** in einer Katastrophe enden **2** (complete failure) Fiasko, *das;* Katastrophe, *die;* **lead to ~:** zu einem Fiasko *od.* einer Katastrophe führen; **prove a ~:** sich als katastrophal erweisen
disaster: ~ area *n.* Katastrophengebiet, *das;* **he/she is a [walking] ~ area** (fig. coll.) er/sie ist eine wandelnde Katastrophe (fig.); **~ fund** *n.* Nothilfefonds, *der;* **~ relief** *n., no pl.* Katastrophenhilfe, *die*
disastrous /dɪ'zɑ:strəs/ *adj.* katastrophal; verhängnisvoll ‹*Irrtum, Entscheidung, Politik*›; verheerend ‹*Überschwemmung, Wirbelsturm, Feuer*›
disastrously /dɪ'zɑ:strəslɪ/ *adv.* katastrophal
disavow /dɪsə'vaʊ/ *v.t.* verleugnen; nicht anerkennen ‹*Rechtsprechung, Vereinbarung*›; **~ responsibility for sth.** die Verantwortung für etwas von sich weisen
disavowal /dɪsə'vaʊəl/ *n.* Verleugnung, *die*
disband /dɪs'bænd/
A *v.t.* auflösen; **the ~ed soldiers** die entlassenen Soldaten
B *v.i.* sich auflösen

disbar /dɪs'bɑ:(r)/ *v.t.* **-rr-** (Law) die Zulassung entziehen (+ *Dat.*)
disbelief /dɪsbɪ'li:f/ *n.* Unglaube, *der;* **be met with ~:** auf Unglauben stoßen; **in ~:** ungläubig
disbelieve /dɪsbɪ'li:v/
A *v.t.* **~ sb./sth.** jmdm. nicht glauben *od.* (geh.) keinen Glauben schenken/etw. nicht glauben
B *v.i.* nicht glauben; **~ in sth.** nicht an etw. (*Akk.*) glauben
disbeliever /dɪsbɪ'li:və(r)/ *n.* Ungläubige, *der/die;* **be a ~ in sth.** nicht an etw. (*Akk.*) glauben
disburden /dɪs'bɜ:dn/ ▸**unburden**
disburse /dɪs'bɜ:s/ *v.t.* ausgeben
disbursement /dɪs'bɜ:smənt/ *n.* Auszahlung, *die;* (expenditure) Ausgabe, *die*
disc /dɪsk/ *n.* **1** Scheibe, *die* **2** (record) [Schall]platte, *die; see also* **compact disc** **3** (Computing) ▸**disk** **4** (Anat.) Bandscheibe, *die; see also* **slipped disc** **5** (Bot.) Körbchen, das
discard
A /dɪ'skɑ:d/ *v.t.* **1** wegwerfen; ablegen ‹*Kleidung*›; fallen lassen ‹*Vorschlag, Idee, Mensch*› **2** (Cards) abwerfen
B /'dɪskɑ:d/ *n.* Ausschuss, *der;* (person) Ausgestoßene, *der/die*
'disc brake *n.* Scheibenbremse, *die*
discern /dɪ'sɜ:n/ *v.t.* wahrnehmen; **sth. can be ~ed** etw. ist zu erkennen; **~ from sth. whether ...:** an etw. (*Dat.*) erkennen, ob ...
discernible /dɪ'sɜ:nɪbl/ *adj.* erkennbar; wahrnehmbar ‹*Stimme, Geruch*›; **a ~ pattern has emerged** ein Schema ist erkennbar geworden
discerning /dɪ'sɜ:nɪŋ/ *adj.* fein ‹*Gaumen, Ohr, Geschmack*›; scharf ‹*Auge*›; urteilsfähig ‹*Richter, Kritiker*›; kritisch ‹*Leser, Kunde, Zuschauer, Kommentar*›; scharfsichtig ‹*Kritik*›
discernment /dɪ'sɜ:nmənt/ *n., no pl.* (act of discerning) Wahrnehmung, *die;* (faculty of discerning) Urteilsfähigkeit, *die*
discharge
A /dɪs'tʃɑ:dʒ/ *v.t.* **1** (dismiss, allow to leave) entlassen (**from** aus); freisprechen ‹*Angeklagte*›; (exempt from liabilities) befreien (**from** von); **the patient ~d himself from hospital** der Patient verließ eigenmächtig das Krankenhaus **2** (send out) abschießen ‹*Pfeil, Torpedo*›; ablassen ‹*Flüssigkeit, Gas*›; absondern ‹*Eiter*›; (unload from ship) ausschiffen; löschen ‹*Ladung*›; (Electr.) entladen **3** (relieve of load) entladen; löschen ‹*Schiff*›; (fire) abfeuern ‹*Gewehr, Kanone*› **4** (acquit oneself of, pay) erfüllen ‹*Pflicht, Verbindlichkeiten, Versprechen*›; bezahlen ‹*Schulden*›
B *v.i.* **1** entladen werden; ‹*Schiff auch:*› gelöscht werden; ‹*Batterie:*› sich entladen; ‹*Gewehr:*› losgehen **2** (flow) münden (**into** in + *Akk.*) **3** ‹*Wunde, Geschwür:*› eitern
C /dɪs'tʃɑ:dʒ, 'dɪstʃɑ:dʒ/ *n.* **1** (dismissal) Entlassung, *die* (**from** aus); (of defendant) Freispruch, *der;* (exemption from liabilities) Befreiung, *die;* (written certificate of release) Entlassungsschein, *der;* (written certificate of exemption) Entlastungsschein, *der;* **be granted a full ~ [by the court]** [vom Gericht] in allen Punkten freigesprochen werden **2** (emission) Ausfluss, *der;* (of gas) Austritt, *der;* (of pus) Absonderung, *die;* (Electr.) Entladung, *die;* (of gun) Abfeuern, *das;* **vaginal ~:** [Scheiden]ausfluss, *der* **3** (of debt) Begleichung, *die;* (of duty) Erfüllung, *die*
'disc harrow *n.* (Agric.) Scheibenegge, *die*
disciple /dɪ'saɪpl/ *n.* **1** (Relig.) Jünger, *der* **2** (follower) Anhänger, *der*/Anhängerin, *die;* Jünger, *der* (geh., oft scherzh.)
disciplinarian /dɪsɪplɪ'neərɪən/ *n.* Zuchtmeister, *der*/-meisterin, *die* (veralt., noch scherzh.); (in school, family also) [strenger] Erzieher; **he is a poor ~:** er kann nicht für Disziplin sorgen
disciplinary /'dɪsɪplɪnərɪ, dɪsɪ'plɪnərɪ/ *adj.* Disziplinar-; disziplinarisch; **~ action** Disziplinarmaßnahmen *Pl.;* **~ proceedings** Disziplinarverfahren, *das*
discipline /'dɪsɪplɪn/
A *n.* **1** (order, branch) Disziplin, *die;* **maintain ~:** die Disziplin aufrechterhalten; **lack of ~:** Mangel an Disziplin; **change ~s** die Disziplin

od. das Fach wechseln **2** (mental training) Schulung, *die;* **the ~ of adversity** die strenge Schule der Not **3** (system of rules) Kanon, *der* **4** (punishment) Strafe, *die;* (physical also) Züchtigung, *die* (geh.); (Relig.) Kasteiung, *die*

B *v.t.* **1** disziplinieren; (train in military exercises) ausbilden; **you must ~ yourself to eat less** Sie müssen sich zwingen, weniger zu essen; **~ one's emotions/feelings** *etc.* seine Emotionen/Gefühle *usw.* unter Kontrolle halten **2** (punish) bestrafen; (physically also) züchtigen (geh.); (Relig.) kasteien

disciplined /ˈdɪsɪplɪnd/ *adj.* diszipliniert; **highly/well ~:** sehr diszipliniert; **badly ~:** undiszipliniert

ˈdisc jockey *n.* Diskjockey, *der*

disclaim /dɪsˈkleɪm/ *v.t.* **1** abstreiten **2** (Law) verzichten auf (+ *Akk.*)

disclaimer /dɪsˈkleɪmə(r)/ *n.* Gegenerklärung, *die;* (Law) Verzichterklärung, *die*

disclose /dɪsˈkləʊz/ *v.t.* **1** (expose to view) den Blick freigeben auf (+ *Akk.*) **2** (make known) enthüllen; bekannt geben ‹*Information, Nachricht*›; **research ~d that …:** Nachforschungen ergaben, dass …; **he didn't ~ why he'd come** er verriet nicht, warum er gekommen war

disclosure /dɪsˈkləʊʒə(r)/ *n.* Enthüllung, *die;* (of information, news) Bekanntgabe, *die;* **for fear of possible ~:** aus Furcht vor einer möglichen Enthüllung; **the newspaper's ~ of bribery** die Enthüllungen der Zeitung über Bestechung

disco /ˈdɪskəʊ/ *n., pl.* **~s** (coll.) **1** (discothèque, party) Disko, *die* **2** (equipment) **travelling ~:** rollende Disko

ˈdisco dancing *n.* Diskotanz, *der*

discolor (Amer.) ▸ **discolour**

discoloration /dɪskʌləˈreɪʃn/ *n.* Verfärbung, *die*

discolour /dɪsˈkʌlə(r)/ (Brit.)

A *v.t.* verfärben; (fade) ausbleichen

B *v.i.* sich verfärben; (fade) ausbleichen

discolouration (Brit.) ▸ **discoloration**

discombobulate /dɪskəmˈbɒbjʊleɪt/ *v.t.* (Amer. joc.) durcheinander bringen

discomfit /dɪsˈkʌmfɪt/ *v.t.* **1** (baffle, disconcert) verunsichern **2** (arch.: overwhelm, thwart) schlagen

discomfiture /dɪsˈkʌmfɪtʃə(r)/ *n.* Verunsicherung, *die*

discomfort /dɪsˈkʌmfət/

A *n.* **1** *no pl.* (uneasiness of body) Beschwerden *Pl.;* **cause/give sb. ~:** jmdm. Beschwerden machen **2** *no pl.* (uneasiness of mind) Unbehagen, *das* **3** (hardship) Unannehmlichkeit, *die*

B *v.t.* zu schaffen machen (+ *Dat.*)

discompose /dɪskəmˈpəʊz/ *v.t.* aus der Fassung bringen; **appear ~d** einen verstörten Eindruck machen

discomposure /dɪskəmˈpəʊʒə(r)/ *n., no pl.* Verstörtheit, *die*

ˈdisco music *n.* Diskomusik, *die*

disconcert /dɪskənˈsɜːt/ *v.t.* irritieren; **I was ~ed to find the gates locked** ich war verwirrt, als ich vor verschlossenen Toren stand

disconcerted /dɪskənˈsɜːtɪd/ *adj.* verstört; irritiert

disconcerting /dɪskənˈsɜːtɪŋ/ *adj.*, **disconcertingly** /dɪskənˈsɜːtɪŋlɪ/ *adv.* irritierend

disconnect /dɪskəˈnekt/ *v.t.* **1** abtrennen; abhängen ‹*Wagen*› **2** (Electr., Teleph.) **~ the electricity from a house** ein Haus von der Stromversorgung abtrennen; **~ the TV** den Stecker des Fernsehers herausziehen; **the loudspeakers have become ~ed** die Lautsprecher sind nicht mehr angeschlossen; **if you don't pay your telephone bill you will be ~ed** wenn Sie Ihre Telefonrechnung nicht bezahlen, wird Ihr Telefon abgestellt; **operator, I've been ~ed** hallo, Vermittlung, die Verbindung ist unterbrochen; **~ a call** ein Gespräch unterbrechen

disconnected /dɪskəˈnektɪd/ *adj.* **1** abgetrennt; abgestellt ‹*Telefon*›; **is the cooker/TV ~?** ist der Stecker beim Herd/Fernseher herausgezogen? **2** (incoherent) unzusammenhängend ‹*Rede, Worte*›

disconnectedly /dɪskəˈnektɪdlɪ/ *adv.* unzusammenhängend

disconnection, (Brit.) **disconnexion** /dɪskəˈnekʃn/ *n.* Abtrennung, *die*

disconsolate /dɪsˈkɒnsələt/ *adj.* **1** (unhappy) unglücklich **2** (inconsolable) untröstlich

disconsolately /dɪsˈkɒnsələtlɪ/ *adv.* **1** (unhappily) unglücklich **2** (inconsolably) untröstlich

discontent /dɪskənˈtent/

A *n.* Unzufriedenheit, *die*

B *v.t.* unzufrieden machen

discontented /dɪskənˈtentɪd/ *adj.* unzufrieden (**with, about** mit)

discontentment /dɪskənˈtentmənt/ *n., no pl.* Unzufriedenheit, *die*

discontinuance /dɪskənˈtɪnjʊəns/, **discontinuation** /dɪskəntɪnjʊˈeɪʃn/ *ns.* Einstellung, *die;* (of subscription) Abbestellung, *die;* (of treatment) Abbruch, *der;* (of habit) Aufgabe, *die*

discontinue /dɪskənˈtɪnjuː/ *v.t.* **1** einstellen; abbestellen ‹*Abonnement*›; abbrechen ‹*Behandlung*›; aufgeben ‹*Gewohnheit*› **2** (Commerc.) **a ~d range** *or* **line** eine auslaufende Serie

discontinuity /dɪskɒntɪˈnjuːɪtɪ/ *n.* Bruch, *der;* **a ~ of style** ein stilistischer Bruch

discontinuous /dɪskənˈtɪnjʊəs/ *adj.* nicht kontinuierlich; diskontinuierlich (geh.)

discontinuously /dɪskənˈtɪnjʊəslɪ/ *adv.* mit Unterbrechungen; nicht kontinuierlich

discord /ˈdɪskɔːd/ *n.* **1** Zwietracht, *die;* (quarrelling) Streit, *der* **2** (Mus.) (chord) Dissonanz, *die;* (interval) Disharmonie, *die;* (single note) Misston, *der* **3** (harsh noise) Missklang, *der*

discordant /dɪˈskɔːdənt/ *adj.* **1** gegensätzlich **2** (dissonant) misstönend; **a ~ note** (lit. or fig.) ein Misston

discordantly /dɪˈskɔːdəntlɪ/ *adv.* **1** gegensätzlich **2** (dissonantly) misstönend

discothèque /ˈdɪskətek/ *n.* Diskothek, *die*

discount

A /ˈdɪskaʊnt/ *n.* (Commerc.) Rabatt, *der;* (on bill of exchange) Diskont, *der;* (discounting) Diskontierung, *die;* **give** *or* **offer [sb.] a ~ on sth.** [jmdm.] Rabatt auf etw. (*Akk.*) geben *od.* gewähren; **~ for cash** Skonto, *der od. das;* Rabatt bei Barzahlung; **at a ~:** mit Rabatt; (St. Exch.) unter dem Nennwert; (fig.) nicht gefragt; **the books were sold at a [big] ~:** die Bücher wurden [weit] unter dem normalen Preis verkauft

B /dɪˈskaʊnt/ *v.t.* **1** (disbelieve) unberücksichtigt lassen; (discredit) widerlegen ‹*Beweis, Theorie*›; (underrate) zu gering einschätzen; (lessen) schmälern ‹*Wert*›; (reduce effect of) einkalkulieren **2** (Commerc.) diskontieren ‹*Wechsel*›

ˈdiscount: ~ broker *n.* (Commerc.) Wechselmakler, *der;* **~ card** *n.* Kundenkarte, *die;* **~ house** *n.* (Commerc.) Diskontbank, *die;* **~ shop, ~ store** *ns.* Discountladen, *der;* Discountgeschäft, *das*

discourage /dɪˈskʌrɪdʒ/ *v.t.* **1** (dispirit) entmutigen; **be** *or* **become ~d [by sth.** *or* **because of sth.]** sich [durch etw.] entmutigen lassen; **be ~d because …:** sich entmutigt fühlen, weil … **2** (advise against) abraten; **~ sb. from sth.** jmdm. von etw. abraten; **~ sb. from doing sth.** jmdm. davon abraten, etw. zu tun **3** (act against) zu unterbinden suchen **4** (disapprove of) nicht gutheißen; **sth. must be ~d** man darf etw. nicht gutheißen **5** (stop) abhalten ‹*Person*›; verhindern ‹*Handlung*›; **~ sb. from doing sth.** jmdn. davon abhalten, etw. zu tun; **not ~d by fear of reprisals** ohne Furcht vor Vergeltungsmaßnahmen

discouragement /dɪˈskʌrɪdʒmənt/ *n.* **1** Entmutigung, *die* **2** (deterrent) Abschreckung, *die;* **act as a ~ to sb.** eine abschreckende Wirkung auf jmdn. haben **3** (depression) Mutlosigkeit, *die*

discouraging /dɪˈskʌrɪdʒɪŋ/ *adj.* **1** (dispiriting) entmutigend; **paint a ~ picture of sth.** ein düsteres Bild von etw. malen; **he was rather ~:** er hat mir/ihm/ihr *usw.* wenig Mut gemacht; **the article makes ~ reading** die Lektüre des Artikels ist entmutigend **2** (deterring) abschreckend

discouragingly /dɪˈskʌrɪdʒɪŋlɪ/ *adv.* entmutigend

discourse

A /ˈdɪskɔːs/ *n.* Diskurs, *der;* **hold a ~** *or* **be in ~ with sb.** einen Diskurs mit jmdm. haben *od.* führen

B /dɪˈskɔːs/ *v.i.* **~ [upon sth.]** sich [über etw. (*Akk.*)] ausführlich äußern; (converse) [über etw.] ausführlich reden

discourteous /dɪsˈkɜːtɪəs/ *adj.*, **discourteously** /dɪsˈkɜːtɪəslɪ/ *adv.* unhöflich

discourtesy /dɪsˈkɜːtəsɪ/ *n.* Unhöflichkeit, *die;* **he did her a ~:** er beging ihr gegenüber eine Unhöflichkeit

discover /dɪˈskʌvə(r)/ *v.t.* **1** (find, notice, get knowledge of, realize) entdecken **2** (by search) herausfinden; **~ a meaning in life** entdecken, dass das Leben einen Sinn hat; **it was never ~ed how …:** es kam nie heraus, wie …; **~ sb.'s identity** herausfinden, wer jmd. ist; **as far as I can ~:** soweit ich feststellen kann **3** (Chess) **~ed check** Abzugsschach, *das*

discoverable /dɪˈskʌvərəbl/ *adj.* auffindbar

discoverer /dɪˈskʌvərə(r)/ *n.* Entdecker, *der*/Entdeckerin, *die*

discovery /dɪˈskʌvərɪ/ *n.* Entdeckung, *die;* **voyage of ~:** Entdeckungsreise, *die;* **for fear of ~:** aus Angst, entdeckt zu werden

ˈdisc parking *n.* (Brit.) Parken mit Parkscheibe

discredit /dɪsˈkredɪt/

A *n.* **1** *no pl.* Misskredit, *der;* **bring ~ on sb./sth., bring sb./sth. into ~:** jmdn./etw. in Misskredit (*Akk.*) bringen; **be to the ~ of sb.** jmdm. keine Ehre machen; **without any ~ to the firm** ohne die Firma in Misskredit zu bringen **2** (sb. or sth. that ~s) **be a ~ to sb./sth.** jmdm./einer Sache keine Ehre machen **3** *no pl.* (doubt) **throw ~ on sth.** etw. unglaubwürdig erscheinen lassen; **fall into ~:** ins Zwielicht geraten

B *v.t.* **1** (disbelieve) keinen Glauben schenken (+ *Dat.*); (discount as unreliable) anzweifeln; (cause to be disbelieved) unglaubwürdig machen; **careful research has ~ed this theory** sorgfältige Untersuchungen haben diese Theorie zweifelhaft werden lassen **2** (disgrace) diskreditieren (geh.); in Verruf bringen; **be ~ed** diskreditiert werden (geh.); in Verruf geraten

discreditable /dɪsˈkredɪtəbl/ *adj.* unehrenhaft

discreditably /dɪsˈkredɪtəblɪ/ *adv.* unehrenhaft; **perform ~ in the examination** bei der Prüfung unrühmlich abschneiden

discreet /dɪˈskriːt/ *adj.*, **~er** /dɪˈskriːtə(r)/, **~est** /dɪˈskriːtɪst/ diskret; taktvoll; (unobtrusive) diskret; dezent ‹*Parfüm, Kleidung*›

discreetly /dɪˈskriːtlɪ/ *adv.* diskret; dezent ‹*gekleidet*›

discreetness /dɪˈskriːtnɪs/ *n., no pl.* Diskretheit, *die*

discrepancy /dɪˈskrepənsɪ/ *n.* Diskrepanz, *die;* **there is a wide ~ between the statements of the two witnesses** die beiden Zeugenaussagen stimmen bei weitem nicht überein

discrepant /dɪˈskrepənt/ *adj.* [voneinander] abweichend

discrete /dɪˈskriːt/ *adj.* eigenständig; (Math., Phys.) diskret; **a ~ whole** ein Ganzes aus eigenständigen Teilen

discreteness /dɪˈskriːtnɪs/ *n., no pl.* Eigenständigkeit, *die*

discretion /dɪˈskreʃn/ *n.* **1** (prudence) Umsicht, *die;* (reservedness) Diskretion, *die;* **use ~:** diskret sein; **reach years** *or* **the age of ~:** mündig werden; **~ is the better part of valour** (prov.) Vorsicht ist besser als Nachsicht (ugs. scherzh.); Vorsicht ist die Mutter der Weisheit **2** (liberty to decide) Ermessen, *das;* **leave sth. to sb.'s ~:** etw. in jmds. Ermessen (*Akk.*) stellen; etw. jmds. Entscheidung (*Dat.*) überlassen; **at sb.'s ~:** nach jmds. Ermessen; **be**

d

within *or* **at** *or* **left to sb.'s ~:** in jmds. Ermessen (*Dat.*) liegen; **use one's ~:** nach eigenem Ermessen *od.* Gutdünken handeln

discretionary /dɪˈskreʃənərɪ/ *adj.* nach freiem Ermessen gewährt ‹*Leistung, Zuschuss usw.*›; Ermessens‹*leistung*›; **~ powers** Entscheidungsgewalt, *die*

discriminate /dɪˈskrɪmɪneɪt/

A *v.t.* unterscheiden

B *v.i.* **1** (distinguish, use discernment) unterscheiden; **~ between [two things]** unterscheiden zwischen [zwei Dingen] **2** **~ against sb.** jmdn. diskriminieren; **~ in favour of sb.** jmdn. bevorzugen

discriminating /dɪˈskrɪmɪneɪtɪŋ/ *adj.* kritisch ‹*Urteil, Auge, Kunde, Kunstsammler*›; fein ‹*Geschmack, Gaumen, Ohr*›

discriminatingly /dɪˈskrɪmɪneɪtɪŋlɪ/ *adv.* kritisch; scharfsichtig ‹*kritisieren*›

discrimination /dɪskrɪmɪˈneɪʃn/ *n.* **1** (act of discriminating) Unterscheidung, *die* **2** (discernment) [kritisches] Urteilsvermögen **3** (differential treatment) Diskriminierung, *die* (**against** *Gen.*); **~ against Blacks/women** Diskriminierung von Schwarzen/Frauen; **~ against foreign imports** die Erschwerung von ausländischen Importen; **~ in favour of** Bevorzugung (+ *Gen.*); **racial ~:** Rassendiskriminierung, *die*

discriminatory /dɪˈskrɪmɪnətərɪ/ *adj.* diskriminierend

discursive /dɪˈskɜːsɪv/ *adj.*, **discursively** /dɪˈskɜːsɪvlɪ/ *adv.* weitschweifig

discursiveness /dɪˈskɜːsɪvnɪs/ *n.*, *no pl.* Weitschweifigkeit, *die*

discus /ˈdɪskəs/ *n.* (Sport) **1** Diskus, *der* **2** (event) Diskuswerfen, *das*

discuss /dɪˈskʌs/ *v.t.* **1** (talk about) besprechen; **~ sth. with sb.** etw. mit jmdm. besprechen; **the children were ~ing the wedding** die Kinder sprachen über die Hochzeit; **I'm not willing to ~ this matter at present** ich möchte jetzt nicht darüber sprechen **2** (debate) diskutieren über (+ *Akk.*); (examine) erörtern; diskutieren

discussion /dɪˈskʌʃn/ *n.* **1** (conversation) Gespräch, *das;* (more formal) Unterredung, *die;* **after much ~:** nach langen Gesprächen/Unterredungen; **let's have a ~ about it** wir wollen darüber reden *od.* sprechen; **there was some ~ before they ...:** sie besprachen sich miteinander, bevor sie ... **2** (debate) Diskussion, *die;* (examination) Erörterung, *die;* **come up for ~:** zur Diskussion gestellt werden; **be under ~:** zur Diskussion stehen; **matter** *or* **topic for ~:** Thema *od.* Gegenstand der Diskussion; **hold** *or* **have a ~ with sb.** mit jmdm. diskutieren

discussion: ~ group *n.* Diskussionsrunde, *die;* **~ programme** *n.* (Radio, Telev.) Diskussionssendung, *die*

disdain /dɪsˈdeɪn/

A *n.* Verachtung, *die;* **with ~:** verächtlich; **a look of ~:** ein verächtlicher *od.* geringschätziger Blick

B *v.t.* verachten; verächtlich ablehnen ‹*Rat, Hilfe*›; **~ to do sth.** zu stolz sein, etw. zu tun

disdainful /dɪsˈdeɪnfl/ *adj.* verächtlich, geringschätzig ‹*Lachen, Ton, Blick, Kommentar*›; **look ~:** verächtlich dreinblicken; **be ~ of advice/simple pleasures** Ratschläge verächtlich ablehnen/einfache Freuden verachten

disdainfully /dɪsˈdeɪnfəlɪ/ *adv.* verächtlich; geringschätzig; voll Verachtung ‹*ignorieren*›; **look ~ at sb./sth.** jmdn./etw. verächtlich *od.* geringschätzig ansehen

disease /dɪˈziːz/ *n.* ▸ **ⓘ p. 1231** (lit. or fig.) Krankheit, *die;* **suffer from a ~:** an einer Krankheit leiden; **the spreading of ~:** die Ausbreitung von Krankheiten

diseased /dɪˈziːzd/ *adj.* (lit. or fig.) krank

disembark /dɪsɪmˈbɑːk/

A *v.t.* ausschiffen

B *v.i.* von Bord gehen; **wait a long time to ~:** lange auf die Ausschiffung warten

disembarkation /dɪsembɑːˈkeɪʃn/ *n.* (of troops) Landung, *die;* (of cargo, passengers) Ausschiffung, *die*

disembodied /dɪsɪmˈbɒdɪd/ *adj.* körperlos ‹*Seele, Geist*›; geisterhaft ‹*Stimme*›

disembowel /dɪsɪmˈbaʊəl/ *v.t.*, (Brit.) **-ll-** die Eingeweide herausnehmen (+ *Dat.*); (by violence) den Bauch aufschlitzen (+ *Dat.*)

disempower /dɪsemˈpaʊə(r)/ *v.t.* (make less powerful) schwächen; kraftlos machen; (make less confident) entmutigen; demoralisieren

disenchant /dɪsɪnˈtʃɑːnt/ *v.t.* **1** entzaubern (geh.) **2** (disillusion) ernüchtern; **he became ~ed with sb./sth.** jmd./etw. hat ihn desillusioniert

disenchantment /dɪsɪnˈtʃɑːntmənt/ *n.* ▸**disenchant**: Entzauberung, *die* (geh.); Ernüchterung, *die* (**with** in Bezug auf)

disenfranchise /dɪsɪnˈfræntʃaɪz/ ▸**disfranchise**

disengage /dɪsɪnˈgeɪdʒ/

A *v.t.* **1** lösen (**from** aus, von); **~ one's hand** seine Hand freibekommen **2** (Mech.) **~ the clutch** auskuppeln; **~ the gear** den Gang herausnehmen **3** (Mil.) abziehen

B *v.i.* **1** sich zurückziehen (**from** aus); ‹*Kupplung:*› sich lösen **2** (Mil.) sich zurückziehen (**from** aus) **3** (Fencing) sich [aus der gegnerischen Bindung] lösen

disengaged /dɪsɪnˈgeɪdʒd/ *adj.* **1** frei **2** (uncommitted) nicht [politisch] engagiert

disentangle /dɪsɪnˈtæŋgl/

A *v.t.* **1** (extricate) befreien (**from** aus); (fig.) herauslösen (**from** aus) **2** (unravel) entwirren; (fig.) ordnen ‹*Gedanken*›; entwirren ‹*Handlung, Hinweise*›

B *v.i.* sich entwirren

disentanglement /dɪsɪnˈtæŋglmənt/ *n.* (lit. or fig.) Entwirrung, *die*

disentomb /dɪsɪnˈtuːm/ *v.t.* ausgraben; freilegen

disequilibrium /dɪsiːkwɪˈlɪbrɪəm/ *n.*, *no pl.* gestörtes Gleichgewicht; Ungleichgewicht, *das*

disestablishment /dɪsɪˈstæblɪʃmənt/ *n.* **the ~ of the Church** die Trennung der Kirche vom Staat

disfavour (*Amer.:* **disfavor**) /dɪsˈfeɪvə(r)/

A *n.* **1** (displeasure, disapproval) Missfallen, *das;* (condition of being out of favour) Ungnade, *die;* **incur sb.'s ~:** jmds. Unwillen erregen **2** (disadvantage) **in sb.'s ~:** zu jmds. Ungunsten

B *v.t.* missbilligen

disfigure /dɪsˈfɪgə(r)/ *v.t.* entstellen; verunstalten ‹*Landschaft*›

disfigurement /dɪsˈfɪgəmənt/ *n.* Entstellung, *die;* (of countryside) Verunstaltung, *die*

disfranchise /dɪsˈfræntʃaɪz/ *v.t.* die Privilegien entziehen (+ *Dat.*); (of right to vote) das Wahlrecht entziehen (+ *Dat.*)

disgorge /dɪsˈgɔːdʒ/ *v.t.* **1** ausspucken; ausspeien (geh.); (fig.) ausspeien (geh.); herausgeben ‹*Gefangene, Beute, Eigentum*› **2** (discharge) ergießen ‹*Wasser*›

disgrace /dɪsˈgreɪs/

A *n.*, *no pl.* **1** (ignominy) Schande, *die;* Schmach, *die* (geh.); (deep disfavour) Ungnade, *die;* **bring ~ on sb./sth.** Schande über jmdn./etw. bringen; **send sb. home in ~:** jmdn. wegen ungebührlichen Verhaltens nach Hause schicken; **he had to resign in ~:** er musste unehrenhaft zurücktreten **2** **be a ~ [to sb./sth.]** [für jmdn./etw.] eine Schande sein

B *v.t.* **1** (bring shame on) ‹*Person:*› Schande machen (+ *Dat.*); ‹*Person, Handlung:*› Schande bringen über (+ *Akk.*); **~ oneself** sich blamieren; ‹*Kind, Hund:*› sich danebenbenehmen (ugs.) **2** **be ~d** (be put out of favour) in Ungnade fallen; (be held up to reproach) bloßgestellt werden

disgraceful /dɪsˈgreɪsfl/ *adj.* erbärmlich; miserabel ‹*Handschrift*›; skandalös ‹*Benehmen, Enthüllung, Bedingungen, Verstoß, Behandlung, Tat*›; **what a ~ thing to say/do!** wie kann man nur so etwas Schändliches sagen/tun!; **it's [absolutely** *or* **really** *or* **quite] ~:** es ist [wirklich] ein Skandal; **how ~!** was für eine Schande!; **you look ~:** du siehst ja furchtbar aus! (ugs.)

disgracefully /dɪsˈgreɪsfəlɪ/ *adv.* erbärmlich; schändlich ‹*verraten, betrügen, behandeln*›; **behave ~:** sich schändlich *od.* (geh.) schimpflich benehmen; **arrive ~ late** (coll.) furchtbar spät eintreffen; **she neglected her duties quite ~:** sie vernachlässigte ihre Pflichten geradezu sträflich

disgruntled /dɪsˈgrʌntld/ *adj.* verstimmt; **be in a ~ mood** verstimmt sein

disguise /dɪsˈgaɪz/

A *v.t.* **1** verkleiden ‹*Person*›; verstellen ‹*Stimme*›; tarnen ‹*Gegenstand*›; **~ oneself** sich verkleiden; **he ~d himself with a false beard** er tarnte sich mit einem falschen Bart **2** (misrepresent) verschleiern; **there is no disguising the fact that ...:** es lässt sich nicht verheimlichen, dass ...; **a ~d tax** eine versteckte Steuer **3** (conceal) verbergen; hinter dem Berg halten mit ‹*Ansichten, Missbilligung*›; **the herbs ~ the taste of the meat** die Kräuter überdecken den Geschmack des Fleisches

B *n.* Verkleidung, *die;* (fig.) Maske, *die;* **adopt/wear a ~:** eine Verkleidung wählen/verkleidet sein; **wear sth. as a ~:** etw. zur Tarnung tragen; **in the ~ of** verkleidet als; **in ~:** verkleidet; **without any attempt at ~:** ohne irgendeinen Versuch, sich zu tarnen; *see also* **blessing 3**

disgust /dɪsˈgʌst/

A *n.* (nausea) Ekel, *der* (**at** vor + *Dat.*); (revulsion) Abscheu, *der* (**at** vor + *Dat.*); (indignation) Empörung, *die* (**at** über + *Akk.*); **in/with ~:** angewidert; (with indignation) empört

B *v.t.* anwidern; (fill with nausea) anwidern; ekeln; (fill with indignation) empören

disgusted /dɪsˈgʌstɪd/ *adj.* angewidert; (nauseated) angewidert; angeekelt; (indignant) empört; **feel ~ at sth./with sb.** angewidert/angeekelt von etw./empört über etw./jmdn. sein

disgustedly /dɪsˈgʌstɪdlɪ/ *adv.* voller Ekel; angewidert; (with nausea) angewidert, angeekelt; (indignantly) empört

disgusting /dɪsˈgʌstɪŋ/ *adj.* widerlich; widerwärtig; (nauseating also) ekelhaft; miserabel (ugs. abwertend) ‹*Prüfungsergebnis, schulische Leistungen*›; **don't be ~:** sei nicht so geschmacklos

disgustingly /dɪsˈgʌstɪŋlɪ/ *adv.* widerlich; (causing nausea also) ekelhaft; unmöglich (ugs.) ‹*sich kleiden*›; (iron.) unverschämt ‹*gut aussehen, reich*›

dish /dɪʃ/

A *n.* **1** (for food) Schale, *die;* (flatter) Platte, *die;* (deeper) Schüssel, *die* **2** *in pl.* (crockery) Geschirr, *das;* **wash** *or* (coll.) **do the ~es** Geschirr spülen; abwaschen **3** (type of food) Gericht, *das;* **it is [not] my/everybody's ~** (fig. coll.) darauf steh ich [nicht]/darauf steht [nicht] jeder (ugs.) **4** (coll.: person) (woman, girl) klasse Frau (ugs.); (man) klasse Typ (ugs.); **be quite a ~:** eine Wucht sein (salopp) **5** (receptacle) Schale, *die;* (concavity) Mulde, *die* **6** (Radio, Telev.) Parabolantenne, *die*

B *v.t.* **1** anrichten ‹*Essen*› **2** (coll.) (outmanœuvre) austricksen (ugs.); (ruin) kleinkriegen (ugs.); zunichte machen ‹*Hoffnung, Chancen*›

Phrasal verbs

- **~ ˈout** *v.t.* **1** austeilen ‹*Essen*› **2** (coll.: distribute) verteilen
- **~ ˈup** *v.t.* auftragen, servieren ‹*Essen*›; (fig.) auftischen (ugs. abwertend)

dishabille /dɪsəˈbiːl/ ▸**déshabillé**

disharmony /dɪsˈhɑːmənɪ/ *n.* (lit. or fig.) Disharmonie, *die*

dish: ~cloth *n.* **1** (for washing) Abwaschlappen, *der;* Spültuch, *das;* **2** (Brit.: for drying) Geschirrtuch, *das;* **~ cover** *n.* Cloche, *die* (Gastr.); (against flies etc.) Fliegenglocke, *die*

dishearten /dɪsˈhɑːtn/ *v.t.* entmutigen; **be ~ed** den Mut verlieren/verloren haben

disheartening /dɪsˈhɑːtənɪŋ/ *adj.*, **dishearteningly** /dɪsˈhɑːtənɪŋlɪ/ *adv.* entmutigend

dished /dɪʃt/ *adj.* konkav

dishevelled (*Amer.:* **disheveled**) /dɪˈʃevld/ *adj.* unordentlich ‹*Kleidung*›; zerzaust ‹*Haar, Bart*›; ungepflegt ‹*Erscheinung*›

ˈdishmop *n.* ≈ Spülbürste, *die*

dishonest /dɪsˈɒnɪst/ *adj.* unehrlich ‹*Person*›; unaufrichtig ‹*Person, Antwort*›; unlauter (geh.)

‹Geschäftsgebaren, Vorhaben›; unredlich ‹Geschäftsmann›; unreell ‹Geschäft, Gewinn›; ~ **goings-on** undurchsichtige Vorgänge; **be ~ with sb.** unehrlich *od.* unaufrichtig gegen jmdn. sein

dishonestly /dɪsˈɒnɪstlɪ/ *adv.* unehrlich; unaufrichtig; unlauter (geh.) ‹*handeln*›; unredlich ‹*sich verhalten*›

dishonesty /dɪsˈɒnɪstɪ/ *n.* Unehrlichkeit, *die;* Unaufrichtigkeit, *die;* (of methods) Unlauterkeit, *die* (geh.)

dishonor *etc.* (*Amer.*) ▸**dishonour** *etc.*

dishonour /dɪsˈɒnə(r)/

A *n.* Schande, *die;* **bring ~ [up]on the nation/sb.** Schande über die Nation/jmdn. bringen

B *v.t.* **1** beleidigen **2** (disgrace) entehren; **~ one's family** seiner Familie (*Dat.*) Schande machen **3** (Commerc.) nicht honorieren ‹*Wechsel*›; nicht einlösen, zurückgehen lassen ‹*Scheck*›; nicht bezahlen ‹*Schulden*›

dishonourable /dɪsˈɒnərəbl/ *adj.* unehrenhaft

dishonourably /dɪsˈɒnərəblɪ/ *adv.* in unehrenhafter Weise

dish: ~ rack *n.* Abtropfgestell, *das;* (in dishwasher) Geschirrwagen, *der;* **~ towel** *n.* Geschirrtuch, *das;* **~washer** *n.* **1** Geschirrspülmaschine, *die;* Geschirrspüler, *der* (ugs.); *attrib.* **~washer detergent** Geschirrreiniger, *der;* **~washer powder** Geschirrreiniger für Spülmaschinen; **~washer salt** Spülmaschinensalz, *das;* **2** (person) Geschirrspüler, *der*/-spülerin, *die;* **~-washing** *n., no pl.* Geschirrspülen, *das;* **~-washing machine** ▸**~washer 1**; **~water** *n., no pl.* Abwaschwasser, *das;* Spülwasser, *das;* **this tea's like ~water** der Tee schmeckt wie Spülwasser

dishy /ˈdɪʃɪ/ *adj.* (Brit. coll.) klasse (ugs.)

disillusion /dɪsɪˈljuːʒn, dɪsɪˈluːʒn/

A *n., no pl.* Desillusion, *die* (**with** über + *Akk.*)

B *v.t.* ernüchtern; **I don't want to ~ you, but ...:** ich möchte dir nicht deine Illusionen rauben, aber ...

disillusioned /dɪsɪˈljuːʒnd, dɪsɪˈluːʒnd/ *adj.* desillusioniert; **become ~ with sth.** seine Illusionen über etw. (*Akk.*) verlieren

disillusionment /dɪsɪˈljuːʒnmənt, dɪsɪˈluːʒnmənt/ *n.* Desillusionierung, *die*

disincentive /dɪsɪnˈsentɪv/ *n.* Hemmnis, *das;* **act as** *or* **be a ~ to sb. to do sth.** jmdn. davon abhalten, etw. zu tun

disinclination /dɪsɪnklɪˈneɪʃn/ *n.* Abneigung, *die* (**for, to** gegen)

disincline /dɪsɪnˈklaɪn/ *v.t.* abgeneigt machen (**for, to** gegen)

disinclined /dɪsɪnˈklaɪnd/ *adj.* abgeneigt

disinfect /dɪsɪnˈfekt/ *v.t.* desinfizieren

disinfectant /dɪsɪnˈfektənt/

A *adj.* desinfizierend

B *n.* Desinfektionsmittel, *das*

disinfection /dɪsɪnˈfekʃn/ *n.* Desinfektion, *die;* Desinfizierung, *die*

disinfest /dɪsɪnˈfest/ *v.t.* von Ungeziefer befreien; entwesen (fachspr.)

disinformation /dɪsɪnfəˈmeɪʃn/ *n.* Desinformation, *die*

disingenuous /dɪsɪnˈdʒenjʊəs/ *adj.* unaufrichtig

disingenuously /dɪsɪnˈdʒenjʊəslɪ/ *adv.* in unaufrichtiger Weise

disinherit /dɪsɪnˈherɪt/ *v.t.* enterben; (fig.) entrechten

disinheritance /dɪsɪnˈherɪtəns/ *n.* Enterbung, *die*

disintegrate /dɪsˈɪntɪgreɪt/

A *v.i.* **1** zerfallen; ‹*Straßenbelag:*› aufbrechen; ‹*Gestein:*› zerbröckeln, zerfallen; (shatter suddenly) zerbersten; (fig.) sich auflösen **2** (Phys.) zerfallen

B *v.t.* **1** zerstören; (by weathering also) zerfressen; (by exploding) sprengen; (fig.) auflösen **2** (Phys.) spalten

disintegration /dɪsɪntɪˈgreɪʃn/ *n.* **1** Zerfall, *der;* (of road surface) Aufbrechen, *das;* (fig.) Auflösung, *die;* (of personality) [allmähliche] Zerstörung; (of hopes) Zusammenbruch, *der* **2** (Phys.) Zerfall, *der*

disinter /dɪsɪnˈtɜː(r)/ *v.t.*, **-rr-** **1** ausgraben **2** (fig.) ans Licht bringen

disinterest /dɪsˈɪntrəst, dɪsˈɪntrɪst/ ▸**disinterestedness**

disinterested /dɪsˈɪntrəstɪd, dɪsˈɪntrɪstɪd/ *adj.* **1** (impartial) unvoreingenommen; unparteiisch; (free from selfish motive) selbstlos; uneigennützig **2** (coll.: uninterested) desinteressiert

disinterestedly /dɪsˈɪntrəstɪdlɪ, dɪsˈɪntrɪstɪdlɪ/ *adv.* ▸**disinterested**: unvoreingenommen; unparteiisch; selbstlos; uneigennützig; desinteressiert

disinterestedness /dɪsˈɪntrəstɪdnɪs, dɪsˈɪntrɪstɪdnɪs/ *n., no pl.* ▸**disinterested**: Unvoreingenommenheit, *die;* Selbstlosigkeit, *die;* Uneigennützigkeit, *die;* Desinteresse, *das* (**in** an + *Dat.*)

disinterment /dɪsɪnˈtɜːmənt/ *n.* **1** Ausgrabung, *die* **2** (fig.) Ausgraben, *das*

disinvestment /dɪsɪnˈvestmənt/ *n.* (Econ.) Desinvestition, *die*

disjoin /dɪsˈdʒɔɪn/ *v.t.* [voneinander] trennen

disjointed /dɪsˈdʒɔɪntɪd/ *adj.*, **disjointedly** /dɪsˈdʒɔɪntɪdlɪ/ *adv.* unzusammenhängend; zusammenhanglos

disjunctive /dɪsˈdʒʌŋktɪv/ *adj.* **1** trennend **2** (Ling., Logic) disjunktiv

disk **1** (Computing) **[floppy] ~:** Floppydisk, *die;* Diskette, *die;* **[hard] ~** Festplatte, *die* **2** ▸**disc 1, 2, 4, 5**

ˈdisk drive *n.* (Computing) Diskettenlaufwerk, *das*

diskette /dɪsˈket/ *n.* (Computing) Diskette, *die*

disk: ~ operating system *n.* (Computing) Plattenbetriebssystem, *das;* **~ space** *n., no pl.* (Computing) Festplattenplatz, *der*

dislike /dɪsˈlaɪk/

A *v.t.* nicht mögen; (a little stronger) nicht leiden können; **~ sb./sth. greatly** *or* **intensely** jmdn./etw. ganz und gar nicht leiden können; **I don't ~ it** ich finde es nicht schlecht; **~ doing sth.** es nicht mögen/nicht leiden können, etw. zu tun; etw. ungern tun; **I ~ your having to stay late** ich sehe es nicht gern, dass du lange bleiben musst

B *n.* **1** *no pl.* Abneigung, *die* (**of, for** gegen); **she took an instant ~ to him/the house** sie empfand sofort eine Abneigung gegen ihn/das Haus; **have a ~ for sb./sth.** eine Abneigung gegen jmdn./etw. haben *od.* (geh.) hegen; **feel ~ for sb./sth.** jmdn./etw. nicht leiden können **2** (object) **one of my greatest ~s is ...:** zu den Dingen, die ich am wenigsten leiden kann, gehört ...

dislocate /ˈdɪsləkeɪt/ *v.t.* **1** (Med.) luxieren (fachspr.); ausrenken; auskugeln ‹*Schulter, Hüfte*› **2** (fig.) beeinträchtigen

dislocation /dɪsləˈkeɪʃn/ *n.* **1** (Med.) Luxation, *die* (fachspr.); Ausrenkung, *die;* (of shoulder, hip) Auskugelung, *die* **2** (fig.) Beeinträchtigung, *die*

dislodge /dɪsˈlɒdʒ/ *v.t.* entfernen (**from** aus); (detach) lösen (**from** von); (Mil.: drive out) vertreiben (**from** aus)

disloyal /dɪsˈlɔɪəl/ *adj.* illoyal (**to** gegenüber); treulos ‹*Freund, Ehepartner*›; **be ~:** nicht loyal sein

disloyalty /dɪsˈlɔɪəltɪ/ *n.* Illoyalität, *die* (**to** gegenüber); (to spouse, friend) Treulosigkeit, *die*

dismal /ˈdɪzməl/ *adj.* trist; düster; trostlos ‹*Landschaft, Ort*›; bedrückend ‹*Niedergang*›; (coll.: feeble) kläglich ‹*Zustand, Leistung, Versuch*›; **in a ~ manner/tone of voice** düster/mit bedrückter Stimme; **a ~ failure** ein völliger Reinfall (ugs.)

dismally /ˈdɪzməlɪ/ *adv.* trostlos; trübe ‹*beleuchtet*›; kläglich ‹*fehlschlagen, jammern*›

dismantle /dɪsˈmæntl/ *v.t.* zerlegen; demontieren; (fig.) demontieren; abbauen ‹*Schuppen, Gerüst*›; (permanently) abreißen, niederreißen ‹*Gebäude*›; schleifen ‹*Befestigungsanlage*›; abwracken ‹*Schiff*›

dismast /dɪsˈmɑːst/ *v.t.* (Naut.) entmasten

dismay /dɪsˈmeɪ/

A *v.t.* bestürzen; **he was ~ed to hear that ...:** mit Bestürzung hörte er, dass ...; **he was ~ed at the news** er war bestürzt über die Nachricht

B *n.* Bestürzung, *die* (**at** über + *Akk.*); **he was filled with ~ at the news** die Nachricht erfüllte ihn mit Bestürzung; **watch in** *or* **with ~:** bestürzt zusehen

dismember /dɪsˈmembə(r)/ *v.t.* **1** verstümmeln **2** (partition) zersplittern

dismemberment /dɪsˈmembəmənt/ *n.* **1** Verstümmelung, *die* **2** (partitioning) Zersplitterung, *die*

dismiss /dɪsˈmɪs/ *v.t.* **1** (send away, ask to leave or disperse) entlassen; auflösen, aufheben ‹*Versammlung*›; **~!** (Mil.) weggetreten! **2** (from employment) entlassen **3** (from the mind) verwerfen; (treat very briefly) abtun **4** (Law) abweisen ‹*Klage*›; entlassen ‹*Geschworene*›; **~ with costs** kostenpflichtig abweisen **5** (Cricket) ausscheiden lassen

dismissal /dɪsˈmɪsl/ *n.* **1** Entlassung, *die;* (of committee, gathering, etc.) Auflösung, *die;* Aufhebung, *die;* **she made a gesture of ~ to the servant** sie entließ den Diener mit einer Handbewegung **2** (from employment) Entlassung, *die;* **give sb. his/her ~:** jmdn. entlassen **3** (from the mind) Aufgabe, *die;* (rejection) Ablehnung, *die;* (very brief treatment) Abtun, *das* **4** (Law) (of a case) Abweisung, *die;* (of jury) Entlassung, *die* **5** (Cricket) Ausscheiden, *das*

dismissive /dɪsˈmɪsɪv/ *adj.* abweisend; (disdainful) abschätzig; **be ~ about sth.** etw. abtun *od.* nicht würdigen

dismissively /dɪsˈmɪsɪvlɪ/ *adv.* abweisend; (disdainfully) abschätzig

dismount /dɪsˈmaʊnt/

A *v.i.* absteigen

B *v.t.* abwerfen ‹*Reiter*›

disobedience /dɪsəˈbiːdɪəns/ *n.* Ungehorsam, *der;* **act of ~:** ungehorsames Verhalten; Ungehorsam, *der;* **~ to orders** Nichtbefolgen der Anordnungen

disobedient /dɪsəˈbiːdɪənt/ *adj.* ungehorsam; **be ~ to orders/to sb.** Anordnungen nicht befolgen/jmdm. nicht gehorchen

disobediently /dɪsəˈbiːdɪəntlɪ/ *adv.* ungehorsam; **act/behave ~:** ungehorsam sein

disobey /dɪsəˈbeɪ/ *v.t.* nicht gehorchen (+ *Dat.*); nicht befolgen, missachten ‹*Befehl, Vorschrift usw.*›; übertreten ‹*Gesetz*›; (Mil.) den Gehorsam verweigern (+ *Dat.*)

disoblige /dɪsəˈblaɪdʒ/ *v.t.* **~ sb.** jmds. Wunsch nicht nachkommen

disobliging /dɪsəˈblaɪdʒɪŋ/ *adj.* ungefällig; **be very/most ~:** wenig/kein bisschen entgegenkommend sein

disorder /dɪsˈɔːdə(r)/

A *n.* **1** Unordnung, *die;* Durcheinander, *das;* **everything was in [complete] ~:** alles war ein einziges[, heilloses] Durcheinander; **the meeting broke up in ~:** die Versammlung endete in einem heillosen Durcheinander; **throw sth. into ~:** etw. in Unordnung bringen; **the marchers were thrown into ~:** die Marschierenden gerieten aus der Reihe; **the troops fled in ~:** die Soldaten flohen in ungeordneten Haufen; **leave the house in a state of ~:** das Haus in großer Unordnung hinterlassen **2** (rioting, disturbance) Unruhen *Pl.* **3** (Med.) [Funktions]störung, *die;* **suffer from a mental ~:** geisteskrank sein; **a stomach/liver ~:** ein Magen-/Leberleiden; **a blood ~:** eine Blutkrankheit

B *v.t.* **1** in Unordnung bringen; durcheinander bringen **2** verwirren ‹*Geist*›

disordered /dɪsˈɔːdəd/ *adj.* **1** unordentlich; ungeordnet ‹*Wortschwall, Gedanken[gang]*›; wirr ‹*Fantasie*› **2** (Med.) gestört; angegriffen ‹*Organ*›; (mentally unbalanced) geistesgestört

disorderly /dɪsˈɔːdəlɪ/ *adj.* **1** (untidy) unordentlich; ungeordnet ‹*Denkweise, Ansammlung*› **2** (unruly) undiszipliniert; disziplinlos; zügellos, unsolide ‹*Lebensweise*›; aufrührerisch ‹*Mob*›; **~ conduct** ungebührliches *od.* ungehöriges Benehmen

d

dis'orderly house *n.* (brothel) öffentliches Haus (verhüll.); (gambling-den) Spielhölle, *die* (abwertend)

disorganization /dɪsɔːɡənaɪˈzeɪʃn/ *n., no pl.* Desorganisation, *die;* (muddle) Durcheinander, *das;* **cause ~ of sth.** etw. durcheinander bringen

disorganize /dɪsˈɔːɡənaɪz/ *v.t.* durcheinander bringen; desorganisieren (geh.)

disorganized /dɪsˈɔːɡənaɪzd/ *adj.* chaotisch; unsystematisch, chaotisch ‹*Arbeiter, Person*›; **he's completely ~:** er geht völlig unsystematisch vor

disorient /dɪsˈɔːrɪənt, dɪsˈɒrɪənt/, **disorientate** /dɪsˈɒrɪənteɪt, dɪsˈɔːrɪənteɪt/ *v.t.* die Orientierung nehmen (+ *Dat.*); (fig.) verwirren

disorientated /dɪsˈɒrɪənteɪtɪd, dɪsˈɔːrɪənteɪtɪd/ *adj.* verwirrt; desorientiert

disorientation /dɪsɒrɪənˈteɪʃn, dɪsɔːrɪənˈteɪʃn/ *n.* (lit. or fig.) Verwirrung, *die;* Desorientiertheit, *die*

disoriented /dɪsˈɔːrɪəntɪd, dɪsˈɒrɪəntɪd/ ▸**disorientated**

disown /dɪsˈəʊn/ *v.t.* **1** (repudiate) verleugnen; **if you do that I'll ~ you** (joc.) wenn du das tust, sind wir geschiedene Leute **2** (renounce allegiance to) nicht anerkennen

disparage /dɪˈspærɪdʒ/ *v.t.* **1** herabsetzen **2** (discredit) in Verruf bringen; diskreditieren (geh.)

disparagement /dɪˈspærɪdʒmənt/ *n.* Herabsetzung, *die;* **speak with ~ of sth./sb.** sich verächtlich über etw./jmdn. äußern

disparaging /dɪˈspærɪdʒɪŋ/ *adj.* abschätzig

disparagingly /dɪˈspærɪdʒɪŋlɪ/ *adv.* abschätzig

disparate /ˈdɪspərət/ *adj.* [völlig] verschieden; disparat (geh.)

disparity /dɪˈspærɪtɪ/ *n.* Disparität, *die* (geh.); (difference also) Unterschied, *der;* (lack of parity) Ungleichheit, *die*

dispassionate /dɪˈspæʃənət/ *adj.* leidenschaftslos; (impartial) unvoreingenommen

dispassionately /dɪˈspæʃənətlɪ/ *adv.* leidenschaftslos; (impartially) unvoreingenommen

dispatch /dɪˈspætʃ/
A *v.t.* **1** (send off) schicken; **~ sb. [to do sth.]** jmdn. entsenden (geh.) [um etw. zu tun] **2** (get through) erledigen; abschließen ‹*Geschäft*›; erfüllen ‹*Pflicht*› **3** (kill) töten **4** (eat) verschlingen; verputzen (ugs.)
B *n.* **1** (official report, Journ.) Bericht, *der;* Depesche, *die* (veralt.); **they were mentioned in ~es** (Mil.) ≈ ihnen wurde förmliche Anerkennung ausgesprochen **2** (sending off) Absenden, *das;* (of troops, messenger, delegation) Entsendung, *die* (geh.) **3** (killing) Tötung, *die* **4** (prompt execution) Erledigung, *die* **5** **act with ~:** prompt handeln

dispatch: ~ box, ~ case *ns.* Aktenkoffer, *der*

dispatcher /dɪˈspætʃə(r)/ *n.* Verkehrsbetriebsregler, *der*

dispatch: ~ note *n.* Versandanzeige, *die;* **~ rider** *n.* Bote, *der;* (Mil.) Meldefahrer, *der*

dispel /dɪˈspel/ *v.t.*, **-ll-** vertreiben; zerstreuen ‹*Besorgnis, Befürchtung*›; verdrängen, unterdrücken ‹*Gefühl, Erinnerung, Vorahnung*›

dispensable /dɪˈspensəbl/ *adj.* entbehrlich

dispensary /dɪˈspensərɪ/ *n.* (Pharm.) Apotheke, *die;* (in hospital) [Krankenhaus]apotheke, *die*

dispensation /dɪspenˈseɪʃn/ *n.* **1** (distribution) Verteilung, *die* (**to** an + *Akk.*); (of grace) Zuteilwerden-Lassen, *das;* (of favours) Gewährung, *die;* **~ of justice** Rechtsprechung, *die* **2** (management) Verfügung, *die;* (Theol.: by Providence) **divine ~:** göttliche Fügung **3** (exemption) Sonderregelung, *die;* **~ from the examination** Erlass der Prüfung **4** (Eccl.) Dispens, *die*

dispense /dɪˈspens/
A *v.i.* **~ with** verzichten auf (+ *Akk.*); (set aside) außer Acht lassen; (do away with) überflüssig machen
B *v.t.* **1** (distribute, administer) verteilen (**to** an + *Akk.*); gewähren ‹*Gastfreundschaft*›; zuteil werden lassen ‹*Gnade*›; spenden ‹*Sakrament*›; **~ justice** Recht sprechen; **the machine ~s hot drinks** der Automat gibt heiße Getränke aus; **the device ~s liquid soap/toilet paper** aus der Vorrichtung kommt flüssige Seife/Toilettenpapier **2** (Pharm.) dispensieren (fachspr.); bereiten und abgeben

dispenser /dɪˈspensə(r)/ *n.* **1** (Pharm.) Apotheker, *der*/Apothekerin, *die* **2** (vending machine) Automat, *der;* (container) Spender, *der*

dispensing 'chemist *n.* ▸**ⓘ p. 1260** Apotheker, *der*/Apothekerin, *die*

dispersal /dɪˈspɜːsl/ *n.* **1** (scattering) Zerstreuung, *die;* (diffusion) Ausbreitung, *die;* (of mist, oil slick) Auflösung, *die;* (Mil.) Auseinanderziehen, *das* **2** (Bot., Zool.) Verbreitung, *die* **3** (Phys.) Dispersion, *die*

dispersant /dɪˈspɜːsənt/ *n.* Dispersionsmittel, *das*

disperse /dɪˈspɜːs/
A *v.t.* **1** (scatter) zerstreuen; (dispel) auflösen ‹*Dunst, Öl*›; vertreiben ‹*Wolken, Gase*›; (Mil.) auseinander ziehen **2** (Phys.) dispergieren (fachspr.); verteilen; zerlegen ‹*Lichtstrahl*›
B *v.i.* sich zerstreuen; (Phys.) sich verteilen

dispersion /dɪˈspɜːʃn/ *n.* **1** (scattering) Zerstreuung, *die;* (diffusion) Ausbreitung, *die;* (Mil.) Auseinanderziehen, *das* **2** **D~** (Jewish Hist.) ▸**Diaspora** **3** (Phys.) Dispersion, *die;* (system) Dispersoid, *das* **4** (Statistics) Streuung, *die;* Dispersion, *die* (fachspr.)

dispirit /dɪˈspɪrɪt/ *v.t.* entmutigen

dispirited /dɪˈspɪrɪtɪd/ *adj.* entmutigt; mutlos ‹*Gesichtsausdruck*›; halbherzig ‹*Versuch*›

dispiritedly /dɪˈspɪrɪtɪdlɪ/ *adv.* entmutigt

dispiriting /dɪˈspɪrɪtɪŋ/ *adj.* entmutigend

displace /dɪsˈpleɪs/ *v.t.* **1** (move from place) verschieben; (force to flee) vertreiben; (remove from office) entlassen **2** (supplant) ersetzen; (crowd out) verdrängen **3** (Phys.: take the place of) verdrängen

displaced 'person *n.* Vertriebene, *der/die*

displacement /dɪsˈpleɪsmənt/ *n.* **1** (moving) Verschiebung, *die;* (removal from office) Entlassung, *die* **2** (supplanting) Ersetzung, *die* **3** (Phys.: [amount] taking the place of sth.) Verdrängung, *die* **4** (Naut.: weight displaced) [Wasser]verdrängung, *die* **5** (Psych.) Verschiebung, *die* **6** (Motor Veh.) Hubraum, *der*

display /dɪˈspleɪ/
A *v.t.* **1** tragen ‹*Abzeichen*›; vorzeigen ‹*Fahrkarte, Einladung*›; aufstellen ‹*Trophäe*›; (to public view) ausstellen; (on noticeboard) aushängen; (standing) aufstellen ‹*Schild*›; (attached) aufhängen ‹*Schild, Fahne*›; (make manifest) zeigen; (depict) zeigen, darstellen **2** (flaunt) zur Schau stellen **3** (Commerc.) ausstellen **4** (reveal involuntarily) zeigen **5** (Printing) hervorheben
B *n.* **1** Aufstellung, *die;* (to public view) Ausstellung, *die;* (manifestation) Demonstration, *die;* **a ~ of ill will/courage** eine Demonstration von jmds. Übelwollen/Mut **2** (exhibition) Ausstellung, *die;* (Commerc.) Auslage, *die;* Display, *das* (Werbespr.); **a military ~:** eine öffentliche militärische Veranstaltung; **a fashion ~:** eine Modenschau; **a ~ of flowers** ein Blumenarrangement; **be on ~:** ausgestellt werden; **[be] for ~:** zur Ansicht [sein]; **put a house on ~:** ein Haus als Musterhaus herrichten **3** (ostentatious show) Zurschaustellung, *die;* **make a ~ of one's knowledge/affection** sein Wissen/seine Gefühle zur Schau stellen **4** (Computing etc.) Display, *das;* Anzeige, *die* **5** (Printing) Hervorhebung, *die;* **~ advertising** [größere] Zeitungsanzeige **6** (Ornith.) Imponiergehabe, *das;* (courtship ~) Balzverhalten, *das*

display: ~ cabinet, ~ case ▸**case² A 4**; **~ window** *n.* Schaufenster, *das*

displease /dɪsˈpliːz/ *v.t.* **1** (earn disapproval of) **~ sb./the authorities** jmds. Missfallen/das Missfallen der Behörden erregen **2** (annoy) verärgern; **be ~d [with sb./at sth.]** [über jmdn./etw.] verärgert sein; **she was most ~d to see that ...:** sie war sehr ärgerlich, als sie sah, dass ...

displeasing /dɪsˈpliːzɪŋ/ *adj.* unangenehm; unerfreulich ‹*Anblick, Aussicht*›; unschön ‹*Akzent*›; **be ~ to sb./to the eye/ear** jmdm. missfallen/keine Freude für das Auge/das Ohr sein

displeasure /dɪsˈpleʒə(r)/ *n., no pl.* Missfallen, *das* (**at** über + *Akk.*); **arouse/cause ~:** Missfallen erregen

disport /dɪˈspɔːt/ *v. refl. & i.* (literary) sich vergnügen

disposable /dɪˈspəʊzəbl/
A *adj.* **1** (to be thrown away after use) Wegwerf-; **~ bottle/container/syringe** Einwegflasche/-behälter/-spritze; **be ~:** nach Gebrauch weggeworfen werden **2** (available) verfügbar; (Finance also) disponibel (fachspr.)
B *n.* Wegwerfartikel, *der*

disposable: ~ 'assets *n. pl.* (Finance) frei verfügbares *od.* disponibles Vermögen; **~ 'income** *n.* (Finance) verfügbares Einkommen

disposal /dɪˈspəʊzl/ *n.* **1** (getting rid of, killing) Beseitigung, *die;* (of waste) Entsorgung, *die;* **~ of sewage** Abwasserbeseitigung, *die* **2** (putting away) Forträumen, *das* **3** (eating up) Aufessen, *das* **4** (settling) Erledigung, *die;* (of argument) Beilegung, *die* **5** (treating) Abhandlung, *die* **6** (bestowal) Übertragung, *die* (**to** auf + *Akk.*) **7** (sale) Veräußerung, *die* **8** (control) Verfügung, *die;* **place** *or* **put sth./sb. at sb.'s [complete] ~:** jmdm. etw./jmdn. [ganz] zur Verfügung stellen; **have sth./sb. at one's ~:** etw./jmdn. zur Verfügung haben; **be at sb.'s ~:** jmdm. zur Verfügung *od.* zu jmds. Verfügung stehen

dispose /dɪˈspəʊz/
A *v.t.* **1** (make inclined) **~ sb. to sth.** jmdn. zu etw. veranlassen; **~ sb. to do sth.** jmdn. dazu veranlassen, etw. zu tun **2** (arrange) anordnen; (Mil.) aufstellen ‹*Truppen*›
B *v.i.* (determine course of events) entscheiden; Entscheidungen treffen; **man proposes, God ~s** (prov.) der Mensch denkt, Gott lenkt (Spr.)

Phrasal verb

• **~ of** *v.t.* **1** (do as one wishes with) **~ of sth./sb.** über etw./jmdn. frei verfügen **2** (kill, get rid of) beseitigen ‹*Rivalen, Leiche, Abfall*›; erlegen, töten ‹*Gegner, Drachen*›; **she ~d of the tea leaves down the sink** sie hat die Teeblätter in den Ausguss getan *od.* den Ausguss hinuntergespült **3** (put away) wegräumen **4** (eat up) aufessen; verputzen (ugs.) **5** (settle, finish) erledigen; **~ of the business** das Geschäftliche erledigen *od.* regeln **6** (disprove) widerlegen

disposed /dɪˈspəʊzd/ *adj.* **be ~ to sth.** zu etw. neigen; **be ~ to do sth.** dazu neigen, etw. zu tun; **be ~ to anger** leicht zornig werden; **I'm not ~/don't feel ~ to help that lazy fellow** ich bin nicht geneigt/fühle mich nicht veranlasst, diesem Faulpelz zu helfen; **feel ~ to make a complaint** meinen, dass man sich beschweren muss; **be well/ill ~ towards sb.** jmdm. wohlgesinnt/übel gesinnt sein; **be well/ill ~ towards sth.** einer Sache (*Dat.*) positiv/ablehnend gegenüberstehen

disposition /dɪspəˈzɪʃn/ *n.* **1** (arrangement; also Mil.: attack plan) Aufstellung, *die;* (of guards etc.) Aufstellung, *die;* Postierung, *die;* (of seating, figures) Anordnung, *die;* **~ of troops** Truppenaufstellung, *die* **2** *in pl.* (preparations; also Mil.) Vorbereitungen *Pl.* **3** (ordinance of Providence, fate, or God) Fügung, *die* **4** (temperament) Veranlagung, *die;* Disposition, *die;* **his boastful ~:** seine prahlerische Art; **she has a/is of a rather irritable ~:** sie ist ziemlich reizbar **5** (inclination) Hang, *der;* Neigung, *die* (**towards** zu); **have a ~ to do sth./to[wards] sth.** dazu neigen, etw. zu tun/zu etw. neigen

dispossess /dɪspəˈzes/ *v.t.* **1** (oust) verdrängen; entthronen ‹*Monarchen*›; stürzen ‹*Diktator*›; enterben ‹*Kind*› **2** (deprive) **~ sb. of sth.** jmdm. etw. entziehen; (fig.) jmdm. etw. rauben

disproportion /dɪsprəˈpɔːʃn/ *n.* Missverhältnis, *das*

disproportionate /dɪsprəˈpɔːʃənət/ *adj.* **1** (relatively too large/small) vom Normalen abweichend; unangemessen; **be [totally] ~ to sth.** in einem [völligen] Missverhältnis *od.* in [gar] keinem Verhältnis zu etw. stehen **2** (lacking proportion) unproportioniert

disproportionately /dɪsprəˈpɔːʃənətlɪ/ *adv.* unverhältnismäßig

disprove /dɪsˈpruːv/ *v.t.* widerlegen; **~ sb.'s innocence** jmds. Schuld beweisen

disputable /dɪˈspjuːtəbl, ˈdɪspjʊtəbl/ *adj.* strittig; disputabel (geh.)

disputant /dɪˈspjuːtənt/ *n.* Disputant, *der*/Disputantin, *die*

disputation /dɪspjʊˈteɪʃn/ *n.* [1] *no pl.* (argument) Meinungsverschiedenheiten *Pl.*; Streit, *der* [2] (arch.: academic debate) Disputation, *die*

disputatious /dɪspjʊˈteɪʃəs/ *adj.* streitlustig; streitbar

dispute /dɪˈspjuːt/

A *n.* [1] *no pl.* (controversy) Streit, *der*; **there has been some ~ as to what ...:** es hat Streit darüber gegeben, was ...; **be a matter/subject of much ~:** eine sehr umstrittene Frage/ein sehr umstrittenes Thema sein; **it is a matter of ~ whether ...:** man kann darüber streiten, ob ...; **that is [not] in ~:** darüber wird [nicht] gestritten; **be beyond ~:** außer Frage stehen [2] (argument) Streit, *der* (**over** um); **a ~ arose as to whether ...:** wegen der Frage, ob ..., kam es zum *od.* zu einem Streit

B *v.t.* [1] (discuss) sich streiten über (+ *Akk.*); **~ whether .../how ...:** sich darüber streiten, ob .../wie ... [2] (oppose) bestreiten; anfechten ‹*Rechtsanspruch*›; angreifen ‹*Entscheidung*› [3] (resist) [an]kämpfen gegen [4] (contend for) streiten um; **they are disputing the leadership of the party** sie machen sich (*Dat.*) gegenseitig die Parteiführung streitig

C *v.i.* (argue) streiten; **~ with sb. on** *or* **about sth.** mit jmdm. über etw. (*Akk.*) diskutieren

disqualification /dɪskwɒlɪfɪˈkeɪʃn/ *n.* [1] (disqualifying) Ausschluss, *der* (**from** von); (Sport) Disqualifikation, *die* [2] (thing that disqualifies) Grund zum Ausschluss

disqualify /dɪsˈkwɒlɪfaɪ/ *v.t.* [1] (debar) ausschließen (**from** von); (Sport) disqualifizieren [2] (make unfit) ungeeignet machen; **~ sb./sth. for sth.** jmdn./etw. für etw. ungeeignet machen [3] (incapacitate) verbieten (+ *Dat.*)

disquiet /dɪsˈkwaɪət/ *n.* Unruhe, *die*

disquieting /dɪsˈkwaɪətɪŋ/ *adj.* beunruhigend

disquisition /dɪskwɪˈzɪʃn/ *n.* Abhandlung, *die*; (long speech) Vortrag, *der*; Sermon, *der* (abwertend)

disregard /dɪsrɪˈgɑːd/

A *v.t.* ignorieren; nicht berücksichtigen ‹*Tatsache*›; **~ a request** einer Bitte (*Dat.*) nicht nachkommen

B *n.* Missachtung, *die* (**of, for** *Gen.*); (of wishes, feelings) Gleichgültigkeit, *die* (**for, of** gegenüber); **he shows a total ~ of** *or* **for other people/others' feelings/wishes** ihm sind andere/die Gefühle anderer/die Wünsche anderer völlig gleichgültig

disrepair /dɪsrɪˈpeə(r)/ *n.* (of building) schlechter [baulicher] Zustand; Baufälligkeit, *die*; (of furniture etc.) schlechter Zustand; **the house is in a state of/has fallen into ~:** das Haus ist baufällig

disreputable /dɪsˈrepjʊtəbl/ *adj.* zwielichtig; übel beleumdet ‹*Person*›; verrufen ‹*Etablissement, Gegend*›; schäbig ‹*Aussehen, Kleidung*›

disrepute /dɪsrɪˈpjuːt/ *n.* Verruf, *der*; (of area) Verrufenheit, *die*; **bring sb./sth. into ~:** jmdn./etw. in Verruf bringen; **fall into ~:** in Verruf kommen *od.* geraten

disrespect /dɪsrɪˈspekt/ *n.* Missachtung, *die*; **show [only] ~ for sb./sth.** [überhaupt] keine Achtung *od.* keinen Respekt vor jmdm./etw. haben; **I meant no ~ [to you]** ich wollte [Ihnen gegenüber] nicht respektlos sein

disrespectful /dɪsrɪˈspektfl/ *adj.* respektlos; **be ~ towards sb.** vor jmdm. keinen Respekt *od.* keine Achtung haben

disrespectfully /dɪsrɪˈspektfəlɪ/ *adv.* respektlos

disrobe /dɪsˈrəʊb/ (formal)

A *v.t.* [1] (divest of robe) das Gewand abnehmen (+ *Dat.*) [2] (undress) ausziehen; entkleiden (geh.)

B *v.i.* [1] (divest oneself of robe, coat, etc.) ablegen [2] (undress) sich ausziehen; sich entkleiden (geh.)

disrupt /dɪsˈrʌpt/ *v.t.* [1] (break up) zerschlagen ‹*Regierung, Partei, System*› [2] (interrupt) unterbrechen; stören ‹*Klasse, Sitzung*›

disruption /dɪsˈrʌpʃn/ *n.* [1] (break-up) Zerschlagung, *die* [2] (interruption) Unterbrechung; (of class, meeting) Störung, *die*

disruptive /dɪsˈrʌptɪv/ *adj.* [1] (breaking up) zerstörerisch [2] (violently interrupting) störend

dissatisfaction /dɪsætɪsˈfækʃn/ *n.*, *no pl.* Unzufriedenheit, *die* (**with, at** mit)

dissatisfied /dɪˈsætɪsfaɪd/ *adj.* **be ~ with** *or* **at sb./sth.** mit jmdm./etw. unzufrieden sein

dissect /dɪˈsekt/ *v.t.* [1] (cut into pieces) zerschneiden, zerlegen (**into** in + *Akk.*) [2] (Med., Biol.) präparieren; sezieren, präparieren ‹*Leiche*› [3] (analyse) zergliedern; sezieren

dissection /dɪˈsekʃn/ *n.* [1] (cutting into pieces) Zerlegung, *die* [2] (Med., Biol.) Präparation, *die*; (of body) Sektion, *die*; Präparation, *die* [3] (Med.: thing cut up) Präparat, *das* [4] (analysis) Zergliederung, *die*; Sezierung, *die*

dissemble /dɪˈsembl/

A *v.t.* (disguise) verbergen ‹*Gefühle, Absichten*›; verheimlichen ‹*Liebe*›

B *v.i.* [1] (conceal one's motives) sich verstellen [2] (talk or act hypocritically) heucheln

disseminate /dɪˈsemɪneɪt/ *v.t.* (lit. or fig.) verbreiten; verstreuen ‹*Samen, Truppen, Flüchtlinge*›; *see also* **sclerosis 1**

dissemination /dɪsemɪˈneɪʃn/ *n.* Verbreitung, *die*

dissension /dɪˈsenʃn/ *n.* Dissens, *der*; Streit, *der* (**on** über + *Akk.*); **~s** Streitigkeiten; Meinungsverschiedenheiten

dissent /dɪˈsent/

A *v.i.* [1] (refuse to assent) nicht zustimmen; **~ from sth.** mit etw. nicht übereinstimmen [2] (disagree) **~ from sth.** von etw. abweichen

B *n.* [1] (difference of opinion) Ablehnung, *die*; (from majority) Abweichung, *die* [2] (refusal to accept) Ablehnung, *die*

dissenter /dɪˈsentə(r)/ *n.* Andersdenkende, *der/die*; **be a ~ from sth.** etw. ablehnen

dissentient /dɪˈsenʃɪənt, dɪˈsenʃənt/

A *adj.* anders denkend ‹*Person, Minderheit*›; abweichend ‹*Meinung, Vorstellung, Standpunkt*›

B *n.* Andersdenkende, *der/die*

dissertation /dɪsəˈteɪʃn/ *n.* (spoken) Vortrag, *der*; (written) Abhandlung, *die*; (for bachelor's degree) Diplomarbeit, *die*; (for master's degree) Magisterarbeit, *die*; (for PhD) Dissertation, *die*

disservice /dɪˈsɜːvɪs/ *n.* **do sb. a ~:** jmdm. einen schlechten Dienst erweisen

dissidence /ˈdɪsɪdəns/ *n.*, *no pl.* Uneinigkeit, *die*; Meinungsverschiedenheit, *die*

dissident /ˈdɪsɪdənt/

A *adj.* [1] (disagreeing) anders denkend; **a ~ person** ein Andersdenkender; **a ~ group/faction** eine Dissidentengruppe [2] (dissentient) **hold a ~ view** *or* **opinion** eine abweichende Meinung vertreten

B *n.* Dissident, *der*/Dissidentin, *die*; Regimekritiker, *der*/-kritikerin, *die*

dissimilar /dɪˈsɪmɪlə(r)/ *adj.* unähnlich; unterschiedlich, verschieden ‹*Ideen, Ansichten, Geschmäcker*›; **be [highly] ~ to sth./sb.** [ganz] anders als etw./jmd. sein

dissimilarity /dɪsɪmɪˈlærɪtɪ/ *n.* Unähnlichkeit, *die*

dissimulate /dɪˈsɪmjʊleɪt/ *v.t.* verbergen ‹*Gefühle*›; verheimlichen ‹*Tatsache, Wahrheit, Ideale*›; verleugnen ‹*Identität*›.

dissipate /ˈdɪsɪpeɪt/

A *v.t.* [1] (dispel) auflösen ‹*Nebel, Dunst*›; vertreiben ‹*Angst, Sorgen, Wolken*›; zerstreuen ‹*Befürchtungen, Zweifel*›; zunichte machen ‹*Begeisterung, Illusion*›; aufhellen, heben ‹*düstere Stimmung*› [2] (bring to nothing) zerstören [3] (break up) auseinander treiben ‹*Gruppe, Truppen, Menge*›; auseinander brechen lassen ‹*Familie, Gemeinde, Volk*› [4] (fritter away) vergeuden; (squander) durchbringen ‹*Vermögen, Erbschaft*›; verschwenden ‹*Geld*›; **~ sb.'s energy** jmdn. entkräften; jmds. Energien aufzehren

B *v.i.* ‹*Nebel, Dunst:*› sich auflösen

dissipated /ˈdɪsɪpeɪtɪd/ *adj.* ausschweifend; zügellos; **~ morals** lockere Moral

dissipation /dɪsɪˈpeɪʃn/ *n.* [1] (scattering) Auflösung, *die* [2] (intemperate living) Ausschweifung, *die* [3] (wasteful expenditure) Verschwendung, *die*; (of fortune, inheritance) Vergeudung, *die*; **~ of money/energy** Geld-/Energieverschwendung, *die* [4] (frivolous amusement) Amüsement, *das*

dissociate /dɪˈsəʊʃɪeɪt, dɪˈsəʊsɪeɪt/ *v.t.* [1] (disconnect) trennen; **~ oneself from sth./sb.** sich von etw./jmdm. distanzieren; **~ oneself from all responsibility** alle Verantwortung ablehnen [2] (Chem.) dissoziieren

dissociation /dɪsəʊsɪˈeɪʃn/ *n.* [1] Distanzierung, *die* (**of** von); (of ideas) Abgrenzung, *die* [2] (Chem.) Dissoziation, *die*

dissolute /ˈdɪsəluːt, ˈdɪsəljuːt/ *adj.* (licentious) ausschweifend; (against morality) lasterhaft; freizügig ‹*Mode*›; zügellos ‹*Benehmen*›

dissolutely /ˈdɪsəluːtlɪ, ˈdɪsəljuːtlɪ/ *adv.* lasterhaft ‹*leben*›; zügellos ‹*sich benehmen*›

dissolution /dɪsəˈluːʃn, dɪsəˈljuːʃn/ *n.* [1] (disintegration) Zersetzung, *die* [2] (undoing, dispersal) Auflösung, *die*; **~ of a bond** Lösung einer Bindung

dissolve /dɪˈzɒlv/

A *v.t.* auflösen; abbrechen ‹*Freundschaft*›; **acid ~s protein** Säure zersetzt Eiweiß

B *v.i.* [1] sich auflösen; (in acid) sich zersetzen; ‹*Vorstellung:*› vorbeigehen; **~ into tears/laughter** in Tränen/Gelächter ausbrechen; **~ into thin air** sich in Luft auflösen [2] (Cinemat.) überblenden

C *n.* (Cinemat.) Überblendung, *die*

dissonance /ˈdɪsənəns/ *n.* (Mus.) Dissonanz, *die*; (fig.) Disharmonie, *die*

dissonant /ˈdɪsənənt/ *adj.* (Mus.) dissonant; (fig.) disharmonisch; voneinander abweichend ‹*Meinungen*›

dissuade /dɪˈsweɪd/ *v.t.* **~ sb. from sth.** jmdn. von etw. abbringen; **~ sb. from doing sth.** jmdn. davon abbringen, etw. zu tun

dissuasion /dɪˈsweɪʒn/ *n.* Abbringen, *das*

distaff /ˈdɪstɑːf/ *n.* [1] (in spinning) Rocken, *der* [2] *attrib.* (concerning women) weiblich; **~ side** weibliche Seite

distance /ˈdɪstəns/ ▸ **p. 1072**

A *n.* [1] Entfernung, *die* (**from** zu); **their ~ from each other** die räumliche Entfernung zwischen ihnen; **keep [at] a [safe] ~ [from sb./sth.]** jmdm./einer Sache nicht zu nahe kommen; **maintain a safe ~ from the car in front** einen Sicherheitsabstand zum Vordermann einhalten [2] (fig.: aloofness) Abstand, *der*; **keep one's ~** *or* **at a ~ [from sb./sth.]** Abstand [zu jmdm./etw.] wahren [3] (way to cover) Strecke, *die*; Weg, *der*; (gap) Abstand, *der*; **accompany sb. for part of the ~:** jmdn. einen Teil des Weges *od.* ein Stück begleiten; **from this ~:** aus dieser Entfernung; von hier aus; **at a ~ of ... [from sb./sth.]** in einer Entfernung von ... [von jmdm./etw.]; **a short ~ away** ganz in der Nähe; **fall a ~ of one metre** einen Meter tief fallen; **that's no [great] ~:** das ist nicht weit; das ist keine Entfernung [4] (remoter field of vision) Ferne, *die*; **in/into the ~:** in der/die Ferne; **run off into the ~:** weit weglaufen; **the car vanished into the ~:** das Auto verschwand in der Ferne; **middle ~** (Art) Mittelgrund, *der* [5] (distant point) Entfernung, *die*; **at a ~/[viewed] from a ~:** von weitem; (fig.) oberflächlich betrachtet; **they remained at a ~:** sie blieben in einiger Entfernung stehen [6] (space of time) Abstand, *der*; **at a ~ of 20 years** aus einem Abstand von 20 Jahren; nach [einem Zeitraum von] 20 Jahren [7] (Racing, Boxing) Distanz, *die*; **go** *or* **stay the ~:** über die volle Distanz gehen; (fig.) [bis zum Schluss] durchhalten

B *v.t.* [1] (leave behind in race) hinter sich (*Dat.*) lassen [2] (fig.) entfremden; **~ oneself from sb./sth.** sich von jmdm./etw. distanzieren

distance: ~ learning *n.* Fernstudium, *das*; **~ runner** *n.* Langstreckenläufer, *der*/-läuferin, *die*

distant /ˈdɪstənt/ *adj.* [1] (far) fern; **from nearby and ~ parts** von *od.* aus nah und fern; **be ~ [from sb.]** weit [von jmdm.] weg sein; **about three miles ~ from here** ungefähr drei

ℹ Distance

1 yard = 0,914 m (null Komma neun eins vier Meter)
1 mile = 1,61 km (eins Komma sechs eins Kilometer)

How far is it or ***What's the distance from London to Edinburgh?***
= Wie weit ist es von London nach Edinburgh?
It's/The distance is 365 miles
= Es sind/Die Entfernung beträgt 588 Kilometer
It's quite a long way [away]
= Es ist ziemlich weit [entfernt]
The house is just a few hundred yards from here
= Das Haus liegt nur ein paar hundert Meter von hier [entfernt]
Manchester is further from the sea than Chester
= Manchester liegt *or* ist weiter vom Meer entfernt als Chester
Reading is nearer to London than Oxford
= Reading liegt näher an London als Oxford
A and B are the same distance away
= A und B sind gleich weit entfernt
He hit the target from a distance of 50 metres
= Er traf das Ziel aus einer Entfernung von 50 Metern
a fifty mile drive
= eine Autofahrt von achtzig Kilometern
an hour's drive
= eine Stunde Fahrt [mit dem Auto], eine Autostunde
It's only a ten minute walk
= Es sind nur zehn Minuten zu Fuß

Meilen von hier [entfernt] **2** (fig.: remote) entfernt ‹*Ähnlichkeit, Verwandtschaft, Verwandte, Beziehung*›; **it's a ~ prospect/possibility** das ist Zukunftsmusik; **~ memories/recollections** weit zurückreichende Erinnerungen; **have a ~ memory of sth.** sich an etw. (*Akk.*) vage erinnern **3** (in time) fern; **in the ~ past/future** in ferner Vergangenheit/Zukunft; **in some ~ era** in fernen Zeiten **4** (cool) reserviert, distanziert ‹*Mensch, Haltung*›; **be ~ with sb.** jmdm. gegenüber reserviert sein

distantly /ˈdɪstəntlɪ/ *adv.* **1** (far) fern **2** (fig.: remotely) entfernt; **~ resemble each other** eine entfernte Ähnlichkeit aufweisen **3** (coolly) reserviert

distaste /dɪsˈteɪst/ *n.* Abneigung, *die;* **[have] a ~ for sb./sth.** eine Abneigung gegen jmdn./etw. [haben]; **in ~:** aus Abneigung; **turn away in ~:** sich angewidert abwenden

distasteful /dɪsˈteɪstfl/ *adj.* unangenehm; **be ~ to sb.** jmdm. zuwider sein

distastefully /dɪsˈteɪstfəlɪ/ *adv.* geschmacklos; **look ~ at sth.** etw. angewidert betrachten

distastefulness /dɪsˈteɪstflnɪs/ *n., no pl.* Widerwärtigkeit, *die*

distemper¹ /dɪˈstempə(r)/
A *n.* **1** (paint) Temperafarbe, *die* **2** (method) Temperamalerei, *die*
B *v.t.* mit Temperafarbe bemalen

distemper² *n.* (animal disease) Staupe, *die*

distend /dɪˈstend/ *v.t.* aufblähen, auftreiben ‹*Leib, Bauch*›; blähen ‹*Nüstern*›; aufblasen ‹*Backen, Ballon*›; erweitern ‹*Gefäße, Darm, Ader*›; aufschwellen ‹*Euter*›

distension /dɪˈstenʃn/ *n.* Aufblähung, *die;* Auftreiben, *das;* (of blood vessel, intestine) Erweiterung, *die*

distich /ˈdɪstɪk/ *n.* (Pros.) Distichon, *das*

distil (*Amer.:* **distill**) /dɪˈstɪl/ *v.t.*, **-ll-** (lit. or fig.) destillieren; brennen ‹*Branntwein*›; **~ sth. from sth.** (fig.) etw. aus etw. [heraus]destillieren;

distillate /ˈdɪstɪleɪt/ *n.* Destillat, *das*

distillation /dɪstɪˈleɪʃn/ *n.* Destillation, *die;* (fig.) Herausdestillieren, *das;* (result) Destillat, *das*

distiller /dɪˈstɪlə(r)/ *n.* Destillateur, *der;* Branntweinbrenner, *der*

distillery /dɪˈstɪlərɪ/ *n.* [Branntwein]brennerei, -destillation, *die;* Destille, *die*

distinct /dɪˈstɪŋkt/ *adj.* **1** (different) verschieden; **keep two things ~:** zwei Dinge auseinander halten; **as ~ from** im Unterschied zu **2** (clearly perceptible, decided) deutlich; klar ‹*Stimme, Sicht*›; ausgeprägt ‹*Falten, Charme*› **3** (separate) unterschiedlich **4** (particular) bestimmt ‹*Gegend, Gebiet*›

distinction /dɪˈstɪŋkʃn/ *n.* **1** (making a difference) Unterscheidung, *die;* **by way of ~, for ~:** zur Unterscheidung **2** (difference) Unterschied, *der;* **there is a clear ~ between A and B** es besteht ein deutlicher Unterschied zwischen A und B; **make** *or* **draw a ~ between A and B** einen Unterschied zwischen A und B machen; **draw a sharp/clear ~ between A and B** streng/klar zwischen A und B trennen; **a ~ without a difference** ein nomineller Unterschied **3** (being different) Andersartigkeit, *die* **4** (distinctive feature) besonderes Merkmal; **have the ~ of being ...:** sich dadurch auszeichnen, dass man ... ist **5** (showing of special consideration) Ehrung, *die;* **be mentioned with special ~:** besonders lobend erwähnt werden; **a mark of ~:** eine Ehre *od.* Auszeichnung **6** (mark of honour) Auszeichnung, *die;* **gain** *or* **get a ~ in one's examination** das Examen mit Auszeichnung bestehen **7** (excellence) hoher Rang; **a scientist of ~:** ein Wissenschaftler von Rang [und Namen]

distinctive /dɪˈstɪŋktɪv/ *adj.* unverwechselbar; **be ~ of sth.** für etw. typisch *od.* charakteristisch sein

distinctively /dɪˈstɪŋktɪvlɪ/ *adv.* unverwechselbar

distinctly /dɪˈstɪŋktlɪ/ *adv.* **1** (clearly) deutlich; **we couldn't see ~ in the mist** in dem Nebel konnten wir nichts deutlich erkennen **2** (decidedly) merklich; **be ~ aware of sth.** etw. deutlich spüren **3** (markedly) ausgeprägt

distinctness /dɪˈstɪŋktnɪs/ *n., no pl.* **1** (difference) Verschiedenheit, *die* **2** (separateness) Getrenntheit, *die*

distinguish /dɪˈstɪŋgwɪʃ/
A *v.t.* **1** (make out) erkennen; (hear) verstehen; (read) lesen; entziffern **2** (differentiate) unterscheiden; (characterize) kennzeichnen; **~ sth./sb. from sth./sb.** etw./jmdn. von etw./jmdm. unterscheiden **3** (divide) einteilen; **~ things/persons into ...:** Dinge/Personen einteilen in (+ *Akk.*) **4** (make prominent) **~ oneself [by sth.]** sich [durch etw.] hervortun; **~ oneself by doing sth.** sich dadurch hervortun, dass man etw. tut; **~ oneself in an exam** in einem Examen glänzen (ugs.); **you've really ~ed yourself, haven't you?** (iron.) na, da hast du vielleicht 'ne Glanzleistung vollbracht!
B *v.i.* unterscheiden; **~ between persons/things** Personen/Dinge auseinander halten *od.* voneinander unterscheiden; **one can barely ~ between the original and the copy** man kann das Original kaum von der Kopie unterscheiden

distinguishable /dɪˈstɪŋgwɪʃəbl/ *adj.* **1** (able to be made out) erkennbar; (audible) hörbar; (readable) lesbar; (decipherable) entzifferbar **2** (able to be differentiated) erkennbar; unterscheidbar **3** (able to be divided) einteilbar

distinguished /dɪˈstɪŋgwɪʃt/ *adj.* **1** (eminent) namhaft, angesehen ‹*Persönlichkeit, Schule, Firma*›; glänzend ‹*Laufbahn*›; hervorragend ‹*Qualität*›; **a ~ politician** ein Politiker von Rang [und Namen] **2** (looking eminent) vornehm, (geh.) distinguiert ‹*Aussehen, Mensch*› **3** (remarkable) **~ [for/by sth.]** sich [durch etw.] auszeichnend *attr.*

distort /dɪˈstɔːt/ *v.t.* **1** verzerren ‹*Gesicht, Stimme, Musik*›; verformen ‹*Gegenstand*›; ‹*Schmerz, Krankheit:*› entstellen **2** (misrepresent) entstellt *od.* verzerrt wiedergeben; verdrehen ‹*Worte, Wahrheit*›

distortion /dɪˈstɔːʃn/ *n.* **1** Verzerrung, *die;* (by disease) Entstellung, *die* **2** (misrepresentation) Entstellung, *die;* (of words, truth) Verdrehung, *die*

distract /dɪˈstrækt/ *v.t.* **1** (divert) ablenken; **~ sb.['s attention/concentration/mind from sth.]** jmdn. [von etw.] ablenken **2** *usu. in pass.* (make mad or angry) wahnsinnig machen; **grow ~ed** außer sich geraten; **~ed with joy/worry** außer sich vor Freude/Sorge **3** (bewilder) irritieren

distracted /dɪˈstræktɪd/ *adj.* **1** (mad) von Sinnen *nachgestellt;* außer sich *nachgestellt;* (worried) besorgt; beunruhigt; **run round like one ~:** wie von Sinnen umherlaufen **2** (mentally far away) abwesend

distraction /dɪˈstrækʃn/ *n.* **1** (frenzy) Wahnsinn, *der;* **love sb. to ~:** jmdn. wahnsinnig *od.* bis zur Raserei lieben; **drive sb. to ~:** jmdn. wahnsinnig machen *od.* zum Wahnsinn treiben; **be worried to ~ by sth.** sich (*Dat.*) wegen etw. wahnsinnige (ugs.) Sorgen machen **2** (confusion) Unruhe, *die* **3** (diversion) Ablenkung, *die* **4** (interruption) Störung, *die;* **I don't want any ~s** ich möchte nicht gestört werden; **be a ~:** ein Störfaktor sein **5** (amusement) Zerstreuung, *die;* (pastime) Zeitvertreib, *der*

distrain /dɪˈstreɪn/ *v.i.* (Law) **~ [upon sb./sth.]** [jmdn. *od.* bei jmdm./etw.] pfänden

distraint /dɪˈstreɪnt/ *n.* (Law) Pfändung, *die*

distraught /dɪˈstrɔːt/ *adj.* aufgelöst (**with** vor + *Dat.*); verstört ‹*Blick, Gesichtsausdruck*›; **tearful and ~:** in Tränen aufgelöst

distress /dɪˈstres/
A *n.* **1** (anguish) Kummer, *der* (**at** über + *Akk.*); **suffer ~:** Leid erdulden; Kummer ertragen; **be in [a state of] ~:** in Sorge sein; **cause sb. much ~:** jmdm. viel Kummer zufügen *od.* bereiten **2** (suffering caused by want) Not, *die;* Elend, *das* **3** (danger) Not, *die;* Gefahr, *die;* **an aircraft/a ship in ~:** ein Flugzeug in Not/ein Schiff in Seenot **4** (exhaustion) Erschöpfung, *die;* (severe pain) Qualen *Pl.;* **be in ~:** Qualen leiden **5** (misfortune) Unglück, *das* **6** (Law) ▸**distraint**
B *v.t.* **1** (worry) bedrücken; bekümmern; (cause anguish to) ängstigen; (upset) nahe gehen (+ *Dat.*); mitnehmen; **don't ~ yourself/try not to ~ yourself** ängstigen Sie sich nicht; **we were most ~ed** wir waren zutiefst betroffen *od.* bestürzt **2** (exhaust) erschöpfen **3** (afflict) plagen; heimsuchen

distressed /dɪˈstrest/ *adj.* **1** (anguished) leidvoll; betrübt; (desperate) gequält; verzweifelt **2** (impoverished) Not leidend ‹*Volkswirtschaft, Dritte Welt*›; verarmt ‹*Adel*›; armselig ‹*Verhältnisse*›

distressed 'area *n.* (Brit.) Notstandsgebiet (*mit hoher Arbeitslosigkeit*)

distressing /dɪˈstresɪŋ/ *adj.* **1** (upsetting) erschütternd; **be ~ to sb.** jmdn. sehr belasten **2** (regrettable) beklagenswert

di'stress signal *n.* Notsignal, *das*

distribute /dɪˈstrɪbjuːt/ *v.t.* **1** verteilen (**to** an + *Akk.*, **among** unter + *Akk.*); austeilen ‹*Sakramente*› **2** (divide, classify) aufteilen; **~ sth. into parts/categories/groups** etw. in Absätze/Kategorien unterteilen/in Gruppen aufteilen **3** (Printing) ablegen

distribution /dɪstrɪˈbjuːʃn/ *n.* **1** Verteilung, *die* (**to** an + *Akk.*, **among** unter + *Akk.*); (of seeds) [Aus]streuen, *das;* (Econ.: of goods) Distribution, *die* (fachspr.); Vertrieb, *der;* (of films) Verleih, *der;* **~ of weight** Gewichtverteilung, *die;* **the ~ of wealth** die Vermögensverteilung **2** (division) Aufteilung, *die;* (classification) Einteilung, *die*

distribution: ~ cost *n., usu. in pl.* Vertriebskosten *Pl.;* **~ list** *n.* Verteiler, *der*

distributive /dɪˈstrɪbjʊtɪv/ (Ling.)
A *n.* Distributivum, *das*
B *adj.* ▸**pronoun**

distributor /dɪˈstrɪbjʊtə(r)/ *n.* [1] Verteiler, *der*/Verteilerin, *die;* (Econ.) Vertreiber, *der;* (firm) Vertrieb, *der;* (of films) Verleih[er], *der* [2] (Motor Veh.) [Zünd]verteiler, *der*

district /ˈdɪstrɪkt/ *n.* [1] (administrative area) Bezirk, *der* [2] (Brit.: part of county) Distrikt, *der* [3] (Amer.: political division) Wahlkreis, *der* [4] (tract of country, area) Gegend, *die;* **country ~s** ländliche Gegenden; **residential ~:** Wohngebiet, *das*

District of Columbia

Der Bundesdistrikt der USA - Abkürzung D.C., postamtlich DC - mit der Bundeshauptstadt Washington, der unmittelbar dem Kongress der USA unterstellt ist. Er wurde 1790 geschaffen, und ursprünglich war das Land ein Geschenk der Bundesstaaten Maryland und Virginia; Virginia nahm das Geschenk später wieder zurück. Die Bewohner durften bis 1961 nicht an den Präsidentschaftswahlen teilnehmen.

district: ~ atˈtorney *n.* ▸ⓘ **p. 1260** (Amer. Law) [Bezirks]staatsanwalt, *der*/-anwältin, *die;* **~ ˈcouncil** *n.* (Brit.) Rat des Distrikts; **Newbury D~ Council** der Rat des Distrikts Newbury; **~ ˈcourt** *n.* (Amer. Law) [Bundes]bezirksgericht, *das;* **~ ˈheating** *n.* Fernheizung, *die;* **~ ˈnurse** *n.* ▸ⓘ **p. 1260** (Brit.) Gemeindeschwester, *die*

distrust /dɪsˈtrʌst/
A *n.* Misstrauen, *das* (**of** gegen); **show ~ of sb.** jmdm. Misstrauen entgegenbringen
B *v.t.* misstrauen (+ *Dat.*); (because of bad experiences) mit Argwohn *od.* Misstrauen begegnen (+ *Dat.*); **I rather ~ his driving ability/his motives** ich traue seinen Fahrkünsten nicht so recht/ich bezweifle seine Motive

distrustful /dɪsˈtrʌstfl/ *adj.* misstrauisch; **be ~ of sb./sth.** jmdm./einer Sache nicht trauen

disturb /dɪˈstɜːb/ *v.t.* [1] (break calm of) stören; aufscheuchen ‹*Vögel*›; aufhalten, behindern ‹*Fortschritt*›; **'do not ~!'** „bitte nicht stören!"; **~ing the peace** Ruhestörung, *die;* **sorry to ~ you at this late hour** entschuldigen Sie bitte die späte Störung; **if you find that the noise ~s you** wenn Sie sich durch den Lärm gestört fühlen; **~ sb.'s sleep** jmdn. im Schlaf stören; **don't let us ~ you** lassen Sie sich [durch uns] nicht stören; **they hoped they would not be ~ed** sie hofften, ungestört zu sein [2] (move from settled position) durcheinander bringen; bewegen ‹*Blätter*›; **could I ~ you for a minute?** dürfte ich Sie einen Augenblick stören? [3] (worry) beunruhigen; (agitate) nervös machen; **be greatly ~ed by the fact that ...:** sehr darüber beunruhigt sein, dass ...; **don't be ~ed** beunruhigen Sie sich nicht

disturbance /dɪˈstɜːbəns/ *n.* [1] (interruption) Störung, *die;* (nuisance) Belästigung, *die;* **be a ~ to sth.** etw. stören; **I don't want any ~s** ich möchte nicht gestört werden [2] (agitation, tumult) Unruhe, *die;* **social/political ~s** soziale/politische Unruhen; **racial ~[s]** Rassenunruhen

disturbed /dɪˈstɜːbd/ *adj.* [1] (worried) besorgt ‹*Eindruck, Ausdruck*›; (restless) unruhig ‹*Nacht*› [2] (Psych.) **be [mentally] ~:** geistig gestört sein; **a ~ person** ein Geistesgestörter/eine Geistesgestörte

disturbing /dɪsˈtɜːbɪŋ/ *adj.* bestürzend

disunity /dɪsˈjuːnɪtɪ/ *n.* Uneinigkeit, *die*

disuse /dɪsˈjuːs/ *n.* [1] (discontinuance) Außer-Gebrauch-Kommen, *das;* (disappearance) Verschwinden, *das;* (abolition) Abschaffung, *die;* **the bicycle was rusty from ~:** das Fahrrad war rostig, weil es nicht benutzt wurde [2] (disused state) **fall into ~:** außer Gebrauch kommen

disused /dɪsˈjuːzd/ *adj.* stillgelegt ‹*Bergwerk, Eisenbahnlinie*›; leer stehend ‹*Gebäude*›; ausrangiert (ugs.) ‹*Fahrzeug, Möbel*›

disyllabic /dɪsɪˈlæbɪk, daɪsɪˈlæbɪk/ *adj.* (Ling.) zweisilbig

ditch /dɪtʃ/
A *n.* Graben, *der;* (at side of road) Straßengraben, *der;* **be driven to the last ~** (fig.) in die Enge getrieben werden; **die in a ~** (lit. or fig.) im Straßengraben sterben
B *v.t.* (coll.) [1] (abandon) sitzen lassen ‹*Familie, Freunde*›; sausen lassen (ugs.) ‹*Plan*› [2] (make forced sea-landing with) im Bach landen mit (salopp)

ˈditchwater *n.* stehendes, fauliges Wasser; **[as] dull as ~:** sterbenslangweilig

dither /ˈdɪðə(r)/
A *v.i.* schwanken; **I'm ~ing** ich bin noch am Schwanken; **~ about doing sth.** lange hin und her überlegen, ob man etw. tun soll [oder nicht]
B *n.* (coll.) **be all of a ~** *or* **in a ~:** am Rotieren (ugs.) sein

dithery /ˈdɪðərɪ/ *adj.* unentschlossen

ditto /ˈdɪtəʊ/ *n., pl.* **~s: p. 5 is missing, p. 19 ~:** S. 5 fehlt, ebenso S. 19; **~ marks** Unterführungszeichen, *das;* **I'm hungry. — D~:** Ich habe Hunger. — Ich auch

ditty /ˈdɪtɪ/ *n.* Weise, *die*

ˈditty bag *n.* (Naut.) *Segeltuchtasche für Werkzeug, Nähzeug, Rasierzeug usw. des Seemanns*

ditzy /ˈdɪtsɪ/ *adj.* (Amer. coll.) duss[e]lig (ugs.)

diuretic /daɪjʊəˈretɪk/ (Med.)
A *adj.* diuretisch (fachspr.); harntreibend; **~ drug/substance/remedy** ▸**B**
B *n.* Diuretikum, *das* (fachspr.); harntreibendes Mittel

diurnal /daɪˈɜːnl/ *adj.* [1] (of the day) Tages- [2] (daily) täglich

diva /ˈdiːvə/ *n.* Primadonna, *die;* Göttin, *die* (fig. geh.)

divan /dɪˈvæn/ *n.* [1] (couch, bed) [Polster]liege, *die* [2] (long seat) Chaiselongue, *die*

diˈvan bed ▸**divan 1**

dive /daɪv/
A *v.i.,* **~d** *or* (Amer.) **dove** /dəʊv/ [1] einen Kopfsprung machen; springen; (when already in water) [unter]tauchen [2] (plunge downwards) ‹*Vogel, Flugzeug usw.:*› einen Sturzflug machen; ‹*Unterseeboot usw.:*› abtauchen (Seemannsspr.), tauchen; ‹*Achterbahn usw.:*› hinunterschießen [3] (dart down) sich hinwerfen; **~ under the table for protection** schnell unter dem Tisch Schutz suchen [4] (dart) **~ [out of sight]** sich schnell verstecken; (when frightened) sich flüchten *od.* verkriechen; sich schnell verstecken [5] (rush) hechten; springen; **~ into the nearest pub** gleich in die nächste Kneipe stürzen; **~ into bed** ins Bett springen [6] (plunge with hand) **~ into sth.** in etw. (*Akk.*) mit der Hand greifen *od.* fassen; (fig.: begin to eat) über etw. (*Akk.*) herfallen
B *n.* [1] (plunge) Kopfsprung, *der;* (of bird, aircraft, etc.) Sturzflug, *der* (**towards** auf + *Akk.*); (of submarine etc.) [Unter]tauchen; (of scuba diver) Tauchgang, *der* [2] (sudden darting movement) Sprung, *der;* Satz, *der;* **make a ~ for cover** schnell in Deckung gehen [3] (coll.: disreputable place) Spelunke, *die* (abwertend)

Phrasal verb

- **~ ˈin** *v.i.* [mit dem Kopf voraus] hineinspringen; (fig.: help oneself) zulangen

dive: ~-bomb *v.t.* (Mil.) im Sturzflug bombardieren; **~-bomber** *n.* (Mil.) Sturzkampfflugzeug, *das*

diver /ˈdaɪvə(r)/ *n.* [1] (Sport) Kunstspringer, *der*/-springerin, *die* [2] ▸ⓘ **p. 1260** (as profession) Taucher, *der*/Taucherin, *die* [3] (diving bird) Taucher, *der*

diverge /daɪˈvɜːdʒ, dɪˈvɜːdʒ/ *v.i.* [1] auseinander gehen; **here the road ~s from the river** hier entfernt die Straße sich vom Fluss [2] (fig.) ‹*Berufswege, Pfade:*› sich trennen; (from norm etc.) abweichen [3] (differ) ‹*Meinungen, Ansichten:*› voneinander abweichen, (geh.) divergieren

divergence /daɪˈvɜːdʒəns, dɪˈvɜːdʒəns/ *n.* [1] Divergenz, *die* (fachspr.); Auseinandergehen, *das* [2] (fig.) Abweichung, *die;* (of careers, lifestyles) Auseinanderstreben, *das;* **~ of opinions/views** Meinungsverschiedenheit, *die* (**over** über + *Akk.*)

divergent /daɪˈvɜːdʒənt, dɪˈvɜːdʒənt/ *adj.* [1] divergent (fachspr.); auseinander gehend, auseinander laufend ‹*Routen, Wege*›; (fig.) auseinander strebend ‹*Berufswege*›; **~ lens** (Optics) Zerstreuungslinse, *die* [2] (differing) unterschiedlich, voneinander abweichend ‹*Ansichten, Methoden*›

diverse /daɪˈvɜːs, dɪˈvɜːs/ *adj.* [1] (unlike) verschieden[artig]; unterschiedlich; **be [very] ~ from sth.** [ganz] anders sein als etw. [2] (varied) vielseitig, breit gefächert ‹[*Aus*]*bildung, Interessen, Kenntnisse*›; umfassend ‹*Wissen*›; vielfältig ‹*Arbeitsgebiet*›; bunt [gewürfelt] ‹*Mischung*›

diversification /daɪvɜːsɪfɪˈkeɪʃn, dɪvɜːsɪfɪˈkeɪʃn/ *n.* [1] (varying) [Auf]fächerung, *die;* breite Fächerung [2] (Econ.) Streuung, *die;* **~ [of production]** Diversifikation, *die*

diversify /daɪˈvɜːsɪfaɪ, dɪˈvɜːsɪfaɪ/
A *v.t.* [1] (vary) abwechslungsreich[er] gestalten; Abwechslung bringen in (+ *Akk.*) [2] (Econ.) diversifizieren (fachspr.)
B *v.i.* sich auf neue Produktions-/Produktbereiche umstellen

diversion /daɪˈvɜːʃn, dɪˈvɜːʃn/ *n.* [1] (diverting of attention) Ablenkung, *die* [2] (feint) Ablenkungsmanöver, *das;* **create a ~:** ein Ablenkungsmanöver durchführen [3] *no pl.* (recreation) Unterhaltung, *die;* (distraction) Zerstreuung, *die;* Abwechslung, *die* [4] (amusement) [Möglichkeit der] Freizeitbeschäftigung; **the ~s of the big city** das Unterhaltungsangebot der Großstadt [5] (deviating) (of river, traffic) Ableitung, *die* [6] (Brit.: alternative route) Umleitung, *die;* **there is a traffic ~ on the road** der Verkehr auf der Straße wird umgeleitet

diversionary /daɪˈvɜːʃənərɪ, dɪˈvɜːʃənərɪ/ *adj.* Ablenkungs‹*angriff, -bombardement, -manöver*›

diversity /daɪˈvɜːsɪtɪ, dɪˈvɜːsɪtɪ/ *n.* Vielfalt, *die;* **~ of opinion, ~ in opinions** *or* **views** Meinungsvielfalt, *die*

divert /daɪˈvɜːt, dɪˈvɜːt/ *v.t.* [1] umleiten ‹*Verkehr, Fluss, Fahrzeug*›; ablenken ‹*Aufmerksamkeit, Gedankengang, Blick*›; ableiten ‹*Lavastrom, Blitz*›; lenken ‹*Energien, Aggressionen*›; **~ sb.'s attention/gaze from sth. to sth. else** jmds. Aufmerksamkeit/Blick von etw. auf etw. anderes lenken [2] (distract) ablenken [3] (entertain) unterhalten

diverting /daɪˈvɜːtɪŋ, dɪˈvɜːtɪŋ/ *adj.* (entertaining) unterhaltsam

divest /daɪˈvest, dɪˈvest/ *v.t.* [1] (formal: unclothe) entkleiden (geh.); **~ sb. of sth.** jmdm. etw. abnehmen; **~ sth. of sth.** etw. einer Sache (*Gen.*) entkleiden; **~ oneself of one's clothing/jewellery** seine Kleidung/seinen Schmuck ablegen [2] **~ sb./sth. of sth.** (deprive) jmdn./etw. einer Sache (*Gen.*) berauben; (rid) jmdn./etw. von einer Sache befreien; **~ sb. of a responsibility** jmdn. einer Verantwortung (*Gen.*) entheben; **~ oneself of sth.** sich einer Sache (*Gen.*) entledigen

divide /dɪˈvaɪd/
A *v.t.* [1] teilen; (subdivide) aufteilen; (with precision) einteilen; (into separated pieces) zerteilen; **~ sth. in[to] parts** (separate) etw. [in Stücke (*Akk.*)] aufteilen; **~ sth. into halves/quarters** etw. halbieren/vierteln; **~ sth. in two** etw. [in zwei Teile] zerteilen [2] (by marking out) **~ sth. into sth.** etw. in etw. (*Akk.*) unterteilen [3] (part by marking) trennen; **~ sth./sb. from** *or* **and sth./sb.** etw./jmdn. von etw./jmdm. trennen [4] (mark off) **~ sth. from sth. else** etw. von etw. anderem abgrenzen; **dividing line** Trennungslinie, *die* [5] (distinguish) unterscheiden [6] (classify) einteilen ‹*Lebewesen, Gegenstände, Gesellschaft*› [7] (cause to disagree) entzweien; **be ~d over an issue** in einer Angelegenheit nicht einig sein; **opinion is ~d** die Meinungen sind geteilt; **be ~d against itself** zerstritten sein [8] (distribute) aufteilen; **~ sth. among/between persons/groups** etw. unter Personen/Gruppen (*Akk. od. Dat.*) aufteilen [9] (share) teilen [10] (Math.) dividieren (fachspr.), teilen (**by** durch); **~ three into nine** neun durch drei dividieren *od.* teilen [11] (part for voting) [durch Hammelsprung] abstimmen lassen
B *v.i.* [1] (separate) **~ [in** *or* **into parts]** sich [in Teile] teilen; ‹*Buch, Urkunde usw.:*› sich [in Teile] gliedern *od.* [in Teile] gegliedert sein; **we ~d into groups for discussion** wir bildeten Diskussionsgruppen; **~ into two** sich in zwei

d

Teile teilen **2** ~ **[from sth.]** von etw. abzweigen **3** (Math.) ~ **[by a number/amount]** sich [durch eine Zahl/einen Betrag] dividieren (fachspr.) *od.* teilen lassen; **3 ~s into 36 to give 12** 3 geht zwölfmal in 36 **4** (be parted in voting) **the council ~d and a vote was taken** der Rat stimmte [durch Hammelsprung] ab

C *n.* **1** (Geog.) Wasserscheide, *die* **2** (fig.) (line) Grenze, *die;* (gulf) Kluft, *die;* (rift) Riss, *der;* **the Great D~:** die Scheidelinie; (euphem.) die Schwelle des Todes (geh.)

Phrasal verbs

- **~ 'off**

A *v.t.* trennen; **~ off an area** einen Bereich abtrennen *od.* abteilen

B *v.i.* **~ off from sth.** sich von etw. trennen

- **~ 'out** *v.t.* **~ sth. out [among/between persons]** etw. unter Personen (*Akk. od. Dat.*) aufteilen; (distribute) etw. an Personen (*Akk.*) verteilen
- **~ 'up**

A *v.t.* aufteilen; **~ persons up into groups** Personen in Gruppen einteilen

B *v.i.* **~ up into sth.** sich in etw. (*Akk.*) aufteilen lassen

divided /dɪˈvaɪdɪd/: **~ 'highway** (Amer.) ▸**dual carriageway**; **~ 'skirt** *n.* Hosenrock, *der*

dividend /ˈdɪvɪdend/ *n.* **1** (Commerc., Finance) Dividende, *die* **2** *in pl.* (fig.: benefit) Vorteil, *der;* **your studying will pay ~s** Ihr Studium wird sich auszahlen *od.* rentieren; **reap the ~s** die Früchte ernten *od.* den Nutzen daraus ziehen

dividend: ~-stripping *n., no pl.* (Finance) Rosinenpickerei, *die* (abwertend); **~ warrant** *n.* (Brit. Finance) Dividendenschein, *der*

divider /dɪˈvaɪdə(r)/ *n.* **1** (screen) Trennwand, *die;* (other means) Abgrenzung, *die* **2** **~s** *pl.* Stechzirkel, *der*

divination /dɪvɪˈneɪʃn/ *n.* **1** (foreseeing) Ahnung, *die;* **powers of ~:** Gabe der Weissagung **2** (discovering) Deutung, *die*

divine /dɪˈvaɪn/

A *adj.*, **~r** /dɪˈvaɪnə(r)/, **~st** /dɪˈvaɪnɪst/ **1** göttlich; (devoted to God) gottgeweiht; **~ service** Gottesdienst, *der;* **the ~ right of kings** das Gottesgnadentum; **have no ~ right to do sth.** kein gottgewolltes Recht haben, etw. zu tun **2** (superhumanly excellent) überragend ‹*Begabung*›; göttlich ‹*Schönheit, Musik*›; (superhumanly gifted) gottbegnadet **3** (coll.: delightful) traumhaft

B *n.* Geistliche, *der/die*

C *v.t.* **1** (discover) deuten; (guess) erraten; **~ what sb. is thinking** *or* **sb.'s thoughts** jmds. Gedanken lesen **2** (locate) aufspüren **3** (foresee) vorhersehen; (foretell) weissagen; **~ the future** in die Zukunft sehen

divinely /dɪˈvaɪnlɪ/ *adv.* **1** (by God/a god) von Gott/von einem Gott **2** (with superhuman excellence) genial; virtuos; (with superhuman giftedness) gottbegnadet **3** (coll.: excellently, extremely well) traumhaft

diving /ˈdaɪvɪŋ/ *n.* (Sport) Kunstspringen, *das*

diving: ~ bell *n.* Taucherglocke, *die;* **~ board** *n.* Sprungbrett, *das;* **~ suit** *n.* Taucheranzug, *der*

divining rod /dɪˈvaɪnɪŋrɒd/ ▸**dowsing rod**

divinity /dɪˈvɪnɪtɪ/ *n.* **1** (god) Gottheit, *die* **2** *no pl.* (being a god) Göttlichkeit, *die* **3** *no pl.* (theology) Theologie, *die*

divisible /dɪˈvɪzɪbl/ *adj.* **1** (separable) aufteilbar; (capable of being marked out) [unter-, ein]teilbar; **be ~ into ...:** sich in ... aufteilen lassen **2** (Math.) **be ~ [by a number/an amount]** [durch eine Zahl/einen Betrag] teilbar sein

division /dɪˈvɪʒn/ *n.* **1** ▸**divide A 1**: Teilung/Auf-/Ein-/Zerteilung, *die* **2** (parting) (of things) Abtrennung, *die;* (of persons) Trennung, *die;* (marking off) Abgrenzung, *die* **3** (distinguishing) Unterscheidung, *die;* Abgrenzung, *die* (**from** gegenüber) **4** (classifying) Einteilung, *die* **5** (distributing) Verteilung, *die* (**between/among** an + *Akk.*); (sharing) Teilen, *das;* **~ of labour** Arbeitsteilung, *die* **6** (disagreement) Unstimmigkeit, *die* **7** (Math.) Teilen, *das;* Dividieren, *das;* Division, *die* (fachspr.); **do ~:** dividieren; **long ~:** ausführliche Division (*mit Aufschreiben der Zwischenprodukte*); **short ~:** verkürzte Division (*ohne Aufschreiben der Zwischenprodukte*) **8** (separation in voting) Abstimmung [durch Hammelsprung] **9** (dividing line) Trennungslinie, *die;* (between states) Grenze, *die;* (partition) Trennwand, *die* **10** (part) Unterteilung, *die;* Abschnitt, *der;* (of drawer) Fach, *das* **11** (section) Abteilung, *die* **12** (group) Gruppe, *die* **13** (Mil. etc.) Division, *die;* (of police) Einheit, *die* **14** (of High Court) Kammer, *die* **15** (Footb. etc.) Liga, *die;* Spielklasse, *die;* (in British football) Division, *die* **16** (administrative district) [Verwaltungs]bezirk, *der*

divisional /dɪˈvɪʒənl/ *adj.* (of section) Abteilungs-

division: ~ bell *n.* (Parl.) Abstimmungsklingel, *die;* **~ sign** *n.* Divisionszeichen, *das*

divisive /dɪˈvaɪsɪv/ *adj.* **1** (dividing in opinion etc.) strittig; umstritten ‹*Vorschlag*› **2** (dividing) spalterisch; **have a ~ effect on sth.** etw. spalten

divisor /dɪˈvaɪzə(r)/ *n.* (Math.) Divisor, *der;* Teiler, *der*

divorce /dɪˈvɔːs/

A *n.* **1** [Ehe]scheidung, *die; attrib.* **~ court** Scheidungsgericht, *das;* **~ proceedings** [Ehe-]scheidungsverfahren, *das;* **~ rate** Scheidungsrate, *die;* **~ settlement** (mutually agreed) Scheidungsvereinbarung, *die;* Scheidungsvergleich, *der;* (imposed by court) Scheidungsurteil, *das;* **want a ~:** sich scheiden lassen wollen; **get** *or* **obtain a ~:** sich scheiden lassen; geschieden werden; **grounds for ~:** Scheidungsgründe **2** (fig.) Trennung, *die*

B *v.t.* **1** (dissolve marriage of) scheiden ‹*Ehepartner*›; **they were ~d last year** sie wurden letztes Jahr geschieden *od.* ließen sich letztes Jahr scheiden **2** **~ one's husband/wife** sich von seinem Mann/seiner Frau scheiden lassen; **get ~d** sich scheiden lassen; **her husband refused to ~ her** ihr Mann willigte nicht in die Scheidung ein **3** (fig.) **~ sth./sb. from sth.** etw./jmdn. von etw. loslösen; **keep sth. ~d from sth.** etw. von etw. getrennt halten

divorcee /dɪvɔːˈsiː/ *n.* Geschiedene, *der/die;* **be a ~:** geschieden sein

divot /ˈdɪvət/ *n.* (Golf) ausgehacktes Rasenstück

divulge /daɪˈvʌldʒ, dɪˈvʌldʒ/ *v.t.* preisgeben; enthüllen ‹*Identität*›; bekannt geben ‹*Nachrichten*›; lüften ‹*Geheimnis*›; verraten ‹*Alter*›

divvy /ˈdɪvɪ/ (coll.) *n.* **1** (share) Anteil, *der* **2** (distribution) Verteilung, *die*

dixie *n.* (Brit.) Kochkessel, *der*

Dixie /ˈdɪksɪ/ *n.* **1** die Südstaaten [der USA] **2** (Mus.) Dixie, *der*

'Dixieland *n.* **1** (Mus.) Dixie[land], *der* **2** ▸**Dixie 1**

DIY *abbr.* **= do-it-yourself**

dizzily /ˈdɪzɪlɪ/ *adv.* **1** (giddily) taumelnd; schwankend; (fig.) benommen **2** (so as to cause giddiness) auf Schwindel erregende Weise

dizziness /ˈdɪzɪnɪs/ *n., no pl.* Schwindelgefühl, *das*

dizzy /ˈdɪzɪ/ *adj.* **1** (giddy) schwind[e]lig; **I feel ~:** mir ist schwindlig; **he felt ~:** ihm wurde schwindlig **2** (making giddy) Schwindel erregend; **the ~ heights of fame** die Schwindel erregenden Höhen des Ruhms

DJ /diːˈdʒeɪ/ *abbr.* **1** **= disc jockey** Diskjockey, *der* **2** (Brit.) **= dinner jacket** Smokingjacke, *die*

DLitt /diː ˈlɪt/ *abbr.* **= Doctor of Letters** ≈ Dr. habil.; *see also* **BSc**

DM, D-mark /ˈdiːmɑːk/ *abbr.* (Hist.) **= Deutschmark** DM; D-Mark, *die*

DMus /diː ˈmʌz/ *abbr.* **= Doctor of Music** Doktor der Musikwissenschaften; *see also* **BSc**

DNA *abbr.* **= deoxyribonucleic acid** DNS

DNA: ~ 'fingerprint *n.* DNA-Fingerabdruck, *der;* genetischer Fingerabdruck; **~ 'fingerprinting** *n., no pl.* DNA-Analyse, *die;* **~ 'profile** *n.* DNA-Profil, *das;* **~ 'profiling** *n., no pl.* DNA-Analyse, *die*

D-notice /ˈdiː nəʊtɪs/ *n.* (Brit.) **the government had issued a ~ to the media** die Regierung hatte den Medien die Veröffentlichung [aus Sicherheitsgründen] untersagt

do¹ /də, *stressed* duː/

A *v.t., neg. coll.* **don't** /dəʊnt/, *pres. t.* **he does** /dʌz/, *neg.* (coll.) **doesn't** /ˈdʌznt/, *p. t.* **did** /dɪd/, *neg.* (coll.) **didn't** /ˈdɪdnt/, *pres. p.* **doing** /ˈduːɪŋ/, *p.p.* **done** /dʌn/ **1** (impart) tun; **do sb. a favour** jmdm. einen Gefallen tun

2 (perform) machen ‹*Hausaufgaben, Hausarbeit, Examen, Striptease, Handstand*›; vollbringen ‹*Tat*›; tun, erfüllen ‹*Pflicht*›; tun, verrichten ‹*Arbeit*›; ausführen ‹*Malerarbeiten*›; vorführen ‹*Trick, Nummer, Tanz*›; durchführen ‹*Test*›; aufführen ‹*Stück*›; singen ‹*Lied*›; mitmachen ‹*Rennen, Wettbewerb*›; spielen ‹*Musikstück, Rolle*›; tun ‹*Buße*›; **do the shopping/washing-up/cleaning/gardening** einkaufen [gehen]/abwaschen/sauber machen/die Gartenarbeit erledigen; **do a test on sb.** jmdn. einem Test unterziehen; **do a lot of reading/walking** *etc.* viel lesen/spazieren gehen *usw.;* **do a dance/the foxtrot** tanzen/Foxtrott tanzen; **do one's round** seine Runde machen; **is there anything we can do to help?** können wir [Ihnen] irgendwie helfen *od.* behilflich sein?; **have nothing to do** nichts zu tun haben; **what are you going/planning to do?** was hast du vor?; **what does he do for a living?** was macht er beruflich?; **what is 'he/'that doing here?** was hat er/das hier zu suchen?; **Don't just sit there! Do something!** Sitz nicht so tatenlos herum! Tu *od.* Unternimm doch etwas!; **have sth. [already] done** etw. fertig haben *od.* mit etw. fertig sein; **what are you doing this evening?** was machst du heute Abend?; **what am I going to do?** (baffled) was mach ich bloß?; **do sth. to sth./sb.** etw. mit etw./jmdm. machen; **what have you done to yourself/the cake?** was hast du bloß mit dir/dem Kuchen gemacht?; **do one or two things to the car** noch ein oder zwei Dinge am Wagen in Ordnung bringen; **how could you do this to me?** wie konntest du mir das nur antun!; **he/it does something** *or* **things to me** (fig. coll.) er/das macht mich an (salopp); **do sth. for sb./sth.** etw. für jmdn./etw. tun; **what can I do for you?** was kann ich für Sie tun?; (in shop) was darfs sein?; **this dress does something/nothing for you** (coll.) dieses Kleid steht dir gut/nicht [gut]; **do sth. about sth./sb.** etw. gegen etw./jmdn. unternehmen; **there's nothing we can do about the noise** wir können nichts gegen den Lärm tun *od.* machen; **why don't you do something about your hair?** tu doch mal was für dein Haar!; **what are you going to do about money while you're on holiday?** wie machst du das mit dem Geld, wenn du im Urlaub bist?; **what shall we do for food?** was machen wir mit dem Essen?; **can you do anything with these apples?** kannst du etwas mit diesen Äpfeln anfangen?; **what's to do?** was ist zu tun?; **not know what to do with oneself** nicht wissen, was man machen soll; **that does it** jetzt reichts (ugs.); **that's done it** das war der ausschlaggebende Faktor; (caused a change for the worse) das hat das Fass zum Überlaufen gebracht; (caused a change for the better) das hätten wir; **that will/should do it** so müsste es gehen; (is enough) das müsste genügen; **he's [really] done it** (ruined things) er hat es [wahrlich] geschafft; (achieved something) er hat es [wirklich] geschafft; **do a Garbo** (coll.) es der Garbo (*Dat.*) gleichtun; **how many miles has this car done?** wie viele Kilometer hat der Wagen gefahren?; **the car does** *or* **can do/was doing about 100 mph/does 45 miles to the gallon** das Auto schafft/fuhr mit ungefähr 160 Stundenkilometer/frisst (ugs.) *od.* braucht sechs Liter pro 100 Kilometer

3 (spend) **do a spell in the armed forces** eine Zeit lang bei der Armee sein; **how much longer have you to do at college?** wie lange musst du noch aufs College gehen?

4 (produce) machen ‹*Übersetzung, Kopie*›; schreiben ‹*Gedicht, Roman, Brief*›; anfertigen ‹*Bild, Skulptur*›; herstellen ‹*Artikel, Produkte*›; schaffen ‹*Pensum*›

5 (provide) haben ‹*Vollpension, Mittagstisch*›; (coll.: offer for sale) führen; (effect) erreichen

6 (deal with) (prepare) machen ‹*Bett, Frühstück*›; (work on) machen (ugs.), fertig machen ‹*Garten, Hecke*›; (clean) sauber machen; putzen ‹*Schuhe,*

Fenster›; machen (ugs.) ‹*Treppe*›; (arrange) [zurecht]machen ‹*Haare*›; fertig machen ‹*Korrespondenz, Akten, Zimmer*›; (make up) schminken ‹*Lippen, Augen, Gesicht*›; machen (ugs.) ‹*Nägel*›; (cut) schneiden ‹*Nägel*›; schneiden ‹*Gras, Hecke, Blumen*›; (paint) machen (ugs.) ‹*Zimmer*›; streichen ‹*Haus, Möbel*›; (attend to) sich kümmern um ‹*Bücher, Rechnungen, Korrespondenz*›; abfertigen ‹*Patienten*›; (repair) in Ordnung bringen; machen ‹*Garten*›; (wash) abwaschen ‹*Geschirr*›; **a living room done in blue** ein blau gestrichenes Wohnzimmer
7 (cook) braten; **how do you like your meat done?** wie hätten Sie gern das Fleisch?; **well done** durch[gebraten]; **the meat isn't/the potatoes aren't done [enough] yet** das Fleisch ist/die Kartoffeln sind noch nicht richtig durch *od.* gar
8 (solve) lösen ‹*Problem, Rätsel*›; machen ‹*Puzzle, Kreuzworträtsel*›
9 (translate) übersetzen
10 (study, work at) machen; haben ‹*Abiturfach*›; durchnehmen ‹*Wissensgebiet*›; **do history at university** Geschichte studieren
11 (play the part of) spielen; (impersonate) imitieren; nachmachen; (act like) spielen; mimen (ugs.)
12 (coll.: rob) einsteigen in (+ *Akk.*) ‹*Haus*› (ugs.)
13 (coll.: prosecute) **do sb. [for sth.]** jmdn. wegen etw. rankriegen (ugs.)
14 (sl.: with sexual intercourse) **do sb.** jmdn. bumsen (salopp); **do it [with sb.]** es [mit jmdm.] machen (salopp)
15 (coll.: swindle) reinlegen (ugs.); **do sb. out of sth.** jmdn. um etw. bringen
16 (sl.) (defeat, kill) fertig machen (ugs.); (ruin) erledigen (ugs.)
17 (coll.: exhaust) schaffen (ugs.); fertig machen (ugs.); **we were completely done [in *or* up]** wir waren total geschafft (ugs.) *od.* fix und fertig (ugs.)
18 (traverse) schaffen ‹*Entfernung*›
19 (sl.: undergo) absitzen, (salopp) abreißen ‹*Strafe*›
20 (coll.: visit) besuchen; **do Europe in three weeks** Europa in drei Wochen absolvieren *od.* abhaken (ugs.)
21 (Brit. coll.: provide sth. for) versorgen; **do oneself well** es sich (*Dat.*) gut gehen lassen
22 (satisfy) zusagen (+ *Dat.*); (suffice for, last) reichen (+ *Dat.*); **do sb. very nicely/better** jmdm. voll und ganz/mehr zusagen; **we've got enough food here to do us for a week** wir haben genug Essen für eine Woche hier

B *v.i., forms as* **A** **1** (act) tun; (perform) spielen; **you can do just as you like** du kannst machen, was du willst; **do as they do** mach es wie sie
2 (perform deeds) **do or die** kämpfen oder untergehen; **do-or-die** verzweifelt ‹*Versuch, Angriff*›; wild entschlossen ‹*Gesichtsausdruck*›
3 (fare) **how are you doing?** wie gehts dir?
4 (get on) vorankommen; (in exams) abschneiden; **how are you doing at school?** wie geht es in der Schule?; was macht die Schule?; **do well/badly at school** gut/schlecht in der Schule sein
5 **how do you do?** (formal) guten Tag/Morgen/Abend!
6 (coll.: manage) **how are we doing for time** *or* **as regards time?** wie steht es mit der Zeit *od.* (ugs.) sieht es mit der Zeit aus?
7 (finish) **have done with** ▸**done 5**
8 (serve purpose) es tun; (suffice) [aus]reichen; (be suitable) gehen; **would that do?** tuts das [auch]?; **that won't do** das geht nicht; **that will never do** das geht einfach nicht; **you won't do, Peter** du bist nicht gut genug, Peter; **nothing but the best will do for her** das Beste ist gerade gut genug für sie; **that will do!** jetzt aber genug!; **it doesn't/wouldn't do to tell lies/be late for work/believe all that one is told** es ist/wäre nicht gut zu lügen/zu spät zur Arbeit zu kommen/alles zu glauben, was einem gesagt wird
9 (be usable) **do for** *or* **as sth.** als etw. benutzt werden können; **make do** ▸**make A 20**
10 (happen) **what's doing?** was ist los?; **what's doing at your place?** was ist bei euch los?; was läuft bei euch? (ugs.); **there's nothing doing on the job market** es tut sich nichts auf dem Arbeitsmarkt (ugs.); **Nothing doing. He's not interested** Nichts zu machen (ugs.). Er ist nicht interessiert; **what's to do?** was ist los? *see also* **doing; done**

C *v. substitute, forms as* **A** **1** *replacing v.: usually not translated;* **you mustn't act as he does** du darfst nicht so wie er handeln; **if you drank as much water as you do coffee** wenn du so viel Wasser trinken würdest, wie du Kaffee trinkst
2 *replacing v. and obj. etc.* **he read the Bible every day as his father did before him** er las täglich in der Bibel, wie es schon sein Vater vor ihm getan hatte *od.* wie schon vor ihm sein Vater; **as they did in the Middle Ages** wie sie es im Mittelalter taten; wie im Mittelalter; **if I ate as much chocolate as you do** wenn ich so viel Schokolade äße wie du; **you might not want to ..., but if you do, ...:** du willst vielleicht nicht ..., falls aber doch, ...
3 *as ellipt. aux.* **You went to Paris, didn't you? — Yes, I did** Du warst doch in Paris, oder *od.* nicht wahr? — Ja[, stimmt *od.* war ich]
4 *with 'so', 'it', 'which', etc.* **I knew John Lennon. — So did I** Ich kannte John Lennon. — Ich auch; **if you want to go abroad then do so** wenn du ins Ausland reisen willst, tu es [ruhig]; **go ahead and do it** nur zu; **then please do so within 10 days** dann [tun Sie das] bitte innerhalb von 10 Tagen
5 *in emphatic repetition* **come in, do!** komm doch herein!; **take a seat, do!** nehmen Sie doch Platz!
6 *in tag questions* **I know you from somewhere, don't I?** wir kennen uns doch irgendwoher, nicht?; **he doesn't by any chance play the guitar, does he?** er spielt nicht zufällig Gitarre, oder?; **so you enjoyed yourself in Spain, did you?** es hat Ihnen also in Spanien gefallen, ja?

D *v. aux. + inf. as pres. or past, forms as* **A** **1** *for special emphasis* **I do love Greece** Griechenland gefällt mir wirklich gut; ich liebe Griechenland ganz einfach; **I do apologize** es tut mir wirklich Leid; **you do look glum** du siehst ja so bedrückt aus; **you do smoke a lot** du rauchst ja wirklich viel; **so we did go after all** also gingen wir schließlich doch; **but I tell you, I did see him** aber ich sage dir doch, dass ich ihn gesehen habe
2 *for inversion* **little did he know that ...** er hatte keine Ahnung, dass ...; **rarely do such things happen** so etwas passiert nur selten; **did he but realize it** wenn ihm das bloß klar wäre!
3 *in questions* **do you know him?** kennst du ihn?; **what does he want?** was will er?; **doesn't/didn't he want** *or* **does/did he not want to accompany us?** will/wollte er uns nicht begleiten?; **didn't they look wonderful?** haben sie nicht wunderhübsch ausgesehen?
4 *in negation* **I don't** *or* **do not wish to take part** ich möchte nicht teilnehmen
5 *in neg. commands* **don't** *or* **do not expect to find him in a good mood** erwarten Sie nicht, dass Sie ihn in guter Stimmung antreffen; **children, do not forget ...:** Kinder, vergesst [ja] nicht ...; **don't be so noisy!** seid [doch] nicht so laut!; **don't worry yourselves** macht euch keine Sorgen; **don't!** tus/tuts/tun Sies nicht!
6 + *inf. as imper. for emphasis etc.* **do sit down, won't you?** bitte setzen Sie sich doch!; wollen Sie sich nicht setzen?; **do let us know how you ...:** sag uns aber Bescheid, wie du ...; **do be quiet, Paul!** Paul, sei doch mal ruhig!; **do look here** schau doch mal her!; **do hurry up** beeil dich doch!; **do cheer up!** Kopf hoch!

Phrasal verbs

- **do a'way with** *v.t.* (coll.) abschaffen
- **'do by** *v.t.* **do well by sb.** jmdn. gut behandeln; **he felt hard done by** er fühlte sich zurückgesetzt *od.* schlecht behandelt; **do as you would be done by** handle so, wie du behandelt werden möchtest
- **do 'down** *v.t.* (coll.) **1** (get the better of) ausstechen **2** (speak ill of) schlecht machen; heruntermachen (ugs.)
- **'do for** *v.t.* **1** ▸**do[1] B 9** **2** (coll.: destroy) **do for sb.** jmdn. fertig machen *od.* schaffen (ugs.); **do for sth.** etw. kaputtmachen (ugs.); **be done for** (exhausted) fix und fertig (ugs.) *od.* ganz geschafft (ugs.) sein; **if we don't do better next time we're done for** wenn wir das nächste Mal nicht besser sind, sind wir erledigt **3** (Brit. coll.: keep house for) **do for sb.** für jmdn. sorgen; ‹*Putzfrau:*› für *od.* bei jmdm. putzen
- **do 'in** *v.t.* (sl.) kaltmachen (salopp); alle machen (derb); *see also* **do[1] A 17**
- **do 'out** *v.t.* (coll.: clean) sauber machen; (redecorate) streichen; (in wallpaper) tapezieren; (decorate, furnish) herrichten
- **do 'over** *v.t.* **1** (sl.: beat) zusammenschlagen **2** (Amer. coll.: do again) noch einmal machen
- **do 'up**
  A *v.t.* **1** (fasten) zumachen; binden ‹*Schnürsenkel, Fliege*› **2** (wrap) einpacken; verpacken; (arrange) zurechtmachen; **she did her hair up in a bun** sie machte sich (*Dat.*) einen Knoten **3** (coll.: adorn) zurechtmachen ‹*Menschen*›; schmücken ‹*Kutsche, Pferd, Haus*›; dekorieren ‹*Haus*›
  B *v.i.* ‹*Kleid, Reißverschluss, Knopf usw.:*› zugehen
- **'do with** *v.t.* **1** (get by with) auskommen mit; (get benefit from) **I could do with a glass of orange juice** ich könnte ein Glas Orangensaft vertragen (ugs.); **he could do with a good hiding** eine Tracht Prügel würde ihm nicht schaden **2** **have to do with** zu tun haben mit; **have something/nothing/little to do with sth./sb.** etwas/nichts/wenig mit etw./jmdm. zu tun haben; **it's to do with that job I applied for** es geht um die Stelle, für die ich mich beworben habe
- **'do without** *v.t.* **do without sth.** ohne etw. auskommen; auf etw. (*Akk.*) verzichten; **he could not do without her** er konnte nicht ohne sie leben; **he can't do without drink** er kann das Trinken nicht lassen; *abs.* **you've never had to do with'out** du hast nie auf etwas verzichten müssen

do[2] /du:/ *n., pl.* **dos** *or* **do's** /du:z/ **1** (coll.: swindle) Schwindel, *der;* krumme Sache (ugs.) **2** (Brit. coll.: festivity) Feier, *die;* Fete, *die* (ugs.) **3** *in pl.* **the dos and don'ts** die Ge- und Verbote (**of** *Gen.*); **the dos and don'ts of bringing up children** was man bei der Kindererziehung tun und lassen sollte **4** *in pl.* (Brit. coll.) **fair dos!** gleiches Recht für alle

do[3] ▸**doh**

do. *abbr.* **= ditto** do.; dto.

doable /'du:əbl/ *adj.* (coll.) machbar; **the job was difficult, but ~:** die Arbeit war schwer, aber sie ließ sich bewältigen

doc /dɒk/ *n.* (coll.) Doktor, *der* (ugs.); *as address* Herr/Frau Doktor

docile /'dəʊsaɪl/ *adj.* sanft; (submissive) unterwürfig

docilely /'dəʊsaɪllɪ/ *adv.* unterwürfig

docility /də'sɪlɪtɪ/ *n., no pl.* Sanftmut, *die;* (submissiveness) Unterwürfigkeit, *die*

dock[1] /dɒk/
A *n.* **1** Dock, *das;* **the ship came into ~:** das Schiff ging in[s] Dock; **be in ~:** im Dock liegen; (coll.: in hospital) im Krankenhaus liegen **2** *usu. in pl.* (area) Hafen, *der;* **at the ~s in Hull** im Hafen von Hull; **down by the ~[s]** unten im Hafen **3** (Amer.) (ship's berth) Kai, *der;* (for trucks etc.) Laderampe, *die*
B *v.t.* **1** (bring into ~) [ein]docken **2** (Astronaut.) docken
C *v.i.* **1** (come into ~) anlegen **2** (Astronaut.) docken

dock[2] *n.* (in lawcourt) Anklagebank, *die;* **stand/be in the ~** (lit. or fig.) ≈ auf der Anklagebank sitzen; **put sb. in the ~** (lit. or fig.) ≈ jmdn. auf die Anklagebank bringen

dock[3] *n.* (Bot.) Ampfer, *der*

dock[4] *v.t.* **1** (cut short) kupieren ‹*Hund, Pferd, Schwanz*› **2** (lessen) kürzen ‹*Lohn, Stipendium usw.*›; **he had his pay ~ed by £14, he had £14 ~ed from his pay** sein Lohn wurde um 14 Pfund gekürzt

docker /'dɒkə(r)/ *n.* ▸ⓘ **p. 1260** Hafenarbeiter, *der;* Schauermann, *der;* Docker, *der*

docket /'dɒkɪt/
A *n.* **1** (Brit. Commerc.: list) Liste, *die* **2** (Brit.: custom-house warrant) Zollquittung, *die* **3** (voucher) Bestellschein, *der;* (delivery note) Lieferschein,

der [4] (endorsement on documents etc.) [Register mit] Inhaltsangabe
B *v.t.* (endorse) mit Inhaltsangabe versehen; (label) etikettieren

dock: ~land *n.* das Hafenviertel; **~yard** *n.* Schiffswerft, *die*

doctor /ˈdɒktə(r)/
A *n.* ▸ p. 1260, ▸ p. 1634 [1] (physician) Arzt, *der*/Ärztin, *die;* Doktor, *der* (*ugs.*); *as title* Doktor, *der; as address* Herr/Frau Doktor; **~'s note** (Brit.) Krankschreibung, *die;* **~'s orders** ärztliche Anweisung; **just what the ~ ordered** [ganz] genau das Richtige!; **an apple a day keeps the ~ away** (prov.) [iss] täglich einen Apfel, und du bleibst gesund; **you're the ~** (coll.) Sie sind der Fachmann; **works ~:** Werksarzt, *der* [2] (Amer.: dentist) Zahnarzt, *der*/-ärztin, *die* [3] (Amer.: veterinary surgeon) Tierarzt, *der*/-ärztin, *die* [4] (holder of degree) Doktor, *der;* **D~ of Medicine/Divinity** Doktor der Medizin/Theologie; **graduate as ~, do one's ~'s degree** promovieren; seinen Doktor machen (ugs.)
B *v.t.* (coll.) [1] (falsify) verfälschen ‹*Dokumente, Tonbänder*›; frisieren (ugs.) ‹*Bilanzen, Bücher*›; (adulterate) panschen (ugs.) ‹*Wein*›; verwürzen ‹*Gericht*›; (improve by altering) verfeinern ‹*Gericht*›; verschönern ‹*Aussehen*›; **her punch had been ~ed with something** ihrem Punsch war etwas beigemischt worden [2] (patch up) zusammenflicken (ugs.) [3] (Brit.: sterilize) sterilisieren ‹*Tier*›

doctoral /ˈdɒktərl/ *adj.* Doktor-; **~ thesis** Dissertation, *die;* Doktorarbeit, *die*

doctor-assisted 'suicide *n.* ärztlich assistierter Suizid

doctorate /ˈdɒktərət/ *n.* Doktorwürde, *die;* **do a ~:** seinen Doktor machen (ugs.); promovieren

doctrinaire /dɒktrɪˈneə(r)/ *adj.* doktrinär

doctrinal /dɒkˈtraɪnl, ˈdɒktrɪnl/ *adj.*, **doctrinally** /dɒkˈtraɪnəlɪ, ˈdɒktrɪnəlɪ/ *adv.* doktrinell

doctrine /ˈdɒktrɪn/ *n.* [1] (principle) Lehre, *die;* **the ~ of free speech/equality** der Grundsatz der Redefreiheit/der Gleichheitsgrundsatz; **educational ~s** pädagogische Grundsätze [2] (body of instruction) Doktrin, *die;* Lehrmeinung, *die*

docudrama /ˈdɒkjuːdrɑːmə/ *n.* Dokudrama, *das*

document
A /ˈdɒkjʊmənt/ *n.* Dokument, *das;* Urkunde, *die;* **all the necessary ~s** alle erforderlichen Unterlagen
B /ˈdɒkjʊment/ *v.t.* [1] (prove by document[s]) dokumentieren; [mit Dokumenten] belegen [2] (furnish with document[s]) **be well ~ed** ‹*Leben, Zeit usw.*›: gut belegt sein

documentary /dɒkjʊˈmentərɪ/
A *adj.* [1] (pertaining to documents) dokumentarisch, urkundlich ‹*Beweis*› [2] (factual) dokumentarisch; **~ film** Dokumentarfilm, *der*
B *n.* (film) Dokumentarfilm, *der*

documentation /dɒkjʊmenˈteɪʃn/ *n.* [1] (documenting) Dokumentation, *die* [2] (material) beweiskräftige Dokumente *Pl.*; Beweisstücke *Pl.*

document: ~ case *n.* Kollegmappe, *die;* **~ holder** *n.* Konzepthalter, *der;* **~ reader** *n.* (Computing) Dokumentenleser, *der;* Dokumentenlesegerät, *das*

docusoap /ˈdɒkjuːsəʊp/ *n.* Dokusoap, *die*

dodder /ˈdɒdə(r)/ *v.i.* [1] (totter) wacklig gehen [2] (tremble) zittern

dodderer /ˈdɒdərə(r)/ *n.* Tattergreis, *der* (ugs.)

doddery /ˈdɒdərɪ/ *adj.* tatterig (ugs.) ‹*alter Mann*›; zittrig ‹*Beine, Bewegungen*›

doddle /ˈdɒdl/ *n.* (Brit. coll.) Kinderspiel, *das* (fig.)

dodecaphonic /dəʊdekəˈfɒnɪk/ *adj.* (Mus.) Zwölfton-

dodge /dɒdʒ/
A *v.i.* [1] (move quickly) ausweichen; **~ [out of sight]** schnell verschwinden; **~ behind the hedge/the trees** hinter die Hecke/die Bäume springen *od.* schlüpfen; **~ out of the way/to the side** zur Seite springen [2] (move to and fro) ständig in Bewegung sein; **~ through the traffic** sich durch den Verkehr schlängeln
B *v.t.* (elude by movement) ausweichen (+ *Dat.*) ‹*Schlag, Hindernis usw.*›; entkommen (+ *Dat.*) ‹*Polizei, Verfolger*›; (avoid) sich drücken vor (+ *Dat.*) ‹*Wehrdienst*›; umgehen ‹*Steuer*›; aus dem Weg gehen (+ *Dat.*) ‹*Frage, Problem*›; (evade by trickery) austricksen (ugs.); **~ doing sth.** es umgehen, etw. zu tun; sich davor drücken, etw. zu tun; *see also* **column**
C *n.* [1] (move) Sprung zur Seite [2] (trick) Trick, *der;* **he's up to all the ~s** er ist mit allen Wassern gewaschen

dodgem /ˈdɒdʒəm/ *n.* [Auto]skooter, *der; in pl.* [Auto]skooterbahn, *die;* **have a ride/go on the ~s** Autoskooter fahren

dodger /ˈdɒdʒə(r)/ *n.* Drückeberger, *der* (ugs. abwertend)

dodgy /ˈdɒdʒɪ/ *adj.* [1] (cunning) gerissen (ugs.); ausgekocht (ugs.) [2] (Brit. coll.) (unreliable) unsicher; schwach ‹*Knie, Herz usw.*›; (awkward) verzwickt; vertrackt; (tricky) knifflig; (risky) gewagt; heikel; **the car's a bit ~ sometimes** das Auto hat hin und wieder seine Mucken (ugs.)

dodo /ˈdəʊdəʊ/ *n., pl.* **~s** *or* **~es** Dodo, *der;* Dronte, *die;* **[as] dead as the** *or* **a ~:** völlig ausgestorben

doe /dəʊ/ *n.* (Zool.) [1] (deer) Damtier, *das;* Damgeiß, *die* [2] (hare) Häsin, *die* [3] (rabbit) [Kaninchen]weibchen, *das*

DOE *abbr.* (Brit. Hist.) **= Department of the Environment** Umweltministerium, *das*

doe-eyed /ˈdəʊaɪd/ *adj.* kulleräugig; **be ~:** [große] Kulleraugen haben

does /dʌz/ ▸ **do¹**

'doeskin *n.* [1] Rehfell, *das* [2] (leather) Rehleder, *das* [3] (fine cloth) Doeskin, *der*

doesn't /ˈdʌznt/ (coll.) **= does not;** ▸ **do¹**

doff /dɒf/ *v.t.* (dated) sich entledigen (+ *Gen.*) ‹*Kleidung*›; lüften, ziehen ‹*Hut*›

dog /dɒg/
A *n.* [1] Hund, *der;* **not [stand** *or* **have] a ~'s chance** nicht die geringste Chance [haben]; **I was as sick as a ~:** mir war hundeelend; (fig.) ich hätte heulen können; **it shouldn't happen to a ~:** das würde man seinem ärgsten Feind nicht wünschen; **dressed up/done up like a ~'s dinner** (coll.) aufgeputzt wie ein Pfau (ugs.); ‹*Frau:*› aufgetakelt wie eine Fregatte (ugs.); **a hair of the ~ [that bit one]** ein Schluck gegen den Kater; **give a ~ a bad name [and hang him]** einmal in Verruf gekommen, bleibt man immer verdächtig; **go to the ~s** vor die Hunde gehen (ugs.); **help a lame ~ over a stile** einem Bedürftigen unter die Arme greifen; **love me, love my ~:** man muss mich so nehmen, wie ich bin; **a ~ in the manger** ein Biest, das keinem was gönnt; **~-in-the-manger** missgünstig ‹*Benehmen*›; **put on ~** (coll.) angeben (ugs.); **be like a ~ with two tails** sich freuen wie ein Schneekönig (ugs.); **see a man about a ~:** etwas erledigen; (visit lavatory) hingehen, wo auch der Kaiser zu Fuß hingeht (scherzh.); **there's life in the old ~ yet** er ist noch ganz schön fit für sein Alter (ugs.); er gehört noch nicht zum alten Eisen (ugs.); **you can't teach an old ~ new tricks** alte Menschen können sich nicht mehr umstellen; **the ~s** (Brit. coll.: greyhound racing) das Windhundrennen; **try it on the ~:** ihn/sie *usw.* als Versuchskaninchen benutzen; *see also* **cat 1**; **day 5**; **hot**; **sleeping** [2] (male ~) Rüde, *der* [3] (despicable person; coll.: fellow) Hund, *der* (derb); **you ~!** du Hund[esohn]! (derb); **wise old ~/clever old ~/sly ~/cunning ~:** schlauer Fuchs (ugs.) [4] (esp. Amer. coll.: sth. poor or mediocre) Schrott, *der* (salopp); **a ~ of a film** ein Schrottfilm (salopp)
B *v.t.*, **-gg-** (follow) verfolgen; (fig.) heimsuchen; verfolgen; **~ sb.'s steps** jmdm. hart auf den Fersen bleiben

dog: ~ basket *n.* Hundekorb, *der;* **~ biscuit** *n.* Hundekuchen, *der;* **~ breeder** ▸ **breeder**; **~cart** *n.* Dogcart, *der;* **~ collar** *n.* [1] [Hunde]halsband, *das;* [2] (joc.: clerical collar) Kollar, *das;* **~ days** *n. pl.* Hundstage *Pl.;* **~ dirt** *n.* (coll.) Hundedreck, *der* (ugs.)

doge /dəʊdʒ/ *n.* (Hist.) Doge, *der*

dog: ~-eared *adj.* **a ~-eared book** ein Buch mit Eselsohren; **~-eat-'~** *adj.* gnadenlos; **~-end** *n.* (coll.) Kippe, *die* (ugs.); **~fight** *n.* [1] Hundekampf, *der;* (fig.) Handgemenge, *das;* [2] (between aircraft) Luftkampf, *der;* **~fish** *n.* **[spotted/spiny] ~fish** Katzen-/Dornhai, *der;* **~ food** *n.* Hundefutter, *das*

dogged /ˈdɒgɪd/ *adj.* hartnäckig ‹*Weigerung, Verurteilung*›; zäh ‹*Durchhaltevermögen, Ausdauer*›; beharrlich ‹*Haltung, Kritik*›

doggedly /ˈdɒgɪdlɪ/ *adv.* ▸ **dogged**: hartnäckig; zäh; beharrlich

doggerel /ˈdɒgərəl/
A *adj.* holp[e]rig, unbeholfen ‹*Übersetzung, Geschreibsel*›; **~ verse** *or* **rhyme** Knittelvers, *der*
B *n.* Knittelvers, *der*

doggie /ˈdɒgɪ/ ▸ **doggy**

doggo /ˈdɒgəʊ/ *adv.* (coll.) **lie ~:** sich nicht mucksen (ugs.) *od.* rühren

doggone /ˈdɒgɒn/ *adj., adv.* (Amer. coll.) verdammt

doggy *n.* (coll.) Hündchen, *das*

'doggy bag *n.* (coll.) *Tüte, in der man Essensreste [bes. von einer Mahlzeit im Restaurant] mit nach Hause nimmt*

'doggy-paddle ▸ **dog-paddle**

dog: ~ handler *n.* Hundeführer, *der*/-führerin, *die;* **~house** *n.* [1] (Amer.) Hundehütte, *die;* [2] **be in the ~house** (coll.: in disgrace) in Ungnade sein; verschissen haben (derb); **he is in the ~house** (in family life) bei ihm hängt der Haussegen schief; **~-leg** *n.* Knick, *der;* **~ licence** *n.* Hundesteuerbescheinigung, *die;* **~like** *adj.* hundeähnlich ‹*Aussehen*›; hündisch ‹*Ergebenheit*›

dogma /ˈdɒgmə/ *n.* Dogma, *das*

dogmatic /dɒgˈmætɪk/ *adj.* dogmatisch; **~ theology** Dogmatik, *die;* **be ~ about sth.** in etw. (*Dat.*) dogmatisch sein

dogmatically /dɒgˈmætɪkəlɪ/ *adv.* dogmatisch

dogmatism /ˈdɒgmətɪzm/ *n.* Dogmatismus, *der*

do-gooder /duːˈgʊdə(r)/ *n.* Wohltäter, *der* (iron.); (reformer) Weltverbesserer, *der* (iron.)

dog: ~-paddle *v.i.* Hundepaddeln machen; **~rose** *n.* (Bot.) Hundsrose, *die;* **~sbody** *n.* (Brit. coll.) Mädchen für alles; **~'s 'breakfast** *n.* (coll.) Bockmist, *der* (salopp); **make a ~'s breakfast of sth.** etw. verbocken (ugs.); **~'s life** *n.* **a ~'s life** ein Hundeleben; **give** *or* **lead sb. a ~'s life** jmdn. schäbig behandeln; **~ star** *n.* Sirius, *der;* Hundsstern, *der;* **~ tag** *n.* (lit. or fig.) Hundemarke, *die;* **~-'tired** *adj.* hundemüde; **~-tooth** *n.* (Archit.) Hundszahnornament, *das;* **~track** *n.* Hunderennbahn, *die;* **~trot** *n.* gemächlicher Trott; **~ violet** *n.* (Bot.) Hundsveilchen, *das;* **~watch** *n.* (Naut.) (from 4 p.m. to 6 p.m./from 6 p.m. to 8 p.m.) 1./2. Plattfuß, *der* (Seemannsspr.); **~wood** *n.* (Bot.) Hartriegel, *der;* Hornstrauch, *der*

doh /dəʊ/ *n.* (Mus.) do

doily /ˈdɔɪlɪ/ *n.* [Spitzen-, Zier]deckchen, *das*

doing /ˈduːɪŋ/
A *pres. p. of* **do¹**
B *n.* [1] *vbl. n. of* **do¹** [2] *no pl.* Tun, *das;* **be [of] sb.'s ~:** jmds. Werk sein; **it was not [of]** *or* **none of his ~:** er hatte nichts damit zu tun; **that takes a lot of/some ~:** da gehört sehr viel/schon etwas dazu [3] *in pl.* **sb.'s ~s** (actions) jmds. Tun und Treiben; **the ~s** (coll.) die Dinger (ugs.); (thing with unknown name) das Dings (ugs.)

do-it-yourself /duːɪtjəˈself/
A *adj.* Do-it-yourself-; **~ equipment** Heimwerkerausrüstung, *die*
B *n.* Heimwerken, *das;* Do-it-yourself, *das*

doldrums /ˈdɒldrəmz/ *n. pl.* [1] (low spirits) Niedergeschlagenheit, *die;* Trübsinn, *der;* **in the ~:** niedergeschlagen [2] (Naut.) **in the ~:** ohne Wind; (fig.) in einer Flaute

dole /dəʊl/
A *n.* (coll.) **the ~:** Stempelgeld, *das* (ugs.); Stütze, *die* (ugs.); **draw the ~:** Stempelgeld *od.* Stütze kriegen; **be/go on the ~:** stempeln gehen (ugs.)

B *v.t.* ~ **out** [in kleinen Mengen] verteilen

doleful /ˈdəʊlfl/ *adj.* traurig ‹*Augen, Blick, Gesichtsausdruck*›

dolefully /ˈdəʊlfəlɪ/ *adv.* (sadly) traurig; trübselig

doll /dɒl/

A *n.* **1** (small model of person, dummy) Puppe, *die* **2** (pretty but silly woman) Dummchen, *das* (ugs.); Püppchen, *das* (ugs.); (sl.: young woman) Mieze, *die* (ugs.)

B *v.t.* ~ **up** herausputzen; herausstaffieren (abwertend); auftakeln ‹*Frau*› (abwertend); **she was all ~ed up** sie war so richtig aufgedonnert (abwertend)

dollar /ˈdɒlə(r)/ *n.* ▸ **p. 1332** Dollar, *der;* **feel/look like a million ~s** (coll.) sich pudelwohl fühlen (ugs.)/tipptopp aussehen (ugs.); **sixty-four [thousand] ~ question** (lit. or fig.) Preisfrage, *die; see also* **bottom B 2**

dollar: ~ ˈ**bill** *n.* ▸ **p. 1332** Dollarnote, *die;* Dollarschein, *der;* ~ **diˈplomacy** *n., no pl.* Dollardiplomatie, *die;* ~ **sign** *n.* Dollarzeichen, *das*

ˈ**dollhouse** (Amer.) ▸ **doll's house**

dollop /ˈdɒləp/

A *n.* (coll.) Klacks, *der* (ugs.)

B *v.t.* (coll.) klatschen (ugs.)

doll's house *n.* Puppenhaus, *das*

dolly /ˈdɒlɪ/ *n.* **1** Puppe, *die;* Püppchen, *das;* (child language) Püppi, *die* (Kinderspr.) **2** ▸ **dolly bird**

ˈ**dolly bird** *n.* (Brit. dated coll.) Mieze, *die* (ugs.)

dolmen /ˈdɒlmən/ *n.* (Archaeol.) Dolmen, *der*

Dolomites /ˈdɒləmaɪts/ *pr. n. pl.* **the ~:** die Dolomiten

dolorous /ˈdɒlərəs/ *adj.* (literary/dated) **1** (dismal) düster; trist; schwermütig ‹*Klang*›; (distressing) bedrückend ‹*Nachricht, Vorstellung*› **2** (distressed) gequält ‹*Blick, Ausdruck, Seufzer*›

dolphin /ˈdɒlfɪn/ *n.* (Zool., Her., Sculpture) Delphin, *der*

dolt /dəʊlt/ *n.* Tölpel, *der;* Tollpatsch, *der*

domain /dəˈmeɪn/ *n.* **1** (estate) Gut, *das;* Ländereien *Pl.;* (of the State; also fig.) Domäne, *die; see also* **public domain** **2** (field) Domäne, *die* (geh.); [Arbeits-, Wissens-, Aufgaben]gebiet, *das* **3** (Computing) Domäne, *die;* Domain, *die;* ~ **name** Domänenname, *der*

dome /dəʊm/ *n.* Kuppel, *die;* (fig.) Gewölbe, *das*

Domesday [Book] /ˈduːmzdeɪ (bʊk)/ *n.: das Reichsgrundbuch Englands aus dem Jahre 1086*

domestic /dəˈmestɪk/

A *adj.* **1** (household) häuslich ‹*Verhältnisse, Umstände*›; (family) familiär ‹*Atmosphäre, Angelegenheit, Reibereien*›; ‹*Wasserversorgung, Ölverbrauch*› der privaten Haushalte; ~ **servant** Hausgehilfe, *der*/-gehilfin, *die;* ~ **help** Haushaltshilfe, *die;* ~ **waste** Hausmüll, *der;* ~ **life** Familienleben, *das* **2** (of one's own country) inländisch; einheimisch ‹*Produkt, Tier-/Pflanzenart*›; innenpolitisch ‹*Problem, Auseinandersetzungen*›; (home-produced) im Inland hergestellt; ~ **economy/trade** Binnenwirtschaft, *die*/Binnenhandel, *der;* ~ **policy** Innenpolitik, *die* **3** (kept by man) ~ **animal** Haustier, *das;* ~ **rabbit/cat** Hauskaninchen, *das*/Hauskatze, *die* **4** (fond of home life) häuslich [veranlagt]

B *n.* Domestik, *der* (veralt.); Hausangestellte, *der/die*

domestic apˈpliance *n.* Haushaltsgerät, *das*

domesticate /dəˈmestɪkeɪt/ *v.t.* **1** (make fond of home life or work) fürs häusliche Leben begeistern; (accustom to home life or work) an häusliches Leben gewöhnen **2** (naturalize) einbürgern ‹*Tier, Pflanze*› **3** (tame) zähmen; domestizieren (fachspr.)

domesticated /dəˈmestɪkeɪtɪd/ *adj.* **1** (fond of home life or work) häuslich **2** (naturalized) eingebürgert **3** (tamed) domestiziert (fachspr.); gezähmt

domesticity /dəʊmesˈtɪsɪtɪ, dɒmesˈtɪsɪtɪ/ *n., no pl.* (being domestic) Häuslichkeit, *die*

domestic ˈscience *n., no pl.* Hauswirtschaftslehre, *die*

domicile /ˈdɒmɪsaɪl, ˈdɒmɪsɪl/ (**domicil** /ˈdɒmɪsɪl/)

A *n.* **1** (home) Heimat, *die* **2** (Law) (place of residence) [ständiger] Wohnsitz; (fact of residing) Aufenthalt, *der*

B *v.t.* ansiedeln

dominance /ˈdɒmɪnəns/ *n., no pl.* Dominanz, *die;* Vorherrschaft, *die* (**over** über + *Akk.*); (of colours etc.) Vorherrschen, *das*

dominant /ˈdɒmɪnənt/

A *adj.* **1** dominierend (geh.); beherrschend; hervorstechend, herausragend ‹[*Wesens*]*merkmal, Eigenschaft*›; vorherrschend ‹*Kultur, Farbe, Geschmack*›; ~ **market position** marktbeherrschende Stellung; **have a ~ position** eine beherrschende Stellung einnehmen; **be ~ over** dominieren über (+ *Akk.*) **2** (imposing) beherrschend ‹*Gebäude, Berg usw.*› **3** (Mus.) dominant; ~ **seventh** Dominantseptakkord, *der* **4** (Genetics) dominant

B *n.* (Mus.) Dominante, *die*

dominate /ˈdɒmɪneɪt/

A *v.t.* beherrschen

B *v.i.* **1** ~ **over sb./sth.** jmdn./etw. beherrschen; ‹*großer Mensch, Turm:*› jmdn./etw. überragen **2** (be the most influential) dominieren

domination /dɒmɪˈneɪʃn/ *n., no pl.* [Vor]herrschaft, *die* (**over** über + *Akk.*); **under Roman ~:** unter römischer Herrschaft; **X's ~ of the car market** die Vorherrschaft von X auf dem Automarkt

dominatrix /dɒmɪˈneɪtrɪks/ *n., pl.* **dominatrices** /-trɪsiːz/ *or* **dominatrixes** **1** (dominating woman) dominante *od.* bestimmende Frau **2** (in sadomasochism) Domina, *die*

domineer /dɒmɪˈnɪə(r)/ *v.i.* despotisch herrschen; ~ **over sb./sth.** jmdn./etw. tyrannisieren

domineering /dɒmɪˈnɪərɪŋ/ *adj.* herrisch, herrschsüchtig ‹*Person*›

Dominican /dəˈmɪnɪkən/ ▸ **p. 1345**

A *adj.* dominikanisch

B *n.* Dominikaner[mönch], *der*

Dominican Reˈpublic *pr. n.* **the ~:** die Dominikanische Republik

dominion /dəˈmɪnjən/ *n.* **1** (control) Herrschaft, *die* (**over** über + *Akk.*); **[be] under Roman ~:** unter römischer Herrschaft [stehen]; **have ~ over sb./a country** Macht über jmdn. haben/ein Land beherrschen **2** *usu. in pl.* (feudal domains) Ländereien *Pl.;* (territory of sovereign or government) Reich, *das* **3** (Commonwealth Hist.) Dominion, *das;* **the D~ of Canada** das Dominion Kanada

domino /ˈdɒmɪnəʊ/ *n., pl.* **~es** **1** (piece for game) Domino[stein], *der* **2** **~es** *sing.* (game) Domino[spiel], *das;* **play ~es** Domino spielen **3** (cloak) Domino, *der*

ˈ**domino effect** *n.* Dominoeffekt, *der*

don¹ /dɒn/ *n.* **1** **D~** (Spanish title) Don **2** (Spanish gentleman) spanischer Edelmann **3** ▸ **p. 1260** (Univ.) [Universitäts]dozent, *der* (bes. in Oxford und Cambridge)

don² *v.t.,* **-nn-** anlegen (geh.); anziehen ‹*Mantel usw.*›; aufsetzen ‹*Hut*›

donate /dəʊˈneɪt/ *v.t.* spenden ‹*Organe*›; stiften, spenden ‹*Geld, Kleidung*›; stiften ‹*Land*›; ~ **money to charity** Geld für wohltätige Zwecke stiften; **he ~d his body to science** er stellte seinen Körper der Wissenschaft zur Verfügung

donation /dəˈneɪʃn/ *n.* Spende, *die* (**to[wards]** für); Schenkung, *die* (Rechtsspr.); (large-scale) Stiftung, *die;* **a ~ of money/clothes** eine Geld-/Kleiderspende; **make a ~ of £1,000 [to charity]** 1000 Pfund [für wohltätige Zwecke] spenden *od.* stiften

done /dʌn/ *adj.* **1** *p.p. of* **do¹**; **what's ~ is ~** geschehen ist geschehen; **well ~!** großartig! **2** (coll.: acceptable) **it's not ~ [in this country]** das macht man [hierzulande] nicht; **it's [not] the ~ thing** es ist [nicht] üblich **3** *as int.* (accepted) abgemacht!; einverstanden! **4** (finished) **be ~:** vorbei sein; **be ~ with sth.** mit etw. fertig sein; (fed up) etw. satt haben; **she's ~ with him** sie ist fertig mit ihm (ugs.); **be ~ with alcohol/cigarettes** das Trinken/Zigarettenrauchen aufgegeben haben; **is your plate ~ with?** brauchen Sie Ihren Teller noch?; **when the operation was ~ with** als die Operation vorbei *od.* beendet war **5** **have ~ [doing sth.]** aufgehört haben, etw. zu tun; **have ~ with sth./doing sth.** mit etw. aufhören/aufhören, etw. zu tun

donjon /ˈdɒndʒən, ˈdʌndʒən/ *n.* Hauptturm, *der;* Wachtturm, *der*

donkey /ˈdɒŋkɪ/ *n.* (lit. or fig.) Esel, *der;* **she could talk the hind leg[s] off a ~!** (fig.) die kann einem die Ohren abreden! (ugs.)

donkey: ~ **jacket** *n.* dicke, wasserundurchlässige Jacke; **~'s years** *n. pl.* (coll.) eine Ewigkeit (ugs.); **for** *or* **in ~'s years** eine Ewigkeit (ugs.); ~ **work** *n.* Schwerarbeit, *die*

donnish /ˈdɒnɪʃ/ *adj.* **1** (of college don) akademisch; professoral (oft abwertend) **2** (pedantic) oberlehrerhaft (abwertend); professoral (abwertend)

donor /ˈdəʊnə(r)/ *n.* **1** (of gift) Schenker, *der*/Schenkerin, *die;* (to institution etc.) Stifter, *der*/Stifterin, *die* **2** (of blood, organ, etc.) Spender, *der*/Spenderin, *die;* **be a ~ of sth.** etw. spenden; **blood ~:** Blutspender, *der*/-spenderin, *die*

Don Quixote /dɒn ˈkwɪksət/ *pr. n.* Don Quichotte

don't /dəʊnt/

A *v.i.* (coll.) = **do not;** ▸ **do¹**

B *n.* Nein, *das;* Verbot, *das;* **dos and ~s** ▸ **do² 3**

don't: **~-ˈcare** *n.* Gleichgültige, *der/die;* **~-ˈknow** *n.* jmd., der keine Meinung hat; **be a ~-know** zu etw. unentschieden sein

doodad /ˈduːdæd/ *n.* (Amer.) **1** (fancy article, trivial ornament) Spielerei, *die; in pl.* Kinkerlitzchen *Pl.* (ugs.); Firlefanz, *der* (ugs.) **2** (gadget) Dingsbums, *das* (ugs.); Apparillo, *der* (ugs.)

doodah /ˈduːdɑː/ *n.* (coll.) **1** (gadget) ▸ **doodad 2** **2** (thingamy) (thing) Dings, *das* (ugs.); Dingsbums, *das* (ugs.); (person) Dingsbums, *der/die;* Dingsda, *der/die* **3** **be all of a ~:** ganz aus dem Häuschen sein (ugs.)

doodle /ˈduːdl/

A *v.i.* ≈ Männchen malen; [herum]kritzeln; doodeln

B *n.* Kritzelei, *die; in pl.* Gekritzel, *das;* Kritzeleien *Pl.*

ˈ**doodlebug** *n.* **1** (Amer. Zool.) (tiger beetle) Ameisenjungfer, *die;* (larva) Ameisenlöwe, *der* **2** (Hist. coll.: flying bomb) V1-Rakete, *die*

doom /duːm/

A *n.* **1** (fate) Schicksal, *das;* (ruin) Verhängnis, *das;* **meet one's ~:** vom Schicksal heimgesucht *od.* (geh.) ereilt werden **2** *no pl., no art.* (Last Judgement) das Jüngste Gericht; *see also* **crack**

B *v.t.* verurteilen; verdammen; **~ sb./sth. to sth.** jmdn./eine Sache zu etw. verdammen *od.* verurteilen; **~ sb. to die** jmdn. dem Tode weihen (geh.); **be ~ed to fail** *or* **failure** zum Scheitern verurteilt sein; **be ~ed to exile** ins Exil verbannt werden; **be ~ed** verloren sein

doomsday /ˈduːmzdeɪ/ *n.* der Jüngste Tag; **till ~** (fig.) bis zum Jüngsten Tag; noch Ewigkeiten

ˈ**doomwatch** *n.* Umweltwache, *die; attrib.* ~ **organization** Umweltüberwachungsorganisation, *die*

door /dɔː(r)/ *n.* **1** Tür, *die;* (of castle, barn) Tor, *das;* (of car, coach) Tür, *die;* [Wagen]schlag, *der;* **'~s open at 7'** „Einlass ab 7 Uhr“; **he popped** (coll.) *or* **put his head round the ~:** er streckte den Kopf durch die Tür; **just pop a note through the ~** (coll.) wirf einfach einen Zettel durch den Briefschlitz; **walk sb. right to the ~:** jmdn. bis vor die *od.* bis zur Haustür begleiten; **I'll drop you at the ~:** ich bringe dich vorbei; **milk is delivered to the ~:** Milch wird an die Haustür geliefert; **lay sth. at sb.'s ~** (fig.) jmdm. etw. anlasten *od.* zur Last legen; **next ~:** nebenan; **the boy/girl next ~:** der Junge/das Mädchen von nebenan; **two/three ~s away [from …]** zwei/drei Türen *od.* Häuser entfernt [von …]; **live next ~ to sb.** neben jmdm. *od.* nebenan wohnen; **next ~ to** (fig.) (beside) neben (+ *Dat.*); (almost) fast; beinahe; **from ~ to ~:** von Haus zu Haus; von Tür zu Tür; **go from ~ to ~:** von Tür zu Tür gehen; Klinken putzen (ugs. abwertend) **2** (fig.: entrance) Zugang, *der* (**to** zu); **all ~s are open/closed to**

d

d

him ihm stehen alle Türen offen/sind alle Türen verschlossen; **close the ~ to sth.** etw. unmöglich machen; **have/get one's foot/keep a foot in the ~:** mit einem Fuß *od.* Bein drin sein/hineinkommen/drinbleiben; **leave the ~ open for sth.** die Tür für *od.* zu etw. offen halten; **leave the ~ open for sb. to do sth.** jmdm. die Tür offen halten, etw. zu tun; **open the ~ to** *or* **for sth.** etw. möglich machen; **packed to the ~s** voll [besetzt]; gerammelt voll (ugs.); **show sb. the ~:** jmdm. die Tür weisen; jmdn. vor die Tür setzen (ugs.) 3 (~way) [Tür]eingang, *der;* **walk through the ~:** zur Tür hineingehen/hereinkommen; **shop ~:** Geschäftseingang, *der* 4 **out of ~s** im Freien; draußen; **go out of ~s** nach draußen gehen; ins Freie gehen. *See also* **darken A 2; indoors**

door: ~bell *n.* Türklingel, *die;* **~ chimes** *n. pl.* Türglocke, *die;* **~frame** *n.* Türrahmen, *der;* **~ handle** *n.* Türklinke, *die;* **~keeper** *n.* Pförtner, *der;* Portier, *der;* **~knob** *n.* Türknopf, -knauf, *der;* **~ knocker** ▸**knocker 1**; **~man** *n.* Portier, *der;* **~mat** *n.* Fußmatte, *die;* (fig.) Fußabtreter, *der;* Putzlappen, *der;* **~nail** *n.* Türnagel, *der;* Tornagel, *der; see also* **dead A 1**; **~post** *n.* Türpfosten, *der;* **~step** *n.* Eingangsstufe, *die;* Türstufe, *die;* (coll.: slice) dicke Scheibe Brot; **on one's/the ~step** (fig.) vor jmds./der Tür; **have sth. right on the ~step** (fig.) etw. direkt vor der [Haus]tür haben; **~stop** *n.* Türanschlag, *der;* (stone, wedge, etc.) Türstopper, *der;* **~-to-~** *adj.* **~-to-~ collection** Haussammlung, *die;* **~-to-~ journey** Fahrt von Haus zu Haus; **~-to-~ selling** Hausverkauf, *der;* **~-to-~ salesman** Vertreter, *der;* Hausierer, *der* (abwertend); **~way** *n.* Eingang, *der;* **~yard** *n.* (Amer.) (garden patch) Vorgarten, *der;* (yard) Vorhof, *der*

dope /dəʊp/

A *n.* 1 (stimulant) Aufputschmittel, *das;* (sl.: narcotic) Stoff, *der* (salopp); **~ test** Dopingkontrolle, *die* 2 (sl.) (information) Informationen *Pl.;* (misleading information) Märchen *Pl.* (ugs.) 3 (coll.: fool) Dussel, *der* (ugs.); **I felt such a ~:** ich kam mir ziemlich dusslig vor (ugs.)

B *v.t.* (administer stimulant to) dopen ‹*Pferd, Athleten*›; (administer narcotic to) Rauschgift verabreichen (+ *Dat.*); (stupefy) betäuben

C *v.i.* Rauschgift *od.* Drogen nehmen

(Phrasal verb)

- **~ 'out** *v.t.* (sl.) rauskriegen (ugs.)

dopey /ˈdəʊpɪ/ *adj.* (coll.) 1 benebelt (ugs.) 2 (stupid) blöd; dämlich; bekloppt

Doppler effect /ˈdɒplər ɪfekt/ *n.* (Phys.) Dopplereffekt, *der*

dork /dɔːk/ *n.* (coll.) Trottel, *der* (ugs. abwertend)

dorm /dɔːm/ (coll.) ▸**dormitory 1, 3**

dormant /ˈdɔːmənt/ *adj.* untätig ‹*Vulkan*›; ruhend ‹*Tier, Pflanze*›; verborgen, schlummernd ‹*Talent, Fähigkeiten*›; **lie ~** ‹*Tier:*› schlafen; ‹*Pflanze, Ei:*› ruhen; ‹*Talent, Fähigkeiten:*› schlummern; **be** *or* **lie ~** ‹*Regel, Gesetz, Anspruch:*› ruhen

dormer /ˈdɔːmə(r)/ *n.* **~ [window]** Mansardenfenster, *das*

dormitory /ˈdɔːmɪtərɪ/ *n.* 1 Schlafsaal, *der* 2 (commuter area) **~ suburb** *or* **town** Schlafstadt, *die* 3 (Amer.: student hostel) Studentenwohnheim, *das*

dormouse /ˈdɔːmaʊs/ *n., pl.* **dormice** /ˈdɔːmaɪs/ Haselmaus, *die*

dorsal /ˈdɔːsəl/ *adj.* (Anat., Zool., Bot.) dorsal (fachspr.); Rücken-

dory *n.* (Naut.) Dory, *das* (fachspr.)

dos *pl. of* **do²**

DOS /dɒs/ *abbr.* (Computing) = **disk operating system** DOS

dosage /ˈdəʊsɪdʒ/ *n.* 1 (giving of medicine) Dosierung, *die* 2 (size of dose) Dosis, *die*

dose /dəʊs/

A *n.* 1 (amount of medicine) Dosis, *die;* (fig.) Dosis, *die;* Quantum, *das;* **take a ~ of medicine** Medizin [ein]nehmen; **in small ~s** (fig.) in kleinen Mengen; **like a ~ of salts** (coll.) in null Komma nichts (ugs.) 2 (amount of radiation) Strahlen-, Bestrahlungsdosis, *die* 3 (sl.: venereal infection) Tripper, *der*

B *v.t.* (give medicine to) Arznei geben (+ *Dat.*); **~ sb. with sth.** jmdm. etw. geben *od.* verabreichen

dosh /dɒʃ/ *n.* (coll.) Knete, *die* (salopp)

doss /dɒs/ (Brit. coll.)

A *n.* (bed) was zum Pennen (salopp); (of down-and-out) Platte, *die* (salopp)

B *v.i.* 1 pennen (salopp) 2 **~ down** sich hinhauen (salopp)

dosser /ˈdɒsə(r)/ *n.* (Brit. coll.) 1 (tramp) Penner, *der*/Pennerin, *die* (salopp) 2 (layabout) Faulenzer, *der*/Faulenzerin, *die*

dosshouse *n.* (Brit. coll.) Nachtasyl, *das*

dossier /ˈdɒsɪə(r), ˈdɒsjeɪ/ *n.* Akte, *die;* (bundle of papers) Dossier, *das;* **compile a ~ of information** ein Dossier anlegen

dot /dɒt/

A *n.* 1 Punkt, *der;* (smaller) Pünktchen, *das* 2 **on the ~:** auf den Punkt genau; **at 5 on the ~, on the ~ of 5** Punkt 5 Uhr; **[in] the year ~** (Brit. coll.) Anno dunnemals (ugs. scherzh.)

B *v.t.*, **-tt-** 1 (mark with ~) mit Punkten/einem Punkt markieren; **~ted with white** weiß gepunktet 2 (place [diacritical] ~ over) **~ one's i's/j's** i-/j-Punkte machen; **~ the i's and cross the t's** (fig.) peinlich genau sein 3 (Mus.) punktieren 4 (mark as with ~s) [be]sprenkeln; **the sky was ~ted with stars** der Himmel war von Sternen übersät 5 (scatter) verteilen; **be ~ted about the place** über den ganzen Ort verstreut sein

dotage /ˈdəʊtɪdʒ/ *n.* Senilität, *die* (abwertend); Altersblödsinn, *der* (fachspr.); **be in one's ~:** senil sein

dotard /ˈdəʊtəd/ *n.* seniler Mensch (abwertend); **that old ~:** der/die senile Alte

dot-com /ˈdɒtkɒm/

A *adj.* Dot-com-.

B *n.* Dot-com-Firma, *die*

dote /dəʊt/ *v.i.* **[absolutely] ~ on sb./sth.** jmdn./etw. abgöttisch lieben

doting /ˈdəʊtɪŋ/ *adj.* vernarrt; **her ~ father/husband** ihr in sie vernarrter Vater/Mann

'dot matrix *n.* (Computing) Punktmatrix, *die;* **~ printer** Nadeldrucker, *der*

dotted /ˈdɒtɪd/ *adj.* gepunktet ‹*Kleid, Linie*›; (Mus.) punktiert ‹*Note usw.*›; **sign on the ~ line** (fig.) unterschreiben

dotty /ˈdɒtɪ/ *adj.* (coll.) 1 (silly) dümmlich; **a ~ female** ein Dumm[er]chen (ugs.); **be ~ over** *or* **about sb./sth.** in jmdn./etw. vernarrt sein; **go ~ over** *or* **about sb./sth.** für jmdn./etw. schwärmen 2 (feeble-minded) schrullig (ugs. abwertend); vertrottelt (ugs. abwertend); **go ~:** vertrotteln 3 (absurd) blödsinnig (ugs.); verrückt ‹*Idee*›; **that was a ~ thing to do** das war Blödsinn (ugs.)

double /ˈdʌbl/

A *adj.* 1 (consisting of two parts etc.) doppelt ‹*Anstrich, Stofflage, Sohle*›; **~ wall** Doppelwand, *die*

2 (twofold) doppelt ‹*Sandwich, Futter, Fenster, Boden*›; **win a ~ gold** zwei Goldmedaillen gewinnen; **give a ~ ring on the phone** das Telefon zweimal klingeln lassen; **underline sth. with a ~ line** etw. doppelt unterstreichen; **~ sink** Doppelspüle, *die;* **sleep with a ~ layer of blankets** unter zwei Bettdecken schlafen

3 (with pl.: two) zwei ‹*Punkte, Klingen*›

4 (for two persons) Doppel-; **~ seat** Doppelsitz, *der;* **~ bed/room/cabin** Doppelbett, *das*/-zimmer, *das*/-kabine, *die*

5 **folded ~:** einmal *od.* einfach gefaltet; **be bent ~ with pain** sich vor Schmerzen krümmen

6 (having some part ~) Doppel‹*adler, -heft, -stecker*›; **~ flower** (Bot.) gefüllte *od.* doppelte Blüte; **~ domino/six** Pasch/Sechserpasch, *der*

7 (dual) doppelt ‹*Sinn, [Verwendungs]zweck*›; **have a ~ meaning** einen doppelten Sinn haben; doppeldeutig sein

8 (twice as much) doppelt ‹*Anzahl*›; **a room ~ the size of this** ein doppelt so großes Zimmer wie dieses; **that's ~ what I usually eat** das ist doppelt so viel, wie ich sonst esse; **be ~ the height/width/length/area/time** doppelt so hoch/breit/lang/groß/lang sein; **be ~ the breadth/weight/cost** doppelt so breit/schwer/teuer sein; **~ the heat/strength** doppelt so heiß/stark; **at ~ the cost** zum doppelten Preis; **have ~ the responsibility** doppelt so große Verantwortung haben

9 (twice as many) doppelt so viele wie

10 (of twofold size etc.) doppelt ‹*Portion, Lautstärke, Kognak, Whisky*›

11 (of extra size etc.) doppelt so groß ‹*Anstrengung, Mühe, Schwierigkeit, Problem, Anreiz*›

12 (deceitful) falsch ‹*Spiel*›

B *adv.* (to twice the amount) doppelt

C *n.* 1 (~ quantity) Doppelte, *das*

2 (~ measure of whisky etc.) Doppelte, *der;* (~ room) Doppelzimmer, *das*

3 (twice as much) das Doppelte; doppelt so viel; (twice as many) doppelt so viele; **~ or quits** doppelt oder nichts

4 (duplicate person) Doppelgänger, *der*/-gängerin, *die;* **I saw somebody today who was your ~:** ich habe heute jemanden gesehen, der Ihnen zum Verwechseln ähnlich sah

5 (duplicate thing) Gegenstück, *das* (**of** zu)

6 **at the ~:** unverzüglich; (Mil.) aufs Schnellste

7 (pair of victories) Doppelerfolg, *der*

8 (pair of championships) Double, *das;* Doppel, *das*

9 (Bridge) Verdoppelung, *die*

10 *in pl.* (Tennis etc.) Doppel, *das;* **women's** *or* **ladies'/men's/mixed ~s** Damen-/Herrendoppel, *das*/gemischtes Doppel

11 (Darts) *Wurf mit doppeltem Punktwert*

12 (Racing) Doppelwette, *die*

D *v.t.* 1 verdoppeln; (make ~) doppelt nehmen ‹*Decke*›

2 (Bridge, Mus.) verdoppeln

3 (Naut.) umschiffen ‹*Kap usw.*›

4 (clench) ballen ‹*Faust*›

5 (bend over upon itself) **~ [over]** doppelt nehmen

E *v.i.* 1 sich verdoppeln

2 (run) laufen; (turn sharply) einen Haken schlagen

3 (have two functions) doppelt verwendbar sein; **the sofa ~s as a bed** man kann das Sofa auch als Bett benutzen

(Phrasal verbs)

- **~ 'back** *v.i.* kehrtmachen (ugs.)
- **~ 'up**

A *v.i.* 1 sich krümmen; **~ up with pain** sich vor Schmerzen (*Dat.*) krümmen 2 (fig.) **~ up with laughter/mirth** sich vor Lachen/Heiterkeit krümmen 3 (share quarters) sich (*Dat.*) eine Unterkunft teilen; (in hotel etc.) sich (*Dat.*) ein Zimmer teilen

B *v.t.* 1 in die Knie zwingen; (fig.) **the sight ~d us up with laughter/mirth** bei dem Anblick krümmten wir uns vor Lachen/Heiterkeit; **be ~d up with laughter/pain** *etc.* sich vor Lachen/Schmerzen *usw.* krümmen 2 (fold) einmal falten

double: ~-'acting *adj.* doppelt wirkend; **~ 'agent** *n.* Doppelagent, *der*/-agentin, *die;* **~-barrelled** (*Amer.:* **~-barreled**) /ˈdʌblbærəld/ *adj.* 1 doppelläufig; **~-barrelled [shot]gun/rifle** Doppelflinte/-büchse, *die;* 2 (fig.: twofold) doppelt; Doppel-; zweifach; 3 (fig.: with two parts) Doppel-; **~-barrelled surname** (Brit.) Doppelname, *der;* **~ bass** /dʌbl ˈbeɪs/ *n.* (Mus.) Kontrabass, *der;* **~-bedded** /dʌblˈbedɪd/ *adj.* ‹*Zimmer*› mit Doppelbett/mit zwei Einzelbetten; **~ 'bend** *n.* S-Kurve, *die;* **~ 'bill** *n.* Doppelprogramm, *das;* **~ 'bind** *n.* Zwickmühle, *die;* **be in a ~ bind** in einer Zwickmühle stecken; **~-'blind** *adj.* (Med., Psych.) Doppelblind-; **~-blind test** Doppelblindversuch, *der;* **~ 'boiler** *n.* (Cookery) Wasserbadtopf, *der;* **~-'book** *v.t.* doppelt reservieren; doppelt buchen ‹*Flug*›; (fig.) sich zweierlei vornehmen für; **~-breasted** /dʌblˈbrestɪd/ *adj.* (Tailoring) zwei- *od.* doppelreihig; **~-breasted jacket** Zweireiher, *der;* **~-'check** *v.t.* 1 (verify twice) zweimal kontrollieren; **~-check sb.'s statements** jmds. Aussagen zweimal überprüfen; 2 (verify in two ways) zweifach überprüfen; **~ 'chin** *n.* Doppelkinn, *das;* **~-click** (Computing) A *v.i.* doppelklicken; B *v.t.* **~-click sth.** auf etw. (*Dat.*)

doppelklicken; ~ **'cream** *n.* Sahne mit hohem Fettgehalt; **~-'cross** **A** *n.* Doppelspiel, *das;* **B** *v.t.* ein Doppelspiel treiben mit; reinlegen (ugs.); **~-'dealer** *n.* Betrüger, *der;* **~-dealing** **A** /-'--/ *n.* Betrügerei, *die;* **B** /'----/ *adj.* betrügerisch; **~-decker** /dʌbldekə(r)/ **A** /'----/ *adj.* Doppeldecker-; Doppelstock- (Amtsspr.); **~-decker bus** Doppeldeckerbus, *der;* Doppelstockomnibus, *der* (Amtsspr.); **~-decker train** Doppelstockzug, *der;* **a ~-decker sandwich** ein doppelter Sandwich; ein Doppeldecker (ugs.); **B** /-'--/ *n.* Doppeldecker, *der;* (train) Doppelstockzug, *der;* **~-de'clutch** ▸**declutch**; **~-density** *adj.* (Computing) mit doppelter Dichte *nachgestellt;* Double-Density-; **~-digit** *adj.* zweistellig; ~ **'door** *n.* (door with two parts) Flügeltür, *die;* (twofold door) Doppeltür, *die;* ~ **'Dutch** ▸**Dutch B 3**; **~-dyed** *adj.* (Textiles) doppelt gefärbt; (fig.) Erz‹*schurke, -ganove*›; unverbesserlich ‹*Heuchler*›; **~-edged** *adj.* (lit. or fig.) zweischneidig

double entendre /du:bl ɑ̃'tɑ̃dr/ *n.* Zweideutigkeit, *die*

double: ~ **'entry** ▸**entry 8**; ~ **ex'posure** *n.* (Photog.) Doppelbelichtung, *die;* (result) doppelt belichtetes Foto; ~ **'fault** ▸**fault A 4**; ~ **'feature** *n.* Doppelprogramm, *das;* ~ **'figures** ▸**figure A 12**; **~-'glazed** *adj.* Doppel‹*fenster*›; ~ **'glazing** *n., no pl.* Doppelverglasung, *die;* ~ **'harness** *n.* **1** (fig.: matrimony) Ehe, *die;* **2** (fig.: close partnership) enge Zusammenarbeit; ~ **'header** *n.* (Amer.) *zwei Spiele zwischen denselben Gegnern an einem Tag;* **~-'jointed** *adj.* sehr gelenkig; ~ **'knot** *n.* Doppelknoten, *der;* ~ **lesson** *n.* Doppelstunde, *die;* ~ **'life** *n.* Doppelleben, *das;* **~-'lock** *v.t.* zweimal abschließen; ~ **'meaning** ▸**double entendre**; ~ **'negative** *n.* doppelte Verneinung; **~-page 'spread** ▸**spread C 11**; **~-'park** *v.t. & i.* in der zweiten Reihe parken; **~-'parking** *n., no pl.* Parken in der zweiten Reihe; ~ **period** *n.* Doppelstunde, *die;* ~ **'play** *n.* (Baseball) doppeltes Ausmachen; **~-quick** **A** /'---/ *adj.* **1** **in ~-quick time/at a ~-quick pace** im Laufschritt; **2** (fig.) ganz schnell; **B** /-'-/ *adv.* (Mil.) im Laufschritt; (fig.) ganz schnell; ~ **'room** *n.* Doppelzimmer, *das;* ~ **'saucepan** ▸**double boiler**; **~-'spaced** *adj.* mit doppeltem Zeilenabstand *nachgestellt;* ~ **'spread** ▸**spread C 11**; ~ **'standard** *n.* (rule) Doppelmoral, *die;* **apply** *or* **operate a ~ standard** *or* **~ standards** mit zweierlei Maß messen; ~ **star** *n.* (Astron.) Doppelstern, *der;* **~-stop** *v.i.* (Mus.) mit Doppelgriff spielen

doublet /'dʌblɪt/ *n.* **1** (Hist.: garment) Wams, *das* **2** (one of pair) Dublette, *die*

double: ~ **'take** *n.* **he did a ~ take a moment after he saw her walk by** nachdem sie vorbeigegangen war, stutzte er und sah er ihr nach; **~-talk** *n.* Doppeldeutigkeiten; **~-think** *n.* zwiespältiges Denken; ~ **'time** *n.* **1** (Econ.) doppelter Stundenlohn; **be on ~ time** 100% Zuschlag bekommen; **2** (Mil.: running pace) Laufschritt, *der;* ~ **'track** ▸**track A 5**; ~ **'vision** *n.* (Med.) Doppeltsehen, *das;* ~ **'wedding** *n.* Doppelhochzeit, *die;* ~ **whammy** /dʌbl 'wæmɪ/ *n.* (coll.) doppelter Schlag; **be hit by a ~ whammy** doppelt *od.* in zweifacher Weise getroffen werden; ~ **yellow 'lines** *n. pl.: am Fahrbahnrand verlaufende gelbe Doppellinie, die ein Halteverbot signalisiert*

doubloon /dʌ'blu:n, də'blu:n/ *n.* (Hist.) Dublone, *die*

doubly /'dʌblɪ/ *adv.* doppelt; **make ~ sure that ...:** [ganz] besonders darauf achten, dass ...; **this response made him ~ angry/upset** diese Antwort hat ihn sehr *od.* besonders geärgert/bestürzt

doubt /daʊt/

A *n.* **1** Zweifel, *der;* **~[s] [about** *or* **as to sth./as to whether ...]** (as to future) Ungewissheit, (as to fact) Unsicherheit [über etw. (*Akk.*)/darüber, ob ...]; **there was no ~** *or* **there were no ~s in our minds about** *or* **as to ...:** uns war ... klar; wir waren uns über ... (*Akk.*) im Klaren; **~[s] about** *or* **as to sth., ~ of sth.** (inclination to disbelieve) Zweifel an etw. (*Dat.*); **there's no ~ that ...:** es besteht kein Zweifel daran, dass ...; **~[s]** (hesitations) Bedenken *Pl.;* **have ~ about doing sth., have [one's] ~s about doing sth.** [seine] Bedenken haben, ob man etw. tun soll [oder nicht]; **he's now having ~s [about whether ...]** ihm kommen jetzt Bedenken[, ob ...]; **have one's ~s [about sb./sth.]** seine Bedenken [gegen jmdn./etw.] haben; **have one's ~s about whether ...:** bezweifeln *od.* daran zweifeln, dass ...; **be in ~ about** *or* **as to sth.** (disbelieve) über etw. (*Akk.*) im Zweifel sein; **be in no ~ about** *or* **as to sth.** nicht an etw. (*Dat.*) zweifeln; **be in ~ about** *or* **as to whether to do sth.** (have reservations) Bedenken haben, ob man etw. tun soll; **when** *or* **if in ~:** im Zweifelsfall; **no ~** (certainly) gewiss; (probably) sicherlich; (admittedly) wohl; **there's no ~ about it** daran besteht kein Zweifel; das steht fest; **cast ~ on sth.** etw. in Zweifel ziehen **2** *no pl.* (uncertain state of things) Ungewissheit, *die;* **be in ~:** ungewiss sein; **beyond [all] ~, without [a] ~:** ohne [jeden] Zweifel; **it is beyond [all] ~ that ...:** es steht [völlig] außer Zweifel, dass ...; **without a shadow of [a] ~:** ohne den geringsten Zweifel

B *v.i.* zweifeln; ~ **of sth./sb.** an etw./jmdm. zweifeln

C *v.t.* anzweifeln; zweifeln an (+ *Dat.*); **she ~ed him** sie zweifelte an ihm; **I don't ~ that** *or* **it** ich zweifle nicht daran; ich bezweifle das nicht; **I ~ whether** *or* **if** *or* **that ...:** ich bezweifle, dass ...; ich zweifle daran, dass ...; **not ~ that** *or* **but that** *or* **but** nicht daran zweifeln, dass ...; nicht bezweifeln, dass ...

doubter /'daʊtə(r)/ *n.* Zweifler, *der*/Zweiflerin, *die*

doubtful /'daʊtfl/ *adj.* **1** (sceptical) skeptisch ‹*Mensch, Wesen*›; **a ~ person** ein Skeptiker/eine Skeptikerin **2** (showing doubt) ungläubig ‹*Gesicht, Blick, Stirnrunzeln*› **3** (uncertain) zweifelnd; **be ~ as to** *or* **about sth.** an etw. (*Dat.*) zweifeln; **be ~ whether ...:** daran zweifeln, dass ...; (be unsure) sich (*Dat.*) nicht sicher sein, ob ...; **be ~ about sth.** hinsichtlich einer Sache unsicher sein **4** (causing doubt) fraglich; **the situation looks ~:** die Lage ist unsicher **5** (uncertain in meaning etc.) ungewiss ‹*Ergebnis, Ausgang, Herkunft, Aussicht*›; (questionable) zweifelhaft ‹*Ruf, Charakter, Organisation, Wert, Tugend, Autorität, Kräfte, Potenzial*›; (ambiguous) unklar ‹*Bedeutung*› **6** (unreliable) zweifelhaft ‹*Person, Maßstab, Stütze*› **7** (giving reason to suspect evil) bedenklich ‹*Gewohnheit, Spiel, Botschaft*›

doubtfully /'daʊtfəlɪ/ *adv.* **1** (with doubt) skeptisch **2** (ambiguously) missverständlich

doubting Thomas /daʊtɪŋ 'tɒməs/ *n.* ungläubiger Thomas

doubtless /'daʊtlɪs/ *adv.* **1** (certainly) gewiss **2** (probably) sicherlich **3** (admittedly) wohl

douche /du:ʃ/ *n.* **1** (jet) Dusche, *die;* (Med.) Spülung, *die* **2** (device) Dusche, *die;* (Med.) Spülapparat, *der*

dough /dəʊ/ *n.* **1** Teig, *der;* **yeast ~:** Hefeteig, *der* **2** (coll.: money) Knete, *die* (salopp)

'doughnut *n.* [Berliner] Pfannkuchen, *der;* Berliner, *der* (landsch.)

doughtily /'daʊtɪlɪ/ *adv.,* **doughty** /'daʊtɪ/ *adj.* (arch./joc.) kühn; wacker (veralt./scherzh.)

doughy /'dəʊɪ/ *adj.* teigig ‹*Konsistenz, Finger, Schüssel, Masse*›

dour /dʊə(r)/ *adj.* hartnäckig ‹*Person, Charakter, Arbeiten*›; düster ‹*Blick, Gesicht*›; finster ‹*Miene, Stirnrunzeln*›

douse /daʊs/ *v.t.* **1** (extinguish) ausmachen ‹*Licht, Laterne, Kerze, Feuer*› **2** (throw water on) übergießen ‹*Feuer, Flamme, Menschen*›; ~ **sth. with water** etw. mit Wasser übergießen

dove¹ /dʌv/ *n.* (Ornith., Polit., Relig.) Taube, *die*

dove² /dəʊv/ ▸**dive A**

dove: **~-coloured** *adj.* taubengrau; **~cot, ~cote** *n.* Taubenschlag, *der;* **flutter the ~cots** (fig.) für einige Aufregung sorgen; **~-grey** ▸**~-coloured**; **~tail** **A** *n.* (Carpentry) **1** (joint) Schwalbenschwanzverbindung, *die;* **2** (tenon) Schwalbenschwanz, *der;* **B** *v.t.* **1** (fig.: fit together) aufeinander abstimmen ‹*Pläne, Verabredungen, Termine*›; **2** (put together with ~tails) verschwalben (**into, with** mit); **C** *v.i.* (fig.: fit together) ‹*Vorbereitungen, Zeitpläne:*› aufeinander abgestimmt sein

dovish /'dʌvɪʃ/ *adj.* gemäßigt; kompromissbereit

dowager /'daʊədʒə(r)/ *n.* **1** ▸ⓘ **p. 1634** (widow with title or property) Witwe von Stand; **Queen ~/~ duchess** Königin-/Herzoginwitwe, *die* **2** (coll.: dignified elderly lady) Matrone, *die*

dowdily /'daʊdɪlɪ/ *adv.* schäbig

dowdiness /'daʊdɪnɪs/ *n.* Unansehnlichkeit, *die;* (shabbiness) Schäbigkeit, *die*

dowdy /'daʊdɪ/ *adj.* (unattractively dull) unansehnlich; (shabby) schäbig

dowel /'daʊəl/ (Carpentry)

A *n.* [Holz]dübel, *der*

B *v.t.,* (Brit.) **-ll-:** ~ **[together]** zusammendübeln

dowelling (Amer.: **doweling**) /'daʊəlɪŋ/ *n.* Verdübelung, *die*

'dower house *n.* (Brit.) Haus einer Witwe (*Teil des Wittums*)

Dow Jones index /daʊ'dʒəʊnz ɪndeks/ *n.* (Econ.) Dow-Jones-Index, *der*

down¹ /daʊn/ *n.* (Geog.) [baumloser] Höhenzug; *in pl.* Downs *Pl.* (*an der Süd- und Südostküste Englands*); **the North/South D~s** die North/South Downs

down² *n.* **1** (of bird) Daunen *Pl.;* Flaum, *der;* **chicks covered in ~:** Vogeljunge im Daunenkleid **2** (hair) Flaum, *der;* **have a covering of ~:** mit Flaum bedeckt sein **3** (fluffy substance) Flausch, *der;* (of thistle, dandelion) Flaum, *der*

down³

A *adv.* **1** (to lower place) runter (bes. ugs.); herunter/hinunter (bes. schriftsprachlich); (in lift) abwärts; (in crossword puzzle) senkrecht; **[right] ~ to sth.** [ganz] bis zu etw. her-/hinunter; **come on ~!** komm [hier/weiter] herunter!

2 (to ~stairs) runter (bes. ugs.); herunter/hinunter (bes. schriftsprachlich)

3 (of money: at once) sofort; **pay ~ for sth., pay for sth. cash ~:** etw. [in] bar bezahlen

4 (into prostration) nieder‹*fallen, -geschlagen werden*›; **shout the place/house ~** (fig.) schreien, dass die Wände zittern

5 (on to paper) **copy sth. ~ from the board** etw. von der Tafel abschreiben

6 (on programme) **put a meeting ~ for 2 p.m.** ein Treffen für *od.* auf 14 Uhr ansetzen; **put oneself ~ for a dental appointment** sich (*Dat.*) einen Termin beim *od.* vom Zahnarzt geben lassen

7 (to place regarded as lower) runter (bes. ugs.); herunter/hinunter (bes. schriftsprachlich); **go ~ to the shops/the end of the road** zu den Läden/zum Ende der Straße hinuntergehen

8 (with current) stromab[wärts]; (with wind) mit/vor dem Wind; **brought ~ by river** flussabwärts befördert

9 (away from major town, city) **go ~ to one's cottage in the country for the weekend** zum Wochenende in sein Ferienhaus auf dem Land fahren

10 (southwards) runter (bes. ugs.); herunter/hinunter (bes. schriftsprachlich); **come ~ from Edinburgh to London** von Edinburgh nach London [he]runterkommen

11 (Brit.: from capital) raus (bes. ugs.); heraus/hinaus (bes. schriftsprachlich); **get ~ to Reading from London** von London nach Reading raus-/hinausfahren

12 (Brit.: from university) **come ~ [from Oxford]** das Studium [in Oxford] abschließen

13 (Naut.: with rudder to windward) in Lee; **put the helm ~:** das Ruder in Lee legen

14 *as int.* runter! (bes. ugs.); (to dog) leg dich!; nieder!; (Mil.) hinlegen!; **~ with imperialism/the president!** nieder mit dem Imperialismus/dem Präsidenten!

15 (in lower place) unten; **~ on the floor** auf dem Fußboden; **low/lower ~:** tief/tiefer unten; **~ at the bottom of the hill** [unten] am Fuß des Berges; **~ under the table** unter dem Tisch; **wear one's hair ~:** sein Haar offen tragen; **~ below the horizon** hinter *od.* unter dem Horizont; **~ at the bottom of the sea/pool** [tief] auf dem Meeresgrund/Grund des

Schwimmbeckens; ~ **there/here** da/hier unten; **X metres ~:** x Meter tief; **his flat is on the next floor ~:** seine Wohnung ist ein Stockwerk tiefer

16 (facing ~wards, bowed) zu Boden; **keep one's eyes ~:** zu Boden sehen

17 (~stairs) unten

18 (in fallen position) unten; **~ [on the floor]** (Boxing) am Boden; auf den Brettern; **~ and out** (Boxing) k. o.; (fig.) fertig (ugs.); *see also* **down-and-out**

19 (prostrate) auf dem Fußboden/der Erde; **be ~ with an illness** eine Krankheit haben

20 (out of action) ausgefallen ‹*Computer*›

21 (on paper) nieder-; **be ~ in writing/on paper/in print** niedergeschrieben/zu Papier gebracht/gedruckt sein

22 (on programme) angesetzt ‹*Termin, Treffen*›; **be ~ for an appointment** einen Termin haben; **be ~ to speak** als Redner vorgesehen sein; **be ~ to run in a race** für ein Rennen gemeldet sein

23 (in place regarded as lower) unten; **~ at the bottom of the garden** am unteren Ende des Gartens; **~ at the doctor's/social security office** beim Arzt/Sozialamt

24 (brought to the ground) **be ~:** am Boden liegen

25 (not in major town, city) **~ in Wales/in the country** weit weg in Wales/draußen auf dem Lande; **~ on the farm** auf dem Bauernhof

26 (Brit.: not in university) nicht mehr im Studium; (for vacation) nicht an der Universität; **how long have you been ~ from Oxford?** seit wann sind Sie nicht mehr an der Universität Oxford?

27 (in position of lagging or loss) weniger; **be three points/games ~:** mit drei Punkten/Spielen zurückliegen; **start the second half 1-0 ~:** mit einem 1:0-Rückstand in die zweite Halbzeit gehen; **we're £3,000 ~ on last year, in terms of profit** was unseren Gewinn angeht, so liegt er um 3 000 Pfund unter dem des letzten Jahres; **be ~ on one's earnings of the previous year** weniger verdienen als im Vorjahr; **be ~ on one's luck** eine Pechsträhne haben. *See also* **heel**[1] **A 2**; **up A 11**

28 (Amer.) **~ south/east** in den Südstaaten/im Osten

29 (in depression) **~ [in the mouth]** niedergeschlagen; **are you [feeling] ~ about something?** bedrückt Sie etwas?

30 **be ~ on sb./sth.** (dislike) etwas gegen jmdn./etw. haben; **be very ~ on sb./sth.** jmdm./einer Sache gegenüber sehr kritisch eingestellt sein

31 **~ to the ground** ▸ **ground**[1] **A 2**

32 (now cheaper) [jetzt] billiger; **prices have gone/are ~:** die Preise sind gesunken

33 **be ~ to ...** (have only ... left) nichts mehr haben außer ...; **we're ~ to our last £100** wir haben nur noch 100 Pfund; **strip off ~ to one's underwear** sich bis auf die Unterwäsche ausziehen; **be [left] ~ to sb.** an jmdm. hängen bleiben; **now it's ~ to him to do something** nun liegt es bei *od.* an ihm, etwas zu tun

34 (to reduced consistency or size) **thin gravy ~:** Soße verdünnen; **the water had boiled right ~:** das Wasser war fast verdampft; **wear the soles ~:** die Sohlen ablaufen

35 (to smoother state) **sand sth. ~:** etw. abschmirgeln

36 (including lower limit) **from ... ~ to ...:** von ... bis zu ... hinunter

37 (from earlier time) weiter-; **last ~ to the present day/our time** bis zum heutigen Tag/bis in unsere Zeit weitergegeben werden

38 (more quietly) leiser; **put the sound/TV ~:** den Ton/Fernseher leiser stellen

B *prep.* 1 (~wards along) runter (bes. ugs.); herunter/hinunter (bes. schriftsprachlich); **lower ~ the river** weiter unten am Fluss; **fall ~ the stairs/steps** die Treppe/Stufen herunterstürzen; **fall ~ the ladder** die Leiter runter-/herunterrutschen; **walk ~ the hill/road** den Hügel/die Straße heruntergehen; **lower sb. ~ a cliff** jmdn. an einem Felsen herunterlassen

2 (~wards through) durch

3 (~wards into) rein in (+ *Akk.*) (bes. ugs.); hinein in (+ *Akk.*) (bes. schriftsprachlich); **fall ~ a hole/well/ditch** in ein Loch/einen Brunnen/einen Graben fallen; **trickle ~ the plughole** ins Abflussloch tröpfeln

4 (~wards over) über (+ *Akk.*); **ivy grew ~ the wall** Efeu wuchs an der Mauer herunter; **spill water all ~ one's skirt** sich (*Dat.*) Wasser über den Rock gießen; **condensation running ~ the windows** an den Fenstern herunterlaufendes Kondenswasser

5 (from top to bottom of) runter (bes. ugs.); herunter/hinunter (bes. schriftsprachlich); **his eye travelled ~ the list** sein Auge wanderte über die Liste; **draw a line ~ the page** eine Linie längs über die Seite ziehen

6 (~wards in time) weiter-; **the tradition has continued ~ the ages** die Tradition ist von Generation zu Generation weitergegeben worden

7 (along) **go ~ the road/corridor/track** die Straße/den Korridor/den Weg hinunter- *od.* entlang- *od.* (ugs.) langgehen; **come ~ the street** die Straße herunter- *od.* entlangkommen; **turn ~ a side street** in eine Seitenstraße einbiegen; **part one's hair ~ the middle** einen Mittelscheitel tragen

8 (Brit. coll.: to) **go ~ the pub/disco** in die Kneipe/Disko gehen

9 (at or in a lower position in or on) [weiter] unten; **further ~ the ladder/coast** weiter unten auf der Leiter/an der Küste; **live in a hut ~ the mountain/hill** in einer Hütte weiter unten am Berg wohnen; **live just ~ the road** ein Stück weiter unten in der Straße wohnen; **a place just ~ the river** eine Stelle etwas weiter flussabwärts; *see also* **downtown**

10 (from top to bottom along) an (+ *Dat.*); **~ the stem of a plant/the side of a house** am Stiel einer Pflanze/an der Seite eines Hauses; **the lines ~ the page** die senkrechten Linien auf der Seite; **the buttons ~ the back of the dress** die senkrechte Knopfreihe auf dem Rücken des Kleides; **there were festivities ~ every road** auf allen Straßen wurde gefeiert

11 (all over) überall auf (+ *Dat.*); **I've got coffee [all] ~ my skirt** mein ganzer Rock ist voll Kaffee; **leave marks ~ sb.'s face** in jmds. ganzem Gesicht Spuren hinterlassen

12 (Brit. coll.: in, at) **~ the pub/café/town** in der Kneipe/im Café/in der Stadt; **be ~ the shops** einkaufen sein (ugs.)

C *adj.* (directed ~wards) nach unten führend ‹*Rohr, Kabel*›; ‹*Rolltreppe*› nach unten; nach unten gerichtet ‹*Kolbenhub, Sog*›; **~ train/line/journey** (Railw.) Zug/Gleis/Fahrt stadtauswärts

D *v.t.* (coll.) 1 (knock ~) auf die Bretter schicken ‹*Boxer*›

2 (fig.: defeat) fertig machen (ugs.) ‹*Gegner*›

3 (drink ~) leer machen (ugs.) ‹*Flasche, Glas*›; schlucken (ugs.) ‹*Getränk*›

4 (throw ~) ‹*Tier:*› abschmeißen (ugs.) ‹*Reiter, Last*›; **~ tools** (cease work) zu arbeiten aufhören; (make a break) die Arbeit unterbrechen; (finish work) Feierabend machen; (go on strike) die Arbeit niederlegen

5 (shoot ~) abschießen, runterholen (ugs.) ‹*Flugzeug*›

6 (stop by shot etc.) zusammenschießen (ugs.)

7 (Footb.) legen (Sportjargon) ‹*Gegenspieler*›

E *n.* 1 (Wrestling) Wurf, *der*

2 (Amer. and Can. Footb.) Versuch, *der*

3 **ups and ~s** ▸ **up D**

4 (coll.) **have a ~ on sb./sth.** jmdn./etw. auf dem Kieker haben (ugs.)

down: ~-and-out *n.* Stadtstreicher, *der*/Stadtstreicherin, *die;* Penner, *der*/Pennerin, *die* (ugs.); **~beat** **A** *n.* (Mus.) erster/betonter Taktteil; **B** *adj.* (coll.) 1 (relaxed) ungezwungen; 2 (pessimistic) düster ‹*Film usw.*›; **~cast** *adj.* 1 (dejected) niedergeschlagen ‹*Blick, Gesicht*›; 2 (directed ~wards) gesenkt ‹*Blick, Kopf*›; **with one's head ~cast** mit gesenktem Kopf **~draught** *n.* [Luft]zug von oben

downer /ˈdaʊnə(r)/ *n.* (coll.) 1 (drug) Downer, *der* 2 (depressing experience) **be a ~ [for sb.]** [bei jmdm.] auf die Stimmung drücken

down: ~fall *n.* (ruin) Untergang, *der;* **be** *or* **mean sb.'s ~fall** jmds. Untergang *od.* Ruin sein; **~ grade** *n.* Gefällstrecke, *die;* **he was on the ~ grade** (fig.) es ging bergab mit ihm; **~grade** *v.t.* niedriger einstufen; **~'hearted** *adj.* niedergeschlagen ‹*Blick, Gesicht*›; **~hill** **A** /ˈ--/ *adj.* bergab führend ‹*Fahrt*›; ‹*Strecke, Weg*› bergab; **the journey was ~hill** die Reise führte bergab; **he's on the ~hill path** (fig.) es geht bergab mit ihm; **a ~hill trend** (fig.) ein Abwärtstrend; **the ~hill course of the economy** (fig.) die Talfahrt der Wirtschaft; **be ~hill all the way** (fig.) ganz einfach sein; **B** /-ˈ-/ *adv.* bergab; **come ~hill** den Berg herunterkommen; **sb./sth. is going ~hill** (fig.) es geht bergab mit jmdm./etw.; **C** /ˈ--/ *n.* 1 (~ward slope) Gefällstrecke, *die;* 2 (Skiing) Abfahrtslauf, *der;* **~land** *n.* [baumloses] Hügelland; **~'load** *v.t.* (Computing) herunterladen; **~loadable** *adj.* (Computing) [he]runterladbar; **~loadable software** Download-Software, *die;* **~market** *adj.* weniger anspruchsvoll; **~ payment** *n.* Anzahlung, *die;* **~pipe** *n.* [Regenab]fallrohr, *das;* **~play** *v.t.* [he]runterspielen; **~pour** *n.* Regenguss, *der;* **~right** **A** *adj.* 1 (utter) ausgemacht ‹*Frechheit, Dummheit, Idiot, Lügner*›; glatt ‹*Lüge*›; 2 (straightforward) ehrlich ‹*Rat, Darstellung, Person*›; offen ‹*Wort*›; **B** *adv.* geradezu; ausgesprochen; **it would be ~right stupid to do that** es wäre eine ausgemachte Dummheit, das zu versuchen; **~shift** **A** *v.i.* 1 (Amer.: change to lower gear) [he]runterschalten; 2 (change to less pressured lifestyle) einen Gang zurückschalten; **B** *n.* 1 (Amer.: change to lower gear) [He]runterschalten, *das;* 2 (to less pressured lifestyle) Kürzertreten, *das;* Zurückstecken, *das;* **~shifter** /ˈdaʊnʃɪftə(r)/ *n.* Teilaussteiger, *der*/-aussteigerin, *die;* **~side** *n.* Kehrseite, *die;* **~size** **A** *v.t.* verschlanken; **B** *v.i.* abspecken; **~sizing** /ˈdaʊnsaɪzɪŋ/ *n., no pl.* (of company) Personalverschlankung, *die*

ˈDown's syndrome *n., no pl.* (Med.) Downsyndrom, *das*

down: ~stage (Theatre) **A** *adv.* im Vordergrund der Bühne; **move ~stage** sich zum Vordergrund der Bühne bewegen; **B** *adj.* **a ~stage door/entrance** eine Vordertür/ein Vordereingang zur Bühne; **~stairs** **A** /-ˈ-/ *adv.* die Treppe hinunter‹*gehen, -fallen, -kommen*›; unten ‹*wohnen, sein*›; **B** /ˈ--/ *adj.* im Parterre *od.* Erdgeschoss *nachgestellt;* Parterre‹*wohnung*›; **C** /-ˈ-/ *n.* Untergeschoss, *das;* **~stream** ▸ℹ **p. 1491** **A** /-ˈ-/ *adv.* flussabwärts; **B** /ˈ--/ *adj.* flussabwärts gelegen ‹*Ort*›; **the ~stream voyage** die Reise flussabwärts; **~stroke** *n.* 1 (in writing) Abstrich, *der;* 2 (Mech.: of piston) Abwärtshub, *der;* **~swing** *n.* (Golf, Commerc.) Abschwung, *der;* **~ time** *n.* (Computing) Ausfallzeit, *die;* **~-to-earth** *adj.* praktisch, nüchtern ‹*Person*›; realistisch ‹*Plan, Vorschlag*›; sachlich ‹*Bemerkung, Antwort*›; **~town** (Amer.) **A** *adj.* im Stadtzentrum *nachgestellt;* in der Innenstadt *nachgestellt;* **~town Manhattan** das Zentrum von Manhattan; **B** *adv.* ins Stadtzentrum, in die Innenstadt ‹*gehen, fahren*›; im Stadtzentrum, in der Innenstadt ‹*leben, liegen, sein*›; **C** *n.* Stadtzentrum, *das;* Innenstadt, *die;* **~trodden** *adj.* geknechtet; unterdrückt; **~turn** *n.* (Econ., Commerc.) Abschwung, *der;* **~ 'under** (coll.) **A** *adv.* in/(to) nach Australien/Neuseeland; **B** *n.* (Australia) Australien (*das*); (New Zealand) Neuseeland (*das*)

Downing Street

Der Name einer Straße in Westminster im Zentrum von London. Das Haus mit der Nummer 10 in der *Downing Street* ist der offizielle Sitz des Premierministers und das mit der Nummer 11 der des Finanzministers. Unter Journalisten ist der Ausdruck *Downing Street* oder *Number 10* gebräuchlich, wenn vom Amtssitz des Premierministers die Rede ist.

downward /ˈdaʊnwəd/

A *adj.* nach unten *nachgestellt;* nach unten gerichtet; **~ movement/trend** (lit. or fig.) Abwärtsbewegung, *die*/-trend, *der;* **~ gradient** *or* **slope** Gefälle, *das;* **move in a ~ direction** sich abwärts *od.* nach unten bewegen; **he was on a/the ~ path** (fig.) mit ihm ging es bergab

B *adv.* abwärts ‹*sich bewegen*›; nach unten ‹*sehen, gehen*›; *see also* **face down[ward]**

downwards /ˈdaʊnwədz/ ▸**downward B**

ˈdownwind
A *adv.* mit dem Wind; vor dem Wind ‹*segeln*›; **be ~ of sb./sth.** in jmds. Windschatten/im Windschatten einer Sache (*Gen.*) sein
B *adj.* in Windrichtung liegend; **the ~ side** die windabgewandte Seite

downy /ˈdaʊnɪ/ *adj.* flaumig; flaumweich ‹*Haar, Haut*›; Flaum‹*haar, -bart*›

dowry /ˈdaʊrɪ/ *n.* Mitgift, *die* (veralt.); Aussteuer, *die*

dowse[1] ▸**douse**

dowse[2] /daʊz/ *v.i.* mit der Wünschelrute suchen (**for** nach)

dowser /ˈdaʊzə(r)/ *n.* (person) Wünschelrutengänger, *der*/-gängerin, *die*

dowsing rod /ˈdaʊzɪŋ rɒd/ *n.* Wünschelrute, *die*

doxology /dɒkˈsɒlədʒɪ/ *n.* (Eccl.) Doxologie, *die*

doyen /ˈdɔɪən, ˈdwɑːjæ̃/ *n.* Doyen, *der*

doyenne /dɔɪˈen, dwɑːjen/ *n.* Doyenne, *die*

doyley ▸**doily**

doz. *abbr.* **= dozen** Dtzd.

doze /dəʊz/
A *v.i.* dösen (ugs.); [nicht tief] schlafen; **lie dozing** im Halbschlaf liegen
B *n.* Nickerchen, *das* (ugs.); **fall into a ~:** eindösen (ugs.)

Phrasal verb
- **~ ˈoff** *v.i.* eindösen (ugs.)

dozen /ˈdʌzn/ *n.* **1** *pl. same* (twelve) Dutzend, *das;* **six ~ bottles of wine** sechsmal zwölf Flaschen Wein; **there were several/a few ~ [people] there** Dutzende von Leuten/ein paar Dutzend Leute waren da; **a ~ times/reasons** (fig. coll.: many) dutzend Mal/Dutzende von Gründen; **half a ~:** sechs; ein halbes Dutzend (veralt.) **2** *pl.* **~s** (set of twelve) Dutzend, *das;* **by the ~** (in twelves) im Dutzend; (fig. coll.: in great numbers) in großen Scharen; **do one's daily ~** (coll.) Frühsport machen **3** *in pl.* (coll.: many) Dutzende *Pl.;* **in [their] ~s** (in great numbers) in großen Scharen; **~s of times** dutzendmal

dozy /ˈdəʊzɪ/ *adj.* (drowsy) dösig (ugs.); schläfrig

DP *abbr.* **= data processing** DV

DPhil /diːˈfɪl/ *abbr.* **= Doctor of Philosophy** Dr. phil.; *see also* **BSc**

DPP *abbr.* (Brit.) **= Director of Public Prosecutions** ≈ Generalstaatsanwalt, *der*

Dr *abbr.* **1** ▸**ⓘ p. 1634 = doctor** (as prefix to name) Dr. **2** **= debtor** Sch.

drab /dræb/ *adj.* **1** (dull brown) gelblich braun; sandfarben; (dull-coloured) matt **2** (dull, monotonous) langweilig ‹*Ort, Gebäude*›; trostlos, öde ‹*Landschaft, Umgebung*›; grau, trist ‹*Stadt*›; farblos ‹*Person*› **3** (fig.) eintönig, trist ‹*Leben*›

drabness /ˈdræbnɪs/ *n., no pl.* **1** (of surroundings) Trostlosigkeit, *die;* Ödheit, *die* **2** (fig.: of life, existence) Eintönigkeit, *die*

drachma /ˈdrækmə/ *n. pl.* **~s** *or* **drachmae** /ˈdrækmiː/ Drachme, *die*

Draconian /drəˈkəʊnɪən/ *adj.* drakonisch

draft /drɑːft/
A *n.* **1** (rough copy) (of speech) Konzept, *das;* (of treaty, parliamentary bill) Entwurf, *der;* **~ copy/version** Konzept, *das;* **~ letter** Entwurf eines Briefes **2** (plan of work) Skizze, *die;* [Bau-, Riss-]zeichnung, *die* **3** (Mil.: detaching for special duty) Sonderkommando, *das;* (Brit.: those detached) Abkommandierte *Pl.;* Sonderkommando, *das* **4** (Amer. Mil.: conscription) Einberufung, *die;* (those conscripted) Wehrpflichtige *Pl.;* Einberufene *Pl.* **5** (Commerc.) Abhebung, *die;* Abheben, *das;* (cheque drawn) Wechsel, *der;* Tratte, *die* **6** (Amer.) ▸**draught**
B *v.t.* **1** (make rough copy of) entwerfen **2** (Mil.) abkommandieren **3** (Amer. Mil.: conscript) einberufen; **be ~ed** eingezogen *od.* einberufen werden **4** (fig.) (call upon) berufen; (select) auswählen

ˈdraft dodger *n.* (Amer. Mil.) *jmd., der sich dem Wehrdienst entzieht*

draftee /drɑːfˈtiː/ *n.* (Amer. Mil.) Wehrpflichtige, *der*

draftsman /ˈdrɑːftsmən/ *n., pl.* **draftsmen** /ˈdrɑːftsmən/ **1** *jemand, der Gesetzesvorlagen usw. verfasst;* ≈ Schreiber, *der* **2** ▸**draughtsman**

drafty (Amer.) ▸**draughty**

drag /dræg/
A *n.* **1** (dredging apparatus) Suchanker, *der* **2** ▸**dragnet** **3** (Hunting) (artificial scent) Fuchs, *der;* (club) Schleppjagd, *die;* Reitjagd, *die* **4** (difficult progress) **it was a long ~ up the hill** der Aufstieg auf den Hügel war ein ganz schöner Schlauch (ugs.) **5** (Aeronaut.) Strömungswiderstand, *der;* **~ coefficient** *or* **factor** [Luft]widerstandszahl, *die* **6** (obstruction) Hindernis, *das* (**on** für); Hemmnis, *das* (**on** für); **be a ~ on sb./sth.** jmdm./für etw. eine Last sein **7** (boring thing) langweilige Sache *od.* Angelegenheit; **be a ~:** langweilig sein **8** (coll.: at cigarette) Zug, *der* **9** *no pl.* (coll.: women's dress worn by men) Frauenkleider *Pl.;* **in ~:** in Frauenkleidung **10** (Amer. coll.: road) **the main ~:** die Hauptstraße **11** (Amer. coll.: influence) Einfluss, *der*
B *v.t.,* **-gg- 1** [herum]schleppen; **~ one's feet** *or* **heels** (fig.) sich (*Dat.*) Zeit lassen (**over, in** mit) **2** (move with effort) **~ oneself** sich schleppen; **~ one's feet** [mit den Füßen] schlurfen; **I could scarcely ~ myself out of bed** ich konnte mich kaum aufraffen aufzustehen **3** (fig. coll.: take despite resistance) **he ~ged me to a dance** er schleifte mich (ugs.) zu einer Tanzveranstaltung; **~ the children away from the television** die Kinder [mit Gewalt] vom Fernsehen losreißen; **he ~s her about with him everywhere** er schleppt sie überall mit sich herum; **~ sb. into sth.** jmdn. in etw. (*Akk.*) hineinziehen; **~ sb. into doing sth.** jmdn. dazu drängen, etw. zu tun **4** (search) [mit einem Schleppnetz] absuchen ‹*Fluss-, Seegrund*› **5** (Naut.) **the ship ~s her anchor** das Schiff treibt vor Anker **6** (Computing) ziehen; **~ and drop** ziehen und ablegen
C *v.i.,* **-gg- 1** schleifen; **~ on** *or* **at a cigarette** (coll.) an einer Zigarette ziehen **2** (fig.: pass slowly) sich [hin]schleppen

Phrasal verbs
- **~ ˈdown** *v.t.* nach unten ziehen; **~ sb. down to one's own level** (fig.) jmdn. auf sein Niveau herabziehen
- **~ ˈin** *v.t.* hineinziehen
- **~ ˈon** *v.i.* (continue) sich [da]hinschleppen; **time ~ged on** die Zeit verstrich; **~ on for months** sich über Monate hinziehen
- **~ ˈout** *v.t.* (protract unduly) hinausziehen; in die Länge ziehen; **~ out [one's days/existence]** [sein Leben/Dasein] fristen
- **~ ˈup** *v.t.* (coll.) wieder ausgraben ‹*alte Geschichte, Skandal*›

drag: ~ hounds *n. pl.* Hunde für die Schleppjagd; **~net** *n.* (lit. or fig.) Schleppnetz, *das;* (fig.) Netz, *das*

dragon /ˈdrægn/ *n.* Drache, *der;* (fig.: fearsome person) Drachen, *der*

ˈdragonfly *n.* (Zool.) Libelle, *die*

dragoon /drəˈguːn/
A *n.* (Mil.) Dragoner, *der*
B *v.t.* zwingen; **~ sb. into doing sth.** jmdn. zwingen, etw. zu tun

drag: ~ queen *n.* (coll.) Dragqueen, *die;* **~ racing** *n.* Beschleunigungsrennen *Pl.*

dragster /ˈdrægstə(r)/ *n.* Dragster, *der; für Beschleunigungsrennen gebautes Fahrzeug*

drain /dreɪn/
A *n.* **1** Abflussrohr, *das;* (underground) Kanalisationsrohr, *das;* (grating at roadside) Gully, *der;* **open ~:** Abflussrinne, *die;* **down the ~** (fig. coll.) für die Katz (ugs.); **go down the ~** (fig. coll.) umsonst *od.* vergeblich *od.* (ugs.) für die Katz sein; **that was money [thrown] down the ~** (fig. coll.) das Geld war zum Teufel (salopp) *od.* zum Fenster hinausgeworfen (ugs.); **be going down the ~:** vor die Hunde gehen (geh.); **laugh like a ~** (fig. coll.) schallend lachen; sich vor Lachen ausschütten wollen **2** (fig.: constant demand) Belastung, *die* (**on** *Gen.*); **be a ~ on sb.'s strength** an jmds. Kräften zehren
B *v.t.* **1** trockenlegen ‹*Teich*›; entwässern ‹*Land*›; ableiten ‹*Wasser*› **2** (Cookery) abgießen ‹*Wasser, Kartoffeln, Gemüse*› **3** (Geog.) **the river ~s the valley** der Fluss nimmt das Wasser des ganzen Tales auf **4** (drink all contents of) austrinken **5** (fig.: deprive) **~ a country of its manpower/wealth** *or* **resources** ein Land ausbluten/auslaugen; **~ sb. of his energy** jmdn. auslaugen
C *v.i.* **1** ‹*Geschirr, Gemüse:*› abtropfen; ‹*Flüssigkeit:*› ablaufen **2** **the colour ~ed from her face** (fig.) die Farbe wich aus ihrem Gesicht

drainage /ˈdreɪnɪdʒ/ *n.* **1** (draining) Entwässerung, *die;* Trockenlegung, *die;* (fig.) Ausbeutung, *die* **2** (Geog.: natural ~) [natürliche] Entwässerung; (artificial ~ of fields etc.) Entwässerung, *die;* Dränung *od.* Dränage, *die* (fachspr.); (system) Entwässerungssystem, *das;* (of city, house, etc.) Kanalisation, *die*

draining board /ˈdreɪnɪŋ bɔːd/ (*Brit.; Amer.:* **ˈdrainboard**) *n.* Abtropfbrett, *das*

drain: ~pipe *n.* **1** (to carry off rainwater) Regen[abfall]rohr, *das;* **2** (to carry off sewage) Abwasserleitung, *die;* (underground) Kanalisationsleitung, *die;* **~pipes, ~pipe ˈtrousers** *ns. pl.* (Fashion) Röhrenhosen

drake /dreɪk/ *n.* Enterich, *der;* Erpel, *der; see also* **duck**[1] **A 1**

dram /dræm/ *n.* **1** (Pharm.) (weight) Drachme, *die;* **fluid ~** (Brit.) 3,5515 cm3; (Amer.) 3,6967 cm^3 **2** (small drink) Schlückchen, *das* (ugs.)

drama /ˈdrɑːmə/ *n.* **1** (play, lit. or fig.) Drama, *das* **2** *no pl.* (genre) Drama, *das;* (dramatic art) Schauspielkunst, *die;* Dramatik, *die;* (fig.: episode as in play) Schauspiel, *das; attrib.* **~ critic** Theaterkritiker, *der;* **~ school** Schauspielschule, *die*

dramatic /drəˈmætɪk/ *adj.* **1** (Theatre) dramatisch; **~ art** Dramatik, *die;* **a ~ critic** ein Theaterkritiker **2** (fig.) dramatisch; (exaggerated) theatralisch; bühnenreif

dramatically /drəˈmætɪkəlɪ/ *adv.* dramatisch; (in exaggerated way) theatralisch

dramatic ˈirony *n.* tragische Ironie (Literaturwiss.)

dramatics /drəˈmætɪks/ *n., no pl.* **1** Theater[spiel], *das;* **amateur ~:** Laientheater, *das* **2** (fig. derog.) Theatralik, *die* (geh. abwertend)

dramatisation, dramatise ▸**dramatiz-**

dramatis personae /dræmətɪs pəˈsəʊniː, dræmətɪs pəˈsəʊnaɪ/ *n. pl., often constr. as sing.* dramatis personae; die Personen; (fig.) Hauptpersonen *Pl.*

dramatist /ˈdræmətɪst/ *n.* Dramatiker, *der*/Dramatikerin, *die*

dramatization /dræmətaɪˈzeɪʃn/ *n.* **1** Dramatisierung, *die;* **a television/stage ~:** eine Fernseh-/Bühnenbearbeitung **2** (fig.) Dramatisieren, *das*

dramatize /ˈdræmətaɪz/ *v.t.* **1** dramatisieren; [für die Bühne/das Fernsehen *usw.*] bearbeiten **2** (fig.) dramatisieren; [künstlich] hochspielen; (emphasize) betonen

drank ▸**drink B, C**

drape /dreɪp/
A *v.t.* **1** (cover, adorn) **~ oneself/sb. in sth.** sich/jmdn. in etw. (*Akk.*) hüllen; **~ an altar/walls with sth.** einen Altar/Wände mit etw. behängen **2** (put loosely) **~ sth. over/round sth.** etw. über etw. (*Akk.*)/um etw. legen *od.* drapieren **3** (rest casually) legen; hängen
B *n.* **1** (cloth) Tuch, *das* **2** *usu. in pl.* (esp. Amer.: curtain) Vorhang, *der*

draper /ˈdreɪpə(r)/ *n.* ▸**ⓘ p. 1260** (Brit.) Textilkaufmann, *der;* **the ~'s [shop]** das Textilgeschäft; *see also* **baker**

drapery /ˈdreɪpərɪ/ *n.* **1** (Brit.: cloth) Stoffe; Textilien *Pl.* **2** (Brit.: trade) Textilgewerbe, *das;* **~ shop** Textilgeschäft, *das* **3** (arrangement of cloth) Draperie, *die* **4** (cloth artistically arranged) Faltenwurf, *der* **5** *usu. in pl.* (Amer.: curtain) Vorhang, *der*

drastic /ˈdræstɪk, ˈdrɑːstɪk/ *adj.* drastisch; erheblich ‹*Wandel, Verbesserung*›; durchgreifend, rigoros ‹*Mittel*›; dringend ‹*Bedarf*›; einschneidend ‹*Veränderung*›; erschreckend ‹*Mangel*›; bedrohlich ‹*Lage*›; **something ~ will have to be done** drastische Maßnahmen müssen ergriffen werden

drastically /ˈdræstɪkəlɪ, ˈdrɑːstɪkəlɪ/ *adv.* drastisch; erheblich; rigoros, hart ‹*durchgreifen*›;

d

be ~ in need of sth. dringenden Bedarf an etw. (*Dat.*) haben

drat /dræt/ *v.t.* (coll.) ~ **[it]/him/the weather!** verflucht!/verfluchter Kerl!/verfluchtes Wetter! (salopp)

dratted /ˈdrætɪd/ *adj.* (coll.) verflucht

draught /drɑːft/ *n.* 1 (of air) [Luft]zug, *der;* **where is the ~ coming from?** woher zieht es?; **be [sitting] in a ~:** im Zug sitzen; **there's a ~ [in here]** es zieht [hier]; **feel the ~** (fig. coll.) [finanziell] in der Klemme sitzen (ugs.) 2 **[beer] on ~:** [Bier] vom Fass 3 (swallowing) (act) Zug, *der;* (amount) Schluck, *der* 4 (Naut.) Tiefgang, *der*

draught: ~ **animal** *n.* Zugtier, *das;* ~ **'beer** *n.* Fassbier, *das;* ~ **board** *n.* (Brit.) Damebrett, *das;* ~ **excluder** *n.* Abdichtvorrichtung, *die;* Zugluftverhinderer, *der;* **~horse** *n.* Zugpferd, *das;* **~proof** A *adj.* winddicht; B *v.t.* winddicht machen

draughts /drɑːfts/ *n., no pl.* (Brit.) Damespiel, *das;* **have a game of ~:** eine Partie Dame spielen; **play ~:** Dame spielen

draughtsman /ˈdrɑːftsmən/ *n., pl.* **draughtsmen** /ˈdrɑːftsmən/ (Brit.) 1 ▸ⓘ **p. 1260** Zeichner, *der*/Zeichnerin, *die* 2 (in game) Damestein, *der*

draughtsmanship /ˈdrɑːftsmənʃɪp/ *n.* (art and practice) Zeichenkunst, *die;* (skill) zeichnerisches Können

draughty /ˈdrɑːftɪ/ *adj.* zugig

Dravidian /drəˈvɪdɪən/ (Ethnol.)

A *adj.* drawidisch

B *n.* 1 (person) Drawide, *der*/Drawidin, *die* 2 (language) Drawidisch, *das*

draw /drɔː/

A *v.t.,* **drew** /druː/, **drawn** /drɔːn/ 1 (pull) ziehen; einholen ‹*Fangnetz*›; spannen ‹*Bogen*›; **~ the curtains/blinds** (open) die Vorhänge aufziehen/die Jalousien hochziehen; (close) die Vorhänge zuziehen/die Jalousien herunterlassen; **~ the bolt** (fasten) den Riegel vorschieben; (unfasten) den Riegel zurückschieben; **~ sth. towards one** etw. zu sich heran- *od.* hinziehen

2 (attract, take in) anlocken ‹*Publikum, Menge, Kunden*›; **all eyes were ~n to him** alle Blicke waren auf ihn gerichtet; **~ the fresh air into one's lungs** die frische Luft tief einatmen; **~ criticism upon oneself** Kritik auf sich (*Akk.*) ziehen; **be ~n to sb.** von jmdm. angezogen werden; **feel ~n to sb.** sich von jmdm. angezogen *od.* zu jmdm. hingezogen fühlen; **~ sb. into sth.** jmdn. in etw. (*Akk.*) mit hineinziehen; **he refused to be ~n** (be provoked) er ließ sich nichts entlocken; **~ sb. out of himself** jmdn. aus sich herauslocken; **~ the enemy's**/(fig.) **sb.'s fire** das feindliche Feuer/jmds. Kritik auf sich (*Akk.*) ziehen; *see also* **breath 1, 2**

3 (take out) herausziehen; ziehen (**from** aus); aufstöbern, aufjagen ‹*Fuchs, Dachs*› (**from** aus); **~ money from the bank/one's account** Geld bei der Bank holen/von seinem Konto abheben; **~ a pistol on sb.** eine Pistole auf jmdn. richten; **~ the cork from the bottle** die Flasche entkorken; **~ water from a well** Wasser an einem Brunnen holen *od.* schöpfen; **~ beer from a barrel** Bier vom Fass zapfen; *see also* **blood A 1**; **~ trumps** Trümpfe ziehen; **~ cards from a pack** Karten von einem Haufen abheben

4 (derive, elicit) finden; **~ an example from a book** ein Beispiel einem Buch entnehmen; **~ a response from sb.** von jmdm. eine Antwort bekommen; (interested) Echo bei jmdm. finden; **~ comfort/sustenance from sth.** Trost/Halt in etw. (*Dat.*) finden; **~ reassurance/encouragement from sth.** Zuversicht/Mut aus etw. schöpfen; **~ inspiration from sth.** sich von etw. inspirieren lassen; Anregungen bei *od.* in etw. (*Dat.*) finden; **~ applause/a smile [from sb.]** Applaus/ein Lächeln [bei jmdm.] hervorrufen; *see also* **conclusion 4**

5 (get as one's due) erhalten; bekommen; beziehen ‹*Gehalt, Rente, Arbeitslosenunterstützung*›

6 (select at random) **~ [straws]** [Lose] ziehen; losen; **~ [for partners]** [die Partner] auslosen; **Italy has been ~n against Spain in the World Cup** Italien ist als Gegner für Spanien im Weltmeisterschaftsspiel ausgelost worden; **~ a winner** ein Gewinnlos ziehen

7 (trace) ziehen ‹*Strich*›; zeichnen ‹*geometrische Figur, Bild*›; (fig.: represent in words) darstellen; **do you ~?** kannst du zeichnen?; **~ the line at sth.** (fig.) bei etw. nicht mehr mitmachen; **the line has to be ~n somewhere** *or* **at some point** (fig.) irgendwo muss Schluss sein; **it's difficult to ~ the line** (fig.) es ist schwierig, die Grenze zu ziehen

8 (Commerc.: write out) ziehen ‹*Wechsel*› (**on** auf + *Akk.*); **~ a cheque on one's bank for £100** einen Scheck über 100 Pfund auf seine Bank ausstellen

9 (formulate) ziehen ‹*Parallele, Vergleich*›; herstellen ‹*Analogie*›; herausstellen ‹*Unterschied*›; *see also* **distinction 2**

10 (end with neither side winner) unentschieden beenden ‹*Spiel*›; **the match was ~n** das Spiel ging unentschieden aus; *abs.* **they drew three-all** sie spielten 3:3 unentschieden

11 (disembowel) ausnehmen ‹*Geflügel, Fisch*›; ausweiden ‹*Wild*›

12 (extend) [aus]dehnen; ziehen ‹*Draht*›; **long ~n death agony** lang dauernder Todeskampf

13 (Naut.) **~ 3 m. [of water]** 3 m Tiefgang haben

14 (Hunting) **~ a covert** [ein Tier aus seinem Versteck] aufjagen. *See also* **blank B 3; hang A 6; lot 7**

B *v.i.,* **drew, drawn** 1 (make one's way, move) ‹*Person:*› gehen; ‹*Fahrzeug:*› fahren; ‹*Flugzeug:*› fliegen; **~ into sth.** ‹*Zug:*› in etw. (*Akk.*) einfahren; ‹*Schiff:*› in etw. (*Akk.*) einlaufen; **~ towards sth.** sich einer Sache (*Dat.*) nähern; **~ together** zusammenkommen; **~ closer together** enger zusammenrücken; **~ to an end** zu Ende gehen

2 (allow draught) ‹*Kamin, Zigarette:*› ziehen; **~ well/badly** einen guten/schlechten Zug haben

3 (infuse) ‹*Tee:*› ziehen

C *n.* 1 (raffle) Tombola, *die;* (for matches, contests) Auslosung, *die;* (of lottery) Ziehung, *die;* **be the luck of the ~** (fig.) Glück[s]sache sein

2 ([result of] drawn game) Unentschieden, *das;* (Chess) Remis, *das;* **end in a ~:** mit einem Unentschieden enden

3 Attraktion, *die;* (film, play) Publikumserfolg, *der*

4 **be quick/slow on the ~:** den Finger schnell/zu langsam am Abzug haben; (fig.) sich geistesgegenwärtig zeigen/nicht geistesgegenwärtig genug sein; ‹*Quizteilnehmer:*› schlagfertig sein/nicht schlagfertig genug sein

5 (Amer.: in smoking) Zug, *der*

Phrasal verbs

• **~ a'side** *v.t.* zur Seite ziehen; **~ sb. aside** jmdn. beiseite nehmen

• **~ a'way**

A *v.i.* 1 (move ahead) **~ away from sth./sb.** sich von etw. entfernen/jmdm. davonziehen 2 (set off) losfahren 3 (recoil) zurückweichen (**from** vor + *Dat.*)

B *v.t.* wegnehmen; wegziehen; weglocken ‹*Person*›

• **~ 'back**

A *v.t.* zurückziehen; aufziehen ‹*Vorhang*›

B *v.i.* zurückweichen; (fig.) sich zurückziehen

• **~ 'in**

A *v.i.* 1 (move in and stop) einfahren; **the car drew in to the side of the road** das Auto fuhr an den Straßenrand heran 2 ‹*Tage:*› kürzer werden; ‹*Abende, Nächte:*› länger werden

B *v.t.* (fig.) hineinziehen ‹*Person*›; zum Mitmachen überreden; **I refuse to be ~n in** ich will nicht mit hineingezogen werden

• **~ 'off** *v.t.* ausziehen ‹*Kleidung*›; ablassen ‹*Flüssigkeit*›

• **~ on**

A /-'-/ *v.i.* ‹*Zeit:*› vergehen, (geh.) fortschreiten; (approach) ‹*Winter, Nacht:*› nahen

B *v.t.* 1 /'--/ anziehen ‹*Kleidung*› 2 /-'-/ (induce) anziehen (fig.) ‹*Person*› 3 /'--/ zurückgreifen auf (+ *Akk.*) ‹*Ersparnisse, Vorräte*›; schöpfen aus ‹*Wissen, Erfahrungen*›; **you may ~ on my account** du kannst von meinem Konto abheben

• **~ 'out**

A *v.t.* (extend) ausdehnen; in die Länge ziehen; **long ~n out** ausgedehnt; in die Länge gezogen

B *v.i.* 1 abfahren; **the train/bus drew out of the station** der Zug fuhr aus dem Bahnhof aus/der Bus verließ den Busbahnhof 2 ‹*Tage:*› länger werden; ‹*Abende:*› kürzer werden

• **~ 'up**

A *v.t.* 1 (formulate) abfassen; aufsetzen ‹*Vertrag*›; aufstellen ‹*Liste*›; entwerfen ‹*Plan, Budget*› 2 heranziehen; **~ up a chair!** holen Sie sich doch einen Stuhl! 3 **~ oneself up [to one's full height]** sich [zu seiner vollen Größe] aufrichten 4 aufstellen ‹*Truppen, Fahrzeuge*›

B *v.i.* [an]halten

• **~ upon** ▸**~ on B 3**

draw: **~back** *n.* (snag) Nachteil, *der;* **~bridge** *n.* Zugbrücke, *die*

drawee /drɔːˈiː/ *n.* (Commerc.) Bezogene, *der;* Trassat, *der* (fachspr.)

drawer *n.* 1 /drɔː(r), ˈdrɔːə(r)/ (in furniture) Schublade, *die* 2 /ˈdrɔːə(r)/ (maker of drawings) Zeichner, *der*/Zeichnerin, *die* 3 (Commerc.) Aussteller, *der;* Trassant, *der* (fachspr.) 4 *in pl.* /drɔːz, ˈdrɔːəz/ (dated/joc.: underpants) Unterhosen *Pl.;* (for women) Schlüpfer *Pl.*

drawing /ˈdrɔːɪŋ/ *n.* 1 (activity) Zeichnen, *das;* **be good at ~:** gut zeichnen können 2 (sketch) Zeichnung, *die*

drawing: **~ board** *n.* Zeichenbrett, *das;* **so it's back to the ~ board, I'm afraid** dann müssen wir wohl wieder von vorne beginnen, fürchte ich; **~ office** *n.* Konstruktionsbüro, *das;* **~ paper** *n.* Zeichenpapier, *das;* **~ pin** *n.* (Brit.) Reißzwecke, *die;* **~ room** *n.* Salon, *der*

'drawknife *n.* Zugmesser, *das*

drawl /drɔːl/

A *v.i.* gedehnt *od.* (ugs.) breit sprechen

B *v.t.* dehnen; gedehnt *od.* (ugs.) breit aussprechen

C *n.* gedehntes *od.* (ugs.) breites Sprechen; **speak with a ~:** gedehnt sprechen

drawn /drɔːn/

A *p.p. of* **draw**

B *adj.* 1 verzogen ‹*Gesicht*›; **look ~** (from tiredness) abgespannt aussehen; (from worries) abgehärmt aussehen 2 (Sport) unentschieden; **~ game** Unentschieden, *das;* (Chess) Remis, *das*

'drawstring *n.* Durchziehband, *das*

dray /dreɪ/ *n.* Tafelwagen, *der;* Rollwagen, *der*

dread /dred/

A *v.t.* sich sehr fürchten vor (+ *Dat.*); große Angst haben vor (+ *Dat.*); **the ~ed day/moment** der gefürchtete *od.* mit Schrecken erwartete Tag/Augenblick; **I ~ the moment when ...:** ich fürchte mich vor dem Augenblick, wenn ...; **I ~ to think [what may have happened]** ich mag gar nicht daran denken[, was passiert sein könnte]; **I ~ the thought of ...:** mich schreckt der Gedanke an (+ *Akk.*) ...

B *n., no pl.* (terror) Angst, *die;* **be** *or* **live** *or* **stand in ~ of sth./sb.** in [ständiger] Furcht vor etw./jmdm. leben

C *adj.* (literary) fürchterlich

dreadful /ˈdredfl/ *adj.* schrecklich; furchtbar; (coll.: very bad) fürchterlich; **I feel ~** (unwell) ich fühle mich scheußlich (ugs.); (embarrassed) es ist mir furchtbar peinlich

dreadfully /ˈdredfəlɪ/ *adv.* 1 schrecklich; entsetzlich, furchtbar ‹*leiden*›; (coll.: very badly) grauenhaft; fürchterlich 2 (coll.: extremely) schrecklich; furchtbar

'dreadlocks *n. pl.* Rastalocken *Pl.*

dream /driːm/

A *n.* 1 Traum, *der;* **sweet ~s!** träume süß!; **have a ~ about sb./sth.** von jmdm./etw. träumen; **I had a bad ~ last night** letzte Nacht habe ich schlecht geträumt; **it was all a bad ~:** das Ganze war wie ein böser Traum; **in a ~:** im Traum; **go/work like a ~** (coll.) wie eine Eins fahren/funktionieren (ugs.) 2 (fig.: reverie) **go** *or* **walk around/be/live in a [complete] ~:** in einer [perfekten] Traumwelt leben 3 (ambition, vision) Traum, *der;* **have ~s of doing sth.** davon träumen, etw. zu tun; **never in one's wildest ~s** nicht in seinen kühnsten Träumen 4 (perfect person) **~ [man/woman]** Traummann, *der*/-frau, *die;* (perfect thing) Traum, der; attrib. traumhaft; Traum‹haus, -auto, -urlaub, -job, -ergebnis›. See also **wet dream**

B v.i., ~t /dremt/ or ~ed träumen; (while awake) vor sich (Akk.) hin träumen; ~ **about** or **of sb./sth.** von jmdm./etw. träumen; ~ **of doing sth.** (fig.) davon träumen, etw. zu tun; **he wouldn't ~ of doing it** (fig.) er würde nicht im Traum daran denken, das zu tun

C v.t., ~t or ~ed träumen; **she never** or **little ~t that she'd win** sie hätte sich (Dat.) nie träumen lassen, dass sie gewinnen würde

Phrasal verb

- ~ **'up** v.t. sich (Dat.) ausdenken; sich (Dat.) einfallen lassen

dreamer /'dri:mə(r)/ n. (in sleep) Träumende, der/die; (day~) Träumer, der/Träumerin, die

dreamily /'dri:mɪlɪ/ adv. verträumt

'dreamland n. Traumland, das; Reich der Träume, das

dreamless /'dri:mlɪs/ adj. traumlos

dreamlike /'dri:mlaɪk/ adj. traumhaft

dreamt ▸ **dream B, C**

'dream team n. ideales Team; Dreamteam, das

dreamy /'dri:mɪ/ adj. **1** verträumt ‹Person, Blick›; träumerisch ‹Stimmung› **2** (dreamlike) traumähnlich **3** (coll.: delightful) traumhaft [schön]

'dreamy-eyed adj. ‹Verliebte, Mädchen, Kind› mit verträumten Augen

drearily /'drɪərɪlɪ/ adv. ▸ **dreary**: monoton; düster

dreary /'drɪərɪ/ adj. trostlos; monoton ‹Musik›; langweilig ‹Unterricht, Lehrbuch›; düster ‹Gemüt, Gedanken›

dredge /dredʒ/ v.t. ausbaggern; (fig.) ausgraben; ~ **up** (fig.) ausgraben

dredger /'dredʒə(r)/ n. Bagger, der; (boat) Schwimmbagger, der; Nassbagger, der

dregs /dregz/ n. pl. **1** [Boden]satz, der; **drain one's glass to the ~**: sein Glas bis zur Neige od. bis zum letzten Tropfen leeren **2** (fig.) Abschaum, der

drench /drenʃ/ v.t. durchnässen; **get completely ~ed, get ~ed to the skin** nass bis auf die Haut werden

drenching /'drenʃɪŋ/

A n. **get a ~**: bis auf die Haut nass werden

B adj. ~ **rain** strömender Regen

Dresden /'drezdn/ pr. n. Dresden (das); ~ **china** or **porcelain** Meißner Porzellan

dress /dres/

A n. **1** (woman's or girl's frock) Kleid, das **2** no pl. (clothing) Kleidung, die; **be in native/formal ~**: nach Art der Einheimischen/formell gekleidet sein; **articles of ~**: Kleidungsstücke **3** no pl. (manner of dressing) Kleidung, die; **she's rather slovenly in her ~**: sie kleidet sich sehr nachlässig **4** (external covering) Kleid, das. See also **evening dress**; **full dress**; **morning dress**

B v.t. **1** (clothe) anziehen; **be ~ed** angezogen sein; **be well ~ed** gut gekleidet sein; **the bride was ~ed in white** die Braut trug Weiß; **get ~ed** sich anziehen **2** (provide clothes for) einkleiden ‹Familie› **3** (deck, adorn) schmücken; beflaggen ‹Schiff›; dekorieren ‹Schaufenster› **4** (arrange) frisieren ‹Haare› **5** (Med.) verbinden, versorgen ‹Wunde› **6** (Cookery) zubereiten **7** (treat, prepare) hobeln ‹Holz›; gerben ‹tierische Häute, Felle›; schleifen ‹Tontöpfe, Metall, Stein›; (put finish on) appretieren ‹Gewebe, Holz, Leder›; polieren ‹Tontöpfe, Metall, Stein› **8** (Mil.) ~ **ranks** die Front ausrichten **9** (Agric.: manure) düngen

C v.i. (wear clothes) sich anziehen; sich kleiden; (get dressed) sich anziehen; sich ankleiden (geh.); **I like to ~ in dark colours** ich trage gerne dunkle Farben; ~ **for dinner** sich zum Abendessen umziehen

Phrasal verbs

- ~ **'down** v.t. (fig.) zurechtweisen
- ~ **'up**

A v.t. **1** (in formal clothes) fein machen; fein anziehen; **sb. is all ~ed up and nowhere to go** (fig.) jmds. ganzer Aufwand ist umsonst (ugs.) **2** (disguise) verkleiden; (elaborately as a game) herausputzen **3** (smarten) verschönern

B v.i. **1** (wear formal clothes) sich fein machen **2** (disguise oneself) sich verkleiden; (elaborately as a game) sich herausputzen

dressage /'dresɑ:ʒ/ n. Dressurreiten, das

dress: ~ **circle** n. (Theatre) erster Rang; ~ **coat** n. Frack, der; ~ **code** n. Kleiderordnung, die; ~**-conscious** adj. modebewusst; ~ **designer** n. ▸ ❶ p. 1260 Modeschöpfer, der/-schöpferin, die; Modedesigner, der/-designerin, die; ~**-down Friday** n.: Freitag, an dem legere Kleidung [im Büro] erlaubt ist; legerer Freitag;

dresser¹ /'dresə(r)/ n. **1** (sideboard) Anrichte, die; Büfett, das **2** (Amer.) ▸ **dressing table**

dresser² n. **1** **he's a careless/elegant/tasteful ~**: er kleidet sich nachlässig/elegant/geschmackvoll **2** ▸ ❶ p. 1260 (Theatre) Garderobier, der/Garderobiere, die **3** ▸ ❶ p. 1260 (Med.) Operationsassistent, der/-assistentin, die

dressing /'dresɪŋ/ n. **1** no pl. Anziehen, das; Ankleiden, das (geh.) **2** (Cookery) Dressing, das **3** (Med.) Verband, der **4** (Agric.) Dünger, der

dressing: ~ **case** n. Kosmetikkoffer, der; ~ **'down** n. **give sb. a ~ down** jmdm. einen Rüffel verpassen od. eine Standpauke halten (ugs.); **get a ~ down** zurechtgewiesen od. (ugs.) heruntergemacht werden; ~ **gown** n. Bademantel, der; ~ **room** n. **1** (of actor or actress) [Schauspieler]garderobe, die; [Künstler]garderobe, die; **2** (for games players) Umkleidekabine, die; **3** (in house) Ankleideraum, der; Ankleidezimmer, das; ~ **table** n. Frisierkommode, die; (with kneehole) Frisiertoilette, die

dress: ~ **length** n.: Stoffstück, das für ein Kleid ausreicht; ~**maker** n. ▸ ❶ p. 1260 Damenschneider, der/-schneiderin, die; ~**making** n. Damenschneiderei, die; ~ **rehearsal** n. (lit. or fig.) Generalprobe, die; ~ **sense** n. **she hasn't much ~ sense** sie hat nicht viel Sinn für Mode; ~ **'shirt** n. Smokinghemd, das; ~ **shop** n. Geschäft für Damenbekleidung; Kleiderladen, der (ugs.); ~ **'suit** n. Abendanzug, der; ~ **uniform** n. (Mil.) Paradeuniform, die

dressy /'dresɪ/ adj. **1** **be ~** ‹Person:› immer schick angezogen sein **2** (smart) fein, elegant ‹Kleidung› **3** (grand, formal) vornehm ‹Veranstaltung›

drew ▸ **draw A, B**

dribble /'drɪbl/

A v.i. **1** (trickle) tropfen **2** (slobber) ‹Baby:› sabbern **3** (Sport) dribbeln

B v.t. **1** ‹Baby:› kleckern **2** (Sport) dribbeln mit ‹Ball›

C n. (trickle) Tröpfeln, das

driblet /'drɪblɪt/ n. Tropfen, der; **in** or **by ~s** in kleinen Mengen; kleckerweise (ugs.)

dribs n. pl. ~ **and drabs** /drɪbz n 'dræbz/ kleine Mengen; **in ~ and drabs** kleckerweise (ugs.)

dried /draɪd/ adj. getrocknet; ~ **fruit[s]** Dörr- od. Backobst, das; ~ **milk/egg/meat** Trockenmilch, die od. Milchpulver, das/Trockenei od. Eipulver, das/Trockenfleisch, das

drier¹ ▸ **dry A**

drier² /'draɪə(r)/ n. (for hair) Trockenhaube, die; (hand-held) Föhn, der; Haartrockner, der; (for laundry) [Wäsche]trockner, der

driest ▸ **dry A**

drift /drɪft/

A n. **1** (flow, steady movement) Wanderung, die **2** (fig.: trend, shift, tendency) Tendenz, die **3** (flow of air or water) Strömung, die; **the North Atlantic D~**: der Nordatlantische Strom **4** (Naut., Aeronaut.: deviation from course) Abdrift, die (fachspr.); Abweichung vom Sollkurs **5** (Motor Veh.: controlled slide) Driften, das **6** (wind-propelled mass) (of snow or sand) Verwehung, die; (of leaves) zusammengewehter Haufen **7** (fig.: gist, import) das Wesentliche; **get** or **catch the ~ of sth.** etw. im Wesentlichen verstehen; **I don't get your ~**: ich kann Ihnen nicht ganz folgen od. verstehe nicht ganz, worauf Sie hinauswollen **8** (Geol.: deposits) Geschiebe, das; **glacial ~**: [Glazial]geschiebe, das

B v.i. **1** (be borne by current; fig.: move passively or aimlessly) treiben; ‹Wolke:› ziehen; ~ **out to sea** aufs Meer hinaustreiben; ~ **off course** abtreiben; vom Kurs abgelenkt werden; **come ~ing along** angetrieben kommen; **the mist ~ed away** der Nebel verwehte; **the smoke ~ed to the east** der Rauch zog nach Osten ab; **his thoughts ~ed** er schweifte mit seinen Gedanken ab; **let things ~**: die Dinge treiben lassen; den Dingen ihren Lauf lassen; ~ **along** (fig.) sich treiben lassen; ~ **into crime** in die Kriminalität [ab]driften; ~ **into unconsciousness** in Bewusstlosigkeit versinken; **months ~ed by** die Monate vergingen **2** (coll.: come or go casually) ~ **in** hereinschneien (ugs.); ~ **out** abziehen (ugs.); ~ **in at 1 a. m.** um ein Uhr nachts eintrudeln (ugs.) **3** (form ~s) zusammengeweht werden; ~**ing sand** Treibsand, der

Phrasal verb

- ~ **a'part** v.i. sich (Dat.) fremd werden; (in marriage) sich auseinander leben

drifter /'drɪftə(r)/ n. **1** (Naut.) Drifter, der **2** (person) jmd., der sich treiben lässt; (vagrant) Gammler, der (ugs.); **be a ~**: sich treiben lassen

drift: ~ **ice** n. Treibeis, das; ~ **net** n. Treibnetz, das; ~**wood** n. Treibholz, das

drill¹ /drɪl/

A n. **1** (tool) Bohrer, der; (Dent.) Bohrinstrument, das; (Metalw.) Drillbohrer, der; (Carpentry, Building) Bohrmaschine, die **2** (Mil.: training) Drill, der **3** (Educ.; also fig.) Übung, die; **lifeboat ~**: Rettungsbootübung, die **4** (Brit. coll.: agreed procedure) Prozedur, die; **know the ~**: wissen, wie es gemacht wird; **what's the ~?** wie wird das gemacht?

B v.t. **1** (bore) bohren ‹Loch, Brunnen›; an-, ausbohren ‹Zahn›; ~ **sth.** (right through) etw. durchbohren **2** (Mil.: instruct) drillen **3** (Educ.; also fig.) ~ **sb. in sth.**, ~ **sth. into sb.** mit jmdm. etw. systematisch einüben; jmdm. etw. eindrillen (ugs.) od. (abwertend) einpauken

C v.i. **1** (bore) bohren (**for** nach); ~ **deep/50 ft. into the ground** tief/15 m tief bohren; **finish ~ing** die Bohrung/Bohrungen beenden; ~ **down a long way** tief bohren; ~ **through sth.** etw. durchbohren **2** (Mil.) exerzieren

drill² n. (Agric.) **1** (furrow) Saatrille, die **2** (machine) Drillmaschine, die

drill³ n. (Textiles) Drillich, der

drill: ~ **bit** n. Bohrer, der; ~ **chuck** n. Bohrfutter, das ~ **core** n. Bohrkern, der

drilling/'drɪlɪŋ/: ~ **platform** n. Bohrturmplattform, die; ~ **rig** n. Bohrturm, der; (in offshore ~) Bohrinsel, die

drily /'draɪlɪ/ adv. (fig.) **1** (coldly) kühl **2** (with dry humour) trocken; **sb. is ~ humorous** jmd. hat einen trockenen Humor

drink /drɪŋk/

A n. **1** (type of liquid) Getränk; das; (class of liquids) Getränke Pl.; **many different sorts of ~s** viele verschiedene Getränke **2** (quantity of liquid) Getränk, das; **have a ~** [etwas] trinken; **would you like a ~ of milk?** möchten Sie etwas Milch [trinken]?; **take a long ~ from sth.** einen großen Schluck aus etwas nehmen; **give sb. a ~ [of fruit juice]** jmdm. etwas [Fruchtsaft] zu trinken geben **3** (glass of alcoholic liquor) Glas, das; (not with food) Drink, der; Glas, das; Gläschen, das; **have a ~** ein Glas trinken; **let's have a ~!** trinken wir einen!; **she likes a ~ now and then** hin und wieder trinkt sie ganz gern einen od. ein Glas; **I think we all need a ~!** ich glaube, wir können alle einen vertragen (ugs.); **he has had a few ~s** er hat einige getrunken (ugs.) **4** no pl., no art. (intoxicating liquor) Alkohol, der; **[strong] ~** scharfe od. hochprozentige Getränke; **in ~, the worse for ~** betrunken; **take to ~** zu trinken anfangen; ~ **was his ruin** der Alkohol war sein Verderben; **the ~ problem** der Alkoholismus od. Alkoholmissbrauch; **have a ~ problem** Probleme mit [dem] Alkohol haben; **drive sb. to ~** jmdn. zum Trinker werden lassen **5** (coll.: sea) **the drink** der große Bach (Flieger-, Seemannsspr.)

B v.t., **drank** /dræŋk/, **drunk** /drʌŋk/ **1** trinken ‹Kaffee, Glas Milch, Flasche Whisky›; ~ **down** or **off [in one gulp]** [in einem od. auf einen Zug] austrinken **2** (absorb) ‹Pflanze, poröses

Material:) aufsaugen; **the car ~s petrol** (fig.) das Auto schluckt viel Benzin 3) **~ oneself to death** sich zu Tode trinken; **~ sb. under the table** jmdn. unter den Tisch trinken

C *v.i.*, **drank, drunk** trinken; **~ from a bottle** aus einer Flasche trinken; **~ of sth.** (literary) von etw. trinken; **~[ing and] driving** Alkohol am Steuer; **~ and drive** unter Alkoholeinfluss fahren; **~ to sb./sth.** auf jmdn./etw. trinken; **I'll ~ to that** (coll.) dem kann ich nur zustimmen; *see also* **fish A 1**

d

(Phrasal verbs)

- **~ 'in** *v.t.* 1) (readily take in) einsaugen (*Luft, fig.: Schönheit*); (*Pflanze:*) aufsaugen (*Wasser*) 2) (absorb eagerly) begierig aufnehmen (*Worte, Geschichten*)
- **~ 'up** *v.t. & i.* austrinken; (*Pflanze:*) aufsaugen

drinkable /'drɪŋkəbl/ *adj.* 1) (suitable for drinking) trinkbar (*Wasser*) 2) (pleasant to drink) trinkbar (ugs.) (*Wein*)

drink: ~-'driver *n.* (Brit.) alkoholisierter Autofahrer/alkoholisierte Autofahrerin; **~-driving** *n., no pl.* Fahren unter Alkoholeinfluss; Alkohol am Steuer; *attrib.* **drink-driving offence** Alkoholdelikt, *das*

drinker /'drɪŋkə(r)/ *n.* Trinker, *der*/Trinkerin, *die*

drinkie /'drɪŋkɪ/ *n.* (coll.) was zu trinken (ugs.); **have ~s** trinken

drinking /'drɪŋkɪŋ/: **~ bout** *n.* Trinkgelage, *das;* **~ chocolate** *n., no pl.* (Brit.) Trinkschokolade, *die;* **~ fountain** *n.* Trinkbrunnen, *der;* **~ glass** *n.* Glas, *das;* **~ song** *n.* Trinklied, *das;* **~-'up time** *n.* (Brit.) *Zeit zwischen Ende des Ausschanks und der Schließung der Gaststätte (meist 10 Minuten);* **~ vessel** ▸ **vessel 1**; **~ water** *n.* Trinkwasser, *das*

drinks: ~ cabinet *n.* Hausbar, *die;* **~ dispenser** *n.* Getränkeautomat, *der;* **~ machine** *n.* Getränkeautomat, *der;* **~ party** *n.* Trinkgelage, *das;* Saufparty, *die* (ugs.)

drip /drɪp/

A *v.i.*, **-pp-** 1) tropfen; (overflow in drops) triefen; **be ~ping with water/moisture** triefend nass sein; **the windows were ~ping with condensation** an den Fenstern lief Kondenswasser herunter; **~ off/down sth.** von etw. [herunter]tropfen 2) (fig.) **be ~ping with** überladen sein mit (*Schmuck*); überlaufen vor (+ *Dat.*) (*Gefühlen*); triefen von *od.* vor (*Ironie, Sentimentalität usw.*)

B *v.t.*, **-pp-** tropfen lassen

C *n.* 1) (act) Tropfen, *das* 2) (liquid) Tropfen, *der* 3) (Med.) Tropfinfusion, *die;* **the patient was on a ~:** der Patient hing am Tropf 4) (coll.: feeble, spineless person) Schlappschwanz, *der* (salopp abwertend)

drip: ~-dry (Textiles) **A** /'-'-/ *v.i.* knitterfrei trocknen; **B** /'--/ *adj.* bügelfrei; schnell trocknend; **~-feed** *v.t.* (Med.) durch parenterale Tropfinfusion ernähren

dripping /'drɪpɪŋ/

A *adj.* tropfend (*Wasserhahn*); **~ bathing costumes** tropfnasse Badeanzüge

B *adv.* **~ wet** tropf- *od.* (ugs.) patsch- *od.* (ugs.) klitschnass

C *n.* 1) Tropfen, *das* 2) (Cookery) Schmalz, *das;* **bread and ~:** Schmalzbrot, *das*

drive /draɪv/

A *n.* 1) (trip) Fahrt, *die;* **take sb. for a ~:** jmdn. *od.* mit jmdm. spazieren fahren

2) (distance travelled) [Auto]fahrt, *die;* **a ~ of 40 kilometres, a 40-kilometre ~:** eine [Auto-]fahrt von 40 Kilometern; **a nine-hour ~, a ~ of nine hours** eine neunstündige Autofahrt; **within an hour's ~ of sth.** keine Autostunde von etw. entfernt; **be an hour's ~ from sth.** eine Autostunde von etw. entfernt sein; **have a long ~ to work** eine lange Anfahrt zur Arbeit haben

3) (street) Straße, *die*

4) (private road) Zufahrt, *die;* (entrance) (to small building) Einfahrt, *die;* (to large building) Auffahrt, *die*

5) (energy to achieve) Tatkraft, *die;* **a salesman with ~:** ein dynamischer Vertreter

6) (Commerc., Polit., etc.: vigorous campaign) Aktion, *die;* Kampagne, *die;* **export/sales/recruiting/charity ~:** Export-/Verkaufs-/Anwerbe-/Wohltätigkeitskampagne, *die*

7) (Mil.: offensive) Vorstoß, *der*

8) (Psych.) Trieb, *der*

9) (Motor Veh.: position of steering wheel) **left-hand/right-hand ~:** Links-/Rechtssteuerung *od.* -lenkung, *die;* **be left-hand ~:** Linkssteuerung haben; ein Linkslenker sein (Kfz-W.)

10) (Motor Veh., Mech. Engin.: transmission of power) Antrieb, *der;* **belt/front-wheel/rear-wheel ~:** Riemen-/Front-/Heckantrieb, *der;* **fluid ~:** hydraulische Kupplung

11) (Computing) Laufwerk, *das*

12) (Cards etc.) **whist/bridge ~:** Whist-/Bridgerunde mit vielen Teilnehmern

13) (Sport) Drive, *der* (fachspr.); Treibschlag, *der*

B *v.t.*, **drove** /drəʊv/, **driven** /'drɪvn/ 1) fahren (*Auto, Lkw, Route, Strecke, Fahrgast*); lenken (*Kutsche, Streitwagen*); treiben (*Tier*); führen (*Pflug*); **this is a nice car to ~/this car is easy to ~:** dieses Auto fährt sich gut/leicht; **~ a carriage** *or* **coach and four through** (fig.) zerfetzen (fig.); zunichte machen (*Argumentation*)

2) (as job) **~ a lorry/train** Lkw-Fahrer/Lokomotivführer sein

3) (compel to move) vertreiben; **~ sb. out of** *or* **from a place/country** jmdn. von einem Ort/aus einem Land vertreiben; **~ sb. out of** *or* **from the house** jmdn. aus dem Haus jagen

4) (chase, urge on) treiben (*Vieh, Wild*)

5) (fig.) **~ sb. to sth.** jmdn. zu etw. treiben; **~ sb. to do sth.** *or* **into doing sth.** jmdn. dazu treiben, etw. zu tun; **~ sb. to suicide** jmdn. zum *od.* in den Selbstmord treiben; **~ sb. out of his mind** *or* **wits** jmdn. in den Wahnsinn treiben *od.* um den Verstand bringen

6) (*Wind, Wasser:*) treiben; **be ~n off course** abgetrieben werden

7) (cause to penetrate) **~ sth. into sth.** etw. in etw. (*Akk.*) treiben; **~ sth. into sb.'s head** (fig.) jmdm. etw. einbläuen *od.* einhämmern (ugs.)

8) (power) antreiben (*Mühle, Maschine*); **be steam-~n** *or* **~n by steam** dampfgetrieben sein; **be ~n by electricity** [einen] Elektroantrieb haben

9) (incite to action) antreiben; **he was hard ~n** er wurde hart herangenommen; **be ~n by ambition** von Ehrgeiz getrieben werden

10) (overwork) **~ oneself [too] hard** sich [zu sehr] schinden

11) (transact) **~ a good bargain** ein gutes Geschäft machen; *see also* **hard A 1**

C *v.i.*, **drove, driven** 1) (conduct motor vehicle) fahren; **in Great Britain we ~ on the left** bei uns in Großbritannien ist Linksverkehr; **he ~s to see her every weekend** er besucht sie jedes Wochenende mit dem Auto; **~ at 30 mph** mit 50 km/h fahren; **learn to ~:** [Auto-]fahren lernen; den Führerschein machen (ugs.); **can you ~?** kannst du Auto fahren?; **~ past** vorbeifahren; **~ into a bollard/the back of a lorry** gegen einen Poller fahren/auf einen Lastwagen fahren

2) (travel) mit dem [eigenen] Auto fahren

3) (rush, dash violently) (*Hagelkörner, Wellen:*) schlagen; **clouds were driving across the sky** Wolken jagten über den Himmel

(Phrasal verbs)

- **~ at** *v.t.* hinauswollen auf (+ *Akk.*); **what are you driving at?** worauf wollen Sie hinaus?
- **~ a'way**

A *v.i.* wegfahren.

- **~ at** *v.t.* hinauswollen auf (+ *Akk.*); **what are you driving at?** worauf wollen Sie hinaus?
- **~ a'way**

A *v.i.* wegfahren

B *v.t.* 1) wegfahren, wegbringen (*Ladung, Fahrzeug*); (chase away) wegjagen 2) (fig.) zerstreuen (*Bedenken, Befürchtungen, Verdacht*)

- **~ 'back** *v.t.* (force to retreat) zurückschlagen (*Eindringlinge*); **be ~n back on doing sth.** (fig.) keine andere Wahl haben, als etw. zu tun
- **~ 'off**

A *v.i.* 1) wegfahren 2) (Golf) abschlagen

B *v.t.* (repel) zurückschlagen (*Angreifer*)

- **~ 'on**

A *v.i.* weiterfahren

B *v.t.* (impel) treiben (**to** zu)

- **~ 'out** *v.t.* 1) hinauswerfen (*Person*); hinausjagen (*Hund*); hinausblasen (*Luft*) 2) (fig.) vertreiben (*Sorgen*); austreiben (*bösen Geist*)
- **~ 'up**

A *v.i.* vorfahren (**to** vor + *Dat.*); **she drove up to the starting line** sie fuhr an die Startlinie heran

B *v.t.* hochtreiben (*Kosten*)

drive: ~ belt *n.* (Mech. Engin.) Treibriemen, *der;* **~-by** (Amer.), **~-by shooting** *ns.* Schießen aus einem fahrenden Auto; **be killed in a ~-by [shooting]** aus einem fahrenden Auto heraus erschossen werden; **~-in** *adj.* Drive-in-; **~-in bank** Bank mit Autoschalter; **~-in cinema** *or* (Amer.) **movie [theater]** Autokino, *das*

drivel /'drɪvl/

A *n.* Gefasel, *das* (ugs. abwertend); **talk ~:** faseln (ugs. abwertend)

B *v.i.*, (Brit.) **-ll-** 1) (talk stupidly) faseln (ugs. abwertend) 2) (slaver) geifern

driven ▸ **drive B, C**

'drive-on *adj.* **~ car ferry** Autofährschiff, *das*

driver /'draɪvə(r)/ *n.* 1) Fahrer, *der*/Fahrerin, *die;* Führer, *der* (Amtsspr.); (of locomotive) Führer, *der*/Führerin, *die;* (of horse-drawn carriage) Kutscher, *der*/Kutscherin, *die;* **be in the ~'s seat** (fig.) das Steuer *od.* die Zügel in der Hand haben (fig.) 2) (Golf) Driver, *der* (fachspr.); Holz 1, *das* 3) (Computing) Treiber, *der*

driverless /'draɪvəlɪs/ *adj.* führerlos

'driver's license (Amer.) ▸ **driving licence**

drive: ~shaft *n.* Antriebswelle, *die;* **~-time** *n. attrib.* (*Sender, Sendung*) für Autofahrer im Berufsverkehr; **~way** ▸ **drive A 4**

'drive-through *adj.* **~ restaurant** Drive-in-Restaurant, *das;* **~ bank** Bank mit Autoschalter; **~ carwash** Autowaschstraße, *die*

driving /'draɪvɪŋ/

A *n., no pl.* Fahren, *das;* **his ~ is awful** er fährt furchtbar

B *adj.* 1) **~ rain** peitschender Regen 2) (fig.) treibend; **~ ambition** brennender Ehrgeiz

driving: ~ force *n.* treibende Kraft; Triebfeder, *die;* **the ~ force behind sth.** die treibende Kraft hinter etw.; **~ gloves** *n. pl.* Autohandschuhe; **~ instructor** *n.* ▸ **i p. 1260** Fahrlehrer, *der*/-lehrerin, *die;* **~ lesson** *n.* Fahrstunde, *die;* **[take] ~ lessons** Fahrunterricht [nehmen]; **~ licence** *n.* Führerschein, *der;* **~ mirror** *n.* Rückspiegel, *der;* **~ range** *n.* (Golf) Drivingrange, *das;* **~ school** *n.* Fahrschule, *die;* **~ seat** *n.* 1) Fahrersitz, *der;* 2) **be in the ~ seat = be in the driver's seat** ▸ **driver 1**; **~ test** *n.* Fahrprüfung, *die;* **take/pass/fail one's ~ test** die Fahrprüfung ablegen/bestehen/nicht bestehen; **~ wheel** *n.* Treibrad, *das*

drizzle /'drɪzl/

A *n.* Sprühregen, *der;* Nieseln, *das;* **there was light ~:** es hat leicht genieselt

B *v.i.* **it's drizzling** es nieselt; **drizzling rain** Nieselregen, *der*

droll /drəʊl/ *adj.* 1) (amusing) drollig 2) (odd) komisch

dromedary /'drɒmɪdərɪ, 'drʌmɪdərɪ/ *n.* (Zool.) Dromedar, *das*

drone /drəʊn/

A *n.* 1) (of bees, flies) Summen, *das;* (of machine) Brummen, *das* 2) (derog.: monotonous tone of speech) Geleier, *das* 3) (Zool.: bee; Aeronaut.) Drohne, *die;* (fig.: idler) Müßiggänger, *der* 4) (of bagpipe) Bordunpfeife, *die*

B *v.i.* 1) (buzz, hum) (*Biene:*) summen; (*Maschine:*) brummen 2) (derog.: monotonously) (*Rezitator:*) leiern; (*Rede, Predigt:*) in einförmigem Tonfall vorgetragen werden

C *v.t.* leiern

drool /dru:l/ *v.i.* 1) (show excessive delight) **~ over sb./sth.** eine kindische Freude an jmdm./etw. haben 2) (slaver) geifern

droop /dru:p/

A *v.i.* 1) herunterhängen; (*Blume:*) den Kopf hängen lassen; (*Stiel:*) sich beugen, sich biegen; **his shoulders ~:** seine Schultern hängen; **her head ~ed forwards** ihr Kopf sank nach vorn; **his eyelids were ~ing** ihm fielen die Augen zu; **the dog's tail ~ed** der Hund ließ den Schwanz hängen 2) (fig.: flag) (*Mut, Moral:*) sinken; (*Mensch:*) ermatten

B *v.t.* [herunter]hängen lassen

drop /drɒp/

A *n.* **1** (of liquid) Tropfen, *der;* **~s of rain/dew/blood/sweat** Regen-/Tau-/Bluts-/Schweißtropfen; **~ by ~,** in **~s** tropfenweise; **be a ~ in the ocean** *or* **in the** *or* **a bucket** (fig.) ein Tropfen auf einen heißen Stein sein

2 (fig.: small amount) **[just] a ~:** [nur] ein kleiner Tropfen; **a ~ too much** (of flavouring etc.) eine Idee zu viel

3 (fig. coll.: of alcohol) Gläschen, *das;* **have had a ~ too much** ein Glas über den Durst getrunken haben (ugs.); **take a ~:** sich *(Dat.)* einen genehmigen (ugs.); **that's a nice ~ of beer/wine** das ist ein feines Bierchen/Weinchen (ugs.)

4 *in pl.* (Med.) Tropfen *Pl.*

5 (sweet) Drops, *der*

6 (vertical distance) **there was a ~ of 50 metres from the roof to the ground below** vom Dach bis zum Boden waren es 50 Meter

7 (abrupt descent of land) plötzlicher Abfall; Absturz, *der;* **there was a sheer** *or* **steep ~ of some 500 ft.** das Gelände fiel etwa 150 m steil ab

8 (Aeronaut.) (of men) Absetzen, *das;* (of supplies) Abwurf, *der*

9 (fig.: decrease) Rückgang, *der;* **~ in temperature/prices/outgoings** Temperatur-/ Preis-/ Ausgabenrückgang, *der;* **a ~ in the price of coffee/in house prices** ein Preisrückgang bei Kaffee/bei Häusern; **a ~ in the cost of living** ein Sinken der Lebenshaltungskosten; **a ~ in salary/wages/income** eine Gehalts-/Lohn-/ Einkommensminderung; **a ~ in value** eine Wertminderung; ein Wertverlust; **a ~ in atmospheric pressure/the voltage/power output** (Phys.) ein Druck-/Spannungs-/Leistungsabfall; **a ~ in crime** ein Rückgang der Kriminalität; **a ~ in turnover/sales/production** ein Umsatz-/Absatz-/Produktionsrückgang

10 (coll.: advantage) **get** *or* **have the ~ on sb.** jmdm. zuvorkommen

11 (pendant, hanging ornament) Gehänge, *das;* (of earring) Ohrgehänge, *das*

12 (underworld sl.: hiding place) Versteck, *das. See also* **hat 2**

B *v.i.,* **-pp- 1** (fall) (accidentally) [herunter]fallen; (deliberately) sich [hinunter]fallen lassen; (have abrupt descent) abstürzen (**to** zu); **~ out of** *or* **from sb.'s hand** jmdm. aus der Hand fallen; **let sth. ~:** etw. fallen lassen

2 (sink to ground) ‹*Person:*› fallen; **~ to the ground** umfallen; zu Boden fallen; **~ like flies** wie die Fliegen umfallen; **~ [down] dead** tot umfallen; **~ dead!** (coll.) scher dich zum Teufel!; **~ into bed/an armchair** ins Bett/in einen Sessel sinken; **be fit** *or* **ready to ~** (coll.) zum Umfallen *od.* Umsinken müde sein; **~ on** *or* **to one's knees** auf die Knie fallen

3 (in amount etc.) sinken; ‹*[An]zahl:*› abnehmen, sinken; ‹*Preis, Wert, Verkaufsziffern:*› sinken, fallen; ‹*Wind:*› abflauen, sich legen; ‹*Stimme:*› sich senken; ‹*Kinnlade:*› herunterfallen *od.* -klappen; **the record has ~ped a place/to third place** die Schallplatte ist um einen Platz/auf Platz drei gefallen

4 (move, go) **~ down stream** [sich] stromabwärts treiben [lassen]; **~ back** (Sport) zurückfallen; **~ behind in one's work** mit seiner Arbeit in Rückstand geraten; **~ behind schedule** hinter dem Zeitplan zurückbleiben; **~ astern** (Naut.) achteraus sacken

5 (fall in ~s) ‹*Flüssigkeit:*› tropfen (**from** aus)

6 (pass into some condition) **~ [back] into one's old routine** in den alten Trott verfallen *od.* zurückfallen; **~ into the habit** *or* **way of doing sth.** die Gewohnheit annehmen *od.* sich *(Dat.)* angewöhnen, etw. zu tun; **~ into a dialect** in einen Dialekt fallen

7 (cease) **the affair was allowed to ~:** man ließ die Angelegenheit auf sich *(Dat.)* beruhen; **and there the matter ~ped** und dabei blieb es

8 **let ~:** beiläufig erwähnen ‹*Termin, Tatsache, Absicht*›; fallen lassen ‹*Bemerkung*›; **let [it] ~ that/when ...:** beiläufig erwähnen, dass/wann ...

C *v.t.,* **-pp- 1** (let fall) fallen lassen; abwerfen ‹*Bomben, Flugblätter, Nachschub*›; absetzen ‹*Fallschirmjäger, Truppen*›; **~ a letter in the letter box** einen Brief einwerfen *od.* in den Briefkasten stecken; **~ the curtain** (Theatre) den Vorhang herablassen; **~ the latch on the door** den Türriegel vorlegen

2 (by mistake) fallen lassen; **she ~ped crumbs on the floor/juice on the table** ihr fielen Krümel auf den Boden/tropfte Saft auf den Tisch; **he ~ped the glass/ball** ihm fiel das Glas/der Ball herunter

3 (let fall in drops) tropfen

4 (utter casually) fallen lassen ‹*Namen*›; **~ a hint** eine Anspielung machen; **~ a word in sb.'s ear [about sth.]** einmal mit jmdm. [über etw.] sprechen

5 (send casually) **~ sb. a note** *or* **line** jmdm. [ein paar Zeilen] schreiben; **~ sb. a postcard** jmdm. eine Karte schreiben

6 (set down, unload from car) absetzen ‹*Mitfahrer, Fahrgast*›; (from ship) an Land gehen lassen; (from aircraft) von Bord gehen lassen

7 (omit) (in writing) auslassen; (in speech) nicht aussprechen; **~ one's h's** das h [im Anlaut] nicht aussprechen; **~ a subject from the syllabus/a name from a list** ein Fach aus dem Lehrplan/einen Namen von einer Liste streichen

8 (discontinue, abandon) fallen lassen ‹*Plan, Thema, Schlagzeile, Anklage*›; einstellen ‹*Untersuchung, Ermittlungen*›; ablegen ‹*Titel*›; absetzen ‹*Fernsehsendung*›; beiseite lassen ‹*Formalitäten*›; aufgeben, Schluss machen mit ‹*Verstellung, Heuchelei*›; **~ it!** lass das!; **~ everything!, ~ whatever you're doing!** lass alles stehen und liegen!; **shall we ~ the subject?** lassen Sie uns [lieber] das Thema wechseln; **~ a case** (Law) einen Fall zu den Akten legen

9 (stop associating with) fallen lassen ‹*Freund, Freundin*›; (exclude) **~ sb. from a team** jmdn. aus einer Mannschaft nehmen; **~ sb. from a committee** jmdn. aus einem Ausschuss entlassen

10 **~ one's voice** die Stimme senken

11 (lower) tiefer hängen ‹*Lampe*›; auslassen ‹*Rocksaum*›; **~ped handlebars** Rennlenker, *der*

12 (knock down, fell) zu Boden strecken

13 (lose by gambling or in business) verlieren

Phrasal verbs

- **~ a'way** *v.i.* ‹*Mitgliedschaft, Einnahmen:*› sinken; ‹*Gelände:*› abfallen
- **~ by**

A /'-'-/ *v.i.* vorbeikommen

B /'--/ *v.t.* **~ by sb.'s house** bei jmdm. vorbeigehen *od.* hereinschauen

- **~ 'in**

A *v.t.* (deliver) vorbeibringen

B *v.i.* **1** hineinfallen **2** (visit) hereinschauen; vorbeikommen; **~ in on sb.** *or* **at sb.'s house** bei jmdm. hereinschauen; **~ in for a pint** auf ein Bier vorbeikommen

- **~ 'off**

A *v.i.* **1** (fall off) abfallen; (become detached) abgehen **2** (fall asleep) einnicken **3** (decrease) ‹*Teilnahme, Geschäft:*› zurückgehen; ‹*Unterstützung, Interesse:*› nachlassen; ‹*Absatz:*› rückläufig sein

B *v.t.* **1** (fall off) abfallen von; **~ off a truck** von einem Lkw herunterfallen **2** (set down) absetzen ‹*Fahrgast*›; **the ship ~ped off the cargo** das Schiff hat seine Ladung gelöscht; **~ a package/the shopping off at sb.'s house** ein Paket/die Einkäufe bei jmdm. vorbeibringen

- **~ 'out** *v.i.* **1** (fall out) herausfallen (**of** aus); **your teeth will ~ out** Ihnen werden die Zähne ausfallen **2** (withdraw beforehand) seine Teilnahme absagen; (withdraw while in progress) aussteigen (ugs.) (**of** aus); (abandon sth.) ausscheiden (**of** aus); (disappear from one's place in a series or group) ausfallen; **~ out of the bidding** aussteigen (ugs.); nicht mehr mitbieten **3** (cease to take part) aussteigen (ugs.) (**of** aus); ‹*Student:*› das Studium abbrechen *od.* aufgeben; **~ out of university/the course** das Studium abbrechen *od.* aufgeben; **~ out [of society]** aussteigen (ugs.) **4** (be omitted) aus-, weggelassen werden (**of** aus). *See also* **~out**
- **~ 'round** *v.i.* vorbeikommen

drop: ~-dead *adv.* (coll.) umwerfend (ugs.) ‹*schön*›; unverschämt (ugs.) ‹*gut aussehen*›; **~-down menu** *n.* (Computing) Dropdown-Menü, *das;* **~-forging** *n.* (Metalw.) Gesenkschmieden, *das;* **~ handlebars** *n. pl.* Rennlenker, *der;* **~head** *n.* (Brit. Motor Veh.) Klappverdeck, *das;* (vehicle) Kabriolett, *das;* **~-in centre** *n.* (*jedermann zugängliche, auch Rat und Hilfe anbietende*) Begegnungsstätte; **~ kick** *n.* (Football) Dropkick, *der;* (Rugby) Sprungtritt, *der;* **~-leaf table** *n.* Klapptisch, *der*

droplet /'drɒplɪt/ *n.* Tröpfchen, *das*

'dropout *n.* (coll.) **1** (act of withdrawing) Aussteigen, *das* (ugs.); (from expedition or trip) Ausfall, *der;* Rücktritt, *der;* **the ~ rate** die Aussteigerquote; (among students or trainees) die Zahl der Abbrecher **2** (person) (from college etc.) Abbrecher, *der*/Abbrecherin, *die;* (from society) Aussteiger, *der*/Aussteigerin, *die* (ugs.)

dropped kerb *n.* (Brit.) Bordsteinabsenkung, *die*

dropper /'drɒpə(r)/ *n.* (esp. Med.) Tropfer, *der;* Guttiole, *die* (fachspr.)

droppings /'drɒpɪŋz/ *n. pl.* Mist, *der;* (of horse) Pferdeäpfel *Pl.;* (of cattle) Kuhfladen *Pl.*

drop: ~ shipment *n.* Direktversand, *der;* Direktlieferung, *die;* **~ shot** *n.* (Tennis etc.) Stoppball, *der*

dropsy /'drɒpsɪ/ *n.* Wassersucht, *die*

dross /drɒs/ *n.* **1** Abfall, *der* **2** (Metallurgy) Gekrätz, *das* **3** (fig.) Tand, *der* (geh. veralt.); **human ~** (derog.) Abschaum, *der* (abwertend)

drought /draʊt/ (*Amer., Scot., Ir./poet.:* **drouth** /draʊθ/) *n.* **1** Dürre, *die;* **a period of ~:** eine Dürreperiode **2** (fig.: shortage) Mangel, *der* (**of** an + *Dat.*)

drove[1] ▸ **drive B, C**

drove[2] /drəʊv/ *n.* **1** (herd) Herde, *die* **2** *usu. in pl.* (fig.: of people) Schar, *die;* **in ~s** scharenweise; in Scharen

drover /'drəʊvə(r)/ *n.* Viehtreiber, *der*

drown /draʊn/

A *v.i.* ertrinken

B *v.t.* **1** ertränken; **be ~ed** ertrinken **2** (fig.) **~ one's sorrows [in liquor]** seine Sorgen [im Alkohol] ertränken **3** (submerge, flood) überfluten; überschwemmen; verwässern ‹*Whisky, Brandy*›; **~ed valley** (Geog.) überflutetes Tal; Ria[s]tal, *das* **4** (make inaudible) übertönen ‹*Geräusch, Musik*›. *See also* **rat A 1**

Phrasal verb

- **~ 'out** *v.t.* (make inaudible) übertönen; niederschreien ‹*Redner*›

drowse /draʊz/ *v.i.* [vor sich hin]dösen; **~ off** eindösen; einnicken

drowsily /'draʊzɪlɪ/ *adv.* (while falling asleep) schläfrig; (on just waking) verschlafen

drowsiness /'draʊzɪnɪs/ *n., no pl.* Schläfrigkeit, *die;* **cause ~:** müde *od.* schläfrig machen

drowsy /'draʊzɪ/ *adj.* **1** (half asleep) schläfrig; (on just waking) verschlafen; **feel ~:** sich schläfrig fühlen **2** (soporific) einschläfernd

drub /drʌb/ *v.t.,* **-bb-** (thrash) verprügeln; verdreschen (ugs.); (beat in fight) schlagen

drubbing /'drʌbɪŋ/ *n.* **1** (thrashing) Tracht Prügel, *die* **2** (fig.) Niederlage, *die*

drudge /drʌdʒ/

A *n.* Schwerarbeiter, *der* (fig.); Kuli, *der* (ugs. abwertend)

B *v.i.* schuften; sich abplacken

drudgery /'drʌdʒərɪ/ *n.* Schufterei, *die;* Plackerei, *die*

drug /drʌg/

A *n.* **1** (Med., Pharm.) Medikament, *das;* [Arznei]mittel, *das;* (as ingredient) Mittel, *das;* **this patient is on ~s** dieser Patient muss Medikamente nehmen **2** (narcotic, opiate, etc.) Droge, *die;* Rauschgift, *das;* **take ~s** Drogen *od.* Rauschgift nehmen; **be on ~s** [regelmäßig] Drogen *od.* Rauschgift nehmen **3** (Commerc. fig.) **a ~ on the market** unverkäufliche Ware; ein Ladenhüter (ugs.)

B *v.t.,* **-gg- 1** (administer ~ to) **he was ~ged and kidnapped** er wurde betäubt und entführt **2** (add ~ to) **~ sb.'s food/drink** jmds. Essen/Getränk *(Dat.)* ein Betäubungsmittel beimischen

drug: ~ **abuse** *n.* Drogenmissbrauch, *der;* ~ **abuser** *n.* Drogenmissbrauch Treibender/Treibende; ~ **addict** *n.* Drogen- *od.* Rauschgiftsüchtige, *der/die;* ~ **addiction** *n.* Drogen- *od.* Rauschgiftsucht, *die;* ~ **culture** *n., no pl.* Drogenkultur, *die;* ~ **dealer** *n.* Drogenhändler, *der*/-händlerin, *die;* Dealer, *der*/Dealerin, *die* (Drogenjargon)

druggist /ˈdrʌgɪst/ *n.* ▸❶ **p. 1260** Drogist, *der*/Drogistin, *die*

drug: ~ **habit** *n.* regelmäßiger Drogenkonsum; **have a** ~ **habit** drogensüchtig *od.* drogenabhängig sein; [gewohnheitsmäßig] Drogen nehmen; ~ **peddler** ▸ **drug dealer**; ~ **offence** *n.* Drogendelikt, *das;* ~ **pusher** *n.* Pusher, *der* (Drogenjargon); Drogen- *od.* Rauschgifthändler, *der;* ~ **raid** *n.* Drogenrazzia, *die;* ~**-related** *adj.* Drogen‹*tote, -kriminalität, -delikt, -probleme*›; ~ **ring**, *n.* Drogenring, *der;* Rauschgiftring, *der;* ~ **runner**, *n.* Drogenschmuggler, *der*/-schmugglerin, *die;* ~ **scene**, *n.* Drogenszene, *die*

drugs charges *n. pl.* Anklage wegen eines Drogendelikts

ˈdrug smuggler ▸ **ˈdrug runner**

drugs: ~ **offence** ▸ **drug offence**; ~ **raid** ▸ **drug raid**; ~ **ring** ▸ **drug ring**; ~ **scene** ▸ **drug scene**; ~ **test** ▸ **drug test**

drug: ~**store** *n.* (Amer.) Drugstore, *der;* ~**-taking** *n., no pl.* Drogeneinnahme, *die;* ~ **test** *n.* Drogentest, *der;* (in Sport) Dopingtest, *der* ~ **trafficker** *n.* Dealer, *der*/Dealerin, *die;* Drogenhändler, *der*/-händlerin, *die;* ~ **trafficking** *n., no pl.* Drogenhandel, *der*

Druid /ˈdru:ɪd/ *n.* Druide, *der*

drum /drʌm/

A *n.* **1** Trommel, *die* **2** *in pl.* (in jazz or pop) Schlagzeug, *das;* (section of band etc.) Trommeln *Pl.* **3** (sound) Trommeln, *das* **4** (Anat.) ▸**eardrum** **5** (container for oil etc.) Fass, *das;* ~ **of paint** Farbenhobbock, *der*

B *v.i.,* **-mm-** trommeln

C *v.t.,* **-mm-:** ~ **one's fingers on the desk** mit den Fingern auf den Tisch trommeln

Phrasal verbs

- ~ **into** *v.t.* ~ **sth. into sb.** jmdm. etw. einhämmern (ugs.) *od.* einbläuen (ugs.)
- ~ **ˈout** *v.t.* (Mil.) ~ **sb. out** jmdn. austrommeln (veralt.); (fig.) jmdn. [mit Schimpf und Schande] ausstoßen; **he was** ~**med out of town** er wurde aus der Stadt gejagt
- ~ **ˈup** *v.t.* (Mil.) zusammentrommeln; (fig.) auftreiben ‹*Kunden, Unterstützung*›; erwecken ‹*Enthusiasmus*›; zusammentrommeln (ugs.) ‹*Helfer, Anhänger*›; anbahnen ‹*Geschäfte*›

drum: ~**beat** *n.* Trommelschlag, *der;* ~ **brake** *n.* Trommelbremse, *die;* ~**fire** *n.* (Mil.; also fig.) Trommelfeuer, *das;* ~**head** *n.* **1** (Mus.) [Trommel]fell, *das;* **2** *attrib.* ~**head court martial** Standgericht, *das;* ~ **kit** *n.* Schlagzeug, *das*

drumlin /ˈdrʌmlɪn/ *n.* (Geol.) Drumlin, *der*

drum: ~ **machine** *n.* Drum-Machine, *die;* ~ **ˈmajor** *n.* (Mil.) Tambourmajor, *der;* ~ **majoˈrette** *n.* Tambourmajorette, *die*

drummer /ˈdrʌmə(r)/ *n.* ▸❶ **p. 1260** **1** Schlagzeuger, *der* **2** (Amer.: sales representative) Vertreter, *der*/Vertreterin, *die*

drum: ~ **roll** *n.* Trommelwirbel, *der;* ~**stick** *n.* **1** (Mus.) Trommelschlägel, *der;* **2** (of fowl) Keule, *die;* Schlegel, *der* (südd., österr., schweiz.)

drunk /drʌŋk/

A ▸**drink B, C**

B *adj.* **be** ~: betrunken sein; **be half** ~: angetrunken sein; **get** ~ **[on gin]** [von Gin] betrunken werden; (intentionally) sich [mit Gin] betrinken; **get sb.** ~: jmdn. betrunken machen; **be** ~ **as a lord** (coll.) voll wie eine Haubitze sein (ugs.); ~ **in charge [of a vehicle]** betrunken am Steuer

C *n.* Betrunkene, *der/die*

drunkard /ˈdrʌŋkəd/ *n.* Trinker, *der*/Trinkerin, *die;* Säufer, *der*/Säuferin, *die* (derb abwertend)

drunken /ˈdrʌŋkn/ *attrib. adj.* **1** betrunken; besoffen (derb); (habitually drunk) ständig besoffen **2** **a** ~ **brawl** *or* **fight** eine Schlägerei zwischen Betrunkenen; **in a** ~ **stupor** im Vollrausch; ~ **driving** Trunkenheit am Steuer

drunkenly /ˈdrʌŋkənlɪ/ *adv.* [wie] betrunken

drunkenness /ˈdrʌŋknnɪs/ *n., no pl.* **1** (temporary) Betrunkenheit, *die* **2** (habitual) Trunksucht, *die*

drupe /dru:p/ *n.* (Bot.) Steinfrucht, *die*

Druze /dru:z/ *n.* Druse, *der*/Drusin, *die*

dry /draɪ/

A *adj.,* **drier** /ˈdraɪə(r)/, **driest** /ˈdraɪɪst/ **1** trocken; trocken, (very dry) herb ‹*Wein*›; ausgetrocknet ‹*Fluss, Flussbett*›; **get** *or* **become** ~: trocken werden; trocknen; ~ **bread** trocken[es] Brot; **go** ~: austrocknen; **my throat is** *or* **feels** ~: meine Kehle ist wie ausgetrocknet; ~ **work** Arbeit, die durstig macht; **as** ~ **as a bone** völlig trocken; **there wasn't a** ~ **eye in the house** da blieb kein Auge trocken; **store sth. in a** ~ **place** etw. trocken lagern **2** (not using liquid) Trocken-; ~ **shave/shampoo** Trockenrasur, *die*/-shampoo, *das* **3** (not rainy) trocken ‹*Wetter, Klima*› **4** (coll.: thirsty) durstig; **I'm a bit** ~: ich habe eine trockene Kehle **5** **go** ~ ‹*Flüssigkeit:*› verdunsten; ‹*Suppe usw.:*› verkochen **6** (not yielding) ausgetrocknet, versiegt ‹*Brunnen*› **7** (teetotal) **go** ~: das Alkoholverbot *od.* die Prohibition einführen **8** (fig.) trocken ‹*Humor*›; (impassive, cold) kühl ‹*Art, Bemerkung usw.*› **9** (fig.: meagre, bare) nüchtern ‹*Fakten, Dankesworte*›; nackt ‹*Tatsachen*›; (dull) trocken ‹*Stoff, Bericht, Vorlesung*›; **be as** ~ **as dust** sterbenslangweilig *od.* (ugs.) stinklangweilig sein

B *n.* **1** **give it a good** ~: trockne es gut ab **2** (place) **in the** ~: im Trock[e]nen

C *v.t.* **1** trocknen ‹*Haare, Wäsche*›; abtrocknen ‹*Geschirr, Baby*›; ~ **oneself** sich abtrocknen; ~ **one's eyes** *or* **tears/hands** sich (*Dat.*) die Tränen abwischen/die Hände abtrocknen **2** (preserve) trocknen ‹*Kräuter, Holz, Blumen*›; dörren ‹*Obst, Fleisch*›

D *v.i.* trocknen; trocken werden; ~ **hard on sth.** ‹*Schlamm:*› an etw. (*Dat.*) an- *od.* festtrocknen

Phrasal verbs

- ~ **ˈout**

A *v.t.* **1** trocknen **2** einer Entziehungskur unterziehen ‹*Alkoholiker, Drogenabhängigen*›; trockenlegen (ugs.) ‹*Alkoholiker*›; ausnüchtern ‹*Betrunkenen*›

B *v.i.* **1** trocknen **2** ‹*Alkoholiker, Drogenabhängiger:*› eine Entziehung[skur] machen; ‹*Alkoholiker:*› trocken werden (ugs.); ‹*Betrunkener:*› ausnüchtern

- ~ **ˈup**

A *v.t.* **1** abtrocknen ‹*Geschirr*› **2** austrocknen ‹*Fluss, Teich*›; versiegen lassen ‹*Brunnen*›

B *v.i.* **1** (~ the dishes) abtrocknen; *see also* **drying-up** **2** ‹*Brunnen, Quelle:*› versiegen; ‹*Fluss, Teich:*› austrocknen; **a dried-up person** ein vertrockneter Typ **3** (fig.) ‹*Initiative, Ideen, Erfindergeist:*› versiegen; ‹*Renten, Ersparnisse:*› schrumpfen **4** (be unable to continue) stecken bleiben **5** (coll.: stop talking) ~ **up!** halt die Klappe! (ugs.); hör auf zu sülzen! (salopp)

dryad /ˈdraɪæd/ *n.* (Mythol.) Dryade, *die*

dry: ~ **ˈbattery** *n.* (Electr.) Trockenbatterie, *die;* ~ **ˈcell** *n.* (Electr.) Trockenelement, *das;* ~**-ˈclean** *v.t.* chemisch reinigen; **have sth.** ~**-cleaned** etw. in die Reinigung geben; **'**~**-clean only'** „chemisch reinigen"; ~**-ˈcleaners** *n. pl.* chemische Reinigung; ~**-ˈcleaning** *n.* chemische Reinigung; ~ **ˈdock** *n.* Trockendock, *das*

dryer ▸**drier²**

dry: ~**-eyed** *adj.* ohne Rührung; ~ **goods** *n. pl.* (Commerc.) Textilwaren *Pl.;* Kurzwaren *Pl.;* ~ **ˈice** *n.* Trockeneis, *das*

drying/ˈdraɪɪŋ/: ~ **cupboard** *n.* Wäschetrockenschrank, *der;* ~**-ˈup** *n.* Abtrocknen, *das;* **do the** ~**-up** abtrocknen; *attrib.* ~**-up cloth** Geschirrtuch, *das*

dry ˈland *n.* Festland, *das;* **be back on** ~: wieder festen Boden unter den Füßen haben

dryly ▸**drily**

dry: ~ **ˈmass** *n.* Trockenmasse, *die;* ~ **ˈmeasure** *n.* Trocken[hohl]maß, *das*

dryness /ˈdraɪnɪs/ *n., no pl.* **1** Trockenheit, *die* **2** (fig.: coldness) Kühle, *die* **3** (fig.: of humour) Trockenheit, *die* **4** (fig.: dullness) Trockenheit, *die;* Langweiligkeit, *die*

dry: ~ **ˈrot** *n.* **1** Trockenfäule, *die;* **2** (fungi) Polyparus, *der* (fachspr.); Hausschwamm, *der;* Holzschwamm, *der;* ~ **ˈrun** *n.* (coll.) Probelauf, *der;* ~ **season** *n.* Trockenzeit, *die;* Trockenperiode, *die;* ~**-shave** *v.i.* sich trocken rasieren; ~ **shaver** *n.* Trockenrasierer, *der;* ~ **ˈski slope** *n.* Trockenskihang, *der;* ~**stone** *adj.* ~**stone wall** Trockensteinmauer, *die;* ~**suit** *n.* Trockenanzug, *der;* ~**-weather tyre** *n.* Trokenreifen, *der*

DSc /di:esˈsi:/ *abbr.* = **Doctor of Science** Dr. rer. nat.; *see also* **BSc**

DTD *abbr.* (Computing) = **document type definition** DTD, *die*

DTI *abbr.* (Brit.) = **Department of Trade and Industry**

DTs /di: ˈti:z/ *n. pl.* (coll.) Delirium, *das;* **have the** ~: [vom Trinken] das Zittern haben (ugs.)

DU *abbr.* = **depleted uranium**

dual /dju:əl/ *adj.* **1** doppelt; Doppel-; ~ **status/role/function** Doppelstatus, *der*/-rolle, *die*/-funktion, *die* **2** (Psych.) ~ **personality** gespaltene Persönlichkeit

dual: ~ **ˈcarriageway** *n.* (Brit.) Straße mit Mittelstreifen; ~ **conˈtrol** *n.* (Aeronaut.) Doppelsteuerung, *die;* (Motor Veh.) doppelte Bedienungselemente *Pl.*

dualism /ˈdju:əlɪzm/ *n.* (Philos., Theol.) Dualismus, *der*

duality /dju:ˈælɪtɪ/ *n.* Dualität, *die*

dual: ~**-purpose** *adj.* zweifach verwendbar; ~**-use** *adj.* (Amer.) Dual-Use-‹*Technologie, Ausrüstung etc.*›

dub¹ /dʌb/ *v.t.,* **-bb-** (Cinemat.) synchronisieren

dub² *v.t.,* **-bb-** **1** ~ **sb. [a] knight** jmdn. zum Ritter schlagen **2** (call, nickname) titulieren

dub³ *n.* (Amer. coll.: novice) Flasche, *die* (ugs.)

dub⁴ *n., no pl.* (Mus.) Dub, *der*

dubbin /ˈdʌbɪn/ *n.* Lederfett, *das*

dubious /ˈdju:bɪəs/ *adj.* **1** (doubting) unschlüssig; **feel** ~ **of sb.'s honesty** an jmds. Ehrlichkeit (*Dat.*) zweifeln; **I'm** ~ **about accepting the invitation** ich weiß nicht recht, ob ich die Einladung annehmen soll **2** (suspicious) dubios; zweifelhaft **3** (questionable) zweifelhaft; fragwürdig **4** (of doubtful result) ungewiss **5** (unreliable) zweifelhaft

dubiously /ˈdju:bɪəslɪ/ *adv.* **1** (doubtingly) unschlüssig **2** (suspiciously) dubios

ducal /ˈdju:kl/ *adj.* herzoglich; Herzogs‹*titel, -krone*›

duchess /ˈdʌtʃɪs/ *n.* ▸❶ **p. 1634** Herzogin, *die*

duchy /ˈdʌtʃɪ/ *n.* Herzogtum, *das*

duck¹ /dʌk/

A *n.* **1** *pl.* ~**s** *or* (*collect.*) *same* (Ornith.; as food) Ente, *die;* **wild** ~: Wildente, *die;* **toy** ~: Schwimmente, *die;* Spielzeugente, *die;* **can a** ~ **swim?** (iron.) und ob!; **it was [like] water off a** ~**'s back** (fig.) das lief alles an ihm/ihr *usw.* ab; **take to sth. like a** ~ **to water** bei etw. gleich in seinem Element sein; **fine weather for** ~**s** (joc./iron.) bei dem Wetter könnte man Flossen gebrauchen (scherzh.); **play [at]** ~**s and drakes** [flache] Steine über die Wasseroberfläche springen lassen; titschern; **play** ~**s and drakes with, make** ~**s and drakes of** (fig.) verschwenden; durchbringen ‹*Ersparnisse, Vermögen*›; zum Fenster hinauswerfen ‹*Geld*› **2** (Brit. coll.: dear) **[my]** ~: Schätzchen **3** (Cricket) **be out for a** ~: ohne einen Punkt zu machen aus sein; **break one's** ~: den ersten Punkt holen. *See also* **dead duck**; **lame duck**

B *v.i.* **1** (bend down) sich [schnell] ducken; ~ **[down] [out of sight]** sich ducken, um nicht gesehen zu werden **2** (under water) tauchen **3** (coll.: move hastily) türmen (ugs.)

C *v.t.* **1** ~ **sb. [in water]** jmdn. untertauchen; jmdn. tunken (landsch.) **2** ~ **one's head** den Kopf einziehen **3** (fig. coll.: evade) ausweichen ‹*einer Frage, einem Problem*›

Phrasal verb

- ~ **ˈout** *v.i.* (coll.) ~ **out [of sth.]** sich [vor etw. (*Dat.*)] drücken (ugs.); [vor etw. (*Dat.*)] kneifen (ugs. abwertend)

duck² *n.* (Textiles) Segeltuch, *das*

duck: ~bill, **~-billed 'platypus** ▸ **platypus**; **~boards** *n. pl.* Lattenrost, *der;* **~ egg** *n.* Entenei, *das;* **~-egg 'blue** *n.* zartes Blaugrau

duckie /'dʌkɪ/ ▸ **duck¹ A 2**

ducking /'dʌkɪŋ/ *n.* (immersion) [Ein-, Unter]tauchen, *das;* **give sb. a ~:** jmdn. untertauchen; jmdn. tunken (landsch.)

'ducking stool *n.* (Hist.) Tauchstuhl, *der*

duckling /'dʌklɪŋ/ *n.* Entenküken, *das;* (as food) junge Ente; *see also* **ugly 1**

'duck pond *n.* Ententeich, *der*

ducks /dʌks/ ▸ **duck¹ A 2**

'duckweed *n.* (Bot.) Wasserlinse, *die;* Entengrütze, *die*

duct /dʌkt/

A *n.* **1** (for fluid, gas, cable) [Rohr]leitung, *die;* Rohr, *das;* (for air) Ventil, *das* **2** (Anat.) Gang, *der;* **hepatic/cystic/acoustic ~:** Leber-/Gallenblasen-/Gehörgang, *der;* **spermatic ~:** Samenleiter, *der;* **tear ~:** Tränenkanal, *der* **3** (Bot.) Gang, *der;* Kanal, *der*

B *v.t.* leiten

ductile /'dʌktaɪl/ *adj.* dehnbar, (fachspr.) duktil ‹*Metall*›

ducting /'dʌktɪŋ/ *n.* Leitungssystem, *das*

dud /dʌd/ (coll.)

A *n.* **1** (useless thing) Niete, *die* (ugs.); (counterfeit) Fälschung, *die;* (banknote) Blüte, *die* (ugs.); (failure) Reinfall, *der* (ugs.); (Cards) Lusche, *die* (ugs.); **this battery/lightbulb/watch/ballpoint is a ~:** diese Batterie/Glühlampe/Uhr/dieser Kugelschreiber taugt nichts; **that cheque was a ~:** der Scheck war faul (ugs.) **2** (bomb etc.) Blindgänger, *der* **3** (ineffectual person) Niete, *die* (ugs.); Versager, *der*

B *adj.* **1** mies (ugs.); schlecht; (fake) gefälscht; geplatzt ‹*Scheck*›; **a ~ banknote** eine Blüte (ugs.) **2** **a ~ bullet/shell/bomb** ein Blindgänger

dude /dju:d, du:d/ *n.* (esp. Amer. coll.) **1** (dandy) feiner Pinkel aus der Stadt (ugs.) **2** (fellow, guy) Typ, *der* (ugs.)

'dude ranch *n.* (Amer.) Ferienranch, *die*

dudgeon /'dʌdʒn/ *n.* **in high ~:** äußerst empört

due /dju:/

A *adj.* **1** (owed) geschuldet; zustehend ‹*Eigentum, Recht usw.*›; **the share/reward ~ to him** der ihm zustehende Anteil/die ihm zustehende Belohnung; der Anteil, der/die Belohnung, die ihm zusteht; **the amount ~:** der zu zahlende Betrag; **there's sth. ~ to me, I've got sth. ~, I'm ~ for sth.** mir steht etw. zu **2** (immediately payable, lit. or fig.) fällig; **be more than ~** (fig.) überfällig sein **3** (that it is proper to give) gebührend, geziemend (geh.); erforderlich ‹*Hilfe*›; entsprechend ‹*Ermutigung*›; angemessen ‹*Belohnung*›; **be ~ to sb.** jmdm. gebühren; **recognition ~ to sb.** Anerkennung, die jmdm. gebührt; **respect ~ from sb. to sb.** Respekt, den jmd. jmdm. schuldet; **with all ~ respect, madam** bei allem gebotenen Respekt, meine Dame; **with ~ allowance** *or* **regard** unter gebührender Berücksichtigung (**for** *Gen.*) **4** (that it is proper to use) gebührend, geziemend (geh.); reiflich ‹*Überlegung*›; **with ~ caution/care** mit der nötigen Vorsicht/Sorgfalt; **they were given ~ warning** sie wurden hinreichend gewarnt; **in ~ time** rechtzeitig; **~ process of law** ordentliches Gerichtsverfahren **5** (attributable) **~ to negligence** aufgrund von Nachlässigkeit; **the mistake was ~ to negligence** der Fehler war durch Nachlässigkeit verursacht; **the discovery is ~ to Newton** die Entdeckung ist Newton (*Dat.*) zu verdanken; **it's ~ to her that we missed the train** ihretwegen verpassten wir den Zug; es lag an ihr, dass wir den Zug verpassten; **his death was ~ to a heart attack** Ursache seines Todes war ein Herzanfall; **the difficulty is ~ to our ignorance** die Schwierigkeit ergibt sich aus unserer Unwissenheit; **be ~ to the fact that ...:** darauf zurückzuführen sein, dass ... **6** (scheduled, expected, under engagement or instructions) **be ~ to do sth.** etw. tun sollen; **I'm ~** (my plan is) **to leave tomorrow** ich werde morgen abfahren; **be ~ [to arrive]** ankommen sollen; **the train is now ~:** der Zug müsste jetzt planmäßig ankommen; **when are we ~ to land/dock?** wann landen wir/laufen wir ein?; **I'm ~ in Paris tonight** ich muss heute Abend in Paris sein; **the baby is ~ in two weeks' time** das Baby kommt in zwei Wochen **7** (likely to get, deserving) **be ~ for sth.** etw. verdienen; **he is ~ for promotion** seine Beförderung ist fällig. *See also* **course A 3**

B *adv.* **1** ▸ **i p. 1013** **~ north** genau nach Norden; **~ north wind** Wind direkt von Norden; **the town is ~ north of us** die Stadt liegt genau nördlich von uns **2** **~ to** aufgrund (+ *Gen.*)

C *n.* **1** *in pl.* (debt) Schulden *Pl.*; **pay one's ~s** seine Schulden bezahlen **2** *no pl.* (fig.: just deserts, reward) **sb.'s ~:** das, was jmdm. zusteht; das, was jmdm. gebührt (geh.); **that was no more than his ~:** das hatte er auch verdient; das stand ihm auch zu; **give sb. his ~:** jmdm. Gerechtigkeit widerfahren lassen; **but to give him** *or* **the Devil his ~ he ...:** aber das muss man ihm lassen, er ... **3** *usu. in pl.* (fee) Gebühr, *die;* (toll) Zoll, *der;* **membership ~s** Mitgliedsbeiträge *Pl.*

duel /'dju:əl/

A *n.* **1** Duell, *das;* (Univ.) Mensur, *die;* **fight a ~:** ein Duell/eine Mensur austragen **2** (fig.: contest) Kampf, *der;* **~ of wits** geistiger Wettstreit; **~ of words** Wortgefecht, *das;* Rededuell, *das;* **propaganda ~:** Propagandagefecht, *das*

B *v.i.*, (Brit.) **-ll-** sich duellieren; (Univ.) eine Mensur austragen *od.* schlagen

duet /dju:'et/ *n.* (Mus.) (for voices) Duett, *das;* (instrumental) Duo, *das*

duettist /dju:'etɪst/ *n.* [Duett]partner, *der*/[Duett]partnerin, *die*

duff /dʌf/ *adj.* (Brit. coll.) mies (ugs.)

duffel bag, duffel coat ▸ **duffle bag, duffle coat**

duffer /'dʌfə(r)/ *n.* Trottel, *der* (ugs. abwertend); **be a ~ at football/school** im Fußball/in der Schule eine Niete sein (ugs.)

duffle/'dʌfl/: **~ bag** *n.* Matchbeutel, *der;* (waterproof, also) Seesack, *der;* **~ coat** *n.* Dufflecoat, *der*

dug ▸ **dig A, B**

'dugout *n.* **1** (canoe) Einbaum, *der* **2** (Mil.: shelter) Unterstand, *der*

duke /dju:k/ *n.* **1** ▸ **i p. 1634** Herzog, *der;* **royal ~:** Herzog und Mitglied des Königshauses **2** *in pl.* (coll.: fists) Flossen *Pl.* (salopp); **put up your ~s** Fäuste hoch! (salopp)

dukedom /'dju:kdəm/ *n.* **1** (territory) Herzogtum, *das* **2** (rank) Herzogswürde, *die*

dulcet /'dʌlsɪt/ *adj.* lieblich; **sb.'s ~ tones** (iron.) jmds. zarte Stimme (iron.)

dulcimer /'dʌlsɪmə(r)/ *n.* (Mus.) Hackbrett, *das;* Zimbal, *das*

dull /dʌl/

A *adj.* **1** (stupid) beschränkt; (slow to understand) begriffsstutzig (abwertend) **2** (boring) langweilig; stumpfsinnig ‹*Arbeit, Routine*›; nichts sagend ‹*Eindruck*› **3** (gloomy) trübe ‹*Wetter, Tag*› **4** (not bright) matt, stumpf ‹*Farbe, Glanz, Licht, Metall*›; trübe ‹*Augen*›; blind ‹*Spiegel*›; (not sharp) dumpf ‹*Geräusch, Aufprall, Schmerz, Gefühl*› **5** (not keen) unscharf; schwach ‹*Augen, Gehör*›; **grow ~** ‹*Geisteskräfte*:› nachlassen **6** (sluggish) träge **7** (listless) lustlos; (dejected) niedergeschlagen; bedrückt **8** (blunt) stumpf **9** (Commerc.) flau. *See also* **ditchwater**

B *v.t.* **1** (make less acute) schwächen; trüben; betäuben ‹*Schmerz*› **2** (make less bright or sharp) stumpf werden lassen; verblassen lassen ‹*Farbe*› **3** (blunt) stumpf machen **4** (fig.) dämpfen ‹*Freude, Enthusiasmus*›; abstumpfen ‹*Geist, Sinne, Verstand, Vorstellungskraft*›; lindern ‹*Kummer, Hass*›; **~ the edge of sth.** (fig.) einer Sache (*Dat.*) ihren Reiz nehmen

dullard /'dʌləd/ *n.* Dummkopf, *der* (ugs.)

dullness /'dʌlnɪs/ *n.*, *no pl.* **1** (stupidity) Beschränktheit, *die;* (slow-wittedness) Begriffsstutzigkeit, *die* (abwertend); [geistige] Trägheit **2** (boringness) Langweiligkeit, *die;* (of work, life, routine) Stumpfsinn, *der* **3** (of weather) Trübheit, *die* **4** (of colour, light, metal) Stumpfheit, *die;* Mattheit, *die* **5** (of sight, hearing etc.) Schwächung, *die;* (of sight, mind, senses) Trübung, *die* **6** (sluggishness) Trägheit, *die*

dull-witted /dʌl'wɪtɪd/ ▸ **dull A 1**

dully /'dʌllɪ/ *adv.* **1** (dimly, indistinctly) trübe ‹*scheinen*›; dumpf ‹*fühlen, aufprallen, tönen, schmerzen*›; **his arm was aching ~:** er spürte einen dumpfen Schmerz im Arm **2** (sluggishly) träge **3** (listlessly) lustlos; (dejectedly) niedergeschlagen; bedrückt

duly /'dju:lɪ/ *adv.* **1** (rightly, properly) ordnungsgemäß **2** (sufficiently) ausreichend; hinreichend; **he was ~ punished** er wurde gehörig bestraft **3** (punctually) pünktlich

dumb /dʌm/

A *adj.*, **~er** /'dʌmə(r)/, **~est** /'dʌmɪst/ **1** stumm; **a ~ person** ein Stummer/eine Stumme; **~ animals** *or* **creatures** die Tiere; die stumme Kreatur (dichter.); **~ friend** vierbeiniger Freund **2** (temporarily speechless) stumm; **he was [struck] ~ with fright/amazement** vor Furcht/Staunen verschlug es ihm die Sprache **3** (inarticulate) sprachlos ‹*Massen, Millionen*›; (saying nothing) stumm; schweigend **4** (coll.: stupid) doof (ugs.); **act ~:** sich dumm stellen (ugs.); **a ~ blonde** eine dümmliche Blondine (ugs.)

B *n. pl.* **the ~:** die Stummen; **the deaf and ~:** die Taubstummen

Phrasal verb

• **~ down** *v.t. & i.* (coll.) verflachen

'dumb-bell *n.* **1** Hantel, *die* **2** (coll.: stupid person) Dummkopf, *der* (ugs.); Dümmling, *der* (ugs.)

dumbfound /dʌm'faʊnd/ *v.t.* sprachlos machen; verblüffen

dumbfounded /dʌm'faʊndɪd/ *adj.* sprachlos; verblüfft; **be ~:** sprachlos sein

dumbly /'dʌmlɪ/ *adv.* stumm

dumb: ~ show *n.* **in ~ show** durch Mimik; **~ 'waiter** *n.* **1** (trolley) stummer Diener; **2** (lift) Speisenaufzug, *der*

dumdum /'dʌmdʌm/ *n.* **~ [bullet]** Dumdum[geschoss], *das*

dummy /'dʌmɪ/

A *n.* **1** (of tailor) Schneiderpuppe, *die;* (in shop) Modepuppe, *die;* Schaufensterpuppe, *die;* (of ventriloquist) Puppe, *die;* (figurehead, person acting for another) Strohmann, *der;* (stupid person) Dummkopf, *der* (ugs.); Doofi, *der* (ugs.); **like a stuffed ~:** wie ein Ölgötze (ugs.) **2** (imitation) Attrappe, *die;* Dummy, *der;* (Commerc.) Schaupackung, *die* **3** (esp. Brit.: for baby) Schnuller, *der* **4** (Bridge etc.) (person) Strohmann, *der;* (hand) Tisch, *der* **5** (Rugby coll.) **sell sb. the** *or* **a ~:** jmdn. antäuschen

B *attrib. adj.* unecht; blind ‹*Tür, Fenster*›; Übungs- (Mil.); **~ gun** Gewehrattrappe, *die;* **~ run** Probelauf, *der*

dump /dʌmp/

A *n.* **1** (place) Müllkippe, *die;* (heap) Müllhaufen, *der;* (permanent) Müllhalde, *die* **2** (Mil.) Depot, *das;* Lager, *das* **3** (coll. derog.: unpleasant place) Schweinestall, *der* (derb abwertend); Dreckloch, *das* (salopp abwertend); (boring town) Kaff, *das* (ugs. abwertend); Nest, *das* (ugs. abwertend)

B *v.t.* **1** (dispose of) werfen; (deposit) abladen, kippen ‹*Sand, Müll usw.*›; (leave) lassen; (place) abstellen **2** (Commerc.: send abroad) zu Dumpingpreisen verkaufen **3** (fig. coll.: abandon) abladen (ugs.)

dumper /'dʌmpə(r)/ *n.* **~ truck** Kipper, *der*

dumping /'dʌmpɪŋ/ *n.* **1** [Schutt]abladen, *das;* **'no ~ [of refuse]'** „Schuttabladen verboten" **2** (Commerc.: sending abroad) Dumping, *das*

'dumping ground *n.* Müllkippe, *die;* Schuttabladeplatz, *der;* (fig.) Abstellplatz, *der*

dumpling /'dʌmplɪŋ/ *n.* **1** (Gastr.) Kloß, *der;* **apple ~:** Apfel im Schlafrock **2** (coll.: short, plump person) Tönnchen, *das* (ugs.)

dumps /dʌmps/ *n. pl.* (coll.) **be** *or* **feel [down] in the ~:** ganz down sein (ugs.)

'dump truck *n.* Kipper, *der*

dumpy /'dʌmpɪ/ *adj.* pummelig (ugs.)

dun¹ /dʌn/

A *adj.* graubraun

B *n.* Graubraun, *das*

d

d

dun² *v.t.*, **-nn-** (demand money due from) [Geld] anmahnen bei; **~ sb. for sth.** bei jmdm. etw. anmahnen

dunce /dʌns/ *n.* Null, *die* (ugs. abwertend); Niete, *die* (ugs. abwertend); **the ~ of the class** das Schlusslicht der Klasse (ugs.); **~'s cap** (Hist.) Spotthut, *der* (*für schlechte Schüler*)

dunderhead /ˈdʌndəhed/ *n.* Schwachkopf, *der* (ugs. abwertend)

dune /dju:n/ *n.* Düne, *die*

dung /dʌŋ/
A *n.* Dung, *der;* Mist, *der*
B *v.t.* mit Mist düngen

dungaree /dʌŋgəˈri:/ *n.* **1** (fabric) grober Kattun **2** *in pl.* (garment) Latzhose, *die;* **a pair of ~s** eine Latzhose

ˈdung beetle *n.* Mistkäfer, *der*

dungeon /ˈdʌndʒn/ *n.* Kerker, *der;* Verlies, *das*

ˈdunghill *n.* Misthaufen, *der*

dunk /dʌŋk/ *v.t.* **1** tunken; stippen (bes. nordd.) **2** (immerse) tauchen

Dunkirk /dʌnˈkɜ:k/ *pr. n.* ▸ⓘ **p. 1643** Dünkirchen (*das*); **~ spirit** Durchhaltevermögen, *das*

dunlin /ˈdʌnlɪn/ *n.* (Ornith.) Alpenstrandläufer, *der*

dunnock /ˈdʌnək/ *n.* (Ornith.) Heckenbraunelle, *die*

duo /ˈdju:əʊ/ *n., pl.* **~s** **1** (Theatre) Paar, *das;* **comedy ~:** Komikerpaar, *das* **2** (Mus.) Duo, *das* **3** (coll.: couple) Duo, *das* (oft iron.); **an odd ~:** ein komisches Gespann (ugs.)

duodecimal /dju:əˈdesɪml/ *adj.* duodezimal; Duodezimal‹*system*›

duodenal /dju:əˈdi:nl/ *adj.* (Anat.) duodenal (fachspr.); Zwölffingerdarm-

duodenal ˈulcer *n.* ▸ⓘ **p. 1231** (Med.) Zwölffingerdarmgeschwür, *das*

duodenum /dju:əˈdi:nəm/ *n.* (Anat.) Duodenum, *das* (fachspr.); Zwölffingerdarm, *der*

dupe /dju:p/
A *v.t.* düpieren (geh.); übertölpeln; **be ~d [into doing sth.]** sich übertölpeln lassen [und etw. tun]; **be ~d into believing sth.** auf etw. (*Akk.*) hereinfallen
B *n.* Düpierte, *der/die* (geh.); Dumme, *der/die;* Gelackmeierte, *der/die* (salopp scherzh.)

duple /ˈdju:pl/ *adj.* **~ time** (Mus.) gerader Takt

duplex /ˈdju:pleks/
A *adj.* **1** (twofold) doppelt; zweifach **2** (esp. Amer.: two-storey) zweistöckig ‹*Wohnung*› **3** (esp. Amer.: two-family) Zweifamilien‹*haus*›
B *n.* (esp. Amer.) zweistöckige Wohnung

duplicate
A /ˈdju:plɪkət/ *adj.* **1** (identical) Zweit-; **~ key** Nach- *od.* Zweitschlüssel, *der;* **~ copy** Zweit- *od.* Abschrift, *die;* Doppel, *das* **2** (twofold) doppelt **3** (Cards) **~ bridge/whist** *Form des Bridge/Whists, bei der das Spiel mit derselben Verteilung der Karten, aber mit anderen Spielern wiederholt wird*
B *n.* **1** Kopie, *die;* (second copy of letter/document/key) Duplikat, *das* **2** **prepare/complete sth. in ~:** etw. in doppelter Ausfertigung machen/ausfüllen; **make sth. in ~:** etw. doppelt anfertigen **3** (Cards) **= ~ bridge** *etc.;* ▸**A 3**
C /ˈdju:plɪkeɪt/ *v.t.* **1** (make a copy of, make in ~) **~ sth.** eine zweite Anfertigung von etw. machen; etw. nachmachen (ugs.); **they have tried to ~ his results** sie haben versucht, zu denselben Ergebnissen wie er zu kommen **2** (be exact copy of) genau gleichen (+ *Dat.*) **3** (on machine) vervielfältigen **4** (unnecessarily) [unnötigerweise] noch einmal tun

duplicating /ˈdju:plɪkeɪtɪŋ/: **~ machine** ▸**duplicator**; **~ paper** *n.* (Printing) Vervielfältigungspapier, *das*

duplication /dju:plɪˈkeɪʃn/ *n.* **1** Wiederholung, *die* **2** (on machine) Vervielfältigung, *die* **3** (unnecessary) [unnötige] Wiederholung; **avoid unnecessary ~!** vermeiden Sie unnötige Wiederholungen!; **~ of effort** doppelte Arbeit

duplicator /ˈdju:plɪkeɪtə(r)/ *n.* (Printing) Vervielfältigungsgerät, *das*

duplicitous /dju:ˈplɪsɪtəs/ *adj.* unaufrichtig

duplicity /dju:ˈplɪsɪtɪ/ *n.* Falschheit, *die*

durability /djʊərəˈbɪlɪtɪ/ *n., no pl.* **1** (permanence) (of friendship, peace, etc.) Dauerhaftigkeit, *die;* (of person) Unverwüstlichkeit, *die* **2** (resistance to wear or decay) (of garment, material) Haltbarkeit, die; Strapazierfähigkeit, *die;* (of metal, rock, component) Widerstandsfähigkeit, *die*

durable /ˈdjʊərəbl/
A *adj.* **1** (lasting) dauerhaft ‹*Friede, Freundschaft usw.*› **2** (resisting wear or decay) solide; strapazierfähig, haltbar ‹*Kleidung, Stoff*›; widerstandsfähig ‹*Metall, Fels, Bauelement*›; **~ goods** ▸**B**
B *n. in pl.* (Econ.) **consumer ~s** langlebige *od.* dauerhafte Konsumgüter

duration /djʊəˈreɪʃn/ *n.* Dauer, *die;* **be of short/long ~:** von kurzer/langer Dauer sein; **the courses are of three years' ~:** die Kurse dauern drei Jahre; **for the ~ of sth.** für die Dauer *od.* während [der Dauer] einer Sache (*Gen.*); **for the ~** (of war) auf Kriegsdauer; **I'm afraid we're here for the ~** (fig. coll.) wir werden wohl bis zum Ende ausharren müssen, fürchte ich

duress /djʊəˈres, ˈdjʊəres/ *n., no pl.* Zwang, *der;* **under ~:** unter Zwang

during /ˈdjʊərɪŋ/ *prep.* während; (at a point in) in (+ *Dat.*); **~ the rehearsal/wedding ceremony** während *od.* bei der Probe/Trauung; **~ the night** während *od.* in der Nacht; **~ the journey** während *od.* auf der Reise

durn /dɜ:n/, **durned** /dɜ:nd/ (Amer.) ▸**darn², darned**

dusk /dʌsk/ *n.* (twilight) [Abend]dämmerung, *die;* Einbruch der Dunkelheit; **at/after/until ~:** bei/nach/bis zum Einbruch der Dunkelheit

dusky /ˈdʌskɪ/ *adj.* (dark-coloured) dunkel; dunkelhäutig ‹*Person, Schönheit*›; **a ~ blue/red** ein dunkles Blau/Rot

dust /dʌst/
A *n., no pl.* **1** Staub, *der;* (pollen) Blütenstaub, *der;* **be covered in ~** ‹*Erde:*› staubbedeckt sein; ‹*Gegenstände:*› eingestaubt *od.* verstaubt sein; **the ~ of ages** der Staub der Jahrhunderte; **make a great deal of ~:** sehr stauben; **throw ~ in sb.'s eyes** (fig.) jmdm. Sand in die Augen streuen; **shake the ~ off one's feet** (fig.) den Staub von den Füßen schütteln (geh.); **turn to ~ and ashes** Staub werden; (fig.) zunichte werden; **wait till the ~ has settled** (fig.) warten, bis sich die Wogen geglättet haben; **you couldn't see him for ~** (fig.) man konnte nur noch seine Staubwolke sehen **2** (~ing) Staubwischen, *das;* **give sth. a ~:** den Staub von etw. abwischen; etw. abstauben. *See also* **bite A**; **raise A 2**
B *v.t.* **1** (clear of ~) abstauben ‹*Möbel*›; **~ a room/house** in einem Zimmer/Haus Staub wischen; **the house/the furniture needs ~ing** *or* **to be ~ed** in dem Haus muss Staub gewischt werden/die Möbel müssen abgestaubt werden **2** (sprinkle; also Cookery) **~ sth. with sth.** etw. mit etw. bestäuben; (with talc etc.) etw. mit etw. pudern; (with grated material) etw. mit etw. bestreuen; **~ sth. over** *or* **on [to] sth.** (using powder) etw. auf etw. (*Akk.*) stäuben; (using grated material) etw. auf etw. (*Akk.*) streuen
C *v.i.* Staub wischen

Phrasal verb
- **~ ˈoff** *v.t.* abstauben; (fig. derog.) aus der Mottenkiste hervorholen

dust: ~ allergy *n.* Stauballergie, *die;* **~bag** *n.* Staubsaugerbeutel, *der;* **~bin** *n.* (Brit.) Mülltonne, *die;* Abfalltonne, *die;* **relegate sth. to the ~bin** (fig.) etw. in *od.* auf den Müll wandern lassen (ugs.); **~bin lid** Mülleimerdeckel, *der;* **~bin liner** Mülleimerbeutel, *der;* **~ bowl** *n.* (Geog.) Trockengebiet, *das* (*mit häufigen Staubstürmen*); **~ cap** *n.* Staubkappe, *die;* **~cart** *n.* (Brit.) Müllwagen, *der;* **~cloth** *n.* Schonbezug, *der;* (duster) Staubtuch, *das;* **~ cloud** *n.* (also Astron.) Staubwolke, *die;* **~coat** *n.* (Brit.) Staubmantel, *der;* **~ cover** *n.* (on record player) Abdeckhaube, *die;* (for clothes) Staubschutz, *der;* (on book) ▸**dust jacket**; **~ devil** ▸**devil A 9**

duster /ˈdʌstə(r)/ *n.* **1** (cloth) Staubtuch, *das* **2** (coat) Staubmantel, *der*

dusting /ˈdʌstɪŋ/ *n.* **1** (removal of dust) ▸**dust B 1**: Abstauben, *das;* Staubwischen, *das;* **give a room a ~:** in einem Zimmer Staub wischen **2** (sprinkling) Bestreuen, *das*

dust: ~ jacket *n.* Schutzumschlag, *der;* **~man** /ˈdʌstmən/ *n., pl.* **~men** /ˈdʌstmən/ ▸ⓘ **p. 1260** (Brit.) Müllwerker, *der;* Müllmann, *der;* **~pan** *n.* Kehrschaufel, *die;* **~proof** *adj.* staubdicht; **~ sheet** *n.* Staubdecke, *die;* **~ storm** *n.* Staubsturm, *der;* **~ trap** *n.* Staubfänger, *der* (abwertend); **~-up** *n.* (coll.) Krach, *der* (ugs.); **~ wrapper** ▸**~ jacket**

dusty /ˈdʌstɪ/ *adj.* **1** staubig ‹*Straße, Stadt, Zimmer*›; verstaubt ‹*Bücher, Möbel*›; **the house is/has got very ~:** das Haus ist sehr verstaubt; im Haus hat sich viel Staub angesammelt **2** (dull) schmutzig ‹*Rosa, Blau, Grün*› **3** (vague) vage **4** (bad-tempered) schroff ‹*Antwort*› **5** **not so ~** (Brit. dated coll.) gar nicht so übel (ugs.)

dutch *n.* (Brit. coll.) **my old ~:** meine gute Alte

Dutch /dʌtʃ/
A *adj.* **1** ▸ⓘ **p. 1277**, ▸ⓘ **p. 1345** holländisch; niederländisch **2** (coll.) **go ~ [with sb.] [on sth.]** getrennte Kasse [mit jmdm.] [bei etw.] machen; **talk to sb. like a ~ uncle** jmdm. ernstlich ins Gewissen reden. *See also* **English A**
B *n.* **1** ▸ⓘ **p. 1345** *constr. as pl.* **the ~:** die Holländer *od.* Niederländer **2** (language) ▸ⓘ **p. 1277** Holländisch, *das;* Niederländisch, *das;* **[Cape] ~:** Kapholländisch, *das* **3** **it was all double ~ to him** das waren alles böhmische Dörfer für ihn. *See also* **English B 1**

Dutch: ~ ˈauction ▸**auction A 1**; **~ ˈbarn** *n.* offene Scheune; **~ ˈcourage** *n.* angetrunkener Mut; **give oneself** *or* **get ~ courage** sich (*Dat.*) Mut antrinken; **~ ˈdoll** *n.* holländische Gliederpuppe; **~ ˈdoor** *n.* (Amer.) quer geteilte Tür; **~ ˈelm disease** *n.* (Bot.) Ulmensterben, *das;* **~ ˈhoe** *n.* (Agric.) Schuffel, *die;* **~man** /ˈdʌtʃmən/ *n., pl.* **~men** /ˈdʌtʃmən/ **1** Holländer, *der;* Niederländer, *der;* **2** (fig. coll.) **or I'm a ~man** oder ich will Emil heißen; **3** (ship) holländisches Schiff; **The Flying ~man** Der Fliegende Holländer; **~ ˈoven** *n.* (Cookery) **1** (box) *Backgefäß mit mehreren Fächern;* **2** (pot) Schmortopf, *der;* **~ ˈtreat** *n.: gemeinsames Vergnügen, bei dem jeder für sich selbst bezahlt;* **~woman** *n.* Holländerin, *die;* Niederländerin, *die*

dutiable /ˈdju:tɪəbl/ *adj.* (Customs) zollpflichtig; abgabenpflichtig

dutiful /ˈdju:tɪfl/ *adj.* pflichtbewusst ‹*Ehefrau, Arbeiter, Bürger*›; gehorsam ‹*Tochter, Sklave*›

dutifully /ˈdju:tɪfəlɪ/ *adv.* pflichtbewusst ‹*handeln*›; treu ‹*dienen*›

duty /ˈdju:tɪ/ *n.* **1** *no pl.* (moral or legal obligation) Pflicht, *die;* Verpflichtung, *die;* **~ calls** die Pflicht ruft; **have a ~ to do sth.** die Pflicht haben, etw. zu tun; **have a ~ to sb.** jmdm. gegenüber eine Verpflichtung haben; **one's ~ to** *or* **towards sb./sth.** seine Pflicht gegenüber jmdm./einer Sache; **do one's ~ [by sb.]** [jmdm. gegenüber] seine Pflicht [und Schuldigkeit] tun; **make it one's ~ to do sth.** es sich (*Dat.*) zur Pflicht machen, etw. zu tun; **be/feel in ~ bound to do sth.** verpflichtet sein/sich verpflichtet fühlen, etw. zu tun; **in ~ bound** pflichtschuldigst **2** (specific task, esp. professional) Aufgabe, *die;* Pflicht, *die;* **do one's ~:** seine Pflicht tun; **take up one's duties** seinen Dienst antreten; **your duties will consist of ...:** zu Ihren Aufgaben gehören ...; **[purely] in [the] line of ~:** [rein] dienstlich; **the ~ nurse/~ porter** die Dienst habende Schwester/der Dienst habende Pförtner; **on ~:** im Dienst; **be on ~:** Dienst haben; **while on ~:** während des Dienstes; im Dienst; **go/come on ~ at seven p.m.** um 19 Uhr seinen Dienst antreten; **off ~:** nicht im Dienst; **be off ~:** keinen Dienst haben; ‹*ab ... Uhr*› dienstfrei sein; **go/come off ~ at eight a.m.** seinen Dienst um acht Uhr beenden; **Dr Smith is off ~ tomorrow** Dr. Smith hat morgen dienstfrei; *see also* **off-duty**; **which is the ~ chemist tonight?** welche Apotheke hat heute Nachtdienst? **3** (Econ.: tax) Zoll, *der;* **pay ~ on sth.** Zoll für etw. bezahlen; etw. verzollen; **be liable to ~:** zollpflichtig sein; **~ on alcohol** Branntweinsteuer, *die;* **free of ~:** zollfrei

‹Ware, Preis› 4 **do ~ as/for sth.** (serve as) als/zu etw. dienen

duty: ~-bound *adj.* **be/feel [oneself] ~-bound to do sth.** verpflichtet sein/sich verpflichtet fühlen, etw. zu tun; *see also* **duty 1**; **~ chemist** *n.* (Brit.) (person) Dienst habender Apotheker/Dienst habende Apothekerin; (shop) Dienst habende Apotheke; **~-free** *adj.* zollfrei ‹Ware, Preis›; **~-frees** *n. pl.* (coll.) zollfreie Waren; **~-free 'shop** *n.* Duty-free-Shop, *der;* **~ officer** *n.* (Mil.) Offizier vom Dienst; **~-paid** *adj.* (Econ.) verzollt ‹Ware›; **~ solicitor** *n.* (Brit.) Dienst habender Rechtsanwalt/Dienst habende Rechstanwaltin [in einer Polizeiwache]; **~ visit** *n.* Pflichtbesuch, *der*

duvet /ˈduːveɪ/ *n.* Federbett, *das;* (quilted) Steppdecke, *die; attrib.* **~ cover** Bettbezug, *der*

DVD *abbr.* = **digital versatile disc, = digital video disc** DVD; *attrib.* **~ drive** DVD-Laufwerk, *das;* **~ player** DVD-Spieler, *der;* DVD-Player, *der;* **~ burner, ~ writer** DVD-Brenner, *der;* **DVD-R** DVD-R, *die;* **DVD-RW** DVD-RW, *die;* **~ video** DVD-Video, *das*

DVT *abbr.* = **deep-vein thrombosis** TVT

dwarf /dwɔːf/

A *n., pl.* **~s** *or* **dwarves** /dwɔːvz/ 1 (person) Liliputaner, *der*/Liliputanerin, *die;* Zwerg, *der*/Zwergin, *die* (auch abwertend) 2 (tree) Zwergbaum, *der;* (plant) Zwergpflanze, *die;* (animal) Zwergtier, *das* 3 (Mythol.) Zwerg, *der*/Zwergin, *die* 4 (Astron.) Zwerg[stern], *der*

B *adj.* 1 Zwerg‹baum, -stern› 2 (stunted) winzig

C *v.t.* 1 (stunt in growth) verkümmern lassen 2 (cause to look small) klein erscheinen lassen; verzwergen (geh.) 3 (fig.) in den Schatten stellen

dwarves *pl. of* **dwarf**

dweeb /dwiːb/ *n.* (esp. Amer. coll.) trübe Tasse (ugs. abwertend)

dwell /dwel/ *v.i.*, **dwelt** /dwelt/ (literary; lit. or fig.) wohnen; weilen (geh.)

Phrasal verb

• **~ [up]on** *v.t.* 1 (in discussion) sich länger *od.* ausführlich befassen mit; (in thought) in Gedanken verweilen bei; **don't ~ upon the past** halten Sie sich nicht bei *od.* mit der Vergangenheit auf 2 (prolong) gedehnt aussprechen ‹Wort, Silbe›

dweller /ˈdwelə(r)/ *n., esp. in comb.* Bewohner, *der*/Bewohnerin, *die;* **city-~s** Großstädter *Pl.;* **caravan-~s** [ständige] Caravaner *Pl.*

dwelling /ˈdwelɪŋ/ *n.* (Admin. lang./literary) Wohnung, *die;* **council ~:** Sozialwohnung, *die*

dwelling: ~ house *n.* Wohnhaus, *das;* **~ place** *n.* Wohnsitz, *der*

dwelt ▸ **dwell**

dwindle /ˈdwɪndl/ *v.i.* 1 **~ [away]** abnehmen; ‹Unterstützung, Interesse:› nachlassen; ‹Güter, Vermögen:› zusammenschrumpfen; ‹Vorräte, Handel, Hoheitsgebiet:› schrumpfen; ‹Macht, Einfluss, Tageslicht:› schwinden (geh.); ‹Gewinn, Umsatz:› rückläufig sein; ‹Bodenschätze:› zur Neige gehen (geh.); ‹Ruhm:› verblassen (geh.); **~ in importance** an Bedeutung abnehmen *od.* verlieren; **~ away to nothing** dahinschwinden 2 (fig.: degenerate) herunterkommen (**into** zu)

DWP *abbr.* = **Department for Work and Pensions**

dye /daɪ/

A *n.* 1 (substance) Färbemittel, *das;* **eyelash ~:** Wimperntusche, *die* 2 (colour) Farbe, *die*

B *v.t.*, **~ing** /ˈdaɪɪŋ/ färben; **~d blond hair** blond gefärbtes Haar; **~d-in-the-wool** (fig.) eingefleischt, (ugs.) in der Wolle gefärbt ‹Konservativer, Gewerkschaftler, Reaktionär›

C *v.i.*, **~ing** sich färben lassen

dyer /ˈdaɪə(r)/ *n.* Färber, *der*/Färberin, *die*

'dyestuff ▸ **dye A 1**

dying /ˈdaɪɪŋ/

A *adj.* 1 sterbend ‹Person, Tier›; eingehend ‹Pflanze›; absterbend ‹Baum›; verendend ‹Tier›; aussterbend ‹Kunst, Kultur, Tradition, [Tier]art, Menschenschlag›; zu Ende gehend ‹Jahr›; erlöschend ‹Glut, Leidenschaft›; **he's a ~ man** (will not recover) er lebt nicht mehr lange 2 (related to time of death) letzt…; **to my ~ day** bis an mein Lebensende

B *n. pl.* **the ~:** die Sterbenden. *See also* **die**[1]

dyke /daɪk/ *n.* 1 (flood wall) Deich, *der* 2 (ditch) Graben, *der* 3 (causeway) Damm, *der* 4 (Mining, Geol.) Gang, *der;* (of igneous rock) Eruptivgang, *der*

dynamic /daɪˈnæmɪk/ *adj.*, **dynamically** /daɪˈnæmɪkəlɪ/ *adv.* (lit. or fig.; also Mus.) dynamisch

dynamics /daɪˈnæmɪks/ *n., no pl.* 1 (Mech.) Dynamik, *die* (fachspr.); Kräftelehre, *die* 2 (in other sciences) -dynamik, *die*

dynamism /ˈdaɪnəmɪzm/ *n.* Dynamik, *die*

dynamite /ˈdaɪnəmaɪt/

A *n.* 1 (explosive) Dynamit, *das* 2 (fig.: politically dangerous person or thing) Sprengstoff, *der;* **these revelations are ~:** diese Enthüllungen sind [politisch] brisant 3 (fig.: sensational person or thing) **be ~** ‹Person:› eine Wucht sein (salopp); ‹Sache:› eine Sensation sein

B *v.t.* mit Dynamit sprengen

dynamo /ˈdaɪnəməʊ/ *n., pl.* **~s** 1 Dynamomaschine, *die;* (of car) Lichtmaschine, *die;* (of bicycle) Dynamo, *der* 2 (fig.) **[human] ~:** Energiebündel, *das* (ugs.)

dynastic /dɪˈnæstɪk/ *adj.* dynastisch; ‹Regierung, Herrschaft, Diktatur› einer Dynastie; **~ families** Familiendynastien *Pl.*

dynasty /ˈdɪnəstɪ/ *n.* (lit. or fig.) Dynastie, *die*

dyne /daɪn/ *n.* (Phys.) Dyn, *das*

dysentery /ˈdɪsəntərɪ/ *n.* (Med.) Ruhr, *die;* Dysenterie, *die* (fachspr.)

dysfunction /dɪsˈfʌŋkʃn/ *n., no pl.* 1 (impairment) Funktionsstörung, *die* 2 (maladjustment) Gestörtheit, *die*

dysfunctional /dɪsˈfʌŋkʃənl/ *adj.* 1 (not working) funktionsgestört 2 (maladjusted) gestört

dyslexia /dɪsˈleksɪə/ *n.* (Med., Psych.) Dyslexie, *die* (fachspr.); Lesestörung, *die*

dyslexic /dɪsˈleksɪk/ (Med., Psych.)

A *adj.* dyslektisch (fachspr.); **a ~ child** ein Kind mit einer Lesestörung

B *n.* Dyslektiker, *der*/Dyslektikerin, *die* (fachspr.); Mensch mit einer Lesestörung

dyspepsia /dɪsˈpepsɪə/ *n.* ▸ⓘ **p. 1231** (Med.) Dyspepsie, *die* (fachspr.); Verdauungsstörung, *die*

dystopia /dɪsˈtəʊpɪə/ *n.* Schreckenswelt, *die*

dystrophy /ˈdɪstrəfɪ/ *n.* ▸ⓘ **p. 1231** (Med.) Dystrophie, *die* (fachspr.); Ernährungsstörung, *die;* **muscular ~:** Muskeldystrophie, *die;* (fortschreitender) Muskelschwund

d

Ee

e

E¹, e /iː/ *n., pl.* **Es** *or* **E's** 1 (letter) E, e, *das* 2 **E** (Mus.) E, e, *das;* **E flat** es, Es, *das* 3 **E** (Sch., Univ.: mark) Fünf, *die;* **he got an E** er bekam „mangelhaft" *od.* eine Fünf

E² *abbr.* 1 ▸❶ **p. 1013 = east** O 2 ▸❶ **p. 1013 = eastern** ö. 3 (sl.) **= Ecstasy** E; XTC

each /iːtʃ/

A *adj.* jeder/jede/jedes; **there's cream between ~ layer** zwischen den einzelnen Schichten ist Sahne; **we have two votes ~, we ~ have two votes** jeder von uns hat zwei Stimmen; **they cost** *or* **are a pound ~:** sie kosten ein Pfund pro Stück *od.* je[weils] ein Pfund; **they ~ have ...:** sie haben jeder ...; jeder von ihnen hat ...; **the houses ~ have their own garage[s]** die Häuser haben alle ihre eigene Garage; **books at £1 ~:** Bücher zu je einem Pfund *od.* für je ein Pfund; **two teams with 10 players ~:** zwei Mannschaften mit je 10 Spielern; **I gave them a book ~** *or* **~ a book** ich habe jedem von ihnen ein Buch *od.* ihnen je ein Buch gegeben; **~ one of them** jeder/jede/jedes Einzelne von ihnen; **~ and every employee** jeder einzelne Mitarbeiter; **I travelled 10 miles ~ way every day** ich habe jeden Tag 16 km pro Weg zurückgelegt; **back a horse ~ way** (Brit. Racing) auf Sieg oder Platz eines Pferdes wetten

B *pron.* 1 jeder/jede/jedes; **they are ~ of them ...** jeder *usw.* von ihnen ist ...; **~ despises the other** jeder verachtet den anderen; sie verachten sich [gegenseitig]; **have some of ~:** von jedem etwas nehmen/haben 2 **~ other** sich [gegenseitig]; einander (meist geh.); **they are cross with ~ other** sie sind böse aufeinander; **we have not seen ~ other in years** wir haben uns jahrelang nicht gesehen; **they wore ~ other's hats** jeder trug den Hut des anderen; **be in love with ~ other** ineinander verliebt sein; **live next door to ~ other** Tür an Tür wohnen

eager /ˈiːɡə(r)/ *adj.* eifrig ‹*Person, Arbeiter, Art*›; rege, lebhaft ‹*Interesse*›; brennend, sehnlich ‹*Wunsch*›; erwartungsvoll ‹*Ton, Gesichtsausdruck, Lächeln*›; begeistert ‹*Anhänger einer Partei*›; **be ~ to do sth.** etw. unbedingt tun wollen; **be ~ to make a good impression** eifrig bemüht sein, einen guten Eindruck zu machen; **be ~ to learn** lernbegierig *od.* -eifrig sein; **be ~ for sth.** etw. unbedingt haben wollen; *see also* **beaver A 1**

eagerly /ˈiːɡəlɪ/ *adv.* eifrig ‹*Ja sagen, zustimmen*›; bereitwillig ‹*Auskunft geben*›; gespannt, ungeduldig ‹*warten, Ausschau halten, aufblicken*›; erwartungsvoll ‹*lächeln*›; begierig ‹*ergreifen*›; **look forward ~ to sth.** sich sehr auf etw. (*Akk.*) freuen; **~ seize an opportunity** eine Gelegenheit beim Schopf ergreifen

eagerness /ˈiːɡənɪs/ *n., no pl.* Eifer, *der;* **~ to learn** Lerneifer, *der;* Lernbegier[de], *die;* **~ to succeed** Erfolgshunger, *der;* **~ to assist** Hilfsbereitschaft, *die*

eagle /ˈiːɡl/ *n.* 1 Adler, *der* 2 (Golf) Eagle, *das*

eagle: ~ 'eye *n.* wachsamer Blick; **have/keep/fix one's ~ eye on sb./sth.** ein wachsames Auge *od.* einen wachsamen Blick auf jmdn./etw. haben; **~-eyed** *adj.* adleräugig

eaglet /ˈiːɡlɪt/ *n.* (Ornith.) Adlerjunge, *das*

E&OE *abbr.* **= errors and omissions excepted**

ear¹ /ɪə(r)/ *n.* 1 ▸❶ **p. 951** Ohr, *das;* (of red deer) Lauscher, *der;* (of red fox) Gehör, *das;* (of rabbit, hare) Löffel, *der;* (of hound) Behang, *der* (Jägerspr.); **his good/bad ~:** sein besseres/schlechteres Ohr; **~, nose, and throat hospital/specialist** Hals-Nasen-Ohren-Klinik, *die*/-Arzt, *der*/-Ärztin, *die;* **smile from ~ to ~:** von einem Ohr zum anderen strahlen (ugs.); **have nothing between one's ~s** (fig. coll.) nichts im Kopf haben (ugs.); **be out on one's ~** (fig. coll.) auf der Straße stehen (ugs.); **this brought a storm of criticism about his ~s** das setzte ihn einem Sturm der Kritik aus; **up to one's ~s in work/debt** bis zum Hals in Arbeit/Schulden; **be pleasing to the ~[s]** sich angenehm anhören; **come to** *or* **reach sb.'s ~s** jmdm. zu Ohren kommen; **have a word in sb.'s ~:** jmdm. ein Wort im Vertrauen sagen; **listen with half an ~:** [nur] mit halbem Ohr zuhören; **keep one's ~s open** (fig.) die Ohren offen halten; **have/keep an ~ to the ground** sein Ohr ständig am Puls der Masse haben (ugs. scherzh.); **be[come] all ~s** [plötzlich] ganz Ohr sein; **go in [at] one ~ and out [at] the other** (coll.) zum einen Ohr herein-, zum anderen wieder hinausgehen; **lend an ~ to sb.** jmdm. Gehör schenken; **give ~ to** ein geneigtes Ohr haben für (geh.); **have sb.'s ~/get** *or* **win the ~ of sb.** bei jmdm. Gehör *od.* ein offenes Ohr finden 2 *no pl.* (sense) Gehör, *das;* **have an ~** *or* **a good ~/no ~ for music** ein [gutes]/kein Gehör für Musik haben; **play by ~** (Mus.) nach dem Gehör spielen; **play it by ~** (fig.) es dem Augenblick/der Situation überlassen

ear² *n.* (Bot.) Ähre, *die;* **~ of corn** Kornähre, *die*

ear: ~ache *n.* ▸❶ **p. 1231** (Med.) Ohrenschmerzen *Pl.;* **~ clip** *n.* Ohr[en]klipp, *der;* **~ drops** *n. pl.* 1 (Med.) Ohrentropfen *Pl.;* 2 (earrings) Ohrgehänge, *das;* **~drum** *n.* (Anat.) Trommelfell, *das*

-eared /ɪəd/ *adj. in comb.* **long-/short-~:** lang-/kurzohrig

'ear flap *n.* Ohrenklappe, *die*

earful /ˈɪəfʊl/ *n.* (coll.) **get an ~:** ordentlich was zu hören bekommen (ugs.); **give sb. an ~ [about sth.]** jmdm. ein paar Takte [über etw.] erzählen (ugs.)

'ear hole *n.* 1 (Anat.) Ohröffnung, *die* 2 (coll.: ear) Löffel, *der* (ugs.)

earl /ɜːl/ *n.* ▸❶ **p. 1634** Graf, *der*

earldom /ˈɜːldəm/ *n.* 1 (territory) Grafschaft, *die* 2 (rank) Grafenwürde, *die*

'earlobe *n.* Ohrläppchen, *das*

early /ˈɜːlɪ/

A *adj.* ▸❶ **p. 894** 1 früh; **they had an ~ lunch** sie aßen früh zu Mittag; **I am a bit ~:** ich bin etwas zu früh gekommen *od.* (ugs.) dran; **the train was 10 minutes ~:** der Zug kam 10 Minuten zu früh; **an ~ train** (earlier than one usually takes) ein früherer Zug; **have an ~ night** früh ins Bett gehen; **~ riser** Frühaufsteher, *der*/-aufsteherin, *die;* **~ to bed, ~ to rise [makes a man healthy, wealthy, and wise]** (prov.) früh zu Bette und auf zu früher Stund, macht den Menschen glücklich, reich, gesund (Spr.); **an ~ reply** eine baldige Antwort; **at the earliest** frühestens; **the ~ part of** der Anfang (+ *Gen.*); **in the ~ afternoon/evening** am frühen Nachmittag/Abend; **into the ~ hours** bis in die frühen Morgenstunden; **at/from an ~ age** in jungen Jahren/von klein auf; **from one's earliest years** von frühester Kindheit an; **at an ~ stage, in its ~ stages** im Frühstadium; **~ Gothic** Frühgotik, *die;* **an ~ work/the ~ writings of an author** ein Frühwerk/die Frühschriften eines Autors; **~ Christian times** die frühchristliche Zeit 2 (of the distant past) vorgeschichtlich ‹*Fund, Fossilien*›; (prehistoric) frühgeschichtlich ‹*Fund, Fossilien*›; **the earliest records of a civilization** die frühesten Spuren einer Zivilisation; **at a very ~ date** schon sehr früh 3 (forward in flowering, ripening, etc.) früh blühend ‹*Pflanze*›; Früh‹*gemüse, -obst*›

B *adv.* früh; **~ next week** Anfang der nächsten Woche; **~ next Wednesday** nächsten Mittwoch früh; **~ in June** Anfang Juni; **the earliest I can come is Friday** ich kann frühestens Freitag kommen; **I cannot come earlier than Thursday** ich kann nicht vor Donnerstag kommen; **from ~ in the morning till late at night** von früh [morgens] bis spät [nachts]; **~ on** schon früh; **earlier on this week/year** früher in der Woche/im Jahr

early: ~ bird *n.* (joc.) *jmd., der etw. frühzeitig tut;* (getting up) Frühaufsteher, *der*/-aufsteherin, *die;* **the ~ bird catches the worm** (prov.) Morgenstunde hat Gold im Munde (Spr.); **~ 'closing** *n.* **it is ~ closing** die Geschäfte haben nachmittags geschlossen; **~-'closing day** *n.* *Tag, an dem die Geschäfte nachmittags geschlossen haben;* **~ 'days** *n. pl.* **in the ~ days** am Anfang (**of** *Gen.*); **it is ~ days [yet]** es ist noch zu früh; **~-'warning** *attrib. adj.* Frühwarn-

ear: ~mark A *n.* Ohrmarke, *die;* (fig.) Kennzeichen, *das;* B *v.t.* 1 (mark, lit. or fig.) [kenn]zeichnen; 2 (assign to definite purpose) bestimmen; vorsehen; **~muffs** *n. pl.* Ohrenschützer *Pl.*

earn /ɜːn/ *v.t.* 1 ‹*Person, Tat, Benehmen:*› verdienen; **~ed income** Einkommen aus Arbeit; **it ~ed him much respect** es trug ihm viel Respekt ein 2 (bring in as income or interest) einbringen 3 (incur) eintragen; einbringen; **he ~ed nothing but ingratitude** er erntete nur Undank

earner /ˈɜːnə(r)/ *n.* **be a nice little ~** (coll.) ganz schön was einbringen (ugs.)

earnest¹ /ˈɜːnɪst/

A *adj.* 1 (serious, zealous) ernsthaft; **be ~ in one's endeavour to do sth.** sich ernsthaft bemühen, etw. zu tun 2 (ardent) innig ‹*Wunsch, Gebet, Hoffnung*›; leidenschaftlich ‹*Appell*›

B *n.* **in ~:** mit vollem Ernst; **this time I'm in ~ [about it]** diesmal ist es mir Ernst *od.* meine ich es ernst [damit]; **it's raining in ~ now** jetzt regnet es richtig

earnest² *n.* 1 (money) Handgeld, *das* 2 (foretaste) Vorgeschmack, *der* (**of** von)

earnestly /ˈɜːnɪstlɪ/ *adv.* ernsthaft

earning /ˈɜːnɪŋ/ *n.* 1 Erreichen, *das;* (of money) Verdienen, *das* 2 *in pl.* (money earned) Verdienst, *der;* (of business etc.) Ertrag, *der*

ear: ~phones *n. pl.* Kopfhörer, *der;* **~piece** *n.* Hörmuschel, *die;* **~-piercing** A *adj.* durch Mark und Bein gehend ‹*Lärm*›; B *n.* Durchstechen der Ohrläppchen; **~plug** *n.* Ohropax, *das* (Wz); **~ring** *n.* Ohrring, *der;* **~shot** *n.* **out of/within ~shot** außer/in Hörweite; **~-splitting** *adj.* ohrenbetäubend

earth /ɜːθ/

A *n.* 1 (land, soil) Erde, *die;* (ground) Boden, *der;* **be brought/come down** *or* **back to ~ [with a**

bump] (fig.) [schnell] wieder auf den Boden der Tatsachen zurückgeholt werden/zurückkommen **2** *or* **E~** (planet) Erde, *die* **3** (world) Erde, *die*; **on ~** (existing anywhere) auf der Welt; auf Erden (geh.); **nothing on ~ will stop me** keine Macht der Welt kann mich aufhalten; **how/what** *etc.* **on ~ ...?** wie/was *usw.* in aller Welt ...?; **who on ~ is that?** wer ist das bloß?; **what on ~ do you mean?** was meinst du denn nur?; **where on ~ has she got to?** wo ist sie denn bloß hingegangen?; **look like nothing on ~** (be unrecognizable) nicht zu erkennen sein; (look repellent) furchtbar aussehen; **be like nothing on ~:** unvergleichlich sein; **feel like nothing on ~:** sich ganz mies fühlen (ugs.); **on ~** (Relig.) auf Erden **4** (land and sea together) Erde, *die*; Welt, *die* **5** (of animal) Bau, *der*; **run to ~:** in seinen Unterschlupf hetzen ‹Tier›; (fig.) aufspüren; **have gone to ~** (fig.) untergetaucht sein **6** (coll.) **charge/cost/pay the ~:** ein Vermögen *od.* (ugs.) eine ganze Stange Geld verlangen/kosten/bezahlen; **it won't cost the ~:** das kostet nicht die Welt (ugs.); **promise sb. the ~:** jmdm. das Blaue vom Himmel versprechen (ugs.) **7** (Chem.) Erde, *die* **8** (Brit. Electr.) Erde, *die*; Erdung, *die*

B *v.t.* (Brit. Electr.) erden

Phrasal verb

• **~ 'up** *v.t.* mit Erde bedecken

'earth closet *n.* (Brit.) Humustoilette, *die*

earthen /'ɜːθn/ *adj.* (made of clay) irden; Ton-

earthenware /'ɜːθnweə(r)/

A *n., no pl.* **1** (vessels etc.) Tonwaren *Pl.*; Irdenware, *die* (selten) **2** (clay) Ton, *der*

B *adj.* Ton-; tönern

earthiness /'ɜːθɪnɪs/ *n., no pl.* **1** Erdigkeit, *die* **2** (of person) Derbheit, *die*

earthly /'ɜːθlɪ/ *adj.* irdisch; **no ~ use** *etc.* (coll.) nicht der geringste Nutzen *usw.*; **this is no ~ use to me** (coll.) das nützt mir nicht im Geringsten *od.* überhaupt nicht; **not an ~** (sl.) nicht die geringste Chance

earth: ~-moving **A** *n.* Erdarbeiten *Pl.*; **B** *adj.* **~-moving vehicle** Fahrzeug für Erdarbeiten; **~quake** *n.* Erdbeben, *das*; **~ sciences** *n. pl.* Geowissenschaften *Pl.*; **~-shaking, ~-shattering** *adjs.* (fig.) weltbewegend; **not of ~-shattering importance** nicht weltbewegend; **~ tremor** *n.* Erdstoß, *der*; leichtes Erdbeben; **~work** *n.* **1** (bank) Wall, *der*; **2** (raising of bank) Erdarbeiten *Pl.*; **~worm** *n.* Regenwurm, *der*

earthy /'ɜːθɪ/ *adj.* **1** erdig **2** derb ‹Person›

ear: ~ trumpet *n.* Hörrohr, *das*; **~wax** *n.* Ohrenschmalz, *das*

earwig /'ɪəwɪg/ *n.* Ohrwurm, *der*

ease /iːz/

A *n.* **1** (freedom from pain or trouble) Ruhe, *die*; **set sb. at ~:** jmdn. beruhigen **2** (leisure) Muße, *die*; (idleness) Müßiggang, *der*; **a life of ~:** ein Leben der Muße **3** (freedom from constraint) Entspanntheit, *die*; **at [one's] ~:** entspannt; behaglich; **she sat there taking her ~:** sie machte es sich (*Dat.*) gemütlich *od.* behaglich; **be** *or* **feel at [one's] ~:** sich wohl fühlen; **put** *or* **set sb. at his ~:** jmdm. die Befangenheit nehmen; **he is always at his ~** (never embarrassed) er ist immer unbefangen *od.* ungezwungen **4** **with ~** (without difficulty) mit Leichtigkeit **5** (relief from pain) Linderung, *die* **6** (Mil.) **[stand] at ~!** rührt euch! *see also* **ill C 3**

B *v.t.* **1** (relieve) lindern ‹Schmerz, Kummer›; (make lighter, easier) erleichtern ‹Last, Arbeit›; entspannen ‹Lage, Person›; verringern ‹Belastung›; **~ sb. of a burden** jmdm. eine Last abnehmen **2** (give mental ~ to) erleichtern; **~ sb.'s mind** jmdn. beruhigen **3** (relax, adjust) lockern ‹Griff, Knoten›; verringern ‹Druck, Spannung, Geschwindigkeit›; beruhigen ‹Verkehr› **4** (joc.: rob) erleichtern (ugs. scherzh.); **~ sb. of sth.** jmdn. um etw. erleichtern **5** (cause to move) behutsam bewegen; **~ the clutch in** die Kupplung langsam kommen lassen; **~ the cap off a bottle** eine Flasche vorsichtig öffnen

C *v.i.* **1** ‹Belastung, Druck, Wind, Sturm:› nachlassen **2** **~ off** *or* **up** (begin to take it easy) sich entspannen; (at work) kürzer treten; **~ off, you're going much too fast** fahre ein bisschen langsamer, du bist viel zu schnell **3** ‹Aktien usw.:› nachgeben

easel /'iːzl/ *n.* Staffelei, *die*

easily /'iːzɪlɪ/ *adv.* **1** (without difficulty) leicht; **more ~ said than done** leichter gesagt als getan **2** (without doubt) zweifelsohne; **it is ~ a hundred metres deep** es ist gut und gerne hundert Meter tief **3** (quite possibly) leicht; **that may ~ be** das kann gut sein

easiness /'iːzɪnɪs/ *n.* Leichtigkeit, *die*

east /iːst/ ▸ℹ **p. 1013**

A *n.* **1** Osten, *der*; **the ~:** Ost (Met., Seew.); **in/to[wards]/from the ~:** im/nach *od.* (geh.) gen/von Osten; **to the ~ of** östlich von; östlich (+ *Gen.*); **~, west, home's best** (prov.) ob Osten oder Westen, zu Hause ists zum Besten **2** *usu.* **E~** (part lying to the ~) Osten, *der*; (Geog., Polit.: world lying ~ of Europe) Osten, *der*; Orient, *der*; Morgenland, *das* (dichter.); **from the E~:** aus dem Osten; **the E~** (Amer.: NE part of US) der Osten; *see also* **Far East**; **Middle East**; **Near East** **3** (Cards) Ost

B *adj.* östlich; Ost‹küste, -wind, -grenze, -tor›

C *adv.* ostwärts; nach Osten; **~ of** östlich von; östlich (+ *Gen.*); **~ and west** nach Osten und Westen ‹verlaufen, sich erstrecken›; **~ by north/south** ▸ **by¹ A 4**

East: ~ 'Africa *pr. n.* Ostafrika (*das*); **~ Anglia** /iːst 'æŋglɪə/ *pr. n. die beiden englischen Grafschaften Norfolk und Suffolk*; **~ Ber'lin** *pr. n.* (Hist.) Ost-Berlin (*das*); Berlin, *das* (DDR); **e~bound** *adj.* ▸ℹ **p. 1013** ‹Zug, Verkehr usw.› in Richtung Osten; **~ 'End** *n.* (Brit.) Londoner Osten; **~-Ender** /iːst'endə(r)/ *n.* (Brit.) Bewohner/Bewohnerin des Londoner Ostens

Easter /'iːstə(r)/ *n.* ▸ℹ **p. 1189** Ostern, *das od. Pl.*; **at ~:** [zu *od.* an] Ostern; **next/last ~:** nächste/letzte Ostern

> **Easter**
>
> Ostern ist ein kirchliches Fest, und Christen gedenken am Ostersonntag der Auferstehung Christi. In Großbritannien bekommen vor allem Kinder Ostereier aus Schokolade zu Ostern. In manchen Teilen Englands und Schottlands ist *egg-rolling* ein Osterbrauch. Dabei rollen alle Mitspieler ein hart gekochtes Ei einen Hügel hinunter. Wenn ihr Ei unten unbeschädigt ankommt, bringt es Glück. Die amerikanischen Kinder glauben, dass der *Easter Bunny* (Osterhase), während sie schlafen, Ostereier für sie versteckt, die sie dann am Morgen suchen. Britische Familien veranstalten bisweilen auch eine *Easter egg hunt*, bei der alle Beteiligten vorher versteckte Schokoladeneier suchen, die anschließend gerecht verteilt werden. *Good Friday* (Karfreitag) ist Feiertag in Großbritannien und Irland, und viele Leute essen *hot cross buns* (mit einem Kreuz verzierte Rosinenbrötchen) zum Frühstück. *Easter Monday* ist ebenfalls ein Feiertag in Großbritannien und Irland.

Easter: ~ 'Day *n.* Ostersonntag, *der*; **~ egg** *n.* Osterei, *das*

easterly /'iːstəlɪ/ ▸ℹ **p. 1013**

A *adj.* **1** (in position or direction) östlich; **in an ~ direction** nach Osten **2** (from the east) ‹Wind› aus östlichen Richtungen; **the wind was ~:** der Wind kam aus östlichen Richtungen

B *adv.* **1** (in position) östlich; (in direction) ostwärts **2** (from the east) aus *od.* von Ost[en]

C *n.* Ost[wind], *der*

Easter 'Monday *n.* Ostermontag, *der*

eastern /'iːstən/ *adj.* ▸ℹ **p. 1013** östlich; Ost‹grenze, -hälfte, -seite, -wind›; **~ Germany** Ostdeutschland; *see also* **bloc**; **Far Eastern**; **Middle Eastern**; **Near Eastern**

Eastern: ~ 'Europe *pr. n.* Osteuropa (*das*); **~ Euro'pean** **A** *adj.* osteuropäisch; **B** *n.* Osteuropäer, *der*/-europäerin, *die*; **~ Germany** *pr. n.* Ostdeutschland (*das*)

easternmost /'iːstənməʊst/ *adj.* ▸ℹ **p. 1013** östlichst...

Easter: ~ 'Sunday ▸ **Easter Day**; **~ term** *n.* (Brit.) **1** (Univ.) ▸ **Trinity term**; **2** (Law) Sitzungsperiode von Ostern bis Pfingsten; **~tide** *n.* (arch.) [Tage *Pl.* nach] Ostern; **~ week** *n.* Osterwoche, *die*

East: ~ 'German (Hist.) **A** *adj.* ostdeutsch; **B** *n.* Ostdeutsche, *der/die*; **~ 'Germany** *pr. n.* (Hist.) Ostdeutschland (*das*); **~ 'Indies** *pr. n. pl.* südostasiatische Inselwelt; **e~-north-'~** ▸ℹ **p. 1013** **A** *n.* Ostnordost[en], *der*; **B** *adj.* ostnordöstlich; **C** *adv.* nach Ostnordost[en]; **~ 'Prussia** *pr. n.* Ostpreußen (*das*); **~ Side** *n.* (Amer.) *Ostteil von Manhattan*; **e~-south-'~** ▸ℹ **p. 1013** **A** *n.* Ostsüdost[en], *der*; **B** *adj.* ostsüdöstlich; **C** *adv.* nach Ostsüdost[en]; **~ Timor** /iːst 'tiːmɔː(r)/ *pr. n.* Osttimor (*das*)

eastward /'iːstwəd/ ▸ℹ **p. 1013**

A *adj.* nach Osten gerichtet; (situated towards the east) östlich; **in an ~ direction** nach Osten; [in] Richtung Osten

B *adv.* ostwärts; **they are ~ bound** sie fahren nach *od.* [in] Richtung Osten

C *n.* Osten, *der*

eastwards /'iːstwədz/ ▸ℹ **p. 1013** ▸ **eastward B**

easy /'iːzɪ/

A *adj.* **1** (not difficult) leicht; **~ to clean/learn/see** *etc.* leicht zu reinigen/lernen/sehen *usw.*; **it is ~ to see that ...:** es ist offensichtlich, dass ...; man sieht sofort, dass ...; **it's as ~ as falling off a log** *or* **as ~ as pie** *or* **as ~ as anything** (coll.) es ist kinderleicht; **be an ~ winner** mit Leichtigkeit siegen; **the ~ fit of a coat** *etc.* der bequeme Sitz eines Mantels *usw.*; **it is ~ for him to talk** er hat leicht *od.* gut reden; **it's ~ for him to complain** er kann sich gut beklagen; **on ~ terms** auf Raten ‹kaufen› **2** (free from pain, anxiety, etc.) sorglos, angenehm ‹Leben, Zeit›; **make life ~ for oneself** sich (*Dat.*) das Leben leicht machen; **make it** *or* **things ~ for sb.** es jmdm. leicht machen; **[not] ~ in one's mind** be[un]ruhigt; **I do not feel altogether ~ about it/her** ich mache mir deswegen/ihretwegen doch Sorgen; *see also* **conscience** **3** (free from constraint, strictness, etc.) ungezwungen; unbefangen ‹Art›; **at an ~ pace** in einem gemütlichen *od.* gemächlichen Tempo; **he is an ~ person** *or* **is ~ to get on with/work with** mit ihm kann man gut auskommen/zusammenarbeiten; **I'm ~** (coll.) es ist mir egal; **be ~ on the eye** (coll.) ansprechend aussehen; **woman** *or* **lady of ~ virtue** (dated euphem.) Freudenmädchen, *das* (verhüll.)

B *adv.* leicht; **easier said than done** leichter gesagt als getan; **~ come ~ go** (coll.) wie gewonnen, so zerronnen (Spr.); **~ does it** immer langsam *od.* sachte; **go ~:** vorsichtig sein; **go ~ on** *or* **with** sparsam sein *od.* umgehen mit; **be** *or* **go ~ on** *or* **with sb.** mit jmdm. nachsichtig sein; **take it ~!** beruhige dich!; **take it** *or* **things** *or* **life ~:** sich nicht übernehmen; **stand ~!** (Brit. Mil.) rührt euch!

easy: ~-care *attrib. adj.* pflegeleicht; **~ 'chair** *n.* Sessel, *der*; **~-going** *adj.* (calm, placid) gelassen; (casually pleasant) gemütlich; (informal) ungezwungen; (lax) nachlässig; (careless) unbekümmert; **~ 'listening** *n., no pl.* Easylistening, *das*; **~ 'meat** *n.* (coll.) leichte Beute; **sth./sb. is ~ meat** man hat [ein] leichtes Spiel mit etw./jmdm.; **~ 'money** *n.* leicht verdientes Geld; **~ 'option** *n.* leichter Weg; **~ 'over** *adv.* (esp. Amer.) beidseitig gebraten ‹Ei, Spiegelei›; **fry an egg ~ over** ein Ei von beiden Seiten braten; **~-peasy** /iːzɪ'piːzɪ/ *adj.* (Brit. coll., child lang.) babyleicht; kinderleicht; **~ street** *n., no pl.* (coll.) **be on ~ street** im Wohlstand leben

eat /iːt/

A *v.t.*, **ate** /et, eɪt/, **eaten** /'iːtn/ **1** ‹Mensch:› essen; ‹Tier:› fressen; **I've had enough to ~:** ich habe genug gegessen; ich bin satt *od.* gesättigt; **I could ~ a horse!** ich habe einen Bärenhunger! (ugs.); **you should ~ regular meals** du solltest regelmäßig essen; **don't be afraid — he won't ~ you!** (fig.) keine Angst, er wird dich schon nicht fressen (ugs.); **I could ~ you** du siehst zum Fressen aus (ugs.); **she looks nice enough to ~:** sie sieht zum Anbeißen aus (ugs.); **~ sb. out of house and home** jmdn. arm essen; jmdm. die Haare vom Kopf fressen (ugs.); **what's ~ing you?** (coll.) was hast du denn?; **~ one's words** seine Worte zurücknehmen **2** (destroy, consume, make hole in) fressen; **~ its way into/through sth.** sich in etw.(*Akk.*)/durch etw. hindurchfressen. *see also*

e

bread A 2; dirt 1; hat 2; heart A 1; humble A 1

B *v.i.*, **ate, eaten** 1 ‹*Person:*› essen; ‹*Tier:*› fressen; **~ out of sb.'s hand** (lit. or fig.) jmdm. aus der Hand fressen (ugs.) 2 (penetrate by gnawing or corrosion) **~ into** sich hineinfressen in (+ *Akk.*); **~ through sth.** sich durch etw. durchfressen

Phrasal verbs

- **~ a'way** *v.t.* ‹*Rost, Säure:*› zerfressen.
- **~ 'out** *v.i.* essen gehen
- **~ 'up**

A *v.t.* 1 (consume) ‹*Person:*› aufessen; ‹*Tier:*› auffressen; **the chickens were ~en up by the fox** die Hühner wurden vom Fuchs gefressen; **the car ~s up a lot of petrol** das Auto verbraucht *od.* (ugs.) frisst viel Benzin; **be ~en up by sth.** (fig.) vor etw. [fast] vergehen 2 (traverse rapidly) **our car ~s up the miles** unser Auto frisst die Meilen nur so (ugs.)

B *v.i.* aufessen

eatable /ˈiːtəbl/

A *adj.* genießbar; essbar

B *n.* in *pl.* Lebensmittel *Pl.*; **have no ~s with one** nichts zu essen dabeihaben

'eat-by date *n.* Verfallsdatum, *das*

eaten ▸ **eat**

eater /ˈiːtə(r)/ *n.* 1 (person) Esser, *der*/Esserin, *die*; **a big ~:** ein guter Esser 2 (apple) Essapfel, *der*

eatery /ˈiːtərɪ/ *n.* (coll.) Esskneipe, *die;* Esslokal, *das*

eating /ˈiːtɪŋ/ *n.* Essen, *das;* **make good ~:** ein gutes Essen sein; **not for ~:** nicht zum Essen [geeignet]

eating: ~ apple *n.* Essapfel, *der;* **~ disorder** *n.* Essstörung, *die* (*meist Pl.*); **~ habits** *n. pl.* Essgewohnheiten *Pl.*; **~ house** *n.* Restaurant, *das;* Speisehaus, *das;* **~ place** *n.* Essgelegenheit, *die*

eats /iːts/ *n. pl.* (coll.) Fressalien *Pl.* (ugs.); **what's for ~?** was gibts zu essen? (ugs.)

'e-auction *n.* E-Auktion, *die*

eau de Cologne /əʊdəkəˈləʊn/ *n.* Eau de Cologne, *das;* Kölnisch Wasser, *das*

eaves /iːvz/ *n. pl.* Dachgesims, *das*

eaves: ~drop *v.i.* lauschen; **~drop on sth./sb.** etw./jmdn. belauschen; **~dropper** *n.* Lauscher, *der*/Lauscherin, *die*

'e-bank *n.* E-Bank, *die*

'e-banking *n.*, *no pl.* E-Banking, *das*

ebb /eb/

A *n.* 1 (of tide) Ebbe, *die;* **the tide is on the ~:** es ist Ebbe 2 (decline, decay) Niedergang, *der;* **be at a low ~** (fig.) ‹*Person, Stimmung, Moral:*› auf dem Nullpunkt sein; **my funds are at a low ~:** in meinem Geldbeutel ist Ebbe (ugs.); **the ~ and flow** das Auf und Ab; **the ~ and flow of life** die Höhen und Tiefen des Lebens

B *v.i.* 1 (flow back) zurückgehen 2 (recede, decline) schwinden; **~ away** dahinschwinden; **his life is ~ing away** mit ihm geht es zu Ende

'ebb tide *n.* Ebbe, *die*

'e-billing *n.*, *no pl.* elektronische Rechnungsabwicklung, *die*

Ebonics /eˈbɒnɪks/ *n.*, *no pl.*, *no art.* Ebonics, *das* (*Sprache der Afroamerikaner*)

ebony /ˈebənɪ/

A *n.* Ebenholz, *das*

B *adj.* Ebenholz‹*baum*›; ebenholzfarben ‹*Haar, Haut*›; **~ box** *etc.* Kiste *usw.* aus Ebenholz

'e-book *n.* E-Buch, *das*

ebullience /ɪˈbʌlɪəns, ɪˈbʊlɪəns/ *n.* Überschwänglichkeit, *die;* **~ of youth** jugendlicher Überschwang

ebullient /ɪˈbʌlɪənt, ɪˈbʊlɪənt/ *adj.* (exuberant) überschwänglich; übersprudelnd, überschäumend ‹*Temperament, Laune*›

'e-business *n.* E-Business, *das*

EC *abbr.* 1 **= European Commission** EK 2 **= European Community** EG

e-cash *n.*, *no pl.* E-Cash, *das;* elektronisches Geld; *attrib.* E-Cash-

e-catalogue *n.* E-Katalog, *der*

ECB *abbr.* **= European Central Bank** EZB

eccentric /ɪkˈsentrɪk/

A *adj.* 1 (odd, whimsical) exzentrisch ‹*Person*›; (differing from the usual) ausgefallen, ungewöhnlich ‹*Person*› 2 (not placed centrally, irregular) exzentrisch; einseitig ‹*Belastung*›

B *n.* Exzentriker, *der*/Exzentrikerin, *die*

eccentrically /ɪkˈsentrɪkəlɪ/ *adv.* exzentrisch

eccentricity /eksənˈtrɪsɪtɪ/ *n.* Exzentrizität, *die*

Eccles cake /ˈeklz keɪk/ *n.* (Brit.) *rundes Rosinengebäck*

Ecclesiastes /ɪkliːzɪˈæstiːz/ *n.* (Bibl.) Ekklesiastes, *der;* Prediger Salomo

ecclesiastic /ɪkliːzɪˈæstɪk/ *n.* Kleriker, *der*/Klerikerin, *die;* Geistliche, *der/die*

ecclesiastical /ɪkliːzɪˈæstɪkl/ *adj.* kirchlich; Kirchen‹*recht, -amt, -jahr*›; **~ music** geistliche Musik; Kirchenmusik, *die*

ECG *abbr.* **= electrocardiogram** EKG

echelon /ˈeʃəlɒn, ˈeɪʃəlɒn/ *n.* 1 (of troops) Echelon, *der;* Staffelstellung, *die;* **in ~:** in Staffelstellung 2 (of ships, aircraft, etc.) Staffel, *die;* **in ~:** in staffelförmiger Formation 3 (group in an organization) Stab, *der;* **the lower ~s** die niedrigeren Ränge; *see also* **upper 9 2**

echinoderm /ɪˈkaɪnədɜːm, ˈekɪnədɜːm/ *n.* (Zool.) Echinoderme, *der* (fachspr.); Stachelhäuter, *der*

echo /ˈekəʊ/

A *n.*, *pl.* **~es** 1 Echo, *das;* **cheer sb. to the ~:** jmdn. begeistert *od.* stürmisch feiern 2 (fig.) Anklang, *der* (**of** an + *Akk.*)

B *v.i.* 1 ‹*Ort:*› hallen (**with** von); **it ~es in here** hier gibt es ein Echo 2 ‹*Geräusch:*› widerhallen

C *v.t.* 1 (repeat) zurückwerfen 2 (repeat words of) echoen; wiederholen; (imitate words or opinions of) widerspiegeln

echo: ~ chamber *n.* Echokammer, *die;* **~ location** *n.*, *no pl.* Echolotung, *die;* **~ sounder** /ˈekəʊ saʊndə(r)/ *n.* Echolot, *das*

ECHR *abbr.*

A **= European Court of Human Rights** EGMR

B **= European Convention on Human Rights** EMRK

ECJ *abbr.* **= European Court of Justice** EuGH

eclair /eɪˈkleə(r), ɪˈkleə(r)/ *n.* Eclair, *das*

eclampsia /ɪˈklæmpsɪə/ *n.*, *no pl.* (Med.) Eklampsie, *die*

eclectic /ɪˈklektɪk/

A *adj.* eklektisch

B *n.* Eklektiker, *der*

eclipse /ɪˈklɪps/

A *n.* 1 (Astron.) Eklipse, *die* (fachspr.); Finsternis, *die;* **~ of the sun, solar ~:** Sonnenfinsternis, *die;* **~ of the moon, lunar ~:** Mondfinsternis, *die;* **in ~:** verfinstert 2 (deprivation of light) Dunkelheit, *die;* Finsternis, *die* 3 (fig.) Niedergang, *der;* **his fame suffered a total ~:** sein Ruhm verblasste völlig; **in ~:** im Dunkel

B *v.t.* 1 verfinstern ‹*Sonne, Mond*› 2 (fig.: outshine, surpass) in den Schatten stellen

ecliptic /ɪˈklɪptɪk/ *n.* (Astron.) Ekliptik, *die*

eco- /ˈiːkəʊ/ *in comb.* öko-/Öko-

eco: ~-audit *n.* Ökoaudit, *das;* **~-car** *n.* Ökoauto, *das;* **~catastrophe** *n.* Umweltkatastrophe, *die;* **~climate** *n.* Ökoklima, *das*

Ecofin /ˈiːkəʊfɪn/ *n.*, *no pl.* (EU) Ecofin, *der;* *attrib.* **~ Council** Ecofin-Rat, *der*

eco: ~-friendly *adj.* umweltfreundlich; **~-label** *n.* Ökoetikett, *das;* **~-labelling** *n.*, *no pl.* Ökoetikettierung, *die*

ecological /iːkəˈlɒdʒɪkl/ *adj.* ökologisch; **~ disaster** Umweltkatastrophe, *die*

eco'logically *adv.* ökologisch; **~ aware/sound/harmful** umweltbewusst/-gerecht/-schädlich

ecologist /iːˈkɒlədʒɪst/ *n.* Ökologe, *der*/Ökologin, *die*

ecology /iːˈkɒlədʒɪ/ *n.* Ökologie, *die;* *attrib.* **~ movement** Ökologiebewegung, *die*

'e-commerce *n.* elektronischer Handel; E-Commerce, *der;* *attrib.* E-Commerce-

economic /iːkəˈnɒmɪk, ekəˈnɒmɪk/ *adj.* 1 (of economics) Wirtschafts‹*politik, -abkommen, -system, -modell*›; ökonomisch, wirtschaftlich ‹*Entwicklung, Zusammenbruch*›; **~ cycle** Konjunkturzyklus, *der;* Konjunkturablauf, *der* 2 (giving adequate return) wirtschaftlich ‹*Miete*› 3 (maintained for profit) wirtschaftlich; Gewinn bringend

economic 'aid *n.*, *no pl.* Wirtschaftshilfe, *die*

economical /iːkəˈnɒmɪkl, ekəˈnɒmɪkl/ *adj.* wirtschaftlich; ökonomisch; sparsam ‹*Person*›; **be ~ with sth.** mit etw. haushalten; **be ~ with the truth** sparsam mit der Wahrheit umgehen; **the car is ~ to run** das Auto ist wirtschaftlich; **~ use of words** knappe Ausdrucksweise

economically /iːkəˈnɒmɪkəlɪ, ekəˈnɒmɪkəlɪ/ *adv.* 1 (with reference to economics) wirtschaftlich 2 (not wastefully) sparsam; **be ~ minded** wirtschaftlich denken

economic: E~ and 'Finance Committee *n.* (EU) Wirtschafts- und Finanzausschuss, *der;* **E~ and Monetary 'Union** *n.* Wirtschafts- und Währungsunion, *die;* **~ 'forecast** *n.* Wirtschaftsprognose, *die;* **~ refu'gee** *n.* Wirtschaftsflüchtling, *der*

economics /iːkəˈnɒmɪks, ekəˈnɒmɪks/ *n.*, *no pl.* 1 Wirtschaftswissenschaft, *die* (*meist Pl.*); [politische] Ökonomie 2 (economic considerations) wirtschaftlicher Aspekt; **the ~ of the situation** die wirtschaftliche *od.* finanzielle Seite der Situation 3 (condition of a country) Wirtschaft, *die*

eco'nomic system *n.* Wirtschaftssystem, *das*

economise ▸ **economize**

economist /ɪˈkɒnəmɪst/ *n.* ▸ **p. 1260** Wirtschaftswissenschaftler, *der*/-wissenschaftlerin, *die;* **political ~:** Wirtschaftspolitiker, *der*/-politikerin, *die*

economize /ɪˈkɒnəmaɪz/ *v.i.* sparen; **~ on sth.** etw. sparen

economy /ɪˈkɒnəmɪ/ *n.* 1 *no pl.* (frugality) Sparsamkeit, *die;* (of effort, motion) Wirtschaftlichkeit, *die;* (of style) Kürze, *die;* Knappheit, *die* 2 (instance) Einsparung, *die;* **make economies** zu Sparmaßnahmen greifen 3 (of country etc.) Wirtschaft, *die*

economy: ~ class *n.* Touristenklasse, *die;* Economyklasse, *die;* **~-class syndrome** *n.*, *no pl.* Economyclasssyndrom, *das;* **~ pack** *n.* Sparpackung, *die;* **~ size** *n.* Haushaltspackung, *die;* Sparpackung, *die;* **an ~-size packet of salt** eine Haushaltspackung Salz; **~ version** *n.* Sparversion, *die*

eco: ~sphere *n.* Ökosphäre, *die;* **~system** *n.* Ökosystem, *das;* **~-tax** *n.* Ökosteuer, *die;* **~terrorism** *n.*, *no pl.* 1 (terrorism carried out by environmentalist groups) Ökoterrorismus, *der;* 2 (damage to the environment) Ökoterror, *der;* **an act of ~terrorism** ein Ökoterrorakt; **~tourism** *n.* Ökotourismus, *der;* **~tourist** *n.* Ökotourist, *der*/-touristin, *die;* **~-warrior** *n.* Ökokrieger, *der*/-kriegerin, *die*

ecstasy /ˈekstəsɪ/ 1 *n.* Ekstase, *die;* Verzückung, *die;* **be in/go into ecstasies [over sth.]** in Ekstase [über etw. (*Akk.*)] sein/geraten 2 **E~** (drug) Ecstasy, *das*

ecstatic /ɪkˈstætɪk/ *adj.*, **ecstatically** /ɪkˈstætɪkəlɪ/ *adv.* ekstatisch; verzückt

ECT *abbr.* **= electroconvulsive therapy** EKT

ectopic /ekˈtɒpɪk/ *adj.* (Med.) **~ pregnancy** ektopische Schwangerschaft; (tubal pregnancy) Eileiterschwangerschaft, *die*

ectopic pregnancy /ekˈtɒpɪk pregnənsɪ/ *n.* (Med.) Bauchhöhlenschwangerschaft, *die*

ECU, ecu /ˈekjuː, ˈeɪkjuː/ *abbr.* (Hist.) **= European currency unit** Ecu, *der od. die*

Ecuador /ekwəˈdɔː(r)/ *pr. n.* Ekuador (*das*)

Ecuadorean /ekwəˈdɔːrɪən/ ▸ **p. 1345**

A *adj.* ecuadorianisch; **sb. is ~:** jmd. ist Ecuadorianer/Ecuadorianerin

B *n.* Ecuadorianer, *der*/Ecuadorianerin, *die*

ecumenical /iːkjʊˈmenɪkl, ekjʊˈmenɪkl/ *adj.* **1** (Relig.) ökumenisch; **E~ Council** ökumenisches Konzil **2** (worldwide) [welt]umfassend; [welt]umspannend

ecumenicalism /iːkjʊˈmenɪkəlɪzm, ekjʊˈmenɪkəlɪzm/ *n.* (Relig.) ökumenische Bewegung; Ökumenismus, *der* (kath. Kirche)

ecumenism /iːˈkjuːmənɪzm/ *n.* (Relig.) Ökumene, *die;* ökumenische Bewegung

eczema /ˈeksɪmə, ˈekzɪmə/ *n.* ▸ℹ **p. 1231** (Med.) Ekzem, *das* (fachspr.); Hautausschlag, *der*

ed. *abbr.* **1** **= edited [by]** hg.; hrsg. **2** **= edition** Ausg. **3** **= editor** Hrsg. **4** **= editor's note** Anm. d. Hrsg.; (in newspaper) Anm. d. Red.

Edam /ˈiːdæm/ *n.* Edamer [Käse], *der*

eddy /ˈedɪ/
A *n.* **1** (whirlpool) Strudel, *der* **2** (of wind, fog, smoke) Wirbel, *der;* **eddies of dust** Staubwirbel *Pl*
B *v.i.* ‹*Blätter:*› wirbeln; ‹*Wasser:*› sprudeln

edelweiss /ˈeɪdlvaɪs/ *n.* Edelweiß, *das*

edema (Amer.) ▸**oedema**

Eden /ˈiːdn/ *n.* Eden *(das);* (fig.) Paradies, *das;* **the Garden of ~:** der Garten Eden

EDF *abbr.* (EU) **= European Development Fund** EEF

edge /edʒ/
A *n.* **1** (of knife, razor, weapon) Schneide, *die;* (sharpness) Schärfe, *die;* (fig.: effectiveness) Schärfe, *die;* Schneidende, *das;* **the knife has lost its ~/has no ~:** das Messer ist stumpf geworden *od.* ist nicht mehr scharf/ist stumpf *od.* schneidet nicht; **take the ~ off sth.** etw. stumpf machen; (fig.) etw. abschwächen; **that took the ~ off our hunger** das nahm uns erst einmal den Hunger; **be on ~ [about sth.]** [wegen etw.] nervös *od.* gereizt sein; **her nerves have been all on ~ lately** in letzter Zeit ist sie schrecklich nervös; **set sb.'s teeth on ~:** jmdn. nervös machen; **give sb. the rough** *or* **sharp ~ of one's tongue** jmdm. gehörig Bescheid sagen (ugs.); **have/get the ~ [on sb./sth.]** (coll.) jmdm./einer Sache überlegen *od.* (ugs.) über sein/jmdn./etw. übertreffen **2** (of solid, bed, brick, record, piece of cloth) Kante, *die;* (of dress) Saum, *der;* **~ of a table** Tischkante, *die;* **roll off the ~ of the table** vom Tisch hinunterrollen; **a book with gilt ~s** ein Buch mit Goldschnitt **3** (boundary) (of sheet of paper, road, forest, desert, cliff) Rand, *der;* (of sea, lake, river) Ufer, *das;* (of estate) Grenze, *die;* **~ of the paper/of a road** Papierrand, *der*/Straßenrand, *der;* **platform ~:** Bahnsteigkante, *die;* **the ~ of the kerb** die Bordsteinkante; **at the ~ of a precipice** am Rande eines Abgrundes; **fall off the ~ of the cliff** die Klippe hinunterfallen; **on the ~ of sth.** (fig.) am Rande einer Sache (*Gen.*); **be on the ~ of disaster/bankruptcy** am Rande des Untergangs/Bankrotts stehen; **go over the ~** (fig. coll.) verrückt werden (salopp)
B *v.i.* (move cautiously) sich schieben; **~ along sth.** sich an etw. (*Dat.*) entlangschieben; **~ away** sich davonstehlen; sich wegschleichen; **~ away from sb./sth.** sich allmählich von jmdm./etw. entfernen; **~ up to sb.** sich an jmdn. heranmachen (ugs.); **~ out of the room** sich aus dem Zimmer stehlen
C *v.t.* **1** (furnish with border) säumen ‹*Straße, Platz*›; besetzen ‹*Kleid, Hut*›; einfassen ‹*Garten, Straße*›; **~ with fur** mit Pelz verbrämen ‹*Kragen*› **2** (push gradually) [langsam] schieben; **~ oneself** *or* **one's way through a crowd** sich [langsam] durch eine Menschenmenge schieben *od.* drängen; **he ~d his chair nearer to the fire** er rückte mit seinem Stuhl etwas näher ans Feuer **3** (Cricket) mit der Kante des Schlägers schlagen ‹*Ball*›

edged /edʒd/ *adj.* mit einer Schneide versehen; **an ~ blade/tool** eine scharfe Klinge/ein Werkzeug mit einer Schneide; **double-** *or* **two-~ blade** zweischneidige Klinge; **sharp-/dull-~:** scharf/stumpf; **black-/rough-~:** schwarzrandig/mit einem unebenen Rand

edgeways /ˈedʒweɪz/, **edgewise** /ˈedʒwaɪz/ *adv.* **1** (with edge uppermost or foremost) mit der Schmalseite voran; **stand sth. ~:** etw. hochkant stellen **2** (edge to edge) Kante an Kante **3** (fig.) **I can't get a word in ~!** ich komme überhaupt nicht zu Wort!

edging /ˈedʒɪŋ/ *n.* (border, fringe) (of dress) Borte, *die;* (of lawn, garden, flower bed) Einfassung, *die;* (lace, ribbon) Paspel, *die;* **fur ~:** Pelzbesatz, *der*

ˈedging shears *n. pl.* Kantenschneider, *der*

edgy /ˈedʒɪ/ *adj.* nervös

EDI *abbr.* **= electronic data interchange** EDA

edible /ˈedɪbl/
A *adj.* essbar; genießbar
B *n. in pl.* Nahrungsmittel *Pl.;* Lebensmittel *Pl.*

edict /ˈiːdɪkt/ *n.* Erlass, *der;* Edikt, *das* (hist.)

edification /edɪfɪˈkeɪʃn/ *n.* Erbauung, *die;* **for the ~ of ...:** zur Erbauung (+ *Gen.*)

edifice /ˈedɪfɪs/ *n.* Gebäude, *das;* (fig.) Gefüge, *das;* Gebäude, *das*

edifying /ˈedɪfaɪɪŋ/ *adj.* erbaulich

Edinburgh /ˈedɪnbərə/ ▸ℹ **p. 1643**
A *pr. n.* Edinburgh *(das);* Edinburg *(das)*
B *attrib. adj.* Edinburger

edit /ˈedɪt/ *v.t.* **1** (act as editor of) herausgeben ‹*Zeitung*› **2** (prepare for publication) redigieren ‹*Buch, Artikel, Manuskript*› **3** (Computing) editieren **4** (prepare an edition of) bearbeiten; **~ the works of Homer** die Werke Homers neu herausgeben **5** (take extracts from and collate) schneiden, cutten ‹*Film, Bandaufnahme*› **6** **~ sth. out** etw. weglassen

edition /ɪˈdɪʃn/ *n.* **1** (form of work, one copy; also fig.) Ausgabe, *die;* **paperback ~:** Taschenbuchausgabe, *die;* **first ~:** Erstausgabe, *die;* **he is a second ~ of his father** er gleicht seinem Vater aufs Haar **2** (from same types or at one time) Auflage, *die;* **the book is in its fourth ~:** das Buch erscheint in seiner vierten Auflage; **the work has already gone through six ~s** das Werk erscheint schon in der sechsten Auflage; **morning/evening ~ of a newspaper** Morgen-/Abendausgabe einer Zeitung

editor /ˈedɪtə(r)/ *n.* ▸ℹ **p. 1260** **1** (who prepares the work of others) Redakteur, *der*/Redakteurin, *die;* (of particular work) Bearbeiter, *der*/Bearbeiterin, *die;* (scholarly) Herausgeber, *der*/-geberin, *die* **2** (who conducts a newspaper or periodical) Herausgeber, *der*/-geberin, *die;* **chief/sports/business ~:** Chef-/Sport-/Wirtschaftsredakteur, *der* **3** (of films etc.) Cutter, *der*/Cutterin, *die*

editorial /edɪˈtɔːrɪəl/
A *n.* Leitartikel, *der*
B *adj.* (of an editor) redaktionell; Redaktions‹*assistent*›; **~ staff** Redaktion[sangestellte *Pl.*], *die;* **~ department** Redaktion, *die;* **~ job/work** Lektorenstelle, *die*/Lektorentätigkeit, *die;* **~ article** Leitartikel, *der*

editorship /ˈedɪtəʃɪp/ *n.* Chefredaktion, *die;* Schriftleitung, *die;* **under the [general] ~ of Mr X** unter Herrn X als Herausgeber

ˈedit suite *n.* Editierraum, *der*

EDP *abbr.* **= electronic data processing** EDV

EDT *abbr.* (Amer.) **= Eastern Daylight Time** östliche Sommerzeit

educable /ˈedjʊkəbl/ *adj.* erziehbar

educate /ˈedjʊkeɪt/ *v.t.* **1** (bring up) erziehen; **~ sb. in sth.** jmdm. etw. beibringen **2** (provide schooling for) **he was ~d at Eton and Cambridge** er hat seine Ausbildung in Eton und Cambridge erhalten **3** (give intellectual and moral training to) bilden; **~ oneself** sich [weiter]bilden; **the public must be ~d in** *or* **about how to save energy** die Öffentlichkeit muss aufgeklärt werden, wie man Energie spart **4** (train) schulen ‹*Geist, Körper*›; [aus]bilden ‹*Geschmack*›; dressieren, abrichten ‹*Tier*›; **~ oneself to do sth.** sich dazu erziehen, etw. zu tun

educated /ˈedjʊkeɪtɪd/ *adj.* gebildet; **make an ~ guess** eine wohl begründete Vermutung anstellen

education /edjʊˈkeɪʃn/ *n.* **1** (instruction) Erziehung, *die;* (course of instruction) Ausbildung, *die;* (system) Erziehungs[- und Ausbildungs]wesen, *das;* (science) Erziehungswissenschaften *Pl.;* Pädagogik, *die;* **~ is free** die Schulausbildung ist kostenlos; **Ministry of E~:** Ministerium für Erziehung und Unterricht; Kultusministerium, *das;* **be a man of ~:** ein gebildeter Mensch sein; **receive a good ~:** eine gute Ausbildung genießen; **sb. with school/a higher** *or* **university ~:** jmd. mit Schulbildung/Universitätsausbildung; **literary/scientific ~:** literarische/naturwissenschaftliche Bildung; **lecturer in ~:** Dozent/Dozentin für Pädagogik; **science/methods of ~:** Erziehungswissenschaften *Pl.*/-methoden *Pl.* **2** (development of character or mental powers) Schulung, *die. see also* **College of Education**

educational /edjʊˈkeɪʃənl/ *adj.* pädagogisch; erzieherisch; Lehr‹*film, -spiele, -anstalt*›; Erziehungs‹*methoden, -arbeit*›; **~ equipment** Unterrichtsmittel *Pl.;* **for ~ purposes** zu Lehr- *od.* Unterrichtszwecken

educationalist /edjʊˈkeɪʃənəlɪst/ *n.* Pädagoge, *der*/Pädagogin, *die;* Erziehungswissenschaftler, *der*/-wissenschaftlerin, *die*

educationally /edjʊˈkeɪʃənəlɪ/ *adv.* pädagogisch; **~ subnormal** lernbehindert; **be ~ backward** ein niedriges Bildungsniveau haben

eduˈcation authority *n.* (Brit.) Bildungsbehörde, *die*

educationist /edjʊˈkeɪʃənɪst/ ▸**educationalist**

eduˈcation system *n.* Bildungssystem, *das*

educative /ˈedjʊkətɪv/ *adj.* (educational) erzieherisch, pädagogisch ‹*Fragen, Gründe*›; (instructive) erzieherisch; Erziehungs-; lehrreich ‹*Film, Buch*›

educator /ˈedjʊkeɪtə(r)/ *n.* Pädagoge, *der*/Pädagogin, *die;* Erzieher, *der*/Erzieherin, *die;* (fig.) Erzieher, *der*

edutainment /edjuːˈteɪnmənt/ *n., no pl.* Edutainment, *das; attrib.* Edutainment-

Edward /ˈedwəd/ *pr. n.* (Hist., as name of ruler etc.) Eduard *(der)*

Edwardian /edˈwɔːdɪən/
A *adj.* edwardianisch
B *n.* Edwardianer, *der*

EEC *abbr.* **= European Economic Community** EWG

eel /iːl/ *n.* Aal, *der;* **be as slippery as an ~:** aalglatt sein

e'en /iːn/ (arch./poet.) ▸**even**[1,2]

e'er /eə(r)/ (poet.) ▸**ever**

eerie /ˈɪərɪ/ *adj.* unheimlich ‹*Ort, Gebäude, Form*›; schaurig ‹*Klang*›; schauerlich ‹*Schrei*›; **give sb. an ~ feeling** jmdn. schaudern lassen

eerily /ˈɪərɪlɪ/ *adv.* ▸**eerie**: unheimlich; schaurig

eff /ef/ *v.i.* (coll.) **~ and blind** fluchen

efface /ɪˈfeɪs/
A *v.t.* **1** (rub out) beseitigen ‹*Inschrift*› **2** (fig.: obliterate) auslöschen; tilgen (geh.)
B *v. refl.* sich im Hintergrund halten

effect /ɪˈfekt/
A *n.* **1** (result) Wirkung, *die* (**on** auf + *Akk.*); **her words had little ~ on him** ihre Worte erzielten bei ihm nur eine geringe Wirkung; **the ~s of sth. on sth.** die Auswirkungen einer Sache (*Gen.*) auf etw. (*Akk.*); die Folgen einer Sache (*Gen.*) für etw.; **the ~ of this was that ...:** das hatte zur Folge, dass ...; **be of no** *or* **to no ~:** erfolglos *od.* ergebnislos sein; **with the ~ that ...:** mit der Folge *od.* dem Resultat, dass ...; **take ~:** wirken; die erwünschte Wirkung erzielen; **in ~:** in Wirklichkeit; praktisch **2** *no art.* (impression) Wirkung, *die;* Effekt, *der;* **solely** *or* **only for ~:** nur des Effekts wegen; aus reiner Effekthascherei (abwertend) **3** (meaning) Inhalt, *der;* Sinn, *der;* **or words to that ~:** oder etwas in diesem Sinne; **a letter to the following ~:** ein Brief folgenden Inhalts; **we received a letter to the ~ that ...:** wir erhielten ein Schreiben des Inhalts, dass ...; **all families received instructions to that ~:** alle Familien bekamen entsprechende Anweisungen; **to the same ~:** desselben Inhalts **4** (validity) Kraft, *die;* Gültigkeit, *die;* **be in ~:** gültig *od.* in Kraft sein; **come into ~:** gültig *od.* wirksam werden; ‹*bes. Gesetz:*› in Kraft treten; **bring** *or* **carry** *or* **put into ~:** in Kraft setzen ‹*Gesetz*›; verwirklichen ‹*Plan*›; verwerten ‹*Erfahrung, Kenntnisse*›; **give ~ to sth.** etw. in Kraft treten

e

e

lassen; **take ~:** in Kraft treten; **with ~ from 2 November/Monday** mit Wirkung vom 2. November/von Montag **5** *in pl.* (in play, film, broadcast) **light ~s** Lichteffekte *Pl.* **6** *in pl.* (property) Vermögenswerte *Pl.*; Eigentum, *das;* **personal ~s** persönliches Eigentum; Privateigentum, *das;* **household ~s** Hausrat, *der*

B *v.t.* durchführen; herbeiführen ‹*Einigung*›; erzielen ‹*Übereinstimmung, Übereinkommen*›; tätigen ‹*Umsatz, Kauf*›; abschließen ‹*Versicherung*›; leisten ‹*Zahlung*›; **payment was ~ed in dollars** die Zahlung erfolgte in Dollar

effective /ɪˈfektɪv/ *adj.* **1** (having an effect) wirksam ‹*Mittel*›; effektiv ‹*Maßnahmen*›; gleichwertig ‹*Ersatz*›; **the measures have not been ~:** die Maßnahmen blieben ohne Wirkung *od.* waren wirkungslos; **be ~** ‹*Arzneimittel:*› wirken **2** (having come into operation) gültig; **~ from/as of** mit Wirkung von; **the law is no longer ~/is ~ as from 1 September** das Gesetz hat keine Gültigkeit mehr *od.* ist außer Kraft/tritt ab 1. September in Kraft *od.* wird ab 1. September wirksam **3** (powerful in effect) überzeugend ‹*Rede, Redner, Worte*›; kraftvoll ‹*Stimme*› **4** (striking) wirkungsvoll; effektvoll **5** (existing) wirklich, tatsächlich ‹*Hilfe*›; effektiv ‹*Gewinn, Umsatz*›; **the ~ strength of the army** die Iststärke der Armee

effectively /ɪˈfektɪvlɪ/ *adv.* (in fact) effektiv; (with effect) wirkungsvoll; effektvoll; **they are ~ the same** effektiv sind sie gleich

effectiveness /ɪˈfektɪvnɪs/ *n., no pl.* Wirksamkeit, *die;* Effektivität, *die*

effectual /ɪˈfektjʊəl/ *adj.* **1** (sufficient) wirksam ‹*Mittel, Maßnahmen*› **2** (valid) [rechts]gültig, bindend ‹*Vertrag, Dokument*›

effectually /ɪˈfektjʊəlɪ/ *adv.* erfolgreich

effectuate /ɪˈfektjʊeɪt/ *v.t.* bewirken; herbeiführen ‹*Änderung*›; erzielen ‹*Übereinstimmung*›

effeminate /ɪˈfemɪnət/ *adj.* unmännlich, (geh.) effeminiert ‹*Mann*›

effervesce /efəˈves/ *v.i.* sprudeln; efferveszieren (fachspr.); (fig.) übersprudeln; überschäumen

effervescence /efəˈvesəns/ *n., no pl.* Sprudeln, *das;* (fig.) Übersprudeln, *das;* Überschäumen, *das*

effervescent /efəˈvesənt/ *adj.* sprudelnd; (fig.) übersprudelnd, überschäumend ‹*Freude, Verhalten*›; überschwänglich ‹*Stimme*›; **~ tablets** Brausetabletten

effete /eˈfiːt/ *adj.* (exhausted, worn out) verbraucht; saft- und kraftlos ‹*Person*›; überlebt ‹*System*›; (soft, decadent) verweichlicht

efficacious /efɪˈkeɪʃəs/ *adj.* wirksam ‹*Methode, Mittel, Medizin*›

efficaciousness /efɪˈkeɪʃəsnɪs/, **efficacy** /ˈefɪkəsɪ/ *ns., no pl.* Wirksamkeit, *die*

efficiency /ɪˈfɪʃənsɪ/ *n.* **1** (of person) Fähigkeit, *die;* Tüchtigkeit, *die;* (of machine, engine, factory) Leistungsfähigkeit, *die;* (of organization, method) gutes Funktionieren **2** (Mech., Phys.) Wirkungsgrad, *der*

efficient /ɪˈfɪʃənt/ *adj.* fähig ‹*Person*›; tüchtig ‹*Arbeiter, Sekretärin*›; leistungsfähig ‹*Maschine, Motor, Fabrik*›; gut funktionierend ‹*Methode, Organisation*›

efficiently /ɪˈfɪʃəntlɪ/ *adv.* gut; effizient (geh.)

effigy /ˈefɪdʒɪ/ *n.* Bildnis, *das;* **hang/burn sb. in ~:** jmdn. in effigie hängen/verbrennen (geh.)

effing /ˈefɪŋ/ *adj.* (sl.) Scheiß- (salopp)

effloresce /efləˈres/ *v.i.* (Chem.) ausblühen

efflorescence /efləˈresəns/ *n.* (Chem.) Ausblühung, *die*

effluent /ˈefluənt/

A *adj.* abfließend ‹*Fluss, Wasser*›; **~ drain** Abfluss, *der*

B *n.* **1** (stream) Abfluss, *der* **2** (outflow from sewage tank, waste etc.) Abwässer *Pl.*

effluvium /eˈfluːvɪəm/ *n., pl.* **effluvia** /eˈfluːvɪə/ Ausdünstung, *die*

effort /ˈefət/ *n.* **1** (exertion) Anstrengung, *die;* Mühe, *die;* **make an/every ~** (physically) sich anstrengen; (mentally) sich bemühen; **without [any]/only with the greatest ~:** ohne Anstrengung *od.* mühelos/nur mit äußerster Anstrengung *od.* größter Mühe; **for all his ~s** trotz all seiner Bemühungen; **vain ~s** vergebliche Bemühungen; **it is an ~ [for me] to get up in the mornings** es kostet [mich] einige Mühe *od.* Anstrengung, morgens aufzustehen; **[a] waste of time and ~:** verlorene *od.* vergebliche Liebesmüh; **make every possible ~ to do sth.** jede nur mögliche Anstrengung unternehmen *od.* machen, etw. zu tun; **he makes no ~ at all** er bemüht sich überhaupt nicht; er gibt sich überhaupt keine Mühe **2** (attempt) Versuch, *der;* **in an ~ to do sth.** beim Versuch, etw. zu tun; **make no ~ to be polite** sich (*Dat.*) nicht die Mühe machen, höflich zu sein; **make one last ~:** einen letzten Versuch unternehmen; **~s are being made to do sth.** es sind Bestrebungen im Gange, etw. zu tun **3** (activity) **research ~[s]** Einsatz in der Forschungsarbeit; **business ~s** geschäftliche Unternehmungen **4** (coll.: result) Leistung, *die;* **that was a pretty poor ~:** das war ein ziemlich schwaches Bild (ugs.); **whose is this rather poor ~?** welcher Stümper hat das denn verbrochen? (ugs.); **the book was one of his first ~s** das Buch war einer seiner ersten Versuche

effortless /ˈefətlɪs/ *adj.* mühelos; leicht; flüssig, leicht ‹*Stil*›

effortlessly /ˈefətlɪslɪ/ *adv.* mühelos; ohne Anstrengung; flüssig ‹*schreiben*›

effrontery /ɪˈfrʌntərɪ/ *n.* Dreistigkeit, *die;* **have the ~ to do sth.** die Frechheit *od.* (geh.) Stirn besitzen, etw. zu tun

effusion /ɪˈfjuːʒn/ *n.* **1** (pouring forth) (of light, sound) Ausströmen, *das;* Entströmen, *das;* (of the Holy Spirit) Ausgießung, *die* **2** (utterance) Überschwang, *der;* **literary/romantic ~s** literarische/romantische Ergüsse

effusive /ɪˈfjuːsɪv/ *adj.* überschwänglich; exaltiert (geh.) ‹*Person, Stil, Charakter*›

effusively /ɪˈfjuːsɪvlɪ/ *adv.* ▸**effusive**: überschwänglich; exaltiert (geh.)

effusiveness /ɪˈfjuːsɪvnɪs/ *n., no pl.* (of speech, action, greeting) Überschwänglichkeit, *die;* (of style) Exaltiertheit, *die* (geh.)

EFL *abbr.* = **English as a foreign language**

'e-form *n.* E-Formular, *das*

EFT *abbr.* = **electronic funds transfer** EZV

Efta, EFTA /ˈeftə/ *n. abbr.* = **European Free Trade Association** EFTA

EFTPOS /ˈeftpɒz/ *abbr.* = **electronic funds transfer at point of sale** EFTPOS

e.g. /iːˈdʒiː/ *abbr.* = **for example** z. B.

egalitarian /ɪgælɪˈteərɪən/

A *adj.* egalitär (geh.) ‹*Person, Einstellung, Gruppe*›; Gleichheits‹*prinzipien*›

B *n.* Verfechter/Verfechterin des Egalitarismus

egg¹ /eg/ *n.* Ei, *das;* **a bad ~** (fig. coll.) (person) eine üble Person; **a good/tough ~** (coll.) (person) ein feiner *od.* (veralt.) famoser/harter Kerl (ugs.); **good ~!** (dated coll.) famos! (veralt.); **have** *or* **put all one's ~s in one basket** (fig. coll.) alles auf eine Karte setzen; **it's like teaching your grandmother to suck ~s** da will das Ei wieder klüger sein als die Henne; **as sure as ~s is** *or* **are ~s** (coll.) so sicher wie das Amen in der Kirche (ugs.); **have ~ on** *or* **all over one's face** (fig.) dumm *od.* blöd dastehen (ugs.); dumm aus der Wäsche gucken (salopp)

egg² *v.t.* **~ sb. on [to do sth.]** jmdn. anstacheln *od.* aufhetzen[, etw. zu tun]

egg: ~-and-'spoon race Eierlaufen, *das;* **~ beater** *n.* **1** (device) Rührbesen, *der;* **2** (Amer. coll.: helicopter) Hubschrauber, *der;* **~ box** *n.* Eierkarton, *der;* **~ cosy** *n.* (Brit.) Eierwärmer, *der;* **~cup** *n.* Eierbecher, *der;* **~ 'custard** *n.* Eierkrem, *die;* **~ donor** *n.* Ei[zellen]spenderin, *die;* **~ 'flip** *n.* Eierlikör, *der;* **~head** *n.* (coll.) Eierkopf, *der* (abwertend); Egghead, *der* (geh. oft scherzhaft od. abwertend); **~ 'nog** ▸**~ flip**; **~plant** *n.* Aubergine, *die;* (fruit also) Eierfrucht, *die;* (plant also) Eierpflanze, *die;* **~ powder** *n.* Eipulver, *das;* **~-shaped** *adj.* eiförmig; **~shell** *n.* **1** Eierschale, *die;* **2** *attrib.* (fragile) **~shell china** Eierschalenporzellan, *das;* **~shell glaze** Mittelglanzglasur, *die;* **~ slice** *n.* ≈ Wender, *der;* **~ spoon** *n.* Eierlöffel, *der;* **~ timer** *n.* Eieruhr, *die;* **~ whisk** *n.* Schneebesen, *der;* **~ white** *n.* Eiweiß, *das;* **~ yolk** *n.* Eigelb, *das;* Eidotter, *der od. das*

EGM *abbr.* = **extraordinary general meeting** aoHV, ao.HV (*außerordentliche Hauptversammlung*); (of club) aoMV, ao.MV (*außerordentliche Mitgliederversammlung*)

ego /ˈegəʊ, ˈiːgəʊ/ *n., pl.* **~s** **1** (Psych.) Ego, *das;* (Metaphys.) Ich, *das* **2** (self-esteem) Selbstbewusstsein, *das;* **inflated ~:** übersteigertes Selbstbewusstsein; **boost sb.'s ~:** jmds. Selbstbewusstsein stärken; jmdm. Auftrieb geben

egocentric /egəʊˈsentrɪk/ *adj.* egozentrisch; ichbezogen

egoism /ˈegəʊɪzm/ *n., no pl.* **1** (systematic selfishness) Egoismus, *der;* Selbstsucht, *die* (abwertend) **2** (opinionatedness) Selbstherrlichkeit, *die* **3** ▸**egotism 1**

egoist /ˈegəʊɪst/ *n.* Egoist, *der*/Egoistin, *die*

egoistic /egəʊˈɪstɪk/, **egoistical** /egəʊˈɪstɪkl/ *adj.* **1** (self-regarding, selfish) egoistisch; selbstsüchtig; eigennützig **2** ▸**egotistic 1**

egomania /iːgəʊˈmeɪnɪə/ *n.* Egomanie, *die*

egomaniac /iːgəʊˈmeɪnɪæk/ *n.* Egomane, *der*/Egomanin, *die*

egotism /ˈegətɪzm/ *n., no pl.* **1** Egotismus, *der* (fachspr.); Ichbezogenheit, *die* **2** (self-conceit) Egotismus, *der;* Selbstgefälligkeit, *die* **3** ▸**egoism 1**

egotist /ˈegətɪst/ *n.* Egotist, *der*/Egotistin, *die* (fachspr.); (self-centred person) Egozentriker, *der*/Egozentrikerin, *die*

egotistic /egəˈtɪstɪk/, **egotistical** /egəˈtɪstɪkl/ *adj.* **1** ichbezogen ‹*Rede, Gespräch*› **2** selbstsüchtig, selbstgefällig (abwertend) ‹*Person*›

'ego trip *n.* (coll.) Egotrip, *der;* **be on an ~:** auf einem Egotrip sein

egregious /ɪˈgriːdʒəs/ *adj.* ungeheuer[lich]; ausgemacht ‹*Trottel*›

egress /ˈiːgres/ *n.* (formal) Ausgang, *der* (**to, into** zu)

egret /ˈiːgrɪt, ˈegrɪt/ *n.* (Ornith.) Reiher, *der*

Egypt /ˈiːdʒɪpt/ *pr. n.* Ägypten (*das*)

Egyptian /ɪˈdʒɪpʃn/ ▸❶ **p. 1277**, ▸❶ **p. 1345**

A *adj.* ägyptisch; **sb. is ~:** jmd. ist Ägypter/Ägypterin; *see also* **English A**

B *n.* **1** (person) Ägypter, *der*/Ägypterin, *die* **2** (language) Ägyptisch, *das; see also* **English B 1**

Egyptologist /iːdʒɪpˈtɒlədʒɪst/ *n.* Ägyptologe, *der*/Ägyptologin, *die*

Egyptology /iːdʒɪpˈtɒlədʒɪ/ *n., no pl.* Ägyptologie, *die*

eh /eɪ/ *int.* (coll.) *expr. inquiry or surprise* wie?; wie bitte?; *inviting assent* nicht [wahr]?; *asking for sth. to be repeated or explained* was?; hä? (salopp); **wasn't that good, eh?** war das nicht gut?; **let's not have any more fuss, eh?** Schluss mit dem Theater, ja? (ugs.)

EIB *abbr.* (EU) = **European Investment Bank** EIB

eiderdown /ˈaɪdədaʊn/ *n.* Daunenbett, *das;* Federbett, *das*

eider/ˈaɪdə(r)/: **~ [duck]** *n.* Eiderente, *die;* **~ [down]** *n.* [Eider]daunen *Pl.*; Flaumfedern *Pl.*

eight /eɪt/ ▸❶ **p. 894**, ▸❶ **p. 1001**, ▸❶ **p. 1358**

A *adj.* acht; **at ~:** um acht; **it's ~ [o'clock]** es ist acht [Uhr]; **half past ~:** halb neun; **~ thirty** acht Uhr dreißig; **~ ten/fifty** zehn nach acht/vor neun; (esp. in timetable) acht Uhr zehn/fünfzig; **around ~ at about ~:** gegen acht [Uhr]; **half ~** (coll.) halb neun; **girl of ~:** Mädchen von acht Jahren; **~-year-old boy** achtjähriger Junge; **an ~-year-old** ein Achtjähriger/eine Achtjährige; **be ~ [years old]** acht [Jahre alt] sein; **at [the age of] ~, aged ~:** mit acht Jahren; im Alter von acht Jahren; **he won ~-six** er hat acht zu sechs gewonnen; **Book/Volume/Part/Chapter E~:** Buch/Band/Teil/Kapitel acht; achtes Buch/achter Band/achter Teil/achtes Kapitel; **~-figure number** achtstellige Zahl; **~-page** achtseitig; **~-storey[ed] building** achtstöckiges *od.* achtgeschossiges

Gebäude; **~-sided polygon** achtseitiges Vieleck; **bet at ~ to one** acht zu eins wetten; **~ times** achtmal
B n. **1** (number, symbol) Acht, *die;* **the first/last ~:** die ersten/letzten acht; **there were ~ of us present** wir waren [zu] acht; **~ of us attended the lecture** wir waren [zu] acht bei der Vorlesung; **come ~ at a time/in ~s** acht auf einmal kommen/zu je acht kommen; **arabic/Roman ~:** arabische/römische Acht; **stack the boxes in ~s** die Kisten zu achten stapeln; **the [number] ~ [bus]** die Buslinie Nr. 8; der Achter (ugs.); **two-~ time** (Mus.) Zweiachteltakt, *der;* **behind the ~ ball** (Amer.) (at a disadvantage) im Nachteil; (in a baffling situation) in einer misslichen Lage **2** (8-shaped figure) **[figure of] ~:** Achter, *der* (ugs.); Acht, *die* **3** (Cards) **~ of hearts/trumps** Herz-/Trumpfacht, *die* **4** (size) **a size ~ dress** ein Kleid [in] Größe 8; **wear size ~ shoes** Schuhgröße 8 haben *od.* tragen; **wear an ~, be size ~:** Größe 8 tragen *od.* haben **5** (Rowing) (crew) Achtermannschaft, *die;* (boat) Achter, *der;* **the Eights** (boat races) Achterrennen, *das* **6** **have had one over the ~** (coll.) einen über den Durst getrunken haben (ugs.)

eighteen /eɪˈtiːn/
A *adj.* ▸ⓘ **p. 894**, ▸ⓘ **p. 1001**, ▸ⓘ **p. 1358** achtzehn; *see also* **eight A**
B n. Achtzehn, *die;* **~ seventy** achtzehnhundertsiebzig; **in the ~ seventies** in den siebziger Jahren des neunzehnten Jahrhunderts; **~ hundred hours** ▸**hundred A 1**; *see also* **eight B 1, 4**

eighteenth /eɪˈtiːnθ/ ▸ⓘ **p. 1047**
A *adj.* ▸ⓘ **p. 1358** achtzehnt...; *see also* **eighth A**
B n. (fraction) Achtzehntel, *das; see also* **eighth B**

eightfold /ˈeɪtfəʊld/
A *adj.* achtfach; **an ~ increase** ein Anstieg auf das Achtfache
B *adv.* achtfach; **multiply ~:** sich verachtfachen; **increase ~:** sich auf das Achtfache erhöhen

eighth /eɪtθ/
A *adj.* ▸ⓘ **p. 1358** acht...; **be/come ~:** Achter sein/als Achter ankommen; **an ~ part/share** ein Achtel; **~ largest** achtgrößt...
B n. ▸ⓘ **p. 1047** (in sequence, rank) Achte, *der/die/das;* (fraction) Achtel, *das;* **be the ~ to do sth.** der/die/das Achte sein, der/die/das etw. tut; (day) **the ~ of May** der achte Mai; **the ~ [of the month]** der Achte [des Monats]

ˈeighth note n. (Amer. Mus.) Achtel, *das;* Achtelnote, *die*

eightieth /ˈeɪtɪɪθ/
A *adj.* ▸ⓘ **p. 1358** achtzigst...; *see also* **eighth A**
B n. (fraction) Achtzigstel, *das; see also* **eighth B**

eighty /ˈeɪtɪ/ ▸ⓘ **p. 894**, ▸ⓘ **p. 1358**
A *adj.* achtzig; *see also* **eight A**
B n. Achtzig, *die;* **be in one's eighties** in den Achtzigern sein; **be in one's early/late eighties** Anfang/Ende achtzig sein; **the eighties** (years) die Achtzigerjahre; **the temperature will be rising [well] into the eighties** die Temperatur steigt auf [gut] über 80 Grad Fahrenheit; *see also* **eight B 1**

eighty: ~-ˈfirst *etc. adj.* ▸ⓘ **p. 1358** einundachtzigst... *usw.; see also* **eighth A**; **~-ˈone** *etc.* **A** *adj.* einundachtzig *usw.; see also* **eight A**; **B** n. ▸ⓘ **p. 1358** Einundachtzig *usw., die; see also* **eight B 1**

Eire /ˈeərə/ *pr. n.* Irland *(das);* Eire *(das)*

eisteddfod /aɪˈsteðvəd/ n., *pl.* **~s** *or* **~au** /aɪsteðˈvədaɪ/ **1** (of Welsh bards) Eisteddfod, *das* **2** (gathering for competitions) Dichter- und Sängerfest, *das*

either /ˈaɪðə(r), ˈiːðə(r)/
A *adj.* **1** (each) **at ~ end of the table** an beiden Enden des Tisches; **on ~ side of the road** auf beiden Seiten der Straße; **~ way** ▸**way A 3** **2** (one or other) [irgend]ein ... [von beiden]; **take ~ one** nimm einen/eine/eins von [den] beiden
B *pron.* **1** (each) beide *Pl.;* **~ is possible** beides ist möglich; **I can't cope with ~:** ich kann mit keinem von beiden fertig werden; **I don't like ~ [of them** *or* **of the two]** ich mag beide nicht *od.* keinen von beiden **2** (one or other) einer/eine/ein[e]s [von beiden]; **~ of the buses** jeder der beiden Busse; beide Busse
C *adv.* **1** (any more than the other) auch [nicht]; **'I don't like that ~:** ich mag es auch nicht; **I don't like ˈthat ~:** auch das mag ich nicht; **she plays the piano badly and she can't sing ~:** sie spielt schlecht Klavier, und singen kann sie auch nicht **2** (moreover, furthermore) noch nicht einmal; **there was a time, and not so long ago ~:** früher, noch gar nicht einmal so lange her
D *conj.* **~ ... or ...** entweder ... oder ...; (after negation) weder ... noch ...; **I've never been to ~ Berlin or Munich** ich bin weder in Berlin noch in München gewesen

ˈeither-or
A *adj.* Entweder-Oder-‹*Problem*›
B n. Entweder-Oder, *das*

ejaculate /ɪˈdʒækjʊleɪt/
A *v.t.* **1** (utter suddenly) ausstoßen ‹*Fluch, Gebet*› **2** (eject) ausstoßen; ejakulieren ‹*Samen*›
B *v.i.* (eject semen) ejakulieren

ejaculation /ɪdʒækjʊˈleɪʃn/ n. **1** (utterance) Ausbruch, *der;* (cry) Ausruf, *der* **2** (ejection) Ausstoß, *der;* (of semen) Ejakulation, *die;* Samenerguss, *der*

eject /ɪˈdʒekt/
A *v.t.* **1** (expel) (from committee, hall, meeting) hinauswerfen **(from** aus) **2** (from machine gun) auswerfen; (from aircraft) hinausschleudern; (from video player etc.) ‹*Gerät:*› auswerfen, ‹*Person:*› herausholen ‹*Kassette*› **3** (dispossess) hinauswerfen; exmittieren (Amtsspr.)
B *v.i.* sich hinauskatapultieren

eˈject button n. Auswurftaste, *die*

ejection /ɪˈdʒekʃn/ n. (of intruder etc.) Vertreibung, *die;* (of heckler, troublesome drunk) Hinauswurf, *der;* (of empty cartridge) Ausstoß, *der;* Auswerfen, *das;* (of pilot) Hinausschleudern, *das*

ejector /ɪˈdʒektə(r)/ n. (of firearm) Auswerfer, *der*

eˈjector seat n. Schleudersitz, *der*

eke /iːk/ *v.t.* **~ out** strecken ‹*Vorräte, Essen, Einkommen*›; **~ out a living** *or* **an existence** sich *(Dat.)* seinen Lebensunterhalt notdürftig *od.* mühsam verdienen

elaborate
A /ɪˈlæbərət/ *adj.* kompliziert; ausgefeilt ‹*Stil*›; durchorganisiert ‹*Studium, Forschung*›; kunstvoll [gearbeitet] ‹*Arrangement, Stickerei, Verzierung, Kleidungsstück*›; üppig, umfangreich ‹*Menü*›
B /ɪˈlæbəreɪt/ *v.t.* weiter ausarbeiten; weiter ausführen ‹*Arbeit, Plan, Thema*›
C *v.i.* mehr ins Detail gehen; **could you ~?** könnten Sie das näher ausführen?; **~ on sth.** etw. ausführlicher erklären *od.* näher ausführen

elaborately /ɪˈlæbərətlɪ/ *adv.* anspruchsvoll ‹*sich kleiden*›; kompliziert ‹*ausarbeiten, planen*›; kunstvoll ‹*entwerfen, verzieren*›; umfangreich ‹*vorbereiten*›

elaboration /ɪlæbəˈreɪʃn/ n. (of plan, theory, etc.) Ausarbeitung, *die* (meist Pl.); (of style) Ausfeilung, *die;* (that which elaborates) Elaborat, *das* (abwertend)

élan /ˈeɪlɑ̃/ n., *no pl.* Energie, *die;* Schwung, *der*

eland /ˈiːlənd/ n. (Zool.) Elenantilope, *die*

elapse /ɪˈlæps/ *v.i.* ‹*Zeit:*› vergehen, ins Land gehen

elastic /ɪˈlæstɪk, ɪˈlɑːstɪk/
A *adj.* **1** elastisch **2** (springy) geschmeidig ‹*Bewegung*›; federnd ‹*Gang*›; elastisch ‹*Muskel*› **3** (fig.: flexible) flexibel; weit ‹*Gewissen*›; weit auslegbar ‹*Klausel, Bestimmung*›; Gummi‹*begriff, -paragraph*› (ugs.)
B n. (**~ band**) Gummiband, *das;* (fabric) elastisches Material

elasticated /ɪˈlæstɪkeɪtɪd, ɪˈlɑːstɪkeɪtɪd/ *adj.* elastisch

elastic ˈband n. Gummiband, *das*

elasticity /elæsˈtɪsɪtɪ, iːlæsˈtɪsɪtɪ/ n., *no pl.* **1** (of material etc.) Elastizität, *die* **2** (springiness) Geschmeidigkeit, *die* **3** (fig.: flexibility) Flexibilität, *die;* (of rules, laws) [weite] Auslegbarkeit **4** (Econ.) Anpassungsfähigkeit, *die*

elastic ˈstocking n. Gummistrumpf, *der*

elate /ɪˈleɪt/ *v.t.* erfreuen; erbauen (geh.); **be ~d by/over sth.** aufgrund einer Sache *(Gen.)*/über etw. *(Akk.)* hocherfreut *od.* in Hochstimmung sein

elated /ɪˈleɪtɪd/ *adj.* freudig erregt; **~ mood** *or* **state of mind** Hochstimmung, *die;* **be** *or* **feel ~:** in Hochstimmung sein

elation /ɪˈleɪʃn/ n., *no pl.* freudige Erregung; **feel ~ at one's success** über seinen Erfolg hocherfreut sein

elbow /ˈelbəʊ/
A n. **1** ▸ⓘ **p. 951** Ell[en]bogen, *der* **2** (of piping) Knie, *das* **3** (bend, corner) Knick, *der;* (of river) Biegung, *die;* Knie, *das;* (of road) Biegung, *die* **4** (of garment) Ellbogen, *der* **5** **at one's ~:** bei sich; in Reichweite; **sth./sb. is at sb.'s ~:** etw. ist in Reichweite/jmd. ist in jmds. Nähe; **bend** *or* **lift one's ~** (coll.: drink) einen heben (ugs.); **give sb. the ~** (coll.) jmdm. den Laufpass geben (ugs.); **out at ~s** an den Ellbogen abgetragen *od.* durchgewetzt ‹*Mantel*›; heruntergekommen ‹*Person*›; **be up to one's** *or* **the ~s in sth./work** mit etw. alle Hände voll zu tun haben/bis über die Ohren in Arbeit stecken
B *v.t.* **~ one's way** sich mit den Ell[en]bogen einen Weg bahnen; sich drängeln (ugs.); **~ sb. aside** jmdn. mit den Ell[en]bogen zur Seite stoßen; **~ sb. out** (fig.) jmdn. hinausdrängeln

elbow: ~ grease n., *no pl.* (joc.) Muskelkraft, *die;* **~ patch** n. [Ellbogen]flicken, *der;* Ellbogenverstärkung, *die* (Textilw.); **~ room** n. (lit. or fig.) Ellbogenfreiheit, *die;* (fig.) Spielraum, *der*

elder[1] /ˈeldə(r)/
A *attrib. adj.* älter...; **Pliny the E~, the ~ Pliny** Plinius der Ältere
B n. **1** (senior) Ältere, *der/die;* **he is my ~ by several years** er ist mehrere Jahre älter als ich **2** *in pl.* Alten *Pl.;* **our ~s and betters** die Älteren mit mehr Lebenserfahrung; **the village ~s** die Dorfältesten; **the ~s of the tribe** die Stammesältesten **3** (official in Church) [Kirchen]älteste, *der/die*

elder[2] n. (Bot.) Holunder, *der*

elder: ~berry n. Holunderbeere, *die;* **~berry ˈwine** n. Holunderbeerwein, *der;* **~care** n., *no pl.* (Amer.) Altenpflege, *die;* Altenbetreuung, *die;* **~flower** n. Holunderblüte, *die;* **~flower ˈwine** n. Holunderblütenwein, *der*

elderly /ˈeldəlɪ/
A *adj.* älter; **my parents are both quite ~ now** meine Eltern sind beide inzwischen ziemlich alt geworden
B n. *pl.* **the ~:** ältere Menschen

elder: ~ ˈstatesman n. Elder statesman, *der* (Politik); **~ ˈwine** ▸**elderberry wine**

eldest /ˈeldɪst/ *adj.* ältest...

eldorado /eldəˈrɑːdəʊ/ n., *pl.* **~s** Eldorado, *das*

ˈe-learning n., *no pl.* E-Learning, *das*

elect /ɪˈlekt/
A *adj.* **1** *postpos.* (chosen but not installed) gewählt; **the President ~:** der gewählte *od.* designierte Präsident **2** (choice) auserlesen, exklusiv ‹*Gruppe*›; (chosen) [aus]erwählt
B *v.t.* **1** (choose by vote) wählen; **~ sb. chairman/MP** *etc.* jmdn. zum Vorsitzenden/Abgeordneten *usw.* wählen; **~ sb. to the chair/to the Senate** jmdn. zum Vorsitzenden/in den Senat wählen **2** (choose) **~ to do sth.** sich dafür entscheiden, etw. zu tun

election /ɪˈlekʃn/ n. Wahl, *die;* **presidential ~s** (Amer.) Präsidentschaftswahlen *Pl.;* **general/local ~:** allgemeine/kommunale Wahlen; **~ as chairman** Wahl zum Vorsitzenden; **~ results** Wahlergebnisse *Pl.;* **~ day** Wahltag, *der; see also* **by-election**

eˈlection campaign n. Wahlkampf, *der;* (in US presidential election) Wahlkampagne, *die*

electioneer /ɪlekʃəˈnɪə(r)/ *v.i.* **be/go ~ing** Wahlkampf machen

electioneering /ɪlekʃəˈnɪərɪŋ/ n., *no pl.* (propaganda) Wahlpropaganda, *die;* (campaign) Wahlkampagne, *die*

elective /ɪˈlektɪv/ *adj.* **1** (chosen or filled by election) gewählt; **an ~ office** ein Amt, das durch Wahl besetzt wird/wurde **2** (having the power to elect) wahlberechtigt **3** (optional) wahlfrei, fakultativ ‹*Kursus, Fach*›

e

elector /ɪˈlektə(r)/ *n.* **1** Wähler, *der*/Wählerin, *die;* Wahlberechtigte, *der/die* **2** E~ (Hist.: prince) Kurfürst, *der*

electoral /ɪˈlektərl/ *adj.* Wahl‹*liste, -zettel, -system, -bezirk, -berechtigung*›; Wähler‹*liste, -verzeichnis, -wille, -gruppe*›

electoral ˈcollege *n.* Wahlmännergremium, *das;* Wahlausschuss, *der*

electorate /ɪˈlektərət/ *n.* Wähler *Pl.;* Wählerschaft, *die*

electric /ɪˈlektrɪk/

A *adj.* elektrisch ‹*Strom, Feld, Licht, Orgel usw.*›; Elektro‹*kabel, -motor, -karren, -herd, -kessel*›; Elektrizitäts‹*lehre, -erzeuger, -werk*›; Strom‹*versorgung*›; (fig.) spannungsgeladen ‹*Atmosphäre*›; elektrisierend ‹*Wirkung*›

B *n. in pl.* elektrische Geräte; Elektrogeräte *Pl.;* (whole system) Elektrik, *die*

electrical /ɪˈlektrɪkl/ *adj.* elektrisch ‹*Defekt, Kontakt*›; Elektro‹*abteilung, -handel, -geräte*›

electrical: ~ engiˈneer *n.* ▸ⓘ **p. 1260** Elektroingenieur, *der*/-ingenieurin, *die;* **~ engiˈneering** *n.* Elektrotechnik, *die*

electrically /ɪˈlektrɪkəlɪ/ *adv.* elektrisch; (fig.) [wie] elektrisiert

electric: ~ ˈblanket *n.* Heizdecke, *die;* **~ ˈblue** *n.* Stahlblau, *das;* **~ ˈchair** *n.* elektrischer Stuhl; **~ cooker** *n.* Elektroherd, *der;* **~ ˈeel** *n.* Zitteraal, *der;* **~ ˈeye** *n.* Photozelle, *die;* **~ ˈfan** *n.* Ventilator, *der;* **~ ˈfence** *n.* elektrischer Zaun; Elektrozaun, *der;* **~ ˈfire** *n.* [elektrischer] Heizofen; Heizstrahler, *der;* **~ guiˈtar** *n.* elektrische Gitarre; E-Gitarre, *die*

electrician /ɪlekˈtrɪʃn/ *n.* ▸ⓘ **p. 1260** Elektriker, *der*/Elektrikerin, *die;* (who sets up electrical apparatus) Elektromechaniker, *der*/-mechanikerin, *die*

electricity /ɪlekˈtrɪsɪtɪ, elekˈtrɪsɪtɪ/ *n., no pl.* **1** Elektrizität, *die* **2** (supply) Strom, *der;* **install ~:** Stromanschlüsse legen **3** (fig.) Spannung, *die*

electricity: ~ bill *n.* Stromrechnung, *die;* **~ man** *n.* (fitter) Elektroinstallateur, *der;* (meter reader, collector) Stromableser, *der;* Strommann, *der* (ugs.); **~ meter** *n.* Stromzähler, *der;* **~ supply** *n.* Stromversorgung, *die*

electric: ~ ˈkettle *n.* [elektrischer] Wasserkocher; **~ ˈshock** *n.* Stromschlag, *der;* [elektrischer] Schlag; (Med.) Elektroschock, *der;* **~ ˈstorm** *n.* Gewitter, *das;* Gewittersturm, *der*

electrification /ɪlektrɪfɪˈkeɪʃn/ *n.* **1** (charging) Unter-Strom-Setzen, *das* **2** (conversion) Elektrifizierung, *die* **3** (fig.) Elektrisierung, *die*

electrify /ɪˈlektrɪfaɪ/ *v.t.* **1** (charge) an das Stromnetz anschließen ‹*Maschine*›; unter Strom setzen ‹*Kabel, Leiter*› **2** (convert) elektrifizieren ‹*Eisenbahnstrecke*› **3** (fig.) elektrisieren

electro- /ɪlektrəʊ/ *in comb.* elektro-/Elektro-

electroˈcardiogram *n.* Elektrokardiogramm, *das*

electroˈchemical *adj.* elektrochemisch

electroconˈvulsive *adj.* Elektrokrampf-; **~ shock/treatment** *or* **therapy** Elektroschock, *der*/Elektroschockbehandlung, *die*

electrocute /ɪˈlektrəkjuːt/ *v.t.* durch Stromschlag töten

electrocution /ɪlektrəˈkjuːʃn/ *n.* **1** (execution) Hinrichtung auf dem elektrischen Stuhl **2** (death) Tod durch Stromschlag

electrode /ɪˈlektrəʊd/ *n.* Elektrode, *die*

electrolyse /ɪˈlektrəlaɪz/ *v.t.* **1** (Chem.) elektrolysieren **2** (Med.) elektroresezieren

electrolysis /ɪlekˈtrɒlɪsɪs, elekˈtrɒlɪsɪs/ *n., pl.* **electrolyses** /ɪlekˈtrɒlɪsiːz, elekˈtrɒlɪsiːz/ **1** (Chem.) Elektrolyse, *die* **2** (Med.) Elektroresektion, *die*

electrolyte /ɪˈlektrəlaɪt/ *n.* Elektrolyt, *der*

electrolytic /ɪlektrəˈlɪtɪk/ *adj.* (Chem.) elektrolytisch

electrolyze (Amer.) ▸**electrolyse**

electroˈmagnet *n.* Elektromagnet, *der*

electromagˈnetic *adj.* elektromagnetisch

electroˈmagnetism *n.* Elektromagnetismus, *der*

electron /ɪˈlektrɒn/ *n.* Elektron, *das*

electron: ~ ˈbeam *n.* Elektronenstrahl, *der;* **~ ˈgun** *n.* Elektronenkanone, *die*

electronic /ɪlekˈtrɒnɪk, elekˈtrɒnɪk/ *adj.* elektronisch; Elektronen‹*uhr, -orgel*›

electronically /ɪlekˈtrɒnɪklɪ/ *adv.* elektronisch

electronic: ~ ˈbrain *n.* (coll.) Elektronen[ge]hirn, *das* (ugs.); **~ ˈcash** *n.* elektronisches Geld; **~ comˈputer** *n.* Computer, *der;* Elektronenrechner, *der;* **~ ˈflash** *n.* Elektronenblitz, *der;* **~ ˈfunds transfer system** *n.* elektronisches Zahlungssystem; **~ ˈmail** *n.* elektronische Post; **~ ˈmedia** *n. pl.* electronische Medien; **~ ˈoffice** *n.* elektronisches Büro; **~ ˈpaper** *n.* elektronisches Papier; **~ ˈpayment** *n.* elektronische Zahlung; **~ ˈpayment terminal** *n.* elektronisches Zahlungsterminal; **~ point of ˈsale** *n.* elektronischer Verkaufspunkt; **~ ˈpublishing** *n.* elektronisches Publizieren

electronics /ɪlekˈtrɒnɪks, elekˈtrɒnɪks/ *n., no pl.* Elektronik, *die*

electronic: ~ ˈshopping *n.* elektronisches Shopping; **~ ˈshopping basket** *n.* elektronischer Warenkorb; **~ ˈstorefront** *n.* elektronisches Schaufenster; **~ ˈtag** *n.* (attached to person) elektronische Fußfessel; (attached to goods) Sicherheitsetikett, *das;* **~ ˈtagging** *n., no pl.* (of person) das Anbringen einer elektronischen Fußfessel; (of goods) das Anbringen eines Sicherheitsetiketts; **use ~ tagging** (for offenders) elektronische Fußfesseln verwenden; (for goods) Sicherheitsetiketten verwenden

electron: ~ ˈmicroscope *n.* Elektronenmikroskop, *das;* **~ ˈoptics** *n.* Elektronenoptik, *die;* **~volt** *n.* (Physics) Elektronvolt, *das*

eˈlectroplate *v.t.* galvanisieren

electroˈstatic *adj.* (Phys.) elektrostatisch

electroˈstatics *n., no pl.* (Phys.) Elektrostatik, *die*

elegance /ˈelɪgəns/ *n., no pl.* Eleganz, *die;* (of lifestyle) Kultiviertheit, *die*

elegant /ˈelɪgənt/ *adj.* elegant; kultiviert ‹*Lebensstil*›

elegantly /ˈelɪgəntlɪ/ *adv.* elegant

elegiac /elɪˈdʒaɪək/

A *adj.* elegisch

B *n. in pl.* elegische Verse

elegy /ˈelɪdʒɪ/ *n.* Elegie, *die*

element /ˈelɪmənt/ *n.* **1** (component part) Element, *das;* **a novel with a strong ~ of religion** ein Roman mit einem stark religiösen Element; **have all the ~s of a real scandal** alle Voraussetzungen für einen richtigen Skandal tragen; **an ~ of truth** ein Körnchen Wahrheit; **an ~ of chance/danger in sth.** eine gewisse Zufälligkeit/Gefahr bei etw.; **when reduced to its ~s** im Grunde [genommen] **2** (Chem.) Element, *das;* Grundstoff, *der* **3** *in pl.* (atmospheric agencies) Elemente *Pl.* **4** (Philos.) **the four ~s** die vier Elemente; **be in one's ~** (fig.) in seinem Element sein; **be out of one's ~** (fig.) sich fehl am Platz fühlen **5** (Electr.) (wire) Heizelement, *das;* (electrode) Elektrode, *die* **6** *in pl.* (rudiments of learning) Grundlagen *Pl.;* Elemente *Pl.* **7** *in pl.* (Relig.) Brot und Wein **8** (Math., Logic) Element, *das*

elemental /elɪˈmentl/ *adj.* **1** (of the four elements) urgewaltig; elementar **2** Natur‹*gottheit, -religion*›; Elementar‹*geist*› **3** (fig.) elementar; natürlich ‹*Größe*›; urwüchsig, ursprünglich ‹*Leben, Fantasie*› **4** (essential) grundlegend

elementary /elɪˈmentərɪ/ *adj.* **1** elementar; grundlegend ‹*Fakten, Wissen*›; schlicht ‹*Fabel, Stil*›; Grundschul‹*lehrer, -bildung*›; Grund‹*stufe, -kurs, -ausbildung, -rechnen, -kenntnisse*›; Ausgangs‹*text, -thema*›; Anfangs‹*stadium*›; **course in ~ German** Grundkurs in Deutsch; **my knowledge is ~:** ich habe nur Anfängerkenntnisse; **be still in its ~ stages** noch in den Anfängen stecken; **an ~ mistake** ein grober Fehler **2** (Chem.) elementar; Elementar-

elementary: ~ ˈparticle *n.* (Phys.) Elementarteilchen, *das;* **~ school** *n.* Grundschule, *die*

> **elementary school**
>
> Die Grundschule in den Vereinigten Staaten. An *elementary schools* werden Kinder im Alter von sechs bis zwölf oder dreizehn Jahren unterrichtet. Diese Schulstufe wird auch als *grade school* oder *primary school* bezeichnet.

elephant /ˈelɪfənt/ *n.* Elefant, *der;* **see pink ~s** weiße Mäuse sehen; *see also* **white elephant**

elephantine /elɪˈfæntaɪn/ *adj.* **1** (of elephants) Elefanten- **2** (huge) massig ‹*Körper, Person, Ringer, Boxer*›; gigantisch ‹*Masse*› **3** (clumsy) schwerfällig

elevate /ˈelɪveɪt/ *v.t.* **1** (bring higher) erhöhen ‹*Temperatur*›; aufschütten ‹*Boden*›; [empor]heben ‹*Gerät, Gegenstand*›; (fig.) aufwerten ‹*Stellung*› **(into** zu) **2** (Eccl.) emporheben, zeigen ‹*Hostie*› **3** (raise) heben ‹*Stimme, Blick*›; aufrichten ‹*Blick, Geschützrohr*›; auf einer Hochtrasse führen ‹*Bahn*› **4** (in rank) befördern; **~ sb. to top management/a professorship/the peerage** jmdn. in die Unternehmensspitze berufen/auf einen Lehrstuhl berufen/in den Adelsstand erheben **5** (morally, intellectually) erbauen ‹*Geist, Person*›; aufrichten ‹*Mut*›; erheben ‹*Seele, Gemüt*›

elevated /ˈelɪveɪtɪd/ *adj.* **1** (raised) gehoben ‹*Stellung*›; erhöht ‹*Lage, Platzierung*›; hoch gelegen ‹*Land*›; aufgeschüttet ‹*Damm, Straße*›; erhoben ‹*Stimme, Blick, Bein, Arm*›; **keep one's arm in an ~ position** den Arm erhoben halten **2** (above ground level) Hoch‹*bahn, -straße*› **3** (noble, refined) erhaben; edel; **feel ~:** sich aufgerichtet fühlen **4** (formal, dignified) gehoben ‹*Stil, Rede, Sprache, Wortwahl*›

elevation /elɪˈveɪʃn/ *n.* **1** (position of house, building, land) erhöhte Lage **2** (Eccl.: of the Host) Elevation, *die* **3** (of temperature) Ansteigen, *das;* Anstieg, *der* **4** (of voice) Heben, *das;* Hebung, *die* **5** (in rank) Beförderung, *die;* (to the peerage) Erhebung, *die;* (to top management, professorship) Berufung, *die* **6** (of mind, thought) Erhebung, *die;* (state) Erhabenheit, *die;* **the ~ of his style** sein gehobener Stil **7** (height) Höhe, *die;* **~ of the ground** Bodenerhebung *od.* Anhöhe, *die* **8** (angle) Elevation, *die;* **angle of ~:** Elevationswinkel, *der;* Erhöhungswinkel, *der* **9** (drawing, diagram) Aufriss, *der*

elevator /ˈelɪveɪtə(r)/ *n.* **1** (machine) Förderwerk, *das;* Elevator, *der* **2** (storehouse) Getreidesilo, *der od. das* **3** (Amer.) ▸**lift C 2** **4** (Aeron.) Höhenruder, *das*

eleven /ɪˈlevn/ ▸ⓘ **p. 894**, ▸ⓘ **p. 1001**, ▸ⓘ **p. 1358**

A *adj.* elf; *see also* **eight A**

B *n.* (number, symbol; also Sport) Elf, *die; see also* **eight B 1, 4**

eleven-ˈplus *n.* (Brit. Educ. Hist.) **~ [examination]** *Prüfung der elf- bis zwölfjährigen Schüler [vor Fortsetzung der schulischen Laufbahn an höherer Schule]*

elevenses /ɪˈlevnzɪz/ *n. sing. or pl.* (Brit. coll.) ≈ zweites Frühstück [gegen elf Uhr]

eleventh /ɪˈlevnθ/ ▸ⓘ **p. 1047**

A *adj.* ▸ⓘ **p. 1358** elft...; **at the ~ hour** im letzten Augenblick; in letzter Minute; **an ~-hour change of plan** eine Planungsänderung in letzter Minute; *see also* **eighth A**

B *n.* (fraction) Elftel, *das; see also* **eighth B**

elf /elf/ *n., pl.* **elves** /elvz/ **1** (Mythol.) Elf, *der*/Elfe, *die* **2** (mischievous creature) [boshafter] Schelm; Kobold, *der*

elfin /ˈelfɪn/ *adj.* elfenhaft

elfish /ˈelfɪʃ/ *adj.* elfenhaft; (mischievous) schalkhaft; koboldhaft

elicit /ɪˈlɪsɪt/ *v.t.* entlocken ‹*Antwort, Auskunft, Wahrheit, Geheimnis*› **(from** *Dat.*); hervorrufen ‹*Begeisterung, Zustimmung*›; gewinnen ‹*Unterstützung*› **(amongst** bei); **the discussion has ~ed some important facts** die Diskussion brachte einige interessante Einzelheiten ans Tageslicht

elide /ɪˈlaɪd/ *v.t.* (Ling.) elidieren (fachspr.); auslassen

eligibility /elɪdʒɪˈbɪlɪtɪ/ *n., no pl.* (fitness) Qualifikation, *die;* (for a job) Eignung, *die;* (entitlement) Berechtigung, *die* **(for** zu)

eligible /ˈelɪdʒɪbl/ *adj.* [1] **be ~ for sth.** (fit) für etw. qualifiziert *od.* geeignet sein; (entitled) zu etw. berechtigt sein; **be ~ for membership/a pension/an office** mitglieds-/pensionsberechtigt sein/für ein Amt infrage kommen; **be ~ to do sth.** etw. tun dürfen; **become ~ to vote** das Wahlrecht erhalten [2] (marriageable) begehrt ‹*Junggeselle*›

eliminate /ɪˈlɪmɪneɪt/ *v.t.* [1] (remove) beseitigen ‹*Zweifel, Fehler*›; ausschließen ‹*Möglichkeit*›; eliminieren, beseitigen ‹*Gegner*› [2] (exclude) ausschließen; (Sport) aus dem Wettbewerb werfen; **the team was ~d at the end of the third round** die Mannschaft schied nach der dritten Runde aus [3] (Physiol.) ausscheiden

elimination /ɪlɪmɪˈneɪʃn/ *n.* [1] (removal) (of doubt, error) Beseitigung, *die;* (of opponent) Eliminierung, *die;* Beseitigung, *die;* **process of ~:** Ausleseverfahren, *das* [2] (exclusion) Ausschluss, *der;* (Sport) Ausscheiden, *das* [3] (Physiol.) Ausscheidung, *die*

elision /ɪˈlɪʒn/ *n.* (Ling.) Elision, *die* (fachspr.); Auslassung, *die*

elite /eɪˈliːt, ɪˈliːt/ *n.* (the best) Elite, *die;* (of society, club) Spitze, *die;* Creme, *die;* (group, class) Elite, *die;* **the ~** (high society) die oberen Zehntausend (ugs.)

elitism /eɪˈliːtɪzm, ɪˈliːtɪzm/ *n.* Elitedenken, *das*

elitist /ɪˈliːtɪst/

A *adj.* elitär; Elite‹*denken*›

B *n.* Anhänger/Anhängerin des Elitedenkens; elitär Denkender/Denkende

elixir /ɪˈlɪksə(r)/ *n.* Heilmittel, *das;* **~ [of life]** [Lebens]elixier, *das*

Elizabeth /ɪˈlɪzəbəθ/ *pr. n.* (Hist., as name of ruler etc.) Elisabeth

Elizabethan /ɪlɪzəˈbiːθn/

A *adj.* elisabethanisch

B *n.* elisabethanischer Zeitgenosse

elk /elk/ *n., pl.* **~s** *or same* [1] (deer) Elch, *der* [2] (moose) Riesenelch, *der*

elk: ~ hound *n.* Jämthund, *der;* **~ test** *n.* Elchtest, *der*

ellipse[1] /ɪˈlɪps/ *n.* (Math.) Ellipse, *die*

ellipsis /ɪˈlɪpsɪs/ (**[2]ellipse**) *n., pl.* **ellipses** /ɪˈlɪpsiːz/ [1] (Ling., Lit.) Ellipse, *die* [2] (set of dots etc.) Auslassungszeichen *Pl.*

elliptic /ɪˈlɪptɪk/, **elliptical** /ɪˈlɪptɪkl/ *adj.* [1] (of ellipses; also Ling.) elliptisch; Ellipsen‹*bogen, -bahn*› [2] (Lit.) kryptisch (geh.) [3] (brief, concise) komprimiert; knapp

elliptically /ɪˈlɪptɪkəlɪ/ *adv.* (Ling., Lit.) in elliptischen Sätzen

elm /elm/ *n.* Ulme, *die*

ˈelmwood *n.* Ulmen- *od.* Rüsternholz, *das*

elocution /eləˈkjuːʃn/ *n.* [1] *no pl.* (art) Sprechkunst, *die;* Vortragskunst, *die;* **teacher of ~:** Sprecherzieher, *der*/-erzieherin, *die;* **give lessons in ~:** Sprechunterricht geben [2] (style of speaking) Redeweise, *die;* Diktion, *die*

elocutionary /eləˈkjuːʃənərɪ/ *adj.* deklamatorisch ‹*Sprechweise, Fertigkeit, Effekt*›

elocutionist /eləˈkjuːʃənɪst/ *n.* Vortragskünstler, *der*/-künstlerin, *die*

elongate /ˈiːlɒŋgeɪt/ *v.t.* länger werden lassen ‹*Schatten*›; strecken ‹*Körper*›; recken ‹*Hals*›

elongated /ˈiːlɒŋgeɪtɪd/ *adj.* lang gestreckt ‹*Gestalt, Gliedmaße*›; lang gereckt ‹*Hals*›

elongation /iːlɒŋˈgeɪʃn/ *n.* Verlängerung, *die;* (of limbs, neck) [Aus]recken, *das;* (of forms, shapes) Strecken, *das*

elope /ɪˈləʊp/ *v.i.* weglaufen; durchbrennen (ugs.)

elopement /ɪˈləʊpmənt/ *n.* Weglaufen, *das;* Durchbrennen, *das* (ugs.)

eloquence /ˈeləkwəns/ *n.* Beredtheit, *die;* Eloquenz, *die* (geh.); **he is a man of great ~:** er ist ein sehr beredter Mann

eloquent /ˈeləkwənt/ *adj.* [1] eloquent (geh.); gewandt ‹*Sprechweise, Ausdruck, Stil, Redner*›; beredt ‹*Person*› [2] (fig.) beredt ‹*Blick, Schweigen*›

eloquently /ˈeləkwəntlɪ/ *adv.* [1] gewandt ‹*sprechen, schreiben, sich ausdrücken, formulieren*› [2] (fig.) beredt ‹*schauen*›

else /els/ *adv.* [1] (besides, in addition) sonst [noch]; **anybody/anything ~?** sonst noch jemand/etwas?; **don't mention it to anybody ~:** erwähnen Sie es gegenüber niemandem sonst; **somebody/something ~:** [noch] jemand anders/noch etwas; **everybody/everything ~:** alle anderen/alles andere; **nobody ~:** niemand sonst; sonst niemand; **nothing ~:** sonst *od.* weiter nichts; **will there be anything ~?** (asked by salesperson) darf es sonst noch etwas sein?; (asked by waiter) haben Sie sonst noch einen Wunsch?; **nothing ~, thank you** das ist alles, danke; **that is something ~ again** das ist wieder etwas anderes; **be something ~** (coll.: very good) schon was Besonderes sein (ugs.); **anywhere ~?** anderswo? (ugs.); woanders?; **not anywhere ~:** sonst nirgendwo; **somewhere ~:** anderswo (ugs.); woanders; **go somewhere ~:** anderswohin (ugs.) *od.* woandershin gehen; **everywhere ~:** [auch] sonst überall; **go everywhere ~:** sonst überallhin gehen; **nowhere ~:** sonst nirgendwo; **go nowhere ~:** sonst nirgendwohin gehen; **little ~:** kaum noch etwas; nur noch wenig; **much ~:** [noch] vieles andere *od.* mehr; **not much ~:** nicht mehr viel; nur noch wenig; **who/what/when/how ~?** wer/was/wann/wie sonst noch?; **where ~?** wo/wohin sonst noch?; **why ~?** warum sonst? [2] (instead) ander…; **sb. ~'s hat** der Hut von jmd. anders *od.* jmd. anderem (ugs.); **anybody/anything ~?** [irgend]jemand anders/etwas anderes?; **anyone ~ but Joe would have realized that** jeder [andere] außer Joe hätte das bemerkt; **somebody/something ~:** jemand anders/etwas anderes; **everybody/everything ~:** alle anderen/alles andere; **nobody/nothing ~:** niemand anders/nichts anderes; **no one ~ but he** nur er; niemand außer ihm; **nothing ~ but the best** nur das Beste; **there's nothing ~ for it** es hilft nichts; **anywhere ~?** anderswo? (ugs.); woanders?; **somewhere ~:** anderswo (ugs.); woanders; **go somewhere ~:** woandershin gehen; **his mind was/his thoughts were somewhere ~:** im Geist/mit seinen Gedanken war er woanders; **everywhere ~:** überall anders; überall sonst; **nowhere ~:** nirgendwo sonst; **go nowhere ~:** nirgendwo sonst hingehen; **there's not much ~ we can do but …:** wir können kaum etwas anderes tun, als …; **who ~ [but]?** wer anders [als]?; **it was John — who ~?** es war John — wer [denn] sonst? **what ~ can I do?** was kann ich anderes machen?; **why ~ would I have done it?** warum hätte ich es sonst getan?; **when/where ~ can we meet?** wann/wo können wir uns stattdessen treffen?; **where ~ could we go?** wohin könnten wir stattdessen gehen?; **how ~ would you do it?** wie würden Sie es anders *od.* sonst machen? [3] (otherwise) sonst; anderenfalls; **or ~:** oder aber; **do it or ~ …!** tun Sie es, sonst …!; **do it or ~!** (coll.) tu es gefälligst!

ˈelsewhere *adv.* woanders; **go ~:** woandershin gehen; **his mind was/his thoughts were ~:** im Geist/mit seinen Gedanken war er woanders

ELT *abbr.* **= English Language Teaching**

elucidate /ɪˈljuːsɪdeɪt, ɪˈluːsɪdeɪt/ *v.t.* erläutern; aufklären ‹*Geheimnis*›

elucidation /ɪljuːsɪˈdeɪʃn, ɪluːsɪˈdeɪʃn/ *n.* Erläuterung, *die;* (of mystery) Aufklärung, *die*

elude /ɪˈljuːd, ɪˈluːd/ *v.t.* sich entziehen (+ *Dat.*); missachten ‹*Befehl, Gesetz, Forderung*›; umgehen ‹*Verpflichtung*›; (avoid) ausweichen (+ *Dat.*) ‹*Person, Schlag, Angriff, Blick, Frage, Gefahr*›; (escape from) entkommen (+ *Dat.*); **the causes of this disease have so far ~d medical science** die Mediziner konnten die Ursachen dieser Krankheit noch nicht herausfinden; **~ the police** sich dem Zugriff der Polizei entziehen; **sleep ~s me** ich kann keinen Schlaf finden; **the name ~s me at the moment** der Name ist mir im Moment entfallen *od.* fällt mir im Moment nicht ein; **the significance of his remark ~s me** die Bedeutung seiner Bemerkung ist mir nicht klar

elusive /ɪˈljuːsɪv, ɪˈluːsɪv/ *adj.* [1] (avoiding grasp or pursuit) schwer zu erreichen ‹*Person*›; schwer zu fassen ‹*Straftäter*›; scheu ‹*Fuchs, Waldbewohner*›; **I have phoned every day but she has been very ~:** ich habe jeden Tag angerufen, aber sie ist sehr schwer zu erreichen [2] (short-lived) flüchtig ‹*Freude, Glück*› [3] (tending to escape from memory) schwer zu behaltend, (präd.) schwer zu behalten ‹*Gedanke, Wort*›; **~ memory** schwache Erinnerung [4] (avoiding definition) schwer definierbar ‹*Begriff, Sinn*› [5] (hard to pin down or identify) schwer zu bestimmend, (präd.) schwer zu bestimmen ‹*Geruch*›; schwer durchschaubar ‹*Person*› [6] (evasive) ausweichend ‹*Antwort*›

elver /ˈelvə(r)/ *n.* (Zool.) Glasaal, *der*

elves *pl. of* **elf**

elvish /ˈelvɪʃ/ ▸ **elfish**

Elysium /ɪˈlɪzɪəm/ *n.* [1] (Greek Mythol.) Elysium, *das* [2] (fig.: place of ideal happiness) Paradies, *das;* Elysium, *das* (dichter.)

em /em/ *n.* (Printing) Cicero, *das*

'em /əm/ *pron.* (coll.) se (*Akk.*) (ugs.); ihnen (*Dat.*)

emaciated /ɪˈmeɪsɪeɪtɪd, ɪˈmeɪʃɪeɪtɪd/ *adj.* ausgemergelt; abgezehrt; **become ~:** abmagern

emaciation /ɪmeɪsɪˈeɪʃn/ *n., no pl.* Ausmergelung, *die;* Abzehrung, *die*

e-mail /ˈiːmeɪl/

A *n.* E-Mail, *die; attrib.* **~ address** E-Mail-Adresse, *die;* **~ message** E-Mail, *die;* **be on ~:** eine E-Mail-Adresse haben; E-Mail haben (ugs.)

B *v.t.* per E-Mail übermitteln ‹*Ergebnisse, Datei usw.*›; **~ sb.** jmdm. eine E-Mail schicken; **~ sb. with sth.** jmdm. etw. per E-Mail mitteilen

emanate /ˈeməneɪt/ *v.i.* [1] (originate) ausgehen (**from** von) [2] (proceed, issue) ausgestrahlt werden (**from** von); ausstrahlen [3] (formal: be sent out) ‹*Befehle:*› erteilt *od.* erlassen werden; ‹*Briefe, Urkunden:*› ausgestellt *od.* ausgefertigt werden

emanation /eməˈneɪʃn/ *n.* [1] (Theol.) Emanation, *die* (**from** aus) [2] *no pl.* (issuing) Ausstrahlen, *das* [3] (sth. proceeding from source) Ausströmung, *die* [4] (fig.) Ausfluss, *der;* **be an ~ of** *or* **from sth.** von etw. ausgehen

emancipate /ɪˈmænsɪpeɪt/ *v.t.* emanzipieren; unabhängig machen; **~ sb. from slavery** jmdn. aus der Sklaverei befreien; **~ oneself from sth./sb.** sich von etw. emanzipieren *od.* frei machen/sich von jmdm. frei machen

emancipated /ɪˈmænsɪpeɪtɪd/ *adj.* emanzipiert ‹*Frau, Vorstellung, Einstellung*›; **become ~:** sich emanzipieren; **~ slave** freigelassener Sklave

emancipation /ɪmænsɪˈpeɪʃn/ *n.* Emanzipation, *die;* (of slave) Freilassung, *die;* **~ from servitude/superstition** Befreiung aus der Knechtschaft/vom Aberglauben

ˈe-marketing *n., no pl.* E-Marketing, *das*

emasculate /ɪˈmæskjʊleɪt/ *v.t.* [1] (Med.: castrate) entmannen; emaskulieren (fachspr.); kastrieren ‹*Tier*› [2] (weaken) schwächen; kastrieren (ugs. scherzh.); verwässern ‹*Plan, Vorschlag, Gesetzentwurf*›

emasculation /ɪmæskjʊˈleɪʃn/ *n.* [1] (Med.: castration) Entmannung, *die;* Emaskulation, *die* (fachspr.); (of animal) Kastration, *die* [2] (weakening) Schwächung, *die;* Kastration, *die;* (of plan, proposal) Verwässerung, *die*

embalm /ɪmˈbɑːm/ *v.t.* einbalsamieren

embankment /ɪmˈbæŋkmənt/ *n.* Damm, *der;* **~ of a river** Uferdamm, *der;* **~ of earth/stone** Erd-/Steindamm, *der;* **~ of a road** Straßendamm, *der;* Böschung, *die;* **~ of a track/railway** Bahndamm, *der;* **the Thames E~:** die Themse-Uferstraße (in London)

embargo /emˈbɑːgəʊ, ɪmˈbɑːgəʊ/

A *n., pl.* **~es** [1] Embargo, *das;* **be under an ~:** mit einem Embargo belegt sein; **put** *or* **lay an ~ on sth., place** *or* **lay sth. under an ~:** etw. mit einem Embargo belegen; **lift** *or* **raise** *or* **remove an ~ [from sth.]** ein Embargo [für etw.] aufheben [2] (impediment) Stopp, *der;* **~ on new appointments** Einstellungsstopp, *der;* Einstellungssperre, *die;* **~ on further spending** Ausgabenstopp, *der*

B *v.t.* mit einem Embargo belegen

embark /ɪmˈbɑːk/

A *v.t.* einschiffen ‹*Passagiere, Waren*›

B *v.i.* [1] sich einschiffen (**for** nach); **the troops**

e

~ed at night die Truppen wurden nachts eingeschifft [2] (engage) **~ [up]on sth.** etw. in Angriff nehmen; **~ [up]on a war** einen Krieg anfangen *od.* beginnen

embarkation /embɑːˈkeɪʃn/ *n.* Einschiffung, *die;* **port of ~:** Einschiffungshafen, *der;* **~ leave** Einschiffungsurlaub, *der*

embarrass /ɪmˈbærəs/ *v.t.* (make feel awkward) in Verlegenheit bringen; **become seriously ~ed** in ernste Verlegenheit kommen; **be ~ed by lack of money** in Geldverlegenheit sein

embarrassed /ɪmˈbærəst/ *adj.* verlegen ‹*Person, Blick, Lächeln, Benehmen, Schweigen*›; **be** *or* **feel/look/get ~:** verlegen sein/aussehen/werden; **now don't be ~!** geniere dich nicht!; **make sb. feel ~:** jmdn. verlegen machen

embarrassing /ɪmˈbærəsɪŋ/ *adj.* peinlich ‹*Benehmen, Schweigen, Situation, Augenblick, Frage, Thema*›; beschämend ‹*Großzügigkeit*›; verwirrend ‹*Auswahl*›; **~ person** jmd., der andere blamiert; **I find it very ~ to have to say this, but ...:** es ist mir sehr peinlich, so etwas sagen zu müssen, aber ...

embarrassingly /ɪmˈbærəsɪŋlɪ/ *adv.* peinlich; irritierend ‹*freimütig*›; unerhört ‹*grob*›; beschämend ‹*großzügig*›

embarrassment /ɪmˈbærəsmənt/ *n.* Verlegenheit, *die;* (instance) Peinlichkeit, *die;* **much to his ~:** zu seiner großen Verlegenheit; **cause sb. ~:** jmdn. verlegen machen; **cause sb. a great deal of ~:** jmdn. in große Verlegenheit bringen; **he was a source of ~ to his family** seine Familie musste sich seinetwegen schämen; **financial ~[s]** Geldverlegenheit, *die;* **~ of riches** verwirrende [Über]fülle

embassy /ˈembəsɪ/ *n.* Botschaft, *die*

embattled /ɪmˈbætld/ *adj.* kampfbereit ‹*Armee*›; befestigt ‹*Turm, Wall, Gebäude*›

embed /ɪmˈbed/ *v.t.*, **-dd-:** [1] (fix) einlassen; **stones ~ded in rock** in Fels eingelagerte Steine; **a brick firmly ~ded in mortar** ein fest in Mörtel gefügter Ziegelstein; **~ sth. in cement/concrete** etw. einzementieren/einbetonieren; **the bullet ~ded itself in the ground** die Kugel bohrte sich in den Boden; **~ded in the mud** im Schlamm versunken; **~ded journalist** eingebetteter Journalist; **~ded sentence** (Ling.) eingeschobener Satz [2] (fig.) **be firmly ~ded in sth.** fest in etw. (*Dat.*) verankert sein

embellish /ɪmˈbelɪʃ/ *v.t.* [1] (beautify) schmücken; beschönigen ‹*Wahrheit*› [2] ausschmücken ‹*Geschichte, Bericht*›

embellishment /ɪmˈbelɪʃmənt/ *n.* [1] *no pl.* (ornamentation) (of church, room) Verschönerung, *die;* (of story) Ausschmückung, *die;* (of truth) Beschönigung, *die* [2] (sth. that embellishes) Verzierung, *die;* (in narrative) Mittel der Ausschmückung [3] (Mus.) Verzierung, *die;* Ornament, *das* (fachspr.)

ember /ˈembə(r)/ *n., usu. in pl.* (lit. or fig.) Glut, *die;* **dying ~s** verlöschende Glut; *see also* **fan**[1] **B**

ˈember day *n.* (Eccl.) Quatember, *der*

embezzle /ɪmˈbezl/ *v.t.* unterschlagen; veruntreuen

embezzlement /ɪmˈbezlmənt/ *n.* Unterschlagung, *die;* Veruntreuung, *die*

embezzler /ɪmˈbezlə(r)/ *n.* Unterschlager, *der*/Unterschlagerin, *die;* Veruntreuer, *der*/Veruntreuerin, *die*

embitter /ɪmˈbɪtə(r)/ *v.t.* vergiften ‹*Beziehungen*›; verschärfen ‹*Auseinandersetzung*›; verbittern ‹*Person*›

emblazon /ɪmˈbleɪzn/ *v.t.* [1] (Her.) verzieren; blasonieren (fachspr.) [2] (mark boldly) **the book covers were ~ed with his name** sein Name prangte auf den Einbänden

emblem /ˈembləm/ *n.* [1] (Her.) Wappenbild, *das* [2] (symbol) Emblem, *das;* Wahrzeichen, *das;* (on national flag etc.) Hoheitszeichen, *das;* **~ of peace** Friedenssymbol, *das*

emblematic /emblɪˈmætɪk/, **emblematical** /emblɪˈmætɪkl/ *adj.* emblematisch; sinnbildlich; **be ~ of sth.** das Sinnbild einer Sache (*Gen.*) sein

embodiment /ɪmˈbɒdɪmənt/ *n.* [1] (act, state) Verkörperung, *die* [2] (incarnation) Inbegriff, *der* [3] (incorporation) Eingliederung, *die;* Integration, *die* (geh.)

embody /ɪmˈbɒdɪ/ *v.t.* [1] (express tangibly) Ausdruck verleihen (+ *Dat.*); **his ideas are embodied in this letter** seine Vorstellungen kommen in diesem Brief zum Ausdruck *od.* erhalten in diesem Brief Form und Gestalt [2] (give concrete form to) verkörpern ‹*Vorstellungen, Gefühle, Ideale*› [3] (be incarnation of) personifizieren; verkörpern; der Inbegriff (+ *Gen.*) sein [4] (include) enthalten

embolden /ɪmˈbəʊldn/ *v.t.* ermutigen; **~ sb. to do sth.** jmdn. [dazu] ermutigen, etw. zu tun

embolism /ˈembəlɪzm/ *n.* (Med.) Embolie, *die*

emboss /ɪmˈbɒs/ *v.t.* prägen ‹*Metall, Papier, Leder usw.*›; (with heat) gaufrieren ‹*Papier, Gewebe usw.*›; **an ~ed design** ein erhabenes Muster; **~ed notepaper** geprägtes Briefpapier; **~ed stamp** im Prägedruck hergestellte Brief-/Wertmarke

embrace /ɪmˈbreɪs/

A *v.t.* [1] (hold in arms) umarmen; **they ~d [each other]** sie umarmten sich *od.* (geh.) einander [2] (fig.: surround) umgeben [3] (accept) wahrnehmen, ergreifen ‹*Gelegenheit*›; annehmen ‹*Angebot*› [4] (adopt) annehmen; **~ a cause** eine Sache zu seiner eigenen machen; **~ Catholicism** sich zum Katholizismus bekennen [5] (include) umfassen

B *n.* Umarmung, *die;* **he held her to him in a close ~:** er hielt sie eng umschlungen

embrasure /ɪmˈbreɪʒə(r)/ *n.* [1] (of door, window) [abgeschrägte] Laibung [2] (in parapet) Schießscharte, *die*

embrocation /embrəˈkeɪʃn/ *n.* Einreibemittel, *das;* Liniment, *das* (fachspr.)

embroider /ɪmˈbrɔɪdə(r)/ *v.t.* sticken ‹*Blumen, Muster*›; besticken ‹*Tuch, Kleid*›; (fig.) ausschmücken ‹*Erzählung, Wahrheit*›

embroiderer /ɪmˈbrɔɪdərə(r)/ *n.* Sticker, *der*/Stickerin, *die*

embroidery /ɪmˈbrɔɪdərɪ/ *n.* [1] Stickerei, *die* [2] *no pl.* (embroidering) Sticken, *das* [3] (fig.: ornament) Ausschmückungen *Pl.;* schmückendes Beiwerk

embroil /ɪmˈbrɔɪl/ *v.t.* **~ sb. in sth.** jmdn. in etw. (*Akk.*) hineinziehen; **become/be ~ed in a war** in einen Krieg verwickelt werden/sein; **~ oneself in a dispute** sich in einen Streit einmischen

embryo /ˈembrɪəʊ/ *n., pl.* **~s** Embryo, *der;* **in ~** (fig.) im Keim; in nuce (geh.); **the plans are as yet in ~:** die Planungen befinden sich erst im Anfangsstadium

embryology /embrɪˈɒlədʒɪ/ *n.* (Biol.) Embryologie, *die*

embryonic /embrɪˈɒnɪk/ *adj.* (Biol., fig.) Embryonal‹*entwicklung, -struktur, -zustand, -stadium*›; unausgereift ‹*Vorstellung*›; **~ membrane** Eihülle, *die;* **~ plant** Pflanzenembryo, *der;* **~ plan** Plan im Embryonalstadium

ˈembryo research *n.* Embryonenforschung, *die*

ˈem dash *n.* (Printing) Geviertstrich, *der*

emend /ɪˈmend/ *v.t.* (Lit.) emendieren (fachspr.); berichtigen

emendation /iːmenˈdeɪʃn/ *n.* (Lit.) Emendation, *die* (fachspr.); Berichtigung, *die*

emerald /ˈemərəld/

A *n.* [1] Smaragd, *der* [2] ▸**emerald green**

B *adj.* [1] smaragdgrün [2] **~ ring** Smaragdring, *der* [3] **the E~ Isle** die Grüne Insel

emerald ˈgreen *n.* Smaragdgrün, *das*

emerge /ɪˈmɜːdʒ/ *v.i.* [1] auftauchen (**from** aus, **from behind** hinter + *Dat.*, **from beneath** *or* **under** unter + *Dat.* hervor); **the sun ~d from behind the clouds** die Sonne trat hinter den Wolken hervor; **~ from the shadow into bright daylight** aus dem Schatten ans helle Tageslicht treten *od.* kommen; **the river ~s from the mountains** der Fluss tritt aus dem Gebirge heraus; **the caterpillar ~d from the egg/as a beautiful butterfly** die Raupe schlüpfte aus dem Ei/wurde zu einem wunderschönen Schmetterling; **difficulties may ~ in this venture** bei diesem Unterfangen können Schwierigkeiten auftreten [2] (become known, evolve) hervorgehen (**from** aus); ‹*Leben:*› entstammen (**from** + *Dat.*); ‹*Wahrheit:*› an den Tag kommen; ‹*Virus usw.:*› entstehen; **it ~s that ...:** es zeigt sich *od.* stellt sich heraus, dass ...; **it ~s from this that ...:** hieraus geht hervor, dass ...; **two essential points ~d from the discussion** aus der Diskussion haben sich zwei wesentliche Punkte ergeben

emergence /ɪˈmɜːdʒəns/ *n.* [1] (out of liquid) Auftauchen, *das* [2] (coming known) Hervortreten, *das;* (of mode, school of thought, new ideas) Aufkommen, *das*

emergency /ɪˈmɜːdʒənsɪ/

A *n.* [1] (serious happening) Notfall, *der;* **in an** *or* **in case of ~:** im Notfall; **be prepared for any ~:** auf den Notfall vorbereitet sein; **~ [case]** (Med.) Notfall, *der;* **be called out on an ~:** zu einem Notfall gerufen werden [2] (Polit.) Ausnahmezustand, *der;* **declare a state of ~:** den Ausnahmezustand ausrufen *od.* erklären

B *adj.* Not‹*bremse, -ruf, -ausgang, -landung, -unterkunft*›; **~ cord** Notbremse, *die;* **~ number** Notrufnummer, *die;* **~ ˈpowers** Sondervollmachten *Pl.* [aufgrund einer Notlage]; **~ services** Hilfsdienste *Pl.;* **~ ward** Unfallstation, *die;* **~ worker** Katastrophenschutzhelfer, *der*/-helferin, *die*

emergent /ɪˈmɜːdʒənt/ *adj.* [1] (rising out) aufragend ‹*Insel, Felsen, Baum*› (**from** aus); jung, sprießend ‹*Vegetation*› [2] jung, aufstrebend ‹*Volk*›

emeritus /ɪˈmerɪtəs/ *adj.* emeritiert ‹*Professor*›; **professor ~:** Professor emeritus

emery /ˈemərɪ/ *n.* Schmirgel, *der*

emery: ~ board *n.* Schleifbrett, *das;* (strip for fingernails) Sandblattfeile, *die;* **~ paper** *n.* Schmirgelpapier, *das*

emetic /ɪˈmetɪk/ (Med.)

A *adj.* emetisch (fachspr.); Brechreiz erregend; **be ~:** Brechreiz erregen

B *n.* Emetikum, *das* (fachspr.); Brechmittel, *das*

EMF *abbr.* **= electromotive force** EMK

emigrant /ˈemɪgrənt/

A *adj.* auswandernd; emigrierend; **the ~ population in the USA** die Einwanderer in den USA

B *n.* (person) Auswanderer, *der*/Auswanderin, *die;* Emigrant, *der*/Emigrantin, *die;* (plant) Wanderpflanze, *die*

emigrate /ˈemɪgreɪt/ *v.i.* auswandern, emigrieren (**to** nach, **from** aus)

emigration /emɪˈgreɪʃn/ *n.* Auswanderung, Emigration, *die* (**to** nach, **from** aus)

émigré /ˈemɪgreɪ/ *n.* Emigrant, *der*/Emigrantin, *die*

eminence /ˈemɪnəns/ *n.* [1] *no pl.* (distinguished superiority) hohes Ansehen; **person of great ~:** bedeutender *od.* hoch angesehener Mensch; **win/reach/attain ~:** hohes Ansehen erwerben/erreichen/erlangen; **rise to** *or* **reach ~:** zu hohem Ansehen gelangen [2] (person) angesehener Mensch [3] (rising ground) Erhebung, *die* [4] **E~** (Eccl.) Eminenz, *die*

éminence grise /eminɑ̃s ˈgriːz/ *n.* graue Eminenz

eminent /ˈemɪnənt/ *adj.* [1] (exalted, distinguished) bedeutend, hoch angesehen ‹*Redner, Gelehrter, Künstler*›; **~ guest** hoher Gast; **the most ~ citizens** die angesehensten Bürger; **be ~ in one's field** eine Koryphäe auf seinem Gebiet sein [2] (remarkable) ausnehmend ‹*Eigenschaft*›

eminently /ˈemɪnəntlɪ/ *adv.* ausnehmend; vorzüglich ‹*geeignet*›; überaus ‹*erfolgreich*›; **~ respectable** hoch angesehen

emir /eˈmɪə(r)/ *n.* Emir, *der*

emirate /ˈemɪərət/ *n.* Emirat, *das*

emissary /ˈemɪsərɪ/ *n.* Emissär, *der*/Emissärin, *die;* Abgesandte, *der/die;* **special ~:** Sonderbotschafter, *der*/-botschafterin, *die*

emission /ɪˈmɪʃn/ *n.* [1] (giving off or out) Aussendung, *die;* (of vapour) Ablassen, *das;* (of liquid) Ausscheidung, *die;* (of sparks) Versprühen, *das;* **~ of light/heat** Licht-/Wärmeausstrahlung, *die;* **~ of fumes** Abgasemission, *die;* **~ of**

smell/gas Geruchs-/Gasausströmung, *die;* ~ **of rays** Strahlenaussendung, *die;* ~ **of sound** Geräuschabgabe, *die;* ~ **of smoke/lava** Rauch-/Lavaausstoß, *der* 2 (thing given off) Abstrahlung, *die;* (effluvium) Ausdünstung, *die;* (of semen) Samenerguss, *der*

emit /ɪ'mɪt/ *v.t.*, **-tt-** aussenden ‹*Strahlen*›; ausstrahlen ‹*Wärme, Licht*›; ausstoßen ‹*Lava, Asche, Rauch, Schrei*›; ausscheiden ‹*Flüssigkeit*›; abgeben ‹*Geräusch*›; versprühen ‹*Funken*›; ausströmen ‹*Geruch, Gas*›; ablassen ‹*Dampf*›

emollient /ɪ'mɒlɪənt/
A *adj.* 1 (softening) weichmachend 2 (conciliatory) versöhnlich
B *n.* Weichmacher, *der*

emolument /ɪ'mɒljʊmənt/ *n., usu. in pl.* Vergütung, *die;* Bezüge *Pl.*

'e-money *n., no pl.* E-Geld, *das*

emoticon /ɪ'məʊtɪkɒn/ *n.* (Computing) Emoticon, *das*

emotion /ɪ'məʊʃn/ *n.* 1 (state) Ergriffenheit, *die;* Bewegtheit, *die;* **speak with deep** ~: tief ergriffen *od.* bewegt sprechen; **charged with** ~: gefühlsgeladen; **be overcome with** ~: von Gefühl übermannt sein; **be touched with/full of** ~: ergriffen/bewegt sein; **show no** ~: keine Gefühlsregung *od.* Emotionen zeigen 2 (feeling) Gefühl, *das;* **conflicting** ~**s** widerstrebende Gefühle

emotional /ɪ'məʊʃənl/ *adj.* 1 (of emotions) emotional; Gefühls‹*ausdruck, -leben, -erlebnis, -reaktion*›; Gemüts‹*zustand, -störung*›; seelisch ‹*Belastung*›; psychologisch ‹*Erpressung*›; gefühlsgeladen ‹*Worte, Musik, Geschichte, Film*›; gefühlsbetont, emotional ‹*Verhalten*›; gefühlsmäßig ‹*Einschätzung, Entscheidung*›; gefühlvoll ‹*Stimme, Ton*›; ~ **appeal** Appell an die Gefühle *od.* Emotionen 2 (liable to excessive emotion) emotiv (geh.); leicht erregbar ‹*Person*›; ~ **character** *or* **nature** *or* **disposition** leichte Erregbarkeit; **get** ~ **over sth.** sich über etw. (*Akk.*) erregen

emotionalism /ɪ'məʊʃənəlɪzm/ *n., no pl.* Gefühlsbetontheit, *die;* Rührseligkeit, *die* (abwertend)

emotionally /ɪ'məʊʃənəlɪ/ *adv.* emotional; gefühlvoll ‹*sprechen, sich verhalten*›; gefühlsmäßig, emotional ‹*reagieren*›; gefühlsbetont ‹*denken*›; **thank sb.** ~: [sich bei] jmdm. von Herzen [be]danken; **be** ~ **exhausted/worn out/disturbed** seelisch erschöpft/ausgelaugt/gestört sein; **get** ~ **involved with sb.** eine gefühlsmäßige Bindung mit jmdm. eingehen

emotionless /ɪ'məʊʃnlɪs/ *adj.* emotionslos; emotionsfrei; ausdruckslos ‹*Gesicht*›; gleichgültig ‹*Stimme*›

emotive /ɪ'məʊtɪv/ *adj.* emotional; gefühlsbetont; emotiv (Psych., Sprachw.)

empathize /'empəθaɪz/ *v.i.* ~ **with sb.** sich in jmdn. hineinversetzen; ~ **with sth.** etw. nachempfinden

empathy /'empəθɪ/ *n.* Empathie, *die* (Psych.); Einfühlung, *die*

emperor /'empərə(r)/ *n.* ▸ℹ **p. 1634** Kaiser, *der;* ~ **penguin** Kaiserpinguin, *der*

emphasis /'emfəsɪs/ *n., pl.* **emphases** /'emfəsi:z/ 1 (in speech etc.) Betonung, *die;* **the** ~ **is on sth.** die Betonung liegt auf etw. (*Dat.*); **lay** *or* **place** *or* **put** ~ **on sth.** etw. betonen 2 (intensity) Nachdruck, *der;* **do sth. with** ~: etw. nachdrücklich tun 3 (importance attached) Gewicht, *das;* **lay** *or* **place** *or* **put [considerable]** ~ **on sth.** [großes] Gewicht auf etw. (*Akk.*) legen; **the school's** ~ **is on languages** die Schule legt das Schwergewicht auf die [Fremd]sprachen; **the** ~ **has shifted** der Akzent hat sich verlagert; **with particular** *or* **special** ~ **on sth.** unter besonderer Berücksichtigung einer Sache (*Gen.*)

emphasize (**emphasise**) /'emfəsaɪz/ *v.t.* (lit. or fig.) betonen; (attach importance to) Gewicht auf etw. (*Akk.*) legen; **sth. cannot be too strongly** ~**d** etw. kann nicht genug betont werden

emphatic /ɪm'fætɪk/ *adj.* nachdrücklich; emphatisch (geh.); eindringlich, emphatisch (geh.) ‹*Redner*›; (forcible) demonstrativ ‹*Rückzug, Ablehnung*›; eindringlich ‹*Demonstration*›; **make sth. more** ~: einer Sache (*Dat.*) Nachdruck verleihen; **be quite** ~ **that ...:** durchaus darauf bestehen, dass …

emphatically /ɪm'fætɪkəlɪ/ *adv.* nachdrücklich; emphatisch (geh.); eindringlich ‹*sprechen*›; (decisively) entschieden ‹*bestreiten usw.*›

emphysema /emfɪ'si:mə/ *n.* ▸ℹ **p. 1231** (Med.) Emphysem, *das*

empire /'empaɪə(r)/ *n.* 1 Reich, *das;* **the E**~ (Hist.) (British) das Empire; das britische Weltreich; (Holy Roman) das Heilige Römische Reich 2 (commercial organization) Imperium, *das* (fig.)

empire: ~ **builder** *n.* (fig.) **be an** ~ **builder** seinen Einflussbereich ausweiten wollen; ~**-building** *n.* (fig.) **it is just** ~**-building** es geht dabei nur um den Aufbau eines kleinen Imperiums

empirical /ɪm'pɪrɪkl/ *adj.* empirisch; empirisch begründet ‹*Entscheidung, Argument, Wissen, Schlussfolgerung*›

empirically /ɪm'pɪrɪkəlɪ/ *adv.* empirisch

empiricism /ɪm'pɪrɪsɪzm/ *n., no pl.* 1 (method) Empirie, *die* 2 (Philos.) Empirismus, *der*

emplacement /ɪm'pleɪsmənt/ *n.* (Mil.) Geschützstand, *der*

employ /ɪm'plɔɪ/
A *v.t.* 1 (take into one's service) einstellen; (keep in one's service) beschäftigen; **are you** ~**ed in London/as a teacher?** arbeiten Sie in London/als Lehrer?; **be** ~**ed by** *or* **with a company** bei einer Firma arbeiten 2 (use services of) ~ **sb. in** *or* **on sth.** jmdn. für etw. einsetzen; ~ **sb. in** *or* **on doing sth.,** ~ **sb. to do sth.** jmdn. dafür einsetzen, etw. zu tun 3 (use) einsetzen (**for, in, on** für); unternehmen ‹*Anstrengungen*›; anwenden ‹*Methode, List*› (**for, in, on** bei); ~ **sth. to do sth.** etw. anwenden, um etwas zu tun; ~ **[one's] time on sth./[on] doing sth.** [seine] Zeit mit etw. verbringen/damit verbringen, etw. zu tun 4 (busy) ~ **oneself/sb. doing sth./in sth.** sich/jmdn. damit beschäftigen, etw. zu tun/mit etw. beschäftigen
B *n., no pl.* **be in the** ~ **of sb.** bei jmdm. beschäftigt sein; in jmds. Diensten stehen (veralt.); **the firm has 500 people in its** ~: bei der Firma sind 500 Leute beschäftigt

employable /ɪm'plɔɪəbl/ *adj.* 1 (fit to be taken into service) **be** ~: zu beschäftigen sein 2 (usable) verwendbar; **be** ~ **as/for sth.** als/für etw. verwendet werden können

employee (*Amer.:* **employe**) /emplɔɪ'i:, em'plɔɪi:/ *n.* Angestellte, *der/die;* (in contrast to employer) Arbeitnehmer, *der*/-nehmerin, *die;* **the firm's** ~**s** die Belegschaft der Firma

employer /ɪm'plɔɪə(r)/ *n.* Arbeitgeber, *der*/-geberin, *die;* **the firm is only a small** ~: die Firma hat nur wenige Beschäftigte

employment /ɪm'plɔɪmənt/ *n., no pl.* 1 (work) Arbeit, *die;* **there's no** ~ **available** es gibt keine freien Stellen *od.* keine Arbeit; **be in gainful** ~: erwerbstätig sein; **be in** ~ **with sb.** bei jmdm. arbeiten; **be in/without regular** ~: eine/keine feste Anstellung haben 2 (regular trade or profession) Beschäftigung, *die;* **what is your** ~? welchen Beruf üben Sie aus? 3 *no art.* (amount of work available) **full** ~: Vollbeschäftigung, *die* 4 **Secretary for E**~ (Brit.) Arbeitsminister, *der*/-ministerin, *die*

employment: ~ **agency** *n.* Stellenvermittlung, *die;* ~ **exchange**, ~ **office** *ns.* (Brit.) Arbeitsamt, *das;* ~ **statistics** *n. pl.* Beschäftigungsstatistik, *die*

emporium /em'pɔ:rɪəm/ *n., pl.* ~**s** *or* **emporia** /em'pɔ:rɪə/ 1 (market) Handelszentrum, *das* 2 (shop) Kaufhaus, *das*

empower /ɪm'paʊə(r)/ *v.t.* 1 (authorize) ermächtigen; (enable) befähigen 2 (make stronger and more confident) ~ **sb.** jmdn. in die Lage versetzen, sein Leben selbst in die Hand zu nehmen

empress /'emprɪs/ *n.* Kaiserin, *die*

emptiness /'emptɪnɪs/ *n., no pl.* (lit. or fig.) Leere, *die*

empty /'emptɪ/
A *adj.* 1 leer; **find an** ~ **seat/parking place** einen freien Sitz-/Parkplatz finden; ~ **of sth.** ohne etw.; ~ **of people** menschenleer; **the street is** ~ **of traffic** in der Straße herrscht kein Verkehr; *see also* **stomach A 1** 2 (coll.: hungry) **I feel a bit** ~: ich bin ein bisschen hungrig; **an hour later you feel quite** ~: eine Stunde später hat man schon wieder Hunger 3 (fig.) (foolish) dumm; hohl ‹*Kopf*›; (meaningless) leer
B *n.* (vehicle) Leerfahrzeug, *das;* (bottle) leere Flasche; (container) leerer Behälter; **sb. is running on** ~: jmdm. geht der Sprit aus; (fig.) jmd. ist am Ende
C *v.t.* 1 (remove contents of) leeren; [aus]leeren ‹*Tasche*›; (finish using contents of) aufbrauchen; (remove people from) räumen; (eat/drink whole contents of) leer essen ‹*Teller*›/leeren ‹*Glas*›; ~ **one's bladder/bowels** die Blase/den Darm entleeren 2 (transfer) umfüllen (**into** in + *Akk.*); (pour) schütten (**over** über + *Akk.*); ~ **sth. into/down the sink** etw. in den Ausguss schütten
D *v.i.* 1 (become ~) sich leeren 2 (discharge) ~ **into** ‹*Fluss, Abwasserkanal:*› münden in (+ *Akk.*)

empty: ~**-'handed** *pred. adj.* mit leeren Händen; ~**-headed** *adj.* hohlköpfig (abwertend)

EMS *abbr.* = **European Monetary System** EWS

emu /'i:mju:/ *n.* (Ornith.) Emu, *der*

EMU *abbr.*
A = **Economic and Monetary Union** WWU
B = **European Monetary Union** EWU

emulate /'emjʊleɪt/ *v.t.* 1 (try to equal or excel) nacheifern (+ *Dat.*) 2 (imitate zealously) nachahmen

emulation /emjʊ'leɪʃn/ *n.* 1 (attempt at equalling or excelling) ~ **of sb.** Bestreben, es jmdm. gleichzutun 2 (zealous imitation) Nachahmung, *die*

emulsifier /ɪ'mʌlsɪfaɪə(r)/ *n.* Emulgator, *der*

emulsify /ɪ'mʌlsɪfaɪ/ *v.t.* emulgieren

emulsion /ɪ'mʌlʃn/ *n.* 1 Emulsion, *die* 2 ▸**emulsion paint**

e'mulsion paint *n.* Dispersionsfarbe, *die*

en /en/ *n.* (Printing) Halbgeviert, *das*

enable /ɪ'neɪbl/ *v.t.* ~ **sb. to do sth.** es jmdm. ermöglichen, etw. zu tun; ~ **sth. [to be done]** etw. ermöglichen; ~ **an investigation to be made** eine Untersuchung ermöglichen; **enabling act** (Law) Ermächtigungsgesetz, *das;* (Amer. Law: legalizing) gesetzliche Sonderregelung

enact /ɪ'nækt/ *v.t.* 1 (ordain, make law) erlassen; ~ **that ...:** verfügen, dass … 2 (act out) aufführen ‹*Theaterstück*›; spielen ‹*Rolle*›; mitwirken bei ‹*Feier*›; **be** ~**ed** ‹*Geschehen, Szene:*› sich abspielen

enamel /ɪ'næml/
A *n.* 1 Emaille, *die;* Email, *das;* (paint) Lack, *der;* (on pottery) Glasur, *die* 2 (~ painting) Email[le]malerei, *die* 3 (Anat.) [Zahn]schmelz, *der*
B *attrib. adj.* 1 (containing ~) Email[le]- 2 (with ~ coating and/or design) emailliert; Email[le]‹*geschirr*›
C *v.t.*, (Brit.) **-ll-** emaillieren; glasieren ‹*Ton, Steinzeug*›

enamoured (*Brit.; Amer.:* **enamored**) /ɪ'næməd/ *adj.* ~ **of sb.** (in love with) in jmdn. verliebt; (liking) von jmdm. angetan; **[not exactly** *or* **particularly]** ~ **of sth.** von etw. [nicht gerade] begeistert

en bloc /ɑ̃ 'blɒk/ *adv.* en bloc

encamp /ɪn'kæmp/ (Mil.)
A *v.t.* **the troops were** ~**ed near the border** die Truppen bezogen ein Lager nahe der Grenze
B *v.i.* ein Lager aufschlagen

encampment /ɪn'kæmpmənt/ *n.* 1 *no pl.* Lagern, *das* 2 (place) Lager, *das*

encapsulate /ɪn'kæpsjʊleɪt/ *v.t.* 1 (in capsule) einkapseln ‹*Medikament*›; in eine[r] Kapsel einschließen; (as in capsule) einschließen 2 (fig.) festhalten; einfangen (geh.)

encase /ɪn'keɪs/ *v.t.* einschließen; fassen ‹*Edelstein*›; **the watch was** ~**d in metal** die Armbanduhr hatte ein Metallgehäuse; ~ **in plaster** eingipsen ‹*Bein, Arm*›

encash /ɪn'kæʃ/ *v.t.* (Brit.) (realize) [in bar] einnehmen; sich (*Dat.*) [bar] auszahlen lassen ‹*Gewinn*›; (convert into cash) [bar] einlösen

encephalitis /ensefə'laɪtɪs/ *n.* (Med.) Enzephalitis, *die* (fachspr.); Gehirnentzündung, *die*

enchant /ɪn'tʃɑ:nt/ *v.t.* **1** (bewitch) verzaubern; **she ~s men with her beauty** (fig.) sie bezaubert die Männer mit ihrer Schönheit **2** (delight) entzücken; **be ~ed by sth.** von etw. entzückt sein; **we were ~ed by the place** wir waren von dem Ort bezaubert

enchanted /ɪn'tʃɑ:ntɪd/ *adj.* **1** (bewitched) verzaubert; **~ forest** Zauberwald, *der;* **~ evening** (fig.) zauberischer Abend (geh.) **2** (delighted) entzückt

enchanting /ɪn'tʃɑ:ntɪŋ/ *adj.* **1** zauberisch (veralt.); **~ power** Zauberkraft, *die* **2** (delightful) entzückend; bezaubernd

enchantingly /ɪn'tʃɑ:ntɪŋlɪ/ *adv.* bezaubernd

enchantment /ɪn'tʃɑ:ntmənt/ *n.* **1** Verzauberung, *die;* (fig.) Zauber, *der;* **world of ~:** Zauberwelt, *die* **2** (delight) Entzücken, *das* (**with** über + *Akk.*)

enchantress /ɪn'tʃɑ:ntrɪs/ *n.* (lit. or fig.) Zauberin, *die*

encipher /ɪn'saɪfə(r)/ *v.t.* verschlüsseln; chiffrieren

encircle /ɪn'sɜ:kl/ *v.t.* **1** umgeben; **the enemy ~d us** der Feind kreiste uns ein *od.* umstellte uns; **~d with** *or* **by bodyguards** von Leibwächtern umringt; **his arms ~d her waist** seine Arme umschlangen ihre Taille **2** (mark with circle) einkreisen ‹*Buchstabe, Antwort*›

encirclement /ɪn'sɜ:klmənt/ *n.* (Mil.) Einkreisung, *die*

encl. *abbr.* **= enclosed a, enclosure[s]** Anl.

enclave /'enkleɪv/ *n.* (lit. or fig.) Enklave, *die*

enclitic /en'klɪtɪk/ (Ling.)

A *adj.* enklitisch

B *n.* Enklitikon, *das*

enclose /ɪn'kləʊz/ *v.t.* **1** (surround) umgeben; (shut up or in) einschließen; **be ~d in a cell/tomb/coffin** in einer Zelle/einem Grab/Sarg eingeschlossen sein; **~d in this casing is ...:** in diesem Gehäuse befindet sich ...; **~ land in** *or* **with barbed wire** Land mit Stacheldraht einzäunen **2** (put in envelope with letter) beilegen (**with,** in *Dat.*); **I [herewith] ~ the completed application form** anbei der ausgefüllte Bewerbungsbogen; **your passport is ~d herewith** Ihr Pass liegt als Anlage bei; **please find ~d, ~d please find** als Anlage übersenden wir Ihnen; anbei erhalten Sie; **a cheque for £10 is ~d** beiliegend finden Sie einen Scheck über 10 Pfund **3** (Math.) einschließen **4** (Hist.: make private) zur privaten Nutzung einfrieden

enclosed /ɪn'kləʊzd/ *adj.* **1** (in a container) darin enthalten; (included with letter) beigelegt; beigefügt; **from the ~ you will see that ...:** aus der Anlage werden Sie ersehen, dass ... **2** (closed off) eingefriedet; (by fence) eingezäunt

enclosure /ɪn'kləʊʒə(r)/ *n.* **1** (action) Einfriedung, *die;* (with fence) Einzäunung, *die* **2** (place) eingefriedeter/eingezäunter Bereich; (in zoo) Gehege, *das;* (paddock) Koppel, *die* **3** (fence) Umzäunung, *die;* (wall etc.) Einfriedung, *die* **4** (with letter in envelope) Anlage, *die*

encode /ɪn'kəʊd/ *v.t.* verschlüsseln; chiffrieren; (Computing) enkodieren

encoding /en'kəʊdɪŋ/ *n., no pl.* (Computing) Enkodierung, *die*

encomium /en'kəʊmɪəm/ *n., pl.* **~s** *or* **encomia** /en'kəʊmɪə/ (formal) Lobpreisung, *die* (geh.); **give sb. an ~:** jmdn. lobpreisen (geh.)

encompass /ɪn'kʌmpəs/ *v.t.* **1** (encircle) umgeben; (surround) umringen **2** (take in) umfassen **3** (contain) einhüllen

encore /ɒŋ'kɔ:(r), 'ɒŋkɔ:(r)/

A *int.* Zugabe!

B *n.* Zugabe, *die;* **receive three ~s** drei Zugaben geben müssen; **give an ~** ‹*Band, Orchester:*› eine Zugabe spielen

C *v.t.* als Zugabe verlangen ‹*Lied, Tanz usw.*›; um eine Zugabe bitten ‹*Sänger, Tänzer, Künstler*›

encounter /ɪn'kaʊntə(r)/

A *v.t.* **1** (as adversary) treffen auf (+ *Akk.*) **2** (by chance) begegnen (+ *Dat.*) **3** (meet with, come across) stoßen auf (+ *Akk.*) ‹*Problem, Schwierigkeit, Kritik, Widerstand usw.*›

B *n.* **1** (in combat) Zusammenstoß, *der;* **have an ~ with the authorities over a matter** mit den Behörden wegen einer Angelegenheit aneinander geraten; **I had a slight ~ with another car yesterday** (coll. iron.) ich hatte gestern eine etwas heftige Begegnung mit einem anderen Auto (iron.); **verbal ~:** Wortgefecht, *das;* **this was not his first ~ with the law** das war nicht das erste Mal, dass er mit dem Gesetz in Konflikt kam **2** (chance meeting, introduction) Begegnung, *die;* **have a chance ~ with sb.** jmdm. zufällig begegnen

en'counter group *n.* Encountergruppe, *die* (Psych.)

encourage /ɪn'kʌrɪdʒ/ *v.t.* **1** (stimulate, incite) ermutigen; **bread ~s rats and mice** Brot lockt Ratten und Mäuse an **2** (promote) fördern; beleben ‹*Verkauf*›; **~ a smile/a response from sb.** jmdm. ein Lächeln/eine Reaktion entlocken; **~ bad habits** schlechte Angewohnheiten unterstützen; **we do not ~ smoking in this office** wir unterstützen es nicht, dass in diesem Büro geraucht wird **3** (urge) **~ sb. to do sth.** jmdn. dazu ermuntern, etw. zu tun **4** (cheer) **be [much] ~d by sth.** durch etw. neuen Mut schöpfen; **we were ~d to hear** *or* **felt ~d when we heard ...:** wir schöpften neuen Mut, als wir hörten ...

encouragement /ɪn'kʌrɪdʒmənt/ *n.* **1** (support, incitement) Ermutigung, *die* (**from** durch); **give sb. ~:** jmdn. ermutigen; **get** *or* **receive ~ from sth.** durch etw. ermutigt werden **2** (urging) Ermunterung, *die* **3** (stimulus) Ansporn, *der;* **be an ~ to rats/moths** *etc.* Ratten/Motten *usw.* anlocken

encouraging /ɪn'kʌrɪdʒɪŋ/ *adj.* ermutigend; **the teacher is very ~** (by nature) der Lehrer hat eine sehr ermutigende Art

encouragingly /ɪn'kʌrɪdʒɪŋlɪ/ *adv.* ermutigend

encroach /ɪn'krəʊtʃ/ *v.i.* (lit. or fig.) **~ [on sth.]** [in etw. (*Akk.*)] eindringen; **the shadows began ~ing on the lawn** die Schatten drangen allmählich auf den Rasen vor; **the sea is ~ing [on the land]** das Meer dringt vor; **~ on sb.'s time** jmds. Zeit über Gebühr in Anspruch nehmen

encroachment /ɪn'krəʊtʃmənt/ *n.* (lit. or fig.) Eindringen, *das* (**on** in + *Akk.*); **make ~s** eindringen; **make ~s on sb.'s time** jmds. Zeit über Gebühr in Anspruch nehmen

encrust /ɪn'krʌst/ *v.t.* überkrusten; **be ~ed with diamonds/beads/gold** über und über mit Diamanten/Perlen besetzt/mit Gold überzogen sein

encrypt /en'krɪpt/ *v.t.* verschlüsseln

encryption /en'krɪpʃn/ *n.* Verschlüsselung, *die*

encumber /ɪn'kʌmbə(r)/ *v.t.* **1** (hamper) behindern; **~ oneself/sb. with sth.** sich/jmdn. mit etw. belasten **2** (burden) **~ sb. with debt** jmdn. mit Schulden belasten

encumbrance /ɪn'kʌmbrəns/ *n.* **1** (burden) Last, *die;* (nuisance) Belastung, *die* **2** (impediment) Hindernis, *das* (**to** für); **be without ~** (without family) ohne Anhang sein **3** (on property) Belastung, *die*

encyclic /en'sɪklɪk/, **encyclical** /en'sɪklɪkl/

A *adj.* **~ letter** Enzyklika, *die*

B *n.* Enzyklika, *die*

encyclopaedia *etc.* ▸ **encyclopedia** *etc.*

encyclopedia /ensaɪklə'pi:dɪə, ɪnsaɪklə'pi:dɪə/ *n.*Lexikon, *das;* Enzyklopädie, *die;* **walking A**

encyclopedic /ensaɪklə'pi:dɪk, ɪnsaɪklə'pi:dɪk/ *adj.* enzyklopädisch

end /end/

A *n.* **1** (extremity, farthest point, limit) Ende, *das;* (of nose, hair, tail, branch, finger) Spitze, *die;* **go to the ~s of the earth** bis ans Ende der Welt gehen; **that was the ~** (coll.) (no longer tolerable) da war Schluss (ugs.); (very bad) das war das Letzte (ugs.); **you are the ~** (coll.) du bist [einfach] unmöglich; **he beat him all ~s up** er hat ihn vernichtend geschlagen; **at an ~:** zu Ende; **come to an ~:** enden; ein Ende nehmen; **have come to the ~ of a task** mit einer Aufgabe fertig sein; **be coming to the ~ of a task** mit einer Aufgabe fast fertig sein; **when you come to the ~ of the page** wenn Sie mit der Seite fertig sind; **my patience has come to** *or* **is now at an ~:** meine Geduld ist jetzt am Ende; **our supplies have come to an ~:** unsere Vorräte sind erschöpft; **come to/be coming to the ~ of the coffee** den Kaffee aufbrauchen/fast aufgebraucht haben; **that's the ~ of the butter** (coll.: is used up) die Butter ist alle (ugs.); **turn sth. ~ for ~:** etw. umdrehen; **look at a building/a pencil ~ on** ein Gebäude von der Schmalseite/einen Bleistift von der Spitze her betrachten; **~ on against** *or* **to sth.** mit dem Ende gegen etw.; **from ~ to ~:** von einem Ende zum anderen; **~ to ~:** längs hintereinander; **lay ~ to ~:** aneinander reihen; **keep one's ~ up** (fig.) seinen Mann stehen; **make an ~ of sth.** etw. abschaffen; **make [both] ~s meet** (fig.) [mit seinem Geld] zurechtkommen; **no ~** (coll.) unendlich viel; **it's been criticized no ~:** es ist über die Maßen kritisiert worden; **have no ~ of trouble/a surprise** nichts als Ärger haben/maßlos überrascht sein; **no ~ of a fuss** ein wahnsinniges Theater (ugs.); **there is no ~ to sth.** (coll.) etw. nimmt kein Ende; **there's no ~ to what you can achieve/learn** du kannst unendlich viel erreichen/lernen; **put an ~ to sth.** einer Sache (*Dat.*) ein Ende machen; **not know** *or* **not be able to tell one ~ of sth. from the other** bei etw. nicht wissen, wo hinten und vorne ist (ugs.)

2 (of box, packet, tube, etc.) Schmalseite, *die;* (top/bottom surface) Ober-/Unterseite, *die;* **on ~** (upright) hochkant; **sb.'s hair stands on ~** (fig.) jmdm. stehen die Haare zu Berge (ugs.); *see also* **7**

3 (remnant) Rest, *der;* (of cigarette, candle) Stummel, *der;* **tie up the/a few [loose] ~s** (fig.) die/ein paar Einzelheiten erledigen

4 (side) Seite, *die;* **how are things at the business/social/at your ~?** wie sieht es geschäftlich/mit den sozialen Kontakten/bei dir aus?; **be on the receiving ~ of sth.** etw. abbekommen *od.* einstecken müssen; **he was on the receiving ~ in the fight** er musste in dem Kampf einiges einstecken

5 (half of sports pitch or court) Spielfeldhälfte, *die;* **change ~s** die Seiten wechseln; **choice of ~s** Seitenwahl, *die*

6 (of swimming pool) **deep/shallow ~ [of the pool]** tiefer/flacher Teil [des Schwimmbeckens]; **go in/be thrown in at the deep ~** (fig.) ins kalte Wasser springen/geworfen werden; **go [in] off the deep ~** (fig. coll.) aus der Haut fahren (ugs.)

7 ▸ **i p. 1047** (conclusion, lit. or fig.) Ende, *das;* (of lesson, speech, story, discussion, meeting, argument, play, film, book, sentence) Schluss, *der;* Ende, *das;* **the ~ is not yet** ein Ende ist noch nicht abzusehen; (there is still hope) es ist noch nicht aller Tage Abend; **by the ~ of the hour/day/week** *etc.* **we were exhausted** als die Stunde/der Tag/die Woche *usw.* herum war, waren wir erschöpft; **at the ~ of 1987/March** Ende 1987/März; **by the ~ of the meeting** als die Versammlung zu Ende war; **until** *or* **till the ~ of time** bis ans Ende aller Tage; **read to the ~ of the page** die Seite zu Ende lesen; **leave before the ~ of the film** gehen, ehe der Film zu Ende ist; **that's the ~ of 'that** (fig.) damit ist die Sache erledigt; **will there never be an ~ to all this?** wird das alles nie ein Ende nehmen?; **want [to see] an ~ to sth.** das Ende einer Sache (*Gen.*) wollen; **I shall never hear the ~ of it** (joc.) das werde ich noch lange zu hören bekommen; **I wonder if there's an ~ to it all** ich frage mich, ob das denn gar kein Ende nimmt; **be at an ~:** zu Ende sein; **bring a meeting/discussion/lesson to an ~:** eine Versammlung/Diskussion/Unterrichtsstunde beenden; **his education/journey was brought to an abrupt ~:** seine Ausbildung/Reise fand ein plötzliches Ende; **in the ~:** schließlich; **on ~:** ununterbrochen; *see also* **2**

8 (downfall, destruction) Ende, *das;* (death) Ende, *das* (geh. verhüll.); **meet one's ~:** den Tod finden

(geh.); **meet its ~** ‹*Sache:*› sein Ende finden (fig.); **sb. is nearing his ~:** mit jmdm. geht es zu Ende (verhüll.); **this will be the ~ of him** das bedeutet das Ende für ihn; **drink will be the ~ of him** der Alkohol wird ihn noch ins Grab bringen; **sb. comes to a bad** *or* **sticky ~:** es nimmt ein böses *od.* schlimmes Ende mit jmdm.
9 (purpose, object) Ziel, *das;* Zweck, *der;* **~ in itself** Selbstzweck, *der;* **be an ~ in itself** (likewise a purpose) auch ein lohnendes Ziel sein; (the only purpose) das eigentliche Ziel sein; **the ~ justifies the means** der Zweck heiligt die Mittel; **with this ~ in view** mit diesem Ziel vor Augen; **as a means to an ~:** als Mittel zum Zweck; **for material ~s** aus materiellen Gründen; **gain** *or* **win** *or* **achieve one's ~s** seine Ziele erreichen; **to** *or* **for this ~:** zu diesem Zweck *od.* (veralt.) Ende; **to** *or* **for what ~[s]** zu welchem Zweck *od.* (veralt.) Ende; **to no ~:** vergebens; ohne Erfolg. *See also* **bitter A 2; East End; tether A 2; West End; without A 1; world 1**
B *v.t.* **1** (bring to an end) beenden; kündigen ‹*Abonnement*›; **~ one's life/days** (spend last part of life) sein Leben/seine Tage beschließen
2 (put an end to, destroy) ein Ende setzen (+ *Dat.*); **~ it [all]** (coll.: kill oneself) [mit dem Leben] Schluss machen (ugs.)
3 (stand as supreme example of) **a car/feast/race** *etc.* **to ~ all cars/feasts/races** *etc.* ein Auto/Fest/Rennen *usw.*, das alles [bisher Dagewesene] in den Schatten stellt
C *v.i.* enden; **where will it all ~?** wo soll das noch hinführen?; **~ by doing sth.** schließlich etw. tun; **the project ~ed in chaos/disaster** das Vorhaben endete im Chaos/in einer Katastrophe; **the discussion ~ed in a quarrel** die Diskussion endete mit einem Streit; **the match ~ed in a draw** das Spiel ging unentschieden aus
Phrasal verb
• **~ 'up** *v.i.* enden; **we ~ed up in a ditch** (coll.) wir landeten in einem Graben (ugs.); **he'll ~ up in prison** (coll.) er wird im Gefängnis landen (ugs.); **we ~ed up at his place** (coll.) wir landeten schließlich bei ihm zu Hause (ugs.); **~ up [as] a teacher/an alcoholic** (coll.) schließlich Lehrer/zum Alkoholiker werden; **I always ~ up doing all the work** (coll.) am Ende bleibt die ganze Arbeit immer an mir hängen

'end-all ▸ **be D**

endanger /ɪnˈdeɪndʒə(r)/ *v.t.* gefährden

endangered /ɪnˈdeɪndʒəd/ *adj.* gefährdet; **an ~ species** eine vom Aussterben bedrohte Art

'en dash *n.* (Printing) Halbgeviertstrich, *der*

endear /ɪnˈdɪə(r)/ *v.t.* **~ sb./sth./oneself to sb.** jmdn./etw./sich bei jmdm. beliebt machen

endearing /ɪnˈdɪərɪŋ/ *adj.* reizend; gewinnend ‹*Lächeln, Art*›

endearingly /ɪnˈdɪərɪŋlɪ/ *adv.* reizend; gewinnend ‹*lächeln*›

endearment /ɪnˈdɪəmənt/ *n.* Zärtlichkeit, *die;* **term of ~:** Kosename, *der*

endeavour (*Amer.:* **endeavor**) /ɪnˈdevə(r)/
A *v.i.* **~ to do sth.** sich bemühen, etw. zu tun
B *n.* Bemühung, *die;* (attempt) Versuch, *der;* **~ to do sth.** Bemühen, etw. zu tun (geh.); **make every ~ to do sth.** alle Anstrengungen unternehmen, um etw. zu tun; **make an ~** *or* **make ~s to do sth.** *or* **at doing sth.** sich bemühen, etw. zu tun; **despite his best ~s** obwohl er sich nach Kräften bemühte; **human ~:** das Streben des Menschen

endemic /enˈdemɪk/ *adj.* (Biol., Med.) endemisch; einheimisch ‹*Pflanze, Tier*›; örtlich begrenzt auftretend ‹*Infektionskrankheit*›; (regularly found) verbreitet ‹*Krankheit*›; [allgemein] verbreitet ‹*Gewalt, Alkoholismus, Rastlosigkeit*›

endemically /enˈdemɪkəlɪ/ *adv.* endemisch

'endgame *n.* Endspiel, *das*

ending /ˈendɪŋ/ *n.* Schluss, *der;* (of word) Endung, *die; see also* **happy ending**

endive /ˈendɪv/ *n.* **1** Endivie, *die* **2** (Amer.: chicory crown) Brüsseler Endivie; Chicorée, *der od. die*

endless /ˈendlɪs/ *adj.* **1** endlos; (coll.: innumerable) unzählig; (eternal) unendlich; **have an ~ wait, wait an ~ time** endlos lange warten; **the journey seemed ~:** die Reise schien kein Ende zu nehmen **2** (infinite) unendlich; endlos ‹*Straße*›; unbegrenzt ‹*Auswahl*›; unendlich lang ‹*Straße, Liste*›

endless 'cable *n.* Umlaufseil, *das*

endlessly /ˈendlɪslɪ/ *adv.* **1** (incessantly) unaufhörlich ‹*streiten, schwatzen*›; (interminably) endlos lange ‹*warten*› **2** (infinitely) endlos ‹*sich erstrecken, lang*›

endmost /ˈendməʊst/ *adj.* letzt…; **the ~ leaves on the branches** die Blätter an den Spitzen der Zweige/Äste

endocrine /ˈendəʊkrɪn/ *adj.* (Physiol.) endokrin

endorse /ɪnˈdɔːs/ *v.t.* **1** (write on back of) auf der Rückseite beschriften; **~ sth. with one's signature** etw. auf der Rückseite signieren; **~ sth. on the [back of the] document** etw. auf die Rückseite des Dokuments schreiben **2** (sign one's name on back of) indossieren ‹*Scheck, Wechsel*›; **~ a cheque** *etc.* **[over] to sb.** einen Scheck *usw.* durch Indossament auf jmdn. übertragen **3** (support, declare approval of) beipflichten (+ *Dat.*) ‹*Meinung, Aussage*›; billigen, gutheißen ‹*Entscheidung, Handlung, Einstellung*›; unterstützen ‹*Antrag, Vorschlag, Kandidaten, Kandidatur*› **4** (Brit.: make entry regarding offence on) einen Strafvermerk machen auf (+ *Akk. od. Dat.*)

endorsement /ɪnˈdɔːsmənt/ *n.* **1** (writing on back) Beschriftung auf der Rückseite; **the ~ of a document with one's signature** das Unterzeichnen eines Dokuments auf der Rückseite **2** (of cheque) Indossament, *das;* **~ to sb.** Übertragung durch Indossament auf jmdn. **3** (support, declaration of approval) Billigung, *die;* (of proposal, move, candidate) Unterstützung, *die* **4** (Brit.: entry regarding offence) Strafvermerk, *der* **(of** auf + *Akk. od. Dat.*)

endow /ɪnˈdaʊ/ *v.t.* **1** (give permanent income to) [über Stiftungen/eine Stiftung] finanzieren ‹*Einrichtung, Krankenhaus usw.*›; mit Geld ausstatten ‹*Person*›; stiften ‹*Preis, Lehrstuhl*›; **~ed school** durch Stiftungen finanzierte Schule **2** (fig.) **nature has ~ed her with great beauty** die Natur hat sie mit großer Schönheit ausgestattet; **be ~ed with charm/a talent for music** *etc.* Charme/musikalisches Talent *usw.* besitzen; **be well ~ed** ‹*Frau:*› Holz vor der Hütte haben (ugs.); ‹*Mann:*› stark gebaut sein (verhüll.)

endowment /ɪnˈdaʊmənt/ *n.* **1** (endowing, property, fund, etc.) Stiftung, *die* **2** (talent etc.) Begabung, *die*

endowment: ~ assurance *n.* abgekürzte *od.* gemischte Lebensversicherung; **~ mortgage** *n.* ≈ Tilgungslebensversicherung, *die;* **~ policy** ▸ **~ assurance**

end: ~paper *n.* Vorsatz, *der;* Vorsatzblatt, *das;* **~ point** *n.* **1** (Chem.) Umschlagspunkt, *der;* **2** (fig.) Endpunkt, *der;* **~ product** *n.* (lit. or fig.; also Chem.) Endprodukt, *das;* (fig.) Resultat, *das;* **~ re'sult** *n.* Endergebnis, *das;* (consequence) Folge, *die*

endue /ɪnˈdjuː/ *v.t.* (literary) **1** (clothe) bekleiden **(with** mit) **2** (furnish) ▸ **endow 2**

endurable /ɪnˈdjʊərəbl/ *adj.* erträglich

endurance /ɪnˈdjʊərəns/ *n.* **1** Widerstandskraft, *die* **(of** gegen); (ability to withstand strain) Ausdauer, *die;* (patience) Geduld, *die;* **the material's ~ [of wear and tear]** die Strapazierfähigkeit des Materials; **past** *or* **beyond ~:** unerträglich **2** (lastingness) Dauerhaftigkeit, *die*

en'durance test *n.* Belastungsprobe, *die*

endure /ɪnˈdjʊə(r)/
A *v.t.* (undergo, tolerate) ertragen; (submit to) über sich ergehen lassen; (suffer) erleiden ‹*Verlust, Unrecht*›; **~ to do sth.** es ertragen, etw. zu tun; **I can't ~ the thought of** *or* **to think of him alone there** der Gedanke, dass er allein dort ist, ist mir unerträglich
B *v.i.* fortdauern; **Shakespeare is a name which will ~:** der Name Shakespeares wird die Zeit überdauern

enduring /ɪnˈdjʊərɪŋ/ *adj.* (lasting) dauerhaft; beständig ‹*Glaube, Tradition*›

'end user **1** *n.* (Econ.) Endverbraucher, *der* **2** (Computing) Endbenutzer, *der*/-benutzerin, *die*

endways /ˈendweɪz/, **endwise** /ˈendwaɪz/ *advs.* **1** (with end towards spectator) **turn sth. ~ towards sb.** jmdm. die Schmalseite einer Sache (*Gen.*) zuwenden **2** (with end foremost) **~ [on]** längs; **let's have the bed facing that wall ~ [on]** lass uns das Bett mit der Schmalseite zu der Wand aufstellen! **3** (with end uppermost) **~ [on]** hochkant **4** (end to end) der Länge nach hintereinander; längs hintereinander

ENE /iːstnɔːθˈiːst/ *abbr.* ▸ⓘ **p. 1013 = east-north-east** ONO

enema /ˈenɪmə/ *n., pl.* **~s** *or* **enemata** /enɪˈmɑːtə/ (Med.) **1** (injection, substance) Einlauf, *der;* Klistier, *das* (Med.) **2** (syringe) Klistierspritze, *die* (Med.)

enemy /ˈenəmɪ/
A *n.* **1** (lit. or fig.) Feind, *der* **(of, to** *Gen.*); **make enemies** sich (*Dat.*) Feinde machen *od.* schaffen; **make an ~ of sb.** sich (*Dat.*) jmdn. zum Feind machen; **~ of the people/state** Volks-/Staatsfeind, *der;* **the ~ at the gate/within** der Feind vor den Toren/in den eigenen Reihen; **the E~:** der böse Feind (verhüll.); **be one's own worst ~, be nobody's ~ but one's own** niemandem schaden als sich (*Dat.*) selbst **2** (member of hostile army or nation, hostile force) Feind, *der;* (ship) feindliches Schiff
B *adj.* feindlich; **destroyed by ~ action** durch Feindeinwirkung zerstört

energetic /enəˈdʒetɪk/ *adj.* **1** (strenuously active) energiegeladen; schwungvoll ‹*Redner*›; tatkräftig ‹*Mitarbeiter*›; lebhaft ‹*Kind*›; **be an ~ person** sehr tatkräftig sein; **I don't feel ~ enough** ich habe nicht genug Energie **2** (vigorous) schwungvoll; entschieden, energisch ‹*Zustimmung, Ablehnung*›; kräftig ‹*Rühren, Schlag, Beifall*›

energetically /enəˈdʒetɪkəlɪ/ *adv.* schwungvoll; entschieden ‹*sich äußern*›

energize (**energise**) /ˈenədʒaɪz/ *v.t.* **1** (infuse energy into) in Schwung bringen (ugs.) **2** (Electr.) mit Strom versorgen

energy /ˈenədʒɪ/ *n.* **1** (vigour) Energie, *die;* (active operation) Kraft, *die;* **save your ~:** schone deine Kräfte!; **I've no ~ left** ich habe keine Energie mehr; **build up one's ~:** Kräfte sammeln **2** *in pl.* (individual's powers) Kraft, *die* **3** (Phys.) Energie, *die;* **sources of ~:** Energiequellen; *see also* **conservation 2; potential A**

energy: ~ audit *n.* Energieaudit, *das;* **~ consumption** *n.* Energieverbrauch, *der;* **~ crisis** *n.* Energiekrise, *die;* **~ efficiency** *n.* Energieeffizienz, *die;* **~-giving** *adj.* Energie spendend; **~ resources** *n. pl.* Energieressourcen *Pl.;* **~-saving** *adj.* Energie sparend; **~-saving lamp** Energiesparlampe, *die;* **~ value** *n.* Nährwert, *der*

enervate /ˈenəveɪt/ *v.t.* schwächen

enervating /ˈenəveɪtɪŋ/ *adj.* enervierend (geh.), ermüdend ‹*Auseinandersetzung, Streben*›; schlapp machend ‹*Klima, Feuchtigkeit*›; kräftezehrend ‹*Krankheit*›; lähmend ‹*Hitze*›

enervation /enəˈveɪʃn/ *n.* Schwächung, *die;* (state) Schwäche, *die*

enfant terrible /ɑ̃fɑ̃ teˈriːbl/ *n., pl.* **enfants terribles** /ɑ̃fɑ̃ teˈriːbl/ Enfant terrible, *das*

enfeeble /ɪnˈfiːbl/ *v.t.* schwächen

enfeeblement /ɪnˈfiːblmənt/ *n.* Schwächung, *die;* (state) Schwäche, *die*

enfold /ɪnˈfəʊld/ *v.t.* **1** (wrap up) **~ sb. in** *or* **with sth.** jmdn. in etw. (*Akk.*) einhüllen *od.* mit etw. umhüllen **2** (clasp) umschließen; **he ~ed her in his arms** er schloss sie in die Arme

enforce /ɪnˈfɔːs/ *v.t.* **1** durchsetzen; sorgen für ‹*Disziplin*›; **~ sth. [up]on sb.** jmdm. etw. aufzwingen; **~ the law** dem Gesetz Geltung verschaffen; das Gesetz durchsetzen **2** (give more force to) Nachdruck verleihen (+ *Dat.*)

enforceable /ɪnˈfɔːsəbl/ *adj.* durchsetzbar

e

enforcement /ɪn'fɔːsmənt/ *n.* Erzwingung, *die;* (of law) Durchsetzung, *die*

enfranchise /ɪn'fræntʃaɪz/ *v.t.* 1 (give vote to) das Wahlrecht verleihen (+ *Dat.*); **be ~d** das Wahlrecht erhalten 2 (invest with municipal rights) einen Parlamentssitz verleihen (+ *Dat.*)

enfranchisement /ɪn'fræntʃɪzmənt/ *n.* 1 (giving of vote to) Verleihung des Wahlrechts (**of** an + *Akk.*) 2 (investing with municipal rights) Verleihung eines Parlamentssitzes (**of** an + *Akk.*)

ENG *abbr.* = **electronic news-gathering** elektronische Berichterstattung; EB

Engadine /'eŋgədiːn/ *pr. n.* **the ~**: das Engadin

engage /ɪn'geɪdʒ/

A *v.t.* 1 engagieren; **a singer was ~d to sing at the wedding** ein Sänger/eine Sängerin wurde engagiert *od.* verpflichtet, der/die bei der Hochzeit singen sollte 2 (hire) einstellen; **we have ~d his services** er arbeitet für uns; wir nehmen seine Dienste in Anspruch 3 (employ busily) beschäftigen (**in** mit); (involve) verwickeln (**in** in + *Akk.*); **~ oneself in sth.** sich mit etw. befassen *od.* beschäftigen; **~ sb. in conversation** jmdn. ins Gespräch ziehen; (more absorbingly) jmdn. in ein Gespräch verwickeln 4 (attract and hold fast) wecken [und wach halten] ‹*Interesse*›; auf sich (*Akk.*) ziehen ‹*Aufmerksamkeit*›; fesseln ‹*Person*›; in Anspruch nehmen ‹*Konzentration*›; gewinnen ‹*Sympathie, Unterstützung*› 5 (arrange to occupy) mieten 6 (enter into conflict with) angreifen; (bring into conflict) **~ sb. in a duel** jmdn. in einen Zweikampf verwickeln 7 (Mech.) **~ one cog with another** die Zahnräder ineinander greifen lassen; **~ the clutch/gears** einkuppeln/einen Gang einlegen 8 (Fencing) **~ [foils]** [die Klingen] kreuzen

B *v.i.* 1 **~ in sth.** sich an etw. (*Dat.*) beteiligen; **~ in politics** sich politisch engagieren; **~ in various sports** verschiedene Sportarten betreiben 2 (pledge) **~ to do sth.** sich verpflichten, etw. zu tun; (vow) geloben, etw. zu tun 3 (Mech.) ineinander greifen; **the clutch would not ~**: die Kupplung ließ sich nicht einrücken *od.* fasste nicht 4 (come into conflict) **~ with the enemy** den Feind angreifen

engaged /ɪn'geɪdʒd/ *adj.* 1 (to be married) verlobt; **be ~ [to be married] [to sb.]** [mit jmdm.] verlobt sein; **become** *or* **get ~ [to be married] [to sb.]** sich [mit jmdm.] verloben 2 (bound by promise) verabredet; **be otherwise ~**: etwas anderes vorhaben; **are you ~ this evening?** bist du für heute Abend verabredet?; hast du [für] heute Abend etwas vor? 3 (occupied with business) beschäftigt; **be** *or* **have become ~ in sth./in doing sth.** mit etw. befasst *od.* beschäftigt sein/damit befasst *od.* beschäftigt sein, etw. zu tun 4 (occupied or used by person) besetzt ‹*Toilette, Taxi*›; **the telephone [line]/number is ~**: der [Telefon]anschluss/die Nummer ist besetzt; **you're always ~**: bei dir ist immer besetzt; **~ signal** *or* **tone** (Brit. Teleph.) Besetztzeichen, *das*

engagement /ɪn'geɪdʒmənt/ *n.* 1 (to be married) Verlobung, *die* (**to** mit); **have a long ~**: lange verlobt sein 2 (appointment made with another) Verabredung, *die;* **have a previous** *or* **prior ~**: schon anderweitig festgelegt sein; **social ~**: gesellschaftliche Verpflichtung; **lunch/dinner ~**: Verabredung zum Mittag-/Abendessen 3 (booked appearance) Engagement, *das* 4 (hiring, appointment) Einstellung, *die* 5 (Mil.) Kampfhandlung, *die* 6 (Mech.: of gears) Ineinandergreifen, *das*

en'gagement ring *n.* Verlobungsring, *der*

engaging /ɪn'geɪdʒɪŋ/ *adj.* bezaubernd; gewinnend ‹*Lächeln*›; einnehmend ‹*Persönlichkeit, Art*›

engagingly /ɪn'geɪdʒɪŋlɪ/ *adv.* gewinnend ‹*lächeln*›

engender /ɪn'dʒendə(r)/ *v.t.* zur Folge haben; erzeugen; ‹*Person:*› hervorrufen

engine /'endʒɪn/ *n.* 1 (mechanical contrivance) Motor, *der;* (of spacecraft, jet aircraft) Triebwerk, *das* 2 (locomotive) Lok[omotive], *die*

'engine driver *n.* ▸ℹ **p. 1260** (Brit.) Lok[omotiv]führer, *der*

engineer /endʒɪ'nɪə(r)/

A *n.* ▸ℹ **p. 1260** 1 Ingenieur, *der*/Ingenieurin, *die;* (service ~, installation ~) Techniker, *der*/Technikerin, *die; see also* **chemical engineer**; **civil engineer**; **electrical engineer**; **mechanical engineer**; **sound engineer** 2 (maker or designer of engines) Maschinenbauingenieur, *der* 3 **[ship's] ~**: Maschinist, *der* 4 (Amer.: engine driver) Lok[omotiv]führer, *der* 5 (Mil.) (designer and constructor of military works) technischer Offizier; (soldier) Pionier, *der; see also* **Royal Engineers**

B *v.t.* 1 (contrive) arrangieren; entwickeln ‹*Plan*› 2 (manage construction of) konstruieren

engineering /endʒɪ'nɪərɪŋ/ *n., no pl.* 1 Technik, *die;* **career in ~**: Ingenieurlaufbahn, *die* 2 *attrib.* technisch ‹*Arbeiten, Fähigkeiten*›; **~ science** Ingenieurwesen, *das;* **~ company** *or* **firm** Maschinenbaufirma, *die*

engine: ~ failure *n.* Motorversagen, *das;* **~ failures** Motorpannen *Pl.;* **~ room** *n.* Maschinenhaus, *das;* Maschinenraum, *der*

England /'ɪŋglənd/ *pr. n.* England (*das*)

Englander /'ɪŋgləndə(r)/ *n.* (Hist.) **Little ~** *Gegner der imperialistischen Politik Englands*

English /'ɪŋglɪʃ/

A *adj.* ▸ℹ **p. 1277**, ▸ℹ **p. 1345** englisch; **he/she is ~**: er ist Engländer/sie ist Engländerin; *see also* **bond A 8**

B *n.* 1 (language) ▸ℹ **p. 1277** Englisch, *das;* **grammar of ~**: englische Grammatik; Grammatik der englischen Sprache; **say sth. in ~**: etw. auf Englisch sagen; **speak ~**: Englisch sprechen; **be speaking ~**: englisch sprechen; **I [can] speak/read ~**: ich spreche Englisch/kann Englisch lesen; **I cannot** *or* **do not speak/read ~**: ich spreche kein Englisch/kann Englisch nicht lesen; **translate into/from [the] ~**: ins Englische/aus dem Englischen übersetzen; **speak a very pure [form of] ~**: ein sehr reines Englisch sprechen; **write sth. in ~**: etw. englisch schreiben; etw. auf *od.* in Englisch schreiben; **is that [good** *or* **correct] ~?** ist das gutes Englisch?; **what you've written is just not ~!** was du da geschrieben hast, ist einfach kein Englisch!; **her ~ is very good** sie schreibt/spricht ein sehr gutes Englisch; **the King's/Queen's ~**: die englische Hochsprache; **British/American ~**: britisches/amerikanisches Englisch; **Northern/Southern ~**: in Nordengland/Südengland gesprochenes Englisch; **Middle ~**: Mittelenglisch, *das;* **Old ~**: Altenglisch, *das;* **in plain ~**: in einfachen Worten; **say sth. in plain ~**: etw. frei heraussagen; **now put it into plain ~**: ≈ nun sag es noch mal auf Deutsch 2 ▸ℹ **p. 1345** *pl.* **the ~**: die Engländer 3 (Amer. Billiards) ▸ **side A 11**. *See also* **pidgin English**

English: ~ 'breakfast *n.* englisches Frühstück; **~ 'Channel** *pr. n.* **the ~ Channel** der [Ärmel]kanal; **~ 'horn** *n.* (Mus.) Englischhorn, *das;* Englisch Horn, *das* (fachspr.); **~man** /'ɪŋglɪʃmən/ *n., pl.* **~men** /'ɪŋglɪʃmən/ Engländer, *der; see also* **castle A 1**

Englishness /'ɪŋglɪʃnɪs/ *n., no pl.* englische Eigenart

'Englishwoman *n.* Engländerin, *die*

engrave /ɪn'greɪv/ *v.t.* 1 gravieren ‹*Platte, Porträt, Illustration*›; **the brass plate had been ~d with his name** sein Name war in die Messingplatte eingraviert worden 2 (carve) **~ figures** *etc.* **[up]on a surface** Figuren *usw.* in eine Oberfläche eingravieren; **~ sth. [up]on a stone** etw. in einen Stein meißeln; **~ one's name on a tree** seinen Namen in einen Baum schnitzen; **the memory of that day has been** *or* **is ~d indelibly on my mind** (fig.) die Erinnerung an diesen Tag hat sich mir unauslöschlich eingeprägt *od.* eingegraben

engraver /ɪn'greɪvə(r)/ *n.* ▸ℹ **p. 1260** (of metal) Graveur, *der;* Stecher, *der;* (of wood) Holzschneider, *der;* (of stone) Steinschneider, *der;* Graveur, *der*

engraving /ɪn'greɪvɪŋ/ *n.* 1 (action) Gravieren, *das* 2 (design, marks) Gravur, *die;* Gravierung, *die* 3 (Art) (form) Gravierkunst, *die;* Kupferstich, *der;* (print) Stich, *der;* (print from wood) Holzschnitt, *der*

engross /ɪn'grəʊs/ *v.t.* (fully occupy) fesseln; völlig in Anspruch nehmen ‹*Zeit, Kraft usw.*›; **be ~ed in sth.** in etw. (*Akk.*) vertieft sein; **become** *or* **get ~ed in sth.** sich in etw. (*Akk.*) vertiefen

engrossing /ɪn'grəʊsɪŋ/ *adj.* fesselnd

engulf /ɪn'gʌlf/ *v.t.* verschlingen (auch fig.); (wrap up) einhüllen; **the house was ~ed in flames** das Haus stand in hellen Flammen

enhance /ɪn'hɑːns/ *v.t.* erhöhen ‹*Wert, [An]reiz, Macht, Aussichten, Schönheit*›; verstärken ‹*Wirkung*›; steigern ‹*Qualität, Wirkung*›; heben ‹*Stimmung, Aussehen*›; betonen ‹*Augen*›

enhancement /ɪn'hɑːnsmənt/ *n.* ▸ **enhance**: Erhöhung, *die;* Verstärkung, *die;* Steigerung, *die;* Hebung, *die;* Betonung, *die*

enigma /ɪ'nɪgmə/ *n.* Rätsel, *das*

enigmatic /enɪg'mætɪk/, **enigmatical** /enɪg'mætɪkl/ *adj.* rätselhaft

enjambement, enjambment /en'dʒæmmənt/ *n.* (Pros.) Enjambement, *das*

enjoin /ɪn'dʒɔɪn/ *v.t.* **~ a duty/restriction on sb.** jmdm. eine Pflicht/Einschränkung auferlegen; **~ silence/obedience [on sb.]** [jmdn.] zum Schweigen ermahnen/Gehorsam [von jmdm.] fordern; **notices on the wall ~ed silence** Schilder an der Wand mahnten zur Ruhe; **~ caution on sb.** jmdn. zur Vorsicht ermahnen; **~ sb. [not] to do sth.** jmdn. eindringlich ermahnen, etw. [nicht] zu tun; **~ that sth. should be done** nachdrücklich fordern, dass etw. getan wird

enjoy /ɪn'dʒɔɪ/

A *v.t.* 1 **I ~ed the book/film/work** das Buch/der Film/die Arbeit hat mir gefallen; **are you ~ing your meal?** schmeckt dir das Essen?; **he ~s reading/travelling** er liest/reist gern; **he ~s music and drama** er mag Musik und Theater; **we really ~ed seeing you again** wir haben uns wirklich gefreut, euch wiederzusehen; **as a rule, people don't actually ~ going to the dentist** im Allgemeinen geht man nicht gerade gern zum Zahnarzt 2 (have use of) genießen ‹*Recht, Privileg, Vorteil*›; sich erfreuen (+ *Gen.*) ‹*hohen Einkommens*›; **~ the right to vote** das Wahlrecht ausüben können 3 (experience) sich erfreuen (+ *Gen.*) ‹*Respekts, guter Gesundheit*›; genießen ‹*Achtung*›

B *v. refl.* sich amüsieren; **you look as if you're ~ing yourself** du siehst ganz vergnügt aus; **we thoroughly ~ed ourselves in Spain** wir hatten viel Spaß in Spanien; **~ yourself at the theatre** viel Spaß im Theater!; **the children ~ed themselves making sandcastles** die Kinder vergnügten sich damit, Sandburgen zu bauen

enjoyable /ɪn'dʒɔɪəbl/ *adj.* schön; angenehm ‹*Empfindung, Unterhaltung, Arbeit*›; unterhaltsam ‹*Buch, Film, Stück*›

enjoyably /ɪn'dʒɔɪəblɪ/ *adv.* angenehm

enjoyment /ɪn'dʒɔɪmənt/ *n.* (delight) Vergnügen, *das* (**of** an + *Dat.*); **don't spoil other people's ~**: verdirb anderen nicht die Freude

enlarge /ɪn'lɑːdʒ/

A *v.t.* vergrößern; (widen) verbreitern ‹*Straße, Durchgang*›; weiter machen ‹*Kleidungsstück*›; erweitern ‹*Wissen*›; **the tumour had become ~d** der Tumor war größer geworden

B *v.i.* 1 sich vergrößern; größer werden; (widen) sich verbreitern 2 **~ [up]on sth.** etw. weiter ausführen

enlargement /ɪn'lɑːdʒmənt/ *n.* 1 Vergrößerung, *die;* (making or becoming wider) Verbreiterung, *die* 2 (further explanation) weitere Ausführung 3 (EU) Erweiterung, *die;* **the ~ of the EU** die EU-Erweiterung

enlarger /ɪn'lɑːdʒə(r)/ *n.* (Photog.) Vergrößerungsapparat, *der*

enlighten /ɪn'laɪtn/ *v.t.* aufklären (**on, as to** über + *Akk.*); **let me ~ you on the matter** lass mich dir die Sache erklären; **be ~ing** erhellend sein

enlightened /ɪn'laɪtnd/ *adj.* aufgeklärt

enlightenment /ɪn'laɪtnmənt/ *n., no pl.* Aufklärung, *die;* **[spiritual] ~**: [geistige] Erleuchtung; **the E~** (Hist.) die Aufklärung; **the Age of E~**: das Zeitalter der Aufklärung

enlist /ɪn'lɪst/
A *v.t.* 1 (Mil.) anwerben; **∼ed person** (Amer.) (soldier) Soldat, *der;* (sailor) Matrose, *der* 2 (secure as means of help) gewinnen
B *v.i.* **∼ [for the army/navy]** in die Armee/Marine eintreten; **∼ [as a soldier]** Soldat werden

enlistment /ɪn'lɪstmənt/ *n.* 1 (Mil.) Anwerbung, *die* 2 (securing as means of help) Gewinnung, *die*

enliven /ɪn'laɪvn/ *v.t.* beleben; anregen ‹*Fantasie*›; in Schwung bringen (ugs.) ‹*Person, Schulklasse usw.*›; lebhafter gestalten ‹*Tanz, Unterricht*›

en masse /ɑ̃ 'mæs/ *adv.* 1 (all together) alle zusammen; **taken ∼:** alles in allem 2 (in a crowd) in Massen

enmesh /ɪn'meʃ/ *v.t.* **∼ sb./sth. [in sth.]** jmdn./etw. [mit etw.] fangen; (fig.) jmdn./etw. [in etw. (*Akk.*)] verstricken; **a fly had become ∼ed in the spider's web** eine Fliege hatte sich in dem Spinnennetz verfangen

enmity /'enmɪtɪ/ *n.* Feindschaft, *die*

ennoble /ɪ'nəʊbl/ *v.t.* 1 adeln 2 (elevate) erheben

ennui /'ɒnwi:/ *n.* Ennui, *der* (geh.)

enormity /ɪ'nɔ:mɪtɪ/ *n.* 1 (atrocity) Ungeheuerlichkeit, *die* (abwertend) 2 ▸ **enormousness**

enormous /ɪ'nɔ:məs/ *adj.* 1 enorm; riesig, gewaltig ‹*Figur, Tier, Meer, Kathedrale, Fluss, Wüste, Menge*›; gewaltig, enorm ‹*Veränderung, Unterschied, Liebe, Hass, Widerspruch, Größe, Ausgabe, Kraft*›; ungeheuer ‹*Mut, Charme, Schmerz, Problem, Gefahr*› 2 (fat) ungeheuer dick

enormously /ɪ'nɔ:məslɪ/ *adv.* ungeheuer; enorm, ungeheuer ‹*groß, hoch, sich ändern, wachsen, sich bessern*›

enormousness /ɪ'nɔ:məsnɪs/ *n., no pl.* ungeheure Größe; Riesenhaftigkeit, *die;* (of size, length, height) ungeheures Ausmaß

enough /ɪ'nʌf/
A *adj.* genug; genügend; **that's ∼ arguing for one evening** für heute [Abend] haben wir uns genug gestritten; **there's ∼ room** *or* **room ∼:** es ist Platz genug *od.* genügend Platz; **be man/fool/miser** *etc.* **∼ to do sth.** Manns/dumm/geizig *usw.* genug sein, etw. zu tun; **he made ∼ fuss about getting it/having got it** (iron.) er hat so einen Wirbel darum gemacht, dass er es haben wollte/er hat großen Wirbel darum gemacht, dass er es bekommen hatte; **more than ∼:** mehr als genug; **∼ noise to wake the dead** ein Lärm, um Tote aufzuwecken
B *n., no pl., no art.* genug; **be ∼ to do sth.** genügen, etw. zu tun; **she says she's not getting ∼ out of her marriage** sie sagt, ihre Ehe gebe ihr nicht genug *od.* fülle sie nicht aus; **are there ∼ of us to lift this heavy weight?** sind wir genug [Leute], um diese schwere Last zu heben?; **four people are quite ∼:** vier Leute genügen völlig; **he's had quite ∼** (is drunk) er hat genug; **that [amount] will be ∼ to go round** das reicht für alle; **you [already] have ∼ to do looking after the baby** du hast schon genug damit zu tun, auf das Baby aufzupassen; **∼ of ...:** genug von ...; **have you had ∼ of the meat dish?** hast du genug Fleisch gehabt?; **I've seen ∼ of Bergman's films** ich habe genug Bergman-Filme gesehen; **are there ∼ of these books to go round?** reichen diese Bücher für alle?; **∼ of that!** genug davon!; **[that's] ∼ [of that]!** [jetzt ist es] genug!; **∼ of your nonsense!** Schluss mit dem Unsinn!; **have had ∼ [of sb./sth.]** genug [von jmdm./etw.] haben; **I've had ∼:** jetzt reichts mir aber!; jetzt habe ich aber genug!; **haven't you had ∼ of travelling?** hast du nicht langsam genug vom Reisen?; **more than ∼, ∼ and to spare** mehr als genug; **[that's] ∼ about ...:** genug über ... (*Akk.*) geredet; **but ∼ about politics** aber Schluss mit der Politik; **∼ about that** genug davon!; Schluss damit!; **∼ said** mehr braucht man dazu nicht zu sagen; **∼ is ∼:** mal muss es auch genug sein (ugs.); **it's ∼ to make you weep** es ist zum Weinen; **it's ∼ to make you sick** da wird einem ganz schlecht; **∼ is as good as a feast** allzu viel ist ungesund (Spr.); **cry '∼'** (fig.) aufgeben; **as if that were not ∼:** als ob das noch nicht genügte; **be ∼ of a man/fool/miser** *etc.* **to do sth.** Manns/dumm/geizig *usw.* genug sein, etw. zu tun
C *adv.* genug; **the meat is not cooked ∼:** das Fleisch ist nicht genügend durch; **you don't express your views ∼:** du sagst zu wenig über deine Ansichten; **he is not trying hard ∼:** er gibt sich nicht genug *od.* genügend Mühe; **they were friendly ∼ towards us** sie waren so weit recht nett zu uns; **she's a pretty ∼ girl** sie ist doch ein recht hübsches Mädchen; **you know well ∼ what we're referring to** ihr wisst recht gut, was wir meinen; **oddly/strangely/funnily ∼:** merkwürdiger-/seltsamer-/(ugs.) komischerweise; **sure ∼:** natürlich; **be good/kind ∼ to do sth.** so gut sein, etw. zu tun; *see also* **fair² A 1; right A 2; true A 1**

en passant /ɑ̃ 'pæsɑ̃/ *adv.* en passant (geh.); beiläufig; **just ∼:** ganz nebenbei

enquire *etc.* ▸ **inquir-**

enrage /ɪn'reɪdʒ/ *v.t.* wütend machen; reizen ‹*wildes Tier*›; **be ∼d by sth.** über etw. (*Akk.*) wütend werden/von etw. gereizt werden; **be ∼d at** *or* **with sb./sth.** auf jmdn./etw. wütend sein; **become** *or* **get ∼d** wütend werden (**at, with** über, auf + *Akk.*); **I was ∼d to hear that ...:** ich war wütend, als ich erfuhr, dass ...

enrapture /ɪn'ræptʃə(r)/ *v.t.* entzücken; ‹*Gesang, Musik:*› bezaubern; **be ∼d by sth./sb.** von etw./jmdm. entzückt sein

enraptured /ɪn'ræptʃəd/ *adj.* entzückt; verzückt

enrich /ɪn'rɪtʃ/ *v.t.* 1 (make wealthy) reich machen; bereichern (veralt.) 2 (fig.) bereichern; anreichern ‹*Nahrungsmittel, Boden, Uran*›; verbessern ‹*Haut, Qualität, Gewebe*›; erweitern ‹*Kenntnisse*›; **we were greatly ∼ed by the experience** diese Erfahrung hat uns sehr bereichert

enrichment /ɪn'rɪtʃmənt/ *n.* (lit. or fig.) Bereicherung, *die;* (of soil, food, uranium) Anreicherung, *die*

enrol (*Amer.:* **enroll**) /ɪn'rəʊl/
A *v.i.*, **-ll-** sich anmelden; sich einschreiben *od.* eintragen [lassen]; (Univ.) sich einschreiben; sich immatrikulieren; **∼ in sth.** in etw. (*Akk.*) eintreten; **∼ for a course/test** sich zu einem Kurs/einer Prüfung anmelden
B *v.t.*, **-ll-** einschreiben ‹*Studenten, Kursteilnehmer*›; anwerben ‹*Rekruten*›; aufnehmen ‹*Schüler, Mitglied, Rekruten*›; **∼ sb. in sth.** jmdn. in etw. (*Akk.*) aufnehmen; **∼ sb. for a course/the army** jmdn. für einen Kurs annehmen/in die Armee aufnehmen; **State E∼led Nurse** (Brit.) ≈ Krankenpflegehelfer, *der*/-helferin, *die*

enrolment (*Amer.:* **enrollment**) /ɪn'rəʊlmənt/ *n.* 1 Anmeldung, *die;* (Univ.) Immatrikulation, *die;* Einschreibung, *die;* (in army) Eintritt, *der* 2 (Amer.: number of students) Studentenzahl, *die*

en route /ɑ̃ 'ru:t/ *adv.* unterwegs; auf dem Weg; **∼ to Scotland/for Edinburgh** unterwegs *od.* auf dem Weg nach Schottland/Edinburgh; **∼ [for] home/to school** auf dem Heim-/Schulweg

ensconce /ɪn'skɒns/ *v.t.* **∼ oneself in sth.** sich in etw. (*Dat.*) niederlassen; (hide) sich in etw. (*Dat.*) verbergen; **be ∼d in/behind sth.** sich in/hinter etw. (*Dat.*) niedergelassen haben

ensemble /ɑ̃'sɑ̃bl/ *n.* Ensemble, *das*

enshrine /ɪn'ʃraɪn/ *v.t.* (lit. or fig.) bewahren

ensign /'ensaɪn, 'ensn/ *n.* 1 (banner) Hoheitszeichen, *das* 2 (Brit.) **blue/red/white ∼:** Flagge der britischen Marinereserve/britischen Handelsschiffe/britischen Marine 3 (standard-bearer) Fähnrich, *der;* (Hist.: infantry officer) Fahnenjunker, *der* 4 (Amer.: naval officer) Fähnrich zur See

enslave /ɪn'sleɪv/ *v.t.* 1 versklaven 2 (fig.) **marriage had ∼d her to the kitchen sink** die Ehe hatte sie an den Spülstein gekettet; **become ∼d to a habit** zum Sklaven einer Gewohnheit werden

ensnare /ɪn'sneə(r)/ *v.t.* (lit. or fig.) fangen; **the questions were designed to ∼ him** (fig.) die Fragen waren als Falle für ihn gedacht

ensue /ɪn'sju:/ *v.i.* 1 (follow) sich daran anschließen; **the discussion which ∼d** die anschließende *od.* folgende Diskussion 2 (result) sich daraus ergeben; **∼ from sth.** sich aus etw. ergeben

ensuing /ɪn'sju:ɪŋ/ *adj.* darauf folgend

en suite /ɑ̃ 'swi:t/
A *adj.* **with ∼ bathroom/toilet** mit eigenem Bad/eigener Toilette
B *adv.* daran anschließend; **rooms arranged ∼:** miteinander verbundene Zimmer

ensure /ɪn'ʃʊə(r)/ *v.t.* 1 **∼ that ...** (satisfy oneself that) sich vergewissern, dass ...; (see to it that) gewährleisten, dass ... 2 (secure) **∼ sth.** etw. gewährleisten; **this will ∼ victory for the Labour Party** dies wird der Labour Party den Sieg sichern; **I cannot ∼ you a good seat** ich kann nicht dafür garantieren, dass Sie einen guten Platz bekommen 3 (make safe) **∼ sb./sth. against sth.** jmdn./etw. vor etw. (*Dat.*) *od.* gegen etw. schützen; **they ∼d themselves against possible disappointment/criticism/hostility** sie sicherten sich gegen eine eventuelle Enttäuschung/Kritik/Anfeindung ab; *abs.* **proper insulation will ∼ against loss of heat** sorgfältige Isolierung schützt gegen Wärmeverlust

ENT *abbr.* (Med.) **= ear, nose, and throat** HNO

entablature /ɪn'tæblətʃə(r)/ *n.* (Archit.) Gebälk, *das*

entail /ɪn'teɪl/
A *v.t.* 1 (involve) mit sich bringen; **what exactly does your job ∼?** worin besteht Ihre Arbeit ganz genau?; **sth. ∼s doing sth.** etw. bedeutet, dass man etw. tun muss 2 (Law) in ein Fideikommiss umwandeln; (leave) als Fideikommiss vererben
B *n.* (Law) Fideikommiss, *das*

entailment /ɪn'teɪlmənt/ *n.* (Law) Umwandlung in ein Fideikommiss

entangle /ɪn'tæŋgl/ *v.t.* 1 (catch) einfangen; sich verfangen lassen; **he got bits of straw ∼d in his hair** Strohhalme verfingen sich in seinem Haar; **he got his trouser leg ∼d in his bicycle chain** sein Hosenbein hat sich in der Fahrradkette verfangen; **get [oneself]** *or* **become ∼d in** *or* **with sth.** sich in etw. (*Dat.*) verfangen; **get [oneself]** *or* **become ∼d in a mass of details** (fig.) sich in einer Unmenge von Einzelheiten verlieren; **be ∼d in sth.** sich in etw. (*Dat.*) verfangen haben 2 (fig.: involve) verwickeln; **get [oneself] ∼d in sth.** sich in etw. (*Akk.*) verwickeln lassen; **be/become ∼d in sth.** in etw. (*Akk.*) verwickelt sein/werden; **get [oneself]/be ∼d with** sich einlassen/eingelassen haben auf (+ *Akk.*) ‹*Probleme*›; in Konflikt geraten/sein mit ‹*Gesetz*›; sich einlassen/eingelassen haben mit ‹*Frau, Mann, politischer Gruppe*› 3 (make tangled) völlig durcheinander bringen; **get sth. ∼d [with sth.]** etw. [mit etw.] durcheinander bringen; **the threads have become** *or* **are ∼d [with each other]** die Fäden haben sich verwirrt

entanglement /ɪn'tæŋglmənt/ *n.* 1 Verwicklung, *die;* Verfangen, *das* 2 (fig.: involvement) **his ∼ in a divorce case** seine Verwicklung in eine Scheidungsaffäre; **get oneself into an ∼ with sb.** sich mit jmdm. einlassen 3 (thing that entangles) Verwicklung, *die;* (entangled things) Durcheinander, *das;* (Mil.) [Draht]verhau, *der*

entente /ɑ̃'tɑ̃t/ *n.* Entente, *die;* **∼ cordiale** /ɑ̃tɑ̃t kɔ:dɪ'ɑ:l/ (Hist.) Entente cordiale, *die*

enter /'entə(r)/
A *v.i.* 1 (go in) hineingehen; ‹*Fahrzeug:*› hineinfahren; (come in) hereinkommen; (walk into room) eintreten; (cross border into country) einreisen; (drive into tunnel etc.) hineinfahren; (come on stage) auftreten; **∼ Macbeth** (Theatre) Auftritt Macbeth; **∼ into a building/another world** ein Gebäude/eine andere Welt betreten; **∼ into the world of entertainment** in die Unterhaltungsbranche einsteigen (ugs.); **someone called 'E∼!'** jemand rief: „Herein!"; **only a small amount of light ∼ed through the windows** durch die Fenster fiel *od.* kam nur wenig Licht
2 (penetrate) eindringen
3 (apply to participate) sich zur Teilnahme

anmelden (**for** an + *Dat.*)

B *v.t.* [1] (go into) [hinein]gehen in (+ *Akk.*); ‹*Fahrzeug:*› [hinein]fahren in (+ *Akk.*); ‹*Flugzeug:*› [hinein]fliegen in (+ *Akk.*); betreten ‹*Gebäude, Zimmer*›; eintreten in (+ *Akk.*) ‹*Zimmer*›; einlaufen in (+ *Akk.*) ‹*Hafen*›; einreisen in (+ *Akk.*) ‹*Land*›; (drive into) hineinfahren in (+ *Akk.*); (come into) [herein]kommen in (+ *Akk.*); **~ a bus/train** in einen Bus/Zug [ein]steigen; **~ the ship/plane** (go/come into) an Bord [des Schiffes/Flugzeugs] gehen/kommen; **a small amount of light ~ed the room** in den Raum fiel *od.* kam wenig Licht; **the poison ~ed the blood** das Gift gelangte ins Blut; **it would never ~ his mind** *or* **head to cheat you** es käme ihm nie in den Sinn, dich zu betrügen; **has it ever ~ed your mind** *or* **head that ...?** ist dir nie der Gedanke gekommen, dass ...?; **~ sb.'s heart/soul** von jmdm. Besitz ergreifen (geh.)

[2] (penetrate) eindringen in (+ *Akk.*)

[3] (become a member of) beitreten (+ *Dat.*) ‹*Verein, Klub, Organisation, Partei*›; eintreten in (+ *Akk.*) ‹*Kirche*›; ergreifen ‹*Beruf*›; **~ the army/[the] university** zum Militär/auf die *od.* zur Universität gehen; **~ school** in die *od.* zur Schule kommen; **~ the legal profession/the medical profession/teaching** die juristische Laufbahn einschlagen/den Arztberuf ergreifen/den Lehrberuf ergreifen; Jurist/Arzt/Lehrer werden; **~ a monastery/nunnery** Mönch/Nonne werden; in ein Kloster eintreten; **~ the House of Commons** Mitglied *od.* Abgeordneter des Unterhauses werden

[4] (participate in) sich beteiligen an (+ *Dat.*) ‹*Diskussion, Unterhaltung*›; teilnehmen an (+ *Dat.*) ‹*Rennen, Wettbewerb*›

[5] (write) **~ sth. in a book/register** *etc.* etw. in ein Buch/Register *usw.* eintragen; **~ a name in** *or* **on a list** einen Namen in eine Liste eintragen *od.* auf eine Liste setzen; **~ sth. in a dictionary/an index** etw. in ein Wörterbuch/ein Register aufnehmen

[6] (record) **~ an action against sb.** gegen jmdn. Klage einreichen *od.* erheben; **~ a caveat** Einspruch einlegen *od.* erheben; **~ a judgement** ein Urteil fällen; **~ one's protest** Protest *od.* Widerspruch erheben; **~ a bid** ein Gebot abgeben

[7] **~ sb./sth./one's name for** jmdn./etw./sich anmelden für ‹*Rennen, Wettbewerb, Prüfung*›

[8] (Computing) eingeben ‹*Daten usw.*›; **press ~:** 'Enter' drücken

(Phrasal verbs)

- **~ into** *v.t.* [1] (engage in) anknüpfen ‹*Gespräch*›; sich beteiligen an (+ *Dat.*) ‹*Diskussion, Debatte, Wettbewerb*›; aufnehmen ‹*Beziehung, Verhandlungen*›; (bind oneself by) eingehen ‹*Verpflichtung, Ehe, Beziehung*›; schließen ‹*Vertrag*›; **~ into details/long-drawn-out explanations** ins Detail gehen/sich in langatmigen Erklärungen ergehen; **it's not worth ~ing into a discussion about it** es lohnt sich nicht, eine Diskussion darüber anzufangen; **~ into an understanding with sb.** mit jmdm. eine Vereinbarung treffen *od.* eingehen; **~ into the pros and cons** auf das Für und Wider eingehen [2] (sympathize with) nachempfinden ‹*jmds. Gefühle*›; nachvollziehen ‹*jmds. Gedanken*›; sich hineinversetzen, einfühlen in (+ *Akk.*) ‹*Person, Rolle, Stimmung*›; **~ into the spirit of Christmas** in Weihnachtsstimmung kommen; **she really ~s into anything she does** sie ist bei allem, was sie tut, ganz bei der Sache [3] (form part of) Bestandteil sein von; **~ into sb.'s considerations** bei jmds. Überlegungen eine Rolle spielen; **having children doesn't ~ into our plans** Kinder sind [bei uns] nicht geplant; **that doesn't ~ into it at all** das hat damit gar nichts zu tun
- **~ on** *v.t.* [1] (Law: assume possession of) in Besitz nehmen [2] (begin) beginnen ‹*Karriere, Laufbahn, Amtsperiode*›; aufnehmen ‹*Studium*›; in Angriff nehmen ‹*Aufgabe, Projekt*›
- **~ 'up** *v.t.* eintragen; **~ up the books** die Bücher auf den letzten Stand bringen
- **~ upon** ▸ **~ on**

enteric /en'terɪk/ *adj.* [1] (Anat.) Darm- [2] ▸ⓘ **p. 1231** **~ fever** (Med.) Typhus, *der;* Typhus abdominalis, *der* (fachspr.)

enteritis /entə'raɪtɪs/ *n.* ▸ⓘ **p. 1231** (Med.) Enteritis, *die* (fachspr.); Dünndarmentzündung, *die*

'enter key *n.* (Computing) Entertaste, *die;* Eingabetaste, *die*

enterprise /'entəpraɪz/ *n.* [1] (undertaking) Unternehmen, *das;* **commercial ~:** Handelsunternehmen, *das;* **free/private ~:** freies/privates Unternehmertum [2] *no indef. art.* (readiness to undertake new ventures) Unternehmungsgeist, *der*

enterprise: ~ 'culture *n., no pl.* Unternehmenskultur, *die;* **~ zone** *n.* wirtschaftliches Fördergebiet

enterprising /'entəpraɪzɪŋ/ *adj.* unternehmungslustig; rührig ‹*Geschäftsmann*›; kühn ‹*Reise, Gedanke, Idee*›

entertain /entə'teɪn/ *v.t.* [1] (amuse) unterhalten; **we were greatly ~ed by ...:** wir haben uns köstlich über ... (*Akk.*) amüsiert [2] (receive as guest) bewirten; **they enjoy ~ing** sie haben gern Gäste; **do some** *or* **a bit of/a lot of ~ing** manchmal/sehr oft Gäste einladen; **~ sb. to lunch/dinner** (Brit.) jmdn. zum Mittag-/Abendessen einladen [3] (have in the mind) haben ‹*Meinung, Vorstellung*›; hegen (geh.) ‹*Gefühl, Vorurteil, Verdacht, Zweifel, Groll*›; (consider) in Erwägung ziehen; **he would never ~ the idea of doing that** er würde es nie ernstlich erwägen, das zu tun; **~ ambitions/ideas** *or* **thoughts of doing sth.** den Ehrgeiz haben/sich mit dem Gedanken tragen, etw. zu tun; **~ hopes of achieving sth.** sich (*Dat.*) Hoffnungen machen, etw. zu erreichen

entertainer /entə'teɪnə(r)/ *n.* ▸ⓘ **p. 1260** Entertainer, *der*/Entertainerin, *die;* Unterhalter, *der*/Unterhalterin, *die*

entertaining /entə'teɪnɪŋ/

A *adj.* unterhaltsam

B *n., no pl., no indef. art.* **she does a lot of ~:** sie bewirtet häufig Gäste; **she's not very good at ~:** sie ist keine sehr gute Gastgeberin

entertainment /entə'teɪnmənt/ *n.* [1] (amusement) Unterhaltung, *die;* **much to our ~, to our great ~:** zu unserem großen Vergnügen; **get ~ from sth.** etw. unterhaltsam finden; **the world of ~:** die Welt des Showbusiness; **~ value** Unterhaltungswert, *der;* **have [great] ~ value** [sehr] unterhaltsam sein; **provide ~ for the children** für die Unterhaltung der Kinder sorgen [2] (public performance, show) Veranstaltung, *die*

entertainment: ~ guide *n.* Freizeitführer, *der;* **~ industry** *n.* Unterhaltungsindustrie, *die*

enthral (*Amer.:* **enthrall**) /ɪn'θrɔːl/ *v.t.*, **-ll-** [1] (captivate) fesseln; gefangen nehmen (fig.) [2] (delight) begeistern; entzücken

enthrone /ɪn'θrəʊn/ *v.t.* inthronisieren; **he was ~d [as] King** er bestieg den Königsthron

enthronement /ɪn'θrəʊnmənt/ *n.* Inthronisation, *die;* Thronbesteigung, *die*

enthuse /ɪn'θjuːz, ɪn'θuːz/ (coll.)

A *v.i.* **~ [about** *or* **over sth./sb.]** [über etw./jmdn.] in Begeisterung ausbrechen

B *v.t.* begeistern

enthusiasm /ɪn'θjuːzɪæzəm, ɪn'θuːzɪæzəm/ *n.* [1] *no pl.* Begeisterung, *die;* Enthusiasmus, *der;* **~ for** *or* **about sth.** Begeisterung für *od.* über etw. (*Akk.*); **for this job we want someone with ~:** wir brauchen einen begeisterungsfähigen Menschen für diese Arbeit; **I've no ~ about going out shopping** ich habe keine Lust, einkaufen zu gehen [2] (thing about which sb. is enthusiastic) Leidenschaft, *die*

enthusiast /ɪn'θjuːzɪæst, ɪn'θuːzɪæst/ *n.* Enthusiast, *der;* (for sport, pop music) Fan, *der;* **a DIY/cookery ~:** ein begeisterter Heimwerker/Koch; **be a great ~ for sth.** sich sehr für etw. begeistern

enthusiastic /ɪnθjuːzɪ'æstɪk, ɪnθuːzɪ'æstɪk/ *adj.* begeistert; enthusiastisch, begeistert ‹*Applaus, Empfang, Lob*›; **be ~ about sth.** von etw. begeistert sein; **not be very ~ about doing sth.** keine große Lust haben, etw. zu tun; **become ~ about sth.** sich für etw. begeistern

enthusiastically /ɪnθjuːzɪ'æstɪkəlɪ, ɪnθuːzɪ'æstɪkəlɪ/ *adv.* begeistert; enthusiastisch, begeistert ‹*empfangen, applaudieren, loben*›

entice /ɪn'taɪs/ *v.t.* locken (**into** in + *Akk.*); **~ sb./sth. [away] from sb./sth.** jmdn./etw. von jmdm./etw. fortlocken; **~ mice from their holes** Mäuse aus ihren Mauselöchern [heraus]locken; **~ sb. into doing** *or* **to do sth.** jmdn. dazu verleiten, etw. zu tun

enticement /ɪn'taɪsmənt/ *n.* [1] *no pl.* Lockung, *die;* (into depravity, immorality) Verleitung, *die* (**into** zu); **~ from sth.** Fortlockung von etw. [2] (thing) Lockmittel, *das*

enticing /ɪn'taɪsɪŋ/ *adj.*, **enticingly** /ɪn'taɪsɪŋlɪ/ *adv.* verlockend

entire /ɪn'taɪə(r)/ *adj.* [1] (whole) ganz; **take an ~ fortnight for one's holiday** volle vierzehn Tage Urlaub machen [2] (intact) vollständig ‹*Buch, Manuskript, Service, Ausgabe*›; **remain ~:** unversehrt bleiben

entirely /ɪn'taɪəlɪ/ *adv.* [1] (wholly) völlig; ganz ‹*wach*›; **not ~ suitable for the occasion** dem Anlass nicht ganz angemessen [2] (solely) ganz ‹*für sich behalten*›; allein, voll ‹*verantwortlich sein*›; **it's up to you ~:** es liegt ganz bei dir; **it's your responsibility ~:** du allein hast die Verantwortung

entirety /ɪn'taɪərətɪ/ *n., no pl.* (completeness) Uneingeschränktheit, *die;* **in its ~:** als Ganzes; in seiner Gesamtheit

entitle /ɪn'taɪtl/ *v.t.* [1] (give title of) **~ a book/film ...:** einem Buch/Film den Titel ... geben [2] (give rightful claim) berechtigen (**to** zu); **~ sb. to do sth.** jmdn. berechtigen *od.* jmdm. das Recht geben, etw. zu tun; **your degree does not ~ you to more pay** aufgrund Ihres akademischen Grades haben Sie noch keinen Anspruch auf höhere Bezahlung; **she is ~d to a bit of respect from you** sie kann ein wenig Respekt von dir verlangen; **be ~d to [claim] sth.** Anspruch auf etw. (*Akk.*) haben; **be ~d to do sth.** das Recht haben, etw. zu tun

entitlement /ɪn'taɪtlmənt/ *n.* (rightful claim) Anspruch, *der* (**to** auf + *Akk.*); **your leave ~ is four weeks** Sie haben Anspruch auf vier Wochen Urlaub

entity /'entɪtɪ/ *n.* (thing that exists) **[separate] ~:** eigenständiges Gebilde; **legal ~:** juristische Person

entomb /ɪn'tuːm/ *v.t.* (place in tomb) beisetzen (geh.); (fig.) einkerkern

entombment /ɪn'tuːmmənt/ *n.* Beisetzung, *die* (geh.); (fig.) Einkerkerung, *die*

entomological /entəmə'lɒdʒɪkl/ *adj.* entomologisch

entomologist /entə'mɒlədʒɪst/ *n.* ▸ⓘ **p. 1260** Entomologe, *der*/Entomologin, *die*

entomology /entə'mɒlədʒɪ/ *n.* Entomologie, *die;* Insektenkunde, *die*

entourage /ɒntʊ'rɑːʒ/ *n.* Gefolge, *das;* **have a permanent ~ of beautiful women** ständig von schönen Frauen umgeben sein

entr'acte /'ɒntrækt/ *n.* (Theatre) [1] (interval) Zwischenakt, *der* [2] (performance in interval) Entreakt, *der*

entrails /'entreɪlz/ *n. pl.* Eingeweide; Gedärm, *das;* (fig.) Innere, *das*

entrain[1] /ɪn'treɪn/ *v.t.* [1] (result in) nach sich ziehen [2] (carry along in flow) mitführen ‹*Tröpfchen, Dampf*›

entrain[2]

A *v.t.* [in einen/den Zug] verladen

B *v.i.* [in einen/den Zug] einsteigen; **~ for London** in den Zug nach London einsteigen

entrance[1] /'entrəns/ *n.* [1] (entering) Eintritt, *der* (**into** in + *Akk.*); (of troops) Einzug, *der;* (of vehicle) Einfahrt, *die;* (into office, position) Antritt, *der* (**into, upon** *Gen.*); **before his ~ into the room** bevor er das Zimmer betrat *od.* ins Zimmer trat; **[ceremonial] ~:** [feierlicher] Einzug [2] (on to stage, lit. or fig.) Auftritt, *der;* **make an** *or* **one's ~:** seinen Auftritt haben; **she likes to make a dramatic ~** (fig.) sie setzt sich gern in Szene [3] (way in) Eingang, *der* (**to** *Gen. od.* zu); (for vehicle) Einfahrt, *die;* **factory ~:** Fabrik- *od.* Werk[s]tor, *das;* **the ~ to the cellar/city is through a trapdoor/large gates** man gelangt durch eine Falltür/große Tore in den Keller/die Stadt **4** no pl., no art. (right of admission) Aufnahme, *die* (**to** in + *Akk.*); **gain ~ to/apply for ~ at a school/university** an einer Schule/Universität aufgenommen werden/sich um die Aufnahme an einer Schule/Universität bewerben; **~ to the concert is by ticket only** man kommt nur mit einer Eintrittskarte in das Konzert; *see also* **common entrance** **5** (fee) Eintritt, *der*

entrance² /ɪn'trɑ:ns/ *v.t.* **1** (throw into trance) in Trance versetzen **2** (carry away as in trance) hinreißen; bezaubern; **become ~d** verzaubert werden; **be ~d by** *or* **with sth.** von etw. hingerissen *od.* bezaubert sein

entrance/'entrəns/: **~ examination** *n.* Aufnahmeprüfung, *die;* **~ fee** *n.* Eintrittsgeld, *das;* (for competition) Teilnahmegebühr, *die;* (on joining club) Aufnahmegebühr, *die;* **~ hall** *n.* Eingangshalle, *die;* **~ money** ▸**~ fee**; **~ requirement** *n.* Aufnahmebedingung, *die;* **~ ticket** *n.* Eintrittskarte, *die*

entrancing /ɪn'trɑ:nsɪŋ/ *adj.* bezaubernd; hinreißend

entrant /'entrənt/ *n.* **1** Eintretende, *der/die;* (into country) Einreisende, *der/die* **2** (immigrant) Einwanderer, *der;* **illegal ~s into the country** illegale Einwanderer **3** (into a profession etc.) Anfänger, *der*/Anfängerin, *die* **4** (for competition, race, etc.) Teilnehmer, *der*/Teilnehmerin, *die* (**for** *Gen.*, an + *Dat.*)

entrap /ɪn'træp/ *v.t.*, **-pp-** **1** (catch in trap) fangen; **be ~ped** gefangen sein; in der Falle sitzen **2** (enclose and retain) einschließen **3** (trick) locken (**to** in + *Akk.*); **~ sb. into doing sth./into sth.** jmdn. verlocken (geh.) *od.* verleiten, etw. zu tun/jmdn. zu etw. verlocken (geh.) *od.* verleiten

entreat /ɪn'tri:t/ *v.t.* (ask) inständig bitten; (beseech) anflehen; **~ sb. to do sth.** jmdn. inständig bitten/jmdn. anflehen, etw. zu tun

entreating /ɪn'tri:tɪŋ/ *adj.*, **entreatingly** /ɪn'tri:tɪŋlɪ/ *adv.* flehentlich

entreaty /ɪn'tri:tɪ/ *n.* ▸**entreat**: inständige/flehentliche Bitte; **make an ~ to sb. to do sth.** jmdn. inständig/flehentlich bitten, etw. zu tun

entrecôte /'ɒntrəkəʊt/ *n.* (Gastr.) **~ [steak]** Entrecote, *das*

entrée /'ɒntreɪ, 'ɑ̃treɪ/ *n.* **1** (right of admission) Zutritt, *der* (**of, to, into** zu); **give sb. an/the ~ to sth.** jmdm. Zutritt zu etw. verschaffen **2** (Gastr.) (Brit.) Entree, *das;* Zwischengericht, *das;* (Amer.: main dish) Hauptgericht, *das*

entrench /ɪn'trenʃ/ *v.t.* **1** in Sicherheit bringen ‹*Person, Besitz*›; **~ oneself in/behind sth.** (lit. or fig.) sich in/hinter etw. (*Dat.*) verschanzen; **become ~ed** (fig.) ‹*Vorurteil, Gedanke:*› sich festsetzen; ‹*Tradition:*› sich verwurzeln **2** (apply extra safeguards to) verankern ‹*Rechte, Privilegien*›

entrenchment /ɪn'trenʃmənt/ *n.* (lit. or fig.) Verschanzung, *die*

entre nous /ɒntrə 'nu:/ *adv.* unter uns; **well, ~, what really happened was …:** nun, unter uns gesagt, was wirklich geschah, war …

entrepôt /'ɒntrəpəʊ/ *n.* **1** (commercial centre) Umschlagplatz, *der* **2** (storehouse) Speicher, *der*

entrepreneur /ɒntrəprə'nɜ:(r)/ *n.* **1** Unternehmer, *der*/Unternehmerin, *die* **2** (middleman) Vermittler, *der*

entrepreneurial /ɒntrəprə'nɜ:rɪəl/ *adj.* unternehmerisch

entropy /'entrəpɪ/ *n.* (Phys.) Entropie, *die*

entrust /ɪn'trʌst/ *v.t.* **~ sb. with sth.** jmdm. etw. anvertrauen; **he could not be ~ed with such responsibility** man konnte ihm keine solche Verantwortung übertragen; **~ sb./sth. to sb./sth.** jmdn./etw. jmdm./einer Sache anvertrauen; **~ a task to sb., ~ sb. with a task** jmdn. mit einer Aufgabe betrauen; **~ sth. to sb.'s safe keeping** jmdm. etw. zur Aufbewahrung anvertrauen

entry /'entrɪ/ *n.* **1** Eintritt, *der* (**into** in + *Akk.*); (of troops) Einzug, *der;* (of foreign matter into wound etc.) Eindringen, *das;* (into organization, cartel) Beitritt, *der* (**into** zu); (into country) Einreise, *die;* (ceremonial entrance) [feierlicher] Einzug; **upon ~ into Britain** bei der Einreise nach Großbritannien; **gain ~ to the house** ins Haus gelangen; **gain ~ to the EU** der EU beitreten; **force an ~:** sich (*Dat.*) [gewaltsam] Zutritt *od.* Zugang verschaffen; *see also* **port¹ A 1** **2** (on to stage) Auftritt, *der* **3** no pl., no art. (liberty to enter) (into car park) Einfahrt, *die* (**into** in + *Akk.*); (into building) Zutritt, *der* (**into** zu); (into country) Einreise, *die* (**to** in + *Akk.*); *see also* **'no entry'** **4** (Law: taking possession) Inbesitznahme, *die;* **make ~ of** *or* **on** in Besitz nehmen **5** (way in) Eingang, *der;* (for vehicle) Einfahrt, *die* **6** (passage between buildings) Durchgang, *der* **7** (Mus.) Einsatz, *der* **8** (registration, item registered) Eintragung, *die* (**in, into** in + *Akk. od. Dat.*); (in dictionary, encyclopedia, yearbook, index) Eintrag, *der;* **make an ~:** eine Eintragung vornehmen; **double/single ~** (Bookk.) doppelte/einfache Buchführung **9** (body of entrants) (for race etc.) Teilnehmerfeld, *das;* (for university/school) [Zahl der] Studienanfänger/Schulanfänger **10** (person or thing in competition) Nennung, *die;* (set of answers etc.) Lösung, *die;* **latest date for entries** Einsendeschluss, *der;* (for sporting event) Meldeschluss, *der*

entry: ~ fee ▸**entrance fee**; **~ form** *n.* Anmeldeformular, *das;* (for competition) Teilnahmeschein, *der;* **~ permit** *n.* Einreiseerlaubnis, *die;* Einreisegenehmigung, *die;* **E~phone** ® *n.* Sprechanlage, *die;* **~ visa** *n.* Einreisevisum, *das*

entwine /ɪn'twaɪn/ *v.t.* **1** (interweave, lit. or fig.) verflechten (**with** mit); **~ one's hair with ribbons** sich (*Dat.*) Bänder ins Haar flechten **2** (wreathe) **~ sth. about** *or* **round sb./sth.** etw. um jmdn./etw. schlingen *od.* (geh.) winden; **~ sth. with sth.** etw. mit etw. umschlingen *od.* (geh.) umwinden

'E number *n.* (Commerc.) E-Nummer, *die*

enumerable /ɪ'nju:mərəbl/ *adj.* zählbar

enumerate /ɪ'nju:məreɪt/ *v.t.* **1** (count) zählen **2** (mention one by one) [einzeln] aufzählen *od.* aufführen

enumeration /ɪnju:mə'reɪʃn/ *n.* **1** (counting) Zählung, *die* **2** (mentioning one by one) Aufzählung, *die;* Auflistung, *die* **3** (list) Auflistung, *die*

enunciate /ɪ'nʌnsɪeɪt/ *v.t.* **1** (pronounce) artikulieren **2** (express) formulieren ‹*Idee, Theorie*›; zum Ausdruck bringen ‹*Überzeugung, Wahrheit*›

enunciation /ɪnʌnsɪ'eɪʃn/ *n.* **1** (pronunciation) Artikulation, *die;* [deutliche] Aussprache **2** (expression) Formulierung, *die*

enure ▸**inure**

envelop /ɪn'veləp/ *v.t.* [ein]hüllen (**in** in + *Akk.*); **we were ~ed in mist** Nebel hüllte uns ein; **be ~ed in flames** ganz von Flammen umgeben sein; **he ~ed her in his arms** er schloss sie in die Arme

envelope /'envələʊp/, 'ɒnvələʊp/ *n.* **1** ▸**❶ p. 1287** (for letter) [Brief]umschlag, *der* **2** (Aeronaut.: gas container) Hülle, *die*

enviable /'envɪəbl/ *adj.* beneidenswert; **be ~ for sth.** um etw. zu beneiden sein

envious /'envɪəs/ *adj.* neidisch (**of** auf + *Akk.*); **speak in ~ tones** in neiderfülltem Ton sprechen; **I'm so ~ of you!** wie ich dich beneide!

enviously /'envɪəslɪ/ *adv.* neidisch; neidererfüllt

environment /ɪn'vaɪərənmənt/ *n.* **1** (natural surroundings) **the ~:** die Umwelt; **the Department of the E~** (Brit.) das Umweltministerium **2** (surrounding objects, region) Umgebung, *die;* (surrounding circumstances) Umwelt, *die;* Umfeld, *das* (bes. Psych., Soziol.); (social surroundings) Milieu, *das;* **physical/working/metropolitan ~:** Umwelt, *die*/Arbeitswelt, *die*/Großstadtmilieu, *das;* **home/family ~:** häusliches Milieu/Familienverhältnisse *Pl.*

environmental /ɪnvaɪərən'mentl/ *adj.* Umwelt‹*verschmutzung, -schutz, -einflüsse*›; **for ~ reasons** aus Gründen des Umweltschutzes; **~ group** Umweltschutzorganisation, *die*

environmental: ~ 'audit *n.* Ökoaudit, *das;* **~ 'health** *n.* Umwelthygiene, *die;* **~ health officer** Umwelthygienebeauftragte, *der;* **~ health department** Umwelthygieneamt, *das*

environmentalism /ɪnvaɪərən'mentəlɪzm/ *n., no pl., no art.* Engagement für die Umwelt; (as political movement) Ökologismus, *der*

environmentalist /ɪnvaɪərən'mentəlɪst/ *n.* Umweltschützer, *der*/-schützerin, *die*

environmentally /ɪnvaɪərən'mentəlɪ/ *adv.* ökologisch; **~ friendly** umweltfreundlich; **~ sensitive** ökologisch sensibel; **~ sound** umweltverträglich; umweltgerecht

Environmental Pro'tection Agency *n.* Umwelt[schutz]behörde, *die*

environs /ɪn'vaɪərənz, 'envɪrənz/ *n. pl.* Umgebung, *die;* **Oxford and its ~:** Oxford und Umgebung

envisage /ɪn'vɪzɪdʒ/, **envision** /ɪn'vɪʒn/ *v.t.* (imagine, contemplate) sich (*Dat.*) vorstellen; **what do you ~ for the future of the department?** wie siehst du die Zukunft der Abteilung?; **what do you ~ doing [about it]?** was gedenkst du [in der Sache] zu tun?; **she doesn't ~ staying in London for much longer** sie hat nicht vor, noch länger in London zu bleiben

envoy /'envɔɪ/ *n.* (messenger) Bote, *der*/Botin, *die;* (Diplom. etc.) Gesandte, *der*/Gesandtin, *die*

envy /'envɪ/

A *n.* **1** Neid, *der;* **feelings of ~:** Neidgefühle; **they could not conceal their ~ of her** sie konnten nicht verbergen, dass sie neidisch auf sie waren **2** (object) **his new sports car was the ~ of all his friends** alle seine Freunde beneideten ihn um seinen neuen Sportwagen; **you'll be the ~ of all your friends** alle deine Freunde werden dich beneiden

B *v.t.* beneiden; **~ sb. sth.** jmdn. um etw. beneiden; **I don't ~ you** dich kann ich nicht beneiden; **I don't ~ you your job** ich beneide dich nicht um deine Tätigkeit

enwrap /ɪn'ræp/ *v.t.*, **-pp-: ~ sb./sth. in sth.** jmdn./etw. in etw. (*Akk.*) [ein]hüllen *od.* [ein]wickeln

enzyme /'enzaɪm/ *n.* (Chem.) Enzym, *das*

EOC *abbr.* (Brit.) **= Equal Opportunities Commission**

Eocene /'i:əsi:n/ (Geol.)

A *adj.* eozän; Eozän-

B *n.* Eozän, *das*

eon ▸**aeon**

EP *abbr.* **= extended-play [record]** EP

epaulette (*Amer.:* **epaulet**) /'epɔ:let, 'epəʊlet, epə'let/ *n.* **1** Epaulette, *die* **2** (shoulder strap) Schulterklappe, *die*

épée /'epeɪ/ *n.* [Fecht]degen, *der*

ephemeral /ɪ'fi:mərl, ɪ'femərl/ *adj.* **1** (short-lived) ephemer[isch] (geh.); kurzlebig **2** (lasting only a day) eintägig

epic /'epɪk/

A *adj.* **1** episch; **~ poet** epischer Dichter; Epiker, *der;* **~ subject** Stoff für ein Epos **2** (of heroic type or scale, lit. or fig.) monumental; groß ‹*Seereise, Entdeckungsfahrt*›; **~ film** Filmepos, *das;* **~ book** monumentaler Roman; Epos, *das* (fig.)

B *n.* Epos, *das;* (film) [Film]epos, *das;* (book) monumentaler Roman; Epos, *das* (fig.); **folk/national ~:** Volks-/Nationalepos, *das*

epicentre (*Brit.; Amer.:* **epicenter**) /'epɪsentə(r)/ *n.* Epizentrum, *das*

epicure /'epɪkjʊə(r)/ *n.* Feinschmecker, *der;* Gourmet, *der*

epicurean /epɪkjʊə'ri:ən/

A *adj.* (devoted to pleasure) epikureisch (geh.); **~ person** ▸**B**

B *n.* (person devoted to pleasure) Epikureer, *der* (geh.); Genussmensch, *der*

epidemic /epɪ'demɪk/ (Med.; also fig.)

A *adj.* epidemisch

B *n.* Epidemie, *die*

epidemiology /epɪdi:mɪ'ɒlədʒɪ/ *n., no pl.* (Med.) Epidemiologie, *die*

epidermal /epɪ'dɜ:ml/ *adj.* (Anat., Biol.) epidermal

epidermis /epɪ'dɜ:mɪs/ *n.* (Anat., Biol.) Epidermis, *die* (fachspr.); Oberhaut, *die*

epidiascope /epɪ'daɪəskəʊp/ *n.* Epidiaskop, *das*

epidural /epɪ'djʊərəl/ *n.* (Med.) Epiduralanästhesie, *die*

epiglottis /epɪ'glɒtɪs/ *n.* (Anat.) Epiglottis, *die* (fachspr.); Kehldeckel, *der*

epigram /'epɪgræm/ *n.* (Lit.) **1** (short poem) Epigramm, *das;* Sinngedicht, *das* **2** (pointed saying) Sinnspruch, *der* **3** (mode of expression) epigrammatischer Ausdruck

epigrammatic /epɪgrə'mætɪk/ *adj.* (Lit.) epigrammatisch

epigraph /'epɪgrɑːf/ *n.* **1** (inscription) Epigraph, *das* **2** (motto) Motto, *das*

epilepsy /'epɪlepsɪ/ *n.* ▸ **p. 1231** (Med.) Epilepsie, *die*

epileptic /epɪ'leptɪk/ (Med.)

A *adj.* epileptisch; *see also* **fit¹ 1**

B *n.* Epileptiker, *der*/Epileptikerin, *die*

epilogue (*Amer.:* **epilog**) /'epɪlɒg/ *n.* (Lit.) Epilog, *der;* (of literary work also) Nachwort, *das*

Epiphany /ɪ'pɪfənɪ/ *n.* (Relig.) Epiphanie, die; **[Feast of the] ~:** Epiphanias, *das;* Dreikönigsfest, *das;* **at ~:** am Dreikönigstag

episcopal /ɪ'pɪskəpl/ *adj.* episkopal; bischöflich; Episkopal‹*system, -kirche*›; Bischofs‹*ornat, -mütze*›

episcopalian /ɪpɪskə'peɪlɪən/

A *adj.* (of episcopal church) der Episkopalkirche *nachgestellt*

B *n.* **1** (member of episcopal church) Episkopale, *der/die* **2** (adherent of episcopacy) Episkopalist, *der*/Episkopalistin, *die*

episcopate /ɪ'pɪskəpət/ ▸ **bishopric 1**

episode /'epɪsəʊd/ *n.* **1** (also Mus.) Episode, *die* **2** (instalment of serial) Folge, *die;* **read next week's exciting ~:** lesen Sie die spannende Fortsetzung in der nächsten Woche!

episodic /epɪ'sɒdɪk/, **episodical** /epɪ'sɒdɪkl/ *adj.* episodisch; episodenhaft ‹*Szene, Ereignis*›

epistemological /epɪstɪmə'lɒdʒɪkl/ *adj.* (Philos.) epistemologisch

epistemology /epɪstɪ'mɒlədʒɪ/ *n.* (Philos.) Epistemologie, *die* (fachspr.); Erkenntnislehre, *die*

epistle /ɪ'pɪsl/ *n.* (Bibl., Lit., or usu. joc.: letter) Epistel, *die*

epistolary /ɪ'pɪstələrɪ/ *adj.* epistolarisch (veralt.); **~ style** Briefstil, *der*

epitaph /'epɪtɑːf/ *n.* Epitaph, *das;* Grab[in-]schrift, *die*

epithet /'epɪθet/ *n.* **1** (expressing quality or characteristic) Beiname, *der;* (as term of abuse) Schimpfname, *der* **2** (Ling.) Epitheton, *das* (fachspr.); Beiwort, *das*

epitome /ɪ'pɪtəmɪ/ *n.* (of quality, type, etc.) Inbegriff, *der*

epitomize /ɪ'pɪtəmaɪz/ *v.t.* (embody) **~ sth.** der Inbegriff einer Sache (*Gen.*) sein

epoch /'iːpɒk, 'epɒk/ *n.* (also Geol.) Epoche, *die;* **a new ~ in British politics** eine neue Ära in der britischen Politik

epochal /'iːpɒkl, 'epɒkl/ *adj.* **1** (of epoch[s]) der Epoche[n] *nachgestellt* **2** ▸ **epoch-making**

'epoch-making *adj.* epochal ‹*Bedeutung*›; Epoche machend ‹*Entdeckung*›

eponymous /ɪ'pɒnɪməs/ *adj.* namengebend

EPOS /'iːpɒz/ *abbr.* **= electronic point of sale** EPOS

epoxy /ɪ'pɒksɪ/ (Chem.)

A *adj.* Epoxid-; Epoxid- (fachspr.); **~ resin** ▸ **B**

B *n.* Epoxidharz, *das;* Epoxidharz, *das* (fachspr.)

epsilon /ep'saɪlən/ *n.* Epsilon, *das*

Epsom salt /epsəm 'sɔːlt, epsəm 'sɒlt/ *n.* **~[s]** (Med.) Bittersalz, *das*

equable /'ekwəbl/ *adj.* **1** (uniform) gleichförmig ‹*Stil*› **2** (balanced) ausgeglichen ‹*Wesen, Person, Klima*› **3** (equally proportioned) ausgewogen ‹*Maße, System, Proportionen*› **4** (fair-minded) sachlich ‹*Einstellung, Art*›

equably /'ekwəblɪ/ *adv.* **1** (in uniform style) gleichförmig **2** (in balanced manner) **~ [disposed** *or* **tempered]** ausgeglichen **3** (in equal proportions) gleichmäßig **4** (in fair-minded manner) sachlich

equal /'iːkwl/

A *adj.* **1** gleich; **~ in** *or* **of ~ height/weight/size/importance/strength** *etc.* gleich hoch/schwer/groß/wichtig/stark *usw.;* **add flour and cornflour in ~ measure** *or* **amounts** gleich viel Mehl und Stärkemehl hinzufügen; **marry sb. of ~ rank** standesgemäß heiraten; **not ~ in length** verschieden lang; **~ rights** gleiche Rechte; Gleichberechtigung, *die;* **divide a cake into ~ parts/portions** einen Kuchen in gleich große Stücke/Portionen aufteilen; **~ amounts of milk and water** gleich viel Milch und Wasser; **she had ~ success with her second novel** mit ihrem zweiten Roman hatte sie ebenso großen Erfolg; **she does both jobs with ~ pleasure/enjoyment** beide Tätigkeiten machen ihr gleich viel Spaß; **all men were created ~:** alle Menschen sind gleich geschaffen; **some are more ~ than others** (joc.) einige sind gleicher; **his salary is ~ to mine** er verdient genauso viel wie ich; **be ~ in size to sth.** ebenso groß wie etw. sein; **three times four is ~ to twelve** drei mal vier ist [gleich] zwölf; **none was ~ to her in beauty/elegance** keine kam ihr an Schönheit/Eleganz gleich; **Britain is now ~ with France in terms of medals won** Großbritannien ist *od.* liegt jetzt im Medaillenspiegel gleichauf mit Frankreich; **Michael came ~ third** *or* **third ~ with Richard in the class exams** bei den Klassenprüfungen kam Michael zusammen mit Richard auf den dritten Platz; **~ pay [for ~ work]** gleicher Lohn für gleiche Arbeit; **have ~ standing [with sb.]** [jmdm.] gleichgestellt sein; **be on ~ terms [with sb.]** [mit jmdm.] gleichgestellt sein; **meet each other/discuss matters on ~ terms** als Gleichgestellte zusammenkommen/Angelegenheiten als Gleichgestellte erörtern; **all/other things being ~:** wenn nichts dazwischen kommt; *see also* **~ opportunity**

2 **~ to** (adequate for): **be ~ to sth./sb.** (strong, clever, etc. enough) einer Sache/jmdm. gewachsen sein; **a job ~ to sb.'s abilities** eine Arbeit, die jmds. Fähigkeiten entspricht; **be ~ to doing sth.** imstande sein, etw. zu tun

3 (impartial) gerecht; **they were all given ~ treatment** sie wurden alle gleich behandelt

4 (evenly balanced) ausgeglichen; **the battle was not ~:** es war ein ungleicher Kampf

B *n.* Gleichgestellte, *der/die;* **be among [one's] ~s** unter seinesgleichen sein; **talk to sb. as [if he were] one's ~:** mit jmdm. wie mit seinesgleichen sprechen; **be sb.'s/sth.'s ~:** jmdm. ebenbürtig sein/einer Sache (*Dat.*) gleichkommen; **he/she/it has no** *or* **is without ~:** er/sie/es hat nicht seines-/ihresgleichen; **he has met an** *or* **his ~ in her** in ihr hat er jemanden gefunden, der ihm ebenbürtig ist

C *v.t.,* (Brit.) **-ll-:** **1** (be equal to) **~ sb./sth. [in sth.]** jmdm./einer Sache [in etw. (*Dat.*)] entsprechen; **three times four ~s twelve** drei mal vier ist [gleich] zwölf; **she easily ~s him in intelligence** so intelligent wie er ist sie allemal; **the square on the hypotenuse ~s the sum of the squares on the other two sides** das Quadrat über der Hypotenuse ist gleich der Summe der Quadrate über den Katheten; **no pop group has ~led the Beatles in terms of success** keine Popgruppe ist je an den Erfolg der Beatles herangekommen

2 (do sth. equal to) **~ sb.** es jmdm. gleichtun; **I don't know if I could ever ~ such a high score/your success/such an achievement** ich weiß nicht, ob ich je eine so hohe Punktzahl erreichen könnte/so erfolgreich sein könnte wie Sie/eine solche Leistung vollbringen könnte

equalisation, equalise, equaliser ▸ **equaliz-**

equality /ɪ'kwɒlɪtɪ/ *n.* Gleichheit, *die;* (equal rights) Gleichberechtigung, *die;* **~ between the races/the religions, racial/religious ~:** Gleichberechtigung der Rassen/Konfessionen; **~ between the sexes** Gleichheit von Mann und Frau; **women are campaigning for ~ with men** die Frauen kämpfen für ihre Gleichstellung den Männern gegenüber

equalization /iːkwəlaɪ'zeɪʃn/ *n.* Angleichung, *die* (**to, with** an + *Akk.*)

equalize /'iːkwəlaɪz/

A *v.t.* ausgleichen ‹*Druck, Temperatur*›; angleichen ‹*Maßstäbe, Einkommen, Chancen*› (**with** *Dat.*); gleichstellen ‹*Personen, gesellschaftliche Gruppen*› (**to, with** *Dat. od.* mit)

B *v.i.* **1** (become equal) sich ausgleichen; **~ with sth.** sich einer Sache (*Dat.*) angleichen **2** (Footb. etc.) den Ausgleich[streffer] erzielen

equalizer /'iːkwəlaɪzə(r)/ *n.* (Footb. etc.) Ausgleich[streffer], *der*

equally /'iːkwəlɪ/ *adv.* **1** ebenso; **rank ~ [with one another]** den gleichen Rang einnehmen; **be ~ close to a and b** von a und b gleich weit entfernt sein; **the two are ~ gifted** die beiden sind gleich begabt **2** (in equal shares) in gleiche Teile ‹*aufteilen*›; gleichmäßig ‹*verteilen*›; **consist ~ of A and B** zu gleichen Teilen aus A und B bestehen **3** (according to the same rule and measurement) in gleicher Weise; gleich ‹*behandeln*›

Equal Opportunities Commission *n.* (Brit.) *Ausschuss für Chancengleichheit;* ≈ Gleichstellungsausschuss, *der*

equal oppor'tunity *n.* Chancengleichheit, *die;* **an ~** *or* **equal opportunities employer** ein Arbeitgeber, der jedem die gleiche Chance gibt (*unabhängig von Geschlecht, Rasse usw.*)

'equals sign *n.* (Math.) Gleichheitszeichen, *das*

equanimity /ekwə'nɪmɪtɪ, iːkwə'nɪmɪtɪ/ *n., no pl.* **1** (composure, resignation) Gelassenheit, *die* **2** (evenness of mind, temper) Gleichmut, *der*

equate /ɪ'kweɪt/ *v.t.* **~ sth. [to** *or* **with sth.]** etw. [einer Sache (*Dat.*) *od.* mit etw.] gleichsetzen

equation /ɪ'kweɪʒn/ *n.* **1** (Math.) Gleichung, *die* **2** (Chem.) [chemische] Gleichung; [Reaktions]gleichung, *die*

equator /ɪ'kweɪtə(r)/ *n.* (Geog., Astron.) Äquator, *der*

equatorial /ekwə'tɔːrɪəl, iːkwə'tɔːrɪəl/ *adj.* (Geog., Astron.) äquatorial ‹*Hitze, Klima*›; Äquatorial‹*gegend, -strom*›; Äquator‹*linie, -durchmesser, -gürtel, -sonne*›; **~ telescope** (Astron.) Äquatoreal, *das*

equerry /'ekwərɪ/ *n.* **1** (in charge of horses) königlicher Stallmeister **2** (of royal household) Kammerherr, *der*

equestrian /ɪ'kwestrɪən/

A *adj.* **1** (of horse riding) reiterlich; Reit‹*turnier, -talent*› **2** (on horseback) Reiter‹*standbild, -bildnis*› **3** (of knights) Ritter-

B *n.* Reiter, *der*/Reiterin, *die;* **circus ~s** Zirkusreiter

equestrianism /ɪ'kwestrɪənɪzm/ ▸ **horsemanship**

equidistant /iːkwɪ'dɪstənt/ *adj.* gleich weit entfernt (**from** von)

equilateral /iːkwɪ'lætərl/ *adj.* (Math.) gleichseitig ‹*Dreieck, Rechteck, Hyperbel*›

equilibrium /iːkwɪ'lɪbrɪəm/ *n., pl.* **equilibria** /iːkwɪ'lɪbrɪə/ *or* **~s** Gleichgewicht, *das;* (sense of balance) Gleichgewichtssinn, *der;* **lose/keep one's ~:** das Gleichgewicht verlieren/nicht verlieren; **mental/emotional ~:** geistige/emotionale Ausgeglichenheit; **in ~:** im Gleichgewicht; **maintain/restore ~:** das Gleichgewicht halten/wieder finden; **~ of power** (fig.) Gleichgewicht der Kräfte; **stable/unstable/neutral ~** (Phys.) stabiles/labiles/indifferentes Gleichgewicht

equine /'ekwaɪn, 'iːkwaɪn/ *adj.* **1** (of horse) Pferde‹*körper*› **2** (like horse) pferdeähnlich ‹*Gang, Haltung, Gesichtszüge, Augen*›

equinoctial /iːkwɪ'nɒkʃl, ekwɪ'nɒkʃl/ *adj.* (Astron., Geog.) Äquinoktial‹*punkt, -kreis, -stürme*›; **~ line** Himmelsäquator, *der*

equinox /'iːkwɪnɒks, 'ekwɪnɒks/ *n.* **1** Tagundnachtgleiche, *die;* Äquinoktium, *das* (fachspr.); **spring** *or* **vernal ~:** Frühjahrs-Tagundnachtgleiche, *die;* **autumn** *or* **autumnal ~:** Herbst-Tagundnachtgleiche, *die* **2** (Astron.: equinoctial point) Äquinoktialpunkt, *der; see also* **precession**

equip /ɪ'kwɪp/ *v.t.,* **-pp-** ausrüsten ‹*Fahrzeug, Armee*›; ausstatten ‹*Zimmer, Küche*›; **fully ~ped** komplett ausgerüstet/ausgestattet; **~ sb./oneself [with sth.] [for a journey** *etc.***]**

jmdn./sich [für eine Reise *usw.*] [mit etw.] ausrüsten; **be ~ped with sth.** (fig.) über etw. (*Akk.*) verfügen; **he is well ~ped for the job** (fig.) er bringt gute Voraussetzungen für den Job mit

equipment /ɪˈkwɪpmənt/ *n.* 1 Ausrüstung, *die;* (of kitchen, laboratory, etc.) Ausstattung, *die;* (sth. needed for activity) Geräte *Pl.*; **breathing ~:** Sauerstoffgerät, *das;* **climbing/diving ~:** Bergsteiger-/Taucherausrüstung, *die;* **fighting/skiing ~:** Kampf-/Skiausrüstung, *die;* **gardening/gymnastics/recording ~:** Garten-/Turn-/Aufnahmegeräte; **mining ~:** Bergbauausrüstung, *die;* **playground ~:** Spielgeräte (*auf einem Spielplatz*); **riding ~:** Reitzeug, *das* (ugs.); **writing ~:** Schreibutensilien *Pl.* 2 (fig.: intellectual resources) **mental/intellectual ~:** geistiges Rüstzeug

equitable /ˈekwɪtəbl/ *adj.* 1 (fair) gerecht; **in an ~ manner** gerecht 2 (valid) billig; **~ jurisdiction** Rechtsprechung nach dem Billigkeitsrecht

equitably /ˈekwɪtəblɪ/ *adv.* gerecht

equity /ˈekwɪtɪ/ *n.* 1 (Law) billiges *od.* natürliches Recht; **in ~:** billigermaßen; **acknowledge a claim in ~:** einen Anspruch billigerweise anerkennen 2 (fairness) Gerechtigkeit, *die;* **with ~:** gerecht 3 (use of justice as well as law) Billigkeit, *die;* **on the basis of ~:** auf der Grundlage der Billigkeit 4 **E~** (Brit. Theatre) *britische Schauspielergewerkschaft* 5 *in pl.* (stocks and shares without fixed interest) [Stamm]aktien 6 (value of shares) Eigenkapital, *das* 7 (net value of mortgaged property) *Wert eines Besitzes nach Abzug der Belastungen*

equity: ~ 'capital *n.* (Commerc.) Eigenkapital, *das;* **~ market** *n.* (Commerc.) Aktienmarkt, *der*

equivalence /ɪˈkwɪvələns/, **equivalency** /ɪˈkwɪvələnsɪ/ *n.* 1 (being equivalent) **~ [of value]** Gleichwertigkeit, *die;* (of two amounts) Wertgleichheit, *die* 2 (having equivalent meaning) **~ [in meaning]** Äquivalenz, *die* (bes. Logik); Bedeutungsgleichheit, *die* 3 (correspondence) Entsprechung, *die* 4 (Chem.) Äquivalenz, *die*

equivalent /ɪˈkwɪvələnt/

A *adj.* 1 (equal, having same result) gleichwertig; **be ~ to sth.** einer Sache (*Dat.*) entsprechen; **be ~ to doing sth.** dasselbe sein, wie wenn man etw. tut; **something of ~ value** etwas Gleichwertiges; **an ~ amount [of money]** ein entsprechender *od.* gleich hoher Betrag; **an ~ amount of flour** gleich viel Mehl 2 (meaning the same) äquivalent (Sprachw.); entsprechend; **these two words are [not] ~ in meaning** diese beiden Wörter sind [nicht] bedeutungsgleich 3 (corresponding) entsprechend; **be ~ to sth.** einer Sache (*Dat.*) entsprechen 4 (Chem.) äquivalent

B *n.* 1 (~ or corresponding thing or person) Pendant, *das;* Gegenstück, *das;* **be the ~ of sb./sth.** das Pendant *od.* Gegenstück zu jmdm./einer Sache sein 2 (word etc. having same meaning) Entsprechung, *die* (**of** zu); Äquivalent, *das* (**of** für) 3 (thing having same result) **be the ~ of sth.** einer Sache (*Dat.*) entsprechen 4 (Chem.) Äquivalent, *das*

equivocal /ɪˈkwɪvəkl/ *adj.* 1 (ambiguous) zweideutig; **~ meaning** Zweideutigkeit, *die* 2 (questionable) zweifelhaft ‹*Person, Erfolg, Glück, Ruf*›

equivocally /ɪˈkwɪvəkəlɪ/ *adv.* (ambiguously) zweideutig

equivocate /ɪˈkwɪvəkeɪt/ *v.i.* zweideutige Aussagen machen; ausweichen

equivocation /ɪkwɪvəˈkeɪʃn/ *n.* zweideutige Formulierungen

er /ɜː(r)/ *int.* äh

ER *abbr.* **= King Edward/Queen Elizabeth**

era /ˈɪərə/ *n.* 1 (system of chronology) Ära, *die* 2 (period) Zeit; **the Adenauer ~:** die Ära Adenauer; **Byzantine/computer ~:** byzantinische Zeit/(ugs.) Computerzeitalter, *das;* **the Renaissance/Beatles ~:** die Zeit der Renaissance/Beatles; **Roman/Viking ~:** Römer-/Wikingerzeit, *die;* **a new ~ in fashion began** in der Mode begann eine neue Ära 3 (Geol.) Ära, *die* (fachspr.); Erdzeitalter, *das*

eradicate /ɪˈrædɪkeɪt/ *v.t.* (remove) ausrotten; gründlich beseitigen ‹*Ursache*›

eradication /ɪrædɪˈkeɪʃn/ *n.* Ausrottung, *die*

erase /ɪˈreɪz/ *v.t.* 1 (rub out) auslöschen; (with rubber, knife) ausradieren 2 (obliterate) tilgen (geh.) (**from** aus) 3 (remove recorded signal from; also Computing) löschen

eraser /ɪˈreɪzə(r)/ *n.* **[pencil] ~:** Radiergummi, *der;* **[blackboard] ~** *Block mit Filzbelag o. Ä. zum Löschen von Kreideschrift;* (sponge) Tafelschwamm, *der*

erasure /ɪˈreɪʒə(r)/ *n.* 1 (rubbing out) Auslöschen, *das;* (with rubber) Ausradieren, *das* 2 (obliteration) Tilgung, *die* (**from** aus) 3 (removal of recorded signal) Löschen, *das;* (place) gelöschte Stelle

ERDF *abbr.* (EU) **= European Regional Development Fund** EFRE

ere /eə(r)/ (poet./arch.)

A *prep.* vor (+ *Dat.*) **~ long** binnen kurzem; **~ now** bereits; **~ then** bis dann

B *conj.* ehe

erect /ɪˈrekt/

A *adj.* 1 (upright, vertical; also fig.) aufrecht; gerade ‹*Rücken, Wuchs*›; **stand ~** ‹*Soldat:*› strammstehen; **with head ~:** mit hoch erhobenem Kopf 2 (Physiol.: enlarged and rigid) erigiert 3 (raised) aufgestellt ‹*Ohren*›

B *v.t.* 1 (build) errichten; aufbauen ‹*Gerüst*›; aufstellen ‹*Standbild, Mast, Verkehrsschild*›; aufschlagen, aufstellen ‹*Zelt*›; konstruieren ‹*Theorie*› 2 (raise) aufrichten ‹*Körper, Ohren, Stacheln*›

erectile /ɪˈrektaɪl/ *adj.* (Physiol.) schwellfähig; erektil (fachspr.)

erection /ɪˈrekʃn/ *n.* 1 (building) ▸**erect B 1**: Errichtung, *die;* Aufbau, *der;* Aufstellen, *das;* Aufschlagen, *das;* Konstruieren, *das* 2 (structure) Bauwerk, *das;* (other than a building) Konstruktion, *die* 3 (raising) Aufstellen, *das* 4 (Physiol.) Anschwellen, *das;* (of penis) Erektion, *die*

erectly /ɪˈrektlɪ/ *adv.* (in upright manner, vertically; also fig.) aufrecht

erectness /ɪˈrektnɪs/ *n., no pl.* (uprightness) **~ [of stance** *or* **bearing** *or* **posture]** aufrechte Haltung

erg /ɜːg/ *n.* (Phys.) Erg, *das*

ergo /ˈɜːgəʊ/ *adv.* (literary) ergo

ergonomic /ɜːgəˈnɒmɪk/ *adj.*, **ergonomically** /ɜːgəˈnɒmɪklɪ/ *adv.* ergonomisch

ergonomics /ɜːgəˈnɒmɪks/ *n., no pl.* Ergonomie, *die;* Ergonomik, *die*

ergot /ˈɜːgət/ *n.* 1 (disease) Mutterkornbefall, *der* 2 (fungus) Mutterkornpilz, *der* 3 (dried mycelium) Mutterkorn, *das*

erica /ˈerɪkə, ɪˈriːkə/ *n.* (Bot.) Erika, *die*

ERM *abbr.* **= exchange rate mechanism** ▸**exchange C 4**

ermine /ˈɜːmɪn/ *n.* 1 (fur; also Her.) Hermelin, *der* 2 (Zool.) Hermelin, *das*

erode /ɪˈrəʊd/

A *v.t.* 1 ‹*Säure, Rost:*› angreifen; ‹*Wasser, Regen, Meer:*› auswaschen; ‹*Wind:*› verwittern lassen; ‹*Wasser, Regen, Meer, Wind:*› erodieren (Geol.) 2 (fig.) unterminieren ‹*Grundlage, Fundament, Beziehung*›

B *v.i.* 1 verwittern 2 (fig.) unterminiert werden

erogenous /ɪˈrɒdʒɪnəs/ *adj.* erogen ‹*Zone*›; **~ stimulation** sexuelle Stimulation

erosion /ɪˈrəʊʒn/ *n.* 1 ▸**erode A 1**: Angreifen, *das;* Auswaschung, *die;* Verwitterung, *die;* Erosion, *die* (Geol.) 2 (fig.) Unterminierung, *die*

erosive /ɪˈrəʊsɪv/ *adj.* (Geol.) erodierend

erotic /ɪˈrɒtɪk/ *adj.* erotisch

erotica /ɪˈrɒtɪkə/ *n. pl.* Erotika

erotically /ɪˈrɒtɪkəlɪ/ *adv.* erotisch

eroticism /ɪˈrɒtɪsɪzm/ *n.* Erotik, *die*

err /ɜː(r)/ *v.i.* sich irren; **to ~ is human** (prov.) Irren ist menschlich; **you ~ in your opinion of him** Sie schätzen ihn falsch ein; **let's ~ on the right** *or* **safe side and ...:** um sicherzugehen, wollen wir ...

errand /ˈerənd/ *n.* 1 Botengang, *der;* (shopping) Besorgung, *die;* **go on** *or* **run an ~:** einen Botengang/eine Besorgung machen; **go** *or* **run ~s** Botengänge/Besorgungen machen; **send sb. on an ~:** jmdn. auf einen Botengang schicken/jmdn. etwas besorgen lassen; **go on an ~ of mercy [for sb.]** Hilfe für jmdn. holen; **send sb. on an ~ of mercy** jmdn. auf eine Rettungsmission entsenden; *see also* **fool's errand** 2 (object of journey) Auftrag, *der* 3 (purpose) Zweck, *der*

errand: ~ boy *n.* (dated) Laufbursche, *der;* Bote[njunge], *der;* **~ girl** *n.* (dated) Laufmädchen, *das;* Botin, *die*

errant /ˈerənt/ *adj.* irrig, falsch ‹*Prinzip, Maßstab, Meinung, Vorstellung*›; fehlgeleitet ‹*Person, Verhalten*›; untreu ‹*Ehemann, Ehefrau*›; *see also* **knight errant**

errata *pl. of* **erratum**

erratic /ɪˈrætɪk/

A *adj.* unregelmäßig; sprunghaft ‹*Wesen, Person, Art*›; unbeständig ‹*Charakter, Leistung, Wetter*›; launenhaft ‹*Verhalten*›; ungleichmäßig ‹*Bewegung, Verlauf*›; **the ~ moods of the weather** die wechselnden Launen des Wetters; **he is rather ~ in the standard of work he produces** das Niveau seiner Arbeiten ist recht unterschiedlich

B *n.* ▸**erratic block**

erratically /ɪˈrætɪkəlɪ/ *adv.* unregelmäßig; launenhaft ‹*sich verhalten*›; ungleichmäßig ‹*sich bewegen, verlaufen*›

erratic 'block *n.* (Geol.) erratischer Block (fachspr.); Findling, *der*

erratum /eˈreɪtəm, eˈrɑːtəm/ *n., pl.* **errata** /eˈreɪtə, eˈrɑːtə/ (Bibliog., Printing) Erratum, *das* (fachspr.); Druckfehler, *der*

erroneous /ɪˈrəʊnɪəs/ *adj.* falsch; irrig ‹*Schlussfolgerung, Eindruck, Ansicht, Auffassung, Annahme*›

erroneously /ɪˈrəʊnɪəslɪ/ *adv.* fälschlich; irrigerweise

error /ˈerə(r)/ *n.* 1 (mistake) Fehler, *der;* **gross ~ of judgement** grobe Fehleinschätzung; **printing/typographical ~:** Druck-/Setzfehler, *der* 2 (wrong opinion) Irrtum, *der;* **lead sb. into ~:** jmdn. irreleiten; **realize the ~ of one's ways** seine Fehler einsehen; **in ~:** irrtümlich[erweise]; **there's an ~ in his calculations** er hat sich verrechnet 3 (Math. etc.) Abweichung, *die*

'error message *n.* (Computing) Fehlermeldung, *die*

ersatz /ˈersæts/ *adj.* (produced as a substitute) Ersatz-; (not real or genuine) unecht; falsch

erstwhile /ˈɜːstwaɪl/ *adj.* einstig; einstmalig (veralt.)

erudite /ˈerʊdaɪt/ *adj.* gelehrt ‹*Abhandlung, Vortrag*›; gebildet, gelehrt ‹*Person*›

erudition /erʊˈdɪʃn/ *n., no pl.* Gelehrsamkeit, *die* (geh.)

erupt /ɪˈrʌpt/ *v.i.* 1 ‹*Vulkan, Geysir:*› ausbrechen; **ashes and lava ~ed from the volcano** Asche und Lava wurden aus dem Vulkan geschleudert; **~ with anger/into a fit of rage** (fig.) einen Wutanfall bekommen 2 (appear) ‹*Hautausschlag:*› ausbrechen

eruption /ɪˈrʌpʃn/ *n.* 1 (of volcano, geyser) Ausbruch, *der;* Eruption, *die* (Geol.) 2 (rash) Eruption, *die* (Med.); Hautausschlag, *der* 3 (fig.) Ausbruch, *der*

eruptive /ɪˈrʌptɪv/ *adj.* eruptiv; **~ rocks** (Geol.) Eruptivgestein, *das*

erythema /erɪˈθiːmə/ *n.* (Med.) Erythem, *das* (fachspr.); Hautrötung, *die*

erythrocyte /ɪˈrɪθrəsaɪt/ *n.* (Anat.) Erythrozyt, *der* (fachspr.); rotes Blutkörperchen

ESA *abbr.* **= European Space Agency** ESA

escalate /ˈeskəleɪt/

A *v.i.* sich ausweiten (**into** zu); eskalieren (geh.) (**into** zu); ‹*Löhne, Preise, Kosten:*› [ständig] steigen

B *v.t.* ausweiten (**into** zu); eskalieren (geh.) (**into** zu); beschleunigen ‹*Anstieg*›

escalation /eskəˈleɪʃn/ *n.* (of rioting, war) Ausweitung, *die;* Eskalation, *die* (geh.); (of wages, prices, costs) Anstieg, *der*

escalator /ˈeskəleɪtə(r)/ *n.* 1 Rolltreppe, *die* 2 (Commerc.) **~ clause** Gleitklausel, *die*

e

e

escalope /'eskələʊp/ *n.* (Gastr.) Schnitzel, *das*

escapade /eskə'peɪd/ *n.* Eskapade, *die* (geh.)

escape /ɪ'skeɪp/

A *n.* **1** (lit. or fig.) Flucht, *die* (**from** aus); (from prison or mental hospital also) Ausbruch, *der* (**from** aus); (of large wild animal) Ausbruch, *der;* (of small animal) Entlaufen, *das;* (of bird) Entfliegen, *das;* **there is no ~** (lit. or fig.) es gibt kein Entkommen; **~ vehicle** Fluchtfahrzeug, *das;* **~ route** (lit. or fig.) Fluchtweg, *der;* **make one's ~ [from sth.]** [aus etw.] entkommen; **have a narrow/miraculous ~:** gerade noch einmal/wie durch ein Wunder davonkommen; **have a lucky ~:** glücklich davonkommen; noch einmal Glück haben; **that was a narrow ~** (joc.) gerade noch mal davongekommen; **you had a lucky ~** (joc.) da haben Sie aber noch mal Glück gehabt; **~ from reality** Flucht vor der Realität **2** (leakage of gas etc.) Austritt, *der;* Entweichen, *das* **3** (plant) verwilderte Pflanze. *See also* **fire escape**

B *v.i.* **1** (lit. or fig.) fliehen (**from** aus); entfliehen (geh.) (**from** *Dat.*); (successfully) entkommen (**from** *Dat.*); (from prison or mental hospital also) ausbrechen (**from** aus); ‹*Großtier:*› ausbrechen; ‹*Kleintier:*› entlaufen (**from** *Dat.*); ‹*Vogel:*› entfliegen (**from** *Dat.*); **~ to freedom** in die Freiheit entkommen; **while trying to ~:** auf der Flucht; **~d prisoner/convict** entflohener Gefangener/Sträfling; **~ to one's room** sich in sein Zimmer zurückziehen; **~ into a dream world** (fig.) in eine Traumwelt flüchten **2** (leak) ‹*Gas:*› ausströmen; ‹*Flüssigkeit:*› auslaufen **3** (avoid harm) davonkommen; **~ alive** mit dem Leben davonkommen; **he ~d, but she was killed** er überlebte, während sie getötet wurde **4** (Computing) **press ~:** 'Escape' drücken

C *v.t.* **1** entkommen (+ *Dat.*) ‹*Verfolger, Angreifer, Feind*›; entgehen (+ *Dat.*) ‹*Bestrafung, Gefangennahme, Tod, Entdeckung, Schicksal*›; verschont bleiben von ‹*Katastrophe, Krankheit, Zerstörung, Reduzierung, Auswirkungen*›; **~ observation/a duty** sich der Beobachtung/einer Pflicht entziehen; **he ~d the consequences** ihm blieben die Konsequenzen erspart; **~ being seen** nicht gesehen werden; **she narrowly ~d being killed** sie wäre fast getötet worden; **the car ~d damage** der Wagen blieb unbeschädigt; **one can't ~ the fact that ...:** es lässt sich nicht leugnen, dass ... **2** (not be remembered by) entfallen sein (+ *Dat.*) **3** **~ sb.['s notice]** (not be seen) jmdm. entgehen; **~ notice** nicht bemerkt werden; **~ sb.'s attention** jmds. Aufmerksamkeit (*Dat.*) entgehen; *see also* **memory 2** **4** (not be understood by) **~ sb.** sich jmds. Verständnis (*Dat.*) entziehen **5** (be uttered involuntarily by) entfahren (+ *Dat.*)

escape: ~ artist ▸**escapologist**; **~ attempt**, **~ bid** *ns.* Fluchtversuch, *der;* (from prison) Ausbruchsversuch, *der;* **~ clause** *n.* (Law) Ausweichklausel, *die*

escapee /ɪskeɪ'piː, e'skeɪpiː/ *n.* Entflohene, *der/die*

escape: ~-hatch *n.* (Naut., Aeronaut.) Notausstieg, *der;* (fig.) Rettungsanker, *der;* **~ key** *n.* (Computing) Escapetaste, *die;* **~ mechanism** *n.* (Psych.) Abwehrmechanismus, *der*

escapement /ɪ'skeɪpmənt/ *n.* (Horol.) Hemmung, *die*

e'scape-proof *adj.* ausbruchsicher

escape: ~ road *n.* Auslaufstrecke, *die;* **~ route** *n.* Fluchtweg, *der;* **~ valve** *n.* Sicherheitsventil, *das*

escapism /ɪ'skeɪpɪzm/ *n.* (Psych.) Eskapismus, *der* (fachspr.); Realitätsflucht, *die*

escapist /ɪ'skeɪpɪst/ (Psych.)

A *n.* Eskapist, *der* (fachspr.); Aussteiger, *der*/Aussteigerin, *die* (ugs.)

B *adj.* eskapistisch (fachspr.); Aussteiger- (ugs.)

escapologist /eskə'pɒlədʒɪst/ *n.* (Brit.) Entfesselungskünstler, *der*

escarpment /ɪ'skɑːpmənt/ *n.* (Geog.) Steilhang, *der*

eschatology /eskə'tɒlədʒɪ/ *n.* (Theol.) Eschatologie, *die*

eschew /ɪs'tʃuː/ *v.t.* (literary) meiden (geh.)

escort

A /'eskɔːt/ *n.* **1** (armed guard) Eskorte, *die;* Geleitschutz, *der* (Milit.); **police ~:** Polizeieskorte, *die;* **with an ~, under ~:** mit einer Eskorte; **fighter ~:** Jagdschutz, *der* **2** (person[s] protecting or guiding) Begleitung, *die;* **be sb.'s ~:** jmdn. begleiten **3** (man accompanying woman socially) Begleiter, *der* **4** (hired companion) Begleiter, *der*/Begleiterin, *die;* (woman also) ≈ Hostess, *die*

B /ɪ'skɔːt/ *v.t.* **1** begleiten; (lead) führen; geleiten (geh.); (as guard of honour; also Mil.) eskortieren; **~ sb. to safety** jmdn. in Sicherheit bringen **2** (take forcibly) bringen

escort/'eskɔːt/: **~ agency** *n. Agentur für Begleiter/Begleiterinnen;* **~ carrier** *n.* (Navy) Geleitflugzeugträger, *der;* **~ duty** *n.* **be on ~ duty** als Geleitschutz eingesetzt sein; **~ vessel** *n.* (Navy) Geleitschiff, *das*

escritoire /eskrɪ'twɑː(r)/ *n.* Sekretär, *der*

escutcheon /ɪ'skʌtʃn/ *n.* (Her.) Schild, *der;* **be a blot on sb.'s ~** (fig.) jmds. Ehre beflecken

ESE /iːstsaʊθ'iːst/ *abbr.* ▸**i p. 1013** = **east-south-east** OSO

ESF *abbr.* (EU) = **European Social Fund** ESF

'e-shopping *n., no pl.* E-Shopping, *das*

Eskimo /'eskɪməʊ/ ▸**i p. 1277**

A *adj.* Eskimo-; *see also* **English A**

B *n.* **1** *no pl.* (language) Eskimoisch, *das; see also* **English B 1** **2** *pl.* **~s** *or same* Eskimo, *der*/Eskimofrau, *die;* **the ~[s]** die Eskimos

Eskimo: ~ dog *n.* Eskimohund, *der;* **~ roll** *n.* (Canoeing) Eskimorolle, *die*

ESN *abbr.* = **educationally subnormal**

esophagus (Amer.) ▸**oesophagus**

esoteric /esə'terɪk, iːsə'terɪk/ *adj.* esoterisch (geh.)

ESP *abbr.* (Psych.) = **extra-sensory perception** ASW

espalier /ɪ'spælɪə(r)/ *n.* **1** (trellis) Spalier, *das* **2** (tree) Spalierbaum, *der*

esparto /ɪ'spɑːtəʊ/ *n.* **~ [grass]** (Bot.) Esparto, *der;* Espartogras, *das*

especial /ɪ'speʃl/ *attrib. adj.* [ganz] besonder...; **have ~ talent** besonders begabt sein; **for your ~ benefit** gerade um deinetwillen

especially /ɪ'speʃəlɪ/ *adv.* besonders; **more ~ because ...:** umso eher, als ...; **what ~ do you want to see?** was möchten Sie insbesondere sehen?; **~ as** zumal; **more ~:** ganz besonders

Esperanto /espə'ræntəʊ/ *n., no pl.* ▸**i p. 1277** Esperanto, *das; see also* **English B 1**

espionage /'espɪənɑːʒ/ *n.* Spionage, *die;* **carry out ~ for sb.** für jmdn. spionieren; *see also* **industrial espionage**

esplanade /esplə'neɪd, esplə'nɑːd/ *n.* Esplanade, *die* (geh.)

espousal /ɪ'spaʊzl/ *n.* Eintreten, *das* (**of** für)

espouse /ɪ'spaʊz/ *v.t.* eintreten für

espresso /e'spresəʊ/ *n., pl.* **~s** (coffee) Espresso, *der*

e'spresso bar *n.* Espressobar, *die;* Espresso, *das*

esprit de corps /espriː də 'kɔː/ *n.* Korpsgeist, *der* (geh.); Gemeinschaftsgeist, *der*

espy /ɪ'spaɪ/ *v.t.* (dated/joc.) entdecken

Esq. *abbr.* ▸**i p. 1634** = **Esquire** ≈ Hr.; (on letter) ≈ Hrn.; **Jim Smith, ~** Hr./Hrn. Jim Smith

essay

A /'eseɪ/ *n.* Essay, *der;* Aufsatz, *der* (bes. Schulw.)

B /ɪ'seɪ/ *v.t.* sich versuchen an (+ *Dat.*); **~ to do sth.** sich bemühen, etw. zu tun

essayist /'eseɪɪst/ *n.* ▸**i p. 1260** Essayist, *der*/Essayistin, *die*

essence /'esəns/ *n.* **1** Wesen, *das;* (gist) Wesentliche, *das;* (of problem, message, teaching) Kern, *der;* **she is the [very] ~ of grace/kindness** sie ist der Inbegriff der Anmut/der Liebenswürdigkeit; **in ~:** im Wesentlichen; **be of the ~:** von entscheidender Bedeutung sein **2** (Cookery) Essenz, *die*

essential /ɪ'senʃl/

A *adj.* **1** (fundamental) wesentlich ‹*Unterschied, Merkmal, Aspekt*›; entscheidend ‹*Frage*›; zentral ‹*Thema*› **2** (indispensable) unentbehrlich; lebenswichtig ‹*Versorgungseinrichtungen, Nahrungsmittel, Güter, Organe*›; unabdingbar ‹*Erfordernis, Qualifikation, Voraussetzung*›; unbedingt notwendig ‹*Bestandteile, Maßnahmen, Ausrüstung*›; wesentlich, entscheidend ‹*Rolle*›; **the ~ thing is for her to be happy** die Hauptsache ist, dass sie glücklich ist; **~ to life** lebensnotwendig *od.* -wichtig; **it is [absolutely** *or* **most] ~ that ...:** es ist unbedingt notwendig, dass ...; **these measures are ~:** diese Maßnahmen sind unbedingt erforderlich

B *n., esp. in pl.* **1** (indispensable element) Notwendigste, *das;* **be an ~ for sth.** für etw. unentbehrlich sein; **the ~s of life** die lebensnotwendigsten Güter; **the bare ~s** das Allernotwendigste **2** (fundamental element) Wesentliche, *das;* **confine oneself to the ~:** sich auf das Wesentliche beschränken; **the ~s of French grammar** die Grundzüge der französischen Grammatik

essentially /ɪ'senʃəlɪ/ *adv.* im Grunde; **my opinion does not ~ differ from yours** ich bin nicht grundsätzlich anderer Meinung als Sie

essential 'oil *n.* (Chem.) ätherisches Öl

establish /ɪ'stæblɪʃ/

A *v.t.* **1** (set up, create, found) schaffen ‹*Einrichtung, Frieden, Präzedenzfall, Ministerposten*›; gründen ‹*Organisation, Institut*›; stiften ‹*Krankenhaus, Frieden*›; errichten ‹*Reich, Geschäft, Lehrstuhl, System*›; einsetzen, bilden ‹*Regierung, Ausschuss*›; einsetzen ‹*Sakrament*›; herstellen ‹*Kontakt, Beziehungen*› (**with** zu); aufschlagen ‹*Hauptquartier*›; aufstellen ‹*Rekord*›; erlassen ‹*Gesetz*›; einführen ‹*Mode, Steuer, neue Methoden*›; ins Leben rufen, begründen ‹*Bewegung*›; **~ a routine** eine Routine entwickeln; **~ one's authority** sich (*Dat.*) Autorität verschaffen; **~ law and order** Recht und Ordnung herstellen **2** (settle, place) unterbringen; **be ~ed in one's new home** sich in seinem neuen Heim eingerichtet haben; **~ sb. in business** jmdm. zum Start im Geschäftsleben verhelfen; **~ sb. in a business of his/her own** jmdm. zur Gründung eines eigenen Geschäfts verhelfen **3** (appoint) einsetzen **4** (secure acceptance for) etablieren; **become ~ed** sich einbürgern; **be firmly ~ed** einen festen Platz haben; **~ one's reputation** sich (*Dat.*) einen Namen machen **5** (prove) beweisen ‹*Schuld, Unschuld, Tatsache*›; unter Beweis stellen ‹*Können*›; nachweisen ‹*Anspruch*›; **an inspection ~ed that ...:** eine Prüfung ergab, dass ... **6** (discover) feststellen; ermitteln ‹*Umstände, Aufenthaltsort*›

B *v. refl.* (take up one's quarters) **~ oneself [at** *or* **in a place]** sich [an einem Ort] niederlassen; **the practice has ~ed itself** der Brauch hat sich eingebürgert; **~ oneself as a carpenter** sich (*Dat.*) als Tischler einen festen Kundenkreis gewinnen

established /ɪ'stæblɪʃt/ *adj.* **1** (entrenched) eingeführt ‹*Geschäft usw.*›; bestehend ‹*Ordnung*›; etabliert ‹*Schriftsteller*›; **long-~ company** alteingeführte *od.* -eingesessene Firma; **this firm has an ~ reputation** diese Firma ist sehr renommiert; **~ civil servant** ≈ Beamter auf Lebenszeit **2** (accepted) üblich; etabliert ‹*Stilrichtung, Gesellschaftsordnung*›; geltend ‹*Norm*›; fest ‹*Brauch*›; feststehend ‹*Tatsache*›; überkommen ‹*Glaube*›; **become ~:** sich durchsetzen **3** (Eccl.) **~ church/religion** Staatskirche/-religion, *die*

establishment /ɪ'stæblɪʃmənt/ *n.* **1** (setting up, creation, foundation) Gründung, *die;* (of government, committee) Einsetzung, *die;* (of democracy, empire) Errichtung, *die;* (of movement) Begründung, *die;* (of peace, relations) Schaffung, *die* **2** (settlement, placement) Unterbringung, *die* **3** (appointment) Einsetzung, *die* **4** (proving) Nachweis, *der* **5** (institution) **[business] ~:** Unternehmen, *das;* **commercial/industrial ~:** Handels-/Industrieunternehmen, *das;* **educational ~:** Lehranstalt, *die* **6** (household, residence) Haus, *das* **7** (organized body) Truppe, *die;* (quota) Personalbestand, *der;* **peace[time]/war ~** (Mil.) Friedens-/Kriegsstärke, *die* **8** (Brit.) **the E~** (social group) das Establishment

estate /ɪ'steɪt/ *n.* **1** (landed property) Gut, *das;* **family/private ~:** Familien-/Privatbesitz, *der;* **~ in the country** Landgut, *das* **2** (Brit.: area with buildings) (housing **~**) [Wohn]siedlung, *die;*

(industrial ~) Industriegebiet, *das;* (trading ~) Gewerbegebiet, *das;* **live on an ~:** in einer Wohnsiedlung leben; **on the industrial/trading ~:** im Industrie-/Gewerbegebiet **3** (plantation) Plantage, *die* **4** (total assets) (of deceased person) Erbmasse, *die* (Rechtsspr.); Nachlass, *der;* (of bankrupt) Konkursmasse, *die* (Wirtsch., Rechtsspr.) **5** (Law: person's interest in landed property) Eigentumsrecht, *das; see also* **personal ~; real ~ 6** (political class) Stand, *der;* **the Three Estates [of the Realm]** die drei [Reichs]stände; **the fourth ~** (joc.) die Zunft der Journalisten (scherzh.) **7** (arch.: condition) Stand, *der;* **the [holy] ~ of matrimony** der heilige Stand der Ehe (geh.) **8** (Brit.) ▸**~ car**

estate: ~ agent *n.* ▸ⓘ **p. 1260** (Brit.) **1** Grundstücksmakler, *der;* Immobilienmakler, *der;* **2** (steward) Gutsverwalter, *der;* **~ car** *n.* (Brit.) Kombiwagen, *der;* **~ duty** (Brit.), **~ tax** (Amer.) *ns.* Erbschaftssteuer, *die*

esteem /ɪˈstiːm/

A *n., no pl.* Achtung, *die* (**for** vor + *Dat.*); Wertschätzung, *die* (geh.) (**for** *Gen.*, für); **hold sb./sth. in [high** *or* **great] ~:** [hohe *od.* große] Achtung vor jmdm./etw. haben; **go up** *or* **rise/go down** *or* **sink in sb.'s ~:** in jmds. Achtung steigen/sinken; **[as a] token** *or* **mark of my ~:** [als] Zeichen meiner Hochachtung *od.* (geh.) Wertschätzung

B *v.t.* **1** (think favourably of) schätzen; **highly** *or* **much** *or* **greatly ~ed** hoch geschätzt (geh.); sehr geschätzt **2** (formal: consider) **~ [as]** erachten für (geh.); ansehen als; **~ sth. an honour** sich (*Dat.*) etw. zur Ehre anrechnen (geh.)

ester /ˈestə(r)/ *n.* (Chem.) Ester, *der*

esthetic *etc.* (*Amer.*) ▸**aesthetic** *etc.*

estimable /ˈestɪməbl/ *adj.* schätzenswert

estimate

A /ˈestɪmət/ *n.* **1** (of number, amount, etc.) Schätzung, *die;* **at a rough ~:** grob geschätzt **2** (of character, qualities, etc.) Einschätzung, *die;* **form an ~ of sb.'s abilities** jmds. Fähigkeiten beurteilen **3** (Commerc.) Kostenvoranschlag, *der;* **give an ~ of £50** die Kosten auf 50 Pfund veranschlagen **4** (Brit. Parl.) **the E~s** der Etat

B /ˈestɪmeɪt/ *v.t.* schätzen ‹*Größe, Entfernung, Zahl, Umsatz*› (**at** auf + *Akk.*); einschätzen ‹*Fähigkeiten, Durchführbarkeit, Aussichten*›; **how far would you ~ the distance to be?** wie groß ist nach Ihrer Schätzung die Entfernung?

estimation /estɪˈmeɪʃn/ *n.* Schätzung, *die;* (of situation etc.) Einschätzung, *die;* Beurteilung, *die;* (esteem) Wertschätzung, *die* (geh.); **in sb.'s ~:** nach jmds. Schätzung; **go up/down in sb.'s ~:** in jmds. Achtung steigen/sinken

estimator /ˈestɪmeɪtə(r)/ *n.* Kalkulator, *der*

Estonia /eˈstəʊnɪə/ *pr. n.* Estland (*das*)

Estonian /eˈstəʊnɪən/ ▸ⓘ **p. 1277,** ▸ⓘ **p. 1345**

A *adj.* estländisch; estnisch; *see also* **English A**

B *n.* **1** (language) Estnisch[e], *das;* Estländisch[e], *das; see also* **English B 1** **2** (person) Este, *der*/Estin, *die;* Estländer, *der*/Estländerin, *die*

estrange /ɪˈstreɪndʒ/ *v.t.* entfremden (**from** *Dat.*); **be/become ~d from sb.** jmdm. entfremdet sein/sich jmdm. entfremden; **they are ~d** sie sind einander fremd geworden; (married couple also) sie haben sich auseinander gelebt; **her ~d husband/his ~d wife** ihr ihr fremd gewordener Mann/seine ihm fremd gewordene Frau; **the ~d couple** die einander fremd gewordenen Ehepartner

estrangement /ɪˈstreɪndʒmənt/ *n.* Entfremdung, *die* (**from** von); **since their ~:** seit sie sich fremd geworden sind; (of married couple also) seit sie sich auseinander gelebt haben

estrogen (Amer.) ▸**oestrogen**

estuary /ˈestjʊərɪ/ *n.* ▸ⓘ **p. 1491** (Geog.) Ästuar, *das* (fachspr.); [Trichter]mündung, *die;* **the Thames ~:** die Mündung der Themse

ˈEstuary English *n.* Estuary-Englisch, *das* (*bes. in Südostengland gesprochene Variante des Englischen mit Elementen des in London gesprochenen Englischs*)

ETA *abbr.* **= estimated time of arrival** voraussichtliche Ankunftszeit

e-tail /ˈiːteɪl/ *n., no pl.* elektronischer Einzelhandel; Internet[einzel]handel, *der; attrib.* Internet-

e-tailer /ˈiːteɪlə(r)/ Interneteinzelhändler, *der*/-händlerin, *die*

e-tailing /ˈiːteɪlɪŋ/ *n., no pl.* elektronischer Einzelhandel; Internet[einzel]handel, *der*

et al. /et ˈæl/ *abbr.* **= and others** et al.

etc. *abbr.* **= et cetera** usw.

et cetera, etcetera /etˈsetərə, ɪtˈsetərə/ und so weiter; et cetera

etch /etʃ/

A *v.t.* **1** ätzen (**on** auf *od.* in + *Akk.*); (on metal also) ‹*bes. Künstler:*› radieren **2** (fig.) einprägen (**in, on** *Dat.*); **be ~ed in** *or* **on sb.'s mind/memory** sich jmdm. eingeprägt haben/ins Gedächtnis eingegraben haben

B *v.i.* ätzen; (on metal also) ‹*bes. Künstler:*› radieren

etching /ˈetʃɪŋ/ *n.* Ätzung, *die;* (piece of art) Radierung, *die;* **come up and see my ~s** (joc.) komm mit rauf, ich zeig dir meine Briefmarkensammlung (ugs. scherzh.)

eternal /ɪˈtɜːnl, iːˈtɜːnl/ *adj.* **1** ewig; **be called to one's ~ rest** in die Ewigkeit abberufen werden (geh. verhüll.); **life ~:** das ewige Leben; **~ triangle** Dreiecksverhältnis, *das* **2** (coll.: unceasing) ewig (ugs.); **you'll have my ~ thanks** *or* **gratitude** ich werde Ihnen ewig dankbar sein

eternally /ɪˈtɜːnəlɪ, iːˈtɜːnəlɪ/ *adv.* **1** ewig; **be ~ damned** auf ewig verdammt sein **2** (coll.: unceasingly) ewig (ugs.)

eternity /ɪˈtɜːnɪtɪ, iːˈtɜːnɪtɪ/ *n.* **1** Ewigkeit, *die;* **for** *or* **in all** *or* **throughout ~, from here to ~:** [bis] in alle Ewigkeit **2** (coll.: long time) Ewigkeit, *die* (ugs.); **wait for [what seemed] an ~:** [scheinbar] eine Ewigkeit warten

ˈe-text *n.* elektronischer Text

ethanol /ˈeθənɒl/ *n., no pl.* (Chem.) Äthanol, *das*

ether /ˈiːθə(r)/ *n.* **1** (Chem.) Äther, *der* **2** (Phys.; also fig.) Äther, *der*

ethereal /ɪˈθɪərɪəl/ *adj.* **1** (delicate, light, airy; also Phys., Chem.) ätherisch **2** (poet.: heavenly) ätherisch (veralt.); himmlisch

ethereal ˈoil *n.* (Chem.) ätherisches Öl

ˈEthernet *n.* (Computing) Ethernet, *das*

ethic /ˈeθɪk/

A *n.* Ethik, *die* (geh.); Ethos, *das* (geh.)

B *adj.* ▸**ethical 1, 2, 4**

ethical /ˈeθɪkl/ *adj.* **1** (relating to morals) ethisch; **~ philosophy** Ethik, *die;* **~ philosopher** Ethiker, *der*/Ethikerin, *die* **2** (morally correct) moralisch einwandfrei; **it is not ~ for a doctor ...:** es entspricht nicht dem Berufsethos eines Arztes ... **3** (Med.) verschreibungspflichtig ‹*Medikament*› **4** (Ling.) **~ dative** Dativus ethicus, *der*

ethical inˈvestment *n.* (Finance) ethische Geldanlage

ethicality /eθɪˈkælɪtɪ/ *n., no pl.* (moral correctness) Sittlichkeit, *die*

ethically /ˈeθɪkəlɪ/ *adv.* **1** (according to ethical rules) ethisch; **be ~ obliged** *or* **bound to do sth.** die moralische Verpflichtung haben, etw. zu tun **2** (in a morally correct way) moralisch einwandfrei

ethics /ˈeθɪks/ *n., no pl.* **1** Moral, *die;* (moral philosophy) Ethik, *die* **2** *usu. constr. as pl.* (moral code of person, group, etc.) Ethik, *die* (geh.); Ethos, *das* (geh.); **medical ~:** ärztliche Ethik; **professional ~:** Berufsethos, *das;* **legal ~:** Standespflichten der Juristen **3** *constr. as pl.* (moral correctness) ethische Berechtigung

Ethiopia /iːθɪˈəʊpɪə/ *pr. n.* Äthiopien (*das*)

Ethiopian /iːθɪˈəʊpɪən/ ▸ⓘ **p. 1277,** ▸ⓘ **p. 1345**

A *adj.* äthiopisch; **sb. is ~:** jmd. ist Äthiopier/Äthiopierin

B *n.* Äthiopier, *der*/Äthiopierin, *die*

ethnic /ˈeθnɪk/ *adj.* **1** (ethnological) ethnisch; Volks‹*gruppe, -musik, -tanz*›; **~ mix** Völkergemisch, *das;* **~ minority** ethnische Minderheit **2** (from specified group) Volks‹*chinesen, -deutsche*›

ethnic ˈcleansing *n.* ethnische Säuberung

ethnicity /eθˈnɪsɪtɪ/ *n.* Ethnizität, *die;* Volksgruppenzugehörigkeit, *die*

ethnology /eθˈnɒlədʒɪ/ *n.* Ethnologie, *die;* vergleichende Völkerkunde

ethology /iːˈθɒlədʒɪ/ *n.* **1** (science of animal behaviour) Verhaltensforschung, *die;* Ethologie, *die* **2** (science of character-formation) Charakterkunde, *die;* Charakterologie, *die*

ethos /ˈiːθɒs/ *n.* (guiding beliefs) Gesinnung, *die;* (fundamental values) Ethos, *das* (geh.); (characteristic spirit) Geist, *der*

ethyl /ˈeθɪl, ˈiːθaɪl/ *n.* (Chem.) Äthyl, *das*

ethyl ˈalcohol *n.* (Chem.) Äthylalkohol, *der*

ethylene /ˈeθɪliːn/ *n.* (Chem.) Äthylen, *das;* **~ ˈglycol** Äthylenglykol, *das*

etiology (Amer.) ▸**aetiology**

etiquette /ˈetɪket, ˈetɪket/ *n.* **1** (social convention, court ceremonial) Etikette, *die;* **breach of ~:** Verstoß gegen die Etikette; **book of ~:** Buch mit Verhaltensregeln; **that's ~:** das gehört sich so; **it's not ~:** das gehört sich nicht **2** (professional code) **professional ~ [of the law]** Berufspraxis [der Juristen]; **medical/legal ~:** Berufspraxis der Ärzte/Juristen

Etna /ˈetnə/ *pr. n.* **[Mount] ~:** der Ätna

> **Eton**
>
> *Eton College* ist die berühmteste und größte **public school** (Privatschule) Englands. Die Jungenschule in der Nähe von Windsor wurde 1440 von König Heinrich VI. gegründet und wird hauptsächlich von den Söhnen reicher Familien besucht. Viele bedeutende Persönlichkeiten des öffentlichen Lebens in Großbritannien haben diese Schule besucht. Ehemalige Schüler von Eton werden als *Old Etonians* bezeichnet.

Etonian /iːˈtəʊnɪən/ *n.* Etonschüler, *der*

Etruscan /ɪˈtrʌskn/ (Ethnol.) ▸ⓘ **p. 1277,** ▸ⓘ **p. 1345**

A *adj.* etruskisch

B *n.* **1** (language) Etruskisch, *das* **2** (person) Etrusker, *der*/Etruskerin, *die*

ETUC *abbr.* **= European Trade Union Confederation**

étude /ˈeɪtjuːd, eɪˈtjuːd/ *n.* (Mus.) Etüde, *die*

etymological /etɪməˈlɒdʒɪkl/ *adj.*, **etymologically** /etɪməˈlɒdʒɪkəlɪ/ *adv.* (Ling.) etymologisch

etymologist /etɪˈmɒlədʒɪst/ *n.* (Ling.) Etymologe, *der*/Etymologin, *die*

etymology /etɪˈmɒlədʒɪ/ *n.* (Ling.) Etymologie, *die; see also* **folk etymology**

EU *abbr.* **= European Union** EU

eucalyptus /juːkəˈlɪptəs/ *n., pl.* **~es** *or* **eucalypti** **1** **~ [oil]** (Pharm.) Eukalyptusöl, *das* **2** (Bot.) Eukalyptus[baum], *der*

Eucharist /ˈjuːkərɪst/ *n.* (Eccl.) Eucharistie, *die*

eugenics /juːˈdʒenɪks/ *n., no pl.* Eugenik, *die* (fachspr.); Erbgesundheitslehre, *die*

eulogise ▸**eulogize**

eulogistic /juːləˈdʒɪstɪk/ *adj.* lobrednerisch

eulogize /ˈjuːlədʒaɪz/ *v.t.* preisen (geh.); rühmen

eulogy /ˈjuːlədʒɪ/ *n.* **1** (speech, writing) Lobrede, *die;* Eloge, *die* (geh.); (Amer.: funeral oration) Grabrede, *die* **2** (praise) Lobspruch, *der*

eunuch /ˈjuːnək/ *n.* Eunuch, *der;* (fig. derog.) Schwächling, *der* (abwertend)

euonymus /juːˈɒnɪməs/ *n.* (Bot.) Spindelstrauch, *der;* Evonymus, *der od. die;* (Euonymus europaeus) Pfaffenhütchen, *das*

euphemism /ˈjuːfəmɪzm/ *n.* Euphemismus, *der* (bes. Sprachw.); verhüllende Umschreibung

euphemistic /juːfəˈmɪstɪk/ *adj.*, **euphemistically** /juːfəˈmɪstɪkəlɪ/ *adv.* euphemistisch (bes. Sprachw.); verhüllend

euphonious /juːˈfəʊnɪəs/ *adj.* **1** (pleasant-sounding) wohlklingend (geh.) **2** (Ling., Phonet.) euphonisch

euphonium /juːˈfəʊnɪəm/ *n.* (Mus.) Euphonium, *das*

euphony /ˈjuːfənɪ/ *n.* **1** (pleasing sound) Wohlklang, *der* (geh.) **2** (Ling., Phonet.) Euphonie, *die*

euphorbia /juːˈfɔːbɪə/ *n.* (Bot.) Euphorbia[pflanze], *die* (fachspr.); Wolfsmilch, *die*

euphoria /juːˈfɔːrɪə/ *n., no pl.* Euphorie, *die* (geh.); (elation also) Hochstimmung, *die*

euphoric /juːˈfɔːrɪk/ *adj.* euphorisch (geh.)

e

Euphrates /juː'freɪtiːz/ *pr. n.* ▸ⓘ **p. 1491** Euphrat, *der*

Eurasia /jʊə'reɪʒə/ *pr. n.* Eurasien *(das)*

Eurasian /jʊə'reɪʒn/
A *adj.* eurasisch
B *n.* Eurasier, *der*/Eurasierin, *die*

eureka /jʊə'riːkə/ *int.* heureka (geh.); ich habs (ugs.)

euro /'jʊərəʊ/ *n.* ▸ⓘ **p. 1332** Euro, *der;* **cost 20 ~s** 20 Euro kosten

Euro- /'jʊərəʊ/ *in comb.* euro-/Euro-

'Eurobond *n.* (Commerc.) Eurobond, *der;* Euroanleihe, *die*

'euro cent, 'eurocent *n.* Eurocent, *der*

Eurocentric /jʊərəʊ'sentrɪk/ *adj.* eurozentrisch

Eurocentrism /jʊərəʊ'sentrɪzm/ *n.* Eurozentrismus, *der*

Euro: ~cheque *n.* (Commerc.) Euroscheck, *der;* **~crat** /'jʊərəkræt/ *n.* Eurokrat, *der*/Eurokratin, *die;* **~currency** *n.* Eurowährung, *die;* **~dollar** *n.* (Econ.) Eurodollar, *der;* **~land** *n.* Euroland *(das);* **~market** *n.* **1** (Commerc.) Euro[geld]markt, *der;* **2** (European Community) europäischer Markt; [EU-]Binnenmarkt, *der;* **~-MP** *n.* Europaabgeordnete, *der/die*

Europe /'jʊərəp/ *pr. n.* **1** Europa *(das);* **the continent of ~:** der europäische Kontinent **2** (Brit.: EC) EG, *die;* **go into ~:** der EG beitreten **3** (Brit. coll.: mainland ~) Kontinent, *der*

European /jʊərə'piːən/ ▸ⓘ **p. 1345**
A *adj.* europäisch; **sb. is ~:** jmd. ist Europäer/Europäerin; **win ~ recognition** in ganz Europa Anerkennung finden
B *n.* Europäer, *der*/Europäerin, *die*

European: ~ Agricultural Guidance and Guaran'tee Fund *n.* (EU) Europäischer Ausrichtungs- und Garantiefonds für die Landwirtschaft; **~ Central 'Bank** *n.* Europäische Zentralbank; **~ Coal and 'Steel Community** *n.* Europäische Kohle- und Stahlgemeinschaft; **~ Com'mission** *n.* (EU) Europäische Kommission; **~ Court of Auditors** (EU) Europäischer Rechnungshof; **~ Court of Human 'Rights** *n.* Europäischer Gerichtshof für Menschenrechte; **~ 'Cup** *n.* (Footb.) Europacup, *der;* Europapokal, *der;* **~ 'currency unit** *n.* Europäische Währungseinheit; **~ De'velopment Fund** *n.* (EU)Europäischer Entwicklungsfonds; **~ Economic Com'munity** *n.* Europäische Wirtschaftsgemeinschaft; **~ Free 'Trade Association** *n.* Europäische Freihandelsassoziation; **~ In'vestment Bank** *n.* Europäische Investitionsbank; **~ 'Monetary System** *n.* Europäisches Währungssystem; **~ Monetary 'Union** *n.* Europäische Währungsunion; **~ 'Parliament** *n.* Europäisches Parlament; **~ plan** *n.* (Amer. Hotel Managem.) *Berechnungssystem für Hotelzimmer ohne Verpflegung*

Europeanise ▸ **Europeanize**

Europeanism /jʊərə'piːənɪzm/ *n.* Europäertum, *das;* (ideal of the unification of Europe) europäischer Gedanke

Europeanize /jʊərə'piːənaɪz/ *v.t.* europäisieren

European: ~ 'Police Office *n.* Europäisches Polizeiamt; **~ Regional De'velopment Fund** *n.* (EU) Europäischer Regionalentwicklungsfonds; **~ 'Social Fund** *n.* (EU) Europäischer Sozialfonds; **~ 'Space Agency** *n.* Europäische Raumfahrtbehörde; **~ 'Union** *n.* Europäische Union

Europol /'jʊərəʊpɒl/ *n.* Europol, *(das) od. die*

Euro: ~-rebel *n.* (esp. Brit.) [innerparteilicher] Europagegner/[innerparteiliche] Europagegnerin; **~sceptic** *n.* Euroskeptiker, *der*/-skeptikerin, *die;* **~scepticism** *n., no pl.* Euroskepsis, *die;* **~star**® *n.* Eurostar, *der;* **go by ~star** mit dem Eurostar fahren; **~vision** *n.* (Telev.) Eurovision, *die;* **e~zone** *n.* Eurozone, *die*

Eustachian tube /juːs'teɪʃn tjuːb/ *n.* (Anat.) eustachische Röhre

euthanasia /juːθə'neɪzɪə/ *n.* Euthanasie, *die;* Sterbehilfe, *die*

evacuate /ɪ'vækjʊeɪt/ *v.t.* **1** (remove from danger, clear of occupants) evakuieren (**from** aus) **2** (esp. Mil.: cease to occupy) räumen **3** (Physiol.) entleeren ‹*Darm*›

evacuation /ɪvækjʊ'eɪʃn/ *n.* **1** (removal of people or things, clearance of place) Evakuierung, *die* (**from** aus) **2** (esp. Mil.: withdrawal from occupation) **the ~ of a territory** die Räumung eines Gebietes; **the ~ of the army** der Abzug der Armee **3** (Physiol.) Entleerung, *die*

evacuee /ɪvækjʊ'iː/ *n.* Evakuierte, *der/die; attrib.* **~ children** evakuierte Kinder

evade /ɪ'veɪd/ *v.t.* **1** ausweichen (+ *Dat.*) ‹*Angriff, Angreifer, Schlag, Blick, Problem, Schwierigkeit, Tatsache, Frage, Hindernis, Thema*›; sich entziehen (+ *Dat.*) ‹*Verhaftung, Ergreifung, Wehrdienst, Einberufung, Gerechtigkeit, Pflicht, Verantwortung, Liebkosung*›; entkommen (+ *Dat.*) ‹*Polizei, Verfolger, Verfolgung, Gegner*›; hinterziehen ‹*Steuern, Zölle*›; umgehen ‹*Zahlungsverpflichtung*›; **~ recognition** nicht erkannt werden; **~ doing sth.** vermeiden, etw. zu tun; **~ giving an answer** der Beantwortung einer Frage ausweichen **2** (circumvent) umgehen ‹*Gesetz, Vorschrift*› **3** (elude) **the significance of his remark ~s me** die Bedeutung seiner Bemerkung ist mir nicht klar; **~ definition** sich einer Definition entziehen

evaluate /ɪ'væljʊeɪt/ *v.t.* **1** (value) schätzen ‹*Wert, Preis, Schaden, Kosten*› **2** (quantify, express numerically) in Zahlen ausdrücken; quantifizieren **3** (appraise) einschätzen; auswerten ‹*Daten*›; (judge) beurteilen

evaluation /ɪvæljʊ'eɪʃn/ *n.* **1** Schätzung, *die;* (quantification) Berechnung, *die;* Quantifizierung, *die* **2** (appraisal) Einschätzung, *die;* (of data) Auswertung, *die*

evanescent /iːvə'nesənt, evə'nesənt/ *adj.* flüchtig ‹*Erscheinung, Vision, Glück*›; vergänglich ‹*Reiz*›

evangelical /iːvæn'dʒelɪkl/ *adj.* **1** (of the Gospels) **~ texts/preaching** Texte/Verkündigung des Evangeliums **2** (Protestant) evangelikal **3** (evangelizing, crusading) missionarisch (fig.)

evangelicalism /iːvæn'dʒelɪkəlɪzm/ *n., no pl.* evangelikale Lehre

evangelise ▸ **evangelize**

evangelism /ɪ'vændʒəlɪzm/ *n., no pl.* **1** (preaching the Gospel) Evangelisation, *die* **2** (crusading zeal) Bekehrungseifer, *der*

evangelist /ɪ'vændʒəlɪst/ *n.* **1** (Gospel-writer) Evangelist, *der* **2** (Gospel-preacher) Evangelist, *der;* Prediger, *der;* (itinerant preacher) Wanderprediger, *der*

evangelize /ɪ'vændʒəlaɪz/ *v.t.* evangelisieren

evaporate /ɪ'væpəreɪt/
A *v.i.* **1** (become vapour) verdunsten **2** (lose liquid) eindicken; (completely) eintrocknen **3** (fig.) sich in Luft auflösen; dahinschwinden (geh.); ‹*Furcht, Begeisterung:*› verfliegen
B *v.t.* **1** (turn into vapour) verdunsten lassen **2** (cause to lose liquid) evaporieren (Chem.); eindampfen (Chem.)

evaporated 'milk *n.* Kondensmilch, *die*

evaporation /ɪvæpə'reɪʃn/ *n.* **1** (changing into vapour) Verdunstung, *die* **2** (losing liquid) Eindickung, *die;* (completely) Eintrocknung, *die*

evasion /ɪ'veɪʒn/ *n.* **1** (avoidance) Umgehung, *die;* (of duty) Vernachlässigung, *die;* (of responsibility, question) Ausweichen, *das* (**of** vor + *Dat.*) **2** (evasive statement) Ausrede, *die;* **~s** Ausflüchte *Pl.* **3** (prevarication) Ausflüchte *Pl.*

evasive /ɪ'veɪsɪv/ *adj.* **1** **be/become [very] ~:** [ständig] ausweichen; **be ~ about sth.** um etw. herumreden **2** (aimed at evasion) ausweichend ‹*Antwort*›; **take ~ action** ein Ausweichmanöver machen

evasively /ɪ'veɪsɪvlɪ/ *adv.* ausweichend

eve *n.* **1** Vorabend, *der;* (day) Vortag, *der;* **the ~ of** der Abend/Tag vor (+ *Dat.*); der Vorabend/Vortag (+ *Gen.*); *see also* **Christmas Eve**; **New Year's Eve** **2** (fig.) **[be] on the ~ of sth.** kurz vor etw. (*Dat.*) [stehen] **3** (arch.: evening) Abend, *der*

Eve /iːv/ *pr. n.* (Bibl.) Eva *(die)*

even[1] /'iːvn/
A *adj.*, **~er** /'iːvənə(r)/, **~est** /'iːvənɪst/ **1** (smooth, flat) eben ‹*Boden, Fläche*›; glatt ‹*Faser, Gewebe*›; **make sth. ~:** etw. ebnen/glätten **2** (level) gleich hoch ‹*Stapel, Stuhl-, Tischbein*›; gleich lang ‹*Vorhang, Stuhl-, Tischbein usw.*›; **be of ~ height/length** gleich hoch/lang sein; **~ with** genauso hoch/lang wie; **on an ~ keel** (Naut., Aeronaut.) auf ebenem Kiel (Seemannsspr.); ≈ ausgetrimmt (Seemannssspr., Fliegerspr.); (fig.) ausgeglichen; **keep the firm on an ~ keel** die Firma über Wasser halten **3** (straight) gerade ‹*Saum, Kante*› **4** (parallel) parallel (**with** zu) **5** (regular) regelmäßig ‹*Zähne*›; ebenmäßig ‹*Gesichtszüge*›; (steady) gleichmäßig ‹*Schrift, Rhythmus, Atmen, Schlagen*›; stetig ‹*Fortschritt*› **6** (equal) gleich [groß] ‹*Menge, Abstand*›; ausgewogen ‹*Kräfteverhältnis*›; gleichmäßig ‹*Verteilung, Aufteilung*›; ausgeglichen ‹*Punktestand*›; **start out ~:** mit den gleichen Voraussetzungen beginnen; **the teams are/the score is ~:** die Mannschaften sind punktgleich/die Punktzahl ist dieselbe *od.* gleich; **we need another goal to make it ~:** wir brauchen noch ein Tor zum Ausgleich; **the match is still ~:** die Begegnung steht noch unentschieden; **~s** (Brit.), **~ money** (Betting) eins zu eins; **an ~s** *or* **~ money favourite [to win]** ein 1 : 1-Favorit; **I have an ~ chance of getting there on time** meine Chancen, pünktlich anzukommen, stehen fünfzig zu fünfzig *od.* (ugs.) fifty-fifty; **the odds are ~, it's ~ odds** *or* **an ~ bet** die Chancen stehen fünfzig zu fünfzig *od.* (ugs.) fifty-fifty; **~ Stephen** /iːvn 'stiːvn/ (coll.) ≈ fifty-fifty (ugs.) **7** (balanced) im Gleichgewicht; **with an ~ hand** (fig.) gerecht **8** (quits, fully revenged) **be** *or* **get ~ with sb.** es jmdm. heimzahlen **9** (uniform) gleichmäßig **10** (calm) ausgeglichen; **have an ~ temper** ausgeglichen sein **11** (divisible by two, so numbered) gerade ‹*Zahl, Seite, Hausnummer*›; **the ~ syllables** die zweite, vierte usw. Silbe **12** (exact) **an ~ dozen** ein rundes Dutzend (ugs.); **let's make it an ~ ten** sagen wir rund zehn (ugs.). *See also* **break even**
B *adv.* **1** sogar; selbst; **~ perhaps ...:** vielleicht sogar ...; **hard, unbearable ~:** hart, sogar *od.* wenn nicht gar unerträglich; **does he ~ suspect the danger?** ahnt er überhaupt die Gefahr?; **do sth. ~ without being told** etw. auch ohne Aufforderung tun; **~ afterwards** selbst *od.* sogar danach; **~ before[hand]** auch schon vorher; **~ today** selbst *od.* sogar heute noch **2** *with negative* **not** *or* **never ~ ...** [noch] nicht einmal ...; **without ~ saying goodbye** ohne wenigstens Auf Wiedersehen zu sagen **3** *with compar. adj. or adv.* sogar noch ‹*komplizierter, weniger, schlimmer usw.*› **4** **~ if** *or* **though Arsenal win** selbst wenn Arsenal gewinnt; **~ if Arsenal won** selbst wenn Arsenal gewinnen würde; (fact) obgleich Arsenal gewann; **~ supposing we had been present** selbst wenn wir dabei gewesen wären; **~ were she to appear** selbst wenn sie auftauchen sollte; **~ as** (just when) gerade als; (in just the way that) geradeso wie; (during the period that) während ... noch; **~ so** [aber] trotzdem *od.* dennoch; (arch.: that is correct) so ist es; **~ now/then** (as well as previously) selbst *od.* sogar jetzt/dann; (at this/that very moment) gerade in diesem Augenblick
C *v.t.* ebnen; (smooth) glätten

Phrasal verbs

• **~ 'out**
A *v.t.* **1** (make smooth) glätten **2** (distribute more equally) gleich verteilen; ausgleichen ‹*Unterschiede*›
B *v.i.* **1** (become smooth) ‹*Boden:*› sich einebnen **2** (become more equal) sich ausgleichen

• **~ 'up**
A *v.t.* ausgleichen; **so as to ~ things up** zum Ausgleich

B v.i. (settle debt, get revenge) abrechnen

even² n. (poet.) Abend, der

even-'handed adj. gerecht

evening /'i:vnɪŋ/ n. [1] ▸❶ p. 1001, ▸❶ p. 1048 Abend, der; attrib. Abend‹vorstellung, -ausgabe, -messe›; this/tomorrow ~: heute/morgen Abend; during the ~: am Abend; [early/late] in the ~: am [frühen/späten] Abend; (regularly) [früh/spät] abends; at eight in the ~: um acht Uhr abends; on the ~ of 2 May am Abend des 2. Mai; on Wednesday ~s/~: Mittwoch abends/am Mittwochabend; ~s, of an ~: abends; one ~: eines Abends; every ~: jeden Abend; ~ came es wurde Abend; two ~s ago vorgestern Abend; the other ~: neulich abends; a good ~'s viewing ein gutes Abendprogramm [im Fernsehen]; the cool of the ~: die Abendkühle; an ~ of cards ein Abend beim Kartenspiel; see also good A 13 [2] ▸❶ p. 1189 (coll: greeting) 'n Abend! (ugs.) [3] (soirée) Abend, der; discussion ~: Diskussionsabend, der [4] (fig.) Abend, der (geh.); (of life) Lebensabend, der (geh.)

evening: ~ class n. Abendkurs, der; take or do ~ classes in pottery etc. Abendkurse im Töpfern usw. besuchen; ~ 'dress n. Abendkleidung, die; in [full] ~ dress in Abendkleidung; ~ dress, ~ gown ns. Abendkleid, das; ~ 'meal n. Abendessen, das; ~ 'paper n. Abendzeitung, die; ~ 'primrose n. Nachtkerze, die; ~ school n. Abendschule, die; ~ 'service n. (Eccl.) Abendandacht, die; (mass) Abendgottesdienst, der; ~ 'star n. Abendstern, der

evenly /'i:vnlɪ/ adv. gleichmäßig; say sth. ~: etw. in ruhigem Ton sagen; be ~ spaced den gleichen Abstand voneinander haben; the runners are ~ matched die Läufer sind einander ebenbürtig

even-numbered /'i:vnnʌmbəd/ adj. gerade; the houses are ~: die Häuser haben gerade Hausnummern

'evensong n. (Eccl.) Abendandacht, die

event /ɪ'vent/ n. [1] in the ~ of his dying or death im Falle seines Todes; falls er stirbt; in the ~ of rain bei Regenwetter; in the ~ of sickness/war im Falle einer Krankheit/im Kriegsfalle; in that ~: in dem Falle; in such an ~: in solch einem Falle; in the unlikely ~ of sb. doing sth. falls, was nicht sehr wahrscheinlich ist, jmd. etw. tut; in the ~ that (Amer.) im Falle, dass [2] (outcome) in any/either ~ = in any case ▸case¹ 1; at all ~s auf jeden Fall; in the ~: letzten Endes [3] (occurrence) Ereignis, das; ~s have proved ...: die Ereignisse haben gezeigt ...; the dramatic ~s in Rome das dramatische Geschehen in Rom; ~s are taking place in Argentina which ...: ~s es geschehen Dinge in Argentinien, die ...; sth. is [quite] an ~: etw. ist schon ein Ereignis; see also course A 1; wise [4] (Sport) Wettkampf, der; showjumping ~: Jagdspringen, das; Springprüfung, die; three-day ~: Military, die; Vielseitigkeitsprüfung, die [5] (public or social occasion) Veranstaltung, die

even-'tempered adj. ausgeglichen

eventful /ɪ'ventfl/ adj. ereignisreich ‹Tag, Zeiten›; bewegt ‹Leben, Jugend, Zeiten›

'eventide n. (arch.) Abendzeit, die (geh.)

eventual /ɪ'ventjʊəl/ adj. predict sb.'s ~ downfall vorhersagen, dass jmd. schließlich zu Fall kommen wird; lead to sb.'s ~ downfall schließlich zu jmds. Sturz führen; the career of Napoleon and his ~ defeat der Aufstieg Napoleons und schließlich seine Niederlage; we are heading towards ~ destruction wir steuern letztlich auf den Untergang zu

eventuality /ɪventjʊ'ælɪtɪ/ n. Eventualität, die; the ~ of war der mögliche Kriegsfall; in certain eventualities in bestimmten [möglichen] Fällen; be ready for all eventualities auf alle Eventualitäten gefasst sein

eventually /ɪ'ventjʊəlɪ/ adv. schließlich; she'll ~ get married sie wird irgendwann od. eines Tages heiraten; I'll do that ~: ich mache das irgendwann [noch]

eve-of-'poll adj. ~ [survey] [Umfrage] kurz vor der Wahl

ever /'evə(r)/ adv. [1] (always, at all times) immer; stets; for ~: für immer ‹weggehen, gelten›; ewig ‹lieben, da sein, leben›; auf ewig (dichter.) ‹unerreichbar›; go on for ~: immer so bleiben; (derog.) ewig dauern; it is for ~ changing es ändert sich dauernd; the traffic lights took for ~ to change (coll.) die Ampeln schalteten erst nach einer Ewigkeit um; Arsenal for ~! es lebe Arsenal!; for ~ and ~: immer und ewig; (in the Lord's Prayer) in Ewigkeit; for ~ and a day eine Ewigkeit; ~ since [then] seit [dieser Zeit]; ~ after[wards] seitdem; I've been frightened of dogs ~ 'since or 'after seitdem od. seit diesem Tag habe ich Angst vor Hunden; ~ since he inherited it von dem Tag an, an dem er das geerbt hat; ~ since I've known her solange ich sie kenne; ~ since I can remember soweit ich zurückdenken kann; ~ since she was a child von Kindheit an; ~ yours or yours ~, Ethel deine/eure Ethel; immer die deine/eure, Ethel (veralt.) [2] in comb. with compar. adj. or adv. noch; immer; get ~ deeper into debt sich noch od. immer mehr verschulden; ~ further noch immer weiter [3] in comb. with participles etc. ~-increasing ständig zunehmend; ~-recurring immer wiederkehrend; ~-present allgegenwärtig; ~-youthful ewig jugendlich; ~-changing rules sich ständig ändernde Vorschriften; an ~-patient mother eine Mutter, die nie die Geduld verliert; go round in ~-decreasing circles (fig. coll.) [mit immer größeren Anstrengungen] immer weniger erreichen [4] (at any time) je[mals]; not ~: noch nie; ~ before je zuvor; never ~: nie im Leben; never ~ before noch nie zuvor; nothing ~ happens es passiert nie etwas; his best performance ~: seine beste Vorstellung überhaupt; it hardly ~ rains es regnet so gut wie nie; don't you ~ do that again! mach das bloß nicht noch mal!; did you ~? (coll.) hast du Töne? (salopp); he's a devil if ~ there was one (coll.) er ist ein Teufel, alles, was recht ist (ugs.); better than ~: besser denn je; more frequently than ~: häufiger als je zuvor; the same as ~ or as it ~ was das Gleiche wie immer; as ~: wie gewöhnlich; (iron.) wie gehabt; yours as ~, Bob (in letter) wie immer, dein Bob; as ... as ~: unverändert ...; I'm as stupid as ~: ich bin immer noch nicht schlauer; he's as kind a man as ~ lived er ist der freundlichste Mensch, den es je gegeben hat; if I ~ catch you doing that again wenn ich dich dabei noch einmal erwische; seldom, if ~, (coll.) seldom ~: so gut wie nie; as if I ~ would! ich doch nicht!; a fool if ~ there was one der größte Narr, den man sich (Dat.) vorstellen kann; is he ~ conceited (Amer. coll.) ist der vielleicht eingebildet! (ugs.); the first men ~ or the first ~ men to reach the moon die Ersten, die je auf dem Mond waren; you're the first ~: du bist der/die Allererste; the greatest tennis player ~: der größte Tennisspieler, den es je gegeben hat; the hottest day ~: der heißeste Tag seit Menschengedenken [5] emphasizing question what ~ does he want? was will er nur?; who/which ~ could it be? wer/welcher könnte das nur sein?; how ~ did I drop it?/could I have dropped it? wie konnte ich es nur fallen lassen?; when ~ did he do it? wann hat er es nur getan?; where ~ in the world have you been? wo in aller Welt hast du bloß gesteckt?; why ~ not? warum denn nicht? [6] intensifier before ~ he opened his mouth noch bevor er seinen Mund aufmachte; as soon as ~ I can so bald wie irgend möglich; I'm ~ so sorry (coll.) mir tut es ja so Leid; ~ so nice (coll.) so ungemein schön; ~ so slightly drunk (coll.) ein ganz klein wenig betrunken; thanks ~ so [much] (coll.) vielen herzlichen Dank; he liked her ~ so (coll.) er mochte sie so sehr; it was ~ such a shame (coll.) es war so schade [7] (arch.: always) all[e]zeit (veralt.); it was ~ thus so ist es immer [8] ~ and again or (literary) anon dann und wann

'everglade n. (Amer. Geog.) Sumpfgebiet, das; the E~s die Everglades

'evergreen
A adj. [1] immergrün ‹Baum, Strauch, Landschaft› [2] (fig.) immer wieder aktuell ‹Problem, Thema›; immer wieder gern gehört ‹Lied, Schlager, Sänger›; ~ song Evergreen, der
B n. immergrüne Pflanze/immergrüner Baum

ever'lasting adj. [1] (eternal) immer während; ewig ‹Leben, Gesetz, Höllenqualen, Gott, Gedenken, Berge, Fels›; unvergänglich ‹Ruhm, Ehre› [2] (incessant) ewig (ugs.); endlos

everlastingly /evə'lɑ:stɪŋlɪ/ adv. [1] (eternally) ewig ‹leben, leiden› [2] (incessantly) ewig (ugs.); ständig

'ever-loving adj. your ~ wife/husband (in letter) deine dich ewig liebende Frau/dein dich ewig liebender Mann

ever'more adv. auf ewig; for ~: in [alle] Ewigkeit

every /'evrɪ/ adj. [1] (each single) jeder/jede/jedes; ~ man will do his duty jeder [Einzelne] wird seine Pflicht tun; have ~ reason allen Grund haben; ~ [single] time/on ~ [single] occasion [aber auch] jedes Mal; ~ [single] time we ...: [aber auch] jedes Mal, wenn wir ...; there was one man for ~ three women auf einen Mann kamen drei Frauen; he ate ~ last or single biscuit (coll.) er hat die ganzen Kekse aufgegessen (ugs.); she's spent ~ last penny (coll.) sie hat das ganze Geld ausgegeben; ~ one jeder/jede/jedes [Einzelne]; ~ time (coll.: without any hesitation) jederzeit; give me or I prefer Switzerland ~ time (coll.) es geht doch nichts über die Schweiz; ~ which way (esp. Amer.) in alle Richtungen [2] after possessive adj. your ~ wish all[e] deine Wünsche; his ~ thought all[e] seine Gedanken [3] (indicating recurrence) she comes [once] ~ day sie kommt jeden Tag [einmal]; ~ three/few days alle drei/paar Tage; ~ third day jeder dritte/jeden dritten Tag; ~ other (every second, or fig.: almost every) jeder/jede/jedes Zweite; ~ now and then or again, ~ so often, ~ once in a while hin und wieder [4] ▸❶ p. 1189 (the greatest possible) unbedingt, uneingeschränkt ‹Vertrauen›; voll ‹Beachtung›; all ‹Respekt, Aussicht›; there's ~ prospect of a victory for England alles deutet auf einen Sieg Englands hin; I wish you ~ happiness/success ich wünsche dir alles Gute/viel Erfolg

'everybody n. & pron. jeder; has ~ seen it? haben es alle od. hat es jeder gesehen?; ~ else alle anderen; ~ knows ~ else round here hier kennt jeder jeden; he asked ~ to be quiet er bat alle um Ruhe; hello, ~! (coll.) Tag, zusammen! (ugs.); would ~ be quiet please? würden Sie bitte alle ruhig sein?; it's not ~ who can ...: nicht jeder kann ...; it's ~'s duty es ist jedermanns Pflicht; jeder[mann] ist verpflichtet; opera isn't [to] ~'s taste Oper ist nicht jedermanns Sache; holidays to suit ~'s purse Urlaub für jeden Geldbeutel; see also anybody 3

'everyday attrib. adj. alltäglich; Alltags‹kleidung, -sprache›; routinemäßig ‹Geschäftsführung›; in ~ life im Alltag; im täglichen Leben; an ~ story of country folk eine Geschichte über den Alltag der Leute vom Lande; ~ reality der Alltag; ~ expressions Ausdrücke der Alltagssprache; it is a matter of ~ knowledge that ... jedermann weiß, dass ...

'Everyman n., no pl. der Durchschnittsbürger; [Herr] Jedermann (veralt.)

everyone /'evrɪwʌn, 'evrɪwən/ ▸everybody

'everyplace (Amer.) ▸everywhere

'everything n. & pron. [1] alles; ~ [that] you have alles, was du hast; ~ else alles andere; some pupils are good at ~: manche Schüler sind in allen Fächern gut; ~ comes to him who waits (prov.) mit Geduld und Spucke fängt man eine Mucke (ugs.); the man who has ~: der Mann, der schon alles hat; ~ interesting/valuable alles Interessante/Wertvolle; there's a [right] time for ~: alles zu seiner Zeit; they bought the house and ~ in it sie kauften das

Haus mit allem Inventar; **he is ~ a man should be** er hat alle Qualitäten, die ein Mann besitzen sollte **2** (coll.: all that matters) alles; **looks aren't ~:** das Aussehen [allein] ist nicht alles; **her child is ~ to her** das Kind ist ihr Ein und Alles; **have ~:** [einfach] alles haben

'everyway *adv.* in jeder Beziehung

'everywhere

A *adv.* **1** (in every place) überall **2** (to every place) **go ~:** überall hingehen/-fahren; **~ you go/look** wohin man auch geht/sieht

B *n.* **from ~:** überallher; von überall [her]; **~ is quiet in Holland on a Sunday** überall in Holland ist es sonntags ruhig

evict /ɪ'vɪkt/ *v.t.* exmittieren (Rechtsspr.); **~ a family [from the house]** eine Familie zur Räumung [des Hauses] zwingen

eviction /ɪ'vɪkʃn/ *n.* Zwangsräumung, *die;* Exmission, *die* (Rechtsspr.); **the ~ of the tenant** die zwangsweise Vertreibung des Mieters [aus seiner Wohnung]; **action for ~** (Law) Räumungsklage, *die;* **~ order** (Law) Räumungsbefehl, *der*

evidence /'evɪdəns/

A *n.* **1** Beweis, *der;* (indication) Anzeichen, *das;* Beweis, *der;* **be ~ of sth.** etw. beweisen; **provide ~ of sth.** den Beweis *od.* Beweise für etw. liefern; **as ~ of sth.** als *od.* zum Beweis für etw.; **we do not have any ~ for this** wir haben nicht einen einzigen Beweis *od.* keinerlei Anhaltspunkte dafür; **there was no ~ of a fight** nichts deutete auf einen Kampf hin; **give ~ of having been damaged** offensichtlich beschädigt worden sein; **hard ~:** durchschlagende Beweise; *see also* **external A 6**; **internal evidence** **2** (Law) Beweismaterial, *das;* (object) Beweisstück, *das;* (testimony) [Zeugen]aussage, *die;* **give ~:** [als Zeuge] aussagen; **give ~ under oath/for sb./against sb.** unter Eid/für jmdn./gegen jmdn. aussagen; **refuse to give ~:** die Aussage verweigern; **hear** *or* **take ~:** Zeugen vernehmen; **hearing** *or* **taking of ~:** Beweisaufnahme, *die;* **because of insufficient ~:** aus Mangel an Beweisen; mangels Beweisen (Amtsspr.); **piece of ~:** Beweisstück, *das;* (statement) Beweis, *der;* **incriminating ~:** Belastungsmaterial, *das;* **[turn] King's/Queen's ~** (Brit.) *or* (Amer.) **State's ~:** [als] Kronzeuge [auftreten]; **the witness said in ~ that ...:** der Zeuge sagte aus, dass ...; **call sb. in ~:** jmdn. als Zeugen benennen *od.* anrufen; **submit sth. in ~:** etw. als Beweis vorlegen; *see also* **circumstantial 1**; **presumptive** **3** **be [much] in ~:** [stark] in Erscheinung treten; **he was nowhere in ~:** er war nirgends zu sehen; **sth. is very much in ~:** überall sieht man etw.

B *v.t.* zeugen von

evident /'evɪdənt/ *adj.* offensichtlich; deutlich ‹*Verbesserung*›; **the effect is still ~:** die Wirkung ist [immer] noch deutlich sichtbar; **be ~ to sb.** jmdm. klar sein; **it soon became ~ that ...:** es stellte sich bald heraus, dass ...

evidently /'evɪdəntlɪ/ *adv.* offensichtlich

evil /'i:vl, 'i:vɪl/

A *adj.* **1** böse; schlecht ‹*Charakter, Beispiel, Einfluss, System*›; übel, verwerflich ‹*Praktiken*›; **with ~ intent** in *od.* aus böser Absicht; **the E~ One** der Böse; **~ doings** Missetaten *Pl.;* **~ tongue** böse Zunge; Lästerzunge, *die* (abwertend); **the ~ eye** der böse Blick **2** (unlucky) verhängnisvoll, unglückselig ‹*Tag, Stunde*›; böse, schlecht ‹*Zeichen*›; schwer, schlimm ‹*Schicksal*›; **~ days** *or* **times** schlechte *od.* schlimme Zeiten; **put off** *or* **postpone the ~ hour** das Unvermeidliche hinauszögern; **fall on ~ days** ins Unglück geraten **3** (disagreeable) übel ‹*Geruch, Geschmack*›; (coll.: unattractive) mies (ugs.) ‹*Kneipe, Wetter*›

B *n.* **1** *no pl.* (literary) Böse, *das;* **the root of all ~:** die Wurzel allen Übels; **deliver us from ~** (Relig.) erlöse uns von dem Übel (bibl.); **he saw the ~ of his ways** er erkannte, dass er auf dem Pfad der Sünde wandelte (geh.); **speak ~ of sb.** schlecht über jmdn. reden; **do ~:** Böses tun; sündigen **2** (bad thing) Übel, *das;* **necessary** *or* **inescapable ~:** notwendiges Übel; **social ~s** soziale Missstände; **the lesser ~:** das kleinere Übel; **choose the lesser of two ~s** von zwei Übeln das kleinere wählen

evil: ~doer /'i:vldu:ə(r)/ *n.* Übeltäter, *der*/-täterin, *die;* **~-'minded** *adj.* bösartig; böswillig; **~-smelling** *adj.* übel riechend; **~-tasting** *adj.* widerlich schmeckend

evince /ɪ'vɪns/ *v.t.* ‹*Person:*› an den Tag legen; ‹*Äußerung, Handlung:*› zeugen von

eviscerate /ɪ'vɪsəreɪt/ *v.t.* ausweiden ‹*Wild*›; ausnehmen ‹*Geflügel, Fisch*›; (fig.) der Substanz berauben

evocation /evə'keɪʃn/ *n.* Heraufbeschwören, *das;* Evokation, *die* (geh.); **the film is an ~ of Edwardian England** in dem Film lebt das England unter Edward VII. noch einmal auf

evocative /ɪ'vɒkətɪv/ *adj.* evokativ (geh.); (thought-provoking) aufrüttelnd (fig.); **be ~ of sth.** an etw. (*Akk.*) erinnern; etw. heraufbeschwören; **an ~ scent** ein Duft, der Erinnerungen weckt

evoke /ɪ'vəʊk/ *v.t.* hervorrufen ‹*Bewunderung, Überraschung, Wirkung*›; erregen ‹*Interesse*›

evolution /i:və'lu:ʃn, evə'lu:ʃn/ *n.* **1** (development) Entwicklung, *die* **2** (Biol.: of species etc.) Evolution, *die;* **theory of ~:** Evolutionstheorie, *die* **3** (Mil., Naut.) Formierung, *die;* Evolution, *die* (veralt.); (Dancing etc.) Figur, *die;* Evolution, *die* (veralt.) **4** (of heat, gas, etc.) Entstehung, *die*

evolutionary /i:və'lu:ʃənərɪ, evə'lu:ʃənərɪ/ *adj.* **1** evolutionär; sich [langsam] entwickelnd; **the ~ process** der Entwicklungsprozess **2** (Biol.) evolutionär; **~ theory** Evolutionstheorie, *die*

evolutionism /i:və'lu:ʃənɪzm, evə'lu:ʃənɪzm/ *n., no pl.* Evolutionismus, *der*

evolutionist /i:və'lu:ʃənɪst, evə'lu:ʃənɪst/ *n.* Evolutionist, *der*/Evolutionistin, *die*

evolve /ɪ'vɒlv/

A *v.i.* **1** (develop) sich entwickeln (**from** aus) **2** (Biol.) sich entwickeln (**into** zu); **~ out of** entstehen aus; sich entwickeln aus

B *v.t.* **1** entwickeln **2** (Biol.) entwickeln ‹*Art usw.*› (**from** aus)

ewe /ju:/ *n.* Mutterschaf, *das*

ewer /'ju:ə(r)/ *n.* [Wasch]krug, *der*

ex[1] /eks/ *n.* (coll.) Verflossene, *der/die* (ugs.)

ex[2] *prep.* **1** (Commerc.) **ex works/store** ‹*Güter*› ab Werk/Lager **2** (Finance) ohne

ex- *pref.* Ex-‹*Freundin, Präsident, Champion*›; Alt-‹*[bundes]kanzler, -bundespräsident, -bürgermeister*›; ehemalig

exacerbate /ek'sæsəbeɪt/ *v.t.* verschlimmern ‹*Schmerz, Krankheit, Wut*›; steigern ‹*Unzufriedenheit, Feindschaft*›; verschlechtern ‹*Zustand*›; verschärfen ‹*Lage*›

exact /ɪg'zækt/

A *adj.* **1** genau; exakt, genau ‹*Daten, Berechnung*›; **those were his ~ words** das waren genau seine Worte; **an ~ copy of the painting/inscription** eine perfekte Kopie des Gemäldes/eine wortgetreue Wiedergabe der Inschrift; **on the ~ spot where ...:** genau an der Stelle, wo ...; **could you give me the ~ money?** könnten Sie mir das Geld passend geben?; **11 to be ~:** 11, um genau zu sein; **be ~ in one's work** es mit der Arbeit genau nehmen **2** (rigorous) streng **3** **~ science** exakte Wissenschaft

B *v.t.* **1** fordern, verlangen; erheben ‹*Gebühr, Zoll*›; **~ from sb. a promise of sth.** von jmdm. verlangen, dass er etw. verspricht **2** (call for) ‹*Sache:*› erfordern, verlangen

exacting /ɪg'zæktɪŋ/ *adj.* anspruchsvoll; streng ‹*Prüfer, Lehrer, Maßstab*›; hoch ‹*Anforderung, Maßstab*›; **be very ~ about punctuality** großen Wert auf Pünktlichkeit legen

exaction /ɪg'zækʃn/ *n.* Forderung, *die* (**of** nach)

exactitude /ɪg'zæktɪtju:d/ *n., no pl.* Genauigkeit, *die;* **with complete ~:** mit letzter Genauigkeit

exactly /ɪg'zæktlɪ/ *adv.* **1** genau; **when ~** *or* **~ when did he leave?** wann genau ging er?; wann ging er genau?; **~ what happened we'll never know** was genau geschehen ist, werden wir nie erfahren; **at ~ the right moment** genau im richtigen Moment; **~!** genau!; **~ a year ago today** heute vor genau einem Jahr; **I'm not ~ sure** ich bin nicht ganz sicher; **at four o'clock ~:** Punkt vier Uhr; **~ as** genau [so] wie; **~ as you wish** ganz wie du willst; **not ~** (coll. iron.) nicht gerade; **I'll tell her ~ what I think of her** ich werde ihr ganz genau sagen, was ich von ihr halte **2** (with perfect accuracy) [ganz] genau; **so ~:** mit solcher Genauigkeit

exactness /ɪg'zæktnɪs/ *n., no pl.* Genauigkeit, *die;* **doubt the ~ of the figure** bezweifeln, dass die Zahl genau stimmt

exaggerate /ɪg'zædʒəreɪt/ *v.t.* **1** übertreiben; **you are exaggerating his importance/its worth** du machst ihn wichtiger, als er ist/so wertvoll ist es nun auch wieder nicht; **the story had been grossly ~d** die Sache war gewaltig aufgebauscht worden (abwertend); **you always ~:** du musst immer übertreiben **2** (accentuate) unterstreichen; betonen

exaggerated /ɪg'zædʒəreɪtɪd/ *adj.* übertrieben; **grossly** *or* **highly ~:** stark übertrieben; **he has an ~ opinion of himself** er hat eine übertrieben hohe Meinung von sich selbst

exaggeratedly /ɪg'zædʒəreɪtɪdlɪ/ *adv.* übertrieben

exaggeration /ɪgzædʒə'reɪʃn/ *n.* Übertreibung, *die;* **it is a wild/is no ~ to say that ...:** es ist stark/nicht übertrieben, wenn man sagt, dass ...; **no ~!** ohne Übertreibung!; **he's prone to ~:** er übertreibt gern; **that, of course, is an ~:** das ist natürlich übertrieben; **that's a bit of an** *or* **a slight ~:** das ist leicht übertrieben

exalt /ɪg'zɔ:lt/ *v.t.* **1** (praise) [lob]preisen; **~ sb. to the skies** jmdn. in den Himmel heben (ugs.) **2** (raise in rank or power) erheben; (raise in estimation) hoch achten

exaltation /egzɔ:l'teɪʃn, eksɔ:l'teɪʃn/ *n.* **1** (fig.: elevation) Erhebung, *die* **2** (elation) Begeisterung, *die*

exalted /ɪg'zɔ:ltɪd/ *adj.* **1** (high-ranking) hoch; **those in ~ positions** hoch gestellte Persönlichkeiten **2** (lofty, sublime) hoch ‹*Ideal*›; erhaben ‹*Thema, Stil, Stimmung, Gedanke*›

exam /ɪg'zæm/ (coll.) ▸ **examination 3**

examination /ɪgzæmɪ'neɪʃn/ *n.* **1** (inspection) Untersuchung, *die;* (of accounts) [Über]prüfung, *die;* **on ~ it was found to contain drugs** die Untersuchung ergab, dass es Drogen enthielt; **on closer** *or* **further ~:** bei genauerer *od.* näherer Untersuchung *od.* Überprüfung; **be under ~:** untersucht *od.* überprüft werden; **give sth. a thorough ~:** etw. gründlich untersuchen *od.* überprüfen; **carry out an ~ of sth./into sth.** etw. untersuchen *od.* überprüfen/eine Untersuchung über etw. (*Akk.*) anstellen *od.* durchführen **2** (Med.) Untersuchung, *die;* **give sb. a thorough ~:** jmdn. gründlich untersuchen; **undergo an ~:** sich untersuchen lassen **3** (test of knowledge or ability) Prüfung, *die;* (final ~ at university) Examen, *das; attrib.* Prüfungs-/Examens-; **~ nerves** Prüfungsangst, *die* **4** (Law) (of witness, accused) Verhör, *das;* Vernehmung, *die;* (of case) Untersuchung, *die;* **he is still under ~:** er wird noch verhört *od.* vernommen; **be subjected to ~:** einem Verhör *od.* einer Vernehmung unterzogen werden

examination: ~ board *n.* Prüfungsgremium, *das;* Prüfungskommission, *die;* **~ paper** *n.* **1** **~ paper[s]** schriftliche Prüfungsaufgaben; **2** (with candidate's answers) ≈ Klausurarbeit, *die*

examine /ɪg'zæmɪn/ *v.t.* **1** (inspect) untersuchen (**for** auf + *Akk.*); prüfen ‹*Dokument, Gewissen, Gefühle, Geschäftsbücher*›; kontrollieren ‹*Ausweis, Gepäck*› **2** (Med.) untersuchen **3** (test knowledge or ability of) prüfen (**in** in + *Dat.*); **~ sb. on his knowledge of French** jmds. Französischkenntnisse prüfen **4** (Law) verhören; vernehmen

examinee /ɪgzæmɪ'ni:/ *n.* Prüfungskandidat, *der*/-kandidatin, *die;* Prüfling, *der;* (Univ. also) Examenskandidat, *der*/-kandidatin, *die;* (to qualify for higher education also) Abiturient, *der*/Abiturientin, *die*

examiner /ɪg'zæmɪnə(r)/ *n.* Prüfer, *der*/Prüferin, *die;* **board of ~s** Prüfungsausschuss, *der*

examining body /ɪg'zæmɪnɪŋ bɒdɪ/ *n.* ≈ Prüfungsamt, *das*

example /ɪg'zɑːmpl/ *n.* **1** Beispiel, *das;* **by way of [an] ~:** als Beispiel; **she is a perfect ~ of how ...:** sie ist das beste Beispiel dafür, wie ...; **take sth. as an ~:** etw. zum Beispiel nehmen; **just to give [you] an** *or* **one ~:** um [dir] nur ein Beispiel zu nennen; **for ~:** zum Beispiel; **she's an ~ to us all** sie gibt uns (*Dat.*) allen ein Beispiel; **set an ~** *or* **a good ~ to sb.** jmdm. ein Beispiel geben; **follow sb.'s ~ [in doing sth.]** sich (*Dat.*) an jmdm. ein Beispiel nehmen [und etw. tun]; (in a particular action) jmds. Beispiel folgen **2** (as warning) [abschreckendes] Beispiel; **make an ~ of sb.** ein Exempel an jmdm. statuieren; **punish sb. as an ~ to others** jmdn. exemplarisch bestrafen; **let that be an ~ to you** lass dir das eine Lehre sein

exasperate /ɪg'zæspəreɪt, ɪg'zɑːspəreɪt/ *v.t.* (irritate) verärgern; (infuriate) zur Verzweiflung bringen; **be ~d at** *or* **by sb./sth.** über jmdn./etw. verärgert/verzweifelt sein; **feel ~d** verärgert/verzweifelt sein; **become** *or* **get ~d [with sb.]** sich [über jmdn.] ärgern

exasperating /ɪg'zæspəreɪtɪŋ, ɪg'zɑːspəreɪtɪŋ/ *adj.* ärgerlich; ‹*Aufgabe*› die einen zur Verzweiflung bringt; **be ~:** einen zur Verzweiflung bringen

exasperatingly /ɪg'zæspəreɪtɪŋlɪ, ɪg'zɑːspəreɪtɪŋlɪ/ *adv.* zum Verzweifeln

exasperation /ɪgzæspə'reɪʃn, ɪgzɑːspə'reɪʃn/ *n.* ▸**exasperate**: Ärger, *der*/Verzweiflung, *die* (**with** über + *Akk.*); **in ~:** verärgert/verzweifelt

excavate /'ekskəveɪt/ *v.t.* **1** ausschachten; (with machine) ausbaggern; fördern, abbauen ‹*Erz, Metall*› **2** (Archaeol.) ausgraben; *abs.* Ausgrabungen vornehmen

excavation /ekskə'veɪʃn/ *n.* **1** Ausschachtung, *die;* (with machine) Ausbaggerung, *die;* (of ore, metals) Förderung, *die;* Abbau, *der* **2** (Archaeol.) Ausgrabung, *die;* **~ work** Ausgrabungsarbeiten *Pl.* **3** (place) [Bau]grube, *die;* (Archaeol.) Ausgrabungsstätte, *die*

excavator /'ekskəveɪtə(r)/ *n.* **1** (machine) Bagger, *der* **2** (Archaeol.: person) Ausgräber, *der*/Ausgräberin, *die*

exceed /ɪk'siːd/ *v.t.* **1** (be greater than) übertreffen (**in** an + *Dat.*); ‹*Kosten, Summe, Anzahl:*› übersteigen (**by** um); **not ~ing** bis zu **2** (go beyond) überschreiten; hinausgehen über (+ *Akk.*) ‹*Auftrag, Befehl*›; (surpass) übertreffen (**in** an + *Dat.*)

exceedingly /ɪk'siːdɪŋlɪ/ *adv.* äußerst; ausgesprochen ‹*hässlich, dumm*›; **fit ~ well** ausgezeichnet passen; **a joke in ~ bad taste** ein ausgesprochen geschmackloser Witz; **it was ~ obvious that she was pregnant** es war überdeutlich zu sehen, dass sie schwanger war

excel /ɪk'sel/

A *v.t.*, **-ll-** übertreffen; **~ oneself** (lit. or iron.) sich selbst übertreffen

B *v.i.*, **-ll-** sich hervortun (**at, in** in + *Dat.*); **~ as an orator** ein hervorragender Redner sein; **she ~s at cookery** sie ist eine glänzende Köchin

excellence /'eksələns/ *n.* hervorragende Qualität; (merit) hervorragende Leistung; **an unusual degree of ~:** eine außergewöhnlich hohe Qualitätsstufe/ein außergewöhnlich hohes Leistungsniveau; **moral/academic ~:** höchster moralischer/wissenschaftlicher Rang; **this school is known for its standards of ~:** diese Schule ist für ihr außerordentlich hohes Niveau bekannt

Excellency /'eksələnsɪ/ *n.* **His/Her ~:** Seine/Ihre Exzellenz

excellent /'eksələnt/ *adj.* ausgezeichnet; hervorragend; exzellent (geh.); vorzüglich ‹*Wein, Koch, Speise*›; **be in an ~ mood** bester Laune sein; **he's an ~ chap** er ist ein Prachtkerl (ugs.)

excellently /'eksələntlɪ/ *adv.* ausgezeichnet; hervorragend; exzellent (geh.)

except /ɪk'sept/

A *prep.* **~ [for]** außer (+ *Dat.*); **~ for** (in all respects other than) bis auf (+ *Akk.*); abgesehen von; **~ [for the fact] that ...,** (coll.) **~ ...:** abgesehen davon, dass ...; **I know little of her ~ that she ...** *or* (coll.) **~ she ...:** ich weiß wenig über sie, nur dass sie ...; **I should buy a new car ~ that** *or* (coll.) **~ I've no money** ich würde mir ein neues Auto kaufen, ich habe nur kein Geld; **I'd come, ~ that** *or* (coll.) **~ I have no time** ich würde kommen, doch ich habe keine Zeit; **there was nothing to be done ~ [to] stay there** man konnte nichts anderes tun als dableiben; **where could he be ~ in the house?** wo könnte er [denn] sonst sein, wenn nicht im Haus?; **she's everywhere ~ where she ought to be** sie ist überall, nur nicht da, wo sie sein soll

B *v.t.* ausnehmen (**from** bei); **~ed** ausgenommen; **nobody ~ed** alle ohne Ausnahme; **errors ~ed** Irrtümer vorbehalten; **present company ~ed** Anwesende ausgenommen

excepting /ɪk'septɪŋ/ *prep.* außer (+ *Dat.*); **not ~ Peter** Peter nicht ausgenommen; **~ that ...,** (coll.) **~ ...:** abgesehen davon, dass ...

exception /ɪk'sepʃn/ *n.* **1** Ausnahme, *die;* **with the ~ of** mit Ausnahme (+ *Gen.*); **with the ~ of her/myself** mit Ausnahme von ihr/mir; **the ~ proves the rule** (prov.) Ausnahmen bestätigen die Regel; **this case is an ~ to the rule** dieser Fall ist die Ausnahme von der Regel; **be no ~ [to the rule]** durchaus keine Ausnahme sein; **there's an ~ to every rule** keine Regel ohne Ausnahme; **make an ~ [of/for sb.]** [bei jmdm.] eine Ausnahme machen; **by way of an ~:** ausnahmsweise **2** *no pl., no art.* **take ~ to sth.** (be offended by sth., object to sth.) an etw. (*Dat.*) Anstoß nehmen; **great ~ is taken to sth.** etw. erregt großen Unwillen

exceptional /ɪk'sepʃənl/ *adj.* außergewöhnlich; **in ~ cases** in Ausnahmefällen

exceptionally /ɪk'sepʃənəlɪ/ *adv.* **1** (as an exception) ausnahmsweise **2** (remarkably) ungewöhnlich; außergewöhnlich

excerpt

A /'eksɜːpt/ *n.* Auszug, *der* (**from, of** aus); (from book also) Exzerpt, *das* (geh.); (from film, speech) Ausschnitt, *der;* (from record) Stück, *das*

B /ɪk'sɜːpt/ *v.t.* exzerpieren (geh.) (**from** aus)

excess /ɪk'ses/ *n.* **1** (inordinate degree or amount) Übermaß, *das* (**of** an + *Dat.*); **such ~ of detail** ein solches Übermaß an Details; **eat/drink/be generous to ~:** übermäßig essen/trinken/großzügig sein; **don't do anything to ~:** man soll nichts übertreiben; **carry sth. to ~:** etw. bis zum Exzess treiben; **in ~:** im Übermaß **2** *esp. in pl.* (act of immoderation, over-indulgence) Exzess, *der;* (sexual or gluttonous also) Ausschweifung, *die;* (savage also) Ausschreitung, *die* **3** **be in ~ of sth.** etw. übersteigen; **a figure in ~ of a million** eine Zahl von über einer Million; **a speed in ~ of ...:** eine Geschwindigkeit von mehr als ... **4** (surplus) Überschuss, *der;* **produce an ~ of sth.** einen Überschuss an etw. (*Dat.*) produzieren; **~ weight** Übergewicht, *das* **5** (esp. Brit. Insurance) Selbstbeteiligung, *die;* Selbstbehalt, *der* (fachspr.)

excess /'ekses/: **~ 'baggage** *n.* Mehrgepäck, *das;* **~ 'fare** *n.* Mehrpreis, *der;* **pay the ~ fare** nachlösen

excessive /ɪk'sesɪv/ *adj.* übermäßig; exzessiv; übertrieben ‹*Forderung, Lob, Ansprüche*›; zu stark ‹*Schmerz, Belastung*›; unmäßig ‹*Esser, Trinker*›; **~ drinking of alcohol** übermäßiger Alkoholgenuss; **an ~ talker/eater** ein Schwätzer (abwertend)/Vielfraß (ugs.); **sb. is being rather ~:** jmd. ist ziemlich extrem

excessively /ɪk'sesɪvlɪ/ *adv.* **1** (immoderately) übertrieben; exzessiv; unmäßig ‹*essen, trinken*›; **~ cautious** übervorsichtig; **talk/spend ~:** [all]zu viel reden/ausgeben **2** (exceedingly) ausgesprochen

excess /'ekses/: **~ 'luggage** ▸**~ baggage**; **~ 'postage** *n.* Nachgebühr, *die*

exchange /ɪks'tʃeɪndʒ/

A *v.t.* **1** tauschen ‹*Plätze, Zimmer, Ringe, Küsse*›; umtauschen, wechseln ‹*Geld*›; austauschen ‹*Adressen, [Kriegs]gefangene, Erinnerungen, Gedanken, Erfahrungen*›; wechseln ‹*Blicke, Worte, Ringe*›; **[no] shots were ~d** es fand [k]ein Schusswechsel statt; **the two men ~d letters** die beiden Männer führten einen Briefwechsel; **~ blows/insults** sich schlagen/sich gegenseitig beleidigen **2** (give in place of another) eintauschen (**for** für, gegen); umtauschen ‹*[gekaufte] Ware*› (**for** gegen); austauschen ‹*Spion*› (**for** gegen); (interchange) austauschen (**for** gegen)

B *v.i.* tauschen

C *n.* **1** Tausch, *der;* (of prisoners, spies, compliments, greetings, insults) Austausch, *der;* **an ~ of ideas/blows** ein Meinungsaustausch/Handgreiflichkeiten *Pl.*; **in ~:** dafür; **in ~ for sth.** für etw.; **fair ~ is no robbery** (prov.; joc./iron.) so kann jeder zufrieden sein (scherzh./iron.) **2** (Educ.) Austausch, *der;* **an ~ of pupils** ein Schüleraustausch; **an ~ student** ein Austauschstudent/eine Austauschstudentin; **the pupils are going on [an] ~ to Paris** die Schüler fahren im Rahmen eines Austauschprogramms nach Paris **3** (quarrel) Wortwechsel, *der* **4** (of money) Umtausch, *der;* **bill of ~:** Wechsel, *der;* Tratte, *die* (Bankw.); **~ [rate], rate of ~:** Wechsel- *od.* Umrechnungskurs, *der* **5** ▸**telephone exchange** **6** (Commerc.: building) Börse, *die*

exchangeable /ɪks'tʃeɪndʒəbl/ *adj.* austauschbar (**for** gegen); **these goods are not ~:** diese Waren sind vom Umtausch ausgeschlossen

exchequer /ɪks'tʃekə(r)/ *n.* **1** (Brit.) Schatzamt, *das;* Finanzministerium, *das; see also* **chancellor 1** **2** (royal or national treasury) Staatsschatz, *der*

excise[1] /'eksaɪz/ *n.* Verbrauchsteuer, *die;* **Customs and E~ Department** (Brit.) *Amt für Zölle und Verbrauchsteuern*

excise[2] /ɪk'saɪz/ *v.t.* **1** (from book, article) entfernen (**from** aus); (from film also) herausschneiden (**from** aus) **2** (Med.) entfernen; exzidieren (fachspr.)

excision /ɪk'sɪʒn/ *n.* **1** Entfernung, *die* (**from** aus) **2** (Med.) Entfernung, *die;* Exzision, *die* (fachspr.)

excitable /ɪk'saɪtəbl/ *adj.* leicht erregbar; **have an ~ temper** reizbar sein

excite /ɪk'saɪt/ *v.t.* **1** (thrill) begeistern; **she was/became ~d by the idea** die Idee begeisterte sie; **it greatly ~d the children** es machte die Kinder ganz aufgeregt **2** (agitate) aufregen; **be/become ~d by sth.** sich über etw. (*Akk.*) aufregen *od.* erregen **3** (elicit) erregen **4** (stimulate; also Physiol.) anregen; (sexually) erregen **5** (provoke) aufstacheln (**to** zu)

excited /ɪk'saɪtɪd/ *adj.* **1** (thrilled) aufgeregt (**at** über + *Akk.*); **you don't seem very ~ [about it]** du scheinst [davon] nicht sehr begeistert zu sein; **I'm ~ to see what happens next** ich bin gespannt, was als Nächstes geschieht; **it's nothing to get ~ about** es ist nichts Besonderes; **don't get ~:** sei nicht gleich so aufgeregt **2** (agitated) erregt; aufgeregt; **it's nothing to get ~ about** es besteht kein Grund zur Aufregung; **don't get ~, it's only Tom** keine Panik, es ist nur Tom; **don't get so ~:** reg dich nicht so auf; **get all ~** (coll.) sich furchtbar aufregen (ugs.) **3** (Physiol.) angeregt; (sexually) erregt

excitedly /ɪk'saɪtɪdlɪ/ *adv.* aufgeregt; gespannt ‹*warten*›; **look forward ~ to the holidays** den Ferien entgegenfiebern

excitement /ɪk'saɪtmənt/ *n.* **1** *no pl.* Aufregung, *die;* (enthusiasm) Begeisterung, *die;* (suspense) Spannung, *die;* **in [a state of] ~:** aufgeregt; **in all the ~/in his ~ he forgot to say thank you** in der Aufregung vergaß er, sich zu bedanken; **full of ~:** ganz aufgeregt; **wild with ~:** wie toll vor Aufregung *od.* Erregung **2** (incident) Aufregung, *die* **3** (Physiol.: sexual) Erregung, *die*

exciting /ɪk'saɪtɪŋ/ *adj.* aufregend; (full of suspense) spannend; **it isn't exactly ~:** es ist nicht gerade berauschend (ugs.)

exclaim /ɪk'skleɪm/

A *v.t.* ausrufen; **~ that ...:** rufen, dass ...

B *v.i.* aufschreien; **~ in delight** vor Freude aufschreien

e

exclamation /ekskləˈmeɪʃn/ *n.* Ausruf, *der;* **utter an ~ of pain/delight** vor Schmerz aufschreien/einen Freudenschrei ausstoßen

exclamation: ~ mark, (Amer.) **~ point** *ns.* Ausrufezeichen, *das*

exclude /ɪkˈskluːd/ *v.t.* **1** (keep out, debar) ausschließen (**from** von); **sb. is ~d from a profession/the Church/a room** jmdm. ist die Ausübung eines Berufes/die Zugehörigkeit zur Kirche/der Zutritt zu einem Raum verwehrt; **the public were ~d from the courtroom** die Verhandlung fand unter Ausschluss der Öffentlichkeit statt; **~ noise/draughts from a room** Lärm von einem Zimmer fernhalten/ein Zimmer gegen Zugluft abdichten; **~ sb. from one's will/the Party** jmdn. im Testament nicht bedenken/aus der Partei ausschließen **2** (make impossible, preclude) ausschließen; **this ~s any [further] question of sth.** damit ist etw. völlig ausgeschlossen **3** (leave out of account) nicht berücksichtigen (**from** bei)

excluding /ɪkˈskluːdɪŋ/ *prep.* **~ drinks/VAT** Getränke ausgenommen/ohne Mehrwertsteuer

exclusion /ɪkˈskluːʒn/ *n.* Ausschluss, *der;* **[talk about sth.] to the ~ of everything else** ausschließlich [über etw. (*Akk.*) sprechen]

exˈclusion order *n.* (Law) Aufenthaltsverbot, *das*

exclusive /ɪkˈskluːsɪv/

A *adj.* **1** (not shared) alleinig ‹*Besitzer, Kontrolle*›; ungeteilt ‹*Aufmerksamkeit*›; einzig ‹*Beschäftigung*›; Allein‹*eigentum*›; (Journ.) Exklusiv‹*bericht, -interview*›; (Fashion) Modell‹*kleid usw.*›; **~ right** Alleinrecht, *das;* (Journ.) Exklusivrecht, *das;* **have ~ rights** die Alleinrechte/Exklusivrechte haben **2** (select, privileged) exklusiv; (unwilling to mix) unnahbar; distanziert **3** (excluding) ausschließlich; **~ of** ohne; **~ of drinks** Getränke ausgenommen; **the price is ~ of postage** Versandkosten sind im Preis nicht inbegriffen; **be mutually ~:** sich gegenseitig ausschließen

B *n.* (Journ.) Exklusivbericht, *der*

exclusively /ɪkˈskluːsɪvlɪ/ *adv.* ausschließlich; (Journ.) exklusiv

exclusiveness /ɪkˈskluːsɪvnɪs/ *n., no pl.* Exklusivität, *die*

exclusivity /eksklu:ˈsɪvɪtɪ/ *n., no pl.* **1** (of product, resort) Exklusivität, *die* **2** (in trading agreements) Exklusivrechte *Pl.;* **~ contract/agreement** Exklusivvertrag, *der;* **grant sb. ~:** jmdm. die Exklusivrechte gewähren

excommunicate /ekskəˈmjuːnɪkeɪt/ *v.t.* (Eccl.) exkommunizieren

excommunication /ekskəmjuːnɪˈkeɪʃn/ *n.* (Eccl.) Exkommunikation, *die*

excoriate /eksˈkɔːrɪeɪt/ *v.t.* (fig.: censure) vernichtend kritisieren

excrement /ˈekskrɪmənt/ *n. in sing. or pl.* Exkremente *Pl.* (bes. Med.); Kot, *der* (geh.)

excrescence /ɪkˈskresəns/ *n.* **1** Auswuchs, *der;* Wucherung, *die;* Exkreszenz, *die* (fachspr.) **2** (fig.) Auswuchs, *der*

excreta /ɪkˈskriːtə/ *n. pl.* Ausscheidungen *Pl.*

excrete /ɪkˈskriːt/ *v.t.* ausscheiden

excretion /ɪkˈskriːʃn/ *n.* Ausscheidung, *die*

excretory /ɪkˈskriːtərɪ/ *adj.* Ausscheidungs-

excruciating /ɪkˈskruːʃɪeɪtɪŋ/ *adj.* unerträglich; qualvoll ‹*Tod*›; quälend ‹*Frage*›; **it is ~:** es ist unerträglich *od.* nicht auszuhalten; **be in ~ pain** unerträgliche Schmerzen haben; **an ~ pun** ≈ ein schlimmer Kalauer

excruciatingly /ɪkˈskruːʃɪeɪtɪŋlɪ/ *adv.* entsetzlich; furchtbar; wahnsinnig ‹*lustig*›

exculpate /ˈekskəlpeɪt/ *v.t.* freisprechen; **he was ~d** seine Unschuld wurde festgestellt; **~ oneself** sich rechtfertigen (**from** gegenüber)

exculpation /ekskəlˈpeɪʃn/ *n., no pl.* Entlastung, *die;* (vindication) Rechtfertigung, *die*

excursion /ɪkˈskɜːʃn/ *n.* **1** Ausflug, *der;* **day ~:** Tagesausflug, *der;* **go on/make an ~:** einen Ausflug machen; **~ rates/fares** Sonderpreis [für Ausflüge] **2** (fig.: digression) Ausflug, *der;* Exkurs, *der* (geh.)

excursionist /ɪkˈskɜːʃənɪst/ *n.* Ausflügler, *der*/Ausflüglerin, *die*

excursion: ~ ticket *n.* Ausflugskarte, *die;* Ausflugsticket, *das;* **~ train** *n.* (Amer.) Sonderzug, *der*

excusable /ɪkˈskjuːzəbl/ *adj.* entschuldbar; verzeihlich

excusably /ɪkˈskuːzəblɪ/ *adv.* verständlicherweise

excuse

A /ɪkˈskjuːz/ *v.t.* **1** ►**i** **p. 908** (forgive, exonerate) entschuldigen; **~ oneself** (apologize) sich entschuldigen; **~ me** Entschuldigung; Verzeihung; **please ~ me** bitte entschuldigen Sie; **~ me[, what did you say]?** (Amer.) Verzeihung[, was haben Sie gesagt]?; **~ me if I don't get up** entschuldigen Sie, wenn ich nicht aufstehe; **~ sth. in sb., ~ sb. sth.** etw. bei jmdm. entschuldigen; **I can be ~d for confusing them** es ist verzeihlich, dass ich sie verwechselt habe; **sb. can be ~d for that** das ist verzeihlich; **acts which nothing can ~:** Taten, die durch nichts zu entschuldigen sind **2** (release, exempt) befreien; **~ sb. [from] sth.** jmdn. von etw. befreien; **they were ~d payment of all taxes** ihnen wurden alle Steuern erlassen; **~ oneself from doing sth.** sich erlauben, etw. nicht zu tun **3** (allow to leave) entschuldigen; **~ oneself** sich entschuldigen; **and now, if I may be ~d** *or* **if you will ~ me** wenn Sie mich jetzt bitte entschuldigen wollen; **you are ~d** ihr könnt gehen; **may I be ~d?** (wishing to leave the table) darf ich aufstehen?; (euphem.: wishing to go to the toilet) darf ich mal verschwinden *od.* austreten?

B /ɪkˈskjuːs/ *n.* **1** Entschuldigung, *die;* **give** *or* **offer an ~ for sth.** sich für etw. entschuldigen; **there is no ~ for what I did** was ich getan habe, ist nicht zu entschuldigen; **what did he give as his ~ this time?** welche Entschuldigung hatte er diesmal?; **I'm not trying to make ~s, but ...:** das soll keine Entschuldigung sein, aber ...; **make one's/sb.'s ~s to sb.** sich/jmdn. bei jmdm. entschuldigen; **any ~ for a drink!** zum Trinken gibt es immer einen Grund; **be as good an ~ as any** ein willkommener Anlass sein **2** (evasive statement) Ausrede, *die;* **make ~s** sich herausreden **3** (pathetic specimen) **this is an ~ for a pencil/letter** *etc.*, **isn't it!** das kann man wohl kaum als Bleistift/Brief *usw.* bezeichnen

ex-diˈrectory *adj.* (Brit. Teleph.) Geheim‹*nummer, -anschluss*›; **famous people are usually ~:** berühmte Leute stehen gewöhnlich nicht im Telefonbuch

ex ˈdividend (Finance) *adv.* abzüglich Dividende

exec /ɪɡˈzek/ *n.* (coll.) ► **executive A 1**

execrable /ˈeksɪkrəbl/ *adj.*, **execrably** /ˈeksɪkrəblɪ/ *adv.* abscheulich

execration /eksɪˈkreɪʃn/ *n.* **1** (act) Fluchen, *das* **2** (curse) Fluch, *der;* Verwünschung, *die* **3** *no pl.* (abhorrence) Abscheu, *der;* **hold sth. in ~:** etw. verabscheuen

executable /ɪɡˈzekjʊtəbl/ *adj.* (Computing) ausführbar

execute /ˈeksɪkjuːt/ *v.t.* **1** (kill) hinrichten; exekutieren (Milit.) **2** (put into effect, perform) ausführen; durchführen ‹*Vorschrift, Gesetz*› **3** (Law: give effect to) vollstrecken; (make legally valid) rechtsgültig machen; unterzeichnen ‹*Urkunde*›

execution /eksɪˈkjuːʃn/ *n.* **1** (killing) Hinrichtung, *die;* Exekution, *die* (Milit.) **2** (putting into effect, performance) Ausführung, *die;* (of instruction, law) Durchführung, *die;* (of will, verdict) Vollstreckung, *die;* **put sth. into ~:** etw. aus- *od.* durchführen/vollstrecken; **in the ~ of one's duty/duties** bei Erfüllung seiner Pflicht; in [treuer] Pflichterfüllung **3** (Mus.) Vortrag, *der* **4** (Law: seizure of property, carrying out) Vollstreckung, *die;* (rendering legally valid) [rechtsgültige] Unterzeichnung

executioner /eksɪˈkjuːʃənə(r)/ *n.* Scharfrichter, *der*

executive /ɪɡˈzekjʊtɪv/

A *n.* **1** (person) leitender Angestellter/leitende Angestellte **2** (administrative body) **the ~** (of government) die Exekutive; (of political organization, trade union) der Vorstand

B *adj.* **1** (Commerc.) leitend ‹*Stellung, Funktion*›; geschäftsführend ‹*Vorsitzende[r]*›; **~ powers** Vollmacht, *die;* (Commerc. Law) Prokura, *die;* **~ ability** Führungsqualitäten *Pl.* **2** (relating to government) exekutiv; **~ powers** Exekutivgewalt, *die*

executive: ~ comˈmittee *n.* [geschäftsführender] Vorstand; **~ ˈcouncil** *n.* Ministerrat, *der;* **~ ˈprivilege** *n., no pl.* (Amer.) *Recht der Regierung, der Öffentlichkeit unter bestimmten Umständen bestimmte Informationen vorzuenthalten;* **~ ˈstress** *n.* Managerstress, *der;* **~ ˈsummary** *n.* Managementsummary, *das;* **~ ˈtoy** *n.* Managerspielzeug, *das*

executor /ɪɡˈzekjʊtə(r)/ *n.* (Law) Testamentsvollstrecker, *der;* **the ~ of his will** sein Testamentsvollstrecker; **literary ~:** Verwalter/Verwalterin des literarischen Nachlasses

exegesis /eksɪˈdʒiːsɪs/ *n., pl.* **exegeses** /eksɪˈdʒiːsiːz/ Auslegung, *die;* Exegese, *die* (auch Theol.)

exemplary /ɪɡˈzemplərɪ/ *adj.* **1** (model) vorbildlich **2** (deterrent) exemplarisch; **~ damages** (Law) Buße, *die* **3** (illustrative) beispielhaft; exemplarisch

exemplification /ɪɡzemplɪfɪˈkeɪʃn/ *n.* Veranschaulichung, *die;* Exemplifikation, *die* (geh.)

exemplify /ɪɡˈzemplɪfaɪ/ *v.t.* veranschaulichen; exemplifizieren (geh.); (serve as example of) als Beispiel dienen für

exempt /ɪɡˈzempt/

A *adj.* **[be] ~ [from sth.]** [von etw.] befreit [sein]; **make sb. ~ from sth.** jmdn. von etw. befreien

B *v.t.* befreien; **be ~ed from sth.** von etw. befreit werden

exemption /ɪɡˈzempʃn/ *n.* Befreiung, *die;* **~ from payment of a fine** Erlass einer Geldstrafe

exercise /ˈeksəsaɪz/

A *n.* **1** *no pl., no indef. art.* (physical exertion) Bewegung, *die;* (of dog also) Auslauf, *der;* (fig.) Training, *das;* **get ~:** Bewegung haben; **take ~:** sich (*Dat.*) Bewegung verschaffen; **provide ~ for sth.** etw. trainieren; eine gute Übung für etw. sein **2** (task set, activity; also Mus., Sch.) Übung, *die;* **the object of the ~:** der Sinn der Übung **3** (to improve fitness) [Gymnastik]übung, *die;* **morning ~s** Morgengymnastik, *die* **4** *no pl.* (employment, application) Ausübung, *die;* **the ~ of tolerance is essential** Toleranz zu üben ist sehr wichtig **5** *usu. in pl.* (Mil.) Übung, *die;* **go on ~s** eine Übung machen **6** *in pl.* (Amer.: ceremony) Feierlichkeiten *Pl*

B *v.t.* **1** ausüben ‹*Recht, Macht, Einfluss*›; walten lassen ‹*Vorsicht*›; **~ restraint/discretion/patience** sich in Zurückhaltung/Diskretion/Geduld üben; **~ one's right of veto** von seinem Vetorecht Gebrauch machen; **~ tact** taktvoll sein; **~ great care** sehr vorsichtig sein **2** (tax the powers of) in Anspruch nehmen; (perplex, worry) beschäftigen; **~ the mind** die geistigen Fähigkeiten herausfordern **3** (physically) trainieren ‹*Körper, Muskeln*›; bewegen ‹*Pferd*› **4** (Mil.) drillen

C *v.i.* sich (*Dat.*) Bewegung verschaffen

exercise: ~ bicycle, (coll.) **~ bike** *ns.* Heimtrainer, *der;* **~ book** *n.* [Schul]heft, *das*

exerciser /ˈeksəsaɪzə(r)/ *n.* (device) Trainingsgerät, *das*

exert /ɪɡˈzɜːt/

A *v.t.* aufbieten ‹*Kraft, Beredsamkeit*›; ausüben ‹*Einfluss, Druck, Macht*›; **~ all one's force on the door** sich mit aller Kraft gegen die Tür stemmen

B *v. refl.* sich anstrengen; **don't ~ yourself** (iron.) überanstrenge dich nur nicht

exertion /ɪɡˈzɜːʃn/ *n.* **1** *no pl.* (exerting) (of strength, force) Aufwendung, *die;* (of influence, pressure, force) Ausübung, *die;* **by the ~ of all sb.'s strength** unter Aufbietung aller Kräfte **2** (effort) Anstrengung, *die;* **by her own ~s she managed ...:** durch eigene Anstrengung gelang es ihr, ...

exeunt /ˈeksɪʌnt/ *v.i.* (Theatre: as stage direction) ab; **~ omnes** /eksɪʌnt ˈɒmniːz/ alle ab

ex gratia /eks 'greɪʃə/ *adj.* freiwillig; ohne Anerkennung einer Rechtspflicht

exhalation /ekshə'leɪʃn/ *n.* 1) (breathing out) Ausatmung, *die;* (of smoke, gas; also Med.) Exhalation, *die* 2) (puff of breath) Atemzug, *der* 3) (gas etc. emitted) exhalierte Dämpfe/Gase

exhale /eks'heɪl/

A *v.t.* 1) (from lungs) ausatmen; exhalieren (Med.) 2) (emit) verströmen ‹*Duft*›; ausstoßen ‹*Rauch, Gas*›

B *v.i.* ausatmen; exhalieren (Med.)

exhaust /ɪg'zɔːst/

A *v.t.* 1) (use up) erschöpfen; erschöpfend behandeln ‹*Thema*›; (try out fully) ausschöpfen; **she ~ed her ideas in her first novel** sie hat den Vorrat ihrer Ideen bereits in ihrem ersten Roman erschöpft 2) (drain of strength, resources, etc.) erschöpfen; **have been ~ed by sth.** von etw. erschöpft sein; **have ~ed oneself** sich völlig verausgabt haben; **this work is ~ing me** diese Arbeit strengt mich sehr an 3) (draw off) herauspumpen; **~ sth. from sth.** etw. aus etw. [heraus]pumpen 4) (empty) auspumpen

B *n.* 1) **~ [system]** Abgasrohr, *das;* (Motor Veh.) Auspuff, *der;* (of train) Abgasleitung, *die* 2) (what is expelled) Abgase *Pl.;* (of car) Auspuffgase *Pl.; attrib.* **~ fumes** Auspuff[ab]gase *Pl.;* **~ emissions** Auspuffemissionen *Pl.;* **~ emissions test** Abgasuntersuchung, *die*

exhausted /ɪg'zɔːstɪd/ *adj.* erschöpft

exhausting /ɪg'zɔːstɪŋ/ *adj.* anstrengend; beschwerlich ‹*Husten*›; ermüdend ‹*Wetter*›; **he is ~ company** *or* **~ to be with** er ist sehr anstrengend

exhaustion /ɪg'zɔːstʃn/ *n., no pl.* Erschöpfung, *die*

exhaustive /ɪg'zɔːstɪv/ *adj.* umfassend

exhaustively /ɪg'zɔːstɪvlɪ/ *adv.* umfassend; **treat a subject ~:** ein Thema erschöpfend *od.* umfassend behandeln

ex'haust pipe *n.* Abzugsrohr, *das;* (of car) Auspuffrohr, *das*

exhibit /ɪg'zɪbɪt/

A *v.t.* 1) (display) vorzeigen; (show publicly) ausstellen; **he has ~ed in London** er hat in London ausgestellt; **~ in court** (Law) dem Gericht vorlegen 2) (manifest) zeigen ‹*Mut, Verachtung, Symptome, Neigung, Angst*›; beweisen ‹*Mut, Können*›

B *n.* 1) Ausstellungsstück, *das* 2) (Law: in court; also fig.) Beweisstück, *das*

exhibition /eksɪ'bɪʃn/ *n.* 1) (public display) Ausstellung, *die;* **~ catalogue** Ausstellungskatalog, *der* 2) (act) Vorführung, *die;* (manifestation) **give an ~ of one's skills** sein Können demonstrieren; **her ~ of grief** die Zurschaustellung ihrer Trauer 3) (derog.) **make an ~ of oneself** sich unmöglich aufführen; **what an ~!** ein unmögliches Benehmen! 4) (Brit. Univ.: scholarship) Stipendium, *das*

exhibitioner /eksɪ'bɪʃənə(r)/ *n.* (Brit. Univ.) Stipendiat, *der*

exhibitionism /eksɪ'bɪʃənɪzm/ *n.* Exhibitionismus, *der*

exhibitionist /eksɪ'bɪʃənɪst/ *n.* Exhibitionist, *der*/Exhibitionistin, *die*

exhibitor /ɪg'zɪbɪtə(r)/ *n.* Aussteller, *der*/Ausstellerin, *die*

exhilarate /ɪg'zɪləreɪt/ *v.t.* erfrischen, beleben; (gladden) fröhlich stimmen; (stimulate) anregen

exhilarated /ɪg'zɪləreɪtɪd/ *adj.* erfrischt; belebt; (gladdened) fröhlich gestimmt; (stimulated) angeregt; **feel ~:** sich erfrischt/angeregt fühlen/fröhlich gestimmt sein

exhilarating /ɪg'zɪləreɪtɪŋ/ *adj.* belebend; fröhlich stimmend ‹*Nachricht, Musik, Anblick*›; **~ feeling** erhebendes Gefühl

exhilaration /ɪgzɪlə'reɪʃn/ *n.* **[feeling of] ~:** Hochgefühl, *das;* **the ~ of hang-gliding** das Hochgefühl beim Drachenfliegen

exhort /ɪg'zɔːt/ *v.t.* **~ sb. to do sth.** jmdn. [ernsthaft] ermahnen, etw. zu tun

exhortation /eksɔː'teɪʃn/ *n.* 1) (exhorting) Ermahnung, *die* 2) (formal address) Appell, *der;* Exhortation, *die* (kath. Rel.)

exhumation /eksjʊ'meɪʃn/ *n.* Exhumierung, *die*

exhume /ɪg'zjuːm/ *v.t.* exhumieren; (fig.) ausgraben

exigence /'eksɪdʒəns/, **exigency** /'eksɪdʒənsɪ/ *n.* 1) *usu. in pl.* (urgent demand) Erfordernis, *das* 2) (emergency) Notlage, *die;* (Polit. also) Krisensituation, *die* 3) (urgency) Dringlichkeit, *die*

exigent /'eksɪdʒənt/ *adj.* 1) (exacting) anspruchsvoll 2) (urgent) dringend ‹*Fall, Lage*›; zwingend ‹*Grund, Notwendigkeit, Umstand*›

exiguous /eg'zɪgjʊəs/ *adj.* gering; schmal (geh.) ‹*Gehalt, Budget*›; dürftig ‹*Kost*›

exile /'eksaɪl, 'egzaɪl/

A *n.* 1) Exil, *das;* (forcible also) Verbannung, *die* (**from** aus); **order sb.'s ~:** jmdn. ins Exil schicken; **live/be in ~:** im Exil leben/sein; **go into ~:** ins Exil gehen; **internal ~:** Verbannung, *die* (*an einen Ort innerhalb des eigenen Landes*); **the E~** (Jewish Hist.) die Babylonische Gefangenschaft 2) (exiled person, lit. or fig.) Verbannte, *der/die;* Exilierte, *der/die* (geh.)

B *v.t.* verbannen; exilieren (geh.); **~d Russian** Exilrusse, *der/*-russin, *die*

exist /ɪg'zɪst/ *v.i.* 1) (be in existence) existieren; ‹*Zweifel, Gefahr, Problem, Zusammenarbeit, Brauch, Einrichtung:*› bestehen; **ever since records have ~ed ...:** seit es Aufzeichnungen gibt, ...; **fairies do ~:** es gibt Feen; **the biggest book that has ever ~ed** das größte Buch, das es je gegeben hat; **the conditions that ~ in the Third World** die Bedingungen, die man in der Dritten Welt vorfindet; **does life ~ on Venus?** gibt es Leben auf der Venus? 2) (survive) existieren; überleben; **~ on sth.** von etw. leben 3) (be found) **sth. ~s only in Europe** es gibt etw. nur in Europa

existence /ɪg'zɪstəns/ *n.* 1) (existing) Existenz, *die;* **doubt sb.'s ~/the ~ of sth.** bezweifeln, dass es jmdn./etw. gibt; **the continued ~ of this tradition** das Fortbestehen dieser Tradition; **be in ~:** existieren; **the only such plant [which is] in ~:** die einzige Pflanze dieser Art, die es gibt; **come into ~:** entstehen; **bring sth. into ~:** etw. einführen; **go out of ~:** verschwinden 2) (mode of living) Dasein, *das;* (survival) Existenz, *die;* **struggle for ~:** Existenzkampf, *der;* **means of ~:** Existenzgrundlage, *die*

existent /ɪg'zɪstənt/ ▸ **existing**

existential /egzɪ'stenʃl/ *adj.* existenziell

existentialism /egzɪ'stenʃəlɪzm/ *n., no pl.* (Philos.) Existenzialismus, *der*

existentialist /egzɪ'stenʃəlɪst/ *n.* (Philos.) Existenzialist, *der*/Existenzialistin, *die; attrib.* existenzialistisch

existing /ɪg'zɪstɪŋ/ *adj.* existierend; (present) bestehend ‹*Ordnung, Schwierigkeiten*›; gegenwärtig ‹*Lage, Führung, Stand der Dinge*›

exit /'eksɪt/

A *n.* 1) (way out) Ausgang, *der* (**from** aus); (from drive, motorway) Ausfahrt, *die* 2) (from stage) Abgang, *der;* **make one's ~:** abgehen 3) (from room) Hinausgehen, *das;* (from group) Weggehen, *das;* **make a speedy ~:** schnell hinausgehen/weggehen; **she made a dramatic ~:** ihr Abgang war dramatisch 4) (departure) **right of ~ from a country** Recht, ein Land zu verlassen

B *v.i.* 1) (make one's ~) hinausgehen (**from** aus); (from stage) abgehen (**from** von) 2) (Theatre: as stage direction) ab; **~ Hamlet** Hamlet ab

exit: ~ permit *n.* Ausreiseerlaubnis, *die;* **~ poll** *n.: Befragung der ein Wahllokal verlassenden Wähler;* **~ ramp** *n.* (Amer.) Abfahrt, *die;* **~ sign** *n.* Ausgangsschild, *das;* **~ visa** *n.* Ausreisevisum, *das;* **~ wound** *n.* Austritswunde, *die*

exodus /'eksədəs/ *n.* Auszug, *der;* Exodus, *der* (geh.); **general ~:** allgemeiner Aufbruch; **[the Book of] E~:** das zweite Buch Mose

ex officio /eks ə'fɪʃɪəʊ/

A *adv.* ex officio (geh.); von Amts wegen

B *adj.* **~ chairman** Vorsitzender von Amts wegen *od.* ex officio (geh.); **be an ~ member** kraft seines Amtes Mitglied sein

exonerate /ɪg'zɒnəreɪt/ *v.t.* entlasten; **~ sb. from a duty/task** jmdn. von einer Pflicht/Aufgabe befreien; **~ sb. from blame** jmdn. von der Schuld freisprechen

exoneration /ɪgzɒnə'reɪʃn/ *n.* Entlastung, *die;* (from task, obligation) Befreiung, *die*

exorbitance /ɪg'zɔːbɪtəns/ *n., no pl.* Maßlosigkeit, *die;* Exorbitanz, *die* (geh.)

exorbitant /ɪg'zɔːbɪtənt/ *adj.* [maßlos] überhöht ‹*Preis, Miete, Gewinn, Anforderung, Rechnung*›; maßlos ‹*Ehrgeiz, Forderung*›; **£10 — that's ~!** 10 Pfund — das ist unverschämt viel! (ugs.); **be ~ in one's demands** [maßlos] überhöhte Ansprüche stellen

exorcise ▸ **exorcize**

exorcism /'eksɔːsɪzm/ *n.* Exorzismus, *der;* Teufelsaustreibung, *die*

exorcist /'eksɔːsɪst/ *n.* Exorzist, *der*

exorcize /'eksɔːsaɪz/ *v.t.* austreiben; exorzieren; **be ~d from** *or* **out of sb./sth.** jmdm./einer Sache ausgetrieben werden

exotic /ɪg'zɒtɪk/

A *adj.* exotisch

B *n.* Exot[e], *der*/Exotin, *die*

exotica /ɪg'zɒtɪkə/ *n. pl.* Exotika *Pl.*

exotically /ɪg'zɒtɪkəlɪ/ *adv.* exotisch; **~ named ...:** mit dem exotischen Namen ...

expand /ɪk'spænd/

A *v.i.* 1) (get bigger) sich ausdehnen; ‹*Unternehmen, Stadt, Staat:*› expandieren; ‹*Verkehrsaufkommen, Wissen:*› zunehmen; ‹*Institution:*› erweitert werden; ‹*geistiger Horizont:*› sich erweitern; **~ into sth.** zu etw. anwachsen; **~ing watch strap** elastisches Gliederband 2) (Commerc.) expandieren; **~ into a large organization** zu einer großen Organisation heranwachsen; **~ into other areas of production** die Produktion um andere Sektoren erweitern 3) **~ on a subject** ein Thema weiter ausführen 4) (spread out) sich öffnen 5) (become genial) freundlich werden

B *v.t.* 1) (enlarge) ausdehnen; erweitern ‹*Horizont, Wissen*›; dehnen ‹*Körper*›; aufblasen ‹*Ballon*›; aufpumpen ‹*Reifen*›; **~ sth. into sth.** etw. zu etw. erweitern; **~ed metal** Streckmetall, *das* (Bauw.) 2) (Commerc.: develop) erweitern; **~ the economy** das Wirtschaftswachstum fördern 3) (amplify) weiter ausführen ‹*Gedanken, Notiz, Idee*›

expandable /ɪk'spændəbl/ *adj.* [aus]dehnbar; (Commerc.) entwicklungsfähig

expanse /ɪk'spæns/ *n.* [weite] Fläche; **~ of water** Wasserfläche, *die;* **surrounded by a huge ~ of desert** umgeben von einer sich weithin erstreckenden Wüste; **she was swathed in an ~ of red silk** sie war in weite Bahnen roter Seide gehüllt

expansion /ɪk'spænʃn/ *n.* 1) Ausdehnung, *die;* (of territorial rule also) Expansion, *die;* (of sphere of influence) Ausweitung, *die;* (of knowledge, building) Erweiterung, *die;* **the ~ of the volume of traffic on the roads** die zunehmende Verkehrsdichte auf den Straßen 2) (Commerc.) Expansion, *die;* **the ~ of this small business into a huge organization** die Erweiterung dieses kleinen Betriebes zu einer großen Firma 3) (amplification) Erweiterung, *die;* **further ~ of the ideas** weitere Ausführung der Ideen

expansionary /ɪk'spænʃənərɪ/ *adj.* (also Commerc.) expansionistisch

expansion: ~ card *n.* (Computing) Erweiterungskarte, *die;* **~ joint** *n.* Dehnungsfuge, *die*

expansive /ɪk'spænsɪv/ *adj.* (effusive) offen; (responsive) zugänglich; **be ~:** aus sich herausgehen

expat /eks'pæt/ (coll.) ▸ **expatriate B,C**

expatiate /ɪk'speɪʃɪeɪt/ *v.i.* **~ [up]on sth.** etw. ausführlich erörtern; sich über etw. (*Akk.*) verbreiten (oft abwertend)

expatiation /ɪkspeɪʃɪ'eɪʃn/ *n.* [ausführliche] Erörterung (**[up]on** *Gen.*)

expatriate

A /eks'pætrɪeɪt, eks'peɪtrɪeɪt/ *v.t.* (exile) ausbürgern; expatriieren

B /eks'pætrɪət, eks'peɪtrɪət/ *attrib. adj.* im Ausland lebend; **~ community** Kolonie, *die*

C *n.* (exile) Exilant, *der*/Exilantin, *die;* (foreigner)

Ausländer, *der*/Ausländerin, *die;* (emigrant) Auswanderer, *der*/Auswanderin, *die*

expatriation /ekspætrɪ'eɪʃn, ekspeɪtrɪ'eɪʃn/ *n.* (forcible) Ausbürgerung, *die;* Expatriation, *die;* (voluntary) [freiwilliges] Exil

expect /ɪk'spekt/ *v.t.* **1** (regard as likely, anticipate) erwarten; **~ to do sth.** damit rechnen, etw. zu tun; **~ sth. from sb.** etw. von jmdm. erwarten; **~ sb. to do sth.** damit rechnen, dass jmd. etw. tut; **I ~ you'd like something to eat** ich nehme an, dass du gern etwas essen möchtest; **don't ~ me to help you out** von mir hast du keine Hilfe zu erwarten; **it is ~ed that ...:** man erwartet, dass ...; **that was [not] to be ~ed** das war [auch nicht] zu erwarten; **I ~ed as much** das habe ich erwartet; **it is everything one ~s** es erfüllt alle Erwartungen; **it is all one can ~:** mehr kann man [auch] nicht erwarten; **~ the worst** mit dem Schlimmsten rechnen; **be ~ing a baby/child** ein Baby/Kind erwarten; **be ~ing** *abs.* schwanger sein; **is he/she ~ing you?** werden Sie erwartet?; **I/we shall not ~ you till I/we see you** wenn du kommst, bist du da (ugs.); **~ me when you see me** (coll.) wenn ich komme, bin ich da (ugs.) **2** (require) erwarten; **~ sb. to do sth.** von jmdm. erwarten, dass er etw. tut; **~ sth. from** *or* **of sb.** etw. von jmdm. erwarten; **they are ~ed to be present** man erwartet [von ihnen], dass sie da sind **3** (coll.: think, suppose) glauben; **I ~ so** ich glaube schon; **I rather ~ not** ich glaube kaum; **I don't ~ so** ich glaube nicht; **I ~ it was/he did** *etc.* das glaube ich gern

expectancy /ɪk'spektənsɪ/ *n.* **1** *no pl.* Erwartung, *die;* **with an air** *or* **a look of ~:** mit erwartungsvoller Miene; **mood of ~:** erwartungsvolle Stimmung **2** (prospective chance) **an ~ of another 28 years of life** eine Lebenserwartung von noch 28 Jahren; *see also* **life expectancy**

expectant /ɪk'spektənt/ *adj.* **1** erwartungsvoll **2** **~ mother** werdende Mutter

expectantly /ɪk'spektəntlɪ/ *adv.* erwartungsvoll; gespannt ‹*warten*›

expectation /ekspek'teɪʃn/ *n.* **1** *no pl.* (expecting) Erwartung, *die;* **in the ~ of sth.** in Erwartung einer Sache (*Gen.*) **2** *usu. in pl.* (thing expected) Erwartung, *die;* **have great ~s for sb./sth.** große Erwartungen in jmdn./etw. setzen; **come up to ~[s]/sb.'s ~s** den/jmds. Erwartungen entsprechen; **contrary to ~** *or* **to all ~s** wider Erwarten; **be a success beyond all ~s** über alles Erwarten erfolgreich sein **3** **~ of life** ▸ **life 5** **4** *in pl.* (prospects of inheritance) **have great ~s** ein großes Erbe in Aussicht haben

expectorate /ɪk'spektəreɪt/ *v.t. & i.* aushusten; (spit) [aus]spucken

expedience /ɪk'spi:dɪəns/, **expediency** /ɪk'spi:dɪənsɪ/ *n.* Zweckmäßigkeit, *die;* **he has sacrificed his integrity for ~:** er hat seine Integrität den so genannten Sachzwängen geopfert

expedient /ɪk'spi:dɪənt/

A *adj., usu. pred.* **1** (appropriate, advantageous) angebracht **2** (politic) zweckmäßig

B *n.* Mittel, *das*

expediently /ɪk'spi:dɪəntlɪ/ *adv.* zweckmäßigerweise; **act ~:** handeln, wie man es für zweckmäßig hält

expedite /'ekspɪdaɪt/ *v.t.* (hasten) beschleunigen; vorantreiben; (execute promptly) umgehend ausführen

expedition /ekspɪ'dɪʃn/ *n.* **1** Expedition, *die* **2** (Mil.) Feldzug, *der;* Expedition, *die* (veralt.); **send an ~ to Egypt** Truppen nach Ägypten schicken **3** (excursion) Ausflug, *der;* **go on a hunting/shopping ~:** einen Jagdausflug/eine Einkaufstour machen **4** *no pl.* (speed) Eile, *die*

expeditionary /ekspɪ'dɪʃənərɪ/ *adj.* **~ force** (Mil.) Expeditionskorps, *das*

expeditious /ekspɪ'dɪʃəs/ *adj.* (doing or done speedily) schnell; (suited for speedy performance) schnell durchführbar

expeditiously /ekspɪ'dɪʃəslɪ/ *adv.* schnell

expel /ɪk'spel/ *v.t.*, **-ll-** **1** ausweisen; **~ sb. from school [for misconduct]** jmdn. [wegen schlechten Betragens] von der Schule verweisen; **~ sb. from a country** jmdn. aus einem Land ausweisen; **~ from a club** aus einem Verein ausschließen **2** (with force) vertreiben (**from** aus); auswerfen ‹*Patrone*›; absaugen ‹*Küchendunst*› **3** (from substance; also Med.) austreiben ‹*Gas, Wasser usw.*›

expend /ɪk'spend/ *v.t.* **1** aufwenden (**[up]on** für); **~ much care in doing sth.** etw. mit viel Sorgfalt tun **2** (use up) aufbrauchen (**[up]on** für)

expendable /ɪk'spendəbl/ *adj.* **1** (inessential) entbehrlich; **be ~** (Mil.; also fig.) geopfert werden können **2** (used up in service) zum Verbrauch bestimmt

expenditure /ɪk'spendɪtʃə(r)/ *n.* **1** (amount spent) Ausgaben *Pl.* (**on** für); (of fuel, effort, etc.) Aufwand, *der* **2** (spending) Ausgabe, *die;* (using up of fuel or effort) Aufwand, *der* (**of** an + *Dat.*); **~ of money/time** Geldausgabe, *die*/Zeitaufwand, *der*

expense /ɪk'spens/ *n.* **1** Kosten *Pl.;* **regardless of ~:** ungeachtet der Kosten; **those who can afford the ~:** diejenigen, die es sich leisten können; **at little ~:** preiswert; **at great ~ to sb./sth.** unter großen Kosten für jmdn./etw.; **living ~s** Lebenshaltungskosten *Pl.;* **at sb.'s ~:** auf jmds. Kosten (*Akk.*); **at one's own ~:** auf eigene Kosten; **go to the ~ of travelling first-class** sogar noch das Geld für die erste Klasse ausgeben; **go to some/great ~:** sich in Unkosten/große Unkosten stürzen; **put sb. to ~:** jmdm. Kosten verursachen; **put sb. to the ~ of sth./of doing sth.** jmdm. die Kosten für etw. zumuten/dafür zumuten, etw. zu tun **2** (expensive item) teure Angelegenheit; **be** *or* **prove a great** *or* **big ~:** mit großen Ausgaben verbunden sein **3** *usu. in pl.* (Commerc. etc.: amount spent [and repaid]) Spesen *Pl.;* **with [all] ~s paid** auf Spesen; **the ~s incurred** die anfallenden Spesen; **he is able to claim ~s** er kann sich (*Dat.*) seine Spesen erstatten lassen; **put sth. on ~s** etw. auf die Spesenabrechnung setzen; **it all goes on to ~s** das geht alles auf Spesen **4** (fig.) Preis, *der;* **[be] at the ~ of sth.** auf Kosten von etw. [gehen]; **at considerable ~ in terms of human lives** unter großem Verlust an Menschenleben; **he achieved it, but at the ~ of his life** er erreichte es, aber es kostete ihn das Leben; **at sb.'s ~:** auf jmds. Kosten (*Akk.*)

ex'pense account *n.* Spesenabrechnung, *die; attrib.* ‹*Essen, Leben*› auf Spesen

expensive /ɪk'spensɪv/ *adj.* teuer; **prove ~ to sb.** jmdn. teuer zu stehen kommen

expensively /ɪk'spensɪvlɪ/ *adv.* teuer; **~ priced** teuer

experience /ɪk'spɪərɪəns/

A *n.* **1** *no pl., no indef. art.* Erfahrung, *die;* **have ~ of sth./sb.** Erfahrung in etw. (*Dat.*) /mit jmdm. haben; **have ~ of doing sth.** Erfahrung darin haben, etw. zu tun; **several years' ~:** mehrjährige Erfahrung; **learn by** *or* **through** *or* **from ~:** durch eigene *od.* aus eigener Erfahrung lernen; **he learnt through** *or* **by ~ that ...:** die Erfahrung hat ihn gelehrt, dass ...; **his first ~ of war/freedom** seine erste Begegnung mit dem Krieg/der Freiheit; **a man of your ~:** ein Mann mit deiner Erfahrung; **in/from my [own] [previous] ~:** nach meiner/aus eigener Erfahrung; **know from** *or* **by ~ that ...:** aus Erfahrung wissen, dass ...; **~ has shown that ...:** die Erfahrung hat gezeigt, dass ...; **chalk it up** *or* **charge it up** *or* **put it down to ~:** durch Schaden wird man klug; **~ of life** Lebenserfahrung, *die* **2** (event) Erfahrung, *die;* Erlebnis, *das;* **have an [unpleasant/odd] ~:** eine [unangenehme/merkwürdige] Erfahrung machen; **he went through some terrible wartime ~s** er hat im Krieg Schreckliches mitgemacht; **it's quite an ~!** das ist [schon] ein Erlebnis! **3** **the American ~ shows how ...:** das Beispiel Amerika zeigt, wie ...

B *v.t.* erleben; stoßen auf (+ *Akk.*), haben ‹*Schwierigkeiten*›; kennen lernen ‹*Lebensweise*›; verspüren, empfinden ‹*Hunger, Kälte, Schmerz, Freude, Trauer, Gefühl*›; **he is unable to ~ things deeply** er ist nicht fähig, etwas tief zu empfinden; **only he who has himself ~d poverty** nur wer Armut selbst erfahren hat

experienced /ɪk'spɪərɪənst/ *adj.* erfahren; **be ~ in sth.** in etw. (*Dat.*) erfahren sein; mit etw. Erfahrung haben; **an ~ eye** ein geschulter Blick

experiment

A /ɪk'sperɪmənt/ *n.* **1** Experiment, *das* (**on** an + *Dat.*); Versuch, *der* (**on** an + *Dat.*); **do an ~:** ein Experiment machen; **series of ~s** Versuchsreihe, *die* **2** (fig.) Experiment, *das;* **by ~:** experimentell; **as an ~:** versuchsweise

B /ɪk'sperɪment/ *v.i.* experimentieren; Versuche anstellen; **~ on sb./sth.** an jmdm./etw. experimentieren *od.* Versuche anstellen; **~ with sth.** mit etw. experimentieren

experimental /ɪksperɪ'mentl/ *adj.* **1** experimentell; (based on experiment) Experimental‹*physik, -psychologie*›; (used for experiments) Experimentier‹*theater, -kino*›; Versuchs‹*labor, -bedingungen*›; (used in experiment) Versuchs‹*tier*›; **at the/an ~ stage** im Versuchsstadium; im Experimentierstadium **2** (fig.: tentative) vorläufig; **~ drilling/flight** Probebohrung, *die*/-flug, *der;* **on an ~ basis** versuchsweise

experimentalist /ɪksperɪ'mentəlɪst/ *n.* Experimentator, *der*

experimentally /ɪksperɪ'mentəlɪ/ *adv.* **1** (as an experiment) versuchsweise **2** (by experiment) experimentell

experimentation /ɪksperɪmen'teɪʃn/ *n.* Experimentieren, *das*

experimenter /ɪk'sperɪmentə(r)/ *n.* Experimentator, *der*

expert /'ekspɜ:t/

A *adj.* **1** ausgezeichnet; **be ~ in** *or* **at sth.** Fachmann *od.* Experte in etw. (*Dat.*) sein; sich in etw. (*Dat.*) sehr gut auskennen; **be ~ in** *or* **at doing sth.** etw. ausgezeichnet können **2** (of an ~) fachmännisch; **~ witness** sachverständiger Zeuge; **an ~ opinion** die Meinung eines Fachmanns; **~ knowledge** Fachkenntnis, *die;* **cast one's ~ eye over sth.** etw. fachmännisch begutachten; **do an ~ job** fachmännisch arbeiten

B *n.* Fachmann, *der;* Experte, *der*/Expertin, *die;* (Law) Sachverständige, *der/die;* **among ~s** unter Fachleuten; in Fachkreisen; **be an ~ in** *or* **at/on sth.** Fachmann *od.* Experte in etw. (*Dat.*)/für etw. sein; **an ~ on the subject** ein Fachmann *od.* Experte auf dem Gebiet; **she's an ~ at solving riddles** sie ist eine Expertin im Rätsellösen; **forensic/mining ~:** Gerichts-/Bergbausachverständige, *der/die*

expertise /ekspɜ:'ti:z/ *n.* Fachkenntnisse *Pl.;* (skill) Können, *das;* **area of ~:** Fachgebiet, *das*

expertly /'ekspɜ:tlɪ/ *adv.* meisterhaft; fachmännisch ‹*reparieren, beraten, beurteilen*›

expert: ~ system *n.* (Computing) Expertensystem, *das;* **~ 'witness** *n.* sachverständiger Zeuge

expiate /'ekspɪeɪt/ *v.t.* sühnen (geh.)

expiation /ekspɪ'eɪʃn/ *n.* Sühne, *die* (geh.); Buße, *die;* **in ~ of** zur *od.* als Buße für

expiatory /'ekspɪeɪtərɪ/ *adj.* **an ~ act** ein Akt der Sühne; **~ sacrifice** Sühneopfer, *das*

expiration /ekspɪ'reɪʃn/ *n.* **1** ▸ **expiry** **2** (of air) Ausatmung, *die*

expire /ɪk'spaɪə(r)/

A *v.i.* **1** (become invalid) ablaufen; ‹*Patent, Titel:*› erlöschen; ‹*Gesetz, Statut:*› außer Kraft treten; ‹*Gutschein:*› verfallen; ‹*Vertrag, Amtszeit:*› auslaufen **2** (literary: die) versterben (geh.)

B *v.t.* (exhale) ausatmen

expiry /ɪk'spaɪərɪ/ *n.* ▸ **expire A 1**: Ablauf, *der;* Erlöschen, *das;* Außerkrafttreten, *das;* Verfall, *der;* **before/at** *or* **on the ~ of sth.** vor/nach Ablauf einer Sache (*Gen.*); **~ date, date of ~** (of contract, credit card, etc.) Ablaufdatum, *das;* (of voucher, medicine, etc.) Verfallsdatum, *das*

explain /ɪk'spleɪn/

A *v.t., also abs.* erklären; erläutern ‹*Grund, Motiv, Gedanken*›; darlegen ‹*Absicht, Beweggrund*›; aufklären ‹*Geheimnis*›; **I need to have it ~ed [to me]** ich brauche eine Erklärung; **be good at ~ing [things]** gut erklären können; **how do you ~ that?** wie erklären Sie sich (*Dat.*) das?

B *v. refl.* **1** *often abs.* (justify one's conduct) **please ~ [yourself]** bitte erklären Sie mir das; **he refused to ~:** er wollte mir keine Erklärung dafür geben; **let me ~ [myself]** lassen Sie mich Ihnen das erklären; **I'd better ~ [myself]** ich sollte Ihnen das erklären; **you've got some ~ing to do** Sie müssen mir da einiges erklären **2** (make one's meaning clear) **please ~ yourself** bitte erklären Sie das [näher]

Phrasal verb

• **~ a'way** *v.t.* eine [plausible] Erklärung finden für

explainable /ɪk'spleɪnəbl/ *adj.* erklärbar; **be ~:** sich erklären lassen

explanation /eksplə'neɪʃn/ *n.* Erklärung, *die;* **need ~:** einer Erklärung (*Gen.*) bedürfen; **in ~ [of sth.]** zur Erklärung [einer Sache (*Gen.*)]; **what is the ~ of this?** wie soll ich mir das erklären?; **some ~ is called for** es bedarf einer Erklärung (*Gen.*)

explanatory /ɪk'splænətərɪ/ *adj.* erklärend; erläuternd ‹*Bemerkung*›

expletive /ɪk'spli:tɪv, ek'spli:tɪv/

A *n.* **1** (oath) Kraftausdruck, *der* **2** (Ling.) Füllwort, *das;* Expletiv, *das* (fachspr.)

B *adj.* (Ling.) füllend; **~ word** Füllwort, *das*

explicable /ɪk'splɪkəbl/ *adj.* erklärbar

explicate /'eksplɪkeɪt/ *v.t.* **1** (explain) erläutern; explizieren (geh.); aufklären ‹*Geheimnis*› **2** (develop meaning of) ausführen

explicit /ɪk'splɪsɪt/ *adj.* **1** (stated in detail) ausführlich; (openly expressed) offen; unverhüllt; (definite) klar; ausdrücklich ‹*Zustimmung, Erwähnung*›; **please would you be more ~:** bitte drücken Sie sich etwas deutlicher aus; **he did not make his meaning very ~:** er wurde nicht sehr deutlich; **make ~ mention of sth.** etw. ausdrücklich erwähnen **2** (Theol.) **~ faith** Fides explicita, *die*

explicitly /ɪk'splɪsɪtlɪ/ *adv.* ausdrücklich; deutlich ‹*beschreiben, ausdrücken*›; (in openly expressed manner) unverhüllt

explicitness /ɪk'splɪsɪtnɪs/ *n., no pl.* Deutlichkeit, *die;* (open expression) **with less ~:** weniger deutlich

explode /ɪk'spləʊd/

A *v.i.* **1** explodieren **2** (fig.) explodieren; ‹*Bevölkerung:*› rapide zunehmen; **~ with laughter** in Gelächter ausbrechen

B *v.t.* **1** zur Explosion bringen **2** (fig.) widerlegen ‹*Vorstellung, Doktrin, Theorie*›

exploded 'view *n.* Explosionsdarstellung, *die;* auseinander gezogene Darstellung

exploit

A /'eksplɔɪt/ *n.* (feat; also joc.: deed) Heldentat, *die*

B /ɪk'splɔɪt/ *v.t.* **1** (derog.) ausbeuten ‹*Arbeiter, Kolonie usw.*›; ausnutzen ‹*Gutmütigkeit, Freund, Unwissenheit*› **2** (utilize) nutzen; nützen; ausnutzen ‹*Gelegenheit, Situation*›; ausbeuten ‹*Grube*›

exploitable /ek'splɔɪtəbl/ *adj.* nutzbar; abbaubar ‹*Bodenschätze usw.*›; ausbeutbar ‹*Ölreserven*›

exploitation /eksplɔɪ'teɪʃn/ *n.* **1** (derog.) (of the working classes) Ausbeutung, *die;* (of genius, good nature) Ausnutzung, *die* **2** (utilization) Nutzung, *die*

exploitative /ɪk'splɔɪtətɪv/, **exploitive** /ɪk'splɔɪtɪv/ *adj.* (derog.) ausbeuterisch

exploration /eksplə'reɪʃn/ *n.* **1** Erforschung, *die;* (of town, house) Erkundung, *die;* **in the course of his ~s** im Verlauf seiner Erforschung/Erkundung; **voyage of ~:** Entdeckungsreise, *die* **2** (fig.) Untersuchung, *die* **3** (Med.) Untersuchung, *die;* Exploration, *die* (fachspr.)

explorative /ɪk'splɒrətɪv/, **exploratory** /ɪk'splɒrətərɪ/ *adjs.* Forschungs-; **~ talks** Sondierungsgespräche; **~ drilling** Suchbohrung, *die;* **~ operation** (Med.) explorative Operation; Operation zu diagnostischen Zwecken

explore /ɪk'splɔ:(r)/ *v.t.* **1** erforschen; erkunden ‹*Stadt, Haus*›; **go exploring/out to ~:** auf Entdeckungsreise gehen **2** (fig.) untersuchen; **~ every avenue** alle möglichen Wege prüfen; **~ how the land lies** das Terrain sondieren

explorer /ɪk'splɔ:rə(r)/ *n.* **1** Entdeckungsreisende, *der/die;* **Arctic ~:** Arktisforscher, *der/* -forscherin, *die;* **~s of the Nile** Erforscher des Nils **2** (Amer.: Scout) Pfadfinder, *der*

explosion /ɪk'spləʊʒn/ *n.* **1** Explosion, *die;* (noise) [Explosions]knall, *der* **2** (fig.: of anger etc.) Ausbruch, *der;* **if the boss gets to hear of this there will be an ~:** wenn das der Chef erfährt, explodiert er **3** (rapid increase) Explosion, *die;* explosionsartiger Anstieg; **~ of population** Bevölkerungsexplosion, *die*

explosive /ɪk'spləʊsɪv, ɪk'spləʊzɪv/

A *adj.* **1** explosiv; **highly ~:** hochexplosiv; **~ substance** Explosivstoff, *der;* **~ device** Sprengkörper, *der* **2** (fig.) explosiv; brisant ‹*Thema*›

B *n.* Sprengstoff, *der;* **high ~:** hochexplosiver Stoff; **~s expert** Sprengstoffexperte, *der/*-expertin, *die*

explosively /ɪk'spləʊsɪvlɪ, ɪk'spləʊzɪvlɪ/ *adv.* (lit. or fig.) explosionsartig

exponent /ɪk'spəʊnənt/ *n.* **1** (of doctrine) Vertreter, *der*/Vertreterin, *die;* (representative also) Exponent, *der*/Exponentin, *die;* (of cause) Verfechter, *der*/Verfechterin, *die* **2** (Math.) Exponent, *der;* Hochzahl, *die* **3** (Mus.) Interpret, *der*/Interpretin, *die*

exponential /ekspə'nenʃl/ *adj.* exponentiell; Exponential-; **~ function** (Math.) Exponentialfunktion, *die;* **~ growth** exponentielles Wachstum

exponentially /ekspə'nenʃəlɪ/ *adv.* exponentiell

export

A /ɪk'spɔ:t, 'ekspɔ:t/ *v.t.* **1** exportieren; ausführen; **~ing country** Ausfuhrland, *das;* **~ to other nations/to South Africa** in andere Länder/nach Südafrika exportieren; **oil-~ing countries** [Erd]öl exportierende Länder **2** (Computing) exportieren ‹*Daten, Datei*›

B /'ekspɔ:t/ *n.* **1** (process, amount exported) Export, *der;* Ausfuhr, *die;* (exported articles) Exportgut, *das;* Ausfuhrgut, *das;* **boost ~s** den Export *od.* die Ausfuhr ankurbeln; **ban on the ~ of grain** Ausfuhrverbot für Getreide; **~s of sugar** Zuckerexporte *od.* -ausfuhren **2** *attrib.* Export‹*leiter, -handel, -markt, -kaufmann*›

exportation /ekspɔ:'teɪʃn/ *n.* Export, *der;* Ausfuhr, *die*

export /'ekspɔ:t/: **~ drive** *n.* Exportkampagne, *die;* **~ duty** *n.* Exportzoll, *der;* Ausfuhrzoll, *der*

exporter /ɪk'spɔ:tə(r), 'ekspɔ:tə(r)/ *n.* Exporteur, *der;* (person also) Exporthändler, *der;* (firm also) Exportfirma, *die;* (country) **be an ~ of coal** Kohle exportieren

export/'ekspɔ:t/: **~ licence** *n.* Ausfuhrlizenz, *die;* **~ permit** *n.* Exporterlaubnis, *die;* Ausfuhrerlaubnis, *die;* **~ 'reject** *n.* [wegen ungenügender Qualität] nicht exportfähige Ware; **~ sales** *n. pl.* Exporte *Pl.;* Ausfuhren *Pl.;* Exportverkäufe *Pl.;* **~ surplus** *n.* Exportüberschuss, *der*

expose /ɪk'spəʊz/

A *v.t.* **1** (uncover) freilegen; bloßlegen ‹*Draht, Nerv*›; entblößen ‹*Haut, Körper, Knie*›; **~ to view** freilegen; sichtbar machen **2** (make known) offenbaren ‹*Schwäche, Tatsache, Geheimnis, Plan*›; aufdecken ‹*Irrtum, Missstände, Verbrechen, Verrat*›; entlarven ‹*Täter, Verräter, Spion*› **3** (subject) **~ to sth.** einer Sache (*Dat.*) aussetzen; (acquaint with sth.) mit etw. vertraut machen; **~ to ridicule** der Lächerlichkeit (*Dat.*) preisgeben **4** (Photog.) belichten **5** (leave out of doors to die) aussetzen

B *v. refl.* sich [unsittlich] entblößen

exposé /ek'spəʊzeɪ/ *n.* **1** (of facts) Exposé, *das* **2** (of sth. discreditable) Enthüllung, *die;* (of crime) Aufdeckung, *die*

exposed /ɪk'spəʊzd/ *adj.* **1** (unprotected) ungeschützt; **~ to the wind/elements** dem Wind/den Elementen ausgesetzt; **~ position** (lit. or fig.) exponierte Stellung **2** (visible) freigelegt; sichtbar ‹*Körperteil*› **3** (Photog.) belichtet

exposition /ekspə'zɪʃn/ *n.* **1** (statement, presentation) Darstellung, *die;* (commentary) Kommentar, *der* (**of** zu); (explanation) Erläuterung, *die* (**of** zu); (act of expounding) **~ of heretical views** Verbreitung ketzerischer Ansichten **2** (Mus., Lit.: of principal themes) Exposition, *die* **3** (exhibition) Ausstellung, *die*

expostulate /ɪk'spɒstjʊleɪt/ *v.i.* protestieren; **~ with sb. about** *or* **on sth.** mit jmdm. über etw. (*Akk.*) debattieren

expostulation /ɪkspɒstjʊ'leɪʃn/ *n.* Protest, *der*

exposure /ɪk'spəʊʒə(r)/ *n.* **1** (to air, cold, etc.) (being exposed) Ausgesetztsein, *das;* (exposing) Aussetzen, *das;* (of goods etc.) Ausstellung, *die;* (of children) Aussetzung, *die;* **die of/suffer from ~ [to cold]** an Unterkühlung (*Dat.*) sterben/leiden; **~ to infection** Kontakt mit Krankheitserregern; **indecent ~:** Entblößung in schamverletzender Weise; **media ~:** Publicity, *die* **2** (unmasking) (of fraud etc.) Enthüllung, *die;* (of criminal) Entlarvung, *die;* (of hypocrite or hypocrisy) Bloßstellung, *die* **3** (Photog.) (exposing time) Belichtung, *die;* (picture) Aufnahme, *die*

ex'posure meter *n.* (Photog.) Belichtungsmesser, *der*

expound /ɪk'spaʊnd/ *v.t.* **1** darlegen ‹*These, Theorie, Doktrin*› (**to** *Dat.*) **2** (explain) auslegen ‹*Schriften, Gesetz*› (**to** *Dat.*)

express /ɪk'spres/

A *v.t.* **1** (indicate) ausdrücken **2** (put into words) äußern, zum Ausdruck bringen ‹*Meinung, Wunsch, Dank, Bedauern, Liebe*›; **~ sth. in another language** etw. in einer anderen Sprache ausdrücken; **~ oneself** sich ausdrücken; **he ~ed himself strongly on that subject** er äußerte sich sehr entschieden zu diesem Thema; **~ one's willingness** *or* **readiness to do sth.** sich bereit erklären, etw. zu tun **3** (represent by symbols) ausdrücken ‹*Zahl, Wert*› **4** (squeeze) [heraus]drücken; [heraus]pressen **5** (send by ~ delivery) als Schnellsendung schicken

B *attrib. adj.* **1** Eil‹*brief, -bote usw.*›; Schnell‹*paket, -sendung*›; *see also* **~ train** **2** (particular) besonder...; bestimmt; ausdrücklich ‹*Absicht*› **3** (stated) ausdrücklich ‹*Wunsch, Befehl usw.*›

C *adv.* als Eilsache ‹*senden*›

D *n.* **1** (train) Schnellzug, *der;* D-Zug, *der;* (messenger) Eilbote, *der;* **by ~:** durch Eilboten **2** (Amer.: company) Transportunternehmen, *das*

express: ~ company *n.* (Amer.) Transportunternehmen, *das;* **~ de'livery** *n.* Eilzustellung, *die*

expression /ɪk'spreʃn/ *n.* **1** Ausdruck, *der;* **find ~ in sth.** in etw. (*Dat.*) Ausdruck finden *od.* zum Ausdruck kommen; **give ~ to one's gratitude** seine Dankbarkeit zum Ausdruck bringen; seiner Dankbarkeit (*Dat.*) Ausdruck verleihen (geh.); **manner** *or* **mode of ~:** Ausdrucksweise, *die;* **profuse ~s of gratitude** überschwängliche Dankesbezeugungen; **the ~ on his face** *or* **his facial ~ was one of deepest hatred** sein Gesichtsausdruck zeugte von tiefstem Hass; tiefster Hass stand ihm im Gesicht geschrieben; **full of/without ~:** ausdrucksvoll/-los; **devoid of all ~:** völlig ausdruckslos; **she put a martyred ~ on her face** sie setzte ihre Duldermiene auf **2** (Art, Mus., Math.) Ausdruck, *der;* **play/sing with ~:** ausdrucksvoll *od.* -stark spielen/singen

expressionism /ɪk'spreʃənɪzm/ *n., no pl.* Expressionismus, *der*

expressionist /ɪk'spreʃənɪst/ *n.* Expressionist, *der*/Expressionistin, *die; attrib.* expressionistisch ‹*Kunst usw.*›

expressionistic /ɪkspreʃə'nɪstɪk/ *adj.* expressionistisch

expressionless /ɪk'spreʃnlɪs/ *adj.* ausdruckslos

ex'pression mark *n.* (Mus.) Vortragsbezeichnung, *die*

expressive /ɪk'spresɪv/ *adj.* **1** **be ~ of sth.** etw. ausdrücken **2** (significant) ausdrucksvoll; viel sagend ‹*Schweigen*›; expressiv (geh.), ausdrucksvoll ‹*Geste*›

expressively /ɪk'spresɪvlɪ/ *adv.* ausdrucksvoll

express: ~ 'letter *n.* Eilbrief, *der;* **~ 'lift** *n.* Schnellaufzug, *der*

e

expressly /ɪk'spreslɪ/ *adv.* **1** (particularly) ausdrücklich **2** (definitely) eindeutig; ausdrücklich

express: ~ **'train** *n.* Schnellzug, *der;* D-Zug, *der;* ~**way** *n.* (Amer.) Schnell[verkehrs]straße, *die*

expropriate /eks'prəʊprɪeɪt/ *v.t.* enteignen; ‹*Staat usw.*:› verstaatlichen

expropriation /eksprəʊprɪ'eɪʃn/ *n.* Enteignung, *die;* Expropriation, *die* (veralt.); (esp. by State) Verstaatlichung, *die*

expulsion /ɪk'spʌlʃn/ *n.* (from school, college) Verweisung, *die* (**from** von); Relegation, *die* (**from** von); (from home, homeland) Vertreibung, *die* (**from** aus); (from country) Ausweisung, *die* (**from** aus); (from club) Ausschluss, *der* (**from** aus); (Med.: from the body) Austreibung, *die* (**from** aus); (of gas, water, etc. from substance) Austreiben, *das* (**from** aus)

expunge /ɪk'spʌndʒ/ *v.t.* [aus]streichen (**from** aus); (fig.) tilgen (**from** aus)

expurgate /'ekspəgeɪt/ *v.t.* (purify) zensieren, (verhüll.) säubern ‹*Text, Buch, Theaterstück*›; ~**d version/edition** zensierte *od.* (verhüll.) bereinigte Fassung/Ausgabe

exquisite /'ekskwɪzɪt, ɪk'skwɪzɪt/ *adj.* **1** erlesen; exquisit, bezaubernd ‹*Aussicht, Landschaft, Muster, Melodie, Frau, Anmut*›; ausgesucht ‹*Höflichkeit*› **2** (acute) heftig ‹*Schmerz, Freude*›; riesig ‹*Triumph*›; unerträglich ‹*Leiden, Schmerzen*›

exquisitely /'ekskwɪzɪtlɪ, ɪk'skwɪzɪtlɪ/ *adv.* **1** (excellently, beautifully) vorzüglich; kunstvoll ‹*verziert, geschnitzt*› **2** (acutely) äußerst; außerordentlich

ex-'service *adj.* (Brit.) Veteranen-; ~**man** ehemaliger Soldat

ext. *abbr.* **1** = **exterior** **2** = **external** **3** = **[telephone] extension** App.

extant /ek'stænt, 'ekstənt/ *adj.* [noch] vorhanden *od.* existent

extemporaneous /ɪkstempə'reɪnɪəs/ *adj.* improvisiert; ~ **translation** Stegreifübersetzung, *die*

extempore /ɪk'stempərɪ/

A *adv.* aus dem Stegreif; ex tempore (Theater, geh.); **speak** ~**:** frei sprechen; extemporieren

B *adj.* improvisiert ‹*Gedicht, Lied*›; **give an** ~ **speech** eine Rede aus dem Stegreif *od.* eine Stegreifrede halten

extemporisation, extemporise ▸ **extemporiz-**

extemporization /ɪkstempəraɪ'zeɪʃn/ *n.* Improvisation, *die;* Extempore, *das*

extemporize /ɪk'stempəraɪz/ *v.t. & i.* improvisieren; extemporieren

extend /ɪk'stend/

A *v.t.* **1** (stretch out) ausstrecken ‹*Arm, Bein, Hand*›; ausziehen ‹*Leiter, Teleskop*›; spannen ‹*Seil*›; ausbreiten ‹*Flügel*›; ~ **one's hand to sb.** jmdm. die Hand reichen *od.* entgegenstrecken; **the table can be** ~**ed** der Tisch ist ausziehbar **2** (make longer) (in space) verlängern; ausdehnen ‹*Grenze*›; ausbauen ‹*Bahnlinie, Straße*›; (in time) verlängern; verlängern lassen ‹*Leihbuch, Visum*›; ~ **a credit** Kreditverlängerung gewähren; ~ **the time limit** den Termin hinausschieben **3** (enlarge) ausdehnen ‹*Einfluss, Macht, Forschung[sgebiet]*›; erweitern ‹*Wissen, Wortschatz, Bedeutung, Freundeskreis, Besitz, Geschäft*›; verlängern ‹*Aufsatz, Referat*›; ausbauen, vergrößern ‹*Haus, Geschäft, Fabrik, Unternehmen*› **4** (offer) gewähren, zuteil werden lassen ‹*[Gast]freundschaft, Schutz, Gunst, Hilfe, Kredit*› (**to** *Dat.*); erweisen ‹*Freundlichkeit, Gefallen*› (**to** *Dat.*); (accord) aussprechen ‹*Dank, Einladung, Glückwunsch*› (**to** *Dat.*); ausrichten ‹*Gruß*› (**to** *Dat.*); ~ **a welcome to sb.** jmdn. willkommen heißen **5** (tax) fordern; ~ **oneself** sich verausgaben

B *v.i.* sich erstrecken; **the wall** ~**s for miles** die Mauer zieht sich meilenweit hin; **the bridge** ~**s over the river** die Brücke führt über den Fluss; **the road** ~**s from X to Y** die Straße führt von X nach Y; **the winter season** ~**s from November to March** die Wintersaison währt von November bis März; **negotiations** ~**ed over weeks** die Verhandlungen zogen sich über Wochen *od.* wochenlang hin; **the problem** ~**s to other fields as well** das Problem berührt auch andere Bereiche

extended /ɪk'stendɪd/: ~ **'family** *n.* Großfamilie, *die;* ~**-play** *adj.* EP-‹*Band*›

extendible /ɪk'stendɪbl/, **extensible** /ɪk'stensɪbl/ *adjs.* [aus]dehnbar ‹*Stoff*›; ausziehbar ‹*Fernrohr, Leiter*›; erweiterungsfähig ‹*Gebäude, Gewerbe, Firma, Industrie*›

extensible 'markup language *n.* (Computing) XML, *die*

extension /ɪk'stenʃn/ *n.* **1** (stretching out) (of arm, leg, hand) [Aus]strecken, *das;* (of wings) Ausbreiten, *das;* (of muscle) Streckung, *die* **2** (extent) Umfang, *der;* (range) Reichweite, *die* **3** (prolonging) Verlängerung, *die;* (of road, railway) Ausbau, *der;* ~ **of time** Fristverlängerung, *die;* **ask for an** ~**:** um Verlängerung bitten; Verlängerung beantragen; **be granted** *or* **get an** ~**:** Verlängerung bekommen **4** (enlargement) (of power, influence, research, frontier) Ausdehnung, *die;* (of enterprise, trade, knowledge) Erweiterung, *die;* (of house, estate) Ausbau, *der* **5** (additional part) (of house) Anbau, *der;* (of office, university, hospital, etc.) Erweiterungsbau, *der;* **build an** ~ **to a hospital** einen Erweiterungsbau zu einem Krankenhaus errichten; ein Krankenhaus ausbauen; **two** ~**s** zwei Anbauten **6** (telephone) Nebenanschluss, *der;* Fernsprechnebenstelle, *die* (fachspr.); (number) Apparat, *der* **7** ~ **course** (correspondence course) Fernstudium, *das*

extension: ~ **cord** (Amer.) ▸ ~ **lead;** ~ **ladder** *n.* Ausziehleiter, *die;* ~ **lead** *n.* (Brit.) Verlängerungsschnur, *die;* ~ **number** *n.* Nebenstellennummer, *die*

extensive /ɪk'stensɪv/ *adj.* ausgedehnt ‹*Ländereien, Reisen, Stadt, Wald, Besitz[tümer], Handel, Forschungen*›; extensiv ‹*Wirtschaft*›; weit ‹*Land[strich], Meer[esfläche], Blick*›; umfangreich ‹*Reparatur, Investitionen, Wissen, Nachforschungen, Studien, Auswahl, Angebot, Sammlung*›; beträchtlich ‹*Schäden, Geldmittel, Anstrengungen*›; weit reichend ‹*Änderungen, Reformen, Einfluss, Machtbefugnis, Unterstützung*›; langwierig ‹*Operation, Unternehmung, Suche*›; ausführlich ‹*Bericht, Einleitung*›; **make** ~ **use of sth.** von etw. ausgiebig Gebrauch machen

extensively /ɪk'stensɪvlɪ/ *adv.* beträchtlich ‹*ändern, beschädigen*›; gründlich ‹*reparieren*›; ausführlich ‹*berichten, schreiben*›; **they used these rooms** ~**:** sie machten ausgiebig von diesen Räumen Gebrauch

extent /ɪk'stent/ *n.* **1** (space over which sth. extends) Ausdehnung, *die;* (of wings) Spannweite, *die* **2** (scope) (of damage, debt, knowledge, power, authority) Umfang, *der;* (of influence, genius) Größe, *die;* (of damage, loss, disaster, power, authority) Ausmaß, *das;* **losses to the** ~ **of £100** Verluste in Höhe von 100 Pfund; **to what** ~**?** inwieweit?; in welchem Maße?; **the full** ~ **of his power** seine ganze Machtfülle; **to a great** *or* **large/small** *or* **slight** ~**:** in hohem/geringem Maße; **to some** *or* **a certain** ~**:** in gewissem Maße; **to the same** ~ **as ...:** im selben Maße wie ...; **to a greater/lesser** ~**:** in höherem/geringerem Maße; **to a greater or lesser** ~**:** mehr oder weniger; **to such an** ~ **that ...:** in solchem Maße, dass ...; **her condition has not improved to any [great]** ~**:** ihr Zustand hat sich [fast] überhaupt nicht gebessert **3** (area of sea, land) Weite, *die;* **you can see the whole** ~ **of the park** man kann den Park in seiner ganzen Ausdehnung sehen

extenuate /ɪk'stenjʊeɪt/ *v.t.* verharmlosen, beschönigen ‹*Vergehen, Verbrechen, Fehler, Schuld*›; entschuldigen ‹*Benehmen*›; **extenuating circumstances** mildernde Umstände

extenuation /ɪkstenjʊ'eɪʃn/ *n.* (of crime, offence, fault, guilt) Verharmlosung, *die;* Beschönigung, *die;* **in** ~ **of sth./sb.** als Entschuldigung für etw./jmdn.

exterior /ɪk'stɪərɪə(r)/

A *adj.* **1** äußer...; Außen‹*fläche, -wand, -anstrich*›; ~ **varnish** Lack für Außenanstriche **2** ([coming from] outside) äußer...; außerhalb gelegen **3** (Cinemat.) ~ **scene** Außenaufnahme, *die*

B *n.* **1** Äußere, *das;* (of house) Außenwände *Pl.* **2** (appearance) Äußere, *das;* **a man with a pleasant/rough** ~**:** ein Mann von angenehmem/ungeschlachtem Äußerem; **judge people by their** ~**:** Menschen nach ihrem Äußeren beurteilen **3** (Cinemat.) Außenaufnahme, *die*

exterminate /ɪk'stɜːmɪneɪt/ *v.t.* ausrotten; vertilgen, vernichten ‹*Ungeziefer*›

extermination /ɪkstɜːmɪ'neɪʃn/ *n.* Ausrottung, *die;* (of pests) Vertilgung, *die;* Vernichtung, *die*

extermi'nation camp *n.* Vernichtungslager, *das*

external /ɪk'stɜːnl/

A *adj.* **1** äußer...; Außen‹*fläche, -wirkung, -druck, -winkel, -durchmesser, -abmessungen*›; **give the** ~ **appearance of ease** äußerlich einen ungezwungenen Eindruck machen; **purely** ~**:** nur *od.* rein äußerlich **2** (applied to outside) äußerlich ‹*Heilmittel*›; **for** ~ **use only** nur äußerlich anzuwenden; nur zur äußerlichen Anwendung **3** (of foreign affairs) Außen‹*minister, -handel, -wirtschaft, -politik*›; **Ministry of E**~ **Affairs** Außenministerium, *das;* Ministerium für auswärtige Angelegenheiten *od.* des Auswärtigen **4** (Univ.) extern; ~ **examiner** externer Prüfer/externe Prüferin; ~ **student** Externe, *der/die;* **do** ~ **studies/an** ~ **degree** ein Fernstudium absolvieren **5** (of world of phenomena) äußer...; **the** ~ **world** die Welt der Erscheinungen **6** ~ **evidence** sich auf äußere Umstände gründender Beweis

B *n. in pl.* Äußerlichkeiten *Pl.*

externalize (externalise) /ɪk'stɜːnəlaɪz/ *v.t.* nach außen projizieren; (Philos.) veräußerlichen; (Psych.) externalisieren

externally /ɪk'stɜːnəlɪ/ *adv.* äußerlich; **the medicine is only to be used** ~**:** die Medizin ist nur zur äußerlichen Anwendung [bestimmt]; **be** ~ **calm** äußerlich *od.* nach außen hin ruhig sein; **the work is done** ~**:** die Arbeit wird außer Haus[e] erledigt

extinct /ɪk'stɪŋkt/ *adj.* erloschen ‹*Vulkan, Feuer, Leidenschaft, Liebe, Hoffnung*›; ausgestorben ‹*Art, Rasse, Volk, Gattung, Leben*›; untergegangen ‹*Volk, Dynastie, Reich, Kultur, Sitte, Brauch*›; abgeschafft ‹*Einrichtung, Amt, Posten, System, Gesetz*›; tot ‹*Sprache*›; **become** ~ ‹*Art, Rasse, Volk, Gattung:*› aussterben; ‹*Vulkan, Hoffnung, Adelstitel:*› erlöschen

extinction /ɪk'stɪŋkʃn/ *n., no pl.* (of fire, light) (extinguishing) Löschen, *das;* (being extinguished) Erlöschen, *das;* Verlöschen, *das;* (abolition) (of religion, system, institution, law, custom) Abschaffung, *die;* (of debt) Tilgung, *die;* (of independence etc.) Aufhebung, *die;* **threatened with** ~**:** vom Aussterben bedroht

extinguish /ɪk'stɪŋgwɪʃ/ *v.t.* **1** löschen; erlöschen lassen ‹*Leidenschaft, Hoffnung*›; auslöschen ‹*Leben*› **2** (destroy) beseitigen

extinguisher /ɪk'stɪŋgwɪʃə(r)/ *n.* **1** (for fire) Feuerlöscher, *der* **2** (for candle) Löschhütchen, *das*

extirpate /'ekstɜːpeɪt/ *v.t.* [mit der Wurzel] ausreißen ‹*Pflanze, Haare*›; entfernen ‹*Tumor*›; ausrotten ‹*Rasse, Volk, Sekte, Gattung*›; aufräumen mit, ausmerzen ‹*Ketzerei, Unsitten, Vorurteil*›

extol /ɪk'stəʊl, ɪk'stɒl/ *v.t.,* **-ll-** rühmen; preisen

extort /ɪk'stɔːt/ *v.t.* erpressen (**out of, from** von); ~ **a secret/confession from sb.** ein Geheimnis/Geständnis aus jmdm. herauspressen

extortion /ɪk'stɔːʃn/ *n., no pl.* (of money, taxes) Erpressung, *die;* **£50? This is sheer** ~**!** 50 Pfund? Das ist ja Wucher!

extortionate /ɪk'stɔːʃənət/ *adj.* **1** (excessive, exorbitant) Wucher‹*preis, -zinsen usw.*›; horrend ‹*Gebühr, Steuer*›; maßlos überzogen ‹*Forderung*› **2** (using extortion) erpresserisch ‹*Methode*›

extortioner /ɪk'stɔːʃənə(r)/ *n.* Erpresser, *der*/Erpresserin, *die*

extra /'ekstrə/

A *adj.* **1** (additional) zusätzlich; Mehr‹*arbeit, -kosten, -ausgaben, -aufwendungen*›; Sonder‹*bus, -zug*›; ~ **hours of work** Überstunden; **all we**

need is an ~ hour/three pounds** wir brauchen nur noch eine Stunde/drei Pfund [zusätzlich]; **~ charge** Aufpreis, *der;* **drinks are ~:** Getränke werden extra bezahlt *od.* (ugs.) gehen extra; **make an ~ effort** sich besonders anstrengen; **take ~ care** besonders vorsichtig sein; **for ~ safety** als zusätzliche *od.* besondere Sicherheitsvorkehrung; **can I have an ~ helping?** kann ich noch eine Portion haben? **2** (more than is necessary) überzählig ‹*Exemplar, Portion*›; **an ~ pair of gloves** noch ein *od.* ein zweites Paar Handschuhe; **have an ~ bed** noch ein Bett frei *od.* ein unbenutztes Bett haben; **we have an ~ ten minutes to kill** wir müssen noch zehn Minuten mehr totschlagen
B *adv.* **1** (more than usually) besonders; extra‹*lang, -stark, -fein*›; überaus ‹*froh*›; **an ~ large blouse** eine Bluse in Übergröße; **an ~ special occasion** eine ganz besondere Gelegenheit **2** (additionally) extra; **packing and postage ~:** zuzüglich Verpackung und Porto
C *n.* **1** (added to services, salary, etc.) zusätzliche Leistung; (on car etc. offered for sale) Extra, *das;* (adornment on dress etc.) besondere Note; (outside normal school curriculum) zusätzliches Angebot **2** (sth. with ~ charge) **be an ~:** zusätzlich berechnet werden **3** (in play, film, etc.) Statist, *der*/Statistin, *die;* Komparse, *der*/Komparsin, *die* **4** (Cricket) *Lauf, der nicht durch Schlag erzielt wird*

extra- /ekstrə/ *pref.* außer-; extra- (*mit Fremdwörtern lateinischen Ursprungs*)

extract
A /'ekstrækt/ *n.* **1** Extrakt, *der* (fachspr. auch: das); **an ~ of certain plants** ein Auszug *od.* Extrakt aus bestimmten Pflanzen **2** (from book, music, etc.) Auszug, *der;* Extrakt, *der* (geh.); **in ~s** auszugsweise; im Extrakt (geh.)
B /ɪk'strækt/ *v.t.* **1** ziehen, (fachspr.) extrahieren ‹*Zahn*›; herausziehen ‹*Dorn, Splitter usw.*›; **~ a bullet from a wound** eine Kugel aus einer Wunde entfernen; **she ~ed herself from his embrace** sie befreite *od.* löste sich aus seiner Umarmung; **~ sth. from sb.** (fig.) etw. aus jmdm. herausholen; **~ a promise/confession from sb.** jmdm. ein Versprechen/Geständnis abpressen; **~ papers from a folder** einem Aktenordner Unterlagen entnehmen **2** (obtain) extrahieren; **~ the juice of apples** Äpfel entsaften; **~ sugar from beet** aus Rüben Zucker gewinnen; **~ oil from the earth** Erdöl fördern; **~ metal from ore/honey from the honeycomb** Metall aus Erz/Honig aus der Wabe gewinnen **3** (derive) erfassen ‹*Bedeutung, Hauptpunkte*›; **~ happiness/pleasure/comfort from sth.** Fröhlichkeit/Freude/Trost aus etw. schöpfen; **~ much pleasure from life** dem Leben viel Freude abgewinnen **4** (Math.) ziehen ‹*Wurzel*›

extraction /ɪk'strækʃn/ *n.* **1** (of tooth; also Chem.) Extraktion, *die;* (of thorn, splinter, etc.) Herausziehen, *das;* (of bullet) Entfernen, *das;* (of juice, honey, metal) Gewinnung, *die;* (of oil) Förderung, *die* **2** (descent) Abstammung, *die;* Herkunft, *die;* **be of German ~:** deutscher Abstammung *od.* Herkunft sein

extractive /ɪk'stræktɪv/ *adj.* **~ industries** Rohstoffindustrie, *die;* **~ processes** Extraktionsverfahren *Pl.*

extractor /ɪk'stræktə(r)/ *n.* (for extracting juice) Entsafter, *der*

ex'tractor fan *n.* Entlüfter, *der;* Exhaustor, *der*

extra-curricular /ekstrəkə'rɪkjʊlə(r)/ *adj.* extracurricular (fachspr.); ‹*Aktivität*› außerhalb des Lehrplans

extraditable /ekstrə'daɪtəbl/ *adj.* **this is an ~ offence** für dieses Vergehen kann man ausgeliefert werden

extradite /'ekstrədaɪt/ *v.t.* **1** ausliefern ‹*Verbrecher*› **2** (obtain extradition of) **~ sb.** jmds. Auslieferung erwirken

extradition /ekstrə'dɪʃn/ *n.* Auslieferung, *die;* **~ treaty** Auslieferungsvertrag, *der*

extra'marital *adj.* außerehelich

extra'mural *adj.* (Univ.) außerhalb der Universität *nachgestellt;* außeruniversitär; **~ courses** *or* **classes** Hochschulkurse außerhalb der Universität; Fernkurse

extraneous /ɪk'streɪnɪəs/ *adj.* **1** (from outside) von außen; (Med.) körperfremd; **free from ~ matter** frei von Fremdstoffen **2** (irrelevant) belanglos; **be ~ to sth.** für etw. ohne Belang sein

extraordinarily /ɪk'strɔːdɪnərɪlɪ, ekstrə'ɔːdɪnərəlɪ/ *adv.* außergewöhnlich; überaus, ungemein ‹*merkwürdig*›

extraordinary /ɪk'strɔːdɪnərɪ, ekstrə'ɔːdɪnərɪ/ *adj.* **1** (exceptional) außergewöhnlich; (unusual, peculiar) ungewöhnlich ‹*Gabe*›; merkwürdig, eigenartig ‹*Zeichen, Benehmen, Angewohnheit*›; außerordentlich ‹*Verdienste, Einfluss*›; (additional) außerordentlich ‹*Versammlung*›; **how ~!** wie seltsam! **2** (more than ordinary) ungewöhnlich; **~ powers** außerordentliche Vollmachten **3** (specially employed) außerordentlich ‹*Gesandte[r], Professor[in]*›; **ambassador ~:** Sonderbotschafter, *der*

extra'ordinary general meeting *n.* (of shareholders) außerordentliche Hauptversammlung; (of club) außerordentliche Mitgliederversammlung

extrapolate /ɪk'stræpəleɪt/ (Math. etc.)
A *v.t.* extrapolieren (**to** auf + *Akk.*, **from** aus); (fig.) ableiten; extrapolieren (geh.)
B *v.i.* extrapolieren

extra: ~-'sensory *adj.* außersinnlich; **~-sensory perception** außersinnliche Wahrnehmung; **~ter'restrial** *adj.* außerirdisch; ex[tra]terrestrisch (fachspr.); **~terri'torial** *adj.* exterritorial; **~'time** *n., no pl.* (Sport) **in ~ time** in der Verlängerung; **after ~ time** nach einer Verlängerung; **the match went to ~ time** das Spiel wurde verlängert; **play ~ time** in die Verlängerung gehen

extravagance /ɪk'strævəgəns/ *n.* **1** *no pl.* (being extravagant) Extravaganz, *die;* (of claim, wish, order, demand) Übertriebenheit, *die;* (of words, thoughts, ideas, etc.) Verstiegenheit, *die;* (with money) Verschwendungssucht, *die;* **the ~ of her tastes** ihr teurer Geschmack **2** (extravagant thing) Luxus, *der*

extravagancy /ɪk'strævəgənsɪ/ ▸ **extravagance 1**

extravagant /ɪk'strævəgənt/ *adj.* **1** (wasteful) verschwenderisch; aufwendig ‹*Lebensstil*›; teuer ‹*Geschmack*› **2** (immoderate) übertrieben ‹*Benehmen, Lob, Eifer, Begeisterung usw.*›; maßlos ‹*Gebrauch, Begeisterung*› **3** (beyond bounds of reason) abwegig ‹*Theorie, Frage, Einfall*›; **it is not ~ to suppose that ...:** die Vermutung liegt nahe, dass ... **4** (exorbitant) überhöht ‹*Preis*›

extravagantly /ɪk'strævəgəntlɪ/ *adv.* extravagant ‹*einrichten, ausstatten, sich kleiden*›; verschwenderisch ‹*benutzen, verbrauchen*›; luxuriös, aufwendig ‹*leben*›; außergewöhnlich ‹*sich benehmen*›; überschwänglich ‹*loben*›; **spend money ~:** mit vollen Händen Geld ausgeben

extravaganza /ɪkstrævə'gænzə/ *n.* (Lit.) fantastische Dichtung; (Mus.) fantastische Komposition; (Theatre) Ausstattungsstück, *das*

'extra-virgin *adj.* [extra]nativ ‹*Olivenöl*›

extreme /ɪk'striːm/
A *adj.* **1** (outermost, utmost) äußerst... ‹*Spitze, Rand, Ende*›; extrem, krass ‹*Gegensätze*›; **the ~ end of the finger** die Fingerspitze *od.* -kuppe; **the ~ points of a line/scale** die Endpunkte einer Linie/Skala; **at the ~ edge/left** ganz am Rand/ganz links; **in the ~ North** im äußersten Norden **2** (reaching high degree) extrem; gewaltig ‹*Entfernung, Unterschied*›; höchst... ‹*Gefahr*›; äußerst... ‹*Notfall, Grenzen, Höflichkeit, Bescheidenheit*›; stärkst... ‹*Schmerzen*›; heftigst... ‹*Zorn*›; tiefst... ‹*Hass, Dankbarkeit*›; größt... ‹*Überraschung, Wichtigkeit, Wunsch*›; stürmisch ‹*Begeisterung*› **3** (not moderate) extrem ‹*Person, Einstellung, Gesinnung, Forderungen, Ideen, Tendenzen, Kritik*›; **~ right-wing views** rechtsextreme Ansichten **4** (RC & Orthodox Ch.) **~ unction** die Letzte Ölung **5** (severe) drastisch ‹*Maßnahme*›; **take ~ action against sb.** rigoros gegen jmdn. vorgehen
B *n.* Extrem, *das;* [krasser] Gegensatz; **~s of heat and cold** extreme Hitze und Kälte; **the ~s of wealth and poverty** größter Reichtum und äußerste Armut; **~s of passion** extreme Pole der Leidenschaft; **~s of temperature** extreme Temperaturunterschiede; **go to the ~ of doing sth.** bis zum Äußersten gehen und etw. tun; **go to ~s** *or* **to any ~** *or* **to the last ~:** vor nichts zurückschrecken; **go to the other ~:** ins andere Extrem verfallen; **go from one ~ to another** von *od.* aus einem Extrem ins andere fallen; **annoying/monotonous in the ~:** äußerst unangenehm/extrem *od.* äußerst eintönig; **run to ~s** einen Hang zum Extremen haben; *see also* **carry A 7**

extremely /ɪk'striːmlɪ/ *adv.* äußerst; **Did you enjoy the party? — Yes, ~:** Hat dir die Party gefallen? — Ja, sehr sogar!

extremeness /ɪk'striːmnɪs/ *n., no pl.* (of views, actions, policies) Extremität, *die;* (of measures) Härte, *die*

extreme: ~ 'sport *n.* Extremsportart, *die;* **~ 'sportsman** *n.* Extremsportler, *der;* **~ 'sportswoman** *n.* Extremsportlerin, *die*

extremism /ɪk'striːmɪzm/ *n., no pl.* Extremismus, *der*

extremist /ɪk'striːmɪst/ *n.* **1** Extremist, *der*/Extremistin, *die;* **right-wing ~:** Rechtsextremist, *der*/-extremistin, *die* **2** *attrib.* extremistisch

extremity /ɪk'stremɪtɪ/ *n.* **1** (of branch, path, road) äußerstes Ende; (of region) Rand, *der;* **the southernmost ~ of a continent** die Südspitze eines Kontinents **2** *in pl.* (hands and feet) Extremitäten *Pl.* **3** (adversity) äußerste *od.* höchste Not; (intensity) Heftigkeit, *die;* **be reduced to ~:** in eine Notlage geraten

extricate /'ekstrɪkeɪt/ *v.t.* **~ sth. from sth.** etw. aus etw. herausziehen; **~ oneself/sb. from sth.** sich/jmdn. aus etw. befreien

extrinsic /ek'strɪnsɪk/ *adj.* **1** äußer...; äußerlich ‹*Wert*›; extrinsisch (Philos.); **be ~ to sth.** einer Sache (*Dat.*) fremd sein **2** (not essential) irrelevant (**to** für)

extrovert /'ekstrəvɜːt/
A *n.* extravertierter Mensch; Extravertierte, *der*/*die;* **be an ~:** extravertiert sein
B *adj.* extravertiert; **have ~ tendencies** zur Extravertiertheit neigen

extroverted /'ekstrəvɜːtɪd/ *adj.* extravertiert

extrude /ɪk'struːd/ *v.t.* ausstoßen; ausstrecken ‹*Fühler*›; extrudieren (fachspr.) ‹*Metall, Kunststoff*›; (Geol.) auswerfen ‹*Gestein*›; (fig.: expel) ausschließen (**from** aus)

extrusion /ɪk'struːʒn/ *n.* (of metal, plastic, etc.) Extrudieren, *das* (fachspr.); (article extruded) Formstück, *das*

exuberance /ɪg'zjuːbərəns/ *n.* **1** (vigour) Überschwang, *der;* (of health) Robustheit, *die;* **~ of joy/spirits** überschwängliche Freude/Stimmung; **~ of youth** jugendlicher Überschwang **2** (of language, style) Lebendigkeit, *die*

exuberant /ɪg'zjuːbərənt/ *adj.* **1** (overflowing, abounding) strotzend ‹*Gesundheit*›; überschäumend ‹*Kraft, Freude, Eifer, Heiterkeit*› **2** (effusive) überschwänglich; sehr lebhaft ‹*Farbe*›; **he was ~ when ...:** er freute sich überschwänglich, als ...

exuberantly /ɪg'zjuːbərəntlɪ/ *adv.* überschwänglich ‹*begrüßen, beschreiben*›; **~ happy** überglücklich

exude /ɪg'zjuːd/
A *v.i.* abgesondert werden (**from** aus); ‹*Blut:*› fließen (**from** aus); (fig.) ausgehen (**from** von)
B *v.t.* absondern ‹*Flüssigkeit, Harz*›; ausströmen ‹*Geruch*›; (fig.) ausstrahlen ‹*Charme, Zuversicht*›

exult /ɪg'zʌlt/ *v.i.* **1** (literary: rejoice) jubeln; frohlocken (geh.) (**in, at, over** über + *Akk.*); **~ to find that ...:** darüber frohlocken, dass ...; **~ with joy** vor Freude jubeln **2** (triumph) triumphieren (**over** über + *Akk.*)

exultant /ɪg'zʌltənt/ *adj.* **1** (literary: exulting) jubelnd ‹*Person, Menge, Lachen*›; unbändig ‹*Freude*›; **be ~:** jubeln; **be in an ~ mood** in Hochstimmung sein **2** (triumphant) triumphierend ‹*Sieger*›

exultantly /ɪg'zʌltəntlɪ/ *adv.* überglücklich

exultation /egzʌl'teɪʃn/ *n.* Jubel, *der*

e

'ex-works
A *adj.* Ab-Werk-
B *adv.* ab Werk

eye /aɪ/
A *n.* 1 ▸ p. 951 Auge, *das;* **as far as the ~ can see** so weit das Auge reicht; **~s** (look, glance, gaze) Blick, *der;* **a pair of blue ~s** zwei blaue Augen; **close** *or* **shut/open one's ~s** die Augen schließen/öffnen; **that will make him open his ~s** (fig.) da wird er Augen machen; **open sb.'s ~s to sth.** (fig.) jmdm. die Augen über etw. (*Akk.*) öffnen; **shut** *or* **close one's ~s to sth.** (fig.) die Augen vor etw. (*Dat.*) verschließen; **the sun/light is [shining] in my ~s** die Sonne/das Licht blendet mich; **I've got the sun in my ~s** die Sonne blendet mich; **out of the corner of one's ~:** aus den Augenwinkeln; **lift up one's ~s** die Augen erheben; aufblicken; **drop** *or* **lower one's ~s** die Augen niederschlagen; den Blick senken; **with one's own** *or* **very ~s** mit eigenen Augen; **under/before sb.'s very ~s** unter/vor jmds. Augen (*Dat.*); **measure a distance by ~** *or* **with one's ~[s]** einen Abstand nach Augenmaß schätzen; **judge sth. by ~:** etw. nach dem Augenschein beurteilen (geh.); **paint/draw sth. by ~:** etw. nach der Natur malen/zeichnen; **with the ~ of an artist, with an artist's ~:** mit den Augen eines Künstlers; **look sb. in the ~:** jmdm. gerade in die Augen sehen; **not be able to look sb. in the ~:** jmdm. nicht ins Gesicht sehen können; **have ~s [only] for sb.** sich [nur] für jmdn. interessieren; **be unable to take one's ~s off sb./sth.** die Augen *od.* den Blick nicht von jmdm./etw. abwenden können; **make [sheep's] ~s at sb.** jmdm. [schöne] Augen machen; **keep an ~ on sb./sth.** auf jmdn./etw. aufpassen; ein Auge auf jmdn./etw. haben; **keep a sharp** *or* **close** *or* **strict ~ on sb./sth.** scharf auf jmdn./etw. aufpassen; streng auf jmdn./etw. achten; **keep one's ~[s] on sb./sth.** jmdn./etw. im Auge behalten; **have [got] an** *or* **one's ~[s] on sb./sth.** ein Auge auf jmdn./etw. geworfen haben; **I've got my ~ on you!** ich lasse dich nicht aus den Augen!; **keep an ~ open** *or* **out [for sb./sth.]** [nach jmdm./etw.] Ausschau halten; **keep one's ~s open** die Augen offen halten; **keep one's ~s skinned** *or* **peeled** (coll.) wie ein Schießhund aufpassen (ugs.); **keep one's ~s open** *or* (coll.) **peeled** *or* (coll.) **skinned for sth.** nach etw. Ausschau halten; **keep one's ~s and ears open** Augen und Ohren offen halten; **with one's ~s open** (fig.) mit offenen Augen; bewusst; **with one's ~s shut** (fig.) (without full awareness) blind; (with great ease) im Schlaf; **with a friendly/jealous/eager/critical ~:** freundlich / eifersüchtig / erwartungsvoll / kritisch; **have you no ~s in your head?** hast du keine Augen im Kopf? (ugs.); bist du blind?; **where are your ~s?, use your ~s!** wo hast du deine Augen?; **I haven't [got] ~s at** *or* **in the back of my head** ich habe hinten keine Augen; **in the ~s of God/the law** vor Gott/nach dem Gesetz; **in sb.'s ~s** in jmds. Augen (*Dat.*); **see sb./sth. through sb.'s ~s** jmdn./etw. mit jmds. Augen sehen; **look at sth. through the ~s of sb.** etw. mit jmds. Augen betrachten; **tire one's ~s out** seine Augen ermüden; **be all ~s** gespannt zusehen; **[all] my ~** (coll.) [alles] Schnickschnack (ugs. abwertend); **do sb. in the ~** (coll.) jmdn. übers Ohr hauen (ugs.); **[an] ~ for [an] ~:** Auge um Auge; **~s front!/right!/left!** (Mil.) Augen geradeaus/rechts/links!; **have an ~ to sth./doing sth.** auf etw. (*Akk.*) bedacht sein/darauf bedacht sein, etw. zu tun; **with an ~ to sth.** im Hinblick auf etw. (*Akk.*); **with an ~ to doing sth.** mit dem Gedanken, etw. zu tun; **hit sb. in the ~** (fig.) jmdm. ins Auge springen *od.* fallen; **that was one in the ~ for him** (coll.) das war ein Schlag ins Kontor (ugs.) für ihn; **see ~ to ~ [on sth. with sb.]** [mit jmdm.] einer Meinung [über etw. (*Akk.*)] sein; **not see ~ to ~ with sb. on sth.** über etw. (*Akk.*) anderer Meinung als jmd. sein; **be up to one's ~s** (fig.) bis über beide Ohren drinstecken (ugs.); **be up to one's ~s in work/debt** bis über beide Ohren in der Arbeit/in Schulden stecken (ugs.); **have an ~ for sth.** ein Auge *od.* einen Blick für etw. haben; **have an ~ for sb.** jmdn. gern haben; **a man with an ~ for the ladies** ein Mann, der die Frauen gern hat; **have a keen/good ~ for sth.** einen geschärften/einen sicheren *od.* den richtigen Blick für etw. haben; **make ~s at sb.** jmdm. [schöne] Augen machen; **see with half an ~ that ...:** auf den ersten Blick sehen, dass ...; **get one's ~ in at shooting/tennis** sich einschießen/sich einspielen; *see also* **open A 1**
2 (sth. like an ~) Auge, *das;* (of peacock's tail) Pfauenauge, *das;* (on butterfly's wing) Augenfleck, *der;* (of needle, fish-hook) Öhr, *das;* (metal loop) Öse, *die*
B *v.t.,* **~ing** *or* **eying** /ˈaɪɪŋ/ beäugen; **~ sb. up and down/from head to foot** jmdn. von oben bis unten/von Kopf bis Fuß mustern

eye: ~ball A *n.* Augapfel, *der;* **~ball to ~ball** (coll.) hautnah ‹*Konfrontation*›; **be** *or* **meet ~ball to ~ball** sich (*Dat.*) Auge in Auge gegenüberstehen; B *v.t.* **~ball sb.** (coll.) jmdn. anstarren; **~bath** *n.* Augenbadewanne, *die;* **~black** *n.* (dated) schwarze Wimperntusche; **~bright** *n.* (Bot.) Augentrost, *der;* **~brow** *n.* Augenbraue, *die;* **raise** *or* **lift an ~brow** *or* **one's ~brows [at sth.]** die [Augen]brauen [wegen etw.] hochziehen; (fig.) (in surprise) die Stirn runzeln (**at** über + *Akk.*); (superciliously) die Nase rümpfen (**at** über + *Akk.*); **it will raise a few ~brows** das wird einiges Stirnrunzeln hervorrufen; **up to the** *or* **one's ~brows [in sth.]** bis über beide Ohren [in etw. (*Dat.*)]; **~brow pencil** Augenbrauenstift, *der;* **~ candy** *n., no pl.* (coll.) Augenweide, *die;* **be ~ candy** schön anzusehen sein; **~-catching** *adj.* ins Auge springend *od.* fallend ‹*Inserat, Plakat, Buchhülle usw.*›; **be [very] ~-catching** ein [wirkungsvoller] Blickfang sein; **she is very ~-catching** sie zieht die Augen aller auf sich (*Akk.*); **~ contact** *n.* Blickkontakt, *der*

-eyed /aɪd/ *adj. in comb.* ▸ **p. 951** -äugig; **big-~/bright-~:** groß-/helläugig; **fierce-~/sad-~:** mit grimmigen/traurigen Augen *od.* grimmigem/traurigem Blick *nachgestellt;* **be sad-~:** traurige Augen haben

eye: ~ dropper *n.* (Med.) Augentropfer, *der;* **~ drops** *n. pl.* (Med.) Augentropfen *Pl.*

eyeful /ˈaɪfʊl/ *n.* (coll.) **be quite an ~** ‹*Person:*› toll *od.* klasse aussehen; **get an ~ [of sth.]** (sight) einiges [von etw.] zu sehen bekommen; **get an ~ of soot** *etc.* eine Ladung Ruß *usw.* in die Auge kriegen

eye: ~glass *n.* (dated) Augenglas, *das* (veralt.); **~ hospital** *n.* Augenklinik, *die;* **~lash** *n.* Augenwimper, *die*

eyeless /ˈaɪlɪs/ *adj.* blind ‹*Person, Tier*›

eyelet /ˈaɪlɪt/ *n.* 1 Öse, *die;* (Naut.) Auge, *das* 2 (to look through) Guckloch, *das*

eye: ~ level *n.* Augenhöhe, *die; attrib.* in Augenhöhe *nachgestellt;* **~lid** *n.* Augenlid, *das;* **~liner** *n.* Eyeliner, *der;* Lidstrich, *der;* **~ make-up** *n.* Augen-Make-up, *das;* **~-opener** *n.* (surprise, revelation) Überraschung, *die;* **the book was an ~-opener to the public** das Buch hat der Öffentlichkeit die Augen geöffnet; **~patch** *n.* Augenklappe, *die;* **~piece** *n.* (Optics) Okular, *das;* **~shade** *n.* Augenschirm, *der;* **~shadow** *n.* Lidschatten, *der;* **~sight** *n.* Sehkraft, *die;* **have good ~sight** gute Augen haben; gut sehen können; **his ~sight is poor** er hat schlechte Augen; **~ socket** *n.* Augenhöhle, *die;* **~sore** *n.* Schandfleck, *der* (abwertend); **the building is an ~sore** das Gebäude beleidigt das Auge; **~ strain** *n.* Überanstrengung der Augen; **be a cause of ~ strain** die Augen überanstrengen; **~ test** *n.* Sehtest, *der;* **~ tooth** *n.* Eckzahn, *der;* **cut one's ~ teeth** (fig.) Erfahrungen sammeln; **she would give her ~ teeth for it/to do it** sie würde alles dafür geben/darum geben, es zu tun; **~wash** *n.* 1 (Med.: lotion) Augenwasser, *das;* 2 (coll.) (nonsense) Gewäsch, *das* (ugs. abwertend); (concealment) Augen[aus]wischerei, *die* (ugs.); **~witness** *n.* Augenzeuge, *der/-zeugin, die;* **be an ~witness of sth.** Augenzeuge einer Sache (*Gen.*) sein; *attrib.* **~witness account** *or* **report** Augenzeugenbericht, *der*

eyrie /ˈɪərɪ/ *n.* (nest) Horst, *der*

e

F, f /ef/ *n., pl.* **Fs** *or* **F's** 1 (letter) F, f, *das* 2 **F** (Mus.) F, f, *das;* **F sharp** fis, Fis, *das* 3 **F** (Sch., Univ.: mark) Sechs, *die;* **he got an F** er bekam „ungenügend" *od.* eine Sechs

f. *abbr.* 1 **= female** weibl. 2 **= feminine** f. 3 **= focal length** f; **f/8** (Photog.) Blende 8 4 **= following [page]** f. 5 **= forte** f 6 **= folio** F.

F. *abbr.* 1 **= Fahrenheit** F 2 **= Fellow** 3 (on pencil) **= firm** F 4 ▸ℹ **p. 1332 = franc** F 5 (Phys.) **= farad[s]** F

fa ▸**fah**

FA *abbr.* (Brit.) **= Football Association** (*Britischer Fußballverband*)

fab /fæb/ *adj.* (Brit. coll.) fabelhaft (ugs.); dufte, toll (salopp)

fable /ˈfeɪbl/ *n.* 1 (story of the supernatural, myth, lie) Märchen, *das;* **land of ~:** Märchen- *od.* Fabelland, *das;* **separate fact from ~:** Dichtung und Wahrheit unterscheiden 2 (thing that does not really exist, brief story) Fabel, *die*

fabled /ˈfeɪbld/ *adj.* 1 (told as in fable) **it is ~ that ...:** es heißt, dass ... 2 (mythical) Fabel‹*land, -wesen, -tier*› 3 (celebrated) berühmt (**for** für)

fabric /ˈfæbrɪk/ *n.* 1 (material, construction, texture) Gewebe, *das;* **woven/knitted/ribbed/coarse/mixed ~:** Web-/Strickware, *die*/Rips, *der*/Grob-/Mischgewebe, *das* 2 (thing put together) Gebilde, *das* 3 (fig.: frame) Gefüge, *das;* **the ~ of society** die Struktur der Gesellschaft; **destroy the ~ of sb.'s life** jmds. Welt zerstören 4 (of building) bauliche Substanz; Bausubstanz, *die*

fabricate /ˈfæbrɪkeɪt/ *v.t.* 1 (invent) erfinden; (forge) fälschen 2 (construct, manufacture) herstellen

fabrication /fæbrɪˈkeɪʃn/ *n.* 1 (of story etc., falsehood) Erfindung, *die;* **the story is [a] pure ~:** die Geschichte ist frei erfunden 2 (construction, manufacture) Herstellung, *die*

fabric: ~ conditioner *n.* Gewebeconditioner, *der;* **~ softener** *n.* Weichspülmittel, *das;* Weichspüler, *der*

fabulous /ˈfæbjʊləs/ *adj.* 1 (unhistorical, legendary, celebrated) sagenhaft; **~ animal/creature** *or* **being** Fabeltier/-wesen, *das* 2 (exaggerated) fantastisch ‹*Geschichte*› 3 (coll.: marvellous) fabelhaft (ugs.)

facade /fəˈsɑːd/ *n.* (lit. or fig.) Fassade, *die;* **that's just a ~** (fig.) das ist alles nur Fassade

face /feɪs/

A *n.* 1 ▸ℹ **p. 951** Gesicht, *das;* **wash one's ~:** sich (*Dat.*) das Gesicht waschen; **blush/be smiling all over one's ~:** bis über die Ohren rot werden/über das ganze Gesicht strahlen; **go purple** *or* **black in the ~** (with strangulation), **go blue in the ~** (with cold) blau im Gesicht werden; **go red** *or* **purple in the ~** (with exertion or passion or shame) rot im Gesicht werden; **the stone struck me on my ~** *or* **in the ~:** der Stein traf mich ins Gesicht; **the ~ of an angel/a devil/a criminal** ein Engels-/Teufels-/Verbrechergesicht; **bring A and B ~ to ~:** A und B einander (*Dat.*) gegenüberstellen; **stand ~ to ~:** sich (*Dat.*) gegenüberstehen; **meet sb. ~ to ~:** jmdn. persönlich kennen lernen; **come** *or* **be brought ~ to ~ with sb.** mit jmdm. konfrontiert werden; **come ~ to ~ with the fact that ...:** vor der Tatsache stehen, dass ...; **fly in the ~ of sb./sth.** jmdn. mit Verachtung strafen/sich über etw. (*Akk.*) hinwegsetzen; **in [the] ~ of sth.** (despite) trotz; (confronted with) vor (+ *Dat.*); **cowardice in the ~ of the enemy** Feigheit vor dem Feind; **slam the door in sb.'s ~:** jmdm. die Tür vor der Nase zuknallen (ugs.); **shine in sb.'s ~:** jmdm. ins Gesicht scheinen; **fall [flat] on one's ~** (lit. or fig.) auf die Nase fallen (ugs.); **look sb./sth. in the ~:** jmdm./einer Sache ins Gesicht sehen; **put one's ~ on** (coll.) sich anmalen (ugs.); **set one's ~ against sb./sth.** sich jmdm./einer Sache entgegenstellen; **show one's ~:** sich sehen *od.* blicken lassen; **tell sb. to his ~ what ...:** jmdm. [offen] ins Gesicht sagen, was ...; **use sb.'s nickname to his ~:** jmds. Spitznamen in seiner Gegenwart benutzen; **talk/scream/complain** *etc.* **till one is blue in the ~:** reden/schreien/klagen *usw.* bis man verrückt wird (ugs.); **shut one's ~** (sl.) die *od.* seine Klappe halten (salopp); **have the ~ to do sth.** die Stirn haben, etw. zu tun; **save one's ~:** das Gesicht wahren *od.* retten; **lose ~ [with sb.] [over sth.]** das Gesicht [vor jmdm.] [wegen etw.] verlieren; **sth. makes sb. lose ~:** etw. kostet jmdn. das Gesicht *od.* Ansehen; **see by sb.'s ~ that ...:** es jmdm. [am Gesicht] *od.* es jmds. Gesicht (*Dat.*) ansehen, dass ...; **make** *or* **pull a ~/~s [at sb.]** (to show dislike) ein Gesicht/Gesichter machen *od.* ziehen; (to amuse or frighten) eine Grimasse/Grimassen schneiden; **don't make a ~!** mach nicht so ein Gesicht!; **with a ~ like thunder** *or* **as black as thunder** schwarz vor Ärger; **on the ~ of it** dem Anschein nach; **change the ~ of sth.** einer Sache (*Dat.*) ein neues Gesicht geben; **put a brave** *or* **good** *or* **bold ~ on it/the matter/the affair** *etc.* gute Miene zum bösen Spiel machen

2 (front) (of mountain, cliff) Wand, *die;* (of building) Stirnseite, *die;* (of clock, watch) Zifferblatt, *das;* (of dice) Seite, *die;* (of coin, medal, banknote, playing card) Vorderseite, *die;* (of tool) Bahn, *die;* (of golf club, cricket bat, hockey stick, tennis racket) Schlagfläche, *die*

3 (surface) **the ~ of the earth** die Erde; **disappear off** *or* **from the ~ of the earth** spurlos verschwinden; **be wiped off the ~ of the earth** ausradiert werden

4 (Geom.; also of crystal, gem) Fläche, *die*

5 ▸**typeface**

6 ▸**coalface.** *See also* **face down[ward]; face up[ward]; fall B 14; laugh B; long[1] A 2; smack[2] A 2; straight face**

B *v.t.* 1 ▸ℹ **p. 1013** (look towards) sich wenden zu; **sb. ~s the front** jmd. sieht nach vorne; **[stand] facing one another** sich (*Dat.*) *od.* (meist geh.) einander gegenüber[stehen]; **the house facing the church** das Haus gegenüber der Kirche; **the window ~s the garden/front** das Fenster geht zum Garten/zur Straße hinaus *od.* liegt zum Garten/zur Straße; **travel/sit facing the engine** mit dem Gesicht in Fahrtrichtung fahren/in Fahrtrichtung sitzen; **sit facing the stage** vor der Bühne *od.* mit dem Gesicht zur Bühne sitzen

2 (fig.: have to deal with) ins Auge sehen (+ *Dat.*) ‹*Tod, Vorstellung*›; gegenübertreten (+ *Dat.*) ‹*Kläger*›; sich stellen (+ *Dat.*) ‹*Anschuldigung, Kritik*›; stehen vor (+ *Dat.*) ‹*Ruin, Entscheidung*›; eingehen ‹*Risiko*›; **~ trial for murder, ~ a charge of murder** sich wegen Mordes vor Gericht verantworten müssen

3 (not shrink from) ins Auge sehen (+ *Dat.*) ‹*Tatsache, Wahrheit*›; mit Fassung gegenübertreten (+ *Dat.*) ‹*Kläger*›; **~ sth. out** etw. durchstehen; **~ sb. down** jmdn. demoralisieren *od.* (ugs.) kleinkriegen; **refuse to be ~d down by threats** sich von Drohungen nicht kleinkriegen lassen (ugs.); **~ the music** (fig.) die Suppe auslöffeln (ugs.); **let's ~ it** (coll.) machen wir uns (*Dat.*) doch nichts vor (ugs.)

4 **be ~d with sth.** sich einer Sache (*Dat.*) gegenübersehen; **~d with these facts** mit diesen Tatsachen konfrontiert; **he was ~d with the possibility** für ihn ergab sich die Möglichkeit; **he is ~d with a lawsuit** gegen ihn wird ein Prozess eingeleitet; **the problems/questions that we are ~d with** die Probleme/Fragen, vor denen wir stehen

5 (coll.: bear) verkraften

6 (dress, trim) besetzen ‹*Kleidungsstück*›; verkleiden, verblenden ‹*Wand*›; **a cloak ~d with white** ein Umhang mit weißem Besatz

C *v.i.* 1 ▸ℹ **p. 1013** (look) **~ backwards/forwards** ‹*Person/Bank, Sitz:*› entgegen der/in Fahrtrichtung sitzen/aufgestellt sein; **in which direction was he facing?** in welche Richtung blickte er?; **~ away [from sb.]** das Gesicht [von jmdm.] abwenden; **stand facing away from sb.** mit dem Rücken zu jmdm. stehen; **~ away from the road/on to the road/east[wards]** *or* **to[wards] the east** ‹*Fenster, Zimmer:*› nach hinten/vorn/Osten liegen; **the side of the house ~s to[wards] the sea** die Seite des Hauses liegt zum Meer

2 (Amer. Mil.) eine Wendung machen; **~ about/to the right/left** eine Kehrt-/Rechts-/Linkswendung machen; **left/right ~!** ganze Abteilung links/rechts um!

Phrasal verb

• **~ ˈup to** *v.t.* ins Auge sehen (+ *Dat.*); sich abfinden mit ‹*Möglichkeit*›; auf sich nehmen ‹*Verantwortung*›

face: ~ card ▸**court card; ~cloth** *n.* (cloth for ~) Waschlappen [für das Gesicht]; **~ cream** *n.* Gesichtscreme, *die*

-faced /feɪst/ *adj. in comb.* -gesichtig

face: ~ ˈdown[ward] *adv.* mit der Vorderseite nach unten; **put one's cards ~ down on the table** seine Karten verdeckt auf den Tisch legen; **lie ~ down[ward]** ‹*Person:*› auf dem Bauch liegen; ‹*Buch:*› auf dem Gesicht liegen; *see also* **face B 3; ~ flannel** (Brit.) ▸**~cloth**

faceless /ˈfeɪslɪs/ *adj.* 1 (without face) gesichtslos 2 (anonymous) anonym (fig.)

face: ~lift *n.* 1 Facelifting, *das;* **have** *or* **get a ~lift** sich liften lassen; 2 (fig.: improvement in appearance) Verschönerung, *die;* **~ mask** 1 (protective mask) Atemschutzmaske, *die;* 2 (face pack) [Gesichts]maske, *die;* **~-off** *n.* (Ice Hockey) Bully, *das;* **~ pack** *n.* [Gesichts]maske, *die;* **~ paint** *n.* Gesichtsfarbe, *die;* **~-painting** *n., no pl.* Gesichtsbemalung, *die;* (at events for children) Kinderschminken, *das;* **~ powder** *n.* Gesichtspuder, *das;* **~-saving** **A** *adj.* zur Wahrung des Gesichts *nachgestellt;* **as a ~-saving gesture** um das Gesicht zu wahren *od.* retten; **B** *n.* Wahrung des Gesichts

facet /ˈfæsɪt/ *n.* 1 (of many-sided body, esp. of cut stone) Facette, *die* 2 (aspect) Seite, *die;* **every ~:** alle Seiten *od.* (geh.) Facetten

faceted /ˈfæsɪtɪd/ *adj.* facettiert ‹*Edelstein, Diamant, Linse*›

'face time *n., no pl.* (coll.) **1** (media exposure) Medienpräsenz, *die;* **television ~:** Bildschirmpräsenz, *die* **2** (face-to-face contact) direkter Kontakt

facetious /fəˈsiːʃəs/ *adj.* [gewollt] witzig; (impudently) frech; **[not] be ~ [about sth.]** [keine] Witze [über etw. (*Akk.*)] machen (ugs.)

facetiously /fəˈsiːʃəslɪ/ *adv.* [gewollt] witzig

face: ~-to-~ *adj.* unmittelbar ‹*Gegenüberstellung*›; **~ 'up[ward]** *adv.* mit der Vorderseite nach oben; **lie ~ up[ward]** ‹*Karte:*› offen *od.* aufgedeckt liegen; ‹*Person:*› auf dem Rücken liegen; (open) ‹*Buch:*› aufgeschlagen liegen; **~ value** *n.* (Finance) Nominalwert, *der* (fachspr.); Nennwert, *der;* **accept sth. at [its] ~ value** (fig.) etw. für bare Münze nehmen; **take sb. at [his/her] ~ value** (fig.) jmdn. nach seinem Äußeren beurteilen; **~worker** *n.* (Mining) Untertagearbeiter, *der*

facia /ˈfeɪʃə/ *n.* **1** (plate) **~ [board]** Firmenschild, *das* **2** (Motor Veh.) **~ [board** *or* **panel]** Armaturenbrett, *das*

facial /ˈfeɪʃl/
A *adj.* Gesichts-
B *n.* Gesichtsmassage, *die;* **have a ~:** sich (*Dat.*) das Gesicht massieren lassen

facile /ˈfæsaɪl, ˈfæsɪl/ *adj.* (often derog.) leicht ‹*Sieg, Arbeit, Aufgabe*›; einfach ‹*Art, Methode, Technik*›; gewandt ‹*Lügner, Schriftsteller*›; nichtssagend, banal ‹*Bemerkung*›; oberflächlich, (abwertend) flach ‹*Person, Einstellung*›

facilitate /fəˈsɪlɪteɪt/ *v.t.* erleichtern

facilitator /fəˈsɪlɪteɪtə(r)/ *n.* Vermittler, *der*/Vermittlerin, *die;* **the company is a ~:** die Firma nimmt eine Vermittlerrolle ein

fa'cilities management *n., no pl.* Liegenschaftsverwaltung, *die;* Gebäudemanagement, *das*

facility /fəˈsɪlɪtɪ/ *n.* **1** *esp. in pl.* Einrichtung, *die;* **cooking/washing facilities** Koch-/Waschgelegenheit, *die;* **sports facilities** Sportanlagen; **drying facilities** (indoor) Trockenraum, *der;* (outdoor) Trockenplatz, *der;* **postal facilities** Postdienste; **shopping facilities** Einkaufsmöglichkeiten; **banking facilities** Banken; **travel facilities** Verkehrsmittel; **a holiday complex with all facilities** eine Ferienanlage mit allem, was dazu gehört **2** (building[s], premises) Anlage, *die;* **research ~:** Forschungseinrichtung, *die* **3** (feature of service or machine) Möglichkeit, *die;* **have the ~ to do sth.** die Möglichkeit haben *od.* bieten, etw. zu tun **4** *no pl.* (ease, aptitude, freedom from difficulty) Leichtigkeit, *die;* (dexterity) Gewandtheit, *die;* **~ in speech/writing** Rede-/Schreibgewandtheit, *die*

facing /ˈfeɪsɪŋ/ *n.* **1** (on garment) Aufschlag, *der;* Besatz, *der* **2** *in pl.* (cuffs, collar, etc. of jacket) [Uniform]aufschläge *Pl.* **3** (covering) Verblendung, *die;* Verkleidung, *die*

facsimile /fækˈsɪmɪlɪ/ *n.* **1** Faksimile, *das* **2** (Telecommunications) ▸**fax A**

fact /fækt/ *n.* **1** (true thing) Tatsache, *die;* **~s and figures** Fakten und Zahlen; **the ~ remains that ...:** Tatsache bleibt: ...; **the true ~s of the case** *or* **matter** der wahre Sachverhalt; **know for a ~ that ...:** genau *od.* sicher wissen, dass ...; **is that a ~?** (coll.) Tatsache? (ugs.); **and that's a ~:** und daran gibts nichts zu zweifeln (ugs.); **the value/reason lies in the ~ that ...:** der Nutzen/Grund besteht darin, dass ...; **look the ~s in the face, face [the] ~s** den Tatsachen ins Gesicht sehen; **it is a proven/an established/an undisputed/an accepted ~ that ...:** es ist erwiesen/steht fest/ist unbestritten/man geht davon aus, dass ...; **the ~ [of the matter] is that ...:** die Sache ist die, dass ...; **[it is a] ~ of life** [das ist die] harte *od.* rauhe Wirklichkeit; **tell** *or* **teach sb. the ~s of life** (coll. euphem.) jmdn. [sexuell] aufklären **2** (reality) Wahrheit, *die;* Tatsachen *Pl.;* **distinguish ~ from fiction** Fakten und Fiktion (geh.) *od.* Dichtung und Wahrheit unterscheiden; **in ~:** tatsächlich; **I don't suppose you did/would do it? — In ~, I did/would** Ich nehme an, Sie haben es nicht getan/würden es nicht tun. — Doch[, ich habe es tatsächlich getan/würde es tatsächlich tun]; **I was planning to go to your party and had in ~ bought a bottle of wine** ich wollte zu deiner Party kommen und hatte sogar *od.* auch schon eine Flasche Wein gekauft; **he was supposed to arrive before eight, but he didn't in ~ get here till after twelve** er sollte vor acht Uhr ankommen, ist dann aber doch erst nach 12 Uhr hier eingetroffen; **he has left us; in ~ he is not coming back** er hat uns verlassen, und er kommt auch nicht mehr zurück; **I don't think he'll come back; in ~ I know he won't** ich glaube nicht, dass er zurückkommt, ich weiß es sogar **3** (thing assumed to be ~) Faktum, *das;* **deny the ~ that ...:** [die Tatsache] abstreiten, dass ... **4** (Law: crime) [Straf]tat, *die;* **be an accessory before/after the ~:** jmdm. Beihilfe leisten/Begünstigung gewähren. *see also* **matter A 4**

fact: ~ finder *n.* **1** (person) Ermittler, *der*/Ermittlerin, *die;* **2** (book) Faktensammlung, *die;* **~-finding** *attrib. adj.* Erkundungs‹*fahrt, -flug, -trupp*›; **~-finding committee/trip/study** Untersuchungsausschuss, *der*/Informationsreise, *die*/Ermittlungsarbeit, *die*

faction /ˈfækʃn/ *n.* **1** (party or group) Splittergruppe, *die;* Faktion, *die* (veralt.) **2** *no pl.* (party strife) Parteihader, *der*

factional /ˈfækʃənl/ *adj.* parteiintern ‹*Konflikt, Uneinigkeit, Streit*›; **a ~ group/splinter group** eine Gruppierung/Splittergruppe

factious /ˈfækʃəs/ *adj.* faktiös; parteisüchtig ‹*Absicht*›

factitious /fækˈtɪʃəs/ *adj.*, **factitiously** /fækˈtɪʃəslɪ/ *adv.* künstlich

factor /ˈfæktə(r)/
A *n.* **1** (Math.; also fact, circumstance) Faktor, *der* **2** (Biol.) Erbfaktor, *der* **3** (merchant) Kommissionär, *der* **4** (Scot.: land agent, steward) Gutsverwalter, *der* **5** (agent, deputy) Vertreter, *der. See also* **common factor**
B *v.t.* **1** (Math.) in Faktoren zerlegen **2** (resolve into components) zerlegen

factoring /ˈfæktərɪŋ/ *n.* (Commerc.) Factoring, *das*

factorize (factorise) /ˈfæktəraɪz/ (Math.)
A *v.t.* in Faktoren zerlegen
B *v.i.* sich in Faktoren zerlegen lassen

factory /ˈfæktərɪ/ *n.* Fabrik, *die;* Werk, *das;* **a ~ for assembling cars/machines** ein Kraftfahrzeug[montage]werk/eine Maschinenfabrik

factory: ~ 'farm *n.* (Agric.) [voll]automatisierter landwirtschaftlicher Betrieb; **~ 'farming** *n., no pl.* [fabrikmäßige] Massentierhaltung; **the ~ farming of salmon** die massenweise Lachsproduktion; **~ 'floor** *n.* Arbeitsplatz (in der Produktion); **on the ~ floor** (amongst the workforce) in der Belegschaft/den Belegschaften; **~-gate** *attrib. adj.* **~-gate prices** Ab-Werk-Preise; **~-made** *adj.* fabrik- *od.* serienmäßig hergestellt; **~-made clothes/furniture** Konfektion[skleidung], *die*/Serienmöbel *Pl.;* **~ outlet** *n.* Factoryoutlet, *das;* Fabrikverkauf, *der;* **~ ship** *n.* Fabrikschiff, *das;* **~ shop** Fabrikverkauf, *der;* Factoryoutlet, *das;* **~ 'unit** *n.* Fabrikeinheit, *die;* Fabrikgebäude, *das;* **~ work** *n.* Fabrikarbeit, *die;* **~ worker** *n.* ▸❶ **p. 1260** Fabrikarbeiter, *der*/-arbeiterin, *die*

factotum /fækˈtəʊtəm/ *n.* Faktotum, *das*

'fact sheet *n.* Infoblatt, *das*

factual /ˈfæktʃʊəl/ *adj.* sachlich ‹*Bericht, Darlegung, Stil*›; auf Tatsachen beruhend ‹*Aspekt, Punkt, Beweis*›; wahr ‹*Geschichte*›; **~ error** Sachfehler, *der*

factually /ˈfæktʃʊəlɪ/ *adv.* sachlich; mit Tatsachen *od.* Fakten ‹*beweisen*›

faculty /ˈfækəltɪ/ *n.* **1** (physical capability) Fähigkeit, *die;* Vermögen, *das;* **~ of sight/speech/hearing/thought** Seh-/Sprach-/Hör-/Denkvermögen, *das* **2** (mental power) **mental ~, ~ of the mind** geistige Kraft; Geisteskraft, *die;* **in [full] possession of [all] one's faculties** im [Voll]besitz [all] seiner [geistigen] Kräfte; **all one's creative faculties** seine ganze Kreativität *od.* schöpferische Kraft **3** (aptitude) Begabung, *die;* Fähigkeit, *die;* **have a ~ for doing sth.** die Fähigkeit *od.* das Talent haben, etw. zu tun **4** (Univ.: department) Fakultät, *die;* Fachbereich, *der;* **~ of arts/sciences/medicine** philosophische/naturwissenschaftliche/medizinische Fakultät **5** (Amer. Sch., Univ.: staff) Lehrkörper, *der*

fad /fæd/ *n.* Marotte, *die;* Spleen, *der* (ugs.); **the latest fashion ~:** die neueste Modetorheit; **a ~ for doing sth.** die Marotte *od.* der Spleen, etw. zu tun

faddish /ˈfædɪʃ/, **faddy** /ˈfædɪ/ *adjs.* heikel ‹*Person, Geschmack*›

fade /feɪd/
A *v.i.* **1** (droop, wither) ‹*Blätter, Blumen, Kränze:*› [ver]welken, welk werden **2** (lose freshness, vigour) verblassen; [v]erlöschen; ‹*Läufer:*› langsamer werden; ‹*Frau, Schönheit:*› verblühen **3** (lose colour) bleichen; **~ [in colour]** [ver]bleichen; verschießen; **guaranteed not to ~:** garantiert farbecht **4** (grow pale, dim) **the light ~d [into darkness]** es dunkelte; **the fading light of evening** das dämmrige Abendlicht (dichter.); die Abenddämmerung **5** (fig.: lose strength) ‹*Erinnerung:*› verblassen; ‹*Eingebung, Kreativität, Optimismus:*› nachlassen; ‹*Freude, Lust, Liebe:*› erlöschen; ‹*Ruhm:*› verblassen; ‹*Traum, Hoffnung:*› zerrinnen; schwinden; **~ from sb.'s mind** jmds. Gedächtnis (*Dat.*) entfallen **6** (disappear, depart, leave) weichen; ‹*Metapher, Bedeutung, Stern:*› verschwinden; (blend) übergehen (**into** in + *Akk.*); (grow faint) ‹*Laut:*› verklingen; **~ into the distance** in der Ferne entschwinden; ‹*Laut, Stimme:*› in der Ferne verklingen; **~ from sight** *or* **sb.'s eyes** dem Blick entschwinden (geh.); **his smile ~d from his face** das Lächeln schwand aus seinem Gesicht **7** (lose power) ‹*Bremskraft, Bremse:*› nachlassen **8** (Radio, Telev., Cinemat.) **~ [down]** ausgeblendet werden; **~ up** eingeblendet werden **9** (deviate) ‹*Golfball usw.:*› einen Bogen beschreiben
B *v.t.* **1** (cause to ~) ausbleichen ‹*Vorhang, Gobelin, Teppich, Farbe*› **2** (Radio, Telev., Cinemat.) einblenden (**into** in + *Akk.*); **~ one scene into another** eine Szene in eine andere überblenden; **~ a sound down/up** ein Geräusch aus-/einblenden
C *n.* (Radio, Telev., Cinemat., Motor Veh.) Fading, *das* (fachspr.)

Phrasal verbs

- **~ a'way** *v.i.* **1** schwinden; ‹*Farbe:*› verblassen; ‹*Laut:*› verklingen (**into** in + *Dat.*); ‹*Erinnerung, Augenlicht, Kraft:*› nachlassen; ‹*Kranke[r]:*› immer schwächer werden; ‹*Interesse, Hoffnung:*› erlöschen; (joc.) ‹*dünne Person:*› immer weniger werden (scherzh.); **the daylight ~d away** es dämmerte **2** (depart, leave) gehen
- **~ 'in** (Radio, Telev., Cinemat.)
A *v.i.* eingeblendet werden
B *v.t.* einblenden. *see also* **fade-in**
- **~ 'out**
A *v.i.* **1** (Radio, Telev., Cinemat.) ausgeblendet werden **2** (disappear, depart) **~ out of sb.'s life/mind** aus jmds. Leben/Bewusstsein verschwinden
B *v.t.* (Radio, Telev., Cinemat.) ausblenden. *see also* **fade-out**

faded /ˈfeɪdɪd/ *adj.* welk ‹*Blume, Blatt, Laub*›; verblichen ‹*Stoff, Jeans, Farbe, Gemälde, Ruhm, Teppich*›; verblüht ‹*Schönheit*›; verblasst ‹*Erinnerung*›

'fade-in *n.* (Radio, Telev., Cinemat.) Einblendung, *die*

fadeless /ˈfeɪdlɪs/ *adj.* farbecht ‹*Stoff*›; echt ‹*Farbe*›

'fade-out *n.* **1** (Radio, Telev., Cinemat.) Ausblendung, *die* **2** (Radio: by ionospheric disturbances) Fading, *das* (fachspr.); Schwund, *der* **3** (fig.: disappearance) Niedergang, *der*

fading /ˈfeɪdɪŋ/ *n.* (Radio) Fading, *das* (fachspr.); Schwund, *der*

faecal /ˈfiːkl/ *adj.* (Physiol.) Kot-; kotig; fäkal (fachspr.)

faeces /ˈfiːsiːz/ *n. pl.* Fäkalien *Pl.*

faff about /fæf əˈbaʊt/ *v.i.* (Brit. coll.) herummachen (ugs.); **stop faffing about!** reg dich ab! (ugs.)

fag[1] /fæg/

A *v.i.*, **-gg-: 1** (toil) sich [ab]schinden (ugs.), sich abrackern (salopp) (**[away] at** mit) **2** (Brit. Sch. dated) **~ for a senior** einen älteren Schüler bedienen

B *v.t.*, **-gg-: ~ sb. [out]** jmdn. schlauchen (ugs.); **~ oneself out** sich [ab]schinden (ugs.); **be ~ged out** geschlaucht sein (ugs.)

C *n.* **1** (Brit. coll.) Schinderei, *die* (ugs. abwertend) **2** (Brit. Sch. dated) Diener, *der; Internatsschüler, der einem älteren bestimmte Dienste leistet* **3** (coll.: cigarette) Glimmstängel, *der* (ugs. scherzh.)

fag[2] *n.* (sl. derog.: homosexual) Schwule, *der* (ugs.)

ˈfag end *n.* **1** (remnant) Schluss, *der;* Ende, *das* **2** (coll.: cigarette end) Kippe, *die* (ugs.)

faggot (*Amer.:* **fagot**) /ˈfægət/ *n.* **1** (sticks, twigs) Reisigbündel, *das* **2** *usu. in pl.* (Gastr.) Leberknödel, *der* **3** (woman) Weib, *das* (abwertend) **4** (sl. derog.: homosexual) Schwule, *der*

fah /fɑː/ *n.* (Mus.) fa

Fahr. *abbr.* **= Fahrenheit** F

Fahrenheit /ˈfærənhaɪt/ *adj.* **▸❶ p. 1620** Fahrenheit; **~ scale** Fahrenheitskala, *die*

fail /feɪl/

A *v.i.* **1** (not succeed) scheitern; **~ in sth.** mit etw. scheitern; **he ~ed in doing it** es gelang ihm nicht, es zu tun; **~ in one's duty** seine Pflicht versäumen; **~ as a human being/a doctor** als Mensch/Arzt versagen; **he ~ed in his attempts to escape** seine Fluchtversuche schlugen fehl *od.* misslangen **2** (miscarry, come to nothing) scheitern; fehlschlagen; **if all else ~s** wenn alle Stricke *od.* Stränge reißen (ugs.) **3** (become bankrupt) Bankrott machen; Bankrott gehen **4** (in examination) nicht bestehen (**in** in + *Dat.*); durchfallen (ugs.) (**in** in + *Dat.*) **5** (be rejected) ‹*Bewerber, Kandidat, Bewerbung:*› abgelehnt werden **6** (become weaker) ‹*Augenlicht, Gehör, Gedächtnis, Stärke, Eifer, Entschlossenheit:*› nachlassen; ‹*Atem:*› schwächer werden; ‹*Mut:*› sinken; **his voice ~ed** ihm versagte die Stimme; **he** *or* **his health is ~ing** sein Gesundheitszustand verschlechtert sich; **the light was ~ing** (fig. literary) es dämmerte **7** (break down, stop) ‹*Versorgung:*› zusammenbrechen; ‹*Motor, Radio:*› aussetzen; ‹*Generator, Batterie, Pumpe:*› ausfallen; ‹*Bremse, Herz:*› versagen **8** (prove misleading) ‹*Prophezeiung, Vorhersage:*› sich nicht bewahrheiten **9** (be insufficient) ‹*Ernte:*› schlecht ausfallen

B *v.t.* **1 ~ to do sth.** (not succeed in doing) etw. nicht tun [können]; **~ to reach a decision** zu keinem Entschluss kommen; **~ to achieve one's purpose/aim** seine Absicht/sein Ziel verfehlen; **~ to pass an exam** eine Prüfung nicht bestehen; in einer Prüfung durchfallen (ugs.); **~ to remember sth.** etw. vergessen; **his hopes ~ed to materialize** seine Hoffnungen haben sich nicht verwirklicht; **the letter ~ed to reach its destination** der Brief ist nicht an seinem Bestimmungsort eingetroffen **2** (be unsuccessful in) nicht bestehen ‹*Prüfung*›; durchfallen in (+ *Dat.*) (ugs.) ‹*Prüfung*› **3** (reject) durchfallen lassen (ugs.) ‹*Prüfling*› **4 ~ to do sth.** (not do) etw. nicht tun; (neglect to do) [es] versäumen, etw. zu tun; **not ~ to do sth.** etw. tun; **he never ~s to send me a card** er schreibt mir immer eine Karte *od.* versäumt es nie, mir eine Karte zu schreiben; **I ~ to see the reason why ...:** ich sehe nicht ein, warum ... **5** (not suffice for) im Stich lassen; **his legs ~ed him** seine Beine ließen ihn im Stich *od.* (geh.) versagten ihm den Dienst; **his heart** *or* **courage ~ed him** ihn verließ der Mut; **words ~ sb.** jmdm. fehlen die Worte; jmd. findet keine Worte **6 the wind ~ed us** (did not blow) wir hatten keinen Wind; (was blowing the wrong way) die Windrichtung war ungünstig

C *n.* **without ~:** auf jeden Fall; garantiert

failed /feɪld/ *attrib. adj.* nicht bestanden ‹*Prüfung*›; durchgefallen (ugs.) ‹*Prüfling*›; gescheitert ‹*Person, Geschäft, Ehe, Versuch*›

failing /ˈfeɪlɪŋ/

A *n.* Schwäche, *die*

B *prep.* **~ that** *or* **this** andernfalls; wenn nicht; **~ which** widrigenfalls (Papierdt.); **..., ~ which you can ...:** ..., ansonsten können Sie ...

C *adj.* sich verschlechternd ‹*Gesundheitszustand*›; nachlassend ‹*Kraft*›; sinkend ‹*Mut*›; dämmrig ‹*Licht*›

ˈfail-safe *adj.* ausfallsicher; abgesichert ‹*Methode*›; Failsafe-‹*Vorkehrung, Prinzip*› (fachspr.)

failure /ˈfeɪljə(r)/ *n.* **1** (omission, neglect) Versäumnis, *das;* **~ to do sth.** Versäumnis, etw. zu tun; **~ to observe** *or* **follow the rule** Nichtbeachtung *od.* Übertretung der Regel; **~ to appear in court** Nichterscheinen (Amtsspr.) vor Gericht; **~ to deliver goods** Nichtlieferung von Waren; **~ to pass an exam** Nichtbestehen einer *od.* (ugs.) Durchfallen bei einer Prüfung **2** (lack of success) Scheitern, *das;* (of an application) Ablehnung, *die;* **be doomed to ~,** **be bound to end in ~:** zum Scheitern verurteilt sein; **end in ~:** scheitern **3** (unsuccessful person or thing) Versager, *der;* **the party/play/film was a ~:** das Fest/Stück/der Film war ein Misserfolg; **our plan/attempt was a ~:** unser Plan/Versuch war fehlgeschlagen; **the cake/dish turned out a ~:** der Kuchen/das Gericht misslang; **be a ~ as a doctor/teacher** als Arzt/Lehrer versagen; **be a ~ at doing sth.** keine glückliche Hand bei etw. haben **4** (non-occurrence of a process) **the ~ of the medicine to have the desired effect** das Ausbleiben der Wirkung der Arznei; **my ~ to understand his motives** mein fehlendes Verständnis für seine Motive; **his ~ to keep in touch/to contact us was ...:** dass er es unterlassen hat, von sich hören zu lassen/mit uns Kontakt aufzunehmen, war ... **5** (running short, breaking down) (of supply) Zusammenbruch, *der;* (of engine, generator) Ausfall, *der;* **signal/pump/engine/generator ~:** Ausfall des Signals/der Pumpe/des Motors/des Generators; **power** *or* **electricity ~:** Stromausfall, *der;* **brake ~:** Versagen der Bremsen; **crop ~, ~ of crops** Missernte, *die* **6** (Med.) Versagen, *das;* Insuffizienz, *die* (fachspr.) **7** (deterioration, weakening) (of health) Verschlechterung, *die;* (of hearing, eyesight, strength) Nachlassen, *das;* (of energy) Erlahmen, *das;* (of courage) Sinken, *das* **8** (absence, non-existence) Fehlen, *das;* **~ of justice** Versagen der Justiz **9** (bankruptcy) Zusammenbruch, *der;* **a bank ~:** der Zusammenbruch einer Bank

fain /feɪn/ (arch.) *adv.* **I would ~ ...** ich möchte gerne ...

faint /feɪnt/

A *adj.* **1** (dim, indistinct, pale) matt ‹*Licht, Farbe, Stimme, Lächeln*›; schwach ‹*Geruch, Duft*›; leise ‹*Flüstern, Geräusch, Stimme, Ton, Ruf, Schritt*›; entfernt ‹*Ähnlichkeit*›; undeutlich ‹*Umriss, Linie, Gestalt, Spur, Stimme, Fotokopie*› **2** (weak, vague) leise ‹*Wunsch, Hoffnung, Verdacht, Ahnung*›; gering ‹*Chance*›; **not have the ~est idea** *or* **notion** nicht die geringste *od.* blasseste Ahnung haben; **Where is he? — I haven't the ~est idea** *or* (coll.) **~est** Wo ist er? — Keine Ahnung! (ugs.) **3** (giddy, weak) matt; schwach; **she felt/looked ~:** sie fühlte sich/schien einer Ohnmacht nahe; ihr war schwindelig/ihr schien schwindelig zu sein; **be ~ with** *or* **feel ~ from hunger** *etc.* vor Hunger *usw.* matt *od.* schwach sein; **his breathing grew ~:** sein Atem wurde schwächer **4** (timid) gering, schwach ‹*Mut*›; **~ heart never won fair lady** (prov.) wer nicht wagt, der nicht gewinnt (Spr.) **5** (feeble) schwach ‹*Lob, Widerstand*›; zaghaft ‹*Versuch, Bemühung*›; *see also* **damn A 1** **6 ▸feint**[2]

B *v.i.* ohnmächtig werden, in Ohnmacht fallen (**from** vor + *Dat.*)

C *n.* Ohnmacht, *die;* **in a [dead] ~:** ohnmächtig; **go off in** *or* **fall into a ~:** ohnmächtig werden; in Ohnmacht fallen

faint: ~-heart *n.* Hasenherz, *das* (abwertend); **~-hearted** *adj.* hasenherzig (abwertend); zaghaft ‹*Versuch*›; **~-heartedly** hasenherzig (abwertend)

faintly /ˈfeɪntlɪ/ *adv.* **1** (indistinctly) undeutlich ‹*markieren, hören*›; kaum ‹*sichtbar*›; schwach ‹*riechen, scheinen*›; entfernt ‹*sich ähneln*› **2** (slightly) leise ‹*hoffen, verdächtigen*›; wenig ‹*interessieren*›; leicht ‹*enttäuschen, herablassend*› **3** (feebly) zaghaft ‹*versuchen, lächeln*›

faintness /ˈfeɪntnɪs/ *n., no pl.* **1** (dimness, feebleness) (of marking, outline, voice) Undeutlichkeit, *die;* (of resemblance) Entferntheit, *die;* (of colour) Mattheit, *die;* (of old photograph) Verblasstheit, *die;* **the ~ of the smell/light** der schwache Geruch/das schwache Licht; **the ~ of his smile/recollection** sein schwaches Lächeln/seine schwache Erinnerung **2** (dizziness) Schwäche, *die;* Mattigkeit, *die;* **feeling of ~:** Schwächegefühl, *das* **3** (cowardice) **~ of spirits** Verzagtheit, *die;* **~ of heart** (literary) Zagheit, *die* (geh.)

fair[1] /feə(r)/ *n.* **1** (gathering) Markt, *der;* (with shows, merry-go-rounds) Jahrmarkt, *der;* **village/cattle ~:** Dorf-/Viehmarkt, *der;* **a day after the ~** (fig.) zu spät **2 ▸funfair 3** (exhibition) Ausstellung, *die;* Messe, *die;* **agricultural/world/industries ~:** Landwirtschafts-/Welt-/Industrieausstellung, *die;* **book/antiques/trade ~:** Buch-/Antiquitäten-/Handelsmesse, *die*

fair[2]

A *adj.* **1** (just) gerecht; begründet ‹*Beschwerde, Annahme*›; berechtigt ‹*Frage*›; fair ‹*Spiel, Kampf, Prozess, Preis, Beurteilung, Handel*›; (representative, typical) typisch, markant ‹*Beispiel, Kostprobe*›; **be ~ with** *or* **to sb.** gerecht gegen jmdn. *od.* zu jmdm. sein; **it's only ~ to do sth./for sb. to do sth.** es ist nur recht und billig, etw. zu tun/dass jmd. etw. tut; **strict but ~:** streng, aber gerecht; **a ~ day's wages for a ~ day's work** anständiger Lohn für anständige Arbeit; **that's not ~, you're not ~:** das ist ungerecht *od.* unfair; **[well, that's] ~ enough!** (coll.) dagegen ist nichts einzuwenden; (OK) na gut; **by ~ means or foul** egal wie (ugs.); auf ehrliche oder unehrliche Weise; **all's ~ in love and war** in der Liebe und im Krieg ist alles erlaubt; **~ play** Fairness, *die;* Fair play, *das;* **~ play in business** anständiges Geschäftsgebaren; **~ and square** ehrlich; *see also* **crack A 1; deal**[1] **C 1; do**[2] **4; field A 5; game**[1] **A 7; share A 1** **2** (not bad, pretty good) ganz gut ‹*Bilanz, Vorstellung, Anzahl, Menge, Kenntnisse, Chance*›; ziemlich ‹*Maß, Geschwindigkeit*›; **a ~ amount of work** ein schönes Stück Arbeit; **she has a ~ amount of sense** sie ist ganz vernünftig; **not all, but a ~ number** nicht alle, aber doch recht viele; **be a ~ judge of character** ein recht guter Menschenkenner sein; *see also* **middling A 2** **3** (favourable) schön ‹*Wetter, Tag, Abend*›; günstig ‹*Wetterlage, Wind*›; heiter ‹*Wetter, Tag, Himmel, Morgen*›; **the barometer/weather is set ~:** das Barometer steht auf Schönwetter/das schöne Wetter hält an; **be in a ~ way to doing sth.** gute Aussichten haben, etw. zu tun; **be in a ~ way to succeed/winning** gute Erfolgs-/Gewinnchancen haben **4** (considerable, satisfactory) ansehnlich ‹*Erbe, Vermögen*› **5** (complimentary) schön ‹*Rede, Worte*› **6** (blond) blond ‹*Haar, Person*›; (not dark) hell ‹*Teint, Haut*›; hellhäutig ‹*Person*›; **very ~:** hellblond; **a ~ head** ein Blondkopf **7** (poet. or literary: beautiful) hold (dichter. veralt.) ‹*Kind, Mädchen, Maid, Prinz, Gesicht*›; schön ‹*Stadt*›; (pure, unsullied) gut, unbescholten ‹*Name, Ruf*›; **the ~ sex** das schöne Geschlecht; **with her own ~ hands** (iron.) mit ihren zarten Händen **8** (clean, clear) sauber ‹*Handschrift*›; **~ copy** Reinschrift, *die;* **make a ~ copy of sth.** etw. ins Reine schreiben

B *adv.* **1** (in a ~ manner) fair ‹*kämpfen, spielen*›; gerecht ‹*behandeln*› **2** (coll.: completely) völlig; **the sight ~ took my breath away** der Anblick hat mir glatt (ugs.) den Atem verschlagen **3 ~ and square** (honestly) offen und ehrlich; (accurately) voll, genau ‹*schlagen, treffen*›. *See also* **bid B 1; dinkum; play B 1**

C *n.* **~'s ~** (coll.) Gerechtigkeit muss sein

fair: ~-faced *adj.* (having light complexion) hellhäutig; **~ground** *n.* Festplatz, *der;* **~-haired** *adj.* blond; **~-haired boy** (Amer. fig.) Liebling, *der;* Favorit, *der*

fairing *n.* (structure) Verkleidung, *die*

fairish /ˈfeərɪʃ/ *adj.* passabel

ˈFair Isle *attrib. adj.* (Textiles) *für die Insel Fair Isle typisch;* ≈ Shetland‹*pullover, -muster*›

fairly /ˈfeəlɪ/ *adv.* **1** fair ‹*kämpfen, spielen*›; gerecht ‹*bestrafen, beurteilen, behandeln*›; **come**

f

by sth. ~: auf ehrliche Weise zu etw. kommen **2** (tolerably) ziemlich **3** (completely) völlig; heftig, sehr ‹*bestürmen, bedrängen*›; **it ~ took my breath away** es hat mir glatt (ugs.) den Atem verschlagen **4** (actually) richtig; **I ~ jumped for joy** ich habe einen regelrechten Freudensprung gemacht **5** **~ and squarely** (honestly) offen und ehrlich; (accurately) voll, genau ‹*schlagen, treffen*›; **look at a situation ~ and squarely** eine Lage nüchtern betrachten; **beat sb. ~ and squarely** jmdn. nach allen Regeln der Kunst (ugs.) besiegen

'fair-minded *adj.* unvoreingenommen

fairness /'feənɪs/ *n., no pl.* Gerechtigkeit, *die;* **sense of ~:** Gerechtigkeitsgefühl, *das;* **in all ~ [to sb.]** fairerweise; um fair [gegen jmdn.] zu sein

fair: ~-sized /'feəsaɪzd/ *adj.* recht ansehnlich; **~way** *n.* **1** (channel) Fahrrinne, *die;* **2** (Golf) Fairway, *das;* **~-weather friend** *n.* Freund, der/Freundin, die nur in guten Zeiten treu ist

f

fairy /'feərɪ/

A *n.* **1** (Mythol.) Fee, *die;* (in a household) Kobold, *der* **2** (sl. derog.: homosexual) Tunte, *die* (salopp); Warme, *der* (salopp)

B *attrib. adj.* feenhaft ‹*Stimme, Wesen*›; Feen‹*reigen, -reich*›

fairy: ~ 'godmother *n.* (lit. or fig.) gute Fee; **F~land** *n.* (land of fairies) Feenland, *das;* (enchanted region) Märchenland, *das;* **winter ~land** winterliche Märchenlandschaft; **~ lights** *n. pl.* kleine farbige Lichter; **~ 'ring** *n.* (Bot.) Hexenring, *der;* **~ story** ▸ **~ tale A;** **~ tale** **A** *n.* (lit. or fig.) Märchen, *das;* **B** *adj.* Märchen‹*landschaft*›; märchenhaft schön ‹*Szene, Wirkung, Kleid, Ball*›; märchenhaft ‹*Schönheit*›

fait accompli /feɪt ə'kɒmplɪ/ *n., pl.* **faits accomplis** /feɪt ə'kɒmplɪ/ vollendete Tatsache; Fait accompli, *das* (geh.)

faith /feɪθ/ *n.* **1** (reliance, trust) Vertrauen, *das;* **have ~ in sb./sth.** Vertrauen zu jmdm./etw. haben; auf jmdn./etw. vertrauen; **have ~ in oneself** Selbstvertrauen haben; **lose ~ in sb./sth.** das Vertrauen zu jmdm./etw. verlieren; **pin one's ~ on** *or* **put one's ~ in sb./sth.** sein Vertrauen auf *od.* in jmdn./etw. setzen **2** (belief) Glaube, *der;* **on ~:** in gutem Glauben **3** (religious belief) Glaube, *der;* **the ~:** der [christliche] Glaube; **different Christian ~s** verschiedene christliche Glaubensrichtungen; **a matter of ~:** eine Glaubenssache **4** (promise) [Ehren]wort, *das;* (pledge of fidelity) Treue, *die;* **pledge one's ~ to sb.** jmdm. Treue geloben; **to do that would be breaking ~:** das zu tun, wäre [ein] Wortbruch; **break ~ with an ally** an einem Verbündeten treubrüchig werden; **keep ~ with sb.** jmdm. treu bleiben *od.* die Treue halten **5** (loyalty) Redlichkeit, *die;* **good/bad ~:** Vertrauen/Misstrauen, *das;* **in good ~:** ohne Hintergedanken; (unsuspectingly) in gutem Glauben; guten Glaubens; **in all good ~:** auf Treu und Glauben; **in bad ~:** in böser Absicht

faithful /'feɪθfl/

A *adj.* **1** (showing faith, loyal) treu; **remain ~ to sb./sth.** jmdm./einer Sache treu bleiben; **remain ~ to one's promise** [sein] Wort halten; sein Versprechen halten **2** (conscientious) pflichttreu; treu ‹*Briefschreiber*›; [ge]treu ‹*Diener*› **3** (accurate) [wahrheits]getreu; originalgetreu ‹*Wiedergabe, Kopie*›

B *n. pl.* **the ~:** die Gläubigen; **the party ~:** treue Anhänger der Partei

faithfully /'feɪθfəlɪ/ *adv.* **1** (loyally) treu ‹*dienen*›; pflichttreu ‹*überbringen, zustellen*›; gewissenhaft ‹*hüten, halten*›; hoch und heilig, fest ‹*versprechen*›; **promise [me] ~ that ...** (coll.: emphatically) versprich mir ganz fest, dass ... **2** (accurately) wahrheitsgetreu ‹*erzählen*›; originalgetreu ‹*wiedergeben*›; genau ‹*befolgen*› **3** ▸ **ⓘ p. 1287 yours ~** (in business letter) mit freundlichen Grüßen; (more formally) hochachtungsvoll

faith: ~ healer *n.* Gesundbeter, *der/*-beterin, *die;* **~ healing** *n.* Gesundbeten, *das*

faithless /'feɪθlɪs/ *adj.* **1** (perfidious, unreliable) untreu ‹*Geliebte[r], Mann, Frau*›; treulos ‹*Untertan, Diener, Freund, Handeln, Verhalten*›; **be ~ to sb./sth.** jmdm./einer Sache untreu sein **2** (unbelieving) ungläubig

fake /feɪk/

A *adj.* unecht; gefälscht ‹*Dokument, Banknote, Münze*›; **~ money** Falschgeld, *das*

B *n.* **1** (thing ~d up) Imitation, *die;* (painting) Fälschung, *die* **2** (trick) Finte, *die;* (fig.) Schwindel, *der* (abwertend) **3** (spurious person) Schwindler, *der*/Schwindlerin, *die*

C *v.t.* **1** (feign, contrive) nachahmen ‹*Akzent*›; fälschen ‹*Unterschrift*›; vortäuschen ‹*Krankheit, Einbruch, Unfall*› **2** (make plausible) **~ [up]** imitieren ‹*Diamanten*›; fälschen ‹*Gemälde*›; erfinden ‹*Geschichte*› **3** (alter so as to deceive) frisieren (ugs.); verfälschen

D *v.i.* simulieren

faker /'feɪkə(r)/ *n.* (swindler) Schwindler, *der*/Schwindlerin, *die;* (pretender) Heuchler, *der*/Heuchlerin, *die*

fakir /'feɪkɪə(r), fə'kɪə(r)/ *n.* Fakir, *der*

falcon /'fɔːlkn, 'fɔːkn/ *n.* (Ornith.) Falke, *der*

falconer /'fɔːlkənə(r), 'fɔːkənə(r)/ *n.* (Hunting) Falkner, *der*/Falknerin, *die*

falconry /'fɔːlknrɪ, 'fɔːknrɪ/ *n., no pl., no indef. art.* Falknerei, *die*

Falkland Islands /'fɔːlklənd aɪləndz/, **Falklands** /'fɔːlkləndz/ *pr. ns. pl.* Falklandinseln *Pl.*

fall /fɔːl/

A *n.* **1** (act or manner of falling) Fallen, *das;* (of person) Sturz, *der;* **~ of leaves/snow/rain** Blatt- *od.* Laub-/Schnee-/Regenfall, *der;* **in a ~:** bei einem Sturz; **have a ~:** stürzen; **a ten-inch ~ of rain/snow** eine Niederschlagsmenge von 254 mm/25 cm Schnee[fall] **2** (collapse, defeat) Fall, *der;* (of culture, dynasty, empire) Untergang, *der;* (of government) Sturz, *der;* **~ from power** Entmachtung, *die* **3** (lapse into sin) [Sünden]fall, *der;* **the F~ [of man]** (Theol.) der Sündenfall **4** (slope) Abfall, *der* (**to** zu, nach) **5** *usu. in pl.* (waterfall) [Wasser]fall, *der;* **Niagara F~s** Niagarafälle; der Niagarafall **6** (fig.: decrease) ▸ **drop A 9** **7** (of night etc.) Einbruch, *der* **8** ▸ **ⓘ p. 1515** (Amer.: autumn) Herbst, *der* **9** (Wrestling) (throw) Schulterwurf, *der;* (wrestling-bout) Ringkampf, *der*

B *v.i.*, **fell** /fel/, **~en** /'fɔːln/ **1** (drop) fallen; **~ off sth., ~ down from sth.** von etw. [herunter]fallen; **~ down [into] sth.** in etw. (*Akk.*) [hinein]fallen; **~ out of sth.** aus etw. [heraus]fallen; **~ to the ground** zu Boden *od.* auf den Boden fallen; **she let sth. ~ [from her hand]** (deliberately) sie hat etw. [aus der Hand] fallen lassen; (by mistake) ihr ist etw. aus der Hand gefallen; **~ down dead** tot umfallen; **~ down the stairs** *or* **downstairs** die Treppe herunter-/hinunterfallen; **~ into the trap** in die Falle gehen; **always ~ on one's feet** (fig.) immer [wieder] auf die Beine (ugs.) *od.* Füße fallen; **nearly** *or* **almost ~ off one's chair** (lit. or fig.) fast vom Stuhl fallen (ugs.); **~ to earth** auf die Erde *od.* zur Erde fallen; **the blossom ~s** die Blüte fällt ab; **the land ~s to sea level** das Gelände fällt auf Meeresspiegelhöhe ab; **~ from a great height** aus großer Höhe abstürzen; **~ing star** (Astron.) Sternschnuppe, *die;* **rain/snow is ~ing** es regnet/schneit **2** (fig.) ‹*Nacht, Dunkelheit:*› hereinbrechen; ‹*Abend:*› anbrechen; ‹*Stille:*› eintreten; **night began to ~:** die Nacht brach herein **3** (fig.: swoop) **~ upon** ‹*Katastrophe, Unglück, Seuche:*› hereinbrechen über (+ *Akk.*) (geh.); ‹*Rache:*› treffen; ‹*Furcht:*› befallen **4** (fig.: be uttered) ‹*Worte, Bemerkungen:*› fallen; **~ from sb.'s lips** *or* **mouth** über jmds. Lippen (*Akk.*) kommen; **let ~ a remark** eine Bemerkung fallen lassen **5** (lose high position) fallen; **~ from power** entmachtet werden; **~ from one's high estate** seinen hohen Rang einbüßen; **~en angel** gefallener Engel; **~en arch** (Med.) Senkfuß, *der* **6** (become detached) ‹*Blätter:*› [ab]fallen; **~ out** ‹*Haare, Federn:*› ausfallen **7** (hang down) fallen; **a lock fell over her face** eine Locke fiel *od.* hing ihr ins Gesicht **8** (be born) ‹*Lamm, Kalb usw.:*› geworfen werden **9** (sink to lower level) sinken; ‹*Barometer:*› fallen; ‹*Absatz, Verkauf:*› zurückgehen; (in pitch) ‹*Musik:*› [in der Tonhöhe] fallen; **~ by 10 per cent/from 10 [°C] to 0 [°C]** um 10%/von 10 [°C] auf 0 [°C] sinken; **[make sb.] ~ in sb.'s esteem** *or* **estimation/eyes** (fig.) [jmdn.] in jmds. Achtung/Augen (*Dat.*) sinken [lassen]; **~ into error/sin/temptation** einen Fehler/eine Sünde begehen/der Versuchung er- *od.* unterliegen **10** ▸ **~ away 2** **11** (subside) ‹*Wasserspiegel, Gezeitenhöhe:*› fallen; ‹*Wind, Sturm:*› sich legen **12** (show dismay) **his/her face** *or* **countenance fell** er/sie machte ein langes Gesicht (ugs.) **13** (look down) **his/her glance/eyes fell** er/sie senkte den Blick/die Augen **14** (no longer stand) fallen; ‹*Baum:*› umstürzen; ‹*Pferd:*› stürzen; **~ to the ground** zu Boden fallen; (fig.) ‹*Plan, Verabredung usw.:*› ins Wasser fallen; ‹*Argument, These:*› in sich zusammenfallen; **~ into one another's arms** einander in die Arme fallen *od.* sinken; **~ on one's knees** auf die Knie fallen; sich auf die Knie werfen; **~ at sb.'s feet** *or* **down before sb.** jmdm. zu Füßen fallen; **~ [flat] on one's face** (lit. or fig.) auf die Nase fallen (ugs.) **15** (be defeated) ‹*Festung, Stadt:*› fallen; ‹*Monarchie, Regierung:*› gestürzt werden; ‹*Reich:*› untergehen; **the fortress fell to the enemy** die Festung fiel dem Feind in die Hände **16** (fail) untergehen; **united we stand, divided we ~:** Einigkeit macht stark (Spr.) **17** (perish) ‹*Soldat:*› fallen; **the ~en [soldiers]** die Gefallenen **18** (collapse, break) einstürzen; **cause a building to ~:** ein Gebäude zum Einsturz bringen; **~ to pieces, ~ apart** ‹*Buch, Wagen:*› auseinander fallen; (fig.) ‹*Unternehmen, jmds. Welt:*› zusammenbrechen; **~ in two** entzweigehen; **~ apart at the seams** an den Nähten aufplatzen; (fig.) ‹*Plan:*› ins Wasser fallen (ugs.) **19** (Cricket) **a wicket ~s** ein Schlagmann wird ausgeschlagen **20** (come by chance, duty, etc.) fallen (**to** an + *Akk.*); **it fell to me** *or* **to my lot to do it** das Los, es tun zu müssen, hat mich getroffen; **~ [in] sb.'s way** jmdm. zufallen; **~ among thieves** unter die Räuber fallen; **~ into an ambush** in einen Hinterhalt fallen; **he has ~en into the role of a mere spectator** er ist in die Rolle des Zuschauers gedrängt worden; **~ into bad company** in schlechte Gesellschaft geraten; **~ into conversation with sb.** mit jmdm. ins Gespräch kommen; **~ into decay** ‹*Gebäude:*› verfallen; (fig.) ‹*Monarchie, Reich, Institution:*› zerfallen; ‹*Gesetz:*› seine Bedeutung verlieren; **~ into parts/sections** in Teile/Abschnitte zerfallen; ‹*Roman:*› sich in Teile/Abschnitte gliedern; **~ into different categories** in *od.* unter verschiedene Kategorien fallen; **~ to doing sth.** anfangen *od.* beginnen, etw. zu tun; **they fell to fighting among themselves** es kam zu einer Schlägerei zwischen ihnen; *abs.* **~ to** beginnen, drauflos zu essen/arbeiten *usw.; see also* **fall on** **21** (take specified direction) ‹*Auge, Strahl, Licht, Schatten:*› fallen (**upon** auf + *Akk.*) **22** (have specified place) liegen (**on, to** auf + *Dat.*, **within** in + *Dat.*); **~ into** *or* **under a category** in *od.* unter eine Kategorie fallen **23** (pass into specified state) **~ into a rage** einen Wutanfall bekommen; **~ into despair** verzweifeln; **~ into a deep sleep** in tiefen Schlaf fallen *od.* (geh.) versinken; **~ ill** krank werden; **~ into a swoon** *or* **faint** in Ohnmacht fallen **24** (occur) fallen (**on** auf + *Akk.*) ‹*Datum*›; **Easter ~s late this year** Ostern fällt dieses Jahr spät. *See also* **asleep 1; astern; flat² A 1, 2; foul A 6; grace A 5; hand A 3; line¹ A 6; love A 1; place A 10; prey A 2; push A 1; short B 3; silent 1; victim 1; wayside**

Phrasal verbs

- **~ a'bout** *v.i.* **~ about [laughing** *or* **with laughter]** sich [vor Lachen] kringeln (ugs.)
- **~ a'way** *v.i.* **1** abfallen (**from** von); ‹*Mit-*

gliedschaft, Einnahmen:) sinken; ‹*Nachfrage, Produktion, Aufträge:*› zurückgehen [2] (have slope) abfallen (**to** zu)

- ~ **'back** *v.i.* zurückweichen; ‹*Armee:*› sich zurückziehen; (lag) zurückbleiben; *see also* **fall-back**
- ~ **'back on** *v.t.* zurückgreifen auf (+ *Akk.*)
- ~ **behind**

[A] /'---/ *v.t.* zurückfallen hinter (+ *Akk.*)

[B] /--'-/ *v.i.* zurückbleiben; ~ **behind with sth.** mit etw. in Rückstand (*Akk.*) geraten

- ~ **'down** *v.i.* [1] ▸ ~ **B 1** [2] (collapse) ‹*Brücke, Gebäude:*› einstürzen; ‹*Person:*› hinfallen; ~ **down [on sth.]** (fig. coll.) [bei etw.] versagen; **the argument ~s down on one point** das Argument sticht in einem Punkt nicht; **the theory fell down for** *or* **on lack of evidence** die Theorie war nicht haltbar, weil es an Beweisen fehlte; ~ **down on the job** der Aufgabe nicht gewachsen sein
- ~ **for** *v.t.* (coll.) [1] (~ in love with) sich verknallen in (ugs.) [2] (be fooled by) hereinfallen auf (+ *Akk.*) (ugs.)
- ~ **'in** *v.i.* [1] hineinfallen [2] (Mil.) antreten (**for** zu); ~ **in!** angetreten! [3] (collapse) ‹*Gebäude, Wand usw.:*› einstürzen
- ~ **'in with** *v.t.* [1] (meet and join) stoßen zu [2] (agree) beipflichten (+ *Dat.*) ‹*Person, Meinung, Vorschlag usw.*›; eingehen auf (+ *Akk.*) ‹*Plan, Person, Bitte, Forderung*›; entsprechen (+ *Dat.*) ‹*Forderung, Bitte*›; einstimmen in (+ *Akk.*) ‹*Ton*›
- ~ **'off** *v.i.* [1] ▸ ~ **B 1** [2] ‹*Nachfrage, Produktion, Aufträge, Anzahl:*› zurückgehen [3] ‹*Mut, Niveau:*› sinken; ‹*Dienstleistungen, Gesundheit, Geschäft:*› sich verschlechtern; ‹*Begeisterung, Eifer, Interesse:*› nachlassen. *See also* **fall-off**
- ~ **on** *v.t.* [1] (lit., or fig.: attack) herfallen über [2] (be borne by) ~ **on sb.** jmdm. zufallen; ‹*Verdacht, Schuld, Los:*› auf jmdn. fallen
- ~ **'out** *v.i.* [1] herausfallen [2] ▸ ~ **B 6** [3] (quarrel) ~ **out [with sb. over sth.]** sich [mit jmdm. über etw. (*Akk.*)] [zer]streiten [4] (come to happen) vonstatten gehen; **see how things ~ out** abwarten, wie sich die Dinge entwickeln; **it [so] fell out that ...** (literary) es begab sich (geh.), dass ... [5] (Mil.) wegtreten; ~ **out!** weggetreten! *see also* **fallout**
- ~ **over**

[A] /'---/ *v.t.* [1] (stumble over) fallen über (+ *Akk.*); **they were ~ing over each other to get the sweets** sie drängelten sich, um die Süßigkeiten zu bekommen; ~ **over oneself** *or* **one's own feet** über seine eigenen Füße stolpern [2] ~ **over oneself to do sth.** (fig. coll.) sich vor Eifer überschlagen, um etw. zu tun (ugs.)

[B] /-'--/ *v.i.* umfallen; (in faint) hinfallen; ~ **over on to sth.** auf etw. (*Akk.*) fallen; *see also* **backwards 1**

- ~ **'through** *v.i.* (fig.) ins Wasser fallen (ugs.); ‹*Einigungsversuch:*› fehlschlagen
- ~ **upon** [1] ▸ ~ **on** [2] ▸ ~ **B 3, 23**

fallacious /fə'leɪʃəs/ *adj.* [1] (containing a fallacy) irrig; ~ **conclusion/syllogism** Fehl- *od.* Trugschluss, *der* [2] (deceptive, delusive) irreführend ‹*Methode, Bericht*›; trügerisch ‹*Hoffnung, Friede*›

fallacy /'fæləsɪ/ *n.* [1] (delusion, error) Irrtum, *der* [2] (unsoundness, delusiveness) Irrigkeit, *die* [3] (Logic) Trugschluss, *der*

'fallback *adj.* ~ **position** Rückfallposition, *die;* ~ **pay** Überbrückungsgeld, *das;* ~ **job** (for seasonal worker) Nebenerwerb, *der* (*zur Überbrückung außerhalb der Saison*)

fallen /'fɔːlṇ/ *adj.* **a ~ woman** (dated) ein gefallenes Mädchen

'fall guy *n.* (coll.) [1] (victim) Lackierte, *der/die* (salopp) [2] (scapegoat) Prügelknabe, *der* (ugs.); **be the ~ for sb.** den Prügelknaben für jmdn. abgeben

fallibility /fælɪ'bɪlɪtɪ/ *n., no pl.* Fehlbarkeit, *die*

fallible /'fælɪbl/ *adj.* [1] (liable to err) fehlbar ‹*Person*›; ~ **human nature** die Fehlbarkeit des Menschen [2] (liable to be erroneous) nicht unfehlbar

'fall-off *n.* (in quality) [Ver]minderung, *die* (**in** *Gen.*); (in quantity) Rückgang, *der* (**in** *Gen.*); ~ **in quality/exports** Qualitäts[ver]minderung, *die*/Exportrückgang, *der*

Fallopian tube /fə'ləʊpɪən tjuːb/ *n.* (Anat.) Eileiter, *der*

'fallout *n.* radioaktiver Niederschlag; (fig.: side effects) Abfallprodukte *Pl.*; ~ **shelter** Atombunker, *der*

fallow[1] /'fæləʊ/

[A] *n.* (Agric.) Brache, *die*

[B] *adj.* (lit. or fig.) brach liegend; ~ **ground** *or* **field/land** Brache, *die*/Brachland, *das;* **lie ~** (lit. or fig.) brach liegen

fallow[2] *adj.* (in colour) rotbraun

'fallow deer *n.* Damhirsch, *der*

false /fɔːls, fɒls/

[A] *adj.* [1] falsch; Fehl‹*deutung, -urteil*›; Falsch‹*meldung, -eid, -aussage, -geld*›; treulos ‹*Geliebte[r]*›; gefälscht ‹*Urkunde, Dokument*›; ~ **doctrine** Irrlehre, *die;* **be ~ to one's wife** seine Frau betrügen; seiner Frau (*Dat.*) untreu sein [2] (sham) falsch ‹*Scham, Bescheidenheit, Stolz*›; künstlich ‹*Wimpern, Auge*›; (deliberate) geheuchelt ‹*Bescheidenheit*›; gekünstelt ‹*Tränen, Lächeln*›; **distinguish the real from the ~:** zwischen Richtigem und Falschem *od.* Echtem und Unechtem unterscheiden; **under a ~ name** unter falschem Namen [3] (deceptive) falsch ‹*Hoffnung, Sparsamkeit*›; unberechtigt ‹*Furcht*›; trügerisch ‹*Wärme, Licht*›

[B] *adv.* unehrlich; **play sb. ~:** mit jmdm. ein falsches Spiel treiben

false: ~ **a'larm** *n.* blinder Alarm; ~ **'bottom** *n.* doppelter Boden; ~ **'card** *n.* *zwecks Irreführung des Gegners gespielte Karte;* ~ **'ceiling** *n.* Zwischendecke, *die;* ~ **'colours** *n. pl.* **sail under ~ colours** (fig.) unter falscher Flagge segeln; ~ **'dawn** *n.* (Astron.) ≈ Zodiakallicht, *das;* (fig.) Täuschung, *die;* ~ **'floor** *n.* Zwischenboden, *der;* ~ **'hair** *n.* falsches Haar

falsehood /'fɔːlshʊd, 'fɒlshʊd/ *n.* [1] *no pl.* (falseness) Unrichtigkeit, *die* [2] (untrue thing) Unwahrheit, *die;* **tell a ~:** die Unwahrheit sagen

false 'keel *n.* (Naut.) Schutzkiel, *der*

falsely /'fɔːlslɪ, 'fɒlslɪ/ *adv.* [1] (dishonestly) unaufrichtig ‹*sprechen*›; falsch ‹*schwören*› [2] (incorrectly, unjustly) falsch ‹*auslegen, verstehen*›; fälschlich[erweise] ‹*annehmen, glauben, behaupten, anklagen, beschuldigen, verurteilen*› [3] (insincerely) gekünstelt ‹*lächeln*›

false 'move ▸ **false step**

falseness /'fɔːlsnɪs, 'fɒlsnɪs/ *n., no pl.* [1] (incorrectness) Unrichtigkeit, *die;* Falschheit, *die* [2] (faithlessness) Treulosigkeit, *die* (**to** gegenüber) [3] (insincerity) Unaufrichtigkeit, *die*

false: ~ **po'sition** *n.* Lage, *in der man scheinbar entgegen seinen Prinzipien handeln muss;* **he was put in a ~ position** er wurde in ein schiefes Licht gerückt; ~ **pre'tences** *n. pl.* Vorspiegelung falscher Tatsachen; ~ **'start** *n.* (Sport; also fig.) Fehlstart, *der;* ~ **'step** *n.* (lit. or fig.) falscher Schritt; **make a ~ step** einen falschen Schritt tun; ~ **'teeth** *n. pl.* [künstliches] Gebiss; Prothese, *die*

falsetto /fɔːl'setəʊ, fɒl'setəʊ/ *n., pl.* **~s** (voice) Kopfstimme, *die;* (Mus.: of man) Falsett, *das;* Fistelstimme, *die*

falsies /'fɔːlsɪz, 'fɒlsɪz/ *n. pl.* (coll.) Gummibusen, *der* (salopp)

falsification /fɔːlsɪfɪ'keɪʃn, fɒlsɪfɪ'keɪʃn/ *n.* [1] (alteration) Fälschung, *die;* (of fact, event, truth, history) Verfälschung, *die;* **lies and ~s** Lügen und Unwahrheiten [2] (showing that sth. is false) Widerlegung, *die*

falsify /'fɔːlsɪfaɪ, 'fɒlsɪfaɪ/ *v.t.* [1] (alter) fälschen; (misrepresent) verfälschen ‹*Tatsache, Geschichte, Ereignis, Wahrheit*› [2] (show to be false) widerlegen; falsifizieren (geh.)

falsity /'fɔːlsɪtɪ, 'fɒlsɪtɪ/ *n., no pl.* [1] (incorrectness) Falschheit, *die* [2] (falsehood) Unwahrheit, *die;* (error) Unrichtigkeit, *die* [3] (deceitfulness, unfaithfulness) Treulosigkeit, *die* [4] (artificiality) Unnatürlichkeit, *die*

falter /'fɔːltə(r), 'fɒltə(r)/

[A] *v.i.* [1] (waver) stocken; ‹*Mut, Hoffnung:*› sinken; ~ **in one's resolve/desire/determination** in seinem Entschluss/Wunsch/seiner Entschlossenheit schwankend werden; **their courage/hopes did not ~:** sie verloren nicht den Mut/die Hoffnung [2] (stumble, stagger) wanken;

with ~ing steps mit [sch]wankenden Schritten

[B] *v.t.* ~ **[out] sth.** etw. stammeln

fame /feɪm/ *n., no pl.* Ruhm, *der;* **rise to ~:** zu Ruhm kommen *od.* gelangen; **win ~ for oneself** Ruhm gewinnen; **a man of [great] literary/political ~:** ein [sehr] berühmter Literat/Politiker; **is that Erich Segal of 'Love Story' ~?** ist das der Erich Segal, der mit „Love Story" berühmt geworden ist?; **ill ~** (dated) schlechter Ruf; *see also* **house A 5**

famed /feɪmd/ *adj.* berühmt (**for** für, wegen); *see also* **far-famed**

familiar /fə'mɪljə(r)/

[A] *adj.* [1] (well acquainted) bekannt; **be ~ with sb.** jmdn. näher kennen; **we never really got ~:** wir lernten uns (*Akk.*) nie richtig kennen *od.* (ugs.) wurden nie so richtig warm miteinander [2] (having knowledge) vertraut; **are you ~ with Ancient Greek?** können Sie Altgriechisch? [3] (well known) vertraut; bekannt ‹*Gesicht, Name, Lied*›; gewohnt ‹*Geruch*›; (common, usual) geläufig ‹*Ausdruck*›; gängig ‹*Vorstellung*›; **be on ~ ground** (fig.) Bescheid wissen; **he looks ~:** er kommt mir bekannt vor; **his name seems ~ [to me]** sein Name kommt mir bekannt vor; **the word is ~ to me** das Wort ist mir geläufig [4] (informal) familiär, freundschaftlich ‹*Ton, Begrüßung*›; ungezwungen ‹*Sprache, Art, Stil*›; **are you on ~ terms with him?** kennt ihr euch gut?; **a ~ term of address** eine vertrauliche Anrede [5] (presumptuous) plump-vertraulich (abwertend) [6] (intimate) intim; **make oneself** *or* **become** *or* **get too ~ with sb.** mit jmdm. zu vertraulich werden; **be on ~ terms with sb.** enge Beziehungen zu jmdm. unterhalten

[B] *n.* (literary: friend, associate) Vertraute, *der/die* (geh.)

familiarity /fəmɪlɪ'ærɪtɪ/ *n.* [1] *no pl.* (acquaintance) Vertrautheit, *die* [2] *no pl.* (relationship) ungezwungenes Verhältnis; familiäres Verhältnis [3] (of action, behaviour) Vertraulichkeit, *die;* **the ~ of their greeting** ihre freundschaftliche Begrüßung; ~ **breeds contempt** (prov.) zu große Vertraulichkeit erzeugt Verachtung [4] *no pl.* (sexual intimacy) Intimität, *die;* Vertraulichkeiten *Pl.*; **attempts at ~:** plumpe Annäherungsversuche [5] *in pl.* (caresses) Intimitäten *Pl.*; Vertraulichkeiten *Pl.*

familiarize (**familiarise**) /fə'mɪljəraɪz/ *v.t.* vertraut machen; einweisen ‹*neuen Mitarbeiter*›; ~ **(familiarise) oneself with a/one's new job** sich einarbeiten

familiarly /fə'mɪljəlɪ/ *adv.* [1] (informally) ungezwungen [2] (presumptuously) plump-vertraulich (abwertend) [3] (commonly) ~ **known as ...** allgemein ... genannt; **more ~ known as** besser bekannt als

family /'fæməlɪ/ *n.* [1] Familie, *die;* **be one of the ~:** zur Familie gehören; **with just the immediate ~:** im engsten Familienkreis; **start a ~:** eine Familie gründen; **give my regards to Mr and Mrs Brown and ~:** grüßen Sie Familie Brown von mir; **run in the ~:** in der Familie liegen; **be in the** *or* **a ~ way** (coll.) in anderen Umständen sein (verhüll.) [2] (ancestry) **of [good] ~:** aus guter Familie [3] (group, race) Geschlecht, *das;* **the ~ of human beings** das Menschengeschlecht [4] (brotherhood) [große] Familie; **the ~ of Christians/of man** die Christenheit/die Menschheit; **the ~ of nations** die Völkerfamilie (geh.) [5] (group of things; also Biol.) Familie, *die;* (Ling.) [Sprach]familie, *die* [6] *attrib.* Familien-; familiär ‹*Hintergrund*›; **in the ~ circle** im Kreis der Familie; *see also* **council 1**

family: ~ **al'lowance** *n.* Kindergeld, *das;* ~ **'Bible** *n.* Familienbibel, *die;* **F~ Division** *n.* (Brit. Law) *Abteilung für Familienrecht im obersten Gericht;* ~ **'doctor** *n.* Hausarzt, *der;* ~ **'income supplement** *n.* (Brit.) ≈ Familienzulage, *die;* ~ **man** *n.* Familienvater, *der;* (home-loving man) häuslich veranlagter Mann; ~ **name** *n.* Familienname, *der;* Nachname, *der;* ~ **'planning** *n.* Familienplanung, *die;* ~ **'planning clinic** *n.* ≈ Familienberatung[sstelle], *die;* ~ **room** *n.* [1] (in a house)

f

Familienzimmer, *das;* 2) (Brit.: in a pub) Familienraum, *der;* ~ **'tree** *n.* Stammbaum, *der;* ~ **viewing** *n.* **be** ~ **viewing/suitable for** ~ **viewing** ‹*Film usw.:*› für die ganze Familie geeignet sein; **this programme is** ~ **viewing** dies ist eine Familiensendung

famine /'fæmɪn/ *n.* 1) Hungersnot, *die* 2) (shortage) Knappheit, *die;* **~-stricken** von Hunger betroffen

famish /'fæmɪʃ/ *v.i.* hungern; **I'm ~ing!** (coll.) ich sterbe vor Hunger (ugs.)

famished /'fæmɪʃt/ *adj.* ausgehungert; halb verhungert; **I'm absolutely** ~ (coll.) ich sterbe vor Hunger (ugs.)

famous /'feɪməs/ *adj.* 1) (well-known) berühmt (**for** wegen, für) 2) (coll.: excellent) prima (ugs.); famos (ugs. veralt.); **a** ~ **victory** ein rühmlicher Sieg

f

famously /'feɪməslɪ/ *adv.* (coll.) prima (ugs.); famos (ugs. veralt.)

fan¹ /fæn/

A *n.* 1) Fächer, *der* 2) (sth. spread out) Fächer, *der;* (of peacock) Rad, *das* 3) (apparatus) Ventilator, *der*

B *v.t.*, **-nn-** fächeln ‹*Gesicht*›; anfachen ‹*Feuer*›; ~ **oneself/sb.** sich/jmdm. Luft zufächeln; ~ **one's face** sich (*Dat.*) das Gesicht fächeln; ~ **the fire into a brisk blaze** das Feuer anfachen, bis es hell lodert; ~ **the flame[s]** *or* **embers** (fig.) das Feuer schüren; Öl ins Feuer gießen; ~ **hatred** Hass schüren

Phrasal verb

• ~ **'out**

A *v.t.* fächern; auffächern ‹*Spielkarten*›

B *v.i.* fächern; ‹*Soldaten:*› ausfächern

fan² *n.* (devotee) Fan, *der;* **she is a Garbo ~:** sie ist ein Garbo-Fan; **I'm quite a** ~ **of yours!** ich bewundere Sie!

fanatic /fə'nætɪk/

A *adj.* fanatisch

B *n.* Fanatiker, *der*/Fanatikerin, *die*

fanatical /fə'nætɪkl/ ▸**fanatic A**

fanatically /fə'nætɪkəlɪ/ *adv.* fanatisch

fanaticism /fə'nætɪsɪzm/ *n.* Fanatismus, *der*

'fan belt *n.* (Motor Veh.) Keilriemen, *der*

fancier /'fænsɪə(r)/ *n.* Liebhaber, *der*/Liebhaberin, *die;* **be a rose/pigeon ~:** Rosen/Tauben züchten

fanciful /'fænsɪfl/ *adj.* 1) (whimsical) versponnen ‹*Person*›; abstrus, überspannt ‹*Vorstellung, Gedanke*› 2) (fantastically designed) fantastisch ‹*Gemälde, Design*›; reich verziert ‹*Kleid, Kostüm*›

fancifully /'fænsɪfəlɪ/ *adv.* fantasievoll ‹*erzählen*›; fantastisch ‹[*aus*]*geschmückt*›

fan: ~ **club** *n.* Fanklub, *der;* **~-cooled** *adj.* gebläsegekühlt

fancy /'fænsɪ/

A *n.* 1) (taste, inclination) **have a** ~ **for sth.** eine augenblickliche Schwäche für etw. haben; **have a** ~ **for a drink/some ice cream** Lust auf einen Drink/ein Eis haben; **he has taken a** ~ **to our plan/a new car/her** unser Plan/ein neues Auto/sie hat es ihm angetan; **take** *or* **catch sb.'s ~:** jmdm. gefallen; jmdn. ansprechen 2) (whim) Laune, *die;* **I just go where the** ~ **takes me** ich fahre einfach drauflos *od.* ins Blaue; **just as the** ~ **takes me** ganz nach Lust und Laune; **he only paints when the** ~ **takes him** er malt nur, wenn ihm [gerade] danach ist; **a passing ~:** eine [vorübergehende] Laune; nur so eine Laune; **tickle sb.'s ~:** jmdn. reizen 3) (notion) merkwürdiges Gefühl; (delusion, belief) Vorstellung, *die;* **a mere ~:** bloße Einbildung; **have a** ~ **that something is wrong** so ein Gefühl haben, dass etwas nicht stimmt 4) (faculty of imagining) Fantasie, *die;* **let one's** ~ **roam** seine Fantasie schweifen lassen (geh.); seiner Fantasie (*Dat.*) freien Lauf lassen; **in** ~ **he saw himself as ...:** in Gedanken sah er sich als ... 5) (mental image) Fantasievorstellung, *die;* **just a ~:** nur Einbildung 6) (cake) fein[st]es Gebäck

B *attrib. adj.* 1) (ornamental) kunstvoll ‹*Arbeit, Muster, Dribbling*›; ausgefallen ‹*Artikel, Design*›; schick ‹*Auto, Laden*›; raffiniert ‹*Gerät*›; fein[st...] ‹*Kuchen, Spitzen*›; ~ **jewellery** Modeschmuck, *der;* **nothing ~:** etwas ganz Schlichtes; **the meal will be nothing ~:** es gibt nichts Besonderes *od.* nur etwas ganz Einfaches zu essen 2) (whimsical) überspannt 3) (extravagant) stolz (ugs.); ~ **prices** Fantasiepreise (ugs.); gepfefferte Preise (ugs.) 4) (based on imagination) fantasievoll 5) (specially bred) speziell gezüchtet ‹*Tier*› 6) (Amer.: high-quality) feinst... ‹*Lebensmittel*›; Delikatess‹*gurke, -senf*›

C *v.t.* 1) (imagine) sich (*Dat.*) einbilden; ~ **oneself [to be] clever** sich einbilden, klug zu sein; sich für klug halten; **a fancied resemblance** eine eingebildete Ähnlichkeit 2) (coll.) *in imper. as excl. of surprise* ~ **meeting you here!** na, so etwas, Sie hier zu treffen!; ~ **his still being so naïve** nicht zu fassen, dass er noch immer so naiv ist; ~ **that!** sieh mal einer an!; also so etwas!; **just ~, she's run off with ...:** stell dir vor, sie ist mit ... durchgebrannt! 3) (suppose) glauben; denken; **..., I ~:** ..., möchte ich meinen 4) (wish to have) mögen; **what do you** ~ **for dinner?** was hättest du gern zum Abendessen?; **I don't** ~ **this house at all** mir gefällt dieses Haus überhaupt nicht; **he fancies [the idea of] doing sth.** er würde gern etw. tun; er hätte Lust, etw. zu tun; **I don't** ~ **a secretarial job** eine Sekretärinnenstelle reizt mich überhaupt nicht; ~ **a walk?** hast du Lust zu einem Spaziergang?; **do you think she fancies him?** glaubst du, er hat es ihr angetan?; (sexually) glaubst du, sie ist scharf auf ihn? (ugs.) 5) (coll.: have high opinion of) ~ **oneself** von sich eingenommen sein; ~ **oneself as a singer** sich für einen [großen] Sänger halten; ~ **one's/sb.'s chances** seine/jmds. Chancen hoch einschätzen; **he fancies his chances with her** er glaubt, bei ihr landen zu können (ugs.)

fancy: ~ **'dress** *n.* [Masken]kostüm, *das;* **in** ~ **dress** kostümiert; **~-dress party** Kostümfest, *das;* **~-dress ball** *or* **dance** Maskenball, *der;* **~-'free** *adj.* frei und ungebunden; *see also* **footloose;** ~ **goods** *n. pl.* Geschenkartikel; ~ **man** *n.* (coll. derog.) 1) (woman's lover) Liebhaber, *der;* 2) (pimp) Zuhälter, *der;* ~ **woman** *n.* (coll. derog.) Geliebte, *die;* **~-work** *n.* feine Handarbeit

fanfare /'fænfeə(r)/ *n.* Fanfare, *die;* **a** ~ **of trumpets** Trompetenstöße *Pl.*

fang /fæŋ/ *n.* 1) (canine tooth) Reißzahn, *der;* Fang[zahn], *der;* (of boar; joc.: of person) Hauer, *der;* (of vampire) Vampirzahn, *der;* **draw sb.'s/sth.'s ~s** (fig.) jmdn./etw. unschädlich machen 2) (of snake) Giftzahn, *der* 3) (root of tooth) Zahnwurzel, *die*

fan: ~ **heater** *n.* Heizlüfter, *der;* **~light** *n.* Oberlicht, *das;* (fan-shaped) Fächerfenster, *das* (Archit.); ~ **mag** (coll.), ~ **magazine** *ns.* Fanmagazin, *das;* ~ **mail** *n.* Fanpost, *die;* Verehrerpost, *die*

fanny /'fænɪ/ *n.* 1) (Amer. sl.: buttocks) Po, *der* (fam.) 2) (Brit. coarse: vulva) Möse, *die* (vulg.)

'fanny pack *n.* (Amer.) Gürteltasche, *die*

fan: ~ **oven** *n.* Heißluftofen, *der;* ~ **palm** *n.* Fächerpalme, *die;* **~-shaped** *adj.* fächerförmig; **~tail** *n.* Fächerschwanz, *der;* (pigeon) Pfautaube, *die*

fantasia /fæn'teɪzɪə, fæntə'ziːə/ *n.* (Mus.) Fantasia, *die* (fachspr.); Fantasie, *die*

fantasist /'fæntəsɪst/ *n.* Fantast, *der*/Fantastin, *die*

fantasize /'fæntəsaɪz/

A *v.i.* träumen

B *v.t.* sich zusammenfantasieren

fantastic /fæn'tæstɪk/ *adj.* 1) (grotesque, quaint) bizarr; skurril; (fanciful) fantastisch; (eccentric) absurd ‹*Gerücht, Plan, Geschichte*› 2) (coll.: magnificent, excellent, extraordinary) fantastisch (ugs.)

fantastically /fæn'tæstɪkəlɪ/ *adv.* 1) fantastisch 2) (coll.: excellently, extraordinarily) fantastisch (ugs.)

fantasy /'fæntəzɪ/ *n.* 1) Fantasie, *die;* (mental image, daydream) Fantasiegebilde, *das* 2) (Lit.) Fantasie, *die* 3) (Mus.) ▸**fantasia**

fan: ~ **'tracery** *n.* (Archit.) fächerförmiges Maßwerk; ~ **'vaulting** *n.* (Archit.) Fächergewölbe, *das*

'fanzine /'fænziːn/*n.* Fanmagazin, *das*

FAQ /fæk/ *abbr.* (Computing) FAQ

far /fɑː(r)/

A *adv.*, **farther, further; farthest, furthest** 1) ▸❶ **p. 1072**, ▸❶ **p. 1699** (in space) weit; ~ **away** weit entfernt (*see also* **d**); ~ **[away] from** weit entfernt von (*see also* **d**); **see sth. from** ~ **away** etw. aus der Ferne sehen; **have you come [from]** ~ *or* **from** ~ **off** *or* **away?** hatten Sie einen weiten Weg?; kommen Sie von weit her?; **how** ~ **have you come?** wie viel Kilometer mussten Sie zurücklegen?; **he travelled** ~ **into Russia/the desert/the jungle** er reiste bis tief ins Innere Russlands/in die Wüste/in den Dschungel; **I won't be** ~ **off** *or* **away** ich werde ganz in der Nähe sein; ~ **above/below** hoch über/tief unter (+ *Dat.*); *adv.* hoch oben/tief unten; **so ~:** bis hierher (*see also* **4**); **fly as** ~ **as Munich** bis [nach] München fliegen; ~ **and near** fern und nah; ~ **and wide** weit und breit; **from** ~ **and near** *or* **wide** von fern und nah

2) (in time) weit; ~ **into the night** bis spät *od.* tief in die Nacht; **the day** *or* **time is not** ~ **off** *or* **distant when ...:** es dauert nicht mehr lange, bis ...; **as** ~ **back as I can remember** soweit ich zurückdenken kann

3) (by much) weit; ~ **too** viel zu; ~ **different from** ganz *od.* völlig anders als; ~ **longer/better** weit[aus] länger/besser; **the rent is** ~ **beyond what I can afford to pay** die Miete übersteigt bei weitem meine Mittel; **they were not** ~ **wrong** sie hatten gar nicht so Unrecht; **you were/I was not** ~ **out** du lagst/ich lag gar nicht so falsch (ugs.); **your guess wasn't** ~ **out** deine Vermutung war gar nicht so abwegig; **your shot/guess wasn't** ~ **off** du hast fast getroffen/richtig vermutet

4) (fig.) **as** ~ **as** (to whatever extent, to the extent of) so weit [wie]; **I haven't got as** ~ **as phoning her** ich bin noch nicht dazu gekommen, sie anzurufen; **not as** ~ **as I know** nicht, dass ich wüsste; **your plans are all right as** ~ **as they go** Ihre Pläne sind so weit gut; **as** ~ **as I remember/know** soweit ich mich erinnere/weiß; **go so** ~ **as to do sth.** so weit gehen und etw. tun; **he's gone so** ~ **as to collect the material** er hat immerhin schon Material gesammelt; **in so** ~ **as** insofern *od.* insoweit als; **so** ~ (until now) bisher; bis jetzt; **so** ~ **so good** so weit, so gut; ~ **away** (in thought) weit weg; ~ **and away** bei weitem; weitaus; **by ~:** bei weitem; **better by ~:** weitaus besser; **by** ~ **the best** der/die/das weitaus Beste; ~ **from easy/good** alles andere als leicht/gut; ~ **from admiring his paintings, I dislike them intensely** nicht nur, dass ich seine Gemälde nicht bewundere, sie gefallen mir ganz und gar nicht; ~ **from it!** ganz im Gegenteil!; ~ **be it from me/us** *etc.* **to do that** es liegt mir/uns *usw.* fern, das zu tun; **go ~:** weit kommen; **I am** ~ **from doing sth.** ich bin weit davon entfernt, etw. zu tun; **he will go** ~ **in life** er wird es im Leben weit bringen; **go** ~ **to** *or* **towards sth./doing sth.** viel zu etw. beitragen/dazu beitragen, etw. zu tun; **not go ~:** nicht weit *od.* lange reichen; **one pound won't go ~:** ein Pfund ist schnell weg *od.* (ugs.) alle; **go too ~:** zu weit gehen; **this has gone** ~ **enough** damit ist jetzt Schluss; **carry** *or* **take sth. too ~:** etw. zu weit treiben; **that's carrying the joke too ~:** da hört der Spaß auf; **you are carrying things too** ~ **by saying that ...:** du übertreibst, wenn du sagst, dass ...; **how** ~ **[can she be trusted]?** inwieweit [kann man ihr trauen]?; **he's too** ~ **gone** er ist nicht mehr in der Lage, etw. zu tun; (drunk) er hat zu viel intus (ugs.); (delirious) er ist nicht mehr ganz bei Sinnen *od.* klar im Kopf. *See also* **few A 1**; **further B**; **furthest B**

B *adj.*, **farther, further; farthest, furthest** 1) (remote) weit entfernt; (remote in time) fern; **in the** ~ **distance** in weiter Ferne 2) (more remote) weiter entfernt; **the** ~ **bank of the river/side of the road** das andere Flussufer/die andere Straßenseite; **the** ~ **door/wall** *etc.* die hintere Tür/Wand *usw. See also* **cry A 1**; **further A**; **furthest A**

'faraway *attrib. adj.* 1) (remote in space) entlegen; abgelegen; (remote in time) fern 2) (dreamy) verträumt ‹*Stimme, Blick, Augen*›

farce /fɑːs/ *n.* **1** Farce, *die;* **become nothing but a ~:** zur reinen Farce werden **2** (Theatre) Posse, *die;* Farce, *die*

farcical /ˈfɑːsɪkl/ *adj.* **1** (absurd) farcenhaft; absurd **2** (Theatre) possenhaft ‹*Stück, Element*›

farcically /ˈfɑːsɪkəlɪ/ *adv.* (absurdly) absurd

fare /feə(r)/

A *n.* **1** (price) Fahrpreis, *der;* (money) Fahrgeld, *das;* **train/boat ~:** Bahnpreis/Preis für die Überfahrt; **what** *or* **how much is the ~?** was kostet die Fahrt/(by air) der Flug/(by boat) die Überfahrt?; **have the exact ~:** das Fahrgeld passend haben; **have one's ~ ready** das Fahrgeld bereithalten; **[all] ~s, please, any more ~s?** noch jemand zugestiegen? noch jemand ohne [Fahrschein]? **2** (passenger) Fahrgast, *der* **3** (food) Kost, *die; see also* **bill³ A 4**

B *v.i.* (get on) **I don't know how he is faring/how he ~d on his travels** ich weiß nicht, wie es ihm geht/wie es ihm auf seinen Reisen ergangen ist

Far: ~ ˈEast *n.* **the ~ East** der Ferne Osten; Fernost *o. Art.;* **~ ˈEastern** *adj.* fernöstlich; des Fernen Ostens *nachgestellt;* ‹*Person*› aus dem Fernen Osten

ˈfare stage *n.* Teilstrecke, *die;* (end of section) Zahlgrenze, *die* (Verkehrsw.)

farewell /feəˈwel/

A *int.* leb[e] wohl (veralt.); **say ~ to sth.** von etw. Abschied nehmen

B *n.* **1** **a few words of ~:** ein paar Worte des Abschieds; **make one's ~s** sich verabschieden; (by visiting) Abschiedsbesuche machen; *see also* **bid A 5** **2** *attrib.* **~ speech/gift** *etc.* Abschiedsrede, *die*/-geschenk, *das usw.*

far: ~-famed *adj.* weithin berühmt; **~-fetched** *adj.* weit hergeholt; an *od.* bei den Haaren herbeigezogen (ugs.); **~-flung** *adj.* (widely spread) weit ausgedehnt; (distant) weit entfernt; abgelegen

farm /fɑːm/

A *n.* **1** [Bauern]hof, *der;* [Land]wirtschaft, *die;* (larger) Gut, *das;* Gutshof, *der;* (in English-speaking countries outside Europe) Farm, *die;* **poultry/chicken ~:** Geflügel-/Hühnerfarm, *die;* **~ bread/eggs** Landbrot, *das*/Landeier *Pl.;* **~ animals** Nutzvieh, *das; see also* **dairy farm** **2** ▸**farmhouse** **3** (place for breeding animals) Zucht, *die;* **trout ~:** Forellenzucht, *die*

B *v.t.* **1** bebauen, bewirtschaften ‹*Land*›; züchten ‹*Lachs, Forellen*›; **be engaged in sheep ~ing** Schafzucht betreiben **2** (take proceeds of) pachten **3** ▸**~ out**

C *v.i.* Landwirtschaft betreiben; **he ~s in Africa** er ist Landwirt in Afrika; er hat eine Farm in Afrika

Phrasal verb

- **~ ˈout** *v.t.* **1** verpachten ‹*Land*› **2** vergeben ‹*Arbeit*› (**to** an + *Akk.*) **3** (hire out) verdingen (veralt.) ‹*Arbeitskräfte*›; in Lohnarbeit geben ‹*Arbeitskräfte*› **4** in Pflege geben ‹*Kinder*› (**to** *Dat.*, bei)

farmer /ˈfɑːmə(r)/ *n.* ▸**i** **p. 1260** Landwirt, *der*/-wirtin, *die;* Bauer, *der*/Bäuerin, *die;* **poultry ~:** Geflügelzüchter, *der*/-züchterin, *die*

farm: ~hand *n.* ▸**i** **p. 1260** Landarbeiter, *der*/-arbeiterin, *die;* (on a small farm) Knecht, *der*/Magd, *die* (veralt.); **~house** *n.* Bauernhaus, *das;* (larger) Gutshaus, *das*

farming /ˈfɑːmɪŋ/ *n, no pl., no indef. art.* Landwirtschaft, *die;* **~ of crops** Ackerbau, *der;* **~ of animals** Viehzucht, *die;* **~ community** Landwirtschaft betreibende Gemeinde; **~ implement** Ackergerät, *das;* landwirtschaftliches Gerät; **go into ~:** Landwirt *od.* Bauer werden

farm: ~stead *n.* Bauernhof, *der;* Gehöft, *das;* **~worker** *n.* ▸**i** **p. 1260** Landarbeiter, *der*/-arbeiterin, *die;* **~yard** *n.* Hof, *der*

Faroes /ˈfeərəʊz/ *pr. n. pl.* Färöer *Pl.*

ˈfar-off *adj.* (in space) [weit] entfernt; (in time) fern

ˈfar out *adj.* **1** (distant) [weit] entfernt **2** (fig. coll.: excellent) toll (ugs.); super (ugs.)

farrago /fəˈrɑːgəʊ/ *n., pl.* **~s** ((Amer.) **~es**) (mixture) Gemisch, *das;* (disordered assemblage) Allerlei, *das*

ˈfar-reaching *adj.* ausgedehnt ‹*Wälder, Felder*›; weit reichend ‹*Konsequenzen, Bedeutung, Wirkung*›

farrier /ˈfærɪə(r)/ *n.* (Brit.: smith) Hufschmied, *der*

farrow /ˈfærəʊ/

A *n.* Wurf, *der* (*von Ferkeln, Frischlingen*)

B *v.t.* werfen ‹*Ferkel, Frischling*›

C *v.i.* ‹*Sau:*› ferkeln; ‹*Bache:*› frischen

far: ~-seeing *adj.* weitblickend; **~sighted** *adj.* **1** (able to see a great distance) scharfsichtig; **2** (having foresight) weitblickend

fart /fɑːt/ (coarse)

A *v.i.* **1** furzen (derb) **2** (fool) **~ about** *or* **around** sich mit jedem Scheißdreck aufhalten (derb)

B *n.* **1** Furz, *der* (derb) **2** (person) Scheißer, *der* (derb)

farther /ˈfɑːðə(r)/ ▸**further A 1, B 1**

farthermost /ˈfɑːðəməʊst/ ▸**furthermost**

farthest /ˈfɑːðɪst/ ▸**furthest**

farthing /ˈfɑːðɪŋ/ *n.* **1** (Brit. Hist.) Farthing, *der;* **to the last ~:** auf Heller und Pfennig **2** (fig. dated) **it doesn't matter a ~:** es macht nicht das Geringste *od.* (ugs.) nicht die Bohne was aus; *see also* **brass farthing**

Far ˈWest *n.* (Amer.) **the ~:** der Westen der USA

fascia /ˈfeɪʃɪə, ˈfeɪʃə/ *n.* **1** (Archit.) Faszie, *die* **2** ▸**facia**

fascicle /ˈfæsɪkl/ *n.* Lieferung, *die;* Faszikel, *der* (Buchw.)

fascinate /ˈfæsɪneɪt/ *v.t.* fesseln; bezaubern; faszinieren (geh.); **it ~s me how ...:** ich finde es erstaunlich *od.* faszinierend, wie ...;

fascinated /ˈfæsɪneɪtɪd/ *adj.* (enchanted) fasziniert; **the audience watched ~:** das Publikum sah gebannt zu

fascinating /ˈfæsɪneɪtɪŋ/ *adj.* faszinierend (geh.); bezaubernd; hochinteressant ‹*Thema, Faktum, Meinung*›; spannend, fesselnd ‹*Buch*›; **there is something ~ about her** sie hat etwas Faszinierendes [an sich (*Dat.*)]

fascinatingly /ˈfæsɪneɪtɪŋlɪ/ *adv.* faszinierend (geh.); hochinteressant, fesselnd ‹*erzählen, beschreiben*›; berauschend, hinreißend ‹*schön*›

fascination /fæsɪˈneɪʃn/ *n., no pl.* Faszination, *die* (geh.); (quality of fascinating) Zauber, *der;* Reiz, *der;* **find a certain ~ in sth.** einen gewissen Reiz an einer Sache verspüren; **have a ~ for sb.** einen besonderen Reiz auf jmdn. ausüben

fascism /ˈfæʃɪzm/ *n.* Faschismus, *der;* **Italian ~:** der italienische Faschismus

fascist /ˈfæʃɪst/

A *n.* Faschist, *der*/Faschistin, *die*

B *adj.* faschistisch

fashion /ˈfæʃn/

A *n.* **1** Art [und Weise]; **talk/behave in a peculiar ~:** merkwürdig sprechen/sich merkwürdig verhalten; **dress in a similar ~:** sich ähnlich kleiden; **she will do it in her own ~:** sie wird es auf ihre [eigene] Art [und Weise] tun; **in the Japanese ~:** im japanischen Stil; **in the usual ~:** in der üblichen Art; *as sentence-modifier* wie üblich; **in this ~:** auf diese Weise; so; **he expresses himself in a striking ~:** er hat eine bemerkenswerte Ausdrucksweise *od.* einen bemerkenswerten Ausdruck; **walk crab-~/in a zigzag ~:** im Krebsgang/Zickzack gehen; **German-~:** nach deutscher Sitte; nach Art der Deutschen; **after** *or* **in the ~ of** im Stil *od.* nach Art von; **in best British ~:** nach guter, alter britischer Art; **after** *or* **in a ~:** schlecht und recht; einigermaßen; **after** *or* **in one's/its ~:** auf seine/ihre Art; **Were you successful? — Well yes, after** *or* **in a ~:** Hast du Erfolg gehabt? — Na ja, so einigermaßen *od.* es geht (ugs.) **2** (custom, esp. in dress) Mode, *die;* **be dressed in the height of** *or* **the latest ~:** hochmodern *od.* nach der neuesten Mode gekleidet sein; **the latest summer/autumn ~s** die neusten Sommer-/Wintermodelle; **~s for men's clothes/women's clothes** die Herrenmode/Damenmode; **the Paris ~s** die Pariser Mode; **it is the ~:** es ist Mode *od.* modern; **hats are the ~ this summer** in diesem Sommer sind Hüte in Mode; **be all the ~:** große Mode *od.* groß in Mode sein; **in ~:** in Mode; modern; **she always follows the/every ~:** sie geht immer nach *od.* mit der Mode/sie macht immer jede Mode mit; **be out of ~:** nicht mehr modern *od.* in Mode sein; **come into/go out of ~:** in Mode/aus der Mode kommen; **bring sth. into ~:** etw. in Mode bringen; **lead** *or* **set the ~:** die Mode vorschreiben; **the ~s in literature/music/art** die Literatur-/Musik-/Kunstrichtungen **3** (usages of society) Sitte, *die;* Brauch, *der;* **it was the ~ in those days** das war damals Sitte *od.* Brauch; **men/women of ~:** Herren/Damen der Gesellschaft. *see also* **old-fashioned**

B *v.t.* **1** formen, gestalten (**after, according to** nach; **out of, from** aus; **[in]to** zu); **~ sth. after sth.** etw. einer Sache (*Dat.*) nachbilden **2** (shape to leg) in Passform bringen ‹*Strümpfe*›

fashionable /ˈfæʃənəbl/ *adj.* modisch ‹*Kleider, Person, Design*›; modern ‹*Sitte*›; vornehm ‹*Gegend, Hotel, Restaurant*›; zur Zeit bevorzugt ‹*Tätigkeit*›; Mode‹*farbe, -krankheit, -wort, -autor*›; **it isn't ~ any more** es ist nicht mehr modern *od.* in Mode; **all the ~ people** die Schickeria

fashionably /ˈfæʃənəblɪ/ *adv.* modisch ‹*sich kleiden*›; modern ‹*leben*›

fashion: ~-conscious *adj.* modebewusst; **~ designer** *n.* ▸**i** **p. 1260** Modemacher, *der*/-macherin, *die;* **~ drug** *n.* Modedroge, *die;* **~ magazine** *n.* Modezeitschrift, *die;* Modemagazin, *das;* **~ parade** *n.* Mode[n]schau, *die;* **~ plate** *n.* **1** (picture) Modezeichnung, *die;* **2** (fig.: man/woman) Modegeck, *der*/-puppe, *die* (abwertend); **~ show** *n.* Mode[n]schau, *die*

fast¹ /fɑːst/

A *v.i.* fasten; **a day of ~ing** ein Fast[en]tag

B *n.* (going without food) Fasten, *das;* (hunger strike) Hungerstreik, *der;* (day) Fast[en]tag, *der;* (season) Fastenzeit, *die;* **break one's ~:** das Fasten brechen; **a 40-day ~:** eine Fastenzeit von 40 Tagen

fast²

A *adj.* **1** (fixed, attached) fest; **the rope is ~:** das Tau ist fest[gemacht]; **make [the boat] ~:** das Boot festmachen *od.* vertäuen; **hard and ~:** fest; bindend, verbindlich ‹*Regeln*›; klar ‹*Entscheidung*› **2** (steady, close) fest ‹*Freundschaft*›; unzertrennlich, treu ‹*Freunde*› **3** (not fading) farbecht ‹*Stoff*›; echt, beständig ‹*Farbe*›; (against light) lichtecht; (against washing) waschecht **4** (rapid) schnell; tempogeladen, aktionsreich ‹*Krimi, Film*›; **~ train** Schnellzug, *der;* D-Zug, *der;* **~ speed** hohe Geschwindigkeit; **he is a ~ worker** (lit. or fig.) er arbeitet schnell; (in amorous activities) er geht mächtig ran (ugs.); **I say, that was ~ work** na, das ging ja sehr schnell; **pull a ~ one [on sb.]** (coll.) jmdn. übers Ohr hauen *od.* reinlegen (ugs.) **5** ▸**i** **p. 1001 be ~ [by ten minutes], be [ten minutes] ~** ‹*Uhr:*› [zehn Minuten] vorgehen **6** schnell ‹*Tennisplatz, Billardtisch usw.*›; **~ road** Straße, auf der man schnell vorankommt; **~ line** (Railw.) Schnellverkehrsgleis, *das* **7** (immoral) flott ‹*Person, Leben*›; locker ‹*Lebenswandel*›; leichtlebig ‹*Frau*› **8** (Photog.) hoch empfindlich ‹*Film*›; lichtstark ‹*Objektiv*›. *See also* **furious**

B *adv.* **1** (lit. or fig.) fest; **the wall stood ~:** die Mauer blieb stehen; **hold ~ to sth.** sich an etw. (*Dat.*) festhalten; (fig.) an etw. (*Dat.*) festhalten; **stand ~ in one's belief** an seiner Meinung festhalten; **stand ~ by sth./sb.** zu etw./jmdm. stehen **2** (soundly) **be ~ asleep** fest schlafen; (when one should be awake) fest eingeschlafen sein **3** ▸**i** **p. 1566** (quickly) schnell; **not so ~!** nicht so hastig! **4** (ahead) **that clock is running ~:** diese Uhr geht vor; **play ~ and loose with sb.** mit jmdm. ein falsches *od.* doppeltes Spiel treiben

fast: ~back *n.* (back of car) Fließheck, *das;* Fastback, *das;* (car) Wagen mit Fließheck; Fastback, *das;* **~ ˈbowler** *n.* (Cricket) schneller Werfer; **~ ˈbreeder [reactor]** *n.* schneller Brüter; **~ ˈbuck** ▸**buck⁴**; **~ day** *n.* Fast[en]tag, *der*

fasten /ˈfɑːsn/

A *v.t.* **1** festmachen, befestigen (**on, to** an + *Dat.*); festmachen, vertäuen (**to** an + *Dat.*) ‹*Boot*›; festziehen, anziehen ‹*Schraube*›; zumachen ‹*Kleid, Spange, Knöpfe, Jacke*›;

f

[ab]schließen, [ver]schließen ‹*Tür*›; schließen ‹*Fenster*›; anstecken ‹*Brosche*› (**to** an + *Akk.*); **~ sth. together with a clip** etw. zusammenheften; **~ the rope to a post** das Tau an einem Pfosten anbinden *od.* festmachen; **~ sth. up with string** etw. zu- *od.* verschnüren; **~ one's safety belt** sich anschnallen; seinen Sicherheitsgurt anlegen; **she ~ed her hair back** sie band ihre Haare zurück **2** heften ‹*Blick*› (**[up]on** auf + *Akk.*); richten ‹*Aufmerksamkeit, Gedanken*› (**[up]on** auf + *Akk.*); setzen ‹*Erwartungen, Hoffnungen*› (**[up]on** auf + *Akk.*); **~ one's attention/affections on sb.** jmdm. seine Aufmerksamkeit zuwenden/Zuneigung schenken **3** (assign) anhängen, beilegen ‹*Spottnamen*› (**[up]on** + *Dat.*); **~ the blame/charge [up]on sb.** die Schuld auf jmdn. schieben; jmdm. die Schuld in die Schuhe schieben (ugs.)

B *v.i.* **1** sich schließen lassen; **the skirt ~s at the back** der Rock wird hinten zugemacht; **the hook and the eye ~ together** der Haken und die Öse werden miteinander verbunden **2** **~ [up]on sth.** (single out) etw. herausgreifen; (seize upon) etw. aufs Korn nehmen (ugs.)

fastener /ˈfɑːsnə(r)/ *n.* Verschluss, *der*

fastening /ˈfɑːsnɪŋ/ *n.* (device) Verschluss, *der*

fast: ~ ˈfood *n. im Schnellrestaurant angebotenes Essen;* Fastfood, *das; attrib.* **~food restaurant** Schnellrestaurant, *das;* **~ ˈforward** *n.* schneller Vorlauf; (playback) Zeitrafferwiedergabe, *die;* **watch sth. on ~ forward** etw. im Zeitraffer ansehen; **~-forward** **A** *attrib. adj.* Vorspul‹*taste, -funktion*›; **B** *v.t. & i.* vorspulen; **~-growing** *adj.* schnell wachsend

fastidious /fæˈstɪdɪəs/ *adj.* (hard to please) heikel, (ugs.) pingelig (**about** in Bezug auf + *Akk.*); (carefully selective) wählerisch (**about** in Bezug auf + *Akk.*)

fastidiously /fæˈstɪdɪəslɪ/ *adv.* **behave ~:** pingelig (ugs.)/wählerisch sein; **dress ~:** in seiner/ihrer Kleidung untadelig sein; **~ clean** peinlich sauber

fast: ~ lane *n.* Überholspur, *die;* **life in the ~ lane** (fig.) schnelles, lockeres Leben; Leben auf vollen Touren (ugs.); **~-moving** *adj.* schnell; spannend, tempogeladen ‹*Film, Drama*›; **a ~-moving train** ein schnell fahrender Zug

fastness /ˈfɑːstnɪs/ *n.* **1** *no pl.* (of colour, dye) [Farb]echtheit, *die;* (against light) Lichtechtheit, *die;* (against washing) Waschechtheit, *die* **2** (stronghold) Feste, *die*

ˈfast track *n.* Überholspur, *die;* **a career on the ~:** eine Blitzkarriere; **the ~ to success** der schnelle Weg zum Erfolg; **be on the ~:** eine Blitzkarriere machen

ˈfast-track

A *v.t.* beschleunigen ‹*Projekt*›

B *attrib. adj.* Schnell-; **~ procedure** Schnellverfahren, *das;* Fast-Track-Verfahren, *das* (Politik)

fat /fæt/

A *adj.* **1** dick; fett (abwertend); rund ‹*Wangen, Gesicht*›; fett ‹*Schwein*›; **grow** *or* **get ~:** dick werden; **grow ~** (fig.) reich werden; **you won't get ~ on that** (fig. coll.) das wird dir nicht viel einbringen **2** **~ cattle** Mast- *od.* Schlachtvieh, *das* **3** (containing much ~) fett ‹*Essen, Fleisch, Brühe*› **4** (fig.) dick ‹*Bündel, Buch, Brieftasche, Zigarre*›; umfangreich ‹*Filmrolle, Band*›; üppig, fett ‹*Gewinn, Gehalt, Bankkonto, Scheck*› **5** (coll. iron.) **~ lot of good ˈyou are** du bist mir 'ne schöne Hilfe (iron.); **a ~ lot [of good it would do me]** [das würde mir] herzlich wenig [helfen]; **~ lot he knows** was der nicht alles weiß (iron.); **a ~ chance** herzlich wenig Aussicht; **~ chance ˈhe's got** da hat er ja Mordschancen (iron.)

B *n.* Fett, *das;* **low in ~:** fettarm ‹*Nahrungsmittel*›; **put on ~:** Fett ansetzen; **lose ~:** abnehmen; **the ~ is in the fire** (fig.) der Teufel ist los (ugs.); **live off** *or* **on the ~ of the land** (fig.) wie die Made im Speck leben (ugs.). *See also* **chew A**

C *v.t.*, **-tt-** mästen; herausfüttern; **~ted cattle** Schlacht- *od.* Mastvieh, *das;* **kill the ~ted calf [for sb.]** [jmdm.] ein Festessen zum Empfang geben

fatal /ˈfeɪtl/ *adj.* **1** (ruinous, disastrous) verheerend (**to** für); fatal; schicksalsschwer ‹*Tag, Moment*›; **it would be ~:** das wäre das Ende; **it is ~ to assume that ...:** es ist ein verhängnisvoller Irrtum anzunehmen, dass ... **2** (deadly) tödlich ‹*Unfall, Verletzung*›; **that sort of thing in her present state would be ~:** das würde in ihrem augenblicklichen Zustand den sicheren Tod für sie bedeuten; **deal sb. a ~ blow** jmdm. einen vernichtenden Schlag versetzen; **be** *or* **come as a ~ blow to sb.** (fig.) ein schwerer Schlag für jmdn. sein **3** (inevitable) unabwendbar; unvermeidlich; schicksalhaft ‹*Tag*› **4** (of destiny) schicksalhaft; Schicksals-

fatalism /ˈfeɪtəlɪzm/ *n., no pl.* Fatalismus, *der* (geh.); Schicksalsergebenheit, *die*

fatalist /ˈfeɪtəlɪst/ *n.* Fatalist, *der*/Fatalistin, *die*

fatalistic /feɪtəˈlɪstɪk/ *adj.* fatalistisch; schicksalsergeben ‹*Person*›

fatality /fəˈtælɪtɪ/ *n.* (death) Todesfall, *der;* (in car crash, war, etc.) [Todes]opfer, *das*

fatally /ˈfeɪtəlɪ/ *adv.* tödlich ‹*verwunden, enden*›; (disastrously) verhängnisvoll; auf verhängnisvolle Weise ‹*beeinflusst*›; unwiderstehlich ‹*attraktiv*›; **be ~ wrong** *or* **mistaken** einem verhängnisvollen Irrtum unterliegen; **be ~ ill** todkrank sein

ˈfat cat *n.* (coll.) Geldsack, *der* (ugs.) (*mit politischem Einfluss*)

fate /feɪt/ *n.* **1** Schicksal, *das;* **an accident** *or* **stroke of ~:** eine Fügung des Schicksals; **~ decided otherwise** das Schicksal hat es anders bestimmt *od.* wollte es anders; **as sure as ~:** todsicher **2** (Mythol.) **the F~s** die Parzen. *see also* **death 1**

fated /ˈfeɪtɪd/ *adj.* (doomed) zum Scheitern verurteilt ‹*Plan, Projekt*›; **be ~ to fail** *or* **to be unsuccessful** zum Scheitern verurteilt sein; **it was ~ that we should never meet again** es war uns (*Dat.*) bestimmt, uns nie wieder zu sehen; **be ~:** unter einem ungünstigen Stern stehen

fateful /ˈfeɪtfl/ *adj.* **1** (important, decisive) schicksalsschwer ‹*Tag, Stunde, Entscheidung*›; entscheidend ‹*Worte*› **2** (controlled by fate) schicksalhaft ‹*Begegnung, Treffen, Ereignis*› **3** (prophetic) prophetisch; (of misfortune) unheilverkündend

fat: ~-free *adj.* fettfrei; **~head** *n.* Dummkopf, *der* (ugs.); Schafskopf, *der* (ugs. abwertend); **~-headed** *adj.* dumm; blöd (ugs.)

father /ˈfɑːðə(r)/

A *n.* ▸ⓘ **p. 1634** **1** Vater, *der;* **become a ~:** Vater werden; **he is a** *or* **the ~ of six** er hat sechs Kinder; **be ~ to sb.** jmds. Vater sein; **be [like] a ~ to sb.** wie ein Vater zu jmdm. sein; **he is his ~'s son** er ist ganz der Vater; **like ~ like son** der Apfel fällt nicht weit vom Stamm (ugs. scherzhaft, Spr.); **the wish is ~ to the thought** der Wunsch ist der Vater des Gedankens; **the ~ and mother of a row/beating** (coll.) ein furchtbarer Krach/eine furchtbare Tracht Prügel (ugs.); *see also* **child 2** *in pl.* (forefathers) Väter *Pl.* **3** (originator) Vater, *der;* Urheber, *der;* **F~s [of the Church]** Kirchenväter *Pl.* **4** (revered person) Vater, *der;* **the ~ of his country** der Landesvater **5** (God) **[our heavenly] F~:** [unser himmlischer] Vater; **God the F~, the Son, and the Holy Ghost** der Vater, der Sohn und der Heilige Geist; **the Our F~:** das Vaterunser **6** (confessor) Beichtvater, *der;* (priest) Pfarrer, *der;* (monk) Pater, *der;* **F~** (as title: priest) Herr Pfarrer; (as title: monk) Pater; **the Holy F~:** der Heilige Vater; **Right/Most Reverend F~ [in God]** Ehrwürdiger Vater; **F~ Superior** Prior, *der* **7** **F~** (venerable person, god) Vater, *der;* **F~ Thames** die Themse; **[Old] F~ Time** der Chronos (geh.) **8** (oldest member) [Dienst]älteste, *der;* **F~ of the House of Commons** (Brit. Polit.) dienstältestes Mitglied des Unterhauses; *see also* **city fathers**; **Pilgrim Fathers**

B *v.t.* **1** (beget) zeugen **2** (originate) ins Leben rufen

father: F~ ˈChristmas *n.* der Weihnachtsmann; **~ figure** *n.* Vaterfigur, *die*

fatherhood /ˈfɑːðəhʊd/ *n., no pl.* Vaterschaft, *die*

father: ~-in-law *n., pl.* **~s-in-law** Schwiegervater, *der;* **~land** *n.* Vaterland, *das*

fatherless /ˈfɑːðəlɪs/ *adj.* vaterlos; **be ~:** keinen Vater haben

fatherly /ˈfɑːðəlɪ/

A *adj.* väterlich; **~ responsibilities** Vaterpflichten *Pl.;* **~ words of advice** väterliche Ratschläge

B *adv.* wie ein Vater; väterlich ‹*belehren*›

ˈFather's Day *n.* Vatertag, *der*

fathom /ˈfæðəm/

A *n.* (Naut.) Fathom, *das* (geh.); Faden, *der*

B *v.t.* **1** (measure) mit dem Lot messen **2** (fig.: comprehend) verstehen; **~ sb./sth. out** jmdn./etw. ergründen; **I just cannot ~ him out** er ist mir ein Rätsel

fathomless /ˈfæðəmlɪs/ *adj.* (immeasurable) unermesslich; grenzenlos, unendlich ‹*Liebe Gottes*›; bodenlos ‹*Abgrund*›

fatigue /fəˈtiːɡ/

A *n.* **1** Ermüdung, *die;* Erschöpfung, *die;* **fight against ~:** gegen die Müdigkeit ankämpfen; **extreme ~:** Übermüdung, *die* **2** (of metal etc.) Ermüdung, *die* **3** (of muscle, organ, etc.) Übermüdung, *die;* Überanstrengung, *die* **4** (task) mühselige Arbeit; Mühsal, *die* (geh.) **5** (Mil.) Arbeitsdienst, *der;* **be put on ~ duty** zum Arbeitsdienst eingeteilt werden; **~s** ▸**fatigue-dress**

B *v.t.* ermüden

fatigued /fəˈtiːɡd/ *adj.* ermüdet; müde ‹*Blick*›; (exhausted) erschöpft

fatigue: ~-dress *n.* (Mil.) Arbeitsanzug, *der;* **~-party** *n.* (Mil.) Arbeitskommando, *das*

fatless /ˈfætlɪs/ *adj.* ohne Fett *nachgestellt;* mager ‹*Fleisch*›

fatness /ˈfætnɪs/ *n., no pl.* (corpulence) Dicke, *die;* Beleibtheit, *die* (verhüll.); Fettheit, *die* (abwertend)

ˈfatstock *n., no pl.* Mastvieh, *das*

fatted /ˈfætɪd/ ▸**fat C**

fatten /ˈfætn/

A *v.t.* herausfüttern ‹*Person*›; mästen ‹*Tier*›

B *v.i.* ‹*Tier:*› fett werden; ‹*Person:*› dick werden; fett werden (abwertend); **~ on sth.** sich mästen mit etw.

fattening /ˈfætnɪŋ/ *adj.* dick machend ‹*Nahrungsmittel*›; **~ foods** Dickmacher *Pl.* (ugs.); **be ~:** dick machen

fatty /ˈfætɪ/

A *adj.* **1** fett ‹*Fleisch, Soße*›; fetthaltig ‹*Speise, Nahrungsmittel*›; fettig ‹*Substanz*› **2** (consisting of fat) Fett-; **~ tissue/tumour** Fettgewebe, *das*/Fettgeschwulst, *die*

B *n.* (coll.) Dicke, *der*/*die;* Dickerchen, *das* (scherzh.)

fatty ˈacid *n.* (Chem.) Fettsäure, *die*

fatuous /ˈfætjʊəs/ *adj.* albern; töricht; einfältig ‹*Grinsen*›

fatuously /ˈfætjʊəslɪ/ *adv.* albern; töricht ‹*handeln*›; einfältig ‹*bewundern*›

fatwa /ˈfætwɑː/ *n.* Fatwa, *die*

faucet /ˈfɔːsɪt/ *n.* **1** (for barrel) Fasszapfen, *der* **2** (Amer.: tap) Wasserhahn, *der*

fault /fɔːlt, fɒlt/

A *n.* **1** (defect) Fehler, *der;* **we all have our little ~s** wir alle haben unsere Schwächen; **confess one's ~s** seine Sünden bekennen; **to a ~:** allzu übertrieben; übermäßig; **meticulous to a ~:** peinlich genau; **find ~ [with sb./sth.]** etw. [an jmdm./etw.] auszusetzen haben; **find ~ with goods** Mängel an Waren feststellen; **[sold] with all ~s** ohne Mängelgewähr [verkauft]; **free from** *or* **without ~:** mangelfrei **2** (responsibility) Schuld, *die;* Verschulden, *das;* **whose ~ was it?** wer war schuld [daran]?; **it's all your own ~!** das ist deine eigene Schuld!; du bist selbst schuld!; **it isn't my ~:** ich habe keine Schuld; es ist nicht meine Schuld; **not through any ~ of mine** nicht durch meine Schuld; **the ~ lies with him** die Schuld liegt bei ihm; **be at ~:** im Unrecht sein; **my memory was at ~:** mein Gedächtnis hat mich getrogen (geh.); **it is difficult to determine who is at ~:** es ist schwierig zu sagen, wer die Schuld daran trägt *od.* wer dafür verantwortlich ist **3** (thing wrongly done) Fehler, *der;* **commit a ~:** einen Fehler begehen **4** (Tennis, Show Jumping etc.) Fehler, *der;* **double ~:** Doppelfehler, *der* **5** (in gas or water supply; also Electr.) Defekt, *der* **6** (Geol.) Verwerfung, *die*

B *v.t.* **1** Fehler finden an (+ *Dat.*); etwas auszusetzen haben an (+ *Dat.*); **he/his argument had been ~ed** er/seine Argumentation war bemängelt *od.* kritisiert worden 2 (declare faulty) bemängeln

fault: ~finder *n.* Krittler, *der*/Krittlerin, *die* (abwertend); **~finding** A *n.* Krittelei, *die* (abwertend); B *adj.* krittelig (abwertend); **~finding critic/criticism** Krittler, *der*/Krittelei, *die*

faultily /ˈfɔːltɪlɪ, ˈfɒltɪlɪ/ *adv.* fehlerhaft; mangelhaft

faultless /ˈfɔːltlɪs, ˈfɒltlɪs/ *adj.* einwandfrei; tadellos ‹*Erscheinung*›; fehlerlos, fehlerfrei ‹*Übersetzung, Englisch*›; untadelig ‹*Betragen*›; ausgezeichnet ‹*Ruf*›

faultlessly /ˈfɔːltlɪslɪ, ˈfɒltlɪslɪ/ *adv.* fehlerfrei; fehlerlos; makellos ‹*schön*›; **the dress fits ~:** das Kleid hat einen tadellosen Sitz

faulty /ˈfɔːltɪ, ˈfɒltɪ/ *adj.* fehlerhaft; unzutreffend ‹*Argument*›; defekt ‹*Gerät usw.*›; **~ design/calculation** Fehlkonstruktion, *die*/Fehlkalkulation, *die*

faun /fɔːn/ *n.* (Mythol.) Faun, *der*

fauna /ˈfɔːnə/ *n.*, *pl.* **~e** /ˈfɔːniː/ *or* **~s** (Zool.) Fauna, *die*

faute de mieux /fəʊt də ˈmjɜː/ *adv.* faute de mieux (geh.); in Ermangelung eines Besseren

faux pas /fəʊ ˈpɑː/ *n.*, *pl. same* /fəʊ ˈpɑːz/ Fauxpas, *der*

favor, favorite *etc.* (*Amer.*) ▸**favour** *etc.*

favour /ˈfeɪvə(r)/ (Brit.)

A *n.* 1 Gunst, *die;* Wohlwollen, *das;* **look with ~ on** mit Wohlwollen betrachten; wohlwollend gegenüberstehen (+ *Dat.*) ‹*Person, Plan, Idee usw.*›; **find ~ in the eyes of sb.** *or* **in sb.'s eyes** (literary) vor jmds. Augen (*Dat.*) Gnade finden; **find/lose ~ with sb.** ‹*Sache:*› bei jmdm. Anklang finden/jmdm. nicht mehr gefallen; ‹*Person:*› jmds. Wohlwollen gewinnen/verlieren; **as a mark of her ~:** als *od.* zum Zeichen ihrer Wertschätzung *od.* Anerkennung; **be in ~ [with sb.]** [bei jmdm.] beliebt *od.* (ugs.) gut angeschrieben sein; ‹*Idee, Kleidung usw.:*› [bei jmdm.] in Mode sein; **be out of ~ [with sb.]** [bei jmdm.] unbeliebt *od.* (ugs.) schlecht angeschrieben sein; [bei jmdm.] in Ungnade sein (oft spött.); ‹*Idee, Kleidung usw.:*› [bei jmdm.] nicht mehr in Mode sein; **get back in[to] sb.'s ~:** jmds. Gunst *od.* Wohlwollen wiedergewinnen 2 (kindness) Gefallen, *der;* Gefälligkeit, *die;* **ask a ~ of sb.** jmdn. um einen Gefallen bitten; **do sb. a ~, do a ~ for sb.** jmdm. einen Gefallen tun; **do me the ~ of shutting up** (iron.) tu mir den Gefallen und halt den Mund; **as a ~:** aus Gefälligkeit; **as a ~ to sb.** jmdm. zuliebe; **get special ~s** besondere Vergünstigungen genießen 3 (aid, support) **be in ~ of sth.** für etw. sein; **in ~ of** zugunsten (+ *Gen.*); **all those in ~:** alle, die dafür sind; **in sb.'s ~:** zu jmds. Gunsten; **the exchange rate is in our ~:** der Wechselkurs steht *od.* ist günstig für uns 4 (preferential treatment) Begünstigung, *die;* **show ~ to[wards] sb.** jmdn. begünstigen 5 (ornament, badge) Andenken, *das;* (ribbon, cockade) Schleife, *die;* Kokarde, *die;* (party-badge) Abzeichen, *das;* Plakette, *die. See also* **fear A 1**

B *v.t.* 1 (approve) für gut halten, gutheißen ‹*Plan, Idee, Vorschlag*›; (think preferable) bevorzugen; **I ~ the first proposal** ich bin für den ersten Vorschlag 2 **~ sb.** (treat sb. kindly) jmdm. günstig gesinnt sein; jmdm. wohl wollen; (encourage or sponsor sb.) jmdn. unterstützen; jmdn. fördern 3 (oblige) beehren (**with** mit) (geh.); **~ sb. with a smile/glance/an interview** jmdm. ein Lächeln/einen Blick schenken/ein Interview gewähren (geh.); **he ~ed me with a visit** (iron.) er beglückte mich mit einem Besuch 4 (treat preferentially) bevorzugen 5 (aid, support) helfen (+ *Dat.*) 6 (confirm) bekräftigen, bestätigen ‹*Ansicht, Meinung, Theorie*› 7 (prove advantageous to) begünstigen; **the weather ~ed our journey** das Wetter trug zum Gelingen unserer Reise [wesentlich] bei

favourable /ˈfeɪvərəbl/ *adj.* (Brit.) 1 günstig ‹*Eindruck, Licht*›; gewogen ‹*Haltung, Einstellung*›; wohlmeinend ‹*Blick, Urteil*›; **~ attitude towards sth.** positive Einstellung einer Sache gegenüber; **be ~ to[wards] sth.** einer Sache (*Dat.*) positiv gegenüberstehen 2 (praising) freundlich ‹*Erwähnung, Empfehlung*›; positiv, günstig ‹*Bericht[erstattung], Bemerkung*› 3 (promising) viel versprechend; gut ‹*Omen, Zeichen*› 4 (helpful) günstig (**to** für) ‹*Wetter, Wind, Umstand*›; **be ~ for doing sth.** günstig sein, um etw. zu tun 5 (giving consent) zustimmend; **give sb. a ~ answer** jmdm. eine Zusage geben

favourably /ˈfeɪvərəblɪ/ *adv.* (Brit.) 1 wohlwollend ‹*ansehen, anhören, denken, urteilen*›; günstig ‹*stimmen*›; **be ~ impressed with sb./sb.'s ideas** von jmdm./jmds. Ideen sehr angetan sein; **be ~ disposed towards sb./sth.** jmdm./einer Sache positiv gegenüberstehen 2 (in praising manner) lobend ‹*erwähnen*›; positiv ‹*vermerken*› 3 (promisingly) viel versprechend 4 (helpfully) günstig 5 (with consent) **answer ~:** eine positive Antwort geben

favoured /ˈfeɪvəd/ *adj.* (Brit.) (privileged) bevorzugt; (well-liked) Lieblings‹*platz, -buch, -gericht*›; **the ~ few** die kleine Gruppe der Auserwählten (iron.); **most-~ nation** meistbegünstigter Staat; **most-~-nation treatment** Meistbegünstigung, *die* (Wirtsch.)

favourite /ˈfeɪvərɪt/ (Brit.)

A *adj.* Lieblings-; **~ son** (Amer. Polit.) Favorit, *der;* Spitzenkandidat, *der;* **sb.'s ~ person** jmds. Liebling

B *n.* 1 (film/food/country/pupil etc.) Lieblingsfilm, *der*/-essen, *das*/-land, *das*/-schüler, *der usw.;* (person in general) Liebling, *der;* **this/he is my ~:** das/ihn mag ich am liebsten; **she's a great ~ with the children** sie wird von den Kindern sehr geliebt 2 (Sport) Favorit, *der*/Favoritin, *die;* **start ~:** als Favorit an den Start gehen 3 (unduly favoured intimate) Günstling, *der* 4 (Computing) **favourites** Favoriten *Pl.*

favouritism /ˈfeɪvərɪtɪzm/ *n.*, *no pl.* (Brit.) Begünstigung, *die;* (when selecting sb. for a post etc.) Günstlingswirtschaft, *die*

fawn[1] /fɔːn/

A *n.* 1 (fallow deer) [Dam]kitz, *das;* (buck) Bockkitz, *das;* (doe) Geißkitz, *das* 2 (colour) Rehbraun, *das*

B *adj.* rehfarben; **~ colour** Rehbraun, *das*

fawn[2] *v.i.* 1 (show affection) seine Freude zeigen; ‹*Hund:*› [bellen und] mit dem Schwanz wedeln; **~ [up]on sb.** um jmdn. herumstreichen 2 (behave servilely) **~ [on** *or* **upon sb.]** sich [bei jmdm.] einschmeicheln; [vor jmdm.] katzbuckeln (abwertend)

ˈfawn-coloured *adj.* rehfarben

fawning /ˈfɔːnɪŋ/ *adj.* (showing affection) schwanzwedelnd [und bellend] ‹*Hund*›; (cringing) sich einschmeichelnd; katzbuckelnd (abwertend)

fax /fæks/

A *n.* Fax, *das*

B *v.t.* faxen; **I'll ~ it [through] to you** ich faxe sie/ihn/es dir zu

fax: ~ machine *n.* Faxgerät, *das;* **~ modem** *n.* (Computing) Faxmodem, *das;* **~ number** *n.* Faxnummer, *die*

faze /feɪz/ *v.t.* (coll.) aus der Fassung bringen; **be ~d** sich aus der Fassung bringen lassen

FBI *abbr.* (Amer.) = **Federal Bureau of Investigation** FBI, *das*

FC *abbr.* = **Football Club** FC, *der*

FCO *abbr.* (Brit.) = **Foreign and Commonwealth Office** [Britisches] Außen- und Commonwealthministerium; ≈ AA

fealty /ˈfiːəltɪ/ *n.* (Hist.) Lehnstreue, *die;* (fig.) Treue, *die*

fear /fɪə(r)/

A *n.* 1 Furcht, Angst, *die* (**of** vor + *Dat.*); (instance) Befürchtung, *die;* **out of ~:** aus Angst; **~ of death** *or* **dying/heights/open spaces** Todes-/Höhen-/Platzangst, *die;* **~ of flying** Flugangst, *die;* Angst vorm Fliegen (ugs.); **~ of doing sth.** Angst *od.* Furcht davor, etw. zu tun; **have a [terrible] ~ of sth./sb.** [furchtbare] Angst vor etw./jmdm. haben; **have a ~** *or* **have ~s of doing sth.** Angst davor haben, etw. zu tun; **in ~:** angstvoll; angsterfüllt; **be in ~:** Angst haben; **in ~ of being caught** in der Angst, gefasst zu werden; **in ~ and trembling** zitternd und zagend (geh.); mit schlotternden Knien (ugs.); **for ~ of waking** *or* **[that] we should wake** *or* **lest we [should] wake the others** aus Angst [davor], die anderen zu wecken *od.* dass wir die anderen wecken könnten; **without ~ or favour** völlig unparteiisch *od.* unvoreingenommen 2 (object of ~) Furcht, *die; in pl.* Befürchtungen *Pl.;* **what are your main ~s?** wovor haben Sie am meisten Angst? 3 (dread and reverence) [Ehr]furcht, *die* (**of** vor + *Dat.*); **put the ~ of God into sb.** (fig.) jmdn. fürchterlich erschrecken; jmdm. gehörig Angst einjagen 4 (anxiety for sb.'s/sth.'s safety) Sorge, *die* (**for** um); **go** *or* **be in ~ of one's life** Angst um sein Leben haben; in Todesangst sein 5 (risk) Gefahr, *die;* **no** *or* **not any ~ of sth./'that happening** keine Gefahr, dass etw./dies geschieht; **there's no ~ of 'that [ever happening]!** (iron.) die Gefahr besteht bestimmt nicht! (iron.); **no ~!** (coll.) keine Bange! (ugs.)

B *v.t.* 1 (be afraid of) **~ sb./sth.** vor jmdm./etw. Angst haben; sich vor jmdm./etw. fürchten; **~ to do** *or* **doing sth.** Angst haben *od.* sich fürchten, etw. zu tun; **you have nothing to ~:** Sie haben nichts zu befürchten; **~ the worst** das Schlimmste befürchten 2 (be worried about) befürchten; **~ [that ...]** fürchten[, dass ...]; **it is to be ~ed that ...:** es steht zu befürchten, dass ...; **we need not ~ that/but [that] he will come** wir brauchen uns keine Sorgen zu machen, dass er kommt/nicht kommt

C *v.i.* sich fürchten; **~ for sb./sth.** um jmdn./etw. bangen (geh.) *od.* fürchten; **never ~** (also joc. iron.) keine Bange (ugs.)

fearful /ˈfɪəfl/ *adj.* 1 (terrible) furchtbar; grauenhaft ‹*Erfahrung, Anblick, Tod, Untier*›; (coll.: very bad) fürchterlich; scheußlich ‹*Farbe, Wetter*›; **we had a ~ wait** wir mussten furchtbar lange warten 2 (frightened) ängstlich; (apprehensive) **~ of sth./sb.** erfüllt von Angst vor etw./jmdm.; **be ~ of sth./sb.** vor etw./jmdm. Angst haben; **be ~ of doing sth.** Angst [davor] haben, etw. zu tun; **be ~ [that** *or* **lest] ...:** Angst haben, dass ...

fearfully /ˈfɪəfəlɪ/ *adv.* 1 (terribly) furchtbar; (coll.: extremely) fürchterlich; schrecklich; furchtbar ‹*nett, gut, laut, heiß*› 2 (in frightened manner) ängstlich

fearless /ˈfɪəlɪs/ *adj.* furchtlos; (through skill) kühn; **be ~ [of sth./sb.]** keine Angst [vor etw./jmdm.] haben *od.* kennen

fearlessly /ˈfɪəlɪslɪ/ *adv.* furchtlos; ohne Angst

fearsome /ˈfɪəsəm/ *adj.* furchteinflößend; furchterregend; grässlich ‹*Anblick*›; **he/it is a ~-looking man/weapon** er/die Waffe sieht furchterregend aus

feasibility /fiːzɪˈbɪlɪtɪ/ *n.*, *no pl.* 1 (practicability) Durchführbarkeit, *die;* (of method) Tauglichkeit, *die;* Anwendbarkeit, *die;* (possibility) Möglichkeit, *die* 2 (coll.) (manageability) Machbarkeit, *die;* (convenience) Annehmlichkeit, *die*

feasiˈbility study *n.* Durchführbarkeitsstudie, *die*

feasible /ˈfiːzɪbl/ *adj.* 1 (practicable) durchführbar ‹*Plan, Vorschlag*›; anwendbar ‹*Methode*›; erreichbar ‹*Ziel*›; gangbar ‹*Weg, Lösung*›; (possible) möglich 2 (manageable) machbar; (convenient) möglich

feast /fiːst/

A *n.* 1 (Relig.) Fest, *das;* **the ~ of Christmas/Easter/Epiphany** das Weihnachts-/Oster-/Erscheinungsfest; **movable/immovable ~:** beweglicher/unbeweglicher Feiertag; **breakfast is a movable ~ in our family** (joc.) wir frühstücken nicht zu festen Zeiten 2 (banquet) Festessen, *das;* Bankett, *das* (geh.); (fig.) Labsal, *das* (geh.); **a ~ for the eyes/ears** eine Augenweide/ein Ohrenschmaus; *see also* **enough B**

B *v.i.* 1 schlemmen; schwelgen; **~ on sth.** sich an etw. (*Dat.*) gütlich tun; (fig.) sich an etw. (*Dat.*) laben (geh.); sich an etw. (*Dat.*) weiden (geh.) 2 (celebrate with festivities) Feste/ein Fest begehen; feiern

C *v.t.* festlich bewirten; **he ~ed his eyes on her beauty** seine Augen labten *od.* weideten sich an ihrer Schönheit (geh.)

ˈfeast day *n.* [kirchlicher] Feiertag

feat /fiːt/ *n.* (action) Meisterleistung, *die;* Bravourleistung, *die;* (thing) Meisterwerk, *das;* **a ~ of intellect/strength** eine intellektuelle/physische Meisterleistung; **no mean** *or* **small ~:** eine beachtliche Leistung

feather /'feðə(r)/
A n. 1 Feder, die; (on arrow) [Pfeil]feder, die; (for hat) [Hut]feder, die; **as light as a ~:** federleicht; herrlich locker ‹Kuchen›; **show the white ~** (fig.) es mit der Angst [zu tun] kriegen (ugs.); kneifen (ugs.); **fine ~s make fine birds** (prov.) Kleider machen Leute (Spr.); **a ~ in sb.'s cap** (fig.) ein Grund für jmdn., stolz zu sein; **ruffle sb.'s ~s** jmdn. reizen od. aufregen; **you could have knocked me down with a ~:** ich war völlig von den Socken (ugs.); **make the ~s fly** hohe Wellen schlagen 2 collect. (plumage) Gefieder, das; Federkleid, das (geh.); **in high** or **full** or **fine ~** (fig.) in guter Form. see also **bird 1**
B v.t. 1 (furnish with ~s) mit Federn versehen; befiedern; **~ one's nest** (fig.) auf seinen finanziellen Vorteil bedacht sein 2 (turn edgeways) aufdrehen ‹Paddel, Ruder›. See also **tar[1] B**

feather: ~ 'bed n. mit Federn gefüllte Matratze; **~-bed** v.t. [ver]hätscheln; **~ 'boa** n. Federboa, die; **~-brain** n. Schwachkopf, der (ugs.); **~-brained** /'feðəbreɪnd/ adj. schwachköpfig (ugs.); **~ 'duster** n. Federwisch, der

feathered /'feðəd/ adj. gefiedert

feather: ~-stitch n. Federstich, der; **~weight** n. 1 (very light thing/person) Fliegengewicht, das; **be a ~weight** federleicht sein; 2 (Boxing etc.) Federgewicht, das; (person also) Federgewichtler, der

feathery /'feðərɪ/ adj. 1 (covered with feathers) befiedert; gefiedert 2 (adorned with feathers) federngeschmückt; Feder‹hut, -schmuck› 3 (feather-like) (in quality) federartig; gefiedert ‹Blatt›; (in weight) federleicht; locker ‹Kuchenteig›

feature /'fiːtʃə(r)/
A n. 1 usu. in pl. (part of face) Gesichtszug, der; **facial ~s** Gesichtszüge 2 (distinctive characteristic) [charakteristisches] Merkmal; Charakteristikum, das; **be a ~ of sth.** charakteristisch für etw. sein; **which ~s of city life attract you most?** was zieht dich am Stadtleben besonders an?; **a/one particular ~:** ein besonderes Merkmal; **make a ~ of sth.** etw. [sehr] betonen od. herausstellen 3 (Journ. etc.) Reportage, die; Dokumentarbericht, der; Feature, das 4 (Cinemat.) **~ [film]** Hauptfilm, der; Spielfilm der 5 (Radio, Telev.) **~ [programme]** Feature, das
B v.t. (make attraction of) vorrangig vorstellen; den Vorrang geben (+ Dat.); (give special prominence to) (in film) in einer Hauptrolle zeigen; (in show) als Stargast präsentieren
C v.i. 1 (be ~) vorkommen 2 (be [important] participant) **~ in sth.** eine [bedeutende] Rolle bei etw. spielen; **~ in a film** eine Hauptrolle in einem Film spielen

featureless /'fiːtʃəlɪs/ adj. eintönig; ereignislos ‹Zeit›

Feb. abbr. = **February** Febr.

febrile /'fiːbraɪl/ adj. fiebrig; Fieber‹schweiß, -schlaf, -zustand›

February /'februərɪ/ n. ▸ⓘ **p. 1047** Februar, der; see also **August**

feces (Amer.) ▸ **faeces**

feckless /'feklɪs/ adj. (feeble) schwächlich ‹Person›; (futile) vergeblich ‹Versuch, Anstrengung›; nutzlos, vertan ‹Leben›; (inefficient) untauglich; (aimless) ziellos

fecund /'fiːkənd, 'fekənd/ adj. (fertile, fertilizing, lit. or fig.) fruchtbar

fecundity /fɪ'kʌndɪtɪ/ n., no pl. (fertility, fertilizing power, lit. or fig.) Fruchtbarkeit, die

fed /fed/
A ▸ **feed A, B**
B pred. adj. (coll.) **be/get ~ up with sb./sth.** jmdn./etw. satt haben (ugs.); **you're looking rather ~ up** du siehst aus, als hättest du die Nase voll (ugs.); **be/get ~ up with doing sth.** es satt haben, etw. zu tun (ugs.); **be/get ~ up to the [back] teeth with sb./sth.** jmdn./etw. zum Kotzen finden (derb)

federal /'fedərl/ adj. 1 Bundes-; föderativ ‹System›; bundesweit ‹Feiertag›; bundeseigen ‹Betrieb›; **~ district/territory** etc. Bundesdistrikt, der/-territorium, das usw.; **~ legislation/representative** Gesetzgebung/Abgeordneter des Bundes 2 (relating to or favouring the central government) föderalistisch ‹Partei usw.›; **~ supporter/tendency** Anhänger des/Neigung zum Föderalismus 3 **F~** (Amer. Hist.: of Northern States in Civil War) der Unionisten nachgestellt 4 (having largely independent units) föderiert

federalism /'fedərəlɪzəm/ n., no pl. Föderalismus, der

federalist /'fedərəlɪst/
A adj. föderalistisch
B n. Föderalist, der/Föderalistin, die

federally /'fedərəlɪ/ adv. von der Bundesregierung; vom Bund

federate /'fedəreɪt/
A v.t. 1 (organize on federal basis) föderalistisch organisieren; föderalisieren 2 (band together in league) zu einem Bund zusammenschließen; föderieren
B v.i. sich [zu einem Bund] zusammenschließen

federation /fedə'reɪʃn/ n. 1 (federating) Zusammenschluss, der 2 (group of states) Bündnis, das; Föderation, die; (society) Bund, der; Verband, der

fee /fiː/ n. 1 Gebühr, die 2 (of doctor, lawyer, etc.) Honorar, das; (of performer) Gage, die; **what ~ do you charge?** was verlangen Sie als Honorar/Gage? 3 in pl. (of company director etc.) Bezüge Pl. 4 ▸ **transfer fee** 5 (entrance money) Gebühr, die; **matriculation/registration ~:** Einschreibe-/Aufnahmegebühr, die 6 (administrative charge) Bearbeitungsgebühr, die 7 in pl. (regular payment for instruction) **school ~s** Schulgeld, das; **tuition ~s** ▸ **tuition 2**

feeble /'fiːbl/ adj., **~r** /'fiːblə(r)/, **~st** /'fiːblɪst/ 1 (weak) schwach 2 (deficient) schwächlich; (in resolve, argument, commitment) halbherzig 3 (lacking energy) schwach ‹Leistung, Kampf, Stimme, Applaus›; wenig überzeugend ‹Argument, Entschuldigung, Erklärung, Vorstellung›; zaghaft, kläglich ‹Versuch, Bemühung›; kraftlos ‹Drohung›; lahm (ugs.) ‹Witz› 4 (indistinct) schwach ‹[Licht]schein, Herzschlag›

'feeble-minded adj. 1 töricht 2 (Psych.) geistesschwach; **~ person** Schwachsinnige, der/die

feebly /'fiːblɪ/ adv. 1 (weakly) mühsam ‹gehen, sich bewegen› 2 (deficiently) schwach; kaum ‹reagieren› 3 (without energy) schwach ‹widerstehen, unterstützen, applaudieren›; zaghaft ‹versuchen, ablehnen, widersprechen, behaupten›

feed /fiːd/
A v.t., **fed** /fed/ 1 (give food to) füttern; **~ sb./an animal with sth.** jmdm. etw. zu essen/einem Tier [etw.] zu fressen geben; **~ a baby/an animal/an invalid on** or **with sth.** ein Baby/Tier/einen Invaliden mit etw. füttern; **the dog is fed every evening at 6 o'clock** der Hund bekommt jeden Abend um 6 Uhr sein Fressen; **~ intravenously** intravenös ernähren; **~ [at the breast]** stillen 2 (provide food for) ernähren; satt machen; **~ sb./an animal on** or **with sth.** jmdn./ein Tier mit etw. ernähren 3 (put food into mouth of) füttern; **~ oneself** allein od. ohne Hilfe essen; **can the child ~ herself/himself with a spoon yet?** kann das Kind schon mit dem Löffel essen?; **be ~ing one's face** (coll. derog.) fressen (abwertend) 4 (graze) weiden lassen; weiden 5 (produce food for) **~ sb. [with sth.]** jmdn. [mit etw.] versorgen 6 (nourish) mit Nährstoffen versorgen; (fig.) verstärken 7 ▸ **feed up** 8 (give out) verfüttern ‹Viehfutter› **(to** an + Akk.) 9 (keep supplied) speisen ‹Wasserreservoir›; unterhalten ‹Feuer›; am Brennen halten ‹Ofen›; (supply with material) versorgen; (supply) **~ a film into the projector** einen Film in das Vorführgerät einlegen; **~ data into the computer** Daten in den Computer eingeben; den Computer mit Daten füttern; **~ sth. to sb., ~ sb. sth.** (fig.) jmdn. mit etw. füttern; **~ sth. to the flames** etw. den Flammen übergeben; see also **meter[1] A 2** 10 (lead) **~ sth. through sth.** etw. durch etw. hindurchführen 11 (Theatre coll.) **~ the actor [with] his cues** or **the cues to the actor** dem Schauspieler das Stichwort geben 12 (Football etc.) zuspielen **(to** Dat.). See also **fed B**
B v.i., **fed** ‹Tier:› fressen **(from** aus); ‹Person:› essen **(off** von); **~ on sth.** ‹Tier:› etw. fressen, mit etw. gefüttert werden; ‹Person:› sich von etw. [er]nähren, etw. essen, etw. futtern (ugs.); (fig.) von etw. leben; **~ off sth.** sich von etw. ernähren; (fig.) von etw. leben
C n. 1 (instance of eating) (of animals) Fressen, das; (of baby) Mahlzeit, die; **when is the baby's next ~ due?** wann muss das Baby wieder gefüttert werden?; **have [quite] a ~** (coll.: feast) [ordentlich] futtern (ugs.); [kräftig] zulangen 2 (horse's oats etc.) [Futter]ration, die; (fodder) **[cattle/sheep/pig] ~:** [Vieh-/Schaf-/Schweine]futter, das; **be off its ~** ‹Tier:› schlecht fressen 3 (of machine) Versorgung, die; (of furnace) Begichtung, die; (supplying of material) Einspeisung, die 4 (material supplied to machine) Nachschub, der; (amount supplied) Nachschub, der; Nachfüllmenge, die; (into computer) Einspeisung, die 5 (hopper) Trichter, der.

Phrasal verbs

• **~ 'back**
A v.t. 1 zurückleiten; weiterleiten, -geben ‹Informationen›; **be fed back** zurückfließen 2 (Electr.) rückkoppeln
B v.i. **~ back into sth.** in etw. (Akk.) zurückfließen; **~ back to sth./sb.** an etw./jmdn. weitergeleitet werden. See also **feedback**

• **~ 'up** v.t. (fatten) mästen; (fill up with food) voll stopfen (ugs.); see also **fed B**

'feedback n. 1 (information about result, response) Reaktion, die; Feedback, das (fachspr.) 2 (Electr.) **[positive/negative] ~:** [positive/negative] Rückkopplung 3 (Biol., Psych., etc.) Reafferenz, die (fachspr.); Rückkopplung, die

feeder /'fiːdə(r)/ n. 1 (animal) Fresser, der; **plankton ~** Planktonfresser, der; **the larvae are voracious ~s** die Larven sind gefräßig 2 (dispenser) Futterspender, der

feeder: ~ road n. Zubringer, der; Zubringerstraße, die; **~ school** n. abgebende Schule

feeding/'fiːdɪŋ/: **~ bottle** n. [Saug]flasche, die; **~ frenzy** n. (of sharks, piranhas) Beuterausch, der; **the remark caused a media ~ frenzy** auf die Bemerkung stürzten sich die Medien; **~ time** n. 1 Fütterungszeit, die; 2 (fig. joc.) Essenszeit, die; **~ time!** Essen!

feed: ~ pipe n. Zuleitungsrohr, das; Füllrohr, das; **~stock** n. Einsatz- od. Ausgangsmaterial, das

feel /fiːl/
A v.t., **felt** /felt/ 1 (explore by touch) befühlen; **~ sb.'s pulse** jmdm. den Puls fühlen; (fig.) bei jmdm. vorfühlen; jmdm. auf den Zahn fühlen (ugs.) **(on, about** hinsichtlich); **~ one's way** sich (Dat.) seinen Weg ertasten; (fig.: try sth. out) vorsichtig vorgehen; sich vorsichtig vor[an]tasten; **be ~ing one's way** versuchen, sich zurechtzufinden; **~ one's way along the corridor/towards the door** sich den Flur entlangtasten/sich zur Tür tasten
2 (perceive by touch) fühlen; (become aware of) bemerken; (be aware of) merken; (have sensation of) spüren; **~ sb.'s temperature** fühlen, ob jmd. Fieber hat
3 ▸ **feel up**
4 (be conscious of) empfinden ‹Mitleid, Dank, Eifersucht›; verspüren ‹Drang, Wunsch›; spüren ‹Gefühle anderer›; **~ the cold/heat** unter der Kälte/Hitze leiden; **~ one's age** sein Alter spüren; **~ pride in sb./sth.** stolz auf jmdn./etw. sein; **~ bitterness/amazement** verbittert/erstaunt sein; **~ the temptation** sich versucht fühlen; **make itself felt** zu spüren sein; (have effect) sich bemerkbar machen; **make one's presence felt** sich bemerkbar machen
5 (experience) empfinden; (be affected by) zu spüren bekommen
6 (be emotionally affected by) leiden unter (+ Dat.); **he felt it terribly when his dog died** er litt ganz furchtbar, als sein Hund starb
7 (have vague or emotional conviction) **~ [that] ...:** das Gefühl haben, dass ...
8 (think) **if that's what you ~ about the matter** wenn du so darüber denkst; **~ it to be one's duty to ...:** es für seine Pflicht halten, zu ...; **~ oneself hard done by** sich schlecht behandelt fühlen; **~ [that] ...:** glauben, dass ...; **if you ~ [that] you would like to know**

more wenn Sie gern mehr wissen möchten. *See also* **bone A 1**; **draught 1**

B *v.i.*, **felt** 1 (search with hand etc.) ~ **[about] in sth. [for sth.]** in etw. (*Dat.*) [nach etw.] [herum]suchen; ~ **[about] in one's bag/pocket [to see whether ...]** in seiner Tasche [herum]kramen[, um festzustellen, ob ...] (ugs.); ~ **[about] [after** *or* **for sth.] with sth.** mit etw. [nach etw.] [umher]tasten
2 (have sense of touch) fühlen
3 (be conscious that one is) sich ... fühlen; ~ **angry/enthusiastic/sure/delighted/disappointed** böse/begeistert/sicher/froh/enttäuscht sein; **she felt quite sick/horrified at the idea** der Gedanke machte sie ganz krank/widerte sie an; **I felt such a fool** ich kam mir wie ein Idiot vor; ~ **[the] better for sth.** (in mind) sich erleichtert fühlen; (in body) sich besser fühlen; ~ **inclined to do sth.** dazu neigen, etw. zu tun; ~ **committed to sth.** sich einer Sache (*Dat.*) verschrieben haben; **the child did not ~ loved/wanted/needed** das Kind hatte das Gefühl, ungeliebt/unerwünscht/überflüssig zu sein; **I ~ dubious about doing that** ich weiß nicht recht, ob ich das machen soll; ~ **quite hopeful** guter Hoffnung sein; **I felt sorry for him** er tat mir leid; ~ **hard done by** sich schlecht behandelt fühlen; ~ **like sth.** sich (*Dat.*) vorkommen wie etw.; **he makes you ~ like a fool/lady** bei ihm kommt man sich (*Dat.*) wie ein Idiot vor/er gibt einem das Gefühl, eine Dame zu sein; ~ **like a new man/woman** sich wie neugeboren fühlen; **what do you ~ like** *or* **how do you ~ today?** wie fühlst du dich *od.* wie geht es dir heute?; **what would you ~ like** *or* **how would you ~ if someone said such a thing to you?** was würdest du empfinden, wenn jemand so etwas zu dir sagte?; **let's see what we ~ like** *or* **how we ~ when ...:** warten wir ab, in welcher Verfassung wir sind *od.* (what we should like to do) wie uns der Sinn steht, wenn ...; ~ **like sth./doing sth.** (coll.: wish to have/do) auf etw. (*Akk.*) Lust haben/Lust haben, etw. zu tun; **do you ~ like a cup of tea?** möchtest du eine Tasse Tee?; **I ~ like a new hairdo** ich könnte eine neue Frisur gebrauchen; **we ~ as if** *or* **as though ...:** es kommt uns vor, als ob ...; (have the impression that) wir haben das Gefühl, dass ...; **how do you ~ about him now/the idea?** was empfindest du jetzt für ihn/was hältst du von der Idee?; **if that's how** *or* **the way you ~ about it** wenn du so darüber denkst; **she just didn't ~ that way about him** sie hatte nun einmal nicht solche Gefühle für ihn; ~ **the same [way] about each other** dasselbe füreinander empfinden; ~ **[quite] one'self** sich wohl fühlen
4 (be emotionally affected) ~ **passionately/bitterly about sth.** sich für etw. begeistern/über etw. (*Akk.*) verbittert sein; ~ **kindly towards sb.** jmdm. wohlgesonnen sein
5 (be consciously perceived as) sich ... anfühlen; ~ **like sth.** sich wie etw. anfühlen; **it ~s funny/strange/nice/uncomfortable** es ist ein komisches / seltsames / angenehmes / unangenehmes Gefühl; **it ~s so good to be away from the hustle** es tut gut, der Hetze entronnen zu sein; **it all ~s so strange here** es kommt einem hier alles so seltsam vor. *see also* **cheap A 3**

C *n.* 1 (sense of touch) [Be]tasten, *das;* **be dry/soft** *etc.* **to the ~:** sich trocken/weich *usw.* anfühlen
2 (act of ~ing) Abtasten, *das;* **let me have a ~:** lass mich mal fühlen
3 (sensation when touched) Gefühl, *das;* **have a silky ~:** sich seidig anfühlen
4 (sensation characterizing a situation, place, etc.) Atmosphäre, *die;* **there is a mysterious/ghostly ~ about the place** der Ort hat etwas Mysteriöses/Gespenstisches [an sich]; **get a [real]/the ~ of sth.** ein [wirkliches] Gespür für etw. bekommen; **get the ~ of things in a firm/of a new job** sich in einer Firma zurechtfinden/sich in eine neue Arbeit hineinfinden; **have a ~ for sth.** (fig.) ein Gespür *od.* einen Blick für etw. haben; (talent) eine Ader für etw. haben

Phrasal verbs
- ~ **for** *v.t.* ~ **for sb.** mit jmdm. Mitleid haben
- ~ **'out** *v.t.* 1 (sound out) ~ **sb. out** jmds. Ansichten feststellen 2 (test practicability of) zur Diskussion stellen; austesten
- ~ **'up** *v.t.* (sl.) befummeln (salopp)
- ~ **with** *v.t.* Mitgefühl haben mit; mitfühlen; **I ~ with you** Sie haben mein Mitgefühl

feeler /'fiːlə(r)/ *n.* Fühler, *der;* **put out ~s** (fig.) seine Fühler ausstrecken

'feeler gauge *n.* Fühlerlehre, *die*

'feel-good *adj.* wohlfühl-; *attrib.* ~ **factor** Feelgood Faktor, *der;* ~ **film/song** Gute-Laune-Film, *der*/Gute-Laune-Lied, *das*

feeling /'fiːlɪŋ/

A *n.* 1 (sense of touch) **[sense of] ~:** Tastsinn, *der;* **have no ~ in one's legs** kein Gefühl in den Beinen haben 2 (physical sensation) Gefühl, *das;* **you'll have a painful ~:** es wird weh tun 3 (emotion) Gefühl, *das;* **what are your ~s for each other?** was empfindet ihr füreinander?; **say sth. with ~:** etw. mit Nachdruck sagen; **~s were running high** Emotionen wurden geweckt; **there were strong ~s about it** es gab sehr entschiedene Ansichten darüber; **bad ~** (jealousy) Neid, *der;* (annoyance) Verstimmung, *die* 4 *in pl.* (sensibilities) Gefühle; **hurt sb.'s ~s** jmdn. verletzen 5 (sympathy) Mitgefühl, *das;* Einfühlungsvermögen, *das* 6 (consciousness) **a ~ of hopelessness/harmony** *etc.* ein Gefühl der Hoffnungslosigkeit/Harmonie *usw.;* **there was a ~ of mystery/peace about the place** der Ort hatte etwas Mysteriöses/Friedvolles [an sich (*Dat.*)] *od.* mutete mysteriös/friedvoll an; **I have a funny ~ that ...:** ich habe das komische Gefühl, dass ... (ugs.) 7 (belief) Gefühl, *das;* (impression) Eindruck, *der;* **have a/the ~ [that] ...:** das Gefühl haben, dass ...; **you get the ~ that ...** man bekommt den Eindruck, dass ... 8 (sentiment) Ansicht, *die;* **air one's ~s** seinem Herzen Luft machen; seine Ansicht äußern; **the general ~ was that ...:** man war allgemein der Ansicht, dass ...; *see also* **mixed 1**

B *adj.* 1 (sensitive) empfindlich 2 (sympathetic) einfühlsam; **be ~ about other people** sich in andere Leute einfühlen können 3 (showing emotion) gefühlvoll

feelingly /'fiːlɪŋlɪ/ *adv.* 1 (sympathetically) mitfühlend ‹*reagieren*› 2 (in manner showing emotion) gefühlvoll; **say sth. ~:** etw. mit Nachdruck sagen

'fee-paying *adj.* ~ **school** schulgeldpflichtige Schule; ~ **pupil/student** Schulgeld/Studiengebühren zahlender Schüler/Student

feet *pl. of* **foot**

feign /feɪn/ *v.t.* vorspiegeln; vortäuschen; ~ **ignorance** sich dumm stellen; ~ **that one is ...:** vorgeben, ... zu sein

feint[1] /feɪnt/

A *n.* 1 (Boxing, Fencing) Finte, *die;* **make a ~:** eine Finte ausführen; fintieren 2 (Mil.) Scheinangriff, *der;* **make a ~ [at** *or* **of attacking sb./sth.]** einen Scheinangriff [auf jmdn./etw.] ausführen

B *v.i.* 1 (Boxing, Fencing) ~ **at sb./sth.** eine Finte gegen jmdn./etw. ausführen 2 (Mil.) ~ **at** *or* **[up]on sb./sth.** einen Scheinangriff auf jmdn./etw. durchführen

feint[2] *adj.* (Commerc.) ~ **lines** feine Linierung; **ruled ~:** fein liniert

feisty /'faɪstɪ/ *adj.* (coll.) beherzt

feldspar /'feldspɑː(r)/ *n.* (Min.) Feldspat, *der*

felicitate /fɪ'lɪsɪteɪt/ *v.t.* (literary) ~ **sb. [on sth.]** jmdn. [zu etw.] beglückwünschen

felicitation /fɪlɪsɪ'teɪʃn/ *n.* Glückwunsch, *der;* Gratulation, *die;* **give sb. one's ~s on sth.** jmdn. zu etw. beglückwünschen; jmdm. zu etw. gratulieren

felicitous /fɪ'lɪsɪtəs/ *adj.* glücklich ‹*Zufall, Nachricht, Umstand, Wahl*›; nett ‹*Bemerkung, Art*›; gelungen ‹*Formulierung, Kommentar, Anspielung*›; geeignet, passend ‹*Worte*›

felicitously /fɪ'lɪsɪtəslɪ/ *adv.* glücklich

felicity /fɪ'lɪsɪtɪ/ *n.* 1 *no pl.* (happiness) Glück, *das* 2 (thing or person causing happiness) Glück, *das* 3 (fortunate trait) glückliche Gabe 4 (in choice of words) Formulierungskunst, *die;* ~ **of expression** glückliche Wahl des Ausdrucks

feline /'fiːlaɪn/

A *adj.* (of cat[s]) Katzen-; (catlike) katzenartig; katzenhaft

B *n.* Katze, *die;* **the ~s** die Katzen *od.* (fachspr.) Feliden

fell[1] ▸ **fall B**

fell[2] /fel/ *v.t.* 1 (cut down) fällen ‹*Baum*› 2 (strike down) niederstrecken ‹*Gegner*›

fell[3] *n.* (Brit.) 1 (hill) Berg, *der* 2 (stretch of high moorland) Hochmoor, *das*

fell[4] *adj.* 1 **at** *or* **in one ~ swoop** auf einen Schlag 2 (poet./rhet.) (fierce) wild; grimmig ‹*Drohung, Feind*›; (destructive) vernichtend

fellatio /fə'lɑːtɪəʊ/ *n.* Fellatio, *die*

fellow /'feləʊ/

A *n.* 1 *usu. in pl.* (comrade) Kamerad, *der;* **~s at school/work** Schulkameraden/Arbeitskollegen; **a good ~:** ein guter Kumpel (ugs.) 2 *usu. in pl.* (equal) Gleichgestellte, *der/die;* **be among one's ~s** unter seinesgleichen sein 3 (contemporary) Zeitgenosse, *der*/-genossin, *die* 4 (counterpart) Gegenstück, *das* 5 (Brit. Univ.) Fellow, *der;* (elected graduate) graduierter Stipendiat/graduierte Stipendiatin; (member of governing body) Mitglied des Verwaltungsrats 6 (member of academy or society) Fellow, *der;* Mitglied, *das* 7 (coll.: man, boy) Bursche, *der* (ugs.); Kerl, *der* (ugs.); (boyfriend) Freund, *der;* **the ~s** die Jungs (ugs.); **well, young ~:** nun, junger Mann; **old** *or* **dear ~:** alter Junge *od.* Knabe (ugs.); **a ~** (anyone) ein Mann; **young ~-my-lad** junger Mann; **I'm not the sort of ~ who ...:** ich bin nicht der Typ, der ...; **a devil of a ~:** ein Teufelskerl; **the other ~** (fig.) der andere 8 (derog.: despised person) Kerl, *der* (*abwertend*). *see also* **hail**[2] **D**; **stout A 3**

B *attrib. adj.* Mit-; ~ **lodger/worker** Mitbewohner/Kollege, *der*/Mitbewohnerin/Kollegin, *die;* ~ **man** *or* **human being** Mitmensch, *der;* ~ **sufferer** Leidensgenosse, *der*/-genossin, *die;* **my ~ teachers/workers** *etc.* meine Lehrer-/Arbeitskollegen *usw.;* ~ **member of the party** Parteigenosse, *der*/-genossin, *die;* ~ **member of the club** Klubkamerad, *der*/-kameradin, *die;* ~ **student** Kommilitone, *der*/Kommilitonin, *die*

fellow: ~ **'countryman** ▸ **countryman 1**; ~ **'feeling** *n.* 1 (sympathy) Mitgefühl, *das;* **have a ~ feeling for sb.** mit jmdm. fühlen; 2 (mutual understanding) Zusammengehörigkeitsgefühl, *das*

fellowship /'feləʊʃɪp/ *n.* 1 *no pl.* (companionship) Gesellschaft, *die;* **in a spirit of good ~:** von Gemeinschaftsgeist erfüllt 2 *no pl.* (community of interest) Zusammengehörigkeit, *die* 3 (association) Verbundenheit, *die* 4 (brotherhood) [Glaubens]gemeinschaft, *die* 5 (Univ. etc.) Status eines Fellows; Fellowship, *die*

fellow-'traveller *n.* 1 (who travels with another) Mitreisende, *der/die* 2 (with Communist sympathies) Sympathisant, *der*/Sympathisantin, *die*

felon /'felən/ *n.* Kapitalverbrecher, *der*/-verbrecherin, *die*

felonious /fə'ləʊnɪəs/ *adj.* verbrecherisch

felony /'felənɪ/ *n.* Kapitalverbrechen, *das*

felspar /'felspɑː(r)/ ▸ **feldspar**

felt[1] /felt/ *n.* (cloth) Filz, *der;* ~ **hat/slippers/mat** Filzhut, *der*/-pantoffeln *Pl.*/-matte, *die*

felt[2] ▸ **feel A, B**

felt[-tip] 'pen *n.* Filzstift, *der*

female /'fiːmeɪl/

A *adj.* 1 weiblich; Frauen‹*stimme, -station, -chor, -verein*›; ~ **animal/bird/fish/insect** Weibchen, *das;* ~ **child/doctor** Mädchen, *das*/Ärztin, *die;* ~ **elephant/whale** [Elefanten-/Wal]kuh, *die;* **a ~ engineer/student/slave** eine Ingenieurin/Studentin/Sklavin; ~ **impersonator** Frauendarsteller, *der* 2 ~ **screw/thread** [Schrauben]mutter, *die*/Innengewinde, *das*

B *n.* 1 (person) Frau, *die;* (fetus, child) Mädchen, *das;* (animal) Weibchen, *das* 2 (derog.: woman) Weib[sbild], *das* (ugs. abwertend)

female 'condom *n.* Frauenkondom, *das*

feminine /'femɪnɪn/

A *adj.* 1 (of women) weiblich; Frauen‹*angelegen-*

heit, -problem, -leiden›; Damen‹*mode*›; (womanly) fraulich; feminin; feminin, (abwertend) weibisch ‹*Mann*›; **she is so very ~ [in her ways]** sie gibt sich so betont fraulich [2] (Ling.) weiblich; feminin (fachspr.)

[B] *n.* (Ling.) Femininum, *das*

feminine 'rhyme *n.* (Pros.) weiblicher Reim

femininity /femɪˈnɪnɪtɪ/ *n.*, *no pl.* Weiblichkeit, *die;* (more mature) Fraulichkeit, *die*

feminism /ˈfemɪnɪzm/ *n.*, *no pl.* Feminismus, *der*

feminist /ˈfemɪnɪst/

[A] *n.* Feministin, *die*/Feminist, *der;* Frauenrechtlerin, *die*/-rechtler, *der*

[B] *adj.* feministisch; Frauen‹*bewegung, -blatt, -gruppe*›

femme fatale /fæm fæˈtɑːl/ *n.* Femme fatale, *die* (geh.)

femoral /ˈfemərl/ *adj.* (Anat.) femoral (fachspr.); Oberschenkel[knochen]-

femur /ˈfiːmə(r)/ *n.*, *pl.* **~s** *or* **femora** /ˈfemərə/ [1] (Anat.) Oberschenkelknochen, *der;* Femur, *der* (fachspr.) [2] (Zool.) Femur, *der*

fen /fen/ *n.* Fenn, *das;* Fehn, *das* (nordd.); **the Fens** die Fens

fence /fens/

[A] *n.* [1] Zaun, *der;* **sunk ~:** Sicherungsgraben, *der;* **mend one's ~s** (fig.) das Kriegsbeil begraben (ugs.); **sit on the ~** (fig.) sich nicht einmischen; sich neutral verhalten [2] (for horses to jump) Hindernis, *das* [3] (sl.: receiver) Hehler, *der*/Hehlerin, *die*

[B] *v.i.* (Sport) fechten

[C] *v.t.* (surround with fence) einzäunen; (surround) umgeben; (fig.) absichern (**with** durch)

(Phrasal verbs)

- **~ 'in** *v.t.* einzäunen; (fig.) einengen (**with** durch)
- **~ 'off** *v.t.* abzäunen; (fig.) absperren

fencer /ˈfensə(r)/ *n.* Fechter, *der*/Fechterin, *die*

fencing /ˈfensɪŋ/ *n.*, *no pl.* [1] Einzäunen, *das* [2] (Sport/Hist.) Fechten, *das; attrib.* Fecht- [3] (enclosure) Zaun, *der;* Einzäunung, *die* [4] (fences) Zäune *Pl.;* Umfriedung, *die* (geh.) [5] (material for fences) Zaun, *der*

fend /fend/ *v.i.* **~ for sb.** für jmdn. sorgen; **~ for oneself** für sich selbst sorgen; (in hostile surroundings) sich allein durchschlagen

(Phrasal verb)

- **~ 'off** *v.t.* abwehren; von sich fern halten; **~ off these criticisms/the flies/fans** sich gegen diese Kritik wehren/sich (*Dat.*) die Fliegen/Fans vom Leib halten

fender /ˈfendə(r)/ *n.* [1] Schutz, *der, o. Pl.;* Schutzvorrichtung, *die* [2] (for fire) Kaminschutz, *der* [3] (for dock wall etc.) Fender, *der;* Dalbe, *die* (Seemannsspr.) [4] (on ship) Fender, *der* [5] (Brit.: car bumper) Stoßstange, *die* [6] (Amer.) (train bumper) Rammbohle, *die;* (car mudguard or wing) Kotflügel, *der;* (bicycle mudguard) Schutzblech, *das*

fenland /ˈfenlənd/ *n.* Marschland, *das*

fennel /ˈfenl/ *n.* (Bot.) Fenchel, *der*

fenugreek /ˈfenjʊɡriːk/ *n.* (Bot.) Griechisch-Heu, *das;* Bockshornklee, *der*

feral /ˈfɪərl, ˈferl/ *adj.* [1] (wild) wild; wild wachsend ‹*Pflanze*› [2] (after escape) verwildert; **become ~:** verwildern

ferment

[A] /fəˈment/ *v.i.* [1] (undergo fermentation) gären; **cause to ~:** in *od.* zur Gärung bringen; **begin to ~:** in Gärung übergehen [2] (be in state of agitation) gären; ‹*Plan, Idee:*› reifen; ‹*Wut, Frustration:*› rumoren, brodeln

[B] *v.t.* [1] (subject to fermentation) zur Gärung bringen [2] (excite) heraufbeschwören ‹*Gewalt, Unzufriedenheit, Unruhe*›

[C] /ˈfɜːment/ *n.* [1] (fermenting agent) Enzym, *das* [2] (fermentation) Gärung, *die;* Fermentation, *die* (fachspr.) [3] (agitation) Unruhe, *die;* Aufruhr, *der;* **in [a] ~:** in Unruhe *od.* Aufruhr

fermentation /fɜːmenˈteɪʃn/ *n.* [1] Gärung, *die;* Fermentation, *die* (fachspr.); **be under** *or* **undergo ~:** gären; sich in Gärung befinden [2] (agitation) (political) Unruhe, *die;* (of ideas) Reifen, *das*

fern /fɜːn/ *n.* Farnkraut, *das; collect.* Farn, *der*

ferocious /fəˈrəʊʃəs/ *adj.* wild ‹*Tier, Person, Aussehen, Blick, Lachen*›; grimmig ‹*Stimme*›; heftig ‹*Schlag, Kampf, Stoß*›; (fig.) scharf ‹*Kritik, Angriff*›; heftig ‹*Bemerkung, Äußerung, Streit, Auseinandersetzung*›; **~-looking** Furcht erregend

ferociously /fəˈrəʊʃəslɪ/ *adv.* wütend ‹*bellen, knurren*›; grimmig ‹*blicken, lachen, sagen*›; heftig ‹*kämpfen, streiten*›; (fig.) scharf, heftig ‹*angreifen, kritisieren*›

ferociousness /fəˈrəʊʃəsnɪs/, **ferocity** /fəˈrɒsɪtɪ/ *ns.*, *no pl.* ▸**ferocious**: Wildheit, *die;* Grimmigkeit, *die;* Heftigkeit, *die;* Schärfe, *die*

ferrel /ˈferl/ ▸**ferrule**

ferret /ˈferɪt/

[A] *n.* Frettchen, *das*

[B] *v.i.* **~ [about** *or* **around]** herumstöbern (ugs.); herumschnüffeln (abwertend); **~ for sth.** nach etw. stöbern (ugs.) *od.* (abwertend) schnüffeln

(Phrasal verb)

- **~ 'out** *v.t.* aufspüren; aufstöbern (ugs.)

Ferris wheel /ˈferɪs wiːl/ *n.* Riesenrad, *das*

ferro- /ferəʊ/ *in comb.* Ferro-

ferro'concrete *n.* Stahlbeton, *der*

ferrous /ˈferəs/ *adj.* (containing iron) eisenhaltig; Eisen-

ferrule /ˈferuːl, ˈferl/ *n.* Zwinge, *die*

ferry /ˈferɪ/

[A] *n.* [1] Fähre, *die* [2] (service) Fährverbindung, *die;* Fähre, *die* (ugs.)

[B] *v.t.* [1] (convey in boat) **~ [across** *or* **over]** übersetzen [2] (transport) befördern, bringen ‹*Güter, Personen*›; **~ the children back and forth to school** die Kinder zur Schule und wieder nach Hause fahren

ferry: ~ boat *n.* Fährboot, *das;* (punt) Stakfähre, *die;* Kahnfähre, *die;* **~man** /ˈferɪmən/ *n.*, *pl.* **~men** /ˈferɪmən/ Fährmann, *der;* **~ service** *n.* [1] Fährverbindung, *die;* [2] (business) Fährbetrieb, *der*

fertile /ˈfɜːtaɪl/ *adj.* [1] (fruitful) fruchtbar (**in** an + *Dat.*); (fig.) produktiv; schöpferisch; **have a ~ imagination** viel Fantasie haben [2] (capable of developing) befruchtet [3] (able to become parent) fortpflanzungsfähig

fertilisation, fertilise, fertiliser ▸**fertiliz-**

fertility /fɜːˈtɪlɪtɪ/ *n.*, *no pl.* [1] Fruchtbarkeit, *die* (auch fig.); Fertilität, *die* [2] (ability to become parent) Fortpflanzungsfähigkeit, *die*

fertility: ~ drug *n.* (Med.) Hormonpräparat, *das* (*zur Steigerung der Fruchtbarkeit*); **~ symbol** *n.* (Anthrop.) Fruchtbarkeitssymbol, *das*

fertilization /fɜːtɪlaɪˈzeɪʃn/ *n.* [1] (Biol.) Befruchtung, *die* [2] (Agric.) Düngung, *die*

fertilize /ˈfɜːtɪlaɪz/ *v.t.* [1] (Biol.) befruchten [2] (Agric.) düngen

fertilizer /ˈfɜːtɪlaɪzə(r)/ *n.* Dünger, *der*

fervency /ˈfɜːvənsɪ/ *n.*, *no pl.* ▸**fervent**: Leidenschaftlichkeit, *die;* Inbrunst, *die;* Glut, *die*

fervent /ˈfɜːvənt/ *adj.* leidenschaftlich; inbrünstig ‹*Gebet, Wunsch, Hoffnung*›; glühend ‹*Leidenschaft, Verehrer, Liebe, Hass*›

fervently /ˈfɜːvəntlɪ/ *adv.* ▸**fervent**: leidenschaftlich; inbrünstig; glühend

fervour (*Brit.; Amer.:* **fervor**) /ˈfɜːvə(r)/ *n.* (of discussion, feeling, person, campaign) Leidenschaftlichkeit, *die;* (of love, belief) Inbrunst, *die;* (of passion) Glut, *die*

fess[e] /fes/ *n.* (Her.) Balken, *der*

fest /fest/ *n.* (esp. Amer.) Fest, *das*

fester /ˈfestə(r)/ *v.i.* [1] (lit. or fig.) eitern; schwären (geh.) [2] (putrefy) verfaulen

festival /ˈfestɪvl/

[A] *n.* [1] (feast day) Fest, *das;* **the ~ of Christmas/Easter** das Weihnachts-/Osterfest [2] (performances, plays, etc.) Festival, *das;* Festspiele *Pl.;* **the Bayreuth F~:** die Bayreuther Festspiele; **the Edinburgh F~:** das Edinburgh-Festival

[B] *attrib. adj.* Fest-

festive /ˈfestɪv/ *adj.* [1] (joyous) festlich; fröhlich [2] (of a feast) Fest-; **the ~ season** die Weihnachtszeit [3] (convivial) gesellig

festivity /feˈstɪvɪtɪ/ *n.* [1] *no pl.* (gaiety) Feststimmung, *die* [2] (festive celebration) Feier, *die;* **festivities** Feierlichkeiten *Pl.*

festoon /feˈstuːn/

[A] *n.* [1] (chain of flowers) Girlande, *die* [2] (carved ornament) Feston, *das*

[B] *v.t.* schmücken (**with** mit)

fetal /ˈfiːtl/ *adj.* fötal; fetal; **the ~ position** die Fötuslage

fetch /fetʃ/

[A] *v.t.* [1] holen; (collect) abholen (**from** von); **~ sb. sth., ~ sth. for sb.** jmdm. etw. holen [2] (be sold for) erzielen ‹*Preis*›; **my car ~ed £5000** ich habe für den Wagen 5000 Pfund bekommen [3] **~ a sigh** aufseufzen; **~ a deep breath** tief Atem *od.* Luft holen; **just give me time to ~ my breath** lass mich erst mal wieder zu Atem kommen [4] (deal) **~ sb. a blow/punch** jmdm. einen Schlag versetzen [5] (draw forth) erregen ‹*Bewunderung, Ärger*›; entlocken ‹*Tränen, Lachen*› (**from** + *Dat.*)

[B] *v.i.* **~ and carry [for sb.]** [bei jmdm.] Mädchen für alles sein (ugs.); **he is always there to ~ and carry for her** (does every little thing) er bedient sie vorn und hinten (ugs.)

(Phrasal verb)

- **~ 'up** (coll.)

[A] *v.t.* erbrechen; wieder von sich geben; (fig.) speien

[B] *v.i.* landen (ugs.)

fetching /ˈfetʃɪŋ/ *adj.* einnehmend, gewinnend ‹*Lächeln, Stimme, Wesen, Benehmen*›; schick ‹*Kleidung*›; **that suit looks very ~ on you** das Kostüm steht dir ausgezeichnet

fetchingly /ˈfetʃɪŋlɪ/ *adv.* einnehmend ‹*lächeln, sich benehmen*›; ausgesprochen ‹*hübsch*›; schick, geschmackvoll ‹*gekleidet, eingerichtet*›

fête /feɪt/

[A] *n.* [1] [Wohltätigkeits]basar, *der* [2] (festival) Fest, *das;* Feier, *die*

[B] *v.t.* feiern

fetid /ˈfetɪd/ *adj.* stinkend; übel riechend; **~ smell/odour/stench** Gestank, *der*

fetish /ˈfetɪʃ/ *n.* [1] Manie, *die* (geh.); Fetisch, *der* (geh.); Fimmel, *der* (ugs.); **she makes something of a ~ of** *or* **has a ~ about tidiness** Sauberkeit ist bei ihr zur Manie geworden; sie hat einen richtigen Sauberkeitsfimmel (ugs.) [2] (inanimate object of worship; also Psych.) Fetisch, *der*

fetishism /ˈfetɪʃɪzm/ *n.* Fetischismus, *der*

fetishist /ˈfetɪʃɪst/ *n.* Fetischist, *der*/Fetischistin, *die*

fetlock /ˈfetlɒk/ *n.* Köte, *die*

fetter /ˈfetə(r)/

[A] *n.* [1] (shackle) Fußfessel, *die* [2] *usu. in pl.* (bond) Fesseln *Pl.; in pl.* (fig.: captivity) Gefangenschaft, *die;* Fesseln *Pl.* [3] *in pl.* (restraint) Fesseln *Pl.*

[B] *v.t.* [1] (bind [as] with **~s**) fesseln; **be ~ed to sth./sb.** (fig.) an etw./jmdn. gekettet sein [2] (impede) einengen ‹*Freiheit, Rechte, Souveränität, Personen*›; hemmen ‹*Fortschritt, Entwicklung, Wachstum, Entfaltung*›; lähmen ‹*Fantasie*›

fettle /ˈfetl/ *n.* **be in good** *or* **fine/poor ~:** sich in guter/schlechter Verfassung befinden; ‹*Sache:*› sich in gutem/schlechtem Zustand befinden

fetus /ˈfiːtəs/ *n.* Fötus, *der;* Fetus, *der*

feud /fjuːd/

[A] *n.* Zwist, *der;* Zwistigkeiten *Pl.;* (Hist./fig.) Fehde, *die;* **carry on a ~ with sb.** eine Fehde mit jmdm. ausfechten *od.* austragen

[B] *v.i.* **~ [with sb./each other]** [mit jmdm./miteinander] im Streit liegen

feudal /ˈfjuːdl/ *adj.* (of or according to feudal system) Feudal-; feudalistisch; **~ overlord** Feudal- *od.* Lehnsherr, *der;* **~ rights** Lehnsherrlichkeit, *die;* **in ~ Britain** im feudalistischen England

feudalism /ˈfjuːdəlɪzm/ *n.*, *no pl.* Feudalismus, *der*

'feudal system *n.* (Hist.) Feudalsystem, *das*

fever /ˈfiːvə(r)/ *n.* ▸ⓘ **p. 1231** [1] *no pl.* (Med.: high temperature) Fieber, *das;* **have a** *or* **suffer from a [high] ~:** [hohes] Fieber haben; **a ~ of 105 °F** 40,5 °C Fieber [2] (Med.: disease) Fieberkrankheit, *die* [3] (nervous excitement) Erregung, *die;* Aufregung, *die;* **the crowd was in a ~ of**

excitement die Menge befand sich in heller Aufregung; **in a ~ of anticipation** im Fieber der Erwartung

fevered /ˈfiːvəd/ *adj.* fiebrig ‹*Stirn, Gesicht, Haut usw.*›

fever: ~ heat *n.* 1▶ (high temperature) Fieberhitze, *die;* 2▶ (fig.) ▶**fever pitch**; **~ hospital** *n.* Seuchenkrankenhaus, *das*

feverish /ˈfiːvərɪʃ/ *adj.* ▶❶ **p. 1231** 1▶ (Med.: having symptoms of fever) fiebrig; Fieber‹*zustand, -schweiß, -traum*›; **be ~:** fiebern; Fieber haben; **spend a ~ night** eine Nacht im Fieber verbringen 2▶ (excited) erregt, aufgeregt ‹*Geschrei, Lachen*›; fiebrig ‹*Erwartung, Nervosität*›; heftig ‹*Andrang*›; fieberhaft ‹*Aufregung, Eifer, Kampf, Eile*›; **make ~ attempts to do sth.** fieberhaft versuchen, etw. zu tun

feverishly /ˈfiːvərɪʃlɪ/ *adv.* 1▶ (Med.) im Fieber; **toss and turn ~:** sich im Fieber hin und her wälzen 2▶ (excitedly) fieberhaft ‹*kämpfen, gestikulieren*›

ˈfever pitch *n.* Siedepunkt, *der* (fig.); **reach ~:** auf dem Siedepunkt angelangt sein; **at ~:** auf dem Siedepunkt

few /fjuː/

A *adj.* 1▶ (not many) wenige; **~ people** [nur] wenige [Leute]; **these ~ euros** die paar Euro; **openings for sociologists are ~:** freie Stellen für Soziologen sind knapp *od.* rar; **trees were ~ in that barren region** es gab nur wenige Bäume in dieser kargen Gegend; **the responsibility of these ~ men** die Verantwortung dieser wenigen; **with very ~ exceptions** mit ganz wenigen Ausnahmen; **very ~ housewives know that** das wissen die wenigsten Hausfrauen; **his ~ belongings** seine paar Habseligkeiten; seine wenige Habe; **how could those ~ people have achieved such a thing?** wie konnten so wenige [Leute] das nur erreicht haben?; **[all] too ~ people** [viel] zu wenig Leute; **~ and far between** rar; **they were ~ in number** sie waren nur sehr wenige *od.* nur ein kleines Häuflein; **these stamps are ~ in number** diese Briefmarken sind selten; **a ~ ...:** wenige ...; **not a ~ ...:** eine ganze Reihe ...; **they made not a ~ criticisms of the idea** sie übten nicht wenig Kritik an der Idee; **[just** *or* **only] a ~ troublemakers** einige [wenige] Störenfriede; **just a ~ words from you** nur ein paar Worte von dir 2▶ (some) wenige; **he said his ~ words** er sagte nur ein paar Worte; **a ~ ...:** einige *od.* ein paar ...; **a very ~:** nur wenige; **a ~ more ...:** noch einige *od.* ein paar ...; **some ~ [...]** einige wenige [...]; **every ~ minutes** alle paar Minuten; **a good ~ [...]/quite a ~ [...]** (coll.) eine ganze Menge [...]/ziemlich viele [...]; **there are a ~ which ...:** es gibt welche *od.* ein paar, die ...

B *n.* 1▶ (not many) wenige; **these are the beliefs of ~:** das glauben nur wenige; **a ~:** wenige; **the ~:** die wenigen; **the wealthy ~:** die wenigen Reichen; **~ of us/them** nur wenige von uns/nur wenige [von ihnen]; **~ of the people** nur wenige [Leute]; **~ of the words meant anything to him** er konnte mit nur wenigen Wörtern etwas anfangen; **they are among** *or* **some of the very ~ who ...:** sie gehören zu den wenigen, die ...; **only a ~ of them/the applicants** nur wenige [von ihnen]/[der] Bewerber; **just a ~ of you/her friends** nur ein paar von euch/ihrer Freunde; **the privilege of [only] a ~:** das Vorrecht von nur wenigen *od.* einiger weniger; **not a ~ of them** eine ganze Reihe von ihnen; **not a ~:** nicht wenige; ziemlich viele 2▶ (some) **the/these/those ~ who** diejenigen, die; **there were a ~ of us who ...:** es gab einige unter uns, die ...; **with a ~ of our friends** mit einigen *od.* ein paar unserer Freunde; **a ~ [more] of these biscuits** [noch] ein paar von diesen Keksen; **a ~ [who]** einige[, die]; **some ~:** einige wenige [Leute]; **some ~ of us/the members** einige wenige von uns/[der] Mitglieder; **a good ~/quite a ~** (coll.) eine ganze Menge/ziemlich viele [Leute]; **a good ~ of us/quite a ~ of us** (coll.) eine ganze Menge von uns/ziemlich viele von uns; **have had a ~** (coll.: be drunk) einen sitzen haben (salopp). *See also* **fewer**; **fewest**

fewer /ˈfjuːə(r)/

A *adj.* weniger; **become ~ and ~:** immer weniger werden; **smokers are ~ in number than twenty years ago** es gibt weniger Raucher als vor zwanzig Jahren

B *n.* **~ of the apples/of us** weniger Äpfel/von uns

fewest /ˈfjuːɪst/

A *adj.* **[the] ~ [...]** die wenigsten [...]

B *n.* **the ~ [of us/them]** die wenigsten [von uns/ihnen]; **at [the] ~:** mindestens

fey /feɪ/ *adj.* 1▶ (other-worldly) entrückt 2▶ (clairvoyant) hellseherisch

fez /fez/ *n.*, *pl.* **~zes** Fes, *der*

ff *abbr.* **= fortissimo** ff

ff. *abbr.* 1▶ **= and following pages** ff. 2▶ **= folios** Bl.

fiancé /fɪˈɑ̃seɪ/ *n.* Verlobte, *der*

fiancée /fɪˈɑ̃seɪ/ *n.* Verlobte, *die*

fiasco /fɪˈæskəʊ/ *n.*, *pl.* **~s** Fiasko, *das*

fiat /ˈfiːæt, ˈfiːət/ *n.* 1▶ (authorization) Genehmigung, *die* 2▶ (decree) Anordnung, *die*

fib /fɪb/

A *n.* Flunkerei, *die* (ugs.); **tell ~s** flunkern (ugs.); schwindeln; **that was a ~:** das war geschwindelt

B *v.i.*, **-bb-** schwindeln; flunkern (ugs.)

C *v.t.*, **-bb-: ~ one's way out [of sth.]** sich [aus etw.] herausschwindeln

fibber /ˈfɪbə(r)/ *n.* Flunkerer, *der* (ugs.); Schwindler, *der*/Schwindlerin, *die*

fibre (*Brit.; Amer.:* **fiber**) /ˈfaɪbə(r)/ *n.* 1▶ Faser, *die;* **with every ~ of his being** (fig.) mit jeder Faser seines Herzens 2▶ (substance consisting of fibres) [Faser]gewebe, *das* 3▶ (roughage) Ballaststoffe *Pl.* 4▶ (character) Wesensart, *die;* (strength) Festigkeit, *die;* (essence) Grundstruktur, *die;* **moral ~:** Charakterstärke, *die. See also* **optical fibre**

fibre: ~board *n.* Holzfaserplatte, *die;* **~glass** (*Amer.:* **fiber glass**) *n.* (fibrous glass) Glasfaser, *die;* (plastic) glasfaserverstärkter Kunststoff; *attrib.* **~glass boat** Kunststoffboot, *das;* **~ optic ˈcable** *n.* Glasfaserkabel, *das;* **~ ˈoptics** *n.* Faseroptik, *die*

fibrillation /fɪbrɪˈleɪʃn/ *n.* (Med.) Zucken, *das;* (esp. of heart muscle) Flimmern, *das*

fibrin /ˈfaɪbrɪn/ *n.* (Med.) Fibrin, *das*

fibrositis /faɪbrəˈsaɪtɪs/ *n.* ▶❶ **p. 1231** (Med.) Rheumatismus der Weichteile; Fibrositis, *die* (fachspr.)

fibrous /ˈfaɪbrəs/ *adj.* faserig ‹*Aufbau, Beschaffenheit, Eigenschaft*›; Faser‹*gewebe, -holz, -stoff*›

fibula /ˈfɪbjʊlə/ *n.*, *pl.* **~e** /ˈfɪbjʊliː/ *or* **~s** 1▶ (Anat.) Wadenbein, *das* 2▶ (Hist.: brooch) Fibel, *die*

fiche /fiːʃ/ *n.*, *pl. same or* **~s** ▶**microfiche**

fickle /ˈfɪkl/ *adj.* unberechenbar, launisch ‹*Glück, Schicksal, Person*›

fiction /ˈfɪkʃn/ *n.* 1▶ (literature) erzählende Literatur; 2▶ (thing feigned or imagined) **a ~/~s** eine Erfindung; **be pure ~** *or* **a mere ~:** [eine] reine Erfindung sein; 3▶ (conventionally accepted falsehood) kleine Unaufrichtigkeit. *See also* **fact 2**; **legal fiction**

fictional /ˈfɪkʃənl/ *adj.* belletristisch; fiktional (fachspr.); erfunden ‹*Inhalt, Geschichte*›; **~ literature** erzählende Literatur; Belletristik, *die* (*ohne Lyrik*); **~ characters** fiktive Figuren

fictionalize /ˈfɪkʃənəlaɪz/ *v.t.* als Fiktion darstellen

ˈfiction writer *n.* ▶❶ **p. 1260** Belletrist, *der*/Belletristin, *die*

fictitious /fɪkˈtɪʃəs/ *adj.* 1▶ (counterfeit) fingiert; vorgetäuscht ‹*Ohnmacht, Verletzung*›; Schein‹*schwangerschaft*›; unwahr ‹*Behauptung, Darstellung*› 2▶ (assumed) falsch ‹*Name, Identität*›; angenommen ‹*Rolle*› 3▶ (imaginary) [frei] erfunden ‹*Person, Figur, Geschichte*›; (of or in novels) fiktiv 4▶ (Law) **~ character** *or* **person** erfundene *od.* fiktive Person; **~ person** (legal entity) juristische Person

fiddle /ˈfɪdl/

A *n.* 1▶ (Mus.) (coll./derog.) Fiedel, *die;* (violin for traditional or folk music) Geige, *die;* Fiedel, *die;* **[as] fit as a ~:** kerngesund; **a face as long as a ~** (fig.) ein Gesicht wie drei *od.* sieben Tage Regenwetter (ugs.); **play first/second ~** (fig.) die erste/zweite Geige spielen (ugs.); **play second ~ to sb.** in jmds. Schatten (*Dat.*) stehen 2▶ (coll.: swindle) Gaunerei, *die;* **it's some sort of ~:** an der Sache ist was faul (ugs.); **it's all a ~:** das ist alles Schiebung (ugs.); **get sth. by a ~:** sich (*Dat.*) etw. ergaunern; **be on the ~:** krumme Dinger machen (ugs.)

B *v.i.* 1▶ (coll.: play the ~) Geige spielen 2▶ **~ about** (coll.: waste time) herumtrödeln (ugs.); (be frivolous) [herum]schludern (ugs.); **~ about with** *or* **away at sth.** (work on to adjust etc.) an etw. (*Dat.*) herumfummeln (ugs.); (tinker with) an etw. (*Dat.*) herumbasteln (ugs.); **~ at sth.** an etw. (*Dat.*) herumspielen *od.* herumfingern; **~ with sth.** (play with) mit etw. herumspielen 3▶ (coll.: deceive) krumme Dinger drehen (ugs.); **he ~d, lied, and cheated** er hat geschoben, gelogen und betrogen

C *v.t.* (coll.) (falsify) frisieren (ugs.) ‹*Bücher, Rechnungen*›; (get by cheating) [sich (*Dat.*)] ergaunern (ugs.); **~ one's way into sth. [by lying/cheating]** sich [mit Lügen/Betrügereien] in etw. (*Akk.*) einschleichen

fiddle-de-dee /fɪdldɪˈdiː/

A *int.* Schnickschnack

B *n.* Schnickschnack, *der* (ugs.)

fiddle-faddle /ˈfɪdlfædl/ *n.* Unsinn, *der;* Unfug, *der*

fiddler /ˈfɪdlə(r)/ *n.* 1▶ ▶❶ **p. 1260** (player) Geiger, *der*/Geigerin, *die* 2▶ (coll.: swindler etc.) Gauner, *der*/Gaunerin, *die* (abwertend)

ˈfiddler crab *n.* Winkerkrabbe, *die*

ˈfiddlestick (coll.)

A *n.* Geigenbogen, *der*

B *int.* **~s** dummes Zeug (ugs.); Schnickschnack (ugs.)

fiddling /ˈfɪdlɪŋ/ *adj.* 1▶ (petty) belanglos 2▶ ▶**fiddly**

fiddly /ˈfɪdlɪ/ *adj.* 1▶ (awkward to do) knifflig 2▶ (awkward to use) umständlich

fidelity /fɪˈdelɪtɪ/ *n.* 1▶ (faithfulness) Treue, *die* (**to** zu); **oath of ~:** Treueid, *der;* **breach of ~:** Treubruch, *der* 2▶ (conformity to truth or fact) Glaubwürdigkeit, *die* 3▶ (exact correspondence to the original) (of photograph, imitation) Naturtreue, *die;* (of translation) [Wort]treue, *die* 4▶ (Radio, Telev., etc.) Wiedergabetreue, *die;* [original]getreue Wiedergabe; (of sound) Klangtreue, *die;* (of picture) Bildtreue, *die*

fidget /ˈfɪdʒɪt/

A *n.* 1▶ **[be] in a [terrible] ~:** [ganz] zappelig [sein] (ugs.); **put sb. in a ~:** jmdn. unruhig machen; **have/get the ~s** zappelig sein/werden (ugs.); **give sb. the ~s** jmdn. zappelig *od.* kribbelig machen (ugs.) 2▶ (restless mood) Unrast, *die;* **be [all] in a ~:** [sehr] unruhig sein; **have/get the ~s** ruhelos sein/werden 3▶ (person) Zappelphilipp, *der* (ugs.)

B *v.i.* 1▶ **~ [about]** [herum]zappeln (ugs.); herumrutschen 2▶ (be uneasy) nervös sein; **make sb. ~:** jmdn. unruhig machen

fidgety /ˈfɪdʒɪtɪ/ *adj.* unruhig ‹*Person, Pferd, Stimmung*›; nervös ‹*Bewegungen, Zuckungen*›

fiduciary /fɪˈdjuːʃərɪ/ *adj.* 1▶ (Law) treuhänderisch; **~ money** Giralgeld, *das* 2▶ (Finance: depending on public confidence or securities) ungedeckt ‹*Papiergeld*›

fief /fiːf/ *n.* 1▶ (feudal benefice) Lehen, *das* 2▶ (sphere of control) Machtbereich, *der*

field /fiːld/

A *n.* 1▶ (cultivated) Feld, *das;* Acker, *der;* (for grazing) Weide, *die;* (meadow) Wiese, *die;* **wheat/tobacco/poppy ~:** Weizen-/Tabak-/Mohnfeld, *das;* **work in the ~s** auf dem Feld arbeiten; **~s of rye** Roggenfelder 2▶ (area rich in minerals etc.) Lagerstätte, *die;* **gas ~:** Gasfeld, *das* 3▶ (battlefield) Schlachtfeld, *das;* (fig.) Feld, *das;* **leave sb. a clear** *or* **the ~** (fig.) jmdm. das Feld überlassen; **hold the ~:** das Feld beherrschen; **win/lose the ~:** siegreich sein/die Schlacht verlieren 4▶ (scene of campaign) [Kriegs]schauplatz, *der;* **enter the ~** (fig.) eingreifen; auf der Bildfläche erscheinen (ugs.); **in the ~:** im Feld; an der Front; (fig.) ‹*Vertreter*› im Außendienst; ‹*Student*› in der Praxis; **be sent out into the ~:**

[hin]ausgeschickt werden; **keep the ~:** weiterkämpfen; **take the ~:** in den Kampf ziehen (*see also* **5**) **5** (playing ~) Sportplatz, *der;* (ground marked out for game) Platz, *der;* [Spiel]feld, *das;* **send sb. off the ~:** jmdn. vom Platz stellen; **take the ~:** das Spielfeld betreten (*see also* **4**) **6** (Sport: area for defence or attack) [Spiel]feld, *das* **7** (competitors in sports event) Feld, *das;* (fig.) Teilnehmerkreis, *der;* **play the ~** (fig. coll.) sich nicht festlegen [wollen]; alles nehmen, wie es kommt; (take advantage of all chances offered) alle gebotenen Chancen wahrnehmen; **lead the ~** (lit. or fig.) das Feld anführen **8** (Her.) Feld, *das;* Grund, *der* **9** (area of operation, subject areas, etc.) Fach, *das;* [Fach]gebiet, *das;* (range of vision or view) Sichtfeld, *das;* **his researches range over a wide ~:** seine Forschungen erstrecken sich über ein großes Gebiet; **in the ~ of medicine** auf dem Gebiet der Medizin; **workers in the ~:** die Leute vom Fach; **he's working in his own ~:** er arbeitet in seinem [erlernten] Beruf; **that is outside my ~:** das fällt nicht in mein Fach; **~ of vision** *or* **view** Blickfeld, *das* **10** (Phys.) **magnetic/gravitational ~:** Magnet-/Gravitationsfeld, *das* **11** *attrib.* (found in open country) Feld-; **~ marigold** [Saat]wucherblume, *die;* **~ mushroom** Wiesenchampignon, *der;* **~ poppy** Klatschmohn, *der* **12** *attrib.* (carried out in natural environment; light and mobile) Feld‹*studie, -forschung, -artillerie, -ausrüstung*›. *See also* **airfield**; **coalfield**; **goldfield**; **minefield**; **oilfield**

B *v.i.* (Cricket, Baseball, etc.) als Fänger spielen; **he ~s well** er ist ein guter Fänger

C *v.t.* **1** (Cricket, Baseball, etc.) (stop) fangen ‹*Ball*›; (stop and return) auffangen und zurückwerfen **2** (put into ~) aufstellen, aufs Feld schicken ‹*Mannschaft, Spieler*› **3** (fig.: deal with) fertig werden mit; parieren ‹*Fragen*›

'field day *n.* **1** (Mil.) Feldübung, *die;* Manöver, *das* **2** (fig.) großer Tag; **have a ~** seinen großen Tag haben

fielder /ˈfiːldə(r)/ *n.* (Cricket, Baseball, etc.) Feldspieler, *der*

'field event *n.* (Sport) technische Disziplin

fieldfare /ˈfiːldfeə(r)/ *n.* (Ornith.) Wacholderdrossel, *die*

field: ~ glasses *n. pl.* Feldstecher, *der;* **~ hockey** (Amer.) ▸**hockey 1**; **~ hospital** *n.* (Mil.) Feldlazarett, *das;* **F~ 'Marshal** *n.* ▸ⓘ **p. 1634** (Brit. Mil.) Feldmarschall, *der;* **~ mouse** *n.* Brandmaus, *die;* **~ officer** *n.* (Mil.) Stabsoffizier, *der;* **~sman** /ˈfiːldzmən/ *n., pl.* **~smen** /ˈfiːldzmən/ ▸**fielder**; **~ sports** *n. pl.* Sport im Freien (bes. Jagen und Fischen); **~ test** *n.* ▸**~ trial**; **~-test** *v.t.* in der Praxis erproben; **~ trial** *n.* Feldversuch, *der;* **~ trip** *n.* Exkursion, *die;* **~work** *n.* **1** (Mil.: temporary fortification) Feldbefestigung, *die;* **2** (outdoor work) (of surveyor etc.) Arbeit im Gelände; (of sociologist, collector of scientific data, etc.) Feldforschung, *die;* **~worker** *n.* ▸ⓘ **p. 1260** Feldforscher, *der/-forscherin, die*

fiend /fiːnd/ *n.* **1** (very wicked person) Scheusal, *das;* Unmensch, *der* **2** **the F~:** der Teufel *od.* Satan **3** (evil spirit) böser Geist **4** (coll.) (mischievous or tiresome person) Plagegeist, *der;* (artful person) Schlaufuchs, *der* **5** (devotee) Fan, *der;* **travel/theatre ~:** Reise-/Theaternarr, *der/-närrin, die;* **motorbike/health food ~:** Motorrad-/Naturkostfreak, *der;* **fresh-air ~:** Frischluftfanatiker, *der/-fanatikerin, die*

fiendish /ˈfiːndɪʃ/ *adj.* **1** (fiendlike) teuflisch **2** (extremely awkward) höllisch

fiendishly /ˈfiːndɪʃlɪ/ *adv.* **1** (in fiendlike manner) teuflisch **2** (extremely awkwardly) höllisch

fierce /fɪəs/ *adj.* **1** (violently hostile) wild; erbittert ‹*Widerstand, Kampf*›; wuchtig ‹*Schlag*›; heftig ‹[*Bomben*]*angriff*›; feindselig ‹*Benehmen*› **2** (raging) wütend; tobend ‹*Wind*›; grimmig ‹*Hass, Wut*›; grausam ‹*Krankheit, Tyrannei*›; scharf ‹*Kritik, Verurteilung*›; wild ‹*Tier*› **3** (ardent) ungestüm ‹*Leidenschaft, Verlangen*›; heftig ‹*Andrang, Streit*›; heiß ‹*Wettbewerb*›; hitzig ‹*Kampagne*›; leidenschaftlich ‹*Ehrgeiz, Stolz, Wille*›; wild ‹*Entschlossenheit, Jagd*› **4** (unpleasantly strong or intense) unerträglich; **the heat is a bit ~:** die Hitze ist ein bisschen zu stark **5** (violent in action) hart ‹*Bremsen, Ruck*›

fiercely /ˈfɪəslɪ/ *adv.* **1** (with violent hostility) heftig ‹*angreifen, Widerstand leisten*›; wütend, grimmig ‹*brüllen*› **2** (with raging force) wütend ‹*toben*›; aufs Heftigste ‹*kritisieren, bekämpfen*›; **the fire burnt ~ for several hours** der Brand wütete mehrere Stunden **3** (ardently) äußerst ‹*stolz, unabhängig sein*›; wild ‹*entschlossen, kämpfen*› **4** (with unpleasant strength or intensity) unerträglich **5** (with violent action) heftig; scharf ‹*bremsen*›

fiery /ˈfaɪərɪ/ *adj.* **1** (consisting of or flaming with fire) glühend; feurig ‹*Atem*› **2** (looking like fire) feurig; (blazing red) feuerrot; glutrot **3** (hot as fire) glühend heiß; **~ temperature** Gluthitze, *die* **4** (producing burning sensation) brennend, juckend ‹*Ausschlag*›; feurig ‹*Geschmack, Gewürz*›; scharf ‹*Getränk*› **5** (fervent, full of spirit) feurig ‹*Liebhaber, Pferd*›; (irascible, impassioned) hitzig ‹*Temperament, Debatte*›; feurig ‹*Rede, Redner*›; **~ zeal** Feuereifer, *der;* **have a ~ temper** ein Hitzkopf sein

fiery 'cross *n.* **1** (Hist.: rallying-signal of Scottish Highlanders) Feuerkreuz, *das* **2** (Amer.: of Ku Klux Klan) Flammenkreuz, *das*

fiesta /fiːˈestə/ *n.* Fest, *das*

FIFA /ˈfiːfə/ *abbr.* **= International Football Federation** FIFA, *die;* Fifa, *die*

fife /faɪf/ *n.* Pfeife, *die*

fifteen /fɪfˈtiːn/ ▸ⓘ **p. 894**, ▸ⓘ **p. 1001**, ▸ⓘ **p. 1358**

A *adj.* fünfzehn; *see also* **eight A**

B *n.* **1** Fünfzehn, *die; see also* **eight B 1, 4**; **eighteen B** **2** (Rugby Football) [Rugby]mannschaft, *die*

fifteenth /fɪfˈtiːnθ/ ▸ⓘ **p. 1047**

A *adj.* ▸ⓘ **p. 1358** fünfzehnt…; *see also* **eighth A**

B *n.* (fraction) Fünfzehntel, *das; see also* **eighth B**

fifth /fɪfθ/

A *adj.* ▸ⓘ **p. 1358** fünft…; *see also* **eighth A**

B *n.* **1** (in sequence, rank) Fünfte, *der/die/das;* (fraction) Fünftel, *das* **2** (~ form) fünfte [Schul]klasse; Fünfte, *die* (Schuljargon) **3** (Mus.) Quinte, *die* **4** ▸ⓘ **p. 1047** (day) **the ~ of May** der fünfte Mai; **the ~ [of the month]** der Fünfte [des Monats] **5** (Amer. coll.) (bottle) ≈ Dreiviertelliterflasche, *die;* (*of a gallon*) *ca. dreiviertel Liter. See also* **eighth B**

fifth: ~ 'column *n.* fünfte Kolonne; **~-'columnist** *n.* Mitglied der fünften Kolonne; **~ form** ▸**form A 4**

fiftieth /ˈfɪftɪɪθ/

A *adj.* ▸ⓘ **p. 1358** fünfzigst…; *see also* **eighth A**

B *n.* (fraction) Fünfzigstel, *das; see also* **eighth B**

fifty /ˈfɪftɪ/ ▸ⓘ **p. 894**, ▸ⓘ **p. 1001**, ▸ⓘ **p. 1358**

A *adj.* **1** fünfzig **2** (large indefinite number) **~ times** hundertmal; zigmal (ugs.). *See also* **eight A**

B *n.* Fünfzig, *die; see also* **eight B 1**; **eighty B**

fifty: ~-~ *adv., adj.* fifty-fifty (ugs.); halbe-halbe (ugs.); **go ~-~:** fifty-fifty *od.* halbpart machen; **on a ~-~ basis** auf der Basis, dass fifty-fifty geteilt wird; **~-'first** *etc. adj.* ▸ⓘ **p. 1358** einundfünfzigst… *usw.; see also* **eighth A**; **~fold** /ˈfɪftɪfəʊld/ *adj., adv.* fünfzigfach; *see also* **eightfold**; **~-'one** *etc.* **A** *adj.* einundfünfzig *usw.; see also* **eight A**; **B** *n.* ▸ⓘ **p. 1358** Einundfünfzig *usw., die; see also* **eight B 1**

fig¹ /fɪg/ *n.* **1** Feige, *die* **2** (valueless thing) **it's not worth a ~:** das ist keinen Pfifferling wert (ugs.); **not care** *or* **give a ~ about** *or* **for sth.** sich nicht die Bohne (ugs.) *od.* keinen Deut für etw. interessieren

fig² *n.* (coll.: attire) **in full ~:** in vollem Staat

fig. *abbr.* **= figure** Abb.

fight /faɪt/

A *v.i.,* **fought** /fɔːt/ **1** (lit. or fig.) kämpfen; (with fists) sich schlagen; **~ to do sth.** darum kämpfen, etw. zu tun; **~ to save sb.'s life** um jmds. Leben kämpfen; **watch animals/people ~ing** Tieren/Menschen beim Kampf zusehen; **~ shy of sb./sth.** jmdm./einer Sache aus dem Weg gehen; **~ shy of doing sth.** sich davor drücken, etw. zu tun (ugs.); es vermeiden, etw. zu tun

2 (squabble) [sich] streiten, [sich] zanken (**about** wegen). *See also* **cat 1**; **cock¹ A 1**; **hand A 1**; **tooth 1**

B *v.t.,* **fought** **1** (in battle) **~ sb./sth.** gegen jmdn./etw. kämpfen; (using fists) **~ sb.** sich mit jmdm. schlagen; (*Boxer:*) gegen jmdn. boxen **2** (seek to overcome) bekämpfen; (resist) **~ sb./sth.** gegen jmdn./etw. ankämpfen

3 (contend in) durchfechten; durchkämpfen; **~ a battle** einen Kampf austragen; **be ~ing a losing battle** (fig.) auf verlorenem Posten stehen *od.* kämpfen; **~ sb.'s battles for him** (fig.) jmdm. alle Schwierigkeiten aus dem Weg räumen; **~ the good fight** (fig.) für die gute *od.* gerechte Sache kämpfen

4 ausfechten ‹*Problem*›; führen ‹*Kampagne*›; kandidieren bei ‹*Wahl*›

5 **~ one's way** sich (*Dat.*) den Weg freikämpfen; (fig.) sich (*Dat.*) seinen Weg bahnen; **~ one's way to the top** (fig.) sich an die Spitze kämpfen; **~ one's way up** (fig.) sich nach oben kämpfen; sich hochkämpfen

C *n.* **1** (combat, campaign, boxing match) Kampf, *der* (**for** um); (brawl) Schlägerei, *die;* (literary: battle) Schlacht, *die;* **their ~ for freedom** ihr Freiheitskampf; **make a ~ of it, put up a ~:** sich wehren; (fig.) sich zur Wehr setzen; **give in without a ~** (fig.) klein beigeben; **aren't you going to make a ~ of it?** (fig.) willst du dir das etwa gefallen lassen?; **world championship title ~:** Titelkampf um die Weltmeisterschaft

2 (squabble) Streit, *der;* **they are always having ~s** zwischen ihnen gibt es dauernd Streit; **he likes a good ~:** er hat nichts gegen einen guten Streit

3 (ability to ~) Kampffähigkeit, *die;* (appetite for ~ing) Kampfgeist, *der;* **have no ~ left in one** nicht mehr zum Kampf fähig sein; (fig.) erledigt *od.* fertig sein; **all the ~ had gone out of him** (fig.) sein Kampfgeist war erloschen; **show ~** (lit. or fig.) Stärke demonstrieren

Phrasal verbs

- **~ against** *v.t.* **1** (in war) kämpfen gegen; (in boxing match) antreten gegen **2** (resist) kämpfen gegen; ankämpfen gegen ‹*Wellen, Wind, Gefühle*›; bekämpfen ‹*Krankheit, Analphabetentum*›
- **~ 'back**

A *v.i.* zurückschlagen; sich zur Wehr setzen

B *v.t.* **1** (suppress) zurückhalten **2** (resist) zurückdrängen; aufhalten ‹*Vormarsch*›

- **~ 'down** *v.t.* zurückhalten
- **~ for** *v.t.* (lit. or fig.) kämpfen für; **~ for one's life** um sein Leben kämpfen
- **~ 'off** *v.t.* (lit. or fig.) abwehren; abwimmeln (ugs.) ‹*Reporter, Fans, Bewunderer*›; widerstehen (+ *Dat.*) ‹*Versuchung*›; bekämpfen ‹*Erkältung*›; **~ off the desire** dem Wunsch widerstehen
- **~ 'out** *v.t.* (lit. or fig.) ausfechten; **~ it out amongst yourselves** macht das unter euch (*Dat.*) aus
- **~ over** *v.t.* **1** (~ with regard to) [sich] streiten über (+ *Akk.*) **2** (~ to gain possession of) kämpfen um; (squabble to gain possession of) [sich] streiten um; [sich] zanken um
- **~ with** *v.t.* **1** kämpfen mit **2** (squabble with) [sich] streiten mit; [sich] zanken mit **3** (~ on the side of) kämpfen [zusammen] mit

fighter /ˈfaɪtə(r)/ *n.* **1** Kämpfer, *der/*Kämpferin, *die;* (warrior) Krieger, *der;* (boxer) Fighter, *der* **2** (aircraft) Kampfflugzeug, *das;* **~ pilot** ▸ⓘ **p. 1260** Jagdflieger, *der*

fighting /ˈfaɪtɪŋ/

A *adj.* Kampf‹*truppen, -schiff, -flugzeug*›; *see also* **cock¹ A 1**

B *n.* Kämpfe *Pl.;* **be in a ~ mood** kämpferisch gestimmt sein

fighting: ~ 'chance *n.* **have a ~ chance of succeeding/of doing sth.** Aussicht auf Erfolg haben/gute Chancen haben, etw. zu tun; **~ 'drunk** *adj.* (coll.) betrunken und streitsüchtig; **~ fish** *n.* Kampffisch, *der;* **~ 'fit** *adj.* topfit (ugs.); **~ fund** *n. Geldmittel* [*aus einer Spendenaktion*] *zur Durchführung einer Kampagne;* **raise a ~ fund** eine Spendenaktion durchführen; **~ 'mad** *adj.* [vor Wut] rasend; **~ 'words** *n. pl.* (coll.) Kampfparolen

'fig leaf *n.* (lit. or fig.) Feigenblatt, *das*

figment /ˈfɪgmənt/ *n.* (imagined thing) Hirngespinst, *das;* **a ~ of one's** *or* **the imagination** pure Einbildung

'fig tree *n.* Feigenbaum, *der*

figurative /ˈfɪgjʊrətɪv, ˈfɪgərətɪv/ *adj.* **1** (metaphorical) bildlich; übertragen; figurativ (Sprachw.);

(in a ~ sense) im übertragenen Sinne [2] (with many figures of speech) bilderreich

figuratively /ˈfɪɡjʊrətɪvlɪ, ˈfɪɡərətɪvlɪ/ *adv.* [1] (metaphorically) bildlich; übertragen; im übertragenen Sinne; figurativ (Sprachw.) [2] (with many figures of speech) bilderreich

figure /ˈfɪɡə(r)/

A *n.* [1] (shape) Form, *die*

[2] (Geom.) Figur, *die*

[3] (one's bodily shape) Figur, *die;* **have to worry about one's ~:** auf seine Figur achten müssen; **keep one's ~:** sich (*Dat.*) seine Figur bewahren; schlank bleiben; **lose one's ~:** dick werden

[4] (person as seen) Gestalt, *die;* (literary ~) Figur, *die;* (historical etc. ~) Persönlichkeit, *die;* **a fine ~ of a man/woman** eine stattliche Erscheinung; **a ~ of fun** eine Spottfigur; **make** *or* **cut a brilliant/poor** *etc.* **~:** eine glänzende/erbärmliche *usw.* Figur machen *od.* abgeben

[5] (image) Bild, *das;* **she looked a ~ of misery** sie bot ein Bild des Jammers

[6] (three-dimensional representation) Figur, *die;* (two-dimensional representation) Gestalt, *die*

[7] (emblem) Symbol, *das;* **a ~ of peace** ein Friedenssymbol

[8] (simile etc.) ~ **[of speech]** Redewendung, *die;* (Rhet.) Redefigur, *die;* **it was just a ~ of speech** das habe ich nicht wirklich gemeint

[9] (illustration) Abbildung, *die*

[10] (decorative pattern) Muster, *das*

[11] (Dancing, Skating) Figur, *die*

[12] (numerical symbol) Ziffer, *die;* (number so expressed) Zahl, *die;* (amount of money) Betrag, *der;* (amount paid for sth.) Erlös, *der;* (value) [Zahlen-]wert, *der;* **double ~s** zweistellige Zahlen; **membership is in double ~s** die Mitgliederzahl ist zweistellig; **three/four** *etc.* **~s** drei-/vierstellige *usw.* Zahlen; **go** *or* **run into three ~s** sich auf dreistellige Zahlen belaufen; **three-/four-** *etc.* **~:** drei-/vierstellig *usw.*

[13] *in pl.* (arithmetical calculations) Rechnen, *das;* (accounts, result of calculations) Zahlen *Pl.;* **can you check my ~s?** kannst du mal nachrechnen?; **do the ~s** den [Jahres-, Rechnungs]abschluss durchführen; **last month's ~s** die Zahlen/Werte des Vormonats; **he is good at ~s** er kann gut rechnen; *see also* **head A 2**

[14] (Ling.) [grammatische] Figur. *see also* **eight B 2; father figure**

B *v.t.* [1] (represent pictorially) darstellen

[2] (esp. Amer. coll.: picture mentally) sich (*Dat.*) vorstellen; **~ sb./oneself as** *or* **for sth.** jmdn./sich selbst als etw. [an]sehen

[3] (be symbol of) versinnbildlichen

[4] (embellish) verzieren ‹*Seide, Samt*›

[5] (Mus.) beziffern ‹*Bass*›; *see also* **bass³ B 3**

[6] (Amer.: calculate) kalkulieren; berechnen

[7] (Amer.: reckon) **I ~ that ...:** ich schätze, dass ...

C *v.i.* [1] (make appearance) vorkommen; erscheinen; (in play) auftreten; **children don't ~ in her plans for the future** Kinder spielen in ihren Zukunftsplänen keine Rolle; **this image often ~d in her dreams** dieses Bild tauchte in ihren Träumen häufig auf; **~ prominently on the music scene/in world politics** in der Musikszene/Weltpolitik eine bedeutende Rolle spielen

[2] (coll.: be likely, understandable) **it ~s that ...:** es kann gut sein, dass ...; **that ~s** das stimmt sicher; ds wird schon stimmen

Phrasal verbs

- **~ on** *v.t.* rechnen mit; **~ on doing sth.** damit rechnen, etw. zu tun
- **~ 'out** *v.t.* [1] (work out by arithmetic) ausrechnen [2] (Amer.: estimate) **~ out that ...:** damit rechnen, dass ... [3] (understand) verstehen; **I can't ~ him out** ich werde nicht schlau aus ihm [4] (ascertain) herausfinden; **it's difficult to ~ out whether ...:** es ist schwer zu sagen, ob ...; **I can't ~ out where we've met before** ich weiß nicht, wo wir uns schon gesehen haben

figure: ~-conscious *adj.* figurbewusst; **she's very ~-conscious** sie achtet sehr auf ihre Figur; **~head** *n.* (lit. or fig.) Galionsfigur, *die;* **~-hugging** *adj.* figurbetont ‹*Kleidung*›; **~-hugging trousers** Hosen, die die Figur betonen; **~ skating** *n.* Eiskunstlauf, *der;* **~work** *n., no pl.* **do some ~work** ein paar Berechnungen anstellen

figurine /ˈfɪɡəriːn/ *n.* Figurine, *die*

Fiji /ˈfiːdʒiː/ *pr. n.* Fidschi (*das*); Fidschiinseln *Pl.*

Fijian /fɪˈdʒiːən/

A *adj.* fidschianisch; **he/she is ~:** er ist Fidschianer/sie ist Fidschianerin

B *n.* Fidschianer, *der*/Fidschianerin, *die*

filament /ˈfɪləmənt/ *n.* [1] Faden, *der;* (Chem.) Filament, *das* (fachspr.); Faser, *die* [2] (conducting wire or thread) Glühfaden, *der* [3] (Bot.) Staubfaden, *der;* Filament, *das* (fachspr.)

filbert /ˈfɪlbət/ *n.* [1] (cultivated hazel) Haselnussstrauch, *der* [2] (nut) Haselnuss, *die*

filch /fɪltʃ/ *v.t.* stibitzen (ugs.)

file¹ /faɪl/

A *n.* Feile, *die;* (nail ~) [Nagel]feile, *die*

B *v.t.* feilen ‹*Fingernägel*›; mit der Feile bearbeiten ‹*Holz, Eisen*›; **~ sth. to make it smooth** etw. glatt feilen

Phrasal verbs

- **~ a'way** *v.t.* abfeilen
- **~ 'down** *v.t.* abfeilen

file²

A *n.* [1] (holder) Ordner, *der;* (box) Kassette, *die;* [Dokumenten]schachtel, *die;* **on ~:** in der Kartei/in *od.* bei den Akten; **on** *or* **in sb.'s ~s** in jmds. Kartei/in *od.* bei jmds. Akten; **put sth. on ~:** etw. in die Akten/Kartei aufnehmen

[2] (set of papers) Akte, *die;* (as cards) Kartei, *die;* (Law) Akten *Pl.;* **reopen/close the ~ on a case** einen Fall wieder aufnehmen/abschließen; **open/keep a ~ on sb./sth.** eine Akte über jmdn./etw. anlegen/führen [3] (series of issues of newspaper etc.) [Zeitungs]bündel, *das* (*von aufeinander folgenden Nummern*) [4] (Computing) Datei, *die* [5] (stiff wire) Zettelspieß, *der*

B *v.t.* [1] (place on a ~) [in die Kartei] einordnen/[in die Akten] aufnehmen; ablegen (Bürow.); (place among public records) archivieren; **~ sth. in drawers** etw. in Schubladen aufbewahren [2] (submit) einreichen ‹*Antrag*› [3] ‹*Journalist:*› einsenden ‹*Bericht*›

C *v.i.* (Law) **to ~ for divorce/bankruptcy** die Scheidung einreichen/Konkurs anmelden

Phrasal verb

- **~ a'way** *v.t.* ablegen (Bürow.)

file³

A *n.* [1] (Mil. etc.) Reihe, *die;* **stand in ~:** in Reih und Glied stehen; **[in] single** *or* **Indian ~:** [im] Gänsemarsch [2] (row of persons or things) Reihe, *die*

B *v.i.* in einer Reihe gehen; nacheinander gehen

Phrasal verbs

- **~ a'way** *v.i.* [einer nach dem anderen] weggehen; [nacheinander] fortgehen
- **~ 'off** ▸ **~ away**

file: ~ card *n.* Karteikarte, *die;* **~ copy** *n.* Belegexemplar, *das;* (of letter) Kopie für die Akten; **~ extension** (Computing) Dateierweiterung, *die;* **~-'management system** *n.* (Computing) Dateimanagementsystem, *das;* **~ name** *n.* (Computing) Dateiname, *der;* **~ server** *n.* (Computing) Dateiserver, *der;* Fileserver, *der;* **~ sharing** /ˈfaɪlʃeərɪŋ/ *n., no pl.* (Computing) Filesharing, *das*

filet /ˈfileɪ/ *n.* (Gastr.) Filet, *das*

file 'transfer protocol *n.* (Computing) Dateitransferprotokoll, *das*

filial /ˈfɪlɪəl/ *adj.* [1] (of or due from son or daughter) kindlich ‹*Gehorsam, Achtung, Treue*›; Kindes-, Sohnes-/Tochter‹*liebe, -pflicht*› [2] (Biol.) **~ generation** Filialgeneration, *die*

filibuster /ˈfɪlɪbʌstə(r)/

A *n.* (obstructionist) Verschleppungstaktiker, *der;* (obstruction) Verschleppungstaktik, *die;* Filibuster, *das*

B *v.i.* obstruieren; Dauerreden halten

filigree /ˈfɪlɪɡriː/ *n.* (lit. or fig.) Filigran, *das*

filing¹ /ˈfaɪlɪŋ/ *n.* **~s** (particles) Späne *Pl.;* **iron ~s** Eisen[feil]späne *Pl.*

filing² *n.* (action of **file B 1**) Ablage, *die;* (documents) [abzulegende] Akten

filing: ~ cabinet *n.* Aktenschrank, *der;* **~ clerk** *n.* ▸ ❶ **p. 1260** Archivkraft, *die;* **~ system** *n.* Ablagesystem, *das*

Filipino /fɪlɪˈpiːnəʊ/ ▸ ❶ **p. 1345**

A *adj.* philippinisch

B *n., pl.* **~s** Filipino, *der*/Filipina, *die*

fill /fɪl/

A *v.t.* [1] (make full) **~ sth. [with sth.]** etw. [mit etw.] füllen; **the room was ~ed** (with people) der Raum war fast voll besetzt; **~ the walls with photos** die Wände mit Fotos vollhängen; **~ sb./sb.'s heart with fear** jmdm. Furcht einflößen; **~ed with** voller ‹*Reue, Bewunderung, Neid, Verzweiflung*› (**at** über + *Akk.*); **be ~ed with envy at sb.'s success** auf jmds. Erfolg (*Akk.*) neidisch sein

[2] (distend) blähen ‹*Segel*›

[3] (stock abundantly) füllen; (fig.) anfüllen; **be ~ed with people/flowers/fish** *etc.* voller Menschen/Blumen/Fische *usw.* sein; **the journey had ~ed his mind with new ideas** die Reise hatte ihm zahlreiche neue Anregungen gegeben

[4] (occupy whole capacity of, spread over) füllen; besetzen ‹*Sitzplätze*›; (fig.) ausfüllen ‹*Gedanken, Zeit*›; **the room was ~ed to capacity** der Raum war voll besetzt *od.* (ugs.) [proppen]voll; **tears suddenly ~ed her eyes** plötzlich standen ihr Tränen in den Augen; **when you've ~ed this notebook ...:** wenn dein Heft voll ist ...; **the fat lady ~ed two seats** die dicke Dame brauchte zwei Plätze; **enough cake to ~ three large plates** genug Kuchen für drei große Teller; **~ the bill** (fig.) den Erwartungen entsprechen; (be appropriate) angemessen sein

[5] (pervade) erfüllen; **light/silence ~ed the room** Licht strömte in das Zimmer/Schweigen breitete sich im Zimmer aus

[6] (block up) füllen ‹*Lücke*›; füllen, (veralt.) plombieren ‹*Zahn*›

[7] (Cookery) (stuff) füllen; (put layer of sth. solid in) belegen; (put layer of sth. spreadable in) bestreichen

[8] (satisfy) sättigen; satt machen

[9] (hold) innehaben ‹*Posten*›; versehen ‹*Amt*›; (take up) ausfüllen ‹*Position*›

[10] (execute) ausführen ‹*Auftrag*›

[11] (appoint sb. to) besetzen ‹*Posten, Lehrstuhl*›

B *v.i.* [1] (become full) **~ [with sth.]** sich [mit etw.] füllen; (fig.) sich [mit etw.] erfüllen

[2] (be distended by wind) sich blähen

C *n.* [1] (as much as one wants) **eat/drink one's ~:** sich satt essen/trinken; **have had one's ~ [of food and drink]** seinen Hunger und Durst gestillt haben; **weep one's ~:** sich ausweinen; **have had one's ~ of sth./doing sth.** genug von etw. haben/etw. zur Genüge getan haben [2] (enough to ~ sth.) **he needs a ~ of tobacco for his pipe/of petrol/of ink** er muss seine Pfeife stopfen/tanken/Tinte nachfüllen

Phrasal verbs

- **~ 'in**

A *v.t.* [1] füllen; zuschütten, auffüllen ‹*Erdloch*› [2] (complete) ausfüllen; ergänzen ‹*Auslassungen*› [3] (insert) einsetzen [4] (find occupation during) überbrücken ‹*Zeit*›; **how did you ~ in your evenings?** was hast du abends unternommen? [5] (coll.: inform) **~ sb. in [on sth.]** jmdn. [über etw. (*Akk.*)] unterrichten *od.* ins Bild setzen

B *v.i.* **~ in for sb.** für jmdn. einspringen

- **~ 'out**

A *v.t.* [1] (enlarge to proper size or extent) ausfüllen; vervollständigen ‹*Essay, Aufsatz*› [2] (Amer.: complete) ausfüllen ‹*Formular usw.*›

B *v.i.* [1] (become enlarged) sich ausdehnen [2] (become plumper) [Fett] ansetzen; voller werden

- **~ 'up**

A *v.t.* [1] (make full) **~ sth. up [with sth.]** etw. [mit etw.] füllen; **put a little milk into the cup and then ~ it up with water** gießen Sie etwas Milch in die Tasse und füllen Sie mit Wasser auf; **~ oneself/sb. up [with sth.]** sich/jmdn. [mit etw.] voll stopfen; **their mother tried to ~ them up** ihre Mutter versuchte, sie satt zu kriegen; **that will ~ you up!** davon wirst du satt! [2] (put petrol into) **~ up [the tank]** tanken; **~ her up!** (coll.) voll [tanken]! [3] auffüllen ‹*Loch*›; zuschmieren ‹*Riss*› [4] (complete) ausfüllen ‹*Formular usw.*›

B *v.i.* ‹*Theater, Zimmer, Zug usw.:*› sich füllen; ‹*Becken, Spülkasten:*› voll laufen

filled /fɪld/ *adj.* gefüllt; **a cream-~ cake** ein Kuchen mit Cremefüllung

filler /ˈfɪlə(r)/ *n.* [1] (to fill cavity) Füllmasse, *die;* Spachtelmasse, *die* [2] (food to increase bulk) Sattmacher, *der* [3] (word) Füllwort, *das*

ˈfiller cap *n.* Tankverschluss, *der*

fillet /ˈfɪlɪt/

A *n.* [1] (Gastr.) Filet, *das;* **~ [steak]** (slice) Filetsteak, *das;* (cut) Filet, *das;* **~ of pork/beef/cod/halibut** Schweine-/Rinder-/Kabeljau-/Heilbuttfilet, *das* [2] (Archit.) (narrow flat band) Leiste, *die;* (between flutes of column) Kannelüre, *die* [3] (headband) Haarband, *das*

B *v.t.* [1] (divide into fillets) filetieren [2] (remove bones from) entgräten ‹*Fisch*›; ausbeinen ‹*Fleisch*›

filling /ˈfɪlɪŋ/

A *n.* [1] (for teeth) Füllung, *die;* Plombe, *die* (veralt.) [2] (for pancakes etc.) Füllung, *die;* (for sandwiches etc.) Belag, *der;* (for spreading) Aufstrich, *der*

B *adj.* sättigend

f

ˈfilling station *n.* Tankstelle, *die*

fillip /ˈfɪlɪp/ *n.* Anreiz, *der;* Ansporn, *der;* **give sb. a ~:** jmdn. anspornen; **give** *or* **be a ~ to the economy** die Wirtschaft beleben

filly /ˈfɪlɪ/ *n.* [1] junge Stute; Stutfohlen, *das* [2] (coll. dated: young woman) Käfer, *der* (ugs. veralt.); Biene, *die* (ugs. veralt.)

film /fɪlm/

A *n.* [1] (thin layer) Schicht, *die;* **~ [of varnish/dust]** [Lack-/Staub]schicht, *die;* **~ [of oil/slime]** [Öl-/Schmier]film, *der* [2] (Photog.) Film, *der;* **put sth. on ~:** etw. ablichten; **the events are all on ~:** die Vorgänge sind alle gefilmt worden [3] (Cinemat.: story etc.) Film, *der;* Streifen, *der* (ugs.); **make/direct a ~:** einen Film drehen/bei einem Film Regie führen [4] *in pl.* (cinema industry) Kino, *das;* Film, *der;* **go into ~s** zum Kino *od.* Film gehen; **she is in ~s** sie ist beim Film [5] *no pl.* (as art form) der Film; **are you interested in ~?** interessieren Sie sich für [den] Film?

B *v.t.* (Cinemat. etc.) [1] (record on motion ~) filmen; (for motion picture) drehen ‹*Kinofilm, Szene*› [2] (make cinema etc. ~ of) verfilmen ‹*Buch usw.*›

C *v.i.* ‹*Szene:*› sich filmen lassen; ‹*Buch, Geschichte:*› sich verfilmen lassen

Phrasal verb

• **~ ˈover** *v.i.* ‹*Spiegel, Glas:*› anlaufen; **her eyes ~ed over with tears** Tränen traten ihr in die Augen

film: ~ clip ▸**clip² B 2**; **~ crew** *n.* Kamerateam, *das;* **~ critic** *n.* Filmkritiker, *der*/-kritikerin, *die;* **~ director** *n.* ▸❶ **p. 1260** Filmregisseur, *der*/-regisseurin, *die;* **~ editor** *n.* ▸❶ **p. 1260** Cutter, *der*/Cutterin, *die;* **~goer** *n.* Kinogänger, *der*/-gängerin, *die;* **~ industry** *n.* Filmindustrie, *die;* **~ library** *n.* Filmarchiv, *das;* **~ poster** *n.* Filmplakat, *das;* **~ projector** *n.* Projektor, *der;* **~ script** *n.* Drehbuch, *das;* **~ set** *n.* Dekoration, *die;* **~setting** *n.* (Printing) Lichtsatz, *der;* **~ show** *n.* Filmvorführung, *die;* **~ star** *n.* ▸❶ **p. 1260** Filmstar, *der;* **~strip** *n.* Filmstreifen, *der;* **~ studio** *n.* Filmstudio, *das*

Filofax ® /ˈfaɪləʊfæks/ *n.* ≈ Terminplaner, *der*

filter /ˈfɪltə(r)/

A *n.* [1] Filter, *der* [2] (Brit.) (route) Abbiegespur, *die;* (light) grünes Licht für Abbieger

B *v.t.* filtern

C *v.i.* [1] (flow through filter) ‹*Flüssigkeiten:*› sickern; ‹*Luft usw.:*› durch einen Filter strömen [2] (make way gradually) **~ through/into/down sth.** durch etw. hindurch-/in etw. (*Akk.*) hinein-/etw. hinuntersickern [3] (at road junction) sich einfädeln; **~ off** sich ausfädeln

Phrasal verbs

• **~ ˈout**

A *v.t.* (lit. or fig.) herausfiltern

B *v.i.* durchsickern

• **~ ˈthrough** ▸**~ out B**

filter: ~ bed *n.* Filterkies, *der;* Filtersand, *der;* **~ ciga'rette** *n.* Filterzigarette, *die;* **~ coffee** *n.* Filterkaffee, *der*

ˈfiltering software *n., no pl.* (Computing) Filtersoftware, *die*

filter: ~ lane *n.* Abbiegespur, *die;* **~ paper** *n.* Filterpapier, *das* **~ tip** *n.* [1] Filter, *der;* [2] **~ tip [cigarette]** Filterzigarette, *die*

filth /fɪlθ/ *n., no pl.* [1] (disgusting dirt) Dreck, *der;* (pollution) Schmutzigkeit, *die* [2] (moral corruption) Verderbtheit, *die;* (vileness) Abscheulichkeit, *die* [3] (obscenity) Schmutz [und Schund] [4] (foul language) unflätige Sprache; Schweinereien *Pl.* (ugs.)

filthiness /ˈfɪlθɪnɪs/ *n., no pl.* [1] Schmutzigkeit, *die;* Verdrecktheit, *die* (ugs.) [2] (obscenity) Unzüchtigkeit, *die*

filthy /ˈfɪlθɪ/

A *adj.* [1] (disgustingly dirty) dreckig (ugs.); schmutzig; (fig.) widerlich ‹*Angewohnheit*›; (fond of filth) im Dreck lebend ‹*Tiere*› [2] (vile) widerlich; gemein ‹*Lügner, Trick*›; schmutzig ‹*Fantasie, Gedanken*›; **~ lucre** schnöder Mammon (abwertend, auch scherzh.) [3] (very unpleasant) ekelhaft; scheußlich; **~ weather** scheußliches Wetter; Dreckwetter, *das* (ugs.) [4] (obscene) schweinisch (ugs.); obszön, unflätig ‹*Sprache*›; **he is ~, he is a ~ devil** er ist ein Schweinigel (ugs.); **a ~-minded person** ein Mensch mit einer schmutzigen Fantasie

B *adv.* **~ dirty** völlig verdreckt (ugs.); **~ rich** (coll.) stinkreich (ugs.)

filtrate /ˈfɪltreɪt/ *n.* Filtrat, *das*

filtration /fɪlˈtreɪʃn/ *n.* Filtrierung, *die;* (percolation) Durchsickern, *das*

fin /fɪn/ *n.* [1] (Zool.; on boat) Flosse, *die;* (flipper) [Schwimm]flosse, *die;* (on car) Heckflosse, *die* [2] (on engine) Kühlrippe, *die;* (on radiator etc.) Rippe, *die. See also* **tail fin**

final /ˈfaɪnl/

A *adj.* [1] (ultimate) letzt...; End‹*spiel, -stadium, -stufe, -ergebnis*›; Schluss‹*bericht, -szene, -etappe, -phase*›; **~ examination** Abschlussprüfung, *die;* **have a ~ swim** ein letztes Mal schwimmen gehen; **give a ~ wave** noch einmal *od.* ein letztes Mal winken; **what will be the ~ outcome of this crisis?** wie wird diese Krise letztendlich ausgehen? [2] (conclusive) endgültig ‹*Urteil, Entscheidung*›; **have the ~ word** das letzte Wort haben; **is this your ~ decision/word/verdict?** ist das Ihr letztes Wort?; **the ~ solution** (Hist. euphem.) die Endlösung; **I'm not coming with you, and that's ~!** ich komme nicht mit, und damit basta! (ugs.) [3] (concerned with goal) **~ cause** Endziel, *das;* **~ clause** (Ling.) Finalsatz, *der*

B *n.* [1] (Sport etc.) Finale, *das;* (of ball game also) Endspiel, *das;* (of quiz game) Endrunde, *die* [2] *in sing. or pl.* (examination) Abschlussprüfung, *die;* (at university) Examen, *das* [3] (newspaper) Spätausgabe, *die*

final ˈdrive *n.* (Motor Veh.) Achsantrieb [mit Gelenkwelle]

finale /fɪˈnɑːlɪ/ *n.* [1] (Mus.) Finale, *das* [2] (close of drama) Schlussszene, *die* [3] (conclusion) Abschluss, *der*

finalise ▸**finalize**

finalist /ˈfaɪnəlɪst/ *n.* Teilnehmer/Teilnehmerin in der Endausscheidung; (Sport) Finalist, *der*/Finalistin, *die*

finality /faɪˈnælɪtɪ/ *n., no pl.* Endgültigkeit, *die;* (of tone of voice) Entschiedenheit, *die*

finalize /ˈfaɪnəlaɪz/ *v.t.* [endgültig] beschließen; unter Dach und Fach bringen ‹*Geschäft, Vertrag*›; (complete) zum Abschluss bringen; **~ sth. with sb.** etw. mit jmdm. [endgültig] absprechen

finally /ˈfaɪnəlɪ/ *adv.* [1] (in the end) schließlich; (expressing impatience etc.) endlich [2] (in conclusion) abschließend; zum Schluss [3] (conclusively) bestimmt, entschieden ‹*sagen*›; (once for all) ein für alle Mal

finance /faɪˈnæns, fɪˈnæns, ˈfaɪnæns/

A *n.* [1] *in pl.* (resources) Finanzen *Pl.* [2] (management of money) Geldwesen, *das;* **high ~:** Hochfinanz, *die;* **be in ~:** im Finanz- und Geldwesen tätig sein [3] (support) Gelder *Pl.* (ugs.); Geldmittel *Pl*

B *v.t.* finanzieren; finanziell unterstützen ‹*Person*›; **how are you going to ~ yourself at university?** wie willst du dein Studium finanzieren?

finance: ~ company *n.* Finanzierungsgesellschaft, *die;* **~ director** *n.* Leiter der Finanzabteilung; **~ house** ▸**~ company**

financial /faɪˈnænʃl, fɪˈnænʃl/ *adj.* finanziell; Finanz‹*mittel, -quelle, -experte, -lage*›; Geld‹*mittel, -geber, -sorgen*›; Finanzierungs‹*last, -geschäft*›; Wirtschafts‹*nachrichten, -bericht*›

financially /faɪˈnænʃəlɪ, fɪˈnænʃəlɪ/ *adv.* finanziell; **be ~ rewarded for sth.** für etw. mit Geld entlohnt werden

financial: ~ ˈplanner *n.* [1] (esp. Amer.: financial advisor) Finanzplaner, *der*/-planerin, *die;* [2] (in diary) Finanzplaner, *der;* **~ ˈyear** *n.* Geschäftsjahr, *das;* (*im öffentlichen Haushalt*) Rechnungsjahr, *das*

financier /faɪˈnænsɪə(r), fɪˈnænsɪə(r)/ *n.* [1] (expert) Finanzexperte, *der*/-expertin, *die* [2] (capitalist) Finanzier, *der*

finback [ˈwhale] ▸**fin whale**

finch /fɪnʃ/ *n.* (Ornith.) Fink[envogel], *der*

find /faɪnd/

A *v.t.*, **found** /faʊnd/ [1] (get possession of by chance) finden; (come across unexpectedly) entdecken; **~ that ...:** herausfinden *od.* entdecken, dass ...; **hope this letter ~s you well** [ich] hoffe, dass dieser Brief dich gesund antreffen wird; **he was found dead/injured** er wurde tot/verletzt aufgefunden [2] (obtain) finden ‹*Zustimmung, Erleichterung, Rückendeckung, Trost, Gegenliebe*›; stoßen auf (+ *Akk.*) ‹*Kritik, Ablehnung*›; erlangen ‹*Popularität*›; **have found one's feet** (be able to walk) laufen können; (be able to act by oneself) selbstständig sein; auf eigenen Füßen stehen [3] (recognize as present) sehen ‹*Veranlassung, Schwierigkeit*›; feststellen ‹*Züge, Ähnlichkeit*›; (acknowledge or discover to be) finden; **~ no difficulty in doing sth.** etw. nicht schwierig finden; **these plants are found nowhere else** diese Pflanzen findet man sonst nirgendwo; **you don't ~ many flowers here** es gibt hier nicht viele Blumen; **~ sb. in/out** jmdn. antreffen/nicht antreffen; **~ sb./sth. to be ...:** feststellen, dass jmd./etw. ... ist/war; **~ oneself somewhere** sich irgendwo wieder finden; **when I came in, I found him opening his/my letters** als ich hineinkam, war er gerade dabei, seine Briefe zu öffnen/ertappte ich ihn dabei, wie er meine Briefe öffnete; **~ oneself doing sth.** sich dabei ertappen, wie man etw. tut; **you must** *or* **will have to take us as you ~ us** du darfst dich nicht daran stören, wie es bei uns aussieht/zugeht *usw.*; **you won't ~ me doing ˈthat** das wirst du nicht erleben, dass ich das tue [4] (discover by trial or experience to be or do) für ... halten; **do you ~ him easy to get on with?** finden Sie, dass sich gut mit ihm auskommen lässt?; **she ~s it hard to come to terms with his death** es fällt ihr schwer, sich mit seinem Tod abzufinden; **she ~s it impossible to discuss the subject** es ist ihr unmöglich, das Thema zu erörtern; **~ sth. necessary** etw. für nötig befinden *od.* erachten; **~ sth./sb. to be ...:** herausfinden, dass etw./jmd. ... ist/war; **sth. has been found to be ...:** man hat herausgefunden, dass etw. ... ist; **I found that it was already noon** ich stellte fest, dass es schon [nach] zwölf war; **we ~ [that] we are struggling all the time** wir sehen, wie wir uns die ganze Zeit abmühen; **you will ~ [that] ...:** Sie werden sehen *od.* feststellen, dass ... [5] (discover by search) finden; **want to ~ sth.** etw. suchen; **~ [again]** wieder finden [6] (Hunting) aufstöbern; *abs.* Wild aufstöbern [7] (reach by natural or normal process) [heraus]finden; **~ one's place in society** seinen Platz in der Gesellschaft finden [8] (succeed in obtaining) finden ‹*Zeit, Mittel und Wege, Worte*›; auftreiben ‹*Geld, Gegenstand*›; aufbringen ‹*Kraft, Energie*›; **when I ~ the opportunity** bei passender Gelegenheit; **~ it in oneself** *or* **one's heart to do sth.** es über sich *od.* übers Herz bringen, etw. zu tun; **~ its mark** sein Ziel finden *od.* treffen [9] (ascertain by study or calculation or inquiry) finden; **love will ~ a way** der Liebe ist kein Ding unmöglich (veralt.); **~ what time the train leaves** herausfinden, wann der Zug [ab]fährt; **~ one's way [to/into sth.]** [zu etw.] hinfinden-/[in etw. (*Akk.*)] hineinfinden; (accidentally) [zu

etw.] hingelangen/[in etw. (*Akk.*)] hineingeraten; ~ **one's way home** nach Hause zurückfinden; ~ **one's way into journalism/films** zum Journalismus/Film kommen; **she found her way into teaching quite by accident** eher zufällig war sie Lehrerin geworden; ~ **its way [into sth.]** [in etw. (*Akk.*)] gelangen; **the disease found its way into other organs** die Krankheit griff auf andere Organe über
10 (Law) ~ **sb. guilty/not guilty [of sth.]** jmdn. [an etw. (*Dat.*)] schuldig sprechen/[von etw.] freisprechen; ~ **a verdict of guilty/innocent** [im Urteil] auf schuldig/nicht schuldig erkennen; **the jury found him not guilty of murder** die Geschworenen entschieden, dass er des Mordes nicht schuldig war
11 (supply) besorgen; ~ **sb. sth.** *or* **sth. for sb.** jmdn. mit etw. versorgen; **all found** bei freier Kost und Logis; bei freier Station (veralt.)
B *v. refl.*, **found** 1 (provide for one's own needs) ~ **oneself [in sth.]** sich selbst [mit etw.] versorgen
2 (discover one's vocation) zu sich selbst finden; seine wahre Bestimmung finden
C *n.* 1 Fund, *der;* **make a ~/two ~s** fündig/zweimal fündig werden
2 (person) Entdeckung, *die*
Phrasal verbs
• ~ **for** *v.t.* (Law) ~ **for the defendant/plaintiff** zugunsten der Verteidigung/des Klägers entscheiden; ~ **for the accused** auf Freispruch erkennen
• ~ **'out** *v.t.* 1 (discover, devise) herausfinden; bekommen ‹*Informationen*›; ~ **out new ways** einen neuen Weg finden; **manage to ~ out how ...:** herausbekommen, wie ...; ~ **out about** (get information on) sich informieren über (+ *Akk.*); (learn of) erfahren von 2 (detect in offence, act of deceit, etc.) erwischen, ertappen ‹*Dieb usw.*›; ~ **out a liar** einem Lügner auf die Schliche kommen; einen Lügner durchschauen; **your sins will ~ you out** deine Sünden werden an den Tag kommen

findable /'faɪndəbl/ *pred. adj.* **be [easily] ~:** [leicht] zu finden sein

finder /'faɪndə(r)/ *n.* 1 (of sth. lost) Finder, *der*/Finderin, *die;* (of sth. unknown) Entdecker, *der*/Entdeckerin, *die;* **~s keepers** (coll.) wers findet, dem gehörts (ugs.) 2 (Photog.) Sucher, *der*

fin de siècle /fæ̃ də 'sjekl/ *adj.* Fin-de-siècle- ‹*Architektur, Atmosphäre usw.*›

finding /'faɪndɪŋ/ *n.* 1 Finden, *das;* ~ **is keeping** wer's findet, dem gehört's (ugs.) 2 *usu. in pl.* (conclusion[s]) Ergebnis, *das;* (verdict) Urteil, *das;* **what were the ~s of the investigations?** was haben die Ermittlungen ergeben? 3 *in pl.* (Amer.) (small parts or tools) Handwerkszeug, *das;* (sewing essentials) Nähzeug, *das*

fine[1] /faɪn/
A *n.* Geldstrafe, *die;* (for minor offence) Bußgeld, *das*
B *v.t.* mit einer Geldstrafe belegen; **we were ~d £10** wir mussten ein Bußgeld von 10 Pfund bezahlen; **be ~d for speeding** ein Bußgeld wegen überhöhter Geschwindigkeit zahlen müssen

fine[2]
A *adj.* 1 (of high quality) gut; hochwertig ‹*Qualität, Lebensmittel*›; fein ‹*Besteck, Gewebe, Spitze*›; edel ‹*Pferd, Holz, Wein*›
2 (pure) rein ‹*Öl, Metall, Wein*›
3 (containing specified proportion of pure metal) fein; **gold 18 carats ~:** 18-karätiges Gold
4 (delicately beautiful) zart ‹*Porzellan, Spitze*›; ansprechend ‹*Beleuchtung, Manuskript*›; fein ‹*Muster, Kristall, Stickerei, Gesichtszüge*›
5 (refined) edel ‹*Empfindungen*›; fein ‹*Taktgefühl, Geschmack*›; **a man of ~ feelings** ein Mann mit viel Feingefühl; **sb.'s ~r feelings** das Gute in jmdm.
6 (delicate in structure or texture) fein
7 (thin) fein; hauchdünn; **cut** *or* **run it ~** knapp kalkulieren; **we'd be cutting it ~ if there are only three minutes to spare** es wird etwas knapp werden, wenn wir nur drei Minuten Zeit haben
8 (in small particles) [hauch]fein ‹*Sand, Staub*›; ~ **rain** Nieselregen, *der*
9 (sharp, narrow-pointed) scharf ‹*Spitze, Klinge*›; spitz ‹*Nadel, Schreibfeder*›
10 ~ **print ▸ small print**
11 (capable of delicate perception, discrimination) fein ‹*Gehör*›; scharf ‹*Auge*›; genau ‹*Waage, Werkzeug*›; empfindlich ‹*Messgerät*›
12 (perceptible only with difficulty) fein ‹*Unterschied, Nuancen*›; (precise) klein ‹*Detail*›; **the ~r points** die Feinheiten
13 (excellent) schön; gut ‹*Ruf, Charakter, Stimmung, Hotel*›; edel ‹*Gesinnung*›; ausgezeichnet ‹*Sänger, Schauspieler*›; nett ‹*Person*›; **a ~ time to do sth.** (iron.) ein passender Zeitpunkt, etw. zu tun (iron.); **well, that's a ~ thing to say** (iron.) das ist wirklich nett *od.* reizend, so was zu sagen (iron.); **that's a ~ excuse/way to treat your father** (iron.) das ist ja eine schöne Entschuldigung/feine Art, seinen Vater zu behandeln (iron.); **you 'are a ~ one!** (iron.) du bist mir vielleicht einer! (ugs.); **[this/that is] all very ~, but ...:** [das ist ja] alles schön und gut, aber ...
14 (satisfactory) schön; gut; **that's ~ with** *or* **by me** ja, ist mir recht; **everything is ~:** es ist alles in Ordnung
15 (well conceived or expressed) schön ‹*Worte, Ausdruck usw.*›; gelungen ‹*Rede, Übersetzung usw.*›
16 (of handsome appearance or size) schön; stattlich ‹*Mann, Baum, Tier*›; **~-looking** gut aussehend; **a ~ body of men** eine vortreffliche Gruppe
17 (in good health or state) gut; **feel ~:** sich wohl fühlen; **she is ~ there now** sie fühlt sich jetzt wohl dort; **they had a few problems, but they're ~ now** es gab Probleme zwischen ihnen, aber jetzt kommen sie klar; **How are you? — F~, thanks. And you?** Wie geht es Ihnen? — Gut, danke. Und Ihnen?; **the car is ~ now** das Auto ist jetzt wieder in Ordnung
18 (bright and clear) schön ‹*Wetter, Sommerabend*›; ~ **and sunny** heiter und sonnig; **one ~ day ...:** eines schönen Tages ...; **one of these ~ days ...:** eines [schönen] Tages
19 (ornate) prächtig ‹*Kleidung*›; ~ **feathers** prächtiges Gefieder; (fig.) prächtige Gewänder; *see also* **feather A 1**
20 (fastidious) vornehm, fein ‹*Dame, Herr, Art, Manieren*›; (affectedly ornate) geziert; schön klingend ‹*Worte*›; gewählt ‹*Ausdrucksweise*›; **his ~ sensibilities** sein Feingefühl; **she's too ~ to associate with us** sie ist sich (*Dat.*) zu fein für uns. *See also* **dandy B**; **point A 2**
B *adv.* 1 (into small particles) fein ‹*mahlen, raspeln, hacken*›
2 (delicately) fein ‹*gewebt, gesponnen usw.*›
3 (coll.: well) gut

fine: ~ **'art** *n.* 1 (subject) bildende Kunst; 2 (skill) **get sth. [down] to a ~ art** etw. zu einer richtigen Kunst entwickeln; **have got sth. [down] to a ~ art** etw. aus dem Effeff beherrschen (ugs.); 3 **the ~ arts** die Schönen Künste; **~-drawn** *adj.* sehnig, hager ‹*Gestalt*›; fein geschnitten ‹*Gesichtszüge*›; (subtle) feinsinnig; **~-grained** *adj.* fein gekörnt ‹*Sand, Salz, Papier*›; fein genarbt ‹*Leder*›; fein gemasert ‹*Holz*›

finely /'faɪnlɪ/ *adv.* 1 (exquisitely) ~ **executed** *or* **crafted jewellery** fein gearbeiteter Schmuck
2 (delicately) fein ‹*gewebt, gehäkelt usw.*›; genau ‹*ausbalanciert*› 3 (to a fine point or edge) **a ~-sharpened blade** eine sorgfältig geschärfte Klinge; **a ~-pointed needle** eine feinspitzige Nadel; eine Nadel mit feiner Spitze; **a ~-drawn line** eine fein *od.* dünn [aus]gezogene Linie 4 (into small particles) fein ‹*mahlen*›
5 (subtly) fein[sinnig]

finery /'faɪnərɪ/ *n., no pl.* Pracht, *die;* (garments etc.) Staat, *der;* **in all her wedding ~:** in ihrem Hochzeitsstaat

finesse /fɪ'nes/
A *n.* 1 (refinement) Feinheit, *die;* (of diplomat) Gewandtheit, *die;* (delicate manipulation) Finesse, *die* 2 (artfulness) Raffinesse, *die;* **the ~ of the negotiators** das Geschick der Verhandlungspartner 3 (Cards) Schneiden, *das*
B *v.i.* 1 mit aller Raffinesse vorgehen 2 (Cards) schneiden
C *v.t.* (Cards) schneiden mit

fine-tooth 'comb *n.* fein gezähnter Kamm; **go through a manuscript** *etc.*/**house** *etc.* **with a ~** (fig.) ein Manuskript *usw.* Punkt für Punkt durchgehen/ein Haus *usw.* gründlich durchkämmen

'fine-tune *v.t.* feinstimmen ‹*Saite*›; feinabstimmen ‹*Kanal*›; aufpolieren ‹*Fertigkeit, Sprachkenntnisse*›

finger /'fɪŋgə(r)/
A *n.* 1 ▸ⓘ **p. 951** Finger, *der;* **sb.'s ~s itch [to do sth.]** es juckt jmdm. in den Fingern[, etw. zu tun] (ugs.); **lay a ~ on sb.** (fig.) jmdm. ein Härchen krümmen (ugs.); **they never lift** *or* **move** *or* **raise a ~ to help her** (fig.) sie rühren keinen Finger, um ihr zu helfen; **they didn't lift** *or* **move** *or* **raise a ~** (fig.) sie haben keinen Finger krumm gemacht; **get** *or* **pull** *or* **take one's ~ out** (fig. coll.) Dampf dahinter machen (ugs.); **point a** *or* **one's ~ at sb./sth.** mit dem Finger/(fig. ugs.) mit Fingern auf jmdn./etw. zeigen; **put the ~ on sb.** (fig. coll.) jmdn. verpfeifen (ugs. abwertend); **have a ~ in sth.** (fig.) die Finger in etw. (*Dat.*) haben; **put** *or* **lay one's ~ on sth.** (fig.) etw. genau ausmachen; **sth. slips through sb.'s ~s** etw. gleitet jmdm. durch die Finger; (fig.) etw. geht jmdm. durch die Lappen (ugs.); **let sth. slip through one's ~s** (fig.) sich (*Dat.*) etw. entgehen *od.* (ugs.) durch die Lappen gehen lassen; **his ~s are [all] thumbs, he is all ~s and thumbs** er hat zwei linke Hände (ugs.); **count the things/people on the ~s of one hand** die Dinge/Menschen an einer Hand abzählen 2 (of glove etc.) Finger, *der* 3 (finger-like object) **chocolate ~:** Löffelbiskuit mit Schokoladeüberzug; **a ~ of toast** ein Streifen Toast; **sponge ~s** schmale Stücke Rührkuchen 4 (coll.: amount of liquor) Fingerbreit, *der;* **a ~ of whisky** ein Fingerbreit Whisky. *See also* **bone A 1**; **burn**[1] **B 3**; **cross B 1**; **fish finger**; **forefinger**; **green A 1**; **index finger**; **little finger**; **middle finger**; **pie**; **ring finger**
B *v.t.* 1 (touch with ~s) berühren ‹*Ware*›; greifen ‹*Akkord*›; (turn about with ~s) anfassen; (toy or meddle with) befingern; herumfingern an (+ *Dat.*)
2 (esp. Amer. coll.: indicate) ~ **sb./sth. to the police** jmdn. bei der Polizei verpfeifen/etw. der Polizei stecken (ugs. abwertend)

finger: **~board** *n.* Griffbrett, *das;* ~ **bowl** *n.* Fingerschale, *die;* ~ **end** Fingerspitze, *die;* ~ **food** Fingerfood *das;* ~ **glass** ▸ ~ **bowl**

fingering /'fɪŋgərɪŋ/ *n.* (Mus.) Fingersatz, *der;* (proper method) Fingertechnik, *die*

finger: **~-licking** *adj.* (esp. Amer.) köstlich; **~-licking good** [einfach] köstlich; **~mark** *n.* Fingerabdruck, *der;* **~nail** *n.* Fingernagel, *der;* ~ **paint** *n.* Fingerfarbe, *die;* **~post** *n.* Wegweiser, *der;* **~print** **A** *n.* Fingerabdruck, *der;* **leave one's ~prints** (fig.) seine Fingerabdrücke hinterlassen; *see also* **take A 9**; **B** *v.t.* einen Fingerabdruck nehmen von; **~print sb.** jmdm. die Fingerabdrücke abnehmen; **~stall** *n.* Fingerling, *der;* **~tip** *n.* Fingerspitze, *die;* **have sth. at one's ~tips** (fig.) etw. aus dem Effeff können *od.* im kleinen Finger haben (ugs.); **to the ~tips** (fig.) durch und durch; **he's a Spaniard to the very ~tips** er ist durch und durch Spanier

finial /'fɪnɪəl/ *n.* (Archit.) Kreuzblume, *die*

finical /'fɪnɪkl/, **finicking** /'fɪnɪkɪŋ/ *adjs.* ▸ **finicky A**

finicky /'fɪnɪkɪ/ *adj.* 1 heikel; **she's so ~ about her appearance** sie ist so heikel, wenn es um ihr Äußeres geht; **he's so ~ about what he eats** in puncto Essen ist er sehr wählerisch 2 (needing much attention to detail) kniff[e]lig ‹*Arbeit, Stickerei*›

finish /'fɪnɪʃ/
A *v.t.* 1 (bring to an end) beenden ‹*Unterhaltung*›; erledigen ‹*Arbeit*›; abschließen ‹*Kurs, Ausbildung*›; **have you ~ed the letter/book?** hast du den Brief/das Buch fertig [geschrieben]?; **have ~ed sth.** etw. fertig haben; mit etw. fertig sein; **have ~ed doing one's homework** seine Hausaufgaben fertig haben; mit seinen Hausaufgaben fertig sein; ~ **writing/reading sth.** etw. zu Ende schreiben/lesen; **haven't you ~ed eating yet?** hast du noch nicht zu Ende gegessen *od.* fertig gegessen?; *abs.* **please**

f

let me ~ [speaking] bitte lassen Sie mich ausreden; have you quite ~ed? sind Sie fertig?; (iron.) nun, bist du jetzt endlich fertig?
2 (get through) aufessen ‹Mahlzeit›; auslesen ‹Buch, Zeitung›; austrinken ‹Flasche, Glas›; I should ~ the book by this evening ich müsste das Buch bis heute Abend durchhaben (ugs.)
3 (kill) umbringen; (destroy) vernichten ‹Ernte›; (coll.: overcome) schaffen (ugs.); (overcome completely) bezwingen ‹Feind›; (ruin) zugrunde richten; any more stress would ~ him noch mehr Stress würde ihn kaputtmachen (ugs.); a cold would ~ her eine Erkältung würde das Ende für sie bedeuten; it almost ~ed me! das hat mich fast geschafft! (ugs.); this scandal ~ed her as an actress dieser Skandal bedeutete das Ende ihrer Schauspielerkarriere
4 (perfect) vervollkommnen; den letzten Schliff geben (+ Dat.); ~ a seam einen Saum vernähen
5 (complete education of) ausbilden; (make highly accomplished) mit allen Fertigkeiten ausstatten; (make polished) verfeinern ‹Umgangsformen›; ausfeilen ‹Sprechweise›
6 (complete with surface treatment) eine schöne Oberfläche geben (+ Dat.); glätten ‹Papier, Holz›; appretieren ‹Gewebe, Leder›; glasieren ‹Tonwaren›; polieren ‹Metall›; verputzen ‹Mauerwerk›; ~ sth. with a coat of varnish/waterproof coating/by polishing it etw. zum Schluss lackieren/imprägnieren/polieren; the ~ed article or product das fertige Produkt

B v.i. 1 (reach the end) aufhören; ‹Geschichte, Episode:› enden; ‹Sturm, Unwetter:› sich legen; when does the concert ~? wann ist das Konzert aus?; coffee to ~: Kaffee zum Abschluss
2 (come to end of race) das Ziel erreichen; ~ first als Erster durchs Ziel gehen; Erster werden; ~ badly/well nicht durchhalten/einen guten Endspurt haben
3 ~ in sth. mit etw. enden; ~ by doing sth. zum Schluss etw. tun

C n. 1 (termination) Ende, das; fight to a ~: bis zur Entscheidung kämpfen; it would be the ~ of him as a politician das würde das Ende seiner Karriere als Politiker bedeuten; be in at the ~ das Ende od. den Schluss miterleben
2 (point at which race etc. ends) Ziel, das; arrive at the ~: das Ziel erreichen; durchs Ziel gehen
3 (what serves to give completeness) letzter Schliff; a ~ to sth. die Vervollkommnung od. Vollendung einer Sache; form a perfect ~ to a memorable evening einen krönenden Abschluss eines unvergesslichen Abends bilden
4 (accomplishment, polished manners) Schliff, der; have ~: Schliff haben
5 (mode of finishing) [technische] Ausführung; Finish, das; (of paper) Oberflächenfinish, das; (of material, fabric) Appretur, die; (of metal) Politur, die; paintwork with a matt/gloss ~: Matt-/Hochglanzlack, der

Phrasal verbs

- ~ 'off v.t. 1 ▸finish A 3, 4 2 (provide with ending) abschließen; beenden; ~ off a story eine Geschichte zu Ende schreiben/erzählen 3 (~ or trim neatly) sauber verarbeiten
- ~ 'up v.i. 1 ▸~ B 3 2 = end up 3 (complete all outstanding work) alles erledigen
- ~ with v.t. 1 (complete one's use of) have you ~ed with the sugar? brauchen Sie den Zucker noch?; have ~ed with a book ein Buch aus- od. fertig gelesen od. zu Ende gelesen haben; are you ~ed with your plate? hast du deinen Teller leer gegessen?; if these things are ~ed with, then throw them away wenn du diese Sachen nicht mehr brauchst, wirf sie weg 2 (end association with) brechen mit; she ~ed with her boyfriend sie hat mit ihrem Freund Schluss gemacht 3 have ~ed with doing sth. es aufgegeben haben, etw. zu tun

finisher /'fɪnɪʃə(r)/ n. 1 (Sport) there were only two ~s es kamen nur zwei Teilnehmer ins Ziel; he/the horse is a fast ~: er/das Pferd ist im Endspurt schnell 2 (Ind.) Fertigbearbeiter, der/-bearbeiterin, die; metal-~: Polierer, der/Poliererin, die; cloth-~: Appretierer, der/Appretiererin, die

finishing: ~ post n. Zielpfosten, der; ~ school n. Mädchenpensionat, das (veralt.) (besonders zur Vorbereitung auf das gesellschaftliche Leben); ~ 'touch n. as a ~ touch to sth. zur Vollendung od. Vervollkommnung einer Sache; um eine Sache abzurunden; put the ~ touches to sth. einer Sache (Dat.) den letzten Schliff geben

finite /'faɪnaɪt/ 1 (bounded) begrenzt; ~ number (Math.) endliche Zahl 2 (Ling.) finit

Finland /'fɪnlənd/ pr. n. Finnland (das)

Finn /fɪn/ n. ▸❶ p. 1345 Finne, der/Finnin, die

Finnish /'fɪnɪʃ/ ▸❶ p. 1277, ▸❶ p. 1345
A adj. finnisch; sb. is ~: jmd. ist Finne/Finnin; the ~ language das Finnische; see also English A
B n. Finnisch, das; see also English B 1

'fin whale n. Finnwal, der

fiord ▸fjord

fir /fɜː(r)/ n. 1 (tree) Tanne, die 2 (wood) Tanne, die; Tannenholz, das. See also Scotch fir; silver fir

'fir cone n. Tannenzapfen, der

fire /'faɪə(r)/
A n. 1 Feuer, das; set ~ to sth. ‹Person:› etw. anzünden; set ~ to oneself sich anzünden; strike ~ from sth. Funken aus etw. schlagen; be on ~: brennen (auch fig.); in Flammen stehen; catch or take ~, (Scot., Ir.) go on ~ (lit. or fig.) Feuer fangen; ‹Wald, Gebäude:› in Brand geraten; set sth. on ~: etw. anzünden; (in order to destroy) etw. in Brand stecken; (deliberately) Feuer an etw. (Akk.) legen; he won't/it's not going to set the world or (Brit.) the Thames on ~: er hat das Pulver nicht erfunden (ugs.)/es ist nichts Weltbewegendes od. Welterschütterndes
2 (in grate) [offenes] Feuer; (electric or gas ~) Heizofen, der; (in the open air) Lagerfeuer, das; open ~: Kaminfeuer, das; round or by the ~: am warmen Ofen; over a low ~: auf kleinem Feuer; make up the ~: nachlegen; turn up the ~ (electric) die Heizung/(gas) das Gas höher drehen od. aufdrehen; switch on another bar of the ~: einen weiteren Heizstab einschalten; have ~ in one's belly (ambition) Ehrgeiz haben; (enthusiasm) begeisterungsfähig sein; play with ~ (lit. or fig.) mit dem Feuer spielen; light the ~: den Ofen anstecken; (in grate) das [Kamin]feuer anmachen; lay a ~: ein Feuer anlegen; make a ~: ein Feuer [an]machen
3 (destructive burning) Brand, der; in case of ~, follow these instructions bei Feuer od. im Brandfall ist diesen Anweisungen Folge zu leisten; insure sth. against ~: etw. gegen Feuer versichern; where's the ~? (coll. iron.) wo brennts denn? (ugs.); F~! Feuer!; es brennt!; go through ~ and water [to help sb.] (fig.) [für jmdn.] durchs Feuer gehen
4 (fervour) Feuer, das; the ~ with which he speaks die Leidenschaft, mit der er spricht; his speech was full of ~: er hielt eine glühende od. feurige od. (geh.) flammende Rede
5 (firing of guns) Schießen, das; Schießerei, die; pistol ~: [Pistolen]schüsse; cannon ~: Kanonenfeuer, das; be exposed to the ~ of critics (fig.) im Kreuzfeuer der Kritik stehen; von den Kritikern unter Beschuss genommen werden; line of ~ (lit. or fig.) Schusslinie, die; running ~ (lit. or fig.) Trommelfeuer, das; between two ~s (lit. or fig.) zwischen zwei Feuern; be/come under ~: beschossen werden/unter Beschuss geraten; (fig.) heftig angegriffen werden/unter Beschuss geraten. See also cease B 2; coal 2; draw A 2; fat B; frying pan; fuel A; hang A 9; hold A 20; iron A 2; open C 3; smoke A 1
B v.t. 1 (set fire to) anzünden; in Brand stecken
2 (kindle) zünden ‹Sprengladung›
3 (fig.: stimulate) beflügeln ‹Fantasie›; anregen ‹Ehrgeiz›; erregen ‹Interesse›; inspirieren, anregen ‹Person›; (fill with enthusiasm) begeistern, in Begeisterung versetzen ‹Person›
4 (bake) brennen ‹Tonwaren, Ziegel›
5 (supply with fuel) befeuern ‹Ofen›; [be]heizen ‹Lokomotive›
6 (cause to explode) zünden ‹Sprengladung›; [in die Luft] sprengen ‹Mine›
7 (discharge) abschießen ‹Gewehr›; abfeuern ‹Kanone›; ~ one's gun/pistol/rifle at sb. auf jmdn. schießen
8 (produce with guns) ~ a 21-gun salute 21 Salutschüsse abgeben
9 (propel from gun etc.) abgeben, abfeuern ‹Schuss›; (fig.) vom Stapel lassen (ugs.) ‹Kritik, Bemerkungen›; ~ a bullet/cartridge einen Schuss abgeben; ~ blank cartridges mit Platzpatronen schießen; two shots were ~d/~d by sb. es fielen zwei Schüsse/zwei Schüsse wurden von jmdm. abgegeben; ~ questions at sb. jmdn. mit Fragen bombardieren; Fragen auf jmdn. abfeuern
10 (coll.: dismiss) feuern (ugs.) ‹Angestellten›
C v.i. 1 (shoot) schießen; feuern; ~! [gebt] Feuer!; be the first to ~: das Feuer eröffnen; ~ at/on sth./sb. auf etw./jmdn. schießen; ~ into the air/at the ground/into the crowd in die Luft/in den Boden/in die Menge schießen; ~ on sth. from above etw. aus der Luft beschießen
2 ‹Motor:› zünden; the engine is not firing properly der Motor läuft nicht richtig

Phrasal verbs

- ~ a'way v.i. (fig. coll.) losschießen (fig. ugs.); ~ away! schieß los!; fang an!
- ~ 'out (Amer.) ▸~ B 10

fire: ~ alarm n. Feuermelder, der; ~arm n. Schusswaffe, die; ~ axe n. Feuerwehraxt, die; ~ ball n. 1 (large meteor) Feuerkugel, die; 2 (ball of flame) Feuerball, der; 3 (globular lightning) Kugelblitz, der; 4 (energetic person) Energiebündel, das (ugs.); ~ bell n. Feuerglocke, die; ~ blanket n. Feuerlöschdecke, die; ~bomb A n. Brandsatz, der; (aerial bomb) Brandbombe, die; attrib. ~bomb attack Brandanschlag, der; B v.t. ~bomb sth. einen Brandanschlag auf etw. (Akk.) verüben; ~brand n. Brandfackel, die; (fig.) Unruhestifter, der/-stifterin, die; Aufwiegler, der/Aufwieglerin, die; ~break n. Brandschneise, die; ~-breathing adj. Feuer speiend; ~brick n. Schamottestein, der; ~ brigade n. (Brit.) Feuerwehr, die; ~ bucket n. Löscheimer, der; ~ chief n. (Amer.) Branddirektor, der; ~clay n. Schamotte, die; ~cracker n. (firework) Kracher, der; ~-damaged adj. durch Brand beschädigt; ~damp n. Grubengas, das; ~ department (Amer.) ▸~ brigade; ~ door n. Feuerschutztür, die; ~ drill n. (for firemen) Feuerwehrübung, die; (for others) Probe[feuer]alarm, der; ~-eater n. 1 (conjuror) Feuerschlucker, der; 2 (fond of fighting) Kampfhahn, der (ugs.); (fond of quarrelling) Streithahn, der (ugs.); ~ engine n. Löschfahrzeug, das; ~ escape n. (staircase) Feuertreppe, die; (ladder) Feuerleiter, die; ~ exit n. Notausgang, der; ~ extinguisher n. Feuerlöscher, der; portable ~ extinguisher Handfeuerlöscher, der; ~fighter n. ▸❶ p. 1260 Feuerwehrmann, der/-frau, die; ~fighting n., no pl. Feuerbekämpfung, die; Brandbekämpfung, die; attrib. ~fighting equipment Feuerlöscheinrichtung, die; ~fly n. Leuchtkäfer, der; Glühwürmchen, das (ugs.); ~guard n. Schutzgitter, das; Kamingitter, das; ~ hazard n. Brandrisiko, das; ~ hose n. Feuerwehrschlauch, der; ~ insurance n. Feuerversicherung, die; Brandversicherung, die; ~ irons n. pl. Kaminbesteck, das; ~light n. Schein des Feuers; Schein der Flammen; ~lighter n. (Brit.) Feueranzünder, der; ~man /'faɪəmən/ n., pl. ~men /'faɪəmən/ ▸❶ p. 1260 1 (member of fire brigade) Feuerwehrmann, der; ~man's lift Feuerwehrgriff, der; 2 (Railw.: on steam engine) Heizer, der; ~place n. Kamin, der; ~power n. Feuerkraft, die; ~ practice ▸~ drill; ~ precautions n. pl. Feuerschutz, der; ~ prevention n., no pl. Brandverhütung, die; attrib. ~ prevention officer Brandschutzbeauftragte, der/die; ~proof A adj. feuerfest; B v.t. feuerfest machen; ~-raiser n. (Brit.) Brandstifter, der/-stifterin, die; ~-raising n. (Brit.) Brandstiftung, die; ~-resistant adj. feuerbeständig; ~-retardant A adj. feuerhemmend. B n. Feuerhemmer, der; ~ risk ▸~ hazard; ~ screen n. Ofenschirm, der; F~ Service n. Feuerwehr, die; ~side n. Kaminecke, die; at or by the ~side am Kamin; at or by one's

own ~side am heimischen Herde; **~side chat** Plauderei am Kamin; **~ station** *n.* Feuerwache, *die;* **~storm** *n.* **1** (intense fire) Feuersturm, *der;* **2** (fig.: outburst) Sturm, *der;* **~ tender** *n.* Gerätewagen (der Feuerwehr); **~ tongs** *n. pl.* Feuerzange, *die;* **a pair of ~ tongs** eine Feuerzange; **~ trap** *n.* Feuerfalle, *die;* **~-walker** *n. jmd., der barfüßig über glühende Steine läuft;* Feuerläufer, *der/-läuferin, die;* **~wall** *n.* **1** Feuer[schutz]wand, *die;* **2** (Computing) Firewall, *die od. der;* **~ warden** *n.* Brandwart, *der/-wartin, die;* **~-watcher** *n.* Feuerposten, *der;* Brandwart, *der/-wartin, die;* (in war) Luftschutzwart, *der/-wartin, die;* **~water** *n.* (coll.) Feuerwasser, *das* (ugs.); **~wood** *n.* Brennholz, *das;* **~work** *n.* **1** Feuerwerkskörper, *der; attrib.* **~work display** Feuerwerk, *das;* **2** *in pl.* (display) Feuerwerk, *das;* (fig.: display of wit) Feuerwerk des Geistes; **intellectual ~works** ein geistiges *od.* intellektuelles Feuerwerk; **there were** *or* **it caused ~works** (fig.) da war was los *od.* flogen die Funken (ugs.)

firing /ˈfaɪərɪŋ/ *n.* **1** (of houses) Anzünden, *das;* (of pottery) Brennen, *das* **2** (fuel) Feuerung, *die;* **the ~ for these furnaces was coal** diese Öfen wurden mit Kohle befeuert **3** *no pl.* (of guns) Abfeuern, *das;* **we could hear ~ in the distance** in der Ferne konnten wir Schüsse hören; **the ~ in the streets** die Schießerei in den Straßen

firing: ~ line *n.* (lit. or fig.) Feuerlinie, *die;* **~ party, ~ squad** *ns.* (at military funeral) Ehrensalutkommando, *das;* (at military execution) Exekutionskommando, *das*

firm¹ /fɜːm/ *n.* Firma, *die;* **~ of architects/decorators** Architektenbüro, *das*/Malerbetrieb, *der*

firm²

A *adj.* **1** fest; stabil ‹*Verhältnis, Konstruktion, Stuhl*›; straff ‹*Busen*›; stramm ‹*Bäckchen*›; verbindlich ‹*Angebot*›; **be on ~ ground again** (lit. or fig.) wieder festen Boden unter den Füßen haben; **do sth. to make a chair/bench ~:** etw. tun, damit ein Stuhl/eine Bank fest steht; **as ~ as a rock** felsenfest; **they are ~ friends** sie sind gut befreundet; **have a ~ grip on sth.** etw. fest in der Hand haben; **the chair is not ~:** der Stuhl wackelt *od.* ist wacklig; **make a ~ date** eine feste Zeit vereinbaren **2** (resolute) entschlossen ‹*Blick*›; bestimmt, entschieden ‹*Ton*›; stark ‹*Widerstand*›; **in ~ pursuit of his goal** in energischer *od.* entschiedener Verfolgung seines Ziels; **be a ~ believer in sth.** fest an etw. (*Akk.*) glauben; **be ~ when you speak to him** sei bestimmt, wenn du mit ihm sprichst; **be ~ in one's beliefs** fest auf seiner Überzeugung beharren; an seiner Überzeugung festhalten; **~ insistence** Beharrlichkeit, *die;* **she has a ~ character** sie besitzt Charakterstärke **3** (insisting on obedience etc.) bestimmt; **be ~ with sb.** jmdm. gegenüber bestimmt auftreten; **a ~ hand** eine feste Hand; **with a ~ hand** mit fester *od.* starker Hand **4** (Commerc.) fest; stabil ‹*Markt*›; **oil is not ~:** der Ölmarkt ist nicht stabil

B *adv.* **stand ~!** (fig.) sei standhaft!; lass dich nicht davon abbringen!; **stand ~ in sth.** (fig.) fest *od.* unerschütterlich bei etw. bleiben; **hold ~ to sth.** (fig.) an einer Sache festhalten

C *v.t.* **1** (make firm or solid) fest werden lassen; festigen, straffen ‹*Muskulatur, Körper*› **2** fest [ein]pflanzen ‹*Pflanzen*›

Phrasal verb

• **~ ˈup**

A *v.t.* konkretisieren ‹*Plan, Geschäft, Vereinbarung*›

B *v.i.* ‹*Plan, Geschäft, Vereinbarung:*› sich konkretisieren

firmament /ˈfɜːməmənt/ *n.* (literary) Firmament, *das*

firmly /ˈfɜːmlɪ/ *adv.* **1** fest; **the jelly has set ~:** der Gelee ist fest geworden; **a ~-built structure** eine stabile Konstruktion; **sth. is ~ under lock and key** etw. ist sicher weggeschlossen **2** (resolutely) beharrlich ‹*unterstützen, sich widersetzen*›; bestimmt, energisch ‹*reden*›; **deal with** *or* **treat sb. ~:** jmdm. gegenüber bestimmt auftreten

firmness /ˈfɜːmnɪs/ *n., no pl.* **1** (solidity) Festigkeit, *die;* (of foundations, building) Stabilität, *die;* (of offer) Verbindlichkeit, *die* **2** (resoluteness) Entschlossenheit, *die;* (of voice) Bestimmtheit, *die;* (of support, belief) Beständigkeit, *die;* Beharrlichkeit, *die;* **the ~ of his resolve** seine feste Entschlossenheit **3** (insistence on obedience etc.) Bestimmtheit, *die;* **use ~ with sb., treat sb. with ~:** jmdm. gegenüber bestimmt auftreten

ˈfirmware *n., no pl., no indef. art.* (Computing) Firmware, *die*

first /fɜːst/

A *adj.* ▸ⓘ **p. 1358** erst...; (for the ~ time ever) Erst‹*aufführung, -besteigung*›; (of an artist's ~ achievement) Erstlings‹*film, -roman, -stück, -werk*›; **he was ~ to arrive** er kam als Erster an; **who was ~?** wer war Erster?; **for the [very] ~ time** zum [aller]ersten Mal; **there's always a ~ time** (coll.) irgendwann passierts dann eben doch (ugs.); **~ thing you know** (coll.) ehe du dich's versiehst; **just buy the ~ thing one sees** das erste Beste kaufen; **I'll do it at the ~ opportunity** ich tue es bei der erstbesten Gelegenheit; **say the ~ thing that comes into one's head** das sagen, was einem zuerst einfällt; **the ~ two** die ersten beiden *od.* zwei; **come in ~** (win race) [das Rennen] gewinnen; **head/feet ~:** mit dem Kopf/den Füßen zuerst *od.* voran; **~ thing after breakfast** (coll.) gleich nach dem Frühstück; **~ thing in the morning** gleich frühmorgens; (coll.: tomorrow) gleich morgen früh; **~ thing on arrival** (coll.) gleich nach der Ankunft; **the ~ thing [to do]** (coll.) das Erste [, was man tun muss]; **~ things ~** (coll.) eins nach dem anderen; immer [hübsch] der Reihe nach; **have [the] ~ claim to sth.** eine Option auf etw. (*Akk.*) haben; **she is ~ in the class** sie ist Klassenbeste *od.* die Beste in der Klasse; **he's always [the] ~ to help** er ist immer als Erster zur Stelle, wenn Hilfe benötigt wird; **not know the ~ thing about sth.** von einer Sache nicht das Geringste verstehen; **~ soprano/cello** (Mus.) erster Sopran/Cellist; *see also* **eighth A**

B *adv.* **1** (before anyone else) zuerst; als Erster/Erste ‹*sprechen, ankommen*›; (before anything else) an erster Stelle ‹*stehen, kommen*›; (when listing: firstly) zuerst; als Erstes; **women and children ~!** Frauen und Kinder zuerst; **ladies ~!** Ladys first!; den Damen der Vortritt!; **you [go] ~** (as invitation) Sie haben den Vortritt; bitte nach Ihnen; **~ come ~ served** wer zuerst kommt, mahlt zuerst (Spr.); **we must put our children's education ~:** die Schulbildung unserer Kinder muss für uns an erster Stelle stehen; **this matter is** *or* **comes ~ on the agenda** diese Angelegenheit ist der erste Punkt unserer Tagesordnung; **come ~ with sb.** (fig.) bei jmdm. zuerst kommen; **say ~ one thing and then another** erst so und dann wieder so sagen (ugs.)

2 (beforehand) vorher; **... but ~ we must ...:** ... aber zuerst *od.* erst müssen wir ...

3 (for the ~ time) zum ersten Mal; das erste Mal; erstmals ‹*bekannt geben, sich durchsetzen*›

4 (in preference) eher; lieber; **I'd [rather] die ~:** eher *od.* lieber würde ich sterben; **I wouldn't give him a penny. I'd see him damned ~:** ich würde ihm keinen Cent geben, soll er zum Teufel gehen! (ugs.)

5 **~ of all** zuerst; (in importance) vor allem; **~ of all let me express my gratitude to you** zu[aller]erst *od.* als Erstes möchte ich Ihnen meinen Dank aussprechen; **~ and foremost** (basically) zunächst einmal; (in importance) vor allem; **~ and last** (almost entirely) in erster Linie; (reckoned altogether) im Ganzen; insgesamt

6 (~-class) **travel ~:** erster Klasse reisen

C *n.* **1** **the ~** (in sequence, rank) der/die/das Erste; **the ~ shall be last** (Bibl.) die Ersten werden die Letzten sein; **be the ~ to arrive** als Erster/Erste ankommen; **she is the ~ in the class** sie ist Klassenbeste *od.* die Beste in der Klasse; **~ among equals** Primus inter pares (geh.); **this is the ~ I've heard of it** das höre ich zum ersten Mal

2 **at ~:** zuerst; anfangs; **from the ~:** von Anfang an; **from ~ to last** von Anfang bis Ende; **I've always said from ~ to last that ...:** ich habe schon immer gesagt, dass ...; **it took five years, from ~ to last** es hat alles in allem fünf Jahre gedauert

3 ▸ⓘ **p. 1047** (day) **the ~ of May** der erste Mai; **the ~ [of the month]** der Erste [des Monats]

4 (Brit. Univ.) Eins, *die;* (person) **he's a ~ [in History]** er hat eine Eins [in Geschichte] bekommen; **get** *or* **take** *or* **be awarded a ~ in one's finals** sein Examen mit [der Note] Eins bestehen

5 (~ form) erste [Schul]klasse; Erste, *die* (Schuljargon)

6 (Motor Veh.) erster Gang; **in ~:** im ersten [Gang]; **change down to ~:** in den ersten [Gang] runterschalten

7 (pioneering feat) **a ~:** eine Pioniertat; **this is a ~ for him/the company** es ist das erste Mal, das er/die Firma so etwas unternimmt

8 *in pl.* (best-quality goods) erstklassige Ware; Ware von erster *od.* bester Qualität. *see also* **eighth B**

first: ~ ˈaid *n.* erste Hilfe; **give [sb.] ~ aid** [jmdm.] erste Hilfe leisten; **~-aid tent/post** *or* **station** Sanitätszelt, *das*/-wache, *die;* **~-aid box/kit** Verbandskasten, *der*/Erste-Hilfe-Ausrüstung, *die;* **~-ˈaider** /fɜːstˈeɪdə(r)/ *n.* Ersthelfer, *der/-helferin, die;* **~ ˈbase** ▸**base¹ A 3**; **~ ˈblood** ▸**blood A 1**; **~-born A** *adj.* erstgeboren; **B** *n.* Erstgeborene, *der/die;* **~ ˈclass** *n.* **1** erste Kategorie; (for produce) Klasse A; **2** (Transport) erste Klasse; **travel in the ~ class** erster Klasse reisen; **3** (Brit. Univ.) ▸**first C 4**; **4** (Post) *bevorzugt beförderte Post;* **~-class A** /ˈ--/ *adj.* **1** (of the ~ class) **~-class carriage** Erste[r]-Klasse-Wagen, *der;* **~-class ticket** Fahrkarte erster Klasse; **~-class compartment** Erste[r]-Klasse-Abteil, *das;* Abteil erster Klasse; **~-class honours degree** (Brit. Univ.) Prädikatsexamen, *das;* **~-class mail** *or* **post** *bevorzugt beförderte Post;* **~-class stamp** *Briefmarke für bevorzugt beförderte Post;* **2** (excellent) erstklassig; **a ~-class idiot** (iron.) ein Vollidiot; **B** /-ˈ-/ *adv.* **1** (by the ~ class) erster Klasse ‹*reisen*›; **send a letter ~-class** *einen Brief bevorzugt befördern lassen;* **2** (coll.: excellently) prima (ugs.); großartig; **~ ˈcoat** *n.* (of paint) erster Anstrich; **~ ˈcousin** ▸**cousin**; **~-degree** *attrib. adj.* **1** (Med.) ‹*Verbrennung*› ersten Grades; **2** (esp. Amer. Law) schwer ‹*Mord*›; **~ eˈdition** *n.* Erstausgabe, *die;* **~ ˈfloor** ▸**floor A 2**; **~ form** ▸**form A 4**; **~ ˈfruits** *n. pl.* Erstlinge *Pl.;* (fig.) erste Ergebnisse; **~ ˈgear** *n., no pl.* (Motor Veh.) erster Gang; *see also* **gear A 1**; **~-hand** *adj.* aus erster Hand *nachgestellt;* **from ~-hand experience** aus eigener Erfahrung; **have ~-hand knowledge of sth.** etw. aus erster Hand wissen; **have ~-hand acquaintance with suffering** viel Leid erfahren haben; *see also* **hand A 10**; **F~ ˈLady** *n.* First Lady, *die;* **~ language** *n.* Erstsprache, *die;* **~ lieuˈtenant** ▸**lieutenant 1**; **~ ˈlight** *n.* **at ~ light** im *od.* beim Morgengrauen

firstly /ˈfɜːstlɪ/ *adv.* zunächst [einmal]; (followed by 'secondly') erstens

first: ~ name *n.* Vorname, *der;* **be on ~-name terms with sb.** jmdn. mit Vornamen anreden; **~-named** *attrib. adj.* erstgenannt...; **~ ˈnight** *n.* (Theatre) Premiere, *die;* **~-night nerves/audience** Premierenfieber, *das*/-publikum, *das;* **~ off** *adv.* (coll.) zuerst; **~ ofˈfender** *n.* Ersttäter, *der;* **~ ˈofficer** *n.* (Naut.) Erster Offizier; **~ ˈperson** ▸**person 4**; **~ person ˈshooter** *n.* Ego-Shooter, *der;* **~ ˈproof** ▸**proof A 6**; **~-rate A** /ˈ--/ *adj.* **1** (excellent) erstklassig; **2** (coll.) **feel a ~-rate fool** (iron.) sich (*Dat.*) wie ein Dummkopf ersten Ranges vorkommen; **B** /-ˈ-/ *adv.* (coll.) prima (ugs.); großartig; **~ ˈreading** ▸**reading 7**; **~ refusal** ▸**refusal**; **~ school** *n.* (Brit.) ≈ Grundschule, *die;* **F~ ˈSecretary** *n.* Erster Sekretär; **~ ˈstrike** *n.* (Mil.) Erstschlag, *der;* Präventivschlag, *der;* **~-strike capability** Präventivschlagkapazität, *die;* **~ ˈstring** ▸**string A 2**; **~-time** *attrib. adj.* **~-time voter** Erstwähler, *der;* **~-time buyer** *jmd., der zum ersten Mal ein eigenes Haus/eine Eigentumswohnung kauft;* **~ ˈwater** ▸**water A 4**

f

first school

► **primary school**

firth /fɜːθ/ *n.* Förde, *die*

'fir tree ►**fir 1**

fiscal /'fɪskl/ *adj.* fiskalisch; finanzpolitisch; **~ policy** Fiskal- *od.* Finanzpolitik, *die;* **~ year** (Brit.) Geschäftsjahr, *das;* Rechnungsjahr, *das;* (Amer.) Finanzjahr, *das;* Etatjahr, *das;* **~ autonomy** Finanzhoheit, *die*

fiscally /'fɪskəlɪ/ *adv.* fiskalisch; finanzpolitisch

fish /fɪʃ/

A *n., pl. same or* (esp. child lang./poet.) **~es** **1** Fisch, *der;* **~ and chips** Fisch mit Pommes frites; **~ and chip shop** ≈ Fischbraterei, *die;* **a big ~ in a little pond** (fig.) ein Großer bei den Kleinen; **a little ~ in a big pond** (fig.) nur einer von vielen; **[be] like a ~ out of water** [sich] wie ein Fisch auf dem Trockenen [fühlen]; **drink like a ~** (coll.) wie ein Loch saufen (derb); **have other ~ to fry** (fig. coll.) Wichtigeres zu tun haben; **neither ~ nor fowl** (fig.) weder Fisch noch Fleisch (ugs.); **there are plenty more ~ in the sea** (fig. coll.) es gibt noch andere auf der Welt **2** (Astrol.) **the F~[es]** die Fische; *see also* **archer 2** **3** (coll.: person) **queer ~:** komischer Kauz; **big ~:** großes Tier; großer *od.* dicker Fisch (ugs., scherzh.); **cold ~:** kalter Fisch (ugs.); **the poor ~!** der arme Tropf!

B *v.i.* **1** fischen; (with rod) angeln; **go ~ing** fischen/angeln gehen; **go trout-~ing** auf Forellenfang gehen; **~ in troubled waters** (fig.) im Trüben fischen **2** (fig. coll.) (try to get information) auf Informationen aus sein; (delve) **~ around in one's bag** in der Tasche herumsuchen

C *v.t.* **1** fischen; fangen ‹*Fisch*›; (with rod) angeln; **~ a river/lake** in einem Fluss/See fischen/angeln **2** (fig.: take, pull) [heraus]fischen (ugs.) **(out of** aus)

(Phrasal verbs)

- **~ for** *v.t.* **1** fischen/angeln; fischen/angeln auf (+ *Akk.*) (Anglerjargon) **2** (fig. coll.) suchen nach; **be ~ing for sth.** auf etw. (*Akk.*) aus sein (ugs.)
- **~ 'out** *v.t.* (fig. coll.) herausfischen (ugs.); **~ sb./a dead body out of the river** jmdn./eine Leiche aus dem Fluss fischen (ugs.)
- **~ 'up** *v.t.* herausfischen

fish: ~ bone *n.* [Fisch]gräte, *die;* **~bowl** *n.* Fischglas, *das;* **~ cake** *n.* (Cookery) Fischfrikadelle, *die;* **~ course** *n.* Fischgang, *der*

fisherman /'fɪʃəmən/ *n., pl.* **fishermen** /'fɪʃəmən/ ►**❶ p. 1260** Fischer, *der;* (angler) Angler, *der;* **~'s story** Seemannsgarn, *das*

fishery /'fɪʃərɪ/ *n.* **1** *no pl., no indef. art.* (fishing) Fischfang, *der;* Fischerei, *die* **2** (fishing grounds) Fischfanggebiet, *das;* Fischereigewässer, *das;* **inshore fisheries** Küstenfischerei, *die;* **deep-sea fisheries** Hochseefischerei, *die*

fishery pro'tection vessel *n.* (Naut.) Fischereischutzboot, *das*

fish: ~eye lens *n.* (Photog.) Fischaugenobjektiv, *das;* **~ farm** *n.* Fischzucht[anlage], *die;* **~ farming** *n.* Fischzucht, *die;* **~ 'finger** *n.* Fischstäbchen, *das;* **~ fork** *n.* Fischgabel, *die;* **~-glue** *n.* Fischleim, *der;* **~-hook** *n.* Angelhaken, *der*

fishing /'fɪʃɪŋ/ *n.* (occupation) Fischen, *das;* (with rod) Angeln, *das; attrib.* Fischerei-; **freshwater ~:** Süßwasserfischerei, *die;* **~ craft** *pl.* Fischereifahrzeuge *Pl.*

fishing: ~ boat *n.* Fischerboot, *das;* **~ expedition** *n.* **1** Fangfahrt, *die;* **go on a ~ expedition** auf Fischfang gehen; **2** (fig.) Schnüffeltour, *die* (ugs.); **~ fleet** *n.* Fischereiflotte, *die;* **~ grounds** *n. pl.* Fischgründe *Pl.;* **~ industry** *n.* Fischerei[industrie], *die;* **~ licence** *ns.* Angelschein, *der;* Fischereischein, *der;* **~ limits** *n. pl.* Fischereigrenze, *die;* **~ line** *n.* Angelschnur, *die;* **~ net** *n.* Fischernetz, *das;* **~ permit** *ns.* Angelschein, *der;* Fischereischein, *der;* **~ rights** *n. pl.* Fischereirecht, *das;* **~ rod** *n.* Angelrute, *die;* **~ smack** *n.* Fischkutter, *der;* **~ story** *n.* Seemannsgarn, *das;* **~ tackle** *n.* Angelgeräte *Pl.;* **~ vessel** *n.* Fischereifahrzeug, *das;* **~ village** *n.* Fischerdorf, *das*

fish: ~ kettle *n.* Fischkessel, *der;* **~ knife** *n.* Fischmesser, *das;* **~ knife and -fork** Fischbesteck, *das;* **~ ladder** *n.* Fischleiter, *die;* Fischpass, *der;* **~like** *adj.* fischartig; **~meal** *n.* Fischmehl, *das;* **~monger** /'fɪʃmʌŋgə(r)/ *n.* ►**❶ p. 1260** (Brit.) Fischhändler, *der*/-händlerin, *die;* **a ~monger's** ein Fischgeschäft; *see also* **baker; ~net** *n.* Fischnetz, *das;* **~net stockings** Netzstrümpfe; **~ paste** *n.* Fischpaste, *die;* **~ pond** *n.* Fischteich, *der;* **~ restaurant** *n.* Fischrestaurant, *das;* **~ shop** *n.* Fischgeschäft, *das;* **~ slice** *n.* Wender, *der;* (carving knife) Fischvorlegemesser, *das;* **~ 'supper** *n.* Fisch[abend]essen, *das;* (fish and chips from a takeaway) Fisch mit Pommes frites; **~ tank** *n.* Fischkasten, *der;* Fischbehälter, *der;* **~wife** *n.* (derog.) Fischweib, *das* (veralt.)

fishy /'fɪʃɪ/ *adj.* **1** fischartig; **~ smell/taste** Fischgeruch/-geschmack, *der* **2** (coll.: questionable) verdächtig; zweifelhaft, fragwürdig ‹*Umstände*›; nicht ganz astrein (ugs.) ‹*Sache*›; **there's something ~ about this whole business** an der ganzen Sache ist was faul (ugs.)

fissile /'fɪsaɪl/ *adj.* (Nucl. Phys.) fissil (fachspr.); spaltbar

fission /'fɪʃn/ *n.* **1** (Nucl. Phys.) [Kern]spaltung, *die;* Fission, *die* (fachspr.) **2** (Biol.) [Zell]teilung, *die;* Fission, *die* (fachspr.)

fissionable /'fɪʃənəbl/ *adj.* (Nucl. Phys.) spaltbar; fissil (fachspr.)

fissure /'fɪʃə(r)/ *n.* Riss, *der;* (Geol.) Erdspalte, *die;* Bodenriss, *der*

fist /fɪst/ *n.* **1** Faust, *die* **2** (coll.: hand) Hand, *die;* Pfote, *die* (salopp); (joc.: handwriting) Handschrift, *die;* Klaue, *die* (ugs. abwertend)

'fist fight *n.* Schlägerei, *die*

fistful /'fɪstfʊl/ *n.* Handvoll, *die;* **a ~ of coins** eine Hand voll Münzen

fisticuffs /'fɪstɪkʌfs/ *n. pl.* Handgreiflichkeiten *Pl.;* **the quarrel ended in ~:** der Streit endete mit einer Schlägerei

fistula /'fɪstjʊlə/ *n.* (Med., Zool.) Fistel, *die*

fit¹ /fɪt/ *n.* **1** Anfall, *der;* **~ of coughing** Hustenanfall, *der;* **fainting ~:** Ohnmachtsanfall, *der;* **collapse in a ~:** einen Kollaps *od.* Anfall erleiden; zusammenbrechen; **epileptic ~:** epileptischer Anfall **2** (fig.) [plötzliche] Anwandlung; **give sb. a ~** (startle sb.) jmdn. einen Schrecken einjagen; (outrage sb.) jmdn. aus der Haut fahren lassen (ugs.); **[almost] have** *or* **throw a ~:** [fast] Zustände kriegen (ugs.); **she'll have a ~ when she hears that** (fig. coll.) sie kriegt einen Anfall, wenn sie das erfährt (ugs.); **have forty ~s** (coll.) Zustände kriegen (ugs.); einen Anfall bekommen (ugs.); **be in ~s of laughter** sich vor Lachen biegen; **sb./sth. has sb. in ~s [of laughter]** jmd. ruft dröhnendes Gelächter bei jmdm. hervor/etw. löst dröhnendes Gelächter bei jmdm. aus; **in a ~ of ...:** in einem Anfall *od.* einer Anwandlung von ...; **in** *or* **by ~s [and starts]** mit [häufigen] Unterbrechungen

fit²

A *adj.* **1** (suitable) geeignet; **~ to eat** *or* **to be eaten/for human consumption** essbar/zum Verzehr geeignet; **be ~ to be seen** sich sehen lassen können; *see also* **survival 1**

2 (worthy) würdig; wert; **a man not ~ to hold high office** ein Mann, der eines hohen Amtes nicht würdig ist; *see also* **candle A 1**

3 (right and proper) richtig; **as is only ~ [and proper]** wie es sich gehört *od.* (geh.) gebührt; **see** *or* **think ~ [to do sth.]** es für richtig *od.* angebracht halten[, etw. zu tun]; **do as you see** *or* **think ~:** tu, was du für richtig hältst

4 (ready) **be ~ to drop** zum Umfallen müde sein

5 (healthy) gesund; fit (ugs.); in Form (ugs.); **keep** *or* **stay ~:** sich fit halten; fit bleiben; **get ~ again after an illness** nach einer Krankheit wieder zu Kräften kommen; **be ~ and well** in guter körperlicher Verfassung sein; **~ for duty** *or* **service** dienstfähig *od.* -tauglich; **~ for work/travel** arbeits-/reisefähig; *see also* **fiddle A 1**

B *n.* Passform, *die;* **it is a good/bad ~:** es sitzt *od.* passt gut/nicht gut; **be an excellent ~:** einen tadellosen Sitz haben; wie angegossen sitzen *od.* passen; **the coat is a tight ~:** das Jackett sitzt stramm *od.* ist eng; **three in the back seat is a tight ~:** drei auf dem Rücksitz ist sehr eng; **I can just get it in the suitcase, but it's a tight ~** (fig.) ich kriege es noch in den Koffer, aber nur gerade so (ugs.)

C *v.t.,* **-tt-** **1** ‹*Kleider:*› passen (+ *Dat.*); ‹*Schlüssel:*› passen in (+ *Akk.*); ‹*Deckel, Bezug:*› passen auf (+ *Akk.*); **the suit ~s him properly** der Anzug passt ihm gut *od.* sitzt gut; **make sth. to ~:** etw. passend machen

2 (Dressm. etc.) anpassen ‹*Kleidungsstück, Brille*›; **when may I come to be ~ted?** wann kann ich zur Anprobe kommen?

3 (correspond to, suit) entsprechen (+ *Dat.*); (make correspond) abstimmen (**to** auf + *Akk.*); anpassen (**to** an + *Akk.*); **the description ~s this man** die Beschreibung passt auf diesen Mann *od.* trifft auf diesen Mann zu; **the translation ~s the context** die Übersetzung wird dem Kontext gerecht; **~ the bill** angemessen sein

4 (put into place) anbringen (**to** an + *Dat. od. Akk.*); einbauen ‹*Motor, Ersatzteil*›; einsetzen ‹*Scheibe, Tür, Schloss*›; (equip) ausstatten

5 (make competent) befähigen (**for** zu); **the experience helped to ~ her for the task** die Erfahrung trug dazu bei, dass sie für die Aufgabe gerüstet war

D *v.i.,* **-tt-** passen; (agree) zusammenpassen; übereinstimmen; **~ well** ‹*Kleidungsstück:*› gut sitzen; **the two pieces ~ together to form a screwdriver** die beiden Teile zusammen ergeben einen Schraubenzieher; **we must find a lid that ~s** wir müssen einen passenden Deckel finden; *see also* **cap A 1; glove 1**

(Phrasal verbs)

- **~ 'in**

A *v.t.* **1** unterbringen **2** (install) einbauen **3** (to a schedule) einen Termin geben (+ *Dat.*); unterbringen, einschieben ‹*Treffen, Besuch, Sitzung*›; **I could ~ you in just before lunch** so kurz vor Mittag hätte ich Zeit für Sie; **the hairdresser usually manages to ~ me in** gewöhnlich kann mich der Friseur zwischendurch drannehmen (ugs.); **~ sth. in with sth.** etw. mit etw. abstimmen

B *v.i.* **1** hineinpassen **2** (be in accordance) **~ in with sth.** mit etw. übereinstimmen; **~ in with sb.'s plan/ideas** in jmds. Plan/Konzept (*Akk.*) passen; **how does that ~ in?** wie passt das dazu *od.* ins Ganze?; **it didn't ~ in with our plans** es ließ sich nicht mit unseren Plänen vereinbaren; **I'll just ~ in with you/your arrangements** ich richte mich ganz nach dir/deinen Plänen **3** (settle harmoniously) ‹*Person:*› sich anpassen (**with** an + *Akk.*); **~ in easily with a group** sich leicht in eine Gruppe einfügen; **he ~s in well here/with the others** er passt gut hierher/mit den anderen zusammen

- **~ 'out** *v.t.* ausstatten; (for expedition etc.) ausrüsten
- **~ 'up** *v.t.* (fix) anbringen ‹*Lampe, Waschbecken*›; (install, mount) aufstellen ‹*Arbeitsbank usw.*›; **~ sb./sth. up with sth.** jmdn./etw. mit einer Sache versehen *od.* ausstatten; **~ a room up as an office** ein Zimmer als Büro einrichten

fitful /'fɪtfl/ *adj.* unbeständig; unruhig ‹*Schlaf*›; vereinzelt ‹*Schüsse*›; ungleichmäßig ‹*Fortgang, Arbeitsweise*›; launisch ‹*Brise*›

fitfully /'fɪtfəlɪ/ *adv.* unregelmäßig; sporadisch ‹*arbeiten*›; unruhig ‹*schlafen*›; **the sun shone ~:** die Sonne kam vereinzelt durch

fitfulness /'fɪtflnɪs/ *n., no pl.* Unbeständigkeit, *die;* (of sleep) Unregelmäßigkeit, *die*

fitment /'fɪtmənt/ *n.* (piece of furniture) Einrichtungsgegenstand, *der;* (piece of equipment) Zubehörteil, *das;* **~s** Ausstattung, *die*

fitness /'fɪtnɪs/ *n., no pl.* **1** (physical) Fitness, *die;* **~ for active service** (Mil.) Wehrdiensttauglichkeit, *die* **2** (suitability) Eignung, *die;* (appropriateness) Angemessenheit, *die;* **have a sense of the ~ of things** ein Gefühl dafür haben, was angebracht *od.* angemessen ist

'fitness centre, 'fitness studio *ns.* Fitnessstudio, *das*

fitted /'fɪtɪd/ *adj.* **1** (suited) geeignet (**for** für, zu) **2** (shaped) tailliert, auf Taille gearbeitet

‹Kleider›; ~ carpet Teppichboden, der; ~ sheet Spannbettuch, das; ~ kitchen/cupboards Einbauküche, die/Einbauschränke

fitter /ˈfɪtə(r)/ n. ▸ⓘ p. 1260 **1** Monteur, der; (of pipes) Installateur, der; (of machines) Maschinenschlosser, der; electrical ~: Elektriker, der; Elektroinstallateur, der **2** (of clothes) Schneider, der/Schneiderin, die (als Zuschneider u. für Änderungen)

fitting /ˈfɪtɪŋ/

A adj. (appropriate) passend; angemessen; geeignet ‹Moment, Zeitpunkt›; günstig, passend ‹Gelegenheit›; (becoming) schicklich (geh.) ‹Benehmen›; I thought it ~ to inform him ich hielt es für angebracht, ihn zu informieren; it is not ~ for a young woman ...: es schickt sich nicht für eine junge Dame, ...

B n. **1** usu. in pl. (fixture) Anschluss, der; (connecting piece used for installations) Fitting, das (Technik); ~s (furniture) Ausstattung, die; a car with luxurious ~s ein Wagen mit Luxusausstattung; electrical ~s Elektroinstallationen Pl.; see also fixture 1 **2** (of clothes) Anprobe, die; go to the tailor's for a ~: zur Anprobe gehen **3** (Brit.: size) Größe, die; shoes of a wide/narrow ~: weite/enge Schuhe

fittingly /ˈfɪtɪŋlɪ/ adv. passend ‹sich kleiden›; angemessen ‹enden›; schicklich ‹sich benehmen›

fitting: ~-room n. Anprobe, die; ~-shop n. Montagehalle, die

five /faɪv/ ▸ⓘ p. 894, ▸ⓘ p. 1001, ▸ⓘ p. 1358

A adj. **1** fünf; see also eight A **2** ~-finger exercise (Mus.: also fig.) Fingerübung, die; ~ o'clock shadow [nachmittäglicher] Stoppelbart (ugs.); see also week

B n. (number, symbol) Fünf, die; see also eight B 1, 3, 4

five-and-ˈdime, five-and-ˈten n. (Amer.) Billigkaufhaus, das

ˈfive-figure adj. fünfstellig

fivefold /ˈfaɪvfəʊld/ adj., adv. fünffach; see also eightfold

fiver /ˈfaɪvə(r)/ n. ▸ⓘ p. 1332 (coll.) (Brit.) Fünfpfundschein, der; (Amer.) Fünfdollarschein, der

fives /faɪvz/ n. sing.: ein Wandballspiel; Eton /ˈiːtn/ ~ Wandballspiel mit drei Wänden; Rugby ~: Wandballspiel mit vier Wänden

five: ~-star adj. Fünf-Sterne-‹Hotel, General›; (fig.) ausgezeichnet; ~-ˈyear plan n. Fünfjahresplan, der

fix /fɪks/

A v.t. **1** (place firmly, attach, prevent from moving) befestigen; festmachen; (fig.: imprint) einprägen; ~ a post in[to] the ground einen Pfosten im Boden verankern; ~ a stone firmly into position einen Stein an der vorgesehenen Stelle einsetzen; ~ sth. to/on sth. etw. an/auf etw. (Dat.) befestigen od. festmachen; ~ shelves to the wall/a handle on the door Regale an der Wand/eine Klinke an der Tür anbringen; ~ bayonets Bajonette aufpflanzen; ~ sth. in one's mind sich (Dat.) etw. fest einprägen

2 (direct steadily) richten ‹Blick, Gedanken, Augen› ([up]on auf + Akk.); setzen ‹Hoffnung› ([up]on auf + Akk.); her mind was [firmly] ~ed on her work sie war ganz auf ihre Arbeit fixiert; his thoughts were ~ed elsewhere er war mit seinen Gedanken [ganz] woanders

3 (decide, specify) festsetzen, festlegen ‹Termin, Preis, Strafe, Grenze›; (settle, agree on) ausmachen; (allocate) übertragen ‹Verantwortung›; zuschieben ‹Schuld› ([up]on + Dat.); ~ the price at £50 den Preis auf 50 Pfund festsetzen; nothing's been ~ed yet es ist noch nichts fest [ausgemacht od. beschlossen]; it was ~ed that ...: es wurde beschlossen od. vereinbart, dass ...

4 (repair) in Ordnung bringen; reparieren; need ~ing repariert werden müssen

5 (arrange) arrangieren; ~ a rehearsal for Friday eine Probe für od. auf Freitag (Akk.) ansetzen; they tried to ~ things so that ...: sie versuchten es so zu arrangieren, dass ...; have you anything ~ed for Saturday evening? hast du [für] Samstagabend schon etwas vor?; nothing definite has been ~ed yet es ist noch nichts Endgültiges vereinbart od. ausgemacht

6 (manipulate fraudulently) manipulieren ‹Rennen, Kampf›; bestechen ‹Zeugen›; the whole thing was ~ed das war eine abgekartete Sache (ugs.)

7 (Amer. coll.: prepare) machen ‹Essen, Kaffee, Drink›; ~ one's hair sich frisieren; ~ one's face sich schminken

8 (coll.: deal with) in Ordnung bringen; regeln; ~ sb. (get even with) es jmdm. heimzahlen; (kill) jmdn. kaltmachen (salopp); Don't bother about that. I'll ~ things with her Mach dir deswegen keine Sorgen. Ich regle das mit ihr od. bringe das mit ihr in Ordnung; I'll soon ~ that (prevent) das werd ich zu verhindern wissen; that'll ~ her dann kann sie nichts mehr machen

9 (make permanent) fixieren ‹Farben, Foto, Gewebe›

10 (coll.: castrate) kastrieren

11 (Bot.: assimilate) ‹Pflanze:› binden

B v.i. **1** (coll.: arrange) ~ for sb. to do sth. es arrangieren, dass jmd. etw. tun kann

2 (Amer. coll.: intend) vorhaben; be ~ing to do sth. vorhaben, etw. zu tun

3 (sl.: inject narcotics) fixen (Drogenjargon)

C v. refl. ▸B 3

D n. **1** (coll.: predicament) Patsche, die (ugs.); Klemme, die (ugs.); be in a ~: in der Klemme sein (ugs.); get oneself in[to] a ~: sich (Dat.) eine schöne Suppe einbrocken (ugs.)

2 (Naut.) Standort, der; Position, die; radio ~: Funkortung, die

3 (sl.: of narcotics) Fix, der (Drogenjargon)

4 (Amer. coll.: bribery) Bestechung, die; (illicit arrangement) abgekartete Sache (ugs.)

Phrasal verbs

- ~ on v.t. **1** /-ˈ-/ anbringen **2** /ˈ--/ (decide on) sich entscheiden für; (determine) festsetzen, festlegen ‹Termin›; ~ on doing sth. beschließen, etw. zu tun
- ~ ˈup v.t. **1** (arrange) arrangieren; festsetzen, ausmachen ‹Termin, Treffpunkt›; we've nothing ~ed up for tonight wir haben noch nichts vor [für] heute Abend; let's ~ up when and where we'll next meet machen wir aus, wann und wo wir uns das nächste Mal treffen; we ~ed up that ...: wir vereinbarten, dass ...; I'll ~ up for you to accompany me ich werde es arrangieren, dass du mich begleiten kannst **2** (provide) versorgen; (provide with accommodation) unterbringen; ~ sb. up with sth. jmdm. etw. verschaffen od. besorgen; ~ sb. up [with a bed] for the night jmdn. für die Nacht unterbringen **3** (establish) get oneself ~ed up sich etablieren; you can stay with us until you get yourself ~ed up du kannst bei uns wohnen, bis du ein Zimmer/eine Wohnung usw. hast; ~ sb. up in the spare room jmdn. im Gästezimmer unterbringen **4** (furnish) einrichten

fixate /fɪkˈseɪt/ v.t. (Psych.) fixieren (upon auf + Akk.)

fixation /fɪkˈseɪʃn/ n. (fixing, being fixed, obsession, Psych.) Fixierung, die; he has a ~ about his mother er ist zu stark auf seine Mutter fixiert

fixed /fɪkst/ adj. **1** pred. (coll.: placed) how are you/is he etc. ~ for cash/fuel? wie siehts bei dir/ihm usw. mit dem Geld/Treibstoff aus? (ugs.); they are better ~ financially than we are sie stehen finanziell besser da als wir; how are you ~ for this evening? was hast du [für] heute Abend vor? **2** (not variable) fest; starr ‹Lächeln, Gesichtsausdruck›; ~ assets Anlagevermögen, das; ~ cost Fixkosten Pl.; ~ price Festpreis, der; ~-interest stocks festverzinsliche Wertpapiere; ~ capital Anlagekapital, das; ~ focus (Photog.) Fixfokus, der; ~ idea fixe Idee; have no ~ ideas on sth. keine feste Vorstellung von etw. haben; ~ income festes Einkommen; ~-income investments Festgeldanlagen Pl.; ~ odds feste od. gleich bleibende Gewinnchancen; ~ salary Fixum, das; ~ star Fixstern, der; ~-wing aircraft Starrflügelflugzeug, das; Starrflügler, der; see also abode[1]; address B 1 **3** (firm, resolute) fest ‹Absicht›; be ~ in one's determination fest entschlossen sein; with the ~ intention of doing sth. in od. mit der festen Absicht, etw. zu tun

fixedly /ˈfɪksɪdlɪ/ adv. starr, unverwandt ‹blicken, lächeln›; stare ~ out of the window aus dem Fenster starren

fixed: ~ ˈpoint n. **1** (Phys.) Fixpunkt, der; Festpunkt, der; **2** (Computing) Festkomma, das; ~ price Festpreis, der; ~-rate attrib. adj. Festzins-; mit festem Zins nachgestellt

fixer /ˈfɪksə(r)/ n. **1** (Photog.) Fixiermittel, das **2** (coll.: person) Organisator, der; (derog.) Mittelsmann, der durch Schmiergeldzahlungen unlautere geschäftliche Transaktionen ermöglicht

fixings /ˈfɪksɪŋz/ n. pl. **1** (Brit.: screws, bolts, etc.) Kleinteile Pl. **2** (Amer. Cookery: trimmings) Beilagen Pl.

fixity /ˈfɪksɪtɪ/ n., no pl. Beständigkeit, die; ~ of purpose Zielstrebigkeit, die

fixture /ˈfɪkstʃə(r)/ n. **1** (furnishing) eingebautes Teil; (pipe etc.) fest verlegtes Rohr usw.; (accessory) festes Zubehörteil; ~s (Law) unbewegliches Inventar; ~s and fittings Ausstattung und Installationen; lighting ~s Beleuchtungskörper Pl. **2** (Sport) Veranstaltung, die; the Derby is an annual ~: das Derby findet jedes Jahr statt; ~ list Spielplan, der **3** (fig. joc.: established person or thing) [lebendes] Inventar (scherzh.); be a ~: zum Inventar gehören (scherzh.)

fizz /fɪz/

A v.i. [zischend] sprudeln

B n. **1** (effervescence) Sprudeln, das; the lemonade has lost its ~: die Limonade sprudelt nicht mehr **2** (coll.: effervescent drink) Sprudel, der; (flavoured) Brause[limonade], die (ugs.); gin ~: Ginfizz, der

fizzle /ˈfɪzl/ v.i. zischen

Phrasal verb

- ~ ˈout v.i. ‹Feuerwerk:› zischend verlöschen; ‹Begeisterung:› sich legen; ‹Kampagne:› im Sande verlaufen

fizzy /ˈfɪzɪ/ adj. sprudelnd; ~ lemonade Brause[limonade], die; ~ drinks kohlensäurehaltige Getränke; be ~: sprudeln

fjord /fjɔːd/ n. Fjord, der

fl. abbr. **1** = floor OG **2** = fluid fl.

flab /flæb/ n. (coll.) Fett, das; Speck, der (ugs.)

flabbergast /ˈflæbəgɑːst/ v.t. verblüffen; umhauen (ugs.); I was [absolutely] ~ed ich war [völlig] verblüfft; es hat mich [einfach] umgehauen (ugs.); she looked at them, ~ed sie sah sie völlig verblüfft an

flabby /ˈflæbɪ/ adj. schlaff ‹Muskeln, Bauch, Fleisch, Hände, Wangen, Brüste›; wabbelig (ugs.), schwammig ‹Bauch, Fleisch›; (fig.) schwammig; schwach ‹Willenskraft›

flaccid /ˈflæksɪd/ adj. schlaff; (fig.) lasch

flag[1] /flæg/

A n. Fahne, die; (small paper etc. device) Fähnchen, das; (national ~, ~ on ship) Flagge, die; red/white ~: rote/weiße Fahne; yellow ~: Quarantäneflagge, die; ~ of convenience billige Flagge (Seew.); ~ of truce Parlamentärflagge, die; keep the ~ flying (fig.) die Fahne hochhalten; show the ~ (fig.) seiner Repräsentationspflicht nachkommen; put the ~[s] out! (fig. coll.) Gott sei's getrommelt und gepfiffen! (salopp)

B v.t., -gg- **1** beflaggen ‹Gebäude›; (mark with ~s) [mit Fähnchen] markieren; (Computing) markieren; kennzeichnen **2** (communicate by ~ signals) [mit Fahne od. Fähnchen] signalisieren **3** ▸~ down

Phrasal verb

- ~ ˈdown v.t. [durch Winken] anhalten

flag[2] v.i., -gg- **1** (lose vigour) erlahmen; business is ~ging die Geschäfte lassen nach **2** ‹Blume:› den Kopf hängen lassen; ‹Pflanze:› schlappen (ugs.), die Blätter hängen lassen

flag[3]

A n. ▸flagstone

B v.t., -gg- mit Fliesen/Steinplatten belegen; fliesen ‹Fußboden›

flag: ~ captain n. (Navy) Kommandant des Flaggschiffs; ~ day n. **1** (Brit.) Tag der Straßensammlung für wohltätige Zwecke; **2** F~ Day (Amer.) 14. Juni als Gedenktag der Einführung der amerikanischen Nationalflagge

flagella pl. of flagellum

flagellate[1] /ˈflædʒəleɪt/ v.t. geißeln

f

f

flagellate² /ˈflædʒələt/ (Zool.)
A adj. geißelförmig; **∼ organism** ▸B
B n. Flagellat, der (fachspr.); Geißeltierchen, das

flagellation /flædʒəˈleɪʃn/ n. Flagellation, die; Geißelung, die

flagellum /fləˈdʒeləm/ n., pl. **flagella** /fləˈdʒelə/ 1 (Bot.: runner) Ausläufer, der 2 (Biol.) Flagellum, das; Geißel, die

flageolet /flædʒəˈlet, ˈflædʒəlet/ n. (Mus.) Flageolett, das

flag: ∼ lieutenant n. (Navy) Flaggleutnant, der; **∼ officer** n. (Navy) Flaggoffizier, der

flagon /ˈflægən/ n. 1 (with handle and spout; for Eucharist) Kanne, die 2 (big bottle) [bauchige] Weinflasche (in Bocksbeutelform)

ˈflagpole ▸**flagstaff**

flagrancy /ˈfleɪgrənsɪ/ n., no pl. Schändlichkeit, die; (of disregard, defiance) Schamlosigkeit, die

ˈflag rank n. (Navy) Rang eines Flaggoffiziers; ≈ Admiralsrang, der

flagrant /ˈfleɪgrənt/ adj. eklatant; flagrant ‹Verstoß›; (scandalous) ungeheuerlich; himmelschreiend ‹Unrecht›; schamlos ‹Verbrecher, Sünder›

flagrante delicto ▸**in flagrante [delicto]**

flagrantly /ˈfleɪgrəntlɪ/ adv. eklatant; flagrant ‹verstoßen›; unverhohlen ‹beleidigen›; **a ∼ criminal act** ein ungeheuerliches Verbrechen

flag: ∼ship n. (Navy) Flaggschiff, das; (fig. attrib.) führend…; **∼staff** n. Flaggenmast, der; Fahnenmast, der; (horizontal) Fahnenstange, die; (on ship) Flaggenstock, der (Seemannsspr.); **∼stone** n. Steinplatte, die; (for floor) Fliese, die; in pl. (pavement) Straßenpflaster, das; **∼ stop** (Amer.) ▸**request stop**

flail /fleɪl/
A v.i. [wild] um sich schlagen; ‹Propeller:› sich rasend drehen; **with arms ∼ing he tried to keep his balance** mit den Armen fuchtelnd, versuchte er, das Gleichgewicht zu halten
B v.t. (strike with ∼) dreschen; (strike as if with ∼) [wild] einschlagen auf (+ Akk.)
C n. Dreschflegel, der

flair /fleə(r)/ n. Gespür, das; (special ability) Talent, das; [natürliche] Begabung; **have ∼** (talent) Talent haben; talentiert sein; (for dress) Stil od. Geschmack haben; **have a ∼ for sth.** (talent) ein Talent od. eine Begabung für etw. haben; (instinct) ein [feines] Gespür für etw. haben; **have [quite] a ∼ for writing/[learning] languages** schriftstellerisch [recht] begabt sein/[recht] sprachbegabt sein; **he has a ∼ for making money** er weiß, wie man zu Geld kommt

flak /flæk/ n. Flakfeuer, das (Milit.); (gun) Flak, die (Milit.); **get a lot of ∼ for sth.** (fig.) wegen etw. [schwer] unter Beschuss geraten; **give sb. a lot of ∼ for sth.** (fig.) jmdn. wegen etw. [schwer] unter Beschuss nehmen

flake /fleɪk/
A n. 1 (of snow, soap, cereals) Flocke, die; (of dry skin) Schuppe, die; (of plaster) ≈ Bröckchen, das; (of metal) ≈ Span, der; (of enamel, paint) ≈ Splitter, der; (of pastry, rust) ≈ Krümel, der; (of chocolate, coconut) Raspel, die 2 (of fish's flesh) ≈ Stück, das 3 (shark as food) Seeaal, der
B v.i. ‹Stuck, Verputz, Stein:› abbröckeln; ‹Farbe, Rost, Emaille:› abblättern; ‹Haut:› sich schuppen

Phrasal verbs
- **∼ ˈoff** v.i. ‹Farbe, Rost, Emaille:› abblättern; ‹Stuck, Verputz, Stein:› abbröckeln
- **∼ ˈout** v.i. (coll.) umkippen (ugs.); **be ∼d out** total erschöpft sein

ˈflak jacket n. kugelsichere Weste

flaky /ˈfleɪkɪ/ adj. bröcklig ‹Farbe, Gips, Rost›; blättrig ‹Kruste›; schuppig ‹Haut›; **∼ pastry** Blätterteig, der

flambé /ˈflɑ̃beɪ/ (Cookery)
A adj. flambiert
B v.t. flambieren

flamboyance /flæmˈbɔɪəns/, **flamboyancy** /flæmˈbɔɪənsɪ/ n. Extravaganz, die; (of plumage) Pracht, die; (of clothes, lifestyle) Pracht, die; Pomp, der (abwertend)

flamboyant /flæmˈbɔɪənt/ adj. 1 extravagant; prächtig ‹Farben, Federkleid›; (derog.) großspurig ‹Wesen, Verhalten, Geste› 2 (Archit.) **∼ style** Flamboyantstil, der

flamboyantly /flæmˈbɔɪəntlɪ/ adv. extravagant; prächtig, extravagant ‹schmücken, kleiden›

flame /fleɪm/
A n. 1 Flamme, die; **be in ∼s** in Flammen stehen; **burst into ∼[s]** in Brand geraten; **go up in ∼s** in Flammen aufgehen 2 (colour) ≈ Rotorange, das 3 (joc.: sweetheart) Flamme, die (ugs.); **old ∼:** alte Flamme (ugs. veralt.). see also **fan¹ B**; **feed A 9** 3 (Computing) Flame, die
B v.i. 1 brennen 2 (glow) glühen
C v.t. (Computing) **∼ sb.** jmdm. eine Flame/Flames schicken; **the PC was ∼d** die PC wurde mit Flames überzogen

Phrasal verb
- **∼ ˈup** v.i. (lit. or fig.) aufflammen; ‹Fett:› anfangen zu brennen

flame: ∼-coloured adj. feuerfarben; **∼ gun** n. Flämmgerät, das

flameless /ˈfleɪmlɪs/ adj. ohne offene Flamme nachgestellt

flamenco /fləˈmeŋkəʊ/ n., pl. **∼s** Flamenco, der

flame: ∼-proof nicht entflammbar; flammfest; **∼-thrower** n. Flammenwerfer, der

flamer /ˈfleɪmə(r)/ n. (Computing sl.) Flamer, der/Flamerin, die

flaming /ˈfleɪmɪŋ/
A adj. 1 (bright-coloured) feuerrot; flammend ‹Rot, Abendhimmel›; hochrot ‹Wangen› 2 (very hot) glühend heiß; (coll.: passionate) heftig, leidenschaftlich ‹Auseinandersetzung›; **be in a ∼ temper** (coll.) geladen sein (salopp); kochen (ugs.); **∼ June** der heiße Juni 3 (coll.: damned) verdammt
B adv. 1 **∼ red** feuerrot 2 (coll.: damned) **he is too ∼ idle** or **lazy** er ist, verdammt noch mal, einfach zu faul (ugs.); **who does he ∼ well think he is?** verdammt noch mal, für wen hält der sich eigentlich? (ugs)
C n., no pl. (Computing sl.) Flaming, das

flamingo /fləˈmɪŋgəʊ/ n., pl. **∼s** or **∼es** (Ornith.) Flamingo, der

flammability /flæməˈbɪlɪtɪ/ ▸**inflammability**

flammable /ˈflæməbl/ ▸**inflammable 1**

flan /flæn/ n. **[fruit] ∼:** [Obst]torte, die; **[cheese] ∼** flache Pastete mit [Käse]füllung oder -belag

ˈflan case n. Tortenboden, der

Flanders /ˈflɑːndəz/ pr. n. Flandern (das)

flange /flændʒ/ n. Flansch, der; (of wheel) Spurkranz, der

flanged /flændʒd/ adj. mit Flansch/Spurkranz versehen

flank /flæŋk/
A n. (of person) Seite, die; (of animal; also Mil.) Flanke, die; (of mountain, building) Seite, die; Flanke, die (selten); (of beef) Dünnung, die; **attack sb.'s ∼** (Mil.) jmdn. von der Flanke her angreifen; **∼ forward** (Rugby) Außenstürmer, der
B v.t. 1 flankieren; **a road ∼ed by** or **with trees** eine von Bäumen flankierte Straße 2 **∼ing movement** Flankenangriff, der

flannel /ˈflænl/
A n. 1 (fabric) Flanell, der 2 in pl. (trousers) Flanellhose, die; (garments) Flanellsachen Pl.; **cricketing ∼s** Kricketkleidung [aus Flanell] 3 (Brit.) (for washing oneself) Waschlappen, der; (for washing the floor) Aufwischlappen, der 4 (Brit. coll.) (verbose nonsense) Geschwafel, das (ugs. abwertend); (flattery) Schmeicheleien Pl
B attrib. adj. Flanell-

flannelette /flænəˈlet/ n. [Baumwoll]flanell, der

flap /flæp/
A v.t., **-pp-** schlagen; **∼ its wings** mit den Flügeln schlagen; (at short intervals) [mit den Flügeln] flattern
B v.i., **-pp-** 1 ‹Flügel:› schlagen; ‹Segel, Fahne, Vorhang:› flattern 2 **sb.'s ears were ∼ping** (fig. coll.) jmd. hat mitgehört; (was very interested) jmd. spitzte die Ohren 3 (fig. coll.: panic) die Nerven verlieren; **stop ∼ping** reg dich ab (ugs.)
C n. 1 Klappe, die; (of leather shorts) Hosenlatz, der; (of saddle) Seitenblatt, das; (envelope seal, tongue of shoe) Lasche, die; (of table) klappbarer Teil 2 (fig. coll.: panic) **be in a ∼:** furchtbar aufgeregt sein; **get [oneself] in[to] a ∼:** sich furchtbar aufregen; durchdrehen (ugs.); **there's a ∼ on** es herrscht große Aufregung

flapjack /ˈflæpdʒæk/ n. 1 (oatcake) süßer Haferkeks 2 (pancake) Pfannkuchen, der

flare /fleə(r)/
A v.i. 1 (blaze) flackern; (fig.) ausbrechen; **tempers ∼d** die Gemüter erhitzten sich 2 (widen) sich erweitern; (Dressm., Tailoring) ausgestellt sein 3 (billow) sich bauschen
B n. 1 (as signal; also Naut.) Leuchtsignal, das; (from pistol) Leuchtkugel, die; (Aeronaut.: to illuminate target) Leuchtbombe, die 2 (blaze of light) Lichtschein, der 3 (widening) **skirt/trousers with ∼s** ausgestellter Rock/ausgestellte Hose 4 in pl. (trousers) Schlaghose, die; ausgestellte Hose

Phrasal verb
- **∼ ˈup** v.i. 1 (burn more fiercely) aufflackern; auflodern 2 (break out) [wieder] ausbrechen; **∼ up again** ‹Kampf, Streit:› wieder aufflackern 3 (become angry) aufbrausen; aus der Haut fahren (ugs.). See also **flare-up**

flared /fleəd/ adj. (Dressm., Tailoring) ausgestellt

flare: ∼-path n. (Aeronaut.) Anflugbefeuerung, die; **∼-up** n. 1 (of fire) Aufflackern, das; Auflodern, das; 2 (of violence, rioting) Ausbruch, der; **a new ∼-up** ein erneutes Aufflackern; 3 (of rage) Aufregung, die

flash /flæʃ/
A n. 1 (of light) Aufleuchten, das; Aufblinken, das; (as signal) Lichtsignal, das; Blinkzeichen, das; **∼es from a gun** Mündungsfeuer eines Gewehrs; **did you see the ∼?** hast du es aufblitzen od. aufleuchten sehen?; **∼ of lightning** Blitz, der; **[as] quick as a ∼** (coll.) schnell wie ein Blitz (ugs.); **reply as quick as a ∼** (coll.) wie aus der Pistole geschossen antworten (ugs.); **give a ∼ of the headlamps** (Motor Veh.) aufblenden; die Lichthupe betätigen; **∼ in the pan** (fig. coll.) Zufallstreffer, der 2 (Photog.) Blitzlicht, das; **use [a] ∼:** mit Blitzlicht fotografieren; **∼ photo** Blitzlichtaufnahme, die 3 (fig.) **∼ of genius** or **inspiration** or **brilliance** Geistesblitz, der; **∼ of wit** geistreicher Einfall; **∼ of insight** or **intuition** Eingebung, die; **∼ of temper** or **anger** Wutausbruch, der 4 (instant) **be over in a ∼:** gleich od. im Nu vorbei sein; **the answer came to me in a ∼:** blitzartig kam mir die Antwort; **it all happened in a ∼:** es geschah alles blitzschnell 5 (Radio, Telev.) ▸**newsflash** 6 (Cinemat.) [kurze] Einblendung 7 (Brit. Mil.: insignia) Abzeichen, das
B v.t. 1 aufleuchten lassen; **∼ a torch in sb.'s face** jmdm. mit einer Taschenlampe ins Gesicht leuchten; **∼ a signal/warning** blinken/zur Warnung blinken; **∼ a message** eine Botschaft blinken; **∼ the/one's headlights** aufblenden; die Lichthupe betätigen; **∼ sb. with one's headlamps** jmdn. anblinken od. mit der Lichthupe anblenden 2 (fig.) **her eyes ∼ed fire** ihre Augen sprühten Feuer od. funkelten böse; **her eyes ∼ed back defiance** ihre Augen funkelten trotzig 3 (give briefly and suddenly) **∼ sb. a smile/glance** jmdm. ein Lächeln/einen Blick zuwerfen 4 (display briefly) kurz zeigen; (flaunt) zur Schau tragen ‹Reichtum›; funkeln lassen ‹Diamanten›; **∼ one's money about** or **around** mit [dem] Geld um sich werfen (ugs.) 5 (Communications) durchgeben; **∼ news across the world** Nachrichten in die ganze Welt ausstrahlen
C v.i. 1 aufleuchten; **the lightning ∼ed** es blitzte; **a signal was ∼ing** ein Lichtsignal blitzte; **the lighthouse ∼es once a minute** der Leuchtturm gibt einmal in der Minute ein Signal; **∼ing light** Blinklicht, das; (device) (Naut.) Blinkfeuer, das; (Motor Veh.) Blinkleuchte, die; **∼ at sb. with one's headlamps** jmdn. anblinken od. mit der Lichthupe anblenden 2 (fig.) **her eyes ∼ed in anger** ihre Augen blitzten vor Zorn 3 (move swiftly) **∼ by** or **past** vorbeiflitzen (ugs.); (fig.) ‹Zeit, Ferien:› wie im Fluge vergehen 4 (burst suddenly into perception) **sth. ∼ed through my mind** etw. schoss mir durch den

Kopf; **the truth ~ed upon me** die Wahrheit kam über mich; **his whole life ~ed before his eyes** sein ganzes Leben rollte noch einmal vor seinen Augen ab **5** (Brit. coll.: expose oneself) sich [unsittlich] entblößen
D *adj.* (coll.) protzig (ugs. abwertend); ~ **Harry** (Brit.) Stenz, *der* (ugs. abwertend)
Phrasal verb
• ~ **'over** *v.i.* (Electr.) überspringen
flash: ~back *n.* (Cinemat. etc.) Rückblende, *die* (**to** auf + *Akk.*); ~ **bulb** *n.* (Photog.) Blitzbirnchen, *das;* ~ **card** *n.* Flashcard, *die;* **~cube** *n.* (Photog.) Blitzwürfel, *der;* Würfelblitz, *der*
flasher /ˈflæʃə(r)/ *n.* **1** (in advertising) blinkende Leuchtreklame; (Motor Veh.) Blinker, *der;* **headlamp ~:** Lichthupe, *die* **2** (Brit. coll.: who exposes himself) Exhibitionist, *der*
flash: ~ flood *n.* Überschwemmung, *die* (*durch heftige Regenfälle*); **~gun** *n.* (Photog.) Blitz[licht]gerät, *das*
flashily /ˈflæʃɪlɪ/ *adv.* auffällig; protzig (ugs. abwertend)
flashing /ˈflæʃɪŋ/ *n.* (Building) Dichtungsblech, *das*
flash: ~ lamp *n.* Blinklampe, *die;* **~light** *n.* **1** (for signals) Blinklicht, *das;* (in lighthouse) Leuchtfeuer, *das;* **2** (Photog.) Blitzlicht, *das;* **3** (Amer.) Taschenlampe, *die;* ~ **memory** *n.* (Computing) Flash-Speicher, *der;* ~ **mob** *n.* Flashmob, *der;* **~point** *n.* Flammpunkt, *der;* (fig.) Siedepunkt, *der*
flashy /ˈflæʃɪ/ *adj.* auffällig; protzig (ugs. abwertend); **he's a ~ dresser** er kleidet sich [sehr] auffällig; ~ **young men** großspurige junge Männer
flask /flɑːsk/ *n.* **1** ▸**Thermos**; **vacuum flask** **2** (for wine, oil) [bauchige] Flasche; (Chem.) Kolben, *der* **3** (hip flask) Taschenflasche, *die;* Flachmann, *der* (ugs. scherzh.)
flat¹ /flæt/ *n.* (esp. Brit.: dwelling) Wohnung, *die*
flat²
A *adj.* **1** flach; eben ‹*Fläche*›; platt ‹*Nase, Reifen*›; (uniform) gleichmäßig ‹*Tönung, Farbton*›; **knock sb. ~:** jmdn. niederstrecken; **the rug is not ~:** der Teppich liegt nicht glatt; **spread the blanket ~ on the ground** die Decke glatt auf dem Boden ausbreiten; **fall ~ on the ground** der Länge nach hinfallen; **fall ~ on one's back** auf den Rücken fallen; **lie ~ on one's stomach** flach auf dem Bauch liegen **2** (fig.) (monotonous) eintönig; (dull) lahm (ugs.); fade; (stale) schal, abgestanden ‹*Bier, Sekt*›; (Electr.) leer ‹*Batterie*›; (Commerc.: inactive) flau; **fall ~:** nicht ankommen (ugs.); seine Wirkung verfehlen; **go ~:** schal werden; **feel ~:** erschöpft sein **3** (downright) glatt (ugs.) ‹*Absage, Weigerung, Widerspruch*›; **[and] that's ~:** und damit basta (ugs.) **4** (Mus.) [um einen Halbton] erniedrigt ‹*Note*› **5** (Phonet.) kurz und offen ‹*Vokal*›
B *adv.* **1** flach **2** (outright) rundweg; glattweg (ugs.) **3** (Mus.) zu tief ‹*spielen, singen*› **4** (coll.: completely) ~ **broke** total pleite **5** (coll.: exactly) **in two hours ~:** in genau zwei Stunden; **in no time ~:** in null Komma nichts (ugs.)
C *n.* **1** flache Seite; ~ **of the hand** Handfläche, *die* **2** (level ground) Ebene, *die;* (shoal) Untiefe, *die;* **walk on the ~:** auf ebener Strecke gehen **3** (Mus.) erniedrigter Ton; (symbol) Erniedrigungszeichen, *das* **4** (Horseracing) **the ~:** das Flachrennen; (season) die Saison für Flachrennen; **on the ~:** bei Flachrennen **5** (coll.: flat tyre) Platte, *der* (ugs.); Plattfuß, *der* (ugs.) **6** (Theatre) Kulisse, *die*
'flatbed *n.* **1** (esp. Amer.: vehicle) Pritschenwagen, *der;* ~ **truck/pickup** Pritschenwagen, *der;* ~ **trailer** Pritschenanhänger, *der* **2** (Printing) ~ **press** Flachbettdruckmaschine, *die* **3** (Computing) Flachbettgerät, *das*
'flatbed scanner *n.* (Computing) Flachbettscanner, *der*
flat: ~-bottomed /ˈflætbɒtəmd/ *adj.* flach; **~car** *n.* (Amer. Railw.) Flachwagen, *der;* **~-chested** /flætˈtʃestɪd/ *adj.* flachbrüstig; flachbusig; ~ **'feet** *n. pl.* Plattfüße *Pl.* **~fish** *n.* Plattfisch, *der;* **~-footed** /flætˈfʊtɪd/ *adj.* plattfüßig; (fig. coll.) (uninspired) fantasielos; platt (abwertend); (unprepared) unvorbereitet; **~-heeled** *adj.* ‹*Schuh*› mit flachem Absatz; flach ‹*Schuh*›; **~-hunting** *n.* (Brit.) Wohnungssuche, *die;* ~ **iron** *n.* Bügeleisen, *das;* Plätteisen, *das*
flatlet /ˈflætlɪt/ *n.* (Brit.) Appartement, *das*
flatly /ˈflætlɪ/ *adv.* rundweg; glatt (ugs.)
'flatmate *n.* (esp. Brit.) Mitbewohner, *der*/Mitbewohnerin, *die;* **they were ~s** sie haben zusammen gewohnt
flatness /ˈflætnɪs/ *n., no pl.* **1** Flachheit, *die;* (of nose) Plattheit, *die* **2** (uniformity) Gleichmäßigkeit, *die* **3** (fig.: monotony) Eintönigkeit, *die;* (dullness) Fadheit, *die*
flat: ~ 'out *adv.* **1** ▸**i** p. 1566 (at top speed) **he ran/worked ~ out** er rannte/arbeitete, so schnell er konnte; **drive ~ out** mit Vollgas fahren; **go ~ out** ‹*Fahrzeug:*› mit Höchstgeschwindigkeit fahren; **2** (exhausted) total erledigt; total erschöpft; **~-pack** *adj.* ‹*Möbel*› zum Selbstbauen; ~ **race** *n.* Flachrennen, *das;* ~ **racing** *n., no pl., no indef. art.* Flachrennen, *das;* ~ **rate** *n.* Einheitstarif, *der;* ~ **screen** *n.* (Computing) Flachbildschirm, *der;* ~ **'spin** *n.* (Aeronaut.) Flachtrudeln, *das;* **go into a ~ spin** ins Flachtrudeln kommen; (fig. coll.) durchdrehen (ugs.)
flatten /ˈflætn/
A *v.t.* **1** flach *od.* platt drücken ‹*Schachtel*›; dem Erdboden gleichmachen ‹*Stadt, Gebäude*›; umknicken ‹*Bäume, Kornähren*›; **~ed against the door** flach *od.* platt gegen die Tür gedrückt **2** (humiliate) **feel ~ed** sich niedergedrückt *od.* niedergeschlagen fühlen **3** (Mus.) erniedrigen
B *v. refl.* ~ **oneself against sth.** sich flach *od.* platt gegen etw. drücken
Phrasal verb
• ~ **'out**
A *v.i.* **1** flacher werden **2** (Aeronaut.) in die Waagerechte gehen
B *v.t.* ganz flach drücken
flatter /ˈflætə(r)/
A *v.t.* **1** schmeicheln (+ *Dat.*); **I'm not just ~ing [you]** das ist keine bloße Schmeichelei; **feel ~ed** sich geschmeichelt fühlen; **be ~ed [by sth.]** sich [durch etw.] geschmeichelt fühlen; **the portrait ~s her/him** das Porträt ist geschmeichelt **2** (falsely encourage) **sth. ~s sb. into doing sth.** etw. verleitet jmdn. dazu, etw. zu tun
B *v. refl.* ~ **oneself [on being/having sth.]** sich (*Dat.*) einbilden[, etw. zu sein/haben]
flatterer /ˈflætərə(r)/ *n.* Schmeichler, *der*/Schmeichlerin, *die*
flattering /ˈflætərɪŋ/ *adj.* schmeichelhaft; schmeichelnd, schmeichlerisch ‹*Person*›; vorteilhaft ‹*Kleid, Licht, Frisur*›
flattery /ˈflætərɪ/ *n.* Schmeichelei, *die;* ~ **will get you nowhere** mit Schmeicheleien erreichst du gar nichts
flat 'tyre *n.* Reifenpanne, *die;* (the tyre itself) platter Reifen
flatulence /ˈflætjʊləns/ *n.* Blähungen *Pl.;* Flatulenz, *die* (Med.); **suffer from ~:** Blähungen haben
flatulent /ˈflætjʊlənt/ *adj.* an Blähungen leidend ‹*Mensch, Tier*›; blähend ‹*Wirkung, Lebensmittel*›
flat: ~ware *n., no pl.* (dishes) Geschirr, *das;* (Amer.: cutlery) Besteck, *das;* **~worm** *n.* Plattwurm, *der*
flaunt /flɔːnt/*v.t.* zur Schau stellen
flautist /ˈflɔːtɪst/ *n.* ▸**i** p. 1260 Flötist, *der*/Flötistin, *die*
flavor *etc.* (*Amer.*) ▸**flavour** *etc.*
flavour /ˈfleɪvə(r)/ (Brit.)
A *n.* **1** Aroma, *das;* (taste) Geschmack, *der;* **the dish lacks ~:** das Gericht schmeckt fade; **add ~ to sth.** einer Sache (*Dat.*) Geschmack geben; **different ~s** verschiedene Geschmacksrichtungen; **~ of the month** (fig.) hoch im Kurs stehen; **I'm not ~ of the month with him at the moment** er ist zur Zeit nicht gut auf mich zu sprechen **2** (fig.) Touch, *der* (ugs.); Anflug, *der;* **nostalgic ~:** nostalgischer Touch; Anflug von Nostalgie
B *v.t.* **1** abschmecken; würzen; **orange-~ed sweets** Bonbons mit Orangengeschmack **2** (fig.) Würze verleihen (+ *Dat.*)
flavour enhancer /ˈfleɪvər ɪnhɑːnsə(r)/ *n.* Geschmacksverstärker, *der*
flavouring /ˈfleɪvərɪŋ/ *n.* (Brit.) Aroma, *das;* **add [more] ~ to sth.** etw. [stärker] würzen
flavourless /ˈfleɪvəlɪs/ *adj.* (Brit.) fade
flavoursome /ˈfleɪvəsəm/ *adj.* (Brit.) schmackhaft
flaw /flɔː/
A *n.* **1** (imperfection) Makel, *der;* (in plan, argument, character, or logic; crack in china, glass, or jewel) Fehler, *der;* (in workmanship, or goods) Mangel, *der* **2** (Law) Formfehler, *der*
B *v.t.* entstellen ‹*Gesicht, Schönheit*›; beschädigen ‹*Porzellan, Glas*›
flawed /flɔːd/ *adj.* fehlerhaft
flawless /ˈflɔːlɪs/ *adj.* **1** makellos ‹*Schönheit*›; untadelig ‹*Verhalten*›; einwandfrei, fehlerlos ‹*Aussprache, Verarbeitung*› **2** (masterly) vollendet ‹*Aufführung, Wiedergabe*› **3** lupenrein ‹*Edelstein*›
flawlessly /ˈflɔːlɪslɪ/ *adv.* ▸**flawless 1, 2**: makellos; untadelig; einwandfrei; fehlerlos; vollendet
flax /flæks/ *n.* **1** (Bot.) Flachs, *der* **2** (Textiles: fibre) Flachsfaser, *die;* Flachs, *der*
flaxen /ˈflæksn/ *adj.* flachsfarben; (made of flax) flächsern; **she's a ~ blonde** sie ist flachsblond
'flaxen-haired *adj.* flachsblond
flay /fleɪ/ *v.t.* **1** häuten; abziehen ‹*Haut*›; abschälen ‹*Rinde*›; ~ **sb. alive** jmdm. bei lebendigem Leibe die Haut abziehen; (fig. coll.) jmdm. das Fell gerben (salopp) **2** (fig.: criticize) heruntermachen (ugs.); **he was ~ed by them** sie ließen kein gutes Haar an ihm (ugs.)
flea /fliː/ *n.* Floh, *der;* **send sb. away** *or* **off with a ~ in his/her ear** (fig. coll.) jmdn. abblitzen lassen (ugs.); **as fit as a ~** (coll.) kerngesund
flea: ~ bite *n.* Flohbiss, *der;* **it's just a ~ bite** (fig.) es ist nur eine Kleinigkeit *od.* (ugs.) ein Klacks; ~ **circus** *n.* Flohzirkus, *der;* ~ **market** *n.* Flohmarkt, *der;* **~pit** *n.* (Brit. coll. derog.) Flohkino, *das* (ugs.)
fleck /flek/
A *n.* **1** Tupfen, *der;* (small) Punkt, *der;* (blemish on skin) Fleck, *der* **2** (speck) Flocke, *die*
B *v.t.* sprenkeln; **the sky is ~ed with wispy clouds** der Himmel ist mit Wölkchen übersät; **green eyes ~ed with brown** braun gesprenkelte grüne Augen
fled ▸**flee**
fledg[e]ling /ˈfledʒlɪŋ/ *n.* Jungvogel, *der;* (fig.) Anfänger, *der;* Grünschnabel, *der* (abwertend); ~ **writer** Jungautor, *der*/-autorin, *die;* ~ **actor** Nachwuchsschauspieler, *der*/-schauspielerin, *die*
flee /fliː/
A *v.i.,* **fled** /fled/ **1** fliehen; ~ **from sth./sb.** aus etw./vor jmdm. flüchten *od.* fliehen; ~ **abroad** [sich] ins Ausland flüchten; ~ **before** *or* **from the storm** vor dem Sturm flüchten *od.* fliehen; ~ **from sth.** (fig.) einer Sache (*Dat.*) entfliehen; **the police arrived and the thieves fled** als die Polizei kam, ergriffen die Diebe die Flucht; **be ~ing from justice** auf der Flucht vor den Richtern sein **2** (vanish) sich verflüchtigen; ‹*Jugend, Zeit:*› vergehen
B *v.t.,* **fled** **1** fliehen aus; ~ **the country** aus dem Land fliehen *od.* flüchten **2** (avoid, shun) sich entziehen (+ *Dat.*); fliehen (geh.) ‹*Gesellschaft, Personen*›
fleece /fliːs/
A *n.* **1** Vlies, *das;* [Schaf]fell, *das;* (quantity shorn) Schur, *die;* (woollen fabric) Flausch, *der;* (artificial fabric) Webpelz, *der;* Fleece, *das; see also* **Golden Fleece** **2** (garment) Fleece, *das*
B *v.t.* (fig.) ausplündern; (charge excessively) neppen (ugs. abwertend); **be ~d of one's money** um sein Geld gebracht werden
fleecy /ˈfliːsɪ/ *adj.* flauschig; ~ **cloud** Schäfchenwolke, *die*
fleet¹ /fliːt/ *n.* **1** (Navy) Flotte, *die;* **the F~:** die Marine; *see also* **admiral 1** **2** (in operation together) (vessels) Flotte, *die;* (aircraft) Geschwader, *das;* (vehicles) ≈ Kolonne, *die;* **a fishing ~:** eine Fischfangflotte; *see also* **merchant fleet**

f

3▸ (under same ownership) Flotte, *die* (fig.); **he owns a ~ of cars** ihm gehört ein ganzer Wagenpark

fleet² *adj.* (poet./literary) flink; **~ of foot, ~-footed** leichtfüßig; schnellfüßig

fleeting /'fli:tɪŋ/ *adj.* flüchtig; vergänglich ‹*Natur, Schönheit*›; **~ visit** Stippvisite, *die* (ugs.)

fleetingly /'fli:tɪŋlɪ/ *adv.* flüchtig; **she was here ~:** sie war kurz hier

'Fleet Street *pr. n.* (Brit. fig.) die [überregionale britische] Presse

Fleming /'flemɪŋ/ *n.* Flame, *der*/Flämin, *die*

Flemish /'flemɪʃ/ ▸❶ **p. 1277**, ▸❶ **p. 1345**

A *adj.* flämisch; *see also* **English A**

B *n.* Flämisch, *das; see also* **English B 1**

flesh /fleʃ/

A *n., no pl., no indef. art.* 1▸ Fleisch, *das;* **he's got no ~ on him** er hat kein Fleisch auf den Rippen; **~ and blood** Fleisch und Blut; **it's more than ~ and blood can stand** das ist mehr, als ein Mensch ertragen kann; **one's own ~ and blood** sein eigen[es] Fleisch und Blut (geh.); *see also* **creep A 2** 2▸ (of fruit, plant) [Frucht]fleisch, *das* 3▸ (fig.: body) Fleisch, *das* (geh.); **and the Word was made ~** (Bibl.) und das Wort ist Fleisch geworden; **go the way of all ~:** den Weg allen Fleisches gehen (geh.); **in the ~:** in natura; **sins of the ~:** fleischliche Sünden; *see also* **spirit A 4** 4▸ (as food) Fleisch, *das;* **human ~:** Menschenfleisch, *das*

B *v.t.* **~ out** ausstatten; untermauern ‹*Plan*›

C *v.i.* **~ out** Fleisch ansetzen

flesh: ~ colour *n.* Fleischfarbe, *die;* **~-coloured** *adj.* fleischfarben; **~-eating** *adj.* Fleisch fressend

fleshly /'fleʃlɪ/ *adj.* (carnal) fleischlich; (mortal, worldly) irdisch

flesh: ~pots *n. pl.* 1▸ (high living) **wallow in the ~pots** wie die Made im Speck leben; 2▸ (striptease clubs etc.) einschlägige Lokale; **~ tints** *n. pl.* (Art) Fleischtöne *Pl.;* **~ wound** *n.* Fleischwunde, *die*

fleshy /'fleʃɪ/ *adj.* 1▸ (fat, boneless) fett; fleischig ‹*Hände*›; **the ~ parts of a fish** die grätenlosen Stücke eines Fisches 2▸ (Bot.) fleischig 3▸ (like flesh) fleischartig

fleur-de-lis /flɜ:də'li:/ *n., pl.* **fleurs-de-lis** /flɜ:də'li:/ 1▸ (Her.) Lilie, *die* 2▸ *in sing. or pl.* (Hist.: arms of France) bourbonische Lilie 3▸ (Bot.) Lilie, *die*

flew ▸**fly² A, B**

flex¹ /fleks/ *n.* (Brit. Electr.) Kabel, *das*

flex² *v.t.* 1▸ (Anat.) beugen ‹*Arm, Knie*› 2▸ **~ one's muscles** (lit. or fig.) seine Muskeln spielen lassen

flexibility /fleksɪ'bɪlɪtɪ/ *n., no pl.* 1▸ Biegsamkeit, *die;* Elastizität, *die* 2▸ (fig.) Flexibilität, *die*

flexible /'fleksɪbl/ *adj.* 1▸ biegsam; elastisch 2▸ (fig.) flexibel; dehnbar ‹*Vorschriften*›; schwach ‹*Wille*›; **~ working hours** *or* **time** gleitende Arbeitszeit

flexibly /'fleksɪblɪ/ *adv.* 1▸ elastisch 2▸ (fig.) flexibel

flexitime /'fleksɪtaɪm/ (Brit.), **flextime** /'flekstaɪm/ (Amer.) *ns.* (Office Managem.) Gleitzeit, *die;* **be on** *or* **work ~:** gleitende Arbeitszeit haben

flibbertigibbet /flɪbətɪ'dʒɪbɪt/ *n.* Leichtfuß, *der* (ugs.); (gossipy person) Klatschbase, *die* (ugs.)

flick /flɪk/

A *n.* 1▸ **~ of the wrist** kurze, schnelle Drehung des Handgelenks; **a ~ of the switch** ein einfaches Klicken des Schalters; **a ~ with the whip** ein Schnalzen mit der Peitsche; **with a ~ of its tongue/tail** mit vorschnellender Zunge/mit einem Schlag des Schwanzes; **he removed the piece of dirt with a ~ of his finger[s]** er schnippte den Schmutz mit den Fingern weg; **give the room a quick ~ with the duster** (coll.) kurz mit dem Staubtuch durchs Zimmer gehen 2▸ (sound) (of switch) Klicken, *das;* (of whip) Schnalzen, *das;* (of fingers) Schnipsen, *das. See also* **flicks**

B *v.t.* schnippen; anknipsen ‹*Schalter*›; verspritzen ‹*Tinte*›; **~ one's fingers/whip** mit den Fingern schnipsen/mit der Peitsche schnalzen; **~ sth. from** *or* **off sth.** (with fingers) etw. von etw. schnippen; (with duster) etw. von etw. wischen; **the cow ~ed her tail** die Kuh schlug mit dem Schwanz; **would you just ~ the duster round the room?** (coll.) würdest du bitte eben mit dem Staubtuch durchs Zimmer gehen? (ugs.)

C *v.i.* **the lizard's tongue ~ed out** die Eidechse ließ die Zunge hervorschnellen

Phrasal verb

• **~ through** *v.t.* durchblättern

flicker /'flɪkə(r)/

A *v.i.* 1▸ flackern; ‹*Fernsehapparat:*› flimmern; **shadows ~ed on the wall** Schatten huschten über die Wand; **a smile ~ed round her lips** ein Lächeln spielte um ihre Lippen 2▸ (quiver) ‹*Zunge:*› züngeln; ‹*Fahne, Lid:*› flattern; ‹*Blatt:*› zittern

B *n.* 1▸ Flackern, *das;* (of TV) Flimmern, *das;* (of shadow) Huschen, *das;* (fig.) Aufflackern, *das;* (of smile) Anflug, *der;* (of hope, life) Funke, *der* 2▸ (of bird's tail) Wippen, *das;* (of eyelid) Flattern, *das*

Phrasal verb

• **~ 'out** *v.i.* (lit. or fig.) verlöschen

'flick knife *n.* (Brit.) Schnappmesser, *das*

flicks /flɪks/ *n. pl.* (coll.) **the ~:** das Kino; **what's on at the ~?** was gibts im Kino?

flier ▸**flyer**

flight¹ /flaɪt/

A *n.* 1▸ (flying) Flug, *der;* **in ~:** im Flug; **whilst in ~:** während des Fluges 2▸ (journey, passage) Flug, *der;* (migration of birds) Zug, *der;* **the six o'clock ~ to ...:** die 6-Uhr-Maschine nach ...; **on [board] a ~ to ...:** an Bord eines Flugzeugs nach ...; **the ~ from Paris to Rome takes about two hours** die Flugzeit von Paris nach Rom beträgt etwa zwei Stunden 3▸ (fig.: of thought) Höhenflug, *der;* **~ of fancy** [geistiger] Höhenflug 4▸ (set of stairs) **~ [of stairs** *or* **steps]** Treppe, *die;* **live two ~s up** zwei Treppen hoch wohnen 5▸ (flock of birds) Schwarm, *der;* Flug, *der* (Jägerspr.); (volley of arrows) [Pfeil]hagel, *der;* (Air Force) ≈ Staffel, *die;* **in the first** *or* **top ~** (fig.) in der Spitzengruppe; **the first** *or* **top ~ of actors** die besten Schauspieler; die Spitzenschauspieler 6▸ (tail of dart) Befiederung, *die*

B *v.t.* (Cricket etc.) **~ the ball** den Ball mit unberechenbarer Flugbahn werfen

flight² *n.* 1▸ (fleeing) Flucht, *die;* **take [to] ~:** die Flucht ergreifen; **put to ~:** in die Flucht schlagen 2▸ (Econ.) **the ~ from the dollar** die Flucht aus dem Dollar

flight: ~ attendant *n.* ▸❶ **p. 1260** Flugbegleiter, *der*/-begleiterin, *die;* **~ bag** *n.* ≈ Reisetasche, *die;* **~ control** *n.* 1▸ (Aeronaut.) ≈ Flugsicherung, *die;* 2▸ (system of levers, cables, etc.) Steuerung, *die;* **~ controller** *n.* ▸❶ **p. 1260** (Aeronaut.) Fluglotse, *der;* **~ control system** *n.* Flugkontrollsystem, *das;* **~ crew** *n.* Flugbesatzung, *die;* **~ deck** *n.* 1▸ (of aircraft carrier) Flugdeck, *das;* 2▸ (of aircraft) Cockpit, *das;* **~ engineer** *n.* ▸❶ **p. 1260** Flugingenieur, *der*/-ingenieurin, *die*

flightless /'flaɪtlɪs/ *adj.* flugunfähig

flight: ~ lieutenant *n.* (Air Force) Hauptmann [der Luftwaffe]; **~ log** *n.* Flugprotokoll, *das;* **~ mechanic** *n.* ▸❶ **p. 1634** Bordmechaniker, *der;* Bordwart, *der;* **~ number** *n.* Flugnummer, *die;* **~ officer** *n.* 1▸ (Brit. Air Force) [weiblicher] Hauptmann; 2▸ (Amer. Air Force) Stabsfeldwebel, *der;* **~ path** *n.* (Aeronaut.) Flugweg, *der;* (Astronaut.) Flugbahn, *die;* **~ plan** *n.* Flugplan, *der;* **~ recorder** *n.* Flugschreiber, *der;* **~ simulator** *n.* Flugsimulator, *der;* **~-test** *v.t.* [im Flug] testen

flighty /'flaɪtɪ/ *adj.* 1▸ (fickle) flatterhaft 2▸ (capricious) kapriziös

flimsily /'flɪmzɪlɪ/ *adv.* dünn; hastig ‹*errichtet*›; schlecht ‹*gebunden, verpackt*›; **a ~ built** *or* **constructed raft** ein flüchtig zusammengezimmertes Floß

flimsy /'flɪmzɪ/

A *adj.* 1▸ dünn; (very thin) hauchdünn ‹*Seide, Papier*›; fadenscheinig ‹*Kleidung, Vorhang*›; (of inadequate material or workmanship) nicht [sehr] haltbar ‹*Verpackung*›; nicht [sehr] stabil ‹*Konstruktion, Haus, Schiff*› 2▸ (fig.) fadenscheinig (abwertend) ‹*Entschuldigung, Argument*›; dürftig (abwertend) ‹*Entwurf, Handlung*›

B *n.* (thin paper) Durchschlagpapier, *das;* (document) Durchschlag, *der*

flinch /flɪnʃ/ *v.i.* 1▸ zurückschrecken; **~ from sth./doing sth.** vor einer Sache zurückschrecken/davor zurückschrecken, etw. zu tun; **~ from one's responsibilities** sich seinen Pflichten entziehen; **don't ~ from the facts** man muss den Tatsachen ins Auge sehen 2▸ (wince) zusammenzucken

fling /flɪŋ/

A *n.* 1▸ (throw) Wurf, *der* 2▸ (fig.: attempt) **have a ~ at sth., give sth. a ~:** es mit etw. versuchen; **have a ~ at doing sth.** es damit versuchen, etw. zu tun 3▸ (fig.: indulgence) **have one's ~:** sich ausleben; **youth must have its ~:** die Jugend muss sich austoben [können]; **have one last ~:** sein Leben noch einmal richtig genießen; (by going on a drinking spree) noch einmal einen draufmachen (ugs.) 4▸ (brief love affair) Affäre, *die* (**with** mit)

B *v.t.*, **flung** /flʌŋ/ 1▸ werfen; **~ open/shut** aufreißen/zuwerfen; **~ back one's head** den Kopf zurückwerfen; **~ one's arms round sb.'s neck** jmdm. die Arme um den Hals werfen; **~ sth. away** (lit. or fig.) etw. fortwerfen; **~ down the money** das Geld hinschmeißen (ugs.); **~ off one's attacker** seinen Angreifer wegstoßen; **~ off one's clothes** die Kleider von sich werfen; **~ on one's jacket** [sich (*Dat.*)] die Jacke überwerfen; **the horse flung him off** das Pferd warf ihn ab 2▸ (fig.) **~ sb. into jail** jmdn. ins Gefängnis werfen; **~ sb. into confusion** jmdn. in Verwirrung stürzen; **~ sb. a despairing look** jmdm. einen verzweifelten Blick zuwerfen; **~ down a challenge to sb.** jmdn. herausfordern; **~ caution/prudence to the winds/~ aside one's scruples** alle Vorsicht/alle Umsicht/seine Skrupel über Bord werfen; **~ off restraints** Fesseln abwerfen

C *v. refl.*, **flung** 1▸ **~ oneself at sb.** sich auf jmdn. stürzen; **~ oneself in front of/upon** *or* **on to sth.** sich vor/auf etw. (*Akk.*) werfen; **~ oneself at sb.'s feet** sich jmdm. zu Füßen werfen; **~ oneself into a chair** sich in einen Sessel fallen lassen *od.* werfen; **~ oneself into sb.'s arms** in jmds. Arme stürzen 2▸ (fig.) **~ oneself into sth.** sich in etw. (*Akk.*) stürzen; **~ oneself at sb.** sich jmdm. an den Hals werfen (ugs.)

flint /flɪnt/ *n.* Feuerstein, *der;* Flint, *der* (veralt.); **as hard as ~:** hart wie Stein

flint: ~ glass *n.* Flintglas, *das;* **~lock** *n.* (Hist.) Steinschlossgewehr, *das*

flinty /'flɪntɪ/ *adj.* 1▸ (containing flint) feuersteinhaltig; (resembling flint) feuersteinartig 2▸ (fig.) unbeugsam; **have a ~ heart** ein Herz aus Stein haben

flip¹ /flɪp/

A *n.* 1▸ Schnipsen, *das;* **give sth. a ~:** etw. hochschnipsen 2▸ (coll.: outing) [kurzer] Ausflug

B *adj.* (coll.) schnodderig (ugs.)

C *v.t.*, **-pp-** schnipsen; **~ [over]** (turn over) umdrehen; **~ one's lid** (fig. coll.) ausflippen (ugs.)

D *v.i.*, **-pp-** 1▸ (coll.) ausflippen 2▸ (turn over) **the plane ~ped [over] on to its back** das Flugzeug drehte sich auf den Rücken

Phrasal verb

• **~ through** ▸**flick through**

flip² *n.* (drink) Flip, *der; see also* **egg flip**

'flip chart *n.* Flipchart, *das*

'flip-flops *n. pl.* Flipflops *Pl.*

flippancy /'flɪpənsɪ/ *n., no pl.* Unernst, *der;* Leichtfertigkeit, *die*

flippant /'flɪpənt/ *adj.*, **flippantly** /'flɪpəntlɪ/ *adv.* unernst; leichtfertig

flipper /'flɪpə(r)/ *n.* 1▸ (Zool.) Flosse, *die* 2▸ (of swimmer) [Schwimm]flosse, *die*

'flip phone *n.* Klapphandy, *das*

flipping /'flɪpɪŋ/ (Brit. coll.)

A *adj.* **it's a ~ nuisance/waste of time** das ist schon verflixt ärgerlich/eine blöde Zeitvergeudung (ugs.); **you're a ~ idiot** du bist wirklich ein Idiot!; **~ heck!** Scheibe! (ugs. verhüll.)

B *adv.* verflixt (ugs.) ‹*lästig, ärgerlich, kalt*›; ganz schön (ugs.) ‹*schlimm, wütend*›

'flip side *n.* B-Seite, *die*

flirt /flɜ:t/

A *n.* **he/she is just a ~:** er/sie will nur flirten;

she looks a bit of a ~: sie scheint einem Flirt nicht abgeneigt zu sein
B *v.i.* 1 ~ **[with sb.]** [mit jmdm.] flirten 2 (fig.) ~ **with sth.** mit etw. liebäugeln; ~ **with the idea of doing sth.** mit dem Gedanken spielen *od.* liebäugeln, etw. zu tun; ~ **with danger/death** die Gefahr [leichtfertig] herausfordern/mit dem Leben spielen

flirtation /flɜːˈteɪʃn/ *n.* Flirt, *der;* **there's a lot of ~ between the two of them** die beiden flirten ganz schön miteinander; **it was merely innocent ~:** es war nur ein unschuldiger Flirt

flirtatious /flɜːˈteɪʃəs/ *adj.* kokett ‹*Blick, Art*›; **their ~ involvement** ihr Flirt; **she's a ~ woman** sie flirtet gern

flirtatiousness /flɜːˈteɪʃəsnɪs/ *n., no pl.* Koketterie, *die*

flit /flɪt/
A *v.i.,* **-tt-** 1 huschen; **thoughts/recollections ~ted through his mind** Gedanken/Erinnerungen schossen ihm durch den Kopf; **his mind ~ted from one thing to another** seine Gedanken eilten von einem Thema zum anderen 2 (depart) ~ **northward** nach Norden ziehen; ~ **away** verschwinden 3 (esp. Scot., N. Engl.: move house) umziehen
B *n.* **do a ~** (coll.) sich absetzen (ugs.); *see also* **moonlight B**

flitch /flɪtʃ/ *n.* ~ **[of bacon]** Speckseite, *die*

float /fləʊt/
A *v.i.* 1 (on water) treiben; ‹*gestrandetes Schiff:*› flott werden; ~ **away** wegtreiben; **she just ~ed for some time** sie ließ sich eine Weile treiben; ~ **to the surface** an die Oberfläche treiben 2 (through air) schweben; ~ **across sth.** ‹*Wolke, Nebel:*› über etw. (*Akk.*) ziehen; ~ **away** fortschweben 3 (fig.) ~ **about** *or* **[a]round** umgehen; im Umlauf sein; **thoughts ~ through my mind** Gedanken gehen mir durch den Kopf 4 (sl.: move casually) ~ **[around** *or* **about]** herumziehen (ugs.); ~ **in and out** rein- und rausgehen (ugs.); ~ **about the area** sich in der Gegend herumtreiben 5 (Finance) floaten
B *v.t.* 1 (convey by water, on rafts) flößen; (set afloat) flottmachen ‹*Schiff*›; (through air) schweben lassen; **the ship was ~ed by the tide** das Schiff kam bei Flut wieder flott; ~ **the cream on top of the soup** die Sahne [vorsichtig] auf die Suppe geben 2 (fig.: circulate) in Umlauf bringen 3 (Finance) floaten lassen; freigeben 4 (Commerc.) ausgeben, auf den Markt bringen ‹*Aktien*›; gründen ‹*Unternehmen*›; lancieren ‹*Plan, Idee*›; lancieren, auflegen ‹*Anleihe*›
C *n.* 1 (for carnival) Festwagen, *der;* (Brit.: delivery cart) Wagen, *der; see also* **milk float** 2 (petty cash) Bargeld, *das;* (to provide change) Wechselgeld, *das* 3 (Angling) Floß, *das* (fachspr.); Schwimmer, *der;* (on net) Schwimmkörper, *der* 4 (in cistern, carburettor; also Aeronaut.) Schwimmer, *der* 5 (of fish) Schwimmblase, *die* 6 *in sing. or pl.* (Theatre: footlights) Rampenlicht, *das* 7 (of plasterer) Reibebrett, *das*

floating /ˈfləʊtɪŋ/ *adj.* treibend; schwimmend ‹*Hotel*›; **the ~ population** (fig.) die mobile Bevölkerung; ~ **exchange rate** flexibler *od.* frei schwankender Wechselkurs

floating: ~ 'bridge *n.* (bridge) Pontonbrücke, *die;* (ferry) Kettenfähre, *die;* ~ **'capital** *n.* frei verfügbares Kapital; ~ **'debt** *n.* (Finance) schwebende Schuld; ~ **'dock** *n.* Schwimmdock, *das;* ~ **'kidney** *n.* (Med.) Wanderniere, *die;* ~ **'point** *n.* (Computing) Fließkomma, *das;* ~ **'rib** *n.* (Anat.) freie Rippe; ~ **'voter** *n.* Wechselwähler, *der*/-wählerin, *die*

flock¹ /flɒk/
A *n.* 1 (of sheep, goats; also Eccl.) Herde, *die;* (of birds) Schwarm, *der* 2 (of people) Schar, *die;* **in ~s** in [großen *od.* hellen] Scharen; scharenweise 3 (of things) Reihe, *die*
B *v.i.* strömen; ~ **round sb.** sich um jmdn. scharen; ~ **in/out/together** [in Scharen] hinein-/heraus-/zusammenströmen; ~ **to Mecca/the seaside** [in Scharen] nach Mekka/ans Meer strömen; **~/come ~ing to hear sb. speak** herbeiströmen/herbeigeströmt kommen, um jmdn. reden zu hören

flock² *n.* 1 (of wool, cotton, etc.) Flocke, *die* 2 *in pl.* (material) Reißwolle, *die*

flock: ~-mattress *n. mit Reißwolle gefüllte Matratze;* ~ **'wallpaper** *n.* Velourstapete, *die;* Flocktapete, *die* (fachspr.)

floe /fləʊ/ *n.* Eisscholle, *die*

flog /flɒg/ *v.t.,* **-gg-** 1 (beat as punishment) auspeitschen; (urge on) [mit der Peitsche] antreiben; ~ **a dead horse** (fig.) seine Kraft und Zeit verschwenden; ~ **sth. to death** (fig.) etw. zu Tode reiten; ~ **oneself to death** (fig.) sich fast zu Tode arbeiten 2 (Brit. coll.: sell) verscheuern (salopp)

flood /flʌd/
A *n.* 1 Überschwemmung, *die;* **the river is in ~:** der Fluss führt Hochwasser; **~s** Überschwemmungen; **we had a ~ in the kitchen** unsere Küche stand unter Wasser; **the F~** (Bibl.) die Sintflut; *attrib.* ~ **area** Überschwemmungsgebiet, *das* 2 (fig.) Flut, *die;* **in full ~:** in voller Stärke; **in ~s of tears** tränenüberströmt 3 (Theatre coll.) ▸**floodlight A** 4 (of tide) Flut, *die;* (poet.: river) Strom, *der;* ~ **and field** (literary) Wasser und Land; **the tide is at the ~:** es ist Flut
B *v.i.* 1 ‹*Fluss:*› über die Ufer treten; **there's danger of ~ing** es besteht Überschwemmungsgefahr; **there's been a lot of ~ing in the area** es ist in dem Gebiet schon zu zahlreichen Überschwemmungen gekommen 2 (fig.) strömen; ~ **through sb.** jmdn. durchströmen *od.* -fluten; **light ~ed into the room** Licht flutete ins Zimmer; **applications for the job ~ed in** eine Flut von Bewerbungen ging ein
C *v.t.* 1 überschwemmen; (with moving liquid) überfluten; (deluge, irrigate) unter Wasser setzen; **the cellar was ~ed** der Keller stand unter Wasser; **be ~ed out** durch eine Überschwemmung obdachlos werden 2 (fig.) überschwemmen; **~ed with light** lichtdurchflutet

flood: ~ control *n.* Hochwasserschutz, *der;* ~ **damage** *n.* Hochwasserschaden, *der;* **the area suffered extensive ~ damage** in dem Gebiet gab es beträchtliche Hochwasserschäden; **~gate** *n.* (Hydraulic Engin.) Schütze, *die;* **open the ~gates to sth.** (fig.) einer Sache (*Dat.*) Tür und Tor öffnen; **~light A** *n.* Scheinwerfer, *der;* (illumination in a broad beam) Flutlicht, *das;* **B** *v.t.,* **~lit** /ˈflʌdlɪt/ anstrahlen ‹*Bauwerk*›; beleuchten ‹*Weg, Straße*›; mit Flutlicht erhellen ‹*Stadion*›; **~lighting** *n., no indef. art.* (lights) Flutlichtanlage, *die;* ~ **plain** *n.* Überschwemmungsgebiet, *das;* ~ **tide** *n.* Flut, *die;* ~ **warning** *n.* Hochwasserwarnung, *die;* (at the seaside) Flutwarnung, *die;* ~ **water** *n.* Hochwasser, *das;* (in motion) anflutendes Wasser

floor /flɔː(r)/
A *n.* 1 Boden, *der;* (of room) [Fuß]boden, *der;* **built-in ~-to-ceiling cupboards** raumhohe Einbauschränke; **wipe the ~ with sb.** (fig. coll.) jmdn. auseinander nehmen (salopp); **take the ~** (dance) sich aufs Parkett begeben; *see also* **c** 2 (storey) Stockwerk, *das;* **first ~** (Amer.) Erdgeschoss, *das;* **first ~** (Brit.), **second ~** (Amer.) erster Stock; **on the top ~:** im obersten Stock; **ground ~:** Erdgeschoss, *das;* Parterre, *das;* **get in on the ground ~ [of sth.]** (fig. coll.) [bei etw.] von Anfang an dabei sein 3 (in debate, meeting) Sitzungssaal, *der;* (Parl.) Plenarsaal, *der;* **cross the ~** (Brit.) mit der Gegenpartei stimmen; **from the ~:** seitens der Anwesenden; (Parl.) seitens des Plenums; **be given** *or* **have the ~:** das Wort haben; **take the ~** (speak) das Wort ergreifen; *see also* **a; hold² A 14** 4 (fig.: of prices/wages) Mindestpreis/-lohn, *der*
B *v.t.* 1 (confound) überfordern; (overcome, defeat) besiegen; **her rejoinder ~ed him completely** mit ihrer Antwort hat sie es ihm ganz schön gegeben (ugs.) 2 (knock down) zu Boden schlagen *od.* strecken 3 (pave) ~ **[with sth.]** mit einem Boden [aus etw.] versehen

floor: ~ area *n.* Grundfläche, *die;* **~board** *n.* Dielenbrett, *das;* **~cloth** *n.* (Brit.) Scheuertuch, *das;* ~ **covering** *n.* Fußbodenbelag, *der*

flooring /ˈflɔːrɪŋ/ *n.* Fußboden[belag], *der;* **parquet ~:** Parkettfußboden, *der*

floor: ~ lamp *n.* (Amer.) Stehlampe, *die;* ~ **manager** *n.* 1 (Telev.) Aufnahmeleiter, *der;* 2 (in shop) ≈ Abteilungsleiter, *der;* ~ **plan** *n.* Grundriss eines/des Stockwerks; ~ **polish** *n.* Bohnerwachs, *das;* ~ **polisher** *n.* Bohnermaschine, *die;* (manual) Bohner, *der;* ~ **show** *n.* ≈ Unterhaltungsprogramm, *das;* ~ **space** *n.* Grundfläche, *die;* ~ **tile** *n.* Fliese, *die;* ~ **trading** *n., no pl.* (St. Exch.) Parketthandel, *der;* **~walker** *n.* (Amer.) ≈ Abteilungsleiter, *der*

floozie (floosie) /ˈfluːzɪ/ *n.* (coll.) Flittchen, *das* (ugs. abwertend)

flop /flɒp/
A *v.i.,* **-pp-** 1 plumpsen; (flap) flattern; **she ~ped into a chair** sie ließ sich in einen Sessel plumpsen; **the fish ~ped about in the boat** der Fisch zappelte im Boot; **he ~ped down on his knees** er ließ sich auf die Knie fallen 2 (coll.: fail) fehlschlagen; ein Reinfall sein (ugs.); ‹*Theaterstück, Show:*› durchfallen
B *n.* 1 (coll.: failure) Reinfall, *der* (ugs.); Flop, *der* (ugs.) 2 (motion, sound) Plumps, *der*

floppy /ˈflɒpɪ/
A *adj.* weich und biegsam; ~ **ears/hat** Schlappohren/Schlapphut, *der*
B *n.* ▸**floppy disk**

floppy 'disk *n.* (Computing) Floppydisk, *die;* Diskette, *die*

flora /ˈflɔːrə/ *n., pl.* **~e** /ˈflɔːriː/ *or* **~s** Flora, *die;* (list, treatise) **a ~ of North America** eine Übersicht/Abhandlung über die Flora Nordamerikas

floral /ˈflɔːrl, ˈflɒrl/ *adj.* geblümt ‹*Kleid, Stoff, Tapete*›; Blumen‹*gesteck, -arrangement, -muster*›; ~ **perfumes** nach Blumen duftende Parfüms; **a ~ tribute to sb.** ein Blumengruß für jmdn.

Florence /ˈflɒrəns/ *pr. n.* ▸ⓘ **p. 1643** Florenz (*das*)

Florentine /ˈflɒrəntaɪn/
A *adj.* florentinisch
B *n.* Florentiner, *der*/Florentinerin, *die*

floret /ˈflɔːrɪt/ *n.* (Bot.) *Einzelblüte eines Blütenstandes*

florid /ˈflɒrɪd/ *adj.* 1 (over-ornate) schwülstig (abwertend); blumig ‹*Stil, Redeweise*›; überladen ‹*Architektur, Stil, Ornament*› 2 (high-coloured) gerötet ‹*Teint*›

florist /ˈflɒrɪst/ *n.* ▸ⓘ **p. 1260** Florist, *der*/Floristin, *die;* (grower of flowers) ≈ Gärtner, *der*/Gärtnerin, *die;* **~'s [shop]** Blumenladen, *der*

floss /flɒs/ *n.* 1 (silk, thread) Rohseide, *die;* (loosely twisted, of silk or cotton) ≈ Sticktwist, *der* 2 (on cocoon) Flockseide, *die. See also* **candyfloss; dental floss**

flotation /fləʊˈteɪʃn/ *n.* 1 (Phys.) Auftrieb, *der* 2 (Metall.) Schwimmaufbereitung, *die;* Flotation, *die* 3 (Commerc.) ▸**float B 4**: Ausgabe, *die;* Gründung, *die;* Lancierung, *die*

flotilla /fləˈtɪlə/ *n.* Flottille, *die*

flotsam /ˈflɒtsəm/ *n.* ~ **[and jetsam]** Treibgut, *das;* ~ **and jetsam** (fig.: of society) menschliches Treibgut

flounce¹ /flaʊns/ *v.i.* stolzieren

flounce² (Dressm.)
A *n.* Volant, *der*
B *v.t.* mit einem Volant besetzen

flounder¹ /ˈflaʊndə(r)/ *v.i.* taumeln; (stumble, lit. or fig.) stolpern; (struggle) sich quälen; ~ **through a speech** eine Rede zusammenstottern

flounder² *n.* (Zool.) Flunder, *die*

flour /flaʊə(r)/
A *n.* Mehl, *das; see also* **cornflour**
B *v.t.* (Cookery) mit Mehl bestäuben; bemehlen (fachspr.)

flourish /ˈflʌrɪʃ/
A *v.i.* 1 gedeihen; ‹*Handel, Geschäft:*› florieren, gut gehen; ‹*Kunst, Musik, Kirche:*› eine Blütezeit erleben *od.* haben; ‹*Zeitung, Firma:*› sich gut entwickeln 2 (be active) seine Blütezeit erleben *od.* haben; ‹*Künstler:*› seine beste Schaffensperiode haben
B *v.t.* schwingen; ~ **a stick at sb.** vor jmdm. mit einem Stock herumfuchteln (ugs.)
C *n.* 1 **do sth. with a ~:** etw. schwungvoll *od.*

f

mit einer schwungvollen Bewegung tun; **with a ~ of his stick/hand** seinen Stock schwenkend/mit einer schwungvollen Handbewegung **2** (in writing) Schnörkel, *der* **3** (ornate language) Ausschmückung, *die;* **a ~ of fine words** ein Feuerwerk von schönen Worten **4** (Mus.: fanfare) Fanfare, *die;* (florid passage) Verzierung, *die;* **~ of trumpets** Fanfarenstoß, *der*

floury /ˈflaʊərɪ/ *adj.* mehlig

flout /flaʊt/ *v.t.* missachten; sich hinwegsetzen über (+ *Akk.*) ‹*Ratschlag, Wunsch, öffentliche Meinung*›

flow /fləʊ/

A *v.i.* **1** ▸ℹ **p. 1491** fließen; ‹*Körner, Sand:*› rinnen, rieseln; ‹*Gas:*› strömen; **two rivers ~ into each other/into the sea** zwei Flüsse fließen zusammen/münden ins Meer; **the river ~ed over its banks** der Fluss trat über die Ufer; **the oil has ~ed out** das Öl ist ausgelaufen; **lava ~ed across the valley** Lava ergoss sich *od.* strömte ins Tal; **blood will ~** (fig.) es wird Blut fließen **2** (fig.) fließen; ‹*Personen:*› strömen; **keep the traffic ~ing smoothly** den Verkehr fließend halten; **keep the conversation ~ing** das Gespräch in Fluss halten; **the writing does not ~:** der Text ist nicht flüssig geschrieben; **talk ~ed freely** das Gespräch war sehr lebhaft; **is the work ~ing smoothly?** geht die Arbeit gut von der Hand? **3** (abound) **~ freely** *or* **like water** reichlich *od.* in Strömen fließen **4** **~ from** (be derived from) sich ergeben aus; (be produced from) fließen aus ‹*Feder*›; fließen von ‹*Lippen*› **5** (rise) ‹*Flut, Wasser:*› steigen; **the tide ~s twice a day** die Flut kommt zweimal am Tag

B *n.* **1** Fließen, *das;* (progress) Fluss, *der;* (volume) Durchflussmenge, *die;* **~ of water/blood/air/gas/lava/money/people** Wasser-/Blut-/Luft-/Gas-/Lava-/Geld-/Menschenstrom, *der;* **~ of electricity/traffic/capital/conversation** Strom-/Verkehrs-/Kapital-/Gesprächsfluss, *der;* **~ of information/news/ideas/thoughts/words** Informations-/Nachrichten-/Ideen-/Gedanken-/Redefluss, *der;* **the elegant ~ of his prose** der elegante Fluss seiner Prosa; **improve the work ~:** den Arbeitsablauf verbessern; (speaker) **be in full ~** (fig.) richtig in Fahrt sein; **go with the ~** (fig.) mit dem Strom schwimmen; *see also* **cash flow** **2** (of tide, river) Flut, *die;* **the tide is on the ~:** die Flut kommt **3** (Phys.: of solid) Fließen, *das*

Phrasal verb

• **~ aˈway** *v.i.* abfließen

ˈ**flow chart** *n.* Flussdiagramm, *das*

flower /ˈflaʊə(r)/

A *n.* **1** (blossom) Blüte, *die;* (plant) Blume, *die;* **send sb. ~s** jmdm. Blumen schicken; **'no ~s [by request]'** „es wird gebeten, von Blumenspenden abzusehen"; **say it with ~s** es mit Blumen sagen; Blumen sprechen lassen; **[be] in [full] ~:** in [voller] Blüte [stehen]; **come into ~:** zu blühen beginnen **2** *no pl.* (fig.: best part) Zierde, *die;* (prime) Blüte, *die;* **in the ~ of youth/her age** in der Blüte der Jugend/ihrer Jahre

B *v.i.* blühen; (fig.) erblühen (**into** zu)

flower: ~ arrangement *n.* **1** ▸**flower arranging**; **2** (result) Blumenarrangement, *das;* (smaller also) Gesteck, *das;* **~ arranging** *n.* Blumenstecken, *das;* **~ bed** *n.* Blumenbeet, *das*

flowered /flaʊəd/ *adj.* geblümt ‹*Stoff, Teppich, Tapete*›; **purple-~:** purpur blühend ‹*Pflanze*›

flower: ~ garden *n.* Blumengarten, *der;* **~ girl** *n.* Blumenverkäuferin, *die;* **~ head** *n.* Köpfchen, *das* (Bot.); (of composite) Körbchen, *das* (Bot.)

flowering /ˈflaʊərɪŋ/ *adj.* **~ cherry/shrub/currant** Zierkirsche, *die*/Blütenstrauch, *der*/Goldjohannisbeere, *die*

flowerless /ˈflaʊəlɪs/ *adj.* blütenlos ‹*Pflanze*›; **~ gardens** Gärten ohne Blumen

flower: ~ people *n. pl.* Blumenkinder; **~pot** *n.* Blumentopf, *der;* **~ shop** *n.* Blumenladen, *der;* **~ show** *n.* Blumenschau, *die*

flowery /ˈflaʊərɪ/ *adj.* ‹*Wiese*› voller Blumen; ‹*Garten*› voller Blumen/Blüten; geblümt ‹*Stoff, Muster*›; blumig ‹*Duft, Wein*›; (fig.) blumig ‹*Sprache, Ausdruck*›

flowing /ˈfləʊɪŋ/ *adj.* fließend; wallend ‹*Haar, Bart, Gewand*›; flüssig ‹*Handschrift*›

ˈ**flow meter** *n.* Durchflussmessgerät, *das*

flown ▸**fly²** **A, B**

flow: ~ rate *n.* Durchflussmenge, *die;* **~-sheet** ▸**flow chart**

fl oz *abbr.* ▸ℹ **p. 1690 = fluid ounce**

flu /fluː/ *n.* ▸ℹ **p. 1231** (coll.) Grippe, *die;* **get** *or* **catch [the] ~:** Grippe bekommen

fluctuate /ˈflʌktjʊeɪt/ *v.i.* schwanken; fluktuieren (bes. Wirtsch., Soziol.); **the level of attendance ~s** die Teilnehmerzahl schwankt *od.* ist schwankend

fluctuation /flʌktjʊˈeɪʃn/ *n.* Schwankung, *die;* Fluktuation, *die* (bes. Wirtsch., Soziol.)

flue /fluː/ *n.* **1** (in chimney) Rauchabzug, *der;* Feuerzug, *der* (Technik) **2** (for passage of hot air) Luftkanal, *der* **3** (in boiler) Flammrohr, *das* (Technik)

fluency /ˈfluːənsɪ/ *n.* Gewandtheit, *die;* (in speaking) Redegewandtheit, *die;* **I was complimented on the ~ of my Greek** mein flüssiges Griechisch wurde gelobt

fluent /ˈfluːənt/ *adj.* ▸ℹ **p. 1277** gewandt ‹*Stil, Redeweise, Redner, Schreiber, Erzähler*›; **be ~ in Russian, speak ~ Russian, be a ~ speaker of Russian** fließend Russisch sprechen; **you'll soon become ~:** du wirst bald fließend sprechen [können]; **my Arabic is ~:** ich spreche fließend Arabisch

fluently /ˈfluːəntlɪ/ *adv.* fließend ‹*sprechen, lesen*›; flüssig ‹*schreiben*›; gewandt ‹*sich ausdrücken*›; ununterbrochen ‹*fluchen*›

fluff /flʌf/

A *n.* **1** Flusen *Pl.*; Fusseln *Pl.*; (on birds, rabbits, etc.) Flaum, *der;* **there are pieces of ~ all over my trousers** meine Hose ist voller Fusseln; **the carpet is covered in ~:** der Teppich ist mit Flusen bedeckt; **bit of ~** (coll.: young woman) Mieze, *die* (ugs.) **2** (coll.: mistake) Patzer, *der* (ugs.)

B *v.t.* **1** **~ out** *or* **up** aufschütteln ‹*Kissen*›; **the bird ~ed itself/its feathers** der Vogel plusterte sich/seine Federn auf **2** (coll.: bungle) verpatzen (ugs.); **~ one's lines** seinen Text verpatzen

fluffy /ˈflʌfɪ/ *adj.* [flaum]weich ‹*Kissen, Küken, Haar*›; flauschig ‹*Spielzeug, Stoff, Decke*›; locker ‹*Haar, Omelett, Brot*›; flockig ‹*Schnee*›; schaumig ‹*Eiweiß*›

flugelhorn /ˈfluːglhɔːn/ *n.* (Mus.) Flügelhorn, *das*

fluid /ˈfluːɪd/

A *n.* **1** (liquid) Flüssigkeit, *die* **2** (liquid or gas) Fluid, *das* (Technik, Chemie)

B *adj.* **1** (liquid) flüssig; *see also* **dram 1** **2** (liquid or gaseous) fluid (Technik, Chemie) **3** (flowing) flüssig ‹*Stil*›; fließend ‹*Linie, Form*› **4** (fig.) ungewiss, unklar ‹*Lage*›; [noch] nicht fest umrissen ‹*Plan*›

fluid: ~ ˈclutch *n.* (Motor Veh.), **~ ˈcoupling** *n.* (Mech. Engin.) hydraulische Kupplung; Flüssigkeitskupplung, *die*

fluidity /fluːˈɪdɪtɪ/ *n.*, *no pl.* Flüssigkeit, *die;* Fluidität, *die* (Technik, Chemie)

fluid: ~ ˈounce *n.* ▸ℹ **p. 1690** (Brit.) 28 ml; **~ˈounce** *n.* (Amer.) 30 ml; **~ pressure** *n.* hydrostatischer Druck (Physik)

fluke¹ /fluːk/ *n.* (piece of luck) Glücksfall, *der;* **by a** *or* **some [pure] ~:** [nur] durch einen glücklichen Zufall; **by some extraordinary ~:** durch außergewöhnliches Glück; **it was a bit of a ~:** es war ein bisschen Glück dabei

fluke² *n.* **1** (Vet. Med.: flatworm) Saugwurm, *der;* Trematode, *die* (fachspr.); **liver ~:** Leberegel, *der* **2** (fish) Flunder, *die*

fluke³ *n.* **1** (of whale's tail) Fluke, *die* (Zool.); Schwanzflosse, *die* **2** (of anchor) Flunke, *die* (Seemannsspr.); Ankerarm, *der* **3** (of lance, harpoon, etc.) Widerhaken, *der*

fluky /ˈfluːkɪ/ *adj.* glücklich ‹*Zufall, Zusammentreffen, Sieg*›; zufällig ‹*Ergebnis, Relikt*›; Zufalls‹*treffer, -ergebnis*›

flume /fluːm/ *n.* **1** (water channel) Kanal, *der* **2** (water slide) [Wendel]röhrenrutsche, *die*

flummox /ˈflʌməks/ *v.t.* (coll.) aus der Fassung bringen; durcheinander bringen; **be ~ed by sth.** durch etw. verwirrt sein

flung ▸**fling** **B, C**

flunk /flʌŋk/ (Amer. coll.)

A *v.i.* durchfallen (ugs.)

B *v.t.* verhauen (ugs.) ‹*Prüfung, Examen*›; durchfallen lassen (ugs.) ‹*Kandidaten*›; **~ the exam** im Examen *od.* bei der Prüfung durchfallen (ugs.); **get ~ed** durchfallen (ugs.)

Phrasal verb

• **~ ˈout** *v.i.* rausfliegen (salopp); [hinaus]fliegen (ugs.); **~ out of school** von der Schule fliegen (ugs.)

flunkey, flunky /ˈflʌŋkɪ/ *n.* (usu. derog.) Lakai, *der* (abwertend)

fluoresce /fluːəˈres/ *v.i.* fluoreszieren

fluorescence /fluːəˈresəns/ *n.* Fluoreszenz, *die*

fluorescent /fluːəˈresənt/ *adj.* fluoreszierend; **~ material** Leuchtstoff, *der;* **~ display** Leuchtanzeige, *die*

fluorescent: ~ ˈlamp, ~ ˈlight *ns.* Leuchtstofflampe, *die* (Elektrot.); ≈ Neonlampe, *die;* **~ ˈlighting** *n.* Neonbeleuchtung, *die;* Neonlicht, *das;* **~ ˈscreen** *n.* Leuchtschirm, *der;* **~ ˈtube** *n.* Leucht[stoff]röhre, *die*

fluoridate /ˈfluːərɪdeɪt/ *v.t.* fluori[si]eren

fluoridation /fluːərɪˈdeɪʃn/ *n.* Fluori[si]erung, *die*

fluoride /ˈfluːəraɪd/ *n.* Fluorid, *das;* **~ toothpaste** fluorhaltige Zahnpasta

fluorine /ˈfluːəriːn/ *n.* (Chem.) Fluor, *das*

fluorspar /ˈfluːəspɑː(r)/ *n.* (Min.) Flussspat, *der;* Fluorit, *der*

flurried /ˈflʌrɪd/ *adj.* nervös

flurry /ˈflʌrɪ/

A *n.* **1** Aufregung, *die;* **there was a sudden ~ of activity** es herrschte plötzlich rege Betriebsamkeit; **a ~ of excitement** helle *od.* große Aufregung **2** (of rain/snow) [Regen-/Schnee]schauer, *der;* **~ [of wind]** Windstoß, *der*

B *v.t.* durcheinander bringen; **don't let yourself be flurried** lass dich nicht nervös machen

flush¹ /flʌʃ/

A *v.i.* (blush) rot werden; erröten (**with** vor + *Dat.*); **~ hotly/bright red** puter-/knallrot anlaufen *od.* werden

B *v.t.* ausspülen ‹*Becken*›; durch-, ausspülen ‹*Rohr*›; **~ the toilet** *or* **lavatory** spülen; **~ sth. down the toilet** etw. die Toilette hinunterspülen

C *n.* **1** (blush) Erröten, *das;* (in fever, menopause) Flush, *der* (Med.); fliegende Hitze; (glow of light or colour) Glühen, *das;* **hot ~es** Hitzewallungen **2** (elation) **in the [first] ~ of victory** *or* **conquest** im [ersten] Siegestaumel; **~ of excitement** Woge der Begeisterung; **~ of enthusiasm** Begeisterungstaumel, *der* **3** (bloom, vigour) Blüte, *die* (geh.); **in the first ~ of youth/romance** in der ersten Blüte der Jugend/in der ersten Liebesglut **4** (of lavatory, drain, etc.) Spülung, *die* **5** (sudden abundance) Flut, *die*

flush² *adj.* **1** (level) bündig; **be ~ with sth.** mit etw. bündig abschließen; (horizontally) auf gleicher Ebene mit etw. liegen **2** *usu. pred.* (plentiful) reichlich vorhanden *od.* im Umlauf ‹*Geld*›; **be ~ [with money]** gut bei Kasse sein (ugs.)

flush³ *v.t.* aufscheuchen ‹*Vögel, Wild*›

Phrasal verb

• **~ ˈout** *v.t.* aufscheuchen (fig.) ‹*Spion, Verbrecher*›

flush⁴ *n.* (Cards) *Karten derselben Farbe;* (Poker) Flush, *der;* **straight ~:** Straight Flush, *der;* Farbsequenz, *die;* **royal ~:** Royal Flush, *der;* höchste Farbsequenz

flushed /flʌʃt/ *adj.* gerötet ‹*Wangen, Gesicht*›; **you're extremely ~:** du bist ganz rot [im Gesicht]; **~ with pride** vor Stolz glühend

flush ˈtoilet *n.* Toilette mit Wasserspülung

fluster /ˈflʌstə(r)/

A *v.t.* aus der Fassung bringen; **she is not easily**

~**ed** sie ist nicht leicht aus der Fassung zu bringen
B *n.* **be [all] in a ~:** [völlig] durcheinander *od.* verstört sein

flustered /ˈflʌstəd/ *adj.* **be/become ~:** nervös sein/werden

flute /fluːt/ *n.* **1** (Mus.) Flöte, *die* **2** (Archit.) Kannelüre, *die;* ~**s** Kannelierung, *die* **3** (wineglass) [Sekt]flöte, *die*

fluted /ˈfluːtɪd/ *adj.* gerüscht ‹*Stoff, Manschette*›; gerillt ‹*Griff, Tischbein, Stiel*›; (Archit.) kanneliert

flutist /ˈfluːtɪst/ ▸**flautist**

flutter /ˈflʌtə(r)/
A *v.i.* **1** ‹*Vogel, Motte, Papier usw.:*› flattern; ~ **down** hinunter-/herunterflattern; **a leaf ~ed down** ein Blatt taumelte zur Erde; ~ **about** umherflattern; **she was ~ing about** (fig.) sie lief unruhig hin und her **2** (flap) ‹*Vorhang, Fahne, Segel, Drachen, Flügel:*› flattern; ‹*Blumen, Gräser usw.:*› schaukeln **3** (beat abnormally) ‹*Herz:*› schneller *od.* höher schlagen; (Med.) ‹*Puls, Herz:*› flattern
B *v.t.* **1** flattern mit ‹*Flügel*›; ~ **one's eyelashes** mit den Wimpern klimpern; ~ **one's eyelashes at sb.** jmdm. mit den Wimpern zuklimpern **2** (agitate) erregen; *see also* **dovecot**
C *n.* **1** Flattern, *das* **2** (fig.) (stir) [leichte] Unruhe; (nervous state) Aufregung, *die;* **put sb. in a ~:** jmdn. in Aufregung versetzen; **be in a [great] ~:** ganz aufgelöst sein; **be all of a ~:** vor Aufregung fast vergehen **3** (Brit. coll.: bet) Wette, *die;* (small speculative venture) kleine Spekulation; **have a ~:** ein paar Scheinchen riskieren (ugs.); **I enjoy an occasional ~:** hin und wieder riskiere ich ganz gern ein paar Scheinchen (ugs.) **4** (Med.) **heart/ventricular ~:** Herz-/Kammerflattern, *das* **5** (Electronics) (in pitch) rasches Schwanken der Tonhöhe; (in loudness) rasches Schwanken der Tonstärke

flux /flʌks/ *n.* **1** (change) **be in a state of ~:** im Fluss sein; sich verändern **2** (Metalw.) Flussmittel, *das* **3** (Phys.) Fluss, *der;* (amount of radiation or particles) Fluss, *der;* Flux, *der*

fly¹ /flaɪ/ *n.* **1** (Zool.) Fliege, *die;* **the only ~ in the ointment** (fig.) der einzige Haken [bei der Sache] (ugs.); **he wouldn't hurt a ~** (fig.) er kann keiner Fliege etwas zuleide tun; **[die** *or* **drop** *or* **fall] like flies** (fig.) [sterben *od.* umfallen] wie die Fliegen; **I'd like to be a ~ on the wall of his classroom** in seiner Klasse möchte ich gern Mäuschen sein *od.* spielen (ugs.); **[there are] no flies on him** (fig. coll.) ihm kann man nichts vormachen (ugs.); *see also* **breed B 1** **2** (Angling) Fliege, *die*

fly²
A *v.i.,* **flew** /fluː/, **flown** /fləʊn/ **1** fliegen; ~ **about/away** *or* **off** umher-/weg- *od.* davonfliegen; ~ **high** (fig.) (be ambitious) hoch hinauswollen; (prosper) Karriere machen; *see also* **crow A 1**; **high-flown** **2** (as or in aircraft or spacecraft) fliegen; (in balloon) fliegen; fahren; ~ **into Heathrow** in Heathrow landen; ~ **under a bridge** unter einer Brücke hindurchfliegen; ~ **past [sth.]** [an etw. (*Dat.*)] vorbeifliegen **3** (float, flutter) fliegen; **rumours are ~ing about** (fig.) es gehen Gerüchte um **4** (move quickly) fliegen; **glass was ~ing everywhere** überall flogen Glassplitter herum; **come ~ing towards sb.** jmdm. entgegengeflogen kommen; ~ **to sb.'s assistance** jmdm. zu Hilfe eilen; ~ **open** auffliegen; (be opened) aufgerissen werden; **knock** *or* **send sb./sth. ~ing** jmdn./etw. umstoßen; **send sth. ~ing to the other side of the room** etw. quer durchs Zimmer schleudern **5** (fig.) ~ **[by** *or* **past]** wie im Fluge vergehen; dahinfliegen (dichter.); **how time flies!, doesn't time ~!** wie die Zeit vergeht! **6** (wave in the air) ‹*Fahne:*› gehisst sein; *see also* **flag¹ A** **7** (attack angrily, react violently) ~ **at sb.** (lit. or fig.) über jmdn. herfallen; **let ~:** zuschlagen; (fig.: become angry) außer sich geraten; (fig.: use strong language) losschimpfen; **let ~ with** abschießen ‹*Pfeil, Rakete, Gewehr*›; werfen ‹*Stein*›; **let ~ at sb. with a gun/hammer** auf jmdn. schießen/mit einem Hammer auf jmdn. losgehen; ~ **into a temper** *or* **rage** *or* **tantrum** einen Wutanfall bekommen; *see also* **face A 1**; **handle A 1** **8** (flee) fliehen; (coll.: depart hastily) eilig aufbrechen; ~ **for one's life** um sein Leben rennen/fahren *usw.;* **I really must ~** (coll.) jetzt muss ich aber schnell los
B *v.t.,* **flew, flown** **1** (operate, transport or perform by ~ing) fliegen ‹*Flugzeug, Fracht, Einsatz*›; fliegen über (+ *Akk.*) ‹*Strecke*›; (travel over) überfliegen; überqueren; ~ **sb./sth. to and from Berlin** jmdn./etw. nach Berlin fliegen und aus Berlin ausfliegen; ~ **sth. into Gatwick** etw. nach Gatwick fliegen; ~ **Lufthansa** mit [der] Lufthansa fliegen **2** (cause to ~) gehisst haben, (as mark of nationality etc.) führen ‹*Flagge*›; fliegen lassen ‹*Taube, Falke*›; ~ **a kite** einen Drachen steigen lassen; (fig.) einen Versuchsballon steigen lassen; **go ~ a kite!** (coll.) hau ab! (salopp) **3** (flee) ~ **the country** aus dem Land fliehen; ~ **one's pursuers** vor seinen Verfolgern fliehen; **the bird has flown its cage** der Vogel ist aus seinem Käfig entflogen; ~ **the coop** (Amer. fig. coll.) sich aus dem Staube machen (ugs.); (leave home) durchbrennen (ugs.)
C *n.* **1** *in sing. or pl.* (on trousers) Hosenschlitz, *der* **2** (of flag) Flugseite, *die;* fliegendes Ende **3** *in pl.* (Theatre) Schnürboden, *der*

Phrasal verbs
• ~ **'in**
A *v.i.* (arrive in aircraft) [mit dem Flugzeug] eintreffen (**from** aus); (come in to land) landen
B *v.t.* (cause to land) landen; (bring by aircraft) einfliegen
• ~ **'off** *v.i.* **1** abfliegen **2** (become detached) abgehen; ‹*Hut:*› wegfliegen
• ~ **'out**
A *v.i.* abfliegen (**of** von); ~ **out there** dort hinfliegen
B *v.t.* ausfliegen; ~ **troops out to the disaster area** Truppen in das Katastrophengebiet fliegen

fly³ *adj.* (esp. Brit. coll.) clever

fly: ~ 'agaric *n.* Fliegenpilz, *der;* **~-away** *adj.* widerspenstig ‹*Haar*›; **~-blown** *adj.* (infested with flies' eggs) ≈ von Fliegenlarven befallen; (fig.) befleckt; **~-by** *n.* (Astronaut.) Vorbeiflug, *der;* **~-by-night** **A** *adj.* zwielichtig; **B** *n.: jmd., der sich nachts heimlich aus dem Staub macht;* **~-by-wire** *n.* (Aeronaut.) elektronische Flugsteuerung; *attrib.* **a ~-by-wire aircraft** ein Flugzeug mit elektronischer Flugsteuerung; **~catcher** *n.* (Ornith.) Schnäpper, *der;* **~-drive** **A** *attrib. adj.* Fly-drive-‹*Paket, Vereinbarung, Urlaub*›; **B** *n.* Fly-drive-Paket, *das;* Fly-drive-Urlaub, *der*

flyer /ˈflaɪə(r)/ *n.* **1** (bird) Flieger, *der* **2** (pilot) Flieger, *der*/Fliegerin, *die* **3** (fast-moving vehicle or animal) Flitzer, *der* (ugs.); (train) Express, *der;* **the horse is a ~:** das Pferd ist pfeilschnell **4** ▸**high-flyer** **5** (handbill) Handzettel, *der;* (Police) Steckbrief, *der* **6** (Amer.: investment) Spekulation, *die;* **take a ~:** spekulieren

fly: ~-fish *v.i.* mit [künstlichen] Fliegen fischen; **~-fishing** *n.* Fliegenfischerei, *die;* ~ **'half** *n.* (Rugby) Halbspieler, *der*

flying /ˈflaɪɪŋ/
A *adj.* Kurz-; (designed for rapid action) fliegend ‹*Verband, Kolonne, Ambulanz*›; ~ **visit** Stippvisite, *die* (ugs.)
B *n.* Fliegen, *das; attrib.* Flug‹*wetter, -zeit, -geschwindigkeit, -erfahrung*›; **an hour's ~ time** eine Flugstunde

flying: ~ 'bomb *n.* V-Waffe, *die;* ~ **'buttress** *n.* (Archit.) Strebebogen, *der;* Schwibbogen, *der;* ~ **'doctor** *n.* ▸ℹ **p. 1260** *Arzt, der seine Patienten mit dem Flugzeug besucht;* **F~ Dutchman** ▸**Dutchman 3**; ~ **field** *n.* Flugfeld, *das;* ~ **'fish** *n.* fliegender Fisch; ~ **'fox** *n.* (Zool.) Flugfuchs, *der;* Fliegender Hund; ~ **instructor** *n.* ▸ℹ **p. 1260** Fluglehrer, *der;* ~ **'jump,** ~ **'leap** *ns.* Sprung mit Anlauf; großer Satz (ugs.); **take a ~ jump** *or* **leap** Anlauf nehmen; ~ **machine** *n.* (Hist.) Luftfahrzeug, *das;* Flugmaschine, *die* (veralt.); ~ **'mare** *n.* (Wrestling) Schulterschwung, *der;* ~ **officer** *n.* (Brit. Air Force) Oberleutnant, *der;* ~ **'picket** *n.* mobiler Streikposten; ~ **'saucer** *n.* fliegende Untertasse; ~ **school** *n.* Fliegerschule, *die;* ~ **squad** *n.* (Police) Überfallkommando, *das;* ~ **'start** *n.* (Sport) fliegender Start; **get off to** *or* **have a ~ start** (fig.) (begin successfully) einen glänzenden Start haben; (have an advantage) die besten Voraussetzungen haben (fig.); **have got a ~ start over others** anderen gegenüber im Vorteil sein; ~ **suit** *n.* Fliegerkombination, *die;* ~ **'tackle** *n.* (Rugby, Amer. Footb.) Fassen, *das* (*im Lauf oder Sprung*); ~ **time** *n.* Flugzeit, *die*

fly: ~leaf *n.* Vorsatzblatt, *das;* Vorsatz, *der;* **~-on-the-wall** *attrib. adj.* von einer bewusst im Hintergrund gehaltenen Kamera aufgenommen ‹*Dokumentarfilm*›; die Kamera bewusst möglichst im Hintergrund haltend ‹*Aufnahmetechnik, -stil*›; **~over** *n.* (Brit.) [Straßen]überführung, *die;* Fly-over, *der;* **~paper** *n.* Fliegenfänger, *der;* **~-past** *n.* Luftparade, *die;* **~-post** *v.i.* illegal Plakate kleben; ~ **screen** *n.* Fliegengitter, *das;* **~sheet** *n.* **1** (of tent) Überzelt, *das;* **2** (circular) Prospekt, *der;* ~ **spray** *n.* Insektenspray, *der od. das;* ~ **swatter** *n.* Fliegenklappe, *die;* Fliegenklatsche, *die;* **~-tipping** *n., no pl., no indef. art.* illegales Deponieren von Bauschutt; **~trap** *n.* (trap) Fliegenfänger, *der;* (plant) [Venus]fliegenfalle, *die;* **~weight** *n.* (Boxing etc.) Fliegengewicht, *das;* (person also) Fliegengewichtler, *der;* **~wheel** *n.* Schwungrad, *das;* **fluid ~wheel** (Motor Veh. dated) Flüssigkeitskupplung, *die;* ~ **whisk** *n.* Fliegenwedel, *der*

FM *abbr.* **1** = **Field Marshal** FM **2** = **frequency modulation** FM

f-number /ˈefnʌmbə(r)/ *n.* (Photog.) Blende[nzahl], *die*

FO *abbr.* (Brit. Hist.) = **Foreign Office** ≈ AA

foal /fəʊl/
A *n.* Fohlen, *das;* **in** *or* **with ~:** trächtig
B *v.i.* fohlen

foam /fəʊm/
A *n.* **1** Schaum, *der* **2** ▸**foam plastic** **3** ▸**foam rubber**
B *v.i.* (lit. or fig.) schäumen (**with** vor + *Dat.*); ~ **at the mouth** Schaum vorm Mund haben; (fig. coll.) [vor Wut] schäumen

foam: ~-backed *adj.* schaumstoffverstärkt; ~ **bath** *n.* Schaumbad, *das;* ~ **extinguisher** *n.* Schaumlöscher, *der;* Schaumlöschgerät, *das;* ~ **'mattress** *n.* Schaumgummimatratze, *die;* ~ **'plastic** *n.* Schaumstoff, *der;* ~ **'rubber** *n.* Schaumgummi, *der*

foamy /ˈfəʊmɪ/ *adj.* schaumig; schäumend ‹*Brandung*›

fob¹ /fɒb/ *v.t.,* **-bb-: ~ sb. off with sth.** jmdn. mit etw. abspeisen (ugs.); ~ **sth. off on [to] sb.** jmdm. etw. andrehen (ugs.)

fob² *n.* Uhrtasche, *die*

f. o. b. *abbr.* = **free on board** fob

focal/ˈfəʊkl/: ~ **'distance,** ~ **'length** *ns.* Brennweite, *die;* ~ **plane** *n.* Brennebene, *die;* ~ **point** *n.* Brennpunkt, *der* (auch fig.); Fokus, *der;* **become the ~ point of interest** *or* **attention** in den Brennpunkt des Interesses rücken

foc's'le /ˈfəʊksl/ ▸**forecastle**

focus /ˈfəʊkəs/
A *n., pl.* **~es** *or* **foci** /ˈfəʊsaɪ/ **1** (Optics, Photog.) Brennpunkt, *der;* (focal length) Brennweite, *die;* (adjustment of eye or lens) Scharfeinstellung, *die;* **depth of ~** (adjustment) Schärfentiefe, *die;* (focal length) Brennweite, *die;* **out of/in ~:** unscharf/scharf eingestellt ‹*Kamera, Teleskop*›; unscharf/scharf ‹*Foto, Film, Vordergrund usw.*›; (fig.) unklar, verschwommen/klar; **see things in ~** (fig.) die Gegebenheiten klar erkennen; **get sth. in ~** (fig.) etw. klarer erkennen; **bring into ~:** scharf einstellen; (fig.) deutlich machen; **come into ~:** scharf werden; (fig.) sich herauskristallisieren **2** (fig.: centre, central object) Mittelpunkt, *der;* (of storm) Zentrum, *das;* (of earthquake) Herd, *der;* Hypozentrum, *das* (Geol.); (Med.: of disease) Herd, *der;* **be the ~ of attention** im Brennpunkt des Interesses stehen; **the principal ~ of research is ...:** im Mittelpunkt der Forschung steht ... **3** (Geom.) Brennpunkt, *der*
B *v.t.,* **-s-** *or* **-ss-** **1** (Optics, Photog.) einstellen (**on** auf + *Akk.*); fokussieren (fachspr.); ~ **a camera properly** *or* **correctly** eine Kamera auf die richtige Entfernung einstellen; **badly ~ed picture** unscharfes Bild; ~ **one's eyes on sth./sb.** die Augen auf etw./jmdn. richten **2** (concentrate) bündeln ‹*Licht, Strahlen*›; (fig.)

konzentrieren (**on** auf + *Akk.*)

C *v.i.*, **-s-** *or* **-ss-** 1 **the camera ~es automatically** die Kamera hat automatische Scharfeinstellung; **he can't** *or* **his eyes don't ~ properly** er sieht nicht klar *od.* nur verschwommen; **I can't ~ on print at that distance** ich kann Gedrucktes auf diese Entfernung nicht klar erkennen; **his eyes ~ed [up]on the window** sein Blick war auf das Fenster gerichtet 2 ‹*Licht, Strahlen:*› sich bündeln; (fig.) sich konzentrieren (**on** auf + *Akk.*)

'focus group *n.* Fokusgruppe, *die*

focus[s]ing /'fəʊkəsɪŋ/ *n.* (Optics, Photog.) Scharfeinstellung, *die*

fodder /'fɒdə(r)/ *n.* [Vieh]futter, *das;* (fig.) Futter, *das;* **~ plant** Futterpflanze, *die; see also* **cannon fodder**

foe /fəʊ/ *n.* (literary) Feind, *der*

FoE *abbr.* = **Friends of the Earth**

foetal ▸**fetal**

foetid /'fi:tɪd/ ▸**fetid**

foetus ▸**fetus**

fog /fɒg/

A *n.* 1 Nebel, *der;* **there are ~s in winter** es herrscht oft dichter Nebel im Winter; **drive in ~:** bei *od.* im Nebel fahren; **London was blanketed in ~:** über London lag eine Nebeldecke; **be in a [complete] ~** (fig.) [völlig] verunsichert sein; **be in a ~ about sth./as to what to do** sich (*Dat.*) im Unklaren über etw. (*Akk.*) sein/darüber sein, was zu tun ist 2 (Photog.) Schleier, *der*

B *v.t.*, **-gg-** 1 in Nebel hüllen; (bewilder) verwirren; **~ [up]** (obscure as if with ~, make confusing) vernebeln ‹*Aussicht, Straße, Sachverhalt*› 2 (Photog.) **the negative is ~ged** das Negativ hat einen Schleier

C *v.i.*, **-gg-** 1 **~ [up]** (mist over) beschlagen 2 (Photog.) einen Schleier bekommen

fog: ~ bank *n.* Nebelbank, *die;* **~bound** *adj.* 1 (surrounded) in Nebel gehüllt; 2 (immobilized) durch Nebel festgehalten

fogey ▸**fogy**; *see also* **young fogey**

foggy /'fɒgɪ/ *adj.* 1 neblig 2 (fig.) nebelhaft ‹*Vorstellung, Sprache, Bewusstsein*›; **[I] haven't the foggiest [idea** *or* **notion]** (coll.) [ich] hab keinen blassen Schimmer (ugs.)

fog: ~horn *n.* (Naut.) Nebelhorn, *das;* **a voice like a ~horn** (fig.) eine dröhnende *od.* durchdringende Stimme; **~ lamp, ~light** *ns.* (Motor Veh.) Nebelscheinwerfer, *der;* **~ signal** *n.* 1 (Railw.) Knallsignal, *das;* 2 (Naut.) Nebelsignal, *das*

fogy /'fəʊgɪ/ *n.* **[old] ~:** [alter *od.* rückständiger] Opa (salopp)/[alte *od.* rückständige] Oma (salopp)

föhn /fɜ:n/ *n.* (Meteorol.) Föhn, *der*

foible /'fɔɪbl/ *n.* 1 Eigenheit, *die* 2 (Fencing) ≈ Klingenschwäche, *die*

foil¹ /fɔɪl/ *n.* 1 (metal as thin sheet) Folie, *die;* **tin ~:** Stanniol[papier], *das;* **aluminium ~:** Alu[minium]folie, *die* 2 (to wrap or cover food etc.) Folie, *die* 3 (behind mirror-glass) Spiegelbelag, *der* (Technik) 4 (sb./sth. contrasting) ≈ Kontrast, *der*

foil² *v.t.* 1 (frustrate) vereiteln ‹*Versuch, Plan, Flucht*›; durchkreuzen ‹*Vorhaben, Plan*›; **they were ~ed in their attempts to escape** ihre Fluchtversuche wurden zunichte gemacht *od.* vereitelt; **[I've been] ~ed again** es war wieder nichts 2 (parry) parieren (auch fig.); abwehren

foil³ *n.* (sword) Florett, *das*

foil⁴ *n.* (hydrofoil) Tragflächenboot, *das;* Gleitboot, *das*

foist /fɔɪst/ *v.t.* 1 (introduce surreptitiously) **~ sth./sb. into sth.** etw./jmdn. in etw. (*Akk.*) einschmuggeln 2 (palm) **~ [off] on to** *or* **[up]on sb.** jmdm. andrehen (ugs.) ‹*schlechte Waren*›; jmdm. zuschieben ‹*Schuld, Verantwortung*›; auf jmdn. abwälzen ‹*Probleme, Verantwortung*›; **~ oneself on [to] sb.** sich jmdm. aufdrängen

fold¹ /fəʊld/

A *v.t.* 1 (double over on itself) [zusammen]falten; zusammenlegen ‹*Laken, Wäsche*› 2 (collapse) zusammenklappen 3 (wrap) **~ sb. in one's arms** jmdn. in die Arme schließen; **~ one's arms about** *or* **[a]round sb.** die Arme um jmdn. schlingen *od.* legen; **~ sth./sb. in sth.** etw./jmdn. in etw. (*Akk.*) einhüllen; **~ed in a handkerchief** in ein Taschentuch eingewickelt 4 **~ one's arms** die Arme verschränken; **~ one's hands** die Hände falten; **the crow ~ed its wings** die Krähe legte die Flügel an

B *v.i.* 1 (become ~ed) sich zusammenlegen; sich zusammenfalten 2 (be able to be ~ed) sich falten lassen; **it ~s easily** es ist leicht zu falten; es lässt sich leicht falten 3 (collapse) zusammenklappen; (fig.) (cease to function) eingehen (ugs.); (go bankrupt) Konkurs *od.* Bankrott machen 4 (be collapsible) sich zusammenklappen lassen

C *n.* 1 (doubling) Falte, *die;* **the baggy ~s of skin under his eyes** die Tränensäcke unter seinen Augen; **~s of flesh** Fettwülste 2 (hollow, nook in mountain, etc.) Falte, *die* (Geol.); [Tal]mulde, *die* 3 (coil of serpent, string, etc.) Windung, *die* 4 (act of ~ing) Faltung, *die* 5 (line made by ~ing) Kniff, *der* 6 (Geol.) [Gebirgs]faltung, *die*

(Phrasal verbs)

• **~ a'way**

A *v.t.* zusammenklappen

B *v.i.* zusammenklappbar sein; sich zusammenklappen lassen. *see also* **foldaway**

• **~ 'back**

A *v.t.* zurückschlagen, aufschlagen ‹*Laken*›; zurückklappen ‹*Rücksitz*›; umknicken ‹*Papier*›

B *v.i.* sich zurückschlagen lassen

• **~ 'down**

A *v.t.* 1 (make more compact) zusammenklappen 2 (bend back part of) ▸**~ back A** 3 (open out) ausklappen

B *v.i.* ▸**A:** sich zusammenklappen lassen; sich zurückschlagen lassen

• **~ 'in** *v.t.* 1 (double over and inwards) nach innen umlegen 2 (Cookery) unterrühren; unterheben, unterziehen ‹*Eischnee*›

• **~ into** *v.t.* (Cookery) unterrühren unter (+ *Akk.*); unterheben unter (+ *Akk.*), unterziehen ‹*Eischnee*› unter (+ *Akk.*)

• **~ 'out** *v.i.* ‹*Landkarte:*› sich auseinander falten lassen; ‹*Tisch:*› sich hochklappen lassen; **the settee ~s out to become a double bed** das Sofa lässt sich zu einem Doppelbett ausklappen; *see also* **fold-out**

• **~ 'over** *v.t.* umlegen ‹*Saum*›; umknicken ‹*Seiten*›

• **~ 'up**

A *v.t.* 1 (make more compact by ~ing) zusammenfalten; zusammenlegen ‹*Laken, Wäsche*› 2 (collapse) zusammenklappen

B *v.i.* 1 (be able to be ~ed up) sich zusammenfalten lassen 2 (collapse) sich zusammenklappen lassen; **how does this table ~ up?** wie wird dieser Tisch zusammengeklappt?; (fig.) ▸**fold¹ B 2** (fig.)

fold² *n.* 1 ▸**sheepfold** 2 (fig.: body of believers) Gemeinde, *die;* Herde, *die* (geh.); **he has left the ~:** er hat den Schoß der Kirche verlassen (geh.)

-fold

A *adj. in comb.* 1 (times) -fach 2 (having so many parts etc.) -fältig

B *adv. in comb.* -fach

'foldaway *adj.* zusammenklappbar; Klapp‹*tisch, -stuhl, -fahrrad, -bett*›

folder /'fəʊldə(r)/ *n.* 1 (cover, holder for loose papers) Mappe, *die* 2 (folded circular etc.) Faltblatt, *das;* (map also) Faltkarte, *die* 3 (Computing) Ordner, *der*

folding /'fəʊldɪŋ/ ▸**foldaway**

folding: ~ 'door *n.* Falttür, *die;* **~ 'doors** *n. pl.* Falttür, *die;* (of hangar, barn, etc.) Falttor, *das*

'fold-out *n.* ausfaltbare Seite

foliage /'fəʊlɪɪdʒ/ *n., no pl.* 1 (leaves) Blätter *Pl.;* (of tree also) Laub, *das* 2 (Art) Laubwerk, *das*

foliage: ~ leaf *n.* [Laub]blatt, *das;* **~ plant** *n.* Blattpflanze, *die*

folio /'fəʊlɪəʊ/

A *n., pl.* **~s** 1 (leaf of paper etc.) [nur auf der Vorderseite nummeriertes] Blatt 2 (leaf- or page number of printed book) Seitenzahl, *die* 3 (sheet folded once) Doppelbogen, *der;* **in ~:** in Folio; im Folioformat 4 (book) Foliant, *der;* **First F~:** erste Folioausgabe

B *adj.* Folio-

folk /fəʊk/ *n., pl. same or* **~s** 1 (a people) Volk, *das* 2 *in pl.* **~[s]** (people) Leute *Pl.;* (people in general) die Leute; **some ~[s]** manche [Leute] 3 *in pl.* **~s** (coll., as address: people, friends) Leute *Pl.* (ugs.) 4 *in pl.* (people of a particular class) **[the] rich/poor ~:** die Reichen/Armen; **old ~[s]** alte Leute; **old ~'s home** ▸**old people's home** 5 *in pl.* **~s** (coll.) (one's relatives) Verwandte *Pl.;* Leute *Pl.* (ugs.); (one's parents) Alte Herrschaften (ugs.) 6 ▸**folk music** 7 *attrib.* (of the people, traditional) Volks-; **~ handicrafts** Volkskunst, *die;* **~ museum** Heimatmuseum, *das*

folk: ~ club *n.* Folkklub, *der;* **~ dance** *n.* Volkstanz, *der;* **~ dancing** *n.* Volkstanz, *der;* **~ etymology** *n.* Volksetymologie, *die;* **~ hero** *n.* Volksheld, *der;* **~lore** *n.* 1 (traditional beliefs) [volkstümliche] Überlieferung; Folklore, *die;* 2 (study) Volkskunde, *die;* Folklore, *die;* **~ memory** *n.* mündliche Überlieferung, *die;* **~ music** *n.* Volksmusik, *die;* **~ 'rock** *n., no pl.* Folkrock, *der;* **~ singer** *n.* Sänger/Sängerin von Volksliedern; (modern) Folksänger, *der*/-sängerin, *die;* **~ singing** *n.* Singen von Volksliedern *od.* (modern) Folksongs; **~ song** *n.* Volkslied, *das;* (modern) Folksong, *der*

folksy /'fəʊksɪ/ *adj.* 1 (sociable, informal) gesellig 2 (having characteristics of folk art) volkstümlich

folk: ~ tale *n.* Volksmärchen, *das;* **~ways** *n. pl.* traditionelle Lebensweise; **~weave** *n.* grob gewebter Stoff

folky /'fəʊkɪ/ ▸**folksy 2**

follicle /'fɒlɪkl/ *n.* Follikel, *der* (Biol., Med.)

follow /'fɒləʊ/

A *v.t.* 1 folgen (+ *Dat.*); **you're being ~ed** Sie werden verfolgt

2 (go along) folgen (+ *Dat.*); entlanggehen/-fahren ‹*Straße usw.*›

3 (come after in order or time) folgen (+ *Dat.*); folgen auf (+ *Akk.*); **A is ~ed by B** auf A folgt B

4 (accompany) [nach]folgen (+ *Dat.*)

5 (provide with sequel) **~ sth. with sth.** einer Sache (*Dat.*) etw. folgen lassen; **~ your meal with a brandy** schließen Sie Ihr Essen mit einem Kognak ab; **his first novel was ~ed by a string of best-sellers** auf seinen ersten Roman folgte eine ganze Reihe von Bestsellern; **that's a hard act to ~** (fig.) das macht ihm/ihr keiner so leicht nach; **~ that!** (coll.) das mach mir erst mal nach!

6 (go after as admirer or suitor) verehren; anhängen (geh.) (+ *Dat.*)

7 (result from) die Folge sein von; hervorgehen aus; **a stroke is often ~ed by permanent paralysis** die Folge eines Schlaganfalls ist oft eine dauernde Lähmung

8 (treat or take as guide or leader) folgen (+ *Dat.*); sich orientieren an (+ *Dat.*); (adhere to) anhängen (+ *Dat.*); sich bekennen zu

9 (act according to) folgen (+ *Dat.*) ‹*Prinzip, Instinkt, Trend*›; verfolgen ‹*Politik*›; befolgen ‹*Vorschrift, Regel, Anweisung, Rat, Warnung*›; handeln nach ‹*Gefühl, Wunsch*›; sich halten an (+ *Akk.*) ‹*Konventionen, Diät, Maßstab*›; **~ one's heart** der Stimme des Herzens folgen; *see also* **example 1**; **fashion A 2**; **lead² C 1**; **nose A 1**

10 (practise) ausüben ‹*Beruf, Handwerk, eine Kunst*›; **~ the teaching/medical profession/the arts** Lehrer/Arzt/Künstler sein

11 (keep up with mentally, grasp meaning of) folgen (+ *Dat.*); **I can't ~ what he says** ich kann ihm nicht folgen; **do you ~ me?, are you ~ing me?** verstehst du, was ich meine?; **I don't ~ you/your meaning** ich verstehe Sie nicht/verstehe nicht, was Sie meinen; **~ the music from the score** die Partitur mitlesen

12 (be aware of the present state or progress of) verfolgen ‹*Ereignisse, Nachrichten, Prozess*›; **~ a TV serial** eine Fernsehserie regelmäßig sehen

B *v.i.* 1 (go, come) **~ after sb./sth.** jmdm./einer Sache folgen

2 (go or come after person or thing) folgen; **you go ahead in the car and I'll ~ on my bike** du fährst mit dem Auto voraus, und ich komme mit dem Fahrrad nach; **~ in the wake of sth.** etw. ablösen; auf etw. (*Akk.*) folgen

3 (come next in order or time) folgen; **in the years**

that ~ed in den darauf folgenden Jahren; **as ~s** wie folgt; **the details are as ~s** die Einzelheiten lauten folgendermaßen; **there are two options, as ~s: ...:** es gibt zwei Möglichkeiten, und zwar folgende: ...; **would you like coffee to ~?** hätten Sie danach *od.* anschließend gerne [einen] Kaffee?; **what ~s next?** was kommt danach?
4 (ensue) folgen
5 **~ from sth.** (result) die Folge von etw. sein; (be deducible) aus etw. folgen; **it ~s [from this] that ...:** daraus folgt, dass ...; das heißt, dass ...

Phrasal verbs

- **~ 'on** *v.i.* **1** (continue) **~ on from sth.** die Fortsetzung von etw. sein **2** (Cricket) sofort zum zweiten Mal schlagen; *see also* **follow-on**
- **~ 'out** *v.t.* **1** (pursue to the end) durchführen ‹*Plan, Projekt*›; sich (*Dat.*) erfüllen ‹*Wunsch*›; zu Ende verfolgen ‹*Ziel, Politik, Idee*› **2** (carry out) [genau] befolgen ‹*Regel, Anweisung*›
- **~ 'through**
A *v.t.* zu Ende verfolgen; durchziehen (ugs.)
B *v.i.* (Sport) durchschwingen; *see also* **follow-through**
- **~ 'up** *v.t.* **1** (pursue steadily) stetig verfolgen **2** (add further action etc. to) ausbauen ‹*Erfolg, Sieg*› **3** (investigate further) nachgehen (+ *Dat.*) ‹*Hinweis*›; (consider further) berücksichtigen ‹*Bitte, Angebot*›. *see also* **follow-up**

follower /'fɒləʊə(r)/ *n.* Anhänger, *der*/Anhängerin, *die*; **be a dedicated ~ of fashion** immer mit der Mode gehen

following /'fɒləʊɪŋ/
A *adj.* **1** *pres. p. of* **follow; on the ~ day** am Tag danach *od.* darauf; **on the ~ Monday** am nächsten Montag **2** (now to be mentioned) folgend; **the ~ items** folgende Gegenstände; **in the ~ way** folgendermaßen; **for the ~ reasons** aus folgenden Gründen; **the ~:** Folgendes; (persons) Folgende **3** (blowing in one's direction of travel) **~ wind** Rückenwind, *der*
B *prep.* nach
C *n.* Anhängerschaft, *die*

follow: ~-my-'leader (*Amer.:* **~-the-'leader**) *n.: Spiel, bei dem alle Mitspieler das nachmachen, was einer vormacht;* **~-on** *n.* (Cricket) ≈ sofortiger zweiter Durchgang (*nachdem man im ersten nicht nahe genug an die Punktzahl des Gegners herangekommen ist*); **~-through** *n.* (Sport) Durchschwung, *der*; **~-up** *n.* Fortsetzung, *die*; (Med.) Nachuntersuchung, *die*; **there's never any ~-up to his promises** er erfüllt *od.* hält seine Versprechen nie; **as a ~-up** im Anschluss (**to** an + *Akk.*); **~-up letter/visit** Nachfassbrief, *der*/-besuch, *der* (Werbespr.)

folly /'fɒlɪ/ *n.* **1** Torheit, *die* (geh.); **it would be [sheer] ~:** es wäre [äußerst] töricht (geh.); **an act of ~:** eine Torheit (geh.) **2** (Archit. structure with no practical purpose) *rein zur Schau dienendes Gebäude, meist im Schlosspark;* ≈ Pavillon, *der*; (temple) Gloriette, *die* **3** *in pl.* **Follies** (dated; Theatre) Revue mit Glamourgirls

foment /fə'ment, fəʊ'ment/ *v.t.* **1** (foster) schüren **2** (bathe) mit feuchter Wärme behandeln

fomentation /fəʊmen'teɪʃn/ *n.* **1** (fostering) Schüren, *das* **2** (warm cloth[s]) heißer Umschlag **3** (application of warm cloth[s]) Behandlung mit feuchter Wärme *od.* mit heißen Umschlägen

fond /fɒnd/ *adj.* **1** (tender) zärtlich; (affectionate) liebevoll ‹*Blick*›; lieb ‹*Erinnerung*›; (in letters) **~[est] love** mit lieben Grüßen; alles Liebe; **say a ~ farewell** sich überschwänglich verabschieden; **be ~ of sb.** jmdn. mögen *od.* gern haben; **be ~ of sth.** etw. mögen; **be ~ of doing sth.** etw. gern tun; **she's very ~ of Greece/the theatre** sie liebt Griechenland/das Theater; **I'm not very ~ of sweets** ich mache mir nicht viel aus Süßigkeiten; **he's become very ~ of living in Spain** er lebt mittlerweile sehr gern in Spanien **2** (foolishly credulous or hopeful) kühn ‹*Hoffnung, Traum*›; gutgläubig ‹*Person*›; allzu zuversichtlich ‹*Glaube*›; voreingenommen ‹*Eltern*›; **he had ~ hopes of becoming an ambassador one day** er glaubte allen Ernstes daran, einmal Botschafter zu werden **3** (over-affectionate) übertrieben liebevoll

fondant /'fɒndənt/ *n.* Fondant, *der od. das*

fondle /'fɒndl/ *v.t.* streicheln

fondly /'fɒndlɪ/ *adv.* **1** (tenderly) zärtlich; (with affection) liebevoll; **he looks ~ back upon his days at university** er erinnert sich gern an seine Studentenzeit **2** (with foolish credulousness or hopefulness) allzu zuversichtlich

fondness /'fɒndnɪs/ *n., no pl.* **1** (tenderness) Zärtlichkeit, *die*; (affection) Liebe, *die*; **look back with great ~ on sth.** sich sehr gern an etw. (*Akk.*) erinnern; **~ for sth./doing sth.** (special liking) Vorliebe für etw./dafür, etw. zu tun; **~ for sb./art/the sea** Liebe zu jmdm./zur Kunst/zum Meer **2** (foolish credulousness or hopefulness) allzu große Gutgläubigkeit; törichte Zuversicht

fondue /'fɒndju:, 'fɒndu:/ *n.* (Gastr.) Fondue, *das od. die*

font¹ /fɒnt/ *n.* (baptismal) Taufstein, *der*

font² *n.* (Computing, Printing) Schrift, *die*; Font, *der* (fachspr.); (attrib.) **~ size** Schriftgröße, *die*; Fontgröße, *die*

food /fu:d/ *n.* **1** *no pl., no art.* Nahrung, *die*; (for animals) Futter, *das*; **take ~:** Nahrung zu sich nehmen; **lack of ~:** Nahrungsmangel, *der*; **nutritious ~:** nahrhafte Kost **2** *no pl., no art.* (as commodity) Lebensmittel *Pl.*; **one's week's shopping for ~** *or* **~ shopping** der wöchentliche Lebensmitteleinkauf **3** *no pl.* (in solid form) Essen, *das*; **some ~:** etwas zu essen; **there was plenty of ~ and drink** es gab reichlich zu essen und zu trinken; **she had prepared some delicious ~ for the party** für die Party hatte sie einige leckere Sachen vorbereitet; **he likes his ~ too much for that!** dazu isst er viel zu gern!; **he's very keen on Italian ~:** er isst sehr gern italienisch **4** (particular kind) Nahrungsmittel, *das*; Kost, *die*; (for animals) Futter, *das*; **nuts are a very nutritious ~:** Nüsse sind sehr nahrhaft; **canned ~s** Konserven *Pl.*; **preserved/imported ~s** eingemachte/importierte Nahrungsmittel **5** (nutriment) Nahrung, *die* **6** (fig.: material for mental work) Stoff, *der*; **~ for thought** Stoff zum Nachdenken; **~ for discussion** Diskussionsstoff, *der*

food: ~ additive *n.* Lebensmittelzusatz[stoff], *der*; **~ chain** *n.* (Ecol.) Nahrungskette, *die*; **~ counter** *n.* Lebensmitteltheke, *die*; **~ court** *n.* (Amer.) (in a shopping mall) Gastronomiebereich, *der*; **~ crop** *n.* Futterpflanze, *die*; **~ fish** *n.* Speisefisch, *der*; **~ hygiene** *n., no pl.* Lebensmittelhygiene, *die*

foodie /'fu:dɪ/ *n.* (Brit. coll.) ≈ Feinschmecker, *der*/-schmeckerin, *die*

food: ~ parcel *n.* Lebensmittelpaket, *das*; **~ poisoning** *n.* Lebensmittelvergiftung, *die*; **~ processor** *n.* Küchenmaschine, *die*; **~ rationing** *n.* Rationierung [von Lebensmitteln]; **~ shop** ▸ **~ store**; **~ stamps** *n. pl.* (Amer.) Lebensmittelgutscheine *Pl.*; **~ store** *n.* Lebensmittelgeschäft, *das*; **~stuff** *n.* Nahrungsmittel, *das*; **perishable ~stuffs** leicht verderbliche Lebensmittel; **~ supplies** *n. pl.* Vorräte *Pl.*; **~ technology** *n., no pl.* Lebensmitteltechnologie, *die*; Lebensmitteltechnik, *die*; **~ value** *n.* Nährwert, *der*

fool¹ /fu:l/
A *n.* **1** Dummkopf, *der* (ugs.); **look a ~:** unmöglich (ugs.) aussehen; (as regards behaviour) dumm dastehen (ugs.); **he's a ~ to believe stories like that** er ist ein Narr *od.* (ugs.) er ist schön dumm, wenn er solche Geschichten glaubt; **what a ~ I am!** wie dumm von mir!; **oh, you 'are a ~!** wie kannst du nur so dumm sein!; **he makes you feel like a ~:** bei ihm kommt man sich (*Dat.*) wie ein Narr vor; **be no** *or* **nobody's ~:** nicht dumm *od.* (ugs.) nicht auf den Kopf gefallen sein; **I would never be such a ~:** so dumm wäre ich nie; **be ~ enough to do sth.** so dumm *od.* (ugs.) so blöd sein *od.* dumm genug sein, etw. zu tun; **make a ~ of oneself** sich lächerlich machen; **there's no ~ like an old ~:** Alter schützt vor Torheit nicht[, ganz im Gegenteil]; **a ~ and his money are soon parted** ein Dummkopf ist sein Geld bald wieder los; **not suffer ~s gladly** Dummheit nicht ertragen können; **~s rush in where angels fear to tread** blinder Eifer schadet nur (Spr.) **2** (Hist.: jester, clown) Narr, *der*; **act** *or* **play the ~:** herumalbern (ugs.); den Clown spielen (abwertend) **3** (dupe) **make a ~ of sb.** jmdn. blamieren. *see also* **all A 2**; **April**
B *v.i.* herumalbern (ugs.); **you're ~ing!** mach keine Witze! (ugs.)
C *v.t.* **1** (cheat) **~ sb. out of sth.** jmdn. um etw. betrügen; **~ sb. into doing sth.** jmdn. [durch Tricks] dazu bringen, etw. zu tun **2** (dupe) täuschen; hereinlegen (ugs.); (play tricks on) foppen; **don't be ~ed by him** lass dich von ihm nicht täuschen *od.* (ugs.) hereinlegen; **you could have ~ed me** (iron.) ach, was du nicht sagst!

Phrasal verbs

- **~ a'bout, ~ a'round** *v.i.* (play the ~) herumalbern (ugs.); Unsinn machen; (idle) herumtrödeln (ugs.); (trifle) Zeit vergeuden; **~ about** *or* **around with sth./sb.** mit etw./jmdm. herumspielen
- **~ with** *v.t.* [herum]spielen mit

fool² *n.* (Gastr.) *Süßspeise aus Kompott, das mit Sahne o. Ä. verrührt ist*

foolery /'fu:lərɪ/ *n., no pl.* Alberei, *die*

foolhardiness /'fu:lhɑ:dɪnɪs/ *n., no pl.* Tollkühnheit, *die*; [unverantwortlicher] Leichtsinn

foolhardy /'fu:lhɑ:dɪ/ *adj.* tollkühn ‹*Handlung, Behauptung, Person*›; draufgängerisch ‹*Person*›; **that was a ~ thing to say** es war sehr riskant, das zu sagen

foolish /'fu:lɪʃ/ *adj.* **1** töricht; verrückt (ugs.) ‹*Idee, Vorschlag*›; **we were ~ to expect miracles** es war töricht von uns, Wunder zu erwarten; **~ minds** Dummköpfe *Pl.* (ugs.); **don't do anything ~:** mach keinen Unsinn; **what a ~ thing to do/say** wie kann man nur so etwas Dummes tun/sagen **2** (ridiculous) albern (ugs.) ‹*Verhalten*›; blöd, dumm (ugs.) ‹*Grinsen, Bemerkung*›; lächerlich ‹*Aussehen*›

foolishly /'fu:lɪʃlɪ/ *adv.* **1** (in foolish manner) törichterweise **2** (in ridiculous manner) lächerlich ‹*sich benehmen*›; blöd, dumm (ugs.) ‹*grinsen*›

fool: ~proof *adj.* (not open to misuse) wasserdicht (fig.); (not open to misinterpretation) unmissverständlich; (infallible) absolut sicher; (that cannot break down) narrensicher (ugs.); **~scap** /'fu:lskæp, 'fu:lzkæp/ *n.* **1** (size of paper) Kanzleiformat, *das*; **2** (paper of this size) Kanzleipapier, *das*; **~'s 'errand** *n.* nutzloses Unternehmen; **go on a ~'s errand** sich vergeblich bemühen; **I was sent on a ~'s errand** man hat mich völlig umsonst losgeschickt; **~'s 'paradise** *n.* Traumwelt, *die*; **be** *or* **live in a ~'s paradise** in einer Traumwelt leben; sich (*Dat.*) Illusionen machen; **~'s 'parsley** *n.* (Bot.) Hundspetersilie, *die*

foot /fʊt/
A *n., pl.* **feet** /fi:t/ **1** ▸ **p. 951** Fuß, *der*; **at sb.'s feet** zu jmds. Füßen; **be at sb.'s feet** (fig.) jmdm. zu Füßen liegen (geh.); **fall/sit at sb.'s feet** jmdm. zu Füßen fallen/sitzen; **sit at sb.'s feet** (fig.) jmds. Jünger sein; **lay the blame for sth. at sb.'s feet** jmdm. etw. anlasten *od.* zur Last legen; **put one's best ~ forward** (fig.) (hurry) sich beeilen; (do one's best) sein Bestes tun; **please wipe your feet** bitte Schuhe abtreten; **do sth. with both feet** (fig.) sich voll in etw. (*Akk.*) reinknien (ugs.); **feet of clay** (fig.) eine Schwachstelle; **feet first** mit den Füßen zuerst *od.* voran; **go into sth. feet first** (fig.) sich Hals über Kopf (ugs.) in etw. hineinstürzen; **have one ~ in the grave** (fig.) mit einem Fuß im Grabe stehen; **have both [one's] feet on the ground** (fig.) mit beiden Beinen [fest] auf der Erde stehen; **keep one's feet** (fig.) nicht hinfallen; **have a ~ in both camps** (fig.) auf beiden Schultern Wasser tragen; **my ~!** (coll.) beileibe nicht!; **on ~:** zu Fuß; **set sth. on ~:** etw. in Gang bringen *od.* setzen; **on one's/its feet** (lit. or fig.) auf den Beinen; **you'll be back on your feet again before long** (fig.) bald wirst du wieder auf die Beine kommen; **put** *or* **get sb. [back] on his feet** (fig.) jmdn. auf die Beine bringen; **put** *or* **get** *or* **set sth. [back] on its feet** (fig.) etw. [wieder] auf die Beine bringen *od.* stellen; **get on one's feet** sich erheben; aufstehen; **put one's ~ down** (fig.) (be firmly insistent or repressive) energisch werden; (accelerate motor vehicle) [Voll]gas geben; **put**

f

one's ~ in it (fig. coll.) ins Fettnäpfchen treten (ugs.); einen Fauxpas begehen; **put one's feet up** die Beine hochlegen; **start [off]** *or* **get off** *or* **begin on the right/wrong ~** (fig.) einen guten/schlechten Start haben; **set ~ in/on sth.** etw. betreten; **go away and never set ~ in here** *or* **in this place again** geh fort und setze keinen Fuß mehr über diese Schwelle; **he had never set ~ in Britain/outside London** er hatte noch nie einen Fuß auf britischen Boden gesetzt/er war noch nie aus London herausgekommen; **be rushed off one's feet** (fig.) in Trab gehalten werden (ugs.); **stand on one's own [two] feet** (fig.) auf eigenen Füßen stehen; **sweep sb. off his/her feet** (fig.) jmdn. *od.* jmds. Herz im Sturm erobern; **rise** *or* **get to one's feet** sich erheben; aufstehen; **help sb. to his feet** jmdm. aufhelfen; **it's a bit muddy under ~:** der Boden ist ein bisschen matschig; **tread sth./sb. under ~:** auf etw./jmdn. treten; (fig.) etw./jmdn. unterdrücken; **get under sb.'s feet** (fig.) jmdm. vor die Füße laufen; **with four children under her feet** mit vier Kindern, die ihr vor den Füßen herumlaufen; **get one's feet wet** (fig.) sich hineinfinden; **never put a ~ wrong** (fig.) nie etwas falsch machen; **get/have cold feet** kalte Füße kriegen (ugs.)/gekriegt haben (ugs.); **catch sb. on the wrong ~** (fig.) jmdn. auf dem falschen Fuß erwischen; **have two left feet** (fig.) zwei linke Füße haben (ugs.)
2) (step) **swift/light of ~:** schnell-/leichtfüßig
3) *pl. same* (Brit. Hist.) Infanterie, *die* (Milit.); **five hundred ~:** fünfhundert Infanteristen (Milit.) *od.* Fußsoldaten
4) (far end) unteres Ende; (of bed) Fußende, *das;* (lowest part) Fuß, *der;* (of sail) Unterliek, *das;* **at the ~ of the list/page** unten auf der Liste/Seite; **the compost heap is at the ~ of the garden** der Komposthaufen ist im hinteren Teil des Gartens
5) (of stocking etc.) Fuß, *der;* Füßling, *der*
6) (Pros.: metrical unit) [Vers]fuß, *der*
7) (Phonet.: unit of speech) ≈ Akzentgruppe, *die*
8) *pl.* **feet** *or same* ▸**i p. 911**, ▸**i p. 1208**, ▸**i p. 1286** (linear measure) Fuß, *der (30,48 cm);* **7 ~** *or* **feet** 7 Fuß
9) (base) Fuß, *der;* (of statue, pillar) Sockel, *der;* Basis, *die*
10) (Zool.: of invertebrate) Fuß, *der*
11) (Bot.) Ansatzstelle, *die. See also* **ball**[1] **A 2**; **cubic 2**; **door 2**; **drag B 1**; **fall B 1, 16**; **find A 2**; **hand A 1**; **square B 2**; **walk B 2**
B *v.t.* **1) ~ it** (dance) tanzen; (walk) zu Fuß gehen
2) (pay) **~ the bill** die Rechnung bezahlen

footage /ˈfʊtɪdʒ/ *n., no pl., no indef. art.* Filmmaterial, *das;* **documentary ~:** Dokumentaraufnahmen *Pl.*

foot-and-ˈmouth [disease] *n.* Maul- und Klauenseuche, *die*

football /ˈfʊtbɔːl/ *n.* **1)** Fußball, *der;* (elongated) [ovaler] Ball; (fig.) Spielball, *der* **2)** (Brit.: soccer) Fußball, *der;* (Amer.: American ~) Football, *der. see also* **American football**; **Rugby football**

ˈfootball boot *n.* Fußballschuh, *der*

footballer /ˈfʊtbɔːlə(r)/ *n.* ▸**i p. 1260** **1)** (Brit.: soccer player) Fußballspieler, *der;* Fußballer, *der* (ugs.) **2)** (Amer.: American football player) Footballspieler, *der*

football: ~ hooligan *n.* Fußballhooligan, *der;* Fußballrowdy, *der;* **~ hooliganism** *n., no pl.* Fußballrowdytum, *das;* **~ pitch** *n.* Fußballplatz, *der;* **~ pools** *n. pl.* **the ~ pools** das Fußballtoto; *see also* **pool**[2] **A 1**

foot: ~bath *n.* **1)** (washing of feet) Fußbad, *das;* **2)** (small bath) Fußwanne, *die;* **~ brake** *n.* Fußbremse, *die;* **~ bridge** *n.* Steg, *der;* (across road, railway, etc.) Fußgängerbrücke, *die*

-footed /fʊtɪd/ *adj. in comb.* -füßig; **nimble-~:** leichtfüßig; **large-/small-~:** mit großen/kleinen Füßen *nachgestellt*

footer /ˈfʊtə(r)/ **1)** (Brit. coll.) ▸**football A 2** **2)** (in printing) Fußzeile, *die*

-footer /fʊtə(r)/ *n. in comb.* **she is a six-~:** sie ist sechs Fuß groß; **the boat was a nine-~:** das Boot war neun Fuß lang

foot: ~fall *n.* Schritt, *der;* **~ fault** (Lawn Tennis) **A** *n.* Fußfehler, *der;* **B** *v.i.* einen Fußfehler machen; **~hill** *n., usu. pl.* [Gebirgs]ausläufer, *der;* **~hold** *n.* Halt, *der;* (fig.) Stützpunkt, *der;* **get a ~hold** (fig.) Fuß fassen

footing /ˈfʊtɪŋ/ *n.* **1)** (fig.: status) Stellung, *die;* **be on an equal ~ [with sb.]** [jmdm.] gleichgestellt sein; **put A on an equal ~ with B** A mit B auf die gleiche Stufe stellen; **place sth. on a firm ~:** etw. auf eine feste Basis stellen; **be on a friendly ~ with sb.** ein freundschaftliches Verhältnis zu jmdm. haben; **be on a war ~:** sich im Kriegszustand befinden **2)** (foothold) Halt, *der;* **lose/miss/keep one's ~:** den Halt verlieren/keinen Halt finden/sich halten **3)** (surface for standing on) Grund, *der;* (fig.) Stellung, *die;* **gain a ~ as a journalist** sich (*Dat.*) eine Position als Journalist schaffen; als Journalist Fuß fassen **4)** (Building) Bankett, *das*

footle /ˈfuːtl/ *v.i.* (coll.) **~ about** (trifle) herumtrödeln (ugs.); (play the fool) Unfug treiben

ˈfootlights *n. pl.* (Theatre) Rampenlicht, *das*

footling /ˈfuːtlɪŋ/ *adj.* läppisch (abwertend); albern (ugs.)

foot: ~loose *adj.* ungebunden; **~loose and fancy-free** frei und ledig; **~man** /ˈfʊtmən/ *n., pl.* **~men** /ˈfʊtmən/ (servant) Lakai, *der;* **~mark** ▸**~print**; **~muff** *n.* Fußsack, *der;* **~note** *n.* Fußnote, *die;* **~ passenger** *n.* Fußpassagier, *der;* **~path** *n.* (path) Fußweg, *der;* (Brit.: pavement) Gehsteig, *der;* Bürgersteig, *der;* **~plate** *n.* (Brit. Railw.) Führerstand, *der;* **~plate workers** Lokomotivführer und Heizer; **~print** *n.* **1)** (of foot) Fußabdruck, *der;* **~prints in the snow** Fußspuren im Schnee; **2)** (Computing) Stellfläche, *die;* **~ race** *n.* Wettlauf, *der;* Wettrennen, *das;* **~rest** *n.* Fußstütze, *die;* (on bicycle or motorcycle) Fußraste, *die;* **~ rot** *n.* (Vet. Med.) Stoppellähme, *die;* **~ rule** *n.* [einen Fuß langes] Lineal; **~ scraper** *n.* Fußabstreifer, *der;* Abtreter, *der*

footsie /ˈfʊtsɪ/ *n.* (coll.) **play ~ [with sb.]** [mit jmdm.] füßeln (landsch.)

foot: ~slog (coll.) **A** *v.i.* latschen (salopp); **B** *n.* Gelaufe, *das* (ugs.); **~ soldier** *n.* Infanterist, *der* (Milit.); Fußsoldat, *der;* **~sore** *pred. adj.* **be ~sore** wunde Füße haben; **~step** *n.* Schritt, *der;* **follow** *or* **tread in sb.'s ~steps** (fig.) in jmds. Fußstapfen (*Akk.*) treten; **~stool** *n.* Fußbank, *die;* Fußschemel, *der;* **~way** *n.* Fußweg, *der;* **~wear** *n., no pl.* Schuhe *Pl.;* Schuhwerk, *das;* Fußbekleidung, *die* (Kaufmannsspr.); **~work** *n., no pl.* (Sport, Dancing) Beinarbeit, *die*

fop /fɒp/ Dandy, *der;* Geck, *der*

foppish /ˈfɒpɪʃ/ *adj.* dandyhaft (geh.); geckenhaft (abwertend)

for /fə(r), *stressed* fɔː(r)/ ▸**i p. 1151**
A *prep.* **1)** (representing, on behalf of, in exchange against) für; (in place of) für; anstelle von; **what is the German ~ 'buzz'?** wie heißt „buzz" auf Deutsch?; **I. Smith ~ B. Jones** (as signature) B. Jones, i. A. I. Smith; *see also* **eye A 1**
2) (in defence, support, or favour of) für; **be ~ doing sth.** dafür sein, etw. zu tun; **the voting was 5 ~ and 10 against** es stimmten 5 dafür und 10 dagegen; **it's each [man]** *or* **every man ~ himself** jeder ist auf sich selbst gestellt
3) (to the benefit of) für; **do sth. ~ sb.** für jmdn. etw. tun; **die ~ one's country** für sein Land sterben
4) (with a view to) für; (conducive[ly] to) zu; **they invited me ~ Christmas/Monday/supper** sie haben mich zu Weihnachten/für Montag/zum Abendessen eingeladen; **meet ~ a discussion** sich zu einer Besprechung treffen; **what is it ~?** wofür/wozu ist das?; **that's what I'm there ~:** dafür/dazu bin ich ja da; **be saving up ~ sth.** auf etw. (*Akk.*) sparen; **he did everything ~ his family's well-being** er tat alles für das Wohlergehen der Familie
5) (being the motive of) für; (having as purpose) zu; **reason ~ living** Grund zu leben; **a dish ~ holding nuts** eine Schale für Nüsse; *see also* ▸**i p. 1151**
6) (to obtain, win, save) **a request ~ help** eine Bitte um Hilfe; **study ~ a university degree** auf einen Hochschulabschluss hin studieren; **go/run ~ a doctor** gehen/laufen, um einen Arzt zu holen; **phone ~ a doctor** nach einem Arzt telefonieren; **take sb. ~ a ride in the car/a walk** jmdn. im Auto spazieren fahren/mit jmdm. einen Spaziergang machen; **work ~ a living** für den Lebensunterhalt arbeiten; **draw on sb. ~ money** jmdn. um Geld angehen; **oh ~ a few minutes' peace!** wäre hier doch *od.* hätte ich doch einmal ein paar Minuten Ruhe!; **run/jump** *etc.* **~ it** loslaufen/-springen *usw.; see also* **life 1**
7) (to reach) nach; **set out ~ England/the north/an island** nach England/Norden/zu einer Insel aufbrechen; **7.30 ~ 8** zwischen halb acht und acht
8) (to be received by) für; **there's** *or* **that's gratitude** *etc.* **~ you!** (iron.) und so was nennt sich Dankbarkeit *usw.!*; **that's Jim ~ you** das sieht Jim mal wieder ähnlich
9) (as regards) **checked ~ accuracy** auf Richtigkeit geprüft; **be dressed/ready ~ dinner** zum Dinner angezogen/fertig sein; **open ~ business** eröffnet; **open ~ lunch [from ... to ...]** Mittagstisch [von ... bis ...]; **have sth. ~ breakfast/pudding** etw. zum Frühstück/Nachtisch essen; **whether you should do it is not ~ me to say** ob du es tun sollst, kann ich dir nicht sagen; **enough ... ~:** genug ... für; **that's quite enough ~ me** das reicht mir völlig; **too ... ~:** zu ... für; **sb. is not long ~ this world** jmd. wird nicht mehr lange unter uns (*Dat.*) weilen; **there is nothing ~ it but to do sth.** es gibt keine andere Möglichkeit, als etw. zu tun
10) (Cricket) **be out ~ a duck/59** ohne Punktgewinn/mit 59 Punkten aus sein; **65 ~ 3 [wickets]** 65 Punkte mit drei Schlägern ausgeschlagen
11) (to the amount of) **cheque/bill ~ £5** Scheck/Rechnung über *od.* in Höhe von 5 Pfund; **the voucher is good ~ 50p** der Gutschein ist 50 p wert
12) (to affect, as if affecting) für; **things don't look very promising ~ the business** was die Geschäfte angeht, sieht das alles nicht sehr vielversprechend aus; **learn to do things ~ oneself** lernen, die Dinge selbstständig zu erledigen; **I think it would work out ~ us to meet some time** ich glaube, es lässt sich machen, dass wir uns einmal treffen; **it is wise/advisable ~ sb. to do sth.** es ist vernünftig/ratsam, dass jmd. etw. tut; **it's always nice ~ us to know that you're well** wir hören immer wieder gern, dass es dir gut geht; **it's hopeless ~ me to try and explain the system** es ist sinnlos, dir das System erklären zu wollen
13) (as being) für; **what do you take me ~?** wofür hältst du mich?; **I/you** *etc.* **~ one** ich/du *usw.* für mein[en]/dein[en] *usw.* Teil; **see sb. ~ what he really is** jmdn. als das erkennen, was er wirklich ist *od.* so sehen, wie er wirklich ist
14) (on account of) wegen; **famous/well-known ~ sth.** berühmt/bekannt wegen *od.* für etw.; **live ~ one's work** für seine *od.* die Arbeit leben; **~ love of his wife** aus Liebe zu seiner Frau; **jump/shout ~ joy** vor Freude in die Luft springen/schreien; **this is ~ being good** das kriegst du, weil du so artig warst; **had it not been ~ him** wäre er nicht gewesen; **but ~ you/your kindness we might not be here today** nur deinetwegen/nur dank deiner Güte sind wir heute hier; **were it not ~ you/your help, I should not be able to do it** ohne dich/deine Hilfe wäre ich nicht dazu in der Lage
15) (on the occasion of) **~ the first time** zum ersten Mal; **why can't you help ~ once?** warum kannst du nicht einmal helfen?; **you are mistaken ~ once** nun hast du dich aber mal geirrt; **what shall I give him ~ his birthday?** was soll ich ihm zum Geburtstag schenken?
16) (in spite of) **~ all ...:** trotz ...; **~ all that, ...:** trotzdem ...; **~ all that he ...:** obwohl er ...
17) (expressing hindrance) vor (+ *Dat.*); **~ fear of ...:** aus Angst vor (+ *Dat.*); **he couldn't see the ring ~ looking at it** (iron.) er sah den Ring einfach nicht, obwohl er doch gerade auf ihn blickte; **but ~ ..., except ~ ...:** wenn nicht ... gewesen wäre, [dann] ...; **but ~ the captain's carelessness** wenn der Kapitän nicht so leichtfertig gewesen wäre; **were it not ~ the**

 **For**

The most frequent translation of the preposition *for*, with the related senses *on behalf of, in place of, in favour of, for the benefit* or *use of* etc., is **für:**

a bed for two
= ein Bett für zwei

I did it for him
= Ich habe es für ihn gemacht*
*This translation works whether the stress is on *him*, meaning "for his benefit", or on *for*, meaning "in his place", which could also be "an seiner Stelle".

Expressing purpose

Where purpose is involved and where a verbal noun or other noun describing action follows, the translation is **zu:**

a device for removing stones from cherries
= ein Gerät zum Entkernen von Kirschen

We met for a discussion
= Wir trafen uns zu einer Besprechung

She did it for pleasure
= Sie machte es zum Vergnügen *or* zum Zeitvertreib

What's that for?
= Wozu dient denn das?

This also applies to meals:

We had meat for lunch/a mousse for dessert
= Bei uns gab es zum Mittagessen Fleisch/zum Nachtisch eine Mousse

But on the other hand:

a dish for nuts
= eine Schale für Nüsse

The construction *for sb.* + infinitive expressing purpose can be rendered by a clause with **damit:**

For him to be able to come we will have to change the date
= Wir werden den Termin ändern müssen, damit er mitkommen kann

I took a piece for her to try
= Ich nahm ein Stück mit, damit sie es probieren konnte, Ich nahm ihr ein Stück zum Probieren mit

Expressing reasons

With the sense *because of*, **wegen** can be used, although **für** is also found with some adjectives:

The area is well known/famous for its wines
= Die Gegend ist bekannt/berühmt für ihre Weine *or* wegen ihrer Weine

He was sentenced to death for murder
= Er wurde wegen Mordes zum Tode verurteilt

aus also occurs with a governing emotion:

for fear of waking her
= aus Angst, sie zu wecken

for love of his country
= aus Liebe zum Vaterland

Expressing direction

Where the sense is simply *going to*, the translation is **nach:**

the train for Bath
= der Zug nach Bath

We left for Scotland
= Wir sind nach Schottland abgefahren

But with a more general indication of direction rather than destination (meaning *towards*), **auf ... zu** or **in Richtung** can be used in German:

The ship was heading for the rocks
= Das Schiff steuerte auf die Felsen zu

They were making for London
= Sie fuhren in Richtung London

Expressing time

The translation will depend on the tense, which is not the same in German in the first case:

PERFECT CONTINUOUS
***I have been living here for two years* (*and am still living here*)**
= Ich wohne seit zwei Jahren hier

PAST CONTINUOUS
***I had been living here for two years* (*and was still living here at the time*)**
= Ich wohnte seit zwei Jahren hier

PAST
***I lived here for two years* (*and no longer live here*)**
= Ich habe zwei Jahre [lang] hier gewohnt

FUTURE
You will have to wait for an hour
= Sie werden eine Stunde warten müssen

I am going to the USA for two weeks
= Ich fahre für zwei Wochen in die USA

Note that **lang** is placed after the noun, and is often omitted in speech, especially referring to short periods:

I was in Paris for a few days
= Ich war ein paar Tage in Paris

However the translation of the phrase *for hours* is **stundenlang:**

I had to wait for hours
= Ich musste stundenlang warten

Similarly
for weeks
= wochenlang
for months
= monatelang
for years
= jahrelang

Except again with a continuous tense (action still going on):

We've been waiting for hours/weeks/months
= Wir warten schon seit Stunden/Wochen/Monaten

With personal pronouns

In most cases *für* can be used, but the dative of the personal pronoun is often found with adjectives and nouns expressing difficulty, impossibility, unpleasantness etc. and also more positive feelings:

It's good for you
= Es ist gut für dich, Es tut dir gut

This makes it impossible for me
= Das macht es mir unmöglich

Your visit is inconvenient for her
= Dein Besuch ist *or* kommt ihr ungelegen

The whole business is very embarrassing for them
= Die ganze Sache ist ihnen sehr peinlich

It's a great pleasure/honour for me
= Es ist mir eine große Freude/Ehre

---

children wenn die Kinder nicht wären; *see also* **wood 1**
18 (corresponding to) für; **~ every cigarette you smoke you are reducing your life expectancy by one day** jede Zigarette, die du rauchst, verkürzt deine Lebenserwartung um einen Tag; **~ fifty fish eggs that die, a hundred survive** auf fünfzig Fischeier, die absterben, kommen hundert, die sich weiterentwickeln; **man ~ man** Mann für Mann
19 (so far as concerns) **~ all I know/care ...:** möglicherweise/was mich betrifft, ...; **~ my part** *or* **~ myself, I ...:** ich für mein[en] Teil ...; **~ one thing, ...:** zunächst einmal ...
20 (considering the usual nature of) für; **not bad ~ a first attempt** nicht schlecht für den ersten Versuch; **very active ~ a man of eighty** sehr rege für einen Achtziger
21 (during) seit; **we've/we haven't been here ~ three years** wir sind seit drei Jahren hier/nicht mehr hier gewesen; **we waited ~ hours/three hours** wir warteten stundenlang/drei Stunden lang; **we have been waiting ~ hours [on end]** wir warten schon seit Stunden; **how long are you here ~?** wie lange bleiben Sie hier?; **stay here ~ a week/some time** eine Woche/einige Zeit hier bleiben; **sit here ~ now** *or* **~ the moment** *or* **~ the present** bleiben Sie im Augenblick hier sitzen; *see also* **ever 1**
22 (to the extent of) **walk ~ 20 miles/~ another 20 miles** 20 Meilen [weit] gehen/weiter gehen
23 **be ~ it** (coll.: face trouble) dran sein (ugs.); sich auf was gefasst machen können (ugs.)
B *conj.* (since, as proof) denn

forage /ˈfɒrɪdʒ/
A *n.* 1 (food for horses or cattle) Futter, *das* 2 (search for ~) Nahrungssuche, *die;* Futtersuche, *die;* **on the ~:** auf Nahrungssuche 3 (fig.: search for thing) **on the ~ for sth.** auf der Jagd nach etw. (ugs.)
B *v.i.* auf Nahrungssuche sein; **~ for sth.** auf der Suche nach etw. sein; (fig.: rummage) nach etw. stöbern; **~ in sb.'s suitcase/among sb.'s papers** jmds. Koffer/Papiere durchstöbern *od.* -wühlen

ˈforage cap *n.* Käppi, *das*

forasmuch /fɒrəzˈmʌtʃ/ *adv.* (Law/arch.) **~ as** insofern [als]

foray /ˈfɒreɪ/
A *n.* Streifzug, *der;* (Mil.) Ausfall, *der;* (brief trip) kurzer Besuch (iron.) (**to** bei); (fig.: venture) Ausflug, *der* (scherzh.); **go on** *or* **make a ~:** einen Streifzug unternehmen; (Mil.) einen Ausfall machen
B *v.i.* plündernd einfallen

forbad, forbade ▸**forbid**

forbear¹ /ˈfɔːbeə(r)/ *n., usu. in pl.* Vorfahr, *der*

forbear² /fɔːˈbeə(r)/
A *v.i.*, **forbore** /fɔːˈbɔː(r)/, **forborne** /fɔːˈbɔːn/ 1 (refrain) **~ from doing sth.** davon Abstand nehmen, etw. zu tun 2 (be patient) sich gedulden; **~ with sth.** etw. geduldig ertragen; **be ~ing** Geduld haben
B *v.t.*, **forbore, forborne: ~ to do sth.** darauf verzichten, etw. zu tun

forbearance /fɔːˈbeərəns/ *n., no pl.* Nachsicht, *die;* (forbearing nature) Nachsichtigkeit, *die;* **show ~:** sich nachsichtig zeigen; Nachsicht üben

forbid /fəˈbɪd/ *v.t.*, **-dd-, forbade** /fəˈbæd, fəˈbeɪd/ *or* **forbad** /fəˈbæd/, **forbidden** /fəˈbɪdn/ 1 **~ sb. to do sth.** jmdm. verbieten, etw. zu tun; **~ [sb.] sth.** [jmdm.] etw. verbieten; **it is ~den [to do sth.]** es ist verboten *od.* nicht gestattet[, etw. zu tun]; **'the taking of photographs is ~den'** „Fotografieren nicht gestattet" 2 (make impossible) nicht zulassen; nicht erlauben; **I'd like to do it but time ~s** ich würde es gern tun, finde aber nicht die

Zeit dazu; **but decency ~s** aber das verbietet [mir] der Anstand; **God/Heaven ~ [that ...]!** Gott/der Himmel bewahre[, dass ...]!; (future) der Himmel verhüte[, dass ...]!

forbidden /fəˈbɪdn/
A ▸**forbid**
B *adj.* verboten; **~ fruit** (fig.) verbotene Früchte; **~ ground** Gebiet, das nicht betreten werden darf; (fig.) **be ~ ground** tabu sein; *see also* **degree 5**

forbidding /fəˈbɪdɪŋ/ *adj.* Furcht einflößend ‹*Aussehen, Stimme*›; unwirtlich ‹*Landschaft*›; (fig.) düster ‹*Aussicht*›

forbiddingly /fəˈbɪdɪŋlɪ/ *adv.* drohend ‹*sich abzeichnen*›; entmutigend ‹*lang, steil, teuer, schwer*›

forbore, forborne ▸**forbear²**

force¹ /fɔːs/
A *n.* **1▸** *no pl.* (strength, power) Stärke, *die;* (of bomb, explosion, attack, storm) Wucht, *die;* (physical strength) Kraft, *die;* **[a wind of] ~ 12** (Meteorol.) Windstärke 12; **destructive ~ of a bomb** Zerstörungskraft einer Bombe; **achieve sth. by brute ~:** etw. mit roher Gewalt erreichen; **in ~** (in large numbers) mit einem großen Aufgebot; (*see also* **2**)
2▸ *no pl.* (fig.: power, validity) Kraft, *die;* (power to convince) Überzeugungskraft, *die;* **by ~ of** aufgrund (+ *Gen.*); kraft (+ *Gen.*) (Papierdt.); **achieve a victory by ~ of numbers** einen Sieg durch zahlenmäßige Überlegenheit erringen; **~ of conviction/will** Überzeugungs-/Willenskraft, *die;* **~ of arms** Waffengewalt, *die;* **~ of character** Charakterstärke, *die;* **~ of evidence** Beweiskraft, *die;* **have the ~ of law** Gesetzeskraft haben; **argue with much ~:** sehr überzeugend argumentieren; **his dramatic sense comes out with great ~:** seine dramatische Begabung zeigt sich [hier] in voller Stärke; **in ~** (in effect) in Kraft; **come into ~** ‹*Gesetz usw.:*› in Kraft treten; **put in[to] ~:** in Kraft setzen; **the methods currently in ~:** die zur Zeit gängigen Methoden; (*see also* **1**)
3▸ (coercion, violence) Gewalt, *die;* **use** *or* **employ ~ [against sb.]** Gewalt [gegen jmdn.] anwenden; **use of ~:** Gewaltanwendung, *die;* **by ~:** gewaltsam; mit Gewalt; **resort to ~:** zur Gewalt greifen; **with the threat of ~:** unter Androhung von Gewalt
4▸ (organized group) (of workers) Kolonne, *die;* Trupp, *der;* (of police) Einheit, *die;* (Mil.) Armee, *die;* Streitmacht, *die* (veralt.); **the ~s** die Armee; **be in the ~s** beim Militär sein; **the ~** (Police) die Polizei; **a large ~ of infantry/naval ~:** starke Infanterie-/Marineverbände; **join ~s [with sb.]** (fig.) sich [mit jmdm.] zusammentun; *see also* **armed**; **labour force**; **police force**; **sales force**; **task force**; **workforce**
5▸ (forceful agency or person) Kraft, *die;* Macht, *die;* **a ~ for evil** ein Handlanger *od.* Werkzeug des Bösen; **the ~s of destiny/evil** die Macht des Schicksals/Bösen; **there are ~s in action/at work here ...:** hier walten Kräfte/sind Kräfte am Werk ...; **he is a ~ in the land** (fig.)/**a ~ to be reckoned with** er ist ein einflussreicher Mann im Land/eine Macht, die nicht zu unterschätzen ist; *see also* **life force**; **spent 2**
6▸ (meaning) Bedeutung, *die*
7▸ (Phys.) Kraft, *die*
B *v.t.* **1▸** (coerce by violent means) **~ sb. to do sth.** jmdn. zwingen, etw. zu tun; **~ sb. into marriage/compliance** jmdn. zur Heirat zwingen/jmds. Einverständnis erzwingen; **be ~d into war** sich zum Krieg gezwungen sehen; **be ~d to do sth.** gezwungen sein *od.* sich gezwungen sehen, etw. zu tun; **~ sb. out of the room [at gunpoint]** jmdn. [mit vorgehaltener Waffe] zwingen, das Zimmer zu verlassen
2▸ (compel by non-violent means) **~ sb./oneself [to do sth.]** jmdn./sich zwingen[, etw. zu tun]; **~ sb./oneself into sth.** (fig.) jmdn./sich zu etw. zwingen; **I was ~d to accept/into accepting the offer** ich fühlte mich verpflichtet/ich war *od.* sah mich gezwungen, das Angebot anzunehmen; **I was ~d to the conclusion** *or* **to conclude that ...** (fig.) ich musste zu dem Schluss gelangen, dass ...; **~ sb.'s hand** (fig.) jmdn. zwingen zu handeln; *see also* **issue A 6**
3▸ (take by ~) **~ sth. from sb.** jmdm. etw. entreißen; **he ~d it out of her hands** er riss es ihr aus der Hand; **~ a promise out of sb.** (fig.) jmdm. ein Versprechen abringen; **~ a confession from sb.** (fig.) jmdn. zu einem Geständnis zwingen; **~ a smile from sb.** (fig.) jmdm. ein Lächeln entlocken
4▸ (push) **~ sth. into sth.** etw. in etw. *Akk.* [hinein]zwängen; **~ sth. [up] through an opening** etw. [nach oben und] durch eine Öffnung pressen; **~ one's way** sich (*Dat.*) [gewaltsam] einen Weg bahnen
5▸ (impose, inflict) **~ sth. [up]on sb.** jmdm. etw. aufzwingen *od.* aufnötigen; **he ~d his attentions on her** er drängte sich ihr mit seinen Aufmerksamkeiten auf
6▸ (break open) **~ [open]** aufbrechen ‹*Tür, Fenster*›
7▸ (storm) stürmen ‹*Festung*›
8▸ (effect by violent means) sich (*Dat.*) erzwingen ‹*Zutritt*›; **~ one's way in[to a building]** sich (*Dat.*) mit Gewalt Zutritt [zu einem Gebäude] verschaffen; **I had to ~ my way out** ich musste Gewalt anwenden, um herauszukommen
9▸ **~ the pace** (lit. or fig.) das Tempo forcieren; **~ the bidding** das Gebot in die Höhe treiben
10▸ (produce with effort) sich zwingen zu; **~ a smile** sich zu einem Lächeln zwingen
11▸ (put strained sense upon) Gewalt antun (+ *Dat.*); vergewaltigen ‹*Sprache*›; überstrapazieren ‹*Vergleich*›
12▸ treiben ‹*Pflanzen*›

Phrasal verbs
- **~ 'down** *v.t.* **1▸** drücken ‹*Preis*› **2▸** (compel to land) zur Landung zwingen ‹*Flugzeug*› **3▸** (make oneself eat) herunterwürgen (ugs.) ‹*Nahrung*›
- **~ 'up** *v.t.* hochtreiben ‹*Preis*›

force² *n.* (N. Engl.) Wasserfall, *der*

forced /fɔːst/ *adj.* **1▸** (contrived, unnatural) gezwungen; gewollt ‹*Geste, Vergleich, Metapher*›; gekünstelt ‹*Benehmen*› **2▸** (compelled by force) erzwungen; Zwangs‹*arbeit, -anleihe*›; **~-labour camp** Arbeitslager, *das* **3▸** (produced artificially) **~ vibration** (Phys.) unfreie *od.* erzwungene Schwingung; **~-air ventilation** Zwangslüftung, *die* (Technik)

forced: ~ 'landing *n.* Notlandung, *die;* **~ 'march** *n.* (Mil.) Gewaltmarsch, *der;* **~ 'marriage** *n.* erzwungene Ehe

'force-feed *v.t.* zwangsernähren; (fig.) voll stopfen (**on** mit)

forceful /ˈfɔːsfl/ *adj.* stark ‹*Persönlichkeit, Charakter*›; energisch ‹*Person, Art, Stimme, Maßnahme*›; überzeugend ‹*Darlegung*›; schwungvoll ‹*Rede-, Schreibweise*›; eindrucksvoll ‹*Sprache*›; eindringlich ‹*Worte*›

forcefully /ˈfɔːsfəlɪ/ *adv.* eindringlich ‹*reden, darlegen*›; energisch ‹*verfolgen, umgehen*›; nachdrücklich ‹*erinnern*›

force majeure /fɔːs mɑˈʒɜː(r)/ *n.* höhere Gewalt

'forcemeat *n.* (Cookery) Farce, *die*

forceps /ˈfɔːseps/ *n., pl. same* **[pair of] ~:** Zange, *die;* **obstetrical ~:** Geburtszange, *die;* **~ baby/delivery** Zangengeburt, *die*

forcible /ˈfɔːsɪbl/ *adj.* **1▸** (done by force) gewaltsam **2▸** ▸**forceful**

forcibly /ˈfɔːsɪblɪ/ *adv.* **1▸** (by force) gewaltsam; mit Gewalt **2▸** ▸**forcefully**

forcing house /ˈfɔːsɪŋhaʊs/ *n.* (lit. or fig.) Treibhaus, *das*

ford /fɔːd/
A *n.* Furt, *die*
B *v.t.* durchqueren; (wade through) durchwaten

fore /fɔː(r)/
A *adj., esp. in comb.* vorder...; Vorder‹*teil, -front usw.*›
B *n.* **[be/come] to the ~:** im Vordergrund [stehen]/in den Vordergrund [rücken]
C *int.* (Golf) Achtung
D *adv.* (Naut.) vorn; **~ and aft** längs[schiffs]

fore-and-'aft (Naut.)
A *adj.* Längs-; **~ sail** Schratsegel, *das*
B *adv.* längs[schiffs]; **~ rigged** längsschiffs getakelt

'forearm¹ *n.* Unterarm, *der*

fore'arm² *v.t.* rüsten; (fig.) **be ~ed** gerüstet *od.* vorbereitet sein; *see also* **forewarn**

forebear ▸**forbear¹**

fore'bode *v.t.* (portend) ankündigen; **these clouds ~ a storm** die Wolken bedeuten *od.* deuten auf Sturm

foreboding /fɔːˈbəʊdɪŋ/ *n.* Vorahnung, *die;* (unease caused by premonition) ungutes Gefühl; (omen) Vorzeichen, *das;* Omen, *das*

'forecast
A *v.t.,* **~** *or* **~ed** vorhersagen
B *n.* Voraussage, *die;* Prognose, *die;* (Meteorol.) [Wetter]vorhersage, *die;* Wetterbericht, *der;* **the ~ is for rain** laut Wettervorhersage wird es regnen

'forecaster *n.* Meteorologe, *der*/Meteorologin, *die*

forecastle /ˈfəʊksl/ *n.* (Naut.) Back, *die;* (Hist.: deck) [Vorder]kastell, *das*

foreclose /fɔːˈkləʊz/ (Law)
A *v.t.* kündigen; **~ a mortgage** eine Hypothekenforderung geltend machen
B *v.i.* **~ on sb./a mortgage** eine Hypothekenforderung gegenüber jmdm./eine Hypothekenforderung geltend machen

'forecourt *n.* Vorhof, *der;* **~ attendant** ≈ Tankwart, *der;* **~ service** Service an der Tankstelle

'foredeck *n.* (Naut.) Vordeck, *das*

fore'doom *v.t.* vorherbestimmen; **be ~ed to failure** zum Scheitern verurteilt sein

'forefather *n., usu. in pl.* Vorfahr, *der;* **our ~s** unsere Vorväter

'forefinger *n.* Zeigefinger, *der*

'forefoot *n.* Vorderfuß, *der*

'forefront *n.* **[be] in the ~ of** in vorderster Linie (+ *Gen.*) [stehen]

foregather /fɔːˈgæðə(r)/ *v.i.* sich treffen; zusammenkommen

forego ▸**forgo**

foregoing /ˈfɔːgəʊɪŋ, fɔːˈgəʊɪŋ/ *adj.* vorhergehend

'foregone *adj.* **be a ~ conclusion** (be predetermined) von vornherein feststehen; (be certain) so gut wie sicher sein

'foreground *n.* Vordergrund, *der*

'forehand (Tennis etc.)
A *adj.* Vorhand-
B *n.* (also part of horse) Vorhand, *die*

forehead /ˈfɒrɪd, ˈfɔːhed/ *n.* ▸❶ **p. 951** Stirn, *die*

foreign /ˈfɒrɪn/ *adj.* **1▸** (from abroad) ausländisch; Fremd‹*herrschaft, -kapital, -sprache*›; fremdartig ‹*Gebräuche*›; fremdländisch ‹*Aussehen*›; **~ word** fremdsprachliches Wort; (used in English) Fremdwort, *das;* **talk ~** (coll.) auswärts reden *od.* sprechen (ugs. scherzh.); **~ worker** Gastarbeiter, *der*/-arbeiterin, *die;* **he is ~:** er ist Ausländer **2▸** (abroad) Auslands‹*reise, -niederlassung, -markt*›; **foreign countries** Ausland, *das;* **from a ~ country** aus einem anderen Land; aus dem Ausland; **~ travel** Reisen ins Ausland; *see also* **part A 7** **3▸** (related to countries abroad) außenpolitisch; Außen‹*politik, -handel*›; **~ affairs** auswärtige Angelegenheiten; **spokesman on ~ affairs** außenpolitischer Sprecher; **~ news** Nachrichten aus dem Ausland **4▸** (from outside) fremd; **~ body** Fremdkörper, *der* **5▸** (alien, unfamiliar) fremd; **be ~ to sb./sb.'s nature** jmdm. fremd sein/nicht jmds. Art sein; **be ~ to sth.** (unrelated) in keiner Beziehung zu etw. stehen

foreign: ~ 'aid *n.* Entwicklungshilfe, *die;* **F~ and 'Commonwealth Office** *n.* (Brit.) Außenministerium, *das;* **~ corre'spondent** *n.* ▸❶ **p. 1260** (Journ.) Auslandskorrespondent, *der*/-korrespondentin, *die*

foreigner /ˈfɒrɪnə(r)/ *n.* Ausländer, *der*/Ausländerin, *die*

foreign: ~ ex'change *n.* (dealings) Devisenhandel, *der;* (currency) fremde Währung; Devisen *Pl.; attrib.* **~ exchange dealer** Devisenhändler, *der*/-händlerin, *die;* **~ exchange market** Devisenmarkt, *der;* **~ 'language** *n.* Fremdsprache, *die; attrib.* **~-language newspaper/broadcast** fremdsprachige Zeitung/Rundfunksendung; **~-language**

teaching Fremdsprachenunterricht, *der;* ~ **'legion** *n.* Fremdenlegion, *die;* **F~ 'Minister** *n.* Außenminister, *der;* **F~ 'Ministry** *n.* Außenministerium, *das;* **F~ Office** *n.* (Brit. Hist./coll.) Außenministerium, *das;* Auswärtiges Amt; **~-owned** *adj.* **~-owned subsidiaries** Tochtergesellschaften in ausländischem Besitz; **F~ 'Secretary** *n.* (Brit.) Außenminister, *der;* ~ **service** ▸**diplomatic service**

fore'knowledge *n.* vorherige Kenntnis; **with the ~ that ...:** im Wissen, dass ...

'forelady (Amer.) ▸**forewoman 1**

foreland /'fɔːlənd/ *n.* (Geog.) Kap, *das*

'foreleg *n.* Vorderbein, *das;* Vorderlauf, *der* (Jägerspr.)

'forelimb *n.* Vordergliedmaße, *die*

'forelock *n.* Stirnlocke, *die;* **touch one's ~** (joc.) einen Diener machen (iron.)

foreman /'fɔːmən/ *n., pl.* **foremen** /'fɔːmən/ **1** ▸ℹ **p. 1260** (chief workman) Vorarbeiter, *der;* Werkmeister, *der* **2** (Law) Sprecher [der Geschworenen]/(in Germany) der Schöffen]

'foremast *n.* (Naut.) Fockmast, *der*

foremost /'fɔːməʊst, 'fɔːməst/

A *adj.* **1** vorderst...; **the two ~ runners** die beiden Läufer an der Spitze; **fall downstairs head ~:** mit dem Kopf zuerst die Treppe hinunterfallen **2** (fig.) führend; **be in the ~ rank** zur Spitze zählen

B *adv.* ▸**first B 5**

'forename *n.* Vorname, *der*

'forenoon *n.* (Naut., Law/arch.) Vormittag, *der;* **in the ~:** am Vormittag

forensic /fə'rensɪk/ *adj.* gerichtlich; forensisch (fachspr.); **~ medicine** Gerichtsmedizin, *die;* **~ science** Kriminaltechnik, *die;* **~ laboratory** kriminaltechnisches Labor

'forepaw *n.* Vorderpfote, *die*

'foreplay *n.* Vorspiel, *das*

'forerunner *n.* **1** (predecessor) Vorläufer, *der*/Vorläuferin, *die* **2** (harbinger, sign) Vorbote, *der*

foresail /'fɔːseɪl, 'fɔːsl/ *n.* (Naut.) Focksegel, *das*

foresaw ▸**foresee**

foresee /fɔː'siː/ *v.t., forms as* **see**[1] voraussehen; **trouble which had not been ~n** unvorhergesehener Ärger; **as far as one can ~** *or* **as can be ~n** aller Voraussicht nach

foreseeable /fɔː'siːəbl/ *adj.* **1** vorhersehbar **2** **in the ~ future** in absehbarer Zeit

foreseen ▸**foresee**

fore'shadow *v.t.* vorausahnen lassen; vorausdeuten auf (+ *Akk.*)

'foreshore *n.* Vorland, *das;* (between high water and low-water marks) ≈ Strand, *der*

fore'shorten *v.t.* **1** (Art, Photog.) [perspektivisch] verkürzen **2** (shorten, condense) verkürzen; verdichten (fig.) ‹*Ereignisse*›

'foresight *n., no pl.* Weitblick, *der;* Voraussicht, *die;* **act with ~:** vorausschauend handeln; **use ~:** vorausschauend sein; Weitblick zeigen; **have the ~ to do sth.** so vorausschauend sein, etw. zu tun

'foreskin *n.* (Anat.) Vorhaut, *die*

forest /'fɒrɪst/ *n.* **1** Wald, *der;* (commercially exploited) Forst, *der; attrib.* Wald‹*brand, -land*›; **covered in ~s** bewaldet; **~ law** Forstrecht, *das;* **~ warden** or (Amer.) **ranger** Förster, *der; see also* **deer forest** **2** (fig.) Wald, *der* (**of** von); (of ideas etc.) Gewirr, *das;* Wust, *der* (abwertend)

fore'stall *v.t.* zuvorkommen (+ *Dat.*); (prevent by prior action) vermeiden; (anticipate) vorhersehen

'forestay *n.* (Naut.) Vorstag, *das*

forested /'fɒrɪstɪd/ *adj.* bewaldet

forester /'fɒrɪstə(r)/ *n.* **1** ▸ℹ **p. 1260** (warden) Förster, *der* **2** (dweller) Waldbewohner, *der*

forestry /'fɒrɪstrɪ/ *n.* Forstwirtschaft, *die;* (science) Forstwissenschaft, *die;* **F~ Commission** (Brit.) *britische Forstbehörde*

'forest tree *n.* Waldbaum, *der;* Forstbaum, *der*

'foretaste *n.* Vorgeschmack, *der;* **have a ~ of sth.** einen Vorgeschmack von etw. bekommen

fore'tell *v.t.,* **foretold** vorhersagen; voraussagen

'forethought *n.* (prior deliberation) [vorherige] Überlegung; (care for the future) Vorausdenken, *das;* (premeditation) Vorausplanung, *die*

foretold ▸**foretell**

forever /fə'revə(r)/ **= for ever;** ▸**ever 1**

fore'warn *v.t.* vorwarnen; **we were ~ed of the difficulties** man hatte uns vor den Schwierigkeiten gewarnt; **~ed is forearmed** (prov.) wer gewarnt ist, ist gewappnet

fore'warning *n.* Vorwarnung, *die;* **be given adequate ~:** hinreichend vorgewarnt sein

'forewoman *n.* **1** (chief workwoman) Vorarbeiterin, *die* **2** (Law) Sprecherin [der Geschworenen]/(in Germany) der Schöffen]

'foreword *n.* Vorwort, *das*

forfeit /'fɔːfɪt/

A *v.t.* verlieren (auch fig.); einbüßen (geh., auch fig.); verlustig gehen (+ *Gen.*) (Amtsspr.); verwirken (geh.) ‹*Recht, jmds. Gunst*›; **he ~ed the good opinion of his friends** er verscherzte sich (*Dat.*) die Sympathien seiner Freunde

B *n.* **1** (penalty) Strafe, *die;* (fig.) Preis, *der* **2** (Games) Pfand, *das;* **pay/redeem a ~:** ein Pfand geben/einlösen **3** (~ing) Verlust, *der;* Einbuße, *die*

C *adj.* **be ~:** verfallen (**to** *Dat.*); ‹*Leben, Recht:*› verwirkt sein (geh.)

forfeiture /'fɔːfɪtʃə(r)/ *n.* Verlust, *der;* Einbuße, *die*

forgather ▸**foregather**

forgave ▸**forgive**

forge[1] /fɔːdʒ/

A *n.* **1** (workshop) Schmiede, *die* **2** (blacksmith's hearth) Esse, *die;* (furnace for melting or refining metal) Schmiedeofen, *der*

B *v.t.* **1** schmieden (**into** zu) **2** (fig.) schmieden ‹*Plan, Verbindung*›; schließen ‹*Vereinbarung, Freundschaft, Frieden*›; prägen ‹*Charakter*›; (fabricate) erfinden; sich (*Dat.*) ausdenken **3** (counterfeit) fälschen; **~d money** Falschgeld, *das*

forge[2] *v.i.* **1** (advance rapidly) **~ into the lead** ausreißen; **~ ahead** [das Tempo] beschleunigen; ‹*Wettläufer:*› vorstoßen; (take substantial lead) ausreißen; (fig.) vorankommen; Fortschritte machen **2** (progress steadily) **~ on** (lit. or fig.) [stetig] vorankommen

forger /'fɔːdʒə(r)/ *n.* Fälscher, *der*/Fälscherin, *die*

forgery /'fɔːdʒərɪ/ *n.* Fälschung, *die;* **commit an act of ~:** eine Fälschung begehen

forget /fə'get/

A *v.t.,* **-tt-, forgot** /fə'gɒt/, **forgotten** /fə'gɒtn/ *or* (Amer./arch./poet.) **forgot** **1** vergessen; (~ learned ability) verlernen; vergessen; **these names are easy to ~** *or* **easily forgotten** diese Namen vergisst man leicht; **gone but not forgotten** in bleibender Erinnerung; (iron.) aus den Augen, aber schwerlich aus dem Sinn; **never-to-be-forgotten** unvergesslich; **I was quite ~ting you know her** ich hatte ganz vergessen, dass du sie ja kennst; **I ~ his name** (have forgotten) ich habe seinen Namen vergessen; **~ doing sth./having done sth.** vergessen, dass man etw. getan hat; **~ to do sth.** vergessen, etw. zu tun; **don't ~ that ...:** vergiss nicht *od.* denk[e] daran, dass ...; **~ how to dance** das Tanzen verlernen; **a thrashing he won't ~ in a hurry** eine Tracht Prügel, die er nicht so schnell vergessen wird **2** (leave) vergessen **3** **and don't you ~ it** (coll.) vergiss das ja nicht; **~ sth.** (decide to ignore) etw. beiseite lassen; **~ it!** (coll.) schon gut!; vergiss es!

B *v.i.,* **-tt-, forgot, forgotten** es vergessen; **I almost forgot** fast hätte ich es vergessen; **I quite forgot** ich habe es ganz vergessen; **~ about sth.** etw. vergessen; **~ about it!** (coll.) schon gut!; **I had forgotten all about his** *or* **him coming today** ich hatte ganz vergessen, dass er heute kommt; **I forgot about Joe** ich habe gar nicht an Joe gedacht

C *v. refl.,* **-tt-, forgot, forgotten** **1** (act unbecomingly or unworthily) sich vergessen **2** (neglect one's own interests) sich selbst vergessen; nicht an sich (*Akk.*) denken

forgetful /fə'getfl/ *adj.* **1** (absent-minded) vergesslich **2** **~ of sth.** ohne an etw. (*Akk.*) zu denken; **be ~ of sth.** etw. vergessen; **be ~ of one's duty** seine Pflicht vernachlässigen

forgetfully /fə'getfəlɪ/ *adv.* in Gedanken

forgetfulness /fə'getflnɪs/ *n., no pl.* Vergesslichkeit, *die;* Zerstreutheit, *die;* **in a moment of ~:** in einem Moment von Geistesabwesenheit

for'get-me-not *n.* (Bot.) Vergissmeinnicht, *das; attrib.* **~ blue** vergissmeinnichtblau

forgettable /fə'getəbl/ *adj.* **easily ~:** leicht zu vergessen

forging /'fɔːdʒɪŋ/ *n.* (object) Schmiedestück, *das*

forgivable /fə'gɪvəbl/ *adj.* verständlich; verzeihlich

forgivably /fə'gɪvəblɪ/ *adv.* verständlicherweise

forgive /fə'gɪv/ *v.t.,* **forgave** /fə'geɪv/, **forgiven** /fə'gɪvn/ **1** ▸ℹ **p. 908** vergeben ‹*Sünden*›; verzeihen ‹*Unrecht*›; entschuldigen, verzeihen ‹*Unterbrechung, Neugier, Ausdrucksweise*›; **~ sb. [sth.** *or* **for sth.]** jmdm. [etw.] verzeihen *od.* (geh.) vergeben; **~ sb. for doing sth.** jmdm. verzeihen, dass er/sie etw. getan hat; **God ~ me** möge Gott mir vergeben; **am I ~n?** verzeihst du mir?; **you are ~n** ich verzeihe dir; **~ us [for] our sins** vergib uns unsere Sünden; **I'll never ~ myself for not having offered to help** ich werde es mir nie verzeihen, nicht wenigstens meine Hilfe angeboten zu haben; **~ me for saying so, but ...:** entschuldigen *od.* verzeihen Sie[, dass ich es sage], [aber] ...; **she doesn't ~ easily** es fällt ihr schwer zu verzeihen; **~ and forget** vergeben und vergessen **2** (remit, let off) erlassen; **~ sb. a debt** jmdm. eine Schuld erlassen

forgiveness /fə'gɪvnɪs/ *n., no pl.* Verzeihung, *die;* (esp. of sins) Vergebung, *die* (geh.); **ask/beg [sb.'s] ~:** [jmdn.] um Verzeihung/(geh.) Vergebung bitten; **grant sb. [one's] ~:** jmdm. verzeihen; **~ of sins** Vergebung der Sünden; Sündenvergebung, *die*

forgiving /fə'gɪvɪŋ/ *adj.,* **forgivingly** /fə'gɪvɪŋlɪ/ *adv.* versöhnlich

forgo /fɔː'gəʊ/ *v.t., forms as* **go**[1] verzichten auf (+ *Akk.*)

forgone ▸**forgo**

forgot, forgotten ▸**forget**

fork /fɔːk/

A *n.* **1** (for eating with) Gabel, *die;* **knife and ~:** Messer und Gabel; Besteck, *das;* **the knives and ~s** das Besteck; **~ lunch** Gabelfrühstück, *das* (veralt.); ≈ kaltes Büfett; **~ supper** ≈ kaltes Büfett **2** (Agric.) Gabel, *die;* Forke, *die* (bes. nordd.) **3** *in sing. or pl.* (on bicycle) Gabel, *die* **4** ([point of] division into branches) Gabelung, *die;* (one branch) Abzweigung, *die;* (of tree) Astgabel, *die*

B *v.i.* **1** (divide) sich gabeln **2** (turn) abbiegen; **~ [to the] left [for]** [nach] links abbiegen [nach]

C *v.t.* gabeln; **~ in manure** Mist [mit einer Gabel] untergraben

Phrasal verbs

• **~ 'out** (coll.)

A *v.t.* lockermachen (ugs.); **~ out money** blechen (ugs.)

B *v.i.* **~ out [for sth.]** [für etw.] blechen (ugs.)

• **~ 'over** *v.t.* lockern ‹*Boden*›

• **~ 'up** ▸ **~ out**

forked /fɔːkt/ *adj.* gegabelt; **speak with ~ tongue** (fig.) mit gespaltener *od.* doppelter Zunge sprechen (geh.)

forked 'lightning *n., no pl., no indef. art.* Linienblitz, *der*

'forklift truck *n.* Gabelstapler, *der*

forlorn /fə'lɔːn/ *adj.* **1** (desperate) verzweifelt; **~ hope** (faint hope) verzweifelte Hoffnung; (desperate enterprise) aussichtsloses Unterfangen **2** (forsaken) [einsam und] verlassen; (wretched) erbärmlich (auch fig.); desolat ‹*Anblick, Zustand*›

form /fɔːm/

A *n.* **1** (type, guise, style) Form, *die;* **~ of address** [Form der] Anrede; **~ of life/government** Lebens-/Regierungsform, *die;* **the reward will take the ~ of a holiday** die Belohnung wird eine Urlaubsreise sein; **malaria takes various ~s** Malaria äußert sich in verschiedenen Formen; **in human ~:** in menschlicher Gestalt; in Menschengestalt; **in the ~ of** in

Form von *od.* + *Gen.*; **in book ~:** in Buchform; als Buch
[2] *no pl.* (shape, visible aspect) Form, *die;* Gestalt, *die;* (Lit., Mus., Art) Form, *die;* **~ without substance** Form ohne Inhalt; **take ~** (lit. or fig.) Gestalt annehmen *od.* gewinnen; **give ~ to sth.** einer Sache (*Dat.*) Gestalt geben *od.* verleihen; **the ~ and content of a novel** Form und Inhalt eines Romans
[3] (printed sheet) Formular, *das*
[4] (Brit. Sch.) Klasse, *die;* **first/second** *etc.* **~:** erste/zweite *usw.* Klasse (*an einer weiterführenden Schule*); *see also* **sixth form**
[5] (bench) Bank, *die*
[6] *no pl., no indef. art.* (Sport: physical condition) Form, *die;* **peak ~:** Bestform, *die;* **improvement in ~:** Formanstieg, *der;* **out of ~:** außer Form; nicht in Form; **in [good] ~** (lit. or fig.) [gut] in Form; **in top ~/at the top of his** *etc.* **~** (lit. or fig.) in Höchstform; **she was in great ~ at the party** (fig.) bei der Party war sie groß in Form; **on/off ~** (lit. or fig.) in/nicht in Form; **be slightly off ~:** nicht ganz in Form sein
[7] (Sport: previous record) bisherige Leistungen; **on/judging by [past/present] ~** (fig.) nach der Papierform; **true to ~** (fig.) wie üblich *od.* zu erwarten
[8] (set procedure) **in due/proper ~:** in angemessener/richtiger Form; **matter of ~:** Routineangelegenheit *od.* -sache, *die;* **as a matter of ~:** der Form halber; **common ~:** übliches Verfahren; **what's the ~?** was ist das übliche Verfahren?; **tell me the ~:** wie wird üblicherweise verfahren?
[9] (etiquette) **for the sake of ~:** der Form halber; um der Form zu genügen; **good/bad ~:** gutes/schlechtes Benehmen; **it's bad** *or* **not good ~ to do this** so etwas gehört sich nicht
[10] (figure) Gestalt, *die*
[11] (Ling.) Form, *die;* **plural ~:** Pluralform, *die;* Plural, *der;* **feminine ~:** Femininum, *das;* **negative ~:** Verneinung, *die;* Negation, *die*
[12] (Philos.) Form, *die*
[13] *no pl.* (coll.: criminal record) Vorstrafe, *die;* **have ~:** vorbestraft sein
[14] (hare's lair) Lager, *das;* Sasse, *die* (Jägerspr.)
[15] ▸**formwork**
B *v.t.* [1] (make; also Ling.) bilden; **be ~ed from sth.** aus etw. entstehen
[2] (shape, mould) formen, gestalten (**into** zu); (fig.) formen ‹*Charakter usw.*›
[3] (construct in the mind) sich (*Dat.*) bilden ‹*Meinung, Urteil*›; gewinnen ‹*Eindruck*›; fassen ‹*Entschluss, Plan*›; kommen zu ‹*Schluss*›; vornehmen ‹*Schätzung*›; (acquire, develop) entwickeln ‹*Vorliebe, Gewohnheit, Wunsch*›; schließen ‹*Freundschaft*›
[4] (constitute, compose, be, become) bilden; **Schleswig once ~ed [a] part of Denmark** Schleswig war einmal ein Teil von Dänemark; **Joe ~ed one of our party** Joe war einer von uns; **young people ~ed the bulk of the protesters** das Gros der Protestierenden bestand aus jungen Leuten
[5] (establish, set up) bilden ‹*Regierung*›; gründen ‹*Bund, Verein, Firma, Partei, Gruppe*›; **the men ~ed themselves into a committee** die Männer gründeten ein Komitee
[6] (take formation as) bilden; **the dancers ~ed [themselves into] a circle** die Tänzer bildeten einen Kreis
C *v.i.* [1] (come into being) sich bilden; ‹*Idee:*› sich formen, Gestalt annehmen
[2] (fully develop) sich ausformen
[3] (Mil.) sich aufstellen (**in[to]** in + *Dat.*); sich formieren (**in[to]** zu); **~ [up]** sich formieren

formal /ˈfɔːml/
A *adj.* [1] formell; förmlich ‹*Person, Art, Einladung, Begrüßung*›; steif ‹*Person, Begrüßung*›; (official) offiziell; (regular) regelmäßig angelegt ‹*Garten*›; **wear ~ dress** *or* **clothes** Gesellschaftskleidung tragen; **~ call** Höflichkeitsbesuch, *der* [2] (explicit) formell; (in recognized form) traditionell; herkömmlich; **a ~ 'yes'/'no'** eine bindende Zusage/endgültige Absage; **~ education/knowledge** ordentliche Schulbildung/reales Wissen; **make a ~ apology** sich in aller Form entschuldigen [3] (of the outward form) formal; äußerlich; (Philos., Logic) formal
B *n.* (Amer.) [1] (event) gesellschaftliches Ereignis [2] (dress) Gesellschaftskleidung, *die*

formaldehyde /fɔːˈmældɪhaɪd/ *n.* (Chem.) Formaldehyd, *der*

formalise ▸**formalize**

formalism /ˈfɔːməlɪzm/ *n.* Formalismus, *der*

formality /fɔːˈmælɪtɪ/ *n.* [1] (requirement) Formalität, *die;* **drop the** *or* **dispense with the formalities** sich nicht mit Formalitäten aufhalten [2] *no pl.* (being formal, ceremony) Förmlichkeit, *die*

formalize /ˈfɔːməlaɪz/ *v.t.* [1] (specify and systematize) formalisieren [2] (make official) formell bekräftigen

formally /ˈfɔːməlɪ/ *adv.* [1] (ceremoniously) formell; förmlich; feierlich ‹*empfangen*›; (officially) offiziell; (regularly) regelmäßig [2] (explicitly) ausdrücklich ‹*formulieren, wünschen*›; in aller Form ‹*sich entschuldigen*› [3] (in form) formal; äußerlich

format /ˈfɔːmæt/
A *n.* [1] (of book) (general appearance, layout) Aufmachung, *die;* (shape and size) Format, *das* [2] (Telev., Radio: of programme) Aufbau, *der* [3] (Computing) Format, *das*
B *v.t.*, **-tt-** (Computing) formatieren

formation /fɔːˈmeɪʃn/ *n.* [1] *no pl.* (forming) (of substance, object) Bildung, *die;* (of character) Formung, *die;* (of handwriting) Ausbildung, *die;* Ausformung, *die;* (of plan) Entstehung, *die;* (Ling.) Bildung, *die;* (establishing) Gründung, *die* [2] (thing formed; also Ling.) Bildung, *die* [3] (Mil., Aeronaut., Dancing) Formation, *die;* (Footb.) Aufstellung, *die;* **battle ~:** Gefechtsordnung, *die;* **in close ~:** in geschlossener Formation; **~ flying** Formationsflug, *der;* **~ dancing** Formationstanz, *der* [4] (Geol.) Formation, *die;* **rock ~s** Gesteinsformationen *Pl.* [5] (structure) Aufbau, *der;* Struktur, *die*

formative /ˈfɔːmətɪv/ *adj.* [1] formend, prägend ‹*Einfluss*›; **the ~ years of life** die entscheidenden Lebensjahre [2] (Ling.) wortbildend; **~ element** Wortbildungselement, *das;* Formativ, *das*

former /ˈfɔːmə(r)/ *attrib. adj.* [1] (earlier) früher; (ex-) ehemalig; Ex-; **in ~ times** früher [2] (first-mentioned) **the ~ ...:** der/die/das erstere ...; *pl.* die ersteren ...; (as noun) *der/die/das* Erstere: *pl. die* Ersteren; **in the ~ case** im ersteren Fall

-former /fɔːmə(r)/ *n. in comb.* (Brit. Sch.) -klässler, *der*/-klässlerin, *die;* **third-~:** Drittklässler, *der*/-klässlerin, *die; see also* **sixth-former**

formerly /ˈfɔːməlɪ/ *adv.* früher; **Mrs Bloggs, ~ Miss Smith** Frau Bloggs, früher Fräulein Smith

ˈform feed *n.* Seitenvorschub, *der*

Formica ® /fɔːˈmaɪkə/ *n.* ≈ Resopal, *das* (Wz); **surfaced with ~:** kunststoffbeschichtet

formidable /ˈfɔːmɪdəbl, fɔːˈmɪdəbl/ *adj.* gewaltig; ungeheuer; bedrohlich, gefährlich ‹*Herausforderung, Gegner*›; (arousing dread) Furcht erregend; (awe-inspiring) formidabel; beeindruckend

formidably /ˈfɔːmɪdəblɪ, fɔːˈmɪdəblɪ/ *adv.* ungeheuer

formless /ˈfɔːmlɪs/ *adj.* formlos; (having no physical existence) immateriell; körperlos

form: ~ letter *n.* vorgedruckter Brief; **~-master** *n.* (Brit. Sch.) Klassenlehrer, *der;* **~-mate** *n.* (Brit. Sch.) Klassenkamerad, *der*/-kameradin, *die;* Mitschüler, *der*/-schülerin, *die;* **~-mistress** *n.* (Brit. Sch.) Klassenlehrerin, *die;* **~-room** *n.* (Brit. Sch.) Klassenraum, *der*

formula /ˈfɔːmjʊlə/ *n., pl.* **~s** *or* (esp. as tech. term) **~e** /ˈfɔːmjʊliː/ [1] (Math., Chem., Phys.) Formel, *die* [2] (fixed form of words) Formel, *die;* **trite ~s** nichtssagende Floskeln; **find a ~** (to reconcile differences) einen gemeinsamen Nenner finden [3] (set form) Schema, *das* [4] (prescription, recipe) Rezeptur, *die;* Formel, *die;* (fig.) Rezept, *das;* Formel, *die;* **no sure ~ exists** es gibt kein Patentrezept [5] (Motor racing) **F~ One, F~ 1** Formel Eins, Formel 1 [6] (infant's food) Säuglingsmilchpräparat, *das*

formulate /ˈfɔːmjʊleɪt/ *v.t.* formulieren; (devise) entwickeln; **~ in words/writing** in Worte fassen/schriftlich formulieren

formulation /fɔːmjʊˈleɪʃn/ *n.* Formulierung, *die;* **the ~ of a question** eine Fragestellung

ˈformwork *n.* Schalung, *die*

fornicate /ˈfɔːnɪkeɪt/ *v.i.* Unzucht treiben; huren (abwertend)

fornication /fɔːnɪˈkeɪʃn/ *n.* Unzucht, *die;* Hurerei, *die* (abwertend)

for-ˈprofit *attrib. adj.* gewinnorientiert ‹*Organisation*›

forsake /fəˈseɪk/ *v.t.*, **forsook** /fəˈsʊk/, **~n** /fəˈseɪkn/ [1] (give up) entsagen (geh.) (+ *Dat.*); verzichten auf (+ *Akk.*) [2] (desert) verlassen

forsaken /fəˈseɪkn/ *adj.* verlassen

forsook ▸**forsake**

forsooth /fəˈsuːθ/ *adv.* (arch./iron./derog.) fürwahr (geh.)

forswear /fɔːˈsweə(r)/ *v.t., forms as* **swear** abschwören (+ *Dat.*); (deny) ableugnen; abschwören (veralt.)

forswore, forsworn ▸**forswear**

forsythia /fɔːˈsaɪθɪə/ *n.* (Bot.) Forsythie, *die*

fort /fɔːt/ *n.* (Mil.) Fort, *das;* **hold the ~** (fig.) die Stellung halten (fig.)

forte¹ /ˈfɔːteɪ, fɔːt/ *n.* Stärke, *die;* starke Seite (ugs.)

forte² /ˈfɔːtɪ/ (Mus.)
A *adj.* laut; forte *nicht attr.*; forte gespielt/gesungen; forte
B *adv.* forte
C *n.* Forte, *das*

fortepiano /fɔːtɪprˈænəʊ/ *n., pl.* **~s** (Mus.) Fortepiano, *das*

forth /fɔːθ/ *adv.* [1] **and so ~:** und so weiter [2] **from this/that day** *etc.* **~:** von diesem/jenem Tag *usw.* an; von Stund an (geh.) [3] (literary) **stretch ~:** ausstrecken; **give ~:** von sich geben; **go ~:** hinausgehen; ‹*Befehl:*› ausgehen; (emerge) hervorgehen; **ride ~:** losreiten; **show ~:** zeigen

Forth Bridge /fɔːθ ˈbrɪdʒ/ *n.* **it's like [painting] the ~** (fig.) es ist eine Sisyphusarbeit

forthcoming /ˈfɔːθkʌmɪŋ, fɔːθˈkʌmɪŋ/ *adj.* [1] (approaching) bevorstehend; (about to appear) in Kürze zu erwartend; in Kürze anlaufend ‹*Film*›; in Kürze erscheinend ‹*Ausgabe, Buch usw.*›; **be ~:** bevorstehen; (about to appear) in Kürze zu erwarten sein/anlaufen/erscheinen; **'~ events'** (Journ.) „Veranstaltungskalender" [2] *pred.* (made available) **be ~** ‹*Geld, Antwort:*› kommen; ‹*Ware:*› geliefert werden; ‹*Hilfe:*› geleistet werden; **not be ~:** ausbleiben [3] (responsive) mitteilsam, gesprächig ‹*Person*›; **she wasn't very ~ with hard facts** mit der Mitteilung von Tatsachen hielt sie sich ziemlich zurück

forthright /ˈfɔːθraɪt/ *adj.* direkt; offen ‹*Blick*›

forthwith /fɔːθˈwɪθ, fɔːθˈwɪð/ *adv.* unverzüglich

fortieth /ˈfɔːtɪɪθ/
A *adj.* ▸**❶ p. 1358** vierzigst...; *see also* **eighth A**
B *n.* (fraction) Vierzigstel, *das; see also* **eighth B**

fortification /fɔːtɪfɪˈkeɪʃn/ *n.* [1] *no pl.* (Mil.: fortifying) Befestigung, *die* [2] *usu. in pl.* (Mil.: defensive works) Befestigung, *die;* Festungsanlage, *die* [3] (of wine) Aufspriten, *das*

fortify /ˈfɔːtɪfaɪ/ *v.t.* [1] (Mil.) befestigen [2] (strengthen, lit. or fig.) stärken [3] aufspriten ‹*Wein*›; anreichern ‹*Nahrungsmittel*›

fortissimo /fɔːˈtɪsɪməʊ/ (Mus.)
A *adj.* fortissimo *nicht attr.*; fortissimo gespielt/gesungen; Fortissimo-
B *adv.* fortissimo
C *n., pl.* **~s** *or* **fortissimi** /fɔːˈtɪsɪmiː/ Fortissimo, *das*

fortitude /ˈfɔːtɪtjuːd/ *n., no pl.* innere Stärke

fortnight /ˈfɔːtnaɪt/ *n.* vierzehn Tage; zwei Wochen; **a ~ [from] today** heute in vierzehn Tagen; **a ~ on Monday** *etc.* Montag *usw.* in vierzehn Tagen; **a ~ ago today** heute vor vierzehn Tagen; **in a ~['s time]** in vierzehn Tagen; **stay/go away for a ~:** vierzehn Tage [lang] bleiben/[für] vierzehn Tage verreisen; **take a ~'s leave** [sich (*Dat.*)] vierzehn Tage Urlaub nehmen; **once a ~, every ~:** alle vierzehn Tage *od.* zwei Wochen

fortnightly /ˈfɔːtnaɪtlɪ/
A *adj.* vierzehntäglich; zweiwöchentlich; **~ magazine** ▸**C**; **at ~ intervals** in Abständen von zwei Wochen; alle zwei Wochen
B *adv.* alle vierzehn Tage; alle zwei Wochen
C *n.* Halbmonatsschrift, *die*

fortress /ˈfɔːtrɪs/ *n.* (lit. or fig.) Festung, *die*

fortuitous /fɔːˈtjuːɪtəs/ *adj.*, **fortuitously** /fɔːˈtjuːɪtəslɪ/ *adv.* zufällig

fortunate /ˈfɔːtʃʊnət, ˈfɔːtʃənət/ *adj.* glücklich; **it is ~ for sb. [that ...]** es ist jmds. Glück[, dass ...]; **sb. is ~ to be alive** jmd. kann von Glück sagen *od.* reden, dass er noch lebt; **it was very ~ that ...:** es war ein Glück, dass ...; **how ~!, this is ~!** welch ein Glück!

fortunately /ˈfɔːtʃʊnətlɪ, ˈfɔːtʃənətlɪ/ *adv.* 1 (luckily) glücklicherweise; zum Glück; **~ for everybody/me** zum Glück [aller]/zu meinem Glück 2 (favourably, advantageously) gut ‹*dastehen, gestellt sein*›

fortune /ˈfɔːtʃən, ˈfɔːtʃuːn/ *n.* 1 (private wealth) Vermögen, *das;* **family/private ~:** Familien-/Privatvermögen, *das;* **make one's ~:** sein Glück machen; **come into a ~:** ein Vermögen erben; **his brains are his/her face is her ~** (fig. joc.) sein Verstand ist sein/ihr Gesicht ist ihr Kapital; **a [small] ~:** ein [kleines] Vermögen; **make a ~:** ein Vermögen machen 2 (prosperous condition) Glück, *das;* (of country) Wohl, *das;* **seek one's ~:** sein Glück suchen 3 (luck, destiny) Schicksal, *das;* **bad/good ~:** Pech/Glück, *das;* **that was a piece of good ~:** das war Glück; **by sheer good ~ there was ...:** es war reines Glück, dass ... war; **he's had a change of ~:** das Blatt hat sich [für ihn] gewendet (ugs.); **thank one's good ~ that ...:** dem Glück dafür danken, dass ...; **F~** (personified) das Glück; Fortuna (*die*); **~ favours the brave** (prov.) das Glück ist auf der Seite der Mutigen; **~ smiles on sb.** das Glück lächelt *od.* lacht jmdm.; **tell sb.'s ~:** jmdm. wahrsagen *od.* sein Schicksal vorhersagen; **tell ~s** wahrsagen; *see also* **soldier A** 4 *in pl.* (ups and downs, good or bad luck befalling sb., sth.) Schicksal, *das;* **the ~s of war** das Kriegsglück (geh.); **the changing ~s of the combatants** der wechselnde Erfolg der Kämpfer

fortune: ~ cookie *n.* (Amer. Cookery) *Plätzchen mit einer eingebackenen Weissagung;* **~ hunter** *n.* (derog.) Mitgiftjäger, *der* (abwertend); **~ teller** *n.* Wahrsager, *der*/Wahrsagerin, *die;* **~ telling** *n., no pl.* Wahrsagerei, *die*

forty /ˈfɔːtɪ/ ▸ⓘ **p. 894**, ▸ⓘ **p. 1001**, ▸ⓘ **p. 1358**
A *adj.* vierzig; **have ~ 'winks** ein Nickerchen (fam.) machen *od.* halten; *see also* **eight A**
B *n.*Vierzig, *die;* **the roaring forties** (Geog.) *stürmisches Ozeangebiet zwischen dem 40. und 50. Breitengrad;* Roaring forties *Pl.*; **the Forties** (Brit. Geog.) *Seegebiet zwischen der Nordostküste Schottlands und der Südwestküste Norwegens; see also* **eight B 1**; **eighty B**

forty: ~-'first *etc. adj.* ▸ⓘ **p. 1358** einundvierzigst... *usw.*; *see also* **eighth A**; **~-'five** *n.* ▸ⓘ **p. 1358** (record) Single[platte], *die;* **~fold** *adj., adv.* vierzigfach; *see also* **eightfold**; **~-'one** *etc.* **A** *adj.* einundvierzig *usw.*; *see also* **eight A**; **B** *n.* ▸ⓘ **p. 1358** Einundvierzig *usw., die; see also* **eight B 1**

forum /ˈfɔːrəm/ *n.* (also Roman Hist.) Forum, *das;* **~ for discussion** [Diskussions]forum, *das;* **the ~ of public opinion** das Forum der Öffentlichkeit

forward /ˈfɔːwəd/
A *adv.* 1 (in direction faced, onwards in progress) vorwärts; **bend ~:** sich vorbeugen; **take three steps ~:** drei Schritte vortreten; **~ march!** (Mil.) vorwärts marsch! 2 (towards end of room etc. faced) nach vorn; vor‹*laufen, -rücken, -schieben*›; **work one's way ~:** sich nach vorn durcharbeiten; **the seat is too far ~:** der Sitz ist zu weit vorn 3 (closer) heran; **rush ~ to help sb.** jmdm. zu Hilfe eilen; **he came ~ to greet me** er kam auf mich zu, um mich zu begrüßen 4 (ahead, in advance) voraus‹*schicken, -gehen*› 5 (into better state) **the country began to move ~:** mit dem Land ging es allmählich aufwärts 6 (into future) voraus‹*schauen, -denken*›; **from that day/time ~:** von dem *od.* jenem Tag an/von da an; **from this day/time ~:** von heute/jetzt an; **date ~** (Commerc.) vordatieren 7 (into prominence) in den Vordergrund; **come ~** (present oneself) ‹*Zeuge, Helfer:*› sich melden 8 (indicating motion) (Naut.) nach vorn [zum Bug]; (Aeronaut.) nach vorn [in den Bug] 9 (Naut., Aeronaut.: indicating position) (inside) vorn [im Bug]; (outside) vorn [am Bug] 10 (Cricket) **play ~:** nach vorn treten, um zu schlagen. *See also* **backward A 2**; **bring forward**; **carry forward**; **go forward**; **go forward with**; **look forward to**; **push forward**; **put forward**; **set forward**
B *adj.* 1 (directed ahead) vorwärts gerichtet; nach vorn *nachgestellt;* **~ movement** Vorwärtsbewegung, *die;* **~ pass** (Rugby) Vorpass, *der;* **~ somersault** Salto vorwärts 2 (at or to the front) Vorder-; vorder... 3 (lying in one's line of motion) vor einem *nachgestellt;* **the ~ horizon** der vor einem liegende Horizont 4 (advanced) frühreif ‹*Kind, Pflanze, Getreide*›; fortschrittlich ‹*Vorstellung, Ansicht, Maßnahme*›; [früh]zeitig, verfrüht ‹*Frühling, Blüte*›; **be well ~ with one's work/in one's plans** mit seiner Arbeit/seinen Plänen gut vorangekommen *od.* weit gediehen sein 5 (bold) dreist 6 (Commerc.) Termin‹*geschäft, -verkauf*›; Zukunfts‹*planung*› 7 (Naut.) zum Vor[der]schiff gehörend
C *n.* (Sport) Stürmer, *der*/Stürmerin, *die*
D *v.t.* 1 (send on) nachschicken ‹*Brief, Paket, Post*› (**to** an + *Akk.*); (dispatch) abschicken ‹*Waren*› (**to** an + *Akk.*); **'please ~', 'to be ~ed'** „bitte nachsenden" 2 (pass on) weiterreichen, weiterleiten ‹*Vorschlag, Plan*› (**to** an + *Akk.*) 3 (Computing) weiterleiten (**to** an + *Akk.*) 4 (promote) voranbringen ‹*Karriere, Vorbereitung*›; **~ one's own interests** seine eigenen Interessen verfolgen 5 (accelerate) beschleunigen ‹*Wachstum*›

forwarding /ˈfɔːwədɪŋ/: **~ address** *n.* Nachsendeanschrift, *die;* **~ agent** *n.* Spediteur, *der;* **~ instructions** *n. pl.* Anweisung über die Nachsendung/(for dispatch) den Versand

forward: ~ line *n.* (Sport) Sturm, *der;* **~-looking** *adj.* vorausschauend

forwardly /ˈfɔːwədlɪ/ *adv.* dreist

forwardness /ˈfɔːwədnɪs/ *n., no pl.* 1 (boldness) Dreistigkeit, *die* 2 (advanced state) (of child, crop) Frühreife, *die;* (of season) verfrühter *od.* [früh]zeitiger Beginn

forward 'planning *n.* Vorausplanung, *die*

forwards /ˈfɔːwədz/ ▸**forward A 1, 2, 3**

'forward slash *n.* Schrägstrich, *der*

forwent ▸**forgo**

fossil /ˈfɒsɪl/
A *n.* 1 Fossil, *das* 2 (fig. derog.) (antiquated person) Fossil, *das;* (antiquated thing) verstaubtes Relikt 3 (Ling.) **[linguistic] ~:** Sprachrelikt, *das*
B *attrib. adj.* fossil (Paläont.); **~ fuel** fossiler Brennstoff; **~ record** Fossilbefund, *der*

fossilisation, fossilise ▸**fossiliz-**

fossilization /fɒsɪlaɪˈzeɪʃn/ *n.* Fossilisation, *die* (Paläont.)

fossilize /ˈfɒsɪlaɪz/
A *v.t.* fossilisieren lassen (Paläont.); versteinern lassen (auch fig.); **become ~d** ▸**B**; **~d** fossil (Paläont.); (fig.) antiquiert; verstaubt (abwertend); **~d remains** Fossilien *Pl*
B *v.i.* fossilisieren (Paläont.); versteinern (auch fig.)

foster /ˈfɒstə(r)/
A *v.t.* 1 (encourage) fördern; pflegen ‹*Freundschaft*›; (harbour) hegen (geh.) 2 (rear as ~-child) in Pflege haben ‹*Kind*›; **the child was ~ed from the age of two** das Kind war seit seinem dritten Lebensjahr in Pflege *od.* bei Pflegeeltern
B *adj.* **~-** Pflege‹*bruder, -eltern, -sohn usw.*›; **~ home** Pflegestelle, *die;* **put a child into ~ care** ein Kind in Pflege geben; **be in ~ care** in Pflege sein

'foster-child *n.* Pflegekind, *das*

'foster-mother *n.* 1 Pflegemutter, *die* 2 (Brit.: for chickens) künstliche Glucke

fought ▸**fight A, B**

foul /faʊl/
A *adj.* 1 (offensive to the senses, loathsome) abscheulich; übel ‹*Geruch, Geschmack*› 2 (polluted) verschmutzt ‹*Wasser, Luft*›; (putrid) faulig ‹*Wasser*›; stickig ‹*Luft*› 3 (coll.: awful) scheußlich (ugs.); mies (ugs. abwertend) 4 (morally vile) anstößig, unanständig ‹*Sprache, Gerede*›; lose ‹*Maul, Mundwerk*›; schmutzig ‹*Fantasie, Gedanke, Gewerbe*›; niederträchtig ‹*Verleumdung, Tat*›; feige, abscheulich ‹*Mord*›; gemein, schäbig ‹*Behandlung*›; böse, (geh.) übel ‹*Streich*›; **~ deed** Schandtat, *die* 5 (unfair) unerlaubt, unredlich ‹*Mittel*›; (Sport) regelwidrig, verboten ‹*Schlag, Hieb*›; **~ play** (Sport) Foulspiel, *das;* (fig.: unfair dealing) Betrug, *der;* **the police do not suspect ~ play** die Polizei vermutet kein Verbrechen; **there was a lot of ~ play** (Sport) es ging recht unfair zu; *see also* **fair² A 1** 6 **fall** *or* **run ~ of** (Naut.) zusammenstoßen *od.* kollidieren mit; (fig.) kollidieren *od.* in Konflikt geraten mit ‹*Vorschrift, Gesetz, Polizei*›; aneinander geraten mit ‹*Person*› 7 (Naut.: entangled) unklar 8 (clogged up) verstopft
B *n.* (Sport) Foul, *das;* Regelverstoß, *der;* **commit a ~:** foulen; ein Foul *od.* einen Regelverstoß begehen
C *v.t.* 1 (make ~) beschmutzen (auch fig.); verunreinigen (abwertend); verpesten ‹*Luft*›; *see also* **nest A 1** 2 (be entangled with) sich verfangen in (+ *Dat.*) 3 ▸**foul up 2** 4 (Sport) foulen

Phrasal verb
• **~ 'up** *v.t.* 1 (coll.: spoil) vermasseln (salopp); verderben ‹*Atmosphäre, Beziehung*› 2 (block) blockieren. *see also* **foul-up**

foully /ˈfaʊllɪ/ *adv.* (wickedly) skrupellos ‹*ermorden, verurteilen*›; schlecht ‹*behandeln*›; böswillig ‹*verleumden*›

foul-mouthed /ˈfaʊlmaʊðd/ *adj.* unanständig; unflätig

foulness /ˈfaʊlnɪs/ *n., no pl.* 1 Abscheulichkeit, *die* 2 (state of being polluted) Verschmutzung, *die;* (putridness) Fauligkeit, *die*

foul: ~-smelling *adj.* übel riechend; **~-up** *n.* Durcheinander, *das;* Schlamassel, *der* (ugs.)

found¹ /faʊnd/ *v.t.* 1 (establish) gründen; stiften ‹*Krankenhaus, Kloster*›; begründen ‹*Wissenschaft, Religion, Glauben, Kirche*›; **F~ing Fathers** *Mitglieder der verfassunggebenden Versammlung der USA von 1787;* Gründerväter *Pl.* 2 (fig.: base) begründen; **~ sth. [up]on sth.** etw. auf etw. (*Akk.*) gründen; **be ~ed [up]on sth.** [sich] auf etw. (*Akk.*) gründen; auf etw. (*Dat.*) beruhen; *see also* **ill-founded**; **well-founded**

found² ▸**find A, B**

found³ *v.t.* (Metallurgy) gießen; (Glassmaking) gießen; (melt) schmelzen

foundation /faʊnˈdeɪʃn/ *n.* 1 (establishing) Gründung, *die;* (of hospital, monastery) Stiftung, *die;* (of school of painting, of religion) Begründung, *die* 2 (institution) Stiftung, *die;* **be on the ~** (Brit.) ein Stipendium erhalten 3 *usu. in pl.* **~[s]** (underlying part, lit. or fig.) (of building) Fundament, *das;* (of road) Unterbau, *der;* **lay the ~s** das Fundament legen; (for road) den Unterbau legen; **be without** *or* **have no ~** (fig.) unbegründet sein; der Grundlage entbehren; **lay the ~ of/for sth.** (fig.) das Fundament *od.* die Grundlage zu etw. legen; **shake sth. to its ~s** (fig.) etw. in seinen Grundfesten erschüttern 4 (cosmetic) Grundierung, *die* 5 ▸**foundation garment**

foundation: ~ course *n.* (Univ. etc.) Grundkurs, *der;* **~ cream** *n.* Grundierungscreme, *die;* **~ garment** *n.* Mieder, *das;* **~ stone** *n.* (lit. or fig.) Grundstein, *der*

founder¹ /ˈfaʊndə(r)/ *n.* Gründer, *der*/Gründerin, *die;* (of hospital, or with an endowment) Stifter, *der*/Stifterin, *die;* (of sect, science, school, religion) Begründer, *der*/Begründerin, *die;* **~ member** Gründungsmitglied, *das*

founder² *v.i.* 1 ‹*Schiff:*› sinken, untergehen; ‹*Pferd:*› straucheln, stürzen; ‹*Erdboden, Gebäude:*› einstürzen 2 (fig.: fail) sich zerschlagen

foundling /ˈfaʊndlɪŋ/ *n.* Findelkind, *das;* Findling, *der*

foundry /ˈfaʊndrɪ/ *n.* (Metallurgy) Gießerei, *die;* (Glass-making) Glashütte, *die*

fount¹ /faʊnt/ *n.* ▸**font²**

fount² /faʊnt/ *n.* (literary: fountain) Born, *der* (dichter., auch fig. geh.)

fountain /ˈfaʊntɪn/ *n.* 1 ▸**drinking fountain** 2 (jet[s] of water) Fontäne, *die;* (structure) Springbrunnen, *der* 3 (fig.: source) Quelle, *die;*

~ **of youth** Jungbrunnen, *der. see also* **soda fountain**

fountain: ~head *n.* Quelle, *die;* ~ **pen** *n.* Füllfederhalter, *der;* Füller, *der* (ugs.)

four /fɔː(r)/ ▸❶ **p. 894,** ▸❶ **p. 1001,** ▸❶ **p. 1358**

A *adj.* vier; *see also* **eight A**

B *n.* **1** (number, symbol) Vier, *die* **2** (set of ~ people) Vierergruppe, *die;* (Rowing) Vierer, *der;* **the ~:** die Vier; **make up a ~ at tennis/bridge** im Doppel Tennis spielen/der vierte Mitspieler beim Bridge sein **3** **on all ~s** auf allen vieren (ugs.); **be/crawl/move on all ~s** auf allen vieren kriechen (ugs.); **get down on all ~s** sich auf alle viere begeben (ugs.). *See also* **eight B 1, 3, 4**

four: ~-ball *n.* (Golf) Vierball, *der;* **~-by-~** **A** *adj.* Allrad-; **B** *n.* Allradler, *der;* Allradfahrzeug, *das;* **~-door** *attrib. adj.* viertürig ‹*Auto*›; **~fold** /ˈfɔːfəʊld/ *adj., adv.* vierfach; *see also* **eightfold**; **~-footed** /ˈfɔːfʊtɪd/ *adj.* vierfüßig; **~-handed** /fɔːˈhændɪd/ *adj.* **1** ‹*Spiel*› mit vier Mitspielern; **2** (Mus.) zu vier Händen *nachgestellt;* vierhändig; **~-in-hand** *n.* Vierspänner, *der;* **~-lane** *adj.* vierspurig; **~-leaf clover**, **~-leaved clover** *n.* vierblättriges Kleeblatt; **~-legged** /ˈfɔːlegɪd, ˈfɔːlegd/ *adj.* vierbeinig; **~-letter ˈword** *n.* vulgärer Ausdruck; (expressing anger) ≈ Kraftausdruck, *der;* **~pence** /ˈfɔːpəns/ *n.* (Brit.) vier Pence; **~penny** /ˈfɔːpənɪ/ *adj.* (Brit.) (costing 4p or 4d) Vier-Pence-; **~-poster [bed]** *n.* Himmelbett, *das;* **~score** *adj.* (arch.) achtzig; **~some** /ˈfɔːsəm/ *n.* **1** Quartett, *das;* **go in** *or* **as a ~some** zu viert gehen; **2** (Golf) Vierer, *der;* **~-square** *adj.* **1** (square) quadratisch; **2** (fig.: resolute) unerschütterlich; tatkräftig ‹*Unterstützung*›; (forthright) direkt ‹*Inangriffnahme*›; unverblümt ‹*Schilderung*›; **~-stroke** *adj.* (Mech. Engin.) Viertakt‹*motor, -verfahren*›

fourteen /fɔːˈtiːn/ ▸❶ **p. 894,** ▸❶ **p. 1001,** ▸❶ **p. 1358**

A *adj.* vierzehn; *see also* **eight A**

B *n.* Vierzehn, *die; see also* **eight B 1, 4; eighteen B**

fourteenth /fɔːˈtiːnθ/ ▸❶ **p. 1047**

A *adj.* ▸❶ **p. 1358** vierzehnt...; *see also* **eighth A**

B *n.* (fraction) Vierzehntel, *das; see also* **eighth B**

fourth /fɔːθ/

A *adj.* **1** ▸❶ **p. 1358** viert...; **the ~ finger** der kleine Finger; *see also* **eighth A** **2** **~ dimension** vierte Dimension; *see also* **estate 6**

B *n.* **1** (in sequence, rank) Vierte, *der/die/das;* (fraction) Viertel, *das* **2** (~ form) vierte [Schul]klasse; Vierte, *die* (Schuljargon) **3** (Motor Veh.) vierter Gang; **in ~:** im vierten [Gang]; **change up [in]to ~:** in den vierten Gang schalten **4** (Mus.) Quarte, *die* **5** (person) vierter Teilnehmer/vierte Teilnehmerin; (in a game) vierter Mitspieler/vierte Mitspielerin; **make a ~:** als Vierter/Vierte mitmachen **6** ▸❶ **p. 1047** (day) **the ~ of May** der vierte Mai; **the ~ [of the month]** der Vierte [des Monats]; **F~ of July** (Amer.) *Unabhängigkeitstag der USA; see also* **eighth B**

fourth: ~ form ▸**form A 4**; **~ ˈgear** *n., no pl.* (Motor Veh.) vierter Gang; *see also* **gear A 4**

fourthly /ˈfɔːθlɪ/ *adv.* viertens

four-wheel ˈdrive *n.* (Motor Veh.) Vier- *od.* Allradantrieb, *der*

fowl /faʊl/

A *n. pl.* **~s** *or same* **1** Haushuhn, *das;* (collectively) Geflügel, *das* **2** (Gastr.) Huhn, *das;* **boiling ~:** Suppenhuhn, *das* **3** (literary: bird) Vogel, *der; see also* **waterfowl**; **wildfowl**

B *v.i.* **go ~ing** auf die Vogeljagd gehen

fowler /ˈfaʊlə(r)/ *n.* Vogeljäger, *der*

fox /fɒks/

A *n., pl.* **~es** **1** Fuchs, *der* (auch fig. ugs.); **as cunning as a ~:** schlau wie ein Fuchs **2** (fur) Fuchs[pelz], *der*

B *v.t.* verwirren; **that's got you ~ed** *or* **that's ~ed you, hasn't it?** jetzt bist du verblüfft, was?

fox: ~ cub *n.* Fuchswelpe, *der;* **~ fur** *n.* Fuchspelz, *der;* **~glove** *n.* (Bot.) Fingerhut, *der;* **~hole** *n.* **1** Fuchsbau, *der;* **2** (Mil.) Schützenloch, *das;* (fig.) Versteck, *das;* **~hound** *n.* Foxhound, *der;* **~ hunt** **A** *n.* Fuchsjagd, *die;* **B** *v.i.* **go ~-hunting** auf die Fuchsjagd gehen; **~-hunter** *n.* Fuchsjäger, *der;* **~-hunting** *n.* Fuchsjagd, *die;* **~tail** *n.* **1** Fuchsschwanz, *der;* **2** (Bot.) (Alopecurus) Fuchsschwanz, *der;* (Hordeum) Gerste, *die;* (Setaria) Borstenhirse, *die;* **~ ˈterrier** *n.* Foxterrier, *der;* **~trot** **A** *n.* Foxtrott, *der;* **B** *v.i.* Foxtrott tanzen

foxy /ˈfɒksɪ/ *adj.* **1** [fuchs]schlau ‹*Augen, Manöver*› **2** (coll.: attractive) dufte (salopp)

ˈfoxy-looking *adj.* fuchsgesichtig

foyer /ˈfɔɪeɪ, ˈfwɑjeɪ/ *n.* Foyer, *das*

FPS *abbr.* **= first person shooter**

fr. *abbr.* **= franc[s]** fr

Fr. *abbr.* **1** (Eccl.) **= Father** P. **2** **= French** frz.; fr.; franz.

fracas /ˈfrækɑː/ *n., pl. same* /ˈfrækɑːz/ [lautstarke] Auseinandersetzung; Krawall, *der*

fractal /ˈfræktl/ *adj.* (Math.) fraktal

fraction /ˈfrækʃn/ *n.* ▸❶ **p. 1358** **1** (Math.) Bruch, *der;* **do ~s** bruchrechnen; *see also* **decimal fraction**; **improper 4**; **proper fraction**; **vulgar 3** **2** (small part) Bruchteil, *der;* (tiny bit) Kleinigkeit, *die* (ugs.); Stückchen, *das;* Idee, *die;* **the car missed the pedestrian by a ~ of an inch** das Auto hätte den Fußgänger um Haaresbreite überfahren **3** (Chem.) Fraktion, *die*

fractional /ˈfrækʃənl/ *adj.* **1** (Math.) Bruch‹*zahl, -rechnen*›; (fig.: very slight) geringfügig; **~ part** Bruchteil, *der* **2** (Chem.) **~ crystallization/distillation** fraktionierte Kristallisation/Destillation

fractionally /ˈfrækʃənəlɪ/ *adv.* (fig.: very slightly) geringfügig

fractious /ˈfrækʃəs/ *adj.* (unruly) aufsässig; ungebärdig (geh.); störrisch ‹*Pferd*›; (peevish) quengelig ‹*Kind*›

fracture /ˈfræktʃə(r)/ ▸❶ **p. 1231**

A *n.* (also Med., Min.) Bruch, *der;* **nose ~:** Nasenbeinbruch, *der*

B *v.t.* (also Med.) brechen; (break up) aufspalten; **~ one's jaw** *etc.* sich (*Dat.*) den Kiefer *usw.* brechen; **~ one's skull** sich (*Dat.*) einen Schädelbruch zuziehen; **have a ~d jaw** *etc.* sich (*Dat.*) den Kiefer *usw.* gebrochen haben

C *v.i.* (Med.) brechen

fragile /ˈfrædʒaɪl/ *adj.* **1** zerbrechlich; zart ‹*Teint, Hand*›; **'~ — handle with care'** „Vorsicht, zerbrechlich!"; **feel ~** (coll.: ill, esp. because of hangover) sich ganz zerschlagen fühlen **2** (fig.) fadenscheinig ‹*Entschuldigung, Grund*›; heikel ‹*Situation*›; unsicher ‹*Frieden*›; zart ‹*Glück, Gesundheit, Konstitution*›; gebrechlich ‹*alte Frau*›; schwach ‹*Selbstvertrauen*›

fragility /frəˈdʒɪlɪtɪ/ *n., no pl.* Zerbrechlichkeit, *die;* (of health, constitution, frame, beauty) Zartheit, *die;* (fig.: of peace, situation) Unsicherheit, *die*

fragment

A /ˈfrægmənt/ *n.* Bruchstück, *das;* (of document, conversation) Fetzen, *der;* (of china) Scherbe, *die;* (of rock) Brocken, *der;* (Lit., Mus.) Fragment, *das;* Bruchstück, *das;* **it was in ~s** es war zerbrochen

B /frægˈment/ *v.t. & i.* zersplittern

fragmentary /ˈfrægməntərɪ/ *adj.* bruchstückhaft; fragmentarisch

fragmentation /frægmənˈteɪʃn/ *n.* Zersplitterung, *die*

fragmenˈtation bomb *n.* (Mil.) Splitterbombe, *die*

fragmented /frægˈmentɪd/ *adj.* bruchstückhaft

fragrance /ˈfreɪgrəns/ *n.* Duft, *der*

fragrant /ˈfreɪgrənt/ *adj.* duftend; (fig.) angenehm ‹*Erinnerung, Gefühl*›; **~ odour** *or* **smell** *or* **aroma** Wohlgeruch, *der;* **be ~ with sth.** nach etw. duften

frail /freɪl/ *adj.* zerbrechlich; zart ‹*Gesundheit*›; gebrechlich ‹*Greis, Greisin*›; (lacking force) schwach ‹*Stimme*›; (morally weak) schwach, labil ‹*Person, Natur, Charakter*›; (transient) vergänglich ‹*Leben, Glück*›; (slender) schwach ‹*Hoffnung*›; gering ‹*Verständnis*›

frailty /ˈfreɪltɪ/ *n.* **1** *no pl.* Zerbrechlichkeit, *die;* (of health) Zartheit, *die;* (moral weakness) Schwachheit, *die;* (transience) Vergänglichkeit, *die* **2** *esp. in pl.* (fault) Schwäche, *die*

frame /freɪm/

A *n.* **1** (of vehicle, bicycle) Rahmen, *der;* (of easel, rucksack, bed, umbrella) Gestell, *das;* (of ship, aircraft) Gerüst, *das;* (of building) Tragwerk, *das* (Bauw.); **timber ~:** Fachwerk, *das;* Gebälk, *das; see also* **climbing frame** **2** (border) Rahmen, *der;* **[spectacle] ~s** [Brillen]gestell, *das* **3** (fig.: established order) Struktur, *die;* **~ of reference** (Phys., Sociol.) Bezugssystem, *das* **4** (of person, animal) Körper, *der;* **a man of gigantic ~:** ein Mann von hünenhafter Gestalt **5** (Photog., Cinemat.) [Einzel]bild, *das;* (Telev.) [einzelnes Fernseh]bild **6** (of comic strip) [Einzel]bild, *das* **7** (Hort.) Frühbeet, *das* **8** (Snooker) (triangle) [dreieckiger] Rahmen; (round of play) Spiel, *das;* [Spiel]runde, *die* **9** (Computing) Frame, *der od. das. See also* **mind A 5**

B *v.t.* **1** rahmen ‹*Bild, Spiegel*›; umrahmen ‹*Text usw. mit Verzierungen*›; **a face ~d in curls** ein von Locken umrahmtes Gesicht **2** (compose) formulieren ‹*Frage, Antwort, Satz*›; aufbauen ‹*Rede, Aufsatz*›; (devise) entwerfen ‹*Gesetz, Politik, Plan*›; ausarbeiten ‹*Plan, Methode, Denksystem*›; aufstellen ‹*Regel, Theorie*›; (shape) konstruieren; schaffen ‹*Bau[werk]*›; gestalten ‹*[Um]welt, Leben*›; **~ one's words** sich ausdrücken; **her lips ~d a curse** ihre Lippen formten einen Fluch **3** (coll.: incriminate unjustly) **~ sb.** jmdm. etwas anhängen (ugs.)

Phrasal verb

• **~ ˈup** *v.t.* (Amer. coll.) manipulieren; türken (ugs.); *see also* **frame-up**

ˈframe house *n.* Haus mit Holzgerüst

framer /ˈfreɪmə(r)/ *n.* Rahmenschreiner, *der;* **picture-~:** Bildereinrahmer, *der*

frame: ~-up *n.* (coll.) abgekartetes Spiel (ugs.); **~work** *n.* (of ship etc.) Gerüst, *das;* (of building) Fachwerk, *das;* Gebälk, *das;* (fig.: of project) Gerüst, *das;* (of novel) Rahmen, *der;* (of essay, lecture, etc.) Aufbau, *der;* Gliederung, *die;* (of society, government, system) [Grund]struktur, *die;* Grundlagen *Pl.;* **[with]in the ~work of** (as part of) im Rahmen (+ *Gen.*); (in relation to) im Zusammenhang mit; **outside the ~work of** (not as part of) außerhalb (+ *Gen.*)

framing /ˈfreɪmɪŋ/ *n.* (Building) Fachwerk, *das*

franc /fræŋk/ *n.* ▸❶ **p. 1332** (Swiss) Franken, *der;* (Hist.: French, Belgian, Luxemburg) Franc, *der*

France /frɑːns/ *pr. n.* Frankreich (*das*)

franchise /ˈfræntʃaɪz/

A *n.* **1** Stimmrecht, *das;* (esp. for Parliament) Wahlrecht, *das* **2** (Commerc.) Lizenz, *die*

B *v.t.* (Commerc.) [die] Lizenz erteilen (+ *Dat.*)

Francis /ˈfrɑːnsɪs/ *pr. n.* (Hist., as name of ruler etc.) Franz (*der*); **St ~:** der hl. Franziskus

Franciscan /frænˈsɪskn/

A *n.* Franziskaner, *der*/Franziskanerin, *die*

B *adj.* franziskanisch/Franziskaner‹*mönch, -kloster*›

Franco- /ˈfræŋkəʊ/ *in comb.* französisch-; franko‹*kanadisch*›; Franko‹*kanadier*›; **~German** deutsch-französisch; **the ~Prussian War** der Deutsch-Französische Krieg

Franconia /fræŋˈkəʊnɪə/ *pr. n.* Franken, *das*

Franconian /fræŋˈkəʊnɪən/

A *adj.* fränkisch

B *n.* (person) Franke, *der*/Fränkin, *die;* (dialect) Fränkisch, *das*

francophone /ˈfræŋkəfəʊn/

A *adj.* frankophon

B *n.* Frankophone, *der/die*

franglais /ˈfrɑ̃gleɪ/ *n.* von englischen Ausdrücken durchsetztes Französisch; Franglais, *das*

frank[1] *adj.* **1** (candid) offen ‹*Bekenntnis, Aussprache, Blick, Gesicht, Person*›; freimütig ‹*Geständnis, Äußerung*›; (undisguised) offen ‹*Abneigung, Widerwille*›; unverhohlen ‹*Bewunderung, Neugier, Verlangen*›; (uninhibited) unbefangen; **give me your ~ opinion** sag mir offen deine Meinung; **be ~ with sb.** zu jmdm. offen sein; jmdm. offen seine Meinung sagen; **to be [quite] ~** (as sentence-modifier) offen gesagt; **~ and open** offen und ehrlich ‹*Gesicht*›; frei und ungezwungen ‹*Benehmen*› **2** (Med.) eindeutig; manifest (fachspr.)

frank²
A *v.t.* (Post) **1** (in lieu of postage stamp) freistempeln **2** (put postage stamp on) frankieren
B *n. Vermerk über Gebührenfreiheit*

frank³ *n.* (Amer. coll.: frankfurter) Frankfurter [Würstchen]

Frank /fræŋk/ *n.* (Hist.) Franke, *der*/Fränkin, *die*

Frankenstein['s 'monster] /'fræŋknstaɪn/ *n. seinen Schöpfer vernichtendes Ungeheuer;* ≈ Monster, *das*

frankfurter /'fræŋkfɜːtə(r)/ (*Amer.*: **frankfurt** /'fræŋkfɜːt/) *n.* Frankfurter [Würstchen]

frankincense /'fræŋkɪnsens/ *n.* Weihrauch, *der;* (turpentine) Terpentin, *das*

franking machine /'fræŋkɪŋməʃiːn/ *n.* (Brit. Post) Frankiermaschine, *die;* Freistempler, *der*

Frankish /'fræŋkɪʃ/ *adj.* (Hist.) fränkisch

frankly /'fræŋklɪ/ *adv.* (candidly) offen; frank und frei; (honestly) offen *od.* ehrlich gesagt; (openly, undisguisedly) unverhohlen ‹*kritisch, materialistisch usw.*›; (uninhibitedly) unbefangen

frankness /'fræŋknɪs/ *n., no pl.* Offenheit, *die;* Freimütigkeit, *die;* (uninhibitedness) Unbefangenheit, *die*

frantic /'fræntɪk/ *adj.* **1** (nearly mad) **be ~ with fear/rage** *etc.* außer sich (*Dat.*) sein vor Angst/Wut *usw.;* **drive sb. ~:** jmdn. in den Wahnsinn treiben *od.* wahnsinnig machen; **she was getting ~:** sie war am Durchdrehen (ugs.); sie geriet außer sich **2** (very anxious, noisy, uncontrolled) hektisch ‹*Aktivität, Suche, Getriebe*›; heftig ‹*Protest*›; tosend, stürmisch, (geh.) frenetisch ‹*Beifall*› **3** (showing that sb. is ~) erregt ‹*Schrei, Wort, Gebärde*›

frantically /'fræntɪkəlɪ/ *adv.* verzweifelt ‹*schreien, suchen, protestieren*›; stürmisch, (geh.) frenetisch ‹*applaudieren*›; wie angestochen, wie wild (ugs.) ‹*herumrennen*›; **the shops are ~ busy** in den Läden herrscht hektische Betriebsamkeit

frappé /'fræpeɪ/ *adj.* geeist

fraternal /frə'tɜːnl/ *adj.* brüderlich; **~ twins** zweieiige Zwillinge

fraternisation, fraternise ▸**fraterniz-**

fraternity /frə'tɜːnɪtɪ/ *n.* **1** (set of men with common interest) Vereinigung, *die;* (guild) Gilde, *die* (hist.); Zunft, *die* (hist.); **the teaching/medical/legal ~:** die Lehrer-/Ärzte-/Juristenzunft; die Zunft der Lehrer/Ärzte/Juristen **2** (Relig.) Bruderschaft, *die;* Fraternität, *die* (kath. Kirche) **3** (Amer. Univ.: society) [studentische] Verbindung **4** *no pl.* (brotherliness) Brüderlichkeit, *die*

> **fraternity**
>
> Eine studentische Verbindung an amerikanischen Universitäten. Studenten, die in eine solche Verbindung eintreten, wohnen im gleichen *house* (College) und nennen sich *Greeks*. Die Namen der einzelnen Studentenverbindungen leiten sich von zwei oder drei Buchstaben des griechischen Alphabets ab (z. B. Lambda Delta Chi). Viele Verbindungen arbeiten für wohltätige Zwecke, und *fraternities* wie Phi Beta Kappa erzielen sehr hohe akademische Leistungen. Allerdings werden manche wegen ihrer berüchtigten Gebräuche und wilden Feste oft heftig kritisiert.

fraternization /frætənaɪ'zeɪʃn/ *n.* Verbrüderung, *die;* **~ [with sb.]** (Mil.) Fraternisierung [mit jmdm.]

fraternize /'frætənaɪz/ *v.i.* **~ [with sb.]** sich verbrüdern [mit jmdm.]; (Mil.) fraternisieren [mit jmdm.]

fratricide /'frætrɪsaɪd/ *n.* **1** *no pl.* (crime) Brudermord, *der* **2** (person) Brudermörder, *der*/-mörderin, *die*

Frau /fraʊ/ *n.* Deutsche, *die;* deutsche Frau

fraud /frɔːd/ *n.* **1** *no pl.* (cheating, deceit) Betrug, *der;* Täuschung, *die;* (Law) [arglistige] Täuschung **2** (trick, false thing) Schwindel, *der;* (Law) Betrug, *der;* **~s** Betrügereien *Pl.;* **pious ~:** frommer Betrug **3** (person) (impostor, sham) Betrüger, *der*/Betrügerin, *die;* Schwindler, *der*/Schwindlerin, *die;* (hypocrite) Heuchler, *der*/Heuchlerin, *die;* **you [old] ~!** (coll.) du alter Schlawiner! (ugs.)

'fraud squad *n.* (Brit.) Betrugsdezernat, *das*

fraudster /'frɔːdstə(r)/ *n.* (Brit.) Betrüger, *der*/Betrügerin, *die*

fraudulence /'frɔːdjʊləns/ *n., no pl.* betrügerische Absicht

fraudulent /'frɔːdjʊlənt/ *adj.* betrügerisch; **with ~ intent** in betrügerischer Absicht; **~ name** falscher Name

fraudulently /'frɔːdjʊləntlɪ/ *adv.* in betrügerischer Weise

fraught /frɔːt/ *adj.* **1** **be ~ with danger** voller Gefahren *od.* sehr gefahrvoll sein; **~ with tension** spannungsgeladen; **~ with meaning/memories** bedeutungsschwer/mit Erinnerungen befrachtet; **~ with obstacles/difficulties** voller Hindernisse/Schwierigkeiten; **silence ~ with menace** bedrohliche Stille **2** (coll.: distressingly tense) stressig (ugs.) ‹*Atmosphäre, Situation, Diskussion*›; gestresst (ugs.) ‹*Person*›

Fräulein /'frɔɪlaɪn/ *n.* [junge] Deutsche; deutsche [junge] Frau

fray¹ /freɪ/ *n.* (fight) [Kampf]getümmel, *das;* (noisy quarrel) Streit, *der;* **in the thick of the ~:** mitten im dicksten Getümmel; **plunge into the ~:** sich ins [Kampf]getümmel stürzen; **in the heat of the ~** (fig.) in der Hitze des Gefechts (fig.); **be eager/ready for the ~** (lit. or fig.) kampflustig/kampfbereit sein; **enter** *or* **join the ~** (lit. or fig.) sich in den Kampf *od.* ins Getümmel stürzen

fray²
A *v.i.* [sich] durchscheuern; ‹*Hosenbein, Teppich, Seilende:*› ausfransen; **our nerves/tempers began to ~** (fig.) wir verloren langsam die Nerven/unsere Gemüter erhitzten sich
B *v.t.* durchscheuern; ausfransen ‹*Hosenbein, Teppich, Seilende*›; (fig.) belasten; strapazieren

frayed /freɪd/ *adj.* durchgescheuert; ausgefranst ‹*Hosenbein, Teppich, Seilende*›; (fig.) strapaziert ‹*Nerven, Geduld*›; erregt, erhitzt ‹*Gemüt*›; **his politeness was by now somewhat ~:** seine Höflichkeit war inzwischen etwas verkrampft

frazzle /'fræzl/ *n.* (coll.) **to a ~:** völlig; total (ugs.); **my nerves were worn to a ~:** ich war mit den Nerven völlig am Ende

freak /friːk/
A *n.* **1** (monstrosity) (person, animal) Missgeburt, *die;* (plant) missgebildete Pflanze; Mutation, *die;* **~ of nature** Laune der Natur **2** (freakish thing or occurrence) Laune, *die;* (attrib.) ungewöhnlich ‹*Wetter, Ereignis*›; völlig überraschend ‹*Sieg, Ergebnis*› **3** (coll.: fanatic) Freak, *der;* **health ~:** Gesundheitsfanatiker, *der;* **health food ~:** Reformköstler, *der* (ugs.); Körnerfresser, *der* (salopp) **4** (coll.: eccentric person) Freak, *der;* Ausgeflippte, *der/die* (salopp); (derog.) komischer Vogel (ugs.) **5** (caprice) Laune, *die*
B *v.i.* **~ [out]** (coll.) (with fury) die Nerven verlieren; durchdrehen (ugs.); (with ecstasy) vor Freude [ganz] außer sich (*Dat.*) sein

freakish /'friːkɪʃ/ *adj.* (capricious) launisch; verrückt (ugs.); (abnormal) absonderlich; **~ trick of fortune** Laune des Schicksals

freaky /'friːkɪ/ *adj.* **1** ▸**freakish** **2** (coll.: bizarre) irre (salopp); verrückt (ugs.)

freckle /'frekl/ *n.* Sommersprosse, *die*

freckled /'frekld/, **freckle-faced** /'freklfeɪst/, **freckly** /'freklɪ/ *adjs.* sommersprossig

Frederick /'fredrɪk/ *pr. n.* (Hist., as name of ruler etc.) Friedrich

free /friː/
A *adj.,* **freer** /'friːə(r)/, **freest** /'friːɪst/ **1** frei; **get ~:** freikommen; sich befreien; **her heart is ~** (fig.) ihr Herz ist noch frei; **go ~** (escape unpunished) straffrei ausgehen; **let sb. go ~** (leave captivity) jmdn. freilassen; (unpunished) jmdn. freisprechen; **set ~:** freilassen; (fig.) erlösen; **as ~ as air** *or* **a bird** *or* **the wind** frei wie ein Vogel
2 (Polit.) frei; **it's a ~ country** (coll.) wir leben in einem freien Land
3 (unrestricted, unconstrained, unrepressed) frei; (untrammelled) frei; ungebunden; (frank, open) offen; freimütig; (improper) freizügig; (forward, familiar) ungezwungen; **~ of sth.** (outside) außerhalb etw.; (without) frei von etw.; **~ of prejudice/imperfections** vorurteils-/fehlerfrei; **~ of debts/tax/charge/cost** schulden-/steuer-/gebührenfrei/kostenlos; **be glad to be ~ of sth./sb.** froh sein, etw./jmdn. los zu sein; **~ and easy** ungezwungen; locker (ugs.); **give sb. a ~ rein to do sth.** jmdm. freie Hand lassen, etw. zu tun; **give ~ rein to sth.** einer Sache (*Dat.*) freien Lauf lassen; **make ~ with sth.** mit etw. sehr großzügig umgehen; (help oneself) etw. ungeniert benutzen; **make [rather too] ~ with sb.** sich (*Dat.*) jmdm. gegenüber etwas [zu viel] herausnehmen; **be ~ with one's hands** (hitting) eine lockere Hand haben; (stroking) sich (*Dat.*) Freiheiten herausnehmen
4 (Commerc., Econ.) frei ‹*Wirtschaft, Wettbewerb*›
5 (not fixed, untied) frei; lose; **work ~** ‹*Teil:*› sich lösen; **she wrenched herself ~ from his arms** sie entwand sich seinen Armen; **get one hand ~:** eine Hand freibekommen
6 (having liberty) **sb. is ~ to do sth.** es steht jmdm. frei, etw. zu tun; **you're ~ to choose** du kannst frei [aus]wählen; **leave sb. ~ to do sth.** es jmdm. ermöglichen, etw. zu tun; **he's not ~ to marry** er kann/darf nicht heiraten; **our thoughts are ~ to roam** die Gedanken sind frei; **feel ~!** nur zu! (ugs.); **Do you mind if I smoke? — Feel ~!** Stört es Sie, wenn ich rauche? — Nein, ganz und gar nicht!; **feel ~ to correct me** du darfst mich gerne korrigieren; **~ from sth.** frei von etw.; **~ from pain/troubles** schmerz-/sorgenfrei
7 (provided without payment) kostenlos; frei ‹*Überfahrt, Unterkunft, Versand, Verpflegung*›; Frei‹*karte, -exemplar, -fahrt*›; Gratis‹*probe, -vorstellung*›; **they get ~ lunches** sie haben freies Mittagessen; **'admission ~'** „Eintritt frei"; **have a ~ ride on the train** umsonst mit der Bahn fahren; **have a ~ ride at sb.'s expense** (fig. coll.) auf jmds. Kosten faulenzen; **be out for a ~ ride** (fig. coll.) Trittbrettfahrer sein (abwertend); **for ~** (coll.) umsonst; **publicity for ~** (coll.) kostenlose Werbung
8 (not occupied, not reserved, not being used) frei; **~ time** Freizeit, *die;* **when would you be ~ to start work?** wann könnten Sie mit der Arbeit anfangen?; **have a ~ period** (Sch.) eine Freistunde haben; **he's ~ in the mornings** er hat morgens Zeit; **when can you arrange to be ~?** wann könnten Sie sich freimachen?
9 (generous) **be** *or* **make ~ with sth.** mit etw. großzügig umgehen; **be a ~ spender** sein Geld mit vollen Händen ausgeben
10 (not strict) frei ‹*Übersetzung, Interpretation, Bearbeitung usw.*›; **draw a ~ likeness of sb.** jmdn. mit künstlerischer Freiheit zeichnen
11 (Chem., Phys.) frei ‹*Elektron, Energie*›
B *adv.* **1** (without cost or payment) gratis; umsonst; **he gets his accommodation ~:** er hat freies Logis
2 (freely) frei
C *v.t.* (set at liberty) freilassen; (disentangle) befreien **(of, from** von); **~ sb./oneself from** jmdn./sich befreien von ‹*Tyrannei, Unterdrückung, Tradition*›; jmdn./sich befreien aus ‹*Gefängnis, Sklaverei, Umklammerung*›; (make secure) jmdn./sich schützen vor (+ *Dat.*) ‹*Gefahr, Infektion*›; **~ oneself from debt/obligations** sich seiner Schulden/Verpflichtungen entledigen; **~ sb./oneself of** jmdn./sich befreien *od.* freimachen von

-free /friː/ *in comb.* -frei

free 'agent *n.* **be a ~** sein eigener Herr sein

'freebase
A *n., no pl.* Freebase, *das*
B *v.i.* Freebase nehmen
C *v.t.* **~ cocaine** Freebase nehmen

freebie /'friːbɪ/ (coll.)
A *n.* Gratisgeschenk, *das*
B *adj.* Gratis‹*essen, -getränk*›; **~ ticket** Freikarte, *die*

'freeboard *n.* (Naut.) Freibord, *der*

freebooter /'friːbuːtə(r)/ *n.* Freibeuter, *der* (hist.)

free: ~-born *adj.* frei (hist.); **F~ 'Church** *n.* Freikirche, *die*

f

f

freedom /'fri:dəm/ *n.* 1 Freiheit, *die;* **give sb. his ~:** jmdn. freigeben; (from prison, slavery) jmdn. freilassen; **~ of the press** Pressefreiheit, *die;* **~ of action/speech/movement/information** Handlungs-/Rede-/Bewegungs-/Informationsfreiheit, *die;* **~ of movement of labour** Freizügigkeit der Arbeit; **~ from taxes/pain** Steuer-/Schmerzfreiheit, *die* 2 (frankness) Ungezwungenheit, *die;* (over-familiarity) Vertraulichkeit, *die* 3 (ease) **~ of operation of the mechanism** Leichtgängigkeit des Mechanismus 4 (privilege) **[give sb.** *or* **present sb. with] the ~ of the city** [jmdm.] die Ehrenbürgerrechte [verleihen] 5 (use) **give sb. the ~ of sth.** jmdm. etw. zur freien Verfügung überlassen. *see also* **conscience**

'freedom fighter *n.* Freiheitskämpfer, *der*/-kämpferin, *die*

free: ~ 'enterprise *n.* freies Unternehmertum; **~ 'fall** *n.* freier Fall; **~-fall parachuting** Fallschirmspringen mit freiem Fall; **~ 'fight** *n.* Kampf jeder gegen jeden; **F~fone** ® /'fri:fəʊn/ *n., no pl.* ≈ Service 130; **F~phone line** *or* **number/hotline** gebührenfreie Servicenummer/Hotline; **phone us on F~fone 0800 343 027** rufen Sie uns unter 0800 343 027 zum Nulltarif an; **~-for-all** A *n.* [allgemeine] Schlägerei; (less violent) [allgemeines] Gerangel; **the discussion soon became a ~-for-all** bei der Diskussion redeten bald alle wild durcheinander; B *adj.* 1 allgemein ‹*Schlägerei, Gerangel*›; 2 (observing no rules) wild ‹*Diskussion, Schlägerei*›; ‹*Spiel*› ohne [feste] Regeln; **~ 'gift** *n.* Gratisgabe, *die;* **~ 'hand** *n.* 1 **I picked it up with my ~ hand** ich hob es mit der freien Hand auf; 2 (fig.) freier [Handlungs]spielraum; **give sb. a ~ hand** jmdm. freie Hand lassen; 3 **with a ~ hand** (generously) großzügig; **~hand** *adj., adv.* freihändig; **~ 'hit** *n.* (Hockey, Polo) Freischlag, *der;* **~hold** A *n.* Besitzrecht, *das;* B *adj.* Eigentums-; **~hold land** freier Grundbesitz; **~holder** *n.* Grundeigentümer, *der;* **~ house** *n.* (Brit.) *brauereiunabhängiges Wirtshaus;* **~ 'kick** *n.* (Footb.) Freistoß, *der;* **~lance** A *n.* 1 freier Mitarbeiter/freie Mitarbeiterin; 2 (Hist.: mercenary) Söldner, *der;* B *adj.* freiberuflich; **~lance translating** freiberufliche Arbeit als Übersetzer; C *v.i.* freiberuflich arbeiten; **~lancer** /'fri:lɑ:nsə(r)/ ▸**~lance A;** **~'loader** *n.* (coll.) Nassauer, *der* (ugs., meist abwertend); **~ 'love** *n.* freie Liebe

freely /'fri:lɪ/ *adv.* 1 (willingly) großzügig; freimütig ‹*eingestehen*› 2 (without restriction, loosely) frei 3 (frankly) offen 4 (abundantly) reichlich

free: ~man /'fri:mən/ *n., pl.* **~men** /'fri:mən/ 1 Freie, *der* (hist.); 2 (who has freedom of city etc.) Ehrenbürger, *der;* **~ 'market** *n.* (Econ.) freier Markt; **F~mason** *n.* Freimaurer, *der;* **~masonry** *n.* 1 **F~masonry** Freimaurerei, *die;* 2 (fig.: corporate feeling) Zusammengehörigkeitsgefühl, *das;* **~ on 'board** A *adv.* frei Schiff; B *adj.* frei Schiff geliefert; **~ 'pass** *n.* Freikarte, *die;* (Railw.) Freifahrschein, *der;* **F~phone** ▸**Freefone;** **~ 'play** *n.* 1 (Mech.) Spiel, *das;* 2 (fig.) **give ~ play to sth.** etw. sich frei entfalten lassen; **allow one's imagination ~ play** der Fantasie freien Lauf lassen; **~ port** *n.* Freihafen, *der;* **~post** *n.* (Brit.) **'~post'** „Gebühr zahlt Empfänger"

freer ▸**free A**

'free radical *n.* freies Radikal

'free-range *adj.* frei laufend ‹*Huhn*›; **~ eggs** Eier von frei laufenden Hühnern

freesia /'fri:zɪə/ *n.* (Bot.) Freesie, *die*

free: ~ 'speech *n.* Redefreiheit, *die;* **~-spoken** *adj.* freimütig

freest ▸**free A**

free: ~-standing *adj.* frei stehend; **~style** *n.* (Sport) Freistil, *der;* **~thinker** *n.* Freidenker, *der;* **~-thinking** A *n.* Freidenkertum, *das;* B *adj.* freidenkerisch; **~-to-'air** *adj.* gebührenfrei; **~ 'trade** *n.* Freihandel, *der;* **~ 'verse** *n.* (Lit.) freie Verse; **~ 'vote** *n.* (Brit. Parl.) [dem Fraktionszwang nicht unterworfene] freie Stimmabgabe; **~ware** /'fri:weə(r)/ *n., no pl., no indef. art.* (Computing) Freeware, *die;* kostenlose Software; **~way** *n.* (Amer.) Autobahn, *die;* **~wheel** A *n.* Freilauf, *der;* B *v.i.* im Freilauf fahren; **~-wheeling** *adj.* unbekümmert; **~ 'will** *n.* 1 *no art.* (power) Willensfreiheit, *die;* 2 (choice) **do sth. of one's own ~ will** etw. aus freiem Willen tun; **be left to sb.'s own ~ will** jmds. freier Entscheidung (*Dat.*) überlassen sein; **~ 'world** *n.* freie Welt

freeze /fri:z/

A *v.i.*, **froze** /frəʊz/, **frozen** /'frəʊzn/ 1 frieren; **it will ~** (Meteorol.) es wird Frost geben; **it froze hard last night** heute Nacht war starker Frost 2 (become covered with ice) ‹*See, Fluss, Teich:*› zufrieren; ‹*Straße:*› vereisen 3 (solidify) ‹*Flüssigkeit:*› gefrieren; ‹*Rohr, Schloss:*› einfrieren; **the pond has frozen solid** der Teich ist ganz zugefroren 4 (become rigid) steif frieren; (fig.) ‹*Lächeln:*› gefrieren (geh.) 5 (become fastened) festfrieren (**to** an + *Dat.*); **~ together** aneinander festfrieren 6 (be or feel cold) sehr frieren; (fig.) erstarren (**with** vor + *Dat.*); ‹*Blut:*› gefrieren (geh.); **he is freezing** er *od.* ihn friert sehr; **my hands are freezing** meine Hände sind eiskalt; **~ to death** erfrieren; (fig.) bitterlich frieren 7 (make oneself motionless) erstarren; **~!** keine Bewegung!

B *v.t.*, **froze, frozen** 1 zufrieren lassen ‹*Teich, Fluss*›; gefrieren lassen ‹*Rohr*›; (fig.) erstarren lassen; **~ sb.'s blood** (fig.) jmdm. das Blut in den Adern gefrieren lassen (geh.); **you look absolutely frozen** (fig.) du siehst ganz durchgefroren aus; **we were frozen stiff** (fig.) wir waren steif gefroren 2 (preserve) tiefkühlen, tiefgefrieren ‹*Lebensmittel*› 3 (make unrealizable or unchangeable) einfrieren ‹*Kredit, Guthaben, Gelder, Löhne, Preise usw.*› 4 (Cinemat.) in einem Stehkader festhalten 5 (stiffen) gefrieren lassen ‹*Erdboden*›; festfrieren lassen ‹*Wäsche*› (**to** an + *Dat.*) 6 (deaden) ‹*Spritze:*› taub machen; ‹*Spray:*› vereisen 7 (kill) erfrieren lassen ‹*Pflanzen*› 8 (fig.) erstarren lassen; gefrieren lassen (geh.) ‹*Lächeln*›

C *n.* 1 ▸**freeze-up 1** 2 (fixing) Einfrieren, *das* (**on** *Gen.*); **price/wage/nuclear ~:** Preis-/Lohn-/Atomwaffenstopp, *der*

Phrasal verbs

- **~ 'out** *v.t.* (socially) hinausekeln
- **~ 'over** *v.i.* ‹*Teich, Fluss:*› zufrieren; ‹*Fenster-, Windschutzscheibe, Straße:*› vereisen
- **~ 'up**

A *v.i.* ‹*Fluss, Teich:*› zufrieren; ‹*Schloss, Rohr:*› einfrieren; ‹*Fenster:*› vereisen

B *v.t.* ▸**A:** zufrieren/einfrieren/vereisen lassen. *see also* **freeze-up**

freeze: ~-dry *v.t.* gefriertrocknen; **~-frame** *n.* Standbild, *das*

freezer /'fri:zə(r)/ *n.* (deep-freeze) Tiefkühltruhe, *die;* Gefriertruhe, *die;* **[upright] ~:** Tiefkühlschrank, *der;* Gefrierschrank, *der;* **~ compartment** Tiefkühlfach, *das;* Gefrierfach, *das;* **~ [room]** Kühlraum, *der;* **[ice cream] ~:** Eismaschine, *die*

'freeze-up *n.* 1 (period) Dauerfrost, *der;* Frostperiode, *die* 2 (fig.) Stillstand, *der*

freezing /'fri:zɪŋ/ ▸❶ **p. 1620**

A *adj.* (lit. or fig.) frostig; **~ temperatures** Temperaturen unter null Grad; **it is ~ in here** es ist eiskalt hier drinnen

B *n.* 1 *no pl.* (**~ point**) **above/below ~:** über/unter dem/den Gefrierpunkt 2 (of food) Einfrieren, *das*

C *adv.* **~ cold** eiskalt

freezing: ~ 'fog *n.* gefrierender Nebel; **~ point** *n.* ▸❶ **p. 1620** Gefrierpunkt, *der*

freight /freɪt/

A *n.* 1 Fracht, *die;* **~ charges** Frachtgeld, *das;* Frachtkosten *Pl.* 2 (transport) Frachtsendung, *die;* **send goods ~:** Waren als Frachtgut senden 3 (hire) Charter, *die*

B *v.t.* 1 befrachten 2 (hire) chartern; (hire out) vermieten

freightage /'freɪtɪdʒ/ *n., no pl.* Frachtkosten *Pl.*

'freight car *n.* (Amer. Railw.) Güterwagen, *der*

freighter /'freɪtə(r)/ *n.* 1 (ship) Frachter, *der;* Frachtschiff, *das;* (aircraft) Frachtflugzeug, *das* 2 (Amer. Railw.) Güterwagen, *der*

freight: ~-liner *n.* (Railw.) [Container]güterzug, *der;* **~ terminal** *n.* Güterterminal, *das;* **~ train** *n.* (Railw.) Güterzug, *der*

French /frentʃ/ ▸❶ **p. 1277,** ▸❶ **p. 1345**

A *adj.* französisch; **he/she is ~:** er ist Franzose/sie ist Französin; **the ~ people** die Franzosen; **~ lessons** (lit. or euphem.) Französischstunden *Pl.; see also* **English A**

B *n.* 1 Französisch, *das* 2 (euphem.: bad language) **pardon** *or* **excuse my ~:** entschuldigen Sie die Ausdrucksweise! 3 *constr. as pl.* **the ~:** die Franzosen. *See also* **English B 1**

French: ~ 'bean *n.* (Brit.) Gartenbohne, *die;* [grüne] Bohne; **~ 'bread** *n.* französisches [Stangen]weißbrot; **~ Ca'nadian** *n.* ▸❶ **p. 1345** Frankokanadier, *der*/-kanadierin, *die;* **~-Ca'nadian** *adj.* frankokanadisch; **~ 'chalk** *n.* Schneiderkreide, *die;* **~ 'door** ▸**~ window;** **~ 'dressing** *n.* Vinaigrette, *die;* **~ fried po'tatoes, ~ 'fries** *ns. pl.* Pommes frites *Pl.;* **~ 'horn** *n.* (Mus.) [Wald]horn, *das*

Frenchified /'frentʃɪfaɪd/ *adj.* französiert

French: ~ 'kiss *n.* französischer Kuss (ugs.); Zungenkuss, *der;* **~ 'leave** *n.* **take ~ leave** (without giving notice) sich auf Französisch empfehlen *od.* verabschieden (ugs.); (without permission) sich heimlich davonstehlen; **~ 'letter** *n.* (Brit. coll.) Pariser, *der* (salopp); **~man** /'frentʃmən/ *n., pl.* **~men** /'frentʃmən/ Franzose, *der;* **~ 'mustard** *n.* (Brit.) französischer Senf; **~ 'polish** *n.* Schellackpolitur, *die;* **~-'polish** *v.t.* [mit Schellackpolitur] polieren; **~ Revo'lution** *n.* (Hist.) Französische Revolution; **~ 'toast** *n.* 1 (toasted) einseitig geröstete Toastscheibe; 2 (fried) arme Ritter; **~ 'vermouth** *n.* trockener Wermut; **~ 'window** *n., in sing. or pl.* französisches Fenster; **~woman** *n.* Französin, *die*

Frenchy /'frentʃɪ/ (coll.)

A *adj.* [betont] französisch

B *n.* Franzose, *der;* Franzmann, *der* (ugs. veraltend)

frenetic /frɪ'netɪk/ *adj.* verzweifelt ‹*Hilferuf, Versuch*›; frenetisch, rasend ‹*Beifall*›

frenzied /'frenzɪd/ *adj.* rasend; wahnsinnig ‹*Tat*›

frenzy /'frenzɪ/ *n.* 1 (derangement) Wahnsinn, *der* 2 (fury, agitation) Raserei, *die;* **in a ~ of despair/passion** in einem Anfall von Verzweiflung/von wilder Leidenschaft übermannt

frequency /'fri:kwənsɪ/ *n.* 1 Häufigkeit, *die* 2 (of pulse) Puls, *der;* [Puls]frequenz, *die* (Med.) 3 (Phys., Statistics) Frequenz, *die*

'frequency: ~ band *n.* (Radio, Telev., Phys.) Frequenzband, *das;* **~ modulation** *n.* (Radio, Telev.) Frequenzmodulation, *die*

frequent

A /'fri:kwənt/ *adj.* 1 häufig; **it's a ~ practice/occurrence** es ist üblich/kommt häufig vor; **become less ~:** seltener werden 2 (habitual, constant) eifrig ‹*[Kino-, Theater]besucher, Briefschreiber*›; **he is a ~ visitor to our restaurant** er ist Stammgast in unserem Restaurant 3 (abundant) zahlreich

B /frɪ'kwent/ *v.t.* frequentieren (geh.); häufig besuchen ‹*Café, Klub usw.*›; häufig aufsuchen ‹*Futterplatz*›; **much ~ed** stark frequentiert (geh.); viel befahren ‹*Straße*›

frequent 'flyer *n.* Vielflieger, *der*/-fliegerin, *die*

frequently /'fri:kwəntlɪ/ *adv.* häufig

fresco /'freskəʊ/ *n., pl.* **~es** *or* **~s** 1 *no pl., no art.* (method) Freskomalerei, *die* 2 (a painting) Fresko, *das*

fresh /freʃ/

A *adj.* 1 neu; frisch, ausgeruht ‹*Truppen*›; frisch, neu ‹*Energie, Mut*›; (lately made or arrived) frisch; (raw, inexperienced) [jung und] unerfahren; **a ~ series of attacks** eine neuerliche Serie von Angriffen; **make a ~ start** noch einmal von vorn anfangen; (fig.) neu beginnen; **~ from school/India** frisch von der Schule/gerade aus Indien gekommen; **~ from** *or* **off the press** druckfrisch; frisch aus der Presse; **~ from the oven** ofenfrisch; frisch aus dem Ofen 2 (not preserved or stale or faded) frisch ‹*Obst, Fisch, Gemüse, Fleisch, Eier, Tee, Blumen usw.*› 3 (clean, bright) frisch ‹*Aussehen, Gesichtsfarbe,*

Hemd, Wäsche› 4 (pure, cool) frisch ‹Luft, Wasser, Wind›; **go out for some ~ air** nach draußen gehen, um Luft zu schöpfen (geh.); **the wind became ~:** der Wind frischte auf 5 (vigorous, fit) frisch; (refreshed) erfrischt; **as ~ as a daisy/as paint** ganz frisch; (in appearance) frisch wie der junge Morgen (meist scherzh.) 6 (cheeky) keck; **get ~ with sb.** jmdm. frech kommen (ugs.). *See also* **ground[1] A 2**
B *adv.* frisch; **we're ~ out of eggs** (coll.) uns sind gerade die Eier ausgegangen; **~-ground/-painted** frisch gemahlen/gestrichen

fresh-'air fiend *n.* (coll. hum) Frischluftfanatiker, *der*/-fanatikerin, *die*

freshen /'freʃn/
A *v.i.* 1 frisch[er] werden; (increase) ‹Wind:› auffrischen 2 (brighten) ein frisch[er]es Aussehen bekommen
B *v.t.* (ventilate) durchlüften ‹Zimmer›
Phrasal verb
• **~ 'up**
A *v.i.* sich frisch machen
B *v.t.* erfrischen; **~ oneself/sb. up** sich/jmdn. frisch machen

fresher /'freʃə(r)/ (Brit. Univ. coll.) ▸**freshman 1**

freshly /'freʃlɪ/ *adv.* frisch

freshman /'freʃmən/ *n., pl.* **freshmen** /'freʃmən/ 1 Erstsemester, *das;* Frischling, *der* (scherzh.) 2 (Amer.) (in school) Anfänger, *der*/Anfängerin, *die;* (person beginning) Neuling, *der*

freshness /'freʃnɪs/ *n., no pl.* Frische, *die;* (of idea, metaphor, etc.) Neuartigkeit, *die;* (originality) Originalität, *die*

'freshwater *adj.* Süßwasser-; **~ sailor** Binnenschiffer, *der*

fresh 'water *n.* Süßwasser, *das*

fret[1] /fret/
A *v.i.,* **-tt-** (worry) sich (Dat.) Sorgen machen; **don't ~:** keine Sorge!; **~ at** *or* **about** *or* **over sth.** sich über etw. (Akk.) *od.* wegen etw. aufregen; **~ and fume** (anxiously/impatiently) voller Unruhe/Ungeduld sein
B *v.t.,* **-tt-** 1 (distress) beunruhigen; quälen; **~ oneself** sich beunruhigen; sich (Dat.) Sorgen machen (**about** wegen) 2 (chafe) [wund] scheuern
C *n.* Ärger, *der;* **be in a ~:** voll Verdruss sein

fret[2] *n.* (Mus.) Bund, *der*

fretful /'fretfl/ *adj.* (peevish) verdrießlich; mürrisch; quengelig (ugs.) ‹Kleinkind›; (restless) unruhig; (impatient) ungeduldig; (ill-humoured) übellaunig

fret: ~saw *n.* Laubsäge, *die;* **~work** *n.* 1 (Archit.) durchbrochene Arbeit; 2 (wood) Laubsägearbeit, *die*

Freudian /'frɔɪdɪən/ *adj.* freudianisch; **~ interpretation** freudsche Interpretation; **~ slip** freudsche Fehlleistung; freudscher Versprecher (ugs.)

Fri. *abbr.* ▸**i** **p. 1048 = Friday** Fr.

friable /'fraɪəbl/ *adj.* bröck[e]lig

friar /'fraɪə(r)/ *n.* Ordensbruder, *der;* **Black/Grey/White F~:** Dominikaner/Franziskaner/Karmeliter, *der;* **F~ Peter** Bruder Peter

fricassee /frɪkəsi:, frɪkə'si:/ (Cookery)
A *n.* Frikassee, *das*
B *v.t.* frikassieren

fricative /'frɪkətɪv/ (Phonet.)
A *adj.* frikativ
B *n.* Frikativ, *der* (fachspr.); Reibelaut, *der*

friction /'frɪkʃn/ *n.* 1 Reibung, *die; attrib.* Reibungs- 2 (fig.: between persons) Reibereien *Pl.* 3 (of body or scalp) Einreibung, *die;* Friktion, *die* (Med.)

Friday /'fraɪdeɪ, 'fraɪdɪ/ ▸**i** **p. 1048**
A *n.* Freitag, *der;* **on ~:** [am] Freitag; **on a ~, on ~s** freitags; **we got married on a ~:** wir haben an einem Freitag geheiratet; **~ 13 August** Freitag, der 13. August; (at top of letter etc.) Freitag, den 13. August; **on ~ 13 August** am Freitag, den *od.* dem 13. August; **next/last ~:** [am] nächsten/letzten *od.* vergangenen Freitag; **[on] ~ next/last** kommenden/vergangenen Freitag; **we were married a year [ago] last/next ~:** vergangenen/kommenden Freitag vor einem Jahr haben wir geheiratet; **[last] ~'s mail/newspaper** die Post/Zeitung vom [letzten] Freitag; **our ~ session** unsere Freitagssitzung; (this ~) unsere Sitzung am Freitag; **Good ~:** Karfreitag, *der;* **man/girl ~:** Mädchen für alles (ugs.)
B *adv.* (coll.) 1 **~ [week]** Freitag [in einer Woche] 2 **~s** freitags; Freitag (ugs.); **she comes ~s** sie kommt freitags

fridge /frɪdʒ/ *n.* (Brit. coll.) Kühlschrank, *der;* **~-freezer** Kühl-und-Gefrierkombination, *die*

fried ▸**fry[1] B, C**

friend /frend/ *n.* 1 Freund, *der*/Freundin, *die;* **~s and relations** Verwandte und Freunde; **be ~s with sb.** mit jmdm. befreundet sein; **I'm not ~s with you any more!** (joc. or child language) du bist nicht mehr mein Freund!; **let's be ~s again** wir wollen uns wieder vertragen; **make ~s [with sb.]** [mit jmdm.] Freundschaft schließen; **he makes ~s easily** er findet leicht Anschluss; **make a ~ of sb.** sich mit jmdm. anfreunden; **a ~ in need is a ~ indeed** (prov.) Freunde in der Not gehn hundert *od.* tausend auf ein Lot (Spr.); **between ~s** unter Freunden 2 (helper, patron) Freund, *der* (**of, to** Gen.); **~s in high places** *or* **at court** einflussreiche Freunde; Freunde höheren Orts; **the F~s of Covent Garden** der Freundes- *od.* Förderkreis des Covent Garden 3 (Quaker) **the Society of F~s** die Quäker; die Gesellschaft der Freunde 4 **my honourable/noble ~** (Brit. Parl.) mein verehrter Freund; **my learned ~** (Law) mein verehrter *od.* werter Kollege

friendless /'frendlɪs/ *adj.* ohne Freund[e] *nachgestellt*

friendliness /'frendlɪnɪs/ *n., no pl.* Freundlichkeit, *die*

friendly /'frendlɪ/
A *adj.* 1 freundlich (**to** zu); freundschaftlich ‹Rat, Beziehungen, Wettkampf, Gespräch›; **be on ~ terms** *or* **be ~ with sb.** mit jmdm. auf freundschaftlichem Fuße stehen; **we're very ~ with our neighbours** wir sind mit unseren Nachbarn sehr gut befreundet; *see also* **neighbourhood 4** 2 (not hostile) freundlich [gesinnt] ‹Bewohner›; befreundet ‹Staat›; zutraulich ‹Tier›; **~ game** (Sport) Freundschaftsspiel, *das* 3 (well-wishing) wohlwollend ‹Erwähnung›; günstig gestimmt ‹Götter›
B *n.* (Sport) Freundschaftsspiel, *das*

friendly 'fire *n.* (Milit.) eigenes Feuer

'Friendly Society *n.* (Brit.) Versicherungsverein auf Gegenseitigkeit

friendship /'frendʃɪp/ *n.* Freundschaft, *die;* **[feelings of] ~:** freundschaftliche Gefühle; **strike up a ~ with sb.** sich mit jmdm. anfreunden

Friends of the Earth *pr. n. sing. or pl.* Friends of the Earth (Umweltschutzvereinigung)

frier ▸**fryer**

fries /fraɪz/ *n. pl.* (Amer.) Pommes frites *Pl.*

Friesian /'fri:zɪən, 'fri:ʒən/ (Agric.)
A *adj.* schwarzbunt
B *n.* Schwarzbunte, *die*

frieze[1] /fri:z/ *n.* (Textiles) Fries, *der;* Friese, *die* (fachspr.)

frieze[2] *n.* (Archit.) Fries, *der*

frigate /'frɪgət/ *n.* (Naut.) Fregatte, *die*

fright /fraɪt/ *n.* 1 Schreck, *der;* Schrecken, *der;* **in his ~:** vor Schreck; **take ~:** erschrecken; **the ~ of one's life** der Schock seines Lebens; **give sb. a ~:** jmdm. einen Schreck[en] einjagen; **get** *or* **have a ~:** einen Schreck[en] bekommen 2 (grotesque person or thing) **be** *or* **look a ~:** zum Fürchten aussehen (ugs.)

frighten /'fraɪtn/ *v.t.* ‹Explosion, Schuss:› erschrecken; ‹Gedanke, Drohung:› Angst machen (+ Dat.); **be ~ed at** *or* **by sth.** vor etw. (Dat.) erschrecken; **she is not easily ~ed** sie fürchtet sich nicht so schnell; **~ sb. out of his wits/life** jmdn. furchtbar/zu Tode erschrecken; **~ sb. to death** (fig.) jmdn. zu Tode erschrecken; **be ~ed to death** (fig.) zu Tode erschrocken sein; **~ sb. into doing sth.** jmdm. solche Angst machen, dass er etw. tut
Phrasal verb
• **~ a'way, ~ 'off** *v.t.* vertreiben; (put off) abschrecken

frightened /'fraɪtnd/ *adj.* verängstigt; angsterfüllt ‹Stimme›; **be ~ [of sth.]** [vor etw. (Dat.)] Angst haben

frightening /'fraɪtnɪŋ/ *adj.* Furcht erregend

frightful /'fraɪtfl/ *adj.* furchtbar; schrecklich; (coll.: terrible) furchtbar (ugs.)

frightfully /'fraɪtfəlɪ/ *adv.* furchtbar; schrecklich; (coll.: extremely) furchtbar (ugs.)

frigid /'frɪdʒɪd/ *adj.* 1 (very cold) eisig kalt 2 (formal, unfriendly) frostig; (sexually unresponsive) frigid[e] ‹Frau›

frigidity /frɪ'dʒɪdɪtɪ/ *n., no pl.* 1 (coldness) eisige Kälte 2 (formality, unfriendliness) Frostigkeit, *die;* (of woman) Frigidität, *die*

frill /frɪl/ *n.* 1 (ruffled edge) Rüsche, *die* 2 (on animal, plant) Kragen, *der;* (on bird) Halskrause, *die* 3 *in pl.* (embellishments) Beiwerk, *das;* Ausschmückungen *Pl.* (fig.); **with no ~s** ‹Ferienhaus, Auto› ohne besondere Ausstattung

frilly /'frɪlɪ/
A *adj.* mit Rüschen besetzt; Rüschen‹kleid, -bluse›
B *n. in pl.* (coll.) Rüschenunterwäsche, *die*

fringe /frɪndʒ/
A *n.* 1 (bordering) Fransen *Pl.;* Fransenkante, *die* (**on** an + Dat.) 2 (hair) [Pony]fransen *Pl.* (ugs.); Pony, *der* 3 (edge) Rand, *der; attrib.* Rand‹geschehen, -gruppe, -gebiet›; **~ benefits** zusätzliche Leistungen; **live on the ~[s] of the city/of society** am Stadtrand *od.* in den Randgebieten der Stadt wohnen/am Rand der Gesellschaft leben; **lunatic ~:** Extremisten *Pl.*
B *v.t.* säumen (auch fig. geh.)

frippery /'frɪpərɪ/ *n.* Putz, *der;* Zierrat, *der* (geh.); (knick-knacks, trifles) Tand, *der* (geh.); Kinkerlitzchen *Pl.* (ugs.)

frisbee ® /'frɪzbɪ/ *n.* Frisbee, *das*

Frisco /'frɪskəʊ/ *pr. n.* (Amer. coll.) San Francisco (*das*)

Frisian /'frɪzɪən, 'frɪ:ʒn/ ▸**i** **p. 1277,** ▸**i** **p. 1345**
A *adj.* friesisch; *see also* **English A**
B *n.* 1 (language) Friesisch, *das* 2 (person) Friese, *der*/Friesin, *die. See also* **English B 1**

frisk /frɪsk/
A *v.i.* **~ [about]** [herum]springen; **~ away** davonspringen
B *v.t.* (coll.) filzen (ugs.)
C *n.* 1 (frolic) Hüpfer, *der* 2 (coll.: body search) Filzung, *die* (ugs.)

frisky /'frɪskɪ/ *adj.* munter; **as ~ as a kitten** so ausgelassen wie ein Füllen (geh.)

frisson /'fri:sɔ̃/ *n.* Schauer, *der*

fritillary /frɪ'tɪlərɪ/ *n.* 1 (Bot.) Fritillaria, *die* (fachspr.); Kaiserkrone, *die* 2 (Zool.) Fleckenfalter, *der*

fritter[1] /'frɪtə(r)/ *n.* (Cookery) **apple/sausage ~s** Apfelstücke/Würstchen in Pfannkuchenteig

fritter[2] *v.t.* **~ away** vergeuden; verplempern (ugs.)

frivolity /frɪ'vɒlɪtɪ/ *n.* 1 *no pl.* Oberflächlichkeit, *die;* Leichtfertigkeit, *die* 2 (thing) Tand, *der* (geh.); (act) **he watched these frivolities with contempt** er beobachtete dieses leichtfertige Treiben mit Verachtung

frivolous /'frɪvələs/ *adj.* 1 (not serious) frivol 2 (trifling, futile) belanglos

frivolously /'frɪvələslɪ/ *adv.* frivol; extravagant ‹gekleidet›

frizzle /'frɪzl/
A *v.i.* brutzeln; braten
B *v.t.* brutzeln (ugs.); braten

frizzy /'frɪzɪ/ *adj.* kraus

fro /frəʊ/ ▸**to B 2**

frock /frɒk/ *n.* Kleid, *das*

'frock coat *n.* Gehrock, *der*

frog[1] /frɒg/ *n.* 1 Frosch, *der;* **have a ~ in the** *or* **one's throat** (coll.) einen Frosch im Hals haben (ugs.) 2 (sl. derog.: Frenchman) Franzmann, *der* (ugs., veralt.)

frog[2] *n.* 1 (coat fastening) Posamentenverschluss, *der* 2 (on belt) Schlaufe, *die*

f

froggy /'frɒgɪ/
A *adj.* Frosch⟨*gesicht, -stimme*⟩
B *n.* (sl. derog.) ▸**frog¹ 2**

frog: ~man /'frɒgmən/ *n., pl.* **~men** /'frɒgmən/ Froschmann, *der;* **~march** *v.t.* (carry) zu viert an Händen und Füßen [mit dem Gesicht nach unten] tragen; (hustle) ≈ im Polizeigriff abführen; **~spawn** *n.* Froschlaich, *der*

frolic /'frɒlɪk/
A *v.i.*, **-ck-: ~ [about** *or* **around]** [herum]springen
B *n.* (prank, lark) Spaß, *der;* (fun, merriment) Ausgelassenheit, *die*

frolicsome /'frɒlɪksəm/ *adj.* (dated) ausgelassen

from /frəm, *stressed* frɒm/ *prep.* **[1]** *expr. starting point* von; (~ within) aus; **[come] ~ Paris/Munich** aus Paris/München [kommen]; **~ Paris to Munich** von Paris nach München; **where have you come ~?** woher kommen Sie?; wo kommen Sie her? **[2]** ▸**❶ p. 1047** *expr. beginning* von; **~ the year 1972 we never saw him again** seit 1972 haben wir ihn nie mehr [wieder] gesehen; **~ tomorrow [until ...]** von morgen an [bis ...]; **start work ~ 2 August** am 2. August anfangen zu arbeiten; vom 2. August an arbeiten; **~ now on** von jetzt an; ab jetzt; **~ then on** seitdem; (relating to a place) von da an; *see also* **as D [3]** *expr. lower limit* von; **blouses [ranging] ~ £2 to £5** Blusen [im Preis] zwischen 2 und 5 Pfund; **dresses ~ £20 [upwards]** Kleider von 20 Pfund aufwärts *od.* ab 20 Pfund; **~ 4 to 6 eggs** 4 bis 6 Eier; **~ the age of 18 [upwards]** ab 18 Jahre *od.* Jahren; **~ a child** (since childhood) schon als Kind **[4]** *expr. distance* von; **be a mile ~ sth.** eine Meile von etw. entfernt sein; **away ~ home** von zu Hause weg **[5]** *expr. removal, avoidance* von; *expr. escape* vor (+ *Dat.*); **release the bomb ~ the aircraft** die Bombe aus dem Flugzeug ausklinken **[6]** *expr. change* von; **~ ... to ...:** von ... zu ...; (relating to price) von ... auf ...; **~ crisis to crisis, ~ one crisis to another** von einer Krise zur anderen **[7]** *expr. source, origin* aus; **pick apples ~ a tree** Äpfel vom Baum pflücken; **buy everything ~ Harrods/the same shop** alles bei Harrods/im selben Laden kaufen; **where do you come ~?, where are you ~?** woher kommen Sie?; **~ the country/another planet** vom Land/von einem anderen Planeten **[8]** *expr. viewpoint* von [... aus] **[9]** *expr. giver, sender* von; **take it ~ me that ...:** lass dir gesagt sein, dass ... **[10]** (after the model of) **painted ~ life/nature** nach dem Leben/nach der Natur gemalt **[11]** *expr. reason, cause* **she was weak ~ hunger/tired ~ so much work** sie war schwach vor Hunger/müde von der vielen Arbeit; **~ his looks you might think ...:** so wie er aussieht, könnte man denken ...; **~ what I can see/have heard ...:** wie ich das sehe/wie ich gehört habe, ...; **~ the look of things ...:** wie es aussieht, ... **[12]** *with adv.* von ⟨*unten, oben, innen, außen*⟩ **[13]** *with prep.* **~ behind/under[neath] sth.** hinter/unter etw. (*Dat.*) hervor; **~ amidst the trees** zwischen den Bäumen hervor; **~ before the marriage** aus der Zeit vor der Heirat; **the cries came ~ inside/outside the house** die Schreie kamen aus dem Inneren des Hauses/von draußen

frond /frɒnd/ *n.* (Bot.) Wedel, *der;* Blatt, *das*

front /frʌnt/
A *n.* **[1]** Vorderseite, *die;* (of door) Außenseite, *die;* (of house) Vorderfront, *die;* Frontseite, *die;* (of dress) Vorderteil, *das;* (of queue) vorderes Ende; (of procession) Spitze, *die;* (of book) vorderer Deckel; (of cloth) rechte Seite; **in** *or* **at the ~ [of sth.]** vorn [in etw. *position: Dat., movement: Akk.*]; **sit in the ~ of the car** vorne sitzen; **the index is at the ~:** das Register ist vorn; **to the ~:** nach vorn; **the living room is at** *or* **in the ~ of the house** das Wohnzimmer liegt zur Straße hin *od.* (ugs.) nach vorn[e] raus; **lie on one's ~:** auf dem Bauch liegen; **a spot on the ~ of her dress** ein Fleck vorne am Kleid; **in ~:** vorn[e]; **be in ~ of sth./sb.** vor etw./jmdm. sein; **walk in ~ of sb.** (preceding) vor jmdm. gehen; (to position) vor jmdn. gehen; **look in ~ of one** nach vorn sehen; **he was murdered in ~ of his wife** er wurde vor den Augen seiner Frau ermordet **[2]** (Mil.; also fig.) Front, *die;* **on the Western ~:** an der Westfront; **send sb. to the ~:** jmdn. an die Front schicken; **be attacked on all ~s** an allen Fronten/(fig.) von allen Seiten angegriffen werden; **change of ~** (fig.) Gesinnungswandel, *der;* Frontwechsel, *der* (Politik); **on the international/home ~:** im Ausland/Inland; **on the sports ~:** im sportlichen Bereich; **on the entertainment ~:** auf dem Unterhaltungssektor; **the workers'/people's ~:** die Arbeiter-/Volksfront **[3]** (promenade) (at seaside) Strandpromenade, *die;* (inland) Uferpromenade, *die* **[4]** (Theatre) **~ of [the] house** Foyer und Zuschauerraum **[5]** (Archit.) ⟨*West-, Garten-* usw.⟩seite, *die* **[6]** (Meteorol.) Front, *die;* **cold/warm ~:** Kalt-/Warmluftfront, *die* **[7]** ▸**shirt front [8]** (outward appearance) Aussehen, *das;* (bluff) Fassade, *die* (oft abwertend); (pretext, facade) Tarnung, *die;* **put on** *or* **show** *or* **present a bold/brave ~:** sich nach außen unerschrocken zeigen/nach außen hin gefasst bleiben; **preserve a calm ~:** nach außen hin ruhig bleiben; **it's all a ~:** das ist alles nur Fassade (abwertend) **[9]** (used as cover) (person) Strohmann, *der;* (organization) Tarnorganisation, *die*
B *adj.* vorder...; Vorder⟨*rad, -zimmer, -zahn, -eingang, -ansicht*⟩; **~ garden** Vorgarten, *der;* **the ~ four coaches of a train** die ersten vier *od.* vier vorderen Wagen eines Zuges; **~ row** erste Reihe
C *v.i.* **[1] ~ on to the street/upon the lake** zur Straße/zum See hin liegen **[2]** (coll.: act as cover) **~ for sb.** für jmdn. den Strohmann spielen
D *v.t.* (furnish with façade) **~ a building with stone** ein Gebäude mit einer Fassade aus Stein versehen

frontage /'frʌntɪdʒ/ *n.* **[1]** (land) Grundstück[steil] zwischen Gebäude und Straße; **river/street ~:** an den Fluss/die Straße grenzender Teil des Grundstücks **[2]** (extent) Frontbreite, *die* **[3]** (façade) Fassade, *die*

frontal /'frʌntl/ *adj.* **[1]** Frontal- **[2]** (Art) frontal ⟨*Darstellung*⟩; **[full] ~:** frontal dargestellt ⟨*Akt*⟩ **[3]** (Anat.) Stirn⟨*bein, -hirn, -höhle, -lappen*⟩

frontally /'frʌntəlɪ/ *adv.* frontal

front: ~ 'bench *n.* (Brit. Parl.) vorderste Bank; **~-bencher** /frʌnt'bentʃə(r)/ *n.* (Brit. Parl.) führender Politiker; **~ 'door** *n.* (of flat) Wohnungstür, *die;* (of house; also fig.) Haustür, *die;* **~-end** (Computing) **A** *adj.* Front-End-; **B** *n.* (*also* **front end**) Front-End, *das*

frontier /'frʌntɪə(r)/ *n.* **[1]** (lit. or fig.) Grenze, *die; attrib.* Grenz⟨*stadt, -posten, -streitigkeiten*⟩; **at** *or* **on the ~:** an der Grenze; **push the ~s of science forward** (fig.) wissenschaftliches Neuland erobern **[2]** (Amer.: borders of civilization) Grenzland, *das*

frontispiece /'frʌntɪspi:s/ *n.* Frontispiz, *das;* Titelbild, *das*

front: ~ 'line *n.* Front[linie], *die;* **~-loading** *adj.* Frontlader-; **~ man** *n.* **[1]** (of criminal organization) [An]führer, *der;* **[2]** (of television programme) Moderator, *der;* **[3]** (of rock group etc.) Frontmann, *der;* **~ 'office** *n.* (esp. Amer.) Geschäftsstelle, *die;* **~ 'page** *n.* Titelseite, *die;* **make the ~ page** auf die Titelseite kommen; **~-page** *adj.* ⟨*Artikel*⟩ auf der ersten Seite; **~-page 'news** *n., no pl.* Topmeldung, *die;* **become ~-page news** auf die Titelseite kommen; **be ~-page news** Schlagzeilen machen; **~ 'passage** *n.* (Anat. coll.) Scheide, *die;* **~-rank** *adj.* (fig.) herausragend; **~ runner** *n.* **[1]** (in race) *Läufer, der gern an der Spitze läuft;* **[2]** (in any competition) Spitzenkandidat, *der;* **~ 'seat** *n.* (in theatre) Platz in den ersten Reihen; (in car) Vordersitz, *der;* (in bus, coach) vorderer Sitzplatz; **~ vowel** *n.* (Phonet.) Vorderzungenvokal, *der;* **~-wheel drive A** *n.* Vorderradantrieb, *der;* Frontantrieb, *der;* **B** *adj.* **a ~-wheel drive vehicle** ein Fahrzeug mit Vorderrad- *od.* Frontantrieb; **the car is ~-wheel drive** das Auto hat Vorderrad- *od.* Frontantrieb

frost /frɒst/
A *n.* **[1]** Frost, *der;* (frozen dew or vapour) Reif, *der;* **windows covered with ~:** vereiste Fensterscheiben; **white/black ~:** Frost mit/ohne Reif; **early/late ~s** Herbst-/Frühlingsfröste; **ten degrees of ~** (Brit.) zehn Grad minus; **there is still ~ in the ground** der Boden ist noch gefroren **[2]** (fig.: hostility) Frostigkeit, *die* **[3]** (dated coll.: failure) Reinfall, *der* (ugs.); Pleite, *die* (salopp)
B *v.t.* **[1]** (esp. Amer. Cookery) mit Zucker bestreuen; (ice) glasieren **[2]** (give ~like surface to) mattieren ⟨*Glas, Metall*⟩; **~ed glass** Mattglas, *das*

(Phrasal verb)

• **~ 'over**
A *v.t.* **be ~ed over** vereist sein
B *v.i.* vereisen

frost: ~bite *n.* Erfrierung, *die;* **~bitten** *adj.* durch Frost geschädigt; **sb. is ~bitten** jmd. hat Erfrierungen; **his toes are ~bitten** er hat Frost *od.* Erfrierungen in den Zehen; **~-free** *adj.* **[1]** selbstabtauend ⟨*Kühlgerät*⟩; **[2]** (free from frost) frostfrei

frostily /'frɒstɪlɪ/ *adv.* frostig

frosting /'frɒstɪŋ/ *n.* (esp. Amer. Cookery) Zucker, *der;* (icing) Glasur, *die*

frosty /'frɒstɪ/ *adj.* (lit. or fig.) frostig; (covered with hoar frost) bereift; (fig.: white) schneeweiß

froth /frɒθ/
A *n.* **[1]** (foam) Schaum, *der* **[2]** (worthless matter) Tand, *der* (geh.)
B *v.i.* schäumen; **~ at the mouth** Schaum vor dem Mund haben; **~ at the mouth with rage** (fig.) vor Wut schäumen (geh.)
C *v.t.* (Cookery) **[beat and] ~ the eggs** die Eier schaumig schlagen

frothy /'frɒθɪ/ *adj.* schaumig; schäumend ⟨*Bier, Brandung, Maul*⟩; (fig.: empty, shallow) oberflächlich ⟨*Person*⟩; seicht (abwertend) ⟨*Unterhaltung, Roman*⟩

frown /fraʊn/
A *v.i.* **[1]** die Stirn runzeln; **~ at sth./sb.** etw./jmdn. stirnrunzelnd ansehen **[2]** (express disapproval) die Stirn runzeln **(at, [up]on** über + *Akk.*); **~ [up]on a suggestion** über einen Vorschlag die Nase rümpfen; **gambling is very much ~ed upon here** das Glücksspiel ist hier streng verpönt **[3]** (present gloomy aspect) **~ [down]** düster herabblicken **(upon** auf + *Akk.*)
B *n.* Stirnrunzeln, *das;* **with a [deep/worried/puzzled] ~:** mit [stark/sorgenvoll/verwirrt] gerunzelter Stirn; **a ~ of disapproval** ein missbilligender Blick

froze ▸**freeze A, B**

frozen /'frəʊzn/
A ▸**freeze A, B**
B *adj.* **[1]** gefroren, zugefroren ⟨*Fluss, See*⟩; erfroren ⟨*Tier, Person, Pflanze*⟩; eingefroren ⟨*Wasserleitung*⟩; **I am ~ stiff/through** (fig.) ich bin ganz steif gefroren/völlig durchgefroren; **my hands are ~** (fig.) meine Hände sind eiskalt **[2]** (to preserve) tiefgekühlt; **~ food** Tiefkühlkost, *die*

FRS *abbr.* = **Fellow of the Royal Society**

fructose /'frʌktəʊs/ *n.* (Chem.) Fructose, *die* (fachspr.); Fruchtzucker, *der*

frugal /'fru:gl/ *adj.* **[1]** (careful, economical) sparsam ⟨*Hausfrau*⟩; genügsam ⟨*Lebensweise, Person, Wesen*⟩ **[2]** (costing little) frugal, karg ⟨*Mahl*⟩; einfach, karg ⟨*Zimmer, Einrichtung*⟩

frugally /'fru:gəlɪ/ *adv.* frugal, genügsam ⟨*leben, essen*⟩; einfach ⟨*eingerichtet*⟩

fruit /fru:t/
A *n.* **[1]** Frucht, *die;* (collectively) Obst, *das;* Früchte; **~s of the earth** Früchte des Feldes; **bear ~** (lit. or fig.) Früchte tragen **[2]** (Bot.: seed with envelope) Frucht, *die* **[3]** (fig.) (product of action) Frucht, *die* (geh.); Früchte (geh.); **~s** (revenues produced) Früchte (geh.); **this book is the ~ of long study** dieses Buch ist die Frucht langjähriger Arbeit (geh.)
B *v.i.* [Früchte] tragen; (fig.) Früchte tragen

fruit: ~ bat *n.* Flughund, *der;* **~ cake** *n.* englischer Teekuchen; **he is as nutty as a ~ cake** (coll.) (eccentric) er ist ein verrücktes Huhn (ugs.); (insane) er ist völlig übergeschnappt (ugs.); **~ 'cocktail** *n.* Früchtecocktail, *der*

fruiterer /'fru:tərə(r)/ *n.* ▸**❶ p. 1260** Obsthändler, *der*/-händlerin, *die*

'fruit fly *n.* Fruchtfliege, *die*

fruitful /'fru:tfl/ *adj.* **[1]** fruchtbar; (fig.) fruchtbar ⟨*Diskussion, Lebensabschnitt, Anregung*⟩; erfolgreich ⟨*Karriere, Leben, Bemühungen*⟩; **be ~ and multiply** (Bibl.) seid fruchtbar und mehret euch **2** (beneficial) ertragreich ‹*Beschäftigung*›; nützlich ‹*Entdeckung*›

fruitfully /ˈfruːtfəlɪ/ *adv.* nutzbringend

fruition /fruːˈɪʃn/ *n.* (of plan, aim) Verwirklichung, *die;* (of hope) Erfüllung, *die;* **bring to ~:** verwirklichen ‹*Plan, Ziel*›; **come to ~** ‹*Plan:*› Wirklichkeit werden; ‹*Hoffnung:*› sich erfüllen

fruit: ~ juice *n.* Fruchtsaft, *der;* **~ knife** *n.* Obstmesser, *das*

fruitless /ˈfruːtlɪs/ *adj.* (unprofitable) nutzlos ‹*Versuch, Gespräch*›; fruchtlos ‹*Verhandlung, Bemühung, Suche*›; **the investigation was ~:** die Untersuchung verlief ergebnislos; **it is ~ to …:** es ist nutzlos zu …

fruitlessly /ˈfruːtlɪslɪ/ *adv.* umsonst ‹*versuchen, sich bemühen, suchen*›; fruchtlos, ergebnislos ‹*verhandeln, diskutieren*›

fruit: ~ machine *n.* (Brit.) Spielautomat, *der;* **~ ˈsalad** *n.* Obstsalat, *der;* **~ salts** *n. pl.* Magenpulver, *das;* **~ tree** *n.* Obstbaum, *der*

fruity /ˈfruːtɪ/ *adj.* **1** fruchtig ‹*Duft, Geschmack, Wein*› **2** (coll.) (rich in tone) volltönend ‹*Stimme*›; herzhaft ‹*Lachen*›; (full of scandalous interest) saftig (ugs.) ‹*Geschichte, Buch, Witz*›

frump /frʌmp/ *n.* (derog.) Vogelscheuche, *die* (ugs.)

frumpy /ˈfrʌmpɪ/ *adj.* (derog.) ohne jeden Schick *nachgestellt*

frustrate /frʌˈstreɪt, ˈfrʌstreɪt/ *v.t.* vereiteln, durchkreuzen ‹*Plan, Vorhaben, Versuch*›; zunichte machen ‹*Hoffnung, Bemühungen*›; enttäuschen ‹*Erwartung, Hoffnung*›; **he was ~d in his attempts/efforts** seine Versuche/Bemühungen waren vergebens

frustrated /frʌˈstreɪtɪd, ˈfrʌstreɪtɪd/ *adj.* frustriert

frustrating /frʌˈstreɪtɪŋ, ˈfrʌstreɪtɪŋ/ *adj.* frustrierend; ärgerlich ‹*Angewohnheit*›; **he is a ~ person to deal with** es ist frustrierend, mit ihm zu tun zu haben

frustration /frʌˈstreɪʃn/ *n.* Frustration, *die;* (defeat) Enttäuschung, *die;* (of plans, efforts) Scheitern, *das*

fry¹ /fraɪ/

A *n.* **1** Pfannengericht, *das* **2** (internal parts of animals) [gebratene] Innereien *Pl.*; *see also* **lamb's fry** **3** (Amer.: social gathering) Grillparty, *die*

B *v.t.* braten; **fried eggs/potatoes** Spiegeleier/Bratkartoffeln *Pl.*; *see also* **fish A 1**

C *v.i.* braten; (coll.: burn) **~ in the sun** in der Sonne schmoren (ugs.)

Phrasal verb

- **~ ˈup** *v.t.* aufbraten ‹*Reste*›; **let's ~ up something** lass uns schnell was brutzeln (ugs.); *see also* **fry-up**

fry² *n.* (young fishes etc.) Brut, *die;* **ˈsmall ~** (fig.) unbedeutende Leute; (children) junges Gemüse (ugs.); **compared with him all the others are ˈsmall ~** (fig.) im Vergleich mit ihm sind alle anderen unbedeutend

fryer /ˈfraɪə(r)/ *n.* **1** (vessel) Fritteuse, *die* **2** (Amer.: chicken) Brathühnchen, *das;* Brathähnchen, *das*

frying pan /ˈfraɪɪŋpæn/ *n.* Bratpfanne, *die;* **[fall/jump] out of the ~ into the fire** vom Regen in die Traufe [kommen] (ugs.)

fry: ~pan (Amer.) ▸**frying pan**; **~-up** *n.* Pfannengericht, *das*

ft. *abbr.* ▸**ⓘ p. 911**, ▸**ⓘ p. 1208**, ▸**ⓘ p. 1286** **= feet, foot** ft.

FT *abbr.* **= Financial Times**

FTP *abbr.* **= file transfer protocol**

fuchsia /ˈfjuːʃə/ *n.* (Bot.) Fuchsie, *die*

fuck /fʌk/ (coarse)

A *v.t.* **1** ficken (vulg.) **2** (damn) **~ …:** zum Teufel mit … (derb); **~ you!** leck mich am Arsch! (derb); **[oh,] ~!, [oh,] ~ it!** [au,] Scheiße! (derb)

B *v.i.* ficken (vulg)

C *n.* **1** (act) Fick, *der* (vulg.) **2** (person) **be a good ~:** gut ficken (vulg.) **3** (damn) **I don't give/care a ~:** es ist mir scheißegal (derb)

Phrasal verbs

- **~ about, ~ around** (coarse)

A *v.i.* rumgammeln (ugs.); **~ about** *or* **around with sth.** an etw. (*Dat.*) rumfummeln (ugs.)

B *v.t.* verarschen (derb)

- **~ ˈoff** *v.i.* (coarse) **~ off!** verpiss dich! (salopp)
- **~ ˈup** (coarse) *v.t.* versauen (derb)

fucking /ˈfʌkɪŋ/ (coarse)

A *adj.* Scheiß- (salopp); **what the ~ hell's that for?** wofür ist das denn, verdammte Scheiße? (derb)

B *adv.* verdammt (ugs.)

fuddle /ˈfʌdl/ *v.t.* **1** (intoxicate) benebeln ‹*Sinne*›; **they were slightly ~d** sie waren [leicht] beschwipst *od.* angesäuselt (ugs.) **2** (confuse) verwirren

fuddy-duddy /ˈfʌdɪdʌdɪ/ (coll.)

A *adj.* verkalkt (ugs.)

B *n.* Fossil, *das* (fig.)

fudge¹ /fʌdʒ/ *n.* (sweet) Karamellbonbon, *der od. das;* [weiche] Karamelle, *die*

fudge²

A *v.t.* frisieren (ugs.) ‹*Geschäftsbücher*›; ausweichen (+ *Dat.*) ‹*Problem*›; sich (*Dat.*) aus den Fingern saugen ‹*Ausrede, Geschichte, Entschuldigung*›

B *v.i.* ausweichen

C *n.* Schwindel, *der*

fuel /ˈfjuːəl/

A *n.* Brennstoff, *der;* (for vehicle) Kraftstoff, *der;* (for ship, aircraft, spacecraft) Treibstoff, *der;* (for cigarette lighter) Gas, *das;* (petrol) Benzin, *das;* (Nucl. Engin.) Kernbrennstoff, *der;* Spaltstoff, *der;* **add ~ to the flames** *or* **fire** (fig.) Öl ins Feuer gießen

B *v.t.*, (Brit.) **-ll-** heizen ‹*Ofen*›; beschicken ‹*Hochofen*›; auftanken ‹*Schiff, Flugzeug*›; betreiben ‹*Kraftwerk, Motor*›; (fig.: stimulate) Nahrung geben (+ *Dat.*) ‹*Verdacht, Hoffnung, Spekulationen*›; anheizen ‹*Inflation*›; fördern ‹*Entwicklung*›

C *v.i.*, (Brit.) **-ll-** auftanken

fuel: ~-ˈair *adj.* Kraftstoff-Luft-; **~-air [explosive] bomb** Benzinbombe, *die;* **~ cap** *n.* (Motor Veh.) Tankdeckel, *der;* **~ cell** *n.* Brennstoffzelle, *die;* **~ consumption** *n.* Brennstoffverbrauch, *der;* (of vehicle) Kraftstoffverbrauch, *der;* (of aircraft, rocket) Treibstoffverbrauch, *der;* **~-efficient** *adj.* sparsam ‹*Motor, Auto usw.*›; **~ element** *n.* (Nucl. Engin.) Brenn[stoff]element, *das;* **~ gauge** *n.* Kraftstoffanzeiger, *der;* **~ injection** *n.* Treibstoffeinspritzung, *die;* (in petrol engine) Benzineinspritzung, *die;* **~ oil** *n.* Heizöl, *das;* **~ pump** *n.* Kraftstoffpumpe, *die;* **~ rod** *n.* (Nucl. Engin.) Brennstab, *der;* **~ tank** *n.* (of motor vehicle) Kraftstofftank, *der;* (of aircraft, spacecraft) Treibstofftank, *der;* (of ship) Treiböltank, *der;* (for storage) Kraftstoffbehälter, *der*

fug /fʌg/ *n.* (coll.) Mief, *der* (salopp)

fugitive /ˈfjuːdʒɪtɪv/

A *adj.* **1** (lit. or fig.) flüchtig **2** (flitting, shifting) unstet ‹*Wesen, Charakter*›

B *n.* **1** Flüchtige, *der/die;* **be a ~ from justice/from the law** auf der Flucht vor der Justiz/dem Gesetz sein **2** (exile) Flüchtling, *der*

fugue /fjuːg/ *n.* (Mus.) Fuge, *die*

fulcrum /ˈfʊlkrəm/ *n.*, *pl.* **fulcra** /ˈfʊlkrə/ **1** (Mech.) Drehpunkt, *der* **2** (fig.: factor) [Dreh- und] Angelpunkt, *der*

fulfil (*Amer.:* **fulfill**) /fʊlˈfɪl/ *v.t.*, **-ll-** erfüllen; stillen ‹*Verlangen, Bedürfnisse*›; entsprechen (+ *Dat.*) ‹*Erwartungen*›; erhören ‹*Gebet*›; ausführen ‹*Befehl*›; beenden ‹*Arbeit, Werk*›; halten ‹*Versprechen*›; **be fulfilled** ‹*Traum:*› in Erfüllung gehen; ‹*Wunsch, Hoffnung, Prophezeiung:*› sich erfüllen; **~ oneself** sich selbst verwirklichen; **be** *or* **feel fulfilled [in one's job]** [in seinem Beruf] Erfüllung finden

fulfilling /fʊlˈfɪlɪŋ/ *adj.* (giving satisfaction) befriedigend

fulfilment (*Amer.:* **fulfillment**) /fʊlˈfɪlmənt/ *n.* ▸**fulfil**: Erfüllung, *die;* Erhörung, *die;* Ausführung, *die;* Beendigung, *die;* **bring sth. to ~:** etw. erfüllen; **sth. reaches ~:** etw. erfüllt sich; **find ~ in one's work** Erfüllung in seiner Arbeit finden

full¹ /fʊl/

A *adj.* **1** voll; **the jug is ~ of water** der Krug ist voll Wasser; **his pockets are ~ of money** er hat die Taschen voller Geld; **the bus was completely ~:** der Bus war voll besetzt; **~ of hatred/holes** voller Hass/Löcher; **my heart is too ~ for words** mir ist das Herz so voll, dass ich keine Worte finde; **be ~ up** voll [besetzt] sein; ‹*Behälter:*› randvoll sein; ‹*Liste:*› voll sein; ‹*Flug:*› völlig ausgebucht sein

2 (engrossed with): **be ~ of oneself/one's own importance** sehr von sich eingenommen sein/sich sehr wichtig nehmen; **ever since this event she's been ~ of it** seit diesem Ereignis spricht sie von nichts anderem [mehr]; **the newspapers are ~ of the crisis** die Zeitungen sind voll von Berichten über die Krise; **he is ~ of his subject** er geht völlig in seinem Fachgebiet auf

3 (replete with food) voll ‹*Magen*›; satt ‹*Person*›; **I'm ~ [up]** (coll.) ich bin voll [bis obenhin] (ugs.)

4 (comprehensive) ausführlich, umfassend ‹*Bericht, Beschreibung*›; (abundant, satisfying) vollwertig ‹*Mahlzeit*›; erfüllt ‹*Leben*›; (complete) geschlagen (ugs.), ganz ‹*Stunde*›; ganz ‹*Jahr, Monat, Semester, Seite*›; voll ‹*Gehalt, Bezahlung, Unterstützung, Mitgefühl, Verständnis*›; **weigh a ~ ten tons** volle zehn Tonnen wiegen; **the event received ~ TV coverage** das Fernsehen berichtete in aller Ausführlichkeit über das Ereignis; **with illustrations in ~ colour throughout** durchgehend farbig illustriert; **the ~ details of the case** alle Einzelheiten des Falls; **in ~ daylight** am helllichten Tag; **the moon is ~:** es ist Vollmond; **in ~ bloom** in voller Blüte; **they were in ~ flight** (fleeing) sie flohen, so schnell sie konnten; (impressive) sie waren in Hochform; **this will require a ~ day's work** dazu braucht man einen ganzen Tag; **~ member** Vollmitglied, *das;* **~ membership** Vollmitgliedschaft, *die;* **in ~ possession of one's faculties** im Vollbesitz seiner Kräfte; **in ~ view of sb.** [direkt] vor jmds. Augen; **we were in ~ view of the house** wir konnten vom Haus aus ohne weiteres gesehen werden; **the ship came into ~ view** man konnte das Schiff allmählich richtig sehen; **at ~ speed** mit Höchstgeschwindigkeit; **~ speed** *or* **steam ahead!** (lit. or fig.) volle Kraft *od.* Volldampf voraus!; **the machine was operating at ~ capacity** die Maschine lief auf Hochtouren; **the team/cabinet was at ~ strength** die Mannschaft spielte in ihrer besten Besetzung/das Kabinett war vollzählig; **bound in ~ leather** in Ganzleder gebunden; **pay the ~ fare** voll bezahlen; den vollen Fahrpreis bezahlen; **~ name** voller Name; **~ sister/brother** leibliche Schwester/leiblicher Bruder

5 (intense in quality) hell, voll ‹*Licht*›; satt ‹*Farbe*›; voll ‹*Klang, Stimme, Aroma*›

6 (rounded, plump) voll ‹*Gesicht, Busen, Lippen, Mund, Segel*›; füllig ‹*Figur*›; weit geschnitten ‹*Rock*›; **be ~ in the face** ein volles Gesicht haben

B *n.* **1** **in ~:** vollständig; **write your name [out] in ~:** schreiben Sie Ihren Namen aus **2** **satisfy sb./enjoy sth. to the ~:** jmdn. vollauf zufrieden stellen/etw. in vollen Zügen genießen **3** **the moon is at/past the ~:** es ist Vollmond/abnehmender Mond

C *adv.* **1** (very) **know ~ well that …:** ganz genau *od.* sehr wohl wissen, dass … **2** (exactly, directly) genau; voll (ugs.); **~ in the face** direkt ins Gesicht ‹*schlagen, scheinen*›; **look sb. ~ in the face** jmdn. voll ansehen

full² *v.t.* (Textiles) walken ‹*Tuche*›

full: ~ ˈage *n.* Volljährigkeit, *die;* **~ back** *n.* (Sport) Verteidiger, *der*/Verteidigerin, *die;* **~-blooded** /ˈfʊlblʌdɪd/ *adj.* **1** (pure-bred) reinrassig ‹*Tier*›; reinblütig ‹*Mensch*›; **2** (vigorous, hearty, sensual) vollblütig; **~-blown** *adj.* **1** (at height of bloom) voll aufgeblüht; **2** (fig.) ausgewachsen ‹*Skandal*›; ausgereift ‹*Theorie, Plan, Gedanke*›; umfassend ‹*Bericht*›; **~-blown AIDS** Vollbild-Aids, *das;* **~ ˈboard** *n.* Vollpension, *die;* **~-bodied** *adj.* vollmundig, (fachspr.) körperreich ‹*Wein*›; voll ‹*Ton, Klang*›; **~-cream** *adj.* **~-cream milk/cheese** Vollmilch, *die*/Vollfettkäse, *der;* **~ ˈdress** *n.* Gesellschaftsanzug, *der;* **~-dress** *adj.* Gala‹*uniform, -diner*›; (fig.) groß angelegt; **~-dress occasion** feierliche Veranstaltung; **~ emˈployment** *n.* Vollbeschäftigung, *die*

fuller's earth /fʊləz ˈɜːθ/ *n.* (Min.) Fullererde, *die;* Walkerde, *die*

full: ~ ˈface *n.* (Art, Photog.) **in ~ face** en face; **~-face** **A** *adv.* (Art, Photog.) en face; **B** *adj.*

1) (Art, Photog.) En-face-; 2) **~-face helmet** Integralhelm, *der;* **~-faced** *adj.* mit vollem Gesicht *nachgestellt;* **~-frontal** *adj.* 1) völlig ‹*Nacktheit*›; **~-frontal shots** Nacktfotos, die alles zeigen; 2) (no holds barred) Frontal‹*angriff*›; **~-grown** *adj.* ausgewachsen ‹*Mensch, Tier*›; **~ 'house** *n.* 1) (Theatre) ausverkauftes *od.* volles Haus; **play to ~ houses every night** jeden Abend vor ausverkauftem Haus spielen; 2) (Poker) Fullhouse, *das;* (Bingo) Voll, *das;* **~ 'length** A *n.* **at ~ length** (in ~ detail) in aller Ausführlichkeit; (unabridged) ungekürzt; **[stretched out] at ~ length** der Länge nach *od.* (ugs.) längelang ausgestreckt; B *adv.* längelang (ugs.), der Länge nach ‹*hinfallen, liegen*›; **~-length** *adj.* abendfüllend ‹*Film, Theaterstück*›; **~-length novel** größerer Roman; **~-length mirror** großer Spiegel (in dem man sich ganz sehen kann); **~-length portrait** Ganzporträt, *das;* **~-length dress** langes Kleid; **~ 'marks** *n. pl., no art.* die höchste Bewertung; (Sch., Univ.) die beste Note; **~ marks!** (fig. coll.) ausgezeichnet!; **you get ~ marks for observation** das hast du ausgezeichnet beobachtet; **give sb. ~ marks** (fig.) jmdm. höchstes Lob zollen; **~ 'moon** *n.* Vollmond, *der*

fullness /ˈfʊlnɪs/ *n., no pl.* (of skirt) weiter Schnitt; (of figure) Fülligkeit, *die;* (of face) Rundheit, *die;* **a feeling of ~:** ein Völlegefühl; **in the ~ of time** (literary) wenn die Zeit dafür gekommen ist; (in past) als die Zeit dafür gekommen war

full: ~-page *adj.* ganzseitig; **~ pitch** ▸ **~ toss; ~ 'play** *n.* **give sth. ~ play** einer Sache (*Dat.*) freien Lauf lassen; **give sb. ~ play** jmdm. völlig freie Hand lassen; **~ 'point** Punkt, *der;* **~ pro'fessor** *n.* ordentlicher Professor; **~-scale** *adj.* 1) in Originalgröße *nachgestellt;* 2) groß angelegt ‹*Werbekampagne, Untersuchung, Suchaktion*›; umfassend ‹*Umarbeitung, Revision*›; **a ~-scale war/novel** ein richtiger Krieg/größerer Roman; **~ 'score** *n.* (Mus.) Partitur, *die;* **~-size, ~-sized** *adjs.* 1) (standard-size) normal groß; **~-size trees** ausgewachsene *od.* große Bäume; **~-size bottle** große Flasche; 2) (not scaled down) in Originalgröße *postpos.;* **~-size portrait** lebensgroßes Porträt; Porträt in Lebensgröße; **~ 'stop** *n.* 1) Punkt, *der;* 2) (fig. coll.) **come to a ~ stop** zum Stillstand kommen; **I'm not going, ~ stop** ich gehe nicht, [und damit] basta! (ugs.); **~ 'time** A *adv.* ganztags ‹*arbeiten*›; B *n.* (Sport) Spielende, *das;* **~-time** *adj.* ganztägig; Ganztags‹*arbeit, -beschäftigung*›; **sb. is ~-time** jmd. arbeitet ganztags; **~-time teacher** Lehrer mit vollem Deputat; **this is a ~-time job** (fig.) das hält einen den ganzen Tag auf Trab (ugs.); **~-'timer** *n.* Ganztagsbeschäftigte, *der/die;* **become a ~-timer** anfangen, ganztags zu arbeiten; **~ 'toss** (Cricket) *n.: Ball, der den Schlagmann erreicht, ohne den Boden zu berühren*

fully /ˈfʊlɪ/ *adv.* 1) voll [und ganz]; fest ‹*entschlossen*›; reich ‹*belohnt*›; ausführlich ‹*erklären usw.*›; **~ convinced** restlos überzeugt 2) (at least) **~ two hours** volle zwei Stunden; **~ three weeks ago** vor gut drei Wochen

fully: ~-fledged *attrib. adj.* flügge ‹*Vogel*›; (fig.) [ganz] selbstständig; **~-qualified** *attrib. adj.* vollqualifiziert

fulmar /ˈfʊlmə(r)/ *n.* (Ornith.) Eissturmvogel, *der*

fulminate /ˈfʌlmɪneɪt/ *v.i.* (protest) **~ against sb./sth.** gegen jmdn./etw. Sturm laufen

fulsome /ˈfʊlsəm/ *adj.* übertrieben, (ugs. abwertend) dick aufgetragen ‹*Lob, Kompliment, Schmeichelei*›

fulsomely /ˈfʊlsəmlɪ/ *adv.* übertrieben ‹*loben, schmeicheln*›

fumble /ˈfʌmbl/

A *v.i.* **~ at** *or* **with** [herum]fingern an (+ *Dat.*); **~ with one's papers** in seinen Papieren kramen (ugs.); **~ in one's pockets for sth.** in seinen Taschen nach etw. fingern *od.* (ugs.) kramen; **~ for the light switch** nach dem Lichtschalter tasten; **~ [about** *or* **around] in the dark** im Dunkeln herumtasten; **~ [about] for the right words** (fig.) nach den richtigen Worten suchen

B *v.t.* 1) nesteln an (+ *Dat.*) 2) (Games) nicht sicher fangen ‹*Ball*›

fume /fjuːm/

A *n.* 1) *in pl.* (from car exhaust) Abgase *Pl.;* **petrol/ammonia ~s** Benzin-/Ammoniakdämpfe *Pl.;* **~s of wine/whisky** Alkohol-/Whiskydunst, *der;* **[cigarette/cigar] ~s** [Zigaretten-/Zigarren]rauch, *der* 2) (fit of anger); **be in a ~:** vor Wut schäumen

B *v.i.* 1) ‹*Feuer, Ofen:*› rauchen 2) (be angry) vor Wut schäumen; **~ at** *or* **over sb.** auf *od.* über jmdn. wütend sein; **~ at** *or* **over** *or* **about sth.** wegen etw. wütend sein

C *v.t.* **~d oak** geräuchertes Eichenholz (Holzverarb.)

fumigate /ˈfjuːmɪgeɪt/ *v.t.* 1) ausräuchern 2) (apply fumes to) begasen ‹*Pflanzen*›

fumigation /fjuːmɪˈgeɪʃn/ *n.* ▸ **fumigate:** Ausräucherung, *die;* Begasung, *die*

fun /fʌn/

A *n.* Spaß, *der;* **be half the ~:** [mit] das Schönste sein; **have ~ doing sth.** Spaß daran haben, etw. zu tun; **I/we had great ~ playing with the dog** es hat [mir/uns] viel Spaß gemacht, mit dem Hund zu spielen; **have ~!** viel Spaß!; **[are you] having ~?** (iron.) macht Spaß, was? (ugs. iron.); **we'll have great ~:** es wird bestimmt sehr lustig; **I was just having a bit of ~:** ich habe nur Spaß gemacht; **be full of ~:** ein fröhliches Wesen haben; ‹*Tier:*› sehr verspielt sein; **make ~ of** *or* **poke ~ at sb./sth.** sich über jmdn./etw. lustig machen; **in ~:** im Spaß; **the things he said were only in ~:** was er gesagt hat, war nur Spaß; **for ~, for the ~ of it** zum Spaß; **what ~!** toll!; wie schön!; **spoil the** *or* **sb.'s ~:** jmdm. den Spaß verderben; **sounds like ~!** das wird sicher toll werden!; **like ~** (very much) wie verrückt (salopp); (iron.: not at all) von wegen!; **sth. is [good** *or* **great/no] ~:** etw. macht [großen/keinen] Spaß; **he is [good** *or* **great] ~ to have at a party** eine Party mit ihm ist immer sehr lustig; **sb. is [great] ~/no ~ to be with** es macht [großen] Spaß/keinen Spaß, mit jmdm. zusammen zu sein; **it's no ~ being unemployed** es ist kein Vergnügen, arbeitslos zu sein; **~ and games** (coll.) Vergnügungen *Pl.;* **we had the usual ~ and games with him** (iron.: trouble) wir hatten wieder das übliche Theater mit ihm (ugs.); **enjoy** *or* **have the ~ of the fair** (fig.) sich vergnügen; *see also* **figure A 4**

B *adj.* (coll.) lustig; amüsant; **have a ~ time at a party** sich auf einer Party gut amüsieren

function /ˈfʌŋkʃn/

A *n.* 1) (role) Aufgabe, *die;* **in his ~ as surgeon** in seiner Funktion *od.* Eigenschaft als Chirurg 2) (mode of action) Funktion, *die* 3) (formal event) Veranstaltung, *die;* (reception) Empfang, *der;* (official ceremony) Feierlichkeit, *die* 4) (Math.) Funktion, *die*

B *v.i.* ‹*Maschine, System, Organisation:*› funktionieren; ‹*Organ:*› arbeiten; **~ as** (have the ~ of) fungieren als; (serve as) dienen als; **I just don't ~ early in the morning** (coll.) am frühen Morgen bin ich zu nichts zu gebrauchen

functional /ˈfʌŋkʃənl/ *adj.* 1) (useful, practical) funktionell; funktional ‹*Erziehung*›; **~ building** Zweckbau, *der* 2) (working) funktionsfähig; **be ~ again** wieder funktionieren 3) (Physiol.) **~ disease** Funktionsstörung eines Organs

functionalism /ˈfʌŋkʃənəlɪzm/ *n.* Funktionalismus, *der*

functionality /fʌŋkʃəˈnælɪtɪ/ *n., no pl.* 1) (of product) Funktionalität, *die* 2) (Computing: range of operations) Funktionalitäten *Pl.*

functionally /ˈfʌŋkʃənəlɪ/ *adv.* funktionell

functionary /ˈfʌŋkʃənərɪ/ *n.* Funktionär, *der*/Funktionärin, *die*

function: ~ key *n.* (Computing) Funktionstaste, *die;* **~ word** *n.* Funktionswort, *das*

fund /fʌnd/

A *n.* 1) (collection of money) Fonds, *der* 2) (fig.: stock, store) Fundus, *der* (**of** von, an + *Dat.*) 3) *in pl.* (resources) Mittel *Pl.;* Gelder *Pl.;* **public ~s** öffentliche Mittel; **be in ~s** bei Kasse sein (ugs.); **be pressed for** *or* **short of ~s** knapp *od.* schlecht bei Kasse sein (ugs.)

B *v.t.* 1) finanzieren 2) (invest) anlegen; investieren

fundamental /fʌndəˈmentl/

A *adj.* 1) grundlegend (**to** für); fundamental, grundlegend ‹*Unterschied, Bedeutung, Bestandteil*›; elementar ‹*Bedürfnisse*›; (primary, original) Grund‹*struktur, -form, -typus*› 2) (Mus.) **~ note** Grundton, *der;* (Acoustics) **~ tone** Grundton, *der*

B *n.* 1) *in pl.* Grundlage, *die;* Fundament, *das* 2) (Mus.) (note) Grundton, *der;* (tone) Fundamentalbass, *der*

fundamentalism /fʌndəˈmentəlɪzm/ *n.* Fundamentalismus, *der*

fundamentalist /fʌndəˈmentəlɪst/ *n.* Fundamentalist, *der*/Fundamentalistin, *die*

fundamentally /fʌndəˈmentəlɪ/ *adv.* grundlegend; von Grund auf ‹*verschieden, ehrlich*›; völlig ‹*abhängig*›; **I am ~ opposed to this** ich bin grundsätzlich dagegen; **man is ~ good/evil** der Mensch ist von Natur aus gut/böse

fundamental 'particle ▸ **elementary particle**

fund: ~holder *n.* (Brit.) *praktischer Arzt mit eigenständig verwaltetem Budget;* **~holding** (Brit.) A *adj.* **~holding practitioner/practice** praktischer Arzt/[Arzt]praxis mit eigenständig verwaltetem Budget; B *n.* Eigenbudgetierung, *die*

funding /ˈfʌndɪŋ/ *n., no pl., no indef. art.* 1) (providing funds) Finanzierung, *die* 2) (resources) Finanzierungsmittel *Pl.*

fund: ~ management *n., no pl.* Vermögensverwaltung, *die; attrib.* **~ management company** Vermögensverwaltungsgesellschaft, *die;* **~ manager** *n.* ▸ ❶ **p. 1260** Fondsverwalter, *der*/-verwalterin, *die;* Fondsmanager, *der*/-managerin, *die* (fachspr.); **~-raise** *v.i.* Geld beschaffen; (for charity) Spenden sammeln; **~-raiser** /ˈfʌndreɪzə(r)/ *n.* 1) (person) Geldbeschaffer, *der*/-beschafferin, *die;* 2) (event) Benefizveranstaltung, *die;* **~-raising** /ˈfʌndreɪzɪŋ/ *n., no pl.* Geldbeschaffung, *die; attrib.* zur Geldbeschaffung *nachgestellt*

funeral /ˈfjuːnərl/ *n.* 1) Beerdigung, *die;* Beisetzung, *die* (geh.) 2) (procession) Leichenzug, *der* (geh.); Trauerzug, *der* 3) *attrib.* **~ director** ▸ ❶ **p. 1260** Bestattungsunternehmer, *der;* **~ home** (Amer.) *or* **parlour** Bestattungsunternehmen, *das;* **~ march** Trauermarsch, *der;* **~ procession** Leichenzug, *der* (geh.); Trauerzug, *der;* **~ service** Trauerfeier, *die;* **~ pile** *or* **pyre** Scheiterhaufen, *der;* **~ expenses** Bestattungskosten *Pl.* 4) (coll.: one's concern) **that's his/not my ~:** das ist sein/nicht mein Problem 5) (Amer.: service) Trauerfeier, *die;* **preach sb.'s ~:** die Trauerfeier für jmdn. abhalten

funereal /fjuːˈnɪərɪəl/ *adj.* 1) (of funeral) Trauer- 2) (gloomy) düster; **~ voice** Grabesstimme, *die* (ugs.); **~ expression** Trauermiene, *die* (ugs.); trauervolle Miene; **~ pace** Kriechtempo, *das*

'funfair *n.* (Brit.) Jahrmarkt, *der*

fungal /ˈfʌŋgl/ (Med.) Hautpilz-; **~ infection** Pilzinfektion, *die*

fungicidal /fʌŋgɪˈsaɪdl/ *adj.* fungizid

fungicide /ˈfʌndʒɪsaɪd/ *n.* (Hort.) Fungizid, *das;* (Pharm.) Antimykotikum, *das*

fungous /ˈfʌŋgəs/ *adj.* pilzartig

fungus /ˈfʌŋgəs/ *n., pl.* **fungi** /ˈfʌŋgaɪ, ˈfʌndʒaɪ/ *or* **~es** 1) Pilz, *der* 2) (Med.) Hautpilz, *der* 3) (disease of fish) Fischschimmel, *der* 4) (coll.: beard) **[face] ~:** Sauerkohl, *der* (salopp scherzh.)

funicular [railway] /fjuːˈnɪkjʊlə(r) (reɪlweɪ)/ *n.* [Stand]seilbahn, *die*

funk /fʌŋk/ (coll.)

A *n.* Bammel, *der* (salopp); Schiss, *der* (salopp); **be in/go into a [blue] ~:** [mächtig] Bammel *od.* Schiss haben/kriegen (salopp); **put sb. in a [blue] ~:** jmdm. Angst einjagen

B *v.t.* kneifen vor (+ *Dat.*) (ugs.); **he ~ed it** er hat gekniffen (ugs.)

funky /ˈfʌŋkɪ/ *adj.* (coll.) irre (salopp) ‹*Musik*›

'fun-loving *adj.* lebenslustig

funnel /ˈfʌnl/

A *n.* 1) (cone) Trichter, *der* 2) (of ship etc.) Schornstein, *der*

B *v.t.*, (Brit.) **-ll-** konzentrieren ‹*Aufmerksamkeit,*

Anstrengung, Bemühungen›; schleusen ‹*Daten, Verkehr*›; lenken ‹*Verkehr*›

C *v.i.*, (Brit.) **-ll-** strömen

funnily /ˈfʌnɪlɪ/ *adv.* komisch; **~ enough** komischerweise (ugs.)

funny /ˈfʌnɪ/

A *adj.* **1** (comical) komisch; lustig; witzig ‹*Person, Einfall, Bemerkung*›; **are you being** *or* **trying to be ~?** das soll wohl ein Witz sein? **2** (strange) komisch; seltsam; **don't get any ~ ideas** (coll.) komm bloß nicht auf komische Gedanken! (ugs.); **be ~ about money** in Gelddingen komisch *od.* eigen sein; **that's ~, he's gone** komisch, er ist weg; **the ~ thing ˈis that ...:** das Komische [daran] ist, dass ...; **have a ~ feeling that ...:** das komische Gefühl haben, dass ...; **there's something ~ going on here** hier ist doch was faul (ugs.) **3** (coll.: unwell) **I feel ~:** mir ist komisch *od.* (ugs.) blümerant; **he's a bit ~ in the head** er ist nicht ganz richtig im Kopf (ugs.)

B *n.* (coll.) **1** *in pl.* (comic section) Comicseite, *die* **2** (joke) Witz, *der*

funny: ~ bone *n.* (Anat.) Musikantenknochen, *der;* **~ business** *n.* **1** (comic behaviour) Alberei, *die;* **2** (coll.: misbehaviour, deception) krumme Touren (ugs.); **~-face** *n.* (joc./coll.) Krümel, *der* (fam.); **~-ha-ˈha** *adj.* (coll.) [zum Lachen] komisch; **~ man** *n.* Komiker, *der;* **~-peˈculiar** *adj.* (coll.) seltsam

ˈfun run *n.* (coll.) Spaßlauf, *der*

fur /fɜː(r)/

A *n.* **1** (coat of animal) Fell, *das;* (for or as garment) Pelz, *der;* **trimmed/lined with ~:** mit Pelz besetzt *od.* verbrämt/gefüttert; **make the ~ fly** (fig.) hohe Wellen schlagen; *attrib.* **~ coat/hat** Pelzmantel, *der*/-mütze, *die;* **~ rug** Fell, *das* (*als Vorleger*) **2** (coating) Belag, *der;* (formed by hard water) Wasserstein, *der;* (in kettle) Kesselstein, *der*

B *v.t.*, **-rr-: hard water will ~ [up] the kettle/pipes** bei hartem Wasser bildet sich Kesselstein im Kessel/Wasserstein in den Rohren

C *v.i.*, **-rr-: the kettle has/pipes have ~red [up]** im Kessel hat sich Kesselstein/in den Rohren hat sich Wasserstein gebildet

furbelow /ˈfɜːbɪləʊ/ *n.* **frills and ~s** (lit. or fig.) Kinkerlitzchen *Pl.* (ugs. abwertend)

ˈfur-clad *adj.* in Pelz gekleidet

furious /ˈfjʊərɪəs/ *adj.* wütend; heftig ‹*Streit, Kampf, Sturm, Lärm*›; wild ‹*Tanz, Sturm, Tempo, Kampf*›; **be ~ with sb./at sth.** wütend auf jmdn./über etw. (*Akk.*) sein; **the fun was fast and ~:** es ging hoch her

furiously /ˈfjʊərɪəslɪ/ *adv.* wütend; wild ‹*kämpfen, tanzen*›; wie wild (ugs.) ‹*arbeiten, in die Pedale treten*›; heftig ‹*erröten, kämpfen*›

furl /fɜːl/ *v.t.* einrollen ‹*Segel, Flagge*›; zusammenrollen ‹*Schirm*›

furlong /ˈfɜːlɒŋ/ *n.* Achtelmeile, *die*

furlough /ˈfɜːləʊ/ *n.* (Mil.) Urlaub, *der;* **be/go on ~:** Urlaub haben/in Urlaub gehen

furnace /ˈfɜːnɪs/ *n.* Ofen, *der;* (blast-~) Hochofen, *der;* (smelting ~) Schmelzofen, *der;* (pottery-kiln) Brennofen, *der;* **this room is like a ~:** hier ist eine Hitze wie im Treibhaus *od.* Backofen

furnish /ˈfɜːnɪʃ/ *v.t.* **1** möblieren; **live in ~ed accommodation** möbliert wohnen; **~ing fabrics** Möbel- und Vorhangstoffe *Pl.* **2** (provide, supply) liefern ‹*Vorräte*›; **~ sb. with sth.** jmdm. etw. liefern; **the army was ~ed with supplies** die Armee wurde mit Vorräten versorgt *od.* beliefert

furnishings /ˈfɜːnɪʃɪŋz/ *n. pl.* Einrichtungsgegenstände *Pl.;* **including ~ and fittings** mit kompletter Einrichtung

furniture /ˈfɜːnɪtʃə(r)/ *n.*, *no pl.* Möbel *Pl.;* **piece of ~:** Möbel[stück], *das;* **the house has hardly any ~:** das Haus ist kaum eingerichtet; **a bed and a chair were all the ~:** ein Bett und ein Stuhl waren das ganze Mobiliar; **he's [a] part of the ~** (fig. coll.) er gehört zum lebenden Inventar (scherzh.)

furniture: ~ beetle *n.* Totenuhr, *die;* **~ polish** *n.* Möbelpolitur, *die;* **~ van** *n.* Möbelwagen, *der*

furore /fjʊəˈrɔːrɪ/ (*Amer.:* **furor** /ˈfjʊərɔː(r)/) *n.* **create** *or* **cause a ~:** Furore machen; (cause a scandal) einen Skandal verursachen; **when the ~ died down** als allmählich Gras über die Sache gewachsen war

furred /fɜːd/ *adj.* (Med.) belegt ‹*Zunge*›

furrier /ˈfʌrɪə(r)/ *n.* ▸ⓘ p. 1260 (dresser) Kürschner, *der*/Kürschnerin, *die;* (dealer) Pelzhändler, *der*/-händlerin, *die*

furrow /ˈfʌrəʊ/

A *n.* (lit. or fig.) Furche, *die;* **cut a ~ through the waves** ‹*Schiff:*› die Wellen durchpflügen; *see also* **plough B 3**

B *v.t.* **1** (plough) pflügen **2** (make ~s in) durchpflügen **3** (mark with wrinkles) **~ed face** zerfurchtes Gesicht

furry /ˈfɜːrɪ/ *adj.* haarig; flauschig ‹*Mantel, Stofftier*›; belegt ‹*Zunge*›; **~ animal** (toy) Plüschtier, *das;* **it has a ~ feel** es fühlt sich weich und flauschig an

further /ˈfɜːðə(r)/

A *adj. compar. of* **far 1** ▸ⓘ p. 1072 (of two) ander...; (in space) weiter entfernt; **on the ~ bank of the river/side of town** am anderen Ufer/Ende der Stadt **2** (additional) weiter...; **till ~ notice/orders** bis auf weiteres; **I could eat this until ~ orders** (fig. joc.) ich könnte das bis in alle Ewigkeit essen (ugs.); **will there be anything ~?** darf es noch etwas sein?; haben Sie sonst noch einen Wunsch?; **~ details** *or* **particulars** weitere *od.* nähere Einzelheiten

B *adv. compar. of* **far 1** weiter; **before it goes any ~:** bevor es sich weiter ausbreitet; **not let it go any ~:** es nicht weitersagen; **he never got ~ than secondary school** er ist über die Hauptschule nicht hinausgekommen; **until you hear ~ from us** bis Sie wieder von uns hören; **nothing was ~ from his thoughts** nichts lag ihm ferner **2** (moreover) außerdem **3** (euphem.: in hell) **I'll see you/him** *etc.* **~ first!** ich denke nicht im Traum daran!

C *v.t.* fördern; **in order to ~ one's career** um beruflich voranzukommen

furtherance /ˈfɜːðərəns/ *n.*, *no pl.* Förderung, *die;* Unterstützung, *die;* **in ~ of sth.** zur Förderung *od.* Unterstützung einer Sache (*Gen.*)

further eduˈcation *n.* Weiterbildung, *die;* (for adults also) Erwachsenenbildung, *die*

> **further education**
>
> In Großbritannien bedeutet *further education* in der Regel jede Form der Fortbildung für Personen über 16 Jahren, mit Ausnahme der Hochschulausbildung, die als *higher education* bezeichnet wird. In den Vereinigten Staaten schließt jedoch der Ausdruck *further education* auch ein Hochschulstudium mit ein.

furthermore /fɜːðəˈmɔː(r)/ *adv.* außerdem; überdies

furthermost /ˈfɜːðəməʊst/ *adj.* äußerst...; entlegenst...; **to the ~ ends of the earth** bis ans Ende der Welt

furthest /ˈfɜːðɪst/

A *adj. superl. of* **far** am weitesten entfernt; **take sb. to ~ Siberia** jmdn. ins hinterste Sibirien bringen; **to the ~ limits of the kingdom** bis in die entlegensten *od.* entferntesten Winkel des Königreichs; **ten miles at the ~:** höchstens zehn Meilen

B *adv. superl. of* **far** am weitesten ‹*springen, laufen*›; am weitesten entfernt ‹*sein, wohnen*›

furtive /ˈfɜːtɪv/ *adj.* verstohlen; **the fox is ~ in its movements** der Fuchs bewegt sich unauffällig; **he is a ~ person** er wirkt schuldbewusst und bemüht, nicht aufzufallen

furtively /ˈfɜːtɪvlɪ/ *adv.* verstohlen

fury /ˈfjʊərɪ/ *n.* **1** Wut, *die;* (of storm, sea, battle, war) Wüten, *das;* **in a ~:** wütend; **in a terrible ~:** in heller Wut; **in a blind ~:** blindwütig; **fly into a/be in a ~:** einen Wutanfall bekommen/haben; **exposed to the ~ of the elements** dem Wüten der Elemente ausgeliefert **2** **like ~** (coll.) wie wild (ugs.) **3** **Furies** (Mythol.) Furien *Pl.;* **[avenging] furies** Rachegeister *Pl.*

furze /fɜːz/ *n.* (Brit. Bot.) Stechginster, *der*

fuse¹ /fjuːz/

A *v.t.* **1** (blend) verschmelzen (**into** zu) **2** (melt) schmelzen

B *v.i.* **1** (blend) **~ together** miteinander verschmelzen; **~ with sth.** (fig.) sich mit etw. verbinden **2** (melt) schmelzen

fuse²

A *n.* **[time] ~:** [Zeit]zünder, *der;* (cord) Zündschnur, *die;* **be on a short ~** (fig.) leicht explodieren (fig.)

B *v.t.* **~ a bomb** *etc.* einen Zünder an einer Bombe *usw.* anbringen

fuse³ (Electr.)

A *n.* Sicherung, *die*

B *v.t.* **1** **~ the lights** die Sicherung [für die Lampen] durchbrennen lassen **2** (provide with ~) mit einer Sicherung versehen; absichern

C *v.i.* **the lights have ~d** die Sicherung [für die Lampen] ist durchgebrannt

ˈfuse box *n.* (Electr.) Sicherungskasten, *der*

fuselage /ˈfjuːzəlɑːʒ/ *n.* (Aeronaut.) [Flugzeug]rumpf, *der*

fusible /ˈfjuːzɪbl/ *adj.* schmelzbar

fusillade /fjuːzɪˈleɪd/ *n.* Gewehrfeuer, *das*

fusion /ˈfjuːʒn/ *n.* **1** (blending) Verschmelzung, *die;* (fig.) (of political groups, enterprises) Verbindung, *die;* Fusion, *die;* (of ideas, ideologies, races) Verschmelzung, *die* **2** (melting) Schmelzen, *das* **3** (Phys.) Fusion, *die*

fuss /fʌs/

A *n.* Theater, *das* (ugs.); **stop this silly ~:** hör mit dem Theater auf! (ugs.); **~ and bother** Rummel, *der* (ugs.); **without any ~:** ohne großes Theater (ugs.); **kick up a ~:** ein großes Theater machen; **make a ~ [about sth.]** Aufhebens [von etw.] *od.* einen Wirbel [um etw.] machen; **make a ~ of** *or* **over** [einen] Wirbel machen um ‹*Person, Tier*›; **he is made a ~ of** um ihn wird Wirbel gemacht

B *v.i.* Wirbel machen; (get agitated) sich [unnötig] aufregen; **she is always ~ing over sb./sth.** sie macht immer ein Theater mit jmdm./etw. (ugs.)

C *v.t.* **don't ~ me!** mach mich nicht verrückt! (ugs.)

fussily /ˈfʌsɪlɪ/ *adv.* **1** (bustlingly) übereifrig; rührig **2** (fastidiously) mäklig (ugs.) **3** (with undue detail) überladen

ˈfusspot *n.* (coll.) **be a ~:** Theater machen (ugs.); **don't be a ~:** mach kein Theater! (ugs.)

fussy /ˈfʌsɪ/ *adj.* **1** (bustling) übereifrig; rührig; (easily flustered) reizbar; überempfindlich; **don't be so ~!** mach nicht so ein Theater! (ugs.) **2** (fastidious) eigen; penibel; **be ~ about one's food** *or* **what one eats** mäklig im Essen sein (ugs.); **I'm not ~** (in answer: I don't mind) ich bin nicht wählerisch **3** (full of undue detail) überladen; (full of unnecessary decoration) verspielt

fusty /ˈfʌstɪ/ *adj.* **1** (mouldy) schimmelig **2** (stuffy) muffig **3** (old-fashioned) verstaubt

futile /ˈfjuːtaɪl/ *adj.* vergeblich ‹*Versuch, Bemühungen, Vorschlag usw.*›; zum Scheitern verurteilt ‹*Plan, Vorgehen usw.*›

futilely /ˈfjuːtaɪllɪ/ *adv.* vergeblich

futility /fjuːˈtɪlɪtɪ/ *n.*, *no pl.* (of effort, attempt, etc.) Vergeblichkeit, *die;* (of plan) Zwecklosigkeit, *die;* (of war) Sinnlosigkeit, *die*

futon /ˈfuːtɒn/ *n.* Futon, *der*

future /ˈfjuːtʃə(r)/

A *adj.* **1** [zu]künftig; **at some ~ date** zu einem späteren Zeitpunkt **2** (Ling.) futurisch; **~ tense** Futur, *das;* Zukunft, *die; see also* **perfect A 8** **3** **the ~ life** das Leben im Jenseits; das Leben nach dem Tod

B *n.* **1** Zukunft, *die;* **sth. is a thing of the ~:** etw. ist Zukunftsmusik; **what will her ~ be?** wie wird ihre Zukunft aussehen?; **a man with a ~:** ein Mann mit Zukunft; **in ~:** in Zukunft; künftig; **in the distant ~:** in ferner Zukunft; **sth. is still very much in the ~:** etw. liegt noch in weiter Ferne; **see sb. in the near ~:** jmdn. demnächst sehen; **there's no/little ~ in it** das hat keine/wenig Zukunft **2** (Ling.) Futur, *das;* Zukunft, *die* **3** *in pl.* (Commerc.) Terminware, *die;* (contracts) Lieferungsverträge *Pl.; attrib.* **~s contract** Terminkontrakt, *der;* **~s**

f

options Termingeschäftsoptionen *Pl.;* **~s trader** ▸❶ p. 1260 Terminhändler, *der*/-händlerin, *die*

future: ~-proof 🅰 *adj.* zukunftssicher; **~ technology** Zukunftstechnologie, *die.* 🅱 *v.t.* zukunftssicher machen; **~ 'shock** *n.* Zukunftsschock, *der*

futurism /ˈfju:tʃərɪzm/ *n.* Futurismus, *der*

futuristic /fju:tʃəˈrɪstɪk/ *adj.* futuristisch

futurology /fju:tʃəˈrɒlədʒɪ/ *n.* Futurologie, *die*

fuze (Amer.) ▸**fuse²**

fuzz /fʌz/ *n.* ① (fluff) Flaum, *der* ② (frizzy hair) Kraushaar, *das;* **a ~ of black curls** schwarzes Kraushaar ③ *no pl.* (sl.) (police) Polente, *die* (salopp); (policeman) Polyp, *der* (salopp)

fuzzy /ˈfʌzɪ/ *adj.* ① (like fuzz) flaumig ② (frizzy) kraus; wuschelig (ugs.) ③ (blurred) verschwommen; unscharf

fuzzy 'logic *n., no pl.* (Computing) Fuzzylogik, *die*

fuzzy-wuzzy /ˈfʌzɪwʌzɪ/ *n.* (sl. derog.) Krauskopf, *der*

fwd *abbr.* = **forward**

F-word /ˈefwɜ:d/ *n.* (coll.) **the ~:** das schlimme Wort mit f

FYI *abbr.* = **for your information**

Gg

g

G, g /dʒiː/ *n., pl.* **Gs** *or* **G's** 1 (letter) G, g, *das* 2 **G** (Mus.) G, g, *das;* **G sharp** gis, Gis, *das;* **G flat** ges, Ges, *das*

g. *abbr.* 1 ▸ℹ p. 1702 = **gram[s]** g 2 = **gravity** g

gab /gæb/ (coll.)
A *n.* Gequatsche, *das* (ugs. abwertend); **have the gift of the ~:** redegewandt sein
B *v.i.*, **-bb-** quatschen (salopp)

gabardine /ˈgæbədiːn/ *n.* ▸ **gaberdine**

gabble /ˈgæbl/
A *v.i.* (inarticulately) brabbeln (ugs.); (volubly) schnattern (fig.)
B *v.t.* herunterschnurren (salopp) ‹*Gebet, Gedicht*›; herunterhaspeln (ugs.) ‹*Entschuldigung*›
C *n.* Gebrabbel, *das* (ugs.)

gaberdine /ˈgæbədiːn/ *n.* Gabardine, *der;* **~ [coat/suit]** Gabardinemantel/-anzug, *der*

gable /ˈgeɪbl/ *n.* 1 Giebel, *der* 2 ▸ **gable end**

gabled /ˈgeɪbld/ *adj.* gegiebelt; Giebel‹*dach, -haus*›

ˈgable end *n.* Giebelseite, *die*

Gabon /gəˈbɒn/ *pr. n.* Gabun (*das*)

gad[1] /gæd/ *int.* **[by] ~!** bei Gott!

gad[2] *v.i.*, **-dd-** (coll.) **~ about** *or* **around** herumziehen; sich herumtreiben (ugs. abwertend); **~ about** *or* **around the country** im Land herumreisen

ˈgadabout (coll.) *n.* Herumtreiber, *der*/-treiberin, *die* (ugs. abwertend)

ˈgadfly *n.* Bremse, *die*

gadget /ˈgædʒɪt/ *n.* Gerät, *das;* (larger) Apparat, *der;* **~s** (derog.: knick-knack) [technischer] Krimskrams (ugs.)

gadgetry /ˈgædʒɪtrɪ/ *n., no pl.* [hoch technisierte] Ausstattung

Gael /geɪl/ *n.* Gäle, *der*/Gälin, *die*

Gaelic /ˈgeɪlɪk, ˈgælɪk/ ▸ℹ **p. 1277**
A *adj.* gälisch; *see also* **English A**
B *n.* Gälisch, *das; see also* **English B 1**

> **Gaelic**
>
> Die alte Sprache der Kelten, wie sie noch von einigen Schotten und Iren gesprochen wird. Obgleich es beträchtliche Unterschiede zwischen dem schottischen und dem irischen Gälisch gibt, können die Sprecher einander verstehen. Das schottische Gälisch wird nur von etwa 40 000 Menschen im schottischen Hochland und auf den westschottischen Inseln gesprochen. Irisches Gälisch, das auch *Erse* oder einfach *Irish* genannt wird, erlebte in den letzten 50 Jahren eine bemerkenswerte Wiederbelebung. Es wird heute von vielen gesprochen und an Schulen als offizielle Sprache neben Englisch unterrichtet.

Gaelic ˈcoffee *n.* Irish coffee, *der*

gaff[1] /gæf/
A *n.* 1 (Fishing) Speer, *der;* (stick with iron hook) Gaff, *das* 2 (Naut.) Gaffel, *die*
B *v.t.* mit dem Speer/Gaff erlegen

gaff[2] *n.* (coll.) **blow the ~:** plaudern (**on** über + *Akk.*); **I'm not going to blow the ~:** ich werde dichthalten (ugs.); **stand the ~** (Amer.) durchhalten; **stand the ~ for sth.** etw. büßen

gaffe /gæf/ *n.* Fauxpas, *der;* Fehler, *der;* **make** *or* **commit a ~:** einen Fauxpas begehen; ins Fettnäpfchen treten (ugs. scherzh.)

gaffer /ˈgæfə(r)/ *n.* (coll.) 1 (old fellow) Alte, *der;* **some old ~:** so'n alter Typ (ugs.) 2 (Brit.: boss) Boss *der* (ugs.)

ˈgaffer tape *n., no pl.* Lassoband, *das*

gag /gæg/
A *n.* 1 Knebel, *der;* (Med.) Mundsperrer, *der* 2 (joke) Gag, *der*
B *v.t.*, **-gg-** 1 **~ sb.** jmdn. knebeln; (Med.) jmdm. einen Mundsperrer anlegen; (fig.: silence sb.) jmdn. zum Schweigen bringen 2 (cause to choke or retch) **~ sb.** jmdn. würgen
C *v.i.*, **-gg-** 1 Späße machen; witzeln 2 (choke, retch) würgen

gaga /ˈgɑːgɑː/ *adj.* (coll.) übergeschnappt (ugs.); (senile) senil, (ugs.) verkalkt; **be [a bit] ~:** nicht mehr ganz dicht sein (ugs.); **go ~:** überschnappen (ugs.); (become senile) senil werden, (ugs.) verkalken; **she is really ~ about him** sie ist total vernarrt in ihn (ugs.)

gage (Amer./Naut.) ▸ **gauge**

gaggle /ˈgægl/ *n.* 1 **~ [of geese]** Schar [Gänse], *die* 2 (fig.: disorderly group) Schwarm, *der;* Pulk, *der*

gaiety /ˈgeɪətɪ/ *n., no pl.* 1 Fröhlichkeit, *die* 2 (merrymaking) Festivität, *die;* Vergnügung, *die*

gaily /ˈgeɪlɪ/ *adv.* 1 (merrily) fröhlich 2 (brightly, showily) in leuchtenden Farben ‹*gekleidet, bemalt, geschmückt*›; **~ coloured** farbenfroh 3 (airily, without thinking) fröhlich; unbekümmert

gain /geɪn/
A *n.* 1 Gewinn, *der;* **be to sb.'s ~:** für jmdn. von Vorteil sein; **ill-gotten ~s** unrechtmäßig erworbener Besitz; *see also* **capital gain** 2 (increase) Zunahme, *die* (**in** an + *Dat.*); **a ~ of ten kilograms in weight** eine Gewichtszunahme von zehn Kilogramm; **a ~ in efficiency/value** eine Effektivitäts-/Wertsteigerung 3 (Electronics) Verstärkung, *die*
B *v.t.* 1 (obtain) gewinnen; finden ‹*Zugang, Zutritt*›; sich (*Dat.*) schaffen ‹*Feind*›; erwerben ‹*Wissen, Ruf*›; erlangen ‹*Freiheit, Ruhm*›; erzielen ‹*Vorteil, Punkte*›; verdienen ‹*Lebensunterhalt, Geldsumme*›; erreichen ‹*Ziel*›; **~ possession of sth.** in den Besitz einer Sache (*Gen.*) kommen; **~ nothing** nichts erreichen; **~ time** Zeit gewinnen 2 (win) gewinnen ‹*Preis, Schlacht*›; erringen ‹*Sieg*› 3 (obtain as increase) **~ weight/five pounds [in weight]** zunehmen/fünf Pfund zunehmen; **~ speed** schneller werden 4 (reach) gewinnen (geh.), erreichen ‹*Gipfel, Ufer*› 5 (become fast by) **my watch ~s two minutes a day** meine Uhr geht pro Tag zwei Minuten vor. *See also* **ground**[1] **A 2**; **upper A 1**
C *v.i.* 1 (make a profit) **~ by sth.** von etw. profitieren; bei etw. gewinnen 2 (obtain increase) **~ in influence/prestige** an Einfluss/Prestige gewinnen; **~ in health/speed/wealth/wisdom** gesünder/schneller/reicher/weiser werden; **~ in knowledge** sein Wissen vergrößern; **~ in weight** zunehmen 3 (be improved) gewinnen; **~ by comparison** durch einen Vergleich gewinnen 4 (become fast) ‹*Uhr:*› vorgehen 5 **~ [up]on sb.** (come closer) jmdm. [immer] näher kommen; (increase lead) den Vorsprung zu jmdm. vergrößern

gainful /ˈgeɪnfl/ *adj.* bezahlt; (profitable) Gewinn bringend; **~ employment** Erwerbstätigkeit, *die*

gainfully /ˈgeɪnfəlɪ/ *adv.* **~ employed** erwerbstätig

gainsay /geɪnˈseɪ/ *v.t.*, **gainsaid** /geɪnˈseɪd, geɪnˈsed/ (arch./literary) leugnen

gait /geɪt/ *n.* 1 Gang, *der;* **with a slow ~:** mit langsamen Schritten 2 (of horse) Gangart, *die*

gaiter /ˈgeɪtə(r)/ *n.* 1 Gamasche, *die* 2 (Amer.) ▸ **galosh**

gal /gæl/ *n.* (coll.) Mädchen, *das;* **you're a nice ~:** du bist ein netter Käfer (ugs.)

gal. *abbr.* ▸ℹ p. 1690 = **gallon[s]** gal.; gall.

gala /ˈgɑːlə, ˈgeɪlə/ *n.* 1 (fête) Festveranstaltung, *die; attrib.* Gala‹*abend, -diner, -vorstellung*› 2 (Brit.: sports festival) Sportfest, *das;* **swimming ~:** Schwimmfest, *das*

galactic /gəˈlæktɪk/ *adj.* (of a galaxy) galaktisch; (of the Galaxy) Milchstraßen-

Galahad /ˈgæləhæd/ *n.* edler Ritter

galantine /ˈgælənti:n/ *n.* (Cookery) Galantine, *die*

galaxy /ˈgæləksɪ/ *n.* 1 (Milky Way) **the G~:** die Galaxis (Astron.); die Milchstraße 2 (independent system of stars) Galaxie, *die* 3 (fig.: outstanding group) illustre Schar (geh.)

gale /geɪl/ *n.* 1 Sturm, *der;* **it's blowing a ~ outside** draußen stürmt es *od.* tobt ein Sturm; **~ force** Sturmstärke, *die;* **~ warning** Sturmwarnung, *die* 2 (fig.: outburst) Sturm, *der;* **~s of laughter** Lachsalven *Pl.*

Galicia[1] /gəˈlɪʃə/ *pr. n.* (in Spain) Galicien (*das*)

Galicia[2] *pr. n.* (in SW Poland and W. Russia) Galizien (*das*)

Galilee /ˈgælɪliː/ *pr. n.* Galiläa (*das*); **Sea of ~:** See Genezareth, *der*

gall[1] /gɔːl/ *n.* 1 (Physiol.) Galle, *die* 2 (fig.: bitterness) Bitternis, *die* (geh.); **be ~ and wormwood** [bitter wie] Galle und Wermut sein 3 (impudence) Unverschämtheit, *die;* Frechheit, *die*

gall[2]
A *n.* 1 *no pl.* (annoyance) Ärger, *der* 2 (sore) Schürfwunde, *die*
B *v.t.* wund scheuern; (fig.) (annoy) ärgern; (vex) schmerzen; **be ~ed by sth.** unter etw. (*Dat.*) leiden

gall[3] *n.* (Bot.) Gallapfel, *der*

gallant /ˈgælənt/
A *adj.* 1 (brave) tapfer; (chivalrous) ritterlich 2 (grand, stately) stattlich ‹*Schiff*› 3 /ˈgælənt, gəˈlænt/ (attentive to women, amatory) galant; **say ~ things** Galanterien *od.* Artigkeiten sagen (geh.)
B /ˈgælənt, gəˈlænt/ *n.* (dated: ladies' man) Kavalier, *der* (veralt.)

gallantly /ˈgæləntlɪ/ *adv.* 1 (bravely) tapfer 2 (grandly) stattlich 3 /ˈgæləntlɪ, gəˈlæntlɪ/ (with courtesy) galant

gallantry /ˈgæləntrɪ/ *n.* 1 (bravery) Tapferkeit, *die* 2 (courtliness, polite act or speech) Galanterie, *die* (geh.)

ˈgall bladder *n.* ▸ℹ **p. 951** (Anat.) Gallenblase, *die*

galleon /ˈgælɪən/ *n.* (Hist.) Galeone, *die*

gallery /ˈgælərɪ/ *n.* 1 (Archit.) Galerie, *die; see also* **shooting gallery** 2 (Theatre) dritter Rang; Olymp, *der* (ugs. scherzh.); (esp. Golf: group of spectators) Zuschauer *Pl.;* **play to the ~** (fig.) für die Galerie spielen 3 (art ~) (building) Galerie, *die;* (room) Ausstellungsraum, *der* 4 (Mining) Stollen, *der*

'gallery tray *n.* Galerietablett, *das*

galley /'gælɪ/ *n.* 1 (Hist.) Galeere, *die* 2 (kitchen) (of ship) Kombüse, *die;* (of aircraft) Bordküche, *die* 3 (Printing) Satzschiff, *das;* ~ **[proof]** [Druck]fahne, *die*

'galley slave *n.* Galeerensklave, *der*

Gallic /'gælɪk/ *adj.* 1 (of the Gauls) gallisch 2 (often joc.: French) französisch; gallisch ‹*Witz*›

Gallicism /'gælɪsɪzm/ *n.* 1 (word or idiom) Gallizismus, *der* 2 (characteristic) französische Eigenart

galling /'gɔːlɪŋ/ *adj.* äußerst unangenehm

gallivant /gælɪ'vænt/ *v.i.* (coll.) herumziehen (ugs.); ~ **about** *or* **around the country/Europe** im Lande/in Europa herumziehen

'gall nut *n.* (Bot.) Gallapfel, *der*

gallon /'gælən/ *n.* ▸ⓘ **p. 1690** Gallone, *die;* **[imperial]** ~ (Brit.) britische Gallone (4,546 l); **wine** ~ (Brit.), ~ (Amer.) amerikanische Gallone (3,785 l); **drink ~s of water** *etc.* (fig. coll.) literweise *od.* eimerweise Wasser *usw.* trinken

galloon /gə'luːn/ *n.* Galone, *die;* Galon, *der*

gallop /'gæləp/

A *n.* 1 Galopp, *der;* **at a ~/at full ~:** im Galopp/in vollem Galopp 2 (ride) Galoppritt, *der* 3 (track) Galopp[renn]bahn, *die*

B *v.i.* 1 ‹*Pferd, Reiter:*› galoppieren 2 (fig.) ~ **through** im Galopp (ugs.) durchlesen ‹*Buch*›; rasch herunterspielen ‹*Musikstück*›; im Galopp (ugs.) erledigen ‹*Arbeit*›; **~ing consumption/inflation** (fig.) galoppierende Schwindsucht/Inflation

gallows /'gæləʊz/ *n. sing.* Galgen, *der;* **be sent to the ~:** zum [Tod am] Galgen verurteilt werden

gallows: ~-bird *n.* Galgenvogel, *der* (ugs. abwertend); ~ **humour** *n.* Galgenhumor, *der*

'gallstone *n.* ▸ⓘ **p. 1231** (Med.) Gallenstein, *der*

Gallup poll ® /'gæləp pəʊl/ *n.* Meinungsumfrage, *die*

galop /'gæləp/ *n.* (Mus.) Galopp, *der*

galore /gə'lɔː(r)/ *adv.* im Überfluss; in Hülle und Fülle

galosh /gə'lɒʃ/ *n.* [Gummi]überschuh, *der;* [Gummi]galosche, *die*

galumph /gə'lʌmf/ *v.i.* (coll.) 1 (in triumph) stolzieren 2 (noisily, clumsily) stapfen

galvanic /gæl'vænɪk/ *adj.* galvanisch; (fig.) (sudden, remarkable) elektrisierend; Blitz‹*wirkung, -reaktion*›

galvanize (galvanise) /'gælvənaɪz/ *v.t.* 1 (fig.: rouse) wachrütteln ‹*Volk, Partei usw.*›; ~ **sb. into action/activity** jmdn. veranlassen, sofort aktiv zu werden; ~ **sb. into life** jmdn. aufrütteln 2 (coat with zinc) verzinken

Gambia /'gæmbɪə/ *pr. n.* **[the] ~:** Gambia (*das*)

gambit /'gæmbɪt/ *n.* (Chess) Gambit, *das;* (fig.: trick, device) Schachzug, *der;* **[opening] ~** (fig.) einleitender Schachzug; (in a conversation) einleitende Bemerkung; **conversational ~** (fig.) Gesprächseinstieg *od.* -aufhänger, *der*

gamble /'gæmbl/

A *v.i.* 1 [um Geld] spielen; ~ **at cards/on horses** um Geld Karten spielen/auf Pferde wetten 2 (fig.) spekulieren; ~ **on the Stock Exchange/in oil shares** an der Börse/in Öl[aktien] spekulieren; ~ **on sth.** sich auf etw. (*Akk.*) verlassen; auf etw. (*Akk.*) spekulieren (ugs.)

B *v.t.* 1 verspielen; ~ **money on horses** Geld für Pferdewetten einsetzen 2 (fig.) riskieren, aufs Spiel setzen ‹*Vermögen*›

C *n.* (lit. or fig.) Glücksspiel, *das;* **he likes the occasional ~:** er spielt gelegentlich ganz gern; **take a ~:** ein Wagnis eingehen *od.* auf sich (*Akk.*) nehmen

(Phrasal verb)

• ~ **a'way** *v.t.* verspielen ‹*Vermögen, Geld, Geschäft, Haus*›; (on the Stock Exchange) verspekulieren ‹*Vermögen*›

gambler /'gæmblə(r)/ *n.* Glücksspieler, *der;* (risk-taker) Glücksritter, *der;* **born ~:** Spieler- *od.* Abenteurernatur, *die*

gambling /'gæmblɪŋ/ *n.* Spiel[en], *das;* Glücksspiel, *das;* (on horses, dogs) Wetten, *das*

gambling: ~ debts *n. pl.* Spielschulden *Pl.;* ~ **den** *n.* Spielhölle, *die* (abwertend); ~ **machine** *n.* Spielautomat, *der*

gambol /'gæmbl/

A *n.* **~[s]** Herumspringen, *das*

B *v.i.,* (Brit.) **-ll-** ‹*Kind, Lamm:*› herumspringen

game[1] /geɪm/

A *n.* 1 (form of contest) Spiel, *das;* (contest) (with ball) Spiel, *das;* (at [table] tennis, chess, cards, billiards, cricket) Partie, *die;* **have** *or* **play a ~ of tennis/chess** *etc.* **[with sb.]** eine Partie Tennis/Schach *usw.* [mit jmdm.] spielen; **give sb. a ~ of tennis/chess** *etc.* eine Partie Tennis/Schach *usw.* mit jmdm. spielen; **have** *or* **play a ~ of football [with sb.]** Fußball [mit jmdm.] spielen; **play a good/poor ~ [of cards** *etc.***]** gut/schlecht [Karten *usw.*] spielen; ein guter [Karten- *usw.*]spieler sein; **be back in/get back into the ~ again** (have a chance of winning) wieder Gewinnchancen haben/bekommen; **it's all in the ~:** das ist alles dabei möglich; das kann alles dazugehören; **be on/off one's ~:** gut in Form/nicht in Form sein; **beat sb. at his own ~** (fig.) jmdn. mit seinen eigenen Waffen schlagen (geh.); **play the ~** (fig.) sich an die Spielregeln halten (fig.); **I'll show her that two can play [at] that ~** *or* **that it's a ~ that two can play** (fig.) was sie kann, kann ich auch; *see also* **name A 1** 2 (fig.: scheme, undertaking) Vorhaben, *das;* **sb.'s ~ is to do sth.** jmd. führt etw. im Schilde; (policy) jmds. Taktik ist es, etw. zu tun; **play a [double] ~:** ein [falsches] Spiel treiben; **play sb.'s ~:** jmdm. in die Hände arbeiten; (for one's own benefit) jmds. Spiel mitspielen; **the ~ is up** (coll.) das Spiel ist aus; **give the ~ away** alles verraten; **so that's your little ~!** ach, das führst du im Schilde!; **what's his ~?** (coll.) was hat er vor?; **what's the ~?** (coll.) was soll das? 3 (business, activity) Gewerbe, *das;* Branche, *die;* **the ~ of politics** die Politik; **the publishing/newspaper ~:** das Verlags-/Zeitungs- *od.* Pressewesen; **be new to the ~** (fig.) neu im Geschäft sein (auch fig. ugs.); **go [out]/be on the ~** (Brit. coll.) ‹*Prostituierte:*› anschaffen *od.* auf die Anschaffe gehen (salopp); *see also* **candle A 1** 4 (diversion) Spiel, *das;* (piece of fun) Scherz, *der;* Spaß, *der;* **don't play ~s with me** versuch nicht, mich auf den Arm zu nehmen (ugs.); **make ~ of sb./sth.** (dated) sich über jmdn./etw. lustig machen; jmdn./etw. zum Gelächter machen (geh. veralt.) 5 *in pl.* (athletic contests) Spiele *Pl.;* (in school) (sports) Schulsport, *der;* (athletics) Leichtathletik, *die;* **good at ~s** gut im Sport 6 (portion of play) Spiel, *das;* (winning score) **21 points is ~:** zum Gewinn eines Spiels sind 21 Punkte erforderlich; **two ~s all** zwei beide; zwei zu zwei; ~ **to Graf** (Tennis) Spiel Graf; **~, set, and match** (Tennis) Spiel, Satz und Sieg; (fig.: complete and decisive victory) voller Erfolg (**to** für); Sieg auf der ganzen Linie (**to** für) 7 *no pl.* (Hunting, Cookery) Wild, *das;* **fair ~:** jagdbares Wild; (fig.) Freiwild, *das;* **easy ~** (fig. coll.) leichte Beute; **big ~:** Großwild, *das*

B *v.i.* [um Geld] spielen

game[2] *adj.* mutig; ~ **spirit/manner** Unverzagtheit, *die;* **remain ~:** sich nicht entmutigen lassen; **be ~ to do sth.** (be willing) bereit sein, etw. zu tun; **are you ~?** machst du mit?; **be ~ for sth./anything** zu etw./allem bereit sein

game[3] *adj.* (crippled) lahm ‹*Arm, Bein*›

game: ~ bag *n.* Tragetasche, *die;* ~ **bird** *n.* **the pheasant is a ~ bird** Fasane sind Federwild; ~ **birds** Federwild, *das;* **~cock** *n.* Kampfhahn, *der;* **~keeper** *n.* ▸ⓘ **p. 1260** Wildheger, *der*

gamely /'geɪmlɪ/ *adv.* mutig ‹*kämpfen*›

game: ~ park *n.* Wildreservat, *das;* ~ **plan** *n.* (Sport) Taktik, *die;* (fig.) Strategie, *die;* ~ **'point** *n.* (Sport) Spielpunkt, *der;* ~ **reserve** *n.* Wildreservat, *das*

'games console *n.* Spielkonsole, *die*

game show *n.* Gameshow, *die;* Spielshow, *die*

gamesmanship /'geɪmzmənʃɪp/ *n., no pl.* Gerissen- *od.* Gewieftheit (ugs.) beim Spiel

games: ~ room *n.* Spieleraum, *der;* ~ **software** *n., no pl.* Spielesoftware, *die*

gamete /'gæmiːt/ *n.* (Biol.) Gamet, *der;* Geschlechtszelle, *die*

'game warden *n.* ▸ⓘ **p. 1260** Wildhüter, *der*

gamin /'gæmɪn, 'gæmæ̃/ *n.* Gamin, *der* (veralt.); Gassenjunge, *der* (abwertend)

gamine /gə'miːn/ *n.* (small mischievous young woman) schelmisches Mädchen; kesse Motte (salopp)

gaming/'geɪmɪŋ/: ~ **house** *n.* Spielbank, *die;* ~ **machine** *n.* Münzspielgerät, *das;* ~ **table** *n.* Spieltisch, *der*

gamma /'gæmə/ *n.* 1 (letter) Gamma, *das* 2 (Sch., Univ.: mark) Drei, *die*

gamma: ~ radiation *n.* (Phys.) Gammastrahlung, *die;* ~ **ray** *n.* (Phys.) Gammastrahl, *der*

gammon /'gæmən/ *n.* (ham cured like bacon) Räucherschinken, *der*

gammy /'gæmɪ/ *adj.* (coll.) lahm ‹*Arm, Bein, Fuß*›

gamut /'gæmət/ *n.* 1 (Mus.) (series of notes, compass) Tonumfang, *der;* (recognized scale) Skala, *die;* Tonleiter, *die* 2 (fig.: range) Skala, *die;* **run the whole ~ of ...:** die ganze Skala von ... durchgehen

gamy /'geɪmɪ/ *adj.* 1 (having flavour or scent of game) nach Wild ‹*schmecken*›; ~ **taste** Wildgeschmack, *der* 2 (spirited) mutig 3 (Amer.: scandalous) pikant

gander /'gændə(r)/ *n.* 1 (Ornith.) Gänserich, *der;* **what's sauce for the goose is sauce for the ~** (prov.) was dem einen recht ist, ist dem andern billig (Spr.) 2 (coll.: look, glance) Blick, *der;* **take** *or* **have a ~ at/round sth.** sich (*Dat.*) etw. ansehen

gang[1] /gæŋ/

A *n.* 1 (of workmen, slaves, prisoners) Trupp, *der* 2 (of criminals) Bande, *die;* Gang, *die;* ~ **of thieves/criminals/terrorists** Diebes-/Verbrecher-/Terroristenbande, *die* 3 (coll.: band causing any kind of disapproval) Gang, *die;* Bande, *die* (abwertend, oft scherzh.) 4 (coll.: group of friends etc.) Haufen, *der;* Bande, *die* (scherzh.)

B *v.i.* 1 ~ **up [with sb.]** (join) sich [mit jmdm.] zusammentun (ugs.) 2 ~ **up against** *or* **on** (coll.: combine against) sich verbünden *od.* zusammenschließen gegen

gang[2] *v.i.* (Scot.: go) gehen; ~ **agley** /ə'gleɪ/ ‹*Plan:*› scheitern

'gang-bang *n.* (sl.) Bandenfick, *der* (derb)

ganger /'gæŋə(r)/ *n.* (Brit.) Vorarbeiter, *der*

gangland:/'gæŋlænd/ ~ **'boss** *n.* Gangsterboss, *der;* ~ **'murder** *n.* Mord in der Unterwelt

gangling /'gæŋglɪŋ/ *adj.* schlaksig (ugs.) ‹*Person, Gang, Gestalt*›

ganglion /'gæŋglɪən/ *n., pl.* **ganglia** /'gæŋglɪə/ *or* **~s** (Anat.) Ganglion, *das* (fachspr.); Nervenknoten, *der*

gangly /'gæŋglɪ/ ▸**gangling**

gang: ~master *n.* Arbeitskräfteverleiher *der;* **~plank** *n.* (Naut.) Laufplanke, *die;* ~ **rape** *n.* Vergewaltigung durch eine Gruppe

gangrene /'gæŋgriːn/ *n.* 1 ▸ⓘ **p. 1231** (Med.) Gangrän, *die od. fachspr. das;* [Faul]brand, *der* 2 (fig.: corruption) Krebsgeschwür, *das* (fig.)

gangrenous /'gæŋgrɪnəs/ *adj.* (Med.) gangränös (fachspr.); brandig

gangsta rap /'gæŋstə ræp/ *n.* Gangsta-Rap, *der*

gangster /'gæŋstə(r)/ *n.* Gangster, *der* (*abwertend*); *attrib.* Gangster‹*film*›

'gang warfare *n.* Bandenkrieg, *der*

'gangway

A *n.* 1 (Naut.: for boarding ship) Gangway, *die* 2 (Brit.: between rows of seats) Gang, *der;* **leave a ~** (fig.) einen Durchgang freilassen

B *int.* Platz

ganja /'gændʒə/ *n.* (Bot.) Indischer Hanf

gannet /'gænɪt/ *n.* 1 (Ornith.) Tölpel, *der* 2 (coll.: greedy person) Raffke, *der* (salopp abwertend)

gantlet /'gæntlɪt/ (Amer.) ▸**gauntlet[2]**

g

gantry /ˈgæntrɪ/ *n.* (crane) Portal, *das;* (on road) Schilderbrücke, *die;* (Railw.) Signalbrücke, *die;* (Astronaut.) Startrampe, *die*

Gantt chart /ˈgænt tʃɑːt/ *n.* (Managem.) Gantt-Diagramm, *das*

gaol /dʒeɪl/ (Brit. in official use) ▸**jail A, B**

gaoler /ˈdʒeɪlə(r)/ (Brit. in official use) ▸**jailer**

gap /gæp/ *n.* 1 Lücke, *die;* (Motor Veh.: in sparking plug etc.) Elektrodenabstand, *der;* **a ~ in the curtains** ein Spalt im Vorhang 2 (Geog.: gorge, pass) Joch, *das* 3 (fig.: contrast, divergence in views etc.) Kluft, *die;* **that is a ~ in his education/knowledge** er hat hier eine Bildungs-/Wissenslücke; **fill a ~:** eine Lücke füllen *od.* schließen; **stop** *or* **close** *or* **bridge a ~:** eine Kluft überbrücken *od.* überwinden; **close the ~ [on sb.]** den Abstand [zu jmdm.] aufholen

gape /geɪp/

A *v.i.* 1 (open mouth) den Mund aufsperren; ([be] open wide) ‹*Schnabel, Mund:*› aufgesperrt sein; ‹*Loch, Abgrund, Wunde:*› klaffen; **gaping** klaffend ‹*Wunde*›; gähnend ‹*Loch*›; **~ at the seams** ‹*Kleid:*› in den Nähten aufgeplatzt sein 2 (stare) Mund und Nase aufsperren (ugs.); **~ at sb./sth.** jmdn./etw. mit offenem Mund anstarren *od.* anstieren; **what are you gaping at?** worauf stierst du so?; **gaping** erstaunt starrend ‹*Person*›

B *n.* stierer Blick

gappy /ˈgæpɪ/ *adj.* 1 (full of gaps) lückenhaft ‹*Gebiss*›; ‹*Zähne*› mit Lücken; schütter ‹*Hecke*›; **a ~ smile** ein Lächeln, das ein lückenhaftes Gebiss entblößt 2 (deficient, lacking) lückenhaft

gap-toothed /ˈgæptuːθt/ *adj.* ‹*Person*› mit Zahnlücken

ˈgap year *n.* (Brit.) Zwischenjahr, *das*

gar /gɑː(r)/ ▸**garfish**

garage /ˈgærɑːʒ, ˈgærɪdʒ/

A *n.* 1 (for parking) Garage, *die;* **bus ~:** Busdepot, *das* 2 (for selling petrol) Tankstelle, *die;* (for repairing cars) [Kfz-]Werkstatt, *die;* (for selling cars) Autohandlung, *die*

B *v.t.* in die Garage stellen ‹*Fahrzeug*›; **be kept ~d** in der Garage stehen; **where do you ~ your car?** wo parken Sie Ihr Auto?

garage: ~ ˈrock *n., no pl.* Garagenrock, *der;* **~ sale** *n.* (Amer.) Garagenverkauf, *der;* **~ ˈstart-up** *n.* Garagenfirma, *die*

garaging /ˈgærɑːdʒɪŋ/ *n., no pl.* Garagenplätze *Pl.;* (for one car) Garagenplatz, *der*

garb /gɑːb/

A *n.* Tracht, *die;* **strange ~:** seltsame Kleidung; **official ~:** Amtstracht, *die*

B *v.t.* kleiden; **~ed in white robes** in Weiß gekleidet

garbage /ˈgɑːbɪdʒ/ *n.* 1 (esp. Amer.) Abfall, *der;* Müll, *der* 2 (fig.: foul or rubbishy literature) Schund, *der* 3 (coll.: nonsense) Quatsch, *der* (salopp); **~ in, ~ out** (Computing coll.) Mist rein, Mist raus (ugs.)

garbage: ~ can (Amer.) ▸**dustbin**; **~ collection** *n.* (Amer.) Müllabfuhr, *die;* **~ collector** (Amer.) ▸**dustman**; **~ disˈposal unit**, **~ disposer** *ns.* Abfallvernichter, *der;* Müllwolf, *der;* **~ truck** *n.* (Amer.) Müllwagen, *der*

garble /ˈgɑːbl/ *v.t.* 1 verstümmeln, entstellen ‹*Bericht, Korrespondenz, Tatsache*› 2 (confuse) durcheinander bringen; durcheinander werfen; **get ~d** durcheinander geraten

garden /ˈgɑːdn/

A *n.* 1 Garten, *der;* **everything in the ~ is lovely** (fig. coll.) es ist alles in Butter (ugs.); **lead sb. up the ~ [path]** (fig. coll.) jmdn. an der Nase herumführen (ugs.); **tea ~:** Gartencafé, *das;* **a small amount of ~:** ein kleines Stück Garten 2 *usu. in pl., with name prefixed* (Brit.) (park) -park, *der;* (street, square) -garten, *der* 3 (land for raising crops) Plantage, *die* 4 (Amer.: large public hall) Halle, *die* 5 *attrib.* (Bot.: cultivated) Garten‹*pflanze, -gemüse*›. *See also* **kitchen garden**; **market garden**; **zoological garden[s]**

B *v.i.* gärtnern

garden: ~ centre *n.* Gartencenter, *das;* **~ chair** *n.* Gartenstuhl, *der;* **~ ˈcity** *n.* Gartenstadt, *die*

gardener /ˈgɑːdnə(r)/ *n.* ▸❶ **p. 1260** Gärtner, *der*/Gärtnerin, *die*

garden: ~ ˈfork *n.* Grab[e]gabel, *die;* **~-fresh** *adj.* gartenfrisch; **~ ˈgnome** *n.* Gartenzwerg, *der;* **~ ˈhose** *n.* Gartenschlauch, *der*

gardenia /gɑːˈdiːnɪə/ *n.* (Bot.) 1 (tree, shrub) Gardenie, *die* 2 (flower) Gardenienblüte, *die*

gardening /ˈgɑːdnɪŋ/ *n.* Gartenarbeit, *die; attrib.* Garten‹*gerät, -buch, -handschuh*›; **he likes ~:** er gärtnert gern

garden: ~ party *n.* Gartenfest, *das;* **~ ˈshears** *n. pl.* Heckenschere, *die;* **~ ˈshed** *n.* Geräteschuppen, *der;* **~ ˈsuburb** *n.* (Brit.) Gartenstadt, *die;* **~ ˈwaste** *n.* Gartenabfälle *Pl.;* Gartenabfall, *der*

garfish /ˈgɑːfɪʃ/ *n., pl. same* (Zool.) (needlefish) Hornhecht, *der;* (gar) Knochenhecht, *der;* (halfbeak) Halbschnabelhecht, *der*

gargantuan /gɑːˈgæntjʊən/ *adj.* gigantisch; riesig ‹*Person, Hunger, Gelächter*›; Riesen‹*größe, -hunger, -gebrüll*›

gargle /ˈgɑːgl/

A *v.i.* gurgeln

B *n.* 1 (liquid) Gurgelmittel, *das;* Gargarisma, *das* (fachspr.) 2 (act) Gurgeln, *das;* **have a ~:** gurgeln

gargoyle /ˈgɑːgɔɪl/ *n.* (Archit.) Wasserspeier, *der*

garish /ˈgeərɪʃ/ *adj.* 1 (bright, showy) grell ‹*Farbe, Licht, Beleuchtung*›; knallbunt ‹*Kleidung, Verzierung*›; protzig (abwertend) ‹*Lebensstil*› 2 (over-decorated) protzig (abwertend) ‹*Gebäude, Baustil, Aussehen*›; grellbunt, knallbunt ‹*Muster*›

garishly /ˈgeərɪʃlɪ/ *adv.* grell ‹*beleuchten*›; protzig (abwertend) ‹*einrichten*›; grellbunt, knallbunt ‹*kleiden, tapezieren*›; grell-, knall‹*bunt*›

garland /ˈgɑːlənd/

A *n.* (wreath of flowers etc.; Art: festoon) Girlande, *die;* (of laurel) Kranz, *der;* **~ of flowers/laurel/oak leaves** Blumen-/Lorbeer-/Eichenkranz, *der*

B *v.t.* bekränzen

garlic /ˈgɑːlɪk/ *n.* Knoblauch, *der*

garlicky /ˈgɑːlɪkɪ/ *adj.* nach Knoblauch riechend ‹*Atem*›; nach Knoblauch ‹*riechen, schmecken*›

garment /ˈgɑːmənt/ *n.* 1 Kleidungsstück, *das; in pl.* (clothes) Kleidung, *die;* Kleider *Pl.* 2 (fig.: covering) Gewand, *das* (geh.)

garner /ˈgɑːnə(r)/ *v.t.* speichern ‹*Getreide*›; (fig.: collect) sammeln ‹*Kenntnisse usw.*›

garnet /ˈgɑːnɪt/ *n.* (Min.) Granat, *der*

garnish /ˈgɑːnɪʃ/

A *v.t.* (lit. or fig.) garnieren

B *n.* (Cookery) Garnierung, *die*

garotte ▸**garrotte**

garret /ˈgærɪt/ *n.* (room on top floor) Dachkammer, *die;* Mansarde, *die;* (attic) [Dach]boden, *der*

garrison /ˈgærɪsn/

A *n.* Garnison, *die*

B *v.t.* (furnish with ~) in Garnison legen; garnisonieren (fachspr.); (occupy as ~) mit einer Garnison belegen; garnisonieren (fachspr.)

garrison: ~ duty *n.* Garnison[s]dienst, *der;* **~ town** *n.* Garnison[s]stadt, *die*

garrotte /gəˈrɒt/ *v.t.* garrottieren

garrulous /ˈgærʊləs/ *adj.* 1 (talkative) gesprächig; geschwätzig 2 (wordy) wortreich; weitschweifig, langatmig ‹*Rede, Kommentar*›

garrulously /ˈgærʊləslɪ/ *adv.* geschwätzig

garter /ˈgɑːtə(r)/ *n.* 1 Strumpfband, *das* 2 **the [Order of the] G~** (Brit.) der Hosenbandorden 3 (Amer.: suspender) Sockenhalter, *der*

ˈgarter stitch *n.* Kraus[gestrick], *das;* **knit in ~:** kraus rechts stricken

gas /gæs/

A *n., pl.* **~es** /ˈgæsɪz/ 1 Gas, *das;* **natural ~:** Erdgas, *das;* **cook by** *or* **with ~:** mit Gas kochen; **on a low/high ~:** auf kleiner/großer Flamme 2 (Amer. coll.: petrol) Benzin, *das;* **step on the ~:** Gas geben; (fig.: hurry) einen Zahn zulegen (salopp) 3 (anaesthetic) Narkotikum, *das;* Lachgas, *das* 4 (for lighting) Leuchtgas, *das* 5 (to fill balloon) [Trag]gas, *das* 6 (Mining) Grubengas, *das* 7 (coll.: idle talk) leeres Geschwätz (abwertend); Blabla, *das* (salopp) 8 (coll.: sb./sth. attractive and impressive) Wucht, *die* (salopp)

B *v.t.*, **-ss-** mit Gas vergiften; (in Third Reich) vergasen; **~ oneself** den Gashahn aufdrehen (ugs. verhüll.)

C *v.i.*, **-ss-** (coll.) schwatzen (abwertend), schwafeln (ugs. abwertend) (**about** von)

gas: ~bag *n.* 1 Gaszelle, *die;* 2 (coll. derog.: talker) Schwätzer, *der*/Schwätzerin, *die* (abwertend); Schwafler, *der*/Schwaflerin, *die* (ugs. abwertend); **~ chamber** *n.* Gaskammer, *die;* **~-cooled** *adj.* gasgekühlt; **~ cylinder** *n.* Gasflasche, *die*

gaseous /ˈgæsɪəs, ˈgeɪsɪəs/ *adj.* gasförmig

gas: ~ ˈfire *n.* Gasofen, *der;* **~-fired** /ˈgæsfaɪəd/ *adj.* mit Gas betrieben; Gas‹*boiler, -ofen usw.*›; **~ fitter** *n.* Gasinstallateur, *der*

gash /gæʃ/

A *n.* (wound) Schnittwunde, *die;* (cleft) [klaffende] Spalte; (in sack etc.) Schlitz, *der*

B *v.t.* eine Schnittwunde beibringen (+ *Dat.*); aufritzen ‹*Haut*›; aufschlitzen ‹*Sack*›; **~ one's finger/knee** sich (*Dat. od. Akk.*) in den Finger schneiden/sich (*Dat.*) das Knie aufschlagen

gas: ~ heater *n.* Gasofen, *der;* **~holder** *n.* Gasometer, *der;* Gasbehälter, *der;* **~ jet** *n.* Gasflamme, *die;* (burner) Gasbrenner, *der*

gasket /ˈgæskɪt/ *n.* 1 (sheet, ring) Dichtung, *die* 2 (packing) Packung, *die*

gas: ~ lamp *n.* Gaslampe, *die;* (in street etc.) Gaslaterne, *die;* **~light** *n.* 1 ▸**~ lamp**; 2 *no pl.* (illumination) Gaslicht, *das;* Gasbeleuchtung, *die;* **~ lighter** *n.* 1 [Gas]anzünder, *der;* 2 (cigarette lighter) Gasfeuerzeug, *das;* **~ main** *n.* Hauptgasleitung, *die;* **~man** *n.* ▸❶ **p. 1260** (fitter) Gasinstallateur, *der;* (meter reader, collector) Gasableser, *der;* Gasmann, *der* (ugs.); **~-mantle** *n.* Glühstrumpf, *der;* **~ mark** *n.* Stufe, *die;* **~ mark 4** Gas Stufe 4; **~ mask** *n.* Gasmaske, *die;* **~ meter** *n.* Gaszähler, *der*

gasoline (**gasolene**)/ˈgæsəliːn/ *n.* (Amer.) Benzin, *das*

gasometer /gæˈsɒmɪtə(r)/ *n.* Gasometer, *der*

ˈgas oven *n.* 1 Gasherd, *der* 2 ▸**gas chamber**

gasp /gɑːsp/

A *v.i.* nach Luft schnappen (**with** vor); **make sb. ~** (fig.) jmdm. den Atem nehmen; **leave sb. ~ing [with sth.]** jmdm. [vor etw.] den Atem verschlagen *od.* rauben; **he was ~ing for air** *or* **breath/under the heavy load** er rang nach Luft/keuchte unter der schweren Last

B *v.t.* **~ out** hervorstoßen ‹*Bitte, Worte*›; **~ [one's] life away, ~ [one's] breath away** sein Leben aushauchen (geh.)

C *n.* Keuchen, *das;* **give a ~ of fear/surprise** vor Furcht/Überraschung die Luft einziehen; **she gave a ~ of joy** es verschlug ihr vor Freude den Atem; **be at one's last ~:** in den letzten Zügen liegen (ugs.); **sth. is at its last ~:** etw. tut's nicht mehr lange (ugs.); **fight** *etc.* **to the last ~** (fig.) bis zum letzten Atemzug kämpfen *usw.*

gas: ~ pipe *n.* Gasleitung, *die;* **~ pipeline** *n.* Gaspipeline, *die;* **~ pistol** *n.* Gasanzünder, *der;* **~ poker** *n.* Gasanzünder, *der* (*für Kohle*); **~-powered** *adj.* gasbetrieben; **~-powered boiler/central heating** Gaskocher, *der*/Gasheizung, *die;* **~-proof** *adj.* gasdicht; **~ ring** *n.* Gasbrenner, *der;* **~ station** *n.* (Amer.) Tankstelle, *die;* **~ stove** *n.* 1 Gasherd, *der;* 2 (portable) Gaskocher, *der*

gassy /ˈgæsɪ/ *adj.* 1 gasig; (containing gas) gashaltig 2 (fizzy) sprudelnd; schäumend ‹*Bier*›; **be ~:** sprudeln

gas: ~ tank *n.* 1 Gastank, *der;* 2 (Amer.: petrol tank) Benzintank, *der;* **~ tap** *n.* Gashahn, *der;* **~-tight** *adj.* gasdicht

gastric /ˈgæstrɪk/ *adj.* gastrisch (fachspr.); Magen‹*beschwerden, -wand, -säfte usw.*›

gastric: ~ ˈflu (coll.), **~ influˈenza** *ns.* ▸❶ **p. 1231** Darmgrippe, *die;* **~ ˈulcer** *n.* ▸❶ **p. 1231** Magengeschwür, *das*

gastritis /ˈgæˈstraɪtɪs/ *n.* ▸❶ **p. 1231** (Med.) Magenschleimhautentzündung, *die;* Gastritis, *die* (fachspr.)

gastro-enteritis /gæstrəʊentəˈraɪtɪs/ *n.* ▸❶ **p. 1231** (Med.) Gastroenteritis, *die* (fachspr.);

Magen-Darm-Katarrh, *der*

gastronomic /gæstrəˈnɒmɪk/ *adj.* gastronomisch; kulinarisch ‹*Genüsse*›

gastronomy /gæˈstrɒnəmɪ/ *n.* Gastronomie, *die;* **French ~:** französische Küche

gastropod /ˈgæstrəpɒd/ *n.* (Zool.) Gastropode, *der*

gas: ~ turbine *n.* Gasturbine, *die;* **~works** *n. sing., pl. same* Gaswerk, *das*

gate /geɪt/ *n.* **1** (lit. or fig.) Tor, *das;* (barrier) Sperre, *die;* (of animal pen) Gatter, *das;* (in garden fence) [Garten]pforte, *die;* (of lift) [Scheren]gitter, *das;* (Railw.: of level crossing) [Bahn]schranke, *die;* (in airport) Flugsteig, *der;* **the ~s of heaven/hell** die Himmelspforte (dichter.)/die Pforten der Hölle (geh.); **pay at the ~:** am Eingang bezahlen **2** (Sport) (number to see match) Besucher[zahl], *die;* (*money*) ▸**gate money** **3** (Amer. coll.: dismissal) **give sb. the ~:** jmdn. vor die Tür setzen (ugs.); jmdn. rausschmeißen (salopp); **get the ~:** vor die Tür gesetzt werden (ugs.); rausgeschmissen werden (salopp) **4** (of gears in vehicle) Kulisse, *die* **5** (Cinemat.) Bildfenster, *das*

gateau /ˈgætəʊ/ *n., pl.* **~s** *or* **~x** /ˈgætəʊz/ Torte, *die*

gate: ~crash **A** *v.t.* ohne Einladung einfach hingehen zu; **B** *v.i.* ohne Einladung einfach hingehen; **~crasher** *n.* Eindringling, *der;* (at party) ungeladener Gast; **~house** *n.* Torhaus, *das;* **~keeper** *n.* (attendant) Torwächter, *der;* Pförtner, *der;* **~leg[ged]** /ˈgeɪtleg(d)/ *adj.* **~leg[ged] table** Klapptisch, *der;* **~man** ▸**~keeper**; **~ money** *n.* Eintrittsgelder *Pl.;* Einnahmen *Pl.;* **~post** *n.* Torpfosten, *der;* **between you and me and the ~post** (coll.) unter uns (*Dat.*) gesagt; **~way** *n.* **1** (gate) Tor, *das;* **2** (Archit.) (structure) Torbau, *der;* (frame) Torbogen, *der;* **3** (fig.) Tor, *das* (**to** zu); **4** (Computing) **[Internet] ~:** Gateway, *das*

gather /ˈgæðə(r)/

A *v.t.* **1** (bring together) sammeln; zusammentragen ‹*Informationen*›; pflücken ‹*Obst, Blumen*›; **~ sth. [together]** etw. zusammensuchen *od.* -sammeln; **~ [in] potatoes/the harvest** Kartoffeln ernten/die Ernte einbringen **2** (infer, deduce) schließen (**from** aus); **~ from sb. that ...:** von jmdm. erfahren, dass ...; **I ~ he's doing a good job** ich höre, dass er gute Arbeit leistet; **not much can be ~ed from the facts/his statement** aus den Fakten/seiner Erklärung lässt sich nicht viel entnehmen; **as far as I can ~:** soweit ich weiß; **as you will have ~ed** wie Sie sicherlich vermutet haben **3** **it is just ~ing dust** das ist bloß ein Staubfänger; **~ speed/force/strength** schneller/stärker werden/zu Kräften kommen **4** (summon up) **~ [together]** zusammennehmen ‹*Kräfte, Mut*›; **~ oneself [together]** sich zusammennehmen; **~ one's thoughts** seine Gedanken ordnen; **~ one's breath/strength** [wieder] zu Atem kommen/Kräfte sammeln **5** (draw) **~ sb. into one's arms** jmdn. in die Arme nehmen *od.* (geh.) schließen; **she ~ed her shawl round her neck** sie schlang den Schal um den Hals; **~ oneself for a jump** sich zum Sprung sammeln **6** (Sewing) ankrausen

B *v.i.* **1** sich versammeln; ‹*Wolken:*› sich zusammenziehen; ‹*Staub:*› sich ansammeln; ‹*Schweißperlen:*› sich sammeln; **be ~ed [together]** versammelt sein; **~ round** zusammenkommen; **~ round sb./sth.** sich um jmdn./etw. versammeln; **tears/beads of perspiration ~ed in her eyes/on her forehead** Tränen/Schweißperlen traten ihr in die Augen/auf die Stirn **2** (increase) zunehmen; **~ing dangers** wachsende Gefahren; **darkness was ~ing round him** es wurde dunkler um ihn [herum] **3** (Sewing) angekraust sein **4** (Med.) ‹*Furunkel:*› reif werden

C *n. in pl.* (Sewing) Kräusel[falten] *Pl.*

Phrasal verb

• **~ 'up** *v.t.* **1** (bring together and pick up) aufsammeln; auflesen; zusammenpacken ‹*Habseligkeiten, Werkzeug*›; **be left to ~ up the pieces of one's life** (fig.) vor dem Scherbenhaufen seines Lebens stehen **2** (draw) hochraffen ‹*Rock*›; **~ oneself up to one's full height** sich zu seiner vollen Größe aufrichten **3** (sum up) zusammentragen ‹*Fakten*› **4** (summon) sammeln ‹*Kräfte, Gedanken usw.*›

gathering /ˈgæðərɪŋ/ *n.* **1** (group) Gruppe, *die* **2** (assembly, meeting) Versammlung, *die;* (in Scottish Highlands) Volksfest, *das;* **social ~:** gesellschaftliches Ereignis **3** (Sewing) Kräusel[falten] *Pl.*

GATT /gæt/ *abbr.* **= General Agreement on Tariffs and Trade** GATT, *das*

gauche /gəʊʃ/ *adj.* linkisch; (clumsy) schwerfällig; (tactless) plump

gaucheness /ˈgəʊʃnɪs/ *n., no pl.* ▸**gauche**: Linkische, *das;* Schwerfälligkeit, *die;* Plumpheit, *die;* **~ of manner** linkische Art

gaucherie /ˈgəʊʃəri:/ *n.* **1** *no pl.* (manner) linkische Art **2** (action) Plumpheit, *die*

gaucho /ˈgaʊtʃəʊ/ *n., pl.* **~s** Gaucho, *der*

gaudily /ˈgɔ:dɪlɪ/ *adv.* prunkvoll ‹*dekoriert*›; übertrieben aufwendig; protzig (abwertend); **~ coloured** knallbunt

gaudy[1] /ˈgɔ:dɪ/ *adj.* protzig (abwertend); grell, (ugs.) knallig ‹*Farben*›

gaudy[2] *n.* (Brit. Univ.) [College]fest für ehemalige Studenten

gauge /geɪdʒ/

A *n.* **1** (standard measure) [Normal]maß, *das;* (of textile) Gauge, das (fachspr.); (of bullet) Kaliber, *das;* (of rail) Spurweite, *die;* **standard/broad/narrow ~:** Normal- *od.* Regel-/Breit-/Schmalspur, *die* **2** (instrument) Messgerät, *das;* (to measure water level) Pegel, *der;* Wasserstandsanzeiger, *der;* (for dimensions of tools or wire) Lehre, *die; see also* **oil gauge**; **petrol gauge** **3** (Naut.) *Schiffsposition in Bezug auf den Wind;* **have the weather ~ [of sb.]** in Luv [von jmdm.] liegen; (fig.) die Oberhand [über jmdn.] haben **4** (fig.: criterion, test) Kriterium, *das;* Maßstab, *der*

B *v.t.* **1** (measure) messen **2** (fig.) beurteilen (**by** nach)

Gaul /gɔ:l/ *n.* (Hist.) **1** (country) Gallien, *das* **2** (person) Gallier, *der*/Gallierin, *die*

gauleiter /ˈgaʊlaɪtə(r)/ *n.* **1** (Hist.) Gauleiter, *der* **2** (fig.: local or petty tyrant) Ortstyrann, *der*

gaunt /gɔ:nt/ *adj.* **1** (haggard) hager; (from suffering) verhärmt **2** (grim, desolate) öde; kahl ‹*Baum*›; karg ‹*Landschaft*›

gauntlet[1] /ˈgɔ:ntlɪt/ *n.* **1** Stulpenhandschuh, *der* **2** (wrist part of glove) Stulpe, *die* **3** (Hist.: armoured glove) Panzerhandschuh, *der* **4** **fling** *or* **throw down the ~** (fig.) jmdm. den Fehdehandschuh hinwerfen *od.* vor die Füße werfen; **pick** *or* **take up the ~** (fig.) den Fehdehandschuh aufnehmen *od.* aufheben

gauntlet[2] *n.* **run the ~:** Spießruten laufen

gauss /gaʊs/ *n., pl. same or* **~es** (Phys.) Gauß, *das*

gauze /gɔ:z/ *n.* **1** Gaze, *die* **2** (of wire etc.) Drahtgeflecht, *das;* Gaze, *die*

gave ▸**give A, B**

gavel /ˈgævl/ *n.* Hammer, *der*

gavotte /gəˈvɒt/ *n.* (Mus.) Gavotte, *die*

gawk /gɔ:k/ *v.i.* (coll.) gaffen (abwertend); **~ at sth./sb.** etw./jmdn. begaffen

gawky /ˈgɔ:kɪ/ *adj.* linkisch; unbeholfen; (with disproportionately long limbs) schlaksig (ugs.)

gawp /gɔ:p/ ▸**gawk**

gay /geɪ/

A *adj.* **1** (homosexual) schwul (ugs.); Schwulen‹*lokal, -blatt*› **2** (dated: happy) fröhlich; fidel (ugs.) ‹*Person, Gesellschaft*› **3** (dated: showy, bright-coloured) farbenfroh ‹*Stoff, Ausstattung*›; fröhlich, lebhaft ‹*Farbe*›; **~ with flowers/flags** mit Blumen/Fahnen fröhlich geschmückt

B *n.* Schwule, *der* (ugs.)

gayety (Amer.) ▸**gaiety**

gay libe'ration *n.* Schwulenemanzipation, *die;* **~ movement** Schwulenbewegung, *die*

gayness /ˈgeɪnɪs/ ▸**gaiety**

gay 'rights *n. pl.* Schwulenrechte *Pl.;* **~ group/demonstration** Schwulengruppe, *die*/-demonstration, *die*

Gaza [Strip] /ˈgɑ:zə (strɪp)/ *pr. n.* Gazastreifen, *der*

gaze /geɪz/

A *v.i.* blicken; (more fixedly) starren; **~ at sb./sth.** jmdn./etw. anstarren *od.* ansehen; **~ after sb./sth.** jmdm./einer Sache hinterhersehen; **~ around** *or* **about** um sich blicken

B *n.* Blick, *der*

gazebo /gəˈzi:bəʊ/ *n.* (building) Aussichtspavillon, *der;* (tent-like) Zeltling, *der*

gazelle /gəˈzel/ *n.* Gazelle, *die*

gazette /gəˈzet/

A *n.* **1** (Brit.: official journal) **London G~:** Londoner Amtsblatt **2** (newspaper) Anzeiger, *der*

B *v.t.* (Brit.: announce) [amtlich] bekannt geben

gazetteer /gæzɪˈtɪə(r)/ *n.* alphabetisches [Orts]verzeichnis

gazump /gəˈzʌmp/ *v.t.* (coll.) *durch nachträgliches Überbieten um die Chance bringen, ein Haus zu kaufen*

GB *abbr.* **= Great Britain** GB

GBH *abbr.* (Brit. Law) **= grievous bodily harm**

Gbyte *abbr.* **= gigabyte(s)** Gbyte

GC *abbr.* (Brit.) **= George Cross**

GCE *abbr.* (Brit. Hist.) **= General Certificate of Education**

GCSE *abbr.* (Brit.) **= General Certificate of Secondary Education**

GCSE – General Certificate of Secondary Education

Ein Examen in einem bestimmten Fach, das gewöhnlich im 5. Schuljahr von den meisten Schülern in England und Wales abgelegt wird. Die Abschlussnoten (*grades*) werden in jedem Fach einzeln vergeben. Die meisten Schüler legen das *GCSE* in mehreren Fächern ab. Schüler, die danach **A levels** machen wollen, brauchen eine bestimmte Anzahl von *GCSEs* mit den erforderlichen Abschlussnoten, um dafür zugelassen zu werden. Es ist möglich, *GCSEs* mit den eher beruflich orientierten **GNVQ**s zu kombinieren.

GDP *abbr.* **= gross domestic product** BIP

GDR *abbr.* (Hist.) **= German Democratic Republic** DDR, *die*

gear /gɪə(r)/

A *n.* **1** (Motor Veh.) Gang, *der;* (transmission) Übersetzung, *die;* **first/second** *etc.* **~** (Brit.) der erste/zweite usw. Gang; **top/bottom ~** (Brit.) der höchste/erste Gang; **high/low ~:** hoher/niedriger Gang; **change** *or* **shift ~:** schalten; **change** *or* **shift [up] a ~** (fig.) einen Gang zulegen (ugs.); **change into second/a higher/lower ~:** in den zweiten Gang/in einen höheren/niedrigeren Gang schalten; **a bicycle with ten-speed ~s** ein Fahrrad mit Zehngangschaltung; **put** *or* **get** *or* **shift the car into ~:** den Wagen in Gang setzen; einen Gang einlegen; **in ~** (fig.) in Ordnung; im Gleis; **out of ~:** im Leerlauf; (fig.) in Unordnung; aus dem Gleis [geraten]; **the car is in/out of ~:** es ist ein/kein Gang eingelegt; **leave the car in ~:** den Gang drin lassen **2** (combination of wheels, levers, etc.) Getriebe, *das* **3** (coll.: clothes, possessions) Sachen *Pl.* (ugs.); **travelling ~:** Reisekleidung, *die; see also* **headgear** **4** (equipment) Ausrüstung, *die;* (tools) Gerät, *das;* (apparatus) Vorrichtung, *die*

B *v.t.* (adjust, adapt) anpassen (**to** *Dat.*); abstimmen, ausrichten (**to** auf + *Akk.*)

Phrasal verb

• **gear 'up** *v.i.* sich rüsten

gear: ~box *ns.* Getriebekasten, *der;* **five-speed ~box** Fünfganggetriebe, *das;* **~ cable** *n.* Schaltzug, *der;* **~ change** *n.* (Brit.) **an upward/a downward ~ change** ein Hoch-/Herunterschalten; **have a smooth/awkward ~ change** ‹*Fahrrad, Auto:*› sich leicht/schlecht schalten

gearing /ˈgɪərɪŋ/ *n.* **1** (gears) Getriebe, *das;* (ratio) Übersetzung, *die;* **high/low ~:** lange/kurze Übersetzung **2** (Brit. Finance) *Verhältnis von Ausschüttung auf Vorzugsaktien zu Ausschüttung auf Stammaktien*

gear: ~ lever, (Amer.) **~ shift, ~stick** *ns.* Schalthebel, *der;* Schaltknüppel, *der;* **~wheel** *n.* Zahnrad, *das*

gecko /ˈgekəʊ/ *n., pl.* **~s** (Zool.) Gecko, *der*

geddit /ˈgedɪt/ *v.i.* (coll.) **~?** verstanden? (ugs.); kapiert? (salopp)

gee¹ /dʒiː/ *int.* (to horse) hü

gee² *int.* (coll.) Mann (salopp); Mensch [Meier] (salopp)

'gee-gee *n.* (Brit. coll.: horse) Hottehü, *das* (Kinderspr.)

geek /giːk/ *n.* (coll.) 1 (socially inept person) Sonderling, *der;* **he's a complete ~:** er ist völlig abgedreht; **you stupid ~!** du Blödmann! 2 (obsessive enthusiast) Fanatiker, *der*/Fanatikerin, *die;* **computer ~:** Computerfreak, *der*

geese *pl. of* **goose**

'gee-up *int.* ▸**gee¹**

gee 'whiz *int.* (coll.) ▸**gee²**

geezer /'giːzə(r)/ *n.* 1 (coll.: old man) Opa, *der* (ugs. scherzh. od. abwertend) 2 (coll.: fellow) Typ, *der* (ugs.)

Geiger counter /'gaɪgə kaʊntə(r)/ *n.* (Phys.) Geigerzähler, *der*

geisha /'geɪʃə/ *n., pl.* **~s** *or same* Geisha, *die*

gel /dʒel/

A *n.* Gel, *das*

B *v.i.,* **-ll-** 1 gelatinieren; gelieren 2 (fig.) Gestalt annehmen

gelatin /'dʒelətɪn/, (esp. Brit.) **gelatine** /'dʒelətiːn/ *n.* Gelatine, *die;* **blasting ~e** Sprenggelatine, *die*

gelatinous /dʒɪ'lætɪnəs/ *adj.* 1 (resembling gelatin) gelatineartig 2 (consisting of gelatin) gelatinös

geld /geld/ *v.t.* kastrieren; (spay) sterilisieren

gelding /'geldɪŋ/ *n.* kastriertes Tier; (male horse) Wallach, *der*

gelignite /'dʒelɪgnaɪt/ *n.* Gelatinedynamit, *das*

gem /dʒem/ *n.* 1 Edelstein, *der;* (cut also) Juwel, *das od. der;* ([semi-]precious stone with engraved design) Gemme, *die* 2 (fig.) Juwel, *das;* Perle, *die;* (choicest part) Glanzstück, *das*

Gemini /'dʒemɪnaɪ, 'dʒemɪnɪ/ *n.* (Astrol., Astron.) Zwillinge *Pl.;* Gemini *Pl.; see also* **Aries**

Geminian /dʒemɪ'niːən/ *n.* (Astrol.) Zwilling, *der*

'gemstone *n.* Edelstein, *der*

gen /dʒen/ (Brit. coll.)

A *n.* notwendige Angaben; **give sb. the ~ on** *or* **about sth.** jmdn. über etw. (*Akk.*) informieren

B *v.t.,* **-nn-:** **~ oneself/sb. up on** *or* **about sth.** sich/jmdn. über etw. (*Akk.*) informieren

C *v.i.,* **-nn-:** **~ up on** *or* **about sth.** sich über etw. (*Akk.*) informieren

Gen. *abbr.* ▸❶ **p. 1634 = General** Gen.

gendarme /'ʒɒndɑːm/ *n.* Gendarm, *der*

gender /'dʒendə(r)/ *n.* 1 (Ling.) [grammatisches] Geschlecht; Genus, *das* 2 (one's sex) Geschlecht, *das;* **~ gap** Unterschied zwischen den Geschlechtern

'gender-specific *adj.* geschlechtspezifisch

gene /dʒiːn/ *n.* (Biol.) Gen, *das*

genealogical /dʒiːnɪə'lɒdʒɪkl, dʒenɪə'lɒdʒɪkl/ *adj.* genealogisch; **~ tree** Stammbaum, *der*

genealogist /dʒiːnɪ'ælədʒɪst, dʒenɪ'ælədʒɪst/ *n.* ▸❶ **p. 1260** Genealoge, *der*/Genealogin, *die;* Ahnenforscher, *der*/-forscherin, *die*

genealogy /dʒiːnɪ'ælədʒɪ, dʒenɪ'ælədʒɪ/ *n.* 1 Genealogie, *die* (fachspr.); (pedigree) Ahnentafel, *die* (geh.); (investigation) Ahnenforschung, *die* 2 (Zool., Bot.) Stammbaum, *der*

gene: **~ bank** *n.* Genbank, *die;* **~ mapping** *n., no pl.* Genkartierung, *die;* **~ pool** *n.* Genpool, *der*

genera *pl. of* **genus**

general /'dʒenrl/

A *adj.* 1 allgemein; **the ~ public** weite Kreise der Öffentlichkeit *od.* Bevölkerung; **in ~ use** allgemein verbreitet; **be in ~ use as sth.** allgemein als etw. benutzt werden; **not for ~ use** (not to be used by everybody) nicht für den allgemeinen Gebrauch bestimmt; **his ~ health/manner** sein Allgemeinbefinden/sein Benehmen im Allgemeinen; **he has had a good ~ education** er hat eine gute Allgemeinbildung; **a ~ view of the building** eine Gesamtansicht des Gebäudes; **come to a ~ agreement** sich grundsätzlich einigen; **reach a ~ decision** eine grundsätzliche Entscheidung treffen; **in a ~ state of decay** in einem Zustand allgemeinen Verfalls; **~ matters** allgemeine Angelegenheiten; **the cold weather has been ~ in England** es ist in ganz England kalt gewesen 2 (prevalent, widespread, usual) allgemein; weit verbreitet ‹*Übel, Vorurteil, Aberglaube, Ansicht*›; häufig ‹*Leiden*›; **it is the ~ custom** *or* **rule** es ist allgemein üblich *od.* ist Sitte *od.* Brauch 3 (not limited in application) allgemein; (true of [nearly] all cases) allgemein gültig; generell; **as a ~ rule** im Allgemeinen; **in the ~ way [of things]** normalerweise; **in ~:** im Allgemeinen; **'G~ Enquiries'** „Auskunft" 4 (not detailed, vague) allgemein; ungefähr, vage ‹*Vorstellung, Beschreibung, Ähnlichkeit usw.*›; allgemein gehalten ‹*Übersetzung, Bestimmung, Vertrag*›; oberflächlich ‹*Ähnlichkeit*›; **in its ~ form** im Großen und Ganzen; **in the most ~ terms, in a very ~ way** nur ganz allgemein; **the ~ idea** *or* **plan is that we ...:** wir haben uns das so vorgestellt, dass wir ...; **yes, that was the ~ idea** ja, so war es gedacht 5 (Mil.) Generals‹*rang, -streifen usw.*›; **~ officer** General, *der* 6 (chief, head) General‹*direktor, -vertretung*›

B *n.* ▸❶ **p. 1634** (Mil.) General, *der;* (tactician, strategist) Stratege, *der;* **~ of the army/air force** (Amer.) Fünfsternegeneral, *der*

general: **G~ A'merican** *n.* General American, *das;* amerikanische Standardsprache; **~ anaes'thetic** ▸**anaesthetic B; G~ As'sembly** *n.* Generalversammlung, *die;* Vollversammlung, *die;* **G~ Certificate of Edu'cation** *n.* (Brit. Hist.) (ordinary level) ≈ mittlere Reife; (advanced level) ≈ Abitur, *das;* **G~ Certificate of Secondary Edu'cation** *n.* (Brit.) *Abschluss der Sekundarstufe;* **~ 'dealer** *n.* Gemischtwarenhändler, *der;* **~ de'livery** *n.* (Amer.) Schalter für postlagernde Sendungen; *written in address* postlagernd; **~ e'lection** *n.* allgemeine Wahlen *Pl.;* **~ head'quarters** *n. sing. or pl.* Generalkommando, *das;* **~ hospital** *n.* Allgemeinkrankenhaus, *das;* (Mil.) Lazarett, *das*

generalisation, generalise ▸**generaliz-**

generalist /'dʒenrəlɪst/ *n.* Generalist, *der*

generality /dʒenə'rælɪtɪ/ *n.* 1 (applicability) allgemeine Anwendbarkeit; (of conclusion) Allgemeingültigkeit, *die;* **a method of great ~:** eine vielseitig anwendbare Methode 2 (vagueness) Allgemeinheit, *die* 3 **talk in/of generalities** verallgemeinern/über Allgemeines sprechen 4 (main, body, bulk, majority) (of mankind, electorate, etc.) Großteil, *der;* (of voters, individuals, etc.) Mehrheit, *die*

generalization /dʒenrəlaɪ'zeɪʃn/ *n.* Generalisierung, *die;* Verallgemeinerung, *die;* **hasty ~:** voreilige Verallgemeinerung

generalize /'dʒenrəlaɪz/

A *v.t.* 1 generalisieren; verallgemeinern 2 (make more widespread) verbreiten

B *v.i.* **~ [about sth.]** [etw.] verallgemeinern; **~ about the French** die Franzosen alle in einen Topf werfen (ugs.) *od.* über einen Kamm scheren; **you can't ~; each one is different** man soll nicht verallgemeinern — jeder Einzelne ist wieder anders

general 'knowledge *n.* Allgemeinwissen, *das;* **it is ~ that ...:** es ist allgemein bekannt, dass ...; **~ exam/questions** das Allgemeinwissen betreffende Prüfung/Fragen

generally /'dʒenrəlɪ/ *adv.* 1 (extensively) allgemein; **~ available** überall erhältlich 2 **~ speaking** im Allgemeinen 3 (usually) im Allgemeinen; normalerweise 4 (summarizing the situation) ganz allgemein

general: **~ 'manager** *n.* ▸❶ **p. 1260** [leitender] Direktor/[leitende] Direktorin; **~ 'meeting** *n.* Generalversammlung, *die;* Hauptversammlung, *die;* **G~ 'Post Office** *n.* (Brit.) Hauptpost[amt, *das*], *die;* **~ 'practice** *n.* (Med.) Allgemeinmedizin, *die;* **~ prac'titioner** *n.* ▸❶ **p. 1260** (Med.) Arzt-/Ärztin für Allgemeinmedizin; **~ 'public** *n.* Öffentlichkeit, *die;* Allgemeinheit, *die;* **the lecture is open to the ~ public** die Vorlesung *od.* der Vortrag ist öffentlich; **~ reader** *n.* Durchschnittsleser, *der*/-leserin, *die*

generalship /'dʒenrlʃɪp/ *n., no pl.* (strategy) Führung, *die;* Kommando, *das;* (fig.) Leitung, *die*

general: **~ shop** ▸**~ store; ~ 'staff** *n.* Generalstab, *der;* **~ store** *n.* Gemischtwarenhandlung, *die* (veralt.); **~ 'strike** *n.* Generalstreik, *der*

generate /'dʒenəreɪt/ *v.t.* (produce) erzeugen (**from** aus); (result in) führen zu

generating station /'dʒenəreɪtɪŋ steɪʃn/ *n.* Elektrizitätswerk, *das*

generation /dʒenə'reɪʃn/ *n.* 1 Generation, *die;* **the present/rising ~:** die heutige/heranwachsende *od.* junge Generation; **~ gap** Generationsunterschied, *der;* **first-/second-~ computers** *etc.* Computer *usw.* der ersten/zweiten Generation 2 (production) Erzeugung, *die;* **~ of electricity** Stromerzeugung, *die* 3 (procreation) **organs of ~:** Geschlechtsorgane *Pl.;* Fortpflanzungsorgane *Pl.*

generative /'dʒenərətɪv/ *adj.* generativ; Zeugungs‹*fähigkeit, -kraft usw.*›

generator /'dʒenəreɪtə(r)/ *n.* 1 Generator, *der;* (in motor car also) Lichtmaschine, *die* 2 (originator) Schöpfer, *der;* **be a ~ of new ideas** neue Ideen entwickeln

generic /dʒɪ'nerɪk/ *adj.* 1 gattungsmäßig; generisch (fachspr.); **~ term** *or* **name** *or* **heading** Ober- *od.* Gattungsbegriff, *der* 2 (Biol.) Gattungs‹*name, -bezeichnung*›

generic 'drug *n.* Generikum, *das*

generosity /dʒenə'rɒsɪtɪ/ *n.* Großzügigkeit, *die;* Generosität, *die* (geh.); (magnanimity) Großmut, *die;* Generosität, *die* (geh.)

generous /'dʒenərəs/ *adj.* 1 großzügig; generös (geh.); (noble-minded) edel (geh.); großmütig; **he is ~ with compliments** er spart nicht mit Komplimenten 2 (ample, abundant) großzügig; reichhaltig ‹*Mahl*›; reichlich ‹*Nachschub, Vorrat, Portion*›; üppig ‹*Figur, Formen, Mahl*›; weit ‹*Ärmel, Kleidungsstück*›; breit ‹*Saum*›; **~ size 12** groß ausgefallene Größe 12

generously /'dʒenərəslɪ/ *adv.* großzügig; generös (geh.); (magnanimously) großmütig; **'please give ~'** „wir bitten um großzügige Spenden"

genesis /'dʒenɪsɪs/ *n., pl.* **geneses** /'dʒenɪsiːz/ 1 **G~** *no pl.* das erste Buch Mose; Schöpfungsgeschichte, *die* 2 (origin) Ursprung, *der;* Herkunft, *die;* (development into being) Entstehung, *die*

'gene therapy *n., no pl.* Gentherapie, *die*

genetic /dʒɪ'netɪk/ *adj.* 1 genetisch; **~ code** genetischer Code 2 (concerning origin) entwicklungsgeschichtlich; **~ development** Entwicklungsgeschichte, *die*

genetically /dʒɪ'netɪkəlɪ/ *adv.* 1 (according to genetics) genetisch; **~ manipulated** genmanipuliert; **~ modified** gentechnisch verändert; **~ engineered** gentechnisch verändert ‹*Organismen, Pflanzen, Tiere, Nahrungsmittel*›; gentechnisch hergestellt ‹*Medikament, Enzym*› 2 (according to origin) entwicklungsgeschichtlich

genetic: **~ engi'neering** *n.* Gentechnologie, *die;* **~ 'fingerprinting, ~ profiling** /'prəʊfaɪlɪŋ/ *ns., no pl.* DNA-Fingerprintmethode, *die*

geneticist /dʒɪ'netɪsɪst/ *n.* ▸❶ **p. 1260** Genetiker, *der*/Genetikerin, *die*

genetic: **~ manipu'lation** *n.* Genmanipulation, *die;* **~ profile** *n.* genetisches Profil; Genprofil, *das*

genetics /dʒɪ'netɪks/ *n., no pl.* Genetik, *die;* Erbbiologie, *die*

genetic 'testing *n., no pl.* Gentests *Pl.*

Geneva /dʒɪ'niːvə/ ▸❶ **p. 1643**

A *pr. n.* Genf (*das*); **Lake ~:** der Genfer See

B *attrib. adj.* Genfer; **the ~ Convention** die Genfer Konvention

genial /'dʒiːnɪəl/ *adj.* (mild) angenehm; mild ‹*Klima, Luft*›; (jovial, kindly) freundlich; (sociable) jovial, leutselig ‹*Person, Art*›; (amiable) liebenswürdig; (cheering, enlivening) anregend; belebend

geniality /dʒiːnɪ'ælɪtɪ/ *n., no pl.* Freundlichkeit, *die;* **hearty ~:** Herzlichkeit, *die*

genially /'dʒiːnɪəlɪ/ *adv.* freundlich

g

genie /ˈdʒiːnɪ/ *n., pl.* **genii** /ˈdʒiːnɪaɪ/ Flaschenteufel, *der*

genital /ˈdʒenɪtl/
A *n. in pl.* ▸ℹ **p. 951** Geschlechtsorgane *Pl.;* Genitalien *Pl*
B *adj.* Geschlechts‹*teile, -organe, -drüse*›

genitalia /dʒenɪˈteɪlɪə/ *n. pl.* Geschlechtsorgane *Pl.;* Genitalia *Pl.*

genitive /ˈdʒenɪtɪv/ (Ling.)
A *adj.* Genitiv-; genitivisch; ~ **case** Genitiv, *der*
B *n.* Genitiv, *der; see also* **absolute 3**

genius /ˈdʒiːnɪəs/ *n., pl.* ~**es** *or* **genii** /ˈdʒiːnɪaɪ/ 1 *pl.* ~**es** (person) Genie, *das* 2 (natural ability; also iron.) Talent, *das;* Begabung, *die;* (extremely great) Genius, *der* (geh.); Genie, *das;* **a man of** ~: ein genialer Mensch; ein Genie; ~ **for languages** Sprachbegabung, *die* 3 (special character) Geist, *der;* (of people) Charakter, *der;* Wesen, *das* 4 (spirit) [Schutz]geist, *der;* Genius, *der;* (of place, country) Geist, *der;* Genius, *der;* **good/evil** ~: guter/böser Geist

Genoa /ˈdʒenəʊə/ *pr. n.* ▸ℹ **p. 1643** Genua *(das)*

genocide /ˈdʒenəsaɪd/ *n.* Völkermord, *der;* Genozid, *der* (geh.)

genome /ˈdʒiːnəʊm/ *n.* (Biol.) Genom, *das*

genomic /dʒiːˈnəʊmɪk/ *adj.* (Biol.) genomisch

genotype /ˈdʒiːnətaɪp/ *n.* (Biol.) Genotyp[us], *der*

genre /ʒɑ̃r/ *n.* 1 Genre, *das;* Gattung, *die* 2 ▸~ **painting 1**

'genre painting *n.* 1 Genremalerei, *die* 2 (picture) Genrebild, *das*

gent /dʒent/ *n.* 1 (coll./joc.) Gent, der (iron.) 2 (in shops etc.) ~**s'** Herren‹*friseur, -ausstatter*› 3 **the G~s** (Brit. coll.) die Herrentoilette

genteel /dʒenˈtiːl/ *adj.* vornehm; fein; **they lived in** ~ **poverty** sie lebten in vornehmer Armut

genteelly /dʒenˈtiːllɪ/ *adv.* vornehm

gentian /ˈdʒenʃn, ˈdʒenʃɪən/ *n.* (Bot.) Enzian, *der*

Gentile /ˈdʒentaɪl/
A *n.* Nichtjude, *der*/-jüdin, *die;* (Bibl.) Heide, *der*/Heidin, *die*
B *adj.* nichtjüdisch; (Bibl.) heidnisch

gentility /dʒenˈtɪlɪtɪ/ *n., no pl.* 1 (condition) Zugehörigkeit zum niederen Adel 2 (members) niederer Adel 3 (genteel behaviour) Vornehmheit, *die;* **appearance of** ~: vornehme Erscheinung

gentle /ˈdʒentl/ *adj.,* ~**r** /ˈdʒentlə(r)/, ~**st** /ˈdʒentlɪst/ 1 sanft; sanftmütig ‹*Wesen*›; liebenswürdig, freundlich ‹*Person, Verhalten, Ausdrucksweise*›; (not stormy, rough, or violent) leicht, schwach ‹*Brise*›; ruhig ‹*Fluss, Wesen*›; (not loud) leise ‹*Geräusch*›; (moderate) gemäßigt ‹*Tempo*›; mäßig ‹*Hitze*›; gemächlich ‹*Tempo, Schritte, Spaziergang*›; (gradual) sanft ‹*Abhang usw.*›; (mild, not drastic) mild ‹*Reinigungsmittel, Shampoo usw.*›; wohlig ‹*Wärme*›; (easily managed) zahm, lammfromm ‹*Tier*›; **be** ~ **with sb./sth.** sanft mit jmdm./etw. umgehen; **with** ~ **care** äußerst vorsichtig *od.* behutsam; **a** ~ **reminder/hint** ein zarter Wink/eine zarte Andeutung; **the** ~ **sex** das zarte Geschlecht (ugs. scherzh.); **the** ~ **art** *or* **craft** die edle Kunst 2 (dated: honourable, well-born) edel (veralt.); **of** ~ **birth** von hoher *od.* edler Geburt 3 ~ **reader** (arch.) lieber *od.* geneigter Leser

'gentlefolk[s] *n. pl.* feine Leute; vornehme Leute

gentleman /ˈdʒentlmən/ *n., pl.* **gentlemen** /ˈdʒentlmən/ 1 (man of good manners and breeding) Herr, *der;* Gentleman, *der;* ~ **scholar** Privatgelehrter; **a country** ~: ein Landedelmann 2 (man) Herr, *der;* **Gentlemen!** meine Herren!; **Ladies and Gentlemen!** meine Damen und Herren!; **Gentlemen, ...** (in formal, business letter) Sehr geehrte Herren!; **the gentlemen of the jury/press** die Herren Geschworenen/von der Presse; **gentlemen's tailor/hairdresser** Herrenschneider/-friseur, *der* 3 (man attached to household of sovereign etc.) Höfling, *der* 4 *in pl., constr. as sing.* **'Gentlemen'** „Herren"

gentleman 'farmer *n.* Gutsherr, *der*

gentlemanly /ˈdʒentlmənlɪ/ *adj.* gentlemanlike *nicht attrib.;* eines Gentlemans *nachgestellt;* ~ **person** Gentleman, *der*

'gentleman's *or* **'gentlemen's agreement** *n.* Gentleman's *od.* Gentlemen's Agreement, *das;* Vereinbarung auf Treu und Glauben

gentleness /ˈdʒentlnɪs/ *n., no pl.* Sanftheit, *die;* (of nature) Sanftmütigkeit, *die;* (of nurse, words, action) Behutsamkeit, *die;* (of shampoo, cleanser, etc.) Milde, *die;* (of animal) Zahmheit, *die*

'gentlepeople ▸**gentlefolk[s]**

'gentlewoman *n.* (arch.) 1 (woman of good birth or breeding) Dame von Stand 2 (lady) Dame, *die*

gently /ˈdʒentlɪ/ *adv.* (tenderly) zart; zärtlich; (mildly) sanft; (carefully) vorsichtig; behutsam; (quietly, softly) leise; (moderately) sanft; (slowly) langsam; **she broke the news to him** ~: sie brachte ihm die Nachricht schonend bei; **a** ~ **teasing/sarcastic manner** eine leicht neckende/sarkastische Art; **she took things very** ~: sie ließ es langsam angehen (ugs.); ~ **does it!** immer sachte! (ugs.); ~! [sachte] sachte!

gentrification /dʒentrɪfɪˈkeɪʃn/ *n.* Aufwertung, *die*

gentrify /ˈdʒentrɪfaɪ/ *v.t.* aufwerten; **a gentrified look** ein vornehmeres Aussehen

gentry /ˈdʒentrɪ/ *n. pl.* niederer Adel; Gentry, *die*

genuflect /ˈdʒenjuːflekt/ *v.i.* (esp. Relig.) das Knie beugen; eine Kniebeuge machen

genuflection, genuflexion /dʒenjuːˈflekʃn/ *n.* (esp. Relig.) Kniebeuge, *die*

genuine /ˈdʒenjʊɪn/ *adj.* 1 (actually from reputed source or author) echt; authentisch ‹*Text*›; **the** ~ **article** die echte Ausgabe (fig.) 2 (true) aufrichtig; wahr ‹*Zuneigung, Grund, Not*›; echt ‹*Tränen*›; ernsthaft, ernst gemeint ‹*Angebot*›; echt, überzeugt ‹*Skeptiker, Kommunist usw.*›

genuinely /ˈdʒenjʊɪnlɪ/ *adv.* wirklich; **it is** ~ **antique** es ist echt antik

genus /ˈdʒiːnəs, ˈdʒenəs/ *n., pl.* **genera** /ˈdʒenərə/ 1 (Biol., Logic) Gattung, die 2 (in popular use) Gattung, *die;* Art, *die*

geocentric /dʒiːəˈsentrɪk/ *adj.* geozentrisch

geodesic /dʒiːəˈdesɪk, dʒiːəˈdiːsɪk/ *adj.* geodätisch

geodesy /dʒiːˈɒdɪsɪ/ *n.* Geodäsie, *die*

geodetic /dʒiːəˈdetɪk, dʒiːəˈdiːtɪk/ ▸**geodesic**

geographer /dʒɪˈɒgrəfə(r)/ *n.* ▸ℹ **p. 1260** Geograph, *der*/Geographin, *die*

geographic /dʒiːəˈgræfɪk/, **geographical** /dʒiːəˈgræfɪkl/ *adj.* geographisch; ~ **latitude** [geographische] Breite

geographically /dʒiːəˈgræfɪkəlɪ/ *adv.* geographisch

geography /dʒɪˈɒgrəfɪ/ *n.* Geographie, *die;* Erdkunde, *die* (Schulw.); **physical/political/regional** ~: physische Geographie *od.* Naturgeographie, *die*/politische Geographie *od.* Staatengeographie, *die*/Landeskunde, *die;* **show sb. the** ~ **of the house** (coll.) jmdm. zeigen, wo sich die einzelnen Räume befinden

geological /dʒiːəˈlɒdʒɪkl/ *adj.,* **geologically** /dʒiːəˈlɒdʒɪkəlɪ/ *adv.* geologisch

geologist /dʒɪˈɒlədʒɪst/ *n.* ▸ℹ **p. 1260** Geologe, *der*/Geologin, *die*

geology /dʒɪˈɒlədʒɪ/ *n.* Geologie, *die;* (features) geologische Beschaffenheit

geometric /dʒiːəˈmetrɪk/, **geometrical** /dʒiːəˈmetrɪkl/ *adj.* geometrisch; ~ **mean** geometrisches Mittel; **geometrical progression** *or* **series** geometrische Reihe

geometrically /dʒiːəˈmetrɪkəlɪ/ *adv.* geometrisch

geometry /dʒɪˈɒmɪtrɪ/ *n.* Geometrie, *die*

ge'ometry set *n.* Reißzeug, *das*

geophysical /dʒiːəˈfɪzɪkl/ *adj.* geophysikalisch

geophysicist /dʒiːəˈfɪzɪsɪst/ *n.* Geophysiker, *der*/Geophysikerin, *die*

geophysics /dʒiːəˈfɪzɪks/ *n., no pl.* Geophysik, *die*

Geordie /ˈdʒɔːdɪ/ *n.* (Brit.) Geordie, *der;* *Einwohner von Tyneside*

George /dʒɔːdʒ/ *n.* 1 (Hist., as name of ruler etc.) Georg 2 **by** ~! (Brit. dated coll.) potz Blitz!; bei Gott!

George: ~ **'Cross** *n.* (Brit.) Georgskreuz, *das;* ~ **'Medal** *n.* (Brit.) Georgsmedaille, *die*

georgette /dʒɔːˈdʒet/ *n.* (Textiles) [Crêpe] Georgette, *der*

Georgia /ˈdʒɔːdʒɪə/ *pr. n.* (in USSR) Georgien *(das);* (in US) Georgia *(das)*

Georgian[1] /ˈdʒɔːdʒɪən/ *adj.* (Brit. Hist.) georgianisch

Georgian[2] *adj.* ▸ℹ **p. 1345** (USSR) georgisch; (US) aus/in/von Georgia *nachgestellt*

geostationary /dʒiːəˈsteɪʃənərɪ/ *adj.* geostationär

geothermal /dʒiːəˈθɜːməl/ *adj.* geothermisch

Ger. *abbr.* = **German** dt.

geranium /dʒəˈreɪnɪəm/ *n.* 1 (in popular use) Geranie, *die;* Pelargonie, *die* 2 (herb or shrub Geranium) Storchschnabel, *der;* Geranie, *die;* Geranium, *das*

gerbil /ˈdʒɜːbɪl/ *n.* (Zool.) Wüstenmaus, *die;* Rennmaus, *die*

gerfalcon ▸**gyrfalcon**

geriatric /dʒerɪˈætrɪk/
A *adj.* geriatrisch
B *n.* (also joc.) Greis, *der*/Greisin, *die*

geriatrician /dʒerɪəˈtrɪʃn/ *n.* ▸ℹ **p. 1260** Geriater, *der*/Geriaterin, *die*

geriatrics /dʒerɪˈætrɪks/ *n., no pl.* Geriatrie, *die;* Altersheilkunde, *die*

germ /dʒɜːm/ *n.* (lit. or fig.) Keim, *der;* **I don't want to catch your** ~**s** ich möchte mich nicht bei dir anstecken; **I don't want you to spread your** ~**s around** behalte deine Bazillen für dich!; **wheat** ~: Weizenkeim, *der;* **a** ~ **of truth is contained in this legend** (fig.) diese Legende enthält einen wahren Kern

German /ˈdʒɜːmən/ ▸ℹ **p. 1277**, ▸ℹ **p. 1345**
A *adj.* deutsch; **a** ~ **person** ein Deutscher/eine Deutsche; **the** ~ **people** die Deutschen; **he/she is** ~: er ist Deutscher/sie ist Deutsche; **have a** ~ **degree** (in subject) einen Universitätsabschluss in Germanistik haben; (from country) einen akademischen Grad von einer deutschen Universität haben; **he is a native** ~ **speaker** seine Muttersprache ist Deutsch; **he is a '**~ **translator** (translator from ~) er ist Übersetzer für Deutsch; **'**~ **teacher/student** Deutschlehrer/-student, *der;* ~ **'teacher/student** deutscher Lehrer/Student; ~ **studies** Germanistik, *die;* ~ **department** Germanistisches Institut. *See also* **East German A; English A; West German A**
B *n.* 1 (person) Deutsche, *der/die;* **he/she is a** ~: er ist Deutscher/sie ist Deutsche 2 (language) Deutsch, *das;* **High** ~: Hochdeutsch, *das;* **Low** ~: Niederdeutsch, *das. See also* **East German B; English B 1; West German B**

German Democratic Re'public *pr. n.* (Hist.) Deutsche Demokratische Republik

germane /dʒɜːˈmeɪn/ *adj.* ~ **to** von Bedeutung für

Germanic /dʒɜːˈmænɪk/
A *adj.* germanisch; (having German characteristics) deutsch; ~ **Confederation/Empire** (Hist.) Deutscher Bund/Deutsches Reich; ~ **people** Germanen *Pl*
B *n.* (Ling.) **East/North/West** ~: Ost-/Nord-/Westgermanisch, *das*

Germanise ▸**Germanize**

Germanism /ˈdʒɜːmənɪzm/ *n.* 1 (word or idiom) Germanismus, *der* 2 (German ideas or actions) deutsche Eigenart *od.* Sitte

Germanist /ˈdʒɜːmənɪst/ *n.* Germanist, *der*/Germanistin, *die*

germanium /dʒɜːˈmeɪnɪəm/ *n.* (Chem.) Germanium, *das*

Germanize /ˈdʒɜːmənaɪz/
A *v.t.* eindeutschen; germanisieren (abwertend)
B *v.i.* deutsch werden

German: ~ **'measles** *n. sing.* ▸ℹ **p. 1231** Röteln *Pl.*; ~ **'sausage** *n.* ≈ Fleischwurst, *die;* ~ **'shepherd [dog]** *n.* [deutscher] Schäferhund; ~ **'silver** *n.* Neusilber, *das*

Germany /'dʒɜːmənɪ/ *pr. n.* Deutschland *(das)*; **Federal Republic of** ~: Bundesrepublik Deutschland, *die; see also* **East Germany**; **West Germany**

'germ cell *n.* Keimzelle, *die*

germicidal /'dʒɜːmɪsaɪdl/ *n.* keimtötend; germizid (fachspr.)

germicide /'dʒɜːmɪsaɪd/ *n.* keimtötendes Mittel; Bakterizid, *das* (fachspr.)

germinal /'dʒɜːmɪnl/ *adj.* [1] (in earliest stage of development) noch unentwickelt; ~ **form** Anfangsstadium, *das* [2] (of germ) germinal (Bot.); Keim-

germinate /'dʒɜːmɪneɪt/

A *v.i.* keimen; (fig.) entstehen

B *v.t.* zum Keimen bringen; (fig.) hervorbringen

germination /dʒɜːmɪ'neɪʃn/ *n.* Keimung, *die;* Keimen, *das;* (fig.) Entstehung, *die*

'germ line *n.* (Biol.) Keimbahn, *die*

germ 'warfare *n.* Bakterienkrieg, *der;* biologische Kriegführung

gerrymander /dʒerɪ'mændə(r)/

A *v.t. willkürlich in Wahlbezirke aufteilen, um einer politischen Partei Vorteile zu verschaffen*

B *n.* Wahlkreisschiebungen *Pl.* (ugs.)

gerund /'dʒerənd/ *n.* (Ling.) Gerundium, *das*

Gestapo /ge'stɑːpəʊ/ *n.* Gestapo, *die*

gestation /dʒe'steɪʃn/ *n.* [1] (of animal) Trächtigkeit, *die;* (of woman) Schwangerschaft, *die;* ~ **period** Tragezeit, *die*/Zeit der Schwangerschaft [2] (fig.) Reifung, *die;* Heranreifen, *das*

gesticulate /dʒe'stɪkjʊleɪt/ *v.i.* gestikulieren; **he** ~**d to the lorry driver to stop reversing** er signalisierte dem Lkw-Fahrer, nicht weiter rückwärts zu fahren

gesticulation /dʒestɪkjʊ'leɪʃn/ *n.* Gesten *Pl.*; **wild** ~: wildes Gestikulieren

gesture /'dʒestʃə(r)/

A *n.* Geste, *die* (auch fig.); Gebärde, *die* (geh.); **a** ~ **of resignation** eine resignierte Geste

B *v.i.* gestikulieren; ~ **to sb. to do sth.** jmdm. zu verstehen geben *od.* (geh.) jmdm. bedeuten, etw. zu tun

C *v.t.* zu verstehen geben; ~ **sb. to do sth.** jmdm. zu verstehen geben *od.* (geh.) jmdm. bedeuten, etw. zu tun

get /get/

A *v.t.*, **-tt-**, *p. t.* **got** /gɒt/, *p. p.* **got** *or (in comb./ arch./Amer. except in sense* **13)** **gotten** /'gɒtn/ (**got** *also coll. abbr. of* **has got** *or* **have got**)

[1] (obtain) bekommen; kriegen (ugs.); (by buying) kaufen; sich *(Dat.)* anschaffen ‹*Auto usw.*›; (by one's own effort for special purpose) sich *(Dat.)* besorgen ‹*Visum, Genehmigung, Arbeitskräfte*›; sich *(Dat.)* beschaffen ‹*Geld*›; einholen ‹*Gutachten*›; (by contrivance) kommen zu; (find) finden ‹*Zeit*›; (extract) fördern ‹*Kohle, Öl*›; ~ **an income from sth.** ein Einkommen aus etw. beziehen; **where did you** ~ **that?** wo hast du das her?; **the bogy man will come and** ~ **you** der schwarze Mann kommt und holt dich; **he got him by the leg/arm** er kriegte ihn am Bein/ Arm zu fassen; ~ **sb. a job/taxi,** ~ **a job/taxi for sb.** jmdm. einen Job verschaffen/ein Taxi besorgen *od.* rufen; ~ **oneself sth./a rich man/a job** sich *(Dat.)* etw. zulegen/einen reichen Mann finden/einen Job finden; **I need to** ~ **some bread** ich muss Brot besorgen *od.* holen; **you can't** ~ **this kind of fruit in the winter months** dieses Obst gibt es im Winter nicht zu kaufen; ~ **water from a well** das Wasser vom Brunnen holen; *see also* **best C 3**; **better C 1**; **kick A 3**; **upper A 1**; **wind[1] A 6**; **worst C 1**

[2] (fetch) holen; **what can I** ~ **you?** was kann ich Ihnen anbieten?; **is there anything I can** ~ **you in town?** soll ich dir etwas aus der Stadt mitbringen?; ~ **sb. from the station** jmdn. vom Bahnhof abholen

[3] ~ **the bus** *etc.* (be in time for, catch) den Bus *usw.* erreichen *od.* (ugs.) kriegen; (travel by) den Bus nehmen

[4] (prepare) machen (ugs.), zubereiten ‹*Essen*›

[5] (coll.: eat) essen; zu sich nehmen ‹*Imbiss*›; ~ **something to eat** etwas zu essen holen; (be given) etwas zu essen bekommen

[6] (gain) erreichen; **what do I** ~ **out of it?** was habe ich davon?

[7] (by calculation) erhalten

[8] (receive) bekommen; erhalten, (ugs.) kriegen ‹*Geldsumme, Belohnung*›; ernten ‹*Lob*›; **the country** ~**s very little sun/rain** die Sonne scheint/es regnet nur sehr wenig in dem Land; **he got the full force of the blow** er bekam die volle Wucht des Schlages ab; **she got some bruises from the fall** sie hat sich *(Dat.)* mehrere Prellungen bei dem Sturz zugezogen; **he got his jaw broken in a fight** bei einer Schlägerei wurde ihm der Kiefer gebrochen; ~ **nothing but ingratitude** nichts als Undank ernten

[9] (receive as penalty) bekommen, (ugs.) kriegen ‹*6 Monate Gefängnis, lebenslänglich, Geldstrafe, Tracht Prügel*›; **that's what I** ~ **for trying to be helpful** (iron.) das hat man nun davon, dass man helfen will; **you'll** ~ **it** (coll.) du kriegst Prügel (ugs.); es setzt was (ugs.); (be scolded) du kriegst was zu hören (ugs.); **you'll really** ~ **it this time** diesmal wirst du nicht ungeschoren davonkommen; *see also* **best C 4**; **boot A 1**; **neck A 1**; **sack[1] A 2**

[10] (kill) töten; erlegen ‹*Wild*›; (hit, injure) treffen; erwischen; **I'll** ~ **you for that** das wirst du mir büßen; **they've got me** jetzt haben sie mich; ich bin getroffen (Milit.); ~ **him, boy!** (to dog) fass!

[11] (win) bekommen; finden ‹*Anerkennung*›; sich *(Dat.)* verschaffen ‹*Ansehen*›; erzielen ‹*Tor, Punkt, Treffer*›; gewinnen ‹*Spiel, Preis, Belohnung*›; belegen ‹*ersten usw. Platz*›; ~ **fame** berühmt werden; ~ **permission** die Erlaubnis erhalten; **he got his fare paid by the firm** seine Firma hat [ihm] die Fahrt bezahlt

[12] (come to have) finden ‹*Schlaf, Ruhe*›; bekommen ‹*Einfall, Vorstellung, Gefühl*›; gewinnen ‹*Eindruck*›; (contract) bekommen ‹*Kopfschmerzen, Grippe, Malaria*›; ~ **some rest** sich ausruhen; ~ **one's freedom** seine Freiheit wiederhaben; ~ **an idea/a habit from sb.** von jmdm. eine Idee/Angewohnheit übernehmen; **I hope I don't** ~ **the flu from you** hoffentlich steckst du mich nicht mit deiner Grippe an; *see also* **brain A 1**; **religion 2**

[13] **have got** (coll.: have) haben; **give it all you've got** gib dein Bestes; **have got a toothache/a cold** Zahnschmerzen/eine Erkältung haben *od.* erkältet sein; **have got to do sth.** etw. tun müssen; **something has got to be done [about it]** dagegen muss etwas unternommen werden

[14] (succeed in bringing, placing, etc.) bringen; kriegen (ugs.); ~ **sth. through the door** *etc.* etw. durch die Tür *usw.* bekommen; **she could hardly** ~ **herself out of bed** sie kam kaum aus dem Bett hoch; **that bike won't** ~ **you very far** mit dem Fahrrad wirst du nicht weit kommen; **I must** ~ **a message to her** ich muss ihr eine Nachricht zukommen lassen; **he's got you where he wants you** er hat dich genau da[hin] gekriegt, wo er dich hin haben wollte (ugs.)

[15] (bring into some state) **this music will** ~ **the party going** diese Musik wird Schwung in die Party bringen; ~ **a project going** ein Projekt in Gang bringen; ~ **a machine going** eine Maschine in Gang setzen *od.* bringen; ~ **things going** *or* **started** die Dinge in Gang bringen; ~ **everything packed/prepared** alles [ein]packen/vorbereiten; ~ **sth. ready/done** etw. fertig machen; ~ **oneself talked about** sich ins Gerede bringen; ~ **one's feet wet** nasse Füße kriegen; ~ **one's hands dirty** sich *(Dat.)* die Hände schmutzig machen; **I want to** ~ **the work done** ich möchte die Arbeit fertig haben; **I didn't** ~ **much done today** ich habe heute nicht viel geschafft; ~ **with child** (dated) schwängern; **he's got his sums right** er hat richtig gerechnet; **I need to** ~ **my house painted** ich muss mein Haus streichen lassen; **you'll** ~ **yourself thrown out/arrested** du schaffst es noch, dass du rausgeworfen/verhaftet wirst; **I got myself lost** ich habe mich verlaufen; ~ **sb. talking/drunk/interested** jmdn. zum Reden bringen/betrunken machen/jmds. Interesse wecken; ~ **one's hair cut/clothes dry-cleaned** sich *(Dat.)* die Haare schneiden lassen/seine Sachen reinigen lassen

[16] (induce) ~ **sb. to do sth.** jmdn. dazu bringen, etw. zu tun; ~ **sth. to do sth.** es schaffen, dass etw. etw. tut; **I can never** ~ **you to listen to me** nie hörst du mir zu!; **I can't** ~ **the car to start/the door to shut** ich kriege das Auto nicht in Gang/die Tür nicht zu

[17] (bring in) einbringen ‹*Ernte*›

[18] (Radio, Telev.: pick up) empfangen ‹*Sender*›; **he's trying to** ~ **BBC 2** er versucht, BBC 2 reinzukriegen (ugs.)

[19] (get in touch with by telephone) ~ **sb. [on the phone]** jmdn. [telefonisch] erreichen; **please** ~ **me this number** bitte verbinden Sie mich mit dieser Nummer

[20] (answer) **I'll** ~ **it!** ich geh schon!; (answer doorbell) ich mach auf; (answer the phone) ich gehe ran (ugs.) *od.* nehme ab

[21] (coll.: perplex) in Verwirrung bringen; **this question will** ~ **him** mit dieser Frage kriegen wir ihn (ugs.); **you've got me there; I don't know** da bin ich überfragt — ich weiß es nicht

[22] (coll.) (understand) kapieren (ugs.); verstehen ‹*Personen*›; (hear) mitkriegen (ugs.); ~ **it?** alles klar? (ugs.)

[23] (coll.: annoy) aufregen (ugs.)

[24] (coll.: attract, involve emotionally) packen

B *v.i.*, **-tt-, got, got** *or* (Amer.) **gotten** [1] (succeed in coming or going) kommen; ~ **to London/the top before dark** London/den Gipfel vor Einbruch der Dunkelheit erreichen; **we got as far as Oxford** wir kamen bis Oxford; **we have got as far as quadratic equations** wir sind bis zu quadratischen Gleichungen gekommen; **how did that** ~ **here?** wie ist das hierher gekommen?

[2] (come to be) ~ **working** sich an die Arbeit machen; ~ **talking [to sb.]** [mit jmdm.] ins Gespräch kommen; ~ **to talking about sth./sb.** auf etw./jmdn. zu sprechen kommen; **I got [to] thinking how nice …:** ich habe mir überlegt, wie nett …; ~ **going** *or* **started** (leave) losgehen; aufbrechen; (start talking) loslegen (ugs.); (become lively or operative) in Schwung kommen; **once he** ~**s going** wenn er einmal anfängt; ~ **going on** *or* **with sth.** mit etw. anfangen; sich hinter etw. *(Akk.)* klemmen (ugs.); ~ **going on sb.** jmdn. bearbeiten; **I can't** ~ **started in the mornings** ich komme morgens nicht in Gang; *see also* **way A 6**

[3] ~ **to know sb.** jmdn. kennen lernen; **he got to like/hate her** mit der Zeit mochte er sie/begann er, sie zu hassen; ~ **to hear of sth.** von etw. erfahren; **I never** ~ **to see you any more** dich sieht man ja gar nicht mehr; dich bekommt man ja gar nicht mehr zu Gesicht; ~ **to do sth.** (succeed in doing) etw. tun können; dazu kommen, etw. zu tun

[4] (become) werden; ~ **ready/washed** sich fertig machen/waschen; ~ **frightened/hungry** Angst/Hunger kriegen; **the time is** ~**ting near** die Zeit naht; ~ **excited about sth.** sich auf etw. *(Akk.)* freuen; ~ **interested in sth.** sich für etw. interessieren; ~ **caught in the rain** vom Regen überrascht werden; ~ **well soon!** gute Besserung!; *see also* **better A**

[5] (coll.: be off, clear out) verschwinden (ugs.)

(Phrasal verbs)

• ~ **a'bout** *v.i.* [1] (move) sich bewegen; (travel) herumkommen [2] (spread) sich herumsprechen; ‹*Gerücht:*› sich verbreiten

• ~ **across**

A /--'-/ *v.i.* [1] (to/from other side) rüberkommen (ugs.) [2] (be communicated) rüberkommen (ugs.); ~ **across [to sb.]** ‹*Person:*› sich [jmdm.] verständlich machen; ‹*Witz, Idee:*› [bei jmdm.] ankommen

B *[stress varies] v.t.* [1] (cross) überqueren; ~ **sb./sth. across [sth.]** (transport to/from other side) jmdn./etw. [über etw. *(Akk.)*] hin-/herüberbringen [2] (communicate) vermitteln, klarmachen (**to** *Dat.*); ~ **a joke across to sb.** mit einem Witz bei jmdm. ankommen

• ~ **a'long** *v.i.* [1] (advance, progress) ~ **along well** [gute] Fortschritte machen; **how is he** ~**ting along with his work/is his work** ~**ting**

g

along? wie kommt er mit seiner Arbeit voran/kommt seine *od.* geht es mit seiner Arbeit voran?; **the patient is ~ting along very well** mit dem Patienten geht es aufwärts [2] (manage) zurechtkommen [3] (agree or live sociably) auskommen; **~ along with each other** *or* **together** miteinander auskommen [4] (leave) sich auf den Weg machen; **~ along with you!** (fig. coll.) ach, geh *od.* komm! (ugs.); ach, erzähl mir doch nichts! (ugs.)

• **~ a'round**

A *v.i.* [1] ▸**~ round A 2** [2] ▸**~ about 1**

B *v.t.* ▸**~ round B 1, 2, 4**

• **~ at** *v.t.* [1] herankommen an (+ *Akk.*); **let sb. ~ at sth.** jmdn. an etw. (*Akk.*) [heran]lassen; **woodworm has got at the wardrobe** in dem Schrank ist der Holzwurm [2] (coll.: start work on) sich machen an (+ *Akk.*) [3] (get hold of; ascertain) [he]rausfinden ‹*Wahrheit, Ursache usw.*› [4] (coll.) **what are you/is he ~ting at?** worauf wollen Sie/will er hinaus?; (referring to) worauf spielen Sie/spielt er jetzt an? [5] (coll.: tamper with) sich zu schaffen machen an (+ *Dat.*); (bribe) bestechen; (influence) unter Druck setzen [6] (coll.: attack, taunt) anmachen (salopp); **I have the feeling that I'm being got at** ich habe das Gefühl, dass man mich anpflaumen will (ugs.)

• **~ a'way**

A *v.i.* [1] wegkommen; (stand back) zurücktreten; **you need to ~ away [from here]** du müsstest einmal [von hier] fort; **I can't ~ away from work** ich kann nicht von der Arbeit weg; **~ away from the field** (Racing) sich vom Feld absetzen; **there is no ~ting away from the fact that ...:** man kommt nicht um die Tatsache *od.* darum herum, dass ...; **~ away from it all** ▸**all A 1** [2] (escape) entkommen; entwischen (ugs.); **that's the one that got away** (fig.) das/der/die ist mir/dir *usw.* durch die Lappen gegangen (ugs.) [3] (start) aufbrechen; ‹*Läufer:*› losrennen; ‹*Schwimmer:*› losschwimmen; ‹*Flugzeug:*› starten; ‹*Rennwagen:*› [vom Start] wegkommen, starten [4] *in imper.* (coll.) **~ away [with you]!** ach, geh *od.* komm! (ugs.); ach, erzähl mir doch nichts! (ugs.)

B *v.t.* [1] (remove, move) wegnehmen; entfernen, (ugs.) wegkriegen ‹*Fleck*›; wegräumen ‹*Besteck, Geschirr*›; **~ sth. away from sb.** jmdm. etw. wegnehmen; **we've got to ~ her away from here/his influence/her boyfriend** wir müssen sie von hier fortbringen/seinem Einfluss entziehen/von ihrem Freund fernhalten [2] (post) zur Post bringen; abschicken; wegkriegen (ugs.). *see also* **~away**

• **~ a'way with** *v.t.* [1] (steal and escape with) entkommen mit [2] (as punishment) davonkommen mit [3] (go unpunished for) ungestraft davonkommen mit; **the things he ~s away with!** was der sich (*Dat.*) alles erlauben kann!; **~ away with it** es sich (*Dat.*) erlauben können; (succeed) damit durchkommen; **he can ~ away with anything** *or* (fig.) **murder** er kann sich (*Dat.*) alles erlauben

• **~ 'back**

A *v.i.* [1] (return) zurückkommen; **~ back home** nach Hause kommen [2] (stand away) zurücktreten

B *v.t.* [1] (recover) wieder- *od.* zurückbekommen; wieder- *od.* zurückkriegen (ugs.); zurückgewinnen ‹*Kraft, Ehefrau, Freund usw.*›; **~ one's strength back** wieder zu Kräften kommen [2] (return) zurücktun; **I can't ~ the lid back on it** ich kriege den Deckel nicht wieder drauf (ugs.); **~ the children back home** die Kinder nach Hause zurückbringen [3] **~ one's 'own back [on sb.]** (coll.) sich [an jmdm.] rächen

• **~ 'back at** *v.t.* (coll.) **~ back at sb. for sth.** jmdm. etw. heimzahlen

• **~ 'back to** *v.t.* **~ back to sb./sb.'s question** auf jmdn./jmds. Frage zurückkommen; **I'll ~ back to you on that** ich komme darauf noch zurück; **~ back to one's work/to work/to the office** wieder an seine Arbeit/an die Arbeit/ins Büro gehen; **~ting back to what I was saying ...:** um [noch einmal] auf das, was ich gesagt habe, zurückzukommen

• **~ behind**

A /-'-/ *v.i.* zurückbleiben; ins Hintertreffen geraten (ugs.); (with payments) in Rückstand geraten

B [*stress varies*] *v.t.* [1] **~ behind sb./sth.** sich hinter jmdn./etw. stellen [2] (not progress as fast as) **~ behind sb./sth.** hinter jmdm./etw. zurückbleiben

• **~ 'by**

A *v.i.* [1] (move past) passieren; vorbeikommen; **let sb. ~ by** jmdn. vorbeilassen [2] (coll.: be acceptable, adequate) **she should [just about] ~ by in the exam** sie müsste die Prüfung [gerade so] schaffen; **his essay isn't very good but it will ~ by** sein Aufsatz ist nicht sehr gut, aber es reicht noch [3] (coll.: survive, manage) über die Runden kommen (ugs.) (**on** mit)

B *v.t.* [1] (move past) **~ by sb./sth.** an jmdm./etw. vorbeikommen; **he got by the car in front** er überholte den vorderen Wagen [2] (pass unnoticed) entgehen (+ *Dat.*); unbemerkt vorbeikommen an (+ *Dat.*)

• **~ down**

A /-'-/ *v.i.* [1] (come down) heruntersteigen; (go down) hinuntersteigen; (from bus etc.) aussteigen (**from** aus); (from horse) absteigen (**from** von); **help sb. ~ down from the horse/bus** jmdm. vom Pferd/aus dem Bus helfen [2] (leave table) aufstehen [3] (bend down) sich bücken; **~ down on one's knees** niederknien; sich hinknien

B [*stress varies*] *v.t.* [1] (come down) heruntersteigen; herunterkommen; (go down) hinuntersteigen; hinuntergehen [2] **~ sb./sth. down** (manage to bring down) jmdn./etw. hin-/herunterbringen; (with some difficulty) jmdn./etw. hin-/herunterbekommen; (take down from above) jmdn./etw. hin-/herunterholen [3] **~ one's trousers down** die Hose herunterziehen [4] (swallow) hinunterschlucken [5] (write, record) **~ sth. down [on paper]** etw. schriftlich festhalten *od.* zu Papier bringen [6] (depress) fertig machen (ugs.) [7] (reduce) kürzen ‹*Aufsatz*› (**to** auf + *Akk.*); senken ‹*Fieber, Preis*›; (by bargaining) herunterdrücken ‹*Preis*›; **I got him down [to £40]** ich habe ihn [auf 40 Pfund] heruntergehandelt

• **~ 'down to** *v.t.* **~ down to sth.** sich an etw. (*Akk.*) machen; **~ down to writing a letter** sich hinsetzen und einen Brief schreiben; **let's ~ down to the facts now** wenden wir uns nun den Fakten zu; *see also* **brass tacks**; **business 6**

• **~ 'in**

A *v.i.* [1] (enter) (into bus etc.) einsteigen; (into bath) hineinsteigen; (into bed) sich hinlegen; (into room, house, etc.) eintreten; (intrude) eindringen [2] (arrive) ankommen; (**~** home) heimkommen [3] (be elected) gewählt werden; **~ in for Islington** als Abgeordneter für Islington ins Unterhaus einziehen [4] (obtain place) (at institution etc.) angenommen werden; (at university) einen Studienplatz bekommen; (as employee) genommen werden [5] (coll.: gain an advantage) **~ in first/before sb.** die Nase vorn haben (ugs.)/schneller als jmd. sein

B *v.t.* [1] (bring in) einbringen ‹*Ernte*›; hineinbringen, ins Haus bringen ‹*Einkäufe, Kind*›; einlagern ‹*Kohlen, Kartoffeln*›; hineinfahren, in die Garage fahren ‹*Auto*›; reinholen ‹*Wäsche*›; einholen ‹*Netze, Hummerkörbe*›; (Brit.: fetch and pay for) holen ‹*Getränke*› [2] (enter) einsteigen in (+ *Akk.*) ‹*Auto, Zug*› [3] (submit) abgeben ‹*Artikel, Hausarbeit*›; einreichen ‹*Bewerbung, Bericht*› [4] (receive) erhalten; reinkriegen (ugs.) [5] (send for) holen; rufen ‹*Arzt, Polizei*›; hinzuziehen ‹*Spezialist*› [6] (plant, sow) in die Erde kriegen (ugs.); auspflanzen ‹*Blumenzwiebeln*›; aussäen ‹*Samen*› [7] (fit in) reinkriegen (ugs.); einschieben ‹*Unterrichtsstunde*›; **try to ~ in a word about sth.** sich zu etw. äußern wollen; *see also* **edgeways 3** [8] (cause to be admitted) **~ sb. in** (as member, pupil, etc.) jmdm. die Aufnahme ermöglichen; jmdn. reinbringen (ugs.); **his good results should ~ him in** mit seinen guten Noten müsste er reinkommen; **you can ~ him in as a guest** du kannst ihn als Gast mitbringen [9] (Boxing) **~ a blow/punch in** einen Schlag *od.* Treffer landen; (fig.: coll.) einen Schlag versetzen. *See also* **eye A 1**; **hand A 11**

• **~ 'in on** *v.t.* (coll.) sich beteiligen an (+ *Dat.*); *see also* **act A 5**

• **~ into** *v.t.* [1] (bring into) fahren ‹*Auto usw.*› in (+ *Akk.*) ‹*Garage*›; bringen in (+ *Akk.*) ‹*Haus, Bett, Hafen*› [2] (enter) gehen/(as intruder) eindringen in (+ *Akk.*) ‹*Haus*›; [ein]steigen in (+ *Akk.*) ‹*Auto usw.*›; [ein]treten in (+ *Akk.*) ‹*Zimmer*›; steigen in (+ *Akk.*) ‹*Wasser*›; **the coach ~s into the station at 9 p.m.** der Bus kommt um 21.00 Uhr am Busbahnhof an; **it's ~ting into the hundreds** das geht schon in die Hunderte [3] (gain admission to) eingelassen werden in (+ *Akk.*); angenommen werden in (+ *Dat.*) ‹*Schule*›; einen Studienplatz erhalten an (+ *Dat.*) ‹*Universität*›; genommen werden von ‹*Firma*›; **~ sb. into a school/firm/club** dafür sorgen, dass jmd. von einer Schule angenommen/einer Firma genommen/einem Verein aufgenommen wird; **~ into Parliament** ins Parlament einziehen [4] (coll.: make put on) hineinkriegen in (+ *Akk.*); **~ into one's clothes** sich anziehen; **I can't ~ into these trousers** ich komme in diese Hose nicht mehr rein (ugs.) [5] (penetrate) [ein]dringen in (+ *Akk.*); **sand got into my eyes** ich habe Sand in die Augen bekommen; **how did the fly ~ into the jam?** wie ist die Fliege in die Marmelade gekommen? [6] (begin to undergo) geraten in (+ *Akk.*); kommen in (+ *Akk.*) ‹*Schwierigkeiten*›; (cause to undergo) stürzen in (+ *Akk.*) ‹*Schulden, Unglück*›; bringen in (+ *Akk.*) ‹*Schwierigkeiten*› [7] (accustom to, become accustomed to) annehmen ‹*Gewohnheit*›; **~ into the job/work** sich einarbeiten; **once you've got into the book, ...:** wenn man sich einmal eingelesen hat, ...; *see also* **habit A 1**; **way A 12, 15** [8] (change in mood to) geraten in (+ *Akk.*) ‹*Wut, Panik*›; (cause to change in mood to) bringen in (+ *Akk.*) ‹*Wut*›; stürzen in (+ *Akk.*) ‹*Verzweiflung, Panik*› [9] **what's got into him?** was ist nur in ihn gefahren?; **something must have got into him** irgendetwas muss in ihn gefahren sein. *See also* **act A 5**

• **~ 'in with** *v.t.* (coll.) **~ in [well] with sb.** sich mit jmdm. gut stellen; **he got in with a bad crowd** er geriet in schlechte Gesellschaft; **he got in with a pretty girl** er bändelte mit einem hübschen Mädchen an

• **~ off**

A /-'-/ *v.i.* [1] (alight) aussteigen; (dismount) absteigen; **tell sb. where he ~s off** *or* **where to ~ off** (fig. coll.) jmdn. in seine Grenzen verweisen; **she told him where to ~ off in no uncertain terms** sie machte ihm unmissverständlich klar, dass er zu weit gegangen war [2] (not remain on sb./sth.) runtergehen; (from chair) aufstehen; (from ladder, tree, table, lawn, carpet) herunterkommen; (let go) loslassen; **~ off, you filthy dog!** verschwinde, du dreckiger Köter! [3] (start) aufbrechen; **~ off to school/to work** zur Schule/Arbeit losgehen/-fahren; **we hope to ~ off before seven** wir hoffen, noch vor sieben wegzukommen; **~ off to an early start** früh aufbrechen *od.* wegkommen; **~ off to a good** *etc.* **start** einen guten *usw.* Start haben; *see also* **foot A 1** [4] (be sent) ‹*Brief:*› abgeschickt werden; ‹*Paket, Telegramm:*› aufgegeben werden [5] (escape punishment or injury) davonkommen; **~ off lightly** glimpflich davonkommen [6] (fall asleep) einschlafen [7] (leave) [weg]gehen; **~ off early** [schon] früh [weg]gehen

B [*stress varies*] *v.t.* [1] (dismount from) [ab]steigen von ‹*Fahrrad*›; steigen von ‹*Pferd*›; (alight from) aussteigen aus ‹*Bus, Zug usw.*›; steigen aus ‹*Boot*› [2] (not remain on) herunterkommen von ‹*Rasen, Teppich, Mauer, Leiter, Tisch*›; aufstehen von ‹*Stuhl*›; verschwinden von, verlassen ‹*Gelände*›; **~ off my toes!** geh von meinem Fuß runter! (ugs.); **~ off the subject** vom Thema abkommen [3] (cause to start) [los]schicken; **it takes ages to ~ the children off to school** es dauert eine Ewigkeit, die Kinder für die Schule fertig zu machen; **~ sth. off to a good** *etc.* **start** einer Sache (*Dat.*) zu einem guten *usw.* Start verhelfen [4] (remove) ausziehen ‹*Kleidung usw.*›; entfernen ‹*Fleck, Farbe usw.*›; abbekommen ‹*Deckel, Ring*›; **~ sth. off sth.** etw. von etw. entfernen/abbekommen; **~ sb./an animal off [sth.]** jmdn./ein Tier [von etw.] wegjagen; **I can't ~ my shoes off** ich kriege die Schuhe nicht aus (ugs.); **~ that cat off my desk/me!** schaff mir die Katze vom Tisch/Leib!; **~ sb. off a subject** jmdn. von einem Thema abbringen [5] (send, dispatch) abschicken; aufgeben ‹*Telegramm, Paket*› [6] (cause to escape punishment) davonkommen lassen; **the lawyer got his client off with a**

small fine der Rechtsanwalt konnte für seinen Klienten ein niedriges Bußgeld durchsetzen **7** (not have to do, go to, etc.) frei haben; ~ **off school/doing one's homework** nicht zur Schule zu gehen/keine Hausaufgaben zu machen brauchen; ~ **time/a day off [work]** frei/einen Tag frei bekommen; ~ **off work [early]** [früher] Feierabend machen; **I have got the afternoon off** ich habe den Nachmittag frei **8** (cause to fall asleep) zum Einschlafen bringen **9** (coll.: obtain from) bekommen von; kriegen von (ugs.); **I got that recipe off my mother** das Rezept habe ich von meiner Mutter

• ~ **'off with** *v.t.* (Brit. coll.) aufreißen (salopp); anbändeln mit (ugs.); ~ **sb. off with sb.** jmdn. mit jmdm. zusammenbringen *od.* verkuppeln

• ~ **on**

A /-'-/ *v.i.* **1** (climb on) (on bicycle) aufsteigen; (on horse etc.) aufsitzen; (enter vehicle) einsteigen; **you can't ~ on, the bus is full** Sie können nicht mehr rein (ugs.), der Bus ist voll **2** (make progress) vorankommen; ~ **on in life/the world** es [im Leben] zu etwas bringen; **you're ~ting on very nicely** Sie machen gute Fortschritte **3** (fare) **how did you ~ on there?** wie ist es dir dort ergangen?; **he's ~ting on well** es geht ihm gut; **I didn't ~ on too well in my exams** meine Prüfungen sind nicht besonders gut gelaufen (ugs.) **4** (become late) vorrücken; **it's ~ting on for five** es geht auf fünf zu; **it's ~ting on for six months since ...:** es sind bald sechs Monate, seit ...; **time is ~ting on** es wird langsam spät **5** ▸**i p. 894** (advance in age) älter werden; **be ~ting on in years/for seventy** langsam älter werden/auf die Siebzig zugehen **6** **there were ~ting on for fifty people** es waren an die fünfzig Leute da **7** (manage) zurechtkommen **8** ▸~ **along X3**

B [*stress varies*] *v.t.* **1** (climb on) steigen auf (+ *Akk.*) ‹*Fahrrad, Pferd*›; (cause to climb on) setzen auf (+ *Akk.*); (enter, board) einsteigen in (+ *Akk.*) ‹*Zug, Bus, Flugzeug*›; gehen auf (+ *Akk.*) ‹*Schiff*›; (cause to enter or board) setzen in (+ *Akk.*) ‹*Bus, Zug, Flugzeug*›; bringen auf (+ *Akk.*) ‹*Schiff*› **2** (put on) anziehen ‹*Kleider, Schuhe*›; aufsetzen ‹*Hut, Kessel*›; (load) [auf]laden auf (+ *Akk.*); ~ **the cover [back] on** den Deckel [wieder] drauftun; (with some difficulty) den Deckel [wieder] draufbekommen **3** (coll.) **have got something on sb.** (discover sth. incriminating) etwas gegen jmdn. in der Hand haben. *See also* **foot A 1**; **move A 6**; **nerve A 2**

• ~ **'on to** *v.t.* **1** ▸~ **on B 1** **2** (contact) sich in Verbindung setzen mit; (by telephone) anrufen; (more insistently) ~ **on to sb.** jmdm. auf die Pelle rücken (ugs.) **3** (trace, find) ausfindig machen; ~ **on to sb.'s trail/scent** jmdm. auf die Spur kommen/jmds. Fährte aufnehmen **4** (realize) ~ **on to sth.** hinter etw. (*Akk.*) kommen; ~ **on to the fact that ...:** dahinter kommen, dass ... **5** (move or pass to) übergehen zu; (unintentionally in conversation) kommen auf (+ *Akk.*); **we don't ~ on to anatomy until next year** zur Anatomie kommen wir erst im nächsten Jahr

• ~ **'on with** *v.t.* **1** weitermachen mit; **let sb. ~ on with it** (coll.) jmdn. [allein weiter]machen lassen; **enough to be ~ting on with** genug für den Anfang *od.* fürs Erste **2** = ~ **along with** ▸~ **along 1, 3**

• ~ **'out**

A *v.i.* **1** (go away) (walk out) rausgehen (**of** aus); (drive out) rausfahren (**of** aus); (alight) aussteigen (**of** aus); (climb out) rausklettern (**of** aus); ~ **out from under** (fig. coll.) noch einmal davonkommen; ~ **out [of my room]!** raus [aus meinem Zimmer]!; **we'd better ~ out, and quick!** wir verschwinden hier besser, und zwar schnell!; **you need to ~ out a bit more** du müsstest hier öfter mal raus; **she likes to ~ out for a breath of fresh air** sie geht gern mal vor die Tür, um frische Luft zu schnappen **2** (leak) austreten (**of** aus); (escape from cage, jail) ausbrechen, entkommen (**of** aus); (fig.) ‹*Geheimnis:*› herauskommen; ‹*Nachrichten:*› durchsickern **3** ~ **out [of it]!** (coll.) ach, geh *od.* komm!; ach, erzähl mir doch nichts! (ugs.) **4** (Cricket) ausgeschlagen werden

B *v.t.* **1** (cause to leave) rausbringen (**of** aus); (send out) rausschicken (**of** aus); (throw out) rauswerfen (**of** aus); ~ **all the passengers out** alle Passagiere aussteigen lassen; ~ **a nail out/out of the wall** einen Nagel herauskriegen/aus der Wand kriegen (ugs.); ~ **a stain out/out of sth.** einen Fleck wegbekommen/aus etw. herausbekommen **2** (bring or take out) herausholen (**of** aus); herausziehen ‹*Korken*›; (drive out) herausfahren (**of** aus); **you only ~ out what you put in** (fig.) man kriegt nur raus, was man reingesteckt hat (ugs.) **3** (withdraw) abheben ‹*Geld*› (**of** von) **4** (publish) herausbringen **5** (speak, utter) hervorbringen ‹*Entschuldigung, Gruß usw.*›; herausbringen ‹*Wort*› **6** (Cricket) ausschlagen **7** (work out) herausbekommen, (ugs.) herauskriegen ‹*Rechenaufgabe, Summe, Rätsel*›. *see also* **~-out**

• ~ **'out of** *v.t.* **1** (leave) verlassen ‹*Zimmer, Haus, Stadt, Land*›; (cause to leave) entfernen aus; (extract from) herausziehen aus; (bring or take out of) herausholen; (leak from) austreten aus; (withdraw from) abheben von; ~ **a book out of the library** ein Buch aus der Bibliothek ausleihen; ~ **a lazy person out of bed** einen Faulpelz aus dem Bett kriegen (ugs.); ~ **him out of my sight!** schaff ihn mir aus den Augen!; ~ **me out of this mess** hol mich aus diesem Schlamassel heraus! (ugs.); ~ **sth. out of one's head** *or* **mind** sich (*Dat.*) etw. aus dem Kopf schlagen; **he can't ~ the idea out of his head** er wird den Gedanken nicht los; *see also* ~ **out A 1, 2, 3, B 1, 2, 3** **2** (draw out of) herausbringen (ugs.) *od.* herausbekommen ‹*Wahrheit, Worte*› aus **3** (escape) herauskommen aus; (avoid) herumkommen um (ugs.); sich drücken vor (+ *Dat.*) (ugs.) ‹*Arbeit*›; **I can't ~ out of it now** jetzt muss ich mich auch daran halten **4** (gain from) herausholen ‹*Geld*› aus; machen (ugs.) *od.* erzielen ‹*Gewinn*› bei; **I couldn't ~ much out of this book** das Buch hat mir nicht viel gegeben; ~ **a word/the truth/a confession out of sb.** aus jmdm. ein Wort/die Wahrheit/ein Geständnis herausbringen; ~ **the best/most/utmost out of sb./sth.** das Beste/Meiste/Äußerste aus jmdm./etw. herausholen. *See also* **bed A 1**; **depth 4**; **habit A 1**; **hand A 2**; **way A 12**

• ~ **outside [of]** *v.t.* (sl.: eat) sich reinziehen (ugs.)

• ~ **'over**

A *v.i.* **1** (cross) ~ **over to the other side** auf die andere Seite gehen; **manage to ~ over to the other side** es schaffen, auf die andere Seite zu kommen; **I need to talk to you. When can you ~ over here?** ich muss dich sprechen — wann kannst du mal vorbeikommen? **2** (coll.) ▸~ **across A 2**

B *v.t.* **1** (cross) gehen über (+ *Akk.*); setzen über (+ *Akk.*) ‹*Fluss*›; (climb) klettern über (+ *Akk.*); (cause to cross) [hinüber]bringen über (+ *Akk.*); **we got ourselves safely over the river** wir kamen sicher über den Fluss; **manage to ~ over the road** es schaffen, über die Straße zu kommen **2** ▸~ **across B 2** **3** (surmount) überwinden **4** (overcome) überwinden; hinwegkommen über (+ *Akk.*) **5** (recover from) überwinden; hinwegkommen über (+ *Akk.*); verwinden (geh.) ‹*Verlust*›; sich erholen von ‹*Krankheit*› **6** (fully believe) **I can't ~ over his cheek/the fact that ...:** seine Frechheit kann ich nicht begreifen/ich kann gar nicht fassen, dass ... **7** (travel over) zurücklegen ‹*Strecke*› **8** (do, so as not to have still to come) hinter sich bringen; **you might as well ~ it over and done with** je eher du es tust, desto schneller hast du es hinter dir

• ~ **'over with** *v.t.* ~ **sth. over with** etw. hinter sich (*Akk.*) bringen

• ~ **'past**

A *v.i.* ▸~ **by A 1**

B *v.t.* ▸~ **by B 1, 2**

• ~ **'round**

A *v.i.* **1** ▸~ **about** **2** ~ **round to doing sth.** dazu kommen, etw. zu tun

B *v.t.* **1** **she got round the shops very quickly** sie erledigte ihre Besorgungen sehr schnell **2** (avoid) umgehen ‹*Gesetz, Bestimmungen*› **3** ~ **sb. round,** ~ **round sb.** (~ one's way with) jmdn. herumkriegen (ugs.); (persuade) jmdn. überzeugen (**to** von) **4** (overcome) lösen ‹*Problem usw.*›; überwinden ‹*Hindernis usw.*›; umgehen ‹*Schwierigkeit usw.*›. *See also* **table A 1**; **tongue 3**

• ~ **there** *v.i.* **1** (reach a place) dorthin kommen **2** (coll.: succeed) es schaffen **3** (understand) verstehen, was gemeint ist; dahinter kommen (ugs.)

• ~ **through**

A /-'-/ *v.i.* **1** (pass obstacle) durchkommen; (make contact by radio or telephone) durchkommen (ugs.); Verbindung bekommen (**to** mit) **2** (be transmitted) durchkommen (ugs.); durchdringen (**to** bis zu *od.* nach) **3** (win heat or round) gewinnen; ~ **through to the finals** in die Endrunde kommen **4** ~ **through [to sb.]** (make sb. understand) sich [jmdm.] verständlich machen **5** (pass) bestehen; durchkommen (ugs.) **6** ~ **through on** auskommen mit ‹*Gehalt*› **7** (be approved) angenommen werden; durchkommen (ugs.)

B [*stress varies*] *v.t.* **1** (pass through) [durch]kommen durch; ~ **sth. through sth.** etw. durch etw. [durch]bekommen *od.* (ugs.) [durch]kriegen **2** (help to make contact) ~ **sb. through to** jmdn. verbinden mit **3** (bring) [durch]bringen; übermitteln ‹*Nachricht*› (**to** *Dat.*); ~ **food/a message through to sb.** jmdm. Nahrungsmittel/eine Nachricht zukommen lassen **4** (bring as far as) ~ **a team through to the finals** eine Mannschaft in die Endrunde bringen **5** (communicate) ~ **sth. through to sb.** jmdm. etw. klarmachen **6** (pass) durchkommen bei (ugs.), bestehen ‹*Prüfung*›; (help to pass) durchbringen ‹*Prüfling*› **7** (Parl.: cause to be approved) durchbringen **8** (consume, use up) verbrauchen; verqualmen (ugs. abwertend) ‹*Zigaretten*›; aufessen ‹*Essen*›; ablatschen (salopp) ‹*Schuhe*›; abtragen ‹*Kleidung*›; (spend) durchbringen ‹*Geld, Vermögen*› **9** (survive) durchstehen; überstehen; kommen durch **10** (manage to deal with) fertig werden mit, erledigen ‹*Arbeit*›; durchkriegen ‹*Buch*›; **let me ~ through this work first** lass mich erst diese Arbeit fertig machen; ~ **through reading a book/writing a letter** ein Buch auslesen/einen Brief fertig schreiben

• ~ **'through with** *v.t.* **1** (finish) fertig werden mit ‹*Arbeit*›; erledigen ‹*Formalitäten*›; auslesen ‹*Buch*› **2** (coll.: finish dealing with sb.) **wait till I ~ through with him!** warte, bis ich mit ihm fertig bin!

• ~ **to** *v.t.* **1** (reach) kommen zu ‹*Gebäude*›; erreichen ‹*Person, Ort*›; **I've got to here** ich bin bis hierher gekommen; **he is ~ting to the age when ...:** er wird bald das Alter erreicht haben, wo ...; **where have you got to in German/in this book?** wie weit bist du gekommen in Deutsch/mit *od.* in dem Buch?; **I haven't got to the end [of the novel] yet** ich habe [den Roman] noch nicht zu Ende gelesen; **where has the child/the book got to?** wo ist das Kind hin/das Buch hingekommen? **2** (begin) ~ **to doing sth.** anfangen, etw. zu tun **3** ~ **to sb.** (coll.: annoy) jmdm. auf die Nerven gehen (ugs.); **don't let him ~ to you!** lass dir von ihm nicht auf den Nerven rumtrampeln! (salopp)

• ~ **to'gether**

A *v.i.* zusammenkommen; **we must ~ together again sometime** wir müssen uns bald mal wieder sehen; **why not ~ together after work?** wollen wir uns nach Feierabend treffen?

B *v.t.* **1** (collect) zusammenbringen; ~ **one's things together** seine Sachen zusammenpacken; ~ **one's thoughts together** seine Gedanken sammeln **2** (coll.: organize) ~ **it** *or* **things together** die Dinge auf die Reihe kriegen (ugs.); ~ **oneself together** sich am Riemen reißen (ugs.). *See also* **get-together**

• ~ **'under** *v.t.* (shelter) gehen unter (+ *Akk.*); kriechen unter (+ *Akk.*) ‹*Decke, Bett*›; ~ **sth. under sth.** etw. unter etw. (*Akk.*) tun; **how did my passport manage to ~ under your books?** wie ist mein Pass nur unter deine Bücher gekommen?

• ~ **up**

A /-'-/ *v.i.* **1** (rise from bed, chair, floor; leave table) aufstehen; **please don't ~ up!** bitte bleiben Sie sitzen! **2** (climb) [auf]steigen, aufsitzen (**on** auf

g

+ *Dat. od. Akk.*) 3▸ (rise, increase in force) zunehmen; **the sea is ~ting up** die See wird immer wilder 4▸ (Cricket) ‹*Ball:*› steil hochfliegen 5▸ **~ up and go** (coll.) in Gang kommen
B [*stress varies*] *v.t.* 1▸ (call, awaken) wecken; (cause to leave bed) aus dem Bett holen; **~ oneself up** aufwachen; (leave bed) aus dem Bett kommen 2▸ (cause to stand up) aufhelfen (+ *Dat.*); hochkriegen (ugs.) 3▸ (cause to mount) **~ sb. up on the horse** jmdm. aufs Pferd helfen 4▸ (climb) hinaufsteigen; **your car will not ~ up that hill** dein Auto kommt den Berg nicht hinauf *od.* schafft den Berg nicht; **water got up my nose** ich habe Wasser in die Nase gekriegt (ugs.) 5▸ (carry up) **~ sb./sth. up [sth.]** jmdn./etw. [etw.] her-/hinaufbringen; (with some difficulty) jmdn. etw. [etw.] her-/hinaufbekommen 6▸ (organize) organisieren; auf die Beine stellen; auf die Beine bringen ‹*Personen*› 7▸ (arrange appearance of, dress up) zurechtmachen; herrichten ‹*Zimmer*›; hübsch aufmachen ‹*Buch, Geschenk*›; **got up as** verkleidet als. *See also* **back A 1**; **~-up**; **~-up-and-go**; **steam A**; **wind[1] A 5**
• **~ 'up to** *v.t.* 1▸ (reach) erreichen ‹*Leistungsniveau*›; (cause to reach) bringen auf (+ *Akk.*) 2▸ (indulge in) aus sein auf (+ *Akk.*); **~ up to mischief** etwas anstellen; **what have you been ~ting up to?** was hast du getrieben *od.* angestellt?

get: ~-'at-able *adj.* zugänglich; **~away** *n.* 1▸ Flucht, *die; attrib.* Flucht‹*plan, -wagen*›; **make one's ~away** entkommen; 2▸ (in race) Start, *der;* **~-out** *n.* 1▸ (coll.: evasion) Ausweg, *der;* 2▸ **as** *or* **like [all] ~-out** (coll.) wie nur irgendetwas; **~-rich-'quick** *adj.* **~-rich-quick manual/methods** Handbuch/Methoden, wie man schnell reich wird

gettable /ˈgetəbl/ *adj.* erhältlich

get: ~-together *n.* (coll.) Zusammenkunft, *die;* (informal social gathering) gemütliches Beisammensein; **have a ~-together** sich treffen; zusammenkommen; **~-'tough** *attrib. adj.* kompromisslos; unnachgiebig ‹*Haltung*›; **~-up** *n.* (coll.) Aufmachung, *die;* **buy a new ~-up** sich neu einkleiden; **~-up-and-'go** *n.* (coll.) Elan, *der;* Schwung, *der;* **~-'well card** *n.* Genesungskarte, *die*

geyser *n.* 1▸ /ˈgiːzə(r), ˈgeɪzə(r)/ (hot spring) Geysir, *der* 2▸ /ˈgiːzə(r)/ (Brit. dated: water heater) Durchlauferhitzer, *der*

Ghana /ˈgɑːnə/ *pr. n.* Ghana (*das*)

Ghanaian /gɑːˈneɪən/ ▸ⓘ p. 1345
A *adj.* ghanaisch; **sb. is ~:** jmd. ist Ghanaer/Ghanaerin
B *n.* Ghanaer, *der*/Ghanaerin, *die*

ghastly /ˈgɑːstlɪ/ *adj.* 1▸ grauenvoll; grässlich; entsetzlich ‹*Verletzungen*›; schrecklich ‹*Geschichte, Fehler, Irrtum*› 2▸ (coll.: objectionable, unpleasant) scheußlich (ugs.); grässlich (ugs.); **I feel ~:** ich fühle mich scheußlich 3▸ (pale) leichenblass; leichenhaft ‹*Blässe*›; gespenstisch ‹*Weiß*› 4▸ (forced) verzerrt ‹*Grinsen, Grimasse*›

Ghent /gent/ *pr. n.* ▸ⓘ p. 1643 Gent (*das*)

gherkin /ˈgɜːkɪn/ *n.* Essiggurke, *die*

ghetto /ˈgetəʊ/ *n., pl.* **~s** Getto, *das*

ghetto blaster /ˈgetəʊblɑːstə(r)/ *n.* (coll.) [großer, tragbarer] Radiorekorder

ghost /gəʊst/
A *n.* 1▸ Geist, *der;* Gespenst, *das* 2▸ **give up the ~:** den *od.* seinen Geist aufgeben (veralt., scherzh.); (fig.: give up hope) die Hoffnung aufgeben 3▸ (shadowy outline) Schatten, *der;* (trace) Spur, *die;* **the ~ of a smile** der Anflug eines Lächelns; **not have the** *or* **a ~ of a chance/an idea** nicht die geringste Chance/Ahnung haben 4▸ (Telev.) Geisterbild, *das*
B *v.t.* **~ sb.'s speech** *etc.* für jmdn. eine Rede *usw.* [als Ghostwriter] schreiben
C *v.i.* **~ [for sb.]** [für jmdn.] als Ghostwriter arbeiten

ghosting /ˈgəʊstɪŋ/ *n., no pl.* (Telev.) ein Geisterbild

'ghostlike *adj.* gespenstisch

ghostly /ˈgəʊstlɪ/ *adj.* gespenstisch; geisterhaft; **a ~ presence** die Anwesenheit eines Geistes

ghost: ~ site *n.* (Computing) Geisterseite, *die;* **~ story** *n.* Gespenstergeschichte, *die;* **~ town** *n.* Geisterstadt, *die;* **~ train** *n.* Geisterbahn, *die;* **~ writer** *n.* Ghostwriter, *der*

ghoul /guːl/ *n. Mensch mit einem Hang zum Makabren*

ghoulish /ˈguːlɪʃ/ *adj.* teuflisch ‹*Freude*›; schaurig ‹*Gelächter*›; makaber ‹*Geschichte*›

GHQ *abbr.* = **General Headquarters** HQ; H.-Qu.

GI /dʒiːˈaɪ, dʒiːˈaɪ/
A *adj.* GI-‹*Uniform, Haarschnitt*›; **GI bride** Amibraut, *die* (ugs.); **GI Joe** Amisoldat, *der* (ugs.)
B *n.* GI, *der*

giant /ˈdʒaɪənt/
A *n.* 1▸ (legendary being) Riese, *der;* (Greek Mythol.) Gigant, *der* 2▸ (person) Riese, *der;* (animal, plant) besonders großes Exemplar; **a ~ of a man/plant** ein Riese von einem Mann/eine riesengroße Pflanze 3▸ (person of extraordinary ability) Größe, *die;* **he was one of the ~s of his time** er war einer der Großen seiner Zeit 4▸ (sth. with power) Koloss, *der;* **a ~ among rivers** ein gigantischer Strom 5▸ (Astron.) Riese[nstern], *der*
B *attrib. adj.* riesig; Riesen- (ugs.); Riesen‹*tier, -pflanze*›

giantess /ˈdʒaɪəntɪs/ *n.* Riesin, *die*

giant: ~-killer *n.* Riesenbezwinger, *der;* **~ 'panda** *n.* Bambusbär, *der;* Riesenpanda, *der;* **~ 'slalom** *n.* Riesenslalom, *der*

Gib. /dʒɪb/ *pr. n.* (coll.) Gibraltar (*das*)

gibber /ˈdʒɪbə(r)/ *v.i.* plappern; ‹*Affe:*› schnattern; **I just stood there like a ~ing idiot** ich stand da wie ein Idiot

gibberish /ˈdʒɪbərɪʃ/ *n.* 1▸ (unintelligible chatter) Kauderwelsch, *das* 2▸ (nonsense) Geschwafel, *das* (ugs.); **talk ~:** schwafeln (ugs.)

gibbet /ˈdʒɪbɪt/ *n.* (Hist.) Galgen, *der*

gibbon /ˈgɪbən/ *n.* (Zool.) Gibbon, *der*

gibbous /ˈgɪbəs/ *adj.* Buckel‹*mond*›

gibe /dʒaɪb/
A *n.* Spöttelei, *die* (ugs.); Stichelei, *die* (ugs.); **make ~s at sb.** jmdn. verspotten; gegen jmdn. sticheln (ugs.)
B *v.i.* **~ at sb./sth.** über jmdn./etw. spötteln; sich über jmdn./etw. lustig machen

giblets /ˈdʒɪblɪts/ *n. pl.* [Geflügel]klein, *das*

Gibraltar /dʒɪˈbrɔːltə(r)/ *pr. n.* ▸ⓘ p. 1643 Gibraltar (*das*); **the Rock/Straits of ~:** der Felsen/die Straße von Gibraltar

giddiness /ˈgɪdɪnɪs/ *n., no pl.* Schwindel, *der;* **a feeling of ~:** ein Schwindelgefühl; **fits of ~:** Schwindelanfälle *Pl.*

giddy /ˈgɪdɪ/ *adj.* 1▸ (dizzy) schwind[e]lig; **I feel ~, I have a ~ feeling** mir ist schwindlig; mir schwindelt 2▸ (causing vertigo) Schwindel erregend ‹*Höhe, Abgrund*›; atemberaubend ‹*Geschwindigkeit*› 3▸ (fig.: frivolous) ausgelassen; verrückt (ugs.) 4▸ **my ~ aunt!** (fig. coll.) ach, du dicker Vater! (ugs.); ach, du dickes Ei! (ugs.); *see also* **goat 1**

gift /gɪft/ *n.* 1▸ (present) Geschenk, *das;* Gabe, *die* (geh.); (to an organization) Schenkung, *die;* **make sb. a ~ of sth., make a ~ of sth. to sb.** jmdm. etw. schenken *od.* zum Geschenk machen; **it was given to me as a ~:** ich habe es geschenkt bekommen; **a ~ box/pack** eine Geschenkpackung; **I wouldn't [even] have it as a ~:** das würde ich nicht mal geschenkt nehmen 2▸ (money given to charity) Spende, *die* 3▸ (talent etc.) Begabung, *die;* **a person of many ~s** ein vielseitig begabter Mensch; **have a ~ for languages/mathematics** sprachbegabt/mathematisch begabt sein; *see also* **gab A**; **tongue 3** 4▸ (easy task, real bargain etc.) **be a ~:** geschenkt sein (ugs.) 5▸ (right to give) **sth. is in the ~ of sb.** jmd. hat das Recht, etw. zu vergeben; etw. kann von jmdm. vergeben werden 6▸ (Law) Schenkung, *die*

'gift coupon *n.* Geschenkgutschein, *der*

gifted /ˈgɪftɪd/ *adj.* begabt (**in, at** für); **highly ~:** hoch begabt; begnadet ‹*Künstler*›; **be ~ in** *or* **at languages** sprachbegabt sein

gift: ~ horse *n.* **never** *or* **don't look a ~ horse in the mouth** (prov.) einem geschenkten Gaul schaut man nicht ins Maul (Spr.); **~ shop** *n.* Geschenkboutique, *die;* Geschenkladen, *der;* **~ tax** *n.* (Amer.) Schenkungssteuer, *die;* **~ token, ~ voucher** *ns.* Geschenkgutschein, *der;* **~-wrap** *v.t.* als Geschenk einpacken; in Geschenkpapier einpacken; **~-wrapped** *adj.* 1▸ (wrapped in decorative paper) als Geschenk verpackt; in Geschenkpapier eingepackt; 2▸ (fig.: easliy gained) unverhofft ‹*Chance*›; **come/arrive/be delivered ~-wrapped** auf einem silbernen Tablett serviert werden

gig[1] /gɪg/ *n.* (boat, vehicle) Gig, *das*

gig[2] *n.* (coll.: performance) Gig, *der*

giga- /ˈgɪgə/ *pref.* giga-/Giga-

'gigabyte *n.* (Computing) Gigabyte, *das*

gigantic /dʒaɪˈgæntɪk/ *adj.* gigantisch; riesig; enorm, gewaltig ‹*Verbesserung, Appetit, Portion*›; **a ~ success/effort** ein Riesenerfolg/eine Riesenanstrengung; **grow to a ~ size** riesengroß werden

'gigawatt *n.* Gigawatt, *das*

giggle /ˈgɪgl/
A *n.* 1▸ Kichern, *das;* Gekicher, *das;* **have a ~ about sth.** über etw. (*Akk.*) kichern; **with a ~:** kichernd; **[a fit of] the ~s** ein Kicheranfall; **get/have the ~s** kichern müssen 2▸ (coll.) (amusing person) Witzbold, *der;* (amusing thing, joke) Spaß, *der;* **it was a bit of a ~:** es war ganz amüsant; **for a ~:** aus Spaß; **we did it for a ~:** wir wollten unseren Spaß haben
B *v.i.* kichern

giggly /ˈgɪglɪ/ *adj.* kicherig; (giggling) kichernd

gigolo /ˈ(d)ʒɪgələʊ/ Gigolo, *der*

gild[1] /gɪld/ *v.t.* vergolden; (with gold-coloured paint) mit Goldbronze überziehen; **~ed cage** (fig.) goldener Käfig (fig.); **~ed youth** Jeunesse dorée, *die* (veralt.); **~ the lily** etwas Vollkommenes [unnötigerweise] noch vervollkommnen [wollen]; des Guten zu viel tun

gild[2] ▸ **guild**

gilding /ˈgɪldɪŋ/ *n.* Goldauflage, *die;* (process) Vergoldung, *die;* (paint) Goldfarbe, *die*

gill[1] /gɪl/ *n., usu. in pl.* 1▸ (of fish etc.) Kieme, *die;* **green about the ~s** (fig.) grün *od.* blass um die Nase[nspitze] (ugs.) 2▸ (of mushroom etc.) Lamelle, *die*

gill[2] *n.* (Brit.) 1▸ (ravine) [bewaldete] Schlucht 2▸ (torrent) Wildbach, *der*

gill[3] /dʒɪl/ *n.* Viertelpint, *das* (*0,142 l*)

gillie /ˈgɪlɪ/ *n.* (Scot.: Hunting) Jagdgehilfe, *der*

gilt /gɪlt/
A *n.* 1▸ (gilding) Goldauflage, *die;* (paint) Goldfarbe, *die;* **take the ~ off the gingerbread** (fig.) der Sache den Reiz nehmen 2▸ *in pl.* = **~-edged securities** ▸ **~-edged**
B *adj.* vergoldet

gilt-edged *adj.* (Commerc.) **~ securities/stocks** mündelsichere Wertpapiere

gimbal /ˈgɪmbəl/ *n.* Kardanaufhängung, *die*

gimcrack /ˈdʒɪmkræk/ *adj.* schäbig

gimlet /ˈgɪmlɪt/ *n.* [Hand]bohrer, *der;* **~ eye** Luchsauge, *das;* (fig.) Scharfblick, *der*

gimme /ˈgɪmɪ/ (coll.) = **give me**

gimmick /ˈgɪmɪk/ *n.* (coll.) Gag, *der;* **a publicity/public relations/promotional ~:** ein Werbegag

gimmickry /ˈgɪmɪkrɪ/ *n.* (coll.) Firlefanz, *der* (ugs.); Pipifax, *der* (ugs.); **advertising ~:** Werbetricks *od.* -gags *Pl.*

gimmicky /ˈgɪmɪkɪ/ *adj.* (coll.) vergagt; **~ publicity stunts** verrückte Werbegags

gin[1] /dʒɪn/ *n.* (drink) Gin, *der;* **~ and tonic** Gin [und] Tonic, *der;* **~ and it** (Brit. coll.) Gin und [italienischer] Wermut; **pink ~:** Gin und Angostura

gin[2] *n.* (trap) Falle, *die;* (snare) Schlinge, *die*

ginger /ˈdʒɪndʒə(r)/
A *n.* 1▸ Ingwer, *der* 2▸ (colour) Rötlichgelb, *das;* **his hair was a bright shade of ~:** er hatte helles rötliches Haar 3▸ (vigour) Feuer, *das;* Schwung, *der*
B *adj.* 1▸ (flavour) Ingwer‹*gebäck, -geschmack*› 2▸ (colour) rötlich gelb; rotblond ‹*Bart, Haare*›
C *v.t.* **~ up** (fig.) in Schwung bringen

ginger: ~ 'ale *n.* Gingerale, *das;* **~ 'beer** *n.* Ingwerbier, *das;* Gingerbeer, *das;* **~ beer plant**

Mischung aus Hefe und Bakterie zur Gärung von Gingerbeer; ~ **'biscuit** *n.* Ingwerkeks, *der;* **~bread** A *n.* 1 Pfefferkuchen, *der; see also* **gilt** A 1; 2 (Archit. etc.) überflüssiger [geschmackloser] Schmuck; B *adj.* (fig.) überladen; zuckerbäckerhaft ‹[Bau]stil›; ~ **group** *n.* (Brit.) Initiative, *die;* Aktionsgruppe, *die*

gingerly /'dʒɪndʒəlɪ/ *adv.* behutsam; [übertrieben] vorsichtig

ginger: ~ **nut**, ~ **snap** *ns.* Ingwerkeks, *der;* ~ **'wine** *n.* Ingwerwein, *der*

gingery /'dʒɪndʒərɪ/ *adj.* ingwerartig

gingham /'gɪŋəm/ *n.* (Textiles) Gingan, *der*

gingivitis /dʒɪndʒɪ'vaɪtɪs/ *n.* ▸ **p. 1231** (Med.) Gingivitis, *die* (fachspr.); Zahnfleischentzündung, *die*

ginormous /dʒaɪ'nɔːməs/ *adj.* (Brit. coll.) elefantös (ugs. scherzh.)

gin: **~-palace** *n.* auffällig aufgemachte Kneipe; ~ **'rummy** *n.* Rommé mit Zehn

ginseng /'dʒɪnseŋ/ *n.* (Bot., Med.) Ginseng, *der*

gin 'sling *n.* Ginsling, *der*

gippy tummy /dʒɪpɪ 'tʌmɪ/ *n.* (coll.) Durchfall, *der;* Durchmarsch, *der* (salopp)

gipsy ▸ **gypsy**

giraffe /dʒɪ'rɑːf, dʒɪ'ræf/ *n.* Giraffe, *die*

gird /gɜːd/ *v.t.*, **~ed** *or* **girt** /gɜːt/ (literary) 1 (encircle) ~ **sb./sb.'s waist with sth.** jmdn./jmds. Taille mit etw. gürten; etw. um jmdn./jmds. Taille als Gürtel legen 2 (surround) umgeben 3 (prepare) ~ **oneself for sth.** sich zu etw. rüsten

Phrasal verb

• ~ **up** *v.t.* gürten; ~ **up one's loins** (literary) seine Lenden gürten (veralt.); sich gürten

girder /'gɜːdə(r)/ *n.* [Eisen-/Stahl]träger, *der*

girdle[1] /'gɜːdl/

A *n.* 1 (corset) Hüfthalter, *der;* Hüftgürtel, *der* 2 (belt, cord, etc.) Gürtel, *der;* (sash) Schärpe, *die;* **a ~ of trees/forests** eine Baumkette *od.* ein Gürtel von Bäumen/ein Waldgürtel 3 (Anat.) ‹*Schulter-, Becken*›gürtel, *der*

B *v.t.* umgeben; ‹*Bäume:*› umstehen

girdle[2] (Scot.) ▸ **griddle**

girl /gɜːl/ *n.* 1 Mädchen, *das;* (teenager) junges Mädchen; ([young] woman) Frau, *die;* (daughter) Mädchen, *das* (ugs.); Tochter, *die;* **baby ~:** kleines Mädchen; (daughter) Töchterchen, *das;* **~s' school** Mädchenschule, *die;* **a ~'s name** ein Mädchenname; **a little Italian ~:** eine kleine Italienerin; ein kleines italienisches Mädchen; **[my] ~** (as address) [mein] Mädchen; **the ~s** (female friends) meine/ihre *usw.* Freundinnen; **the Smith ~s** die Mädchen von Smiths; *see also* **old girl** 2 (worker) Mädchen, *das;* (secretary) Sekretärin, *die;* (maid) [Haus-/Dienst]mädchen, *das;* **the ~ at the cash desk/switchboard** die Kassiererin/Telefonistin 3 (sweetheart) Mädchen, *das;* Freundin, *die*

girl: ~ **band** *n.* Girlgroup, *die;* ~ **'Friday** *n.* ▸ **Friday** A; **~friend** *n.* Freundin, *die;* ~ **'guide** ▸ **guide** A 5

girlhood /'gɜːlhʊd/ *n.* Kindheit, *die*

girlie /'gɜːlɪ/

A *adj.* 1 (usu. derog.: appropriate to a girl) **talk about ~ things** Weiberkram reden (ugs.); **~ talk** Gerede über Weiberkram (ugs.); **that's a bit ~, isn't it?** das ist doch ehe was für Mädchen, oder? 2 (featuring nudes) ‹*Kalender, Zeitschrift usw.*› mit nackten Mädchen *nachgestellt*

B *n.* [kleines] Mädchen

girlish /'gɜːlɪʃ/ *adj.* mädchenhaft; **a ~ voice** eine Mädchenstimme; **~ laughter** Mädchenlachen, *das*

girl: ~ **power** *n.* (coll.) Girlpower, *die;* ~ **'scout** *n.* (Amer.) Pfadfinderin, *die*

giro /'dʒaɪərəʊ/ *n., pl.* **~s** Giro, *das; attrib.* Giro‹*bank, -geschäft, -konto, -scheck*›; **post office/bank ~:** Postgiro- *od.* (veralt.) Postscheck-/Giroverkehr, *der*

girt ▸ **gird**

girth /gɜːθ/ *n.* 1 (circumference) Umfang, *der;* (at waist) Taillenumfang, *der;* (at belly) Bauchumfang, *der;* (of ship) Spantumfang, *der;* **in ~:** im Umfang *usw.* 2 (band round horse) Bauchgurt, *der*

gismo ▸ **gizmo**

gist /dʒɪst/ *n.* Wesentliche, *das;* (of tale, argument, question, etc.) Kern, *der;* **this is the ~ of what he said** das hat er im Wesentlichen gesagt; **get the ~ of sth.** das Wesentliche einer Sache mitbekommen; **could you give me the ~ of it/what's been going on?** könntest du mir sagen, worum es hier geht?/was los gewesen ist?

git /gɪt/ *n.* (Brit. sl. derog.) Idiot, *der* (salopp); **stupid ~:** Blödmann, *der* (derb); (woman) blöde Kuh (derb)

give /gɪv/

A *v.t.*, **gave** /geɪv/, **given** /'gɪvn/ 1 (hand over, pass) geben; (transfer from one's authority, custody, or responsibility) überbringen; übergeben (**to** an + *Akk.*); **she gave him her bag to carry** sie gab ihm ihre Tasche zum Tragen; **G~ it to me! I'll do it** Gib her! Ich mache das; **~ me ...** (on telephone) geben Sie mir ...; verbinden Sie mich mit ...

2 (as gift) schenken; (donate) spenden; geben; (bequeath) vermachen; **~ sb. sth., ~ sth. to sb.** jmdm. etw. schenken; **~ sb. sth.** *or* **~ sth. [to] sb. as a present** jmdm. etw. schenken; (sth. of great value) jmdm. etw. zum Geschenk machen; **each of the boys was ~n a book** die Jungen bekamen jeder ein Buch [geschenkt]; **the book was ~n me by my son** das Buch hat mir mein Sohn geschenkt; **I was ~n it by my son** mein Sohn hat es mir geschenkt; ich habe es von meinem Sohn [geschenkt] bekommen; **I wouldn't have it if it was ~n [to] me** ich würde es nicht mal geschenkt nehmen; *abs.* **it is more blessed to ~ than to receive** (Bibl.) Geben ist seliger denn Nehmen (Spr.); **~ alms/to the poor** Almosen/den Armen geben; **~ towards sth.** zu etw. beisteuern; **~ blood** Blut spenden; **~ [a donation] to charity** für wohltätige Zwecke spenden; **'please ~ generously'** „wir bitten um großzügige Spenden"; **~ and take** (fig.) Kompromisse eingehen; (in marriage etc.) geben und nehmen

3 (sell) verkaufen; geben; (pay) zahlen; geben (ugs.); (sacrifice) geben; opfern; **I'll ~ you the machine for £2** für 2 Pfund gebe ich dir *od.* hast du die Maschine; **what will you ~ me for this watch?** was *od.* wie viel geben Sie mir für diese Uhr?; **I'll ~ you anything you ask for it** ich zahle Ihnen jeden Preis dafür; **~ sb. sth. [in exchange] for sth.** jmdm. etw. für etw. [im Tausch] geben; **I would ~ anything** *or* **my right arm/a lot to be there** ich würde alles/viel darum geben, wenn ich dort sein könnte

4 (assign) aufgeben ‹*Hausaufgaben, Strafarbeit usw.*›; (sentence to) geben ‹*10 Jahre Gefängnis usw.*›; **~ sb. a translation to do/an essay to write for homework** jmdm. eine Übersetzung/einen Aufsatz aufgeben; **he was ~n ten years** er bekam zehn Jahre

5 (grant, award) geben ‹*Erlaubnis, Arbeitsplatz, Interview, Rabatt, Fähigkeit, Kraft*›; verleihen ‹*Preis, Titel, Orden usw.*›; **be ~n sth.** etw. bekommen; **he was ~n the privilege/honour of doing it** ihm wurde das Vorrecht/die Ehre zuteil, es zu tun; **~ me strength to do it** gib mir Kraft, es zu tun; **it is ~n to few/her** es ist wenigen/ihr gegeben *od.* (geh.) beschieden; **~ sb. to understand** *or* **believe that ...:** jmdn. glauben lassen, dass ...; **he gave me to understand** *or* **believe that ...** (unintentionally) was er sagte, ließ mich glauben, dass ...

6 (entrust sb. with) übertragen (**to** *Dat.*); **~ sb. the power to do sth.** jmdn. ermächtigen, etw. zu tun

7 (allow sb. to have) geben ‹*Recht, Zeit, Arbeit*›; überlassen ‹*seinen Sitzplatz*›; lassen ‹*Wahl, Zeit*›; **be ~n little freedom** wenig Freiheit haben; **~ sb./a horse a rest** jmdm./einem Pferd eine Pause gönnen; **they gave me [the use of] their car for the weekend** sie überließen mir übers Wochenende ihr Auto; **~ it time and it will work out well** gut Ding will Weile haben (Spr.); **I will ~ you a day to think it over** ich lasse dir einen Tag Bedenkzeit; **I can ~ you an hour. Then I must go** Ich habe [für Sie] eine Stunde Zeit. Dann muss ich gehen; **~ yourself time to think about it** lass dir Zeit und denk darüber nach; **~ me the good old times** (fig. coll.) es geht doch nichts über die guten alten Zeiten; **~ me London any day** *or* **time** *or* **every time** (fig. coll.) London ist mir zehnmal lieber; **I['ll] ~ you/him** *etc.* **that** (fig. coll.: grant) das gebe ich zu; zugegeben; **you've got to ~ it to him** (fig. coll.) das muss man ihm lassen; **~ or take** (coll.) mehr oder weniger; **it cost £5, ~ or take a few pence** es hat fünf Pfund gekostet, vielleicht ein paar Pence mehr oder weniger; **~ or take a few errors, this book is ...:** abgesehen von ein paar Fehlern ist dieses Buch ...; **~ oneself to sb.** (yield sexually) sich jmdm. hingeben; **~n that** (because) da; (if) wenn; **~n the right tools** mit dem richtigen Werkzeug; **~n time/the cash, I'll do/buy it** wenn ich Zeit/das nötige Geld habe, mache/kaufe ich es

8 (offer to sb.) geben, reichen ‹*Arm, Hand usw.*›; **~ sb. one's attention/confidence** jmdm. seine Aufmerksamkeit/sein Vertrauen schenken; **please ~ me your attention** ich bitte um Ihre Aufmerksamkeit; **~ sb. in marriage** jmdn. verheiraten; **my heart is ~n to another** mein Herz gehört einer/einem anderen; **she gave him an infection/a cold** sie hat ihn angesteckt/mit ihrer Erkältung angesteckt; **she gave him four sons** sie hat ihm vier Söhne geschenkt (geh.); *see also* **~ way**

9 (cause sb./sth. to have) geben; verleihen ‹*Charme, Reiz, Gewicht, Nachdruck*›; bereiten, machen ‹*Freude, Mühe, Kummer*›; bereiten, verursachen ‹*Schmerz*›; bieten ‹*Abwechslung, Schutz*›; leisten ‹*Hilfe*›; gewähren ‹*Unterstützung*›; erteilen ‹*Absolution*›; **~ sb. sth./be ~n sth. to eat** jmdm. etw. zu essen geben/etw. zu essen bekommen; **~ sb. some refreshment** jmdm. eine Erfrischung reichen; **~ sb. pork for dinner** jmdm. Schweinefleisch zum Abendessen geben *od.* reichen; **I was ~n the guest room** man gab mir das Gästezimmer; **~ a clear picture/~ good reception** (Telev.) ein gutes Bild/einen guten Empfang haben; **the answer was ~n me in a dream** die Antwort kam mir im Traum; **her words gave me much pain/quite a shock** ihre Worte schmerzten/schockierten mich sehr; **~ hope to sb.** jmdm. Hoffnung machen; **~ sb. the name of Jim** jmdn. Jim nennen; jmdm. den Namen Jim geben; **the village gave its name to the battle** die Schlacht wurde nach dem Dorf benannt; **Latin, which has ~n the English language so many words** das Lateinische, aus dem so viele englische Wörter stammen; **~ sb. something to cry for/to complain about** jmdm. einen Grund zum Weinen/Klagen geben; **~ one's labour [free of charge]** unbezahlt arbeiten; seine Arbeit unentgeltlich machen; **~ sb. what for** (coll.) es jmdm. geben (ugs.)

10 (convey in words, tell, communicate) angeben ‹*Namen, Anschrift, Alter, Grund, Zahl*›; nennen ‹*Grund, Einzelheiten, Losungswort*›; geben ‹*Rat, Beispiel, Befehl, Anweisung, Antwort*›; fällen ‹*Urteil, Entscheidung*›; sagen ‹*Meinung*›; erlassen ‹*Gesetze*›; bekannt geben ‹*Nachricht, Ergebnis*›; machen ‹*Andeutung*›; erteilen ‹*Verweis, Rüge*›; (present, set forth) ‹*Wörterbuch, Brief:*› enthalten; ‹*Zeitung:*› bringen ‹*Bericht*›; **~ details of sth.** Einzelheiten einer Sache (*Gen.*) darlegen; **~ sth. a mention** etw. erwähnen; **~ a brief history of sth.** einen kurzen Abriss der Geschichte einer Sache (*Gen.*) geben; **~ sb. the facts** jmdn. mit den Fakten vertraut *od.* bekannt machen; **she gave us the news/the news of her engagement** sie teilte es uns mit/teilte uns ihre Verlobung mit; **~ it as one's opinion that ...:** die Meinung äußern, dass ...; **~ sb. a decision** jmdm. eine Entscheidung mitteilen; **~ sb. the right time** jmdm. die genaue Zeit sagen; **~ him my best wishes** richte ihm meine besten Wünsche aus; **the average wage is ~n as £6,000** der Durchschnittslohn wird mit 6 000 Pfund angegeben; **don't ~ me 'that** (coll.) erzähl mir [doch] nichts! (ugs.); **don't ~ me that legal jargon** lass mich mit deinem Juristenkauderwelsch in Ruhe!; **~!** (coll.: disclose what you know) [nun] red schon!

11 **~n** (specified) gegeben

12 (perform, read, sing, etc.) geben ‹*Vorstellung, Konzert*›; halten ‹*Vortrag, Seminar*›; vorlesen

g

‹*Gedicht, Erzählung*›; singen ‹*Lied*›; spielen ‹*Schauspiel, Oper, Musikstück*›; **~ us a song** sing mal was
13 (in speeches) ausbringen ‹*Toast, Trinkspruch*›; (as toast) **ladies and gentlemen, I ~ you the Queen** meine Damen, meine Herren, auf die Königin *od.* das Wohl der Königin; (as speaker) **I ~ you the Lord Mayor** das Wort hat der Oberbürgermeister
14 (produce) geben ‹*Licht, Milch*›; tragen ‹*Früchte*›; ergeben ‹*Zahlen, Resultat*›; erbringen ‹*Ernte*›; **~ your answer to the third decimal place** berechnen Sie das Ergebnis auf die dritte Stelle hinter dem Komma; **~ a high yield** sehr ertragreich sein; reichen Ertrag bringen
15 (cause to develop) machen; **sth. ~s me a headache** von etw. bekomme ich Kopfschmerzen; **running ~s me an appetite** Laufen macht mich hungrig; **he did this to ~ himself courage** er tat das, um sich (*Dat.*) Mut zu machen
16 (make sb. undergo) geben; versetzen ‹*Schlag, Stoß*›; verabreichen (geh.), geben ‹*Arznei*›; **~ sb. a hammering** (Sport) jmdm. eine schwere Schlappe beibringen; **~ sb. a [friendly] look** jmdm. einen [freundlichen] Blick zuwerfen; **he gave her hand a squeeze** er drückte ihr die Hand; **~ it to sb.** (thrash or scold him) es jmdm. geben (ugs.); **~ as good as one gets** (coll.) es jmdm. mit gleicher Münze heimzahlen
17 (execute, make, show) geben ‹*Zeichen, Stoß, Tritt*›; machen ‹*Satz, Ruck*›; ausstoßen ‹*Schrei, Seufzer, Pfiff*›; **~ a [little] smile** [schwach] lächeln; **the flame gave a final flicker** die Flamme flackerte noch einmal auf; **~ sth./sb. a look** sich (*Dat.*) etw./jmdn. ansehen
18 (devote, dedicate) widmen; **be ~n to sth./doing sth.** zu etw. neigen/etw. gern tun; **~ [it] all one's got** (coll.) sein Möglichstes tun
19 (be host at) geben ‹*Party, Ball, Empfang, Essen usw.*›
20 (predict time remaining as) **~ sb./sth. two months/a year** jmdm./einer Sache zwei Monate/ein Jahr geben
21 **~ birth, ~ chase,** *etc. see the nouns*
B *v.i.*, **gave, given** 1 (yield, bend) nachgeben (auch fig.); ‹*Knie:*› weich werden; ‹*Bett:*› federn; (break down) zusammenbrechen; ‹*Eisdecke, Boden:*› einbrechen; ‹*Brücke:*› einstürzen; (fig.) nachlassen; **something's got to ~:** irgendwo muss man zurückstecken
2 (lead) **~ on to the street/garden/into a room** ‹*Tür usw.:*› auf die Straße hinaus-/in den Garten/ein Zimmer führen
3 **what ~s [with you]?** (coll.) was ist los [bei dir]?
4 **~ of sth.** etw. opfern; **~ of oneself** sich [auf]opfern
C *n.* 1 Nachgiebigkeit, *die;* (elasticity) Elastizität, *die;* **have [no] ~:** [nicht] nachgeben
2 **~ and take** (exchange of ideas) Gedankenaustausch, *der;* (compromise) Kompromiss, *der;* Entgegenkommen, *das;* (exchange of benefits or mutual concessions) Geben und Nehmen, *das;* **with a bit of ~ and take** mit etwas Kompromissbereitschaft

Phrasal verbs

• **~ a'way** *v.t.* 1 (without charge, as gift) verschenken; (fig.: lose by negligence) verschenken ‹*Punkt, Tor usw.*›; vergeben ‹*Chance, Tor, Elfmeter*› 2 (in marriage) dem Bräutigam zuführen 3 (distribute) verteilen, vergeben ‹*Preise*›; überreichen ‹*Zeugnisse usw.*› 4 (fig.: betray) verraten. *see also* **game[1] A 2; ~away**
• **~ 'back** *v.t.* (lit. or fig.) zurückgeben; wiedergeben
• **~ 'forth** ▸**forth 3**
• **~ in**
A /'--/ *v.t.* abgeben; **~ sb.'s name in for sth.** jmdn. zu etw. anmelden
B /-'-/ *v.i.* nachgeben (**to** *Dat.*); (in guessing game) aufgeben; **~ in to temptation/blackmail/a superior force** der Versuchung (*Dat.*) erliegen/auf Erpressung (*Akk.*) eingehen/sich der Übermacht (*Dat.*) ergeben; **~ in to persuasion** sich überzeugen lassen
• **~ 'off** *v.t.* ausströmen ‹*Rauch, Geruch*›; aussenden ‹*Strahlen*›
• **~ out**
A /'--/ *v.t.* 1 (distribute) verteilen ‹*Prospekte, Flugblätter, Karten, Preise*›; austeilen ‹*Stifte, Hefte, Papier usw.*›; vergeben ‹*Arbeit*› 2 (declare) bekannt geben ‹*Nachricht*›; (pretend) vorgeben; **~ oneself out to be …:** sich als … ausgeben
B /-'-/ *v.i.* ‹*Vorräte:*› ausgehen; ‹*Maschine:*› versagen; ‹*Kraft:*› nachlassen; **my patience/voice gave out** ich war mit meiner Geduld am Ende/mir versagte die Stimme
• **~ 'over** *v.t.* 1 **be ~n over to sth.** für etw. beansprucht werden; **the rest of the day was ~n over to pleasure** der Rest des Tages war dem Vergnügen gewidmet 2 (abandon) **~ sth./sb. over to sb.** etw. jmdm. überlassen/jmdn. jmdm. ausliefern; **~ oneself over to sb./sth.** sich jmdm./einer Sache ergeben *od.* hingeben; jmdm./einer Sache verfallen
3 (coll.: stop) **~ over [doing sth.]** aufhören[, etw. zu tun]
• **~ 'up**
A *v.i.* aufgeben
B *v.t.* 1 (abandon, renounce) aufgeben; ablegen ‹*Gewohnheit*›; abschaffen ‹*Auto, Fernsehgerät, Putzfrau*›; widmen ‹*Zeit*›; (relinquish, stop using) verzichten auf (+ *Akk.*) ‹*Territorium, Kinder, Süßigkeiten*›; **~ sth. up/~ up doing sth.** (abandon habit) sich (*Dat.*) etw. abgewöhnen/sich abgewöhnen, etw. zu tun; **~ sb./sth. up as a bad job** (coll.) jmdn./etw. abschreiben (ugs.); **~ oneself up to sth.** sich einer Sache (*Dat.*) hingeben 2 **~ sb. up** (as not coming) jmdn. nicht mehr erwarten; mit jmdm. nicht mehr rechnen; (as beyond help) jmdn. aufgeben; **~ up for lost/dead** verloren geben/für tot halten
3 (hand over to police etc.) übergeben (**to** *Dat.*); ausliefern ‹*Spion usw.*›; **~ oneself up [to sb.]** sich [jmdm.] stellen
• **~ 'way** *v.i.* 1 (yield, lit. or fig.) nachgeben; (collapse) ‹*Brücke, Balkon:*› einstürzen; **his legs gave way under him** er knickte [in den Knien] ein; **~ way to sth.** einer Sache (*Dat.*) nachgeben; **~ way to tears** seinen Tränen freien Lauf lassen; **~ way to anger** seinem Ärger Luft machen; **~ way to persuasion** sich überzeugen lassen; **~ way to fear** der Angst erliegen; **his health gave way under this stress** seine Gesundheit hielt dieser Belastung nicht stand
2 (in traffic) **~ way [to traffic from the right]** [dem Rechtsverkehr] die Vorfahrt lassen; **'Give Way'** „Vorfahrt beachten" 3 (be succeeded by) **~ way to sth.** einer Sache (*Dat.*) weichen; von etw. abgelöst werden; **winter ~s way to spring** auf den Winter folgt der Frühling

'giveaway *n.* (coll.) 1 (what betrays) **the tremble in her voice was the ~:** mit ihrer zitternden Stimme hat sie sich verraten; **it was a dead ~:** es verriet alles 2 *attrib.* (Commerc.) **~ prices** Schleuderpreise *Pl.*

given ▸**give A, B**

'given name *n.* (Amer.) Vorname, *der*

giver /'gɪvə(r)/ *n.* Geber, *der*/Geberin, *die;* (donor) Spender, *der*/Spenderin, *die*

give-'way sign *n.* (Brit.) Vorfahrtsschild, *das*

gizmo /'gɪzməʊ/ *n.* (coll.) Ding, *das* (ugs.)

gizzard /'gɪzəd/ *n.* (of bird) Muskelmagen, *der;* (of insect, fish, etc.) Kaumagen, *der;* **stick in sb.'s ~** (fig.) jmdm. gegen den Strich gehen (ugs.)

Gk. *abbr.* **= Greek** griech./Griech.

glacé /'glæseɪ/ *adj.* 1 glasiert ‹*Früchte*›; (candied) kandiert 2 **~ leather** Glacéleder, *das;* **~ kid gloves** Glacéhandschuhe *Pl.*

glacial /'gleɪsɪəl, 'gleɪʃl/ *adj.* 1 (icy) eisig; (fig.) eiskalt 2 (Geol.) Gletscher-; **~ epoch** *or* **period** Eiszeit, *die;* Glazialzeit, *die* (fachspr.)

glaciation /gleɪsɪ'eɪʃn/ *n.* (Geol.) Vergletscherung, *die*

glacier /'glæsɪə(r)/ *n.* Gletscher, *der*

glad /glæd/ *adj.* 1 *pred.* froh; **be ~ about sth.** sich über etw. (*Akk.*) freuen; **be ~ that …:** sich freuen, dass …; (be relieved) froh sein [darüber], dass …; **[I'm] ~ to meet you** es freut mich *od.* ich freue mich, Sie kennen zu lernen; **be ~ to hear sth.** sich freuen, etw. zu hören; (relieved) froh sein, etw. zu hören; **I am always ~ to see her** ich freue mich jedes Mal, wenn ich sie sehe; **Don't mention it. I was ~ to be of assistance** Keine Ursache. Das habe ich doch gern [für Sie] getan; **I'm ~ to know that …:** zu meiner Freude erfahre ich, dass …; **he's ~ to be alive** er ist froh, dass er lebt; **I'd be ~ to [help you]** aber gern [helfe ich Ihnen]; **we shall be ~ to come/give further information** wir werden gern kommen/wir geben Ihnen gerne weitere Informationen; **be ~ of sth.** über etw. (*Akk.*) froh sein; für etw. dankbar sein; **Take your gloves. You'll be ~ of them** Nimm deine Handschuhe mit. Du wirst sie gebrauchen können; **a sight which makes one ~ to be alive** ein Anblick, der einem Freude am Leben gibt; **I'd be ~ if you'd do some work** (iron.) ich hätte nichts dagegen, wenn du dich jetzt etwas nützlich machst (iron.) 2 (giving joy) froh ‹*Botschaft*›; freudig ‹*Nachricht, Ereignis, Tag usw.*›; (marked by joy) fröhlich; (bright, beautiful) herrlich ‹*Morgen*›

gladden /'glædn/ *v.t.* erfreuen

glade /gleɪd/ *n.* Lichtung, *die*

glad 'eye *n.* **give sb. the ~** (coll.) jmdm. schöne Augen machen (ugs.)

glad 'hand *n.* **give sb. the ~** (coll.) jmdm. die Hand schütteln

gladiator /'glædɪeɪtə(r)/ *n.* (Roman Ant.) Gladiator, *der*

gladiolus /glædɪ'əʊləs/ *n., pl.* **gladioli** /glædɪ'əʊlaɪ/ *or* **~es** (Bot.) Gladiole, *die*

gladly /'glædlɪ/ *adv.* 1 (willingly) gern 2 (with joy) freudig

gladness /'glædnɪs/ *n., no pl.* Freude, *die;* (of voice etc.) Fröhlichkeit, *die*

'glad rags *n. pl.* (coll.) Festkleidung, *die*

Gladstone bag /glædstən 'bæg/ *n.* zweiteiliger Reisehandkoffer

glamor (Amer.) ▸**glamour**

glamorize (**glamorise**) /'glæməraɪz/ *v.t.* (add glamour to) [mehr] Glanz verleihen (+ *Dat.*); (idealize) verherrlichen (**into** zu); glorifizieren

glamorous /'glæmərəs/ *adj.* glanzvoll; glamourös ‹*Filmstar, Lebenswandel usw.*›; schillernd ‹*Name, Persönlichkeit*›; mondän ‹*Kleidung*›; **a ~ job** ein Traumberuf

glamorously /'glæmərəslɪ/ *adv.* mondän ‹*gekleidet sein*›; glanzvoll ‹*darstellen*›

glamour /'glæmə(r)/ *n.* Glanz, *der;* (of person) Ausstrahlung, *die*

glamour: ~ boy *n.* Schönling, *der;* **~ girl** *n.* Glamourgirl, *das*

glamourize (Brit.) ▸**glamorize**

glamour: ~ model *n.* Glamourmodel, *das;* **~ photography** *n., no pl.* Glamourfotografie, *die;* **~ puss** *n.* (coll.) Glamourweib, *die*

glance /glɑːns/
A *n.* 1 (quick look) Blick, *der;* **cast** *or* **take** *or* **have a [quick] ~ at sth./sb.** einen [kurzen] Blick auf etw./jmdn. werfen; **cast** *etc.* **a quick ~ at the newspaper/letter** die Zeitung durchblättern/den Brief überfliegen; **cast** *etc.* **a hasty ~ round the room** sich hastig im Zimmer umsehen; **give sb. a [knowing/quick** *etc.***] ~:** jmdm. einen [wissenden/kurzen *usw.*] Blick zuwerfen; **not give sb./sth. so much as a ~:** jmdn./eine Sache keines Blickes würdigen; **at a ~:** auf einen Blick; **at first/a casual ~:** auf den ersten Blick/wenn man flüchtig hinsieht
2 (Cricket) Streifschlag, *der*
B *v.i.* 1 blicken; schauen; **~ at sb./sth.** jmdn./etw. anblicken; **~ at one's watch** auf seine Uhr blicken; **she ~d at herself in the mirror** sie warf einen Blick in den Spiegel; **~ over/across at sb. [nervously** *etc.***]** jmdm. einen [nervösen *usw.*] Blick zuwerfen; **~ down/up [at sth.]** [auf etw. (*Akk.*)] hinunter-/[zu etw.] aufblicken; **~ over** *or* **through the newspaper** *etc.* die Zeitung *usw.* durchblättern; **~ at the newspaper** *etc.* einen Blick in die Zeitung *usw.* werfen; **~ round [the room]** sich [im Zimmer] umsehen; **~ around/from one thing to another** ‹*Augen, Blick:*› umherwandern/von einem Gegenstand zum anderen wandern
2 (allude briefly) **~ at sth.** etw. nur kurz streifen *od.* ansprechen 3 **~ [off sth.]** abprallen [an etw. (*Dat.*)]; ‹*Messer, Schwert:*› abgleiten [an etw. (*Dat.*)]; **he struck me a glancing blow** sein Schlag streifte mich nur

gland[1] /glænd/ *n.* Drüse, *die*

gland² *n.* (Mech.) Dichtung, *die*

glandular /ˈglændjʊlə(r)/ *adj.* Drüsen-; ~ **swelling** geschwollene Drüse/Drüsen

glandular 'fever *n.* ▸ℹ **p. 1231** Drüsenfieber, *das*

glans /glænz/ *n.* ~ **[penis]** (Anat.) Eichel, *die*

glare /gleə(r)/

A *n.* **1** (dazzle) grelles Licht; **shine with a ~:** grell scheinen; **the ~ of the sun** die grelle Sonne; das grelle Sonnenlicht; **amidst the ~/in the full ~ of publicity** (fig.) im Rampenlicht der Öffentlichkeit **2** (hostile look) feindseliger Blick; **with a ~:** feindselig **3** (gaudiness) Grellheit, *die*

B *v.i.* **1** (glower) [finster] starren; **~ at sb./sth.** jmdn./etw. anstarren **2** ‹*Licht:*› grell scheinen; (shine by reflection) ‹*Strand, Straße:*› flimmern; **~ down** ‹*Sonne:*› herunterbrennen

C *v.t.* **~ contempt/defiance/hate** *etc.* **at sb.** jmdn. verächtlich/herausfordernd/hasserfüllt *usw.* anstarren

glaring /ˈgleərɪŋ/ *adj.* **1** (dazzling) grell [strahlend/scheinend]; gleißend hell ‹*Licht*› **2** (fig.: conspicuous) schreiend; eklatant ‹*Beispiel*›; grob ‹*Fehler*›; krass ‹*Gegensatz*›; **the most ~ omission was ...** was/wer am meisten fehlte, war ...; **there was one ~ omission from the proposal** eines fehlte bei dem Vorschlag völlig

glaringly /ˈgleərɪŋlɪ/ *adv.* **1** grell; **~ bright** gleißend hell **2** (fig.) **be ~ obvious** überdeutlich sein

glasnost /ˈglæsnɒst/ *n.* Glasnost, *die*

glass /glɑːs/

A *n.* **1** *no pl.* (substance) Glas, *das;* **pieces of/broken ~:** Glasscherben *Pl.;* (smaller) Glassplitter *Pl.;* **a pane/sheet of ~:** eine Glasscheibe/Glasplatte **2** (drinking ~) Glas, *das;* **a ~ of milk** ein Glas Milch; **a friendly ~:** ein Gläschen unter Freunden; **he's fond of his ~:** er trinkt gern ein Gläschen; **wine by the ~:** offener Wein; **raise one's ~ [to sb.]** (fig.) [auf jmdn.] das Glas erheben **3** (of spectacles, watch) Glas, *das;* (pane, covering picture) [Glas]scheibe, *die* **4** *in pl.* (spectacles) **[a pair of] ~es** eine Brille; **she wears thick ~es** sie trägt eine Brille mit dicken Gläsern; **driving/reading ~es** Fahr-/Lesebrille, *die* **5** (binoculars) Fernglas, *das;* **~es** *pl.* ein Fernglas **6** (barometer) Barometer, *das. See also* **dark glasses; eyeglass; field glasses; ground glass; hourglass; magnifying glass; opera glasses; plate glass; water glass**

B *attrib. adj.* Glas-; **people who live in ~ houses should not throw stones** (prov.) wer im Glashaus sitzt, soll nicht mit Steinen werfen (Spr.)

C *v.t., usu. in p. p.* verglasen; **~ed in** verglast

glass: ~-blower *n.* ▸ℹ **p. 1260** Glasbläser, *der*/Glasbläserin, *die;* **~-blowing** *n.* Glasblasen, *das;* **~ 'case** *n.* Vitrine, *die;* Glaskasten, *der;* **~ 'ceiling** *n.* (fig.) unsichtbare Barriere; **~cloth** *n.* Gläsertuch, *das;* **~ 'door** *n.* Glastür, *die;* **~ 'fibre** *n.* Glasfaser, *die*

glassful /ˈglɑːsfʊl/ *n.* Glas, *das* (**of** von); **a ~ of milk** ein Glas Milch

glass: ~house *n.* **1** (~works) Glashütte, *die;* **2** (Brit.: greenhouse) Gewächshaus, *das;* Glashaus, *das;* **3** (Brit. sl.: military prison) Bunker, *der* (Soldatenspr. salopp); **~-making** *n.* Glasherstellung, *die;* **~-paper** *n.* Glaspapier, *das;* **~ware** *n.* Glas, *das;* **~ wool** *n.* Glaswolle, *die;* **~works** *n. sing.* Glashütte, *die*

glassy /ˈglɑːsɪ/ *adj.* gläsern; (fig.) glasig ‹*Blick*›; spiegelglatt ‹*Wasseroberfläche*›

'glassy-eyed *adj.* glasig; ‹*Person*› mit glasigem Blick; **begin to look ~:** einen glasigen Blick bekommen

Glaswegian /glæzˈwiːdʒn/

A *adj.* Glasgower

B *n.* Glasgower, *der*/Glasgowerin, *die*

glaucoma /glɔːˈkəʊmə/ *n.* ▸ℹ **p. 1231** (Med.) Glaukom, *das* (fachspr.); grüner Star

glaze /gleɪz/

A *n.* (on food or pottery) Glasur, *die;* (of paint) Lasur, *die;* (on paper, fabric) Appretur, *die*

B *v.t.* **1** (cover with ~) glasieren ‹*Esswaren, Töpferwaren*›; satinieren ‹*Papier, Leder, Kunststoff, Tuch*›; lasieren ‹*Farbe, bemalte Fläche*›; **~d tile** Kachel, *die* **2** (fit with glass) **~ [in]** verglasen ‹*Fenster, Haus usw.*›; hinter Glas setzen ‹*Bild*›

C *v.i.* **~ [over]** ‹*Augen:*› glasig werden

glazed /gleɪzd/ *adj.* glasig ‹*Blick*›

glazier /ˈgleɪzɪə(r), ˈgleɪʒə(r)/ *n.* ▸ℹ **p. 1260** Glaser, *der*

glazing /ˈgleɪzɪŋ/ *n.* (pane) [Glas]scheibe, *die;* (layer) Glasur, *die; see also* **double glazing**

gleam /gliːm/

A *n.* **1** Schein, *der;* (fainter, transient, or more subdued) Schimmer, *der;* **~ of light** Lichtschein, *der* **2** (fig.: faint trace) Anflug, *der* (**of** von); **~ of hope/truth** Hoffnungsschimmer, *der*/Funke Wahrheit; **there was a ~ of anticipation in his eyes** seine Augen leuchteten erwartungsvoll

B *v.i.* ‹*Sonne, Licht:*› scheinen; ‹*Fußboden, Fahrzeug, Stiefel:*› glänzen; ‹*Zähne:*› blitzen; ‹*Augen:*› leuchten

gleaming /ˈgliːmɪŋ/

A *adj.* glänzend ‹*Wasser, Metall, Fahrzeug*›; schimmernd ‹*Licht*›; leuchtend ‹*Augen*›

B *adv.* **~ white** leuchtend *od.* strahlend weiß; blendend *od.* blitzend weiß ‹*Zähne*›

glean /gliːn/

A *v.t.* **1** zusammentragen ‹*Angaben, Informationen, Nachrichten usw.*›; herausfinden ‹*Inhalt eines Briefes, Gesprächs usw.*›; **~ sth. from sth.** einer Sache (*Dat.*) etw. entnehmen **2** (Agric.) nachlesen ‹*Getreide, Feld*›

B *v.i.* Ähren lesen

gleaner /ˈgliːnə(r)/ *n.* Ährenleser, *der*/Ährenleserin, *die*

gleanings /ˈgliːnɪŋz/ *n. pl.* **1** (of news) zusammengeklaubte Informationen; (of research, study) Ausbeute, *die* **2** (of corn etc.) Nachlese, *die*

glee /gliː/ *n.* **1** Freude, *die;* (gloating joy) Schadenfreude, *die;* Häme, *die;* **do sth. with** *or* **in ~:** etw. voll [Schaden]freude tun **2** (Mus.) Glee, *der*

'glee club *n.* Männergesangverein, *der*

gleeful /ˈgliːfl/ *adj.* freudig; vergnügt; (gloatingly joyful) schadenfroh; hämisch; **be ~:** sich [hämisch] freuen

gleefully /ˈgliːfəlɪ/ *adv.* freudig; vor Freude ‹*lachen usw.*›; (gloatingly) schadenfroh; hämisch

glen /glen/ *n.* [schmales] Tal

glib /glɪb/ *adj.* (derog.) aalglatt ‹*Person*›; (impromptu, offhand) leicht dahingesagt, unbedacht ‹*Antwort*›; (unreflecting) vorschnell ‹*Schluss, Verallgemeinerung*›; (voluble) gewandt, geschickt ‹*Redner, Politiker, Verkäufer*›; (facile in the use of words) zungenfertig ‹*Person*›; flink ‹*Zunge*›; flinkzüngig ‹*Antwort*›; **be ~ in finding excuses** schnell Entschuldigungen bei der Hand haben

glide /glaɪd/

A *v.i.* **1** gleiten; (through the air) schweben; (slip, steal, creep) schleichen; ‹*Gespenst:*› huschen **2** (Aeronaut.) ‹*Segelflugzeug:*› gleiten, schweben; ‹*Flugzeug:*› im Gleitflug fliegen; ‹*Person:*› segelfliegen; **~ down** im Gleitflug niedergehen

B *n.* **1** (Dancing) Schleifschritt, *der* **2** (Mus.) Portamento, *das* (fachspr.) **3** (Phonet.) Gleitlaut, *der*

'glide path *n.* (Aeronaut.) Gleitflugbahn, *die*

glider /ˈglaɪdə(r)/ *n.* Segelflugzeug, *das;* **~ [pilot]** Segelflieger, *der*/-fliegerin, *die*

gliding /ˈglaɪdɪŋ/ *n.* (Sport) Segelfliegen, *das; attrib.* Segelflug-

glimmer /ˈglɪmə(r)/

A *n.* (of light etc.) [schwacher] Schein; Glimmer, *der* (selten); Schimmer, *der* (**of** von) (auch fig.); (of fire, candle) Glimmen, *das;* **~ of light** Lichtschimmer, *der;* **~ of hope** Hoffnungsschimmer, *der*

B *v.i.* glimmen; ‹*Satin usw.:*› schimmern

glimmering /ˈglɪmərɪŋ/ *n.* (lit. or fig.) Schimmer, *der* (**of** von)

glimpse /glɪmps/

A *n.* [kurzer] Blick; **catch** *or* **have** *or* **get a ~ of sb./sth.** jmdn./etw. [kurz] zu sehen *od.* zu Gesicht bekommen; (fig.) einen Eindruck von jmdm./Einblick in etw. (*Akk.*) bekommen; **it gives us a ~ of what life must have been like then** es gibt uns einen Einblick in das damalige Leben

B *v.t.* flüchtig sehen; (fig.) einen Einblick bekommen in (+ *Akk.*); einen Eindruck gewinnen von

glint /glɪnt/

A *n.* Schimmer, *der;* (reflected flash) Glitzern, *das;* (of eyes) Funkeln, *das;* (of knife, dagger) Blitzen, *das*

B *v.i.* blinken; glitzern

glissando /glɪˈsændəʊ/ *n., pl.* **glissandi** /glɪˈsændiː/ *or* **~s** (Mus.) Glissando, *das*

glisten /ˈglɪsn/ *v.i.* glitzern; *see also* **glitter A 1**

glitch /glɪtʃ/ *n.* (coll.) Panne, *die*

glitter /ˈglɪtə(r)/

A *v.i.* **1** glitzern; ‹*Augen, Juwelen, Sterne:*› funkeln; **the sky ~s with stars, stars ~ in the sky** am Himmel funkeln Sterne; **all that ~s** *or* **glistens is not gold** (prov.) es ist nicht alles Gold, was glänzt (Spr.) **2** *esp. in pres. p.* (fig.) glänzen; **~ing prizes** verlockende *od.* attraktive Preise

B *n.* **1** Glitzern, *das;* (of diamonds) Funkeln, *das* **2** (fig.: ~ing attractiveness) verlockende Aussicht (**of** auf + *Akk.*) **3** (tinsel etc.) Flitterwerk, *das;* Glitzerwerk, *das*

glitterati /glɪtəˈrɑːtɪ/ *n. pl.* Schickeria, *die* (Jargon)

glitz /glɪts/ *n.* Glanz, *der*

glitzy /ˈglɪtsɪ/ *adj.* glanzvoll

gloaming /ˈgləʊmɪŋ/ *n., no pl.* **the ~:** die Abenddämmerung

gloat /gləʊt/ *v.i.* **~ over sth.** (look at with selfish delight) sich an etw. (*Dat.*) weiden *od.* ergötzen; (derive sadistic pleasure from) sich hämisch über etw. (*Akk.*) freuen

gloatingly /ˈgləʊtɪŋlɪ/ *adv.* (with delight) selbstgefällig; genüsslich; (with sadistic pleasure) hämisch

global /ˈgləʊbl/ *adj.* **1** (worldwide) global; weltweit; weltumspannend ‹*Kommunikationssystem*›; **~ peace/warfare** Weltfrieden/-krieg, *der;* **~ strategy** Globalstrategie, *die;* **the ~ village** das Weltdorf **2** (comprehensive) Gesamt-; umfassend ‹*Berichterstattung*›; **take a ~ view** die Dinge global betrachten

global e'conomy *n.* globale Wirtschaft

globalization /gləʊbəlaɪˈzeɪʃn/ *n.* Globalisierung, *die*

globalize /ˈgləʊbəlaɪz/ *v.t.* globalisieren

globally /ˈgləʊbəlɪ/ *adv.* **1** (on a worldwide basis) global; weltweit **2** (comprehensively) umfassend

global: ~ po'sitioning system *n.* **1** (navigation system) GPS, *das;* GPS-[Navigations-]system, *das;* **2** (device) GPS[-Gerät], *das;* **~ 'search** *n.* (Computing) globale Suche; **~ 'warming** *n., no pl.* globaler Temperaturanstieg

globe /gləʊb/ *n.* **1** (sphere, spherical object) Kugel, *die* **2** (sphere with map) Globus, *der* **3** (world) **the ~:** der Erdball; **from all over the ~:** aus der ganzen Welt

globe: ~ 'artichoke ▸ **artichoke; ~fish** *n.* Kugelfisch, *der;* **~flower** *n.* Trollblume, *die;* **~trotter** *n.* Globetrotter, *der;* Weltenbummler, *der;* **~trotting** *n.* Globetrotten, *das;* Weltreisen, *das*

globular /ˈglɒbjʊlə(r)/ *adj.* kugelförmig

globule /ˈglɒbjuːl/ *n.* Kügelchen, *das;* (of liquid) Tröpfchen, *das*

globulin /ˈglɒbjʊlɪn/ *n.* (Biochem.) Globulin, *das*

glockenspiel /ˈglɒkənspiːl, ˈglɒkənʃpiːl/ *n.* (Mus.) Glockenspiel, *das*

gloom /gluːm/ *n.* **1** (darkness) Dunkel, *das* (geh.) **2** (despondency) düstere Stimmung; **cast a ~ over sth.** einen Schatten auf etw. (*Akk.*) werfen (fig.)

gloomily /ˈgluːmɪlɪ/ *adv.* finster; düster

gloomy /ˈgluːmɪ/ *adj.* **1** (dark) düster; finster; dämmrig ‹*Tag, Nachmittag usw.*› **2** (depressing) düster, finster [stimmend]; bedrückend; (depressed) trübsinnig ‹*Person*›; bedrückt ‹*Gesicht*›; **he always tends to see the ~ side of things** er sieht immer gleich schwarz; **have a ~ outlook on life** dem Leben erwartungslos *od.* pessimistisch gegenüberstehen; **feel ~ about the future** der Zukunft pessimistisch entgegensehen; **be in a ~ mood** düsterer Stimmung *od.* niedergeschlagen sein; **look ~:** niedergeschlagen *od.* bedrückt aussehen; ein bedrücktes Gesicht machen

g

g

glorification /glɔːrɪfɪˈkeɪʃn/ *n.* **1** (praise) Verherrlichung, *die;* Glorifizierung, *die* **2** (worship) Verehrung, *die;* Anbetung, *die* **3** (exaltation) Verehrung, *die*

glorify /ˈglɔːrɪfaɪ/ *v.t.* **1** (extol) verherrlichen; glorifizieren; (exalt) verehren; ehren ‹*Helden, Andenken*› **2** (worship) verehren; anbeten **3** **glorified** (fig.) besser… (ugs.); **he's no more than a glorified messenger boy** er ist nichts weiter als *od.* doch nur ein besserer Botenjunge;

glorious /ˈglɔːrɪəs/ *adj.* **1** (illustrious) ruhmreich ‹*Held, Sieg, Geschichte*›; rühmlich ‹*Tat, Rolle*›; verehrungswürdig ‹*Heilige*› **2** (honourable) ehrenhaft ‹*Sache, Angelegenheit*›; ehrenvoll, rühmlich ‹*Tod, Kampf, Sieg, Tat*›; glorreich, glanzvoll ‹*Ende einer Karriere, Errungenschaft*› **3** (delightful) wunderschön; herrlich; (iron.) schön; **it was ~ fun** es war ein prächtiger *od.* köstlicher Spaß

gloriously /ˈglɔːrɪəslɪ/ *adv.* **1** (honourably) rühmlich; (illustriously) glanzvoll; **die ~:** in Ehren sterben **2** (splendidly) wunderschön; herrlich

glory /ˈglɔːrɪ/

A *n.* **1** (splendour) Schönheit, *die;* (majesty) Herrlichkeit, *die;* **the Empire at the height of its ~:** das Imperium auf dem Höhepunkt seiner Macht; **a lily in all its ~:** eine Lilie in ihrer vollen Pracht; **in all one's ~** (iron.) in all seiner Pracht und Herrlichkeit (iron.) **2** (honour) Ehre, *die;* (credit) Verdienst, *das;* (fame) Ruhm, *der;* **they did all the work and he got all the ~:** sie haben die ganze Arbeit getan, und ihm wird es als Verdienst angerechnet; **cover oneself with ~:** sich mit Ruhm bedecken (geh.); sich mit Ruhm bekleckern (ugs., iron.) **3** (worshipful praise) Ehre, *die;* Ruhm, *der;* **~ [be] to God in the highest** Ehre sei Gott in der Höhe; **[built] to the ~ of God** [erbaut] zur Ehre/zum Ruhme Gottes; **~ be!** (dated coll.) *expr. surprise* ach du lieber Himmel! (ugs.); *expr. annoyance* Himmel noch mal! (ugs.); *expr. delight* himmlisch! **4** (source of distinction) Größe, *die;* (deed) Ruhmestat, *die;* (achievement) Glanzleistung, *die;* **be the ~ of a nation** der Stolz *od.* die Zierde eines Volkes sein; *see also* **Old Glory** **5** (heavenly bliss) ewige Seligkeit; **Christ in ~:** Christus in seiner Herrlichkeit; **go/send to ~** (arch. coll.) abfahren (veralt.)/ins Jenseits befördern (salopp)

B *v.i.* **~ in sth./doing sth.** (be pleased by) etw. genießen/es genießen, etw. zu tun; (be proud of) sich einer Sache (*Gen.*) rühmen/sich rühmen, etw. zu tun; **~ in the name/title of …:** den stolzen Namen/Titel … besitzen *od.* führen

ˈglory hole *n.* (coll.) Rumpelkammer, *die*

gloss¹ /glɒs/

A *n.* **1** (sheen) Glanz, *der;* **~ paint** Lackfarbe, *die;* **~ finish** Glanz, *der;* **paper/photo with a ~ finish** Glanzpapier, *das*/Glanzabzug, *der;* **give sth. a high ~:** einer Sache (*Dat.*) Hochglanz verleihen **2** (fig.) Anstrich, *der*

B *v.t.* polieren; auf Hochglanz bringen

(Phrasal verb)

• **~ over** *v.t.* bemänteln; beschönigen ‹*Fehler*›; (conceal) unter den Teppich kehren (ugs.)

gloss²

A *n.* **1** (comment) [Wort]erklärung, *die;* (Ling.) Glosse, *die* (fachspr.) **2** (misrepresentation of another's words) [bewusst] falsche Auslegung **3** (glossary) Glossar, *das;* (translation) Interlinearübersetzung, *die;* (continuous explanation) Kommentar, *der*

B *v.t.* glossieren

glossary /ˈglɒsərɪ/ *n.* Glossar, *das*

glossy /ˈglɒsɪ/

A *adj.* **1** glänzend; (printed on ~ paper) Hochglanz-; auf Glanzpapier gedruckt; **~ paper, paper with a ~ finish** Glanzpapier, *das;* **~ print** (Photog.) Glanzabzug, *der;* **~ magazine** Hochglanzzeitschrift, *die* **2** (fig.) glanzvoll

B *n.* (coll.) **1** (magazine) auf [Hoch]glanzpapier gedruckte Zeitschrift; Hochglanzzeitschrift, *die* **2** (photograph) Glanzabzug, *der*

glottal /ˈglɒtl/ *adj.* (Phonet.) glottal; Stimmritzen‹*laut, -verschluss usw.*›

glottal ˈstop *n.* (Phonet.) Glottisschlag, *der;* Knacklaut, *der*

glottis /ˈglɒtɪs/ *n.* (Anat.) Glottis, *die*

glove /glʌv/ *n.* **1** Handschuh, *der;* **sth. fits sb. like a ~:** etw. passt jmdm. wie angegossen (ugs.); (fig.) etw. trifft auf jmdn. haargenau zu; **throw down/take up the ~** (fig.) den Fehdehandschuh werfen/aufnehmen (geh.) **2** ▸**boxing glove**; **argue sth. with the ~s off** sich in allem Ernst *od.* offen und ehrlich über etw. (*Akk.*) auseinander setzen. *See also* **hand A 1**

glove: ~ box *n.* **1** ▸**~ compartment**; **2** (for toxic material etc.) Handschuhkasten, *der;* **~ compartment** *n.* Handschuhfach, *das*

gloved /glʌvd/ *adj.* behandschuht

ˈglove puppet *n.* Handpuppe, *die*

glow /gləʊ/

A *v.i.* **1** glühen; ‹*Lampe, Leuchtfarbe:*› schimmern, leuchten **2** (fig.) (with warmth or pride) ‹*Gesicht, Wangen:*› glühen (**with** vor + *Dat.*); (with health or vigour) strotzen (**with** vor + *Dat.*); (with pleasure or excitement) strahlen (**with** vor + *Dat.*); (with rage or fervour) glühen (**with** vor + *Dat.*) **3** (be suffused with warm colour) [warm] leuchten; **~ with the tints of autumn** in allen Herbstfarben leuchten

B *n.* **1** Glühen, *das;* (of candle, lamp) Schein, *der;* (of embers, lava, sunset) Glut, *die* **2** (fig.) Glühen, *das;* **feel a ~ of pride** vor Stolz glühen; **his cheeks had a healthy ~:** seine Wangen hatten eine blühende Farbe; **~ of youth/health** blühende Jugend/Gesundheit; **feel a ~ of happiness/passion** ein warmes Glücksgefühl/glühende Leidenschaft verspüren

glower /ˈglaʊə(r)/ *v.i.* finster dreinblicken; **~ at sb.** jmdn. finster anstarren

glowing /ˈgləʊɪŋ/ *adj.* glühend (auch fig.); [warm] leuchtend ‹*Herbstfarben*›; (fig.: enthusiastic) begeistert ‹*Bericht, Beschreibung*›; überschwänglich ‹*Lob*›; **be in ~ health** sich blühender Gesundheit (*Gen.*) erfreuen; **describe sth. in ~ colours/terms** (fig.) etw. in glühenden *od.* leuchtenden Farben/glühenden Worten beschreiben; **~ promises** glänzende Versprechungen

glow: ~-lamp *n.* (Electr.) Glühlampe, *die;* **~-worm** *n.* Glühwürmchen, *das*

gloxinia /glɒkˈsɪnɪə/ *n.* (Bot.) Gloxinie, *die*

glucose /ˈgluːkəʊs, ˈgluːkəʊz/ *n.* Glucose, *die;* **~ [powder]** (Med.) Traubenzucker, *der*

glue /gluː/

A *n.* Klebstoff, *der;* Leim, *der;* Kleber, *der* (ugs.); **like ~** (fig.) wie festgeklebt; **cling like ~ to sth./sb.** (fig.) an etw./jmdm. kleben (ugs.)

B *v.t.* **1** kleben; leimen; **~ sth. together/on** etw. zusammen-/ankleben; **~ sth. to sth.** etw. an etw. (*Dat.*) an- *od.* festkleben; **as though ~d to the spot** wie angewurzelt **2** (fig.) **be ~d to sth./sb.** an etw./jmdm. kleben (ugs.); **their eyes** *or* **they were ~d to the TV screen** sie starrten auf den Bildschirm

glue: ~ pot *n.* Leimtopf, *der;* **~-sniffing** *n.* Schnüffeln, *das* (ugs.); Sniefen, *das* (ugs.)

glug /glʌg/ *v.i.*, **-gg-** gluckern; glucksen

glum /glʌm/ *adj.*, **glumly** /ˈglʌmlɪ/ *adv.* verdrießlich; missgelaunt

glut /glʌt/

A *n.* (Commerc.) Überangebot, *das* (**of** an, von + *Dat.*); **a ~ of apples/talent** eine Apfelschwemme/eine Menge Talente

B *v.t.*, **-tt-:** **1** (Commerc.) überschwemmen **2** (gorge) **~ oneself** sich voll stopfen (ugs.) (**with, on** mit); **be ~ted with sth.** (fig.) einer Sache (*Gen.*) überdrüssig sein

glutamate /ˈgluːtəmeɪt/ *n.* (Chem.) Glutamat, *das;* **monosodium ~:** [Mono]natriumglutamat, *das*

gluten /ˈgluːtən/ *n.* Gluten, *das;* Kleber, *der* (fachspr.); **~ bread** Glutenbrot, *das*

glutinous /ˈgluːtɪnəs/ *adj.* klebrig

glutton /ˈglʌtən/ *n.* **1** Vielfraß, *der* (ugs.); **a ~ for books/punishment** (iron.)/**work** (fig.) eine Leseratte (ugs.)/ein Masochist (fig.)/ein Arbeitstier (fig.) **2** (Zool.) Vielfraß, *der*

gluttonous /ˈglʌtənəs/ *adj.* gefräßig

gluttony /ˈglʌtənɪ/ *n.* Gefräßigkeit, *die*

glycerine /ˈglɪsəriːn/ (*Amer.:* **glycerin** /ˈglɪsərɪn/) *n.* Glyzerin, *das*

glycogen /ˈglaɪkədʒən/ *n.* (Med., Biol.) Glykogen, *das*

glycol /ˈglaɪkɒl/ *n.* (Chem.) Glykol, *das*

gm. *abbr.* ▸**ⓘ p. 1702 = gram[s]** g

GM *abbr.* **= genetically modified** *attrib.* **~ crops/food** gentechnisch veränderte Feldfrüchte *Pl.*/Nahrungsmittel *Pl.*

G-man /ˈdʒiːmæn/ *n., pl.* **G-men** /ˈdʒiːmen/ (Amer. coll.) G-Man, *der*

GMO *abbr.* **= genetically modified organism** GVO

GMT *abbr.* **= Greenwich mean time** GMT; WEZ

gnarled /nɑːld/, **gnarly** /ˈnɑːlɪ/ *adjs.* knorrig; knotig ‹*Finger, Hand*›

gnash /næʃ/ *v.t.* **~ one's teeth [in anger]** [vor Zorn] mit den Zähnen knirschen; **~ing of teeth** Zähneknirschen, *das*

gnat /næt/ *n.* [Stech]mücke, *die; see also* **strain¹ C 2**

gnaw /nɔː/

A *v.i.* **1** **~ [away] at sth.** an etw. (*Dat.*) nagen; **~ through a rope/sack** ein Seil/einen Sack durchnagen **2** (fig.) **~ [away] at sth./sb.'s savings** an etw. (*Dat.*) nagen/an jmds. Ersparnissen zehren

B *v.t.* **1** nagen an (+ *Dat.*); abnagen ‹*Knochen*›; kauen an *od.* auf (*Dat.*) ‹*Fingernägeln*›; **~ a hole in sth.** ein Loch in etw. (*Akk.*) nagen **2** (fig.) nagen an (+ *Dat.*) ‹*Gewissen*›; zehren an ‹*Herzen*›

gnawing /ˈnɔːɪŋ/ *adj.* nagend ‹*Hunger, Schmerz, Zweifel, Kummer usw.*›; quälend ‹*Zahnschmerzen, Angst*›

gneiss /gnaɪs, naɪs/ *n.* (Geol.) Gneis, *der*

gnome /nəʊm/ *n.* **1** Gnom, *der;* (in garden) Gartenzwerg, *der* **2** (fig. coll.) **the ~s of Zurich** die Zürcher Gnome; die Schweizer Bankiers

gnomic /ˈnəʊmɪk/ *adj.* gnomisch

gnostic /ˈnɒstɪk/

A *adj.* **1** (relating to or having knowledge) kognitiv; (Relig.) erleuchtet **2** **G~** (Relig. Hist.) gnostisch

B *n.* **G~** (Relig. Hist.) Gnostiker, *der*

Gnosticism /ˈnɒstɪsɪzm/ *n.* (Relig. Hist.) Gnostizismus, *der*

GNP *abbr.* **= gross national product** BSP

gnu /nuː, njuː/ *n.* (Zool.) Gnu, *das*

GNVQ *abbr.* **= General National Vocational Qualification**

go¹ /gəʊ/

A *v.i., pres.* **he goes** /gəʊz/, *p. t.* **went** /went/, *pres. p.* **going** /ˈgəʊɪŋ/, *p. p.* **gone** /gɒn, gɔːn/ **1** gehen; ‹*Fahrzeug:*› fahren; ‹*Flugzeug:*› fliegen; ‹*Vierfüßer:*› laufen; ‹*Reptil:*› kriechen; (on horseback etc.) reiten; (on skis, roller skates) laufen; (in wheelchair, pram, lift) fahren; **go by bicycle/car/bus/train** *or* **rail/boat** *or* **sea** *or* **ship** mit dem [Fahr]rad/Auto/Bus/Zug/Schiff fahren; **go by plane** *or* **air** fliegen; **go by Lufthansa** mit [der] Lufthansa fliegen; **go on foot** zu Fuß gehen; laufen (ugs.); **as one goes [along]** (fig.) nach und nach; **do sth. as one goes [along]** (lit.) etw. beim Gehen *od.* unterwegs tun; **go on a journey** eine Reise machen; verreisen; **go first-class/at 50 mph** erster Klasse reisen *od.* fahren/80 Stundenkilometer fahren; **go with sb.** mit jmdm. gehen; jmdn. begleiten; ‹*Hund:*› jmdm. folgen; **have far to go** weit zu gehen *od.* zu fahren haben; es weit haben; **the doll/dog goes everywhere with her** sie hat immer ihre Puppe/ihren Hund dabei; **who goes there?** (sentry's challenge) wer da?; **there you go** (coll., giving sth.) bitte!; da! (ugs.) **2** (proceed as regards purpose, activity, destination, or route) ‹*Bus, Zug, Lift, Schiff:*› fahren; (use means of transportation) fahren; (fly) fliegen; (proceed on outward journey) weg-, abfahren; (travel regularly) ‹*Verkehrsmittel:*› verkehren (**from … to** zwischen + *Dat.* … und); **know where one is going** (fig.) wissen, was man will; **his hand went to his pocket** er griff nach seiner Tasche; **go to the toilet/cinema/moon/a museum/a funeral** auf die Toilette/ins Kino gehen/zum Mond fliegen/ins Museum/zu einer Beerdigung gehen; **go to a dance** tanzen gehen; **go [along] to the doctor['s]** *etc.* zum Arzt *usw.* gehen; **go [out] to China** nach China gehen; **go [over] to**

America nach Amerika [hinüber]fliegen/-fahren; **go [off] to London** nach London [ab]fahren/[ab]fliegen; **go [over** *or* **across] to the mainland** zum Festland [hinüber]fahren/-fliegen; **last year we went to Italy** letztes Jahr waren wir in Italien; **go this/that way** hier/da entlanggehen/-fahren; **go out of one's way** einen Umweg machen; (fig.) keine Mühe scheuen; **go towards sth./sb.** auf etw./jmdn. zugehen; **don't go on the grass** geh nicht auf den Rasen; **go by sth./sb.** ‹*Festzug usw.*:› an etw./jmdm. vorbeiziehen; ‹*Bus usw.*:› an etw./jmdm. vorbeifahren; **go in/out** hinein-/hinausgehen; **go in and out [of sth.]** [in etw. (*Dat.*)] ein- und ausgehen; **go into sth.** in etw. (*Akk.*) [hinein]gehen; **I'd never go on motorways** ich würde niemals [auf der] Autobahn fahren; **go out for some fresh air** frische Luft schöpfen gehen; **go out to the postbox** zum Briefkasten gehen; **go [out] for a walk** einen Spaziergang machen; spazieren gehen; **go bathing** baden gehen; **go cycling** Rad fahren; **go looking for sb.** jmdn. suchen gehen; **go chasing after sth./sb.** hinter etw./jmdm. herrennen (ugs.); **go to do sth.** gehen, um etw. zu tun; (while standing still) etw. tun wollen; **go to live in Berlin** nach Berlin ziehen; **go to sea** in See stechen; (become sailor) zur See gehen (ugs.); **go to see sb.** jmdn. aufsuchen; **I went to water the garden** ich ging den Garten sprengen; **go and do sth.** [gehen und] etw. tun; **you ought to go and find a flat** du solltest dir eine Wohnung suchen; **I'll go and get my coat** ich hole jetzt meinen Mantel; **I'll just go and put my shoes on** ich ziehe mir nur eben Schuhe an; **go and see whether ...:** nachsehen [gehen], ob ...; **go on a pilgrimage** *etc.* eine Pilgerfahrt *usw.* machen; **go on TV/the radio** im Fernsehen/Radio auftreten; **I'll go!** ich geh schon!; (answer phone) ich geh ran *od.* nehme ab; (answer door) ich mache auf; **'you go** (to the phone) geh du mal ran!

3▸ (start) losgehen; (in vehicle) losfahren; **let's go!** (coll.) fangen wir an!; **here goes!** (coll.) dann mal los!; **whose turn is it to go?** (in game) wer ist an der Reihe?; **go first** (in game) anfangen; **from the word go** (fig. coll.) [schon] von Anfang an

4▸ (pass, circulate, be transmitted) gehen; **a shiver went up** *or* **down my spine** ein Schauer lief mir über den Rücken *od.* den Rücken hinunter; **go to** (be given to) ‹*Preis, Sieg, Gelder, Job:*› gehen an (+ *Akk.*); ‹*Titel, Krone, Besitz:*› übergehen auf (+ *Akk.*); ‹*Ehre, Verdienst:*› zuteil werden (*Dat.*); **go towards** (be of benefit to) zugute kommen (+ *Dat.*); **go according to** (be determined by) sich richten nach; *see also* **head A 1**

5▸ (make specific motion, do something specific) **go round** ‹*Rad:*› sich drehen; **there he** *etc.* **goes again** (coll.) da, schon wieder!; **here we go again** (coll.) jetzt geht das wieder los!

6▸ (act, work, function effectively) gehen; ‹*Mechanismus, Maschine:*› laufen; **get the car to go** das Auto ankriegen (ugs.) *od.* starten; **at midnight we were still going** um Mitternacht waren wir immer noch dabei *od.* im Gange; **go by electricity** mit Strom betrieben werden; **the clock doesn't go** die Uhr geht nicht; **go to it!** (coll.) an die Arbeit!; **keep going** (in movement) weitergehen/-fahren; (in activity) weitermachen; (not fail) sich aufrecht halten; **the car still keeps going** das Auto läuft noch immer; **keep oneself going** durchhalten; **keep sb. going** (enable to continue) jmdn. aufrecht halten; **that'll keep me going** das reicht mir; damit komme ich aus; **keep sth. going** etw. in Gang halten; **make sth. go, get/set sth. going** etw. in Gang bringen; **set sb. going** (iron.) jmdn. aufs Thema bringen (ugs.); jmdn. in Fahrt bringen (ugs.)

7▸ **go to** (attend): **go to work** zur Arbeit gehen; **go to church/kindergarten/school** in die Kirche/den Kindergarten/die Schule gehen; **go to Eton/Oxford** Eton besuchen/in Oxford studieren; **go to a comprehensive school** eine Gesamtschule besuchen; auf eine Gesamtschule gehen; **go as a witch** *etc.* als Hexe *usw.* gehen; **what should I go in?** was soll ich anziehen?

8▸ (have recourse) **go to the police** zur Polizei gehen; **go to the originals** auf die Quellen zurückgreifen; **go to the relevant authority/UN** sich an die zuständige Behörde/UN wenden; **go on hunger strike** in den Hungerstreik treten; **go into the army** zur Armee gehen; **where do we go from here?** (fig.) und was nun? (ugs.)

9▸ (depart) gehen; ‹*Bus, Zug:*› [ab]fahren; ‹*Post:*› rausgehen (ugs.); (resign) zurücktreten; (abdicate) abdanken; **go away** weggehen; (move away) wegziehen; **he/the bus has gone** er/der Bus ist schon weg (ugs.); **I must go** ich muss gehen; **I must be going now** ich muss allmählich gehen; **time to go!** wir müssen/ihr müsst *usw.* gehen!; **'gone away'** (on envelope) „verzogen"; **Oh no! There goes my quiet weekend** Oh nein, jetzt ist mein geruhsames Wochenende dahin!; **to go** (Amer.) ‹*Speisen, Getränke*› zum Mitnehmen; **pizza to ~** (esp. Amer.) Pizza zum Mitnehmen; **my headache has gone** mein Kopfweh ist weg

10▸ (euphem.: die) sterben; **be dead and gone** tot sein; **after I go** wenn ich einmal nicht mehr bin

11▸ (fail) ‹*Gedächtnis, Kräfte:*› nachlassen; (cease to function) kaputtgehen; ‹*Maschine, Computer usw.:*› ausfallen; ‹*Sicherung:*› durchbrennen; (break) brechen; ‹*Seil usw.:*› reißen; (collapse) einstürzen; ‹*Mast:*› umstürzen; (fray badly) ausfransen; **the jacket has gone at the elbows** die Jacke ist an den Ellbogen durchgescheuert *od.* abgewetzt; **his memory is going** sein Gedächtnis lässt nach

12▸ (disappear) weggehen; ‹*Mantel, Hut, Fleck:*› verschwinden; ‹*Zahn:*› ausfallen; ‹*Kultur:*› vergehen; ‹*Geruch, Rauch:*› sich verziehen; ‹*Geld, Zeit:*› draufgehen (ugs.) **(in, on** für); (be relinquished) aufgegeben werden; ‹*Absatz usw.:*› gestrichen werden; ‹*Unterrichtsfach:*› entfallen; ‹*Tradition:*› abgeschafft werden; (be dismissed) ‹*Arbeitskräfte:*› entlassen werden; (Cricket) (be out) aus sein; **be gone from sight** außer Sicht geraten sein; **my coat/the stain has gone** mein Mantel/der Fleck ist weg; **where has my hat gone?** wo ist mein Hut [geblieben]?; **I don't know where my money goes** ich weiß nicht, wo das Geld bleibt; **that aid to developing countries goes on the growing of food** diese Entwicklungshilfe wird für den Anbau von Nahrungsmitteln verwendet; **this paragraph will have to go** dieser Absatz muss gestrichen werden; **all his money goes on women** er gibt sein ganzes Geld für Frauen aus; **all hope has gone** alle Hoffnung ist dahin

13▸ (elapse) ‹*Zeit:*› vergehen; ‹*Interview usw.:*› vorüber-, vorbeigehen; **that has all gone by** das ist jetzt alles vorbei; **in days gone by** in längst vergangenen Zeiten

14▸ **to go** (still remaining) **have sth. [still] to go** [noch] etw. übrig haben; **he has two years to go before he can retire** an der Rente fehlen ihm noch zwei Jahre; **there's hours to go** es dauert noch Stunden; **one week** *etc.* **to go to ...:** noch eine Woche *usw.* bis ...; **there's only another mile to go** [es ist] nur noch eine Meile; **still have a mile to go** noch eine Meile vor sich (*Dat.*) haben; **one down, two to go** einer ist bereits erledigt, bleiben noch zwei übrig (salopp)

15▸ (be sold) weggehen (ugs.); verkauft werden; **it went for £1** es ging für 1 Pfund weg; **I shan't let it go for less** für weniger gebe ich es nicht her; **go to sb.** an jmdn. gehen; **going! going! gone!** Zum Ersten! zum Zweiten! zum Dritten!

16▸ (run) ‹*Grenze, Straße usw.:*› verlaufen, gehen; (afford access, lead) gehen; führen; (extend) reichen; (fig.) gehen; **go high[er]** ‹*Preis:*› [noch weiter] steigen, [noch weiter] in die Höhe gehen; **the line goes across the page/to the corner/upwards** der Strich geht quer über die Seite/bis in die Ecke/verläuft nach oben; **my holiday goes from ... to ...:** ich habe Urlaub von ... bis ...; **as** *or* **so far as he/it goes** so weit; **sth. is correct as** *or* **so far as it goes** etw. ist so weit in Ordnung; **go a long way** ‹*Geld, Vorräte:*› lange reichen; **he will go a long way** (fig.) er wird es weit bringen; **go some/a long way to[wards] achieving sth.** ein kleines/ganzes Stück weiterhelfen *od.* einiges/eine Menge dazu beitragen, etw. zu erreichen; **ten pounds in those days went a long way** damals waren zehn Pfund noch etwas wert; **a little of his company goes a long way** (coll. derog.) wenn man nur kurze Zeit mit ihm verbracht hat, reicht das erst mal für eine Weile *od.* (salopp) ist man erst mal für eine Weile bedient

17▸ (fig.: advance) **we'll go halfway to meet the cost** wir kommen ihnen *usw.* bei den Kosten halbwegs entgegen; **I'll go as high as £100** (at auction) ich gehe *od.* biete bis zu 100 Pfund [mit]; *see also* **bother C 2**; **expense A 1**; **trouble 1**; **way A 5**

18▸ (turn out, progress) ‹*Ereignis, Projekt, Interview, Abend:*› verlaufen; **go for/against sb./sth.** ‹*Wahl, Kampf:*› zu jmds./einer Sache Gunsten/Ungunsten ausgehen; ‹*Entscheidung, Urteil:*› zu jmds./einer Sache Gunsten/Ungunsten ausfallen; ‹*Rechtsfall:*› zu jmds./einer Sache Gunsten/Ungunsten entschieden werden; **how did your holiday/party go?** wie war Ihr Urlaub/Ihre Party?; **how is the book going?** was macht [denn] das Buch?; **how are the rehearsals going?** was machen die Proben?; wie läuft es mit den Proben?; **go according to plan** nach Plan gehen; planmäßig verlaufen; **things have been going well/badly/smoothly** *etc.* **of late** in der letzten Zeit läuft alles gut/schief/glatt *usw.*; **the way things are going, ...:** so wie es aussieht *od.* so wie die Dinge liegen, ...; **how are things going?, how is it going?,** (coll. joc.) **how goes it?** wie stehts *od.* (ugs.) läufts?

19▸ (be, have form or nature, be in temporary state) sein; ‹*Sprichwort, Gedicht, Titel:*› lauten; **this is how things go, that's the way it goes** so ist es nun mal; **go against sth.** mit etw. nicht übereinstimmen; **go against one's principles** gegen seine Prinzipien gehen; **go against logic** der Logik widersprechen; gegen alle Logik sein; **go armed/naked** bewaffnet sein/nackt herumlaufen; **go in rags** in Lumpen *od.* zerlumpt gehen; **go hungry** hungern; hungrig bleiben; **go without food/water** es ohne Essen/Wasser aushalten; **go in fear of one's life** in beständiger Angst um sein Leben leben; **may the blessings of God go with you** möge der Segen des Herrn dich begleiten; der Segen des Herrn sei mit dir; **how does the tune/song/wording go [now]?** wie geht die Melodie/das Lied/lauten die Worte [denn nun]?; **the argument goes like this** das Argument ist folgendes; **now the tale/rumour/theory goes that ...:** es wird erzählt/es geht das Gerücht/es wird die Theorie vertreten, dass ...; **go to the tune of ...:** der Melodie von ... folgen; **this noun/verb goes like ...:** dieses Substantiv/Verb geht genauso wie ...; **as things/canteens/actors** *etc.* **go** verglichen mit anderen Dingen/Kantinen/Schauspielern *usw.*; **as things go, it's not expensive** das ist verhältnismäßig billig; **go by** *or* **under the name of ...:** unter dem Namen ... bekannt sein

20▸ (become) werden; **the tyre has gone flat** der Reifen ist platt; **the phone has gone dead** die Leitung ist tot; **go on the blink** kaputtgehen (ugs.); **go all freaky/Indian** *etc.* völlig ausflippen (ugs.)/ganz auf indisch *usw.* machen; **go serious/arty on sb.** jmdm. auf die ernste Tour/Künstlertour kommen (ugs.); **go nuclear/metric** (coll.) zur Atommacht werden/das metrische System einführen; **the constituency/York went Tory** der Wahlkreis/York ging an die Tories

21▸ (have usual place) kommen; (belong) gehören; **where does the box go?** wo kommt *od.* gehört die Kiste hin?; **where do you want this chair to go?** wo soll *od.* kommt der Stuhl hin?; **that chair will go nicely in the corner** dieser Stuhl macht sich gut in der *od.* passt gut in die Ecke; **this goes under a different heading** das gehört unter eine andere Überschrift; **each drink goes** *or* **all drinks go on the bill** alle Getränke kommen *od.* gehen auf die Rechnung; **the cheque is to go in[to] my account** der Scheck geht auf mein Konto

22▸ (fit) passen; **go in[to] sth.** in etw. (*Akk.*) gehen *od.* [hinein]passen; **it won't go [in]** es geht nicht rein (ugs.); **go through sth.** durch etw. [hindurch]gehen *od.* [hindurch]passen; **six into twelve goes twice** sechs geht zweimal in

g

zwölf; **five goes into forty exactly** vierzig durch fünf geht auf

23 (harmonize, match) passen (**with** zu); **the two colours don't go** die beiden Farben passen nicht zusammen *od.* beißen sich

24 (serve, contribute) dienen; **the qualities that go to make a leader** die Eigenschaften, die einen Führer ausmachen; **the sounds that go to make up a language** die Laute, aus denen eine Sprache besteht; **this fact goes to prove that ...** folgende Tatsache belegt, dass ...; **it just goes to show that ...:** daran zeigt sich, dass ...

25 (make sound of specified kind) machen; (emit sound) ‹*Turmuhr, Gong:*› schlagen; ‹*Glocke:*› läuten; **There goes the bell. School is over** Es klingelt. Die Schule ist aus; **the fire alarm went at 3 a. m.** der Feueralarm ging um 3 Uhr morgens los; **a police car with its siren going** ein Polizeiwagen mit eingeschalteter Sirene

26 *as intensifier* (coll.) **don't go making** *or* **go and make him angry** verärgere ihn bloß nicht; **he might go and hang himself** nachher hängt er sich womöglich auf; **don't go and make a fool of yourself** mach dich doch nicht lächerlich; **don't go looking for trouble** such keinen Streit; **don't go thinking ...:** glaube doch ja nicht, dass ...; **I gave him a £10 note and, of course, he had to go and lose it** (iron.) ich gab ihm einen 10-Pfund-Schein, und er musste ihn natürlich prompt verlieren; **now you've been and gone and done it** (coll.) du hast ja was Schönes angerichtet! (ugs. iron.); **go tell him I'm ready** (coll./Amer.) geh und sag ihm, dass ich fertig bin; **she said to her dog 'Go fetch it'** sie sagte zu ihrem Hund: „Los, hols!"; **let's go get ourselves a drink** (coll./Amer.) holen wir uns was zu trinken

27 (coll.: be acceptable or permitted) erlaubt sein; gehen (ugs.); **everything/anything goes** es ist alles erlaubt; **it/that goes without saying** es/das ist doch selbstverständlich; es/das versteht sich von selbst; **what he** *etc.* **says, goes** was er *usw.* sagt, gilt; wenn er *usw.* etwas sagt, dann gilt es auch; *see also* **let¹ A 1**

28 (coll. euphem.: defecate or urinate) auf die Toilette gehen; **have to go** müssen (ugs.); **I want to go somewhere** ich muss mal wohin *od.* verschwinden (ugs.)

29 **go astray, go into action, go blackberrying, go to the country,** *etc. see the noun, adverb, etc. See also* **going**; **gone**

B *v.t., forms as* **A** **1** (Cards) spielen

2 (coll.) **go it** es toll treiben; (work hard) rangehen; **he has been going it a bit too hard** er hat es etwas zu weit getrieben; **go it!** los!; weiter!; **100 mph? That's really going it** *or* **some!** 160 km/h? Das ist wirklich ein tolles Tempo; *see also* **alone A**

C *n., pl.* **goes** /gəʊz/ (coll.) **1** (attempt, try) Versuch, *der;* (chance) Gelegenheit, *die;* **have a go** es versuchen *od.* probieren; **have a go at doing sth.** versuchen, etw. zu tun; **have a go at sth.** sich an etw. (*Dat.*) versuchen; **someone has had a go at this lock** jmd. hat sich an dem Schloss zu schaffen gemacht; **he's had several goes at the driving test** er hat schon mehrere Anläufe genommen, den Führerschein zu bekommen; **have a good go with the vacuum cleaner** gründlich saugen; **let me have/can I have a go?** lass mich [auch ein]mal/kann ich [auch ein]mal? (ugs.); **it's my go** ich bin an der Reihe *od.* dran; **I've had my go already** ich hab[e] schon (ugs.); ich war schon dran (ugs.); **it's your turn to have a go** du bist jetzt dran (ugs.); **now 'you have a go** jetzt mach d<u>u</u> mal; **you missed one go** du hast einmal ausgesetzt; du bist einmal übersprungen worden; **in two/three goes** bei zwei/drei Versuchen; **at one go** auf einmal; **at the first go** auf Anhieb; **give sth. a go** etw. mal versuchen (ugs.)

2 **have a go at sb.** (scold) sich (*Dat.*) jmdn. vornehmen *od.* vorknöpfen (ugs.); (attack) über jmdn. herfallen; **have a go at a policeman** sich mit einem Polizisten anlegen (ugs.)

3 (period of activity) **in one go** auf einmal; **he downed his beer in one go** er trank sein Bier in einem Zug aus; **the dentist said he'd fill the teeth in two goes** der Zahnarzt meinte, dass er die Füllungen in zwei Sitzungen machen würde

4 (energy) Schwung, *der;* **be full of go** voller Schwung *od.* Elan sein; **have plenty of** *or* **a lot of go** einen enormen Schwung *od.* Elan haben

5 (vigorous activity) **it's all go** es ist alles eine einzige Hetzerei (ugs.); **it's all go at work** es ist ganz schön was los bei der Arbeit; wir müssen ganz schön ran bei der Arbeit; **be on the go** auf Trab sein (ugs.); **keep sb. on the go** jmdn. auf Trab halten (ugs.); **have two jobs** *etc.* **on the go** zwei Jobs *usw.* gleichzeitig haben

6 (success) Erfolg, *der;* **make a go of sth.** (turn sth. into a success) mit etw. Erfolg haben; eine Sache zum Erfolg führen; (not let sth. be a failure) das Beste aus etw. machen; **it's no go** da ist nichts zu machen; **it's a go** (dated coll.) [es ist] abgemacht; *see also* **no-go**

7 **be all the go** der letzte Schrei sein (ugs.); groß in Mode sein

8 **that was a near go** das war knapp; das wäre beinahe schief gegangen

9 (dated coll.: incident) Geschichte, *die;* **a rum go** eine komische Geschichte

D *adj.* (coll.) **all systems go** alles in Ordnung; alles klar

Phrasal verbs

• **go about**

A /--'-/ *v.i.* **1** (move from place to place) herumgehen; (by vehicle) herumfahren; **go about in groups** in Gruppen herumziehen; **go about in leather gear/dressed like a tramp** in Lederkleidung/wie ein Landstreicher herumlaufen; **go about doing sth.** (be in the habit of) etw. immer tun **2** (circulate) ‹*Gerücht, Geschichte, Grippe:*› umgehen **3** (Naut.) wenden

B /'---/ *v.t.* **1** (set about) erledigen ‹*Arbeit*›; angehen ‹*Problem*›; **how does one go about it?** wie geht man da vor?; wie stellt man das am besten an?; **go about it [in] the right way** es richtig angehen; **go about it tactfully** *etc.* taktvoll *usw.* vorgehen **2** (busy oneself with) nachgehen (+ *Dat.*) ‹*Arbeit usw.*›

• **'go after** *v.t.* (hunt) jagen; zu stellen versuchen; (fig.) anstreben; sich bemühen um ‹*Job*›; **decide what you want and go after it** werd dir darüber klar, was du willst, und dann versuche, es auch zu bekommen

• **'go against** *v.t.* zuwiderhandeln (+ *Dat.*); handeln gegen ‹*Prinzip, Gesetz*›; **go against sb.** sich jmdm. in den Weg stellen *od.* widersetzen; *see also* **go¹ A 18, 19**

• **go a'head** *v.i.* **1** (in advance) vorausgehen (**of** *Dat.*); (Sport) an die Spitze gehen; die Führung übernehmen; **the runner went ahead of the others** der Läufer zog an den anderen vorbei; **You go ahead. I'll meet you there** Geh mal schon vor. Wir treffen uns dann dort **2** (proceed) weitermachen; (make progress) ‹*Arbeit:*› fortschreiten, vorangehen; **go ahead with a plan** einen Plan durchführen; **go ahead and do it** es einfach machen; **go ahead!** nur zu!; **May I explain it to you? — OK. Go ahead** Darf ich es Ihnen erklären? — Ja, schießen Sie nur los (ugs.). *See also* **go-ahead**

• **go a'long**

A *v.i.* dahingehen/-fahren; (attend) hingehen

B *v.t.* entlanggehen/-fahren

• **go a'long with** *v.t.* **1** **go along with sth.** (share sb.'s opinion) einer Sache (*Dat.*) zustimmen; (agree to) sich einer Sache (*Dat.*) anschließen **2** **go along with you!** (coll.) ach, geh *od.* komm (ugs.); ach, erzähl mir doch nichts! (ugs.)

• **go a'round** ▸**go about A 1, 2**; **go round**

• **'go at** *v.t.* **go at sb.** (attack) über jmdn. herfallen; auf jmdn. losgehen; **go at sth./it** (work at) sich hinter etw. (*Akk.*) klemmen/sich dahinter klemmen (ugs.); sich an etw. (*Akk.*) machen/sich dranmachen

• **go a'way** *v.i.* weggehen; (on holiday or business) wegfahren; verreisen; **what did the bride wear to go away in?** was trug die Braut, als sie auf Hochzeitsreise ging?; **the problem won't go away** das Problem kann man nicht einfach ignorieren; *see also* **go¹ A 9**; **going-away**

• **go 'back** *v.i.* **1** (return) zurückgehen/-fahren; (restart) ‹*Schule, Fabrik:*› wieder anfangen; (fig.) zurückgehen; **I wouldn't want to go back to that place** dorthin wollte ich auf keinen Fall wieder zurück; **go back to a subject** auf ein Thema zurückkommen; **go back to the beginning** noch mal von vorne anfangen; **there'll be/there's no going back** da gibt es kein Zurück mehr **2** (be returned) zurückgegeben werden; ‹*Waren:*› zurückgehen (**to** an + *Akk.*) **3** (be put back) ‹*Uhren:*› zurückgestellt werden

• **go 'back on** *v.t.* nicht [ein]halten ‹*Versprechen, Wort*›

• **go before**

A /--'-/ *v.i.* (live before) früher leben; (happen before) vorher *od.* früher geschehen

B /'---/ *v.t.* **1** (live before) **go before sb.** vor jmds. Zeit (*Dat.*) leben **2** (appear before) **go before sth./sb.** ‹*Person:*› vor etw./jmdm. erscheinen; ‹*Sache:*› vor etw./jmdm. kommen

• **'go by** *v.t.* **go by sth.** sich nach etw. richten; (adhere to) sich an etw. (*Akk.*) halten; **if the report is anything to go by** wenn man nach dem Bericht gehen kann; **go by appearances** nach dem Äußeren gehen *od.* urteilen; *see also* **go¹ A 2, 13**; **go-by**

• **go 'down** *v.i.* **1** hinuntergehen/-fahren; ‹*Taucher:*› [hinunter]tauchen; (set) ‹*Sonne:*› untergehen; (sink) ‹*Schiff:*› sinken, untergehen; (drown) ‹*Person:*› untergehen, ertrinken; (fall to ground) ‹*Flugzeug usw.:*› abstürzen; **go down to the bottom of the garden/to the doctor/to the beach** zum hinteren Ende des Gartens gehen/zum Arzt gehen/an den Strand gehen **2** (be digested) verdaut werden; (be swallowed) hinuntergeschluckt werden; **go down the wrong way** in die falsche Kehle geraten; **sugar helps the medicine go down** mit Zucker kriegt man die Arznei besser hinunter (ugs.) **3** (become less) sinken; ‹*Umsatz, Schwellung:*› zurückgehen; ‹*Vorräte usw.:*› abnehmen; ‹*Währung:*› fallen; (become lower) fallen; (subside) ‹*Wind usw.:*› nachlassen; **go down in sb.'s estimation/in the world** in jmds. Achtung (*Dat.*) sinken/sich verschlechtern **4** **go down well/all right** *etc.* **[with sb.]** [mit jmdm.] gut *usw.* klarkommen (ugs.); ‹*Film, Schauspieler, Vorschlag:*› [bei jmdm.] gut *usw.* ankommen (ugs.); **that didn't go down [at all] well with his wife** das hat ihm seine Frau nicht abgenommen **5** (be defeated) unterliegen; **go down to sb.** gegen jmdn. verlieren **6** (be recorded in writing) niedergeschrieben werden; schriftlich vermerkt werden **7** (Bridge) den Kontrakt nicht erfüllen; (Cards) [seine Karten] aufdecken **8** (Brit. Univ.) abgehen; (at end of term) in die Semesterferien gehen **9** ‹*Maschine, Computer usw.:*› ausfallen

• **go 'down with** *v.t.* bekommen ‹*Krankheit*›; *see also* **go down 4**

• **'go for** *v.t.* **1** (go to fetch) **go for sb./sth.** jmdn./etw. holen **2** (apply to) **go for sb./sth.** für jmdn./etw. gelten; **that goes for me too** das gilt auch für mich; ich auch; **what goes for me goes for you too** was für mich gilt, gilt auch für dich **3** (attack) **go for sb. [with a knife** *etc.***]** [mit einem Messer *usw.*] auf jmdn. losgehen **4** (pass for) **go for sth.** als etw. durchgehen **5** (like) **go for sb./sth.** jmdn./etw. gut finden; **I could go for for 'him** d<u>e</u>r könnte mir gefallen **6** (count for) **go for nothing/little** nichts/wenig gelten *od.* zählen **7** (aim at) es abgesehen haben auf (+ *Akk.*). *See also* **go¹ A 15, 18**; **going B 6**

• **go 'forth** ▸**forth 3**

• **go 'forward** *v.i.* weitergehen/-fahren; (fig.) voranschreiten; ‹*Uhren:*› vorgestellt werden

• **go 'forward with** *v.t.* weiter durchführen; weiter verfolgen ‹*Plan usw.*›

• **go 'in** *v.i.* **1** (go indoors) hineingehen; reingehen (ugs.) **2** (be covered by cloud) verschwinden; weggehen (ugs.) **3** (be learnt) [in den Kopf] reingehen (ugs.); **it just won't go in** es will einfach nicht in den Kopf **4** (Cricket) zum Schlagen drankommen **5** **go in and win!** Bangemachen gilt nicht! (fam.); nur Mut! *See also* **go¹ A 2, 22**

• **go 'in for** *v.t.* **go in for sth.** (choose as career)

g

etw. [er]lernen wollen; (enter) an etw. (*Dat.*) teilnehmen; (indulge in, like) für etw. zu haben sein; (have as one's hobby, pastime, etc.) sich auf etw. (*Akk.*) verlegen; **go in for sport** Sport treiben; **so you'd like to go in for teaching** du willst also Lehrer/Lehrerin werden; **I don't really go in for jogging** ich habe nicht viel übrig fürs Joggen; **go in for wearing loud colours** gern knallige Farben tragen

- **'go into** *v.t.* 1 (join) eintreten in (+ *Akk.*) ‹*Orden, Geschäft usw.*›; gehen in (+ *Akk.*) ‹*Industrie, Politik*›; gehen zu ‹*Film, Fernsehen, Armee*›; beitreten (+ *Dat.*) ‹*Bündnis*›; **go into law/the church** Jurist/Geistlicher werden; **go into nursing** Krankenschwester/-pfleger werden; **go into publishing** ins Verlagswesen gehen; **go into general practice** (Med.) sich als allgemeiner Mediziner niederlassen 2 (go and live in) gehen in (+ *Akk.*) ‹*Krankenhaus, Heim usw.*›; ziehen in (+ *Akk.*) ‹*Wohnung, Heim*›; **go into digs/lodgings** sich (*Dat.*) eine Bude (ugs.)/ein Zimmer nehmen 3 (consider) eingehen auf (*Akk.*); (investigate, examine) sich befassen mit; (explain) darlegen 4 (crash into) [hinein]fahren in (+ *Akk.*); fahren gegen ‹*Baum usw.*› 5 (pass into specified state) verfallen in (+ *Akk.*); **go into hysterics/a fit** hysterisch werden/einen Anfall bekommen; **go [off] into laughter** *etc.* in Lachen *usw.* ausbrechen; **the book is going into paperback/its fifth edition** das Buch erscheint als Paperback/in der fünften Auflage 6 ([begin to] wear) tragen. *see also* **go¹ A 2, 22**
- **go 'in with** *v.t.* **go in with sb.** [mit jmdm.] mitmachen
- **go off**

A /'-'-/ *v.i.* 1 (Theatre) abgehen 2 **go off with sb./sth.** sich mit jmdm./etw. auf- und davonmachen (ugs.); **his wife has gone off with the milkman** seine Frau ist mit dem Milchmann durchgebrannt (ugs.) 3 ‹*Alarm, Schusswaffe, Klingel:*› losgehen; ‹*Wecker:*› klingeln; ‹*Bombe:*› hochgehen 4 (turn bad) schlecht werden; (turn sour) sauer werden; (fig.) sich verschlechtern 5 ‹*Strom, Gas, Wasser:*› ausfallen 6 **go off [to sleep]** einschlafen 7 (be sent) abgehen (**to** an + *Akk.*) 8 **go off well** *etc.* gut *usw.* verlaufen. *see also* **go¹ A 2**

B /'--, -'-/ *v.t.* 1 (begin to dislike) **go off sth.** von etw. abkommen; **go off sb.** jmdn. nicht mehr mögen; **go off beer/the cinema** sich (*Dat.*) nichts mehr aus Bier/Kino machen 2 **go off the gold standard** vom Goldstandard abgehen 3 **go off into** ▸**go into e**

- **go on**

A /'-'-/ *v.i.* 1 weitergehen/-fahren; (by vehicle) die Reise/Fahrt *usw.* fortsetzen; (go ahead) vorausgehen; (drive ahead) vorausfahren 2 (continue) weitergehen; ‹*Kämpfe:*› anhalten; ‹*Verhandlungen, Arbeiten:*› [an]dauern; (continue to act) weitermachen; (continue to live) weiterleben; **I can't go on** ich kann nicht mehr; ich weiß nicht mehr weiter; **go on for weeks** *etc.* Wochen *usw.* dauern; **this has been going on for months** das geht schon seit Monaten so; **the case went on for years** der Prozess hat sich jahrelang hingezogen; **go on to say** *etc.* fortfahren und sagen *usw.*; **'moreover', he went on, ...:** „außerdem“, fuhr er fort, ...; **go on and on** dauern und dauern; kein Ende nehmen wollen; sich endlos hinziehen; **go on [and on]** (coll.) (chatter) reden und reden; **she does go on so** sie redet unaufhörlich; **go on about sb./sth.** stundenlang von jmdm./etw. erzählen; (complain) sich ständig über jmdn./etw. beklagen; **go on at sb.** (coll.) auf jmdm. herumhacken (ugs.) 3 (elapse) ‹*Zeit:*› vergehen; **as time/the years went on** im Laufe der Zeit/Jahre 4 (happen) passieren; vor sich gehen; **there's more going on in the big cities** in den großen Städten ist mehr los; **the things that go on there** die Dinge, die da vor sich gehen; **what's going on?, what goes on?** was geht vor?; was ist los? 5 **be going on [for]** ... (be nearly) fast ... sein; **he is going on [for] ninety** er geht auf die Neunzig zu; **he is seven going on [for] eight** er ist fast acht; **it is going on [for] ten o'clock** es geht auf 10 Uhr zu 6 (behave) sich benehmen; sich aufführen 7 ‹*Kleidung:*› passen; **my dress wouldn't go on** ich kriegte mein Kleid nicht an (ugs.); ich kam nicht in mein Kleid rein (ugs.); **this hat won't go on** diesen Hut kriege ich nicht auf (ugs.) 8 (Theatre) auftreten; (Cricket) mit dem Werfen beginnen 9 ▸**go forward** 10 (be lit) ‹*Licht:*› angehen; (be supplied) ‹*Strom, Wasser:*› kommen; **go on again** ‹*Strom, Gas, Wasser:*› wiederkommen 11 **go on!** (proceed) los, mach schon! (ugs.); (resume) fahren Sie fort!; (coll.: stop talking nonsense) ach, geh *od.* komm (ugs.); ach, erzähl mir doch nichts! (ugs.); *see also* **goings-on**

B /'--/ *v.t.* 1 (ride on) fahren mit; **go on the roundabout/swings/Big Dipper** Karussell/Schiffschaukel/Achterbahn fahren 2 (continue) **go on working/talking** *etc.* weiterarbeiten/weiterreden *usw.*; **go on trying** es weiter[hin] versuchen 3 (coll.: be guided by) sich stützen auf (+ *Akk.*); **there's little evidence to go on** es gibt wenig Beweismaterial, auf das man sich stützen kann 4 (begin to receive) bekommen, erhalten ‹*Arbeitslosengeld, Sozialfürsorge*›; *see also* **dole A** 5 ▸**go on to 2** 6 (start to take) nehmen ‹*Medikament, Drogen*›; **go on a diet** eine Abmagerungs- *od.* Schlankheitskur machen 7 (coll.: like) ▸**much B**. *See also* **go¹ A 12**; **stage A 2**

- **go 'on for** ▸**go on A 5**
- **go 'on to** *v.t.* 1 (proceed to) übergehen zu; **he went on to become ...:** er wurde schließlich ... 2 (change working arrangements to) übergehen zu ‹*Kurzarbeit, Überstunden*›
- **go 'on with** *v.t.* 1 **go on with sth.** mit etw. weitermachen; **something/enough to go on with** *or* **be going on with** etwas/genug für den Anfang *od.* fürs Erste; **here's something to be going on with** hiermit kann man schon [ein]mal anfangen; **here's £10 to be going on with** hier sind erst [ein]mal 10 Pfund [für den Anfang] (ugs.); **here's a cup of tea to be going on with** hier hast du erst einmal eine Tasse Tee 2 ▸**go along with 2**
- **go 'out** *v.i.* 1 (from home) ausgehen; **go out to work/go out charring/for a meal** arbeiten/putzen/essen gehen; **go out and about** unterwegs sein; auf den Beinen sein; **out you go!** hinaus *od.* (ugs.) raus mit dir!; **go out with sb.** (regularly) mit jmdm. gehen (ugs.) 2 **go out [on strike]** in den Ausstand treten 3 (be extinguished) ‹*Feuer, Licht, Zigarre usw.:*› ausgehen; **go out like a light** (fig. coll.: fall asleep) sofort weg sein (ugs.) *od.* einschlafen 4 (ebb) ‹*Ebbe, Wasser:*› ablaufen, zurückgehen; **the tide has gone out** es ist Ebbe 5 (Polit.) [aus der Regierung] ausscheiden; ‹*Regierung:*› abgelöst werden 6 (be issued) verteilt werden; (Radio, Telev.: be transmitted) übertragen werden; ausgestrahlt werden 7 (euphem.: die) [hinüber]gehen (verhüll.); **he went out peacefully in his sleep** er ist sanft entschlafen (geh.) 8 (end) ‹*Monat, Jahr:*› zu Ende gehen 9 (of fashion) unmodern werden; ‹*Brauch:*› aussterben 10 (Sport: be defeated) unterliegen (**to** *Dat.*). *See also* **go¹ A 2**; **business 2**; **walk C 1**
- **go 'out to** *v.t.* ‹*Sympathie:*› sein mit; **my heart/sympathy goes out to them** ich fühle mit ihnen mit. *See also* **go out 10**
- **go over**

A /'-'--/ *v.i.* 1 **he went over to the fireplace/man in the corner** er ging zum Kamin/zu dem Mann in der Ecke hinüber; **we're going over to our friends** wir fahren zu unseren Freunden; **I'm just going over to the shop** ich gehe kurz ins Geschäft hinüber 2 (be received) ‹*Rede, Ankündigung, Plan:*› ankommen (**with** bei) 3 (Radio, Telev.) **go over to sb./sth./Belfast** zu jmdm./in etw. (*Akk.*)/nach Belfast umschalten. *See also* **go¹ A 2**; **go over to**

B /'---/ *v.t.* 1 (re-examine, think over, rehearse) durchgehen; **go over sth./the facts in one's head** *or* **mind** etw. im Geiste durchgehen/die Fakten überdenken 2 (clean) sauber machen; (inspect and repair) durchsehen ‹*Maschine, Auto usw.*›; **go over the house with the Hoover/duster** durchsaugen/mit dem Staubtuch durchs Haus gehen 3 (survey) begutachten; sich (*Dat.*) ansehen 4 **go over sth. with a pen** etw. mit dem Stift nachziehen. *See also* **going-over**

- **go 'over to** *v.t.* 1 hinübergehen zu; übertreten zu ‹*Glauben, Partei*›; überwechseln zu ‹*Revolutionären*›; ‹*Verräter:*› überlaufen zu ‹*Feind*›; überlaufen in (+ *Akk.*) ‹*Lager des Feindes*› 2 (change to) übergehen zu. *See also* **go¹ A 2, 8**; **go over A**
- **go round**

A /'-'-/ *v.i.* 1 (call) **go round and** *or* **to see sb.** jmdn. besuchen; bei jmdm. vorbeigehen (ugs.); **go round to sb.'s house** (call at) jmdn. aufsuchen 2 (look round) sich umschauen 3 (suffice) reichen; langen (ugs.); **enough coffee to go round** genug Kaffee für alle 4 (spin) sich drehen; **my head is going round** mir dreht sich alles 5 (circulate) **the word went round that ...:** es ging die Parole um, dass ... 6 (Golf) **go round in 70** eine 70er Runde spielen

B /'--/ *v.t.* 1 (inspect) besichtigen 2 (encompass) ‹*Gürtel:*› herumreichen um ‹*Taille*›; **the trousers won't go round my waist** die Hose passt mir nicht in der Taille *od.* um die Taille herum 3 **have enough food to go round [so many people]** [für so viele Leute] genügend zu essen haben

- **go through**

A /'-'-/ *v.i.* ‹*Ernennung, Gesetzesvorlage:*› durchkommen; ‹*Geschäft:*› [erfolgreich] abgeschlossen werden; ‹*Antrag, Bewerbung:*› durchgehen; **go through to the final** in die Endrunde kommen; **as soon as his divorce has gone through** sobald seine Scheidung durch ist

B /'--/ *v.t.* 1 (execute, undergo) erledigen ‹*Formalität, Anforderung*›; abwickeln ‹*Geschäft*›; absolvieren ‹*Kurs, Lehre*›; durchziehen (ugs.) ‹*Programm*›; **go through a marriage ceremony/divorce proceedings** sich trauen lassen/die Scheidung durchmachen 2 (rehearse) durchgehen 3 (examine) durchsehen ‹*Post, Unterlagen*›; (search) durchsuchen ‹*Taschen*› 4 (endure) durchmachen ‹*schwere Zeiten*›; durchstehen ‹*Belastung*›; (suffer) erleiden ‹*Schmerzen*› 5 (use up) verbrauchen; durchbringen ‹*Erbschaft*›; aufbrauchen ‹*Vorräte*› 6 (be published in) erleben ‹*Auflagen*›. *See also* **go¹ A 22**

- **go 'through with** *v.t.* zu Ende führen; ausführen ‹*Hinrichtung*›; **she realized that she would have to go through with it** sie sah ein, dass sie jetzt nicht mehr zurückkonnte; **she told him that she couldn't go through with the wedding** sie sagte ihm, dass aus der Hochzeit nichts würde
- **go to'gether** *v.i.* 1 (coincide) zusammengehen 2 (match) zusammenpassen 3 (date regularly) miteinander gehen (ugs.)
- **go 'under** *v.i.* (sink below surface) untergehen; (fig.: fail) ‹*Geschäftsmann:*› scheitern; ‹*Unternehmen:*› eingehen; **go under to sth.** einer Sache (*Dat.*) zum Opfer fallen
- **go 'up** *v.i.* 1 hinaufgehen/-fahren; ‹*Ballon:*› aufsteigen; ‹*Flugzeug, Flieger:*› fliegen; (Theatre) ‹*Vorhang:*› aufgehen, hochgehen; ‹*Lichter:*› angehen 2 (increase) ‹*Bevölkerung, Zahl:*› wachsen; ‹*Preis, Wert, Zahl, Niveau:*› steigen; **everything is going up these days** heutzutage wird alles teurer 3 (be constructed) ‹*Gebäude, Barrikade:*› errichtet werden 4 (be destroyed) in die Luft fliegen (ugs.); hochgehen (ugs.); *see also* **flame A 1**; **smoke A 1** 5 (Brit. Univ.) sein Studium aufnehmen; **go up to Oxford** sein Studium in Oxford aufnehmen; (at beginning of term) nach den Semesterferien nach Oxford zurückkehren 6 **go up to sb.** (approach for talk) auf jmdn. zugehen 7 **go up in the world** [gesellschaftlich] aufsteigen
- **'go with** *v.t.* 1 (be concomitant with) einhergehen mit 2 (be included with) gehören zu 3 (date regularly) gehen mit (ugs.). *See also* **go¹ A 1, 23**
- **go without**

A /'---/ *v.t.* verzichten auf (+ *Akk.*); **have to go without sth.** ohne etw. auskommen müssen

B /-'-'-/ *v.i.* (receive nothing) **if you won't eat that dinner, you'll have to go without** wenn du das Essen nicht isst, musst du eben ohne auskommen

go² *n.* (game) Go, *das*

goad /gəʊd/

A *v.t.* 1 **~ sb. into sth./doing sth.** jmdn. zu etw. anstacheln/dazu anstacheln, etw. zu tun; **~ sb. into a fury** jmdn. in Wut bringen 2 antreiben ‹*Vieh usw.*›

B *n.* Stachelstock, *der*; (fig.) Stachel, *der*; (stimulus) Ansporn, *der*

g

(Phrasal verb)
• ~ 'on v.t. ~ sb. on jmdn. anstiften

'go-ahead
A adj. (enterprising) unternehmungslustig; (progressive) fortschrittlich; ~ **spirit** Unternehmungsgeist, der
B n. grünes Licht (fig.); **give sb./sth. the ~:** jmdm./einer Sache grünes Licht geben

goal /gəʊl/ n. **1** (aim) Ziel, das; **what do you have as your ~?** welches Ziel hast du dir gesetzt?; **attain** or **reach** or **accomplish one's ~:** sein Ziel erreichen **2** (Assoc. Footb., Hockey) Tor, das; (Rugby) Mal, das; **keep ~:** das Tor hüten; **[play] in ~:** im Tor [stehen]; **score/kick a ~:** einen Treffer erzielen; **win by two ~s to one** zwei zu eins gewinnen

goal: ~ area n. Torraum, der; ~ **average** n. **on ~ average** nach Toren; ~ **difference** n. Tordifferenz, die

goalie /'gəʊlɪ/ n. (coll.) Tormann, der; Schlussmann, der (ugs.)

goal: ~keeper n. ▸ p. 1260 Torwart, der; ~ **kick** n. (Assoc. Footb.) Abstoß, der; (Rugby) Tritt nach dem Mal

goalless /'gəʊllɪs/ adj. torlos; **end in a ~ draw** torlos [unentschieden] enden

goal: ~-line n. (Assoc. Footb., Hockey) Torlinie, die; (Rugby) Mallinie, die; **~minder** n. (Amer.) Torwart, der; **~mouth** n. Raum unmittelbar vor dem Tor; **~post** n. Torpfosten, der; **move the ~posts** (fig. coll.) sich nicht an die Spielregeln halten; **~-tender** n. (Amer.) Torwart, der

go-as-you-'please adj. ungezwungen

goat /gəʊt/ n. **1** Ziege, die; **act** or **play the [giddy] ~:** den Clown spielen; herumalbern; **get sb.'s ~** (coll.) jmdn. aufregen (ugs.) **2** (Astrol.) **the G~:** der Steinbock; see also **archer 2** **3** (coll.: fool) Idiot, der (ugs. abwertend); Esel, der (ugs.) **4** (coll.: licentious man) **old ~:** alter [geiler] Bock (salopp) **5** (Amer.: scape~) Sündenbock, der (ugs.)

goatee /gəʊ'ti:/ n. ~ **[beard]** Kinnbart, der; Spitzbart, der

'goatherd n. Ziegenhirt[e], der

goatish /'gəʊtɪʃ/ adj. (fig.) geil

goat: ~skin n. Ziegenleder, das; (bottle) Ziegenlederflasche, die; **~'s milk** n. Ziegenmilch, die; **~sucker** ▸ **nightjar**

gob¹ /gɒb/ n. (sl.) Gosche, die (landsch. derb); Schnauze, die (derb abwertend); Maul, das (derb abwertend); **shut your ~!** halts Maul! (derb); halt die Schnauze! (derb)

gob² v.i. (sl.: spit) rotzen (derb)

gobble¹ /'gɒbl/
A v.t. ~ **[down** or **up]** hinunterschlingen
B v.i. schlingen

(Phrasal verb)
• ~ **up** v.t. (fig. coll.) verschlingen; ‹Land, Imperium:› sich (Dat.) einverleiben ‹kleineres Land usw.›

gobble² v.i. (make sound) kollern

gobbledegook, gobbledygook /'gɒbldɪgu:k, 'gɒbldɪgʊk/ n. Kauderwelsch, das

'go-between n. Vermittler, der/Vermittlerin, die; (in love affair) Postillon d'Amour, der

Gobi /'gəʊbɪ/ pr. n. **the ~ [Desert]** die [Wüste] Gobi

goblet /'gɒblɪt/ n. Kelchglas, das

goblin /'gɒblɪn/ n. Kobold, der

gobsmacked /'gɒbsmækt/ adj (Brit. coll.) geplättet (salopp); baff (salopp)

'gobstopper n. (Brit.) Riesenlutscher, der; Maulstopfer, der (ugs.)

goby /'gəʊbɪ/ n. (Zool.) Grundel, die

'go-by n. **give the ~ to sb., give sb. the ~:** jmdn. schneiden

'go-cart n. **1** ▸ **go-kart** **2** (handcart) Handwagen, der; (soapbox) Seifenkiste, die

god /gɒd/ n. **1** Gott, der; **the drink of the ~s** der Göttertrank; **be** or **lie in the lap** or **on the knees of the ~s** im Schoß der Götter liegen; **a feast [fit] for the ~s** ein göttliches Mahl; **a gift from the ~s** ein Geschenk des Himmels; **a sight [fit] for the ~s** eine Augenweide; (with grandeur) ein majestätischer Anblick; (iron.) ein Bild für die Götter (ugs. scherzh.); **ye ~s [and little fishes]!** mein Gott! **2** **G~** no pl. (Theol.) Gott; **Almighty G~:** der allmächtige Gott; **G~ the Father, Son, and Holy Ghost** Gott Vater, Sohn und Heiliger Geist; **G~ moves in a mysterious way** (prov.) die Wege des Herrn sind unerforschlich; **G~ helps those who help themselves** (prov.) hilf dir selbst, so hilft dir Gott (Spr.); **G~ knows** (as G~ is witness) weiß Gott (ugs.); **G~ knows, I tried** ich habe es, weiß Gott, versucht; **G~ [only] knows** (coll.: nobody knows) weiß der Himmel (ugs.); **G~ willing, if it is G~'s will** so Gott will; **an act of G~:** höhere Gewalt; **before G~:** bei Gott; **play G~:** sich zum Gott aufwerfen; **under G~:** auf Erden (geh.); **G~'s gift** ein Geschenk Gottes; ein Gottesgeschenk; **she thinks she's G~'s gift to men** sie denkt, sie ist der Traum aller Männer; **G~'s truth** [nichts als] die reine Wahrheit (geh.); **be with G~:** bei Gott sein (bibl.); **G~'s [own] country** Paradies auf Erden; **G~'s earth** Gottes [weite] Erde; **G~!/good G~!/my G~!/oh G~!/G~ in Heaven!** [ach] Gott!/großer od. allmächtiger od. guter Gott!/mein Gott!/o Gott!/[guter] Gott im Himmel!; **dear G~!** lieber Gott!; **for G~'s sake!** um Himmels od. Gottes willen!; **I hope to G~ that ...:** ich hoffe bei Gott, dass ...; **G~ be with you** Gott mit euch; **G~, he's so stupid!** [mein] Gott, ist er dumm!; **by G~:** bei Gott; **thank G~!** Gott sei Dank!; **G~ damn it!** zum Teufel noch mal! (ugs.); **G~ damn you/him** etc. Gott verfluche dich/ihn usw.; **G~ help you/him** etc. möge Gott dir/ihm usw. helfen; Gott steh dir/ihm usw. bei; **G~ grant ...:** Gott gebe ...; **please G~!** so es Gott gefällt; **as G~ is my witness/judge** Gott ist mein Zeuge; see also **bless 1**; **forbid 2**; **help A 5**; **man A 1, 2**; **name A 4** **3** (fig.) Gott, der; Götze, der (geh., abwertend); see also **tin ~** **4** (Theatre) **the ~s** der Olymp (ugs. scherzh.)

'God-awful adj. (sl.) fürchterlich

god: ~child n. Patenkind, das; **~dam, ~damn, ~damned** **A** adj. gottverdammt (derb); **[it is] none of your ~dam business** das geht dich einen Dreck an (salopp); **B** adv. gottverdammt (derb); **you're ~dam right!** du hast, verdammt noch mal, Recht! (derb); **~-daughter** n. Patentochter, die

goddess /'gɒdɪs/ n. Göttin, die

'godfather n. **1** Pate, der; Patenonkel, der; **my ~s!** [ach] du meine od. liebe Güte! **2** (fig.) Boss, der (ugs.); (of Mafia etc.) Pate, der

'God-fearing adj. gottesfürchtig

'godforsaken adj. gottverlassen

'God-given adj. gottgegeben

godhead /'gɒdhed/ n. Göttlichkeit, die; **the G~:** die Gottheit; Gott, der

godless /'gɒdlɪs/ adj. gottlos

godlike /'gɒdlaɪk/ adj. göttlich; göttergleich (geh.)

godliness /'gɒdlɪnɪs/ n., no pl. Gottgefälligkeit, die

godly /'gɒdlɪ/ adj. gottgefällig; gottergeben

god: ~mother n. Patin, die; Patentante, die; **~parent** n. (male) Pate, der; (female) Patin, die; **~parents** Paten Pl.; **~send** n. Gottesgabe, die; **be a ~send to sb.** für jmdn. ein Geschenk des Himmels sein; **~son** n. Patensohn, der

God'speed n. (dated) **wish** or **bid sb. ~:** jmdm. eine glückliche Reise wünschen

godwit /'gɒdwɪt/ n. (Ornith.) Pfuhlschnepfe, die

goer /'gəʊə(r)/ n. **1** (horse) Geher, der; **be a good ~:** gut gehen **2** (active person) Energiebündel, das (ugs.) **3** in comb. -gänger, der; -besucher, der; see also **churchgoer, filmgoer,** etc.

goes ▸ **go¹ A, B**

Goethian (Goethean) /'gɜ:tɪən/ adj. goethisch; goethesch

'go-getter n. Draufgänger, der

'go-getting adj. draufgängerisch; Ellbogen gebrauchend

goggle /'gɒgl/
A n. in pl. **[a pair of] ~s** eine Schutzbrille
B adj. ~ **eyes** Glupschaugen Pl. (nordd.); Froschaugen Pl. (ugs.)
C v.i. glotzen (ugs.); ~ **at sb./sth.** jmdn./etw. anglotzen (ugs.)

goggle: ~-box n. (Brit. coll.) Glotze, die (salopp); Glotzkiste, die (salopp); **~-eyed** adj. glotzäugig (ugs.)

'go-go adj. (coll.) Go-go-; ~ **dancer** or **girl** Go-Go-Girl, das

going /'gəʊɪŋ/
A n. **1** vbl. n. of **go¹ A, B** **2** (progress) Vorankommen, das; (Horseracing, Hunting, etc.) Geläuf, das; **150 miles in two hours, that is good ~:** 150 Meilen in zwei Stunden, das ist wirklich gut; **the ~ was slow/heavy** man kam nur langsam/schwer voran; **the journey was slow ~:** die Reise zog sich [in die Länge]; **interviewing her is heavy ~:** ein Gespräch mit ihr ist ganz schön mühsam od. ein schwieriges Geschäft; **this book is heavy ~:** dieses Buch liest sich schwer; **while the ~ is good** solange noch Zeit dazu ist od. es noch geht
B adj. **1** pres. p. of **go¹** **2** (available) erhältlich; **there is sth. ~:** es gibt etw.; **take any job ~:** jede Arbeit annehmen, die es nur gibt; **this cabbage was the best one ~:** das war der beste Kohl, den man bekommen konnte **3** **be ~ to do sth.** etw. tun [werden/wollen]; **he's ~ to be a ballet dancer when he grows up** wenn er groß ist, wird er Balletttänzer; **I was ~ to say** ich wollte sagen; **I was not ~** (did not intend) **to do sth.** ich hatte nicht die Absicht, etw. zu tun; **it's ~ to snow** es wird schneien **4** (current) [derzeit/damals/dann] geltend; **the ~ rate of exchange** der augenblickliche Wechselkurs **5** **a ~ concern** eine gesunde Firma **6** **have a lot/nothing** etc. **~ for one** (coll.) viel/nichts usw. haben, was für einen spricht; **it has a lot ~ for it** vieles spricht dafür; es hat viele Vorteile **7** **to be ~ on with** ▸ **go on with**; **set/keep sth. ~, keep sb. ~** ▸ **go¹ A 6**; **get ~** ▸ **get A 15, B 2**; **be ~ on fifteen** etc. ▸ **go on A 5**; ~ **strong** ▸ **strong B**; ~ **great guns** ▸ **gun A 1**

going: ~-a'way attrib. adj. ‹Ausstattung, Kleid› für die Hochzeitsreise; **~-over** n. **1** (coll.: overhaul) (of list etc.) Durchsicht, die; (of engine etc.) (overhaul) Überholung, die; (check) Überprüfung, die; **give sth. a [good etc.] ~-over** eine Sache [gründlich usw.] durchgehen od. durchsehen; **give the room a ~-over with the Hoover/duster** das Zimmer durchsaugen/im Zimmer Staub wischen; **2** (coll.: thrashing) **give sb. a [good] ~-over** jmdn. [ordentlich] verprügeln (ugs.); **3** (Amer. coll.: scolding) **give sb. a [good] ~-over** sich (Dat.) jmdn. [einmal ordentlich] vorknöpfen (ugs.)

goings-on /gəʊɪŋz'ɒn/ n. pl. Ereignisse Pl.; Vorgänge pl.; **there have been some strange ~:** es sind seltsame Dinge passiert; **be disgusted by sb.'s ~:** empört über jmds. Treiben od. Geschichten (Akk.) sein

goitre (Brit.; Amer.: **goiter**) /'gɔɪtə(r)/ n. (Med.) Kropf, der

'go-kart n. Gokart, der

gold /gəʊld/
A n. **1** no pl., no indef. art. Gold, das; **the price of ~:** der Goldpreis; **be worth one's weight in ~:** nicht mit Gold aufzuwiegen sein; **a heart of ~:** ein goldenes Herz; **she is pure ~:** sie ist Gold wert **2** no pl., no indef. art. (wealth) Geld, das; (coins) Goldmünzen Pl.; **a crock or pot of ~ at the end of the rainbow** ein Krug/Topf voll Gold am Ende des Regenbogens (ein unerfüllbarer Wunsch) **3** (colour) Gold, das; **the ~ of her hair** ihr goldenes Haar **4** (medal) Gold, das; **win six Olympic ~s** sechsmal olympisches Gold gewinnen **5** (Archery: bullseye) Gold, das. See also **glitter A 1**; **good A 6**
B attrib. adj. golden; Gold‹münze, -stück, -kette, -krone usw.›

gold: ~ 'brick n. **1** (coll.: fraud) Schwindel, der; **sell sb. a ~ brick** jmdn. übers Ohr hauen (ugs.); jmdm. etwas andrehen (ugs.); **2** (Amer. coll.: shirker) Drückeberger, der (ugs. abwertend); ~ **'card** n. Goldkarte, die; **G~ coast** pr. n. Goldküste, die; **~-coloured** adj. goldfarben; **~crest** n. (Ornith.) Wintergoldhähnchen, das;

~-digger *n.* Goldgräber, *der;* **she's a ~-digger** (fig. coll.) sie ist nur auf das Geld der Männer aus; **~ 'disc** *n.* Goldene Schallplatte; **~ dust** *n.* [1] Goldstaub, *der;* **be like ~ dust** eine Rarität sein; [2] (Bot.) Felsensteinkraut, *das*

golden /'gəʊldn/ *adj.* [1] golden; **~ brown/yellow** goldbraun/goldgelb [2] (fig.) golden; einmalig ‹*Gelegenheit*›

golden: ~ age *n.* goldenes Zeitalter; **~ boy** *n.* Goldjunge, *der;* **~ 'calf** *n.* Goldenes Kalb; **~ 'disc** ▸**gold disc;** **~ 'eagle** *n.* Steinadler, *der;* **G~ 'Fleece** *n.* (Greek Mythol.) Goldenes Vlies; **G~ 'Gate** *pr. n.* (Geog.) Goldenes Tor; **the ~ Gate Bridge** die Golden-Gate-Brücke; **~ girl** *n.* Goldmädchen, *das;* **~-haired** *adj.* mit goldenem Haar *nachgestellt* (dichter.); **~ 'hamster** *n.* Goldhamster, *der;* **~ 'handshake** *n.* Abfindung[ssumme], *die;* **~ hel'lo** *n.* Einstellungsprämie, *die;* **~ 'jubilee** *n.* goldenes Jubiläum; **~ 'mean** *n.* goldene Mitte; **~ 'parachute** *n.* (coll.) goldener Fallschirm; **~ re'triever** *n.* Golden Retriever, *der;* **~ rod** *n.* (Bot.) Goldrute, *die;* **~ 'rule** *n.* goldene Regel; **~ 'syrup** *n.* (Brit.) Sirup, *der;* **~ 'wedding** *n.* goldene Hochzeit

gold: ~ fever *n.* Goldrausch, *der;* **~field** *n.* Goldfeld, *das;* **~finch** *n.* Stieglitz, *der;* Distelfink, *der;* **~fish** *n.* Goldfisch, *der;* **~fish bowl** *n.* Goldfischglas, *das;* **like being in a ~fish bowl** (fig.) wie auf dem Präsentierteller; **~ 'foil** *n.* Goldfolie, *die*

goldilocks /'gəʊldɪlɒks/ *n.* Blondkopf, *der*

gold: ~ 'leaf *n.* Blattgold, *das;* **~ 'medal** *n.* Goldmedaille, *die;* **~ 'medallist** *n.* Goldmedaillengewinner, *der*/-gewinnerin, *die;* **~ mine** *n.* Goldmine, *die;* (fig.) Goldgrube, *die;* **~ 'plate** *n., no pl., no indef. art.* [1] vergoldete Ware; (coating) Goldauflage, *die;* **be ~ plate** vergoldet sein; [2] (vessels, tableware) Goldgeschirr, *das;* **~-plate** *v.t.* vergolden; **~ reserve** *n.* Goldreserve, *die;* **~ rush** *n.* **the ~ rush to Alaska** der Strom von Goldgräbern nach Alaska; **~smith** *n.* ▸❶ **p. 1260** Goldschmied, *der*/-schmiedin, *die;* **~ standard** *n.* Goldstandard, *der; see also* **go off B 2;** **~ 'thread** *n.* Goldfaden, *der*

golf /gɒlf/

A *n., no pl.* Golf, *das; attrib.* Golf‹*platz, -schlag usw.*›

B *v.i.* Golf spielen; **his ~ing friends** seine Golffreunde

golf: ~ bag *n.* Golftasche, *die;* **~ ball** *n.* [1] Golfball, *der;* [2] (in typewriter) Kugelkopf, *der;* **~ buggy** *n.* Golfbuggy, *der;* **~ cart** Golfwagen, *der;* **~ club** *n.* [1] (implement) Golfschläger, *der;* [2] (association) Golfklub, *der;* **~ course** *n.* Golfplatz, *der*

golfer /'gɒlfə(r)/ *n.* Golfer, *der*/Golferin, *die;* Golfspieler, *der*/Golfspielerin, *die*

golf links *n. pl.* Golfplatz, *der*

Goliath /gə'laɪəθ/ *n.* (lit. or fig.) Goliath, *der*

golliwog /'gɒlɪwɒg/ *n.* Negerpuppe, *die;* **have hair like a ~:** einen Krauskopf haben

golly[1] /'gɒlɪ/ ▸**golliwog**

golly[2] *int.* meine Güte!; **by ~:** Menschenskind!

golosh (Brit.) ▸**galosh**

gonad /'gəʊnæd/ *n.* (Anat., Zool.) Gonade, *die*

gondola /'gɒndələ/ *n.* [1] (boat) Gondel, *die* [2] (Amer. Railw.) **~ [car]** offener Güterwagen; offener Flachwagen [3] (of ski lift, airship) Gondel, *die* [4] (in shop) Gondel, *die;* Verkaufsregal, *das*

gondolier /gɒndə'lɪə(r)/ *n.* ▸❶ **p. 1260** Gondoliere, *der*

gone /gɒn/

A *p. p. of* **go**[1] **A, B**

B *pred. adj.* [1] (away) weg; **it's time you were ~:** es ist *od.* wird Zeit, dass du gehst; **he has been ~ ten minutes** er ist seit zehn Minuten fort *od.* weg; **he will be ~ a year** er wird ein Jahr lang weg sein; **no, it's ~ again** (fig.: forgotten) es ist mir schon wieder entfallen [2] ▸❶ **p. 1001** (of time: after) nach; **not be back until ~ ten o'clock** erst nach zehn Uhr zurückkommen; **it's ~ ten o'clock** es ist zehn Uhr vorbei; **at ~ midnight** nach Mitternacht [3] (used up) **be all ~:** alle sein (ugs.) [4] (coll.: pregnant) **be six** *etc.* **months ~:** im sechsten *usw.* Monat sein [5] **be ~ on sb./sth.** (coll.) ganz weg von jmdm./etw. sein (ugs.). *See also* **far A 4; forget A 1; go**[1] **A 11**

goner /'gɒnə(r)/ *n.* (coll.) **he is a ~:** er hat die längste Zeit gelebt (ugs.); **the ship is a ~:** das Schiff macht es nicht mehr lange *od.* wird bald seinen Geist aufgeben (ugs.)

gong /gɒŋ/ *n.* [1] Gong, *der* [2] (Brit coll.: medal) Orden, *der; in pl.* Blech, *das* (ugs.); Lametta, *das* (ugs.)

gonna /'gɒnə/ (coll./Amer.) **= going to;** ▸**going B 3**

gonorrhoea (*Amer.:* **gonorrhea**) /gɒnə'rɪə/ *n.* ▸❶ **p. 1231** (Med.) Gonorrhö, *die* (fachspr.); Tripper, *der*

goo /gu:/ *n.* (coll.) Schmiere, *die* (ugs.); (fig.) Gefühlsduselei, *die* (ugs. abwertend); (in film etc.) Schmalz, *der* (ugs. abwertend)

good /gʊd/

A *adj.,* **better** /'betə(r)/, **best** /best/ [1] (satisfactory) gut; (reliable) gut; zuverlässig; (sufficient) gut; ausreichend ‹*Vorrat*›; ausgiebig ‹*Mahl*›; (competent) gut; geeignet; **his ~ eye/leg** sein gesundes Auge/Bein; **in ~ health** bei guter Gesundheit; **come in a ~ third** einen guten dritten Platz belegen; **come ~** (coll.) groß rauskommen (ugs.); **Late again! It's just not ~ enough** (coll.) Schon wieder zu spät. So geht es einfach nicht!; **your excuse is not ~ enough** diese Entschuldigung reicht nicht; **in ~ time** frühzeitig; **all in ~ time** alles zu seiner Zeit; **take ~ care of sb.** gut für jmdn. sorgen; **be ~ at sth.** in etw. (*Dat.*) gut sein; **be ~ at doing sth.** etw. gut können; **speak ~ English** gut[es] Englisch sprechen; **be ~ with people** *etc.* mit Menschen *usw.* gut *od.* leicht zurechtkommen; **the ~ ship 'Victory'** die gute alte „Victory“ [2] (favourable, advantageous) gut; günstig ‹*Gelegenheit, Augenblick, Angebot*›; **a ~ chance of succeeding** gute Erfolgschancen; **too ~ to be true** zu schön, um wahr zu sein; **in the ~ sense** im positiven Sinn; **I've heard so many ~ things about you** ich habe schon so viel Gutes von Ihnen gehört; **the ~ thing about it is that ...:** das Gute daran ist, dass ...; **be on to a ~ thing** was Gutes aufgetan haben (ugs.); **be too much of a ~ thing** zu viel des Guten sein; **you can have too much of a ~ thing** man kann es auch übertreiben; **be ~ for sb./sth.** gut für jmdn./etw. sein; **apples are ~ for you** Äpfel sind gesund; **eat more than is ~ for one** mehr essen, als einem gut tut; **know what is ~ for one** wissen, was sich gehört; **it's a ~ thing you told him** nur gut, dass du es ihm gesagt hast; **make a ~ death** *or* **end** einen schönen Tod haben; **the water isn't ~ to drink** das Wasser kann man nicht trinken [3] (prosperous) gut; **~ times** eine schöne Zeit; **have it ~:** es gut haben [4] (enjoyable) schön ‹*Leben, Urlaub, Wochenende*›; **the ~ things** alles, was gut und schön ist; **the ~ things in life** Annehmlichkeiten; **the ~ old days** die gute alte Zeit; **the ~ life** das angenehme[, sorglose] Leben; **have a ~ time!** viel Spaß *od.* Vergnügen!; **did you have a ~ time in Spain?** war es schön in Spanien?; **be after a ~ time** auf sein Vergnügen aus sein; **have a ~ journey!** gute Reise!; **it's ~ to be alive** es ist eine Lust zu leben; **it's ~ to be home again** es ist schön, wieder zu Hause zu sein; **ox liver is not very ~ to eat** Rinderleber ist nicht gut zum Verzehr geeignet; **Did you have a ~ day at the office?** Wie war es heute im Büro? [5] (cheerful) gut; angenehm ‹*Patient*›; **~ humour** *or* **spirits** *or* **mood** gute Laune; **feel ~:** sich wohl fühlen; **I'm not feeling too ~** (coll.) mir geht es nicht sehr gut [6] (well-behaved) gut; brav; **be ~!, be a ~ girl/boy!** sei brav *od.* lieb!; **[as] ~ as gold** ganz artig *od.* brav [7] (virtuous) rechtschaffen; (kind) nett; gut ‹*Absicht, Wünsche, Benehmen, Tat*›; **the ~ guy** der Gute; **be ~ to sb.** gut zu jmdm. sein; **would you be so ~ as to** *or* **~ enough to do that?** wären Sie so freundlich *od.* nett, das zu tun?; **how ~ of you!** wie nett von Ihnen!; **that/it is ~ of you** das/es ist nett *od.* lieb von dir; **he has a very ~ nature** er ist sehr gutmütig; **~ works** gute Taten *od.* Werke; *see also* **turn A 12** [8] (commendable) gut; **~ for 'you** *etc.* (coll.), **~ 'on you** *etc.* (esp. Austral. and NZ coll.) bravo!; **~ old Jim** *etc.* (coll.) der gute alte Jim *usw.* (ugs.); **~ man!** (coll.) mein lieber Mann!; alle Achtung!; **my ~ man/friend** (coll.) mein lieber Herr/Freund (ugs.; auch iron.); **the ~ man/woman** (dated) der werte Herr/die werte Dame (geh.); **your ~ man/lady** Ihr lieber Mann/Ihre liebe Frau; Ihr werter Gatte/Ihre werte Gattin; **~ men and true** rechtschaffene Leute; **that's a ~ one** (coll.) der ist gut! (ugs.); (iron.) das ist'n Ding! (ugs.); *see also* **fellow A 1** [9] (attractive) schön; gut ‹*Figur, Haltung*›; gepflegt ‹*Erscheinung, Äußeres*›; wohlgeformt ‹*Nase, Beine*›; **look ~** gut aussehen; **~ looks** gutes Aussehen; **have ~ looks** gut aussehen [10] (thorough) gut; **take a ~ look round** sich gründlich umsehen; **give sb. a ~ beating/scolding** jmdn. tüchtig verprügeln/ausschimpfen; **give sth. a ~ polish** etw. ordentlich polieren; **have a ~ weep/rest/sleep** sich richtig ausweinen/ausruhen/[sich] richtig ausschlafen (ugs.) [11] (considerable) [recht] ansehnlich ‹*Menschenmenge*›; ganz schön, ziemlich (ugs.) ‹*Stück Wegs, Entfernung, Zeitraum, Strecke*›; gut, anständig ‹*Preis, Erlös*›; hoch ‹*Alter*›; **a ~ bit better** (coll.) ein ganzes Stück besser; **a ~ dose of ...:** eine gute Dosis ...; (fig.) eine gehörige Portion ...; **take a ~ long time** ziemlich *od.* recht lange dauern; seine Zeit brauchen; **have a ~ long sleep** [sich] richtig ausschlafen; **live to a ~ old age** ein recht hohes Alter erreichen; **a ~ four hours** *etc.* volle *od.* ganze vier Stunden *usw.*; gut vier Stunden *usw.*; **a ~ half pound** ein gutes halbes Pfund; **he is a ~ seventy** (coll.) er ist gute siebzig (ugs.) [12] (sound, valid) gut ‹*Grund, Rat, Gedanke*›; berechtigt ‹*Anspruch*›; (Commerc.) solide ‹*Kunde*›; sicher ‹*Anleihe, Kredit*›; gedeckt ‹*Scheck*›; **~ sense** Vernünftigkeit, *die;* **have the ~ sense to do sth.** so vernünftig sein, etw. zu tun; **be ~ for a year** es ein Jahr machen; ‹*Gerät usw.:*› ein Jahr halten; ‹*Ticket:*› ein Jahr gelten; **~ for five journeys** gültig für fünf Fahrten; **I'm ~ for another hour's walk** ich kann noch eine Stunde weiterlaufen; **he's ~ for £5,000** er wird bestimmt 5 000 Pfund geben (ugs.); **how much is he ~ for?** wie viel wird er wohl geben? (ugs.); **the draft is ~ for ...:** der Wechsel ist auf ... (*Akk.*) ausgestellt [13] ▸❶ **p. 1189** *in greeting* gut; **~ afternoon/day** guten Tag!; **~ evening/morning** *or* (Brit. arch.) **morrow** guten Abend/Morgen!; **~ night** gute Nacht!; **a ~-night kiss** ein Gutenachtkuss [14] *in exclamation* gut; **very ~, sir** sehr wohl!; **~ God/Lord** *etc. see the nouns* [15] (best) gut ‹*Geschirr, Anzug*› [16] (correct, fitting) gut; (appropriate) angebracht; ratsam [17] (socially prestigious) gut; **be of a ~/very ~ family** aus guter Familie/bestem Hause stammen [18] **as ~ as** so gut wie; *see also* **give A 16** [19] **make ~** (succeed) erfolgreich sein; (effect) in die Tat umsetzen; ausführen ‹*Plan*›; erfüllen ‹*Versprechen*›; (compensate for) wieder gutmachen ‹*Fehler*›; (indemnify) ersetzen ‹*Schaden, Ausgaben*›; (prove) belegen ‹*Behauptung, Anschuldigung*›; **the film made ~ at the box office** der Film war ein Kassenerfolg; **they soon made ~ in Australia** sie brachten es bald zu was in Australien (ugs.). *See also* **best A; better A; egg**[1]**; form A 6, 8; luck 1; temper A 1**

B *adv.* [1] (coll.) *as intensifier* **~ and ...** richtig ...; **~ and angry** (Amer.) richtig böse; **~ and proper** ordentlich; **it was raining ~ and hard** es hat [so] richtig gegossen [2] (Amer. coll.: well) gut; **get along ~** gut zurechtkommen; **he's doing pretty ~ these days** es geht ihm in letzter Zeit sehr gut. *See also* **best B; better B**

C *n.* [1] (use) Nutzen, *der;* **be some ~ to sb./sth.** jmdm./einer Sache nützen; **he'll never be any ~** aus dem wird nichts Gutes werden; **is this book any ~?** taugt dieses Buch etwas?; **you're**

a lot of ~, I must say! (iron.) du bist mir vielleicht einer! (ugs.); **be no ~ to sb./sth.** für jmdn./etw. nicht zu gebrauchen sein; **not be any ~ for work** nicht zur Arbeit taugen *od.* geeignet sein; **it is no/not much ~ doing sth.** es hat keinen/kaum einen Sinn, etw. zu tun; **what's the ~ of ...?, what ~ is ...?** was nützt ...?; **what's the ~ of knowing Latin?** was nützt einem Latein?; wozu ist Latein gut?; *see also* **no-~**

2▸ (benefit) **for your/his** *etc.* **own ~** zu deinem/seinem *usw.* Besten *od.* eigenen Vorteil; **for the ~ of mankind/the country** zum Wohl[e] der Menschheit/des Landes; **for ~ or ill** ▸**ill B 1**; **do no/little ~:** nichts/wenig helfen *od.* nützen; **do sb./sth. ~** jmdm./einer Sache nützen; ‹*Ruhe, Erholung:*› jmdm./einer Sache gut tun; ‹*Arznei:*› jmdm./einer Sache helfen; **I'll tell him, but what ~ will that do?** ich sag es ihm, aber was nützt *od.* hilft das schon?; **do sb. a lot/a world of ~** jmdm. sehr gut tun; **just sitting there won't do you any ~** einfach dasitzen hilft dir auch nicht weiter; **you aren't doing yourself any ~** du tust dir keinen Gefallen; **much ~ may it do you** (iron.) [na, dann] viel Vergnügen; **look what ~** *or* **a lot of ~** *or* **much ~ it did him** (iron.) [und] was hat es ihm genützt?; und das hat er nun davon gehabt (iron.); **to the ~** (for the best) zum Guten; (in profit) plus; **this development was all to the ~** diese Entwicklung war nur von Vorteil; **the delay was partly to the ~** die Verspätung hatte auch ihr Gutes; **end up [in a game** *etc.***] £10 to the ~:** [bei einem Spiel *usw.*] 10 Pfund gutmachen; **come home £10 to the ~:** mit 10 Pfund plus nach Hause kommen; **be 4 points/wins to the ~** 4 Punkte/Siege voraus *od.* im Vorteil sein; **come to no ~** kein gutes Ende nehmen

3▸ (goodness) Gute, *das;* **the highest ~** (Philos.) das Höchste Gut; **there's ~ and bad in everyone** in jedem steckt Gutes und Böses; **the difference between ~ and bad** *or* **evil** der Unterschied zwischen Gut und Böse

4▸ (kind acts) Gute, *das;* **be up to** *or* **after no ~** nichts Gutes im Sinn haben *od.* im Schilde führen; **do ~** Gutes tun

5▸ **take the ~ with the bad** die Dinge so hinnehmen wie sie eben sind; **for ~ [and all]** (finally) ein für alle Mal; (permanently) für immer [und ewig]; endgültig

6▸ *constr. as pl.* (virtuous people) **the ~** die Guten

7▸ *in pl.* (wares etc.) Waren *Pl.;* (belongings) Habe, *die;* (Brit. Railw.) Fracht, *die; attrib.* Fracht‹*büro, -tarif, -schiff, -flugzeug, -zettel usw.*›; Güter‹*abfertigung, -bahnhof, -produktion, -verkehr, -wagen, -zug usw.*›; **~s and chattels** Sachen *Pl.;* **canned/manufactured ~s** Konserven/Fertigwaren *Pl.;* **stolen ~s** gestohlene Waren; Diebesgut, *das;* **by ~s** per Bahnfracht; als Frachtgut

8▸ *in pl.* **the ~s** (coll.: what is wanted) das Gewünschte; das Verlangte; **deliver the ~s** (fig.) halten, was man verspricht; **sb. is the ~s** jmd. ist der Richtige; **he's got the ~s** er ist der richtige Mann

good: ~'bye (*Amer.:* **~'by**) /gʊd'baɪ/ ▸❶ **p. 1189** **A** *int.* auf Wiedersehen!; (on telephone) auf Wiederhören!; **B** *n., pl.* **~'byes** (*Amer.:* **~'bys**) (farewell remark or gesture) Lebewohl, *das* (geh.); (parting) Abschied, *der;* **say ~bye to sb.** jmdm. Auf Wiedersehen sagen; **say ~bye, say one's ~byes** sich verabschieden; **nod/wave ~bye** zum Abschied nicken/winken; **kiss sb. ~bye** jmdm. einen Abschiedskuss geben; **say ~bye to sth.** Abschied nehmen von etw.; **say ~bye to sth., kiss sth. ~bye** (fig.: accept its loss) etw. abschreiben (ugs.); **~ 'fellowship** *n.* Kameradschaftlichkeit, *die;* **~-for-nothing** (derog.) **A** *adj.* nichtsnutzig; **B** *n.* Taugenichts, *der;* **G~ 'Friday** ▸**Friday A**; **~-hearted** /'gʊdhɑːtɪd/ *adj.* gutherzig; gut gemeint ‹*Bemühungen*›; **~-humoured** /gʊd'hjuːməd/ *adj.*, **~-humouredly** /gʊd'hjuːmədlɪ/ *adv.* gutmütig

goodie bag /'gʊdɪ bæg/ *n.* Tasche mit Gratis[produkt]proben

goodies /'gʊdɪz/ *n. pl.* (coll.) (food) Naschereien *Pl.;* (sweets) Süßigkeiten *Pl.;* (attractive things) Attraktionen *Pl.;* tolle Sachen

goodish /'gʊdɪʃ/ *adj.* 1▸ (quite good) ganz gut; recht gut 2▸ (considerable) ganz schön

good: ~-looker *n.* flotte Erscheinung (ugs.); **be a ~-looker** gut aussehen; **~-'looking** *adj.* gut aussehend

goodly /'gʊdlɪ/ *adj.* stattlich; ansehnlich

good: ~-'natured *adj.* gutwillig; gutmütig; **~-naturedly** /gʊd'neɪtʃədlɪ/ *adv.* gutmütig; **~-'neighbour** *attrib. adj.* gutnachbarlich; **a ~-neighbour policy** eine Politik der guten Nachbarschaft

goodness /'gʊdnɪs/

A *n., no pl.* 1▸ (virtue) Güte, *die;* **have the ~ to do sth.** die Güte haben, etw. zu tun (geh., auch iron.) 2▸ (of food) Nährgehalt, *der;* Güte, *die;* (of soil) Fruchtbarkeit, *die;* Güte, *die*

B *int.* **[my] ~** *expr. surprise* meine Güte! (ugs.); **[oh] my ~** *expr. shock* lieber Himmel!; **~ gracious** *or* **me!** [ach] du lieber Himmel *od.* liebe Güte! (ugs.); **for ~' sake** um Himmels willen; **~ [only] knows** weiß der Himmel (ugs.); **I hope to ~ that ...:** gebe Gott, dass ...; **I wish to ~ I'd never met him** wenn ich ihn doch bloß nie kennen gelernt hätte!; **surely to ~ you don't mean that** das ist doch wohl nicht dein Ernst?; **thank ~:** Gott sei Dank

good: ~-o, ~-oh *int.* (coll.) toll! prima!

goods ▸**good C 7, 8**

good: ~-sized ▸**-sized**; **~s station** *n.* (Brit. Railw.) Güterbahnhof, *der;* **~s train** *n.* (Brit. Railw.) Güterzug, *der;* **~s vehicle** *n.* Nutzfahrzeug, *das;* **~s yard** *n.* (Brit. Railw.) Güterbahnhof, *der;* **~-'tempered** *adj.* ausgeglichen; gutmütig; verträglich ‹*Person*›; **~-time** *adj.* **a ~-time girl** ein leichtes Mädchen (abwertend); **~ 'will** *n.* gute Absicht; **~'will** *n.* 1▸ (friendly feeling) guter Wille; *attrib.* Goodwill‹*botschaft, -reise usw.*›; **men of ~will** Menschen, die guten Willens sind; 2▸ (willingness) Bereitwilligkeit, *die;* **with ~will** bereitwillig; 3▸ (Commerc.) Goodwill, *der*

goody[1] /'gʊdɪ/ *n.* (coll.: hero) Gute, *der/die; see also* **goodies**

goody[2] *int.* (coll.) toll; prima; **~, ~ gumdrops!** juhu!; juchhe!

goody: ~-~ **A** *n.* Tugendbold, *der* (iron.); **B** *adj.* [scheinheilig] tugendhaft; musterhaft (iron.); **~-'two-shoes** *n.* Tugendlamm, *das* (iron.)

gooey /'guːɪ/ *adj.*, **gooier** /'guːɪə(r)/, **gooiest** /'guːɪɪst/ (coll.) klebrig; (fig.: sentimental) rührselig; schnulzig (ugs. abwertend)

goof /guːf/ (coll.)

A *n.* 1▸ (fool) Döskopp, *der* (salopp); Doofi, *der* (ugs.) 2▸ (gaffe) Schnitzer, *der* (ugs.); Patzer, *der* (ugs.)

B *v.i.* Mist machen *od.* bauen (salopp)

C *v.t.* vermasseln (salopp); Murks machen bei (salopp)

Phrasal verb

• **~ about, ~ around** *v.i.* (coll.) herumpfuschen (ugs. abwertend); (spend time idly) herumhängen (salopp); herumtrödeln

goofy /'guːfɪ/ *adj.* (coll.) 1▸ dämlich (ugs.); bescheuert (salopp) 2▸ vorstehend ‹*Zähne*›

google /'guːgl/ (coll.)

A *v.t.* **~ sb.** das Internet nach Informationen über jmdn. durchsuchen

B *v.i.* googeln

googly /'guːglɪ/ *n.* (Cricket) (zur Täuschung des Schlagmanns) gedrehter Ball

gook /guːk, gʊk/ *n.* (Amer. sl. derog.) Schlitzauge, *das* (salopp abwertend)

goolies /'guːliːz/ *n. pl.* (Brit. coarse) Eier *Pl.* (derb)

goon /guːn/ *n.* (coll.) 1▸ (hatchet man) Schläger, *der* (abwertend) 2▸ (fool) Blödmann, *der* (salopp)

goosander /guː'sændə(r)/ *n.* (Ornith.) Gänsesäger, *der*

goose /guːs/ *n., pl.* **geese** /giːs/ 1▸ Gans, *die;* **roast ~:** Gänsebraten, *der;* **all mothers think their geese are swans** jede Mutter glaubt, ihre Kinder seien etwas Besonderes; **kill the ~ that lays the golden eggs** (fig.) das Huhn, das goldene Eier legt, schlachten; *see also* **boo A**; **cook B 1** 2▸ (simpleton) Gans, *die* (ugs.)

gooseberry /'gʊzbərɪ/ *n.* 1▸ (berry, shrub) Stachelbeere, *die* 2▸ **play ~:** das fünfte Rad am Wagen sein (ugs.)

'gooseberry bush *n.* Stachelbeerstrauch, *der;* **we found you under a ~** (fig.) dich hat uns der Klapperstorch gebracht (Kinderspr.)

goose: ~ bumps *n. pl.* (Amer.) Gänsehaut, *die;* **~ egg** *n.* Gänseei, *das;* **~flesh** *n., no pl.* Gänsehaut, *die;* **~foot** *n., pl.* **~foots** (Bot.) Gänsefuß, *der;* **~grass** *n.* Klebkraut, *das;* **~neck** *n.* Schwanenhals, *der* (fig.); **~ pimples** *n. pl.* **have ~ pimples** eine Gänsehaut haben; **~step** **A** *n.* Stechschritt, *der;* **B** *v.i.* im Stechschritt marschieren

gopher /'gəʊfə(r)/ *n.* 1▸ (Zool.) Taschenratte, *die;* (Amer.: ground squirrel) Ziesel, *der* 2▸ (Computing) Gopher, *der*

gorblimey /gɔː'blaɪmɪ/ *int.* (Brit. sl.) Mensch! (salopp)

Gordian knot /gɔːdɪən 'nɒt/ *n.* gordischer Knoten; **cut the ~:** den gordischen Knoten durchhauen

gore[1] /gɔː(r)/ *v.t.* [mit den Hörnern] aufspießen *od.* durchbohren; **be ~d to death by a bull** von den Hörnern eines Stieres durchbohrt [und tödlich verletzt] werden

gore[2] *n.* (blood) Blut, *das*

gore[3] *n.* Keil, *der;* (of skirt) [Rock]bahn, *die*

gorge /gɔːdʒ/

A *n.* 1▸ Schlucht, *die;* Klamm, *die* 2▸ **sb.'s ~ rises at sth.** (fig.) jmdm. wird schlecht *od.* übel von *od.* bei etw

B *v.i.* sich voll stopfen (**on** mit) (ugs.); ‹*Tier:*› sich voll fressen (**on** mit)

C *v.t.* (satiate) voll stopfen (ugs.); **~ oneself with** *or* **on sth.** sich mit etw. voll stopfen (ugs.)

gorgeous /'gɔːdʒəs/ *adj.* 1▸ (magnificent) prächtig; hinreißend ‹*Frau, Mann, Lächeln*›; (richly coloured) farbenprächtig; **the ~ colours of sth.** die Farbenpracht einer Sache 2▸ (coll.: splendid) sagenhaft (ugs.); prächtig ‹*Wetter*›

gorgeously /'gɔːdʒəslɪ/ *adv.* 1▸ prächtig; hinreißend ‹*lächeln*› 2▸ (coll.: splendidly) sagenhaft (ugs.)

gorgon /'gɔːgən/ *n.* 1▸ (Greek Mythol.) Gorgo, *die* 2▸ (person) Drachen, *der* (ugs. abwertend)

gorilla /gə'rɪlə/ *n.* Gorilla, *der*

gormandize (**garmandise**) /'gɔːməndaɪz/ *v.i.* prassen; schlemmen

gormless /'gɔːmlɪs/ *adj.* (Brit. coll.) dämlich (ugs.)

gorse /gɔːs/ *n.* Stechginster, *der*

gory /'gɔːrɪ/ *adj.* 1▸ blutbefleckt ‹*Hände*›; blutbeschmiert ‹*Waffe*›; blutig ‹*Schlacht*› 2▸ (fig.: sensational) blutrünstig

gosh /gɒʃ/ *int.* (coll.) Gott

goshawk /'gɒshɔːk/ *n.* (Ornith.) [Hühner]habicht, *der*

gosling /'gɒzlɪŋ/ *n.* Gänseküken, *das;* Gössel, *das* (nordd.)

'go-slow *n.* (Brit.) Bummelstreik, *der*

gospel /'gɒspl/ *n.* 1▸ (Relig.) Evangelium, *das;* (reading) Lesung, *die* 2▸ (fig.) Evangelium, *das;* **take sth. for** *or* **as ~:** etw. für bare Münze nehmen; **preach the ~ of non-violence** Gewaltlosigkeit predigen

gospel: ~ music *n.* Gospelmusik, *die;* **~ 'oath** *n.* Eid auf die Bibel; **~ singer** *n.* Gospelsänger, *der/-sängerin, die;* **~ 'truth** *n.* absolute *od.* reine Wahrheit

gossamer /'gɒsəmə(r)/ *n.* 1▸ Altweibersommer, *der;* **like ~:** wie Spinnfäden 2▸ (fig.) Spinnfäden *Pl.* (fig.); *attrib.* hauchdünn ‹*Flügel*›

gossip /'gɒsɪp/

A *n.* 1▸ (person) Klatschbase, *die* (ugs. abwertend) 2▸ (talk) Schwatz, *der;* (esp. malicious) Klatsch, *der* (ugs. abwertend); **the latest ~ is that ...:** seit neustem wird geklatscht, dass ...

B *v.i.* schwatzen; (esp. maliciously) klatschen (ugs. abwertend)

gossip: ~ column *n.* Klatschspalte, *die* (ugs. abwertend); **~ columnist** *n.* ▸❶ **p. 1260** Klatschspaltenkolumnist, *der/-kolumnistin, die* (abwertend)

gossiper /'gɒsɪpə(r)/ ▸**gossip A 1**

'gossipmonger *n.* (derog.) Klatschmaul, *das* (ugs. abwertend)

gossipy /ˈgɒsɪpɪ/ *adj.* geschwätzig (abwertend); (conversational) plaudernd ‹*Ton, Stil*›; im Plauderton geschrieben ‹*Buch, Brief*›

got ▸**get**

gotcha /ˈgɒtʃə/ *int.* (coll.) hab ich dich!

Goth /gɒθ/ *n.* Gote, *der*

Gothic /ˈgɒθɪk/

A *adj.* **1** gotisch **2** (Lit.) *für den Schauerroman charakteristisch;* ~ **novel** Schauerroman, *der* **3** (Printing) gotisch

B *n.* **1** (Ling.) Gotisch[e], *das* **2** (Archit.) Gotik, *die* **3** (type, script) Gotisch, *das*

Gothic Re'vival *n.* (Archit.) Neugotik, *die*

gotta /ˈgɒtə/ (coll.) **= got to, got a; I['ve]** ~ **go** ich muss gehen; **I['ve]** ~ **present for you** ich habe da ein Geschenk für dich

gotten ▸**get**

gouache /guːˈɑːʃ/ *n.* (Art) Gouache, *die*

gouge /gaʊdʒ/

A *v.t.* **1** aushöhlen; ausmeißeln; ~ **a channel** ‹*Fluss:*› eine Rinne auswaschen **2** (Amer.: overcharge) betrügen

B *n.* **1** Hohleisen, *das;* Hohlmeißel, *der* **2** (Amer.: overcharging) Betrug, *der*

Phrasal verb

• ~ **out** *v.t.* ausschneiden; ausstechen; ~ **sb.'s eye out** jmdm. ein Auge ausstechen

goulash /ˈguːlæʃ/ *n.* (Gastr.) Gulasch, *das od. der*

gourd /gʊəd/ *n.* **1** (fruit, plant) [Flaschen]kürbis, *der* **2** (bottle, bowl) Kürbisflasche, *die;* Kalebasse, *die*

gourmand /ˈgʊəmənd/ *n.* (glutton) Gourmand, *der*

gourmet /ˈgʊəmeɪ/ *n.* Gourmet, *der; attrib.* ~ **meal/restaurant** Feinschmeckergericht, *das*/-lokal, *das*

gout /gaʊt/ *n.* ▸**i** **p. 1231** (Med.) Gicht, *die*

gouty /ˈgaʊtɪ/ *adj.* (Med.) gichtkrank; gichtig

Gov. *abbr.* **1** = **Government** Reg.; Rg. **2** = **Governor** Gouv.

govern /ˈgʌvn/

A *v.t.* **1** (rule) regieren ‹*Land, Volk*›; (administer) verwalten ‹*Provinz, Kolonie*› **2** (dictate) bestimmen; **be** ~**ed by sth.** sich von etw. leiten lassen; **self-interest** ~**s all his actions** Eigennutz beherrscht all sein Tun **3** (regulate proceedings of) leiten ‹*Geschäft, Unternehmen*›; ‹*Vorschriften:*› regeln **4** (be in command of) den Befehl haben über (+ *Akk.*) ‹*Festung, Stadt*› **5** (restrain) zügeln ‹*Temperament, Leidenschaften*› **6** (constitute a law or principle for) ‹*Prinzipien:*› die Grundlage bilden für; **the laws which** ~ **the animal kingdom** die Gesetze, denen das Tierreich unterworfen ist **7** (Ling.) verlangen; regieren ‹*Kasus*›

B *v.i.* regieren

governable /ˈgʌvənəbl/ *adj.* regierbar

governance /ˈgʌvənəns/ *n.* Regieren, *das;* (office, function) Regierungsgewalt, *die;* (control) Herrschaft, *die*

governess /ˈgʌvənɪs/ *n.* ▸**i** **p. 1260** Gouvernante, *die* (veraltet); Hauslehrerin, *die*

governing /ˈgʌvənɪŋ/ *adj.* **1** (ruling) regierend **2** (guiding) dominierend ‹*Einfluss*›; geltend ‹*Vorschriften*›; **sb.'s** ~ **principle** das Prinzip, von dem jmd. sich leiten lässt; ~ **body** leitendes Gremium

government /ˈgʌvnmənt/ *n.* **1** Regierung, *die;* **form a G**~: die Regierung bilden **2** (system, form) Regierungsform, *die* **3** (an administration or ministry) **[central]** ~: Zentralregierung, *die; attrib.* Regierungs-; ~ **money** Staatsgelder *Pl.;* ~ **securities** *or* **stocks** Staatspapiere *od.* -anleihen *Pl.;* ~**-controlled establishment** staatlich kontrollierte Einrichtung; *see also* **body A 4**

governmental /gʌvnˈmentl/ *adj.* Regierungs-

government: ~ **department** *n.* Regierungsstelle, *die;* ~**-funded** *adj.* staatlich finanziert; ~ **official** *n.* Regierungsbeamte, *der*/Regierungsbeamtin, *die;* ~ **'surplus** *n.* Waren aus Regierungsbeständen; *attrib.* ~ **surplus radio** Radio aus Regierungsbeständen

governor /ˈgʌvənə(r)/ *n.* ▸**i** **p. 1260** **1** (ruler) Herrscher, *der* **2** (of province, town, etc.) Gouverneur, *der;* Statthalter, *der* (hist.) **3** (of State of US) Gouverneur, *der* **4** (of institution) Direktor, *der*/Direktorin, *die;* **[board of]** ~**s** Vorstand, *der;* (of school) Schulleitung, *die;* (of bank, company) Direktorium, *das;* Direktion, *die* **5** (of prison) Gefängnisdirektor, *der*/-direktorin, *die* **6** (commandant) Kommandant, *der;* Gouverneur, *der* **7** (coll.) (employer) Boss, *der* (ugs.); (father) Alte, *der* (salopp); **hey,** ~**!** (as voc.: mister) hallo, Chef! (salopp) **8** (Mech.) Regler, *der*

Governor-'General *n.* Generalgouverneur, *der*

governorship /ˈgʌvənəʃɪp/ *n.* Gouverneursamt, *das*

Govt. *abbr.* **= Government** Reg.; Rg.

gown /gaʊn/ *n.* **1** [elegantes] Kleid; **bridal/baptismal** ~: Braut-/Taufkleid, *das* **2** (official or uniform robe) Talar, *der;* Robe, *die;* **town and** ~: Bürger und Studenten **3** (surgeon's overall) [Operations]kittel, *der*

GP *abbr.* **1** = **general practitioner** **2** = **Grand Prix**

> **GP — general practitioner**
>
> Ein *GP*, oft auch *family doctor* (Hausarzt) genannt, ist ein Arzt für Allgemeinmedizin in Großbritannien. Die meisten *GPs* arbeiten mit mehreren Kollegen zusammen in einer Gemeinschaftspraxis. Die Patienten der Praxis können den behandelnden Arzt frei wählen. Durch den **National Health Service** müssen Patienten ihren Arzt nicht bezahlen, die Praxis wird direkt oder indirekt aus staatlichen Geldern finanziert. Wenn nötig, kann ein *GP* einen Patienten zu einem Spezialisten überweisen oder ins Krankenhaus einweisen. Die Praxis wird *surgery* genannt.

GPO *abbr.* **1** (Hist.) = **General Post Office** Post, *die* **2** (Amer.) = **Government Printing Office** Staatsdruckerei, *die*

GPS *abbr.* **= Global Positioning System**

gr. *abbr.* **1** = **grain[s]** Gran, *der* (veralt.) **2** = **gram[s]** g **3** = **gross** bto.

grab /græb/

A *v.t.,* **-bb-:** **1** greifen nach; (seize) packen; (capture, arrest) schnappen (ugs.); ~ **sth. away from sb.** jmdm. etw. entreißen; ~ **sb. by the arm** *etc.* jmdn. am Arm *usw.* packen; **should we** ~ **some food** *or* **a bite to eat?** (coll.) sollen wir schnell etwas essen?; **could you** ~ **a table while I ...** (coll.) versuch du, einen Tisch zu ergattern, während ich ... (ugs.); **I managed to** ~ **her before she got on the bus** (stop her) ich konnte sie gerade noch aufhalten, bevor sie in den Bus stieg; ~ **the chance** die Gelegenheit ergreifen; **I would** ~ **an offer like that** ein solches Angebot würde ich mir nicht entgehen lassen; ~ **hold of sb./sth.** sich (*Dat.*) jmdn./etw. schnappen (ugs.) **2** (coll.: impress) **how does that** ~ **you?** wie findest du das?; **this doesn't [really]** ~ **me** das lässt mich [im Grunde] kalt

B *v.i.,* **-bb-** **1** ~ **at sth.** nach etw. greifen; **don't** ~ **like that!** grapsch nicht so! (ugs.) **2** (act jerkily) ‹*Bremse:*› ruckartig greifen

C *n.* **1** **make a** ~ **at** *or* **for sb./sth.** nach jmdm./etw. greifen *od.* (ugs.) grapschen; **be up for** ~**s** (coll.) zu erwerben sein; ‹*Posten:*› frei sein **2** (coll.: robbery) Raubüberfall, *der;* (burglary) Bruch, *der* (ugs.) **3** (Mech.) Greifer, *der. See also* **smash-and-grab [raid]**

grab: ~ **bag** *n.* (Amer.) Grabbelsack, *der* (ugs.); ~ **handle** *n.* Haltegriff, *der;* ~ **rail** *n.* Haltestange, *die*

grace /greɪs/

A *n.* **1** (charm) Anmut, *die* (geh.); Grazie, *die* **2** (attractive feature) Charme, *der;* **airs and** ~**s** vornehmes Getue (ugs. abwertend); affektiertes Benehmen **3** (accomplishment) **social** ~**s** Umgangsformen *Pl.* **4** (decency) Anstand, *der;* **have the** ~ **to do sth.** so anständig sein und etw. tun; **he didn't even have the** ~ **to apologize** er brachte es nicht einmal fertig, sich zu entschuldigen; (civility) **with [a] good/bad** ~: bereitwillig/widerwillig; **he accepted my criticism with good/bad** ~: er trug meine Kritik mit Fassung/nahm meine Kritik mit Verärgerung hin **5** (favour) Wohlwollen, *das;* Gunst, *die;* (Theol.) Gnade, *die;* **be in sb.'s good** ~**s** in jmds. Gunst stehen; bei jmdm. gut angeschrieben sein (ugs.); ~ **and favour house/residence** *etc. von der Regierung od. Krone zur Verfügung gestelltes Haus/gestellte Residenz usw.;* **act of** ~: Gnadenakt, *der;* **there, but for the** ~ **of God, go I** es hätte leicht auch mich erwischen können; **by the** ~ **of God Queen of ...:** von Gottes Gnaden Königin von ...; **state of** ~ (Theol.) Stand der Gnade; **he fell from** ~: er fiel in Ungnade; **in the year of** ~ **1892** (literary) im Jahr des Herrn 1892 **6** (favour shown by granting delay) Frist, *die;* (Commerc.) Zahlungsfrist, *die;* **give sb. a day's** ~: jmdm. einen Tag Aufschub gewähren; **we will grant you two weeks'** ~: wir lassen Ihnen zwei Wochen Zeit **7** (prayers) Tischgebet, *das;* **say** ~: das Tischgebet sprechen **8** ▸**i** **p. 1634** *in address* **Your G**~: Euer Gnaden **9** (Mus.) ▸~ **note** **10** (Greek Mythol.) **the Graces** die Grazien. *See also* **saving grace**

B *v.t.* **1** (adorn) zieren (geh.); schmücken **2** (honour) auszeichnen; ehren; ~ **a premiere by** *or* **with one's presence** eine Premiere mit seiner Anwesenheit beehren (geh.)

graceful /ˈgreɪsfl/ *adj.* elegant; graziös ‹*Bewegung, Eleganz*›; geschmeidig ‹*Katze, Pferd*›

gracefully /ˈgreɪsfəlɪ/ *adv.* elegant; graziös ‹*tanzen, sich bewegen*›; **grow old** ~: mit Würde alt werden

gracefulness /ˈgreɪsflnɪs/ *n., no pl.* Eleganz, *die;* (of movement, form, style) Grazie, *die*

graceless /ˈgreɪslɪs/ *adj.* (lacking sense of decency) taktlos; (lacking charm and elegance) ungehobelt, schroff ‹*Benehmen, Person*›

'grace note *n.* (Mus.) Verzierung, *die;* Manier, *die* (fachspr.)

gracious /ˈgreɪʃəs/

A *adj.* **1** liebenswürdig; freundlich; (iron./joc.) gütig; ~ **living** kultivierter Lebensstil; **our** ~ **Queen** unsere gnädige Königin **2** (merciful) gnädig

B *int.* ~**!, good[ness]** ~**!, [goodness]** ~ **me!** [ach] du meine *od.* liebe Güte!

graciously /ˈgreɪʃəslɪ/ *adv.* liebenswürdig; freundlich; (with condescension) gnädig

gradation /grəˈdeɪʃn/ *n.* **1** *usu. in pl.* (stage) ~**s of madness/an illness** Stufen *od.* Grade des Wahnsinns/einer Krankheit **2** (degree in rank, merit, intensity, etc.) Stufung, *die;* ~**s of colour** Farbskala, *die;* ~ **on a thermometer** Gradeinteilung, *die*

grade /greɪd/

A *n.* **1** Rang, *der;* (Mil.) Dienstgrad, *der;* (salary ~) Gehaltsstufe, *die;* (in things: degree of quality, size, or value) [Handels-, Güte]klasse, *die;* (of textiles) Qualität, *die;* (position, level) Stufe, *die;* (intensity of illness) Grad, *der;* **what** ~ **is your job?** in welcher Gehaltsklasse sind Sie?; **a high** ~ **of intelligence** ein hohes Maß an Intelligenz **2** (Amer. Sch.: class) Klasse, *die* **3** (Sch., Univ.: mark) Note, *die;* Zensur, *die;* **attain** ~ **B or a higher** ~: eine Zwei oder eine bessere Note erreichen **4** (Amer.: gradient) (ascent) Steigung, *die;* (descent) Neigung, *die;* **at** ~: auf gleicher Höhe; ebenerdig ‹*Wohnung usw.*› **5** **on the up/down** ~ (lit.) ansteigend/abfallend; (fig.) auf dem auf-/absteigenden Ast; **make the** ~: es schaffen

B *v.t.* **1** einstufen ‹*Arbeit nach Gehalt, Schüler nach Fähigkeiten, Leistungen*›; [nach Größe/Qualität] sortieren ‹*Eier, Kartoffeln*› **2** (mark) benoten; zensieren

C *v.i.* (pass gradually) übergehen (**into** in + *Akk.*)

'grade crossing *n.* (Amer.) Kreuzung, *die;* (of railroad tracks and road) schienengleicher Bahnübergang

grader /ˈgreɪdə(r)/ *n.* (Amer. Sch.) **a ninth/tenth-**~: ein Schüler der 9./10. Klasse; ein Neunt-/Zehntklässler (südd., schweiz.)

'grade school *n.* (Amer.) Grundschule, *die*

> **grade school**
>
> ▸ **elementary school.**

gradient /ˈgreɪdɪənt/ *n.* **1** (amount of slope) (ascent) Steigung, *die;* (descent) Gefälle, *das;* (inclined part of road) Neigung, *die;* **a** ~ **of 1 in 10** eine Steigung/ein Gefälle von 10% **2** ([rate of] rise or fall of temperature etc.) Gradient, *der* (bes.

Math.); (ascent) Anstieg, *der;* (descent) Abfall, *der*

gradual /ˈgrædʒʊəl/ *adj.* allmählich; sanft ‹*Steigung, Gefälle usw.*›

gradually /ˈgrædʒʊəlɪ/ *adv.* allmählich; sanft ‹*ansteigen, abfallen*›

graduate

A /ˈgrædʒʊət/ *n.* 1 Graduierte, *der/die;* (who has left university) Akademiker, *der*/Akademikerin, *die;* **university ~:** Hochschulabsolvent, *der*/-absolventin, *die;* **he is an Oxford ~:** er hat seinen Universitätsabschluss in Oxford gemacht 2 (Amer. Sch.) Schulabgänger, *der*/-abgängerin, *die*

B /ˈgrædʒʊeɪt/ *v.i.* 1 einen akademischen Grad/Titel erwerben; **he ~d from Oxford University** er schloss sein Studium an der Universität von Oxford ab 2 (Amer. Sch.) die [Schul]abschlussprüfung bestehen (**from** an + *Dat.*) 3 (move up) **he's ~d from comics to detective stories** er hat sich vom Comicleser zum Krimileser entwickelt 4 (pass by degrees) **~ into** allmählich übergehen in (+ *Akk.*)

C /ˈgrædʒʊeɪt/ *v.t.* 1 (mark out) mit Gradeinteilung versehen; graduieren (bes. Technik) ‹*Thermometer*›; (arrange in gradations) gradweise abstufen 2 (Amer. Univ.) graduieren; (Amer. Sch.) aus der Schule entlassen

graduated /ˈgrædʒʊeɪtɪd/ *adj.* (marked with lines) mit einer Skala versehen; (arranged in grades) abgestuft; **~ markings** unterteilte Markierung

graduate school /ˈgrædʒʊət skuːl/ *n.* (Amer.) *Hochschulabteilung für Fortgeschrittenenstudium*

> **graduate school**
>
> Das Seminar einer Universität in den USA, das Kurse und Betreuung für graduierte Studierende organisiert, die ihr Studium und/oder ihre Forschung nach dem ersten Examen (nach ungefähr 3-4 Jahren Universitätsstudium) fortsetzen wollen.

graduation /grædʒʊˈeɪʃn/ *n.* 1 (Univ.) Graduierung, *die* 2 (Amer. Sch.) Entlassung, *die* 3 *attrib.* Abschluss- 4 (mark on a scale) Graduation, *die* (bes. Technik)

graffiti /grəˈfiːtiː/ *n. sing. or pl.* Graffiti *Pl.; attrib.* **~ artist** Graffitikünstler, *der*/-künstlerin, *die*

graft¹ /grɑːft/

A *n.* 1 (Bot.) (shoot, scion) Edelreis, *das;* Pfropfreis, *das;* (process) Pfropfung, *die;* (place) Pfropfstelle, *die* 2 (Med.) Transplantat, *das* 3 (Brit. coll.: work) Plackerei, *die* (ugs.)

B *v.t.* 1 (Bot.) pfropfen 2 (fig.) **~ sth. on to sth.** etw. einer Sache (*Dat.*) aufpfropfen 3 (Med.) transplantieren (fachspr.); verpflanzen

C *v.i.* 1 (Bot.) pfropfen 2 (Brit. coll.: work) schuften (ugs.)

graft²

A *n., no pl.* (dishonesty) Gaunerei, *die;* (profit) Fischzug, *der*

B *v.i.* mit kleinen Gaunereien Geld machen

grafter /ˈgrɑːftə(r)/ *n.* 1 (dishonest person) Gauner, *der* 2 (Brit. coll.: worker) Wühler, *der* (ugs.); Arbeitstier, *das* (ugs.)

Grail /greɪl/ *n.* **[Holy] ~:** [Heiliger] Gral

grain /greɪn/

A *n.* 1 Korn, *das;* (collect.: [species of] corn) Getreide, *das;* Korn, *das* 2 (particle) Korn, *das* 3 (unit of weight) Gran, *das* (veralt.); (fig.: small amount) **a ~ of truth** ein Gran *od.* Körnchen Wahrheit; **not a ~ of love/sense** kein Fünkchen Liebe/Funke [von] Verstand 4 (texture, also Photog.) Korn, *das* (fachspr.); Griff, *der;* (of fibre in wood) Maserung, *die;* (in paper) Faser, *die;* Faserverlauf, *der;* (in leather) Narbung, *die;* **go against the ~ [for sb.]** (fig.) jmdm. gegen den Strich gehen (ugs.)

B *v.t.* körnen ‹*Papier*›; masern ‹*Holz*›; narben ‹*Leder*›

grained /greɪnd/ *adj.* gekörnt ‹*Papier*›; genarbt ‹*Leder*›; maserig, gemasert ‹*Holz*›

ˈ**grain elevator** *n.* Getreideheber, *der*

grainy /ˈgreɪnɪ/ *adj.* körnig ‹*Foto, Papier, Leder*›; gemasert ‹*Holz*›; genarbt ‹*Leder*›

gram /græm/ *n.* ▸ ❶ **p. 1702** Gramm, *das*

grammar /ˈgræmə(r)/ *n.* 1 (also book) Grammatik, *die;* **sth. is [bad] ~:** etw. ist grammat[ikal]isch [nicht] richtig *od.* korrekt 2 (Brit. coll.) ▸ **grammar school 1**

ˈ**grammar book** *n.* Grammatik, *die;* Sprachlehre, *die*

grammarian /grəˈmeərɪən/ *n.* Grammatiker, *der*/Grammatikerin, *die*

ˈ**grammar school** *n.* 1 (Brit.) ≈ Gymnasium, *das* 2 (Amer.) ≈ Realschule, *die*

> **grammar school**
>
> Eine dem Gymnasium ähnliche Form der weiterführenden Schule in einigen Gebieten Englands und Wales' für Schüler zwischen 11 und 18 Jahren. Schüler im Alter von 11 oder 12 Jahren werden nach bestandener Aufnahmeprüfung zugelassen. *Grammar schools* wurden seit 1965 größtenteils von **comprehensive schools** ersetzt. In den USA ist *grammar school* ein anderer Name für **elementary school**.

grammatical /grəˈmætɪkl/ *adj.* 1 grammat[ikal]isch richtig *od.* korrekt 2 (of grammar) grammatisch

grammatically /grəˈmætɪkəlɪ/ *adv.* grammat[ikal]isch ‹*richtig, falsch*›; **speak English ~:** grammatisch richtiges *od.* korrektes Englisch sprechen

gramme ▸ **gram**

Grammy /ˈgræmɪ/ *n.* Grammy, *der*

gramophone /ˈgræməfəʊn/ *n.* (dated) Plattenspieler, *der*

ˈ**gramophone record** *n.* (dated) Schallplatte, *die*

gran /græn/ *n.* (coll./child lang.) Oma, *die* (Kinderspr./ugs.)

granary /ˈgrænərɪ/ *n.* 1 Getreidesilo, *der od. das;* Kornspeicher, *der* 2 **~ [loaf]** Vollkornbrot, *das* (*mit in die Kruste eingebackenen Getreidekörnern*)

ˈ**granary bread** *n.* Ganzkornbrot, *das*

grand /grænd/

A *adj.* 1 (in official titles: chief) Groß‹*meister, -herzog usw.*›; *see also* **cross A 7**; **lodge A 3** 2 (most or very important) groß; **~ finale** großes Finale; *see also* **slam² 3** (final) **~ total** Gesamtsumme, *die* 4 (main) Haupt‹*eingang, -raum, -halle usw.*› 5 (great) groß ‹*Armee, Leidenschaft usw.*› 6 (splendid) grandios; (impressive) eindrucksvoll ‹*Erscheinung, Figur, Person*›; (conducted with solemnity, splendour, etc.) glanzvoll; **live in ~ style** auf großem Fuß leben 7 (distinguished) vornehm; **put on a ~ air** die Nase hoch tragen (ugs. abwertend) 8 (dignified, lofty) erhaben; groß ‹*Versprechungen, Pläne, Worte*›; (noble, admirable) ehrwürdig 9 (coll.: excellent) großartig

B *n.* 1 (piano) Flügel, *der* 2 *pl. same* (*coll.: thousand pounds or* (*Amer.*) *dollars*) Riese, *der* (salopp)

grandad /ˈgrændæd/ *n.* (coll./child lang.) Großpapa, *der* (fam.); Opa, *der* (Kinderspr./ugs.)

grand: ~aunt *n.* Großtante, *die;* **~child** *n.* Enkel, *der*/Enkelin, *die;* Enkelkind, *das;* **~dad[dy]** /ˈgrændæd(ɪ)/ *n.* (coll./child lang.) *see* **grandad**; **~daughter** *n.* Enkelin, *die;* Enkeltochter, *die;* **~ ˈduchess** *n.* Großherzogin, *die;* **~ ˈduchy** *n.* Großherzogtum, *das;* **~ ˈduke** *n.* Großherzog, *der*

grandee /grænˈdiː/ *n.* Grande, *der*

grandeur /ˈgrændʒə(r), ˈgrændjə(r)/ *n.* 1 Erhabenheit, *die* 2 (splendour of living, surroundings, etc.) Großartigkeit, *die;* Glanz, *der;* **live a life of ~:** in Glanz und Herrlichkeit leben 3 (nobility of character) Größe, *die;* Erhabenheit, *die* 4 (power, rank) Größe, *die;* Macht, *die*

ˈ**grandfather** *n.* Großvater, *der;* **~ clock** Standuhr, *die*

grandiloquence /grænˈdɪləkwəns/ *n., no pl.* Großsprecherei, *die* (abwertend); (of style) Pathos, *das*

grandiloquent /grænˈdɪləkwənt/ *adj.* großtönend (geh. abwertend); hochtrabend (abwertend) ‹*Stil, Worte, Rede*›

grandiose /ˈgrændɪəʊs/ *adj.* 1 (impressive) grandios 2 (pompous) bombastisch (abwertend); großtönend (geh. abwertend) ‹*Worte, Art*›

grand ˈjury *n.* (Hist./Amer.) Großes Geschworenengericht

grandly /ˈgrændlɪ/ *adv.* großartig; aufwendig ‹*sich kleiden*›; in großem Stil ‹*leben*›

grand: ~ma[ma] *n.* (coll./child lang.) Großmama, *die* (fam.); Oma, *die* (Kinderspr./ugs.); **~ˈmaster** *n.* Großmeister, *der;* **~mother** *n.* Großmutter, *die; see also* **egg¹**; **G~ ˈNational** *n.* (Brit. Horseracing) Grand National, *das;* **~nephew** *n.* Großneffe, *der*

grandness /ˈgrændnɪs/ *n., no pl.* Großartigkeit, *die;* (pomp) Pracht[fülle], *die*

grand: ~niece *n.* Großnichte, *die;* **~ old man** *n.* Grand Old Man, *der; älteste bedeutende männliche Persönlichkeit in einem bestimmten Bereich;* **G~ Old Party** *n.* (Amer.) Republikanische Partei; **~ ˈopera** *n.* große Oper; **~pa[pa]** *n.* (coll./child lang.) Großpapa, *der* (fam.); Opa, *der* (Kinderspr./ugs.); **~parent** *n.* (male) Großvater, *der;* (female) Großmutter, *die;* **~parents** Großeltern *Pl.;* **~ piˈano** *n.* [Konzert]flügel, *der;* **G~ Prix** /grɑ̃ ˈpriː/ *n.* Grand Prix, *der;* **~son** *n.* Enkel, *der;* Enkelsohn, *der;* **~stand** *n.* [Haupt]tribüne, *die;* **~stand finish** packendes Finish; **~stand view** guter Überblick (**of** über + *Akk.*); **~stand play** (Amer.) Effekthascherei, *die;* **~ ˈtour** *n.* 1 (Hist.) Bildungsreise, *die;* Kavalierstour, *die;* 2 (fig.) große Fahrt *od.* Reise (scherzh.); **make the ~ tour of** auf große Fahrt *od.* Reise gehen zu (scherzh.); **~uncle** *n.* Großonkel, *der*

grange /greɪndʒ/ *n.* Gutshof, *der;* Landsitz, *der*

granite /ˈgrænɪt/ *n.* 1 Granit, *der* 2 (fig.: unyieldingness) Unnachgiebigkeit, *die*

granny (grannie) /ˈgrænɪ/ *n.* 1 (coll./child lang.) Großmama, *die* (fam.); Oma, *die* (Kinderspr./ugs.) 2 ▸ **granny knot**

granny: ~ flat *n.* Einliegerwohnung, *die;* **~ knot** *n.* Altweiberknoten, *der* (Seemannsspr.)

grant /grɑːnt/

A *v.t.* 1 (consent to fulfil) erfüllen ‹*Wunsch*›; erhören ‹*Gebet, Flehen*›; stattgeben (+ *Dat.*) ‹*Gesuch*›; gewähren ‹*Gunst*›; **~ sb. his wish** jmdm. seinen Wunsch erfüllen 2 (concede, give) gewähren; gestatten ‹*Blick*›; geben ‹*Zeit*›; bewilligen ‹*Geldmittel*›; verleihen ‹*akademischen Grad, Auszeichnung*›; zugestehen ‹*Recht*›; erteilen ‹*Erlaubnis*›; (transfer legally) übertragen (**to** auf + *Akk.*) 3 (in argument) zugeben; einräumen (geh.); **~ed that ...:** zugegeben, dass ...; **~ing this to be true** *or* **that this is true** nehmen wir einmal an, dass das stimmt; **take sb./sth. [too much] for ~ed** sich (*Dat.*) jmds. [allzu] sicher sein/etw. für [allzu] selbstverständlich halten; **nobody likes to be taken for ~ed** keiner mag es, wenn man sich nicht um ihn bemüht; **he's a good fellow, [that] I ~ you** er ist ein guter Kumpel *od.* Kerl, das gebe ich zu; **I beg your pardon — G~ed** Entschuldigen Sie! — Bitte

B *n.* 1 (sum of money) Zuschuss, *der;* (financial aid [to student]) [Studien]beihilfe, *die;* (scholarship) Stipendium, *das* 2 (conceding, allowing) (of request, respite) Gewährung, *die;* (of pension, holiday) Bewilligung, *die;* (of award, degree) Verleihung, *die;* (of permission) Erteilung, *die*

ˈ**grant-aided school** *n.* (Brit.) subventionierte Schule

grant-in-ˈaid *n., pl.* **grants-in-aid** (Educ.) [staatlicher Schul]zuschuss

> **grant-maintained school**
>
> Eine Form der weiterführenden Schule in England und Wales, die von der Regierung in London und nicht von der lokalen Regierung finanziert wird.

granular /ˈgrænjʊlə(r)/ *adj.* körnig; granulös (Med.)

granulate /ˈgrænjʊleɪt/ *v.t.* granulieren (bes. Technik); **~d sugar** [Zucker]raffinade, *die;* Kristallzucker, *der*

granule /ˈgrænjuːl/ *n.* Körnchen, *das*

grape /greɪp/ *n.* Weintraube, *die;* Weinbeere, *die;* **a bunch of ~s** eine Traube; **the juice of the ~** (literary) der Saft der Rebe[n] (dichter.); **[it's] sour ~s** (fig.) die Trauben hängen zu hoch

grape: ~fruit *n., pl. same* Grapefruit, *die;* **~ harvest** *n.* Weinlese, *die;* **~ ˈhyacinth** *n.*

Traubenhyazinthe, *die;* ~ **juice** *n.* Traubensaft, *der;* ~**shot** *n., pl. same* (Mil. Hist.) Kartätsche, *die;* ~**vine** *n.* 1 Wein, *der;* 2 (fig.) **the** ~**vine** die Flüsterpropaganda; **I heard [it] on the** ~**vine that they were getting married** es wird geflüstert, dass sie heiraten wollen

graph /græf, grɑːf/
A *n.* grafische Darstellung; Graph, *der* (Math.)
B *v.t.* grafisch darstellen

graphic /ˈgræfɪk/
A *adj.* 1 grafisch; ~ **art** Grafik, *die;* ~ **artist** Grafiker, *der*/Grafikerin, *die;* ~ **display** Grafikdisplay, *das* 2 (clear, vivid) plastisch; anschaulich; **in** ~ **detail** in allen Einzelheiten
B *n.* 1 (product) Grafik, *die* 2 *in pl.* ▸ **graphics**

graphical /ˈgræfɪkl/ ▸ **graphic A**

graphically /ˈgræfɪkəlɪ/ *adv.* 1 (clearly, vividly) plastisch; anschaulich 2 (by use of graphic methods) grafisch

graphical user ˈinterface *n.* (Computing) grafische Benutzeroberfläche

graphic: ~ **arts** *n. pl.* Grafik, *die;* ~ **deˈsign** *n., no pl.* Grafikdesign, *das;* ~ **deˈsigner** *n.* ▸ⓘ **p. 1260** Grafikdesigner, *der*/-designerin, *die;* Grafiker, *der*/Grafikerin, *die*

graphics /ˈgræfɪks/ *n.* (design and decoration) grafische Gestaltung; (use of diagrams) grafische Darstellung; **computer** ~: Computergrafik, *die*

ˈgraphics board, ˈgraphics card *ns.* (Computing) Grafikkarte, *die*

graphite /ˈgræfaɪt/ *n.* Graphit, *der*

graphologist /grəˈfɒlədʒɪst/ *n.* ▸ⓘ **p. 1260** Graphologe, *der*/Graphologin, *die*

graphology /grəˈfɒlədʒɪ/ *n., no pl.* Graphologie, *die*

ˈgraph paper *n.* Diagrammpapier, *das*

grapnel /ˈgræpnəl/ *n.* 1 (anchor) Draggen, *der;* Dreghaken, *der* 2 (grappling hook) Enterhaken, *der*

grapple /ˈgræpl/
A *v.i.* (in fighting) handgemein werden; **they** ~**d together** (Wrestling) sie rangen miteinander; ~ **with** (fig.) sich auseinander setzen *od.* (ugs.) herumschlagen mit; ~ **with death** mit dem Tode ringen
B *v.t.* 1 (seize, fasten) [mit Enterhaken] festhaken ‹*Schiff*›; (drag) [mit Dreghaken] absuchen ‹*Fluss*› 2 (grip with hands) packen

grappling /ˈgræplɪŋ/: ~**-hook**, ~**-iron** *n.* (Naut. Hist.) Enterhaken, *der*

grasp /grɑːsp/
A *v.i.* ~ **at** greifen nach; (esp. fig.) ergreifen ‹*Gelegenheit*›; sich stürzen auf (+ *Akk.*) ‹*Angebot*›; *see also* **straw 2**
B *v.t.* 1 (seize) ergreifen (auch fig.); **manage to** ~: zu fassen bekommen 2 (hold firmly) festhalten; ~ **sb. in one's arms** jmdn. [fest] in den Armen halten; ~ **the nettle** (fig.) das Problem beherzt anpacken 3 (understand) verstehen; erfassen ‹*Bedeutung*›
C *n.* 1 (firm hold) Griff, *der;* **twist from sb.'s** ~: sich jmds. Griff (*Dat.*) entwinden; **he had my hand in a firm** ~: er hielt meine Hand mit festem Griff; **tighten/loosen one's** ~: fester zupacken/den Griff lockern; **sth. is within/beyond sb.'s** ~: etwas ist in/außer jmds. Reichweite (*Dat.*); **success was almost within/was completely beyond his** ~ (fig.) der Erfolg war zum Greifen nah/in unerreichbarer Ferne 2 (mental hold) **have a good** ~ **of sth.** etw. gut beherrschen; **his** ~ **of this subject is remarkable** er beherrscht das Thema außergewöhnlich gut; **sth. is beyond/within sb.'s** ~: etw. überfordert jmds. [intellektuelle] Fähigkeiten/kann von jmdm. verstanden werden

graspable /ˈgrɑːspəbl/ *adj.* (fig.) verständlich

grasping /ˈgrɑːspɪŋ/ *adj.* (greedy) habgierig

grass /grɑːs/
A *n.* 1 Gras, *das;* **be as green as** ~ (fig.) noch feucht hinter den Ohren sein (ugs.); **not let the** ~ **grow under one's feet** (fig. coll.) die Sache nicht auf die lange Bank schieben (ugs.); **the** ~ **is always greener on the other side [of the hill** *or* **fence]** (prov.) die Kirschen aus Nachbars Garten schmecken immer viel besser 2 *no pl.* (lawn) Rasen, *der* 3 *no pl.* (grazing, pasture) Weide, *die;* (pastureland) Weideland, *das;* **be out at** ~: auf der Weide sein; **put** *or* **turn out to** ~: auf die Weide treiben *od.* führen; (fig.) in den Ruhestand versetzen; nicht mehr zur Arbeit einsetzen ‹*Pferd*› 4 (coll.: marijuana) Grass, *das* (ugs.) 5 (Brit. coll.: police informer) Spitzel, *der*
B *v.t.* 1 (cover with turf) mit Rasen bedecken 2 (Brit. coll.: betray) verpfeifen (ugs.)
C *v.i.* (Brit. coll.: inform police) singen (salopp); ~ **on sb.** jmdn. verpfeifen (ugs.)

grass: ~**box** *n.* Grasfangkorb, *der;* ~ **ˈcourt** *n.* Rasenplatz, *der;* Grasplatz, *der;* ~**-green** *adj.* grasgrün; ~**hopper** *n.* Grashüpfer, *der; see also* **knee-high;** ~**land** *n.* Grasland, *das;* (for grazing) Weideland, *das;* ~**-root[s]** *attrib. adj.* (Polit.) Basis-; **at the** ~**-roots/at** ~**-roots level** an der Basis; ~ **ˈroots** *n. pl.* (fig.) (source) Wurzeln *Pl.;* (Polit.) Basis, *die;* **the** ~ **roots of the party** die Parteibasis; ~ **seed** *n.* Grassamen, *der;* ~ **ˈskirt** *n.* Baströckchen, *das;* ~ **snake** *n.* 1 (Brit.: ringed snake) Ringelnatter, *die;* 2 (Amer.: green snake) Grasnatter, *die;* ~ **widow** *n.* Strohwitwe, *die* (ugs. scherzh.); ~ **widower** *n.* Strohwitwer, *der* (ugs. scherzh.)

grassy /ˈgrɑːsɪ/ *adj.* mit Gras bewachsen

grate¹ /greɪt/ *n.* Rost, *der;* (fireplace) Kamin, *der*

grate²
A *v.t.* 1 (reduce to particles) reiben; (less finely) raspeln 2 (grind) ~ **one's teeth in anger/in one's sleep** vor Wut/im Schlaf mit den Zähnen knirschen 3 (utter in harsh tone) [durch die Zähne] knirschen
B *v.i.* 1 (rub) knirschen; **the door** ~**s [up]on its hinges** die Tür knirscht in den Angeln 2 (have irritating effect) ~ **[up]on sb./sb.'s nerves** jmdm. auf die Nerven gehen 3 (sound harshly) knirschen; **her shrill voice** ~**d [up]on our ears** ihre schrille Stimme gellte uns in den Ohren

grateful /ˈgreɪtfl/ *adj.* 1 dankbar (**to** *Dat.*); **a** ~ **word of thanks** ein herzliches Wort des Dankes 2 (pleasant, agreeable) wohltuend

gratefully /ˈgreɪtfəlɪ/ *adv.* dankbar; **thank sb.** ~: jmdm. aufrichtig danken

grater /ˈgreɪtə(r)/ *n.* Reibe, *die;* (less fine) Raspel, *die*

gratification /grætɪfɪˈkeɪʃn/ *n.* 1 (pleasure) Genugtuung, *die;* **the** ~ **of doing sth.** die Genugtuung, etw. zu tun 2 (satisfaction) ▸ **gratify 2**: Befriedigung, *die;* Erfüllung, *die;* Stillung, *die*

gratify /ˈgrætɪfaɪ/ *v.t.* 1 (please) freuen; **be gratified by** *or* **with** *or* **at sth.** über etw. (*Akk.*) erfreut sein; **I was gratified** *or* **it gratified me to hear that ...:** mit Genugtuung erfuhr ich, dass ... 2 (satisfy) befriedigen ‹*Neugier, Bedürfnis, Eitelkeit*›; erfüllen ‹*Wunsch*›; stillen ‹*Sehnsucht, Verlangen*›

gratifying /ˈgrætɪfaɪɪŋ/ *adj.* erfreulich

gratin /ˈgrætæ̃/ *n.* (Cookery) Gratin, *das;* **cauliflower au** ~ /əʊ ˈgrætæ̃/ gratinierter Blumenkohl

grating /ˈgreɪtɪŋ/ *n.* (framework) Gitter, *das*

gratis /ˈgrætɪs, ˈgrɑːtɪs, ˈgreɪtɪs/
A *adv.* gratis, kostenlos ‹*bekommen, abgeben*›; umsonst, unentgeltlich ‹*tun*›
B *adj.* gratis *nicht attr.;* Gratis‹*mahlzeit, -vorstellung usw.*›

gratitude /ˈgrætɪtjuːd/ *n., no pl.* Dankbarkeit, *die* (**to** gegenüber); **show one's** ~ **to sb.** sich jmdm. gegenüber dankbar zeigen

gratuitous /grəˈtjuːɪtəs/ *adj.* 1 (uncalled for, motiveless) grundlos; unnötig; (without logical reason) unbegründet 2 (got or given free) unentgeltlich ‹*Dienstleistung*›

gratuitously /grəˈtjuːɪtəslɪ/ *adv.* 1 (without motive or reason) ohne Grund 2 (free of cost) unentgeltlich

gratuity /grəˈtjuːɪtɪ/ *n.* 1 (formal: tip) Trinkgeld, *das* 2 (Brit.: bounty) Sonderzuwendung, *die*

graunch /grɔːnʃ/
A *v.t.* ~ **the gears** knirschend schalten
B *v.i.* (make grinding sound) knirschen
C *n.* Knirschen, *das*

grave¹ /greɪv/ *n.* Grab, *das;* **the house was as quiet** *or* **silent** *or* **still as the** ~: im Haus herrschte Grabesstille; **dig one's own** ~ (fig.) sich (*Dat.*) selbst sein Grab graben (fig.); **he would turn in his** ~ (fig.) er würde sich im Grabe herumdrehen; **sb. is walking on** *or* **over my/his** *etc.* ~ (fig.) es überläuft mich/ihn *usw.* eiskalt; **carry a scar** *etc.* **to one's** ~: eine Narbe *usw.* bis an sein Lebensende tragen; **a message from beyond the** ~: eine Botschaft aus dem Jenseits; **take a secret to the** ~: ein Geheimnis mit ins Grab nehmen; *see also* **cradle A 1; foot A 1**

grave² *adj.* 1 (important, dignified, solemn) ernst 2 (formidable, serious) schwer, gravierend ‹*Fehler, Irrtum, Verfehlung*›; ernst ‹*Situation, Lage, Schwierigkeit*›; groß ‹*Gefahr, Risiko, Verantwortung*›; schlimm ‹*Nachricht, Zeichen*›

grave³ /grɑːv/ *adj.* (Ling.) ~ **accent** Accent grave, *der;* Gravis, *der*

gravedigger /ˈgreɪvdɪgə(r)/ *n.* ▸ⓘ **p. 1260** Totengräber, *der*

gravel /ˈgrævl/
A *n.* 1 (small stones) Kies, *der; attrib.* ~ **path/pit** Kiesweg, *der*/-grube, *die* 2 (Geol., Mining) Geröll, *das* 3 (Med.) **[bladder/kidney]** ~: Harn-/Nierengrieß, *der*
B *v.t.,* (Brit.) **-ll-** kiesen

gravelly /ˈgrævəlɪ/ *adj.* 1 kieshaltig ‹*Boden*› 2 rau, heiser ‹*Stimme*›

gravely /ˈgreɪvlɪ/ *adv.* 1 (in grave manner) ernst 2 (seriously) ernstlich; **be** ~ **mistaken** sich schwer irren (ugs.)

graven image /greɪvn ˈɪmɪdʒ/ *n.* Götzenbild, *das*

grave /greɪv/: ~**side** *n.* **at the** ~**side** am Grab; ~**stone** *n.* Grabstein, *der;* ~**yard** *n.* Friedhof, *der;* **be a** ~**yard of reputations** manch einen guten Ruf zerstört haben; ~**yard shift** *n.* Nachtschicht, *die* (*zwischen Mitternacht und 8 Uhr*)

graving dock /ˈgreɪvɪŋ dɒk/ ▸ **dry dock**

gravitas /ˈgrævɪtɑːs/ *n.* Gravität, *die* (veralt.)

gravitate /ˈgrævɪteɪt/ *v.i.* gravitieren (Phys., Astron., geh.); **young people** ~ **to[wards] the cities** junge Leute zieht es in die Städte

gravitation /grævɪˈteɪʃn/ *n.* Gravitation, *die;* Schwerkraft, *die;* (fig.) Streben, *das*

gravitational /grævɪˈteɪʃənl/ *adj.* Gravitations‹*feld, -energie usw.*›; ~ **pull** Anziehungskraft, *die;* ~ **force** Schwerkraft, *die*

gravity /ˈgrævɪtɪ/ *n.* 1 (solemnity) Feierlichkeit, *die* 2 (importance) (of mistake, offence) Schwere, *die;* (of situation) Ernst, *der* 3 (seriousness, staidness) Ernst, *der;* **the** ~ **of his manner** seine Ernsthaftigkeit; **keep** *or* **preserve one's** ~: ernst bleiben 4 (Phys., Astron.) Gravitation, *die;* Schwerkraft, *die;* **the law/force of** ~: das Gravitationsgesetz/die Schwerkraft; **centre of** ~ (lit. or fig.) Schwerpunkt, *der;* **specific** ~ (Phys.) spezifisches Gewicht; Wichte, *die* (fachspr.)

ˈgravity feed *n.* Schwerkraftzufuhr, *die* (Technik)

gravy /ˈgreɪvɪ/ *n.* 1 (juices) Bratensaft, *der* 2 (dressing) [Braten]soße, *die* 3 (coll.: money) Nebenverdienst, *der;* (tip) Trinkgeld, *das*

gravy: ~ **boat** *n.* Sauciere, *die;* Soßenschüssel, *die;* ~ **train** *n.* **ride/board the** ~ **train** (coll.) leichtes Geld machen (ugs.)

gray *etc.* (*Amer.*) ▸ **grey** *etc.*

grayling /ˈgreɪlɪŋ/ *n., pl. same* (Zool.) Äsche, *die*

graze¹ /greɪz/
A *v.i.* 1 grasen; weiden 2 (coll.: snack) zwischendurch dies und jenes naschen; **I had been grazing all day** ich hatte den ganzen Tag herumgenascht (ugs.); ~ **on sth.** etw. naschen
B *v.t.* 1 (feed) weiden ‹*Schafe, Rinder*› 2 (feed on) abweiden ‹*Feld, Wiese*›

graze²
A *n.* Schürfwunde, *die*
B *v.t.* 1 (touch lightly) streifen 2 (scrape) abschürfen ‹*Haut*›; zerkratzen ‹*Oberfläche*›; ~ **one's knee/elbow** sich (*Dat.*) das Knie/den Ellbogen aufschürfen
C *v.i.* ~ **against/by** *or* **past the wall** an der Mauer entlang-/vorbeischrammen

grazier /ˈgreɪzɪə(r)/ *n.* 1 Viehzüchter, *der* 2 (Austral.: sheep farmer) Schafzüchter, *der*

grazing /ˈgreɪzɪŋ/
A *n.* (feeding) Weiden, *das;* (land) Weide, *die;* Weideland, *das*

B *adj.* weidend; ~ **land** Weideland, *das;* ~ **rights** Weiderecht, *das*

grease
A *n.* /gri:s/ Fett, *das;* (lubricant) Schmierfett, *das*
B *v.t.* /gri:z, gri:s/ einfetten; einreiben ‹*Haut, Rücken usw.*›; (lubricate) schmieren; **like ~d lightning** (coll.) wie ein geölter Blitz (ugs.); ~ **sb.'s palm** (fig. coll.) jmdn. schmieren (salopp abwertend); ~ **the wheels** (fig. coll.) der Sache (*Dat.*) nachhelfen

grease: ~ **gun** *n.* Fettpresse, *die* (Technik); ~ **monkey** *n.* (dated coll.) Schmiermaxe, *der* (ugs.); **~paint** *n.* [Fett]schminke, *die;* **~proof** *adj.* fettdicht; **~proof paper** Pergament- *od.* Butterbrotpapier, *das*

greasy /ˈgri:zɪ, ˈgri:sɪ/ *adj.* **1** fettig; fett ‹*Essen*›; speckig ‹*Kleidung*›; (lubricated) geschmiert; (slippery, dirty with lubricant) schmierig **2** (fig.: unctuous) schmierig (abwertend)

great /greɪt/
A *adj.* **1** (large) groß; ~ **big** (coll.) riesengroß (ugs.); ~ **thick** (coll.) mordsdick (ugs.); **give sb. a ~ big hug** (coll.) jmdn. mit großer Herzlichkeit umarmen; **a ~ many** sehr viele; **a ~ amount of patience** eine Menge Geduld (ugs.); *see also* **deal²** **2** (beyond the ordinary) groß; sehr gut ‹*Freund*›; sehr schwer ‹*Krise*›; **a ~ [old] age** ein hohes Alter; **take ~ care of/a ~ interest in** sich sehr kümmern um/interessieren für **3** (important) groß ‹*Tag, Ereignis, Attraktion, Hilfe*›; (powerful, influential, of remarkable ability) groß ‹*Person, Komponist, Schriftsteller*›; (impressive) großartig; **the ~ thing is** die Hauptsache ist; *in titles or names* **Peter the G~:** Peter der Große; *in excl.* **G~ Scott!** großer Gott!; (having much skill) **be ~ at sth.** in etw. (*Dat.*) ganz groß sein (ugs.); (having much knowledge) **be ~ on modern music** in zeitgenössischer Musik sehr beschlagen sein (ugs.); **be a ~ one for sth.** etw. sehr gern tun; *see also* **spirit A 8** **4** (coll.: splendid) großartig **5** (in relationship) Groß‹*onkel, -tante, -neffe, -nichte*›; Ur‹*großmutter, -großvater, -enkel, -enkelin*›; **~-~-** Urgroß‹*onkel, -tante, -neffe, -nichte*›; Urur‹*großmutter, -großvater, -enkel, -enkelin*›
B *n.* **1** (person) Größe, *die;* **literary/football ~s** literarische Größen/Fußballgrößen; *as pl.* **the ~:** die Großen [der Geschichte/Literatur *usw.*]; **the ~est** (coll.) der/die Größte/die Größten (ugs.) **2** **G~s** (Brit. Univ.) klassische Philologie

Great: ~ **'Bear** *n.* (Astron.) Großer Bär; ~ **'Britain** *pr. n.* Großbritannien (*das*); **g~coat** *n.* [Winter]mantel, *der;* ~ **'Dane** *n.* Deutsche Dogge

Greater: ~ **'London** *pr. n.* Groß-London; ~ **London 'Council** *n.* (Hist.) Stadtrat von Groß-London

great: **~-hearted** *adj.* hochherzig; großmütig; ~ **'house** *n.* Gutshaus, *das;* Herrenhaus, *das;* **the ~ houses of England** englische Schlösser und Adelssitze; **G~ 'Lakes** *pr. n. pl.* Große Seen *Pl.*

greatly /ˈgreɪtlɪ/ *adv.* sehr; höchst ‹*verärgert*›; stark ‹*beeinflusst, beunruhigt*›; weit ‹*überlegen*›; bedeutend ‹*verbessert*›; **sth. is ~ to be feared** etw. muss ernstlich befürchtet werden; **it doesn't ~ matter** es ist nicht so wichtig

greatness /ˈgreɪtnɪs/ *n., no pl.* Größe, *die;* (extent, degree) Ausmaß, *das;* **~ of heart/mind/soul** Hochherzigkeit, *die*/Großmut, *die*/ Seelengröße, *die*

Great: ~ **'Power** *n.* Großmacht, *die;* ~ **Salt 'Lake** *pr. n.* Großer Salzsee; **g~ tit** *n.* (Ornith.) Kohlmeise, *die;* **g~ 'toe** *n.* großer Zeh; ~ **'War** *n.* Erster Weltkrieg

grebe /gri:b/ *n.* (Ornith.) Lappentaucher, *der*

Grecian /ˈgri:ʃn/
A *adj.* griechisch
B *n.* Grieche, *der*/Griechin, *die*

Greece /gri:s/ *pr. n.* Griechenland (*das*)

greed /gri:d/ *n.* Gier, *die* (**for** nach); (gluttony) Gefräßigkeit, *die* (abwertend); (of animal) Fressgier, *die;* ~ **for money/power** Geld-/Machtgier, *die*

greedily /ˈgri:dɪlɪ/ *adv.* gierig

greediness /ˈgri:dɪnɪs/ *n., no pl.* Gier, *die*

greedy /ˈgri:dɪ/ *adj.* gierig; (gluttonous) gefräßig (abwertend); (eager) begierig; **be ~ for sth.** nach etw. gieren; ~ **for money/power/success** geldgierig/machthungrig/erfolgshungrig; **be ~ to do/get sth.** etw. unbedingt tun/bekommen wollen

'greedy-guts *n. sing.* (coll.) Vielfraß, *der* (ugs.)

Greek /gri:k/ ▸**ℹ p. 1277**, ▸**ℹ p. 1345**
A *adj.* griechisch; **sb. is ~:** jmd. ist Grieche/Griechin; *see also* **calends**; **English A**
B *n.* **1** (person) Grieche, *der*/Griechin, *die* **2** (language) Griechisch, *das;* **modern ~:** Neugriechisch, *das;* **it's all ~ to me** (fig.) das sind mir *od.* für mich böhmische Dörfer; *see also* **English B 1**

Greek: ~ **'Church** ▸~ **Orthodox Church**; ~ **'god** *n.* (fig.) Adonis, *der;* ~ **Orthodox 'Church** *n.* griechisch-orthodoxe Kirche

green /gri:n/
A *adj.* **1** grün; **have ~ fingers** *or* (Amer.) **a ~ thumb** (fig.) eine grüne Hand haben (ugs.); ~ **vegetables** Grüngemüse, *das* **2** (Polit.) **G~:** grün; **he/she is ~:** er ist ein Grüner/sie ist eine Grüne; **the Greens** die Grünen **3** (environmentally safe) ökologisch; ~ **electricity** Ökostrom, *der* **4** (unripe, young, tender) grün ‹*Obst, Apfel, Banane, Zweig*› **5** (not dried, seasoned, smoked, or tanned) grün ‹*Holz, Speck, Heringe*›; nicht gegerbt ‹*Fell*› **6** (pale) **his face turned ~ at the sight of the blood** beim Anblick des Blutes wurde er ganz grün im Gesicht; **be/turn ~ with envy/jealousy** vor Neid/Eifersucht grün sein/werden **7** (immature, naïve) unreif; (gullible) naiv; einfältig; (inexperienced) grün
B *n.* **1** (colour) Grün, *das* **2** (piece of land) Grünfläche, *die;* **village ~:** Dorfanger, *der* **3** *in pl.* (~ vegetables) Grüngemüse, *das* **4** (verdure, vegetation) Grün, *das* **5** (Snooker) grüne Kugel **6** (~ clothes) **dressed in ~:** grün gekleidet **7** (traffic light) Grün, *das;* **the traffic light is at ~:** die Ampel steht auf Grün
C *v.i.* grünen

green: **~back** *n.* (Amer.) Dollarschein, *der;* ~ **'belt** *n.* Grüngürtel, *der;* ~ **'card** *n.* **1** (Brit. Insurance) grüne Karte (Verkehrsw.); **2** (Amer.) Aufenthaltsgenehmigung [mit Arbeitserlaubnis]

> **green card**
>
> Ein offizielles Dokument, das nichtamerikanische Bürger zur Erwerbstätigkeit in den USA berechtigt. Die *green card* braucht jeder, der beabsichtigt, eine feste Stelle in den USA anzutreten.

greenery /ˈgri:nərɪ/ *n., no pl.* Grün, *das*

green: **~-eyed** *adj.* grünäugig; (fig.) neidisch; **be ~-eyed** grüne Augen haben; **~'field site** *n.* Bauplatz im Grünen; **~finch** *n.* Grünfink, *der;* **~fly** *n.* (Brit.) grüne Blattlaus; **~gage** *n.* Reineclaude, *die;* **~grocer** *n.* ▸**ℹ p. 1260** (Brit.) Obst- und Gemüsehändler, *der*/-händlerin, *die; see also* **baker**; **~grocery** *n.* (Brit.) **1** Obst- und Gemüsehandlung, *die;* **2** *in sing. or pl.* (goods) Obst und Gemüse; **~horn** *n.* (esp. Amer. coll.) Greenhorn, *das;* **~house** *n.* Gewächshaus, *das;* **~house effect** Treibhauseffekt, *der;* **~house gas** Treibhausgas, *das*

greenish /ˈgri:nɪʃ/ *adj.* grünlich

'greenkeeper *n.* (Golf) Golfwart, *der*

Greenland /ˈgri:nlənd/ *pr. n.* Grönland (*das*)

Greenlander /ˈgri:nləndə(r)/ *n.* ▸**ℹ p. 1345** Grönländer, *der*/Grönländerin, *die*

green 'light *n.* **1** grünes Licht; (as signal) Grün, *das;* **it's a ~:** die Ampel ist grün **2** (fig. coll.) **give sb./get the ~:** jmdm. grünes Licht geben/grünes Licht erhalten

greenness /ˈgri:nnɪs/ *n., no pl.* **1** (of colour) Grün, *das;* grüne Farbe **2** (of sth. covered with herbage) Grün, *das* **3** (unripeness) grüner Zustand **4** (fig.: youth, immaturity) Unreife, *die;* (inexperience) Unerfahrenheit, *die;* (gullibility) Naivität, *die;* Einfalt, *die*

green: **G~ 'Paper** *n.* (Brit.) *öffentliches Diskussionspapier über die Regierungspolitik;* **G~ Party** *n.* (Polit.) die Grünen; ~ **'pepper** ▸**pepper A 2**; ~ **revo'lution** *n.* grüne Revolution; ~ **room** *n.* (Theatre) Künstlerzimmer, *das;* **~stick fracture** *n.* (Med.) Grünholzfraktur, *die;* **~sward** *n.* (literary) Grünfläche, *die;* ~ **'tea** *n.* grüner Tee; **~way** *n.* (Amer.) Grüngürtel, *der;* ~ **'welly brigade** *n.* (Brit. coll.) Schickeria vom Lande

> **Green Party**
>
> Eine politische Partei in Großbritannien, die sich dem Umweltschutz verpflichtet und Kritik an Industrien, Transportmitteln und Energiequellen übt, die sie für umweltschädlich hält. Die Grünen sprechen sich beispielsweise gegen die Nutzung von Atomenergie aus.

Greenwich /ˈgrenɪtʃ, ˈgrɪnɪdʒ/ *n.* ~ **[mean] time** Greenwicher Zeit; [mittlere] Greenwich-Zeit

'greenwood *n.* [grüner] Wald

greet /gri:t/ *v.t.* **1** begrüßen; (in passing) grüßen; (receive) empfangen; ~ **sb. with sth.** jmdn. mit etw. begrüßen/grüßen/empfangen **2** (meet) empfangen; ~ **sb.'s eyes/ears** sich jmds. Augen (*Dat.*) darbieten/an jmds. Ohr (*Akk.*) dringen

greeting /ˈgri:tɪŋ/ *n.* ▸**ℹ p. 1189** Begrüßung, *die;* (in passing) Gruß, *der;* (words) Grußformel, *die;* (reception) Empfang, *der;* **please give my ~s to your parents** grüßen Sie bitte Ihre Eltern von mir; **my husband also sends his ~s** mein Mann lässt auch grüßen

greeting: **~[s] card** *n.* Grußkarte, *die;* (for anniversary, birthday) Glückwunschkarte, *die;* **~[s] telegram** *n.* Glückwunschtelegramm, *das*

gregarious /grɪˈgeərɪəs/ *adj.* **1** (Zool.) gesellig; Herden‹*tier, -trieb*› **2** (fond of company) gesellig

gregariousness /grɪˈgeərɪəsnɪs/ *n., no pl.* **1** (Zool.) Herdenleben, *das* **2** (of person) Geselligkeit, *die*

Gregorian /grɪˈgɔ:rɪən/ *adj.* gregorianisch; ~ **calendar/chant** gregorianischer Kalender/ Gesang

Gregory /ˈgregərɪ/ *pr. n.* (Hist., as name of pope) Gregor

gremlin /ˈgremlɪn/ *n.* (coll. joc.) *böser Geist, der für Maschinendefekte usw. verantwortlich gemacht wird;* (unexplained fault) rätselhafter Fehler

grenade /grɪˈneɪd/ *n.* Granate, *die; see also* **hand grenade**

Grenadier Guards /grenədɪə(r) ˈgɑ:dz/ *n. pl.* (Brit.) Grenadiergarde, *die*

grew ▸**grow**

grey /greɪ/
A *adj.* **1** (lit. or fig.) grau; **he** *or* **his hair went** *or* **turned ~:** er wurde grau *od.* ergraute; **grow ~ in sb.'s service** (fig.) in jmds. Diensten ergrauen; ~ **area** (fig.) Grauzone, *die* **2** (anonymous) gesichtslos ‹*Person*›
B *n.* **1** Grau, *das* **2** (~ clothes) **dressed in ~:** grau gekleidet **3** (horse) Grauschimmel, *der*

grey: **~beard** *n.* Graubart, *der* (ugs.); ~ **cells** *n. pl.* graue Substanz (Anat.); ~ **e'conomy** *n.* graue Wirtschaft; ~ **'eminence** ▸**éminence grise**; **G~ Friar** *n.* Franziskaner, *der;* ~ **goose** *n.* Graugans, *die;* **~-haired**, **~-headed** *adjs.* grauhaarig; **~-hen** *n.* Birkhenne, *die*

'greyhound *n.* Windhund, *der*

> **Greyhound bus**
>
> Ein Bus der *Greyhound Lines Company*, der größten Busgesellschaft in den Vereinigten Staaten. *Greyhound*-Busse verkehren zwischen größeren und kleineren Städten in den gesamten Vereinigten Staaten und sind vor allem bei jungen Leuten und Touristen beliebt, die oft lange Strecken mit ihnen zurücklegen.

'greyhound racing *n.* Windhundrennen, *das*

greyish /ˈgreɪɪʃ/ *adj.* gräulich

greylag /ˈgreɪlæg/ *n.* ~ **[goose]** Graugans, *die*

grey: ~ **matter** *n.* graue Substanz (Anat.); (fig.: intelligence) graue Zellen; ~ **'seal** *n.* Kegelrobbe, *die;* ~ **'squirrel** *n.* Grauhörnchen, *das*

grid /grɪd/ *n.* **1** (grating) Rost, *der* **2** (of lines) Gitter[netz], *das* **3** (for supply) [Versorgungs-]netz, *das* **4** ▸**gridiron 1** **5** (Motor racing)

Greetings (See also ◻ Letter-writing)

On a postcard

Greetings or ***Best wishes from Freiburg***
= Schöne *or* Herzliche Grüße aus Freiburg

Having a wonderful time
= Es gefällt uns hier ausgezeichnet

Wish you were here!
≈ Das hättest Du alles sehen sollen!

See you soon
= Bis bald

All best wishes, Steve and Cathy
= Herzlichst *or* Herzliche Grüße *or* Es grüßen recht herzlich Steve und Cathy

For a birthday

Many happy returns [of the day], Happy birthday
= Herzlichen Glückwunsch zum Geburtstag

All good or ***best wishes for your birthday***
= Alles Gute zum Geburtstag

For Christmas and the New Year

Happy Christmas!
= Frohe Weihnachten!

[Best wishes for] a Merry or ***Happy Christmas and a Prosperous New Year***
= Frohe Weihnachten *or* Fröhliche Weihnachten *or* Ein gesegnetes Weihnachtsfest und viel Glück im neuen Jahr

Happy New Year!
= Glückliches neues Jahr!; (*when drinking*) Prost *or* Prosit Neujahr!

For Easter

[Best wishes for a] Happy Easter
= Frohe Ostern *or* Ein fröhliches Osterfest

For a wedding

Every good wish to the happy couple or to the bride and groom on their wedding day and in the years to come
= Dem glücklichen Paar alles Schöne am Hochzeitstag und viel Glück in der Zukunft

For an exam

Every success in your [forthcoming] exams
= Viel Erfolg bei deiner *or* der bevorstehenden Prüfung

All good wishes for your A levels/GCSEs
≈ Alles Gute zum Abitur

For a house move

Every happiness in your new home
= Viel Glück im neuen Heim

For an illness

Get well soon!
= Gute Besserung!

Best wishes for a speedy recovery
= Die besten Wünsche zur baldigen Genesung

Spoken greetings

Equivalents can only be approximate in some cases, and in others do not really exist.

Meeting someone

Hello or ***Hallo*** or ***Hullo [there]!, Hi!***
= Hallo! (*more colloquial*); Guten Tag! (*more formal*); Grüß Gott! (*South German*)

Good morning!
= Guten Morgen!

Good afternoon!
= *no equivalent; say* Guten Tag!

Good evening!
= Guten Abend!

How are you?
= Wie geht es Ihnen? (*formal*); Wie gehts? (*more colloquial*)

How do you do?
≈ (*when being introduced*) Freut mich!; Angenehm! (*dated*)

Saying goodbye

Goodbye!
= Auf Wiedersehen!

Bye now!
= Wiedersehen!; Tschüs! (*more colloquial*)

Look after yourself!, Take care!
= Machs gut!

Startmarkierung, *die* 6 (of town streets) rechtwinkliges Straßennetz; **~ pattern** rechtwinkliges Straßensystem 7 (Electronics) Gitter, *das*

griddle /ˈgrɪdl/ *n.* [*beheizbare*] *runde Eisenplatte zum Backen;* **~ cake** Crêpe, *die*

grid: ~iron *n.* 1 (Cookery) Bratrost, *der;* 2 (Amer.: football field) Footballfeld, *das;* **~lock** *n.* Verkehrsinfarkt, *der;* (fig.) völliger Stillstand; **save the city centre from the threat of ~lock** das Stadtzentrum vor dem Verkehrsinfarkt bewahren; **~locked** /ˈgrɪdlɒkt/ *adj.* total verstopft ‹*Straße, Stadt*›; (fig.) festgefahren; **the traffic is ~locked** der Verkehr ist völlig zusammengebrochen; **~ reference** *n.* Positionsangabe, *die*

grief /griːf/ *n.* 1 Kummer, *der* (**over, at** über + *Akk.,* um); (at loss of sb.) Trauer, *die* (**for** um); **she felt [real] ~:** es bekümmerte sie sehr; **be a [great] ~ to sb.** jmdm. [großen *od.* viel] Kummer machen; **come to ~** (fail) scheitern; **the car came to ~:** das Auto wurde beschädigt 2 **good** *or* **great ~!** guter *od.* großer Gott!

ˈgrief-stricken *adj.* untröstlich (**at** über + *Akk.*); **say sth. in a ~ voice** etw. mit vor Kummer erstickter Stimme sagen; **the ~ look on his face** sein gramvolles Gesicht

grievance /ˈgriːvəns/ *n.* (complaint) Beschwerde, *die;* Klage, *die;* (resentment, grudge) Groll, *der;* **air one's ~s** seine Beschwerden vorbringen/seinem Groll Luft machen; **I have no ~s against him personally** ich habe nichts gegen ihn persönlich

ˈgrievance procedure *n.* Schlichtungsverfahren, *das*

grieve /griːv/
A *v.t.* betrüben; bekümmern
B *v.i.* trauern (**for** um) ; **my heart ~s** *or* **I ~ for you** (sympathize) ich trauere mit dir; **~ over sb./sth.** jmdm./einer Sache nachtrauern

grievous /ˈgriːvəs/ *adj.* 1 (causing grief) schmerzlich 2 (flagrant, heinous) schwer; **~ wrong[s]** schreiendes Unrecht 3 (severe) schwer ‹*Verwundung, Krankheit*›; groß ‹*Schmerz*› 4 (bringing serious trouble) folgenschwer ‹*Irrtum, Dummheit*›; schwer ‹*Autounfall*›; **~ bodily harm** (Brit. Law) schwere Körperverletzung

grievously /ˈgriːvəslɪ/ *adv.* 1 (seriously) schwer ‹*verletzt, benachteiligt*› 2 (strongly, exceedingly) stark, ernstlich ‹*beunruhigt*›

griffin /ˈgrɪfɪn/ *n.* Greif, *der*

grill¹ /grɪl/
A *v.t.* 1 (cook) grillen 2 (fig.: question) in die Mangel nehmen (ugs.)
B *v.i.* grillen; **be ~ing in the hot sun** (fig.) sich von *od.* in der heißen Sonne braten lassen (ugs.)
C *n.* 1 (Gastr.) Grillgericht, *das;* **mixed ~:** Mixed Grill, *der;* gemischte Grillplatte 2 (restaurant) Grillrestaurant, *das* 3 (on cooker) Grill, *der* 4 ▸ **gridiron 1**

grille (**grill²**) *n.* 1 (grating) Gitter, *das* 2 (Motor Veh.) [Kühler]grill, *der*

grill: ~ lighter *n.* Grillanzünder, *der;* **~ room** ▸ **grill¹ C 2**

grim /grɪm/ *adj.* (stern) streng; grimmig ‹*Lächeln, Gesicht, Blick, Schweigen, Humor*›; Furcht erregend ‹*Krieger*›; (unrelenting, merciless, severe) erbittert ‹*Widerstand, Kampf, Schlacht*›; grimmig ‹*Entschlossenheit, Winter*›; eisern ‹*Vorsatz*›; (sinister, ghastly) grauenvoll ‹*Aufgabe, Anblick, Nachricht*›; grausig ‹*Wetter, Zeiten*›; trostlos ‹*Wetter, Winter, Tag, Landschaft, Aussichten*›; (mirthless) grimmig ‹*Humor, Spaß*›; **hold** *or* **hang** *or* **cling on [to sth.] like ~ death** sich mit aller Kraft [an etw. (*Dat.*)] festklammern; *see also* **reaper 2**

grimace /ˈgrɪməs, grɪˈmeɪs/
A *n.* Grimasse, *die;* **make a ~:** eine Grimasse machen *od.* schneiden
B *v.i.* Grimassen machen *od.* schneiden; **~ with pain/disgust** vor Schmerz/Ekel das Gesicht verziehen

grime /graɪm/ *n.* Schmutz, *der;* (soot) Ruß, *der*

grimly /ˈgrɪmlɪ/ *adv.* grimmig; eisern ‹*entschlossen sein, sich festhalten*›; verbissen, erbittert ‹*kämpfen*›

Grimm's Law /ˈgrɪmz lɔː/ *n.* (Ling.) germanische *od.* erste Lautverschiebung

grimy /ˈgraɪmɪ/ *adj.* schmutzig; schwarz (ugs.); **buildings ~ with soot** rußgeschwärzte Gebäude

grin /grɪn/
A *n.* Grinsen, *das*
B *v.i.,* **-nn-** grinsen; **~ at sb.** jmdn. angrinsen; **~ and bear it** gute Miene zum bösen Spiel machen; *see also* **Cheshire cat**
C *v.t.,* **-nn-: ~ approval/satisfaction** *etc.* beifällig/zufrieden *usw.* grinsen

grind /graɪnd/
A *v.t.,* **ground** /graʊnd/ 1 (reduce to small particles) **~ [up]** zermahlen; pulverisieren ‹*Metall*›; mahlen ‹*Kaffee, Pfeffer, Getreide*›; **~ sth. to dust/[a] powder/into flour** *etc.* etw. zu Staub/[einem] Pulver/zu Mehl *usw.* zermahlen 2 (sharpen) schleifen ‹*Schere, Messer*›; schärfen ‹*Klinge*›; (smooth, shape) schleifen ‹*Linse, Edelstein*›; **~ sth. to a sharp edge** etw. scharf schleifen; *see also* **axe A 1** 3 (rub harshly) zerquetschen; **~ a cigarette end into the ground** einen Zigarettenstummel austreten; **~ facts into pupils** Schülern Fakten einhämmern; **~ dirt into sth.** Schmutz in etw. (*Akk.*) treten; **~ one's teeth** mit den Zähnen knirschen 4 (produce by grinding) mahlen ‹*Mehl*› 5 (turn, cause to work) drehen ‹*Leier*›; **~ the coffee mill** den Kaffee mahlen; **~ a barrel organ** eine Drehorgel spielen 6 (fig.: oppress, harass) **~ the faces of the poor** (literary) die Armen [grausam] ausbeuten; **~ing poverty/tyranny** erdrückende Armut/Tyrannei
B *v.i.,* **ground** 1 **~ up the hill** sich bergauf schleppen 2 (rub gratingly) knirschen (**on** auf + *Dat.*); **bring sth. ~ing to a halt** etw. lahm legen; **~ to a halt, come to a ~ing halt** ‹*Fahrzeug:*› quietschend zum Stehen kommen; (fig.) ‹*Verkehr:*› zum Erliegen kommen; ‹*Maschine:*› stehen bleiben; ‹*Projekt:*› sich festfahren
C *n.* Plackerei, *die* (ugs.); **the daily ~** (coll.) der alltägliche Trott

(Phrasal verbs)

• **~ aˈway**
A *v.t.* abschleifen
B *v.i.* (fig.) hart arbeiten (**at** an + *Dat.*); (study) büffeln (ugs.) (**at** *Akk.*)

• **~ ˈdown** *v.t.* 1 zermahlen; pulverisieren ‹*Metall*›; mahlen ‹*Kaffee*› 2 (fig.: oppress) ‹*Tyrann, Regierung:*› unterdrücken; ‹*Armut, Verantwortung:*› erdrücken 3 (sharpen) abschleifen

• ~ **'in** *v.t.* **1** (Mech.) einschleifen ‹*Ventil*› **2** ~ **the dirt in** den Schmutz ein- *od.* festtreten; ~ **in facts** (fig. coll.) Fakten einhämmern

• ~ **'on** *v.i.* sich mühsam voranarbeiten

• ~ **'out** *v.t.* (fig.) sich (*Dat.*) abquälen ‹*Verse, Melodie, Aufsatz*›

grinder /'graɪndə(r)/ *n.* **1** Schleifmaschine, *die;* (pulverizing machine) Mühle, *die* **2** *in comb.* (person) ‹*Messer-, Scheren*›schleifer, *der* **3** (tooth) Mahlzahn, *der* **4** (millstone) Läufer, *der. See also* **organ-grinder**

'grindstone *n.* Schleifstein, *der;* **hold** *or* **keep one's/sb.'s nose to the** ~ (fig.) sich dahinter klemmen (ugs.)/dafür sorgen, dass jmd. sich dahinter klemmt (ugs.); **get back to the** ~: sich wieder an die Arbeit machen

gringo /'grɪŋgəʊ/ *n., pl.* ~**s** (often derog.) Gringo, *der* (abwertend)

grip /grɪp/

A *n.* **1** (firm hold) Halt, *der;* (fig.: power) Umklammerung, *die;* **hold sth. with a firm** ~: etw. mit festem Griff halten; **have a** ~ **on sth.** etw. festhalten; **loosen one's** ~: loslassen; **take a** ~: festhalten (**on** *Akk.*); **get** *or* **take a** ~ **on oneself** (fig.) sich zusammenreißen (ugs.); **gain a** ~: einen Halt finden; ‹*Reifen:*› greifen; **have/get a** ~ **on sth.** (fig.) etw. im Griff haben/in den Griff bekommen; **winter tightened its** ~: der Winter wurde noch strenger; **come** *or* **get to** ~**s with sth./sb.** (fig.) mit etw. fertig werden/sich (*Dat.*) jmdn. vorknöpfen *od.* vornehmen (ugs.); **be in the** ~ **of** (fig.) beherrscht werden von ‹*Angst, Leidenschaft, Furcht*›; heimgesucht werden von ‹*Naturkatastrophe, Armut, Krieg*›; **lose one's** ~ (fig.) nachlassen; **lose one's** ~ **on reality** (fig.) den Bezug zur Realität verlieren; **the Prime Minister is losing his** ~ (fig.) der Premierminister hat die Situation nicht mehr richtig im Griff **2** (strength or way of ~ping) Griff, *der* **3** (holding device) Klammer, *die;* (part which is held) Griff, *der;* (of oar) Holm, *der* **4** ▸**hairgrip** **5** (bag) Reisetasche, *die*

B *v.t.,* **-pp-** festhalten; packen; ‹*Reifen:*› greifen; (fig.) ergreifen; fesseln ‹*Publikum, Aufmerksamkeit*›; ~ **sb.'s collar/hand** *or* **sb. by the collar/hand** jmdn. am Kragen packen/sich an jmds. Hand (*Akk.*) klammern; ~ **sb.'s imagination** (fig.) jmdn. fesseln

C *v.i.,* **-pp-** ‹*Räder, Bremsen usw.:*› greifen

gripe /graɪp/

A *n.* **1** (coll.: complaint) Meckern, *das* (ugs. abwertend); **one more** ~ **about my driving ...:** noch ein Wort über meinen Fahrstil ...; **his favourite** ~ **is ...:** am liebsten schimpft er über (+ *Akk.*) ...; **have a good** ~ **about sth./at sb.** sich über etw. (*Akk.*) ausschimpfen/jmdn. tüchtig ausschimpfen **2** *in pl.* (colic) **get/have the** ~**s** Bauchschmerzen *od.* (ugs.) Bauchweh bekommen/haben

B *v.i.* (coll.) meckern (ugs. abwertend) (**about** über + *Akk.*)

gripping /'grɪpɪŋ/ *adj.* (fig.) packend

grisly /'grɪzlɪ/ *adj.* grausig

Grisons /'gri:zɔ̃/ *pr. n.* Graubünden (*das*)

grist /grɪst/ *n.* **1** Mahlgut, *das;* (Brewing) Malzschrot, *der od. das* **2** (fig.) **it's all** ~ **to the/sb.'s mill** man kann aus allem etwas machen/jmd. versteht es, aus allem etwas zu machen

gristle /'grɪsl/ *n.* Knorpel, *der*

gristly /'grɪslɪ/ *adj.* knorp[e]lig

grit /grɪt/

A *n.* **1** Sand, *der* **2** ▸**gritstone** **3** (coll.: courage, endurance) Schneid, *der* (ugs.)

B *v.t.,* **-tt-** **1** streuen ‹*vereiste Straßen*› **2** ~ **one's teeth** die Zähne zusammenbeißen (ugs.)

grits /grɪts/ *n. pl.* **1** (oats) geschälte Haferkörner **2** (oatmeal) Haferschrot, *der od. das*

'gritstone *n.* (Geol.) Grit, *der* (fachspr.); Sandstein, *der*

gritter [lorry] /'grɪtə(r)/ *n.* Streuwagen, *der*

gritty /'grɪtɪ/ *adj.* **1** (containing grit) sandig ‹*Weg, Boden, Butterbrot*›; (full of hard particles) grobkörnig ‹*Struktur, Sand*› **2** (fig.: courageous) **be** ~: Schneid haben

grizzle /'grɪzl/ *v.i.* (Brit. coll.) quengeln (ugs.)

grizzled /'grɪzld/ *adj.* grau ‹*Haar, Bart*›; grauhaarig ‹*Person*›; (partly grey) grau meliert ‹*Haar*›

grizzly /'grɪzlɪ/ *n.* ~ **[bear]** Grislybär, *der*

groan /grəʊn/

A *n.* (of person) Stöhnen, *das;* (of thing) Ächzen, *das* (fig.); **give a** ~ **of pain** vor Schmerz stöhnen; **a** ~ **rose from the crowd** die Menge stöhnte auf

B *v.i.* **1** ‹*Person:*› [auf]stöhnen (**at** bei); ‹*Tisch, Planken:*› ächzen (fig.); ~ **inwardly** innerlich aufstöhnen; **a** ~**ing board** (literary) ein reich gedeckter Tisch **2** (fig.: be oppressed) stöhnen

C *v.t.* stöhnen

groats /grəʊts/ *n. pl.* (hulled) geschälte [Hafer]körner; (hulled and crushed) [Hafer]grütze, *die*

grocer /'grəʊsə(r)/ *n.* Lebensmittelhändler, *der*/-händlerin, *die; see also* **baker**

grocery /'grəʊsərɪ/ *n.* **1** *in pl.* (goods) Lebensmittel *Pl.* **2** ~ **[store]** Lebensmittelgeschäft, *das* **3** (trade) Lebensmittelhandel, *der*

grog /grɒg/ *n.* Grog, *der;* (Austral. and NZ coll.) (beer) Bier, *das;* (spirits) Schnaps, *der* (ugs.)

groggily /'grɒgɪlɪ/ *adv.* benommen ‹*sprechen, gehen*›; auf unsicheren *od.* (ugs.) auf wackeligen Beinen ‹*gehen*›

groggy /'grɒgɪ/ *adj.* wackelig auf den Beinen (ugs.) *präd.;* groggy (ugs.) *präd.*

groin /grɔɪn/ *n.* **1** ▸ℹ **p. 951** (Anat.) Leistengegend, *die;* (euphem.: genitals) Weichteile *Pl.* (verhüll.) **2** (Archit.) Grat, *der* (fachspr.)

grommet /'grɒmɪt/ *n.* **1** (Naut.) Grummet, *das;* Grummetstropp, *der* **2** (washer) Durchführung, *die* **3** (in cap) Versteifungsring, *der*

groom /gru:m, grʊm/

A *n.* **1** (stable boy) Stallbursche, *der;* (stable girl) Stallgehilfin, *die* **2** (bride~) Bräutigam, *der* **3** (Brit.: officer of Royal Household) *Bediensteter des britischen Hofes*

B *v.t.* **1** striegeln ‹*Pferd*›; (smarten) pflegen ‹*Kleidung*›; ~ **oneself** sich zurechtmachen; **well/badly** ~**ed** gepflegt/ungepflegt **2** (fig.: prepare) ~ **sb. for/as sth.** jmdn. für/als etw. aufbauen; ~ **sb. for a career** jmdn. auf *od.* für eine Laufbahn vorbereiten

groove /gru:v/

A *n.* **1** (channel) Nut, *die* (bes. Technik); (of record) Rille, *die* **2** (fig.: routine) **get into a** ~ ‹*Arbeit:*› routinemäßig ablaufen; ‹*Person:*› zum Gewohnheitsmenschen werden; **be stuck in a** ~: aus dem Trott nicht mehr herauskommen **3** **be in the** ~ (dated coll.) gut drauf sein (salopp); (perform excellently) groß in Form sein (ugs.); (be appreciative) ‹*Publikum:*› begeistert mitgehen

B *v.t.* nuten

groovy /'gru:vɪ/ *adj.* (coll.) (excellent, very good) klasse (ugs.); **be** ~ (Jazz) in Form sein (ugs.); gut drauf sein (salopp)

grope /grəʊp/

A *v.i.* tasten (**for** nach); ~ **for the right word/truth** nach dem richtigen Wort/der Wahrheit suchen; ~ **after sth.** (fig.) etw. herauszufinden versuchen

B *v.t.* **1** ~ **one's way [along]** sich [entlang]tasten; (fig.) [sich durch]lavieren (ugs. abwertend) **2** (coll.: caress) ~ **sb.** jmdn. betatschen (ugs. abwertend)

grosgrain /'grəʊgreɪn/ *n.* (Textiles) grob gerippter Stoff; Grosgrain, *der* (fachspr.)

gros point /'grəʊ pwæ̃/ *n.* **1** (embroidery) Kreuzstichstickerei, *die* **2** (stitch) Kreuzstich, *der*

gross¹ /grəʊs/

A *adj.* **1** (flagrant) grob ‹*Fahrlässigkeit, Fehler, Irrtum*›; übel ‹*Laster, Beleidigung*›; schwer ‹*Verbrechen, Beleidigung*›; schreiend ‹*Ungerechtigkeit*› **2** (obese) fett (abwertend); (luxuriant) üppig, dicht ‹*Vegetation*› **3** (coarse, rude) ordinär (abwertend); (coll.: disgusting) **that's really** ~! das ist wirklich ekelhaft! **4** (total) Brutto-; Gesamt‹*umsatz, -absatz*›; **earn £20,000** ~: 20 000 Pfund brutto verdienen; ~ **national product** Bruttosozialprodukt, *das* **5** (dull, not delicate) grob ‹*Person, Geschmack*› **6** (coarse) deftig ‹*Mahlzeit, Essen*›

B *v.t.* **1** (yield) [insgesamt] einbringen ‹*Geld*› **2** ~ **up** einbeziehen; ~**ed up** Brutto‹*dividende, -rendite*›

Phrasal verb

• ~ **'out** *v.t.* (Amer. sl.) schocken (ugs.)

gross² *n., pl. same* Gros, *das;* **by the** ~: en gros

grossly /'grəʊslɪ/ *adv.* **1** (flagrantly) äußerst; grob ‹*übertreiben*›; schwer ‹*beleidigen*› **2** (coarsely, rudely) ordinär ‹*sich benehmen, sprechen*›; ohne Manieren ‹*essen*›

grotesque /grəʊ'tesk/

A *adj.* grotesk

B *n.* **1** (decoration) Groteske, *die* **2** (Printing) Grotesk, *die*

grotesquely /grəʊ'tesklɪ/ *adv.* grotesk

grotto /'grɒtəʊ/ *n., pl.* ~**es** *or* ~**s** Grotte, *die*

grotty /'grɒtɪ/ *adj.* (Brit. coll.) mies (ugs.); heruntergekommen ‹*Haus, Gegend*›; (dirty) dreckig (ugs.); **the bathroom looks** ~: das Bad ist total versifft (salopp)

grouch /graʊtʃ/ (coll.)

A *v.i.* schimpfen; mosern (ugs.)

B *n.* **1** (person) Miesepeter, *der* (ugs. abwertend) **2** (cause) Ärger, *der;* **have a** ~ **against sb.** auf jmdn. sauer sein (salopp)

grouchy /'graʊtʃɪ/ *adj.* (coll.) griesgrämig

ground¹ /graʊnd/

A *n.* **1** Boden, *der;* **work above/below** ~: über/unter der Erde arbeiten; **1,000 feet above the** ~: 1000 Fuß über dem Erdboden; **deep under the** ~: tief unter der Erde; **uneven, hilly** ~: unebenes, hügeliges Gelände; **on high** ~: in höheren Lagen; **cover much** ~ (distance) eine weite Strecke zurücklegen

2 (fig.) **cut the** ~ **from under sb.'s feet** jmdm. den Wind aus den Segeln nehmen (ugs.); **be** *or* **suit sb. down to the** ~ (coll.) genau das Richtige für jmdn. sein; **Friday suits me down to the** ~: Freitag passt mir prima (ugs.); **that's Billy down to the** ~ (coll.) das ist typisch Billy (ugs.); **fall to the** ~: zunichte werden; **be dashed to the** ~: [mit einem Schlag] zunichte werden; **from the** ~ **up** (coll.) (thoroughly) von der Pike auf (ugs.) ‹*lernen*›; (from scratch) ganz von vorne ‹*anfangen*›; **get off the** ~ (coll.) konkrete Gestalt annehmen; **get sth. off the** ~ (coll.) etw. in die Tat umsetzen; **hit the** ~ **running** (coll.) voll durchstarten (ugs.); **go to** ~ ‹*Fuchs usw.:*› im Bau verschwinden; ‹*Person:*› untertauchen; **run to** ~: aufstöbern; **run sb./oneself into the** ~ (coll.) jmdn./sich kaputtmachen (ugs.); **run a car into the** ~ (coll.) ein Auto so lange fahren, bis es schrottreif ist; **on the** ~ (in practice) an Ort und Stelle; **be/not be on firm** *or* **solid** ~: sich auf sicherem/schwankendem Boden bewegen; **thin/thick on the** ~: dünn/dicht gesät; **break fresh** *or* **new** ~: Neuland betreten; **cover much** *or* **a lot of** ~: weit vorankommen; **cover the** ~ ‹*Student:*› den Stoff erarbeiten; ‹*Buch:*› eine umfassende Darstellung geben; **cover the same** ~ ‹*Vorträge, Buch:*› denselben Stoff behandeln; **gain** *or* **make** ~: Boden gewinnen (**on** gegenüber); (become established) Fuß fassen; **give** *or* **lose** ~: an Boden verlieren; **hold** *or* **keep** *or* **stand one's** ~: nicht nachgeben; **shift one's** ~: umschwenken; *see also* **foot A 1**

3 (special area) Gelände, *das;* **[sports]** ~: Sportplatz, *der;* **[cricket]** ~: Cricketfeld, *das; see also* **common ground**; **forbidden B**

4 *in pl.* (attached to house) Anlage, *die*

5 (Brit.: floor) Boden, *der*

6 (motive, reason) Grund, *der;* **on the** ~**[s] of, on** ~**s of** aufgrund (+ *Gen.*); (giving as one's reason) unter Berufung auf (+ *Akk.*); **on the** ~**s that ...:** unter Berufung auf die Tatsache, dass ...; **on health/religious** *etc.* ~**s** aus gesundheitlichen/religiösen *usw.* Gründen; **on what** ~**s do you suspect him?** mit welcher Begründung verdächtigen Sie ihn?; **the** ~**s for divorce are ...:** als Scheidungsgrund gilt ...; **there are no** ~**s for this assumption** es besteht kein Grund zu dieser Annahme; **have/give [no]** ~**s for sth.** [k]einen Grund für etw. haben/[keine] Gründe für etw. angeben; **have no** ~**s for sth./to do sth.** keinen Grund für etw. haben/keinen Grund haben, etw. zu tun; **have no** ~**s for complaint** keinen Grund zur Klage haben; **have good** ~**s for doing sth.** allen Grund haben, etw. zu tun

7 (in embroidery, painting, etc.) Grund, *der;* **on a white** ~: auf weißem Grund

8 *in pl.* (sediment) ~**s** Satz, *der;* (of coffee) Kaffeesatz, *der*

9 (Electr.) Erde, *die;* **~ed plug** (Amer.) Schukostecker, *der*
10 (bottom of sea) Grund, *der*
B *v.t.* **1** (Aeronaut.) am Boden festhalten; (prevent from flying) nicht fliegen lassen ‹*Piloten*›; **be ~ed by bad weather/owing to a defect** *etc.* wegen schlechten Wetters/eines Defekts *usw.* nicht starten können
2 (cause to run ashore) auf Grund setzen ‹*Schiff*›; **be ~ed** auf Grund gelaufen sein
3 (base, establish) gründen (**on** auf + *Akk.*); **be ~ed on** gründen auf (+ *Dat.*); **well ~ed** wohl begründet
4 (instruct) **~ sb. [in the essentials]** jmdn. in die Anfangsgründe einführen; **be well/not well ~ed in a subject** über gute/keine guten Grundkenntnisse auf einem Gebiet verfügen
5 (Electr.) erden
6 (coll.: confine to home) **be ~ed** Stubenarrest *od.* Hausarrest haben
C *v.i.* (run ashore) ‹*Schiff:*› auf Grund laufen

ground²
A ▸**grind A, B**
B *adj.* gemahlen ‹*Kaffee, Getreide*›; pulverisiert ‹*Holz, Gummi*›; **~ meat** (Amer.) Hackfleisch, *das;* **~ coffee** Kaffeepulver, *das;* **fine-/coarse-/medium-~ coffee** fein/grob/mittelfein gemahlener Kaffee

ground: ~bait *n.* Grundköder, *der;* **~ bass** /ˈgraʊnd beɪs/ *n.* (Mus.) Basso ostinato, *der;* Ground, *der;* **~breaking** *adj.* bahnbrechend; **~ control** *n.* (Aeronaut.) **1** (personnel, equipment, etc.) Flugsicherungskontrolldienst, *der;* **2** (directing) **~ control approach** GCA-Verfahren, *das;* **~ crew** *n.* (Aeronaut.) Bodenpersonal, *das;* **~ effect** *n.* Bodeneffekt, *der* (Technik); **~ ˈfloor** Erdgeschoss, *das;* **~ forces** *n. pl.* Bodentruppen *Pl.;* **~ frost** *n.* Bodenfrost, *der;* **~ ˈglass** *n.* Mattglas, *das;* **~hog** *n.* (Amer.) Waldmurmeltier, *das*

grounding /ˈgraʊndɪŋ/ *n.* **1** Grundkenntnisse *Pl.;* Grundwissen, *das* **2** (Aeronaut.) **the ~ of the plane was ordered** dem Flugzeug wurde Startverbot erteilt

ground: ~ ivy *n.* Gundelrebe, *die;* **~keeper** (Amer.) ▸**groundsman**

groundless /ˈgraʊndlɪs/ *adj.* unbegründet; **these reports/rumours/statements are ~:** diese Berichte/Gerüchte/Aussagen entbehren jeder Grundlage

ground: ~ level *n.* **above/below ~ level** oberhalb/unterhalb der ebenen Erde; **on** *or* **at ~ level** ebenerdig; ‹*Wohnung, Fenster*› zu ebener Erde; **~nut** *n.* (Brit.) Erdnuss, *die;* **~ plan** *n.* Grundriss, *der;* (fig.) Grundstruktur, *die;* **~ rent** *n.* Grundrente, *die;* **~ ˈrice** *n.* Reismehl, *das;* **~ rule** *n.* **1** (Sport) Platzregel, *die;* **2** (basic principle) Grundregel, *die*

groundsel /ˈgraʊnsl/ *n.* (Bot.) Greiskraut, *das*

ground: ~sheet *n.* Bodenplane, *die;* **~sman** /ˈgraʊndzmən/ *n., pl.* **~smen** /ˈgraʊndzmən/ (Sport) Platzwart, *der;* **~ speed** *n.* (Aeronaut.) Grundgeschwindigkeit, *die;* **~ squirrel** *n.* Erdhörnchen, *das;* **~ staff** *n.* (Aeronaut.) Bodenpersonal, *das;* **~ station** *n.* (Astronaut., Communications) Bodenstation, *die;* **~swell** *n.* schwere Dünung; **the ~swell of public opinion** (fig.) der wachsende Druck der öffentlichen Meinung; **~ traffic** *n.* Bodenverkehr, *der;* **~ water** *n.* Grundwasser, *das;* **~work** *n.* Vorarbeiten *Pl.;* (fig.) Grundlage, *die;* **do the ~work for sth.** die Vorarbeiten für etw. machen; **~ ˈzero** *n.* [Boden]nullpunkt, *der*

group /gruːp/
A *n.* **1** Gruppe, *die; attrib.* Gruppen‹*verhalten, -dynamik, -bewusstsein*›; **~ of houses/trees/islands** Häuser-/Baum-/Inselgruppe, *die;* **the Germanic ~ of languages** die germanische Sprachfamilie **2** (Commerc.) [Unternehmens]gruppe, *die* **3** (Polit.) Gruppe, *die;* (Parl.) Fraktion, *die* **4** ▸**pop group** **5** (Math., Chem.) Gruppe, *die*
B *v.t.* gruppieren; **~ books according to their subjects** Bücher nach ihrer Thematik ordnen; **~ flowers together** Blumen zusammenstellen; **you can't ~ all criminals together** man kann nicht alle Verbrecher in einen Topf werfen (ugs.); **be ~ed into classes** Klassen zugeordnet werden

group: ~ booking *n.* Gruppenbuchung, *die;* **~ captain** *n.* (Air Force) Oberst der Luftwaffe; **~ discussion** *n.* Gruppendiskussion, *die*

groupie /ˈgruːpɪ/ *n.* (coll.) Groupie, *das*

grouping /ˈgruːpɪŋ/ *n.* (placing in groups) Gruppierung, *die;* (classification) Klassifizierung, *die;* **blood ~:** Bestimmung der Blutgruppe; ([belonging to a] blood group) Blutgruppe[nzugehörigkeit], *die*

group: ~ practice *n.* Gemeinschaftspraxis, *die;* **~ sex** *n.* Gruppensex, *der;* **~ therapy** *n.* Gruppentherapie, *die;* **~ware** *n., no pl.* (Computing) Groupware, *die*

grouse¹ /graʊs/ *n.* **1** *pl. same* Raufußhuhn, *das;* **[red] ~** (Brit.) Schottisches Moorschneehuhn **2** *no pl.* (as food) Waldhuhn, *das;* schottisches Moorhuhn

grouse² (coll.)
A *v.i.* meckern (ugs.), mosern (ugs.) (**about** über + *Akk.*)
B *n.* Meckerei, *die* (ugs.); Moserei, *die* (ugs.); **my only ~ is that ...:** mir stinkt nur, dass ... (salopp)

grouser /ˈgraʊsə(r)/ *n.* (coll.) Meckerer, *der;* Meckerfritze, *der*/-liese, *die* (ugs.)

ˈgrouse-shooting *n.* Jagd auf Moorhühner

grout /graʊt/
A *n.* Mörtelschlamm, *der*
B *v.t.* verstreichen ‹*Fugen, Löcher*›; [aus]fugen ‹*Mauer, Fliesen*›

grouting /ˈgraʊtɪŋ/ *n., no pl.* **1** (action) Verspachteln, *das* **2** (material) Spachtelmasse, *die*

grove /grəʊv/ *n.* Wäldchen, *das;* Hain, *der* (dichter. veralt.)

grovel /ˈgrɒvl/ *v.i.,* (Brit.) **-ll-** **1** (lie prone) auf dem Bauch liegen; (go down on one's knees) sich auf die Knie werfen; **be ~ling on the floor** auf dem Fußboden kriechen **2** (fig.: be subservient) katzbuckeln (abwertend); (in apology) zu Kreuze kriechen (abwertend) (**before** vor + *Dat.*)

grovelling (*Amer.:* **groveling**) /ˈgrɒvəlɪŋ/ *adj.* kriechend; (fig.) kriecherisch (abwertend)

grow /grəʊ/
A *v.i.,* **grew** /gruː/, **grown** /grəʊn/ **1** (sprout) ‹*Pflanze:*› wachsen; **leaves are beginning to ~ on the trees** an den Bäumen bilden sich allmählich Blätter **2** (in size etc.) wachsen; **haven't you ~n!** du bist aber gewachsen *od.* groß geworden!; **~ing lad** Junge, der noch im Wachsen ist *od.* noch wächst; **it just ~ed** (coll.) es hat sich einfach so entwickelt **3** (develop, expand) wachsen; (increase numerically) ‹*Bevölkerung:*› zunehmen, wachsen; **~ out of** *or* **from sth.** sich aus etw. entwickeln; (from sth. abstract) aus etw. erwachsen; von etw. herrühren; ‹*Situation, Krieg usw.:*› die Folge von etw. sein; ‹*Plan:*› aus etw. erwachsen; **~ in** zunehmen *od.* gewinnen an (+ *Dat.*) ‹*Größe, Bedeutung, Autorität, Ansehen, Weisheit*›; gewinnen an (+ *Dat.*) ‹*Popularität, Format*› **4** (become) werden; **~ used to sth./sb.** sich an etw./jmdn. gewöhnen; **~ like sb.** jmdm. ähnlich werden; **~ apart** (fig.) sich auseinander leben; **~ away from sb.** (fig.) sich jmdm. entfremden; **~ to be sth.** allmählich etw. werden; **he grew to be a man** er wuchs zum Manne heran (geh.); **~ to love/hate** *etc.* **sb./sth.** jmdn./etw. lieben/hassen *usw.* lernen; **~ to like sb./sth.** nach und nach Gefallen an jmdm./etw. finden; **~ old [gracefully]** [mit Würde] alt werden. *See also* **growing; grown B**
B *v.t.,* **grew, grown** **1** (cultivate) (on a small scale) ziehen; (on a large scale) anpflanzen; züchten ‹*Blumen*›; (produce) züchten ‹*Kristalle*› **2** **~ one's hair [to a great length]** sich (*Dat.*) die Haare [sehr lang] wachsen lassen; **~ a beard** sich (*Dat.*) einen Bart wachsen lassen; **the lizard will ~ a new tail** der Eidechse wächst ein neuer Schwanz

Phrasal verbs

- **~ into** *v.t.* **1** (become) werden zu **2** (become big enough for) hineinwachsen in (+ *Akk.*) ‹*Kleidungsstück*›
- **~ on** *v.t.* **it ~s on you** man findet mit der Zeit Geschmack *od.* Gefallen daran; **he grew on us** wir haben ihn schätzen gelernt
- **~ ˈout of** *v.t.* **1** (become too big for) herauswachsen aus ‹*Kleidungsstück*› **2** (lose in the course of time) ablegen ‹*Angewohnheit*›; entwachsen (+ *Dat.*) ‹*Kindereien*›; überwinden ‹*Zustand*›; *see also* **~ A 3**
- **~ ˈup** *v.i.* **1** (spend early years) aufwachsen; (become adult) erwachsen werden; **she grew up to be a gifted pianist** sie wuchs zu einer begabten Pianistin heran; **what do you want to be** *or* **do when you ~ up?** was willst du denn mal werden, wenn du groß bist? **2** (fig.: behave more maturely) erwachsen werden; **~ up!** werde endlich erwachsen! **3** (develop) ‹*Freundschaft, Feindschaft, Streit:*› sich entwickeln; ‹*Legende:*› entstehen, sich bilden; ‹*Tradition, Brauch:*› sich herausbilden
- **~ ˈup into** *v.t.* werden *od.* sich entwickeln zu

ˈgrowbag *n.* (Brit.) Pflanzbeutel, *der*

grower /ˈgrəʊə(r)/ *n.* **1** *usu. in comb.* (person) Produzent, *der*/Produzentin, *die;* **fruit/apple/vegetable ~:** Obst-/Apfel-/Gemüsebauer, *der;* **coffee/tobacco ~:** Kaffee-/Tabakpflanzer, *der* **2** (plant) **be a slow/free ~:** langsam/schnell wachsen; eine langsam/schnell wachsende Pflanze sein

growing /ˈgrəʊɪŋ/
A *adj.* wachsend; sich verdichtend ‹*Anzeichen*›; immer umfangreicher werdend ‹*Sachgebiet*›; sich immer mehr verbreitend ‹*Praktik*›
B *n.* Anbau, *der; attrib.* **~ season** Vegetationsperiode, *die;* **good/bad ~ weather** dem Pflanzenwachstum förderliches/abträgliches Wetter

ˈgrowing pains *n. pl.* Wachstumsschmerzen *Pl.;* (fig.) Anfangsschwierigkeiten *Pl.*

growl /graʊl/
A *n.* (of dog, lion) Knurren, *das;* (of bear) Brummen, *das;* **a ~ of disapproval** ein missbilligendes Knurren
B *v.i.* **1** ‹*Hund, Löwe:*› knurren; ‹*Bär:*› [böse] brummen; **~ at sb.** jmdn. anknurren/anbrummen **2** (murmur angrily) knurren
C *v.t.* **~ [out]** knurren

grown /grəʊn/
A ▸**grow**
B *adj.* erwachsen; **fully ~:** ausgewachsen

ˈgrown-up
A *n.* Erwachsene, *der/die*
B *adj.* erwachsen; **~ books/clothes** Bücher/Kleider für Erwachsene; **act in a ~ way** sich wie ein Erwachsener verhalten

growth /grəʊθ/ *n.* **1** (of industry, economy, population) Wachstum, *das* (**of, in** *Gen.*); (of interest, illiteracy) Zunahme, *die* (**of, in** *Gen.*); *attrib.* Wachstums‹*hormon, -rate*› **2** (growing of organisms, crystals) Wachstum, *das;* (cultivation) Anbau, *der* **3** (amount grown) Wachstum, *das* **4** (thing grown) Vegetation, *die;* Pflanzenwuchs, *der;* (in classification of vineyards) Lage, *die;* **a thick ~ of weeds** dicht wucherndes Unkraut; **cut away the old ~:** die alten Triebe ab- *od.* wegschneiden; **a four days' ~ [of beard]** ein vier Tage alter Bart **5** (Med.) Geschwulst, *die;* Gewächs, *das*

growth: ~ area *n.* Wachstumsbereich, *der;* **~ hormone** *n.* Wachstumshormon, *das;* **~ ˈindustry** *n.* Wachstumsindustrie, *die;* **~ rate** *n.* Wachstumsrate, *die;* **~ ring** *n.* Wachstumsring, *der;* **~ stock** *n.* Wachstumsaktien *Pl.*

groyne /grɔɪn/ *n.* Buhne, *die*

grub /grʌb/
A *n.* **1** Larve, *die;* (maggot) Made, *die;* (ugs.) Wurm, *der;* (caterpillar) Raupe, *die;* (larva of cockchafer etc.) Engerling, *der* **2** (coll.: food) Futterage, *die* (ugs.); Fressen, *das* (salopp); (victuals) Fressalien *Pl.* (ugs.); **~['s] up!** ran an die Futterkrippe! (ugs.); **lovely ~!** ein Spitzenfraß! (salopp); **pub ~** (Brit.) Kneipenessen, *das* (ugs.)
B *v.i.,* **-bb-** **1** (dig) wühlen, buddeln (ugs.) (**for** nach) **2** (search) (in bag, cupboard, etc.) wühlen, kramen (**for** nach); **~ about** [herum]wühlen; [herum]kramen; **~ about for sth.** nach etw. wühlen *od.* kramen
C *v.t.,* **-bb-** **1** (dig) umgraben ‹*Land, Boden*›; ‹*Tier:*› aufwühlen; (remove roots or stumps from) roden ‹*Land*›; (extract by digging) ausgraben; (uproot) [aus]roden ‹*Buschwerk, Baum*› **2** (fig.)

g

barely **∼bing a subsistence** gerade eben in der Lage zu existieren

Phrasal verbs

- **∼ 'out** *v.t.* roden ‹*Land*›; [aus]roden ‹*Wurzelstock*›;
- **∼ 'up** *v.t.* ausgraben; [aus]jäten ‹*Unkraut*›; [aus]roden ‹*Wurzelstock*›

grubby /ˈgrʌbɪ/ *adj.* (dirty) schmudd[e]lig (ugs. abwertend); (slovenly) schlampig (ugs. abwertend)

'grub screw *n.* (Mech. Engin.) Gewindestift, *der*

grudge /grʌdʒ/

A *v.t.* **∼ sb. sth.** jmdm. etw. missgönnen *od.* nicht gönnen; **I don't ∼ him his success** ich gönne ihm seinen Erfolg; **∼ every penny that is taken in tax** der Steuer jeden Cent missgönnen; **∼ doing sth.** (be unwilling to do sth.) nicht bereit sein, etw. zu tun; (do sth. reluctantly) etw. ungern tun; **I ∼ paying £20 for this** es geht mir gegen den Strich, dafür 20 Pfund zu zahlen (ugs.)

B *n.* Groll, *der;* **have** *or* **hold a ∼ against sb.** einen Groll *od.* (ugs.) Hass auf jmdn. haben; jmdm. grollen; **I owe him a ∼:** den habe ich gefressen (ugs.); *see also* **bear² A 8**

grudging /ˈgrʌdʒɪŋ/ *adj.* widerwillig ‹*Lob, Bewunderung, Unterstützung*›; widerwillig gewährt ‹*Zuschuss*›; **be ∼ in one's approval** nur widerwillig zustimmen

grudgingly /ˈgrʌdʒɪŋlɪ/ *adv.* widerwillig

gruel /ˈgruːəl/ *n.* [Hafer]schleim, *der;* Schleimsuppe, *die*

gruelling (*Amer.:* **grueling**) /ˈgruːəlɪŋ/*adj.* aufreibend; zermürbend; [äußerst] strapaziös ‹*Reise, Marsch*›; mörderisch (ugs.) ‹*Tempo, Rennen*›

gruesome /ˈgruːsəm/ *adj.*, **gruesomely** /ˈgruːsəmlɪ/ *adv.* grausig; schaurig

gruff /grʌf/ *adj.* barsch; schroff; ruppig, bärbeißig ‹*Benehmen, Wesen*›; (low-pitched, hoarse) rau ‹*Stimme, Lachen*›

gruffly /ˈgrʌflɪ/ *adj.* barsch; schroff; (with a gruff voice) mit rauer Stimme

grumble /ˈgrʌmbl/

A *v.i.* **1** murren; **∼ at sb. about** *or* **over sth.** sich bei jmdm. über etw. (*Akk.*) *od.* wegen etw. beklagen; **put up with sth. without grumbling** etw. ohne Murren ertragen **2** (rumble) ‹[*Geschütz*]*donner:*› grollen

B *n.* **1** (act) Murren, *das;* (complaint) Klage, *die;* **without a ∼:** ohne Murren; **she's always full of ∼s** sie hat immer etwas zu murren; **my chief ∼ is that ...:** vor allem missfällt mir, dass ...; am meisten stört mich, dass ... **2** (rumble of thunder, cannon) Grollen, *das*

grumbler /ˈgrʌmblə(r)/ *n.* Querulant, *der*/Querulantin, *die*

grumbling a'ppendix *n.* (Med.) Blinddarmreizung, *die*

grumpily /ˈgrʌmpɪlɪ/ *adv.* unleidlich; grantig (ugs.)

grumpiness /ˈgrʌmpɪnɪs/ *n.*, *no pl.* Unleidlichkeit, *die;* Grantigkeit, *die* (ugs.)

grumpy /ˈgrʌmpɪ/ *adj.* unleidlich; grantig (ugs.)

grunge /grʌndʒ/ *n.*, *no. pl.* **1** (coll.: grime) Dreck, *der* (ugs.); Siff, *der* (salopp) **2** (music) Grunge, *der* **3** (fashion) Grunge[look], *der*/-[stil], *der*

grunt /grʌnt/

A *n.* Grunzen, *das;* **give a ∼:** grunzen

B *v.i.* grunzen; **he only ∼ed in answer** er gab nur ein Grunzen zur Antwort

C *v.t.* **∼ [out]** grunzen

gruyère /ˈgruːjeə(r)/ *n.* Gruyère[käse], *der;* Greyerzer [Käse], *der*

gryphon /ˈgrɪfn/ ▸ **griffin**

GSOH *abbr.* (in advertisements) = **good sense of humour** Humor, *der;* **outgoing, friendly, GSOH:** kontaktfreudig, freundlich, humorvoll

'G-string *n.* **1** (Mus.) G-Saite, *die* **2** (garment) (of showgirl) ≈ Cachesexe, *das;* G-String, *die od. der*

'G-suit *n.* (Aeronaut.) Anti-g-Anzug, *der*

Gt. *abbr.* = **Great** Gr.

guacamole /gwɑːkəˈməʊleɪ/ *n.*, *no pl.* Guacamole, *die*

guano /ˈgwɑːnəʊ/ *n.*, *pl.* **∼s** Guano, *der*

guarantee /gærənˈtiː/

A *v.t.* **1** garantieren; garantieren für, bürgen für ‹*Echtheit usw.*›; **∼ sth. to sb.** jmdm. etw. zusichern **2** (by formal agreement) garantieren für; [eine] Garantie geben auf (+ *Akk.*); **∼ sth. for a year** auf etw. (*Akk.*) ein Jahr Garantie geben; **is the clock ∼d?** hat die Uhr Garantie?; gibt es auf die Uhr Garantie?; **the clock is ∼d for a year** die Uhr hat ein Jahr Garantie; **∼ sb. regular employment** jmdm. eine Beschäftigungsgarantie geben; **∼d wage** Garantielohn, *der;* **∼d genuine** *etc.* garantiert echt *usw.* **3** (Law: take responsibility for) bürgen für ‹*Darlehen, Schuld usw.*› **4** (promise) garantieren (ugs.); (ensure) bürgen für ‹*Qualität*›; garantieren ‹*Erfolg*›; **be ∼d to do sth.** etw. garantiert tun; **there's no ∼ing he'll get a work permit** es ist gar nicht gesagt, dass er eine Arbeitserlaubnis kriegt

B *n.* **1** (Commerc. etc.) Garantie, *die;* (document) Garantieschein, *der;* (Law) Bürgschaft, *die;* **there's a year's ∼ on this radio, this radio has** *or* **carries a year's ∼:** auf dieses Radio gibt es *od.* dieses Radio hat ein Jahr Garantie; **is it still under ∼?** ist noch Garantie darauf?; **come under** *or* **be covered by the ∼:** unter die Garantie fallen **2** (guarantor) Garant, *der;* (Law) Bürge, *der*/Bürgin, *die* **3** (promise) Garantie, *die* (ugs.); **give sb. a ∼ that ...:** jmdm. garantieren, dass ...; **you have my ∼:** das garantiere ich dir; **be a ∼ of sth.** (ensure) eine Garantie für etw. sein

guarantor /ˈgærəntə(r), gærənˈtɔː(r)/ *n.* Bürge, *der*/Bürgin, *die;* **be** *or* **stand ∼ for sb., be sb.'s ∼:** eine Bürgschaft für jmdn. übernehmen; für jmdn. bürgen

guaranty /ˈgærəntɪ/ *n.* **1** (undertaking to pay another's debt) Bürgschaft, *die* **2** (basis of security) Garantie, *die;* Gewähr, *die*

guard /gɑːd/

A *n.* ▸ ℹ **p. 1260** **1** (Mil.: **∼sman**) Wachtposten, *der* **2** *no pl.* (Mil.: group of soldiers) Wache, *die;* Wachmannschaft, *die;* **∼ of honour** Ehrenwache, *die;* Ehrengarde, *die;* **change ∼:** Wachablösung machen; **relieve ∼:** die Wache ablösen; **mount ∼:** Wache beziehen; *see also* **old guard** **3** **Guards** (Brit. Mil.: household troops) Garderegiment, *das;* Garde, *die; see also* **Horse Guards**; **Life Guards** **4** (watch; also Mil.) Wache, *die;* **be on ∼:** Wache haben; **keep** *or* **stand ∼:** Wache halten *od.* stehen; **keep** *or* **mount** *or* **stand ∼ over sth./sb.** etw./jmdn. bewachen; **be on [one's] ∼ [against sb./sth.]** (lit. or fig.) [vor jmdm./etw.] auf der Hut sein; sich [vor jmdm./etw.] hüten; **be off [one's] ∼** (fig.) nicht auf der Hut sein; **be caught** *or* **taken off [one's] ∼ [by sth.]** (fig.) [von etw.] überrascht werden; **put sb. on [his/her] ∼:** jmdn. misstrauisch machen; **put** *or* **throw sb. off [his/her] ∼:** jmdn. überrumpeln (ugs.); **under ∼:** unter Bewachung; **be [kept/held] under ∼:** bewacht werden; unter Bewachung stehen; **keep** *or* **hold/put under ∼:** bewachen/unter Bewachung stellen; **put a ∼ on sb./sth.** jmdn./etw. bewachen lassen **5** (Brit. Railw.) [Zug]schaffner, *der*/-schaffnerin, *die* **6** (Amer.: prison warder) [Gefängnis]wärter, *der*/-wärterin, *die* **7** (safety device) Schutz, *der;* Schutzvorrichtung, *die;* (worn on body) Schutz, *der;* Schützer, *der;* (crossbar on sword) Parierstange, *die;* (of rapier) Stichblatt, *das;* (Fencing: of weapon) Glocke, *die* **8** (posture) (Boxing, Fencing) Deckung, *die;* (Cricket) Abwehrhaltung, *die;* **on ∼!** (Fencing) en garde!; **take ∼:** in Verteidigungsstellung gehen; **drop** *or* **lower one's ∼:** die Deckung fallen lassen; (fig.) seine Reserve aufgeben; **have one's ∼ down** (fig.) sich ungezwungen verhalten *od.* bewegen. *See also* **security guard**

B *v.t.* **1** (watch over) bewachen; (keep safe) hüten ‹*Geheimnis, Schatz, Juwelen*›; schützen ‹*Leben*›; beschützen ‹*Blinden, Schwächeren, Prominenten*›; **∼ sb./oneself against sth.** jmdn. vor etw. (*Dat.*) beschützen/sich vor etw. (*Dat.*) schützen **2** (keep in check) hüten, im Zaum halten ‹*Zunge*›; mäßigen ‹*Worte*›

Phrasal verb

- **∼ against** *v.t.* sich hüten vor (+ *Dat.*); verhüten ‹*Unfall*›; vorbeugen (+ *Dat.*) ‹*Krankheit, Gefahr, Irrtum*›; **∼ against doing sth.** sich [davor] hüten, etw. zu tun

guard: ∼ dog *n.* Wachhund, *der;* **∼ duty** *n.* Wachdienst, *der;* **be on** *or* **do ∼ duty** Wachdienst haben

guarded /ˈgɑːdɪd/ *adj.*, **guardedly** /ˈgɑːdɪdlɪ/ *adv.* zurückhaltend; vorsichtig

'guardhouse *n.* (Mil.) Wache, *die;* Wach[t]haus, *das*

guardian /ˈgɑːdɪən/ *n.* **1** Hüter, *der;* Wächter, *der* **2** (Law) Vormund, *der;* **place sb. under the care of a ∼:** jmdm. einen Vormund geben

> **The Guardian**
>
> Eine britische überregionale Tageszeitung. Der *Guardian* ist eine **broadsheet**-Zeitung und zählt zur seriösen Presse. Politisch steht der *Guardian* links von der Mitte; er berichtet ausführlich über soziale und kulturelle Themen.

guardian 'angel *n.* Schutzengel, *der*

> **Guardian Angels**
>
> Eine Jugendorganisation in den USA, die gegründet wurde, um Menschen vor Verbrechen zu schützen. Ihre Mitglieder tragen rote Kappen und T-Shirts mit dem Motto '*Dare to Care*' ('Trau dich zu helfen'). Sie arbeiten mit der Polizei zusammen und sind unbewaffnet.

guardianship /ˈgɑːdɪənʃɪp/ *n.* **1** *no pl.* Schutz, *der* **2** (Law) Vormundschaft, *die;* **have [legal] ∼ of sb.** jmds. Vormund sein

guard: ∼ rail *n.* Geländer, *das;* (Railw.) Radlenker, *der;* **∼room** *n.* (Mil.) Wachstube, *die;* Wachlokal, *das*

guardsman /ˈgɑːdzmən/ *n.*, *pl.* **guardsmen** /ˈgɑːdzmən/ ▸ ℹ **p. 1260** (belonging to guard) Wachtposten, *der;* (belonging to Guards) Gardist, *der;* Gardesoldat, *der*

'guard's van *n.* (Brit. Railw.) Gepäckwagen (*mit Dienstabteil*)

Guatemala /gwɑːtəˈmɑːlə/ *pr. n.* Guatemala (*das*)

Guatemalan /gwɑːtəˈmɑːlən/ ▸ ℹ **p. 1345**

A *adj.* guatemaltekisch; **sb. is ∼:** jmd. ist Guatemalteke/Guatemaltekin

B *n.* Guatemalteke, *der*/Guatemaltekin, *die*

guava /ˈgwɑːvə/ *n.* **1** (fruit) Guave, *die;* Guajave, *die* **2** (tree) Guajavabaum, *der*

gubbins /ˈgʌbɪnz/ *n.* (Brit.) **1** *no pl.* (trash) Schund, *der* (ugs. abwertend); Ramsch, *der* (ugs. abwertend); (personal effects) Kram, *der* (ugs.); Krempel, *der* (ugs.); (gadgetry) Zeug, *das* **2** (coll.: fool) Simpel, *der* (ugs.)

gubernatorial /gjuːbənəˈtɔːrɪəl/ *adj.* (esp. Amer.) Gouverneurs-

gudgeon /ˈgʌdʒn/ *n.* (Zool.) Gründling, *der*

'gudgeon pin *n.* (Mech. Engin.) Kolbenbolzen, *der*

guelder rose /ˈgeldə rəʊz/ *n.* (Bot.) Schneeball, *der*

guerilla ▸ **guerrilla**

Guernsey /ˈgɜːnzɪ/ *n.* **1** *pr. n.* Guernsey (*das*) **2** (animal) Guernseyrind, *das*

guerrilla /gəˈrɪlə/ *n.* Guerillakämpfer, *der*/-kämpferin, *die;* (in Latin America) Guerillero, *der*/Guerillera, *die; attrib.* Guerilla-

guess /ges/

A *v.t.* **1** (estimate) schätzen; (surmise) raten; (surmise correctly) erraten; raten ‹*Rätsel*›; **I ∼ her [age] to be ten** ich schätze sie auf zehn; **can you ∼ his weight?** schätz mal, wie viel er wiegt; **∼ who's here!** rate mal, wer da ist!; **∼ what!** (coll.) stell dir vor!; **he ∼ed from their manner that ...:** er entnahm aus ihrem Verhalten, dass ...; **you'd never ∼ that ...:** man würde nie vermuten, dass ...; **I ∼ed as much** das habe ich mir schon gedacht **2** (esp. Amer.: suppose) **I ∼:** ich glaube; ich schätze (ugs.); **I ∼ I ought to apologize** ich sollte mich wohl entschuldigen; **I ∼ we'll have to** wir müssen wohl; **I ∼ so/not** ich glaube schon *od.* ja/nicht *od.* kaum

B *v.i.* (estimate) schätzen; (make assumption) vermuten; (surmise correctly) es erraten; **∼ at sth.** etw. schätzen; (surmise) über etw. (*Akk.*) Vermutungen anstellen; **I'm just ∼ing** das ist nur eine Schätzung/eine Vermutung; **you've ∼ed right/wrong** deine Vermutung ist richtig/

falsch; **Do you know what he said? — No, but I can ~:** Weißt du, was er gesagt hat? — Nein, aber ich kann es mir denken; **well, ~!** na, rate mal!; **keep sb. ~ing** (coll.) jmdn. im Unklaren *od.* Ungewissen lassen; **how did you ~?** wie hast du das nur erraten?; **you'll never ~!** darauf kommst du nie!

C *n.* Schätzung, *die;* (supposition) Vermutung, *die;* **at a ~:** schätzungsweise; **what's your ~?** was schätzen Sie?; **make** *or* **have a ~:** schätzen; **have a ~!** rate *od.* schätz mal!; **my ~ is [that] ...:** ich schätze *od.* vermute, dass ...; **miss one's ~** (Amer.) sich verschätzen; **I'll give you three ~es** (coll.) dreimal darfst du raten (ugs.); **have another ~ coming** (coll.) sich verrechnet haben (ugs.); *see also* **anybody 2**

guessing game /ˈgesɪŋgeɪm/ *n.* Ratespiel, *das*

guesstimate /ˈgestɪmət/ *n.* (coll.) grobe Schätzung

ˈguesswork *n., no pl., no indef. art.* **be ~:** eine Vermutung sein; **rely largely on ~:** [weitgehend] auf Vermutungen angewiesen sein; **How did you know? — Oh, it was only [by] ~:** Woher wusstest du das? — Ach, ich habe nur geraten

guest /gest/ *n.* Gast, *der; attrib.* Gast‹*auftritt, -spiel, -vortrag, -redner*›; Gäste‹*handtuch*›; **be my ~** (fig. coll.) tun Sie sich/tu dir keinen Zwang an; (go on!) nur zu!; (help yourself) bedienen Sie sich/bedien dich; **as [the] ~ of** als Gast (+ *Gen.*); **~ of honour** Ehrengast, *der*

guest: ~ artist *n.* Gast, *der;* **today's ~ artist is ...** zu Gast ist heute ...; **~ house** *n.* Pension, *die;* **~ list** *n.* Gästeliste, *die* (**at** *Gen.*); **~ night** *n.* Gästeabend, *der;* **~ room** *n.* Gästezimmer, *das;* **~ worker** *n.* Gastarbeiter, *der*/-arbeiterin, *die*

guff /gʌf/ *n.* (coll.) Mumpitz, *der* (ugs.)

guffaw /gʌˈfɔː, ˈgʌfɔː/

A *n.* brüllendes Gelächter; **give a [great] ~:** in brüllendes Gelächter ausbrechen

B *v.i.* brüllend lachen

GUI /ˈguːɪ/ *abbr.* (Computing) = **graphical user interface** GUI

guidance /ˈgaɪdəns/ *n., no pl., no indef. art.* [1] (leadership, direction) Führung, *die;* (by teacher, tutor, etc.) [An]leitung, *die;* **pray for God's ~:** Gott bitten, einem den rechten Weg zu weisen [2] (advice) Rat, *der;* **turn to sb. for ~:** jmdn. um Rat fragen *od.* bitten; **give sb. ~ on sth.** jmdn. in etw. (*Dat.*) beraten; **financial/vocational ~:** Finanz-/Berufsberatung, *die*

guide /gaɪd/

A *n.* [1] Führer, *der*/Führerin, *die;* (Tourism) [Fremden]führer, *der*/-führerin, *die;* (professional mountain climber) [Berg]führer, *der*/-führerin, *die* [2] (fig.: mentor) Berater, *der*/Beraterin, *die;* **God is my ~:** Gott leitet mich [3] (directing principle) Richtschnur, *die;* **always let your conscience be your ~:** lass dich stets von deinem Gewissen leiten [4] (indicator) **be a [good/bad] ~ to sth.** ein [guter/schlechter] Anhaltspunkt für etw. sein; **be no/little ~ to sth.** keine/nur begrenzte Rückschlüsse auf etw. (*Akk.*) zulassen [5] (Brit.: member of girls' organization) **[Girl] G~:** Pfadfinderin, *die;* **the G~s** (organization) die Pfadfinderinnen; **King's/Queen's G~** (im Britischen Commonwealth) *Pfadfinderin der höchsten Rangstufe* [6] (handbook) Handbuch, *das;* **a ~ to healthier living** ein Ratgeber für ein gesünderes Leben [7] (book for tourists) [Reise]führer, *der;* (on entertainment, with dates) Veranstaltungskalender, *der;* **a ~ to York/the cathedral/the museum** ein Führer für *od.* durch York/für die Kathedrale/ein Museumsführer [8] (Mech. Engin.) Führung, *die*

B *v.t.* [1] führen ‹*Personen, Pflug, Maschinenteil usw.*› [2] (fig.) bestimmen ‹*Handeln, Urteil*›; anleiten ‹*Schüler, Lehrling*›; **be ~d by sth./sb.** sich von etw./jmdm. leiten lassen; **guiding star** (fig.) Leitstern, *der* (geh.); **guiding hand** (fig.) leitende Hand [3] (conduct affairs of) führen, lenken ‹*Land, Staat*›; lenken ‹*Angelegenheit*›; führen ‹*Finanzen*›

ˈguidebook ▸ **guide A 7**

guided missile /gaɪdɪd ˈmɪsaɪl/ *n.* Lenkflugkörper, *der*

ˈguide dog *n.* **~ [for the blind]** Blinden[führ]hund, *der*

guided tour /gaɪdɪd ˈtʊə(r)/ *n.* Führung, *die* (**of** durch)

guide: ~line *n.* (fig.) Richtlinie, *die;* (model) Vorlage, *die;* **~post** *n.* Wegweiser, *der*

Guider /ˈgaɪdə(r)/ *n.* (Brit.) Pfadfinderführerin, *die*

guild /gɪld/ *n.* [1] Verein, *der;* Vereinigung, *die* [2] (Hist.) (of merchants) Gilde, *die;* (of artisans) Zunft, *die*

ˈguildhall *n.* [1] (town hall) Rathaus, *das;* **[the] Guildhall** (Brit.) die Guildhall (in London) [2] (Hist.) (for merchants) Gildehaus, *das;* (for artisans) Zunfthaus, *das*

guile /gaɪl/ *n., no pl.* Arglist, *die* (geh.); Hinterlist, *die;* (wiliness) List, *die;* **be without ~:** ohne Arg *od.* Falsch sein (geh.)

guileful /ˈgaɪlfl/ *adj.* arglistig (geh.); hinterlistig; (wily) listig

guileless /gaɪllɪs/ *adj.* arglos

guillemot /ˈgɪlɪmɒt/ *n.* (Ornith.) (Uria) Lumme, *die;* (Cepphus) Teiste, *die*

guillotine /ˈgɪlətiːn/

A *n.* [1] Guillotine, *die;* Fallbeil, *das* [2] (for paper) Papierschneidemaschine, *die;* (for metal) Schlagschere, *die* [3] (Brit. Parl.) Begrenzung der Beratungszeit (*im Gesetzgebungsverfahren*)

B *v.t.* [1] (behead) guillotinieren; mit der Guillotine *od.* dem Fallbeil hinrichten [2] (cut) schneiden

guilt /gɪlt/ *n., no pl.* [1] Schuld, *die* (**of, for** an + *Dat.*); **bear the ~ of** *or* **for sth.** die Schuld für etw. auf sich (*Akk.*) tragen [2] (awareness of being in the wrong) Schuldbewusstsein, *das;* (guilty feeling) Schuldgefühle *Pl.;* **feel [full of] ~:** [starke] Schuldgefühle haben; **~ was written all over his face** sein schlechtes Gewissen stand ihm im Gesicht geschrieben; **~ complex** (Psych.) Schuldkomplex, *der*

guiltily /ˈgɪltɪlɪ/ *adv.* schuldbewusst

guiltless /ˈgɪltlɪs/ *adj.* unschuldig (**of** an + *Dat.*)

guilty /ˈgɪltɪ/ *adj.* [1] schuldig; **the ~ person** der/die Schuldige; **be ~ of murder** des Mordes schuldig sein; **find sb. ~/not ~ [of sth.]** jmdn. [an etw. (*Dat.*)] schuldig sprechen/[von etw.] freisprechen; **the jury found him not ~ of murder** die Geschworenen entschieden, dass er des Mordes nicht schuldig war; **~ thoughts** böse Gedanken; **[return** *or* **find a verdict of] ~/not ~:** [auf] „schuldig"/„nicht schuldig" [erkennen]; **feel ~ about sth./having done sth.** ein schlechtes Gewissen haben wegen etw./, weil man etw. getan hat; **everyone is/we're all ~ of that** (coll.) das tut jeder/das tun wir alle; **I've often been ~ of that myself** (coll.) das habe ich auch schon oft gemacht; **be ~ of bad taste** eine Geschmacklosigkeit begangen haben [2] (prompted by guilt) schuldbewusst ‹*Miene, Blick, Verhalten*›; schlecht ‹*Gewissen*›; **~ feeling[s]** Schuldgefühle *Pl.*

guinea /ˈgɪnɪ/ *n.* (Hist.) Guinee, *die*

Guinea /ˈgɪnɪ/ *pr. n.* Guinea (*das*)

guinea: ~fowl, ~ hen *ns.* Perlhuhn, *das*

Guinean /ˈgɪnɪən/

A *adj.* guineisch

B *n.* Guineer, *der*/Guineerin, *die*

ˈguinea pig *n.* [1] (animal) Meerschweinchen, *das* [2] (fig.: subject of experiment) (person) Versuchsperson, *die;* Versuchskaninchen, *das* (ugs. abwertend); (thing) Versuchsobjekt, *das;* **act as ~:** Versuchskaninchen spielen

guise /gaɪz/ *n.* [1] (semblance) Gestalt, *die;* **in** *or* **under the ~ of** in Gestalt (+ *Gen.*) [2] (pretence) Vorwand, *der* [3] (external appearance) Äußere, *das*

guitar /gɪˈtɑː(r)/ *n.* Gitarre, *die; attrib.* Gitarren‹*musik, -spieler, -konzert*›; **electric ~:** elektrische Gitarre; Elektrogitarre, *die*

guitarist /gɪˈtɑːrɪst/ *n.* ▸ⓘ **p. 1260** Gitarrist, *der*/Gitarristin, *die*

Gujarati /guːdʒəˈrɑːtɪ/ ▸ⓘ **p. 1277**

A *adj.* gudscharatisch

B *n.* [1] (person) Gudscharate, *der*/Gudscharatin, *die* [2] (language) Gudscharati, *das*

gulch /gʌltʃ/ *n.* (Amer.) Schlucht, *die;* Klamm, *die*

gulf /gʌlf/ *n.* [1] (portion of sea) Golf, *der;* Meerbusen, *der;* **the [Arabian** *or* **Persian] G~:** der Persische Golf; **the G~ of Bothnia/Mexico** der Bottnische Meerbusen/der Golf von Mexiko [2] (wide difference, impassable gap) Kluft, *die;* **there is a great ~ between them** es besteht eine tiefe Kluft zwischen ihnen [3] (chasm) Abgrund, *der*

Gulf: ~ States *pr. n. pl.* Golfstaaten *Pl.;* **~ Stream** *pr. n.* Golfstrom, *der;* **~ War** *n.* Golfkrieg, *der; attrib.* **~ War syndrome** Golfkriegssyndrom, *das*

gull /gʌl/ *n.* Möwe, *die*

gullet /ˈgʌlɪt/ *n.* [1] (food passage) Speiseröhre, *die* [2] (throat) Kehle, *die;* Gurgel, *die*

gullible /ˈgʌlɪbl/ *adj.* leichtgläubig; (trusting) gutgläubig

ˈgull-wing *adj.* **~ door** Flügeltür, *die*

gully /ˈgʌlɪ/ *n.* [1] (artificial channel) Abzugskanal, *der;* Abzugsrinne, *die* [2] (drain) Gully, *der* [3] (water-worn ravine) [Erosions]rinne, *die;* Runse, *die* (Geol.) [4] (Cricket) *Position/Feldspieler seitlich hinter dem Schlagmann*

ˈgully hole ▸ **gully 2**

gulp /gʌlp/

A *v.t.* hinunterschlingen; hinuntergießen ‹*Getränk*›

B *v.i.* (swallow with difficulty) würgen; (choke, swallow on account of shock) schlucken; **~ for air** nach Luft ringen *od.* schnappen

C *n.* [1] (act of ~ing, effort to swallow) Schlucken, *das;* **swallow in** *or* **at one ~:** mit einem Schluck herunterstürzen ‹*Getränk*›; in einem Bissen herunterschlingen ‹*Speise*› [2] (large mouthful) (of drink) kräftiger Schluck; (of food) großer Bissen [3] (act of swallowing due to shock) **give a ~:** schlucken

Phrasal verbs

- **~ ˈback** *v.t.* hinunterschlucken ‹*Tränen*›; unterdrücken ‹*Schluchzer*›
- **~ ˈdown** *v.t.* hinunterschlingen; hinuntergießen ‹*Getränk*›

gum¹ /gʌm/ *n., usu. in pl.* ▸ⓘ **p. 951** (Anat.) **~[s]** Zahnfleisch, *das*

gum²

A *n.* [1] (viscous secretion) Gummi, *das;* (glue) Klebstoff, *der* [2] (sweet) Gummibonbon, *der od. das* [3] (chewing ~) Kaugummi, *der* [4] (tree) ▸ **gum tree**

B *v.t.*, **-mm-** [1] (smear with ~) mit Klebstoff bestreichen; gummieren ‹*Briefmarken, Etiketten usw.*›; **~med envelopes** gummierte Briefumschläge [2] (fasten with ~) kleben

Phrasal verb

- **~ ˈup** *v.t.* aufkleben; **~ up the works** (fig. coll.) alles vermasseln (salopp)

gum: ~ ˈarabic ▸ **Arabic A; ~boil** *n.* ▸ⓘ **p. 1231** Zahnfleischabszess, *der;* **~boot** *n.* Gummistiefel, *der*

gummy /ˈgʌmɪ/ *adj.* [1] (sticky) klebrig [2] (covered with gum) mit Klebstoff verschmiert

gumption /ˈgʌmpʃn/ *n., no pl., no indef. art.* (coll.) [1] (resourcefulness) Grips, *der* (ugs.); **she had the ~ to open the door** sie war clever genug, die Tür zu öffnen [2] (practical sense) praktische Veranlagung; **have a lot of ~:** sehr praktisch veranlagt sein

gum: ~shield *n.* Mundschutz, *der;* **~ tree** *n.* Gummiharz liefernder Baum; (eucalyptus) [Australischer] Gummibaum; **be up a ~ tree** (fig.) in der Klemme sitzen (ugs.)

gun /gʌn/

A *n.* [1] Schusswaffe, *die;* (piece of artillery) Geschütz, *das;* (rifle) Gewehr, *das;* (pistol) Pistole, *die;* (revolver) Revolver, *der;* **big ~** (coll.: important person) hohes *od.* großes Tier (ugs.); **be going great ~s** laufen wie geschmiert (ugs.); ‹*Person:*› toll in Schwung sein (ugs.); **son of a ~** (coll.) Hund, *der* (salopp); (joc.) alter Hund (salopp); **stick to one's ~s** auf seinem Posten bleiben; (fig.) auf seinem Standpunkt beharren; **give it the ~!** (coll.) drück auf die Tube! (ugs.); **~s or butter** (fig.) Macht oder Wohlleben [2] (starting pistol) Startpistole, *die;* **wait for the ~:** auf den Startschuss warten; **beat** *or* **jump the ~:** einen

g

Fehlstart verursachen; (fig.) vorpreschen; (by saying sth.) vorzeitig etwas bekannt werden lassen **3** (member of shooting party) Schütze, *der*
B *v.t.*, **-nn-: 1** (Amer. coll.) erschießen; umlegen (salopp) **2** (coll.) **~ the engine** den Motor hochdrehen
(Phrasal verbs)
• **~ 'down** *v.t.* niederschießen
• **~ for** *v.t.* **1** (seek with ~) Jagd machen auf (+ *Akk.*) **2** (fig.) **be ~ning for sb.** jmdn. auf dem Kieker haben (ugs.)

gun: ~ barrel *n.* Kanonenrohr, *das;* (of rifle) Gewehrlauf, *der;* **~ battle** *n.* Schießerei, *die;* **~boat** *n.* Kanonenboot, *das;* **~boat diplomacy** Kanonenbootpolitik, *die;* **~ carriage** *n.* [fahrbare] Geschützlafette; **~ control** *n.* Bestimmungen *Pl.* über den Besitz und den Gebrauch von Schusswaffen; *attrib.* **~ control law** Waffengesetz, *das;* **~ control legislation** Waffengesetze *Pl.;* **~cotton** *n.* Schießbaumwolle, *die;* **~ crew** *n.* Geschützbedienung, *die;* **~ dog** *n.* Jagdhund, *der;* **~fight** *n.* (Amer. coll.) Schießerei, *die;* **~fighter** *n.* Revolverheld, *der;* **~fire** *n.* Geschützfeuer, *das;* (of small arms) Schießerei, *die*

gunge /gʌndʒ/ (Brit. coll.)
A *n.* Schmiere, *die*
B *v.t.* **~ up** verschmieren; **be/get ~d up** schmierig werden

gung-ho /gʌŋ'həʊ/ *adj.* wild entschlossen; **be very ~ for sth.** ein leidenschaftlicher Verfechter einer Sache (*Gen.*) sein

gungy /'gʌndʒɪ/ *adj.* (Brit. coll.) schmierig

gunk /gʌŋk/ *n.* (coll.) Schmiere, *die*

gun: ~ laws *pl.* Waffengesetze *Pl.;* **~man** /'gʌnmən/ *n., pl.* **~men** /'gʌnmən/ [mit einer Schusswaffe] bewaffneter Mann; **~metal** *n.* Geschützbronze, *die;* (colour) Metallgrau, *das;* **~ moll** *n.* (Amer. coll.) **1** (armed woman criminal) Revolverbraut, *die* (salopp); **2** ▸ **moll**

gunnel /'gʌnl/ ▸ **gunwale**

gunner /'gʌnə(r)/ *n.* Artillerist, *der;* (private soldier) Kanonier, *der;* (on an aircraft) Bordschütze, *der;* (on a ship) Geschützführer, *der*

gunnery /'gʌnərɪ/ *n., no pl.* Geschützwesen, *das*

gunny /'gʌnɪ/ *n.* Rupfen, *der;* **~ cloth** Rupfenleinwand, *die;* **~-sack** Rupfensack, *der*

gun: ~play *n., no pl., no indef. art.* Schießereien *Pl.;* (single fight) Schießerei, *die;* **~point** ▸ **point A 2; ~powder** *n.* Schießpulver, *das;* **Gunpowder Plot** (Hist.) Pulververschwörung, *die;* **~room** *n.* **1** (in house) Waffenkammer, *die;* **2** (in warship) Kadettenmesse, *die;* **~-runner** *n.* Waffenschmuggler, *der*/-schmugglerin, *die;* **~-running** *n.* Waffenschmuggel, *der;* **~ship** *n.* Kampfhubschrauber, *der;* **~shot** *n.* **1** (shot) Schuss, *der;* **~shot wound** Schusswunde, *die;* **2** **within/out of ~shot** in/außer Schussweite; **~slinger** ▸ **gunman; ~smith** *n.* ▸ **i p. 1260** Büchsenmacher, *der*

gunwale /'gʌnl/ *n.* (Naut.) Schandeck, *das;* Schandeckel, *der;* (of rowing boat) Dollbord, *der*

guppy /'gʌpɪ/ *n.* (Zool.) Guppy, *der*

gurgle /'gɜ:gl/
A *n.* Gluckern, *das;* (of brook) Plätschern, *das;* (of baby) Lallen, *das;* (with delight) Glucksen, *das*
B *v.i.* gluckern; ‹*Bach:*› plätschern; ‹*Baby:*› lallen/glucksen
C *v.t.* glucksen

Gurkha /'gɜ:kə, 'gʊəkə/ *n.* Gurkha, *der*

gurnard /'gɜ:nəd/, **gurnet** /'gɜ:nɪt/ *n.* (Zool.) Knurrhahn, *der*

guru /'gʊru:/ *n.* **1** Guru, *der* **2** (mentor) Mentor, *der*

gush /gʌʃ/
A *n.* **1** (sudden stream) Schwall, *der* **2** (effusiveness) Überschwänglichkeit, *die* **3** (sentimental affectation) Schmalz, *der* (abwertend)
B *v.i.* **1** strömen; schießen; (fig.: speak or act effusively) überschwänglich sein; **~ out** herausströmen; herausschießen; **water ~ed down through the ceiling** das Wasser floss in Strömen durch die Decke **2** (fig.: speak or act with sentimental affectation) schwärmen
C *v.t.* **1** **sth. ~es water/oil/blood** Wasser/Öl/Blut schießt aus etw. hervor **2** **'...' she ~ed** „...", sagte sie begeistert

gusher /'gʌʃə(r)/ *n.* **1** (oil well) [natürlich sprudelnde] Ölquelle **2** (person) exaltierter Mensch

gushing /'gʌʃɪŋ/ *adj.* **1** reißend ‹*Strom*›; strömend ‹*Regen*› **2** (effusive) exaltiert

gusset /'gʌsɪt/ *n.* (strengthening) Verstärkung, *die;* (enlarging) Einsatz, *der;* (triangular) Zwickel, *der;* Keil, *der*

gust /gʌst/
A *n.* **~ [of wind]** Windstoß, *der;* Bö[e], *die*
B *v.i.* böig wehen

gusto /'gʌstəʊ/ *n., no pl.* (enjoyment) Genuss, *der;* (vitality) Schwung, *der*

gusty /'gʌstɪ/ *adj.* böig; **~ rain** Regenböen *Pl.*

gut /gʌt/
A *n.* **1** (material) Darm, *der;* (for fishingline) Seidenwurmdarm, *der;* (Med.: for stitches) Katgut, *das* **2** *in pl.* (bowels) Eingeweide *Pl.;* Gedärme *Pl.;* **hate sb.'s ~s** (coll.) jmdn. auf den Tod nicht ausstehen können; **sweat** *or* **work one's ~s out** (coll.) sich dumm und dämlich schuften (ugs.) **3** *in pl.* (fig.: substantial contents) Innereien *Pl.* (scherzh.); (of problem, matter) Kern, *der;* **sth. has no ~s in it** etw. ist ohne Saft und Kraft; etw. ist fad[e] **4** *in pl.* (coll.: pluck) Schneid, *der* (ugs.); Mumm, *der* (ugs.) **5** (intestine) Darm, *der;* **large/small ~:** Dick-/Dünndarm, *der;* **bust a ~** (coll.) sich totarbeiten (ugs.) **6** (narrow water passage) (of sea) Meerenge, *die;* Sund, *der;* (of river) Fluss-, Stromenge, *die*
B *v.t.*, **-tt-: 1** (take out ~s of) ausnehmen **2** (remove or destroy fittings in) ausräumen; **the fire ~ted the house** bei dem Feuer ist das Haus ausgebrannt; **it was ~ted [by the fire]** es brannte aus **3** (extract essence of) ≈ exzerpieren ‹*Buch*›
C *attrib. adj.* **1** (fundamental) grundlegend ‹*Problem*› **2** (instinctive) gefühlsmäßig ‹*Reaktion*›; **~ feeling** instinktives Gefühl; **have a ~ feeling that ...** es im Gefühl *od.* (salopp) Urin haben, dass...; **rely on one's ~ feelings** sich auf seine Gefühle *od.* (ugs.) seinen Bauch verlassen

gutless /'gʌtlɪs/ *adj.* feige; **be ~:** keinen Mumm haben (ugs.)

gutsy /'gʌtsɪ/ *adj.* (coll.: courageous) mutig

gutta-percha /gʌtə'pɜ:tʃə, gʌtə'pɜ:kə/ *n.* Guttapercha, *die od. das*

gutted /'gʌtɪd/ *adj.* (Brit. coll.) **be/feel ~:** am Boden zerstört sein (ugs.)

gutter /'gʌtə(r)/
A *n.* **1** (below edge of roof) Dach- *od.* Regenrinne, *die;* (at side of street) Rinnstein, *der;* Gosse, *die;* (open conduit) Rinne, *die;* **the ~** (fig.) die Gosse **2** (track worn by water) Rinne, *die*
B *v.i.* ‹*Kerze:*› tropfen; ‹*Flamme:*› [immer schwächer] flackern

guttering /'gʌtərɪŋ/ *n.* (on roof) Dachrinnen *Pl.;* (in floor) Rinnen *Pl.*

gutter: ~ press *n.* Sensationspresse, *die* (abwertend); **~snipe** *n.* Gassenjunge, *der* (abwertend)

guttural /'gʌtərl/
A *adj.* **1** (from the throat) guttural; kehlig **2** (of the throat) Kehl-; (of the larynx) Kehlkopf- **3** (Phonet.) Kehl-; guttural (Sprachw. veralt.)
B *n.* (Phonet.) Gaumensegellaut, *der;* Guttural[laut], *der* (Sprachw. veralt.)

guv /gʌv/, **guv'nor** /'gʌvnə(r)/ (Brit. coll.) ▸ **governor 7**

guy[1] /gaɪ/ *n.* (rope, wire) Halteseil, *das;* (for hoisted things) Lenkseil, *das*

guy[2]
A *n.* **1** (coll.: man) Typ, *der* (ugs.) **2** *in pl.* (esp. Amer.: everyone) **[listen,] you ~s!** [hört mal,] Kinder! (ugs.) **3** (Brit.: effigy) Guy-Fawkes-Puppe, *die;* **Guy Fawkes Night** ▸ **Bonfire Night;**
B *v.t.* (ridicule) sich lustig machen über (+ *Akk.*)

Guy Fawkes Night
▸ **Bonfire Night.**

Guyana /gaɪ'ænə/ *pr. n.* Gu[a]yana *(das)*

Guyanese /gaɪə'ni:z/ ▸ **i p. 1345**
A *adj.* gu[a]yanisch
B *n.* Gu[a]yaner, *der*/Gu[a]yanerin, *die*

guy: ~-rope *n.* Zelt[spann]leine, *die;* **~-wire** *n.* Spanndraht, *der;* Drahtseilabspannung, *die*

guzzle /'gʌzl/
A *v.t.* (eat) hinunterschlingen; (drink) hinuntergießen; (eat or drink up) wegputzen (ugs.)
B *v.i.* schlingen

gybe /dʒaɪb/ (Naut.)
A *v.i.* **1** (swing across) übergehen **2** (change course) halsen; (accidentally) eine Patenthalse machen
B *n.* (change of course) Halse, *die;* (accidental) Patenthalse, *die;* (swing of boom) Schwenken, *das*

gym /dʒɪm/ *n.* (coll.) **1** (gymnasium) Turnhalle, *die;* (fitness studio) Fitnessstudio, *das* **2** *no pl., no indef. art.* (gymnastics) Turnen, *das;* **~ teacher** Turnlehrer, *der*/Turnlehrerin, *die*

gymkhana /dʒɪm'kɑ:nə/ *n.* Gymkhana, *das*

gymnasium *n.* **1** /dʒɪm'neɪzɪəm/ *pl.* **~s** *or* **gymnasia** /dʒɪm'neɪzɪə/ Turnhalle, *die* **2** /dʒɪm'neɪzɪəm, gɪm'nɑ:zɪʊm/ *pl.* **~s** (European grammar school) Gymnasium, *das*

gymnast /'dʒɪmnæst/ *n.* Turner, *der*/Turnerin, *die*

gymnastic /dʒɪm'næstɪk/ *adj.* turnerisch ‹*Können*›; **~ exercise** gymnastische Übung; (esp. with apparatus) Turnübung, *die;* **~ equipment** Turngeräte *Pl.;* (portable) gymnastische Geräte

gymnastics /dʒɪm'næstɪks/ *n., no pl.* **1** (exercise) Gymnastik, *die;* (esp. with apparatus) Turnen, *das; attrib.* Gymnastik-/Turn‹*stunde, -lehrer*› **2** (fig.) **mental ~:** Gehirnakrobatik, *die* (ugs. scherzh.); **verbal ~:** Wortakrobatik, *die* (ugs. scherzh.)

gym: ~ shoe *n.* Turnschuh, *der;* **~slip, ~ tunic** *ns.* Trägerrock, *der (für die Schule)*

gynaecological /gaɪnɪkə'lɒdʒɪkl/ *adj.* (Med.) gynäkologisch

gynaecologist /gaɪnɪ'kɒlədʒɪst/ *n.* ▸ **i p. 1260** (Med.) Gynäkologe, *der*/Gynäkologin, *die;* Frauenarzt, *der*/Frauenärztin, *die*

gynaecology /gaɪnɪ'kɒlədʒɪ/ *n.* (Med.) Gynäkologie, *die;* Frauenheilkunde, *die*

gynecological *etc.* (Amer.) ▸ **gynaec-**

gyp /dʒɪp/ *n.* **give sb. ~** (coll.: pain sb.) jmdm. sehr zu schaffen machen (ugs.)

gypsophila /dʒɪp'sɒfɪlə/ *n.* (Bot.) Gipskraut, *das*

gypsum /'dʒɪpsəm/ *n.* Gips, *der*

gypsy, Gypsy /'dʒɪpsɪ/ *n.* Zigeuner, *der*/Zigeunerin, *die;* **family of gypsies** Zigeunerfamilie, *die*

gypsy: ~ moth *n.* (Zool.) Schwammspinner, *der;* **~ rose** *n.* (Bot.) Krätz[en]kraut, *das*

gyrate /dʒaɪ'reɪt/ *v.i.* sich drehen; kreiseln

gyration /dʒaɪ'reɪʃn/ *n.* Drehung, *die;* kreiselnde Bewegung

gyratory /dʒaɪ'reɪtərɪ, 'dʒaɪərətərɪ/ *adj.* kreiselnd

gyrfalcon /'dʒɜ:fɔ:lkn, 'dʒɜ:fɒlkn/ *n.* (Ornith.) Gerfalke, *der*

gyro /'dʒaɪrəʊ/ *n., pl.* **~s** (coll.) ▸ **gyroscope**

'gyrocompass *n.* Kreiselkompass, *der*

gyroscope /'dʒaɪrəskəʊp/ *n.* (Phys., Naut., Aeronaut.) Kreisel, *der;* (for scientific purposes) Gyroskop, *das*

gyroscopic /dʒaɪrə'skɒpɪk/ *adj.* Kreisel-

'gyrostabilizer *n.* Schiffskreisel, *der*

Hh

H¹, h /eɪtʃ/ *n., pl.* **Hs** *or* **H's** /ˈeɪtʃɪz/ (letter) H, h, *das; see also* **drop C 7**

H² *abbr.* (on pencil) = **hard** H

h. *abbr.* **1** = **hecto-** h **2** = **hour[s]** Std[n].; **at 1700h** um 17.00 h

ha /hɑː/
A *int. expr. surprise, triumph* ha; *expr. hesitation* hm
B *v.i.* ▸**hum A 1**
C *n., pl.* **ha's** ▸**hum C 2**

ha. *abbr.* = **hectare[s]** ha

habeas corpus /heɪbɪəs ˈkɔːpəs/ *n., no pl.* (Law) Anordnung eines Haftprüfungstermins; **Habeas Corpus Act** Habeaskorpusakte, *die*

> **habeas corpus**
>
> 'Du habest den Körper' sind die Anfangsworte eines mittelalterlichen Erlasses, der anordnet, den Verhafteten dem Gericht vorzuführen. Die Habeaskorpusakte ist das grundlegende englische Gesetz von 1679 zum Schutz der persönlichen Freiheit, nach dem niemand ohne richterliche Überprüfung in Haft genommen und gehalten werden darf, ohne dass ein Gerichtsbeschluss darüber vorliegt. Sie entstand als Reaktion auf willkürliche Verhaftungen unter Karl II. Die US-Verfahrensordnung, die in Artikel 1 der amerikanischen Verfassung festgelegt ist, beruht auch auf der Habeaskorpusakte von 1679.

haberdasher /ˈhæbədæʃə(r)/ *n.* ▸**i p. 1260** **1** (Brit.) Kurzwarenhändler, *der*/-händlerin, *die* **2** (Amer.) (dealer in men's accessories) Inhaber eines Geschäfts für Herrenartikel; (dealer in menswear) Herrenausstatter, *der* **3** **~'s** ▸**haberdashery 2**

haberdashery /ˈhæbədæʃərɪ/ *n.* **1** (goods) (Brit.) Kurzwaren *Pl.;* (Amer.: men's accessories) Herrenartikel *Pl.;* (Amer.: menswear) Herrenmoden **2** (shop) (Brit.) Kurzwarengeschäft, *das;* Kurzwarenhandlung, *die;* (Amer.) Geschäft für Herrenartikel/Herrenmodengeschäft, *das* **3** (department) (Brit.) Kurzwarenabteilung, *die;* (Amer.) Abteilung für Herrenartikel/Herrenmodenabteilung, *die*

habit /ˈhæbɪt/ *n.* **1** (set practice) Gewohnheit, *die;* **good/bad ~:** gute/schlechte [An]gewohnheit; **the ~ of smoking** das [gewohnheitsmäßige] Rauchen; **have a** *or* **the ~ of doing sth.** die Angewohnheit haben, etw. zu tun; **the sun has a ~ of disappearing at the weekend** (iron.) zum Wochenende verzieht sich die Sonne regelmäßig; **make a [regular] ~ of doing sth.** sich (*Dat.*) angewöhnen, etw. [regelmäßig] zu tun; **you shouldn't make a ~ of it** du solltest es nicht zur Gewohnheit werden lassen; **let sth. become** *or* (coll.) **get to be a ~:** etw. zur Gewohnheit werden *od.* (ugs.) einreißen lassen; **out of ~, from [force of] ~:** aus Gewohnheit; **old ~s die hard** der Mensch ist ein Gewohnheitstier (ugs.); **be in the ~ of doing sth.** die Gewohnheit haben, etw. zu tun; **not be in the ~ of doing sth.** es nicht gewohnt sein, etw. zu tun; **I'm not in the ~ of accepting lifts from strangers** ich pflege mich nicht von Fremden im Auto mitnehmen zu lassen; **get** *or* **fall into a** *or* **the ~ of doing sth.** [es] sich (*Dat.*) angewöhnen, etw. zu tun; **get into** *or* **form** *or* **acquire good ~s** gute Angewohnheiten annehmen; **get** *or* **fall into** *or* (coll.) **pick up bad ~s** schlechte [An]gewohnheiten annehmen; **get out of** *or* **give up** *or* **stop a/the ~:** sich (*Dat.*) etwas/das abgewöhnen; eine/die Angewohnheit ablegen; **get out of the ~ of doing sth.** [es] sich (*Dat.*) abgewöhnen, etw. zu tun **2** (coll.) (addiction) Süchtigkeit, *die;* [Drogen]abhängigkeit, *die;* (craving) Sucht, *die;* **have got the ~:** süchtig sein; User sein (Drogenjargon) **3** (dress) Habit, *der od. das;* (woman's riding dress) Reitkostüm, *das;* (arch.: clothing) Gewand, *das* **4** (Psych.) Habit, *das od. der* **5** (Biol., Bot.) Habitus, *der.*

habitable /ˈhæbɪtəbl/ *adj.* bewohnbar

habitat /ˈhæbɪtæt/ *n.* **1** (of animals, plants) Habitat, *das* (Zool., Bot.); Lebensraum, *der;* Standort, *der* (Bot.); (of humans) Lebensraum, *der* **2** ▸**habitation 2**

habitation /hæbɪˈteɪʃn/ *n.* **1** (inhabiting) [Be]wohnen, *das;* **fit/unfit** *or* **not fit for human ~:** bewohnbar/unbewohnbar **2** (place) Wohnstätte, *die* (geh.)

habit-forming /ˈhæbɪtfɔːmɪŋ/ *adj.* Abhängigkeit erzeugend; **be ~:** Abhängigkeit erzeugen; abhängig machen; (fig.) leicht zur Gewohnheit werden [können]

habitual /həˈbɪtjʊəl/ *adj.* **1** (customary) gewohnt; üblich **2** (continual, recurring) ständig; **that's a ~ problem of hers** das ist immer wieder ihr Problem **3** (given to habit) gewohnheitsmäßig; Gewohnheits⟨*trinker*⟩; notorisch (abwertend), gewohnheitsmäßig ⟨*Lügner*⟩

habitually /həˈbɪtjʊəlɪ/ *adv.* **1** (regularly, recurrently) regelmäßig **2** (incessantly) ständig

habituate /həˈbɪtjʊeɪt/ *v.t.* **~ sb./oneself to sth./sb.** jmdn./sich an etw./jmdn. gewöhnen; **~ sb./oneself to doing sth.** jmdn./sich daran gewöhnen, etw. zu tun; **become [too] ~d to sth.** sich [zu sehr] an etw. (*Akk.*) gewöhnen

habitué /həˈbɪtjʊeɪ/ *n.* Habitué, *der* (veralt.); regelmäßiger Besucher; (of hotel, casino, etc.) Stammgast, *der*

Habsburg /ˈhæpsbɜːg/ *pr. n.* **1** (place) Habsburg (*das*) **2** (family name) Habsburger, *der;* **the ~ family** die Habsburger *Pl.;* **the ~ emperors** die habsburgischen Kaiser; die Habsburgerkaiser

hack¹ /hæk/
A *v.t.* **1** (cut) hacken ⟨*Holz*⟩; **~ sb./sth. to bits** *or* **pieces** jmdn. zerstückeln/etw. in Stücke hacken; **~ to bits** *or* **pieces** (fig.) zerpflücken; kaputtmachen ⟨*Ruf*⟩; verreißen ⟨*Artikel*⟩; **~ sth. out of sth.** etw. aus etw. heraushacken; **~ one's way [through/along/out of sth.]** sich (*Dat.*) einen Weg [durch etw./etw. entlang/aus etw. heraus] [frei]schlagen **2** (Footb.) **~ sb.'s shin** jmdm. *od.* jmdn. vors *od.* gegen das Schienbein treten
B *v.i.* **1** (deal blows) **~ at** herumhacken auf (+ *Dat.*); **~ through the undergrowth** sich (*Dat.*) einen Weg durchs Unterholz schlagen **2** (Computing) **~ into sth.** in etw. (*Akk.*) eindringen **3** **~ it** (coll.: manage, cope) es schaffen

Phrasal verbs

• **~ a'bout** *v.t.* verpfuschen (ugs.); (fig.) zurechtstutzen
• **~ a'way**
A *v.i.* **~ away at sth.** auf etw. (*Akk.*) einhacken; (fig.) etw. aushöhlen
B *v.t.* weghacken
• **~ 'off** *v.t.* **1** abhacken; abschlagen **2** **~ sb. off** (coll.: annoy) jmdn. stocksauer machen (salopp)
• **~ 'out** *v.t.* heraushauen (**from** aus); (fig.: work out) zustande bringen

hack²
A *n.* **1** (drudge) ≈ Gelegenheitsarbeiter, *der;* Mietling, *der* (veralt. abwertend); (uninspired worker) Arbeitstier, *das;* (writer) Schreiberling, *der* (abwertend); **newspaper ~:** Zeitungsschreiber, *der;* **publisher's ~:** Lohnschreiber, *der;* Auftragsschreiber, *der* **2** (hired horse) Mietpferd, *das;* (horse for ordinary riding) Reitpferd, *das* **3** (derog.: worn-out horse) alter Klepper (abwertend) **4** (Amer.) (taxi) Taxi, *das;* (taxi driver) Taxifahrer, *der*
B *adj.* **1** **~ writer** Lohnschreiber, *der* **2** (mediocre) Nullachtfünfzehn- (ugs. abwertend)

hacker /ˈhækə(r)/ *n.* (Computing) Hacker, *der*

hackette /hæˈket/ *n.* (joc. derog.) mittelmässige Journalistin; Schreiberling, *der* (abwertend)

hacking /ˈhækɪŋ/: **~ 'cough** *n.* trockener Husten; Reizhusten, *der;* **~ jacket,** *n.* Reitjackett, *das;* (sports jacket) Sportjacke, *die*

hackle /ˈhækl/ *n.* **1** (long feather/feathers) Schmuckfeder, *die*/Schmuckfedern; (neck plumage) Kragen, *der;* Kragenfedern; **a cock's ~s are up** ein Hahn sträubt die Federn *od.* stellt die Federn auf **2** *in pl.* (animal's hair) Nacken[- und Rücken]haare *Pl.;* **a dog's ~s are up** einem Hund sträubt sich das Fell; **sb.'s ~s rise/are up** (fig.) jmd. gerät/ist in Harnisch; **get sb.'s ~s up, make sb.'s ~s rise** (fig.) jmdn. wütend machen; **that kind of thing always gets his ~s up** bei so was sieht er immer rot (ugs.); so etwas bringt ihn immer in Harnisch **3** (comb) Hechel, *die* (Landw.)

hackney /ˈhæknɪ/ *n.* [gewöhnliches] Pferd; Gaul, *der* (ugs.)

hackney: **~ 'cab, ~ 'carriage** *ns.* Droschke, *die* (veralt.); Taxe, *die;* **~ 'coach** *n.* (Hist.) [Pferde]droschke, *die*

hackneyed /ˈhæknɪd/ *adj.* abgegriffen; abgedroschen (ugs.)

'hacksaw *n.* [Metall]bügelsäge, *die*

had ▸**have A, B**

haddie /ˈhædɪ/ (Scot.) ▸**haddock**

haddock /ˈhædək/ *n., pl. same* Schellfisch, *der;* **smoked ~:** Haddock, *der*

Hades /ˈheɪdiːz/ *n., no pl.* **1** (Greek Mythol.) Hades, *der;* **to/in ~:** in den/im Hades **2** (coll. euphem.) ▸**hell 1**

hadji /ˈhædʒɪ/ *n.* Hadschi, *der*

hadn't /ˈhædnt/ (coll.) = **had not;** ▸**have A, B**

Hadrian's Wall /heɪdrɪənz ˈwɔːl/ *n.* (Hist.) Hadrianswall, *der*

haematology /hiːməˈtɒlədʒɪ/ *n.* (Med.) Hämatologie, *die*

haemoglobin /hiːməˈgləʊbɪn/ *n.* (Anat., Zool.) Hämoglobin, *das*

haemophilia /hiːməˈfɪlɪə/ *n.* ▸**i p. 1231** (Med.) Hämophilie, *die* (fachspr.); Bluterkrankheit, *die*

haemophiliac /hiːməˈfɪlɪæk/ *n.* (Med.) Bluter, *der*/Bluterin, *die*

haemorrhage /ˈhemərɪdʒ/ (Med.)
A *n.* Hämorrhagie, *die* (fachspr.); Blutung, *die*
B *v.i.* starke Blutungen haben

haemorrhoid /ˈhemərɔɪd/ *n., usu. in pl.* (Med.) Hämorrhoide, *die*

haft /hɑːft/ *n.* Griff, *der;* Heft, *das* (geh.)

hag /hæg/ *n.* 1 (old woman) [alte] Hexe 2 (witch) Hexe, *die* 3 ▸**hagfish**

'hagfish *n.* Inger, *der;* Schleimaal, *der*

haggard /'hægəd/ *adj.* (worn) ausgezehrt; (with worry) abgehärmt; (tired) abgespannt

haggis /'hægɪs/ *n.* (Gastr.) Haggis, *der; gefüllter Schafsmagen*

haggle /'hægl/

A *v.i.* sich zanken (**over, about** wegen); (over price) feilschen (abwertend) (**over, about** um)

B *n.* Gezänk, *das* (abwertend); (over price) Gefeilsche, *das* (abwertend)

hagiography /hægɪ'ɒgrəfɪ/ *n.* Hagiographie, *die*

'hag-ridden *adj.* **be ~ by sth.** von etw. geplagt *od.* gequält werden; **look ~:** niedergedrückt aussehen

Hague /heɪg/ *pr. n.* ▸ℹ **p. 1643 The ~:** Den Haag (*das*); der Haag (geh.); **The ~ Conventions** die Haager Konventionen

ha ha /hɑ: 'hɑ:/ *int.* haha!

ha-ha /'hɑ:hɑ:/ *n.* Umfassungsgraben, *der;* Aha, *das* (Bauw.)

haiku /'haɪku:/ *n., pl. same* (Lit.) Haiku, *das*

hail[1] /heɪl/

A *n.* 1 *no pl., no indef. art.* (Meteorol.) Hagel, *der* 2 (fig.: shower) Hagel, *der;* (of curses, insults, questions, praise) Schwall, *der;* Flut, *die;* **a ~ of bullets/missiles/stones/arrows** ein Kugel-/Geschoss-/Stein-/Pfeilhagel *od.* -regen

B *v.i.* 1 *impers.* (Meteorol.) **it ~s** *or* **is ~ing** es hagelt 2 (fig.: descend) **~ down** niederprasseln (**on** auf + *Akk.*); **~ down on sb.** ‹*Beschimpfungen, Vorwürfe usw.:*› auf jmdn. einprasseln

C *v.t.* niederhageln *od.* niederprasseln lassen

hail[2]

A *v.t.* 1 (call out to) anrufen, (fachspr.) anpreien ‹*Schiff*›; (signal to) heranwinken, anhalten ‹*Taxi*›; **within/not within ~ing distance** in/außer Rufweite 2 (salute) grüßen; (receive, welcome) begrüßen; empfangen 3 (acclaim) zujubeln (+ *Dat.*); bejubeln (**as** als); **~ sb. king** jmdm. als König zujubeln

B *v.i.* 1 rufen 2 **where does the ship ~ from?** woher kommt das Schiff?; **where do you ~ from?** woher kommst du?; wo bist du her? (ugs.)

C *n.* 1 (salutation) Gruß, *der;* (shout of acclamation) Jubelruf, *der* 2 (call) [Zu]ruf, *der;* **within/out of ~:** in/außer Rufweite

D *int.* (arch.) sei gegrüßt (geh.); **~ Macbeth/to thee, O Caesar** Heil Macbeth/dir, o Cäsar; **H~ Mary** ▸**Ave Maria**; **say ~ and farewell to sb.** jmdn. begrüßen und von ihm [zugleich] Abschied nehmen; *see also* **all A 1**

hail: ~-fellow-well-met *adj.* kumpelhaft; **be ~-fellow-well-met with sb.** jmdn. kumpelhaft behandeln; **~stone** *n.* (Meteorol.) Hagelkorn, *das;* **~storm** *n.* (Meteorol.) heftiger Hagelfall; Hagelschauer, *der*

hair /heə(r)/ *n.* 1 (one strand) Haar, *das;* **a dog's ~:** ein Hundehaar; **without turning a ~** (fig.) ohne eine Miene zu verziehen; **not harm a ~ of sb.'s head** (fig.) jmdm. kein Haar krümmen; *see also* **dog A 1; hang B 1; short A 1; split C 2** 2 ▸ℹ **p. 951** *collect., no pl.* (many strands, mass) Haar, *das;* Haare *Pl.; attrib.* Haar-; (horse~) Rosshaar-; **the cat has a lovely coat of black ~:** die Katze hat ein wunderschönes schwarzes Fell; **do one's/sb.'s ~:** sich/jmdm. das Haar machen (ugs.); **do one's own ~:** sich (*Dat.*) das Haar selbst machen (ugs.); **have** *or* **get one's ~ done** sich (*Dat.*) das Haar *od.* die Haare machen lassen (ugs.); **where did you get your ~ done?** bei welchem Friseur warst du?; **pull sb.'s ~:** jmdn. an den Haaren ziehen; **he's losing his ~:** ihm gehen die Haare aus; **he has still not lost his ~:** er hat seine Haare noch [alle]; **keep your ~ on!** (coll.), **don't lose your ~!** (coll.) geh [mal] nicht gleich an die Decke! (ugs.); **let one's ~ down** sein Haar aufmachen *od.* lösen; (fig. coll.) [ganz] locker sein (ugs.); sich [ganz] locker geben (ugs.); (give free expression to one's feelings etc.) aus sich herausgehen; (have a good time) auf den Putz hauen (ugs.); die Sau rauslassen (salopp); **sb.'s ~ stands on end** (fig.) jmdm. stehen die Haare zu Berge (ugs.); **get in sb.'s ~** (fig. coll.) jmdm. auf die Nerven *od.* den Wecker gehen *od.* fallen (ugs.); **get out of my ~!** (coll.) lass mich in Ruhe! (ugs.); **keep out of sb.'s ~** (coll.) jmdn. in Ruhe lassen; *see also* **bad 2; curl A 1, B 1; tear**[1] **B 2** 3 (Bot.) Haar, *das* 4 (thin filament) Faden, *der* 5 (minute amount) **by a ~:** knapp ‹*gewinnen*›

hair: ~band *n.* Haarband, *das;* **~breadth** ▸**~'s breadth**; **~brush** *n.* Haarbürste, *die;* **~care** *n., no pl.* Haarpflege, *die; attrib.* Haarpflege-; **~ conditioner** *n.* Pflegespülung *die;* **~ cream** *n.* Haarcreme, *die;* Pomade, *die;* **~ curler** *n.* Lockenwickler, *der;* **~cut** *n.* 1 (act) Haareschneiden, *das;* **go for/need a ~cut** zum Friseur gehen/müssen; **give sb. a ~cut** jmdm. die Haare schneiden; **get** *or* **have a ~cut** sich (*Dat.*) die Haare schneiden lassen; 2 (style) Haarschnitt, *der;* **~do** *n.* (coll.) 1 **get a ~do** sich (*Dat.*) das Haar machen lassen (ugs.); **give sb. a ~do** jmdm. das Haar machen (ugs.); 2 (style) Frisur, *die;* **~dresser** *n.* ▸ℹ **p. 1260** Friseur, *der*/Friseuse, *die;* **men's ~dresser** Herrenfriseur, *der*/-friseurin, *die;* **ladies' ~dresser** Damenfriseur, *der*/-friseurin, *die;* **go to the ~dresser['s]** zum Friseur gehen; **~dressing** *n., no pl.* der Friseurberuf; *attrib.* **~dressing salon** Friseursalon, *der;* **~drier, ~dryer** *ns.* Haartrockner, *der;* Fön Ⓦ, *der;* (with a hood) Trockenhaube, *die;* **~ dye** *n.* Haarfärbemittel, *das;* **use ~ dye** sich (*Dat.*) das Haar färben

-haired /heəd/ *adj. in comb.* ▸ℹ **p. 951 black-/dark-/frizzy-~:** schwarz-/dunkel-/kraushaarig; **greasy-~:** mit fettigem Haar *nachgestellt*

hair: ~ extension *n., usu. pl.* Haarverlängerung, *die;* **~ follicle** *n.* Haarbalg, *der;* **~grip** *n.* (Brit.) Haarklammer, *die;* **~ lacquer** ▸**~spray**

hairless /'heəlɪs/ *adj.* unbehaart ‹*Körper[teil], Pflanze, Blatt*›; kahlköpfig ‹*Person*›; kahl ‹*Kopf*›

hair: ~line *n.* 1 (edge of hair) Haaransatz, *der;* **his ~line is receding, he has a receding ~line** er bekommt eine Stirnglatze; 2 (narrow line) haarfeine Linie; haarfeiner Strich; 3 (crack) haarfeiner Riss; **~line crack** (esp. Metallurgy, Mech. Engin.) Haarriss, *der;* **~line fracture** (Med.) Fissur, *die;* 4 (in writing or printing) Haarstrich, *der;* **~net** *n.* Haarnetz, *das;* **~piece** *n.* Haarteil, *das;* **~pin** *n.* Haarnadel, *die;* **~pin 'bend** *n.* Haarnadelkurve, *die;* **~-raising** /'heəreɪzɪŋ/ *adj.* Furcht erregend; (very bad) haarsträubend; mörderisch ‹*Rennstrecke; Abstieg vom Berg usw.*›; **~-restorer** *n.* Haarwuchsmittel, *das;* **~'s breadth** A *n.* winzige Kleinigkeit; **by [no more than] a ~'s breadth** [nur] um Haaresbreite ‹*verfehlen*›; nur knapp ‹*gewinnen*›; **the firm was within a ~'s breadth of bankruptcy** die Firma wäre um ein Haar (ugs.) bankrott gegangen; B *adj.* minimal; hauchdünn (ugs.) ‹*Chance*›; **that was a ~'s breadth escape** das war äußerst *od.* (ugs.) verdammt knapp; **~ 'shirt** *n.* härenes Hemd (geh.); Härenhemd, *das* (veralt.); (worn as a penance) Büßerhemd, *das;* **~slide** *n.* (Brit.) Haarspange, *die;* **~-space** *n.* (Printing) Haarspatium, *das;* **~-splitting** (derog.) A *adj.* haarspalterisch (abwertend); B *n.* Haarspalterei, *die* (abwertend); **~spray** *n.* Haarspray, *das;* **~spring** *n.* (Horol.) Unruhfeder, *die;* **~style** *n.* Frisur, *die;* **~stylist** *n.* ▸ℹ **p. 1260** Friseur, *der*/Friseurin, *die;* Hair-Stylist, *der*/-Stylistin, *die;* **~-trigger** *n.* (Arms) Stecher, *der*

hairy /'heərɪ/ *adj.* 1 (having hair) behaart; flauschig ‹*Schal, Pullover, Teppich*›; **you're beginning to get a ~ chest** du bekommst Haare auf der Brust; **a very ~ dog** ein Hund mit einem dichten Fell; (having very long hair) ein sehr langhaariger Hund; **be all ~:** voller Haare sein 2 (made of hair) aus Haar (nachgestellt); hären (geh.) ‹*Gewand*› 3 (coll.: alarming and difficult) haarig

Haiti /hɑ:'i:tɪ, 'heɪtɪ/ *pr. n.* Haiti (*das*)

Haitian /hɑ:'i:ʃn, 'heɪʃn/ ▸ℹ **p. 1345**

A *adj.* haitianisch; **sb. is ~:** jmd. ist Haitianer/Haitianerin

B *n.* Haitianer, *der*/Haitianerin, *die*

hajji ▸**hadji**

hake /heɪk/ *n., pl. same* (Zool.) Seehecht, *der*

halal /hɑ:'lɑ:l/ (Islam)

A *adj.* ‹*Fleisch*› von einem nach muslimischem Ritus geschlachteten Tier

B *n.* Fleisch von einem nach muslimischem Ritus geschlachteten Tier

halberd /'hælbəd/, **halbert** /'hælbət/ *ns.* (Arms Hist.) Hellebarde, *die*

'halcyon days /'hælsɪən deɪz/ *n. pl.* (happy days) glückliche Tage *Pl.*; glückliche Zeiten *Pl.*

hale /heɪl/ *adj.* kräftig ‹*Körper, Konstitution*›; rege ‹*Geist*›; **~ and hearty** gesund und munter

half /hɑ:f/

A *n., pl.* **halves** /hɑ:vz/ 1 ▸ℹ **p. 894,** ▸ℹ **p. 1001,** ▸ℹ **p. 1358** (part) Hälfte, *die;* **~ [of sth.]** die Hälfte [von etw.]; **~ of Europe** halb Europa; **I've only ~ left** ich habe nur noch die Hälfte; **~ [of] that** die Hälfte [davon]; **I don't believe ~ of it!** ich glaube nicht die Hälfte davon; **cut sth. in ~** *or* **into [two] halves** etw. in zwei Hälften schneiden; **divide sth. in ~** *or* **into halves** etw. halbieren; **one/two and a ~ hours, one hour/two hours and a ~:** anderthalb *od.* eineinhalb/zweieinhalb Stunden; **she is three and a ~:** sie ist dreieinhalb; **that was a performance/game/job and a ~** (fig. coll.) das war vielleicht eine Vorstellung/ein Spiel/eine Arbeit (ugs.); **an idiot/a joker/a fool/a woman and a ~** (fig. coll.) ein Oberidiot/-witzbold/-trottel (ugs.)/eine Superfrau (ugs.); **not/never do anything/things by halves** keine halben Sachen machen; **you don't do things by halves, do you?** (iron.) du meinst wohl, wenn schon, denn schon?; **be too cheeky/big by ~:** entschieden zu frech/groß sein; **be too clever by ~** (iron.) oberschlau (ugs. iron.) *od.* superklug (ugs. iron.) sein; **go halves** *or* **go ~ and ~ [with sb.] in** *or* (coll.) **on sth.** sich (*Dat.*) etw. [mit jmdm.] teilen; bei etw. halbe-halbe [mit jmdm.] machen (ugs.); **how the other ~ lives** wie andere Leute leben; **that's only** *or* **just** *or* **not the ~ of it** das ist noch nicht alles; **you don't know the ~ of it** [ja,] wenn es nur das wäre!; **my other ~** (coll.) meine bessere Hälfte (ugs.); *see also* **better A**

2 (coll.: ~ pint) kleines Glas; ≈ Viertel, *das;* (of beer) kleines Bier; Kleine, *das* (ugs.); **a ~ of bitter/lager/cider** ein kleines Bitter/ein kleines Lager/ein kleiner Apfelmost

3 (child's ticket) Fahrkarte zum halben Preis; halbe Fahrkarte; **one and a ~ to Oxford** eineinhalbmal nach Oxford; **two halves to Oxford** zwei halbe [Fahrkarten] nach Oxford

4 (Footb. etc.) (period) Halbzeit, *die;* (of pitch) [Spielfeld]hälfte, *die;* (coll.: ~-back) Läufer, *der*/Läuferin, *die*

5 (Golf) halbiertes Loch; **the outward/inward ~:** die Löcher 1-9/10-18

B *adj.* 1 (equal to a ~) halb; **~ the house/books/staff/time** die Hälfte des Hauses/der Bücher/des Personals/der Zeit; **~ the world** die halbe Welt; **he is drunk ~ the time** (very often) er ist fast immer betrunken; **she knits ~ the time/the day** (a lot of, a good deal of) sie strickt die ganze Zeit/den halben Tag; **~ an hour** eine halbe Stunde; **be only ~ the man/woman one used to be** (fig.) längst nicht mehr der/die alte sein

2 (forming a ~) **they each have a ~ share in the boat** das Boot gehört jedem [von ihnen] zur Hälfte; **be given a ~ day's holiday** einen halben Tag freibekommen

3 (Bookbinding) Halb‹*leder, -leinen*›; *see also* **battle A 3; ear**[1] **1; eye A 1; mind A 2**

C *adv.* 1 (to the extent of ~) zur Hälfte; halb ‹*öffnen, schließen, aufessen, fertig, voll, geöffnet*›; (almost) fast ‹*fallen, ersticken, tot sein*›; **our journey was now ~ done** die Hälfte der Reise lag hinter uns; **~ as much/many/big/heavy** halb so viel/viele/groß/schwer; **~ run [and] ~ walk** teils laufen, teils gehen; **~ cough and ~ sneeze** halb husten, halb niesen; **we had only ~ entered the room when ...:** wir waren noch nicht ganz eingetreten, als ...; **I ~ wished/hoped that ...:** ich wünschte mir/hoffte fast, dass ...; **only ~ hear what ...:** nur zum Teil hören, was ...; **~ listen for/to** mit halbem Ohr horchen auf (+ *Akk.*)/zuhören (+ *Dat.*); **I ~ laughed** (almost) ich hätte fast [los]gelacht; **I felt ~ dead** (fig.) ich war halbtot; **be only ~ ready** *or* **done** (Cookery) erst halb gar sein; **~ cook sth.** etw. halb gar werden lassen;

be ~ happy, ~ worried about sth. teils glücklich, teils besorgt über etw. (*Akk.*) sein; **leave the food ~ eaten** die Hälfte von dem Essen übrig lassen; **go ~ crazy/wild** halb verrückt (ugs.) werden; **not ~ cooked yet** noch lange nicht gar; **not ~ finished yet** noch lange nicht fertig; **not ~ long/strong enough** bei weitem nicht lang/stark genug; **not ~** (coll.) (most certainly) und ob!; (extremely) irrsinnig (ugs.); **not ~ bad** (coll.) toll (ugs.); **not ~ a bad fellow/meal** (coll.) ein toller Typ/ein tolles Essen (ugs.); **not ~ he wouldn't!** (coll.) und ob er das wäre/tun würde!; **it wasn't ~ a problem** (coll.) es war ein großes *od.* (ugs.) wahnsinniges Problem; **she can't ~ be stubborn** (coll.) sie ist wahnsinnig (ugs.) dickköpfig; **there won't ~ be trouble** (coll.) es wird einen Riesenkrach geben; *see also* **again 1**

[2] ▸ ❶ **p. 1001** (in time expressions) halb; **at ~ past the hour** um halb; **from eight o'clock till ~ past** von acht bis halb neun; **~ past** *or* (coll.) **~ twelve/one/two/three** *etc.* halb eins/zwei/drei/vier *usw.*; **~ past midday/midnight** halb eins mittags/nachts

half- *in comb.* ▸ ❶ **p. 1001** halb ‹*gar, verbrannt, betrunken, voll, leer*›; **~cold** fast kalt; **~starved** halb verhungert; **a ~dozen** ein halbes Dutzend; **~pound bag/~litre glass** Halbpfundtüte, *die*/-literglas, *das;* **a ~mile** eine halbe Meile; **~year** Halbjahr, *das;* halbes Jahr

half: ~-and-'~ **A** *n.* **Does it contain a or b? — H~-and-~:** Enthält es a oder b? — Halb und halb; **it is all silver, not ~-and-~:** es ist reines Silber, nicht halb Silber und halb etwas anderes; **settle for ~-and-~:** sich für eine Kombination aus beidem entscheiden; **B** *adj.* [1] (equal) **~-and-~ mixture of a and b** Mischung, die je zur Hälfte aus a und b besteht; [2] (indecisive) halb ‹*Maßnahme*›; **C** *adv.* zu gleichen Teilen; **they divide their earnings/share the duties ~-and-~:** sie teilen ihre Einkünfte/die Pflichten gleichmäßig untereinander auf; **~-arse[d]** /'hɑːfɑːs(t)/ *adj.* (sl.) bescheuert (salopp); beknackt (salopp); **do a ~-arse[d] job** Murks machen (ugs.); pfuschen (ugs.); **~-back** *n.* (Footb., Hockey) Läufer, *der*/Läuferin, *die;* **~-baked** /hɑːf'beɪkt/ *adj.* [1] (Cookery) nicht richtig durchgebacken; [2] (fig.) unausgegoren (abwertend), unausgereift ‹*Plan, Aufsatz, Idee*›; [3] (~-witted) nicht ganz gar *od.* dicht (ugs.); **~-binding** *n.* (Bookbinding) Halbledereinband, *der;* Halbfranzeinband, *der;* **~-blood** ▸ **~-breed 1**; **~-'blue** *n.* (Brit. Univ.) **get a** *or* **one's ~-blue** *die Universität bei weniger wichtigen Sportwettkämpfen oder als Reservespieler vertreten;* **~-'board** *n.* Halbpension, *die;* **~-board accommodation** [Unterkunft mit] Halbpension; **~-boot** *n.* Halbstiefel, *der;* **~-breed** *n.* [1] Mischling, *der;* Halbblut, *das;* [2] ▸ **cross-breed A**; **~-brother** *n.* Halbbruder, *der;* **be ~-brother to sb.** jmds. Halbbruder sein; **~-caste** **A** *n.* Mischling, *der;* Halbblut, *das;* **B** *adj.* Mischlings-; **~ 'cock** ▸ **cock¹ A 5**; **~-cocked** /hɑːf'kɒkt/ *adj., adv.* (Amer.) = **at ~ cock** ▸ **cock¹ A 5**; **~-conscious** *adj.* [nur] halb bewusst ‹*Wunsch, Wahrnehmung usw.*›; **be only ~-conscious** ‹*Person:*› nicht bei vollem Bewusstsein sein; **~-'crown** *n.* (Brit. Hist.) Halfcrown, *die;* **~-day** *n.* halber Tag; *attrib.* halbtägig ‹*Kurs, Test*›; **take a ~-day's holiday** einen halben Tag Urlaub nehmen; **it's ~-day closing today** heute ist nur halbtägig geöffnet; **~-'hardy** *adj.* (Hort.) [bedingt] winterhart; **~-hearted** /hɑːf'hɑːtɪd/ *adj.*, **~-heartedly** /hɑːf'hɑːtɪdlɪ/ *adv.* halbherzig; **~ hitch** ▸ **hitch C 2**; **~ 'holiday** *n.* halber freier Tag; **I'll take a ~ holiday on Wednesday** ich werde [am] Mittwoch einen halben Tag Urlaub nehmen; **there will be a ~ holiday in May** im Mai gibt es einen halben Tag frei; **~-hose** ▸ **hose A 2**; **~-'hour** *n.* ▸ ❶ **p. 1001** halbe Stunde; **at the ~-hour** um halb; **the clock chimes at the ~-hour** die Uhr schlägt jeweils um halb; **~-'hourly** ▸ ❶ **p. 1001** **A** *adj.* halbstündlich; halbstündlich verkehrend ‹*Bus usw.*›; **the bus service is ~-hourly** der Bus verkehrt halbstündlich; **B** *adv.* jede halbe Stunde; halbstündlich; **~-hunter** ▸ **hunter 5**; **~-'inch** **A** *n.* halber Inch; halber Zoll; *attrib.* /'--/ halbzollig; Halbzoll‹*bohrer, -schraube*›; **B** *v.t.* (Brit. sl.) klauen (ugs.); klemmen (salopp); **~-landing** *n.* Treppenabsatz, *der;* Zwischenpodest, *das* (Bauw.); **~-life** *n.* (Phys.) Halbwertszeit, *die;* **~-light** *n.* Halblicht, *das;* **~ 'mast** *n.* **be [flown] at ~ mast** ‹*Flagge:*› auf halbmast gehisst sein *od.* stehen; **raise/lower to ~ mast** auf halbmast hissen/setzen ‹*Flagge*›; **~ measure** *n.* [1] **a ~ measure of whisky** ein halber Whisky; [2] *in pl.* halbe Maßnahme; Halbheit, *die* (abwertend); **there are no ~ measures with him** er macht keine halben Sachen (ugs.); bei ihm gibt es keine Halbheiten; **~ 'moon** *n.* [1] Halbmond, *der;* [2] (Anat.) Möndchen, *das;* **the ~ moons of his nails** seine Nagelmöndchen; **~ 'nelson** *n.* (Wrestling) Halbnelson, *der;* **~ note** (Amer. Mus.) ▸ **minim 1**; **~ 'pay** *n.* (~ wages) halber Lohn; (~ salary) halbes Gehalt; **be on ~ pay** den halben Lohn/das halbe Gehalt bekommen; **~penny** /'heɪpnɪ/, *pl. usu.* **~pennies** /'heɪpnɪz/ *for separate coins,* **~pence** /'heɪpəns/ *for sum of money* (Brit. Hist.) (coin) Halfpenny, *der;* (sum) halber Penny; **~pennyworth** /'heɪpəθ/ *n.* (Brit.) [1] (Hist.: amount) **a ~pennyworth of ...:** für einen halben Penny ...; [2] (fig. dated: small amount) **not a** *or* **one ~pennyworth of** nicht für fünf Pfennig (ugs.) ‹*Verstand*›; nicht das kleinste bisschen ‹*Ruhe, Gastfreundschaft, Entgegenkommen usw.*›; **~-'pint** *n.* [1] (quantity) halbes Pint; [2] (coll.: small or insignificant person) halbe Portion (ugs. spött.); **~-'price** **A** *n.* halber Preis; **all articles are at ~-price** alle Artikel gibt es zum halben Preis; **bring sth. down** *or* **reduce sth. to ~-price** etw. um die Hälfte heruntersetzen *od.* reduzieren; **B** *adj.* zum halben Preis *nachgestellt;* **~-price air fares** um die Hälfte herabgesetzte Flugpreise; **C** *adv.* zum halben Preis; **~-seas-over** /hɑːfsiːz'əʊvə(r)/ *adj.* (coll.) angesäuselt (ugs.); **~-shell** *n.* Austernschale, *die:* **lobster on the ~-shell** (Gastr.) auf einer Austernschale servierter Hummer; **~-sister** *n.* Halbschwester, *die;* **be ~-sister to sb.** jmds. Halbschwester sein; **~-size** **A** *n.* Zwischengröße, *die;* halbe Größe; **a ~-size larger** eine halbe Nummer größer; **B** *adj.* halb ‹*Portion*›; klein ‹*Blumentopf, Spaten*›; **~ 'staff** (Amer.) ▸ **~ mast**; **~ step** (Amer. Mus.) ▸ **semitone**; **~-'term** *n.* (Brit.) [1] **it is nearly ~-term** das Trimester ist fast zur Hälfte vorüber; **by/at/towards ~-term** bis zur/in der/gegen die Mitte des Trimesters; **before ~-term** in der ersten Trimesterhälfte; [2] (holiday) **~-term [holiday/break]** Ferien in der Mitte des Trimesters; **~-timbered** /hɑːf'tɪmbəd/ *adj.* Fachwerk‹*haus, -bauweise*›; **be ~-timbered** ein Fachwerkbau sein; **~-'time** **A** *n.* [1] (Sport) Halbzeit, *die; attrib.* /'--/ Halbzeit‹*pfiff, -stand*›; **blow the whistle for ~-time** die erste Halbzeit abpfeifen; **by/to ~-time** bis zur Halbzeit; **at ~-time** bei *od.* bis zur Halbzeit; (during interval) in der Halbzeitpause; **~-time score** Halbzeitergebnis, *das;* [2] (Industry) Kurzarbeit, *die* (*mit um 50 Prozent gekürzter Arbeitszeit*); **~-time working** Kurzarbeit, *die;* **several cotton mills were put on ~-time** in mehreren Baumwollspinnereien wurde Kurzarbeit eingeführt; **1,150 workers were put on ~-time** *or* **had to go on ~-time schedules** 1150 Arbeiter mussten kurzarbeiten; **B** *adv.* (Industry) kurz‹*arbeiten*›; **~-title** *n.* (Printing) [1] Schmutztitel, *der;* Vortitel, *der;* [2] (section title) Zwischentitel, *der;* **~-tone** *n.* [1] (Printing etc.) Rasterbild, *das;* [2] (Amer. Mus.) ▸ **semitone**; **~-track** *n.* [1] (system) Halbkettenantrieb, *der;* [2] (vehicle) Halbkettenfahrzeug, *das;* **~-truth** *n.* Halbwahrheit, *die;* **you've only told us a ~-truth** du hast uns nur die halbe Wahrheit gesagt; **~-'volley** ▸ **volley A 3**; **~'way** **A** *adj.* halb ‹*Maßnahme*›; **~way point** Mitte, *die;* **we're well over the ~way mark** wir haben gut die Hälfte geschafft; **~way house** Gasthaus auf halbem Weg; (fig.: compromise) Kompromiss, *der;* Mittelweg, *der;* **~way line** (Footb.) Mittellinie, *die;* **B** *adv.* die Hälfte des Weges ‹*begleiten, fahren*›; **not ~way satisfactory** nicht einmal halbwegs zufrieden stellend; **by midday they had climbed ~way up the mountain** bis zum Mittag hatten sie den halben Aufstieg hinter sich; *see also* **go¹ A 17**; **meet¹ A 2**; **~wit** *n.* Schwachkopf, *der;* (scatterbrain) Schussel, *der;* **~-witted** /hɑːf'wɪtɪd/ *adj.* dumm; (mentally deficient) debil; schwachsinnig; **~-witted person** Schwachkopf, *der;* **~-'yearly** **A** *adj.* halbjährlich; **at ~-yearly intervals** in halbjährigen Abständen; halbjährlich; **B** *adv.* halbjährlich; jedes halbe Jahr

halibut /'hælɪbət/ *n., pl. same* (Zool.) Heilbutt, *der*

halide /'heɪlaɪd/ *n.* (Chem.) Halogenid, *das;* Halid, *das*

halitosis /hælɪ'təʊsɪs/ *n., pl.* **halitoses** /hælɪ'təʊsiːz/ (Med.) Halitose, *die* (fachspr.); schlechter Atem

hall /hɔːl/ *n.* [1] (entrance passage) Diele, *die;* Flur, *der* [2] (Amer.: corridor) Korridor, *der;* Flur, *der* [3] (large [public] room) Saal, *der;* (public building) Halle, *die;* (for receptions, banquets) Festsaal, *der;* (in medieval house: principal living room) Wohnsaal, *der;* **school/church ~:** Aula, *die*/Gemeindehaus, *das; see also* **servants' hall** [4] (mansion) Herrenhaus, *das;* Herrensitz, *der* [5] (Univ.) (residential building) **~ [of residence]** Studentenwohnheim, *das;* (Hist.: college) Kolleg, *das;* **live in ~:** im [Studenten]wohnheim wohnen [6] (Univ.: dining room) Speisesaal, *der;* Mensa, *die;* **in ~:** im Speisesaal; in der Mensa [7] *no art.* (dinner taken in ~) Abendessen in der Mensa [8] *in pl.* (Hist.: music ~s) Varietee, *das;* **be on the ~s** im Varietee auftreten; **do a turn on the ~s** mit einer Nummer im Varietee auftreten

hallal ▸ **halal**

hallelujah /hælɪ'luːjə/
A *int.* hallelujah
B *n.* Hallelujah, *das*

halliard ▸ **halyard**

'hallmark
A *n.* [Feingehalts]stempel, *der;* Repunze, *die;* (fig.: distinctive mark) Kennzeichen, *das;* **be the ~ of quality/perfection** (fig.) für Qualität/Vollkommenheit bürgen *od.* stehen
B *v.t.* stempeln; repunzieren

hallo /hə'ləʊ/
A *int.* [1] (to call attention) hallo! [2] (Brit.) **hello**
B *n., pl.* **~s** Hallo, *das;* Halloruf, *der;* **give a ~:** Hallo rufen

hall of 'fame *n.* Ruhmeshalle, *die*

halloo /hə'luː/
A *int.* [1] (Hunting) horrido! [2] ▸ **hallo A 1**
B *n.* [1] (Hunting) Horrido, *das* [2] ▸ **hallo B**

hallow /'hæləʊ/
A *n.* **All H~s, H~mas = All Saints' Day** ▸ **all A 2**
B *v.t.* [1] (sanctify) heiligen; **~ed** geheiligt (auch fig.); heilig ‹*Boden*› [2] (honour) als heilig verehren; **~ed be Thy Name** (in Lord's Prayer) geheiligt werde dein Name

Hallowe'en /hæləʊ'iːn/ *n.* Halloween, *das; Abend vor Allerheiligen;* **on** *or* **at ~:** [an] Halloween

hall: ~ 'porter *n.* (Brit.) [Hotel]portier, *der;* **~ stand** *n.* [Flur]garderobe, *die*

hallucinant /hə'luːsɪnənt/
A *adj.* ▸ **hallucinogenic**
B *n.* ▸ **hallucinogen**

hallucinate /hə'luːsɪneɪt/ *v.i.* halluzinieren (Med., Psych.); Halluzinationen haben

hallucination /həluːsɪ'neɪʃn/ *n.* (act) Halluzinieren, *das;* (instance, imagined object) Halluzination, *die;* Sinnestäuschung, *die*

hallucinatory /hə'luːsɪnətərɪ/ *adj.* [1] (producing hallucinations) ▸ **hallucinogenic** [2] (associated with hallucinations) halluzinatorisch (Med., Psych.) [3] (unreal) imaginär (geh.); **be purely ~:** reine Einbildung sein

hallucinogen /hə'luːsɪnədʒen/ *n.* (Med.) Halluzinogen, *das*

hallucinogenic /həluːsɪnə'dʒenɪk/ *adj.* (Med.) halluzinogen

'hallway *n.* [1] ▸ **hall 8** [2] (corridor) Flur, *der;* Korridor, *der;* Gang, *der* (bes. südd., österr., schweiz.)

halo /'heɪləʊ/ *n., pl.* **~es** [1] (Meteorol.) Halo, *der* (fachspr.); Hof, *der;* **there was a ~ round** *or* **a ~ surrounded the moon** der Mond hatte einen

Hof *od.* (fachspr.) Halo **2** (circle) Ring, *der;* (of light) Lichthof, *der* **3** (around head) Heiligen-, Glorienschein, *der* **4** (fig.: aura) Nimbus, *der;* **put a romantic ~ about sth.** etw. mit einer romantischen Gloriole umgeben

halogen /ˈhælədʒən/ *n.* (Chem.) Halogen, *das; attrib.* **~ lamp** Halogenlampe, *die*

halon /ˈheɪlɒn/ *n.* (Chem.) Halon, *das*

halt /hɔːlt/

A *n.* **1** (temporary stoppage) Pause, *die;* (on march or journey) Rast, *die;* Pause, *die;* (esp. Mil. also) Halt, *der;* **make a ~:** Rast/eine Pause machen/Halt machen; **call a ~:** eine Pause machen lassen/Halt machen lassen; **let's call a ~:** machen wir eine Pause! **2** (interruption) Unterbrechung, *die;* **come to a ~** zum Stehen kommen; ‹*Produktion, Verkehr:*› zum Stillstand kommen; *see also* **call B 6**; **come A 8**; **grind B 2** **3** (Brit. Railw.) Haltepunkt, *der*

B *v.i.* **1** (stop) ‹*Fußgänger, Tier:*› stehen bleiben; ‹*Fahrer:*› anhalten; (for a rest) eine Pause machen; (esp. Mil.) Halt machen; (to collect one's thoughts etc.) innehalten; **~, who goes there?** (Mil.) halt, wer da? **2** (end) eingestellt werden

C *v.t.* **1** (cause to stop) anhalten; Halt machen lassen ‹*Marschkolonne usw.*›; **he could not be ~ed** (fig.) er war nicht aufzuhalten *od.* (ugs.) zu bremsen **2** (cause to end) stoppen ‹*Inflation, Diskussion*›; beenden ‹*Herrschaft*›; einstellen ‹*Projekt*›

halter /ˈhɔːltə(r)/ *n.* **1** (for horse) Halfter, *das;* (for cattle) **[rope] ~:** Strick, *der* **2** (Dressmaking) (strap) Nackenträger, *der;* Nackenband, *das;* (top with a ~) Oberteil *od.* Top mit Nackenträger; **~ dress/bodice/top/bra** Kleid/Mieder/Oberteil *od.* Top/Büstenhalter mit Nackenträger; **~ neck** Nackenband, *das*

halting /ˈhɔːltɪŋ/ *adj.* schleppend ‹*Stimme, Redeweise, Fortschritt*›; holprig ‹*Verse*›; zögernd ‹*Antwort*›; schwach ‹*Argument*›; **in a ~ing way** *or* **manner** schleppend ‹*sprechen*›

haltingly /ˈhɔːltɪŋlɪ/ *adv.* schleppend ‹*vorankommen*›; (with uncertain steps) mit unsicheren Schritten ‹*gehen*›; (hesitantly) zögernd; **come ~ to the point** nur auf Umwegen zur Sache kommen

halve /hɑːv/ *v.t.* **1** (divide) halbieren **2** (share) [ehrlich] teilen; **they ~d the cake [between them]** sie haben sich (*Dat.*) den Kuchen ehrlich geteilt **3** (reduce) halbieren; auf *od.* um die Hälfte verringern; **'sale — all prices ~d!'** „Ausverkauf — alles zum halben Preis!"; **~ the amount of beer one drinks/number of nights one goes out** nur noch halb so viel Bier trinken/halb so oft abends ausgehen **4** (Golf) mit der gleichen Anzahl von Schlägen erreichen ‹*Loch*› (**with** wie); **the hole was ~d in 5** beide Spieler erreichten das Loch mit fünf Schlägen

halves *pl. of* **half**

halyard /ˈhæljəd/ *n.* (Naut.) Fall, *das;* (for flag) Flagg[en]leine, *die*

ham /hæm/

A *n.* **1** ([meat from] thigh of pig) Schinken, *der* **2** *usu. in pl.* (back of thigh) Hinterseite des Oberschenkels; **squat** *or* **sit on one's ~s** in der Hocke sitzen **3** (coll.) (amateur) Amateur, *der;* (poor actor) Schmierenkomödiant, *der* (abwertend); **radio ~:** Funkamateur, *der* **4** *no pl., no art.* (coll.: inexpert acting) Schmierentheater, *das* (abwertend)

B *adj.* (coll.) überzogen; **a very ~ performance** ein ziemliches Schmierentheater (abwertend)

C *v.i.*, **-mm-** (coll.) überziehen

D *v.t.*, **-mm-** (coll.) überzogen spielen

(Phrasal verb)

- **~ 'up** *v.t.* (coll.) überzogen spielen ‹*Stück*›; **~ it up** überziehen

hamadryad /hæməˈdraɪæd/ *n.* **1** (Greek and Roman Mythol.) Hamadryade, *die* **2** (Zool.: cobra) Königskobra, *die* **3** (Zool.: baboon) Mantelpavian, *der*

Hamburg /ˈhæmbɜːg/ ▸**❶ p. 1643**

A *pr. n.* Hamburg (*das*)

B *attrib. adj.* Hamburger

hamburger /ˈhæmbɜːgə(r)/ *n.* **1** (beef cake) Hacksteak, *das;* (filled roll) Hamburger, *der* **2** **H~** (person) Hamburger, *der*/Hamburgerin, *die*

Hamelin /ˈhæmlɪn/ *pr. n.* Hameln (*das*)

ham: ~-fisted /hæmˈfɪstɪd/, **~-handed** /hæmˈhændɪd/ *adjs.* (coll.) tollpatschig (ugs.) ‹*Mensch, Art*›; dilettantisch ‹*Bearbeitung, Vorgehensweise*›; plump (abwertend) ‹*Vorstellung, Humor*›; **~-fisted** *or* **~-handed actions** Tollpatschigkeiten

hamlet /ˈhæmlɪt/ *n.* Weiler, *der*

hammer /ˈhæmə(r)/

A *n.* **1** (tool; also Anat.) Hammer, *der;* **the H~ and Sickle** (Hist.) Hammer und Sichel; **go** *or* **be at sth. ~ and tongs** sich bei etw. schwer ins Zeug legen (ugs.); **go** *or* **be at it ~ and tongs** (quarrel) sich streiten, dass die Fetzen fliegen **2** (of gun) Hahn, *der* **3** (auctioneer's mallet) Hammer, *der;* **come under the ~:** unter den Hammer kommen **4** (Athletics) [Wurf]hammer, *der;* **[throwing] the ~** (event) das Hammerwerfen

B *v.t.* **1** (strike with ~) hämmern; (fig.) hämmern auf (*Akk.*) ‹*Tasten, Tisch*›; einhämmern auf (*Akk.*) ‹*Gegner, Opfer*›; **~ a nail into sth.** einen Nagel in etw. (*Akk.*) hämmern *od.* schlagen; **~ sth. into sb.['s head]** (fig.) jmdm. etw. einhämmern; **~ home** einschlagen ‹*Nagel, Bolzen usw.*›; **He must not do that. We'll ~ it home** Er darf das nicht tun. Wir werden es ihm einbläuen **2** (coll.: inflict heavy defeat on) abservieren (ugs.) ‹*Gegner*›; vernichtend schlagen ‹*Feind*›; ausstechen ‹*Konkurrenten*› **3** (St. Exch.) für zahlungsunfähig erklären

C *v.i.* **1** (give blows) hämmern; klopfen; **~ at sth.** an etw. (*Dat.*) [herum]hämmern; **~ at** *or* **on the door** an *od.* gegen die Tür hämmern **2** (fig. coll.: travel fast) düsen (ugs.); kacheln (salopp)

(Phrasal verbs)

- **~ a'way** *v.i.* hämmern; **~ away at** herumhämmern *od.* (ugs.) -kloppen auf (+ *Dat.*); (fig.: work hard at) sich hineinknien in (+ *Akk.*) (ugs.) ‹*Tätigkeit*›; [herum]bosseln an (+ *Dat.*) (ugs.) ‹*Aufsatz*›
- **~ 'down** *v.t.* festhämmern, -klopfen
- **~ 'out** *v.t.* **1** (make smooth) ausklopfen ‹*Delle, Beule*›; ausbeulen ‹*Kotflügel usw.*›; glatt klopfen ‹*Blech usw.*› **2** (fig.: devise) ausarbeiten ‹*Plan, Methode, Vereinbarung*›; kommen zu ‹*Entscheidung, Entschluss*›

hammock /ˈhæmək/ *n.* Hängematte, *die*

hammy /ˈhæmɪ/ *adj.* **1** (resembling ham) schinkenartig; Schinken‹*geschmack, -geruch*›; **have a ~ taste** nach Schinken schmecken **2** (coll.: of ham actors) theatralisch (abwertend) ‹*Nummer, Rolle, Aufführung, Darstellung*›

hamper¹ /ˈhæmpə(r)/ *n.* **1** (basket) [Deckel]korb, *der* **2** (consignment of food) Präsentkorb, *der;* **Christmas ~:** Weihnachtsgeschenkkorb, *der*

hamper² *v.t.* behindern; hemmen ‹*Entwicklung, Wachstum usw.*›; **~ sb. in his progress, ~ sb.'s progress** ‹*Hindernis:*› jmdn. aufhalten; **~ sb. in his movements** jmdn. behindern *od.* in seiner Bewegungsfreiheit beeinträchtigen

hamster /ˈhæmstə(r)/ *n.* Hamster, *der; see also* **golden hamster**

'hamstring

A *n.* (Anat.) **1** (in man, ape) Kniesehne, *die* **2** (in quadruped) Achillessehne, *die*

B *v.t.*, **hamstrung** **1** (cripple) die Kniesehnen/Achillessehnen durchtrennen (+ *Dat.*) **2** (fig.: destroy efficiency of) lähmen

hand /hænd/

A *n.* **1** ▸**❶ p. 951** (Anat., Zool.) Hand, *die;* **eat from** *or* **out of sb.'s ~** (lit. or fig.) jmdm. aus der Hand fressen; **I need an extra/a strong pair of ~s** ich brauche noch jmdn., der/eine kräftige Person, die mir hilft; **get one's ~s dirty, dirty** *or* **soil one's ~s** (lit. or fig.) sich (*Dat.*) die Hände schmutzig machen; **give sb. one's ~** (reach, shake) jmdm. die Hand geben *od.* reichen; **give** *or* **lend [sb.] a ~ [with** *or* **in sth.]** [jmdm.] [bei etw.] helfen; **not/never do a ~'s turn** keine/niemals eine Hand rühren (ugs.); keinen/niemals einen Finger krumm machen (ugs.); **pass** *or* **go through sb.'s ~s** (fig.) durch jmds. Hand *od.* Hände gehen; **pass through many/several ~s** durch viele/etliche Hände gehen; **many ~s make light work** (prov.) viele Hände machen der Arbeit bald ein Ende (Spr.); **~ in ~:** Hand in Hand; **go ~ in ~ [with sth.]** (fig.) [mit etw.] Hand in Hand gehen; **the problem/project/matter in ~:** das vorliegende Problem/Projekt/die vorliegende Angelegenheit; *see also* **4**; **~ hands** Händchen halten (ugs. scherzh.); sich bei den Händen halten; **hold sb.'s ~:** jmds. Hand halten; jmdm. die Hand halten; (fig.: give sb. close guidance) jmdn. bei der Hand nehmen; (fig.: give sb. moral support or backing) jmdn. moralisch unterstützen; jmdm. das Händchen halten (iron.); **take one's child's/big brother's ~** ‹*Erwachsener:*› sein Kind an die Hand nehmen/‹*Kind:*› sich von seinem großen Bruder an die Hand nehmen lassen; **~s off!** Hände *od.* Finger weg!; **~s off my wife/Chile!** Hände weg von meiner Frau/Chile!; **take/keep one's ~s off sb./sth.** jmdn./etw. loslassen/nicht anfassen; **take your ~s off me this instant!** nimm sofort die Finger weg!; **keep one's ~s off sth.** (fig.) die Finger von etw. lassen (ugs.); **show of ~s** Handzeichen, *das;* **~s up [all those in favour]** (as sign of assent) wer dafür ist, hebt die Hand!; **~s up!** (as sign of surrender) Hände hoch!; **win ~s down** (fig.) (easily) mit links gewinnen; (by a large margin) ganz klar gewinnen; **be good with one's ~s** [handwerklich] geschickt sein; **change** *or* (coll.) **swap ~s** die Hand wechseln; die andere Hand nehmen; *see also* **3**; **turn one's ~ to sth.** sich einer Sache (*Dat.*) zuwenden; **put** *or* **set one's ~ to** sich machen an (+ *Akk.*) ‹*Arbeit, Aufgabe*›; *see also* **12**; **put** *or* **set one's ~ to doing sth.** sich daran machen, etw. zu tun; **have sth. at ~:** etw. zur Hand haben; **have sb. at ~:** jmdn. bei sich haben; **be at ~** (be nearby) in der Nähe sein; (be about to happen) unmittelbar bevorstehen; **out of ~** (without delay) unverzüglich; (summarily) kurzerhand; *see also* **2**; **be to ~** (be readily available, within reach) zur Hand sein; (be received) ‹*Brief, Notiz, Anweisung:*› vorliegen; **come to ~** (turn up) sich finden; (be received) ‹*Brief, Mitteilung:*› eingehen; **she uses whatever comes to ~:** sie nimmt, was gerade da ist; **fight ~ to ~:** Mann gegen Mann kämpfen; **go/pass from ~ to ~:** von Hand zu Hand gehen; **~ over ~** *or* **fist** Zug um Zug ‹*hinaufklettern, einziehen*›; **~ over fist** (fig.) (with steady progress) laufend; (with rapid progress) rapide; **live from ~ to mouth** von der Hand in den Mund leben; **be ~ in glove [with]** unter einer Decke stecken [mit]; **bind sb. ~ and foot** jmdn. an Händen und Füßen fesseln; **wait on** *or* **serve sb. ~ and foot** (fig.) jmdn. vorn und hinten bedienen (ugs.); **on [one's] ~s and knees** auf Händen und Knien; **crawl on [one's] ~s and knees** auf allen vieren kriechen (ugs.); **get down on one's ~s and knees** auf die Knie gehen; **his ~s are tied** (fig.) ihm sind die Hände gebunden; **have one's ~s full** die Hände voll haben; (fig.: be fully occupied) alle Hände voll zu tun haben (ugs.); **~ on** *or* **over heart** (fig.) Hand aufs Herz; **get one's ~s on sb./sth.** jmdn. erwischen *od.* (ugs.) in die Finger kriegen/etw. auftreiben; **lay** *or* **put one's ~ on sth.** etw. finden; **lay [one's] ~s on sth.** sich einer Sache bemächtigen; **everything** *or* **anything** *or* **all they could lay [their] ~s on** alles, wessen sie habhaft werden konnten; **lay ~s on sb.** jmdm. etw. tun; Hand an jmdn. legen (geh.); (violate) sich an jmdm. vergreifen; **by ~** (manually) mit der *od.* von Hand; (in ~writing) handschriftlich; (by messenger) durch Boten; **be made by ~:** Handarbeit sein; **bring up by ~:** mit der Flasche aufziehen; **I could do that with one ~ tied behind my back** das mache ich doch mit links (ugs.); *see also* **banana 1**; **clean A 2**; **finger A 1**; **hand-to-hand**; **hand-to-mouth**; **join A 1**; **shake B 1**; **sit A 2**; **wash A 1** **2** (fig.: authority) **with a strict/firm/iron ~:** mit fester/starker Hand/eiserner Faust ‹*regieren*›; **with a heavy ~:** mit eiserner Strenge; **he needs a father's ~:** er braucht die väterliche Hand; **hold one's ~:** abwarten; **hold one's ~ and not do sth.** davon Abstand nehmen, etw. zu tun; **keep in ~:** unter Kontrolle behalten ‹*Schüler, Demonstranten*› (*see also* **4**); **get out of ~:** außer Kontrolle geraten; *see also* **1**; **give sb. a free ~:** jmdm. freie Hand lassen; **have a**

free ~ to do sth. freie Hand haben, etw. zu tun; *see also* **free hand**; **take A 1**; **upper A 1**
3 *in pl.* (custody) **in sb.'s ~s, in the ~s of sb.** (in sb.'s possession) in jmds. Besitz; (in sb.'s care) in jmds. Obhut; **I am in your ~s** die Entscheidungen überlasse ich Ihnen; **put oneself in sb.'s ~s** sich jmdm. anvertrauen; **be in the ~s of the police** ‹*Verdächtiger:*› sich in Polizeigewahrsam befinden; **may I leave the matter in your ~s?** darf ich die Angelegenheit Ihnen überlassen?; **the matter/the decision is now out of my ~s** ich bin für die Angelegenheit/die Entscheidung nicht mehr zuständig; **take sth. out of sb.'s ~s** (withdraw sth. from sb.) jmdm. etw. entziehen *od.* aus der Hand nehmen; (relieve sb. of sth.) jmdm. etw. abnehmen; **fall into sb.'s ~s** ‹*Person, Geld:*› jmdm. in die Hände fallen; ‹*Verantwortung:*› jmdm. zufallen; **be in good/bad ~s** in guten/schlechten Händen sein; **have [got] sth./sb. on one's ~s** sich um etw./jmdn. kümmern müssen; **he's got such a lot/enough on his ~s at the moment** er hat augenblicklich so viel/genug um die Ohren (ugs.); **suddenly we had a riot on our ~s** plötzlich sahen wir uns mit Ausschreitungen konfrontiert; **have time on one's ~s** [viel] Zeit haben; (too much) mit seiner Zeit nichts anzufangen wissen; **they are off our ~s at last** endlich sind wir sie los (ugs.); **have [got] sth./sb. off one's ~s** etw./jmdn. los sein (ugs.); **take sb./sth. off sb.'s ~s** jmdm. jmdn./etw. abnehmen; **change ~s** den Besitzer wechseln; *see also* **1**
4 (disposal) **have sth. in ~:** etw. zur Verfügung haben; (not used up) etw. [übrig] haben; **keep in ~:** in Reserve halten ‹*Geld*› (*see also* **2**); **have on ~:** dahaben; **be on ~:** da sein
5 (share) **have a ~ in sth.** bei etw. seine Hände im Spiel haben; **take a ~ [in sth.]** sich [an etw. (*Dat.*)] beteiligen; **take a ~ [at bridge]** [Bridge] mitspielen; *see also* **bear² A 11**
6 (agency) Wirken, *das* (geh.); **the ~ of a thief/artist/craftsman has been at work here** hier war ein Dieb/Künstler/Handwerker am Werk; **the ~ of God** die Hand Gottes; **these two paintings are by the same ~:** diese beiden Gemälde stammen von derselben Hand; **suffer/suffer injustice at the ~s of sb.** unter jmdm./jmds. Ungerechtigkeit zu leiden haben; **die by one's own ~[s]** (literary) Hand an sich (*Akk.*) legen (geh.)
7 (pledge of marriage) **ask for** *or* **seek sb.'s ~ [in marriage]** um jmds. Hand bitten *od.* (geh.) anhalten; um jmdn. anhalten (geh.); **ask sb. for his daughter's ~:** jmdn. um die Hand seiner Tochter bitten; bei jmdm. um die Hand seiner Tochter anhalten (geh.); **win sb.'s ~:** jmdn. zur Frau *od.* jmds. Hand gewinnen
8 (worker) Arbeitskraft, *die;* Arbeiter, *der;* (Naut.: seaman) Hand, *die* (fachspr.); Matrose, *der;* **the ship sank with all ~s** das Schiff sank mit der gesamten Mannschaft
9 (person having ability) **be a good/poor/rotten ~ at [playing] tennis** ein guter/schwacher/miserabler Tennisspieler sein; **I'm no ~ at painting** ich kann nicht malen; *see also* **old A 2**
10 (source) Quelle, *die;* **at first/second/third ~:** aus erster/zweiter/dritter Hand; *see also* **firsthand**; **second-hand**
11 (skill) Geschick, *das;* (characteristic style) Handschrift, *die;* **get one's ~ in** wieder in Übung kommen *od.* (ugs.) reinkommen; **get one's ~ in at sth.** etw. lernen; **keep one's ~ in [at singing/dancing]** [im Singen/Tanzen] in der Übung bleiben *od.* nicht aus der Übung kommen; *see also* **try B 2**
12 (style of ~writing) Handschrift, *die;* Hand, *die* (veralt.); (signature) Unterschrift, *die;* **set one's ~ to sth.** seine Unterschrift unter etw. (*Akk.*) setzen; *see also* **A**
13 (of clock or watch) Zeiger, *der*
14 (side) Seite, *die;* **on the right/left ~:** rechts/links; rechter/linker Hand; **on sb.'s right/left ~:** rechts/links von jmdm.; zu jmds. Rechten/Linken; **on either ~:** zu *od.* auf beiden Seiten; **on every ~:** von allen Seiten ‹*umringt sein*›; ringsum ‹*etw. sehen*›; von überallher ‹*eintreffen*›; **on the one ~ ..., [but] on the other [~] ...:** einerseits ..., andererseits ...; auf der einen Seite ..., auf der anderen Seite ...; **[but] on the other ~:** aber andererseits *od.* auf der anderen Seite; *see also* **left-hand**; **right-hand**
15 (measurement) Handbreit, *die*
16 (Cards) Karte, *die;* (player) Mitspieler, *der*/-spielerin, *die;* (period of play) Runde, *die;* **have a good/bad ~:** ein gutes/schlechtes Blatt haben; eine gute/schlechte Karte haben; **play a good ~:** gut spielen; *see also* **force¹ B 2**; **play B 1**; **show B 1**
17 (coll.: applause) Beifall, *der;* Applaus, *der;* **give him a big ~, let's have a big ~ for him** viel Applaus *od.* Beifall für ihn!
B *v.t.* **1** (deliver) reichen, geben (**to sb** jmdm.); ‹*Überbringer:*› übergeben ‹*Sendung, Lieferung*›; **~ sth. from one to another** etw. von einem zum anderen weitergeben *od.* -reichen; **~ sth. [a]round [to sb.]** (offer for distribution) [jmdm.] etw. anbieten; **~ sth. [a]round** (pass round, circulate) etw. herumgeben *od.* -reichen; (among group) etw. herumgehen lassen; **you've got to ~ it to them/her** *etc.* (fig. coll.) das muss man ihnen/ihr *usw.* lassen
2 (help) helfen; **~ sb. out of/into/over sth.** jmdm. aus etw./in etw. (*Akk.*)/über etw. (*Akk.*) helfen

Phrasal verbs

- **~ 'back** *v.t.* (return) zurückgeben
- **~ 'down** *v.t.* **1** (pass on) überliefern ‹*Geschichte, Information, Tradition*›; weitergeben ‹*Gegenstand*› (**to** an + *Akk.*); [weiter]vererben ‹*Erbstück*› (**to** an + *Akk.*); **that ring has been ~ed down from your great-great-grandmother** der Ring ist ein Erbstück von deiner Ururgroßmutter **2** (Law) verhängen ‹*Strafe*› (**to** über + *Akk.*); fällen ‹*Entscheidung*›; verkünden ‹*Urteil*›; **~ down a fine to sb.** jmdn. mit einer Geldstrafe belegen **3** (give to person below) hinunter-/herunterreichen
- **~ 'in** *v.t.* abgeben ‹*Klausur, Arbeit, Aufsatz*› (**to, at** bei); einreichen ‹*Petition, Bewerbung*› (**to, at** bei)
- **~ 'on** *v.t.* weitergeben ‹*Rundschreiben, Nachricht, Erfahrungen, Information*› (**to** an + *Akk.*); **at 65 he ~ed the business on to his son** mit 65 hat er das Geschäft seinem Sohn übergeben
- **~ 'out** *v.t.* aus-, verteilen (**to** an + *Akk.*, **among** unter + *Dat.*); geben ‹*Ratschläge, Tipps, Winke*› (**to** an + *Akk.*); verteilen ‹*Komplimente, Lob*› (**to** an + *Akk.*); *see also* **handout**
- **~ 'over**

A *v.t.* **1** (deliver) übergeben (**to** *Dat.*); freilassen ‹*Geisel*›; **~ over your guns/money!** Waffen/Geld her!; gebt eure Waffen/euer Geld her!; **he ~ed the housekeeping money over to his wife** er händigte seiner Frau das Haushaltsgeld aus **2** (transfer) übergeben *od.* -reichen (**to** *Dat.*); (pass) herüber- *od.* rübergeben *od.* -reichen (**to** *Dat.*); (allow to have) abgeben
B *v.i.* (to next speaker/one's successor) das Wort/die Arbeit übergeben (**to** an + *Akk.*)

- **~ 'up** *v.t.* heraufreichen (**to** *Dat.*)

hand- *in comb.* **1** (operated by hand, held in the hand) Hand‹*hammer, -hebel, -gepäck, -werkzeug, -mixer*› **2** (done by hand) hand‹*gestickt*›; mit der Hand *od.* von Hand ‹*glasiert, verziert, gebacken*›

hand: ~bag A *n.* Handtasche, *die.* **B** *v.t.* (Brit. coll. joc.) abkanzeln (ugs.); **~ baggage** *n.* Handgepäck, *das;* **~ball** *n.* **1** *no pl.* (game) Handball, *der;* **2** (Soccer: foul) Handspiel, *das;* **~bell** *n.* Handglocke, *die;* (musical instrument) Glocke, *die;* **~bill** *n.* Handzettel, *der;* **~book** *n.* Handbuch, *das;* (guidebook) Führer, *der;* **~brake** *n.* Handbremse, *die*

h & c *abbr.* **= hot and cold running water** fl. h. u. k. W.

hand: ~cart *n.* Handwagen, *der;* **~clap** *n.* **1** (single clap) In-die-Hände-Klatschen, *das;* **give three ~claps** dreimal in die Hände klatschen; **2** (applause) [Hände]klatschen, *das; see also* **slow handclap**; **~clasp** *n.* Händedruck, *der;* **~craft A** *n.* ▸**handicraft 1**; **B** *v.t.* in Handarbeit herstellen; **~ cream** *n.* Handcreme, *die;* **~cuff A** *n., usu. in pl.* Handschelle, *die;* **B** *v.t.* in Handschellen (*Akk.*) legen ‹*Hände*›; **~cuff sb.** jmdm. Handschellen anlegen; **~ drier, ~ dryer** *ns.* Händetrockner, *der*

handed-'down *adj.* abgelegt ‹*Kleidungsstück*›; (to posterity) überliefert

hand-'finished *adj.* ▸**finish A 6**: mit der Hand *od.* von Hand geglättet/appretiert/glasiert/poliert/lackiert *usw.*

handful /'hændfʊl/ *n.* **1** (quantity, or fig.: small number) Handvoll, *die;* **a few ~s of nuts** ein paar Hand voll *od.* ein paar Hände voll Nüsse; **they picked them up by the ~:** sie sammelten ganze Hände voll davon auf; **come out in ~s** *or* **by the ~** ‹*Haar:*› büschelweise ausgehen **2** (fig. coll.: troublesome person[s] or thing[s]) **these children are/this dog is a real ~:** die Kinder halten/der Hund hält einen ständig auf Trab (ugs.); **it's quite a ~ looking after the children** mit der Versorgung der Kinder hat man alle Hände voll zu tun; **that car is quite a ~ to steer** das Auto zu lenken ist Schwerarbeit (ugs.)

hand: ~ grenade *n.* (Mil.) Handgranate, *die;* **~gun** *n.* (Arms) Faustfeuerwaffe, *die;* **~-held** *adj.* **~-held camera** Handkamera, *die;* **~-held device** Handgerät, *das;* (electronic) Handheld, *das;* **~hold** *n.* Halt, *der;* **provide ~holds/a ~hold for sb.** jmdm. Halt bieten; **use sth. as a ~hold** sich an etw. (*Dat.*) festhalten; **~-hot** *adj.* handwarm

handicap /'hændɪkæp/
A *n.* **1** (Sport) (advantage) Handikap, *das* (fachspr.); Vorgabe, *die;* (disadvantage) **carry a ~** ‹*Jockey:*› ein Ergänzungsgewicht mitführen; ‹*Pferd:*› ein Ergänzungsgewicht tragen **2** (race, competition) Handikaprennen, *das;* Ausgleichsrennen, *das* **3** (fig.: hindrance) Handikap, *das;* **have a mental/physical ~:** geistig behindert/körperbehindert sein; **be a ~/more of a ~ than a help** hinderlich/eher hinderlich als eine Hilfe sein; **don't let the child become a ~ to you** lass dich durch das Kind nicht zu sehr einschränken
B *v.t.*, **-pp- 1** (Sport: impose a ~ on) ein Handikap festlegen für **2** (fig.: put at a disadvantage) benachteiligen; handikapen (ugs.); (fig.: obstruct) ein Hemmnis darstellen für

handicapped /'hændɪkæpt/
A *adj.* behindert; **mentally/physically ~:** geistig behindert/körperbehindert
B *n. pl.* **the [mentally/physically] ~:** die [geistig/körperlich] Behinderten; **a home for the ~:** ein Heim für Behinderte; ein Behindertenheim

handicapper /'hændɪkæpə(r)/ *n.* (Sport) (person) Handikapper, *der*/Handikapperin, *die;* Ausgleicher, *der*/Ausgleicherin, *die*

handicraft /'hændɪkrɑːft/ *n.* **1** (craft) [Kunst-]handwerk, *das;* (knitting, weaving, needlework) Handarbeit, *die* **2** *no pl.* (manual skill) Handfertigkeit, *die*

handily /'hændɪlɪ/ *adv.* praktisch; günstig ‹*gelegen*›; deutlich ‹*gewinnen, schlagen*›

handiness /'hændɪnɪs/ *n., no pl.* **1** (convenience) Vorteil, *der;* (nearness) günstige Lage **2** (adroitness) Geschicklichkeit, *die*

handiwork /'hændɪwɜːk/ *n., no pl., no indef. art.* **1** (working) handwerkliche Arbeit; **he enjoys ~:** er arbeitet gern handwerklich; **a nice piece of ~!** (fig.) gute Arbeit! **2** (piece of work) [Hand]arbeit, *die;* **this painting is the ~ of a master** dieses Bild ist das Werk eines Meisters *od.* ein Meisterwerk; **this ring/newly decorated kitchen is all my own ~:** diesen Ring habe ich selbst gemacht *od.* (geh.) gearbeitet/diese Küche habe ich selbst renoviert **3** (derog.: bad piece of work) Werk, *das* (ugs.); **whose ~ is this?** wer hat das [denn] verbrochen? (ugs.)

handkerchief /'hæŋkətʃɪf, 'hæŋkətʃiːf/ *n., pl.* **~s** *or* **handkerchieves** /'hæŋkətʃiːvz/ Taschentuch, *das*

handle /'hændl/
A *n.* **1** (part held) [Hand]griff, *der;* (of bag etc.) [Trag]griff, *der;* (of knife, chisel) Heft, *das;* Griff, *der;* (of axe, brush, comb, broom, saucepan) Stiel, *der;* (of handbag) Bügel, *der;* (of door) Klinke, *die;* (of bucket, watering can, cup, jug) Henkel, *der;* (of pump) Schwengel, *der;* **fly off the ~** (fig. coll.) an die Decke gehen (ugs.); ausflippen (salopp) **2** (coll.) (title) Titel, *der;* (name) Name, *der;* **have a ~ to one's name** einen Titel haben **3** (fact used

against one) Handhabe, *die* [4] (feel) Griff, *der;* **have a natural/give a warm ~:** sich natürlich/warm anfühlen

[B] *v.t.* [1] (touch, feel) anfassen; **'Fragile! H~ with care!'** „Vorsicht! Zerbrechlich!"; **mind how you ~ those glasses** geh bitte vorsichtig mit den Gläsern um [2] (deal with) umgehen mit ‹*Person, Tier, Situation*›; führen ‹*Verhandlung*›; erledigen ‹*Korrespondenz, Telefonat usw.*›; (cope with) fertig werden *od.* zurechtkommen mit ‹*Person, Tier, Situation*›; **train sb. to ~ dogs** jmdn. zum Hundeführer ausbilden [3] (control) handhaben ‹*Fahrzeug, Flugzeug*› [4] (treat) behandeln ‹*Person*› [5] (process, transport) umschlagen ‹*Fracht*›; **Heathrow ~s x passengers per year** in Heathrow werden pro Jahr x Passagiere abgefertigt; **the railway ~s x tons of coal a week** die Bahn befördert wöchentlich x Tonnen Kohle [6] (discuss) behandeln ‹*Thema, Ansicht, Frage*› [7] (deal in) handeln mit

[C] *v.i.* ‹*Gerät:*› sich handhaben lassen; ‹*Fahrzeug, Boot:*› sich fahren; ‹*Flugzeug:*› sich fliegen

handlebar /'hændlbɑ:(r)/ *n.* Lenkstange, *die;* Lenker, *der; attrib.* **~ moustache** Schnauzbart, *der*

'handlebar tape *n.* Lenkerband, *das*

handler /'hændlə(r)/ *n.* [1] **▸ⓘ p. 1260** (of police dog) Hundeführer, *der/*-führerin, *die* [2] (dealer) **a ~ of stolen goods** ein Hehler

handling /'hændlɪŋ/ *n., no pl.* [1] (management) Handhabung, *die;* (of troops, workforce, bargaining, discussion) Führung, *die;* (of situation, class, crowd) Umgang, *der* (**of** mit) [2] (use) Handhabung, *die;* (Motor Veh.) Fahrverhalten, *das;* Handling, *das;* **what's your car's ~ like?** wie fährt sich dein Auto? [3] (treatment) Behandlung, *die;* **the child needs firm/considerate ~:** das Kind braucht eine feste Hand/muss rücksichtsvoll behandelt werden; **come in for some rough ~** ‹*Sache:*› schlecht behandelt werden; ‹*Person:*› ganz schön etwas abbekommen (ugs.) [4] (processing) Beförderung, *die;* (of passengers) Abfertigung, *die*

'handling charge *n.* (Commerc.) Bearbeitungsgebühr, *die*

hand: ~list *n.* Aufstellung, *die;* Liste, *die;* **~ lotion** *n.* Handlotion, *die;* **~ luggage** *n.* Handgepäck, *das;* **~made** *adj.* handgearbeitet; in Handarbeit hergestellt; handgeschöpft ‹*Papier*›; **~maid, ~maiden** *ns.* [1] (arch.: female attendant) Kammerfrau, *die;* [Kammer]zofe, *die;* [2] (fig.: subordinate) Dienerin, *die;* **~-me-down** [A] *n.* [1] (garment handed down) abgelegtes *od.* getragenes *od.* gebrauchtes Kleidungsstück (**from** *Gen.*); **I got the hat/ring as a ~-me-down from my aunt** den Hut/Ring habe ich von meiner Tante übernommen *od.* (scherzh.) geerbt; [2] (ready-made garment) [billiges] Kleidungsstück von der Stange; [B] *adj.* gebraucht; alt; **~out** *n.* [1] (alms) Almosen, *das;* Gabe, *die;* [2] (information) Handout, *das;* (press release) Presseerklärung, *die;* **~over** *n.* Übergabe, *die;* **~-painted** *adj.* handbemalt ‹*Gegenstand*›; handgemalt ‹*Muster, Bild*›; **~-'picked** *adj.* sorgfältig ausgewählt; handverlesen (ugs. scherzh.); **~rail** *n.* Geländer, *das;* Handlauf, *der* (Bauw.); (on ship) Handläufer, *der;* **~set** *n.* (Teleph.) Handapparat, *der*

hands: ~-free *adj.* Freisprech‹*einrichtung, -betrieb*›; **~-free kit** Freisprechanlage, *die;* Freisprecheinrichtung, *die;* **~-'off** *adj.* **have a ~-off approach** sich heraushalten (**to** aus); **be a ~ manager** seinen Mitarbeitern freie Hand lassen

'handshake *n.* Händedruck, *der;* Handschlag, *der; see also* **golden handshake**

handsome /'hænsəm/ *adj.*, **~r** /'hænsəmə(r)/, **~st** /'hænsəmɪst/ [1] (good-looking) gut aussehend ‹*Mann, Frau*›; schön, edel ‹*Tier, Möbel, Vase usw.*›; **~ is as ~ does** (prov.) man soll nicht nach dem Äußeren urteilen [2] (generous) großzügig ‹*Geschenk, Belohnung, Mitgift*›; nobel ‹*Behandlung, Verhalten, Empfang*›; (considerable) stattlich, ansehnlich ‹*Vermögen, Summe, Preis*›; stolz ‹*Preis, Summe*›

handsomely /'hænsəmlɪ/ *adv.* großzügig; mit großem Vorsprung ‹*gewinnen*›

hand: ~s-'on *adj.* praktisch; **~spring** *n.* Handstandüberschlag, *der;* **~stand** *n.* Handstand, *der;* **~-to-~** *adj.* **~-to-~ combat** ein Kampf Mann gegen Mann; **~-to-mouth** *adj.* [1] (meagre) kärglich, kümmerlich ‹*Leben, Dasein*›; **eke out/lead a ~-to-mouth life/existence** von der Hand in den Mund leben; [2] (precarious) Gelegenheits‹*arbeit*›; **operate on a ~-to-mouth basis** von der Hand in den Mund leben (fig.); **~ towel** *n.* [Hände]handtuch, *das;* **~work** *n., no pl.* Handarbeit, *die;* **~writing** *n.* [Hand]schrift, *die;* **his style of ~writing** seine [Hand]schrift; **~'written** *adj.* handgeschrieben; handschriftlich

handy /'hændɪ/ *adj.* [1] (ready to hand) griffbereit; greifbar; **keep/have sth. ~:** etw. griffbereit *od.* greifbar haben; **there is a ~ socket just by my bed** ich habe direkt am Bett eine Steckdose; **the house is very ~ for the market/town centre** *etc.* von dem Haus aus ist man sehr schnell auf dem Markt/in der Stadt *usw.* [2] (useful) praktisch; nützlich; **come in ~:** sich als nützlich erweisen; **that'll come in ~!** das kann ich gebrauchen! [3] (adroit) geschickt; **be ~ about the house** handwerklich geschickt sein; **be [quite/very] ~ with sth.** [ganz gut/sehr gut] mit etw. umgehen können; **he is too ~ with his fists** ihm sitzen die Fäuste allzu locker

'handyman *n.* Handwerker, *der;* **[home] ~:** Heimwerker, *der;* **be a ~:** handwerklich geschickt sein

hang /hæŋ/

[A] *v.t.*, **hung** /hʌŋ/ (*see also* **5**): [1] (support from above) hängen; aufhängen ‹*Gardinen*›; **~ sth. from sth.** etw. an etw. (*Dat.*) aufhängen; **~ sth. on sb.** (fig. coll.) jmdm. etw. anhängen (ugs. abwertend)

[2] (place on wall) aufhängen ‹*Bild, Gemälde, Zeichnung*›; **~ a picture from a nail** ein Bild an *od.* mit einem Nagel aufhängen

[3] (paste up) ankleben ‹*Tapete*›; **~ [the] wallpaper** tapezieren

[4] (install) aufhängen ‹*Glocke*›; einhängen ‹*Tür, Tor*›

[5] (Cookery) abhängen lassen ‹*Fleisch, Wild*›; **be well hung** gut abgehangen sein

[6] *p.t., p.p.* **hanged** (execute) hängen, (ugs.) aufhängen (**for** wegen); **~ oneself** sich erhängen *od.* (ugs.) aufhängen; **be ~ed, drawn, and quartered** (Hist.) gehängt werden(, die Eingeweide herausgenommen bekommen) und gevierteilt werden; **I'll be** *or* **I am ~ed if …** (fig.) der Henker soll mich holen, wenn …; **[well,] I'm ~ed!** beim *od.* zum Henker! (derb); **I'm ~ed if I will** (said as a retort) den Teufel werd' ich (salopp); **~ it!** zum Henker! (derb); **~ the expense!** die Kosten interessieren mich nicht

[7] (let droop) **~ one's head [in** *or* **for shame]** [beschämt] den Kopf senken

[8] (decorate) schmücken (**with** mit)

[9] **~ fire** (fig.) zögern; **he won't ~ fire** er wird keinen Augenblick zögern

[B] *v.i.*, **hung** [1] (be supported from above) hängen; ‹*Kleid usw.*› fallen; **~ from the ceiling** an der Decke hängen; von der Decke [herab]hängen; **~ by a rope** an einem Strick hängen; **~ in folds** ‹*Haut, Segel, Markise, Zelt:*› Falten werfen; **~ loose** lose sein; **~ tough** (Amer. coll.) hart bleiben; **~ in there!** (coll.) halte durch!; **~ by a hair** (fig.) an einem seidenen Faden hängen; **he had the threat of prison ~ing over his head** ihm drohte eine Gefängnisstrafe; **time ~s heavily** *or* **heavy** die Zeit wird einem lang; **time ~s heavily** *or* **heavy on sb.** die Zeit wird jmdm. lang; *see also* **balance A 3**; **lip 1**; **thereby**; **thread A 2**

[2] (be executed) hängen; **let sth. go ~** (coll.) etw. schleifen lassen (ugs.); **let things go ~:** alles schleifen lassen (ugs.); **let sb. go ~:** jmdn. abschreiben (ugs.)

[3] (droop) **the dog's ears and tail hung [down]** der Hund ließ die Ohren und den Schwanz hängen; **his head hung** er hielt den Kopf gesenkt; **with his head ~ing** mit gesenktem Kopf

[C] *n., no pl.* [1] (how sth. hangs) Sitz, *der;* **the ~ of those clothes is perfect** die Kleider sitzen perfekt; **get the ~ of** (fig. coll.) (get the knack of, understand) klarkommen mit (ugs.) ‹*Gerät, Arbeit*›; (see the meaning of) kapieren (ugs.) ‹*Sprache, Argument*›; **you'll soon get the ~ of it/doing it** du wirst den Bogen bald raushaben (ugs.)/wirst bald raushaben, wie man es macht

[2] **I don't give** *or* **care a ~ about that/him** (coll.) das/er kümmert mich nicht die Bohne (ugs.)

Phrasal verbs

• **~ about** (Brit.), **~ around**

[A] /--'-/ *v.i.* [1] (loiter about) herumlungern (salopp); **we ~ about** *or* **around there all evening** wir hängen da den ganzen Abend rum (ugs.) [2] (coll.: wait) warten; **keep sb. ~ing about** *or* **around** jmdn. warten lassen; **don't ~ about, get a move on!** trödel nicht, beeile dich!; **~ about!** (coll.) wart mal!; Sekunde mal! (ugs.)

[B] /'---/ *v.t.* herumlungern an/in/*usw.* (+ *Dat.*) (salopp); **~ about the exit** am Ausgang herumlungern

• **~ 'back** *v.i.* [1] (be reluctant) sich zieren; **don't ~ back!** na komm schon! [2] (keep rearward position) zurückbleiben

• **~ on**

[A] /-'-/ *v.i.* [1] (hold fast) sich festhalten; **~ on to** (lit.: grasp) sich festhalten an (+ *Dat.*) ‹*Gegenstand*›; (fig. coll.: retain) behalten ‹*Eigentum, Stellung*› [2] (stand firm, survive) durchhalten [3] (coll.: wait) warten; **~ on [a minute]!** Moment *od.* (ugs.) Sekunde mal! [4] (coll.: not ring off) dranbleiben (ugs.)

[B] /'--/ *v.t.* **~ on sth.** (fig.) von etw. abhängen; **~ on sb.'s words** jmdm. gespannt zuhören

• **~ 'out**

[A] *v.t.* [1] (suspend) aufhängen ‹*Wäsche*› [2] (cause to protrude) heraushängen lassen ‹*Zunge, Tentakel*›

[B] *v.i.* [1] (protrude) heraushängen; **the dog's tongue hung out** dem Hund hing die Zunge heraus; **let it all ~ out** (fig. coll.) die Sau rauslassen (ugs.); **just let it all ~ out!** mach einfach das, wozu du lustig bist! (ugs.) [2] (coll.) (reside) wohnen; seine Bude haben (ugs.); (be often present) sich herumtreiben (ugs.); rumhängen (ugs.)

• **~ to'gether** *v.i.* [1] (be coherent) ‹*Handlung:*› stimmig sein; ‹*Teile eines Ganzen:*› sich zusammenfügen; ‹*Aussagen:*› zusammenstimmen [2] (be or remain associated) zusammenhalten

• **~ 'up**

[A] *v.t.* [1] (suspend) aufhängen; **~ up sth. on a hook** etw. an einen Haken hängen *od.* an einem Haken aufhängen [2] (fig.: put aside) an den Nagel hängen (ugs.) [3] (postpone) aufschieben, vertagen ‹*Entscheidung*›; (indefinitely) auf die lange Bank schieben [4] (cause delay to) aufhalten ‹*Person*›; **the negotiations were hung up for a week** die Verhandlungen kamen für eine Woche zum Stillstand [5] (coll.: cause inhibition to) **be hung up about sth.** ein gestörtes Verhältnis zu etw. haben. *See also* **hang-up**

[B] *v.i.* (Teleph.) einhängen; auflegen; **~ up on sb.** einfach einhängen *od.* auflegen

hangar /'hæŋə(r), 'hæŋgə(r)/ *n.* Hangar, *der;* Flugzeughalle, *die*

'hangdog *adj.* zerknirscht

hanger /'hæŋə(r)/ *n.* [1] (for clothes) Bügel, *der* [2] (loop on clothes etc.) Aufhänger, *der*

hanger-'on *n.* **there are many hangers-on in every political party** in jeder politischen Partei gibt es viele, denen es nur um den persönlichen Vorteil geht; **the rock group with its usual [crowd of] hangers-on** die Rockgruppe mit ihrem üblichen Anhang

hang: ~-glider *n.* Hängegleiter, *der;* Drachen, *der;* **~-glider pilot** Drachenflieger, *der/*-fliegerin, *die;* **~-gliding** *n.* Drachenfliegen, *das*

hanging /'hæŋɪŋ/

[A] *n.* [1] **▸hang A:** [Auf]hängen, *das;* Ankleben, *das;* Einhängen, *das;* Abhängen, *das* [2] (execution) Hinrichtung [durch den Strang]; **~ is too good for sb.** der Strang wäre noch eine zu milde Strafe [für jmdn.]; **this is a ~ matter** *or* **crime** darauf steht der Tod durch Erhängen; **it's/that's not a** *or* **no ~ matter** (fig.) das ist doch kein Beinbruch! (ugs.) [3] *in pl.* (drapery) Behang, *der*

[B] *adj.* **~ basket/staircase/balcony** Hängekorb, *der*/freitragende Treppe/vorstehender Balkon

hanging: ~ **'gardens** *n. pl.* hängende Gärten; ~ **judge** *n. Richter, der schnell mit der Todesstrafe bei der Hand ist;* ~ **'paragraph** *n.* (Printing) *Absatz mit ausgerückter erster Zeile;* ~ **'valley** *n.* (Geog.) Hängetal, *das;* ~ **'wardrobe** *n.* Kleiderschrank, *der*

hang: ~**man** /'hæŋmən/ *n., pl.* ~**men** /'hæŋmən/ Henker, *der;* ~**over** *n.* **1** (aftereffects) Kater, *der* (ugs.); **2** (remainder) Relikt, *das;* ~**-up** *n.* (coll.) **1** (difficulty) Problem, *das;* **we have no ~-ups about morals** die Moral ist bei uns kein Thema; **2** (inhibition) Macke, *die* (ugs.); **have a ~-up about sth.** ein gestörtes Verhältnis zu etw. haben; **3** (fixation) Komplex, *der* (**about** wegen); **he has a ~-up about his mother** er hat einen Mutterkomplex

hank /hæŋk/ *n.* Strang, *der*

hanker /'hæŋkə(r)/ *v.i.* ~ **after** *or* **for** ein [heftiges] Verlangen haben nach ‹*Person, etwas Neuem, Zigarette*›; sich (*Dat.*) sehnlichst wünschen ‹*Gelegenheit*›

hankering /'hæŋkərɪŋ/ *n.* (craving) Verlangen, *das* (**after, for** nach); (longing) Sehnsucht, *die* (**after, for** nach)

hanky /'hæŋkɪ/ *n.* (coll.) Taschentuch, *das*

hanky-panky /hæŋkɪ'pæŋkɪ/ *n., no pl., no indef. art.* (coll.) **1** (underhand dealing) Mauschelei, *die* (abwertend); **there's been some ~, there was some ~ going on** es ist gemauschelt worden (ugs. abwertend) **2** (love affair) Techtelmechtel, *das;* **be involved in some ~ with sb.** ein Techtelmechtel mit jmdm. haben **3** (illicit sexual activity) Knutscherei, *die* (ugs.); Gefummel, *das* (ugs. abwertend); **there was some ~ going on** es wurde geknutscht *od.* gefummelt (ugs.)

Hanover /'hænəʊvə(r)/ *pr. n.* ▸ℹ **p. 1643** Hannover (*das*); **the House of ~** (Hist.) das Haus Hannover

Hanoverian /hænə'vɪərɪən/ ▸ℹ **p. 1643**
A *n.* (Hist.: person) Hannoveraner, *der*/Hannoveranerin, *die;* **be a ~:** aus dem Haus Hannover sein
B *adj.* hannoversch

Hansard /'hænsɑːd/ *n.* Hansard, *der: die britischen Parlamentsberichte*

Hanse /'hæns/ *n.* (Hist.) Hanse, *die*

Hanseatic /hænsɪ'ætɪk/ *adj.* (Hist.) hansisch; ~ **town** Hansestadt, *die;* **the ~ League** der Hansebund

hansom [cab] /'hænsəm (kæb)/ *n.* (Hist.) Hansom, *der*

Hants *abbr.* = **Hampshire**

haphazard /hæp'hæzəd/
A *adj.* willkürlich ‹*Auswahl*›; unbedacht ‹*Bemerkung*›; **arranged in a ~ fashion** willkürlich *od.* wahllos angeordnet; **the whole thing was rather ~:** das Ganze geschah ziemlich planlos
B *adv.* (at random) willkürlich; wahllos

haphazardly /hæp'hæzədlɪ/ *adv.* willkürlich; wahllos; ~ **planned** planlos

hapless /'hæplɪs/ *adj.* unglückselig

ha'p'orth /'heɪpəθ/ ▸ **halfpennyworth**

happen /'hæpn/ *v.i.* **1** (occur) geschehen; ‹*Vorhergesagtes:*› eintreffen; **these things [do] ~:** das kommt vor; **it was the only thing that 'could ~:** es konnte [gar] nicht anders kommen; **what's ~ing?** was ist los?; **what's ~ing this evening?** was ist für heute Abend geplant?; **I can't** *or* **don't see 'that ~ing** das kann ich mir nicht vorstellen; **it all ~ed like this ...:** das war so ...; **nothing ever ~s here** hier ist nichts los; **don't let it ~ again!** dass mir das nicht wieder vorkommt!; **that's what ~s!** das kommt davon!; **~ to sb.** jmdm. passieren; **what has ~ed to him/her arm?** was ist mit ihm/ihrem Arm?; **what can have ~ed to him?** was mag mit ihm los sein?; **it all ~ed so quickly that ...:** es ging alles so schnell, dass ...; **it's all ~ing** (coll.) es ist was los (ugs.); **it's all ~ing for him** (coll.) es läuft gut bei ihm (ugs.) **2** (chance) **~ to do sth./be sb.** zufällig etw. tun/jmd. sein; **it so ~s** *or* **as it ~s I have ...:** zufällig habe ich *od.* ich habe zufällig ...; **how does it ~ that ...?** wie kommt es, dass ...?; **do you ~ to know him?** kennen Sie ihn zufällig?

(Phrasal verbs)
- ~ **'by** *v.i.* zufällig vorbeikommen
- ~ **[up]on** *v.t.* zufällig treffen ‹*Person*›; stoßen auf, zufällig finden ‹*Gegenstand*›

happening /'hæpnɪŋ/ *n.* **1** *usu. in pl.* (event) Ereignis, *das;* **a regrettable ~:** ein bedauerlicher Vorfall; **such ~s cannot be tolerated** solche Vorfälle können nicht toleriert werden **2** (improvised performance) Happening, *das*

happenstance /'hæpnstæns, 'hæpnstɑːns/ *n.* (Amer.) Zufall, *der*

happily /'hæpɪlɪ/ *adv.* **1** glücklich ‹*lächeln*›; fröhlich, vergnügt ‹*spielen, lachen*›; gut ‹*zurechtkommen*›; **they lived ~ ever after[wards]** (at end of fairy tale) sie lebten fortan glücklich und zufrieden[, und wenn sie nicht gestorben sind, dann leben sie noch heute] **2** (gladly) mit Vergnügen **3** (aptly) gut; treffend, passend ‹*ausdrücken, formulieren*› **4** (fortunately) glücklicherweise; zum Glück; **it ended ~:** es ging gut aus

happiness /'hæpɪnɪs/ *n., no pl.* ▸ℹ **p. 1189** ▸ **happy 1**: Glück, *das;* Heiterkeit, *die;* Zufriedenheit, *die;* **I wish you every ~:** [ich wünsche Ihnen] alles Gute

happy /'hæpɪ/ *adj.* **1** ▸ℹ **p. 1189** (joyful) glücklich; heiter ‹*Bild, Veranlagung, Ton*›; (contented) zufrieden; (causing joy) erfreulich ‹*Gedanke, Erinnerung, Szene*›; froh ‹*Ereignis*›; glücklich ‹*Zeiten*›; **I'm not ~ with her work** ich bin mit ihrer Arbeit nicht zufrieden; **not be ~ about sth./doing sth.** nicht froh über etw. (*Akk.*) sein/etw. nicht gern tun; **are you ~?** (not needing help) kommen Sie allein zurecht?; **~ birthday!** herzlichen Glückwunsch zum Geburtstag!; **~ anniversary!** herzlichen Glückwunsch! (*zum Jahrestag*); **~ Christmas!** frohe Weihnachten!; **~ New Year!** ein glückliches neues Jahr!; **~ days/landings!** (dated coll.) viel Glück!; **~ event** (euphem.: birth) freudiges Ereignis (verhüll.); **[strike] a ~ medium** den goldenen Mittelweg [wählen]; **~ release** (death) Erlösung, *die; see also* **day 1**; **lark**[1]; **return C 1**; **sandboy** **2** (glad) **be ~ to do sth.** etw. gern *od.* mit Vergnügen tun; **[I'm] ~ to meet you** [es] freut mich, Sie kennen zu lernen; **I'm ~ for you** das freut mich für dich; **make sb. ~:** jmdn. zufrieden stellen; **yes, I'd be ~ to** (as reply to request) ja, gern *od.* mit Vergnügen; **I'd be only too ~ to do that** ich würde das nur zu gern tun **3** (lucky) glücklich; **by a ~ chance/accident/coincidence** durch einen glücklichen Zufall **4** (apt) glücklich ‹*Einfall*›; gut ‹*Wahl, Methode*› **5** *in comb.* (quick to use sth.) **bomb-~:** mit Bomben schnell bei der Hand *nur präd.*; **gun-~:** schießwütig (ugs.); *see also* **slap-happy**; **trigger-happy**

happy: ~ **'ending** *n.* Happy End, *das;* ~ **'families** *n. sing.* (Cards) Quartett, *das;* **~-go-'lucky** *adj.* sorglos; unbekümmert; ~ **hour** *n. Zeitspanne am frühen Abend, in der die Getränke in einer Bar o. Ä. billiger verkauft werden;* ~ **'hunting ground[s]** *n.* [*pl.*] **1** (N. Amer. Ind. Mythol.) **the ~ hunting grounds** die ewigen Jagdgründe; **2** (fig.) Eldorado, *das;* (shop, market, etc.) Fundgrube, *die*

hara-kiri /hærə'kɪrɪ/ *n.* Harakiri, *das*

harangue /hə'ræŋ/
A *n.* Tirade, *die* (abwertend)
B *v.t.* eine Ansprache halten an (+ *Akk.*); **stop haranguing me about how ...:** hör auf, mir ständig zu predigen (ugs.), wie ...

harass /'hærəs/ *v.t.* schikanieren; **constantly ~ the enemy** den Feind nicht zur Ruhe kommen lassen; **~ sb. with complaints** jmdn. mit [ständigen] Beschwerden belästigen; **~ sb. into doing sth.** jmdm. so sehr zusetzen, dass er etw. tut

harassed /'hærəst/ *adj.* geplagt (**with** von); gequält ‹*Blick, Ausdruck*›

harassment /'hærəsmənt/ *n.* Schikanierung, *die;* **constant ~ of/by the enemy** ständiger Kleinkrieg mit dem Feind; **sexual ~:** [sexuelle] Belästigung

harbinger /'hɑːbɪndʒə(r)/ *n.* Vorbote, *der*/Vorbotin, *die*

harbour (*Brit.; Amer.:* **harbor**) /'hɑːbə(r)/
A *n.* **1** (for ships) Hafen, *der;* **in ~:** im Hafen **2** (shelter) Unterschlupf, *der*
B *v.t.* beherbergen; Unterschlupf gewähren (+ *Dat.*) ‹*Verbrecher, Flüchtling*›; (fig.) hegen (geh.) ‹*Hoffnung, Groll, Verdacht*›

'harbour master *n.* Hafenmeister, *der*

hard /hɑːd/
A *adj.* **1** hart; fest ‹*Gelee, Eiscreme, Preis*›; stark, heftig ‹*Regen*›; hart, streng ‹*Frost*›; gesichert ‹*Beweis, Zahlen, Daten, Information*›; **~ water area** Gebiet mit hartem Wasser; **drive a ~ bargain** hart verhandeln; **[a drop of] the ~ stuff** (coll.) [etwas] Hochprozentiges; **the ~ fact is that ...:** es ist einfach eine Tatsache, dass ...; **~ facts** nackte *od.* unumstößliche Tatsachen; *see also* **cheese 3**; **iron A 1**; **liquor 1**; **nail A 2**; **nut 1**
2 (difficult) schwer; schwierig; **this is ~ to believe** das ist kaum zu glauben; es fällt schwer, das zu glauben; **it is ~ to do sth.** es ist schwer, etw. zu tun; **he's ~ to get on with** mit ihm ist schwer auszukommen; **this is a [very] ~ thing [for me] to say** es fällt mir [sehr] schwer, das zu sagen; **make it ~ for sb. [to do sth.]** es jmdm. schwer machen[, etw. zu tun]; **make sth. ~ for sb.** jmdm. etw. schwer machen; **[choose to] go about/do sth. the ~ way** es sich (*Dat.*) bei etw. unnötig schwer machen; **learn sth. the ~ way** etw. durch schlechte Erfahrungen lernen; **be [a] ~ [person] to please/prove wrong/catch out** schwer zufrieden zu stellen/zu widerlegen/zu überführen sein; **be ~ to convince [of sth.]** schwer [von etw.] zu überzeugen sein; **be ~ to understand** schwer zu verstehen sein; **have a ~ row to hoe** (fig. dated) es nicht leicht haben; **be ~ of hearing** schwerhörig sein; **be ~ going** ‹*Buch:*› sich schwer lesen; ‹*Arbeit:*› anstrengend sein; **play ~ to get** (coll.) so tun, als sei man nicht interessiert; **have a ~ time doing sth.** Schwierigkeiten haben, etw. zu tun; **give sb. a ~ time** jmdm. das Leben schwer machen; **it's a ~ life** (joc.) das Leben ist schwer
3 (involving suffering) hart, anstrengend, beschwerlich ‹*Marsch*›; **it is [a bit] ~ on him** es ist [schon] schlimm für ihn; **~ luck** Pech; *see also* **line**[1] **A 1**
4 (strenuous) hart; beschwerlich ‹*Reise*›; konzentriert ‹*Gespräch, Diskussion*›; leidenschaftlich ‹*Spieler*›; **be a ~ drinker** viel trinken; **this is really ~ work!** (coll.) das ist wirklich nicht leicht; **go in [too much] for ~ drinking/gambling** zu viel trinken/spielen; **be a ~ worker** sehr viel arbeiten; **try one's ~est to do sth.** sich nach Kräften bemühen, etw. zu tun; **I worked my very ~est** ich arbeitete, so hart ich konnte
5 (vigorous) heftig ‹*Angriff, Schlag*›; kräftig ‹*Schlag, Stoß, Tritt, Klaps*›; (severe) streng ‹*Winter*›; (strong) hart, hochprozentig ‹*alkoholisches Getränk*›
6 (unfeeling) hart; streng ‹*Kritiker*›; **be ~ [up]on sb.** streng mit jmdm. sein; **take a ~ line [with sb. on sth.]** [in Bezug auf etw. (*Akk.*)] eine harte Linie [gegenüber jmdm.] vertreten; *see also* **nail A 2**
7 (harsh) hart; **be ~ on sb./sth.** jmdn./etw. strapazieren
8 (Phonet.) hart
B *adv.* **1** (strenuously) hart ‹*arbeiten, trainieren*›; schnell ‹*laufen*›; fleißig ‹*lernen, studieren, üben*›; genau ‹*überlegen, beobachten, ansehen*›; scharf ‹*nachdenken*›; gut ‹*aufpassen, zuhören, sich festhalten*›; fest ‹*kleben*›; **he drinks ~:** er ist ein starker Trinker; **concentrate ~/~er** sich sehr/mehr konzentrieren; **try ~:** sich sehr bemühen; **work ~ and play ~:** intensiv arbeiten und leben; **be ~ at work on sth.** an etw. (*Dat.*) intensiv *od.* konzentriert arbeiten; **go ~ at it** sich richtig hineinknien (ugs.); **be ~ 'at it** schwer arbeiten; **we found him already ~ 'at it** wir fanden ihn schon mitten in der Arbeit; **it's freezing ~ outside** es friert Stein und Bein draußen (ugs.)
2 (vigorously) heftig; herzhaft ‹*küssen*›; laut ‹*rufen*›; fest ‹*schlagen, drücken, klopfen*›
3 (severely, drastically) hart; streng ‹*zensieren*›; **come down ~ on sb.** jmdn. zusammenstauchen (ugs.); **cut back** *or* **down ~ on sth.** etw. drastisch einschränken; **he took the news**

very ~: die Nachricht traf ihn hart *od.* sehr; **be ~ up** knapp bei Kasse sein (ugs.); **be ~ up for sth.** um etw. verlegen sein
4 (with difficulty) **it goes ~ with sb.** jmd. bekommt Schwierigkeiten; **be ~ put to it [to do sth.]** große Schwierigkeiten haben[, etw. zu tun]
5 hart ‹*kochen*›; fest ‹*gefrieren [lassen]*›; **bake ~:** abbacken; **set ~:** fest werden
6 (close) **~ by** in nächster Nähe; **~ by sth.** nahe an etw. (*Dat.*); **follow ~ upon sth.** unmittelbar auf etw. (*Akk.*) folgen; *see also* **heel¹ A 1; trail A 2**
7 (Naut.) hart; **~ a-port!** hart backbord!

hard: ~ and 'fast ▸**fast² A 1**; **~back** (Printing) **A** *n.* gebundene Ausgabe; Hardcoverausgabe, *die; attrib.* Hardcover‹*verlag, -verkäufe*›; **in ~back** gebunden; mit festem Einband; **B** *adj.* gebunden; Hardcover-; **~backed** /'hɑːdbækt/ *adj.* ▸**~back B**; **~bitten** *adj.* hartgesotten; abgebrüht (ugs.) ‹*Veteran, Journalist, Karrieremacher*›; **~board** *n.* Hartfaserplatte, *die; attrib.* Hartfaser‹*trennwand, -unterlage*›; **~-boiled** *adj.* **1** (boiled solid) hart gekocht; **2** (fig.) (shrewd) ausgekocht (ugs.); (realistic, unsentimental) realistisch; (tough) hartgesotten; **~ 'case** *n.* (intractable person) ausgebuffter Typ (ugs.); (criminal) Gangster, *der;* **~ 'cash** *n.* **1** (coins) Hartgeld, *das;* **2** (actual money) Bargeld, *das;* **in ~ cash** in bar ‹*bezahlen*›; **~ 'coal** *n.* Anthrazit, *der;* **~ 'copy** *n.* (Computing) Hardcopy, *die;* Papierausdruck, *der;* **~ core** *n.* **1** /-'-/ (nucleus) harter Kern; (of a problem) Kern, *der;* **2** /'--/ (Brit.: material) Packlage, *die* (Bauw.); **~-core** *attrib. adj.* hart ‹*Pornographie*›; zum harten Kern gehörend ‹*Terrorist, Parteimitglied*›; **~ 'court** *n.* (Tennis) Hartplatz, *der;* **~ 'cover** *n.* Hardcovereinband, *der; attrib.* Hardcover‹*ausgabe*›; **in ~ covers** als Hardcover ‹*herauskommen*›; **~ 'currency** *n.* (Econ.) harte Währung; *attrib.* ‹*Markt, Land*› mit harter Währung; *attrib.* **~-currency shop** Geschäft, in dem nur harte Währungen angenommen werden; **~ 'disk** *n.* (Computing) Festplatte, *die;* **~-drinking** *attrib. adj.* ‹*Mann/Frau,*› der/die viel [Alkohol] trinkt; **~ drive** *n.* (Computing) Festplattenlaufwerk, *das;* **~ drug** *n.* harte Droge; **~-earned** *adj.* schwer verdient

harden /'hɑːdn/
A *v.t.* **1** (make hard) härten **2** (fig.: reinforce) bestärken (**in** in + *Dat.*); **~ sb.'s attitude/conviction** jmdn. in seiner Haltung/Überzeugung bestärken **3** (make robust) abhärten (**to** gegen) **4** (make tough) unempfindlich machen (**to** gegen); **~ sb./oneself to sth.** jmdn./sich gegenüber etw. hart machen; **~ sb. to killing** jmdn. an das Töten gewöhnen; **he ~ed his heart against her** er verhärtete sich gegen sie
B *v.i.* **1** (become hard) hart werden; härten **2** (become confirmed) sich verhärten **3** ‹*Preis:*› sich festigen **4** (become severe) ‹*Gesicht:*› einen harten Ausdruck annehmen; ‹*Gesichtsausdruck:*› hart werden; **his face ~ed into anger** sein Gesicht verhärtete sich zornig
Phrasal verb
• **~ 'off** *v.t.* widerstandsfähig machen ‹*Pflanze*›

hardened /'hɑːdnd/ *adj.* **1** verhärtet ‹*Arterie*› **2** (grown tough) abgehärtet, unempfindlich (**to, against** gegen); hartgesotten ‹*Verbrecher, Sünder, Krieger*›; **be ~ to sth.** gegen etw. unempfindlich sein; **become** *or* **get ~ to sth.** gegen etw. unempfindlich werden; **a ~ drinker** Gewohnheitstrinker, der viel verträgt **3** (seasoned) eingefleischt

hardener /'hɑːdnə(r)/ *n.* Härter, *der*

hardening /'hɑːdnɪŋ/ *n.* **1** (of steel) Härten, *das;* (of arteries) Verhärtung, *die* **2** (making callous) Verhärtung, *die*

hard: ~-featured *adj.* ‹*Person*› mit harten Gesichtszügen; hart ‹*Gesicht*›; **~ 'feelings** *n. pl.* (coll.) **no ~ feelings** schon gut; **make sure there are no ~ feelings** dafür sorgen, dass er/sie/*usw.* nicht mehr böse ist; **with no ~ feelings on either side** ohne dass es einer dem anderen nachtrug; **~-fought** *adj.* heftig ‹*Kampf*›; hart ‹*Spiel, Wettbewerb*›; **~ 'hat** *n.* (protective headgear) Schutzhelm, *der;* **~-headed** *adj.* sachlich; nüchtern; **be ~-headed about what one wants** genau wissen, was man will; **~-hearted** /hɑːd'hɑːtɪd/ *adj.* hartherzig (**towards** gegenüber); **~-'hitting** *adj.* schlagkräftig; (fig.) aggressiv ‹*Rede, Politik, Kritik*›

hardiness /'hɑːdɪnɪs/ *n., no pl.* Widerstandsfähigkeit, *die*

hard: ~ 'labour *n.* Zwangsarbeit, *die;* **~ 'landing** *n.* (Astronaut.) harte Landung; **~line** *adj.* kompromisslos; **~'liner** *n.* Befürworter einer harten Linie (**on** gegenüber); **~-'luck story** *n.* Leidensgeschichte, *die*

hardly /'hɑːdlɪ/ *adv.* kaum; **he can ~ have arrived yet** er kann kaum jetzt schon angekommen sein; **~ anyone** *or* **anybody/anything** kaum jemand/etwas; fast niemand/nichts; **~ any wine/beds** kaum Wein/Betten; fast kein Wein/keine Betten; **~ ever** so gut wie nie; **~ at all** fast überhaupt nicht

hard 'money *n.* (Amer.) Hartgeld, *das*

hardness /'hɑːdnɪs/ *n., no pl.* Härte, *die;* (of blow) Heftigkeit, *die;* (of person) Strenge, *die;* **~ of hearing** Schwerhörigkeit, *die*

hard: ~ 'news *n. sing.* gesicherte Fakten; **~-nose[d]** /'hɑːdnəʊz(d)/ *adj.* (coll.) abgebrüht; **~-on** *n.* (sl.) Ständer, *der* (ugs.); **~ 'palate** *n.* (Anat.) harter Gaumen; **~ 'porn** (coll.), **~ por'nography** *ns.* harte Pornographie; harte Pornos *Pl.* (ugs.); **~ 'pressed** *adj.* hart bedrängt; **be ~ pressed** große Schwierigkeiten haben; **~ 'rock** *n.* (Mus.) Hardrock, *der;* **~-scrabble** (Amer.) **A** *n.* karger Boden; **B** *adj.* ertragsarm ‹*Bauernhof*›; karg ‹*Boden, Feld, Acker*›; **~ 'sell** *n.* aggressive Verkaufsmethoden; *attrib.* aggressiv ‹*Werbung, [Verkaufs]methode*›

hardship /'hɑːdʃɪp/ *n.* **1** *no pl., no indef. art.* Not, *die;* Elend, *das;* **life of ~:** entbehrungsreiches *od.* hartes Leben **2** (instance) Notlage, *die;* **~s** Not, *die;* Entbehrungen; **if it's not too much of a ~ for you** wenn es nicht zu viel verlangt ist **3** (sth. causing suffering) Unannehmlichkeit, *die*

hard: ~ 'shoulder *n.* Standspur, *die;* **~ 'standing** *n., no pl., no indef. art.* befestigter Abstellplatz; **~ stuff** *n., no pl.* (coll.) **the ~ stuff** Hochprozentiges; **~ 'tack** *n.* Schiffszwieback, *der;* **~ top** *n.* Hardtop, *das;* **~ware** *n., no pl., no indef. art.* **1** (goods) Eisenwaren *Pl.;* (for domestic use also) Haushaltswaren *Pl.; attrib.* Eisen-/Haushaltswaren‹*geschäft*›; **2** (coll.: weapons) Schießeisen (ugs.); **military ~ware** Waffen *Pl.;* **3** (Computing) Hardware, *die;* **~-wearing** *adj.* strapazierfähig; **~ 'wheat** *n.* Hartweizen, *der;* **~-wired** *adj.* (Computing) festverdrahtet; **~-won** *adj.* schwer errungen *od.* erkämpft ‹*Sieg*›; mühsam gewonnen ‹*Schlacht*›; schwer erarbeitet ‹*Reichtum*›; **~wood** *n.* Hartholz, *das; attrib.* Hartholz‹*möbel, -fußboden, -baum*›; **~ 'words** *n. pl.* **1** (difficult to understand) schwierige Wörter; **2** (angry) harte Worte; **~-working** *adj.* fleißig ‹*Person*›

hardy /'hɑːdɪ/ *adj.* **1** (robust) abgehärtet; zäh, robust ‹*Rasse*› **2** (Hort.) winterhart

hardy: ~ 'annual *n.* **1** (Hort.) winterharte einjährige Pflanze; **2** (fig. joc.) nicht totzukriegendes Thema (scherzh.); **~ per'ennial** *n.* **1** (Hort.) winterharte mehrjährige Pflanze; **2** (fig. joc.) Dauerbrenner, *der* (ugs.)

hare /heə(r)/
A *n.* Hase, *der;* **run like a ~:** wie ein geölter Blitz laufen (ugs.); **[as] mad as a March ~** (fig.) völlig verrückt (ugs.); **run with the ~ and hunt with the hounds** (fig.) auf beiden Schultern *od.* Achseln Wasser tragen (veralt.)
B *v.i.* sausen (ugs.); **go haring about** herumsausen (ugs.)

hare: ~ and 'hounds *n. sing.* Schnitzeljagd, *die;* **~bell** *n.* (Bot.) **1** (Scottish bluebell) Rundblättrige Glockenblume; **2** (English bluebell) Hasenglöckchen, *das;* **~-brained** *adj.* unüberlegt; **~'lip** *n.* Hasenscharte, *die*

harem /'hɑːriːm, hɑː'riːm/ *n.* Harem, *der*

haricot /'hærɪkəʊ/, **haricot bean** *ns.* Gartenbohne, *die;* (pod also) grüne Bohne; (seed also) weiße Bohne

hark /hɑːk/ *v.i.* **1** (arch., literary: listen) **~!** horch!/horcht! **2** (coll.) **just ~ at him!** hör ihn dir/hört ihn euch nur an!
Phrasal verb
• **~ 'back** *v.i.* **~ back to** (come back to) zurückkommen auf (+ *Akk.*); zurückgreifen auf (+ *Akk.*) ‹*Tradition*›; wieder anfangen von ‹*alten Zeiten*›; (go back to) ‹*Idee, Brauch:*› zurückgehen auf (+ *Akk.*)

Harlequin /'hɑːlɪkwɪn/ *n.* Harlekin, *der*

harlot /'hɑːlət/ (arch./derog.) *n.* Metze, *die* (veralt.)

harlotry /'hɑːlətrɪ/ *n.* (arch./derog.) Prostitution, *die*

harm /hɑːm/
A *n.* Schaden, *der;* **do ~:** Schaden anrichten; **do ~ to sb., do sb. ~:** jmdm. schaden; (injure) jmdn. verletzen; **the blow didn't do him any ~:** der Schlag war harmlos; **the dog won't do you any ~:** der Hund tut dir nichts; **it would do you no** *or* **wouldn't do you any ~** (iron.) es würde dir nichts schaden; **do ~ to sth.** einer Sache (*Dat.*) schaden; **sb./sth. comes to no ~:** jmdm./einer Sache passiert nichts; **there is no ~ done** nichts ist passiert; **there's no ~ in doing sth., it will do no ~ to do sth.** (could be of benefit) es kann nicht schaden, etw. zu tun; **there's no ~ in asking** Fragen kostet nichts; **it will do more ~ than good** es wird mehr schaden als nützen; **where's** *or* **what's the ~ in it?** was ist denn schon dabei?; **see no ~ in it/sth./doing sth.** nichts dabei/bei etw. finden/dabei finden, etw. zu tun; **let's hope no ~ will come of it** wir wollen hoffen, dass es sich nicht negativ auswirkt; **stay here, out of ~'s way** bleib hier, wo dir nichts passieren kann; **keep out of ~'s way** der Gefahr fernbleiben; an einem sicheren Ort aufbewahren ‹*Medikamente*›; von der Gefahr fern halten ‹*Person*›; **get sb. out of ~'s way** jmdn. in Sicherheit bringen; *see also* **intend 1; mean³ 1**
B *v.t.* etwas [zuleide] tun (+ *Dat.*); schaden (+ *Dat.*) ‹*Beziehungen, Land, Karriere, Ruf*›

harmful /'hɑːmfl/ *adj.* schädlich (**to** für); schlecht ‹*Angewohnheit*›

harmfulness /'hɑːmflnɪs/ *n., no pl.* Schädlichkeit, *die*

harmless /'hɑːmlɪs/ *adj.* harmlos; **make** *or* **render ~:** unschädlich machen; entschärfen ‹*Bombe*›

harmlessly /'hɑːmlɪslɪ/ *adv.* ohne Schaden anzurichten

harmlessness /'hɑːmlɪsnɪs/ *n., no pl.* Harmlosigkeit, *die*

harmonic /hɑː'mɒnɪk/
A *adj.* (also Mus., Math.) harmonisch
B *n.* **1** (Mus.) Oberton, *der* **2** (component frequency) Harmonische, *die* (Physik); **upper ~s** harmonische Oberschwingungen (Physik)

harmonica /hɑː'mɒnɪkə/ *n.* (Mus.) Mundharmonika, *die*

harmonious /hɑː'məʊnɪəs/ *adj.*, **harmoniously** /hɑː'məʊnɪəslɪ/ *adv.* harmonisch

harmonise ▸**harmonize**

harmonium /hɑː'məʊnɪəm/ *n.* (Mus.) Harmonium, *das*

harmonize /'hɑːmənaɪz/
A *v.t.* **1** (bring into harmony) aufeinander abstimmen; **~ sth. with sth.** etw. mit etw. in Einklang bringen *od.* auf etw. (*Akk.*) abstimmen **2** (Mus.) harmonisieren
B *v.i.* (be in harmony) harmonieren (**with** mit); ‹*Interessen, Ansichten, Wort und Tat:*› miteinander im *od.* in Einklang stehen; **~ well together** ‹*Farben, Klänge:*› gut harmonieren

harmony /'hɑːmənɪ/ *n.* **1** Harmonie, *die;* **live in perfect ~:** völlig harmonisch *od.* in vollkommener Harmonie zusammenleben; **peace and ~:** Friede und Eintracht; **be in ~** ▸**harmonize B**; **be in ~ with sth.** mit etw. im *od.* in Einklang stehen; **be out of ~ with sth.** mit etw. nicht im *od.* in Einklang stehen **2** (Mus.) Harmonie, *die;* (theory of ~) Harmonielehre, *die;* **sing in ~:** mehrstimmig singen; *see also* **sphere 3**

harness /'hɑːnɪs/
A *n.* **1** (for horse) Geschirr, *das* **2** (on parachute) Gurtzeug, *das;* (for toddler, dog) Laufgeschirr, *das;*

(for window cleaner, steeplejack, etc.) Sicherheitsgürtel, *der;* **in ~** (fig.) (in the daily routine) in der Tretmühle (ugs. abwertend); (together) gemeinsam; **die in ~:** in den Sielen sterben; **out of ~** (fig.) außer Dienst; *see also* **double harness**
B *v.t.* **1** (put ~ on) anschirren; **~ a horse to a cart** ein Pferd vor einen Wagen spannen **2** (fig.) nutzen

'harness racing *n., no pl.* Trabrennen, *das*

harp /hɑːp/
A *n.* Harfe, *die*
B *v.i.* **~ on [about] sth.** [immer wieder] von etw. reden; (critically) auf etw. (*Dat.*) herumreiten (salopp); (complainingly) über etw. (*Akk.*) lamentieren (ugs.); **don't ~ on about it!** hör auf damit!

harpist /ˈhɑːpɪst/ *ns.* Harfenist, *der*/ Harfenistin, *die;* Harfenspieler, *der*/-spielerin, *die*

harpoon /hɑːˈpuːn/
A *n.* Harpune, *die*
B *v.t.* harpunieren

harpoon-'gun *n.* Harpunengeschütz, *das*

'harp seal *n.* (Zool.) Sattelrobbe, *die*

harpsichord /ˈhɑːpsɪkɔːd/ *n.* (Mus.) Cembalo, *das*

harpy /ˈhɑːpɪ/ *n.* **1** (grasping woman) Hyäne, *die* (ugs. abwertend) **2** (Greek and Roman Mythol.) Harpyie, *die*

harridan /ˈhærɪdən/ *n.* Schreckschraube, *die* (ugs. abwertend)

harrier /ˈhærɪə(r)/ *n.* **1** (Ornith.) Weihe, *die* **2** (Hunting) Harrier, *der* (*Hund für die Hasenjagd*)

Harris tweed /hærɪs ˈtwiːd/ *n.* Harristweed, *der; attrib.* Harristweed‹*jackett*›

harrow /ˈhærəʊ/
A *n.* Egge, *die*
B *v.t.* **1** eggen **2** (distress) quälen

harrowing /ˈhærəʊɪŋ/ *adj.* entsetzlich; (horrific) grauenhaft ‹*Anblick, Geschichte*›

harry /ˈhærɪ/ *v.t.* **1** **~ [continuously]** wiederholt angreifen **2** (harass) bedrängen

harsh /hɑːʃ/ *adj.* **1** rau ‹*Gewebe, Oberfläche, Gegend, Land, Klima*›; schrill ‹*Ton, Stimme*›; grell ‹*Licht, Farbe, Ton*›; schroff, stark ‹*Kontrast*›; scharf ‹*Geschmack*›; stechend, streng ‹*Geruch*›; hart ‹*Bedingungen, Leben*› **2** (excessively severe) [sehr] hart; [äußerst] streng ‹*Richter, Disziplin*›; rücksichtslos ‹*Tyrann, Herrscher, Verhalten, Politik*›; **back to ~ reality** zurück zur grauen Wirklichkeit; **don't be ~ on him** sei nicht zu streng mit ihm

harshly /ˈhɑːʃlɪ/ *adv.* **1** (disagreeably) grell ‹*klingen*›; in schroffem Ton ‹*reden*› **2** (extremely severely) [sehr] hart; [sehr] streng ‹*strafen*›

harshness /ˈhɑːʃnɪs/ *n., no pl.* **1** ▸ **harsh 1**: Rauheit, *die;* schriller Klang; Grelle, *die;* Schroffheit, *die;* Schärfe, *die;* (of life conditions) Härte, *die* **2** ▸ **harsh 2**: Härte, *die;* Strenge, *die;* Rücksichtslosigkeit, *die*

hart /hɑːt/ *n.* Hirsch, *der*

harum-scarum /heərəmˈskeərəm/ (coll.)
A *adj.* unbesonnen
B *n.* Wildfang, *der*

harvest /ˈhɑːvɪst/
A *n.* **1** Ernte, *die;* **grape ~:** Weinlese, *die;* **find/reap a [rich] ~** (fig.) einen [tollen] Fang machen **2** (time) Ernte[zeit], *die*
B *v.t.* ernten; schlagen ‹*Holz*›; lesen ‹*Weintrauben*›; fangen ‹*Fisch*›; (fig.) gewinnen ‹*Energie*›; ansammeln ‹*Vermögen*›; **~ the crops** die Ernte einbringen; **~ the fruits of one's labours** (fig.) die Früchte seiner Arbeit ernten

harvester /ˈhɑːvɪstə(r)/ *n.* **1** (machine) Erntemaschine, *die; see also* **combine C 2** **2** (person) Erntearbeiter, *der*/-arbeiterin, *die*

harvest: ~ 'festival *n.* Erntedankfest, *das;* **~ 'home** *n.* Erntefest, *das;* **~man** /ˈhɑːvɪstmən/ *n., pl.* **-men** /ˈhɑːvɪstmən/ (Zool.) Weberknecht, *der;* **~ 'moon** *n.* Vollmond zur Zeit der Herbst-Tagundnachtgleiche; **~ mouse** *n.* Zwergmaus, *die*

has ▸ **have A, B**

has-been /ˈhæzbiːn/ *n.* (coll.) **be [a bit of] a ~:** seine besten Jahre hinter sich haben; **a seedy ~ of an actor** ein abgetakelter Schauspieler

hash¹ /hæʃ/
A *n.* (Cookery) Haschee, *das;* (fig.) Aufguss, *der* (abwertend); **make a ~ of sth.** (coll.) etw. verpfuschen *od.* verpatzen (ugs.); **settle sb.'s ~** (coll.) jmdn. zur Vernunft bringen; (by forceful methods) jmdn. unschädlich machen; **I'll settle his ~:** dem werd ichs zeigen (ugs.)
B *v.t.* haschieren; (fig. coll.) verpfuschen (ugs.); verpatzen (ugs.); **~ and rehash sth.** etw. x-mal durchkauen (ugs.)

Phrasal verb
- **~ 'up** *v.t.* zerkleinern; (fig. coll.) verpfuschen (ugs.); verpatzen (ugs.)

hash² *n.* (coll.: drug) Hasch, *das* (ugs.)

'hash browns *n. pl.:* *Bratkartoffeln mit Zwiebeln;* ≈ Rösti mit Zwiebeln

hashish /ˈhæʃɪʃ/ *n.* Haschisch, *das od. der*

Hasidic /həˈsɪdɪk/ *adj.* chassidisch

hasn't /ˈhæznt/ = **has not;** ▸ **have A, B**

hasp /hɑːsp/ *n.* Haspe, *die;* (fastener snapping into a lock) [Schnapp]schloss, *das;* (fastener for book or cape) Schließe, *die*

hassle /ˈhæsl/ (coll.)
A *n.* **~[s]** Krach, *der* (ugs.); (trouble, problem) Ärger, *der;* **get involved in ~s with sb.** mit jmdm. Ärger kriegen (ugs.); **no end of ~[s]** nichts als Ärger; **it's a real ~:** das ist ein echtes Problem; **it's too much [of a]/such a ~:** das macht zu viel/so viel Umstände
B *v.t.* schikanieren; **don't ~ me** nerv mich nicht (ugs.)

hassock /ˈhæsək/ *n.* **1** (cushion) Kniekissen, *das* **2** (tuft of grass) Grasbüschel, *das*

haste /heɪst/ *n., no pl.* Eile, *die;* (rush) Hast, *die;* **in his ~:** in seiner Hast; **no need for ~:** kein Grund zur Eile; **more ~, less speed** (prov.) eile mit Weile (Spr.); **do sth. in ~:** etw. eilig tun; **yours in ~** (at end of letter) in Eile, Dein/Deine; **make ~:** sich beeilen

hasten /ˈheɪsn/
A *v.t.* (cause to hurry) drängen; (accelerate) beschleunigen
B *v.i.* eilen; (precipitately) hasten (geh.); **~ away** davoneilen; **~ to do sth.** sich beeilen, etw. zu tun; **I ~ to add/say** ich muss *od.* möchte gleich hinzufügen/sagen

hastily /ˈheɪstɪlɪ/ *adv.* (hurriedly) eilig; (precipitately) hastig; (rashly) übereilt; (quick-temperedly) heftig; hitzig; **judge sb. too ~:** jmdn. vorschnell beurteilen

hasty /ˈheɪstɪ/ *adj.* (hurried) eilig; flüchtig ‹*Skizze, Blick*›; (precipitate) hastig; (rash) übereilt; (quick-tempered) heftig; hitzig; **beat a ~ retreat** sich schnellstens zurückziehen *od.* (ugs.) aus dem Staub machen; (fig.) schnell einen Rückzieher machen; **he's a man of ~ temper/disposition** er hat eine recht hitzige Art

hasty 'pudding *n.* (Brit.) Mehlbrei, *der;* (Amer.) Maismehlbrei, *der*

hat /hæt/ *n.* **1** Hut, *der;* **[sailor's/woollen/knitted] ~:** [Matrosen-/Woll-/Strick]mütze, *die;* **without a ~:** ohne Hut/Mütze; **raise** *or* (dated) **doff one's ~ to sb.** vor jmdm. den Hut ziehen; **take off one's ~, take one's ~ off** seinen *od.* den Hut abnehmen; **take one's ~ off** *or* **take off one's ~ to sb./sth.** (lit. or fig.) vor jmdm./etw. den Hut ziehen; **~s off to him!** Hut ab vor ihm! **2** (fig.) **at the drop of a ~:** auf der Stelle; **sb. will/would eat his ~ if ...:** jmd. frisst einen Besen/will einen Besen fressen, wenn ... (salopp); **somewhere** *or* **a place to hang [up] one's ~:** ein Ort, an dem man zu Hause ist; **throw one's ~ in the ring** seine Kandidatur anmelden; **my ~!** *expr. surprise* ist es/[denn] das die Möglichkeit! (ugs.); *expr. disbelief* dass ich nicht lache!; **be old ~** (coll.) ein alter Hut sein (ugs.); **become old ~** (coll.) aus der Mode kommen; **they pulled his name out of a ~:** er wurde ganz zufällig ausgewählt; **produce sth. out of a ~:** etw. aus dem Ärmel schütteln; **pass** *or* **send round the ~** *or* **the ~ round** (coll.) den Hut herumgehen lassen; **with ~ in hand** demütig; **talk through one's ~** (coll.) dummes Zeug reden (ugs.); **keep sth. under one's ~:** etw. für sich behalten; **[when he is] wearing his ... ~:** in seiner Rolle als ...; **switch ~s** die Rollen vertauschen; **wear two ~s** zwei Interessen gleichzeitig vertreten

hat: ~band *n.* Hutband, *das;* **~box** *n.* Hutschachtel, *die*

hatch¹ /hætʃ/ *n.* **1** (opening) Luke, *die;* **under ~es** unter Deck; **down the ~!** (fig. coll.) runter damit! (ugs.) **2** (serving ~) Durchreiche, *die. see also* **escape-hatch**

hatch²
A *v.t.* (lit. or fig.) ausbrüten
B *v.i.* [aus]schlüpfen; *see also* **chicken A 1**
C *n.* **1** (act of ~ing) Schlüpfen, *das* **2** (brood ~ed) Brut, *die*

Phrasal verbs
- **~ 'out**
A *v.i.* ausschlüpfen; **the eggs have ~ed out** die Eier sind ausgebrütet
B *v.t.* ausbrüten
- **~ 'up** *v.t.* ausbrüten (fig.); aushecken (ugs.)

hatch³ *v.t.* (Art) schraffieren

'hatchback *n.* **1** (door) Heckklappe, *die;* **a ~ model** ein Modell mit Heckklappe **2** (vehicle) Schrägheckllimousine, *die*

hatchery /ˈhætʃərɪ/ *n.* (for birds) Brutplatz, *der;* (for fish) Laichplatz, *der*

hatchet /ˈhætʃɪt/ *n.* Beil, *das;* **bury the ~** (fig.) das Kriegsbeil begraben

hatchet: ~ face *n.* scharf geschnittenes Gesicht; **~-faced** *adj.* mit scharfen Gesichtszügen *nachgestellt;* **~ job** *n.* **do a ~ job on sb./sth.** jmdn./etw. in der Luft zerreißen (salopp); **~ man** **1** (professional killer) Killer, *der;* **be a real ~ man** (fig.) kein Pardon kennen; **2** (henchman) Erfüllungsgehilfe, *der* (fig. abwertend)

hatchling /ˈhætʃlɪŋ/ *n.* Junge, *das*

'hatchway *n.* Luke, *die*

hate /heɪt/
A *n.* **1** Hass, *der;* **~ for sb.** Hass auf *od.* gegen jmdn. **2** (coll.: object of dislike) **be sb.'s great/particular ~:** jmdm. besonders verhasst sein; **my pet ~ at the moment is ...:** ... hasse ich zurzeit am meisten
B *v.t.* hassen; **I ~ having to get up at seven** ich hasse es, um sieben Uhr aufstehen zu müssen; **I ~ to say this** (coll.) ich sage das nicht gern; **I ~ [having] to trouble you** (coll.) tut mir Leid, dass ich Sie damit behelligen muss; **I ~ to think what would have happened if .../I ~ the thought of having to leave this job** (coll.) ich darf gar nicht daran denken, was geschehen wäre, wenn .../wie es wäre, wenn ich die Stelle aufgeben müsste

hateful /ˈheɪtfl/ *adj.* abscheulich; verabscheuenswürdig (geh.); **that would be a ~ thing to do** das [zu tun] wäre abscheulich

'hate mail *n.* hasserfüllte Briefe *Pl.*

hatful /ˈhætfʊl/ *n.* (considerable number/amount) eine ganze Menge (ugs.)

hatless /ˈhætlɪs/ *adj.* ohne Hut *nachgestellt*

hat: ~ peg *n.* Huthaken, *der;* **~pin** *n.* Hutnadel, *die*

hatred /ˈheɪtrɪd/ *n.* Hass, *der;* **feel ~ for** *or* **of sb./sth.** Hass auf *od.* gegen jmdn./etw. empfinden

'hatstand *n.* Hutständer, *der*

hatter /ˈhætə(r)/ *n.* Hutmacher, *der;* **[as] mad as a ~** (fig.) völlig verrückt (ugs.)

'hat trick *n.* Hattrick, *der;* **make** *or* **score a ~:** einen Hattrick erzielen; **be on a ~:** vor einem Hattrick stehen

haughtily /ˈhɔːtɪlɪ/ *adv.* hochmütig

haughtiness /ˈhɔːtɪnɪs/ *n., no pl.* Hochmut, *der*

haughty /ˈhɔːtɪ/ *adj.* hochmütig

haul /hɔːl/
A *v.t.* **1** (pull) ziehen; schleppen; (Fishing) einholen ‹*Netze*›; **~ sth. up the wall** etw. die Mauer hochziehen; **~ the boat up on the beach** das Boot auf den Strand ziehen; **be ~ed before the court** (fig. coll.) vor Gericht gestellt werden; **~ down** einholen ‹*Flagge, Segel*›; *see also* **coal 2** **2** (transport) transportieren; befördern
B *v.i.* **~ [up]on** *or* **at sth.** an etw. (*Dat.*) [kräftig] ziehen
C *n.* **1** Ziehen, *das;* Schleppen, *das;* (Fishing) Einholen, *das* **2** (catch) Fang, *der;* (fig.) Beute, *die* **3** (distance) Strecke, *die; see also* **long haul; short haul**

h

h

haulage /ˈhɔːlɪdʒ/ *n., no pl.* **1** (hauling) Transport, *der;* (business) Spedition, *die* **2** (charges) Transportkosten *Pl.*

ˈhaulage company *n.* Spedition[sfirma], *die;* Fuhrunternehmen, *das*

hauler /ˈhɔːlə(r)/ (Amer.), **haulier** /ˈhɔːlɪə(r)/ (Brit.) *n.* (person) Spediteur, *der;* (firm) Spedition[sfirma], *die*

haulm /hɔːm, hɑːm/ *n.* (stem) (of grass, straw) Halm, *der;* (of leaf, fruit) Stiel, *der*

haunch /hɔːnʃ/ *n.* **1** **sit on one's/its ~es** auf seinem Hinterteil sitzen **2** (Gastr.) Keule, *die* **3** (Archit.) [Bogen]schenkel, *der*

haunt /hɔːnt/

A *v.t.* **1** **~ a house/castle** in einem Haus/Schloss spuken *od.* umgehen; **the old farmhouse is ~ed by ghosts** in dem alten Bauernhaus spuken Geister **2** (fig.: trouble) ‹*Erinnerung, Gedanke:*› plagen, verfolgen **3** (frequent) häufig besuchen ‹*Ort, Lokal*›

B *n.* **a favourite ~ of artists** ein beliebter Treffpunkt für Künstler; **these are my old ~s** hier habe ich mich früher immer herumgetrieben (ugs.)

haunted /ˈhɔːntɪd/ *adj.* **1** **a ~ house** ein Haus, in dem es spukt; **a ~ castle** ein Spukschloss **2** (fig.: troubled) gehetzt ‹*Blick, Eindruck*›

haunting /ˈhɔːntɪŋ/ *adj.* sehnsüchtig ‹*Klänge, Musik*›; lastend ‹*Erinnerung*›; drückend ‹*Schuld*›

Hausa /ˈhaʊsə/ *n., pl. same* **1** (person) Haus[s]a, *der*/Haus[s]afrau, *die* **2** (language) Hausa, *das*

hausfrau /ˈhaʊsfraʊ/ *n.* [biedere] Hausfrau

haute couture /əʊt kuːˈtjʊə(r)/ *n., no pl.* Haute Couture, *die*

haute école /əʊt eɪˈkɒl/ *n., no pl.* (dressage) [die] hohe Schule

hauteur /əʊˈtɜː(r)/ *n., no pl.* Stolz, *der*

Havana /həˈvænə/ *n.* **1** (cigar) Havanna, *die* **2** *pr. n.* ▸ℹ **p. 1643** Havanna *(das)*

have

A /hæv/ *v.t., pres.* **he has** /hæz/, *p.t. & p.p.* **had** /hæd/ **1** (possess) haben; **I ~ it!** ich habs[!]; **and what ~ you** (coll.) und so weiter; **I ~ something to say [to you]** ich habe Ihnen etwas zu sagen; **~ nothing to do/wear/say** nichts zu tun/anzuziehen/zu sagen haben; **they ~ some French** sie können etwas Französisch; **I still ~ some work to do** ich muss noch etwas arbeiten; **you ~ some explaining to do** du schuldest mir eine Erklärung; **you ~ five minutes [in which] to do it** Sie haben fünf Minuten [Zeit], um es zu tun

2 (obtain) bekommen; **there was no money/help to be had** es war kein Geld/keine Hilfe zu bekommen *od.* (ugs.) aufzutreiben; **we shall ~ snow** es wird schneien; **let's not ~ any ...:** lass uns ... vermeiden; **come on, let's ~ it!** (coll.) rück schon raus damit! (ugs.)

3 (take) nehmen; **~ a cigarette** nehmen Sie eine Zigarette; *see also* **5**

4 (keep) behalten; haben; **you can ~ that pencil** Sie können den Bleistift behalten *od.* haben

5 (eat, drink, etc.) **~ breakfast/dinner/lunch** frühstücken/zu Abend/zu Mittag essen; **~ a cup of tea** eine Tasse Tee trinken; **~ a cigarette** eine Zigarette rauchen; *see also* **3**

6 (experience) haben ‹*Spaß, Vergnügen*›

7 (suffer) haben ‹*Krankheit, Schmerz, Enttäuschung, Abenteuer*›; erleiden ‹*Schock*›; (feel) haben ‹*Gefühl, Idee*›; (show) haben ‹*Güte, Freundlichkeit, Frechheit*›; **let him/them ~ it** (coll.) gibs ihm/ihnen (ugs.)

8 (engage in) **~ a game of football** Fußball spielen; **~ a try** es [einmal] versuchen

9 (accept) **I won't ~ it** das lasse ich mir nicht bieten; **I won't ~ him in the house** er kommt mir nicht ins Haus; **I won't ~ you behaving like that** so kannst du dich nicht benehmen

10 (give birth to) **~ a baby/children** ein Baby/Kinder bekommen; **~ pups** *etc.* Junge bekommen

11 (sl.: copulate with) **he had her on the sofa** er machte es mit ihr auf dem Sofa (salopp); **~ it [with sb.]** es [mit jmdm.] machen (salopp)

12 (coll.: beat) **you ~ me there** da bringen Sie mich aber in Verlegenheit

13 (coll.: swindle) **I was had** ich bin [he]reingelegt worden (ugs.); **ever been had!** da bist du ganz schön reingefallen (ugs.)

14 (know) **I ~ it on good authority that ...:** ich weiß es aus zuverlässiger Quelle, dass ...; **she ˈwill ~ it that ...:** sie besteht darauf, dass ...; **she won't ~ it that ...:** sie will nichts davon hören, dass ...; **rumour/legend/tradition has it that they escaped** einem Gerücht/der Legende/der Überlieferung zufolge sind sie entkommen; **as Goethe has it** wie Goethe sagt

15 (as guest) **~ sb. to stay** jmdn. zu Besuch haben; **thanks for having me** danke für die Einladung

16 (summon) **he had me into his office** er hat mich in sein Büro beordert

17 **~ had it** (coll.): **you've had it now** jetzt ist es aus (ugs.); **if you want another drink, you've had it** falls du noch was trinken willst, da geht nichts mehr (ugs.); **this car/dress has had it** dieser Wagen/dieses Kleid hat ausgedient

B /həv, əv, *stressed* hæv/ *v. aux.*, **he has** /həz, əz, *stressed* hæz/, **had** /həd, əd, *stressed* hæd/ **1** *forming past tenses* **I've** *or* **I ~/I had read** ich habe/hatte gelesen; **I've** *or* **I ~/I had gone** ich bin/war gegangen; **having seen him** (because) weil ich ihn gesehen habe/hatte; (after) wenn ich ihn gesehen habe/nachdem ich ihn gesehen hatte; **if I had known ...:** wenn ich gewusst hätte ...

2 (cause to be) **~ sth. made/repaired** etw. machen/reparieren lassen; **~ the painters in** die Maler haben; **~ sb. do sth.** jmdn. etw. tun lassen; **~ a tooth extracted** sich *(Dat.)* einen Zahn ziehen lassen; **~ oneself tattooed** sich tätowieren lassen

3 **she had her purse stolen** man hat ihr das Portemonnaie gestohlen

4 *expr. obligation* **~ to** müssen; **you don't ~ to** du brauchst *od.* musst nicht; **I only ~ to do the washing-up** ich muss nur noch den Abwasch machen; **I ~ only to see him to feel annoyed** ich brauche ihn nur zu sehen, und ich ärgere mich; **he ˈhas to be guilty** er ist fraglos schuldig

C /hæv/ *n. in pl.* **the ~s and the ~-nots** die Besitzenden und die Besitzlosen

Phrasal verbs

- **~ aˈway** ▸**~ off b**
- **~ ˈoff** *v.t.* **1** abmachen **2** **~ it off [with sb.]** (sl.) es [mit jmdm.] treiben (salopp)
- **~ ˈon** *v.t.* **1** **~ the light on** das Licht anhaben **2** (wear) **~ a dress/hat on** ein Kleid/einen Hut tragen; ein Kleid anhaben/einen Hut aufhaben (ugs.) **3** (Brit. coll.: deceive) **~ sb. on** jmdn. auf den Arm nehmen (ugs.)
- **~ ˈout** *v.t.* **1** entfernen; **~ a tooth/one's tonsils out** sich *(Dat.)* einen Zahn ziehen lassen/sich *(Dat.)* die Mandeln herausnehmen lassen **2** (discuss and settle) **~ sth. out** sich über etw. *(Akk.)* offen [mit jmdm.] aussprechen; **~ it out with sb.** mit jmdm. offen sprechen
- **~ ˈup** *v.t.* **1** aufgehängt haben ‹*Vorhang, Bild*› **2** (coll.: bring to court) **~ sb. up** jmdn. rankriegen (ugs.)

haven /ˈheɪvn/ *n.* (mooring) geschützte Anlegestelle, *die;* (fig.: refuge) Zufluchtsort, *der;* **a ~ of peace** eine Insel des Friedens

have-not /ˈhævnɒt/ ▸**have C**

haven't /ˈhævnt/ = **have not;** ▸**have A, B**

haver /ˈheɪvə(r)/ *v.i.* **1** (talk foolishly) **~ [on] about sth.** über etw. *(Akk.)* schwafeln (ugs.) **2** (vacillate) zögern

haversack /ˈhævəsæk/ *n.* Brotbeutel, *der*

havoc /ˈhævək/ *n., no pl.* **1** (devastation) Verwüstungen *Pl.;* **cause** *or* **create** *or* **wreak ~:** Verwüstungen anrichten; **play ~ with** ruinieren ‹*Gesundheit, Frisur usw.*› **2** (confusion) Chaos, *das;* **play ~ with sth.** etw. völlig durcheinander bringen

haw¹ /hɔː/ *n.* (Bot.) **1** (tree) (white) Weißdorn, *der;* (red) Rotdorn, *der* **2** (fruit) Weißdorn-/Rotdornfrucht, *die*

haw² ▸**hum A 1, C 2**

Hawaii /həˈwaɪiː/ *pr. n.* Hawaii *(das)*

Hawaiian /həˈwaɪən/ ▸ℹ **p. 1277,** ▸ℹ **p. 1345**

A *adj.* hawaiisch

B *n.* **1** (person) Hawaiianer, *der*/Hawaiianerin, *die* **2** (language) Hawaiisch, *das*

ˈhawfinch *n.* [Kirsch]kernbeißer, *der*

haw-haw /ˈhɔːhɔː/

A *int.* (laughter) haha

B *n.* **let out a loud ~:** laut auflachen

hawk¹ /hɔːk/

A *n.* (Ornith., Polit.) Falke, *der;* **watch sb. like a ~:** jmdn. mit Argusaugen beobachten; **have eyes like a ~:** Augen wie ein Luchs *od.* Adleraugen haben

B *v.i.* mit dem Falken jagen; beizen (Jägerspr.)

hawk² *v.t.* (peddle) **~ sth.** (at door) mit etw. hausieren [gehen]; (in street) etw. [auf der Straße] verkaufen; **~ sth. around** (fig.) mit etw. hausieren [gehen]

hawk³

A *v.t.* **~ [up] phlegm** Schleim auswerfen

B *v.i.* Schleim hochziehen [im Hals]

hawker /ˈhɔːkə(r)/ *n.* Hausierer, *der*/Hausiererin, *die;* (in street) fliegender Händler

ˈhawk-eyed *adj.* adleräugig; **be ~:** Falkenaugen *od.* Adleraugen haben

hawkish /ˈhɔːkɪʃ/ *adj.* raubvogelartig ‹*Aussehen*›; (Polit.) militant

ˈhawklike *adj.* falkenartig

hawk: ~moth *n.* (Zool.) Schwärmer, *der;* **~-nosed** *adj.* hakennasig; **be ~-nosed** eine Hakennase *od.* Habichtsnase haben; **~weed** *n.* (Bot.) Habichtskraut, *das*

hawser /ˈhɔːzə(r)/ *n.* (Naut.) Trosse, *die*

hawthorn /ˈhɔːθɔːn/ *n.* (Bot.) (white) Weißdorn, *der;* (red) Rotdorn, *der*

hay /heɪ/ *n., no pl.* Heu, *das;* **make ~:** Heu machen; **make ~ while the sun shines** (prov.) die Zeit nutzen; *see also* **hit A 9**

hay: ~cock *n.* Heuhaufen, *der;* **~ fever** *n., no pl.* ▸ℹ **p. 1231** Heuschnupfen, *der;* **~field** *n.* Heuwiese, *die;* **~maker** *n.* **1** Heumacher, *der;* **2** (coll.: blow) weit ausholender Schlag; Heumacher, *der* (Boxen Jargon); **~making** *n., no pl.* Heuernte, *die;* **~rick** ▸**~stack;** **~seed** *n.* **1** Heublumen *Pl.;* **2** (Amer. derog.: yokel) Bauerntölpel, *der;* **~stack** *n.* Heuschober, *der* (südd.); Heudieme, *die* (nordd.); *see also* **needle A**

haywire /ˈheɪwaɪə(r)/ *adj.* (coll.) **go ~** ‹*Instrument:*› verrückt spielen (ugs.); ‹*Plan:*› über den Haufen geworfen werden (ugs.); ‹*Person:*› durchdrehen (ugs.)

hazard /ˈhæzəd/

A *n.* **1** (danger) Gefahr, *die;* (on road) Gefahrenstelle, *die;* **occupational ~:** Berufsrisiko, *das; see also* **fire hazard** **2** (chance) Schicksal, *das* **3** (Golf) Hindernis, *das*

B *v.t.* **1** (endanger) in Gefahr bringen **2** (venture) riskieren; **~ a guess** es mit Raten probieren

ˈhazard lights *ns. pl.* (Motor Veh.) Warnblinkanlage, *die*

hazardous /ˈhæzədəs/ *adj.* (dangerous) gefährlich; (risky) riskant; **~ waste** Sondermüll, *der*

hazardously /ˈhæzədəslɪ/ *adv.* (dangerously) gefährlich; (riskily) riskant

hazard ˈwarning lights ▸**hazard lights**

haze /heɪz/

A *n.* Dunst[schleier], *der;* (fig.) Nebel, *der*

B *v.t.* vernebeln

hazel /ˈheɪzl/

A *n.* **1** (Bot.) Haselnussstrauch, *der;* (wood) Haselholz, *das* (veralt.) **2** (colour) Haselnussbraun, *das*

B *adj.* haselnussbraun

ˈhazelnut *n.* Haselnuss, *die*

hazily /ˈheɪzɪlɪ/ *adv.* (lit. or fig.) verschwommen; unscharf; vage ‹*verstehen*›; unklar ‹*sich vorstellen*›

haziness /ˈheɪzɪnɪs/ *n., no pl.* Dunst, *der;* (fig.) Vagheit, *die*

hazy /ˈheɪzɪ/ *adj.* dunstig, diesig ‹*Wetter, Tag[eszeit]*›; verschwommen, unscharf ‹*Konturen*›; (fig.) vage; **I have a ~ recollection that ...:** ich erinnere mich dunkel, dass ...

H-bomb /ˈeɪtʃbɒm/ *n.* H-Bombe, *die*
HDTV *abbr.* = **high-definition television** HDTV
he¹ /hɪ, *stressed* hiː/
A *pron.* er; *referring to personified things or animals which correspond to German feminines/neuters* sie/es; **it was he** (formal) er war es; **he who** wer; (Games) **be 'he'** dran sein; *see also* **him**; **himself**; **his**
B *n., pl.* **hes** /hiːz/ Er, *der* (ugs.)
he² /hiː/ *int.* haha!
he- /hiː/ *pref.* männlich; **he-goat** [Ziegen]bock, *der*
HE *abbr.* **1** = **high explosive** **2** = **His Eminence** **3** = **His/Her Excellency**
head /hed/
A *n.* **1** ▸ⓘ **p. 951** Kopf, *der;* Haupt, *das* (geh.); **count ~s** die Anzahl feststellen; **mind your ~!** Vorsicht, dein Kopf!; (on sign) Vorsicht — geringe Durchgangshöhe!; **turn sb.'s ~** (fig.) jmdm. den Kopf verdrehen; **laugh/scream one's ~ off** wie verrückt lachen/schreien; **from ~ to foot** von Kopf bis Fuß; **get one's ~ down** (coll.) sich aufs Ohr hauen (ugs.); **keep one's ~ down** (lit. or fig.) in Deckung bleiben; **stand on one's ~:** [einen] Kopfstand machen; **I could do that [standing] on my ~** (fig. coll.) das kann *od.* mache ich mit links (ugs.); **he has a price on his ~:** auf seinen Kopf ist eine Belohnung *od.* ein Preis ausgesetzt; **have a [bad] ~** (fig. coll.: headache) einen Brummschädel haben (ugs.); **the crowned ~s of Europe** die gekrönten Häupter Europas; **taller by a ~, a ~ taller** einen Kopf größer; **win by a ~/short ~:** mit einer Kopflänge/Nasenlänge gewinnen; **be** *or* **stand ~ and shoulders above sb.** (fig.) jmdm. haushoch überlegen sein; **give a horse its ~:** einem Pferd die Zügel schießen lassen; **give sb.** *or* **let sb. have his/her ~** (fig.) jmdm. freie Hand lassen; **go to sb.'s ~:** jmdm. in den *od.* zu Kopf steigen; **have a [good] ~ for heights** schwindelfrei sein; **~ first** mit dem Kopf zuerst/voran; (fig.) kopfüber; **not know whether one is [standing] on one's ~ or one's heels** nicht wissen, wo einem der Kopf steht; **~ over heels** kopfüber; **~ over heels in love** bis über beide Ohren verliebt (ugs.); **I can hold up my ~ [again]** ich brauche mich nicht [mehr] zu schämen; **keep one's ~:** einen klaren Kopf behalten; **keep one's ~ above water** (fig.) sich über Wasser halten; **put our/your/their ~s together [on sth.]** sich [wegen etw.] zusammensetzen; **lose one's ~:** enthauptet werden; (fig.) den Kopf verlieren; **~ to tail** in einer Reihe dicht hintereinander; (**~** beside tail) nebeneinander in umgekehrter Richtung; **be unable to make ~ or tail of sth./sb.** aus etw./jmdm. nicht klug werden; **be off one's ~** (coll.) übergeschnappt sein (ugs.); **off the top of one's ~** (coll.) aus dem Stegreif; (as estimate) über den Daumen gepeilt; **on your** *etc.* **[own] ~ be it** das hast du *usw.* selbst zu verantworten; **promote sb. over sb.'s ~:** jmdn. jmdm. bei der Beförderung vorziehen; **go over sb.'s ~:** jmdn. übergehen; *see also* **ear¹ 1**; **hole A 1**; **raise A 1**
2 (mind) Kopf, *der;* **in one's ~:** im Kopf; **enter sb.'s ~:** jmdm. in den Sinn kommen; **two ~s are better than one** (prov.) zwei Köpfe sind besser als einer; **it went right out of my ~:** ich habe das völlig vergessen; **take it into one's ~ [to do sth.]** auf die Idee kommen[, etw. zu tun]; **put sth. into sb.'s ~:** jmdn. auf etw. (*Akk.*) bringen; **it went above** *or* **over my ~** (fig.) das war zu hoch für mich (ugs.); **talk over sb.'s ~:** sich zu kompliziert für jmdn. ausdrücken; **I've got a good/bad ~ for figures** ich kann gut rechnen/rechnen kann ich überhaupt nicht; **use your ~:** gebrauch deinen Verstand; **not quite right in the ~** (coll.) nicht ganz richtig [im Kopf] (ugs.); **get sth. into one's ~:** etw. begreifen; **get this into your ~!** schreib dir das hinter die Ohren! (ugs.); **have got it into one's ~ that ...:** fest [davon] überzeugt sein, dass ...; **the first thing that comes into sb.'s ~:** das Erste, was jmdm. einfällt; **you ought to have your ~ examined** (joc.) ich glaube, du musst mal deinen Kopf untersuchen lassen (ugs. scherzh.); **the ~ rules the heart** der Verstand kontrolliert die Gefühle
3 (person) **a** *or* **per ~:** pro Kopf
4 *pl. same* (in counting) Stück [Vieh], *das*
5 *in pl.* (on coin) **~s or tails?** Kopf oder Zahl?; **~s [it is]** Kopf; **~s I go, tails I stay** bei Kopf gehe ich, bei Zahl bleibe ich; **~s I win, tails you lose** es läuft auf dasselbe hinaus
6 (working end etc.; also Mus.) Kopf, *der;* (of axe) Blatt, *das;* (of spear) Spitze, *die;* (of cylinder) Zylinderkopf, *der;* **drilling/cutting ~:** Bohr-/Schneidkopf, *der;* **playback/erasing ~:** Wiedergabe-/Löschkopf, *der*
7 (of plant) Kopf, *der;* (of grain) Ähre, *die;* **~ of lettuce** Salatkopf, *der*
8 (on beer) Blume, *die*
9 (highest part) Kopf, *der;* (of stairs) oberes Ende; (of list, column) oberste Reihe; (of mast) Topp, *der*
10 (upper or more important end) Kopf, *der;* (of table) Kopf, *der;* Kopfende, *das;* (of lake, valley) oberes Ende; (of river) Quelle, *die;* (of bed) Kopfende, *das*
11 (of boil etc.) Spitze, *die;* (fig.: crisis) **come to a ~:** sich zuspitzen; **bring matters to a ~:** die Sache auf die Spitze treiben; (force a decision) die Entscheidung herbeiführen
12 (leader) Leiter, *der*/Leiterin, *die;* (of church, family) Oberhaupt, *das;* **~ of government** Regierungschef, *der*/-chefin, *die;* **~ of state** Staatsoberhaupt, *das*
13 ▸**~master**; **~mistress**
14 (leadership) Spitze, *die;* **he is at the ~ of his profession** er hat eine Spitzenstellung in seinem Beruf
15 (of ship) Bug, *der*
16 ▸**~land**
17 **~ [of water]** gestautes Wasser; Oberwasser, *das;* (height of liquid) Höhe, *die;* (pressure) Druck, *der;* **under a full ~ of steam** mit Volldampf
18 (title) Überschrift, *die;* (fig.: category) Rubrik, *die*
B *attrib. adj.* (senior) **~ boy/girl** ≈ Schulsprecher, *der*/-sprecherin, *die* (*vom Lehrkörper eingesetzt*); **~ waiter** Oberkellner, *der;* **~ clerk** Bürovorsteher, *der;* (main) **~ office** Hauptverwaltung, *die;* (Commerc.) Hauptbüro, *das;* (Banking, Insurance) Hauptgeschäftsstelle, *die*
C *v.t.* **1** (provide with heading) überschreiben; betiteln; **~ed notepaper** Briefpapier mit Kopf
2 (stand at top of) anführen ‹*Liste*›; (lead) leiten; führen ‹*Bewegung*›
3 (precede) anführen
4 (direct) **~ sth. towards sth.** etw. auf etw. zusteuern; **we were ~ed towards Plymouth** wir fuhren mit Kurs auf Plymouth
5 (Football) köpfen
6 (overtake and stop) **~ sb./sth. [off]** jmdn./etw. abdrängen
7 (surpass) überholen
D *v.i.* steuern; **~ for London** ‹*Flugzeug, Schiff:*› Kurs auf London nehmen; ‹*Auto:*› in Richtung London fahren; **~ towards** *or* **for sb./the buffet** auf jmdn./das Büfett zusteuern; **where are you ~ing?** wo gehst du hin?; **you're ~ing in the wrong direction** (fig.) du bist auf dem Holzweg; **you're ~ing for trouble** du wirst Ärger bekommen
Phrasal verb
• **~ 'up** *v.t.* (be in charge of) leiten
head: ~ache *n.* ▸ⓘ **p. 1231** Kopfschmerzen *Pl.;* (fig. coll.) Problem, *das;* **~achy** *adj.* (coll.) drückend ‹*Wetter*›; **feel ~achy** einen Druck im Kopf haben; **~band** *n.* Stirnband, *das;* **~board** *n.* (of bed) Kopfende, *das;* **~butt** **A** *n.* Kopfstoß, *der;* **B** *v.t.* einen Kopfstoß geben (+ *Dat.*); **~ case** *n.* (coll.) Hirni, *der* (ugs.); **be some sort of ~ case** sie nicht alle haben (ugs.); **~ count** *n.* **1** **take a ~ count** abzählen; die Anzahl feststellen; **2** (number of people) Kopfzahl, *die;* **~ covering** *n.* Kopfbedeckung, *die;* **~dress** *n.* Kopfschmuck, *der*
-headed /ˈhedɪd/ *adj. in comb.* -köpfig
header /ˈhedə(r)/ *n.* **1** (Footb.) Kopfball, *der* **2** (dive) Kopfsprung, *der* **3** (Building) Binder, *der*
head: ~gear *n., no pl.* **1** Kopfbedeckung, *die;* (hats) Kopfbedeckungen *Pl.;* **protective ~gear** Kopfschutz, *der;* **2** (Mining) Fördergerüst, *das;* **~hunt** *v.t.* (for job) abwerben; **~hunter** *n.* (lit. or fig.) Kopfjäger, *der*
heading /ˈhedɪŋ/ *n.* **1** (title) Überschrift, *die;* (in encyclopedia) Stichwort, *das;* (fig.: category) Rubrik, *die;* **come under the ~ [of] X** unter die Rubrik X fallen; **let's discuss these problems under separate ~s** diese Probleme sollten gesondert behandelt werden **2** (direction) Kurs, *der*
head: ~lamp *n.* Scheinwerfer, *der;* **~land** /ˈhedlənd, ˈhedlænd/ *n.* **1** (Geog.) Landspitze, *die;* **2** (Agric.) Vorgewende, *das*
headless /ˈhedlɪs/ *adj.* ohne Kopf; **run around like a ~ chicken** herumrennen wie ein aufgescheuchtes Huhn/wie aufgescheuchte Hühner
head: ~light *n.* Scheinwerfer, *der;* **~line** *n.* Schlagzeile, *die;* **be ~line news, make [the] ~lines,** (coll.) **hit the ~lines** Schlagzeilen machen; **the [news] ~lines** (Radio, Telev.) die Kurznachrichten; (within news programme) der [Nachrichten]überblick; *see also* **running head[line]**; **~liner** *n.* (Amer.) Star (der ständig in den Schlagzeilen ist); **~lock** *n.* (Wrestling) Schwitzkasten, *der*
ˈheadlong
A *adv.* **1** (head first) **fall/plunge ~ into sth.** kopfüber in etw. fallen/springen **2** (uncontrollably) blindlings; **rush ~ into sth.** (fig.) etw. überstürzen
B *adj.* **1** (head first) **~ dive** Kopfsprung, *der* **2** (impetuous) überstürzt ‹*Flucht, Entscheidung*›
head: ~man *n.* Häuptling, *der;* **~ˈmaster** *n.* ▸ⓘ **p. 1260**, ▸ⓘ **p. 1634** Schulleiter, *der;* (in secondary school) Direktor, *der;* (in primary school) Rektor, *der;* **~ˈmistress** *n.* ▸ⓘ **p. 1260**, ▸ⓘ **p. 1634** ▸**~master**: Schulleiterin, *die;* Direktorin, *die;* Rektorin, *die;* **~ office** Hauptverwaltung, *die;* **~-on** **A** /ˈ--/ *adj.* frontal; offen ‹*Konfrontation, Konflikt*›; **a ~-on collision** *or* **crash** ein Frontalzusammenstoß; **B** /-ˈ-/ *adv.* frontal; **meet sth./sb. ~-on** (fig.: resolutely) einer Sache/jmdm. entschieden entgegentreten; **~phones** *n. pl.* Kopfhörer, *der;* **~ˈquarters** *n. sing. or pl.* Hauptquartier, *das;* (of firm) Zentrale, *die;* **police ~quarters** Polizeidirektion, *die;* **~rest** *n.* Kopfstütze, *die;* **~ restraint** *n.* (Motor Veh.) Kopfstütze, *die;* **~room** *n., no pl.* [lichte] Höhe, *die;* (in car) Kopffreiheit, *die;* **low ~room** (of arch, tunnel) geringe Durchfahrtshöhe; **~scarf** *n.* Kopftuch, *das;* **~set** *n.* Kopfhörer, *der*
headship /ˈhedʃɪp/ *n.* Posten des Schulleiters/der Schulleiterin
head: ~shrinker *n.* **1** Kopfjäger, *der;* **2** (coll.: psychiatrist) Seelenklempner, *der* (salopp); **~square** *n.* [viereckiges] Kopftuch; **~ ˈstart** *n.* **a ~ start [over sb.]** eine Vorgabe [gegenüber jmdm.]; **~stock** *n.* Spindelstock, *der;* **~stone** *n.* **1** (gravestone) Grabstein, *der;* **2** (of building) Grundstein, *der;* (fig.) Grundpfeiler, *der;* **~strong** *adj.* eigensinnig; störrisch ‹*Pferd, Esel*›; **~ tax** *n.* (Amer.) Kopfsteuer, *die;* **~ ˈteacher** *n.* ▸**headmaster**; **headmistress**; **~-to-ˈhead** **A** *adj.* direkt ‹*Wettbewerb*›; **~-to-head debate** Streitgespräch, *das;* **B** *adv.* direkt ‹*konkurrieren*›; **the winners of the heats then rode ~-to-head** die Sieger der Vorläufe fuhren dann gegeneinander; **C** *n.* Zweikampf, *der;* (debate) [Rede]duell, *das;* **~-ˈup display** *n.* Head-up-Display, *das;* **~ voice** *n.* Kopfstimme, *die;* **~water** *n., usu. in pl.* Quellfluss, *der;* **~way** *n., no pl.* (progress) **make ~way** Fortschritte machen; **~ wind** *n.* Gegenwind, *der;* **~word** *n.* **1** Stichwort, *das;* **2** (Ling.) Nukleus, *der;* **~work** *n., no pl.* Kopfarbeit, *die*
heady /ˈhedɪ/ *adj.* **1** vorschnell; unbesonnen **2** (intoxicating) berauschend
heal¹ /hiːl/
A *v.t.* **1** (lit. or fig.) heilen; **time ~s all** (fig.) die Zeit heilt [alle] Wunden **2** (arch.) ▸**cure B 1**
B *v.i.* **~ [up]** [ver]heilen
heal² ▸**hele**
healer /ˈhiːlə(r)/ *n.* (person) Heilkundige, *der/die;* **time is a great ~:** die Zeit heilt alle Wunden
healing /ˈhiːlɪŋ/
A *n.* Heilung, *die;* **powers of ~:** Heilkräfte
B *attrib. adj.* **~ effect** Heilwirkung, *die;* **~ influence** heilsamer Einfluss; **~ ointment** Heilsalbe, *die*

h

health /helθ/ *n.* [1] *no pl.* (state) Gesundheitszustand, *der;* (healthiness) Gesundheit, *die;* **in good/very good ~:** bei guter/bester Gesundheit; **sb. suffers from poor** *or* **bad** *or* **ill ~:** jmdm. geht es gesundheitlich schlecht; **be restored to ~:** wieder hergestellt sein; **be in poor ~:** in schlechtem gesundheitlichen Zustand sein; **[not] be in the best of ~:** [nicht] bei bester Gesundheit sein; **in my state of ~:** in meinem Gesundheitszustand; **I'm not doing it for [the good of] my ~:** ich mache das nicht meiner Gesundheit zuliebe *od.* (fig.) nicht zum Vergnügen; **at least you have your ~:** du bist wenigstens gesund [2] (toast) **drink sb.'s ~** *or* **a ~ to sb.** auf jmds. Gesundheit trinken; **good** *or* **your ~!** auf deine Gesundheit!; zum Wohl!; pros[i]t!

health: ~ authority *n.* Gesundheitsbehörde, *die;* **~ care** *n.* Gesundheitsfürsorge, *die; attrib.* **~-care worker** im Gesundheitswesen Beschäftigte, *der/die;* **inadequate ~ care** unzureichende medizinische Versorgung; **~ centre** *n.* medizinisches Versorgungszentrum; Poliklinik, *die;* **~ certificate** *n.* Gesundheitszeugnis, *das;* **~ check** *n.* Gesundheitsuntersuchung, *die;* **~ education** *n.* Gesundheitslehre, *die;* **~ farm** *n.* Gesundheitsfarm, *die* (ugs.); **~ food** *n.* Reformhauskost, *die; attrib.* **~ food shop** Reformhaus, *das;* **~-giving** *adj.* gesund; **~ hazard** *n.* Gesundheitsrisiko, *das*

healthily /ˈhelθɪlɪ/ *adv.* gesund

healthiness /ˈhelθɪnɪs/ *n., no pl.* (lit. or fig.) Gesundheit, *die*

health: ~ insurance *n.* Krankenversicherung, *die;* **~ ˈphysics** *n.* Strahlenhygiene, *die;* **~ resort** *n.* Kurort, *der;* **~ salts** *n. pl.* leichtes Magenmittel; **H~ Secretary** *n.* (Brit.) Gesundheitsminister, *der/*-ministerin, *die;* **~ service** *n.* Gesundheitsdienst, *der;* **~ visitor** *n.* ▸ **p. 1260** Krankenschwester/Krankenpfleger im Sozialdienst; **~ warning** *n.* Warnhinweis, *der; Hinweis auf die Gesundheitsgefährdung*

healthy /ˈhelθɪ/ *adj.* [1] gesund; (fig.) **the engine sounds ~:** der Motor hat einen gesunden Klang; **a ~ attitude towards sex** ein gesundes *od.* natürliches Verhältnis zum Sex [2] (salutary) gut ‹*Zeichen*›; **~ living** ein gesundes Leben; (safe) **stay at a ~ distance** in sicherer Entfernung bleiben

heap /hi:p/

A *n.* [1] (pile) Haufen, *der;* **a ~ of clothes** ein Kleiderhaufen; **lying in a ~/in ~s** auf einem/in Haufen liegen; **he was lying in a ~ on the ground** er lag zusammengesackt am Boden; **at the bottom/top of the ~** (fig.) bei den Verlierern/Gewinnern [2] (fig. coll.: quantity) **a [whole] ~ of** eine [ganze] Menge; **~s of** jede Menge (ugs.) [3] (fig. coll. derog.: vehicle) Klapperkiste, *die* (ugs.)

B *v.t.* (pile) aufhäufen; **a ~ed spoonful of sugar** ein gehäufter Löffel Zucker; **~ sth. up** etw. aufhäufen; **~ sth. with sth.** etw. mit etw. [hoch] beladen; **~ sth. on sb.** (fig.) jmdn. mit etw. überhäufen

hear /hɪə(r)/

A *v.t.,* **heard** /hɜ:d/ [1] hören; **they ~d the car drive away** sie hörten den Wagen abfahren; **did you ~ him leaving** *or* **leave?** hast du ihn weggehen gehört *od.* hören?; **I have ~d it said that ...:** ich habe sagen hören, dass ...; **I can hardly ~ myself think/speak** ich kann keinen klaren Gedanken fassen/kann mein eigenes Wort nicht verstehen; **let's ~ it!** nun sags schon!; **from what one ~s** wie man hört; **what's this I ~?** was muss ich da hören?; **you haven't ~d the last of this matter** das letzte Wort in dieser Sache ist noch nicht gesprochen; *see also* **end A 7; last¹ C 1** [2] (understand) verstehen [3] (Law) [an]hören; verhandeln ‹*Fall*› [4] (answer) **our prayers have been ~d** unsere Gebete sind erhört worden

B *v.i.,* **heard: ~ about sb./sth.** von jmdm./etw. [etwas] hören; **I've ~d all aˈbout you** ich habe schon viel von Ihnen gehört; **~ from sb.** von jmdm. hören; **have you ~d from Tokyo/Smith yet?** haben Sie schon Nachricht aus Tokio/von Smith?; **I never ~d of such a thing!** hat man so was schon gehört!; **he was never ~d of again** von ihm hat man nie wieder [etwas] gehört; **he wouldn't ~ of it** er wollte davon nichts hören

C *int.* **H~! H~!** bravo!; richtig!

Phrasal verb

• **~ ˈout** *v.t.* ausreden lassen

heard ▸ **hear A, B**

hearer /ˈhɪərə(r)/ *n.* Hörer, *der*/Hörerin, *die*

hearing /ˈhɪərɪŋ/ *n.* [1] *no pl., no art.* (faculty) Gehör, *das;* **have good ~:** gut hören können; **be hard of ~:** schwerhörig sein [2] *no pl.* (distance) **within/out of ~:** in/außer Hörweite [3] *no pl.* **a fair ~:** eine faire Chance zu sprechen; **get a ~:** sich (*Dat.*) Gehör verschaffen können [4] (Law etc.) Hearing, *das*

ˈhearing aid *n.* Hörgerät, *das*

hearken /ˈhɑ:kn/ *v.i.* (arch./literary) **~ to sb./sth.** jmdm./einer Sache lauschen

hearsay /ˈhɪəseɪ/ *n., no pl., no indef. art.* Gerücht, *das;* Klatsch, *der* (abwertend); **~ evidence** (Law) Beweis vom Hörensagen

hearse /hɜ:s/ *n.* Leichenwagen, *der*

heart /hɑ:t/ *n.* [1] ▸ **p. 951** (Anat.; also **~**-shaped object) Herz, *das;* **he has a weak ~** (Med.) er hat ein schwaches Herz; **know/learn sth. by ~:** etw. auswendig wissen/lernen [2] (seat of feeling) **at ~:** im Grunde seines/ihres Herzens; **sb. has sth. at ~, sth. is near** *or* **close to sb.'s ~:** jmdm. liegt etw. am Herzen; **a matter near** *or* **close to sb.'s ~:** ein Herzensanliegen; **go to sb.'s ~:** jmdm. ans Herz gehen; **in one's ~ [of ~s]** im tiefsten Herzen; **from the** *or* **one's ~:** von Herzen; **from the bottom of one's ~:** aus tiefstem Herzen; **with all one's ~ [and soul]** von ganzem Herzen; **put one's ~ and soul into sth.** etw. mit Leib und Seele tun; **put one's ~ into sth.** mit ganzem Herzen bei einer Sache sein; **cry one's ~ out** sich (*Dat.*) die Augen ausweinen *od.* aus dem Kopf weinen; **eat one's ~ out** sich vor Gram/Sehnsucht/Trauer *usw.* verzehren; **eat your ~ out!** da kannst du grün vor Neid werden!; **set one's ~ on sth./on doing sth.** sein Herz an etw. (*Akk.*) hängen/daran hängen, etw. zu tun; **to one's ~'s content** nach Herzenslust; **take sth. to ~:** sich (*Dat.*) etw. zu Herzen nehmen; (accept) beherzigen ‹*Rat*›; **take sb. to one's ~:** jmdn. in sein *od.* ins Herz schließen; **my ~ goes out to them** ich verspüre großes Mitleid mit ihnen; **my ~ bleeds for him** ich habe tiefstes Mitgefühl mit ihm; (iron.) mir blutet das Herz; **it does my ~ good** es erfreut mein Herz; **somebody after my own ~:** jemand ganz nach meinem Herzen; **have a ~ to ~ talk** offen und ehrlich miteinander sprechen; **her ~ is in the right place** sie hat das Herz auf dem rechten Fleck; **lose one's ~ to sb./sth.** sein Herz an jmdn./etw. verlieren; **give one's ~:** sein Herz schenken; **be sick at ~:** verzweifelt sein; **with a light/heavy ~:** leichten/schweren Herzens; **his ~ is not in it** er ist nicht mit dem Herzen dabei; **all the ~ could desire** alles, was das Herz begehrt; **bless his/her ~:** das liebe Kind!; **wear one's ~ [up]on one's sleeve** das Herz auf der Zunge tragen; **find it in one's ~ to do sth.** es übers Herz bringen, etw. zu tun; **have a ~!** hab' Erbarmen!; **not have the ~ to do sth.** nicht das Herz haben, etw. zu tun [3] (seat of courage) **take ~:** Mut schöpfen (**from** bei); **put new ~ into sb.** jmdm. neuen Mut geben; **in good ~:** voll Zuversicht; **lose ~:** den Mut verlieren; **his ~ stood still** ihm stand das Herz still; **my ~ was in my boots** ich war am Boden zerstört (ugs.); **my ~ sank** mein Mut sank [4] (Cards) Herz, *das; see also* **club A 4** [5] (centre) (of cabbage) Strunk, *der;* (of lettuce) Herz, *das;* (of tree) Kernholz, *das;* **the ~ of the matter** der wahre Kern der Sache; **go to the ~ of a problem** zum Kern eines Problems kommen; **in the ~ of the forest/England** mitten im Wald/im Herzen Englands. *See also* **break¹ A 8, B 1; change A 1; dear A 1; desire A 3; gold A 1; stone A 1**

heart: ~ache *n.* [seelische] Qual; **~ attack** *n.* ▸ **p. 1231** Herzanfall, *der;* (fatal) Herzschlag, *der;* **~beat** *n.* Herzschlag, *der;* **~['s]-blood** *n.* (fig.) Herzblut, *das* (geh.); **~break** *n.* Herzeleid, *das* (geh.); tiefer Kummer; **~breaking** *adj.* herzzerreißend; **~broken** *adj.* **she was ~broken** ihr Herz war gebrochen; **~burn** *n., no pl.* ▸ **p. 1231** (Med.) Sodbrennen, *das;* **~ disease** *n., no pl.* ▸ **p. 1231** Herzkrankheiten *Pl.;* **die of** *or* **from ~ disease** einem Herzleiden erliegen

hearten /ˈhɑ:tn/ *v.t.* ermutigen

heartening /ˈhɑ:tənɪŋ/ *adj.* ermutigend; **~ news** erfreuliche Nachrichten

heart: ~ failure *n.* ▸ **p. 1231** Herzversagen, *das;* **~felt** *adj.* tief empfunden ‹*Beileid*›; aufrichtig ‹*Dankbarkeit*›; **a ~felt wish** ein Herzenswunsch

hearth /hɑ:θ/ *n.* [1] [*gekachelter o. ä.*] *Platz vor dem Kamin;* **~ and home** (fig.) der heimische Herd [2] (in furnace) Ofenraum, *der;* (smith's **~**) Esse, *die*

hearthrug *n.* Kaminvorleger, *der*

heartily /ˈhɑ:tɪlɪ/ *adv.* von Herzen; **eat ~:** tüchtig essen; **be ~ sick of sth.** etw. herzlich leid sein

ˈheartland *n.* Landesinnere, *das*

heartless /ˈhɑ:tlɪs/ *adj.,* **heartlessly** /ˈhɑ:tlɪslɪ/ *adv.* herzlos; unbarmherzig

heartlessness /ˈhɑ:tlɪsnɪs/ *n., no pl.* Unbarmherzigkeit, *die*

heart: ~-ˈlung machine *n.* (Med.) Herz-Lungen-Maschine, *die;* **~ rate** *n.* Herzfrequenz, *die;* **an abnormally rapid ~ rate** ein abnorm schneller Herzschlag; **~-rending** *adj.* herzzerreißend; **~-searching** *n.* Gewissenserforschung, *die;* **~'s-ease** *n.* (Bot.) Veilchen, *das;* (Viola tricolor) Stiefmütterchen, *das;* **~-shaped** *adj.* herzförmig; **~sick** *adj.* verzweifelt; **~strings** *n. pl.* **touch sb.'s ~strings** jmdm. zu Herzen gehen; **~-throb** *n.* (person) Idol, *das;* **~-to-~** *n.* **have a ~-to-~:** offen und ehrlich miteinander sprechen; **~ transplant** *n.* (operation) Herztransplantation, *die* (fachspr.); Herzverpflanzung, *die;* (transplanted heart) Herztransplantat, *das* (fachspr.); **receive a ~ transplant from sb.** jmds. Herz eingepflanzt *od.* implantiert bekommen; **~ trouble** *n.* ▸ **p. 1231** Probleme mit dem Herzen; **~-warming** *adj.* herzerfreuend; **~wood** *n.* (Bot.) Kernholz, *das*

hearty /ˈhɑ:tɪ/

A *adj.* [1] (wholehearted) ungeteilt ‹*Unterstützung, Zustimmung*›; (enthusiastic, unrestrained) herzlich; begeistert ‹*Gesang*›; **a ~ eater** ein starker Esser [2] (large) herzhaft ‹*Mahlzeit*›; gesund ‹*Appetit*› [3] (vigorous) herzhaft ‹*Ruck, Tritt*›; *see also* **hale¹**

B *n.* (Naut.) **come on, my hearties!** auf gehts, Jungs!

heat /hi:t/

A *n.* [1] (hotness) Hitze, *die;* (temperature) Temperatur, *die;* (temperature setting) Temperaturstufe, *die;* (fig.: sensation) Brennen, *das;* **remove sth. from/return sth. to the ~:** etw. vom Feuer nehmen/wieder erhitzen [2] (Phys.) Wärme, *die;* **latent ~:** Umwandlungswärme, *die;* **specific ~:** spezifische Wärme [3] (fig.) (anger) Erregung, *die;* **generate a lot of ~/more ~ than light** die Gemüter erregen/mehr Erregung als Erleuchtung erzeugen; **take the ~ out of a situation** eine Situation entschärfen; **in the ~ of the moment** in der Hitze des Gefechts; (coll.: pressure) **the ~ is on** die Sache ist heiß (ugs.); **put the ~ on** Druck machen; **put the ~ on sb.** jmdn. unter Druck setzen; **the ~ is off** die Lage hat sich entspannt [4] (Zool.) Brunst, *die;* **come into** *or* **on/be in** *or* **on ~:** brünstig werden/sein; ‹*Stute:*› rossig werden/sein; ‹*Hündin:*› läufig werden/sein; ‹*Katze:*› rollig werden/sein [5] (Sport) Vorlauf, *der; see also* **dead heat**

B *v.t.* heizen ‹*Raum*›; erhitzen ‹*Substanz, Lösung*›; vorheizen ‹*Backofen*›

C *v.i.* warm werden

Phrasal verb

• **~ ˈup** *v.t.* heiß machen ‹*Essen, Wasser*›

heated /ˈhi:tɪd/ *adj.* erhitzt; (fig.: angry) hitzig; **a ~ exchange** ein heftiger Schlagabtausch (fig.)

heatedly /ˈhi:tɪdlɪ/ *adv.* hitzig

heater /ˈhiːtə(r)/ *n.* **1** Ofen, *der;* (for water) Boiler, *der* **2** (dated coll.: firearm) Kanone, *die* (salopp)

ˈ**heat exchanger** *n.* Wärmetauscher, *der*

heath /hiːθ/ *n.* **1** Heide, *die* **2** (Bot.) (Calluna) Heidekraut, *das;* (Erica) Erika, *die;* Glockenheide, *die*

ˈ**heat haze** *n.* Hitzeschleier, *der;* **sth. shimmers in the ~** etw. flimmert in der Hitze; **through the shimmering ~:** durch die flimmernde Hitze

heathen /ˈhiːðn/
A *adj.* heidnisch
B *n.* Heide, *der*/Heidin, *die;* (fig. derog.) gottloser Mensch

heather /ˈheðə(r)/ *n.* **1** (plant) Heidekraut, *das* **2** (colour) Erikarot, *das*

heating /ˈhiːtɪŋ/ *n., no pl.* Heizung, *die*

heat: ~proof *adj.* feuerfest; **~ pump** *n.* Wärmepumpe, *die;* **~ rash** *n.* (Med.) Hitzebläschen *Pl.;* **~-resistant** *adj.* hitzebeständig; **~-seeking** *adj.* wärmesuchend; **~ shield** *n.* (Astronaut.) Hitzeschild, *der;* **~stroke** *n.* Hitzschlag, *der;* **~-treat** *v.t.* (Metall., Med.) wärmebehandeln; **~ treatment** *n.* (Metallurgy, Med.) Wärmebehandlung, *die;* **~wave** *n.* Hitzewelle, *die*

heave /hiːv/
A *v.t.* **1** (lift) heben; wuchten (ugs.) **2** *p.t. & p.p.* (esp. Naut.) **hove** /həʊv/ (coll.: throw) werfen; schmeißen (ugs.); (Naut.: cast, haul up) hieven **3** (utter) **~ a sigh [of relief]** [erleichtert] aufseufzen
B *v.i.* **1** (pitch) [auf und nieder] schwanken; ‹*Schiff:*› stampfen (Seemannsspr.); (rise [and fall]) sich heben [und senken] **2** (pull) ziehen; **~ ho!** hau ruck!; holt auf (Seemannsspr.) **3** (pant) keuchen **4** (retch) **my stomach ~d** mein Magen drehte such um **5** *p.t. & p.p.* **hove** (move) **~ into sight** *or* **view** in Sicht kommen; **~ to** (Naut.) beidrehen
C *n.* **1** (pull) Zug, *der* **2** (throw) Schwung, *der*

heaven /ˈhevn/ *n.* **1** Himmel, *der;* **in ~:** im Himmel; **go** *or* **ascend to ~:** in den Himmel kommen; **~ on earth** (fig.) der Himmel auf Erden; **be sent from ~** (fig.) ein Geschenk des Himmels sein; **it was ~ [to her]** (fig.) es war der Himmel auf Erden [für sie]; **seventh ~** (fig.) der siebte Himmel; **move ~ and earth** (fig.) Himmel und Erde in Bewegung setzen **2** *in pl.,* (*poet.*) *in sing.* (sky) Firmament, *das;* Himmelszelt, *das* (dichter.); **in the ~s** am Himmel; **the ~s opened** es prasselte los **3** (God, Providence) **by H~!** bei Gott; **[good] H~s!** gütiger Himmel!; **H~s above!** du lieber Himmel!; **H~ [only] knows** weiß der Himmel; **H~ help us** der Himmel steh uns bei; **for H~'s sake** um Gottes *od.* Himmels willen; **thank H~[s]** Gott sei Dank; **I hope to H~ that …:** ich hoffe zu Gott, dass …; *see also* **forbid 2**; **name A 4**

heavenly /ˈhevnlɪ/ *adj.* **1** (also coll.: delightful) himmlisch **2** **~ body** Himmelskörper, *der* **3** (of heaven) himmlisch; **the H~ City** das Himmelreich

ˈ**heaven-sent** *adj.* **a ~ opportunity** eine Gelegenheit, die wie gerufen kommt/kam

heavenward[s] /ˈhevnwəd(z)/ *adv.* himmelwärts

heavily /ˈhevɪlɪ/ *adj.* **1** (with great weight, severely, with difficulty) schwer ‹*beladen, bestraft, atmen*›; **~ guarded** streng bewacht **2** (to a great extent) stark; schwer ‹*bewaffnet*›; tief ‹*schlafen*›; dicht ‹*bevölkert*›; **smoke/drink ~:** ein starker Raucher/Trinker sein; **eat too ~:** zu schwer essen; **gamble ~:** ein [leidenschaftlicher] Spieler sein; **rely ~ on sb./sth.** von jmdm./etw. [vollkommen] abhängig sein **3** (with great force) **it rained/snowed ~:** es regnete/schneite stark; **fall ~:** hart fallen; **~ underlined** dick unterstrichen; **weigh ~ [up]on sb.** (fig.) schwer auf jmdm. lasten; **~ built** kräftig gebaut

heaviness /ˈhevɪnɪs/ *n., no pl.* **1** (weight) Gewicht, *das* **2** (great extent) Ausmaß, *das;* (severity) Härte, *die* **3** (clinging quality) Schwere, *die* **4** (tiredness) Schwerfälligkeit, *die*

heaving /ˈhiːvɪŋ/ *adj.* **1** wogend ‹*Meer*› **2** (Brit. coll.: very crowded) knall[e]voll (ugs.)

heavy /ˈhevɪ/
A *adj.* **1** ▸ⓘ **p. 1702** (in weight) schwer; dick ‹*Mantel*›; fest ‹*Schuh*›; **~ traffic** (trucks) Schwerlastverkehr, *der;* (dense traffic) starker Verkehr; hohes Verkehrsaufkommen; **~ work** Schwerarbeit, *die;* **a ~ crop** (fig.) eine [sehr] reiche Ernte; **a ~ silence** eine atemlose Stille **2** (severe) schwer ‹*Schaden, Verlust, Strafe, Kampf*›; hoch ‹*Steuern, Schulden, Anforderungen*›; massiv ‹*Druck, Unterstützung*›; **~ responsibilities** schwere Verantwortung **3** (excessive) unmäßig ‹*Trinken, Essen, Rauchen*›; ausgiebig ‹*Necking, Petting*›; **be ~ on the sugar/petrol** (coll.) viel Zucker nehmen/viel Benzin verbrauchen; **a ~ smoker/drinker** ein starker Raucher/Trinker; **a ~ gambler** ein [leidenschaftlicher] Spieler; **be a ~ sleeper** sehr fest schlafen **4** (violent) schwer ‹*Schlag, Sturm, Regen, Sturz, Seegang*›; hart ‹*Aufprall*›; **~ weather** ungünstiges Wetter; **make ~ weather of sth.** (fig.) die Dinge unnötig komplizieren **5** (clinging) schwer ‹*Boden*›; *see also* **going A 2** **6** (hard to digest) schwer ‹*Mahlzeit*› **7** (overcast) bedeckt ‹*Himmel*› **8** (in sound) **~ footsteps** schwere Schritte **9** (clumsy) plump; (intellectually slow) schwerfällig; **~ with sleep** schlaftrunken; **our eyes were ~ with sleep** wir konnten [vor Müdigkeit] kaum noch die Augen offen halten **10** (tedious) schwerfällig; (serious) seriös ‹*Zeitung*›; ernst ‹*Musik, Theaterrolle*›; **lie ~ on sb.'s stomach/conscience** jmdm. schwer im Magen liegen/auf der Seele liegen; **time lies ~ on my hands** mir wird die Zeit lang; *see also* **hand A 2** **11** (Phys.) **~ hydrogen/water** schwerer Wasserstoff/schweres Wasser
B *n.* (coll.) **1** (newspaper) seriöse Zeitung **2** (coll.: thug) Schlägertyp, *der* (ugs.)

heavy: ~-duty *adj.* strapazierfähig ‹*Kleidung, Material*›; schwer ‹*Werkzeug, Maschine*›; **~-ˈfooted** *adj.* schwerfällig; **~ ˈgoods vehicle** *n.* Schwerlastwagen, *der;* **~-ˈhanded** *adj.* (clumsy) ungeschickt ‹*Person*›; umständlich ‹*Stil*›; (oppressive) unbarmherzig ‹*Tyrannei, Diktatur*›; **~-ˈhearted** *adj.* traurig; **~ hitter** *n.* (coll.) Prominente, *der/die;* **~ ˈindustry** *n.* Schwerindustrie, *die;* **~ ˈmetal** *n.* **1** Schwermetall, *das;* **2** (Mus.) Heavy-Metal, *das; attrib.* **a ~-metal band** eine Heavy-Metal-Band; **~ ˈpetting** *n., no pl.* [schweres] Petting; **~ ˈtype** *n.* (Printing) fette Schrift; **~weight** *n.* (Boxing etc.) Schwergewicht, *das;* (person also) Schwergewichtler, *der;* (fig.) Größe, *die*

Hebraic /hiːˈbreɪɪk/ *adj.* hebräisch

Hebrew /ˈhiːbruː/ ▸ⓘ **p. 1277**
A *adj.* hebräisch; *see also* **English A**
B *n.* **1** (Israelite) Hebräer, *der*/Hebräerin, *die* **2** *no pl.* (language) Hebräisch, *das;* **a ~ scholar** ein Hebraist; *see also* **English B 1**

Hebrides /ˈhebrɪdiːz/ *pr. n. pl.* Hebriden *Pl.;* **Inner/Outer ~:** Innere/Äußere Hebriden

heck /hek/ (coll. euphem.) ▸**hell 2**

heckle /ˈhekl/ *v.t.* **~ sb./a speech** jmdn./eine Rede durch Zwischenrufe unterbrechen

heckler /ˈheklə(r)/ *n.* Zwischenrufer, *der*

hectare /ˈhekteə(r), ˈhektɑː(r)/ *n.* ▸ⓘ **p. 911** Hektar, *das od. der*

hectic /ˈhektɪk/ *adj.* hektisch

hecto- /ˈhektə/ *pref.* hekto-/Hekto-

hector /ˈhektə(r)/
A *v.t.* einschüchtern
B *v.i.* bramarbasieren (geh.)

hectoring /ˈhektərɪŋ/ *adj.* überheblich

he'd /hɪd, *stressed* hiːd/ **1** = **he had** **2** = **he would**

hedge /hedʒ/
A *n.* (of bushes, trees, etc.) Hecke, *die;* (fig.: barrier) Mauer, *die;* (fig.: means of protection) Schutzwall, *der;* (against financial loss) Absicherung, *die*
B *v.t.* **1** (surround with **~**) mit einer Hecke umgeben; **~ sb. [in** *or* **round]** (fig.) jmdn. in seiner Handlungsfreiheit einschränken **2** (protect) **~ one's bets** mit verteiltem Risiko wetten; (fig.) nicht alles auf eine Karte setzen
C *v.i.* (avoid commitment) sich nicht festlegen; **stop hedging and give me a straight answer** weich nicht dauernd aus, und gib mir eine klare Antwort

ˈ**hedge clippers** *n. pl.* Heckenschere, *die*

hedgehog /ˈhedʒhɒg/ *n.* Igel, *der*

ˈ**hedge-hop** *v.i.* im Tiefflug fliegen

hedge: ~row *n.* Hecke, *die* [als Feldbegrenzung]; **~ sparrow** *n.* Heckenbraunelle, *die*

hedonism /ˈhiːdənɪzm/ *n., no pl.* Hedonismus, *der*

hedonist /ˈhiːdənɪst/ *n.* Hedonist, *der*/Hedonistin, *die*

hedonistic /hiːdəˈnɪstɪk/ *adj.* hedonistisch

heebie-jeebies /hiːbɪˈdʒiːbɪz/ *n. pl.* (coll.) **give sb. the ~:** jmdn. kribblig machen (ugs.)

heed /hiːd/
A *v.t.* beachten; beherzigen ‹*Rat, Lektion*›; **~ the danger/risk** sich (*Dat.*) der Gefahr/des Risikos bewusst sein
B *n., no art., no pl.* **give** *or* **pay ~ to, take ~ of** Beachtung schenken (+ *Dat.*); **give** *or* **pay no ~ to, take no ~ of** nicht beachten

heedful /ˈhiːdfl/ *adj.* achtsam; **be ~ of sth.** etw. beachten; **be ~ of the danger/necessity** sich (*Dat.*) der Gefahr/Notwendigkeit (*Gen.*) bewusst sein; **be ~ of sb.'s warning** jmds. Warnung beherzigen

heedless /ˈhiːdlɪs/ *adj.* unachtsam; **be ~ of sth.** auf etw. (*Akk.*) nicht achten; **be ~ of the danger/risks** die Gefahr/Risiken nicht beachten

hee-haw /ˈhɪːhɔː/
A *int.* iah
B *n.* Iah, *das*
C *v.i.* iahen; (fig.) wiehern

heel[1] /hiːl/
A *n.* **1** ▸ⓘ **p. 951** Ferse, *die;* **~ of the hand** Handballen, *der;* **Achilles' ~** (fig.) Achillesferse, *die;* **bring a dog to ~:** einen Hund bei Fuß rufen; **bring sb. to ~** (fig.) jmdn. auf Vordermann bringen (ugs.); **come to ~:** bei Fuß gehen; (fig.) parieren (ugs.); **[to] ~!** bei Fuß!; **at ~:** bei Fuß; **be on sb.'s ~s** (fig.) jmdm. auf den Fersen sein (ugs.); **[hard** *or* **close] on** *or* **at the ~s of sb./sth.** [dicht] hinter jmdm./etw.; (in time or quality) gleich nach jmdm./etw.; **show a clean pair of ~s** (fig.) sich aus dem Staub machen (ugs.); **show sb. a clean pair of ~s** (fig.) jmdn. abhängen (ugs.); **take to one's ~s** (fig.) Fersengeld geben (ugs.); **cool one's ~s** (fig. coll.) lange warten [müssen]; **kick one's ~s** (fig. coll.) rumhängen (ugs.); **be under the ~ of sb.** (fig.) unter jmds. Herrschaft sein; *see also* **dig in B 2** **2** (of shoe) Absatz, *der;* (of stocking) Ferse, *die;* **down at ~:** abgetreten; (fig.) heruntergekommen (ugs.); **turn on one's ~:** auf dem Absatz kehrtmachen; *see also* **high heel** **3** (of violin bow) Frosch, *der;* (of golf club) Ferse, *die;* (of ski) hinteres Ende; (of loaf) Endstück, *das* **4** (coll.: person) Schuft, *der* (abwertend)
B *v.t.* **1** **~ a shoe** einen Schuh mit einem [neuen] Absatz versehen **2** (Golf) mit der Ferse schlagen **3** (Rugby) mit dem Absatz spielen

heel[2] (Naut.)
A *v.i.* **~ [over]** krängen
B *v.t.* **~ [over]** zum Krängen bringen
C *n.* Krängung, *die*

heel[3] *v.t.* (Hort.) **~ sth. [in]** etw. einpflanzen

heel: ~ bar *n.* Absatzschnelldienst, *der;* **~ bone** *n.* (Anat.) Fersenbein, *das*

heelless /ˈhiːllɪs/ *adj.* ‹*Schuhe*› ohne Absatz

heft /heft/
A *v.t.* wuchten ‹*Kisten*›; (test weight of) anheben (*und dabei das Gewicht feststellen*)
B *n.* (Amer.) Gewicht, *das*

heftily /ˈheftɪlɪ/ *adv.* kräftig; (fig.) stark

hefty /ˈheftɪ/ *adj.* kräftig; (heavy) schwer; (fig.: large) hoch ‹*Rechnung, Summe, Strafe, Anteil*›; deutlich ‹*Mehrheit*›; stark ‹*Erhöhung*›

Hegelian /heˈgiːlɪən, heɪˈgiːlɪən/ (Philos.)
A *adj.* hegelianisch
B *n.* Hegelianer, *der*/Hegelianerin, *die*

hegemony /hɪˈdʒemənɪ/ *n.* Hegemonie, *die*

Hegira /ˈhedʒɪrə/ *n.* Hedschra, *die*

heh /heɪ/ *int.* he

he-he /hiːˈhiː/ *int.* haha

heifer /ˈhefə(r)/ *n.* Färse, *die*

ℹ Height and depth

1 inch = 25,4 mm
1 foot = 30,48 cm

Height

People

How tall is she?, What height is she?
= Wie groß ist sie?
She's five foot six
= Sie ist ein Meter achtundsechzig (1,68 m) groß
He's smaller or ***less tall than his brother***
= Er ist kleiner als sein Bruder
A is the same height or ***as tall as B***
= A ist [genau] so groß wie B
They are the same height
= Sie sind gleich groß
an athlete six feet tall
= ein 1,80 Meter großer Athlet

Things

How high is it?, What height is it?
= Wie hoch ist es?
It's about thirty feet high or ***in height***
= Es ist ungefähr neun Meter hoch
A is lower/higher than B
= A ist niedriger/höher als B
A is the same height or ***as high as B***
= A ist [genau]so hoch wie B
The towers are the same height
= Die Türme sind gleich hoch
The aircraft was flying at a height or an altitude of 10,000 feet
= Die Maschine flog in einer Höhe von 3 000 Metern
The treeline is at a height of about 6,500 feet
= Die Baumgrenze liegt bei etwa 2 000 Meter Höhe *or* bei etwa 2 000 Metern
waves ten feet high
= drei Meter hohe Wellen
a mountain of over 20,000 feet or ***over 20,000 feet in height***
= ein Berg von über 6 000 Metern *or* von über 6 000 Meter Höhe

Depth

How deep or ***What depth is the river?***
= Wie tief ist *or* Welche Tiefe hat der Fluss?
It's ten feet deep
≈ Er ist drei Meter tief *or* hat eine Tiefe von drei Metern
The treasure is at a depth of fifty feet or ***is fifty feet down***
≈ Der Schatz liegt in einer Tiefe von fünfzehn Metern *or* fünfzehn Meter tief
A is the same depth as B
= A hat die gleiche Tiefe wie B
A and B are the same depth
= A und B sind gleich tief
A is shallower than B
= A ist flacher *or* seichter als B
a hole ten feet deep
≈ ein drei Meter tiefes Loch

heigh-ho /heɪˈhəʊ/ *int.* ach ja

height /haɪt/ *n.* **1** ▸ℹ **p. 1208** Höhe, *die;* (of person, animal, building) Größe, *die;* **lose ~** (Aeron.) an Höhe verlieren; **be three metres in ~:** drei Meter hoch sein; **at a ~ of three metres** in einer Höhe von drei Metern; **be six feet in ~** ‹*Person:*› 1,80 m groß sein; **what is your ~?** wie groß sind Sie? **2** *usu. in pl.* (high place) **the ~s** die Anhöhe; **be afraid of ~s** nicht schwindelfrei sein; **~ of land** (Amer. Geog.) Wasserscheide, *die* **3** (fig.: highest point) Höhepunkt, *der;* **at the ~ of one's fame** auf dem Gipfel seines Ruhms; **the ~ of luxury** das Nonplusultra an Luxus; **the ~ of folly** der Gipfel der Dummheit; **at the ~ of summer** im Hochsommer; *see also* **fashion A 2**

heighten /ˈhaɪtn/
A *v.t.* aufstocken; (fig.: intensify) verstärken
B *v.i.* (fig.) sich verstärken

heinous /ˈheɪnəs, ˈhiːnəs/ *adj.* schändlich; ruchlos (geh., veralt.)

heir /eə(r)/ *n.* (lit. or fig.) Erbe, *der*/Erbin, *die;* **the ~ to the throne** der Thronerbe/die Thronerbin; *see also* **apparent 1; presumptive**

heiress /ˈeərɪs/ *n.* Erbin, *die* (*bes. eines Vermögens*); *see also* **heir**

heirloom /ˈeəluːm/ *n.* **1** Erbstück, *das;* (fig.) Erbe, *das* **2** (Law) *von einem Erbe nicht abtrennbarer Teil*

heist /haɪst/ (coll.)
A *n.* Raubüberfall, *der*
B *v.t.* (Amer.) (steal) rauben; (rob) ausrauben

hejira ▸**hegira**

held ▸**hold² A, B**

Helen /ˈhelən/ *pr. n.* **~ of Troy** [die schöne] Helena

heli- /ˈhelɪ/ *in comb.* Heli-

helical /ˈhelɪkl/ *adj.* spiralförmig; spiralig; **~ gear** Schrägstirnrad, *das;* **~ spring** Schraubenfeder, *die*

helices *pl. of* **helix**

helicopter /ˈhelɪkɒptə(r)/ *n.* Hubschrauber, *der*

helicopter ˈgunship *n.* Kampfhubschrauber, *der*

Heligoland /ˈhelɪgəlænd/ *pr. n.* Helgoland (*das*)

helio- /ˈhiːlɪə/ *in comb.* helio-/Helio-

ˈheliograph
A *n.* Heliograph, *der*
B *v.t.* mit dem Heliographen übermitteln

heliotrope /ˈhiːlɪətrəʊp, ˈhelɪətrəʊp/
A *n.* **1** (Bot., Min.) Heliotrop, *das* **2** (colour) Bläulichviolett, *das;* Heliotrop, *das*
B *adj.* bläulich violett; heliotrop

helipad /ˈhelɪpæd/ *n.* Hubschrauberlandeplatz, *der;* Helipad, *der*

heliport /ˈhelɪpɔːt/ *n.* Heliport, *der*

helium /ˈhiːlɪəm/ *n.* Helium, *das*

helix /ˈhiːlɪks/ *n., pl.* **helices** /ˈhiːlɪsiːz/ **1** Spirale, *die* **2** (Archit.) Volute, *die* **3** (Anat.) Helix, *die*

hell /hel/ *n.* **1** Hölle, *die;* **suffer the torments of ~:** Höllenqualen erleiden; **make sb.'s life [a] ~, make life ~ for sb.** jmdm. das Leben zur Hölle machen; **all ~ was let loose** (fig.) es war die Hölle los; **~ on earth** (fig.) die Hölle auf Erden **2** (coll.: in imprecations and phrases) **[oh] ~!** verdammter Mist! (ugs.); **what the ~!** ach, zum Teufel! (ugs.); **to** *or* **the ~ with it!** ich habs satt (ugs.); **who the ~ are you?** wer, zum Teufel, sind Sie? (ugs.); **~'s bells!** (coll.) Mensch, Scheiße! (salopp); **get the ~ ˈout of here!, go to ~!** scher dich zum Teufel! (ugs.); **play [merry] ~ with sth.** etw. [ganz schön] ins Schleudern bringen (ugs.); **there'll be ~ to pay if you get caught** wenn sie dich erwischen, ist der Teufel los (ugs.); **as tired/angry as ~:** unheimlich müde/wütend; **a** *or* **one ~ of a** *or* **a helluva [good] party** eine unheimlich gute Party (ugs.); **a ~ of a** *or* **a helluva noise** ein Höllenlärm (salopp); **like sb./sth. a ~ of a lot** jmdn./etw. wahnsinnig gern mögen (ugs.); **a ~ of a lot of money** wahnsinnig viel Geld (ugs.); **he thinks he's a ~ of a fellow** er denkt, er ist ein Teufelskerl (ugs.); **that was a ~ of a thing to do** das war ungeheuerlich (abwertend)/(*praising*) grandios; **work/run like ~:** wie der Teufel arbeiten/rennen (ugs.); **like ~!** nie im Leben! (ugs.); **it hurt like ~:** es tat höllisch weh (ugs.); **beat** *or* **knock [the] ~ out of sb.** jmdn. grün und blau schlagen (ugs.); **give sb. ~:** jmdm. die Hölle heiß machen (ugs.); ‹*Schmerzen usw.:*› jmdn. verrückt machen (ugs.); **get ~:** großen Ärger kriegen (ugs.); **come ~ or high water** [völlig] egal, was passieren sollte (ugs.); **do sth. [just] for the ~ of it** etw. [nur so] aus Jux und Tollerei tun (ugs.); **~ for leather** wie der Teufel (ugs.); **I'll see you in ~ first** ich denke nicht im Traum daran!; *see also* **hope A; raise A 7**

he'll /hɪl, *stressed* hiːl/ = **he will**

hell: ~bender *n.* (Amer. Zool.) Schlammteufel, *der;* **~-ˈbent** *adj.* **be ~-bent on doing sth.** (coll.) wild entschlossen sein, etw. zu tun (ugs.); **~cat** *n.* (derog.) Wildkatze, *die*

hellebore /ˈhelɪbɔː(r)/ *n.* (Bot.) Nieswurz, *die*

Hellenic /heˈlenɪk/ *adj.* hellenisch

Hellenist /ˈhelɪnɪst/ *n.* Hellenist, *der*/Hellenistin, *die*

Hellenistic /helɪˈnɪstɪk/ *adj.* hellenistisch

hell: ~fire *n.* Höllenfeuer, *das;* **~hole** *n.* (room) [scheußliches] Loch; (place) Schreckensort, *der;* **~hound** *n.* Höllenhund, *der;* (fig.) Teufel, *der*

hellish /ˈhelɪʃ/
A *adj.* höllisch ‹*Qual, Schmerz*›; scheußlich ‹*Arbeit, Zeit*›
B *adv.* (coll.) verdammt (ugs.)

hellishly /ˈhelɪʃlɪ/ *adv.* höllisch; scheußlich; (coll. as intensive) verdammt (ugs.)

hello /həˈləʊ, heˈləʊ/ ▸ℹ **p. 1189**
A *int.* (greeting) hallo!; (surprise) holla!
B *n.* Hallo, *das*

hellraiser /ˈhelreɪzə(r)/ *n.* Rabauke, *der*

Hell's ˈAngel *n.* Rocker, *der*

helluva /ˈheləvə/ = **hell of a;** ▸**hell 2**

helm¹ /helm/ *n.* (Naut.) Ruder, *das;* **be at the ~** (lit. or fig.) am Ruder sein; **take the ~** (lit. or fig.) das Ruder übernehmen

helm² *n.* (arch.: helmet) Helm, *der*

helmet /ˈhelmɪt/ *n.* Helm, *der*

helmeted /ˈhelmɪtɪd/ *adj.* behelmt

helmsman /ˈhelmzmən/ *n., pl.* **helmsmen** /ˈhelmzmən/ (Naut.) Rudergänger, *der*

help /help/
A *v.t.* **1** **~ sb. [to do sth.]** jmdm. helfen[, etw. zu tun]; **~ [sb.] with sth.** [jmdm.] bei etw. helfen; **~ oneself** sich (*Dat.*) selbst helfen (*see also* **2**); **can I ~ you?** was kann ich für Sie tun?; (in shop also) was möchten Sie bitte?; **~ sb. over a difficulty** jmdm. über eine Schwierigkeit hinweghelfen; **~ sb. on/off with his coat** jmdm. in den/aus dem Mantel helfen; **every little ~s** auch der kleinste Beitrag hilft weiter; **it would ~ [matters], if ...:** es wäre von Nutzen, wenn ...; **how does that ~?** was sollte *od.* könnte das nützen? **2** (serve) **~ oneself** sich bedienen; **~ oneself to sth.** sich (*Dat.*) etw. nehmen; (coll.: steal) etw. mitgehen lassen (ugs.); **~ sb. to some soup** jmdm. etwas Suppe geben (*see also* **1**) **3** (avoid) **if I/you can ~ it** wenn es irgend zu vermeiden ist; **not if I can ~ it** nicht wenn ich es verhindern kann; **it can't be ~ed** es lässt sich nicht ändern; (remedy) **I can't ~ it** ich kann nichts dafür (ugs.) **4** (refrain from) **I can't ~ it** *or* **myself** ich kann mir nicht helfen; **I can't ~ thinking** *or* **can't ~ but think that ...:** ich kann mir nicht helfen, ich glaube, ...; **I couldn't ~ hearing what you said** ich konnte nicht umhin zu hören, was Sie sagten; **I can't ~ laughing** ich muss einfach lachen **5** (in oath) **so ~ me [God]** so wahr mir Gott helfe
B *n.* **1** Hilfe, *die;* **can I be of ~?** kann ich Ihnen behilflich sein?; **a cry for ~:** ein Hilferuf; **give sb. some ~:** jmdm. helfen (**with** bei); **be of [some]/no/much ~ to sb.** jmdm. eine gewisse/keine/eine große Hilfe sein; **with the ~ of sth./sb.** mit Hilfe einer Sache/mit jmds. Hilfe; mit Hilfe von etw./jmdm.; **walk without the**

~ of a stick ohne Stock gehen; **that's no ~:** das hilft nicht; **there's no ~ for it** daran lässt sich nichts ändern; **be a great ~ to sb.** jmdm. eine große Hilfe sein **2** (employee) Aushilfskraft, *die;* **home ~** (Brit.) Haushaltshilfe, *die*

Phrasal verb

• **~ 'out**

A *v.i.* aushelfen

B *v.t.* **~ sb. out** jmdm. helfen

'help desk *n.* Help Desk, *das* (fachspr.); *Auskunftsstelle für Computerbenutzer*

helper /'helpə(r)/ *n.* Helfer, *der*/Helferin, *die;* (paid assistant) Aushilfskraft, *die*

helpful /'helpfl/ *adj.* (willing) hilfsbereit; (useful) hilfreich; nützlich

helpfully /'helpfəlɪ/ *adv.* hilfsbereit

helpfulness /'helpflnɪs/ *n., no pl.* (willingness) Hilfsbereitschaft, *die;* (usefulness) Nützlichkeit, *die*

helping /'helpɪŋ/

A *adj.* **lend [sb.] a ~ hand [with sth.]** (fig.) [jmdm.] [bei etw.] helfen; **need a ~ hand** jmdn. brauchen, der einem hilft; **be ready with a ~ hand** bereit sein zu helfen

B *n.* Portion, *die*

helpless /'helplɪs/ *adj.* hilflos; (powerless) machtlos

helplessly /'helplɪslɪ/ *adv.* hilflos

helplessness /'helplɪsnɪs/ *n., no pl.* Hilflosigkeit, *die;* (powerlessness) Machtlosigkeit, *die*

'helpline *n.* Hotline, *die;* **a ~ for parents** ein telefonischer Beratungsdienst für Eltern; **the AIDS ~:** das AIDS-Telefon

helpmate /'helpmeɪt/, **helpmeet** /'helpmi:t/ *n.* Gefährte, *der*/Gefährtin, *die* (geh.)

helter-skelter /'heltəskeltə(r)/

A *adv.* in wildem Durcheinander

B *adj.* unkontrolliert

C *n.* **1** wildes Durcheinander **2** (in funfair) [spiralförmige] Rutschbahn

helve /helv/ *n.* Stiel, *der*

hem[1] /hem/

A *n.* Saum, *der*

B *v.t.*, **-mm-:** **1** säumen **2** (surround) **~ sb./sth. in** *or* **about** jmdn./etw. einschließen; **feel ~med in** (fig.) sich eingeengt fühlen

hem[2] /hem, həm, hm/

A *int.* hm!

B *n.* (sound) Räuspern, *das;* **give a loud ~:** sich laut räuspern

C *v.i.*, **-mm-** sich räuspern; **~ and haw** (coll.) herumdrucksen (ugs.)

he-man /'hi:mæn/ *n.* (coll.) **a real ~:** ein richtiger Mann; (muscular) ein echter Kraftmeier (ugs.)

hematology (Amer.) ▸**haematology**

hemi- /'hemɪ/ *pref.* hemi-/Hemi-

hemiplegia /hemɪ'pli:dʒɪə/ *n.* (Med.) Halbseitenlähmung, *die;* Hemiplegie, *die* (fachspr.)

hemiplegic /hemɪ'pli:dʒɪk/ *adj.* (Med.) halbseitig gelähmt

'hemisphere *n.* **1** Halbkugel, *die;* Hemisphäre, *die;* **the Southern ~** (Geog., Astron.) die südliche Halbkugel **2** (Anat.) Hemisphäre, *die*

hemi'spherical *adj.* halbkugelig; halbkugelförmig

'hemline *n.* Saum, *der;* **~s are up/down** die Röcke sind kürzer/länger [geworden]; **Yves St. Laurent's new ~:** die neue Rocklänge bei Yves St. Laurent

hemlock /'hemlɒk/ *n.* Schierling, *der*

hemlock ['fir, 'spruce] *ns.* (Amer. Bot.) Hemlocktanne, *die*

hemo- (Amer.) ▸**haemo-**

hemp /hemp/ *n.* **1** (Bot., Textiles) Hanf, *der* **2** (drug) Haschisch, *das od. der*

'hem-stitch

A *n.* Hohlsaum, *der*

B *v.t.* mit Hohlsaum versehen

hen /hen/ *n.* **1** (Ornith.) Huhn, *das;* (as opposed to cock) Henne, *die* **2** (Zool.) (lobster, crab) weiblicher Hummer/Krebs; (salmon) Lachsweibchen, *das*

'henbane *n., no pl.* (Bot., Med.) Bilsenkraut, *das*

hence /hens/ *adv.* **1** (therefore) daher **2** (from this time) **a week/ten years ~:** in einer Woche/zehn Jahren **3** (arch./poet.: from here) **[from] ~:** von hinnen (veralt.)

hence'forth, hence'forward *advs.* von nun an; fürderhin (veralt.)

henchman /'hentʃmən/ *n., pl.* **henchmen** /'hentʃmən/ (derog.) Handlanger, *der*

'hen-coop *n.* Hühnerstall, *der*

hendeca- /hen'dekə/ *in comb.* elf-/Elf-

'hen house *n.* Hühnerhaus, *das;* Hühnerstall, *der*

henna /'henə/ *n.* (dye) Henna, *das*

hen: ~ night *n.* (Brit. coll.) Brautabend, *der;* **~ party** *n.* (coll.) [Damen]kränzchen, *das;* **~pecked** /'henpekt/ *adj.* **a ~pecked husband** ein Pantoffelheld (ugs.); **be ~pecked** unter dem Pantoffel stehen (ugs.); **~-run** *n.* [Hühner]auslauf, *der*

Henry /'henrɪ/ *pr. n.* (Hist., as name of ruler etc.) Heinrich *(der)*

hep *adj.* (dated coll.) **hip[4]**

hepatic /hɪ'pætɪk/ *adj.* (Anat., Med.) Leber-

hepatitis /hepə'taɪtɪs/ *n.* ▸ⓘ **p. 1231** (Med.) Leberentzündung, *die;* Hepatitis, *die* (fachspr.)

heptagon /'heptəgən/ *n.* (Geom.) Siebeneck, *das;* Heptagon, *das* (fachspr.)

heptagonal /hep'tægənl/ *adj.* (Geom.) siebeneckig; heptagonal (fachspr.)

heptathlete /hep'tæθli:t/ *n.* Siebenkämpfer, *der*/-kämpferin, *die*

heptathlon /hep'tæθlɒn/ *n.* Siebenkampf, *der*

her[1] /hə(r), *stressed* hɜ:(r)/ *pron.* sie; *as indirect object* ihr; *reflexively* sich; *referring to personified things or animals which correspond to German masculines/neuters* ihn/es; *as indirect object* ihm; **it was ~:** sie wars; **~ and me** (coll.) sie und ich; **if I were ~** (coll.) wenn ich sie wäre

her[2] *poss. pron. attrib.* ihr; *referring to personified things or animals which correspond to German masculines/neuters* sein; **she opened ~ eyes/mouth** sie öffnete die Augen/den Mund; **~ father and mother** ihr Vater und ihre Mutter; **she has problems of ~ own** sie hat ihre eigenen Probleme; **she has a room of ~ own** sie hat ein eigenes Zimmer; **he complained about ~ being late** er beklagte sich darüber, dass sie zu spät kam; er beklagte sich über ihr Zuspätkommen

herald /'herəld/

A *n.* **1** Herold, *der* **2** (messenger) Bote, *der;* (fig.: forerunner) Vorbote, *der* **3** (Brit.: official of Heralds' College) *Beamter des Heroldamtes*

B *v.t.* (lit. or fig.) ankündigen

heraldic /he'rældɪk/ *adj.* heraldisch; **~ animal** Wappentier, *das*

heraldry /'herəldrɪ/ *n., no pl.* **1** Wappenkunde, *die;* Heraldik, *die* **2** (armorial bearings) Wappenschmuck, *der*

herb /hɜ:b/ *n.* **1** Kraut, *das;* (Cookery) Gewürzkraut, *das* **2** (Med.) [Heil]kraut, *das*

herbaceous /hɜ:'beɪʃəs/ *adj.* (Bot.) krautartig ‹*Pflanze*›; krautig ‹*Stiel*›; **~ border** Staudenrabatte, *die*

herbage /'hɜ:bɪdʒ/ *n., no pl.* (Agric.) (herbs) Weide, *die;* (succulent parts) Kraut, *das*

herbal /'hɜ:bl/

A *attrib. adj.* Kräuter‹*tee, -arznei*›; ‹*Behandlung*› mit Heilkräutern

B *n.* Pflanzenbuch, *das*

herbalist /'hɜ:bəlɪst/ *n.* **1** ▸ⓘ **p. 1260** Kräuterhändler, *der*/Kräuterhändlerin, *die* [für Heilkräuter] **2** (Hist.) Herbalist, *der*

herbarium /hɜ:'beərɪəm/ *n., pl.* **herbaria** /hɜ:'beərɪə/ Herbarium, *das*

'herb garden *n.* Kräutergarten, *der*

herbicide /'hɜ:bɪsaɪd/ *n.* Unkrautvertilgungsmittel, *das;* Herbizid, *das*

herbivore /'hɜ:bɪvɔ:(r)/ *n.* (Zool.) Pflanzenfresser, *der;* Herbivore, *der* (fachspr.)

herbivorous /hɜ:'bɪvərəs/ *adj.* Pflanzen fressend; herbivor (fachspr.)

'herb tea *n.* Kräuteraufguss, *der*

herby /'hɜ:bɪ/ *adj.* **a ~ taste/smell** ein Geschmack/Geruch nach Kräutern

Herculean /hɜ:kjʊ'li:ən, hɜ:'kju:lɪən/ *adj.* übermenschlich ‹*Anstrengung*›; bärenstark ‹*Person*›; herkulisch (geh.), ungeheuer ‹*Kraft*›; **~ labour** Herkulesarbeit, *die*

Hercules /'hɜ:kjʊli:z/ *pr. n.* Herakles, *der;* Herkules, *der* (auch fig.); **the labours of ~:** die zwölf Arbeiten des Herakles

herd /hɜ:d/

A *n.* **1** Herde, *die;* (of wild animals) Rudel, *das;* **a ~ of sheep/elephants** eine Herde Schafe/Elefanten; eine Schaf-/Elefantenherde; **ride ~ on sb.** (Amer.) jmdn. im Auge behalten **2** (fig.) Masse, *die;* **the common ~** (derog.) die breite Masse; **the ~ instinct** der Herdentrieb; **follow the ~** (fig.) der Herde folgen; mit der Herde laufen

B *v.t.* **1** (lit. or fig.) treiben; **~ [people] together** (fig.) [Menschen] zusammenpferchen **2** (tend) hüten

C *v.i.* sich zu einer Herde zusammenschließen; (fig.) sich drängen

'herdsman /'hɜ:dzmən/ *n., pl.* **herdsmen** /'hɜ:dzmən/ ▸ⓘ **p. 1260** Hirt[e], *der*

here /hɪə(r)/

A *adv.* **1** (in or at this place) hier; **Schmidt ~** (on telephone) Schmidt; **spring is ~:** der Frühling ist da; **stay ~:** hier bleiben; **down/in/up ~:** hier unten/drin/oben; **~ below** (fig. literary) hienieden (geh.); auf dieser Erde; **~ goes!** (coll.) dann mal los! (ugs.); **~'s to you!** auf dein Wohl!; **~, there, and everywhere** überall; **that's neither ~ nor there** (coll.) das ist völlig nebensächlich; **~ today and gone tomorrow** (of traveller) heute hier, morgen dort; (of money) wie gewonnen, so zerronnen; **~ you are** (giving sth.) hier; **~ we are** (on arrival) da sind *od.* wären wir; **~ we go again** (coll.) jetzt geht das wieder los! (ugs.) **2** (to this place) hierher; **in[to] ~:** hierherein; **come/bring ~:** herkommen/-bringen; hierher kommen/bringen; **put sth. ~:** etw. hierhin *od.* hierher tun; **~ comes the bus** hier *od.* da kommt der Bus

B *n.* **leave ~:** von hier abreisen; **near ~:** hier in der Nähe; **up to ~, as far as ~:** bis hierhin; **he is up to ~ in problems** die Probleme sind ihm über den Kopf gewachsen; **from ~ on** von nun an; **where do we go from ~?** (fig.) was machen wir jetzt?

C *int.* (attracting attention) he; (at roll-call) hier

here: ~a'bout[s] *adv.* hier [in dieser Gegend]; **~'after** *adv.* (formal) im Folgenden; (in the future) fürderhin (veralt.); (literary: in the next world) dereinst (geh.); **the life ~after** das Leben im Jenseits; **~'by** *adv.* (formal) hiermit

hereditary /hɪ'redɪtərɪ/ *adj.* **1** erblich ‹*Titel, Amt*›; ererbt ‹*Reichtum*›; **~ monarchy/right** Erbmonarchie, *die*/Erbrecht, *das* **2** (Biol.) angeboren ‹*Instinkt, Verhaltensweise*›; **~ disease** Erbkrankheit, *die* **3** (of a family) **~ feud/enemy** Erbfehde, *die*/-feind, *der*

heredity /hɪ'redɪtɪ/ *n.* (Biol.) **1** (transmission of qualities) Vererbung, *die* **2** (genetic constitution) Erbgut, *das*

here: ~'in *adv.* (formal) hierin; **~in'after** *adv.* (formal) im Folgenden; **~'of** *adv.* (formal) davon

heresy /'herɪsɪ/ *n.* Ketzerei, *die*

heretic /'herɪtɪk/ *n.* Ketzer, *der*/Ketzerin, *die*

heretical /hɪ'retɪkl/ *adj.* ketzerisch

here: ~'to /hɪə'tʊ, hɪə'tu:/ *adv.* (formal) darauf/hierauf; **~to'fore** *adv.* (formal) (up to now) bisher; (up until that time) bis dahin; **~'under** *adv.* (formal) im Folgenden; **~u'pon** *adv.* hierauf; **~'with** *adv.* **1** (with this letter) in der Anlage; **we enclose ~with your cheque** wir legen Ihren Scheck diesem Schreiben bei; **2** ▸▸**~by**

heritage /'herɪtɪdʒ/ *n.* (lit. or fig.) Erbe, *das*

> **heritage centre**
>
> Ein Museumstyp in Großbritannien, der einem bestimmten Thema wie z.B. der Geschichte der lokalen Architektur oder einer bestimmten traditionellen Industrie oder Aktivität gewidmet ist. *Heritage centres* werden manchmal um alte Gebäude herum entwickelt.

heritage 'tourism *n., no pl.* Kulturtourismus, *der*

h

hermaphrodite /hɜːˈmæfrədaɪt/ **A** *n.* Zwitter, *der* (auch fig.); Hermaphrodit, *der* **B** *adj.* zwittrig; hermaphroditisch

hermeneutics /hɜːmɪˈnjuːtɪks/ *n., no pl.* Hermeneutik, *die*

hermetic /hɜːˈmetɪk/ *adj.* (airtight) luftdicht; (fig.) hermetisch (geh.)

hermetically /hɜːˈmetɪkəlɪ/ *adv.* hermetisch

hermit /ˈhɜːmɪt/ *n.* **1** Einsiedler, *der*/Einsiedlerin, *die* **2** (Relig.) Eremit, *der*

hermitage /ˈhɜːmɪtɪdʒ/ *n.* Einsiedelei, *die*

ˈhermit crab *n.* Einsiedlerkrebs, *der*

hernia /ˈhɜːnɪə/ *n., pl.* **~s** *or* **~e** /ˈhɜːnɪiː/ (Med.) Bruch, *der*; Hernie, *die* (Med.)

hero /ˈhɪərəʊ/ *n., pl.* **~es** Held, *der*; (demigod) Heros, *der*; **~ of the hour** Held des Tages

heroic /hɪˈrəʊɪk/ *adj.* **1** heldenhaft; heroisch (geh.) **2** (Lit.) **~ epic/legend** Heldenepos, *das*/-legende, *die*; **~ couplet** Heroic Couplet, *das*; **~ verse** heroischer Vers **3** (high-flown) erhaben; (very large) gewaltig

heroically /hɪˈrəʊɪkəlɪ/ *adv.* heldenhaft

heroics /hɪˈrəʊɪks/ *n. pl.* **1** (language) Theatralische, *das*; (foolhardiness) Draufgängertum, *das* **2** (Lit.) heroischer Vers

heroin /ˈherəʊɪn/ *n., no pl.* Heroin, *das*

heroine /ˈherəʊɪn/ *n.* Heldin, *die*; Heroin, *die* (geh.); Heroine, *die* (Theater)

heroism /ˈherəʊɪzm/ *n., no pl.* Heldentum, *das*

heron /ˈhern/ *n.* Reiher, *der*

hero: ~ ˈsandwich *n.* (Amer.) ▸ **hoagie**; **~-worship A** *n.* Heldenverehrung, *die*; **B** *v.t.* vergöttern; **~-worshipper** *n.* Heldenverehrer, *der*/-verehrerin, *die*

herpes /ˈhɜːpiːz/ *n.* ▸ **i p. 1231** (Med.) Herpes, *der*

herring /ˈherɪŋ/ *n.* Hering, *der*

herring: ~bone A *n.* **1** (Textiles) (stitch) Fischgrätenstich, *der*; (cloth) Fischgrat, *der*; **2** (Archit.) Fischgrätenverband, *der*; **B** *adj.* **~bone pattern** (Textiles) Fischgrätenmuster, *das*; **~ gull** *n.* Silbermöwe, *die*; **~ pond** *n.* (joc.) Atlantik, *der*

hers /hɜːz/ *poss. pron. pred.* ihrer/ihre/ihres; der/die/das ihre *od.* ihrige (geh.); **the book is ~:** das Buch gehört ihr; **that car is ~:** das ist ihr Wagen; der Wagen gehört ihr; **some friends of ~:** ein paar Freunde von ihr; **a book of ~:** ein Buch von ihr; eins ihrer Bücher; **those children of ~:** ihre Kinder; **~ is a difficult job** sie hat einen schwierigen Job (ugs.)

herself /hɜːˈself/ *pron.* **1** *emphat.* selbst; **she ~ said so** sie selbst hat das gesagt; **she saw it ~:** sie hat es selbst gesehen; **she wanted to be ~:** sie wollte sie selbst sein; **she was just being ~:** sie gab sich einfach so, wie sie ist; **she is [quite] ~ again** sie ist wieder ganz die Alte; (after an illness) sie ist wieder auf der Höhe (ugs.); **all right in ~:** im Wesentlichen gesund; **she's not quite ~:** sie ist nicht ganz in Ordnung; **[all] by ~** (on her own, by her own efforts) [ganz] allein[e] **2** *refl.* sich; allein[e] ‹*tun, wählen*›; **she wants to see for ~** sie will [es] selbst sehen; **she wants it for ~:** sie will es für sich [selbst]; **she won't believe anything that she hasn't seen for ~:** sie glaubt nichts, was sie nicht selbst gesehen hat; **younger than/as heavy as ~:** jünger als/so schwer wie sie selbst; **... she thought to ~:** ... dachte sie sich [im Stillen]; ... dachte sie bei sich

hertz /hɜːts/ *n., pl. same* (Phys.) Hertz, *das*

he's /hɪz, *stressed* hiːz/ **1** **= he is 2** **= he has**

hesitance /ˈhezɪtəns/, **hesitancy** /ˈhezɪtənsɪ/ *n., no pl.* Zögern, *das*; (indecision) Unschlüssigkeit, *die*

hesitant /ˈhezɪtənt/ *adj.* zögernd ‹*Politik, Reaktion*›; stockend ‹*Rede*›; unschlüssig, unsicher ‹*Person, Stimme*›; **be ~ to do sth.** *or* **about doing sth.** Bedenken haben, etw. zu tun

hesitantly /ˈhezɪtəntlɪ/ *adv.* zögernd ‹*handeln, reagieren*›; stockend ‹*sprechen*›

hesitate /ˈhezɪteɪt/ *v.i.* **1** (show uncertainty) zögern; **he who ~s is lost** (prov.) man muss die Gelegenheit beim Schopfe fassen **2** (falter) ins Stocken geraten **3** (show reluctance) **~ to do sth.** Bedenken haben, etw. zu tun

hesitation /hezɪˈteɪʃn/ *n.* **1** *no pl.* Zögern, *das*; (indecision) Unentschlossenheit, *die*; **without the slightest ~:** ohne im Geringsten zu zögern; **have no ~ in doing sth.** nicht zögern, etw. zu tun **2** (instance of faltering) Unsicherheit, *die* **3** *no pl.* (reluctance) Bedenken *Pl.*

Hesse /ˈhesə/ *pr. n.* Hessen (*das*)

hessian *n.* Sackleinen, *das*; Hessian, *das* (fachspr.)

Hessian /ˈhesɪən/ **A** *adj.* hessisch **B** *n.* Hesse, *der*/Hessin, *die*

hetero /ˈhetərəʊ/*n.* (coll.) **A** *n.* Hetero *der/die*; **be a ~:** hetero sein **B** *adj.* heterosexuell; *attrib. also* Hetero-

hetero- /ˈhetərəʊ/ *in comb.* hetero-/Hetero-

heterodox /ˈhetərədɒks/ *adj.* heterodox

heterodoxy /ˈhetərədɒksɪ/ *n.* Heterodoxie, *die*

heterogeneity /hetərədʒɪˈniːɪtɪ/ *n.* Ungleichartigkeit, *die*; Heterogenität, *die*

heterogeneous /hetərəˈdʒiːnɪəs, hetərəˈdʒenɪəs/ *adj.* ungleichartig; heterogen

heterosexual /heterəˈseksjʊəl/ **A** *adj.* heterosexuell **B** *n.* Heterosexuelle, *der/die*

heterosexuality /hetərəseksjʊˈælətɪ/ *n., no pl.* Heterosexualität, *die*

het up /het ˈʌp/ *adj.* (coll.) aufgeregt; **get ~ over sth.** sich über etw. (*Akk.*) aufregen

heuristic /hjʊəˈrɪstɪk/ **A** *adj.* heuristisch **B** *n.* (procedure) heuristische Methode

hew /hjuː/ **A** *v.t., p. p.* **~n** /hjuːn/ *or* **~ed** /hjuːd/ **1** (cut) hacken ‹*Holz*›; fällen ‹*Baum*›; losschlagen ‹*Kohle, Gestein*›; **~ away** *or* **off** abschlagen **2** (shape) hauen ‹*Stufen*›; behauen ‹*Holz, Stein*› **B** *v.i., p. p.* **~n** *or* **~ed 1** zuschlagen; **~ at sth.** auf etw. (*Akk.*) einschlagen **2** (Amer.: conform) **~ to sth.** sich an etw. (*Akk.*) halten

hex /heks/ (Amer.) **A** *v.t.* (lit. or fig.) verhexen **B** *n.* **1** **put a ~ on sb./sth.** jmdn./etw. verhexen **2** (witch, lit. or fig.) Hexe, *die*

hexagon /ˈheksəgən/ *n.* (Geom.) Sechseck, *das*; Hexagon, *das* (fachspr.)

hexagonal /hekˈsægənl/ *adj.* (Geom.) sechseckig; hexagonal (fachspr.)

hexameter /hekˈsæmɪtə(r)/ *n.* (Pros.) Hexameter, *der*

hey /heɪ/ *int.* he!; **~ presto!** simsalabim!

heyday /ˈheɪdeɪ/ *n., no pl.* Blütezeit, *die*

hf. *abbr.* **= half**

HF *abbr.* **= high frequency** HF

HGV *abbr.* (Brit.) **= heavy goods vehicle**

HH *abbr.* ▸ **i p. 1634 1** **= Her/His Highness** I. H./S. H. **2** **= His Holiness**

hi /haɪ/ *int.* ▸ **i p. 1189** hallo (ugs.)

hiatus /haɪˈeɪtəs/ *n.* **1** (gap) Bruch, *der*; (interruption) Unterbrechung, *die* **2** (Ling.) Hiatus, *der*

hibernate /ˈhaɪbəneɪt/ *v.i.* Winterschlaf halten

hibernation /haɪbəˈneɪʃn/ *n.* Winterschlaf, *der*; **go into/come out of ~:** sich zum Winterschlaf zurückziehen/aus dem Winterschlaf erwachen

Hibernian /haɪˈbɜːnɪən/ **A** *adj.* irisch **B** *n.* Ire, *der*/Irin, *die*

hibiscus /hɪˈbɪskəs/ *n.* (Bot.) Hibiskus, *der*

hic /hɪk/ *int.* hick (ugs.)

hiccup /ˈhɪkʌp/ **A** *n.* **1** Schluckauf, *der*; **have/get [the] ~s** [den] Schluckauf haben/bekommen; **give a ~:** schlucksen (ugs.); hick machen (ugs.); **an attack of [the] ~s** ein Schluckaufanfall **2** (fig.: stoppage) Störung, *die*; **without any ~s** reibungslos **B** *v.i.* schlucksen (ugs.); hick machen (ugs.); (many times) den Schluckauf haben

hick /hɪk/ *n.* (Amer. coll.) **[country] ~:** Provinzler, *der* (ugs. abwertend); Hinterwäldler, *der* (spött.); **~ town** Provinzstadt, *die*; Provinznest, *das* (ugs. abwertend)

hickey /ˈhɪkɪ/ *n.* (Amer.) Dings, *das* (ugs.)

hickory /ˈhɪkərɪ/ *n.* **1** (tree) Hickory[baum], *der* **2** (wood) Hickory[holz], *das*

hid ▸ **hide¹ A, B**

hidden ▸ **hide¹ A, B**

hidden reˈserve *n.* (Econ.) stille Reserve *od.* Rücklage

hide¹ /haɪd/ **A** *v.t.*, **hid** /hɪd/, **hidden** /ˈhɪdn/ **1** (put or keep out of sight) verstecken ‹*Gegenstand, Person usw.*› (**from** vor + *Dat.*); **~ one's head [in embarrassment/shame]** (fig.) sich [vor Verlegenheit/Scham (*Dat.*)] verstecken; **~ one's face in one's hands** sein Gesicht in den Händen bergen; *see also* **bushel 2** (keep secret) verbergen ‹*Gefühle, Sinn, Freude usw.*› (**from** vor + *Dat.*); verheimlichen ‹*Tatsache, Absicht, Grund usw.*› (**from** *Dat.*); **have nothing to ~:** nichts zu verbergen haben; **the future is hidden from us** die Zukunft ist uns verborgen **3** (obscure) verdecken; **~ sth. [from view]** etw. verstecken; (by covering) etw. verdecken; ‹*Nebel, Rauch usw.*:› etw. einhüllen **B** *v.i.*, **hid, hidden** sich verstecken *od.* verbergen (**from** vor + *Dat.*); **where is he hiding?** wo hält er sich versteckt *od.* verborgen? **C** *n.* (Brit.) Versteck, *das*; (hunter's **~**) Ansitz, *der* (Jägerspr.)

Phrasal verbs

- **~ aˈway** *v.i.* sich verstecken *od.* verbergen; *see also* **hideaway**
- **~ ˈout, ~ ˈup** *v.i.* sich versteckt *od.* verborgen halten; *see also* **hideout**

hide² *n.* (animal's skin) Haut, *die*; (of furry animal) Fell, *das*; (dressed) Leder, *das*; (joc.: human skin) Haut, *die*; Fell, *das*; **tan sb.'s ~:** jmdm. das Fell gerben *od.* versohlen (salopp); **save one's own ~:** die eigene Haut retten (ugs.); **when I returned I could find neither ~ nor hair of them** als ich zurückkam, waren sie spurlos verschwunden

hide: ~-and-ˈseek (*Amer.:* **~-and-go-ˈseek**) *n.* Versteckspiel, *das*; **play ~-and-seek** Verstecken spielen; **~away** ▸ **~out**; **~bound** *adj.* engstirnig, borniert (abwertend) ‹*Person, Ansicht*›

hideous /ˈhɪdɪəs/ *adj.* **1** (extremely ugly, offensive to the ear) scheußlich; (repulsive, horrific) entsetzlich; grauenhaft **2** (coll.: unpleasant) furchtbar (ugs.), schrecklich (ugs.)

hideously /ˈhɪdɪəslɪ/ *adv.* **1** entsetzlich, grauenhaft ‹*verstümmelt, entstellt, schreien*› **2** (coll.: unpleasantly) furchtbar (ugs.), schrecklich (ugs.) ‹*langweilig, teuer, kalt, laut usw.*›

ˈhideout *n.* Versteck, *das*; (of bandits, partisans, etc.) Versteck, *das*; Unterschlupf, *der*; (retreat) Refugium, *das*

hidey-hole /ˈhaɪdɪhəʊl/ *n.* (coll.) Versteck, *das*

hiding¹ /ˈhaɪdɪŋ/ *n.* **go into ~:** sich verstecken; (to avoid police, public attention) untertauchen; **be/stay in ~:** sich versteckt halten/sich weiterhin versteckt halten; (to avoid police, public attention) untergetaucht sein/bleiben; **come out of ~:** aus seinem Versteck kommen; (no longer avoid police, public attention) wieder auftauchen

hiding² *n.* (coll.: beating) Tracht Prügel; (fig.) Schlappe, *die*; **give sb. a [good] ~:** jmdm. eine [ordentliche] Tracht Prügel verpassen; (fig.) jmdm. eine [klare] Abfuhr erteilen; **get/be given/take a real ~ [from sb.]** [von jmdm.] gehörige Prügel beziehen *od.* einstecken müssen; (fig.) sich (*Dat.*) [von jmdm.] eine klare Abfuhr holen; **be on a ~ to nothing** eine undankbare Rolle haben

ˈhiding place *n.* Versteck, *das*

hidy-hole ▸ **hidey-hole**

hierarchic /haɪəˈrɑːkɪk/, **hierarchical** /haɪəˈrɑːkɪkl/ *adj.* hierarchisch

hierarchy /ˈhaɪərɑːkɪ/ *n.* Hierarchie, *die*

hieroglyph /ˈhaɪərəglɪf/ *n.* **1** Hieroglyphe, *die* **2** *in pl.* (joc.: scrawl) Hieroglyphen (scherzh.)

hieroglyphic /haɪərəˈglɪfɪk/ **A** *adj.* **1** (composed of hieroglyphs) hieroglyphisch **2** (symbolical) geheimnisvoll ‹*Zeichen*› **B** *n. in pl.* (also joc.) Hieroglyphen

hi-fi /ˈhaɪfaɪ/ (coll.)
A *adj.* Hi-Fi-
B *n.* **1** (equipment) Hi-Fi-Anlage, *die* **2** (use of ~) Hi-Fi, *das; attrib.* Hi-Fi-‹*Fan usw.*›

higgledy-piggledy /hɪɡldɪˈpɪɡldɪ/
A *adv.* wie Kraut und Rüben (ugs.)
B *adj.* wirr, kunterbunt ‹*Ansammlung usw.*›

high /haɪ/
A *adj.* **1** ▸❶ **p. 1208** (reaching far up) hoch ‹*Berg, Gebäude, Mauer*›; **a wall eight feet** *or* **foot ~:** eine acht Fuß hohe Mauer; **I've known him since he was only so ~** (coll.) ich kannte ihn schon, als er [noch] so [klein] war
2 (above normal level) hoch ‹*Stiefel*›; **a dress with a ~ neckline** ein hochgeschlossenes Kleid; **the river/water is ~:** der Fluss/das Wasser steht hoch; **~ and dry** ‹*Boot:*› auf dem Trockenen; hoch und trocken (Seemannsspr.); **be left ~ and dry** (fig.) auf dem Trock[e]nen sitzen (ugs.); (be stuck without transport) festsitzen (ugs.)
3 (far above ground or sea level) hoch ‹*Gipfel, Punkt*›; groß ‹*Höhe*›; Hoch‹*ebene, -moor*›; **be ~** ‹*Ort:*› hoch liegen; ‹*Sonne, Mond:*› hoch stehen
4 (to or from far above the ground) hoch ‹*Aufstieg, Sprung*›; **~ diving** Turmspringen, *das;* **a ~ dive** ein Sprung vom Turm; *see also* **bar¹ A 2**
5 (of exalted rank) hoch ‹*Beamter, Amt, Gericht*›; **the Most H~** (Bibl.) der Allerhöchste; **~ and low** Arm und Reich (veralt.); **a ~er court** eine höhere Instanz; **~er mammals/plants** höhere Säugetiere/Pflanzen; **~ and mighty** (coll.: high-handed) selbstherrlich; (coll.: self-important) wichtigtuerisch; (coll.: superior) hochnäsig (ugs.); (arch.: exalted) hoch ‹*Adlige*›; groß ‹*Häuptling*›; **aim for ~er things** (fig.) nach Höherem streben; **be born** *or* **destined for ~er things** zu Höherem geboren *od.* bestimmt sein; **in ~ places** an höherer Stelle; höheren Orts; **people in ~ places** Leute in hohen Positionen; **those in ~ places** die Oberen
6 (great in degree) hoch; groß ‹*Gefallen, Bedeutung*›; stark ‹*Wind*›; **be ~ in iodine** einen hohen Jodgehalt aufweisen; **be held in ~ regard/esteem** hohes Ansehen/hohe Wertschätzung genießen; hoch angesehen/geschätzt sein; **~ blood pressure** Bluthochdruck, *der;* **~ vacuum** Hochvakuum, *das;* **her ~est aspiration** ihr größter Wunsch; **get a nice ~ polish on the car** das Auto auf Hochglanz polieren; **a/his** *etc.* **~ colour** ein/sein *usw.* rotes Gesicht; **have a ~ opinion of sb./sth.** eine hohe Meinung von jmdm./etw. haben (geh.); viel von jmdm./etw. halten
7 (extreme in opinion) extrem
8 (noble, virtuous) hoch ‹*Ideal, Ziel, Prinzip, Berufung*›; edel ‹*Charakter*›; **of ~ birth** von hoher Geburt (geh.); **~ art/comedy** hohe Kunst/Komödie
9 (Geog.) **~ latitudes** hohe Breiten
10 (of time, season) **it is ~ time you left** es ist *od.* wird höchste Zeit, dass du gehst; **~ noon** Mittag; **it was ~ noon** es war genau Mittag; **~ summer** Hochsommer, *der*
11 (fully developed) hoch; Hoch‹*mittelalter, -renaissance usw.*›
12 (Mech.) **~ gear** hoher Gang; **~ gearing** *or* **ratio** lange Übersetzung; **engage a ~er gear** hochschalten
13 (enjoyable) **have a ~ [old] time** sich bestens amüsieren; **have a ~ [old] time doing sth.** Spaß damit haben, etw. zu tun
14 (coll.) (under the influence) (of a drug) high *nicht attr.* (ugs.) **(on** von); angeturnt (ugs.) **(on** von); (on cannabis) bekifft (ugs.); (on alcohol) blau (ugs.) **(on** von); **get ~ on** sich anturnen mit (ugs.) ‹*Haschisch, Ecstasy usw.*›; sich besaufen mit (salopp) ‹*Whisky, Bier usw.*›
15 (in pitch) hoch ‹*Ton, Stimme, Lage, Klang usw.*›
16 (slightly decomposed) angegangen (landsch.) ‹*Fleisch*›; ‹*Wild*› mit Hautgout
17 (Cards) hoch; **ace is ~:** Ass ist hoch; **I'm queen** *etc.* **~:** Dame *usw.* ist das Höchste, was ich habe
18 (Ling.) ▸**close A 14.** *See also* **horse A 1**
B *adv.* **1** (in or to a ~ position) hoch; **~ on our list of priorities** weit oben auf unserer Prioritätenliste; **~er up the valley** weiter oben im Tal; **we climbed ~er up the cliff** wir kletterten das Kliff ein Stück höher hinauf; **search** *or* **hunt** *or* **look ~ and low** überall suchen; **search** *or* **hunt** *or* **look ~ and low for sb./sth.** jmdn./etw. suchen wie eine Stecknadel; *see also* **aim B 1**
2 (to a ~ level) hoch; **prices have gone too ~:** die Preise sind zu stark gestiegen; **I'll go as ~ as two thousand pounds** ich gehe bis zweitausend Pfund
3 (at or to a ~ pitch) hoch ‹*singen*›
4 **play ~** (Cards) etwas Hohes spielen; (Gambling) mit hohen Einsätzen spielen
C *n.* **1** (~est level/figure) Höchststand, *der; see also* **all-time**
2 ▸❶ **p. 1620** (Meteorol.) Hoch, *das*
3 (Amer. coll.: ~ school) Oberschule, *die;* **in junior ~:** in der Unterstufe [der Oberschule]
4 (coll.: drug-induced euphoria) Rausch[zustand], *der;* **give sb. a ~** ‹*Droge:*› jmdn. high machen (ugs.)
5 (Motor Veh.) höchster Gang
6 (~ position) **on ~:** hoch oben *od.* (geh., südd., österr.) droben; (in heaven) im Himmel; **from on ~:** von hoch oben; (from heaven) vom Himmel; (fig.: from a ~ authority) von oben; **a judgement from on ~:** eine Strafe des Himmels

high: ~ 'altar *n.* (Eccl.) Hochaltar, *der;* **~-altitude** *adj.* Höhen-; **~ball** *n.* (Amer.) **1** (drink) Highball, *der;* **2** (Railw.: signal) Freie-Fahrt-Signal, *das;* **~ 'beam** *n.* Fernlicht, *das;* **I was on ~ beam** ich fuhr mit Fernlicht; **~binder** *n.* (Amer.) **1** (thug) Schläger, *der;* **2** (assassin) [chinesischer] Killer; **3** (swindler) Schwindler, *der;* Ganove, *der* (ugs.); **~-born** *adj.* hochgeboren (veralt.); **~boy** *n.* (Amer.) (hochbeinige) hohe Kommode; Highboy, *der* (fachspr.); **~brow** **A** *n.* Intellektuelle, *der/die;* **B** *adj.* intellektuell ‹*Person, Gerede usw.*›; hochgestochen (abwertend) ‹*Person, Gerede, Musik, Literatur usw.*›; hochgeistig ‹*Interessen, Beschäftigung, Gerede*›; **~ chair** *n.* (for baby) Hochstuhl, *der;* **H~ 'Church** *n.* High Church, *die;* Hochkirche, *die; attrib.* hochkirchlich; **~-class** *adj.* hochwertig ‹*Erzeugnis*›; erstklassig ‹*Unterkunft, Konditor usw.*›; **~ com'mand** *n.* (Mil.) Oberkommando, *das;* **H~ Com'mission** *n.* Hohe Kommission; **H~ Com'missioner** *n.* Hoher Kommissar; **H~ 'Court [of Justice]** *n.* (Brit. Law) *oberster Gerichtshof für Zivil- und Strafsachen;* **~ day** *n.* **on ~ days and holidays** zu besonderen Anlässen; **~-definition 'television** *n.* hoch auflösendes Fernsehen; **~-density 'housing** *n., no pl.* hoch verdichtete Wohnbebauung; **~ 'diving** *n., no pl.* Turmspringen, *das;* **~-energy 'physics** *n., no pl.* Hochenergiephysik, *die*

higher /ˈhaɪə(r)/: **~ edu'cation** *n., no pl., no art.* Hochschul[aus]bildung, *die;* **he works in ~ education** er ist im Hochschulbereich tätig; **more funds are needed for ~ education** das Hochschulwesen braucht mehr Mittel; **~ mathe'matics** *n.* höhere Mathematik

high: ~ ex'plosive ▸**explosive B;** **~-faluting** /haɪfəˈluːtɪŋ/, **~-falutin'** /haɪfəˈluːtɪn/ *adj.* (coll. derog.) hochtrabend ‹*Gerede, Stil, Sprache usw.*›; aufgeblasen (ugs. abwertend) ‹*Person*›; **~ 'fashion** ▸**haute couture;** **~ fi'delity** *n.* High Fidelity, *die;* **reproduce sth. in ~ fidelity** etw. in Hi-Fi-Qualität wiedergeben; **~ fi'nance** *n.* Hochfinanz, *die;* **~ 'five** *n.* (esp. Amer. coll.) Highfive, *die* (Jargon); **give sb. a ~ five** jmdn. abklatschen (ugs.); **exchange ~ fives** sich abklatschen (ugs.); **~-'flier** ▸**~-flyer;** **~-flown** *adj.* geschwollen (abwertend) ‹*Stil, Ausdrucksweise*›; hochfliegend ‹*Ideen, Pläne*›; **~-'flyer** *n.* **1** (ambitious person) Ehrgeizling, *der* (ugs., abwertend); **be a ~-flyer** große Rosinen im Kopf haben (ugs.); hoch hinaus wollen; **2** (successful person) Senkrechtstarter, *der;* (person with great potential) Hochbegabte, *der/die;* **~-'flying** *adj.* hoch fliegend; (fig.) hochfliegend ‹*Pläne, Ideen*›; erfolgreich ‹*Person*›; **~ 'frequency** *n.* hohe Frequenz; (radio frequency) Hochfrequenz, *die;* **~-frequency** *adj.* hochfrequent ‹*Welle, Schwingung, Strahlung, Strom, Ton, Signal*›; Hochfrequenz‹*welle, -schwingung, -signal, -gerät, -sender usw.*›; ‹*Sendung*› ≈ auf Kurzwelle; ‹*Verluste*› im Hochfrequenzbereich; **~ 'German** ▸**German B 2;** **~-grade** *adj.* hochwertig; **~-grade ore** hochhaltiges Erz; Reicherz, *das;* **~-grade steel** Edelstahl, *der;* **~-handed** /haɪˈhændɪd/ *adj.* selbstherrlich; **~ 'hat** *n.* **1** (tall hat) Zylinder, *der;* **2** (fig.: snobbish person) dünkelhafter Mensch; **~ 'heel** *n.* **1** hoher Absatz; **2** *in pl.* (shoes) hochhackige Schuhe; **~-heeled** /haɪˈhiːld/ *adj.* ‹*Schuhe*› mit hohen Absätzen; **~ 'holiday** *n.* (Relig.) *einer der beiden höchsten jüdischen Feiertage;* höchster Feiertag; **~-income** *adj.* einkommensstark; **~-income earners** Bezieher hoher Einkommen; **~-income area/country** Gebiet/Land mit hohem Pro-Kopf-Einkommen; **~-income investment** Investition mit hoher Rendite; **~ jinks** /ˈhaɪ dʒɪŋks/ *n. pl.* [übermütige] Ausgelassenheit; **~ jump** *n., no pl.* **1** (Sport) Hochsprung, *der;* **2** (fig.: reprimand, punishment) **he is for the ~ jump, it's the ~ jump for him** er kann sich auf was gefasst machen (ugs.); **~ jumper** *n.* (Sport) Hochspringer, *der*/-springerin, *die;* **~-'key** *adj.* (Photog.) High-Key-‹*Bild, Aufnahme usw.*› (fachspr.); **~ 'kick** *n.* hoher Beinwurf; **~land** /ˈhaɪlənd/ **A** *n., usu. in pl.* Hochland, *das;* **the H~lands** (in Scotland) die Highlands; **B** *adj.* hochländisch; **H~land 'cattle** *n. pl.* schottische Hochlandrinder; **H~land 'dress** *n., no pl.* [schottische] Hochlandtracht; **~lander** /ˈhaɪləndə(r)/ *n.* Hochländer, *der*/-länderin, *die;* **H~lander** schottischer Hochländer/schottische Hochländerin; **H~land 'fling** *n.* Highlandfling, *der;* **~-level** *adj.* ‹*Verhandlungen usw.*› auf hoher Ebene; **~-level talks** Spitzengespräche; **~-level computer language** problemorientierte Programmiersprache; **~ life** *n., no pl.* **1** (life of upper class) das Leben der Oberschicht; **2** (luxurious living) **the ~ life** das Leben auf großem Fuße; **~light** **A** *n.* **1** (outstanding moment) Höhepunkt, *der;* **the ~light of the week's events** das herausragende Ereignis der Woche; **2** (bright area) Licht, *das;* **3** (in hair) *usu. pl.* Strähnchen, *das;* **B** *v.t.,* **~ed** ein Schlaglicht werfen auf (+ *Akk.*) ‹*Probleme usw.*›; markieren ‹*Text, Wort etc.*› **~lighter** *n.* Textmarker, *der*

highly /ˈhaɪlɪ/ *adv.* **1** (to a high degree) sehr; äußerst; hoch‹*interessant, -gebildet, -modern, -aktuell*›; hoch ‹*begabt, bezahlt, angesehen*›; leicht ‹*entzündlich*›; stark ‹*gewürzt*›; **feel ~ honoured** sich hoch geehrt fühlen; **I can ~ recommend the restaurant** ich kann dieses Restaurant sehr empfehlen; *see also* **polish A 2** **2** (favourably) **think ~ of sb./sth., regard sb./sth. ~:** eine hohe Meinung von jmdm./etw. haben; **speak/write ~ of sb./sth.** jmdn./etw. sehr loben

'highly strung *adj.* übererregbar

high: ~ 'mass ▸**mass¹;** **~-minded** /haɪ ˈmaɪndɪd/ *adj.* hochgesinnt ‹*Person*›; hoch, (geh.) hehr ‹*Prinzipien, Dienstauffassung usw.*›; **~-necked** *adj.* hochgeschlossen ‹*Kleidungsstück*›

Highness /ˈhaɪnɪs/ *n.* ▸❶ **p. 1634** Hoheit, *die;* **His/Her/Your [Royal] ~:** Seine/Ihre/Eure [Königliche] Hoheit

high: ~-octane *adj.* hochoktanig; **~-performance** *adj.* Hochleistungs-; **~-pitched** *adj.* **1** hoch ‹*Ton, Stimme*›; **2** (Archit.) steil ‹*Dach*›; **3** (lofty) anspruchsvoll; hochgeistig ‹*Unterhaltung*›; **be too ~-pitched intellectually for sb.** jmdm. *od.* für jmdn. zu hoch sein (ugs.); **~ point** *n.* Höhepunkt, *der;* Gipfelpunkt, *der;* **~-powered** /ˈhaɪpaʊəd/ *adj.* **1** (powerful) stark ‹*Fahrzeug, Motor, Glühbirne usw.*›; **2** (forceful) dynamisch ‹*Geschäftsmann, Manager usw.*›; **3** (authoritative) mit umfangreichen Vollmachten ausgestattet; (intellectually excellent) [äußerst] fähig; hochkarätig (ugs.) ‹*Examen*›; **~ 'pressure** *n.* **1** (Meteorol.) Hochdruck, *der;* **an area of ~ pressure** ein Hochdruckgebiet; **2** (Mech. Engin.) Überdruck, *der;* **3** (fig.: high degree of activity) Hochdruck, *der;* **work at ~ pressure** mit Hochdruck arbeiten (ugs.); **~-pressure** *adj.* Hochdruck-; (fig.: persuasive) aggressiv ‹*Verkaufsmethoden*›; aufdringlich ‹*Vertreter*›; **~-priced** /haɪˈpraɪst/ *adj.* teuer; **~ 'priest** *n.* Hohepriester, *der;* **~ 'profile** ▸**profile A 7;** **~-protein** *adj.* eiweißreich; **~-ranking** *adj.* hochrangig; von hohem Rang *nachgestellt;* hoch ‹*Beamter, Offizier*›; **~ re'lief** ▸**relief² 1;** **~-rise** *adj.* Hochhaus-; **~-rise building** Hochhaus, *das;*

h

~-rise [block of] flats/office block Wohn-/Bürohochhaus, *das;* **~-risk** *attrib. adj.* risikoreich; Risiko‹*gruppe, -sportart*›; hochgradig gefährdet ‹*Person*›; **take a ~-risk gamble** viel aufs Spiel setzen; viel riskieren; **a ~-risk investment** eine Geldanlage mit hohem Risiko; **~ road** *n.* Hauptstraße, *die;* **the ~ road to ruin** der sichere Weg zum Ruin; **a ~ road to happiness** ein sicherer Weg zum Glück; **~ 'roller** *n.* (esp. Amer. coll.) (gambler) Zocker, *der*/Zockerin, *die* (Gaunerspr.); (person who spends large sums of money) Geldprotz, *der* (ugs.); **~ school** *n.* ≈ Oberschule, *die;* **~-scoring** *adj.* (Sport) punktreich; (with many goals) torreich; **~ 'seas** *n. pl.* **the ~ seas** die hohe See; **~ season** *n.* Hochsaison, *die;* **~-security** *adj.* Hochsicherheits‹*trakt, -gefängnis*›; **~-sided vehicle** *n.* hohes Fahrzeug; **~ sign** *n.* (Amer. coll.) **give sb. the ~ sign** jmdm. signalisieren, dass die Luft rein ist; **~-sounding** *adj.* hochtönend; hochtrabend (abwertend); **~-speed** *adj.* **1** schnell [fahrend]; **~-speed train** Hochgeschwindigkeitszug, *der;* **~-speed steel** Schnell[arbeits-]stahl, *der;* **2** (Photog.) ▸**fast²** **A 8;** **~-spirited** ▸**spirited 2;** **~ 'spirits** ▸**spirit A 8;** **~ spot** *n.* (coll.) Höhepunkt, *der;* **~ street** *n.* Hauptstraße, *die;* **~ street shop/office** Geschäft/Büro in der Hauptstraße; **~ street banks** Großbanken; **~-'strung** ▸**highly strung;** **~ 'table** *n.* **1** (at public dinner) erhöhte Speisetafel; **2** (table for college fellows) Dozententisch, *der;* **~tail** *v.i. & t.* (Amer. coll.) **~tail [it]** abhauen (salopp); verduften (ugs.); sich aus dem Staub machen (ugs.); **~ 'tea** ▸**tea 2;** **~-tech** *adj.* (coll.) Hightech-; **~ 'tech** (coll.), **~ tech'nology** *ns.* Spitzentechnologie, *die;* Hochtechnologie, *die;* **~-technology** *adj.* hoch technisiert; Hightech-; **~-'tensile** *adj.* [hoch]zugfest; **~ 'tension** *n.* (Electr.) Hochspannung, *die;* **~-'tension** (Electr.) Hochspannungs-; **~ 'tide** *n.* Flut, *die;* **~ 'treason** ▸**treason 1;** **~-up** *n.* (coll.) hohes Tier (ugs.); **~ 'voltage** (Electr.) Hochspannung, *die;* **~-'voltage** *adj.* (Electr.) Hochspannungs-; **~ 'water** *n.* Flut, *die;* **~ 'water mark** *n.* **1** (level reached by tide) Hochwassermarke, *die;* **2** (maximum value) höchster Stand; Höchststand, *der;* (highest point of excellence) Höhepunkt, *der;* **~way** *n.* **1** (Amer.) ≈ Autobahn, *die;* (public path) öffentlicher Weg; **H~ways Department** Straßenbauamt, *das;* **the King's/Queen's ~way** (Brit.) *eine öffentliche Straße;* **2** (main route) Verkehrsweg, *der;* **3** (fig.: course of action) **the ~way to ruin** der sichere Weg zum Ruin; **H~way 'Code** *n.* (Brit.) Straßenverkehrsordnung, *die;* **~way 'maintenance** *n., no pl.* (Brit.) Straßeninstandhaltung, *die; attrib.* **H~way Maintenance Department** ≈ Straßenmeisterei, *die;* **~wayman** /'haɪweɪmən/ *n., pl.* **~waymen** /'haɪweɪmən/ (Hist.) Straßenräuber, *der;* Wegelagerer, *der;* **~ 'wire** *n.* [Hoch]seil, *das*

> **high school**
>
> Eine weiterführende Schule in den USA, normalerweise für Schüler von 14 bis 18 Jahren, die vorher eine *intermediate school* oder **middle school** besucht haben. Schüler erwerben einen Highschoolabschluss durch Nachweis von *credits* (Punkten) in bestimmten Pflicht- und Wahlkursen. Der Abschluss ist Voraussetzung zum Besuch der Hochschule. Auch in Großbritannien werden einige weiterführende Schulen als *high schools* bezeichnet.

hijack /'haɪdʒæk/
A *v.t.* **1** (seize) in seine Gewalt bringen; entführen ‹*Flugzeug*›; **they ~ed an aircraft to Cuba** sie haben ein Flugzeug nach Kuba entführt; **he ~ed the lorry to London** er zwang den Fahrer des LKWs, nach London zu fahren **2** (coll.: steal) sich (*Dat.*) unter den Nagel reißen (ugs.)
B *n.* (of aircraft) Entführung, *die* (**of** *Gen.*); (of vehicle) Überfall, *der* (**of** auf + *Akk.*)

hijacker /'haɪdʒækə(r)/ *n.* Entführer, *der;* (of aircraft) Hijacker, *der;* Flugzeugentführer, *der;* **be seized by ~s** entführt werden

hike /haɪk/
A *n.* **1** (long walk) Wanderung, *die;* **go on a ~:** eine Wanderung machen; wandern gehen; **be on a ~:** auf einer Wanderung sein; eine Wanderung machen **2** (esp. Amer.: increase) Anstieg, *der;* Erhöhung, *die* (**in** *Gen.*)
B *v.i.* **1** wandern; eine Wanderung machen **2** (walk vigorously) wandern; marschieren
C *v.t.* **1** (hoist) hieven (ugs.) **2** (esp. Amer.: raise) erhöhen, anheben ‹*Preise usw.*› (**to** auf + *Akk.*)

Phrasal verb
• **~ 'up** *v.t.* hochziehen ‹*Hose, Rock*›; (fig.) hochschrauben ‹*Preise*›

hiker /'haɪkə(r)/ *n.* Wanderer, *der*/Wanderin, *die*

hiking boot /'haɪkɪŋ bu:t/ *n.* Wanderstiefel, *der*

hilarious /hɪ'leərɪəs/ *adj.* (extremely funny) urkomisch; rasend komisch (ugs.)

hilariously /hɪ'leərɪəslɪ/ *adv.* **be ~ funny** rasend komisch sein (ugs.); zum Schreien sein (ugs.)

hilarity /hɪ'lærɪtɪ/ *n., no pl.* **1** (gaiety) Fröhlichkeit, *die* **2** (merriment) übermütige Ausgelassenheit; (loud laughter) Heiterkeit, *die*

Hilary term /'hɪlərɪ tɜ:m/ *n.* (Brit. Univ.) Frühjahrstrimester, *das*

hill /hɪl/ *n.* **1** Hügel, *der;* (higher) Berg, *der;* **walk in the ~s** in den Bergen wandern; **built on a ~:** am Hang gebaut; **be over the ~** (fig. coll.) auf dem absteigenden Ast sein (ugs.); (past the crisis) über den Berg sein (ugs.); **[as] old as the ~s** (fig.) uralt; ‹*Person*› [so] alt wie Methusalem; *see also* **up B 1; up~ 2** (heap) Hügel, *der;* (ant~, dung~, mole~) Haufen, *der* **3** (sloping road) Steigung, *die;* **park on a ~:** am Berg parken

hill: ~billy *n.* (Amer.) **1** Hinterwäldler, *der*/Hinterwäldlerin, *die* (spött.); Landpomeranze, *die* (ugs. abwertend, auch scherzh.); (of the SE US) Hillbilly, *der;* **2** (Mus.) Hillbilly, *der;* **~ climb** *n.* (Motor Racing) Bergrennen, *das;* **~ fort** *n.* Bergfestung, *die;* (Archaeol.) Hillfort, *das;* **~man** *n.* Bergbewohner, *der*

hillock /'hɪlək/ *n.* [kleiner] Hügel

hill: ~side *n.* Hang, *der;* **~ start** *n.* (Motor Veh.) Anfahren am Berg, *das;* **do a ~ start** am Berg anfahren; **~top** *n.* [Berg]gipfel, *der;* **~ walker** *n.* Bergwanderer, *der*/-wanderin, *die;* **~walking** *n., no pl.* Bergwandern, *das*

hilly /'hɪlɪ/ *adj.* hüg[e]lig; (higher) bergig

hilt /hɪlt/ *n.* Griff, *der;* Heft, *das* (geh., fachspr.); **[up] to the ~** (fig.) voll und ganz ‹*unterstützen usw.*›; schlagend, stichhaltig ‹*beweisen*›

him /ɪm, *stressed* hɪm/ *pron.* ihn; *as indirect object* ihm; *reflexively* sich; *referring to personified things or animals which correspond to German feminines/neuters* sie/es; *as indirect object* ihr/ihm; **it was ~:** er wars; *see also* **her¹**

Himalayan /hɪmə'leɪən/ *adj.* Himalaja-

Himalayas /hɪmə'leɪəz/ *pr. n. pl.* Himalaja, *der*

himself /hɪm'self/ *pron.* **1** *emphat.* selbst **2** *refl.* sich. *see also* **herself**

hind¹ /haɪnd/ *n.* Hirschkuh, *die*

hind² *adj.* hinter...; **~ legs** Hinterbeine; **get up on one's ~ legs** (fig. joc.) sich hinstellen; *see also* **donkey**

hinder /'hɪndə(r)/
A *v.t.* (impede) behindern; (delay) verzögern ‹*Vollendung einer Arbeit, Vorgang*›; aufhalten ‹*Person*›; **~ sb. in his work** jmdn. bei der Arbeit behindern; **~ sb. from doing sth.** jmdn. daran hindern, etw. zu tun
B *v.i.* **will it help or ~?** bedeutet es eine Erleichterung oder eine Erschwernis?

Hindi /'hɪndi:/ ▸**i** **p. 1277**
A *adj.* Hindi-; *see also* **English A**
B *n.* Hindi, *das; see also* **English B 1**

hind: ~most *adj.* (furthest behind) hinterst...; *see also* **devil A 3; ~quarters** *n. pl.* Hinterteil, *das;* (of large quadruped) Hinterteil, *das;* Hinterhand, *die* (fachspr.)

hindrance /'hɪndrəns/ *n.* **1** (action) Behinderung, *die; see also* **let² 1 2** (obstacle) Hindernis, *das* (**to** für); **he is more of a ~ than a help** er stört mehr, als dass er hilft; **be a ~ to navigation** ein Hindernis für die Schifffahrt sein *od.* darstellen

'hindsight *n.* **in ~, with [the benefit of] ~:** im Nachhinein

Hindu /'hɪndu:, hɪn'du:/ ▸**i** **p. 1345**
A *n.* Hindu, *der*
B *adj.* hinduistisch; Hindu‹*gott, -tempel*›

Hinduism /'hɪndu:ɪzm/ *n., no pl.* Hinduismus, *der*

Hindustani /hɪndə'stɑ:ni:/ ▸**i** **p. 1277**
A *adj.* **1** hindustanisch **2** (Ling.) Hindustani-; hindustanisch; *see also* **English A**
B *n.* Hindustani, *das; see also* **English B 1**

hinge /hɪndʒ/
A *n.* **1** Scharnier, *das;* (piano ~) Klavierband, *das;* **off its ~s** ‹*Tür*› aus den Angeln gehoben **2** (Zool.: of bivalve) Schloss, *das*
B *v.t.* mit Scharnieren/einem Scharnier versehen; **~ sth. to sth.** etw. mit Scharnieren/einem Scharnier an etw. (*Dat.*) befestigen
C *v.i.* **1** (hang and turn) **~ [up]on sth.** mit Scharnieren/einem Scharnier an etw. (*Dat.*) befestigt sein **2** (fig.: depend) abhängen (**[up]on** von); hängen (ugs.) (**[up]on** an + *Dat.*)

hinged /hɪndʒd/ *adj.* mit Scharnieren/einem Scharnier versehen; **~ lid** Klappdeckel, *der*

hinny /'hɪnɪ/ *n.* (Zool.) Maulesel, *der*

hint /hɪnt/
A *n.* **1** (suggestion) Wink, *der;* Hinweis, *der;* **give a ~ that ...:** andeuten, dass ...; **give no ~ that ...:** nicht einmal andeutungsweise zu erkennen geben, dass ...; **is that a ~?** ist das ein Wink mit dem Zaunpfahl? (scherzh.); **~, ~!** (joc.) wenn ich mal mit dem Zaunpfahl winken darf (scherzh.); *see also* **broad A 2; drop C 4; take A 22 2** (slight trace) Spur, *die* (**of** von); **the ~/no ~ of a smile** der Anflug/nicht die Spur eines Lächelns; **there was a ~ of sadness in his smile** in seinem Lächeln zeigte sich ein Anflug von Traurigkeit; **a ~ of aniseed** ein Hauch von Anis **3** (practical information) Tipp, *der* (**on** für); **car repair ~s** Tips für die Autoreparatur
B *v.t.* **~ that ...**andeuten, dass ...; **nothing has yet been ~ed about it** darüber hat man noch nichts herausgelassen (ugs.)
C *v.i.* **~ at** andeuten

hinterland /'hɪntəlænd/ *n.* Hinterland, *das;* (area surrounding city) Umland, *das*

hip¹ /hɪp/ *n.* **1** ▸**i** **p. 951** Hüfte, *die;* **with one's hands on one's ~s** die Arme in die Hüften gestemmt; **shoot from the ~** (lit. or fig.) aus der Hüfte schießen **2** *in sing. or pl.* (~ measurement) Hüftumfang, *der;* Hüftweite, *die;* (of man, boy) Gesäßumfang, *der;* Gesäßweite, *die;* **have thirty-seven-inch ~s** *or* **a thirty-seven-inch ~:** eine Hüftweite/Gesäßweite von vierundneunzig Zentimetern haben; **how large are your ~s?** welche Hüftweite/Gesäßweite hast du? **3** (Archit.) Grat, *der*

hip² *n.* (Bot.) Hagebutte, *die*

hip³ *int.* ▸**hurrah A**

hip⁴ *adj.* (coll.) **1** (fashionable) [sehr] modisch **2** **be ~ to sth.** über etw. (*Akk.*) auf dem Laufenden sein

hip: ~ bath *n.* Sitzbad, *das;* **~ bone** *n.* (Anat.) Hüftbein, *das;* Hüftknochen, *der;* **~ flask** *n.* Taschenflasche, *die;* Flachmann, *der* (ugs. scherzh.); **~ hop** *n.* Hip-Hop, *der;* **~ joint** *n.* (Anat.) Hüftgelenk, *das;* **~-length** *adj.* hüftlang ‹*Kleidungsstück*›; **~ measurement** *n.* Hüftumfang, *der;* Hüftweite, *die;* (of man, boy) Gesäßumfang, *der;* Gesäßweite, *die*

hippie /'hɪpɪ/ *n.* (coll.) Hippie, *der*

hippo /'hɪpəʊ/ *n., pl.* **~s** (coll.) ▸**hippopotamus**

hip 'pocket *n.* Gesäßtasche, *die*

Hippocratic oath /hɪpəkrætɪk 'əʊθ/ *n.* (Med.) Eid des Hippokrates

hippopotamus /hɪpə'pɒtəməs/ *n., pl.* **~es** *or* **hippopotami** /hɪpə'pɒtəmaɪ/ (Zool.) Nilpferd, *das;* Flusspferd, *das*

hippy /'hɪpɪ/ ▸**hippie**

hip: ~ roof *n.* (Archit.) Walmdach, *das;* **~ size** ▸**~ measurement**

hipster /'hɪpstə(r)/
A *adj.* auf der Hüfte sitzend ‹*Hose*›
B *in pl.* Hüfthose, *die*

hire /haɪə(r)/
A *n.* **1** (action) Mieten, *das;* (of worker) Einstellen, *das;* **conditions of ~:** Mietbedingungen **2** (condition) **be on ~ [to sb.]** [an jmdn.] vermietet sein; **for** *or* **on ~:** zu vermieten; **'for ~'** „frei"; **there are boats for** *or* **on ~:** man kann Boote mieten **3** (amount) Leihgebühr, *die*
B *v.t.* **1** (employ) anwerben; engagieren ‹*Anwalt, Berater usw.*›; **~d assassin** gedungener Mörder **2** (obtain use of) mieten; **~ sth. from sb.** etw. bei jmdm. mieten **3** (grant use of) vermieten; **~ sth. to sb.** etw. jmdm. *od.* an jmdn. vermieten
Phrasal verb
• **~ 'out** *v.t.* vermieten

'hire car *n.* Mietwagen, *der;* Leihwagen, *der*

hired /haɪəd/: **~ car** ▸**hire car**; **~ girl** *n.* (Amer.) Hausmädchen, *das;* (on farm) Magd, *die* (veralt.); **~ man** *n.* (Amer.) Gehilfe, *der;* (on farm) Knecht, *der* (veralt.)

hireling /ˈhaɪəlɪŋ/ *n.* Söldling, *der* (abwertend); Mietling, *der* (abwertend)

hire 'purchase *n., no pl., no art.* (Brit.) Ratenkauf, *der;* Teilzahlungskauf, *der; attrib.* Raten-; Teilzahlungs-; **pay for/buy sth. on ~:** etw. in Raten bezahlen/auf Raten *od.* Teilzahlung kaufen

hirer /ˈhaɪərə(r)/ *n.* Mieter, *der*/Mieterin, *die;* (who grants use) Vermieter, *der*/Vermieterin, *die*

hirsute /ˈhɜːsjuːt/ *adj.* behaart; (unkempt) zottelig; struppig

his /ɪz, *stressed* hɪz/ *poss. pron.* **1** *attrib.* sein; *referring to personified things or animals which correspond to German feminines/neuters* ihr/sein; *see also* **her²** **2** *pred.* (the one[s] belonging to him) seiner/seine/sein[e]s; der/die/das seine *od.* seinige (geh.); **towels labelled '~' and 'hers'** mit „Er" und „Sie" gekennzeichnete Handtücher; *see also* **hers**

Hispanic /hɪˈspænɪk/
A *adj.* lateinamerikanisch; **~ studies** Hispanistik, *die;* **~ Americans** Hispanoamerikaner
B *n.* Lateinamerikaner, *der*/-amerikanerin, *die;* Hispanoamerikaner, *der*/-amerikanerin, *die*

Hispanicist /hɪˈspænɪsɪst/, **Hispanist** /ˈhɪspənɪst/ *n.* Hispanist, *der*/Hispanistin, *die*

hiss /hɪs/
A *n.* (of goose, snake, escaping steam, crowd, audience) Zischen, *das;* (of cat, locomotive) Fauchen, *das*
B *v.i.* ‹*Gans, Schlange, Dampf, Publikum, Menge:*› zischen; ‹*Katze, Lokomotive:*› fauchen
C *v.t.* **1** (express disapproval of) auszischen ‹*Redner, Schauspieler*› **2** (utter with a hiss) zischen

histamine /ˈhɪstəmiːn/ *n.* (Physiol.) Histamin, *das*

histogram /ˈhɪstəgræm/ *n.* (Statistics) Histogramm, *das*

histology /hɪˈstɒlədʒɪ/ *n.* (Biol.) Histologie, *die*

historian /hɪˈstɔːrɪən/ *n.* **1** ▸**i** **p. 1260** (writer of history) Geschichtsschreiber, *der*/schreiberin, *die* **2** (scholar of history) Historiker, *der*/Historikerin, *die*

historic /hɪˈstɒrɪk/ *adj.* **1** (famous) historisch **2** (Ling.) historisch ‹*Tempus usw.*›

historical /hɪˈstɒrɪkl/ *adj.* **1** historisch; geschichtlich ‹*Belege, Hintergrund*›; **~ research** Geschichtsforschung, *die;* **of ~ interest** von historischem *od.* geschichtlichem Interesse **2** (belonging to the past) in früheren Zeiten üblich ‹*Methode*›; **be ~:** der Geschichte angehören

historically /hɪˈstɒrɪkəlɪ/ *adv.* **1** (with respect to history) historisch **2** (as a matter of history) in der Geschichte

historiography /hɪstɒrɪˈɒgrəfɪ/ *n., no pl.* Geschichtsschreibung, *die;* Historiographie, *die*

history /ˈhɪstərɪ/ *n.* **1** (continuous record) Geschichte, *die;* **histories** historische Darstellungen **2** *no pl., no art.* Geschichte, *die;* (study of past events) Geschichte, *die;* Geschichtswissenschaft, *die;* **~ relates ...:** die Geschichte erzählt ...; **that's [all] [past] ~:** das ist [alles] [längst] vergangen [und vergessen]; das gehört [alles] [längst] der Vergangenheit an; **~ repeats itself** die Geschichte wiederholt sich; **make [boxing] ~:** Geschichte [im Boxen] machen; **go down in ~:** in die Geschichte eingehen; **and the rest is ~:** und das Weitere ist [ja] bekannt **3** (train of events) Geschichte, *die;* (of person) Werdegang, *der;* **have a ~ of asthma/shoplifting** schon lange an Asthma leiden/eine Vorgeschichte als Ladendieb haben **4** (eventful past career) Geschichte, *die;* **he has quite a ~:** er hat eine bewegte Vergangenheit **5** (Theatre) historisches Drama; **Shakespeare's histories** Shakespeares Historien. *See also* **ancient A 1**; **case history**; **life history**; **medieval history**; **natural history**

'history book *n.* Geschichtsbuch, *das*

histrionic /hɪstrɪˈɒnɪk/
A *adj.* **1** schauspielerisch ‹*Talent, Fähigkeiten*›; **~ art** Schauspielkunst, *die* **2** (stagy) theatralisch (abwertend)
B *n. in pl.* (melodramatic behaviour) theatralisches Getue (abwertend); **forget the ~s!** lass die Schauspielerei! (ugs. abwertend)

hit /hɪt/
A *v.t.*, **-tt-**, **hit** **1** (strike with blow) schlagen; (strike with missile) treffen; ‹*Geschoss, Ball usw.:*› treffen; **I've been ~!** (struck by bullet) ich bin getroffen!; **I could ~ him** (fig. coll.) ich könnte ihm eine runterhauen (ugs.); **the ball ~ me in the face** der Ball traf mich ins Gesicht; **~ sb. over the head** jmdm. eins überziehen (ugs.); **~ one's thumb** sich (*Dat.*) auf den Daumen schlagen; **~ by lightning** vom Blitz getroffen; **~ a man when he's down** (fig.) jmdn. treten, der schon am Boden liegt; *see also* **belt A 1**; **nail A 2**; **note A 1**
2 (come forcibly into contact with) ‹*Fahrzeug:*› prallen gegen ‹*Mauer usw.*›; ‹*Schiff:*› laufen gegen ‹*Felsen usw.*›; **the aircraft ~ the ground** das Flugzeug schlug auf den Boden auf; **the noise of the hammer ~ting the anvil** das Geräusch des Hammers beim Auftreffen auf den Amboss; **~ the roof** *or* **ceiling** (fig. coll.: become angry) an die Decke *od.* in die Luft gehen (ugs.)
3 (cause to come into contact) [an]stoßen; [an]schlagen; **~ one's head on sth.** mit dem Kopf gegen etw. stoßen; sich (*Dat.*) den Kopf an etw. (*Dat.*) stoßen
4 (deliver) **~ sb. a blow** jmdm. einen Schlag verpassen (ugs.)
5 (fig.: cause to suffer) **~ sb. badly** *or* **hard** jmdn. schwer treffen; **I will ~ them very hard** (take severe measures against) ich werde mit aller Schärfe gegen sie vorgehen
6 (fig.: affect) treffen; **have been ~ by frost/rain** *etc.* durch Frost/Regen *usw.* gelitten haben
7 (fig.: light upon) finden; stoßen *od.* treffen auf (+ *Akk.*); finden ‹*Bodenschätze*›; **you've ~ it!** du sagst es!
8 (fig.: characterize) ▸**~ off**
9 (fig. coll.) (encounter) Bekanntschaft machen mit (+ *Dat.*) (ugs.); (arrive at) erreichen ‹*Höchstform, bestimmten Ort, bestimmte Höhe, bestimmtes Alter usw.*›; **I think we've ~ a snag** ich glaube, jetzt gibts Probleme; **~ a pool of water** ‹*Auto:*› in eine [Wasser]pfütze fahren; **~ an all-time high** ‹*Preis:*› eine Rekordhöhe erreichen; **the car can ~ 100 miles an hour** das Auto schafft 100 Meilen in der Stunde (ugs.); **they ~ all the night spots** sie statteten allen Nachtlokalen einen Besuch ab (ugs.); **~ town** ankommen; **~ the trail** (Amer. coll.) *or* **the road** sich auf den Weg *od.* (ugs.) die Socken machen; **~ the hay** (coll.) in die Falle gehen (ugs.); sich in die Falle hauen (ugs.)
10 (fig. coll.: indulge in) **[begin to] ~ the bottle** das Trinken anfangen
11 (Cricket) erzielen ‹*Lauf*›; **~ the ball for six** (Brit.) sechs Läufe auf einmal erzielen; **~ sb. for six** (Brit.) gegen jmdn. sechs Läufe erzielen; (fig.: defeat) jmdn. übertrumpfen; **~ the enemy for six** (Brit.) den Feind zerschmettern
B *v.i.*, **-tt-**, **hit** **1** (direct a blow) schlagen; **~ hard** fest *od.* hart zuschlagen; **~ at sb./sth.** auf jmdn./etw. einschlagen; (fig.: criticize) jmdn./etw. kritisieren; **~ at sth. as being extravagant** etw. als verschwenderisch geißeln; **~ and run** ‹*Autofahrer:*› Fahrer- *od.* Unfallflucht begehen; ‹*Angreifer:*› einen Blitzüberfall machen; *see also* **~-and-run**
2 (come into forcible contact) **~ against** *or* **upon sth.** gegen *od.* auf etw. (*Akk.*) stoßen
C *n.* **1** (blow) Schlag, *der*
2 (sarcastic remark) Seitenhieb, *der* (**at** gegen); Spitze, *die* (**at** gegen); (censure, rebuke) Angriff, *der;* **that's a ~ at me** das geht gegen mich
3 (shot or bomb striking target) Treffer, *der*
4 (success) Erfolg, *der;* Knüller, *der* (ugs.); (success in entertainment) Schlager, *der;* Hit, *der* (ugs.); **make a ~:** gut ankommen; **make** *or* **be a ~ with sb.** bei jmdm. einschlagen *od.* gut ankommen; **I'm sure she'll be** *or* **make a [big] ~:** ich bin sicher, sie wird [ganz] groß herauskommen (ugs.)
5 (stroke of luck) Glückstreffer, *der*
6 (Computing) (in search) Treffer, *der;* (on Web site) Hit, *der*
Phrasal verbs
• **~ 'back**
A *v.t.* zurückschlagen
B *v.i.* zurückschlagen; (verbally) kontern; sich wehren; **~ back at sb.** (fig.) jmdm. Kontra geben
• **~ 'off** *v.t.* **1** (characterize) genau treffen; treffend charakterisieren **2** **~ it off [with each other]** gut miteinander auskommen; **~ it off with sb.** gut mit jmdm. auskommen
• **~ on** ▸**~ upon**
• **~ 'out** *v.i.* **1** (aim blows) drauflosschlagen **2** **~ out at** *or* **against sb./sth.** (fig.) jmdn./etw. scharf angreifen *od.* attackieren
• **~ upon** *v.t.* stoßen auf (+ *Akk.*); finden ‹*richtige Antwort, Methode*›; kommen auf (+ *Akk.*) ‹*Idee*›

hit: ~-and-'miss ▸**~-or-miss**; **~-and-'run** *adj.* **1** unfallflüchtig ‹*Fahrer*›; **~-and-run accident** Unfall mit Fahrerflucht; **2** Blitz‹*-angriff, -überfall*›; **~-and-run tactics** Taktik des Blitzüberfalls

hitch /hɪtʃ/
A *v.t.* **1** (move by a jerk) rücken **2** (fasten) [fest]binden ‹*Tier*› (**to** an + *Akk.*); binden ‹*Seil*› (**round** um + *Akk.*); [an]koppeln ‹*Anhänger usw.*› (**to** an + *Akk.*); spannen ‹*Zugtier, -maschine usw.*› (**to** vor + *Akk.*); **get ~ed** (coll.) heiraten; *see also* **wagon 1** **3** **~ a lift** *or* **ride** (coll.) per Anhalter fahren; trampen; **he was trying to ~ a lift** *or* **ride** er wollte mitgenommen werden
B *v.i.* ▸**hitch-hike A**
C *n.* **1** (jerk) Ruck, *der;* **give sth. a ~:** an etw. (*Dat.*) rucken **2** (Naut.: knot) Stek, *der* (Seemannsspr.); **half ~:** halber Schlag; *see also* **clove hitch** **3** (stoppage) Unterbrechung, *die;* **go off without a ~:** glatt *od.* reibungslos über die Bühne gehen **4** (impediment) Problem, *das;* Schwierigkeit, *die;* **have one ~:** einen Haken haben (ugs.) **5** ▸**hitch-hike B**
Phrasal verb
• **~ 'up** *v.t.* **1** hochheben ‹*Rock*›; **~ up one's trousers** seinen Hosenbund hochziehen **2** (attach) anspannen

hitch: ~-hike **A** *v.i.* per Anhalter fahren; trampen; **B** *n.* Tramptour, *die;* **~-hiker** *n.* Anhalter, *der*/Anhalterin, *die;* Tramper, *der*/Tramperin, *die;* **~-hiking** *n.* Trampen, *das*

hitching post /ˈhɪtʃɪŋpəʊst/ *n.* Pfosten, *der* (*zum Anbinden von Zug- und Reittieren*)

hi-tech ▸**high-tech**

hither /ˈhɪðə(r)/ *adv.* (literary) hierher; **~ and thither** hierhin und dorthin; *see also* **come-~**

hitherto /ˈhɪðətʊ, hɪðəˈtuː/ *adv.* (literary) bisher; bislang; (up to that time) bis dahin

hit: ~ list *n.* **1** (charts) ▸**~ parade**; **2** (victims) Abschussliste, *die* (fig.); **~ man** *n.* (coll.) Killer, *der* (salopp); **~-or-'miss** *adj.* (coll.) (random) unsicher, unzuverlässig ‹*Methode*›; (careless) schlampig, schluderig (ugs. abwertend) ‹*Arbeit*›; **it was a very ~-or-miss affair** das ging alles aufs Geratewohl (ugs.); **~ parade** *n.* Hitparade, *die;* Schlagerparade, *die;* **~ 'record** *n.* Hit, *der* (ugs.); **~ squad** *n.* **1** (team of assassins) Killerkommando, *das;* **2** (Brit.: government commission) Spezialeinheit, *die;* Sonderkommission, *die*

Hittite /ˈhɪtaɪt/ ▸**i** **p. 1277**, ▸**i** **p. 1345**
A *n.* **1** Hethiter, *der*/Hethiterin, *die* **2** (Ling.) Hethitisch, *das*
B *adj.* hethitisch

h

HIV *abbr.* (Med.) = **human immunodeficiency virus** HIV; **~-positive/-negative** HIV-positiv/-negativ; **~-infected** HIV-infiziert

hive /haɪv/

A *n.* **1** [Bienen]stock, *der;* (of straw) Bienenkorb, *der;* **frame ~:** Bienenkasten, *der* **2** (fig.: busy place) **what a ~ of industry!** der reinste Bienenstock! (ugs.); **the office is a [regular] ~ of industry** in dem Büro geht es zu wie in einem Bienenstock

B *v.t.* in einen Stock bringen, einfangen ‹*Bienen*›

Phrasal verb

• **~ 'off** *v.t.* (Brit.) (separate and make independent) verselbstständigen; (assign) zuweisen, übertragen ‹*Aufgabe usw.*› (**to** *Dat.*); **the firm was ~d off from the parent company** die Firma wurde aus der Muttergesellschaft ausgegliedert

hiya /'haɪjə/ *int.* (coll.) hallo!

HM *abbr.* **1** = **Her/His Majesty** I. M./S. M. **2** = **Her/His Majesty's 3** = **headmaster/headmistress** ≈ Dir.

HMG *abbr.* (Brit.) = **Her/His Majesty's Government**

HMI *abbr.* (Brit.) = **Her/His Majesty's Inspector [of Schools]**

HMS *abbr.* (Brit.) = **Her/His Majesty's Ship** H.M.S.

HMSO *abbr.* (Brit.) = **Her/His Majesty's Stationery Office**

HNC *abbr.* (Brit.) = **Higher National Certificate**

HND *abbr.* (Brit.) = **Higher National Diploma**

ho /həʊ/ *int.* **1** *expr. surprise* oh; nanu; *expr. admiration* oh; *expr. triumph* ha; *drawing attention* he; heda; *expr. derision* haha; **land ho!** Land in Sicht! **2** (Naut. Hist.: rallying cry) **westward ho!** auf nach Westen!

ho. *abbr.* = **house**

hoagie /'həʊgɪ/ *n.* (esp. Amer.) Schlemmerbaguette, *das*

hoard /hɔːd/

A *n.* **1** (store laid by) Vorrat, *der;* **make/collect a ~ of sth.** etw. horten **2** (fig.: amassed stock) Sammlung, *die;* **he had accumulated a ~ of grievances** bei ihm hatten sich eine Menge Klagen angehäuft *od.* angestaut **3** (Archaeol.) Hort, *der* (fachspr.)

B *v.t.* **~ [up]** horten ‹*Geld, Brennmaterial, Lebensmittel usw.*›; hamstern ‹*Lebensmittel*›

C *v.i.* horten

hoarder /'hɔːdə(r)/ *n.* Hamsterer, *der*/Hamsterin, *die*

hoarding¹ /'hɔːdɪŋ/ *n.* Horten, *das;* Hamstern, *das*

hoarding² *n.* **1** (fence) Bretterzaun, *der;* Bretterwand, *die;* (round building site) Bauzaun, *der* **2** (Brit.: for advertisements) Reklamewand, *die;* Plakatwand, *die*

hoar frost /'hɔːfrɒst/ *n.* [Rau]reif, *der*

hoarse /hɔːs/ *adj.* **1** (rough, husky) heiser ‹*Laut*›; heiser, rau ‹*Stimme*›; (croaking) krächzend ‹*Laut*›; (with emotion) belegt ‹*Stimme*› **2** (having a dry, husky voice) heiser; **shout oneself ~:** sich heiser schreien

hoarsely /'hɔːslɪ/ *adv.* (in a hoarse voice) heiser ‹*sprechen*›; mit heiserer Stimme ‹*reden, schreien, singen*›; (in an emotional voice) mit belegter Stimme

hoarseness /'hɔːsnɪs/ *n.* Heiserkeit, *die*

hoary /'hɔːrɪ/ *adj.* **1** (grey) grau; ergraut (geh.); (white) [schloh]weiß; **become ~:** grau werden, (geh.) ergrauen/weiß werden **2** (having grey hair) grauhaarig; ergraut (geh.); (having white hair) weißhaarig **3** (very old) **~ [old] joke** uralter Witz

hoax /həʊks/

A *v.t.* anführen (ugs.); foppen; zum Besten haben *od.* halten; **I'd been ~ed** ich hatte mich anführen (ugs.) *od.* foppen lassen; **~ sb. into believing sth.** jmdm. etw. weismachen

B *n.* (deception) Schwindel, *der;* (false report) Falschmeldung, *die;* Ente, *die* (ugs.); (practical joke) Streich, *der;* (false alarm) blinder Alarm

'hoax call *n.* Scherzanruf, *der;* (to emergency services) falscher Notruf

hoaxer /'həʊksə(r)/ *n.* Schwindler, *der*/Schwindlerin, *die*

hob /hɒb/ *n.* **1** (of cooker) Kochmulde, *die* (Fachspr.); [Koch]platte, *die;* Kochstelle, *die* **2** (at side of fireplace) Kamineinsatz, *der* **3** (peg) Zielpflock, *der*

hobble /'hɒbl/

A *v.i.* **~ [about]** [herum]humpeln *od.* -hinken

B *v.t.* **1** (cause to ~) [beim Gehen] behindern **2** (tie together legs of) an den Füßen fesseln ‹*Pferd usw.*› **3** (tie together) fesseln ‹*Vorderbeine*›

C *n.* **1** *no pl.* (uneven gait) Humpeln, *das;* Hinken, *das* **2** (device for hobbling) [Fuß]fessel, *die*

hobby¹ /'hɒbɪ/ *n.* Hobby, *das;* Steckenpferd, *das;* **do sth. as a ~:** etw. als Hobby tun

hobby² *n.* (Ornith.) Baumfalke, *der*

'hobby horse *n.* **1** (wicker horse) Pferdemaske, *die* **2** (child's toy) Steckenpferd, *das* **3** ▸**rocking horse 4** (favourite topic) Lieblingsthema, *das;* **get on to/start on one's ~:** anfangen, sein Steckenpferd zu reiten (scherzh.)

hob: ~goblin *n.* **1** (mischievous imp) Kobold, *der;* Puck, *der;* **2** (bogy) Schreckgespenst, *das;* **~nail** *n.* [starker] Schuh- *od.* Stiefelnagel; **~nailed** /'hɒbneɪld/ *adj.* Nagel‹*schuh, -stiefel*›; **~-nob** *v.i.*, **-bb-: I've seen them ~-nobbing [together] a lot recently** ich habe sie in letzter Zeit viel zusammen gesehen; **he's always ~-nobbing with the aristocracy** er verkehrt viel in adeligen Kreisen

hobo /'həʊbəʊ/ *n.*, *pl.* **~es** (Amer.) Landstreicher, *der*/-streicherin, *die*

Hobson's choice /hɒbsnz 'tʃɔɪs/ *n.* **it was [a case of] ~:** es gab eigentlich gar keine Wahl

hock¹ /hɒk/ (joint of quadruped's leg) Sprunggelenk, *das*

hock² *n.* (Brit.: wine) Rheinwein, *der*

hock³ (Amer. coll.)

A *v.t.* versetzen

B *n.* **be in ~** (in pawn) versetzt sein; (in prison) [im Kittchen *od.* Knast] sitzen (ugs.); Knast schieben (salopp); (in debt) in Schulden stecken; **put sth. in ~:** etw. versetzen; **put sb. in ~** (in debt) jmdn. in Schulden stürzen; (in prison) jmdn. einlochen (salopp); **be in ~ to sb.** bei jmdm. in der Kreide stehen (ugs.)

hockey /'hɒkɪ/ *n.* **1** Hockey, *das* **2** (Can.: ice ~) Eishockey, *das*

hockey: ~ player *n.* Hockeyspieler, *der*/-spielerin, *die;* **~ stick** *n.* Hockeystock, *der;* Hockeyschläger, *der*

hocus-pocus /həʊkəs'pəʊkəs/ *n.* (deception) Zauberei, *die*

hod /hɒd/ *n.* **1** (Building) Tragmulde, *die* **2** (for coal) Kohlenschütte, *die*

hodgepodge /'hɒdʒpɒdʒ/ ▸**hotchpotch**

hoe /həʊ/

A *n.* Hacke, *die; see also* **Dutch hoe**

B *v.t.* hacken ‹*Beet, Acker*›; **~ up** weg- *od.* heraushacken ‹*Unkraut*›; **~ in** einhacken; *see also* **hard A 2**

C *v.i.* hacken

'hoedown *n.* (Amer.) **1** (dance) Hoedown, *der* **2** (party) Schwof, *der* (ugs.)

hog /hɒg/

A *n.* **1** (domesticated pig) [Mast]schwein, *das;* **go the whole ~** (coll.) Nägel mit Köpfen machen (ugs.); **go the whole ~ with sb.** so weit wie jmd. gehen; **live high off** *or* **on the ~** (Amer.) aus dem Vollen leben **2** (Zool.: animal of family Suidae) Schwein, *das* **3** (fig.: person) Schwein, *das* (derb); Sau, *die* (derb); Ferkel, *das* (derb)

B *v.t.*, **-gg-** (coll.) sich (*Dat.*) unter den Nagel reißen; **~ the middle of the road** ‹*Fahrer:*› die Mitte der Straße für sich beanspruchen; **~ the bathroom** das Badezimmer mit Beschlag belegen

'hogback *n.* (Geog.) [scharfer, steiler und langer] Grat

hoggish /'hɒgɪʃ/ *adj.* verfressen (salopp abwertend)

Hogmanay /'hɒgməneɪ/ *n.* (Scot., N. Engl.) Silvester, *der od. das*

hog's back /'hɒgz bæk/ ▸**hogback**

hogshead /'hɒgzhed/ *n.* **1** (cask) [großes] Fass; Oxhoftfass, *das* **2** (measure) Oxhoft, *das*

hog: ~-tie *v.t.* (Amer.) **1** (secure) an Händen und Füßen fesseln ‹*Person*›; an allen vieren fesseln ‹*Tier*›; **2** (fig.: impede) in ein zu enges Korsett zwängen; **sb. is ~-tied** jmdm. sind Hände und Füße gebunden; **~-wash** *n.* **1** (coll.: nonsense) Quatsch, *der* (salopp); **2** (pigswill) Schweinefutter, *das;* **~weed** *n.* (Bot.) Wiesenbärenklau, *der*

ho-'ho *int. expr. surprise* ach ne!; *expr. triumph, derision* haha!

hoick /hɔɪk/ *v.t.* (Brit. coll.) wuchten ‹[*schweren*] *Gegenstand*› (**over** über + *Akk.*, **into** in + *Akk.*)

hoi polloi /hɔɪ pɒ'lɔɪ/ *n. pl.* (derog.) **[the] ~:** das [gemeine] Volk; die Masse; der Pöbel (abwertend)

hoist /hɔɪst/

A *v.t.* **1** (raise aloft) hoch-, aufziehen, hissen ‹*Flagge usw.*›; heißen (Seemannsspr.) ‹*Flagge usw.*›; setzen (Seemannsspr.) ‹*Signal usw.*›; **~ sth. up a mast** etw. an einem Mast hoch-/aufziehen/hissen/heißen/setzen **2** (raise by tackle etc.) hieven ‹*Last*›; setzen ‹*Segel*›

B *n.* **1** (act of hoisting) [Hoch]hieven, *das* **2** (part of flag) Liek, *das* **3** (goods lift) [Lasten]aufzug, *der*

C *adj.* **be ~ with one's own petard** sich in seiner eigenen Schlinge fangen

hoity-toity /hɔɪtɪ'tɔɪtɪ/ *adj.* (coll.) hochnäsig (abwertend); eingebildet; (petulant) pikiert

hokum /'həʊkəm/ *n.* (coll.) Humbug, *der*

hold¹ /həʊld/ *n.* (of ship) Laderaum, *der;* (of aircraft) Frachtraum, *der*

hold²

A *v.t.*, **held** /held/ **1** (grasp) halten; (carry) tragen; (keep fast) festhalten; **~ sb. by the arm** jmdn. am Arm festhalten; **they held each other tight** sie hielten sich fest umschlungen; **~ one's belly/head** *etc.* sich (*Dat.*) den Bauch/Kopf *usw.* halten; **~ tight!** (in bus etc.) festhalten!; *see also* **baby A 1**; **clock A 1**; **hand A 1**; **nose A 1**

2 (support) ‹*tragendes Teil:*› halten, stützen, tragen ‹*Decke, Dach usw.*›; aufnehmen ‹*Gewicht, Kraft*›

3 (keep in position) halten; **~ the door open for sb.** jmdm. die Tür aufhalten; **~ sth. in place** etw. halten; **~ sth. over sb.** (fig.) jmdm. ständig mit etw. drohen; *see also* **candle A 1**

4 (grasp to control) halten ‹*Kind, Hund, Zügel*›

5 (keep in particular attitude) **~ oneself well/badly/straight** sich gut/schlecht/gerade halten; **~ oneself still** stillhalten; **~ oneself ready** *or* **in readiness** sich bereit *od.* in Bereitschaft halten; **~ oneself ready** *or* **in readiness to do sth.** jederzeit bereit sein, etw. zu tun; **~ one's head high** (fig.) (be confident) selbstbewusst sein *od.* auftreten; (be proud) den Kopf hoch tragen

6 (contain) enthalten; bergen ‹*Gefahr, Geheimnis*›; (be able to contain) fassen ‹*Liter, Personen usw.*›; **the bag ~s flour** in dem Sack wird Mehl aufbewahrt; **the room ~s ten people** in dem Raum haben 10 Leute Platz; der Raum bietet 10 Leuten Platz; **the box won't ~ these books** diese Bücher gehen nicht in die Kiste; **the disaster may ~ lessons for the future** aus dem Unglück kann man vielleicht Lehren für die Zukunft ziehen; **no one knows what the future will ~:** niemand weiß, was die Zukunft bringt *od.* bringen wird; **~ water** ‹*Behälter:*› wasserdicht sein; Wasser halten; (fig.) ‹*Argument, Theorie:*› stichhaltig sein, hieb- und stichfest sein; ‹*Annahme, Theorie, Alibi:*› haltbar sein

7 (not be intoxicated by) **he can/can't ~ his drink** *or* **liquor** er kann etwas/nichts vertragen

8 (possess) besitzen; haben; halten (Wirtsch.) ‹*Aktien, Anteile*›

9 (Cards: have in one's hand) [auf der Hand] haben

10 (have gained) halten ‹*Rekord*›; haben ‹*Diplom, Doktorgrad*›

11 (keep possession of) halten ‹*Stützpunkt, Stadt, Stellung*›; (Mus.: sustain) [aus]halten ‹*Ton*›; **~ one's own** (fig.) sich behaupten; **~ one's position** (fig.) auf seinem Standpunkt beharren; **~ the line on the price/over one's demands**

den Preis [stabil] halten/in seinen Forderungen hart *od.* fest bleiben; *see also* **12**; **fort**; **ground¹ A 2**

12 (occupy) innehaben, (geh.) bekleiden ‹*Posten, Amt, Stellung*›; ~ **office** im Amt sein; ~ **the line** (Teleph.) am Apparat bleiben; *see also* **11**; ~ **the road well** ‹*Auto:*› eine gute Straßenlage haben

13 (engross) fesseln, (geh.) gefangen halten ‹*Aufmerksamkeit, Publikum*›

14 (dominate) ~ **the stage** *or* **house** das Publikum *od.* ganze Haus in Bann halten (geh.); ~ **the floor** das Wort führen; das Gespräch/die Diskussion/Debatte *usw.* beherrschen *od.* bestimmen; *see also* **field A 5**

15 (keep in specified condition) halten; ~ **the ladder steady** die Leiter festhalten; ~ **the audience in suspense** das Publikum fesseln; *see also* **bay⁴ A**; **ransom A**

16 (detain) (in custody) in Haft halten, festhalten; (imprison) festsetzen; inhaftieren; (arrest) festnehmen; **be held in a prison** in einem Gefängnis einsitzen; ~ **a [connecting] train** einen [Anschluss]zug warten lassen; **there was nothing to ~ me there** da hielt mich nichts mehr

17 (oblige to adhere) ~ **sb. to the terms of the contract/to a promise** darauf bestehen, dass jmd. sich an die Vertragsbestimmungen hält/dass jmd. ein Versprechen hält *od.* einlöst; **You can have the car when I go abroad — I'll ~ you to that** Du kannst das Auto haben, wenn ich ins Ausland gehe — Ich werde dich beim Wort nehmen

18 (Sport: restrict) ~ **one's opponent [to a draw]** ein Unentschieden [gegen den Gegner] halten *od.* verteidigen; ~ **one's opponents to three goals** die Zahl der gegnerischen Tore bei drei halten

19 (cause to take place) stattfinden lassen; abhalten ‹*Veranstaltung, Konferenz, Gottesdienst, Sitzung, Prüfung*›; veranstalten ‹*Festival, Auktion*›; austragen ‹*Meisterschaften*›; führen ‹*Unterhaltung, Gespräch, Korrespondenz*›; durchführen ‹*Untersuchung*›; geben ‹*Empfang*›; halten ‹*Vortrag, Rede*›; **be held** stattfinden; ~ **a conversation with sb.** eine Unterhaltung mit jmdm. führen *od.* haben; sich mit jmdm. unterhalten; *see also* **court A 3**

20 (restrain) [fest]halten; ~ **sb. from doing sth.** jmdn. davon abhalten, etw. zu tun; ~ **one's fire** [noch] nicht schießen; (fig.: refrain from criticism) mit seiner Kritik zurückhalten; ~ **your fire!** nicht schießen!; (fig.) nun mal sachte! (ugs.); **there is/was no ~ing sb.** jmd. ist/war nicht mehr zu halten *od.* (ugs.) bremsen; für jmdn. gibt/gab es kein Halten mehr; *see also* **breath 1**; **hand A 2**; **peace 2**

21 (coll.: withhold) zurückhalten; ~ **one's payments** die Zahlungen einstellen; ~ **it!** [einen] Moment mal!; ~ **everything!** stopp! (ugs.); *see also* **horse A 1**

22 (think, believe) ~ **a view** *or* **an opinion** eine Ansicht haben (**on** über + *Akk.*); ~ **that ...:** dafürhalten, dass ...; der Ansicht sein, dass ...; ~ **sb. to be ...:** jmdn. für ... halten; glauben, dass jmd. ... ist; ~ **sb./oneself guilty/blameless** jmdn./sich für schuldig/unschuldig halten (**for** an + *Dat.*); ~ **sb. responsible for sth.** jmdn. für etw. verantwortlich machen; ~ **sb. in high/low regard** *or* **esteem** viel/wenig von jmdm. halten; jmdn. hoch schätzen (geh.)/gering schätzen; ~ **sth. against sb.** jmdm. etw. vorwerfen; ~ **it against sb. that ...:** jmdm. vorwerfen, dass ...; *see also* **cheap A 3**; **dear A 1**

23 (Law: pronounce) ~ **that ...:** entscheiden, dass ...

B *v.i.*, **held 1** (not give way) ‹*Seil, Nagel, Anker, Schloss, Angeklebtes:*› halten; ‹*Damm:*› [stand]halten

2 (remain unchanged) anhalten; [an]dauern; ‹*Wetter:*› sich halten, so bleiben; ‹*Angebot, Versprechen:*› gelten; **his luck held** er hatte auch weiterhin Glück

3 (remain steadfast) ~ **to sth.** bei etw. bleiben; an etw. (*Dat.*) festhalten; ~ **to** *or* **by one's family** zur Familie stehen *od.* halten; ~ **by one's beliefs/convictions** tun, was man für richtig hält; **he still ~s to the view that ...:** er ist nach wie vor der Ansicht, dass ...; *see also* **aloof A**

4 (be valid) ~ **[good** *or* **true]** gelten; Gültigkeit haben

C *n.* **1** (grasp) Griff, *der*; **grab** *or* **seize ~ of sth.** etw. ergreifen; **get** *or* **lay** *or* **take ~ of sth.** etw. fassen *od.* packen; (manage to grip on sth.) etw. zu fassen kriegen (ugs.) *od.* bekommen; (in order to carry it) etw. nehmen; **keep ~ of sth.** etw. festhalten; **keep/lose one's ~:** den Halt nicht verlieren/den Halt verlieren; **lose one's ~ on reality** den Sinn für die Realität verlieren; **take ~** (fig.) sich durchsetzen; ‹*Krankheit:*› fortschreiten; **get ~ of sth.** (fig.) etw. bekommen *od.* auftreiben; **if the newspapers get ~ of the story** wenn die Zeitungen Wind von der Sache bekommen (ugs.); **get ~ of sb.** (fig.) jmdn. erreichen; **get a ~ on oneself** sich fassen; **have a ~ over sb.** jmdn. in der Hand halten; *see also* **catch A 1**

2 (influence) Einfluss, *der* (**on, over** auf + *Akk.*); **lose one's ~:** seinen Einfluss verlieren; **gain a ~:** zu Einfluss gelangen

3 (Sport) Griff, *der*; **there are no ~s barred** (fig.) alles ist erlaubt

4 (thing to ~ by) Griff, *der*

5 **put on ~:** auf Eis legen ‹*Plan, Programm*›

Phrasal verbs

- ~ **'back**

A *v.t.* **1** (restrain) zurückhalten; ~ **sb. back from doing sth.** jmdn. [daran] hindern, etw. zu tun **2** (impede progress of) hindern; **nothing can ~ him back** er ist nicht mehr aufzuhalten **3** (withhold) zurückhalten; zurückhalten mit ‹*Bekanntgabe von Ergebnissen, Veröffentlichung eines Berichts*›; ~ **sth. back from sb.** jmdm. etw. vorenthalten

B *v.i.* zögern; ~ **back from doing sth.** zögern, etw. zu tun

- ~ **'down** *v.t.* **1** festhalten; (repress) unterdrücken; niederhalten ‹*Volk*›; (fig.: keep at low level) niedrig halten ‹*Preise, Löhne usw.*› **2** (keep) sich halten in (+ *Dat.*) ‹*Stellung, Position*›
- ~ **'forth**

A *v.t.* (offer) anpreisen

B *v.i.* sich in langen Reden ergehen (oft abwertend); ~ **forth about** *or* **on sth.** sich über etw. (*Akk.*) auslassen (abwertend)

- ~ **'in** *v.t.* zügeln ‹*Pferd, Temperament*›; einziehen ‹*Bauch*›; ~ **oneself in** (temper, emotions) sich beherrschen; an sich (*Akk.*) halten; (stomach) den Bauch einziehen
- ~ **'off**

A *v.t.* (keep at bay) von sich fernhalten, (ugs.) sich (*Dat.*) vom Leib halten ‹*Fans, Presse*›; in Schach halten ‹*gegnerische Stürmer*›; abwehren ‹*Angriff*›; Einhalt gebieten (+ *Dat.*) ‹*Inflation, Arbeitslosigkeit*›; **he's been ~ing her off for years** er hat sie jahrelang immer wieder abgewiesen; ~ **your dog off!** halten Sie Ihren Hund zurück!

B *v.i.* (restrain oneself) ‹*Käufer usw.:*› sich zurückhalten; ‹*Feind:*› sich ruhig verhalten; (be delayed) ‹*Regen, Monsun, Winter:*› ausbleiben, auf sich (*Akk.*) warten lassen

- ~ **'on**

A *v.t.* (keep in position) [fest]halten

B *v.i.* **1** (grip) sich festhalten; ~ **on to sb./sth.** sich an jmdm./etw. festhalten; (fig.: retain) jmdn./etw. behalten; **the firm should make every effort to ~ on to him** die Firma sollte alles versuchen, ihn zu halten **2** (continue) andauern; weitergehen **3** (stand firm) durchhalten; aushalten; ‹*Regierung:*› sich halten **4** (Teleph.) am Apparat bleiben; dranbleiben (ugs.) **5** (coll.: wait) warten; ~ **on!** einen Moment!; **just [you] ~ on now!** (calm yourself) nun mal ganz ruhig!; Moment mal!

- ~ **'out**

A *v.t.* **1** (stretch forth) ausstrecken ‹*Hand, Arm usw.*›; ausbreiten ‹*Arme*›; hinhalten ‹*Tasse, Teller*› **2** (fig.: offer) in Aussicht stellen (**to** *Dat.*); **he did not ~ out much hope** er hat mir/dir usw. nicht viel Hoffnung gemacht

B *v.i.* **1** (maintain resistance) sich halten **2** (last) ‹*Vorräte:*› vorhalten; ‹*Motor:*› halten; durchhalten (ugs.) **3** ~ **out for sth.** etw. herauszuschinden versuchen (ugs.) **4** ~ **out [on sb.]** (coll.: withhold knowledge) [jmdm.] etwas verschweigen

- ~ **'over** *v.t.* vertagen (**till** auf + *Akk.*)
- ~ **to'gether**

A *v.t.* zusammenhalten

B *v.i.* (lit. or fig.) zusammenhalten

- ~ **'under** *v.t.* unter Wasser drücken; (fig.) unterdrücken ‹*Land, Volk, usw.*›
- ~ **'up**

A *v.t.* **1** (raise) hochhalten; hochheben ‹*Person*›; [hoch]heben ‹*Hand, Kopf*›; ~ **sth. up to the light** etw. ins Licht/(to see through it) gegen das Licht halten; ~ **up one's head** (fig.) seine Selbstachtung nicht verlieren; **he'd never be able to ~ his head up again** er könnte seine Selbstachtung niemals mehr wiedergewinnen **2** (fig.: offer as an example) ~ **sb. up as ...:** jmdn. als ... hinstellen; ~ **sb. up as an example** jmdn. als [leuchtendes] Vorbild hinstellen; ~ **sb./sth. up to ridicule/scorn** jmdn./etw. dem Spott/Hohn preisgeben **3** (support) stützen; tragen ‹*Dach usw.*›; (fig.: give support to) stützen ‹*Regime*›; ~ **sth. up with sth.** etw. mit etw. abstützen **4** (delay) aufhalten; behindern ‹*Verkehr, Versorgung*›; verzögern ‹*Friedensvertrag*›; (halt) ins Stocken bringen ‹*Produktion*› **5** (rob) überfallen [und ausrauben]. *see also* **~-up**

B *v.i.* **1** (under scrutiny) sich als stichhaltig erweisen **2** ‹*Wetter:*› schön bleiben, sich halten

- ~ **with** *v.t.* **~/not ~ with sth.** mit etw. einverstanden sein/etw. ablehnen

holdall /ˈhəʊldɔːl/ *n.* Reisetasche, *die*

holder /ˈhəʊldə(r)/ *n.* **1** (of post) Inhaber, *der*/Inhaberin, *die* **2** (of title) Träger, *der*/Trägerin, *die*; Inhaber, *der*/Inhaberin, *die*; (Sport) Titelhalter, -inhaber, *der*; (share~) Aktionär, *der*; Aktieninhaber, *der*; **in the Cup Final, the ~s were beaten** im Pokalendspiel wurden die Pokalverteidiger geschlagen **3** ‹*Zigaretten*›spitze, *die*; ‹*Schirm*›ständer, *der*; ‹*Papier-, Feder-, Zahnputzglas*›halter, *der*; **flowerpot ~:** Übertopf, *der*

holding /ˈhəʊldɪŋ/ *n.* **1** (tenure) Land-, Grundbesitz, *der* **2** (land held) Gut, *das*; *see also* **small-holding** **3** (property held) Besitz, *der*; (stocks or shares) Anteil, *der*

holding: ~ company *n.* (Commerc.) Holding[gesellschaft], *die*; **~ operation** *n.* Aktion zur Schadensbegrenzung

'hold-up *n.* **1** (robbery) [Raub]überfall, *der* **2** (stoppage) Unterbrechung, *die*; (delay) Verzögerung, *die*; **run into a traffic ~:** in einen [Verkehrs]stau geraten; **there are ~s on the motorway** auf der Autobahn kommt es zu erheblichen Behinderungen

hole /həʊl/

A *n.* **1** Loch, *das*; **make a ~ in sth.** (fig.) eine ganze Menge von etw. verschlingen; **be a round/square peg in a square/round ~** (fig.) es nicht gut getroffen haben; **be in ~s** voller Löcher sein; **pick ~s in** Löcher machen in (+ *Akk.*) ‹*Pullover usw.*›; (fig.: find fault with) zerpflücken (ugs.); auseinander nehmen (ugs.); madig machen (ugs.) ‹*Person*›; **be full of ~s** (fig.) viele Schwächen haben; **~ in the heart** Loch in der Herzscheidewand; Septumdefekt, *der* (fachspr.); **they need it like a ~ in the head** (coll.) das ist das Letzte, was sie gebrauchen können (ugs.) **2** (burrow) (of fox, badger, rabbit) Bau, *der*; (of mouse) Loch, *das* **3** (coll.) (dingy abode) Loch, *das* (salopp abwertend); (wretched place) Kaff, *das* (ugs. abwertend); Nest, *das* (ugs. abwertend) **4** (coll.: awkward situation) Klemme, *die* (ugs.); Patsche, *die* (ugs.); **be in a ~:** in der Klemme sein; in der Patsche sitzen **5** (Golf) Loch, *das*; (space between tee and ~) [Spiel]bahn, *die*; (point scored) Loch, *das*; **~ in one** Hole-in-One, *das*; Ass *das. see also* **burn¹ B 1**

B *v.t.* **1** Löcher/ein Loch machen in (+ *Akk.*); **be ~d** Löcher/ein Loch haben **2** (Naut.: pierce side of) **be ~d** leckschlagen (Seemannsspr.) **3** (Golf) ▸ **~ out**

Phrasal verbs

- ~ **'out** *v.t.* (Golf) einlochen; *abs.* **~ out in one** ein Hole-in-One *od.* As spielen
- ~ **'up** *v.i.* (coll.) sich verkriechen (ugs.)

hole-and-'corner *adj.* zwielichtig; anrüchig

'hole-in-the-wall *adj.* **~ [cash] machine** Geldautomat, *der*

holiday /ˈhɒlɪdeɪ, ˈhɒlɪdɪ/

A *n.* **1** (day of recreation) [arbeits]freier Tag; (day of

h

festivity) Feiertag, *der;* **the whole country was given a ~:** das ganze Land bekam einen Tag [arbeits]frei; **tomorrow is a ~:** morgen ist frei/Feiertag; *see also* **bank holiday**; **national holiday**; **public holiday** **2** *in sing. or pl.* (Brit.: vacation) Urlaub, *der;* (Sch.) [Schul]ferien *Pl.;* **need a ~:** urlaubsreif sein; **have a good ~!** schönen Urlaub!; (at Christmas etc.) schöne Feiertage!; **go to Cornwall for one's ~[s]** im Urlaub/in den Ferien nach Cornwall fahren; in Cornwall urlauben (ugs.); **take** *or* **have a/one's ~:** Urlaub nehmen *od.* machen/seinen Urlaub nehmen; **on ~, on one's ~s** im *od.* in seinem Urlaub; **be [away] on ~** *or* **on one's ~s** in *od.* im *od.* auf Urlaub sein; **go on [a] ~** *or* **on one's ~s** (leave work) in Urlaub gehen; (go away) in Urlaub fahren; *see also* **busman**

B *attrib. adj.* Urlaubs-/Ferien‹*stimmung, -pläne*›; Freizeit‹*kleidung*›

C *v.i.* Urlaub/Ferien machen; urlauben (ugs.)

holiday: ~ camp *n.* Feriendorf, *das;* Ferienpark, *der;* **~ centre** *n.* **1** (holiday destination) Urlaubs-/Ferienziel, *das;* **2** (purpose-built centre) Ferienzentrum, *das;* **~ home** *n.* Feriendomizil, *das;* **~ job** *n.* Ferienjob, *der;* **~maker** *n.* Urlauber, *der*/Urlauberin, *die;* **~ resort** *n.* Ferienort, *der;* **~ season** *n.* Urlaubszeit, *die*

holier-than-thou /həʊlɪəðən'ðaʊ/ *adj.* selbstgerecht

holiness /'həʊlɪnɪs/ *n., no pl.* ▸ⓘ **p. 1634** Heiligkeit, *die;* **His H~:** Seine Heiligkeit

holism /'hɒlɪzm, 'həʊlɪzm/ *n., no pl.* (Philos.) Holismus, *der*

holistic /hɒ'lɪstɪk, həʊ'lɪstɪk/ *adj.* (Philos.) holistisch

Holland /'hɒlənd/ *pr. n.* Holland (*das*)

hollandaise /'hɒləndeɪz/ *n.* (Gastr.) **~ [sauce]** holländische Soße; Sauce hollandaise, *die*

holler /'hɒlə(r)/ (coll.)

A *v.i.* schreien; brüllen

B *v.t.* schreien

hollow /'hɒləʊ/

A *adj.* **1** (not solid) hohl; Hohl‹*ziegel, -mauer, -zylinder, -kugel*›; **have ~ legs** (joc.) nicht satt zu kriegen sein (ugs.) **2** (sunken) eingefallen ‹*Wangen, Schläfen*›; hohl, tief liegend ‹*Augen*›; nach innen gewölbt ‹*Stück Blech usw.*›; **a ~ place in the ground/road** *etc.* eine Vertiefung im Boden/in der Straße *usw.* **3** (hungry) **feel ~:** ein Loch im Bauch haben (ugs.) **4** (echoing) hohl ‹*Ton, Klang*›; **speak with a ~ voice** mit Grabesstimme sprechen **5** (fig.: empty) wertlos; eitel (geh.) ‹*Reichtum*›; oberflächlich ‹*Person*› **6** (fig.: cynical) verlogen; leer ‹*Versprechen*›; gequält ‹*Lachen*›

B *n.* [Boden]senke, *die;* [Boden]vertiefung, *die;* (area below general level) Niederung, *die;* **hold sth. in the ~ of one's hand** etw. in der hohlen Hand halten

C *adv.* **beat sb. ~** (coll.) jmdn. um Längen schlagen (ugs.)

D *v.t.* **~ out** aushöhlen; graben ‹*Höhle*›; bohren, graben ‹*Tunnel*›

'hollow-eyed *adj.* hohläugig

hollowly /'hɒləʊlɪ/ *adv.* hohl ‹*widerhallen*›

hollowness /'hɒləʊnɪs/ *n. no pl.* **1** Hohlheit, *die* **2** (of voice) Hohlheit, *die* **3** (fig.) (emptiness) Hohlheit, *die;* (falseness) Verlogenheit, *die*

'hollowware *n., no pl.* Geschirr, *das;* Gefäße *Pl.*

holly /'hɒlɪ/ *n.* **1** (tree) Stechpalme, *die;* Ilex, *der* (fachspr.) **2** (foliage) Stechpalmenzweige *Pl.*

'hollyhock *n.* (Bot.) Stockrose, *die*

holm¹ /həʊm/ *n.* (Brit.) (islet) kleine Insel; Holm, *der* (nordd.); (in a river) Werder, *der*

holm² *n.* **~ [oak]** (Bot.) Steineiche, *die*

holocaust /'hɒləkɔ:st/ *n.* (destruction) Massenvernichtung, *die;* **the H~:** der Holocaust; die Judenvernichtung; **nuclear ~:** atomarer Holocaust

Holocene /'hɒləsi:n/ *n.* (Geol.) Holozän, *das*

hologram /'hɒləgræm/ *n.* Hologramm, *das*

holographic /hɒlə'græfɪk/ *adj.* holografisch; Hologramm‹*aufkleber*›

holography /hɒ'lɒgrəfɪ/ *n., no pl., no art.* Holographie, *die*

hols /hɒlz/ *n. pl.* (Brit. coll.) Ferien *Pl.*

holster /'həʊlstə(r)/ *n.* [Pistolen]halfter, *die od. das*

holy /'həʊlɪ/ *adj.* heilig; fromm ‹*Zweck*›; **~ saints** Heilige; **~ smoke** *or* **cow!** (coll.) heiliger Bimbam (ugs.) *od.* (salopp) Strohsack!

holy: H~ 'Bible *n.* Heilige Schrift; **H~ 'City** *n.* Heilige Stadt; **H~ Com'munion** ▸**communion 1**; **~ 'cross** *n.* Kreuz Christi, *das;* **the sign of the ~ cross** das Kreuzzeichen; **~ day** *n.* religiöser Feiertag; **H~ 'Family** *n.* Heilige Familie; **H~ 'Father** ▸**father A 6**; **H~ 'Ghost** ▸**H~ Spirit**; **H~ Grail** ▸**Grail**; **~ 'Joe** *n.* (coll. derog.) Pfaffe, *der* (abwertend); **H~ Land** *n.* **the H~ Land** das Heilige Land; **~ of 'holies** *n.* (inner chamber, fig.: sacred place) Allerheiligste, *das;* **~ 'orders** ▸**order A 8**; **~ place** *n.* **1** Heilige, *das;* **2** *in pl.* (places of pilgrimage) heilige Stätten *Pl.;* **H~ Roman 'Empire** ▸**Roman Empire**; **H~ 'Sacrament** ▸**sacrament 1**; **H~ 'Saturday** *n.* Karsamstag, *der;* **H~ 'Scripture** ▸**scripture**; **H~ 'See** ▸**see²**; **H~ 'Spirit** *n.* (Relig.) Heiliger Geist; **~ 'terror** ▸**terror 3**; **H~ 'Trinity** ▸**Trinity 1**; **~ 'war** *n.* heiliger Krieg; **~ 'water** *n.* (Eccl.) Weihwasser, *das;* **H~ Week** *n.* Karwoche, *die*

homage /'hɒmɪdʒ/ *n.* (tribute) Huldigung, *die* (**to** an + *Akk.*); **pay** *or* **do ~ to sb./sth.** jmdm./einer Sache huldigen

Homburg /'hɒmbɜ:g/ *n.* **~ [hat]** Homburg, *der*

home /həʊm/

A *n.* **1** (place of residence) Zuhause, *das;* Heim, *das;* (flat) Wohnung, *die;* (house) Haus, *das;* (parental ~) Elternhaus, *das;* **my ~ is in Leeds** ich bin in Leeds zu Hause *od.* wohne in Leeds; **a ~ of one's own** ein eigenes Zuhause; **give sb./an animal a ~:** jmdm./einem Tier ein Zuhause geben; **work/be away from ~:** auswärts arbeiten/nicht zu Hause sein; **leave/have left ~:** aus dem Haus gehen/sein; **have a good ~:** ein gutes Zuhause haben; **live at ~:** im Elternhaus wohnen; **they had no ~/~s [of their own]** sie hatten kein Zuhause; **safety in the ~:** Sicherheit im Haus[halt]; **make one's ~ in the country/abroad** aufs Land ziehen/ins Ausland gehen; **at ~:** zu Hause; (not abroad) im Inland; **be at ~ [to sb.]** (be available to caller) [für jmdn.] zu sprechen sein *od.* da sein; (Sport: play on one's own ground) auf eigenem Platz *od.* zu Hause [gegen jmdn.] spielen; **is our next match at ~ or away?** ist unser nächstes Spiel ein Heimspiel oder ein Auswärtsspiel?; **who/what is X when he's/it's at ~?** (joc.) wer/was ist das denn?; **be/feel at ~** (fig.) sich wohl fühlen; **make sb. feel at ~:** es jmdm. behaglich machen; **make yourself at ~:** fühl dich wie zu Hause; **he is quite at ~ in French** er ist im Französischen ganz gut zu Hause; *see also* **4**; **at-~**; **there's no place like ~** (prov.) es geht [doch] nichts über das eigene Zuhause; **~ from ~:** zweites Zuhause

2 (fig.) **this was something very near ~:** das war etwas, das einen sehr direkt betraf; **to take an example nearer ~, ...:** um ein Beispiel zu nehmen, das uns näher liegt, ...; *see also* **from 4**; **second ~**

3 (Amer., Austral., NZ: dwelling house) Haus, *das*

4 (native country) die Heimat; **at ~:** zu Hause; in der Heimat; *see also* **1**

5 (place where thing is native) Heimat, *die*

6 (institution) Heim, *das;* (coll.: mental home) Anstalt, *die* (salopp); **you ought to be in a ~:** du gehörst in die Klapsmühle; *see also* **mental ~**; **nursing ~**

7 *no art.* (Games: safe place) das Mal; (in Ludo etc.) das Haus; (finishing point) das Ziel

B *adj.* **1** (connected with home) Haus-; Haushalts‹*gerät usw.*›; **she enjoyed her ~ life** sie genoss das Zuhausesein

2 (done at home) häuslich; Selbst‹*backen, -brauen usw.*›

3 (in the neighbourhood of home) nahe gelegen

4 (Sport) Heim‹*spiel, -sieg, -mannschaft*›; ‹*Anhänger, Spieler*› der Heimmannschaft; **~ ground** eigener Platz

5 (not foreign) [ein]heimisch; inländisch; *see also* **trade**

C *adv.* **1** (to home) nach Hause; **find one's way ~:** nach Hause finden; **on one's way ~:** auf dem Weg nach Hause *od.* Nachhauseweg; **get ~:** nach Hause kommen; (to the finishing point) das Ziel erreichen; **get ~ by inches** um eine Nasenlänge gewinnen; **Pierre is going ~ to France tomorrow** Pierre fährt morgen nach Frankreich zurück; **be going ~** (fig.: be becoming unserviceable) den Geist aufgeben (ugs.); **he takes ~ £200 a week after tax** er verdient 200 Pfund netto in der Woche; **nothing to write ~ about** (coll.) nichts Besonderes *od.* Aufregendes

2 (arrived at home) zu Hause; **the first competitor ~ was Paul** als erster [Teilnehmer] traf Paul am Ziel ein *od.* ging Paul durchs Ziel; **be ~ and dry** (fig.) aus dem Schneider sein (ugs.)

3 (at home) zu Hause

4 (to the point aimed at) **go ~** ‹*Schlag usw.:*› sitzen (ugs.); ‹*Schuss:*› treffen; (fig.) ‹*Bemerkungen usw.:*› ins Schwarze treffen, (ugs.) sitzen

5 (as far as possible) **push ~:** [ganz] hineinschieben ‹*Schublade*›; forcieren ‹*Angriff*›; ausnutzen ‹*Vorteil*›; **press ~:** [ganz] hinunterdrücken ‹*Hebel*›; forcieren ‹*Angriff*›; [voll] ausnutzen ‹*Vorteil*›; **drive ~:** [ganz] einschlagen ‹*Nagel*›

6 **come** *or* **get ~ to sb.** (become fully realized) jmdm. in vollem Ausmaß bewusst werden; **bring sth. ~ to sb.** jmdm. etw. klarmachen *od.* vor Augen führen; *see also* **roost A**

D *v.i.* **1** ‹*Vogel usw.:*› zurückkehren

2 (be guided) **these missiles ~ [in] on their targets** diese Flugkörper suchen sich (*Dat.*) ihr Ziel

3 **~ in on sth.** (fig.) etw. herausgreifen

home: ~ address *n.* Privatanschrift, *die;* **~ 'banking** *n., no pl.* Homebanking, *das;* **~-based** /'həʊmbeɪst/ *adj.* zu Hause arbeitend; **be ~-based** zu Hause arbeiten; seinen Arbeitsplatz zu Hause haben; **~ bird** *n.* häuslicher Mensch; **~ brew** *n.* selbst gebrautes Bier; **~-brewed** /'həʊmbru:d/ *adj.* selbst gebraut; **~buyer** *n.* Eigenheimkäufer, *der*/-käuferin, *die;* **~ 'comforts** *n. pl.* häuslicher Komfort; **~coming** *n.* Heimkehr, *die;* **~ com'puter** *n.* Heimcomputer, *der;* **H~ Counties** *n. pl.* (Brit.) **the Home Counties** die Home Countys; *die Grafschaften um London;* **~ 'country** *n.* Heimatland, *das;* Herkunftsland, *das;* **America is his ~ country** er stammt aus Amerika; **~ eco'nomics** *n. sing.* ▸**domestic science**; **~ enter'tainment** *n., no pl.* Heimunterhaltung, *die;* **~ enter'tainment centre** *n.* Heimunterhaltungsanlage, *die;* **~ farm** *n.* (Brit.) Herrenhof, *der;* **~ 'ground** *n.* **on [one's] ~ ground** auf heimischem Boden; (fig.) zu Hause (ugs.); **~-grown** *adj.* selbst gezogen ‹*Gemüse, Obst*›; **H~ 'Guard** *n.* (Brit. Hist.) **1** (army) Bürgerwehr, *die;* **2** (person) Mitglied der Bürgerwehr; **~ 'help** (Brit.) ▸**help B 2**; **~land** *n.* **1** (native land) Heimat, *die;* Heimatland, *das;* **2** (in South Africa) Homeland, *das;* **~land security** *n., no pl.* (esp. Amer.) Heimatschutz, *der;* **~ leave** *n.* Heimaturlaub, *der*

> **Home Counties**
>
> Die britischen *Home Counties* sind die Grafschaften um London – Buckinghamshire, Essex, Hertfordshire, Kent, Berkshire, Surrey und das frühere Middlesex. Die *Home Counties* gelten als die wohlhabendsten Gebiete in Großbritannien.

homeless /'həʊmlɪs/

A *adj.* obdachlos; **~ person** Obdachlose, *der/die*

B *n.* **the ~:** die Obdachlosen

homelessness /'həʊmlɪsnɪs/ *n.* Obdachlosigkeit, *die*

'homelike *adj.* wohnlich

'home-loving *adj.* häuslich

homely /'həʊmlɪ/ *adj.* **1** (unpretentious, simple) einfach, schlicht ‹*Worte, Stil, Sprache usw.*›; warmherzig ‹*Person*›; bescheiden ‹*kleines Haus*› **2** (Amer.: not attractive) nicht sehr attraktiv; wenig attraktiv

home: ~-made *adj.* selbst gemacht; selbst gebacken ‹*Brot*›; hausgemacht ‹*Lebensmittel*›; **~maker** *n.* Hausfrau, *die;* (man) Hausmann, *der;* **~ 'movie** *n.* Amateurfilm, *der;*

H~ Office *n.* (Brit.) Innenministerium, *das*

homeopathic /həʊmɪə'pæθɪk, hɒmɪə'pæθɪk/ *adj.* homöopathisch

homeopathy /həʊmɪ'ɒpəθɪ, hɒmɪ'ɒpəθɪ/ *n.* Homöopathie, *die*

home: ~owner *n.* Eigenheimbesitzer, *der*/-besitzerin, *die*; **~ page** *n.* (Computing) Homepage *die*; **~ 'perm** *n.* selbst gemachte Dauerwelle; **~ 'plate** ▸**plate A 12**; **~ 'port** *n.* Heimathafen, *der*

Homer *pr. n.* Homer (*der*)

Homeric /həʊ'merɪk/ *adj.* homerisch

home: ~ 'rule *n.* Autonomie, *die*; Selbstbestimmung, *die*; **~ 'run** *n.* (Baseball) Homerun, *der*; **H~ 'Secretary** *n.* (Brit.) Innenminister, *der*; **~ 'shopping** *n., no pl.* Homeshopping, *das*; **~sick** *adj.* heimwehkrank; **become/be ~sick** Heimweh bekommen/haben; **~sickness** *n., no pl.* Heimweh, *das*; **~spun** *adj.* **1** (spun [and woven] at ~) selbst gesponnen [und gewoben]; (of ~ manufacture) in Heimarbeit gesponnen; **2** (unsophisticated) schlicht; einfach; **~spun philosophy** Lebensweisheiten; **~stead** *n.* **1** (house with land) Anwesen, *das*; (farm) Gehöft, *das*; **2** (Austral., NZ: residence) Herrenhaus, *das*; **3** (Amer.: area of land) Parzelle, *die*; ≈ Heimstätte, *die*; **~ 'straight** (*Amer.*: **~ 'stretch**) *n.* (lit. or fig.) Zielgerade, *die*; **~ 'town** *n.* Heimatstadt, *die*; Vaterstadt, *die* (geh.); (town of residence) Wohnort, *der*; **~ 'truth** *n.* unangenehme Wahrheit; **tell** *or* **give sb. a few ~ truths** jmdm. [gehörig] die Meinung sagen; **now you're going to listen to a few ~ truths** jetzt hörst du mir mal zu!; **~ 'video** *n.* **1** *no pl.* (video equipment) Videoausrüstung, *die*; **2** *no pl.* (activity) Videofilmen, *das*; **3** (camera, recorder) [Heim]videokamera, *die*; **4** (recording) Amateurvideo, *das*; **~ 'visit** Hausbesuch, *der*

homeward /'həʊmwəd/

A *adj.* nach Hause *nachgestellt*; Nachhause⟨*weg*⟩; (return) Rück⟨*fahrt, -reise, -weg*⟩; *see also* **bound**[3]

B *adv.* nach Hause; heimwärts

homewards /'həʊmwədz/ ▸**homeward B**

home: ~work *n.* (Sch.) Hausaufgabe, *die*; **Latin ~work** Hausaufgaben in Latein; **be given ~work** Hausaufgaben aufbekommen *od.* aufhaben; **give/set sb. too much ~work** jmdm. zu viel [Hausaufgaben] aufgeben; **for ~work** als Hausaufgabe; **do one's ~work** (fig.) sich mit der Materie vertraut machen; seine Hausaufgaben machen (scherzh.); **~worker** *n.* Heimarbeiter, *der*/-arbeiterin, *die*; **~working** *n., no pl.* Heimarbeit, *die*

homey /'həʊmɪ/ *adj.* wohnlich; heimelig (veralt.) ⟨*Zimmer, Haus*⟩; vertraut ⟨*Anblick*⟩

homicidal /hɒmɪ'saɪdl/ *adj.* gemeingefährlich; **~ tendency** Drang zum Töten

homicide /'hɒmɪsaɪd/ *n.* **1** (act) Tötung, *die*; (manslaughter) Totschlag, *der* **2** (person) *jemand, der einen Menschen getötet hat*

homily /'hɒmɪlɪ/ *n.* **1** (sermon) Homilie, *die* (Theol.) **2** (tedious discourse) Moralpredigt, *die*; Predigt, *die* (ugs.); **give sb. a ~:** jmdm. eine [Moral]predigt halten

homing /'həʊmɪŋ/ *attrib. adj.* zielsuchend ⟨*Flugkörper, Torpedo*⟩; Zielsuch⟨*einrichtung, -kopf*⟩; **~ instinct/sense** Heimfindevermögen, *das*

'homing pigeon *n.* Brieftaube, *die*

hominid /'hɒmɪnɪd/ (Zool.)

A *adj.* zu den Hominiden gehörend

B *n.* Hominide, *der*

homo /'həʊməʊ/ (coll.)

A *adj.* homosexuell; homo *nicht attr.* (ugs.)

B *n., pl.* **~s** Homo, *der* (ugs.)

homo- /həʊməʊ, hɒməʊ/ *in comb.* homo-/Homo-

homoeopathic *etc.* ▸**homeo-**

homoe'rotic *adj.* homoerotisch

homogeneity /hɒmədʒɪ'niːɪtɪ, həʊmədʒɪ'niːɪtɪ/ *n., no pl.* Homogenität, *die*

homogeneous /hɒmə'dʒiːnɪəs, həʊmə'dʒiːnɪəs/ *adj.* homogen

homogenisation, homogenise, homogeniser ▸**homogeniz-**

homogenization /həmɒdʒɪnaɪ'zeɪʃn/ *n.* Homogenisierung, *die*

homogenize /hə'mɒdʒɪnaɪz/ *v.t.* (lit. or fig.) homogenisieren

homogenizer /hə'mɒdʒɪnaɪzə(r)/ *n.* Homogenisator, *der*

'homograph *n.* (Ling.) Homograph, *das*

homologous /hə'mɒləgəs/ *adj.* homolog

homonym /'hɒmənɪm/ *n.* (Ling.) Homonym, *das*

homonymous /hə'mɒnɪməs/ *adj.* homonym

homophobia /hɒmə'fəʊbɪə/ *n., no pl.* Homophobie, *die*

homophobic /hɒmə'fəʊbɪk/ *adj.* homophob

'homophone *n.* (Ling.) Homophon, *das*

Homo sapiens /hɒməʊ 'sæpɪenz/ *n., no pl.* Homo sapiens, *der*

homo'sexual

A *adj.* homosexuell

B *n.* Homosexuelle, *der/die*; **he is a ~:** er ist homosexuell

homosexu'ality *n.* Homosexualität, *die*

homy ▸**homey**

Hon. /ɒn/ *abbr.* **1** = **Honorary** **2** ▸❶ **p. 1634 = Honourable**

honcho /'hɒntʃəʊ/ *n.* (Amer. coll.) Boss, *der* (ugs.)

Honduran /hɒn'djʊərən/ ▸❶ **p. 1345**

A *adj.* honduranisch; **sb. is ~:** jmd. ist Honduraner/Honduranerin

B *n.* Honduraner, *der*/Honduranerin, *die*

Honduras /hɒn'djʊərəs/ *pr. n.* Honduras (*das*)

hone /həʊn/

A *n.* Wetzstein, *der*

B *v.t.* **1** wetzen ⟨*Messer, Klinge usw.*⟩; **~ a razor to a sharp edge** ein Rasiermesser wetzen, bis die Schneide scharf ist **2** (fig.: perfect) vervollkommnen ⟨*Fähigkeiten*⟩

honest /'ɒnɪst/ *adj.* **1** (acting fairly) ehrlich; **~ broker** ehrlicher Makler **2** (sincere) ehrlich; **the ~ truth** die reine Wahrheit; **to be ~ [with you]** offen *od.* ehrlich gesagt **3** (showing righteousness) redlich; ehrenhaft ⟨*Absicht, Tat, Plan*⟩; ehrlich ⟨*Arbeit*⟩ **4** (blameless) rechtschaffen; **he made an ~ woman of her** (joc.) er heiratete sie **5** (got by fair means) ehrlich erworben ⟨*Besitz*⟩; ehrlich verdient ⟨*Geld*⟩; ehrlich erwirtschaftet ⟨*Gewinn*⟩; **make an ~ living** sein Leben auf ehrliche Weise verdienen; **earn** *or* **turn an ~ penny** sich (*Dat.*) sein Brot ehrlich verdienen **6** (unsophisticated) [gut und] einfach; (unadulterated) rein; **~ bread** gutes, einfaches Brot **7** **~ [to God], ~ to goodness!** (coll.) ehrlich! (ugs.); *see also* **honest-to-God**

honestly /'ɒnɪstlɪ/ *adv.* **1** (fairly) ehrlich; redlich ⟨*handeln*⟩ **2** (frankly) ehrlich; offen **3** (genuinely, really) ehrlich (ugs.); wirklich; **~!** ehrlich!; (annoyed) also wirklich!

honest: ~-to-God, ~-to-goodness *adjs.* echt

honesty /'ɒnɪstɪ/ *n.* **1** (truthfulness) Ehrlichkeit, *die*; Aufrichtigkeit, *die*; **in all ~:** ganz ehrlich; **in all ~, I have to admit ...:** ich muss ehrlicherweise zugeben ... **2** (upright conduct) Redlichkeit, *die*; Anständigkeit, *die*; **~ is the best policy** (prov.) ehrlich währt am längsten (Spr.) **3** (Bot.) Silberblatt, *das*

honey /'hʌnɪ/ *n.* **1** Honig, *der* **2** (colour) Honiggelb, *das* **3** (fig.: sweetness) Lieblichkeit, *die* **4** (darling) Schatz, *der* (ugs.); **sb. is a [real] ~:** jmd. ist ein Schatz (ugs.)

honey: ~ bee *n.* Honigbiene, *die*; **~ blonde** *adj.* honigblond; **~-coloured** *adj.* honigfarben; **~comb** *n.* Bienenwabe, *die*; (filled with honey) Honigwabe, *die*; **~combed** /'hʌnɪkəʊmd/ *adj.* (with cavities) wabenartig durchsetzt *od.* durchzogen; **~dew** *n.* (lit. or fig.) Honigtau, *der*; **~dew [melon]** Honigmelone, *die*

honeyed /'hʌnɪd/ *adj.* honigsüß ⟨*Worte*⟩

honey: ~moon **A** *n.* **1** Flitterwochen *Pl.*; Honigmond, *der* (scherzh.); (journey) Hochzeitsreise, *die*; **where did you go for your ~moon?** wohin habt ihr eure Hochzeitsreise gemacht?; **be a ~moon couple** sich auf der Hochzeitsreise befinden; **2** (fig.: initial period) anfängliche Begeisterung; **the ~moon period** die Phase der Begeisterung; **B** *v.i.* seine Flitterwochen verbringen; flittern (ugs. scherzh.); **~pot** *n.* Honigtopf, *der*; **~suckle** *n.* (Bot.) Geißblatt, *das*; **~-sweet** *adj.* honigsüß

honeymooner /'hʌnɪmuːnə(r)/ *n.* Hochzeitsreisende, *der/die*; Honeymooner, *der*/Honeymoonerin, *die*

honk /hɒŋk/

A *n.* **1** (of horn) Hupen, *das*; **I gave him a ~ [on my horn]** ich hupte ihn an; **~s** Hupsignale **2** (of goose or seal) Schrei, *der*

B *v.i.* **1** ⟨*Fahrzeug, Fahrer:*⟩ hupen **2** ⟨*Gans, Seehund:*⟩ schreien

C *v.t.* **~ one's horn** ▸**horn A 4**

honky-tonk /'hɒŋkɪtɒŋk/ *n.* (coll.) **1** (nightclub) Schuppen, *der* (ugs.) **2** (music) Ragtime, *der*

honor, honorable, honorably (Amer.) ▸**honour** *etc.*

honorarium /ɒnə'reərɪəm/ *n., pl.* **~s** *or* **honoraria** /ɒnə'reərɪə/ Honorar, *das*

honorary /'ɒnərərɪ/ *adj.* **1** ehrenamtlich; Ehren⟨*mitglied, -präsident, -doktor, -bürger*⟩ **2** (conferred as an honour) Ehren-; **~ degree** ehrenhalber verliehener akademischer Grad; **the position is an ~ one** der Posten ist ehrenamtlich

honour /'ɒnə(r)/ (Brit.)

A *n.* **1** *no indef. art.* (reputation) Ehre, *die*; **win/achieve ~:** zu Ehren kommen; **to his ~, he refused** es ehrt ihn, dass er abgelehnt hat; **do ~ to sb./sth.** jmdm./einer Sache zur Ehre gereichen (geh.); jmdm./einer Sache Ehre machen **2** (respect) Hochachtung, *die*; **he was treated with** *or* **shown ~:** ihm wurde große Achtung entgegengebracht; **hold sb./sth. in ~:** jmdn./etw. achten; **do sb. ~, do ~ to sb.** jmdm. Ehre erweisen; (show appreciation of) jmdn. würdigen; **do ~ to sth.** etw. würdigen; **in ~ of sb.** jmdm. zu Ehren; **in ~ of sth.** um etw. gebührend zu feiern **3** (privilege) Ehre, *die*; **have the ~ to do** *or* **of doing sth.** die Ehre haben, etw. zu tun; **may I have the ~ [of the next dance]?** darf ich [um den nächsten Tanz] bitten?; **do sb. an ~:** jmdm. eine Ehre erweisen; **you do me too great an ~:** Sie tun mir zu viel Ehre an; **do sb. the ~ of doing sth.** jmdm. die Ehre erweisen, etw. zu tun **4** *no art.* (ethical quality) Ehre, *die*; **he is a man of ~** *or* **with a sense of ~:** er ist ein Ehrenmann *od.* Mann von Ehre; **feel [in] ~ bound to do sth.** sich moralisch verpflichtet fühlen, etw. zu tun; **promise [up]on one's ~:** sein Ehrenwort geben; **be on one's ~:** sein Ehrenwort gegeben haben; **[up]on my ~!** Ehrenwort!; bei meiner Ehre! (geh.); **the prisoner was put [up]on his ~ not to escape** der Gefangene musste sich auf Ehrenwort verpflichten, nicht zu fliehen; **~ bright** (coll.) großes Ehrenwort! (ugs.); **[there is] ~ among thieves** [es gibt so etwas wie] Ganovenehre **5** (chastity) Ehre, *die* (veralt.) **6** (distinction) Auszeichnung, *die*; (title) Ehrentitel, *der*; *see also* **birthday**; **new year** **7** *in pl.* (recognition) Auszeichnungen **8** *in pl.* (Univ.) **she gained ~s in her exam, she passed [the exam] with ~s** sie hat das Examen mit Auszeichnung bestanden **9** *in pl.* **do the ~s** (coll.) (introduce guests) die Honneurs machen; (serve guests) den Gastgeber spielen **10** (ceremony) **funeral** *or* **last ~s** Trauerfeierlichkeiten *Pl.*; **pay the last ~s to sb.** jmdm. die letzte Ehre erweisen (geh.); **military ~s** militärische Ehren **11** *in title* **your H~** (Brit. Law) hohes Gericht; Euer Ehren **12** (person or thing that brings credit) **be an ~ to sb./sth.** jmdm./einer Sache Ehre machen **13** (Cards) Honneur, *das*; (fig.) **~s are even** es gibt keinen Verlierer. *See also* **affair 6**; **code A 1**; **companion**[1] **3**; **debt**; **guard A 2**; **guest**; **legion 3**; **maid of honour**; **matron 2**; **point A 3**; **word A 3**

B *v.t.* **1** ehren; würdigen ⟨*Verdienste, besondere Eigenschaften*⟩; **be ~ed as an artist** als Künstler Anerkennung finden; **~ your father and your mother** du sollst Vater und Mutter ehren; **be ~ed with a knighthood** in den Ritterstand erhoben werden; **~ sb. with one's presence** (iron.) jmdn. mit seiner Gegenwart beehren **2** (acknowledge) beachten ⟨*Vorschriften*⟩; respektieren ⟨*Gebräuche, Rechte*⟩ **3** (fulfil) sich halten an (+ *Akk.*); (Commerc.) honorieren; begleichen ⟨*Rechnung, Schuld*⟩

h

honourable /ˈɒnərəbl/ *adj.* (Brit.) **1** (worthy of respect) ehrenwert (geh.); ehrbar (geh.) **2** (bringing credit) achtbar; (consistent with honour) ehrenvoll ‹*Frieden, Rückzug, Entlassung*› **3** (ethical) rechtschaffen; redlich ‹*Geschäftsgebaren*›; **sb.'s intentions are ~:** jmd. hat ehrliche Absichten **4** ▸ℹ **p. 1634** *in title* **the H~ …** ≈ der/die ehrenwerte …; **the ~ gentleman/lady, the ~ member [for X]** (Brit. Parl.) der Herr/die Frau Abgeordnete [für den Wahlkreis X]; ≈ der [verehrte] Herr Kollege/die [verehrte] Frau Kollegin; **the Most H~ …** (Brit.) ≈ der/die höchst ehrenwerte …; **the Right H~ …** (Brit.) ≈ der/die sehr ehrenwerte … *see also* **mention A 2**

honourably /ˈɒnərəblɪ/ *adv.* (Brit.) **1** (with credit) ehrenvoll **2** (ethically) ehrenhaft ‹*handeln*›

honours: ~ degree *n.* Examen mit Auszeichnung; **~ list** *n.* **1** (Univ.) *Liste der Kandidaten, die das Examen mit Auszeichnung bestanden haben;* **2** (of sovereign) *Liste der Titel- und Rangverleihungen*

Hon. Sec. /ɒn ˈsek/ *abbr.* = **Honorary Secretary**

hooch /huːtʃ/ *n.* (Amer. coll.) [schwarz gebrannter] Schnaps; Fusel, *der* (ugs. abwertend)

hood¹ /hʊd/ *n.* **1** Kapuze, *die* **2** (of vehicle) (Brit.: waterproof top) Verdeck, *das;* (Amer.: bonnet) [Motor]haube, *die;* (of pram) Verdeck, *das;* **drive with the ~ down** mit offenem Verdeck fahren **3** (over hearth) [Rauch]abzug, *der;* (over stove) Abzugshaube, *die*

hood² /hʊd, huːd/ *n.* (coll.: gangster) Gangster, *der*

hooded /ˈhʊdɪd/ *adj.* (wearing hood) mit einer Kapuze bekleidet; (with hood attached) ‹*Mantel usw.*› mit Kapuze; **a ~ figure** eine Gestalt mit [einer] Kapuze

hooded ˈcrow *n.* (Ornith.) Nebelkrähe, *die*

hoodlum /ˈhuːdləm/ *n.* **1** (young thug) Rowdy, *der* (abwertend) **2** (gangster) Gangster, *der*

hoodoo /ˈhuːduː/ *n.* **1** (bad spell) Fluch, *der;* **there is a ~ on that house** es liegt ein Fluch über diesem Haus; **put a ~ on sb.** ‹*Hexe:*› jmdn. verwünschen **2** (bringer of bad luck) **be a ~:** Unglück bringen

hoodwink /ˈhʊdwɪŋk/ *v.t.* hinters Licht führen; täuschen

hooey /ˈhuːɪ/ (coll.)

A *n.* Quatsch, *der* (ugs.); Blödsinn, *der* (ugs.)

B *int.* Quatsch [mit Soße]! (ugs.)

hoof /huːf/

A *n., pl.* **~s** *or* **hooves** /huːvz/ **1** Huf, *der;* (coll. derog.: human foot) Pedal, *das* (ugs. scherzh.) **2** **buy cattle on the ~** (for meat) Lebendvieh kaufen; **make decisions on the ~:** Entscheidungen auf der Stelle *od.* ohne Überlegung treffen. *See also* **cloven B**

B *v.t.* (coll.) **1** (kick) **he ~ed him out of** *or* **through the door** er gab ihm einen Tritt, dass er durch die Tür flog; **get ~ed out of the army** (fig.) aus der Armee fliegen (ugs.) **2** (walk) **~ it** tippeln (ugs.)

ˈhoofbeat *n.* Hufschlag, *der*

hoofed /huːft/ *adj.* behuft; **~ animal** Huftier, *das*

hoo-ha /ˈhuːhɑː/ *n.* (coll.) Wirbel, *der;* **make a [lot of** *or* **big] ~ [about sth.]** [viel] Wind [um etw.] machen (ugs.)

hook /hʊk/

A *n.* **1** Haken, *der;* (Fishing) [Angel]haken, *der;* **~ and eye** Haken und Öse; **swallow sth. ~, line, and sinker** (fig.) etw. blind glauben; **they fell for it ~, line, and sinker** (fig.) sie sind voll und ganz darauf hereingefallen; **get sb. off the ~** (fig. coll.) jmdn. herauspauken (ugs.); **get oneself off the ~** (fig. coll.) den Kopf aus der Schlinge ziehen; **that lets me/him off the ~** (fig. coll.) da bin ich/ist er noch einmal davongekommen; **by ~ or by crook** mit allen Mitteln **2** (telephone cradle) Gabel, *die;* **the telephone was off the ~:** das Telefon war ausgehängt **3** (Agric.) (for cutting grass or grain) Sense, *die;* (for cutting and lopping) Hippe, *die* **4** (Boxing) Haken, *der* **5** (Baseball, Bowling, Cricket, Golf) Hook, *der* **6** (Geog., Geol.) (in river) [scharfe] Krümmung; (sand spit) spitz zulaufende Sandbank; (projecting land) gekrümmte Landzunge; **the H~** (coll.) ▸**Hook of Holland** **7** (Mus.) [Noten]fähnchen, *das*

B *v.t.* **1** (grasp) mit Haken/mit einem Haken greifen **2** (fasten) mit Haken/mit einem Haken befestigen (**to** an + *Dat.*); festhaken ‹*Tor*› (**to** an + *Akk.*); haken ‹*Bein, Finger*› (**over** über + *Akk.*, **in** in + *Akk.*) **3** **be ~ed [on sth./sb.]** (coll.) (addicted harmfully) [von etw./jmdm.] abhängig sein; (addicted harmlessly) [auf etw./jmdn.] stehen (ugs., bes. Jugendspr.); (captivated) [von etw./jmdm.] fasziniert sein; **be ~ed on heroin/drugs** heroin-/drogenabhängig sein **4** (catch) an die Angel bekommen ‹*Fisch*›; (fig.) sich (*Dat.*) angeln **5** **~ it** (dated coll.: leave) abhauen (salopp) **6** (Boxing) einen Haken versetzen *od.* geben (+ *Dat.*) **7** (Rugby) hakeln; (Golf) ‹*Rechtshänder:*› einen Linksdrall geben (+ *Dat.*), nach links verziehen ‹*Ball*›; ‹*Linkshänder:*› einen Rechtsdrall geben (+ *Dat.*), nach rechts verziehen ‹*Ball*›; (Cricket) *mit waagerechtem Schläger in Schulterhöhe hinter sich schlagen* ‹*Ball*›

(Phrasal verbs)

• **~ ˈon**

A *v.t.* anhaken (**to** an + *Akk.*); anhängen ‹*Wagen, Anhänger, Schiff*› (**to** an + *Akk.*)

B *v.i.* angehakt werden (**to** an + *Akk.*)

• **~ ˈup**

A *v.t.* **1** festhaken (**to** an + *Akk.*); zuhaken ‹*Kleid*› **2** (Radio and Telev. coll.) zusammenschalten ‹*Sender*›; *see also* **hook-up**

B *v.i.* ‹*Kleid:*› mit Haken geschlossen werden

hookah /ˈhʊkə/ *n.* Huka, *die;* [indische] Wasserpfeife

hooked /hʊkt/ *adj.* **1** (hook-shaped) hakenförmig; **~ nose** Hakennase, *die* **2** (having hook[s]) mit Haken/mit einem Haken versehen. *See also* **hook B 3**

hooker /ˈhʊkə(r)/ *n.* **1** (Rugby) Hakler, *der* **2** (esp. Amer. coll.: prostitute) Nutte, *die* (salopp)

hookey /ˈhʊkɪ/ *n.* (Amer. coll.) **play ~:** [die] Schule schwänzen (ugs.)

hook: ~ ˈnose *n.* Hakennase, *die;* **~-nosed** /ˈhʊknəʊzd/ *adj.* mit einer Hakennase *nachgestellt;* hakennasig; **be ~-nosed** eine Hakennase haben; **H~ of ˈHolland** *pr. n.* Hoek van Holland (*das*); **~-up** *n.* (Radio and Telev. coll.) Zusammenschaltung, *die* (*zu einer Gemeinschaftssendung*); **~worm** *n.* **1** (worm) Hakenwurm, *der;* **2** *no art.* (disease) die Hakenwurmkrankheit

hooky ▸**hookey**

hooligan /ˈhuːlɪɡən/ *n.* Rowdy, *der*

hooliganism /ˈhuːlɪɡənɪzm/ *n., no pl.* Rowdytum, *das*

hoop /huːp/ *n.* **1** (circular band) Reifen, *der;* (of barrel) Fassreifen, *der;* Fassband, *das* **2** (toy) Reifen, *der* **3** (Croquet) [Krocket]tor, *das* **4** (in circus, show, etc.) Springreifen, *der;* **go** *or* **be put/put sb. through the ~[s]** (fig.) durch die Mangel gedreht werden/jmdn. durch die Mangel drehen (salopp)

hoop-la /ˈhuːplɑː/ *n.* Ringwerfen, *das*

hoopoe /ˈhuːpuː/ *n.* (Ornith.) Wiedehopf, *der*

hooray ▸**hurray**

Hooray ˈHenry *n.* (Brit.) [reicher, extrovertierter] Schickimicki (ugs.)

hoosegow /ˈhuːsɡaʊ/ *n.* (Amer. coll.) Knast, *der* (ugs.)

hoot /huːt/

A *v.i.* **1** (call out) johlen; **~ with laughter** in johlendes Gelächter ausbrechen **2** ‹*Eule:*› schreien **3** ‹*Fahrzeug, Fahrer:*› hupen, tuten; ‹*Sirene, Nebelhorn usw.:*› heulen, tuten; **~ at sb./sth.** jmdn./etw. anhupen

B *v.t.* heulen *od.* tuten lassen ‹*Sirene, Nebelhorn*›; **~ one's horn** ▸**horn A 4**

C *n.* **1** (shout) **~s of derision/scorn** verächtliches Gejohle; **~s of laughter** johlendes Gelächter **2** (owl's cry) Schrei, *der* **3** (signal) (of vehicle) Hupen, *das;* (of siren, foghorn) Heulen, *das;* Tuten, *das;* **give a ~ of** *or* **on one's horn** ‹*Fahrer:*› hupen **4** (coll.) **I don't care** *or* **give a ~** *or* **two ~s what you do** es ist mir völlig piepegal *od.* schnuppe (ugs.), was du tust; **not matter a ~** *or* **two ~s [to sb.]** [jmdm.] völlig schnuppe sein (ugs.) **5** (coll.: cause of laughter) **what a ~!** zum Kaputtlachen! (ugs.); **be a ~:** zum Schießen sein (ugs.)

hooter /ˈhuːtə(r)/ *n.* (Brit.) **1** (siren) Sirene, *die* **2** (motor horn) Hupe, *die;* **sound one's ~:** hupen **3** (coll.: nose) Zinken, *der* (ugs. scherzh.)

hoots /huːts/ *int.* (Scot., N. Engl. arch. or joc.) ach was!

hoover /ˈhuːvə(r)/ (Brit.)

A *n.* **1** **H~** ® [Hoover]staubsauger, *der* **2** (made by any company) Staubsauger, *der*

B *v.t.* staubsaugen; saugen ‹*Boden, Teppich*›; absaugen ‹*Möbel*›

C *v.i.* [staub]saugen

hooves *pl. of* **hoof**

hop¹ /hɒp/ *n.* **1** (Bot.) (plant) Hopfen, *der; in pl.* (cones) Hopfendolden **2** *in pl.* (Brewing) Hopfen, *der*

hop²

A *v.i.,* **-pp-:** **1** hüpfen; ‹*Hase:*› hoppeln; **be ~ping mad [about** *or* **over sth.]** (coll.) [wegen etw.] fuchsteufelswild sein (ugs.) **2** (fig. coll.) **~ out of bed** aus dem Bett springen; **~ into the car/on [to] the bus/train/bicycle** sich ins Auto/in den Bus/Zug/aufs Fahrrad schwingen (ugs.); **~ into bed with sb.** mit jmdm. ins Bett steigen (ugs.); **~ off/out** aussteigen **3** (coll.: change location) **be always ~ping [about] from place to place/country to country** ständig unterwegs sein

B *v.t.,* **-pp-:** **1** (jump over) springen über (+ *Akk.*) **2** (coll.: jump aboard) aufspringen auf (+ *Akk.*) **3** **~ it** (Brit. coll.: go away) sich verziehen (ugs.). *see also* **hedge-hop**

C *n.* **1** (action) Hüpfer, *der;* Hopser, *der* (ugs.); **~, step, and jump** ▸**triple jump** **2** **be on the ~** (Brit. coll.: be bustling about) auf Trab sein (ugs.); **keep sb. on the ~** (Brit. coll.) jmdn. in Trab halten (ugs.) **3** **catch sb. on the ~** (Brit. coll.) (unprepared) jmdn. überraschen *od.* überrumpeln; (in the act) jmdn. auf frischer Tat ertappen **4** (coll.: dance) Schwof, *der* (ugs.) **5** (distance flown) Flugstrecke, *die;* (stage of journey) Teilstrecke, *die;* Etappe, *die;* (flight) kurzer Flug; (trip) kurze Reise

hope /həʊp/

A *n.* Hoffnung, *die;* **~ springs eternal [in the human breast]** (prov.) der Mensch hofft, solange er lebt; **give up ~:** die Hoffnung aufgeben; **that is my [dearest] ~:** darauf setze ich meine [ganze] Hoffnung; **hold out ~ [for sb.]** [jmdm.] Hoffnung machen; **I don't hold out much ~ for his recovery** ich habe nicht viel Hoffnung, dass er sich wieder erholt; **beyond** *or* **past ~:** hoffnungslos; **in the ~/in ~[s] of sth./doing sth.** in der Hoffnung auf etw. (*Akk.*)/, etw. zu tun; **live in ~[s] of sth.** in der Hoffnung auf etw. (*Akk.*) leben; **sb.'s ~[s] of sth.** jmds. Hoffnung auf etw. (*Akk.*); **I have some ~[s] of success** *or* **of succeeding** *or* **that I shall succeed** es besteht die Hoffnung, dass ich Erfolg habe; **set** *or* **put** *or* **place one's ~s on** *or* **in sth./sb.** seine Hoffnung auf etw./jmdn. setzen; **raise sb.'s ~s** jmdm. Hoffnung machen; **raise sb.'s ~s too much** *or* **high** jmdm. zu große Hoffnungen machen; **high ~s** große Hoffnungen; **have high ~s of sth./doing sth.** sich (*Dat.*) große Hoffnungen auf etw. (*Akk.*) machen/sich (*Dat.*) große Hoffnungen machen, etw. zu tun; **there is no/some/little ~ that …:** es besteht keine/einige/wenig Hoffnung, dass …; **not have a ~ [in hell] [of sth.]** (coll.) sich (*Dat.*) keine[rlei] Hoffnung [auf etw. (*Akk.*)] machen können; **there's not a ~ in hell that …** (coll.) es besteht nicht die leiseste Chance, dass …; **not a ~ [in hell]!** (coll. iron.) völlig ausgeschlossen!; **what a ~!** (coll.), **some ~[s]!** (coll. iron.) schön wärs!; **be hoping against ~ that …:** trotz allem die Hoffnung nicht aufgeben, dass …; **be the great new tennis ~:** die große neue Hoffnung im Tennis sein; **hard work is our only ~ for** *or* **of a better way of life** nur wenn wir hart arbeiten, können wir auf ein besseres Leben hoffen; **my ~ is that …:** ich hoffe, dass …; *see also* **alive 1; forlorn 1**

B *v.i.* hoffen (**for** auf + *Akk.*); **I ~ so/not** hoffentlich/hoffentlich nicht; ich hoffe es/ich hoffe nicht; **~ for the best** das Beste hoffen

C *v.t.* **~ to do sth./that it may be so** hoffen, etw. zu tun/dass das der Fall ist; **I ~ to go to Paris** (am planning) ich habe vor, nach Paris zu fahren; **I ~ [that] that is true** hoffentlich stimmt das;

hoping to see you soon in der Hoffnung, Sie bald zu sehen

'hope chest *n.* (Amer.) Aussteuertruhe, *die*

hoped-for /'həʊptfɔː(r)/ *attrib. adj.* erhofft

hopeful /'həʊpfl/

A *adj.* **1** zuversichtlich; **I'm ~/not ~ that ...:** ich hoffe zuversichtlich/bezweifle, dass ...; **feel ~:** zuversichtlich sein; **be** *or* **feel ~ about the future** hoffnungsvoll *od.* zuversichtlich in die Zukunft blicken; **if you think he will help you, you are very ~ indeed** wenn du denkst, dass er dir helfen wird, dann bist du wirklich ein Optimist; **be ~ of sth./of doing sth./that it may be so** auf etw. (*Akk.*) hoffen/voller Hoffnung sein, etw. zu tun/dass das der Fall ist **2** (promising) viel versprechend; aussichtsreich ‹*Kapitalanlage, Kandidat*›

B *n.* **[young] ~:** hoffnungsvoller junger Mensch

hopefully /'həʊpfəlɪ/ *adv.* **1** (expectantly) voller Hoffnung **2** (promisingly) viel versprechend **3** (coll.: it is hoped that) hoffentlich; **~, our problems should now be over** wir wollen hoffen, dass unsere Probleme jetzt beseitigt sind; **~, it will be available in the autumn** wir hoffen, dass es im Herbst zur Verfügung steht

hopeless /'həʊplɪs/ *adj.* **1** hoffnungslos **2** (inadequate, incompetent) miserabel; **be ~, be a ~ case** ein hoffnungsloser Fall sein (ugs.) (**at** in + *Dat.*); **be ~ at doing sth.** etw. überhaupt nicht können

hopelessly /'həʊplɪslɪ/ *adv.* **1** hoffnungslos; **be ~ in love** (fig.) rettungslos verliebt sein (ugs.); **I'm ~ bad at maths** in Mathematik bin ich ein hoffnungsloser Fall (ugs. scherzh.) **2** (inadequately) miserabel

hopelessness /'həʊplɪsnɪs/ *n.*, *no pl.* Hoffnungslosigkeit, *die*

'hop garden *n.* (Brit. Agric.) Hopfengarten, *der*

hopper /'hɒpə(r)/ *n.* (Mech.) Trichter, *der*

hop: ~sack *n.* **1** (bag) Hopfensack, *der*; **2** (Textiles) Sackleinen, *das*; Sackleinwand, *die*; **~scotch** *n.* Himmel-und-Hölle-Spiel, *das*; **play ~scotch** „Himmel und Hölle" spielen

horde /hɔːd/ *n.* (huge number) große Menge; (derog./of wild animals) Horde, *die*; **in [their] ~s** in Scharen; **~s of tourists** Scharen von Touristen

horizon /hə'raɪzn/ *n.* **1** Horizont, *der*; **on/over the ~:** am Horizont; **the sun dropped below the ~:** die Sonne verschwand hinter dem Horizont; **there is trouble on the ~** (fig.) am Horizont tauchen Probleme auf; **there's nothing on the ~** (fig.) da ist nichts in Sicht (ugs.); *see also* **artificial horizon** **2** (fig.: perceptual limit) Horizont, *der*; Gesichtskreis, *der*; **broaden one's/sb.'s ~s** seinen/jmds. Horizont erweitern **3** (Geol.) Horizont, *der* **4** (Archaeol.) Kulturschicht, *die* **5** (Soil Science) Bodenhorizont, *der*

horizontal /hɒrɪ'zɒntl/

A *adj.* horizontal; waagerecht; *see also* **bar¹ A 2**; **integration 4**

B *n.* Horizontale, *die*; Waagerechte, *die*

horizontally /hɒrɪ'zɒntəlɪ/ *adv.* horizontal; (flat) waagerecht; flach ‹*liegen*›

hormonal /hɔː'məʊnl/ *adj.* (Biol., Pharm.) hormonal; hormonell; **~ deficiency** Hormonmangel, *der*

hormone /'hɔːməʊn/ *n.* (Biol., Pharm.) Hormon, *das*

hormone: ~ re'placement therapy *n.*, *no pl.* (Med.) Hormonsubstitutionstherapie, *die*; **~ treatment** *n.*, *no pl.* (Med) Hormonbehandlung, *die*

horn /hɔːn/

A *n.* **1** (of animal or devil) Horn, *das*; (of deer) Geweihstange, *die* (Jägerspr.); **~s** Geweih, *das*; **lock ~s [with sb.]** (fig.) [mit jmdm.] die Klinge[n] kreuzen (geh.) **2** (substance) Horn, *das*; *attrib.* Horn- **3** (Mus.) Horn, *das*; **[French] ~:** [Wald]horn, *das*; *see also* **English horn** **4** (of vehicle) Hupe, *die*; (of ship) [Signal]horn, *das*; (of factory) [Fabrik]sirene, *die*; **sound** *or* **blow** *or* **hoot** *or* **honk the** *or* **one's ~ [at sb.]** ‹*Fahrer:*› [jmdn. an]hupen **5** (of snail) Horn, *das*; (of insect) Fühler, *der*; **draw in one's ~s** (fig.) sich zurückhalten; (restrain one's ambition) zurückstecken **6** (receptacle) Horn, *das*; (to drink from) Trinkhorn, *das* (hist.); (for gunpowder) Pulverhorn, *das* (hist.); **~ of plenty** Füllhorn, *das* **7** (loudspeaker) [Schall]trichter, *der* **8** (of crescent) Horn, *das*; **the ~s of the moon** die Hörnerspitzen des Mondes **9** (Geog.) (of land) Horn, *das* (veralt.); **the H~:** das Kap Hoorn **10** (coarse: erect penis) Latte, *die* (*salopp*). *See also* **bull¹ A 1**; **dilemma**; **foghorn**; **shoehorn**

B *v.i.* (coll.: intrude) **~ in [on sth.]** sich [in etw. (*Akk.*)] reinhängen (salopp)

horn: ~beam *n.* (Bot.) Hainbuche, *die*; Hornbaum, *der*; **~bill** *n.* (Ornith.) Nashornvogel, *der*

horned /hɔːnd/ *adj.* **1** gehörnt; (with antlers) Geweih tragend **2** (poet.: crescent-shaped) sichelförmig

horned: ~ 'owl *n.* Ohreule, *die*; **~ 'toad** *n.* Texaskrötenechse, *die*

hornet /'hɔːnɪt/ *n.* Hornisse, *die*; **stir up** *or* **walk into a ~s' nest** (fig.) in ein Wespennest stechen *od.* greifen (ugs.); **bring a ~s' nest about one's ears** (fig.) sich in ein Wespennest setzen (ugs.)

hornless /'hɔːnlɪs/ *adj.* hornlos; (without antlers) geweihlos

'hornpipe *n.* (Mus.) Hornpipe, *die*

'horn-rimmed *adj.* **~ spectacles** *or* **glasses** Hornbrille, *die*

horny /'hɔːnɪ/ *adj.* **1** (hard) hornig ‹*Fußsohlen, Haut, Hände*› **2** (made of horn) aus Horn *nachgestellt*; (like horn) hornartig **3** (sl.: sexually aroused) spitz (ugs.); geil (oft abwertend)

horology /hɒ'rɒlədʒɪ/ *n.*, *no pl.* **1** (science) Lehre von der Zeitmessung **2** (clock-making) Uhrmacherkunst, *die*

horoscope /'hɒrəskəʊp/ *n.* (Astrol.) Horoskop, *das*; **draw up** *or* **cast sb.'s ~:** jmdm. das Horoskop stellen

horrendous /hə'rendəs/ *adj.* (coll.) schrecklich (ugs.); entsetzlich (ugs.) ‹*Dummheit*›; horrend ‹*Preis*›

horrendously /hə'rendəslɪ/ *adv.* (coll.) entsetzlich (ugs.); horrend ‹*teuer*›

horrible /'hɒrɪbl/ *adj.* **1** grauenhaft; grausig ‹*Monster, Geschichte*›; grauenvoll ‹*Verbrechen, Albtraum*›; schauerlich ‹*Maske*›; **I find all insects ~:** mir graust vor jeder Art von Insekten **2** (coll.: unpleasant, excessive) grauenhaft (ugs.); horrend ‹*Ausgaben, Kosten*›; **have a ~ surprise** eine ganz böse Überraschung erleben (ugs.); **don't be so ~ to me** sei nicht so gemein zu mir; **I have a ~ feeling that ...:** ich habe das ungute Gefühl, dass ...

horribly /'hɒrɪblɪ/ *adv.* **1** entsetzlich ‹*entstellt*›; scheußlich ‹*grinsen*›; **it was a ~ frightening story** es war eine überaus grausige Geschichte **2** (coll.: unpleasantly, excessively) entsetzlich (ugs.); fürchterlich (ugs.) ‹*aufregen*›; horrend ‹*teuer*›

horrid /'hɒrɪd/ *adj.* scheußlich; **don't be so ~ to me** (coll.) sei nicht so gemein zu mir

horrific /hə'rɪfɪk/ *adj.* schrecklich; grausig ‹*Geistergeschichte*›; (coll.) horrend ‹*Preis*›

horrify /'hɒrɪfaɪ/ *v.t.* **1** (excite horror in) mit Schrecken erfüllen; **it horrifies me to think what ...:** ich denke mit Schrecken daran, was ...; **I was horrified to see my car rolling into the river** voller Entsetzen sah ich, wie mein Auto in den Fluss rollte **2** (shock, scandalize) **be horrified** entsetzt sein (**at, by** über + *Akk.*)

horrifying /'hɒrɪfaɪɪŋ/ *adj.* grauenhaft; grausig ‹*Film*›; **it is ~ to think that ...:** der Gedanke, dass ..., ist schrecklich

horrifyingly /'hɒrɪfaɪɪŋlɪ/ *adv.* erschreckend

horror /'hɒrə(r)/

A *n.* **1** Entsetzen, *das* (**at** über + *Akk.*); (repugnance) Grausen, *das*; **she screamed in ~:** sie schrie voller Entsetzen; **there was [an expression of] ~ on her face** Entsetzen/Grauen stand ihr im Gesicht geschrieben; **have a ~ of sb./sth./doing sth.** einen Horror vor jmdm./etw. haben/einen Horror davor haben, etw. zu tun (ugs.); **have a fit of the ~s** weiße Mäuse sehen (ugs.); **spiders gave her the ~s** vor Spinnen hatte sie eine panische Angst; **he gives me the ~s** er ist mir unheimlich **2** (coll.: dismay) Entsetzen, *das* (**at** über + *Akk.*) **3** (horrifying quality) Grauenhaftigkeit, *die*; (horrifying thing) Gräuel, *der*; (horrifying person) Scheusal, *das*; **'Six Die in Blaze H~'** „Sechs Tote in flammendem Inferno"; **Chamber of H~s** (lit. or fig.) Schreckenskabinett, *das*

B *attrib. adj.* Horror‹*comic, -film, -geschichte*›

C *int.* **~[s]!** wie schrecklich!; o Graus! (ugs. scherzh.); **~ of ~s!** o Schreck, o Graus! (ugs. scherzh.)

horror: ~-stricken, ~-struck *adjs.* von Entsetzen gepackt; **be ~-stricken** *or* **-struck at sth.** über etw. (*Akk.*) furchtbar entsetzt sein

hors de combat /ɔː də 'kɒ̃bɑː/ *pred. adj.* kampfunfähig; **put** *or* **render sb./sth. ~:** jmdn./etw. außer Gefecht setzen

hors d'oeuvre /ɔː'dɜːvr, ɔː'dɜːv/ *n.* (Gastr.) Horsd'oeuvre, *das*; ≈ Vorspeise, *die*

horse /hɔːs/

A *n.* **1** Pferd, *das*; (adult male) Hengst, *der*; **be/get on one's high ~** (fig.) auf dem hohen Ross sitzen/sich aufs hohe Ross setzen (ugs.); **get [down] off one's high ~** (fig.) von seinem hohen Ross herunterkommen *od.* -steigen (ugs.); **hold your ~s!** (fig.) immer sachte mit den jungen Pferden! (ugs.); **he ought to hold his ~s** er sollte erst einmal abwarten; **as strong as a ~:** bärenstark (ugs.); **eat/work like a ~:** wie ein Scheunendrescher essen (salopp)/wie ein Pferd arbeiten; **I could eat a ~** (coll.) ich habe einen Bärenhunger (ugs.); **[right** *or* **straight] from the ~'s mouth** (fig.) aus erster Hand *od.* Quelle; **change** *or* **swap ~s in midstream** (fig.) auf halbem Wege die Richtung ändern; **to ~!** aufgesessen!; **it's [a question** *or* **matter of] ~s for courses** (fig.) jeder sollte die Aufgaben übernehmen, für die er am besten geeignet ist; **you can lead** *or* **take a ~ to water, but you can't make it drink** (prov.) man kann ein Pferd zur Tränke bringen, aber es nicht zwingen zu trinken **2** *constr. as pl.* (Mil. Hist.) Kavallerie, *die*; Reiterei, *die*; **800 ~:** 800 Reiter *od.* Berittene **3** (Gymnastics) **[vaulting] ~:** [Sprung]pferd, *das* **4** (framework) Gestell, *das*; (for planks or beams) [Auflager]bock, *der*; **[clothes] ~:** Wäscheständer, *der* **5** *in pl.* (coll.: ~power) PS, *das*. *See also* **cart A**; **carthorse**; **dark ~**; **flog 1**; **gift ~**; **hobby ~**; **light ~**; **lock² B 1**; **marine B 1**; **pommel ~**; **rocking ~**; **sea ~**; **Trojan ~**; **white ~**; **wild ~**; **wooden ~**

B *v.i.* **~ about** *or* **around** (coll.) herumalbern (ugs.)

horse: ~-and-'buggy *adj.* (Amer. fig.) aus der Zeit der Postkutschen (fig.) *nachgestellt*; **~back** **A** *n.* **1** **on ~back** zu Pferd; **ride on ~back** reiten; **2** *attrib.* (Amer.) **~back riding** Reiten, *das*; **go in for** *or* **enjoy ~back rides** gerne reiten; **B** *adv.* **go ~back** reiten; **~box** *n.* (trailer) Pferdeanhänger, *der*; (Motor Veh.) Pferdetransporter, *der*; **~ brass** ▸ **brass A 3**; **~breaker** *n.* Zureiter, *der*; **~ breeder** ▸ **breeder**; **~ 'chestnut** *n.* (Bot.) Rosskastanie, *die*; **~-drawn** *attrib. adj.* pferdebespannt; von Pferden gezogen; **~-drawn vehicle** Pferdewagen, *der*; Pferdefuhrwerk, *das*; **~flesh** *n.* **1** (meat) Pferdefleisch, *das*; **2** (horses) Pferde; **~fly** *n.* (Zool.) Pferdebremse, *die*; **H~ Guards** *n. pl.* (Brit. Mil.) (brigade) Gardekavallerie, *die*; **~hair** *n.* **1** (single hair) Pferdehaar, *das*; **2** *no pl.*, *no indef. art.* (mass of hairs) Rosshaar, *das*; **3** (fabric) Rosshaar, *das*; **~ latitudes** *n. pl.* (Geog.) Rossbreiten *Pl.*; **~ laugh** *n.* laute Lache (ugs.); **~man** /'hɔːsmən/ *n.*, *pl.* **~men** /'hɔːsmən/ **1** ([skilled] rider) [guter] Reiter; **2** (Amer.: breeder) Pferdezüchter, *der*

horsemanship /'hɔːsmənʃɪp/ *n.*, *no pl.* **[skills of] ~:** reiterliches Können

horse: ~ opera *n.* (Amer. coll.) Pferdeoper, *die* (ugs.); **~play** *n.* Balgerei, *die*; Alberei, *die*; **~power** *n.*, *pl. same* (Mech.) Pferdestärke, *die*; **a 100 ~power car** ein Auto mit 100 PS; **what ~power does the engine produce?** wie viel PS liefert der Motor?; **~ race** *n.* Pferderennen, *das*; **~racing** *n.* Pferderennsport, *der*; **~radish** *n.* Meerrettich, *der*; **~ sense** *n.* (coll.) [gesunder Menschen]verstand; **~shoe**

h

n. Hufeisen, *das;* (Archit.) Hufeisenbogen, *der; attrib.* hufeisenförmig; **~shoe magnet** Hufeisenmagnet, *der;* **~shoe crab** (Amer. Zool.) Königskrabbe, *die;* **~ show** *n.* Pferdeschau, *die;* **~tail** *n.* **1** (Bot.) Schachtelhalm, *der;* **2** ▸**ponytail**; **~-trader** *n.* Pferdehändler, *der;* **~-trading** *n., no pl.* **1** (dealing in horses) Pferdehandel, *der;* **2** (fig.: bargaining) Kuhhandel, *der* (ugs. abwertend); **~whip** **A** *n.* Reitpeitsche, *die;* **B** *v.t.* auspeitschen; **~woman** *n.* Reiterin, *die*

horsy (horsey) /'hɔːsɪ/ *adj.* **1** (horselike) pferdeähnlich; **~ face/laugh** Pferdegesicht, *das*/wieherndes Lachen (ugs.) **2** (much concerned with horses) pferdenärrisch; **~ people** Pferdenarren

horticultural /hɔːtɪ'kʌltʃərl/ *adj.* gartenbaulich; Gartenbau‹*zeitschrift, -ausstellung*›; **~ society** Gesellschaft für Gartenbau; **~ show** Gartenschau, *die*

horticulture /'hɔːtɪkʌltʃə(r)/ *n.* Gartenbau, *der*

horticulturist /hɔːtɪ'kʌltʃərɪst/ *n.* ▸❶ **p. 1260** Gärtner, *der*/Gärtnerin, *die*

hosanna /həʊ'zænə/ (Bibl.)
A *int.* hosianna
B *n.* Hosianna, *das*

hose /həʊz/
A *n.* **1** (flexible tube) Schlauch, *der;* **garden ~:** Gartenschlauch, *der* **2** *constr. as pl.* (stockings) Strümpfe; **half-~:** Socken **3** *constr. as pl.* (Hist.) (tights) Strumpfhose, *die;* (breeches) Kniehose, *die; see also* **doublet 1**
B *v.t.* sprengen
Phrasal verb
• **~ 'down** *v.t.* abspritzen

'hosepipe ▸**hose A 1**

hosiery /'həʊʒərɪ/ *n., no pl.* Strumpfwaren *Pl.*

hospice /'hɒspɪs/ *n.* **1** (Brit.) (for the destitute) Heim für Mittellose; (for the terminally ill) Sterbeklinik, *die* **2** (for travellers or students) Hospiz, *das*

hospitable /'hɒspɪtəbl/ *adj.* (welcoming) gastfreundlich ‹*Person, Wesensart*›; gastlich ‹*Haus, Hotel*›; freundlich ‹*Klima, Einladung*›; **be ~ to sb.** jmdn. gastfreundlich *od.* gastlich aufnehmen

hospitably /'hɒspɪtəblɪ/ *adv.* (welcomingly) gastlich; gastfreundlich

hospital /'hɒspɪtl/ *n.* Krankenhaus, *das;* **in ~** (Brit.), **in the ~** (Amer.) im Krankenhaus; **into** *or* **to ~** (Brit.), **to the ~** (Amer.) ins Krankenhaus ‹*gehen, bringen*›; **veterinary/dolls' ~:** Tier-/Puppenklinik, *die*

hospital: ~ bed *n.* Krankenhausbett, *das;* **~ case** *n.* Fall fürs Krankenhaus

hospitalisation, hospitalise ▸**hospitaliz-**

hospitality /hɒspɪ'tælɪtɪ/ *n., no pl.* (of person) Gastfreundschaft, *die;* (of thing, action, environment) Freundlichkeit, *die*

hospi'tality tent *n.* Bewirtungszelt, *das*

hospitalization /hɒspɪtəlaɪ'zeɪʃn/ *n.* Einweisung ins Krankenhaus; **long periods of ~:** lange Krankenhausaufenthalte

hospitalize /'hɒspɪtəlaɪz/ *v.t.* ins Krankenhaus einweisen

hospital: ~ 'nurse *n.* ▸❶ **p. 1260** Krankenschwester, *die*/Krankenpfleger, *der;* **~ 'porter** *n.* ▸❶ **p. 1260** ≈ Krankenpflegehelfer, *der*/-helferin, *die;* **~ ship** *n.* Lazarettschiff, *das;* **~ trust** *n.: für ein od. mehrere NHS-Krankenhäuser zuständiges Verwaltungsgremium*

host¹ /həʊst/ *n.* **1** (large number) Menge, *die;* **in [their] ~s** in Scharen; **a ~ of people/children** eine Menge Leute/eine Schar von Kindern; **he has ~s** *or* **a ~ of things to do/friends** er hat eine Menge zu erledigen/eine Menge Freunde **2** (arch.: army) Heer, *das* **3** (Bibl.) **the Lord [God] of ~s** der Herr der Heerscharen; **the heavenly ~** (angels) die himmlischen Heerscharen (bibl.)

host²
A *n.* **1** Gastgeber, *der*/Gastgeberin, *die;* **be** *or* **play ~ to sb.** jmdn. zu Gast haben; **~ country** Gastland, *das* **2** (landlord) [Gast]wirt, *der;* **mine ~** (arch./joc.) der Herr Wirt **3** (compère) Moderator, *der;* **your ~ for the show is ...:** durch die Show führt Sie ...; (for chat show) Gastgeber ist heute Abend ... **4** (Computing) Host, *der* **5** (Biol.: of parasite) Wirt, *der;* **~ organism/animal/cell** Wirtsorganismus, *der*/-tier, *das*/-zelle, *die* **6** (Biol./Med.: recipient) Empfänger [eines Transplantats]; (of organ) [Organ]empfänger, *der*
B *v.t.* **1** (act as host at) Gastgeber sein bei; **China is to ~ the Olympic Games** China soll die Olympischen Spiele ausrichten **2** (compère) moderieren; **~ a programme** durch ein Programm führen **3** (Computing) hosten ‹*Website*›

host³ *n.* (Eccl.: bread) Hostie, *die*

hostage /'hɒstɪdʒ/ *n.* Geisel, *die;* **hold/take sb. ~:** jmdn. als Geisel festhalten/nehmen; **a ~ to fortune** (fig.) etwas, was einem das Schicksal nehmen kann

'host country *n.* Gastland, *das*

hostel /'hɒstl/ *n.* (Brit.) **1** Wohnheim, *das* **2** ▸**youth hostel**

hostelry /'hɒstlrɪ/ *n.* (arch./literary) Herberge, *die* (veralt.)

hostess /'həʊstɪs/ *n.* **1** Gastgeberin, *die;* **take flowers for the ~:** der Dame des Hauses Blumen mitbringen **2** (in nightclub) Animierdame, *die* **3** (euphem.: prostitute) Hostess, *die* (verhüll.) **4** (in passenger transport) Hostess, *die; see also* **air hostess** **5** (compère) Moderatorin, *die*

'hostess gown *n.* Hausmantel, *der*

hostile /'hɒstaɪl/ *adj.* **1** feindlich **2** (unfriendly) feindselig (**to[wards]** gegenüber); **give sb. a ~ look** jmdn. feindselig ansehen; **be ~ to** *or* **towards sb.** jmdm. mit Feindseligkeit begegnen; **be ~ to sth.** etw. ablehnen; **a government ~ to change** eine Veränderungen ablehnende Regierung **3** (inhospitable) unwirtlich; feindselig ‹*Atmosphäre*›; rau ‹*Wirklichkeit*›

hostility /hɒ'stɪlɪtɪ/ *n.* **1** *no pl.* (enmity) Feindschaft, *die* **2** *no pl.* (antagonism) Feindseligkeit, *die* (**to[wards]** gegenüber); **feel no ~ towards anybody** niemandem feindlich gesinnt sein; **show ~ to sth.** einer Sache (*Dat.*) feindlich gegenüberstehen **3** (state of war, act of warfare) Feindseligkeit, *die;* **an act of ~:** eine feindselige Handlung

hot /hɒt/
A *adj.* **1** heiß; (cooked) warm ‹*Mahlzeit, Essen*›; (fig.: potentially dangerous, difficult) heiß (ugs.) ‹*Thema, Geschichte*›; ungemütlich, gefährlich ‹*Lage*›; **bake in a ~ oven** bei hoher Temperatur backen; **the room is much too ~:** in dem Zimmer ist es viel zu heiß; **~ and cold running water** fließend warm und kalt Wasser; **I've climbed more mountains than you've had ~ dinners** (coll.) ich habe schon mehr Berge bestiegen, als du dir vorstellen kannst; **be too ~ to handle** (fig.) eine zu heiße Angelegenheit sein (ugs.); **things were getting too ~ for him [to handle]** (fig.) die Sache wurde ihm zu brenzlig (ugs.); **make it** *or* **things [too] ~ for sb.** (fig.) jmdm. die Hölle heiß machen (ugs.) **2** (feeling heat) **I am/feel ~:** mir ist heiß; **I got ~:** mir wurde heiß; **I went ~ and cold all over** es überlief mich heiß und kalt **3** (pungent) scharf ‹*Gewürz, Senf usw.*›; scharf gewürzt ‹*Essen*› **4** (suggesting heat) grell, flammend ‹*Farbe*› **5** (passionate, lustful) glühend ‹*Begeisterung*›; heiß ‹*Küsse, Tränen, Umarmung*›; **be ~ for sth.** heiß auf etw. (*Akk.*) sein (ugs.); **be ~ on sth./sb.** (keen) auf etw./jmdn. wild sein (ugs.); von etw./jmdm. seht angetan sein; **he's really ~ on her** (sexually) er ist richtig scharf auf sie (ugs.); **have a ~ temper** ein hitziges Temperament haben **6** (agitated, angry) hitzig; **get ~ over sth.** sich an etw. (*Dat.*) erhitzen; **be [all] ~ and bothered** ganz aufgelöst sein; **get [all] ~ and bothered** sich [fürchterlich (ugs.)] aufregen **7** (intense) heiß ‹[*Wett*]*kampf, Auseinandersetzung*› **8** (coll.: good, skilful) toll (ugs.); **be ~ at sth.** in etw. (*Dat.*) [ganz] groß sein (ugs.); **I'm not too ~ at that** darin bin ich nicht besonders umwerfend (ugs.); **be ~ on sth.** (knowledgeable) sich in *od.* mit etw. (*Dat.*) gut auskennen; **not so** *or* **too ~** (coll.) nicht gerade berauschend (ugs.) **9** (recent) (Hunting) warm, frisch ‹*Fährte*›; (fig.) noch warm ‹*Nachrichten*›; **this is really ~ [news]** das ist wirklich das Neueste vom Neuen; **~ off the press[es]** (Journ., Printing) frisch aus der Presse **10** (close) **you are getting ~/are ~** (in children's games) es wird schon wärmer/[jetzt ist es] heiß; **follow ~ on sb.'s heels** jmdm. dicht auf den Fersen folgen (ugs.); **be ~ on sb.'s track** *or* **trail, be in ~ pursuit of sb.** jmdm. dicht auf den Fersen sein (ugs.) **11** (Mus.: rhythmical) heiß; schräg (ugs.) ‹*Musik*›; **he is a really ~ saxophonist** er spielt ein heißes Saxophon **12** (coll.: in demand) zugkräftig; **they are the ~test items just now** sie sind die augenblicklichen Renner (ugs.); **a ~ property** (singer, actress, etc.) eine ertragreiche Zugnummer; (company, invention, etc.) eine ertragreiche Geldanlage **13** (coll.: radioactive) heiß (Kernphysik) **14** (Sport; also fig.) heiß (ugs.) ‹*Tipp, Favorit*› **15** (coll.: illegally obtained) heiß ‹*Ware, Geld*›. **16** (coll.: strict) **be ~ on sth.** hart gegen etw. durchgreifen. *See also* **blow¹ A 2; cake A 2; collar A 1; potato 1; red-hot; white-hot**
B *adv.* heiß
C *n. in pl.* **have the ~s for sb.** (coll.) richtig scharf auf jmdn. sein (ugs.)
Phrasal verb
• **~ 'up** (Brit. coll.)
A *v.t.* **1** (heat) warm machen **2** (make more exciting) in Schwung bringen; (make more dangerous) verschärfen **3** (Motor Veh.) frisieren (ugs.)
B *v.i.* **1** (rise in temperature) heiß werden; **the weather ~s up** es wird wärmer **2** (become exciting) in Schwung kommen; (become dangerous) sich verschärfen **3** (become more intense) sich verstärken; ‹*Wortgefecht:*› zunehmend heißer *od.* hitziger werden

hot: ~ 'air *n.* (coll.: idle talk) leeres Gerede (ugs.); **talk ~ air** dummes Gewäsch von sich geben (ugs. abwertend); *see also* **balloon A 1**; **~bed** *n.* (Hort.) Mistbeet, *das;* Frühbeet, *das;* (fig.: place favouring growth) Nährboden, *der* (**of** für); (of vice, corruption, etc.) Brutstätte, *die* (**of** für); **~-blooded** /'hɒtblʌdɪd/ *adj.* heißblütig; **~ button** *n.* (Amer. coll.) brisantes [Schlüssel]thema; brisanter [Streit]punkt; *attrib.* **~ button issue** Reizthema, *das*

hotchpotch /'hɒtʃpɒtʃ/ *n.* (mixture) Mischmasch, *der* (ugs.) (**of** aus); **a ~ of people** eine bunte Mischung von Leuten (scherzh.)

hot: ~ cross 'bun *n.: mit einem Kreuz aus Teig verziertes Rosinenbrötchen, das traditionsgemäß am Karfreitag gegessen wird;* **~-'desking** *n., no pl. Mehrfachnutzung von Arbeitsplätzen;* **~ dog** *n.* (coll.) Hotdog, *das od. der; attrib.* **~-dog stand** ≈ Würstchenbude, *die*

hotel /hə'tel, həʊ'tel/ *n.* **1** Hotel, *das; see also* **private hotel** **2** (Austral., NZ: public house) Wirtshaus, *das*

hotelier /hə'telɪə(r)/ *n.* ▸❶ **p. 1260** Hotelier, *der*

hotel: ~ 'manager *n.* ▸❶ **p. 1260** Hoteldirektor, *der*/-direktorin, *die;* Hotelmanager, *der*/-managerin, *die;* **~ re'ceptionist** *n.* ▸❶ **p. 1260** Empfangschef, *der*/-dame, *die;* **~ room** *n.* Hotelzimmer, *das;* **~ 'staff** *n.* Hotelpersonal, *das*

hot: ~ 'flush *n.* (Med.) **suffer from ~ flushes** unter fliegender Hitze leiden; **~foot** **A** *adv.* stehenden Fußes; **B** *adj.* **be in ~foot pursuit of sb.** jmdm. dicht auf den Fersen sein (ugs.); **C** *v.i.* (Amer. coll.) **~foot home** machen, dass man nach Hause kommt (ugs.); **D** *v.t.* **~foot it** sich hastig davonmachen; **~head** *n.* Hitzkopf, *der;* **~-headed** *adj.* hitzköpfig; **~house** *n.* Treibhaus, *das; attrib.* (lit. or fig.) Treibhaus-; **~ key** *n.* (Computing) Hotkey, *der;* **~line** *n.* Hotline, *die;* (Polit.) heißer Draht; **~ link** *n.* (Computing) **1** (connection) Hotlink, *der;* **2** (hypertext) Hyperlink, *der*

hotly /'hɒtlɪ/ *adv.* heftig; **they were ~ pursued by the police** die Polizei war ihnen dicht auf den Fersen (ugs.); **his cheeks flushed ~:** er wurde über und über rot

hot: ~-'metal *adj.* (Printing) Bleisatz-; **~ 'money** *n.* (Finance) heißes Geld

hotness /ˈhɒtnɪs/ *n., no pl.* [1] (temperature) Hitze, *die;* **test the ~:** die Wärme prüfen [2] (hot sensation) Hitze, *die* [3] (pungency) Schärfe, *die* [4] (ardour) Feuer, *das;* Glut, *die* (geh.)

hot: ~ pants *n. pl.* Hotpants *Pl.;* **~plate** *n.* Kochplatte, *die;* (for keeping food ~) Warmhalteplatte, *die;* **~pot** *n.* (Gastr.) **[Lancashire] ~pot** *Fleischeintopf mit Kartoffeleinlage;* **~ rod** *n.* (Motor Veh.) hochfrisiertes Auto (ugs.); **~ seat** *n.* (coll.) [1] (electric chair) elektrischer Stuhl; [2] (uneasy situation) Folterbank, *die* (fig.); (involving heavy responsibility) **be in the ~ seat** den Kopf hinhalten müssen (ugs.); **~ shoe** *n.* (Photog.) [Blitzlicht]mittenkontakt, *der;* **~shot** *n.* (coll.) Ass, *das* (ugs.); **~ spot** *n.* [1] heiße Gegend; [2] **a ~ spot of political instability** (fig.) ein politischer Krisenherd; [3] (nightclub) Nachtlokal, *das;* [4] (difficult situation) **find oneself** *or* **be in/get into a ~ spot** in der Bredouille sein/in die Bredouille kommen *od.* geraten (ugs.); [5] (Computing) Hotspot, *der;* **~ 'spring** *n.* heiße Quelle; Thermalquelle, *die;* **~ 'stuff** *n., no pl., no art.* (coll.) **sb./sth. is ~ stuff** jmd./etw. ist große Klasse (ugs.); **~-tempered** *adj.* heißblütig

Hottentot /ˈhɒtntɒt/ *n.* (person) Hottentotte, *der*/Hottentottin, *die; attrib.* ‹*Gebräuche, Lebensweise*› der Hottentotten

hot: ~ 'ticket *n.* (coll.) (person) Hit, *der* (ugs.); (concept, event) Knaller, *der* (ugs.); **be a ~ ticket** angesagt sein; **the latest ~ ticket** der letzte Schrei; **~ 'water** *n.* (fig. coll.) **be in/get into ~ water** in der Bredouille sein/in die Bredouille geraten (ugs.); **he got into ~ water with the authorities** er bekam Ärger mit den Behörden; **~-'water bag** (Amer.), **~-'water bottle** *ns.* Wärmflasche, *die;* **~-wire** *v.t.* (coll.) kurzschließen

hound /haʊnd/

A *n.* [1] Jagdhund, *der;* **the [pack of] ~s** (Brit. Hunting) die Meute (Jägerspr.); **ride to ~s** mit der Meute jagen [2] (despicable man) Lump, *der*

B *v.t.* jagen; (fig.) verfolgen; **they were ~ed from country to country** sie wurden von einem Land ins andere gejagt

Phrasal verbs

- **~ 'down** *v.t.* (lit. or fig.) zur Strecke bringen
- **~ 'out** *v.t.* [1] (hunt out) aufspüren [2] (force to leave) vertreiben (**of** aus); verjagen (**of** aus)

hound's-tooth *n.* (Textiles) (pattern) Hahnentritt, *der;* (fabric) Stoff mit Hahnentrittmuster

hour /ˈaʊə(r)/ *n.* ►**i** p. 1001 [1] Stunde, *die;* **half an ~:** eine halbe Stunde; **an ~ and a half** anderthalb Stunden; **be paid by the ~:** stundenweise bezahlt werden; **it takes her ~s to get ready** sie braucht Stunden, bis sie fertig ist; **I did two ~s' work** ich habe zwei Stunden [lang] gearbeitet; **there aren't enough ~s in the day** der Tag hat nicht genug Stunden [für all die Dinge, die man erledigen möchte]; **an eight-~ day** ein Achtstundentag; **a two-~ session** eine zweistündige Sitzung; **the 24-~ clock** die Vierundzwanzigstundenuhr; *see also* **lunch hour** [2] (time o'clock) Zeit, *die;* **the ~ grows late** (literary) es wird spät; **strike the ~:** die volle Stunde schlagen; **on the ~:** zur vollen Stunde; **every ~ on the ~:** jede volle Stunde; **at this late ~:** zu so später Stunde (geh.); **at an early/a late ~:** zu früher/später *od.* vorgerückter Stunde (geh.); **at all ~s** zu jeder [Tages- oder Nacht]zeit; (late at night) spät in der Nacht; **till all ~s [of the morning/night]** bis zum Morgengrauen/bis in die späte Nacht; **the small ~s [of the morning]** die frühen Morgenstunden; **0100/0200/1700/1800 ~s** (on 24-~ clock) 1.00/2.00/17.00/18.00 Uhr [3] *in pl.* **doctor's ~s** Sprechstunde, *die;* **post office ~s** Schalterstunden der Post; **what ~s do you work?, what are your working ~s?** wie ist deine Arbeitszeit?; **strike for shorter ~s** für eine kürzere Arbeitszeit streiken; **work long ~s** einen langen Arbeitstag haben; **during school ~s** während der Schulstunden *od.* des Unterrichts; **out of/after ~s** (in office, bank, etc.) außerhalb der Dienstzeit; (of doctor) außerhalb der Sprechstunde; (in shop) außerhalb der Geschäftszeit; (in pub) außerhalb der Ausschankzeit; (in school) außerhalb der Unterrichtszeit; **keep regular/irregular ~s** geregelte/keine geregelten Zeiten einhalten; **what sort of ~s do you keep?** was hast du für einen Tagesrhythmus?; **be accustomed to late ~s** gewöhnlich lange aufbleiben [4] (particular time) Stunde, *die;* **don't desert me in my ~ of need** verlass mich nicht in der Stunde der Not; **~ of glory** Stunde des Ruhmes; **sb.'s finest ~:** jmds. größte Stunde; **one's dying** *or* **final ~** *or* **~ of death** jmds. letzte Stunde *od.* Todesstunde; **at an unhappy/a happy ~:** in einer unglücklichen/glücklichen Stunde [5] (present) **the question** *etc.* **of the ~:** das Problem *usw.* der Stunde [6] (distance) Stunde, *die;* **they are two ~s from us by train** sie wohnen zwei Bahnstunden von uns entfernt; **he lives an ~ from the sea** er wohnt eine Stunde vom Meer entfernt [7] *in pl.* (RC Ch.) (times) Gebetsstunden; (prayers) Stundengebete; **book of ~s** Stundenbuch, *das. See also* **eleventh A**

hour: ~glass *n.* Sanduhr, *die;* Stundenglas, *das* (veralt.); **a woman with an ~glass figure** eine kurvenreiche Frau (ugs. scherzh.); **~ hand** *n.* Stundenzeiger, *der;* kleiner Zeiger

houri /ˈhʊərɪ/ *n.* (Muslim Mythol.) Huri, *die*

'hour-long

A *attrib. adj.* einstündig

B *adv.* eine Stunde [lang]

hourly /ˈaʊəlɪ/

A *adj.* [1] (happening every hour) stündlich; **at ~ intervals** jede Stunde; stündlich; **there are ~ trains to London** jede *od.* alle Stunde fährt ein Zug nach London; **the bus service is ~:** der Bus verkehrt stündlich [2] (reckoned by the hour) **he is paid an ~ rate of £6** er hat einen Stundenlohn von 6 Pfund; **on an ~ basis** stundenweise ‹*mieten*› [3] (continual) ständig [4] **two-~:** zweistündlich

B *adv.* stündlich; **be paid ~:** stundenweise bezahlt werden

house

A /haʊs/ *n., pl.* **~s** /ˈhaʊzɪz/ [1] (dwelling, occupants) Haus, *das;* **a collection from ~ to ~:** eine Haussammlung; **to/at my ~:** zu mir [nach Hause]/bei mir [zu Hause]; **~ of cards** (lit. or fig.) Kartenhaus, *das;* **H~ of God** Gotteshaus, *das;* **~ and home** Haus und Hof; **keep ~ [for sb.]** [jmdm.] den Haushalt führen; **keep open ~:** ein offenes Haus haben *od.* führen; **set up ~:** einen eigenen Hausstand gründen; **put** *or* **set one's ~ in order** (fig.) seine Angelegenheiten in Ordnung bringen; **[as] safe as ~s** absolut sicher; **[get on] like a ~ on fire** (fig.) prächtig [miteinander auskommen]; **go all [a]round the ~s** (fig.) überall herumlaufen; (in discussion) sich lange im Kreise drehen; **man/lady** *or* **woman of the ~:** Hausherr, *der*/Dame des Hauses [2] *in comb.* (for animals) **lion/reptile/monkey ~:** Löwen-/Reptilien-/Affenhaus, *das* [3] (Parl.) (building) Parlamentsgebäude, *das;* (assembly) Haus, *das;* **the H~** (Brit.) das Parlament; **H~ of Keys** *Unterhaus der Insel Man; see also* **commons 1; lord A 3; Lower House; parliament; representative A 2; Upper House** [4] (institution) Haus, *das;* **fashion ~:** Modehaus, *das;* **Broadcasting H~:** das Funkhaus; **Congress H~:** das Gewerkschaftshaus [5] (inn etc.) Wirtshaus, *das;* **keep a good ~:** ein gepflegtes Haus führen; **on the ~:** auf Kosten des Hauses; **~ of ill fame** *or* **repute** (arch./joc.: brothel) öffentliches Haus (verhüll.); *see also* **free house; tied** [6] (Relig.) (residence) Ordenshaus, *das;* (members) Ordensgemeinschaft, *die;* Orden, *der;* **a ~ of friars** ein Mönchskloster; **she entered a ~ of nuns** sie ging in ein Kloster [7] (Sch.) *eine von mehreren Schülergruppen innerhalb einer Privatschule* [8] (Theatre) (building) Haus, *das;* (audience) Publikum, *das;* (performance) Vorstellung, *die;* **an empty ~:** ein leeres Haus; **a good/bad ~:** eine gut/schlecht besuchte Vorstellung; **bring the ~ down, bring down the ~:** stürmischen Beifall auslösen; (cause laughter) Lachstürme entfesseln; *see also* **full house 1** [9] (family) Haus, *das;* Geschlecht, *das;* **the H~ of Windsor** das Haus Windsor [10] (Astrol.) Haus, *das*

B /haʊz/ *v.t.* [1] (provide with home) ein Heim geben (+ *Dat.*); **be ~d in sth.** in etw. (*Dat.*) untergebracht sein [2] (receive in ~) beherbergen; **be ~d by sb.** bei jmdm. unterkommen *od.* Unterkunft finden [3] (keep, store) unterbringen; einlagern ‹*Waren*› [4] (fig.: encase) in sich (*Dat.*) bergen (geh.)

house/haʊs/: **~ agent** *n.* ►**i** p. 1260 (Brit.) Häusermakler, *der;* **~ arrest** *n.* Hausarrest, *der;* **~boat** *n.* Hausboot, *das;* **~-bound** *adj.* ans Haus gefesselt; **~boy** *n.* Boy, *der;* **~breaker** *n.* (burglar) Einbrecher, *der;* **~breaking** *n., no pl.* (burglary) Einbruch, *der;* **~coat** *n.* Hausmantel, *der;* Morgenmantel, *der;* **~craft** *n., no pl., no art.* (Brit.) Hauswirtschaft, *die;* **~father** *n.* Hausvater, *der;* **~ flag** *n.* (Naut.) Hausflagge, *die;* **~fly** *n.* Stubenfliege, *die*

houseful /ˈhaʊsfʊl/ *n.* **a ~ of guests** ein Haus voll[er] Gäste; **we've already got a ~:** wir haben das Haus schon voll (ugs.)

house guest /ˈhaʊs gest/ *n.* Logiergast, *der*

household /ˈhaʊshəʊld/ *n.* [1] Haushalt, *der; attrib.* Haushalts-; **~ chores** Hausarbeit, *die* [2] **the H~** (Brit.: royal family) die königliche Hofhaltung

household 'cavalry *n.* (Brit. Mil.) berittene königliche Leibgarde

householder /ˈhaʊshəʊldə(r)/ *n.* [1] (homeowner) Wohnungsinhaber, *der*/-inhaberin, *die* [2] (head of household) Haushaltsvorstand, *der*

household: ~ 'gods *n. pl.* (Roman Ant.; also fig.) Hausgötter; **~ 'management** *n.* Hauswirtschaft, *die;* **~ 'name** *n.* geläufiger Name; **be a ~ name** ein Begriff sein; **~ 'troops** *n. pl.* (Brit. Mil.) königliche Leibgarde; **~ 'word** *n.* geläufiger Ausdruck

house /haʊs/: **~-hunter** *n.* Haussuchende, *der/die;* **~-hunting** *n., no pl.* Suche nach einem Haus; **go ~-hunting** sich nach einem Haus umsehen; **~ husband** *n.* Hausmann, *der;* **~keep** *v.i.* (coll.) den Haushalt führen (**for** *Dat.*); **~keeper** *n.* ►**i** p. 1260 (woman managing household affairs) Haushälterin, *die;* Wirtschafterin, *die;* (person running own home) Hausfrau, *die*/Hausmann, *der;* (person in charge) Hausmeister, *der*/-meisterin, *die;* **~keeping** *n., no pl.* [1] (management) Hauswirtschaft, *die;* Haushaltsführung, *die;* **he does most of/helps with the ~keeping** er besorgt fast den ganzen Haushalt/hilft im Haushalt; **~keeping money,** (coll.) **~keeping** Haushalts- *od.* Wirtschaftsgeld, *das;* [2] (fig.: maintenance, record-keeping, etc.) Wirtschaften, *das;* **~leek** *n.* (Bot.) Hauswurz, *die;* **~ lights** *n. pl.* (Theatre) Lichter im Zuschauerraum; **~ magazine** *n.* Hauszeitschrift, *die;* **~maid** *n.* ►**i** p. 1260 Hausgehilfin, *die;* **~maid's 'knee** *n.* (Med.) Dienstmädchenknie, *das;* **~man** /ˈhaʊsmən/ *n., pl.* **~men** ►**i** p. 1260 /ˈhaʊsmən/ [1] (Amer.) Hausdiener, *der;* [2] (Brit. Med.) Medizinalassistent, *der;* **~ martin** *n.* (Ornith.) Mehlschwalbe, *die;* **~master** *n.* (Sch.) *für ein „house" zuständiger Lehrer;* **~mistress** *n.* (Sch.) *für ein „house" zuständige Lehrerin;* **~mother** *n.* Hausmutter, *die;* **~ officer** *n.* ►**i** p. 1260 (Brit. Med.) Medizinalassistent, *der;* **~ painter** *n.* ►**i** p. 1260 Maler, *der*/Malerin, *die;* Anstreicher, *der*/Anstreicherin, *die;* **~ party** *n.* ≈ Gesellschaft, *die; mehrtägiges Fest in einem Landhaus;* **~ physician** *n.* (in hospital) *im Krankenhaus wohnender Arzt;* (elsewhere) Hausarzt, *der;* Anstaltsarzt, *der;* **~ plant** *n.* Zimmerpflanze, *die;* **~ prices** *n. pl.* Immobilienpreise; **~-proud** *adj.* **he/she is ~-proud** Ordnung und Sauberkeit [im Haushalt] gehen ihm/ihr über alles; **~room** *n., no pl., no indef. art.* **find ~room for sth.** einen Platz für etw. [in der Wohnung] finden; **I wouldn't give it ~room** das käme mir nicht ins Haus; **~-sit** *v.i.* das Haus hüten; **~-sitter** *n.* House-sitter, *der* (ugs.); *Person, die für jemanden das Haus hütet;* **~-sitting** *n., no pl.* Haussitting, *das;* **~ 'style** *n.* (Printing, Publishing) hauseigener Stil; **~ surgeon** *n.* (in hospital) *im Krankenhaus wohnender Chirurg;* (elsewhere) Hauschirurg, *der;* Anstaltschirurg, *der;* **~-to-~** **A** *adj.* **make ~-to-~ enquiries** von Haus zu Haus gehen und fragen; **a ~-to-~ delivery** eine Lieferung von Haus zu Haus; **B** *adv.* von Haus zu Haus ‹gehen usw.›; **~-train** v.t. (Brit.) **~-train a cat/child** eine Katze/ein Kleinkind dazu bringen, dass sie/es stubenrein/sauber wird; **~-trained** adj. (Brit.) stubenrein ‹Hund, Katze›; sauber ‹Kleinkind›; **~-training** n., no pl. (of pet) Stubenreinmachen, das; (of child) Sauberkeitserziehung, die; Sauberkeitsgewöhnung, die; **~-warming** /ˈhaʊswɔːmɪŋ/ n. **~-warming [party]** Einzugsfeier, die; **~wife** n. Hausfrau, die; **~wifely** adj. hausfraulich; **~work** n., no pl. Hausarbeit, die

Houses of Parliament

Die zwei Häuser des britischen Parlaments: **House of Commons** und **House of Lords**. Der *Westminster Palace* (Westminsterpalast), der Gebäudekomplex an der Themse in London, wo beide Häuser untergebracht sind, ist auch als *Houses of Parliament* bekannt.

housey-housey, housie-housie /haʊsɪ ˈhaʊsɪ/ n. Lotto, das

housing /ˈhaʊzɪŋ/ n. **1** no pl. (dwellings collectively) Wohnungen; (provision of dwellings) Wohnungsbeschaffung, die; attrib. Wohnungs-; **there was insufficient ~:** es gab zu wenig Wohnungen; **this piece of land has been set aside for ~:** auf diesem Stück Land sollen neue Wohnungen gebaut werden; **~ programme** Wohnungsbauprogramm, das **2** no pl. (shelter) Unterkunft, die **3** (Mech. Engin.) Gehäuse, das

housing: ~ association n. (Brit.) Gesellschaft für sozialen Wohnungsbau; **~ benefit** n. (Brit.) Wohngeld, das; **~ estate** n. (Brit.) Wohnsiedlung, die; **~ market** n. Wohnungsmarkt, der; **~ shortage** n. Wohnraummangel, der

HOV abbr. (Amer.) = **high occupancy vehicle** Fahrzeug mit mehreren Insassen; attrib. **~ lane** Spur für Fahrzeuge mit mehreren Insassen

hove ▸**heave A 2, B 5**

hovel /ˈhɒvl/ n. [armselige] Hütte; (joc.) Bruchbude, die (ugs. abwertend)

hover /ˈhɒvə(r)/ v.i. **1** (hang in air) schweben **2** (linger) sich herumdrücken (ugs.); **~ about** or **round sb./sth.** um jmdn./etw. herumschleichen (ugs.) **3** (move to and fro) herumstrolchen (ugs. abwertend) **4** (waver) schwanken; **~ between doing this and doing that** schwanken, ob man dieses oder jenes tun soll; **~ between life and death** (fig.) zwischen Leben und Tod schweben

hover: ~craft n., pl. same Hovercraft, das; Luftkissenfahrzeug, das; **~ mower** n. Luftkissenmäher, der; **~port** n. Anlegestelle [für Hovercrafts]; **~train** n. Luftkissenzug, der; (magnetic) Magnetschwebebahn, die

how /haʊ/

A ▸**❶ p. 1189** adv. wie; **learn ~ to ride a bike/swim** etc. Rad fahren/schwimmen usw. lernen; **this is ~ to do it** so macht man das; **~ do you know that?** woher weißt du das?; **~ does one find the answer?** wie soll man die Lösung finden?; **~ should I know?** woher soll ich das wissen?; **~ 'could you?** wie konntest du nur?; **here's ~!** (as toast) zum Wohl!; **~ is it/does it happen that ...?** wie kommt es, dass ...?; **~'s that?** (~ did that happen?) wie kommt das [denn]?; (is that as it should be?) ist es so gut?; (will you agree to that?) was hältst du davon?; (Cricket) ist der Schlagmann aus?; **~'s that for impudence?** ist das nicht eine Unverschämtheit?; **~ so?** wieso [das]?; **~ can that be?** wie kommt das?; **~ would it be if ...?** wie wäre es, wenn ...?; **~ would this dress be?** wie wäre es mit diesem Kleid?; **[I know/see] ~ it is** [ich weiß,] wie das ist; **~ is she/the car?** (after accident) wie geht es ihr?/was ist mit dem Auto?; **~ 'are you?** wie geht es dir?; (greeting) guten Morgen/Tag/Abend!; **~ do you 'do?** (formal) guten Morgen/Tag/Abend!; **~ 'do?** (coll.) Morgen/Tag/'n Abend! (ugs.); **~ much?** wie viel?; (joc.: I did not hear) wie bitte?; **~ many?** wie viel?; wie viele?; **~ many times?** wie oft?; **~ crazy** etc. **can you get?** verrückter usw. gehts wohl nicht! (ugs.); **~ far** (to what extent) inwieweit; **~ marvellous/perfect!** wie herrlich od. wunderbar!; **~ right/wrong you are!** da hast du völlig Recht/da irrst du dich gewaltig!; **~ naughty of him** das war aber frech von ihm; **and ~!** (coll.) und wie! (ugs.); **we must earn a living ~ [best] we can** wir müssen uns unseren Lebensunterhalt, so gut es geht, verdienen; **~ about ...?** wie ist es mit ...?; (in invitation, proposal, suggestion) wie wäre es mit ...?; **~ about all the overtime I've done?** wie ist das eigentlich mit meinen ganzen Überstunden?; **~ about having a drink?** wie wäre es mit etwas zu trinken?; **~ about getting up?** wie wäre es, wenn du aufstehst/wir aufstehen?; **~ about [giving me] a lift?** wie sieht's aus, kannst du mich mitnehmen? (ugs.); **~ about tomorrow?** wie siehts morgen aus? (ugs.); **~ about it/that?** na, wie ist das?/was sagst du nun?; (is that acceptable?) was hältst du davon?; see also **come 13**; **do¹ B 6**; **ever 5**; **go¹ A 18, 19**

B n. Wie, das

howdah /ˈhaʊdə/ n. [baldachinartig überdachter] Sitz auf einem Elefanten

how-de-do /haʊdɪˈduː/, **how-do-you-do** /haʊdjʊˈduː/ ns. **[this is] a fine** or **pretty ~ [we have landed in]** das ist ja eine schöne Bescherung (ugs. iron.)

howdy /ˈhaʊdɪ/ int. (Amer.) = **how do;** ▸**how A**

how-d'ye-do /haʊdjəˈduː/ ▸**how-de-do**

however /haʊˈevə(r)/ adv. **1** wie ... auch; egal, wie (ugs.); **it's a long journey ~ you choose to travel, whether by train or by car** es ist eine lange Fahrt, ganz gleich, ob du mit dem Zug oder mit dem Auto fährst; **~ beautiful she is** wie schön sie auch ist; ganz gleich, wie schön sie ist; **I shall never win this race, ~ hard I try** ich werde dieses Rennen nie gewinnen, und wenn ich mich noch so anstrenge od. wie sehr ich mich auch anstrenge **2** (nevertheless) jedoch; aber; **I don't like him very much. H~, he has never done me any harm** Ich mag ihn nicht sehr. Er hat mir allerdings noch nie etwas getan; **~, the rain soon stopped, and ...:** es hörte jedoch od. aber bald auf zu regnen, und ...; **this, ~, seems not to be true** das scheint jedoch od. aber nicht wahr zu sein **3** (coll.) = **how ever** ▸**ever 5**

howitzer /ˈhaʊɪtsə(r)/ n. (Mil.) Haubitze, die

howl /haʊl/

A n. **1** (of animal, wind) Heulen, das; (of distress) Schrei, der; **the repeated ~s of the dog** das wiederholte Heulen des Hundes; **a ~ of pain** or **agony** ein Schmerzensschrei; **~s of protest/rage** Protestgeschrei, das/wütendes Geschrei; **~s of laughter** brüllendes Gelächter; **~s of delight/merriment** Freudengeheul, das; **~s of derision/scorn** verächtliches Gejohle **2** (in loudspeaker) Pfeifgeräusch, das

B v.i. ‹Tier, Wind:› heulen; (with distress) schreien; **~ in** or **with pain/hunger** etc. vor Schmerz/Hunger usw. schreien; **~ with laughter** vor Lachen brüllen

C v.t. [hinaus]schreien

Phrasal verb

• **~ 'down** v.t. niederbrüllen

howler /ˈhaʊlə(r)/ n. **1** (coll.: blunder) Schnitzer, der (ugs.); **make a ~:** sich (Dat.) einen Schnitzer leisten **2** (Zool.) ▸**~ monkey**

'howler monkey n. (Zool.) Brüllaffe, der

howling /ˈhaʊlɪŋ/

A n. Heulen, das; (of distress) Schreien, das

B adj. **1** heulend ‹Tier, Wind›; (crying with distress) schreiend; (with laughter) johlend; **the ~ mob** der johlende Pöbel; **five ~ brats/children** fünf Schreihälse (ugs.); **there is a ~ draught in this room** (coll.) hier im Zimmer zieht es höllisch (ugs.) **2** (coll.: extreme) enorm; fürchterlich ‹Katastrophe›; **a ~ mistake** ein Riesenfehler (ugs.)

howso'e'er (poet.), **howso'ever** adv. **1** (arch.) wie auch immer **2** (to whatsoever extent) wie ... auch immer

hoy /hɔɪ/ int. he! (ugs.)

HP abbr. **1** /eɪtʃˈpiː/ (Brit.) = **hire purchase; on HP** auf Teilzahlungsbasis **2** = **horsepower** PS **3** = **high pressure**

HQ abbr. = **headquarters** HQ

HR abbr. = **human resources**

HRH abbr. = **Her/His Royal Highness** I./S. Kgl. H.

hr[s]. abbr. = **hour[s]** Std[n].; **at 0800 hrs.** um 8.00 Uhr

HRT abbr. = **hormone replacement therapy**

HT abbr. = **high tension**

HTML abbr. (Computing) = **hypertext markup language** HTML

HTTP abbr. = **Hypertext Transport** (or **Transfer) Protocol** (Computing) HTTP

hub /hʌb/ n. **1** (of wheel) [Rad]nabe, die **2** (fig.: central point) Mittelpunkt, der; Zentrum, das; **the ~ of the universe** (fig.) der Nabel der Welt (geh.) **3** (Computing) Hub, der

hubbub /ˈhʌbʌb/ n. **1** (din) Lärm, der; **a ~ of conversation/voices** ein Stimmengewirr **2** (disturbance) Tumult, der; **be in a ~:** sich in Aufruhr befinden

hubby /ˈhʌbɪ/ n. (coll.) Mann, der; (iron./joc.) der Herr des Hauses

hub: ~cap n. Radkappe, die; **~ dynamo** n. Nabendynamo, der **~ gear** n. Nabenschaltung, die

hubris /ˈhjuːbrɪs/ n., no pl. Überheblichkeit, die; Hybris, die (geh.)

huckleberry /ˈhʌklbərɪ/ n. (Bot.) **1** (Gaylussacia) Gaylussacie, die (fachspr.); ≈ Heidelbeere, die; attrib. ≈ Heidelbeer- **2** (Vaccinium) Heidel- od. Blaubeere, die

huckster /ˈhʌkstə(r)/ n. **1** (pedlar) Straßenhändler, der; (from door to door) Hausierer, der **2** (mercenary person) Profitjäger, der (abwertend) **3** (Amer.) (salesman using showmanship) Werbefachmann, der; (Radio, Telev.: presenter) Propagandist, der

huddle /ˈhʌdl/

A v.i. sich drängen; (curl up, nestle) sich kuscheln; **~ against each other/together** sich aneinander drängen/sich zusammendrängen; **a few cottages ~d on the hillside** ein paar kleine Häuser kauerten sich an den Hang

B v.t. [eng] zusammendrängen; **the sheep were ~d against the fence/together** die Schafe drängten sich gegen den Zaun/aneinander

C v. refl. **~ oneself against sb./sth.** sich an jmdn./etw. kuscheln; **~ oneself up** sich zusammenkauern

D n. **1** (tight group) dicht gedrängte Menge od. Gruppe; **[stand] in a ~:** dicht zusammengedrängt [stehen] **2** (coll.: conference) Besprechung, die; **be in a ~/go [off] in[to] a ~:** die Köpfe zusammenstecken (ugs.)

Phrasal verb

• **~ 'up** v.i. (nestle up) sich zusammenkauern; (crowd together) sich [zusammen]drängen; **~ up to sb./sth.** sich an jmdn./etw. kuscheln

hue¹ /hjuː/ n. **1** Farbton, der; **his face was of** or **had** or **looked a very sickly ~:** er hatte eine sehr ungesunde Gesichtsfarbe; **the sky took on a reddish ~:** der Himmel färbte sich rötlich **2** (fig.: aspect) Schattierung, die; Couleur, die

hue² n. **~ and cry** (outcry) lautes Geschrei; (protest) Gezeter, das (abwertend); **raise a ~ and cry against sb./sth.** ein lautes Geschrei/Gezeter über jmdn./etw. anstimmen

huff /hʌf/

A v.i. **~ and puff** schnaufen und keuchen; (fig.: speak threateningly and bombastically) sich aufblasen (ugs.)

B n. **be in a ~:** beleidigt od. (ugs.) eingeschnappt sein; **get into a ~:** einschnappen (ugs.); den Beleidigten/die Beleidigte spielen (ugs.); **go off in a ~:** beleidigt od. eingeschnappt abziehen (ugs.)

huffy /ˈhʌfɪ/ adj. **1** (indignant) ungehalten (geh.); **get ~ [about** or **over sth.]** [wegen etw.] beleidigt od. (ugs.) eingeschnappt sein; (become irritated) [über etw. (Akk.)] aufgebracht sein **2** (easily offended) empfindlich; gereizt ‹Stimmung, Laune›

hug /hʌg/

A n. (squeeze) Umarmung, die; (of animal) Umklammerung, die; **give sb. a ~:** jmdn. umarmen

B v.t., **-gg-** **1** (squeeze) umarmen; ‹Tier:› umklammern; **~ sb./sth. to oneself** jmdn./etw. an sich (Akk.) drücken od. pressen; **~**

one's knees seine Knie umfassen; **the bear ~ged him to death** der Bär drückte ihn zu Tode **2** (keep close to) sich dicht halten an (+ *Dat.*); ‹*Schiff, Auto usw.*:› dicht entlangfahren an (+ *Dat.*) **3** (fit tightly around) eng anliegen an (+ *Dat.*); **a pullover that ~s the figure** ein Pullover, der die Figur betont

C *v. refl.*, **-gg-** die Arme um sich schlagen; **we ~ged ourselves for** *or* **on managing to win** (fig.) wir beglückwünschten uns dazu, den Sieg errungen zu haben

huge /hju:dʒ/ *adj.* riesig; gewaltig ‹*Unterschied, Verbesserung, Interesse*›; **the problem is ~:** das Problem ist außerordentlich schwierig; **he is not just fat: he is ~:** er ist nicht einfach dick: er ist ein Monstrum; **tell ~ lies** wie gedruckt lügen (ugs.)

hugely /ˈhju:dʒlɪ/ *adv.* gewaltig; riesig ‹*sich freuen, sich amüsieren*›; außerordentlich ‹*intelligent*›; ungeheuer ‹*erfolgreich*›

Huguenot /ˈhju:gənəʊ/ *pr. n.* Hugenotte, *der*/Hugenottin, *die*; *attrib.* Hugenotten-

huh /hʌ/ *int.* pah!

hula hoop /ˈhu:lə hu:p/ *n.* Hula-Hoop-Reifen, *der*

hulk /hʌlk/ *n.* **1** (body of old ship) [Schiffs]rumpf, *der*; (as store etc.) Hulk, *die od. der* (Seew.) **2** (wreck) (of car, machine, etc.) Wrack, *das*; (of house) Ruine, *die* **3** (unwieldy ship) dicker Pott (ugs.) **4** (fig.) (big thing) Klotz, *der*; (big person) Koloss, *der* (ugs. scherzh.); **a ~ of a man** ein Klotz von [einem] Mann (fig. ugs.)

hulking /ˈhʌlkɪŋ/ *adj.* (coll.) (bulky) wuchtig; (clumsy) klotzig (abwertend); **a ~ great person/thing** ein klobiger Mensch/ein klobiges Etwas; **a ~ great brute of a man/dog** ein grobschlächtiger, brutaler Kerl/ein scheußliches Ungetüm von einem Hund

hull[1] /hʌl/ *n.* (Naut.) Schiffskörper, *der*; (Aeronaut.) Rumpf, *der*

hull[2]

A *n.* (Bot.) (pod, husk) Hülse, *die*; (of peas) Schote, *die*; (of barley, oats, etc.) Spelze, *die*

B *v.t.* enthülsen ‹*Erbsen, Bohnen, Korn*›; entstielen ‹*Erdbeeren*›

hullabaloo /hʌləbəˈlu:/ *n.* **1** (noise) Radau, *der* (ugs.); Lärm, *der*; (of show business life, city) Trubel, *der* **2** (controversy) Aufruhr, *der*; **make a ~ about sth.** viel Lärm um etw. machen; **I don't see what all the ~ is about** ich verstehe nicht, was das ganze Theater (ugs.) eigentlich soll

hullo /həˈləʊ/ ▸**hallo**; **hello**

hum /hʌm/

A *v.i.*, **-mm-**: **1** summen; ‹*Motor, Maschine, Kreisel*:› brummen; **~ and ha** *or* **haw** (coll.) herumdrucksen (ugs.); **the workshop was ~ming with the noise of machinery** die Werkstatt war vom Brummen der Maschinen erfüllt **2** (coll.: be in state of activity) voller Leben *od.* Aktivität sein; **things are ~ming** die Sache ist in Schwung gekommen *od.* läuft (ugs.); **make things ~, set things ~ming** die Sache in Schwung bringen (ugs.) **3** (Brit. coll.: smell) riechen

B *v.t.*, **-mm-** summen ‹*Melodie, Lied*›

C *n.* **1** Summen, *das*; (of spinning top, machinery, engine) Brummen, *das* **2** (inarticulate sound) Hm, *das*; **~s and ha's** *or* **haws** verlegenes Geräusper **3** (of voices, conversation) Gemurmel, *das*; (of insects and small creatures) Gesumme, *das*; (of traffic) Brausen, *das* **4** (Electronics) Brummen, *das* **5** (Brit. coll.: smell) Geruch, *der*

D *int.* hm

human /ˈhju:mən/

A *adj.* menschlich; **~ biology** Humanbiologie, *die*; **result in a terrible loss of ~ life** ‹*Katastrophe*:› erschreckend viele Menschenleben fordern (geh.); **untouched by ~ hand** ≈ hygienisch verpackt ‹*Lebensmittel*›; **the ~ condition** das Menschsein; **the ~ race** die menschliche Rasse; das Menschengeschlecht (geh.); **~ sacrifice** Menschenopfer, *das*; **~ dustbin** (joc.) Resteesser, *der*; **they formed a ~ chain** sie bildeten eine Kette; (as demonstration) sie bildeten eine Menschenkette; **do everything within ~ power** alles Menschenmögliche tun; **that is not ~:** das ist unmenschlich; **I sometimes wonder if he's ~** (iron.) manchmal frage ich mich, ob er überhaupt ein Mensch ist; **I'm only ~:** ich bin auch nur ein Mensch; **it's only ~:** es ist menschlich; **~ error** menschliches Versagen; **the ~ element** *or* **factor** das menschliche Element; der menschliche Faktor; **lack the ~ touch** menschliche Wärme vermissen lassen; **be ~!** sei kein Unmensch!; *see also* **nature 4**

B *n.* Mensch, *der*

human: ~ ˈbeing *n.* Mensch, *der*; **~ ˈcomedy** *n.* menschliche Komödie (fig.)

humane /hju:ˈmeɪn/ *adj.* **1** human **2** (tending to civilize) humanistisch

humane ˈkiller *n. Instrument zur schmerzlosen Tötung von Tieren* (bes. im Schlachthof)

humanely /hju:ˈmeɪnlɪ/ *adv.* human

human: ~ engiˈneering *n.*, *no pl.* (Industry) Human engineering, *das*; Ergonomie, *die*; **~ ˈinterest** *n.*, *no pl.* **a story full of/an occupation with a lot of ~ interest** eine Geschichte, in der/ein Beruf, in dem das Menschliche eine große Rolle spielt; **~-interest story** Geschichte aus dem Leben

humanise ▸**humanize**

humanism /ˈhju:mənɪzm/ *n.*, *no pl.* Humanismus, *der*

humanist /ˈhju:mənɪst/ *n.* Humanist, *der*/Humanistin, *die*

humanistic /hju:məˈnɪstɪk/ *adj.* humanistisch

humanitarian /hju:mænɪˈteərɪən/

A *adj.* humanitär

B *n.* (philanthropist) Menschenfreund, *der*; (promoter of human welfare) Humanitarist, *der*/Humanitaristin, *die*

humanitarianism /hju:mænɪˈteərɪənɪzm/ *n.*, *no pl.* Humanitarismus, *der*

humanity /hju:ˈmænɪtɪ/ *n.* **1** *no pl.* Menschsein, *das*; **he was a pathetic specimen of ~:** er war ein jämmerliches Exemplar der Gattung Mensch **2** *no pl.*, *no art.* (mankind) Menschheit, *die*; (people collectively) Menschen **3** *no pl.* (being humane) Humanität, *die*; Menschlichkeit, *die* **4** *in pl.* (cultural learning) **[the] humanities** [die] Geisteswissenschaften; (study of Latin and Greek classics) [die] Altphilologie; [die] klassische Philologie

humanize /ˈhju:mənaɪz/ *v.t.* **1** (make human) vermenschlichen **2** (adapt to human use) den menschlichen Bedürfnissen anpassen; humanisieren ‹*Industrie*› **3** (make humane) humanisieren ‹*Strafvollzug*›; zivilisieren ‹*Wilde*›; geistig bilden ‹*Gesellschaft*›

ˈhumankind *n.*, *no pl.*, *no art.* die Menschheit; **all ~:** die ganze Menschheit

humanly /ˈhju:mənlɪ/ *adv.* menschlich; (by human means) mit menschlichen Mitteln; **do everything ~ possible** alles Menschenmögliche tun; **would it be ~ possible to obtain a copy?** wäre es irgendwie möglich, ein Exemplar zu bekommen?

humanoid /ˈhju:mənɔɪd/

A *adj.* humanoid

B *n.* Humanoide, *der*

human: ~ reˈlations *n. pl.* (Social Psych., Industry) Human Relations *Pl.*; **~ reˈsources** *n.* **1** *pl.* [Arbeits]kräfte *Pl.*; Personal, *das*; **2** *sing.* (department) Personalabteilung, *die*; *attrib.* **~ resources manager** ▸❶ **p. 1260** Personalleiter, *der*/-leiterin, *die*; Personalchef, *der*/-chefin, *die*; **~ ˈright** *n.* Menschenrecht, *das*; **~ rights** Menschenrechte *Pl.*; **fundamental ~ right** Grundrecht, *das*; **Court of H~ Rights** Europäischer Gerichtshof für Menschenrechte; *attrib.* **~ rights activist** Menschenrechtsaktivist, *der*/-aktivistin, *die*; **~ rights campaign** Menschenrechtskampagne, *die*; **~ rights campaigner** Menschenrechtler, *der*/-rechtlerin, *die*; **~ rights group** Menschenrechtsorganisation, *die*; **~ ˈshield** *n.* menschlicher Schutzschild

humble /ˈhʌmbl/

A *adj.* **1** ▸❶ **p. 908** (modest) bescheiden; ergeben ‹*Untertan, Diener, Gefolgsmann*›; bescheiden ‹*Vorschlag, Meinung*›; demütig ‹*Gebet*›; ehrfurchtsvoll ‹*Bewunderung*›; unterwürfig (oft abwertend) ‹*Haltung, Knechtschaft*›; **when I look up at the vast universe, it makes me feel very ~:** wenn ich das unermessliche Universum betrachte, komme ich mir sehr klein und unbedeutend vor; **may I offer** *or* **please accept my ~ apologies** ich bitte ergebenst um Verzeihung; **eat ~ pie** klein beigeben; *see also* **servant 3** **2** (low-ranking) einfach; niedrig ‹*Status, Rang usw.*›; **he stems from very ~ stock/origins** er ist von sehr niedriger Geburt *od.* Herkunft **3** (unpretentious) einfach; bescheiden ‹*Zuhause, Wohnung, Anfang*›; **the meal/gift was a very ~ offering** es war ein sehr einfaches Essen/nur eine bescheidene Gabe

B *v.t.* **1** (abase) demütigen; **feel ~d** sich (*Dat.*) klein vorkommen; **~ oneself** sich demütigen *od.* erniedrigen **2** (remove power of) entmachten; (defeat decisively) [vernichtend] schlagen

ˈhumble-bee *n.* Hummel, *die*

humbly /ˈhʌmblɪ/ *adv.* **1** (with humility) demütig; ergebenst ‹*um Verzeihung bitten*›; ergeben ‹*dienen*›; (meekly) unterwürfig; (in formal address) höflichst ‹*bitten, ersuchen*› **2** (in low rank) **~ born** von niedriger Herkunft **3** (unpretentiously) einfach; bescheiden; spärlich ‹*ausgestattet*›

humbug /ˈhʌmbʌg/ *n.* **1** *no pl.*, *no art.* (deception, nonsense) Humbug, *der* (ugs. abwertend) **2** (fraud) Schwindel, *der*; Betrug, *der* **3** (impostor) Schwindler, *der*/Schwindlerin, *die* (abwertend) **4** (Brit.: sweet) [Pfefferminz]bonbon, *der od. das*

humdinger /ˈhʌmdɪŋə(r), hʌmˈdɪŋə(r)/ *n.* (coll.) **be a ~:** Spitze *od.* große Klasse sein (ugs.); **she's a real ~:** sie ist absolute Spitze; **when we have a quarrel, it's a real ~:** wenn wir uns streiten, fliegen die Fetzen (ugs.)

humdrum /ˈhʌmdrʌm/ *adj.* **1** alltäglich; eintönig ‹*Leben*›; langweilig ‹*Person*› **2** (monotonous) stumpfsinnig; **the ~ routine of life/things** das tägliche Einerlei

humerus /ˈhju:mərəs/ *n.*, *pl.* **humeri** /ˈhju:məraɪ/ (Anat., Zool.) Humerus, *der*

humid /ˈhju:mɪd/ *adj.* feucht; humid (Geogr.)

humidifier /hju:ˈmɪdɪfaɪə(r)/ *n.* Luftbefeuchter, *der*

humidify /hju:ˈmɪdɪfaɪ/ *v.t.* befeuchten

humidity /hju:ˈmɪdɪtɪ/ *n.* **1** *no pl.* Feuchtigkeit, *die*; **I don't mind the heat but I cannot stand ~:** die Hitze macht mir nichts aus, aber die [hohe] Luftfeuchtigkeit kann ich nicht vertragen **2** (degree of moisture) **~ [of the atmosphere]** Luftfeuchtigkeit, *die* (Met.); Luftfeuchte, *die* (bes. fachspr.)

humiliate /hju:ˈmɪlɪeɪt/ *v.t.* demütigen; **I was** *or* **felt totally ~d** ich war zutiefst beschämt

humiliation /hju:mɪlɪˈeɪʃn/ *n.* Demütigung, *die*

humility /hju:ˈmɪlɪtɪ/ *n.* Demut, *die*; (of servant) Ergebenheit, *die*; (absence of pride or arrogance) Bescheidenheit, *die*

humming/ˈhʌmɪŋ/: **~bird** *n.* Kolibri, *der*; **~-top** *n.* Brummkreisel, *der*

hummock /ˈhʌmək/ *n.* **1** (hillock) [kleiner] Hügel **2** (Amer.: rise) Waldinsel, *die* **3** (in ice field) Eishügel, *der*

humor (Amer.) ▸**humour**

humoresque /hju:məˈresk/ *n.* (Mus.) Humoreske, *die*

humorist /ˈhju:mərɪst/ *n.* **1** (facetious person) Spaßvogel, *der*; Komiker, *der* (fig.) **2** (talker, writer) Humorist, *der*/Humoristin, *die*

humorless (Amer.) ▸**humourless**

humorous /ˈhju:mərəs/ *adj.* **1** (comic) lustig, komisch ‹*Geschichte, Name, Situation*›; witzig ‹*Bemerkung*›; **I fail to see anything ~ in the situation** ich finde die Situation überhaupt nicht komisch *od.* lustig; **the ~ side of the situation** das Komische der Situation; **stop trying to be ~:** hör auf damit, komisch wirken zu wollen! **2** (showing sense of humour) humorvoll ‹*Person*›; **be/not be in a ~ mood** in heiterer Stimmung sein/nicht zum Lachen aufgelegt sein

humorously /ˈhju:mərəslɪ/ *adv.* **1** (comically) komisch; lustig; **his remarks were meant ~, not offensively** seine Bemerkungen sollten belustigen und nicht verletzen; **~ enough, ...:**

h

lustigerweise ... 2 (with sense of humour) humorvoll; **look ~ at the problems of life** den Problemen des Alltags mit Humor begegnen

humour /'hju:mə(r)/ (Brit.)

A *n.* 1 *no pl., no indef. art.* (faculty, comic quality) Humor, *der;* (of situation) Komische, *das;* **see the ~ of sth.** einer Sache (*Dat.*) die komische Seite abgewinnen; **sense of ~:** Sinn für Humor; **he has no sense of ~:** er hat keinen Humor 2 *no pl., no indef. art.* (facetiousness) Witzigkeit, *die;* **a funeral is no place for ~:** bei einer Beerdigung macht man keine Witze 3 (mood) Laune, *die;* **be in a good/bad ~:** in guter Stimmung sein/schlechte Laune haben; **what sort of ~ are you in?** wie ist deine Stimmung?; **in good ~:** gut gelaunt; **be out of ~:** schlechte Laune haben; **a fit of ill ~:** ein Anfall von schlechter Laune; **have recovered one's good ~:** wieder bei Laune sein 4 (Hist.: body fluid) Körpersaft, *der;* Humor, *der* (Med. veralt.); **the cardinal ~s** die Hauptsäfte des Körpers; *see also* **aqueous humour**; **vitreous 2**

B *v.t.* (indulge) willfahren (geh.) (+ *Dat.*); **~ sb.** jmdm. seinen Willen lassen; **~ sb.'s taste** jmds. Geschmack *od.* Vorliebe (*Dat.*) entsprechen; **don't [try to] ~ me!** sei nicht so übertrieben rücksichtsvoll!; **do it just to ~ her/him** tus doch, damit sie ihren/er seinen Willen hat

humourless /'hju:məlɪs/ *adj.* (Brit.) humorlos; todernst ‹*Gesicht*›; trocken ‹*Buch*›

humous /'hju:məs/ *adj.* humos (Bodenk.)

hump /hʌmp/

A *n.* 1 (human) Buckel, *der;* Höcker, *der* (ugs.); (of animal) Höcker, *der;* **he has a ~ on his back** er hat einen Buckel; **live on one's ~** (fig.) von seinen Reserven leben 2 (mound) Hügel, *der;* (Railw.) Ablaufberg, *der* 3 (fig.: critical point) **be over the ~:** über den Berg sein (ugs.) 4 (Brit. coll.) **have the ~:** sauer sein (ugs.); **get the ~:** [stink]sauer werden (ugs.)

B *v.t.* (Brit. coll.) (carry) schleppen; (hoist) **~ a sack on to one's shoulders** einen Sack buckeln *od.* auf den Buckel nehmen (ugs.)

hump: ~back *n.* 1 ▸**hunchback**; 2 ▸**~back whale**; **~back 'bridge** *n.* gewölbte Brücke; **~backed** /'hʌmpbækt/ *adj.* ▸**hunchbacked**; **~back 'whale** *n.* Buckelwal, *der*

humph /hmf/

A *int.* hm

B *n.* Hm, *das;* Grunzen, *das* (ugs.)

humus /'hju:məs/ *n.* Humus, *der*

Hun /hʌn/ *n.* 1 (Hist.) Hunne, *der*/Hunnin, *die; attrib.* Hunnen- 2 (derog.: German) Sauerkrautfresser, *der* (ugs. abwertend); **the ~** (collect.) der Teutone (abwertend)

hunch[1] /hʌntʃ/

A *v.t.* hochziehen ‹*Schultern*›; **sit ~ed in a corner** zusammengekauert in einer Ecke sitzen; **he/the cat ~ed his/its back** er/die Katze machte einen Buckel

B *v.i.* (adopt bent posture) sich krümmen; (curl up) sich zusammenrollen; **~ in a chair** gebeugt *od.* mit krummem Rücken auf einem Stuhl sitzen

Phrasal verb

• **~ 'up**

A *v.t.* hochziehen; **don't sit ~ed up like that** sitz nicht so krumm da!; **~ oneself up** einen Buckel machen

B *v.i.* ▸**hunch**[1] **B**

hunch[2] *n.* (intuitive feeling) Gefühl, *das;* **I have a ~ that ..., my ~ is that ...:** ich habe das [leise] Gefühl, dass ...; **the detective followed a ~:** der Detektiv folgte einem inneren Gefühl

hunch: ~back *n.* 1 (back) Buckel, *der;* 2 (person) Bucklige, *der/die;* **be a ~back** einen Buckel haben; **the H~back of Notre Dame** der Glöckner von Notre-Dame; **~backed** /'hʌntʃbækt/ *adj.* buck[e]lig

hundred /'hʌndrəd/ ▸**i p. 894**, ▸**i p. 1001**, ▸**i p. 1358**

A *adj.* 1 hundert; **a** *or* **one ~:** [ein]hundert; **two/several ~:** zweihundert/mehrere hundert; **a** *or* **one ~ and one** [ein]hundert[und]eins; **a** *or* **one ~ and one people** hundert[und]ein Menschen *od.* Mensch; **the ~ metres race** der Hundertmeterlauf; **the H~ Years War** (Hist.) der Hundertjährige Krieg; **eighteen ~ hours** 18.00 Uhr 2 **a ~ [and one]** (fig.: innumerable) hundert (ugs.); **I've told you a ~ times** ich habe es dir schon hundertmal gesagt; **never** *or* **not in a ~ years** nie im Leben; **I've got a ~ [and one] things to do** ich habe hunderterlei zu tun (ugs.) 3 **a** *or* **one ~ per cent** hundertprozentig; **I'm not a ~ per cent at the moment** (fig.) momentan geht es mir nicht sehr gut. *See also* **eight A**; **mile 1**

B *n.* 1 (number) hundert; **a** *or* **one/two ~:** [ein]hundert/zweihundert; **count up to a** *or* **one ~:** bis hundert zählen; **not if I live to be a ~:** nie im Leben; **in** *or* **by ~s** hundertweise; **the seventeen-~s** *etc.* das achtzehnte *usw.* Jahrhundert; **a ~ and one** *etc.* [ein]hundert[und]eins *usw.*; **a** *or* **one/two ~ of the men died** einhundert/zweihundert der Männer starben; **there are five ~ of us** wir sind zu fünfhundert; **it's a ~ to one that ...:** die Chancen stehen hundert zu eins, dass ... 2 (symbol, written figure) Hundert, *die; in adding numbers by columns* Hunderter, *der* (Math.); (set or group of 100) Hundert, *das;* (~-pound etc. note) Hunderter, *der* 3 (indefinite amount) **~s** Hunderte *Pl.*; **tourists flock to Rome by the ~[s]** *or* **in their ~s** die Touristen reisen zu Hunderten nach Rom; **~s of times** mehrere hundertmal 4 (Brit. Hist.: county division) Zent, *die; see also* **Chiltern Hundreds**. *See also* **eight B 1**

hundredfold /'hʌndrədfəʊld/

A *adv.* hundertfach

B *adj.* hundertfach

C *n.* Hundertfache, *das;* **improve a ~** (fig.) sich um ein Vielfaches verbessern; **she had repaid his kindness a ~:** sie hatte seine Güte tausendfach vergolten; **by a ~:** um das Hundertfache. *See also* **eightfold**

hundreds and 'thousands *n. pl.* (sweets) Liebesperlen *Pl.*

hundredth /'hʌndrədθ/

A *adj.* hundertst...; **the one-/two-~ person** der [ein]hundertste/zweihundertste Mensch; **a ~ part** ein Hundertstel; *see also* **eighth A**

B *n.* 1 (fraction) Hundertstel, *das;* **a ~ of a second** eine Hundertstelsekunde 2 (in sequence, rank) Hundertste, *der/die/das;* **Old H~** (Eccl.) der hundertste Psalm. *see also* **eighth B**

hundredweight /'hʌndrədweɪt/ *n., pl. same or* **~s** ▸**i p. 1702** 1 (Brit.) **[long] ~:** 50,8 kg; ≈ Zentner, *der* 2 (in metric weight) **[metric] ~:** Zentner, *der* 3 (Amer.) **[short] ~:** 45,36 kg; ≈ Zentner, *der (45,36 kg)*

hung ▸**hang A, B**

Hungarian /hʌŋ'geərɪən/ ▸**i p. 1277**, ▸**i p. 1345**

A *adj.* ungarisch; **sb. is ~:** jmd. ist Ungar/Ungarin; *see also* **English A**

B *n.* 1 (person) Ungar, *der*/Ungarin, *die* 2 (language) Ungarisch, *das; see also* **English B 1**

Hungary /'hʌŋgərɪ/ *pr. n.* Ungarn (*das*)

hunger /'hʌŋgə(r)/

A *n.* (lit. or fig.) Hunger, *der;* **pang[s] of ~:** quälender Hunger; **the pangs of ~ were getting stronger** der Hunger plagte mich *usw.* immer mehr; **~ is the best sauce** (prov.) Hunger ist der beste Koch (Spr.); **die of ~:** verhungern; (fig.: be very hungry) vor Hunger sterben (ugs.); **~ for sth.** (lit. or fig.) Hunger nach etw. (geh.); **~ for revenge/knowledge** Rache-/Wissensdurst, *der*

B *v.i.* (have craving); **~ after** *or* **for sb./sth.** [heftiges] Verlangen nach jmdm./etw. haben

hunger: ~ march *n.* Hungermarsch, *der;* **~ marcher** *n.* Hungermarschierer, *der;* **~ strike** A *n.* Hungerstreik, *der;* **stage a/go on ~ strike** in den Hungerstreik treten. B *v.i.* in den Hungerstreik treten; **be ~ striking** sich im Hungerstreik befinden; **~ striker** *n.* Hungerstreikende, *der/die*

hung: ~ 'jury *n.: Geschworenengericht, das zu keinem einstimmigen Urteil/keinem Mehrheitsurteil gelangen kann;* **~-'over** *adj.* (coll.) verkatert (ugs.); **~ 'parliament** *n.: Parlament, in dem keine Partei die absolute Mehrheit hat*

hungrily /'hʌŋgrɪlɪ/ *adv.* 1 hungrig; **my stomach was rumbling/growling ~:** mir knurrte vor Hunger der Magen 2 (fig.: longingly) sehnsüchtig ‹*an etw. denken*›; [be]gierig ‹*etw. verfolgen*›

hungry /'hʌŋgrɪ/ *adj.* 1 (feeling hunger) hungrig; (regularly feeling hunger or lacking food) hungernd; (showing hunger) hungrig, gierig ‹*Augen, Blick*›; **be ~:** Hunger haben; hungrig sein; **we were poor and ~:** wir waren arm und litten Hunger; **[as] ~ as a hunter** *or* **lion** *or* **wolf** hungrig wie ein Löwe *od.* Wolf; **go ~:** hungern; hungrig bleiben; **I don't like fish. — Go ~, then!** Ich mag keinen Fisch. — Dann musst du eben hungern; **~ years** Hungerjahre *Pl.* 2 (inducing hunger) hungrig machend 3 (fig.: eager, avaricious) [hab]gierig ‹*Spekulant*›; stürmisch ‹*Liebhaber*›; brennend, glühend ‹*Verlangen*›; hungrig ‹*Ozean, Kriegsmaschine usw.*›; **be ~ for sb./sth.** sich nach jmdm. sehnen/nach etw. hungern (geh.); **be ~ to do sth.** darauf brennen, etw. zu tun; **~ for success/power/knowledge/love** erfolgs-/macht-/bildungs-/liebeshungrig; **~ to learn** lernbegierig; **be ~ after sth.** nach etw. hungern (geh.); **success-/war-/freedom-~:** erfolgshungrig/kriegslustig/freiheitsdurstig 4 (barren) karg

hunk /hʌŋk/ *n.* 1 (large piece) [großes] Stück; (clumsy piece) Brocken, *der;* (of bread) Brocken, *der;* Ranken, *der* (landsch.); **~s of wood** große Holzscheite 2 (coll.: large person) stattliche Erscheinung; **he is a gorgeous great ~:** er ist ein blendend aussehender, stattlicher Mann; **a great ~ of a weightlifter** ein Koloss (ugs. scherzh.) von einem Gewichtheber

hunky /'hʌŋkɪ/ *adj.* (coll.) stattlich

hunky-dory /hʌŋkɪ'dɔ:rɪ/ *adj.* (coll.) prima (ugs.); **everything's ~, it's all ~:** es ist alles in [bester] Ordnung

hunt /hʌnt/

A *n.* 1 (pursuit of game) Jagd, *die;* **the ~ is up** (Sport) die Jagd ist eröffnet; Jagd frei! (Jägerspr.); **badger-/deer-~:** Dachs-/Hirschjagd, *die* 2 (search) Suche, *die;* (strenuous search) Jagd, *die;* **be on the ~ for sb./sth.** auf der Suche/Jagd nach jmdm./etw. sein; **the ~ is on/up [for sb./sth.]** die Suche/Jagd [nach jmdm./etw.] hat begonnen/die Jagd [nach jmdm./etw.] ist eröffnet 3 (body of fox-hunters) Jagd[gesellschaft], *die;* (association) Jagdverband, *der;* **the local ~:** der örtliche Jägerverein 4 (district) Jagd, *die;* Jagdrevier, *das*

B *v.t.* 1 jagen; Jagd machen auf (+ *Akk.*); **he spends his weekends ~ing foxes** am Wochenende geht er auf die Fuchsjagd 2 (search for) Jagd machen auf (+ *Akk.*) ‹*Mörder usw.*›; fahnden nach ‹*vermisster Person*›; **~ the thimble/slipper** (Games) Fingerhutverstecken, *das*/Pantoffelverstecken, *das* 3 (drive, lit. or fig.) jagen; **he was ~ed from office/out of society** er wurde aus dem Amt gejagt/aus der Gesellschaft ausgestoßen 4 (Amer.: shoot) schießen ‹*Wildenten*›

C *v.i.* 1 jagen; **go ~ing** jagen; auf die Jagd gehen; **~ after** *or* **for** Jagd machen auf (+ *Akk.*), jagen ‹*Tier*› 2 (seek) **~ after** *or* **for sb./sth.** nach jmdm./etw. suchen; **he ~ed through his pockets for a coin** er durchsuchte seine Taschen nach einer Münze; **the police are ~ing for him** die Polizei ist auf der Suche nach ihm 3 (Mech.: operate irregularly) abwechselnd zu schnell und zu langsam laufen; pendeln (Technik)

Phrasal verbs

• **~ a'bout, ~ a'round** *v.i.* **~ about** *or* **around for sb./sth.** [überall] nach jmdm./etw. suchen

• **~ 'down** *v.t.* 1 (bring to bay) hetzen und stellen; **the animal was finally ~ed down** das Tier wurde schließlich zur Strecke gebracht (Jägerspr.) 2 (pursue and overcome) zur Strecke bringen ‹*Person*›; abschießen ‹*feindliches Flugzeug*› 3 (fig.: track down) aufstöbern

• **~ 'out** *v.t.* 1 (drive from cover) aufstöbern 2 (seek out) suchen 3 (fig.: track down) ausfindig machen ‹*Tatsachen, Antworten*›

• **~ 'up** *v.t.* aufspüren

hunt 'ball *n. Ball eines Jagdverbandes*

hunted /'hʌntɪd/ *adj.* 1 (pursued) gejagt; **the deer is a much ~ beast** der Hirsch ist ein viel bejagtes *od.* intensiv bejagtes Tier 2 (fig.:

h

sought) gesucht **3** (expressing fear) gejagt, gehetzt ‹*Blick, Gesichtsausdruck*›

hunter /ˈhʌntə(r)/ *n.* **1** Jäger, *der;* **big-game ~:** Großwildjäger, *der;* **whale ~:** Walfänger, *der* **2** (fig.: seeker) **be a ~ after glory/truth** dem Ruhm nachjagen/der Wahrheit nachspüren; **autograph ~:** Autogrammjäger, *der;* **treasure ~:** Schatzsucher, *der; see also* **fortune hunter** **3** (horse) Jagdpferd, *das* **4** (dog) Jagdhund, *der* **5** (watch) Sprungdeckeluhr, *die;* **half-~** *Sprungdeckeluhr mit teilweise durchsichtigem Deckel*

hunter-ˈkiller *n.: zur Jagd auf Schiffe eingesetztes U-Boot*

hunter's ˈmoon *n. Vollmond nach dem „harvest moon"*

hunting /ˈhʌntɪŋ/

A *n., no pl.* **1** die Jagd (**of** auf + *Akk.*); das Jagen (**of** *Gen.*); **there's good ~** *or* **the ~ is good in this forest** dieser Wald ist ein gutes Jagdgebiet; **~, shooting, [and] fishing,** (iron.) **huntin', shootin', and fishin'** Fischen und Jagen; **otter-~:** Otterjagd, *die; see also* **fox-hunting** **2** (fig.: searching) Suche, *die* (**for** nach); **the ~ of a criminal** die Verbrecherjagd; **after months of/much ~:** nach monatelanger/langer Suche; **[I wish you] good ~** (fig.) [ich wünsche dir] viel Glück bei der Suche; *see also* **house-hunting**; **job-hunting** **3** (searching through) (of house) Durchsuchen, *das;* (of area) Absuchen, *das;* (in pursuit of game) Jagen, *das* (**of** in + *Dat.*) **4** (Amer.: shooting) Schießen, *das*

B *adj.* jagend

hunting: ~ box *n.* (Brit.) Jagdhütte, *die;* **~ crop** ▸ **crop A 3**; **~ ground** *n.* (lit. or fig.) Jagdrevier, *das; see also* **happy hunting ground[s]**; **~ horn** *n.* Jagdhorn, *das;* **~ lodge** *n.* Jagdhaus, *das;* **~ ˈpink** *n.* Rot des Jagdrocks

ˈhunt saboteur *n.* Jagdsaboteur, *der*

huntsman /ˈhʌntsmən/ *n., pl.* **huntsmen** /ˈhʌntsmən/ **1** (hunter) Jäger, *der;* (riding to hounds) Jagdreiter, *der* **2** (manager of hunt) Rüdemeister, *der* (Jagdw. hist.); (in fox-hunting) Pikör, *der* (Jagdw. hist.)

huntswoman /ˈhʌntswʊmən/ *n.* Jägerin, *die;* (riding to hounds) Jagdreiterin, *die*

hurdle /ˈhɜːdl/

A *n.* **1** (Athletics) Hürde, *die;* **~ race, ~s** Hürdenlauf, *der;* (for horses) Hürdenrennen, *das;* **the 400 metres ~s** der 400-m-Hürdenlauf; die 400m Hürden (Sportjargon) **2** (fig.: obstacle) Hürde, *die;* **fall at the last ~:** an der letzten Hürde scheitern; **get over** *or* **negotiate a ~:** eine Hürde nehmen **3** (for fence) Hürde, *die*

B *v.t.* überspringen ‹*Zaun, Hecke usw.*›

hurdler /ˈhɜːdlə(r)/ *n.* (Athletics) Hürdenläufer, *der*/-läuferin, *die*

hurdy-gurdy /ˈhɜːdɪgɜːdɪ/ *n.* **1** (Mus. Hist.) Drehleier, *die* (hist.) **2** (coll.: barrel organ) Drehorgel, *die;* Leierkasten, *der* (ugs.)

hurl /hɜːl/

A *v.t.* **1** (throw) werfen; (violently) schleudern; (throw down) stürzen; **~ sb. [down] into the street** jmdn. auf die Straße hinunterstürzen; **she ~ed herself to her death from a 15th-floor window** sie stürzte sich aus einem Fenster im 15. Stock zu Tode **2** (fig.) **~ insults at sb.** jmdm. Beleidigungen ins Gesicht schleudern; **~ defiant looks/glances at sb.** trotzige Blicke auf jmdn. schleudern **3** (drive) werfen; **be ~ed around the ship/against each other** durch das Schiff geschleudert/gegeneinander geschleudert werden; **~ oneself at** *or* **upon sb.** sich auf jmdn. stürzen; **~ oneself into a new job** (fig.) sich in eine neue Arbeit stürzen

B *n.* (throwing) Stürzen, *das;* (violent) Schleudern, *das*

hurling /ˈhɜːlɪŋ/ *n.* (Sport) Hurling, *das;* irisches Hockey; *attrib.* Hurling-

hurly-burly /ˈhɜːlɪbɜːlɪ/ *n.* Tumult, *der;* **the ~ of city life** der Großstadtrummel (ugs.)

hurrah /həˈrɑː, hʊˈrɑː/, **hurray** /həˈreɪ, hʊˈreɪ/

A *int.* hurra; **~ for sb./sth.!** jmd./etw. lebe hoch!; **~ for the Queen!** ein Hoch der Königin!; **hip, hip, ~!** hipp, hipp, hurra!

B Hurra, *das;* **their joyous ~s** ihre freudigen Hurrarufe

C *v.i.* Hurra rufen

hurricane /ˈhʌrɪkən/ *n.* **1** (tropical cyclone) Hurrikan, *der;* (storm, lit. or fig.) Orkan, *der;* **it's/the wind is blowing a ~ outside** draußen tobt ein Orkan **2** (Meteorol.) Orkan, *der; attrib.* **~ force** Orkanstärke, *die;* **~ force winds** Winde, die Orkanstärke erreichen

hurricane: ~ lamp *n.* Sturmlaterne, *die;* **~ season** *n.: Jahreszeit, in der Hurrikane am häufigsten auftreten*

hurried /ˈhʌrɪd/ *adj.* eilig; überstürzt ‹*Abreise*›; eilig *od.* hastig geschrieben ‹*Brief, Aufsatz*›; eilig vollzogen ‹*Zeremonie*›; in Eile ausgeführt ‹*Arbeit*›; **our farewells were ~:** wir verabschiedeten uns eilig

hurriedly /ˈhʌrɪdlɪ/ *adv.* eilig; überstürzt ‹*abreisen*›; in Eile ‹*ausführen*›

hurry /ˈhʌrɪ/

A *n.* **1** (great haste) Eile, *die;* **what is** *or* **why the [big] ~?** warum die Eile?; **amongst all the ~ at the airport** in der allgemeinen Hetze am Flughafen; **in a ~:** eilig; **be in a [great** *or* **terrible] ~:** es [furchtbar] eilig haben; in [großer] Eile sein; **do sth. in a ~:** etw. in Eile tun; **leave in a ~:** davoneilen; **I have to get there in a ~:** ich muss so schnell wie möglich dort sein; **I need it in a ~:** ich brauche es dringend; **the handle won't come off again in a ~** (coll.) der Griff wird so schnell nicht wieder abgehen; **I shall not ask again in a ~** (coll.) ich frage so schnell nicht wieder; **be in a/not be in a** *or* **be in no ~ to do sth.** es eilig/nicht eilig haben, etw. zu tun **2** (urgent requirement) **there is a ~ for sth.** etw. ist sehr gefragt; **there is a ~ for us to get out** wir müssen uns beeilen, hinauszukommen; **there's no ~:** es eilt nicht; es hat keine Eile; **is there any ~ for this letter [to be sent off]?** ist dieser Brief eilig?

B *v.t.* (transport fast) schnell bringen; (urge to go or act faster) antreiben; (quicken process of) beschleunigen; (consume fast) hinunterschlingen ‹*Essen*›; hinunterstürzen ‹*Getränk*›; **~ sb. out of the house** dafür sorgen, dass jmd. bald aus dem Haus herauskommt; **~ dinner** sich mit dem Abendessen beeilen; **~ a soufflé** ein Soufflé zu schnell zubereiten; **~ one's work** seine Arbeit in zu großer Eile erledigen

C *v.i.* sich beeilen; (to or from place) eilen; **~ downstairs/out/in** nach unten/nach draußen/nach drinnen eilen; **she hurried from shop to shop** sie hastete von einem Laden zum andern

Phrasal verbs

• **~ aˈlong**

A *v.i.* sich beeilen

B *v.t.* zur Eile antreiben; beschleunigen ‹*Vorgang*›

• **~ ˈon**

A *v.i.* weitereilen; **the teacher is ~ing on too fast** (fig.) der Lehrer geht zu schnell weiter; **I must ~ on** ich muss [rasch] weiter

B *v.t.* antreiben; beschleunigen ‹*Vorgang*›

• **~ through** *v.t.* **1** /--ˈ-/ beschleunigen **2** /ˈ---/ schnell durcheilen; (fig.) möglichst schnell durchziehen (ugs.); (Parl.) durchpeitschen ‹*Gesetz*›

• **~ ˈup**

A *v.i.* sich beeilen

B *v.t.* antreiben; beschleunigen, vorantreiben ‹*Vorgang*›

hurt /hɜːt/

A *v.t.,* **hurt** **1** ▸ **i** **p. 1231** (cause pain to) wehtun (+ *Dat.*); (injure physically) verletzen; **~ one's arm/leg/head/back** sich (*Dat.*) am Arm/Bein/Kopf/Rücken wehtun; (injure) sich (*Dat.*) den Arm/das Bein/am Kopf/am Rücken verletzen; **you are ~ing me/my arm** du tust mir weh/am Arm weh; **my arm is ~ing me** mein Arm tut [mir] weh; mir tut der Arm weh; **it ~s me to move my arm** es tut [mir] weh, wenn ich den Arm bewege; **it ~s my ears to listen to that noise** dieser Lärm tut meinen Ohren weh; **he wouldn't ~ a fly** (fig.) er tut keiner Fliege etwas zuleide; **sth. won't** *or* **wouldn't ~ sb.** etw. tut nicht weh; (fig.) etw. würde jmdm. nichts schaden (ugs.); **~ oneself** sich (*Dat.*) wehtun; (injure oneself) sich verletzen **2** (damage, be detrimental to) schaden (+ *Dat.*); **sth. won't** *or* **wouldn't ~ sth.** etw. würde einer Sache (*Dat.*) nichts schaden **3** (distress emotionally) verletzen, kränken ‹*Person*›; verletzen ‹*Ehrgefühl, Stolz*›; **~ sb.'s feelings** jmdn. verletzen; **it ~s me to have to tell you this** es ist mir schmerzlich, Ihnen dies sagen zu müssen; **~ sb.'s sense of honour** jmdn. in seiner Ehre kränken

B *v.i.,* **hurt** **1** ▸ **i** **p. 1231** (cause pain) wehtun; schmerzen **2** (cause damage, be detrimental) schaden; **does it ~ to drive the car with the handbrake on?** schadet es dem Auto, wenn man mit angezogener Handbremse fährt?; **I don't think it really ~s** ich glaube nicht, dass es wirklich etwas schadet; **publicity never ~s** Publicity kann nie schaden (ugs.); **sth. won't** *or* **wouldn't ~** (also iron.) etw. würde nichts schaden (ugs.); **it won't ~ to have another biscuit** noch ein Keks kann doch nichts schaden **3** (cause emotional distress) wehtun; ‹*Worte, Beleidigungen:*› verletzen; ‹*Person:*› verletzend sein **4** (suffer) **I ~ all over** es tut mir überall weh; **my leg ~s** mein Bein tut [mir] weh; **does your hand ~?** tut dir die Hand weh?; **I ~ inside** (emotionally) es tut mir innerlich weh

C *adj.* gekränkt ‹*Tonfall, Miene*›

D *n.* **1** (bodily injury) Verletzung, *die* **2** (detriment) Schaden, *der* **3** (emotional pain) Schmerz, *der;* (emotional injury) Kränkung, *die*

hurtful /ˈhɜːtfl/ *adj.* **1** (physically harmful, detrimental) schädlich (**to** für); **be ~ to sb./sth.** jmdm./einer Sache schaden **2** (fig.: painful) schmerzlich **3** (emotionally wounding) verletzend; **be ~ [in what one says] about sth.** sich in verletzender Form über etw. äußern; **what a ~ thing to say/do!** wie kann man nur so etwas Verletzendes sagen/tun!

hurtle /ˈhɜːtl/

A *v.i.* **1** (move rapidly) rasen (ugs.); **he went hurtling down the street/round the corner** er raste die Straße hinunter/um die Ecke; **the car was hurtling along** das Auto brauste *od.* sauste dahin **2** (move with clattering sound) **the saucepans came hurtling to the floor** die Kochtöpfe fielen mit lautem Klappern auf den Boden

B *v.t.* schleudern

husband /ˈhʌzbənd/

A *n.* Ehemann, *der;* **my/your/her ~:** mein/dein/ihr Mann; **give my regards to your ~:** grüßen Sie Ihren Mann *od.* (geh.) Gatten von mir; **~ and wife** Mann und Frau; **they are a ~-[and-]wife team of interior decorators** die Eheleute arbeiten gemeinsam als Innenarchitekten

B *v.t.* regeln ‹*Angelegenheiten*›; haushalten mit ‹*Mitteln*›; bewirtschaften ‹*Land*›

husbandry /ˈhʌzbəndrɪ/ *n., no pl.* **1** (farming) Landwirtschaft, *die;* (application of farming technique) Bewirtschaftung, *die;* **animal/dairy ~:** Viehzucht, *die*/Milchviehhaltung, *die* **2** (management) **bad/good ~:** schlechtes/sparsames Wirtschaften; **bad/good ~ of sth.** verschwenderischer/haushälterischer Umgang mit etw. **3** (careful management) sparsames Wirtschaften

hush /hʌʃ/

A *n.* **1** (silence) Schweigen, *das;* **a sudden ~ fell over them** sie verstummten plötzlich; **can we have a bit of ~ now, please?** (coll.) ein bisschen mehr Ruhe jetzt, wenn ich bitten dürfte! **2** (stillness) Stille, *die;* **dead ~:** Totenstille, *die* **3** (secrecy) Geheimhaltung, *die;* **why all the ~?** wozu die ganze Geheimnistuerei? (ugs.)

B *v.t.* (silence) zum Schweigen bringen; zum Verstummen bringen ‹*Vogelgesang, Gerüchte*›; (still) beruhigen; besänftigen; (quieten) dämpfen ‹*Stimme*›; **she tried to ~ her baby to sleep/her baby's crying** sie versuchte, ihr Baby zum Schlafen zu bringen/ihr schreiendes Baby zu beruhigen

C *v.i.* still sein; (become silent) verstummen; **~!** still!

Phrasal verb

• **~ ˈup** *v.t.* **1** (make silent) zum Schweigen bringen **2** (keep secret) **~ sth. up** etw. vertuschen

hushaby[e] /ˈhʌʃəbaɪ/ *int.* eiapopeia

hushed /hʌʃt/ *adj.* schweigend ‹*Publikum*›; gedämpft ‹*Flüstern, Stimme*›; **~ atmosphere**

Stille, *die;* **there was a ~ silence** alles schwieg; **with ~ respect/attention** mit respektvollem/gespanntem Schweigen

hush: ~-~ *adj.* (coll.) geheim; **strictly/terribly/very ~-~:** streng geheim; **keep sth. ~-~:** etw. geheim halten; **~ money** *n.* Schweigegeld, *das*

husk /hʌsk/
A *n.* Schale, *die;* (of wheat, grain, rice) Spelze, *die;* (Amer.: of maize) Hüllblatt, *das;* Liesche, *die* (Bot.); (fig.: useless remainder) Hülse, *die*
B *v.t.* schälen

huskily /ˈhʌskɪlɪ/ *adv.* heiser

husky[1] /ˈhʌskɪ/
A *adj.* **1** (hoarse) heiser; **her voice has a natural/an attractive ~ quality** ihre Stimme ist von Natur aus rau/sie hat eine anziehende rauchige Stimme **2** (coll.: tough) bärenstark (ugs.)
B *n.* (Amer. coll.: strong person) bärenstarker Typ (ugs.)

husky[2] *n.* (dog) Eskimohund, *der;* (Siberian ~) Husky, *der;* (sledge dog) Schlittenhund, *der*

hussar /hʊˈzɑː(r)/ *n.* (Mil.) Husar, *der*

hussy /ˈhʌsɪ, ˈhʌzɪ/ *n. fem.* **1** (improper woman) Flittchen, *das* (ugs. abwertend) **2** (pert girl) Göre, *die* (nordd.); Fratz, *der* (fam.)

hustings /ˈhʌstɪŋz/ *n. pl.* **1** *constr. as sing. or pl.* (proceedings) Wahlveranstaltungen **2** (Hist.: platform) *Rednerbühne für die Kandidaten einer Wahl* **3** (fig.) **he gave a good speech from the ~:** er hielt eine gute Wahlrede

hustle /ˈhʌsl/
A *v.t.* **1** drängen (**into** zu) **2** (jostle) anrempeln (salopp); schubsen (ugs.); (thrust) [hastig] drängen; **the guide ~d the tourists along/from one church to another** der Führer scheuchte die Touristen voran/von einer Kirche zur anderen (ugs.); **~ a Budget through the Senate** ein Budget im Senat durchpeitschen (ugs.) **3** (coll.: exert pressure on) bedrängen; **~ sb. to do sth.** jmdn. dazu bringen wollen, etw. zu tun
B *v.i.* **1** (push roughly) **~ against sb./sth.** jmdn. anrempeln/gegen etw. stoßen; **~ through the crowds** sich durch die Menge drängeln **2** (hurry) hasten; **~ about the house** durchs Haus wirbeln; **we'll have to ~:** wir müssen uns beeilen; **~ and bustle about** geschäftig hin und her eilen *od.* sausen **3** (coll.: strive for business) **~ for sth.** etw. zu kriegen versuchen (ugs.) **4** (Amer. coll.: solicit) **~ [on the street]** auf den Strich gehen (salopp); **he ~s for her** er besorgt ihr die Freier (ugs.)
C *n.* **1** (jostling) Gedränge, *das* **2** (hurry) Hetze, *die;* **~ and bustle** Geschäftigkeit, *die;* (in street) geschäftiges Treiben

hustler /ˈhʌslə(r)/ *n.* (Amer. coll.: prostitute) Strichmädchen, *das*/Strichjunge, *der* (salopp)

hut /hʌt/ *n.* Hütte, *die;* (Mil.) Baracke, *die*

hutch /hʌtʃ/ *n.* **1** (for rabbit) Stall, *der;* (for guinea pig) Käfig, *der* **2** (derog.: hut, small house) Hütte, *die*

hyacinth /ˈhaɪəsɪnθ/ *n.* **1** (Bot.) Hyazinthe, *die;* **wild** *or* **wood ~:** Hasenglöckchen, *das; see also* **grape hyacinth 2** (colour) **~ [blue]** Hyazinthblau, *das*

hybrid /ˈhaɪbrɪd/
A *n.* **1** (Biol.) Hybride, *die od. der* (**between** aus); Kreuzung, *die* **2** (Ethnol.) Mischling, *der* **3** (fig.: mixture) Mischung, *die* **4** (Ling.) hybride Bildung
B *adj.* **1** (Biol.) hybrid ‹*Züchtung*›; **this is a ~ rose** diese Rose ist eine Hybride; **a ~ species/animal/plant** eine Hybridzüchtung; ein[e] Hybride **2** (Ethnol.) mischerbig **3** (fig.: mixed) gemischt; Misch‹*kultur, -sprache*› **4** (Ling.) hybrid

hybrid: ~ bike *n.* Crossrad, *das;* **~ car** *n.* Hybridauto, *das*

hybridize (**hybridise**) /ˈhaɪbrɪdaɪz/ *v.t.* **1** (Biol.) hybridisieren (fachspr.); kreuzen **2** (Ling.) **~ words** hybride Wörter bilden

hydra /ˈhaɪdrə/ *n.* **1** (Greek Mythol.) Hydra, *die* **2** (Zool.: polyp) Süßwasserpolyp, *der;* Hydra, *die*

hydrangea /haɪˈdreɪndʒə/ *n.* (Bot.) Hortensie, *die;* Hydrangea, *die* (fachspr.)

hydrant /ˈhaɪdrənt/ *n.* Hydrant, *der*

hydrate /ˈhaɪdreɪt/ *n.* (Chem.) Hydrat, *das*

hydration /haɪˈdreɪʃn/ *n.* **1** (addition of fluid) Flüssigkeitszufuhr, *die* **2** (Chem.) Hydra[ta]tion, *die*

hydraulic /haɪˈdrɔːlɪk/ *adj.* (Mech. Engin.) hydraulisch; **~ engineer** Wasserbauingenieur, *der;* **~ engineering** Wasserbau, *der*

hydraulically /haɪˈdrɔːlɪklɪ/ *adv.* (Mech. Engin.) hydraulisch

hydraulic: ~ 'brake *n.* (Mech. Engin.) hydraulische Bremse; **~ 'fluid** *n.* (Mech. Engin.) hydraulische Flüssigkeit; (in brake system) Bremsflüssigkeit, *die;* **~ 'ram** *n.* (Mech. Engin.) **1** (pump) hydraulischer Widder; **2** (piston) Hydraulikkolben, *der*

hydride /ˈhaɪdraɪd/ *n.* (Chem.) Hydrid, *das*

hydrocarbon /haɪdrəˈkɑːbən/ *n.* (Chem.) Kohlenwasserstoff, *der*

hydrochloric acid /haɪdrəklɔːrɪk ˈæsɪd/ *n.* (Chem.) Salzsäure, *die*

hydrodynamic /haɪdrəʊdaɪˈnæmɪk/ *adj.* (Phys.) hydrodynamisch

hydrodynamics /haɪdrəʊdaɪˈnæmɪks/ *n., no pl.* (Phys.) Hydrodynamik, *die*

hydroelectric /haɪdrəʊɪˈlektrɪk/ *adj.* (Electr.) hydroelektrisch; **~ power plant** *or* **station** Wasserkraftwerk, *das*

hydroelectricity /haɪdrəʊɪlekˈtrɪsɪtɪ/ *n., no pl.* (Electr.) Hydroelektrizität, *die*

hydrofoil /ˈhaɪdrəfɔɪl/ *n.* (Naut.) **1** (structure) Tragfläche, *die;* Tragflügel, *der* **2** (vessel) Tragflächenboot, *das;* Tragflügelboot, *das*

hydrogen /ˈhaɪdrədʒən/ *n.* Wasserstoff, *der;* Hydrogen[ium], *das* (fachspr.); **a ~-filled balloon** ein mit Wasserstoff gefüllter Ballon; *see also* **peroxide A 2**

'hydrogen bomb *n.* Wasserstoffbombe, *die*

hydrological /haɪdrəˈlɒdʒɪkl/ *adj.* hydrologisch

hydrology /haɪˈdrɒlədʒɪ/ *n., no pl.* Hydrologie, *die*

hydrolyse /ˈhaɪdrəlaɪz/ *v.t.* (Chem.) hydrolysieren

hydrolysis /haɪˈdrɒlɪsɪs/ *n., pl.* **hydrolyses** /haɪˈdrɒlɪsiːz/ (Chem.) Hydrolyse, *die*

hydrolyze (Amer.) ▸**hydrolyse**

hydrometer /haɪˈdrɒmɪtə(r)/ *n.* Hydrometer, *das*

hydrophobia /haɪdrəˈfəʊbɪə/ *n.* ▸**ⓘ p. 1231** **1** (Med.) (rabies) Tollwut, *die;* (symptom) Hydrophobie, *die* (Med.) **2** (Psych.) Hydrophobie, *die* (fachspr.); krankhafte Wasserscheu

hydrophobic /haɪdrəˈfəʊbɪk/ *adj.* **1** (Med.) tollwutkrank, tollwutinfiziert ‹*Tier, Person*›; tollwütig ‹*Tier*›; **be ~:** Tollwut haben **2** (water-resistant) hydrophob (Chemie, Technik)

hydroplane /ˈhaɪdrəpleɪn/ *n.* **1** (Naut.: finlike device) Gleitfläche, *die;* (of submarine) Tiefenruder, *das* **2** (motor boat) Gleitboot, *das*

hydroponics /haɪdrəˈpɒnɪks/ *n., no pl.* (Hort.) Hydroponik, *die* (fachspr.); Hydrokultur, *die*

hydrosphere /ˈhaɪdrəsfɪə(r)/ *n.* (Geog.) Hydrosphäre, *die*

hydrostatic /haɪdrəˈstætɪk/ *adj.* (Phys.) hydrostatisch

hydrostatics /haɪdrəˈstætɪks/ *n., no pl.* (Phys.) Hydrostatik, *die*

hydrothermal /haɪdrəˈθɜːml/ *adj.* hydrothermal

hydrous /ˈhaɪdrəs/ *adj.* (Chem., Min.) wasserhaltig ‹*Salz, Substanz*›

hydroxide /haɪˈdrɒksaɪd/ *n.* (Chem.) Hydroxid, *das*

hydrozoan /haɪdrəˈzəʊən/ (Zool.)
A *adj.* zu den Hydrozoen gehörend; **~ polyp** Hydroidpolyp, *der*
B *n.* Hydrozoon, *das*

hyena /haɪˈiːnə/ *n.* **1** (Zool.) Hyäne, *die;* **laughing** *or* **spotted ~:** Tüpfel- *od.* Fleckenhyäne, *die;* **laugh like a ~:** wie eine Hyäne kreischen; ≈ wiehernd lachen **2** (fig.: person) Hyäne, *die* (ugs. abwertend) **3** (Austral. Zool.) Beutelwolf, *der*

hygiene /ˈhaɪdʒiːn/ *n., no pl.* **1** Hygiene, *die;* **conditions of bad ~:** schlechte hygienische Verhältnisse; **domestic ~:** häusliche Hygiene; **feminine ~:** Monatshygiene, *die* **2** *no art.* (science) Hygiene, *die* (Med.); **dental ~:** Zahnhygiene, *die*

hygienic /haɪˈdʒiːnɪk/ *adj.* hygienisch; **not ~:** unhygienisch

hygienically /haɪˈdʒiːnɪkəlɪ/ *adv.* hygienisch

hygienist /haɪˈdʒiːnɪst/ *n.* ▸**ⓘ p. 1260** Hygieniker, *der*/Hygienikerin, *die;* **dental ~:** Zahnhygieniker, *der*/-hygienikerin, *die*

hygrometer /haɪˈgrɒmɪtə(r)/ *n.* (Meteorol.) Hygrometer, *das*

hymen /ˈhaɪmen/ *n.* (Anat.) Hymen, *das od. der* (fachspr.); Jungfernhäutchen, *das*

hymn /hɪm/
A *n.* **1** (Relig.) Hymne, *die;* Loblied, *das;* (sung in service) Kirchenlied, *das;* **Easter ~, ~ for Easter** Osterlied, *das* **2** (song of praise, lit. or fig.) Hymne, *die;* **a ~ to nature** eine Hymne an die Natur; **a ~ to Venus/England/the new age** eine Hymne auf Venus/England/das neue Zeitalter
B *v.t.* (praise with songs) besingen (geh.); lobpreisen (dichter.) ‹*Gott, Werke Gottes*›; (fig.: praise) preisen (geh.)

hymnal /ˈhɪmnl/, **hymnary** /ˈhɪmnərɪ/ *ns.* Gesangbuch, *das;* Hymnar[ium], *das*

'hymn book *n.* Gesangbuch, *das*

hyoid /ˈhaɪɔɪd/ (Anat.) *adj. & n.* **~ [bone]** Zungenbein, *das*

hype /haɪp/ (coll.)
A *n.* **1** (deception) Schwindel, *der* (ugs.) **2** (misleading publicity) Reklameschwindel, *der* (ugs.); **media ~:** Medienrummel, *der*
B *v.t.* **1** (cheat) reinlegen (ugs.); **~ sb. into sth./doing sth.** jmdn. [durch Tricks] zu etw. bringen/jmdn. [durch Tricks] dazu bringen, etw. zu tun **2** **~ [up]** (publicize excessively) groß herausbringen

Phrasal verb

• **~ up** *v.t.* (coll. stimulate) hochputschen (ugs.); **feel ~d up** überdreht sein (ugs.)

hyper /ˈhaɪpə(r)/ *adj.* (coll.) aufgedreht (ugs.); überdreht (ugs.); **there's no need to get so ~:** kein Grund zur Panik! (ugs.)

hyperactive /haɪpəˈræktɪv/ *adj.* überaktiv

hyperactivity /haɪpəræk'tɪvɪtɪ/ *n., no pl.* Überaktivität, *die*

hyperbola /haɪˈpɜːbələ/ *n., pl.* **~s** *or* **~e** /haɪˈpɜːbəliː/ (Geom.) Hyperbel, *die*

hyperbole /haɪˈpɜːbəlɪ/ *n.* (Rhet.) Hyperbel, *die*

hyperbolic /haɪpəˈbɒlɪk/ *adj.* **1** (Geom.) hyperbolisch **2** ▸**hyperbolical 1**

hyperbolical /haɪpəˈbɒlɪkl/ *adj.* **1** (Rhet.) hyperbolisch ‹*Stil, Wendung usw.*› **2** ▸**hyperbolic 1**

hypercritical /haɪpəˈkrɪtɪkl/ *adj.* hyperkritisch; übertrieben kritisch

hyperlink /ˈhaɪpəlɪŋk/ *n.* (Computing) Hyperlink, *der*

hypermarket /ˈhaɪpəmɑːkɪt/ *n.* Verbrauchermarkt, *der*

hypersensitive /haɪpəˈsensɪtɪv/ *adj.* hypersensibel; überempfindlich; **be ~ to sth.** überempfindlich auf etw. (*Akk.*) reagieren

hypersensitivity /haɪpəsensɪˈtɪvɪtɪ/ *n., no pl.* Überempfindlichkeit, *die*

hypersonic /haɪpəˈsɒnɪk/ *adj.* Überschall-

hypertension /haɪpəˈtenʃn/ *n.* (Med.) Hypertonie, *die* (fachspr.); Bluthochdruck, *der*

hypertensive /haɪpəˈtensɪv/ *adj.* (Med.) hypertonisch

hypertext *n., no pl.* (Computing) Hypertext, *der; attrib.* **~ link** Hyperlink, *der;* **H~ Markup Language** HTML, *das;* **H~ Transport** (*or* **Transfer**) **Protocol** Hypertext-Transferprotokoll, *das*

hypertrophied /haɪˈpɜːtrəfɪd/ *adj.* hypertroph ‹*Organ*›

hyper'ventilate *v.i.* hyperventilieren (Med.)

hyperventilation /haɪpəventɪˈleɪʃn/ *n., no pl.* Hyperventilation, *die*

hypha /ˈhaɪfə/ *n., pl* **~e** /ˈhaɪfiː/ (Bot.) Hyphe, *die* (fachspr.); Pilzfaden, *der*

hyphen /ˈhaɪfn/ *n.* **1** Bindestrich, *der* **2** (connecting separate syllables) Trennungsstrich, *der;* Divis, *das* (fachspr.)

hyphenate /ˈhaɪfəneɪt/ *v.t.* mit Bindestrich schreiben; koppeln

hyphenation /haɪfəˈneɪʃn/ *n., no pl.* Kopplung, *die*

hypnosis /hɪpˈnəʊsɪs/ *n., pl.* **hypnoses** /hɪpˈnəʊsi:z/ Hypnose, *die;* (act, process) Hypnotisierung, *die;* **under ~:** in Hypnose (*Dat.*)

hypnotic /hɪpˈnɒtɪk/
A *adj.* hypnotisch; (producing hypnotism) hypnotisch; hypnotisierend ‹*Wirkung, Blick*›; **have a ~ effect on sb.** hypnotisierend *od.* einschläfernd auf jmdn. wirken
B *n.* Schlafmittel, *das;* (Med. also) Hypnotikum, *das* (fachspr.)

hypnotically /hɪpˈnɒtɪklɪ/ *adv.* hypnotisch

hypnotism /ˈhɪpnətɪzm/ *n.* Hypnotik, *die;* (act) Hypnotisieren, *das*

hypnotist /ˈhɪpnətɪst/ *n.* Hypnotiseur, *der*/Hypnotiseuse, *die*

hypnotize /ˈhɪpnətaɪz/ *v.t.* (lit. or fig.) hypnotisieren; (fig.: fascinate) faszinieren

hypo /ˈhaɪpəʊ/ *n.* (Photog.) Fixiernatron, *das;* Fixiersalz, *das*

hypocaust /ˈhaɪpəkɔ:st/ *n.* (Roman Ant.) Hypokaustum, *das*

hypochondria /haɪpəˈkɒndrɪə/ *n.* Hypochondrie, *die*

hypochondriac /haɪpəˈkɒndrɪæk/
A *adj.* hypochondrisch
B *n.* Hypochonder, *der*

hypocrisy /hɪˈpɒkrɪsɪ/ *n.* **1** Heuchelei, *die;* Hypokrisie, *die* (geh.) **2** (simulation of virtue) Scheinheiligkeit, *die*

hypocrite /ˈhɪpəkrɪt/ *n.* **1** Heuchler, *der*/Heuchlerin, *die;* Hypokrit, *der* (geh. veralt.) **2** (person feigning virtue) Scheinheilige, *der/die*

hypocritical /hɪpəˈkrɪtɪkl/ *adj.* **1** heuchlerisch **2** (feigning virtue) scheinheilig; hypokritisch (geh. veralt.)

hypodermic /haɪpəˈdɜ:mɪk/ (Med.)
A *adj.* subkutan ‹*Injektion*›; subkutan verabreicht ‹*Medikament*›; **~ syringe** Injektionsspritze, *die*
B *n.* **1** (injection) subkutane Injektion **2** (syringe) Injektionsspritze, *die*

hypotension /haɪpəʊˈtenʃn/ *n.* (Med.) Hypotonie, *die* (fachspr.); zu niedriger Blutdruck

hypotensive /haɪpəʊˈtensɪv/ *adj.* (Med.) hypotonisch; (tending to lower the blood pressure) blutdrucksenkend ‹*Medikament*›

hypotenuse /haɪˈpɒtənju:z/ *n.* (Geom.) Hypotenuse, *die;* **square on the ~:** Hypotenusenquadrat, *das*

hypothermia /haɪpəˈθɜ:mɪə/ *n.* (Med.) Hypothermie, *die* (fachspr.); Unterkühlung, *die*

hypothesis /haɪˈpɒθɪsɪs/ *n., pl.* **hypotheses** /haɪˈpɒθɪsi:z/ Hypothese, *die;* (unproved assumption also) Annahme, *die*

hypothesize (**hypothesise**) /haɪˈpɒθɪsaɪz/
A *v.i.* eine Hypothese aufstellen; mutmaßen; spekulieren
B *v.t.* annehmen

hypothetical /haɪpəˈθetɪkl/ *adj.* hypothetisch; angenommen; **it will remain ~:** darüber wird man nur mutmaßen *od.* spekulieren können

hypothetically /haɪpəˈθetɪkəlɪ/ *adv.* hypothetisch

hyrax /ˈhaɪəræks/ *n.* (Zool.) Klippschliefer, *der*

hyssop /ˈhɪsəp/ *n.* (Bot.) Ysop, *der*

hysterectomy /hɪstəˈrektəmɪ/ *n.* (Med.) Hysterektomie, *die* (fachspr.); operative Entfernung der Gebärmutter

hysteria /hɪˈstɪərɪə/ *n.* Hysterie, *die*

hysterical /hɪˈsterɪkl/ *adj.* hysterisch

hysterically /hɪˈsterɪkəlɪ/ *adv.* hysterisch; **~ funny** urkomisch

hysterics /hɪˈsterɪks/ *n. pl.* (laughter) hysterischer Lachanfall; (crying) hysterischer Weinkrampf; **have ~:** hysterisch lachen/weinen

Hz *abbr.* **= hertz** Hz

i

I[1], **i** /aɪ/ *n., pl.* **Is** *or* **I's** 1 (letter) I, i, *das; see also* **dot B 2** 2 (Roman numeral) I

I[2]

A *pron.* ich; **it was I** (formal) ich war es; **it was I who locked the door** (formal) ich war es, der die Tür abgeschlossen hat; *see also* **me**[1]; **mine**[2]; **my**; **myself**

B *n., no pl.* **the I** (Philos.) das Ich

I. *abbr.* 1 **= Island[s]** I. 2 **= Isle[s]** I.

iamb /ˈaɪæm/ ▸**iambus**

iambic /aɪˈæmbɪk/ (Pros.)

A *adj.* jambisch; **~ pentameter** fünffüßiger Jambus

B *n. in pl.* Jamben

iambus /aɪˈæmbəs/ *n., pl.* **~es** *or* **iambi** /aɪˈæmbaɪ/ (Pros.) Jambus, *der*

IATA /ɪˈɑːtə, aɪˈɑːtə/ *abbr.* **= International Air Transport Association** IATA, *die*

IBA *abbr.* (Brit.) **= Independent Broadcasting Authority** *Kontrollgremium für den privaten Rundfunk und das Privatfernsehen*

Iberia /aɪˈbɪərɪə/ *pr. n.* (Hist., Geog.) Iberische Halbinsel

Iberian /aɪˈbɪərɪən/

A *adj.* iberisch

B *n.* (inhabitant of [ancient] Iberia) Iberer, *der*/Ibererin, *die*

Iberian Peˈninsula *pr. n.* (Geog.) Iberische Halbinsel

ibex /ˈaɪbeks/ *n.* (Zool.) Steinbock, *der*

ibid. *abbr.* **= ibidem** ib.; ibd.; ibid.

ibidem /ˈɪbɪdem, ɪˈbaɪdəm/ *adv.* ibidem; ebenda; ebendort

ibis /ˈaɪbɪs/ *n.* (Ornith.) Ibis, *der*

i/c *abbr.* 1 **= in charge** 2 **= in command**

ICBM *abbr.* **= intercontinental ballistic missile**

ice /aɪs/

A *n.* 1 *no pl.* Eis, *das;* **become ~:** [zu Eis] gefrieren; **feel/be like ~** (be very cold) eiskalt sein; **there was ~ over the pond** eine Eisschicht bedeckte den Teich; **fall through the ~:** auf dem Eis einbrechen; **be on ~** (coll.) (be held in reserve) ‹*Plan:*› auf Eis (*Dat.*) liegen (ugs.); **put on ~** (coll.) auf Eis (*Akk.*) legen (ugs.); **be on thin ~** (fig.) sich auf dünnes Eis begeben haben; **break the ~** (fig.: make a beginning) den Anfang machen; (break through reserve) das Eis brechen; *see also* **cut A 2**; **skate**[2] **B** 2 (confection) [Speise]eis, *das;* Eiscreme, *die;* **an ~/two ~s** ein/zwei Eis 3 *no pl., no indef. art.* (Amer. coll.: diamonds) Diamanten

B *v.t.* 1 (freeze) einfrieren, tiefkühlen ‹*Lebensmittel*›; *see also* **lolly 1** 2 (cool with ~) [mit Eis] kühlen; **~d coffee/tea** Eiskaffee, *der*/Tee mit Eis; **be ~d** eisgekühlt sein 3 (cover in icing) glasieren ‹*Kuchen*›

Phrasal verbs

• **~ ˈover** *v.i.* ‹*Gewässer:*› zufrieren; ‹*Straße, Flugzeug:*› vereisen

• **~ ˈup** *v.i.* 1 (freeze) ‹*Wasserleitung:*› einfrieren 2 ▸**~ over**

ice: ~ age *n.* Eiszeit, *die;* **~ axe** *n.* Pickel, *der;* **~ beer** *n.* Eisbier, *das*

iceberg /ˈaɪsbɜːg/ *n.* Eisberg, *der;* **the tip of the ~** (fig.) die Spitze des Eisbergs

ice: ~ blue A /ˈ-ˈ-/ *n.* Eisblau, *das;* B /ˈ--/ *adj.* eisblau; **~-bound** *adj.* eingefroren ‹*Schiff*›; durch Vereisung abgeschnitten ‹*Hafen, Küste*›; **~box** *n.* (Amer. dated) Kühlschrank, *der;* (Brit.: ice-making compartment) Eisfach, *das;* Gefrierfach, *das;* **~-breaker** *n.* (Naut.) Eisbrecher, *der;* **~ bucket** *n.* Eisbehälter, *der;* **~ cap** *n.* Eisdecke, -schicht, *die;* (polar) Eiskappe, *die;* **~-cold** *adj.* eiskalt; **~ ˈcream** *n.* Eis, *das;* Eiscreme, *die;* **one ~ cream/two/too many ~ creams** ein/zwei/zu viel Eis; **~ ˈcream parlour** *n.* Eisdiele, *die;* Eiscafé, *das;* **~ cube** *n.* Eiswürfel, *der*

iced /aɪst/ *adj.* 1 (cooled) eisgekühlt; **~ coffee/tea** Eiskaffee, *der*/Tee mit Eis 2 (with icing) glasiert

ice: ~ field *n.* Eisfeld, *das;* **~ floe** ▸**floe**; **~ hockey** *n.* Eishockey, *das*

Iceland /ˈaɪslənd/ *pr. n.* Island (*das*)

Icelander /ˈaɪsləndə(r)/ *n.* ▸ⓘ **p. 1345** Isländer, *der*/Isländerin, *die*

Icelandic /aɪsˈlændɪk/ ▸ⓘ **p. 1277**, ▸ⓘ **p. 1345**

A *adj.* isländisch; *see also* **English A**

B *n.* Isländisch, *das; see also* **English B 1**

ice: ~ ˈlolly ▸**lolly 1**; **~ machine** *n.* Gefrierapparat, *der;* **~ pack** *n.* 1 (to relieve pain) Eispackung, *die;* 2 (to keep food cool) Kälteakku *od.* Kühlakku, *der* (ugs.); 3 (sea ~) [Pack]eisdecke, *die;* **~ rink** *n.* Schlittschuh-, Eisbahn, *die;* **~ shelf** *n.* Eisschelf, *der od. das;* **~ skate** *n.* Schlittschuh, *der;* **~-skate** *v.i.* Schlittschuh laufen; Eis laufen; **~ skater** *n.* Schlittschuhläufer, *der;* **~ skating** *n., no pl.* Schlittschuhlaufen, *das;* **~ water** *n.* Eiswasser, *das*

ichthyologist /ɪkθɪˈɒlədʒɪst/ *n.* Ichthyologe, *der*/Ichthyologin, *die;* Fischkundler, *der*/-kundlerin, *die*

ichthyology /ɪkθɪˈɒlədʒɪ/ *n.* Ichthyologie, *die;* Fischkunde, *die*

icicle /ˈaɪsɪkl/ *n.* Eiszapfen, *der*

icily /ˈaɪsɪlɪ/ *adv.* eisig; (fig.) kalt ‹*ablehnend, lächelnd*›; eisig, frostig ‹*empfangen, begrüßen, anblicken*›; **~ cold** eiskalt

iciness /ˈaɪsɪnɪs/ *n., no pl.* Eis[es]kälte, *die;* (of road) Eisglätte, *die*

icing /ˈaɪsɪŋ/ *n.* 1 *no pl.* (formation of ice) Vereisen, *das;* (cooling) Kühlen, *das;* (of cake) Überziehen mit Zuckerguss 2 (Cookery: sugar coating) Zuckerguss, *der;* Zuckerglasur, *die;* **[the] ~ on the cake** (fig.) das Tüpfelchen auf dem i

ˈicing sugar *n.* (Brit.) Puderzucker, *der*

icon /ˈaɪkən, ˈaɪkɒn/ *n.* 1 (statue) Standbild, *das* 2 (Orthodox Ch.) Ikone, *die* 3 (Computing) Icon, *das* 4 (representative symbol) Kultsymbol, *das;* (Person) Ikone, *die*

iconic /aɪˈkɒnɪk/ *adj.* ikonisch; **achieve ~ status** zur Ikone werden; **an ~ figure** eine Ikone

iconoclast /aɪˈkɒnəklæst/ *n.* (lit. or fig.) Bilderstürmer, *der*

iconoclastic /aɪkɒnəˈklæstɪk/ *adj.* (lit. or fig.) bilderstürmerisch

ICT *abbr.* **= Information and Communication Technology**

icterus /ˈɪktərəs/ *n.* (Med.) Ikterus, *der* (fachspr.); Gelbsucht, *die*

icy /ˈaɪsɪ/ *adj.* 1 vereist ‹*Berge, Landschaft, Straße, See*›; eisreich ‹*Region, Land*›; **in ~ conditions** bei Eis 2 (very cold) eiskalt; eisig; (fig.) frostig ‹*Benehmen, Ton*›

id /ɪd/ *n.* (Psych.) Es, *das*

I'd /aɪd/ 1 **= I had** 2 **= I would**

ID /aɪˈdiː/ *n.* **ID card/disc/badge** ▸**identification 3**; **have you [got] some** *or* **any ID?** können Sie sich ausweisen?

idea /aɪˈdɪə/ *n.* 1 (conception) Idee, *die;* Gedanke, *der;* **arrive at an ~:** auf eine Idee *od.* einen Gedanken kommen; **get one's** *or* **the ~ from sth.** sich durch etw. anregen *od.* inspirieren lassen; **the ~ of going abroad** der Gedanke *od.* die Vorstellung, ins Ausland zu fahren; **have a good ~ of sth.** über etw. (*Akk.*) Bescheid wissen; **give/get some ~ of sth.** einen Überblick über etw. (*Akk.*) geben/einen Eindruck von etw. bekommen; **get the ~ [of sth.]** verstehen, worum es [bei etw.] geht; **be getting the ~ quickly** schnell [damit] zurechtkommen; **sb.'s ~ of sth.** (coll.) jmds. Vorstellung von etw.; **not my ~ of …** (coll.) nicht, was ich mir unter … (*Dat.*) vorstelle; **he has no ~** (coll.) er hat keine Ahnung (ugs.) 2 (mental picture) Vorstellung, *die;* **what gave you ˈthat ~?** wie bist du darauf gekommen?; **get the ~ that …:** den Eindruck bekommen, dass …; **I don't want her to get the ~ that …:** ich will nicht, dass sie glaubt *od.* den Eindruck bekommt, dass …; **he's got the ~ that …:** er bildet sich (*Dat.*) ein, dass …; **get** *or* **have ~s** (coll.) (be rebellious) auf dumme Gedanken kommen (ugs.); (be ambitious) sich (*Dat.*) Hoffnungen machen; **put ~s into sb.'s head** jmdn. auf dumme Gedanken bringen 3 (vague notion) Ahnung, *die;* Vorstellung, *die;* **have you any ~ [of] how …?** weißt du ungefähr, wie …?; **have no ~ [of] where …:** keine Ahnung haben, wo …; **you can have no ~ [of] how …:** du kannst dir gar nicht vorstellen, wie …; **not have the remotest** *or* **slightest** *or* **faintest** *or* (coll.) **foggiest ~:** nicht die entfernteste *od.* mindeste *od.* leiseste Ahnung haben; keinen blassen Schimmer haben (ugs.); **I suddenly had the ~ that …:** mir kam plötzlich der Gedanke, dass …; **I've an ~ that …:** ich habe so eine Ahnung, dass …; **the ~ of his having committed a murder** die Vorstellung, dass er einen Mord begangen hat *od.* er könne einen Mord begangen haben; **the [very] ~!, what an ~!** (coll.) unvorstellbar!; allein die Vorstellung! 4 (way of thinking) Vorstellung, *die* 5 (plan) Idee, *die;* **man of ~s** kluger Kopf; einfallsreicher Mensch; **have you any ~s for the future?** hast du [irgendwelche] Zukunftspläne?; **be full of good/new ~s** viele gute/neue Ideen haben; voller guter/neuer Ideen sein; **good ~!** [das ist eine] gute Idee!; **ˈthat's an ~** (coll.) das ist eine gute Idee; **that gives me an ~:** das hat mich auf eine Idee gebracht; **the ~ was that …:** der Plan war, dass …; **have big ~s** große Rosinen im Kopf haben; **what's the big ~?** (iron.) was soll das?; was soll der Blödsinn? (ugs.) 6 (archetype) Leitgedanke, *der;* (Platonic Philos.) Idee, *die*

ideal /aɪˈdɪəl/

A *adj.* 1 ideal; vollendet ‹*Genuss, Ehemann, Gastgeber, Rittertum*›; vollkommen ‹*Glück, Welt*› 2 (embodying an idea, existing only in idea) ideell; gedacht 3 (visionary) idealistisch

B *n.* 1 (perfect type) Ideal, *das;* Idealvorstellung, *die* 2 (standard for imitation) Vorbild, *das*

ideal ˈgas *n.* (Phys.) ideales Gas

idealise ▸**idealize**

idealism /aɪˈdɪəlɪzm/ *n., no pl.* 1 Idealismus, *der* 2 (representation in idealized form) Idealisierung, *die*

idealist /aɪˈdɪəlɪst/ *n.* Idealist, *der*/Idealistin, *die*

idealistic /aɪdɪə'lɪstɪk/ *adj.* idealistisch; ~ **young people** junge Idealisten *Pl.*

idealize /aɪ'dɪəlaɪz/ *v.t.* [1] (exalt) idealisieren; verklären [2] (represent in ideal form) idealisieren; idealisierend darstellen

ideally /aɪ'dɪəlɪ/ *adv.* ideal; ~, **the work should be finished in two weeks** im Idealfalle *od.* idealerweise sollte die Arbeit in zwei Wochen abgeschlossen sein

idée fixe /i:deɪ 'fi:ks/ *n., pl.* **idées fixes** /i:deɪ 'fi:ks/ fixe Idee; Idée fixe, *die* (geh.)

identical /aɪ'dentɪkl/ *adj.* [1] (same) identisch; **the ~ species** dieselbe Art; **he is the ~ convict who ...:** er ist genau der Sträfling, der ... [2] (agreeing in every detail) identisch; sich (*Dat.*) gleichend; **be ~:** sich (*Dat.*) völlig gleichen; ~ **twins** eineiige Zwillinge

identically /aɪ'dentɪkəlɪ/ *adv.* völlig, genau ‹*gleich, übereinstimmend*›; völlig gleich, völlig einheitlich ‹*bauen usw.*›

identifiable /aɪ'dentɪfaɪəbl/ *adj.* erkennbar (**by** an + *Dat.*); nachweisbar ‹*Stoff, Substanz*›; bestimmbar ‹*Pflanzen-, Tierart*›; diagnostizierbar ‹*Krankheit*›

identification /aɪdentɪfɪ'keɪʃn/ *n.* [1] (treating as identical) Gleichsetzung, *die* [2] (association) Identifikation, *die;* Identifizierung, *die* [3] (determination of identity) (of person) Identifizierung, *die;* Wiedererkennen, *das;* (of plants or animals) Bestimmung, *die;* **means of ~:** Ausweispapiere *Pl.;* **have you any means of ~?** können Sie sich ausweisen?; ~ **card** [Personal]ausweis, *der;* ~ **disc** Erkennungsmarke, *die;* ~ **plate** Kennzeichenschild, *das;* ~ **badge** Ausweisplakette, *die;* Legitimationsabzeichen, *das*

identifi'cation parade *n.* (Brit.) Gegenüberstellung [zur Identifizierung], *die*

identifier /aɪ'dentɪfaɪə(r)/ *n.* [1] (device) Identifikationsmerkmal, *das;* (number) Identifikationsnummer, *die* [2] (Computing) Identifikationskode, *der*

identify /aɪ'dentɪfaɪ/

A *v.t.* [1] (treat as identical) gleichsetzen (**with** mit) [2] (associate) identifizieren (**with** mit); **Guy Fawkes will always be identified with the Gunpowder Plot** bei Guy Fawkes wird jeder sofort an die Pulververschwörung denken [3] (recognize) identifizieren; bestimmen ‹*Pflanze, Tier*› [4] (establish) ermitteln

B *v.i.* ~ **with sb.** sich mit jmdm. identifizieren

Identikit ® /aɪ'dentɪkɪt/ *n.* Phantombild, *das*

identity /aɪ'dentɪtɪ/ *n.* [1] (sameness) Übereinstimmung, *die* [2] (individuality, being specified person) Identität, *die;* **proof of ~:** Identitätsnachweis, *der;* **[case of] mistaken ~:** [Personen]verwechslung, *die* [3] (Math.) Identität, *die;* identische Gleichung [4] ~ **badge/disc/plate** *etc.* ▸ **identification 3**

identity: ~ **card** *n.* [Personal]ausweis, *der;* ~ **crisis** *n.* Identitätskrise, *die;* ~ **parade** ▸ **identification parade**; ~ **theft** *n., no pl.* Identitätsdiebstahl, *der*

ideogram /'ɪdɪəgræm/, **ideograph** /'ɪdɪəgrɑ:f/ *ns.* Ideogramm, *das;* Begriffszeichen, *das*

ideological /aɪdɪə'lɒdʒɪkl, ɪdɪə'lɒdʒɪkl/ *adj.*, **ideologically** /aɪdɪə'lɒdʒɪkəlɪ, ɪdɪə'lɒdʒɪkəlɪ/ *adv.* ideologisch; weltanschaulich

ideologue /'aɪdɪəlɒg, 'ɪdɪəlɒg/ *n.* Ideologe, *der*/Ideologin, *die*

ideology /aɪdɪ'ɒlədʒɪ, ɪdɪ'ɒlədʒɪ/ *n.* Ideologie, *die;* Weltanschauung, *die*

ides /aɪdz/ *n. pl.* Iden *Pl.;* **the ~ of March** die Iden des März

idiocy /'ɪdɪəsɪ/ *n.* [1] (foolishness) Dummheit, *die;* Idiotie, *die* (abwertend) [2] *no pl.* (Med.) Idiotie, *die;* hochgradiger Schwachsinn

idiolect /'ɪdɪəlekt/ *n.* (Ling.) Idiolekt, *der*

idiom /'ɪdɪəm/ *n.* [1] (set phrase) [Rede]wendung, *die;* idiomatischer Ausdruck [2] (expression peculiar to a group) Ausdrucksweise, *die;* (expression peculiar to a person) Stil, *der;* Diktion, *die* (geh.); **the legal ~:** die Juristensprache [3] (national language) Idiom, *das;* [National]sprache, *die* [4] (style of artistic expression) Ausdrucksform, *die;* **the New Orleans ~:** der New-Orleans-Stil

idiomatic /ɪdɪə'mætɪk/ *adj.*, **idiomatically** /ɪdɪə'mætɪkəlɪ/ *adv.* idiomatisch

idiosyncrasy /ɪdɪə'sɪŋkrəsɪ/ *n.* [1] (mental constitution) [geistige] Einstellung [2] (view, behaviour) Eigentümlichkeit, *die;* Eigenheit, *die*

idiosyncratic /ɪdɪəsɪŋ'krætɪk/ *adj.*, **idiosyncratically** /ɪdɪəsɪŋ'krætɪkəlɪ/ *adv.* eigenwillig

idiot /'ɪdɪət/ *n.* [1] (coll.: fool) Idiot, *der* (ugs.); Trottel, *der* (ugs.) [2] (Med.) Schwachsinnige, *der/die;* Idiot, *der*/Idiotin, *die* (veralt.)

idiot: ~ **board** *n.* (Telev. coll.) Neger, *der* (Jargon); ~ **box** *n.* (Amer. coll.) Glotze, *die* (ugs.); Glotzkiste, *die* (ugs.)

idiotic /ɪdɪ'ɒtɪk/ *adj.* idiotisch (ugs. abwertend); schwachsinnig (abwertend); **what an ~ thing to do/say** was für ein Schwachsinn

idiotically /ɪdɪ'ɒtɪkəlɪ/ *adv.* idiotisch (ugs.); schwachsinnig

idle /'aɪdl/

A *adj.* [1] (lazy) faul; träge [2] (not in use) außer Betrieb *nachgestellt;* **be** *or* **stand ~** ‹*Maschinen, Fabrik:*› stillstehen; *see also* **lie² B 2** [3] (having no special purpose) bloß ‹*Neugier*›; nutzlos, leer ‹*Geschwätz*› [4] (groundless) unbegründet ‹*Annahme, Mutmaßung*›; bloß, rein ‹*Spekulation, Angeberei, Gerücht, Behauptung*›; **no ~ jest** kein Scherz; **no ~ boast** (iron.) kein leeres Versprechen [5] (ineffective) sinnlos, (geh.) müßig ‹*Diskussion, Streit*›; fruchtlos, vergeblich ‹*Versuch*›; leer ‹*Versprechen*› [6] (unoccupied) frei ‹*Zeit, Stunden, Tag*›; **Satan** *or* **the devil finds** *or* **makes work for ~ hands [to do]** (prov.) Müßiggang ist aller Laster Anfang (Spr.). [7] (unemployed) arbeitslos; **be made ~** ‹*Arbeiter:*› arbeitslos werden. **be ~ for an hour** eine Stunde lang untätig sein *od.* nichts tun

B *v.i.* [1] faulenzen [2] ‹*Motor:*› leer laufen, im Leerlauf laufen

Phrasal verb

• ~ **a'way** *v.t.* vertun ‹*Zeit, Leben, Chancen*›

idleness /'aɪdlnɪs/ *n., no pl.* (being unoccupied) Untätigkeit, *die;* (avoidance of work) Müßiggang, *der* (geh.)

idler /'aɪdlə(r)/ *n.* [1] (person) Faulenzer, *der*/Faulenzerin, *die;* Faulpelz, *der* (fam.) [2] (Tech.) (pulley) Losscheibe, *die;* (wheel) Zwischenrad, *das*

idly /'aɪdlɪ/ *adv.* [1] (carelessly) leichtsinnig; gedankenlos [2] (inactively) untätig; **stand ~ by while ...** (fig.) untätig zusehen, wie ... [3] (indolently) faul; **spend one's time ~:** seine Zeit mit Faulenzen verbringen

idol /'aɪdl/ *n.* [1] (false god) Götze, *der;* (image of deity) Götzenbild, *das* [2] (person venerated) Idol, *das;* (thing venerated) Götze, *der*

idolater /aɪ'dɒlətə(r)/ *n.* [1] (worshipper of idols) Götzendiener, *der* [2] (devoted admirer) Verehrer, *der*/Verehrerin, *die*

idolatrous /aɪ'dɒlətrəs/ *adj.* götzendienerisch ‹*Religion, Person*›; abgöttisch, götzenhaft ‹*Verehrung*›

idolatry /aɪ'dɒlətrɪ/ *n.* [1] (worship of false gods) Götzenverehrung, *die* [2] (veneration of person or thing) Vergötterung, *die*

idolize (**idolise**) /'aɪdəlaɪz/ *v.t.* [1] (make an idol of) anbeten; verehren [2] (fig.: venerate) vergöttern; zum Idol erheben

idyll (**idyl**) /'ɪdɪl/ *n.* [1] (description of scene) Idylle, *die;* **prose ~** Idylle in Prosa [2] (episode) Idyll, *das*

idyllic /aɪ'dɪlɪk, ɪ'dɪlɪk/ *adj.* idyllisch

i.e. /aɪ'i:/ *abbr.* = **that is** d. h.; i. e.

if /ɪf/

A *conj.* [1] wenn; **if anyone should ask ...:** falls jemand fragt, ...; wenn jemand fragen sollte, ...; **if you were a bird ...:** wenn du ein Vogel wärest; **if you would lend me some money ...:** wenn du mir Geld leihen würdest, ...; **if I knew what to do ...:** wenn ich wüsste, was ich tun soll ...; **if I were you** an deiner Stelle; **if and when ...:** im Falle, dass ...; unter der Voraussetzung, dass ...; **write down the items you wish to buy, if any** schreib auf, welche Artikel du kaufen willst, wenn *od.* falls du etwas möchtest; **better, if anything** vielleicht etwas besser; **tell me what I can do to help, if anything** falls ich irgendwie helfen kann, sag es mir; **if so/not** wenn ja/nein *od.* nicht; **if then/that/at all** wenn überhaupt; **if only for today** wenn auch nur für heute; **if only because/to ...:** schon allein, weil/um ... zu ...; **as if** als ob; **he nodded, as if to say ...:** er nickte, als ob er sagen wollte ...; **as if you didn't know!** als ob du es nicht gewusst hättest!; **it isn't** *or* **it's not as if we were** *or* (coll.) **we're rich** es ist nicht etwa so, dass wir reich wären [2] (whenever) [immer] wenn; **if I mention that, he blushes** [immer *od.* jedesmal] wenn ich das erwähne, errötet er [3] (whether) ob; **ask him if he knows her** frag ihn, ob er sie kennt [4] *in excl. of wish* **if I only knew, if only I knew!** wenn ich das nur wüsste!; das wüsste ich gern!; **if only he arrives in time!** wenn er nur rechtzeitig ankommt!; **if only you could** *or* **if you could only have seen it!** wenn du es nur hättest sehen können! [5] *expr. surprise etc.* **if it isn't Ronnie!** das ist doch Ronnie!; **and if he didn't try to knock me down!** und er hat doch tatsächlich versucht, mich niederzuschlagen! [6] *in polite request* **if you will wait a moment** wenn Sie einen Augenblick warten wollen; **if you wouldn't mind holding the door open** wenn Sie so freundlich wären und die Tür aufhielten; wenn Sie freundlicherweise die Tür aufhielten [7] (though) und wenn; auch *od.* selbst wenn; **if I'm mistaken, you're mistaken too** wenn ich mich auch irre, du irrst dich genauso; **even if he did say that, ...:** selbst wenn er das gesagt hat, ... [8] (despite being) wenn auch; **likeable, if somewhat rough** liebenswürdig, wenn auch etwas derb

B *n.* Wenn, *das;* Einschränkung, *die;* **ifs and buts** Wenn und Aber, *das*

iffish /'ɪfɪʃ/, **iffy** /'ɪfɪ/ *adjs.* (coll.) ungewiss; zweifelhaft

IGC *abbr.* (EU) = **Intergovernmental Conference** RK

igloo /'ɪglu:/ *n.* Iglu, *der od. das*

igneous /'ɪgnɪəs/ *adj.* ~ **rock** (Geol.) Extrusivgestein, *das;* Eruptivgestein, *das*

ignite /ɪg'naɪt/

A *v.t.* [1] anzünden; entzünden (geh.) [2] (Chem.: heat) [bis zur Verbrennung] erhitzen

B *v.i.* sich entzünden

ignition /ɪg'nɪʃn/ *n.* [1] (igniting) Zünden, *das;* Entzünden, *das* (geh.); (being ignited) Entzündung, *die;* **we have ~:** wir haben gezündet [2] (Motor Veh.) Zündung, *die*

ignition: ~ **key** *n.* (Motor Veh.) Zündschlüssel, *der;* ~ **system** *n.* (Motor Veh.) Zündanlage, *die*

ignoble /ɪg'nəʊbl/ *adj.* niedrig ‹*Geburt, Herkunft*›; niederträchtig ‹*Person*›; schändlich ‹*Tat*›

ignominious /ɪgnə'mɪnɪəs/ *adj.* [1] verwerflich (geh.) ‹*Tat, Idee, Praktik*›; schändlich, verworfen ‹*Person*› [2] (humiliating) schändlich; schmachvoll (geh.)

ignominiously /ɪgnə'mɪnɪəslɪ/ *adv.* (in a humiliating manner) auf entehrende *od.* erniedrigende Weise; schmachvoll (geh.)

ignominy /'ɪgnəmɪnɪ/ *n.* Schande, *die*

ignoramus /ɪgnə'reɪməs/ *n.* Ignorant, *der;* Nichtswisser, *der*

ignorance /'ɪgnərəns/ *n., no pl.* Ignoranz, *die* (abwertend); Unwissenheit, *die;* **keep sb. in ~ of sth.** jmdn. in Unkenntnis über etw. (*Akk.*) lassen; ~ **is bliss** das ist das Glück der Unwissenden; was ich nicht weiß, macht mich nicht heiß (Spr.); **his ~ of physics** seine mangelnden Kenntnisse in Physik

ignorant /'ɪgnərənt/ *adj.* [1] (lacking knowledge) unwissend; ungebildet [2] (behaving in uncouth manner) unkultiviert (abwertend) [3] (uninformed) **be ~ of sth.** über etw. (*Akk.*) nicht informiert sein; von etw. keine Ahnung haben; **remain ~ of sth.** über etw. (*Akk.*) nie etwas erfahren; **be ~ in** *or* **of mathematics** mangelnde Kenntnisse in Mathematik haben *od.* (geh.) aufweisen

ignorantly /'ɪgnərəntlɪ/ *adv.* unwissend; in Unwissenheit; **behave ~** (in an uncouth manner) sich ungehobelt benehmen

ignore /ɪg'nɔ:(r)/ v.t. ignorieren; nicht beachten; nicht befolgen ‹*Befehl, Rat*›; übergehen, überhören ‹*Frage, Bemerkung*›; **he ~d me in the street** er ist [auf der Straße] einfach an mir vorbeigegangen; **I shall ~ that remark!** ich habe das nicht gehört!

iguana /ɪ'gwɑ:nə/ n. (Zool.) Leguan, *der*

ikon ▸**icon**

Iliad /'ɪlɪæd/ n. Ilias, *die*

ilk /ɪlk/ n. 1▸ **Bill and [others of] his ~:** Bill und seinesgleichen; **... and that ~:** ... und dergleichen; **he's another of the same ~:** er gehört auch zu *od.* ist auch von derselben Sorte; **people of that ~:** solche Leute 2▸ **of that ~** (Scot. esp. arch.) aus dem Clan/Ort gleichen Namens

ill /ɪl/

A *adj.* 1▸ ▸ⓘ **p. 1231** (sick) krank; **be ~ with flu** an Grippe (*Dat.*) erkrankt sein; [die] Grippe haben; **be ~ with worry** vor Sorgen [ganz] krank sein; sich vor Sorgen verzehren (geh.); *see also* **health A 1** 2▸ **worse** /wɜ:s/, **worst** /wɜ:st/ (bad) schlecht; **~ effects** schädliche Wirkungen; **~ health** schlechte Gesundheit; **~ temper** *or* **humour** schlechte Laune; **do an ~ turn to sb.** (dated) jmdm. Schaden zufügen; **~ manners** (dated) schlechte Manieren; *see also* **fame**; **house A 5**; **repute B** 3▸ **worse** /wɜ:s/, **worst** /wɜ:st/ (unfavourable) ungünstig ‹*Zeitpunkt*›; widrig ‹*Schicksal, Umstand*›; **~ fate** *or* **fortune** *or* **luck** Pech, *das;* **it's an ~ wind that blows nobody [any] good** (prov.) des einen Leid, des andern Freud' (Spr.); **as ~ luck would have it** wie es das Unglück wollte

B *n.* 1▸ (evil) Übel, *das;* **for good or ~:** komme, was will; **through good and ~:** im Glück wie im Unglück 2▸ (harm) Schlechte, *das;* Unglück, *das;* **wish sb. ~:** jmdm. nichts Gutes *od.* nur das Schlechteste wünschen; **think/speak ~ of sb.** Schlechtes über jmdn. *od.* von jmdm. denken/sagen; **let's not speak ~ of the dead** die Toten soll man ruhen lassen 3▸ *in pl.* (misfortunes) Missstände *Pl.;* **the ~s that flesh is heir to** die Leiden, mit denen die Menschheit geschlagen ist

C *adv.*, **worse, worst** 1▸ (badly) schlecht, unschicklich ‹*sich benehmen*› 2▸ (unfavourably) ungünstig ‹*gelegen*›; **it goes ~ with sb.** (dated) es geht jmdm. schlecht 3▸ (imperfectly) schlecht, unzureichend ‹*versorgt, ausgestattet*›; **he can ~ afford it** er kann es sich (*Dat.*) kaum leisten; **it ~ becomes sb. to do sth.** (formal) es ist nicht jmds. Sache *od.* steht jmdm. nicht zu, etw. zu tun; **be ~ at ease** sich nicht wohl fühlen

I'll /aɪl/ 1▸ **= I shall** 2▸ **= I will**

ill: ~-advised *adj.* unklug; schlecht beraten ‹*Kunde*›; **be ~-advised** ‹*Person:*› schlecht beraten sein; **~-ad'visedly** *adv.* (without thinking) unklug, unüberlegt ‹*handeln*›; **~-assorted** *adj.* schlecht zusammenpassend; nicht harmonierend, unverträglich ‹*Ehepaar usw.*›; bunt zusammengewürfelt ‹*Sammlung*›; **~-behaved** /'ɪlbɪheɪvd/ *adj.* ungezogen; **~-bred** *adj.* schlecht erzogen ‹*Kind, Jugendlicher*›; unkultiviert (abwertend) ‹*Leute, Kerl usw.*›; **~-conceived** /'ɪlkənsi:vd/ *adj.* schlecht durchdacht; **~-defined** /'ɪldɪfaɪnd/ *adj.* ungenau definiert, unklar ‹*Verfahren, Vorgehen*›; verschwommen [formuliert] ‹*Gesetz, Verordnung*›; nicht klar *od.* fest umrissen ‹*Aufgabenbereich*›; **~-disposed** /'ɪldɪspəʊzd/ *adj.* ▸**disposed**

illegal /ɪ'li:gl/ *adj.* ungesetzlich; illegal; (Games, Sport: contrary to rules) regelwidrig; unerlaubt; **it is ~ to drive a car without a licence** es ist verboten, ohne Führerschein Auto zu fahren

il'legal immigrant *n.* illegaler Einwanderer/illegale Einwanderin

illegality /ɪlɪ'gælɪtɪ/ *n.* 1▸ *no pl.* Ungesetzlichkeit, *die;* **be unaware of the ~ of sth.** nicht wissen, dass etw. gegen das Gesetz *od.* ungesetzlich ist 2▸ (illegal act) Gesetzesübertretung, *die*

illegally /ɪ'li:gəlɪ/ *adv.* illegal; **bring sth. into the country ~:** etw. illegal *od.* auf illegalem Wege einführen

illegibility /ɪledʒɪ'bɪlɪtɪ/ *n.*, *no pl.* Unleserlichkeit, *die*

illegible /ɪ'ledʒɪbl/ *adj.*, **illegibly** /ɪ'ledʒɪblɪ/ *adv.* unleserlich

illegitimacy /ɪlɪ'dʒɪtɪməsɪ/ *n.*, *no pl.* ▸**illegitimate**: 1▸ Unehelichkeit, *die;* Illegitimität, *die* 2▸ Unrechtmäßigkeit, *die* 3▸ Unzulässigkeit, *die*

illegitimate /ɪlɪ'dʒɪtɪmət/ *adj.* 1▸ (not from wedlock) unehelich; illegitim 2▸ (not authorized by law) unrechtmäßig ‹*Machtergreifung, Geschäft*›; mit dem Gesetz unvereinbar ‹*Maßnahme, Vorgehen, Beweggrund*› 3▸ (wrongly inferred) unzulässig

illegitimately /ɪlɪ'dʒɪtɪmətlɪ/ *adv.* ▸**illegitimate**: 1▸ unehelich 2▸ zu Unrecht 3▸ auf unzulässige Weise

ill: ~-'fated *adj.* unglückselig; verhängnisvoll ‹*Entscheidung, Stunde, Tag*›; **~-'favoured** *adj.* (unattractive) unansehnlich ‹*Person*›; **~ 'feeling** *n.* Verstimmung, *die;* **cause ~ feeling** böses Blut machen *od.* schaffen; **no ~ feeling[s]?** sind Sie jetzt verstimmt *od.* (fam.) böse?; **no ~ feeling[s]** das macht [doch] nichts; ich nehme es nicht übel; **~-founded** /'ɪlfaʊndɪd/ *adj.* unbegründet;haltlos ‹*Theorie, Gerücht*›; **be ~-founded** völlig haltlos sein; jeder Grundlage entbehren; **~-gotten** *adj.* unrechtmäßig erworben; **~ humour** *n.* schlechte Laune; Gereiztheit, *die;* **~-humoured** /ɪl'hju:məd/ *adj.* schlecht gelaunt

illicit /ɪ'lɪsɪt/ *adj.* verboten ‹*Glücksspiel*›; unerlaubt ‹*[Geschlechts]verkehr, Beziehung*›; Schwarz‹*handel, -verkauf, -arbeit, -brennerei*›; **~ traffic in drugs** illegaler Drogenhandel

illicitly /ɪ'lɪsɪtlɪ/ *adv.* illegal ‹*Handel treiben, Schnaps brennen*›

'ill-informed *adj.* schlecht informiert; auf Unkenntnis beruhend ‹*Bemerkung, Schätzung, Urteil*›

illiteracy /ɪ'lɪtərəsɪ/ *n.*, *no pl.* Analphabetentum, *das;* Analphabetismus, *der*

illiterate /ɪ'lɪtərət/

A *adj.* 1▸ des Lesens und Schreibens unkundig; analphabetisch ‹*Bevölkerung*›; **he is ~:** er ist Analphabet 2▸ (showing lack of learning) primitiv (abwertend); **musically ~:** auf musikalischem Gebiet *od.* musikalisch völlig unbedarft; **he is politically ~:** er ist ein politischer Analphabet

B *n.* Analphabet, *der*/Analphabetin, *die*

ill: ~-judged /ɪl'dʒʌdʒd/ *adj.* unklug; (rash) unüberlegt; leichtfertig; **~-mannered** /ɪl'mænəd/ *adj.* rüpelhaft (abwertend); ungezogen ‹*Kind*›; **an ~-mannered fellow** ein Rüpel; **~-matched** *adj.* schlecht zusammenpassend; **~-natured** /ɪl'neɪtʃəd/ *adj.*, **~-naturedly** /ɪl'neɪtʃədlɪ/ *adv.* übellaunig

illness /'ɪlnɪs/ *n.* ▸ⓘ **p. 1231** 1▸ (a disease) Krankheit, *die;* Erkrankung, *die;* **children's ~:** Kinderkrankheit, *die* 2▸ *no pl.* Krankheit, *die;* **because of ~:** wegen [einer] Krankheit

illogical /ɪ'lɒdʒɪkl/ *adj.* unlogisch; unbegründet ‹*Ärger, Verstimmung*›

illogicality /ɪlɒdʒɪ'kælɪtɪ/ *n.* 1▸ *no pl.* Unlogik, *die* 2▸ (illogical thing) Ungereimtheit, *die;* logischer Fehler

illogically /ɪ'lɒdʒɪkəlɪ/ *adv.* auf unlogische Weise; ohne jede Logik

ill: ~-omened /ɪl'əʊmənd/ *adj.* unheilvoll; **~-starred** /'ɪlstɑ:d/ *adj.* unglücklich ‹*Liebesverhältnis*›; unheilvoll, verhängnisvoll ‹*Tag, Jahr, Zufall*›; **the trip was ~-starred** die Reise stand unter einem Unstern *od.* ungünstigen Stern; **~ 'temper** ▸**ill humour**; **~-tempered** /ɪl'tempəd/ ▸**ill-humoured**; **~-timed** /ɪl'taɪmd/ *adj.* [zeitlich] ungelegen; ungünstig; unpassend, unbesonnen ‹*Bemerkung*›; **~-'treat** *v.t.* misshandeln ‹*Lebewesen*›; nicht schonend behandeln, schlecht umgehen mit ‹*Gegenstand*›; **~-'treatment** *n.*, *no pl.* (of living thing) Misshandlung, *die;* (of object) wenig pflegliche Behandlung; **suffer/receive ~-treatment** misshandelt/wenig schonend *od.* pfleglich behandelt werden

illuminate /ɪ'lju:mɪneɪt, ɪ'lu:mɪneɪt/ *v.t.* 1▸ (light up) ‹*Lampe usw.:*› beleuchten; ‹*Mond, Sonne:*› erleuchten 2▸ (give enlightenment to) erleuchten 3▸ (help to explain) erhellen; [näher] beleuchten; **~ a period of history** Licht in eine Geschichtsepoche bringen 4▸ (decorate with lights) festlich beleuchten; illuminieren; **~d advertisements** Leuchtreklamen 5▸ (decorate with colours) ausmalen, (fachspr.) illuminieren ‹*Handschriften usw.*›; **~d initial letters** verzierte *od.* ausgemalte Initialen

illuminating /ɪ'lju:mɪneɪtɪŋ, ɪ'lu:mɪneɪtɪŋ/ *adj.* aufschlussreich

illumination /ɪlju:mɪ'neɪʃn, ɪlu:mɪ'neɪʃn/ *n.* 1▸ (lighting) Beleuchtung, *die* 2▸ (enlightenment) Erleuchtung, *die* 3▸ (decorative lights) *often in pl.* **~[s]** Festbeleuchtung, *die;* Illumination, *die* 4▸ (of manuscript) Buchmalerei, *die;* Illumination, *die* (fachspr.)

illumine /ɪ'lju:mɪn, ɪ'lu:mɪn/ *v.t.* (literary) 1▸ (light up) erhellen; illuminieren (geh.) 2▸ (enlighten) erleuchten; Erleuchtung bringen (+ *Dat.*); illuminieren (geh.)

ill-use

A /ɪl'ju:z/ *v.t.* ▸**ill-treat**

B /ɪl'ju:s/ *n.* ▸**ill-treatment**

illusion /ɪ'lju:ʒn, ɪ'lu:ʒn/ *n.* 1▸ (false sense-perception) [Sinnes]täuschung, *die;* Illusion, *die;* **have the ~ of seeing sth.** sich (*Dat.*) einbilden, etw. zu sehen; etw. zu sehen glauben; **the ointment produces an ~ of warmth** die Salbe ruft die Empfindung *od.* Illusion von Wärme hervor 2▸ (deception) Wunschbild, *das;* Illusion, *die;* (misapprehension) falsche Vorstellung; Illusion, *die;* **be under an ~:** sich Illusionen (*Dat.*) hingeben; sich (*Dat.*) Illusionen machen; **be under the ~ that ...:** sich (*Dat.*) einbilden, dass ...; **have no ~s about sb./sth.** sich (*Dat.*) über jmdn./etw. keine Illusionen machen *od.* nichts vormachen

illusionist /ɪ'lju:ʒənɪst, ɪ'lu:ʒənɪst/ Zauberkünstler, *der*/-künstlerin, *die*

illusory /ɪ'lju:sərɪ, ɪ'lu:sərɪ/ *adj.* 1▸ (deceptive) illusorisch; trügerisch 2▸ (of the nature of an illusion) imaginär (geh.) ‹*Gestalt*›; Wahn‹*bild, -idee, -vorstellung*›; irrig ‹*Lehre, Ansicht, Annahme*›

illustrate /'ɪləstreɪt/ *v.t.* 1▸ (serve as example of) veranschaulichen; illustrieren 2▸ (elucidate by pictures) [bildlich] darstellen ‹*Vorgang, Ablauf*›; illustrieren ‹*Buch, Erklärung*› 3▸ (explain) verdeutlichen; erläutern; (make clear by examples) anschaulicher machen; illustrieren 4▸ (ornament) illustrieren; bebildern

illustration /ɪlə'streɪʃn/ *n.* 1▸ (example) Beispiel, *das* (**of** für) 2▸ (picture) Abbildung, *die;* Illustration, *die* 3▸ *no pl.* (action of illustrating) (with example) Illustration, *die;* Erläuterung, *die;* (with picture) Illustration, *die;* Illustrierung, *die;* **by way of ~:** zur Illustration *od.* Verdeutlichung

illustrative /'ɪləstrətɪv/ *adj.* erläuternd; illustrativ; **be ~ of sth.** beispielhaft *od.* typisch für etw. sein; **~ material** Beispielmaterial, *das*

illustrator /'ɪləstreɪtə(r)/ *n.* ▸ⓘ **p. 1260** Illustrator, *der*/Illustratorin, *die*

illustrious /ɪ'lʌstrɪəs/ *adj.* berühmt ‹*Person*› (**for** wegen); ruhmreich ‹*Tat, Herrschaft*›

ill 'will *n.* Böswilligkeit, *die*

I'm /aɪm/ **= I am**

image /'ɪmɪdʒ/ *n.* 1▸ Bildnis, *das* (geh.); (statue) Standbild, *das;* Statue, *die* 2▸ (Optics, Math.) Bild, *das* 3▸ (semblance) Bild, *das;* (counterpart) Ebenbild, *das* (geh.); (archetype) Verkörperung, *die;* **God created man in his own ~** (Bibl.) Gott schuf den Menschen nach seinem Bilde; **she is the [very] ~ of her mother** sie ist das [getreue] Ebenbild ihrer Mutter 4▸ (Lit.: simile, metaphor) Bild, *das;* Metapher, *die* (fachspr.) 5▸ (mental representation) Bild, *das;* (conception) Vorstellung, *die* 6▸ (perceived character) Image, *das;* **improve one's ~:** sein Image aufbessern; **public ~:** Image [in der Öffentlichkeit], *das*

image: ~-conscious *adj.* imagebewusst; **~ consultant** *n.* Imageberater, *der*/-beraterin, *die*

imagery /'ɪmɪdʒərɪ, 'ɪmɪdʒrɪ/ *n.*, *no pl.* 1▸ (images) Bilder *Pl.;* bildliche Darstellungen *Pl.* 2▸ (mental images) Vorstellungen *Pl.* 3▸ (Lit.: figurative illustration) Metaphorik, *die*

imaginable /ɪ'mædʒɪnəbl/ *adj.* erdenklich; **the biggest lie ~:** die unverschämteste Lüge,

i

ℹ Illnesses, aches and pains

Injuries

Where does it hurt?
= Wo haben Sie Schmerzen?; (*to child*) Wo tut es weh?

My right arm is hurting
= Der rechte Arm tut mir weh, Mir tut der rechte Arm weh

She has hurt her foot
= (*e.g. twisted it*) Sie hat sich am Fuß weh getan; (*wounded it, e.g. cut it or stuck something into it*) Sie hat sich am Fuß verletzt

I have sprained my ankle
= Ich habe mir den Fuß verstaucht

He has broken his leg
= Er hat sich das Bein gebrochen

She has a fractured skull/pelvis
= Sie hat einen Schädelbruch/Beckenbruch

You've burnt your hand
= Du hast dir die Hand verbrannt

Note the number of expressions where the English possessive with a part of the body is translated by a definite article and a personal pronoun in the dative (*see also* ◻ **The body**).

Aches and pains

I've got toothache/a headache/a stomach ache
= Ich habe Zahnschmerzen/Kopfschmerzen/Magenschmerzen *or* (*coll.*) Zahnweh/Kopfweh/Magenweh

She has a pain in her knee
= Sie hat Schmerzen im Knie

something to relieve the pain
= etwas gegen die Schmerzen

a stab of pain
= ein stechender Schmerz

A gnawing pain went right through him
= Ein bohrender Schmerz durchfuhr ihn

Note that **Schmerz** referring to physical pain is mostly used in the plural for continuing or repeated pain, and in the singular only when a single occurrence is meant.

Being ill

I feel ill
= Ich fühle mich krank; (*esp. sick*) Mir ist übel *or* schlecht

He is ill with flu, He has [got] flu
= Er ist an Grippe erkrankt, Er hat [die] Grippe

He is seriously/terminally ill
= Er ist schwer krank/unheilbar krank

She has caught* or *gone down with a cold
= Sie hat sich erkältet *or* sich (*Dat.*) eine Erkältung zugezogen

You'll catch pneumonia
= Du holst dir eine Lungenentzündung

They suffer from asthma/bronchitis
= Sie leiden an Asthma/Bronchitis

a bout of malaria
= ein Malariaanfall

an asthma attack
= ein Asthmaanfall

Illnesses and conditions

More permanent illnesses are usually translated as **-leiden:**

He has a heart condition/a stomach complaint
= Er hat ein Herzleiden/ein Magenleiden

But:

a skin complaint
= eine Hautkrankheit

Indicating often general and less well defined pain or discomfort, the German **-beschwerden** (plural) corresponds approximately to the English "trouble" (also translated by **-probleme**):

heart/stomach trouble
= Herzbeschwerden *or* Herzprobleme/Magenbeschwerden *or* Magenprobleme

She suffers from back trouble
= Sie hat Rückenprobleme, Sie hats mit dem Rücken (*coll.*)

In some cases, the noun describing the person is used rather than the word for the illness:

He has epilepsy
= Er ist Epileptiker

German forms many words for people with certain illnesses by adding **-kranke(r):**

people with Aids* or *Aids sufferers
= Aidskranke

a cancer patient* or *victim
= ein Krebskranker/eine Krebskranke

Treatment

She is having* or *receiving treatment [from a specialist]
= Sie ist [bei einem Facharzt] in Behandlung

He is being treated for cancer/a stomach ulcer
= Er wird wegen Krebs/eines Magengeschwürs behandelt

In this last example **auf** + accusative can also be used, but this gives the phrase the sense "given the treatment for", i.e. the condition has not necessarily been diagnosed (or not correctly):

They treated him for a stomach ulcer, but it turned out that he had cancer
= Sie haben ihn auf ein Magengeschwür behandelt, aber es stellte sich heraus, dass er Krebs hatte

What can I take for hay fever?
= Was kann ich gegen Heuschnupfen nehmen?

To be taken three times a day
= Dreimal täglich einzunehmen

Shake the bottle
= Vor Gebrauch schütteln

There is no cure for Aids
= Aids ist nicht heilbar

I had four operations
= Ich bin viermal operiert worden

Have you been vaccinated against cholera?
= Sind Sie gegen Cholera geimpft [worden]?

She gave me an injection
= Sie gab mir eine Spritze

Recovery

He is getting better* or *is on the mend* or *on the road to recovery
= Er ist auf dem Wege der Besserung

She is much better
= Es geht ihr *or* Sie fühlt sich viel besser

I am completely cured/fully recovered
= Ich bin völlig geheilt/habe mich vollständig erholt

---

die man sich (*Dat.*) vorstellen kann

imaginary /ɪˈmædʒɪnərɪ/ *adj.* **1** imaginär (geh.); konstruiert ‹*Bildnis*›; eingebildet ‹*Krankheit*› **2** (Math.) imaginär

imagination /ɪmædʒɪˈneɪʃn/ *n.* **1** *no pl., no art.* Fantasie, *die;* **do/see sth. in one's ~:** sich (*Dat.*) vorstellen, etw. zu tun/etw. vor seinem geistigen Auge sehen; **use your ~!** hab doch ein bisschen Fantasie! (ugs.); entwickel doch mal etwas Fantasie! **2** *no pl., no art.* (fancy) Einbildung, *die;* **catch sb.'s ~:** jmdn. begeistern; **it's just your ~:** das bildest du dir nur ein; **it's all in your ~:** das bildest du dir alles [nur] ein

imaginative /ɪˈmædʒɪnətɪv/ *adj.* **1** fantasievoll ‹*Person*›; **be too ~:** zu viel Fantasie haben **2** einfallsreich ‹*Idee, Vorschlag, Geschichte usw.*›

imaginatively /ɪˈmædʒɪnətɪvlɪ/ *adv.* **1** einfallsreich **2** (using imagination) fantasievoll

imagine /ɪˈmædʒɪn/ *v.t.* **1** (picture to oneself) sich (*Dat.*) vorstellen; **can you ~?** stell dir vor!; **it cannot be ~d** es ist unvorstellbar; **~ things** sich (*Dat.*) Dinge einbilden[, die gar nicht stimmen]; **..., or am I imagining things?** ..., oder bilde ich mir das bloß ein? **2** (think) sich (*Dat.*) vorstellen; **~ sb./sth. to be/do ...:** denken *od.* sich (*Dat.*) vorstellen, dass jmd./etw. ... ist/tut; **~ sth. to be easy/difficult** *etc.* sich (*Dat.*) etw. leicht/schwer *usw.* vorstellen; **~ oneself to be sth.** sich (*Dat.*) einbilden, etw. zu sein; **do not ~ that ...:** bilden Sie sich (*Dat.*) bloß nicht ein, dass ... **3** (guess) sich (*Dat.*) vorstellen; **as you can ~, as may be ~d** wie du dir denken *od.* vorstellen kannst/wie man sich denken *od.* vorstellen kann **4** (suppose) glauben; **I ~ she will be coming** ich nehme an, dass sie kommen wird **5** (get the impression) **~ [that ...]:** sich (*Dat.*) einbilden[, dass ...]

imago /ɪˈmeɪgəʊ/ *n., pl.* **imagines** /ɪˈmeɪdʒɪniːz/ *or* **~s** *or* (Amer.) **~es** (Biol., Psych.) Imago, *die*

imam /ɪˈmɑːm/ *n.* (Muslim Rel.) Imam, *der*

imbalance /ɪmˈbæləns/ *n.* Unausgeglichenheit, *die*

imbecile /ˈɪmbɪsiːl/
A *adj.* **1** (stupid) schwachsinnig (ugs. abwertend) **2** (Med.) imbezil[l]
B *n.* **1** (stupid person) Idiot, *der* (ugs.); Schwachkopf, *der* **2** (Med.) Imbezil[l]e, *der/die*

imbibe /ɪmˈbaɪb/ *v.t.* **1** (drink) trinken **2** (fig.: assimilate) in sich (*Akk.*) aufsaugen

imbroglio /ɪmˈbrəʊljəʊ/ *n., pl.* **~s** **1** **a financial ~:** ein finanzielles Chaos; ein Finanzchaos **2** (dramatic situation) Verwicklungen *Pl.;* (political situation) Wirrwarr, *das*

imbue /ɪmˈbjuː/ *v.t.* **1** (tinge) färben **2** (permeate) durchdringen; **~d with sth.** von etw. durchdrungen

IMF *abbr.* = **International Monetary Fund** IWF, *der*

imitate /ˈɪmɪteɪt/ *v.t.* **1** (mimic) nachahmen; nachmachen (ugs.); **~ sb.** (follow example of) es jmdm. gleichtun **2** (produce sth. like) kopieren **3** (be like) imitieren

imitation /ɪmɪˈteɪʃn/
A *n.* **1** (imitating) Nachahmung, *die;* **Tim's ~ of his brother** die Art und Weise, wie Tim seinen Bruder nachahmt/nachahmte; **a style developed in ~ of classical models** ein nach klassischen Vorbildern entwickelter Stil; **do ~s of sb.** jmdn. imitieren *od.* nachahmen; **he sings, tells jokes, and does ~s** er singt, erzählt Witze und ahmt andere Leute nach; **~ is the sincerest [form of] flattery** nachgeahmt zu werden ist das größte Kompliment **2** (copy) Kopie, *die;* Nachbildung, *die;* (counterfeit) Imitation, *die*

B *adj.* imitiert; Kunst‹*leder, -horn*›; ~ **marble/ivory/teak/fur** *etc.* Marmor-/Elfenbein-/Teak-/Pelzimitation *usw., die*

imitative /ˈɪmɪtətɪv, ˈɪmɪteɪtɪv/ *adj.* **1** uneigenständig; epigonal (geh.); **be ~ of sb./sth.** jmdn./etw. nachahmen; **~ arts** bildende Künste **2** (prone to copy) imitativ (geh.)

imitator /ˈɪmɪteɪtə(r)/ *n.* Nachahmer, *der*/Nachahmerin, *die*; (one who mimics another) Imitator, *der*/Imitatorin, *die*; **be an ~ of sb.** jmdn. nachahmen

immaculate /ɪˈmækjʊlət/ *adj.* **1** (spotless) makellos ‹*Kleidung, Weiß*› **2** (faultless) tadellos

Immaculate Conˈception *n.* (RC Ch.) Unbefleckte Empfängnis

immaculately /ɪˈmækjʊlətlɪ/ *adv.* **1** (spotlessly) makellos; **~ white** blütenweiß **2** (faultlessly) tadellos

immanence /ˈɪmənəns/ *n., no pl.* Immanenz, *die*

immanent /ˈɪmənənt/ *adj.* **1** immanent; **be ~ in sth.** einer Sache (*Dat.*) innewohnen (geh.) **2** (Theol.) allgegenwärtig

immaterial /ɪməˈtɪərɪəl/ *adj.* **1** (unimportant) unerheblich; **it's quite ~ to me** das ist für mich vollkommen uninteressant **2** (not consisting of matter) immateriell (geh.); körperlos ‹*Wesen*›

immature /ɪməˈtjʊə(r)/ *adj.* **1** noch nicht voll entwickelt ‹*Lebewesen*›; noch nicht voll ausgereift ‹*Begabung, Talent*›; unausgegoren ‹*Kunststil*›; unreif ‹*Persönlichkeit, Einstellung*› **2** (Biol.: unripe) unreif; noch nicht voll entwickelt ‹*Organ*›

immaturity /ɪməˈtjʊərɪtɪ/ *n.* **1** *no pl.* Unreife, *die* **2** *no pl.* (Biol.: unripeness) Unreife, *die*; **in ~:** vor der Reife

immeasurable /ɪˈmeʒərəbl/ *adj.* unermesslich; unmessbar ‹*Entfernung*›

immeasurably /ɪˈmeʒərəblɪ/ *adv.* **1** unmessbar; unendlich ‹*lang*› **2** (immensely) ungeheuer

immediate /ɪˈmiːdjət/ *adj.* **1** unmittelbar; (nearest) nächst... ‹*Nachbar[schaft], Umgebung, Zukunft*›; engst... ‹*Familie*›; unmittelbar ‹*Kontakt*›; **your ~ action must be to ...:** als Erstes müssen Sie ...; **~ inference** direkter Schluss; **his ~ plan is to ...:** zunächst einmal will er ... **2** (occurring at once) prompt; unverzüglich ‹*Handeln, Maßnahmen*›; umgehend ‹*Antwort*›

immediately /ɪˈmiːdjətlɪ/
A *adv.* **1** unmittelbar; direkt **2** (without delay) sofort
B *conj.* sobald

immemorial /ɪmɪˈmɔːrɪəl/ *adj.* undenklich; **from time ~:** seit undenklichen Zeiten

immense /ɪˈmens/ *adj.* **1** ungeheuer; immens **2** (coll.: great) enorm

immensely /ɪˈmenslɪ/ *adv.* **1** ungeheuer **2** (coll.: very much) unheimlich (ugs.)

immensity /ɪˈmensɪtɪ/ *n., no pl.* (great size) Ungeheuerlichkeit, *die*

immerse /ɪˈmɜːs/ *v.t.* **1** (dip) [ein]tauchen; **he ~d his head in cold water** er tauchte den Kopf in kaltes Wasser **2** (cause to be under water) versenken; (Eccl.) untertauchen; **~d in water** unter Wasser **3** **be ~d in thought/one's work** (fig.: involved deeply) in Gedanken versunken/in seine Arbeit vertieft sein

immersion /ɪˈmɜːʃn/ *n.* **1** Eintauchen, *das* **2** (Relig.) Untertauchen, *das* **3** (fig.) (in work) Vertiefung, *die*; (in thought) Versunkenheit, *die* (geh.)

imˈmersion heater *n.* Heißwasserbereiter, *der*; (small, portable) Tauchsieder, *der*

immigrant /ˈɪmɪgrənt/
A *n.* Einwanderer, *der*/Einwanderin, *die*; Immigrant, *der*/Immigrantin, *die*
B *adj.* Einwanderer-; **~ population** Einwanderer *Pl.*; **~ workers** ausländische Arbeitnehmer

immigrate /ˈɪmɪgreɪt/ *v.i.* einwandern, immigrieren (**into** nach, **from** aus)

immigration /ɪmɪˈgreɪʃn/ *n.* Einwanderung *die*, Immigration, *die* (**into** nach, **from** aus); *attrib.* Einwanderungs‹*kontrolle, -beschränkung, -gesetz*›; **go through ~:** durch die Einwanderungskontrolle gehen; *attrib.* **~ officer** Beamte/Beamtin der Einwanderungsbehörde; **~ authorities** Einwanderungsbehörden *Pl.*; **~ Service** Einwanderungsbehörde, *die*

imminence /ˈɪmɪnəns/ *n., no pl.* Bevorstehen, *das*

imminent /ˈɪmɪnənt/ *adj.* unmittelbar bevorstehend; drohend ‹*Gefahr*›; **be ~:** unmittelbar bevorstehen/drohen

imminently /ˈɪmɪnəntlɪ/ *adv.* unmittelbar; **the President's arrival is expected ~:** die Ankunft des Präsidenten wird jeden Moment erwartet

immiscible /ɪˈmɪsɪbl/ *adj.* nicht mischbar

immobile /ɪˈməʊbaɪl/ *adj.* **1** (immovable) unbeweglich; (Mil.) immobil **2** (motionless) bewegungslos

immobilisation, immobilise ▸**immobiliz-**

immobility /ɪməˈbɪlɪtɪ/ *n., no pl.* **1** (immovableness) Unbeweglichkeit, *die*; (of army) Immobilität, *die* **2** (motionlessness) Bewegungslosigkeit, *die*

immobilization /ɪməʊbɪlaɪˈzeɪʃn/ *n.* **1** (fixing immovably) Verankerung, *die* **2** (Med.: restricting in movement) Ruhigstellung, *die*

immobilize /ɪˈməʊbɪlaɪz/ *v.t.* **1** (fix immovably) verankern; (fig.) lähmen **2** (restrict movement of) feststellen ‹*Tür usw.*›; ruhig stellen ‹*Tier, Körperteil, Patienten*› **3** gegen Wegfahren sichern ‹*Fahrzeug*›

immobilizer /ɪˈməʊbɪlaɪzə(r)/ *n.* (Motor Veh.) Wegfahrsperre, *die*

immoderate /ɪˈmɒdərət/ *adj.* **1** (excessive) unmäßig ‹*Rauchen, Trinken*›; überhöht ‹*Geschwindigkeit, Preis*›; übermäßig ‹*Lärm*› **2** (extreme) extrem ‹*Ansichten, Politiker*›; maßlos ‹*Lebensstil*›

immoderately /ɪˈmɒdərətlɪ/ *adv.* **1** (excessively) übermäßig ‹*hoch*›; unmäßig ‹*essen, trinken usw.*›; übertrieben ‹*schnell, laut*› **2** (to an extreme degree) extrem

immodest /ɪˈmɒdɪst/ *adj.* **1** (impudent) unbescheiden **2** (improper) unanständig

immodestly /ɪˈmɒdɪstlɪ/ *adv.* **1** (impudently) unbescheidenerweise **2** (improperly) unanständig

immodesty /ɪˈmɒdɪstɪ/ *n., no pl.* **1** (impudence) Unbescheidenheit, *die* **2** (impropriety) Unanständigkeit, *die*; **the ~ of her short skirt** ihr unanständig kurzer Rock

immolate /ˈɪməleɪt/ *v.t.* (literary) **1** (kill) opfern (**to** *Dat.*) **2** (fig.: sacrifice) zum Opfer bringen, aufopfern (geh.) (**to** *Dat.*)

immolation /ɪməˈleɪʃn/ *n.* (literary) **1** Opferung, *die* **2** (fig.) Aufopferung, *die*

immoral /ɪˈmɒrəl/ *adj.* **1** (not conforming to morality) unmoralisch; unsittlich; sittenwidrig (Rechtsspr.) **2** (morally evil) pervers; (unchaste) sittenlos **3** (dissolute) zügellos

immoral ˈearnings *n. pl.* (Law) Einkünfte aus gewerbsmäßiger Unzucht

immorality /ɪməˈrælɪtɪ/ *n.* **1** *no pl.* Unsittlichkeit, *die*; Unmoral, *die*; Sittenwidrigkeit, *die* (Rechtsspr.) **2** *no pl.* (wickedness) Verdorbenheit, *die*; (unchastity) Sittenlosigkeit, *die* **3** *no pl.* (dissoluteness) Zügellosigkeit, *die* **4** (morally evil or unchaste act) Unsittlichkeit, *die* **5** (dissolute act) Ausschweifung, *die*

immorally /ɪˈmɒrəlɪ/ *adv.* **1** (without regard for morality) unmoralisch; unsittlich **2** (wickedly) unmoralisch; (unchastely) sittenlos **3** (dissolutely) ausschweifend; zügellos

immortal /ɪˈmɔːtl/
A *adj.* **1** (living for ever) unsterblich **2** (divine) ewig; **~ life, the life ~:** das ewige Leben **3** (incorruptible) unvergänglich **4** (famous for all time) unsterblich, unvergänglich ‹*Kunstwerk*›
B *n.* **1** Unsterbliche, *der/die* **2** *in pl.* (Greek and Roman Mythol.) Unsterbliche; Götter

immortality /ɪmɔːˈtælɪtɪ/ *n., no pl.* ▸**immortal A 1, 3, 4**: Unsterblichkeit, *die*; Unvergänglichkeit, *die*

immortalize /ɪˈmɔːtəlaɪz/ *v.t.* unsterblich machen

immortally /ɪˈmɔːtəlɪ/ *adv.* **1** (eternally) ewig[lich] **2** (perpetually) [immer und] ewig

immovable /ɪˈmuːvəbl/ *adj.* **1** (also Law) unbeweglich; **be ~:** sich nicht bewegen lassen **2** (motionless) bewegungslos **3** (not subject to change) unveränderbar; *see also* **feast A 1** **4** (steadfast) unerschütterlich; unverrückbar ‹*Entschluss*›

immovably /ɪˈmuːvəblɪ/ *adv.* **1** fest; **be ~ stuck** feststecken **2** (in a motionless manner) bewegungslos **3** (unchangeably) unveränderbar **4** (steadfastly) unerschütterlich; **be ~ resolved** fest entschlossen sein

immune /ɪˈmjuːn/ *adj.* **1** (exempt) sicher (**from** vor + *Dat.*); geschützt (**from, against** vor + *Dat.*); gefeit (geh.) (**from, against** gegen); **~ from criminal liability** nicht strafmündig; **make oneself ~ from criticism** sich gegen Kritik abschirmen **2** (insusceptible) unempfindlich (**to** gegen); (to hints, suggestions, etc.) unempfänglich (**to** für); immun (**to** gegen) **3** (Med.) (resistant to disease) immun (**to** gegen); (relating to immunity) Immun‹*defekt, -körper, -schwäche, -serum*›; **~ system** Immunsystem, *das*

imˈmune therapy *n., no pl.* Immuntherapie, *die*

immunisation, immunise ▸**immuniz-**

immunity /ɪˈmjuːnɪtɪ/ *n.* **1** (freedom) **~ from criminal liability** Strafunmündigkeit, *die*; **~ from prosecution** Schutz vor Strafverfolgung; **give sb. ~ from punishment** ‹*Person:*› jmdn. von der Bestrafung ausnehmen; ‹*Umstand:*› jmdn. vor Strafe schützen; *see also* **diplomatic immunity** **2** ▸**immune 2**: Unempfindlichkeit, *die* (**to** gegen); Unempfänglichkeit, *die* (**to** für); Immunität, *die* (**to** gegen) **3** (Law) Immunität, *die* (**from** vor + *Dat.*) **4** (Med.: capacity to resist disease) Immunität, *die*; **have ~ to infection** gegen Infektion immun sein

immunization /ɪmjʊnaɪˈzeɪʃn/ *n.* (Med.) Immunisierung, *die*

immunize /ˈɪmjʊnaɪz/ *v.t.* (Med.) immunisieren

immunodeficiency /ɪˈmjuːnəʊdɪfɪʃənsɪ/ *n., no pl.* (Med.) Immunschwäche, *die*

immunodeficient /ɪˈmjuːnəʊdɪfɪʃənt/ *adj.* (Med.) immunschwach

immunological /ɪmjʊnəˈlɒdʒɪkl/ *n.* (Med.) immunologisch

immunologist /ɪmjʊˈnɒlədʒɪst/ *n.* ▸**❶ p. 1260** Immunologe, *der*/Immunologin, *die*

immunology /ɪmjʊˈnɒlədʒɪ/ *n., no pl.* (Med.) Immunologie, *die*

immunotherapy /ɪmjuːnəʊˈθerəpɪ/ *n., no pl.* Immuntherapie, *die*

immure /ɪˈmjʊə(r)/ (literary)
A *v.t.* einkerkern (geh.)
B *v. refl.* **~ oneself** sich abkapseln

immutability /ɪmjuːtəˈbɪlɪtɪ/ *n., no pl.* Unveränderlichkeit, *die*

immutable /ɪˈmjuːtəbl/ *adj.* unveränderlich

imp /ɪmp/ *n.* **1** Kobold, *der* **2** (fig.: mischievous child) Racker, *der* (fam.)

impact
A /ˈɪmpækt/ *n.* **1** Aufprall, *der* (**on, against** auf + *Akk.*); (of shell or bomb) Einschlag, *der*; (collision) Zusammenprall, *der* **2** (fig.: effect) Wirkung, *die*; **the ~ of plastics on modern life** die Auswirkung von Kunststoffen auf das moderne Leben; **have an ~ on sb./sth.** Auswirkungen auf jmdn./etw. haben; **make an ~ on sb./sth.** Eindruck auf jmdn./etw. machen
B /ɪmˈpækt/ *v.t.* pressen

impacted /ɪmˈpæktɪd/ *adj.* **1** (Dent.) impaktiert ‹*Zahn*› **2** (Med.) **~ fracture** Knocheneinkeilung, *die*

ˈimpact strength *n.* (Metallurgy) Stoßfestigkeit, *die*

impair /ɪmˈpeə(r)/ *v.t.* **1** (damage) beeinträchtigen; schaden (+ *Dat.*) ‹*Gesundheit*› **2** (weaken) beeinträchtigen; **~ed vision** Sehschwäche, *die*; **~ed hearing** Schwerhörigkeit, *die*

impairment /ɪmˈpeəmənt/ *n.* Beeinträchtigung, *die*; **~ of memory** Gedächtnisschwäche, *die*

impala /ɪmˈpɑːlə/ *n., pl. same* (Zool.) Impala, *die*

impale /ɪmˈpeɪl/ *v.t.* **1** aufspießen; (Hist.) pfählen **2** (Her.) spalten ‹*Wappen*›

impalpable /ɪmˈpælpəbl/ *adj.* [1] (imperceptible to touch) nicht fühlbar [2] (not easily grasped by the mind) unfassbar

impart /ɪmˈpɑːt/ *v.t.* [1] (give) [ab]geben (**to** an + *Akk.*); vermachen (**to** *Dat.*) [2] (communicate) kundtun (geh.) (**to** *Dat.*); vermitteln ‹*Kenntnisse*› (**to** *Dat.*)

impartial /ɪmˈpɑːʃl/ *adj.* unparteiisch; gerecht ‹*Entscheidung, Behandlung, Urteil*›

impartiality /ɪmpɑːʃɪˈælɪtɪ/ *n., no pl.* Unparteilichkeit, *die*

impartially /ɪmˈpɑːʃəlɪ/ *adv.* unparteiisch

impassable /ɪmˈpɑːsəbl/ *adj.* unpassierbar (**to** für); (to vehicles) unbefahrbar (**to** für)

impasse /ˈæmpɑːs/ *n.* (lit. or fig.) Sackgasse, *die*; **the negotiations have reached an ~:** die Verhandlungen sind in eine Sackgasse geraten

impassioned /ɪmˈpæʃnd/ *adj.* leidenschaftlich

impassive /ɪmˈpæsɪv/ *adj.* [1] ausdruckslos [2] (incapable of feeling emotion) leidenschaftslos

impassively /ɪmˈpæsɪvlɪ/ *adv.* ▸**impassive**: [1] ausdruckslos [2] leidenschaftslos

impatience /ɪmˈpeɪʃəns/ *n., no pl.* [1] Ungeduld, *die* (**at** über + *Akk.*) [2] (intolerance) Unduldsamkeit, *die* (**of** gegen) [3] (eager desire) [ungeduldige] Erwartung (**for** *Gen.*)

impatient /ɪmˈpeɪʃənt/ *adj.* [1] ungeduldig; **~ at sth./with sb.** ungeduldig über etw. (*Akk.*)/mit jmdm. [2] (intolerant) unduldsam (**of** gegen); **be ~ of sth.** etw. nicht ertragen können [3] (eagerly desirous) **be ~ for sth.** etw. kaum erwarten können; **be ~ to do sth.** unbedingt etw. tun wollen

impatiently /ɪmˈpeɪʃəntlɪ/ *adv.* [1] ungeduldig [2] (intolerantly) unduldsam [3] (with eager desire) begierig

impeach /ɪmˈpiːtʃ/ *v.t.* [1] (call into question) infrage stellen [2] (Law) **~ sb.** jmdn. anklagen (**for, with** *Gen.*, wegen); (Brit.: accuse of treason) jmdn. des Hochverrats beschuldigen; (Amer.: charge with misconduct while in office) jmdm. eine Verletzung seiner Amtspflichten vorwerfen

impeachment /ɪmˈpiːtʃmənt/ *n.* [1] (calling in question) Infragestellung, *die* [2] (Law) Anklage, *die*; (Brit.: accusation of treason) Beschuldigung des Hochverrats; (Amer.) Impeachment, *das*

impeccable /ɪmˈpekəbl/ *adj.* makellos; tadellos ‹*Manieren*›

impeccably /ɪmˈpekəblɪ/ *adv.* tadellos; makellos ‹*rein*›

impecunious /ɪmpɪˈkjuːnɪəs/ *adj.* mittellos

impedance /ɪmˈpiːdəns/ *n.* (Electr.) Impedanz, *die*

impede /ɪmˈpiːd/ *v.t.* behindern

impediment /ɪmˈpedɪmənt/ *n.* [1] Hindernis, *das* (**to** für) [2] (speech defect) Sprachfehler, *der*

impedimenta /ɪmpedɪˈmentə/ *n. pl.* [klobiges] Gepäck, *das*

impel /ɪmˈpel/ *v.t.*, **-ll-** [1] (force) treiben; **feel ~led to do sth.** sich genötigt *od.* gezwungen fühlen, etw. zu tun; **~ sb. to greater efforts** jmdn. zu größeren Bemühungen anspornen [2] (drive forward) treiben; antreiben ‹*Turbine usw.*›

impending /ɪmˈpendɪŋ/ *adj.* (about to happen) bevorstehend; drohend ‹*Gefahr*›

impenetrable /ɪmˈpenɪtrəbl/ *adj.* [1] undurchdringlich (**by, to** für); unbezwingbar, uneinnehmbar ‹*Festung*› [2] (inscrutable) unergründlich

impenetrably /ɪmˈpenɪtrəblɪ/ *adv.* [1] undurchdringlich [2] (inscrutably) unergründlich

impenitent /ɪmˈpenɪtənt/ *adj.* reu[e]los; **be quite ~:** keine Spur von Reue zeigen

impenitently /ɪmˈpenɪtəntlɪ/ *adv.* reu[e]los

imperative /ɪmˈperətɪv/

A *adj.* [1] (commanding) gebieterisch (geh.) ‹*Stimme, Geste*› [2] (urgent) dringend erforderlich [3] (obligatory) zwingend ‹*Verpflichtung*› [4] (Ling.) imperativisch; **~ mood** Imperativ, *der*

B *n.* [1] (necessity) Notwendigkeit, *die* [2] (Ling.) Imperativ, *der*; Befehlsform, *die*

imperceptible /ɪmpəˈseptɪbl/ *adj.* [1] nicht wahrnehmbar (**to** für); unsichtbar ‹*Schranke*›; **be ~ to sb./the senses** von jmdm./den Sinnen nicht wahrgenommen werden können [2] (very slight or gradual) unmerklich; (subtle) kaum zu erkennen *nicht attr.*; kaum zu erkennend; minimal ‹*Unterschied*›

imperceptibly /ɪmpəˈseptɪblɪ/ *adv.* unmerklich; kaum wahrnehmbar ‹*sich bewegen*›; (very slightly) geringfügig

imperfect /ɪmˈpɜːfɪkt/

A *adj.* [1] (not fully formed) unfertig; (incomplete) unvollständig; **drainage in this region is ~:** die Entwässerung in dieser Gegend ist mangelhaft; **slightly ~ stockings/pottery** *etc.* Strümpfe/Keramik *usw.* mit kleinen Fehlern [2] (faulty) mangelhaft; **human beings are ~:** der Mensch ist unvollkommen [3] (Ling.) Imperfekt-; **the ~ tense** das Imperfekt

B *n.* (Ling.) Imperfekt, *das*

imperfection /ɪmpəˈfekʃn/ *n.* [1] *no pl.* (incompleteness) Unvollständigkeit, *die* [2] *no pl.* (faultiness) Mangelhaftigkeit, *die*; (of human beings) Unvollkommenheit, *die* [3] (fault) Mangel, *der*

imperfectly /ɪmˈpɜːfɪktlɪ/ *adv.* [1] (incompletely) unvollständig [2] (faultily) fehlerhaft; mangelhaft

imperial /ɪmˈpɪərɪəl/ *adj.* [1] kaiserlich; imperial (geh.); Reichs‹*adler, -insignien*›; **I~ Rome** das Rom der Kaiserzeit; das kaiserliche Rom [2] (Brit. Hist.) des Britischen Weltreiches *nachgestellt* [3] (of an emperor) Kaiser-; **the I~ Court** der Kaiserhof; der kaiserliche Hof; **Her I~ Majesty** Ihre Kaiserliche Hoheit [4] (majestic) majestätisch; (haughty) hochmütig; erhaben (iron.) [5] (magnificent) fürstlich; glanzvoll ‹*Stadt*› [6] (fixed by statute) britisch ‹*Maße, Gewichte*›; *see also* **gallon**

imperialism /ɪmˈpɪərɪəlɪzm/ *n., no pl.* (derog.) Imperialismus, *der*; **US/Soviet ~:** der US-/Sowjetimperialismus

imperialist /ɪmˈpɪərɪəlɪst/ *n.* (derog.) Imperialist, *der*/Imperialistin, *die*; **~ countries** imperialistische Länder

imperialistic /ɪmpɪərɪəˈlɪstɪk/ *adj.* (derog.) imperialistisch

imperil /ɪmˈperəl/ *v.t.*, (Brit.) **-ll-** gefährden

imperious /ɪmˈpɪərɪəs/ *adj.* [1] (overbearing) herrisch; gebieterisch [2] (urgent) zwingend; mächtig ‹*Triebe usw.*›

imperiously /ɪmˈpɪərɪəslɪ/ *adv.* [1] (overbearingly) herrisch [2] (urgently) zwingend

imperishable /ɪmˈperɪʃəbl/ *adj.* [1] (immortal) unvergänglich [2] (not decaying) alterungsbeständig ‹*Material*›; unverderblich ‹*Lebensmittel*›

imperishably /ɪmˈperɪʃəblɪ/ *adv.* unvergänglich

impermanence /ɪmˈpɜːmənəns/ *n., no pl.* Vergänglichkeit, *die*

impermanent /ɪmˈpɜːmənənt/ *adj.* vorübergehend; vergänglich ‹*Leben*›

impermeable /ɪmˈpɜːmɪəbl/ *adj.* undurchlässig; impermeabel (fachspr.)

impermissible /ɪmpəˈmɪsɪbl/ *adj.* unzulässig

impersonal /ɪmˈpɜːsənl/ *adj.* unpersönlich; **an ~ thing** etwas [rein] Dingliches

impersonality /ɪmpɜːsəˈnælɪtɪ/ *n., no pl.* Unpersönlichkeit, *die*

impersonally /ɪmˈpɜːsənəlɪ/ *adv.* unpersönlich

impersonal: ~ ˈpronoun ▸**pronoun**; **~ ˈverb** *n.* (Ling.) unpersönliches Verb; Impersonale, *das* (fachspr.)

impersonate /ɪmˈpɜːsəneɪt/ *v.t.* (pretend to be) (for entertainment) imitieren; nachahmen; (for purpose of fraud) sich ausgeben als

impersonation /ɪmpɜːsəˈneɪʃn/ *n.* [1] (personification) Verkörperung, *die* [2] (imitation) Imitation, *die*; Nachahmung, *die*; **he does ~s** er ist Imitator; **his ~ of Churchill** seine Churchill-Imitation; **do an ~ of sb.** jmdn. imitieren *od.* nachahmen; **~ of sb.** (for purpose of fraud) Auftreten als jmd.

impersonator /ɪmˈpɜːsəneɪtə(r)/ *n.* (entertainer) Imitator, *der*/Imitatorin, *die*; (sb. with fraudulent intent) Betrüger, *der*/Betrügerin, *die*; **an ~ posing as a policeman** jemand, der sich als Polizist ausgibt; *see also* **female A 1**

impertinence /ɪmˈpɜːtɪnəns/ *n.* Unverschämtheit, *die*; Impertinenz, *die* (geh.)

impertinent /ɪmˈpɜːtɪnənt/ *adj.* unverschämt; impertinent (geh.)

impertinently /ɪmˈpɜːtɪnəntlɪ/ *adv.* unverschämterweise; **behave ~:** sich unverschämt benehmen

imperturbability /ɪmpətɜːbəˈbɪlɪtɪ/ *n., no pl.* Gelassenheit, *die*

imperturbable /ɪmpəˈtɜːbəbl/ *adj.* gelassen; **be completely ~:** durch nichts zu erschüttern sein; die Ruhe weghaben (ugs.)

imperturbably /ɪmpəˈtɜːbəblɪ/ *adv.* gelassen; **..., he said ~:** ..., sagte er in aller Ruhe

impervious /ɪmˈpɜːvɪəs/ *adj.* [1] undurchlässig; **~ to water/bullets/rain** wasserdicht/kugelsicher/regendicht [2] (fig.: impenetrable) unergründlich [3] **be ~ to sth.** (fig.) unempfänglich für etw. sein; **be ~ to argument** Argumenten unzugänglich sein

impetigo /ɪmpɪˈtaɪgəʊ/ *n.* ▸ⓘ **p. 1231** (Med.) Impetigo, *die* (fachspr.); Eiterflechte, *die*

impetuosity /ɪmpetjʊˈɒsɪtɪ/ *n.* [1] *no pl.* (quality) Impulsivität, *die* [2] (act, impulse) Ausbruch, *der*

impetuous /ɪmˈpetjʊəs/ *adj.* impulsiv ‹*Person*›; unüberlegt ‹*Handlung, Entscheidung*›; (vehement) stürmisch; ungestüm ‹*Person, Angriff*›

impetuously /ɪmˈpetjʊəslɪ/ *adv.* unüberlegt ‹*handeln, entscheiden*›

impetuousness /ɪmˈpetjʊəsnɪs/ ▸**impetuosity 1**

impetus /ˈɪmpɪtəs/ *n.* [1] Kraft, *die*; (of impact) Wucht, *die* [2] (fig.: impulse) Motivation, *die*; **give an ~ to sth.** einer Sache (*Dat.*) Impulse geben; **give sth. new** *or* **fresh ~:** einer Sache (*Dat.*) neuen Auftrieb geben; **the ~ behind the development of nuclear power** die treibende Kraft bei der Entwicklung der Kernkraft

impiety /ɪmˈpaɪətɪ/ *n.* [1] *no pl.* (ungodliness) Gottlosigkeit, *die* [2] (irreverence) Pietätlosigkeit, *die*

impinge /ɪmˈpɪndʒ/ *v.i.* (encroach, affect) **~ [up]on sth.** auf etw. (*Akk.*) Einfluss nehmen

impious /ˈɪmpɪəs/ *adj.* [1] (ungodly) gottlos [2] (irreverent) pietätlos

impish /ˈɪmpɪʃ/ *adj.* lausbübisch; diebisch ‹*Freude*›; verschmitzt ‹*Grinsen, Blick*›

impishly /ˈɪmpɪʃlɪ/ *adv.* lausbübisch; diebisch ‹*sich freuen*›; verschmitzt ‹*grinsen*›

implacable /ɪmˈplækəbl/ *adj.* unversöhnlich; erbittert ‹*Gegner*›; erbarmungslos ‹*Verfolgung*›; unerbittlich ‹*Schicksal*›

implacably /ɪmˈplækəblɪ/ *adv.* unerbittlich; unaufhaltsam ‹*voranschreiten*›

implant

A /ɪmˈplɑːnt/ *v.t.* [1] (Med.) implantieren (fachspr.), einpflanzen (**in** *Dat.*); **~ sb./sth. with sth.** jmdm./einer Sache etw. einpflanzen [2] (Physiol.) **be ~ed** sich einnisten [3] (fig.: instil) einpflanzen (**in** *Dat.*)

B /ˈɪmplɑːnt/ *n.* (Med.) Implantat, *das*

implantation /ɪmplɑːnˈteɪʃn/ *n.* [1] (Med.) Implantation, *die* (fachspr.); Einpflanzung, *die* [2] (fig.: instilling) Einpflanzung, *die*

implausibility /ɪmplɔːzɪˈbɪlɪtɪ/ *n., no pl.* Unglaubwürdigkeit, *die*

implausible /ɪmˈplɔːzɪbl/ *adj.*, **implausibly** /ɪmˈplɔːzɪblɪ/ *adv.* unglaubwürdig

implement

A /ˈɪmplɪmənt/ *n.* Gerät, *das*

B /ˈɪmplɪment/ *v.t.* [1] (fulfil, complete) erfüllen ‹*Versprechen, Vertrag*›; einhalten ‹*Termin usw.*›; vollziehen ‹*Erlass usw.*› [2] (put into effect) [in die Tat] umsetzen ‹*Politik, Plan usw.*›

implementation /ɪmplɪmenˈteɪʃn/ *n.* ▸**implement B**: Erfüllung, *die*; Einhaltung, *die*; Vollzug, *der*; Umsetzung [in die Tat], *die*

implicate /ˈɪmplɪkeɪt/ *v.t.* [1] (show to be involved) belasten ‹*Verdächtigen usw.*›; **be ~d in a scandal** in einen Skandal verwickelt sein [2] (affect) **be ~d in sth.** von etw. betroffen sein

implication /ɪmplɪˈkeɪʃn/ *n.* 1 (implying, thing implied) Implikation, *die* (geh.); **by ~:** implizit; implizite (geh.) 2 *no pl.* (being involved) Verwicklung, *die* (**in** in + *Akk.*) 3 *no pl.* (being affected) Betroffenheit, *die* (**in** von)

implicit /ɪmˈplɪsɪt/ *adj.* 1 (implied) implizit (geh.); unausgesprochen ‹*Drohung, Zweifel*› 2 (virtually contained) **be ~ in sth.** in etw. (*Dat.*) enthalten sein 3 (resting on authority) unbedingt; blind ‹*Vertrauen*›

implicitly /ɪmˈplɪsɪtlɪ/ *adv.* 1 (by implication) implizit (geh.) 2 (unquestioningly) blind ‹*vertrauen, gehorchen usw.*›

implode /ɪmˈpləʊd/
A *v.i.* implodieren
B *v.t.* implodieren lassen; **be ~d** implodieren

implore /ɪmˈplɔː(r)/ *v.t.* 1 (beg for) erflehen (geh.); flehen um; **'please', she ~d** „bitte", flehte sie 2 (entreat) anflehen (**for** um); **~ sb. to do/not to do sth.** jmdn. anflehen *od.* inständig bitten, etw. zu tun/nicht zu tun

imploring /ɪmˈplɔːrɪŋ/ *adj.* flehend

imploringly /ɪmˈplɔːrɪŋlɪ/ *adv.* flehentlich (geh.)

implosion /ɪmˈpləʊʒn/ *n.*, *no pl.* Implosion, *die*

imply /ɪmˈplaɪ/ *v.t.* 1 (involve the existence of) implizieren (geh.); (by inference) schließen lassen auf (+ *Akk.*); **be implied in sth.** in etw. (*Dat.*) enthalten sein; **silence sometimes implies consent** Schweigen bedeutet manchmal Zustimmung 2 (express indirectly) hindeuten auf (+ *Akk.*); (insinuate) unterstellen; **are you ~ing that ...?** willst du damit etwa sagen, dass ...?

impolite /ɪmpəˈlaɪt/ *adj.*, **~r** /ɪmpəˈlaɪtə(r)/, **~st** /ɪmpəˈlaɪtɪst/ unhöflich; ungezogen ‹*Kind*›

impolitely /ɪmpəˈlaɪtlɪ/ *adv.* unhöflich

impoliteness /ɪmpəˈlaɪtnɪs/ *n.*, *no pl.* Unhöflichkeit, *die;* (of child) Ungezogenheit, *die*

impolitic /ɪmˈpɒlɪtɪk/ *adj.* (inexpedient) unklug; unratsam

imponderable /ɪmˈpɒndərəbl/
A *adj.* unwägbar; imponderabel (geh. veralt.)
B *n.* Unwägbarkeit, *die;* **~s** Unwägbarkeiten; Imponderabilien (geh.)

import
A /ɪmˈpɔːt/ *v.t.* 1 importieren, einführen ‹*Waren*› (**from** aus, **into** nach); importieren ‹*Kulturgüter*›; **~ing country** Einfuhrland, *das;* **oil-~ing countries** [Erd]öl importierende Länder 2 (signify) bedeuten
B /ˈɪmpɔːt/ *n.* 1 (process, amount imported) Import, *der;* Einfuhr, *die;* **~s of beef/sugar** Zucker-/Rindfleischimporte *od.* -einfuhren; **ban on the ~ of sth.** Einfuhrverbot für etw. 2 (article imported) Importgut, *das* 3 (meaning) Bedeutung, *die;* Sinn, *der;* **the ~ of his speech was that ...:** was aus seiner Rede hervorging, war, dass ... 4 (importance) Bedeutung, *die;* **an event of great ~:** ein sehr bedeutungsvolles Ereignis

importance /ɪmˈpɔːtəns/ *n.*, *no pl.* 1 Bedeutung, *die;* Wichtigkeit, *die;* **be of great ~ to sb./sth.** für jmdn./etw. äußerst wichtig sein 2 (significance) Bedeutung, *die;* (of decision) Tragweite, *die;* **increase in ~:** an Bedeutung zunehmen; **be of/without ~:** wichtig/unwichtig sein; **a man of considerable ~:** ein sehr wichtiger Mann; **speak with an air of ~:** mit gewichtiger Miene sprechen; **full of one's own ~:** von seiner eigenen Wichtigkeit überzeugt

important /ɪmˈpɔːtənt/ *adj.* 1 bedeutend; (in a particular matter) wichtig (**to** für); **the most ~ thing is ...:** die Hauptsache ist ... 2 (momentous) wichtig ‹*Entscheidung*›; bedeutsam ‹*Tag*› 3 (having high rank) wichtig ‹*Persönlichkeit*›; **very ~ person** wichtige Persönlichkeit; VIP; **pretend to be ~:** wichtig tun

importantly /ɪmˈpɔːtəntlɪ/ *adv.* 1 **bear ~ [up]on sth.** auf etw. bedeutsame Auswirkungen haben; **more/most ~** *as sentence-modifier* was noch wichtiger/am wichtigsten ist 2 (pompously) wichtigtuerisch; **act ~:** wichtig tun

importation /ɪmpɔːˈteɪʃn/ ▸ **import B 1**

ˈ**import duty** *n.* Einfuhrzoll, *der*

importer /ɪmˈpɔːtə(r)/ *n.* Importeur, *der;* **be an ~ of cotton** Baumwollimporteur sein; ‹*Land:*› Baumwolle importieren

ˈ**import permit** *n.* Einfuhrerlaubnis, *die*

importunate /ɪmˈpɔːtjʊnət/ *adj.* aufdringlich

importunately /ɪmˈpɔːtʃʊnətlɪ/ *adv.* aufdringlich; nachdrücklich ‹*beharren auf, instruieren*›

importune /ɪmpɔːˈtjuːn/ *v.t.* 1 behelligen; **she ~d her neighbours and relatives for money** sie belästigte ihre Nachbarn und Verwandten mit Bitten um Geld 2 (solicit for immoral purpose) belästigen

importunity /ɪmpɔːˈtjuːnɪtɪ/ *n.* Aufdringlichkeit, *die*

impose /ɪmˈpəʊz/
A *v.t.* 1 auferlegen (geh.) ‹*Bürde, Verpflichtung*› (**[up]on** *Dat.*); erheben ‹*Steuer, Zoll*› (**on** auf + *Akk.*); verhängen ‹*Kriegsrecht*›; anordnen ‹*Rationierung*›; verhängen ‹*Sanktionen*› (**on** gegen); **~ a ban on sth.** etw. mit einem Verbot belegen; **~ a tax on sth.** etw. mit einer Steuer belegen; **~ a nervous strain on sb.** jmdn. nervlich belasten 2 (compel compliance with) **~ sth. [up]on sb.** jmdm. etw. aufdrängen; **~ one's company [up]on sb.** sich jmdm. aufdrängen; **~ restraints [up]on sb.** jmdm. Grenzen setzen 3 (Printing) ausschießen ‹*Seiten*›
B *v.i.* (take advantage) **I would** *or* **do not want** *or* **wish to ~:** ich will nicht aufdringlich sein
C *v. refl.* **~ oneself on sb.** sich jmdm. aufdrängen

Phrasal verbs

- **~ on** *v.t.* 1 (take advantage of) ausnutzen ‹*Gutmütigkeit, Toleranz usw.*›; **~ on sb. for help** jmdn. mit der Bitte um Hilfe belästigen 2 (force oneself on) **~ on sb.** sich jmdm. aufdrängen
- **~ upon** ▸ **~ on**

imposing /ɪmˈpəʊzɪŋ/ *adj.* imposant

imposition /ɪmpəˈzɪʃn/ *n.* 1 *no pl.* (action) Auferlegung, *die;* (of tax) Erhebung, *die* 2 *no pl.* (enforcement) Durchsetzung, *die* 3 *no pl.* (Printing) Ausschießen, *das* 4 (tax) Abgabe, *die;* Steuer, *die* 5 (piece of advantage-taking) Ausnützung, *die;* **I am weary of the ~s of my relatives** ich bin es leid, mich von meinen Verwandten ausnützen zu lassen; **I hope it's not too much of an ~:** ich hoffe, es macht nicht zu viele Umstände 6 (Brit. Sch.: work set as punishment) Strafarbeit, *die*

impossibility /ɪmpɒsɪˈbɪlɪtɪ/ *n.* 1 *no pl.* Unmöglichkeit, *die;* **the ~ of a man's flying** die Tatsache, dass der Mensch nicht fliegen kann *od.* dass es dem Menschen nicht möglich ist zu fliegen 2 **go after impossibilities** das Unerreichbare wollen; **that's an absolute ~:** das ist völlig unmöglich *od.* ausgeschlossen *od.* ein Ding der Unmöglichkeit (ugs.)

impossible /ɪmˈpɒsɪbl/
A *adj.* 1 unmöglich; **it is ~ for me to do it** es ist mir nicht möglich, es zu tun 2 (not easy) schwer; (not easily believable) unmöglich (ugs.); **his car is becoming ~ to start** sein Auto lässt sich kaum noch starten 3 (coll.: intolerable) unmöglich (ugs.)
B *n.* **the ~:** das Unmögliche; Unmögliches; **achieve the ~:** das Unmögliche erreichen

impossibly /ɪmˈpɒsɪblɪ/ *adv.* 1 unmöglich; **the stone was ~ heavy to lift** der Stein war so schwer, dass man ihn unmöglich anheben konnte 2 (to an unbelievable degree) unglaublich (ugs.) ‹*schwierig, teuer usw.*› 3 (coll.: intolerably) unmöglich (ugs.); **he is ~ idealistic** er ist unmöglich mit seinem Idealismus (ugs.)

impost /ˈɪmpəʊst/ *n.* 1 (tax) Abgabe, *die* 2 (Archit.) Kämpfer[stein], *der*

impostor /ɪmˈpɒstə(r)/ *n.* Hochstapler, *der*/-staplerin, *die;* (swindler) Betrüger, *der*/Betrügerin, *die*

imposture /ɪmˈpɒstʃə(r)/ *n.* 1 *no pl.* (practice of deception) Hochstapelei, *die;* (swindling) Betrügerei, *die* 2 (act of deception) Betrug, *der;* Schwindel, *der*

impotence /ˈɪmpətəns/, **impotency** /ˈɪmpətənsɪ/ *n.*, *no pl.* 1 (powerlessness) Machtlosigkeit, *die* 2 (helplessness) Hilflosigkeit, *die* 3 (lack of sexual power; in popular use: sterility) Impotenz, *die*

impotent /ˈɪmpətənt/ *adj.* 1 (powerless) machtlos; kraftlos ‹*Argument*›; **be ~ to do sth.** nicht in der Lage sein, etw. zu tun 2 (helpless) hilflos 3 (lacking in sexual power; sterile) impotent

impotently /ˈɪmpətəntlɪ/ *adv.* 1 (powerlessly) machtlos 2 (helplessly) hilflos

impound /ɪmˈpaʊnd/ *v.t.* 1 (shut up) einpferchen ‹*Vieh*›; einsperren ‹*streunende Hunde usw.*›; (fig.: confine) einsperren ‹*Person*› 2 (take possession of) beschlagnahmen; requirieren (Milit.)

impoverish /ɪmˈpɒvərɪʃ/ *v.t.* 1 verarmen lassen; **be/become ~ed** verarmt sein/verarmen 2 (exhaust) auslaugen ‹*Boden*›

impoverishment /ɪmˈpɒvərɪʃmənt/ *n.*, *no pl.* 1 (making poor) Verarmung, *die;* (being poor) Armut, *die* 2 (exhaustion) (process) Auslaugung, *die;* (state) Ausgelaugtheit, *die*

impracticability /ɪmpræktɪkəˈbɪlɪtɪ/ *n.* 1 *no pl.* (of plan) Undurchführbarkeit, *die;* (of prediction) Unmöglichkeit, *die* 2 (thing) **be an ~:** undurchführbar sein; **it's an ~:** es lässt sich nicht durchführen

impracticable /ɪmˈpræktɪkəbl/ *adj.* undurchführbar; impraktikabel (geh.)

impractical /ɪmˈpræktɪkl/ 1 unpraktisch ‹*Person*› 2 ▸ **impracticable**

impracticality /ɪmpræktɪˈkælɪtɪ/ ▸ **impracticability**

imprecation /ɪmprɪˈkeɪʃn/ *n.* Verwünschung, *die*

imprecise /ɪmprɪˈsaɪs/ *adj.*, **imprecisely** /ɪmprɪˈsaɪslɪ/ *adv.* ungenau; unpräzise (geh.)

imprecision /ɪmprɪˈsɪʒn/ *n.* Ungenauigkeit, *die*

impregnability /ɪmpregnəˈbɪlɪtɪ/ *n.*, *no pl.* Uneinnehmbarkeit, *die;* (of strongroom etc.) Einbruch[s]sicherheit, *die;* (fig.) Unanfechtbarkeit, *die*

impregnable /ɪmˈpregnəbl/ *adj.* uneinnehmbar ‹*Festung, Bollwerk*›; einbruch[s]sicher ‹*Tresorraum usw.*›; (fig.) unanfechtbar ‹*Ruf, Tugend, Stellung*›

impregnate /ˈɪmpregneɪt, ɪmˈpregneɪt/ *v.t.* 1 imprägnieren 2 (make pregnant) schwängern; (Biol.: fertilize) befruchten; **Mary was ~d by the Holy Ghost** Maria empfing vom Heiligen Geist

impregnation /ɪmpregˈneɪʃn/ *n.*, *no pl.* 1 Imprägnierung, *die* 2 (making pregnant) Schwängerung, *die;* (Biol.: fertilization) Befruchtung, *die*

impresario /ɪmprɪˈsɑːrɪəʊ/ *n.*, *pl.* **~s** Impresario, *der*

impress
A /ɪmˈpres/ *v.t.* 1 (apply) drücken; **~ a pattern** *etc.* **on/in sth.** ein Muster *usw.* auf etw. (*Akk.*) aufdrücken *od.* aufprägen/in etw. (*Akk.*) eindrücken *od.* einprägen 2 (arouse strong feeling in) beeindrucken; Eindruck machen auf (+ *Akk.*); *abs.* Eindruck machen (**with** mit); **be ~ed by** *or* **with sth.** von etw. beeindruckt sein 3 (affect favourably) beeindrucken; *abs.* Eindruck machen; **~ sb. favourably/unfavourably** auf jmdn. einen günstigen/ungünstigen Eindruck machen 4 (mark) stempeln ‹*Dokument*›; **~ a child with the right attitude** (fig.) einem Kind die richtige Einstellung vermitteln
B /ˈimpres/ *n.* 1 Druck, *der* 2 (mark) Abdruck, *der;* **bear the ~ of sth.** (fig.) den Stempel *od.* (geh.) das Gepräge von etw. tragen

Phrasal verb

- **~ [up]on** *v.t.* einprägen, einschärfen (+ *Dat.*); **they have had ~ed [up]on them the danger of doing that** ihnen ist eingeschärft worden, wie gefährlich es sei, das zu tun; **~ sth. [up]on sb.'s memory** jmdm. etw. einprägen *od.* einschärfen

impression /ɪmˈpreʃn/ *n.* 1 (impressing) Druck, *der* 2 (mark) Abdruck, *der* 3 (print) Druck, *der;* **take an ~ of sth.** einen Abzug von etw. machen; (of painting, engraving, etc.) Druck, *der* 4 (Printing) (quantity of copies) Auflage, *die;* (unaltered reprint) Nachdruck, *der* 5 (effect on persons) Eindruck, *der* (**of** von); (effect on inanimate things) Wirkung, *die;* **make an ~ on sb.** Eindruck auf jmdn. machen; **make a good/bad/strong** *etc.* **~ on sb.** einen guten/schlechten/starken *usw.* Eindruck auf jmdn. machen; bei jmdm. einen guten/schlechten/starken *usw.* Eindruck hinterlassen; **he had made quite an ~ on the weed-choked flower bed** nachdem er sich des im Unkraut erstickenden Blumenbeets angenommen hatte, war es kaum noch wieder zu erkennen; **first ~/~s** erster Eindruck/erste Eindrücke **6** (impersonation) **do an ~ of sb.** jmdn. imitieren; **do ~s** andere Leute imitieren **7** (notion) Eindruck, *der;* **it's my ~ that ...:** ich habe den Eindruck, dass ...; **what's your ~ of him?** welchen Eindruck hast du von ihm *od.* macht er auf dich?; **form an ~ of sb.** sich (*Dat.*) ein Bild von jmdm. machen; **it's only an ~:** es ist nur ein Gefühl; **give [sb.] the ~ that .../of being bored** [bei jmdm.] den Eindruck erwecken, als ob .../als ob man sich langweile; **be under the ~ that ...:** der Auffassung sein, dass ...; (less certain) den Eindruck haben, dass ...

impressionable /ɪmˈpreʃənəbl/ *adj.* beeinflussbar; **have an ~ mind, be ~:** sich leicht beeinflussen lassen; **children at an ~ age** Kinder in einem Alter, in dem sie noch formbar sind

impressionism /ɪmˈpreʃənɪzm/ *n., no pl.* Impressionismus, *der*

impressionist /ɪmˈpreʃənɪst/ *n.* Impressionist, *der*/Impressionistin, *die; attrib.* impressionistisch ‹*Kunst usw.*›

impressionistic /ɪmpreʃəˈnɪstɪk/ *adj.* impressionistisch

impressive /ɪmˈpresɪv/ *adj.* beeindruckend; imponierend; **be ~ on account of** *or* **~ for sth.** durch etw. beeindrucken

impressively /ɪmˈpresɪvlɪ/ *adv.* beeindruckend; imponierend

imprimatur /ɪmprɪˈmɑːtə(r), ɪmprɪˈmeɪtə(r)/ *n.* **1** (RC Ch.) Imprimatur, *das* **2** (fig.: sanction) **put the ~ of approval on sth.** etw. gutheißen *od.* billigen; **bear the ~ of sb./an institution** jmds. Plazet/das Plazet einer Institution haben (geh.)

imprint

A /ˈɪmprɪnt/ *n.* **1** Abdruck, *der;* **publisher's/printer's ~:** Impressum, *das* **2** (fig.) Stempel, *der;* **leave one's ~ on sb./sth.** jmdm./einer Sache seinen Stempel aufdrücken; **the ~ of suffering upon sb.'s face** die Spuren des Leidens in jmds. Gesicht

B /ɪmˈprɪnt/ *v.t.* **1** (stamp) aufdrucken; aufdrücken ‹*Poststempel*›; (on metal) aufprägen **2** (fix indelibly) **sth. is ~ed in** *or* **on sb.'s memory** etw. hat sich jmdm. [unauslöschlich] eingeprägt **3** (Ethol.) **~ on** *or* **to** prägen ‹*Tier*› auf (+ *Akk.*)

imprison /ɪmˈprɪzn/ *v.t.* **1** in Haft nehmen; **be ~ed** sich in Haft befinden; eine Freiheitsstrafe verbüßen; **be ~ed for three months** (be sentenced to three months in prison) eine dreimonatige Freiheitsstrafe erhalten **2** (fig.: confine) einsperren; (hold) festhalten

imprisonment /ɪmˈprɪznmənt/ *n.* **1** Haft, *die;* **a long term** *or* **period of ~:** eine langjährige Haft- *od.* Freiheitsstrafe; **serve a sentence of ~:** eine Gefängnisstrafe verbüßen **2** (fig.: being confined) Gefangenschaft, *die;* **~ by sb./sth.** Gefangensein durch jmdn./etw.

improbability /ɪmprɒbəˈbɪlɪtɪ/ *n.* Unwahrscheinlichkeit, *die*

improbable /ɪmˈprɒbəbl/ *adj.* **1** (not likely) unwahrscheinlich **2** (incongruous) unmöglich (ugs.); **he is an ~ person to be in charge of a large company** es ist eigentlich erstaunlich, dass er der Chef einer großen Firma ist

impromptu /ɪmˈprɒmptjuː/

A *adj.* improvisiert; **an ~ speech** eine Stegreifrede; **an ~ visit** ein Überraschungsbesuch; ein unangekündigter Besuch

B *adv.* aus dem Stegreif

C *n.* **1** Improvisation, *die* **2** (Mus.) Impromptu, *das*

improper /ɪmˈprɒpə(r)/ *adj.* **1** (wrong) unrichtig; ungeeignet ‹*Werkzeug*› **2** (unseemly) ungehörig; unpassend; (indecent) unanständig **3** (not in accordance with rules of conduct) unangebracht; unzulässig ‹*Gebühren*› **4** **~ fraction** (Math.) unechter Bruch

improperly /ɪmˈprɒpəlɪ/ *adv.* **1** (wrongly) unrichtig; **use sth. ~:** etw. unsachgemäß gebrauchen **2** (in unseemly fashion) unpassend; (indecently) unanständig **3** (in contravention of rules of conduct) unzulässigerweise; **use sth. ~:** etw. missbrauchen

impropriety /ɪmprəˈpraɪətɪ/ *n.* **1** *no pl.* Unrichtigkeit, *die;* (unfitness) Ungeeignetheit, *die* **2** *no pl.* (unseemliness) Unpassende, *das;* (indecency) Unanständigkeit, *die;* **the ~ of sb.'s clothing** jmds. unpassende/unschickliche Kleidung **3** *no pl.* (lack of accordance with rules of conduct) Unrechtmäßigkeit, *die;* Unredlichkeit, *die;* **see no ~ in doing sth.** nichts Unrechtmäßiges *od.* Unredliches darin sehen, etw. zu tun **4** (instance of improper conduct) Unanständigkeit, *die;* **moral ~:** moralisches Fehlverhalten

improvable /ɪmˈpruːvəbl/ *adj.* verbesserungsfähig

improve /ɪmˈpruːv/

A *v.i.* sich verbessern; besser werden; ‹*Person, Wetter:*› sich bessern; (become more attractive) sich zu seinem Vorteil verändern; **he was ill, but he's improving now** er war krank, aber es geht ihm jetzt schon besser; **things are improving** es sieht schon besser aus

B *v.t.* verbessern; erhöhen, steigern ‹*Produktion*›; ausbessern ‹*Haus usw.*›; verschönern ‹*öffentliche Anlage usw.*›; **~d health** ein besserer Gesundheitszustand; **~ one's mind** sich [weiter]bilden; **~ one's situation** sich verbessern

C *v. refl.* **~ oneself** sich weiterbilden

Phrasal verb

• **~ [up]on** *v.t.* überbieten ‹*Rekord, Angebot*›; verbessern ‹*Leistung*›

improvement /ɪmˈpruːvmənt/ *n.* **1** *no pl.* Verbesserung, *die;* Besserung, *die;* (in trading) Steigerung, *die;* **there is need for ~ in your handwriting** deine Handschrift müsste besser werden; **an ~ on** *or* **over sth.** eine Verbesserung gegenüber etw. **2** (addition) Verbesserung, *die;* **make ~s to sth.** Verbesserungen an etw. (*Dat.*) vornehmen

improver /ɪmˈpruːvə(r)/ *n.* **1** (person above novice level) Person mit Vorkenntnissen; *attrib.* **~ course** Kurs für Teilnehmern mit Vorkenntnissen **2** (food additive) Zusatz[stoff], *der*

improvidence /ɪmˈprɒvɪdəns/ *n., no pl.* **1** Sorglosigkeit, *die* **2** (heedlessness) Leichtsinn, *der* **3** (extravagance) Verschwendungssucht, *die*

improvident /ɪmˈprɒvɪdənt/ *adj.* **1** sorglos; leichtsinnig; **he is ~:** er ist ein unbekümmerter Mensch; **~ action** unbedachtes Handeln **2** (heedless) leichtsinnig **3** (extravagant) verschwenderisch

improvidently /ɪmˈprɒvɪdəntlɪ/ *adv.* **1** leichtsinnigerweise **2** (extravagantly) verschwenderisch

improvisation /ɪmprəvaɪˈzeɪʃn/ *n.* **1** *no pl.* Improvisieren, *das;* (composing while performing) Improvisation, *die;* **his talent for ~:** sein Improvisationstalent; (in speaking) sein Talent für Stegreifreden **2** (thing) Improvisation, *die;* **the speech was an ~:** die Rede war improvisiert *od.* aus dem Stegreif vorgetragen; **the bench was only an ~:** die Bank war nur ein Provisorium

improvise /ˈɪmprəvaɪz/ *v.t.* improvisieren; aus dem Stegreif vortragen ‹*Rede*›

imprudence /ɪmˈpruːdəns/ *n.* **1** *no pl.* Unklugheit, *die;* **with great ~:** sehr unklug **2** (rash act) Unbesonnenheit, *die*

imprudent /ɪmˈpruːdənt/ *adj.* unklug; (showing rashness) unbesonnen

imprudently /ɪmˈpruːdəntlɪ/ *adv.* unbesonnenerweise; bedenklich ‹*nah, schnell*›

impudence /ˈɪmpjʊdəns/ *n.* **1** Unverschämtheit, *die* **2** (brazenness) Dreistigkeit, *die*

impudent /ˈɪmpjʊdənt/ *adj.*, **impudently** /ˈɪmpjʊdəntlɪ/ *adv.* unverschämt; (brazen) dreist

impugn /ɪmˈpjuːn/ *v.t.* in Zweifel ziehen; anfechten ‹*Anspruch*›

impulse /ˈɪmpʌls/ *n.* **1** (act of impelling) Stoß, *der;* Impuls, *der;* (fig.: motivation) Impuls, *der;* **give an ~ to sth.** einer Sache (*Dat.*) neue Impulse geben **2** (mental incitement) Impuls, *der;* **be seized with an irresistible ~ to do sth.** von einem unwiderstehlichen Drang ergriffen werden, etw. zu tun **3** (tendency to act without reflection) Impulsivität, *die;* **from pure ~:** rein impulsiv; **be ruled/guided by ~:** impulsiv sein; **be a creature of ~:** ein impulsives Wesen haben; **act/do sth. on [an] ~:** impulsiv handeln/etw. tun **4** (impetus) Stoßkraft, *die* **5** (Biol., Electr., Phys.) Impuls, *der*

ˈimpulse buying *n.* Spontankäufe *Pl.*

impulsion /ɪmˈpʌlʃn/ *n.* **1** (impelling push) Stoß, *der* **2** (mental impulse) Antrieb, *der* **3** (impetus) Impuls, *der*

impulsive /ɪmˈpʌlsɪv/ *adj.* **1** impulsiv **2** (driving) vorwärts treibend; **~ force** Antriebskraft, *die* **3** (Phys.) stoßartig

impulsively /ɪmˈpʌlsɪvlɪ/ *adv.* impulsiv

impulsiveness /ɪmˈpʌlsɪvnɪs/ *n., no pl.* Impulsivität, *die*

impunity /ɪmˈpjuːnɪtɪ/ *n., no pl.* Straffreiheit, *die;* **be able to do sth. with ~:** etw. gefahrlos tun können; (without being punished) etw. ungestraft tun können

i

impure /ɪmˈpjʊə(r)/ *adj.* **1** (dirty) unsauber; schmutzig ‹*Wasser*› **2** (unchaste) unrein; unanständig ‹*Person, Sprache*›; schmutzig ‹*Gedanke*› **3** (mixed with extraneous substance) unrein; (fig.: of mixed nature) unrein; uneinheitlich ‹*Stilform*›

impurity /ɪmˈpjʊərɪtɪ/ *n.* **1** *no pl.* (being dirty) Unsauberkeit, *die;* (of water) Verschmutzung, *die* **2** *no pl.* (not being chaste) Unreinheit, *die;* **moral ~:** moralische Verfehlung **3** *no pl.* (being mixed with extraneous substance) Unreinheit, *die* **4** *in pl.* (dirt) Schmutz, *der* **5** (foreign matter) Fremdkörper, *der;* Fremdstoff, *der*

imputation /ɪmpjʊˈteɪʃn/ *n.* **1** *no pl.* Zuschreibung, *die;* (accusing) Bezichtigung, *die;* [ungerechtfertigte] Beschuldigung; Imputation, *die* (veralt.) **2** (charge) Anschuldigung, *die;* Beschuldigung, *die*

impute /ɪmˈpjuːt/ *v.t.* **~ sth. to sb./sth.** jmdm./einer Sache etw. zuschreiben; **~ bad intentions to sb.** jmdm. schlechte Absichten unterstellen

in /ɪn/

A *prep.* **1** (position; also fig.) in (+ *Dat.*); **I looked into all the boxes, but there was nothing in them** ich sah in alle Kisten hinein, aber es war nichts darin; **in the 'Mauretania'** auf der „Mauretania"; **in the fields** auf den Feldern; **a ride in a motor car** eine Autofahrt; **shot/wounded in the leg** ins Bein geschossen/am Bein verwundet; **in this heat** bei dieser Hitze; **the highest mountain in the world** der höchste Berg der Welt; *see also* **bed A 1**; **clover**; **country 2**; **dark B 1**; **prison 2**; **rage A 1**; **sky A**; **sleep A 2**; **street 1**; **tear**[2]

2 (wearing as dress) in (+ *Dat.*); (wearing as headgear) mit; **in brown shoes** mit braunen Schuhen; **a lady in black** eine Dame in Schwarz; **a group of youths in leather jackets** eine Gruppe Jugendlicher in *od.* mit Lederjacken; *see also* **shirtsleeve A**

3 (with respect to) **two feet in diameter** mit einem Durchmesser von zwei Fuß; **young in years** jung an Jahren; **a change in attitude** eine Änderung der Einstellung; *see also* **herself 1**; **itself 1**

4 (as a proportionate part of) **eight dogs in ten** acht von zehn Hunden; **pay 33 pence in the pound as interest** 33 Prozent Zinsen zahlen; **a ~ of 1 in 10** eine Steigung von 10%

5 (as a member of) in (+ *Dat.*); **be in the Scouts** bei den Pfadfindern sein; **be employed in the Civil Service** als Beamter/Beamtin beschäftigt sein

6 (as content of) **there are three feet in a yard** ein Yard hat drei Fuß; **is there anything in the notion of ...?** ist an der Vorstellung ... etwas dran?; **what is there in this deal for me?** was springt für mich bei dem Geschäft heraus? (ugs.); **there is nothing of the hero in him** er hat nichts von einem Helden an sich (*Dat.*);

there is nothing/not much *or* **little in it** (difference) da ist kein/kein großer Unterschied [zwischen ihnen]; **there is something in what you say** an dem, was Sie sagen, ist etwas dran (ugs.)
7 (as a kind of) in (+ *Dat.*); **the latest thing in fashion/in luxury** der letzte Modeschrei/der neueste Luxus
8 *expr. identity* in (+ *Dat.*); **have a faithful friend in sb.** an jmdm. einen treuen Freund haben; **we have lost a first-rate teacher in Jim** wir haben mit Jim einen erstklassigen Lehrer verloren
9 (concerned with) in (+ *Dat.*); **what line of business are you in?** in welcher Branche sind Sie?; **he's in politics** er ist Politiker; **she's in insurance** sie ist in der Versicherungsbranche tätig
10 **be [not] in it** (as competitor) [nicht] dabei *od.* im Rennen sein
11 (Mus.) in; **in [the key of] D flat** in Des
12 (Ling.) (ending with) [endend] auf (+ *Akk.*); (beginning with) beginnend mit
13 (with arrangement of) in (+ *Dat.*); **sell eggs in half-dozens** Eier im halben Dutzend verkaufen; *see also* **order A 1**
14 (with the means of; having as material, colour) **a message in code** eine verschlüsselte Nachricht; **in writing** schriftlich; **in this way** auf diese Weise; so; **in a few words** mit wenigen Worten; **bind in leather** in Leder binden; **a dress in velvet** ein Kleid aus Samt; **this sofa is also available in leather/blue** dieses Sofa gibt es auch in Leder/Blau; **write sth. in red** etw. in Rot schreiben; **write in red** mit Rot schreiben; **pay in pounds/dollars** in Pfund/Dollar bezahlen; **draw in crayon/ink** *etc.* mit Kreide/Tinte *usw.* zeichnen; **be cast in brass** *etc.* aus Messing *usw.* gegossen sein; *see also* **English B 1**
15 ▸ⓘ **p. 1047** (while, during) **in crossing the river** beim Überqueren des Flusses; **in fog/rain** *etc.* bei Nebel/Regen *usw.*; **in the 20th century** im 20. Jahrhundert; **in the eighties/nineties** in den Achtzigern/Neunzigern; **4 o'clock in the morning/afternoon** 4 Uhr morgens/abends; **in 1990** [im Jahre] 1990
16 (after a period of) in (+ *Dat.*); **in three minutes/years** in drei Minuten/Jahren
17 (within the ability of) **have it in one [to do sth.]** fähig sein[, etw. zu tun]; **I didn't know you had it in you** das hätte ich dir nicht zugetraut; **he has in him the makings of a good soldier** er hat das Zeug zu einem guten Soldaten; **be in human nature** in der menschlichen Natur liegen; **there is no malice in him** er hat nichts Bösartiges an sich (*Dat.*)
18 (into) in (+ *Akk.*); **get the whole of sth. in a photo** etwas ganz auf ein Foto kriegen (ugs.) *od.* bekommen
19 **in that** insofern als; *see also* **far A 4**
20 **in doing this** (by so doing) indem jmd. das tut/tat; dadurch; hierdurch

B *adv.* 1 (inside) hinein‹*gehen usw.*›; (towards speaker) herein‹*kommen usw.*›; **when the animal is in, shut the cage door** wenn das Tier drin ist, mach die Käfigtür zu; **is everyone in?** sind alle drin? (ugs.); **in with you!** rein mit dir! (ugs.); **'In'** „Einfahrt"/„Eingang"; **the children have been in and out all day** die Kinder sind den ganzen Tag raus- und reingerannt (ugs.)
2 (at home, work, etc.) **be in** da sein; **find sb. in** jmdn. antreffen; **ask sb. in** jmdn. hereinbitten; **he's been in and out all day** er war den ganzen Tag über mal da und mal nicht da
3 (included) darin; drin (ugs.); **cost £50 all in** 50 Pfund kosten, alles inbegriffen; **the word is not in** das Wort ist nicht aufgeführt; **your article is not in** dein Artikel steht nicht drin (ugs.)
4 (inward) innen
5 (in fashion) in (ugs.); in Mode
6 (elected) **be in** gewählt sein; **the Tories are in** die Tories sind am Ruder; **the Tories are in by three votes** die Tories haben die Wahl mit einer Mehrheit von drei Stimmen gewonnen
7 (Cricket) **our team is in** unsere Mannschaft ist am Schlag
8 (Brit.: burning) **be in** ‹*Feuer:*› an sein, brennen; **keep the fire in** das Feuer brennen lassen
9 (having arrived) **be in** ‹*Zug, Schiff, Ware, Bewerbung:*› da sein; ‹*Ernte:*› eingebracht sein; **the coach is not due in for another hour** der Bus wird nicht vor einer Stunde da sein
10 (present) **be in at the start/climax** beim Start/Höhepunkt dabei sein
11 **sb. is in for sth.** (about to undergo sth.) jmdm. steht etw. bevor; (in competition for sth.) jmd. nimmt im Wettbewerb um etw. teil; (taking part in sth.) jmd. nimmt an etw. (*Dat.*) teil; **we're in for it now!** (coll.) jetzt blüht uns was! (ugs.); **have it in for sb.** es auf jmdn. abgesehen haben (ugs.)
12 (coll.: as participant, accomplice, observer, etc.) **be in on the secret/discussion** in das Geheimnis eingeweiht sein/bei der Diskussion dabei sein; **be in on the action** dabei sein; **be [well] in with sb.** mit jmdm. [gut] auskommen; **be in with the right/wrong people** mit den richtigen/falschen Leuten verkehren
13 (Sport) **be in** ‹*Ball:*› drin sein. *See also* **all C; eye A 1; far A 4; luck 2; penny 3; tide A 1**

C *attrib. adj.* (fashionable) Mode-; **the in crowd** die Clique, die gerade in ist (ugs.); **in joke** Insiderwitz, *der*

D *n.* **know the ins and outs of a matter** sich in einer Sache genau auskennen; **I don't know the ins and outs of the argument** ich weiß nicht [genau], worum es bei diesem Streit geht

in. *abbr.* ▸ⓘ **p. 1208**, ▸ⓘ **p. 1286 = inch[es]**

inability /ɪnəˈbɪlɪtɪ/ *n., no pl.* 1 (being unable) Unfähigkeit, *die* 2 (lack of power) Unvermögen, *das*

in absentia /ɪn æbˈsentiə, ɪn æbˈsenʃɪə/ *adv.* in absentia (bes. Rechtsw.)

inaccessibility /ɪnəksesɪˈbɪlɪtɪ/ *n., no pl.* 1 (unreachableness) Unzugänglichkeit, *die* 2 (unapproachableness) Unnahbarkeit, *die*

inaccessible /ɪnəkˈsesɪbl/ *adj.* 1 (that cannot be reached) unzugänglich 2 (unapproachable) unnahbar; unzugänglich

inaccuracy /ɪnˈækjʊrəsɪ/ *n.* 1 (incorrectness) Unrichtigkeit, *die*; **an example of ~ in the use of ...:** ein Beispiel für den unrichtigen Gebrauch von ... 2 (imprecision) Ungenauigkeit, *die*

inaccurate /ɪnˈækjʊrət/ *adj.* 1 (incorrect) unrichtig 2 (imprecise) ungenau

inaccurately /ɪnˈækjʊrətlɪ/ *adv.* 1 (incorrectly) falsch 2 (imprecisely) ungenau

inaction /ɪnˈækʃn/ *n., no pl., no indef. art.* 1 Untätigkeit, *die* 2 (sluggishness) Trägheit, *die*

inactive /ɪnˈæktɪv/ *adj.* 1 untätig 2 (sluggish) träge

inactivity /ɪnækˈtɪvɪtɪ/ *n., no pl.* 1 Untätigkeit, *die* 2 (sluggishness) Trägheit, *die*

inadequacy /ɪnˈædɪkwəsɪ/ *n.* 1 Unzulänglichkeit, *die* 2 (incompetence) mangelnde Eignung

inadequate /ɪnˈædɪkwət/ *adj.* 1 unzulänglich; **his response was ~ [to the situation]** seine Antwort war [der Situation] nicht angemessen; **the resources are ~ to his needs** die Mittel reichen für seine Bedürfnisse nicht aus 2 (incompetent) ungeeignet; **feel ~:** sich überfordert fühlen

inadequately /ɪnˈædɪkwətlɪ/ *adv.* 1 unzulänglich 2 (incompetently) mangelhaft

inadmissibility /ɪnədmɪsɪˈbɪlɪtɪ/ *n., no pl.* Unzulässigkeit, *die*

inadmissible /ɪnədˈmɪsɪbl/ *adj.* unzulässig

inadvertent /ɪnədˈvɜːtənt/ *adj.* ungewollt; versehentlich

inadvertently /ɪnədˈvɜːtəntlɪ/ *adv.* versehentlich

inadvisability /ɪnədvaɪzəˈbɪlɪtɪ/ *n., no pl.* (inappropriateness) Unangebrachtheit, *die*; (foolishness) Unvernünftigkeit, *die*; **see the ~ of sth.** sehen, dass etw. nicht ratsam ist

inadvisable /ɪnədˈvaɪzəbl/ *adj.* nicht ratsam; unratsam

inalienable /ɪnˈeɪlɪənəbl/ *adj.* unveräußerlich ‹*Recht*›

inane /ɪˈneɪn/ *adj.*, **inanely** /ɪˈneɪnlɪ/ *adv.* dümmlich

inanimate /ɪnˈænɪmət/ *adj.* unbelebt

inanity /ɪˈnænɪtɪ/ *n.* Dümmlichkeit, *die*

inapplicability /ɪnæplɪkəˈbɪlɪtɪ/ *n., no pl.* Nichtanwendbarkeit, *die*

inapplicable /ɪnˈæplɪkəbl, ɪnəˈplɪkəbl/ *adj.* nicht anwendbar (**to** auf + *Akk.*); **delete if ~:** Unzutreffendes [bitte] streichen

inappropriate /ɪnəˈprəʊprɪət/ *adj.* unpassend; **be ~ for sth.** für etw. nicht geeignet sein; **be ~ to the occasion** dem Anlass nicht angemessen sein; **this translation is ~:** diese Übersetzung ist nicht angemessen

inappropriately /ɪnəˈprəʊprɪətlɪ/ *adv.* unpassend

inapt /ɪnˈæpt/ *adj.*, **inaptly** /ɪnˈæptlɪ/ *adv.* unpassend

inarticulate /ɪnɑːˈtɪkjʊlət/ *adj.* 1 **she's rather/very ~:** sie kann sich ziemlich schlecht/sehr schlecht ausdrücken; **a clever but ~ mathematician** ein kluger Mathematiker, der sich aber nur schlecht ausdrücken kann 2 (indistinct) unverständlich; inartikuliert (geh.) 3 (dumb) unfähig zu sprechen

inarticulately /ɪnɑːˈtɪkjʊlətlɪ/ *adv.* inartikuliert (geh.); unverständlich ‹*murmeln*›

inartistic /ɪnɑːˈtɪstɪk/ *adj.* unkünstlerisch ‹*Person*›

inasmuch /ɪnəzˈmʌtʃ/ *adv.* **~ as** 1 insofern als 2 (because) da

inattention /ɪnəˈtenʃn/ *n., no pl.* Unaufmerksamkeit, *die* (**to** gegenüber); **~ to detail** Ungenauigkeit im Detail

inattentive /ɪnəˈtentɪv/ *adj.* unaufmerksam (**to** gegenüber)

inattentiveness /ɪnəˈtentɪvnɪs/ *n., no pl.* Unaufmerksamkeit, *die*

inaudible /ɪnˈɔːdɪbl/ *adj.*, **inaudibly** /ɪnˈɔːdɪblɪ/ *adv.* unhörbar

inaugural /ɪˈnɔːgjʊrl/ *adj.* 1 (first in series) Eröffnungs- 2 (given at inauguration) **~ lecture** *or* **address** Antrittsrede, *die*; (of professor) Antrittsvorlesung, *die*

inaugurate /ɪˈnɔːgjʊreɪt/ *v.t.* 1 (admit to office) in sein Amt einführen; inaugurieren (geh.) 2 (begin) einführen; aufnehmen ‹*Frachtverkehr usw.*›; in Angriff nehmen ‹*Projekt*› 3 (officially open) seiner Bestimmung übergeben; (with ceremony) einweihen

inauguration /ɪnɔːgjʊˈreɪʃn/ *n.* 1 (admission to office) Amtseinführung, *die*; Inauguration, *die* (geh.) 2 (beginning) Einführung, *die*; (of service) Aufnahme, *die*; (of project) Inangriffnahme, *die* 3 (official opening) Übergabe, *die*; (with ceremony) Einweihung, *die*

inauspicious /ɪnɔːˈspɪʃəs/ *adj.* 1 (ominous) Unheil verkündend; unheilvoll; **we made an ~ start to the project** schon der Beginn des Projekts verhieß nichts Gutes 2 (unlucky) unglücklich

ˈinboard (Naut., Aeronaut., Motor Veh.)
A *adv.* binnenbords
B *adj.* Innen[bord]-

ˈinborn *adj.* angeboren (**in** *Dat.*)

ˈinbound *adj.* ankommend; eingehend ‹*Post*›

ˈin-box *n.* (Computing) Inbox, *die*; Posteingang, *der*

inˈbred *adj.* 1 angeboren 2 (impaired by inbreeding) **they are/have become ~:** bei ihnen herrscht Inzucht

inˈbreeding *n.* Inzucht, *die*

ˈinbuilt *adj.* jmdm./einer Sache eigen

Inc. *abbr.* (Amer.) **= Incorporated** e. G.

Inca /ˈɪŋkə/
A *n.* Inka, *der/die*
B *adj.* der Inkas *nachgestellt*

incalculable /ɪnˈkælkjʊləbl/ *adj.* 1 (very great) unermesslich 2 (unpredictable) unabsehbar; unberechenbar ‹*Person, Temperament*›

in camera ▸ **camera 2**

incandescent /ɪnkænˈdesənt/ *adj.* glühend; **~ lamp** Glühlampe, *die*

incantation /ɪnkænˈteɪʃn/ *n.* 1 (words) Zauberspruch, *der* 2 (spell) Beschwörung, *die*

incapability /ɪnkeɪpəˈbɪlɪtɪ/ *n., no pl.* Unvermögen, *das*; Unfähigkeit, *die*

incapable /ɪnˈkeɪpəbl/ *adj.* 1 (lacking ability) **be ~ of doing sth.** außerstande sein, etw. zu tun; **be ~ of sth.** zu etw. unfähig sein; **she is ~ of such an act** sie ist zu einer solchen Tat nicht fähig 2 **be ~ of** (not allow) nicht zulassen ‹*Beweis, Messung usw.*›; **sb. is ~ of any improvement** jmd. ist zu keiner Besserung fähig; **a statement that is ~ of proof** eine Feststellung, die nicht beweisbar ist 3 (incompetent) unfähig; **he was drunk to the point of being completely ~:** er war so betrunken, dass er zu nichts mehr fähig war

incapacitate /ɪnkəˈpæsɪteɪt/ *v.t.* 1 (render unfit) unfähig machen; **~ sb. for** *or* **from doing sth.** es jmdm. unmöglich machen, etw. zu tun; **physically ~d/~d by illness** körperlich/durch Krankheit behindert 2 (disqualify) ausschließen (**for** von)

incapacity /ɪnkəˈpæsɪtɪ/ *n., no pl.* Unfähigkeit, *die* (**for** zu); **civil ~** (Law) Geschäftsunfähigkeit, *die*

incarcerate /ɪnˈkɑːsəreɪt/ *v.t.* einkerkern (geh.)

incarceration /ɪnkɑːsəˈreɪʃn/ *n.* Einkerkerung, *die* (geh.)

incarnate /ɪnˈkɑːnət/ *adj.* 1 **be the devil ~:** der leibhaftige Satan *od.* der Teufel in Person sein; **the Word I~** (Theol.) das Fleisch gewordene Wort 2 (in perfect form) **be beauty/wisdom** *etc.* **~:** die personifizierte Schönheit/Weisheit *usw.* sein

incarnation /ɪnkɑːˈneɪʃn/ *n.* Inkarnation, *die*

incautious /ɪnˈkɔːʃəs/ *adj.*, **incautiously** /ɪnˈkɔːʃəslɪ/ *adv.* unbedacht

incendiary /ɪnˈsendɪərɪ/

A *adj.* 1 **~ attack** Brandstiftung, *die;* **~ device** Brandsatz, *der;* **~ bomb** ▸B 2 2 (fig.) aufwieglerisch; Hetz-

B *n.* 1 (person) Brandstifter, *der*/-stifterin, *die;* (fig.) Aufwiegler, *der*/Aufwieglerin, *die* 2 (bomb) Brandbombe, *die*

incense¹ /ˈɪnsens/ *n.* Weihrauch, *der*

incense² /ɪnˈsens/ *v.t.* erzürnen; erbosen; **be ~d at** *or* **by sth./with sb.** über etw./jmdn. erbost *od.* erzürnt sein

incentive /ɪnˈsentɪv/ *n.* 1 (motivation) Anreiz, *der;* **~ to achievement** Leistungsanreiz, *der;* *attrib.* **~ payment system** System des finanziellen Anreizes 2 (payment) finanzieller Anreiz

inception /ɪnˈsepʃn/ *n.* Einführung, *die;* **from** *or* **since/at its ~:** von Beginn an/zu Beginn

incessant /ɪnˈsesənt/ *adj.*, **incessantly** /ɪnˈsesəntlɪ/ *adv.* unablässig; unaufhörlich

incest /ˈɪnsest/ *n.* Inzest, *der;* Blutschande, *die*

incestuous /ɪnˈsestjʊəs/ *adj.* (lit. or fig.) inzestuös

inch /ɪnʃ/

A *n.* 1 ▸❶ **p. 911**, ▸❶ **p. 1208**, ▸❶ **p. 1286** Inch, *der;* Zoll, *der* (veralt.); **a 2½-~ map** eine Landkarte im Maßstab 1 Meile : 2½ Inches; **he could hardly see an ~ in front of him** er konnte kaum die Hand vor Augen sehen; **miss sth./sb. by ~es** etw./jmdn. um Haaresbreite verfehlen 2 (small amount) **~ by ~:** ≈ Zentimeter um Zentimeter; **by ~es** ≈ zentimeterweise; **escape death by an ~:** dem Tod mit knapper Not entrinnen; **she came within an ~ of winning** sie hätte um ein Haar gewonnen; **give him an ~ and he will take a mile** wenn man ihm den kleinen Finger reicht, nimmt er gleich die ganze Hand; **not give** *or* **yield an ~:** keinen Fingerbreit nachgeben; keinen Zoll weichen (geh.); **he is every ~ a soldier** er ist Zoll für Zoll ein Soldat (geh.); **he was flogged within an ~ of his life** er wurde fast zu Tode geprügelt 3 *in pl.* (stature) Körpergröße, *die*

B *v.t.* ≈ zentimeterweise bewegen; **~ one's way forward** sich Zoll für Zoll vorwärts bewegen

C *v.i.* ≈ sich zentimeterweise bewegen; **~ along/forward** sich ganz langsam entlangbewegen/vorwärts bewegen

inchoate /ˈɪnkəʊət/ *adj.* 1 (just begun) beginnend 2 (undeveloped) unausgereift

incidence /ˈɪnsɪdəns/ *n.* 1 (occurrence) Auftreten, *das;* Vorkommen, *das* 2 (manner or range of occurrence) Häufigkeit, *die;* **~ of crime/accidents** Verbrechens-/Unfallrate, *die* 3 (Phys.) Einfall, *der;* **angle of ~:** Einfall[s]winkel, *der;* Inzidenzwinkel, *der* (fachspr.)

incident /ˈɪnsɪdənt/

A *n.* 1 (notable event) Vorfall, *der;* (minor occurrence) Begebenheit, *die;* Vorkommnis, *das;* **the evening passed without ~:** der Abend verging ohne besondere Vorkommnisse 2 (clash) Zwischenfall, *der;* **frontier ~:** Grenzzwischenfall, *der* 3 (in play, novel, etc.) Episode, *die*

B *adj.* 1 (attaching) **~ to** verbunden mit 2 (falling) einfallend ‹*Licht, Strahl*›

incidental /ɪnsɪˈdentl/

A *adj.* 1 (casual) beiläufig ‹*Art, Bemerkung*›; Neben‹*ausgaben, -einnahmen, -gewinn*› 2 (attaching) **~ to** verbunden mit

B *n., in pl.* Nebensächlichkeiten; (expenses) Nebenausgaben

incidentally /ɪnsɪˈdentəlɪ/ *adv.* 1 (by the way) nebenbei [bemerkt] 2 (by chance) zufällig 3 (as not essential) am Rande

inci'dental music *n.* Begleitmusik, *die*

'incident room *n.* Einsatzzentrum, *das*

incinerate /ɪnˈsɪnəreɪt/ *v.t.* verbrennen

incineration /ɪnsɪnəˈreɪʃn/ *n., no pl.* Verbrennung, *die*

incinerator /ɪnˈsɪnəreɪtə(r)/ *n.* Verbrennungsofen, *der;* (in garden) Abfallverbrenner, *der*

incipient /ɪnˈsɪpɪənt/ *adj.* anfänglich; einsetzend ‹*Schmerzen*›; aufkommend ‹*Zweifel, Angst*›

incise /ɪnˈsaɪz/ *v.t.* einschneiden

incision /ɪnˈsɪʒn/ *n.* 1 (cutting) Einschneiden, *das* 2 (cut) Einschnitt, *der;* **abdominal ~:** Bauchschnitt, *der*

incisive /ɪnˈsaɪsɪv/ *adj.* schneidend ‹*Ton*›; scharf ‹*Verstand*›; scharfsinnig ‹*Genie, Kritik, Methode, Frage, Bemerkung, Argument*›; präzise ‹*Sprache, Stil*›

incisively /ɪnˈsaɪsɪvlɪ/ *adv.* scharfsinnig; präzise ‹*sich ausdrücken*›

incisor /ɪnˈsaɪzə(r)/ *n.* (Anat., Zool.) Schneidezahn, *der*

incite /ɪnˈsaɪt/ *v.t.* anstiften; aufstacheln, aufwiegeln ‹*Massen, Volk*›

incitement /ɪnˈsaɪtmənt/ *n.* 1 (act) Anstiftung, *die;* (of masses, crowd) Aufstachelung, *die;* Aufwiegelung, *die* 2 (encouragement) Antrieb, *der*

incivility /ɪnsɪˈvɪlɪtɪ/ *n.* Unhöflichkeit, *die;* **it is gross ~ to refuse** es ist eine grobe Unhöflichkeit abzulehnen

incl. *abbr.* = **including** inkl.; einschl.

inclement /ɪnˈklemənt/ *adj.* unfreundlich ‹*Wetter*›

inclination /ɪnklɪˈneɪʃn/ *n.* 1 (slope) [Ab]hang, *der;* (of roof) Neigung, *die* 2 (preference, desire) Neigung, *die;* **have a strong ~ to[wards]** *or* **for sth.** eine ausgeprägte Neigung für etw. haben; **my ~ is to let the matter rest** ich neige dazu, die Sache auf sich beruhen zu lassen; **by ~ he tended to be a recluse** er hatte eine Neigung zum Einsiedlertum; **have neither the time nor the ~ to pursue the matter** weder die Zeit noch die Lust haben, die Sache zu verfolgen; **my immediate ~ was to throw him out** mein erster Gedanke war, ihn hinauszuwerfen; **show no ~ to go to bed** keine Anstalten machen, ins Bett zu gehen 3 (liking) **~ for sb.** Zuneigung für jmdn. 4 (bow, nod) Neigung, *die*

incline

A /ɪnˈklaɪn/ *v.t.* 1 (bend) neigen 2 (dispose) veranlassen; **all her instincts ~d her to stay** alles in ihr drängte sie zu bleiben

B *v.i.* 1 (be disposed) neigen (**to[wards]** zu); **~ to believe that ...:** geneigt sein zu glauben, dass ...; **~ to suppose that ...:** zu der Annahme neigen, dass ... 2 (lean) sich neigen

C /ˈɪnklaɪn/ *n.* Steigung, *die*

inclined /ɪnˈklaɪnd/ *adj.* 1 (disposed) geneigt; **be mathematically ~:** sich für Mathematik interessieren; **he is not very much ~ to believe me** er zeigt wenig Neigung, mir zu glauben; **they are ~ to be slow** sie neigen zur Langsamkeit; **if you feel [so] ~:** wenn Sie Lust dazu haben; **if you are that way ~:** wenn das Ihren Neigungen entspricht; **he is that way ~:** er neigt dazu; **be ~ to believe that ...:** geneigt sein zu glauben, dass ...; **the door is ~ to bang** die Tür schlägt leicht zu 2 (sloping) abfallend

inclined 'plane *n.* (Phys.) schiefe Ebene

inclose ▸**enclose**

include /ɪnˈkluːd/ *v.t.* einschließen; (contain) enthalten; **his team ~s a number of people who ...:** zu seiner Mannschaft gehören einige, die ...; **..., [the] children ~d ...**, [die] Kinder eingeschlossen; **does that ~ 'me?** gilt das auch für mich?; **the list ~d several prominent politicians** die Liste enthielt mehrere prominente Politiker; **your name is not ~d in the list** dein Name steht nicht auf der Liste; **have you ~d the full amount?** haben Sie den vollen Betrag einbezogen?; **~ sth. in an essay** *etc.* etw. in einen Aufsatz *usw.* aufnehmen; **~d in the price** im Preis inbegriffen; **postage ~d** einschließlich Porto

Phrasal verb

- **~ 'out** *v.t.* (coll. joc.) auslassen; **[you can] ~ me out** ohne mich!

including /ɪnˈkluːdɪŋ/ *prep.* einschließlich; **I make that ten ~ the captain** mit dem Kapitän sind das nach meiner Rechnung zehn; **up to and ~ the last financial year** bis einschließlich des letzten Geschäftsjahres; **~ VAT** inklusive Mehrwertsteuer; **the lights cost me £10, ~ the batteries** die Lampen kosteten mich, einschließlich Batterien, 10 Pfund

inclusion /ɪnˈkluːʒn/ *n.* Aufnahme, *die*

inclusive /ɪnˈkluːsɪv/ *adj.* 1 inklusive (bes. Kaufmannsspr.); einschließlich; **be ~ of sth.** etw. einschließen; **the rent is not ~ of gas and electricity charges** in der Miete sind Gas und Strom nicht enthalten; **from 2 to 6 January ~:** vom 2. bis einschließlich 6. Januar; **pages 7 to 26 ~:** Seite 7 bis 26 einschließlich 2 (including everything) Pauschal-; Inklusiv-; **~ terms** Pauschalpreis, *der;* **it costs £50 ~:** es kostet 50 Pfund, alles inbegriffen

incognito /ɪnkɒgˈniːtəʊ/

A *adj., adv.* inkognito

B *n.* Inkognito, *das*

incoherent /ɪnkəʊˈhɪərənt/ *adj.* zusammenhanglos; **~ person/talk** sich ohne Zusammenhang ausdrückende Person/zusammenhangloses Gerede

incoherently /ɪnkəʊˈhɪərəntlɪ/ *adv.* zusammenhanglos

incombustible /ɪnkəmˈbʌstɪbl/ *adj.* unbrennbar

income /ˈɪnkəm/ *n.* Einkommen, *das;* **~s** (receipts) Einkünfte *Pl.;* **live within/beyond one's ~:** entsprechend seinen Verhältnissen/über seine Verhältnisse leben

income: ~ bracket, ~ group *ns.* Einkommensklasse, *die;* **~s policy** *n.* Einkommenspolitik, *die;* **~ sup'port** *n.* (Brit.) zusätzliche Hilfe zum Lebensunterhalt; **~ tax** *n.* Einkommensteuer, *die;* (on wages, salary) Lohnsteuer, *die;* *attrib.* **~ tax return** Einkommensteuererklärung, *die*/Lohnsteuererklärung, *die*

'incomer *n.* (Brit.) Zuzügler, *der*/Zuzüglerin, *die*

'incoming *adj.* 1 (arriving) ankommend; einlaufend ‹*Zug, Schiff*›; landend ‹*Flugzeug*›; einfahrend ‹*Zug*›; eingehend ‹*Telefongespräch, Auftrag*›; **the ~ post** *or* **mail** der Posteingang (Bürow.); **the ~ tide** die Flut 2 (succeeding) neu ‹*Vorsitzender, Präsident, Mieter, Regierung*›

incomings /ˈɪnkʌmɪŋz/ *n. pl.* (revenue, income) Einnahmen *Pl.;* Einkünfte *Pl.*

incommensurable /ɪnkəˈmenʃərəbl/ *adj.* inkommensurabel

incommensurate /ɪnkəˈmenʃərət/ *adj.* (not comparable) **be ~ with** *or* **to sth.** einer Sache (*Gen.*) unangemessen sein

incommode /ɪnkəˈməʊd/ *v.t.* (formal) 1 (annoy) belästigen; inkommodieren (geh. veralt.) 2 (inconvenience) behindern

incommunicado /ɪnkəmjuːnɪˈkɑːdəʊ/ *pred. adj.* von der Außenwelt abgeschnitten; **hold sb. ~:** jmdn. ohne Verbindung zur Außenwelt halten

incomparable /ɪn'kɒmpərəbl/ *adj.*, **incomparably** /ɪn'kɒmpərəblɪ/ *adv.* unvergleichlich

incompatibility /ɪnkəmpætɪ'bɪlɪtɪ/ *n.*, *no pl.* **1** (inability to harmonize) Unverträglichkeit, *die;* **divorce on grounds of ~:** Scheidung wegen unüberwindlicher Abneigung **2** (unsuitability for use together) Nichtübereinstimmung, *die;* (of medicines) Unverträglichkeit, *die* **3** (inconsistency) Unvereinbarkeit, *die*

incompatible /ɪnkəm'pætɪbl/ *adj.* **1** (unable to harmonize) unverträglich; **they were ~ and they separated** sie passten nicht zueinander und trennten sich **2** (unsuitable for use together) unvereinbar; inkompatibel (Technik); unverträglich ‹*Medikamente*› **3** (inconsistent) unvereinbar

incompetence /ɪn'kɒmpɪtəns/, **incompetency** /ɪn'kɒmpɪtənsɪ/ *n.* Unfähigkeit, *die;* Unvermögen, *das*

incompetent /ɪn'kɒmpɪtənt/
A *adj.* unfähig; unzulänglich ‹*Arbeit*›; **he was ~ at his job** in seinem Beruf war er völlig unfähig
B *n.* Unfähige, *der/die*

incompetently /ɪn'kɒmpɪtəntlɪ/ *adv.* stümperhaft

incomplete /ɪnkəm'pli:t/ *adj.*, **incompletely** /ɪnkəm'pli:tlɪ/ *adv.* unvollständig

incompleteness /ɪnkəm'pli:tnɪs/ *n.*, *no pl.* Unvollständigkeit, *die*

incomprehensible /ɪnkɒmprɪ'hensɪbl/ *adj.* unbegreiflich; unverständlich ‹*Sprache, Rede, Theorie, Argument*›

incomprehension /ɪnkɒmprɪ'henʃn/ *n.*, *no pl.* Verständnislosigkeit, *die* (**of** gegenüber)

inconceivable /ɪnkən'si:vəbl/ *adj.*, **inconceivably** /ɪnkən'si:vəblɪ/ *adv.* unvorstellbar

inconclusive /ɪnkən'klu:sɪv/ *adj.* ergebnislos; nicht schlüssig ‹*Beweis, Argument*›; **the result was ~:** das Ergebnis gab keinen Aufschluss

inconclusively /ɪnkən'klu:sɪvlɪ/ *adv.* ergebnislos; nicht schlüssig ‹*argumentieren*›

incongruity /ɪnkɒŋ'gru:ɪtɪ/ *n.* **1** *no pl.* (quality) Deplatziertheit, *die;* **without ~:** ohne deplatziert zu wirken **2** (instance) Absurdität, *die*

incongruous /ɪn'kɒŋgrʊəs/ *adj.* **1** (inappropriate) unpassend; deplatziert **2** (inharmonious) unvereinbar; nicht zusammenpassend ‹*Farben, Kleidungsstücke*›

incongruously /ɪn'kɒŋgrʊəslɪ/ *adv.* (inappropriately) unpassend; *as sentence-modifier* unpassenderweise

incongruousness /ɪn'kɒŋgrʊəsnɪs/ ▸**incongruity 1**

inconsequent /ɪn'kɒnsɪkwənt/ *adj.* **1** (irrelevant) sprunghaft ‹*Abweichung, Eingebung*›; zusammenhanglos ‹*Bemerkung*› **2** (illogical) unlogisch **3** (disconnected) unzusammenhängend

inconsequential /ɪnkɒnsɪ'kwenʃl/ *adj.* **1** (unimportant) belanglos **2** ▸**inconsequent 1**

inconsiderable /ɪnkən'sɪdərəbl/ *adj.* unbeträchtlich; unerheblich; **the costs were not ~:** die Kosten waren nicht unerheblich

inconsiderate /ɪnkən'sɪdərət/ *adj.* **1** (unkind) rücksichtslos **2** (rash) unbedacht; unüberlegt

inconsiderately /ɪnkən'sɪdərətlɪ/ *adv.* (unkindly) rücksichtslos; *as sentence-modifier* rücksichtsloserweise

inconsistency /ɪnkən'sɪstənsɪ/ *n.* **1** (incompatibility, self-contradiction) Widersprüchlichkeit, *die* (**with** zu) **2** (illogicality) Inkonsequenz, *die* **3** (irregularity) Unbeständigkeit, *die;* Inkonsistenz, *die* (geh.)

inconsistent /ɪnkən'sɪstənt/ *adj.* **1** (incompatible, self-contradictory) widersprüchlich; **be ~ with sth.** zu etw. im Widerspruch stehen; **results ~ with the others** Ergebnisse, die nicht zu den anderen passen **2** (illogical) inkonsequent **3** (irregular) unbeständig; inkonsistent (geh.)

inconsistently /ɪnkən'sɪstəntlɪ/ *adv.* **1** (in a self-contradictory manner) widersprüchlich **2** (illogically) inkonsequent **3** (irregularly) unbeständig; inkonsistent (geh.)

inconsolable /ɪnkən'səʊləbl/ *adj.* untröstlich

inconspicuous /ɪnkən'spɪkjʊəs/ *adj.* unauffällig; **make oneself ~:** sich so verhalten, dass man nicht auffällt

inconspicuously /ɪnkən'spɪkjʊəslɪ/ *adv.* unauffällig

inconstancy /ɪn'kɒnstənsɪ/ *n.*, *no pl.* ▸**inconstant**: Unstetigkeit, *die;* Wankelmut, *der* (geh.); Ungleichmäßigkeit, *die*

inconstant /ɪn'kɒnstənt/ *adj.* **1** (fickle) unstet; wankelmütig (geh.) **2** (irregular) ungleichmäßig

incontestable /ɪnkən'testəbl/ *adj.* unbestreitbar; unwiderlegbar ‹*Beweis*›

incontinence /ɪn'kɒntɪnəns/ *n.* (Med.) Inkontinenz, *die*

incontinent /ɪn'kɒntɪnənt/ *adj.* (Med.) inkontinent; **be ~:** an Inkontinenz leiden

incontrovertible /ɪnkɒntrə'vɜ:tɪbl/ *adj.* unbestreitbar; unwiderlegbar ‹*Beweis*›

incontrovertibly /ɪnkɒntrə'vɜ:tɪblɪ/ *adv.* unbestreitbar; unwiderlegbar ‹*beweisen*›

inconvenience /ɪnkən'vi:nɪəns/
A *n.* **1** *no pl.* (discomfort, disadvantage) Unannehmlichkeiten (**to** für); **put sb. to a lot of ~:** jmdm. große Unannehmlichkeiten bereiten; **go to a great deal of ~:** große Unannehmlichkeiten auf sich (*Akk.*) nehmen **2** (instance) **if it's no ~:** wenn es keine Umstände macht; **it is rather an ~ to have to wait** es ist ziemlich unangenehm, warten zu müssen
B *v.t.* Unannehmlichkeiten bereiten (+ *Dat.*); (disturb) stören; **don't ~ yourself just for me** *or* **on my account** mach [dir] meinetwegen nur keine Umstände!

inconvenient /ɪnkən'vi:nɪənt/ *adj.* unbequem; ungünstig ‹*Lage, Standort*›; unpraktisch ‹*Design, Konstruktion, Schnitt*›; **a very ~ time** eine sehr ungünstige Zeit; **come at an ~ time** zu ungelegener Zeit kommen; **if it is not ~ [to you]** wenn es Ihnen recht ist

inconveniently /ɪnkən'vi:nɪəntlɪ/ *adv.* ungünstig ‹*gelegen*›; unbequem ‹*klein*›

incorporate /ɪn'kɔ:pəreɪt/ *v.t.* **1** (make a legal corporation) vereinigen; **~ a company** eine Gesellschaft gründen; **be ~d as a company** zu einer Gesellschaft zusammengeschlossen sein **2** (include) aufnehmen (**in[to], with** in + *Akk.*); **your suggestion will be ~d in the plan** dein Vorschlag wird in den Plan eingehen; **the new plan ~s many of your suggestions** in dem neuen Plan sind viele deiner Vorschläge enthalten **3** (unite) verbinden (**into** zu); **~ one's ideas in an essay** seine Gedanken in einem Essay zusammenfassen

incorporated /ɪn'kɔ:pəreɪtɪd/ *adj.* eingetragen ‹[*Handels*]*gesellschaft*›

incorporation /ɪnkɔ:pə'reɪʃn/ *n.* **1** (formation) Gründung, *die* **2** (inclusion) Eingliederung, *die;* (of material, chemical) Aufnahme, *die* **3** (union) Verbindung, *die* (**into** zu)

incorporeal /ɪnkɔ:'pɔ:rɪəl/ *adj.* (not composed of matter; also Law) unkörperlich; geisterhaft ‹*Erscheinung, Wesen*›

incorrect /ɪnkə'rekt/ *adj.* **1** unrichtig; inkorrekt; **be ~:** nicht stimmen; **it is ~ to say that ...:** es stimmt nicht, dass ...; **you are ~ in believing that ...:** du irrst, wenn du glaubst, dass ... **2** (improper) inkorrekt; unschicklich

incorrectly /ɪnkə'rektlɪ/ *adv.* **1** unrichtigerweise; falsch ‹*beantworten, aussprechen*› **2** (improperly) inkorrekt; unschicklich

incorrectness /ɪnkə'rektnɪs/ *n.*, *no pl.* **1** Unrichtigkeit, *die;* Inkorrektheit, *die* **2** (impropriety) Inkorrektheit, *die;* Unschicklichkeit, *die*

incorrigible /ɪn'kɒrɪdʒɪbl/ *adj.*, **incorrigibly** /ɪn'kɒrɪdʒɪblɪ/ *adv.* unverbesserlich

incorruptible /ɪnkə'rʌptɪbl/ *adj.* **1** (upright) unbestechlich **2** (not subject to decay) unzerstörbar

increase
A /ɪn'kri:s/ *v.i.* zunehmen; ‹*Schmerzen:*› stärker werden; ‹*Lärm:*› größer werden; ‹*Verkäufe, Preise, Nachfrage:*› steigen; **~ in skill** größere Fertigkeit gewinnen; **~ in weight/size/price** schwerer/größer/teurer werden; **~ in maturity/value/popularity** an Reife/Wert/Popularität (*Dat.*) gewinnen
B *v.t.* **1** (make greater) erhöhen; vermehren ‹*Besitz*›; **wages are ~d** die Löhne steigen **2** (intensify) verstärken; **~ one's efforts/commitment** sich mehr anstrengen/engagieren
C /'ɪnkri:s/ *n.* **1** (becoming greater) Zunahme, *die* (**in** *Gen.*); (in measurable amount) Anstieg, *der* (**in** *Gen.*); (deliberately caused) Steigerung, *die* (**in** *Gen.*); **~ in weight/size** Gewichtszunahme, *die*/Vergrößerung, *die;* **~ in popularity** Popularitätsgewinn, *der;* **be on the ~:** [ständig] zunehmen **2** (by reproduction) Zunahme, *die;* Zuwachs, *der* **3** (amount) Erhöhung, *die;* (of growth) Zuwachs, *der*

increasing /ɪn'kri:sɪŋ/ *adj.* steigend; wachsend; **an ~ number of people** mehr und mehr Menschen

increasingly /ɪn'kri:sɪŋlɪ/ *adv.* in zunehmendem Maße; **become ~ apparent** immer deutlicher werden; **I am ~ of the opinion that ...:** ich bin immer mehr der Meinung, dass ...; **~, the husband looks after the children** immer häufiger kümmert sich der Mann um die Kinder

incredibility /ɪnkredɪ'bɪlɪtɪ/ *n.*, *no pl.* Unglaublichkeit, *die*

incredible /ɪn'kredɪbl/ *adj.* **1** (beyond belief) unglaublich **2** (coll.) (remarkable) unglaublich (ugs.); (wonderful) toll (ugs.)

incredibly /ɪn'kredɪblɪ/ *adv.* **1** unglaublich **2** (coll.: remarkably) unglaublich (ugs.); unwahrscheinlich (ugs.) **3** *as sentence-modifier* es ist/war kaum zu glauben, aber ...

incredulity /ɪnkrɪ'dju:lɪtɪ/ *n.*, *no pl.* Ungläubigkeit, *die*

incredulous /ɪn'kredjʊləs/ *adj.* ungläubig; **be ~ of sth.** einer Sache (*Dat.*) keinen Glauben schenken

incredulously /ɪn'kredjʊləslɪ/ *adv.* ungläubig

increment /'ɪnkrɪmənt/ *n.* Erhöhung, *die;* (amount of growth) Zuwachs, *der*

incremental /ɪnkrɪ'mentl/ *adj.* schrittweise; **be ~/ an ~ process** schrittweise erfolgen; **~ increases** regelmäßige Erhöhungen; **a pay scale with eleven ~ points** eine elfstufige Gehaltsskala

incriminate /ɪn'krɪmɪneɪt/ *v.t.* belasten; **incriminating evidence** belastendes Material

incriminatory /ɪn'krɪmɪnətərɪ/ *adj.* belastend

incrustation /ɪnkrʌs'teɪʃn/ *n.* **1** (encrusting) Überkrustung, *die* **2** (deposit) Inkrustation, *die* (Geol.); Verkrustung, *die*

incubate /'ɪnkjʊbeɪt/
A *v.t.* bebrüten; (to hatching; also fig.) ausbrüten
B *v.i.* ‹*Henne:*› brüten

incubation /ɪnkjʊ'beɪʃn/ *n.* **1** Inkubation, *die* (Biol.); Bebrütung, *die;* (fig.) Ausbrüten, *das* **2** (Med.) Inkubation, *die;* **~ period** Inkubationszeit, *die*

incubator /'ɪnkjʊbeɪtə(r)/ *n.* Inkubator, *der* (Biol., Med.); (for babies also) Brutkasten, *der;* (for eggs) Brutapparat, *der*

incubus /'ɪŋkjʊbəs/ *n.*, *pl.* **~es** *or* **incubi** /'ɪnkjʊbaɪ/ **1** Albdruck, *der* **2** (spirit) Inkubus, *der*

inculcate /'ɪnkʌlkeɪt/ *v.t.* **~ sth. in[to] sb., ~ sb. with sth.** jmdm. etw. einpflanzen

inculpate /'ɪnkʌlpeɪt/ *v.t.* **1** (accuse) **~ sb. [for a crime]** jmdn. [eines Verbrechens] beschuldigen **2** (incriminate) belasten

inculpation /ɪnkʌl'peɪʃn/ *n.* Beschuldigung, *die*

incumbency /ɪn'kʌmbənsɪ/ *n.* Amt, *das*

incumbent /ɪn'kʌmbənt/
A *n.* **1** (Eccl.) **the ~ of the parish** der Inhaber der Pfarrstelle **2** (office-holder) Amtsinhaber, *der*
B *adj.* (imposed) **the duty ~ on me** die mir obliegende Pflicht; **it is ~ on sb. to do it** es ist jmds. Pflicht *od.* obliegt jmdm., es zu tun; **I**

feel it ~ on me ich sehe es als meine Pflicht an

incur /ɪn'kɜː(r)/ *v.t.*, **-rr-** sich (*Dat.*) zuziehen ‹*Unwillen, Ärger*›; **~ a loss** einen Verlust erleiden; **~ debts/expenses/risks** Schulden machen/Ausgaben haben/Risiken eingehen; **they had ~red fines** sie waren mit Geldstrafen belegt worden

incurable /ɪn'kjʊərəbl/
A *adj.* **1** (Med.) unheilbar **2** (fig.) unheilbar (ugs.); unstillbar ‹*Sehnsucht, Verlangen*›; unüberwindbar ‹*Scheu, Zurückhaltung*›
B *n.* unheilbar Kranker/Kranke

incurably /ɪn'kjʊərəblɪ/ *adv.* unheilbar ‹*krank*›

incurious /ɪn'kjʊərɪəs/ *adj.* uninteressiert

incursion /ɪn'kɜːʃn/ *n.* (invasion) Eindringen, *das;* (by sudden attack) Einfall, *der*

indebted /ɪn'detɪd/ *pred. adj.* **1** **be/feel deeply ~ to sb.** tief in jmds. Schuld (*Dat.*) stehen (geh.); **he was ~ to the book/a friend for this information** er verdankte dem Buch/einem Freund diese Information; **be [much] ~ to sb. for sth.** jmdm. für etw. [sehr] verbunden sein (geh.) *od.* zu Dank verpflichtet sein **2** (owing money) **be ~ to the bank for a large sum** bei der Bank mit einer hohen Summe verschuldet sein; **be [heavily] ~ to a friend** bei einem Freund [große] Schulden haben

indebtedness /ɪn'detɪdnɪs/ *n.* **1** (something owed) Dankesschuld, *die* (geh.) (**to** bei) **2** (condition of owing money) Verschuldung, *die*

indecency /ɪn'diːsənsɪ/ *n.* Unanständigkeit, *die*

indecent /ɪn'diːsənt/ *adj.* **1** (immodest, obscene) unanständig; *see also* **exposure 1** **2** (unseemly) ungehörig; **with ~ haste** mit unziemlicher Hast (geh.)

indecent as'sault *n.* (Law) Notzucht, *die* (Rechtsw.)

indecently /ɪn'diːsəntlɪ/ *adv.* unanständig

indecipherable /ɪndɪ'saɪfərəbl/ *adj.* unentzifferbar

indecision /ɪndɪ'sɪʒn/ *n.*, *no pl.* Unentschlossenheit, *die*

indecisive /ɪndɪ'saɪsɪv/ *adj.* **1** (not conclusive) ergebnislos ‹*Streit, Diskussion*›; nichts entscheidend ‹*Krieg, Schlacht*›; nichts sagend ‹*Ergebnis, Beobachtung*› **2** (hesitating) unentschlossen; **be ~ about one's plans** keine festen Pläne haben; **~ about which line of action to choose** unschlüssig, wie man vorgehen soll

indecisively /ɪndɪ'saɪsɪvlɪ/ *adv.* **1** (inconclusively) ohne Entscheidung **2** (hesitatingly) unentschlossen

indecisiveness /ɪndɪ'saɪsɪvnɪs/ *n.*, *no pl.* **1** Ergebnislosigkeit, *die;* Unentschlossenheit, *die* **2** (hesitation) **~ over a crucial issue** Unentschlossenheit in einer äußerst wichtigen Sache

indeclinable /ɪndɪ'klaɪnəbl/ *adj.* (Ling.) indeklinabel

indecorous /ɪn'dekərəs/ *adj.* (improper) ungehörig; (in bad taste) unschicklich

indeed /ɪn'diːd/ *adv.* **1** (in truth) in der Tat; tatsächlich; **~ that is correct** das stimmt tatsächlich *od.* in der Tat **2** *emphat.* **thank you very much ~:** haben Sie vielen herzlichen Dank; **it was very kind of you ~:** es war wirklich sehr freundlich von Ihnen; **I shall be very glad ~ when ...:** ich bin wirklich sehr froh, wenn ...; **~ it is** in der Tat; allerdings; **yes ~, it certainly is/I certainly did** *etc.* ja, das kann man wohl sagen; **no, ~:** nein, ganz bestimmt nicht **3** (in fact) ja sogar; **~, he can ...:** ja, er kann sogar ...; **if ~ such a thing is possible** wenn so etwas überhaupt möglich ist; **I feel, ~ I know, she will come** ich habe das Gefühl, [ja] ich weiß sogar, dass sie kommen wird **4** (admittedly) zugegebenermaßen; zwar **5** *interrog.* **~?** wirklich?; ist das wahr? **6** *expr. irony, surprise, interest, etc.* **He expects to win — Does he ~!** Er glaubt, dass er gewinnt — Tatsächlich?; **I want a fortnight off work — [Do you] ~!** Ich möchte 14 Tage freihaben — Ach wirklich?; **smoked salmon, ~!** soso *od.* sieh mal einer an, geräucherter Lachs [also]! **7** *echoing question* **Who is this Mr Smith? — Who is he, ~!** (you may well ask) Wer ist denn dieser Mr. Smith? — Ja, wer ist er eigentlich?

indefatigable /ɪndɪ'fætɪgəbl/ *adj.* unermüdlich

indefensible /ɪndɪ'fensɪbl/ *adj.* **1** (insecure) unhaltbar **2** (untenable) unvertretbar; unhaltbar **3** (intolerable) unverzeihlich

indefinable /ɪndɪ'faɪnəbl/ *adj.* undefinierbar; **have a certain ~ something** etwas Gewisses haben

indefinite /ɪn'defɪnɪt/ *adj.* **1** (vague) unbestimmt; **she was rather ~ about it** sie äußerte sich ziemlich vage darüber **2** (unlimited) unbegrenzt; **~ leave** Urlaub auf unbestimmte Zeit **3** (Ling.) unbestimmt; indefinit (fachspr.); infinit (fachspr.) ‹*Verbform*›; *see also* **article A 3; pronoun**

indefinitely /ɪn'defɪnɪtlɪ/ *adv.* **1** (vaguely) unbestimmt **2** (unlimitedly) unbegrenzt; **it can't go on ~:** es kann nicht endlos so weitergehen; **postponed ~:** auf unbestimmte Zeit verschoben; **it would be easy to prolong the list ~:** die Liste ließe sich beliebig verlängern

indelible /ɪn'delɪbl/ *adj.* unauslöschlich (auch fig.); nicht zu entfernend ‹*Fleck*›; **~ ink** Wäschetinte, *die;* **~ pencil** Kopierstift, *der;* Tintenstift, *der*

indelibly /ɪn'delɪblɪ/ *adv.* unauslöschlich

indelicacy /ɪn'delɪkəsɪ/ *n.* ▸**indelicate**: Ungehörigkeit, *die;* Geschmacklosigkeit, *die;* Mangel an Feingefühl

indelicate /ɪn'delɪkət/ *adj.* (coarse) ungehörig; (almost indecent) geschmacklos; (slightly tactless) nicht sehr feinfühlig

indelicately /ɪn'delɪkətlɪ/ *adv.* ▸**indelicate**: ungehörig; geschmacklos; wenig feinfühlend

indemnification /ɪndemnɪfɪ'keɪʃn/ *n.* Entschädigung, *die*

indemnify /ɪn'demnɪfaɪ/ *v.t.* **1** (protect) **~ sb. against sth.** jmdn. gegen etw. absichern **2** (compensate) entschädigen

indemnity /ɪn'demnɪtɪ/ *n.* **1** (security) Absicherung, *die* **2** (compensation) Entschädigung, *die*

in'demnity policy *n.* Haftpflichtversicherung, *die*

indent[1]
A /'ɪndent/ *n.* **1** (incision) Einschnitt, *der* **2** (Brit.: requisition) Requisition, *die* **3** ▸**indentures**
B /ɪn'dent/ *v.t.* **1** (make notches in) einkerben **2** (form recesses in) einschneiden in (+ *Akk.*); **an ~ed coastline** eine Küste mit tiefen Einschnitten **3** (Printing: from margin) einrücken **4** (Brit.: order) requirieren
C *v.i.* (Brit.: make requisition) **~ [on sb.] for sth.** etw. [bei jmdm.] requirieren

indent[2] /ɪn'dent/ *v.t.* (imprint) eindrücken

indentation /ɪnden'teɪʃn/ *n.* **1** (indenting, notch) Einkerbung, *die* **2** (recess) Einschnitt, *der*

indentures /ɪn'dentʃəz/ *n. pl.* Ausbildungsvertrag, *der*

independence /ɪndɪ'pendəns/ *n.* Unabhängigkeit, *die;* **declaration of ~:** Unabhängigkeitserklärung, *die;* **~ of mind/spirit** geistige Selbstständigkeit

Inde'pendence Day *n.* (Amer.) Unabhängigkeitstag, *der*

> **Independence Day**
>
> In den USA ist der 4. Juli ein Nationalfeiertag. Die Unabhängigkeitserklärung des Jahres 1776 wird mit Umzügen, Feuerwerken und Beflaggung gefeiert. Freunde und Verwandte treffen sich zum Essen im Freien oder zu Grillfesten.

independent /ɪndɪ'pendənt/
A *adj.* **1** unabhängig; **~ income/means** eigenes Einkommen **2** (not wanting obligations) selbstständig
B *n.* (Polit.) Unabhängige, *der/die*

> **The Independent**
>
> Eine britische überregionale Tageszeitung. Ihr Pendant am Sonntag heißt *The Independent on Sunday*. Obgleich der *Independent* politisch eher links steht, strebt er, wie der Name schon andeutet, eine unabhängige überparteiliche Berichterstattung an.

independently /ɪndɪ'pendəntlɪ/ *adv.* unabhängig (**of** von); **they work ~:** sie arbeiten unabhängig voneinander

inde'pendent school *n.* (Brit.) *Schule in nichtstaatlicher Trägerschaft;* Privatschule, *die*

> **independent school**
>
> Eine Privatschule in Großbritannien, die sich selbst finanziert, und zwar durch Elternbeiträge. Sie erhält keine staatliche Unterstützung. **Public schools** und **preparatory schools** fallen in diese Kategorie.

Independent 'Television *n.* kommerzielles britisches Fernsehprogramm

'in-depth ▸**depth 3**

indescribable /ɪndɪ'skraɪbəbl/ *adj.*, **indescribably** /ɪndɪ'skraɪbəblɪ/ *adv.* unbeschreiblich

indestructible /ɪndɪ'strʌktɪbl/ *adj.* unzerstörbar; unerschütterlich ‹*Glaube*›

indeterminable /ɪndɪ'tɜːmɪnəbl/ *adj.* unbestimmbar

indeterminacy /ɪndɪ'tɜːmɪnəsɪ/ *n.*, *no pl.* Unbestimmtheit, *die*

indeterminate /ɪndɪ'tɜːmɪnət/ *adj.* **1** (not fixed, vague) unbestimmt ‹*Form, Menge*›; unklar ‹*Konzept, Bedeutung*› **2** (left undecided) ergebnislos; offen ‹*Rechtsfrage*› **3** (Math.) unbestimmt

index /'ɪndeks/
A *n.* **1** (list) Index, *der;* Register, *das;* **~ of sources** Quellenverzeichnis, *das; see also* **card index** **2** *pl.* **indices** /'ɪndɪsiːz/ (Phys.) **refractive ~:** Brechzahl, *die;* Brechungsindex, *der* **3** *pl.* **indices** (Math.) Index, *der;* (exponent) Exponent, *der* **4** (pointer on scale) Zeiger, *der* **5** (Econ.) Index, *der* **6** *pl.* **indices** (indication) [An]zeichen, *das* **7** **the I~** (RC Ch. Hist.) der Index; **put on the I~:** auf den Index setzen
B *v.t.* **1** (furnish with ~) mit einem Register *od.* Index versehen **2** (enter in ~) ins Register aufnehmen **3** (Econ.) indexieren; **~ pensions** Renten dynamisieren

indexation /ɪndek'seɪʃn/ *n.* (Econ.) Indexierung, *die*

'index card *n.* Karteikarte, *die*

indexer /'ɪndeksə(r)/ *n.* Verfasser eines Registers/von Registern

index: ~ finger *n.* Zeigefinger, *der;* Index, *der* (Anat.); **~ gears** *pl.* (of bicycle etc.) Indexschaltung, *die;* **~-linked** *adj.* (Econ.) indexiert; dynamisch ‹*Rente*›; **~-linking** *n.* (Econ.) Indexierung, *die;* **~-linking of pensions** ≈ Rentenanpassung, *die;* **~ number** *n.* Indexzahl, *die* (bes. Statistik)

India /'ɪndɪə/ *pr. n.* Indien (*das*); **~ ink** (Amer.) ▸**Indian ink**

Indian /'ɪndɪən/ ▸ ❶ **p. 1345**
A *adj.* **1** indisch; **sb. is ~:** jmd. ist Inder/Inderin **2** **[American] ~:** indianisch. *See also* **file**[3] **A 1; Red Indian; West Indian A**
B *n.* **1** Inder, *der*/Inderin, *die* **2** **[American] ~:** Indianer, *der*/Indianerin, *die*

Indian: ~ 'club *n.* Keule, *die;* **~ 'corn** *n.* Mais, *der;* **~ 'ink** *n.* (Brit.) Tusche, *die;* **~ 'Ocean** *pr. n.* Indischer Ozean; **~ 'rope-trick** *n.* indischer Seiltrick; **~ 'summer** *n.* Altweibersommer, *der;* Nachsommer, *der* (auch fig.)

'India rubber ▸**rubber**[1] **1, 2**

indicate /'ɪndɪkeɪt/
A *v.t.* **1** (be a sign of) erkennen lassen; **this ~s something about his attitude** dies gibt Aufschlüsse über seine Haltung **2** (state briefly) andeuten; **~ the rough outlines of a project** ein Projekt kurz umreißen *od.* in groben Umrissen darstellen; **they ~d that they might take action** sie gaben zu verstehen, dass sie Schritte unternehmen könnten **3** (mark, point

out) anzeigen 4▸ (suggest, make evident) zum Ausdruck bringen (**to** gegenüber) 5▸ (Med.) **be ~d** indiziert sein

B *v.i.* blinken (bes. Verkehrsw.)

indication /ɪndɪˈkeɪʃn/ *n.* 1▸ (sign, guide) [An]zeichen, *das* (**of** *Gen.*, für); **he gave no ~ that he understood** nichts wies darauf hin, dass er verstand; **there is every/no ~ that ...:** alles/nichts weist darauf hin, dass ...; **give a clear ~ of one's intentions** seine Absichten klar zum Ausdruck bringen; **first ~s are that ...:** die ersten Anzeichen deuten darauf hin, dass ...; **that is some ~ of his feelings/the seriousness of the situation** das lässt seine Gefühle erkennen/das deutet darauf hin, wie ernst die Lage ist; **give me a rough ~ of when you will arrive** sagen Sie mir ungefähr, wann Sie kommen 2▸ (Med.) Indikation, *die*

indicative /ɪnˈdɪkətɪv/

A *adj.* 1▸ (suggestive) **be ~ of sth./that ...:** auf etw. (*Akk.*) schließen lassen/darauf schließen lassen, dass ... 2▸ (Ling.) indikativisch; **~ mood** Indikativ, *der*

B *n.* (Ling.) Indikativ, *der*

indicator /ˈɪndɪkeɪtə(r)/ *n.* 1▸ (instrument) Anzeiger, *der* 2▸ (board) Anzeigetafel, *die* 3▸ (on vehicle) Blinker, *der* 4▸ (fig.: pointer) Indikator, *der* (bes. Wirtsch.) 5▸ (Chem.) Indikator, *der*

indices *pl. of* **index A 2, 3, 6**

indict /ɪnˈdaɪt/ *v.t.* anklagen (**for, on a charge of** *Gen.*)

indictable /ɪnˈdaɪtəbl/ *adj.* strafrechtlich verfolgbar ‹*Person*›; strafbar ‹*Handlung*›

indictment /ɪnˈdaɪtmənt/ *n.* 1▸ (esp. Amer. Law) Anklageerhebung, *die;* **~ for** *or* **on a charge of murder** Mordanklage, *die;* **bring an ~ against sb.** Anklage gegen jmdn. erheben; **[bill of] ~:** Anklageschrift, *die* 2▸ (fig.) **~ of sth.** (thing serving as condemnation) Anklage gegen etw. (geh.); (critical statement) vernichtende Kritik einer Sache

indie /ˈɪndɪ/ (coll.)

A *adj.* Indie-‹*Gruppe, Szene, Charts usw.*›

B *n.* (record company) Indie-Label, *das;* (band) Indie-Band, *die*

indifference /ɪnˈdɪfərəns/ *n., no pl.* 1▸ (unconcern) Gleichgültigkeit, *die* (**to[wards]** gegenüber) 2▸ (neutrality) Indifferenz, *die* 3▸ (unimportance) **a matter of ~:** eine Belanglosigkeit; **this is a matter of complete ~ to** *or* **for him** das ist für ihn völlig belanglos

indifferent /ɪnˈdɪfərənt/ *adj.* 1▸ (without concern or interest) gleichgültig; unbeteiligt ‹*Beobachter*›; **be ~ to[wards] sb./sth.** sich für jmdn./etw. nicht interessieren 2▸ (not good) mittelmäßig; (fairly bad) mäßig; (neither good nor bad) durchschnittlich; **very ~:** sehr schlecht; ganz miserabel

indifferently /ɪnˈdɪfərəntlɪ/ *adv.* 1▸ (unconcernedly) gleichgültig 2▸ (badly) mäßig

indigence /ˈɪndɪdʒəns/ *n., no pl.* Armut, *die*

indigenous /ɪnˈdɪdʒɪnəs/ *adj.* einheimisch; eingeboren ‹*Bevölkerung*›; **a species ~ to India** eine in Indien heimische *od.* beheimatete Art; **~ inhabitant** Ureinwohner, *der*

indigent /ˈɪndɪdʒənt/ *adj.* arm

indigestible /ɪndɪˈdʒestɪbl/ *adj.* (lit. or fig.) unverdaulich

indigestion /ɪndɪˈdʒestʃn/ *n., no pl., no indef. art.* Magenverstimmung, *die;* (chronic) Verdauungsstörungen *Pl.*; **[acid] ~:** Sodbrennen, *das*

indignant /ɪnˈdɪgnənt/ *adj.* entrüstet (**at, over, about** über + *Akk.*); indigniert ‹*Blick, Geste*›; **grow ~:** sich entrüsten; **it makes me ~:** es regt mich auf; **he was ~ with his wife** er ärgerte sich über seine Frau; **it's no use getting ~:** es hat keinen Zweck, sich aufzuregen

indignantly /ɪnˈdɪgnəntlɪ/ *adv.* entrüstet; indigniert

indignation /ɪndɪgˈneɪʃn/ *n., no pl.* Entrüstung, *die* (**about, at, against, over** über + *Akk.*); **feel great ~ at sb.** sehr entrüstet über jmdn. sein

indignity /ɪnˈdɪgnɪtɪ/ *n.* Demütigung, *die;* **be treated with great ~:** äußerst demütigend behandelt werden; **the ~ of my position** das Demütigende [an] meiner Situation; **oh, the ~ of it!** o Schmach und Schande!; **the ~ of having to do sth.** die Demütigung, etw. tun zu müssen

indigo /ˈɪndɪgəʊ/

A *n., pl.* **~s** 1▸ (dye) Indigo, *der od. das* 2▸ (plant) Indigopflanze, *die* 3▸ (colour) **~ [blue]** Indigoblau, *das*

B *adj.* **~ [blue]** indigoblau

indirect /ɪndɪˈrekt, ɪndaɪˈrekt/ *adj.* indirekt; (long-winded) umständlich; **follow an ~ route** nicht den direkten Weg nehmen; **that's the more ~ way** das ist der weniger direkte *od.* geradlinige Weg; **that road is rather ~:** diese Straße ist ein ziemlicher Umweg; **by ~ means** auf Umwegen (fig.)

indirectly /ɪndɪˈrektlɪ, ɪndaɪˈrektlɪ/ *adv.* indirekt; auf Umwegen ‹*hören, herausfinden*›

indirect: ~ ˈobject *n.* (Ling.) indirektes Objekt; (in German) Dativobjekt, *das;* **~ ˈquestion** *n.* (Ling.) indirekte Frage; **~ ˈspeech** *n.* (Ling.) indirekte Rede

indiscernible /ɪndɪˈsɜːnɪbl/ *adj.* unmerklich; **the sound was virtually ~:** das Geräusch war kaum wahrnehmbar

indiscipline /ɪnˈdɪsɪplɪn/ *n., no pl., no indef. art.* Disziplinlosigkeit, *die*

indiscreet /ɪndɪˈskriːt/ *adj.* indiskret; taktlos ‹*Benehmen*›; **she was ~ to do that** es war indiskret von ihr, das zu tun

indiscreetly /ɪndɪˈskriːtlɪ/ *adv.* indiskret; taktlos ‹*sich benehmen*›

indiscretion /ɪndɪˈskreʃn/ *n.* 1▸ (conduct) Indiskretion, *die;* (tactlessness) Taktlosigkeit, *die* 2▸ (imprudence) Unbedachtheit, *die* 3▸ (action) Unbedachtsamkeit, *die;* (love affair) Seitensprung, *der* 4▸ (revelation of official secret etc.) Indiskretion, *die*

indiscriminate /ɪndɪˈskrɪmɪnət/ *adj.* 1▸ (undiscriminating) unkritisch; **hand out ~ condemnations** unterschiedslos alles verurteilen 2▸ (unrestrained, promiscuous) wahllos; willkürlich ‹*Anwendung*›; unüberlegt ‹*Ausgaben*›

indiscriminately /ɪndɪˈskrɪmɪnətlɪ/ *adv.* ▸**indiscriminate**: unkritisch; wahllos; willkürlich; unüberlegt

indispensability /ɪndɪspensəˈbɪlɪtɪ/ *n., no pl.* Unentbehrlichkeit, *die* (**to** für)

indispensable /ɪndɪˈspensəbl/ *adj.* unentbehrlich (**to** für); unabdingbar ‹*Voraussetzung*›; **make oneself ~:** sich unentbehrlich machen

indisposed /ɪndɪˈspəʊzd/ *adj.* 1▸ (unwell) unpässlich; indisponiert ‹*Sänger, Schauspieler*› 2▸ (disinclined) **be ~ to do sth.** abgeneigt sein, etw. zu tun; **she was ~ to be polite** sie war nicht geneigt, höflich zu sein

indisposition /ɪndɪspəˈzɪʃn/ *n.* 1▸ (ill health) Unpässlichkeit, *die;* (of singer, actor) Indisposition, *die* 2▸ (disinclination) **an ~ to do sth.** eine Abneigung dagegen, etw. zu tun

indisputable /ɪndɪˈspjuːtəbl/ *adj.*, **indisputably** /ɪndɪˈspjuːtəblɪ/ *adv.* unbestreitbar

indissoluble /ɪndɪˈsɒljʊbl/ *adj.*, **indissolubly** /ɪndɪˈsɒljʊblɪ/ *adv.* unauflöslich

indistinct /ɪndɪˈstɪŋkt/ *adj.* undeutlich; (blurred) verschwommen; **grow ~ in the twilight** in der Dämmerung verschwimmen

indistinctly /ɪndɪˈstɪŋktlɪ/ *adv.* undeutlich ‹*sprechen*›; verschwommen ‹*sich erinnern*›

indistinguishable /ɪndɪˈstɪŋgwɪʃəbl/ *adj.* 1▸ (not distinguishable) nicht unterscheidbar; **the twins are ~:** die Zwillinge sind nicht voneinander zu unterscheiden 2▸ (imperceptible) nicht erkennbar; nicht wahrnehmbar ‹*Geräusch*›

individual /ɪndɪˈvɪdjʊəl/

A *adj.* 1▸ (single) einzeln 2▸ (special, personal) besonder... ‹*Vorteil, Merkmal*›; **give ~ attention to one's pupils** seine Schüler individuell betreuen; **~ case** Einzelfall, *der* 3▸ (intended for one) für eine [einzelne] Person bestimmt; **~ portions** Einzelportionen; **~ pie** Pastete für eine [einzelne] Person 4▸ (distinctive) eigentümlich; individuell; **be ~ in one's view** individuelle *od.* eigene Ansichten vertreten

B *n.* 1▸ (one member) Einzelne, *der/die;* (animal) Einzeltier, *das;* einzelnes Tier; **~s** Einzelne 2▸ (one being) Individuum, *das;* Einzelne, *der/die;* **the rights of the ~:** die Rechte des Individuums *od.* des Einzelnen 3▸ (coll.: person) Individuum, *das* (abwertend); **who is that ~?** wer ist dieser Typ?

individualise ▸**individualize**

individualist /ɪndɪˈvɪdjʊəlɪst/ *n.* Individualist, *der*/Individualistin, *die*

individualistic /ɪndɪvɪdjʊəˈlɪstɪk/ *adj.* individualistisch

individuality /ɪndɪvɪdjʊˈælɪtɪ/ *n., no pl.* 1▸ (character) eigene Persönlichkeit; Individualität, *die* 2▸ (separate existence) individuelle Existenz

individualize /ɪndɪˈvɪdjʊəlaɪz/ *v.t.* **~ sth.** einer Sache (*Dat.*) einen eigenen Charakter geben

individually /ɪndɪˈvɪdjʊəlɪ/ *adv.* 1▸ (singly) einzeln 2▸ (distinctively) individuell 3▸ (personally) persönlich

indivisibility /ɪndɪvɪzɪˈbɪlɪtɪ/ *n., no pl.* Unteilbarkeit, *die*

indivisible /ɪndɪˈvɪzɪbl/ *adj.* 1▸ (not divisible) unteilbar 2▸ (not distributable) nicht aufteilbar

indivisibly /ɪndɪˈvɪzɪblɪ/ *adv.* unteilbar

Indo- /ɪndəʊ/ *in comb.* Indo-

Indo-ˈChina *pr. n.* (Hist.) Indochina (*das*)

indoctrinate /ɪnˈdɒktrɪneɪt/ *v.t.* indoktrinieren (abwertend)

indoctrination /ɪndɒktrɪˈneɪʃn/ *n.* Indoktrination, *die* (abwertend)

Indo: ~-Euroˈpean, ~-Gerˈmanic

A *adjs.* indoeuropäisch; indogermanisch. **B** *ns.* (Ling.) Indogermanisch, *das*

indolence /ˈɪndələns/ *n., no pl.* Trägheit, *die;* Indolenz, *die* (geh.)

indolent /ˈɪndələnt/ *adj.*, **indolently** /ˈɪndələntlɪ/ *adv.* träge; indolent (geh.)

indomitable /ɪnˈdɒmɪtəbl/ *adj.* unbeugsam; unbezähmbar ‹*Begeisterung*›

Indonesia /ɪndəˈniːʒə, ɪndəˈniːzɪə/ *pr. n.* Indonesien (*das*)

Indonesian /ɪndəˈniːʒən, ɪndəˈniːzɪən/ ▸❶ **p. 1277**, ▸❶ **p. 1345**

A *adj.* indonesisch; **sb. is ~:** jmd. ist Indonesier/Indonesierin; *see also* **English A**

B *n.* 1▸ (person) Indonesier, *der*/Indonesierin, *die* 2▸ (language) Indonesisch, *das; see also* **English B 1**

ˈindoor *adj.* **~ shoes** Schuhe für zu Hause; **~ swimming pool/sports/tennis** Hallenbad, *das*/-sport, *der*/-tennis, *das;* **~ plants** Zimmerpflanzen; **~ games** Spiele im Haus; (Sport) Hallenspiele; **~ aerial** Innenantenne, *die;* (in room) Zimmerantenne, *die;* **I don't enjoy ~ work** ich arbeite nicht gern drinnen *od.* im Haus/Büro *usw.*; **he's not one for [the] ~ life** er ist lieber draußen als drinnen

indoors /ɪnˈdɔːz/ *adv.* drinnen; im Haus; **come/go ~:** nach drinnen *od.* ins Haus kommen/gehen

indorse ▸**endorse**

indubitable /ɪnˈdjuːbɪtəbl/ *adj.* unzweifelhaft

indubitably /ɪnˈdjuːbɪtəblɪ/ *adv.* zweifellos; zweifelsohne

induce /ɪnˈdjuːs/ *v.t.* 1▸ (persuade) **~ sb. to do sth.** jmdn. dazu bringen, etw. zu tun 2▸ (bring about) hervorrufen; verursachen, führen zu ‹*Krankheit*› 3▸ (Med.) einleiten ‹*Wehen, Geburt*›; herbeiführen ‹*Schlaf*› 4▸ (Electr., Phys., Philos.) induzieren

inducement /ɪnˈdjuːsmənt/ *n.* (incentive) Anreiz, *der;* **as an added ~:** als besonderer Anreiz *od.* Ansporn; **no ~ would persuade her to give up her home** kein noch so verlockendes Angebot könnte sie dazu bewegen, ihr Zuhause aufzugeben

induct /ɪnˈdʌkt/ *v.t.* 1▸ einführen (**to** in + *Akk.*) 2▸ (Amer. Mil.) einziehen; einberufen

inductance /ɪnˈdʌktəns/ *n.* (Electr.) Induktanz, *die*

inductee /ɪndʌkˈtiː/ *n.* (Amer. Mil.) Einberufene, *der/die*

induction /ɪnˈdʌkʃn/ *n.* 1▸ (formal introduction) Amtseinführung, *die* 2▸ (initiation) Einführung, *die* (**into** in + *Akk.*); **~ course** Einführungskurs, der **3** (Med.) Einleitung, *die;* (of sleep) Herbeiführen, *das* **4** (Electr., Phys., Math., Philos.) Induktion, *die* **5** (Amer. Mil.) Einberufung, *die*

induction: ~ coil *n.* (Electr.) Induktionsspule, *die;* **~ heating** *n.* Induktionsheizung, *die*

inductive /ɪnˈdʌktɪv/ *adj.*, **inductively** /ɪnˈdʌktɪvlɪ/ *adv.* (Electr., Phys., Math., Logic) induktiv

indue ▸ **endue**

indulge /ɪnˈdʌldʒ/

A *v.t.* **1** (yield to) nachgeben (+ *Dat.*) ‹*Wunsch, Verlangen, Verlockung*›; frönen (geh.) (+ *Dat.*) ‹*Leidenschaft, Neigung*› **2** (please) verwöhnen; **~ sb. in sth.** jmdm. in etw. (*Dat.*) nachgeben; **~ oneself in** schwelgen in (geh.) (+ *Dat.*); sich gütlich tun an (+ *Dat.*) ‹*Speisen, Leckereien*›

B *v.i.* **1** (allow oneself pleasure) **~ in** frönen (geh.) (+ *Dat.*) ‹*Leidenschaft, Neigung*›; sich gütlich tun an (+ *Dat.*) ‹*Speisen, Leckereien*› **2** (coll.: take alcoholic drink) sich (*Dat.*) einen genehmigen (ugs.); **I'd better not ~:** ich halte mich besser zurück

indulgence /ɪnˈdʌldʒəns/ *n.* **1** Nachsicht, *die;* (humouring) Nachgiebigkeit, *die* (**with** gegenüber) **2** **constant ~ in bad habits** ständiges Nachgeben gegenüber schlechten Gewohnheiten **3** (thing indulged in) Luxus, *der* **4** (privilege) Vorrecht, *das* **5** (Relig. Hist.: remission) Ablass, *der*

indulgent /ɪnˈdʌldʒənt/ *adj.* nachsichtig (**with, to[wards]** gegenüber); (to oneself) [zu] nachgiebig; **she's so ~ with that dog of hers** sie verhätschelt ihren Hund so sehr

indulgently /ɪnˈdʌldʒəntlɪ/ *adv.* nachsichtig

industrial /ɪnˈdʌstrɪəl/ *adj.* **1** industriell; betrieblich ‹*Ausbildung, Forschung*›; Arbeits‹*unfall, -medizin, -psychologie*› **2** (intended for industry) Industrie‹*alkohol, -diamant usw.*› **3** (characterized by industry) industrialisiert; **the ~ nations** die Industrienationen. *see also* **archaeology; estate 2**

industrial: ~ 'action *n.* Arbeitskampfmaßnahmen *Pl.*; **take ~ action** in den Ausstand treten; **~ area** *n.* Industriegebiet, *das;* **~ di'sease** *n.* Berufskrankheit, *die;* **~ dispute** *n.* Arbeitskonflikt, *der;* **~ 'espionage** *n.* Industriespionage, *die;* **~ estate** *n.* Industriegebiet, *das;* **~ exhibition** *n.* Industrieausstellung, *die;* **~ 'injury** *n.* Arbeitsverletzung, *die*

industrialisation, industrialise ▸ **industrializ-**

industrialist /ɪnˈdʌstrɪəlɪst/ *n.* Industrielle, *der/die*

industrialization /ɪndʌstrɪəlaɪˈzeɪʃn/ *n.* Industrialisierung, *die*

industrialize /ɪnˈdʌstrɪəlaɪz/ *v.i. & t.* industrialisieren

industrially /ɪnˈdʌstrɪəlɪ/ *adv.* industriell

industrial: ~ park *n.* Industriegebiet, *das;* **~ plant** *n.* Industrieanlage, *die;* **~ re'lations** *n. pl.* Industrialrelations *Pl.* (*Wirtsch.*); *Beziehungen zwischen Arbeitgebern und Arbeitern;* **I~ Revo'lution** *n.* (Hist.) industrielle Revolution; **~ town** *n.* Industriestadt, *die;* **~ tribunal** *n.* Arbeitsgericht, *das;* **~ un'rest** *n.* Unruhe in der Arbeitnehmerschaft; **~ 'waste** *n.* Industriemüll, *der;* **~ wastes** Industrieabfälle *Pl.*

industrious /ɪnˈdʌstrɪəs/ *adj.* fleißig; (busy) emsig

industriously /ɪnˈdʌstrɪəslɪ/ *adv.* fleißig; (busily) emsig

industry /ˈɪndəstrɪ/ *n.* **1** Industrie, *die;* **several industries** mehrere Industriezweige; **steel/coal ~:** Stahl-/Kohleindustrie, *die;* **the nation's ~:** die Industrie des Landes; **incentives to ~:** Maßnahmen zur Förderung des industriellen Wachstums; **the leaders of ~:** die Industriebosse (ugs.); die Industriekapitäne; **~ is thriving** die Industrie blüht; **his experience of ~:** seine Erfahrungen auf dem industriellen Sektor; **the Shakespeare/abortion ~** (coll.) die Vermarktung Shakespeares/das Geschäft mit der Abtreibung **2** ▸ **industrious**: Fleiß, *der;* Emsigkeit, *die*

inebriated /ɪˈniːbrɪeɪtɪd/ *adj.* **1** (drunk) betrunken **2** (fig.) berauscht (**with** von); trunken (geh.) (**with** von, vor + *Dat.*)

inebriation /iniːbrɪˈeɪʃn/ *n., no pl.* Betrunkenheit, *die*

inedible /ɪnˈedɪbl/ *adj.* ungenießbar

ineducable /ɪnˈedjʊkəbl/ *adj.* lernunfähig

ineffable /ɪnˈefəbl/ *adj.* unbeschreiblich

ineffective /ɪnɪˈfektɪv/ *adj.* **1** unwirksam; ineffektiv; fruchtlos ‹*Anstrengung, Versuch*›; ineffizient ‹*Produktionsmethoden*›; wirkungslos ‹*Argument*› **2** (inefficient) untauglich **3** (lacking artistic effect) reizlos

ineffectively /ɪnɪˈfektɪvlɪ/ *adv.* unwirksam; ineffektiv

ineffectiveness /ɪnɪˈfektɪvnɪs/ *n., no pl.* ▸ **ineffective**: Unwirksamkeit, *die;* Ineffizienz, *die;* Fruchtlosigkeit, *die;* Wirkungslosigkeit, *die;* Untauglichkeit, *die;* Reizlosigkeit, *die*

ineffectual /ɪnɪˈfektjʊəl/ *adj.* unwirksam; ineffektiv; fruchtlos ‹*Versuch, Bemühung*›; ineffizient ‹*Methode, Person*›

ineffectually /ɪnɪˈfektjʊəlɪ/ *adv.* vergebens; ohne Aussagekraft ‹*schreiben*›

inefficacious /ɪnefɪˈkeɪʃəs/ *adj.* unwirksam; wirkungslos

inefficacy /ɪnˈefɪkəsɪ/ *n., no pl.* (of measures) Unwirksamkeit, *die;* Wirkungslosigkeit, *die*

inefficiency /ɪnɪˈfɪʃənsɪ/ *n.* Ineffizienz, *die;* (incapability) Unfähigkeit, *die*

inefficient /ɪnɪˈfɪʃənt/ *adj.* ineffizient; (incapable) unfähig; **the worker/machine is ~:** der Arbeiter/die Maschine leistet nicht genug

inefficiently /ɪnɪˈfɪʃəntlɪ/ *adv.* ineffizient; **do one's job too ~:** zu wenig leisten

inelastic /ɪnɪˈlæstɪk, ɪnɪˈlɑːstɪk/ *adj.* **1** (not elastic) unelastisch **2** (unadaptable) nicht flexibel

inelegance /ɪnˈelɪgəns/ *n., no pl.* **1** (of dress) Mangel an Eleganz; (of gestures, movements, gait) Schwerfälligkeit, *die* **2** (lack of refinement, polish) Ungeschliffenheit, *die* (abwertend)

inelegant /ɪnˈelɪgənt/ *adj.* **1** unelegant; schwerfällig ‹*Bewegung, Gang*› **2** (unrefined, unpolished) ungeschliffen (abwertend)

inelegantly /ɪnˈelɪgəntlɪ/ *adv.* **1** unelegant; schwerfällig ‹*sich bewegen*› **2** (without refinement or polish) ungeschliffen (abwertend)

ineligible /ɪnˈelɪdʒɪbl/ *adj.* **be ~ for** nicht infrage kommen für ‹*Beförderung, Position, Mannschaft*›; nicht berechtigt sein zu ‹*Leistungen des Staats usw.*›; **be ~ for a pension** nicht pensionsberechtigt sein

ineluctable /ɪnɪˈlʌktəbl/ *adj.* (literary) unausweichlich; unentrinnbar (geh.) ‹*Schicksal*›

inept /ɪˈnept/ *adj.* **1** (unskilful) ungeschickt; (clumsy) unbeholfen **2** (inappropriate) unangemessen, unpassend ‹*Vergleich*›; unpassend, unangebracht ‹*Bemerkung, Eingreifen*› **3** (foolish) albern

ineptitude /ɪˈneptɪtjuːd/ *n., no pl.* **1** (unskilfulness) Ungeschicktheit, *die;* (clumsiness) Unbeholfenheit, *die* **2** (inappropriateness) (of comparison) Unangemessenheit, *die;* (of remark, intervention) Unangebrachtheit, *die* **3** (foolishness) Albernheit, *die*

ineptly /ɪˈneptlɪ/ *adv.* **1** (unskilfully) ungeschickt; (clumsily) unbeholfen **2** (inappropriately) **intervene ~:** in unangebrachter Weise eingreifen **3** (foolishly) albern

ineptness ▸ **ineptitude**

inequable /ɪnˈekwəbl/ *adj.* **1** (not uniform) ungleichmäßig **2** (not fair) ungleich

inequality /ɪnɪˈkwɒlɪtɪ/ *n.* **1** (lack of equality) Ungleichheit, *die;* **great inequalities between rich and poor** große Ungleichheit zwischen arm und reich; **educational ~:** Ungleichheit der Bildungschancen; **the inequalities in income** die ungleiche Einkommensverteilung **2** (variableness) Veränderlichkeit, *die;* (in time) Unbeständigkeit, *die* **3** (irregularity) Unebenheit, *die* **4** (Math.) Ungleichheit, *die;* (expression) Ungleichung, *die*

inequitable /ɪnˈekwɪtəbl/ *adj.*, **inequitably** /ɪnˈekwɪtəblɪ/ *adv.* ungerecht

inequity /ɪnˈekwɪtɪ/ *n.* Ungerechtigkeit, *die*

ineradicable /ɪnɪˈrædɪkəbl/ *adj.* unausrottbar ‹*Vorurteil, Aberglaube*›

inert /ɪˈnɜːt/ *adj.* **1** reglos; (sluggish) träge; (passive) untätig **2** (Chem.: neutral) inert

inert 'gas *n.* (Chem.) Edelgas, *das*

inertia /ɪˈnɜːʃə, ɪˈnɜːʃjə/ *n.* (also Phys.) Trägheit, *die; see also* **moment 3**

inertial /ɪˈnɜːʃl/ *adj.* **1** (esp. Phys.) Trägheits- **2** (performed automatically) Automatik-

inertia: ~ reel *n.* Aufrollautomatik, *die;* **~ reel seat belt** Automatikgurt, *der;* **~ selling** *n.* unverlangte Warenzusendung

inertly /ɪˈnɜːtlɪ/ *adv.* reglos; (sluggishly) träge; (passively) untätig

inescapable /ɪnɪˈskeɪpəbl/ *adj.* unausweichlich ‹*Schlussfolgerung, Logik*›; **the facts were ~:** man konnte sich den Tatsachen nicht entziehen

inessential /ɪnɪˈsenʃl/

A *adj.* (not necessary) unwesentlich; (dispensable) entbehrlich

B *n.* Nebensächlichkeit, *die*

inestimable /ɪnˈestɪməbl/ *adj.* unschätzbar

inevitability /ɪnevɪtəˈbɪlɪtɪ/ *n., no pl.* Unvermeidlichkeit, *die;* (of fate, event) Unabwendbarkeit, *die*

inevitable /ɪnˈevɪtəbl/ *adj.* unvermeidlich; unabwendbar ‹*Ereignis, Krieg, Schicksal*›; zwangsläufig ‹*Ergebnis, Folge*›; **bow to the ~:** sich in das Unvermeidliche fügen

inevitably /ɪnˈevɪtəblɪ/ *adv.* zwangsläufig

inexact /ɪnɪgˈzækt/ *adj.* ungenau

inexactitude /ɪnɪgˈzæktɪtjuːd/ ▸ **inexactness**

inexactly /ɪnɪgˈzæktlɪ/ *adv.* ungenau

inexactness /ɪnɪgˈzæktnɪs/ *n.* Ungenauigkeit, *die*

inexcusable /ɪnɪkˈskjuːzəbl/ *adj.*, **inexcusably** /ɪnɪkˈskjuːzəblɪ/ *adv.* unverzeihlich; unentschuldbar

inexhaustible /ɪnɪgˈzɔːstɪbl/ *adj.* unerschöpflich ‹*Reserven, Quelle, Energie*›; unverwüstlich ‹*Person*›

inexorable /ɪnˈeksərəbl/ *adj.*, **inexorably** /ɪnˈeksərəblɪ/ *adv.* unerbittlich

inexpediency /ɪnɪkˈspiːdɪənsɪ/ *n., no pl.* Unklugheit, *die;* (of plan, measure) Ungeeignetheit, *die*

inexpedient /ɪnɪkˈspiːdɪənt/ *adj.* unklug ‹*Entscheidung, Politik*›; ungeeignet ‹*Plan, Maßnahme*›; **she thought it somewhat ~ to reveal the names** es erschien ihr wenig ratsam, die Namen preiszugeben

inexpensive /ɪnɪkˈspensɪv/ *adj.* preisgünstig; **the car is ~ to run** der Wagen ist sparsam im Verbrauch

inexpensively /ɪnɪkˈspensɪvlɪ/ *adv.* günstig ‹*kaufen*›; unaufwendig ‹*leben*›; ohne viel Geld ‹*einrichten*›

inexperience /ɪnɪkˈspɪərɪəns/ *n.* Unerfahrenheit, *die;* Mangel an Erfahrung; **his ~ with this machine** seine mangelnde Vertrautheit mit dieser Maschine

inexperienced /ɪnɪkˈspɪərɪənst/ *adj.* unerfahren; **~ at doing sth.** wenig damit vertraut, etw. zu tun; **~ in sth.** wenig vertraut mit etw.

inexpert /ɪnˈekspɜːt/ *adj.* unerfahren; (unskilled) ungeschickt; unsachgemäß ‹*Behandlung*›

inexpertly /ɪnˈekspɜːtlɪ/ *adv.* ungeschickt; unsachgemäß ‹*behandeln*›

inexplicable /ɪnekˈsplɪkəbl/ *adj.* unerklärlich

inexplicably /ɪnekˈsplɪkəblɪ/ *adv.* (*with adj.*) unerklärlich; (*with verb*) unerklärlicherweise

inexpressible /ɪnɪkˈspresɪbl/ *adj.*, **inexpressibly** /ɪnɪkˈspresɪblɪ/ *adv.* unbeschreiblich

inextinguishable /ɪnɪkˈstɪŋgwɪʃəbl/ *adj.* nicht löschbar ‹*Feuer, Flamme*›; unauslöschlich ‹*Liebe, Hoffnung, Sehnsucht, Verlangen*›

in extremis /ɪn ekˈstriːmɪs/ *adv.* **1** (in great difficulties) in äußerster Not **2** (at point of death) in extremis (Med.); **be ~:** im Sterben liegen

inextricable /ɪnˈekstrɪkəbl/ *adj.* **1** (that cannot be unravelled) unentwirrbar **2** unüberschaubar ‹*Durcheinander*›

inextricably /ɪn'ekstrɪkəblɪ/ *adv.* **become ~ entangled** sich vollkommen verheddern (ugs.); **[be] ~ linked** untrennbar verbunden [sein]

INF *abbr.* **= intermediate-range nuclear force** Mittelstrecken-Nuklearkräfte *Pl.*

infallibility /ɪnfælɪ'bɪlɪtɪ/ *n., no pl.* Unfehlbarkeit, *die;* **Papal I~:** päpstliche Unfehlbarkeit; Infallibilität, *die* (kath. Kirche)

infallible /ɪn'fælɪbl/ *adj.*, **infallibly** /ɪn'fælɪblɪ/ *adv.* unfehlbar

infamous /'ɪnfəməs/ *adj.* 1 berüchtigt; **of ~ repute** (literary) verrufen 2 (wicked) infam; niederträchtig

infamy /'ɪnfəmɪ/ *n.* 1 Verrufenheit, *die* 2 (wickedness) Infamie, *die;* Niederträchtigkeit, *die*

infancy /'ɪnfənsɪ/ *n.* 1 frühe Kindheit 2 (fig.: early state) Frühzeit, *die;* **be in its ~:** noch in den Anfängen *od.* Kinderschuhen stecken 3 (Law) Minderjährigkeit, *die*

infant /'ɪnfənt/
A *n.* 1 kleines Kind; **teach ~s** ≈ Vorschulklassen unterrichten 2 (Law) Minderjährige, *der/die*
B *adj.* 1 kindlich 2 (fig.: not developed) in den Anfängen steckend

infanta /ɪn'fæntə/ *n.* (Hist.) Infantin, *die*

infanticide /ɪn'fæntɪsaɪd/ *n.* Kindesmord, *der;* (custom) Kindestötung, *die*

infantile /'ɪnfəntaɪl/ *adj.* 1 (relating to infancy) kindlich 2 (childish) kindisch (abwertend); infantil (abwertend)

infant: ~ mor'tality *n.* Säuglingssterblichkeit, *die;* **~ 'prodigy** *n.* Wunderkind, *das*

infantry /'ɪnfəntrɪ/ *n. constr. as sing. or pl.* Infanterie, *die*

infantryman /'ɪnfəntrɪmən/ *n., pl.* **infantrymen** /'ɪnfəntrɪmən/ Infanterist, *der*

'infant school *n.* (Brit.) ≈ Vorschule, *die; Grundschule für die ersten beiden Jahrgänge*

> **infant school**
>
> Eine Grundschule in Großbritannien, die für die ersten drei Jahre der Schulausbildung sorgt. Schulpflichtiges Alter in Großbritannien ist fünf. Oft ist die *infant school* Teil einer **primary school**, zusammen mit einer **junior school**, die Kinder bis zu ihrem 11. Lebensjahr betreut.

infarction /ɪn'fɑ:kʃn/ *n.* (Med.) Infarkt, *der*

infatuated /ɪn'fætjʊeɪtɪd/ *adj.* betört (geh.); verzaubert; **be ~ with sb./oneself** in jmdn./sich selbst vernarrt sein

infatuation /ɪnfætjʊ'eɪʃn/ *n.* Vernarrtheit, *die* (**with** in + *Akk.*)

infect /ɪn'fekt/ *v.t.* 1 (contaminate) verseuchen 2 (affect with disease) infizieren (Med.); **~ sb. with sth.** jmdn. mit etw. infizieren *od.* anstecken; **the wound became ~ed** die Wunde entzündete sich; **be ~ed with sth.** (fig.) von etw. infiziert sein 3 (imbue) anstecken

infection /ɪn'fekʃn/ *n.* ▸❶ **p. 1231** Infektion, *die;* **throat/ear/eye ~:** Hals-/Ohren-/Augenentzündung, *die*

infectious /ɪn'fekʃəs/ *adj.* 1 ▸❶ **p. 1231** infektiös (Med.), ansteckend ‹*Krankheit*›; **be ~** ‹*Person:*› eine ansteckende Krankheit haben; ansteckend sein (ugs.) 2 (fig.) ansteckend ‹*Heiterkeit, Begeisterung, Lachen*›

infectiously /ɪn'fekʃəslɪ/ *adv.* ansteckend ‹*lachen usw.*›

infectiousness /ɪn'fekʃəsnɪs/ *n., no pl.* 1 Infektiosität, *die* (Med.); Ansteckungsfähigkeit, *die* 2 (fig.) **the ~ of her enthusiasm** ihre ansteckend wirkende *od.* mitreißende Begeisterung

infelicitous /ɪnfɪ'lɪsɪtəs/ *adj.*, **infelicitously** /ɪnfɪ'lɪsɪtəslɪ/ *adv.* unangebracht

infelicity /ɪnfɪ'lɪsɪtɪ/ *n.* Unangebrachtheit, *die;* **infelicities of style** stilistische Ungeschicklichkeiten

infer /ɪn'fɜ:(r)/ *v.t.*, **-rr-** schließen (**from** aus); erschließen ‹*Voraussetzung*›; gewinnen ‹*Kenntnisse*›; ziehen ‹*Schlussfolgerung*›

inference /'ɪnfərəns/ *n.* [Schluss]folgerung, *die;* **make ~s** [Schluss]folgerungen ableiten *od.* ziehen; **by ~:** schlussfolgernd

inferential /ɪnfə'renʃl/ *adj.* 1 auf [Schluss]folgerungen beruhend; schlussfolgernd 2 (deduced by inference) gefolgert

inferior /ɪn'fɪərɪə(r)/
A *adj.* 1 (of lower quality) minderwertig ‹*Ware*›; minder… ‹*Qualität*›; gering ‹*Kenntnis*›; unter…, nieder… ‹*Klasse, Kaste*›; unterlegen ‹*Gegner*›; **~ to sth.** schlechter als etw.; **feel ~:** Minderwertigkeitsgefühle haben; **feel ~ to sb.** sich jmdm. gegenüber unterlegen fühlen 2 (having lower rank) untergeordnet (**to** *Dat.*) 3 (Printing) tiefgestellt ‹*Buchstabe, Zahl*›
B *n.* Untergebene, *der/die;* **his social ~s** die gesellschaftlich unter ihm Stehenden

inferiority /ɪnfɪərɪ'ɒrɪtɪ/ *n., no pl.* Unterlegenheit, *die* (**to** gegenüber); (of goods) schlechtere Qualität

inferi'ority complex *n.* (Psych.) Minderwertigkeitskomplex, *der*

infernal /ɪn'fɜ:nl/ *adj.* 1 (of hell) höllisch; ‹*Regionen, Geister, Götter*› der Unterwelt 2 (hellish) teuflisch 3 (coll.: detestable) verdammt (salopp)

infernally /ɪn'fɜ:nəlɪ/ *adv.* (coll.) verdammt; **he is too ~ clever for me** er ist, verdammt noch mal, zu clever für mich (ugs.)

inferno /ɪn'fɜ:nəʊ/ *n., pl.* **~s** Inferno, *das;* **a blazing ~:** ein flammendes Inferno; **the ~ of the blazing house** das Flammenmeer des brennenden Hauses

infertile /ɪn'fɜ:taɪl/ *adj.* unfruchtbar

infertility /ɪnfɜ:'tɪlɪtɪ/ *n., no pl.* Unfruchtbarkeit, *die*

infer'tility clinic *n.* Fertilitätsklinik, *die*

infest /ɪn'fest/ *v.t.* ‹*Ungeziefer, Schädlinge:*› befallen; ‹*Unkraut:*› überwuchern; (fig.) heimsuchen; **~ed with** befallen/überwuchert/heimgesucht von

infestation /ɪnfes'teɪʃn/ *n.* **~ of rats/insects** Ratten-/Insektenplage, *die*

infidel /'ɪnfɪdəl/ *n.* (Relig. Hist.) Ungläubige, *der/die*

infidelity /ɪnfɪ'delɪtɪ/ *n.* Untreue, *die* (**to** gegenüber); **infidelities** (to lover, wife, husband) Seitensprünge

'infighting *n.* 1 (in organization) interne Machtkämpfe 2 (Boxing) Nahkampf, *der*

infiltrate /'ɪnfɪltreɪt/
A *v.t.* 1 (penetrate into) infiltrieren ‹*feindliche Reihen*›; unterwandern ‹*Partei, Organisation*› 2 (cause to enter) einschleusen ‹*Agenten*› 3 (esp. Biol., Med.: pass into, permeate) infiltrieren
B *v.i.* 1 (penetrate) einsickern (fig.); **~ into** unterwandern ‹*Partei, Organisation*›; infiltrieren ‹*feindliche Reihen*› 2 ‹*Flüssigkeit:*› eindringen

infiltration /ɪnfɪl'treɪʃn/ *n.* 1 (penetration) (of enemy lines) Infiltration, *die;* (of party, organization) Unterwanderung, *die* (**into** *Gen.*) 2 (of spies, agents) Einschleusung, *die* 3 (of liquid) Einsickern, *das*

infiltrator /'ɪnfɪltreɪtə(r)/ *n.* Eindringling, *der;* (of party, organization) Unterwanderer, *der*

infinite /'ɪnfɪnɪt/ *adj.* 1 (endless) unendlich; **I don't have an ~ amount of time/money** ich habe nicht unbegrenzt Zeit/keine unbegrenzten Mittel 2 (very great) ungeheuer; unendlich groß 3 (very many) endlos; **his problems seemed to be ~:** seine Probleme schienen kein Ende zu nehmen 4 (Math.) unendlich

infinitely /'ɪnfɪnɪtlɪ/ *adv.* 1 (endlessly) unendlich ‹*mitfühlend, dumm usw.*›; endlos ‹*sich erstrecken, teilbar*› 2 (vastly) unendlich; unendlich viel ‹*weiser, stärker, besser*›

infinitesimal /ɪnfɪnɪ'tesɪml/ *adj.* 1 (Math.) infinitesimal; *see also* **calculus 1** 2 (very small) äußerst gering; winzig ‹*Menge*›; **be of ~ value** so gut wie wertlos sein

infinitesimally *adv.* um eine Winzigkeit; **~ small** winzig klein

infinitive /ɪn'fɪnɪtɪv/ (Ling.)
A *n.* Infinitiv, *der*
B *adj.* Infinitiv-

infinity /ɪn'fɪnɪtɪ/ *n.* 1 (boundlessness, boundless extent) Unendlichkeit, *die* 2 (indefinite amount) **an ~ of [stars *etc.*]** unendlich viele [Sterne *usw.*] 3 (Geom.: infinite distance) **at ~:** im Unendlichen ‹*sich schneiden*›; **focus on ~** (Photog.) auf unendlich stellen 4 (Math.: infinite quantity) unendliche Menge

infirm /ɪn'fɜ:m/ *adj.* 1 (weak) gebrechlich 2 (irresolute) schwach

infirmary /ɪn'fɜ:mərɪ/ *n.* 1 (hospital) Krankenhaus, *das* 2 (sick-quarters) Krankenstation, *die;* (room) Krankenzimmer, *das*

infirmity /ɪn'fɜ:mɪtɪ/ *n.* 1 *no pl.* (feebleness) Gebrechlichkeit, *die* 2 (malady) Gebrechen, *das* (geh.) 3 (weakness of character) Schwäche, *die*

in flagrante [delicto] /ɪn flæ'græntɪ (de 'lɪktəʊ)/ *adv.* in flagranti

inflame /ɪn'fleɪm/ *v.t.* 1 (excite) entflammen (geh.); **~d with patriotic fever** in patriotischem Fieber entbrannt 2 (aggravate) schüren ‹*Feindschaft, Hass*› 3 (Med.) **become/be ~d** ‹*Auge, Wunde:*› sich entzünden/entzündet sein 4 (make hot) erhitzen; **his face was ~d with anger/passion** sein Gesicht glühte vor Zorn/Leidenschaft

inflammability /ɪnflæmə'bɪlɪtɪ/ *n., no pl.* Feuergefährlichkeit, *die;* Entflammbarkeit, *die* (Chemie)

inflammable /ɪn'flæməbl/ *adj.* 1 (easily set on fire) feuergefährlich; leicht entzündlich *od.* entflammbar; **'highly ~'** „feuergefährlich" 2 explosiv ‹*Situation*›

inflammation /ɪnflə'meɪʃn/ *n.* 1 (Med.) Entzündung, *die;* Inflammation, *die* (fachspr.) 2 (fig.: of feeling etc.) Entfachung, *die* (geh.)

inflammatory /ɪn'flæmətərɪ/ *adj.* 1 aufrührerisch; **an ~ speech** eine Hetzrede (abwertend) 2 (Med.) entzündlich

inflatable /ɪn'fleɪtəbl/
A *adj.* aufblasbar; **~ dinghy** Schlauchboot, *das*
B *n.* 1 (boat) Schlauchboot, *das* 2 (mattress) Luftmatratze, *die*

inflate /ɪn'fleɪt/ *v.t.* 1 (blow up) aufblasen; (with pump) aufpumpen 2 (Econ.) in die Höhe treiben ‹*Preise, Kosten*›; inflationieren ‹*Währung*›; **~ the economy** Inflationspolitik betreiben 3 (fig.: puff up) **be ~d with pride** von Stolz geschwellt sein

inflated /ɪn'fleɪtɪd/ *adj.* (lit or fig.) aufgeblasen; geschwollen ‹*Stil*›; **have an ~ opinion of oneself** aufgeblasen sein (ugs. abwertend); **have an ~ ego** ein übertriebenes Selbstbewusstsein haben

inflation /ɪn'fleɪʃn/ *n.* 1 Aufblasen, *das;* (with pump) Aufpumpen, *das* 2 (Econ.) Inflation, *die*

inflationary /ɪn'fleɪʃənərɪ/ *adj.* (Econ.) inflationär; **~ policies** Inflationspolitik, *die*

in'flation-proofed *adj.* mit Inflationsausgleich *nachgestellt*

inflect /ɪn'flekt/ *v.t.* 1 (Ling.) flektieren; beugen 2 (change pitch) modulieren ‹*Stimme*›

inflection ▸ **inflexion**

inflectional ▸ **inflexional**

inflective /ɪn'flektɪv/ ▸ **inflexional**

inflexibility /ɪnfleksɪ'bɪlɪtɪ/ *n., no pl.* 1 (stiffness) Unbiegsamkeit, *die* 2 (obstinacy) [geistige] Unbeweglichkeit; (lack of versatility) mangelnde Flexibilität

inflexible /ɪn'fleksɪbl/ *adj.* 1 (stiff) unbiegsam 2 (obstinate) [geistig] unbeweglich ‹*Person*›; wenig flexibel ‹*Einstellung, Meinung*›

inflexion /ɪn'flekʃn/ *n.* (Brit.) 1 (in voice) Tonfall, *der;* **a rising ~:** ein Heben der Stimme 2 (bending) Biegung, *die* 3 (Ling.) (form) Flexionsform, *die;* (suffix) Flexionsendung, *die*

inflexional /ɪn'flekʃənl/ *adj.* (Brit. Ling.) flektierend ‹*Sprache*›; **~ ending** Flexionsendung, *die*

inflict /ɪn'flɪkt/ *v.t.* zufügen ‹*Leid, Schmerzen*›, beibringen ‹*Wunde*›, versetzen ‹*Schlag*› (**on** *Dat.*); **~ punishment [on sb.]** eine Strafe [über jmdn.] verhängen; [jmdm.] eine Strafe auferlegen (geh.); **~ oneself** *or* **one's company on sb.** sich jmdm. aufdrängen

infliction /ɪn'flɪkʃn/ *n.:* ▸ **inflict**: Zufügen, *das;* Beibringen, *das;* Versetzen, *das;* Verhängung, *die*

'in-flight *adj.* Bord‹*verpflegung, -programm*›

inflorescence /ɪnflə'resəns/ *n.* (Bot.) Blütenstand, *der*

'inflow *n.* Zustrom, *der*

influence /ˈɪnflʊəns/
A *n.* (also thing, person) Einfluss, *der;* **exercise ~:** Einfluss ausüben (**over** auf + *Akk.*); **owe sth. to ~:** etw. seinen guten Beziehungen verdanken; **have ~ with/over sb.** Einfluss bei jmdm./auf jmdn. haben; **use one's ~ to do sth.** seinen Einfluss nutzen, um etw. zu tun; **you have to have ~ to get a job** man muss Beziehungen haben, um eine Stelle zu bekommen; **a person of ~:** eine einflussreiche Persönlichkeit; **be a good/bad/major ~ [on sb.]** einen guten/schlechten/bedeutenden Einfluss [auf jmdn.] ausüben; **under the ~ of alcohol** unter Alkoholeinfluss; **be under the ~** (coll.) betrunken sein; **steal a car while under the ~** (coll.) in betrunkenem Zustand ein Auto stehlen
B *v.t.* beeinflussen; **be too easily ~d** sich zu leicht beeinflussen lassen

influential /ɪnflʊˈenʃl/ *adj.* einflussreich ‹*Person*›; **be ~ in sb.'s decision/on sb.'s career** jmdn. in seiner Entscheidung beeinflussen/jmds. Karriere beeinflussen; **have been ~ in the successful outcome of sth.** den erfolgreichen Ausgang einer Sache (*Gen.*) beeinflusst haben

influenza /ɪnflʊˈenzə/ *n.* ▸**ⓘ p. 1231** Grippe, *die; see also* **gastric influenza**

influx /ˈɪnflʌks/ *n.* Zustrom, *der*

info /ˈɪnfəʊ/ *n., no pl.* (coll.) Infos *Pl.* (ugs.)

infomercial /ɪnfəʊˈmɜːʃl/ *n.* Infomercial, *das*

inform /ɪnˈfɔːm/
A *n.* **1** informieren (**of, about** über + *Akk.*); **I am pleased to ~ you that ...:** ich freue mich, Ihnen mitteilen zu können, dass ...; **keep sb./oneself ~ed** jmdn./sich auf dem Laufenden halten; **he is not very well ~ed** er ist nicht besonders gut informiert; **why wasn't I ~ed?** warum wurde ich nicht [darüber] informiert? **2** (animate, inspire) durchdringen **3** (give character or essence to) prägen
B *v.i.* **~ against** *or* **on sb.** jmdn. anzeigen *od.* (abwertend) denunzieren (**to** bei)

informal /ɪnˈfɔːml/ *adj.* **1** (without formality) zwanglos; ungezwungen ‹*Ton, Sprache*›; leger ‹*Kleidungsstück*›; **'dress: ~'** „keine festliche Garderobe" **2** (unofficial) informell ‹*Gespräch, Treffen*›

informality /ɪnfɔːˈmælɪtɪ/ *n. no pl.* Zwanglosigkeit, *die;* Ungezwungenheit, *die*

informally /ɪnˈfɔːməlɪ/ *adv.* **1** (casually) zwanglos; leger ‹*gekleidet*› **2** (unofficially) informell; **talks are proceeding ~:** die Gespräche laufen auf informeller Ebene

informant /ɪnˈfɔːmənt/ *n.* Informant, *der*/Informantin, *die;* Gewährsmann, *der*

informatics /ɪnfəˈmætɪks/ *n., no pl.* Informatik, *die*

information /ɪnfəˈmeɪʃn/ *n., no pl.no indef. art.* Informationen; **give ~ on sth.** Auskunft über etw. (*Akk.*) erteilen; **piece** *or* **bit of ~:** Information, *die;* **some/any ~:** einige/irgendwelche Informationen; **source of ~:** Informationsquelle, *die;* **where can we get hold of some ~?** wo können wir uns informieren?; wo können wir Auskunft bekommen?; **have ~ about sth.** über etw. (*Akk.*) informiert sein; **have no ~ on sb.** nichts über jmdn. wissen; **we have ~ that ...:** uns (*Dat.*) liegen Informationen [darüber] vor, dass ...; **for your ~:** zu Ihrer Information; (iron.) damit du Bescheid weißt!

information: ~ bureau, ~ centre *ns.* Auskunftsbüro, *das;* **~ desk** *n.* Informationsschalter, *der;* **~ economy** *n.* Informationswirtschaft, *die;* **~ explosion** *n.* Informationsflut, *die;* **~ highway** *n.* (Computing) Datenautobahn, *die;* **~ office** ▸ **~ bureau; ~ pack** *n.* Informationspaket, *das;* (folder etc.) Informationsmappe, *die;* (for journalists) Pressemappe, *die;* **~ retrieval** *n., no pl.* (Computing) Retrieval, *das; attrib.* **~ retrieval system** Retrievalsystem, *das;* **~ revolution** *n.* Informationsrevolution, *die;* **~ science** *n., no pl.* Informatik, *die;* **~ scientist** *n.* Informatiker, *der*/Informatikerin, *die;* **~ society** *n.* Informationsgesellschaft, *die;* **~ superhighway** *n.* (Computing) Datenautobahn, *die;* Datensuperhighway, *der;* **~ system** *n.* Informationssystem, *das;* **management ~ system** Managementinformationssystem, *das;* **~ technology** *n.* Informationstechnologie, *die;* Informationstechnik, *die;* **~ theory** *n.* Informationstheorie, *die*

informative /ɪnˈfɔːmətɪv/ *adj.* informativ; **not very ~:** nicht sehr aufschlussreich ‹*Dokument, Schriftstück*›; **he was not very ~ about his qualifications** er war nicht sehr mitteilsam, was seine Qualifikationen anbelangte

informed /ɪnˈfɔːmd/ *adj.* **1** informiert; fundiert ‹*Schätzung*›; **very ~:** sehr gut informiert; *see also* **ill-informed; well-informed** **2** (educated) kultiviert; **~ opinion suggests that ...:** Kundige meinen, dass ...

informer /ɪnˈfɔːmə(r)/ *n.* Denunziant, *der*/Denunziantin, *die* (abwertend); Informant, *der*/Informantin, *die;* **police ~:** Polizeispitzel, *der* (abwertend)

infotainment /ɪnfəʊˈteɪnmənt/ *n., no pl.* Infotainment, *das*

infotech /ˈɪnfəʊtek/ *n., no pl.* Infotechnik, *die; attrib.* IT-

infraction /ɪnˈfrækʃn/ *n.* Übertretung, *die;* Regelverstoß, *der* (Sport)

infra dig. /ɪnfrəˈdɪɡ/ *pred. adj.* (coll.) unter meiner/seiner *usw.* Würde

infra-red /ɪnfrəˈred/ *adj.* **1** infrarot **2** (using ~ radiation) Infrarot-

infrasound /ˈɪnfrəsaʊnd/ *n., no pl.* Infraschall, *der*

infrastructure /ˈɪnfrəstrʌktʃə(r)/ *n.* Infrastruktur, *die*

infrequency /ɪnˈfriːkwənsɪ/ *n., no pl.* Seltenheit, *die*

infrequent /ɪnˈfriːkwənt/ *adj.* **1** (uncommon) selten **2** (sparse) vereinzelt

infrequently /ɪnˈfriːkwəntlɪ/ *adv.* selten

infringe /ɪnˈfrɪndʒ/
A *v.t.* verstoßen gegen
B *v.i.* **~ [up]on** verstoßen gegen ‹*Recht, Gesetz usw.*›; **~ upon sb.'s privacy** jmds. Privatsphäre verletzen

infringement /ɪnˈfrɪndʒmənt/ *n.* **1** (violation) Verstoß, *der* (**of** gegen); **~ of the contract** Vertragsverletzung, *die;* Vertragsbruch, *der* **2** (encroachment) Übergriff, *der* (**on** auf + *Akk.*); (on privacy) Eingriff, *der* (**on** in + *Akk.*)

infuriate /ɪnˈfjʊərɪeɪt/ *v.t.* wütend machen; **be ~d** wütend sein (**by** über + *Akk.*)

infuriating /ɪnˈfjʊərɪeɪtɪŋ/ *adj.* **she is an ~ person** sie kann einen zur Raserei bringen; **it is ~ when/that ...:** es ist wahnsinnig ärgerlich, wenn/dass ... (ugs.); **he has some ~ habits** er hat einige Angewohnheiten, die einen rasend machen können; **~ calmness/slowness** aufreizende Gelassenheit/Langsamkeit

infuriatingly /ɪnˈfjʊərɪeɪtɪŋlɪ/ *adv.* aufreizend ‹*gleichgültig, langsam*›

infuse /ɪnˈfjuːz/
A *v.t.* **1** (instil) **~ sth. into sb., ~ sb. with sth.** jmdm. etw. einflößen *od.* (geh.) eingeben; **~ new life into an ancient institution** eine altehrwürdige Institution mit neuem Leben erfüllen; **~ vitality into** mit Vitalität erfüllen; **be ~d with new hope** neue Hoffnung schöpfen **2** (steep) aufgießen ‹*Tee usw.*›
B *v.i.* ‹*Tee usw.:*› ziehen; **let the tea [stand to] ~:** den Tee ziehen lassen

infusion /ɪnˈfjuːʒn/ *n.* **1** (Med.) Infusion, *die;* **an ~ of new blood into the organization is essential** (fig.) die Organisation braucht dringend frisches Blut **2** (imparting) Einflößen, *das* **3** (steeping) Aufgießen, *das* **4** (liquid) Aufguss, *der*

ingenious /ɪnˈdʒiːnɪəs/ *adj.* **1** (resourceful) einfallsreich; (skilful) geschickt **2** (cleverly constructed) genial ‹*Methode, Idee*›; raffiniert ‹*Spielzeug, Werkzeug, Maschine*›

ingeniously /ɪnˈdʒiːnɪəslɪ/ *adv.* genial; raffiniert ‹*konstruiert*›

ingénue /ˈæʒemjuː/ *n.* unschuldiges junges Mädchen; (Theatre) Naive, *die*

ingenuity /ɪndʒɪˈnjuːɪtɪ/ *n., no pl.* **1** (resourcefulness) Einfallsreichtum, *der;* (skill) Geschicklichkeit, *die* **2** (cleverness of construction) Genialität, *die;* **a plan of some ~:** ein recht raffinierter Plan

ingenuous /ɪnˈdʒenjʊəs/ *adj.* **1** (frank) freimütig **2** (innocent) naiv; unschuldig ‹*Augen, Lächeln*›

ingenuously /ɪnˈdʒenjʊəslɪ/ *adv.* freimütig

ingest /ɪnˈdʒest/ *v.t.* (formal) aufnehmen

ingestion /ɪnˈdʒestʃn/ *n.* (formal) Aufnahme, *die;* **~ of food** Nahrungsaufnahme, *die*

inglenook /ˈɪŋɡlnʊk/ *n.* Kaminecke, *die*

inglorious /ɪnˈɡlɔːrɪəs/ *adj.* unrühmlich; schmählich (geh.) ‹*Niederlage*›

ingot /ˈɪŋɡət/ *n.* Ingot, *der* (Metall.)

ingrained /ˈɪnɡreɪnd, ɪnˈɡreɪnd/ *adj.* **1** (embedded) **the stain was deeply ~ in the fibres** der Fleck war tief in die Fasern eingedrungen; **hands ~ with dirt** stark verschmutzte Hände **2** (fig.) tief eingewurzelt ‹*Vorurteil usw.*› **3** (thorough) eingefleischt ‹*Skeptiker usw.*›

ingratiate /ɪnˈɡreɪʃɪeɪt/ *v. refl.* **~ oneself with sb.** sich bei jmdm. einschmeicheln

ingratiating /ɪnˈɡreɪʃɪeɪtɪŋ/ *adj.* schmeichlerisch

ingratitude /ɪnˈɡrætɪtjuːd/ *n., no pl.* Undankbarkeit, *die* (**to[wards]** gegenüber)

ingredient /ɪnˈɡriːdɪənt/ *n.* Zutat, *die;* Ingredienz, *die;* **the ~s of a successful marriage** (fig.) die Voraussetzungen für eine gute Ehe; **all the ~s of success** (fig.) alles, was man zum Erfolg braucht

'in-group *n.* Ingroup, *die* (Soziol.); Eigengruppe, *die* (Soziol.)

ingrowing /ˈɪnɡrəʊɪŋ/ *adj.* eingewachsen ‹*Zehennagel usw.*›

'ingrown *adj.* (Med.) eingewachsen

inhabit /ɪnˈhæbɪt/ *v.t.* bewohnen; **the region was ~ed by penguins/the Celts** in der Gegend lebten Pinguine/die Kelten; **a region ~ed by a rich flora** eine Gegend mit einer reichen Flora

inhabitable /ɪnˈhæbɪtəbl/ *adj.* bewohnbar

inhabitant /ɪnˈhæbɪtənt/ *n.* Bewohner, *der*/Bewohnerin, *die;* (of village etc. also) Einwohner, *der*/Einwohnerin, *die;* **that district has few ~s** in diesem Bezirk leben nur wenige Menschen

inhalant /ɪnˈheɪlənt/ *n.* (Med.) Inhalationsmittel, *das*

inhalation /ɪnhəˈleɪʃn/ *n.* (Med.) Inhalation, *die*

inhale /ɪnˈheɪl/
A *v.t.* (breathe in) einatmen; (take into the lungs) inhalieren (ugs.) ‹*Zigarettenrauch usw.*›; (Med.) inhalieren
B *v.i.* einatmen; (Med.) inhalieren; ‹*Raucher:*› inhalieren (ugs.), über die Lunge rauchen

inhaler /ɪnˈheɪlə(r)/ *n.* (Med.) Inhalationsapparat, *der*

inharmonious /ɪnhɑːˈməʊnɪəs/ *adj.* **1** disharmonisch; misstönend **2** (fig.) unharmonisch

inharmoniously /ɪnhɑːˈməʊnɪəslɪ/ *adv.* **1** disharmonisch **2** (fig.) unharmonisch

inherent /ɪnˈhɪərənt, ɪnˈherənt/ *adj.* (belonging by nature) innewohnend (geh.); natürlich ‹*Anmut, Eleganz*›; inhärent (Philos.); **our ~ indolence** die uns (*Dat.*) innewohnende Trägheit

inherently /ɪnˈhɪərəntlɪ, ɪnˈherəntlɪ/ *adv.* von Natur aus

inherit /ɪnˈherɪt/ *v.t.* erben

inheritable /ɪnˈherɪtəbl/ *adj.* erblich; **~ disease** Erbkrankheit, *die*

inheritance /ɪnˈherɪtəns/ *n.* **1** (what is inherited) Erbe, *das;* **come into one's ~:** sein Erbe antreten **2** *no pl.* (inheriting) Erbschaft, *die*

in'heritance tax *n.* Erbschaftssteuer, *die*

inhibit /ɪnˈhɪbɪt/ *v.t.* hemmen; **~ sb. from doing sth.** jmdn. daran hindern, etw. zu tun

inhibited /ɪnˈhɪbɪtɪd/ *adj.* gehemmt

inhibition /ɪnhɪˈbɪʃn/ *n.* 1 (stopping) Unterdrückung, *die* 2 (Psych.) Hemmung, *die* 3 (emotional resistance) Hemmung, *die;* **without ~:** hemmungslos; **have no ~s about doing sth.** keine Hemmungen haben, etw. zu tun

inhomogeneity /ɪnhɒmədʒɪˈniːɪtɪ, ɪnhəʊmədʒɪˈniːɪtɪ/ *n.* 1 *no pl.* (lack of homogeneity) Inhomogenität, *die* 2 (irregularity) Unregelmäßigkeit, *die*

inhomogeneous /ɪnhɒməˈdʒiːnɪəs, ɪnhəʊməˈdʒiːnɪəs/ *adj.* inhomogen

inhospitable /ɪnhɒsˈpɪtəbl/ *adj.* 1 ungastlich ‹*Person, Verhalten*› 2 unwirtlich ‹*Gegend, Klima*›

ˈin-house *adj.* hausintern

inhuman /ɪnˈhjuːmən/ *adj.* 1 (brutal) unmenschlich ‹*Tyrann, Grausamkeit, Strenge*›; inhuman (geh.) ‹*Arbeitgeber, Verhalten*› 2 (not human) nicht menschlich

inhumane /ɪnhjuːˈmeɪn/ *adj.* unmenschlich; inhuman (geh.); menschenunwürdig ‹*Zustände, Behandlung*›

inhumanity /ɪnhjuːˈmænɪtɪ/ *n.* ▸ **inhumane**: Unmenschlichkeit, *die;* Inhumanität, *die* (geh.); Menschenunwürdigkeit, *die;* **man's ~ to man** die Unmenschlichkeit unter den Menschen

inimical /ɪˈnɪmɪkl/ *adj.* 1 (hostile) feindselig ‹*Blick, Beziehungen*›; feindlich [gesinnt] ‹*Macht*›; **be ~ to sb.** jmdm. feindlich gesinnt sein; jmdm. Feind sein (geh.) 2 (harmful) abträglich (**to** *Dat.*) (geh.); nachteilig (**to** für); schädlich (**to** für)

inimitable /ɪˈnɪmɪtəbl/ *adj.* unnachahmlich ‹*Gabe, Fähigkeit*›; einzigartig ‹*Persönlichkeit*›

iniquitous /ɪˈnɪkwɪtəs/ *adj.* 1 (wicked) schändlich 2 (unjust) ungerecht ‹*Urteil*›; ungeheuer hoch ‹*Preis*›

iniquity /ɪˈnɪkwɪtɪ/ *n.* 1 (wickedness) Schändlichkeit, *die;* (sin) Missetat, *die* 2 (injustice) Ungerechtigkeit, *die*

initial /ɪˈnɪʃl/

A *adj.* anfänglich; zu Anfang auftretend ‹*Symptome*›; Anfangs‹*stadium, -schwierigkeiten*›; **~ costs** *or* **expenses** Startkosten

B *n. esp. in pl.* Initiale, *die;* **what do the ~s OUP stand for?** wofür steht *od.* was bedeutet die Abkürzung OUP?

C *v.t.,* (Brit.) **-ll-** abzeichnen ‹*Scheck, Quittung, Beleg*›; paraphieren ‹*Vertrag, Abkommen usw.*›

initial ˈletter *n.* Anfangsbuchstabe, *der*

initially /ɪˈnɪʃəlɪ/ *adv.* anfangs; am *od.* zu Anfang

initiate

A /ɪˈnɪʃɪeɪt/ *v.t.* 1 (admit) [feierlich] aufnehmen; initiieren (Soziol., Völkerk.); (introduce) einführen (**into** in + *Akk.*); **~ sb. into sth.** (into club, group, etc.) jmdn. in etw. (*Akk.*) aufnehmen; (into knowledge, mystery, etc.) jmdn. in etw. (*Akk.*) einweihen 2 (begin) initiieren (geh.); in die Wege leiten ‹*Vorhaben*›; einleiten ‹*Verhandlungen, Reformen*›; eröffnen ‹*Diskussion, Verhandlung, Feierlichkeiten, Feindseligkeiten*›; anstrengen ‹*Prozess, Klage*›

B /ɪˈnɪʃɪət/ *n.* Eingeweihte, *der/die*

initiation /ɪnɪʃɪˈeɪʃn/ *n.* 1 (beginning) Initiierung, *die* (geh.); (of hostilities, discussion, negotiation, festivities) Eröffnung, *die;* (of reforms, negotiations) Einleitung, *die* 2 (admission) Aufnahme, *die* (**into** in + *Akk.*); (into knowledge, mystery, etc.) Einweihung, *die;* Initiation, *die* (Soziol., Völkerk.); (introduction) Einführung, *die* (**into** in + *Akk.*); **~ ceremony** Aufnahmezeremonie, *die;* Initiationsritus, *der* (Soziol., Völkerk.)

initiative /ɪˈnɪʃətɪv, ɪˈnɪʃɪətɪv/ *n.* 1 (power) **the ~ is ours/lies with them** die Initiative liegt bei uns/ihnen; **have the ~:** die Überhand haben; (Mil.) den Kampf bestimmen 2 *no pl., no indef. art.* (ability) Initiative, *die;* **lack ~:** keine Initiative haben *od.* besitzen 3 (first step) Initiative, *die;* **take the ~:** die Initiative ergreifen; den ersten Schritt tun; **on one's own ~:** aus eigener Initiative 4 (citizen's right to initiate legislation) Gesetzesinitiative, *die*

initiator /ɪˈnɪʃɪeɪtə(r)/ *n.* Initiator, *der/*Initiatorin, *die*

inject /ɪnˈdʒekt/ *v.t.* 1 [ein]spritzen; injizieren (Med.) 2 (put fluid into) **~ a vein with sth.** etw. in eine Vene spritzen *od.* (Med.) injizieren; **~ a mould with plastic** Plastik in eine Form spritzen 3 (administer sth. to) **~ sb. with sth.** jmdm. etw. spritzen *od.* (Med.) injizieren; **~ sb. against smallpox** jmdn. gegen Pocken impfen 4 (fig.) pumpen ‹*Geld*›; **~ new life/vigour into sth.** einer Sache (*Dat.*) neues Leben geben/neue Kraft verleihen

injection /ɪnˈdʒekʃn/ *n.* ▸ ❶ **p. 1231** 1 (injecting) Einspritzung, *die;* Injektion, *die* (Med.); **give sb. an ~:** jmdm. eine Spritze *od.* Injektion geben 2 (liquid injected) Injektion, *die;* Injektionslösung, *die* 3 (fig.) **~ of money/capital, financial ~:** Geldzuschuss, *der;* Finanzspritze, *die* (ugs.); *see also* **fuel injection**

inˈjection moulding *n.* Spritzguss, *der*

injudicious /ɪndʒuːˈdɪʃəs/ *adj.* unklug; ungünstig ‹*Moment*›

Injun /ˈɪndʒən/ *n.* (Amer. coll. offensive) Indianer, *der*/Indianerin, *die*

injunction /ɪnˈdʒʌŋkʃn/ *n.* 1 (order) Verfügung, *die* 2 (Law) [richterliche] Verfügung; **a court ~:** eine richterliche Verfügung

injure /ˈɪndʒə(r)/ *v.t.* 1 (hurt) verletzen; (fig.) verletzen ‹*Stolz, Gefühle*›; kränken ‹*Person*›; **his leg was ~d** er wurde/(state) war am Bein verletzt; **six people were badly ~d** es gab sechs Schwerverletzte 2 (impair) schaden (+ *Dat.*); schädigen ‹*Gesundheit*›; beeinträchtigen ‹*Beziehungen*› 3 (do harm to) schädigen ‹*Ruf, Ansehen*›

injured /ˈɪndʒəd/ *adj.* 1 (hurt, lit. or fig.) verletzt; verwundet ‹*Soldat*›; **because of his ~ hand** wegen seiner Handverletzung; **the ~:** die Verletzten/Verwundeten 2 (wronged) geschädigt; hintergangen, betrogen ‹*Ehemann*›; **the ~ party** (Law) der/die Geschädigte 3 (offended) gekränkt ‹*Stimme, Blick*›; verletzt, beleidigt ‹*Person*›; **with an ~ air** mit gekränkter Miene; **speak in an ~ voice** mit gekränkter Stimme sprechen

injurious /ɪnˈdʒʊərɪəs/ *adj.* 1 (wrongful) ungerecht ‹*Behandlung*› 2 (hurtful) schädlich; **be ~ to sb./sth.** jmdm./einer Sache schaden; **smoking is ~ to health** Rauchen schadet der Gesundheit

injury /ˈɪndʒərɪ/ *n.* 1 (harm) Verletzung, *die* (**to** *Gen.*); **risk ~ to life and limb** Leben und Gesundheit aufs Spiel setzen 2 (instance of harm) Verletzung, *die* (**to** *Gen.*); (fig.) Kränkung, *die* (**to** *Gen.*); **add insult to ~:** das Ganze noch schlimmer machen; **do sb./oneself an ~:** jmdm./sich wehtun; **I'll do him an ~ if he doesn't shut up!** (coll.) ich tu ihm jetzt [gleich] was, wenn er nicht ruhig ist! 3 (wrongful action) Verletzung, *die* (**to** *Gen.*)

ˈinjury time *n.* (Brit. Footb.) Nachspielzeit, *die;* **be into/play ~:** nachspielen

injustice /ɪnˈdʒʌstɪs/ *n.* 1 (unfairness) Ungerechtigkeit, *die;* **fight against ~:** gegen die Ungerechtigkeit *od.* das Unrecht kämpfen; **protest at the ~ of a statement** gegen eine ungerechte Behauptung protestieren 2 (wrong act) Ungerechtigkeit, *die;* **do sb. an ~:** jmdm. unrecht tun

ink /ɪŋk/

A *n.* 1 Tinte, *die;* (for stamp pad) Farbe, *die;* (for drawing) Tusche, *die;* **my ballpoint has run out of ~:** meine [Kugelschreiber]mine ist leer 2 (in printing) Druckfarbe, *die;* (in duplicating, newsprint) Druckerschwärze, *die* 3 (Zool.) Tinte, *die*

B *v.t.* 1 **~ in** mit Tinte/Tusche nachziehen ‹*Bleistiftstrich usw.*›; mit Tusche ausmalen ‹*Teil eines Bildes*›; **~ over** mit Tusche übermalen ‹*Papier, Blatt*› 2 (apply ink to) einfärben ‹*Druckform*›; mit Farbe schwärzen ‹*Stempel*›

ˈink bottle *n.* Tintenfass, *das*

ˈink-jet printer *n.* Tintenstrahldrucker, *der*

inkling /ˈɪŋklɪŋ/ *n.* Ahnung, *die;* **I haven't an ~:** ich habe nicht die leiseste Ahnung *od.* (ugs.) keinen blassen Schimmer; **have an ~ of sth.** etw. ahnen; **get an ~ of sth.** Wind von etw. bekommen (ugs.)

ink: ~-pad *n.* Stempelkissen, *das;* **~well** *n.* [eingelassenes] Tintenfass

inky /ˈɪŋkɪ/ *adj.* 1 (covered with ink) tintenbeschmiert; tintig; **I have ~ fingers** meine Finger sind voller Tinte 2 (black) tintenschwarz; tintig

inlaid ▸ **inlay A**

inland

A /ˈɪnlənd, ˈɪnlænd/ *adj.* 1 (placed ~) Binnen-; binnenländisch; **~ town** Stadt im Landesinneren; **an ~ state** ein Binnenstaat 2 (carried on ~) inländisch; Binnen‹*handel, -verkehr*›; Inlands‹*brief, -paket, -gebühren*›

B /ɪnˈlænd/ *adv.* landeinwärts; im Landesinneren ‹*leben*›

inland: ~ naviˈgation *n.* Binnenschifffahrt, *die;* **~ ˈrevenue** *n.* Steuereinnahmen *Pl.;* **I~ ˈRevenue** *n.* (Brit.) ≈ Finanzamt, *das;* **~ ˈsea** *n.* Binnenmeer, *das*

ˈin-law *n., usu. in pl.* (coll.) angeheirateter Verwandter/angeheiratete Verwandte; **~s** (parents-in-law) Schwiegereltern

inlay

A /-ˈ-/ *v.t.,* **inlaid** 1 (embed) einlassen 2 (ornament) einlegen

B /ˈ--/ *n.* 1 (work) Einlegearbeit, *die;* Intarsie, *die* 2 (material) **~s** Intarsien *Pl.* (**of** aus) 3 (Dent.) Inlay, *das*

inlet /ˈɪnlet, ˈɪnlɪt/ *n.* 1 [schmale] Bucht 2 (piece inserted) eingelegtes Stück; Einsatz, *der* 3 (way of entry) Einlassöffnung, *die;* **~ pipe** Zuleitungsrohr, *das;* Zuleitung, *die;* **~ valve** Einlassventil, *das*

in-liners /ɪnˈlaɪnəz/, **ˈin-line skates** *ns. pl.* Inliner, *Pl.;* Inlineskates, *Pl.*

ˈinmate *n.* (of hospital, prison, etc.) Insasse, *der*/Insassin, *die;* (of house) Bewohner, *der*/Bewohnerin, *die*

in memoriam /ɪn mɪˈmɔːrɪæm/

A *n.* Gedenkschrift, *die*

B *prep.* in memoriam

inmost /ˈɪnməʊst, ˈɪnməst/ *adj.* 1 (deepest) tiefst... 2 (fig.: most inward) innerst... ‹*Gefühle, Wesen*›

inn /ɪn/ *n.* 1 (hotel) Herberge, *die* (veralt.); Gasthof, *der;* **no room at the ~** (fig.) alles ausgebucht (scherzh.) 2 (pub) Wirtshaus, *das;* Gastwirtschaft, *die;* **'The Swan Inn'** „Wirtshaus zum Schwan"

innards /ˈɪnədz/ *n. pl.* (coll.) Eingeweide *Pl.;* (in animals for slaughter) Innereien *Pl.*

innate /ɪˈneɪt, ˈɪneɪt/ *adj.* 1 (inborn) angeboren; natürlich ‹*Schönheit, Fähigkeit*›; **be ~ in sb.** jmdm. angeboren sein; **we all have an ~ desire for happiness** das Streben nach Glück ist uns allen angeboren 2 (Philos.) angeboren ‹*Ideen*›

innately /ɪˈneɪtlɪ/ *adv.* von Natur aus; **he is ~ honest** er ist seinem Wesen nach ehrlich

inner /ˈɪnə(r)/ *adj.* 1 inner...; Innen‹*hof, -tür, -fläche, -seite usw.*›; **~ ear** (Anat.) Innenohr, *das* 2 (fig.) inner... ‹*Gefühl, Wesen, Zweifel, Ängste*›; verborgen ‹*Bedeutung*›; **~ life** Seelenleben, *das;* **~ circle of friends** engster Freundeskreis; *see also* **bar¹ A 9**

inner: ~ ˈcity *n.* Innenstadt, *die;* City, *die;* **~ city areas** Innenbezirke; Innenstadtgebiete; **~ man** *n.* 1 (soul, mind) Innere, *das;* **the needs of the ~ man** die inneren Bedürfnisse; 2 (joc.: stomach) Magen, *der;* **satisfy the ~ man** für sein leibliches Wohl sorgen

innermost /ˈɪnəməʊst/ *adj.* innerst...; **one's ~ thoughts** seine geheimsten Gedanken; **in the ~ depths of the forest** im tiefsten Wald

inner: ~-spring (Amer.) ▸ **interior-sprung**; **~ tube** *n.* Schlauch, *der;* **~ woman** *n.* 1 (soul, mind) Innere, *das;* **the needs of the ~ woman** die inneren Bedürfnisse 2 (joc.: stomach) Magen, *der;* **satisfy the ~ woman** für ihr leibliches Wohl sorgen

inning /ˈɪnɪŋ/ *n.* (Amer. Baseball) Inning, *das*

innings /ˈɪnɪŋz/ *n., pl. same or* (coll.) **~es** 1 (Cricket) Durchgang, *der;* Innings, *das* (fachspr.) 2 (period of office) Amtszeit, *die;* (dominance of political party) Legislaturperiode, *die* 3 (period of life etc.) **he had a good/long ~:** er hatte ein langes/ausgefülltes Leben

ˈinnkeeper *n.* [Gast]wirt, *der*/-wirtin, *die*

innocence /ˈɪnəsəns/ *n., no pl.* 1 Unschuld, *die;* **a presumption of ~:** eine Unschuldsvermutung; **lose one's ~:** die Unschuld verlieren 2 (lack of knowledge) Unkenntnis, *die;* **in all ~:** in aller Unschuld; **in all ~ of the fact that ...:**

ohne die leiseste Ahnung davon zu haben, dass ...

innocent /ˈɪnəsənt/

A *adj.* **1** unschuldig (**of** an + *Dat.*); **be ~ of the charge/accusation** unschuldig sein; **the ~ party** der/die Unschuldige; **he is not as ~ as he appears** er ist nicht der Unschuldsengel, der er scheint (ugs.) **2** (simple) einfältig; naiv ‹*Wortwahl*› **3** (harmless) harmlos **4** (naïve) unschuldig; **he is ~ about the ways of the world** er ist völlig unerfahren **5** (pretending to be guileless) arglos, unschuldig ‹*Blick, Erscheinung*›; **adopt an ~ air** eine Unschuldsmiene aufsetzen

B *n.* (innocent person) Unschuldige, *der/die;* **he was such an ~ when he went to London** er war noch so unschuldig *od.* unverdorben, als er nach London ging

innocently /ˈɪnəsəntlɪ/ *adv.* unschuldig ‹*blicken*›; in aller Unschuld ‹*etw. sagen, tun*›

innocuous /ɪˈnɒkjʊəs/ *adj.* (not injurious) unschädlich ‹*Tier, Mittel*›; (inoffensive) harmlos

innocuously /ɪˈnɒkjʊəslɪ/ *adv.* harmlos

Inn of 'Court *n., pl.* **Inns of Court** (Brit.) (society) *englischer Anwaltsverband;* (*building*) *Gebäude dieses Verbandes*

innovate /ˈɪnəveɪt/ *v.i.* **1** (bring in novelties) Innovationen vornehmen; innovieren (fachspr.) **2** (make changes) Änderungen vornehmen

innovation /ɪnəˈveɪʃn/ *n.* **1** (introduction of something new) Innovation, *die* (geh., fachspr.); (thing introduced) Neuerung, *die* **2** (change) [Ver]änderung, *die;* Neuerung, *die;* Innovation, *die* (geh., fachspr.)

innovative /ˈɪnəvətɪv/ *adj.* innovativ

innovator /ˈɪnəveɪtə(r)/ *n.* Neuerer, *der*/Neuerin, *die*

'inn sign *n.* Gasthausschild, *das*

innuendo /ɪnjuːˈendəʊ/ *n., pl.* **~es** *or* **~s** versteckte Andeutung; Anspielung, *die;* Innuendo, *das* (geh.); **make ~es about sb.** über jmdn. Andeutungen fallen lassen *od.* machen

innumerable /ɪˈnjuːmərəbl/ *adj.* unzählig; zahllos; (uncountable) unzählbar

innumeracy /ɪˈnjuːmərəsɪ/ *n., no pl.* (Brit.) Nicht-rechnen-Können, *das*

innumerate /ɪˈnjuːmərət/ *adj.* (Brit.) **be ~:** nicht rechnen können; des Rechnens unkundig sein (geh.)

inoculate /ɪˈnɒkjʊleɪt/ *v.t.* **1** (treat by injection) impfen (**against, for** gegen) **2** (implant) einimpfen (**into** in + *Akk.*); **~ sb. with a virus** jmdm. einen Virus einimpfen

inoculation /ɪnɒkjʊˈleɪʃn/ *n.* Impfung, *die,* Inokulation, *die* (Med.) (**against, for** gegen); **give sb. an ~:** jmdn. impfen

inoffensive /ɪnəˈfensɪv/ *adj.* **1** (unoffending) harmlos; gutartig ‹*Tier*› **2** (not objectionable) harmlos ‹*Bemerkung*›; unaufdringlich ‹*Geruch, Art, Person*›; **be ~ to the eye** dem Auge nicht wehtun

inoffensively /ɪnəˈfensɪvlɪ/ *adv.* harmlos

inoperable /ɪnˈɒpərəbl/ *adj.* **1** (Surg.) inoperabel (fachspr.); nicht operierbar **2** (fig.) undurchführbar ‹*Politik*›

inoperative /ɪnˈɒpərətɪv/ *adj.* ungültig; außer Kraft *nicht attr.*; **render sth. ~:** etw. außer Betrieb setzen

inopportune /ɪnˈɒpətjuːn/ *adj.* inopportun (geh.); unpassend, unangebracht ‹*Bemerkung*›; ungelegen, unpassend ‹*Augenblick, Besuch*›; **it was very ~ that ...:** es kam sehr ungelegen, dass ...

inopportunely /ɪnˈɒpətjuːnlɪ/ *adv.* zur Unzeit ‹*kommen*›; unpassenderweise, im unpassenden Moment ‹*vorbringen, äußern*›

inordinate /ɪˈnɔːdɪnət/ *adj.* (immoderate) unmäßig; ungeheuer ‹*[Menschen]menge*›; überzogen, übertrieben ‹*Forderung*›; **an ~ amount of work/money** ungeheuer viel Arbeit/eine Unmenge Geld

inordinately /ɪˈnɔːdɪnətlɪ/ *adv.* unmäßig; ungeheuer ‹*groß, hoch, weit usw.*›; **he is ~ fond of ...:** seine Zuneigung zu ... ist übertrieben

inorganic /ɪnɔːˈgænɪk/ *adj.* **1** (Chem.) anorganisch **2** (fig.) unorganisch (geh.)

inorganic 'chemist *n.* Anorganiker, *der*/Anorganikerin, *die*

'inpatient *n.* stationär behandelter Patient/behandelte Patientin; **be an ~:** stationär behandelt werden

'input

A *n.* **1** (esp. Computing: what is put in) Input, *der od. das;* (of capital) Investition, *die;* (of manpower) [Arbeits]aufwand, *der;* (of electricity) Energiezufuhr, *die;* **his ~ into the project** sein Beitrag zum Projekt **2** (esp. Computing: place where information etc. enters system) Eingang, *der*

B *v.t.,* **-tt-, ~** *or* **~ted** (esp. Computing) eingeben ‹*Daten, Programm*›; zuführen ‹*Strom, Energie*›; **~ data to the computer** Daten in den Computer eingeben

input: ~ circuit *n.* Eingangsstromkreis, *der;* Primärstromkreis, *der;* **~ data** *n. pl.* Eingabedaten *Pl.*; Rechnerdaten *Pl.*; **~ mask** *n.* (Computing) Eingabemaske, *die*

inquest /ˈɪnkwest, ˈɪŋkwest/ *n.* **1** (legal inquiry) gerichtliche Untersuchung **2** (inquiry by coroner's court) **~ [into the causes of death]** gerichtliche Untersuchung der Todesursache **3** (coll.: discussion) ▸**post-mortem C 2** **4** (inquisition) Untersuchung, *die* (**into** *Gen.*)

inquietude /ɪnˈkwaɪɪtjuːd, ɪŋˈkwaɪɪtjuːd/ *n., no pl.* Unruhe, *die*

inquire /ɪnˈkwaɪə(r), ɪŋˈkwaɪə(r)/

A *v.i.* **1** (make search) Untersuchungen anstellen (**into** über + *Akk.*); **~ into a matter** eine Angelegenheit untersuchen *od.* prüfen **2** (seek information) sich erkundigen (**about, after** nach, **of** bei) **3** (ask) fragen (**for** nach)

B *v.t.* sich erkundigen nach, fragen nach ‹*Weg, Namen*›; **~ how/whether** *etc.* **...:** fragen *od.* sich erkundigen, wie/ob *usw.* ...

inquirer /ɪnˈkwaɪərə(r), ɪŋˈkwaɪərə(r)/ *n.* (for the way, a name, etc.) Fragende, *der/die;* (into a matter) Untersuchende, *der/die;* Nachforschende, *der/die*

inquiring /ɪnˈkwaɪərɪŋ, ɪŋˈkwaɪərɪŋ/ *adj.* fragend; forschend ‹*Geist*›

inquiry /ɪnˈkwaɪərɪ, ɪŋˈkwaɪərɪ/ *n.* **1** (asking) Anfrage, *die;* **on ~:** auf Anfrage; **give sb. a look of ~:** jmdn. fragend ansehen **2** (question) Erkundigung, *die* (**into** über + *Akk.*); **make inquiries** Erkundigungen einziehen; Nachforschungen anstellen **3** (investigation) Untersuchung, *die;* (research) Forschung, *die;* **hold an ~:** eine Untersuchung durchführen (**into** *Gen.*); **court of ~** (Mil.) Untersuchungskommission, *die*

inquiry: ~ agent *n.* (Brit.) Privatdetektiv, *der;* **~ desk, ~ office** *ns.* Auskunft, *die*

inquisition /ɪnkwɪˈzɪʃn, ɪŋkwɪˈzɪʃn/ *n.* **1** (search) Nachforschung, *die* (**into** über + *Akk.*) **2** (judicial inquiry) gerichtliche Untersuchung; (fig. coll.) Verhör, *das* **3** **I~** (Hist.) Inquisition, *die*

inquisitive /ɪnˈkwɪzɪtɪv, ɪŋˈkwɪzɪtɪv/ *adj.* **1** (unduly inquiring) neugierig **2** (inquiring) wissbegierig; **be ~ about sth.** alles über etw. (*Akk.*) wissen wollen; **give sb. an ~ look** jmdn. forschend ansehen

inquisitively /ɪnˈkwɪzɪtɪvlɪ, ɪŋˈkwɪzɪtɪvlɪ/ *adv.* ▸**inquisitive 1, 2**: neugierig; wissbegierig

inquisitiveness /ɪnˈkwɪzɪtɪvnɪs, ɪŋˈkwɪzɪtɪvnɪs/ *n., no pl.* ▸**inquisitive 1, 2**: Neugier[de], *die;* Wissbegier[de], *die*

inquisitor /ɪnˈkwɪzɪtə(r)/ *n.* Inquisitor, *der*/Inquisitorin, *die*

inquorate /ɪnˈkwɔːreɪt, ɪŋˈkwɔːreɪt/ *adj.* nicht beschlussfähig

'inroad *n.* **1** (intrusion) Eingriff, *der* (**on, into** in + *Akk.*); **make ~s into the market** in den Markt eindringen; **make ~s into sb.'s savings** jmds. Ersparnisse angreifen **2** (hostile incursion) Einfall, *der* (**into** in + *Akk.*); Überfall, *der* (**[up]on** auf + *Akk.*); **make ~s on a country** in ein Land einfallen

'inrush *n.* Zustrom, *der;* (of water) Einbruch, *der;* **an ~ of air/water** ein Luftzug/Wassereinbruch

insalubrious /ɪnsəˈluːbrɪəs/ *adj.* **1** (unhealthy) ungesund; der Gesundheit abträglich **2** (disreputable) verrufen

insane /ɪnˈseɪn/ *adj.* **1** (not of sound mind) geisteskrank **2** (extremely foolish) wahnsinnig (ugs.); irrsinnig (ugs.)

insanely /ɪnˈseɪnlɪ/ *adv.* **1** (in a mad manner) wahnsinnig (ugs.) ‹*eifersüchtig*›; irr[e] ‹*reden*› **2** (very foolishly) verrückt ‹*sich benehmen*›

insanitary /ɪnˈsænɪtərɪ/ *adj.* unhygienisch

insanity /ɪnˈsænɪtɪ/ *n.* **1** Geisteskrankheit, *die;* Wahnsinn, *der* **2** (extreme folly) Irrsinn, *der;* Wahnsinn, *der* (ugs.); (instance) Verrücktheit, *die*

insatiable /ɪnˈseɪʃəbl/ *adj.* unersättlich; unstillbar ‹*Verlangen, Neugierde*›; **he has an ~ thirst for knowledge** er ist unersättlich in seinem Wissensdurst

inscribe /ɪnˈskraɪb/ *v.t.* **1** (write) schreiben; (on ring etc.) eingravieren; (on stone, rock) einmeißeln; **~ sth. on sth.** etw. auf etw. (*Akk.*) schreiben/in etw. (*Akk.*) eingravieren/einmeißeln **2** (enter) eintragen ‹*Namen*› (**on** in + *Akk.*); **~ one's name in the Visitors' Book** sich in das Gästebuch eintragen **3** (mark) mit einer Inschrift versehen ‹*Denkmal, Grabstein*›; **~ a tombstone/locket with a name** einen Namen in einen Grabstein einmeißeln/ein Medaillon eingravieren **4** (with informal dedication) **~ sth. to sb.** jmdm. etw. widmen

inscription /ɪnˈskrɪpʃn/ *n.* **1** (words inscribed) Inschrift, *die;* (on coin) Aufschrift, *die* **2** (informal dedication) Widmung, *die*

inscrutability /ɪnskruːtəˈbɪlɪtɪ/ *n., no pl.* Unergründlichkeit, *die;* (of facial expression) Undurchdringlichkeit, *die*

inscrutable /ɪnˈskruːtəbl/ *adj.* **1** (mysterious) unergründlich; geheimnisvoll ‹*Lächeln*›; undurchdringlich ‹*Miene*›; **he remained ~:** seine Miene *od.* sein Gesichtsausdruck blieb undurchdringlich **2** (incomprehensible) unerforschlich (geh.)

inscrutably /ɪnˈskruːtəblɪ/ *adv.* unergründlich; geheimnisvoll ‹*lächeln*›

insect /ˈɪnsekt/ *n.* Insekt, *das*

insect: ~ bite *n.* Insektenstich, *der;* **~-borne** *adj.* durch Insekten übertragen ‹*Krankheit*›; **~ control** *n.* Insektenbekämpfung, *die*

insecticide /ɪnˈsektɪsaɪd/ *n.* Insektizid, *das*

insectivore /ɪnˈsektɪvɔː(r)/ *n.* (Zool.) Insektenfresser, *der*

insectivorous /ɪnsekˈtɪvərəs/ *adj.* insektenfressend; insektivor (fachspr.)

insect: ~ powder *n.* Insektenpulver, *das;* **~-proof** *adj.* insektensicher; **~ repellent** *n.* Insektenschutzmittel, *das*

insecure /ɪnsɪˈkjʊə(r)/ *adj.* **1** (unsafe) unsicher **2** (not firm, liable to give way) nicht sicher; nicht fest ‹*Knoten*›; unstabil, instabil ‹*Regal*› **3** (Psych.) unsicher; **feel ~:** sich nicht sicher fühlen

insecurely /ɪnsɪˈkjʊəlɪ/ *adv.* nicht sicher ‹*befestigt*›; nicht fest ‹*verschlossen*›

insecurity /ɪnsɪˈkjʊərɪtɪ/ *n., no pl.* (also Psych.) Unsicherheit, *die;* **the ~ of his job** sein unsicherer Arbeitsplatz

inseminate /ɪnˈsemɪneɪt/ *v.t.* inseminieren (Med., Zool., Landw.); befruchten ‹*Frau*›; besamen ‹*Vieh*›

insemination /ɪnsemɪˈneɪʃn/ *n.* Insemination, *die* (Med., Zool., Landw.); (of woman) Befruchtung, *die;* (of animal) Besamung, *die;* *see also* **artificial insemination**

insensibility /ɪnsensɪˈbɪlɪtɪ/ *n., no pl.* **1** (lack of emotional feeling, indifference) Gefühllosigkeit, *die* (**to** gegenüber) **2** (unconsciousness) Bewusstlosigkeit, *die* **3** (lack of physical feeling) Unempfindlichkeit, *die* (**to** gegen); **~ to pain** Schmerzunempfindlichkeit, *die*

insensible /ɪnˈsensɪbl/ *adj.* **1** (imperceptible) unmerklich; nicht wahrnehmbar **2** (unconscious) bewusstlos; **they drank themselves ~:** sie betranken sich bis zur Bewusstlosigkeit **3** (unaware) **be ~ of** *or* **to sth.** sich (*Dat.*) einer Sache (*Gen.*) nicht bewusst sein **4** (deprived of sensation) unempfindlich (**to** gegen); **be ~ to the cold/to pain** keine Kälte/keinen Schmerz empfinden **5** (emotionless) gefühllos ‹*Person, Art*›; unempfindlich (**to** für)

insensitive /ɪn'sensɪtɪv/ *adj.* 1 (lacking feeling) gefühllos ‹*Person, Art*›; **be ~ to the needs of others** kein Gefühl für die Bedürfnisse anderer haben 2 (unappreciative) unempfänglich (**to** für) 3 (not physically sensitive) unempfindlich (**to** gegen); **~ to light/heat** licht-/hitzeunempfindlich

insensitively /ɪn'sensɪtɪvlɪ/ *adv.* gefühllos, ohne Gefühl ‹*reagieren, sprechen*›

insensitiveness /ɪn'sensɪtɪvnɪs/, **insensitivity** /ɪnsensɪ'tɪvɪtɪ/ *ns., no pl.* 1 (lack of feeling) Gefühllosigkeit, *die* (**to** gegenüber) 2 (unappreciativeness) Unempfindlichkeit, *die* (**to** für) 3 (lack of physical sensitiveness) Unempfindlichkeit, *die* (**to** gegen); **~** *or* **insensitivity to heat** Hitzeunempfindlichkeit, *die*

inseparable /ɪn'sepərəbl/ *adj.* 1 untrennbar; (fig.) unzertrennlich ‹*Freunde, Zwillinge usw.*›; **sth. is ~ from sth.** etw. ist mit etw. untrennbar verbunden; **he is ~ from his teddy bear** der Junge und sein Teddybär sind unzertrennlich 2 (Ling.) untrennbar

inseparably /ɪn'sepərəblɪ/ *adv.* untrennbar

insert

A /ɪn'sɜ:t/ *v.t.* 1 einlegen ‹*Film*›; einwerfen ‹*Münze*›; einsetzen ‹*Herzschrittmacher*›; einstechen ‹*Nadel*›; **~ a piece of paper into the printer** ein Blatt Papier in den Drucker einlegen; **~ sth. in/between sth.** etw. in/zwischen etw. (*Akk.*) stecken/legen *usw.*; **~ the key [into the lock]** den Schlüssel ins Schloss stecken; **~ a page into a book** ein Blatt in ein Buch einlegen 2 (introduce into) einfügen ‹*Wort, Satz usw.*› (**in** in + *Akk.*); **~ an advertisement in 'The Times'** eine Anzeige in die „Times" setzen; in der „Times" inserieren 3 (Computing) einfügen; **~ key** Einfügetaste, *die*

B /'ɪnsɜ:t/ *n.* (in magazine, newspaper) Beilage, *die;* (in garment) Einsatz, *der;* (in book) Einlage, *die*

insertion /ɪn'sɜ:ʃn/ *n.* 1 (inserting) ▸ **insert A 1**: Einlegen, *das;* Einwerfen, *das;* Einsetzen, *das;* Einstechen, *das* 2 (thing inserted) (words, sentences in a text) Einfügung, *die;* Beifügung, *die;* (advertisement in newspaper) Inserat, *das* 3 (each appearance of an advertisement) Insertion, *die*

in-service 'training *n.* Fort- *od.* Weiterbildung [für Berufstätige]; (in firm) innerbetriebliche Fort- *od.* Weiterbildung

inset

A /'--/ *n.* (small map) Nebenkarte, *die;* (small photograph, diagram) Nebenbild, *das*

B /-'-/ *v.t.*, **-tt-**, **~** *or* **~ted** einfügen ‹*Karte, Seite*› (**in** in + *Akk.*)

inshore

A /'--/ *adj.* Küsten‹*fischerei, -gewässer, -schifffahrt*›; **~ currents** sich auf die Küste zubewegende Strömungen

B /-'-/ *adv.* auf die Küste zu ‹*treiben*›; in Küstennähe ‹*sein, fischen*›; **close ~:** dicht an der Küste ‹*sein, liegen*›; dicht an die Küste ‹*heranfahren*›

inside

A /-'-, '--/ *n.* 1 (internal side) Innenseite, *die;* **on the ~:** innen; **to/from the ~:** nach/von innen; **overtake on the ~** (driving on the left) auf der linken Seite überholen; (driving on the right) auf der rechten Seite überholen; **on the ~ of the door** innen an der Tür; **lock the door from the ~:** die Tür von innen abschließen 2 (inner part) Innere, *das;* **the ~ of the cupboard needs a good clean-out** der Schrank muss innen richtig sauber gemacht werden 3 *in sing. or pl.* (coll.: stomach and bowels) Eingeweide *Pl.;* Innere, *das;* **have a pain in one's ~[s]** Bauch- *od.* Leibschmerzen haben 4 (position affording ~ information) **he knows Parliament from the ~:** er kennt das Parlament von innen; **be on the ~:** eingeweiht *od.* ein Insider sein 5 **the wind blew her umbrella ~ out** der Wind hat ihren Regenschirm umgestülpt; **wear one's sweater ~ out** seinen Pullover verkehrt *od.* falsch herum anhaben; **turn a jacket ~ out** eine Jacke nach links wenden; **turn sth. ~ out** (fig.) etw. auf den Kopf stellen (ugs.); **know sth. ~ out** etw. in- und auswendig kennen

B /'--/ *adj.* (of, on, nearer the ~) inner...; Innen‹*wand, -einrichtung, -ansicht, -reparatur, -durchmesser*›; (fig.) intern; **be on an ~ page** im Inneren [der Zeitung] stehen; **give the ~ story of sth.** etw. von innen beleuchten (fig.); **~ information** interne Informationen; **the burglary was an ~ job** (coll.) der Einbruch war das Werk von Insidern; **~ pocket** Innentasche, *die;* **~ lane** Innenspur, *die;* **~ track** (Racing) Innenbahn, *die*

C /-'-/ *adv.* 1 (on or in the ~) innen; (to the ~) nach innen hinein/herein; (indoors) drinnen; **come ~:** hereinkommen; **take a look ~:** hineinsehen; (in search of sth.) innen nachsehen; **go ~:** [ins Haus] hineingehen; **see ~ for further details** weitere Informationen finden Sie in diesem Brief/in dieser Broschüre 2 (sl.: in prison) **be ~:** sitzen (ugs.); **put sb. ~:** jmdn. einlochen (salopp) 3 **~ of** ▸ **D**

D /-'-/ *prep.* 1 (on inner side of) [innen] in (+ *Dat.*); (with direction) in (+ *Akk.*) hinein; **sit/get ~ the house** im Haus sitzen/ins Haus hineinkommen; **what's ~ that package?** was ist in diesem Paket?; **leave your shoes just ~ the door** lass deine Schuhe gerade [innen] an der Tür stehen 2 (in less than) **~ an hour** innerhalb [von] einer Stunde; in weniger als einer Stunde

inside: ~ edge *n.* (Skating, Cricket) Innenkante, *die;* **~ examiner** *n.* (Sch., Univ.) interner Prüfer/interne Prüferin, *die;* **~ 'forward** *n.* (Footb., Hockey) Halbstürmer, *der;* Innenstürmer, *der;* Inside, *der* (schweiz. Fußball); **~ 'left** *n.* (Footb., Hockey) Halblinke, *der/die;* **~-leg** *adj.* **~-leg measurement** Schrittlänge, *die*

insider /ɪn'saɪdə(r)/ *n.* 1 (within a society) Mitglied, *das;* Zugehörige, *der/die* 2 (person privy to secret) Eingeweihte, *der/die;* Insider, *der;* **~ dealing** *or* **trading** (Stock Exch.) Insiderhandel, *der*

inside 'right *n.* (Footb., Hockey) Halbrechte, *der/die*

insidious /ɪn'sɪdɪəs/ *adj.* heimtückisch; **an ~ disease** eine heimtückische *od.* (fachspr.) insidiöse Krankheit

insidiously /ɪn'sɪdɪəslɪ/ *adv.* auf heimtückische Weise

insidiousness /ɪn'sɪdɪəsnɪs/ *n., no pl.* Heimtücke, *die*

'insight *n.* 1 (penetration, discernment) Verständnis, *das;* **be lacking in ~:** einen Mangel an Verständnis zeigen; **~ into human nature** Menschenkenntnis, *die* 2 (instance) Einblick, *der* (**into** in + *Akk.*); **be** *or* **give an ~ into sth.** einen Einblick in etw. (*Akk.*) geben; **gain an ~ into sth.** [einen] Einblick in etw. (*Akk.*) gewinnen *od.* bekommen

insignia /ɪn'sɪgnɪə/ *n., pl. same* Insigne, *das*

insignificance /ɪnsɪg'nɪfɪkəns/ *n., no pl.* 1 (unimportance) Bedeutungslosigkeit, *die;* Unwichtigkeit, *die* 2 (contemptibility) Unscheinbarkeit, *die* 3 (meaninglessness) Belanglosigkeit, *die*

insignificant /ɪnsɪg'nɪfɪkənt/ *adj.* 1 (unimportant) unbedeutend; geringfügig ‹*Summe*›; unbedeutend, geringfügig ‹*Unterschied*›; unscheinbar ‹*Äußeres*› 2 (contemptible) unscheinbar ‹*Person*› 3 (meaningless) belanglos ‹*Bemerkung*›

insincere /ɪnsɪn'sɪə(r)/ *adj.* unaufrichtig; falsch ‹*Lächeln*›

insincerely /ɪnsɪn'sɪəlɪ/ *adv.* unaufrichtig; falsch ‹*lächeln*›

insincerity /ɪnsɪn'serɪtɪ/ *n.* Unaufrichtigkeit, *die;* (of smile, person) Falschheit, *die*

insinuate /ɪn'sɪnjʊeɪt/ *v.t.* 1 (introduce) [auf geschickte Art] einflößen ‹*Propaganda*›; insinuieren (veralt.); **~ doubts into sb.'s mind** jmdm. geschickt Zweifel einpflanzen 2 (convey) andeuten (**to sb.** jmdm. gegenüber); unterstellen; insinuieren (geh.); **how dare you ~ that ...?** wie können Sie es wagen, zu behaupten, dass ...?; **insinuating remarks** Andeutungen; Unterstellungen 3 **~ oneself into sb.'s favour** sich bei jmdm. einschmeicheln

insinuation /ɪnsɪnjʊ'eɪʃn/ *n.* Anspielung, *die* (**about** auf + *Akk.*); versteckte Andeutung; **by ~:** andeutungsweise

insipid /ɪn'sɪpɪd/ *adj.* 1 (tasteless) fad[e] ‹*Essen*›; schal ‹*Getränk*› 2 (lacking liveliness) fad[e] (ugs.), geistlos ‹*Person*›; schal, fad[e] (ugs.) ‹*Witz, Spaß*›; geistlos ‹*Gespräch*›; langweilig ‹*Farbe, Musik*›

insist /ɪn'sɪst/

A *v.i.* bestehen (**[up]on** auf + *Dat.*); **~ on doing sth./on sb.'s doing sth.** darauf bestehen, etw. zu tun/dass jmd. etw. tut; **if you ~:** wenn du darauf bestehst; **he 'will ~ on ringing us late at night** er ruft uns beharrlich spätabends an; **she ~s on her innocence** sie behauptet beharrlich, unschuldig zu sein

B *v.t.* 1 **~ that ...:** darauf bestehen, dass ... 2 (maintain positively) **they keep ~ing that ...:** sie beharren *od.* bestehen beharrlich darauf, dass ...; **he ~ed that he was right** er bestand darauf, dass er Recht habe

insistence /ɪn'sɪstəns/, **insistency** /ɪn'sɪstənsɪ/ *n., no pl.* Bestehen, *das* (**on** auf + *Dat.*); **I only came here at your ~:** ich kam nur auf dein Drängen hierher

insistent /ɪn'sɪstənt/ *adj.* 1 beharrlich, hartnäckig ‹*Person*›; aufdringlich ‹*Musik*›; nachdrücklich ‹*Forderung*›; **be most ~ that .../about sth.** hartnäckig darauf bestehen, dass .../auf etw. (*Dat.*) bestehen 2 ([annoyingly] persistent) penetrant (abwertend)

insistently /ɪn'sɪstəntlɪ/ *adv.* 1 mit Nachdruck ‹*betonen, fordern*› 2 (persistently) penetrant (abwertend)

in situ /ɪn 'sɪtju:/ *adv.* in situ; in natürlicher Lage (Med.); in originaler Lage (Archäol.)

insobriety /ɪnsə'braɪətɪ/ *n., no pl.* Trunkenheit, *die*

insofar /ɪnsəʊ'fɑ:(r)/ *adv.* = **in so far;** ▸ **far A 4**

insole /'ɪnsəʊl/ *n.* 1 Einlegesohle, *die* 2 (part of shoe or boot) Brandsohle, *die*

insolence /'ɪnsələns/ *n., no pl.* Unverschämtheit, *die;* Frechheit, *die*

insolent /'ɪnsələnt/ *adj.*, **insolently** /'ɪnsələntlɪ/ *adv.* 1 (contemptuous[ly]) anmaßend; überheblich 2 (insulting[ly]) unverschämt; frech

insolubility /ɪnsɒljʊ'bɪlɪtɪ/ *n., no pl.* ▸ **insoluble**: Unlösbarkeit, *die;* Unlöslichkeit, *die*

insoluble /ɪn'sɒljʊbl/ *adj.* 1 unlösbar ‹*Problem, Rätsel usw.*› 2 unlöslich ‹*Substanz*›; insolubel (Chem.) ‹*Verbindung*›

insolvency /ɪn'sɒlvənsɪ/ *n.* Insolvenz, *die* (bes. Wirtsch.); Zahlungsunfähigkeit, *die*

insolvent /ɪn'sɒlvənt/

A *adj.* (unable to pay debts) insolvent (bes. Wirtsch.); zahlungsunfähig

B *n.* zahlungsunfähiger Schuldner

insomnia /ɪn'sɒmnɪə/ *n.* Schlaflosigkeit, *die;* Insomnie, *die* (Med.)

insomniac /ɪn'sɒmnɪæk/ *n.* an Schlaflosigkeit Leidender/Leidende; **be an ~:** an Schlaflosigkeit leiden

insomuch /ɪnsəʊ'mʌtʃ/ *adv.* 1 (to such an extent) **~ that** so sehr *od.* dermaßen, dass 2 (inasmuch) insofern (**as** als)

insouciance /ɪn'su:sɪəns/ *n., no pl.* Unbekümmertheit, *die;* Sorglosigkeit, *die*

insouciant /ɪn'su:sɪənt/ *adj.* unbekümmert; sorglos

inspect /ɪn'spekt/ *v.t.* 1 (view closely) prüfend betrachten; **let me ~ your hands** lass mich mal deine Hände sehen; zeig mal deine Hände vor; **~ a cat for fleas** eine Katze auf Flöhe untersuchen 2 (examine officially) überprüfen; inspizieren, kontrollieren ‹*Räumlichkeiten*›; abschreiten ‹*Ehrenformation*›

inspection /ɪn'spekʃn/ *n.* Überprüfung, *die;* (of premises) Kontrolle, *die;* Inspektion, *die;* **tour of ~:** Inspektionsrunde, *die;* (on foot also) Inspektionsgang, *der* (**of** durch); **present/show/submit sth. for ~:** etw. zur Prüfung vorlegen; **hold out your hands for ~:** zeigt eure Hände vor; **on [closer] ~:** bei näherer Betrachtung *od.* Prüfung

in'spection copy *n.* Ansichtsexemplar, *das;* (for teachers) Lehrerprüfstück, *das*

inspector /ɪn'spektə(r)/ *n.* 1 (official) (on bus, train etc.) Kontrolleur, *der*/Kontrolleurin, *die;* **~ [of schools]** Schulrat, *der*/-rätin, *die;* **health ~** Beamter/Beamtin in der Gesundheitsfürsorge 2 (Brit.: police officer) ≈ Polizeiinspektor, *der*

inspectorate /ɪnˈspektərət/ *n.* (esp. Brit.) Inspektion, *die;* Inspektorat, *das* (österr., schweiz.)

inspector: ~ 'general *n.* Oberinspektor, *der;* **~ of 'taxes** *n.* (Brit.) Finanzbeamte, *der*/Finanzbeamtin, *die*

inspiration /ɪnspəˈreɪʃn/ *n.* **1** Inspiration, *die* (geh.); **get one's ~ from sth.** sich von etw. inspirieren lassen; **I have just had an ~:** ich hatte gerade eine [plötzliche] Eingebung; mir ist gerade eine Erleuchtung gekommen (oft iron.); **sth. is an ~ to sb.** etw. inspiriert jmdn. **2** (drawing in of breath) Inspiration, *die* (Med.); Einatmung, *die*

inspirational /ɪnspɪˈreɪʃənl/ *adj.* inspirativ

inspire /ɪnˈspaɪə(r)/ *v.t.* **1** (instil thought or feeling into) inspirieren (geh.); **in an ~d moment** (coll.) in einem Augenblick der Erleuchtung **2** (breathe in) einatmen ‹*Luft*› **3** (animate) inspirieren; anregen; (encourage) anspornen; **~ sb. with hope/confidence/respect** jmdn. mit Hoffnung/Vertrauen/Respekt erfüllen; **~d playing** beseeltes Spiel; **~d idea** genialer Gedanke; **~d guess** intuitiv richtige Vermutung **4** (instil) einflößen ‹*Mut, Angst, Respekt*› (**in** *Dat.*); [er]wecken ‹*Vertrauen, Gedanke, Hoffnung*› (**in** in + *Dat.*); hervorrufen ‹*Hass, Abneigung*› (**in** bei); (incite) anstiften; anzetteln (abwertend) ‹*Unruhen usw.*›; **what ~d this piece of music?** woher kamen die Anregungen zu diesem Musikstück?

inspiring /ɪnˈspaɪərɪŋ/ *adj.* inspirierend (geh.); **his speech was not particularly ~:** seine Rede riss einen nicht gerade vom Stuhl (ugs.)

inst. *abbr.* (Commerc.) = **instant** d. M.

instability /ɪnstəˈbɪlɪtɪ/ *n.* (mental, physical) Labilität, *die;* (inconstancy) Instabilität, *die*

install, install /ɪnˈstɔːl/ *v.t.* **1** (establish) **~ oneself** sich installieren; (in a chair etc.) sich niederlassen; sich pflanzen (ugs.); (in a house etc.) sich einrichten; **when we're ~ed in our new house** wenn wir in unserem neuen Haus eingerichtet sind **2** (set up for use) installieren ‹*Heizung, Leitung, Software*›; anschließen ‹*Telefon*›; einbauen ‹*Badezimmer*›; aufstellen, anschließen ‹*Herd*› **3** (place ceremonially) installieren (geh.); **~ sb. in an office/a post** jmdn. in ein Amt einführen *od.* einsetzen

installation /ɪnstəˈleɪʃn/ *n.* **1** (installing) (in an office or post) Amtseinsetzung, *die;* Amtseinführung, *die;* Installation, *die* (schweiz., sonst veralt.); (setting up for use) Installation, *die;* (of bathroom etc.) Einbau, *der;* (of telephone, cooker) Anschluss, *der;* **~ charges** Installationskosten **2** (apparatus etc. installed) Anlage, *die;* **kitchen ~:** Kücheneinrichtung, *die*

instalment (*Amer.:* **installment**) /ɪnˈstɔːlmənt/ *n.* **1** (part payment) Rate, *die;* **pay by** *or* **in ~s** in Raten *od.* ratenweise zahlen; **monthly ~:** Monatsrate, *die* **2** (of serial, novel) Fortsetzung, *die;* (of film, radio programme) Folge, *die* **3** **installment plan** (Amer.) Ratenzahlung, *die;* Teilzahlung, *die;* **buy on an installment plan** auf Raten kaufen

instance /ˈɪnstəns/

A *n.* **1** (example) Beispiel, *das* (**of** für); **as an ~ of ...:** als [ein] Beispiel für ...; **for ~:** zum Beispiel **2** (particular case) **in your/this ~:** in deinem/diesem Fall[e]; **in many ~s** in vielen Fällen; **isolated ~s** Einzelfälle **3** **at the ~ of ...:** auf Ersuchen *od.* Betreiben (+ *Gen.*); **at his ~:** auf seine Veranlassung [hin]; auf sein Betreiben; **court of first ~** (Law) erste Instanz **4** **in the first ~:** zuerst *od.* zunächst einmal; (at the very beginning) gleich zu Anfang; **it will be for six months in the first ~:** es ist zunächst auf sechs Monate befristet

B *v.t.* **1** (cite as an ~) anführen **2** *usu. in pass.* (exemplify) exemplifizieren

instant /ˈɪnstənt/

A *adj.* **1** (occurring immediately) unmittelbar; sofortig ‹*Wirkung, Linderung, Ergebnis*›; **these new showers give you ~ hot water** mit diesen neuen Duschen hat man sofort heißes Wasser **2** **~ coffee/tea** Instant- *od.* Pulverkaffee/Instanttee, *der;* **~ potatoes** fertiger Kartoffelbrei; **~ cake mix** fertige Backmischung; **~ meal** Fertiggericht, *das* **3** (fig.: hurriedly produced) eilig angefertigt/geschrieben *usw.* **4** (Commerc.) **the 14th ~:** der vierzehnte *od.* 14. dieses Monats

B *n.* Augenblick, *der;* **at that very ~:** genau in dem Augenblick; **come here this ~:** komm sofort *od.* auf der Stelle her; **we were just this ~ talking about you** wir haben gerade eben von dir gesprochen; **the ~ he walked in at the door ...:** in dem Augenblick, als er hereintrat, ...; **in an ~:** augenblicklich; sofort; **not [for] an ~:** keinen Augenblick

instantaneous /ɪnstənˈteɪnɪəs/ *adj.* unmittelbar; **his reaction was ~:** er reagierte sofort; **death was ~:** der Tod trat sofort *od.* unmittelbar ein

instantaneously /ɪnstənˈteɪnɪəslɪ/ *adv.* sofort; unverzüglich

instantly /ˈɪnstəntlɪ/ *adv.* sofort; **he is ~ likeable** er ist einem sofort sympathisch

instant 'replay *n.* (Sport) [sofortige] Wiederholung

instead /ɪnˈsted/ *adv.* stattdessen; **~ of doing sth.** [an]statt etw. zu tun; **~ of sth.** anstelle einer Sache (*Gen.*); **I will go ~ of you** ich gehe an deiner Stelle; **Friday ~ of Saturday** Freitag anstelle von *od.* [an]statt Sonnabend

'instep *n.* **1** (of foot) Spann, *der;* Fußrücken, *der* **2** (of shoe) Blatt, *das*

instigate /ˈɪnstɪgeɪt/ *v.t.* **1** (urge on) anstiften (**to** zu); **~ sb. to do sth.** jmdn. dazu anstiften, etw. zu tun **2** (bring about) initiieren (geh.) ‹*Reformen, Projekt usw.*›; anzetteln (abwertend) ‹*Streik usw.*›

instigation /ɪnstɪˈgeɪʃn/ *n.* **1** (urging) Anstiftung, *die;* **at sb.'s ~:** auf jmds. Betreiben (*Akk.*) **2** (bringing about) Anzettelung, *die* (abwertend); (of reforms etc.) Initiierung, *die* (geh.)

instigator /ˈɪnstɪgeɪtə(r)/ *n.* **1** (of bank raid etc.) Anstifter, *der*/Anstifterin, *die* **2** (of riot, strike) Anzettler, *der*/Anzettlerin, *die* (abwertend); (of reforms) Initiator, *der*/Initiatorin, *die* (geh.)

instil (*Amer.:* **instill**) /ɪnˈstɪl/ *v.t.*, **-ll-** **1** (introduce gradually) einflößen (**in** *Dat.*); einimpfen (**in** *Dat.*); beibringen ‹*gutes Benehmen, Wissen*› (**in** *Dat.*) **2** (put in by drops) einträufeln (**into** in + *Akk.*)

instinct /ˈɪnstɪŋkt/ *n.* **1** Instinkt, *der;* **~ for survival, survival ~:** Überlebenstrieb, *der; see also* **herd A 2** **2** (intuition) Instinkt, *der;* instinktives Gefühl (**for** für); (unconscious skill) natürliche Begabung (**for** für); Sinn, *der* (**for** für); **~ warns them when danger is near** der Instinkt warnt sie bei drohender Gefahr; **have an ~ for business** Geschäftssinn *od.* -instinkt haben **3** (innate impulse) angeborener *od.* natürlicher *od.* instinktiver Drang

instinctive /ɪnˈstɪŋktɪv/ *adj.*, **instinctively** /ɪnˈstɪŋktɪvlɪ/ *adv.* instinktiv

institute /ˈɪnstɪtjuːt/

A *n.* Institut, *das; see also* **Women's Institute**

B *v.t.* einführen ‹*Reform, Brauch, Beschränkung*›; einleiten ‹*Suche, Verfahren, Untersuchung*›; gründen ‹*Gesellschaft*›; anstrengen ‹*Prozess, Klage*›; schaffen ‹*Posten*›; einrichten ‹*Ausstellung*›; **his wife ~d divorce proceedings against him** seine Ehefrau reichte die Scheidung [gegen ihn] ein

institution /ɪnstɪˈtjuːʃn/ *n.* **1** (instituting) Einführung, *die* **2** (law, custom) Institution, *die* **3** (coll.: familiar object) Institution, *die;* **become an ~:** zur Institution werden; **he's one of the ~s of the place** er gehört dort/hier schon zum Inventar (scherzh.) **4** (institute) Heim, *das;* Anstalt, *die;* **charitable/educational ~:** Wohltätigkeitseinrichtung/Erziehungsanstalt, *die*

institutional /ɪnstɪˈtjuːʃənl/ *adj.* **1** (of, like, organized through institutions) institutionell (geh.) **2** (suggestive of typical charitable institutions) Heim-; Anstalts-; **~ care/catering** Heim-/Anstaltsfürsorge, *die*/Heim-/Anstaltsverpflegung, *die* **3** (Amer.) **~ advertising** Prestigewerbung, *die;* institutionelle Werbung (fachspr.)

institutionalize /ɪnstɪˈtjuːʃənəlaɪz/ *v.t.* **1** (establish) institutionalisieren **2** (place in an institution) verheimen

instruct /ɪnˈstrʌkt/ *v.t.* **1** (teach) unterrichten ‹*Klasse, Fach*› **2** (direct, command) anweisen; die Anweisung erteilen (+ *Dat.*); instruieren; **we were ~ed to do it in this way** wir hatten Weisung (Amtsspr.) *od.* Anweisung, es so zu machen **3** (inform) unterrichten; in Kenntnis setzen; instruieren (geh.) **4** (Law: appoint) beauftragen ‹*Anwalt*›

instruction /ɪnˈstrʌkʃn/ *n.* **1** (teaching) Unterricht, *der;* **a course of ~:** ein Lehrgang; **give ~ in judo** Judounterricht erteilen; **'Driver under ~'** ≈ „Fahrschule" **2** *esp. in pl.* (direction, order) Anweisung, *die;* Instruktion, *die;* **~ manual/~s for use** Gebrauchsanleitung, *die;* (for machine etc.) Betriebsanleitung, *die;* **they had precise ~s as to where to go** sie hatten genaue Anweisung, wo sie hinzugehen hatten; **under ~s from** *or* **on the ~s of the committee** auf Anweisung *od.* Anordnung des Komitees; **be under strict ~s to do sth.** strenge Anweisung haben, etw. zu tun **3** (Computing) Befehl, *der*

instructional /ɪnˈstrʌkʃənl/ *adj.* Schulungs-; lehrreich ‹*Erfahrung*›; **an ~ film** ein Lehrfilm

instructive /ɪnˈstrʌktɪv/ *adj.* aufschlussreich; instruktiv; lehrreich ‹*Erfahrung, Buch*›

instructively /ɪnˈstrʌktɪvlɪ/ *adv.* aufschlussreich; instruktiv; **an ~ written book** ein lehrreiches Buch

instructor /ɪnˈstrʌktə(r)/ *n.* ▸ⓘ **p. 1260** **1** Lehrer, *der*/Lehrerin, *die;* (Mil.) Ausbilder, *der;* **riding ~:** Reitlehrer, *der*/-lehrerin, *die* **2** (Amer. Univ.) Dozent, *der*/Dozentin, *die*

instrument /ˈɪnstrʊmənt/ *n.* **1** (tool, implement) Instrument, *das;* **~s of torture** Folterwerkzeuge *od.* -instrumente **2** (measuring device) Instrument, *das;* **~ failure** Versagen der Instrumente **3** (Mus.) Instrument, *das* **4** (person) Werkzeug, *das;* Instrument, *das* (geh.) **5** (means, cause) Mittel, *das* **6** (Law) Urkunde, *die;* **~ of abdication** Abdankungsurkunde, *die*

instrumental /ɪnstrʊˈmentl/ *adj.* **1** (serving as instrument or means) dienlich (**to** *Dat.*); förderlich (**to** *Dat.*); **he was ~ in finding me a post** er hat mir zu einer Stelle verholfen **2** (Mus.) instrumental; Instrumental‹*musik*, *-version*, *-nummer*› **3** (Ling.) instrumental

instrumentalist /ɪnstrʊˈmentəlɪst/ *n.* Instrumentalist, *der*/Instrumentalistin, *die*

instrumentation /ɪnstrʊmenˈteɪʃn/ *n.* **1** (Mus.) Instrumentation, *die* **2** (provision) Instrumentierung, *die;* (use) Anwendung von Instrumenten

instrument: ~ board, ~ panel *ns.* Instrumentenbrett, *das*

insubordinate /ɪnsəˈbɔːdɪnət/ *adj.* aufsässig; widersetzlich; (Mil.) ungehorsam; **~ behaviour** Widersetzlichkeit, *die;* (Mil.) Ungehorsam, *der*

insubordination /ɪnsəbɔːdɪˈneɪʃn/ *n.*, *no pl.* Aufsässigkeit, *die;* Widersetzlichkeit, *die;* (Mil.) Gehorsamsverweigerung, *die*

insubstantial /ɪnsəbˈstænʃl/ *adj.* **1** (lacking solidity) wenig substanziell (geh.); gegenstandslos ‹*Anschuldigung*›; dürftig ‹*Essen, Kleidung*›; gering[fügig] ‹*Menge, Betrag*› **2** (not real) unwirklich; gegenstandslos ‹*Hoffnung, Angst*›

insufferable /ɪnˈsʌfərəbl/ *adj.* **1** (unbearably arrogant) unausstehlich **2** (intolerable) unerträglich

insufferably /ɪnˈsʌfərəblɪ/ *adv.* unerträglich

insufficiency /ɪnsəˈfɪʃənsɪ/ *n.* **1** Unzulänglichkeit, *die;* (of money, provisions, information) Mangel, *der* (**of** an + *Dat.*); (inability, incompetence) Unfähigkeit, *die;* mangelnde Eignung; **an ~ of money** Geldknappheit, *die* **2** (Med.) Insuffizienz, *die;* **cardiac/renal ~:** Herz-/Niereninsuffizienz, *die*

insufficient /ɪnsəˈfɪʃənt/ *adj.* nicht genügend ‹*Arbeit, Gründe, Geld*›; unzulänglich ‹*Beweise*›; unzureichend ‹*Versorgung, Beleuchtung*›; **we have ~ membership** wir haben nicht genügend *od.* zu wenig Mitglieder; **give sb. ~ notice** jmdm. nicht rechtzeitig Bescheid geben

insufficiently /ɪnsəˈfɪʃəntlɪ/ *adv.* ungenügend; unzulänglich; unzureichend ‹*versorgen*›

insular /ˈɪnsjʊlə(r)/ *adj.* **1** (of an island) Insel-; insular (fachspr.); **an ~ people** *or* **race** ein Inselvolk **2** (fig.: narrow-minded) provinziell (abwertend)

insularity /ɪnsjʊ'lærɪtɪ/ *n.* Provinzialität, *die* (abwertend)

insulate /'ɪnsjʊleɪt/ *v.t.* [1] (isolate) isolieren (**against, from** gegen); ~ **floors against noise** Fußböden schallisolieren *od.* gegen Schall isolieren [2] (detach from surrounding) isolieren (**from** von)

insulating/'ɪnsjʊleɪtɪŋ/: ~ **material** *n.* Isoliermaterial, *das;* ~ **tape** *n.* Isolierband, *das*

insulation /ɪnsjʊ'leɪʃn/ *n.* Isolierung, *die;* **put ~ in the loft** den Dachboden isolieren

insulator /'ɪnsjʊleɪtə(r)/ *n.* Isolator, *der*

insulin /'ɪnsjʊlɪn/ *n.* (Med.) Insulin, *das*

'insulin shock *n.* (Med.) Insulinschock, *der*

insult

A /'ɪnsʌlt/ *n.* Beleidigung, *die* (**to** *Gen.*); **fling an ~ in sb.'s face** jmdm. eine Beleidigung an den Kopf werfen (ugs.); *see also* **injury 2**

B /ɪn'sʌlt/ *v.t.* beleidigen

insulting /ɪn'sʌltɪŋ/ *adj.* beleidigend

insuperable /ɪn'su:pərəbl, ɪn'sju:pərəbl/ *adj.*, **insuperably** /ɪn'su:pərəblɪ, ɪn'sju:pərəblɪ/ *adv.* unüberwindlich

insupportable /ɪnsə'pɔ:təbl/ *adj.* [1] (unendurable) unerträglich [2] (unjustifiable) nicht zu rechtfertigen *präd.*; nicht zu rechtfertigend

insurance /ɪn'ʃʊərəns/ *n.* [1] (insuring) Versicherung, *die;* (fig.) Sicherheit, *die;* Gewähr, *die;* **take out ~ against/on sth.** eine Versicherung gegen etw. abschließen/etw. versichern lassen; **travel ~:** Reisegepäck- und -unfallversicherung, *die;* ~ **against fire/theft/accident** Feuer-/Diebstahl-/Unfallversicherung, *die* [2] (sum received) Versicherungssumme, *die;* (sum paid) Versicherungsbetrag, *der;* **I got £50 ~ when my bike was stolen** ich bekam 50 Pfund von der Versicherung, als mein Fahrrad gestohlen wurde; **I've been paying ~ for the last 15 years** ich zahle jetzt schon 15 Jahre in die Versicherung ein; **claim the ~:** den Versicherungsanspruch geltend machen

insurance: ~ agent *n.* ▸ⓘ **p. 1260** Versicherungsvertreter, *der*/-vertreterin, *die;* Versicherungsagent, *der*/-agentin, *die;* ~ **broker** *n.* ▸ⓘ **p. 1260** Versicherungsmakler, *der;* ~ **claim** *n.* Versicherungsanspruch, *der;* **make an ~ claim** eine Versicherung in Anspruch nehmen; ~ **company** *n.* Versicherungsgesellschaft, *die;* ~ **policy** *n.* Versicherungspolice, *die;* (fig.) Sicherheit, *die;* Gewähr, *die;* **take out an ~ policy** eine Versicherung abschließen; ~ **stamp** *n.* (Brit.) Versicherungsmarke, *die*

insure /ɪn'ʃʊə(r)/ *v.t.* [1] (secure payment to) versichern ‹*Person*› (**against** gegen); ~ **[oneself] against sth.** sich gegen etw. versichern; **the ~d** der/die Versicherte; der Versicherungsnehmer/die Versicherungsnehmerin (fachspr.) [2] (secure payment for) ‹*Versicherungsgesellschaft:*› versichern; ‹*Versicherungsnehmer:*› versichern lassen ‹*Gepäck, Gemälde usw.*›; ~ **one's life** eine Lebensversicherung abschließen [3] (Amer.) ▸**ensure**

insurer /ɪn'ʃʊərə(r)/ *n.* Versicherer, *der;* Versicherungsgeber, *der* (fachspr.)

insurgency /ɪn'sɜ:dʒənsɪ/ *n.* Unruhe, *die;* (rebellion) Aufstand, *der*

insurgent /ɪn'sɜ:dʒənt/

A *attrib. adj.* aufständisch

B *n.* Aufständische, *der/die*

insurmountable /ɪnsə'maʊntəbl/ *adj.* unüberwindlich

insurrection /ɪnsə'rekʃn/ *n.* (uprising) Aufstand, *der*

intact /ɪn'tækt/ *adj.* [1] (entire) unbeschädigt; unversehrt; intakt ‹*Uhr, Maschine usw.*›; **keep one's capital ~:** sein Kapital unangetastet lassen [2] (unimpaired) unversehrt; **keep one's reputation ~:** sich (*Dat.*) seinen guten Ruf bewahren [3] (untouched) unberührt; unangetastet; **the package was returned to me ~:** das Paket wurde ungeöffnet an mich zurückgesandt

intaglio /ɪn'tælɪəʊ, ɪn'tɑ:lɪəʊ/ *n., pl.* **~s** [1] (engraved design) eingeschnittene Figur [2] (carving in hard material) Steinschneidekunst, *die;* Glyptik, *die;* **in ~:** in negativer Gravierung [3] (printing process) Tiefdruck, *der* [4] (gem with incised design) Intaglio, *das*

'intake *n.* [1] (action) Aufnahme, *die;* ~ **of breath** Atemholen, *das* [2] (where water enters channel or pipe) Einströmungsöffnung, *die;* (where air or fuel enters engine) Ansaugöffnung, *die;* (airway into mine) Einziehschacht, *der* [3] (persons or things taken in) Neuzugänge; (amount taken in) aufgenommene Menge; (number of persons taken in) Zahl der aufgenommenen Personen; ~ **of alcohol** Alkoholkonsum, *der;* ~ **of calories** Kalorienzufuhr, *die;* aufgenommene Kalorienmenge; ~ **of students** Zahl der Studienanfänger

intangible /ɪn'tændʒɪbl/ *adj.* [1] (that cannot be touched) nicht greifbar; **feel an ~ presence in the room** spüren, dass etwas Unwirkliches anwesend ist [2] (that cannot be grasped mentally) unbestimmbar; unbestimmt ‹*Gefühl*›; vage ‹*Vorstellung*›; ~ **assets** (Econ.) immaterielle Anlagewerte

integer /'ɪntɪdʒə(r)/ *n.* (Math.) ganze Zahl

integral /'ɪntɪgrl/

A *adj.* [1] (of a whole) wesentlich, integral ‹*Bestandteil*› [2] (whole, complete) vollständig; vollkommen [3] (forming a whole) ein Ganzes bildend; integrierend; **an ~ group** eine aus verschiedenen integrierenden Teilen zusammengesetzte Gruppe [4] (Math.) (of or denoted by an integer) ganzzahlig; (involving only integers) Integral-; *see also* **calculus 1**

B *n.* (Math.) Integral, *das*

integrate /'ɪntɪgreɪt/

A *v.t.* [1] (combine into a whole) integrieren; **an ~d Europe** ein vereintes Europa; **an ~d personality** eine in sich (*Dat.*) ausgewogene Persönlichkeit [2] (into society) integrieren; ~ **sb. into a society** jmdn. in eine Gesellschaft integrieren *od.* eingliedern [3] (open to all racial groups) ~ **a school/college** eine Schule/ein College für alle Rassen zugänglich machen; **an ~d school** eine Schule ohne Rassentrennung [4] (Math.) integrieren

B *v.i.* integrieren; ‹*Schulen:*› auch für Farbige zugänglich werden

integrated 'circuit *n.* (Electronics) integrierter Schaltkreis

integrated services digital network *n.* ISDN, *das*

integration /ɪntɪ'greɪʃn/ *n.* [1] (integrating; also Math.) Integration, *die* [2] (ending of segregation) Integration, *die* (**into** in + *Akk.*); **the ~ of the schools** die Aufhebung der Rassentrennung an den Schulen; **racial ~:** Rassenintegration, *die* [3] (Psych.) Integration, *die* [4] (Commerc.) **horizontal ~:** horizontale Integration; **vertical ~:** Vertikalkonzentration, *die*

integrationist /ɪntɪ'greɪʃənɪst/ *n.* Integrationist, *der*/Integrationistin, *die*

integrity /ɪn'tegrɪtɪ/ *n.* [1] (uprightness, honesty) Redlichkeit, *die;* (of business, venture) Seriosität, *die;* (of style) Echtheit, *die;* Unverfälschtheit, *die;* **intellectual ~:** intellektuelle Redlichkeit *od.* Integrität; **business ~:** honoriges Geschäftsgebaren; **a writer of ~:** ein redlicher Autor [2] (wholeness) (of country, empire) Einheit, *die;* (of person) Ganzheit, *die;* (of fossil etc.) Unversehrtheit, *die;* **territorial ~:** territoriale Integrität [3] (soundness) Intaktheit, *die*

integument /ɪn'tegjʊmənt/ *n.* (Biol.) Integument, *das*

intellect /'ɪntəlekt/ *n.* [1] (faculty) Verstand, *der;* Intellekt, *der;* ~ **distinguishes man from the animals** das Denkvermögen unterscheidet den Menschen vom Tier [2] (understanding) Intelligenz, *die;* **powers of ~:** Verstandeskräfte; intellektuelle Fähigkeiten [3] (person) großer Geist

intellectual /ɪntə'lektjʊəl/

A *adj.* [1] (of intellect) intellektuell; geistig ‹*Klima, Interessen, Waffe, Arbeit*›; abstrakt ‹*Mitgefühl, Sympathie*›; ~ **powers** intellektuelle Fähigkeiten [2] (possessing good understanding or intelligence) geistig anspruchsvoll ‹*Person, Publikum*›

B *n.* Intellektuelle, *der/die*

intellectually /ɪntə'lektjʊəlɪ/ *adv.* intellektuell; geistig; **it's ~ stimulating** es regt den Geist an

intellectual 'property *n., no pl.* (Law) geistiges Eigentum; *attrib.* ~ **rights** gewerblicher Rechtsschutz und Urheberrecht

intelligence /ɪn'telɪdʒəns/ *n.* [1] (quickness of understanding) Intelligenz, *die;* **have the ~ to do sth.** so intelligent sein, etw. zu tun; **have ~:** intelligent sein [2] (intellect, understanding) Intelligenz, *die;* **a man of no mean ~:** ein sehr intelligenter Mann [3] (being) Geist, *der;* (spirit) Geistwesen, *das* [4] (information) Informationen *Pl.*; (news) Nachrichten *Pl.*; Meldungen *Pl.*; **a source of ~:** eine Informationsquelle [5] ([persons employed in] collecting information) Nachrichtendienst, *der;* **military ~:** militärischer Geheimdienst; **be in ~:** dem Nachrichtendienst angehören

intelligence: ~ department *n.* Nachrichtendienst, *der;* ~ **officer** *n.* Nachrichtenoffizier, *der;* ~ **quotient** *n.* Intelligenzquotient, *der;* ~ **service** *n.* Nachrichtendienst, *der;* ~ **test** *n.* Intelligenztest, *der*

intelligent /ɪn'telɪdʒənt/ *adj.* intelligent; intelligent geschrieben, geistreich ‹*Buch*›; (clever also) klug; gescheit; **is there ~ life on other planets?** gibt es intelligente *od.* vernunftbegabte Lebewesen auf anderen Planeten?

intelligently /ɪn'telɪdʒəntlɪ/ *adv.* intelligent

intelligentsia /ɪntelɪ'dʒentsɪə/ *n.* Intelligenzija, *die* (geh.); Intelligenz, *die*

intelligibility /ɪntelɪdʒɪ'bɪlɪtɪ/ *n., no pl.* Verständlichkeit, *die*

intelligible /ɪn'telɪdʒɪbl/ *adj.* verständlich (**to** für); intelligibel (Philos.); **is their language ~ to you?** verstehst du ihre Sprache?

intelligibly /ɪn'telɪdʒɪblɪ/ *adv.* in verständlicher Form; (clearly) deutlich

intemperance /ɪn'tempərəns/ *n.* Maßlosigkeit, *die;* Unmäßigkeit, *die;* (addiction to drinking) Trunksucht, *die*

intemperate /ɪn'tempərət/ *adj.* [1] (immoderate) maßlos; überzogen, übertrieben ‹*Verhalten, Bemerkung*›; unmäßig, maßlos ‹*Verlangen, Appetit, Konsum*›; übermäßig ‹*Eifer*›; ausschweifend ‹*Leben*›; **his ~ conduct** seine Maßlosigkeit [2] (addicted to drinking) trunksüchtig

intemperately /ɪn'tempərətlɪ/ *adv.* unmäßig

intend /ɪn'tend/ *v.t.* [1] (have as one's purpose) beabsichtigen; ~ **doing sth.** *or* **to do sth.** beabsichtigen, etw. zu tun; **did you ~ that [to happen]?** hast du das beabsichtigt?; **we ~ed no harm** wir haben nichts Böses damit bezweckt; (we didn't mean to cause offence) wir haben es nicht böse gemeint; **it isn't really what we ~ed** es ist eigentlich nicht das, was wir wollten; **longer than was ~ed** länger als geplant *od.* beabsichtigt [2] (design, mean) **we ~ed it as a stopgap** das sollte eine Notlösung sein; **we ~ him to go** wir wollen, dass er geht; er soll gehen; **this dish is ~ed to be cooked slowly** dieses Gericht soll langsam gekocht werden; **it was ~ed as a joke** das sollte ein Witz sein; **what do you ~ by that remark?** was willst du mit dieser Bemerkung sagen?; **what does the author ~ here?** was will der Autor hier sagen? *See also* **intended**

intended /ɪn'tendɪd/

A *adj.* beabsichtigt ‹*Wirkung*›; erklärt ‹*Ziel*›; absichtlich ‹*Beleidigung*›; **be ~ for sb./sth.** für jmdn./etw. bestimmt *od.* gedacht sein; ~ **for adults/beginners** für Erwachsene/Anfänger; ~ **for drinking** zum Trinken [gedacht]

B *n.* (coll.) Zukünftige, *der/die* (ugs.)

intense /ɪn'tens/ *adj.*, **~r** /ɪn'tensə(r)/, **~st** /ɪn'tensɪst/ [1] intensiv; groß ‹*Hitze, Belastung*›; stark ‹*Schmerzen*›; kräftig, intensiv ‹*Farbe*›; äußerst groß ‹*Aufregung*›; ungeheuer ‹*Kälte, Helligkeit*›; **the day before the play opens is a period of ~ activity** am Tag vor der Premiere herrscht große Geschäftigkeit [2] (eager, ardent) eifrig, lebhaft ‹*Diskussion*›; stark, ausgeprägt ‹*Interesse*›; brennend, glühend ‹*Verlangen*›; äußerst groß ‹*Empörung, Aufregung, Betrübnis*›; tief ‹*Gefühl*›; rasend ‹*Hass, Eifersucht*› [3] (with strong emotion) stark gefühlsbetont ‹*Person, Brief*›; (earnest) ernst

intensely /ɪn'tenslɪ/ *adv.* äußerst ‹*schwierig, verärgert, enttäuscht, kalt*›; ernsthaft, intensiv ‹studieren›; intensiv ‹fühlen›

intensification /ɪntensɪfɪ'keɪʃn/ *n.* Intensivierung, *die*

intensifier /ɪn'tensɪfaɪə(r)/ *n.* (Ling.) intensivierendes Adverb

intensify /ɪn'tensɪfaɪ/

A *v.t.* intensivieren

B *v.i.* zunehmen; ‹*Hitze, Schmerzen:*› stärker werden; ‹*Kampf:*› sich verschärfen

intensity /ɪn'tensɪtɪ/ *n.* **1** Intensität, *die;* (of feeling also) Heftigkeit, *die;* **the heat had lost some of its ~:** die Hitze hatte etwas abgenommen *od.* nachgelassen **2** (measurable amount) Intensität, *die*

intensive /ɪn'tensɪv/

A *adj.* **1** (vigorous, thorough) intensiv; Intensiv‹*kurs*› **2** (Ling.) verstärkend; intensivierend **3** (concentrated, directed to a single point or area) intensiv; heftig ‹*Beschuss*›; gezielt ‹*Entwicklung*› **4** (Econ.) intensiv ‹*Landwirtschaft*› **5** *in comb.* **capital-~/labour-~:** kapital-/arbeitsintensiv

B *n.* ▸ **intensifier**

intensive 'care *n.* Intensivpflege, *die* (Med.); **be in ~:** auf der Intensivstation sein; **~ unit** Intensivstation, *die*

intensively /ɪn'tensɪvlɪ/ *adv.* intensiv

intent /ɪn'tent/

A *n.* Absicht, *die;* **by ~:** beabsichtigt; **with good/malicious ~:** in guter/schlechter Absicht; **with ~ to do sth.** (Law) in der Absicht *od.* mit dem Vorsatz, etw. zu tun; **do sth. with ~:** etw. vorsätzlich tun; **to all ~s and purposes** im Grunde; praktisch; *see also* **loiter**

B *adj.* **1** (resolved) erpicht, versessen (**[up]on** auf + *Akk.*); **be ~ on achieving sth.** etw. unbedingt erreichen wollen; **be ~ upon revenge** auf Rache sinnen **2** (attentively occupied) eifrig beschäftigt (**on** mit); **be ~ on one's work** auf seine Arbeit konzentriert sein; in seine Arbeit vertieft sein **3** (earnest, eager) aufmerksam; konzentriert; forschend ‹*Blick*›

intention /ɪn'tenʃn/ *n.* **1** Absicht, *die;* Intention, *die;* **have no ~/every ~ of doing sth.** nicht die Absicht haben/die feste Absicht haben, etw. zu tun; **it was my ~ to visit him** ich hatte die Absicht *od.* beabsichtigte, ihn zu besuchen; **with the best of ~s** in der besten Absicht; **the road to hell is paved with good ~s** (prov.) der Weg zur Hölle ist mit guten Vorsätzen gepflastert (Spr.); **what is the author's ~ here?** was will der Autor hier sagen? **2** *in pl.* (coll.: in respect of marriage) [Heirats]absichten

intentional /ɪn'tenʃənl/ *adj.* absichtlich; vorsätzlich (bes. Rechtsspr.); **it wasn't ~:** es war keine Absicht

intentionally /ɪn'tenʃənəlɪ/ *adv.* absichtlich; mit Absicht

intently /ɪn'tentlɪ/ *adv.* aufmerksam ‹*zuhören, lesen, beobachten*›

inter /ɪn'tɜː(r)/ *v.t.*, **-rr-** (literary) bestatten (geh.) ‹*Leichnam*›

interact /ɪntər'ækt/ *v.i.* **1** ‹*Ideen:*› sich gegenseitig beeinflussen; ‹*Chemikalien usw.:*› aufeinander einwirken, miteinander reagieren **2** (Sociol., Psych.) interagieren

interaction /ɪntər'ækʃn/ *n.* **1** gegenseitige Beeinflussung; (Chem., Phys.) Wechselwirkung, *die;* Reaktion, *die* **2** (Sociol., Psych.) Interaktion, *die*

interactive /ɪntər'æktɪv/ *adj.* **1** (Chem.) miteinander reagierend **2** (Sociol., Psych., Computing) interaktiv; **~ 'learning** interaktives Lernen; **~ television** interaktives Fernsehen

inter alia /ɪntər'eɪlɪə/ *adv.* unter anderem

interbreed /ɪntə'briːd/

A *v.t.*, **interbred** /ɪntə'bred/ bastardieren (fachspr.); kreuzen ‹*Pflanzen, Tiere*›

B *v.i.*, **interbred** bastardisieren (fachspr.); sich kreuzen

intercede /ɪntə'siːd/ *v.i.* sich einsetzen (**with** bei; **for, on behalf of** für)

intercept /ɪntə'sept/ *v.t.* **1** (seize) abfangen; **~ the enemy** dem Feind den Weg abschneiden **2** (check, stop) abwehren ‹*Schlag, Angriff*› **3** (listen in to) abhören ‹*Gespräch, Funkspruch*›

interception /ɪntə'sepʃn/ *n.* ▸ **intercept**: Abfangen, *das;* Abwehr, *die;* Abhören, *das*

interceptor /ɪntə'septə(r)/ *n.* (Air Force) Abfangjäger, *der*

intercession /ɪntə'seʃn/ *n.* (mediation) Vermittlung, *die,* (entreaty) Fürsprache, *die* (**for, on behalf of** für)

interchange

A /'ɪntətʃeɪndʒ/ *n.* **1** (reciprocal exchange) Austausch, *der* **2** (road junction) [Autobahn]kreuz, *das*

B /ɪntə'tʃeɪndʒ/ *v.t.* **1** (exchange with each other) austauschen; wechseln ‹*Briefe, Blicke, Worte, Grüße*› **2** (put each in the other's place) [miteinander] vertauschen; **they can be ~d** sie sind austauschbar **3** (alternate) wechseln; [aus]wechseln ‹*Kulissen usw.*›

interchangeable /ɪntə'tʃeɪndʒəbl/ *adj.* austauschbar; synonym ‹*Wörter, Ausdrücke*›

intercity /ɪntə'sɪtɪ/ *adj.* Intercity-; **~ train** Intercity[zug], *der*

intercom /'ɪntəkɒm/ *n.* Gegensprechanlage, *die;* (Aeronaut.) Eigenverständigungsanlage, *die*

intercommunicate /ɪntəkə'mjuːnɪkeɪt/ *v.i.* **1** ‹*Räume:*› miteinander verbunden sein **2** ‹*Personen, Organisationen:*› Kontakt haben zueinander

interconnect /ɪntəkə'nekt/

A *v.t.* miteinander verbinden; zusammenschalten ‹*Stromkreise, Verstärker, Lautsprecher*›; **~ed facts/results** zusammenhängende Tatsachen/Ergebnisse; **the events are ~ed** es besteht ein Zusammenhang zwischen den Ereignissen

B *v.i.* miteinander in Zusammenhang stehen; **~ing rooms** miteinander verbundene Zimmer

interconnection /ɪntəkə'nekʃn/ *n.* (of parts, components) Zusammenwirken, *das;* (of circuits) Zusammenschalten, *das;* (of facts, events, ideas) Zusammenhang, *der*

intercontinental /ɪntəkɒntɪ'nentl/ *adj.* interkontinental; Interkontinental‹*rakete, -flug, -reise*›

intercourse /'ɪntəkɔːs/ *n., no pl.* **1** (social communication) Umgang, *der;* **social ~:** gesellschaftlicher Verkehr; **human ~:** menschliche Kontakte; die Beziehungen der Menschen **2** (sexual ~) [Geschlechts]verkehr, *der*

interdenominational /ɪntədɪnɒmɪ'neɪʃənl/ *adj.* interkonfessionell

interdepartmental /ɪntədiːpɑːt'mentl/ *adj.* ‹*Konferenz, Zusammenarbeit, Streit*› zwischen den Abteilungen/Fachbereichen

interdependence /ɪntədɪ'pendəns/ *n.* gegenseitige Abhängigkeit; Interdependenz, *die*

interdependent /ɪntədɪ'pendənt/ *adj.* voneinander abhängig; interdependent

interdict /'ɪntədɪkt/ *n.* **1** (authoritative prohibition) Verbot, *das* **2** (RC Ch.) Interdikt, *das*

interdisciplinary /ɪntədɪsɪ'plɪnərɪ/ *adj.* fachübergreifend; interdisziplinär

interest /'ɪntrəst, 'ɪntrɪst/

A *n.* **1** (concern, curiosity) Interesse, *das;* Anliegen, *das;* **take** *or* **have an ~ in sb./sth.** sich für jmdn./etw. interessieren; **show/develop a [lively] ~ in sb./sth.** [lebhaftes] Interesse an jmdm./etw. zeigen/entwickeln; **take** *or* **have/show no further ~ in sb./sth.** das Interesse an jmdm./etw. verloren haben/kein Interesse mehr an jmdm./etw. zeigen; **[just] for** *or* **out of ~:** [nur] interessehalber; **with ~:** interessiert (*see also* **5**); **lose ~ in sb./sth.** das Interesse an jmdm./etw. verlieren; **~ in life/food** Lust am Leben/Essen **2** (quality of sth.) Interesse, *das;* Bedeutung, *die;* **this has no great ~ for me** das interessiert mich nicht besonders; **be of ~:** interessant *od.* von Interesse sein (**to** für); **this is of no ~ to me** das interessiert mich nicht **3** (advantage, profit) Interesse, *das;* **act in one's own/sb.'s ~[s]** im eigenen/in jmds. Interesse handeln; **it is in your ~ to go** es liegt in deinem Interesse zu gehen; **in the ~[s] of humanity** zum Wohle der Menschheit **4** (thing in which one is concerned) Angelegenheit, *die;* Belange *Pl.;* **have a wide range of ~s** viele Interessen haben **5** (Finance) Zinsen *Pl.;* **rate of ~, ~ rate** Zinssatz, *der;* **~ on one's capital** Zinsen auf sein Kapital; **~ on a mortgage** Hypothekenzinsen *Pl.;* **at ~:** gegen *od.* auf Zinsen; **at 6% ~:** zu 6% Zinsen; **with ~** (fig.: with increased force etc.) überreichlich; doppelt und dreifach (ugs.) (*see also* **1**); **give back** *or* **return blows with ~** (fig.) Schläge mit doppelter Härte zurückgeben **6** (financial stake) Beteiligung, *die;* Anteil, *der;* **have [financial] ~s all over the world** an Firmen *od.* Unternehmungen in der ganzen Welt finanziell beteiligt sein; **American ~s in the Caribbean** amerikanische Interessen in der Karibik; **declare an ~:** seine Interessen darlegen **7** (legal concern) [Rechts]anspruch, *der* **8** (party having common ~) Interessengruppe, *die;* **banking ~s** Bankkreise *Pl.;* die Banken; **business ~s** die Großindustrie. *See also* **compound ~; simple ~; vested**

B *v.t.* interessieren (**in** für); **be ~ed in sb./sth.** sich für jmdn./etw. interessieren; **~ oneself in ...:** sich für ... interessieren; **sb. is ~ed by sb./sth.** jmd./etw. erregt jmds. Interesse; *see also* **interested**

interested /'ɪntrəstɪd, 'ɪntrɪstɪd/ *adj.* **1** (taking or showing interest) interessiert; **be ~ in music/football/sb.** sich für Musik/Fußball/jmdn. interessieren; **I shall be ~ to hear about your trip** ich bin gespannt darauf, von deiner Reise zu hören; **I should be ~ to know why ...:** es würde mich interessieren, warum ...; **be ~ in doing sth.** sich dafür interessieren, etw. zu tun; **he is ~ in buying a car** er würde gern ein Auto kaufen; **not ~ in his work** nicht an seiner Arbeit interessiert; **the ~ parties** die beteiligten Parteien; **he looked ~:** er zeigte sich interessiert **2** (not impartial) voreingenommen; eigennützig ‹*Beweggründe*›; befangen ‹*Zeuge*›

interest: ~-free *adj.* unverzinslich ‹*Schuldverschreibung*›; zinsfrei ‹*Darlehen*›; **~ group** *n.* Interessengruppe, *die*

interesting /'ɪntrəstɪŋ, 'ɪntrɪstɪŋ/ *adj.* interessant

interestingly /'ɪntrəstɪŋlɪ, 'ɪntrɪstɪŋlɪ/ *adv.* interessant; **~ [enough], ...:** interessanterweise ...

'interest rate *n.* Zinssatz, *der;* Zinsfuß, *der*

interface /'ɪntəfeɪs/ *n.* **1** (surface) Grenzfläche, *die* **2** (place where interaction occurs) Nahtstelle, *die;* (fig.) Verbindung, *die;* Kontakt, *der* **3** (Computing) Schnittstelle, *die*

interfacing /'ɪntəfeɪsɪŋ/ *n.* (Dressm.) Einlage, *die*

interfere /ɪntə'fɪə(r)/ *v.i.* **1** (meddle) sich einmischen (**in** in + *Akk.*); **~ with sth.** sich an etw. (*Dat.*) zu schaffen machen **2** (disrupt) in Konflikt geraten (**with** mit); **~ with sth.** (do harm to) etw. beeinträchtigen; **~ with sb.'s plans** jmds. Pläne durchkreuzen **3** (Radio, Telev.) stören (**with** *Akk.*) **4** **~ with sb.** (sexually) jmdn. sexuell missbrauchen **5** (Phys.) interferieren

interference /ɪntə'fɪərəns/ *n.* **1** (interfering) Einmischung, *die* **2** (Radio, Telev.) Störung, *die;* **~ suppressor** Siebkreis, *der;* Entstörgerät, *das* **3** (sexual) Notzucht, *die* (veralt.); Missbrauch, *der* **4** (Phys.) Interferenz, *die*

interfering /ɪntə'fɪərɪŋ/ *attrib. adj.* sich einmischend; **she is an ~ old busybody** sie mischt sich in alles und jedes ein

interferon /ɪntə'fɪərɒn/ *n., no pl.* (Biochem.) Interferon, *das*

intergovernmental /ɪntəgʌvn'mentl/ *adj.* zwischenstaatlich; **~ agreement/conference** Regierungsabkommen, *das*/-konferenz, *die;* **~ discussions** Gespräche auf Regierungsebene; **~ cooperation** internationale Zusammenarbeit

Intergovernmental 'Conference *n.* (EU) Regierungskonferenz, *die*

interim /'ɪntərɪm/

A *n.* **in the ~:** in der Zwischenzeit

B *adj.* **1** (intervening) dazwischenliegend; **the ~ period** die Zwischenzeit **2** (temporary, provisional) vorläufig ‹*Vereinbarung, Bericht, Anordnung, Zustand, Maßnahme*›; Zwischen‹*lösung, -abkommen, -kredit, -finanzierung, -zinsen*›; Übergangs‹*regierung, -regelung, -hilfe*›

interim 'dividend *n.* (Finance) Abschlagsdividende, *die*

interior /ɪnˈtɪərɪə(r)/
A *adj.* **1** inner...; Innen‹*fläche, -einrichtung, -wand*› **2** (inland) im Landesinneren befindlich **3** (internal, domestic) Inlands-; Binnen‹*markt, -handel*› **4** (Cinemat.) ~ **shots/photography** Innenaufnahmen *Pl*
B *n.* **1** (inland region) [Landes]innere, *das* **2** (~ part) Innere, *das;* **redecorate the ~ of the shop** den Laden innen renovieren **3** ([picture of] inside of building, room, etc.) Innere, *das;* (picture) Interieur, *das* **4** (Cinemat.) Innenaufnahme, *die;* (Theatre) Szene eines Innenraumes **5** (home affairs) **Department of the I~** (US, Canada), **Ministry of the I~** (France, Germany, etc.) Innenministerium, *das;* Ministerium des Innern

interior: ~ **decoˈration** *n.* Raumgestaltung, *die;* ~ **ˈdecorator** *n.* Raumgestalter, *der*/-gestalterin, *die;* ~ **deˈsign** *n.* Innenarchitektur, *die;* ~ **deˈsigner** *n.* Innenarchitekt, *der*/-architektin, *die;* **~-sprung** *adj.* (Brit.) **~-sprung mattress** Federkernmatratze, *die*

interject /ɪntəˈdʒekt/ *v.t.* **1** (interpose) einwerfen ‹*Behauptung, Bemerkung, Frage*›; ~ **remarks** Einwürfe *od.* Zwischenbemerkungen machen; **..., he ~ed ...,** rief er dazwischen **2** (remark parenthetically) einflechten; nebenbei bemerken

interjection /ɪntəˈdʒekʃn/ *n.* **1** (exclamation) Ausruf, *der;* (Ling.) Interjektion, *die* **2** (interposed remark) Einwurf, *der;* Zwischenbemerkung, *die*

interlace /ɪntəˈleɪs/ *v.t.* **1** (bind together) zusammenfügen **2** (interweave) [miteinander] verflechten; (fig.) [miteinander] verbinden; **cloth ~d with gold threads** mit Goldfäden durchwirktes Tuch **3** (mingle) [miteinander] kombinieren ‹*zwei Muster*›; spicken ‹*Rede, Schreiben*› (**with** mit)

interlard /ɪntəˈlɑːd/ *v.t.* spicken (**with** mit); **be heavily ~ed with quotations** von Zitaten strotzen

interleave /ɪntəˈliːv/ *v.t.* (Printing) durchschießen (**with** mit); (fig.) abwechseln (**with** mit)

inter-library loan /ɪntəlaɪbrərɪ ˈləʊn/ *n.* Fernleihe, *die;* **get a book on ~:** ein Buch über die Fernleihe bekommen

interlink /ɪntəˈlɪŋk/ *v.t.* miteinander verbinden

interlock /ɪntəˈlɒk/
A *v.i.* sich ineinander haken; ‹*Teile eines Puzzles:*› sich zusammenfügen
B *v.t.* **1** (lock together) zusammenfügen; verflechten ‹*Fasern*› **2** (connect) (Railw.) verriegeln; (Cinemat.) synchronisieren

interloper /ˈɪntələʊpə(r)/ *n.* Eindringling, *der*

interlude /ˈɪntəluːd, ˈɪntəljuːd/ *n.* **1** (Theatre: break) Pause, *die* **2** (occurring in break) Zwischenspiel, *das;* Intermezzo, *das;* **musical ~:** musikalisches Zwischenspiel **3** (intervening time) kurze Phase *od.* Periode; **a few brief ~s of sleep** wenige kurze Schlafpausen **4** (event interposed) Intermezzo, *das*

intermarriage /ɪntəˈmærɪdʒ/ *n.* **1** (between groups) Mischehen *Pl.* **2** (within groups) Heirat untereinander; (between related persons) Verwandtenehe, *die*

intermarry /ɪntəˈmærɪ/ *v.i.* **1** (between groups) Mischehen schließen **2** (within groups) untereinander heiraten; (between related persons) Verwandtenehen schließen

intermediary /ɪntəˈmiːdɪərɪ/ *n.* Vermittler, *der*/Vermittlerin, *die*

intermediate /ɪntəˈmiːdjət/
A *adj.* **1** Zwischen-; ~ **level/point between ...:** Niveau/Punkt zwischen ... **2** (Educ.) Mittel‹*stufe, -schule*›; ~ **education** ≈ Realschulausbildung, *die;* mittlere Reife; ~ **French** Französisch für fortgeschrittene Anfänger
B *n.* **1** fortgeschrittener Anfänger **2** (Chem.) Zwischenprodukt, *das*

intermediate-range [ballistic] ˈmissile *n.* Mittelstreckenrakete, *die*

interment /ɪnˈtɜːmənt/ *n.* (literary) Bestattung, *die* (geh.); Beisetzung, *die* (geh.)

intermesh /ɪntəˈmeʃ/ *v.i.* ‹*Zahnräder:*› ineinander greifen; ‹*Fäden, Garne:*› sich ineinander fügen

intermezzo /ɪntəˈmetsəʊ/ *n., pl.* **intermezzi** /ɪntəˈmetsiː/ *or* **~s** Intermezzo, *das*

interminable /ɪnˈtɜːmɪnəbl/ *adj.*, **interminably** /ɪnˈtɜːmɪnəblɪ/ *adv.* (lit. or fig.) endlos

intermingle /ɪntəˈmɪŋgl/
A *v.i.* sich vermischen; ‹*Personen:*› miteinander in Kontakt treten
B *v.t.* vermischen

intermission /ɪntəˈmɪʃn/ *n.* **1** (pause) Unterbrechung, *die* **2** (period of inactivity) Pause, *die* **3** (Amer.: interval in performance) Pause, *die*

intermittent /ɪntəˈmɪtənt/ *adj.* in Abständen auftretend ‹*Signal, Fehler, Geräusch*›; **be ~:** in Abständen auftreten; **there was ~ rain all day** es hat den ganzen Tag mit kurzen Unterbrechungen geregnet; ~ **fever** Wechselfieber, *das;* intermittierendes Fieber (fachspr.)

intermittently /ɪntəˈmɪtəntlɪ/ *adv.* in Abständen

intern
A /ɪnˈtɜːn/ *v.t.* gefangen halten; internieren ‹*Kriegsgefangenen usw.*›
B /ˈɪntɜːn/ *n.* (Amer.) **1** (Med.) Medizinalassistent, *der*/-assistentin, *die* **2** (teacher) Lehramtskandidat, *der*/-kandidatin, *die*

internal /ɪnˈtɜːnl/ *adj.* **1** inner...; Innen‹*winkel, -durchmesser, -fläche, -druck, -gewinde, -abmessungen*› **2** (Physiol.) inner... ‹*Blutung, Sekretion, Verletzung*›; ~ **temperature** Innentemperatur, *die* **3** (intrinsic) inner... ‹*Logik, Stimmigkeit*› **4** (within country) inner... ‹*Angelegenheiten, Frieden, Probleme*›; Binnen‹*handel, -markt*›; innenpolitisch ‹*Angelegenheiten, Streitigkeiten, Probleme*›; (within organization) [betriebs-/partei]intern ‹*Auseinandersetzung, Post, Praxis, Verfahren[sweise]*›; inner[betrieblich/-kirchlich/-gewerkschaftlich usw.] ‹*Streitigkeiten*›; ~ **telephone** Haustelefon, *das* **5** (Med.) innerlich ‹*Anwendung*› **6** (of the mind) inner... ‹*Monolog, Bewegung, Regung, Widerstände, Groll*› **7** (Univ.) ordentlich ‹*Student*›; ~ **examiner** interner Prüfer/interne Prüferin; ~ **examination** *an der Universität, an der man immatrikuliert ist, abgelegte Prüfung*

internal: ~ **ˈclock** *n.* innere Uhr; **~-comˈbustion engine** *n.* Verbrennungsmotor, *der;* ~ **ˈevidence** *n.* impliziter Beweis

internalize (internalise) /ɪnˈtɜːnəlaɪz/ *v.t.* (Psych.) verinnerlichen; internalisieren (fachspr.)

internally /ɪnˈtɜːnəlɪ/ *adv.* innerlich; (within organization) [partei-/betriebs]intern; **not to be taken ~:** nicht zum Einnehmen; nur zur äußerlichen Anwendung; **bleed ~:** innere Blutungen haben; ~ **inconsistent** in sich (*Dat.*) unstimmig

internal: ~ **ˈmarket** *n.* (Econ) **1** (single European market) Binnenmarkt, *der;* **2** (Brit.: NHS funding system) *vertraglich geregelter Austausch von Dienstleistungen;* ~ **ˈmedicine** *n.* innere Medizin; ~ **ˈrevenue** *n.* (Amer.) Steuereinnahmen *Pl.;* **I~ ˈRevenue Service** *n.* (Amer.) ≈ Finanzamt, *das;* ~ **ˈrhyme** *n.* (Pros.) Binnenreim, *der*

international /ɪntəˈnæʃənl/
A *adj.* international; **it was a very ~ gathering** das Treffen hatte ausgesprochen internationalen Charakter; ~ **travel** Auslandsreisen *Pl.;* ~ **team** (Sport) Nationalmannschaft, *die*
B *n.* **1** (Sport: contest) Länderkampf, *der;* (in team sports) Länderspiel, *das* **2** (Sport: participant) Internationale, *der/die;* (in team sports) Nationalspieler, *der*/-spielerin, *die* **3** **I~** (Polit.) Internationale, *die*

international: ~ **call** *n.* (Teleph.) Auslandsgespräch, *das;* ~ **ˈcode** *n.* (Naut.) internationales Signalbuch; **I~ Court of ˈJustice** *n.* Internationaler Gerichtshof; ~ **date line** ▸**date line**; ~ **ˈdriving licence** *or* **permit** *n.* internationaler Führerschein

> **The International Herald Tribune**
>
> Eine internationale amerikanische Zeitung. Sie hat ihren Sitz in Paris, wird täglich in 180 Ländern veröffentlicht und hat eine exzellente Reputation für seriöse und gründliche Berichterstattung. Sie ist eine **broadsheet**-Zeitung.

internationalism /ɪntəˈnæʃənəlɪzm/ *n.* Internationalismus, *der*

internationalize (internationalise) /ɪntəˈnæʃənəlaɪz/ *v.t.* internationalisieren

international ˈlaw *n.* Völkerrecht, *das*

internationally /ɪntəˈnæʃənəlɪ/ *adv.* international

international: I~ ˈMonetary Fund *n.* Internationaler Währungsfonds; ~ **reˈply coupon** *n.* (Post) internationaler Antwortschein; ~ **system of ˈunits** *n.* (Phys.) Internationales Einheitensystem

internecine /ɪntəˈniːsaɪn/ *adj.* (mutually destructive) [für beide Seiten] vernichtend; (bloody) Vernichtungs‹*krieg, -feldzug*›; (internal) intern ‹*Streitigkeiten, Zwist*›

internee /ɪntɜːˈniː/ *n.* Internierte, *der/die*

Internet /ˈɪntənet/ *n.* **the ~** das Internet; **on the ~:** im Internet

Internet: ~ **acˈcess** *n., no pl.* Internetzugang, *der;* ~ **ˈaccess provider** *n.* Internetzugangsanbieter, *der;* ~ **address** *n.* Internetadresse, *die;* ~ **ˈadvertising** *n., no pl.* Internetwerbung, *die;* ~ **ˈbanking** *n., no pl.* Internetbanking, *das;* ~ **ˈcafé** *n.* Internetcafé, *das;* ~ **ˈchat** *n.* **1** *no pl.* (facility) Chat, *der;* **2** (online communication) Chat, *der;* ~ **ˈcommerce** *n., no pl.* Internethandel, *der;* ~ **connection** *n.* Internetanschluss, *der;* **~-eˈnabled** *adj.* internetfähig; Internet‹*dienstleistung, -arbeiter*›; ‹*Person*› mit Internetzugang; ~ **ˈhost** *n.* Internethost, *der;* ~ **ˈhosting** *n., no pl.* Webhosting, *das;* ~ **ˈphone** *n.* Internettelefon, *das;* ~ **ˈpresence provider** *n.* Internetpräsenzanbieter, *der;* ~ **ˈprotocol** *n.* Internetprotokoll, *das;* ~ **Relay ˈChat** *n.* IRC, *das;* ~ **search** *n.* Internetsuche, *die;* ~ **ˈservice provider** *n.* Internetprovider, *der;* Internetanbieter, *der;* ~ **site** *n.* Internetseite, *die;* ~ **ˈstart-up** *n.* Internet-Start-up, *das;* ~ **user** *n.* Internetnutzer, *der*/-nutzerin, *die*

internist /ɪnˈtɜːnɪst/ *n.* **1** (specialist) Facharzt-/-ärztin für innere Krankheiten; Internist, *der*/Internistin, *die* **2** (Amer.: general practitioner) praktischer Arzt/praktische Ärztin

internment /ɪnˈtɜːnmənt/ *n.* Internierung, *die;* ~ **camp** Internierungslager, *das*

interpersonal /ɪntəˈpɜːsənl/ *adj.* interpersonal; interpersonell

interplanetary /ɪntəˈplænɪtərɪ/ *adj.* (Astron., Astronaut.) interplanetar[isch] ‹*Rakete, Raum, Raumfahrt*›

interplay /ˈɪntəpleɪ/ *n.* **1** (interaction) Wechselwirkung, *die* **2** (reciprocal action) Zusammenspiel, *das*

Interpol /ˈɪntəpɒl/ *n.* Interpol, *die*

interpolate /ɪnˈtɜːpəleɪt/ *v.t.* **1** (interpose orally) einwerfen ‹*Satz, Bemerkung*›; (in programme) einschieben ‹*Warnung usw.*› **2** (introduce by insertion) einfügen ‹*Worte*› **3** (Math.) interpolieren

interpolation /ɪntɜːpəˈleɪʃn/ *n.* **1** Einfügung, *die;* **his ~ of that remark** sein Einwurf **2** (Math.) Interpolation, *die*

interpose /ɪntəˈpəʊz/
A *v.t.* **1** (insert) dazwischenlegen; ~ **sth. between sb./sth. and sb./sth.** etw. zwischen jmdn./etw. und jmdn./etw. bringen **2** (say as interruption) einwerfen ‹*Frage, Bemerkung*› **3** (exercise, advance) ~ **one's veto** sein Veto einlegen; von seinem Veto[recht] Gebrauch machen; ~ **one's authority** seinen Einfluss geltend machen; ~ **an objection** einen Einwand vorbringen; Einspruch einlegen (Rechtsw.)
B *v.i.* ~ **on sb.'s side** *or* **behalf** sich für jmdn. einsetzen; ~ **in sth.** in etw. (*Akk.*) [vermittelnd] eingreifen

interpret /ɪnˈtɜːprɪt/
A *v.t.* **1** interpretieren; deuten ‹*Traum, Zeichen*›; auslegen ‹*Heilige Schrift*› **2** (between languages) dolmetschen **3** (decipher) entziffern ‹*Schrift, Inschrift*›
B *v.i.* dolmetschen

interpretation /ɪntɜːprɪˈteɪʃn/ *n.* **1** Interpretation, *die;* (of dream, symptoms) Deutung, *die;* (of biblical passage) Auslegung, *die* **2** (deciphering) Entzifferung, *die*

interpretative /ɪn'tɜ:prɪtətɪv/ *adj.* erläuternd ‹*Artikel, Aufsatz*›; interpretativ ‹*Kraft, Talent*›; interpretierend ‹*Künstler*›

interpreter /ɪn'tɜ:prɪtə(r)/ *n.* [1] (between languages) Dolmetscher, *der*/Dolmetscherin, *die* [2] (of dreams, hieroglyphics) Deuter, *der* [3] (performer on stage etc.) Interpret, *der*/Interpretin, *die*

interpretive /ɪn'tɜ:prɪtɪv/ ▸ **interpretative**

interracial /ɪntə'reɪʃl/ *adj.* rassenübergreifend; Rassen‹*konflikt, -unruhen*›

interregnum /ɪntə'regnəm/ *n.*, *pl.* **~s** *or* **interregna** /ɪntə'regnə/ [1] (period) Zwischenregierung, *die;* Interregnum, *das* (Politik) [2] (interval) Unterbrechung, *die*

interrelated /ɪntərɪ'leɪtɪd/ *adj.* zusammenhängend ‹*Tatsachen, Ereignisse, Themen*›; verwandt ‹*Sprachen, Fachgebiete*›; **be ~:** zusammenhängen/verwandt sein

interrelation /ɪntərɪ'leɪʃn/ *n.* Wechselbeziehung, *die;* (between events) Zusammenhang, *der*

interrogate /ɪn'terəgeɪt/ *v.t.* vernehmen ‹*Zeugen, Angeklagten*›; verhören ‹*Angeklagten, Verdächtigen, Spion, Gefangenen*›; ausfragen ‹*Freund, Kind, Schüler usw.*›

interrogation /ɪnterə'geɪʃn/ *n.* (interrogating) Verhör, *das; attrib.* Verhör-; **under ~:** beim Verhör; **be under ~:** verhört werden

interrogative /ɪntə'rɒgətɪv/ *adj.* [1] (having question form) Frage-; fragend ‹*Tonfall*› [2] (inquiring) fragend ‹*Ton, Blick*› [3] (Ling.) Interrogativ-‹*pronomen, -adverb, -form*›

interrogator /ɪn'terəgeɪtə(r)/ *n.* Vernehmer, *der*

interrupt /ɪntə'rʌpt/

A *v.t.* unterbrechen; **~ sb.'s sleep** jmds. Schlaf stören; **don't ~ me when I'm busy** stör mich nicht, wenn ich zu tun habe; **~ sb.'s view** jmdm. die Sicht versperren

B *v.i.* unterbrechen; stören; **stop ~ing!** unterbrich *od.* stör nicht dauernd!

interruption /ɪntə'rʌpʃn/ *n.* (of work etc.) Unterbrechung, *die;* Störung, *die;* (of peace, sleep) Störung, *die;* (of services) [zeitweiliger] Ausfall; **without ~:** ohne Unterbrechung; ununterbrochen

intersect /ɪntə'sekt/

A *v.t.* [1] ‹*Kanäle, Schluchten, [Quarz]adern:*› durchziehen ‹*Land, Boden*›; **streets ~ing each other** einander kreuzende Straßen [2] (Geom.) schneiden; **~ each other** sich schneiden

B *v.i.* [1] ‹*Straßen:*› sich kreuzen [2] (Geom.) sich schneiden

intersection /ɪntə'sekʃn/ *n.* [1] (intersecting; road etc. junction) Kreuzung, *die* [2] (Geom.) **[point of] ~:** Schnittpunkt, *der* [3] (Logic, Math.) Schnittmenge, *die*

intersperse /ɪntə'spɜ:s/ *v.t.* [1] (scatter) [hier und da] einfügen [2] **be ~d with** durchsetzt sein mit; ‹*Erzählung, Arbeit, Routine:*› unterbrochen werden durch ‹*Pausen, Ruhe, Aufregungen*›

interstate /'ɪntəsteɪt/ *adj.* zwischen den [Bundes]staaten *nachgestellt;* zwischenstaatlich; **~ highway** Fernstraße (*die durch mehrere Bundesstaaten führt*)

> **interstate (highway)**
>
> Durch mehr als einen Bundesstaat führende Autobahn in den USA. *Interstates* haben ein rotblaues Zeichen, auf dem 'I' steht. Nord-Süd-*interstates* haben ungerade Nummern und Ost-West-*interstates* haben gerade. Sie sind in jeder Richtung vierspurig.

interstellar /ɪntə'stelə(r)/ *adj.* interstellar ‹*Materie, Staub, Raum*›; **~ travel** [Welt-]raumfahrt, *die*

interstice /ɪn'tɜ:stɪs/ *n.* (intervening space) Zwischenraum, *der;* (of net) Masche, *die;* (between panels etc.) Fuge, *die*

intertribal /ɪntə'traɪbl/ *adj.* ‹*Krieg, Streitigkeiten usw.*› zwischen verschiedenen Stämmen

intertwine /ɪntə'twaɪn/

A *v.t.* flechten (**in** in + *Akk.*); **he ~d his fingers with hers** er schlang *od.* flocht seine Finger zwischen ihre *od.* die ihren (geh.)

B *v.i.* sich [ineinander] verschlingen

interval /'ɪntəvl/ *n.* [1] (intervening space) Zwischenraum, *der;* (intervening time) [Zeit]abstand, *der;* **at ~s** in Abständen; **at 20-minute ~s** in Abständen von 20 Minuten; **at frequent** *or* **short/wide ~s** in kurzen/weiten Abständen; **at ~s along the road/river** hier und da an der Straße/am Flussufer; **after an ~ of three years** nach [Ablauf von] drei Jahren [2] (break; also Brit. Theatre etc.) Pause, *die;* **an ~ of silence** eine Schweige- *od.* Gedenkminute; **an ~ in the shooting** eine Unterbrechung der Schießereien; **sunny** *or* **bright ~s** (Meteorol.) Aufheiterungen *Pl.*; **~ music** Pausenmusik, *die* [3] (period) Pause, *die;* **~s of sanity** lichte Momente [4] (Mus.) Intervall, *das;* **perfect ~:** reines Intervall

'interval signal *n.* (Broadcasting) Pausenzeichen, *das*

intervene /ɪntə'vi:n/ *v.i.* [1] [vermittelnd] eingreifen (**in** in + *Akk.*); (come between persons) vermitteln (**between** zwischen + *Dat.*); **if nothing ~s** wenn nichts dazwischenkommt; **if fate had not ~d** wenn das Schicksal nicht eingegriffen hätte [2] (occur) **the years that ~d, the intervening years** die dazwischenliegenden Jahre [3] (Law) **~ in** eintreten in (+ *Akk.*) ‹*Vertrag usw.*›; beitreten (+ *Dat.*) ‹*Verfahren*›

intervention /ɪntə'venʃn/ *n.* Eingreifen, *das;* Intervention, *die* (bes. Politik); **surgical ~:** chirurgischer Eingriff; **at my ~:** auf mein Eingreifen/meine Intervention [hin]; **I~ Board** ≈ Interventionsstelle, *die*

interventionist /ɪntə'venʃənɪst/

A *n.* Interventionist, *der*

B *adj.* interventionistisch

interview /'ɪntəvju:/

A *n.* [1] (for job etc.) Vorstellungsgespräch, *das* [2] (Journ., Radio, Telev.) Interview, *das* [3] (discussion) Gespräch, *das;* Unterredung, *die*

B *v.t.* ein Vorstellungsgespräch/Vorstellungsgespräche führen mit ‹*Stellen-, Studienbewerber*›; interviewen ‹*Politiker, Filmstar, Konsumenten usw.*›; vernehmen ‹*Zeugen*›

interviewee /ɪntəvju:'i:/ *n.* (for opinion poll) Befragte, *der/die;* (candidate, applicant) [Stellen-, Studien]bewerber, *der*/-bewerberin, *die;* (politician, celebrity, etc.) Interviewpartner, *der*/-partnerin, *die;* Interviewte, *der/die*

interviewer /'ɪntəvju:ə(r)/ *n.* (reporter, pollster, etc.) Interviewer, *der*/Interviewerin, *die;* (for job etc.) Leiter/Leiterin des Vorstellungsgesprächs

inter-war /'ɪntəwɔ:(r)/ *attrib. adj.* ‹*Zeit, Jahre*› zwischen den [Welt]kriegen

interweave /ɪntə'wi:v/ *v.t.*, **interwove** /ɪntə'wəʊv/, **interwoven** /ɪntə'wəʊvn/ [miteinander] verweben ‹*Fäden, Wolle, Seide usw.*›; [miteinander] verflechten ‹*Zweige, Bänder*›; **our lives are interwoven** unsere Lebenswege sind miteinander verschlungen

intestacy /ɪn'testəsɪ/ *n.* Sterben ohne Hinterlassung eines Testaments

intestate /ɪn'testət/ *adj.* Intestat‹*erbe, -erbfolge, -nachlass*›; **die ~:** ohne Hinterlassung eines Testaments sterben

intestinal /ɪn'testɪnl, ɪnte'staɪnl/ *adj.* (Med.) Darm-; intestinal (fachspr.)

intestine /ɪn'testɪn/ *n.* ▸ ❶ **p. 951** *in sing. or pl.* (Anat.) Darm, *der;* Gedärme *Pl.*; **large/small ~:** Dick-/Dünndarm, *der*

intimacy /'ɪntɪməsɪ/ *n.* [1] (state) Vertrautheit, *die;* (close personal relationship) enges [Freundschafts]verhältnis [2] (euphem.: sexual intercourse) Intimität, *die;* **~ took place** es kam zu Intimitäten [3] *in pl.* (caresses) Intimitäten; Vertraulichkeiten

intimate

A /'ɪntɪmət/ *adj.* [1] (close, closely acquainted) eng ‹*Freund, Freundschaft, Beziehung, Verhältnis*›; vertraulich ‹*Ton*›; **be on ~ terms with sb.** zu jmdm. ein enges *od.* vertrautes Verhältnis haben [2] (euphem.: having sexual intercourse) intim ‹*Beziehungen*›; **be/become ~ with sb.** mit jmdm. intim sein/werden [3] (from close familiarity) **~ knowledge of sth.** genaue *od.* intime Kenntnis einer Sache; **~ acquaintance with sth.** enge Vertrautheit mit etw. [4] (closely personal) persönlich ‹*Problem*›; privat ‹*Angelegenheit, Gefühl, Dinge*›; geheim ‹*Gedanken*›; (euphem.) Intim‹*bereich, -spray*› [5] innig ‹*Verbindung, Verschmelzung, Zusammenhang*› [6] intim ‹*Tagebuch, Brief, Darstellung, Raum, Theater, Restaurant, Musik, Feier, Treffen*›; **the party was a small, ~ affair** die Feier fand im intimsten Kreis statt

B *n.* (close friend) Vertraute, *der/die*

C /'ɪntɪmeɪt/ *v.t.* [1] **~ sth. [to sb.]/[to sb.] that ...** (make known) [jmdm.] etw. mitteilen/[jmdm.] mitteilen, dass ...; (show clearly) [jmdm.] etw. deutlich machen *od.* zu verstehen geben/[jmdm.] zu verstehen geben, dass ... [2] (imply) andeuten

intimately /'ɪntɪmətlɪ/ *adv.* genau[estens] ‹*kennen*›; bestens ‹*vertraut*›; gründlich ‹*vermischen*›; eng ‹*verbinden*›; **he is ~ involved in the planning of the project** er ist an der Planung des Projekts maßgeblich beteiligt; **we know each other, but not ~:** wir kennen uns, aber nicht näher

intimation /ɪntɪ'meɪʃn/ *n.* [1] Mitteilung, *die;* (of sb.'s death etc.) Anzeige, *die;* **give an ~:** eine Mitteilung machen [2] (hint) Andeutung, *die;* (of trouble, anger, pain) Anzeichen, *das;* **give ~s** Andeutungen machen

intimidate /ɪn'tɪmɪdeɪt/ *v.t.* einschüchtern; **~ sb. into doing sth.** jmdn. einschüchtern *od.* unter Druck setzen, damit er etw. tut; **use intimidating behaviour** zum Mittel der Einschüchterung greifen

intimidation /ɪntɪmɪ'deɪʃn/ *n.* Einschüchterung, *die*

into /*before vowel* 'ɪntʊ, *before consonant* 'ɪntə/ *prep.* [1] *expr. motion or direction* in (+ *Akk.*); (against) gegen; **I went out ~ the street** ich ging auf die Straße hinaus; **they disappeared ~ the night** sie verschwanden in die Nacht hinein; **you don't have to go ~ London** (coll.) du brauchst nicht nach London rein (ugs.); **he was [straight] ~ the biscuit tin** er machte sich über die Keksdose her; **baptized ~ the Catholic Church** katholisch getauft; **they were soon ~ their clothes and on deck** sie waren in kurzer Zeit angekleidet auf Deck; **4 [divided] ~ 20 = 5** 20 [geteilt] durch 4 = 5; **until well ~ that century** bis weit in das Jahrhundert hinein; **it was 15 minutes ~ the second half before ...:** erst in der 15. Minute der zweiten Halbzeit ... [2] *expr. change, result* **translate sth. ~ English** etw. ins Englische übersetzen; **the book is ~ its third edition** das Buch liegt schon in dritter Auflage vor; **poke the fire ~ a blaze** das Feuer [durch Schüren] zum Auflodern bringen [3] (coll.) **be ~ sth./sb.** (interested in) auf etw./jmdn. stehen (ugs.); auf etw./jmdn. abfahren (salopp); **be ~ sth.** (knowledgeable about) mit etw. vertraut sein; **he's heavily ~ meditation** er ist völlig auf Meditation abgefahren (salopp)

intolerable /ɪn'tɒlərəbl/ *adj.* unerträglich; **it's ~:** es ist nicht auszuhalten; **an ~ place to live in** ein Ort, an dem das Leben unerträglich ist

intolerably /ɪn'tɒlərəblɪ/ *adv.* unerträglich

intolerance /ɪn'tɒlərəns/ *n.*, *no pl.* Intoleranz, *die;* Unduldsamkeit, *die* (**of** gegenüber); (Med.) [Über]empfindlichkeit, *die* (**to, of** gegen)

intolerant /ɪn'tɒlərənt/ *adj.* intolerant, unduldsam (**of** gegenüber)

intonation /ɪntə'neɪʃn/ *n.* (modulation) Intonation, *die* (Sprachw.); Sprachmelodie, *die;* **speak with a Russian ~:** in russischem Tonfall sprechen

intone /ɪn'təʊn/ *v.t.* intonieren; psalmodieren (Rel.)

intoxicant /ɪn'tɒksɪkənt/

A *n.* Rauschmittel, *das*

B *adj.* berauschend

intoxicate /ɪn'tɒksɪkeɪt/ *v.t.* [1] (make drunk) betrunken machen; **be/become ~d** betrunken sein/werden [2] (excite) berauschen; **be ~d by/with sth.** durch/von etw. berauscht sein

intoxicating /ɪn'tɒksɪkeɪtɪŋ/ *adj.* berauschend ‹*Wirkung, Schönheit*›; mitreißend ‹*Worte, Rhythmus*›; **~ liquors** alkoholische Getränke

intoxication /ɪntɒksɪ'keɪʃn/ *n.* [1] Rausch, *der;* **in a state of ~:** in betrunkenem Zustand;

im Rausch **2** (excitement) Hochgefühl, *das;* Euphorie, *die* (geh.)

intra- /ɪntrə/ *pref.* inner-; (*mit Fremdwörtern meist*) intra-

intractable /ɪn'træktəbl/ *adj.* widerspenstig ‹*Verhalten, Kind, Tier*›; aufrührerisch ‹[*Menschen-*]*menge, -masse*›; unbeugsam ‹*Wille*›; hartnäckig ‹*Krankheit, Schmerzen, Problem*›

intra'mural *adj.* (Univ.) innerhalb der Universität; inneruniversitär

intra'muscular *adj.* (Med.) intramuskulär

'Intranet *n.* (Computing) Intranet, *das*

intransigence /ɪn'trænsɪdʒəns, ɪn 'trænzɪdʒəns/ *n.*, *no pl.* ▸**intransigent**: Kompromisslosigkeit, *die;* Unnachgiebigkeit, *die;* Intransigenz, *die* (geh.); Unerschütterlichkeit, *die*

intransigent /ɪn'trænsɪdʒənt, ɪn 'trænzɪdʒənt/

A *adj.* kompromisslos, unnachgiebig, (geh.) intransigent ‹*Haltung, Einstellung*›; unerschütterlich ‹*Wille, Grundsätze, Glaube*›

B *n.* (in politics) Radikale, *der/die*

intransitive /ɪn'trænsɪtɪv, ɪn'trɑːnsɪtɪv/ *adj.*, **intransitively** /ɪn'trænsɪtɪvlɪ, ɪn'trɑːnsɪtɪvlɪ/ *adv.* (Ling.) intransitiv

intrapreneur /ɪntrəprə'nɜː(r)/ *n.* Intrapreneur, *der*/Intrapreneurin, *die*

intra-uterine /ɪntrə'juːtəraɪn/ *adj.* (Med.) intrauterin; **~ [contraceptive] device** Intrauterinpessar, *das*

intravenous /ɪntrə'viːnəs/ *adj.* (Med.) intravenös; **~ drip** intravenöse Tropfinfusion

intravenously /ɪntrə'viːnəslɪ/ *adv.* (Med.) intravenös

'in-tray *n.* Ablage für Eingänge

intrepid /ɪn'trepɪd/ *adj.*, **intrepidly** /ɪn 'trepɪdlɪ/ *adv.* unerschrocken

intricacy /'ɪntrɪkəsɪ/ *n.* **1** *no pl.* (quality) Kompliziertheit, *die;* **increase the ~ of sth.** etw. [noch] komplizierter machen **2** *in pl.* (things) Feinheiten *Pl.*

intricate /'ɪntrɪkət/ *adj.* verschlungen ‹*Pfad, Windung*›; kompliziert ‹*System, Muster, Fabel, Werkstück, Maschinenteil, Aufgabe*›; (obscure) schwer verständlich

intricately /'ɪntrɪkətlɪ/ *adv.* kompliziert; **an ~ designed pattern** ein kompliziertes Muster

intrigue /ɪn'triːg/

A *v.t.* faszinieren; **I'm ~d to find out what ...:** ich bin gespannt darauf, zu erfahren, was ...

B *v.i.* **~ against sb.** gegen jmdn. intrigieren; **~ with sb.** mit jmdm. Ränke schmieden *od.* Intrigen spinnen

C /ɪn'triːg, 'ɪntriːg/ *n.* Intrige, *die;* **~s** Machenschaften *Pl.* (abwertend)

intriguer /ɪn'triːgə(r)/ *n.* Intrigant, *der*/Intrigantin, *die*

intriguing /ɪn'triːgɪŋ/ *adj.*, **intriguingly** /ɪn'triːgɪŋlɪ/ *adv.* faszinierend

intrinsic /ɪn'trɪnsɪk, ɪn'trɪnzɪk/ *adj.* (inherent) innewohnend; inner... ‹*Verdorbenheit, Aufbau, Logik*›; immanent (geh.); (essential) wesentlich, (Philos.) essenziell ‹*Eigenschaft, Bestandteil, Mangel*›; **be ~ in** *or* **to a thing** wesentliches Merkmal einer Sache sein; **~ value** innerer Wert; (of sth. concrete) Eigenwert, *der*

intrinsically /ɪn'trɪnsɪkəlɪ, ɪn'trɪnzɪkəlɪ/ *adv.* im Wesentlichen; (Philos.) essenziell

intro /'ɪntrəʊ/ *n.*, *pl.* **~s** (coll.) (presentation) Vorstellung, *die;* (Mus.) Einleitung, *die;* Intro, *das* (fachspr.)

introduce /ɪntrə'djuːs/ *v.t.* **1** (bring in) [erstmals] einführen ‹*Ware, Tier, Pflanze*› (**into** in + *Akk.*, **from ... into** von ... nach); einleiten ‹*Maßnahmen*›; einflechten ‹*Episoden in Roman*›; einschleppen ‹*Krankheit*›; **~ irrelevancies into the discussion** Unwesentliches in die Diskussion bringen **2** einführen ‹*Katheter, Schlauch*› (**into** in + *Akk.*); stecken ‹*Schlüssel, Draht, Rohr, Schlauch*› (**into** in + *Akk.*); **~ sth. into the flame** etw. der Flamme aussetzen **3** (bring into use) einführen ‹*Neuerung, Verfahren, Brauch, Mode, Kalender, Nomenklatur*›; aufbringen ‹*Gerücht, Schlagwort, Mode*› **4** (make known) vorstellen; einführen ‹*Vortragenden*›; **~ oneself/sb. [to sb.]** sich/jmdn. [jmdm.] vorstellen; **I ~d them to each other** ich machte sie miteinander bekannt *od.* stellte sie einander vor; **I don't think we've been ~d** ich glaube, wir kennen uns noch nicht; **~ sb. to a hobby/to drugs** jmdn. in ein Hobby einführen/mit Drogen bekannt machen **5** (usher in, begin, precede) einleiten ‹*Buch, Thema, Musikstück, Epoche*› **6** (present) ankündigen ‹*Programm, Darsteller*› **7** (Parl.) einbringen ‹*Antrag, Entwurf, Gesetz*›; einleiten ‹*Reform*›

introduction /ɪntrə'dʌkʃn/ *n.* **1** (of methods, measures, process, machinery) Einführen, *das;* Einführung, *die;* (of rules) Aufstellung, *die;* (of fashion) Aufbringen, *das* **2** (of tube, catheter) Einführen, *das* **3** **an ~ to London nightlife** eine Einführung ins Londoner Nachtleben; **~ to heroin** erste Bekanntschaft mit Heroin **4** (formal presentation) Vorstellung, *die;* (into society) Einführung, *die;* (of reform) Einleiten, *das;* (of parliamentary bill) Einbringen, *das;* **X needs no ~ from me** ich brauche X nicht vorzustellen; **do the ~s** die Anwesenden miteinander bekannt machen; **letter of ~:** Empfehlungsschreiben, *das* **5** (preliminary matter) Einleitung, *die;* Introduktion, die (Musik) **6** (introductory treatise) Einführung, *die* (**to** in + *Akk.*); Leitfaden, *der* (**to** *Gen.*) **7** (thing introduced) Eingeführte, *das;* (exotic plant or animal) Eingebürgerte, *der/die/das;* **mechanized sowing was a later ~:** [die] maschinelle Aussaat wurde [erst] später eingeführt

intro'duction agency *n.* Partnervermittlung[sagentur], *die;* **join an ~:** sich bei einer Partnervermittlung registrieren lassen

introductory /ɪntrə'dʌktərɪ/ *adj.* einleitend; Einführungs‹*kurs, -vortrag*›; Einleitungs‹*kapitel, -rede*›

introspection /ɪntrə'spekʃn/ *n.* Selbstbeobachtung, *die;* Introspektion, *die* (geh., Psych.)

introspective /ɪntrə'spektɪv/ *adj.* in sich (*Akk.*) gerichtet; verinnerlicht; introspektiv (geh., Psych.)

introvert /'ɪntrəvɜːt/

A *n.* Introvertierte, *der/die;* introvertierter Mensch; **be an ~:** introvertiert sein

B *adj.* introvertiert; **have ~ tendencies** zur Introvertiertheit neigen

introverted /'ɪntrəvɜːtɪd/ *adj.* introvertiert

intrude /ɪn'truːd/

A *v.i.* stören; **~ [up]on sb.'s grief/leisure time/privacy** jmdn. in seiner Trauer stören/ jmds. Freizeit beanspruchen/in jmds. Privatsphäre (*Akk.*) eindringen; **~ [up]on sb.'s time** jmds. Zeit in Anspruch nehmen; **~ in[to] sb.'s affairs/conversation** sich in jmds. Angelegenheiten/Unterhaltung (*Akk.*) einmischen

B *v.t.* aufdrängen (**into, [up]on** *Dat.*); **the idea** *or* **thought ~d itself into my mind** der Gedanke drängte sich mir auf; **~ oneself** *or* **one's presence upon sb.** sich jmdm. aufdrängen

intruder /ɪn'truːdə(r)/ *n.* Eindringling, *der;* (Mil.) Intruder, *der*

in'truder alarm *n.* Einbruchmeldeanlage, *die*

intrusion /ɪn'truːʒn/ *n.* **1** (intruding) Störung, *die;* **an ~/numerous ~s upon** *or* **into sb.'s privacy** ein/wiederholtes Eindringen in jmds. Privatsphäre (*Akk.*); **~ on sb.'s leisure time** Inanspruchnahme von jmds. Freizeit **2** (into building, country, etc.) [gewaltsames] Eindringen; (Mil.) Einmarsch, *der* (**into** in + *Akk.*) **3** (forcing oneself in) Einmischung, *die* (**upon** in + *Akk.*) **4** (Geol.) Intrusion, *die*

intrusive /ɪn'truːsɪv/ *adj.* **1** aufdringlich ‹*Person*›; aggressiv ‹*Bemerkung, Kultur, Journalismus*› **2** (Phonet.) intrusiv **3** (Geol.) **~ rock** Intrusivgestein, *das*

intuition /ɪntjuː'ɪʃn/ *n.* Intuition, *die;* **know sth. by ~:** etw. intuitiv wissen; **have an ~ that ...:** eine Eingebung haben *od.* intuitiv spüren, dass ...

intuitive /ɪn'tjuːɪtɪv/ *adj.* intuitiv; gefühlsmäßig ‹*Ablehnung, Beurteilung*›; instinktiv ‹*Annahme, Gefühl*›

intuitively /ɪn'tjuːɪtɪvlɪ/ *adv.* intuitiv; gefühlsmäßig

Inuit /'ɪnjʊɪt/

A **1** *n. pl.* (people) Inuit *Pl.* **2** *no pl.* (language) Inuit, *das*

B *adj.* **he/she is ~:** er/sie ist Inuk

inundate /'ɪnəndeɪt/ *v.t.* überschwemmen; ‹*Meer:*› überfluten; (fig.) (with inquiries, letters, complaints, goods, information) überschwemmen; (with work, praise, advice) überhäufen; **~d with tourists** von Touristen überlaufen; **we've been ~d with letters** eine Flut von Zuschriften ist bei uns eingegangen

inundation /ɪnən'deɪʃn/ *n.* Überschwemmung, *die;* (by the sea) Überflutung, *die;* (fig.) Flut, *die*

inure /ɪ'njʊə(r)/ *v.t.* gewöhnen (**to** an + *Akk.*); (toughen) abhärten (**to** gegen); **become ~d to/~ oneself to sth.** sich an etw. (*Akk.*) gewöhnen

in vacuo /ɪn 'vækjʊəʊ/ *adv.* (fig.) im luftleeren Raum; (lit.) in einem Vakuum

invade /ɪn'veɪd/ *v.t.* **1** einfallen in (+ *Akk.*) ‹*Gebiet, Staat*›; **Poland was ~d by the Germans** die Deutschen marschierten in Polen (*Akk.*) ein **2** (swarm into) ‹*Touristen, Kinder:*› überschwemmen ‹*Land, Strand, Schwimmbad*› **3** (fig.) ‹*unangenehmes Gefühl, Krankheit, Schwäche:*› befallen ‹*Personen, Gewebe, Körper*›; ‹*Krankheit, Seuche, Unwetter:*› heimsuchen ‹*Person, Stadt, Gebiet*›; ‹*Glücksgefühl, Geruch:*› durchströmen ‹*Person, Raum*›; ‹*Thema, Vorstellung:*› Eingang finden in (+ *Akk.*) ‹*Literatur, Sprache*› **4** (encroach upon) verletzen ‹*Rechte*›; stören ‹*Ruhe, Frieden*›; eindringen in (+ *Akk.*) ‹*Haus, Bereich, Privatsphäre*›

invader /ɪn'veɪdə(r)/ *n.* (hostile) Angreifer, *der;* Invasor, *der* (bes. Milit.); (intruder) Eindringling, *der* (**of** in + *Akk.*)

invalid[1]

A /'ɪnvəlɪd/ *n.* (Brit.) Kranke, *der/die;* (disabled person) Körperbehinderte, *der/die;* (from war injuries) Kriegsinvalide *der*/-invalidin, *die*

B *adj.* (Brit.) körperbehindert; (from war injuries) kriegsbeschädigt; kriegsinvalide

C /'ɪnvəliːd/ *v.t.* **~ home** *or* **out** als dienstuntauglich entlassen; **~ out of the army** wegen Dienstuntauglichkeit aus der Armee entlassen

invalid[2] /ɪn'vælɪd/ *adj.* nicht schlüssig ‹*Argument, Behauptung, Folgerung, Theorie*›; nicht zulässig ‹*Annahme*›; ungerechtfertigt ‹*Forderung, Vorwurf*›; nichtig ‹*Entschuldigung*›; ungültig ‹*Fahrkarte, Garantie, Vertrag, Testament, Ehe*›

invalidate /ɪn'vælɪdeɪt/ *v.t.* aufheben; widerlegen ‹*Theorie, These, Behauptung*›

invalid/'ɪnvəlɪd/: **~ carriage** *n.* Kranken[fahr]stuhl, *der;* **~ chair** *n.* Rollstuhl, *der;* **~ diet** *n.* Krankenkost, *die*

invalidity /ɪnvə'lɪdɪtɪ/ *n.*, *no pl.* ▸**invalid[2]**: mangelnde Schlüssigkeit; Unzulässigkeit, *die;* Ungerechtigkeit, *die;* Nichtigkeit, *die;* Ungültigkeit, *die*

invalidly /ɪn'vælɪdlɪ/ *adv.* nicht ordnungsgemäß

invaluable /ɪn'væljʊəbl/ *adj.* unbezahlbar; unersetzlich ‹*Mitarbeiter, Person*›; unschätzbar ‹*Dienst, Verdienst, Hilfe, Bedeutung*›; außerordentlich wichtig ‹*Rolle, Funktion*›; außerordentlich wertvoll ‹*Rat[schlag]*›; **be ~ to sb.** für jmdn. von unschätzbarem Wert sein

invariable /ɪn'veərɪəbl/ *adj.* **1** (fixed) unveränderlich ‹*Wert, Einheit*› **2** (always the same) [stets] gleich bleibend ‹*Druck, Temperatur, Höflichkeit, gute Laune*›; ständig ‹*Pech*›

invariably /ɪn'veərɪəblɪ/ *adv.* immer; ausnahmslos ‹*falsch, richtig*›; **it's ~ wet when I am on holiday** wenn ich Urlaub habe, regnet es garantiert

invasion /ɪn'veɪʒn/ *n.* **1** (of troops, virus, locusts) Invasion, *die;* (of weeds etc.) massenweise Ausbreitung; (intrusion) [überfallartiges] Eindringen (**of** in + *Akk.*); **the ~ of Belgium by German troops** der Einmarsch deutscher Truppen in Belgien; **the Viking ~ of Britain** der Einfall der Wikinger in Britannien **2** (encroachment) ▸**invade 4**: Verletzung, *die;* Störung, *die;* Eindringen, *das*

invasive /ɪn'veɪzɪf/ *adj.* **1** (Med.) invasiv; **minimally ~:** minimalinvasiv **2** invasiv ‹*Pflanze*› **3** (intrusive) störend

invective /ɪn'vektɪv/ *n.* **1** (abusive language) Beschimpfungen *Pl.* **2** (violent attack in words) Schmähung, *die;* Invektive, *die* (geh.)

inveigh /ɪn'veɪ/ *v.i.* **~ against sb./sth.** über jmdn./etw. schimpfen *od.* sich empören; **~ against fate/the elements** gegen das Schicksal/die Elemente aufbegehren

inveigle /ɪn'vi:gl, ɪn'veɪgl/ *v.t.* **1** (entice) **~ sb. into sth./doing sth.** jmdn. zu etw. verleiten/dazu verleiten, etw. zu tun; **~ sb. into the house** jmdn. ins Haus locken **2** (cajole) **~ sb. into doing sth.** jmdn. überreden *od.* (ugs.) beschwatzen, etw. zu tun

invent /ɪn'vent/ *v.t.* **1** (create) erfinden ‹*Maschine, Verfahren, Spiel*›; ersinnen ‹*Melodie*›; entwickeln ‹*Schrift*› **2** (concoct) erfinden; sich (*Dat.*) ausdenken

invention /ɪn'venʃn/ *n.* **1** (thing invented, inventing) Erfindung, *die;* (concept) Idee, *die;* **it's a device of my own ~:** das habe ich mir selbst ausgedacht; **a story of his own ~:** eine von ihm [selbst] erfundene Geschichte **2** (inventiveness) Erfindungsgabe, *die;* [schöpferische] Fantasie **3** (fictitious story) Erfindung, *die;* Lüge, *die*

inventive /ɪn'ventɪv/ *adj.* **1** schöpferisch ‹*Person, Kraft, Geist, Begabung*›; fantasievoll ‹*Künstler, Kind*› **2** (produced with originality) originell; einfallsreich

inventiveness /ɪn'ventɪvnɪs/ *n., no pl.* Erfindungsgabe, *die;* Kreativität, *die*

inventor /ɪn'ventə(r)/ *n.* Erfinder, *der/*Erfinderin, *die*

inventory /'ɪnvənt(ə)rɪ/

A *n.* **1** (list) Bestandsliste, *die;* **make** *or* **take an ~ of sth.** von etw. ein Inventar aufstellen; Inventur machen **2** (stock) Lagerbestand, *der* **3** (Amer.: trader's stock) Warenbestand, *der*

B *v.t.* **1** (make ~ of) eine Bestandsliste *od.* ein Inventar aufstellen von **2** (enter in ~) inventarisieren

inverse /ɪn'vɜ:s, 'ɪnvɜ:s/

A *adj.* umgekehrt ‹*Reihenfolge*›

B *n.* (opposite) Gegenteil, *das;* (inversion) Umkehrung, *die*

inversely /ɪn'vɜ:slɪ, 'ɪnvɜ:slɪ/ *adv.* umgekehrt

inverse: ~ pro'portion *n.* umgekehrtes Verhältnis; **be in ~ proportion to sth.** im umgekehrten Verhältnis zu etw. stehen; **~ 'ratio** *n.* umgekehrtes Verhältnis; **~ 'square law** *n.* (Phys.) [quadratisches] Abstandsgesetz

inversion /ɪn'vɜ:ʃn/ *n.* **1** (turning upside down) Umdrehen, *das* **2** (reversal of role, relation) Umkehrung, *die* **3** (Ling., Meteorol., Mus.) Inversion, *die*

invert /ɪn'vɜ:t/ *v.t.* **1** (turn upside down) umstülpen; **~ sth. over sth.** etw. über etw. (*Akk.*) stülpen **2** umkehren ‹*Wortstellung*›; vertauschen ‹*Wörter, Filmrollen usw.*› **3** (Mus.) umkehren

invertebrate /ɪn'vɜ:tɪbrət/ (Zool.)

A *adj.* wirbellos

B *n.* wirbelloses Tier; Evertebrat, *der* (fachspr.)

inverted: ~ 'commas *n. pl.* (Brit.) Anführungszeichen *Pl.;* Gänsefüßchen *Pl.* (ugs.); **in ~ commas** (also iron.) in Anführungszeichen; **~ 'pleat** *n.* Kellerfalte, *die;* **~ 'snob** *n.* Edelproletarier, *der* (salopp); **~ 'snobbery** *n.* Edelproletariertum, *das* (salopp)

invest /ɪn'vest/

A *v.t.* **1** (Finance) anlegen (**in** in + *Dat.*); investieren (**in** in + *Dat. od. Akk.*); **~ time and effort in sth.** Zeit und Mühe in etw. (*Akk.*) investieren **2** **~ sb. with** (cause to have) jmdm. übertragen ‹*Aufgabe, Amt, Leitung*›; jmdm. verleihen ‹*Orden, Titel, Amt, Rechte, Kraft*›; jmdn. ausstatten mit ‹*Geldmitteln, Vollmacht, Insignien*› **3** **~ sth. with sth.** einer Sache (*Dat.*) etw. verleihen; **be ~ed with [an air of] mystery** den Anschein des Geheimnisvollen haben **4** (Mil.) belagern

B *v.i.* investieren (**in** in + *Akk.*, **with** bei); **~ in sth.** (coll.: buy) sich (*Dat.*) etw. zulegen (ugs.)

investigate /ɪn'vestɪgeɪt/

A *v.t.* untersuchen; überprüfen; prüfen ‹*Rechtsfrage, Material, Methode*›; ermitteln ‹*Produktionskosten*›; **~ a case** einen Fall untersuchen; in einem Fall ermitteln; **~ a crime** ein Verbrechen untersuchen; wegen eines Verbrechens ermitteln

B *v.i.* nachforschen; ‹*Kripo, Staatsanwaltschaft:*› ermitteln; **~ into sth.** etw. untersuchen

investigation /ɪnvestɪ'geɪʃn/ *n.* ▸ **investigate**: Untersuchung, *die* (**into** *Gen.*); Überprüfung, *die;* Prüfung, *die;* Ermittlung, *die;* **sth. is under ~:** etw. wird überprüft; **sb. is under ~:** gegen jmdn. wird ermittelt; **a scientific ~:** eine wissenschaftliche Untersuchung

investigative /ɪn'vestɪgətɪv/ *adj.* detektivisch; **~ journalism** Enthüllungsjournalismus, *der*

investigator /ɪn'vestɪgeɪtə(r)/ *n.* Ermittler, *der/*Ermittlerin, *die;* (government official) Untersuchungsbeamte, *der/*-beamtin, *die;* **[private] ~:** [Privat]detektiv, *der/*-detektivin, *die*

investigatory /ɪn'vestɪgeɪtərɪ/ *adj.* **~ proceedings/tests/studies** Untersuchungen *Pl.*

investiture /ɪn'vestɪtʃə(r)/ *n.* Investitur, *die;* **~ with the Order of the Garter** Verleihung des Hosenbandordens

investment /ɪn'vestmənt/ *n.* **1** (of money) Investition, *die* (auch fig.); Anlage, *die;* (fig.) Einsatz, *der;* Aufwand, *der; attrib.* Investitions-; Anlage-; **~ of capital** Kapitalanlage, *die;* **make an ~ [of £1,000 in sth.]** [1000 Pfund in etw. (*Akk.*)] investieren; **~ advice** Anlageberatung, *die;* **~ income** Kapitaleinkommen, *das;* **~ capital** Anlagekapital, *das;* **~ trust** Investmenttrust, *der;* Investmentgesellschaft, *die* **2** (money invested) angelegtes Geld; **his large ~ in the company** seine hohe Beteiligung an dem Unternehmen **3** (property) Kapitalanlage, *die;* **be a good ~** (fig.) sich bezahlt machen; eine gute Investition sein **4** ▸ **investiture** **5** (Mil.) (siege) Belagerung, *die;* (blockade) Blockade, *die*

investor /ɪn'vestə(r)/ *n.* Investor, *der/*Investorin, *die;* [Kapital]anleger, *der/*-anlegerin, *die;* **~s in that company** Anteilseigner dieser Firma; **small ~s** Kleinanleger

inveterate /ɪn'vetərət/ *adj.* **1** (deep-rooted) unüberwindbar ‹*Vorurteil, Misstrauen*›; unversöhnlich ‹*Hass*›; unverbesserlich ‹*Faulheit usw.*› **2** (habitual) eingefleischt ‹*Trinker, Raucher, Individualist, Spieler*›; unverbesserlich ‹*Lügner*›

invidious /ɪn'vɪdɪəs/ *adj.* undankbar ‹*Aufgabe*›; unpassend, unfair ‹*Vergleich, Bemerkung*›

invidiously /ɪn'vɪdɪəslɪ/ *adv.* ▸ **invidious**: auf eine undankbare/unpassende *od.* unfaire Art; *as sentence-modifier* unfairerweise

invigilate /ɪn'vɪdʒɪleɪt/ *v.i.* (Brit.: in examination) Aufsicht führen

invigilation /ɪnvɪdʒɪ'leɪʃn/ *n.* (Brit.) Aufsichtführung, *die*

invigilator /ɪn'vɪdʒɪleɪtə(r)/ *n.* (Brit.) Aufsichtsperson, *die;* Aufsichtführende, *der/die;* **there were no ~s** es gab keine Aufsicht

invigorate /ɪn'vɪgəreɪt/ *v.t.* **1** (make vigorous) stärken; (physically) kräftigen **2** (animate) beleben; anregen ‹*Fantasie*›

invigorating /ɪn'vɪgəreɪtɪŋ/ *adj.* kräftigend ‹*Getränk, Mahlzeit, Klima*›; stärkend ‹*Schlaf, Mittel*›; belebend ‹*Brise, Dusche, Rasierwasser*›; (fig.) anregend ‹*Idee, Erfahrung*›

invincibility /ɪnvɪnsɪ'bɪlɪtɪ/ *n., no pl.* Unbesiegbarkeit, *die*

invincible /ɪn'vɪnsɪbl/ *adj.* unbesiegbar; unerschütterlich ‹*Entschlossenheit, Mut, Überzeugung, Stolz*›; unüberwindlich ‹*Schwierigkeiten, Unwissenheit, Skepsis*›

inviolable /ɪn'vaɪələbl/ *adj.* **1** (not to be violated) unantastbar; **maintain ~ secrecy** unverbrüchliches Stillschweigen bewahren **2** (to be kept sacred) unantastbar; sakrosankt (geh.)

inviolate /ɪn'vaɪələt/ *adj.* **1** (not violated) unversehrt; ungestört ‹*Friede, Ruhe*›; nicht verletzt ‹*Abkommen*› **2** (unbroken) ungetrübt ‹*Freundschaft*›; unerschüttert ‹*Glaube*› **3** (unprofaned) unangetastet

invisibility /ɪnvɪzɪ'bɪlɪtɪ/ *n.* Unsichtbarkeit, *die*

invisible /ɪn'vɪzɪbl/ *adj.* (also Econ.) unsichtbar; (hidden because of fog etc.; too small) nicht sichtbar; **almost ~:** kaum zu sehen; **~ mending** Kunststopfen, *das;* **~ earnings** (Commerc.) unsichtbare Einkünfte

invisibly /ɪn'vɪzɪblɪ/ *adv.* [für das Auge] nicht sichtbar; **~ repaired** *or* **mended** so repariert, dass man nichts [davon] sieht; kunstgestopft ‹*Gewebe*›

invitation /ɪnvɪ'teɪʃn/ *n.* (lit. or fig.) Einladung, *die;* **at sb.'s ~:** auf jmds. Einladung (*Akk.*); **admission by ~ only** Einlass nur mit Einladung; **an [open] ~ to thieves** eine Aufforderung zum Diebstahl

invite

A /ɪn'vaɪt/ *v.t.* **1** (request to come) einladen; **~ oneself** (iron.) sich selbst einladen; **before an ~d audience** vor geladenen Gästen; **~ sb. in/over/round** jmdn. hereinbitten/herüberbitten/[zu sich] einladen (**for, to** zu) **2** (request to do sth.) auffordern; **she ~d him to accompany her** sie forderte ihn auf *od.* lud ihn ein, sie zu begleiten; **they ~d him to ascend the throne** sie boten ihm an, den Thron zu besteigen; sie trugen ihm den Thron an (geh.) **3** (make formal request for) erbitten; bitten um **4** (bring on) herausfordern ‹*Kritik, Verhängnis, Spott, Verachtung, Protest*›; **you're inviting ridicule** du machst dich lächerlich *od.* zum Gespött **5** (attract) einladen; **~ interest in sth.** Interesse an etw. (*Dat.*) wecken

B /'ɪnvaɪt/ *n.* (coll.) Einladung, *die*

invitee /ɪnvaɪ'ti:/ *n.* geladener Gast

inviting /ɪn'vaɪtɪŋ/ *adj.* einladend; verlockend ‹*Gedanke, Vorstellung, Aussicht*›; freundlich ‹*Klima*›; ansprechend ‹*Anblick, Schriftbild*›; **make sth. ~ to sb.** etw. für jmdn. attraktiv machen

invitingly /ɪn'vaɪtɪŋlɪ/ *adv.* einladend

in vitro /ɪn 'vi:trəʊ/ (Biol.)

A *adj.* In-vitro-

B *adv.* in vitro

in-vitro fertili'zation *n.* künstliche Befruchtung [im Reagenzglas]; In-vitro-Fertilisation, *die* (fachspr.)

invocation /ɪnvə'keɪʃn/ *n.* Anrufung, *die;* Invokation, *die* (geh.)

invoice /'ɪnvɔɪs/

A *n.* (bill) Rechnung, *die;* (list) Lieferschein, *der*

B *v.t.* **1** (make ~ for) eine Rechnung ausstellen für; (enter in ~) in Rechnung stellen ‹*Waren*› **2** (send ~ to) **~ sb.** jmdm. eine Rechnung schicken; **~ sb. for sth.** jmdm. etw. in Rechnung stellen; **be ~d for sth.** für etw. eine Rechnung erhalten

invoke /ɪn'vəʊk/ *v.t.* **1** (call on) anrufen **2** (appeal to) sich berufen auf (+ *Akk.*); **~ an example/sth. as an example** ein Beispiel/etw. als Beispiel anführen; **~ sth. to justify/explain sth.** etw. bemühen, um etw. zu rechtfertigen/erklären **3** (summon) beschwören **4** (ask earnestly for) erbitten; bitten um

involucre /'ɪnvəlu:kə(r)/ *n.* (Bot.) Hülle, *die*

involuntarily /ɪn'vɒləntərɪlɪ/ *adv.*, **involuntary** /ɪn'vɒləntərɪ/ *adj.* unwillkürlich

involve /ɪn'vɒlv/ *v.t.* **1** (implicate) verwickeln; **~ sb. in a charge** jmdn. zum Mitangeklagten machen **2** (draw in as a participant) **~ sb. in a game/fight** jmdn. an einem Spiel beteiligen/in eine Schlägerei [mit] hineinziehen; **become** *or* **get ~d in a fight** in eine Schlägerei verwickelt *od.* hineingezogen werden; **be ~d in a project** (employed) an einem Projekt mitarbeiten; **get ~d with sb.** sich mit jmdm. einlassen; (sexually, emotionally) eine Beziehung mit jmdm. anfangen; **sth. is ~d** (concerned) etw. kommt mit ins Spiel; **no other vehicle was ~ in the accident** kein anderes Fahrzeug war an dem Unfall beteiligt **3** (include) enthalten; (contain implicitly) beinhalten; **this event ~s us all** dieses Ereignis betrifft uns alle *od.* geht uns alle an **4** (be necessarily accompanied by) mit sich bringen; (require as accompaniment) erfordern; (cause, mean) bedeuten

involved /ɪn'vɒlvd/ *adj.* verwickelt; (complicated) kompliziert; (complex) komplex

involvement /ɪn'vɒlvmənt/ *n.* **1** **my ~ in this affair began only recently** ich habe mit

i

dieser Angelegenheit erst seit kurzem zu tun; **his ~ in the company** seine Beteiligung an der Firma; **I don't know the extent of his ~ in this affair** ich weiß nicht, inwieweit er mit dieser Sache zu tun hat **2** (implication) **~ in a conflict** Einmischung in einen Konflikt; **his increasing ~ in public life** die Rolle, die er in zunehmendem Maße im öffentlichen Leben spielt; **have an ~ with sb.** (sexually) eine Affäre mit jmdm. haben; **you may not take on any other ~:** Sie dürfen sich nicht anderweitig engagieren

invulnerable /ɪnˈvʌlnərəbl/ *adj.* unverwundbar ‹*Lebewesen, Waffensystem*›; (impregnable) uneinnehmbar ‹*Festung, Stadt usw.*›; (fig.) unantastbar ‹*Würde, Stellung*›; **be ~ to sth.** gegen etw. gefeit sein (geh.)

inward /ˈɪnwəd/
A *adj.* **1** (situated within) inner… **2** (mental, spiritual) inner… ‹*Impuls, Regung, Friede, Kampf*›; innerlich (geh.) ‹*Leben*›; **his ~ thoughts** seine innersten *od.* geheimsten Gedanken **3** (directed inside) nach innen gehend; nach innen gerichtet; **'goods ~'** „Eingänge"; **~ slope** Innenneigung, *die;* Neigung nach innen
B *adv.* einwärts ‹*gerichtet, gebogen*›; **open ~:** nach innen öffnen; **an ~-looking person** (fig.) ein in sich (*Akk.*) gekehrter Mensch

inwardly /ˈɪnwədlɪ/ *adv.* im Inneren; innerlich

inwards /ˈɪnwədz/ ▸**inward B**

in-your-ˈface *adj.* (coll) (deliberately provocative) provokativ; provokant; (uncompromisingly direct) ultrabrutal (ugs.)

iodide /ˈaɪədaɪd/ *n.* (Chem.) Jodid, *das*

iodine /ˈaɪədiːn, ˈaɪədɪn/ *n.* Jod, *das*

IOM *abbr.* **= Isle of Man**

ion /ˈaɪən/ *n.* (Phys., Chem.) Ion, *das*

ion exˈchange *n.* Ionenaustausch, *der*

ionic /aɪˈɒnɪk/ *adj.* (Phys., Chem.) Ionen-; in Ionenform vorliegend ‹*Grundstoff*›; ionisch ‹*Bindung, Verbindung usw.*›

ionisation, ionise ▸**ioniz-**

ionization /aɪənaɪˈzeɪʃn/ *n.* Ionisation, *die*

ionize /ˈaɪənaɪz/ *v.t.* ionisieren

ionosphere /aɪˈɒnəsfɪə(r)/ *n.* Ionosphäre, *die*

iota /aɪˈəʊtə/ *n.* **1** (smallest amount) Jota, *das* (geh.); **not an** *or* **one ~:** nicht ein Jota (geh.); kein Jota (geh.); **there's not an ~ of truth in that** daran ist nicht ein Fünkchen Wahrheit **2** (Greek letter) Jota, *das*

IOU /aɪəʊˈjuː/ *n.* Schuldschein, *der*

IOW *abbr.* **= Isle of Wight**

IPA *abbr.* **= International Phonetic Alphabet/Association** IPA

i.p.s. *abbr.* **= inches per second** inch/s

ipso facto /ɪpsəʊ ˈfæktəʊ/ *adv.* **1** (by that very fact) eo ipso (geh.); eben dadurch **2** (thereby) aufgrund dessen **3** (by the very nature of the case) eo ipso; naturgemäß

IQ *abbr.* **= intelligence quotient** IQ, *der;* **IQ-test** IQ-Test, *der*

IRA *abbr.* **= Irish Republican Army** IRA, *die*

> **IRA**
>
> Abkürzung für *Irish Republican Army.* Die Irisch-Republikanische Armee ist eine radikalnationalistische Untergrundorganisation, die die Angliederung von Nordirland an die Republik Irland zu erreichen versucht. Die *IRA* wurde 1919 gegründet und kämpfte für die Unabhängigkeit Irlands von Großbritannien. Nach der Gründung des irischen Freistaats spaltete sich die Organisation; ein Teil trat der regulären irischen Armee bei, ein anderer kämpfte als *IRA* illegal weiter. Seit der Stationierung britischer Soldaten in Nordirland im Jahre 1968 hat die *IRA* wieder zunehmend Anhängerschaft gefunden. Die religiös-sozialen Unruhen haben zu Gewalttätigkeiten und Terrorakten in Nordirland und England geführt. Das Karfreitags-Abkommen von 1998 hat bewirkt, dass Nationalisten und Unionisten in Nordirland in letzter Zeit relativ friedlich zusammenleben. Anhänger der ▸▸▸
>
> ▸▸▸ paramilitärischen *IRA* werden oft auch als *Provos* oder *Provisionals* (provisorische *IRA*) bezeichnet. *Sinn Fein* ist der politische Teil der *IRA.*

Iran /ɪˈrɑːn/ *pr. n.* Iran, *der*

Iranian /ɪˈreɪnɪən/ ▸**ⓘ p. 1277**, ▸**ⓘ p. 1345**
A *adj.* iranisch; **sb. is ~:** jmd. ist Iraner/Iranerin
B *n.* **1** (person) Iraner, *der*/Iranerin, *die* **2** (Ling.) Iranisch, *das;* **speak ~:** eine iranische Sprache sprechen

Iraq /ɪˈrɑːk/ *pr. n.* Irak, *der*

Iraqi /ɪˈrɑːkɪ/, ▸**ⓘ p. 1277**, ▸**ⓘ p. 1345**
A *adj.* irakisch; **sb. is ~:** jmd. ist Iraker/Irakerin
B *n.* **1** (person) Iraker, *der*/Irakerin, *die* **2** (dialect) Irakisch, *das*

Iraq ˈWar *n.* Irakkrieg, *der*

irascible /ɪˈræsɪbl/ *adj.* (hot-tempered) aufbrausend; (irritable) reizbar

irate /aɪˈreɪt/ *adj.* wütend ‹*Person, Tier, Menge*›; erbost (geh.) ‹*Person*›

irately /aɪˈreɪtlɪ/ *adv.* wütend

IRC *abbr.* **= Internet Relay Chat** IRC

ire /ˈaɪə(r)/ *n.* (literary) Zorn, *der*

Ireland /ˈaɪələnd/ *pr. n.* **[Republic of] ~:** Irland (*das*)

iridescence /ɪrɪˈdesəns/ *n.* Schillern, *das;* Irisieren, *das*

iridescent /ɪrɪˈdesənt/ *adj.* regenbogenfarben; (changing colour with position) schillernd; irisierend

iridium /ɪˈrɪdɪəm/ *n.* (Chem.) Iridium, *das*

iris /ˈaɪərɪs/ *n.* **1** (Anat.) Iris, *die;* Regenbogenhaut, *die* **2** (Bot.) Iris, *die;* Schwertlilie, *die* **3** (Optics) Irisblende, *die*

Irish /ˈaɪərɪʃ/ ▸**ⓘ p. 1277**, ▸**ⓘ p. 1345**
A *adj.* **1** irisch; **sb. is ~:** jmd. ist Ire/Irin; **~ joke** Irenwitz, *der; see also* **English A 2** (offensive coll.: contradictory) widersprüchlich; unlogisch
B *n.* **1** (language) Irisch, *das; see also* **English B 1** **2** *constr. as pl.* **the ~:** die Iren

Irish: ~ ˈbull *n.* Widerspruch in sich; Paradox, *das* (geh.); **~ ˈcoffee** *n.* Irishcoffee, *der;* **~ ˈGaelic** *n.* Irisch-Gälisch, *das;* **~man** /ˈaɪərɪʃmən/ *n., pl.* **~men** /ˈaɪərɪʃmən/ Ire, *der;* **~ Reˈpublic** *pr. n.* Irische Republik; **~ ˈSea** *pr. n.* Irische See; **~ ˈstew** *n.* Irishstew, *das;* **~ ˈwhisk[e]y** *n.* irischer Whisk[e]y; **~woman** *n.* Irin, *die*

irk /ɜːk/ *v.t.* ärgern

irksome /ˈɜːksəm/ *adj.* lästig

iron /ˈaɪən/
A *n.* **1** (metal) Eisen, *das;* **~ tablets** Eisentabletten; **man of ~** (fig.) stahlharter Mann; **with a grip of ~:** mit eisernem Griff; **as hard as ~:** eisenhart; **will of ~:** eiserner Wille; **strike while the ~ is hot** (prov.) das Eisen schmieden, solange es heiß ist (Spr.); *see also* **pyrites; rod 3** **2** (tool) Eisen, *das;* **have several ~s in the fire** mehrere Eisen im Feuer haben (ugs.); **have too many ~s in the fire** sich verzetteln; sich (*Dat.*) zu viel auf einmal vornehmen **3** (Golf) Eisen, *das;* Eisenschläger, *der* **4** (for smoothing) Bügeleisen, *das* **5** *in pl.* (Hist.: fetters) Eisen *Pl.;* **put sb. in ~s** jmdn. in Eisen legen (dichter., veralt.)
B *attrib. adj.* **1** (of iron) eisern; Eisen‹*platte usw.*› **2** (very robust) eisern ‹*Konstitution*›; stählern ‹*Muskeln*› **3** (unyielding) eisern; ehern (geh.) ‹*Stoizismus*›; **~ rule/his ~ rule** ein/sein eisernes Regiment
C *v.t.* bügeln
D *v.i.* **1** ‹*Kleidungsstück:*› sich bügeln lassen **2** ‹*Person:*› bügeln

Phrasal verbs

- **~ ˈon** *v.t.* aufbügeln; *see also* **iron-on**
- **~ ˈout** *v.t.* herausbügeln ‹*Falten*›; (flatten) glätten ‹*Papier*›; (fig.) beseitigen ‹*Kurve, Unregelmäßigkeit*›; aus dem Weg räumen ‹*Schwierigkeit, Problem*›; ausgleichen ‹*Interessengegensatz*›

Iron: ~ Age *n.* Eisenzeit, *die;* **i~clad** **A** *adj.* **1** (clad in iron) eisenbewehrt; gepanzert ‹*Schiff*›; **2** (fig.) (rigorous) eisern; unverbrüchlich ‹*Eid*›; unnachsichtig ‹*Kontrolle*›; **there are no ~clad rules in this matter** dafür gibt es keine starren Regeln; **B** *n.* (Navy Hist.) Panzerschiff, *das;* **~ ˈCross** *n.* Eisernes Kreuz; **~ ˈCurtain** *n.* (fig.) Eiserner Vorhang; **i~-grey** **A** *adj.* eisengrau; grau ‹*Herbsttag*›; **B** *n.* Eisengrau, *das*

ironic /aɪˈrɒnɪk/, **ironical** /aɪˈrɒnɪkl/ *adj.* ironisch; **it is ~ that …:** es ist paradox, dass …

ironically /aɪˈrɒnɪkəlɪ/ *adv.* ironisch; *as sentence-modifier* ironischerweise

ironing /ˈaɪənɪŋ/ *n.* Bügeln, *das;* (things [to be] ironed) Bügelwäsche, *die;* **do the ~:** bügeln

ˈironing board *n.* Bügelbrett, *das*

iron ˈlung *n.* eiserne Lunge

ironmonger /ˈaɪənmʌŋgə(r)/ *n.* ▸**ⓘ p. 1260** (Brit.) Eisenwarenhändler, *der*/-händlerin, *die; see also* **baker**

ironmongery /ˈaɪənmʌŋgərɪ/ *n.* (Brit.) **1** (hardware) Eisenwaren *Pl.* **2** (coll.: firearms) Schießeisen (ugs.)

iron: ~-on *adj.* aufbügelbar; zum Aufbügeln *nachgestellt;* **~ ore** *n.* Eisenerz, *das;* **~ ˈration** *n.* eiserne Ration; **~ware** *n., no pl.* Eisenwaren *Pl.;* (household utensils) Haushaltswaren *Pl.;* **~work** *n., no pl.* Eisenarbeit, *die;* (part) Eisenwerk, *das;* (articles) Eisenwaren *Pl.;* **~works** *n. sing., pl. same* Eisenhüttenwerk, *das;* Eisenhütte, *die*

irony /ˈaɪrənɪ/ *n.* Ironie, *die;* **one of life's [little] ironies** eine Ironie des Schicksals; **the ~ was that …:** die Ironie lag darin, dass …; das Ironische war, dass …; *see also* **tragic 2**

irradiate /ɪˈreɪdɪeɪt/ *v.t.* **1** (shine upon) bescheinen **2** (light up) erstrahlen lassen; zum Leuchten bringen **3** (Phys., Med., Gastr.) bestrahlen

irradiation /ɪreɪdɪˈeɪʃn/ *n.* **1** (illumination) Leuchten, *das* **2** (fig.) Erleuchtung, *die* **3** (Phys., Med.) Bestrahlung, *die* **4** **[food] ~:** [Lebensmittel]bestrahlung, *die*

irrational /ɪˈræʃənl/ *adj.* **1** (unreasonable) irrational (geh.); vernunftwidrig **2** (incapable of reasoning) nicht vernunftbegabt **3** (Math.) irrational ‹*Zahl*›

irrationality /ɪræʃəˈnælɪtɪ/ *n.* Irrationalität, *die* (geh.); (of situation) Absurdität, *die*

irrationally /ɪˈræʃənəlɪ/ *adv.* irrationalerweise (geh.); ohne vernünftigen Grund

irreconcilable /ɪˈrekənsaɪləbl/ *adj.* **1** (implacably hostile) unversöhnlich; unüberwindlich ‹*Abneigung*› **2** (incompatible) unvereinbar; unversöhnlich ‹*Gegensätze*›; **theory and practice are completely ~:** Theorie und Praxis widersprechen sich total

irrecoverable /ɪrɪˈkʌvərəbl/ *adj.* unwiederbringlich verloren; endgültig ‹*Verlust*›; nicht eintreibbar ‹*Schuld*›; **the situation was ~:** die Situation war nicht mehr zu retten

irredeemable /ɪrɪˈdiːməbl/ *adj.* nicht wieder gutzumachend ‹*Fehler*›; **be ~:** nicht wieder gutzumachen sein; **the mistake is not yet ~:** noch kann der Fehler wieder gutgemacht werden

irreducible /ɪrɪˈdjuːsɪbl/ *adj.* nicht [mehr *od.* weiter] reduzierbar; Mindest‹*menge*›

irrefutable /ɪˈrefjʊtəbl, ɪrɪˈfjuːtəbl/ *adj.* unwiderlegbar

irregular /ɪˈregjʊlə(r)/
A *adj.* **1** (not conforming) unkorrekt ‹*Verhalten, Handlung usw.*›; **this is most ~!** das ist eigentlich nicht erlaubt! **2** (uneven in duration, order, etc.) unregelmäßig; *see also* **hour 3** **3** (abnormal) sonderbar; eigenartig **4** (not symmetrical) unregelmäßig; uneben ‹*Oberfläche, Gelände*› **5** (disorderly) ungeregelt ‹*Leben[sweise]*›; (lawless) zwielichtig **6** (Mil.) irregulär ‹*Truppen*› **7** (Ling., Bot.) unregelmäßig
B *n. in pl.* (Mil.) Irreguläre *Pl.*

irregularity /ɪregjʊˈlærɪtɪ/ *n.* **1** (of behaviour, action) Unkorrektheit, *die;* (instance also) Unregelmäßigkeit, *die* **2** (unevenness in duration, order, etc.) Unregelmäßigkeit, *die* **3** (abnormality) Sonderbarkeit, *die;* Eigenartigkeit, *die* **4** (disorderliness) Ungeregeltheit, *die;* (lawlessness) Zwielichtigkeit, *die* **5** (lack of symmetry) Unregelmäßigkeit, *die;* (of surface) Unebenheit, *die*

irregularly /ɪˈregjʊləlɪ/ *adv.* **1** (not in conformity) unkorrekt; (lawlessly) unzulässigerweise **2** (unevenly) unregelmäßig

irrelevance /ɪ'relɪvəns/ *n.* (being irrelevant) Belanglosigkeit, *die;* Irrelevanz, *die* (geh.); (irrelevant detail, information, etc.) Belanglosigkeit, *die*

irrelevant /ɪ'relɪvənt/ *adj.* belanglos; irrelevant (geh.); **be ~ to a subject** für ein Thema ohne Belang *od.* (geh.) irrelevant sein

irreligious /ɪrɪ'lɪdʒəs/ *adj.* irreligiös (geh.), ungläubig ‹*Person*›; gottlos ‹*Verhaltensweise, Idee, Person*›

irremediable /ɪrɪ'mi:dɪəbl/ *adj.* nicht wieder gutzumachend ‹*Tat, Verlust, Schaden, Fehler, Irrtum*›; nicht wettzumachend ‹*Verschlechterung*›; nicht zu behebend ‹*Mangel*›; nicht zu verbessernd ‹*Situation*›; **be ~:** nicht wieder gutzumachen/wettzumachen/zu beheben/zu verbessern sein

irreparable /ɪ'repərəbl/ *adj.* nicht wieder gutzumachend; irreparabel (geh., Med.)

irreparably /ɪ'repərəblɪ/ *adv.* irreparabel (geh.); **be ~ damaged** einen nicht behebbaren *od.* (geh.) irreparablen Schaden haben

irreplaceable /ɪrɪ'pleɪsəbl/ *adj.* **1** (not replaceable) nicht ersetzbar; nicht nachlieferbar ‹*Waren*› **2** (of which the loss cannot be made good) unersetzlich

irrepressible /ɪrɪ'presɪbl/ *adj.* nicht zu unterdrückend; unbezähmbar ‹*Neugier, Verlangen*›; unerschütterlich ‹*Optimismus*›; unbändig ‹*Freude, Entzücken*›; unbezwingbar ‹*Neigung*›; sonnig ‹*Gemüt*›; **he/she is ~:** er/sie ist nicht unterzukriegen (ugs.); **an ~ chatterbox** eine unentwegte Quasselstrippe (ugs.)

irreproachable /ɪrɪ'prəʊtʃəbl/ *adj.* untadelig ‹*Charakter, Lebenswandel, Benehmen*›; unanfechtbar ‹*Ehrlichkeit*›; tadellos ‹*Kleidung, Manieren*›; makellos ‹*Vergangenheit [eines Menschen]*›

irresistible /ɪrɪ'zɪstɪbl/ *adj.* unwiderstehlich; bestechend ‹*Argument*›

irresistibly /ɪrɪ'zɪstɪblɪ/ *adv.* unwiderstehlich; unaufhaltsam ‹*näher kommen*›

irresolute /ɪ'rezəlu:t, ɪ'rezəlju:t/ *adj.* **1** (undecided) unentschlossen; unschlüssig **2** (lacking in resoluteness) unentschlossen

irresolutely /ɪ'rezəlu:tlɪ, ɪ'rezəlju:tlɪ/ *adv.* unentschlossen; unschlüssig

irresoluteness /ɪ'rezəlu:tnɪs, ɪ'rezəlju:tnɪs/, **irresolution** /ɪrezə'lu:ʃn, ɪrezə'lju:ʃn/ *ns., no pl.* **1** (being undecided) Unentschlossenheit, *die;* Unschlüssigkeit, *die* **2** (lack of resoluteness) Unentschlossenheit, *die;* Entschlusslosigkeit, *die*

irrespective /ɪrɪ'spektɪv/ *adj.* **~ of** ungeachtet (+ *Gen.*); (independent of) unabhängig von; **~ of what ...:** unabhängig davon, was ...; **~ of the consequences** ungeachtet der *od.* ohne Rücksicht auf die Folgen

irresponsibility /ɪrɪspɒnsɪ'bɪlɪtɪ/ *n., no pl.* ▸**irresponsible:** Verantwortungslosigkeit, *die;* Unverantwortlichkeit, *die;* **it is sheer ~ to ...:** es ist einfach unverantwortlich, zu ...

irresponsible /ɪrɪ'spɒnsɪbl/ *adj.* verantwortungslos ‹*Person*›; unverantwortlich ‹*Benehmen*›; **[financially] ~:** verschwenderisch

irresponsibly /ɪrɪ'spɒnsɪblɪ/ *adv.* verantwortungslos; unverantwortlich; in verantwortungsloser Weise

irretrievable /ɪrɪ'tri:vəbl/ *adj.* nicht mehr wiederzubekommen *nicht attr.;* nicht mehr korrigierbar ‹*Fehler*›; (irreversible) endgültig ‹*Ruin, Verfall, Verlust*›; unheilbar ‹*Zerrüttung einer Ehe*›; ausweglos ‹*Situation*›

irretrievably /ɪrɪ'tri:vəblɪ/ *adv.* unwiederbringlich ‹*verloren*›; (for ever) endgültig; für alle Zeiten; **the marriage has ~ broken down** die Ehe ist unheilbar zerrüttet

irreverence /ɪ'revərəns/ *n.* ▸**irreverent:** Respektlosigkeit, *die;* Pietätlosigkeit, *die* (geh.); **an [act of] ~:** eine Respektlosigkeit/Pietätlosigkeit (geh.)

irreverent /ɪ'revərənt/ *adj.*, **irreverently** /ɪ'revərəntlɪ/ *adv.* respektlos; (towards religious values or the dead) pietätlos (geh.)

irreversible /ɪrɪ'vɜ:sɪbl/ *adj.* **1** (unalterable) unabänderlich, unumstößlich ‹*Entscheidung, Entschluss, Tatsache*›; unwiderruflich ‹*Entschluss, Entscheidung, Anordnung, Befehl usw.*› **2** (not reversible) irreversibel (geh.) ‹*Vorgang*›; (inexorable) unaufhaltsam ‹*Entwicklung, Verfall*›; **~ damage** nicht wieder gutzumachender *od.* (geh.) irreparabler Schaden

irreversibly /ɪrɪ'vɜ:sɪblɪ/ *adv.* irreversibel

irrevocable /ɪ'revəkəbl/ *adj.* **1** (unalterable, final) unwiderruflich ‹*Gelübde, Entscheidung, Entschluss, Befehl*›; unabänderlich ‹*Entschluss*› **2** (gone beyond recall) unwiederbringlich ‹*Vergangenheit, Augenblick*›

irrevocably /ɪ'revəkəblɪ/ *adv.* unwiederbringlich, unwiderruflich ‹*verloren, vorüber*›

irrigate /'ɪrɪgeɪt/ *v.t.* **1** bewässern **2** (Med.) [aus]spülen

irrigation /ɪrɪ'geɪʃn/ *n.* **1** Bewässerung, *die;* **overhead ~:** Beregnung, *die* **2** (Med.) Spülung, *die;* Irrigation, *die* (fachspr.)

irritability /ɪrɪtə'bɪlɪtɪ/ *n.* ▸**irritable 1:** Reizbarkeit, *die;* Gereiztheit, *die*

irritable /'ɪrɪtəbl/ *adj.* **1** (quick to anger) reizbar; (temporarily) gereizt **2** (of organ) empfindlich; **~ to the touch** empfindlich gegen Berührung **3** (Biol.) reizbar

irritably /'ɪrɪtəblɪ/ *adv.* gereizt

irritant /'ɪrɪtənt/
A *adj.* Reiz-; **be ~:** reizen
B *n.* Reizstoff, *der;* **the spicy food proved to be an ~ to his stomach** sein Magen vertrug das scharf gewürzte Essen nicht; **be an ~ to sb./sb.'s nerves** (fig.) jmdm. auf die Nerven gehen (ugs.)

irritate /'ɪrɪteɪt/ *v.t.* **1** ärgern; **get ~d** ärgerlich werden; **be ~d** sich ärgern; ungehalten sein (geh.); **be ~d by** *or* **feel ~d at sth.** sich über etw. (*Akk.*) ärgern; **be ~d with sb.** sich über jmdn. aufregen *od.* ärgern; **be ~d that ...:** verärgert *od.* (geh.) ungehalten [darüber] sein, dass ...; **she was ~d to hear this** sie war ärgerlich *od.* (geh.) ungehalten, als sie dies hörte **2** (Med., Biol.) reizen

irritating /'ɪrɪteɪtɪŋ/ *adj.* lästig; **I find him ~:** er geht mir auf die Nerven (ugs.)

irritatingly /'ɪrɪteɪtɪŋlɪ/ *adv.* ärgerlich; *as sentence-modifier* ärgerlicherweise; **the tap was dripping ~:** der Wasserhahn tropfte nervtötend

irritation /ɪrɪ'teɪʃn/ *n.* **1** Ärger, *der;* **[source** *or* **cause of] ~:** Ärgernis, *das* **2** (Med., Biol.) Reizung, *die;* (itch) Juckreiz, *der*

is ▸**be**

Is. *abbr.* = **Island[s]; Isle[s]** I[n].

Isaac /'aɪzək/ *pr. n.* (Bibl.) Isaak *(der)*

Isaiah /aɪ'zaɪə/ *pr. n.* (Bibl.) Jesaja *(der)*

ISBN *abbr.* = **international standard book number** ISBN

ISDN *abbr.* = **integrated services digital network** ISDN

isinglass /'aɪzɪŋglɑ:s/ *n.* Hausenblase, *die;* Fischleim, *der*

Islam /'ɪzlɑ:m, 'ɪzlæm, ɪz'lɑ:m/ *n.* Islam, *der*

Islamic /ɪz'læmɪk/ *adj.* islamisch

Islamist /'ɪzləmɪst/
A *n.* Islamist, *der*/Islamistin, *die*
B *adj.* islamistisch

island /'aɪlənd/ *n.* (lit. or fig.) Insel, *die; see also* **traffic island**

islander /'aɪləndə(r)/ *n.* Inselbewohner, *der*/-bewohnerin, *die;* Insulaner, *der*/Insulanerin, *die*

island: **~-hop** *v.i.* **go ~ping** eine Inselhoppingtour machen; **~-hopping** *n.; no pl.* Inselhopping, *das; attrib.* **an ~-hopping holiday** eine Urlaubsreise von Insel zu Insel

isle /aɪl/ *n.* Insel, *die;* Eiland, *das* (dichter.)

Isle of Man /aɪl əv 'mæn/ *pr. n.* Insel Man, *die*

Isle of Wight /aɪl əv 'waɪt/ *pr. n.* Insel Wight, *die*

islet /'aɪlɪt/ *n.* **1** (little island) kleine Insel; kleines Eiland (dichter.) **2** (isolated spot) Insel, *die* **3** (Anat.) Insel, *die*

ism /ɪzm/ *n.* (derog.) Ismus, *der* (abwertend)

isn't /'ɪznt/ (coll.) = **is not;** ▸**be**

ISO *abbr.* = **International Organization for Standardization** ISO, *die*

isobar /'aɪsəbɑ:(r)/ *n.* (Meteorol., Phys.) Isobare, *die*

isolate /'aɪsəleɪt/ *v.t.* isolieren; (Electr.) vom Stromkreis trennen; **~ sb. from sb.** jmdn. von jmdm. trennen; **he felt completely ~d** er kam sich (*Dat.*) völlig verloren vor

isolated /'aɪsəleɪtɪd/ *adj.* **1** (single) einzeln; (occasional) vereinzelt; (unique) einmalig; **~ instances/cases** Einzelfälle **2** (solitary) einsam; (remote) abgelegen (**from** von); (cut off) abgeschnitten (**from** von)

isolation /aɪsə'leɪʃn/ *n.* **1** (act) Isolierung, *die;* Absonderung, *die* **2** (state) Isoliertheit, *die;* Isolation, *die;* Abgeschnittenheit, *die;* (remoteness) Abgeschiedenheit, *die;* **examine/look at/treat sth. in ~:** etw. isoliert *od.* gesondert betrachten; *attrib.* **~ hospital** Infektionskrankenhaus, *das;* **~ ward** Isolierstation, *die;* Infektionsabteilung, *die*

isolationism /aɪsə'leɪʃənɪzm/ *n.* (Polit.) Isolationismus, *der*

isolationist /aɪsə'leɪʃənɪst/ *n.* (Polit.) Isolationist, *der*/Isolationistin, *die*

isomer /'aɪsəmə:(r)/ *n.* (Chem.) Isomer[e], *das*

isometric /aɪsə'metrɪk/ *adj.* (Geom., Physiol.) isometrisch

isometrics /aɪsə'metrɪks/ *n., no pl.* isometrisches Muskeltraining; Isometrik, *die*

isomorph /'aɪsəmɔ:f/ *n.* Isomorphe, *die*

isomorphic /aɪsə'mɔ:fɪk/ *adj.* isomorph

isomorphism /aɪsə'mɔ:fɪzm/ *n.* Isomorphie, *die;* (of crystals) Isomorphismus, *der*

isomorphous /aɪsə'mɔ:fəs/ *adj.* isomorph

isosceles /aɪ'sɒsəli:z/ *adj.* (Geom.) gleichschenklig

isotherm /'aɪsəθɜ:m/ *n.* (Meteorol., Phys.) Isotherme, *die*

isothermal /aɪsə'θɜ:ml/ *adj.* (Meteorol., Phys.) isotherm

isotonic /aɪsə'tɒnɪk/ *adj.* (Physiol.) isotonisch; **~ drink** Isodrink, *der*

isotope /'aɪsətəʊp/ *n.* (Chem., Phys.) Isotop, *das*

isotropic /aɪsə'trɒpɪk/ *adj.* (Phys.) isotrop

ISP *abbr.* = **Internet service provider** ISP

Israel /'ɪzreɪl/ *pr. n.* Israel *(das)*

Israeli /ɪz'reɪlɪ/ ▸❶ **p. 1345**
A *adj.* israelisch; **sb. is ~:** jmd. ist Israeli
B *n.* Israeli, *der/die*

Israelite /'ɪzrɪəlaɪt/ *n.* (Bibl.) Israelit, *der*/Israelitin, *die*

issue /'ɪʃu:, 'ɪsju:/
A *n.* **1** (point in question) Frage, *die;* **the ~ of the day** das Thema des Tages; **contemporary ~s** aktuelle Fragen *od.* Themen; **make an ~ of sth.** etw. aufbauschen; **the real ~s in today's world** die Kernprobleme der heutigen Zeit; **become an ~:** zum Problem werden; **evade** *or* **dodge** *or* **duck the ~:** ausweichen; **~ of fact** (Law) Tatsachenfrage, *die;* **the point at ~:** der strittige Punkt; worum es geht; **what is at ~ here?** worum geht es hier eigentlich?; **that's not at ~:** das steht nicht zur Debatte; darum geht es nicht; **be at ~ over sth.** wegen etw. miteinander im Streit liegen; wegen etw. Meinungsverschiedenheiten haben; **join** *or* **take ~ with sb. over sth.** sich mit jmdm. auf eine Diskussion über etw. (*Akk.*) einlassen **2** (giving out) Ausgabe, *die;* (of document) Ausstellung, *die;* (of shares) Emission, *die;* **date of ~:** Ausgabedatum, *das;* Ausgabetag, *der;* (of document) Ausstellungsdatum, *das;* (of stamps) Ausgabetag, *der* **3** (of magazine, journal, etc.) Ausgabe, *die* **4** (total number of copies) Auflage, *die* **5** (quantity of coins) Emissionszahl, *die;* (quantity of stamps) Auflage, *die* **6** (result, outcome) Ergebnis, *das;* Ausgang, *der;* **decide the ~:** den Ausschlag geben; **force the ~:** eine Entscheidung erzwingen **7** (termination) Ende, *das* **8** (Law:

It

The tendency when translating *it* into German is to put **es** whatever it refers to. This is of course correct if *it* refers back to a neuter noun (**Brot, Messer, Auto** etc.). Remember the dative form is **ihm.**

Where's the knife? It's on the table
= Wo ist das Messer? Es liegt auf dem Tisch

The car is stuck. Can you give it a shove?
= Das Auto sitzt fest. Kannst du ihm einen Schubs geben?

The translation is also **es** where it stands for an idea which may be expressed in a whole sentence or clause (which is the case with actions, statements and impersonal subjects):

Who did it/said it?
= Wer hat es getan/gesagt?

It was very kind of you
= Es war sehr nett von Ihnen

It's true that I can't stand him
= Es stimmt, ich kann ihn nicht leiden

There are also impersonal verbs and constructions which always have *it* as the subject:

It's snowing/raining
= Es schneit/regnet

It was ten o'clock
= Es war zehn Uhr

But if *it* refers back to a noun which is masculine in German, it must be translated by **er** (or **ihn** if it is accusative and **ihm** in the dative):

The winter was over; it had been cold
= Der Winter war vorüber; er war kalt gewesen

That's my pencil — give it to me
= Das ist mein Bleistift — gib ihn mir

There's the river; the road follows it
= Dort ist der Fluss; die Straße folgt ihm

Similarly, if the noun referred to is feminine *it* must be translated by **sie** (or **ihr** in the dative):

The flower is wilting — it needs water/you must water it
= Die Blume ist welk — sie braucht Wasser/du musst sie begießen

He found a track and followed it
= Er fand eine Spur und folgte ihr

There are some exceptions to this requirement for agreement, in particular when the noun referred to follows *it's* or *it was:*

It's a good film
= Es ist ein guter Film

It was a lovely evening
= Es war ein schöner Abend

In other cases, an expression with **es** may be seen as a set phrase which does not need to reflect the gender of the noun referred to. In the example with the pencil above, *give it to me* could also be translated by 'gibs her'.

After prepositions

Combinations such as *with it, from it, to it* etc. are translated by the prepositions with the prefix **da-** (**damit, davon, dazu** etc.). Prepositions beginning with a vowel insert an **r** (**daran, darauf, darunter, darüber** etc., in which the **a** is elided in colloquial speech to give **dran, drauf, drunter, drüber** etc.). This makes it possible to distinguish between a person and a thing in examples such as:

It suits him
= Es passt zu ihm

and:

It goes well with it
= Es passt dazu

Other examples:

I can't do anything with it
= Ich kann nichts damit anfangen

Don't lean on it!
= Lehn dich nicht daran!

Put something under it/on top of it
= Leg etwas darunter *or* drunter/darauf *or* drauf

Sometimes the separable verb prefixes with **hin-** are sufficient:

It won't fit into it
= Es passt nicht hinein

Add sugar to it
= Geben Sie Zucker hinzu

---

progeny) Nachkommen (Pl.) **9** (outgoing, outflow) Austritt, *der*

B *v.t.* **1** (give out) ausgeben; ausstellen ‹*Pass, Visum, Zeugnis, Haft-, Durchsuchungsbefehl*›; erteilen ‹*Lizenz, Befehl*›; **~ sb. with sth.** etw. an jmdn. austeilen **2** (publish) herausgeben ‹*Publikation*›; herausbringen ‹*Publikation, Münze, Briefmarke*›; emittieren ‹*Wertpapiere*›; geben ‹*Warnung*› **3** (supply) ausgeben (**to** an + *Akk.*); **~ sb. with sth.** jmdn. mit etw. ausstatten; **be ~d with sth.** etw. erhalten

C *v.i.* **1** (go or come out) ‹*Personen:*› herausströmen (**from** aus); ‹*Gas, Flüssigkeit:*› austreten (**from** aus); ‹*Rauch:*› heraus-, hervorquellen (**from** aus); ‹*Ton, Geräusch:*› hervor-, herausdringen (**from** aus) **2** (be derived) entspringen (**from** *Dat.*) **3** (result) sich ergeben (**from** aus)

isthmus /ˈɪsməs, ˈɪsθməs/ *n.* (Geog.) Landenge, *die;* Isthmus, *der*

it[1] /ɪt/ *pron.* ▸ⓘ p. 1256 **1** (the thing, animal, young child previously mentioned) er/sie/es; *as direct obj.* ihn/sie/es; *as indirect obj.* ihm/ihr/ihm; **behind/under it** dahinter/darunter; **the book was not in the cupboard but behind it** das Buch war nicht im Schrank, sondern dahinter; **the animal turned and snarled at the huntsman behind it** das Tier drehte sich um und knurrte den Jäger hinter sich (*Dat.*) an; **the cathedral and the buildings around it** der Dom und die umliegenden Gebäude **2** (the person in question) **who is it?** wer ist da?; **it was the children** es waren die Kinder; **is it you, father?** bist du es, Vater?; **Are you the one responsible for all this mess? — No, it's him** Sind Sie für dieses Durcheinander verantwortlich? — Nein, er **3** *subj. of impers. v.* es; **it is snowing/warm** es schneit/ist warm; **it is winter/midnight/ten o'clock** es ist Winter/Mitternacht/zehn Uhr; **it is ten miles to Oxford** es sind zehn Meilen bis Oxford; **it says in the Bible that ...:** in der Bibel heißt es, dass ...; in der Bibel steht, dass ...; **had it not been a Sunday ...:** wenn nicht Sonntag gewesen wäre ...; **if it hadn't been for you ...:** wenn du nicht gewesen wärst, ... **4** *anticipating subj. or obj.* es; **it is typical of her to do that** es ist typisch für sie, so etwas zu tun; **it is absurd talking** *or* **to talk like that** es ist absurd, so zu reden; **it is a difficult time, winter** es ist eine schwierige Zeit, der Winter; **it is not often that we see them** wir sehen sie nicht oft; **it was for our sake that he did it** um unseretwillen hat er es getan; **it is to him that you must apply** an ihn musst du dich wenden **5** *as antecedent to relative* es; **it was us who saw him** wir waren es, die ihn gesehen haben; wir haben ihn gesehen; **it was a large sum of money that he found** was er fand, war ein großer Geldbetrag **6** *as indef. obj.* es; **I can't cope with it any more** ich halte das nicht mehr länger aus; **have a hard time of it** eine schwere Zeit haben; **what is it?** was ist los?; was ist denn? **7** (exactly what is needed) **That's it! That's exactly what I've been looking for** Das ist es! Genau das habe ich gesucht; **a gift that is really 'it** das ideale Geschenk (ugs.); **he thinks he's really 'it** er denkt, er ist der Größte (ugs.) **8** (the extreme limit of achievement) **this is really 'it** das ist wirklich [einsame *od.* absolute] Spitze (ugs.) **9** (coll.: sexual appeal) das gewisse Etwas (ugs.) **10** **that's 'it** (coll.) (that's the problem) das ist es [eben]; (that's the end) jetzt ist Schluss; (my patience is at an end) jetzt reichts [mir]; (that's true) genau (ugs.); **when you've done your stint, that's 'it!** wenn du deinen Anteil geleistet hast, dann fertig *od.* dann wars das; **this is 'it** (coll.) (the time for action) es ist so weit; (the real problem) das ist es [eben] **11** (in children's games) **you're 'it!** du bist! (ugs.). *See also* **its; itself**

it[2] *n.* (Brit. coll.) [italienischer] Wermut

IT *abbr.* **= information technology**

Italian /ɪˈtæljən/ ▸ⓘ p. 1277, ▸ⓘ p. 1345

A *adj.* italienisch; **sb. is ~:** jmd. ist Italiener/Italienerin; *see also* **English A**

B *n.* **1** (person) Italiener, *der*/Italienerin, *die* **2** (language) Italienisch, *das; see also* **English B 1**

Italianate /ɪˈtæljənət, ɪˈtæljəneɪt/ *adj.* italienisch beeinflusst

italic /ɪˈtælɪk/

A *adj.* kursiv

B *n. in pl.* Kursivschrift, *die;* **in ~s** kursiv; **my ~s** Hervorhebung von mir

italicize (**italicise**) /ɪˈtælɪsaɪz/ *v.t.* kursiv setzen

italic: ~ 'script *n.* Kursive, *die;* **~ 'type** *n.* (Printing) Kursivschrift, *die*

Italy /ˈɪtəlɪ/ *pr. n.* Italien (*das*)

itch /ɪtʃ/

A *n.* **1** Juckreiz, *der;* Jucken, *das;* **I have an ~:** es juckt mich; ich habe einen Juckreiz; **when you get an ~:** wenn es [dich] juckt **2** (disease) Krätze, *die* **3** (restless desire) Drang, *der;* **I have an ~ to do it** es juckt (ugs.) *od.* reizt mich, es zu tun; **an ~ for money/success** ein Verlangen nach Geld/Erfolg

B *v.i.* **1** einen Juckreiz haben; **I'm ~ing** es juckt mich; **woollen jumpers make me ~:** Wollpullover jucken mich; **this heat makes me ~ all over** bei der Hitze juckt es mich überall; **it ~es** es juckt; **my back ~es** mein Rücken juckt; es juckt mich am Rücken; *see also* **finger A 1** **2** (feel a desire) **~** *or* **be ~ing to do sth.** darauf brennen, etw. zu tun; **~ for sth.** sich nach etw. sehnen; **he is ~ing for a fight** er ist nur darauf aus, sich zu prügeln

itching powder /ˈɪtʃɪŋpaʊdə(r)/ *n.* Juckpulver, *das*

itchy /ˈɪtʃɪ/ *adj.* kratzig ‹*Socken, Laken*›; **be ~** ‹*Körperteil:*› jucken; **I feel ~:** es juckt mich; **I've got ~ feet** (fig. coll.) mich hält es hier nicht länger; (by temperament) mich hält es nirgends lange

it'd /ˈɪtəd/ (coll.) **1** **= it had** **2** **= it would**

item /ˈaɪtəm/ *n.* **1** Ding, *das;* Sache, *die;* (in shop, catalogue) Artikel, *der;* (in variety show, radio, TV) Nummer, *die;* **~ of clothing/furniture** Kleidungs-/Möbelstück, *das;* **~ of equipment** Ausrüstungsgegenstand, *der* **2** **~ [of news]** Nachricht, *die* **3** (in account or bill) Posten, *der;* (in list, programme, agenda) Punkt, *der*

itemize (**itemise**) /ˈaɪtəmaɪz/ *v.t.* einzeln aufführen; spezifizieren ‹*Rechnung*›; **~ the stock** den Bestand auflisten

iteration /ɪtəˈreɪʃn/ *n.* **1** *no pl.* (repetition) Wiederholung, *die* **2** (Computing) Iteration, *die*

iterative /ˈɪtərətɪv/ *adj.*, **iteratively** /ˈɪtərətɪvlɪ/ *adv.* (Ling.) iterativ

itinerant /ɪˈtɪnərənt, aɪˈtɪnərənt/

A *adj.* reisend; umherziehend; Wander‹*prediger, -arbeiter*›; fahrend ‹*Sänger*›

B *n.* Landfahrer, *der*/Landfahrerin, *die*

itinerary /aɪˈtɪnərərɪ, ɪˈtɪnərərɪ/ *n.* **1** (route) [Reise]route, *die;* [Reise]weg, *der* **2** (record of travel) Reisebericht, *der;* Reisebeschreibung, *die*

it'll /ɪtl/ (coll.) **=it will**

its /ɪts/ *poss. pron. attrib.* sein/ihr/sein; *see also* **her²**

it's /ɪts/ **1** = **it is** **2** = **it has**

itself /ɪtˈself/ *pron.* **1** *emphat.* selbst; **by ~** (automatically) von selbst; (alone) allein; (taken in isolation) für sich; **in ~:** für sich genommen; **which ~ is reason enough** was allein schon Grund genug ist; **he is generosity ~:** er ist die Großzügigkeit in Person **2** *refl.* sich; **the rocket destroys ~:** die Rakete zerstört sich selbst; **the machine switches ~ off** die Maschine schaltet sich [von] selbst aus.

itsy-bitsy /ɪtsɪˈbɪtsɪ/, **itty-bitty** /ɪtɪˈbɪtɪ/ *adjs.* (coll.) klitzeklein (ugs.); **~ little** klitzeklitzeklein (ugs.)

ITV *abbr.* (Brit.) = **Independent Television** *kommerzielles britisches Fernsehprogramm*

ITV — Independent Television

Die Gruppe von Fernsehgesellschaften, die in Großbritannien auf *Channel 3* senden. Es gibt fünfzehn Regionen, von denen jede ihre eigenen Programme und Nachrichten empfangen kann. Daneben werden auf *Channel 3* aber auch viele Gemeinschaftssendungen ausgestrahlt.

IUD *abbr.* = **intrauterine device**

Ivan /ˈaɪvn/ *pr. n.* (Hist., as name of ruler etc.) Iwan (*der*); **~ the Terrible** Iwan der Schreckliche

I've /aɪv/ = **I have**

IVF *abbr.* = **in-vitro fertilization**

ivory /ˈaɪvərɪ/ *n.* **1** (substance) Elfenbein, *das; attrib.* elfenbeinern; Elfenbein- **2** (object) Elfenbeinschnitzerei, *die* **3** (colour) Elfenbein, *das; attrib.* elfenbeinfarbig **4** **tickle the ivories** (coll.) ein bisschen auf dem Klavier spielen

ivory: I~ 'Coast *pr. n.* Elfenbeinküste, *die;* **~ 'tower** *n.* Elfenbeinturm, *der*

ivy /ˈaɪvɪ/ *n.* Efeu, *der; see also* **ground ivy**

'ivy-clad *adj.* efeubewachsen

'Ivy League *n.* (Amer.) *Eliteuniversitäten im Osten der USA*

Ivy League

Amerikanische Universitäten sind in Gruppen von Institutionen aufgeteilt, die gemeinsam sportliche Veranstaltungen durchführen. Die exklusivste Gruppe ist die *Ivy League* (Efeuliga; der Name bezieht sich auf den Efeu, der sich an den alten Universitätsgebäuden hochrankt). Die acht Eliteuniversitäten im Nordosten der USA, die seit 1870 sportlich die besten Leistungen erzielten, bis 1913 im **American Football** eine führende Rolle spielten und den besten akademischen Ruf haben, sind: Harvard, Yale, Columbia University, Cornell University, Dartmouth College, Brown University, Princeton University und die Universität von Pennsylvania. Wer von der *Ivy League* kommt, hat beste Berufsaussichten; viele bedeutende amerikanische Politiker studierten an einer *Ivy-League*-Universität.

Jj

J, j /dʒeɪ/ *n., pl.* **Js** *or* **J's** J, j, *das*

J. *abbr.* **1** (Cards) = **jack** B **2** (Phys.) = **joule[s]** J

jab /dʒæb/

A *v.t.*, **-bb-** **1** (poke roughly) stoßen; **he ~bed my arm with his finger** er pikste mir mit dem Finger in den Arm; **he ~bed his elbow into my side** er stieß mir den Ellbogen in die Seite **2** (stab) stechen; **he ~bed the needle into my leg** er stach mir mit der Nadel ins Bein **3** (thrust abruptly) stoßen

B *v.i.*, **-bb-: ~ at sb. [with sth.]** auf jmdn. [mit etw.] einhauen; (stab at) auf jmdn. [mit etw.] einstechen

C *n.* **1** (abrupt blow) Schlag, *der;* (with stick, elbow) Stoß, *der;* (with needle) Stich, *der;* (Boxing) Jab, *der;* **give sb. a ~:** jmdm. einen Schlag/Stoß/Stich versetzen **2** (Brit. coll.: hypodermic injection) Spritze, *die;* **give sb./oneself a ~:** jmdm./sich eine Spritze verpassen (ugs.); **have you had your cholera ~s yet?** bist du schon gegen Cholera geimpft worden?

jabber /ˈdʒæbə(r)/

A *v.i.* plappern (ugs.); **~ at sb.** auf jmdn. einreden

B *v.t.* brabbeln (ugs.)

C *n.* **1** (fast) Geplapper, *das* (ugs.) **2** (unclear) Gebrabbel, *das* (ugs. abwertend); Kauderwelsch, *das*

jabot /ˈʒæbəʊ/ *n.* Jabot, *das*

jack /dʒæk/

A *n.* **1** (Cards) Bube, *der;* **~ of hearts** Herzbube, *der* **2** (for lifting vehicle wheel) Wagenheber, *der* **3** **J~** (man) Hans; **every man ~ [of them]** (coll.) alle miteinander; allesamt; **on one's J~ [Jones]** (Brit. sl.) ganz allein; **all work and no play makes J~ a dull boy** (prov.) zu viel Arbeit ist ungesund; **I'm all right, J~** (fig. coll.) was kümmern *od.* interessieren mich die anderen? **4** ▸**Jack tar** **5** (for turning spit) Bratenwender, *der* **6** (on clock) Glockenschläger, *der* **7** (Teleph. etc.) Buchse, *die;* Klinke, *die* (Postw.); (wall socket) Steckdose, *die* **8** (Bowls) Malkugel, *die* **9** (Zool.) Männchen, *das* **10** (ship's flag) Gösch, *die* (*Seemannsspr.*). *See also* **Union Jack**

B *v.t.* **1** **~ in** *or* **up** (Brit. coll.: abandon) [auf]stecken (ugs.) **2** **~ up** (lift) aufbocken ‹*Fahrzeug*›; (fig. coll.: increase) was draufsatteln auf (+ *Akk.*) (ugs.)

jackal /ˈdʒækl/ *n.* (Zool.) Schakal, *der*

jackanapes /ˈdʒækəneɪps/ *n.* (arch.: impertinent fellow) Laffe, *der* (veralt. abwertend)

jackass /ˈdʒækæs/ *n.* **1** (male ass) Eselhengst, *der* **2** (stupid person) Esel, *der* (ugs.) **3** **laughing ~** (Austral. Ornith.) Lachender Hans

jack: ~boot *n.* **1** [Stulpen]stiefel, *der;* **2** (fig.) **be under the ~boot** brutalen *od.* rücksichtslosen Methoden ausgeliefert sein; **~daw** /ˈdʒækdɔː/ *n.* (Ornith.) Dohle, *die*

jacket /ˈdʒækɪt/ *n.* **1** Jacke, *die;* (of suit) Jackett, *das;* **sports ~:** Sakko, *der;* **a new ~ and trousers** ein neues Jackett und Hosen; eine neue Kombination; **~ pocket** Jackentasche, *die*/Jacketttasche, *die* **2** (round a boiler etc.) Mantel, *der* **3** (of book) Schutzumschlag, *der* **4** (of a potato) Schale, *die;* **~ potato** in der Schale gebackene Kartoffel **5** (Amer.) ▸**sleeve 2**

jack: J~ 'Frost *n.* Väterchen Frost (scherzh.); **~-in-the-box** *n.* Schachtelteufel, *der;* Kastenteufel, *der;* **~-knife** **A** *n.* **1** (large clasp knife) Klappmesser, *das;* **2** (dive) Hechtsprung, *der;* **3** (Motor Veh.) Querstellen des Anhängers; **B** *v.i.* **the lorry ~-knifed** der Anhänger des Lastwagens stellte sich quer; **~ of 'all trades** *n.* Hansdampf [in allen Gassen]; **he is a ~ of all trades and master of none** er versteht von allem ein bisschen was, aber von nichts sehr viel; **~pot** *n.* Jackpot, *der;* **hit the ~pot** (fig.) das große Los ziehen; **J~ Robinson** /dʒæk ˈrɒbɪnsn/ *n.* **before you can/could say J~ Robinson** im Nu (ugs.); in null Komma nichts (ugs.); **J~ Russell** /dʒæk ˈrʌsl/ *n.: eine Terrierart;* **J~ 'tar** *n.* Teerjacke, *die* (scherzh.)

Jacob /ˈdʒeɪkəb/ *pr. n.* (Bibl.) Jakob (*der*); **~'s ladder** (Bot.) Jakobsleiter, *die;* Sperrkraut, *das*

Jacobean /dʒækəˈbiːən/ *adj.* (Hist.) [aus] der Zeit Jakobs I. *nachgestellt*

Jacobite /ˈdʒækəbaɪt/ *n.* (Hist.) Jakobit, *der*

Jacquard [loom] /ˈdʒækɑːd (luːm)/ *n.* Jacquardwebstuhl, *der*

jacuzzi (*Amer.:* ®) /dʒəˈkuːzɪ/ *n.* ≈ Whirlpool, *der*

jade¹ /dʒeɪd/

A *n.* (arch. derog.) **1** (horse) alter Klepper (abwertend); Schindmähre, *die* (abwertend) **2** (woman) Weib, *das;* Weibsbild, *das* (abwertend)

B *v.t.*, *esp. in p.p.* (tire) ermüden; abstumpfen ‹*Geschmacksnerven*›; **look ~d** abgespannt *od.* erschöpft aussehen

jade² *n.* **1** (stone) Jade, *der od. die;* (carvings) Jade[arbeiten], *die* **2** (colour) Jadegrün, *das*

Jaffa /ˈdʒæfə/, **Jaffa orange** /dʒæfə ˈɒrɪndʒ/ *n.* Jaffaapfelsine, *die*

jag¹ *n.* Zacke, *die;* Spitze, *die*

jag² *n.* (sl.: drinking bout) Besäufnis, *das* (salopp); Sauferei, *die* (derb abwertend); **go on a ~:** saufen (derb); **be on a ~:** am Saufen sein (derb)

Jag /dʒæg/ *n.* (Brit. coll.: car) Jaguar, *der*

jagged /ˈdʒægɪd/ *adj.* **1** (irregularly cut) gezackt; ausgefranst ‹*Loch/Riss in Kleidungsstücken*›; ‹*Wunde*› mit [unregelmäßig] gezackten *od.* zerfetzten Rändern **2** (deeply indented) zerklüftet ‹*Küste*›

jaguar /ˈdʒægjʊə(r)/ *n.* (Zool.) Jaguar, *der*

jail /dʒeɪl/

A *n.* (place) Gefängnis, *das;* (confinement) Haft, *die;* **in ~:** im Gefängnis; **be sent to ~:** ins Gefängnis kommen; eingesperrt werden; **go to ~:** ins Gefängnis gehen

B *v.t.* ins Gefängnis bringen; einsperren

jail: ~bird *n.* Knastbruder, *der* (ugs.); **~break** *n.* Gefängnisausbruch, *der*

jailer, jailor /ˈdʒeɪlə(r)/ *n.* Gefängniswärter, *der*/-wärterin, *die*

jalopy /dʒəˈlɒpɪ/ *n.* (coll.) Klapperkiste, *die* (ugs.)

jam¹ /dʒæm/

A *v.t.*, **-mm-** **1** (squeeze and fix between two surfaces) einklemmen; **~ sth. into sth.** etw. in etw. (*Akk.*) zwängen; **the key had become ~med in the lock** der Schlüssel hatte sich im Schloss verklemmt **2** (make immovable) blockieren; (fig.) lähmen; lahm legen; **I seem to ~ the car door every time I lock it** die Autotür verklemmt sich anscheinend jedes Mal, wenn ich sie abschließe **3** (squeeze together in compact mass) stopfen (**into** in + *Akk.*); **~ together** zusammenpferchen ‹*Personen*› **4** (thrust into confined space) stopfen (**into** in + *Akk.*); stecken ‹*Schlüssel, Münze*› (**into** in + *Akk.*) **5** (block by crowding) blockieren; versperren, blockieren ‹*Eingang*›; verstopfen, blockieren ‹*Rohr*›; **the switchboard was ~med with calls** sämtliche Leitungen waren durch Anrufe blockiert **6** (Radio) stören

B *v.i.*, **-mm-** **1** (become tightly wedged) sich verklemmen **2** (become unworkable) ‹*Maschine:*› klemmen **3** (coll.: improvise music) jammen (Jargon)

C *n.* **1** (crush, stoppage) Blockierung, *die;* Klemmen, *das* **2** (crowded mass) Stau, *der* **3** (coll.: dilemma) Klemme, *die* (ugs.); Patsche, *die* (ugs.); **be in a ~:** in der Klemme stecken; in der Patsche sitzen; **get into a ~:** in die Klemme geraten **4** ▸**jam session**. *See also* **logjam**; **traffic jam**

Phrasal verbs

- **~ 'in** *v.t.* hineinzwängen; **we were ~med in** wir waren eingepfercht
- **~ 'on** *v.t.* **~ the brakes [full] on** [voll] auf die Bremse steigen (ugs.); eine Vollbremsung machen
- **~ 'up** *v.t.* verstopfen ‹*Straße usw.*›; lahm legen ‹*System*›; verklemmen ‹*Mechanismus*›

jam² *n.* **1** Marmelade, *die;* Konfitüre, *die* (bes. Kaufmannsspr.); **make ~:** Marmelade einmachen; **[promises of] ~ tomorrow** (fig.) schöne Zukunftsverheißungen; **sb. wants ~ on it** (fig. coll.) jmdm. genügt etw. noch nicht **2** (Brit. coll.: sth. easy) kinderleichte Sache (fam.); Kinderspiel, *das; see also* **money 1**

Jamaica /dʒəˈmeɪkə/ *pr. n.* Jamaika (*das*)

Jamaican /dʒəˈmeɪkən/ ▸❶ **p. 1345**

A *adj.* jamaik[an]isch; **sb. is ~:** jmd. ist Jamaikaner/Jamaikanerin

B *n.* Jamaikaner, *der*/Jamaikanerin, *die*

jamb /dʒæm/ *n.* (of doorway, window) Pfosten, *der*

jamboree /dʒæmbəˈriː/ *n.* **1** fröhliches Beisammensein; Fete, *die* (ugs. scherzh.); (carousal) Zechgelage, *das* (veralt.) **2** (large rally of Scouts) Jamboree, *das*

James /dʒeɪmz/ *pr. n.* (Hist., as name of ruler etc.) Jakob (*der*)

'jam jar *n.* Marmeladenglas, *das*

jammy /ˈdʒæmɪ/ *adj.* **1** (sticky with jam) von Marmelade klebrig; marmeladeverklebt **2** (Brit. coll.) (easy) kinderleicht (fam.); (lucky) **that was ~:** das war Schwein (ugs.); **~ beggar** Glückspilz, *der* (ugs.)

jam: ~-packed *adj.* (coll.) knallvoll (ugs.), proppenvoll (ugs.) (**with** von); **~ session** *n.* (Jazz coll.) Jamsession, *die;* **~ 'tart** *n.* Marmeladentörtchen, *das*

Jan. *abbr.* = **January** Jan.

jane /dʒeɪn/ *n.* (sl.) Mieze, *die* (*salopp*); *see also* **plain A 4**

jangle /ˈdʒæŋgl/

A *v.i.* klimpern; ‹*Klingel:*› bimmeln

B *v.t.* **1** (sound) rasseln mit; bimmeln mit ‹*Glocke*›; klimpern mit ‹[*Klein*]*geld*› **2** (irritate) **~ sb.'s nerves** jmdn. nerven (salopp); jmdm. auf die Nerven gehen

C *n.* Geklapper, *das;* (of bell) Schrillen, *das*

janitor /ˈdʒænɪtə(r)/ *n.* **1** (doorkeeper) Portier, *der* **2** (caretaker) Hausmeister, *der*

January /ˈdʒænjʊərɪ/ *n.* ▸❶ **p. 1047** Januar, *der; see also* **August**

Jap /dʒæp/ *n.* (coll., often derog.) Japs, *der* (ugs., oft abwertend)

j

japan
A *n.* Japanlack, *der*
B *v.t.*, **-nn-** mit Japanlack überziehen; **a ~ned table** ein Lacktisch
Japan /dʒəˈpæn/ *n.* Japan (*das*)
Japanese /dʒæpəˈniːz/ ▸ⓘ **p. 1277,** ▸ⓘ **p. 1345**
A *adj.* japanisch; **sb. is ~:** jmd. ist Japaner/Japanerin; *see also* **English A**
B *n., pl. same* **1** (person) Japaner, *der*/Japanerin, *die* **2** (language) Japanisch, *das; see also* **English B 1**
Japanese: ~ [flowering] ˈcherry *n.* Japanische Kirsche; **~ ˈquince** *n.* Japanische Quitte; **~ ˈsilk** *n.* Japanseide, *die*
jape /dʒeɪp/
A *v.i.* spotten (**with** über + *Akk.*); **~ at** verspotten
B *n.* Scherz, *der*; Spaß, *der*; (practical joke) Streich, *der*
japonica /dʒəˈpɒnɪkə/ *n.* (Bot.) Japanische Quitte
jar¹ /dʒɑː(r)/
A *n.* **1** (harsh or grating sound) Quietschen, *das* **2** (jolt) Stoß, *der*; (thrill of nerves, shock) Schlag, *der*; **stop with a ~:** mit einem Ruck halten **3** (lack of harmony) Misston, *der*
B *v.i.*, **-rr-** **1** (sound discordantly) quietschen; (rattle) ‹*Fenster:*› scheppern (ugs.); **~ on** *or* **against sth.** über etw. (*Akk.*) knirschen; **a ~ring sound** ein Geräusch, das einem durch und durch geht **2** (have discordant or painful effect) **~ [up]on sb./sb.'s nerves** jmdm. auf die Nerven gehen; **~ on the ears** durch Mark und Bein gehen (ugs. scherzh.); **these two colours ~:** diese beiden Farben beißen sich (ugs.) **3** (fig.: be out of harmony) **~ with sth.** sich mit etw. nicht vertragen
C *v.t.*, **-rr-** **1** (cause to vibrate) erschüttern **2** (send shock through) **~ sb.'s nerves** jmdm. auf die Nerven gehen; **~ one's elbow** sich (*Dat.*) den Ellbogen anschlagen
jar² *n.* **1** (vessel) Topf, *der*; (of glass) Glas, *das*; **~ of jam** *etc.* Topf/Glas Marmelade *usw.* **2** (Brit. coll.: glass of beer) Bierchen, *das* (fam.)
jar³ *n.* (arch./coll.) **on the ~** (ajar) angelehnt
jardinière /ʒɑːdɪˈnjeə(r)/ *n.* Jardiniere, *die*
jarful /ˈdʒɑːfʊl/ *n.* Topf, *der*; (contents of glass jar) Glas, *das*; **a ~ of jam** ein Topf/Glas Marmelade; **a ~ of pebbles** ein Topf/Glas voll Kieselsteine
jargon /ˈdʒɑːgən/ *n.* **1** (speech familiar only to a particular group) Jargon, *der* **2** (unintelligible words) Gebrabbel, *das* (ugs. abwertend)
Jas. *abbr.* = **James**
jasmin[e] /ˈdʒæsmɪn, ˈdʒæzmɪn/ *n.* Jasmin, *der*; **common** *or* **white ~:** echter Jasmin; Kletterjasmin, *der*; **red ~:** rot blühende Plumeria; **winter ~:** Winterjasmin, *der*
jasper /ˈdʒæspə(r)/ *n.* (Min.) Jaspis, *der*
jaundice /ˈdʒɔːndɪs/
A *n.* ▸ⓘ **p. 1231** (Med.) Gelbsucht, *die*
B *v.t.* **1** ▸ⓘ **p. 1231** (Med.) **be [badly] ~d** eine [schwere] Gelbsucht haben **2** *usu. in p.p.* (fig.: affect with bitterness) verbittern; **~d** verbittert; (cynical) zynisch; **~ sb. against sth./towards sb.** jmdn. gegen etw./jmdn. einnehmen; **with [a] ~d eye** (enviously) neidvoll; mit Neid; **have a very ~d view of life** dem Leben voller Verbitterung gegenüberstehen
jaunt /dʒɔːnt/
A *n.* Ausflug, *der*; **be off on/go for a ~:** einen Ausflug machen
B *v.i.* **~ [about]** herumziehen; **are you ~ing off again on some new trip?** geht es mal wieder auf Tour?
jauntily /ˈdʒɔːntɪlɪ/ *adv.* unbeschwert
jaunty /ˈdʒɔːntɪ/ *adj.* unbeschwert; keck ‹*Hut*›; **with a ~ gait** beschwingten Schrittes; **he wore his hat at a ~ angle** er hatte sich (*Dat.*) den Hut keck aufs Ohr gesetzt
Java /ˈdʒɑːvə/ *pr. n.* Java (*das*)
javelin /ˈdʒævəlɪn, ˈdʒævlɪn/ *n.* **1** Speer, *der*; **throwing the ~** (Sport) Speerwerfen, *das* **2** (Sport: event) Speerwerfen, *das*
javelin: ~ thrower *n.* (Sport) Speerwerfer, *der*/-werferin, *die*; **~-throwing** *n., no pl.* Speerwerfen, *das*

jaw /dʒɔː/
A *n.* **1** ▸ⓘ **p. 951** (Anat.) Kiefer, *der*; **his ~ dropped** er ließ die Kinnlade herunterfallen; **upper/lower ~:** Ober-/Unterkiefer, *der*; **set one's ~:** ein entschlossenes Gesicht machen **2** *in pl.* (of valley, channel) Schlund, *der* **3** (of machine) [Klemm]backe, *die* **4** *in pl.* (large dangerous mouth) Rachen, *der*; (fig.: of fate, death, etc.) Klauen; **snatch sb. from the ~s of death** jmdn. vor dem sicheren Tod retten; **snatch victory from the ~s of defeat** kurz vor der drohenden Niederlage doch noch den Sieg erringen
B *v.i.* (coll.) quatschen (ugs.); **~ at sb.** jmdn. voll quatschen (ugs.)
jaw: ~bone *n.* ▸ⓘ **p. 951** Kieferknochen, *der*; **~-breaker** *n.* (coll.) Zungenbrecher, *der*
jay /dʒeɪ/ *n.* (Ornith.) **1** (Garrulus glandarius) Eichelhäher, *der* **2** (Garrulinae) Häher, *der*
jay: ~-walk *v.i.* als Fußgänger im Straßenverkehr unachtsam sein; **~walker** *n.* im Straßenverkehr unachtsamer Fußgänger
jazz /dʒæz/
A *n.* Jazz, *der*; *attrib.* Jazz‹*musik, -musiker*›; **and all that ~** (coll.) und der ganze Kram (ugs)
B *v.t.* **~ up** aufpeppen (ugs.); aufmotzen (ugs.)
jazz: ~ band *n.* Jazzband, *die*; **~ dance** *n., no pl.* Jazztanz, *der*; **~ ˈrock** *n., no pl.* Jazzrock, *der*
jazzy /ˈdʒæzɪ/ *adj.* poppig; **a ~ sports car** ein aufgemotzter Sportwagen (ugs.)
JCB ® *n.* [JCB-]Bagger, *der*
JCR *abbr.* (Brit. Univ.) = **Junior Common Room; Junior Combination Room**
jealous /ˈdʒeləs/ *adj.* **1** (feeling resentment) eifersüchtig (**of** auf + *Akk.*) **2** (possessive) eifersüchtig ‹*Liebe*›; **be ~ of sth.** eifersüchtig über etw. (*Akk.*) wachen; **be ~ for sth.** peinlich auf etw. (*Akk.*) bedacht sein; **he kept a ~ eye on her** er wachte eifersüchtig über sie
jealously /ˈdʒeləslɪ/ *adv.* eifersüchtig
jealousy /ˈdʒeləsɪ/ *n.* Eifersucht, *die*; **little jealousies** [kleine] Eifersüchteleien
jean /dʒiːn/ *n.* **1** (cloth) Baumwolldrell, *der* **2** *in pl.* (trousers) Jeans *Pl.*; Jeans, *die*; **a pair of ~s** ein Paar Jeans; eine Jeans; *see also* **blue jeans**
Jeep ® /dʒiːp/ *n.* Jeep Ⓦⓩ, *der*
jeer /dʒɪə(r)/
A *v.i.* höhnen (geh.); **~ at sb.** jmdn. verhöhnen; **~ing** höhnisch johlend ‹*Menge, Mob*›
B *v.t.* verhöhnen; **the crowd ~ed every tackle he made** die Menge johlte höhnisch bei jedem Tackling, das er machte
C *n.* höhnisches Johlen; (remark) höhnische Bemerkung; **~s** höhnisches Gejohle/höhnische Bemerkungen
jehad ▸ **jihad**
Jehovah /dʒɪˈhəʊvə/ *n.* (Relig.) Jehova (*der*)
Jehovah's ˈWitness *n.* (Relig.) Zeuge Jehovas
jejune /dʒɪˈdʒuːn/ *adj.* **1** (intellectually unsatisfying) unergiebig; unzulänglich ‹*Erklärung, Begründung, Leistung*› **2** (puerile) läppisch (abwertend); infantil (abwertend)
jejunum /dʒɪˈdʒuːnəm/ *n.* (Anat.) Leerdarm, *der*
jell /dʒel/ *v.i.* **1** (set as jelly) fest werden; gelieren **2** (fig.: take definite form) Gestalt annehmen; **not ~ as a group** als Gruppe nicht zusammenpassen
Jell-O ®, **jello** /ˈdʒeləʊ/ *n.* (esp. Amer.) Götterspeise, *die*
jelly /ˈdʒelɪ/
A *n.* **1** Gelee, *das*; (dessert) Götterspeise, *die* **2** (substance of similar consistency) gallertartige Masse; **her legs felt like ~:** ihr schlotterten die Knie; sie hatte Pudding in den Knien (ugs.) **3** (coll.: gelignite) Plastiksprengstoff, *der*
B *v.t.* **1** zu einer gallertartigen Masse erstarren lassen; Gelee machen aus ‹*Obst*› **2** **jellied eels** Aal in Aspik
C *v.i.* (become ~) gelieren
jelly: ~ baby *n.* ≈ Gummibärchen, *das*; **~ bean** *n.* [bohnenförmiges] Geleebonbon; **~fish** *n.* Qualle, *die*; **~-like** *adj.* gallertartig; gallertig ‹*Konsistenz*›
jemmy /ˈdʒemɪ/ *n.* (Brit.) Brecheisen, *das*

jeopardize (jeopardise) /ˈdʒepədaɪz/ *v.t.* gefährden
jeopardy /ˈdʒepədɪ/ *n., no pl.* Gefahr, *die*; **put** *or* **place sth./sb. in ~:** etw. aufs Spiel setzen/jmdn. in Gefahr bringen; etw./jmdn. gefährden; **in ~:** in Gefahr; gefährdet; **her life is in ~:** sie schwebt in Lebensgefahr
jerbil ▸ **gerbil**
jerboa /dʒɜːˈbəʊə/ *n.* (Zool.) Springmaus, *die*
Jeremiah /dʒerɪˈmaɪə/ *n.* **1** (Bibl.) Jeremia[s] (*der*) **2** (fig.) Schwarzseher, *der*
Jericho /ˈdʒerɪkəʊ/ *pr. n.* ▸ⓘ **p. 1643** (Geog.) Jericho (*das*)
jerk /dʒɜːk/
A *n.* **1** (sharp sudden pull) Ruck, *der*; ruckartige Bewegung; **with a series of ~s** ruckartig; ruckend; **with a ~ of his thumb, he indicated the direction in which …:** mit einer kurzen Daumenbewegung zeigte er die Richtung, in die …; **give sth. a ~:** einer Sache (*Dat.*) einen Ruck geben; an etw. (*Dat.*) rucken **2** (involuntary movement) Zuckung, *die*; Zucken, *das* **3** (coll.: person) Null, *die* (ugs.); Blödmann, *der* (ugs.)
B *v.t.* **1** reißen an (+ *Dat.*) ‹*Seil usw.*›; **~ sth. away/back** *etc.* etw. weg-/zurückreißen *usw.*; **~ sth. off/out of sth.** *etc.* etw. von etw. [herunter]reißen/aus etw. [heraus]reißen *usw.*; **he ~ed his thumb in the direction of the town** er zeigte mit einer kurzen Bewegung seines Daumens in Richtung Stadt; **a noise ~ed him out of his reverie** ein Geräusch riss ihn aus seinen Träumereien **2** (Weightlifting) stoßen
C *v.i.* ruckeln; (move in a spasmodic manner) zucken; **the lever ~ed out of his hand** der Hebel sprang ihm aus der Hand; **his head ~ed back** sein Kopf zuckte zurück
Phrasal verb
• **~ ˈoff** (coarse)
A *v.t.* **~ sb. off** jmdm. einen abwichsen (vulg.)
B *v.i.* wichsen (derb)
jerkily /ˈdʒɜːkɪlɪ/ *adv.* ruckartig; eckig ‹*gehen, sich verbeugen*›
jerkin /ˈdʒɜːkɪn/ *n.* ≈ Wams, *das*; (modern) Weste, *die*
jerky /ˈdʒɜːkɪ/ *adj.* **1** abgehackt, holprig ‹*Art zu schreiben/sprechen*›; holprig ‹*Busfahrt*›; holpernd ‹*Fahrzeug*›; ruckartig ‹*Bewegung*› **2** (spasmodic) zuckend; **the ~ movements of a puppet** die eckigen Bewegungen einer Marionette
Jerome /dʒəˈrəʊm/ *pr. n.* **St ~:** der heilige Hieronymus
jerrican ▸ **jerrycan**
Jerry /ˈdʒerɪ/ *n.* (Brit. dated coll.) **1** (soldier) Deutsche, *der* **2** *no pl.* (Germans collectively) der Deutsche
jerry: ~-builder *n.* Baupfuscher, *der* (ugs. abwertend); **~-building** *n.* Pfusch am Bau (ugs. abwertend); **~-built** *adj.* unsolide gebaut; **~can** *n.* Kanister, *der*
jersey /ˈdʒɜːzɪ/ *n.* **1** Pullover, *der*; (Sport) Trikot, *das*; Jersey, *das* **2** (vest) Unterhemd, *das* **3** (fabric) Jersey, *der* **4** **J~** (cow) Jerseyrind, *das* **5** **J~** *pr. n.* (island) Jersey (*das*)
Jerusalem /dʒəˈruːsələm/ *pr. n.* ▸ⓘ **p. 1643** Jerusalem (*das*)
Jerusalem ˈartichoke *n.* Topinambur, *der*
jest /dʒest/
A *n.* **1** (joke) Scherz, *der*; Witz, *der*; **make ~s** scherzen; Witze machen **2** *no pl.* (fun) Spaß, *der*; **in ~:** im Scherz
B *v.i.* scherzen; Witze machen
jester /ˈdʒestə(r)/ *n.* Spaßmacher, *der*; (at court) Hofnarr, *der*; (fool) Hanswurst, *der*
Jesu /ˈdʒiːzjuː/ *pr. n. voc.* Jesu
Jesuit /ˈdʒezjʊɪt/ *n.* Jesuit, *der*
Jesuitical /dʒezjʊˈɪtɪkl/ *adj.* jesuitisch
Jesus /ˈdʒiːzəs/
A *pr. n.* Jesus (*der*); **Society of ~:** Jesuitenorden, *der*
B *int.* (sl.) **~ [Christ]!** Herrgott noch mal! (ugs.)
jet¹ /dʒet/
A *n.* **1** (stream) Strahl, *der*; **~ of flame/steam/water** Feuer-/Dampf-/Wasserstrahl, *der*

ℹ Jobs

What's your job?, What do you do [for a living]?
= Was machen Sie beruflich?, Was sind Sie von Beruf?
I work in a bank/in a bookshop
= Ich arbeite bei einer Bank/in einer Buchhandlung
He is in insurance/in the City
= Er ist in der Versicherungsbranche/in der City tätig
I am with a small company or firm/a large combine or group/a multinational
= Ich bin bei einem kleinen Unternehmen/einem großen Konzern/einem Multi
She owns/runs a small business
= Sie hat/führt einen kleinen Betrieb
My husband works for or is employed by the same firm
= Mein Mann ist bei derselben Firma angestellt
She works full time/part time
= Sie arbeitet ganztags *or* hat eine Ganztagsbeschäftigung/ist als Teilzeitkraft angestellt *or* hat eine Teilzeitbeschäftigung
I work freelance/am self-employed
= Ich arbeite freiberuflich/bin selbständig

There is no article in German when giving someone's specific trade or profession. Also there are feminine forms for all nouns denoting professions, usually with the **-in** ending:

He's a baker
= Er ist Bäcker
She's a teacher
= Sie ist Lehrerin
George wants to be a systems analyst
= George will Systemanalytiker werden
Jane works as a journalist
= Jane ist als Journalistin tätig

However if an adjective is included, then there is an indefinite article as in English:

She is a good teacher
= Sie ist eine gute Lehrerin

Looking for a job

I'm looking for a job as a childminder
= Ich suche eine Stellung als Tagesmutter
I didn't find anything suitable in the situations vacant
= Ich habe in den Stellenangeboten nichts Geeignetes gefunden
I want to apply for this job
= Ich will mich um diese Stellung bewerben
A CV should be sent with the application
= Der Bewerbung ist ein Lebenslauf beizufügen
Could you come for an interview on March 24th?
= Könnten Sie bitte am 24. März zu einem Vorstellungsgespräch kommen?
What is the earliest you could start work?
= Wann könnten Sie frühestens anfangen?

[2] (spout, nozzle) Düse, *die* [3] (aircraft) Düsenflugzeug, *das;* Jet, *der;* (engine) Düsentriebwerk, *das*
B *v.i.,* **-tt-** [1] (spurt out) ‹*Wasser:*› herausschießen (**from** aus); ‹*Gas, Dampf:*› ausströmen (**from** aus) [2] (coll.: travel by ~ plane) jetten (ugs.); **~ in/out** *or* **off** [per Jet] einfliegen/abfliegen

jet² *n.* (Min.) Jett, *der od. das;* Gagat, *der*

jet: ~-black *adj.* pechschwarz; kohlrabenschwarz; **~ engine** *n.* Düsen- *od.* Strahltriebwerk, *das;* **~ fighter** *n.* Düsenjäger, *der;* **~foil** *n.* [Jetfoil-]Tragflügelboot, *das;* **~ lag** *n.* Jetlag, *der;* **~-lagged** *adj.* **sb. is ~-lagged** jmdm. macht der Jetlag zu schaffen; **~ plane** *n.* Düsenflugzeug, *das;* **~-propelled** *adj.* düsen- *od.* strahlgetrieben; mit Düsen- *od.* Strahlantrieb *nachgestellt;* **~ pro'pulsion** *n.* Düsen- *od.* Strahlantrieb, *der*

jetsam /ˈdʒetsəm/ *n.* sinkendes Seewurfgut (Seew.); (on seashore) Strandgut, *das; see also* **flotsam**

jet: ~ set *n.* Jetset, *der;* **~-setter** *n.* Jetsetter, *der*/-setterin, *die;* **~-setting** *adj.* (coll.) Jetset-; **~-setting lifestyle** Jetsetleben, *das;* **~ ski** *n.* Jetski, *der;* **~-ski** *v.i.* Jetski fahren; **~-skiing** *n., no pl.* Jetskifahren, *das;* **~ stream** *n.* [1] (Meteorol.) Jetstream, *der;* Strahlstrom, *der;* [2] (of jet engine) Düsenstrahl, *der*

jettison /ˈdʒetɪsən/ *v.t.* [1] (from ship) über Bord werfen; (from aircraft) abwerfen ‹*Ballast, Bombe*›; (discard) wegwerfen; (Astronaut.) (separate) abtrennen; (blast off) absprengen [2] (fig.: abandon) aufgeben; über Bord werfen ‹*Plan*›

jetty /ˈdʒetɪ/ *n.* [1] (protecting harbour or coast) [Hafen]mole, *die* [2] (landing pier) Landungsbrücke, *die;* Anleger, *der* (Seemannsspr.); (smaller) [Landungs]steg, *der*

Jew /dʒuː/ *n.* Jude, *der*/Jüdin, *die; see also* **wandering Jew**

'Jew-baiting *n.* Judenhetze, *die;* Judenverfolgung, *die*

jewel /ˈdʒuːəl/
A *n.* [1] (ornament) [kostbares] Schmuckstück; **~s** *collect.* Schmuck, *der;* Juwelen *Pl.* [2] (precious stone) Juwel, *das od. der;* [wertvoller] Edelstein; (of watch) Stein, *der* [3] (fig.) (person) Goldstück, *das;* Juwel, *das;* (thing) Kleinod, *das*
B *v.t.,* (Brit.) **-ll-;** *esp. in p.p.* [1] (adorn with jewels) mit Juwelen besetzen; **~led hand** juwelengeschmückte Hand [2] (fit with jewels) mit Steinen versehen

jewel: ~ box, ~ case *ns.* Schmuckkasten, *der*

jeweller (*Amer.:* **jeweler**) /ˈdʒuːələ(r)/ *n.* ▸ ℹ **p. 1260** Juwelier, *der;* **~'s rouge** Polierrot, *das; see also* **baker**

jewellery (Brit.), **jewelry** /ˈdʒuːəlrɪ/ *n.* Schmuck, *der;* **~ box** Schmuckkasten, *der*

Jewess /ˈdʒuːɪs/ *n.* Jüdin, *die*

Jewish /ˈdʒuːɪʃ/ *adj.* jüdisch; **he/she is ~:** er ist Jude/sie ist Jüdin

Jewry /ˈdʒʊərɪ/ *n.* Judentum, *das;* Judenheit, *die*

Jew's 'harp *n.* (Mus.) Maultrommel, *die*

jib¹ /dʒɪb/ *n.* [1] (Naut.) (on sailing ship) Stagsegel, *das* (Seew.); (on sailing yacht or dinghy) Fock, *die* (Seew.); **I don't like the cut of his ~** (fig.) mir gefällt sein Gesicht *od.* (ugs.) seine Nase nicht [2] (of crane) Ausleger, *der*

jib² *v.i.,* **-bb-** [1] (refuse to go on) ‹*Pferd usw.:*› bocken; (because of fright) scheuen [2] (fig.) sich sträuben; streiken (ugs.); **~ at sth./at doing sth.** sich gegen etw. sträuben/sich dagegen sträuben, etw. zu tun; **he ~bed at the idea** er wollte nichts davon wissen

jibe¹ /dʒaɪb/ *v.i.* (Amer.) (fit) sich decken; (match) zusammenpassen

jibe² ▸ **gibe; gybe**

jiff /dʒɪf/, **jiffy** /ˈdʒɪfɪ/ *n.* (coll.) Augenblick, *der;* Moment, *der;* **in a ~:** sofort; gleich; **half a ~:** ein Momentchen!

'Jiffy bag ® *n.* gefütterte Versandtasche

jig /dʒɪg/
A *n.* [1] (dance, music) Jig, *die;* (movement of suite) Gigue, *die;* **dance** *or* **do a ~:** einen Freudentanz vollführen [2] (appliance) Einspannvorrichtung, *die*
B *v.i.,* **-gg-** (dance a ~/gigue) eine Jig/eine Gigue tanzen; (fig.) herumhüpfen; **~ up and down** herumhüpfen

jigger /ˈdʒɪgə(r)/ *n.: Messbecher für alkoholische Getränke*

jiggered /ˈdʒɪgəd/ *adj.* (coll.) **I'll be ~:** gibts denn so was! (ugs.); **I'll be ~ if ...:** der Teufel soll mich holen, wenn ... (salopp)

jiggery-pokery /dʒɪgərɪˈpəʊkərɪ/ *n.* (Brit. coll.) [1] (underhand scheming) Schmu, *der* (ugs.); **there is some [sort of] ~ going on** hier ist was faul; **he's up to some [sort of] ~:** er hat 'n krummes Ding vor (ugs.) [2] (nonsense) Stuss, *der* (ugs. abwertend)

jiggle /ˈdʒɪgl/
A *v.t.* rütteln an, wackeln an (+ *Dat.*)
B *v.i.* rütteln; wackeln

'jigsaw *n.* [1] Dekupiersäge, *die;* (electric) Stichsäge, *die* [2] **~ [puzzle]** Puzzle, *das*

jihad /dʒɪˈhæd, dʒɪˈhɑːd/ *n.* (war) Dschihad, *der*

jilt /dʒɪlt/ *v.t.* sitzen lassen (ugs.)

Jim Crow /dʒɪm ˈkrəʊ/ *n.* (Amer. derog.) [1] (a Black) Nigger, *der* (abwertend) [2] *no pl.* (racial segregation) Rassentrennung, *die;* (racial discrimination) Rassendiskriminierung, *die*

jim-jams¹ /ˈdʒɪmdʒæmz/ *n. pl.* (Brit. coll.: pyjamas) Pyjama, *der*

jim-jams² *n. pl.* (coll.: fit of depression, nervousness) Muffe, *die* (ugs.); **she got [an attack of] the ~:** ihr ging die Muffe

jimmy /ˈdʒɪmɪ/ (Amer.) ▸ **jemmy**

jimson [weed] /ˈdʒɪmsən (wiːd)/ *n.* (Amer. Bot.) Stechapfel, *der*

jingle /ˈdʒɪŋgl/
A *n.* [1] Klingeln, *das;* Bimmeln, *das* (ugs.); (of cutlery, chains, spurs) Klirren, *das;* (of coins, keys) Geklimper, *das* [2] (repetition) Aneinanderreihen lautähnlicher Wörter; (trivial verse) Wortgeklingel, *das* (abwertend); (Commerc.) Werbespruch, *der;* Jingle, *der* (Werbespr.) [3] (thing designed to ~) Schelle, *die*
B *v.i.* [1] ‹*Metallgegenstände:*› klimpern; ‹*Kasse, Schelle:*› klingeln; ‹*Glöckchen:*› bimmeln [2] (be full of alliterations, rhymes, etc.) ‹*Text:*› sich reimen und stabreimen
C *v.t.* klingeln mit, (ugs.) bimmeln mit ‹*Glöckchen*›; klimpern mit ‹*Münzen, Schlüsseln, Armreifen*›

'jingle-jangle *n.* Geklimper, *das* (abwertend)

jingo /ˈdʒɪŋgəʊ/ *n., pl.* **~es** (dated) [1] Chauvinist, *der* (abwertend); Hurrapatriot, *der* (ugs. abwertend) [2] **by ~!** beim Zeus!; bei Gott!

jingoism /ˈdʒɪŋgəʊɪzm/ *n., no pl.* Chauvinismus, *der* (abwertend); Hurrapatriotismus, *der* (ugs. abwertend)

jingoist /ˈdʒɪŋgəʊɪst/ Chauvinist, *der*

jingoistic /dʒɪŋgəʊˈɪstɪk/ *adj.* chauvinistisch

jink ▸ **high jinks**

jinx /dʒɪŋks/
A *n.* (coll.) Fluch, *der;* **there seemed to be a ~ on him** er schien vom Pech verfolgt zu sein; **break the ~:** den Bann brechen
B *v.t.* verhexen

jitterbug /ˈdʒɪtəbʌg/
A *n.* [1] Nervenbündel, *das* (ugs.) [2] (dance) Jitterbug, *der*
B *v.i.* Jitterbug tanzen

jitters /ˈdʒɪtəz/ *n. pl.* (coll.) großes Zittern; Bammel, *der* (salopp); **an attack** *or* **a case of the ~:** ein Bammel (salopp); **give sb. the ~:** jmdm. Schiss machen (salopp)

jittery /ˈdʒɪtərɪ/ *adj.* (nervous) nervös; (frightened) verängstigt

jive /dʒaɪv/
A *n.* Jive, *der*
B *v.i.* Jive tanzen

Jnr. *abbr.* **= Junior** jr.; jun.

Joan of Arc /dʒəʊn əv ˈɑːk/ *pr. n.* die Jungfrau von Orleans

job /dʒɒb/
A *n.* [1] (piece of work) **~ [of work]** Arbeit, *die;* **we have five ~s to do today** wir haben heute fünf Dinge zu erledigen; (orders to be fulfilled) wir haben heute fünf Aufträge zu erledigen; **I have a little ~ for you** ich habe eine kleine Aufgabe *od.* einen kleinen Auftrag für dich; **do a ~ for sb.** für jmdn. etw. erledigen; **try to do sb.'s ~ for him** (fig. coll.) jmdm. ins Handwerk pfuschen (ugs.); **it is sb.'s ~ to do sth.** es ist jmds. Arbeit, etw. zu tun; **you've got a really tough ~ on your hands!** da hast du aber eine

Heidenarbeit *od.* ein schönes Stück Arbeit!; **you're doing an excellent ~:** Sie machen das ausgezeichnet; **nose ~** (coll.) Nasenoperation, *die* 2 ▸❶ **p. 1260** (position of employment) Stelle, *die;* Anstellung, *die;* Job, *der* (ugs.); **he is, after all, only doing his ~!** er tut schließlich nur seine Pflicht; **he knows his ~:** er versteht sein Handwerk *od.* versteht etwas von der Sache; **~ vacancies** offene Stellen; (in newspaper) „Stellenangebote"; **have ~ security** einen sicheren Arbeitsplatz haben; **~ situation** Arbeitsmarktsituation, *die;* **it's as much as my ~'s worth** es würde mich meinen Job kosten; **it's not my ~** (fig.) es ist nicht meine Sache *od.* Aufgabe; **the man for the ~:** der richtige Mann; **~s for the boys** (coll.) ≈ wer gute Beziehungen hat, kriegt einen Job (ugs.); **it is a case** *or* **matter of ~s for the boys** alle Posten *od.* (ugs.) Jobs werden unter der Hand vergeben; **just the ~** (fig. coll.) genau das Richtige; die Sache (ugs.); **on the ~:** bei der Arbeit; **out of a ~:** arbeitslos; ohne Stellung 3 (coll.: crime) [krummes] Ding (ugs.); **do a [bank] ~:** ein Ding [in einer Bank] drehen (ugs.); **this was a professional ~:** hier war ein Profi/hier waren Profis am Werk 4 (result of work) Ergebnis, *das;* **make a [good] ~ of sth.** bei etw. gute Arbeit leisten; **make a thorough ~ of it** ganze Arbeit machen; **be a good** *etc.* **~:** gut *usw.* sein; **this respray/rebuilt car is a superb ~!** diese Neulackierung/dieses restaurierte Auto ist großartig geworden! 5 (coll.: difficult task) [schönes] Stück Arbeit; **I had a [hard** *or* **tough] ~ convincing** *or* **to convince him** es war gar nicht so einfach für mich *od.* ich hatte [einige] Mühe, ihn zu überzeugen 6 (state of affairs) **a bad ~:** eine schlimme *od.* üble Sache; **it's a bad ~: the company is virtually bankrupt** es sieht schlecht aus: die Firma ist praktisch pleite; **give sb./sth. up as a bad ~** ▸**give up B 1**; **a good ~:** ein Glück; **we've finished, and a good ~ too!** wir sind fertig, zum Glück; **what** *or* **it's a good ~ he doesn't know about it!** nur gut, dass er nichts davon weiß!

B *v.i.*, **-bb-** 1 (do jobs) Gelegenheitsarbeiten verrichten; jobben (ugs.) 2 (deal in stocks) als Börsenhändler arbeiten 3 (turn position of trust to private advantage) sein Amt [zum eigenen Vorteil] missbrauchen 4 (buy and sell as middleman) als Vermittler Geschäfte machen; (Amer.: trade in wholesale lots) als Zwischenhändler tätig sein

C *v.t.*, **-bb-** im Zwischenhandel verkaufen; makeln ‹*Häuser, Grundstücke*›

Job /dʒəʊb/ *pr. n.* Hiob (*der*); **he would try the patience of ~:** bei ihm braucht man eine Engelsgeduld; **~'s 'comforter** schlechter Trostspender

'job advert *n.* Stellenanzeige, *die*

jobber /'dʒɒbə(r)/ *n.* 1 (Amer.: wholesaler) Zwischenhändler, *der* 2 (stock~) Börsen- *od.* Effektenhändler, *der;* Jobber, *der*

jobbery /'dʒɒbərɪ/ *n., no pl.* Schiebung, *die*

jobbing /'dʒɒbɪŋ/ *adj.* Gelegenheits-; **~ gardener** Gelegenheits- *od.* Aushilfsgärtner, *der;* **~ printer** Akzidenzdrucker, *der*

job: ~centre *n.* (Brit.) Arbeitsvermittlungsstelle, *die;* **~ creation** *n., no pl.* Schaffung von Arbeitsplätzen; **~ creation scheme** *n.* Beschäftigungsprogramm, *das;* Arbeitsbeschaffungsprogramm, *das;* **~ description** *n.* Arbeitsplatzbeschreibung, *die;* Tätigkeitsbeschreibung, *die;* **~ evaluation** *n.* Arbeitsbewertung, *die;* **~-hunt** *v.i.* **go/be ~-hunting** auf Arbeits- *od.* Stellensuche gehen/sein; **~-hunter** *n.* Stellen- *od.* Arbeitssuchende, *der/die;* **~-hunting** *n., no pl.* Arbeitssuche, *die;* Stellensuche, *die;* **~ interview** *n.* Vorstellungsgespräch, *das*

> **jobcentre**
>
> In den meisten britischen Städten gibt es Beratungszentren, die verschiedene Dienste für Arbeitssuchende anbieten, z.B. werden freie Stellen ausgehängt und Bewerbungsgespräche mit Arbeitgebern vermittelt. *Jobcentres* werden vom *Employment Service* betrieben.

jobless /'dʒɒblɪs/ *adj.* beschäftigungslos; arbeitslos

job: ~ 'lot *n.* Partieware, *die* (Kaufmannsspr.); (fig.) Sammelsurium, *das* (abwertend); **~ market** *n.* Arbeitsmarkt, *der;* Stellenmarkt, *der;* **~ offer** *n.* Stellenangebot, *das;* **~ satisfaction** ▸**satisfaction 2**; **~ security** *n., no pl.* Arbeitsplatzsicherheit, *die;* **there is no ~ security in this industry** in dieser Branche gibt es keine sicheren Arbeitsplätze; **~-seeker** *n.* Arbeitssuchende, *der/die;* **~-share A** *n.* geteilter Arbeitsplatz; **look for a ~-share** eine Jobsharing-Stelle suchen; **B** *v.t.* aufteilen ‹*Arbeitsplatz*›; **C** *v.i.* sich (*Dat.*) einen Arbeitsplatz teilen (**with** mit); **~-sharing** *n., no pl.* Jobsharing, *das;* Arbeitsplatzteilung, *die;* **~sheet** *n.* Arbeitsbericht, *der*

> **jobseeker's allowance**
>
> Eine staatliche Beihilfe, die Arbeitssuchenden in Großbritannien gewährt wird, wenn sie nachweisen können, dass sie sich um eine Anstellung bemühen.

jobsworth /'dʒɒbzwɜːθ/ *n.* (Brit. coll.) Beamtenseele, *die* (abwertend); sturer Bürokratentyp

'job title *n.* Berufsbezeichnung, *die*

jock (coll.) ▸**jockey**

Jock /dʒɒk/ *n.* (Brit. coll., often derog.) Schotte, *der*

jockey /'dʒɒkɪ/

A *n.* ▸❶ **p. 1260** Jockei, *der;* Jockey, *der*

B *v.i.* rangeln (**for** um); **~ for position** (lit. or fig.) alles daransetzen, eine möglichst gute Position zu erringen; **all the ~ing behind the scenes** das ganze Gerangel hinter den Kulissen

C *v.t.* **~ sb. into/out of doing sth.** jmdn. dazu bringen, etw. zu tun/nicht mehr zu tun

jockey: ~ cap *n.* Jockeymütze, *die;* **J~ Club** *n.* (Brit.) *oberste Behörde des Galoppsports in England;* **~ shorts** *n. pl.* (Amer.) Unterhose, *die;* Unterhosen *Pl.*

jockstrap /'dʒɒkstræp/ *n.* [Sport]suspensorium, *das*

jocose /dʒə'kəʊs/ *adj.* 1 (playful, fond of joking) launig ‹*Stimmung, Bemerkung, Wesensart*›; **~ person** Spaßvogel, *der* 2 (waggish) schalkhaft

jocular /'dʒɒkjʊlə(r)/ *adj.* lustig, witzig ‹*Bemerkung, Antwort*›; spaßig, scherzhaft ‹*Person*›; **his ~ conversation bored her** seine Witze langweilten sie

jocularly /'dʒɒkjʊləlɪ/ *adv.* scherzhaft

jocund /'dʒɒkənd/ *adj.* (literary) fröhlich

jodhpurs /'dʒɒdpəz/ *n. pl.* Reithose, *die;* Jodhpur[hose], *die*

Joe /dʒəʊ/ *n.* **~ Public** (coll.) Otto Normalverbraucher (*der*) (ugs.)

joey /'dʒəʊɪ/ *n.* (Austral.) junges Känguru

jog /dʒɒg/

A *v.t.*, **-gg-** 1 (shake with push or jerk) rütteln; schütteln; **the horse ~ged its rider up and down** das Pferd schüttelte seinen Reiter durch 2 (nudge) [an]stoßen; **~ sb.'s elbow** jmdn. [am Ellbogen] anstoßen 3 (stimulate) **~ sb.'s memory** jmds. Gedächtnis (*Dat.*) auf die Sprünge helfen

B *v.i.*, **-gg-** 1 (move up and down) auf und ab hüpfen; **~ around/about** herumhüpfen; **his holster was ~ging against his hip** sein Halfter schlug ihm im Rhythmus gegen die Hüfte 2 (move at ~trot) ‹*Pferd:*› [dahin]trotten 3 (run at slow pace) [in mäßigem Tempo] laufen; traben (Sport); (for physical exercise) joggen; [einen] Dauerlauf machen; laufen; **~ along** *or* **on** (fig.) ‹*Geschäft, Projekt:*› laufen, seinen Gang gehen; ‹*Person:*› vor sich hin wursteln (ugs.)

C *n.* 1 (shake, nudge) Stoß, *der;* Schubs, *der* (ugs.) 2 (slow walk or trot) (of horse) Trott, *der;* (of person for physical exercise) Dauerlauf, *der;* **go for a ~:** joggen gehen; **he went off at a ~:** er trabte davon

jogger /'dʒɒgə(r)/ *n.* Jogger, *der*/Joggerin, *die*

jogging /'dʒɒgɪŋ/ *n.* Jogging, *das;* Joggen, *das*

joggle /'dʒɒgl/

A *v.t.* schütteln; wackeln an (+ *Dat.*) ‹*Tisch*›

B *v.i.* wackeln (**to and fro** hin und her); wippen (**up and down** auf und ab); (in the air) taumeln

C *n.* (slight shake) Holpern, *das*

'jogtrot *n.* (lit. or fig.) Trott, *der*

john *n.* (Amer. sl.: lavatory) Lokus, *der* (salopp)

John /dʒɒn/ *pr. n.* (Hist., as name of ruler etc.) Johann (*der*); *see also* **Baptist 2**

John: ~ 'Bull *n.* John Bull (*der*); **a real ~ Bull** ein typischer Engländer; **~ 'Citizen** *n.* Otto Normalverbraucher (*der*); **~ 'Doe** *n.* 1 (Law) ≈ Meier (*der*); ≈ die Partei A; *fiktiver Name einer Prozesspartei;* 2 (Amer.: average man) Otto Normalverbraucher (*der*)

johnny /'dʒɒnɪ/ *n.* (Brit. coll.: chap) Heini, *der* (ugs.)

Johnny-come-'lately *n.* (coll.) Neuankömmling, *der*

joie de vivre /ʒwɑː də 'viːvr/ *n.* Lebensfreude, *die;* Lebenslust, *die*

join /dʒɔɪn/

A *v.t.* 1 (put together, connect) verbinden (**to** mit); **~ two things [together]** zwei Dinge miteinander verbinden; zwei Dinge zusammenfügen; **~ hands** sich (*Dat.*) die Hände reichen; **~ hands [with sb.]** (fig.) ‹*Nation, Partei usw.:*› sich [mit jmdm.] vereinen; **~ sb. [with** *or* **to sb.] in marriage/in holy matrimony** jmdn. [mit jmdm.] ehelich verbinden/durch das heilige Band der Ehe vereinen (geh.); *see also* **force¹ A 4** 2 (come into company of) sich gesellen zu; sich zugesellen (+ *Dat.*); (meet) treffen; (come with) mitkommen mit; sich anschließen (+ *Dat.*); **you go on ahead — I'll ~ you in a minute** geh nur schon voraus — ich komme gleich nach; **may I ~ you [at the table]?** kann ich mich zu euch [an den Tisch] setzen?; **do ~ us for lunch** iss doch mit uns zu Mittag; **would you like to ~ me in a drink?** hast du Lust, ein Glas mit mir zu trinken?; **if you can't beat them, ~ them** wenn man mit dem Gegner nicht fertig wird, läuft man eben zu ihm über 3 (become member of) eintreten in (+ *Akk.*) ‹*Armee, Firma, Orden, Verein, Partei*›; beitreten (+ *Dat.*) ‹*Verein, Partei, Orden*›; **I thought of ~ing the Army/the Scouts** ich dachte daran, zur Armee/zu den Pfadfindern zu gehen 4 (take one's place in) sich einreihen in (+ *Akk.*) ‹*Umzug, Demonstrationszug*›; **~ one's ship** an Bord seines Schiffs gehen; **~ one's regiment** sich bei seinem Regiment einfinden 5 ‹*Fluss, Straße:*› münden in (+ *Akk.*). *See also* **battle A 1**

B *v.i.* 1 (come together) ‹*Flüsse:*› sich vereinigen, zusammenfließen; ‹*Straßen:*› sich vereinigen, zusammenlaufen; ‹*Grundstücke:*› aneinander grenzen, aneinander stoßen; ‹*gebrochener Knochen:*› zusammenwachsen; ‹*Einzelteile:*› zusammenpassen 2 (take part) **~ with sb.** sich jmdm. anschließen; **my wife ~s with me in wishing you ...:** auch meine Frau wünscht Ihnen ... 3 (become member) Mitglied werden; (become employee) in die Firma eintreten

C *n.* Verbindung, *die;* (line) Nahtstelle, *die*

Phrasal verbs

• **~ in**

A /-'-/ *v.i.* mitmachen (**with** bei); (in conversation) sich beteiligen (**with** an + *Dat.*); (in singing) einstimmen; mitsingen; **they all ~ed in together** sie machten/sangen alle mit

B /'--/ *v.t.* mitmachen bei ‹*Spiel, Spaß*›; sich beteiligen an (+ *Dat.*) ‹*Spiel, Festlichkeiten, Gespräch*›; mitsingen ‹*Refrain*›; sich einreihen in (+ *Akk.*), sich anschließen (+ *Dat.*) ‹*Demonstrations-, Umzug*›

• **~ 'on** *v.i.* befestigt werden (**to** an + *Dat.*); ‹*Grundstück:*› [an]grenzen (**to** an + *Akk.*)

• **~ 'up**

A *v.i.* 1 (Mil.) einrücken; Soldat werden 2 ‹*Straßen:*› zusammenlaufen; ‹*Nebenstraße:*› [ein]münden (**with** in + *Akk.*); ‹*Straße:*› zusammenlaufen (**with** mit)

B *v.t.* miteinander verbinden

joiner /'dʒɔɪnə(r)/ *n.* ▸❶ **p. 1260** Tischler, *der*/Tischlerin, *die*

joinery /'dʒɔɪnərɪ/ *n., no pl.* 1 *no art.* (craft) Tischlerei, *die;* Tischlerhandwerk, *das* 2 *no indef. art.* (products) Tischlerarbeiten

joint /dʒɔɪnt/

A *n.* 1 (place of joining) Verbindung, *die;* (line) Nahtstelle, *die;* (Building) Fuge, *die* 2 ▸❶ **p. 951** (Anat.) Gelenk, *das;* **be out of ~** ‹*Körperteil:*› ausgerenkt sein; (fig.: be out of order) ‹*Zeit, Welt:*› aus den Fugen sein; *see also* **nose A 1** 3 (Bot.) Knoten, *der* 4 (Mech. Engin. etc.) Gelenk, *das* 5 (part of carcass) **a ~ [of meat]** ein Stück

j

Fleisch; (for roasting, roast) ein Braten; **a roast ~:** ein Braten; **a ~ of roast beef** ein Rinderbraten; **chicken ~s** Hähnchenteile *Pl.*; **carve/cut sth. into ~s** etw. tranchieren/zerlegen **6** (coll.) (place) Laden, *der* (ugs.); (pub) Kaschemme, *die* (abwertend); (dwelling) Bude, *die* (ugs.); **jazz ~:** Jazzschuppen, *der* (ugs.) **7** (coll.: marijuana cigarette) Joint, *der* **8** (Amer. sl.: prison) Knast, *der* (ugs.)

B *adj.* **1** (of two or more) gemeinsam ‹*Anstrengung, Bericht, Besitz, Projekt, Ansicht, Konto*›; **~ venture** Gemeinschaftsunternehmen, *das;* Jointventure, *das* (*Wirtsch.*); *see also* **several A 2** **2** Mit‹*autor, -erbe, -besitzer*›

C *v.t.* **1** (connect) verbinden **2** (Building) [aus-, ver-]fugen ‹*Wand, Decke, Belag*› **3** (divide) zerlegen ‹*Tier*›

jointed /ˈdʒɔɪntɪd/ *adj.* Glieder‹*puppe, -tier*›; knotig ‹*Stamm*›

jointly /ˈdʒɔɪntlɪ/ *adv.* gemeinsam; **he is ~ responsible** er ist mitverantwortlich

joint: ~ ˈstock *n.* (Econ.) Gesellschafts- *od.* Aktienkapital, *das;* **~ stock bank/company** Aktienbank, *die*/Aktiengesellschaft, *die;* **~ ˈventure** *n.* (Commerc.) Jointventure, *das*

joist /dʒɔɪst/ *n.* (Building) Deckenbalken, *der;* (steel) [Decken]träger, *der*

joke /dʒəʊk/

A *n.* **1** Witz, *der;* Scherz, *der;* **sb.'s little ~** (iron.) jmds. Scherzchen; **make a ~:** einen Scherz machen; **do sth. for a ~:** etw. spaßeshalber *od.* zum Spaß tun; **tell a ~:** einen Witz erzählen; **have a ~ with sb.** mit jmdm. scherzen *od.* spaßen; **play a ~ on sb.** jmdm. einen Streich spielen; **he can/can't take a ~:** er versteht Spaß/keinen Spaß; **the ~ was on him** er war der Narr; **a ~ is a ~:** das ist gar nicht so komisch; **this is getting beyond/is** *or* **goes beyond a ~:** da hört der Spaß auf/das ist kein Spaß mehr; **this is no ~:** das ist nicht zum Lachen **2** (ridiculous thing or circumstance) Witz, *der* (ugs.); (ridiculous person) Witzfigur, *die;* **he/it is a standing ~:** alle Welt lacht nur noch über ihn/darüber; **treat sth. as a ~:** etw. nicht weiter ernst nehmen

B *v.i.* scherzen, Witze machen (**about** über + *Akk.*); **I was only joking** ich habe nur Spaß gemacht (ugs.); **joking apart** Scherz *od.* Spaß beiseite!; **you are/must be** *or* (coll.) **have [got] to be joking!** das soll wohl ein Witz sein!; mach keine Witze!

joker /ˈdʒəʊkə(r)/ *n.* **1** (person fond of making jokes) Spaßvogel, *der;* Witzbold, *der* (ugs.) **2** (coll.: person) Vogel, *der* (salopp) **3** (Cards) Joker, *der;* **~ in the pack** (fig.) Unsicherheitsfaktor, *der* **4** (Amer.: clause) versteckte Klausel **5** (unexpected factor) Pferdefuß, *der;* Haken, *der* (ugs.)

jokey /ˈdʒəʊkɪ/ *adj.* witzig; spaßig

jokingly /ˈdʒəʊkɪŋlɪ/ *adv.* im Scherz; **..., he said ~:** ..., scherzte er

joky ▸ **jokey**

jollification /dʒɒlɪfɪˈkeɪʃn/ *n.* (coll.) Vergnügen, *das*

jollity /ˈdʒɒlɪtɪ/ *n.* Fröhlichkeit, *die;* Lustigkeit, *die;* (merrymaking, festivity) Festlichkeit, *die*

jolly /ˈdʒɒlɪ/

A *adj.* **1** (cheerful) fröhlich; knallig ‹*Farbe*›; (multicoloured) bunt **2** (euphem.: drunk) angeheitert **3** (festive) lustig **4** (coll.: delightful) klasse (ugs.); prima (ugs.)

B *adv.* (Brit. coll.) ganz schön (ugs.); sehr ‹*nett*›; **~ good** wirklich gut; **~ good!** ausgezeichnet! **I should ~ well think so!** das möchte ich auch meinen!; **we ~ well ˈare coming!** und ob wir kommen!

C *v.t.* (coll.) aufmuntern; **~ sb. into doing sth.** jmdn. dazu überreden, etw. zu tun

Phrasal verbs

- **~ aˈlong** *v.t.* bei Laune halten
- **~ ˈup** *v.t.* aufmuntern

ˈjolly boat *n.* Jolle, *die*

Jolly ˈRoger *n.* Piratenflagge, *die;* Totenkopfflagge, *die*

jolt /dʒəʊlt/

A *v.t.* **1** (shake) ‹*Fahrzeug:*› durchrütteln, durchschütteln; **~ sb./sth. out of/on to sth.** jmdn./etw. aus etw./auf etw. (*Akk.*) schleudern *od.* werfen **2** (shock) aufschrecken; **~ sb. into action** jmdn. auf Trab bringen (ugs.); **~ sb. into doing sth.** jmdn. so aufschrecken, dass er etw. tut

B *v.i.* ‹*Fahrzeug:*› holpern, rütteln, rumpeln (ugs.)

C *n.* **1** (jerk) Stoß, *der;* Ruck, *der* **2** (fig.) (shock) Schock, *der;* Schreck, *der;* (surprise) Überraschung, *die;* **give sb. a ~:** jmdm. einen Schock versetzen *od.* einen Schreck[en] einjagen/jmdn. überraschen

Jonah /ˈdʒəʊnə/ *n.* **1** Unglücksvogel, *der* **2** (Bibl.) Jonas (*der*)

Joneses /ˈdʒəʊnzɪz/ ▸ **keep up A 1**

jonquil /ˈdʒɒŋkwɪl/ *n.* (Bot.) Jonquille, *die*

Jordan /ˈdʒɔːdn/ *pr. n.* **1** ▸ **❶ p. 1491** (river) Jordan, *der* **2** (country) Jordanien (*das*)

Jordanian /dʒɔːˈdeɪnɪən/ ▸ **❶ p. 1345**

A *adj.* jordanisch; **sb. is ~:** jmd. ist Jordanier/Jordanierin

B *n.* Jordanier, *der*/Jordanierin, *die*

josh /dʒɒʃ/ (coll.)

A *v.t.* aufziehen

B *v.i.* scherzen

joss stick /ˈdʒɒs stɪk/ *n.* Räucherstäbchen, *das*

jostle /ˈdʒɒsl/

A *v.i.* **1** (knock) **~ [against each other]** aneinander stoßen **2** (struggle) [sich] streiten (**for** um, **with** mit); **~ with each other** [miteinander *od.* sich] streiten

B *v.t.* **1** anrempeln; **~ sb.'s arm** jmdn. [am Arm] anstoßen; **~ sb. aside/off the pavement** jmdn. zur Seite/vom Bürgersteig stoßen; **the defender ~d the forward off the ball** der Verteidiger trennte den Stürmer mit einem Rempler vom Ball **2** (Racing) behindern

jot /dʒɒt/

A *n.* **[not] a ~:** [k]ein bisschen; (of truth, sympathy also) [k]ein Fünkchen; **not one ~ or tittle** (coll.) nicht das kleinste bisschen

B *v.t.*, **-tt-** [rasch] aufschreiben *od.* notieren; **~ sth. on a piece of paper** etw. rasch auf einen Zettel schreiben

Phrasal verb

- **~ ˈdown** *v.t.* [rasch] aufschreiben *od.* notieren; **~ down notes** [sich (*Dat.*)] rasch Notizen machen

jotter /ˈdʒɒtə(r)/ *n.* (pad) Notizblock, *der;* (notebook) Notizbuch, *das*

jotting /ˈdʒɒtɪŋ/ *n.*, *usu. pl.* Notiz, *die*

joule /dʒuːl/ *n.* (Phys.) Joule, *das*

journal /ˈdʒɜːnl/ *n.* **1** (newspaper) Zeitung, *die;* (periodical) Zeitschrift, *die;* **weekly ~:** Wochenzeitung, *die;* **Official Journal** (EU) Amtsblatt, *das* **2** (Bookk.) Journal, *das;* Tagebuch, *das* **3** (daily record of events) Tagebuch, *das* **4** (Naut.) **[captain's/ship's] ~:** Schiffstagebuch, *das;* Journal, *das* (veralt.) **5** (part of shaft or axle) Zapfen, *der*

ˈjournal bearing *n.* (Mech. Engin.) Zapfenlager, *das*

journalese /dʒɜːnəˈliːz/ *n.* (derog.) [schlechter] Zeitungsstil

journalism /ˈdʒɜːnəlɪzm/ *n.* Journalismus, *der*

journalist /ˈdʒɜːnəlɪst/ *n.* ▸ **❶ p. 1260** Journalist, *der*/Journalistin, *die*

journalistic /dʒɜːnəˈlɪstɪk/ *adj.* journalistisch ‹*Stil*›; **~ circles** Journalistenkreise

journey /ˈdʒɜːnɪ/

A *n.* **1** Reise, *die;* (distance) Weg, *der;* **go on a ~:** verreisen; eine Reise machen; **a ~ by car/train/ship** eine Auto-/Bahn-/Schiffsreise; eine Reise mit dem Auto/der Bahn/dem Schiff; **go on a train/car ~:** eine Reise mit dem Zug *od.* Zugreise/eine Reise mit dem Auto *od.* Autoreise machen; **~'s end** die Endstation (fig.); **a three-hour ~:** eine Fahrt von drei Stunden; eine dreistündige Fahrt; (on foot) ein dreistündiger Weg; **London is three hours' ~ from here** man fährt drei Stunden von hier nach London; **a fruitless ~:** ein vergeblicher Gang **2** (fig.) Weg, *der;* **~ through life** Lebensreise, *die* (geh.); **a ~ into history** ein Ausflug in die Geschichte **3** (of vehicle) Fahrt, *die;* **~ time** Fahrtzeit, *die*

B *v.i.* (formal/literary) fahren; ziehen

journeyman /ˈdʒɜːnɪmən/ *n.*, *pl.* **journeymen** /ˈdʒɜːnɪmən/ Geselle, *der;* **a ~ butcher** ein Fleischergeselle

joust /dʒaʊst/

A *n.* Tjost, *die*

B *v.i.* tjostieren

Jove /dʒəʊv/ *n.* **1** (Mythol.) Jupiter (*der*) **2** **by ~!** (dated coll.) *expr. surprise* potztausend! (veralt.); *expr. approval* Hut ab! (ugs.); alle Achtung!

jovial /ˈdʒəʊvɪəl/ *adj.* (hearty) herzlich, freundlich ‹*Gruß*›; (merry) fröhlich ‹*Ausdruck, Person*›; launig ‹*Bemerkung*›; (convivial) lustig ‹*Versammlung, Gesellschaft*›

jovially /ˈdʒəʊvɪəlɪ/ *adv.* fröhlich ‹*zustimmen, rufen*›; herzlich, freundlich ‹*begrüßen*›

jowl /dʒaʊl/ *n.* (jaw) Unterkiefer, *der;* (lower part of face) Kinnbacken *Pl.*; (double chin) Doppelkinn, *das;* (flabby cheek) Hängebacke, *die;* (of cattle) Wamme, *die;* (of bird) Kehllappen, *der; see also* **cheek A 1**

joy /dʒɔɪ/ *n.* **1** Freude, *die;* **wish sb. ~:** jmdm. viel Spaß *od.* Vergnügen wünschen; **I wish you ~ of it** (also iron.) ich wünsche dir viel Vergnügen damit; **sing for/weep with ~:** vor Freude (*Dat.*) singen/weinen; **we heard with ~ that ...:** wir haben zu unserer Freude erfahren, dass ...; **the ~s of cycling** das Vergnügen des Radfahrens; **be full of the ~s of spring** (fig. coll.) vor Freude ganz aus dem Häuschen sein (ugs.); **that is the ~ of the Highlands** das ist der Reiz *od.* das Reizvolle an den Highlands; **it was a ~ to look at** es war eine Augenweide; *see also* **jump B 3** **2** *no pl.*, *no art.* (coll.: success, satisfaction) Erfolg, *der;* **he didn't get much ~ out of it** es hat ihm nicht viel gebracht; **any ~?** Erfolg gehabt?; was erreicht? (ugs.)

joyful /ˈdʒɔɪfl/ *adj.* froh [gestimmt] ‹*Person*›; froh ‹*Gesicht*›; freudig ‹*Blick, Ereignis, Umarmung, Gesang, Beifall*›; freudig, froh ‹*Nachricht, Kunde*›; erfreulich ‹*Nachricht, Ergebnis, Anblick*›; Freuden‹*tag, -schrei*›; **she was ~ [at his return]** sie freute sich [über seine Rückkehr]

joyfully /ˈdʒɔɪfəlɪ/ *adv.* freudig

joyless /ˈdʒɔɪlɪs/ *adj.* traurig ‹*Ausdruck, Nachricht, Ergebnis, Anlass*›; freudlos ‹*Zeit, Leben*›; verdrossen ‹*Person*›

joyous /ˈdʒɔɪəs/ *adj.* freudig ‹*Anlass, Ereignis*›; froh ‹*Lachen, Herz*›; Freuden‹*tag, -schrei*›

joy: ~ride *n.* (coll.) Spritztour [im gestohlenen Auto]; **~rider** *n.* Autodieb (der den Wagen nur für eine Spritztour gestohlen hat); **~riding** *n.*, *no pl.* Spritztouren *Pl.*; **they went ~riding** sie machten eine Spritztour; **~stick** *n.* **1** (Aeronaut. coll.) Knüppel, *der;* **2** (on computer etc.) Hebel, *der;* Joystick, *der* (DV)

JP *abbr.* ▸ **❶ p. 1260 = Justice of the Peace**

Jr. *abbr.* **= Junior** jun.; jr.

jt. *abbr.* **= joint;** ▸ **joint B**

jubilant /ˈdʒuːbɪlənt/ *adj.* jubelnd; (exultingly glad) freudestrahlend ‹*Miene*›; (triumphant) triumphierend ‹*Miene*›; **be ~** ‹*Person:*› frohlocken

jubilation /dʒuːbɪˈleɪʃn/ *n.* Jubel, *der*

jubilee /ˈdʒuːbɪliː/ *n.* (anniversary) Jubiläum, *das; see also* **diamond jubilee**; **golden jubilee**; **silver jubilee**

Judaism /ˈdʒuːdeɪɪzm/ *n.*, *no pl.*, *no art.* Judentum, *das;* Judaismus, *der*

Judas /ˈdʒuːdəs/ *n.* (traitor) Judas, *der*

ˈJudas tree *n.* (Bot.) Judasbaum, *der*

judder /ˈdʒʌdə(r)/

A *v.i.* rattern

B *n.* Rattern, *das;* **give a ~:** rattern; **with a ~:** ratternd

judge /dʒʌdʒ/

A *n.* **1** ▸ **❶ p. 1260**, ▸ **❶ p. 1634** Richter, *der*/Richterin, *die;* **[the Book of] Judges** (Bibl.) das Buch der Richter; **~ and jury** (fig.) sich zum alleinigen Richter aufwerfen; *see also* **sober 1** **2** (in contest) Juror, *der*/Jurorin, *die;* Preisrichter, *der*/-richterin, *die;* (Sport) Kampfrichter, *der*/-richterin, *die;* Schiedsrichter, *der*/-richterin, *die;* (in cycle racing) Zielrichter, *der*/-richterin, *die;* (in dispute) Schiedsrichter, *der*/-richterin, *die* **3** (fig.: connoisseur, critic) Kenner, *der*/Kennerin, *die;* **~ of character/poetry** Menschen-/Lyrikkenner, *der;* **be a good ~ of sth.** etw. gut beurteilen können; **if I'm any ~/any ~ of sth.** soweit ich das/etw. beurteilen kann **4** (person who decides question) Schiedsrichter, *der;* **be the ~ of sth.** über etw. (*Akk.*) entscheiden *od.* befinden

B *v.t.* **1** (pronounce sentence on) richten (geh.); **~ sb.** (Law) jmds. Fall entscheiden; in jmds. Fall das Urteil fällen **2** (try) verhandeln ‹*Fall*› **3** (act as adjudicator of) Juror/Jurorin *od.* Preisrichter/-richterin sein bei; (Sport) Kampfrichter/-richterin *od.* Schiedsrichter/-richterin sein bei **4** (form opinion about) urteilen *od.* ein Urteil fällen über (+ *Akk.*); beurteilen; **~ a book to be worth reading** ein Buch für lesenswert erachten *od.* befinden; **~ sth. [to be] necessary** etw. für *od.* als notwendig erachten; **be good at judging distances** gut Entfernungen schätzen können; **~d by modern standards** nach heutigen Maßstäben **5** (decide) entscheiden ‹*Angelegenheit, Frage*› **6** (conclude) **I ~d that the meat was done** ich war der Meinung, dass das Fleisch gar war; **I can't ~ whether it's any good** ich kann nicht beurteilen, ob er/sie/es etwas taugt

C *v.i.* **1** (form a judgement) urteilen; **to ~ by its size, ...:** der Größe nach zu urteilen, ...; **judging** *or* **to ~ by the look on his face ...:** nach dem Gesicht zu schließen, das er macht/machte, ...; **judging from what you say, ...:** nach dem, was du sagst, ...; **as far as I can ~, ...:** soweit ich es beurteilen kann, ...; **as near as I could ~, ...:** nach meiner Schätzung ... **2** (act as ~) ▸ **A 1, 2**: Richter/Richterin sein; Kampfrichter/-richterin sein; Schiedsrichter/-richterin sein

judgement, judgment /ˈdʒʌdʒmənt/ *n.* **1** Urteil, *das;* **the J~ of Paris** (Greek Mythol.) das Urteil des Paris; **~ was given in favour of/against sb.** das Urteil fiel zu jmds. Gunsten/Ungunsten aus; **pass [a] ~:** ein Urteil abgeben (**on** über + *Akk.*); **give one's ~:** ein Urteil fällen; **in** *or* **according to my ~:** meines Erachtens; **in the ~ of most people** nach Meinung der meisten Leute; **form a ~:** sich (*Dat.*) ein Urteil *od.* eine Meinung bilden; **against one's better ~:** entgegen seiner besseren Einsicht; *see also* **sit A 2**; **Solomon** **2** (critical faculty) Urteilsfähigkeit, *die;* Urteilsvermögen, *das;* **error of ~:** Fehlurteil, *das;* Fehleinschätzung, *die;* **a man of ~:** ein urteilsfähiger Mann; **critical ~:** Kritikfähigkeit, *die;* **I leave it to your ~:** ich stelle das in Ihr Ermessen; **use your own ~:** verfahren Sie nach Ihrem Gutdünken **3** (trial by God) Gericht, *das;* **day of ~, J~ Day** Tag des Jüngsten Gerichts; (fig.) Stunde der Wahrheit; **the last ~:** das Jüngste *od.* Letzte Gericht **4** (misfortune) **it's a ~ on you for ...** (joc.) das ist die Strafe dafür, dass du ...

judgemental, judgmental /dʒʌdʒˈmentl/ *adj.* (critical) ablehnend

judicature /ˈdʒuːdɪkətʃə(r)/ *n.* (Law) Judikatur, *die* (fachspr.); Rechtsprechung, *die;* **Supreme Court of J~** (Brit.) *Oberster Gerichtshof*

judicial /dʒuːˈdɪʃl/ *adj.* **1** gerichtlich; richterlich ‹*Gewalt*›; Recht sprechend ‹*Versammlung*›; **~ error** Justizirrtum, *der;* **~ murder** Justizmord, *der;* **take** *or* **bring ~ proceedings against sb.** gegen jmdn. gerichtlich vorgehen **2** (of a judge) richterlich; **in his ~ capacity** in seiner Eigenschaft als Richter **3** (expressing judgement) kritisch **4** (impartial) unvoreingenommen

judiciary /dʒuːˈdɪʃərɪ/ *n.* (Law) Richterschaft, *die*

judicious /dʒuːˈdɪʃəs/ *adj.* **1** (discerning) klar blickend **2** (sensible) besonnen

judiciously /dʒuːˈdɪʃəslɪ/ *adv.* mit Bedacht

judo /ˈdʒuːdəʊ/ *n., pl.* **~s** Judo, *das*

jug /dʒʌg/

A *n.* **1** Krug, *der;* (with lid, water ~) Kanne, *die;* (small milk ~) Kännchen, *das;* **a ~ of water** ein Krug/eine Kanne Wasser **2** (sl.: prison) Loch, *das* (salopp); **put/be in ~:** ins Loch stecken/im Loch sitzen

B *v.t.,* **-gg-** (Cookery) schmoren; **~ged hare** Hasenpfeffer, *der*

jug-eared /ˈdʒʌgɪəd/ *adj.* (derog.) mit Segelohren *nachgestellt;* **be ~:** Segelohren haben

jugful /ˈdʒʌgfʊl/ *n.* ▸ **jug A 1**: Krug, *der;* Kanne, *die;* Kännchen, *das;* **a ~ of ...:** ein Krug/eine Kanne/ein Kännchen [voll] ...

juggernaut /ˈdʒʌgənɔːt/ *n.* **1** (institution, notion) Moloch, *der* (geh.) **2** (large object) Ungetüm, *das;* **~ [lorry]** (Brit.) schwerer Brummer (ugs.)

juggins /ˈdʒʌgɪnz/ *n.* (Brit. coll. dated) Dämel, *der* (salopp); Dämlack, *der* (salopp)

juggle /ˈdʒʌgl/

A *v.i.* **1** jonglieren; (perform conjuring tricks) zaubern **2** **~ with** (misrepresent) jonglieren mit ‹*Fakten, Zahlen*›

B *v.t.* (lit., or fig.: manipulate) jonglieren [mit]

juggler /ˈdʒʌglə(r)/ *n.* **1** Jongleur, *der*/Jongleurin, *die* **2** (conjuror) Zauber[künstl]er, *der*/Zauber[künstler]in, *die* **3** (trickster) Betrüger, *der*/Betrügerin, *die*

Jugoslav *etc.* ▸ **Yugoslav** *etc.*

jugular /ˈdʒʌgjʊlə(r)/ (Anat.)

A *adj.* jugular (fachspr.); **~ vein** Jugularvene, *die* (fachspr.); Drosselvene, *die*

B *n.* Jugularvene, *die* (fachspr.); Drosselvene, *die;* **go for the ~** (fig.) versuchen, den Lebensnerv zu treffen

juice /dʒuːs/ *n.* **1** Saft, *der; see also* **stew C 1** **2** (sl.) (electricity) Saft, *der* (salopp); (petrol) Sprit, *der* (ugs.)

juicy /ˈdʒuːsɪ/ *adj.* **1** saftig **2** (coll.) (racy) saftig (ugs.) ‹*Anekdote, Witz, Geschichte, Skandal*›; (suggestive) schlüpfrig; (profitable) fett (ugs.) ‹*Vertrag, Geschäft usw.*›

ju-jitsu /dʒuːˈdʒɪtsuː/ *n.* Jiu-Jitsu, *das*

jukebox /ˈdʒuːkbɒks/ *n.* Jukebox, *die;* Musikbox, *die*

Jul. *abbr.* **= July** Jul.

julep /ˈdʒuːlep/ *n.* Julep, *das od. der*

Julian /ˈdʒuːlɪən/ *adj.* **~ calendar** julianischer Kalender

July /dʒʊˈlaɪ/ *n.* ▸ **❶ p. 1047** Juli, *der; see also* **August**

jumble /ˈdʒʌmbl/

A *v.t.* **~ up** *or* **together** *or* **about** durcheinander bringen; durcheinander werfen; **~ sth. up with sth.** etw. mit etw. durcheinander bringen *od.* -werfen; **they've got my clothes ~d up with yours** sie haben meine und deine Sachen durcheinander gebracht

B *n.* **1** Wirrwarr, *der;* Gewirr, *das;* (muddle) Durcheinander, *das;* **the cupboard was in a complete ~:** im Schrank herrschte ein heilloses Durcheinander; **a ~ of clothes, books, and toys** ein kunterbuntes Durcheinander von Kleidungsstücken, Büchern und Spielsachen **2** *no pl., no indef. art.* (Brit.: articles for ~ sale) alte *od.* gebrauchte Sachen

ˈjumble sale *n.* (Brit.) Trödelmarkt, *der;* (for charity) Wohltätigkeitsbasar, *der*

jumbo /ˈdʒʌmbəʊ/

A *n., pl.* **~s** **1** (very large specimen) riesiges Exemplar **2** (jet) Jumbo, *der*

B *adj.* **~[-sized]** riesig; Riesen- (ugs.)

jumbo ˈjet *n.* Jumbojet, *der*

jump /dʒʌmp/

A *n.* **1** Sprung, *der;* **be on the ~** (fig. coll.) in Bewegung *od.* in Aktion sein; **keep sb. on the ~** (fig. coll.) jmdn. auf Trab halten (ugs.); **take a running ~ [at oneself]** (fig. coll.) verschwinden; **get the ~ on sb.** (coll.) sich (*Dat.*) einen Vorsprung vor jmdm. verschaffen; **always be one ~ ahead of sb.** jmdm. immer um eine Nasenlänge voraus sein (ugs.)

2 (sudden movement) **give a ~:** zusammenzucken *od.* -fahren; **have got the ~s** (coll.) ganz zapp[e]lig *od.* (landsch.) fick[e]rig sein; **give sb. the ~s** (coll.) jmdn. ganz zapp[e]lig *od.* (landsch.) fick[e]rig machen

3 (sudden transition) Sprung, *der;* sprunghafter Wechsel; (gap) Lücke, *die*

4 (abrupt rise) sprunghafter Anstieg; **~ in value/temperature** plötzliche Wertsteigerung/plötzlicher Temperaturanstieg; **there has been a considerable ~ in prices** die Preise sind beträchtlich in die Höhe geschnellt

5 (Sport: obstacle) (in steeplechase) Sprung, *der;* (in athletics) Hindernis, *das;* **set of ~s** Sprungkombination, *die*

6 (Parachuting) Absprung, *der. See also* **broad jump; high jump; long jump**

B *v.i.* **1** springen; ‹*Fallschirmspringer:*› abspringen; **~ to one's feet/from one's seat** aufspringen/vom Sitz aufspringen; **~ down sb.'s throat** (fig. coll.) jmdn. anblaffen (salopp); **~ in the lake** *or* **off a cliff** (fig. coll.) sich zum Teufel scheren (ugs.); **~ on sb.** *or* (Amer.) **all over sb.** (fig. coll.) jmdn. zur Minna machen (salopp); *see also* **skin A 1**

2 (fig.: come over-hastily) voreilig gelangen (**to** zu) ‹*Annahme, Lösung*›; **~ to the conclusion that ...:** den voreiligen Schluss ziehen, dass ...; **~ to conclusions** voreilige Schlüsse ziehen

3 (make sudden movement) springen; (start) zusammenzucken; **~ for joy** einen Freudensprung/Freudensprünge machen; (fig.) vor Freude ganz aus dem Häuschen sein; wahre Freudentänze vollführen; **~ up and down with excitement** aufgeregt herumspringen *od.* -hüpfen; **her heart ~ed** ihr Herz machte einen Sprung

4 (rise suddenly) ‹*Kosten, Preise usw.*› sprunghaft steigen, in die Höhe schnellen

5 (rise in status, prominence) plötzlich aufsteigen

6 **~ to it** (coll.) zupacken; **~ to it!** (coll.) mach/macht schon!

C *v.t.* **1** springen über (+ *Akk.*); überspringen ‹*Mauer, Zaun usw.*›

2 springen lassen ‹*Pferd*›; **~ one's horse over a fence** mit dem Pferd über einen Zaun setzen

3 (move to point beyond) überspringen

4 (not stop at) überfahren ‹*rote Ampel*›; **~ the lights** bei Rot [durch]fahren

5 **~ the rails** *or* **track** ‹*Zug:*› entgleisen

6 **~ ship** ‹*Seemann:*› [unter Bruch des Heuervertrages vorzeitig] den Dienst quittieren

7 **~ the starting signal by half a second** eine halbe Sekunde vor dem Startsignal starten; **~ the [bus] queue** (Brit.) sich [an der Bushaltestelle] vordrängeln

8 (skip over) überspringen ‹*Seite, Kapitel usw.*›

9 (attack) herfallen über (+ *Akk.*). *See also* **bail[1] A 1**; **gun A 2**

Phrasal verbs

- **~ aˈbout, ~ aˈround** *v.i.* herumspringen (ugs.)
- **~ at** *v.t.* **1** anspringen; (fig.: rebuke) anfahren **2** (fig.: seize, accept eagerly) sofort [beim Schopf] ergreifen ‹*Gelegenheit*›; sofort zugreifen *od.* (ugs.) zuschlagen bei ‹*Angebot*›; sofort aufgreifen *od.* (ugs.) anspringen auf ‹*Vorschlag*›
- **~ ˈin** *v.i.* reinspringen (ugs.)
- **~ ˈoff**

A *v.i.* **1** abspringen; **he ~ed off from his horse/bicycle** er sprang vom Pferd/Rad **2** (Showjumping) am Stechen teilnehmen; *see also* **jump-off**

B *v.t.* **~ off sth.** von etw. springen

- **~ on**

A /-ˈ-/ *v.i.* aufspringen; **~ on to a bus/train** in einen Bus/Zug springen; **~ on to one's bicycle/horse** sich aufs Fahrrad/Pferd schwingen

B /ˈ--/ *v.t.* **~ on a bus/train** in einen Bus/Zug springen; **~ on one's bicycle** sich aufs Fahrrad schwingen

- **~ ˈout** *v.i.* hinaus-/herausspringen; **~ out of** springen aus
- **~ ˈup** *v.i.* aufspringen (**from** von); **the dog ~ed up at him** der Hund sprang an ihm hoch; **~ up on to sth.** auf etw. (*Akk.*) springen; *see also* **~ B 3**

jumped-up /ˈdʒʌmptʌp/ *adj.* (coll.) emporgekommen

jumper /ˈdʒʌmpə(r)/ *n.* **1** (Brit.: pullover) Pullover, *der;* Pulli, *der* (ugs.) **2** (loose jacket) Jumper, *der;* Buseruntje, *die* (Seemannsspr.) **3** (Sport) Springer, *der*/Springerin, *die* **4** (Amer.: pinafore dress) Trägerkleid, *das*

jumping /ˈdʒʌmpɪŋ/: **~ bean** *n.* Springbohne, *die;* **~ jack** *n.* **1** Hampelmann, *der;* **2** (firework) Knallfrosch, *der;* **~-ˈoff place** *n.* Ausgangsbasis, *die*

jump: ~ jet *n.* (Aeronaut.) Senkrechtstarter, *der;* **~ leads** *n. pl.* (Brit. Motor Veh.) Starthilfekabel, *das;* **~-off** *n.* (Showjumping) Stechen, *das;* **~ seat** *n.* (Amer. Motor Veh.) Klappsitz, *der;* **~-start** **A** *v.t.* **1** **~-start a car** einem Auto Starthilfe geben; **2** (fig.) [wieder] in Gang bringen; [wieder] ankurbeln ‹*Wirtschaft, Industrie*›; **B** *n.* Start durch Starthilfe; (fig.) neuer Impuls *od.* Auftrieb; **the car needs a ~-start** das Auto braucht Starthilfe; **the economy received a ~-start** die Wirtschaft erfuhr [einen] neuen Aufschwung; **~suit** *n.* Overall, *der*

jumpy /'dʒʌmpɪ/ *adj.* nervös; aufgeregt

Jun. *abbr.* **1** = **June** Jun. **2** = **Junior** jun.

junction /'dʒʌŋkʃn/ *n.* **1** Verbindungspunkt, *der;* Verbindungsstelle, *die;* (of rivers) Zusammenfluss, *der;* (of railway lines, roads) ≈ Einmündung, *die;* (of motorway) Anschlussstelle, *die;* (crossroads) Kreuzung, *die;* **the ~ of two roads** ≈ eine Straßeneinmündung **2** (Electr.) [Leitungs]verbindung, *die;* (Electronics) Übergang, *der*

'junction box *n.* (Electr.) Verteilerkasten, *der*

juncture /'dʒʌŋktʃə(r)/ *n.* **at this ~:** unter diesen Umständen; (at this point in time) zu diesem Zeitpunkt

June /dʒu:n/ *n.* ▸**i** **p. 1047** Juni, *der; see also* **August**

'June bug *n.* Gartenlaubkäfer, *der*

jungle /'dʒʌŋgl/ *n.* Dschungel, *der* (auch fig.); Urwald, *der;* **tropical ~:** tropischer Urwald; **~ life** das Leben im Dschungel; **the law of the ~:** das Gesetz des Dschungels; **concrete ~:** Betondschungel, *der* (ugs.)

jungle: ~ music *n., no pl.* Junglemusik, *die;* **~ 'warfare** *n., no pl.* Dschungelkrieg, *der*

junior /'dʒu:nɪə(r)/

A *adj.* **1** ▸**i** **p. 894** (below a certain age) jünger; **~ team** Juniorenmannschaft, *die;* **~ member** ≈ Mitglied der Jugendabteilung; **be ~ to sb.** jünger sein als jmd. **2** (of lower rank) rangniedriger ‹*Person*›; niedriger ‹*Rang*›; einfach ‹*Angestellter*›; **be ~ to sb.** eine niedrigere Stellung haben als jmd.; **be ~ to sb. by two years** zwei Jahre kürzer im Dienst sein als jmd. **3** (Brit. Sch.) Grundschul‹*klasse*›; Grund‹*schule*› **4** (Brit. Univ.) **~ combination** *or* **common room** Gemeinschaftsraum für Studenten **5** (Amer. Sch., Univ.) **~ year** vorletztes Jahr vor der Abschlussprüfung

B *n.* **1** ▸**i** **p. 894** (younger person) Jüngere, *der/die;* (person of lower rank) Untergebene, *der/die;* (*in an office*) *jmd., der in einem Büro die niedrigste Stellung hat;* **be sb.'s ~ [by six years]** *or* **[six years] sb.'s ~:** [sechs Jahre] jünger sein als jmd. **2** (Brit. Sch.) (at primary school) Grundschüler, *der/*-schülerin, *die;* (at secondary school) Unterstufenschüler, *der/*-schülerin, *die* **3** (Amer.) (Univ.) Student/Studentin im vorletzten Studienjahr; (Sch.) Schüler/Schülerin im vorletzten Schuljahr **4** *no art.* (Amer. coll.: son in the family) der Junge; der Junior (scherzh.); **come on, ~:** komm, Junior (scherzh.) *od.* Junge!

junior: ~ 'doctor *n.* (Brit.) Assistenzarzt, *der/*-ärztin, *die;* **~ 'minister** *n.* (Brit.) ≈ Ministerialdirektor, *der/*-direktorin, *die;* **~ 'partner** *n.* Juniorpartner, *der/*-partnerin, *die*

> **junior high school**
>
> Eine Schule in den USA, die für die Ausbildung zwischen der **elementary school** und der **high school** sorgt und normalerweise an eine *high school* angeschlossen ist.

> **junior school**
>
> Eine staatliche Schule in Großbritannien für Kinder von 7 bis 11 Jahren.

juniper /'dʒu:nɪpə(r)/ *n.* (Bot.) Wacholder, *der;* **oil of ~:** Wacholderöl, *das*

junk¹ /dʒʌŋk/

A *n.* **1** (discarded material) Trödel, *der* (ugs.); Gerümpel, *das;* (trash) Plunder, *der* (ugs.); Ramsch, *der* (ugs.) **2** (Naut.) (cables or ropes) [altes] Tauwerk; Junk, *der* (fachspr.); (cable or rope) [alter] Tampen (fachspr.) **3** (sl.: drug, esp. heroin) Junk, *der* (Drogenjargon)

B *v.t.* wegwerfen; ausmisten (ugs.); (fig.) aufgeben

junk² *n.* (ship) Dschunke, *die*

junk: ~ 'bonds *n. pl.* (Finance) Junk bonds *Pl.;* **~ 'e-mail** *n.* Junkmail, *die*

junket /'dʒʌŋkɪt/

A *n.* **1** *no pl.* (dessert of set milk) Dickmilchdessert, *das* **2** (extravagat trip) Vergnügungsfahrt, *die;* (by official[s]) Vergnügungsreise auf Kosten des Steuerzahlers

B *v.i.* eine Vergnügungsreise/Vergnügungsreisen machen

junketing /'dʒʌŋkɪtɪŋ/ *n., no pl.* (by official[s]) Vergnügungsreisen auf Kosten des Steuerzahlers

junk: ~ food *n.* minderwertige Kost; **~ heap** *n.* **1** ▸**scrap heap**; **2** (sl.: old car etc.) Schrotthaufen, *der* (ugs.)

junkie /'dʒʌŋkɪ/ *n.* (sl.) Junkie, *der* (Drogenjargon)

junk: ~ mail *n.* Postwurfsendungen *Pl.;* Reklame, *die;* **~ shop** *n.* Trödelladen, *der* (ugs.); **~yard** ▸**scrapyard**

junta /'dʒʌntə/ *n.* Junta, *die;* **military ~:** Militärjunta, *die*

Jupiter /'dʒu:pɪtə(r)/ *pr. n.* **1** (Astron.) Jupiter, *der* **2** (Roman Mythol.) Jupiter (*der*)

Jura /'dʒʊərə/ *pr. n.* Jura, *der*

Jurassic /dʒʊə'ræsɪk/ (Geol.)

A *adj.* jurassisch; Jura-

B *n.* Jura, *der*

juridical /dʒʊə'rɪdɪkl/ *adj.* **1** (of judicial proceedings) gerichtlich **2** (of law) juristisch

jurisdiction /dʒʊərɪs'dɪkʃn/ *n.* (authority) Jurisdiktion, *die;* Gerichtsbarkeit, *die;* (authority of a sovereign power) Hoheit, *die;* (extent) Zuständigkeit, *die;* (territory) Zuständigkeitsbereich, *der;* **fall** *or* **come under** *or* **within the ~ of sth./sb.** in die Zuständigkeit *od.* den Zuständigkeitsbereich von etw./jmdm. fallen; **have ~ over sb./in a matter** für jmdn./in einer Angelegenheit zuständig sein

jurisprudence /dʒʊərɪs'pru:dəns/ *n., no pl.* Rechtswissenschaft, *die;* Jurisprudenz, *die*

jurist /'dʒʊərɪst/ *n.* ▸**i** **p. 1260** **1** Rechtswissenschaftler, *der/*-wissenschaftlerin, *die;* Jurist, *der/*Juristin, *die* **2** (Amer.: lawyer) [Rechts]anwalt, *der/*-anwältin, *die*

juror /'dʒʊərə(r)/ *n.* Geschworene, *der/die;* (in Germany, in some Austrian courts) Schöffe, *der/*Schöffin, *die*

jury /'dʒʊərɪ/ *n.* **1** (in court) **the ~:** die Geschworenen; (in Germany, in some Austrian courts) die Schöffen; **sit on the ~:** auf der Geschworenen-/Schöffenbank sitzen; **do ~ service** das Amt eines Geschworenen/Schöffen ausüben; **a ~ consists of ...:** eine Geschworenen-/Schöffenbank besteht aus ...; **trial by ~:** Schwurgerichtsverfahren, *das;* **the ~ of public opinion** (fig.) die Instanz der öffentlichen Meinung; *see also* **grand jury**; **judge A 1** **2** (in competition) Jury, *die;* Preisgericht, *das;* (Sport) Schiedsgericht, *das;* Kampfgericht, *das*

jury: ~ box *n.* Geschworenenbank, *die;* (in Germany, in some Austrian courts) Schöffenbank, *die;* **~man** /'dʒʊərɪmən/ *n., pl.* **~men** /'dʒʊərɪmən/ Geschworene, *der;* (in Germany, in some Austrian courts) Schöffe, *der;* **~woman** *n.* Geschworene, *die;* (in Germany, in some Austrian courts) Schöffin, *die*

just /dʒʌst/

A *adj.* **1** (morally right, deserved) gerecht; anständig, korrekt ‹*Verhalten, Benehmen*›; *see also* **desert¹ 1**

2 (legally right) rechtmäßig

3 (well-grounded) berechtigt ‹*Angst, Zorn, Groll*›; gerechtfertigt ‹*Verhalten*›; begründet ‹*Verdacht, Ansicht*›

4 (right in amount) recht, richtig ‹*Proportion, Maß, Verhältnis*›

B *adv.* **1** (exactly) genau; **~ then/enough** gerade da/genug; **~ as** (exactly as, in the same way as) genauso wie; (when) gerade, als; **~ as you like** *or* **please** ganz wie Sie wünschen/du magst; **~ as good/tidy** *etc.* genauso gut/ordentlich *usw.;* **come ~ as you are** komm so, wie du bist; **~ as fast as I can** so schnell wie ich nur kann; **~ about** (coll.) so ziemlich (ugs.); **it'll ~ about be enough** (coll.) es wird in etwa reichen; **I've had ~ about enough of you** (coll.) ich hab langsam genug von dir; **that is ~ 'it** das ist es ja gerade; genau das ist es ja; **that's ~ like him** das ist typisch er *od.* für ihn; **~ 'so** (in an orderly manner) ordentlich; *expr. agreement* ganz recht; **be ~ 'so** (be exactly arranged) tadellos in Ordnung sein; **~ what ...?** was genau ...?; **I wonder ~ how good he is** ich frage mich, wie gut er eigentlich wirklich ist

2 (barely) gerade [eben]; (with very little time to spare) gerade [eben] noch; (no more than) nur; **~ under £10** nicht ganz zehn Pfund; **we had only ~ enough time for a cup of tea** wir hatten gerade [genug] Zeit, eine Tasse Tee zu trinken; **it's ~ possible** das ist gerade noch möglich; **there will be enough, but only ~:** es wird reichen, aber [nur] gerade eben *od.* [nur] gerade so; **it's ~ on/before/after 8 a.m.** es ist fast 8 Uhr/es ist kurz vor/nach 8 Uhr; **it's ~ after/before the traffic lights** es ist direkt hinter/vor der Verkehrsampel

3 (exactly or nearly now or then, in immediate past) gerade [eben]; [so]eben; (at this moment) gerade; **I have ~ seen him** (Brit.), **I ~ saw him** (Amer.) ich habe ihn gerade [eben] *od.* eben gesehen; **~ now** (at this moment) [im Moment] gerade; (a little time ago) gerade eben; **not ~ now** im Moment nicht

4 (coll.) (simply) einfach; (only) nur; *esp. with imperatives* mal [eben]; **it ~ so happens that ...:** es ist ganz zufällig, dass ...; **it is ~ that I don't like them** ich mag sie einfach nicht; **I've come here ~ to see you** ich bin nur gekommen, um dich zu besuchen; **~ [you] wait till I catch you!** warte nur *od.* na warte, wenn ich dich erwische!; **~ anybody** irgendjemand; **~ another car** ein ganz gewöhnliches Auto; **~ look at that!** guck dir das mal an!; **could you ~ turn round?** kannst du dich mal [eben] umdrehen?; **~ come here a moment** komm [doch] mal einen Moment her; **~ a moment, please** einen Moment mal; **~ like that** einfach so; ohne weiteres; **~ in case** für alle Fälle; **~ in case it rains** falls es regnet

5 (coll.: positively) einfach; echt (ugs.); **that's ~ ridiculous/fantastic** das ist einfach lächerlich/fantastisch

6 (quite) **not ~ yet** noch nicht ganz; **it is ~ as well that ...:** [es ist] nur gut *od.* es ist doch gut, dass ...; **you might ~ as well ...:** du könntest genauso gut ...

7 (coll.: really, indeed) wirklich; echt (ugs.); **You wouldn't dare do that! — Oh, wouldn't I ~?** Das würdest du nicht wagen! — Und ob!; **That's lovely. — Isn't it ~?** Das ist schön. — Ja, und wie; **~ the same** (nevertheless) trotzdem; **that's ~ too bad** das ist Pech

C *n. pl.* **the ~:** die Gerechten; *see also* **sleep C 1**

justice /'dʒʌstɪs/ *n.* **1** Gerechtigkeit, *die;* **administer ~:** Recht sprechen; **poetic[al] ~:** ausgleichende Gerechtigkeit; **treat sb. with ~:** jmdn. gerecht behandeln; **do ~ to sth.** einer Sache (*Dat.*) gerecht werden; (to food or drink) einer Sache (*Dat.*) gebührend zusprechen; **~ was done in the end** der Gerechtigkeit wurde schließlich Genüge getan; **do oneself ~:** sich richtig zur Geltung bringen; **in ~ to sb.** um jmdm. gerecht zu werden; **with ~:** mit Recht; **in all ~:** um gerecht zu sein; *see also* **rough justice** **2** (judicial proceedings) **bring sb. to [a court of] ~:** jmdn. vor Gericht bringen *od.* stellen; **let ~ take its course, not interfere with the course of ~:** der Gerechtigkeit ihren Lauf lassen; **Department of J~** (Amer.) Justizministerium, *das* **3** ▸**i** **p. 1260** (magistrate) Schiedsrichter, *der/*-richterin, *die;* Schiedsmann, *der/*-männin, *die;* (*Brit.: judge of Supreme Court*) *Richter/Richterin des Obersten Gerichtshofs;* **Mr/Mrs J~ Smith** (Brit.) Richter/Richterin Smith; **J~ of the Peace** Friedensrichter, *der/*-richterin, *die; see also* **chief B 1**

justifiable /dʒʌstɪ'faɪəbl/ *adj.* berechtigt; gerechtfertigt ‹*Maßnahme, Handlung*›; **it is ~ to state that ...:** man kann mit Recht behaupten, dass ...

justifiably /dʒʌstɪ'faɪəblɪ/ *adv.* zu Recht; berechtigterweise (Papierdt.); **and ~ so** und das zu Recht

justification /dʒʌstɪfɪ'keɪʃn/ *n.* **1** Rechtfertigung, *die;* (condition of being justified) Berechtigung, *die;* **with some ~:** mit einigem Recht; **in sb.'s ~:** zu jmds. Rechtfertigung **2** (Printing) Randausgleich, *der*

justify /'dʒʌstɪfaɪ/ *v.t.* **1** (show justice of, vindicate) rechtfertigen; (demonstrate correctness of) belegen, beweisen ‹*Behauptung, Argument, Darstellung*›; (offer adequate grounds for) begründen ‹*Verhalten, Vorstellung, Behauptung*›; **~ oneself/sth. to sb.** sich/etw. jmdm. gegenüber *od.* vor jmdm. rechtfertigen; **the end justifies the means** der Zweck heiligt die Mittel; **be justified in doing sth.** etw. zu Recht tun; **this cannot be justified** das ist nicht zu rechtfertigen **2** (Printing) ausschließen

just-in-'time *adj.* just-in-time-‹*Produktion, Lieferung usw.*›

justly /'dʒʌstlɪ/ *adv.* (with justice, fairly) gerecht; (rightly) mit *od.* zu Recht

jut /dʒʌt/ *v.i.*, **-tt-: ~ [out]** [her]vorragen; herausragen; **his chin ~s out rather a lot** er hat ein ziemlich stark vorspringendes Kinn

jute *n.* Jute, *die*

Jute /dʒu:t/ *n.* (Ethnol., Hist.) Jüte, *der*/Jütin, *die*

Jutland /'dʒʌtlənd/ *pr. n.* Jütland *(das)*

juvenile /'dʒu:vənaɪl/

A *adj.* **1** (young, characteristic of youth) jugendlich, (geh.) juvenil ‹*Geschmack, Einstellung*›; Jugend‹*literatur, -mode*›; **~ crime** Jugendkriminalität, *die* **2** (immature) kindisch (abwertend); infantil (abwertend)

B *n.* Jugendliche, *der/die; attrib.* **~ lead** (Theatre) jugendlicher Held

juvenile: ~ court *n.* (Law) Jugendgericht, *das;* **~ de'linquency** *n.* Jugendkriminalität, *die;* **~ de'linquent, ~ offender** *ns.* jugendlicher Straftäter/jugendliche Straftäterin

juxtapose /dʒʌkstə'pəʊz/ *v.t.* nebeneinander stellen (**with, to** und)

juxtaposition /dʒʌkstəpə'zɪʃn/ *n.* (action) Nebeneinanderstellung, *die;* (condition) Nebeneinander, *das;* **be in ~:** nebeneinander gestellt sein

j

Kk

K¹, k¹ /keɪ/ *n., pl.* **Ks** *or* **K's** K, k, *das*
k² *abbr.* = **kilo-** k-
K² *abbr.* 1 = **King['s]** kgl. 2 (Phys.) = **kelvin[s]** K 3 (Computing) = **kilobyte** K 4 (Chess) = **king** K 5 (£1,000) Tsd. £; **earn 35K a year** 35 000 im Jahr verdienen
Kaffir /ˈkæfə(r)/
A *n.* 1 (Ethnol.) Kaffer, *der*/Kaffernfrau, *die* 2 (derog.: South African Black) Kaffer, *der*/Kaffernweib, *das* (abwertend)
B *adj.* Kaffern-
Kafkaesque /kæfkəˈesk/ *adj.* kafkaesk (geh.)
kaftan /ˈkæftæn/ *n.* Kaftan, *der*
kale /keɪl/ *n.* (Bot.) **[curly/Scotch] ~:** Grünkohl, *der;* Krauskohl, *der; see also* **seakale**
kaleidoscope /kəˈlaɪdəskəʊp/ *n.* (lit. or fig.) Kaleidoskop, *das*
kaleidoscopic /kəlaɪdəˈskɒpɪk/ *adj.* (lit. or fig.) kaleidoskopisch
kamikaze /kæmɪˈkɑːzɪ/ *n.* (Hist.) 1 (pilot) Kamikaze[flieger], *der* 2 (aircraft) Kamikazeflugzeug, *das*
Kampuchea /kæmpʊˈtʃiːə/ *pr. n.* Kamputschea (*das*)
kangaroo /kæŋgəˈruː/ *n.* Känguru, *das*
kangaˈroo court *n.* Femegericht, *das;* Feme, *die*
Kantian /ˈkæntɪən/ (of Kant) Kantisch; (of Kantianism) kant[ian]isch
kaolin /ˈkeɪəlɪn/ *n.* Kaolin, *das od.* (fachspr.) *der*
kapok /ˈkeɪpɒk/ *n., no pl.* Kapok, *der*
kaput /kæˈpʊt/ *pred. adj.* (coll.) kaputt (ugs.)
karaoke /kærɪˈəʊkɪ/ *n., no pl., no indef. art.* Karaoke, *das; attrib.* Karaoke-; *attrib.* **~ bar** Karaokebar, *die;* **~ machine** Karaokegerät, *das*
karate /kəˈrɑːtɪ/ *n., no pl., no indef. art.* Karate, *das*
kaˈrate chop *n.* Karateschlag, *der;* Handkantenschlag, *der*
karma /ˈkɑːmə/ *n.* (Buddhism, Hinduism) Karma[n], *das*
karst /kɑːst/ *n.* (Geog.) Karst, *der*
kart /kɑːt/ ▸**go-kart**
Kashmir /kæʃˈmɪə(r)/ *pr. n.* Kaschmir (*das*)
Katherine /ˈkæθrɪn/ *pr. n.* (Hist., as name of ruler etc.) Katharina (*die*)
kayak /ˈkaɪæk/ *n.* Kajak, *der*
kazoo /kəˈzuː/ *n.* Kazoo, *das*
KB *abbr.* = **kilobyte** KB
Kbyte *abbr.* = **Kilobyte** Kbyte; KByte
kc *abbr.* = **kilocycle[s]** kHz
KC *abbr.* (Brit.) = **King's Counsel**
kc/s *abbr.* = **kilocycles per second** kHz
kebab /kɪˈbæb/ *n.* Kebab, *der*
kedgeree /ˈkedʒəriː, kedʒəˈriː/ *n.* Kedgeree, *das; indisches Reisgericht mit Hülsenfrüchten, Zwiebeln, Eiern; (European dish) Reisgericht mit Fisch und Eiern*
keel /kiːl/
A *n.* (Naut.) Kiel, *der;* **lay down a ~:** ein Schiff auf Kiel legen; *see also* **even¹ A 2**
B *v.i.* **~ over** 1 (overturn) umstürzen; ‹*Schiff:*› kentern 2 (fall) ‹*Person:*› umkippen; **he ~ed over on to the bed** er fiel aufs Bett
C *v.t.* **~ over** (Naut.) zum Kentern bringen; kieloben legen (Seemannsspr.); (on one side) kielholen (Seemannsspr.)
ˈkeelhaul *v.t.* kielholen (Seemannsspr.); (fig.) zusammenstauchen (ugs.)
keen¹ /kiːn/ *adj.* 1 (sharp) scharf ‹*Messer, Klinge, Schneide*›; (fig.) scharf ‹*Hohn, Spott*›; beißend ‹*Sarkasmus*› 2 (piercingly cold) scharf, schneidend ‹*Wind, Kälte*›; (penetrating, strong) grell ‹*Licht*›; durchdringend, stechend ‹*Geruch*› 3 (eager) begeistert, leidenschaftlich ‹*Fußballfan, Amateurfotograf, Sportler*›; ausgeprägt, lebhaft ‹*Interesse*›; heftig ‹*Konkurrenz, Verlangen*›; **be ~ to do sth.** darauf erpicht sein, etw. zu tun; **he's really ~ to win** er will unbedingt gewinnen; **be ~ on doing sth.** etw. gern[e] tun; **although he's inexperienced, he's really ~:** obwohl er unerfahren ist, ist er doch wirklich sehr interessiert; **she was not particularly ~ to see the play** sie war nicht besonders scharf darauf, das Stück zu sehen (ugs.); **be [as] ~ as mustard** mit Feuereifer dabei sein; **not be ~ on sth.** nicht gerade begeistert von etw. sein; **I'm not too** *or* **not very** *or* **not madly ~ on it** ich bin nicht so wild darauf (ugs.); **my father's very ~ on my going to college** mein Vater will unbedingt, dass ich aufs College gehe; **be ~ on sb.** scharf auf jmdn. sein (ugs.) 4 (highly sensitive) scharf ‹*Augen*›; fein ‹*Sinne*›; ausgeprägt ‹*Sinn für etw.*› 5 (intellectually sharp) scharf ‹*Verstand, Intellekt*›; clever ‹*Geschäftsmann*›; scharfsinnig, geistreich ‹*Bemerkung, Frage usw.*›; rasch ‹*Auffassungsgabe*›; **~ wit** Scharfsinn, *der* 6 (acute) heftig, stark ‹*Schmerzen, Qualen*› 7 (Brit.: exceptionally low) niedrig, günstig ‹*Preis*›; günstig ‹*Angebot*› 8 (coll.: excellent) [einfach] klasse (ugs.)
keen²
A *n.* Totenklage, *die*
B *v.i.* die Totenklage halten *od.* singen (**over** für)
keenly /ˈkiːnlɪ/ *adv.* 1 (sharply) scharf ‹*geschliffen*› 2 (coldly) scharf 3 (eagerly) eifrig ‹*arbeiten*›; brennend ‹*interessiert sein*›; **look forward ~ to sth.** auf etw. (*Akk.*) sehr gespannt sein 4 (piercingly) scharf ‹*ansehen*› 5 (acutely) **be ~ aware of sth.** sich (*Dat.*) einer Sache (*Gen.*) voll bewusst sein; **feel sth. ~:** etw. deutlich fühlen
keenness /ˈkiːnnɪs/ *n., no pl.* 1 (sharpness, coldness, acuteness of sense) Schärfe, *die* 2 (eagerness) Eifer, *der* 3 (of intellect) Schärfe, *die;* **the ~ of his wit** seine Scharfsinnigkeit 4 (of pain etc.) Heftigkeit, *die*
keep /kiːp/
A *v.t.,* **kept** /kept/ 1 (observe) halten ‹*Versprechen, Schwur usw.*›; einhalten ‹*Verabredung, Vereinbarung, Vertrag, Sonntagsruhe, Zeitplan*›; begehen, feiern ‹*Fest*›; halten, einhalten ‹*Sabbat, Fasten*›; *see also* **hour 3**
2 (guard) behüten, beschützen ‹*Person*›; hüten ‹*Herde, Schafe*›; schützen ‹*Stadt, Festung*›; verwahren ‹*Wertgegenstände*›; **may God ~ you!** Gott beschütze dich!; **~ sb. [safe] from sth.** jmdn. vor etw. (*Dat.*) bewahren; **~ sb. safe** jmdn. beschützen; **~ sth. locked away** etw. unter Verschluss halten *od.* aufbewahren
3 (have charge of) aufbewahren; verwahren
4 (retain possession of) behalten; (not lose or destroy) aufheben ‹*Quittung, Rechnung*›; **I'll give you that book to ~:** ich schenke dir das Buch; **~ one's position** seine Stellung behaupten *od.* halten; **you can ~ it** (coll.: I do not want it) das kannst du behalten *od.* dir an den Hut stecken (ugs.); **Another talk on architecture? You can ~ it** Noch ein Vortrag über Architektur? Nein danke, kein Bedarf (ugs.)
5 (maintain) unterhalten, instand halten ‹*Gebäude, Straße usw.*›; pflegen ‹*Garten*›; **neatly kept** gut gepflegt
6 (carry on, manage) unterhalten, führen, betreiben ‹*Geschäft, Lokal, Bauernhof*›
7 halten ‹*Schweine, Bienen, Hund, Katze usw*›; sich (*Dat.*) halten ‹*Diener, Auto*›
8 führen ‹*Tagebuch, Liste usw.*›; **~ an account of expenditure** über seine Ausgaben Buch führen; **~ the books** die Bücher führen
9 (provide for sustenance of) versorgen, unterhalten ‹*Familie*›; **~ sb./oneself in cigarettes** *etc.* jmdn./sich mit Zigaretten *usw.* versorgen; **~ sb. in luxury** jmdm. ein Leben in Luxus bieten; **~ sb. in the style to which he is accustomed** jmdm. den gewohnten Lebensstil bieten; **she has to ~ herself on £20 a week** sie muss mit 20 Pfund pro Woche auskommen
10 sich (*Dat.*) halten ‹*Geliebte, Mätresse usw.*›; sich (*Dat.*) als Geliebte halten ‹*Frau*›; sich (*Dat.*) als Liebhaber halten ‹*Mann*›; **she is a kept woman** sie lässt sich von einem Mann aushalten
11 (have on sale) führen ‹*Ware*›; **~ a stock of sth.** etw. [am Lager] haben; **we always ~ a bit of cheese** wir haben immer ein bisschen Käse da
12 (maintain in quality, state, or position) halten ‹*Rhythmus*›; **~ one's hands in one's pockets** die Hände in den Taschen behalten; **~ sth. in one's head** etw. [im Kopf] behalten; sich (*Dat.*) etw. merken; **~ sth. in a cool place** etw. an einem kühlen Ort aufbewahren; **a cold kept her in bed** eine Erkältung zwang sie, im Bett zu bleiben; **~ sb. to his word/promise** jmdn. beim Wort nehmen; **~ sb. waiting** jmdn. warten lassen; **~ the water boiling** das Wasser am Kochen halten; **~ the office running smoothly** dafür sorgen, dass im Büro weiterhin alles reibungslos [ab]läuft; **~ sb. alive** jmdn. am Leben halten; **~ the traffic moving** den Verkehr in Fluss halten; **~ a plant watered** eine Pflanze feucht halten; **~ sth. shut/tidy** etw. geschlossen/in Ordnung halten; **~ the engine running** den Motor laufen lassen; **~ sth. under [the] water** etw. unter Wasser halten
13 (maintain as quality) **~ silence** schweigen; **~ its shape** seine Form nicht verlieren; **~ one's beauty** sich (*Dat.*) seine Schönheit bewahren
14 (detain) festhalten; **there was no longer anything to ~ him there** es hielt ihn dort nichts mehr; **what kept you [so long]?** wo bleibst du denn [so lange]?; **don't let me ~ you, I mustn't ~ you** lass dich [von mir] nicht aufhalten; **~ sb. in prison** jmdn. in Haft halten; **~ sb. in hospital a few days longer** jmdn. noch ein paar Tage länger im Krankenhaus behalten; **~ sb. indoors** jmdn. nicht aus dem Haus lassen; **the teacher kept Peter behind after the lesson** der Lehrer rief Peter nach der Stunde zu sich; **~ sb. from doing sth.** jmdn. davon abhalten *od.* daran hindern, etw. zu tun; **~ sth. from doing sth.** verhindern, dass etw. etw. tut; **to ~ myself from falling** um nicht zu fallen; **I couldn't ~ myself from laughing** [ich konnte mir nicht helfen,] ich musste einfach lachen; **we must ~ them from seeing each other** wir müssen verhindern, dass sie sich sehen
15 (reserve) aufheben; aufsparen; **I asked him**

to ~ a seat for me ich bat ihn, mir einen Platz freizuhalten; **~ it for oneself** es für sich behalten; **~ sth. for later** *etc.* sich (*Dat.*) etw. für später *usw.* aufheben *od.* aufsparen; **let's ~ the business talk for later** verschieben wir das Geschäftliche erst mal auf später
16 (conceal) **~ sth. to oneself** etw. für sich behalten; **~ sth. a mystery** ein Geheimnis aus etw. machen; **~ sth. from sb.** jmdm. etw. verheimlichen; **he kept the news from them** er verschwieg ihnen die Neuigkeit
17 (continue to follow) folgen (+ *Dat.*) ‹*Straße, Weg*›; **~ a straight path** immer geradeaus gehen
B *v.i.*, **kept** **1** (remain in specified place, condition) bleiben; **~ together** zusammenbleiben; **~ warm/clean** sich warm/sauber halten; **how are you ~ing?** (coll.) wie gehts [dir] denn so? (ugs.); **are you ~ing well?** gehts dir gut?; *see also* **calm B 1**; **cool A 2**; **fit² A 5**; **silent 1**
2 (continue in course, direction, or action) **~ [to the] left/[to the] right/straight ahead** *or* **straight on** sich links/rechts halten/immer geradeaus fahren/gehen *usw.*; **~ on until you get to the traffic lights** geh/fahr *usw.* weiter bis zur Ampel; **'~ left'** (traffic sign) „links vorbeifahren"; (sign to pedestrians) „links gehen"; **traffic in Britain ~s [to the] left** in Großbritannien herrscht Linksverkehr *od.* fährt man links; **the lorry kept to the middle of the road** der Lastwagen fuhr die ganze Zeit auf der Straßenmitte; **~ behind me** halte dich *od.* bleib hinter mir; **~ doing sth.** (not stop) etw. weiter tun; (repeatedly) etw. immer wieder tun; (constantly) etw. dauernd *od.* immer tun; **~ talking/working** *etc.* **until ...:** weiterreden/-arbeiten *usw.*, bis ...; *see also* **smile B**
3 (remain good) ‹*Lebensmittel:*› sich halten; (fig.) ‹*Geheimnis:*› gewahrt bleiben; **that story can ~:** diese Geschichte kann warten *od.* eilt nicht; **your report will have to ~ until the next meeting** mit Ihrem Bericht müssen wir bis zum nächsten Treffen warten; **what I have to say won't ~:** was ich zu sagen habe, ist eilig *od.* eilt; **will your news ~ till tomorrow?** haben ihre Neuigkeiten Zeit bis morgen? *See also* **go¹ A 6**; **touch C 8**
C *n.* **1** (maintenance) Unterhalt, *der*; **I get £100 a month and my ~:** ich bekomme 100 Pfund monatlich und Logis; **you don't earn your ~:** du bist nichts als ein unnützer Esser; **sth. doesn't earn its ~:** etw. zahlt sich nicht aus (ugs.)
2 **for ~s** (coll.) auf Dauer; (to be retained) zum Behalten; **you can have it** *or* **it's yours for ~s** du kannst es behalten
3 (Hist.: tower) Bergfried, *der*

(Phrasal verbs)

- **~ 'after** *v.t.* verfolgen; jagen; (fig.: chivvy) antreiben
- **~ at** *v.t.* **1** (work persistently) weitermachen mit; **~ 'at it!** nicht nachlassen! **2** (cause to work at) **~ sb. at sth.** jmdn. dazu anhalten, dass er etw. weitermacht **3** /-'-/ (nag) nicht in Ruhe lassen; [ständig] zusetzen (+ *Dat.*); **don't ~ at me all the time!** lass mich endlich einmal in Ruhe!; **they kept at him for the money he owed** sie lagen ihm ständig wegen des Geldes, das er ihnen schuldete, in den Ohren (ugs.)
- **~ a'way**
A *v.i.* wegbleiben (ugs.) (**from** von); sich fern halten (**from** von); **I just can't ~ away** es zieht mich immer wieder hin
B *v.t.* fern halten (**from** von); **~ them away from each other!** halte sie auseinander!; **~ him away from me!** halte ihn mir vom Hals! (ugs.); **what kept you away?** warum bist du nicht gekommen?
- **~ 'back**
A *v.i.* zurückbleiben; **~ back from sth.** sich von etw. fern halten; von etw. wegbleiben (ugs.); **~ back!** bleib, wo du bist!; **~ back and wait your turn** halte dich zurück und warte, bis du an der Reihe bist
B *v.t.* **1** (restrain) zurückhalten ‹*Menschenmenge, Tränen*›; **~ sb. back from sb./sth.** jmdn. von jmdm./etw. fern halten **2** (withhold) verschweigen ‹*Informationen, Tatsachen*› (**from** *Dat.*); einbehalten ‹*Geld, Zinsen, Zahlung*›; **don't try to ~ any secrets back** versuch nicht, etwas zu verheimlichen
- **~ 'down**
A *v.i.* unten bleiben; (Mil.: lie low in skirmishing) in Deckung bleiben; ‹*Wind:*› nicht stärker werden; **~ down!** bleib unten!; duck dich!
B *v.t.* **1** (oppress, suppress) unterdrücken ‹*Volk, Person, Tränen*›; bändigen ‹*Hund*›; niederhalten ‹*rebellische Person*›; **you can't ~ a good man down** (prov.) er/sie *usw.* lässt/lassen sich nicht unterkriegen (ugs.) **2** (prevent increase of) niedrig halten ‹*Steuern, Preise, Zinssatz, Ausgaben, usw.*›; eindämmen ‹*Epidemie*›; **~ one's weight down** nicht zunehmen; **~ the weeds down** dafür sorgen, dass das Unkraut nicht überhand nimmt; **~ down insects** Insekten bekämpfen **3** (not raise) unten lassen ‹*Kopf*›; **~ that noise/your voice down** sei/rede nicht so laut; **could you ~ the volume down on your radio?** könntest du dein Radio leiser stellen? **4** (not vomit) bei sich behalten ‹*Essen*›
- **~ from** *v.t.* **~ from doing sth.** etw. nicht tun; (avoid doing) es vermeiden, etw. zu tun; **I couldn't ~ from smiling** ich musste einfach lächeln *od.* konnte ein Lächeln nicht unterdrücken; **it is impossible to ~ from getting wet** es ist nicht zu vermeiden, dass man nass wird
- **~ 'in**
A *v.i.* **1** (remain indoors) drinnen bleiben; im Haus bleiben **2** (remain in favour) **~ in with sb.** sich mit jmdm. gut stellen; sich (*Dat.*) jmdn. warm halten (ugs.)
B *v.t.* **1** (confine) unterdrücken ‹*Gefühle*›; verbergen ‹*Überraschung*›; einziehen ‹*Bauch*› **2** (keep burning) am Brennen halten ‹*Feuer*›; (not extinguish) anlassen ‹*Feuer*› **3** (Sch.) nachsitzen lassen ‹*Schüler*›; **be kept in [after school]** nachsitzen müssen. *See also* **hand A 11**
- **~ 'off**
A *v.i.* ‹*Person:*› wegbleiben; ‹*Regen, Sturm usw.:*› ausbleiben; **let's hope the snow ~s off** hoffen wir, dass es nicht anfängt zu schneien *od.* keinen Schnee gibt; **'~ off'** (on building site etc.) „Betreten verboten"
B *v.t.* **1** fern halten ‹*Person, Tier*›; abhalten ‹*Sonne*›; **~ sb./sth. off sth.** jmdn./etw. von etw. fern halten/abhalten; **~ your dog off our lawn** lassen Sie Ihren Hund nicht auf unseren Rasen **2** (not go on) nicht betreten; nicht begehen/befahren ‹*Weg, Straße usw.*›; **~ off the flower beds** nicht in die Blumenbeete treten; **'~ off the grass'** „Betreten des Rasens verboten" **3** (not touch) **~ off my whisky!** Hände *od.* Finger weg von meinem Whisky! **4** (not eat or drink) **~ off chocolates/brandy** keine Schokolade essen/keinen Weinbrand trinken; **~ off cigarettes** keine Zigaretten rauchen; **~ off the drink** keinen Alkohol *od.* (ugs.) nichts trinken; **if you don't ~ off drugs ...:** wenn du die Finger nicht von den Drogen lässt, ... (ugs.); wenn du Drogen nimmst, ... **5** (not mention) **~ off a subject** ein Thema vermeiden; **do ~ off religion when the vicar comes to tea** sprich nicht über Religion, wenn der Pfarrer zum Tee kommt
- **~ 'on**
A *v.i.* **1** (continue, persist) weitermachen (**with** *Akk.*); **~ on doing sth.** etw. [immer] weiter tun; (repeatedly) etw. immer wieder tun; (constantly) etw. dauernd *od.* immer tun; **I ~ on telling you this** das sage ich dir ja immer; **~ on driving down this road until ...:** fahr diese Straße immer weiter [entlang], bis ...; **I hope you'll ~ on coming to visit us** ich hoffe, du wirst uns auch weiterhin besuchen kommen **2** (Brit.: talk tiresomely) **he does ~ on** er redet von nichts anderem; **~ on about sth.** immer wieder von etw. anfangen; **~ on at sb. about sth.** jmdm. mit etw. ständig in den Ohren liegen (ugs.)
B *v.t.* **1** weiterbeschäftigen, behalten ‹*Angestellten*›; behalten ‹*Wohnung, Auto*›; verlängern ‹*Ausstellung, Film*›; anlassen, laufen lassen ‹*Radio, Fernseher*›; **the film was kept on for another three months/till Easter** der Film blieb drei weitere Monate/bis Ostern im Programm **2** anbehalten, anlassen ‹*Kleid, Mantel*›; aufbehalten ‹*Hut*›; *see also* **hair 2**
- **~ 'out**
A *v.i.* draußen bleiben; **'~ out'** „Zutritt verboten"
B *v.t.* **1** (not let enter) nicht hereinlassen ‹*Person, Tier*› **2** abhalten ‹*Kälte*›; abweisen ‹*Nässe*›; **central heating helps ~ out the cold** eine Zentralheizung sorgt dafür, dass es nie zu kalt wird
- **~ 'out of** *v.t.* **1** (stay outside) **~ out of a room/an area/a country** ein Zimmer/eine Gegend nicht betreten/nicht in ein Land reisen **2** (avoid) **~ out of danger** Gefahren meiden; sich nicht in Gefahr begeben; **~ out of the rain/sun** *etc.* nicht in den Regen/die Sonne *usw.* gehen; **~ out of a quarrel** sich aus einem Streit heraushalten; **~ out of sb.'s way** jmdm. aus dem Weg gehen; **~ out of the way of those boys!** halt dich von diesen Jungen fern!; **~ out of trouble** zurechtkommen **3** (not let enter) nicht hereinlassen in (+ *Akk.*) **4** (cause to avoid) **~ him/the dog out of my way** halte mir ihn/den Hund vom Leibe (salopp); **~ sb. out of danger** jmdn. vor Gefahr bewahren; **~ the plants out of the sun** die Pflanzen vor Sonne schützen; **I want to ~ him out of it** ich möchte ihn da heraushalten; **he wanted his name to be kept out of the papers** er wollte, dass sein Name in den Zeitungen nicht erwähnt wird
- **~ to** *v.t.* **1** (not leave) bleiben auf (+ *Dat.*) ‹*Straße, Weg*›; **~ to the left!** halte dich links!; bleib links! **2** (follow, observe) sich halten an (+ *Akk.*) ‹*Regeln, Muster, Gesetz, Diät usw.*›; einhalten ‹*Zeitplan*›; halten ‹*Versprechen*›; **~ to one's word** Wort halten **3** (remain in) **~ to one's bed** im Bett bleiben **4** **~ [oneself] to oneself** für sich bleiben; **they ~ themselves to themselves** sie bleiben unter sich; **he ~s to himself [most of the time]** er bleibt [meist] für sich allein. *See also* **~ A 12, B 2**
- **~ 'under** *v.t.* **1** (hold in subjection) unterdrücken **2** (maintain in state of unconsciousness etc.) unter Narkose halten
- **~ 'up**
A *v.i.* **1** (proceed equally) **~ up with sb./sth.** mit jmdm./etw. Schritt halten; **he can't ~ up with the rest** er kommt mit den anderen nicht mit; **~ up with the Joneses** mit den andern gleichziehen **2** (maintain contact) **~ up with sb.** mit jmdm. Kontakt halten; **~ up with sth.** sich über etw. (*Akk.*) auf dem Laufenden halten; **~ up with fashions/the times** (follow) mit der Mode/Zeit gehen **3** ‹*Regen, Wetter:*› anhalten
B *v.t.* **1** (prevent from falling) festhalten ‹*Leiter, Zelt usw.*›; **wear a belt to ~ one's trousers up** einen Gürtel tragen, damit die Hosen nicht rutschen **2** (prevent from sinking) aufrechterhalten ‹*Produktion, Standard usw.*›; auf gleichem Niveau halten ‹*Preise, Löhne usw.*› **3** (maintain) aufrechterhalten ‹*Bräuche, Traditionen, Freundschaft, Lebensstil, Tempo, jmds. Moral*›; (provide means for the maintenance of) unterhalten ‹*Anwesen*›; (**~** in repair) instand *od.* (ugs.) in Schuss halten ‹*Haus*›; (**~** in proper condition) in Ordnung *od.* (ugs.) in Schuss halten ‹*Garten*› **4** (continue) fortsetzen ‹*Angriff, Belagerung*›; weiterhin zahlen ‹*Raten*›; **such old customs are no longer kept up** solche alten Bräuche werden nicht mehr gepflegt; **~ one's courage/spirits up** den Mut nicht sinken lassen; **~ one's strength up** sich bei Kräften halten; **~ it up** weitermachen; **~ it up!** weiter so!; **he'll never be able to ~ it up** er wird es nicht durchhalten [können]; **I'm trying to ~ up my French** ich versuche, mit meinem Französisch nicht aus der Übung zu kommen; **~ up one's chess/painting** weiterhin Schach spielen/malen; **they kept up a correspondence for many years** sie haben jahrelang [miteinander] im Briefwechsel gestanden; *see also* **appearance 2**; **chin**; **end A 1** **5** (prevent from going to bed) am Schlafengehen hindern; **are we ~ing you up?** halten wir dich vom Schlafengehen ab?; **they kept me up all night** sie haben mich die ganze Nacht nicht schlafen lassen; **they were kept up by their baby crying** wegen ihres schreienden Babys kamen sie nicht zum Schlafen

keeper /'ki:pə(r)/ *n.* **1** ▸ ❶ **p. 1260** ▸ **gamekeeper** **2** ▸ ❶ **p. 1260** ▸ **goalkeeper**;

k

wicketkeeper 3 ▸ℹ p. 1260 (custodian) Wärter, *der*/Wärterin, *die;* (zoo~) Tierwärter, *der*/-wärterin, *die;* **~ of the keys** Schlüsselverwahrer, *der* (veralt.); **am I my brother's ~?** (Bibl.) soll ich meines Bruders Hüter sein? (bibl.) 4 (fruit that keeps) **these apples are good ~s** diese Äpfel halten sich gut

keep-'fit *n.* Fitnesstraining, *das*

keep-'fit class *n.* Fitnessgruppe, *die;* **go to ~es** zu Fitnessübungen gehen

keeping /'ki:pɪŋ/ *n., no pl.* 1 *no art.* **be in ~ with sth.** einer Sache (*Dat.*) entsprechen; (be suited to sth.) zu etw. passen; **be out of ~ with sth.** einer Sache (*Dat.*) nicht entsprechen; **the dress she wore was rather out of ~:** das Kleid, das sie anhatte, war ziemlich unpassend 2 (custody) **give sth. into sb.'s ~:** jmdm. etw. zur Aufbewahrung [über]geben; **the keys are in his ~:** er bewahrt die Schlüssel auf; **take sth. into one's ~:** etw. in Gewahrsam nehmen; **leave sb. in sb.'s ~:** jmdn. jmds. Obhut anvertrauen 3 **the apples will improve with ~:** die Äpfel werden besser, wenn man sie eine Zeit lang liegen lässt

'keepsake *n.* Andenken, *das;* **take it as** *or* **for a ~ [to remind you] of me** nimm es als *od.* zum Andenken an mich

keg /keg/ *n.* 1 (barrel) [kleines] Fass; Fässchen, *das* 2 *attrib.* **~ beer** *aus luftdichten Metallbehältern gezapftes, mit Kohlensäure versetztes Bier;* ≈ Fassbier, *das*

kelp /kelp/ *n.* [See]tang, *der*

kelvin /'kelvɪn/ *n.* (Phys.) Kelvin, *das*

'Kelvin scale *n.* (Phys.) Kelvinskala, *die*

ken¹ /ken/ *n.* **this is beyond** *or* **outside my ~:** das geht über meinen Horizont; das ist zu hoch für mich (ugs.); (beyond range of knowledge) das übersteigt mein Wissen

ken² *v.t.*, **~ned** *or* **kent** /kent/, **~ned** (Scot.) ▸ **know A**

kennel /'kenl/ *n.* 1 Hundehütte, *die* 2 *in pl.* **[boarding] ~s** Hundepension, *die;* **[breeding] ~s** Zwinger, *der*

Kentish /'kentɪʃ/ *adj.* kentisch

Kenya /'kenjə, 'ki:njə/ *pr. n.* Kenia (*das*)

Kenyan /'kenjən, 'ki:njən/ ▸ℹ p. 1345
A *adj.* kenianisch; **sb. is ~:** jmd. ist Kenianer/Kenianerin
B *n.* Kenianer, *der*/Kenianerin, *die*

kepi /'kepɪ, 'keɪpɪ/ *n.* Käppi, *das*

kept ▸ **keep A, B**

keratin /'kerətɪn/ *n., no pl.* Keratin, *das*

kerb /kɜ:b/ *n.* (Brit.) Bordstein, *der*

kerb: ~-crawling *n., no pl.* (Brit.) *(langsames) Fahren auf dem Autostrich zur Kontaktaufnahme mit einer Prostituierten;* **~ drill** *n.* (Brit.) richtiges [Verhalten beim] Überqueren der Fahrbahn; **~side** *n.* Straßenrand, *der; attrib.* **~side collection** Straßensammlung, *die;* **~stone** *n.* (Brit.) Bordstein, *der;* **~ weight** *n.* (Brit.) [Fahrzeug]leergewicht, *das*

kerchief /'kɜ:tʃɪf, 'kɜ:tʃi:f/ *n.* (worn on the head) Kopftuch, *das;* (worn around the neck) [Hals]tuch, *das*

kerfuffle /kə'fʌfl/ *n.* (Brit. coll.) Wirbel, *der;* Affenzeck, *der* (ugs. abwertend)

kernel /'kɜ:nl/ *n.* (lit. or fig.) Kern, *der;* **a ~ of truth** ein Körnchen Wahrheit

kerosene, kerosine /'kerəsi:n/ *n.* (Amer., Austral., NZ/as tech. term) Paraffin[öl], *das;* (for jet engines) Kerosin, *das;* (for lamps etc.) Petroleum, *das;* **~ lamp** Petroleumlampe, *die*

kestrel /'kestrəl/ *n.* (Ornith.) Turmfalke, *der*

ketch /ketʃ/ *n.* (Naut.) Ketsch, *die*

ketchup /'ketʃʌp/ *n.* Ketchup, *der od. das*

ketone /'ki:təʊn/ *n.* (Chem.) Keton, *das*

kettle /'ketl/ *n.* [Wasser]kessel, *der;* **a pretty** *or* **fine ~ of fish** (iron.) eine schöne Bescherung (ugs. iron.); **a different** *or* **another ~ of fish** eine ganz andere Sache

kettle: ~drum *n.* (Mus.) [Kessel]pauke, *die;* **~-drummer** *n.* (Mus.) Paukist, *der*/Paukistin, *die*

kettleful /'ketlfʊl/ *n.* Kessel, *der;* **a ~ of water** ein Kessel [voll] Wasser

key¹ /ki:/
A *n.* 1 (lit. or fig.) Schlüssel, *der;* **the ~ to success** der Schlüssel zum Erfolg; **the ~ to the mystery** des Rätsels Lösung; der Schlüssel zum Geheimnis 2 (place) Schlüsselstellung, *die* (Milit.) 3 (set of answers) [Lösungs]schlüssel, *der;* (to map etc.) Zeichenerklärung, *die;* (to cipher) Schlüssel, *der* 4 (translation) [wörtliche] Übersetzung 5 (on piano, typewriter, etc.) Taste, *die;* (on wind instrument) Klappe, *die* 6 (Electr.) Taste, *die* 7 (Mus.) Tonart, *die;* (fig.: of speech or writing) Ton, *der;* Tonart, *die;* **sing/play in/off ~:** richtig/falsch singen/spielen 8 (Bot.) Flügelfrucht, *die* 9 (for grasping screws etc.) [Schrauben]schlüssel, *der;* (for winding a clock etc.) Schlüssel, *der. See also* **house A 3**
B *attrib. adj.* entscheidend; Schlüssel(*frage, -position, -rolle, -figur, -industrie*)
C *v.t.* (Computing) **~ [in]** eintasten

Phrasal verb

• **~ up** *v.t.* 1 (stimulate) **key sb. up to sth./to a state of excitement** jmdn. zu etw. hinreißen/in einen Zustand der Erregung versetzen; **the crowd was keyed up for the match** die Menge war auf das Spiel eingestimmt 2 (make extremely tense) **be all keyed up** ganz aufgeregt sein; **he was all keyed up for the great event** er fieberte dem großen Ereignis entgegen

key² *n.* (Geog.) [Korallen]insel, *die*

key: ~board A *n.* (of piano etc.) Klaviatur, *die;* (of typewriter, computer, etc.) Tastatur, *die; attrib.* **~board instrument** Tasteninstrument, *das;* **~board operator** Taster, *der*/Tasterin, *die;* **~board shortcut** Tastaturkürzel, *das;* **~board skills** Kenntnisse im Umgang mit Computertastaturen; B *v.t.* tasten; **~boarder** *n.* ▸ℹ p. 1260 Taster, *der*/Tasterin, *die;* **~boarding** *n., no pl.* Tasten, *das; attrib.* **~boarding error** Tastfehler, *der;* **~ card** *n.* Schlüsselkarte, *die;* **~ holder** *n.* Schlüsselverwalter, *der*/-verwalterin, *die;* **are you the ~ holder?** haben Sie einen Schlüssel?; **~hole** *n.* Schlüsselloch, *das;* **~hole saw** *n.* Schlüssellochsäge, *die;* **~hole 'surgery** *n., no pl.* Schlüssellochchirurgie, *die;* Knopflochchirurgie, *die*

'keying *n., no pl.* ▸ **keyboarding**

key: ~note *n.* 1 (Mus.) Grundton, *der;* 2 (fig.) Grundgedanke, *der;* [Grund]tenor, *der; attrib.* **~note speaker** Programmredner, *der*/-rednerin, *die;* **~note speech** programmatische Rede; **~pad** *n.* Tastenfeld, *das;* **~ring** *n.* Schlüsselring, *der;* **~ signature** *n.* (Mus.) Tonartvorzeichnung, *die;* **~stone** *n.* (Archit.) Schlussstein, *der;* (fig.) Grundpfeiler, *der;* **~stroke** *n.* (Computing) Anschlag, *der;* **~word** *n.* 1 (key to cipher) Schlüsselwort, *das;* 2 (significant word in indexing) Stichwort, *das;* Schlüsselwort, *das* (bes. DV)

kg. *abbr.* ▸ℹ p. 1702 **= kilogram[s]** kg

KG *abbr.* (Brit.) **= Knight [of the Order] of the Garter**

khaki /'kɑ:kɪ/
A *adj.* khakifarben; **~ colour/cloth** Khaki, *das*/Khaki, *der*
B *n.* (cloth) Khaki, *der;* **~-coloured** khakifarben

kHz *abbr.* **= kilohertz** kHz

kibbutz /kɪ'bʊts/ *n., pl.* **kibbutzim** /kɪbʊt'si:m/ Kibbuz, *der*

kibitzer /'kɪbɪtsə(r), kɪ'bɪtsə(r)/ *n.* (coll.) Kiebitz, *der* (ugs.); (meddlesome person) wichtigtuerischer Besserwisser

kibosh /'kaɪbɒʃ/ *n.* (coll.) **put the ~ on sth.** etw. vermasseln (salopp); **that's put the ~ on his hopes, hasn't it?** damit sind seine Hoffnungen wohl im Eimer, was? (salopp)

kick /kɪk/
A *n.* 1 [Fuß]tritt, *der;* (Footb.) Schuss, *der;* **give sb. a ~:** jmdm. einen Tritt geben *od.* versetzen; **give a ~ at sth., give sth. a ~:** gegen etw. treten; **give sb. a ~ in the pants** (fig. coll.) jmdm. Feuer unterm Hintern machen (salopp); **a ~ in the teeth** (fig.) ein Schlag ins Gesicht; **give sb. a ~ in the teeth** (fig. coll.) jmdn. vor den Kopf stoßen
2 (Sport: burst of speed) Spurt, *der*
3 (coll.: sharp effect, thrill) Kitzel, *der;* (of wine) Feuer, *das;* **give sb. a ~:** jmdm. Spaß machen; **this beer has plenty of ~ in it** dieses Bier hat es in sich (*Dat.*); **he gets a ~ out of it** er hat Spaß daran; es macht ihm Spaß; **do sth. for ~s** etw. zum Spaß tun
4 (coll.: temporary interest) Fimmel, *der* (ugs. abwertend); Tick, *der* (ugs.); **be on a** *or* **the fitness ~:** auf einem *od.* dem Fitnesstrip sein (ugs.)
5 (recoil of gun) Rückstoß, *der*
B *v.i.* 1 treten; (*Pferd:*) ausschlagen; (*Baby:*) strampeln; (*Tänzer:*) das Bein hochwerfen; **~ at sth.** gegen etw. treten; **you have to ~ with your legs when doing the crawl** beim Kraulen musst du mit den Beinen schlagen; **~ing and screaming** (fig.) in heftigem *od.* wildem Protest
2 (show opposition) sich zur Wehr setzen (**at, against** gegen). *See also* **alive 4; prick C 5; trace²**
C *v.t.* 1 einen Tritt geben (+ *Dat.*) (*Person, Hund*); treten gegen (*Gegenstand*); kicken (ugs.), schlagen, schießen (*Ball*); **~ the door open/shut** die Tür auf-/zutreten; **he ~ed the ball straight at me** er kickte den Ball genau in meine Richtung; **~ sb. in the teeth** (fig. coll.) jmdn. vor den Kopf stoßen; **~ sb. upstairs** (fig. coll.) *jmdm. eine nach außen bessere Position geben, aber seinen Einflussbereich einschränken;* ≈ jmdn. fortloben; **I could ~ myself!** (coll.) ich könnte mir *od.* mich in den Hintern beißen (salopp)
2 (coll.: abandon) ablegen (*schlechte Angewohnheit*); aufgeben (*Rauchen*); **~ the habit** es aufstecken (ugs.). *See also* **bucket A 1; heel¹ A 1**

Phrasal verbs

• **~ a'bout, ~ a'round**
A *v.t.* 1 [in der Gegend] herumkicken (ugs.) 2 (treat badly) herumstoßen; schikanieren 3 (coll.: discuss unsystematically) bekakeln (ugs.); bequatschen (salopp)
B *v.i.* 1 (coll.: wander about) rumziehen (ugs.) 2 **be ~ing about** *or* **around** (coll.: be present, alive) rumhängen (ugs.); **old Thompson is still ~ing around** (is still alive) der alte Thompson machts immer noch (ugs.) 3 **be ~ing about** *or* **around** (coll.: lie scattered) rumliegen (ugs.); rumfliegen (salopp); **is there a sandwich ~ing around?** gibts hier irgendwo 'n Sandwich? (ugs.)

• **~ 'back**
A *v.i.* 1 (~ in retaliation) zurücktreten; (fig.) zurückschlagen 2 (recoil) (*Gewehr:*) zurückschlagen
B *v.t.* 1 zurückschlagen (*Ball*); mit dem Fuß zurückschlagen (*Bettdecke*) 2 (~ in retaliation) wieder treten. *See also* **kickback**

• **~ 'in** *v.t.* (break, damage) eintreten

• **~ 'off**
A *v.t.* von sich schleudern (*Kleidungsstück, Schuhe*)
B *v.i.* (Footb.) anstoßen; (*Spiel:*) beginnen; (fig. coll.: start) anfangen; *see also* **kick-off**

• **~ 'out** *v.t.* (force to leave) hinauswerfen; rausschmeißen (ugs.); **get ~ed out** rausfliegen (ugs.); **get ~ed out of one's job** [aus der Stellung] fliegen (ugs.)

• **~ 'up** *v.t.* 1 (raise by ~ing) [mit den Füßen] aufwirbeln (*Sand, Staub*); (*Autoreifen:*) hochschleudern (*Steine*); mit dem Fuß umschlagen (*Teppich*) 2 (coll.: create) **~ up a fuss/row** Krach schlagen/anfangen (ugs.); **~ up a stink** Rabatz machen (ugs.)

kick: ~back *n.* (coll.: bribe) Prozente (fig. ugs.); **~-down** *n.* (Motor Veh.) Kickdown, *der;* **~-off** *n.* 1 (Footb.) Anstoß, *der;* (fig.: start) Beginn, *der;* **for a ~-off** (coll.) zunächst einmal; 2 (inaugural event) Eröffnung, *die;* **~-start** A *n.* 1 Kickstarter, *der;* 2 (fig.) [neuer] Auftrieb; B *v.t.* 1 [mit dem Kickstarter] starten; 2 (fig.) ankurbeln (*Industrie, Wirtschaft*); vorantreiben, forcieren (*Friedensprozess, Entwicklung*); **~-start sb.'s career** jmds. Karriere einen [neuen] Schub geben; **~-starter** *n.* (Motor Veh.) Kickstarter, *der;* **~-turn** *n.* (Skiing) Spitzkehre, *die*

kid /kɪd/
A *n.* 1 (young goat) Kitz, *das;* Zickel, *das* 2 (leather) Ziegenleder, *das; attrib.* Ziegenleder- 3 (coll.) (child) Kind, *das;* (young person) Jugendliche, *der/die;* Kid, *das* (ugs.); **these ~s are driving me mad today** diese Bälger machen mich heute verrückt (ugs.); **you're still only a ~:** du bist noch zu jung [dazu]; **OK, ~s, let's go** also gut, Leute, gehen wir (ugs.); **college ~** (Amer.) Student, *der*/Studentin, *die;* **what a**

great ~ she is! sie ist wirklich schwer in Ordnung (ugs.); **it's ~[s'] stuff** (easy) das ist ein Kinderspiel; **I'm too old for that ~s' stuff** ich bin zu alt für diese Kindereien; **~ brother/sister** kleiner Bruder/kleine Schwester; Brüderchen, *das*/Schwesterchen, *das*

B *v.t.*, **-dd-** (coll.) (hoax) anführen (ugs.); auf den Arm nehmen (ugs.); (deceive) was vormachen (+ *Dat.*) (ugs.); (tease) aufziehen (ugs.); **I ~ you 'not** ehrlich!; **~ oneself** sich (*Dat.*) was vormachen (ugs.)

C *v.i.*, **-dd-** (coll.) **be ~ding** Spaß machen (ugs.); **you've got to be ~ding!** das ist doch nicht dein Ernst!; **no ~ding** [ganz] im Ernst *od.* ohne Scherz

kiddie /ˈkɪdɪ/ (coll.) Kindchen, *das;* **all right ~s, off to bed with you** okay, Kinder, ab ins Bett (ugs.); **I wish I had some ~s of my own** ich wünschte, ich hätte selbst kleine Kinder

kid 'glove *n.* Glacéhandschuh, *der;* **handle** *or* **treat sb. with ~s** (fig.) jmdn. mit Samt- *od.* Glacéhandschuhen anfassen (ugs.)

kid-'glove *adj.* sanft; behutsam; **give sb. the ~ treatment** jmdn. mit Samt- *od.* Glacéhandschuhen anfassen (ugs.)

kidnap /ˈkɪdnæp/ *v.t.*, (Brit.) **-pp-** entführen ‹*Person*›; stehlen ‹*Tier*›; (to obtain ransom) kidnappen; entführen

kidnapper /ˈkɪdnæpə(r)/ *n.* Entführer, *der*/Entführerin, *die;* Kidnapper, *der*/Kidnapperin, *die*

kidnapping /ˈkɪdnæpɪŋ/ *n.* Entführung, *die*

kidney /ˈkɪdnɪ/ *n.* **1** ▸ⓘ **p. 951** (Anat., Gastr.) Niere, *die;* **steak and ~ pie/pudding** ▸**steak** **2** (fig.: temperament) [Menschen]schlag, *der;* **of the same/right** *etc.* **~:** vom gleichen/richtigen *usw.* Schlag

kidney: ~ bean *n.* Gartenbohne, *die;* (scarlet runner bean) Feuerbohne, *die;* **red ~ bean** Kidneybohne, *die;* **~ di'alysis** *n., no pl.* (Med.) [Nieren]dialyse, *die;* **a patient on ~ dialysis** ein Dialysepatient/eine Dialysepatientin; **~ dish** *n.* Nierenschale, *die;* **~ donor** *n.* Nierenspender, *der*/-spenderin, *die;* **~ failure** *n.* ▸ⓘ **p. 1231** Nierenversagen, *das;* **~ machine** *n.* künstliche Niere; Dialysegerät, *das;* **~-shaped** *adj.* nierenförmig; **~ stone** *n.* ▸ⓘ **p. 1231**Nierenstein, *der;* **~ table** *n.* Nierentisch, *der;* **~ vetch** *n.* Gemeiner Wundklee; gelber Klee

Kiel Canal /kiːl kəˈnæl/ *pr. n.* Nord-Ostsee-Kanal, *der*

Kilkenny cat /kɪlkenɪ ˈkæt/ *n.* **fight like ~s** wie zwei Wildkatzen kämpfen; (fig.) sich bis zum letzten Blutstropfen bekämpfen

kill /kɪl/

A *v.t.* **1** töten; (deliberately) umbringen; ‹*Rauchen usw.:*› tödliche Folgen haben für; sterben lassen ‹*Romanfigur usw.*›; **be ~ed in action/war** im Kampf/Krieg fallen; **shoot to ~:** gezielt schießen; **too much drink can ~ you** zu viel Alkohol kann tödlich sein; **~ or cure sb./sth.** jmdn./etw. entweder umbringen oder wieder auf die Beine bringen; **be ~ed in a car crash** bei einem Autounfall umkommen *od.* ums Leben kommen; **grief/the shock almost ~ed her** sie wäre vor Gram/Schreck fast gestorben; **it won't ~ you** (iron.) es wird dich [schon] nicht *od.* nicht gleich umbringen; **that last stretch [nearly] ~ed me!** das letzte Stück hat mich fast umgebracht; **~ oneself** sich umbringen; **I'm ~ing myself with this work** ich arbeite mich [dabei] zu Tode; **~ oneself laughing** (fig.) sich totlachen **2** (coll.: cause severe pain to) **it is ~ing me** das bringt mich noch um; **my feet are ~ing me** meine Füße tun wahnsinnig weh (ugs.) **3** abtöten ‹*Krankheitserreger, Schmerz, Ungeziefer, Hefe*›; erfolgreich bekämpfen ‹*Krankheit*›; absterben lassen ‹*Bäume, Pflanzen*›; totschlagen ‹*Geschmack, Farbe*›; verderben ‹*Witz*›; (put an end to) [ab]töten ‹*Gefühl*›; zerstören ‹*Glauben*›; **~ sb.'s ambition** jmdn. resignieren lassen; jmds. Ehrgeiz erkalten lassen (geh.) **4** **~ time** sich (*Dat.*) die Zeit vertreiben; die Zeit totschlagen (abwertend); **I've got such a lot of time to ~ at the moment** ich habe zur Zeit so viel Leerlauf; **~ an hour** sich (*Dat.*) eine Stunde lang die Zeit vertreiben **5** (obtain meat from) schlachten ‹*Tier*›; **~ meat** schlachten **6** (overwhelm) überwältigen; **dress to ~:** sich herausputzen **7** (switch off) ausschalten; (extinguish) ausdrücken, (ugs.) töten ‹*Zigarette*› **8** (coll.) (eat) verdrücken (ugs.); (drink) leer machen ‹*Flasche*› **9** (Footb.) stoppen ‹*Ball*›; (Tennis) unretournierbar schlagen ‹*Ball*› **10** (defeat, veto) zu Fall bringen; abschmettern (ugs.). *See also* **bird 1**

B *n.* **1** (~ing of game) Abschuss, *der;* (prey) Beute, *die;* **the tiger has made a ~/is on the ~:** der Tiger hat eine Beute geschlagen/ist auf der Jagd; **move in for the ~** ‹*Raubtier:*› die Beute anschleichen, zum Sprung auf die Beute ansetzen; (fig.) zum entscheidenden Schlag ausholen; **be in at the ~ = be in at the death** ▸**death 1** **2** (Hunting: amount) Strecke, *die* (Jägerspr.) **3** (destruction) (of aircraft) Abschuss, *der;* (of ship) Versenkung, *die*

(Phrasal verb)

• **~ 'off** *v.t.* vernichten ‹*Feinde, Konkurrenz*›; ausrotten ‹*Tierart*›; abschlachten ‹*Vieh*›; sterben lassen ‹*Romanfigur usw.*›; vertilgen ‹*Ungeziefer, Unkraut*›; scheitern lassen ‹*Projekt*›; ‹*Frost:*› eingehen lassen ‹*Pflanze*›

killer /ˈkɪlə(r)/ *n.* Mörder, *der*/Mörderin, *die;* (murderous ruffian) Killer, *der* (salopp); **be a ~** ‹*Krankheit:*› tödlich sein; *attrib.* **the ~ instinct** der Instinkt zum Töten; der Killerinstinkt (Sportjargon); *see also* **humane killer**

killer: ~ appli'cation *n.* (Computing) Killerapplikation, *die;* **~ cell** *n.* (Biol.) Killerzelle, *die* (Jargon); **~ whale** *n.* Mörderwal, *der*

killing /ˈkɪlɪŋ/

A *n.* **1** Töten, *das;* Tötung, *die;* **the ~ of the three children** der Mord an den drei Kindern **2** (instance) Mord[fall], *der* **3** (fig. coll.: great success) Coup, *der* (ugs.); **make a ~** (make a great profit) einen [Mords]reibach machen (ugs.)

B *adj.* **1** tödlich **2** (coll.: exhausting) mörderisch (ugs.) **3** (coll.: attractive, amusing etc.) umwerfend

killingly /ˈkɪlɪŋlɪ/ *adv.* **~ funny** zum Totlachen [komisch] (ugs.)

'killjoy *n.* Spielverderber, *der*/-verderberin, *die*

kiln /kɪln/ *n.* (for burning/drying) [Brenn-/Trocken]ofen, *der;* (hop-~) Darre, *die*

'kiln-dry *v.t.* [im Ofen] brennen ‹*Keramik*›; darren ‹*Hopfen, Getreide usw.*›

kilo /ˈkiːləʊ/ *n., pl.* **~s** ▸ⓘ **p. 1702** Kilo, *das*

kilo- /ˈkɪlə/ *pref.* kilo-/Kilo-

'kilobyte *n.* (Computing) Kilobyte, *das*

'kilocycle *n.* (frequency unit) Kilohertz, *das*

'kilogram, 'kilogramme *n.* ▸ⓘ **p. 1702** Kilogramm, *das*

'kilohertz *n.* (Phys.) Kilohertz, *das*

kilometre (*Brit.;* *Amer.:* **kilometer**) /ˈkɪləmiːtə(r)/ (Brit.), /kɪˈlɒmɪtə(r)/ *n.* ▸ⓘ **p. 1566** Kilometer, *der*

'kilovolt *n.* (Electr., Phys.) Kilovolt, *das*

'kilowatt *n.* (Electr., Phys.) Kilowatt, *das*

'kilowatt-hour *n.* (Electr., Phys.) Kilowattstunde, *die*

kilt /kɪlt/ *n.* **1** (Scot.) Kilt, *der* **2** (women's garment) Schottenrock, *der;* Kiltrock, *der*

kilted /ˈkɪltɪd/ *adj.* kiltbekleidet; kilttragend; **be ~:** einen Kilt tragen

kilter /ˈkɪltə(r)/ *n.* **be out of ~** (out of order) nicht in Ordnung sein; (out of alignment) schief sein

kimono /kɪˈməʊnəʊ/ *n., pl.* **~s** Kimono, *der*

kin /kɪn/

A *n.* (ancestral stock) Geschlecht, *das;* (relatives) Verwandte, (relation) Verwandte, *der/die; see also* **kith; next C 3**

B *pred. adj.* verwandt (**to** mit)

kind¹ /kaɪnd/ *n.* **1** (class, sort) Art, *die;* **several ~s of apples** mehrere Sorten Äpfel; **all ~s of things/excuses** alles Mögliche/alle möglichen Ausreden; **all ~s of people enjoy that programme** das Programm gefällt den verschiedensten Leuten; **no ... of any ~:** keinerlei ...; **good of its ~:** auf seine Art ganz gut; **books of every ~:** Bücher aller Art; **be [of] the same ~:** von derselben Sorte *od.* Art sein; **I know [you and] your ~:** deine Sorte kenne ich; **people/things of this ~:** diese Art Leute/solche Dinge; **she's not the ~ [of person] to talk scandal** es ist nicht ihre Art, zu tratschen; **something/nothing of the ~:** so etwas Ähnliches/nichts dergleichen; **you'll do nothing of the ~!** das kommt gar nicht in Frage!; **two of a ~:** zwei Gleiche; **they differ** *or* **are different in ~:** sie unterscheiden sich wesentlich; **I suppose it was art of a ~** (derog.) das sollte wohl Kunst sein; **Was there any entertainment? — Well, of a ~** (derog.) Gab es irgendwelche Unterhaltung? — Na ja, es sollte wohl so was sein; **what ~ is it?** was für einer/eine/eins ist es?; **what ~ of [a] tree is this?** was für ein Baum ist das?; **what ~ of people are they?** was für Leute sind sie?; **what ~ of thing are you going to wear?** was ziehst du an?; **what ~ of [a] fool do you take me for?** für wie dumm hältst du mich?; **what ~ of [a] person do you think I am?** für wen hältst du mich?; **the ~ of person we need** der Typ, den wir brauchen; **this is exactly the ~ of house we're looking for** genau so ein Haus suchen wir; **they are the ~ of people who ...:** sie gehören zu der Sorte von Leuten, die ...; das sind solche Leute, die ...; **this ~ of food/atmosphere** diese Art *od.* solches Essen/solch *od.* so eine Stimmung; **these ~ of people/things** (coll.) solche Leute/Sachen **2** (implying vagueness) **a ~ of ...:** [so] eine Art ...; **~ of interesting/cute** *etc.* (coll.) irgendwie interessant/niedlich *usw.* (ugs.) **3** (race) **the human ~:** die Menschheit; das Menschengeschlecht; **one's own ~:** seinesgleichen **4** **in ~** (not in money) in Sachwerten; **pay in ~:** in Naturalien zahlen/bezahlen; **benefits in ~:** Sachbezüge *Pl.;* **pay back** *or* **repay sth. in ~** (fig.) etw. mit *od.* in gleicher Münze zurückzahlen

kind² *adj.* (of gentle nature) liebenswürdig; (showing friendliness) freundlich; (affectionate) lieb; **if the weather is ~:** bei schönem Wetter; **have a ~ heart** gutherzig sein; **would you be so ~ as to** *or* **~ enough to do that?** wären Sie so freundlich *od.* nett, das zu tun?; **be ~ to animals/children** gut zu Tieren/Kindern sein; **oh, you 'are ~!, that 'is ~ of you** sehr nett *od.* liebenswürdig von Ihnen; **how ~ !** wie nett [von ihm/ihr/Ihnen *usw.*]!

kinda /ˈkaɪndə/ (coll.) **= kind of; I ~ like that** ich mag das irgendwie *od.* (ugs.) irgendwo; **that ~ thing** so was (ugs.)

kindergarten /ˈkɪndəgɑːtn/ *n.* Kindergarten, *der;* (forming part of a school) ≈ Vorklasse, *die*

kind-hearted /kaɪndˈhɑːtɪd/ *adj.* gutherzig; liebenswürdig ‹*Geste, Handlung*›

kindle /ˈkɪndl/

A *v.t.* **1** (light) anzünden, (geh.) entzünden ‹*Holz, Feuer*›; entfachen (geh.) ‹*Flamme*›; (fig.: inflame) entzünden, entfachen (geh.) ‹*Zorn, Leidenschaft*›; wecken ‹*Interesse, Gefühl*› **2** (make bright) erglühen lassen (geh.)

B *v.i.* **1** (catch fire) sich entzünden; (fig.: become animated) aufleben; (fig.: flare up) aufflammen; entbrennen (geh.) **2** (become bright) ‹*Augen:*› aufflammen (geh.) (**with** vor + *Dat.*); ‹*Licht:*› aufscheinen (geh.); (start to glow) erglühen (geh.)

kindliness /ˈkaɪndlɪnɪs/ *n., no pl.* Freundlichkeit, *die;* (gentleness of nature) Liebenswürdigkeit, *die*

kindling /ˈkɪndlɪŋ/ *n., no pl., no indef. art.* (for lighting fire) Anmachholz, *das*

kindly /ˈkaɪndlɪ/

A *adv.* **1** freundlich; nett; **..., she said ~:** ..., sagte sie freundlich **2** *in polite request etc.* freundlicherweise **3** **take sth. ~:** etw. gern annehmen; **take ~ to sth./sb.** sich mit etw./jmdm. schnell anfreunden; **he didn't take at all ~ to the suggestion** er konnte sich mit dem Vorschlag gar nicht recht anfreunden; **I wouldn't take ~ to anything like that** für dergleichen könnte ich mich kaum erwärmen **4** **thank sb. ~:** jmdm. herzlich danken; **thank you ~:** herzlichen Dank

B *adj.* **1** freundlich; nett; liebenswürdig; (good-natured, kind-hearted) gütig; wohlwollend; gut ‹*Herz, Tat*› **2** (pleasant) angenehm ‹*Wetter, Klima*›; (favourable) günstig; gut

kindness /ˈkaɪndnɪs/ *n.* **1** *no pl.* (kind nature) Freundlichkeit, *die;* Liebenswürdigkeit, *die;* **do sth. out of ~:** etw. aus Gefälligkeit tun; **out of the ~ of one's heart** aus reiner Freundlichkeit **2** (kind act) Gefälligkeit, *die;* **do sb. a ~:**

K

jmdm. eine Gefälligkeit erweisen *od.* einen Gefallen tun

kindred /ˈkɪndrɪd/
A *n., no pl.* **1** (blood relationship) Blutsverwandtschaft, *die* **2** (one's relatives) Verwandtschaft, *die;* Verwandte
B *adj.* **1** (related by blood) blutsverwandt **2** (fig.) (connected) verwandt; (similar) ähnlich

kindred ˈspirit *n.* Gleichgesinnte, *der/die;* verwandte Seele (geh.)

kinetic /kɪˈnetɪk, kaɪˈnetɪk/ *adj.* kinetisch

king /kɪŋ/ *n.* **1** ▸ **p. 1634** König, *der;* **live like a ~:** leben wie ein Fürst; **a feast fit for a ~:** ein königliches Mahl; **[the First/Second Book of] K~s** (Bibl.) [das erste/zweite Buch der] Könige; **K~ of ~s** (God) König aller Könige; **K~ of the Castle** *ein Kinderspiel, bei dem man versucht, den Gegner von einem Hügel zu verdrängen;* **be the ~ of the castle** (fig.) das Sagen haben; **~ of beasts/birds** König der Tiere/Vögel **2** (great merchant, player, etc.) König, *der;* **oil ~:** Ölkönig, *der;* Ölmagnat, *der* **3** (Chess, Cards) König, *der;* (Draughts) Dame, *die;* **~'s bishop/knight/pawn/rook** Königsläufer/-springer/-bauer/-turm, *der;* **~ of hearts** Herzkönig, *der. See also* **bench 8; colour A 10; counsel A 3; English B 1; evidence A 2; guide A 5; highway 1; messenger 2; ransom A; save A 3; scout¹ A 1; shilling**

king: ~ ˈcobra *n.* Königskobra, *die;* **~ crab** *n.* **1** Königskrabbe, *die;* **2** (Amer.: edible spider crab) Steinkrabbe, *die;* **~cup** *n.* (Bot.) **1** (buttercup) Hahnenfuß, der; **2** (Brit.: marsh marigold) Sumpfdotterblume, *die*

kingdom /ˈkɪŋdəm/ *n.* **1** Königreich, *das;* **the ~ of Naples** das Königreich Neapel; *see also* **United Kingdom 2** (reign of God, sphere of reign) Reich, *das;* **the ~ of God** das Reich Gottes; **thy ~ come** dein Reich komme; **the ~ of heaven** das Himmelreich; **wait till ~ come** (coll.) bis in alle Ewigkeit warten (ugs.); **blast sb. to ~ come** (coll.) jmdn. umnieten (salopp) **3** (domain) Welt, *die;* **the ~ of thought** das Reich der Gedanken **4** (province of nature) Reich, *das;* **animal/vegetable/mineral ~:** Tier-/Pflanzen-/Mineralreich, *das;* **~ of nature** Naturreich, *das*

king: ~fisher *n.* (Ornith.) Eisvogel, *der;* **K~ ˈJames[ʼs] Bible** *or* **Version = Authorized Version** ▸ **authorize 2**

kingly /ˈkɪŋlɪ/ *adj.* königlich

king: ~maker *n.* Königsmacher, *der;* **~ ˈpenguin** *n.* Königspinguin, *der;* **~pin** *n.* (lit., or fig.: essential person or thing) Hauptstütze, *die;* (most prominent person or organization) Nummer eins; **he's the ~pin in the team** mit ihm steht und fällt die Mannschaft

kingship /ˈkɪŋʃɪp/ *n.* **1** *no pl., no art.* (office of king) Königsamt, *das* **2** (rule of king) Königtum, *das*

ˈking-size[d] *adj.* extragroß; Kingsize-⟨*Zigaretten*⟩

kink /kɪŋk/
A *n.* **1** (in pipe, wire, etc.) Knick, *der;* (in rope) Kink, *der* (Seemannsspr.); (in hair, wool) Welle, *die* **2** (fig.: mental peculiarity) Tick, *der* (ugs.); Spleen, *der*
B *v.i.* Knicke kriegen; ⟨*Haar:*⟩ sich wellen
C *v.t.* knicken; Knicke machen in (+ *Akk.*); einen Kink machen in (+ *Akk.*) (Seemannsspr.)

kinkajou /ˈkɪŋkədʒuː/ *n.* (Zool.) Kinkaju, *der;* Wickelbär, *der*

kinky /ˈkɪŋkɪ/ *adj.* **1** geknickt; wellig ⟨*Haar*⟩ **2** (coll.: bizarre, perverted) spleenig; (sexually) abartig

kinsfolk /ˈkɪnzfəʊk/ *n. pl.* Verwandtschaft, *die;* Verwandte

kinship /ˈkɪnʃɪp/ *n.* **1** (blood relationship) Blutsverwandtschaft, *die* **2** (similarity) Ähnlichkeit, *die;* (spiritual) Verwandtschaft, *die*

kinsman /ˈkɪnzmən/ *n., pl.* **kinsmen** /ˈkɪnzmən/ Verwandte, *der*

kinswoman /ˈkɪnzwʊmən/ *n.* Verwandte, *die*

kiosk /ˈkiːɒsk/ *n.* **1** (outdoor structure) Kiosk, *der;* (Brit.: indoor structure) [Verkaufs]stand, *der* **2** (public telephone booth) [Telefon]zelle, *die*

kip /kɪp/ (Brit. coll.)
A *n.* **1** (sleep) Schlaf, *der;* **have a** *or* **get some ~:** eine Runde pennen (salopp) **2** (bed) Falle, *die* (salopp)
B *v.i.*, **-pp-** pennen (salopp); **~ down** sich hinhauen (salopp)

kipper /ˈkɪpə(r)/
A *n.* Kipper, *der;* ≈ Bückling, *der*
B *v.t.* räuchern ⟨*Fisch*⟩; **~ed** Räucher⟨*fisch, -lachs, -hering*⟩

kirk /kɜːk/ *n.* (Brit.) **1** (Scot., N. Engl.: church) Kirche, *die* **2** **the K~ [of Scotland]** die Kirche von Schottland

kirsch[wasser] /ˈkɪəʃ(vɑsə(r))/ *n.* Kirsch, *der;* Kirschwasser, *das*

kiss /kɪs/
A *n.* Kuss, *der;* **the ~ of death** (apparently friendly act causing ruin) ein Danaergeschenk; (act putting an end to sth.) der Todesstoß; **give sb.** (fig.) **sth. the ~ of life** (Brit.) jmdn. von Mund zu Mund beatmen/versuchen, etw. wieder zu beleben; **by administering the ~ of life** durch Mund-zu-Mund-Beatmung; **the ~ of peace** der Friedenskuss; *see also* **blow¹ B 2**
B *v.t.* küssen; **~ sb. good night/goodbye** jmdm. einen Gutenacht-/Abschiedskuss geben; **it hurts, mummy — ~ it better** (child lang.) es tut weh, Mami — puste mal; **~ sb.'s hand** jmdm. einen Handkuss geben
C *v.i.* sich küssen; **~ and make up** sich mit einem Kuss versöhnen

Phrasal verb
• **~ aˈway** *v.t.* wegküssen; **~ away sb.'s tears** jmdm. die Tränen wegküssen

kissable /ˈkɪsəbl/ *adj.* **~ lips/mouth** Kussmund, *der*

kiss-and-ˈtell
A *adj.* Klatsch-; (in politics) Enthüllungs-; **~ memoirs** indiskrete Bekenntnisse
B *n.* (story) Klatschgeschichte, *die;* (book) Klatschbuch, *das*

kisser /ˈkɪsə(r)/ *n.* (sl.: mouth, face) Fresse, *die* (derb); Schnauze, *die* (derb)

kissing /ˈkɪsɪŋ/
A *adj.* Kuss-
B *n.* Küsserei, *die* (ugs.); Geküsse, *das* (oft abwertend)

kissogram /ˈkɪsəgræm/ *n.: Glückwunsch o. Ä., der mit Küssen überbracht wird*

ˈkiss-proof *adj.* kussecht

kit /kɪt/
A *n.* **1** (personal equipment) Sachen; **have you got all your ~ together?** hast du deine Siebensachen beisammen? (ugs.) **2** (Brit.: set of items) Set, *das;* **construction/self-assembly ~:** Bausatz, *der;* **repair ~:** Reparatursatz, *der;* Reparaturset, *das; see also* **tool kit 3** (Brit.: clothing etc.) **sports ~:** Sportzeug, *das;* Sportsachen *Pl.;* **riding/skiing/shooting ~:** Reit-/Ski-/Jagdausrüstung, *die* **4** (Brit. Mil.) Ausrüstung, *die;* (pack) [Feld]gepäck, *das;* (uniform) Montur, *die*
B *v.t.*, **-tt-** (Brit.) **~ out** *or* **up** (equip) ausrüsten; (give clothes or uniforms to) einkleiden

kit: ~bag *n.* (knapsack) Knappsack, *der* (veralt.); Tornister, *der;* (travelling bag) Reisetasche, *die;* **~car** *n.* Bausatzauto, *das*

kitchen /ˈkɪtʃɪn/ *n.* Küche, *die; attrib.* Küchen-; *see also* **soup kitchen**

kitchen-ˈdiner *n.* Essküche, *die*

kitchenette /kɪtʃɪˈnet/ *n.* kleine Küche; Kitchenette, *die;* (alcove) Kochnische, *die*

kitchen: ~ ˈgarden *n.* Küchengarten, *der;* Nutzgarten, *der;* **~ maid** *n.* Küchenmädchen, *das;* Küchenhilfe, *die;* **~ paper** *n.* Küchenkrepp, *der;* Küchentücher *Pl.;* **~ police** *n. pl.* (Amer. Mil.) Küchendienst, *der;* **~ roll** *n.* Küchenrolle, *die;* (kitchen paper) Küchenkrepp, *der;* **~ ˈsink** *n.* [Küchen]ausguss, *der;* Spüle, *die;* **everything but the ~ sink** (fig.) der halbe Hausrat; *attrib.* (Brit.) ≈ neonaturalistisch ⟨*Drama, Kunst usw.*⟩; **~ unit** *n.* Küchenelement, *das;* **~ units** Küchenmöbel *Pl.;* **~ utensil** *n.* Küchengerät, *das;* **~ware** *n., no pl.* Küchengeräte *Pl.;* **~ ˈwaste** *n., no pl.* Küchenabfall, *der;* Küchenabfälle *Pl.*

kite /kaɪt/ *n.* **1** (toy) Drachen, *der* **2** (Ornith.) habichtartiger Greifvogel; (species) Roter Milan; Gabelweihe, *die* **3** (Brit. coll. dated: aeroplane) Vogel, *der;* Kiste, *die (salopp). See also* **fly² B 2**

kite: ~ surfer *n.* Kitesurfer, *der*/-surferin, *die;* **~-surfing** *n., no pl.* Kitesurfen, *das*

kith /kɪθ/ *n.* **~ and kin** Freunde und Verwandte

kitsch /kɪtʃ/ *n.* Kitsch, *der;* **it's a piece of ~:** es ist Kitsch

kitschy /ˈkɪtʃɪ/ *adj.* kitschig

kitten /ˈkɪtn/ *n.* **1** [Katzen]junge, *das;* Kätzchen, *das;* **the cat has had ~s** die Katze hat Junge bekommen; **as weak as a ~:** schwach und matt; **be as nervous as a ~:** furchtbar ängstlich sein; (be easily startled) vor dem eigenen Schatten erschrecken **2** (coll.) **have ~s** (be upset) Zustände kriegen (ugs.); **be having ~s** (be nervous) am Rotieren sein (ugs.)

kittenish /ˈkɪtənɪʃ/ *adj.* verspielt; kokett ⟨*junges Mädchen*⟩

kittiwake /ˈkɪtɪweɪk/ *n.* (Ornith.) Dreizehenmöwe, *die*

kitty¹ /ˈkɪtɪ/ *n.* (kitten) Kätzchen, *das;* (child lang.) Miez[e], *die* (fam.); Miezekätzchen, *das* (fam.); **~, ~, ~!** Miez, Miez, Miez!

kitty² *n.* **1** (Cards) [Spiel]kasse, *die* **2** (joint fund) Kasse, *die;* **raid the ~:** die Kasse plündern (scherzh.)

kiwi /ˈkiːwiː/ *n.* **1** (Ornith.) Kiwi, *der* **2** **K~** (coll.: New Zealander) Neuseeländer, *der*/Neuseeländerin, *die*

kiwi: ~ berry, ~ fruit *ns.* Kiwi[frucht], *die*

klaxon ® /ˈklæksn/ *n.* Horn, *das*

Kleenex ® /ˈkliːneks/ *n.* Papier[taschen]tuch, *das*

kleptocracy /klepˈtɒkrəsɪ/ *n.* Kleptokratie, *die*

kleptocrat /ˈkleptəkræt/ *n.* Kleptokrat, *der*/Kleptokratin, *die*

kleptocratic /kleptəˈkrætɪk/ *adj.* kleptokratisch

kleptomania /kleptəˈmeɪnɪə/ *n., no pl.* Kleptomanie, *die*

kleptomaniac /kleptəˈmeɪnɪæk/ *n.* Kleptomane, *der*/Kleptomanin, *die*

km. *abbr.* **= kilometre[s]** km

knack /næk/ *n.* **1** (faculty) Talent, *das;* **have a ~ for** *or* **of doing sth.** das Talent haben, etw. zu tun; **get the ~ [of doing sth.]** den Bogen rauskriegen[, wie man etw. macht] (ugs.); **there's a [real] ~ in doing sth.** es gehört schon [einiges] Geschick dazu, etw. zu tun; **have lost the ~:** es nicht mehr zustande bringen *od.* (ugs.) hinkriegen **2** (habit) **have a ~ of doing sth.** es [mit seltenem Talent] verstehen, etw. zu tun (iron.)

knacker /ˈnækə(r)/ *n.* (Brit.) (horse slaughterer) Abdecker, *der;* **~'s yard** Abdeckerei, *die*

knackered /ˈnækəd/ *adj.* (Brit. coll.) geschlaucht (ugs.)

knapsack /ˈnæpsæk/ *n.* Rucksack, *der;* (Mil.) Tornister, *der*

knave /neɪv/ *n.* **1** (rogue) Schurke, *der* **2** (Cards) ▸ **jack A 1**

knavery /ˈneɪvərɪ/ *n.* Schurkerei, *die*

knavish /ˈneɪvɪʃ/ *adj.* schurkisch

knead /niːd/ *v.t.* **1** kneten; **~ sth. with sth.** etw. mit etw. verkneten; **~ together** miteinander verkneten **2** (manipulate) kneten ⟨*Muskeln*⟩

knee /niː/ *n.* **1** ▸ **p. 951** Knie, *das;* **the ~s of his trousers were torn** seine Hose war an den Knien zerrissen; **bend** *or* **bow the ~:** das Knie beugen (**to** vor + *Dat.*); (fig.: behave humbly) sich beugen (**to** *Dat.*); **on one's ~s/on bended ~[s]** auf Knien; **be on one's ~s** knien; (fig.: be defeated) in die Knie gezwungen sein (geh.); **bring** *or* **force sb. to his ~s** (fig.) jmdn. in die Knie zwingen (geh.); **go down on one's ~s [to** *or* **before sb.]** [vor jmdm.] auf die Knie sinken (geh.) **2** (of animal) Kniegelenk, *das* **3** (thigh) **hold a child** *etc.* **on one's ~:** ein Kind *usw.* auf den Knien *od.* auf dem Schoß haben; **put a child** *etc.* **over one's ~:** ein Kind *usw.* übers Knie legen (ugs.)

knee: ~ breeches *n. pl.* Kniebundhose, *die;* **~cap** *n.* **1** (Anat.) Kniescheibe, *die;* **2** (protective covering) Knieschoner, *der;* **~capping** *n.* Knieschuss, *der;* **~-deep** *adj.* **1** knietief;

2 (fig.: deeply involved) **be ~-deep in sth.** bis über den Hals in etw. (*Dat.*) stecken (ugs.); **~-high** *adj.* kniehoch; **be ~-high to a grasshopper** (coll.) ein Dreikäsehoch sein (ugs. scherzh.); **~-jerk** *n.* Kniesehnenreflex, *der; attrib.* **~-jerk reaction** (fig.) automatische Reaktion; **~ joint** *n.* Kniegelenk, *das*

kneel /ni:l/ *v.i.*, **knelt** /nelt/ *or* (esp. Amer.) **~ed** knien; **~ down** niederknien; **~ [down] to do sth.** niederknien *od.* sich [hin]knien, um etw. zu tun; **~ to sb.** vor jmdm. [nieder]knien

'knee-length *adj.* knielang

kneeler /'ni:lə(r)/ ▸**hassock 1**

knees-up /'ni:zʌp/ *n.* (coll.) Schwof, *der* (ugs.)

knell /nel/ *n.* Glockengeläut, *das;* (at funeral) Totengeläut, *das;* **ring** *or* **sound the ~ of sth.** (fig.) das Ende einer Sache (*Gen.*) einläuten

knelt ▸**kneel**

knew ▸**know A**

knickerbockers /'nɪkəbɒkəz/ *n. pl.* Knickerbocker *Pl.*

knickers /'nɪkəz/

A *n. pl.* 1 (Brit.: undergarment) [Damen]schlüpfer, *der;* **get one's ~ in a twist** (Brit. fig. coll.) sich aufregen 2 (Amer.) ▸**knickerbockers**

B *int.* (Brit. coll.) was solls (ugs.)

knick-knack /'nɪknæk/ *n.* 1 (dainty thing) **~s** Schnickschnack, *der* (ugs.) 2 (ornament) Nippfigur, *die*

knife /naɪf/

A *n., pl.* **knives** /naɪvz/ Messer, *das;* **put a ~ into sb.** jmdm. ein Messer zwischen die Rippen jagen; **like a ~ through butter** mühelos; **have got one's ~ into sb.** (fig.) einen Hass auf jmdn. haben (ugs.); **you could [have] cut the atmosphere** (fig.)/**air with a ~** (coll.) die Atmosphäre war zum Zerreißen gespannt/die Luft war zum Schneiden; **before you can say ~** (coll.) ehe man sichs versieht; **turn** *or* **twist the ~ [in the wound]** (fig.) Salz in die Wunde streuen; **the knives are out [for sb.]** (fig.) das Messer wird [für jmdn.] gewetzt; *see also* **fork A 1**

B *v.t.* (stab) einstechen auf (+ *Akk.*); (kill) erstechen; **~ sb. in the chest** jmdm. ein/das Messer in die Brust stoßen

knife: ~-edge *n.* Schneide, *die;* **be [balanced] on a ~-edge** (fig.) auf des Messers Schneide stehen; **~ grinder** *n.* Messerschleifer, *der;* **~ pleat** *n.* (Dressm.) Plisseefalte, *die;* **~point** ▸**point A 2**; **~ sharpener** *n.* Messerschärfer, *der;* (steel) Wetzstahl, *der;* **~-throwing** *n., no pl., no indef. art.* Messerwerfen, *das*

knifing /'naɪfɪŋ/ *n.* **there were three ~s on one day** an einem Tag wurden drei Menschen niedergestochen

knight /naɪt/

A *n.* 1 *Träger des Titels „Sir"* 2 (Hist.) Ritter, *der;* **~ in shining armour** (fig.) Märchenprinz, *der* 3 (Chess) Springer, *der* 4 **~ of the road** (lorry driver) Kapitän der Landstraße (ugs.). *See also* **bachelor 3; Templar**

B *v.t.* adeln; zum Ritter schlagen (hist.); in den Ritterstand erheben (hist.)

knight: ~ 'errant *n.* (lit. or fig.) fahrender Ritter; (fig.) Don Quichotte, *der;* **~-'errantry** /naɪt'erəntrɪ/ *n., no pl.* ≈ höfisches Rittertum; (fig.: quixotic behaviour) Donquichotterie, *die*

knighthood /'naɪthʊd/ *n.* 1 (rank) Ritterwürde, *die;* **receive one's ~:** geadelt werden; in den Ritterstand erhoben werden (hist.) 2 (Hist.: vocation) Rittertum, *das* 3 (Hist.: body of knights) Ritterschaft, *die*

knightly /'naɪtlɪ/ *adj.* ritterlich

knit /nɪt/

A *v.t.*, **-tt-, knitted** *or* (esp. fig.) **knit** 1 stricken ‹*Kleidungsstück usw.*› 2 **~ a stitch** eine [rechte] Masche stricken; **~ 2, purl 2** zwei rechts, zwei links [stricken] 3 **~ one's brow** die Stirn runzeln 4 (make compact) zusammenfügen (**into** zu); **closely** *or* **tightly ~** (fig.) festgefügt; hieb- und stichfest ‹*Argument*›; *see also* **well-knit**

B *v.i.* sich verbinden; ‹*Teile:*› zusammenhalten; ‹*Knochenbruch:*› verheilen; ‹*Knochen:*› zusammenwachsen

C *n.* (garment) Strickware, *die;* **this pattern is for a heavy ~:** dieses Muster eignet sich für Grobgestricktes

Phrasal verb

• **~ to'gether**

A *v.t.* zusammenhalten ‹*Familie, Gemeinschaft*›

B *v.i.* ‹*Knochen:*› zusammenwachsen; ‹*Knochenbruch:*› zusammenheilen

knitter /'nɪtə(r)/ *n.* Stricker, *der*/Strickerin, *die*

knitting /'nɪtɪŋ/ *n., no pl., no indef. art.* Stricken, *das;* (work in process of being knitted) Strickarbeit, *die;* **do one's/some ~:** stricken; **carry on with one's ~:** weiterstricken

knitting: ~ machine *n.* Strickmaschine, *die;* **~ needle** *n.* Stricknadel, *die;* **~ pattern** *n.* Strickmuster, *das*

'knitwear *n., no pl., no indef. art.* Strickwaren *Pl.*

knives *pl. of* **knife A**

knob /nɒb/ *n.* 1 (protuberance) Verdickung, *die;* (on club, tree trunk, etc.) Knoten, *der* 2 (on door, walking stick, etc.) Knauf, *der;* (control on radio etc.) Knopf, *der;* **the same to you with [brass] ~s on!** (coll.) danke gleichfalls! (iron.) 3 (of butter, sugar) Klümpchen, *das;* (of coal) Brocken, *der*

knobbly /'nɒblɪ/ *adj.* knotig ‹*Finger, Stock*›; knorrig ‹*Baum*›; **~ knees competition** Knubbelkniewettbewerb, *der*

knock /nɒk/

A *v.t.* 1 (strike) (lightly) klopfen gegen *od.* an (+ *Akk.*); (forcefully) schlagen gegen *od.* an (+ *Akk.*); *see also* **wood 2**

2 (make by striking) schlagen; **~ two rooms/houses into one** zwei Zimmer/Häuser zu einem umbauen; **~ a hole in sth.** ein Loch in etw. (*Akk.*) schlagen

3 (drive by striking) schlagen; **~ sb.'s brains out** jmdm. den Schädel einschlagen; **I'll ~ those ideas out of your head** (fig.) diese Flausen werde ich dir austreiben (ugs.); **~ the handle off a cup** von einer Tasse den Henkel abschlagen; **I'd like to ~ their heads together** (lit.) ich könnte ihre Köpfe gegeneinander schlagen; (fig.: reprove them) ich möchte ihnen mal gehörig die Leviten lesen; **~ sb. into the middle of next week** (coll.) jmdm. ein Ding verpassen, dass ihm Hören und Sehen vergeht (ugs.); **~ for six = hit for six** ▸**hit A 11**; *see also* **bottom A 1; cock¹ B 3; spot A 4**

4 **~ sb. cold** jmdn. bewusstlos schlagen; (fig.) jmdn. am Boden zerstören; **~ sb. on the head** jmdm. eins über *od.* auf den Schädel geben; **~ sth. on the head** (fig.: put an end to) einer Sache (*Dat.*) ein Ende setzen

5 (coll.: criticize) herziehen über (+ *Akk.*) (ugs.); **don't ~ it** halt dich zurück

6 (Brit. coll.: astonish) umhauen (salopp)

B *v.i.* 1 (strike) (lightly) klopfen; (forcefully) schlagen; *see also* **wood 2**

2 (seek admittance) klopfen (**at** an + *Akk.*)

3 (Mech. Engin.) klappern

4 (Motor Veh.) klopfen

C *n.* 1 (rap) Klopfen, *das;* **there was a ~ on** *or* **at the door** es klopfte an der Tür; **give sb. a ~:** bei jmdm. klopfen

2 (blow) Schlag, *der;* (gentler) Stoß, *der;* **have had a ~:** einen Schlag/Stoß abbekommen haben; **he got a bad ~ when he fell** er schlug beim Fallen hart auf; **~ for ~ agreement** (Insurance) gegenseitige Regressverzichtserklärung

3 (fig.: blow of misfortune) [Schicksals]schlag, *der;* **take a [bad** *or* **hard] ~:** einen [schweren *od.* harten] Schlag erleiden

4 (Mech. Engin.) Klappern, *das;* **make a ~:** klappern

5 (Motor Veh.: high-pitched explosive sound) Klopfen, *das*

Phrasal verbs

• **~ a'bout**

A *v.t.* 1 schlagen; verprügeln; **be ~ed about** Schläge *od.* Prügel einstecken müssen; **the building has been ~ed about** das Haus ist ziemlich ramponiert worden 2 **~ about the world** in der Welt herumkommen

B *v.i.* herumhängen (ugs.); ‹*Gegenstand:*› herumfliegen (ugs.); **he's ~ed about a bit** er hat sich in der Welt umgetan; **~ about with sb.** sich mit jmdm. herumtreiben (ugs.). *See also* **knockabout**

• **~ against** *v.t.* stoßen gegen; **~ against each other** gegeneinander stoßen; gegeneinander prallen

• **~ a'round** ▸**~ about**

• **~ 'back** *v.t.* (coll.) 1 (eat quickly) verputzen (ugs.); (drink quickly) hinunterkippen (ugs.) 2 (cost) **~ sb. back a thousand** jmdn. um einen Tausender ärmer machen 3 (disconcert) einen Schlag versetzen (+ *Dat.*)

• **~ 'down** *v.t.* 1 (strike to the ground) niederreißen, umstürzen ‹*Zaun, Hindernis*›; (with fist or weapon) niederschlagen; (with car etc.) umfahren 2 (demolish) abreißen; abbrechen 3 (fig.: defeat) bezwingen 4 (sell by auction) zuschlagen; **~ sth. down to sb.** jmdm. etw. zuschlagen 5 (coll.: lower) heruntersetzen (ugs.) ‹*Preis*›; herunterdrücken (ugs.) ‹*Kosten*› 6 (Amer. coll.: steal) mitgehen lassen (ugs.); klauen (salopp). *See also* **feather A 1; knock-down**

• **~ 'off**

A *v.t.* 1 (leave off) aufhören mit; **~ off painting** zu malen *od.* mit dem Malen aufhören; **~ off work** Feierabend machen; **~ it off!** (coll.) hör auf [damit]! 2 (coll.) (produce rapidly) aus dem Ärmel schütteln (ugs.); (dispatch rapidly) schnell erledigen 3 (deduct) **~ five pounds off the price** es fünf Pfund billiger machen; **how much will you ~ off for me?** wie viel billiger kriege ich es denn? 4 (coll.) (steal) mitgehen lassen (ugs.); klauen (salopp); (rob) ausräumen ‹*Bank, Laden, Kasse*› 5 (sl.: copulate with) bumsen (salopp) 6 (sl.: kill) umlegen (salopp)

B *v.i.* Feierabend machen; **~ off for an hour/for lunch** eine Stunde aussetzen/Mittag machen

• **~ 'on** *v.t.* (Rugby) **~ on a pass** bei der Annahme eines Passes ein Vorfallen verursachen; *see also* **knock-on A**

• **~ 'out** *v.t.* 1 (make unconscious) bewusstlos umfallen lassen; **he collided with a lamp post and ~ed himself out** er stieß mit einem Laternenpfahl zusammen und fiel bewusstlos um 2 (Boxing) k.o. schlagen; kampfunfähig schlagen 3 (fig.: defeat) **be ~ed out [of the Cup]** [aus dem Pokal] ausscheiden *od.* (ugs.) rausfliegen; **they ~ed us out of the Cup** sie warfen uns aus dem Pokal 4 (make useless) außer Funktion setzen 5 (coll.: astonish) umhauen (salopp); **be [completely** *or* **totally] ~ed out** [völlig] fertig sein (ugs.) 6 (coll.: exhaust) kaputtmachen (ugs.) 7 (coll.: produce rapidly) aus dem Ärmel schütteln 8 (empty) ausklopfen ‹*Pfeife*›; **~ the ashes out** die Asche herausklopfen. *See also* **knockout**

• **~ 'over** *v.t.* umstoßen; ‹*Fahrer, Fahrzeug:*› umfahren ‹*Person*›

• **~ to'gether**

A *v.t.* zusammenzimmern (ugs.) ‹*Hütte, Tisch, Bühne*›; *see also* **knock A 3**

B *v.i.* **my knees were ~ing together** mir schlotterten die Knie

• **~ 'up**

A *v.t.* 1 (make hastily) zusammenzimmern (ugs.) ‹*Hütte, Schrank*›; [her]zaubern ‹*Mahlzeit, Imbiss*›; grob skizzieren ‹*Plan*› 2 (score) erzielen 3 (Brit.: awaken) durch Klopfen wecken; (unexpectedly) herausklopfen 4 (exhaust) fertig machen (ugs.); **be ~ed up** fertig *od.* groggy sein (ugs.) 5 (sl.: make pregnant) dick machen (derb)

B *v.i.* (Sport) sich warm spielen; *see also* **knock-up**

knock: ~about *adj.* 1 (boisterous) Klamauk‹*film, -stück, -szene*›; burlesk ‹*Komödie, Komik*›; wild ‹*Spiel*›; 2 (for rough use) strapazierfähig; **~-down** *adj.* 1 (low) **~-down cost/prices** minimale Kosten/Schleuderpreise; 2 (minimum) Mindest‹*preis, -gebot*›; 3 (easily disassembled) zerlegbar ‹*Möbelstück, Boot*›; 4 niederschmetternd ‹*Schlag, Hieb*›; (fig.: conclusive) hieb- und stichfest, schlagend ‹*Argument*›

knocker /'nɒkə(r)/ *n.* 1 (on door) [Tür]klopfer, *der* 2 *in pl.* (coarse: breasts) **[pair of] ~s** Vorbau, *der* (salopp scherzh.); Titten (derb) 3 (coll.: critic) Beckmesser, *der*

knock-for-'knock agreement *n.* (Insurance) Teilungsabkommen, *das*

knocking-'off time *n.* (coll.) Feierabend, *der*

'knocking shop *n.* (Brit. sl.) Puff, *der od. das* (salopp)

k

knock: ~-kneed /'nɒkni:d/ *adj.* x-beinig ‹*Person usw.*›; kuhhessig ‹*Pferd*›; **~ 'knees** *n. pl.* X-Beine *Pl.*; **~-on** **A** *n.* (Rugby) Vorfallen, *das;* **B** *attrib. adj.* **~-on effect** mittelbare Auswirkung; **~out** **A** *n.* **1** (blow) Knockout[-Schlag], *der;* K.-o.[-Schlag], *der;* (to armed forces) vernichtender Schlag; **2** (competition) Ausscheidungs[wett]kampf, *der;* **3** (coll.: outstanding person or thing) **sb./sth. is a [real] ~out** jmd./etw. ist eine Wucht (salopp); **B** *adj.* **1** (that stuns) betäubend; (that incapacitates) vernichtend; **~out blow** K.-o.-Schlag, *der;* **~out drops** K.-o.-Tropfen (ugs.); **2** Ausscheidungs‹*spiel, -[wett]kampf, -runde*›; **~-up** *n.* (Sport) Warmspielen, *das;* **have a ~-up** sich warm spielen

knoll /nəʊl/ *n.* Anhöhe, *die*

knot /nɒt/

A *n.* **1** Knoten, *der;* **the wool has got into a [complete] ~:** die Wolle hat sich völlig verheddert; **tie sb. [up] in ~s** (fig. coll.) jmdn. in Widersprüche verwickeln **2** (ornament) Schleife, *die;* (cockade) Kokarde, *die;* (epaulette) Schulterstück, *das* **3** (problem) Verwicklung, *die;* Haken, *der* (ugs.) **4** (cluster) Pulk, *der* **5** (in wood) Ast, *der* **6** (speed unit) Knoten, *der;* **make** *or* **log ten ~s** zehn Knoten machen *od.* fahren; **at a rate of ~s** (coll.) mit einem Affenzahn (salopp) **7** (Naut.: unit of length) Knotenlänge, *die* **8** (in popular use: nautical mile) Seemeile, *die* **9** (bond) Bund, *der;* **tie the ~** (marry) den Bund der Ehe eingehen (geh.); den Bund fürs Leben schließen (geh.) **10** (lump) Knoten, *der;* Verdickung, *die*

B *v.t.*, **-tt-** **1** (tie) knoten ‹*Seil, Faden usw.*›; knoten ‹*Schnürsenkel*›; knoten, binden ‹*Krawatte*›; **~ threads together** Fäden verknoten; **~ clothes into a bundle** Kleider zu einem Bündel zusammenknoten; **~ a rope** Knoten in ein Seil machen **2** (entangle) verfilzen **3** **get ~ted!** (coll.) rutsch mir den Buckel runter! (ugs.) **4** ▸ **knit A 3** **5** (unite closely) verknüpfen (**into** zu)

knot: ~ garden *n.* Boskettgarten, *der;* **~hole** *n.* Astloch, *das*

knotty /'nɒtɪ/ *adj.* **1** (full of knots) ‹*Seil, Peitsche*› mit Knoten; knotig ‹*Stock, Gewebe, Finger*›; ineinander gewachsen ‹*Gestrüpp, Kriechpflanzen, Ausläufer*›; knorrig, astig ‹*Holz, Baumstamm*› **2** (fig.: puzzling) verwickelt

know /nəʊ/

A *v.t.*, **knew** /nju:/, **~n** /nəʊn/ **1** (recognize) erkennen (**by** an + *Dat.*, **for** als + *Akk.*) **2** (be able to distinguish) **~ sth. from sth.** etw. von etw. unterscheiden können; **~ right from wrong, ~ the difference between right and wrong** den Unterschied zwischen Gut und Böse kennen; **he wouldn't ~ the difference** er wüsste den Unterschied nicht; *see also* **Adam** **3** (be aware of) wissen; kennen ‹*Person*›; **I ~ who she is** ich weiß, wer sie ist; **I ~ for a fact that ...:** ich weiß ganz bestimmt, dass ...; **it is ~n that ...:** man weiß, dass ...; es ist bekannt, dass ...; **they knew they could never become rich** sie wussten [nur zu gut], dass sie niemals reich werden konnten; **~ sb./sth. to be ...:** wissen, dass jmd./etw. ... ist; **I ~ him to be an honest man** ich weiß, dass er ein ehrlicher Mensch ist; **that's/that might be worth ~ing** das ist gut/wäre wichtig zu wissen; **it's worth ~ing whether ...:** es ist wichtig zu wissen, ob ...; **he doesn't want to ~:** er will nichts davon wissen *od.* hören; **not if I ~ it** nicht mit mir; **I 'knew it** ich habs ja geahnt; **'I ~ what** ich weiß was (ugs.); **you ~** (coll.) (as reminder) weißt du [noch]; (as conversational filler) **they think we might be, you ~, glamorous or something** sie meinen, wir wären vielleicht, na ja, superschick oder so (ugs.); **I went to see the doctor, you ~:** ich war beim Arzt, weißt du; **you ~ something** *or* **what?** weißt du was?; **you never ~:** man kann nie wissen (ugs.); **sb. has [never] been ~n to do sth.** jmd. hat bekanntlich [noch nie] etw. getan; **for all I ~ they may be looking for us** ich könnte mir gut denken, dass sie uns suchen; **and I don't ~ what [all]** (coll.) und ich weiß nicht, was noch alles (ugs.); **and he ~s it** und er weiß das auch; **don't I ~ it!** (coll.) das weiß ich nur zu gut; **I don't ~ that ...** (coll.: don't believe) ich glaube nicht, dass ...; **before sb. ~s where he is** ehe jmd. sichs versieht; **what do you ~ [about that]?** (coll.: that is surprising) was sagst du dazu?; **sb. is not to ~** (is not to be told) jmd. soll nichts wissen (**about, of** von); (has no way of learning) jmd. kann nicht wissen; **I was not to ~ until years later** ich sollte erst Jahre später davon erfahren; **not ~ what hit one** (fig.) gar nicht begreifen, was geschehen ist; **that's all 'you ~ [about it]** das glaubst du vielleicht; **I'll have you ~ that ...:** ich möchte Sie darauf hinweisen, dass ...; **if you 'must ~:** wenn du es unbedingt wissen willst; **~ different** *or* **otherwise** es besser wissen; **~ what's what** wissen, wie es in der Welt zugeht; **how should I ~?** woher soll ich das wissen?; **I might have ~n** das hätte ich mir denken können; **do you ~, ...:** stell dir [mal] vor, ...; *see also* **best B**; **better B 4**; **god 2**; **heaven 3**; **let¹ A 2**; **lord A 2**; **thing 3**; **who 1**; **you 1** **4** (have understanding of) können ‹*ABC, Einmaleins, Deutsch usw.*›; beherrschen ‹*Grundlagen, Regeln, Grammatik*›; sich auskennen mit ‹*Gerät, Verfahren, Gesetz*›; **they ~ their Latin well** sie haben gute Kenntnisse in Latein; **do you ~ any German?** können Sie etwas Deutsch?; **~ 'how** wissen, wie das geht; **~ how to mend fuses** wissen, wie man Sicherungen repariert; **~ how to drive a car** Auto fahren können; **~ how to write vividly** [es] verstehen, lebendig zu schreiben; **he doesn't ~ much about computers** er hat nicht viel Ahnung von Computern; **do all one ~s [how]** sein Bestes geben; *see also* **onion**; **rope A 3**; **stuff A 5** **5** (be acquainted with) kennen; **we have ~n each other for years** wir kennen uns [schon] seit Jahren; **surely you ~ me better than that** du müsstest mich eigentlich besser kennen; **you don't really ~ him** du kennst ihn nicht gut genug; **you ~ what he/it is** (is like) du kennst ihn ja/du weißt ja, wie es ist; **you ~ what it is to be an adolescent** du weißt ja, wie man als Jugendlicher ist; *see also* **get B 3**; **sight A 1** **6** (have experience of) erleben; erfahren; **he ~s no fear, he doesn't ~ what it is to be afraid** er kennt keine Furcht; **~ what it is to be hungry** wissen, was es heißt, Hunger zu haben

B *n.* (coll.) **be in the ~:** Bescheid wissen; **those in the ~:** die Eingeweihten

Phrasal verbs

- **~ about** *v.t.* wissen über (+ *Akk.*); **oh, I didn't ~ about it/that** oh, das habe ich nicht gewusst; **did you ~ about your son's behaviour?** haben Sie gehört, wie sich Ihr Sohn benommen hat?; **not much is ~n about some of the tribes** über einige Stämme weiß man fast nichts; **I didn't ~ anything about any committee meeting** ich habe nichts von irgendeiner Ausschusssitzung gewusst; **I don't ~ about 'that** na, ich weiß nicht [so recht]; **I don't ~ about beautiful, but it certainly is old** schön — na, ich weiß nicht, auf jeden Fall ist es alt
- **~ of** *v.t.* wissen von ‹*Plänen, Vorhaben*›; kennen, wissen ‹*Lokal, Geschäft*›; **~ of sb.** von jmdm. gehört haben; **~ of sb. who ...:** jmdn. wissen, der ...; **not that I ~ of** nicht, dass ich wüsste

knowable /'nəʊəbl/ *adj.* [mit dem Verstand] erkennbar

'know-all *n.* (derog.) Neunmalkluge, *der/die* (spöttisch)

knowbot /'nəʊbɒt/ *n.* (Computing) Knowbot, *der*

'know-how *n.*, *no pl.*, *no indef. art.* praktisches Wissen; (technical expertise) Know-how, *das*

knowing /'nəʊɪŋ/

A *adj.* **1** (shrewd) verschmitzt ‹*Blick, Lachen, Lächeln*›; ‹*Person*› mit wachem Verstand; (indicating possession of inside information) viel sagend, wissend ‹*Blick, Lächeln*›; beredt (iron.) ‹*Schweigen*› **2** (derog.: cunning) verschlagen (abwertend)

B *n.* **there is no ~:** niemand weiß; es lässt sich nicht vorhersagen

knowingly /'nəʊɪŋlɪ/ *adv.* **1** (intentionally) wissentlich ‹*lügen, verletzen*›; bewusst ‹*planen*› **2** (in a shrewd manner) verschmitzt ‹*lachen, blicken*›; (indicating possession of inside information) viel sagend ‹*lächeln, anblicken, zwinkern, nicken*› **3** (derog.: cunningly) verschlagen (abwertend)

'know-it-all ▸ **know-all**

knowledge /'nɒlɪdʒ/ *n.*, *no pl.* **1** (familiarity) Kenntnisse (**of** in + *Dat.*); **a ~ of this field** Kenntnisse auf diesem Gebiet; **a little ~ is a dangerous thing** (prov.) Halbwissen ist gefährlich; **gain ~ of sb./sth.** Kenntnisse über jmdn./etw. gewinnen; **~ of human nature** Menschenkenntnis, *die;* *see also* **carnal knowledge** **2** (awareness) Wissen, *das;* **have no ~ of sth.** nichts von etw. wissen; keine Kenntnis von etw. haben (geh.); **she had no ~ of it** sie wusste nichts davon; sie war völlig ahnungslos; **the ~ that it was really important** die Gewissheit, dass es wirklich wichtig war; **sth. came to my ~:** etw. ist mir zu Ohren gekommen; **[not] to my** *etc.* **~:** meines *usw.* Wissens [nicht]; **to my certain ~:** wie ich mit Bestimmtheit weiß; **without sb.'s ~:** ohne jmds. Wissen **3** (understanding) **[a] ~ of languages/French** Sprach-/Französischkenntnisse *Pl.*; **sb. with [a] ~ of computers** jmd., der sich mit Computern auskennt **4** *no art.* (what is known) Wissen, *das;* **in the present state of ~:** beim derzeitigen Wissensstand; **branch of ~:** Wissenszweig, *der*

knowledgeable /'nɒlɪdʒəbl/ *adj.* sachkundig; **be ~ about** *or* **on sth.** viel über etw. (*Akk.*) wissen

'knowledge economy *n.* Wissensökonomie, *die*

known /nəʊn/

A ▸ **know**

B *adj.* bekannt; (generally recognized) anerkannt

knuckle /'nʌkl/ *n.* **1** ▸ **❶ p. 951** (Anat.) [Finger-]knöchel, *der* **2** (joint of meat) (pork) Eisbein, *das;* (veal or pork) Hachse, *die;* Haxe, *die* (südd.) **3** **near the ~** (coll.) hart an der Grenze [des guten Geschmacks]. *See also* **rap¹ A 1, B 1**

Phrasal verbs

- **~ 'down** *v.i.* (apply oneself) **~ down to sth.** sich hinter etw. (*Akk.*) klemmen (ugs.)
- **~ 'under** *v.i.* klein beigeben (**to** gegenüber)

knuckle: ~ bone *n.* **1** (Anat.) Fingerknochen, *der;* **2** (Zool.) Knochen [mit Gelenkkopf]; **~duster** *n.* Schlagring, *der*

knurled /nɜ:ld/ *adj.* geriffelt; kordiert (Technik)

KO *abbr.* **1** = **kick-off** **2** = **knockout** K. o. **3** = **knocked out** k. o.

koala /kəʊ'ɑ:lə/ *n.* **~ [bear]** (Zool.) Koala, *der;* Beutelbär, *der*

KO'd /keɪ'əʊd/ ▸ **KO 3**

kohlrabi /kəʊl'rɑ:bɪ/ *n.* Kohlrabi, *der*

kook /ku:k/ (Amer. coll.)

A *n.* Spinner, *der*/Spinnerin, *die* (ugs. abwertend)

B *adj.* ▸ **kooky**

kookaburra /'kʊkəbʌrə/ *n.* (Austral. Ornith.) Lachender Hans

kooky /'ku:kɪ/ *adj.* (Amer. coll.) überkandidelt (ugs.); idiotisch (ugs. abwertend) ‹*Leben*›

Koran /kɔ:'rɑ:n, kə'rɑ:n/ *n.* (Muslim Relig.) Koran, *der*

Koranic /kə'rænɪk, -'rɑ:nɪk/ *adj.* koranisch

Korea /kə'rɪə/ *pr. n.* Korea (*das*)

Korean /kə'ri:ən/ ▸ **❶ p. 1277**, ▸ **❶ p. 1345**

A *adj.* koreanisch; **sb. is ~:** jmd. ist Koreaner/Koreanerin; *see also* **English A**

B *n.* **1** (person) Koreaner, *der*/Koreanerin, *die* **2** (language) Koreanisch, *das;* *see also* **English B 1**

kosher /'kəʊʃə(r), 'kɒʃə(r)/

A *adj.* (lit. or fig.) koscher

B *n.*, *no pl.*, *no art.* (food) Koschere, *das;* **eat ~:** koscher essen

Kosovan /'kɒsəvən/

A *adj.* kosovarisch; **~ town/immigrant** Stadt im Kosovo/Einwanderer aus dem Kosovo; **~ Albanian** Kosovoalbaner, *der*/-albanerin, *die;* **he/she is ~:** er ist Kosovare/sie ist Kosovarin.

B *n.* (person) Kosovare, *der*/Kosovarin, *die*

Kosovar /'kɒsəvɑ:(r)/

A *adj.* kosovarisch

B *n.* Kosovare, *der*/Kosovarin, *die*

Kosovo /'kɒsəvə, 'kɒsəvəʊ/ *pr. n.* Kosovo, *der* *od.* *das* *od.* (*das*)

kowtow /kaʊˈtaʊ/ (**kotow** /kəʊˈtaʊ/) *v.i.* ~ **[to sb./sth.]** [vor jmdm./etw.] [s]einen Kotau machen

k.p.h. *abbr.* ▸ℹ p. 1566 = **kilometres per hour** km/h

kraal /krɑːl/ *n.* Kral, *der*

Kraut /kraʊt/ *n. & adj.* (sl. derog.) *angelsächsische abwertende Bez. für „Deutscher" und „deutsch"*

Kremlin /ˈkremlɪn/ *n.* **the** ~: der Kreml

Kremlinology /kremlɪˈnɒlədʒɪ/ *n., no pl., no indef. art.* Sowjetforschung, *die;* Kremlastrologie, *die* (ugs.)

krill /krɪl/ *n., no pl., no indef. art.* (Zool.) Krill, *der*

kris /kriːs/ *n.* Kris, *der*

krugerrand /ˈkruːgərɑːnt/ *n.* Krügerrand, *der*

krypton /ˈkrɪptɒn/ *n.* (Chem.) Krypton, *das*

Kt. *abbr.* = **knight**

kudos /ˈkjuːdɒs/ *n., no pl., no indef. art.* Prestige, *das*

Ku-Klux-Klan

Ein amerikanischer Geheimbund mit ordensähnlichem Ritual, dessen Mitglieder weiße Kapuzen tragen. Die erste *Ku-Klux-Klan*-Organisation wurde 1866 in Tennessee gegründet. Der *Klan* hatte sich die Aufrechterhaltung der kolonialen Lebensform in den Südstaaten zum Ziel gesetzt und ging mit Gewalt und Einschüchterung gegen emanzipierte Sklaven und radikale Republikaner vor. Obwohl die Organisation 1871 für verfassungswidrig erklärt wurde, knüpfte 1915 ein neuer *Ku-Klux-Klan* an den Vorläufer an. Jetzt verfolgte der *Klan* nicht nur **African Americans**, sondern auch Juden, Intellektuelle und Gegner der **Prohibition**. Um 1920 soll der *Klan* über 4 Millionen Mitglieder in den Staaten des Mittleren Westens gehabt haben. Während der Weltwirtschaftskrise gingen die Mitgliederzahlen wieder zurück. Erneuten Zulauf brachte die Einführung der Bürgerrechtsgesetze im Süden in den 60er Jahren, doch der Versuch des ▸▸▸

▸▸▸ *Ku-Klux-Klan*, die Durchsetzung gewaltsam zu verhindern, scheiterte. Heute besteht der *Klan* nur noch aus kleinen militanten Gruppen mit einigen tausend Mitgliedern, die kaum Einfluss haben.

kümmel /ˈkʊml/ *n.* Kümmellikör, *der*

kung fu /kʊŋˈfuː, kʌŋˈfuː/ *n.* Kung-Fu, *das*

Kurd /kɜːd/ *n.* Kurde, *der*/Kurdin, *die*

Kurdish /ˈkɜːdɪʃ/ ▸ℹ **p. 1277**
A *adj.* kurdisch
B *n.* Kurdisch, *das*

Kurdistan /kɜːdɪˈstɑːn/ *pr. n.* Kurdistan (*das*)

Kuwait /kʊˈweɪt/ *pr. n.* Kuwait (*das*)

Kuwaiti /kʊˈweɪtɪ/ ▸ℹ **p. 1345**
A *adj.* kuwaitisch; **sb. is** ~: jmd. ist Kuwaiti
B *n.* Kuwaiti, *der*/*die*

kW *abbr.* = **kilowatt[s]** kW

kWh *abbr.* = **kilowatt-hour[s]** kWh

L l

L, l /el/ *n., pl.* **Ls** *or* **L's** 1 (letter) L, l, *das* 2 (Roman numeral) L

£ *abbr.* **= pound[s]** £; **cost £5** 5 £ *od.* Pfund kosten

l. *abbr.* 1 ▸ p. 1690 **= litre[s]** l 2 **= left** l. 3 **= line** Z.

L. *abbr.* 1 **= Lake** 2 **= Liberal** Lib.

la ▸ **lah**

LA *abbr.* **= Los Angeles** L. A.

lab /læb/ *n.* (coll.) Labor, *das*

Lab. *abbr.* **= Labour**

label /ˈleɪbl/

A *n.* 1 (slip) Schildchen, *das;* (on goods, bottles, jars, in clothes) Etikett, *das;* (tied/stuck to an object) Anhänger/Aufkleber, *der* 2 (on record) Label, *das;* (record company) Plattenfirma, *die;* **record on a new ~:** die Plattenfirma *od.* (Fachjargon) das Label gewechselt haben 3 (fig.: classifying phrase) Etikett, *das;* **hang the ~ ... on sb.** jmdn. als ... etikettieren; **acquire/be given the ~ of ...:** als ... etikettiert werden

B *v.t.,* (Brit.) **-ll-** 1 (attach ~ to) etikettieren; (attach price tag to) auszeichnen ‹*Waren*›; (write on) beschriften; (attach stamp or sticker to) mit einem Aufkleber versehen; (tie ~ to) mit einem Anhänger versehen 2 (fig.: classify) **~ sb./sth. [as] sth.** jmdn./etw. als etw. etikettieren; **he doesn't like being ~led** er lässt sich nicht gern etikettieren

labial /ˈleɪbɪəl/

A *adj.* Lippen-; (Anat., Zool., Phonet.) labial; **~ consonant** ▸ **B**

B *n.* (Phonet.) Labial, *der;* Lippenlaut, *der*

labia majora/minora /leɪbɪə məˈdʒɔːrə/mɪˈnɔːrə/ *n. pl.* (Anat.) äußere *od.* große/innere *od.* kleine Schamlippen

labor (Amer.) ▸ **labour**

laboratory /ləˈbɒrətərɪ/ *n.* (lit. or fig.) Labor[atorium], *das; attrib.* **~ animal** Versuchstier, *das;* **~ technician** Labortechniker, *der*/-technikerin, *die; see also* **language laboratory**

labored, laborer (Amer.) ▸ **labour-**

laborious /ləˈbɔːrɪəs/ *adj.* 1 mühsam; mühevoll ‹*Forschung, Aufgabe usw.*› 2 (not fluent) schwerfällig, umständlich ‹*Stil*›; schleppend ‹*Rede*›

laboriously /ləˈbɔːrɪəslɪ/ *adv.* 1 (with difficulty) mühevoll; **~ slow** mühsam und schleppend 2 (not fluently) schwerfällig; schleppend ‹*vorangehen*›

laborite (Amer.) ▸ **labourite**

ˈlabor union (Amer.) ▸ **trade union**

labour /ˈleɪbə(r)/ (Brit.)

A *n.* 1 (task) Arbeit, *die;* **sth. is/they did it as a ~ of love** etw. geschieht/sie taten es aus Liebe zur Sache; **~ of Hercules** Herkulesarbeit, *die* 2 (exertion) Mühe, *die;* **~ in vain, lost ~:** vergebliche *od.* verlorene Mühe; *see also* **hard labour** 3 (work) Arbeit, *die;* **cost of ~:** Arbeitskosten *Pl.;* **withdraw one's ~:** die Arbeit niederlegen 4 (body of workers) Arbeiterschaft, *die;* **immigrant ~:** ausländische Arbeitskräfte 5 **L~** (Polit.) die Labour Party 6 (childbirth) Wehen *Pl.;* **be in ~:** in den Wehen liegen; **go into ~:** die Wehen bekommen. *See also* **intensive A 5**

B *v.i.* 1 (work hard) hart arbeiten (**at, on** an + *Dat.*); (slave away) sich abmühen (**at, over** mit) 2 (strive) sich einsetzen (**for** für); **~ to do sth.** sich bemühen, etw. zu tun 3 (be troubled) leiden; sich quälen; **~ under sth.** sich mit etw. quälen; **~ under a delusion** sich einer Täuschung (*Dat.*) hingeben 4 (Naut.: pitch) ‹*Schiff:*› stampfen (Seemannsspr.) 5 (advance with difficulty) sich quälen *od.* kämpfen; (run too slowly) ‹*Motor:*› untertourig laufen; **~ up the stairs** sich die Treppe hinaufquälen

C *v.t.* (elaborate needlessly) auswalzen (ugs.); **~ the point** sich lange darüber verbreiten; **there's no need to ~ the point** du brauchst dich nicht lange darüber zu verbreiten

labour: ~ camp *n.* Arbeitslager, *das;* **L~ Day** *n.* Tag der Arbeit (*in Amerika: erster Montag im September*)

> **Labor Day**
>
> Der Tag der Arbeit wird in den USA am ersten Montag im September mit Umzügen und Picknicks begangen. Der Feiertag, der zu Ehren der Arbeiter 1894 eingeführt wurde, ist der letzte große Ferientag vor Anfang des Schuljahrs.

laboured /ˈleɪbəd/ *adj.* (Brit.) mühsam; schwerfällig ‹*Stil*›; mühsam zusammengetragen ‹*Argumente*›; **his breathing was ~:** er atmete schwer

labourer /ˈleɪbərə(r)/ *n.* ▸ p. 1260 (Brit.) Arbeiter, *der*/Arbeiterin, *die;* (assisting skilled worker) Hilfsarbeiter, *der*/-arbeiterin, *die;* **bricklayer's ~:** Maurergehilfe, *der;* **builder's ~:** Bau[hilfs]arbeiter, *der*

labour: L~ Exchange (Hist./coll.) ▸ **employment exchange; ~ force** *n.* Arbeitskräfte *Pl.;* **a considerable ~ force** eine beträchtliche Anzahl von Arbeitskräften

labourite /ˈleɪbəraɪt/ *n.* (Brit. Polit.) Anhänger/Anhängerin der Labour Party; (member) Mitglied der Labour Party

labour: ~ market *n.* Arbeitsmarkt, *der;* **~ pains** *n. pl.* Wehenschmerzen; **L~ Party** *n.* (Polit.) Labour Party, *die;* **~ relations** *n. pl.* Beziehungen zwischen Arbeitgebern und Arbeitnehmern; (within one company) Betriebsklima, *das;* **~-saving** *adj.* arbeit[s]sparend ‹*Methode, Vorrichtung*›

> **Labour Party**
>
> Eine der drei großen politischen Parteien in Großbritannien. 1924 übernahm die *Labour Party* zum ersten Mal die Regierung. Ihr Ziel war, die Interessen der Arbeiter und Gewerkschaften zu vertreten. In den letzten 20 Jahren ist die Partei generell von ihren linken Positionen abgerückt. Sie wird daher heute oft als *New Labour* bezeichnet. 1997, 2001 und 2005 wurde die Partei unter der Führung von Tony Blair in die Regierungsverantwortung gewählt. Die Farbe der Partei ist rot.

Labrador /ˈlæbrədɔː(r)/ *n.* **~ [dog** *or* **retriever]** Labrador[hund], *der*

laburnum /ləˈbɜːnəm/ *n.* (Bot.) Goldregen, *der*

labyrinth /ˈlæbərɪnθ/ *n.* Labyrinth, *das*

labyrinthine /læbəˈrɪnθaɪn/ *adj.* 1 labyrinthisch; labyrinthartig 2 (complex) verschachtelt

lac[1] /læk/ *n.* Stocklack, *der;* **~ insect** Lackschildlaus, *die*

lac[2] ▸ **lakh**

lace /leɪs/

A *n.* 1 (for shoe) Schuhband, *das* (bes. südd.); Schnürsenkel, *der* (bes. nordd.) 2 (fabric) Spitze, *die; attrib.* Spitzen- 3 (braid) **gold/silver ~:** Gold-/ Silberlitze, *die*

B *v.t.* 1 (fasten) **~ [up]** [zu]schnüren 2 (interlace) durchwirken (geh.) 3 (pass through) [durch]ziehen 4 **~ sth. with alcohol** einen Schuss Alkohol in etw. (*Akk.*) geben; **~d with brandy** mit einem Schuss Weinbrand; **~ sb.'s drink** einen Schuss Alkohol/eine Droge in jmds. Getränk (*Akk.*) geben

lacerate /ˈlæsəreɪt/ *v.t.* 1 (tear) aufreißen; **her arm was badly ~d** sie hatte tiefe Wunden am Arm 2 (fig.: afflict) verletzen

laceration /læsəˈreɪʃn/ *n.* 1 *no pl.* Verletzung, *die* (*durch Aufreißen*) 2 (wound) Risswunde, *die;* (from glass) Schnittwunde, *die*

lace: ~-up A *attrib. adj.* zum Schnüren *nachgestellt;* **~-up boot** Schnürstiefel, *der;* **B** *n.* Schnürschuh/-stiefel, *der;* **~wing** *n.* (Zool.) Netzflügler, *der*

lachrymal /ˈlækrɪml/ *adj.* (Anat.) Tränen-

lachrymose /ˈlækrɪməʊs/ *adj.* weinerlich; tränenselig, rührselig ‹*Geschichte, Theaterstück, Abschied*›

lacing /ˈleɪsɪŋ/ *n.* 1 Schnur, *die;* (on shoes) Schuhband, *das* (bes. südd.); Schnürsenkel, *der* (bes. nordd.); (of corset) Schnüre *Pl.* 2 (quantity of spirits) Schuss, *der;* **coffee with a ~ of whisky** Kaffee mit einem Schuss Whisky

lack /læk/

A *n.* Mangel, *der* (**of** an + *Dat.*); **his ~ of enemies makes his task easier** dass er keine Feinde hat, macht seine Aufgabe leichter; **her ~ of aggression makes her easy to live with** da ihr jegliche Aggressivität abgeht, kann man gut mit ihr zusammenleben; **~ of self-consciousness** Unbefangenheit, *die;* **~ of obedience** mangelnder Gehorsam; **~ of work** Arbeitsmangel, *der;* **there is no ~ of it [for them]** es fehlt [ihnen] nicht daran; **he has no ~ of confidence** an Vertrauen mangelt *od.* fehlt es ihm nicht; **for ~ of sth.** aus Mangel an etw. (*Dat.*); **for ~ of time** aus Zeitmangel

B *v.t.* **sb./sth. ~s sth.** jmdm./einer Sache fehlt es an etw. (*Dat.*); **sb. ~s the creativity/ability to do sth.** jmdm. fehlt die Kreativität/Fähigkeit, etw. zu tun; **what he ~s is ...:** woran es ihm fehlt, ist ...; **his life ~ed something** seinem Leben fehlte etwas; **~ content** inhaltsarm sein

C *v.i.* **sb. ~s for sth.** (formal) jmdm. fehlt es an etw. (*Dat.*); **I ~ for nothing** mir fehlt es an nichts; *see also* **lacking**

lackadaisical /lækəˈdeɪzɪkl/ *adj.* (unenthusiastic) gleichgültig; desinteressiert; (listless) lustlos

lackadaisically /lækəˈdeɪzɪkəlɪ/ *adv.* ▸ **lackadaisical**: gleichgültig; desinteressiert; lustlos

lackey /ˈlækɪ/ *n.* 1 (footman) Lakai, *der* 2 (servant) Diener, *der* 3 (toady) Speichellecker, *der* (abwertend) 4 (derog.: political follower) Lakai, *der* (fig.: abwertend)

lacking /ˈlækɪŋ/ *adj.* 1 **be ~** ‹*Geld, Ressourcen usw.:*› fehlen; **he was found to be ~** (incapable) es erwies sich, dass er den Ansprüchen nicht genügte; **he is ~ in stamina/confidence** ihm fehlt es an Stehvermögen (*Dat.*)/er hat nicht genug Selbstvertrauen 2 (coll.: deficient in intellect) **be ~:** [geistig] unterbelichtet sein (salopp)

ˈlacklustre *adj.* trüb; glanzlos ‹*Augen*›; matt ‹*Lächeln*›; langweilig ‹*Aufführung, Party*›

laconic /lə'kɒnɪk/ *adj.* **1** (concise) lakonisch **2** wortkarg ‹*Person, Naturell*›

laconically /lə'kɒnɪkəlɪ/ *adv.* lakonisch

lacquer /'lækə(r)/
A *n.* Lack, *der*
B *v.t.* lackieren; **~ed wood** Lackholz, *das*

lacrosse /lə'krɒs/ *n.* (Sport) Lacrosse, *das*

lactate /læk'teɪt/ *v.i.* (Physiol.) laktieren

lactation /læk'teɪʃn/ *n.* (Physiol.) Laktation, *die*

lactic acid /læktɪk 'æsɪd/ *n.* (Chem.) Milchsäure, *die*

lactose /'læktəʊs/ *n.* (Chem.) Laktose, *die;* Milchzucker, *der*

lacto-vegetarian /læktəʊvedʒɪ'teərɪən/
A *n.* Laktovegetarier, *der*/Laktovegetarierin, *die*
B *adj.* laktovegetarisch

lacuna /lə'kju:nə/ *n., pl.* **~e** /lə'kju:ni:/ *or* **~s** Lücke, *die;* (in text) Lakune, *die* (Sprachw.); Textlücke, *die*

lacy /'leɪsɪ/ *adj.* Spitzen-; (of metalwork) spitzenartig; Filigran-

lad /læd/ *n.* **1** (boy) Junge, *der;* **young ~:** kleiner Junge; **when I was a ~:** als ich noch ein Junge war; **these are my ~s** das sind meine Jungen *od.* (ugs.) Jungs **2** (man) Typ, *der;* **the ~s** die Jungs (ugs.); **he always goes out for a drink with the ~s** er geht immer mit seinen Kumpels einen trinken (ugs.); **my ~:** mein Junge (ugs.) **3** **be a bit of** *or* **quite a ~** (coll.) (spirited) kein Kind von Traurigkeit sein (ugs.); (one for the ladies) es mit den Mädchen/Frauen haben (ugs.) **4** ▸ **stable lad**

ladder /'lædə(r)/
A *n.* **1** (lit. or fig.) Leiter, *die;* (fig.: means of advancement) Aufstiegsmöglichkeit, *die;* **the ~ to political power** der Weg zu politischer Macht; **have a foot on the ~:** die erste Sprosse auf der Leiter des Erfolgs erklommen haben (geh.); *see also* **rung**[1] **1; snake A 1; stepladder; top**[1] **A 1** **2** (Brit.: in tights etc.) Laufmasche, *die*
B *v.i.* (Brit.) Laufmaschen/eine Laufmasche bekommen
C *v.t.* (Brit.) Laufmaschen/eine Laufmasche machen in (+ *Akk.*)

'ladder-proof *adj.* (Brit. Textiles) maschenfest; laufmaschensicher

laddie /'lædɪ/ *n.* Jungchen, *das* (fam.); Bubi, *der* (bes. südd.)

laddish /'lædɪʃ/ *adj.* machohaft; **~ behaviour** Machogehabe, *das* (abwertend); **~ magazine** Männermagazin, *das*

lade /leɪd/ *v.t., p. p.* **~n** /'leɪdn/ (Naut.) **1** (load with cargo) laden **2** (load on to ship) verladen

laden /'leɪdn/ *adj.* **1** (loaded) beladen (**with** mit); **the air was ~ with moisture** die Luft war schwer von Feuchtigkeit; **trees ~ with blossom** Bäume, schwer von Blüten **2** (burdened) bedrückt; lastend ‹*Stille*›; bedrückend ‹*Schweigen*›; **~ with grief/guilt** gramerfüllt/schuldbeladen (geh.)

ladette /læ'det/ *n.* Mannweib, *das* (abwertend)

la-di-da /lɑ:dɪ'dɑ:/ *adj.* affektiert; **~ manners** Vornehmtuerei, *die* (abwertend)

ladies'/'leɪdɪz/: **~ man** *n.* Frauenheld, *der;* **~ night** *n.* Damenabend, *der;* **~ room** *n.* Damentoilette, *die*

ladified ▸ **ladyfied**

lading /'leɪdɪŋ/ *n.* **1** (loading) Laden, *das; see also* **bill**[3] **A 8** **2** (freight) Ladung, *die*

ladle /'leɪdl/
A *n.* **1** (utensil) Schöpfkelle, *die;* Schöpflöffel, *der* **2** (Metallurgy) Pfanne, *die*
B *v.t.* schöpfen

Phrasal verb
• **~ 'out** *v.t.* (lit. or fig.) austeilen

'lad mag *n.* Männermagazin, *das*

lady /'leɪdɪ/ *n.* **1** Dame, *die;* (English, American, etc. also) Lady, *die;* **~-in-waiting** (Brit.) Hofdame, *die;* **ladies' hairdresser** Damenfriseur, *der* **2** *in pl., constr. as sing.* **the Ladies[']** (Brit.) die Damentoilette; **'Ladies'** „Damen" **3** *as form of address in sing.* (poet.) Herrin (veralt.); *in pl.* meine Damen; **Ladies and Gentlemen!** meine Damen und Herren!; **my dear** *or* **good ~:** meine Gnädigste **4** ▸ⓘ **p. 1634** (Brit.) *as title* **L~:** Lady; **my ~:** Mylady **5** (ruling woman) Herrin, *die;* **~ of the house** Dame des Hauses; **Our L~** (Relig.) Unsere Liebe Frau; **6** (object of a man's devotion) Angebetete, *die;* (**~-love**) Herzenskönigin, *die* (dichter.); Liebste, *die* (veralt.); **your/his** *etc.* **~:** die Dame deines/seines *usw.* Herzens **7** (titled married woman) Gemahlin, *die* (geh.) **8** **my/your ~ wife** meine Frau/Ihre Gattin *od.* (geh.) Frau Gemahlin; **your good ~:** die Frau Gemahlin (geh.) **9** *attrib.* (female) **~ clerk** Angestellte, *die;* **~ doctor** Ärztin, *die;* **~ friend** Freundin, *die;* **~ dog** Hundedame, *die* (*scherzh.*). *See also* **easy A 3; first B 1; mayoress; old lady; painted lady; young lady**

lady: ~bird, (Amer.) **~bug** *ns.* (Zool.) Marienkäfer, *der;* **L~ chapel** *n.* (Eccl.) Marienkapelle, *die;* **L~ Day** *n., no art.* Mariä Verkündigung; **~ fern** *n.* (Bot.) Waldfrauenfarn, *der*

ladyfied /'leɪdɪfaɪd/ *adj.* [aufgesetzt] damenhaft; **be ~:** sich [allzu] damenhaft geben

lady: ~killer *n.* (coll.) Herzensbrecher, *der;* Ladykiller, *der* (scherzh.); **~like** *adj.* **1** damenhaft; **be ~like** sich wie eine Dame benehmen; **2** (effeminate) feminin (abwertend); **~-love** *n.* Liebste, *die* (veralt.); **~'s 'bedstraw** ▸ **bedstraw**

ladyship /'leɪdɪʃɪp/ *n.* ▸ⓘ **p. 1634 her/your ~/their ~s** Ihre/Eure Ladyschaft/Ihre Ladyschaften

lady: ~'s maid *n.* [Kammer]zofe, *die;* **~'s man** ▸ **ladies' man; ~-smock** ▸ **cuckoo flower; ~'s 'slipper** *n.* (Bot.) Frauenschuh, *der*

lag[1] /læg/
A *v.i.*, **-gg-** (lit. or fig.) zurückbleiben; *see also* **behind A 2, B 3**
B *n.* **1** (delay) Verzögerung, *die;* (falling behind) Zurückbleiben, *das;* **there was a ~ before ...:** es verging einige Zeit, bevor ... **2** (Phys.: retardation) Verzögerung, *die* (**behind** gegenüber); (amount of retardation) Verzögerungszeit, *die. See also* **jet lag; time lag**

lag[2] *n.* (Brit. coll.: convict) Knastbruder, *der* (ugs.); Knacki, *der* (ugs.); **old ~:** alter Knastbruder (ugs.)

lag[3] *v.t.*, **-gg-** (insulate) isolieren

lager /'lɑ:gə(r)/ *n.* Lagerbier, *das;* **a small ~:** ≈ ein kleines Helles

'lager lout *n.* Bier trinkender Rüpel

laggard /'lægəd/
A *n.* Nachzügler, *der;* (with work) Bummelant, *der* (ugs. abwertend)
B *adj.* langsam

lagging[1] *n.* **no ~!** nicht zurückbleiben!

lagging[2] *n.* (insulation) Isolierung, *die*

lagoon /lə'gu:n/ *n.* **1** Lagune, *die* **2** (Amer., Austral., NZ: small lake) kleiner [abflussloser] See **3** (in sewage works) Klärteich, *der*

lah /lɑ:/ *n.* (Mus.) la

laid ▸ **lay**[2] **A, B**

'laid-back *adj.* (coll.) gelassen

lain ▸ **lie**[2] **B**

lair /leər/ *n.* (of wild animal) Unterschlupf, *der;* Lager, *das* (*Jägerspr.*); (fig.: hiding place) (of pirates, bandits) Schlupfwinkel, *der;* (of children etc.) Versteck, *das*

laird /leəd/ *n.* (Scot.) Gutsbesitzer, *der*

laisser-faire, laissez-faire /leɪseɪ'feə(r)/ *n., no pl., no indef. art.* Laisser-faire, *das; attrib.* Laisser-faire‹*-Kapitalismus, -Einstellung*›

laity /'leɪɪtɪ/ *n. pl.* Laien; **many of the ~:** viele aus dem Laienstand

lake[1] /leɪk/ *n.* See, *der;* **the Great L~s** die Großen Seen

lake[2] *n.* (pigment from cochineal) Koschenillerot, *das;* Karmin, *das*

lake: L~ Constance /leɪk 'kɒnstəns/ *pr. n.* der Bodensee; **L~ District** *pr. n.* (Brit.) Lake District, *der* (*Seenlandschaft im Nordwesten Englands*); **~ dwelling** *n.* Pfahlbau, *der;* **L~land** /'leɪklənd/ ▸ **L~ District; L~ Lucerne** ▸ **Lucerne; L~ Lugano** /leɪk lu:'gɑ:nəʊ/ *pr. n.* der Luganer See; **~side** *n.* Seeufer, *das;* **by the ~side** am See[ufer]; **a ~side hotel/promenade** ein Hotel am See/eine Seeuferpromenade; **L~ Su'perior** *pr. n.* der Obere See

lakh /læk/ *n.* (Ind.) Lakh, *der;* **a ~ of rupees** [ein]hunderttausend Rupien

lam /læm/ (coll.)
A *v.i.*, **-mm-: ~ into sb.** auf jmdn. eindreschen (ugs.); (verbally) jmdn. zur Schnecke machen (ugs.)
B *v.t.*, **-mm-** dreschen (salopp) ‹*Ball*›; verdreschen (salopp) ‹*Person*›

lama /'lɑ:mə/ *n.* Lama, *der*

lamasery /'lɑ:məserɪ/ *n.* Lamakloster, *das*

lamb /læm/
A *n.* **1** Lamm, *das;* **as gentle/meek as a ~:** sanft wie ein Lamm; **one may** *or* **might as well be hanged** *or* **hung for a sheep as [for] a ~** (fig.) darauf kommt es jetzt auch nicht mehr an; **like a ~ [to the slaughter]** wie ein Lamm [zur Schlachtbank (geh.)] **2** *no pl.* (flesh) Lamm[fleisch], *das* **3** (mild person) Lamm, *das;* (dear person) Schatz, *der* (ugs.); (pitiable person) armes Geschöpf; **the L~ [of God]** (Bibl.) das Lamm Gottes
B *v.i.* lammen; **~ing season** Lammzeit, *die*

lambaste /læm'beɪst/ (**lambast** /læm'bæst/) *v.t.* (coll.: thrash, lit. or fig.) fertig machen (ugs.)

lamb: ~ 'chop *n.* Lammkotelett, *das;* **~ 'cutlet** *n.* Kammkotelett vom Lamm

Lambda probe /'læmdə prəʊb/ *n.* (Motor Veh.) Lambdasonde, *die*

lambkin /'læmkɪn/ *n.* **1** (animal) Lämmchen, *das* **2** (person) Schäfchen, *das* (fam.)

lamb: ~like *adj.* sanftmütig ‹*Wesen, Aussehen*›; **~'s fry** *n., no pl., no indef. art.* Gekröse vom Lamm; **~skin** *n.* (with wool on) Lammfell, *das;* (as leather) Schafleder, *das;* **~'s 'lettuce** *n., no pl., no indef. art.* (Bot.) Feldsalat, *der;* **~'s-tails** *n. pl.* (Brit. Bot.) Haselkätzchen; **~swool** *n.* Lambswool, *die* (Textilw.)

lame /leɪm/
A *adj.* **1** (disabled) lahm; **go ~:** lahm werden; **be ~ in one's right leg** ein lahmes rechtes Bein haben; **the horse was ~ in one leg** das Pferd lahmte auf einem Bein **2** (fig.: unconvincing) lahm (ugs. abwertend) **3** (fig.: halting) holprig ‹*Vers, Versmaß*›
B *v.t.* lahm reiten ‹*Pferd usw.*›; (fig.: hinder) lähmen ‹*Person, Fähigkeiten, Kraft*›

lamé /'lɑ:meɪ/ (Textiles)
A *n.* Lamé, *der*
B *adj.* lamé; Lamé-

lame: ~brain *n.* (coll.) Schwachkopf, *der* (abwertend); **~ dog** ▸ **dog A 1; ~ 'duck** *n.* **1** (incapable person) Versager, *der*/Versagerin, *die;* **2** (firm) zahlungsunfähige Firma; **the ~ ducks of industry** die bankrotten Industrieunternehmen; **3** (Amer.: official about to retire) *Politiker, der nicht wieder gewählt worden ist*

lamella /lə'melə/ *n., pl.* **~e** /lə'meli:/ Lamelle, *die*

lamely /'leɪmlɪ/ *adv.* **1** hinkend; **the horse walks ~:** das Pferd geht lahm **2** (fig.: unconvincingly) lahm (ugs. abwertend); **she ~ mumbled an excuse** sie murmelte eine lahme Entschuldigung

lameness /'leɪmnɪs/ *n., no pl.* (lit.; also fig.: unconvincingness) Lahmheit, *die*

lament /lə'ment/
A *n.* **1** (expression of grief) Klage, *die* (**for** um); **his great ~ is ...:** sein großer Kummer ist ... **2** (dirge) Klagegesang, *der*
B *v.t.* klagen über (+ *Akk.*) (geh.); klagen um (geh.) ‹*Freund, Heimat, Glück*›; **~ that ...:** beklagen, dass ...
C *v.i.* klagen (geh.); **~ over** *or* **for sth.** etw. beklagen (geh.); etw. beweinen; **~ over** *or* **for sb.** jmdn. beweinen; um jmdn. weinen

lamentable /'læməntəbl/ *adj.* beklagenswert; kläglich ‹*Versuch, Leistung*›

lamentably /'læməntəblɪ/ *adv.* beklagenswert; kläglich ‹*scheitern*›; **be ~ ignorant of sth.** beklagenswert wenig über etw. (*Akk.*) wissen

lamentation /læmən'teɪʃn/ *n.* **1** *no pl., no art.* (lamenting) Wehklagen, *das* (geh.) **2** (lament) [Weh]klage, *die* (geh.)

lamented /lə'mentɪd/ *adj.* betrauert; **the late ~ President** der verschiedene Präsident

laminate
A /'læmɪneɪt/ v.t. 1 (construct) lamellieren (Technik) 2 (make into thin plates) laminieren (Metall.) 3 (split) in [flache] Platten spalten 4 (overlay) beschichten; laminieren (Technik)
B v.i. sich [in flache Platten] spalten
C /'læmɪnət/ n. Schicht[press]stoff, *der* (Technik); Laminat, *das* (Technik); **fibreglass ~:** Glasfaserschichtstoff, *der* (Technik)
laminated /'læmɪneɪtɪd/ adj. lamelliert (Technik); **~ glass** Verbundglas, *das;* **~ fibreglass** Glasfasergewebe, *das*
lamination /læmɪ'neɪʃn/ n. 1 (process) Laminierung, *die* (Technik) 2 (layer of material) Schicht, *die*
lammergeyer /'læməgaɪə(r)/ n. (Ornith.) Lämmergeier, *der;* Bartgeier, *der*
lamp /læmp/ n. Lampe, *die;* (in street) [Straßen]laterne, *die;* [Straßen]lampe, *die;* (of vehicle) Licht, *das;* (car headlamp) Scheinwerfer, *der;* (fig.: source of hope etc.) Licht, *das; see also* **fluorescent lamp**; **neon lamp**; **spirit lamp**; **sunlamp**
lamp: ~black n. Lampenruß, *der;* **~holder** n. [Glühlampen]fassung, *die;* **~light** n. Lampenlicht, *das;* **~lighter** n. Laternenanzünder, *der*
lampoon /læm'pu:n/
A n. Spottschrift, *die;* Pasquill, *das* (geh.)
B v.t. verhöhnen; verspotten
'lamp post n. Laternenpfahl, *der;* (taller) Lichtmast, *der*
lamprey /'læmprɪ/ n. (Zool.) Neunauge, *das*
lamp: ~shade n. Lampenschirm, *der;* **~standard** n. Lichtmast, *der*
LAN /læn/ abbr. = **local area network** LAN
Lancastrian /læŋ'kæstrɪən/
A adj. 1 (of Lancashire) Lancashire-; ‹*Abstammung*› aus Lancashire 2 (Hist.) zum Hause Lancaster gehörig; des Hauses Lancaster *nachgestellt*
B n. 1 (native of Lancashire) **be a ~:** aus Lancashire stammen 2 (Hist.) Mitglied/Anhänger des Hauses Lancaster; **the ~s** die Partei der Lancaster
lance /lɑ:ns/
A n. 1 (weapon) Lanze, *die* 2 (Fishing) Stoßharpune, *die* 3 (pipe) Sprührohr, *das;* (for burning a hole) **[oxygen] ~:** [Sauerstoff]lanze, *die* 4 (Mil.) ▸ **lancer 1**
B v.t. 1 (Med.) mit der Lanzette öffnen 2 (pierce with ~) mit der Lanze durchbohren
lance: ~ bombar'dier n. ▸❶ **p. 1634** (Mil.) Obergefreiter der Artillerie; **~ 'corporal** n. ▸❶ **p. 1634** (Mil.) Obergefreite, *der*
lancer /'lɑ:nsə(r)/ n. 1 (Mil. Hist.) Lanzenreiter, *der* 2 in pl. (dance) Lancier, *der*
lancet /'lɑ:nsɪt/ n. 1 (Med.) Lanzette, *die* 2 (Archit.) **~ [arch/light** *or* **window]** Lanzettbogen, *der*/Lanzettfenster, *das*
land /lænd/
A n. 1 no pl., no indef. art. (solid part of the earth) Land, *das;* **by ~:** auf dem Landweg; **by ~ or by sea** zu Lande oder zu Wasser ‹*reisen*›; auf dem Landweg oder auf dem Seeweg ‹*schicken, transportieren*›; **on ~:** zu Lande; (not in air) auf dem Boden; (not in or on water) an Land; **~ travel** das Reisen zu Lande 2 no indef. art. (expanse of country) Land, *das;* **see/find out how the ~ lies** (fig.) herausfinden, wie die Dinge liegen; **how does the ~ lie?** (fig.) wie ist die Lage?; *see also* **lay² C 2**; **lie² A 1** 3 no pl., no indef. art. (ground for farming or building) Land, *das;* **work the ~:** das Land bebauen; **back to the ~:** zurück aufs Land; **live off the ~:** sich von dem ernähren, was das Land hergibt 4 (country) Land, *das;* **the greatest in the ~:** der/die Größte im ganzen Land; **out of the ~ of Egypt** (Bibl.) aus Ägyptenland (bibl.); **~ of hope and glory** Land der Hoffnung und des Ruhms; *see also* **living A 5**; **promised land** 5 no indef. art. (landed property) Land, *das;* **have** *or* **own ~:** Grundbesitz haben; **~s** (estates) Ländereien *Pl*
B v.t. 1 (set ashore) [an]landen ‹*Truppen, Passagiere, Waren, Fang*› 2 (Aeronaut.) landen ‹[*Wasser*]*flugzeug*›; **they were ~ed at an airstrip** ihr Flugzeug landete auf einer Piste 3 (bring into a situation) **~ oneself in trouble** sich in Schwierigkeiten bringen; sich (*Dat.*) Ärger einhandeln (ugs.); **this will ~ him in bankruptcy** das wird ihn [noch] bankrott machen; **his recklessness ~ed him in danger** durch seinen Leichtsinn hat er sich in Gefahr gebracht; **~ sb. in [the thick of] it** jmdn. [ganz schön] reinreiten (salopp) 4 (deal) landen ‹*Schlag*›; **~ a blow on sb., ~ sb. one** jmdm. einen Schlag versetzen *od.* (ugs.) verpassen; **~ sb. one right in the eye** jmdm. eins aufs Auge geben (ugs.) 5 (burden) **~ sb. with sth., ~ sth. on sb.** jmdm. etw. aufhalsen (ugs.); **be ~ed with sb./sth.** jmdn. auf dem Hals haben (ugs.)/etw. aufgehalst bekommen (ugs.); **this ~ed me with a huge problem** dies stellte mich vor ein ungeheures Problem 6 **~ a fish** einen Fisch an Land ziehen 7 (fig.: obtain in face of competition) an Land ziehen (ugs.)
C v.i. 1 ‹*Boot usw.*:› anlegen, landen; ‹*Passagier*:› aussteigen (**from** aus); **we ~ed at Dieppe** wir gingen in Dieppe an Land 2 (Aeronaut.) landen; (on water) [auf dem Wasser] aufsetzen; wassern; **be about to ~:** zur Landung angesetzt haben; gerade landen 3 (alight) landen; ‹*Ball*:› aufkommen; **~ on one's feet** auf den Füßen landen; (fig.) [wieder] auf die Füße fallen 4 (find oneself in a situation) landen (ugs.) **(at, in** in + *Dat.*); **~ in the middle of a dispute** [mitten] in eine Auseinandersetzung hineingeraten

Phrasal verbs
- **~ 'back** v.i. wieder landen (ugs.)
- **~ on** v.t. **~ on sb.** (impose oneself) jmdn. heimsuchen (fig.)
- **~ 'up** v.i. landen (ugs.)

'land agent n. ▸❶ **p. 1260** 1 (Brit.: steward) Liegenschaftsverwalter, *der*/-verwalterin, *die* 2 (selling land) Grundstücksmakler, *der*/-maklerin, *die*
landau /'lændɔ:/ n. Landauer, *der*
land: ~ breeze n. Landwind, *der;* **~ crab** n. (Zool.) Landkrabbe, *die*
landed /'lændɪd/ adj. 1 (having land) **~ gentry/aristocracy** Landadel, *der;* **the ~ interest** die Großgrundbesitzer 2 (consisting of land) Land‹*besitz, -gut*›
lander /'lændə(r)/ n. (Astronaut.) Landefahrzeug, *das;* Landefähre, *die*
land: ~fall n. (Naut.) Landfall, *der;* **~fill** n. 1 (material) Müll, *der;* Schutt, *der* (*zur Geländeauffüllung*); 2 (process) Geländeauffüllung, *die; attrib.* **~fill site** (*mit Erde wieder aufgefüllte*) Müllgrube; **~ force** n. **~ force[s** *pl.*] Landstreitkräfte *Pl.;* **~form** n. Geländeform, *die;* **~ girl** n. (Brit.) Landarbeiterin, *die;* Landwirtschaftsgehilfin, *die*
landing /'lændɪŋ/ n. 1 (of ship) Landung, *die;* **on ~** (disembarkation) beim Verlassen des Schiffs 2 (of aircraft) Landung, *die;* **emergency ~:** Notlandung, *die; see also* **hard landing**; **soft landing** 3 (place for disembarkation) Anlegestelle, *die* 4 (between flights of stairs) Treppenabsatz, *der;* (passage) Treppenflur, *der*
landing: ~ card n. Landekarte, *die;* **~ craft** n. (Navy) Landungsboot, *das;* **~ flap** n. Landeklappe, *die;* **~ gear** n. Fahrwerk, *das;* **~ lights** n. pl. 1 (on aircraft) Landescheinwerfer *Pl.;* 2 (on runway) Landebahnbeleuchtung, *die;* Landelichter *Pl.;* **~ net** n. Kescher, *der;* **~ place** ▸ **landing 3**; **~ stage** n. Landungssteg, *der;* Landungsbrücke, *die;* (floating) Anlegeponton, *der;* **~ strip** ▸ **airstrip**; **~ wheels** n. pl. Landeräder *Pl.*
land: ~lady n. 1 (of rented property) Vermieterin, *die;* (of flat also) Hauswirtin, *die;* (of room also) Zimmerwirtin, *die;* 2 (of public house) [Gast]wirtin, *die;* 3 (of lodgings etc.) [Pensions]wirtin, *die;* **~less** /'lændlɪs/ adj. landlos; **~line** n. Landkabel, *das;* **~locked** adj. vom Land eingeschlossen ‹*Bucht, Hafen*›; ‹*Staat*› ohne Zugang zum Meer; **~lord** n. 1 (of rented property) Vermieter, *der;* [Haus]wirt, *der;* 2 (of public house) [Gast]wirt, *der;* 3 (of lodgings etc.) [Pensions-]wirt, *der;* **~lubber** /'lændlʌbə(r)/ n. (Naut.) Landratte, *die* (ugs.); **~mark** n. 1 (boundary mark) Grenzzeichen, *das;* (stone) Grenzstein, *der;* 2 (conspicuous object) Orientierungspunkt, *der;* (Naut.) Landmarke, *die;* 3 (fig.: significant event) Markstein, *der;* **stand as a ~mark** einen Meilenstein bedeuten; **~ mass** n. (Geog.) Landmasse, *die;* **~mine** n. (Mil.) 1 (on ground) Landmine, *die;* 2 (parachute mine) Fallschirmmine, *die;* **~owner** n. **[large** *or* **big] ~owner** [Groß]grundbesitzer, *der*/-besitzerin, *die*
landscape /'lændskeɪp, 'lænskeɪp/
A n. 1 Landschaft, *die* 2 (picture) Landschaftsbild, *das;* Landschaft, *die*
B v.t. landschaftsgärtnerisch gestalten ‹*Garten, Park*›
landscape: ~ architect n. ▸❶ **p. 1260** Landschaftsarchitekt, *der*/-architektin, *die;* **~ architecture** n. Landschaftsgestaltung, *die;* **~ format** n. (also Computing) Querformat, *das; attrib.* **~ format sketchbook** Block im Querformat; **~ gardener** n. ▸❶ **p. 1260** Landschaftsgärtner, *der*/-gärtnerin, *die;* **~ gardening** n., no pl. Landschaftsgärtnerei, *die;* **~ painter** n. Landschaftsmaler, *der*/-malerin, *die;* **~ painting** n. Landschaftsmalerei, *die*
land: ~slide n. 1 Erdrutsch, *der;* 2 (fig.: majority) Erdrutsch[wahl]sieg, *der; attrib.* **a ~slide victory** ein Erdrutsch[wahl]sieg; **~slip** ▸ **~slide 1**; **~ tax** n. (Admin.) Grundsteuer, *die*
landward /'lændwəd/
A adj. **~ side** Landseite, *die;* **~ view** Blick zur Landseite hin
B adv. land[ein]wärts
C n. **to [the] ~:** zur Landseite hin
landwards /'lændwədz/ ▸ **landward B**
'land wind n. Landwind, *der*
lane /leɪn/ n. 1 (in the country) Landsträßchen, *das;* (unmetalled) [Hecken]weg, *der;* **it's a long ~ that has no turning** (prov.) alles muss einmal ein Ende haben 2 (in town) Gasse, *die;* **lovers' ~:** Seufzerallee, *die* (scherzh.) 3 (part of road) [Fahr]spur, *die;* **slow/inside ~** (in Britain) linke Spur; (on the continent) rechte Spur; **outside ~:** Überholspur, *die;* **'get in ~'** „bitte einordnen"; *see also* **fast lane** 4 **aircraft ~:** Flugroute, *die;* **shipping ~:** Schifffahrtsweg, *der;* **ocean ~:** Schifffahrtsstraße, *die* 5 (for race) Bahn, *die*
-lane[d] /leɪn(d)/ adj. *in comb.* -spurig
lane: ~ discipline n., no pl.: *Benutzung der richtigen Fahrspur und Vermeidung gefährlicher Spurwechsel;* **~ markings** n. pl. Fahrbahnmarkierungen *Pl.*
language /'læŋgwɪdʒ/ n. ▸❶ **p. 1277** 1 Sprache, *die;* **speak the same ~** (fig.) die gleiche Sprache sprechen; *see also* **artificial language**; **dead language**; **foreign language**; **sign language** 2 no pl., no art. (words, wording) Sprache, *die;* **[style of] ~:** [Sprach]stil, *der;* **use of ~:** Sprachgebrauch, *der* 3 (style) Ausdrucksweise, *die;* Sprache, *die;* **use uncompromising ~:** eine unmissverständliche Sprache sprechen; **mind your ~:** drück dich gefälligst anständig aus; **~ of the gutter** Gossensprache, *die; see also* **bad A 4**; **strong language** 4 (professional vocabulary) [Fach]sprache, *die;* **the ~ of diplomacy** die Sprache der Diplomatie; **medical ~:** medizinische Fachsprache 5 (Computing) Sprache, *die;* **computer ~s** Computersprachen 6 no pl., no art. (faculty of speech) Sprachfähigkeit, *die*
language: ~ course n. Sprachkurs[us], *der;* **~ degree** n. Sprachdiplom, *das;* Sprachzertifikat, *das;* **~ engi'neering** n., no pl. Sprachtechnologie, *die;* **~ lab** (coll.), **~ laboratory** ns. Sprachlabor, *das;* **~ school** n. Sprachenschule; *die;* **~ skills** n. pl. sprachliche Gewandtheit; **~ student** n. Sprachstudent, *der*/-studentin, *die;* Sprachschüler, *der*/-schülerin, *die;* **~ studies** n. pl. Fremdsprachenstudium, *das;* **~ teacher** n. ▸❶ **p. 1260** Sprachlehrer, *der*/-lehrerin, *die*
languid /'læŋgwɪd/ adj. 1 (indisposed to exertion, sluggish) träge 2 (inert) matt 3 (apathetic) lahm
languidly /'læŋgwɪdlɪ/ adv. 1 (without vigour, sluggishly) träge 2 (inertly) matt 3 (apathetically) lustlos
languish /'læŋgwɪʃ/ v.i. 1 (lose vitality) ermatten (geh.); ‹*Pflanzen*:› kümmern 2 (live wretchedly) **~ under sth.** unter etw. (*Dat.*) schmachten (geh.); **~ in prison** im Gefängnis schmachten (geh.) 3 (pine) dahinvegetieren; **~ for sth.**

ℹ Languages

With the major European languages, the noun has the same form as the nationality adjective but with a capital, much as in English. All languages are neuter.

German is difficult to learn
= Deutsch ist schwer zu lernen

She writes faultless/cultivated English
= Sie schreibt ein fehlerloses *or* perfektes Englisch/ein gepflegtes Englisch

He speaks Spanish without an accent
= Er spricht akzentfrei Spanisch

My daughter speaks fluent Russian
= Meine Tochter spricht fließend Russisch

in with a language is usually **auf:**

Say it in German
= Sagen Sie es auf Deutsch

But **in** is also used, especially where there is an adjective:

a speech in fluent French
= eine Rede in fließendem Französisch

The brochure is in English and German
= Der Prospekt ist in Englisch und Deutsch

Furthermore when the features of a language are being discussed, **im** with the nominalized form of the adjective should be used:

In English there are fewer endings than in German
= Im Englischen gibt es weniger Endungen als im Deutschen

The adjective as a noun is also used in relation to translations:

a translation from German into English
= eine Übersetzung aus dem Deutschen ins Englische

There are however cases where the adverb is used, which is written with a small letter. This happens because the word or phrase in question answers the question *how:*

The speech was given in English
= Die Rede wurde englisch *or* auf Englisch gehalten

They spoke German (*i.e. on this occasion, answering the question 'how did they speak?'*)
= Sie sprachen deutsch

They speak German (*i.e. can speak it, answering the question 'what do they speak?'*)
= Sie sprechen Deutsch

---

nach etw. schmachten (geh.); ~ **for sb.** sich nach jmdm. verzehren (geh.)

languor /ˈlæŋgə(r)/ *n.* ► **languorous**: Mattigkeit, *die;* Trägheit, *die;* Verträumtheit, *die*

languorous /ˈlæŋgərəs/ *adj.* **1** (faint) matt **2** (inert) träge **3** (dreamy) verträumt

lank /læŋk/ *adj.* **1** (tall) hager **2** (thin) abgemagert **3** (limp) glatt herabhängend ‹*Haar*›

lanky /ˈlæŋkɪ/ *adj.* schlaksig (ugs.); [dürr und] lang ‹*Arm, Bein*›

lanolin /ˈlænəlɪn/ *n.* Lanolin, *das*

lantern /ˈlæntən/ *n.* Laterne, *die; see also* **Chinese lantern; magic lantern**

lantern: ~-jawed /ˈlæntəndʒɔːd/ *adj.* mit lang geschnittenem Gesicht; ~ **slide** *n.* (Hist.) *bemalte Glasplatte oder Dia für die Laterna magica*

lanyard /ˈlænjəd/ *n.* **1** (Naut.) Bändsel, *das;* (in tackle) Taljenreep, *das* **2** (loop of cord) Kordel, *die* **3** (to fire gun) Abzugsleine, *die*

Laos /laʊs, ˈlɑːɒs/ *pr. n.* Laos (*das*)

Laotian /laʊʃn/ ►ℹ **p. 1345**
A *adj.* laotisch; **sb. is ~:** jmd. ist Laote/Laotin; *see also* **English A**
B *n.* **1** (person) Laote, *der*/Laotin, *die* **2** (language) laotische Sprache

lap¹ /læp/ *n.* **1** (part of body) Schoß, *der;* **live in the ~ of luxury** (fig.) im Überfluss leben; **fall** *or* **drop** *or* **be dropped into sb.'s ~** (fig.) jmdm. in den Schoß fallen; **end up on** *or* **in sb.'s ~** (fig.) bei jmdm. landen (ugs.); bei jmdm. abgeladen werden (fig.); *see also* **god 1** **2** (flap) [Rock]schoß, *der*

lap²
A *n.* **1** (Sport) Runde, *die;* **on the last ~** (fig. coll.) auf der Zielgeraden (fig.); **~ of honour** Ehrenrunde, *die* **2** (amount of overlap) Überlappung, *die* (**of** um); (overlapping part) überlappender Teil
B *v.t.*, **-pp-** **1** (Sport) überrunden **2** (cause to overlap) überlappen **3** (wrap) wickeln (**[a]round** um) **4** (swathe) umwickeln (**in** mit); wickeln ‹*Baby*› (**in** in + *Akk.*)
C *v.i.*, **-pp-:** ~ **over sth.** etw. überlappen

lap³
A *v.i.*, **-pp-** **1** (drink) schlappen; schlecken **2** ‹*See, Wasser, Wellen:*› plätschern
B *v.t.*, **-pp-** **1** (drink) ~ **[up]** [auf]schlappen; [auf]schlecken **2** ► ~ **up 2** **3** ► ~ **up 3** **4** ‹*See, Wasser, Wellen:*› plätschern an (+ *Akk.*)

Phrasal verb

• ~ **ˈup** *v.t.* **1** (drink) ► ~ **B 1** **2** (consume greedily) hinunterschütten **3** (fig.: receive eagerly) schlucken (ugs.); begierig aufnehmen ‹*Lob*›; sich stürzen auf (+ *Akk.*) ‹*Sensation*›

laparoscopy /læpəˈrɒskəpɪ/ *n.* (Med.) Laparoskopie, *die*

lap: ~ belt *n.* Beckengurt, *der;* ~ **dance** *n.* Lapdance, *der;* **~-dance** *v.i.* einen Lapdance vollführen; ~ **dancer** *n.* Lapdancer, *der*/-dancerin, *die;* ~ **dancing** *n., no pl.* Lapdancing, *das;* **~dog** *n.* Schoßhund, *der;* Schoßhündchen, *das*

lapel /ləˈpel/ *n.* Revers, *das od.* (österr.) *der; attrib.* ~ **microphone** Reversmikrofon, *das*

lapidary /ˈlæpɪdərɪ/ *adj.* **1** (of gems) ~ **art** (cutting gems) Steinschneidekunst, *die;* (polishing gems) Kunst des Steinschleifens **2** (engraved) in Stein gehauen **3** (dignified and concise) lapidar

lapis [lazuli] /ˈlæpɪs (ˈlæzjʊlɪ)/ *n., no pl., no indef. art.* **1** (gem) Lapislazuli, *der;* Lasurstein, *der* **2** (pigment, colour) Ultramarin, *das;* Lasurblau, *das*

ˈlap joint *n.* Überlappung, *die;* Überlappungsverbindung, *die*

Lapland /ˈlæplænd/ *pr. n.* Lappland (*das*)

Laplander /ˈlæplændə(r)/ *n.* ►ℹ **p. 1345** Lappländer, *der*/Lappländerin, *die*

Lapp /læp/ ►ℹ **p. 1277**, ►ℹ **p. 1345**
A *n.* **1** (person) Lappe, *der*/Lappin, *die* **2** (language) lappische Sprache
B *adj.* **1** lappisch; lappländisch **2** (of language) lappisch

Lappish /ˈlæpɪʃ/ ► **Lapp B**

lapse /læps/
A *n.* **1** (interval) **a/the ~ of ...:** eine/die Zeitspanne von ...; **a ~ in the conversation** eine Gesprächspause **2** (mistake) Fehler, *der;* Lapsus, *der* (geh.); ~ **of memory** Gedächtnislücke, *die* **3** (deviation) Verstoß, *der* (**from** gegen); **momentary ~ of concentration** momentane Konzentrationsschwäche; **a ~ from his high standard** eine Abweichung von seinem hohen Standard; ~ **from good taste** Geschmacksverirrung, *die* **4** (Law: termination of right) (of patent) Erlöschen, *das;* (of legacy) Heimfall, *der*
B *v.i.* **1** (fail) versagen; ~ **from sth.** etw. vermissen lassen **2** (sink) ~ **into** verfallen in (+ *Akk.*); fallen in (+ *Akk.*) ‹*Schlaf, Koma*›; verfallen (+ *Dat.*) ‹*Sucht, Ketzerei*› **3** (become void) ‹*Vertrag, Versicherungspolice usw.:*› ungültig werden; ‹*Plan, Projekt:*› hinfällig werden; ‹*Anspruch:*› verfallen **4** ~ **to sb.** (Law) auf jmdn. übergehen; an jmdn. fallen

lapsed /læpst/ *adj.* **1** (disused) in Vergessenheit geraten **2** (having defected) abgefallen ‹*Christ, Katholik usw.*› **3** abgelaufen, ungültig ‹*Pass, Führerschein, Versicherungspolice*›; frei geworden ‹*Lehen*›

lap: ~top **A** *adj.* tragbar, Laptop‹*gerät, -PC*›; **B** *n.* Laptop, *der;* tragbarer PC; ~ **weld** (Metalw.) *n.* Überlapp[schweiß]naht, *die;* **~-weld** (Metalw.) *v.t.* überlappt schweißen; **~wing** *n.* (Ornith.) Kiebitz, *der*

larboard /ˈlɑːbəd/ ► **port¹ A 3, B**

larcenous /ˈlɑːsənəs/ *adj.* diebisch

larceny /ˈlɑːsənɪ/ *n.* (Law) Diebstahl, *der*

larch /lɑːtʃ/ *n.* Lärche, *die*

lard /lɑːd/
A *n.* Schweineschmalz, *das;* Schweinefett, *das*
B *v.t.* **1** (Cookery) spicken **2** (fig.: garnish) spicken (ugs.)

larder /ˈlɑːdə(r)/ *n.* (room) Speisekammer, *die;* (cupboard) Speiseschrank, *der*

lardy /ˈlɑːdɪ/ *adj.* fett

ˈlardy cake *n.* ≈ Rosinenbrot, *das*

large /lɑːdʒ/
A *adj.* **1** groß; **a ~ lady** eine stattliche Dame; ~ **importer/user** Großimporteur, *der*/Großverbraucher, *der; see also* **intestine; life 4** **2** (comprehensive, broad) umfassend; **taking the ~ view** im großen Ganzen gesehen
B *n.* **1** **at ~** (at liberty) frei; (not in prison etc.) auf freiem Fuß; in Freiheit; (at full length) ausführlich; (as a body) insgesamt; (Amer. Polit.: representing whole State) für den ganzen Staat ‹*gewählt*›; **society at ~:** die Gesellschaft in ihrer Gesamtheit; **students/teachers/doctors at ~:** die [gesamte] Studenten-/Lehrer-/Ärzteschaft; **ambassador at ~** (Amer.) Sonderbotschafter, *der*/-botschafterin, *die* **2** **in [the] ~:** im Großen
C *adv.* ► **bulk B; by¹ B 4; loom²; write B 4**

ˈlarge-hearted *adj.* großherzig (geh.)

largely /ˈlɑːdʒlɪ/ *adv.* weitgehend

largeness /ˈlɑːdʒnɪs/ *n., no pl.* Größe, *die;* (of person) Stattlichkeit, *die*

larger-than-ˈlife *attrib. adj.* überlebensgroß

large: ~-scale *attrib. adj.* groß angelegt; groß ‹*Erfolg, Misserfolg*›; ‹*Katastrophe*› großen Ausmaßes; ‹*Modell*› in großem Maßstab; **~-scale manufacture** Massenproduktion, *die;* **~-size** ► **-size**

largess[e] /lɑːˈʒes/ *n., no pl.* **1** (gifts) Geschenke *Pl.;* **government ~:** staatliche Geschenke **2** (bestowal) [großzügige] Unterstützung *od.* Förderung

largish /ˈlɑːdʒɪʃ/ *adj.* ziemlich groß; recht stattlich ‹*Person*›

largo /ˈlɑːgəʊ/ (Mus.)
A *adv. & adj.* largo
B *n., pl.* **~s** Largo, *das*

lariat /ˈlærɪət/ *n.* **1** (lasso) (lateinamerikanisches) Lasso **2** (tethering-rope) Seil zum Anpflocken

lark¹ /lɑːk/ *n.* (Ornith.) Lerche, *die;* **be up with the ~:** beim *od.* mit dem ersten Hahnenschrei aufstehen; **gay** *or* **happy as a ~:** lustig und vergnügt

lark² (coll.)
A *n.* **1** (frolic) Jux, *der* (ugs.); **they were only having a ~:** sie haben sich (*Dat.*) nur einen Jux gemacht (ugs.); **be a real ~:** eine Mordsgaudi sein (ugs.); **it'll be a bit of a ~:** es wird bestimmt lustig; **do sth. for a ~:** etw. aus Jux machen (ugs.); **what a ~!** das ist/war spitze (ugs.) **2** (Brit.) (form of activity) Blödsinn, *der* (ugs.); (affair) Geschichte, *die* (ugs.); **blow** *or* (sl.) **sod** *or* (coarse) **bugger this for a ~:** zum Teufel!; verdammte Scheiße (derb)
B *v.i.* ~ **[about** *or* **around]** herumalbern (ugs.)

ˈlarkspur *n.* (Bot.) Rittersporn, *der*

larva /ˈlɑːvə/ *n., pl.* **~e** /ˈlɑːviː/ Larve, *die*

larval /ˈlɑːvl/ *adj.* Larven-; larval (fachspr.); **a ~ fly/frog** eine Fliegen-/Froschlarve

laryngeal /ləˈrɪndʒɪəl/
A *adj.* **1** (Anat.) Kehlkopf-; laryngeal (fachspr.) **2** (Ling.) Kehl[kopf]-; laryngal (fachspr.)
B *n.* (Ling.) Kehl[kopf]laut, *der;* Laryngal, *der* (fachspr.)

laryngitis /lærɪnˈdʒaɪtɪs/ *n.* ►ℹ **p. 1231** (Med.) Kehlkopfentzündung, *die;* Laryngitis, *die* (fachspr.)

larynx /ˈlærɪŋks/ *n., pl.* **larynges** /ləˈrɪndʒiːz/ ▸ⓘ **p. 951** (Anat.) Kehlkopf, *der;* Larynx, *der* (fachspr.)

lasagne /ləˈsænjə, ləˈsɑːnjə/ *n.* (Gastr.) Lasagne *Pl.*

lascivious /ləˈsɪvɪəs/ *adj.* **1** (lustful) lüstern (geh.) **2** (inciting to lust) lasziv

lasciviously /ləˈsɪvɪəslɪ/ *adv.* ▸ **lascivious**: lüstern (geh.); lasziv

lasciviousness /ləˈsɪvɪəsnɪs/ *n., no pl.* ▸ **lascivious**: Lüsternheit, *die* (geh.); Laszivität, *die*

laser /ˈleɪzə(r)/ *n.* Laser, *der*

laser: ~ **beam** *n.* Laserstrahl, *der;* ~**disc** *n.* Laserplatte, *die;* ~**-guided** *adj.* lasergesteuert; ~ **gun** *n.* Laserpistole, *die;* ~ **pointer** *n.* Laserpointer, *der;* ~ **printer** *n.* Laserdrucker, *der;* ~ **show** *n.* Lasershow, *die;* ~ **surgery** *n., no pl.* Laserchirurgie, *die;* **have ~ surgery** sich einer Laserbehandlung unterziehen; sich lasern lassen (ugs.); ~ **treatment** *n.* Laserbehandlung, *die*

lash /læʃ/

A *n.* **1** (stroke) [Peitschen]hieb, *der* **2** (part of whip) *biegsamer Teil der Peitsche;* (whipcord) Peitschenschnur, *die;* (as punishment) **the ~:** die Peitsche **3** (on eyelid) Wimper, *die*

B *v.i.* **1** (make violent movement) schlagen; ‹*Peitsche, Schlange:*› zuschlagen **2** (strike) ‹*Welle, Regen:*› peitschen (**against** gegen, **on** auf + *Akk.*); ‹*Person:*› [mit der Peitsche] schlagen (**at** nach)

C *v.t.* **1** (fasten) festbinden (**to** an + *Dat.*); (Naut.) festzurren (bes. Seemannsspr.); laschen (Seemannsspr.); ~ **together** zusammenbinden **2** (flog) mit der Peitsche schlagen; (as punishment) auspeitschen; ~ **oneself** sich geißeln **3** (rebuke) abkanzeln; geißeln ‹*Missstand, Laster, Fehler*›; (satirize) verhöhnen **4** (move violently) schlagen mit **5** (beat upon) peitschen; **the rain ~ed the windows/roof** der Regen peitschte gegen die Fenster/auf das Dach **6** (drive) ~ **sb. into sth.** jmdn. zu etw. anstacheln

(Phrasal verbs)

- ~ **aˈbout** *v.i.* wild um sich schlagen
- ~ **ˈdown**

A *v.t.* festbinden; (Naut.) festzurren (bes. Seemannsspr.)

B *v.i.* ‹*Regen:*› niederprasseln

- ~ **ˈinto** *v.t.* ~ **into sb.** über jmdn. herfallen
- ~ **ˈout** *v.i.* **1** (hit out) um sich schlagen; ‹*Pferd:*› ausschlagen; ~ **out at sb.** nach jmdm. schlagen; (fig.) über jmdn. herziehen (ugs.) **2** ~ **out on sth.** (coll.) (spend freely) sich (*Dat.*) etw. leisten *od.* gönnen; (pay a lot) viel Geld für etw. ausgeben

lashing /ˈlæʃɪŋ/ *n.* **1** ▸ **lash B**: Schlagen, *das usw.* **2** (cord) Zurring, *der* (Seemannsspr.) **3** *in pl.* (large amounts) ~**s of sth.** Unmengen von etw.

ˈlash-up

A *adj.* behelfsmäßig; ~ **procedures** provisorische Maßnahmen

B *n.* (improvised structure) Notbehelf, *der*

lass /læs/ *n.* **1** (Scot./N. Engl./poet.: girl) Mädchen, *das;* Maid, *die* (dichter.) **2** (sweetheart) Liebste, *die* (veralt.); Mädchen, *das* (ugs.)

lassie /ˈlæsɪ/ *n.* (Scot., N. Engl.) Mädchen, *das;* (sweetheart) Schätzchen, *das* (ugs.)

lassitude /ˈlæsɪtjuːd/ *n.* Mattigkeit, *die*

lasso /ləˈsuː, ˈlæsəʊ/

A *n., pl.* ~**s** *or* ~**es** Lasso, *das*

B *v.t.* mit dem Lasso fangen

last[1] /lɑːst/

A *adj.* ▸ⓘ **p. 1047**, ▸ⓘ **p. 1048** letzt...; **be ~ to arrive** als Letzter/Letzte ankommen; **for the [very] ~ time** zum [aller]letzten Mal; **who was ~?** wer war Letzter?; **the ~ two/three** *etc.* die letzten beiden/drei *usw.*; **he came ~ in the race** er war Letzter bei dem Rennen; **second ~, ~ but one** vorletzt...; **~ but not least** last, not least; nicht zuletzt; **~ evening/night was windy** gestern Abend/gestern *od.* heute Nacht war es windig; **~ week/month/year was cold** letzte Woche/letzten Monat/letztes Jahr war es kalt; **~ month was a memorable one** der letzte Monat war bedeutungsvoll; **~ evening/week we were out** gestern Abend/letzte Woche waren wir aus; **I thought my ~ hour had come** ich dachte, mein letztes Stündlein hätte geschlagen; **sb.'s ~ crust** (fig.) jmds. letztes Stück Brot (fig.); **I was down to my ~ crust** (fig.) ich war völlig abgebrannt (ugs.); **I should be the '~ person to do such a thing** ich wäre der Letzte, der so etwas täte; **the '~ thing** das Letzte; **that would be the '~ thing to do in this situation** das wäre das Letzte, was man in dieser Situation tun würde; *see also* **ditch A**; **honour A 10**; **judgement 3**; **leg A 1**; **quarter A 10**; **resort A 1**; **respect A 5**; **straw 2**

B *adv.* **1** [ganz] zuletzt; als Letzter/Letzte ‹*sprechen, ankommen*›; **come ~ with sb.** (fig.) für jmdn. an letzter Stelle rangieren **2** (on ~ previous occasion) das letzte Mal; zuletzt; **when did you ~ see him** *or* **see him ~?** wann hast du ihn zuletzt *od.* das letzte Mal gesehen?

C *n.* **1** (mention, sight) **I shall never hear the ~ of it** das werde ich ständig zu hören bekommen; **you haven't heard the ~ of this matter** das letzte Wort in dieser Sache ist noch nicht gesprochen; **I hope we shall soon see the ~ of him** ich hoffe, wir werden ihn hoffentlich bald zum letzten Mal gesehen haben; **that's the ~ we'll see of that old car** jetzt sehen wir dieses alte Auto wohl zum letzten Mal; **that was the ~ we ever saw of him** das war das letzte Mal, dass wir ihn gesehen haben **2** (person or thing) letzt...; **these ~:** Letztere; **be the ~ to arrive** als Letzter/Letzte ankommen; **which ~:** welch letzt...; **I'm always the ~ to be told** ich bin immer der Letzte, der etwas erfährt; **she was the ~ to know about it** sie erfuhr es als Letzte; **the ~ shall be first** (Bibl.) die Letzten werden die Ersten sein **3** (day, moment[s]) **towards** *or* **at the ~ he was serene** (just before his death) am Ende war er gelassen; **to** *or* **till the ~:** bis zuletzt **4** **look one's ~ on** einen letzten Blick werfen auf (+ *Akk.*); *see also* **breathe B 1** **5** **at [long] ~:** endlich; schließlich [doch noch]

last[2] *v.i.* **1** (continue) andauern; ‹*Wetter, Ärger:*› anhalten; ~ **all night** die ganze Nacht dauern; ~ **till** dauern bis; ~ **from ... to ...:** von ... bis ... dauern; **built to ~:** dauerhaft gebaut; **a book that will ~:** ein Buch, das bleibt; **he will not ~ very much longer** (live) er hat nicht mehr lange zu leben; (in job) ihm wird bald gekündigt werden; **make one's money ~:** mit seinem Geld haushalten; **it can't/won't ~:** das geht nicht mehr lange so; **it's too good to ~:** es ist zu schön, um von Dauer zu sein; ~ **sb.'s time** halten, solange jmd. es braucht **2** (manage to continue) es aushalten **3** (suffice) reichen; **while stocks ~:** solange Vorrat reicht; **this knife will ~ [me] a lifetime** dies Messer hält mein ganzes Leben; **memories to ~ a lifetime** Erinnerungen für das ganze Leben

(Phrasal verb)

- ~ **ˈout**

A *v.t.* (complete task) durchhalten; (survive) überstehen; ~ **out the winter/journey** ‹*Vorräte usw.:*› den Winter über/für die Reise ausreichen; **he would probably not ~ out the afternoon** er würde wahrscheinlich den Nachmittag nicht überleben

B *v.i.* durchhalten; ‹*Vorräte usw:*› ausreichen

last[3] *n.* (for shoemaker) Leisten, *der;* **the cobbler should stick to his ~** (prov.) Schuster, bleib bei deinem Leisten

last: **L~ ˈDay** *n.* (Relig.) **the L~ Day** der Jüngste Tag; ~**-ditch** *adj.* ~**-ditch attempt** letzter verzweifelter Versuch; ~**-ˈgasp** *adj.* in letzter Minute *nachgestellt*

lasting /ˈlɑːstɪŋ/ *adj.* **1** (permanent) bleibend; dauerhaft ‹*Beziehung*›; nachhaltig ‹*Eindruck, Wirkung, Bedeutung*›; nicht nachlassend ‹*Interesse*›; **be of no ~ benefit to sb.** sich für jmdn. auf die Dauer nicht auszahlen **2** (durable) haltbar; **[made] in a ~ material** aus haltbarem Material

lastly /ˈlɑːstlɪ/ *adv.* schließlich

last: ~**-mentioned** *attrib. adj.* letztgenannt; ~ **ˈminute** *n.* **at the ~ minute** in letzter Minute; **up to the ~ minute** bis zum letzten Augenblick; ~**-minute** *attrib. adj.* in letzter Minute vorgebracht ‹*Plan, Aufruf, Ergänzung, Gesuch, Bewerbung*›; ‹*Sinneswandel*› in letzter Minute; **make a ~-minute dash to the airport** in letzter Minute zum Flughafen rasen; **in the ~-minute rush** kurz vor Toresschluss; ~ **name** *n.* Zuname, *der;* Nachname, *der;* ~**-named** *attrib. adj.* zuletzt genannt; ~ **number ˈredial** *n., no pl.* Wahlwiederholung, *die;* ~ **ˈrites** *n. pl.,* ~ **ˈsacrament** *n.* (Relig.) Letzte Ölung; ~ **ˈsleep** *n., no pl.* (literary) ewiger Schlaf (geh.); **L~ ˈSupper** *n., no pl.* (Relig.) **the L~ Supper** das Abendmahl; ~ **ˈthing** *adv.* (coll.) als Letztes; ~ **ˈtrump** *n.* (Relig.) letzte Posaune; ~ **ˈwill** *n.* ~ **will [and testament]** letzter Wille; ~ **ˈword** *n., no pl., no indef. art.* **1** letztes Wort; **be the ~ word** (fig.) nicht zu überbieten sein (**in** an + *Dat.*); das Letzte sein (**in** an + *Dat.*); **sth. is the ~ word on sth.** mit etw. ist das letzte Wort über etw. (*Akk.*) gesprochen; **2** (latest fashion) **the ~ word** das Allerneueste; der letzte Schrei (ugs.); ~ **ˈwords** *n. pl.* **her/his ~ words** ihre/seine letzten Worte; **[there's] famous ~ words [for you]** (joc. iron.) das wollen wir erst mal sehen

lat. *abbr.* **= latitude** Br.

latch /lætʃ/

A *n.* **1** (bar) Riegel, *der* **2** (spring lock) Schnappschloss, *das* **3** **on the ~** (held by bar) nur mit einem Riegel verschlossen; (with lock not in use) nur eingeklinkt

B *v.t.* zuschnappen lassen

C *v.i.* zuschnappen

(Phrasal verbs)

- ~ **ˈon** *v.i.* (coll.) **1** (attach oneself) sich [ungefragt] anschließen **2** (understand) es mitkriegen (ugs.)
- ~ **ˈon to** *v.t.* (coll.) **1** (attach oneself to) ~ **on to sb.** sich an jmdn. hängen (ugs.) **2** (understand) kapieren (ugs.) **3** (be enthusiastic about) abfahren auf (+ *Akk.*) (salopp)

ˈlatchkey *n.* Hausschlüssel, *der;* ~ **child** (fig.) Schlüsselkind, *das*

late /leɪt/

A *adj.* ▸ⓘ **p. 894** **1** spät; (after proper time) verspätet; **am I ~?** komme ich zu spät?; **I am rather ~:** ich bin ziemlich spät dran (ugs.) *od.* habe mich ziemlich verspätet; **be ~ for the train** den Zug verpassen; **the train is [ten minutes] ~:** der Zug hat [zehn Minuten] Verspätung; **spring is ~ this year** dieses Jahr haben wir einen späten Frühling; **be [very] ~ for dinner** mit [großer] Verspätung zum Essen kommen; **what makes you so ~ today?** warum kommst du heute so spät?; ~ **riser** Spätaufsteher, *der*/-aufsteherin, *die;* ~ **entry** verspätete Anmeldung; ~ **shift** Spätschicht, *die;* **in the ~ evening** spät am Abend; spätabends; **it is ~:** es ist [schon] spät; **have a ~ dinner** [erst] spät zu Abend essen; ~ **summer** Spätsommer, *der;* ~ **spring holidays** Ferien im späten Frühjahr; **in ~ July** Ende Juli; ~ **Gothic/Victorian** spätgotisch/-viktorianisch; ~ **seventeenth-century paintings** Gemälde aus dem späten siebzehnten Jahrhundert; *see also* **hour 2** **2** (deceased) verstorben; *see also* **lamented** **3** (former) ehemalig; vormalig **4** (recent) letzt...; **in ~ times** in letzter Zeit; **of ~ years** in den letzten Jahren **5** (backward in flowering, ripening, etc.) spät ‹*Sorte, Nelken*›; **be ~** ‹*Blumen:*› spät blühen. *See also* **later**; **latest**

B *adv.* **1** (after proper time) verspätet; **[too] ~:** zu spät; **they got home very ~:** sie kamen [erst] sehr spät nach Hause; **better ~ than never** lieber spät als gar nicht **2** (far on in time) spät; **not until quite ~ this year** dieses Jahr erst recht spät; ~ **in August** Ende August; ~ **last century** [gegen] Ende des letzten Jahrhunderts; ~ **in life** erst spät im Leben; erst im fortgeschrittenen Alter **3** (at or till a ~ hour) spät; **be up/sit up ~:** bis spät in die Nacht *od.* lange aufbleiben; **work ~ at the office** [abends] lange im Büro arbeiten; **wait up ~ for sb./sth.** jmds./einer Sache wegen lange aufbleiben **4** (formerly) ~ **of ...:** ehemals wohnhaft in ...; ehemaliger Mitarbeiter (*einer Firma*) **5** (at ~ stage) **traces remained as ~ as the seventeenth century** Überreste blieben noch bis ins siebzehnte Jahrhundert erhalten; **she was seen as ~ as yesterday** sie wurde gestern

noch gesehen; **[a bit** *or* **somewhat** *or* **rather] ~ in the day** (fig. coll.) reichlich spät; **too ~ in the day** (lit. or fig.) zu spät
C *n.* **of ~:** in letzter Zeit

late: ~ bird *n.* (fig. coll.) Nachtmensch, *der;* Nachteule, *die* (ugs. scherzh.); **~comer** *n.* Zuspätkommende, *der/die*

lateen /lə'ti:n/ *adj.* (Naut.) [1] **~ sail** Lateinersegel, *das* [2] (rigged with a ~ sail) Lateinersegel-; mit Lateinersegel *nachgestellt*

lately /'leɪtlɪ/ *adv.* in letzter Zeit; **only ~:** erst vor kurzem; **till ~:** bis vor kurzem

latency /'leɪtənsɪ/ *n.* (Computing) Latenz, *die*

lateness /'leɪtnɪs/ *n., no pl.* [1] (being after due time) Verspätung, *die* [2] (being far on in time) **the ~ of the performance** der späte Beginn der Vorstellung; **the ~ of the hour** die späte *od.* vorgerückte Stunde

'late-night *attrib. adj.* Spät‹programm, -vorstellung›

latent /'leɪtənt/ *adj.* [1] latent [vorhanden] [2] (Med.) latent. *See also* **heat A 2**

latent 'image *n.* (Photog.) latentes Bild

later /'leɪtə(r)/
A *adv.* später; **~ on** später; **it must be ready no ~ than next week** es muss bis spätestens nächste Woche fertig sein; **~ [on] the same day** im weiteren Verlauf des Tages; später am Tag; **see you ~:** bis nachher; bis später; *see also* **soon 2**
B *adj.* später; (more recent) neuer; jünger; **at a ~ date/time** zu einem späteren Zeitpunkt; später; **be ~, be of ~ date** neueren *od.* jüngeren Datums sein

lateral /'lætərəl/ *adj.* [1] seitlich (**to** von); Seiten‹flügel, -ansicht›; **~ thinking** Querdenken, *das* [2] (Anat.) lateral [3] (Bot.) seitenständig; **~ shoot** Seitentrieb, *der*

laterally /'lætərəlɪ/ *adv.* seitlich

latest /'leɪtɪst/ *adj.* [1] (modern) neu[e]st...; **the very ~ thing** das Allerneu[e]ste; **the ~ in fashion** der letzte Schrei (ugs.); die neu[e]ste Mode [2] (most recent) letzt...; **have you heard the ~?** wissen Sie schon das Neu[e]ste?; **what's the ~?** was gibts Neues? [3] **at [the] ~/the very ~:** spätestens/allerspätestens

latex /'leɪteks/ *n., pl.* **~es** *or* **latices** /'leɪtɪsi:z/ Latex, *der*

lath /lɑ:θ/ *n., pl.* **~s** /lɑ:θs, lɑ:ðz/ Latte, *die;* **~s** (arrangement) Lattung, *die;* **~ and plaster** Putzträger und Putz

lathe /leɪð/ *n.* Drehbank, *die;* Drehmaschine, *die* (Technik)

lather /'lɑ:ðə(r), 'læðə(r)/
A *n.* [1] (froth) [Seifen]schaum, *der* [2] (sweat) Schweiß, *der;* Schaum, *der* (veralt.); **get [oneself] into a ~ [about sth.]** (fig.) sich [über etw. (*Akk.*)] aufregen
B *v.t.* [1] (cover with froth) einschäumen; einseifen [2] (coll.: thrash) verprügeln

Latin /'lætɪn/
A *adj.* [1] lateinisch; *see also* **English A** [2] (of ancient Romans) römisch [3] (of RC Ch.) lateinisch [4] (of Southern Europeans) romanisch; südländisch ‹*Temperament, Charme*›
B *n.* ▸ⓘ **p. 1277** Latein, *das;* **medieval ~:** Mittellatein, *das;* **modern ~:** Neulatein, *das;* **thieves' ~:** Gaunersprache, *die; see also* **English B 1**

Latina /læ'ti:nə/ *n.* Latina, *die*

Latin: ~ A'merica *pr. n.* Lateinamerika (*das*); **~ A'merican A** *adj.* lateinamerikanisch; **B** *n.* Lateinamerikaner, *der*/Lateinamerikanerin, *die*

Latinate /'lætɪneɪt/ *adj.* (derived from Latin) aus dem Lateinischen stammend

'Latin Church *n.* lateinische Kirche

Latinism /'lætɪnɪzm/ *n.* Latinismus, *der*

Latinist /'lætɪnɪst/ *n.* Latinist, *der*/Latinistin, *die*

Latinize /'lætɪnaɪz/ *v.t.* latinisieren

Latino /lə'ti:nəʊ/ *n., pl.* **~s** (Amer.) Lateinamerikaner/-amerikanerin [in den USA]

Latin: ~ Quarter *n.* Quartier Latin, *das;* **~ rite** *n.* (Eccl.) lateinischer Ritus

latish /'leɪtɪʃ/ *adj. & adv.* ziemlich spät

latitude /'lætɪtju:d/ *n.* [1] (freedom) Freiheit, *die;* (for differences) Spielraum, *der* [2] (Geog.) [geographische] Breite; (of a place) Breite, *die;* **~s** (regions) Breiten *Pl.;* **~ 40° N.** 40° nördlicher Breite [3] (Astron.) Breite, *die*

latrine /lə'tri:n/ *n.* Latrine, *die*

latte /'læteɪ, 'lɑ:teɪ/ *n.* Latte, *der*

latter /'lætə(r)/ *attrib. adj.* [1] letzter...; **the ~ ...:** der/die/das letztere ...; *pl.* die letzteren ...; (as noun) der/die/das Letztere; *pl.* die Letzteren [2] (later) letzt...; **the ~ half of the century** die zweite Hälfte des Jahrhunderts; **the ~ part of the year** die zweite Jahreshälfte; **the ~ end** das Ende

latter: ~ 'day *n.* Jüngster Tag; **~-day** *adj.* modern; **L~-day 'Saints** *n. pl.* Heilige der Letzten Tage

latterly /'lætəlɪ/ *adv.* [1] (later) später; gegen Ende [2] (lately) in letzter Zeit

lattice /'lætɪs/ *n.* (also fig., Phys.) Gitter, *das*

lattice: ~ frame, ~ girder *ns.* Gitterträger, *der;* **~work** *n., no pl.* Gitterwerk, *das*

Latvia /'lætvɪə/ *pr. n.* Lettland (*das*)

Latvian /'lætvɪən/ ▸ⓘ **p. 1277**, ▸ⓘ **p. 1345**
A *adj.* lettisch; **sb. is ~:** jmd. ist Lette/Lettin; *see also* **English A**
B *n.* [1] (person) Lette, *der*/Lettin, *die* [2] (language) Lettisch, *das; see also* **English B 1**

laud /lɔ:d/ *v.t.* (literary) preisen (geh.); rühmen; **much-~ed** viel gepriesen

laudable /'lɔ:dəbl/ *adj.* lobenswert

laudably /'lɔ:dəblɪ/ *adv.* lobenswert; löblich

laudanum /'lɔ:dnəm, 'lɒdnəm/ *n.* (Pharm.) Laudanum, *das*

laugh /lɑ:f/
A *n.* [1] Lachen, *das;* (loud and continuous) Gelächter, *das;* **have a [good] ~ about sth.** [herzlich] über etw. (*Akk.*) lachen; **give a loud ~:** laut auflachen; **this line in the play always gets/raises a ~:** diese Zeile im Stück bringt immer einen Lacher; **join in the ~:** mitlachen; **have the last ~:** derjenige sein, der zuletzt lacht (fig.); **have** *or* **get the ~ of** *or* **on sb.** jmdn. auslachen können; **the ~ is on me** ich stehe dumm da (ugs.); **he is always good for a ~:** bei ihm gibt es immer etwas zu lachen; **it should be good for a ~:** dabei gibt es sicher etwas zu lachen; **sb./sth. is a ~ a minute** bei jmdm./etw. muss man alle Augenblicke lachen; **that sounds like a ~ a minute** (iron.) da wird man sicher viel zu lachen haben; **for ~s** zum *od.* aus Spaß; **play Mephisto for ~s** (Theatre coll.) aus Mephisto eine komische Figur machen; **for a ~:** [so] zum Spaß; **anything for a ~:** ich bin für alles *od.* für jeden Spaß zu haben (ugs.) [2] (type of ~) Lachen, *das;* Art zu lachen [3] (coll.: comical thing) **it would be a ~ if ...:** es wäre ja zum [Tot]lachen, wenn ... (ugs.); **that's a** *or* **what a ~!** das ist ja zum [Tot]lachen! (ugs.); (iron.) das ist zum Lachen (ugs.); dass ich nicht lache!; **he's a [good] ~:** er ist urkomisch
B *v.i.* lachen; **~ out loud** laut auflachen; **I thought I'd die ~ing** ich hätte mich beinahe totgelacht (ugs.); **I ~ed till I cried** ich habe Tränen gelacht; **be ~ing all over one's face** über das ganze Gesicht lachen; **~ at sb./sth.** (in amusement) über jmdn./etw. lachen; (jeer) jmdn. auslachen/etw. verlachen; über jmdn./etw. lachen; **~ in sb.'s face** jmdm. ins Gesicht lachen; **~ in** *or* **up one's sleeve** sich (*Dat.*) ins Fäustchen lachen; **he'll ~ on the other side of his face when ...:** ihm wird das Lachen [noch] vergehen, wenn ...; **he who ~s last ~s longest** (prov.) wer zuletzt lacht, lacht am besten (Spr.); **don't make me ~** (coll. iron.) dass ich nicht lache!; **~ and the world ~s with you, weep and you weep alone** (prov.) Freunde in der Not gehn hundert *od.* tausend auf ein Lot (Spr.); *see also* **laughing**
C *v.t.* lachen; **he was ~ed out of town/off the stage** mit Hohnlachen wurde er aus der Stadt/von der Bühne gejagt; **~ oneself sick** *or* **silly** sich krank- *od.* schieflachen (ugs.)

Phrasal verb

• **~ 'off** *v.t.* mit einem Lachen abtun

laughable /'lɑ:fəbl/ *adj.* lachhaft (abwertend); lächerlich

laughing /'lɑ:fɪŋ/
A *n.* **be no ~ matter** nicht zum Lachen sein
B *adj.* (coll.: fortunate) **be ~ [all over one's face]** fein raus sein (ugs.); *see also* **hyena 1**; **jackass 3**

'laughing gas *n.* Lachgas, *das*

laughingly /'lɑ:fɪŋlɪ/ *adv.* lachend; **what is ~ called ...** (iron.) was sich ... nennt (spött.)

'laughing stock *n.* **make sb. a ~, make a ~ of sb.** jmdn. zum Gespött machen; **he became the ~ of the whole neighbourhood** er wurde zum Gespött der ganzen Nachbarschaft

laughter /'lɑ:ftə(r)/ *n.* Lachen, *das;* (loud and continuous) Gelächter, *das;* **~ is the best medicine** (prov.) Lachen ist die beste Medizin

'laughter lines *n. pl.* Lachfältchen

launch¹ /lɔ:nʃ/
A *v.t.* [1] zu Wasser lassen, aussetzen ‹*Rettungsboot, Segelboot*›; vom Stapel lassen ‹*neues Schiff*›; (propel) werfen, abschießen ‹*Harpune*›; schleudern ‹*Speer*›; abschießen ‹*Torpedo*›; **~ a rocket into space** eine Rakete ins All schießen [2] (fig.) lancieren (bes. Wirtsch.); auf den Markt bringen ‹*Produkt*›; vorstellen ‹*Buch, Schallplatte, Sänger*›; auf die Bühne bringen ‹*Theaterstück*›; gründen ‹*Firma*›; **~ an attack** einen Angriff durchführen
B *v.i.* **~ into a song** ein Lied anstimmen; **~ into a long speech/a stream of insults** eine lange Rede/eine Flut von Beschimpfungen vom Stapel lassen *od.* loslassen (ugs.)
C *n.* [1] (of spacecraft) Start, *der;* (of rocket) Abschuss, *der;* (of new ship) Stapellauf, *der;* (of boat) Aussetzen, *das* [2] (of product) Lancieren, *das;* (of book, record, singer) Vorstellung, *die;* (of play) Premiere, *die;* (of firm) Gründung, *die*

Phrasal verb

• **~ 'out** *v.i.* (fig.) **~ out into films/a new career/on one's own** sich beim Film versuchen/beruflich etwas ganz Neues anfangen/sich selbstständig machen; **we can really ~ out now** jetzt können wir aus dem Vollen schöpfen *od.* brauchen wir nicht zu sparen; **~ out at sb.** jmdn. anfahren

launch² *n.* (boat) Barkasse, *die*

launcher /'lɔ:nʃə(r)/ *n.* [1] (rocket) Trägerrakete, *die* [2] (structure) Startrampe, *die*

launching: ~ pad *n.* [Raketen]abschussrampe, *die;* **~ site** *n.* [Raketen]abschussbasis, *die*

launch: ~ pad ▸ **launching pad**; **~ site** ▸ **launching site**

launder /'lɔ:ndə(r)/ *v.t.* [1] waschen und bügeln; **I have sent the sheets away to be ~ed** ich habe die Bettlaken zum Waschen weggegeben [2] (fig.) waschen ‹*Geld*›

launderette /lɔ:ndə'ret/, **laundrette** /lɔ:n'dret/, (Amer.) **laundromat** /'lɔ:ndrəmæt/ *ns.* Waschsalon, *der*

laundry /'lɔ:ndrɪ/ *n.* [1] (place) Wäscherei, *die* [2] (clothes etc.) Wäsche, *die;* **do the ~:** Wäsche waschen

laundry: ~ bag *n.* Wäschebeutel, *der;* **~ basket** *n.* Wäschekorb, *der;* **~man** *n.* ▸ⓘ **p. 1260** Wäschemann, *der*

laureate /'lɔ:rɪət, 'lɒrɪət/ *n.* Laureat, *der;* **[Poet] L~:** Hofdichter, *der;* Poeta laureatus, *der;* **Nobel ~:** Nobelpreisträger, *der*

laurel /'lɒrl/ *n.* [1] (emblem of victory) Lorbeer[kranz], *der;* **win one's ~[s]** (fig.) Lorbeeren ernten; **have to look to one's ~s** (fig.) sich nicht auf seinen Lorbeeren ausruhen dürfen; **rest on one's ~s** (fig.) sich auf seinen Lorbeeren ausruhen (ugs.) [2] (Bot.) **[cherry] ~:** Kirschlorbeer, *der;* Lorbeerkirsche, *die;* **mountain ~:** Lorbeerrose, *die*

lav /læv/ *n.* (coll.) Klo, *das* (ugs.)

lava /'lɑ:və/ *n.* Lava, *die*

'lava flow *n.* [1] (lava mass) Lavastrom, *der* [2] *no pl.* (process) Lavafluss, *der*

lavage /'lævɪdʒ/ *n.* (Med.) Spülung, *die*

'lava lamp *n.* Lavalampe, *die*

lavatorial /lævə'tɔ:rɪəl/ *adj.* (esp. Brit.) fäkalisch; Fäkal‹*humor*›

lavatory /'lævətərɪ/ *n.* Toilette, *die; see also* **toilet 1**

l

lavatory: ~ **attendant** *n.* ▸ ⓘ **p. 1260** Toilettenmann, *der*/Toilettenfrau, *die*; ~ **humour** *n.* Fäkalhumor, *der*; ~ **paper** ▸ **toilet paper**; ~ **seat** ▸ **toilet seat**

lavender /ˈlævɪndə(r)/
A *n.* **1** (Bot.) Lavendel, *der* **2** (colour) Lavendel[blau], *das*
B *adj.* lavendel[blau]

ˈlavender water *n.* Lavendel[wasser], *das*

lavish /ˈlævɪʃ/
A *adj.* (generous) großzügig; überschwänglich ‹*Lob, Liebe*›; verschwenderisch ‹*Ausgaben*›; (abundant) üppig; **be** ~ **of** *or* **with sth.** nicht mit etw. geizen; **be too** ~ **with sth.** mit etw. übertreiben
B *v.t.* ~ **sth. on sb.** jmdn. mit etw. überhäufen *od.* überschütten; ~ **too much time and money on a project** zu viel Zeit und Geld an ein Projekt verschwenden; ~ **care on sth.** seine ganze Mühe auf etw. (*Akk.*) verwenden

lavishly /ˈlævɪʃlɪ/ *adv.* großzügig; überschwänglich ‹*loben, lieben*›; verschwenderisch ‹*Geld ausgeben*›; herrschaftlich ‹*eingerichtet*›

law /lɔː/ *n.* **1** *no pl.* (body of established rules) Gesetz, *das*; Recht, *das*; **the** ~ **forbids/allows sth. to be done** nach dem Gesetz ist es verboten/erlaubt, etw. zu tun; **the** ~ **is an ass** das Gesetz ist absurd; **according to/under British** *etc.* ~: nach britischem *usw.* Recht; **break the** ~: gegen das Gesetz verstoßen; **be against the** ~: gegen das Gesetz sein; **the** ~ **is the** ~: Gesetz ist Gesetz; **be well versed in the** ~: gesetzeskundig *od.* rechtskundig sein; sich gut mit den Gesetzen auskennen; **history of** ~: Rechtsgeschichte, *die*; **laid down by [the]** ~: gesetzlich festgelegt; **under the** *or* **by** *or* **in** ~: nach dem Gesetz; **be/become** ~: vorgeschrieben sein/werden; **one** ~ **for the rich and another for the poor** zweierlei Recht für Reiche und Arme; **his word is** ~ (fig.) sein Wort ist Gesetz; **lay down the** ~ **[about politics]** (fig.) [in Sachen Politik] den Ton angeben; **lay down the** ~ **to sb.** (fig.) jmdm. Vorschriften machen; **point** *or* **issue of** ~: Rechtsfrage, *die* (Rechtsw.); ~ **enforcement** Durchführung der Gesetze/des Gesetzes
2 *no pl., no indef. art.* (control through ~) Gesetz, *das*; ~ **and order** Ruhe und Ordnung; **be above the** ~: über dem Gesetz stehen; **outside the** ~: außerhalb der Legalität
3 (statute) Gesetz, *das*; **what are the** ~**s on drinking and driving?** wie sind die gesetzlichen Bestimmungen bei Trunkenheit am Steuer?; **there ought to be a** ~ **against it/people like you** so etwas sollte/Leute wie du sollten verboten werden; **be a** ~ **unto itself** seinen eigenen Gesetzen folgen; **be a** ~ **unto oneself** machen, was man will; **necessity knows** *or* **has no** ~**[s]** (prov.) Not kennt kein Gebot (Spr.)
4 *no pl., no indef. art.* (litigation) Rechtswesen, *das*; Gerichtswesen, *das*; **go to** ~ **[over sth.]** [wegen etw.] vor Gericht gehen; [wegen etw.] den Rechtsweg beschreiten; **have the** ~ **on sb.** (coll.) jmdm. die Polizei auf den Hals schicken (ugs.) jmdn. vor den Kadi schleppen (ugs.); **take the** ~ **into one's own hands** sich (*Dat.*) selbst Recht verschaffen
5 *no pl., no indef. art.* (profession) **practise** ~: Jurist/Juristin sein; **go into [the]** ~: die juristische Laufbahn einschlagen; Jurist/Juristin werden
6 *no pl., no art.* (Univ.: jurisprudence) Jura *Pl.*; Rechtswissenschaft, *die*; *attrib.* Rechts-; **Faculty of L**~: juristische Fakultät; ~ **school** (Amer.) juristische Fakultät; ~ **student** Jurastudent, *der*/-studentin, *die*
7 *no indef. art.* (branch of ~) **commercial** ~: Handelsrecht, *das*; ~ **of contract** Vertragsrecht, *das*; ~ **of nations** Völkerrecht, *das*; **bachelor/doctor of** ~**s** Bakkalaureus/Doktor der Rechte
8 (Sci., Philos., etc.) Gesetz, *das*; (regularity in nature) Gesetzmäßigkeit, *die*; ~ **of nature, natural** ~ (lit., or fig. iron.) Naturgesetz, *das*; ~ **of supply and demand** Gesetz von Angebot und Nachfrage; ~ **of gravity** *or* **gravitation** Gravitationsgesetz, *das*
9 (rule of game, etiquette, or art) Regel, *die*; ~**s of tennis/chess** Tennis-/Schachregeln
10 (Relig.) Gebot, *das*; Gesetz, *das*; **Divine/God's** ~: göttliche Gebote/Gebote Gottes
11 (enforcing agent) **the** ~: die Rechtsordnung; (coll.: police, policeman) Polente, *die* (salopp); **be in trouble with the** ~: mit dem Gesetz in Konflikt geraten; **I'll set the** ~ **on you!** ich hole die Polizei!; **the long arm of the** ~ (rhet./iron.) der Arm des Gesetzes; **officer of the** ~: Vertreter des Gesetzes

law: ~**-abiding** *adj.* gesetzestreu; ~ **agent** (Scot.) ▸ **solicitor 1**; ~**breaker** *n.* Gesetzesbrecher, *der*/-brecherin, *die*; Rechtsbrecher, *der*/-brecherin, *die*; ~ **court** *n.* Gerichtsgebäude, *das*; (room) Gerichtssaal, *der*; **L**~ **Courts** *n. pl.* (Brit.) *Gebäudekomplex von Gerichtshöfen*; ~ **firm** *n.* (Amer.) Anwaltskanzlei, *die*

lawful /ˈlɔːfl/ *adj.* rechtmäßig, legitim ‹*Besitzer, Erbe*›; legitim, ehelich ‹*Tochter, Sohn, Nachkomme*›; legal, gesetzmäßig ‹*Vorgehen, Maßnahme*›; **by** ~ **means** mit legitimen Mitteln; *see also* **wife**

lawfully /ˈlɔːfəlɪ/ *adv.* legal; auf legalem Weg[e] ‹*erwerben*›

ˈlawgiver *n.* Gesetzgeber, *der*

lawless /ˈlɔːlɪs/ *adj.* **1** gesetzlos **2** (unbridled) zügellos

lawlessness /ˈlɔːlɪsnɪs/ *n., no pl.* Gesetzlosigkeit, *die*

law: **L**~ **Lord** *n.* (Brit.) *Mitglied des obersten brit. Berufungsgerichts*; Law Lord, *der*; ~**maker** *n.* Gesetzgeber, *der*; ~**man** *n.* (Amer.) Vertreter des Gesetzes

> **Law Lords**
>
> Die bis zu elf Mitglieder des britischen **House of Lords**, die mit dem **Lord Chancellor** das oberste Berufungsgericht (*Court of Appeal*) in England und Wales bilden.

lawn /lɔːn/ *n.* (grass) Rasen, *der*; ~**s** Rasenflächen; **area of** ~: Rasenfläche, *die*

lawn: ~ **edger** /ˈlɔːn edʒə(r)/ *n.* Rasenkantenschneider, *der*; ~**mower** *n.* Rasenmäher, *der*; ~ **seed** *n.* Grassamen, *der*; ~ **sprinkler** *n.* Rasensprenger, *der*; ~ **ˈtennis** *n.* Rasentennis, *das*

law: ~ **officer** *n.* **1** Justizbeamte, *der*/Justizbeamtin, *die*; **2** (Brit.: member of Government) Kronanwalt, *der*/Kronanwältin, *die*; ~**suit** *n.* Prozess, *der*

lawyer /ˈlɔːjə(r), ˈlɔɪə(r)/ *n.* ▸ ⓘ **p. 1260** **1** (solicitor etc.) Rechtsanwalt, *der*/Rechtsanwältin, *die* **2** (expert in law) Jurist, *der*/Juristin, *die*

lax /læks/ *adj.* lax; **be** ~ **about hygiene/paying the rent** *etc.* es mit der Hygiene/der Zahlung der Miete *usw.* nicht sehr genau nehmen; **the guards are** ~ **about whom they allow to enter** die Wachen nehmen es nicht so genau damit, wen sie hineinlassen

laxative /ˈlæksətɪv/ (Med.)
A *adj.* abführend; stuhlgangfördernd
B *n.* Abführmittel, *das*; Laxativ[um] *das* (fachspr.)

laxity /ˈlæksɪtɪ/, **laxness** /ˈlæksnɪs/ *ns.* Laxheit, *die*; **moral** ~: laxe Moral

lay[1] /leɪ/ *adj.* **1** (Relig.) laikal; Laien‹*bruder, -schwester, -predigt*›; *see also* **vicar** **2** (inexpert) laienhaft; **in** ~ **opinion** nach Ansicht des Laien; **to the** ~ **mind** für den Nichtfachmann *od.* Laien

lay[2]
A *v.t.*, **laid** /leɪd/ **1** (deposit, put) legen, verlegen ‹*Teppichboden, Rohr, Gleis, Steine, Kabel, Leitung*›; legen ‹*Parkett, Fliesen, Fundament*›; anlegen ‹*Straße, Gehsteig*›; ~ **to rest** (euphem.: bury) zur letzten Ruhe betten (geh. verhüll.); ~ **eyes on sb.** jmdn. sehen *od.* erblicken; *see also* **hand A 1**
2 (fig.) **feel oneself laid under an obligation** sich verpflichtet fühlen; ~ **one's case before sb.** jmdm. seinen Fall vortragen; ~ **one's plans/ideas before sb.** jmdm. seine Pläne/Vorstellungen unterbreiten; **the facts are laid before us** die Fakten liegen vor uns; ~ **sth. before the Commons** *or* **on the table** (Brit. Parl.) etw. dem Unterhaus vorlegen; ~ **damages at £900** (Law) 900 Pfund Schadensersatz fordern
3 (impose) auferlegen ‹*Verantwortung, Verpflichtung, Geldbuße, Steuern*› (**on** *Dat.*); verhängen ‹*Strafe*› (**on** über + *Akk.*); ~ **a penalty/a tax on sth.** etw. mit einer Strafe/einer Steuer belegen; ~ **a burden of responsibility on sb.'s shoulders** jmdm. Verantwortung aufbürden; **that** ~**s an obligation on me to do it** das verpflichtet mich, es zu tun; ~ **weight on sth.** Gewicht auf etw. (*Akk.*) legen
4 (wager) **I'll** ~ **you five to one that …:** ich wette mit dir fünf zu eins, dass …; **I'll** ~ **you £10 that he'll come** ich wette mit dir um 10 Pfund, dass er kommt; ~ **a wager on sth.** eine Wette auf etw. (*Akk.*) abschließen; auf etw. (*Akk.*) wetten
5 (prepare) ~ **the table/cloth** den Tisch decken/die Tischdecke auflegen; ~ **three places for lunch** drei Gedecke zum Mittagessen auflegen; ~ **[for] breakfast,** ~ **the breakfast things** den Frühstückstisch decken; *see also* **fire A 4**
6 (Biol.) legen ‹*Ei*›
7 (apply) auftragen ‹*Farbe usw.*› (**on to, over** auf + *Akk.*); (cover) ~ **a floor with lino** *etc.* einen Boden mit Linoleum *usw.* auslegen
8 (devise) schmieden, ersinnen ‹*Plan*›
9 (bring into a state) ~ **idle** stilllegen ‹*Fabrik*›; ~ **land under water** Land überfluten
10 (cause to subside) glätten ‹*See*›; binden ‹*Staub*›; beruhigen ‹*Sturm*›; (fig.) zerstreuen ‹*Bedenken, Befürchtungen*›; bannen ‹*Geist, Gespenst*›
11 (bring down) ~ **one on sb.** (coll.: hit sb.) jmdm. eine reinschlagen (salopp); **the crops were laid [flat] by the rain** der Regen hat das Getreide zu Boden gedrückt
12 (sl.: copulate with) ~ **a woman** eine Frau vernaschen *od.* aufs Kreuz legen (salopp)
13 (make by twisting) drehen ‹*Seil*›
B *v.i.*, **laid** **1** (Naut.) liegen; ~ **at anchor** vor Anker liegen
2 (used erroneously for 'lie') liegen; ~ **down** sich hinlegen
C *n.* **1** (sl.: sexual partner) **she's a good/an easy** ~: sie ist gut im Bett/steigt mit jedem ins Bett (ugs.)
2 (way sth. lies) Lage, *die*; **the** ~ **of the land** (Amer.) ≈ **the lie of the land** ▸ **lie**[2] **A 1**

Phrasal verbs

- ~ **aˈbout** *v.t.* (coll.) ~ **about sb.** auf jmdn. einschlagen; (scold) jmdn. ausschimpfen; ~ **about one** um sich schlagen; *see also* **layabout**
- ~ **aˈside** *v.t.* beiseite *od.* zur Seite legen, weglegen ‹*angefangene Arbeit*›; (fig.) beilegen ‹*Streit, Differenzen*›; beiseite *od.* auf die Seite legen ‹*Geld*›; ablegen ‹*Gewohnheiten, Untugenden*›
- ~ **ˈback** *v.t.* zurückstellen ‹*Autositz, Behandlungsstuhl*›; *see also* **laid-back**
- ~ **ˈby** *v.t.* beiseite *od.* auf die Seite legen; **have some money laid by** etwas [Geld] auf der hohen Kante haben (ugs.)
- ~ **ˈdown** *v.t.* **1** hinlegen; ~ **sth. down on the table** etw. auf den Tisch legen **2** (give up) niederlegen ‹*Amt, Waffen*›; ablegen ‹*Amtskette*›; (deposit) hinterlegen ‹*Geld*›; (wager) wetten ‹*Betrag*›; ~ **down one's arms** sich ergeben; die Waffen strecken (geh.); ~ **down one's life for sth./sb.** sein Leben für etw./jmdn. [hin]geben **3** (build) bauen; auf Kiel legen ‹*Schiff*› **4** (formulate) festlegen ‹*Regeln, Richtlinien, Bedingungen*›; aufstellen ‹*Grundsätze, Regeln, Norm*›; festsetzen ‹*Preis*›; (in a contract, constitution) verankern; niederlegen **5** ~ **the land/field down to pasture** das Land/Feld in Weideland umwandeln **6** (store) einlagern ‹*Wein*›
- ~ **ˈin** *v.t.* einlagern; sich eindecken mit
- ~ **into** *v.t.* (coll.) ~ **into sb.** auf jmdn. losgehen; über jmdn. herfallen; (fig.) jmdn. zusammenstauchen (ugs.)
- ~ **ˈoff**

A *v.t.* **1** (from work) vorübergehend entlassen; **be laid off [from one's job]** Feierschichten einlegen müssen **2** (coll.) (stop) ~ **off shouting!** hör auf zu schreien!; ~ **off it!** lass das!; hör auf damit!; (stop attacking, lit. or fig.) ~ **off him!** lass ihn in Ruhe!
B *v.i.* (coll.: stop) aufhören. *See also* **lay-off**

- ~ **ˈon** *v.t.* **1** (provide) sorgen für ‹*Getränke, Erfrischungen, Unterhaltung*›; bereitstellen ‹*Auto, Transportmittel*›; organisieren ‹*Theaterbesuch,*

Stadtrundfahrt›; anschließen ‹*Gas, Wasser, Strom*› 2 (apply) auftragen ‹*Farbe usw.*›; ~ **it on** (fig.: exaggerate) dick auftragen (ugs.); *see also* **thick A 1**; **trowel 1** 3 (impose) erheben ‹*Steuer, Gebühr*›; verhängen ‹*Strafe*› 4 **~ing on of hands** (Eccl.) Handauflegung, *die*

• **~ 'out**

A *v.t.* 1 (spread out) ausbreiten; (ready for use) zurechtlegen; **the books were laid out on the table** die Bücher waren *od.* lagen auf dem Tisch ausgebreitet; **~ out sth. for sb. to see** etw. vor jmdm. ausbreiten 2 (for burial) aufbahren 3 (arrange) anlegen ‹*Garten, Park, Wege*›; das Layout machen für ‹*Buch*›; *see also* **layout** 4 (coll.: knock unconscious) **~ sb. out** jmdn. außer Gefecht setzen 5 (spend) ausgeben; investieren (ugs.)

B *v. refl.* **~ oneself out to do sth.** sich anstrengen *od.* (ugs.) sich mächtig ins Zeug legen, etw. zu tun

• **~ 'up** *v.t.* 1 (store) lagern; **you're ~ing up trouble/problems for yourself [later on]** (fig.) du handelst dir [für später] nur Ärger/Schwierigkeiten ein 2 (put out of service) [vorübergehend] aus dem Verkehr ziehen ‹*Fahrzeug*›; (through illness) außer Gefecht setzen; **I was laid up in bed for a week** ich musste eine Woche das Bett hüten

lay³ *n.* 1 (of medieval minstrel) Leich, *der* (Literaturw.) 2 (narrative poem, song) Ballade, *die*

lay⁴ ▸ **lie² B**

lay: ~about *n.* (Brit.) Gammler, *der* (ugs. abwertend); Nichtstuer, *der* (abwertend); **~-by** *n., pl.* **~s** (Brit.) Parkbucht, *die;* Haltebucht, *die;* **~ clerk** *n.* Kantoreisänger, *der*

layer /'leɪə(r)/ *n.* 1 Schicht, *die;* **wear several ~s of clothing** mehrere Kleidungsstücke übereinander tragen; **several ~s of paper** mehrere Lagen Papier; **~ of dust** Staubschicht, *die* 2 (Hort.) Ableger, *der* 3 (poultry) Leg[e]henne, *die;* **this hen is a poor ~:** dieses Huhn legt schlecht

'layer cake *n.* Schichttorte, *die*

layered /'leɪəd/ *adj.* stufig ‹*Haarschnitt*›; **three-~ cake** dreischichtige Torte; **~ skirt** Stufenrock, *der;* **~ clouds** Schichtwolken *Pl.*

layette /leɪ'et/ *n.* **[baby's] ~:** Babyausstattung, *die*

lay: ~ figure *n.* 1 (Art) Gliederpuppe, *die;* 2 (in dramatic work) Phantom, *das;* **~man** /'leɪmən/ *n., pl.* **~men** /'leɪmən/ Laie, *der;* **~-off** *n.* 1 (temporary dismissal) vorübergehende Entlassung; **the ~-offs lasted longer than expected** es mussten länger als erwartet Feierschichten gefahren werden; 2 (Sport; coll.: break from work) Pause, *die;* **take a ~-off** [eine] Pause machen; **~out** *n.* (of house, office) Raumaufteilung, *die;* (of garden, park) Gestaltung, *die;* Anlage, *die;* (of book, magazine, poster, advertisement) Gestaltung, *die;* Layout, *das;* (of letter) äußere Form; **~ reader** *n.: Laie, der Teile des Gottesdienstes halten darf;* ≈ Lektor, *der* (ev. Kirche); ≈ Diakon, *der* (kath. Kirche); **~shaft** *n.* (Mech. Engin.) Vorgelegewelle, *die* (Technik)

laze /leɪz/

A *v.i.* faulenzen; **~ around** *or* **about** herumfaulenzen (ugs.); **spend the whole day lazing in bed** den ganzen Tag faul im Bett liegen

B *v.t.* **~ the day/one's life away** den ganzen Tag/sein ganzes Leben vertrödeln *od.* verbummeln (ugs. abwertend)

lazily /'leɪzɪlɪ/ *adv.* faul; (sluggishly) träge

laziness /'leɪzɪnɪs/ *n., no pl.* Faulheit, *die;* (sluggishness) Trägheit, *die*

lazy /'leɪzɪ/ *adj.* faul; träge ‹*Rhythmus, Musik, Geste, Sprechweise*›; träge fließend ‹*Fluss*›; **physically ~:** träge; **mentally ~:** geistig träge; denkfaul; **have a ~ day on the beach** einen Tag am Strand faulenzen; **be in a ~ mood** sich träge fühlen; **be ~ about writing [letters]** schreibfaul sein

lazy: ~bones *n. sing.* Faulpelz, *der;* **~ 'eye** *n.: Auge mit Sehschwäche, das [beim Schielen] weniger belastet wird und deshalb in der Sehkraft weiter nachlässt*

lb. *abbr.* ▸ ℹ **p. 1702 = pound[s]** ≈ Pfd.

l.b.w. /elbi:'dʌblju/ *abbr.* (Cricket) **= leg before wicket**

LCD *abbr.* **= liquid crystal display** LCD

L/Cpl. *abbr.* **= Lance-Corporal** OG

L-driver /'eldraɪvə(r)/ (Brit.) ▸ **learner driver**

> **L-driver - learner driver**
>
> Eine Person in Großbritannien, die Auto- oder Motorradfahren lernt, indem sie schon vor dem Erwerb eines entsprechenden Führerscheins als Lenker oder Lenkerin eines Kraftfahrzeugs am öffentlichen Straßenverkehr teilnimmt. *L-drivers* müssen von einer Person begleitet werden, die eine gültige *driving licence* (Führerschein) besitzt und müssen so lange *L-plates* vorne und hinten am Auto haben, bis sie ihren *driving test* (Führerscheinprüfung) bestanden haben. *L-plates* sind viereckige weiße Schilder mit einem roten 'L'.

lea /li:/ *n.* (poet.) Wiese, *die*

LEA *abbr.* **= Local Education Authority** ≈ Schulamt, *das*

leach /li:tʃ/

A *v.t.* (make percolate) durchsickern lassen; (subject to percolation) auslaugen; (remove by percolation) extrahieren; auslaugen

B *v.i.* (percolate through) durchsickern; (be removed by percolation) ausgelaugt werden

lead¹ /led/

A *n.* 1 (metal) Blei, *das;* **white ~:** Bleiweiß, *das;* **[as] heavy as ~:** schwer wie Blei; bleischwer; **go down like a ~ balloon** mit Pauken und Trompeten durchfallen (ugs.); ‹*Rede, Vorschlag usw.:*› überhaupt nicht ankommen; *see also* **blacklead**; **red lead** 2 (in pencil) [Bleistift]mine, *die* 3 (bullets) Blei, *das* (veralt.); **I'll fill** *or* **pump you full of ~:** ich pumpe dich mit Blei voll 4 (Naut.) Lot, *das;* Senkblei, *das;* **cast** *or* **heave the ~:** das Lot [aus]werfen; **swing the ~** (fig. Brit. coll.) sich drücken 5 *in pl.* (of window) Bleifassung, *die* 6 (Printing) Reglette, *die*

B *attrib. adj.* Blei-

C *v.t.* 1 in Blei fassen ‹*Fenster*›; **~ed** bleigefasst 2 **~ed petrol** bleihaltiges Benzin

lead² /li:d/

A *v.t.,* **led** /led/ 1 führen; **~ sb. a miserable life** *or* **existence** jmdm. das Leben zur Qual machen; **~ sb. through the procedures** (fig.) jmdn. mit dem Verfahren vertraut machen; **~ sb. to do sth.** (fig.) jmdn. dazu bringen, etw. zu tun; **~ sb. by the hand** jmdn. an der Hand führen; **~ sb. by the nose** (fig.) jmdn. nach seiner Pfeife tanzen lassen; **let oneself be led by the nose** (fig.) sich an der Nase herumführen lassen; **~ sb. into trouble/difficulties** (fig.) jmdm. Ärger einbringen/jmdn. in Schwierigkeiten bringen; **this is ~ing us nowhere** (fig.) das führt zu nichts; *see also* **astray A**; **dance C 1**; **garden A 1**; **way A 2**

2 (fig.: influence, induce) **~ sb. to do sth.** jmdn. veranlassen, etw. zu tun; **be easily led** sich leicht beeinflussen lassen; **~ sb. into bad habits** jmdn. zu schlechten Gewohnheiten verleiten; **children are easier led than driven** bei Kindern erreicht man im Guten mehr als im Bösen; **that ~s me to believe that ...:** das lässt mich glauben, dass ...; **I was led to the conclusion that ...:** ich gelangte zu dem Schluss, dass ...; **this ~s me to the conclusion that ...:** daraus schließe ich, dass ...; **Is it true that she was married before? — So I am led to believe** Stimmt es, dass sie schon einmal verheiratet war? — Soweit ich weiß, ja; **he led me to suppose/believe that ...:** er gab mir Grund zu der Annahme/er machte mich glauben, dass ...

3 führen ‹*Leben*›; **~ a life of misery/a wretched existence** ein erbärmliches Dasein führen/eine kümmerliche Existenz fristen

4 (be first in) anführen; **~ the world in electrical engineering** auf dem Gebiet der Elektrotechnik in der ganzen Welt führend sein; **Smith led Jones by several yards/seconds** (Sport) Smith hatte mehrere Yards/Sekunden Vorsprung vor Jones; *see also* **field A 9**

5 (direct, be head of) anführen ‹*Bewegung, Abordnung*›; leiten ‹*Diskussion, Veranstaltung, Ensemble*›; ‹*Dirigent:*› leiten ‹*Orchester, Chor*›; ‹*Konzertmeister:*› führen ‹*Orchester*›; **~ a party** Vorsitzender/Vorsitzende einer Partei sein; **~ the government** an der Spitze der Regierung stehen; Regierungschef/-chefin sein; **Napoleon led his army into Italy/to a great victory** Napoleon führte seine Armee nach Italien/zu einem großen Sieg

6 (cause to pass) **~ water through sth.** Wasser durch etw. [hindurch]leiten; **~ a rope through a pulley** ein Seil über die Rolle[n] eines Flaschenzugs führen

7 (Cards) ausspielen; **~ a spade** Pik ausspielen

B *v.i.,* **led** 1 ‹*Straße usw., Tür:*› führen; **~ to the town/to the sea/out of the town** zur Stadt/ans Meer/aus der Stadt führen; **~ to confusion** Verwirrung stiften; **one thing led to another** es kam eins zum anderen; **what will it all ~ to?** wo soll das alles [noch] hinführen?

2 (be first) führen; (go in front) vorangehen; (fig.: be leader) an der Spitze stehen; **~ by 3 metres** mit 3 Metern in Führung liegen; 3 Meter Vorsprung haben; **~ in the race** das Rennen anführen; **it's Smith ~ing from Jones and Brown** Smith führt vor Jones und Brown

3 (Journ.) **a good story to ~ with** eine gute Titelgeschichte; **~ with the latest spy scandal** die jüngste Spionageaffäre groß herausbringen

4 (Cards) ausspielen; **~ with a spade** Pik ausspielen

C *n.* 1 (precedent) Beispiel, *das;* (clue) Anhaltspunkt, *der;* **follow sb.'s ~, take one's ~ from sb.** jmds. Beispiel (*Dat.*) folgen; **give sb. a ~** (precedent) jmdm. mit gutem Beispiel vorangehen; (clue) jmdm. einen Anhaltspunkt geben

2 (first place) Führung, *die;* **be in the ~:** in Führung liegen; an der Spitze liegen; **move** *or* **go into the ~:** sich an die Spitze setzen; in Führung gehen; **keep one's ~:** sich an der Spitze *od.* seine Führungsposition behaupten; **we mustn't lose our ~:** wir dürfen unsere Führungsposition nicht verlieren; **hold the ~ in export sales** mit seinen Exportgeschäften die Spitze halten; **take the ~ from sb.** jmdm. den Rang ablaufen; (in race) sich vor jmdm. an die Spitze setzen; vor jmdm. in Führung gehen

3 (amount) Vorsprung, *der;* **have a ~ of two metres/minutes over sb.** einen Vorsprung von zwei Metern/Minuten vor jmdm. haben

4 (on dog etc.) Leine, *die;* **on a ~:** an der Leine; **let a dog off the** *or* **its ~:** einen Hund von der Leine losmachen; **put a dog on the ~:** einen Hund anleinen

5 (Electr.) Kabel, *das;* Leitung, *die*

6 (Theatre) Hauptrolle, *die;* (player) Hauptdarsteller, *der*/-darstellerin, *die*

7 (Cards) **whose ~ is it?** wer spielt aus?; **the ~ was the jack of clubs** Kreuzbube war gespielt

D *adj.* Lead‹*gitarre, -gitarrist usw.*›

Phrasal verbs

• **~ a'way** *v.t.* abführen ‹*Gefangenen, Verbrecher*›

• **~ 'off**

A *v.t.* 1 (take away) abführen 2 (begin) beginnen

B *v.i.* beginnen

• **~ 'on**

A *v.t.* 1 (entice) **~ sb. on** jmdn. reizen; **he's ~ing you on** er versucht, dich zu reizen 2 (deceive) auf den Leim führen (ugs.); **she's just ~ing him on** sie hält ihn nur zum Narren 3 (take further) **that ~s me on to my next point** das bringt mich zu meinem nächsten Punkt; **~ sb. on to do sth.** jmdn. darauf bringen, etw. zu tun

B *v.i.* 1 *imper.* (go first) **~ on!** geh vor! 2 **~ing on from what you have just said, ...:** um fortzuführen, was Sie eben sagten, ...; **~ on to the next topic** *etc.* zum nächsten Thema *usw.* führen; **~ on to better things** jmdn. weiterbringen

• **~ 'up to** *v.t.* [schließlich] führen zu; (aim at) hinauswollen auf (+ *Akk.*); **~ up to a very funny punch line** in einer köstlichen Pointe gipfeln; **just as I was ~ing up to the main point of my speech** gerade als ich zum Hauptpunkt meiner Rede kommen wollte

leaden /'ledn/ *adj.* 1 bleiern 2 (fig.) (heavy) bleiern ‹*Schlaf, Augenlider, Glieder*›; schleppend ‹*Tempo*›; bang ‹*Herz*›; (oppressive) drückend

‹*Atmosphäre*›; lähmend ‹*Einfluss*›; starr ‹*Regeln, Haltung*›

leader /ˈliːdə(r)/ *n.* [1] Führer, *der*/Führerin, *die;* (of political party) Vorsitzende, *der/die;* (of gang, hooligans, rebels) Anführer, *der*/Anführerin, *die;* (of expedition, project, troupe) Leiter, *der*/Leiterin, *die;* (of deputation) Sprecher, *der*/Sprecherin, *die;* (of tribe) [Stammes]häuptling, *der;* Stammesführer, *der;* **the Egyptian/Labour ~:** der ägyptische Präsident/der Vorsitzende der Labour Party; **union/the Labour ~s** Gewerkschaftsvorsitzende/die Führenden der Labour Party; **L~ of the House of Commons/Lords** (Brit. Polit.) Führer des Unterhauses/Oberhauses; **have the qualities of a ~:** Führungsqualitäten haben; *see also* **follow-my-leader** [2] (one who is first) **this scientist is a ~ in his field** dieser Wissenschaftler ist eine führende Kapazität auf seinem Gebiet; **be the ~ in a race** in einem Rennen in Führung liegen; **catch up with the ~s** (in race) sich an die Spitze des Feldes vorarbeiten; **be no longer amongst the ~s of world tennis** nicht mehr zur internationalen Spitze[nklasse] im Tennis gehören [3] (Brit. Journ.) Leitartikel, *der* [4] (tab on film or tape) Startband, *das* [5] (Mus.) (leading performer) Leader, *der*/Leaderin, *die;* (Brit.: principal first violinist) Konzertmeister, *der*/-meisterin, *die;* (Amer.: conductor) Dirigent, *der*/Dirigentin, *die* [6] (Hort.) Haupttrieb, *der*

ˈleader board *n.* Anzeigetafel, *die*

leaderless /ˈliːdəlɪs/ *adj.* führerlos

leadership /ˈliːdəʃɪp/ *n.* [1] Führung, *die;* (capacity to lead) Führungseigenschaften *Pl.;* **under the ~ of** unter [der] Führung von [2] (leaders) Führung[sspitze], *die;* **~ of the party** Parteivorsitz, *der*

ˈleader writer *n.* Leitartikelschreiber, *der*/-schreiberin, *die;* Leitartikler, *der*/-artiklerin, *die* (Pressejargon)

lead-free /ˈledfriː/ *adj.* bleifrei

lead-in /ˈliːdɪn/ *n.* Einleitung, *die* (**to** *Gen.*); **as a ~ to the film/programme** zur Einleitung des Films/Programms

leading /ˈliːdɪŋ/ *adj.* führend; (in first position) ‹*Läufer, Pferd, Auto*› an der Spitze; **~ role** Hauptrolle, *die;* (fig.) führende Rolle

leading: ~ ˈarticle *n.* (Brit. Journ.) Leitartikel, *der;* **~ ˈcounsel** *n.* (Brit. Law) Kronanwalt, *der*/-anwältin, *die;* (of the defence) Hauptverteidiger, *der*/-verteidigerin, *die;* **~ ˈedge** *n.* (foremost edge) Vorderkante, *die;* (of sail) Vorliek, *das;* **~ ˈlady** *n.* Hauptdarstellerin, *die;* **his ~ lady** seine Partnerin (*als Hauptdarstellerin*); **~ ˈlight** *n.* herausragende Persönlichkeit; (expert) führende Kapazität; **~ ˈman** *n.* Hauptdarsteller, *der;* **her ~ man** ihr Partner (*als Hauptdarsteller*); **~ ˈquestion** *n.* Suggestivfrage, *die;* **~ rein** *n.* Leitzügel, *der*

lead: ~ pencil /led ˈpensl/ *n.* Bleistift, *der;* **~ poisoning** /ˈled pɔɪzənɪŋ/ *n.* Bleivergiftung, *die;* **~ screw** /ˈliːd skruː/ *n.* Leitspindel, *die* (Technik); **~ shot** /led ˈʃɒt/ *n.* [1] *no pl.* (Angling) Bleikugeln *Pl.;* [2] *no pl.* (for shotgun) Schrot, *der od. das;* [3] (single projectile) Blei- *od.* Schrotkugel, *die;* **~ singer** /liːd ˈsɪŋə(r)/ *n.* Leadsänger *der*/-sängerin, *die;* **~ story** /ˈliːd stɔːrɪ/ *n.* (Journ.) Titelgeschichte, *die;* **~ time** /ˈliːd taɪm/ *n.* (Econ.) Entwicklungszeit, *die;* **~-up** /ˈliːdʌp/ *n.* Vorfeld, *das* (fig.); **in/during the ~-up to the election/revolution** im Vorfeld der Wahlen/der Revolution

leaf /liːf/

A *n., pl.* **leaves** /liːvz/ [1] Blatt, *das;* **the falling leaves** die fallenden Blätter; das fallende Laub; **shake like a ~:** zittern wie Espenlaub; **be in ~:** grün sein; **come into ~:** grün werden; ausschlagen [2] (of paper) Blatt, *das;* **a ~ of paper** ein Blatt Papier; **turn over a new ~** (fig.) einen neuen Anfang machen; sich ändern; *see also* **book A 1** [3] (of door) Flügel, *der;* (of table) (hinged/sliding flap) Platte, *die;* (for inserting) Einlegebrett, *das*

B *v.i.* **~ through sth.** etw. durchblättern; in etw. (*Dat.*) blättern

leaf: ~ green A /ˈ--/ *adj.* laubgrün; **B** /-ˈ-/ *n.* Laubgrün, *das;* **~ insect** *n.* Wandelndes Blatt

leafless /ˈliːflɪs/ *adj.* blattlos, kahl ‹*Baum*›

leaflet /ˈliːflɪt/

A *n.* [1] [Hand]zettel, *der;* (with manufacturer's instructions) Gebrauchsanweisung, *die;* Bedienungsanleitung, *die;* (advertising) Reklamezettel, *der;* (political) Flugblatt, *das* [2] (Bot.) Blättchen, *das*

B *v.t.* [Hand]zettel verteilen an (+ *Akk.*)

leaf: ~ mould *n.* Laubkompost, *der;* **~ spring** *n.* (Mech. Engin.) Blattfeder, *die* (Technik); **~-stalk** *n.* Blattstiel, *der*

leafy /ˈliːfɪ/ *adj.* belaubt; **~ vegetable** Blattgemüse, *das;* **a ~ country lane** eine baumbestandene Landstraße

league[1] /liːg/ *n.* [1] (agreement) Bündnis, *das;* Bund, *der;* (in history) Liga, *die;* **enter into** *or* **form a ~:** ein Bündnis eingehen *od.* schließen; einen Bund schließen; **be in ~ with sb.** mit jmdm. im Bunde sein *od.* stehen; **those two are in ~ [together]** die beiden stecken unter einer Decke (ugs.) [2] (Sport) Liga, *die;* **the ~ championship** die Ligameisterschaft; **I am not in his ~, he is out of my ~** (fig.) ich komme nicht an ihn heran; mit ihm kann ich mich nicht messen; **be in the big ~** (fig.) es geschafft haben; *see also* **Rugby League**

league[2] *n.* (arch.: distance) ≈ drei Meilen; **travel many a ~:** viele Meilen reisen

league: ~ ˈfootball *n.* Ligafußball, *der;* **~ game** *n.* Ligaspiel, *das;* **~ ˈleaders** *n. pl.* (Sport) Tabellenführer, *der;* **~ ˈmatch** *n.* Ligaspiel, *das;* **L~ of ˈNations** *n.* (Hist.) Völkerbund, *der;* **~ table** *n.* Tabelle, *die* (Sport); **be at the top/bottom of the ~ table** an der Tabellenspitze/am Tabellenende sein (fig.); an der Spitze rangieren/das Schlusslicht bilden (ugs.) (**of** unter + *Dat.*)

leak /liːk/

A *n.* [1] (hole) Leck, *das;* (in roof, ceiling, tent) undichte Stelle; **there's a ~ in the tank** der Tank ist leck; der Tank hat ein Leck; **spring a ~** ‹*Schiff:*› leckschlagen (Seemannsspr.); ‹*Gas-, Flüssigkeitsbehälter:*› ein Leck bekommen; **stop the ~:** das Leck abdichten *od.* stopfen [2] (escaping fluid/gas) durch ein Leck austretende Flüssigkeit/austretendes Gas; **I can smell a gas ~:** hier riecht es nach Gas [3] (instance) **a gas/oil ~, a ~ of gas/oil** ein Austreten von Gas/Öl; **there has been a gas/oil ~:** es ist Gas/Öl ausgetreten [4] (fig.: of information) undichte Stelle; **government ~s** undichte Stellen in der Regierung; **there has been a ~ to the press/from reliable sources** der Presse sind Informationen zugespielt worden/aus verlässlichen Quellen sind Informationen durchgesickert; **who was responsible for the ~?** wer war dafür verantwortlich, dass Informationen durchgesickert sind? [5] (Electr.) Elektrizitätsverlust, *der;* (path or point) Fehlerstelle, *die* [6] **have a/go for a ~** (sl.) pinkeln/pinkeln gehen (salopp)

B *v.t.* [1] austreten lassen; **the pipe is ~ing water/gas** aus dem lecken Rohr tritt Wasser/Gas aus [2] (fig.: disclose) durchsickern lassen; **~ sth. to sb.** jmdm. etw. zuspielen; **details of the plan have been ~ed** man hat Einzelheiten des Plans durchsickern lassen

C *v.i.* [1] (escape) austreten (**from** aus); (enter) eindringen (**in** in + *Akk.*) [2] ‹*Fass, Tank, Schiff:*› lecken; ‹*Rohr, Leitung, Dach:*› undicht sein; ‹*Gefäß, Füller:*› auslaufen; **the roof ~s** es regnet durch das Dach [3] (fig.) **~ [out]** durchsickern

leakage /ˈliːkɪdʒ/ *n.* [1] Auslaufen, *das;* (of fluid, gas) Ausströmen, *das;* (fig.: of information) Durchsickern, *das* [2] (substance, amount) **the ~ is increasing** das Leck wird größer; **mop up the ~:** das ausgelaufene Wasser *usw.* aufwischen; **~ to the Press** (fig.) Indiskretionen der Presse gegenüber

leaky /ˈliːkɪ/ *adj.* undicht; leck ‹*Schiff, Boot, Tank*›

lean[1] /liːn/

A *adj.* [1] mager; hager ‹*Person, Gesicht*›; **we had a ~ time [of it] during the War** es ging uns sehr schlecht während des Krieges [2] (Commerc.) schlank

B *n.* (meat) Magere, *das*

lean[2]

A *v.i.*, **~ed** /liːnd, lent/ *or* (Brit.) **~t** /lent/ [1] sich beugen; **~ against the door** sich gegen die Tür lehnen; **~ out of the window** sich aus dem Fenster lehnen *od.* beugen; **~ down/forward** sich herab-/vorbeugen; **~ backwards** sich zurückbeugen; sich nach hinten beugen; **~ back in one's chair** sich im Sessel zurücklehnen [2] (support oneself) **~ against/on sth.** sich gegen/an etw. (*Akk.*) lehnen; **~ on sth.** (from above) sich auf etw. (*Akk.*) lehnen; **~ on sb.'s arm** sich auf jmds. Arm (*Akk.*) stützen [3] (be supported) lehnen (**against** an + *Dat.*) [4] (fig.: rely) **~ [up]on sb.** auf jmdn. bauen; **I ~ on my friends for moral support** ich baue auf den Beistand meiner Freunde [5] (stand obliquely) sich neigen; **the Leaning Tower of Pisa** der Schiefe Turm von Pisa [6] (fig.: tend) **~ to[wards] sth.** zu etw. neigen; **he ~s to the left politically** er tendiert politisch nach links

B *v.t.*, **~ed** *or* (Brit.) **~t** lehnen (**against** gegen *od.* an + *Akk.*)

C *n.* Neigung, *die;* **have a definite ~ to the right** deutlich nach rechts geneigt sein; eine deutliche Neigung nach rechts aufweisen; **be on the ~:** schief sein; **have a ~ of 15°** einen Neigungswinkel von 15° haben

(Phrasal verbs)

- **~ on** *v.t.* (fig. coll.) unter Druck setzen; **he just needs ~ing on a little** man muss ihm nur ein bisschen gut zureden (iron.); *see also* **~[2] A 2, 4**
- **~ over**

A /ˈ---/ *v.t.* sich neigen über (+ *Akk.*)

B /-ˈ--/ *v.i.* ‹*Person:*› sich hinüberbeugen; (forwards) sich vorbeugen; ‹*Gegenstand:*› sich neigen; **he ~ed over backwards/sideways** er beugte sich nach hinten/zur Seite; *see also* **backwards 1**

lean-burn ˈengine *n.* (Motor Veh.) Mager[mix-]motor, *der*

leaning /ˈliːnɪŋ/ *n.* Hang, *der;* Neigung, *die;* **have Marxist/homosexual ~s** zum Marxismus tendieren/homosexuelle Neigungen haben

leanness /ˈliːnnɪs/ *n., no pl.* Hagerkeit, *die;* (of times) Dürftigkeit, *die*

leant ▸ **lean**[2]

lean-to /ˈliːntuː/ *n., pl.* **~s** Anbau, *der*

leap /liːp/

A *v.i.*, **~ed** /liːpt, lept/ *or* **~t** /lept/ [1] springen; ‹*Herz:*› hüpfen; **~ to one's feet** aufspringen; **~ out of/up from one's chair** aus seinem Sessel/von seinem Stuhl aufspringen; **~ down off the table** vom Tisch herunterspringen; **~ back in shock** vor Entsetzen zurückspringen; **~ up and down in excitement** aufgeregt herumspringen; **~ around** *or* **about** herumspringen [2] (fig.) **~ to conclusions** voreilige Schlüsse ziehen; **~ to sb.'s defence** jmdm. beispringen (geh.); **~ at the chance** *or* **opportunity** die Gelegenheit beim Schopf packen; **~ to stardom/into prominence** mit einem Schlag zum Star/berühmt werden; **~ at an offer** sofort zugreifen; **~ to the eye** ins Auge *od.* in die Augen springen. *See also* **look A 1**

B *v.t.*, **~ed** *or* **~t** [1] (jump over) überspringen; springen *od.* setzen über (+ *Akk.*) [2] (cause to ~) springen lassen

C *n.* Sprung, *der;* **take a [great] ~ at the fence** [mit einem großen Satz] am Zaun hochspringen; (successfully) einen [großen] Satz über den Zaun machen; **with** *or* **in one ~:** mit einem Satz; **by ~s and bounds** (fig.) mit Riesenschritten ‹*vorangehen*›; sprunghaft ‹*zunehmen*›; *see also* **dark B 3**

ˈleapfrog

A *n.* Bockspringen, *das*

B *v.i.*, **-gg-** Bockspringen machen; **~ over sb.** einen Bocksprung über jmdn. machen

C *v.t.*, **-gg-** (fig.) überspringen

leapt ▸ **leap**

ˈleap year *n.* Schaltjahr, *das*

learn /lɜːn/

A *v.t.*, **~t** /lɜːnt/ *or* **~ed** /lɜːnd, lɜːnt/ [1] lernen; (with emphasis on completeness of result) erlernen; **~ sth. by** *or* **from experience** etw. durch [die] *od.* aus der Erfahrung lernen; **~ sth. from** *or* **of sb./from a book/an example** etw. von jmdm./aus einem Buch/am Beispiel lernen; **~ one's craft from** *or* **through hard study** seine beruflichen Fähigkeiten durch fleißiges Lernen erwerben; **have you never ~ed any manners/sense?** hat man dir keine Manieren beigebracht/wo hast du nur deinen Verstand?; **I am ~ing [how] to play tennis** ich lerne Tennis spielen; **Can you swim? — No, I never ~ed how [to]** Kannst du schwimmen? — Nein, ich habe es nie gelernt; *see also* **lesson 3**; **rope A 5** [2] (find out) erfahren; lernen; (by oral information) hören; (by observation) erkennen; merken; (by thought) erkennen; (be informed of) erfahren; **I ~ed from the newspaper that ...:** ich habe in der Zeitung gelesen *od.* aus der Zeitung erfahren, dass ...; **I ~ed from his manner what sort of person he was** seine Art verriet mir, was für ein Mensch er war [3] (arch./joc./uneducated: teach) lernen (+ *Dat.*) (mundartl., ugs. [standardsprachlich nicht korrekt]); **that'll ~ you!** das wird dir 'ne Lehre sein!; **I'll ~ you!** (threat) ich werd dir helfen! (ugs.)

B *v.i.*, **~t** *or* **~ed** [1] lernen; **be slow to ~:** langsam lernen; **you'll soon ~:** du wirst es bald lernen; **will you never ~?** du lernst es wohl nie!; **~ from the experience/mistakes of others** aus den Erfahrungen/Fehlern anderer lernen; **some people never ~:** mancher lernts nie; **~ by one's mistakes** aus seinen Fehlern lernen; **I had to ~ by my mistakes** ich konnte nur aus meinen eigenen Fehlern lernen; **~ about sth.** etwas über etw. (*Akk.*) lernen; **you're never too old** *or* **it's never too late to ~:** man kann immer noch [etwas] dazulernen; zum Lernen ist es nie zu spät [2] (get to know) erfahren (**of** von); **I have ~t about what you get up to** ich habe erfahren, was du so treibst

Phrasal verb

• **~ 'up** *v.t.* [1] **~ up some law** sich (*Dat.*) einige juristische Kenntnisse aneignen; einiges über das Rechtswesen lernen [2] (refresh knowledge of) **~ up one's history** seine Geschichtskenntnisse auffrischen

learned /'lɜːnɪd/ *adj.* [1] gelehrt; **very ~ in ancient history** in Alter Geschichte sehr bewandert [2] (associated with ~ persons) wissenschaftlich ‹*Gesellschaft, Zeitschrift*›; akademisch ‹*Stil*›; *see also* **profession 1** [3] (Brit. Law: in address or reference) verehrt; geschätzt; **my ~ colleague** *etc.* mein verehrter Herr Kollege/meine verehrte Frau Kollegin *usw.*; *see also* **friend 4**

learnedly /'lɜːnɪdlɪ/ *adv.* gelehrt

learner /'lɜːnə(r)/ *n.* Lernende, *der/die;* (beginner) Anfänger, *der*/Anfängerin, *die;* **be a slow/quick ~:** langsam/schnell lernen; **the car is driven by a ~:** ein Fahrschüler steuert den Wagen; **I'm only a ~ still** ich lerne noch

learner 'driver *n.* (Brit.) Fahrschüler/-schülerin (*der/die unter Aufsicht fährt*)

learning /'lɜːnɪŋ/ *n.* (scholarship) Wissen, *das;* (of person) Gelehrsamkeit, *die;* **the new ~:** der Humanismus

learning: L~ and 'Skills Council *n.* (Brit.) Beirat für Bildung und Qualifikationserwerb; **~ curve** *n.* Lernkurve, *die;* **~ difficulties** *n. pl.* Lernschwierigkeiten *Pl.*; **~ disability** *n.* Lernbehinderung, *die;* **~ resources centre** *n.* Lernmittelzentrum, *das;* **~ support teacher** *n.* (Brit. Educ.) Stützlehrer, *der*/-lehrerin, *die*

learnt ▸ **learn**

lease /liːs/

A *n.* (of land, business premises) Pachtvertrag, *der;* (of house, flat, office) Mietvertrag, *der;* **be on [a] ~:** gepachtet/gemietet sein; **have sth. on a 99-year** *etc.* **~:** etw. auf 99 Jahre *usw.* gepachtet/gemietet haben; **take a ~ on** pachten ‹*Grundstück, Geschäft*›; mieten ‹*Haus, Wohnung, Büro*›; **enjoy a new ~ of** *or* (Amer.) **on life** neuen Auftrieb bekommen; **give sb./sth. a new ~ of life** jmdm. Auftrieb geben/etw. wieder in Schuss bringen (ugs.)

B *v.t.* [1] (grant ~ on) verpachten ‹*Grundstück, Geschäft, Rechte*›; vermieten ‹*Haus, Wohnung, Büro*› [2] (take ~ on) pachten ‹*Grundstück, Geschäft, Rechte*›; mieten ‹*Haus, Wohnung, Büro*›; leasen ‹*Auto*›

lease: ~back *n.* Verpachtung an den Verkäufer; **~hold** ▸ **lease B**: **A** *n.* **have the ~hold of** *or* **on sth.** etw. gepachtet *od.* in Pacht/gemietet haben; **B** *adj.* gepachtet/gemietet; **C** *adv.* **own a property ~hold** einen Besitz in Pacht/gemietet haben; **~holder** *n.* ▸ **lease B**: Pächter, *der*/Pächterin, *die;* Mieter, *der*/Mieterin, *die*

leash /liːʃ/ *n.* [1] ▸ **lead² C 4** [2] **be straining at the ~ to do sth.** (fig.) darauf brennen, etw. zu tun; **he was straining at the ~:** er war voller Ungeduld

least /liːst/

A *adj.* [1] (smallest) kleinst...; (in quantity) wenigst...; (in status) geringst...; **be ~ in size** am kleinsten sein; **every ~ indication** jedes noch so geringe Anzeichen; **I haven't the ~ idea** ich habe nicht die geringste Ahnung; **not the ~ bit hungry** kein bisschen hungrig; **that's the ~ of our problems** das ist unser geringstes Problem; *see also* **common denominator**; **common multiple**; **last¹ A**; **resistance 1** [2] (Bot., Ornith., Zool.) Zwerg-

B *n.* Geringste, *das;* **the ~ I can do** das Mindeste, was ich tun kann; **the ~ he could do would be to apologize** er könnte sich wenigstens entschuldigen; **pay the ~:** den niedrigsten Preis zahlen; **to say the ~ [of it]** gelinde gesagt; **~ said, soonest mended** (prov.) vieles Reden macht die Sache nur schlimmer; **at ~:** mindestens; (if nothing more; anyway) wenigstens; **at the [very] ~:** [aller]mindestens; **not [in] the ~:** nicht im Geringsten

C *adv.* am wenigsten; **not ~ because ...:** nicht zuletzt deshalb, weil ...; **~ of all** am allerwenigsten; **the ~ likely answer** die unwahrscheinlichste Lösung

leastways /'liːstweɪz/, **leastwise** /'liːstwaɪz/ *adv.* (dial.) wenigstens

leather /'leðə(r)/

A *n.* [1] Leder, *das;* (things made of ~) Lederwaren *Pl.*; **these shoes are genuine ~:** diese Schuhe sind echt Leder *od.* aus echtem Leder; *see also* **chamois 2**; **hell 2**; **patent leather** [2] (used for polishing) Leder, *das;* Lederlappen, *der* [3] (strap) Lederriemen, *der;* (for stirrup) Steigriemen, *der*

B *adj.* ledern; Leder‹*jacke, -mantel, -handschuh*›

C *v.t.* [1] (polish) [ab]ledern [2] (thrash, whip) **~ sb.** jmdm. das Leder gerben

'leatherjacket *n.* (Brit. Zool.) Schnakenlarve, *die*

leathery /'leðərɪ/ *adj.* ledern

leave¹ /liːv/ *n., no pl.* [1] (permission) Erlaubnis, *die;* (official approval) Genehmigung, *die;* **grant** *or* **give sb. ~ to do sth.** jmdm. gestatten, etw. zu tun; **beg ~ to do sth.** um Erlaubnis bitten, etw. tun zu dürfen; **be absent without ~:** sich unerlaubt entfernt haben; **get ~ from sb. to do sth.** von jmdm. die Erlaubnis bekommen, etw. zu tun; **by ~ of sb.** mit jmds. Genehmigung; **by your ~** (formal) mit Ihrer Erlaubnis; (iron.) mit Ihrer gütigen Erlaubnis (iron.); **without so much as a by your ~** (coll.) ohne auch nur zu fragen; **take ~ to do sth.** sich (*Dat.*) erlauben, etw. zu tun [2] (from duty or work) Urlaub, *der;* **~ [of absence]** Beurlaubung, *die;* Urlaub, *der* (auch Mil.); **a fortnight's ~:** vierzehn Tage Urlaub; **book one's ~:** seinen Urlaub anmelden; **when do you intend to go on ~?** wann nehmen Sie Ihren *od.* gehen Sie in Urlaub?; **I've got ~ [of absence] for a couple of days** ich bin für einige Tage beurlaubt; **be on ~:** Urlaub haben; in Urlaub sein [3] **take one's ~** (say farewell) sich verabschieden; Abschied nehmen (geh.); **take [one's] ~ of sb.** sich von jmdm. verabschieden; von jmdm. Abschied nehmen (geh.); **have you taken ~ of your senses?** bist du noch bei Sinnen?; **he must have taken ~ of his senses** er muss von Sinnen sein. *See also* **French leave**; **sick leave**

leave² *v.t.*, **left** /left/ [1] (make or let remain, lit. or fig.) hinterlassen; **may I ~ my dog/son with you?** kann ich meinen Hund/Sohn bei dir lassen?; **he left a message with me for Mary** er hat bei mir eine Nachricht für Mary hinterlassen; **~ sb. to do sth.** es jmdm. überlassen, etw. zu tun; **I am always left to make the decisions** ich muss immer alles entscheiden; **if he likes the work, ~ him to get on with it** wenn ihm die Arbeit Spaß macht, überlässt du ihn am besten sich (*Dat.*) selbst; **~ be** (coll.) sich raushalten (ugs.); **6 from 10 ~s 4** 10 weniger 6 ist 4; (in will) **~ sb. sth.**, **~ sth. to sb.** jmdm. etw. hinterlassen; *see also* **desire B 3** [2] (by mistake) vergessen; **I left my gloves in your car/my umbrella at the butcher's** ich habe meine Handschuhe in deinem Auto liegen lassen *od.* vergessen/meinen Schirm beim Fleischer stehen lassen *od.* vergessen [3] **be left with** nicht loswerden ‹*Gefühl, Verdacht*›; übrig behalten ‹*Geld*›; zurückbleiben mit ‹*Schulden, Kind*›; **I was left with the job/task of clearing up** es blieb mir überlassen, aufzuräumen [4] (refrain from doing, using, etc., let remain undisturbed) stehen lassen ‹*Abwasch, Essen*›; sich (*Dat.*) entgehen lassen ‹*Gelegenheit*›; (spare) verschonen [5] (let remain in given state) lassen; **~ the door open/the light on** die Tür offen lassen/das Licht anlassen; **~ the curtains drawn/the water running** die Vorhänge zugezogen lassen/das Wasser laufen lassen; **~ the book lying on the table** das Buch auf dem Tisch liegen lassen; **~ sb. in the dark** (fig.) jmdn. im Dunkeln lassen; **~ sb. unharmed** jmdm. nichts zuleide tun; **~ one's clothes around** *or* **about/all over the room** seine Kleider überall/im ganzen Zimmer herumliegen lassen; **this ~s me free to do sth.** das erlaubt mir, etw. zu tun; **~ sb. alone** (allow to be alone) jmdn. allein lassen; (stop bothering) jmdn. in Ruhe lassen; **~ sth. alone** etw. in Ruhe lassen; **~ sb. be** jmdn. in Ruhe *od.* Frieden lassen; **~ him** *etc.* **'be** lass ihn *usw.* [in Ruhe]; **~ go [of] sth.** (coll.), **~ hold of sth.** etw. loslassen; **~ it at that** (coll.) es dabei bewenden lassen; **how shall we ~ it?** wie verbleiben wir?; **we left it that he'd phone me tomorrow** wir sind so verblieben, dass er mich morgen anruft; *see also* **well² B 2** [6] (station for a purpose) postieren [7] (refer, entrust) **~ sth. to sb./sth.** etw. jmdm./einer Sache überlassen; **I ~ the matter entirely in your hands** ich lege diese Angelegenheit ganz in Ihre Hand/Hände; **I ~ the decision to** *or* **with you** ich überlasse dir die Entscheidung; **sit back and ~ the worrying to me** lass mich nur machen; **~ it to me** lass mich nur machen; **~ sb. to himself** *or* **to his own devices** *or* **resources** *or* **to it** jmdn. sich (*Dat.*) selbst überlassen [8] (go away from) verlassen; **~ home at 6 a.m.** um 6 Uhr früh von zu Hause weggehen/-fahren; **the plane ~s Bonn at 6 p.m.** das Flugzeug fliegt um 18 Uhr von Bonn ab; **~ Bonn at 6 p.m.** (by car, in train) um 18 Uhr von Bonn abfahren; (by plane) um 18 Uhr in Bonn abfliegen; **please may I ~ the room?** (to go to toilet) darf ich bitte mal austreten? (ugs.); **~ the road** (crash) von der Fahrbahn abkommen; **~ the rails** *or* **tracks** entgleisen; **the train ~s the station** der Zug rollt aus dem Bahnhof; **let's ~ here** lass uns hier weggehen; **I left her at the bus stop** (parted from) an der Bushaltestelle haben wir uns getrennt; (set down) ich habe sie an der Bushaltestelle abgesetzt; **I left her much happier/I left her in tears** als ich ging, war sie schon wieder viel zuversichtlicher/weinte sie; **~ the table** vom Tisch aufstehen; *abs.* **the train ~s at 8.30 a.m.** der Zug fährt *od.* geht um 8.30 Uhr; **~ for Paris** nach Paris fahren/fliegen; **it is time to ~:** wir müssen gehen *od.* aufbrechen; **we're just leaving** wir wollen gerade weggehen; **~ on the 8 a.m. train/flight** mit dem Achtuhrzug fahren/der Achtuhrmaschine fliegen [9] (quit permanently) verlassen; **~ school** die Schule verlassen; (prematurely) von der Schule abgehen; **~ work** aufhören zu arbeiten; **~ this world for the next** diese Welt verlassen (geh. verhüll.); **all my children have left home now** meine Kinder sind jetzt alle aus dem Haus; *abs.* **I am leaving at Easter** ich gehe zu Ostern [10] (desert) verlassen; **~ sb. for another man/woman** jmdn. wegen eines anderen Mannes/einer anderen Frau verlassen; **~ a house to rot** ein Haus dem Verfall überlassen; **she was**

left at the altar der Bräutigam erschien nicht zur Trauung; **~ one's studies halfway through the course** das Studium mittendrin abbrechen; **he was left for dead** man ließ ihn zurück, weil man ihn für tot hielt; *see also* **mercy A 2; post¹ A 3** [11] (pass) **branch off, leaving the farm on one's right** den Bauernhof rechts liegen lassen und abbiegen

(Phrasal verbs)

- **~ a'side** *v.t.* beiseite lassen
- **~ be'hind** *v.t.* [1] zurücklassen [2] (by mistake) ▸ **leave 2**
- **~ 'off** *v.t.* [1] (cease to wear) auslassen (ugs.); nicht anziehen; **in summer we can ~ off our coats** im Sommer brauchen wir keine Mäntel [anzuziehen] [2] (discontinue) aufhören mit; *abs.* aufhören; **~ off smoking** mit dem Rauchen aufhören; aufhören zu rauchen; **~ off the habit of smoking** sich (*Dat.*) das Rauchen abgewöhnen; **has it left off raining?** hat es aufgehört zu regnen?
- **~ 'out** *v.t.* auslassen
- **~ 'over** *v.t.* [1] (Brit.: not deal with till later) zurückstellen [2] **be left over** übrig [geblieben] sein; *see also* **leftover; leftovers**

-leaved /li:vd/ *adj. in comb.* -blätt[e]rig

leaven /'levn/
A *n.* [1] Treibmittel, *das;* (fermenting dough) Sauerteig, *der* [2] (fig.) (transforming influence) Sauerteig, *der* (geh. veralt.)
B *v.t.* [1] mit Treibmittel/Sauerteig ansetzen ‹*Teig*› [2] (fig.: transform) durchsetzen

leaves *pl. of* **leaf**

'leave-taking *n.* Abschied, *der; attrib.* Abschieds-

leaving /'li:vɪŋ/
A *n. in pl.* Überbleibsel, *das* (ugs.); Rest, *der*
B *attrib. adj.* Abschieds‹*party, -geschenk*›; **~ certificate** Abschlusszertifikat, *das;* (from school) Abgangszeugnis, *das*

Lebanese /lebə'ni:z/ ▸❶ **p. 1345**
A *adj.* libanesisch; **sb. is ~:** jmd. ist Libanese/Libanesin; *see also* **English A**
B *n., pl. same* Libanese, *der*/Libanesin, *die*

Lebanon /'lebənən/ *pr. n.* **[the] ~:** [der] Libanon; *see also* **cedar 1**

lecher /'letʃə(r)/ *n.* Wüstling, *der* (abwertend)

lecherous /'letʃərəs/ *adj.*, **lecherously** /'letʃərəslɪ/ *adv.* lüstern (geh.); geil (abwertend)

lechery /'letʃərɪ/ *n.* Wollust, *die* (geh.)

lecithin /'lesɪθɪn/ *n.* (Chem.) Lezithin, *das*

lectern /'lektɜ:n/ *n.* [1] (in church) (for Bible etc.) Lektionar[ium], *das;* (for singers) Notenpult, *das* [2] (for lecturer etc.) Katheder, *das od. der;* Pult, *das*

lector /'lektə(r)/ *n.* Lektor, *der*/Lektorin, *die*

lecture /'lektʃə(r)/
A *n.* [1] Vortrag, *der;* (Univ.) Vorlesung, *die;* **give [sb.] a ~ on sth.** [vor jmdm.] einen Vortrag/eine Vorlesung über etw. (*Akk.*) halten [2] (reprimand) Strafpredigt, *die* (ugs.); **give** *or* **read sb. a ~:** jmdm. eine Strafpredigt halten (ugs.); jmdm. die Leviten lesen (ugs.)
B *v.i.* **~ [to sb.] [on sth.]** [vor jmdm.] einen Vortrag/(Univ.) eine Vorlesung [über etw. (*Akk.*)] halten; (give **~s**) [vor jmdm.] Vorträge/(Univ.) Vorlesungen [über etw. (*Akk.*)] halten
C *v.t.* (scold) **~ sb.** jmdm. eine Strafpredigt halten (ugs.); **he ~d me about** *or* **for** *or* **over being lazy** er hielt mir eine Strafpredigt wegen meiner Faulheit; **stop lecturing me all the time!** mach mir nicht dauernd Vorhaltungen!

lecture: ~ hall *n.* Hörsaal, *der;* **~ notes** *n. pl.* Manuskript, *das*

lecturer /'lektʃərə(r)/ *n.* ▸❶ **p. 1260** [1] Vortragende, *der/die* [2] (Univ.) Lehrbeauftragte, *der/die;* **senior ~:** Dozent, *der*/Dozentin, *die;* **be a ~ in French** Dozent/Dozentin für Französisch sein

'lecture room *n.* Vortragsraum, *der;* (Univ.) Vorlesungsraum, *der;* Hörsaal, *der*

lectureship /'lektʃəʃɪp/ *n.* Dozentur, *die*

lecture: ~ theatre *n.* Hörsaal, *der;* **~ tour** *n.* Vortragsreise, *die;* **a ~ tour of America** eine Vortragsreise durch Amerika

led ▸ **lead² A, B**

LED *abbr.* = **light-emitting diode** LED

ledge /ledʒ/ *n.* [1] (of window) Sims, *der od. das* [2] (of rock) [schmaler] Vorsprung; Band, *das* (Bergsteigen)

ledger /'ledʒə(r)/
A *n.* (Commerc.) Hauptbuch, *das*
B *adj.* (Mus.) **~ line** Hilfslinie, *die*

lee /li:/ *n.* [1] (shelter) Schutz, *der;* **in/under the ~ of** im Schutz (+ *Gen.*) [2] **~ [side]** (Naut.) Leeseite, *die*

'leeboard *n.* Seitenschwert, *das* (Seew.)

leech /li:tʃ/ *n.* [1] [Blut]egel, *der;* **stick like a ~** (fig.) jmdm. nicht von der Pelle gehen (ugs.) [2] (fig.: sponger) Blutsauger, *der* (abwertend)

leek /li:k/ *n.* Stange Porree *od.* Lauch; (as Welsh emblem) Lauch, *der;* **~s** Porree, *der;* Lauch, *der;* **I like ~s** ich mag Porree *od.* Lauch; **three ~s** drei Stangen Porree/Lauch

leek 'soup *n.* Lauch[creme]suppe, *die*

leer /lɪə(r)/
A *n.* **[suggestive/sneering] ~:** anzüglicher/spöttischer Blick; **give sb. a ~ of desire** jmdn. begehrlich ansehen
B *v.i.* [anzüglich/spöttisch/begehrlich] blicken; **he just ~ed in reply** ein anzüglicher/spöttischer/begehrlicher [Seiten]blick war seine ganze Antwort; **~ at sb.** jmdm. einen anzüglichen/spöttischen/begehrlichen [Seiten]blick zuwerfen

leery /'lɪərɪ/ *adj.* (coll.) misstrauisch (**of** gegenüber)

lees /li:z/ *n. pl.* Bodensatz, *der*

leeward /'li:wəd, (Naut.) 'lu:əd/ (esp. Naut.)
A *adj.* **to/on the ~ side of the ship** nach/in Lee; **to/on the ~ side of the mountain** in den/im Windschatten des Berges; in das Lee/im Lee (Geogr.); **L~ Islands** *pr. n. pl.* Inseln unter dem Winde
B *adv.* leewärts; nach Lee
C *n.* Leeseite, *die;* **to ~:** leewärts; nach Lee

'leeway *n.* [1] (Naut.) Leeweg, *der;* Abdrift, *die* [2] (fig.) Spielraum, *der;* **allow** *or* **give sb. ~:** jmdm. Spielraum lassen; **make up ~:** den Zeitverlust aufholen; **have a great deal of ~ to make up** einiges aufzuholen haben

left¹ ▸ **leave²**

left² /left/
A *adj.* [1] ▸❶ **p. 1699** (opposite of right) link...; **on the ~ side** auf der linken Seite; links; **~ field** (Baseball) linkes Außenfeld; **have two ~ feet** (fig.) zwei linke Füße haben (ugs.); *see also* **turn A 3** [2] **L~** (Polit.) link...; **her views are very L~:** sie hat sehr linke Ansichten
B *adv.* nach links; **~ of the road** links von der Straße; *see also* **right D 2**
C *n.* [1] (**~-hand side**) linke Seite; **move to the ~:** nach links rücken; **crowds lined the street to ~ and right** eine Menschenmenge säumte links und rechts die Straße; **on** *or* **to the ~ [of sb./sth.]** links [von jmdm./etw.]; **on** *or* **to my ~, to the ~ of me** links von mir; zu meiner Linken [2] (Polit.) **the L~:** die Linke; (radicals) die Linken; **be on the L~ of the Party** dem linken Flügel der Partei angehören [3] (Theatre) **[stage] ~:** rechte Bühnenseite [4] (Boxing) Linke, *die* [5] (in marching) **~, right, ~, right, ~, ...** (Mil.) links, zwo, drei, vier, links, ...

left: ~ 'back *n.* (Footb.) linker Verteidiger/linke Verteidigerin; **~ 'bank** *n.* linkes Ufer; (in Paris) Rive Gauche; **~-click** (Computing) **A** *v.i.* linksklicken; **B** *v.t.* mit der linken Maustaste anklicken; **~-click the mouse** die linke Maustaste drücken; **~-'footed** *adj.* mit dem linken Fuß geschickter; linksfüßig ‹*Fußballspieler*›; **~ 'hand** *n.* [1] linke Hand; Linke, *die;* [2] (left side) **on** *or* **at sb.'s ~ hand** zu jmds. Linken; links von jmdm.; **on sb.'s ~ hand** (not close) linker Hand; links; **~-hand** *adj.* link...; linksgängig, linksdrehend ‹*Schraube*›; **~-hand bend** Linkskurve, *die;* **on your ~-hand side you see ...:** links *od.* zur Linken sehen Sie ...; **drive on the ~-hand side** links *od.* auf der linken Seite fahren; *see also* **drive A 9; ~-handed** /left'hændɪd/ **A** *adj.* [1] linkshändig; ‹*Werkzeug*› für Linkshänder; ‹*Schlag*› mit der Linken; **be ~-handed** Linkshänder/Linkshänderin sein; [2] (turning to left) links angeschlagen ‹*Tür*›; Links‹*gewinde, -drehung*›; linksgängig, linksdrehend ‹*Schraube*›; [3] (fig.: ambiguous) zweifelhaft ‹*Kompliment, Gefallen*›; [4] (fig.: clumsy) ungeschickt; unbeholfen; **B** *adv.* linkshändig; mit der linken Hand; **~-handedness** /left'hændɪdnɪs/ *n., no pl.* Linkshändigkeit, *die;* **~-hander** /left'hændə(r)/ *n.* [1] (person) Linkshänder, *der*/-händerin, *die;* [2] (blow) Schlag mit der Linken; (Boxing) Linke, *die*

leftie ▸ **lefty**

leftish /'leftɪʃ/ *adj.* (Polit.) nach links tendierend; **be ~, have ~ opinions/views** links angehaucht sein; nach links tendieren

leftism /'leftɪzm/ *n., no pl.* (Polit.) linksorientierte Haltung; (movement) linke [politische] Strömungen

leftist /'leftɪst/ (Polit.)
A *adj.* linksorientiert
B *n.* Linke, *der/die*

left: ~ 'luggage [office] *n.* (Brit. Railw.) Gepäckaufbewahrung, *die;* **~over** *attrib. adj.* übrig geblieben; **~overs** *n. pl.* Reste; (fig.) Relikte; Überbleibsel (ugs.)

leftward /'leftwəd/
A *adv.* [nach] links ‹*abbiegen*›; nach links ‹*blicken, sich wenden*›; **lie ~ of sth.** links von etw. liegen
B *adj.* linker Hand *nachgestellt*

leftwards /'leftwədz/ ▸ **leftward A**

left: ~ 'wing *n.* linker Flügel; **~-wing** *adj.* [1] (Sport) Linksaußen‹*spieler, -position*›; [2] (Polit.) link...; linksgerichtet; Links‹*intellektueller, -extremist, -radikalismus*›; **~-'winger** *n.* [1] (Sport) Linksaußen, *der;* [2] (Polit.) Linke, *der/die;* **extreme ~-winger** Linksaußen, *der/die* (Jargon); Linksradikale, *der/die*

lefty /'leftɪ/ *n.* (coll.) [1] (Polit.) Linke, *der/die;* Rote, *der/die* (ugs., oft abwertend) [2] ▸ **left-hander 1**

leg /leg/
A *n.* [1] ▸❶ **p. 951** Bein, *das;* **upper/lower ~:** Ober-/Unterschenkel, *der;* **artificial ~:** Beinprothese, *die;* **wooden ~:** Holzbein, *das;* **as fast as my ~s would carry me** so schnell mich die Füße trugen; **give sb. a ~ up on to a horse/into the saddle/over the gate** jmdm. auf ein Pferd/in den Sattel/über das Gatter helfen; **give sb. a ~ up in his career** (fig.) jmds. Karriere fördern; **be on one's last ~s** sich kaum noch auf den Beinen halten können; (be about to die) mit einem Fuß *od.* Bein im Grabe stehen; **the car is on its last ~s** das Auto macht es nicht mehr lange (ugs.); **the firm is on its last ~s** die Firma liegt in den letzten Zügen; **on one's ~s** auf den Beinen; **pull sb.'s ~** (fig.) jmdn. auf den Arm nehmen (ugs.); **pull the other ~, it's got bells on** (coll.) das kannst du einem andern erzählen; **be all ~s** staksig sein; **shake a ~** (fig. coll.) das Tanzbein schwingen (ugs. scherzh.); **show a ~!** (coll.) aus den Federn! (ugs.); **not have a ~ to stand on** (fig.) nichts in der Hand haben (fig.); **stretch one's ~s** sich (*Dat.*) die Beine vertreten; **get one's ~ over** (sl.) einen wegstecken (ugs.) [2] (of table, chair, etc.) Bein, *das;* (of machine) Stütze, *die* [3] (of garment) Bein, *das;* (of boot) Schaft, *der;* **trouser ~s** Hosenbeine [4] (Gastr.) Keule, *die;* Schlegel, *der* (südd., österr.); **~ of lamb/veal** Lamm-/Kalbskeule, *die* [5] (of journey) Etappe, *die;* Teilstrecke, *die* [6] (of forked object) Schenkel, *der* [7] (Sport coll.) Durchgang, *der;* (of relay race) Teilstrecke, *die* [8] (Cricket) *Spielfeldhälfte rechts bzw., bei linkshändigem Schlagmann, links vom Werfer* [9] (Geom.) Schenkel, *der* [10] (straight run) (Naut.) Schlag, *der;* (Aeronaut.) Etappe, *die*
B *adj.* (Cricket) ‹*Seite, Torstab*› rechts vom Werfer, (if batsman is left-handed) links vom Werfer
C *v.t.*, **-gg-: ~ it** die Beine in die Hand *od.* unter die Arme nehmen (ugs.)

legacy /'legəsɪ/ *n.* Vermächtnis, *das* (Rechtsspr.); Erbschaft, *die;* (fig.) Erbe, *das;* **leave sb. sth. as a ~** (lit. or fig.) jmdm. etw. hinterlassen; **leave sb. a ~ of £30,000** jmdm. 30 000 Pfund vermachen *od.* hinterlassen

legal /'li:gl/ *adj.* [1] (concerning the law) juristisch; Rechts‹*beratung, -berater, -streit, -experte, -angelegenheit, -schutz*›; gesetzlich ‹*Vertreter*›; rechtlich ‹*Gründe, Stellung*›; (of the law) Gerichts‹*kosten*›; **in**

~ matters/affairs in Rechtsfragen/-angelegenheiten; **seek ~ advice** sich juristisch beraten lassen; **he is a member of the ~ profession** er ist Jurist; **a ~ friend of mine** ein Freund von mir, der Jurist ist **2** (required by law) gesetzlich vorgeschrieben ‹*Mindestalter, Zeitraum*›; gesetzlich ‹*Verpflichtung*›; gesetzlich verankert ‹*Recht*›; **I know my ~ rights** ich kenne meine Rechte **3** (lawful) legal; rechtsgültig ‹*Vertrag, Testament*›; gesetzlich zulässig ‹*Grenze, Höchstwert*›; **it is ~/not ~ to do sth.** es ist rechtlich zulässig/gesetzlich verboten, etw. zu tun; **it is not ~ for children to marry** nach dem Gesetz dürfen Kinder nicht heiraten; **make sth. ~:** etw. legalisieren. *See also* **proceeding 3**; **separation 1**; **tender³ C 2**

legal: ~ 'action *n.* Gerichtsverfahren, *das;* Prozess, *der;* **take ~ action against sb.** gerichtlich gegen jmdn. vorgehen; eine Klage gegen jmdn. anstrengen; **take/have recourse to ~ action** den Rechtsweg beschreiten *od.* einschlagen; **~ 'aid** *n.* ≈ Prozesskostenhilfe, *die;* **~ eagle** *n.* (coll.) Rechtsverdreher, *der*/-verdreherin, *die* (scherzh.)

legalese /liːɡəˈliːz/ *n., no pl.* (coll.) Juristenchinesisch, *das* (ugs.)

legal: ~ 'fiction *n.* juristische Fiktion (Rechtsw.); **~ 'holiday** (Amer.) ▸ **bank holiday 2**

legalistic /liːɡəˈlɪstɪk/ *adj.* legalistisch (geh.); stur legalistisch (abwertend)

legality /lɪˈɡælɪtɪ/ *n.* Legalität, *die;* Rechtmäßigkeit, *die*

legalization /liːɡəlaɪˈzeɪʃn/ *n.* (lit. or fig.) Legalisierung, *die*

legalize /ˈliːɡəlaɪz/ *v.t.* (lit. or fig.) legalisieren

legally /ˈliːɡəlɪ/ *adv.* rechtlich ‹*zulässig, verpflichtet, begründet, unhaltbar, möglich*›; gesetzlich ‹*verankert, verpflichtet*›; vor dem Gesetz ‹*verantwortlich*›; legal ‹*durchführen, abwickeln, erwerben*›; **~ and morally** aus rechtlicher und moralischer Sicht; **~ speaking** rechtlich gesehen; vom rechtlichen Standpunkt aus; **~ valid/binding** rechtsgültig/-verbindlich; **be ~ entitled to sth.** einen Rechtsanspruch auf etw. (*Akk.*) haben

legate /ˈleɡət/ *n.* (RC Ch.) Legat, *der*

legatee /leɡəˈtiː/ *n.* Legatar, *der*/Legatarin, *die* (Rechtsw.); Vermächtnisnehmer, *der*/-nehmerin, *die* (Rechtsw.)

legation /lɪˈɡeɪʃn/ *n.* (Diplom.) Gesandtschaft, *die;* (residence also) Gesandtschaftsgebäude, *das*

legato /lɪˈɡɑːtəʊ/ (Mus.)
A *adj.* Legato-
B *adv.* legato
C *n., pl.* **~s** Legato, *das*

legend /ˈledʒənd/ *n.* **1** (myth) Sage, *die;* (of life of saint etc.; unfounded belief) Legende, *die;* **read sb. tales from** *or* **out of Greek ~:** jmdm. aus den griechischen Sagen vorlesen; **~ has it that ...:** es geht die Sage, dass ...; **become a ~ in one's own lifetime** (fig.) schon zu Lebzeiten zur Legende werden; **turn sb. into a ~** (fig.) jmdn. zur Legende machen **2** (inscription) Inschrift, *die;* (Num.) Randinschrift, *die* **3** (Printing) (caption) Bildunterschrift, *die;* (on map) Legende, *die*

legendary /ˈledʒəndərɪ/ *adj.* **1** legendenhaft; (described in legend) legendär; sagenhaft **2** (coll.: famous) sagenhaft (ugs.); legendär; **become ~:** zur Legende werden

legerdemain /ˈledʒədəmeɪn/ *n.* Taschenspielerei, *die;* **diplomatic ~** (fig.) diplomatische Kunstgriffe

leger line /ˈledʒə laɪn/ *n.* (Mus.) Hilfslinie, *die*

-legged /leɡd, leɡɪd/ *adj. in comb.* ▸❶ **p. 951** -beinig; **two-~:** zweibeinig

leggings /ˈleɡɪŋz/ *n. pl.* Leggings *Pl.;* (of child) Gamaschenhose, *die;* (of baby) Strampelhose, *die*

leggy /ˈleɡɪ/ *adj.* langbeinig; hochbeinig; ‹*Junge, Fohlen, Welpe*› mit [staksigen] langen Beinen

legibility /ledʒɪˈbɪlɪtɪ/ *n., no pl.* Leserlichkeit, *die*

legible /ˈledʒɪbl/ *adj.* leserlich; **easily/scarcely ~:** leicht/kaum lesbar

legibly /ˈledʒɪblɪ/ *adv.* leserlich

legion /ˈliːdʒn/ *n.* **1** (Roman Ant.) Legion, *die* **2** **[Royal] British L~** *Veteranenvereinigung der britischen Streitkräfte;* **American L~** *Veteranenvereinigung der amerikanischen Streitkräfte* **3** **L~ of Honour** Ehrenlegion, *die* **4** (vast number) Legion, *die;* **they are ~** (rhet.) sie sind Legion (geh.). *See also* **foreign legion**

legionary /ˈliːdʒənərɪ/ *n.* **1** (Mil.) Legionär, *der* **2** (of Legion of Honour) Ritter der Ehrenlegion

legionnaire /liːdʒəˈneə(r)/ *n.* Legionär, *der;* (of British or American Legion) ≈ Veteran, *der*

legion'naires' disease *n., no pl., no art.* (Med.) Legionärskrankheit, *die*

legislate /ˈledʒɪsleɪt/ *v.i.* Gesetze verabschieden; **it is the job of Parliament to ~:** dem Parlament obliegt die Gesetzgebung *od.* (fachspr.) Legislatur; **~ for/against sth.** Gesetze zum Schutz von/gegen etw. einbringen; **you cannot ~ for everything** (fig.) man kann nicht für alles Vorschriften erlassen

legislation /ledʒɪsˈleɪʃn/ *n.* **1** (laws) Gesetze *Pl.;* **in German ~:** in den deutschen Gesetzen; **rent-control ~ was extended for another year** die Gesetze zur Mietkontrolle blieben ein weiteres Jahr in Kraft **2** (legislating) Gesetzgebung, *die;* Legislatur, *die* (fachspr.)

legislative /ˈledʒɪslətɪv/ *adj.* gesetzgebend; legislativ (fachspr.); (created by legislature) gesetzgeberisch

legislative: ~ as'sembly *n.* gesetzgebende Versammlung; **~ 'council** *n.* [gesetzgebender] Rat

legislator /ˈledʒɪsleɪtə(r)/ *n.* Mitglied der Legislative; (lawgiver) Gesetzgeber, *der*

legislature /ˈledʒɪsleɪtʃə(r)/ *n.* Legislative, *die*

legit /lɪˈdʒɪt/ (coll.) ▸ **legitimate A 1**

legitimacy /lɪˈdʒɪtɪməsɪ/ *n., no pl.* **1** Rechtmäßigkeit, *die;* Legitimität, *die* **2** (of child) Ehelichkeit, *die*

legitimate
A /lɪˈdʒɪtɪmət/ *adj.* **1** (lawful) legitim; rechtmäßig ‹*Besitzer, Regierung*›; legal ‹*Vorgehen, Weg, Geschäft, Gewinn*›; **I've turned ~:** ich bin jetzt ein gesetzestreuer Bürger **2** (valid) berechtigt; stichhaltig; legitim (geh.) ‹*Argument*›; ausreichend ‹*Entschuldigung*›; triftig ‹*Grund*› **3** (from wedlock) ehelich, legitim ‹*Kind*›; leiblich ‹*Vater*›
B /lɪˈdʒɪtɪmeɪt/ *v.t.* **1** legitimieren **2** (justify) rechtfertigen

legitimately /lɪˈdʒɪtɪmətlɪ/ *adv.* **1** (lawfully) legal; **be ~ entitled to sth.** einen legitimen Anspruch auf etw. (*Akk.*) haben **2** (justifiably) zu Recht **3** (in wedlock) ehelich, legitim ‹*geboren*›

legitimatize (**legitimatise**) /lɪˈdʒɪtɪmətaɪz/, **legitimize** (**legitimise**) /lɪˈdʒɪtɪmaɪz/ *v.t.* legitimieren; [durch Heirat] ehelich machen ‹*Kind*›

legless /ˈleɡlɪs/ *adj.* **1** (without legs) ohne Beine *nachgestellt* **2** (coll.: drunk) sternhagelvoll (salopp)

leg: ~man *n.* (Journ.) Reporter, *der;* **~-of-mutton** *adj.* **~-of-mutton sleeve** Keulenärmel, *der;* Gigot, *das* (Mode); **~-pull** *n.* (coll.) Jux, *der* (ugs.); **~-pulling** *n., no pl., no indef. art.* Aufziehen, *das;* **~room** *n., no pl., no indef. art.* Beinfreiheit, *die;* **~-show** *n.* Revue, *die*

leguminous /lɪˈɡjuːmɪnəs/ *adj.* (Bot.) **~ plant** Hülsenfrucht, *die;* Leguminose, *die* (fachspr.)

leg: ~ warmer *n.* Überstrumpf, *der;* Legwarmer, *der;* **~work** *n., no pl., no indef. art.* Lauferei, *die* (ugs.); (running errands) Botengänge *Pl.;* **do a lot of ~work** viel herumlaufen

leisure /ˈleʒə(r)/ *n.* Freizeit, *die;* (for relaxation) Muße, *die; attrib.* Freizeit‹*kleidung, -beschäftigung, -zentrum, -industrie*›; **a life/day of ~:** ein Leben/Tag der Muße (geh.); **I haven't a moment's ~:** ich habe keine freie Minute; **have [the] ~ to do sth./for sth.** [die] Zeit haben, etw. zu tun/Zeit für etw. haben; **lady/gentleman of ~:** Müßiggängerin, *die*/Müßiggänger, *der;* **she has become a lady of ~:** sie verbringt jetzt ihr Leben im Müßiggang; **do sth. at ~:** etw. in Ruhe tun; **do sth. at one's ~:** sich (*Dat.*) Zeit mit etw. lassen; **~ time** *or* **hours** Freizeit, *die*

'leisure centre *n.* (Brit.) [Sport- und] Freizeitzentrum, *das*

leisured /ˈleʒəd/ *adj.* müßig (geh.); **the ~ classes** das Müßiggängertum

'leisure industry *n.* Freizeitindustrie, *die*

leisurely /ˈleʒəlɪ/
A *adj.* gemächlich; **walk in a ~ manner** gemächlich gehen; **work at a more ~ rate** langsamer *od.* geruhsamer arbeiten; **they made a ~ start** sie ließen es gemächlich angehen
B *adv.* langsam; ohne Hast

'leisurewear *n., no pl., no indef. art.* Freizeitkleidung, *die*

leitmotiv (**leitmotif**) /ˈlaɪtməʊtiːf/ *n.* (Mus. etc.; also fig.) Leitmotiv, *das*

lemma /ˈlemə/ *n., pl.* **~ta** /ˈlemətə/ *or* **~s** (Math., Logic, etc.) Lemma, *das*

lemming /ˈlemɪŋ/ *n.* (Zool.; also fig.) Lemming, *der;* **rush like ~s** rennen wie die Lemminge

lemon /ˈlemən/
A *n.* **1** (fruit) Zitrone, *die* **2** (tree) Zitronenbaum, *der* **3** (colour) Zitronengelb, *das* **4** (coll.: fool) Trottel, *der* (ugs. abwertend) **5** (dud) Reinfall, *der*
B *adj.* **1** (in colour) zitronengelb; zitronenfarben **2** (in taste) Zitronen‹*geschmack, -tee*›. *See also* **verbena**

lemonade /leməˈneɪd/ *n.* [Zitronen]limonade, *die*

lemon: ~ 'balm *n.* (Bot.) Zitronenmelisse, *die;* **~ 'cheese**, **~ 'curd** *ns.* Zitronencreme, *die;* **~ grass** *n.* Zitronengras, *das;* **~ juice** *n.* Zitronensaft, *der;* **~ meringue 'pie** *n.* Zitronenbaisertorte, *die;* **~ 'sole** *n.* Seezunge, *die;* **~ 'squash** *n.* (Brit.) Zitronensaftgetränk, *das;* (concentrated) Zitronensaftkonzentrat, *das;* **~ squeezer** *n.* Zitronenpresse, *die;* **~ tree** ▸ **lemon A 2**; **~ yellow** *adj.* zitronengelb

lemur /ˈliːmə/ *n.* (Zool.) Lemure, *der*

lend /lend/
A *v.t.*, **lent** /lent/ **1** leihen; **~ sth. to sb.** jmdm. etw. leihen **2** (give, impart) geben; zur Verfügung stellen ‹*Dienste*›; verleihen ‹*Würde, Glaubwürdigkeit, Zauber*›; **~ one's support to sth.** etw. unterstützen; **~ one's name/authority to sth.** seinen Namen/guten Namen für etw. hergeben; *see also* **credence 1**; **ear¹ 1**; **hand A 1**
B *v. refl.*, **lent: ~ oneself to sth.** sich für etw. zur Verfügung stellen; (degradingly) sich für etw. hergeben; **the book ~s itself/does not ~ itself to use as a learning aid** das Buch eignet sich/eignet sich nicht als Lehrmittel; **the system ~s itself to manipulation** das System bietet sich zur Manipulation an
C *n.* (coll.) **give me a ~ of your bicycle** leih mir mal dein Fahrrad

lender /ˈlendə(r)/ *n.* Verleiher, *der*/Verleiherin, *die*

lending /ˈlendɪŋ/
A *n.* **~ charge** Leihgebühr, *die*
B *adj.* **~ library** (esp. Brit.) Leihbücherei, *die. See also* **public lending right**

'lending rate *n.* (Finance) Kreditzins, *der*

length /leŋθ, leŋkθ/ *n.* **1** ▸❶ **p. 1286** (also Horseracing, Rowing, Swimming, Phonet., Pros., Tennis, Fashion) Länge, *die;* **the river was navigable for most of its ~:** der Fluss war fast in seiner ganzen Länge schiffbar; **a road four miles in ~:** eine vier Meilen lange Straße; **be six feet** *etc.* **in ~:** sechs Fuß *usw.* lang sein; **the room is twice the ~ of yours** das Zimmer ist doppelt so lang wie deins; **travel the ~ and breadth of the British Isles** überall auf den Britischen Inseln herumreisen; **walk the ~ of the street** die ganze Straße entlanglaufen; **a list the ~ of my arm** (fig.) eine ellenlange Liste; **win by a ~:** mit einer Länge siegen **2** (of time) Länge, *die;* **a short ~ of time** kurze Zeit; **in that ~ of time** in dieser Zeit; **for some ~ of time** für einige Zeit; **I shouldn't care to live here for any ~ of time** auf die Dauer möchte ich hier nicht wohnen; **spend a ridiculous ~ of time in the bath** unmöglich viel Zeit im Badezimmer verbringen; **the play was three hours in ~:** das Stück dauerte drei Stunden; **depend on ~ of service with the company** von der Dauer der

ℹ Length and width

1 inch (in.)	= 25,4 mm (fünfundzwanzig Komma vier Millimeter)		
12 inches	= 1 foot (ft)	= 30,48 cm (dreißig Komma vier acht Zentimeter)	
3 feet	= 1 yard (yd)	= 0,914 m (null Komma neun eins vier Meter)	
1,760 yards	= 1 mile	= 1,61 km (eins Komma sechs eins Kilometer)	

What width/length is it?
= Wie breit/lang ist es?
The room is 12 feet [wide] by 15 feet [long]
= Das Zimmer ist zwölf mal fünfzehn Fuß [groß]
A is the same length/width as B
= A hat die gleiche Länge/Breite wie B
They are the same length or ***are equal in length***
= Sie haben die gleiche Länge *or* sind gleich lang
They are not the same width or ***are different widths***
= Sie sind nicht gleich breit *or* sind verschieden breit
a drive 100 metres long or ***in length***
= eine 100 Meter lange Einfahrt
a plank five centimetres wide or ***in width***
= ein fünf Zentimeter breites Brett

German usually puts such measurements before the noun, with the adjective agreeing. However especially if the measurement is more complicated it may also come after:
a car 14 feet 2 inches long
= ein Auto von 4,32 Meter Länge

Note that the translations for *wide* and *width* are nearly always **breit** and **Breite; weit** and **Weite** may occasionally occur in relation to clothing, but mainly in compounds such as **Hüftweite** (hip measurement) and **Taillenweite** (waist measurement), or referring to loose fit.

Material is sold in German-speaking countries *by the metre* (**meterweise**):
three metres of material at £3.50 a metre
= drei Meter Stoff zu 3,50 Pfund das Meter
a four-metre length of silk
= ein vier Meter langes Stück Seide
two ten-foot lengths of rope
≈ zwei drei Meter lange Stücke Seil

NB There is no translation of the English *of* after a quantity.

Betriebszugehörigkeit abhängen **3** **at ~** (for a long time) lange; (eventually) schließlich; **at [great] ~** (in great detail) lang und breit; sehr ausführlich; **at some ~:** ziemlich ausführlich; **write at undue ~:** übertrieben ausführlich schreiben **4** **go to any/great** *etc.* **~s** alles nur/alles Erdenkliche tun; **she went to absurd ~s to save money** sie kam auf die seltsamsten Ideen, nur um Geld zu sparen; **carry sth. to dangerous ~s** mit etw. gefährlich weit gehen; **he even went to the ~ of phoning the police** er ging sogar so weit, die Polizei anzurufen **5** (piece of material) Länge, *die;* Stück, *das;* **six-foot ~s of wood** sechs Fuß lange Holzstücke **6** (full extent of body) [Körper-]länge, *die.* *See also* **arm[1] 1**; **full length**; **measure A 1, B 5**

-length *adj. in comb.* -lang

lengthen /ˈleŋθən, ˈleŋkθən/
A *v.i.* länger werden
B *v.t.* **1** verlängern; länger machen ‹*Kleid*› **2** (Phonet., Pros.) längen

lengthily /ˈleŋθɪlɪ, ˈleŋkθɪlɪ/ *adv.* ausführlich; lange und gründlich ‹*planen*›

lengthiness /ˈleŋθɪnɪs, ˈleŋkθɪnɪs/ *n., no pl.* Überlänge, *die*

ˈlength mark *n.* (Phonet.) Längezeichen, *das*

lengthways /ˈleŋθweɪz, ˈleŋkθweɪz/ *adv.* der Länge nach

lengthwise /ˈleŋθwaɪz, ˈleŋkθwaɪz/
A *adv.* ▸ **lengthways**
B *adj.* längs angeordnet/verlaufend *usw.*

lengthy /ˈleŋθɪ, ˈleŋkθɪ/ *adj.* überlang

leniency /ˈliːnɪənsɪ/ *n., no pl.* Nachsicht, *die;* Milde, *die;* **show ~:** Milde walten lassen; Nachsicht zeigen

lenient /ˈliːnɪənt/ *adj.* **1** (tolerant) nachsichtig; milde, nachsichtig ‹*Richter*›; **take a ~ view of sth.** Verständnis für etw. haben **2** (mild) mild ‹*Urteil, Strafe*›

leniently /ˈliːnɪəntlɪ/ *adv.* nachsichtig; mit Nachsicht

lens /lenz/ *n.* **1** (Optics, Phys., Anat.) Linse, *die;* (in spectacles) Glas, *das* **2** (Photog.) Objektiv, *das* **3** (Zool.) Einzelauge, *das*

lens: ~ cap *n.* (Photog.) Objektivdeckel, *der;* **~ hood** *n.* (Photog.) Gegenlichtblende, *die*

lent ▸ **lend A, B**

Lent /lent/ *n.* Fastenzeit, *die;* **~ term** (Brit. Univ.) Frühjahrstrimester, *das*

Lenten /ˈlentən/ *attrib. adj.* Fasten-; **~ fare** Fastenspeise, *die*

lentil /ˈlentɪl/ *n.* Linse, *die*

lentil ˈsoup *n.* Linsensuppe, *die*

lentivirus /ˈlentɪvaɪərəs/ *n.* (Biol.) Lentivirus, *das od. der*

Leo /ˈliːəʊ/ *n., pl.* **~s** (Astrol., Astron.) der Löwe; der Leo; *see also* **Aries**

leopard /ˈlepəd/ *n.* (Zool.) Leopard, *der;* **hunting ~:** Gepard, *der;* **a ~ can't change** *or* **never changes its spots** niemand kann aus seiner Haut heraus (ugs.)

ˈleopard skin *n.* Leopardenfell, *das*

leotard /ˈliːətɑːd/ *n.* Turnanzug, *der*

leper /ˈlepə(r)/ *n.* Leprakranke, *der/die;* Aussätzige, *der/die* (auch fig.)

ˈleper colony *n.* Leprakolonie, *die*

lepidopterist /lepɪˈdɒptərɪst/ *n.* Lepidopterologe, *der*/Lepidopterologin, *die*

leprechaun /ˈleprəkɔːn/ *n.* (Ir. Mythol.) Kobold, *der*

leprosy /ˈleprəsɪ/ *n.* **1** (Med.) Lepra, *die* **2** (fig.) Seuche, *die*

leprous /ˈleprəs/ *adj.* (Med.) leprös; lepros

lesbian /ˈlezbɪən/
A *n.* Lesbierin, *die*
B *adj.* lesbisch

lesbianism /ˈlezbɪənɪzm/ *n., no pl.* lesbische Liebe; Lesbianismus, *der* (geh.)

lèse-majesté /leɪzˈmæʒesteɪ/, **lese-majesty** /liːzˈmædʒɪstɪ/ *n.* (Law) Majestätsbeleidigung, *die* (auch scherzh.); (treason) Majestätsverbrechen, *das* (Rechtsw.)

lesion /ˈliːʒn/ *n.* (Med.) Läsion, *die* (fachspr.); Verletzung, *die;* (abnormal change) krankhafte Veränderung

less /les/
A *adj.* weniger; **of ~ value/importance/account** *or* **note** weniger wertvoll/wichtig/bedeutend; von geringerem Wert/geringerer Wichtigkeit/Bedeutung; **his chances are ~ than mine** seine Chancen sind geringer als meine; **for ~ time** kürzere Zeit; **the pain is getting ~:** der Schmerz lässt nach; **~ talking, please** etwas mehr Ruhe, bitte
B *adv.* weniger; **I like him ~ than I used to** ich mag ihn [heute] weniger als früher; **I think ~/no ~ of him after what he did** ich halte nicht mehr so viel/nicht weniger von ihm, seit er das getan hat; **~ and ~:** immer weniger; **~ and ~ [often]** immer seltener; **~ so** weniger; **the ~ so because ...:** umso weniger, als *od.* weil ...; **even** *or* **still/far** *or* **much ~:** noch/viel weniger; **not ..., even** *or* **still** *or* **far** *or* **much ~ ...:** ..., geschweige denn ...; *see also* **more C 7**; **no B 1**; **none B**
C *n., no pl., no indef. art.* weniger; **~ and ~:** immer weniger; **the ~ said [about it] the better** je weniger man darüber sagt, umso besser; **this is ~ of a house than a cottage** das ist weniger ein Haus als ein Cottage *od.* Häuschen; **parking is ~ of a problem with a small car** mit einem kleinen Auto ist das Parken weniger problematisch; **in ~ than no time** (joc.) in null Komma nichts (ugs.); **~ of that!** (coll.) Schluss damit!; **[I'll have] ~ of your clever remarks** (coll.) deine schlauen Bemerkungen kannst du dir sparen (ugs.); **~ of your cheek!** (coll.) sei nicht so frech!; *see also* **little C**; **more B 3**
D *prep.* (deducting) **ten ~ three is seven** zehn weniger drei ist sieben; **work every weekend ~ two Saturdays** bis auf zwei Sonnabende an jedem Wochenende arbeiten; **~ £2/tax** abzüglich 2 Pfund/Steuer

-less /lɪs/ *adj. suf.* (without) -los; **error~:** fehlerlos; **parent~:** elternlos; **window~:** fensterlos; **hat~/trouser~:** ohne Hut/Hose

lessee /leˈsiː/ *n.* ▸ **lease B**: Pächter, *der*/Pächterin, *die;* Mieter, *der*/Mieterin, *die*

lessen /ˈlesn/
A *v.t.* (reduce) verringern; lindern ‹*Schmerz*›; dämpfen ‹*Lärm*›; abschwächen ‹*Aufprall*›
B *v.i.* (become less) sich verringern; ‹*Fieber:*› sinken, fallen; ‹*Schwierigkeiten:*› abnehmen; ‹*Zorn:*› sich legen; ‹*Schmerz:*› nachlassen

lesser /ˈlesə(r)/ *attrib. adj.* geringer...; weniger bedeutend... ‹*Schauspieler, Werk*›; **~ in rank, of ~ rank** rangniedriger; **be a ~ man than ...:** kein so großer Mensch sein wie ...; *see also* **evil B 2**

lesson /ˈlesn/ *n.* **1** (class) [Unterrichts]stunde, *die;* (teaching unit in textbook) Lektion, *die;* **I like her ~s** mir gefällt ihr Unterricht; **give ~s** Privatstunden *od.* -unterricht geben; **give Italian ~s** Italienischunterricht *od.* -stunden geben; **give [sb.] a [riding] ~:** [jmdm.] eine [Reit-]stunde geben; **[give] ~s in/on** Unterricht [erteilen] in (+ *Dat.*); **take piano ~s with sb.** bei jmdm. Klavierstunden nehmen **2** (thing to be learnt) Lektion, *die;* **the first ~ to be learnt** das Erste, was man lernen muss **3** (fig.: example, warning) Lektion, *die;* Lehre, *die;* **teach sb. a ~:** jmdm. eine Lektion erteilen; ‹*Vorfall usw.:*› jmdm. eine Lehre sein; **he needs to be taught a ~:** er braucht einen Denkzettel; **do that again and I'll teach you a ~ you won't forget!** wenn du das noch mal machst, verpasse ich dir einen Denkzettel, den du nicht vergisst!; **be a ~ to sb.** jmdm. eine Lehre sein; **learn one's** *or* **a ~ from sth.** aus etw. eine Lehre ziehen; **I have learnt my ~:** das soll mir eine Lehre sein; **let that be a ~ to you** lass dir das eine Lehre sein! **4** (Eccl.) Lesung, *die;* **read the ~:** die Lesung halten

ˈlesson plan *n.* Unterrichtsplan, *der*

lessor /leˈsɔː(r)/ *n.* ▸ **lease B**: Verpächter, *der*/Verpächterin, *die;* Vermieter, *der*/Vermieterin, *die*

lest /lest/ *conj.* (literary) damit ... nicht; [auf] dass ... nicht (geh.); **he ran away ~ he [should] be seen** er rannte weg, um nicht gesehen zu werden; **I was afraid ~ he [should] come back before I was ready** ich fürchtete, dass er zurückkommen würde, bevor ich fertig war

let[1] /let/
A *v.t.,* **-tt-, let** **1** (allow to) lassen; **~ sb. do sth.** jmdn. etw. tun lassen; **don't ~ things get you down/worry you** lass dich nicht entmutigen/mach dir keine Sorgen; **don't ~ him upset you** reg dich seinetwegen nicht auf; **I'll come if you will ~ me** ich komme, wenn ich darf; **~ sb./sth. alone** jmdn./etw. in Ruhe lassen; **~ alone** (far less) geschweige denn; **~ sb. be** jmdn. in Ruhe *od.* Frieden lassen; **L~ it be. We can't alter things** Lass doch! Wir können die Dinge nicht ändern; **~ go [of] sth./sb.** (release

ℹ Letter-writing

Addressing the envelope

German addresses look different.
Line 1: the person's basic title (*Mr* = Herrn*, *Mrs* or *Ms* = Frau, *Miss* = Fräulein), followed by any other title or rank (Professor, Major etc.), except Dr. and Dipl.-Ing. (Diplomingenieur) which precede the name on ***Line 2.***
Line 3: the street, with the house number after it. ***Line 4*** has the place, preceded by the postcode (**die Postleitzahl**). Finally comes the country on ***Line 5.***

Herrn* Professor	Frau	Fräulein
Manfred Bauer	Dr. Erika Engelsbach	Inge Walz
Fritz-Busch-Str. 48	Ahornweg 6	bei Wolf
D-86163 Augsburg-Hochzoll	A-4924 Waldzell	Hauptstr. 21
Germany	Austria	48637 Coesfeld

*There is an **n** after **Herr** in addresses (and only in addresses) because this is an accusative.

The Postleitzahl may be preceded by D for Germany, A for Austria or CH for Switzerland on letters from outside the country. A district of a large town will often be added after the name of the town and joined with a hyphen.

Writing to someone staying with a family or friend, use **bei** plus the surname, e.g. bei Wolf.

Writing to a firm, **Firma** may precede the name. The name of the department or person you want follows the firm's name (**z.H. = zu Händen**, 'for the attention of'). **Postfach** = P.O. Box. And in typed or printed business mail there is a blank line before the place.

Firma	Müller-Versand KG
Willi Müller	Verkaufsabteilung
z.H. Herrn Nesseldorn	Postfach 21 08 03
Endenicher Straße 218	
	20408 Hamburg
53121 Bonn	

The sender's address should also be given on the back of the envelope, preceded by **Abs.** or **Absender.**

Layout

There is usually no address at the top, just the name of the place and the date:

Rastatt, [den] 7.4.2005

Beginnings

Dear Hans
= Lieber Hans
Dear Karen
= Liebe Karen
Dear Hilde and Erwin
= Liebe Hilde, lieber Erwin
Dear Mr Engel/Mrs Schulz
= (*personal letter*) Lieber Herr Engel/Liebe Frau Schulz; (*formal business letter*) Sehr geehrter Herr Engel/Sehr geehrte Frau Schulz
***Dear Sir or Madam* (formal)**
= Sehr geehrte Damen und Herren

To someone with a title, omit the name:
Dear Professor Wolf
= Sehr geehrter Herr Professor/Sehr geehrte Frau Professor
An exception is the title **Doktor**, where the name is omitted when writing to a doctor of medicine but not when writing to someone who holds the academic title of **Doktor**.

All these greetings can either be followed by a comma, with the first line then starting with a small letter, or by an exclamation mark, with the first line starting with a capital. In the letter itself, **du, dein, ihr, euer** used to be written with a capital, but this is no longer necessary.

... and Endings

Informal:
Yours
= Herzliche Grüße
All my/our love
= Alles Liebe
With best wishes, Kind regards
= Mit herzlichen Grüßen
More formal, standard ending:
Yours sincerely* or (Amer.) *truly
= Mit freundlichen Grüßen
Formal business letter:
Yours faithfully
= Mit freundlichen Empfehlungen, Hochachtungsvoll

hold) etw./jmdn. loslassen; ~ **sb. go** (from captivity) jmdn. freilassen; ~ **go** (release hold) loslassen; (abandon self-restraint) sich gehen lassen; (neglect) herunterkommen lassen ‹*Haus*›; (~ pass) durchgehen lassen ‹*Bemerkung*›; ~ **it go [at that]** es dabei belassen *od.* bewenden lassen; ~ **oneself go** (neglect oneself) sich vernachlässigen; nicht auf sich achten; (abandon self-restraint) sich gehen lassen; ~ **loose** loslassen
2 (cause to) ~ **sb. know** jmdn. wissen lassen; ~ **sb. think that ...:** jmdn. in dem Glauben lassen, dass ...; **I will ~ you know as soon as ...:** ich gebe Ihnen Bescheid, sobald ...; **I have ~ it be known that ...:** ich habe alle wissen lassen, dass ...
3 (release) ablassen ‹*Wasser*› (**out of, from** aus); lassen ‹*Luft*› (**out of** aus); **the practice of ~ting blood** der Brauch des Aderlasses
4 (Brit.: rent out) vermieten ‹*Haus, Wohnung, Büro*›; verpachten ‹*Gelände, Grundstück*›; ~ **a flat to sb. for a year** jmdm. *od.* an jmdn. eine Wohnung für ein Jahr vermieten; **there were plenty of houses to ~:** es gab viele Häuser, die zu vermieten waren; **'to ~'** „zu vermieten"
5 (award) vergeben ‹*Arbeit, Rechte usw.*›. *See also* **fly[2] A 7**; **rip[1] C 2**; **see[1] A 6, B 3**; **slip A 2**; **well[2] B 2**
B *v. aux.*, **-tt-, let** **1** *in exhortations* lassen; ~ **us [just] suppose that ...:** lassen Sie uns einmal annehmen, dass ...; nehmen wir [nur] einmal an, dass ...; **Let's go to the cinema. — Yes, ~'s/No, ~'s not** *or* **don't ~'s** Komm/Kommt, wir gehen ins Kino. — Ja, gut/Nein, lieber nicht; **~'s pretend** tun wir so, als ob; **~'s have a go on your bike** (coll.) lass mich mal mit deinem Rad fahren
2 *in command, challenge, prayer* lassen; ~ **them come in** sie sollen hereinkommen; lassen Sie sie herein; ~ **there be light** (Bibl.) es werde Licht!; ~ **the bells be rung** lasst die Glocken erklingen; ~ **him go to the devil!** er soll zum Teufel gehen!; ~ **it be said that ...:** es muss gesagt werden, dass ...; **never ~ it be thought/said that ...:** keiner soll glauben/sagen, dass ...; **[just] ~ him try!** das soll er [nur] mal wagen!; ~ **him get well** (in prayer) lass ihn gesund werden; ~ **x be equal to 3 a + b²** (Math.) x sei $3a + b^2$; *see also* **pray A**
C *n.* (Brit.) **holiday ~s** ≈ Ferienwohnungen; **rent a flat on a short ~:** eine Wohnung für kurze Zeit mieten

Phrasal verbs

• ~ **'down** *v.t.* **1** (lower) herunter-/hinunterlassen; herunterkurbeln ‹*Autofenster*›; ~ **sb. down gently** (fig.) es jmdm. schonend beibringen (ugs.); *see also* **hair 2** **2** (deflate) die Luft [heraus]lassen aus **3** (Dressm.) auslassen ‹*Saum, Ärmel, Kleid, Hose*› **4** (disappoint, fail) im Stich lassen; ~ **oneself down** sich unter sein Niveau begeben; **I ~ myself down in the exam** ich habe in der Prüfung enttäuschend abgeschnitten; *see also* **let-down**
• ~ **'in** *v.t.* **1** (admit) herein-/hineinlassen; (fig.) die Tür öffnen (+ *Dat.*); ~ **oneself/sb. in** sich (*Dat.*) [die Tür] aufschließen/jmdm. aufmachen; **my shoes are ~ting in water** meine Schuhe sind undicht **2** (Dressm.) enger machen; einnähen **3** ~ **oneself in for sth.** sich auf etw. (*Akk.*) einlassen; ~ **oneself in for a lot of work/trouble** sich (*Dat.*) viel Arbeit aufhalsen (ugs.)/Ärger einhandeln; ~ **sb. in for sth.** jmdm. etw. einbrocken (ugs.) **4** ~ **sb. in on a secret/plan** *etc.* jmdn. in ein Geheimnis/einen Plan *usw.* einweihen
• ~ **into** *v.t.* **1** (admit into) lassen in (+ *Akk.*) **2** (fig.: acquaint with) ~ **sb. into a secret** jmdn. in ein Geheimnis einweihen **3** (set into) **a safe ~ into the wall** ein in die Wand eingelassener Safe
• ~ **'off** *v.t.* **1** (excuse) laufen lassen (ugs.); (allow to go) gehen lassen; ~ **sb. off lightly/with a fine** jmdn. glimpflich/mit einer Geldstrafe davonkommen lassen; ~ **sb. off sth.** jmdm. etw. erlassen; *see also* **let-off** **2** (fire, explode) abbrennen ‹*Feuerwerk*›; abfeuern ‹*Kanone, Gewehrsalve*› **3** (allow to escape) ablassen ‹*Dampf, Flüssigkeit*› **4** (Brit.: rent out) einzeln vermieten **5** (allow to alight) aussteigen lassen
• ~ **'on** (coll.)
A *v.i.* ~ **on about sth. [to sb.]** [jmdm.] etwas verraten; **don't ~ on!** nichts verraten!
B *v.t.* **1** **sb. ~ on to me that ...:** man hat mir gesteckt, dass ... (ugs.) **2** (pretend) ~ **on that ...:** so tun, als ob ... (ugs.); **she's not as sick as she ~s on** sie ist nicht so krank, wie sie tut (ugs.)
• ~ **'out** *v.t.* **1** (open door for) ~ **sb./an animal out** jmdn./ein Tier heraus-/hinauslassen; **Don't get up. I'll ~ myself out** Bleiben Sie sitzen. Ich finde schon allein hinaus **2** (allow out) rauslassen (ugs.); gehen lassen **3** (emit) ausstoßen ‹*Schrei*›; hören lassen ‹*Lachen, Seufzer*›; ~ **out a groan** aufstöhnen **4** (reveal) verraten, ausplaudern ‹*Geheimnis*›; ~ **out that ...:** durchsickern lassen, dass ... **5** (Dressm.) auslassen **6** (Brit.: rent out) ▸ **let[1] A 4** **7** (from duty) **On Saturday? That ~s me out** Samstag? Da falle ich schon mal aus; **that ~s me out of having to go** dann muss ich nicht hin (ugs.); *see also* **let-out**
• ~ **'through** *v.t.* durchlassen
• ~ **'up** *v.i.* (coll.) nachlassen; **don't you ever ~ up?** wirst du überhaupt nicht müde?; *see also* **let-up**

let[2] *n.* **1** **without ~ [or hindrance]** (formal/Law) ohne jede Behinderung **2** (Tennis) Let, *der*

'let-down *n.* Enttäuschung, *die*

lethal /ˈliːθl/ *adj.* tödlich; letal (Med.); (fig.) vernichtend; **that knife looks ~:** das Messer sieht sehr gefährlich aus

lethargic /lɪˈθɑːdʒɪk/ *adj.* **1** träge; (apathetic) lethargisch; (causing lethargy) träge machend; einschläfernd ‹*Atmosphäre, Musik*› **2** (Med.) lethargisch

lethargically /lɪˈθɑːdʒɪkəlɪ/ *adv.* träge; (apathetically) lethargisch

lethargy /ˈleθədʒɪ/ *n.* **1** Trägheit, *die*; (apathy) Lethargie, *die* **2** (Med.) Lethargie, *die*

let: ~-off *n.* **have a ~-off** noch einmal davonkommen; **that was a [lucky] ~-off** da habe ich/hast du *usw.* noch einmal Glück gehabt; **~-out** *n.* Ausrede, *die*; **~-out clause** *n.* Rücktrittsklausel, *die*; Ausweichklausel, *die*

Lett /let/ *n.* **1** (person) Lette, *der*/Lettin, *die* **2** (language) Lettisch, *das*

letter /ˈletə(r)/
A *n.* **1** ▸ℹ **p. 1287** (written communication) Brief, *der* (**to** an + *Akk.*); (official communication) Schreiben, *das*; **a ~ of appointment** eine [briefliche] Anstellungszusage; **by ~:** brieflich; schriftlich; **'~s to the editor'** „Leserbriefe"; *see also*

credit A 5 [2] (of alphabet) Buchstabe, *der;* **how many ~s are there in the word?** wie viele Buchstaben hat das Wort?; **learn one's ~s** die Buchstaben lernen; **write in capital/small ~s** mit Groß-/Kleinbuchstaben schreiben; **have ~s after one's name** Ehrentitel/einen Ehrentitel haben [3] (fig.) **to the ~:** buchstabengetreu; aufs Wort; **the ~ of the law** der Buchstabe des Gesetzes; **in ~ and in spirit** in Geist und Buchstabe [4] *in pl.* (literature) Literatur, *die;* **world of ~s** literarische Welt; **man of ~s** Homme de lettres, *der;* Literat, *der;* **Doctor of L~s** Lit[t]erarum Humaniorum Doctor [5] (Printing: type fount) Letter, *die;* Type, *die* [6] (Amer. Sport: mark of proficiency) Leistungsabzeichen, *das*

B *v.t.* [1] (classify alphabetically) mit Buchstaben kennzeichnen [2] (inscribe on) beschriften

letter: ~ bomb *n.* Briefbombe, *die;* **~ box** *n.* Briefkasten, *der;* (slit) Briefschlitz, *der;* **come** *or* **be put through the ~ box** in den Briefkasten gesteckt werden; **~-card** *n.* Kartenbrief, *der*

lettered /ˈletəd/ *adj.* [1] (well read, educated) gebildet [2] (inscribed) beschriftet

letter: ~head, ~-heading *ns.* Briefpapier mit Briefkopf; (heading) Briefkopf, *der*

lettering /ˈletərɪŋ/ *n.* (letters) Typographie, *die;* (on book cover) Aufschrift, *die;* (carved) Inschrift, *die*

letter: ~ pad *n.* Briefblock, *der;* **~ paper** *n.* Briefpapier, *das;* **~ post** *n.* (Brit. Post) Briefpost, *die* (veralt.); **~press** *n.* [1] (Brit.: text) Text, *der;* [2] (Printing) Hochdruck, *der;* **~s page** *n.* Leserbriefseite, *die;* **~s 'patent** *n. pl.* Patent, *das;* **~-writer** *n.* Briefschreiber, *der*/Briefschreiberin, *die*

Lettish /ˈletɪʃ/

A *adj.* lettisch; *see also* **English A**

B *n.* ▸ **Lett 2**

lettuce /ˈletɪs/ *n.* [Kopf]salat, *der;* [grüner] Salat; **a [head of] ~:** ein Kopf Salat

'let-up *n.* (coll.) (in fighting) Nachlassen, *das;* (in work) Pause, *die;* **there was no ~ in the fighting/bombardment** die Kämpfe ließen/der Beschuss ließ nicht nach

leucocyte /ˈluːkəsaɪt/ *n.* (Anat.) Leukozyt, *der* (fachspr.); weißes Blutkörperchen

leucotomy /luːˈkɒtəmɪ/ *n.* (Med.) Leukotomie, *die*

leukaemia (*Amer.:* **leukemia**) /luːˈkiːmɪə/ *n.* ▸ⓘ **p. 1231** (Med.) Leukämie, *die*

Levant /lɪˈvænt/ *pr. n.* **the ~:** die Levante

Levantine /lɪˈvæntaɪn, ˈlevəntaɪn/

A *adj.* levantinisch

B *n.* Levantiner, *der*/Levantinerin, *die*

levee /ˈlevɪ/ *n.* (Amer. Geog.) Fluss-, Uferdamm, *der*

level /ˈlevl/

A *n.* [1] Höhe, *die;* (storey) Etage, *die;* (fig.: steady state) Niveau, *das;* (fig.: basis) Ebene, *die;* **the water rose to the ~ of the doorsteps** das Wasser stieg bis zur Türschwelle; **live on the same ~:** in *od.* auf derselben Etage wohnen; **prices are at a high/low ~:** die Preise sind hoch/niedrig; **be on a ~ [with sb./sth.]** sich auf gleicher *od.* einer Höhe [mit jmdm./etw.] befinden; (fig.) auf dem gleichen Niveau sein *od.* der gleichen Stufe stehen [wie jmd./etw.]; **on the ~** (fig. coll.) ehrlich; **he's on the ~:** man kann ihm durchaus trauen; **water finds/seeks its ~:** Wasser verteilt sich gleichmäßig; **find one's ~** (fig.) seinen Platz finden

[2] (height) **at waist/rooftop** *etc.* **~:** in Taillen-/Dachhöhe *usw.*

[3] (relative amount) **sugar/alcohol ~:** [Blut]zucker-/Alkoholspiegel, *der;* **noise ~:** Geräuschpegel, *der;* **high ~s of CO_2 in the atmosphere** ein hoher CO_2-Gehalt in der Atmosphäre

[4] (social, moral, or intellectual plane) Niveau, *das;* (degree of achievement etc.) Grad, *der* (**of** an + *Dat.*); (plane of significance) Ebene, *die;* **the lower ~s** die unteren Schichten; **on a personal/moral ~:** auf persönlicher/moralischer Ebene; **expenditure is running at high ~s** die Aufwendungen bewegen sich auf einem hohen Niveau; **high ~ of intellect** hoher Intelligenzgrad; **pupils of varying ~s of ability** Schüler unterschiedlicher Begabung; **he has reached an advanced ~ in his course** er hat in seinem Kurs ein fortgeschrittenes Niveau erreicht; **talks at the highest ~ [of government]** Gespräche auf höchster [Regierungs-]ebene

[5] (instrument to test horizontal) Wasserwaage, *die*

[6] (Surv.: telescope) Nivellierinstrument, *das*

[7] (Mining) Sohle, *die*

B *adj.* [1] waagerecht; flach 〈*Land*〉; eben 〈*Boden, Land*〉; **a ~ spoonful of flour** ein gestrichener Löffel Mehl; **the picture is not ~:** das Bild hängt nicht gerade

[2] (on a ~) **be ~ [with sth./sb.]** auf gleicher Höhe [mit etw./jmdm.] sein; (fig.) [mit etw./jmdm.] gleichauf liegen; **the two pictures are not ~:** die beiden Bilder hängen nicht gleich hoch; **draw/keep ~ with a rival** mit einem Gegner gleichziehen/auf gleicher Höhe bleiben; **~ race** Kopf-an-Kopf-Rennen, *das; see also* **peg B 3**

[3] (fig.: steady, even) ausgeglichen 〈*Leben, Temperament*〉; ausgewogen 〈*Stil*〉; **keep a ~ head** einen kühlen Kopf bewahren

[4] **do one's ~ best** (coll.) sein Möglichstes tun

C *v.t.*, (Brit.) **-ll-** [1] (*make ~* **B 1**) ebnen

[2] (aim) richten 〈*Blick, Gewehr, Rakete*〉 (**at, against** auf + *Akk.*); (fig.) richten 〈*Kritik usw.*〉 (**at, against** gegen); erheben 〈*Anklage, Vorwurf*〉 (**at, against** gegen)

[3] (raze) dem Erdboden gleichmachen 〈*Stadt, Gebäude*〉

[4] (knock down) zu Boden schlagen 〈*Person*〉

[5] (abolish) aufheben, nivellieren 〈*Unterschiede*〉

[6] (Surv.) nivellieren

D *v.i.*, (Brit.) **-ll-** (coll.) **I'll ~ with you** ganz im Ernst; ehrlich (ugs.); **~ with sb.** mit jmdm. ehrlich sein

(Phrasal verbs)

• **~ 'down** *v.t.* herabsetzen; abbauen 〈*Privilegien, Gehälter, Einkommen*〉

• **~ 'off**

A *v.t.* glattmachen

B *v.i.* (Aeronaut.) die Flughöhe beibehalten

• **~ 'out**

A *v.t.* einebnen

B *v.i.* [1] ▸ **~ off B** [2] (fig.) sich ausgleichen; 〈*Preise, Markt:*〉 sich beruhigen

• **~ 'up** *v.t.* anheben 〈*Niveau, Leistungsstand, Gehalt, Einkommen*〉

level 'crossing *n.* (Brit. Railw.) [schienengleicher] Bahnübergang

leveler (Amer.) ▸ **leveller**

level-'headed *adj.* besonnen; **remain ~:** einen kühlen Kopf bewahren

leveller /ˈlevələ(r)/ *n.* Gleichmacher, *der*

levelling screw (*Amer.:* **leveling screw**) /ˈlevəlɪŋ skruː/ *n.* Stellschraube, *die*

lever /ˈliːvə(r)/

A *n.* [1] Hebel, *der;* (crowbar) Brechstange, *die;* (Mech.) Hebel[arm], *der* [2] (fig.: means of persuasion) Druckmittel, *das*

B *v.t.* **~ sth. open** etw. aufhebeln; **~ sth. up** etw. hochhebeln

leverage /ˈliːvərɪdʒ/ *n.* [1] Hebelwirkung, *die;* (action of lever) Hebelkraft, *die;* (system of levers) Hebelwerk, *das;* **I need more ~ to move this cupboard** ich brauche einen günstigeren Ansatzpunkt, um den Schrank bewegen zu können [2] (fig.: influence) **give sb. [a lot of] ~:** jmds. Position [sehr] stärken

leveraged buyout /liːvərɪdʒd ˈbaɪaʊt/ *n.* (Commerc.) Leveraged-Buy-out, *das* (Wirtsch.)

leveret /ˈlevərɪt/ *n.* (Zool.) Junghase, *der*

leviathan /lɪˈvaɪəθən/ *n.* [1] (sea monster) Seeungeheuer, *das* [2] (fig.: huge thing) Riese, *der;* (ship) Ozeanriese, *der*

Levis ® /ˈliːvaɪz/ *n. pl.* Levis, *die* (Wz)

levitate /ˈlevɪteɪt/ *v.i. & t.* levitieren

levitation /levɪˈteɪʃn/ *n.* Levitation, *die*

levity /ˈlevɪtɪ/ *n.* [1] (frivolity) Unernst, *der* [2] (inconstancy) Unbeständigkeit, *die;* Wankelmut, *der* (geh.) [3] (undignified behaviour) Leichtfertigkeit, *die*

levy /ˈlevɪ/

A *n.* [1] [Steuer]erhebung, *die* [2] (tax) Steuer, *die;* **make** *or* **impose a ~ on sth.** eine Steuer auf etw. (*Akk.*) erheben [3] (Mil.: conscription) Einberufung, *die;* (number of conscripts) Anzahl von Einberufenen; *in pl.* (conscripts) Einberufene

B *v.t.* [1] (exact) erheben 〈*Steuern, Beträge*〉; (seize) beschlagnahmen; einziehen; (extort) erpressen 〈*Geld*〉; **~ a fine on sb./a tax on sth.** jmdn. mit einer Geldstrafe/etw. mit einer Steuer belegen [2] (Mil.: conscript) aufstellen 〈*Armee, Truppe*〉; einberufen 〈*Soldat*〉

lewd /ljuːd/ *adj.* geil (oft abwertend), lüstern (geh.) 〈*Person*〉; anzüglich 〈*Blick, Geste*〉; schlüpfrig, unanständig 〈*Lied, Ausdruck, Witz*〉

lewdly /ˈljuːdlɪ/ *adv.* lüstern (geh.); anzüglich

lewdness /ˈljuːdnɪs/ *n., no pl.* (of person) Geilheit, *die* (oft abwertend); Lüsternheit, *die* (geh.); (of look, remark) Anzüglichkeit, *die;* (of language, joke) Schlüpfrigkeit, *die*

lexical /ˈleksɪkl/ *adj.* lexikalisch

lexicographer /leksɪˈkɒgrəfə(r)/ *n.* ▸ⓘ **p. 1260** Lexikograph, *der*/Lexikographin, *die*

lexicography /leksɪˈkɒgrəfɪ/ *n., no pl.* Lexikographie, *die*

lexicon /ˈleksɪkən/ *n.* [1] (dictionary) Wörterbuch, *das;* Lexikon, *das* (veralt.) [2] (vocabulary) Wortschatz, *der*

lexis /ˈleksɪs/ *n.* Wortschatz, *der*

l. h. *abbr.* **= left hand** l.

liability /laɪəˈbɪlɪtɪ/ *n.* [1] *no pl.* (legal obligation) Haftung, *die;* **limited ~** (Brit.) beschränkte Haftung; **~ to pay tax[es]** *or* **for taxation** Steuerpflicht, *die;* **~ for military service** Dienstpflicht, *die* [2] *no pl.* (proneness) (to disease etc.) Anfälligkeit, *die* (**to** für) [3] (sth. one is liable for) Verpflichtung, *die;* **liabilities** (debts) Verbindlichkeiten (Kaufmannsspr.) [4] (cause of disadvantage) Belastung, *die* (**to** für)

liable /ˈlaɪəbl/ *pred. adj.* [1] (legally bound) **be ~ for sth.** für etw. haftbar sein *od.* haften; **~ for military service** militärdienstpflichtig; **be ~ to pay tax[es]** steuerpflichtig sein [2] (prone) **be ~ to sth.** 〈*Sache:*〉 leicht etw. haben; 〈*Person:*〉 zu etw. neigen; **be ~ to do sth.** 〈*Sache:*〉 leicht etw. tun; 〈*Person:*〉 dazu neigen, etw. zu tun [3] (likely) **difficulties are ~ to occur** mit Schwierigkeiten muss man rechnen; **she is ~ to change her mind** es kann durchaus sein, dass sie ihre Meinung ändert; **it is ~ to be cold there** im Allgemeinen ist es dort kalt

liaise /lɪˈeɪz/ *v.i.* eine Verbindung herstellen; **~ on a project** bei einem Projekt zusammenarbeiten; **they ~ on a regular basis** sie haben regelmäßig Kontakt

liaison /lɪˈeɪzɒn/ *n.* [1] (cooperation) Zusammenarbeit, *die;* (connection) Verbindung, *die;* **be in ~ with** in Verbindung stehen mit [2] (illicit relation) Verhältnis, *das;* Liaison, *die* (geh.); **form** *or* **enter into a ~:** ein Verhältnis anfangen [3] (Phonet.) Liaison, *die*

li'aison officer *n.* Verbindungsmann, *der;* (Mil.) Verbindungsoffizier, *der*

liana /lɪˈɑːnə/ *n.* (Bot.) Liane, *die*

liar /ˈlaɪə(r)/ *n.* Lügner, *der*/Lügnerin, *die*

Lib /lɪb/ *abbr.* [1] **= Liberal** Lib. [2] **= liberation**

libation /laɪˈbeɪʃn, lɪˈbeɪʃn/ *n.* Libation, *die;* Trankopfer, *das*

libel /ˈlaɪbl/

A *n.* [1] [schriftliche] Verleumdung; **[public] ~:** [blasphemische, obszöne, aufrührerische od. landesverräterische] Verleumdung [2] (misrepresentation that discredits) diffamierende Entstellung (**on** *Gen.*)

B *v.t.*, (Brit.) **-ll-** [schriftlich] verleumden

libellous (*Amer.:* **libelous**) /ˈlaɪbələs/ *adj.* verleumderisch

liberal /ˈlɪbərl/

A *adj.* [1] (generous, abundant) großzügig; freigebig, großzügig 〈*Person, Wesen*〉; **a ~ amount of** reichlich [2] (generally educative) allgemein bildend; **~ education** *or* **culture** Allgemeinbildung, *die;* **~ studies** *geisteswissenschaftliches Nebenfach bei naturwissenschaftlicher, technischer oder berufsspezifischer Ausbildung* [3] (not strict) liberal; frei 〈*Auslegung*〉 [4] (open-minded) liberal;

aufgeschlossen 5 (Polit.) liberal
B *n.* 1 liberal denkender Mensch 2 **L~** (Polit.) Liberale, *der/die*

liberal 'arts *n. pl.* 1 (Hist.) Artes liberales *Pl.*; die sieben freien Künste 2 (Amer.: arts) Geisteswissenschaften *Pl.*

Liberal 'Democrat *n.* Liberaldemokrat, *der/*-demokratin, *die*

> **Liberal Democratic Party**
>
> Inoffiziell oft auch als *Lib Dems* bezeichnet. Die drittgrößte politische Partei Großbritanniens. Sie ging 1988 aus einem Zusammenschluss der *Liberal Party* und Mitgliedern der *Social Democratic Party* hervor.

liberalism /'lɪbərəlɪzm/ *n.* 1 Liberalität, *die* 2 **L~** (Polit.) Liberalismus, *der*

liberality /lɪbə'rælɪtɪ/ *n., no pl.* 1 (generosity) Großzügigkeit, *die* (**to** gegenüber); Freigebigkeit, *die* 2 (open-mindedness) Liberalität, *die*; **~ of mind** liberale Gesinnung

liberalize /'lɪbərəlaɪz/ *v.t.* liberalisieren

liberally /'lɪbərəlɪ/ *adv.* (generously) großzügig; (abundantly) reichlich

liberate /'lɪbəreɪt/ *v.t.* 1 befreien (**from** aus) 2 (Chem.) freisetzen 3 (joc. coll.: steal) mitgehen lassen (ugs.)

liberation /lɪbə'reɪʃn/ *n.* 1 Befreiung, *die*; **~ theology** Theologie der Befreiung; *see also* **Women's Liberation** 2 (Chem.) Freisetzung, *die*

liberator /'lɪbəreɪtə(r)/ *n.* Befreier, *der/*Befreierin, *die*

Liberia /laɪ'bɪərɪə/ *pr. n.* Liberia (*das*)

Liberian /laɪ'bɪərɪən/ ▸ℹ **p. 1345**
A *adj.* liber[ian]isch; *see also* **English A**
B *n.* Liberi[an]er, *der/*Liberi[an]erin, *die*

libertarian /lɪbə'teərɪən/ (Polit.)
A *n.* Libertarianer, *der/*Libertarianerin, *die*
B *adj.* libertarianisch

libertine /'lɪbətiːn/ *n.* Libertin, *der*

liberty /'lɪbətɪ/ *n.* Freiheit, *die*; **the Statue of L~**: die Freiheitsstatue; **you are at ~ to come and go as you please** es steht Ihnen frei, zu kommen und zu gehen, wie Sie wollen; **be at ~**: auf freiem Fuß sein; **set sb. at ~**: jmdn. auf freien Fuß setzen; **~ of the subject** Recht als Staatsbürger; **~ of action/movement** Handlungs-/Bewegungsfreiheit, *die*; **take the ~ to do** *or* **of doing sth.** sich (*Dat.*) die Freiheit nehmen, etw. zu tun; **take liberties with sb.** sich (*Dat.*) Freiheiten gegen jmdn. herausnehmen (ugs.); **take liberties with sth.** mit etw. allzu frei umgehen; **if you'll pardon the ~**: wenn ich mir die Bemerkung erlauben darf; *see also* **conscience**

liberty: L~ Bell *n.* (Amer.) Freiheitsglocke, *die*; **~ boat** *n.* (Brit. Naut.) *Boot, mit dem Seeleute zu einem kurzen Landurlaub an Land gebracht werden*; **~ horse** *n.* Freiheitsdressurpferd, *das*

libidinal /lɪ'bɪdɪnl/ *adj.* (Psych.) libidinös

libidinous /lɪ'bɪdɪnəs/ *adj.* triebhaft

libido /lɪ'biːdəʊ/ *n.* (Psych.) Libido, *die*

Libra /'liːbrə, 'lɪbrə/ *n.* (Astrol., Astron.) die Waage; die Libra; *see also* **Aries**

Libran /'liːbrən, 'lɪbrən/ *n.* (Astrol.) Waage, *die*

librarian /laɪ'breərɪən/ *n.* ▸ℹ **p. 1260** Bibliothekar, *der/*Bibliothekarin, *die*

librarianship /laɪ'breərɪənʃɪp/ *n.* 1 (subject) Bibliothekswesen, *das*; Bibliothekskunde, *die* 2 (work) bibliothekarische Tätigkeit

library /'laɪbrərɪ/ *n.* 1 Bibliothek, *die*; Bücherei, *die*; **reference ~**: Präsenzbibliothek, *die*; **public ~**: öffentliche Bücherei 2 (collection of films, records, etc.) Sammlung, *die*. *See also* **lending B**; **rental library**

library: ~ book *n.* Buch aus der Bibliothek *od.* Bücherei; **~ edition** *n.* Ausgabe mit Bibliothekseinband; **~ school** *n.* Bibliotheksschule, *die*; **~ science** *n.* Bibliothekswissenschaft, *die*; **~ ticket** *n.* Lesekarte, *die*

librettist /lɪ'bretɪst/ *n.* Librettist, *der/*Librettistin, *die*

libretto /lɪ'bretəʊ/ *n., pl.* **libretti** /lɪ'bretiː/ *or* **~s** Libretto, *das*

Libya /'lɪbɪə/ *pr. n.* Libyen (*das*)

Libyan /'lɪbɪən/ ▸ℹ **p. 1345**
A *adj.* libysch; **sb. is ~**: jmd. ist Libyer/Libyerin; *see also* **English A**
B *n.* Libyer, *der/*Libyerin, *die*

lice *pl. of* **louse A 1**

licence /'laɪsəns/
A *n.* 1 (official permit) [behördliche] Genehmigung; Lizenz, *die*; Konzession, *die* (Amtsspr.); **hunting ~**: Jagdschein, *der*; **gun ~**: Waffenschein, *der*; **~ to marry** ▸ **marriage licence** 2 ([excessive] liberty of action) [uneingeschränkte] Handlungsfreiheit 3 (licentiousness) Unzüchtigkeit, *die*; Zügellosigkeit, *die* 4 (artist's irregularity) Freiheit, *die*; **poetic ~**: dichterische Freiheit
B *v.t.* ▸ **license A**

licence: ~ agreement *n.* Lizenzvereinbarung, *die*; **~ dodger** *n.* (car owner) Schwarzfahrer, *der*; (TV) Schwarzseher, *der*; **~ fee** *n.* Lizenzgebühr, *die*

license /'laɪsəns/
A *v.t.* ermächtigen; **~ a building for use as a theatre** ein Gebäude zur Nutzung als Theater freigeben; **~d to sell alcoholic beverages** (formal) [für den Ausschank von alkoholischen Getränken] konzessioniert; **~d to sell tobacco** berechtigt, Tabakwaren zu verkaufen; **the restaurant is ~d to sell drinks** das Restaurant hat eine Schankerlaubnis *od.* -konzession; **~d** ‹*Händler, Makler, Buchmacher*› mit [einer] Lizenz; **~d house** Gastwirtschaft, *die*; **licensing hours** (in public house) Ausschankzeiten; **licensing laws** Schankgesetze; ≈ Gaststättengesetz, *das*; **~d premises** Gaststätte mit Schankerlaubnis; **get a car ~d, ~ a car** ≈ die Kfz-Steuer für ein Auto bezahlen; **~ a book/play** *etc.* **[for publication]** ein Buch/Stück *usw.* [zur Veröffentlichung] freigeben; *see also* **victualler**
B *n.* (Amer.) ▸ **licence A**

licensee /laɪsən'siː/ *n.* Lizenzinhaber, *der*; Konzessionsinhaber, *der*; (of bar) Wirt, *der/*Wirtin, *die*

'license plate *n.* (Amer.) Nummernschild, *das*

licentiate /laɪ'senʃɪət/ *n.* 1 (person) Inhaber eines Diploms 2 (certificate) Diplom, *das*

licentious /laɪ'senʃəs/ *adj.* zügellos, ausschweifend ‹*Leben, Person*›; unzüchtig ‹*Benehmen, Reden*›; freizügig ‹*Buch, Theaterstück*›

lichen /'laɪkn, 'lɪtʃn/ *n.* Flechte, *die*

lichgate /'lɪtʃgeɪt/ *n.* überdachtes Friedhofstor

licit /'lɪsɪt/ *adj.* legal

lick /lɪk/
A *v.t.* 1 lecken; **~ a stamp** eine Briefmarke anlecken *od.* belecken; **~ one's chops** (coll.) *or* **lips** (lit. or fig.) sich (*Dat.*) die Lippen lecken; **~ sth./sb. into shape** (fig.) etw./jmdn. auf Vordermann bringen (ugs.); **~ sb.'s boots** (fig.) jmdm. die Stiefel lecken; **~ sb.'s arse** (fig. coarse) jmdm. hinten reinkriechen (derb); **~ one's wounds** (lit. or fig.) seine Wunden lecken 2 (play gently over) ‹*Flammen, Feuer:*› [empor]züngeln an (+ *Dat.*); ‹*Wasser, Wellen:*› plätschern über (+ *Akk.*) 3 (coll.: beat) verdreschen (ugs.); (fig.) bewältigen, meistern ‹*Problem*›; (in contest) eine Abfuhr erteilen (+ *Dat.*); **this crossword/problem has [got] me ~ed** bei diesem Kreuzworträtsel/Problem steck ich fest (ugs.)
B *n.* 1 (act) Lecken, *das*; **have a ~ at sth.** an etw. (*Dat.*) lecken; **give a door a ~ of paint** eine Tür [oberflächlich] überstreichen; **give the shoes a ~ of polish** die Schuhe flüchtig putzen; **give sth./oneself a ~ and a promise** (fig. coll.) kurz über etw. (*Akk.*) hinhuschen/Katzenwäsche machen (ugs.) 2 (coll.: fast pace) **at a great** *or* **at full ~**: mit einem Affenzahn (ugs.); **at quite a ~**: mit einem ganz schönen Zahn (ugs.) 3 ▸ **salt lick**

Phrasal verbs
- **~ 'off** *v.t.* ablecken; **~ the cream off the cake** die Sahne vom Kuchen lecken
- **~ 'up** *v.t.* auflecken

lickety-split /lɪkətɪ'splɪt/ *adv.* (coll.) wie der Blitz (ugs.)

licking /'lɪkɪŋ/ *n.* (coll.: beating) Abreibung, *die* (ugs.); **give sb. a good ~**: jmdn. kräftig durchbläuen (ugs.); **take a ~**: eine Abreibung kriegen (ugs.)

'lickspittle *n.* Speichellecker, *der* (abwertend)

licorice ▸ **liquorice**

lid /lɪd/ *n.* 1 Deckel, *der*; **with the ~ off** (fig.) unter Aufdeckung aller Mängel/Schwächen/Missstände; **take the ~ off sth.** (fig.) etw. aufdecken; **keep the ~ on sth.** (fig.) (keep under control) etw. unter Kontrolle halten; (keep secret) etw. geheim halten *od.* abschirmen; **put the [tin] ~ on sth.** (Brit. coll.) (be the final blow) einer Sache (*Dat.*) die Krone aufsetzen; (put an end to) etw. stoppen; **that [really] puts the tin ~ on it** das schlägt dem Fass den Boden aus; *see also* **flip**[1] **C** 2 (eyelid) Lid, *das*

lido /'liːdəʊ/ *n., pl.* **~s** Freibad, *das*

lie[1] /laɪ/
A *n.* 1 (false statement) Lüge, *die*; **tell ~s/a ~**: lügen; **no, I tell a ~, …** (coll.) nein, nicht dass ich jetzt lüge, … (ugs.); **white ~**: Notlüge, *die*; **tell a white ~**: eine Notlüge gebrauchen; **give sb. the ~ [in his throat]** jmdn. der Lüge bezichtigen; **give the ~ to sth.** etw. Lügen strafen 2 (thing that deceives) [einzige] Lüge (fig.); Schwindel, *der* (abwertend); **he lived a ~**: sein Leben war eine einzige Lüge
B *v.i.*, **lying** /'laɪɪŋ/ lügen; **~ to sb.** jmdn. be- *od.* anlügen; **~ through one's teeth** (joc.) das Blaue vom Himmel herunterlügen (ugs.)
C *v.t.*, **lying: ~ one's way out of sth.** sich aus etw. herauslügen

lie[2]
A *n.* 1 (direction, position) Lage, *die*; **the ~ of the land** (Brit. fig.: state of affairs) die Lage der Dinge; die Sachlage 2 (Golf) Lage [des Balles]
B *v.i.*, **lying** /'laɪɪŋ/, **lay** /leɪ/, **lain** /leɪn/ 1 liegen; (assume horizontal position) sich legen; **many obstacles ~ in the way of my success** (fig.) viele Hindernisse verstellen mir den Weg zum Erfolg; **~ resting** ruhen; **she lay asleep/resting on the sofa** sie lag auf dem Sofa und schlief/ruhte sich aus; **~ still/dying** still liegen/im Sterben liegen; **~ sick** [krank] daniederliegen; **~ dead/helpless** tot/hilflos [da]liegen 2 (be or remain in specified state) **~ in prison** im Gefängnis sitzen; **~ idle** ‹*Feld, Garten:*› brachliegen; ‹*Maschine, Fabrik:*› stillstehen; ‹*Gegenstand:*› [unbenutzt] herumstehen (ugs.); **the money is lying idle in the bank** das Geld liegt ungenutzt auf der Bank; **let sth./things ~**: etw./die Dinge ruhen lassen; **how do things ~?** wie liegen die Dinge?; *see also* **close A 11**; **doggo**; **fallow**[1] **B**; **heavy A 10**; **low**[1] **B 5**; **wait C 2**; **waste D 2** 3 (be buried) [begraben] liegen; *see also* **state A 7** 4 (be situated) liegen; **Austria ~s to the south of Germany** Österreich liegt südlich von Deutschland; **our road ~s northwards/along the river** unsere Straße führt nach Norden/verläuft entlang dem Fluss; *see also* **land A 2** 5 (be spread out to view) **the valley/plain/desert lay before us** vor uns lag das Tal/die Ebene/die Wüste; **a brilliant career lay before him** (fig.) eine glänzende Karriere lag vor ihm; **these suggestions now ~ open to discussion** (fig.) diese Vorschläge können jetzt diskutiert werden 6 (Naut.) **~ at anchor/in harbour** vor Anker/im Hafen liegen 7 (fig.) ‹*Gegenstand:*› liegen; **her interest ~s in languages** ihr Interesse liegt auf sprachlichem Gebiet; **I will do everything that ~s in my power to help** ich werde alles tun, was in meiner Macht steht, um zu helfen; **it ~s with you** es liegt bei dir 8 (Law: be admissible or sustainable) zulässig sein; **no objection will ~**: Einspruch kann nicht erhoben werden 9 **~ with sb.** (arch.: have sexual intercourse) jmdm. beiliegen (geh. veraltet)

Phrasal verbs
- **~ a'bout, ~ a'round** *v.i.* herumliegen (ugs.)
- **~ 'back** *v.i.* (recline against sth.) sich zurücklegen; (in sitting position) sich zurücklehnen
- **~ 'down** *v.i.* sich hinlegen; **take sth. lying down** (fig.) etw. ruhig *od.* tatenlos hinnehmen; *see also* **lie-down**
- **~ 'in** *v.i.* 1 (arch.: labour in childbirth) im

Wochenbett liegen (veralt.) **2** (Brit.: stay in bed) liegen bleiben; *see also* **lie-in**
- **~ 'over** *v.i.* ‹*Arbeit:*› liegen bleiben; ‹*Tagesordnungspunkt, Entscheidung:*› vertagt werden
- **~ 'to** *v.i.* (Naut.) beidrehen
- **~ 'up** *v.i.* **1** (hide) sich versteckt halten **2** (stay in bed) das Bett hüten

'lie-abed *n.* Langschläfer, *der*/-schläferin, *die*

lied /li:t/ *n.*, *pl.* **~er** /'li:də(r)/ Lied, *das;* (genre) Kunstlied, *das*

lie: **~ detector** *n.* Lügendetektor, *der;* **~-down** *n.* **have a ~-down** sich hinlegen

liege /li:dʒ/ *n.* (Hist.) **1** (lord) Lehnsherr, *der;* **my ~** *as form of address* mein gnädiger Herr **2** *usu. in pl.* (vassal) Lehnsmann, *der*

Liège /lɪ'eɪʒ/ *pr. n.* Lüttich (*das*)

'lie-in *n.* **1** (Brit.: extra time in bed) **have a ~:** [sich] ausschlafen **2** (protest) *Demonstration, bei der sich die Protestierenden auf den Boden legen;* Lie-in, *das*

lien /'li:ən/ *n.* (Law) Zurückbehaltungsrecht, *das;* Retentionsrecht, *das*

lieu /lju:, lu:/ *n.* **in ~ of sth.** anstelle einer Sache (*Gen.*); **get money/holidays in ~:** stattdessen Geld/Urlaub bekommen

Lieut. *abbr.* = **Lieutenant**

lieutenant /lef'tenənt, ləf'tenənt/ *n.* ▸ **i p. 1634** **1** (Army) Oberleutnant, *der;* (Navy) Kapitänleutnant, *der;* **first ~** (Amer. Air Force) Oberleutnant, *der* **2** (Amer.: policeman) ≈ Polizeioberkommissar, *der*

lieutenant: **~ 'colonel** *n.* ▸ **i p. 1634** Oberstleutnant, *der;* **~ com'mander** *n.* ▸ **i p. 1634** Korvettenkapitän, *der;* **~ 'general** *n.* ▸ **i p. 1634** Generalleutnant, *der;* **~ 'governor** *n.* ▸ **i p. 1634** Vizegouverneur, *der*

life /laɪf/ *n.*, *pl.* **lives** /laɪvz/ **1** Leben, *das;* **sign of ~:** Lebenszeichen, *das;* **essential for ~:** lebensnotwendig; **it is a matter of ~ and death** es geht [dabei] um Leben und Tod; (fig.: it is of vital importance) es ist äußerst wichtig (**to** für); **come to ~** ‹*Bild, Statue:*› lebendig werden; ‹*die Natur:*› zu neuem Leben erwachen; (after unconsciousness) wieder zu sich kommen; **then the match came to ~:** dann kam Leben in das Spiel; **run** *etc.* **for one's ~:** um sein Leben rennen *usw.;* **I cannot for the ~ of me** ich kann beim besten Willen nicht; **lay down one's ~:** sein Leben [hin]geben; **lose one's ~:** sein Leben verlieren; **they lost their lives** sie verloren ihr Leben; **many lives were lost** viele Menschen kamen ums Leben; **risk [losing] one's ~:** sein Leben riskieren; **without loss of ~:** ohne Todesopfer; **~ begins at forty** das Leben beginnt mit 40; **~ is not worth living** das Leben ist nicht lebenswert; **not on your ~** (coll.) nie im Leben! (ugs.); **save one's/sb.'s ~:** sein Leben/jmdm. das Leben retten; **sth. is as much as sb.'s ~ is worth** mit etw. setzt jmd. sein Leben aufs Spiel; **take [sb.'s] ~:** jmdn. töten; **take one's [own] ~:** sich (*Dat.*) das Leben nehmen; **take one's ~ in one's hands** sein Leben riskieren; **upon my ~:** meiner Treu (veralt.); bei Gott; **get a ~** (coll.) was aus seinem Leben machen; *see also* **book A 1**; **lease A**; **limb 1**; **price A 1**; **sell A 1**; **staff A 7**
2 (energy, animation) Leben, *das;* **be the ~ and soul of the party** der Mittelpunkt der Party sein; **full of ~:** energiegeladen ‹*Person*›; lebendig ‹*Stadt, Straße*›; **there is still ~ in sth.** in etw. (*Dat.*) steckt noch Leben; **put some ~ into it!** (coll.) ein bisschen flotter!
3 (living things and their activity) Leben, *das;* **is there ~ on Mars?** gibt es Leben auf dem Mars?; **support ~:** organisches Leben tragen; **bird/insect ~:** die Vogelwelt/die Insekten
4 (living form or model) **draw sb. from ~:** jmdn. nach dem Leben zeichnen; **as large as ~** (life-size) lebensgroß; (in person) in voller Schönheit (ugs. scherzh.); **larger than ~:** überzeichnet; **larger-than-~ faces** überlebensgroße Gesichter; **true to ~:** wahrheitsgetreu; **to the ~:** lebensgetreu
5 (period from birth to death, from specified time to death) Leben, *das;* **marry early in ~:** früh heiraten; **late in ~:** erst im fortgeschrittenen Alter; **sb.'s ~ and times** jmds. Leben und die Zeit, in der er *usw.* lebte; **for ~:** auf Lebenszeit; lebenslänglich ‹*inhaftiert*›; **he's doing ~** (coll.) er sitzt lebenslänglich (ugs.); **get ~** (coll.) lebenslänglich kriegen (ugs.); **expectation of ~:** Lebenserwartung, *die;* **get the fright/shock of one's ~** (coll.) zu Tode erschrecken/den Schock seines Lebens bekommen (ugs.); **have the time of one's ~:** sich hervorragend amüsieren
6 (chance, fresh start) **a cat has nine lives** eine Katze hat neun Leben; **a player has three lives** (Sport) ein Spieler hat drei Versuche
7 (form of existence) Leben, *das;* **he will do anything for a quiet ~:** für ihn ist die Hauptsache, dass er seine Ruhe hat; **nothing in ~:** nichts auf der Welt; **make ~ easy for oneself/sb.** es sich (*Dat.*)/jmdm. leicht machen; **make ~ difficult for oneself/sb.** sich (*Dat.*)/jmdm. das Leben schwer machen; **this is the ~!** *expr. content* so lässt sichs leben!; **what a ~!** *expr. discontent* so ein Hundeleben! (ugs.); **that's ~, ~'s like that** so ist das Leben [nun mal]
8 (specific aspect) ‹*Privat-, Wirtschafts-, Dorf*›leben, *das;* **military/national ~:** das militärische/öffentliche Leben; **the bustle of street ~:** das pulsierende Leben in den Straßen; **in this ~** (on earth) in diesem Leben; **the other** *or* **the future** *or* **the next ~** (in heaven) das zukünftige Leben [nach dem Tode]; **eternal** *or* **everlasting ~:** ewiges Leben; *see also* **depart A 4, B**; **simple 1**
9 (biography) Lebensbeschreibung, *die*
10 (active part of existence) das Leben; **daily ~:** das Alltagsleben; **see ~:** etwas von der Welt sehen; *see also* **high life**
11 (of battery, lightbulb, etc.) Lebensdauer, *die*

life: **~-and-death** *adj.* ‹*Kampf*› auf Leben und Tod; (fig.) überaus wichtig ‹*Frage, Brief*›; **~ an'nuity** *n.* Leibrente, *die;* **~ assurance** *n.* (Brit.) Lebensversicherung, *die;* **~belt** *n.* Rettungsring, *der;* **~blood** *n.* Blut, *das;* Lebenssaft, *der* (dichter.); (fig.) Lebensnerv, *der;* **~boat** *n.* Rettungsboot, *das;* **~buoy** *n.* (ring-shaped) Rettungsring, *der;* **~ coach** *n.* Lebenscoach, *der;* **~ cycle** *n.* Lebenszyklus, *der;* **~ expectancy** *n.* Lebenserwartung, *die;* **~ force** *n.* Elan vital, *der;* **~ form** *n.* Lebensform, *die;* **~-giving** *adj.* Leben spendend (geh.); **~guard** *n.* ▸ **i p. 1260** **1** (soldiers) Leibwache, *die;* **2** (expert swimmer) Rettungsschwimmer, *der*/-schwimmerin, *die;* **L~ Guards** *n. pl.* (Brit.: regiment) [Leib]garde, *die;* **~ 'history** *n.* **1** (of person) Lebensgeschichte, *die;* **2** (of organism) Entwicklungsgeschichte, *die;* **~ insurance** *n.* Lebensversicherung, *die;* **~ jacket** *n.* Schwimmweste, *die*

lifeless /'laɪflɪs/ *adj.* **1** leblos; unbelebt ‹*Gegend, Planet*› **2** (lacking animation) farblos ‹*Stimme, Rede, Aufführung*›; ‹*Stadt*› ohne Leben

life: **~like** *adj.* lebensecht; **~line** *n.* **1** (rope) Rettungsleine, *die;* Manntau, *das;* (of diver) Signalleine, *die;* **2** (fig.) [lebenswichtige] Verbindung; (support) Rettungsanker, *der;* **3** (Palmistry) Lebenslinie, *die;* **~long** *adj.* lebenslang; **sb.'s ~long friend** (future) jmds. Freund fürs Leben; (past) jmds. Freund seit der Kindheit; **~ 'member** *n.* Mitglied auf Lebenszeit; **~ 'membership** *n.* lebenslange Mitgliedschaft; Mitgliedschaft auf Lebenszeit; **~ 'peer** *n.* Peer auf Lebenszeit; **~ 'peerage** *n.* nicht erbliche Peerswürde; **~ preserver** *n.* **1** (~ jacket) Schwimmweste, *die;* (~buoy) Rettungsring, *der;* **2** (stick) Totschläger, *der*

lifer /'laɪfə(r)/ *n.* (coll.) Lebenslängliche, *der/die* (ugs.)

life: **~ raft** *n.* Rettungsfloß, *das;* **~saver** *n.* **1** (Austral., NZ: ~guard) Rettungsschwimmer, *der;* **2** (thing that saves) Lebensretter, *der* (fig.); **it's been a ~saver** es war die letzte Rettung; **~-saving** *n.* Rettungsschwimmen, *das; attrib.* Rettungs‹*gerät, -technik*›; lebensrettend ‹*Medikament*›; **~ sciences** *n. pl.* Biowissenschaften *Pl.;* **~ sentence** *n.* lebenslängliche Freiheitsstrafe; **get a ~ sentence** lebenslänglich bekommen; **~-size**, **~-sized** *adj.* lebensgroß; in Lebensgröße *nachgestellt;* **~span** *n.* Lebenserwartung, *die;* (Biol.) Lebensdauer, *die;* **~ story** *n.* Lebensgeschichte, *die;* **~style** **A** *n.* **1** Lebensstil, *der;* **2** (Commerc.) Lifestyle, *der;* **B** *adj.* (Commerc.) Lifestyle-; **~ support system** *n.* lebenserhaltende Apparate; **~-threatening** *adj.* lebensbedrohend; **~time** *n.* Lebenszeit, *die;* (Phys.) Lebensdauer, *die; attrib.* lebenslang; **once in a ~time** einmal im Leben; **during my ~time** während meines Lebens; **the chance of a ~time** eine einmalige Gelegenheit; die Chance meines/deines *usw.* Lebens; **~ vest** *n.* Schwimmweste, *die;* **~ work** *n.* Lebenswerk, *das*

lift /lɪft/
A *v.t.* **1** heben; (slightly) anheben; (fig.) erheben ‹*Seele, Gemüt, Geist*›; **have one's face ~ed** sich (*Dat.*) das Gesicht liften lassen; **~ sb.'s spirits** jmds. Stimmung heben; **not ~ a hand to do sth.** keine Hand rühren (ugs.); **~ a hand against sb.** die Hand gegen jmdn. heben; *see also* **finger A 1** **2** (coll.: steal) klauen (salopp) **3** (coll.: plagiarize) abkupfern (salopp) (**from** aus) **4** (dig up) ernten ‹*Kartoffeln*›; aus der Erde nehmen ‹*Blumenzwiebeln, -knollen*› **5** (end) aufheben ‹*Verbot, Beschränkung, Blockade*›
B *v.i.* **1** (disperse) sich auflösen; (fig.) ‹*schlechte Stimmung, Unmut:*› verfliegen **2** (rise) ‹*Stimmung:*› sich aufhellen; ‹*Herz:*› höher schlagen
C *n.* **1** (free ride in vehicle) Mitfahrgelegenheit, *die;* **get a ~ [with** *or* **from sb.]** [von jmdm.] mitgenommen werden; **give sb. a ~:** jmdn. mitnehmen; **would you like a ~?** möchtest du mitfahren? **2** (Brit.: machine for vertical movement) Aufzug, *der;* Fahrstuhl, *der* **3** (~ing) Heben, *das;* (of eyebrow) Hochziehen, *das;* (of prices) Anstieg, *der* **4** (Mil.) Lufttransport, *der* **5** (emotional boost) Auftrieb, *der;* **give sb. a ~:** jmdm. Auftrieb geben; ‹*Droge:*› jmdn. anturnen (ugs.); **get a ~ from sth.** durch etw. Aufschwung bekommen **6** (Mech. Engin.) Hub, *der* **7** (upward pressure of air) Auftrieb, *der*

Phrasal verbs
- **~ 'down** *v.t.* herunterheben
- **~ off** *v.t. & i.* abheben; *see also* **lift-off**
- **~ 'up**
  A *v.i.* ‹*Sitz:*› hochklappbar sein
  B *v.t.* (raise) hochheben; (turn upwards) heben ‹*Kopf*›; **~ up one's hands** die Hände erheben (geh.); **~ up your hearts** erhebet die Herzen! (geh.); **~ up one's voice** die Stimme erheben

lift: **~ attendant**, **~ boy**, **~ man** *ns.* (Brit.) Aufzugführer, *der;* **~-off** **A** *adj.* abhebbar; (from backing) abnehmbar; **B** *n.* (Aeronaut., Astronaut.) Abheben, *das;* **soon after ~-off** bald nach dem Abheben; **we have ~-off** wir haben abgehoben

ligament /'lɪgəmənt/ *n.* (Anat.) Band, *das;* Ligament[um], *das* (fachspr.)

ligature /'lɪgətʃə(r)/
A *n.* **1** Bandage, *die;* (in surgery) Ligaturfaden, *der* **2** (Med.: tying; Mus., Printing) Ligatur, *die*
B *v.t.* (bind) abbinden

light[1] /laɪt/
A *n.* **1** Licht, *das;* **in a good ~:** bei gutem Licht; *see also* **10**; **be in sb.'s ~:** jmdm. im Licht sein; **get out of my ~:** geh mir aus dem Weg!; **stand in sb.'s ~** (fig.) jmdm. im Weg stehen (fig.); **at first ~:** bei Tagesanbruch; **while the ~ lasts** solange es [noch] hell ist; noch bei Tageslicht; **~ of day** (lit. or fig.) Tageslicht, *das;* **she was the ~ of his life** (fig.) sie war die Sonne seines Lebens **2** (electric lamp) Licht, *das;* (fitting) Lampe, *die;* **~s out** (in school etc.) Bettruhe *die;* (Mil.) Zapfenstreich, *der;* **go out like a ~** (fig.) sofort weg sein (ugs.) **3** (signal to ships) Leuchtfeuer, *das* **4** *in sing. or pl.* (signal to traffic) Ampel, *die;* **at the third set of ~s** an der dritten Ampel; *see also* **green light**; **red light**; **traffic lights** **5** (to ignite) Feuer, *das;* **have you got a ~?** haben Sie Feuer?; **put a/set ~ to sth.** etw. anzünden; **strike a ~** (produce spark or flame) Feuer schlagen; (with match) ein Streichholz anzünden; (Brit. dated. coll. int.) *expr. surprise* potz Blitz! (veralt.) **6** (eminent person) Größe, *die;* **be a literary ~:** eine literarische Berühmtheit sein; **lesser ~s** weniger berühmte *od.* bekannte Personen; *see also* **leading light** **7** (look in eyes) Leuchten, *das* **8** (fig.: mental illumination) **throw** *or* **shed ~ [up]on sth.** Licht in etw. (*Akk.*) bringen ; **the ~ of nature** *or* **reason** natürliche Verstandeskräfte; **bring sth. to ~:** etw. ans [Tages]licht bringen; **come to ~:** ans

[Tages]licht kommen; see also **see[1] A 1** **9** in pl. (beliefs, abilities, convictions) **according to one's ~s** nach bestem Wissen [und Gewissen] **10** (aspect) **in that ~:** aus dieser Sicht; **seen in this ~:** so gesehen; wenn man es so sieht; **in the ~ of** (taking into consideration) angesichts (+ Gen.); **show sb. in a bad ~:** ein schlechtes Licht auf jmdn. werfen; **put sb. in a good/bad ~:** jmdn. in einem guten/schlechten Licht erscheinen lassen **11** (Crosswords) Lösung, die **12** (Theol.) Erleuchtung, die; Licht, das **13** (window) Fenster, das; (sky~) Oberlicht, das; (division in mullion) Teilfenster, das

B adj. hell; licht (geh.); **~-blue/-brown** etc. hellblau/-braun usw.; see also **blue[1] B 5**

C v.t., **lit** /lɪt/ or **~ed** **1** (ignite) anzünden **2** (illuminate) erhellen; **~ sb.'s/one's way** jmdm./sich leuchten

D v.i., **lit** or **~ed** ‹Feuer, Zigarette:› brennen, sich anzünden lassen

Phrasal verb

• **~ 'up**

A v.i. **1** (become lit) erleuchtet werden **2** (become bright) aufleuchten (**with** vor); (become flushed) aufglühen (**with** vor); **his face lit up in a smile** sein Gesicht hellte sich zu einem Lächeln auf **3** (begin to smoke) sich (Dat.) eine anstecken (ugs.)

B v.t. **1** (illuminate) erleuchten; **~ up with floodlights** mit Flutlicht anstrahlen **2** (make bright) erhellen **3** (ignite) anzünden ‹Zigarette usw.› **4** **lit up** (coll.: drunk) blau (ugs.); sternhagelvoll (salopp)

light[2]

A adj. **1** leicht; Leicht‹metall, -öl, -benzin›; **[for] ~ relief** [als] kleine Abwechslung; **be a ~ sleeper** einen leichten Schlaf haben **2** (small in amount) gering; **traffic is ~ on these roads** auf diesen Straßen herrscht nur wenig Verkehr **3** (Printing) mager ‹Schrift› **4** (not important) leicht; **sth. is no ~ matter** etw. ist keine leichte Sache; **make ~ of sth.** etw. bagatellisieren **5** (jesting, frivolous) leichtfertig **6** (nimble) leicht ‹Schritt, Bewegungen›; gewandt ‹Hände›; **be ~ of foot** leichtfüßig sein; **have ~ fingers** (steal) gern lange Finger machen (ugs.) **7** (easily borne) leicht ‹Krankheit, Strafe›; gering ‹Steuern›; unbedeutend ‹Missgeschick›; (Law) mild ‹Strafe, Urteil› **8** **with a ~ heart** (carefree) leichten od. frohen Herzens **9** **feel ~ in the head** (giddy) leicht benommen sein

B adv. **travel ~:** mit wenig od. leichtem Gepäck reisen

light[3] v.i., **lit** /lɪt/ or **~ed** **1** (come by chance) **~ [up]on sth.** auf etw. (Akk.) kommen od. stoßen **2** (coll.: attack) **~ into sb./sth.** über jmdn./etw. herfallen **3** (coll.: depart) sich auf den Weg machen (**for** nach/zu)

light: ~ 'aircraft n. Leichtflugzeug, das; **~bulb** n. Glühbirne, die; Glühlampe, die (fachspr.); **~-coloured** adj. hell

lighted /'laɪtɪd/ adj. brennend ‹Kerze, Zigarette›; angezündet ‹Streichholz›; beleuchtet ‹Zimmer, Pfad, Schild, Vitrine›

light-emitting 'diode /'daɪəʊd/ n. Leuchtdiode, die

lighten[1] /'laɪtn/

A v.t. **1** (make less heavy) leichter machen; leichtern ‹Schiff› **2** (make less oppressive) lindern ‹Not›; mildern ‹Zorn, Erregung›; leichter machen ‹Arbeit, Aufgabe›; verringern ‹Arbeitslast›; kurzweilig gestalten ‹Weg, Reise›; erleichtern ‹Gewissen›; **~ sb.'s burden** jmdn. entlasten; **~ sb.'s duties** jmdm. leichtere Aufgaben zuteilen

B v.i. (become less heavy) leichter werden; (fig.) ‹Stimmung:› sich aufheitern

lighten[2]

A v.t. **1** (make brighter) aufhellen; heller machen ‹Raum› **2** (arch.: illuminate) erhellen

B v.i. **1** (become brighter) sich aufhellen; ‹Auge:› aufleuchten **2** (emit lightning) blitzen

lighter[1] /'laɪtə(r)/ n. (device) Feuerzeug, das; (in car) Zigarettenanzünder, der

lighter[2] n. (boat) Leichter, der

lighter: ~ fuel n. Feuerzeugbenzin, das; (gas) Feuerzeuggas, das; **~man** /'laɪtəmən/ n., pl. **~men** /'laɪtəmən/ Leichterschiffer, der; **~ socket** n. Zigarettenanzünder, der

light: ~er-than-'air adj. **~er-than-air aircraft/dirigible** Luftschiff, das/lenkbares Luftschiff; **~-face** ▸ **light[2] A 4**; **~-fingered** /'laɪtfɪŋgəd/ adj. langfing[e]rig; **~ fitting** n. Lampe, die; **~-footed** /'laɪtfʊtɪd/ adj. leichtfüßig; **~-'headed** adj. **1** (slightly giddy) leicht benommen; **2** (frivolous) leichtfertig; **~-hearted** adj. **1** (gay, humorous) unbeschwert; heiter; **2** (optimistic, casual) unbekümmert; **~-heartedly** /laɪt'hɑːtɪdlɪ/ adv. unbeschwert ‹lachen›; unbekümmert ‹sich verhalten›; **~ 'heavyweight** n. (Boxing) Halbschwergewicht, das; (person also) Halbschwergewichtler, der; **~ 'horse** n., constr. as pl. (Mil.) leichte Kavallerie; **~ 'horseman** n. (Mil.) leichter Kavallerist; **~house** n. Leuchtturm, der; **~house-keeper** n. ▸❶ p. 1260 Leuchtturmwärter, der; **~ 'industry** n. Leichtindustrie, die; **~ 'infantry** n. (Mil.) leichte Infanterie

lighting /'laɪtɪŋ/ n. **1** (supply of light) Beleuchtung, die **2** (setting alight) Anzünden, das

lighting-'up time n. Zeit zum Einschalten der Beleuchtung; **at ~:** ≈ wenn es dunkel wird

lightish /'laɪtɪʃ/ adj. **1** (in colour) ziemlich hell; hell ‹Farbe, Haare usw.›; **~-blue/-skinned** [eher] hellblau/-häutig **2** (in weight) ziemlich leicht

lightly /'laɪtlɪ/ adv. **1** (not heavily) leicht; **sleep ~:** einen leichten Schlaf haben; **fall ~:** sacht fallen; **touch ~ on a topic** ein Thema kurz streifen **2** (in a small degree) leicht **3** (without serious consideration) leichtfertig **4** (cheerfully, deprecatingly) leichthin; **not treat sth. ~:** etw. nicht auf die leichte Schulter nehmen; **take sth. ~:** etw. nicht [so] ernst nehmen **5** (nimbly) behänd **6** **get off ~** (not receive heavy penalty) glimpflich davonkommen; **let sb. off ~** (not inflict heavy penalty) jmdn. mit Nachsicht behandeln

light: ~ meter n. Lichtmesser, der; (exposure meter) Belichtungsmesser, der; **~-minded** adj. gedankenlos; oberflächlich

lightness[1] /'laɪtnɪs/ n., no pl. **1** (having little weight, lit. or fig.) Leichtigkeit, die; **the pianist's ~ of touch** der weiche Anschlag des Pianisten **2** (of penalty, weather) Milde, die; (of infection) Geringfügigkeit, die **3** (absence of anxiety) **~ of heart/spirit** Heiterkeit/Unbekümmertheit, die **4** (lack of concern) Leichtfertigkeit, die **5** (agility of movement) Leichtigkeit, die

lightness[2] n. (brightness, paleness of colour) Helligkeit, die

lightning /'laɪtnɪŋ/

A n., no pl., no indef. art. Blitz, der; **flash of ~:** Blitz, der; **like ~** (coll.) wie der Blitz (ugs.); **[as] quick as ~** (coll.) schnell wie der Blitz (ugs.); **like greased ~** (coll.) wie ein geölter Blitz (ugs.); **~ never strikes twice [in the same place]** (prov.) der Blitz schlägt nie[mals] zweimal am selben Platz od. Ort ein; see also **ball lightning; sheet lightning; summer lightning**

B adj. Blitz-; **with ~ speed** blitzschnell; **events moved with ~ speed** die Ereignisse überschlugen sich

lightning: ~ bug n. (Amer.) Leuchtkäfer, der; Glühwürmchen, das (ugs.); **~ conductor** n. (lit. or fig.) Blitzableiter, der; **~ rod** n. (Amer.) Blitzableiter, der; **~ strike[1]** n. (~ hitting object) Blitzschlag, der; **~ 'strike[2]** n. (Industry) überraschender [Kurz]streik

light: ~ 'opera ▸ **opera[1] 3**; **~ pen** n. Lichtstift, der; **~proof** adj. lichtundurchlässig; **~ 'railway** n. Kleinbahn, die

lights /laɪts/ n. pl. (lungs) Lunge, die

light: ~ship n. Feuerschiff, das; **~ show** n. Lightshow, die

light: ~-tight adj. lichtdicht; **~weight**

A adj. **1** leicht; **2** (fig.: of little consequence) unmaßgeblich; **3** (Boxing etc.) Leichtgewichts‹boxer, -kampf›; **B** n. **1** (Boxing etc.) Leichtgewicht, das; (person also) Leichtgewichtler, der; **2** (fig.: person of little ability or importance) Leichtgewicht, das (fig.); **~ year** n. Lichtjahr, das; **~ years [removed] from sth.** (fig.) meilenweit von etw. entfernt

ligneous /'lɪgnɪəs/ adj. (Bot.) holzig; **~ plants** Holzgewächse

lignite /'lɪgnaɪt/ n. Braunkohle, die

like[1] /laɪk/

A adj. **1** (resembling) wie; **your dress is ~ mine** dein Kleid ist so ähnlich wie meins; dein Kleid gleicht meinem (geh.); **your dress is very ~ mine** dein Kleid ist meinem sehr ähnlich; **in a case ~ that** in so einem Fall; **there was nothing ~ it** es gab nichts Vergleichbares; **who do you think he's ~?** wem sieht er deiner Ansicht nach ähnlich?; **what is sb./sth. ~?** wie ist jmd./etw.?; **what's he ~ to talk to?** wie redet es sich mit ihm?; **what's it ~ to go up in a balloon?** wie ist es, wenn man im Ballon aufsteigt?; **more ~ twelve** eher zwölf; **that's [a bit] more ~ it** (coll.: better) das ist schon [etwas] besser; (coll.: nearer the truth) das stimmt schon eher; **a man ~ you** ein Mann [so] wie du; **they are nothing ~ each other** sie sind sich (Dat.) nicht im Geringsten ähnlich; **nothing ~ as** or **so good/bad/many** etc. **as ...:** bei weitem nicht so gut/schlecht/viele usw. wie ...; **no, nothing ~:** nein, längst od. bei weitem nicht; **Have you finished it yet? — Nothing ~:** Bist du schon damit fertig? — Noch längst nicht; see also **feel B 3; look A 4; something 6** **2** (characteristic of) typisch für ‹dich, ihn usw.›; **it's just ~ you to be late!** du musst natürlich wieder zu spät kommen!; **it would be [just] ~ her to do that** das sähe ihr [wieder einmal] ähnlich; **just ~ a woman** typisch Frau (ugs.) **3** (similar) ähnlich; **in ~ manner** auf die gleiche Weise; **be as ~ as two peas in a pod** sich (Dat.) gleichen wie ein Ei dem andern; **~ father, ~ son** (prov.) der Apfel fällt nicht weit vom Stamm (Spr.) **4** (Math., Phys.) **~ signs** gleiche Vorzeichen; **~ charges** gleiche Ladungen; **~ quantities** gleiche Größen

B prep. (in the manner of) wie; **[just] ~ that** [einfach] so; **you do it ~ so** (coll.) so musst du das machen; see also **hell 2; mad 1, 6; shot A 4**

C adv. **1** (arch./coll.) **[as] ~ as not, ~ enough** wahrscheinlich **2** (coll.: so to speak) also; irgendwie; **he kind of hit me, ~:** also, der hat mich irgendwie geschlagen (ugs.); **all friendly ~:** ganz freundlich und so (ugs.)

D conj. (coll.) **1** (in same or similar manner as) wie; **he is not shy ~ he used to be** er ist nicht mehr so schüchtern wie früher **2** (coll.: for example) etwa; beispielsweise **3** (Amer.: as if) als ob **4** **tell it ~ it is** sagen Sie die ganze Wahrheit!

E n. **1** (equal) **his/her ~:** seines-/ihresgleichen; **the ~ of it** so etwas; dergleichen; **I've never known the ~ [of it]** so etwas habe ich noch nie gehört; **~ attracts ~:** gleich und gleich gesellt sich gern; **compare ~ with ~:** Vergleichbares miteinander vergleichen; **the ~s of me/you** (coll.) meines-/deinesgleichen; Leute wie ich/du; **if it weren't for the ~s of them ...** (coll.) wenn solche wie die nicht wären, ... (ugs.); **that's not for the ~s of us** (coll.) das ist nichts für unsereinen (ugs.); **I know you and your ~** or **the ~s of you** (coll.) deine Sorte/Leute von deiner Sorte kenne ich (ugs.) **2** (similar things) **the ~:** so etwas; **and the ~:** und dergleichen; **or the ~:** oder so etwas; oder so (salopp)

like[2]

A v.t. (be fond of, wish for) mögen; **~ it or not** ob es dir/ihm usw. gefällt oder nicht; **~ vegetables** Gemüse mögen; gern Gemüse essen; **~ doing sth.** etw. gern tun; **would you ~ a drink/to borrow the book?** möchtest du etwas trinken/dir das Buch leihen?; **would you ~ me to do it?** möchtest du, dass ich es tue?; **I'd ~ it back soon** ich hätte es gern bald zurück; **I don't ~ this affair** die Sache gefällt mir nicht; **I didn't ~ to disturb you** ich wollte dich nicht stören; **perhaps you would ~ time to consider it** vielleicht brauchst du etwas Bedenkzeit; **I ~ 'that!** (iron.) so was hab ich gern! (ugs. iron.); **I ~ his cheek!** (iron.) der hat vielleicht Nerven! (ugs. iron.); **how do you ~ it?** wie gefällt es dir?; **how does he ~ living in America?** wie gefällt es ihm in Amerika?; **how would you ~ an ice cream?** was hältst du von einem Eis?; **how would 'you ~ it if ...?**

wie würdest du es [denn] finden, wenn ...?; **how do you ~ 'that?** was sagst du dazu?; **but what happens 'then, I should ~ to know** (iron.) aber was dann passiert, wüsste ich gern; **I'd ~ to see you try!** (iron.) das möchte ich sehen!; **I should ~ to see them do it** ich möchte mal sehen, wie sie das machen wollen; **if you ~** *expr. assent* wenn du willst *od.* möchtest; *expr. limited assent* wenn man so will; **if one ~s that sort of thing** wenn einem so was gefällt (ugs.)

B *n., in pl.* **~s and dislikes** Vorlieben und Abneigungen; **tell me your ~s and dislikes** sag mir, was du magst und was nicht

-like *adj. suf.* -artig; **bird~:** wie ein Vogel *nachgestellt*

likeable /'laɪkəbl/ *adj.* nett; sympathisch

likelihood /'laɪklɪhʊd/ *n.* Wahrscheinlichkeit, *die;* **what is the ~ of this happening?** wie wahrscheinlich ist es, dass dies geschieht?; **there is little ~ of his seeing this** *or* **that he will see this** es ist kaum anzunehmen, dass er das sieht; **he saw no ~ of the plan being approved** er hielt es für ausgeschlossen, dass der Plan Zustimmung finden könnte; **in all ~:** aller Wahrscheinlichkeit nach

likely /'laɪklɪ/

A *adj.* **1** (probable) wahrscheinlich; glaubhaft ‹*Geschichte*›; voraussichtlich ‹*Bedarf, Zukunft*›; **be the ~ reason/source** wahrscheinlich der Grund/die Ursache sein; **do you think it ~?** hältst du es für wahrscheinlich?; **is it ~ that he'd do that?** ist ihm so etwas zuzutrauen?; *see also* **story¹ 1** **2** (to be expected) wahrscheinlich; **there are ~ to be [traffic] hold-ups** man muss mit [Verkehrs]staus rechnen; **he is ~ to meet the same fate** er könnte leicht das gleiche Schicksal erleiden; **they are [not] ~ to come** sie werden wohl *od.* wahrscheinlich [nicht] kommen; **am I ~ to do something like that?** sehe ich aus, als ob ich so etwas tun würde?; **is it ~ to rain tomorrow?** wird es morgen wohl regnen?; **this is not ~ to happen** es ist unwahrscheinlich, dass das geschieht; das wird wohl kaum geschehen; **he is ~ to be our next president** er wird voraussichtlich unser nächster Präsident sein; **it seems ~ to have been an accident** es dürfte wohl ein Unfall gewesen sein; **the candidate most ~ to succeed** der Kandidat mit den größten Erfolgsaussichten **3** (promising, apparently suitable) geeignet ‹*Person, Ort, Methode, Weg*›; **we've looked in all the ~ places** wir haben an allen infrage kommenden Stellen gesucht; **this looks a ~ place to find mushrooms** es sieht so aus, als ob man hier Pilze finden könnte; **this restaurant seems a ~-looking place** dieses Restaurant sieht ganz annehmbar aus **4** (strong, capable-looking) fähig; (showing promise) viel versprechend ‹*Kandidat, Anwärter*›; begabt ‹*Student usw.*›; **we need a couple of ~ lads** wir brauchen ein paar tüchtige Burschen

B *adv.* (probably) wahrscheinlich; **very** *or* **more than** *or* **quite** *or* **most ~:** höchstwahrscheinlich; sehr wahrscheinlich; **as ~ as not** höchstwahrscheinlich; **not ~!** (coll.) auf keinen Fall!

'like-minded *adj.* gleich gesinnt; **~ people** Gleichgesinnte

liken /'laɪkn/ *v.t.* **~ sth./sb. to sth./sb.** etw./jmdn. mit etw./jmdm. vergleichen

likeness /'laɪknɪs/ *n.* **1** (resemblance) Ähnlichkeit, *die* (**to** mit) **2** (guise) Aussehen, *das;* Gestalt, *die;* **take on the ~ of a swan** die Gestalt eines Schwanes annehmen **3** (portrait) Bild, *das;* Bildnis, *das* (geh.); **take sb.'s ~** (arch.) jmdn. porträtieren

likewise /'laɪkwaɪz/ *adv.* ebenso; **do ~:** das Gleiche tun; **if we all did ~:** wenn [wir] das alle machen würden; **I'm not going — L~:** Ich gehe nicht hin — Ich auch nicht

liking /'laɪkɪŋ/ *n.* Vorliebe, *die;* **they expressed a ~ for her cakes** sie lobten ihre Kuchen; **take a ~ to sb./sth.** an jmdm./etw. Gefallen finden; **sth. is [not] to sb.'s ~:** etw. ist [nicht] nach jmds. Geschmack

lilac /'laɪlək/

A *n.* **1** (Bot.) Flieder, *der* **2** (colour) Zartlila, *das*

B *adj.* zartlila; fliederfarben

Lilliputian /lɪlɪ'pju:ʃn/

A *adj.* Liliput-; winzig ‹*Format, Figur*›

B *n.* Liliputaner, *der*/Liliputanerin, *die*

Lilo ® /'laɪləʊ/ *n.* Luftmatratze, *die*

lilt /lɪlt/ (Scot./literary)

A *n.* **1** (cadence, swing) schwingender Rhythmus; (of voice) singender Tonfall; **speak with a ~:** mit singendem Tonfall sprechen **2** (song, tune) [fröhliche] Weise; Lied[chen], *das*

B *v.t.* trällern ‹*Lied, Melodie*›

lilting /'lɪltɪŋ/ *adj.* heiter, beschwingt ‹*Melodie, Walzer, Lied*›; singend ‹*Tonfall*›

lily /'lɪlɪ/ *n.* Lilie, *die;* **~ of the valley** Maiglöckchen, *das; see also* **gild¹**

lily: ~-livered /'lɪlɪlɪvəd/ *adj.* (literary) feige; **~ pad** *n.* Seerosenblatt, *das;* **~-white** *adj.* lilienweiß

limb /lɪm/ *n.* **1** ▸ ❶ **p. 951** (Anat.) Glied, *das;* **~s** Glieder; Gliedmaßen; **a danger to life and ~:** eine Gefahr für Leib und Leben; **tear sb. ~ from ~** (lit. or fig.) jmdm. alle Glieder einzeln ausreißen **2** (of tree) Ast, *der;* **be out on a ~** (fig.) exponiert sein; **go out** *or* **put oneself out on a ~:** sich exponieren **3** (of cross, sea) Arm, *der*

limber¹ /'lɪmbə(r)/ (Mil.) *n.* Protze, *die*

limber²

A *adj.* **1** (flexible) biegsam ‹*Zweig*›; elastisch ‹*Seil, Leder*› **2** (nimble) geschmeidig; elastisch

B *v.t. & i.* ▸ **limber up**

Phrasal verb

• **~ up**

A *v.i.* sich einlaufen/einspielen *usw.;* (loosen up) die Muskeln lockern; (fig.) sich fit machen (fig.) (**for** für); sich vorbereiten (**for** auf + *Akk.*)

B *v.t.* warm machen; aufwärmen (Sport)

limbic /'lɪmbɪk/ *adj.* (Anat.) **~ system** limbisches system

limbless /'lɪmlɪs/ *adj.* ‹*Person, Tier*› ohne Gliedmaßen; ‹*Baum*› ohne Äste

limbo¹ /'lɪmbəʊ/ *n., pl.* **~s** **1** (region) Vorhölle, *die;* Limbus, *der* (Rel.) **2** (fig.) Vergessenheit, *die;* **vanish into ~:** spurlos verschwinden; **be in ~** (be pending) in der Schwebe sein; (be abandoned) abgeschrieben sein; **live in ~:** in einer Art Niemandsland leben

limbo² *n., pl.* **~s** (dance) Limbo, *der*

lime¹ /laɪm/ *n.* **1** **[quick]~:** [ungelöschter] Kalk; **slaked ~:** gelöschter Kalk; Löschkalk, *der* **2** ▸ **birdlime**

lime² *n.* **1** (fruit) Limone, *die* **2** (juice) Limonensaft, *der* **3** ▸ **lime green**

lime³ ▸ **lime tree**

lime: ~ green **A** *adj.* [leuchtend] hellgrün; **B** *n.* Hellgrün, *das;* **~ juice** *n.* Limonensaft, *der;* **~kiln** *n.* Kalkofen, *der;* **~light** *n.* **1** (light) Kalklicht, *das;* **2** (fig.: attention) **be in the ~light** im Rampenlicht [der Öffentlichkeit] stehen

limerick /'lɪmərɪk/ *n.* Limerick, *der*

lime: ~scale *n., no pl.* (Brit.) (in bath, shower head) Kalk, *der;* (in kettle) Kesselstein, *der; attrib.* **~scale build-up** Kalkablagerungen *Pl.;* **~stone** *n.* Kalkstein, *der;* **~ tree** *n.* Linde, *die;* Lindenbaum, *der* (geh.); **~wood** *n.* Lindenholz, *das*

Limey /'laɪmɪ/ *n.* (Amer. sl. derog.) Engländer, *der;* (esp. soldier) Tommy, *der; attrib.* englisch

limit /'lɪmɪt/

A *n.* **1** *usu. in pl.* (boundary) Grenze, *die;* **within [the] city ~s** innerhalb der Stadtgrenzen **2** (point or line that may not be passed) Limit, *das;* (of ability, love, etc.) Grenze, *die;* **set** *or* **put a ~ on sth.** etw. begrenzen *od.* beschränken; **be over the ~** ‹*Autofahrer:*› zu viel Promille haben; ‹*Reisender:*› Übergepäck haben; **£400 is my upper ~:** 400 Pfund sind für mich das Äußerste; **there is a ~ to what I can spend/do** ich kann nicht unbegrenzt Geld ausgeben/meine Möglichkeiten sind auch nur begrenzt; **there is a ~ to everything** alles hat seine Grenzen; **there is a ~ to my patience** meine Geduld ist begrenzt; **there is no ~ to his impudence, his impudence knows no ~s** seine Unverschämtheit kennt keine Grenzen; **lower/upper ~:** Untergrenze/Höchstgrenze, *die;* **without ~:** unbegrenzt; **within ~s** innerhalb gewisser Grenzen; **'off ~s'** (esp. Amer.) „Zutritt [für Soldaten] verboten"; **this bar is off ~s** zu dieser Bar haben Soldaten keinen Zutritt **3** (coll.) **this is the ~!** das ist [doch] die Höhe!; **he/she is the [very] ~:** er/sie ist [einfach] unmöglich (ugs.) **4** (Math.) Grenzwert, *der*

B *v.t.* begrenzen (**to** auf + *Akk.*); einschränken ‹*Freiheit*›

limitation /lɪmɪ'teɪʃn/ *n.* **1** (act) Beschränkung, *die;* (of freedom) Einschränkung, *die* **2** (condition) (of extent) Begrenzung, *die;* (of amount) Beschränkung, *die;* **know one's ~s** seine Grenzen kennen **3** (restrictive circumstance) Beschränkung, *die;* **due to ~s of space** aus Platzmangel *od.* Platzgründen **4** (Law) Verjährung, *die*

limited /'lɪmɪtɪd/ *adj.* **1** (restricted) begrenzt; **~ company** (Brit.) Gesellschaft mit beschränkter Haftung; **~ edition** limitierte Auflage; **~ train** (Amer.) ≈ Schnellzug, *der* **2** (intellectually narrow) beschränkt (abwertend); **~ outlook/mind** beschränkter Horizont/Verstand

limitless /'lɪmɪtlɪs/ *adj.* grenzenlos

limo /'lɪməʊ/ *n., pl.* **~s** (coll.) Limousine, *die*

limousine /'lɪmʊzi:n/ *n.* Limousine, *die* (*mit Trennscheibe*)

limp¹ /lɪmp/

A *v.i.* (lit. or fig.) hinken; **the ship managed to ~ into port** das Schiff schaffte es mit Müh und Not *od.* gerade so in den Hafen

B *n.* Hinken, *das;* **walk with a ~:** hinken; **have a slight/pronounced ~:** leicht/stark hinken

limp² *adj.* **1** (not stiff, lit. or fig.) schlaff; welk ‹*Blumen*›; **I feel ~ at the thought of it** beim bloßen Gedanken daran wird mir schwach (ugs.) **2** (flexible) flexibel ‹*Einband*›

limpet /'lɪmpɪt/ *n.* (Zool.) Napfschnecke, *die*

'limpet mine *n.* Haftmine, *die*

limpid /'lɪmpɪd/ *adj.* klar

limply /'lɪmplɪ/ *adv.* schlaff; (weakly) schwach

limpness /'lɪmpnɪs/ *n., no pl.* Schlaffheit, *die;* (weakness) Schwäche, *die*

linchpin /'lɪntʃpɪn/ *n.* **1** (pin) Lünse, *die;* Achsnagel, *der* **2** (fig.: essential element) Kernstück, *das;* **he is the ~ of the company** er ist das Herz der Firma; mit ihm steht und fällt die Firma

linctus /'lɪŋktəs/ *n.* (Med.) Hustensaft, *der*

linden /'lɪndən/ *n.* Linde, *die;* Lindenbaum, *der* (geh.)

line¹ /laɪn/

A *n.* **1** (string, cord, rope, etc.) Leine, *die;* **[fishing] ~:** [Angel]schnur, *die;* **the ~s** (Amer.: reins) die Zügel; **hard ~s** (coll.) ein schwerer Schlag; **[that's] hard ~s, old chap!** Schicksal, alter Junge!

2 (telephone or telegraph cable) Leitung, *die;* **our company has 20 ~s** unsere Firma hat 20 Anschlüsse; **get me a ~ to Washington** verbinden Sie mich mit Washington; **bad ~:** schlechte Verbindung; **be on the ~:** am Apparat sein; *see also* **cross B 1**; **hold² A 12**; **party line 1**

3 (long mark; also Math., Phys.) Linie, *die;* (less precise or shorter) Strich, *der;* (Telev.) Zeile, *die;* **capture sth. in a few ~s** etw. mit wenigen Strichen einfangen; **the L~:** die Linie (Seemannsspr.); der Äquator; **~ of force** (Phys.) Kraftlinie, *die;* **~ of life/fortune** (Palmistry) Lebenslinie, *die*/Schicksalslinie, *die;* **straight ~:** gerade Linie; (Geom.) Gerade, *die;* **walk in a straight ~:** in einer geraden Linie gehen; **~ of sight** *or* **vision** Blickrichtung, *die;* **the ~s of her face** ihre Gesichtszüge/(wrinkles) ihre Falten; *see also* **yellow line**

4 *in pl.* (outline of car, ship, etc.) Linien *Pl.*

5 (boundary) Linie, *die;* (fig.) **somewhere on the ~:** irgendwo dazwischen; **lay sth. on the ~ [for sb.]** [jmdm.] etw. rundheraus sagen; **put sth. on the ~:** etw. aufs Spiel setzen; **put oneself on the ~:** ein Risiko eingehen; **your job is on the ~:** deine Stelle steht auf dem Spiel; *see also* **draw A 7**

6 (row) Reihe, *die;* (Amer.: queue) Schlange, *die;* **~ of trees** Baumreihe, *die;* **arrange the chairs in a straight ~:** die Stühle in einer Reihe aufstellen; **bring sb. into ~:** dafür sorgen, dass jmd. nicht aus der Reihe tanzt (ugs.); **come** *or* **fall into ~:** sich in die Reihe stellen; ‹*Gruppe:*› sich in einer Reihe aufstellen; (fig.) nicht mehr aus der Reihe tanzen (ugs.); **be in ~ [with sth.]** [mit etw.] in einer Linie liegen; **be in ~ for promotion** Aussicht auf Beförderung haben; **be in/out of ~ with sth.** (fig.) mit etw. in/nicht in Einklang stehen; **all along the ~:** auf der ganzen Linie; **somewhere along the ~:** irgendwann einmal; **stand in ~** (Amer.: queue) Schlange stehen; *see also* **toe B**

7 (Naut.) **~ abreast** Dwarslinie, *die;* **~ ahead** Kiellinie, *die;* **~ [of battle]** [Kampf]linie, *die*

8 (row of words on a page) Zeile, *die;* **~s** (actor's part) Text, *der;* **drop me a ~:** schreib mir ein paar Zeilen; **she has only a few ~s** (Theatre) sie hat nur ein paar Worte zu sprechen; **he gave the boy 100 ~s** (Sch.) er ließ den Jungen 100 Zeilen abschreiben; *see also* **read A 3**

9 (system of transport) Linie, *die;* **[shipping] ~:** Schifffahrtslinie, *die*

10 (series of persons or things) Reihe, *die;* (generations of family) Linie, *die;* **be third in ~ to the throne** Dritter in der Thronfolge sein

11 (direction, course) Richtung, *die;* **on these ~s** in dieser Richtung; **on the ~s of** nach Art (+ *Gen.*); **on similar ~s** auf ähnliche Art; **be on the right/wrong ~s** in die richtige/falsche Richtung gehen; **along** *or* **on the same ~s** in der gleichen Richtung; **be on the same ~s** die gleiche Richtung verfolgen; **~ of thought/march** Gedankengang, *der*/Marschrichtung, *die;* **what ~ shall we take with her?** wie sollen wir uns ihr gegenüber verhalten?; **take a strong ~ with sb.** jmdm. gegenüber bestimmt *od.* energisch auftreten; **~ of action** Vorgehensweise, *die;* **get a ~ on sb./sth.** (coll.) etwas über jmdn./etw. herausfinden; *see also* **assembly line; hard A 6; hardline; party line 2; resistance 1**

12 (Railw.) Bahnlinie, *die;* (track) Gleis, *das;* **cross the ~:** die Gleise überqueren; **the ~ was blocked** die Strecke war blockiert; **the Waterloo ~, the ~ to Waterloo** die Linie nach Waterloo; **this is the end of the ~ [for you]** (fig.) dies ist das Aus [für dich]

13 (field of activity) Branche, *die;* (academic) Fachrichtung, *die;* **what's your ~?** in welcher Branche sind Sie?/was ist Ihre Fachrichtung?; **he's in the building ~:** er ist in der Baubranche; **that's not my ~:** das ist nicht mein Gebiet; **be in the ~ of duty/business** zu den Pflichten/zum Geschäft gehören; *see also* **shoot B 4**

14 (Commerc.: product) Artikel, *der;* Linie, *die* (fachspr.)

15 (Fashion) Linie, *die*

16 (Mil.: series of defences) Linie, *die;* **draw the ~s** Stellungen beziehen; **enemy ~s** feindliche Stellungen *od.* Linien; *see also* **hold² A 11**

17 (wrinkle) Falte, *die*

B *v.t.* **1** (mark with lines) linieren ‹*Papier*›; **a ~d face** ein faltiges Gesicht; **a face ~d with worry** ein von Sorgen gezeichnetes Gesicht **2** (stand at intervals along) säumen (geh.) ‹*Straße, Strecke*›

Phrasal verb

- **~ 'up**

A *v.t.* antreten lassen ‹*Gefangene, Soldaten usw.*›; [in einer Reihe] aufstellen ‹*Gegenstände*›; (fig.) **I've got a nice little job/a surprise ~d up for you** ich hab da eine nette kleine Beschäftigung/eine Überraschung für dich (ugs.); **have you got anything ~d up for this evening?** haben Sie heute Abend schon etwas vor?; *see also* **line-up**

B *v.i.* ‹*Gefangene, Soldaten:*› antreten; ‹*Läufer:*› Aufstellung nehmen; (queue up) sich anstellen

line² *v.t.* füttern ‹*Kleidungsstück*›; auskleiden ‹*Magen, Nest*›; ausschlagen ‹*Schublade usw.*›; **~ one's pockets** (fig.) sich (*Dat.*) die Taschen füllen

lineage /ˈlɪnɪɪdʒ/ *n.* Abstammung, *die*

lineal /ˈlɪnɪəl/ *adj.* **1** (in direct line of descent) geradlinig ‹*Abstammung*›; direkt ‹*Nachkomme, Vorfahr*› **2** (linear) linear

lineament /ˈlɪnɪəmənt/ *n., usu. in pl.* [Gesichts-]zug, *der;* (distinctive feature) Grundzug, *der*

linear /ˈlɪnɪə(r)/ *adj.* linear; **~ perspective** Linearperspektive, *die;* **~ extent** Längenausdehnung, *die;* **~ measure** Längenmaß, *das*

linear ac'celerator *n.* (Phys.) Linearbeschleuniger, *der*

line: ~backer *n.* (Amer. Footb.) Gedrängehalbspieler, *der;* **~ dance A** *n.* Linedance, *der;* **B** *v.i.* Linedance tanzen; **~ dancer** *n.* Linedance-Tänzer, *der*/-Tänzerin, *die;* **~ dancing** *n., no pl.* Linedance-Tanzen, *das;* **~ drawing** *n.* Strichzeichnung, *die;* **~ engraving** *n.* Strichätzung, *die;* **~ fishing** *n., no pl.* Angeln, *das;* **~man** /ˈlaɪnmən/ *n., pl.* **~men** /ˈlaɪnmən/ ▸ **p. 1260** (Amer. Footb.) Stürmer, *der;* **~ 'management** *n., no pl.* Linienmanagement, *das;* **~ 'manager** *n.* [unmittelbarer] Vorgesetzter; Linienmanager, *der*

linen /ˈlɪnɪn/

A *n.* **1** Leinen, *das* **2** (shirts, sheets, clothes, etc.) Wäsche, *die;* **wash one's dirty ~ in public** (fig.) seine schmutzige Wäsche vor anderen Leuten waschen

B *adj.* Leinen‹*faden, -bluse, -laken*›; Lein‹*tuch*›

linen: ~ basket *n.* (Brit.) Wäschekorb, *der;* **~ cupboard** *n.* Wäscheschrank, *der*

line: ~-out *n.* (Sport) Gasse, *die;* **~ printer** *n.* (Computing) Zeilendrucker, *der*

liner¹ /ˈlaɪnə(r)/ *n.* (removable metal lining) Auskleidung, *die;* (in engine) Laufbuchse, *die;* **carpet ~:** rutschfeste Teppichunterlage; **[bin] ~:** Müllbeutel, *der*

liner² *n.* (ship) Linienschiff, *das;* (aircraft) Linienflugzeug, *das;* **ocean ~:** [Ozean]liner, *der*

'liner train *n.* Containerzug, *der*

linesman /ˈlaɪnzmən/ *n., pl.* **linesmen** /ˈlaɪnzmən/ ▸ **p. 1260** **1** (Sport) Linienrichter, *der* **2** (Brit. Railw.) Streckenarbeiter, *der* **3** ▸ **lineman**

'line-up *n.* **1** Aufstellung, *die;* **~ of cabaret acts** Zusammenstellung von Kabarettauftritten **2** (Amer.) ▸ **identification parade**

ling¹ /lɪŋ/ *n.* (Zool.) Leng[fisch], *der*

ling² *n.* (Bot.) Heidekraut, *das*

linger /ˈlɪŋɡə(r)/ *v.i.* **1** (remain, wait) verweilen (geh.); bleiben; (persist) fortbestehen; ‹*Erkältung, Diskussion, Schmerzen:*› andauern; ‹*Lied:*› nachklingen; **her scent still ~ed in the room** ihr Duft hing noch im Raum **2** (dwell) **~ over** *or* **up[on] a subject** *etc.* bei einem Thema *usw.* verweilen; **~ over a meal** lange beim Essen sitzen

lingerie /ˈlæ̃ʒəriː/ *n.* **[women's] ~:** Damenunterwäsche, *die*

lingering /ˈlɪŋɡərɪŋ/ *adj.* anhaltend; verbleibend ‹*Zweifel*›; langwierig ‹*Krankheit*›; langsam ‹*Tod*›; nachklingend ‹*Melodie*›; **one last ~ look** ein letzter sehnsuchtsvoller Blick; **any ~ hope was abandoned** alle noch vorhandene Hoffnung schwand dahin (geh.)

lingo /ˈlɪŋɡəʊ/ *n., pl.* **~es** **1** (derog./joc.: language) Sprache, *die;* Kauderwelsch, *das* (abwertend) **2** (jargon) Fachjargon, *der*

lingua franca /lɪŋɡwə ˈfræŋkə/ *n.* Lingua franca, *die* (geh.); Verkehrssprache, *die*

linguist /ˈlɪŋɡwɪst/ *n.* **1** Sprachkundige, *der/die;* **she's a good ~:** sie kann mehrere Sprachen; **I'm no ~:** Sprachen liegen mir nicht **2** (philologist) Linguist, *der*/Linguistin, *die;* Sprachwissenschaftler, *der*/-wissenschaftlerin, *die*

linguistic /lɪŋˈɡwɪstɪk/ *adj.* (of **~s**) linguistisch; sprachwissenschaftlich; (of language) sprachlich; Sprach-; **~ science** *see* **linguistics**; **~ skills** Sprachbegabung, *die;* **~ fluency** Sprachgewandtheit, *die*

linguistically /lɪŋˈɡwɪstɪkəlɪ/ *adv.* sprachwissenschaftlich; linguistisch

linguistics /lɪŋˈɡwɪstɪks/ *n., no pl.* Linguistik, *die;* Sprachwissenschaft, *die*

liniment /ˈlɪnɪmənt/ *n.* Liniment, *das* (Med.); Einreib[e]mittel, *das*

lining /ˈlaɪnɪŋ/ *n.* (of clothes) Futter, *das;* (of stomach) Magenschleimhaut, *die;* (of objects, containers, machines, etc.) Auskleidung, *die*

'lining paper *n.* Schrankpapier, *das*

link /lɪŋk/

A *n.* **1** (of chain) Glied, *das* **2** ▸ **cuff link** **3** (connecting part) Bindeglied, *das;* Verbindung, *die;* **radio ~:** Funkverbindung, *die;* **road/rail ~:** Straßen-/Zugverbindung, *die;* **what is the ~ between these two?** was verbindet diese beiden?; **~ between two countries** Verbindung zwischen zwei Ländern; **sever all ~s with sb.** alle Bindungen zu jmdm. lösen; **have ~s with the Mafia** Verbindungen zur Mafia haben; *see also* **cut A 2** **4** ▸ **linkman**

B *v.t.* **1** (connect) verbinden; **how are these events ~ed?** was haben diese Ereignisse miteinander zu tun?; **~ sb. with sth.** jmdn. mit etw. in Verbindung bringen; **his name has been ~ed with hers** sein Name wurde mit ihrem in Verbindung gebracht; **be ~ed by telephone to Oslo** telefonisch mit Oslo verbunden sein **2** (clasp or hook together) **~ hands** sich bei den Händen halten; **~ arms** sich unterhaken

C *v.i.* **~ together** sich zusammenfügen; **~ with sth.** sich verbinden mit etw.; ‹*Firma:*› sich zusammenschließen mit etw.

Phrasal verb

- **~ 'up**

A *v.t.* miteinander verbinden; ankoppeln ‹*Wagen, Raumschiff usw.*› **(to** an + *Akk.*); miteinander in Verbindung bringen ‹*Fakten usw.*›; **~ up A with B** A mit B verbinden

B *v.i.* **~ up with sb.** sich mit jmdm. zusammentun *od.* zusammenschließen; **~ up with American TV** sich dem amerikanischen Fernsehen anschließen; **the spacecraft ~ed up** die Raumschiffe wurden angekoppelt; **this road ~s up with the M3** diese Straße mündet in die M3 *od.* geht in die M3 über. *See also* **link-up**

linkage /ˈlɪŋkɪdʒ/ *n.* **1** Verbindung, *die* **2** (system of links or bars) Gestänge, *das;* **steering ~:** Lenkgestänge, *das* **3** (Chem.) Verknüpfung, *die;* Verbindung, *die* **4** (Genetics) Kopplung, *die*

linkman /ˈlɪŋkmən/ *n., pl.* **linkmen** /ˈlɪŋkmən/ **1** Verbindungsmann, *der* **2** (Radio, Telev.) Moderator, *der*/Moderatorin, *die* **3** (Hockey, Footb.) Mittelfeldspieler, *der*

links /lɪŋks/ *sing. or pl.* **[golf] ~:** Golfplatz, *der*

'link-up *n.* Verbindung, *die;* (of spacecraft etc.) Ankopplung, *die*

linnet /ˈlɪnɪt/ *n.* (Ornith.) Hänfling, *der*

lino /ˈlaɪnəʊ/ *n., pl.* **~s** Linoleum, *das*

linocut *n.* Linolschnitt, *der*

linoleum /lɪˈnəʊlɪəm/ *n.* Linoleum, *das*

linseed /ˈlɪnsiːd/ *n.* Leinsamen, *der*

linseed: ~ cake *n.* (Agric.) Leinkuchen, *der;* **~ 'oil** *n.* Leinöl, *das*

lint /lɪnt/ *n.* **1** Mull, *der* **2** (fluff) Fussel, *die*

lintel /ˈlɪntl/ *n.* (Archit.) Sturz, *der*

lion /ˈlaɪən/ *n.* **1** Löwe, *der;* **put one's head into the ~'s mouth** (fig.) sich in höchste Gefahr begeben; **the ~'s share** der Löwenanteil **2** (celebrity) **literary ~ [of the day]** literarischer Löwe des Tages (veralt.) **3** (Astrol.) **the L~:** der Löwe; *see also* **archer 2**

lioness /ˈlaɪənɪs/ *n.* Löwin, *die*

lion: ~heart *n.* Löwenherz, *das* (dichter. veralt.); **Richard [the] L~heart** Richard Löwenherz; **~-hearted** *adj.* wagemutig; löwenherzig (dichter. veralt.)

lionize (**lionise**) /ˈlaɪənaɪz/ *v.t.* [als Berühmtheit] feiern

'lion tamer *n.* ▸ **p. 1260** Löwenbändiger, *der*

lip /lɪp/ *n.* **1** ▸ **p. 951** Lippe, *die;* **lower/upper ~:** Unter-/Oberlippe, *die;* **bite one's ~** (lit. or fig.) sich (*Dat.*) auf die Lippen beißen; **escape sb.'s ~s** jmds. Lippen (*Dat.*) entschlüpfen; **hang on sb.'s ~s** an jmds. Lippen (*Dat.*) hängen; **lick one's ~s** (lit. or fig.) sich (*Dat.*) die Lippen lecken; **not let a word pass one's ~s** kein Wort über seine Lippen kommen lassen; **not a morsel passed his ~s** er rührte nichts an; **keep a stiff upper ~** (fig.) Haltung bewahren; *see also* **button B; seal² B 2; smack² B 2** **2** (of saucer, cup, crater) [Gieß]rand, *der;* (of jug) Schnabel, *der;* Tülle, *die* **3** (coll.: impudence) **give sb. some ~:** jmdm. gegenüber eine dicke Lippe riskieren (ugs.); **none of your ~!** keine frechen Bemerkungen!

l

'lipgloss *n., no pl.* Lipgloss, *das*

lipid /ˈlɪpɪd/ *n.* (Chem.) Lipid, *das*

liposuction /ˈlaɪpəʊsʌkʃn, ˈlɪpəʊsʌkʃn/ **A** *n.* Fettabsaugung, *die;* Liposuktion, *die* (Med) **B** *v.t.* absaugen ‹Fett›

lipped /lɪpt/ *adj.* **thick-/thin-~:** dick-/dünnlippig; **~ vessel** Gefäß mit Schnabel *od.* Gießrand

lippy /ˈlɪpɪ/ **A** *adj.* (coll.) frech; vorlaut; **get ~:** eine [dicke *od.* große] Lippe riskieren (salopp) **B** *n., no pl.* (coll.) Lippenstift, *der*

lip: ~-read A *v.i.* von den Lippen lesen; **B** *v.t.* **be able to ~-read what sb. says** jmdm. von den Lippen ablesen können, was er/sie sagt; **~-reading** *n., no pl.* Lippenlesen, *das;* **~salve** *n., no pl.* (Brit.) Lippenpflege, *die;* **~ service** *n., no pl.* **pay** *or* **give ~ service to sth.** ein Lippenbekenntnis zu etw. ablegen; **~stick** *n.* Lippenstift, *der*

liquefaction /lɪkwɪˈfækʃn/ *n.* Verflüssigung, *die*

liquefier /ˈlɪkwɪfaɪə(r)/ *n.* Verflüssiger, *der*

liquefy /ˈlɪkwɪfaɪ/ **A** *v.t.* verflüssigen **B** *v.i.* sich verflüssigen

liqueur /lɪˈkjʊə(r)/ *n.* Likör, *der*

liqueur: ~ 'brandy *n.: gut gealterter, hochwertiger Brandy;* **~ 'chocolate** *n.* Likörpraline, *die;* **~ glass** *n.* Likörglas, *das*

liquid /ˈlɪkwɪd/ **A** *adj.* [1] flüssig; glänzend ‹*Augen*›; hell klingend ‹*Töne, Laute*›; **~ air** Flüssigluft, *die;* **~ blue** wasserblau [2] (Commerc.) liquid; **~ assets** flüssige Mittel [3] (Phonet.) **~ consonant** Fließlaut, *der;* Liquida, *die* (fachspr.) **B** *n.* [1] Flüssigkeit, *die;* **he can only take ~s** er kann nur Flüssiges zu sich nehmen [2] (Phonet.) Fließlaut, *der;* Liquida, *die* (fachspr.)

liquidate /ˈlɪkwɪdeɪt/ **A** *v.t.* [1] (Commerc.) liquidieren; tilgen ‹*Schuld*›; **~d damages** (Law) Konventionalstrafe, *die* [2] (eliminate, kill) liquidieren; beseitigen **B** *v.i.* (Commerc.) liquidieren

liquidation /lɪkwɪˈdeɪʃn/ *n.* [1] (Commerc.) Liquidation, *die;* (of debt) Tilgung, *die;* **go into ~:** in Liquidation gehen [2] (eliminating, killing) Liquidierung, *die;* Beseitigung, *die*

liquidator /ˈlɪkwɪdeɪtə(r)/ *n.* (Commerc.) Liquidator, *der*

liquid: ~ 'crystal *n.* Flüssigkristall, *der;* **~ crystal dis'play** *n.* Flüssigkristallanzeige, *die*

liquidity /lɪˈkwɪdɪtɪ/ *n., no pl.* [1] flüssiger Zustand [2] (Commerc.) Liquidität, *die*

liquidize /ˈlɪkwɪdaɪz/ *v.t.* auflösen; (Cookery) [im Mixer] pürieren

liquidizer /ˈlɪkwɪdaɪzə(r)/ *n.* Mixer, *der*

liquid 'measure *n.* Flüssigkeitsmaß, *das*

liquor /ˈlɪkə(r)/ *n.* [1] (drink) Alkohol, *der;* Spirituosen *Pl.;* **be able to carry** *or* **hold one's ~:** etwas vertragen können; **hard** *or* **strong ~:** hochprozentiger Alkohol; scharfe Sachen (ugs.); **be the worse for ~:** betrunken sein [2] (Industry) Beize, *die*

Phrasal verb

• **~ 'up** (sl.) *v.t.* besoffen machen (derb); **get/be ~ed up** sich (*Dat.*) einen ansaufen/besoffen sein (derb)

liquorice /ˈlɪkərɪs/ *n.* [1] (root) Süßholz, *das;* (preparation) Lakritze, *die* [2] (plant) Süßholzstrauch, *der*

'liquor store *n.* (Amer.) Spirituosenladen, *der*

lira /ˈlɪərə/ *n., pl.* **lire** /ˈlɪərə, ˈlɪərɪ/ *or* **~s** Lira, *die*

Lisbon /ˈlɪzbən/ *pr. n.* ▸ **ⓘ p. 1643** Lissabon (*das*)

lisle /laɪl/ *n.* **~ [thread]** Florgarn, *das* (Textilw.)

lisp /lɪsp/ **A** *v.i. & t.* lispeln **B** *n.* Lispeln, *das;* **speak with a ~:** lispeln; **have a bad ~:** stark lispeln

lissom[e] /ˈlɪsəm/ *adj.* geschmeidig

list¹ /lɪst/ **A** *n.* [1] Liste, *die;* **active ~** (Mil.) Liste der Reserve; **publisher's ~:** Verlagsprogramm, *das;* **shopping ~:** Einkaufszettel, *der* [2] *in pl.* **enter the ~s [against sb./sth.]** (fig.) zum Kampf [gegen jmdn./etw.] antreten **B** *v.t.* aufführen; auflisten; (verbally) aufzählen; **~ed securities/stock** an der Börse zugelassene Wertpapiere/Aktien

list² **A** *n.* [1] (Naut.: tilt) Schlagseite, *die;* **have/develop a pronounced ~:** deutlich Schlagseite haben/bekommen [2] (of building, fence, etc.) Neigung, *die;* **develop a ~:** sich neigen **B** *v.i.* [1] (Naut.) **~ [to port/starboard]** Schlagseite [nach Backbord/Steuerbord] haben [2] ‹*Gebäude, Zaun usw.:*› sich neigen

listed 'building *n.* (Brit.) Gebäude unter Denkmalsschutz

listen /ˈlɪsn/ *v.i.* zuhören; **~ to music/the radio** Musik/Radio hören; **just ~ to the noise they are making!** hör dir bloß mal an, was sie für einen Lärm machen!; **~, nitwit** hör zu, du Trottel; **they ~ed to his words** sie hörten ihm zu; **you never ~ to what I say** du hörst mir nie zu; **we stopped and ~ed** wir hielten inne und horchten; **~ [out] for sth./sb.** auf etw. (*Akk.*) horchen/horchen, ob jmd. kommt; **~ to sth./sb.** (pay heed) auf etw./jmdn. hören; **he wouldn't ~** (heed) er wollte nicht hören; **~ to sb.'s grievances** sich (*Dat.*) jmds. Beschwerden anhören

Phrasal verb

• **~ 'in** *v.i.* [1] (Radio) hören (**on, to** *Akk.*) [2] (tap line) mithören [3] (eavesdrop) mithören (**on, to** *Akk.*)

listener /ˈlɪsnə(r)/ *n.* [1] Zuhörer, *der*/Zuhörerin, *die;* **be a good ~:** ein guter Zuhörer sein [2] (Radio) Hörer, *der*/Hörerin, *die*

listening post /ˈlɪsnɪŋ pəʊst/ *n.* (Mil.; also fig.) Horchposten, *der*

listeria /lɪˈstɪərɪə/ *n., no pl.* (Med.) Listeria, *die*

listing /ˈlɪstɪŋ/ *n.* Aufführung, *die;* Auflistung, *die;* (verbal) Aufzählung, *die*

listless /ˈlɪstlɪs/ *adj.,* **listlessly** /ˈlɪstlɪslɪ/ *adv.* lustlos

listlessness /ˈlɪstlɪsnɪs/ *n., no pl.* Lustlosigkeit, *die*

'list price *n.* Katalogpreis, *der*

lit /lɪt/ ▸ **light¹ D; light³**

litany /ˈlɪtənɪ/ *n.* (lit. or fig.) Litanei, *die;* **the L~:** *die Litanei im Book of Common Prayer*

litchi /ˈlaɪtʃɪ, ˈlɪtʃɪ/ *n.* Litschi, *die*

lite, Lite ® /laɪt/ **A** *adj.* kalorienreduziert ‹*Bier, Käse etc.*› **B** *n.* Leichtbier, *das*

liter (Amer.) ▸ **litre**

literacy /ˈlɪtərəsɪ/ *n., no pl.* Lese- und Schreibfertigkeit, *die;* **adult ~ classes** Kurse für Analphabeten; **~ is low** das Analphabetentum ist groß

literacy: ~ hour *n.* (Brit. Educ.) Lese-Schreib-Förderunterricht, *der;* **~ test** *n.* Lese- und Schreibtest, *der*

literal /ˈlɪtərl/ **A** *adj.* [1] wörtlich; **take sth. in a ~ sense** etw. wörtlich nehmen [2] (not exaggerated) buchstäblich; **the ~ truth** die reine Wahrheit [3] (coll.: with some exaggeration) wahr [4] (prosaic) nüchtern; prosaisch [5] (in text) **~ error** Tippfehler, *der;* (misprint) Druckfehler, *der* **B** *n.* [1] (error) Tippfehler, *der;* (misprint) Druckfehler, *der* [2] (Computing) Literal, *das*

literally /ˈlɪtərəlɪ/ *adv.* [1] wörtlich; **take sth./sb. ~:** etw./was jmd. sagt, wörtlich nehmen [2] (actually) buchstäblich [3] (coll.: with some exaggeration) geradezu

literal: ~-'minded *adj.* nüchtern [denkend]; **~-'mindedness** /lɪtərlˈmaɪndɪdnɪs/ *n., no pl.* Nüchternheit [des Denkens]

literary /ˈlɪtərərɪ/ *adj.* literarisch; (not colloquial) gewählt; **be of a ~ turn of mind** sich für Literatur interessieren

literary: ~ 'agent *n.* Literaturagent, *der*/-agentin, *die;* **~ 'critic** *n.* Literaturkritiker, *der*/-kritikerin, *die;* **~ ex'ecutor** ▸ **executor; ~ gent** *n.* (coll.) Literat, *der* (oft abwertend); **~ hi'storian** *n.* Literaturhistoriker, *der*/-historikerin, *die;* **~ 'history** *n.* Literaturgeschichte, *die;* **~ 'luncheon** *n.* literarischer Lunch (*mit Schriftstellern und Verlegern*); **~ man** *n.* Schriftsteller, *der;* (versed in literature) Literaturkenner, *der*

literate /ˈlɪtərət/ **A** *adj.* (able to read and write) des Lesens und Schreibens kundig; (educated) gebildet; **not be ~:** nicht lesen und schreiben können **B** *n.* Alphabet, *der*

literati /lɪtəˈrɑːtɪ/ *n., no pl.* Bildungsbürger *Pl.*

literature /ˈlɪtərətʃə(r), ˈlɪtrətʃə(r)/ *n.* [1] Literatur, *die* [2] (writings on a subject) [Fach]literatur, *die* (**on zu**) [3] (coll.: printed matter) Literatur, *die;* Informationsmaterial, *das;* **advertising ~:** Werbeschriften *od.* -material

lithe /laɪð/ *adj.* geschmeidig

lithium /ˈlɪθɪəm/ *n.* (Chem.) Lithium, *das*

litho /ˈlaɪθəʊ/ (coll.) **A** *n., pl.* **~s** Litho, *das* **B** *adj.* Litho-; **~ print/printing** Litho, *das* **C** *v.t.* lithographieren

lithograph /ˈlɪθəgrɑːf/ **A** *n.* Lithographie, *die* **B** *v.t.* lithographieren

lithographer /lɪˈθɒgrəfə(r)/ *n.* Lithograph, *der*/Lithographin, *die*

lithographic /lɪθəˈgræfɪk/ *adj.* lithographisch

lithography /lɪˈθɒgrəfɪ/ *n.* Lithographie, *die*

Lithuania /lɪθjʊˈeɪnɪə/ *pr. n.* Litauen (*das*)

Lithuanian /lɪθjʊˈeɪnɪən/ ▸ **ⓘ p. 1277,** ▸ **ⓘ p. 1345** **A** *adj.* litauisch; **sb. is ~:** jmd. ist Litauer/Litauerin; *see also* **English A** **B** *n.* [1] (person) Litauer, *der*/Litauerin, *die* [2] (language) Litauisch, *das; see also* **English B 1**

litigant /ˈlɪtɪgənt/ **A** *n.* Prozesspartei, *die* **B** *adj.* **~ party** Prozesspartei, *die*

litigate /ˈlɪtɪgeɪt/ **A** *v.i.* prozessieren **B** *v.t.* vor Gericht verhandeln

litigation /lɪtɪˈgeɪʃn/ *n.* Rechtsstreit, *der;* **in ~:** rechtshängig

litigious /lɪˈtɪdʒəs/ *adj.* prozesssüchtig; **a ~ person** ein Prozesshansel (ugs.)

litmus /ˈlɪtməs/ *n.* Lackmus, *das od. der*

litmus: ~ paper *n.* Lackmuspapier, *das;* **~ test** *n.* (also fig.) Lackmustest, *der*

litotes /ˈlaɪtətiːz/ *n.* (Rhet.) Litotes, *die*

litre /ˈliːtə(r)/ *n.* ▸ **ⓘ p. 1690** (Brit.) Liter, *der od. das*

Litt. D. /lɪt ˈdiː/ ▸ **D. Litt.**

litter /ˈlɪtə(r)/ **A** *n.* [1] (rubbish) Abfall, *der;* Abfälle; **'do not leave ~'** „bitte keine Abfälle zurücklassen"; **her desk was strewn with a ~ of books** ihr Schreibtisch war mit Büchern übersät [2] (vehicle) Sänfte, *die* [3] (stretcher) Trage, *die;* Tragbahre, *die* [4] (bedding for animals) Streu, *die;* Einstreu, *die* (Landw.) [5] (young) Wurf, *der* **B** *v.t.* verstreuen; **papers were ~ed about the room** im Zimmer lagen überall Zeitungen herum; **~ the room with one's books** seine Bücher im Zimmer verstreuen **C** *v.i.* **'do not ~'** „bitte keine Abfälle zurücklassen"

litter: ~ basket *n.* Abfallkorb, *der;* **~ bin** *n.* Abfalleimer, *der;* **~bug, ~ lout** *ns.* Schmutzfink, *der* (ugs.)

little /ˈlɪtl/ **A** *adj.,* **~r** /ˈlɪtlə(r)/, **~st** /ˈlɪtlɪst/ (*Note: it is more common to use the compar. and superl. forms* **smaller, smallest**) [1] (small) klein; **~ town/book/dog** kleine Stadt/kleines Buch/kleiner Hund; (showing affection or amusement) Städtchen, *das*/Büchlein, *das*/Hündchen, *das;* **~ toe** kleine Zehe; **the ~ woman** (coll.: my wife) mein kleines Frauchen (ugs.); **you poor ~ thing!** du armes kleines Ding!; **don't worry your ~ head** zerbrich dir nicht dein Köpfchen!; **I know your ~ ways** ich kenne deine Tricks; **do one's ~ best** sein Bestes tun; **L~ Venice** Klein-Venedig, *das;* **the ~ people** (fairies) die Elfen; *see also* **bear¹ 3; slam² 1**

[2] (young) klein; **the ~ Joneses** die Jones-Kinder; **~ man/woman** (child) Kleiner/Kleine; **the ~ ones** die Kleinen; **my ~ sister** meine kleine Schwester
[3] (short) klein ‹*Person*›; **a ~ way** ein kleines *od.* kurzes Stück; **after a ~ while** nach kurzer Zeit; nach einer kleinen Weile (veralt.)
[4] (not much) wenig; **you have ~ time left** dir bleibt nicht mehr viel Zeit; **there is very ~ tea left** es ist kaum noch Tee *od.* nur noch ganz wenig Tee da; **make a nice ~ profit** (coll. iron.) einen hübschen Gewinn machen (ugs.); **a ~ ...** (a small quantity of) etwas ...; ein wenig *od.* bisschen ...; **speak a ~ German** etwas Deutsch sprechen; **speak only a ~ German** nur wenig Deutsch sprechen; **a ~ goes a long way** ein bisschen reicht lange; (fig.) ein bisschen hat eine große Wirkung; **no ~ ...:** nicht wenig ...
[5] (trivial) klein; **get annoyed about ~ things** sich über Kleinigkeiten aufregen; **of course, this 'would occur to your mean ~ mind** einem miesen Kleingeist wie dir muss natürlich so etwas einfallen; **~ things please ~ minds** kleine Geister erfreuen sich an kleinen Dingen. *See also* **Englander**; **old A 5**; **Russian B 2**

B *n.* wenig; **but ~:** nur wenig; **~ or nothing** kaum etwas; so gut wie nichts; **[do] not a ~:** einiges [tun]; **not a ~ angry** *etc.* ziemlich verärgert *usw.*; **there was ~ we could do** wir konnten nur wenig tun; **a ~** (a small quantity) etwas; ein wenig *od.* bisschen; (somewhat) ein wenig; **too ~ too late** zu wenig [und] zu spät; **think ~ of sb.** gering von jmdm. denken; **after a ~:** nach einer Weile; **a ~ after eight** kurz nach acht; **for a ~:** ein Weilchen; (a short way) ein Stückchen; **we see very ~ of one another** wir sehen sehr wenig voneinander; **~ by ~:** nach und nach; **the ~ I know** das wenige, was ich weiß; *see also* **help A 1**; **make A 13**; **what F 1**

C *adv.*, **less** /les/, **least** /li:st/ [1] (not at all) **she ~ thought that ...:** sie dachte nicht im Geringsten daran, dass ...; **he ~ suspected/knew what ...:** er hatte nicht die geringste Ahnung/wusste überhaupt nicht, was ...
[2] (to only a small extent) **~ as he liked it** sowenig es ihm auch gefiel; **he writes ~ now** er schreibt nur noch wenig; **~ more/less than ...:** kaum mehr/weniger als ...; **that is ~ less than ...:** das grenzt schon an (+ *Akk.*) ...; **the holiday was ~ less than a disaster** der Urlaub war ein ziemlicher Reinfall (ugs.); **his behaviour is ~ less than disgraceful** sein Benehmen ist schon fast skandalös zu nennen

little: ~ end *n.* (Brit. Motor Veh.) Pleuelauge, *das* (Technik); **~ 'finger** *n.* kleiner Finger; **twist sb. round one's ~ finger** jmdn. um den [kleinen] Finger wickeln (ugs.); **~-known** *adj.* wenig bekannt

Little Englander /lɪtl 'ɪŋgləndə(r)/ *n.:* *Verfechter[in] eines mit Europa- und Fremdenfeindlichkeit verbundenen britischen Isolationismus*

littleness /'lɪtlnɪs/ *n., no pl.* Kleinheit, *die*

'little theatre *n.* Kleinbühne, *die*

littoral /'lɪtərl/
A *adj.* litoral (Geogr.)
B *n.* Litoral, *das* (Geogr.); Küstengebiet, *das*

liturgical /lɪ'tɜ:dʒɪkl/ *adj.* liturgisch

liturgy /'lɪtədʒɪ/ *n.* [1] Liturgie, *die* [2] (Book of Common Prayer) **the ~:** das Book of Common Prayer

live¹ /laɪv/
A *adj.* [1] *attrib.* (alive) lebend [2] (Radio, Telev.) **~ performance** Live-Aufführung, *die;* **~ broadcast** Livesendung, *die;* Direkt- *od.* Originalübertragung, *die;* **we go ~ tomorrow** (fig.) morgen machen wir Ernst [3] (topical) aktuell ‹*Thema, Frage*› [4] (Electr.) Strom führend [5] (unexploded) scharf ‹*Munition usw.*› [6] (glowing) glühend ‹*Kohle*› [7] (joc.: actual) **real ~:** richtig [8] (Mech. Engin.) Trieb‹*rad, -feder*›; Antriebs‹*achse, -rad, -welle*›
B *adv.* (Radio, Telev.) live ‹*übertragen usw.*›

live² /lɪv/
A *v.i.* [1] leben; **~ and let ~:** leben und leben lassen; **~ by sth.** von etw. leben; **will he ~?** wird er am Leben bleiben?; **you'll ~** (iron.) du wirsts [schon] überleben (iron.); **as long as I ~ I shall never understand why ...:** mein Leben lang werde ich nicht begreifen, warum ...; **~ to see** [mit]erleben; **she will ~ to regret her stupidity** sie wird ihre Dummheit noch bereuen; **you ~ and learn** man lernt nie aus; **~ for sth./sb.** für etw./jmdn. leben; **~ through sth.** etw. durchmachen (ugs.); (survive) etw. überleben; **~ to a ripe old age/to be a hundred** ein hohes Alter erreichen/hundert Jahre alt werden; **long ~ the queen!** lang lebe die Königin!; **they ~d violently** ihr Leben stand im Zeichen der Gewalt; **~ beyond one's means** über seine Verhältnisse leben; **~ well** (eat well) es sich (*Dat.*) gut gehen lassen; *see also* **hand A 1** [2] (make permanent home) wohnen; leben; **the room seems ~d in** das Zimmer scheint bewohnt zu sein; **~ together** zusammenleben; **~ with sb.** mit jmdm. zusammenleben; **~ with sth.** (lit. or fig.) mit etw. leben
B *v.t.* [1] leben; **~ one's own life** sein eigenes Leben leben; **~ an honest life** ein ehrbares Leben führen; **~ it up** das Leben in vollen Zügen genießen; (have a good time) einen draufmachen (ugs.) [2] (express) **~ one's convictions** nach seiner Überzeugung leben; **what others were preaching, he ~d** was andere nur predigten, lebte er vor

Phrasal verbs

- **~ 'down** *v.t.* Gras wachsen lassen über (+ *Akk.*); **he will never be able to ~ it down** das wird ihm ewig anhängen
- **~ 'in** *v.i.* (Brit.) ‹*Personal, Koch usw.:*› im Haus wohnen; ‹*Student, Krankenschwester:*› im Wohnheim wohnen
- **~ on**
A /'-‐/ *v.t.* leben von; (fig.) zehren von ‹*Ruf*›; leben von ‹*Hoffnung*›; **~ on air** (joc.) von der Luft *od.* (ugs. scherzh.) von Luft und Liebe leben; *see also* **fat B**
B /-'-/ *v.i.* weiterleben
- **~ out**
A /-'-/ *v.i.* (Brit.) außerhalb wohnen
B /'--/ *v.t.* [1] (survive) überleben; überstehen ‹*Winter, Woche*› [2] (complete, spend) verbringen; **they had ~d out their lives as fishermen** sie waren ihr Leben lang Fischer gewesen
- **~ 'up to** *v.t.* gerecht werden (+ *Dat.*); **~ up to one's principles/faith** nach seinen Prinzipien/seinem Glauben leben; **he's a bright lad — I hope he ~s up to his promise** er ist ein aufgeweckter Bursche — ich hoffe, er hält, was er verspricht; **~ up to one's reputation** seinem Ruf Ehre machen; **~ up to one's income** seinen Verhältnissen entsprechend leben

liveable /'lɪvəbl/ *adj.* lebenswert, erträglich ‹*Leben*›

live birth /laɪv 'bɜ:θ/ *n.* Lebendgeburt, *die*

live-in /'lɪvɪn/ *attrib. adj.* im Haus wohnend ‹*Personal*›; **~ cook** Hauskoch *der*/Hausköchin, *die;* **~ lover** Geliebter, der/Geliebte, die bei ihr/ihm *usw.* wohnt

livelihood /'laɪvlɪhʊd/ *n.* Lebensunterhalt, *der;* **gain a ~ from sth.** sich (*Dat.*) seinen Lebensunterhalt mit etw. verdienen; **her ~ is her painting** sie lebt von der Malerei

liveliness /'laɪvlɪnɪs/ *n., no pl.* Lebhaftigkeit, *die*

livelong /'lɪvlɒŋ/ *adj.* (poet./rhet.) **all the ~ day/night** den lieben langen Tag/die ganze Nacht [hindurch]

lively /'laɪvlɪ/ *adj.* [1] lebhaft; lebendig ‹*Gegenwart*›; rege ‹*Handel*›; **things start to get ~ at 9 a.m.** um 9 Uhr wird es lebhaft; **have a ~ sense of humour** immer zu Späßen aufgelegt sein; **look ~** (coll.) sich ranhalten (ugs.) [2] (vivid) lebendig, anschaulich ‹*Bericht, Schilderung*› [3] (joc.: exciting, dangerous, difficult) **things were getting ~:** die Sache wurde gefährlich; **give sb. a ~ time, make things ~ for sb.** jmdm. zu schaffen machen [4] (fresh) lebhaft ‹*Farbe*›

liven ▸ **~ up A**

liven up /laɪvn 'ʌp/
A *v.t.* Leben bringen in (+ *Akk.*)
B *v.i.* ‹*Person:*› aufleben; **things will ~ up when ...:** es wird Leben in die Bude kommen (ugs.), wenn ...

liver¹ /'lɪvə(r)/ *n.* ▸ **p. 951** (Anat., Gastr.) Leber, *die*

liver² *n.* **be a fast/clean ~:** ein flottes/solides Leben führen

'live rail *n.* Stromschiene, *die*

'liver-coloured *adj.* leberbraun

liveried /'lɪvərɪd/ *adj.* livriert

liverish /'lɪvərɪʃ/ *adj.* [1] (unwell) elend; unwohl [2] (grumpy) mürrisch

Liverpudlian /lɪvə'pʌdlɪən/
A *adj.* Liverpooler
B *n.* Liverpooler, *der*/Liverpoolerin, *die*

liver: ~ salts *n. pl.* (Brit.) ≈ Magenmittel, *das;* **~ sausage** *n.* Leberwurst, *die;* **~wort** *n.* Lebermoos, *das;* **~wurst** /'lɪvəwɜ:st/ (Amer.) ▸ **~ sausage**

livery /'lɪvərɪ/ *n.* Livree, *die;* **in/out of ~:** livriert/nicht livriert

livery: ~ company *n.* (Brit.) *Londoner Zunft;* **~ stable** *n.* Mietstall, *der*

lives /laɪvz/ *pl. of* **life**

live /laɪv/: **~stock** *n. pl.* Vieh, *das;* **large number of ~stock** großer Viehbestand; **~ weight** *n.* Lebendgewicht, *das;* **~ 'wire** *n.* (Electr.) Strom führender Draht; (fig.) Energiebündel, *das* (ugs.)

livid /'lɪvɪd/ *adj.* [1] (bluish) bleigrau [2] (Brit. coll.: furious) fuchtig (ugs.)

living /'lɪvɪŋ/
A *n.* [1] Leben, *das; see also* **cost of living**; **standard A 2** [2] (livelihood) Lebensunterhalt, *der;* **make a ~:** seinen Lebensunterhalt verdienen; **earn one's [own] ~:** sich (*Dat.*) seinen Lebensunterhalt [selbst] verdienen; **make one's ~ out of farming** von der Landwirtschaft leben; **make a good ~:** viel verdienen; **it's a ~** (joc.) man kann davon leben [3] (Brit. Eccl.) Pfründe, *die* [4] (way of life) Lebensstil, *der;* **the art of ~:** die Kunst zu leben; **good ~:** üppiges Leben; (pious) guter Lebenswandel; **high ~:** hoher Lebensstandard [5] *in pl.* **the ~:** die Lebenden; **be still/back in the land of the ~:** noch/wieder unter den Lebenden weilen
B *adj.* [1] lebend; **~ things** Lebewesen *Pl.*; **not a ~ soul** keine Menschenseele; **no man ~:** niemand auf der Welt; **it was a ~ death for him** er fühlte sich dort wie lebendig begraben; **within ~ memory** seit Menschengedenken; **be the ~ image of sb.** jmds. Ebenbild sein; **a ~ monument** ein lebendiges Zeugnis (**to** *Gen.*); *see also* **daylight 3** [2] (uncut, unquarried) gewachsen ‹*Stein, Fels*› [3] (still in vernacular use) lebend ‹*Sprache*›

living: ~ 'dead *n. pl* lebendige Tote; **~ expenses** *n. pl.* Lebenshaltungskosten *Pl.;* **~ room** *n.* Wohnzimmer, *das;* **~ space** *n.* [1] Lebensraum, *der;* [2] (in dwelling) Wohnraum, *der;* **~ 'wage** *n.* Lohn, von dem man leben kann; **~ 'will** *n.* Patientenverfügung, *die*

Livy /'lɪvɪ/ *pr. n.* Livius (*der*)

lizard /'lɪzəd/ *n.* Eidechse, *die*

ll. *abbr.* **= lines** Zz.

'll /l/ (coll.) **= shall; will¹**

llama /'lɑ:mə/ *n.* (Zool., Textiles) Lama, *das*

LLB/LLD/LLM *abbrs.* **= Bachelor/Doctor/Master of Laws;** *see also* **BSc**

lo /ləʊ/ *int.* [1] **lo and behold** (joc.) sieh[e] da [2] (arch.) siehe/seh[e]t

loach /ləʊtʃ/ *n.* (Zool.) Schmerle, *die*

load /ləʊd/
A *n.* [1] (burden, weight) Last, *die;* (amount carried) Ladung, *die;* **a ~ of hay** eine Ladung Heu; **barrow~ of apples** Karre voll Äpfel; **a ~ of [old] rubbish** *or* **tripe** (fig. coll.) ein einziger Mist (ugs.); **talk a ~ of rubbish** eine Menge Blödsinn reden (ugs.); **what a ~ of rubbish!** was für ein Quatsch (ugs.) *od.* (ugs. abwertend) Schmarren!; **get a ~ of this!** (coll.) (listen) hör einmal gut *od.* genau zu! (ugs.); (look) guck mal genau hin! (ugs.) [2] (weight) Last, *die;* (Electr.) Belastung, *die* [3] (fig.) Last, *die;* Bürde, *die* (geh.); **a heavy ~ of work** eine große Arbeitsbelastung; **take a ~ off sb.'s mind** jmdm. eine Last von der Seele nehmen; **that's a ~ off my mind** damit fällt mir ein Stein vom Herzen; **teaching ~** (Sch.) Deputat, *das* [4] *usu. in pl.*

(coll.: plenty) **~s of** jede Menge *od.* massenhaft (ugs.) ‹*Nahrungsmittel usw.*›; **have ~s of sense** sehr vernünftig sein
B *v.t.* **1** (put ~ on) beladen; **~ sb. with work** (fig.) jmdm. Arbeit auftragen *od.* (ugs. abwertend) aufhalsen *od.* (geh.) aufbürden **2** (put as ~) laden **3** (weight with lead) mit Blei beschweren; **~ed dice** präparierte Würfel; **the dice were ~ed against him** (fig.) er hatte schlechte Karten **4** (charge) laden ‹*Gewehr*›; **~ a camera** einen Film [in einen Fotoapparat] einlegen **5** (insert) einlegen ‹*Film, Tonband usw.*› (**into** in + *Akk.*); laden ‹*Datei, Dokument*› **6** (strain) schwer belasten; **a table ~ed with food** ein mit Speisen beladener Tisch **7** (overwhelm) (with praise, presents, etc.) überhäufen; (with abuse) überschütten
C *v.i.* laden (**with** *Akk.*); Ladung übernehmen
Phrasal verb
• **~ 'up** *v.i.* laden (**with** *Akk.*)

'load-bearing *adj.* tragend ‹*Wand, Balken, Konstruktion*›

loaded /'ləʊdɪd/ *adj.* **1** (coll.: rich) **be ~:** [schwer] Kohle haben (salopp) **2** (coll.: drunk) voll (ugs.) **3** (Amer. sl.: drugged) high (Jargon verhüll.); **be ~ [up] on heroin** sich mit Heroin voll gepumpt haben (ugs.) **4** **~ for bear** (Amer. coll.) für alles gerüstet **5** **emotionally ~ words** emotional befrachtete Wörter; **a ~ question** eine suggestive Frage. *See also* **load B**

loader /'ləʊdə(r)/ *n.* **1** (person who loads gun) [Gewehr]lader, *der* **2** (machine) Lader, *der* **3** *in comb.* (gun etc.) ‹*Vorder-, Hinter*›lader, *der*

'loading bay *n.* Ladeplatz, *der*

load: ~ line *n.* Ladelinie, *die* (Seew.); **~-shedding** *n.* (Electr.) Stromabschaltung, *die;* **~star** ▸ **lodestar**; **~stone** *n.* **1** (oxide) Magnetit, *der;* **2** (piece) Magnet[eisen]stein, *der;* **3** (fig.) Magnet, *der*

loaf¹ /ləʊf/ *n., pl.* **loaves** /ləʊvz/ **1** Brot, *das;* [Brot]laib, *der;* **a ~ of bread** ein Laib Brot; **a brown/white ~:** ein dunkles Brot/Weißbrot; **half a ~ is better than no bread** *or* **none** (prov.) wenig ist besser als gar nichts **2** (coll.: head) **use one's ~:** seinen Grips anstrengen (ugs.) **3** **~ sugar** Hutzucker, *der*

loaf²
A *v.i.* **1** **~ round town/the house** in der Stadt/zu Hause herumlungern (ugs.) **2** (saunter) trödeln (ugs.)
B *v.t.* **~ away** vertrödeln ‹*Zeit*›

loafer /'ləʊfə(r)/ *n.* **1** (idler) Faulenzer, *der* **2** **L~** ® *bequemer [mokassinartiger] Halbschuh*

loam /ləʊm/ *n.* **1** (paste) Lehm, *der* **2** (soil) Lehmboden, *der*

loamy /'ləʊmɪ/ *adj.* lehmig

loan /ləʊn/
A *n.* **1** (thing lent) Leihgabe, *die* **2** (lending) **let sb. have/give sb. the ~ of sth.** jmdm. etw. leihen; **may I have the ~ of your mower?** könnte ich mir mal Ihren Rasenmäher ausleihen?; **be [out] on ~** ‹*Buch, Schallplatte:*› ausgeliehen sein; **have sth. on ~ [from sb.]** etw. [von jmdm.] geliehen haben **3** (money lent) Darlehen, *das;* Kredit, *der;* (public ~) Anleihe, *die*
B *v.t.* **~ sth. to sb.** jmdm. etw. leihen; etw. an jmdn. verleihen

loan: ~ collection *n.* Leihgaben *Pl;* **~ shark** *n.* (coll.) Kredithai, *der* (ugs. abwertend); **~ translation** *n.* Lehnübersetzung, *die;* **~word** *n.* Lehnwort, *das*

loath /ləʊθ/ *pred. adj.* **be ~ to do sth.** etw. ungern tun; **be nothing ~:** nicht abgeneigt sein

loathe /ləʊð/ *v.t.* verabscheuen; nicht ausstehen können; **he ~s eggs** er mag Eier überhaupt nicht; **I ~ ironing** ich kann Bügeln nicht ausstehen; **I ~d having to tell her** ich fand es grässlich, ihr das sagen zu müssen

loathing /'ləʊðɪŋ/ *n.* Abscheu, *der* (**of, for** vor + *Dat.*); **have a ~ of sth.** Abscheu vor etw. (*Dat.*) haben; etw. verabscheuen

loathsome /'ləʊðsəm/ *adj.* abscheulich; widerlich; verhasst ‹*Tätigkeit, Pflicht*›

loaves *pl. of* **loaf¹**

lob /lɒb/
A *v.t.,* **-bb-** in hohem Bogen werfen; (Tennis) lobben
B *n.* (Tennis) Lob, *der*

lobby /'lɒbɪ/
A *n.* **1** (pressure group) Lobby, *die;* Interessenvertretung, *die* **2** (of hotel) Eingangshalle, *die;* (of theatre) Foyer, *das;* (anteroom) (narrow) Flur, *der;* (larger) Vorraum, *der* **3** (esp. Brit. Parl.: hall) Lobby, *die;* Wandelhalle, *die*
B *v.t.* (als Lobby) zu beeinflussen suchen ‹*Abgeordnete*›
C *v.i.* (als Lobby) seinen Einfluss geltend machen; **~ for/against sth.** (als Lobby) sich für etw. einsetzen/gegen etw. wenden

lobbyist /'lɒbɪɪst/ *n.* Lobbyist, *der*/Lobbyistin, *die*

lobe /ləʊb/ *n.* (ear~) Ohrläppchen, *das;* (of liver, lung, brain) Lappen, *der;* Lobus, *der* (fachspr.); (of leaf) Ausbuchtung, *die*

lobed /ləʊbd/ *adj.* gelappt

lobelia /lə'biːlɪə/ *n.* (Bot.) Lobelie, *die*

lobotomy /lə'bɒtəmɪ/ (Med.) Lobotomie, *die*

lobster /'lɒbstə(r)/ *n.* Hummer, *der*

'lobster pot *n.* Hummerkorb, *der*

local /'ləʊkl/
A *adj.* **1** lokal (bes. Zeitungsw.); Lokal‹*teil, -nachrichten, -sender*›; Kommunal‹*politiker, -wahl, -abgaben*›; (of this area) hiesig; (of that area) dortig; ortsansässig ‹*Firma, Familie*›; ‹*Wein, Produkt, Spezialität*› [aus] der Gegend; (Bot.) örtlich begrenzt [vorkommend]; lokal [verbreitet]; **~ knowledge** Ortskenntnis, *die;* **go into your ~ branch** gehen Sie zu Ihrer Filiale; **our ~ hairdresser** der Friseur bei uns in der Nähe/(in village) bei uns im Dorf; **she's a ~ girl** sie ist von hier/dort; **~ resident** Anwohner, *der*/Anwohnerin, *die;* **~ bus** hiesiger/dortiger Bus; (serving immediate area) Nahverkehrsbus, *der;* **your ~ candidate** der Kandidat Ihres Wahlkreises; **~ opinion** die Meinung der unmittelbar betroffenen Bevölkerung **2** (Med.) lokal ‹*Schmerzen, Entzündung*›; örtlich ‹*Betäubung*› **3** (Post) innerstädtisch ‹*Briefzustellung, Post*›
B *n.* **1** (inhabitant) Einheimische, *der/die* **2** (Brit. coll.: pub) [Stamm]kneipe, *die*

local: ~ anaes'thetic *n.* Lokalanästhetikum, *das* (Med.); **[be treated] under a ~ anaesthetic** unter örtlicher Betäubung *od.* (Med.) Lokalanästhesie [behandelt werden]; **~ area 'network** *n.* (Computing) lokales Netzwerk; **~ au'thority** *n.* (Brit.) Kommunalverwaltung, *die; attrib.* kommunal; **~ call** *n.* (Teleph.) Ortsgespräch, *das;* Nahbereichsgespräch, *das* (Postw.); **~ 'colour** ▸ **colour A 7**; **~ 'Derby** ▸ **Derby 1**

locale /ləʊ'kɑːl/ *n.* Ort, *der;* (of crime etc.) Schauplatz, *der*

local 'government *n.* Kommunalverwaltung, *die;* **~ elections/officials** Kommunalwahlen/-beamte

localise ▸ **localize**

locality /lə'kælɪtɪ/ *n.* **1** (position) (of thing) Position [im Raum]; (of person) Aufenthaltsort, *der;* (of mineral) Vorkommen, *das* **2** (district) Ort, *der;* Gegend, *die*

localization /ləʊkəlaɪ'zeɪʃn/ *n., no pl.* (Computing) Lokalisierung, *die*

localize /'ləʊkəlaɪz/ *v.t.* (restrict) eingrenzen (**to** auf + *Akk.*); lokalisieren (bes. Politik, DV, Med.)

locally /'ləʊkəlɪ/ *adv.* im/am Ort; in der Gegend

'local time *n.* Ortszeit, *die;* **[it's] 3 p.m. ~:** [es ist] 15 Uhr Ortszeit

locate /lə'keɪt/ *v.t.* **1** (position) platzieren; **be ~d** liegen; gelegen sein; **the factory is to be ~d on the edge of the town** die Fabrik soll am Stadtrand errichtet werden **2** (determine position of) ausfindig machen; lokalisieren (fachspr.); orten (Flugw., Seew.)

location /lə'keɪʃn/ *n.* **1** (position) Lage, *die;* (place) Ort, *der;* (of ship, aircraft, police car) Position, *die;* (of person, building, etc.) Standort, *der;* **discover the ~ of sth.** etw. ausfindig machen **2** (positioning) Positionierung, *die* **3** (determination of position of) Lokalisierung, *die;* **succeed in the ~ of the buried treasure** den vergrabenen Schatz ausfindig machen **4** (Cinemat.) Drehort, *der;* **be on ~:** bei Außenaufnahmen sein; **shoot on ~:** Außenaufnahmen drehen **5** (S. Afr.) [Bantu]siedlung, *die*

loc. cit. /lɒk 'sɪt/ *abbr.* **= in the passage already quoted** loc. cit.; a. a. O.

loch /lɒx, lɒk/ *n.* (Scot.) See, *der;* (in Scotland) Loch, *der;* (arm of sea) Meeresarm, *der;* (in Scotland) Loch, *der*

Loch Ness /lɒx 'nes, lɒk 'nes/ *pr. n.* Loch Ness (*der*); **~ monster** Ungeheuer von Loch Ness

lock¹ /lɒk/ *n.* **1** (tress of hair) [Haar]büschel, *das;* [Haar]strähne, *die;* (ringlet) Locke, *die* **2** *in pl.* (hair) Haar, *das* **3** (of wool, cotton, etc.) Flocke, *die*

lock²
A *n.* **1** (of door etc.) Schloss, *das;* **under ~ and key** unter [strengem] Verschluss **2** (on canal etc.) Schleuse, *die* **3** (on wheel) Sperrvorrichtung, *die;* Sperre, *die* **4** (Wrestling) Fesselgriff, *der;* Klammergriff, *der* **5** (of gun) Schloss, *das;* **~, stock, and barrel** (fig.) mit allem Drum und Dran (ugs.); **condemn sth. ~, stock, and barrel** (fig.) etw. in Bausch und Bogen verurteilen **6** (Motor Veh.) Lenkeinschlag, *der;* **full [left/right] ~:** voller Lenk[rad]einschlag [nach links/rechts] **7** (Rugby) **~ [forward]** Gedrängespieler in der zweiten Reihe **8** ▸ **airlock 2**
B *v.t.* **1** (fasten) zuschließen; abschließen; **~** *or* **shut the stable door after the horse has bolted** (fig.) den Brunnen erst zudecken, wenn das Kind hineingefallen ist **2** (shut) **~ sb./sth. in sth.** jmdn./etw. in etw. (*Akk.*) [ein]schließen; **~ sb./sth. out of sth.** jmdn./etw. aus etw. aussperren **3** (Mech. Engin.: engage) befestigen (**in** in + *Dat.*) **4** *in p.p.* (joined) **the wrestlers were ~ed in combat** die Ringer hielten sich im Fesselgriff; **the lovers were ~ed in an embrace** die Liebenden hielten sich fest umschlungen. *See also* **horn A 1**
C *v.i.* ‹*Tür, Kasten usw.:*› sich ab-/zuschließen lassen
Phrasal verbs
• **~ a'way** *v.t.* einschließen; wegschließen; einsperren ‹*Person, Tier*›; **he ought to be ~ed away** er gehört hinter Schloss und Riegel
• **~ 'in** *v.t.* einschließen; (deliberately) einsperren ‹*Person, Tier*›
• **~ 'on to** *v.t.* **1** ‹*Rakete:*› erfassen ‹*Ziel*› **2** ‹*Teleskop:*› sich einstellen auf (+ *Akk.*) ‹*Objekt*›
• **~ 'out** *v.t.* **1** aussperren; **~ oneself out** sich aussperren **2** (Industry) aussperren ‹*Arbeiter*›; *see also* **lockout**
• **~ 'up**
A *v.i.* abschließen
B *v.t.* **1** abschließen ‹*Haus, Tür*› **2** (imprison) einsperren; **he ought to be ~ed up** er gehört hinter Schloss und Riegel **3** (store inaccessibly) binden ‹*Kapital*›; (fig.) unterdrücken ‹*Gefühle*›; **~ sth. up in one's heart** (fig.) etw. ganz für sich behalten. *see also* **lock-up**

'lockdown *n.* Zellenarrest, *der*

locker /'lɒkə(r)/ *n.* **1** Schließfach, *das* **2** (Naut.) Schapp, *das od. der* (Seemannsspr.)

'locker room *n.* Umkleideraum, *der*

locket /'lɒkɪt/ *n.* Medaillon, *das*

lock: ~ gate *n.* Schleusentor, *das;* **~jaw** *n.* (Med.) Kieferklemme, *die;* (disease) Wundstarrkrampf, *der;* **~-keeper** *n.* Schleusenwärter, *der;* **~nut** *n.* (Mech.) Kontermutter, *die;* **~out** *n.* Aussperrung, *die;* **~smith** *n.* ▸ℹ **p. 1260** Schlosser, *der*/Schlosserin, *die;* **~ stitch** **A** *n.* Doppelsteppstich, *der;* **B** *v.t. & i.* steppen; **~-up** **A** *n.* **1** (closing time) Toresschluss, *der;* **2** (jail) Gewahrsam, *das* (veralt.); **B** *adj.* **1** (Brit.) **~-up shop/garage** *Laden in einem Gebäude, in dem der Inhaber nicht wohnt/nicht unmittelbar bei der Wohnung gelegene Garage;* **2** **~-up time** Torresschluss, *der*

locomotion /ləʊkə'məʊʃn/ *n.* Fortbewegung, *die;* Lokomotion, *die* (fachspr.)

locomotive /'ləʊkəməʊtɪv, ləʊkə'məʊtɪv/
A *n.* Lokomotive, *die*
B *adj.* **1** (of locomotion) lokomotorisch (fachspr.) **2** (not stationary) fahrbar ‹*Kran*›; **~ engine** Lokomotive, *die*

locum /'ləʊkəm/ *n.* (coll.), **locum tenens** /ləʊkəm 'tenenz/ *n.*, *pl.* **~ tenentes** /ləʊkəm te'nenti:z/ [Stell]vertreter, *der*/-vertreterin, *die*

locus /'ləʊkəs/ *n.*, *pl.* **loci** /'ləʊsaɪ/ 1 (Math.) geometrischer Ort 2 (Biol.) Genort, *der*

locust /'ləʊkəst/ *n.* 1 [Wander]heuschrecke, *die* 2 (Amer.: cicada) Zikade, *die* 3 (Bot.) **~ [bean]** Johannisbrot, *das*; **~ [tree]** (carob tree) Johannisbrotbaum, *der*; (false acacia) Robinie, *die*; Scheinakazie, *die*

locution /lə'kju:ʃn/ *n.* Lokution, *die* (geh.); (style) Ausdrucksweise, *die*; (idiom) Ausdruck, *der*; Redewendung, *die*

lode /ləʊd/ *n.* (Min.) Erzgang, *der*

loden /'ləʊdn/ *n.* (cloth) Loden, *der*

lode: ~star *n.* Leitstern, *der*; (esp.) Polarstern, *der*; (fig.) Leitbild, *das*; **~stone** ▸ **load-stone**

lodge /lɒdʒ/

A *n.* 1 (servant's cottage) Pförtner-/Gärtnerhaus, *das*; (Sport) [Jagd-/Ski]hütte, *die*; (hotel) Hotel, *das* 2 (porter's room) [Pförtner]loge, *die*; (at gate of school etc.) Pedellloge, *die* 3 (Freemasonry) Loge, *die*; **grand ~:** Großloge, *die* 4 (lair) Bau, *der* 5 (of trade union) Ortsgruppe, *die*

B *v.t.* 1 (deposit formally) einlegen ‹*Beschwerde, Protest, Berufung usw.*›; (bring forward) erheben ‹*Einspruch, Protest*›; einreichen ‹*Klage*›; **~ information against sb.** jmdn. anzeigen 2 (house) unterbringen; (receive as guest) beherbergen; bei sich unterbringen; (establish as resident) einquartieren 3 (leave) **~ sth. with sb./in a bank** *etc.* etw. bei jmdm./in einer Bank *usw.* hinterlegen *od.* deponieren 4 **~ power** *etc.* **in the hands of** *or* **with sb.** jmdm. Macht *od.* Befugnis[se] *usw.* übertragen 5 (put, fix) stecken; [hinein]stoßen ‹*Schwert, Messer usw.*›; **be ~d in sth.** in etw. (*Dat.*) stecken; **become ~d in sth.** ‹*Kugel, Messer:*› stecken bleiben in etw. (*Dat.*); **the idea became ~d in his mind** der Gedanke setzte sich in ihm fest

C *v.i.* 1 (be paying guest) [zur Miete] wohnen 2 (enter and remain) stecken bleiben (**in** in + *Dat.*); hängen bleiben (**on** an + *Dat.*); **~ in sb.'s memory** jmdm. im Gedächtnis bleiben 3 (reside) wohnen; (pass the night) übernachten; nächtigen (geh.)

lodger /'lɒdʒə(r)/ *n.* Untermieter, *der*/Untermieterin, *die*; *see also* **take in 4**

lodging /'lɒdʒɪŋ/ *n.* 1 *usu. in pl.* (rented room) [möbliertes] Zimmer 2 (accommodation) Unterkunft, *die*; **board** *or* **food and ~:** Unterkunft und Verpflegung; Kost und Logis

'lodging house *n.* Pension, *die*

loess /'ləʊes/ *n.* (Geol.) Löss, *der*

loft /lɒft/

A *n.* 1 (attic) [Dach]boden, *der*; (Amer.: room) Dachzimmer, *das* 2 (converted warehouse or factory) Loft, *der od. das* 3 (pigeon house) Taubenschlag, *der* 4 (gallery in church) Empore, *die*

B *v.t.* (Sport) hochspielen ‹*Ball*›; **~ a ball over sth.** einen Ball über etw. (*Akk.*) heben

loft: ~ conversion *n.* Dachausbau, *der*; **~ hatch** *n.* Dachbodenluke, *die*

loftily /'lɒftɪlɪ/ *adv.* 1 (grandiosely) feierlich ‹*schreiben, sprechen*› 2 (haughtily) hochmütig; überheblich

'loft ladder *n.* Dachbodenleiter, *die*

lofty /'lɒftɪ/ *adj.* 1 (exalted, grandiose) hoch; hehr (geh.); hochfliegend ‹*Ideen*›; hoch gesteckt ‹*Ziele*›; (fig.: elevated) feierlich ‹*Stil*› 2 (high) hoch [aufragend]; hoch ‹*Flug, Raum*› 3 (haughty) hochmütig; überheblich

log[1] /lɒg/

A *n.* 1 (rough piece of timber) [geschlagener] Baumstamm; (part of tree trunk) Klotz, *der*; (as cut for firewood) [Holz]scheit, *das*; **be as easy as falling off a ~:** kinderleicht sein; **sleep like a ~:** schlafen wie ein Klotz 2 **~[book]** Tagebuch, *das*; (Naut.) Logbuch, *das*; (Aeronaut.) Bordbuch, *das* 3 (Naut.: float etc.) Log, *das*

B *v.t.*, **-gg-:** 1 (record) Buch führen über (+ *Akk.*); (Naut.) ins Logbuch eintragen 2 (achieve) verbuchen

Phrasal verbs

- **~ 'in** ▸ **~ on**
- **~ 'off** *v.i.* (Computing) sich abmelden
- **~ 'on** *v.i.* (Computing) sich anmelden
- **~ 'out** ▸ **~ off**

log[2] *n.* (Math.) Logarithmus, *der*

loganberry /'ləʊgnbərɪ/ *n.* Loganbeere, *die*

logarithm /'lɒgərɪðm/ *n.* (Math.) Logarithmus, *der*

logarithmic /lɒgə'rɪðmɪk/ *adj.* (Math.) logarithmisch

log: ~book *n.* 1 (Brit.: of car) Zulassung, *die*; 2 ▸ **log**[1] **A 2**; **~ 'cabin** *n.* Blockhütte, *die*; **~ 'fire** *n.* Holzfeuer, *das*

loggerheads /'lɒgəhedz/ *n. pl.* **be at ~ with sb.** mit jmdm. im Clinch liegen; **they were constantly at ~:** sie lagen ständig miteinander im Clinch

loggia /'ləʊdʒjə, 'lɒdʒjə/ *n.* Loggia, *die*

logging /'lɒgɪŋ/ *n.*, *no pl.*, *no indef. art.* Holzeinschlag, *der* (Forstw.)

logic /'lɒdʒɪk/ *n.* Logik, *die*

logical /'lɒdʒɪkl/ *adj.* 1 logisch; **she has a ~ mind** sie denkt logisch 2 (clear-thinking) logisch denkend; klar denkend

logicality /lɒdʒɪ'kælɪtɪ/ *n.* Logik, *die*

logically /'lɒdʒɪkəlɪ/ *adv.* logisch

logical 'positivism *n.* (Philos.) logischer Empirismus

'logic circuit *n.* logischer Schaltkreis

logician /lə'dʒɪʃn/ *n.* (Philos.) Logiker, *der*/Logikerin, *die*

'login *n.* (Computing) Log-in, *das*

logistic /lə'dʒɪstɪk/ *adj.*, **logistical** /lə'dʒɪstɪkl/ *adj.* logistisch

logistically /lə'dʒɪstɪklɪ/ *adv.* logistisch

logistics /lə'dʒɪstɪks/ *n. pl.* Logistik, *die*

'logjam *n.: Stau von treibendem Holz/Flößholz;* **the talks failed to move** *or* **break the ~** (fig.) die Gespräche haben keinen Durchbruch gebracht

logo /'lɒgəʊ, 'ləʊgəʊ/ *n.*, *pl.* **~s** Signet, *das*; Logo, *das*

log: ~off *n.* (Computing) ▸ **logout**; **~out** *n.* (Computing) Log-out, *das*

'log tables *n. pl.* Logarithmentafeln

loin /lɔɪn/ *n.* 1 *in pl.* (Anat.) Lende, *die*; *see also* **gird up** 2 (meat) Lende, *die*

'loincloth *n.* Lendenschurz, *der*

loiter /'lɔɪtə(r)/ *v.i.* trödeln; bummeln; (linger suspiciously) herumlungern; **~ with intent** sich mit gesetzwidriger Absicht herumtreiben

Phrasal verb

- **~ a'way** *v.t.* vertrödeln ‹*Zeit*›

loiterer /'lɔɪtərə(r)/ *n.* Herumtreiber, *der*; Herumlungerer, *der* (salopp)

loll /lɒl/ *v.i.* 1 (lounge) sich lümmeln (ugs. abwertend); **don't ~!** lümmel dich nicht so! 2 (droop) ‹*Zunge:*› heraushängen; ‹*Kopf:*› hängen

Phrasal verb

- **~ a'bout, ~ a'round** *v.i.* sich herumlümmeln (ugs. abwertend)

lollipop /'lɒlɪpɒp/ *n.* Lutscher, *der*

lollipop: ~ man/lady *ns.* ▸ **i p. 1260** (Brit. coll.) *Mann/Frau in der Funktion eines Schülerlotsen*

lollop /'lɒləp/ *v.i.* (coll.) (bob up and down) ‹*Kaninchen usw.:*› hoppeln; (proceed by clumsy bounds) zotteln (ugs.); trotten

lolly /'lɒlɪ/ *n.* 1 (Brit. coll.: lollipop) Lutscher, *der*; **ice[d] ~:** Eis am Stiel 2 *no pl.*, *no indef. art.* (coll.: money) Kohle, *die* (salopp)

Lombardy /'lɒmbədɪ/ *pr. n.* Lombardei, *die*; **~ poplar** (Bot.) Pyramidenpappel, *die*

London /'lʌndən/ ▸ **i p. 1643**

A *pr. n.* London (*das*)

B *attrib. adj.* Londoner

Londoner /'lʌndənə(r)/ *pr. n.* ▸ **i p. 1643** Londoner, *der*/Londonerin, *die*

lone /ləʊn/ *attrib. adj.* 1 (poet./rhet.: solitary) einsam 2 (lonesome) einsam 3 **~ hand** (Cards: player) Einzelspieler, *der*/-spielerin, *die*; **play** *or* **hold a ~ hand** allein spielen; **play a ~ hand** (fig.) einen Alleingang machen

loneliness /'ləʊnlɪnɪs/ *n.*, *no pl.* Einsamkeit, *die*; (remoteness) Abgeschiedenheit, *die*

lonely /'ləʊnlɪ/ *adj.* einsam; (remote) abgeschieden; **~ heart** einsames Herz

lone 'parent *n.* allein erziehender Elternteil; Alleinerziehende, *der/die*; **she/he is a ~:** sie/er ist allein erziehend

loner /'ləʊnə(r)/ *n.* Einzelgänger, *der*/-gängerin, *die*

lonesome /'ləʊnsəm/ *adj.* einsam; **by** *or* **on one's ~:** ganz allein

lone 'wolf *n.* (fig.) Einzelgänger, *der*/-gängerin, *die*

long[1] /lɒŋ/

A *adj.*, **~er** /'lɒŋgə(r)/, **~est** /'lɒŋgɪst/ 1 ▸ **i p. 1286** lang; weit ‹*Reise, Weg*›; **be ~ in the tooth** nicht mehr der/die Jüngste sein; **she's getting a bit ~ in the tooth for that** dafür ist sie allmählich vielleicht doch etwas zu alt; **in two days at the ~est** in spätestens zwei Tagen; **it will take two hours at the ~est** es wird höchstens zwei Stunden dauern; **take a ~ view of sth.** etw. auf lange *od.* weite Sicht sehen; **two inches/weeks ~:** zwei Zoll/Wochen lang; *see also* **law 11**; **way A 5** 2 (elongated) länglich; schmal; **pull** *or* **make a ~ face** (fig.) ein langes Gesicht ziehen *od.* machen (ugs.) 3 (of extended duration) lang; **~ service** (esp. Mil.) langjähriger Dienst; **in the '~ run** auf die Dauer; auf lange Sicht; **in the '~ term** auf lange Sicht; langfristig; **for a '~ time** lange; (still continuing) seit langem; **what a ~ time you've been away!** du warst aber lange [Zeit] fort!; **~ time no see!** (coll.) lange nicht gesehen! (ugs.) 4 (tediously lengthy) lang[atmig]; weitschweifig 5 (lasting) lang; langjährig ‹*Gewohnheit, Freundschaft*›; alt ‹*Brauch, Gewohnheit*› 6 klein, gering ‹*Chance*›; **it would be a ~ chance that ...:** es ist ziemlich unwahrscheinlich, dass ... 7 (seemingly more than stated) lang ‹*Minute, Tag, Jahre usw.*› 8 (coll.: tall) lang (ugs.) ‹*Person*›; hoch ‹*Fenster*› 9 lang ‹*Gedächtnis*›; **have a ~ memory for sth.** etw. nicht so schnell vergessen 10 *qualifying number or measure:* **~ dozen** dreizehn [Stück]; **~ hundred** hundertzwanzig [Stück]; Großhundert, *das* (veralt.); **~ hundredweight** englischer Zentner; **~ ton** Longton, *die* 11 (consisting of many items) lang ‹*Liste usw.*›; hoch ‹*Zahl*› 12 (Phonet., Pros.) lang 13 (Cards) **~ suit** lange Farbe; **be sb.'s ~ suit** (fig.) jmds. Stärke sein 14 **be ~ on sth.** (coll.) ein Ausbund an etw. (*Dat.*) sein (ugs.)

B *n.* 1 (long interval) **take ~:** lange dauern; **for ~:** lange; (since ~ ago) seit langem; **before ~:** bald; **it is ~ since ...:** es ist lange her, dass ... 2 **the ~ and the short of it is ...:** der langen Rede kurzer Sinn ist ...

C *adv.*, **~er**, **~est** 1 lang[e]; **as** *or* **so ~ as** so lange wie; *see also* **C 2** 2 ; **the shop hasn't ~ been open** den Laden gibt es noch nicht lange; **you should have finished ~ before now** du hättest schon längst *od.* viel früher fertig sein sollen; **I knew her ~ before I met you** ich kenne sie schon viel länger als dich; **not ~ before that** kurz davor *od.* zuvor; **not ~ before I ...:** kurz bevor ich ...; **~ since** [schon] seit langem; **all day/night/summer ~:** den ganzen Tag/die ganze Nacht/den ganzen Sommer [über *od.* lang]; **a quiet resort, ~ the gathering place of ...:** ein ruhiger Ferienort, lange/(still continuing) schon lange Versammlungsort von ...; **not be ~ for this world** nicht mehr lange zu leben haben; **I shan't be ~:** ich bin gleich fertig; (departing) bis gleich!; **don't be ~!** beeil dich!; **don't be ~ about [doing] it!** lass dir nicht zu viel Zeit damit!; **sb. is ~ [in** *or* **about doing sth.]** jmd. braucht lange *od.* viel Zeit[, um etw. zu tun]; **the opportunity was not ~ in coming** es dauerte nicht lange, bis sich die Gelegenheit bot; **much ~er** viel länger; **not wait any/much ~er** nicht mehr länger/viel länger warten; **no ~er** nicht mehr; nicht länger ‹*warten usw.*›; **we no ~er had any hope** wir hatten keine

Hoffnung mehr; **play can't go on much ~er** das Spiel muss bald abgebrochen werden; **how much ~er is he going to sleep?** wie lange schläft er denn noch?; *see also* **ago**; **so¹ A 1**
2▸ as *or* **so ~ as** (provided that) solange; wenn

long² *v.i.* **~ for sb./sth.** sich nach jmdm./etw. sehnen; **~ for the end of sth./for the summer to come** das Ende einer Sache/den Sommer herbeisehnen; **~ for sb. to do sth.** sich (*Dat.*) [sehr] wünschen, dass jmd. etw. tut; **I ~ for you to come home** ich warte sehnsüchtig darauf, dass du nach Hause kommst; **~ to do sth.** sich danach sehnen, etw. zu tun; **he ~ed to ask his mother the meaning of it** es drängte ihn, seine Mutter zu fragen, was das bedeutete; **[much] ~ed-for** [lang] ersehnt

long. *abbr.* **= longitude** Lg.

long: ~ ago **A** *n.* längst vergangene Zeit[en]; **B** *adj.* längst vergangen; **~boat** *n.* Barkasse, *die;* Langboot, *das;* **~bow** *n.* (Mil.) Langbogen, *der;* **~-case 'clock** *n.* Standuhr, *die;* **~-dated** *adj.* (Finance) langfristig; **~-distance** **A** /'--/ *adj.* Fern‹*gespräch, -verkehr usw.*›; Langstrecken‹*lauf, -läufer, -flug usw.*›; **~-distance coach** Reise- *od.* Überlandbus, *der;* **~-distance lorry driver** ▸ⓘ **p. 1260** Fern[last]fahrer, *der;* **B** /-'--/ *adv.* **phone ~-distance** ein Ferngespräch führen; **~ division** ▸ **division 7**; **~-drawn[-out]** *adj.* lang gezogen ‹*Schrei, Ton*›; langatmig ‹*Erklärung, Diskussion*›; ausgedehnt ‹*Wanderung*›; **~ drink** *n.* Longdrink, *der*

longevity /lɒn'dʒevɪtɪ/ *n., no pl.* Langlebigkeit, *die*

long: ~-forgotten *adj.* längst vergessen; **~-haired** *adj.* langhaarig; Langhaar‹*dackel, -katze*›; **~hand** *n.* Langschrift, *die;* **~ haul** *n.* Langstreckentransport, *der;* [Güter]ferntransport, *der;* **it's a ~ haul** das ist ein weiter Weg; **~-haul** *adj.* Fern‹*verkehr, -lastwagen*›; Langstrecken‹[*flug*]*verkehr*›; Fernverkehrs‹*bus, -verbindung*›; **~ hop** *n.* (Cricket) *kurz aufgesetzter und dann weit fliegender Ball;* **~horn** *n.* **1▸** (cattle) Longhorn, *das;* **2▸** (beetle) Bockkäfer, *der*

longing /'lɒŋɪŋ/
A *n.* Verlangen, *das;* Sehnsucht, *die;* (craving) Gelüst, *das* (geh.); **I had a sudden ~ for a cigarette** ich hatte plötzlich Lust auf eine Zigarette
B *adj.* sehnsüchtig

longingly /'lɒŋɪŋlɪ/ *adv.* voll Sehnsucht; sehnsüchtig

longish /'lɒŋɪʃ/ *adj.* ziemlich lang

longitude /'lɒndʒɪtju:d, 'lɒŋgɪtju:d/ *n.* **1▸** (Geog.) [geographische] Länge; (of a place) Länge, *die;* **~ 40° E** 40° östlicher Länge **2▸** (Astron.) Länge, *die*

longitudinal /lɒndʒɪ'tju:dɪnl, lɒŋgɪ'tju:dɪnl/ *adj.* **1▸** Längen‹*ausdehnung, -messung*› **2▸** (running lengthwise) längs gerichtet; **~ stripe** Längsstreifen, *der* **3▸** **~ wave** (Phys.) Longitudinalwelle, *die*

long: ~ johns *n. pl.* (coll.) lange Unterhosen; **~ jump** *n.* (Brit. Sport) Weitsprung, *der;* **~-lasting** *adj.* lang andauernd; anhaltend ‹*Niederschläge, Schneefälle usw.*›; dauerhaft ‹*Beziehung, Freundschaft*›; **~-legged** *adj.* langbeinig; **~ 'lens** *n.* (Photog.) Fernobjektiv, *das;* **~-life** *adj.* haltbar [gemacht]; **~-life battery** Batterie mit langer Lebensdauer; **~-life milk** H-Milch, *die;* **~-lived** /'lɒŋlɪvd/ *adj.* (durable) andauernd; (having long life) langlebig; **be ~-lived** sehr alt werden; **a ~-lived family** eine Familie, in der alle sehr alt werden; **~ 'odds** *n. pl.* (Racing, also fig.) geringe Gewinnchancen; **~ 'player, ~-playing 'record** *ns.* Langspielplatte, *die;* **~-range** *adj.* **1▸** (having a long range) Langstrecken‹*flugzeug, -rakete usw.*›; ‹*Geschütz*› mit großer Reichweite; **2▸** (relating to the future) langfristig; **~-running** *adj.* anhaltend; Langzeit‹*versuch*›; wochen-/monate-/jahrelang ‹*Debatte, Streit usw.*›; lange laufend ‹*Theaterstück*›; **~ ship** *n.* (Hist.) Wikingerschiff, *das;* **~shoreman** /'lɒŋʃɔ:mən/ *n., pl.* **~shoremen** /'lɒŋʃɔ:mən/ Schauermann, *der;* **~ shot** *n.* **1▸** (wild guess) reine Spekulation; **2▸** (bet at long odds) gewagter Versuch; **3▸** (Cinemat.) Fernaufnahme, *die;* **4▸** **not by a ~ shot** bei weitem nicht; **~ 'sight** *n.* Weitsichtigkeit, *die;* **have ~ sight** weitsichtig sein; **~-sighted** *adj.* weitsichtig; (fig.) weitblickend; vorausschauend; **~-sleeved** /'lɒŋsli:vd/ *adj.* langärmelig; **~-standing** *attrib. adj.* seit langem bestehend; langjährig ‹*Freundschaft usw.*›; alt ‹*Schulden, Rechnung, Streit*›; **~stop** *n.* (fig.) Notnagel, *der;* **~-suffering** *adj.* schwer geprüft; (meek) geduldig; **~-term** *adj.* langfristig; **~-time** *adj.* seit langem bestehend; alt ‹*Zwist, Freund*›; **~ 'trousers** *n. pl.* lange Hosen; **~ va'cation** *n.* (Brit.) Sommer[semester]ferien *Pl.;* (Law) Sommerpause, *die;* **~ wave** *n.* (Radio) Langwelle, *die;* **~-wave** *adj.* (Radio) Langwellen-; **~ways** *adv.* längs; in Längsrichtung; **~-winded** /lɒŋ 'wɪndɪd/ *adj.* langatmig; weitschweifig

loo /lu:/ *n.* (Brit. coll.) Klo, *das* (ugs.) **go to/be on the ~:** aufs Klo gehen/auf dem Klo sein; *attrib.* **~ seat** Klobrille, *die* (ugs.)

loofah /'lu:fə/ *n.* **1▸** (sponge) Luffaschwamm, *der* **2▸** (Bot.) Luffa, *die*

look /lʊk/
A *v.i.* **1▸** sehen; gucken (ugs.); schauen (bes. südd., sonst geh.); **~ down at one's feet** zu Boden blicken; **don't ~ now, but ...:** sieh jetzt nicht hin, aber ...; **~ before you leap** (prov.) erst wägen, dann wagen (Spr.); **~ the other way** (fig.) die Augen verschließen; **not know which way to ~:** nicht wissen, wohin man sehen soll; **as quick** *or* **soon as ~ [at you]** (coll.: very readily) ohne zu zögern; *see also* **eye A 1**
2▸ (search) nachsehen
3▸ (face) zugewandt sein **(to[wards]** *Dat.*); **the windows ~ north** die Fenster liegen *od.* gehen nach Norden; **the room ~s on to the road/into the garden** das Zimmer liegt zur Straße/zum Garten hin *od.* geht zur Straße/zum Garten
4▸ (appear) aussehen; **~ as if** [so] aussehen, als ob; **~ well/ill** gut *od.* gesund/schlecht *od.* krank aussehen; **~ like** aussehen wie; **it ~s like rain** es sieht nach Regen aus; **he ~s like winning** es sieht so aus, als ob er gewinnt; **make sb. ~ small** jmdn. herabsetzen; jmdn. heruntermachen (salopp); *see also* **alive 4**; **black A 4**; **fool¹ A 1**
5▸ (seem to be) **she ~s her age/her 40 years** man sieht ihr ihr Alter/die 40 Jahre an; **you ~ yourself again** es scheint dir wieder gut zu gehen; **you don't ~ yourself** du siehst schlecht aus; **~ the part** (lit. or fig.) so aussehen; **she ~ed the part to perfection** sie war für die Rolle wie geschaffen
6▸ (inquire) **you haven't ~ed deep enough into it** du hast dich nicht eingehend genug damit befasst; **~ [here]!** (demanding attention) hören Sie/hör zu; (protesting) passen Sie/pass ja *od.* bloß auf!; **~ sharp [about sth.]** (hurry up) sich [mit etw.] beeilen; **~ inwards** in sich (*Akk.*) hineinblicken; nach innen blicken
7▸ (take care, make sure) **~ that ...:** dafür sorgen *od.* zusehen *od.* darauf achten, dass ...; **~ to do sth.** (expect) erwarten *od.* hoffen, etw. zu tun
B *v.t.* **1▸** (ascertain by sight) nachsehen; *in exclamation of surprise etc.* sich (*Dat.*) ansehen; **~ what you've done!** sieh [dir mal an], was du getan *od.* angerichtet hast!; **~ who's here!** sieh mal, wer da ist *od.* gekommen ist!
2▸ (express by one's ~s) **~ a question at sb.** jmdn. fragend ansehen; **she ~ed her surprise** die Überraschung stand ihr im Gesicht geschrieben; *see also* **dagger 1**
C *n.* **1▸** Blick, *der;* **get a good ~ at sb.** jmdn. gut *od.* genau sehen [können]; **have** *or* **take a ~ at sb./sth.** sich (*Dat.*) jmdn./etw. ansehen; einen Blick auf jmdn./etw. werfen; **have a ~ at a town** sich (*Dat.*) eine Stadt ansehen; **let sb. have a ~ at sth.** jmdn. etw. sehen lassen; **if ~s could kill** wenn Blicke töten könnten
2▸ *in sing. or pl.* (person's appearance) Aussehen, *das;* (facial expression) [Gesichts]ausdruck, *der;* **from** *or* **by the ~[s] of sb.** von jmds. Aussehen zu schließen; **good ~s** gutes Aussehen; **have good ~s** gut aussehen; **she's lost her ~s** sie hat ihre Schönheit verloren; **have a hungry ~:** hungrig aussehen; **have the ~ of an artist** wie ein Künstler aussehen; **put on a ~ of innocence** eine Unschuldsmiene aufsetzen; **there were angry ~s from them** sie guckten *od.* (geh.) blickten böse; *see also* **black A 6**
3▸ (thing's appearance) Aussehen, *das;* (Fashion) Look, *der;* **have a neglected ~:** verwahrlost aussehen; **from** *or* **by the ~ of the furniture** *etc.* [so] wie die Möbel *usw.* aussehen; **by the ~[s] of it** *or* **things** [so] wie es aussieht; **the house is empty, by the ~ of it** das Haus steht allem Anschein nach leer; **I don't like the ~ of this** das gefällt mir gar nicht; **the place has a European ~:** der Ort wirkt europäisch; **for the ~ of the thing** (coll.) um den Schein zu wahren

Phrasal verbs

- **~ a'bout**
A *v.t.* **~ about a room** sich in einem Zimmer umsehen; **~ about one** sich umsehen *od.* umschauen
B *v.i.* **1▸** sich umsehen; **~ about everywhere** (search) überall gucken **2▸** (be watchful) sich vorsehen; **~ about for sth.** sich nach etw. umsehen
- **~ 'after** *v.t.* **1▸** (follow with one's eyes) nachsehen (+ *Dat.*) **2▸** (attend to) sich kümmern um **3▸** (care for) sorgen für; **~ after oneself** allein zurechtkommen; für sich selbst sorgen; **~ 'after yourself!** pass auf dich auf!
- **~ a'head** *v.i.* **1▸** nach vorne sehen **2▸** (fig.: plan for future) an die Zukunft denken; vorausschauen; **~ ahead five years/to next year** an die Zeit in fünf Jahren/an nächstes Jahr denken
- **~ a'round** ▸ **~ about**
- **~ at** *v.t.* **1▸** (regard) ansehen; **~ at one's watch** auf seine Uhr sehen; **~ directly at the light** direkt ins Licht sehen; **don't ~ at me like that!** sieh mich nicht so an!; **be pleasing to ~ at** [recht] nett aussehen; **be good/not much to ~ at** nach etwas/nach nichts *od.* nicht nach viel aussehen (ugs.); **to ~ at him, you'd think ...:** wenn man ihn so sieht, würde man meinen, ... **2▸** (examine) sich (*Dat.*) ansehen **3▸** (consider) betrachten; in Betracht ziehen ‹*Angebot*›; **that's the proper way to ~ at it** so muss man es sehen; **I wouldn't even ~ at such an offer** so ein Angebot wäre für mich völlig indiskutabel; **I can't ~ at any more caviare** ich kann Kaviar nicht mehr sehen
- **~ a'way** *v.i.* weggucken (ugs.); wegsehen
- **~ 'back** *v.i.* **1▸** (glance behind) sich umsehen; sich umblicken (geh.); (fig.: hesitate) zurückschauen; **he's never ~ed back since then** seitdem läuft bei ihm alles bestens **2▸** (cast one's mind back) **~ back [up]on** *or* **to sth.** an etw. (*Akk.*) zurückdenken; auf etw. (*Akk.*) zurückblicken
- **~ 'down [up]on** *v.t.* **1▸** herunter-/hinuntersehen, (ugs.) runtergucken auf (+ *Akk.*) **2▸** (fig.: despise) herabsehen auf (+ *Akk.*)
- **~ for** *v.t.* **1▸** (expect) erwarten **2▸** (seek) suchen nach; auf der Suche sein nach ‹*neuen Ideen*›; **~ for trouble** Streit suchen; (unintentionally) sich (*Dat.*) Ärger einhandeln
- **~ 'forward to** *v.t.* sich freuen auf (+ *Akk.*); **~ forward to doing sth.** sich darauf freuen, etw. zu tun
- **~ 'in** *v.i.* **1▸** hin-/hereinsehen; (visit) vorbeikommen **(on** bei); vorbei- *od.* hereinschauen **(on** bei) (bes. südd. ugs.); **~ in at the butcher's** beim Fleischer vorbeigehen; **the doctor ~ed in frequently** der Arzt kam häufig vorbei; **the nurse ~ed in on the patient every hour** die Schwester sah jede Stunde nach dem Patienten **2▸** (coll.: watch television) fernsehen. *See also* **look-in**
- **~ into** *v.t.* **1▸** sehen in (+ *Akk.*) **2▸** (fig.: investigate) [eingehend] untersuchen; unter die Lupe nehmen (ugs.); prüfen ‹*Beschwerde*›
- **~ on**
A /-'-/ *v.i.* zusehen; zugucken (ugs.); *see also* **looker-on**
B /'--/ *v.t.* **~ on sb. as a hero** *etc.* jmdn. als Held[en] *usw.* betrachten; **~ on sb. with distrust/suspicion** jmdn. mit Misstrauen/Argwohn betrachten
- **~ 'out**
A *v.i.* **1▸** hinaus-/heraussehen **(of** aus); rausgucken (ugs.) **2▸** (take care) aufpassen **3▸** (have view) **~ out on sth.** ‹*Zimmer, Wohnung usw.*:› zu etw. gehen (ugs.); zu etw. hin liegen; **the house ~s**

out over the river von dem Haus hat man einen Blick auf den Fluss; **a room ~ing out on the green** ein Zimmer mit Blick auf die Wiese

B *v.t.* (Brit.: select) [her]aussuchen. *See also* **look-out**

- **~ 'out for** *v.t.* (be prepared for) aufpassen *od.* achten auf (+ *Akk.*); sich in Acht nehmen vor (+ *Dat.*) ‹*gefährliche Person, Sturm*›; (keep watching for) Ausschau halten nach ‹*Arbeit, Gelegenheit, Partner, Sammelobjekt usw.*›
- **~ 'out of** *v.t.* sehen *od.* (ugs.) gucken aus
- **~ 'over** *v.t.* **1** sehen über (+ *Akk.*) ‹*Mauer usw.*›; überblicken ‹*Tal usw.*› **2** (survey) inspizieren, sich (*Dat.*) ansehen ‹*Haus, Anwesen*› **3** (scrutinize) mustern ‹*Person*›; durchsehen ‹*Text*›
- **~ 'round** *v.i.* sich umsehen; sich umgucken (ugs.); **~ round in search of sth.** nach etw. Ausschau halten
- **~ through** *v.t.* **1** **~ through sth.** durch etw. [hindurch]sehen **2** (inspect) durchsehen ‹*Papiere*›; prüfen ‹*Antrag, Vorschlag, Aussage*› **3** (glance through) sich (*Dat.*) ansehen ‹*Buch, Notizen*› **4** (fig.: ignore deliberately) **~ straight 'through sb.** durch jmdn. hindurchsehen; jmdn. einfach übersehen **5** (penetrate) durchschauen ‹*Person, Verhaltensweise*›
- **~ to** *v.t.* **1** (rely on, count upon) **~ to sb./sth. for sth.** etw. von jmdm./etw. erwarten; **~ to sb./sth. to do sth.** von jmdm./etw. erwarten, dass er/es etw. tut; **we ~ to him for help/to help us** wir zählen auf seine *od.* rechnen mit seiner Hilfe/zählen darauf *od.* rechnen damit, dass er uns hilft **2** (be careful about) sorgen für; (keep watch upon) aufpassen auf (+ *Akk.*); **~ to it that ...:** zusehen *od.* dafür sorgen, dass ...; **~ to your manners!** benimm dich! (ugs.); *see also* **laurel** 1 **3** (consider) **~ to sth.** etw. beachten; einer Sache (*Dat.*) Beachtung schenken; **~ more to quality than to quantity** mehr auf Qualität als auf Quantität achten **4** (take care of) sich kümmern um ‹*Wunde, Kind usw.*›
- **~ towards** *v.t.* **1** sehen *od.* (ugs.) gucken nach/zu **2** (face) **the balcony/room ~s towards the sea** der Balkon/das Zimmer liegt zum Meer hin **3** (consider) **~ towards the future** an die Zukunft denken **4** (hope for and expect) sich (*Dat.*) erhoffen **5** (aim at) abzielen auf (+ *Akk.*)
- **~ 'up**

A *v.i.* **1** aufblicken; **~ up into the sky** in den Himmel [hinauf]blicken **2** (improve) besser werden; ‹*Aktien, Chancen:*› steigen; **things are ~ing up** es geht bergauf; **business is ~ing up again** das Geschäft läuft wieder besser

B *v.t.* **1** (search for) nachschlagen ‹*Wort*›; heraussuchen ‹*Telefonnummer, Zugverbindung usw.*› **2** (coll.: visit) **~ sb. up** bei jmdm. reingucken (ugs.); bei jmdm. vorbeischauen (bes. südd. ugs.) **3** **~ sb. up and down** jmdn. von Kopf bis Fuß mustern

- **~ upon** ▸ **~ on B**
- **~ 'up to** *v.t.* **~ up to sb.** (lit. or fig.) zu jmdm. aufschauen *od.* aufsehen

'lookalike *n.* Doppelgänger, *der*/-gängerin, *die;* **be ~s** wie Zwillinge aussehen

looker /'lʊkə(r)/ *n.* (coll.: attractive woman) gut aussehende Frau; **she's a ~:** sie sieht gut aus; *see also* **good-looker**

looker-'on *n.* Zuschauer, *der*/Zuschauerin, *die*

'look-in *n.* **1** (visit) kurzer Besuch **2** (opportunity) Chance, *die;* **we didn't get a ~:** wir hatten überhaupt keine Chance

-looking /lʊkɪŋ/ *adj. in comb.* aussehend; **dirty-~:** schmutzig wirkend; **European-/oriental-~:** europäisch/orientalisch aussehend; *see also* **good-looking**

'looking glass *n.* (dated) Spiegel, *der*

'lookout *n., pl.* **~s** **1** (keeping watch) (Naut.) Ausschauhalten, *das;* (guard) Wache, *die;* **keep a ~ or be on the ~ [for sth./sb.]** (wanted) [nach etw./jmdm.] Ausschau halten; (not wanted) [auf etw./jmdn.] aufpassen **2** (observation post) Ausguck, *der;* Beobachtungsstand, *der;* (crow's nest) Krähennest, *das* (Seemannsspr.); Mastkorb, *der* (Seemannsspr.); (belvedere) Aussichtsturm, *der* **3** (person) Wache, *die;* (Mil.) Wach[t]posten, *der;* Beobachtungsposten, *der;* (scout, scouts) Wachtposten, *der* **4** (view) Ausblick, *der;* (esp. Brit. fig.: prospect) Aussichten *Pl.;* **that's a bad ~:** das sind schlechte Aussichten; **it's a poor/bleak etc. ~ for sb./sth.** es sieht schlecht/düster *usw.* aus für jmdn./etw. **5** (concern) Sache, *die;* Problem, *das;* **that's his [own] ~:** das ist [allein] sein Problem *od.* seine Sache

loom[1] /lu:m/ *n.* (Weaving) Webstuhl, *der*

loom[2] *v.i.* auftauchen; (as impending occurrence) sich [bedrohlich] abzeichnen; **~ large** [bedrohlich] auftauchen; (fig.) eine große Rolle spielen

(Phrasal verbs)

- **~ a'head** *v.i.* **1** auftauchen (**of** vor + *Dat.*) **2** ‹*Prüfung:*› unausweichlich bevorstehen (**of** *Dat.*); ‹*Hindernis, Schwierigkeit, Problem:*› sich [bedrohlich] abzeichnen (**of** für)
- **~ 'up** *v.i.* **~ up [in front of sb.]** [unmittelbar] [vor jmdm.] auftauchen

loon /lu:n/ *n.* **1** (crazy person) Idiot, *der* (ugs. abwertend) **2** (Ornith.) [See]taucher, *der*

loony /'lu:nɪ/ (coll.)

A *n.* Verrückte, *der/die* (ugs.)

B *adj.* verrückt (ugs.); irr; **the ~ Left/Right** die hundertfünfzigprozentigen Linken/Rechten

'loony bin *n.* (sl.) Klapsmühle, *die* (salopp)

loop /lu:p/

A *n.* **1** Schleife, *die;* **to be in/out of the ~** (coll.) Bescheid wissen/nicht Bescheid wissen; **to keep sb. in the ~:** jmdn auf dem Laufenden halten; **be kept out of the ~:** in Unkenntnis gelassen werden **2** (cord) Schlaufe, *die* **3** (for lifting or fastening) Schlaufe, *die;* (eye) Öse, *die; attrib.* **~ aerial** *or* (Amer.) **antenna** Rahmenantenne, *die* **4** (contraceptive coil) Spirale, *die*

B *v.t.* **1** (form into a loop) zu einer Schlaufe/Öse formen **2** (enclose) umschlingen **3** (fasten) **~ up/together** *etc.* mit einer Schlaufe hoch-/zusammenbinden *usw.* **4** (Aeronaut.) **~ the ~:** einen Looping fliegen; loopen (fachspr.)

'loophole *n.* **1** (in wall) Maueröffnung, *die;* (for shooting through) Schießscharte, *die* **2** (fig.) Lücke, *die;* **~ in the law** Gesetzeslücke, *die;* Lücke im Gesetz; **tax ~:** Lücke im Steuergesetz

loopy /'lu:pɪ/ *adj.* (coll.) verrückt (ugs.)

loose /lu:s/

A *adj.* **1** (unrestrained) frei laufend ‹*Tier*›; (escaped) ausgebrochen; (bolted) durchgegangen ‹*Pferd*›; **he finally got one hand ~:** er bekam schließlich eine Hand frei; **run** *or* **be ~:** los sein; **set** *or* **turn ~:** freilassen; **cut the boat/dog ~:** das Boot/den Hund losschneiden; **cut ~ from sb.** (fig.) sich von jmdm. lösen; **cut ~** (coll.: behave wildly) verrückt spielen (ugs.); *see also* **cast A 1**; **fast**[2] **A 1**; **let**[1] **A 1** **2** (not firm) locker ‹*Zahn, Schraube, Mutter, Knopf, Messerklinge*›; **come/get/work ~** ‹*Schraube, Mutter, Knoten, Knopf usw.:*› sich lockern; *see also* **screw A 1** **3** (not fixed) lose ‹*Knopf, Buchseite, Brett, Stein*›; **the pages have come ~:** die Seiten haben sich gelöst **4** (not bound together) lose; offen ‹*Haar*› **5** (slack) locker; schlaff ‹*Haut, Gewebe usw.*›; beweglich ‹*Glieder*›; **~ tongue** loses Mundwerk (salopp); **~ bowels** [Neigung zu] Durchfall; **~ build** *or* **frame** schlaksige Gestalt **6** (not dense) locker ‹*Boden, Gewebe usw.*› **7** (hanging free) lose; **be at a ~ end** *or* (Amer.) **at ~ ends** (fig.) beschäftigungslos sein; (not knowing what to do with oneself) nichts zu tun haben; nichts anzufangen wissen; **tie up the ~ ends** *or* **threads** (fig.) die letzten Kleinigkeiten erledigen **8** (inexact) ungenau; schief ‹*Vergleich*›; frei ‹*Stil*›; unsauber ‹*Denken*›; unklar, verwaschen ‹*Aussage*› **9** (morally lax) lose ‹*Mundwerk, Person*›; liederlich ‹*Leben[swandel], Person*›; locker ‹*Moral, Lebenswandel, Mundwerk*›; **a ~ woman** ein leichtes Mädchen **10** *in comb.* lose; locker; **~-flowing hair** locker fallendes Haar

B *v.t.* **1** loslassen ‹*Hund usw.*› **2** (untie) lösen; aufmachen (ugs.) **3** **~ [off]** abschießen ‹*Pfeil*›; abfeuern ‹*Feuerwaffe, Salve*›; abgeben ‹*Schuss, Salve*› **4** (relax) lockern; **~ [one's] hold** loslassen **5** (detach from moorings) losmachen ‹*Schiff*›; loswerfen (Seemannsspr.) ‹*Tau*›

C *n.* **1** **be on the ~:** frei herumlaufen **2** (Rugby) **in the ~:** beim offenen Kombinationsspiel

loose: ~ box Box, *die;* **~ 'cannon** *n.* (fig. coll.) Chaot, *der*/Chaotin, *die;* **~ 'change** ▸ **change A 4**; **~ 'cover** *n.* (Brit.) Überzug, *der;* Schoner, *der;* **~-fitting** *adj.* bequem geschnitten; **~-knit** *adj.* lose zusammenhängend ‹*Organisation, Gemeinschaft usw.*›; **~-leaf** *attrib. adj.* Loseblatt-; **~-leaf binder, ~-leaf file, ~-leaf folder** Loseblatthefter, *der;* **~-limbed** /'lu:slɪmd/ *adj.* gelenkig; geschmeidig; (gawky) schlaksig; **~-lipped** /'lu:slɪpt/ *adj.* geschwätzig; **~-living** *adj.* mit lockerem *od.* liederlichem Lebenswandel *nachgestellt*

loosely /'lu:slɪ/ *adv.* **1** (not tightly) locker; lose **2** (not strictly) locker ‹*gruppieren*›; lose ‹*zusammenhängen*›; frei ‹*übersetzen*›; **~ speaking** grob gesagt; **use a word ~:** ein Wort in einem weiteren Sinne gebrauchen

loosen /'lu:sn/

A *v.t.* **1** (make less tight etc.) lockern **2** (Med.) lösen ‹*Husten*›; **~ the/sb.'s bowels** abführend wirken **3** (fig.: relax) lockern ‹*Bestimmungen, Reglement usw.*›; **~ sb.'s tongue** (fig.) jmds. Zunge lösen

B *v.i.* (become looser) sich lockern

(Phrasal verb)

- **~ up**

A /'---/ *v.t.* lockern ‹*Glieder, Muskeln*›

B /--'-/ *v.i.* sich auflockern; (relax) auftauen

looseness /'lu:snɪs/ *n., no pl.* **1** Lockerheit, *die* **2** (Med.) **~ of the bowels** [Neigung zu] Durchfall

loot /lu:t/

A *v.t.* **1** (plunder) plündern **2** (carry off) rauben

B *n.* **1** (in war) [Kriegs]beute, *die* **2** (gain, esp. illicit) Beute, *die* **3** (coll.: money) Zaster, *der* (salopp); Knete, *die* (salopp)

looter /'lu:tə(r)/ *n.* Plünderer, *der*

lop /lɒp/ *v.t.*, **-pp-** **1** stutzen, beschneiden ‹*Baum, Hecke*› **2** **~ sth. [off** *or* **away]** etw. abhauen *od.* abhacken

lope /ləʊp/ *v.i.* ‹*Hase, Kaninchen:*› springen; ‹*Wolf, Fuchs:*› laufen; ‹*Person:*› beschwingten Schrittes gehen

lop-eared /'lɒpɪəd/ *adj.* schlappohrig (ugs.); hängeohrig

lopsided /lɒp'saɪdɪd/ *adj.* schief; (fig.) einseitig

loquacious /lə'kweɪʃəs/ *adj.* redselig; schwatzhaft (abwertend)

loquacity /lə'kwæsɪtɪ/ *n., no pl.* Redseligkeit, *die;* Geschwätzigkeit, *die* (abwertend)

lord /lɔ:d/

A *n.* **1** (master) Herr, *der;* **the ~s of creation** (fig.: mankind) die Krone der Schöpfung; **~ and master** (joc.) Herr und Gebieter *od.* Meister (scherzh.) **2** **L~** (Relig.) Herr, *der;* **L~ God [Almighty]** unser Herr[, der allmächtige Gott]; **the L~ [God]** [Gott] der Herr; **Our/the L~** (Christ) unser Herr Jesus/der Herr; **in the year of Our L~ ...:** im Jahre des Herrn ...; **the L~'s Prayer** das Vaterunser; **the 'L~'s Day** der Tag des Herrn; **the L~'s Supper** das [heilige] Abendmahl; **L~ only knows** (coll.) weiß der Himmel (ugs.) **3** ▸ **i** **p. 1634** (Brit.: nobleman, or as title) Lord, *der;* **live like a ~** (fig.) fürstlich leben; **treat sb. like a ~:** jmdn. fürstlich bewirten; **the L~s** (Brit.) die Lords; das Oberhaus; **the House of L~s** (Brit.) das Oberhaus; *see also* **drunk A** **4** ▸ **i** **p. 1634** **My L~** (Brit.) *form of address* (to earl, viscount) Graf; (to baron) Baron; (to bishop) Exzellenz; (to ~ mayor, ~ provost) Herr Oberbürgermeister; (to judge) /mlʌd/ Herr Richter **5** (Brit.: feudal superior) Lord, *der;* Lehnsherr, *der*

B *int.* (coll.) Gott!; **oh/good L~!** du lieber Himmel *od.* Gott!; großer Gott!; **L~ bless my soul/me/us** *etc.* allmächtiger Gott!

C *v.t.* **~ it** (rule) das Zepter *od.* Regiment führen; (put on airs) sich groß aufspielen; **~ it over sb.** bei jmdm. den großen Herrn/die große Dame spielen

Lord Chancellor

Der Lordkanzler ist der Vorsitzende der Richter des britischen Oberhauses, die die höchste gerichtliche Instanz sind. Der *Lord Chancellor*, der oberste Richter in England und Wales, ist zugleich der Sprecher des Oberhauses und sitzt auf dem *woolsack*, einem großen, mit Wolle gefüllten Sitzkissen.

House of Lords

Eines der zwei Häuser der britischen **Houses of Parliament**, das Oberhaus des britischen Parlaments. Seine Mitglieder werden nicht gewählt, sondern haben als **Peers** (Adelige), durch Geburt, Amt oder Erhebung in den Adelsstand, ein Anrecht auf einen Sitz im Oberhaus. Aufgrund entsprechender Reformbestrebungen ist es wahrscheinlich, dass der Anspruch der 92 erblichen Peers, die es noch gibt, auf Sitz und Stimme im Oberhaus abgeschafft werden wird. Das *House of Lords* hat die Aufgabe, Gesetze, die vom **House of Commons** verabschiedet wurden, zu diskutieren und sie entweder anzunehmen oder Änderungen vorzuschlagen. Allerdings hat es nur noch die Macht, Gesetze zu verzögern, und bei Etat-Vorlagen hat es überhaupt kein Mitspracherecht mehr. Das *House of Lords* fungiert auch als oberstes Gericht in Großbritannien.

Lord: ~ 'Advocate *n.* (Scot. Law) Kronanwalt, *der;* **~ 'Bishop** *n.* (Brit.) Lordbischof, *der;* **~ 'Chamberlain** *n.* (Brit.) Haushofmeister, *der;* **~ 'Chancellor** *n.* (Brit.) Lord[groß]kanzler, *der;* **~ Chief 'Justice** ▸ **chief B 1**; **~ Lieu'tenant** *n.* (Brit.) Lord Lieutenant, *der; Vertreter der Krone in einer Grafschaft*

lordly /'lɔːdlɪ/ *adj.* [1] (grand) herrschaftlich; edel ‹*Gegenstand*›; herrschaftlich ‹*Gebäude*›; stattlich ‹*Vermögen*› [2] (haughty) anmaßend; hochmütig

Lord: ~ 'Mayor ▸ **mayor**; **~ President of the 'Council** *n.* (Brit.) Lordpräsident, *der;* **~ Privy 'Seal** *n.* (Brit.) Lordsiegelverwalter, *der;* **~ 'Provost** *n.* (Scot.) ≈ Oberbürgermeister, *der*

lordship /'lɔːdʃɪp/ *n.* [1] ▸❶ **p. 1634** (title) Lordschaft, *die;* **his/your ~/their/your ~s** seine/Eure Lordschaft/ihre/Eure Lordschaften [2] (dominion) Herrschaft, *die* (**of, over** über + *Akk.*)

lore /lɔː(r)/ *n.* Wissen, *das;* Kunde, *die;* (body of traditions) Überlieferung, *die;* (of a people, an area) Folklore, *die;* **animal/bird/plant ~**: Tier-/Vogel-/Pflanzenkunde, *die*

lorgnette /lɔː'njet/ *n. in sing. or pl.* Lorgnette, *die*

Lorraine /lɒ'reɪn/ *pr. n.* Lothringen *(das)*

lorry /'lɒrɪ/ *n.* (Brit.) Lastwagen, *der;* Lkw, *der;* Laster, *der* (ugs.); **it fell off the back of a ~** (joc.) das ist mir/ihm *usw.* zugelaufen (ugs. scherzh.)

'lorry driver *n.* ▸❶ **p. 1260** (Brit.) Lastwagenfahrer, *der;* Lkw-Fahrer, *der*

The Los Angeles Times

Eine in Los Angeles verlegte Tageszeitung, die zu den besten Zeitungen in den USA gezählt wird. Sie verkauft Artikel an Zeitungen in aller Welt.

lose /luːz/

A *v.t.*, **lost** /lɒst/ [1] verlieren; kommen um, verlieren ‹*Leben, Habe*›; **sb. has something/nothing to ~ [by doing sth.]** es kann jmdm. schaden/nicht schaden[, wenn er etw. tut]; *see also* **face A 1**; **grip A 1**; **ground¹ A 2**; **hold C 1, 2**; **sight A 2**; **temper A 1** [2] (fail to maintain) verlieren; (become slow by) ‹*Uhr:*› nachgehen ‹*zwei Minuten täglich usw.*› [3] (become unable to find) verlieren; **~ one's way** sich verlaufen/verfahren; **be lost/~ oneself in sth.** (fig.) ganz in etw. (*Dat.*) aufgehen [4] (waste) vertun ‹*Zeit*›; (miss) versäumen, verpassen ‹*Zeitpunkt, Gelegenheit, Ereignis*›; *see also* **time A 2** [5] (fail to obtain) nicht bekommen ‹*Preis, Vertrag usw.*›; (fail to hear) nicht mitbekommen ‹*Teil einer Rede usw.*›; (fail to catch) verpassen, versäumen ‹*Zug, Bus*›; **the motion was lost** der Antrag kam nicht durch *od.* scheiterte [6] (forfeit) verlieren; verlieren, (geh.) verwirken ‹*Recht*› [7] (be defeated in) verlieren ‹*Kampf, Spiel, Wette, Prozess usw.*›; *see also* **fight B 3**; **toss C 1** [8] (cause loss of) **~ sb. sth.** jmdn. um etw. bringen; **you['ve] lost me** (fig.) ich komme nicht mehr mit [9] (get rid of) abschütteln ‹*Verfolger*›; loswerden ‹*Erkältung*›; **~ weight** abnehmen. *See also* **lost**

B *v.i.*, **lost** [1] (suffer loss) einen Verlust erleiden; (in business) Verlust machen (**on** bei); (in match, contest) verlieren; **heads you win, tails you ~**: bei Kopf hast du gewonnen, bei Zahl verloren; **~ in freshness** an Frische verlieren; **the story didn't ~ in the telling** die Geschichte wurde beim Weitererzählen eher noch aufgebauscht; **his poetry ~s in translation** seine Gedichte verlieren durch die Übersetzung; **you can't ~** (coll.) du kannst nur profitieren *od.* gewinnen [2] (become slow) ‹*Uhr:*› nachgehen

(Phrasal verb)

• **~ 'out** *v.i.* verdrängt werden (**to** von)

loser /'luːzə(r)/ *n.* Verlierer, *der*/Verliererin, *die;* (failure) Versager, *der*/Versagerin, *die;* **we'd be the ~s by it** wir wären dabei die Dummen (ugs.)

loss /lɒs/ *n.* [1] (process) Verlust, *der* (**of** *Gen.*) [2] *in sing. or pl.* (what is lost) Verlust, *der;* **sell at a ~**: mit Verlust verkaufen; *see also* **cut A 11** [3] (state) Verlust, *der;* **be a great/no ~ to sb.** für jmdn. ein großer *od.* schwerer/kein Verlust sein [4] **be at a ~**: nicht [mehr] weiterwissen; **be at a ~ what to do** nicht wissen, was zu tun ist; **be at a ~ [how] to do sth.** nicht wissen, wie man etwas machen soll; **be at a ~ to understand sth.** etw. nicht verstehen können; **be at a ~ for words/an answer** um Worte/eine Antwort verlegen sein. *See also* **dead loss**; **life 1**; **profit A 1**

loss: ~ adjuster *n.* (Finance) Schaden[s]regulierer, *der*/Schaden[s]reguliererin, *die;* **~-leader** *n.* (Commerc.) [unter dem Selbstkostenpreis angebotener] Lockartikel; **~-making** *adj.* mit Verlust arbeitend

lost /lɒst/ *adj.* [1] (perished) verloren; ausgestorben ‹*Kunst[fertigkeit]*› [2] (astray) verloren; vermisst ‹*Person*›; **get ~**: sich verlaufen *od.* verirren/verfahren; **get ~!** (coll.) verdufte! (salopp); **he can get ~!** (coll.) er soll verduften! (salopp); **I'm ~** (fig.) ich verstehe gar nichts mehr; **feel ~ without sb./sth.** (fig.) sich (*Dat.*) ohne jmdn./etw. hilflos vorkommen; **~ generation** verlorene Generation; Lostgeneration, *die* (Literaturw.) [3] (wasted) vertan ‹*Zeit, Gelegenheit*›; verschwendet ‹*Zeit, Mühe*›; verpasst, versäumt ‹*Gelegenheit*› [4] (not won) verloren; aussichtslos ‹*Sache*›; *see also* **all B 4**; **cause A 4** [5] **~ in admiration** überwältigt; **be ~ to sb.** für jmdn. verloren sein; **be ~ [up]on sb.** (unrecognized by) bei jmdm. keine Anerkennung finden; von jmdm. nicht gewürdigt werden; **sarcasm was ~ on him** mit Sarkasmus konnte er nichts anfangen; **be ~ to all sense of duty** jedes Pflichtgefühl vermissen lassen. *See also* **lose**; **property 1**

lot /lɒt/ *n.* [1] (method of choosing) Los, *das;* **by ~**: durch das Los [2] (destiny) Los, *das;* **fall to the ~ of sb.** jmdm. bestimmt sein [3] (item to be auctioned) Posten, *der;* **bad ~** (fig.: disreputable person) üble Person [4] (set of persons) Haufen, *der;* **the ~**: [sie] alle; **'our/'your/'their ~** (coll.) wir/ihr/die; **not an honest man among the '~ [of them]** kein einziger anständiger Kerl in dem ganzen Haufen; **I'm bored with the '~ of you** *or* **with 'you ~**: ihr langweilt mich alle [5] (set of things) Menge, *die;* **we received a new ~ of hats** wir haben eine neue Sendung Hüte erhalten; **divide sth. into five ~s** etw. in fünf Stapel/Haufen *usw.* teilen; **the ~** (whole set) alle/alles; **that's the ~** (coll.) das ist alles; das wärs (ugs.); **'that little ~** (coll. iron.) diese Kleinigkeit [6] (coll.: large number or quantity) **~s** *or* **a ~ of money** *etc.* viel *od.* eine Menge Geld *usw.*; **~s of books/coins** eine Menge Bücher/Münzen; **he has a ~ to learn** er muss noch viel lernen; **I have a ~ to be thankful for** ich muss für vieles dankbar sein; **have ~s to do** viel zu tun haben; **we have ~s of time** wir haben viel *od.* (ugs.) massenweise Zeit; **sing** *etc.* **a ~**: viel singen *usw.*; **~s** *or* **a ~ better** viel besser; **not a ~ better** nicht viel besser; **like sth. a ~**: etw. sehr mögen; **Did you like it? — Not a ~**: Hat es dir gefallen? — Nicht sehr [7] (for choosing) Los, *das;* **draw/cast/throw ~s [for sth.]** das Los [über etw. (*Akk.*)] entscheiden lassen; [um etw.] losen; **cast/throw in one's ~ with sb.** sich mit jmdm. zusammentun; **draw ~s to determine sth.** etw. durch das Los entscheiden [8] (plot of land) Gelände, *das;* Platz, *der;* (measured piece of land) Parzelle, *die;* **building ~** (Amer.) Bauplatz, *der;* **across ~s** (Amer.) querfeldein

lotion /'ləʊʃn/ *n.* Lotion, *die*

lottery /'lɒtərɪ/ *n.* Lotterie, *die;* (fig.) Glücksspiel, *das*

lottery: ~ number *n.* Lottozahl, *die;* **~ ticket** *n.* Lotterielos, *das*

lotto /'lɒtəʊ/ *n., no pl.* Lotto, *das*

lotus /'ləʊtəs/ *n.* (Nymphaea) Seerose, *die;* (Nelumbo) Lotusblume, *die*

'lotus position *n.* Lotussitz, *der*

louche /luːʃ/ *adj.* halbseiden

loud /laʊd/

A *adj.* [1] laut; schreiend ‹*Reklame*›; lautstark ‹*Protest, Kritik*›; **he was ~ in his praise/criticism of the government** er lobte die Regierung in den höchsten Tönen/er äußerte scharfe Kritik an der Regierung; *see also* **pedal A 1** [2] (conspicuous) aufdringlich; laut, aufdringlich ‹*Farbe, Muster usw.*›; grell, schreiend ‹*Farbe*›

B *adv.* laut; **laugh out ~**: laut auflachen; **laugh ~ and long** in lautes, anhaltendes Gelächter ausbrechen; **say sth. out ~**: etw. aussprechen; (fig.) etw. laut verkünden

loudhailer /laʊd'heɪlə(r)/ *n.* Megaphon, *das;* Flüstertüte, *die* (ugs. scherzh.)

loudly /'laʊdlɪ/ *adv.* [1] (in a loud voice, clamorously) laut; **he insisted ~ on his rights** er bestand entschieden auf seinen Rechten [2] (flashily) aufdringlich

loud: ~mouth *n.* Großmaul, *das;* **~-mouthed** /'laʊdmaʊðd/ *adj.* großmäulig (ugs. abwertend); großsprecherisch (abwertend)

loudness /'laʊdnɪs/ *n., no pl.* Lautstärke, *die;* (flashiness) Aufdringlichkeit, *die*

loud'speaker *n.* Lautsprecher, *der*

lough /lɒx, lɒk/ *n.* (Ir.) See, der

lounge /laʊndʒ/

A *v.i.* **~ [about** *or* **around]** [faul] herumliegen/-sitzen/-stehen; [faul] herumhängen (ugs.); (in chair etc.) sich lümmeln (ugs.)

B *n.* [1] (public room) Lounge, *die;* (in hotel) Lounge, *die;* [Hotel]halle, *die;* (at station) Wartesaal, *der;* (in theatre) Foyer, *das;* (at airport) Lounge, *die;* Wartehalle, *die* [2] (sitting room) Wohnzimmer, *das* [3] (Brit.: bar) **~ [bar]** ▸ **saloon bar**

'lounge lizard *n.* (coll.) Salonlöwe, *der*

lounger /'laʊndʒə(r)/ *n.* [1] Nichtstuer, *der* [2] (sunbed) Liege, *die*

'lounge suit *n.* (Brit.) Straßenanzug, *der*

lour /'laʊə(r)/ *v.i.* missmutig [drein]blicken; ein finsteres Gesicht machen; (fig.) ‹*Wolken, Gewitter:*› sich [bedrohlich] zusammenziehen; ‹*Himmel:*› sich [bedrohlich] verfinstern

louse /laʊs/

A *n.* [1] *pl.* **lice** /laɪs/ Laus, *die* [2] *pl.* **~s** (sl.: person) Ratte, *die* (derb)

B *v.t.* **~ up** (coll.) vermasseln (salopp)

lousy /'laʊzɪ/ *adj.* [1] (infested) verlaust; **be ~ with money** (coll.) im Geld schwimmen (ugs.); lausig viel Geld haben (ugs.); **places ~ with foreigners** von Ausländern wimmelnde Orte [2] (coll.) (disgusting) ekelhaft; widerlich; (very poor) lausig (ugs.); mies (ugs.); **feel ~**: sich mies (ugs.) *od.* miserabel fühlen; **men are ~ at housework** Männer stellen sich bei der Hausarbeit miserabel an

lout /laʊt/ *n.* Rüpel, *der;* Flegel, *der;* (bumpkin) Tollpatsch, *der* (ugs.); Tölpel, *der*

loutish /'laʊtɪʃ/ *adj.* rüpelhaft; flegelhaft

louvre, ((Amer. also) **louver**) /'luːvə(r)/ *n.* [1] (roof turret) Laterne, *die* (Bauw.) [2] (slat) Jalousiebrettchen, *das;* **~ door** Jalousietür, *die;* **~ window** Jalousiefenster, *das* [3] *in pl.* (blind) Jalousie, *die;* (for cooling engine etc.) Lüftungslamellen *Pl.*

l

lovable /ˈlʌvəbl/ *adj.* liebenswert

love /lʌv/

A *n.* **1** (affection, sexual ~) Liebe, *die* (**for** zu); **~ is blind** (prov.) die Liebe ist blind; **~'s young dream** junges Liebesglück; **in ~ [with]** verliebt [in (+ *Akk.*)]; **fall in ~ [with]** sich verlieben [in (+ *Akk.*)]; **be/fall out of ~ with sb.** jmdn. nicht mehr lieben; **be/fall out of ~ with sth.** einer Sache (*Gen.*) überdrüssig sein/etw. nicht mehr mögen; **make ~ to sb.** (court) um jmdn. werben; jmdm. den Hof machen (veralt., noch scherzh.); (have sex) mit jmdm. schlafen; jmdn. lieben; **they made ~:** sie schliefen miteinander; sie liebten sich; **for ~:** aus Liebe; (free) unentgeltlich; umsonst; (for pleasure) aus Spaß an der Freude (ugs.); nur zum Vergnügen *od.* Spaß; **not for ~ or money** um nichts in der Welt; **[Happy Christmas,] ~ from Beth** [fröhliche Weihnachten und] liebe Grüße von Beth; **give my ~ to her** grüß sie von mir; **send one's ~ to sb.** jmdn. grüßen lassen; **Peter sends [you] his ~:** Peter lässt [dich] grüßen; **there is no ~ lost between them** sie sind sich (*Dat.*) nicht grün (ugs.); **sb.'s life and ~s** jmds. Lebens- und Liebesgeschichte; see also **fair² A 1** **2** (devotion) Liebe, *die* (**of, for, to[wards]** zu); **~ of life/eating/learning** Freude am Leben/Essen/Lernen; **for [the] ~ of sb.** jmdm. zu Liebe; um jmds. willen; **for the ~ of God** um Gottes willen; *see also* **Mike** **3** (sweetheart) Geliebte, *der/die;* Liebste, *der/die* (veraltet); **[my] ~** (coll.: form of address) [mein] Liebling *od.* Schatz; (to sb. less close) mein Lieber/meine Liebe; **sth. is sb.'s first ~:** etw. ist jmds. größte Leidenschaft; **can I help you, ~?** (in shop) was darfs denn sein? **4** (Tennis) **fifteen/thirty ~:** fünfzehn/dreißig null; **win the set six games to ~:** den Satz mit sechs zu null Spielen gewinnen; **~ all** null beide; **~ game/victory** *etc.* Zu-null-Spiel, *das*/-Sieg, *der usw*

B *v.t.* **1** lieben; **our/their ~d ones** unsere/ihre Lieben **2** (like) **I'd ~ a cigarette** ich hätte sehr gerne eine Zigarette; **~ to do** *or* **doing sth.** etw. [leidenschaftlich] gern tun

C *v.i.* lieben

love: **~ affair** *n.* [Liebes]verhältnis, *das;* Liebschaft, *die;* **~bird** *n.* (Ornith.) Unzertrennliche, *der;* (fig.) Turteltaube, *die* (ugs. scherzh.); **~ child** *n.* (euphem.) Kind der Liebe (geh. verhüll.); uneheliches Kind; **~-ˈhate** *adj.* von Hassliebe geprägt; **~-hate relationship** Hassliebe, *die;* **~-in-a-ˈmist** *n.* (Bot.) Jungfer im Grünen; Gretel im Busch; **~ interest** *n.* **1** *no pl.* (romantic sub-plot) Liebesgeschichte, *die* **2** (character, role) Geliebte der Hauptfigur; **~ knot** ▸ **true-love knot**

loveless /ˈlʌvlɪs/ *adj.* **1** (unloving) lieblos; hart **2** (unloved) ohne Liebe *nachgestellt*

love: **~ letter** *n.* Liebesbrief, *der;* **~-lies-ˈbleeding** *n.* (Bot.) Fuchsschwanz, *der;* **~ life** *n.* Liebesleben, *das*

loveliness /ˈlʌvlɪnɪs/ *n., no pl.* Schönheit, *die*

lovelorn /ˈlʌvlɔːn/ *adj.* liebeskrank (geh.)

lovely /ˈlʌvlɪ/

A *adj.* **1** [wunder]schön; herrlich ‹*Tag, Essen*› **2** (lovable) liebenswert **3** (coll.: delightful) toll (ugs.); wunderbar; **~ and warm/cool** *etc.* (coll.) schön warm/kühl *usw*

B *n.* Schönheit, *die;* Schöne, *die*

love: **~making** *n.* **1** (courtship) Liebeswerben, *das* (geh.); **2** (sexual intercourse) körperliche Liebe; **~ match** *n.* Liebesheirat, *die;* **~ nest** *n.* Liebesnest, *das;* **~ potion** *n.* Liebestrank, *der*

lover /ˈlʌvə(r)/ *n.* **1** Liebhaber, *der;* Geliebte, *der;* (woman) Geliebte, *die;* **be ~s** ein Liebespaar sein; **~'s knot** ▸ **true-love knot** **2** (person devoted to sth.) Liebhaber, *der*/Liebhaberin, *die;* Freund, *der*/Freundin, *die;* **~ of the arts** Kunstliebhaber, *der*/-liebhaberin, *die;* Kunstfreund, *der*/-freundin, *die;* **dog ~:** Hundefreund, *der*/-freundin, *die*

love: **~sick** *adj.* an Liebeskummer leidend; liebeskrank (geh.); **be ~sick** Liebeskummer haben; liebeskrank sein (geh.); **~ song** *n.* Liebeslied, *das;* **~ story** *n.* Liebesgeschichte, *die;* **~ token** *n.* Liebespfand, *das*

lovey /ˈlʌvɪ/ *n.* (coll.) *usu. as form of address* Liebling, *der;* Schatz, *der*

lovey-dovey /lʌvɪˈdʌvɪ/ *adj.* **be ~:** den Verliebten/die Verliebte spielen (ugs.); **be ~ with sb.** jmdn. umschmeicheln

loving /ˈlʌvɪŋ/ *adj.* **1** (affectionate) liebend **2** (expressing love) liebevoll; **your ~ father** (in letter) dein dich liebender Vater; in Liebe dein Vater

loving: **~ cup** *n.* Pokal, *der;* **~ ˈkindness** *n.* Güte, *die*

lovingly /ˈlʌvɪŋlɪ/ *adv.* liebevoll; (painstakingly) mit viel Liebe

low¹ /ləʊ/

A *adj.* **1** ▸ **i p. 1208** (not reaching far up) niedrig; niedrig, flach ‹*Absätze, Stirn*›; flach ‹*Relief*›; gering ‹*Körpergröße*› **2** (below normal level) niedrig; tief ‹*Flug*›; flach ‹*Welle*›; tief ausgeschnitten ‹*Kleid*›; tief ‹*Ausschnitt*› **3** (not elevated) tief liegend ‹*Wiese, Grund, Land*›; tief hängend ‹*Wolke*›; tief stehend ‹*Gestirne*›; tief ‹*Verbeugung*›; **the river/water is ~:** der Fluss/das Wasser ist niedrig; **the sun/moon is ~:** die Sonne/der Mond steht tief **4** (of humble rank) nieder; niedrig; *see also* **high A 5** **5** (inferior) niedrig; gering ‹*Intelligenz, Bildung*›; gewöhnlich ‹*Geschmack*›; (vulgar) gewöhnlich **6** (not fair) gemein **7** (Cards) niedrig **8** ▸ **i p. 1620** (small in degree) niedrig; gering ‹*Sichtweite, Wert*›; leicht ‹*Fieber*›; **be ~ in iodine** einen geringen Jodgehalt aufweisen; **have a ~ opinion of sb./sth.** von jmdm./etw. keine hohe Meinung haben; **temperatures will be in the ~ forties** die Temperaturen werden knapp über 40° [Fahrenheit] liegen; *see also* **common denominator** **9** (in pitch) tief ‹*Ton, Stimme, Lage, Klang*›; (in loudness) leise ‹*Ton, Stimme*› **10** (Ling.) ▸ **open A 13** **11** (weak) schwach; **~ vitality** Kraftlosigkeit, *die;* **he is very ~** (physically) er ist sehr geschwächt; (emotionally) er ist sehr niedergeschlagen; **in a ~ state of mind** niedergeschlagen; in gedrückter Stimmung **12** (nearly gone) fast verbraucht *od.* aufgebraucht; **run ~:** allmählich ausgehen *od.* zu Ende gehen; **we are ~/getting ~ on petrol** wir haben nur noch wenig/bald kein Benzin mehr; **the bottle is getting ~:** die Flasche geht allmählich zu Ende *od.* ist bald leer **13** (Geog.) **~ latitudes** niedere Breiten. *See also* **lower² A**

B *adv.* **1** (in or to a ~ position) tief; niedrig, tief ‹*hängen*›; **that comes ~ on my list of priorities** das hat für mich keine hohe Priorität; *see also* **high B 1** **2** (to a ~ level) **prices have gone too ~:** die Preise sind zu weit gefallen; **if the temperature drops any ~er** wenn die Temperatur weiter sinkt **3** (not loudly) leise **4** (at ~ pitch) tief **5** **lay sb. ~** (prostrate) jmdn. niederstrecken (geh.); (confine to sickbed) jmdn. aufs Krankenlager werfen (geh.); **lie ~:** am Boden liegen; (hide) untertauchen. *See also* **bring 1; lower² B**

C *n.* **1** ▸ **i p. 1620** (Meteorol.) Tief, *das* **2** **hit** *or* **reach a new/an all-time ~:** einen neuen/absoluten Tiefststand erreichen

low² *v.i.* ‹*Kuh:*› muhen

low: **~-alcohol** *adj.* alkoholarm ‹*Getränk*›; **~brow** **A** *n.* Nichtintellektuelle, *der/die;* **B** *adj.* schlicht ‹*Person*›; [geistig] anspruchslos ‹*Buch, Programm*›; **~-budget** *adj.* Lowbudget-, Billig‹*film, -produktion usw.*›; **~-calorie** *adj.* kalorienarm ‹*Kost, Getränk*›; **Low ˈChurch** *n.* Low Church, *die;* **~-class** *adj.* (Brit.) (of low quality) drittklassig; (of low social class) Unterschicht[s]-; **~ ˈcomedy** *n.* Schwank, *der;* Posse, *die;* **~-cost** *adj.* preiswert; **Low Countries** *pr. n. pl.* (Hist.) Niederlande *Pl.;* **~-cut** *adj.* [tief] ausgeschnitten ‹*Kleid*›; **~-cut neck** tiefer Ausschnitt; **~-cut shoes** Halbschuhe; **~-down** **A** *adj.* (mean) mies (ugs.); **B** *n.* (coll.) **give [sb.]/get the ~-down on sb./sth.** [jmdm.] sagen/rauskriegen, was es mit jmdm./etw. [wirklich] auf sich hat; **~-end** *adj.* Lowend-; **~-energy house** *n.* Niedrigenergiehaus, *das*

lower¹ /ˈləʊə(r)/

A *v.t.* **1** (let down) herab-/hinablassen; zu Wasser lassen ‹*Boot*›; einholen ‹*Flagge, Segel*›; **~ oneself into** hinuntersteigen in (+ *Akk.*) ‹*Kanalschacht, Keller*›; **~ oneself into a chair** sich in einen Sessel sinken lassen; *abs.* **~ [away]** (Naut.) (**~** boat) das Boot aussetzen *od.* zu Wasser lassen; (**~** sail) das Segel einholen **2** (reduce in height) senken ‹*Blick*›; niederschlagen ‹*Augen*›; niedriger machen ‹*Wand*›; absenken ‹*Zimmerdecke*›; tiefer hängen ‹*Bild*›; auslassen ‹*Saum*›; *see also* **sight A 8** **3** (lessen) senken ‹*Preis, Miete, Zins usw.*› **4** (degrade) herabsetzen; verderben ‹*Geschmack*›; **~ oneself** sich erniedrigen; **~ oneself to do sth.** sich so weit erniedrigen, etw. zu tun **5** (weaken) schwächen; dämpfen ‹*Licht, Stimme, Lärm*›; **~ one's voice** leiser sprechen; die Stimme senken (geh.)

B *v.i.* **1** (weaken) ‹*Stimme:*› leiser werden; ‹*Licht:*› dunkler werden **2** (sink) sinken; ‹*Wasservorrat:*› weniger werden, abnehmen

lower²

A *compar. adj.* **1** unter... ‹*Nil, Themse usw., Atmosphäre*›; Unter‹*jura, -devon usw., -arm, -lippe usw.*›; Nieder‹*rhein, -kalifornien*›; *see also* **jaw A 1** **2** (in rank) unter...; **~ mammals/plants** niedere Säugetiere/Pflanzen; **the ~ orders/classes** die Unterschichten/die unteren Klassen; **~ middle class** untere Mittelschicht

B *compar. adv.* tiefer ‹*sinken, hängen usw.*›

lower³ /ˈlaʊə(r)/ ▸ **lour**

lower: **~ case** **A** *n.* Kleinbuchstaben *Pl.;* **in ~ case** in Kleinbuchstaben; **B** *adj.* klein ‹*Buchstabe*›; **L~ ˈChamber** *n.* (Parl.) Unterhaus, *das;* **~ court** *n.* unteres *od.* untergeordnetes Gericht; **~ ˈdeck** *n.* **1** (of ship) Unterdeck, *das;* (of bus) unteres Deck; **2** (Brit.: seamen) Mannschaft, *die;* **L~ House** *n.* (Parl.) Unterhaus, *das;* **~most** *adj.* unterst...; **be ~most** zuunterst liegen; **~ ˈregions** *n. pl.* (Mythol.) Unterwelt, *die;* **L~ ˈSaxon** *adj.* niedersächsisch; **L~ ˈSaxony** *pr. n.* Niedersachsen (*das*); **~ ˈsixth** *n.* (Brit.) ≈ Unterprima, *die;* **~ ˈworld** *n.* **1** (the earth) Erde, *die;* **2** (hell) Unterwelt, *die*

low: **~-fat** *adj.* fettarm; **~-flying** *adj.* tief fliegend; **~-flying aircraft** Tiefflieger, *der;* **~ ˈfrequency** *n.* Niederfrequenz, *die;* **~-frequency** *adj.* niederfrequent; **Low ˈGerman** ▸ **German B 2**; **~-grade** *adj.* minderwertig; leicht ‹*Infektion*›; **~-grade steel** Stahl minderer Güte; **~-heeled** *adj.* flach ‹*Schuh*›; ‹*Schuhe*› mit flachen Absätzen; **~-income** *adj.* einkommensschwach; **~-income families** Familien mit niedrigem Einkommen; **a ~-income country** ein Land mit niedrigem Nationaleinkommen; **~-key** *adj.* zurückhaltend; unaufdringlich ‹*Beleuchtung, Unterhaltung*›; unauffällig ‹*Einsatz*›; **~land** /ˈləʊlənd/ **A** *n.* Tiefland, *das;* **the Lowlands of Scotland** die Lowlands; das schottische Tiefland; **B** *adj.* tiefländisch; Tiefland‹*rasse, -farm*›; **~lander** /ˈləʊləndə(r)/ *n.* Tieflandbewohner, *der*/-bewohnerin, *die;* (Scot.) Bewohner/Bewohnerin der Lowlands; **~-level** *adj.* **1** (in lower than normal position) tief; niedrig ‹*Möbel*›; tiefhängend ‹*Spülkasten*›; **~-level flying** Tiefffliegen, *das;* **2** (moderate) leicht ‹*Kriminalität, Lärm*›; **3** (of low importance) untergeordnet ‹*Position, Stellung*›; klein ‹*Angestellter, Beamter*›; **4** (Computing) Low-Level-; **5** (Phys.) Niedrig‹*strahlung*›; niedrigstrahlend ‹*Abfälle*›; **~ life** *n., no pl.* (disreputable people, milieu) gesellschaftlicher Bodensatz; **~life** *n., pl* **~lifes** (coll.: disreputable person) zweifelhaftes Element (abwertend); **~lights** *n. pl.* (in hair) dunkel getönte Strähnen

lowly /ˈləʊlɪ/ *adj.* **1** (modest) bescheiden **2** (not highly evolved) nieder...

low: **~-lying** *adj.* tief liegend; **~-necked** *adj.* [tief] ausgeschnitten; **~-nicotine** *adj.* nikotinarm; **~-paid** *adj.* niedrig bezahlt; **~-paid families** Familien mit geringem Einkommen; **~-ˈpitched** *adj.* **1** tief ‹*Stimme*›; **2** (Archit.) wenig geneigt ‹*Dach*›; **~ point** *n.* Tiefpunkt, *der;* **~-powered** /ˈləʊpaʊəd/ *adj.* schwach ‹*Motor, Glühbirne*›; **~ ˈpressure** *n.* Tiefdruck, *der;* **an area of ~ pressure** ein Tiefdruckgebiet; **~-priced** /ləʊˈpraɪst/ *adj.* preisgünstig; **~ ˈprofile** ▸ **profile A 7**; **~ reˈlief** ▸ **relief² 1**; **~-rise** *adj.* ‹*Gebäude*› mit wenigen Stockwerken; **~-risk** *adj.* risikoarm; **~ season** *n.* Nebensaison, *die;* **~-ˈspirited** *adj.* niedergeschlagen; **~-tar** *adj.* teerarm; **~-tech** *adj.* Lowtech‹*system,*

-ausrüstung *etc.*›; ~ **'tension** ▸ ~ **voltage**; ~**-tension** ▸ ~**-voltage**; ~ **'tide** ▸ **tide** A 1; ~ **'voltage** *n.* (Electr.) Niederspannung, *die;* ~**-voltage** *adj.* (Electr.) Niederspannungs-; ~**-wage** *attrib. adj.* schlecht bezahlt; Niedriglohn‹*land*›; ~ **'water** *n.* Niedrigwasser, *das;* (fig.) Tiefpunkt, *der;* ~**-'water mark** *n.* Niedrigwassermarke, *die*

loyal /'lɔɪəl/ *adj.* (to person) treu; (to government etc.) treu [ergeben]; loyal; ~ **address** Ergebenheitsadresse, *die*

loyalist /'lɔɪəlɪst/

A *n.* Loyalist, *der*/Loyalistin, *die*

B *adj.* loyalistisch

loyally /'lɔɪəlɪ/ *adv.* treu; loyal

loyalty /'lɔɪəltɪ/ *n.* Treue, *die;* Loyalität, *die;* **brand** ~: Markentreue, *die*

'loyalty card *n.* Treuekarte, *die* (*für Kunden*)

lozenge /'lɒzɪndʒ/ *n.* **1** (tablet) Pastille, *die* **2** (diamond shape) Raute, *die;* Rhombus, *der*

LP *abbr.* = **long-playing record** LP, *die*

'L-plate *n.* (Brit.) 'L'-Schild, *das;* ≈ „Fahrschule"-Schild, *das*

LSC *abbr.* = **Learning and Skills Council**

LSD *abbr.* = **lysergic acid diethylamide** LSD, *das*

LSE *abbr.* = **London School of Economics**

Lt. *abbr.* = **Lieutenant**

Ltd. *abbr.* = **Limited** GmbH; **... Company** ~ ...gesellschaft mbH

lubricant /'lu:brɪkənt/

A *n.* Schmiermittel, *das*

B *adj.* Schmier-

lubricate /'lu:brɪkeɪt/ *v.t.* schmieren; einfetten ‹*Haut*›

'lubricating oil *n.* Schmieröl, *das*

lubrication /lu:brɪ'keɪʃn/ *n.* Schmierung, *die;* *attrib.* Schmier‹*system, -vorrichtung*›

lucerne *n.* (Brit. Bot.) [Blaue] Luzerne

Lucerne /lu:'sɜ:n/ *pr. n.* ▸ⓘ **p. 1643** Luzern (*das*); **Lake** ~: der Vierwaldstätter See

lucid /'lu:sɪd/ *adj.* klar; [leicht] verständlich; einleuchtend ‹*Argumentation*›; ~ **interval** (period of sanity) lichter Augenblick *od.* Moment

lucidity /lu:'sɪdɪtɪ/ *n., no pl.* Klarheit, *die*

lucidly /'lu:sɪdlɪ/ *adv.* klar [und verständlich] ‹*formulieren usw.*›

luck /lʌk/ *n.* **1** (good or ill fortune) Schicksal, *das;* **as** ~ **would have it** wie das Schicksal es wollte; **good** ~: Glück, *das;* **bad** ~: Pech, *das;* **bring [sb.] good/bad** ~: [jmdm.] Glück/Pech bringen; **better** ~ **next time** mehr Glück beim nächsten Mal; **good** ~ **[to you]!** viel Glück!; alles Gute!; viel Erfolg!; **good** ~ **to him, I say** ich wünsche ihm viel Glück; (iron.) na, dann viel Glück!; **it's the** ~ **of the game** Glück/Pech gehabt!; **just my** ~: typisch für mich; **try one's** ~: sein Glück versuchen; **you never know your** ~: vielleicht hast du ja Glück; *see also* **down³** A 27; **draw** C 1; **hard** A 3; **push** A 3; **worse** A **2** (good fortune) Glück, *das;* **with [any]** ~: mit ein bisschen *od.* etwas Glück; ~ **was with us all the way** wir hatten die ganze Zeit Glück; **I was in** ~**'s way** das war wirklich Glück; **wear sth. for** ~: etw. als Glücksbringer tragen; **do sth. for** ~: etw. tun, damit es einem Glück bringen soll; **have the** ~ **to do sth.** das Glück haben, etw. zu tun; **be in/out of** ~: Glück/kein Glück haben; **sb.'s** ~ **is in/out** jmd. hat Glück/kein Glück; **no such** ~: schön wärs; *see also* **stroke¹** A 3

Phrasal verb

• ~ **'out** *v.i.* (Amer. coll.) großes *od.* (ugs.) unverschämtes Glück haben; Schwein haben (ugs.)

luckily /'lʌkɪlɪ/ *adv.* glücklicherweise; ~ **for her** zu ihrem Glück

luckless /'lʌklɪs/ *adj.* glücklos; (unlucky, unfortunate) unglücklich

lucky /'lʌkɪ/ *adj.* **1** (favoured by chance) glücklich; **be** ~ **[in love/at games]** Glück [in der Liebe/im Spiel] haben; **be** ~ **to be alive** von Glück sagen können, dass man noch am Leben ist; **be** ~ **enough to be rescued** das [große] Glück haben, gerettet zu werden; **I should be so** ~: schön wärs; **get** ~: Glück haben; **Could you lend me £100? — 'You'll be** ~**!**: Könntest du mir 100 Pfund leihen? — So siehst du aus!; **it was** ~ **[for you/him** *etc.*] **the car stopped in time** dein/sein *usw.* Glück, dass das Auto rechtzeitig gehalten hat; **be a** ~ **dog** ein Glückspilz sein (ugs.) **2** (favouring sb. by chance) glücklich ‹*Umstand, Zufall, Zusammentreffen usw.*›; *see also* **escape** A 1 **3** (bringing good luck) Glücks‹*zahl, -tag usw.*›; ~ **charm** Glücksbringer, *der;* **be born under a** ~ **star** ein Glückskind sein; **you can thank your** ~ **stars** du kannst von Glück sagen

lucky: ~ **bag**, (Brit.) ~ **'dip** *ns.* Glückstopf, *der;* (fig.) Glücksspiel, *das*

lucrative /'lu:krətɪv/ *adj.* einträglich; lukrativ

lucre /'lu:kə(r)/ *n.* (derog.) Profit, *der; see also* **filthy** A 2

Luddite /'lʌdaɪt/ *n.* **1** Maschinenstürmer, *der* **2** (Hist.) Luddit, *der*

ludicrous /'lu:dɪkrəs/ *adj.* lächerlich ‹*Anblick, Lohn, Argument, Vorschlag, Idee*›; lachhaft ‹*Angebot, Ausrede*›; **a** ~ **speed/price** (low) eine lächerliche Geschwindigkeit/ein lächerlicher Preis; (high) eine haarsträubende Geschwindigkeit/ein haarsträubender Preis

ludicrously /'lu:dɪkrəslɪ/ *adv.* lächerlich ‹*wenig, billig, langsam, klein*›; haarsträubend ‹*schnell, teuer*›

ludo /'lu:dəʊ/ *n., no pl., no art.* Mensch-ärgere-dich-nicht[-Spiel], *das*

luff /lʌf/ (Naut.)

A *v.t.* **1** (bring nearer wind) luven ‹*Schiff*› **2** (turn) ~ **the helm** anluven **3** (Yacht racing) durch Luven den Wind nehmen (+ *Dat.*)

B *v.i.* anluven

C *n.* Vorliek, *das*

lug¹ /lʌg/

A *v.t.*, **-gg-** **1** (drag) schleppen **2** (force) ~ **sb. along** jmdn. mit herumschleppen (ugs.)

B *v.i.*, **-gg-** ziehen, zerren (**at** an + *Dat.*)

lug² ▸ **lugworm**

lug³ *n.* **1** (projection) Henkel, *der* **2** (coll./joc.: ear) Löffel, *der* (ugs.)

luge /lu:ʒ/ *n.* [Rodel]schlitten, *der*

luggage /'lʌgɪdʒ/ *n.* Gepäck, *das*

luggage: ~ **carrier** *n.* Gepäckträger, *der;* ~ **label** *n.* Gepäckanhänger, *der;* ~ **locker** *n.* [Gepäck]schließfach, *das;* ~ **rack** *n.* Gepäckablage, *die;* ~ **trolley** *n.* Kofferkuli, *der;* ~ **van** *n.* Gepäckwagen, *der*

lugger /'lʌgə(r)/ *n.* (Naut.) Logger, *der*

'lughole *n.* (coll.: ear) Löffel, *der* (ugs.)

lugubrious /lu:'gu:brɪəs, lʊ'gu:brɪəs/ *adj.* (mournful) kummervoll; traurig; (dismal) düster; trübselig

lugubriously /lu:'gu:brɪəslɪ, lʊ'gu:brɪəslɪ/ *adv.* (mournfully) kummervoll; traurig; (dismally) düster

'lugworm *n.* Köderwurm, *der*

Luke /lu:k/ *pr. n.* **St** ~: der hl. Lukas

lukewarm /'lu:kwɔ:m, lu:k'wɔ:m/ *adj.* **1** lauwarm **2** (fig.) lau[warm]; halbherzig

lull /lʌl/

A *v.t.* **1** (soothe) lullen; ~ **a child to sleep** ein Kind in den Schlaf lullen **2** (fig.) einlullen; einschläfern ‹*Misstrauen*›; ~ **sb. into a false sense of security** jmdn. in einer trügerischen Sicherheit wiegen

B *n.* Pause, *die;* **the** ~ **before the storm** (fig.) die Ruhe vor dem Sturm; **a** ~ **in the storm** ein vorübergehendes *od.* kurzes Nachlassen des Sturms

lullaby /'lʌləbaɪ/ *n.* Schlaflied, *das;* Wiegenlied, *das*

lulu /'lu:lu:/ *n.* (coll.) (thing) Hammer, *der* (salopp); (person) bombige Type (ugs.)

lumbago /lʌm'beɪgəʊ/ *n., pl.* ~**s** (Med.) Hexenschuss, *der;* Lumbago, *die* (fachspr.)

lumbar /'lʌmbə(r)/ *adj.* (Anat.) Lenden-; lumbal (fachspr.); ~ **puncture** (Med.) Lumbalpunktion, *die*

lumber¹ /'lʌmbə(r)/ *v.i.* ‹*Person:*› schwerfällig gehen; ‹*Fahrzeug:*› rumpeln

lumber²

A *n.* **1** (furniture) Gerümpel, *das* **2** (useless material) Kram, *der* (ugs. abwertend); Krempel, *der* (ugs. abwertend) **3** (Amer.: timber) [Bau]holz, *das*

B *v.t.* (fill up, encumber) voll stopfen (ugs.); voll stellen ‹*Zimmer*›; überladen ‹*Stil, Buch*›; ~ **sb. with sth./sb.** jmdm. etw./jmdn. aufhalsen (ugs.); **get** ~**ed with sth./sb.** etw./jmdn. aufgehalst kriegen (ugs.); ~ **oneself with too many things** (lit. or fig.) sich (*Dat.*) zu viel Krempel (ugs.) anschaffen

lumbering /'lʌmbərɪŋ/ *adj.* schwerfällig; (graceless in appearance) plump

lumber: ~**jack** *n.* ▸ⓘ **p. 1260** (Amer.) Holzfäller, *der;* ~**jacket** *n.* Lumberjack, *der;* ~**man** ▸ ~**jack**; ~ **room** *n.* Abstellkammer, *die;* Rumpelkammer, *die* (ugs.)

luminary /'lu:mɪnərɪ/ *n.* (person) Koryphäe, *die*

luminescence /lu:mɪ'nesəns/ *n.* Leuchten, *das;* (Phys.) Lumineszenz, *die*

luminescent /lu:mɪ'nesənt/ *adj.* leuchtend; (Phys.) lumineszierend

luminosity /lu:mɪ'nɒsɪtɪ/ *n.* (also Astron.) Helligkeit, *die*

luminous /'lu:mɪnəs/ *adj.* **1** (bright) hell ‹*Feuer, Licht usw.*›; [hell] leuchtend; Leucht‹*anzeige, -zeiger usw.*›; ~ **paint** Leuchtfarbe, *die* **2** (of light) Leucht‹*kraft, -stärke usw.*› **3** (fig.) brillant; (enlightening) erhellend

lumme /'lʌmɪ/ *int.* (Brit. dated. coll.) großer Gott

lummox /'lʌməks/ *n.* (Amer. coll.) Tölpel, *der;* Tollpatsch, *der* (ugs.)

lump¹ /lʌmp/

A *n.* **1** (shapeless mass) Klumpen, *der;* (of sugar, butter, etc.); Stück, *das;* (of wood) Klotz, *der;* (of dough) Kloß, *der;* (of bread) Brocken, *der;* **a** ~ **of sugar/dough/bread** ein Stück Zucker/ein Teigkloß/ein Brocken Brot; **a** ~ **of wood/clay** ein Holzklotz/ein Klumpen Lehm *od.* Lehmklumpen; **have/get a** ~ **in one's throat** (fig.) einen Kloß im Hals haben (ugs.) **2** (swelling) Beule, *die;* (caused by cancer) Knoten, *der* **3** (coll.: heap) Haufen, *der* **4** (thickset person) Klotz, *der* (ugs.); **a great** ~ **of a woman** ein Koloss von Frau **5** **the** ~ (Brit.: workers) die Schwarzarbeiter im Baugewerbe **6** **[taken] in the** ~ im Ganzen [gesehen]; **get payment in a** ~ die gesamte Summe auf einmal erhalten

B *v.t.* (mass together) zusammentun; ~ **sth. with sth.** etw. und etw. zusammentun; ~ **sb./sth. with the rest** jmdn./etw. mit dem Rest in einen Topf werfen (ugs.); ~ **the archaeology books under History** die Archäologiebücher mit zur Geschichte stellen

Phrasal verb

• ~ **to'gether** *v.t.* zusammenfassen

lump² *v.t.* (coll.) sich abfinden mit; **he can [like it or]** ~ **it** er muss sich [wohl oder übel] damit abfinden; **if you don't like it you can** ~ **it** du musst dich wohl oder übel damit abfinden

lumpenproletariat /'lʌmpənprəʊləteərɪət/ *n.* (derog.) Lumpenproletariat, *das*

lumpish /'lʌmpɪʃ/ *adj.* (derog.) **1** (clumsy) plump; (in movement, speech, action) schwerfällig **2** (dull) dumpf; stumpf

lump: ~ **payment** *n.* einmalige Zahlung [einer größeren Summe]; ~**sucker** *n.* (Zool.) Scheibenbauch, *der;* Lumpfisch, *der;* (Cyclopterus lumpus) Seehase, *der;* ~ **'sugar** *n.* Würfelzucker, *der;* ~ **'sum** *n.* (covering several items) Pauschalsumme, *die;* (paid at once) einmalige Pauschale

lumpy /'lʌmpɪ/ *adj.* klumpig ‹*Brei, Lehm*›; ‹*Kissen, Matratze*› mit klumpiger Füllung

lunacy /'lu:nəsɪ/ *n.* **1** (insanity) Wahnsinn, *der;* (Law) geistige Unzurechnungsfähigkeit **2** (mad folly) Wahnsinn, *der* (ugs.); Irrsinn, *der*

lunar /'lu:nə(r)/ *adj.* Mond-; lunar (fachspr.)

lunar: ~ **e'clipse** *n.* (Astron.) Mondfinsternis, *die;* ~ **'module** *n.* Mond[lande]fähre, *die*

lunatic /'lu:nətɪk/

A *adj.* **1** (mad) wahnsinnig; irre (veralt.); *see also* **fringe** A 3 **2** (foolish) wahnwitzig; Wahnsinns- (ugs.); idiotisch (ugs. abwertend)

B *n.* Wahnsinnige, *der/die;* Irre, *der/die;* **be a** ~: wahnsinnig *od.* (veralt.) irre sein

'lunatic asylum *n.* (Hist.) Irrenanstalt, *die* (veralt., ugs. abwertend)

lunch /lʌnʃ/

A *n.* Mittagessen, *das;* **have** *or* **eat** *or* (formal) **take [one's]** ~: zu Mittag essen; das Mittagessen einnehmen (geh.); **get an hour for ~:** eine Stunde Mittag[spause] haben; **have sth. for ~:** etw. zu Mittag essen; **be at** *or* **eating** *or* **having [one's] ~:** gerade beim Mittagessen sein; zu Tisch sein; **there's no such thing as a free ~** (fig.) es wird einem nichts geschenkt

B *v.i.* zu Mittag essen

lunch: ~ box *n.* Lunchbox, *die;* **~ break** ▸ **~ hour**

luncheon /ˈlʌnʃn/ *n.* (formal) **1** (midday meal) Mittagessen, *das* **2** (Amer.: light meal) Imbiss, *der*

luncheon: ~ meat *n.* Frühstücksfleisch, *das;* **~ voucher** *n.* (Brit.) Essenmarke, *die;* Essensbon, *der*

lunch: ~ hour *n.* Mittagspause, *die;* **~room** *n.* Imbissraum, *der;* **~time** *n.* Mittagszeit, *die;* **at ~time** mittags

lung /lʌŋ/ *n.* ▸**i p. 951** Lunge, *die;* (right or left) Lungenflügel, *der;* **have good/weak ~s** eine gute *od.* kräftige/schwache Lunge haben; **the ~s of a city** (fig.) die grünen Lungen einer Stadt

ˈlung cancer *n.* ▸**i p. 1231** (Med.) Lungenkrebs, *der*

lunge /lʌndʒ/

A *n.* **1** (Sport) Ausfall, *der* **2** (sudden forward movement) Sprung nach vorn; **make a ~ at sb.** sich auf jmdn. stürzen

B *v.i.* **1** (Sport) einen Ausfall machen (**at** gegen) **2** **~ at sb. with a knife** jmdn. mit einem Messer angreifen

Phrasal verb

• **~ ˈout** *v.i.* einen Ausfall machen (**at** gegen); **~ out at sb.** (make sudden forward movement) sich auf jmdn. stürzen

lungfish *n.* Lungenfisch, *der*

lungful /ˈlʌŋfəl/ *n.* **a ~ of air** eine Lunge voll Luft; **he blew out a ~ of smoke** er blies den Rauch aus der Lunge; **take in several ~s of smoke** mehrere Male Rauch einatmen

lung power *n.* Stimmkraft, *die*

lupin, lupine¹ /ˈluːpɪn/ *n.* [Edel]lupine, *die*

lupine² /ˈluːpaɪn, ˈljuːpaɪn/ *adj.* Wolfs-; wölfisch; **have ~ features/a ~ appearance** ein Wolfsgesicht haben/wie ein Wolf aussehen

lupus /ˈluːpəs/ *n.* (Med.) Zehrflechte, *die;* Lupus, *der* (fachspr.)

lurch¹ /lɜːtʃ/ *n.* **leave sb. in the ~:** jmdn. im Stich lassen; jmdn. hängen lassen (ugs.)

lurch²

A *n.* Rucken, *das;* (of ship) Schlingern, *das;* **give a ~:** rucken; ‹*Schiff:*› schlingern

B *v.i.* rucken; ‹*Betrunkener:*› torkeln; ‹*Schiff:*› schlingern

lurcher /ˈlɜːtʃə(r)/ *n.* (Brit.) *Kreuzung zwischen Collie und Windhund [besonders als Spürhund eines Wilderers];* ≈ Spürhund, *der*

lure /ljʊə(r), lʊə(r)/

A *v.t.* locken; **~ away from/out of/into sth.** von etw. fortlocken/aus etw. [heraus]locken/in etw. (*Akk.*) [hinein]locken; **~ sb. away from his duty** jmdn. [durch Lockungen] von seinen Pflichten abbringen

B *n.* **1** (Falconry) Federspiel, *das* **2** (Hunting) Lockvogel, *der;* (fig.: thing) Lockmittel, *das* **3** **the ~ of the sea** der Ruf *od.* die Lockung des Meeres (geh.)

lurid /ˈljʊərɪd, ˈlʊərɪd/ *adj.* **1** (ghastly) gespenstisch; (highly coloured) grell ‹*Licht, Schein, Himmel*› **2** (fig.) (horrifying) grässlich, schaurig ‹*Einzelheiten, Beispiele*›; (sensational) reißerisch (abwertend); (showy, gaudy) reißerisch [aufgemacht] (abwertend) ‹*Umschlag, Bild*›

luridly /ˈljʊərɪdlɪ, ˈlʊərɪdlɪ/ *adv.* **1** (glaringly) grell **2** (fig.) (horrifyingly) grässlich; schaurig; (showily, gaudily) reißerisch

lurk /lɜːk/ *v.i.* **1** lauern; ‹*Raubtier:*› auf Lauer liegen; **~ about a place** an einem Ort herumschleichen **2** (fig.) **~ in sb.'s** *or* **at the back of sb.'s mind** ‹*Zweifel, Verdacht, Furcht:*› an jmdm. nagen

lurker /lɜːkə(r)/ *n.* (Computing sl.) Lurker, *der*/Lurkerin, *die*

lurking /ˈlɜːkɪŋ/ *attrib. adj.* heimlich ‹*Zweifel, Verdacht, Angst, Mitgefühl*›

luscious /ˈlʌʃəs/ *adj.* **1** (sweet in taste or smell) köstlich [süß]; saftig [süß] ‹*Obst*› **2** (excessively sweet) aufdringlich süß ‹*Parfüm*› **3** (appealing to senses) üppig ‹*Figur, Kurven*›; knackig (ugs.) ‹*Mädchen*›; voll ‹*Lippen*›; satt ‹*Farbe*›

lush /lʌʃ/ *adj.* saftig ‹*Wiese*›; grün ‹*Tal*›; üppig ‹*Vegetation*›; (fig.) luxuriös, (ugs.) feudal ‹*Atmosphäre, Räumlichkeiten*›

lust /lʌst/

A *n.* **1** (sexual drive) Sinnenlust, *die;* sinnliche Begierde **2** (passionate desire) Gier, *die* (**for** nach); **~ for power/glory/of battle** Machtgier, *die*/Ruhmsucht, *die*/Kampf[es]lust, *die* **3** (Bibl., Theol.) Fleischeslust, *die* (geh.); **~s of the flesh** fleischliche Gelüste (geh.)

B *v.i.* **~ after** [lustvoll] begehren (geh.); **he ~s after ...:** es gelüstet ihn nach ... (geh.); **~ for glory** ruhmbegierig (geh.) *od.* ruhmsüchtig sein

luster (Amer.) ▸ **lustre**

lustful /ˈlʌstfl/ *adj.* lüstern (geh.)

lustily /ˈlʌstɪlɪ/ *adv.* kräftig; forsch ‹*sich bewegen, etw. angehen*›; herzhaft ‹*lachen, gähnen*›; aus voller Kehle ‹*rufen, singen*›; **he tucked ~ into his dinner** er langte kräftig *od.* tüchtig *od.* herzhaft zu

lustre /ˈlʌstə(r)/ *n.* (Brit.) **1** Schimmer, *der;* [schimmernder] Glanz; **shine with a ~:** einen schimmernden Glanz haben **2** (fig.: splendour) Glanz, *der;* **add ~ to** *or* **shed ~ on sth.** einer Sache (*Dat.*) Glanz verleihen; **lack ~** ‹*Augen:*› glanzlos sein; ‹*Lächeln:*› matt sein **3** (glaze) Glasurglanz, *der;* Lüster, *der* (fachspr.)

lustreless /ˈlʌstəlɪs/ *adj.* glanzlos; stumpf

ˈlustreware *n.* Lüsterkeramik, *die*

lustrous /ˈlʌstrəs/ *adj.* schimmernd; (fig.) glanzvoll; erhaben (geh.) ‹*Geist*›

lusty /ˈlʌstɪ/ *adj.* **1** (healthy) gesund; frisch ‹*Gesichtsfarbe*›; (strong, powerful) kräftig **2** (vigorous) herzhaft ‹*Applaus, Tritt*›; tüchtig, zupackend ‹*Arbeiter*›; **a ~ girl from the country** ein strammes Landmädchen

lutanist /ˈluːtənɪst, ˈljuːtənɪst/ *n.* ▸**i p. 1260** (Mus.) Lautenist, *der*/Lautenistin, *die*

lute /luːt, ljuːt/ *n.* (Mus.) Laute, *die*

lutenist ▸ **lutanist**

Lutheran /ˈluːθərən, ˈljuːθərən/

A *adj.* lutherisch

B *n.* Lutheraner, *der*/Lutheranerin, *die*

luvvy (luvvie) /ˈlʌvɪ/ *n.* (coll. derog.) Luvvy, *der*/*die* (*affektierter Schickeriatyp, der seinesgleichen mit 'love' anredet*)

Luxembourg /ˈlʌksəmbɜːg/ *pr. n.* ▸**i p. 1643** Luxemburg (*das*)

Luxembourger /ˈlʌksəmbɜːgə(r)/ *n.* ▸**i p. 1345** Luxemburger, *der*/Luxemburgerin, *die*

Luxembourgian /ˈlʌksəmbɜːgɪən/

A *adj.* luxemburgisch

B *n.* Luxemburgisch, *das;* Letzeburgesch, *das* (fachspr.)

Luxemburg *etc.* ▸ **Luxembourg** *etc.*

luxuriance /lʌgˈzjʊərɪəns, lʌkˈsjʊərɪəns/ *n., no pl.* (superabundance) Üppigkeit, *die;* (of hair) Fülle, *die*

luxuriant /lʌgˈzjʊərɪənt, lʌkˈsjʊərɪənt/ *adj.* **1** (growing profusely, exuberant) üppig ‹*Vegetation, Farbenpracht, Blattwerk*›; voll ‹*Haar*›; ertragreich ‹*Ernte*› **2** (richly ornamented) reich ausgeschmückt

luxuriantly /lʌgˈzjʊərɪəntlɪ, lʌkˈsjʊərɪəntlɪ/ *adv.* üppig

luxuriate /lʌgˈzjʊərɪeɪt, lʌkˈsjʊərɪeɪt/ *v.i.* **~ in** sich aalen in (+ *Dat.*) ‹*Sonne, Bett usw.*›; **~ in the bath** sich genüsslich in der Badewanne rekeln (ugs.)

luxurious /lʌgˈzjʊərɪəs, lʌkˈsjʊərɪəs/ *adj.* luxuriös; Luxus-; (self-indulgent) verwöhnt; luxuriös, verschwenderisch ‹*Lebensstil*›

luxuriously /lʌgˈzjʊərɪəslɪ, lʌkˈsjʊərɪəslɪ/ *adv.* luxuriös; mit allem Luxus; feudal (ugs.) ‹*wohnen, essen*›

luxury /ˈlʌkʃərɪ/

A *n.* **1** Luxus, *der;* **live** *or* **lead a life of ~:** ein Leben im Luxus führen; *see also* **lap¹ 1** **2** (article) Luxusgegenstand, *der;* **luxuries** Luxus, *der* **3** (sth. one enjoys) Luxus, *der*

B *attrib. adj.* Luxus-

LV *abbr.* (Brit.) **= luncheon voucher**

LW *abbr.* (Radio) **= long wave** LW

lychee /ˈlaɪtʃɪ, ˈlɪtʃɪ/ *n.* Litschi, *die*

lychgate ▸ **lichgate**

Lycra ® /ˈlaɪkrə/ *n., no pl.* Lykra (Wz), *das*

lye /laɪ/ *n.* Lauge, *die*

lying /ˈlaɪɪŋ/

A *adj.* **1** (given to falsehood) verlogen; **~ scoundrel** Lügenbold, *der* **2** (false, untrue) lügnerisch; lügenhaft; erlogen ‹*Geschichte*›; falsch, verlogen ‹*Sentimentalität*›

B *n.* Lügen, *das;* **that would be ~:** das wäre gelogen. *See also* **lie¹ B, C**

lymph /lɪmf/ *n.* **1** (Physiol.) Lymphe, *die* (fachspr.); Gewebsflüssigkeit, *die* **2** (Med.: exudation from sore) Blutwasser, *das*

lymphatic /lɪmˈfætɪk/

A *adj.* (Physiol., Anat.) Lymph-; lymphatisch

B *n.* (Anat.) Lymphgefäß, *das*

lymph: ~ gland, ~ node *ns.* (Anat.) Lymphknoten, *der*

lymphocyte /ˈlɪmfəsaɪt/ *n.* (Anat.) Lymphozyt, *der*

lynch /lɪnʃ/ *v.t.* lynchen

ˈlynch law *n.* Lynchjustiz, *die*

lynx /lɪŋks/ *n.* (Zool.) Luchs, *der*

ˈlynx-eyed *adj.* (fig.) luchsäugig; mit Luchsaugen *nachgestellt;* **be ~:** Luchsaugen haben

Lyons /ˈliːɔ̃/ *pr. n.* ▸**i p. 1643** Lyon (*das*)

lyre /ˈlaɪə(r)/ *n.* (Mus.) Lyra, *die;* Leier, *die*

ˈlyrebird *n.* (Ornith.) Leierschwanz, *der*

lyric /ˈlɪrɪk/

A *adj.* lyrisch; **~ poet** Lyriker, *der*/Lyrikerin, *die;* **~ poetry** Lyrik, *die*

B *n.* **1** (poem) lyrisches Gedicht **2** *in pl.* (verses) lyrische Passagen; (of song) Text, *der*

lyrical /ˈlɪrɪkl/ *adj.* **1** ▸ **lyric A** **2** (like lyric poetry) lyrisch **3** (coll.: enthusiastic) gefühlvoll; **become** *or* **grow** *or* **wax ~ about** *or* **over sth.** über etw. (*Akk.*) ins Schwärmen geraten

lyrically /ˈlɪrɪkəlɪ/ *adv.* lyrisch

lyricism /ˈlɪrɪsɪzm/ *n.* **1** (lyric character, a lyrical expression) Lyrismus, *der* **2** (high-flown sentiments) Gefühlsbetontheit, *die;* Gefühlsseligkeit, *die;* Schwärmerei, *die*

lyricist /ˈlɪrɪsɪst/ *n.* ▸**i p. 1260** Texter, *der*/Texterin, *die*

M, m /em/ *n., pl.* **Ms** *or* **M's** 1 (letter) M, m, *das* 2 (Roman numeral) M

m. *abbr.* 1 **= male** männl. 2 **= masculine** m. 3 **= married** verh. 4 ▸ⓘ **p. 1286 = metre[s]** m 5 ▸ⓘ **p. 1690 = milli-** m 6 **= million[s]** Mill. 7 ▸ⓘ **p. 1001 = minute[s]** Min. 8 **= mile[s]** M

M. *abbr.* 1 **= Master/Member of/Monsieur** M. 2 **= mega-** M 3 (Brit.) **= motorway** A

m' /mə/ *poss. pron.* mein

ma /mɑː/ *n.* (coll.) Mama, *die;* Mutti, *die* (fam.)

MA *abbr.* **= Master of Arts** M. A.; *see also* **BSc**

ma'am /mɑːm, mæm/ *n.* gnädige Frau; (in addressing Queen) Majestät

mac /mæk/ *n.* (Brit. coll.) Regenmantel, *der;* Kleppermantel Ⓦⓩ, *der* (ugs. veralt.)

Mac /mæk/ *n.* (coll.) 1 (Scotsman) Schotte, *der;* (in address) Mac 2 (Amer.: fellow) Kumpel, *der* (ugs.); **hi, ~!** Tag, Kumpel!

macabre /məˈkɑːbr/ *adj.* makaber

macaque /məˈkæk/ *n.* (Zool.) Makak, *der*

macaroni /mækəˈrəʊnɪ/ *n.* Makkaroni *Pl.;* **~ and cheese** (Amer.) ▸**macaroni cheese**

macaroni 'cheese *n.* (Brit.) Käsemakkaroni *Pl.*

macaroon /mækəˈruːn/ *n.* Makrone, *die*

macaw /məˈkɔː/ *n.* (Ornith.) Ara, *der;* Langschwanzpapagei, *der*

mace¹ /meɪs/ *n.* 1 (Hist.: weapon) Keule, *die* 2 (staff of office) Amtsstab, *der*

mace² *n.* (Bot., Cookery) Mazis, *der;* Mazisblüte, *die;* Muskatblüte, *die*

'mace-bearer *n.* Träger/Trägerin des Amtsstabes

macédoine /ˈmæsɪdwɑːn/ *n.* (Cookery) Macedoine, *das*

Macedonia /mæsɪˈdəʊnɪə/ *pr. n.* Makedonien (*das*)

macerate /ˈmæsəreɪt/ *v.t.* aufweichen ‹*Papier*›

Mach /mæk, mɑːk/ *n.* (Phys., Aeronaut.) **~ [number]** Machzahl, *die;* machsche Zahl; **~ one/two** *etc.* Geschwindigkeit von 1/2 *usw.* Mach

machete /məˈtʃetɪ, məˈtʃeɪtɪ/ *n.* Machete, *die;* Buschmesser, *das*

Machiavellian /mækɪəˈvelɪən/ *adj.* machiavellistisch

machination /mækɪˈneɪʃn, mæʃɪˈneɪʃn/ *n.* Machenschaft, *die* (abwertend)

machine /məˈʃiːn/

A *n.* 1 Maschine, *die;* **be made by ~:** maschinell hergestellt werden 2 (bicycle) [Fahr]rad, *das;* (motorcycle) Maschine, *die* (ugs.) 3 (computer) Computer, *der* 4 (fig.: person) Roboter, *der;* Maschine, *die* 5 (system of organization) Apparat, *der;* **party/propaganda ~:** Partei-/Propagandaapparat, *der*

B *v.t.* (make with ~) maschinell herstellen; (operate on with ~) maschinell bearbeiten ‹*Werkstück*›; (sew) mit *od.* auf der Maschine nähen

machine: ~ age *n.* Maschinenzeitalter, *das;* **~ code** *n.* (Computing) Maschinensprache, *die;* **~ gun** *n.* Maschinengewehr, *das;* **~ language** ▸**~ code**; **~-made** *adj.* maschinell hergestellt; **~-minder** *n.* Maschinenwärter, *der;* **~ operator** *n.* [Maschinen]bediener, *der*/-bedienerin, *die;* **~ pistol** *n.* Maschinenpistole, *die;* **~-readable** *adj.* (Computing) maschinenlesbar; **~ room** *n.* Maschinenraum, *der*

machinery /məˈʃiːnərɪ/ *n.* 1 (machines) Maschinen *Pl.* 2 (mechanism) Mechanismus, *der* 3 (organized system) Maschinerie, *die* 4 (Lit.) Kunstmittel *Pl.*

machine: ~ tool *n.* Werkzeugmaschine, *die;* **~ trans'lation** *n.* maschinelle Übersetzung; **~-wash** *v.t.* in der Waschmaschine waschen; **~-washable** *adj.* waschmaschinenfest

machinist /məˈʃiːnɪst/ *n.* ▸ⓘ **p. 1260** (who makes machinery) Maschinenbauer, *der;* (who controls machinery) Maschinist, *der*/Maschinistin, *die;* **[sewing] ~:** [Maschinen]näherin, *die*/-näher, *der*

machismo /məˈtʃɪzməʊ, məˈkɪzməʊ/ *n., no pl.* Machismo, *der;* Männlichkeitswahn, *der*

macho /ˈmætʃəʊ/

A *n., pl.* **~s** Macho, *der*

B *adj.* Macho-; **he is really ~:** er ist wirklich ein Macho

mack ▸**mac**

mackerel /ˈmækrəl/ *n., pl. same or* **~s** (Zool.) Makrele, *die*

mackerel 'sky *n.* (Meteorol.) Zirrokumulusbewölkung, *die;* Schäfchenwolken *Pl.*

mackintosh /ˈmækɪntɒʃ/ *n.* Regenmantel, *der*

macramé /məˈkrɑːmɪ/ *n.* Makramee, *das*

macro /ˈmækrəʊ/ *n.* (Computing) Makro, *das*

macro- /ˈmækrəʊ/ *in comb.* makro-/Makro-

macrobiotic /mækrəʊbaɪˈɒtɪk/ *adj.* makrobiotisch

macrocosm /ˈmækrəkɒzm/ *n.* Makrokosmos, *der*

macro: ~economic *adj.* makroökonomisch; **~economics** *n.* Makroökonomie, *die*

macron /ˈmækrɒn/ *n.* übergesetzter waagerechter Strich (*zur Kennzeichnung langer Vokale*)

macroscopic /mækrəʊˈskɒpɪk/ *adj.* makroskopisch

mad /mæd/ *adj.* 1 (insane) geisteskrank; irr ‹*Blick, Ausdruck*›; **you must be ~!** du bist wohl verrückt! (ugs.); **are you ~?** bist du völlig verrückt geworden? (ugs.); **like a ~ thing** (coll.) wie ein Verrückter/eine Verrückte (ugs.) 2 (frenzied) wahnsinnig; verrückt (ugs.); **it's one ~ rush** (coll.) es ist eine einzige Hetze; **make a ~ dash for sth.** sich auf etw. (*Akk.*) stürzen; **drive sb. ~:** jmdn. um den Verstand bringen *od.* (ugs.) verrückt machen; **this noise is enough to drive anyone ~!** dieser Lärm ist ja zum Verrücktwerden! (ugs.); **~ with joy/fear** außer sich vor Freude/Angst 3 (foolish) verrückt (ugs.); **that was a ~ thing to do** das war eine Dummheit *od.* (ugs.) verrückt; **a ~ hope** eine wahnwitzige Hoffnung 4 (very enthusiastic) **be/go ~ about** *or* **on sb./sth.** auf jmdn./etw. wild sein/werden (ugs.); **be ~ keen on sth.** (coll.) auf etw. (*Akk.*) ganz scharf *od.* wild sein (ugs.); **be ~ keen to do sth.** (coll.) ganz scharf *od.* wild darauf sein, etw. zu tun 5 (coll.: annoyed) **~ [with** *or* **at sb.]** sauer [auf jmdn.] (ugs.); **be ~ about/at missing the train** wütend sein, weil man den Zug verpasst hat 6 (with rabies) toll; **~ dog** (fig.) Verrückte, *der/die* (ugs.); **[run** *etc.***] like ~** (coll.) wie wild *od.* wie ein Wilder/eine Wilde (ugs.) [laufen *usw.*] 7 (frivolous) ausgelassen, (ugs.) verrückt ‹*Stimmung*›

Madagascan /mædəˈgæskən/

A *adj.* madagassisch

B *n.* Madagasse, *der*/Madagassin, *die*

Madagascar /mædəˈgæskə(r)/ *pr. n.* Madagaskar (*das*)

madam /ˈmædəm/ *n.* 1 ▸ⓘ **p. 1287,** ▸ⓘ **p. 1634** (formal address) gnädige Frau; **M~ Chairman** Frau Vorsitzende; **Dear M~** (in letter) Sehr verehrte gnädige Frau 2 (euphem.: woman brothel-keeper) Bordellwirtin, *die;* Puffmutter, *die* (salopp) 3 (derog.: conceited, pert young woman) Kratzbürste, *die* (ugs. scherzh.)

Madame /məˈdɑːm, ˈmædəm/ *n., pl.* **Mesdames** /meɪˈdæm, meɪˈdɑːm/ 1 (title) Madame, *die;* **[the] Mesdames A and B** Madame A und Madame B 2 (formal address) gnädige Frau; meine Dame

'madcap

A *adj.* unbesonnen

B *n.* Heißsporn, *der*

mad 'cow disease *n.* (coll.) Rinderwahnsinn, *der*

madden /ˈmædn/ *v.t.* 1 (make mad) wahnsinnig machen (ugs.); um den Verstand bringen; **~ed with grief/loneliness** wahnsinnig vor Kummer/Einsamkeit 2 (irritate) [ver]ärgern; **be ~ed by sth.** sich über etw. (*Akk.*) [maßlos] aufregen; **it ~s me to think that ...:** es fuchst mich (ugs.), wenn ich daran denke, dass ...

maddening /ˈmædənɪŋ/ *adj.* 1 (irritating, tending to infuriate) [äußerst] ärgerlich 2 (tending to craze) unerträglich

maddeningly /ˈmædənɪŋlɪ/ *adv.* ▸**maddening 1, 2**: [äußerst] ärgerlich; unerträglich

madder /ˈmædə(r)/ *n.* 1 (Bot.) Krapp, *der;* Färberröte, *die* 2 (dye) Krappfarbstoff, *der* 3 (Chem.) synthetisches Alizarin

made ▸**make A, B**

Madeira /məˈdɪərə/

A *n.* Madeira[wein], *der*

B *pr. n.* Madeira (*das*)

Ma'deira cake *n.* Madeirakuchen, *der*

madeleine /ˈmædleɪn/ *n.: Butterkeks in Form einer Muschel*

made-to-'measure *attrib. adj.* Maß-; **a ~ suit** ein Maßanzug *od.* maßgeschneiderter Anzug; *see also* **measure A 1**

'made-up *attrib. adj.* erfunden ‹*Geschichte*›

'madhouse *n.* Irrenanstalt, *die;* Irrenhaus, *das;* (fig.) Tollhaus, *das*

Madison Avenue /mædɪsən ˈævənjuː/ *n.* die amerikanische Werbeindustrie

madly /ˈmædlɪ/ *adv.* 1 wie ein Verrückter/eine Verrückte (ugs.) 2 (coll.: passionately, extremely) wahnsinnig (ugs.)

madman /ˈmædmən/ *n., pl.* **madmen** /ˈmædmən/ Wahnsinnige, *der;* Irre, *der*

madness /ˈmædnɪs/ *n., no pl.* Wahnsinn, *der; see also* **method 2**

madonna /məˈdɒnə/ *n.* (Art, Relig.) Madonna, *die*

madrigal /ˈmædrɪgl/ *n.* (Lit., Mus.) Madrigal, *das*

'madwoman *n.* Wahnsinnige, *die;* Irre, *die*

maelstrom /ˈmeɪlstrəm/ *n.* (lit. or fig.) Mahlstrom, *der;* Strudel, *der;* Sog, *der*

maestro /'maɪstrəʊ/ *n., pl.* **maestri** /'maɪstri:/ *or* **~s** (Mus.) Maestro, *der;* (fig.: great performer) Meister, *der*

Mae West /meɪ 'west/ *n.* aufblasbare Schwimmweste

MAFF *abbr.* (Brit. Hist.) = **Ministry of Agriculture, Fisheries, and Food** Landwirtschaftsministerium, *das*

Mafia /'mæfɪə/ *n.* 1 (secret criminal organization) Mafia, *die* 2 **m~** (organization exerting influence) Mafia, *die*

mag /mæg/ *n.* (coll.: magazine) Zeitschrift, *die;* **porno ~:** Pornoheft, *das*

magazine /mægə'zi:n/ *n.* 1 (periodical) Zeitschrift, *die;* (news ~, fashion ~, etc.) Magazin, *das* 2 (Mil.: store) (for arms) Waffenkammer, *die;* (for ammunition) Munitionsdepot, *das;* (for provisions) Proviantlager, *das;* (for explosives) Sprengstofflager, *das* 3 (Arms, Photog.) Magazin, *das*

magenta /mə'dʒentə/
A *n.* 1 (dye) Fuchsin, *das;* Rosanilin, *das* 2 (colour) Magenta, *das;* Purpur, *das*
B *adj.* purpurrot

maggot /'mægət/ *n.* Made, *die*

maggoty /'mægətɪ/ *adj.* madig

Magi /'meɪdʒaɪ/ *n. pl.* **the [three] ~:** die drei Weisen aus dem Morgenland; die Heiligen Drei Könige

magic /'mædʒɪk/
A *n.* 1 (witchcraft, lit. or fig.) Magie, *die;* **do ~:** zaubern; **as if by ~:** wie durch Zauberei; **black/white ~:** schwarze/weiße Magie; **work like ~:** wie ein Wunder wirken; **like ~** (rapidly) blitzartig 2 (conjuring tricks) Zauberei, *die;* **make sth. appear/disappear by ~:** etw. herbei-/wegzaubern 3 (fig.: charm, enchantment) Zauber, *der*
B *adj.* 1 (of ~) magisch ‹*Eigenschaft, Kraft*›; (resembling ~) zauberhaft; (used in ~) Zauber‹*spruch, -trank, -wort, -bann*›; **cast a ~ spell on sb.** jmdn. verzaubern 2 (fig.: producing surprising results) wunderbar
C *v.t.,* **-ck-** zaubern; **~ sth./sb. away** ‹*Zauberspruch:*› etw./jmdn. verschwinden lassen; ‹*Person:*› etw./jmdn. wegzaubern

magical /'mædʒɪkl/ *adj.* (of magic) magisch; (resembling magic) zauberhaft; **the effect was ~:** das wirkte [wahre] Wunder

magically /'mædʒɪkəlɪ/ *adv.* auf wunderbare Weise ‹*schützen, verwandeln, befördern*›; zauberhaft ‹*beleuchten*›

magic: ~ 'carpet *n.* fliegender Teppich; **~ 'eye** *n.* 1 (Electr.: control device) Photozelle, *die;* 2 (Radio) magisches Auge

magician /mə'dʒɪʃn/ *n.* (lit. or fig.) Magier, *der*/Magierin, *die;* (conjuror) Zauberer, *der*/Zauberin, *die;* **I'm not a ~:** ich kann doch nicht zaubern *od.* hexen (ugs.)

magic: ~ 'lantern *n.* (Optics) Laterna Magica, *die;* **~ 'square** *n.* (Math.) magisches Quadrat; **~ 'wand** *n.* Zauberstab, *der*

magisterial /mædʒɪ'stɪərɪəl/ *adj.* 1 (invested with authority) gebieterisch (geh.) 2 (dictatorial) diktatorisch (abwertend); herrisch 3 (authoritative) maßgebend

magistracy /'mædʒɪstrəsɪ/ *n., no pl.* (position) Amt des Friedensrichters

magistrate /'mædʒɪstreɪt/ *n.* ▸❶ **p. 1260** Friedensrichter, *der*/Friedensrichterin, *die;* **~s' court** ≈ Schiedsgericht, *das*

maglev /'mæglev/ *n.* **~ [system]/train** Magnetschwebebahn, *die*

magma /'mægmə/ *n., pl.* **~ta** /'mægmətə/ *or* **~s** (Geol.) Magma, *das*

Magna Carta /mægnə 'kɑ:tə/, (Amer.) **Magna Charta** /'tʃɑ:rtə/ *n.* (Hist.; also fig.) Magna Charta, *die*

magnanimity /mægnə'nɪmɪtɪ/ *n., no pl.* Großmut, *die;* **with ~:** großmütig

magnanimous /mæg'nænɪməs/ *adj.,* **magnanimously** /mæg'nænɪməslɪ/ *adv.* großmütig (**towards** gegen)

magnate /'mægneɪt/ *n.* Magnat, *der*/Magnatin, *die;* **cotton/steel ~:** Baumwoll-/Stahlmagnat, *der*

magnesia /mæg'ni:ʃə/ *n.* Magnesiaweiß, *das; see also* **milk A**

magnesium /mæg'ni:zɪəm/ *n.* (Chem.) Magnesium, *das*

magnet /'mægnɪt/ *n.* (lit. or fig.) Magnet, *der*

magnetic /mæg'netɪk/ *adj.* (lit. or fig.) magnetisch; (fig.: very attractive) sehr anziehend, unwiderstehlich ‹*Person*›; **~ power** (fig.) magnetische Anziehungskraft

magnetically /mæg'netɪklɪ/ *adv.* magnetisch

magnetic: ~ at'traction *n.* (Phys.) magnetische Anziehungskraft; **~ 'compass** *n.* Magnetkompass, *der;* **~ 'disc** ▸**disc 3**; **~ 'field** *n.* (Phys.) Magnetfeld, *das;* **~ 'mine** *n.* Magnetmine, *die;* **~ 'needle** *n.* Magnetnadel, *die;* **~ 'north** *n.* magnetisch Nord, *das;* **~ 'pole** *n.* (Phys.) Magnetpol, *der;* (Geog.) magnetischer Pol; **~ 'storm** *n.* (Phys.) erdmagnetischer Sturm; **~ 'tape** *n.* Magnetband, *das*

magnetise ▸**magnetize**

magnetism /'mægnɪtɪzm/ *n.* 1 (Phys.) (science) Magnetik, *die;* (force, lit. or fig.) Magnetismus, *der;* **terrestrial ~:** Erdmagnetismus, *der* 2 (fig.: personal charm and attraction) Attraktivität, *die;* Anziehungskraft, *die;* Attraktion, *die*

magnetize /'mægnɪtaɪz/ *v.t.* 1 (Phys.) magnetisieren 2 (fig.: attract) in seinen Bann schlagen *od.* ziehen (geh.); **be ~d by sth.** von etw. ganz gebannt sein

magneto /mæg'ni:təʊ/ *n., pl.* **~s** Magnetzünder, *der*

magnification /mægnɪfɪ'keɪʃn/ *n.* Vergrößerung, *die;* **under high/low ~/at x ~s** in starker/geringer/x-facher Vergrößerung

magnificence /mæg'nɪfɪsəns/ *n., no pl.* (lavish display) Pracht, *die;* Üppigkeit, *die;* (splendour) Prunk, *der;* Pracht, *die;* (grandeur) Stattlichkeit, *die;* Großartigkeit, *die;* (beauty) Herrlichkeit, *die*

magnificent /mæg'nɪfɪsənt/ *adj.* 1 (stately, sumptuously constructed or adorned) prächtig; prachtvoll; (sumptuous) prunkvoll; grandios, großartig ‹*Pracht, Herrlichkeit, Anblick*›; (beautiful) herrlich ‹*Garten, Umgebung, Kleidung, Vorhang, Kunstwerk, Wetter, Gestalt*›; (lavish) üppig ‹*Freigebigkeit, Mahl*› 2 (coll.: fine, excellent) fabelhaft (ugs.)

magnificently /mæg'nɪfɪsəntlɪ/ *adv.* 1 (with great stateliness and grandeur) prächtig; prachtvoll; (sumptuously) prunkvoll ‹*einrichten, schmücken*›; (with lavishness) üppig ‹*zubereitet*› 2 (coll.: in fine manner) fabelhaft (ugs.)

magnifier /'mægnɪfaɪə(r)/ *n.* (Optics) Lupe, *die*

magnify /'mægnɪfaɪ/ *v.t.* 1 vergrößern 2 (exaggerate) aufbauschen; übertrieben darstellen ‹*Gefahren*›

'magnifying glass *n.* Lupe, *die;* Vergrößerungsglas, *das*

magnitude /'mægnɪtju:d/ *n.* 1 (largeness, vastness) Ausmaß, *das;* (of explosion, earthquake) Stärke, *die* 2 (size) Größe, *die;* **problems of this ~:** Probleme dieser Größenordnung; **order of ~:** Größenordnung, *die* 3 (importance) Wichtigkeit, *die;* (of person) Bedeutung, *die;* **sth. of the first ~:** etw. von höchster Wichtigkeit; **a writer of the first ~:** ein sehr bedeutender Schriftsteller 4 (Astron.) Helligkeit, *die*

magnolia /mæg'nəʊlɪə/ *n.* (Bot.) Magnolie, *die*

magnum /'mægnəm/ *n.* (bottle) Magnum, *die;* (measure) 1,5 l; **two ~s** drei Liter

magnum 'opus ▸**opus 2**

magpie /'mægpaɪ/ *n.* (Ornith.) Elster, *die;* **chatter like a ~:** unaufhörlich schnattern (ugs.); **be like a ~** (fig.) alles Mögliche sammeln [wie eine Elster]

Magyar /'mægjɑ:(r)/ ▸❶ **p. 1277**, ▸❶ **p. 1345**
A *adj.* madjarisch
B *n.* 1 (person) Madjar, *der*/Madjarin, *die* 2 (language) Madjarisch, *das*

maharaja[h] /mɑ:hə'rɑ:dʒə/ *n.* (Ind. Hist.) Maharadscha, *der*

mah-jong[g] /mɑ:'dʒɒŋ/ *n.* Mah-Jongg, *das*

mahogany /mə'hɒgənɪ/ *n.* 1 (wood) Mahagoni[holz], *das; attrib.* Mahagoni- 2 (tree) Mahagonibaum, *der* 3 (colour) Mahagonibraun, *das*

maid /meɪd/ *n.* 1 (servant) Dienstmädchen, *das;* Dienstmagd, *die* (veralt.); **~ of 'all work** (servant) Hausangestellte, *die;* Hausmädchen, *das;* (fig.: person doing many jobs) Mädchen für alles (ugs.) 2 (arch.: unmarried woman) unverheiratete Frau; Jungfer, *die* (veralt., oft abwertend) 3 (arch./poet.) (girl) Maid, *die* (dichter. veralt.); (young unmarried woman, virgin) Jungfrau, *die* 4 (rhet.: young woman) Maid, *die* (dichter. veralt.); **the M~ [of Orleans]** die Jungfrau von Orleans. *See also* **old maid**

maiden /'meɪdn/
A *n.* 1 ▸**maid 3**; **the answer to a ~'s prayer** genau das Richtige; (attractive man) der Traum aller Frauen 2 ▸**maiden over**
B *adj.* 1 (unmarried) unverheiratet; (befitting a maid) jungfräulich ‹*Unschuld, Schönheit, Anmut*›; mädchenhaft ‹*Bescheidenheit, Erröten*› 2 (first) **~ voyage/speech** Jungfernfahrt/-rede, *die* 3 (unmated) nicht gedeckt, nicht begattet ‹*Tier*› 4 (that has never won) sieglos; **~ horse** Maiden, *das;* **~ race** Maidenrennen, *das*

maiden: ~hair *n.* (Bot.) Frauenhaarfarn, *der;* **~hair tree** Gingko[baum], *der;* Fächerbaum, *der;* **~head** *n.* 1 (virginity) Jungfräulichkeit, *die;* 2 (hymen) Jungfernhäutchen, *das;* **~ name** *n.* Mädchenname, *der;* **~ 'over** *n.* (Cricket) *Serie von sechs Würfen ohne erzielten Lauf*

maid: ~ of 'honour *n., pl.* **~s of honour** 1 (attendant of queen or princess) Hof- *od.* Ehrendame, *die;* 2 (Amer.: chief bridesmaid) Brautjungfer, *die;* **~servant** *n.* (arch.) Hausangestellte, *die;* Hausmädchen, *das*

mail[1] /meɪl/
A *n.* 1 ▸**post**[2] **A** 2 (vehicle carrying ~) Postbeförderungsmittel, *das;* (train) Postzug, *der*
B *v.t.* ▸**post**[2] **B 1**

mail[2] *n.* 1 (armour) Panzer, *der;* Rüstung, *die;* (chain ~) Kettenpanzer, *der;* **coat of ~:** Panzer- *od.* Kettenhemd, *das* 2 (Zool.) Panzer, *der*

mail: ~bag *n.* (postman's bag) Zustelltasche, *die;* (sack for transporting ~) Postsack, *der;* **~boat** *n.* Postschiff *od.* -boot, *das;* Postdampfer, *der;* **~ bomb** *n.* 1 (Amer.) Briefbombe, *die;* 2 (Computing) Mailbombe, *die;* E-Mail-Bombe, *die;* **~box** *n.* (Amer.) Briefkasten, *der;* (slot) Briefschlitz, *der;* **~ coach** *n.* 1 (Hist.) Postkutsche, *die;* 2 (Railw.) Post- *od.* Paketwagen, *der*

mailed /meɪld/ *adj.* 1 (armed with mail) gepanzert 2 **~ fist** ([threat of] armed force) gepanzerte Faust

mailing /'meɪlɪŋ/ *n.* 1 *no pl.* (action) Postversand, *der* 2 (mailed item) [Werbe]brief, *der*

mailing /'meɪlɪŋ/: **~ address** *n.* Postanschrift, *die;* **~ list** *n.* Adressenliste, *die*

mail: ~man *n.* ▸❶ **p. 1260** (Amer.) Briefträger, *der;* Postbote, *der* (ugs.); **M~merge** ®, **~merge** *n.* (Computing) Mailmerge, *das;* Serienbrieffunktion, *die; attrib.* Mailmerge-; **~ order** *n.* postalische Bestellung; Mailorder, *die* (Werbespr., Kaufmannsspr.); **by ~ order** durch Bestellung *od.* Mailorder; **~-order business** *n.* (trading) Versandhandel, *der;* (firm) Versandhaus, *das;* **~-order catalogue** *n.* Versandhauskatalog, *der;* **~-order firm, ~ order house** *ns.* Versandhaus, *das;* **~ room** *n.* Poststelle, *die;* **~shot** *n.* Mailing, *das;* **send out a ~shot** ein Mailing durchführen; **~ train** *n.* Postzug, *der;* **~ van** *n.* (Railw.) Post- *od.* Paketwagen, *der*

maim /meɪm/ *v.t.* (mutilate) verstümmeln; (cripple) zum Krüppel machen; **~ sb. for life** jmdn. zeitlebens zum Krüppel machen

main /meɪn/
A *n.* 1 (channel, pipe) Hauptleitung, *die;* **sewage ~:** Kanalisation, *die;* **~s [system]** öffentliches Versorgungsnetz; (of electricity) Stromnetz, *das;* **turn the gas/water off at the ~[s]** den Haupthahn [für das Gas/Wasser] abstellen; **turn the electricity off at the ~s** [den Strom] am Hauptschalter abschalten; **~s-operated** für Netzbetrieb *nachgestellt;* **the radio works on battery and on ~s** das Radio funktioniert mit Batterie- und Netzstrom 2 **in the ~:** im Allgemeinen; im Großen und Ganzen
B *attrib. adj.* Haupt-; **the ~ body of troops** das Gros der Truppen; **the ~ doubt/principle** der entscheidende Zweifel/oberste Grundsatz; **~ office** Zentrale, *die;* **~ theme** Hauptthema, *das;* **the ~ points of the news** die wichtigsten Meldungen; **the ~ thing is that …:** die Hauptsache *od.* das Wichtigste ist, dass …; **by ~**

force gewaltsam; **have an eye to the ~ chance** auf den eigenen Vorteil bedacht sein; **he married her with an eye to the ~ chance** er war auf seinen eigenen Vorteil bedacht, als er sie heiratete

main: ~ beam *n.* (Motor Veh.) **on ~ beam** aufgeblendet; **~ brace** *n.* (Naut.) Großbrasse, *die;* **splice the ~ brace** (Hist.) eine Extraration Rum austeilen; **~ 'clause** *n.* (Ling.) Hauptsatz, *der;* **~ course** *n.* Hauptgang, *der;* Hauptgericht, *das;* **~frame** *n.* (Computing) Großrechner, *der;* **~land** /'meɪnlənd/ *n.* Festland, *das;* **~ 'line** *n.* 1 (principal line of a railway) Hauptstrecke, *die; attrib.* **~-line station/train** Fernbahnhof/-zug, *der;* **~-line train service** Fernverkehr, *der;* 2 (Amer.: chief road or street) Hauptstraße, *die;* **~line** (sl.) A *v.i.* an der Spritze hängen (ugs.); B *v.t.* spritzen (ugs.) ‹Heroin›

mainly /'meɪnlɪ/ *adv.* hauptsächlich; in erster Linie; (for the most part) vorwiegend

main: ~ 'man *n.* (Amer. coll.) 1 (close friend) Vertraute, *der;* **he has always been my ~ man** er ist immer mein bester Freund gewesen; 2 (principal figure) Hauptperson, *die;* **the team's ~ man** der wichtigste Mann im Team; **~mast** *n.* (Naut.) Großmast, *der;* **~ 'road** Hauptstraße, *die;* **~sail** /'meɪnseɪl, 'meɪnsl/ *n.* (Naut.) Großsegel, *das;* **~spring** *n.* Hauptfeder, *die;* (of clock, watch, etc.; also fig.) Triebfeder, *die;* **~stay** *n.* (Naut.) Großstag, *das;* (fig.) [wichtigste] Stütze; **~ 'stem** *n.* (Amer. coll.) (street) Hauptstraße, *die;* (Railw.) Hauptstrecke, *die;* **~stream** *n.* 1 (principal current) Hauptstrom, *der;* (fig.) Hauptrichtung, *die;* **the ~stream of fashion** der vorherrschende Trend in der Mode; **be in the ~stream** der Hauptrichtung angehören; 2 (Jazz) Mainstream, *der;* **~ 'street** *n.* /(Amer.) '--/ Hauptstraße, *die;* **M~ Street** *n., no pl., no art.* (Amer. fig.) Kleinbürgertum, *das*

m

maintain /meɪn'teɪn/ *v.t.* 1 (keep up) aufrechterhalten; bewahren ‹*Anschein, Haltung, Einstellung, Frieden, Fassung*›; unterhalten ‹*Beziehungen, Briefwechsel*›; [beibe]halten ‹*Preise, Geschwindigkeit, Standard, Temperatur*›; wahren ‹*Rechte, Ruf*›; **in order to ~ security** aus Sicherheitsgründen; 2 (provide for) **~ sb.** für jmds. Unterhalt aufkommen 3 (preserve) instand halten; warten ‹*Maschine, Gerät*›; unterhalten ‹*Straße*›; **the car is too expensive to ~:** der Wagen ist in der Unterhaltung *od.* im Unterhalt zu teuer 4 (give aid to) unterstützen ‹*Partei, Wohlfahrtsorganisation, Sache*› 5 (assert as true) vertreten ‹*Meinung, Lehre*›; beteuern ‹*Unschuld*›; **~ that ...:** behaupten, dass ...

main'tained school *n.* (Brit.) staatliche Schule

maintenance /'meɪntənəns/ *n.* 1 ▸**maintain 1**: Aufrechterhaltung, *die;* Bewahrung, *die;* Unterhaltung, *die;* [Beibe]halten, *das;* Wahrung, *die* 2 (furnishing with means of subsistence) Unterhaltung, *die* 3 (assertion as true) Vertretung, *die;* (of innocence) Beteuerung, *die* 4 (Law: money paid to support sb.) Unterhalt, *der; see also* **separate maintenance** 5 (preservation) Instandhaltung, *die;* (of machinery) Wartung, *die;* **~ instructions** (for car) Wartungs- und Pflegeanleitung, *die* 6 (aiding) Unterstützung, *die*

maintenance: ~-free *adj.* wartungsfrei; **~ manual** *n.* Wartungsbuch, *das;* **~ order** *n.* Unterhaltsurteil, *das;* **~ worker** *n.* Wartungsmonteur, *der*

main 'verb *n.* Hauptverb, *das*

maison[n]ette /meɪzə'net/ *n.* [zweistöckige] Wohnung; Maison[n]ette, *die*

maize /meɪz/ *n.* Mais, *der;* **~ cob** Maiskolben, *der;* **grain of ~:** Maiskorn, *das;* **field of ~:** Maisfeld, *das*

Maj. *abbr.* = **Major[-]** Maj.

majestic /mə'dʒestɪk/ *adj.* majestätisch; hoheitsvoll (geh.); erhaben ‹*Erscheinung, Schlichtheit, Schönheit*›; gemessen ‹*Auftreten, Schritt*›; getragen ‹*Musik*›; (stately) stattlich; (possessing grandeur) grandios

majestically /mə'dʒestɪkəlɪ/ *adv.* majestätisch; gemessen[en Schritts] ‹*gehen*›

majesty /'mædʒɪstɪ/ *n.* ▸**i p. 1634** 1 Majestät, *die* (geh.); (of verse, music) Erhabenheit, *die;* (of appearance) Stattlichkeit, *die;* (of person, bearing) Würde, *die* 2 (sovereign power) Hoheit, *die;* Majestät, *die* 3 **Your/His/Her M~:** Eure/Seine/Ihre Majestät

major /'meɪdʒə(r)/

A *adj.* 1 *attrib.* (greater of two) größer...; **~ part** Großteil, *der* 2 *attrib.* (important) bedeutend...; (serious) schwer ‹*Unfall, Krankheit, Unglück, Unruhen*›; größer... ‹*Krieg, Angriff, Durchbruch*›; **not a ~ poet** kein bedeutender Dichter; kein Dichter von Bedeutung; **of ~ interest/importance** von größerem Interesse/von größerer Bedeutung; **~ road** (important) Hauptverkehrsstraße, *die;* (having priority) Vorfahrtsstraße, *die* 3 *attrib.* (Med.) schwer, größer... ‹*Operation*› 4 (Brit. Sch.) **Jones ~:** der ältere Jones; Jones Nr. 1 (ugs.) 5 (Mus.) Dur-; **~ key/scale/chord** Durtonart, *die*/Durtonleiter, *die*/Durakkord, *der;* **C ~:** C-Dur; **in a ~ key** in Dur; **~ third** *etc.* große Terz *usw*

B *n.* 1 ▸**i p. 1634** (Mil.) (officer above captain) Major, *der;* (*officer in charge of section of band instruments*) *Leiter der Trommler/Trompeter usw. einer Regimentskapelle; see also* **sergeant major** 2 (Amer. Univ.) Hauptfach, *das;* **with ~ in maths** mit Mathematik als Hauptfach; **be an economics ~:** Wirtschaftswissenschaft als Hauptfach studieren

C *v.i.* (Amer. Univ.) **~ in sth.** etw. als Hauptfach studieren

major 'axis *n.* (Geom.) große Achse; Hauptachse, *die*

Majorca /mə'jɔːkə/ *pr. n.* Mallorca (*das*)

major-domo /meɪdʒə'dəʊməʊ/ *n., pl.* **~s** (butler, house steward) Haushofmeister, *der*

majorette /meɪdʒə'ret/ ▸**drum majorette**

major-'general *n.* ▸**i p. 1634** (Mil.) Generalmajor, *der*

majority /mə'dʒɒrɪtɪ/ *n.* 1 (greater number or part) Mehrheit, *die;* **the great ~:** die überwiegende Mehrheit; der größte Teil; **the ~ of people think ...:** die meisten Menschen denken ...; **be in the ~:** in der Mehr- *od.* Überzahl sein; überwiegen 2 (in vote) [Stimmen-]mehrheit, *die;* Majorität, *die;* (party with greater/greatest number of votes) Mehrheitspartei, *die;* **two-thirds ~:** Zweidrittelmehrheit, *die;* **be elected by a narrow** *or* **small ~/a ~ of 3,000** mit knapper Mehrheit/einer Mehrheit von 3 000 Stimmen gewählt werden 3 (full age) Volljährigkeit, *die;* **attain** *or* **reach one's ~:** volljährig werden; **the age of ~:** das Volljährigkeitsalter

majority: ~ de'cision *n.* Mehrheitsentscheid, *der;* **~ 'holding** *n.* (Finance) Mehrheitsanteile *Pl.;* **~ 'rule** *n.* Mehrheitsregierung, *die;* **~ 'verdict** *n.* Mehrheitsentscheid, *der;* **return a ~ verdict** mehrheitlich zu einem Urteil kommen

major: ~ 'league *n.* (Amer.) Oberliga, *die;* **~ 'planet** *n.* Riesenplanet, *der;* **~ 'prophet** *n.* (Bibl.) Großer Prophet; **~ 'suit** *n.* (Bridge) hohe Farbe

make /meɪk/

A *v.t.,* **made** /meɪd/ 1 (construct) machen, anfertigen (**of** aus); bauen ‹*Damm, Straße, Flugzeug, Geige*›; anlegen ‹*See, Teich, Weg usw.*›; zimmern ‹*Tisch, Regal*›; basteln ‹*Spielzeug, Vogelhäuschen, Dekoration usw.*›; nähen ‹*Kleider*›; durchbrechen ‹*Türöffnung*›; (manufacture) herstellen; (create) [er]schaffen ‹*Welt*›; (prepare) zubereiten ‹*Mahlzeit*›; machen ‹*Frühstück, Grog*›; machen, kochen ‹*Kaffee, Tee, Marmelade*›; backen ‹*Brot, Kuchen*›; (compose, write) schreiben, verfassen ‹*Buch, Gedicht, Lied, Bericht*›; machen ‹*Eintrag, Zeichen, Kopie, Zusammenfassung, Testament*›; anfertigen ‹*Entwurf*›; aufsetzen ‹*Bewerbung, Schreiben, Urkunde*›; **~ a film** einen Film drehen; **as tough/clever/stupid as they ~ them** (coll.) zäh/schlau/dumm wie sonst was (ugs.); **~ a dress out of the material, ~ the material into a dress** aus dem Stoff ein Kleid machen; **~ wine from grapes/a frame with timber** aus Trauben Wein/Holz einen Rahmen machen; **~ milk into butter** aus Milch Butter machen; **~ a sofa into a bed** aus einem Sofa ein Bett machen; **a table made of wood/of the finest wood** ein Holztisch/ein Tisch aus feinstem Holz; **made in Germany** in Deutschland hergestellt; **be German-made** deutsche Ware sein; **show what one is made of** zeigen, was in einem steckt (ugs.); **see what sb. is made of** sehen, was in jmdm. steckt (ugs.); **be [simply] 'made of money** (coll.) ein [wahrer] Krösus sein (ugs.); im Geld [nur so] schwimmen (ugs.); **be 'made for sth./sb.** (fig.: ideally suited) wie geschaffen für etw./jmdn. sein; **'made for one another** wie für einander geschaffen; **that's the way he's made** so ist er nun einmal; **be 'made for doing sth.** (fig.) dazu geschaffen sein, etw. zu tun; **be made [so as] to ...:** so beschaffen sein, dass ...; **a made dish** ein aus mehreren Zutaten bereitetes Gericht; **made road** befestigte *od.* gepflasterte Straße; **~ a bed** (for sleeping) ein Bett bauen (ugs.); **~ the bed** (arrange after sleeping) das Bett machen; **have it made** (coll.) ausgesorgt haben (ugs.); **she has it made** (is sure of success) ihr ist der Erfolg sicher; *see also* **best C 5; hash[1] A; hay; head A 5; light[2] A 6; meal[1]; measure A 1; most B 3; nothing A 1; order A 5**

2 (combine into) sich verbinden zu; bilden; **blue and yellow ~ green** aus Blau und Gelb wird Grün; **~ it a foursome** eine Vierergruppe bilden

3 (cause to exist) machen ‹*Ärger, Schwierigkeiten, Lärm, Aufhebens*›; **~ enemies** sich (*Dat.*) Feinde machen *od.* schaffen; **~ time for sb./sth.** sich (*Dat.*) für jmdn./etw. Zeit nehmen; **~ time for doing** *or* **to do sth.** sich (*Dat.*) die Zeit dazu nehmen, etw. zu tun; *see also* **bone A 1, 4; book A 7; conversation; friend 1; fun A; game[1] A 4; mark[1] A 1, 2; name A 5; peace 2; point A 7; room A 2; sport A 4; stir[1] C 1**

4 (result in, amount to) machen ‹*Unterschied, Summe*›; ergeben ‹*Resultat*›; **it ~s a difference** es ist ein *od.* (ugs.) macht einen Unterschied; **two and two ~ four** zwei und zwei ist *od.* macht *od.* sind vier; **twelve inches ~ a foot** zwölf Inches sind ein Fuß; **these two gloves don't ~ a pair** diese beiden Handschuhe ergeben kein Paar *od.* gehören nicht zusammen; **that would ~ a nice Christmas present** das wäre ein schönes Weihnachtsgeschenk; **~ an unusual sight** ein ungewöhnlicher Anblick sein; **they ~ a handsome pair** sie geben ein hübsches Paar ab; sie sind ein hübsches Paar; **qualities that ~ a man** Eigenschaften, die einen Mann ausmachen; *see also* **change A 1, 3, 4; swallow[2]**

5 (establish, enact) bilden ‹*Gegensatz*›; treffen ‹*Unterscheidung, Übereinkommen*›; ziehen ‹*Vergleich, Parallele*›; erlassen ‹*Gesetz, Haftbefehl*›; aufstellen ‹*Regeln, Behauptung*›; stellen ‹*Forderung*›; geben ‹*Bericht*›; schließen ‹*Vertrag*›; vornehmen ‹*Zahlung*›; machen ‹*Geschäft, Vorschlag, Geständnis*›; erheben ‹*Anschuldigung, Protest, Beschwerde*›

6 (cause to be or become) **~ angry/happy/known** *etc.* wütend/glücklich/bekannt *usw.* machen; **~ sb. captain/one's wife** jmdn. zum Kapitän/(veralt.) zu seiner Frau machen; **~ a good husband of sb.** aus jmdm. einen guten Ehemann machen; **~ a star of sb.** aus jmdm. einen Star machen; **~ a friend of sb.** sich mit jmdm. anfreunden; **~ something of oneself/sth.** etwas aus sich/etw. machen; **~ oneself heard/respected** sich (*Dat.*) Gehör/Respekt verschaffen; **~ oneself understood** sich verständlich machen; **~ oneself/sb. feared** bewirken, dass man/jmd. gefürchtet ist; **~ a weekend of it** ein Wochenende daraus machen; es zu einem Wochenende verlängern; **he was made director/the heir** er wurde Direktor/zum Erben; **shall we ~ it Tuesday then?** sagen wir also Dienstag?; **that ~s it one pound exactly** das macht genau ein Pfund; **~ it a round dozen** ein rundes Dutzend daraus machen; das Dutzend voll machen; **~ it a shorter journey by doing sth.** die Reise abkürzen, indem man etw. tut; *see also* **example 2; exhibition 3; fool[1] A 1; habit A 1; night 1; practice[1] 1, 4; scarce A 2**

7 **~ sb. do sth.** (cause) jmdn. dazu bringen, etw. zu tun; (compel) jmdn. zwingen, etw. zu tun; **he made her cry** seinetwegen musste sie

weinen; er brachte sie zum Heulen (ugs.); **~ sb. repeat the sentence** jmdn. den Satz wiederholen lassen; **be made to do sth.** etw. tun müssen; **you can't ~ me** du kannst mich nicht zwingen; **~ oneself do sth.** sich überwinden, etw. zu tun; **what ~s you think that?** wie kommst du darauf?; **~ sth. do sth.** es fertig bringen, dass etw. etw. tut

8 (form, be counted as) **this ~s the tenth time you've failed** das ist nun [schon] das zehnte Mal, dass du versagt hast; du hast nun schon zum zehnten Mal versagt; **will you ~ one of the party?** wirst du dabei *od.* (ugs.) mit von der Partie sein?

9 (serve for) abgeben; **this story ~s good reading** diese Geschichte ist guter Lesestoff

10 (become by development or training) **the site would ~ a good playground** der Platz würde einen guten Spielplatz abgeben *od.* würde sich gut als Spielplatz eignen; **he will ~ a good officer/husband** aus ihm wird noch ein guter Offizier/Ehemann; **~ a reliable partner** ein verlässlicher Partner sein

11 (gain, acquire, procure) machen ‹*Vermögen, Profit, Verlust*›; machen (ugs.) ‹*Geld*›; verdienen ‹*Lebensunterhalt*›; sich (*Dat.*) erwerben ‹*Ruf*›; (obtain as result) kommen zu *od.* auf, herausbekommen ‹*Ergebnis, Endsumme*›; (Cricket: score) erzielen; (Cards: win) machen ‹*Stich*›; erfüllen ‹*Kontrakt*›; **how much did you ~?** wie viel hast du verdient?; **that ~s one pound exactly** das macht genau ein Pfund; **that ~s a hundred you've scored** damit hast du insgesamt 100 Punkte

12 (execute by physical movement) machen ‹*Geste, Bewegung, Verbeugung, Knicks, Satz*›; schlagen ‹*Purzelbaum*›; (perform as action) machen ‹*Reise, Besuch, Ausnahme, Fehler, Angebot, Entdeckung, Witz, Bemerkung*›; begehen ‹*Irrtum*›; vornehmen ‹*Änderung, Stornierung*›; vorbringen ‹*Beschwerde*›; tätigen, machen ‹*Einkäufe*›; geben ‹*Versprechen, Kommentar*›; halten ‹*Rede*›; ziehen ‹*Vergleich*›; durchführen, machen ‹*Experiment, Analyse, Inspektion*›; (wage) führen ‹*Krieg*›; (accomplish) schaffen ‹*Strecke pro Zeiteinheit*›; **~ a good breakfast** *etc.* (dated: eat) gut frühstücken *usw.*; *see also* **back A 1**; **bow² C**; **face A 1**; **love A 1**; **shift C 4**

13 **~ much of sth.** etw. betonen; **~ little of sth.** (play down) etw. herunterspielen; **they could ~ little of his letter** (understand) sie konnten mit seinem Brief nicht viel anfangen; **I couldn't ~ much of the book** (understand) ich konnte mit dem Buch nicht viel anfangen; das Buch sagte mir nicht viel; **I don't know what to ~ of him/it** ich werde aus ihm/daraus nicht schlau *od.* klug; **what do you ~ of him?** was hältst du von ihm?; wie schätzt du ihn ein?

14 (arrive at) erreichen ‹*Bestimmungsort*›; (achieve place in) kommen in (+ *Akk.*) ‹*Hitparade*›; aufsteigen in (+ *Akk.*) ‹*1. Liga usw.*›; (coll.: catch) [noch] kriegen (ugs.) ‹*Zug usw.*›; (coll.: seduce) ins Bett kriegen (ugs.); **~ it** (succeed in arriving) es schaffen; **~ it in business** es geschäftlich zu etwas bringen; **~ it through the winter/night** über den Winter/durch die Nacht kommen; **I can't ~ it tomorrow** (coll.) morgen passt es mir nicht; **~ it with sb.** (coll.: seduce) es mit jmdm. machen (ugs.); mit jmdm. ins Bett steigen (ugs.)

15 (frame in mind) **~ a judgement/an estimate of sth.** sich (*Dat.*) ein Urteil über etw. (*Akk.*) bilden/etw. [ab- *od.* ein]schätzen

16 (secure advancement of) machen (ugs.) ‹*Popstar usw.*›; zum Erfolg verhelfen (+ *Dat.*); **a made man** ein gemachter Mann; **sth. ~s or breaks** *or* **mars sb.** etw. entscheidet über jmds. Glück oder Verderben (*Akk.*); **~ sb.'s day** jmdm. einen glücklichen Tag bescheren

17 (consider to be) **What do you ~ the time? — I ~ it five past eight** Wie spät hast du es *od.* ist es bei dir? — Auf meiner Uhr ist es fünf nach acht; **he made the answer/total £10** er bekam 10 Pfund als Antwort heraus/kam zu einer Gesamtsumme von 10 Pfund

18 (Electr.) herstellen ‹*Kontakt*›; schließen ‹*Stromkreis*›

19 (Naut.) (discern) sichten ‹*Land, Hafen usw.*›; **~ sail** Segel setzen; (start on voyage) lossegeln

20 **~ do** vorlieb nehmen; **~ do and mend** mit den vorhandenen Sachen vorlieb nehmen und sie ausbessern; **~ do with/without sth.** mit/ohne etw. auskommen

B *v.i.*, **made** **1** (proceed) **~ toward sth./sb.** auf etw./jmdn. zusteuern

2 (act as if with intention) **~ to do sth.** Anstalten machen, etw. zu tun; **~ as if** *or* **as though to do sth.** so tun, als wolle man etw. tun

3 (profit) **~ on a deal** bei einem Geschäft Gewinn machen. *See also* **bold 2**; **certain 2**; **free A 3**; **good A 21**; **merry 1**; **sure A 5**

C *n.* **1** (kind of structure) Ausführung, *die;* (of clothes) Machart, *die*

2 (type of manufacture) Fabrikat, *das;* (brand) Marke, *die;* **~ of car** Automarke, *die;* **a camera of Japanese ~:** eine Kamera japanischer Herstellung *od.* Fabrikation

3 **on the ~** (coll.: intent on gain) hinter dem Geld her (abwertend)

Phrasal verbs

- **~ a'way with** ▸ **~ off with**
- **~ for** *v.t.* **1** (move towards) zusteuern auf (+ *Akk.*); zuhalten auf (+ *Akk.*); (rush towards) losgehen auf (+ *Akk.*); zustürzen auf (+ *Akk.*); **~ for home** heimwärts steuern **2** (be conducive to) führen zu, herbeiführen ‹*gute Beziehungen, Erfolg, Zuversicht*›
- **~ 'off** *v.i.* sich davonmachen
- **~ 'off with** *v.t.* **~ off with sb./sth.** sich mit jmdm./etw. [auf und] davonmachen
- **~ 'out**

A *v.t.* **1** (write) ausstellen ‹*Scheck, Dokument, Rechnung*›; aufstellen ‹*Liste*›; ausfertigen (Amtsspr.) ‹*Schreiben, Antrag*› **2** (claim, assert) behaupten; **the novel wasn't as good as the review had made it out to be** *or* **made out** der Roman war nicht so gut, wie in der Rezension behauptet wurde; **~ out a case for/against sth.** für/gegen etw. argumentieren; **you've made out a convincing case** deine Argumente sind überzeugend; **you ~ me out to be a liar** du stellst mich als Lügner hin; **how do you ~ that out?** wie kommst du darauf? **3** (understand) verstehen; **~ out what sb. wants/whether sb. wants help or not** herausbekommen, was jmd. will/ob jmd. Hilfe möchte oder nicht **4** (manage to see or hear) ausmachen; (manage to read) entziffern **5** (pretend, assert falsely) vorgeben

B *v.i.* (coll.) (progress) zurechtkommen (**at** bei); **how are you making out with your girlfriend?** wie läuft es denn so mit deiner Freundin? (ugs.)

- **~ 'over** *v.t.* **1** (transfer) übereignen, überschreiben ‹*Geld, Geschäft, Eigentum*› (**to** *Dat.*) **2** (change, convert) umändern, umarbeiten ‹*Kleidung*›; umbauen ‹*Haus*› (**into** zu); umgestalten ‹*Garten, Zimmer*›
- **~ 'up**

A *v.t.* **1** (replace) ausgleichen ‹*Fehlmenge, Verluste*›; **~ up lost ground/time** Boden gut- *od.* wettmachen (ugs.)/den Zeitverlust aufholen **2** (complete) komplett machen **3** (prepare, arrange) zubereiten ‹*Arznei usw.*›; zusammenstellen ‹*Picknickkorb usw.*›; zurechtmachen ‹*Bett*›; (prepare by mixing) vermischen (**into** zu); (process material) verarbeiten (**into** zu); **~ up into bundles** bündeln **4** (apply cosmetics to) schminken; **~ up one's face/eyes** sich schminken/sich (*Dat.*) die Augen schminken; *see also* **make-up 1** **5** (assemble, compile) zusammenstellen; aufstellen ‹*Liste usw.*›; bilden ‹*ein Ganzes*› **6** (Printing) umbrechen; *see also* **make-up 4** **7** (invent) erfinden; sich (*Dat.*) ausdenken; **you're just making it up!** das hast du dir doch nur ausgedacht! **8** (reconcile) beilegen ‹*Streit, Meinungsverschiedenheit*›; **~ up the quarrel** *or* **~ it up with sb.** sich wieder mit jmdm. vertragen; sich mit jmdm. aus- *od.* versöhnen; **they've made it up [again]** sie vertragen sich wieder *od.* haben sich ausgesöhnt; *see also* **mind A 2** **9** (form, constitute) bilden; **~ up a man's character** den Charakter eines Menschen ausmachen; **be made up of ...:** bestehen aus ...; *see also* **make-up 2, 3** **10** **~ up the fire** [Holz *usw.* aufs Feuer] nachlegen

B *v.i.* **1** (apply cosmetics etc.) sich schminken; *see also* **make-up 1** **2** (be reconciled) sich wieder vertragen

- **~ 'up for** *v.t.* **1** (outweigh, compensate) wettmachen **2** (make amends for) wieder gutmachen **3** **~ up for lost time** Versäumtes nachholen *od.* (ugs.) wettmachen
- **~ 'up to** *v.t.* **1** (raise to, increase to) bringen auf (+ *Akk.*) **2** (coll.: act flirtatiously towards) sich heranmachen an (+ *Akk.*) (ugs.) **3** (coll.: give compensation to) **~ it/this up to sb.** jmdn. dafür entschädigen
- **~ with** *v.t.* (Amer. coll.: supply, produce) **~ with the drinks!** [los,] her mit den Getränken!; **start making with the ideas!** lass dir mal was einfallen!

'make-believe

A *n.* **it's only ~:** das ist bloß Fantasie; **a world of ~:** eine Scheinwelt

B *adj.* nicht echt; **a ~ world/story** eine Scheinwelt/Fantasiegeschichte

make-or-'break *attrib. adj.* alles entscheidend

'makeover *n.* Umgestaltung, *die;* **have a ~:** umgestaltet *or* (ugs.) umgemodelt werden; **give sb. a ~:** jmdm. ein neues Äußeres geben; **give sth. a [complete] ~:** etw. [total] umgestalten *or* (ugs.) ummodeln

maker /ˈmeɪkə(r)/ *n.* **1** (manufacturer) Hersteller, *der;* **~ of laws/rules/regulations** *jmd., der Gesetze macht/Regeln aufstellt/Verordnungen erlässt* **2** **M~** (God) Schöpfer, *der;* **meet one's M~:** vor seinen Schöpfer treten (verhüll.)

-maker *n. in comb.* -macher, *der*/-macherin, *die;* (by machine) -hersteller, *der*/-herstellerin, *die*

make: ~shift **A** *adj.* behelfsmäßig; **a ~shift shelter/bridge** eine Behelfsunterkunft/-brücke; **B** *n.* Notbehelf, *der;* **~-up** *n.* **1** (Cosmetics) Make-up, *das;* (Theatre) Maske, *die;* **put on one's ~-up** Make-up auflegen; sich schminken; (Theatre) Maske machen; *attrib.* **~-up bag** Kosmetiktasche, *die;* **~-up girl** Maskenbildnerin, *die;* **~-up remover** Make-up-Entferner, *der;* **wear heavy ~-up/one's stage ~-up** stark geschminkt/in Maske sein; **2** (composition) Zusammensetzung, *die;* **3** (character, temperament) Veranlagung, *die;* **physical ~-up** Konstitution, *die;* **national ~-up** Nationalcharakter, *der;* **honesty is/is not part of his ~-up** er ist seinem Wesen nach aufrichtig/Aufrichtigkeit liegt nicht in seinem Wesen; **4** (Printing: arrangement of type) Umbruch, *der;* **~weight** *n.* Gewichtszugabe, *die;* (fig.: insignificant thing or person) Lückenbüßer, *der;* (*unimportant point*) *unbedeutender Punkt zur Unterstützung eines Arguments;* **use X as [a] ~weight to Y** Y durch X schwerer machen; (fig.) Y durch X mehr Gewicht verleihen

making /ˈmeɪkɪŋ/ *n.* **1** (production) Herstellung, *die;* **the ~ of the English working class** die Entstehung der englischen Arbeiterklasse; **in the ~:** im Entstehen; im Werden; **a minister in the ~:** ein angehender Minister; **be the ~ of victory/sb.'s career/sb.'s future** zum Sieg/zu jmds. Karriere führen/jmds. Zukunft sichern **2** *in pl.* (profit) Gewinn, *der* (**from** aus); (earnings) Verdienst, *der* (**on** für) **3** *in pl.* (qualities) Anlagen; Voraussetzungen; **have all the ~s of sth.** alle Voraussetzungen für etw. haben; **have the ~s of a leader** über Führerqualitäten verfügen; das Zeug zum Führer haben (ugs.) **4** (Amer., Austral.) **the ~s for cigarettes** Zigarettenpapier und Tabak

malachite /ˈmæləkaɪt/ *n.* (Min.) Malachit, *der; attrib.* aus Malachit *nachgestellt*

maladjusted /mæləˈdʒʌstɪd/ *adj.* (Psych., Sociol.) **[psychologically/socially] ~:** verhaltensgestört

maladjustment /mæləˈdʒʌstmənt/ *n.* (Psych., Sociol.) **[psychological/social] ~:** Verhaltensgestörtheit, *die*

maladministration /mælədmɪnɪˈstreɪʃn/ *n.* Misswirtschaft, *die*

maladroit /mæləˈdrɔɪt, ˈmælədrɔɪt/ *adj.* ungeschickt; taktlos ‹*Bemerkung*›

malady /ˈmælədɪ/ *n.* Leiden, *das;* (fig.: of society, epoch) Übel, *das*

Malaga /ˈmæləgə/ *n.* (wine) Malaga, *der*

Malagasy /mæləˈgæsɪ/ ▸ **i p. 1277**, ▸ **i p. 1345**

A *adj.* madagassisch

B *n.* (person) Madagasse, *der*/Madagassin, *die;* (lan-

m

guage) Malagassi, *das;* Madagassisch, *das*

malaise /mə'leɪz/ *n.* (bodily discomfort) Unwohlsein, *das;* (feeling of uneasiness) Unbehagen, *das;* Malaise, *die* (geh.)

malapropism /'mæləprɒpɪzm/ *n.* Malapropismus, *der* (*Literaturw.*); *irrtümlicher Gebrauch eines [schwierigen] Wortes anstelle eines ähnlich klingenden*

malaria /mə'leərɪə/ *n.* **▸ℹ p. 1231** Malaria, *die*

malarkey /mə'lɑːkɪ/ *n., no pl., no indef. art.* (coll.) Blabla, *das* (salopp); **a load of ~:** reinstes Geschwafel (ugs.)

Malawi /mə'lɑːwɪ/ *pr. n.* Malawi (*das*)

Malawian /mə'lɑːwɪən/ **▸ℹ p. 1345**
A *adj.* malawisch
B Malawier, *der*/Malawierin, *die*

Malay /mə'leɪ/ **▸ℹ p. 1277, ▸ℹ p. 1345**
A *adj.* malaiisch; **sb. is ~:** jmd. ist Malaie/Malaiin; *see also* **English A**
B *n.* **1** (person) Malaie, *der*/Malaiin, *die* **2** (language) Malaiisch, *das; see also* **English B 1**

Malaya /mə'leɪə/ *pr. n.* Malaya (*das*)

Malayan /mə'leɪən/ **▸Malay A, B 1**

Malaysia /mə'leɪzɪə/ *pr. n.* Malaysia (*das*)

Malaysian /mə'leɪzɪən/ **▸ℹ p. 1345**
A *adj.* malaysisch
B *n.* Malaysier, *der*/Malaysierin, *die*

malcontent /'mælkəntent/
A *adj.* unzufrieden; malkontent (landsch., sonst veralt.)
B *n.* Nörgler, *der*/Nörglerin, *die* (abwertend)

Maldives /'mɔːldiːvz/ *pr. n. pl.* Malediven *Pl.*

male /meɪl/
A *adj.* **1** männlich; Männer‹*stimme, -chor, -verein*›; **~ child/dog/cat/doctor/nurse/student** Junge/Rüde/Kater/Arzt/Krankenpfleger/Student, *der;* **~ prostitute** *Mann, der der Prostitution nachgeht;* Strichjunge, *der* (salopp); Stricher, *der* (salopp); **~ animal/bird/fish/insect** Männchen, *das;* **~ ward** Männerstation, *die* **2** **~ screw** Schraube, *die;* **~ thread** Außengewinde, *das. See also* **chauvinism; chauvinist; menopause 1**
B *n.* (person) Mann, *der;* (fetus, child) Junge, *der;* (animal) Männchen, *das*

malediction /mælɪ'dɪkʃn/ *n.* Fluch, *der;* Verwünschung, *die*

'male-dominated *adj.* von Männern dominiert; **a ~ field** eine Männerdomäne

malefactor /'mælɪfæktə(r)/ *n.* Übeltäter, *der*

maleficent /mə'lefɪsənt/ *adj.* böse ‹*Geist, Macht*›

male voice 'choir *n.* Männerchor, *der*

malevolence /mə'levələns/ *n., no pl.* **▸malevolent**: Bosheit, *die;* Übelwollen, *das;* Böswilligkeit, *die;* Boshaftigkeit, *die;* **feel ~ towards sb.** Missgunst gegenüber jmdm. empfinden

malevolent /mə'levələnt/ *adj.* böse ‹*Macht, Tat*›; übel wollend ‹*Gott*›; boshaft, hämisch ‹*Gelächter*›; böswillig ‹*Lüge*›; boshaft ‹*Person*›

malevolently /mə'levələntlɪ/ *adv.* boshaft ‹*anstarren*›; böswillig ‹*verhindern, durchkreuzen*›; in böser Absicht ‹*überreden*›; hämisch ‹*lachen*›

malformation /mælfɔː'meɪʃn/ *n.* (Med.) Missbildung, *die*

malformed /mæl'fɔːmd/ *adj.* (Med.) missgebildet

malfunction /mæl'fʌŋkʃn/
A *n.* Störung, *die;* (Med.) Dysfunktion, *die* (fachspr.); Funktionsstörung, *die*
B *v.i.* ‹*Mechanismus, System, Gerät:*› nicht richtig funktionieren; ‹*Prozess, Vorgang:*› nicht richtig ablaufen; **the nervous system/liver ~s** die Funktion des Nervensystems/der Leber ist gestört

Mali /'mɑːlɪ/ *pr. n.* Mali (*das*)

Malian /'mɑːlɪən/ **▸ℹ p. 1345**
A *adj.* malisch
B *n.* Malier, *der*/Malierin, *die*

malice /'mælɪs/ *n.* **1** (active ill will) Bosheit, *die;* Böswilligkeit, *die;* (desire to tease) Schalkhaftigkeit, *die* (geh.); **bear ~ to** *or* **towards** *or* **against sb.** jmdm. übel wollen **2** (Law) böse Absicht; Dolus, *der* (fachspr.); böser Vorsatz; *see also* **aforethought**

malicious /mə'lɪʃəs/ *adj.* **1** böse ‹*Klatsch, Tat, Person, Wort*›; böswillig ‹*Gerücht, Lüge, Verleumdung*›; boshaft ‹*Person*›; hämisch ‹*Vergnügen, Freude*› **2** (Law) böswillig ‹*Sachbeschädigung, Verleumdung*›

maliciously /mə'lɪʃəslɪ/ *adv.* **1** mit [böser] Absicht; böse ‹*lächeln*› **2** (Law) böswillig

malign /mə'laɪn/
A *v.t.* (slander) verleumden; (speak ill of) schlecht machen; **~ sb.'s character** jmdm. Übles nachsagen; ‹*Klatsch, Verleumdung:*› jmdn. in Verruf bringen
B *adj.* **1** (injurious) böse ‹*Macht, Geist*›; schlecht, unheilvoll ‹*Eigenschaft, Einfluss*› **2** (Med.: malignant) maligne (fachspr.), bösartig ‹*Krankheit*›; schwer ‹*Verletzung*› **3** (malevolent) böse ‹*Absicht*›; niederträchtig ‹*Motiv*›

malignancy /mə'lɪgnənsɪ/ *n.* (Med.) Bösartigkeit, *die;* Malignität, *die* (fachspr.)

malignant /mə'lɪgnənt/ *adj.* **1** (Med.) maligne (fachspr.), bösartig ‹*Krankheit, Geschwür*›; **~ cancer** Karzinom, *das* (fachspr.); Krebs, *der* **2** (harmful) böse ‹*Macht*›; ungünstig ‹*Einfluss*› **3** (feeling or showing ill will) böse ‹*Geist, Zunge, Klatsch*›; bösartig, boshaft ‹*Verleumdung*›

malinger /mə'lɪŋgə(r)/ *v.i.* simulieren

malingerer /mə'lɪŋgərə(r)/ *n.* Simulant, *der*/Simulantin, *die*

mall /mæl, mɔːl/ *n.* **1** (promenade) Promenade, *die* **2** (esp. Amer.: shopping precinct) Einkaufszentrum, *das;* Einkaufsstraße, *die*

mallard /'mælɑːd/ *n.* (Ornith.) Stockente, *die*

malleable /'mælɪəbl/ *adj.* formbar ‹*Material, Person*›

mallet /'mælɪt/ *n.* **1** (hammer) Holzhammer, *der;* Schlegel, *der;* (of stonemason) Klöpfel, *der;* (of carpenter) Klopfholz, *das* **2** (Croquet) Hammer, *der;* (Polo) Schläger, *der*

mallow /'mæləʊ/ *n.* (Bot.) Malve, *die*

malnourished /mæl'nʌrɪʃt/ *adj.* unterernährt

malnutrition /mælnjuː'trɪʃn/ *n.* Unterernährung, *die*

malodorous /mæl'əʊdərəs/ *adj.* übel riechend

malpractice /mæl'præktɪs/ *n.* **1** (wrongdoing) Übeltat, *die* (geh.) **2** (Law, Med.: improper treatment of patient) Kunstfehler, *der* **3** (Law: wrongdoing by official etc.) Amtsvergehen, *das*

malt /mɔːlt, mɒlt/
A *n.* **1** Malz, *das* **2** (coll.: malt whisky) Malzwhisky, *der*
B *v.t.* mälzen ‹*Gerste*›

Malta /'mɔːltə, 'mɒltə/ *pr. n.* Malta (*das*)

malted /'mɔːltɪd, 'mɒltɪd/ *attrib. adj.* Malz-

Maltese /mɔːl'tiːz, mɒl'tiːz/ **▸ℹ p. 1277, ▸ℹ p. 1345**
A *adj.* maltesisch; **sb. is ~:** jmd. ist Malteser/Malteserin
B *n., pl. same* **1** (person) Malteser, *der*/Malteserin, *die* **2** (language) Maltesisch (*das*)

Maltese: ~ 'cat *n.: blaugraue, kurzhaarige Hauskatze;* **~ 'cross** *n.* Malteserkreuz, *das*

malt: ~ 'extract *n.* Malzextrakt, *der;* **~house** *n.* Mälzerei, *die;* **~ 'liquor** *n.* Bier, *das*

maltreat /mæl'triːt/ *v.t.* misshandeln

maltreatment /mæl'triːtmənt/ *n.* Misshandlung, *die*

malt 'whisky *n.* Malzwhisky, *der*

mam /mæm/ *n.* (Brit. coll./child lang.) Mama, *die* (fam.); Mami, *die* (fam.)

mama **▸mamma**

mamba /'mæmbə/ *n.* (Zool.) Mamba, *die*

mamma /mə'mɑː/ *n.* (coll./child lang.) Mama, *die* (fam.); Mami, *die* (fam.); **~'s boy** (coll.) Muttersöhnchen, *das* (ugs.)

mammal /'mæml/ *n.* (Zool.) Säugetier, *das;* Säuger, *der*

mammalian /mə'meɪlɪən/ (Zool.)
A *adj.* Säugetier-; eines Säugetiers *nachgestellt*
B *n.* Säugetier, *das;* Säuger, *der*

mammary /'mæmərɪ/ *adj.* (Anat., Zool.) Brust-; **~ gland** Brustdrüse, *die*

mammography /mæ'mɒgrəfɪ/ *n., no pl.* (Med.) Mammographie, *die*

Mammon /'mæmən/ *n.* **1** (wealth regarded as idol) Mammon, *der;* **ye cannot serve God and ~** (Bibl.) ihr könnt nicht Gott dienen und dem Mammon **2** (the rich) die Reichen

mammoth /'mæməθ/
A *n.* (Zool., Palaeont.) Mammut, *das*
B *adj.* Mammut-; riesig ‹*Menge*›; gigantisch ‹*Vorhaben*›

mammy /'mæmɪ/ *n.* **1** (child lang.: mother) Mama, *die* (fam.); Mami, *die* (fam.) **2** (Amer.: black nurse) schwarze Kinderfrau

man /mæn/
A *n., pl.* **men** /men/ **1** *no art., no pl.* (human being, person) Mensch, *der;* (the human race) der Mensch; **as a ~:** als Mensch; **God was made ~:** Gott ward Mensch (bibl.); **~ is a political animal** der Mensch ist ein politisches Wesen; **everything a ~ needs** alles, was der Mensch braucht; **what can a ~ do?** was kann man tun?; **every ~ for himself** rette sich, wer kann; **as one ~:** wie ein Mann; (unanimously) geschlossen; **any ~ who ...:** wer ...; jeder, der ...; **no ~:** niemand; **always get one's ~:** den Täter immer finden; **[all] to a ~:** allesamt; **to the last ~:** bis zum letzten Mann; **they were killed to a ~:** sie wurden bis auf den letzten Mann getötet; **the ~ in** *or* (Amer.) **on the street** der Mann auf der Straße; **the rights of ~:** die Menschenrechte; **Heidelberg M~:** der Homo heidelbergensis; der Heidelbergmensch; **Java/Peking M~:** der Java-/Pekingmensch
2 (adult male, individual male) Mann, *der;* **every ~, woman, and child** ausnahmslos jeder *od.* alle; **the right ~:** der richtige Mann; der Richtige; **the [very] ~ for sth.** der richtige Mann *od.* der Richtige; **he is your ~:** er ist der richtige Mann *od.* der Richtige für dich; **you have arrested the wrong ~:** Sie haben den Falschen verhaftet; **a ~'s life** ein Leben für Männer; **a ~'s ~:** ein Mann, der sich nur in männlicher Gesellschaft wohl fühlt; **make a ~ out of sb.** (fig.) einen Mann aus jmdm. machen; **be only half a ~:** nur ein halber Mann sein; **like a ~:** wie ein Mann; **that's just like a ~:** typisch Mann!; **a ~ of property/great strength** ein vermögender/sehr kräftiger Mann; **that ~ Oakfield** dieser Oakfield; **play the ~:** ein Mann sein; **men's clothing/outfitter** Herrenkleidung, *die*/Herrenausstatter, *der;* **be ~ enough to ...:** Manns genug sein, um zu ...; **a 'man's voice** eine männliche Stimme; **'the deodorant for men'** „das Herrendeodorant"; **I have lived here, ~ and boy** ich habe hier von frühester Jugend an gewohnt; **sth. sorts out** *or* **separates the men from the boys** (coll.) an etw. (*Dat.*) zeigt sich, wer ein ganzer Kerl ist und wer nicht; **~ of God** Gottesmann, *der* (geh.); **the ~ in the moon** der Mann im Mond; **he's a local ~:** er ist von hier; **a whisky ~:** ein Whiskytrinker; **he's [not] a drinking ~:** er trinkt [nicht]; **be one's own ~:** wissen, was man will; **you've come to the right ~:** bei mir sind Sie richtig; **men's toilet** Herrentoilette, *die;* **'Men'** „Herren"; **my [good] ~:** mein Guter; **fight ~ to ~:** Mann gegen Mann kämpfen; **~ friend** Freund, *der*
3 (husband) Mann, *der;* **be ~ and wife** verheiratet sein
4 (work~) Mann, *der*
5 *usu. in pl.* (soldier, sailor, etc.) Mann, *der*
6 (Chess) Figur, *die;* (Draughts) Stein, *der*
7 (coll.: as int. of surprise or impatience, as mode of address) Mensch! (salopp); **nonsense, ~!** Unsinn!; **hurry up, ~!** Mensch, beeil dich!
8 (type of ~) Mann, *der;* Typ, *der;* **a ~ of the people/world/of action** ein Mann des Volkes/von Welt/der Tat; **he is not a** *or* **the ~ to do something like that** er ist nicht der Mann *od.* Typ, der so etwas tut; **he is not a ~ I could trust** ihm könnte ich nicht trauen; **be an Oxford ~:** aus Oxford kommen; (Univ.) in Oxford studiert haben
9 (~servant) Diener, *der. See also* **action 1; alive 1; best man; Clapham; handyman; honour A 4; house A 1; inner man; jack A 3; letter A 4; little A 2; moment 1; old man; outer 2; part A 9; substance 2;**

town 1; word A 2; world 1
B *v.t.*, **-nn-** bemannen ‹*Schiff, Spill*›; besetzen ‹*Büro, Stelle, Posten, Pumpe, Kontrollpunkt*›; bedienen ‹*Telefon, Geschütz*›; ‹*Soldaten:*› Stellung beziehen in (+ *Dat.*) ‹*Festung*›; mit Personal besetzen ‹*Fabrik, Werk*›; **be ~ned by a crew of 50** ‹*Schiff:*› eine Besatzung von 50 Mann haben

manacle /'mænəkl/
A *n., usu. in pl.* [Hand]fessel, *die;* Kette, *die*
B *v.t.* Handfesseln anlegen (+ *Dat.*)

manage /'mænɪdʒ/
A *v.t.* **1** (handle, wield) handhaben ‹*Werkzeug, Segel, Boot*›; bedienen ‹*Schaltbrett*›; **the tool is too heavy for him to ~:** er kommt mit dem schweren Gerät nicht zurecht **2** (conduct, organize) durchführen ‹*Operation, Unternehmen*›; erledigen ‹*Angelegenheit*›; verwalten ‹*Geld, Grundstück*›; leiten ‹*Geschäft, Büro, Schule, Krankenhaus*›; führen ‹*Haushalt*› **3** (Sport etc.: be manager of) managen, betreuen ‹*Team, Mannschaft*› **4** (cope with) schaffen; **I could/couldn't ~ another apple** (coll.) ich könnte noch einen Apfel schaffen/noch einen Apfel schaffe ich nicht; **I can/can't ~ this suitcase** den Koffer kann ich [alleine] tragen/ich werde mit diesem Koffer nicht fertig; **we can ~ another person in the car** einer hat noch Platz im Wagen; **he can't ~ the stairs** er kommt die Treppe nicht rauf/runter **5** (gain one's ends with) für sich gewinnen ‹*Person*› **6** (succeed in achieving) zustande bringen ‹*Lächeln*› **7** (contrive) **~ to do sth.** (also iron.) es fertig bringen, etw. zu tun; **he ~d to do it** es gelang ihm, es zu tun; **I don't know how you ~d it** ich weiß nicht, wie du das bewerkstelligt hast; **I'll ~ it somehow** ich werde es schon irgendwie hinkriegen (ugs.); **I ~d to get a word in** ich kam endlich zu Wort; **can you ~ to be there at 10 a.m.?** (coll.) kannst du um 10 Uhr dort sein?; **how could you ~ to eat all that?** (coll.) wie hast du es [bloß] geschafft, das alles zu essen?; **can you ~ 7 [o'clock]?** passt dir 7 Uhr? **8** (be in charge of) hüten ‹*Herde*› **9** (control) bändigen ‹*Person, Tier, Haar*›
B *v.i.* zurechtkommen; **~ without sth.** ohne etw. auskommen; **~ on** zurecht- *od.* auskommen mit ‹*Geld, Einkommen*›; **~ by oneself** allein zurechtkommen; **I can ~:** es geht; **can you ~?** gehts?; geht es?

manageable /'mænɪdʒəbl/ *adj.* leicht frisierbar ‹*Haar*›; fügsam ‹*Person, Tier*›; regierbar ‹*Land, Staat*›; überschaubar ‹*Größe, Menge*›; zu bewältigend ‹*Portion*›; lenkbar ‹*Firma*›

management /'mænɪdʒmənt/ *n.* **1** Durchführung, *die;* (of a business) Leitung, *die;* Management, *das;* (of money) Verwaltung, *die; attrib.* **~ studies** Betriebsführung und -organisation (*als Teilgebiet der Betriebswirtschaftslehre*); **it was bad ~ to ...:** es war ein Fehler der Geschäftsleitung, zu ... **2** (managers) Leitung, *die;* Management, *das;* (of theatre etc.) Direktion, *die;* **the ~:** die Geschäftsleitung; **'under new ~'** „unter neuer Leitung" **3** (Med.) Behandlung, *die*

management: ~ 'buyout *n.* Management-Buy-out, *das;* **~ committee** *n.* geschäftsführender Ausschuss; **~ consultancy** *n.* Unternehmensberatung, *die;* **~ consultant** *n.* ▸**i** p. 1260 Unternehmensberater, *der/*-beraterin, *die*

manager /'mænɪdʒə(r)/ *n.* ▸**i** p. 1260 (of branch of shop or bank) Filialleiter, *der/*-leiterin, *die;* Geschäftsstellenleiter, *der/*-leiterin, *die;* (of football team) [Chef]trainer, *der/*-trainerin, *die;* (of tennis player, boxer, pop group) Manager, *der/*Managerin, *die;* (of restaurant, shop, hotel) Geschäftsführer, *der/*-führerin, *die;* (of estate, grounds) Verwalter, *der/*Verwalterin, *die;* (of department; sales or publicity ~) Leiter, *der/*Leiterin, *die;* (of theatre) Direktor, *der/*Direktorin, *die*

manageress /'mænɪdʒəres, mænɪdʒə'res/ *n.* (of restaurant, shop, hotel) Geschäftsführerin, *die; see also* **manager**

managerial /mænə'dʒɪərɪəl/ *adj.* führend, leitend ‹*Stellung*›; geschäftlich ‹*Aspekt, Seite*›; ‹*Pflicht, Fähigkeiten*› als Führungskraft; **~ skills** Führungsqualitäten; **the ~ class** die Führungsschicht

managing /'mænɪdʒɪŋ/ *attrib. adj.* geschäftsführend; leitend; **~ director** Geschäftsführer, *der*

manatee /'mænəti:/ *n.* Manati, *der*

Manchuria /mæn'tʃʊərɪə/ *pr. n.* die Mandschurei

Mancunian /mæŋ'kju:nɪən/
A *adj.* Manchesterer
B *n.* Manchesterer, *der/*Manchesterin, *die*

mandala /'mændələ/ *n.* (Hinduism, Buddhism, Psych.) Mandala, *das*

mandarin¹ /'mændərɪn/ *n.* **~ [orange]** Mandarine, *die*

mandarin² *n.* **1** (Hist.: Chinese official) Mandarin, *der* **2** ▸**i** p. 1277 **M~** (language) Hochchinesisch, *das* **3** (party leader) Parteiboss, *der* (ugs.); [Partei]bonze, *der* (abwertend) **4** (bureaucrat) Bürokrat, *der/*Bürokratin, *die* (abwertend); Apparatschik, *der* (abwertend)

mandarin: ~ 'collar *n.* Mandarinkragen, *der;* **~ 'duck** *n.* Mandarinente, *die*

mandarine /'mændəri:n/ ▸**mandarin¹**

mandarin 'sleeve *n.* Bouffonärmel, *der*

mandate
A /'mændeɪt/ *n.* **1** (judicial or legal command) Verfügung, *die* **2** (commission to act for another) Mandat, *das* **3** (Polit.) Mandat, *das;* **electoral ~:** Wählerauftrag, *der*
B /mæn'deɪt/ *v.t.* **~ a territory to a country** ein Gebiet der Verwaltung eines Landes unterstellen

mandatory /'mændətərɪ/ *adj.* obligatorisch; **be ~:** Pflicht od. obligatorisch sein; **it is ~ for sb. to do sth.** jmd. muss etw. tun

'man-day *n.* (Work Study) Manntag, *der;* Arbeitstag pro Mann

mandible /'mændɪbl/ *n.* (Zool.) **1** (of mammal, fish) Unterkiefer, *der* **2** (of bird) Schnabel, *der;* **lower ~:** Unterschnabel, *der* **3** (of insect) Zange, *die;* Kiefer, *der*

mandolin, mandoline /mændə'lɪn/ *n.* (Mus.) Mandoline, *die*

mandrake /'mændreɪk/ *n.* (Bot.) Mandragore, *die;* Alraunwurzel, *die*

mandrel /'mændrəl/ *n.* (Mech. Engin.) **1** (shaft in lathe) Drehspindel, *die* **2** (rod) Horn, *das*

mandrill /'mændrɪl/ *n.* (Zool.) Mandrill, *der*

mane /meɪn/ *n.* (lit. or fig.) Mähne, *die*

man: ~eater *n.* (tiger) Menschen fressender Tiger; (shark) Menschenhai, *der;* (cannibal) Kannibale, *der/*Kannibalin, *die;* (fig.: woman) Frau, die Männer aussaugt; **~-eating** *adj.* Menschen fressend ‹*Löwe, Tiger*›; **a ~-eating shark** ein Menschenhai

maneuver, maneuverable (Amer.) ▸**manoeuvr-**

man 'Friday ▸**Friday A**

manful /'mænfl/ *adj.* mannhaft

manfully /'mænfəlɪ/ *adv.* mannhaft; wie ein Mann

manganese /'mæŋgəni:z, mæŋgə'ni:z/ *n.* **1** (Min.) Braunstein, *der;* Manganoxid, *das* (fachspr.) **2** (Chem.) Mangan, *das*

mange /meɪndʒ/ *n.* (Vet. Med.) Räude, *die*

mangel[-wurzel] /'mæŋgl(wɜ:zl)/ *n.* (Agric.) Runkelrübe, *die*

manger /'meɪndʒə(r)/ *n.* Futtertrog, *der;* (Bibl.) Krippe, *die; see also* **dog A 1**

mangetout /mɑ̃ʒ'tu:/ *n.* Zuckererbse, *die*

mangle¹ /'mæŋgl/
A *n.* Mangel, *die*
B *v.t.* mangeln ‹*Wäsche*›

mangle² *v.t.* verstümmeln, [übel] zurichten ‹*Person*›; demolieren ‹*Sache*›; verstümmeln, entstellen ‹*Zitat, Musikstück*›

mango /'mæŋgəʊ/ *n., pl.* **~es** *or* **~s** **1** (tree) Mangobaum, *der* **2** (fruit) Mango[frucht], *die*

mangrove /'mæŋgrəʊv/ *n.* (Bot.) Mangrovebaum, *der*

mangy /'meɪndʒɪ/ *adj.* **1** (Vet. Med.) räudig **2** (squalid, shabby) verwahrlost, schäbig ‹*Äußeres, Kleidung*›; abgenutzt, schäbig ‹*Teppich, Decke, Stuhl*›

man: ~handle *v.t.* **1** (move by human effort) von Hand bewegen ‹*Gegenstand*›; **2** (handle roughly) grob behandeln ‹*Person*›; **~-hater** *n.* (misanthrope) Menschenhasser, *der/*-hasserin, *die;* (hater of male sex) Männerfeind, *der/*-feindin, *die;* **~hole** *n.* Mannloch, *das;* (in tank) Einstiegsluke, *die;* (to cables under pavement) Kabelschacht, *der*

manhood /'mænhʊd/ *n., no pl.* **1** (state) Mannesalter, *das* **2** (courage) Männlichkeit, *die* **3** (men of a country) Männer *Pl.*

man: ~-hour *n.* (Work Study) Arbeitsstunde, *die;* **~hunt** *n.* Menschenjagd, *die;* (for criminal) Verbrecherjagd, *die*

mania /'meɪnɪə/ *n.* **1** (madness) Wahnsinn, *der* **2** (enthusiasm) Manie, *die;* **~ for detective novels** Leidenschaft für Krimis; **have a ~ for doing sth.** etw. wie besessen *od.* leidenschaftlich gern tun; **there was a ~ at that time for wearing earrings** damals waren die Leute ganz verrückt auf Ohrringen

-mania *n. in comb.* (Psych.) -manie, *die*

maniac /'meɪnɪæk/
A *adj.* wahnsinnig; krankhaft, (geh.) manisch ‹*Fantasie, Verlangen*›
B *n.* **1** (Psych.) Besessene, *der/die;* (madman/-woman) Wahnsinnige, *der/die* **2** (person with passion for sth.) Fanatiker, *der/*Fanatikerin, *die;* **a nation of tennis ~s** ein Volk von Tennisfanatikern

maniacal /mə'naɪəkl/ *adj.* wahnsinnig

manic /'mænɪk/ *adj.* (Psych.) manisch

manic de'pression *n., no pl.* manische Depression

manic-de'pressive (Psych.)
A *adj.* manisch-depressiv
B *n.* manisch-depressiver Mensch; **be a ~:** manisch-depressiv sein

manicure /'mænɪkjʊə(r)/
A *n.* Maniküre, *die;* **give sb. a ~:** jmdn. maniküren
B *v.t.* maniküren

manicurist /'mænɪkjʊərɪst/ *n.* ▸**i** p. 1260 Maniküre, *die*

manifest /'mænɪfest/
A *adj.* offenkundig; offenbar ‹*Missverständnis*›; sichtbar ‹*Erfolg, Fortschritt*›; sichtlich ‹*Freude*›
B *v.t.* **1** (show, display) zeigen, bekunden (geh.) ‹*Interesse, Missfallen, Begeisterung, Zuneigung*› **2** (reveal) offenbaren (meist geh.); **~ itself** ‹*Geist:*› erscheinen; ‹*Natur, Wahrheit:*› sich offenbaren; ‹*Symptom, Krankheit:*› manifest werden
C *n.* **1** (cargo list) Frachtgutliste, *die;* Ladeverzeichnis, *das;* **ship's ~:** [Schiffs]manifest, *das* **2** (list) (of passengers in aircraft) Passagierliste, *die;* (of trucks etc. in goods train) Fahrzeugliste, *die*

manifestation /mænɪfe'steɪʃn/ *n.* (of ill will, favour, disapproval) Ausdruck, *der;* Bekundung, *die* (geh.); Bezeugung, *die;* (appearance) Erscheinung, *die; in pl.* Erscheinungsformen; (visible expression, sign) [An]zeichen, *das* (**of** von)

manifestly /'mænɪfestlɪ/ *adv.* offenkundig; **it is ~ unjust that ...:** es ist ganz offensichtlich ungerecht, dass ...

manifesto /mænɪ'festəʊ/ *n., pl.* **~s** Manifest, *das*

manifold /'mænɪfəʊld/
A *adj.* (literary) mannigfaltig (geh.); vielfältig; vielseitig ‹*Erzählperspektive, Gehalt, Verwendung*›
B (Mech. Engin.) Verteilerrohr, *das;* **[inlet] ~:** [Ansaug]krümmer, *der;* **[exhaust] ~:** [Auspuff-]krümmer, *der*

manikin /'mænɪkɪn/ *n.* **1** (dwarf) Zwerg, *der* **2** (Art) Gliederpuppe, *die* **3** (Med.) anatomisches Modell

Manila /mə'nɪlə/ *n.* **1** (cigar) Manilazigarre, *die* **2** (fibre) **~ [hemp]** ▸**hemp 1 3** (paper) **~ [paper]** Manilapapier, *das;* **~ [envelope]** Briefumschlag aus Manilapapier; brauner Briefumschlag

manioc /'mænɪɒk/ *n.* **1** (plant) Maniok, *der* **2** (flour) Mandioka, *die*

manipulate /mə'nɪpjʊleɪt/ *v.t.* **1** (also Med.) manipulieren; **~ sb. into doing sth.** jmdn. dahin gehend manipulieren, dass er etw. tut **2** (handle) handhaben

manipulation /mənɪpjʊˈleɪʃn/ *n.* 1) (also Med.) Manipulation, *die* 2) (handling) Handhabung, *die*

manipulative /məˈnɪpjʊlətɪv/ *adj.* manipulativ

mankind /mænˈkaɪnd/ *n.* Menschheit, *die*

ˈmanlike *adj.* 1) (like a male, mannish) männlich 2) (like a human) menschenähnlich

manly /ˈmænlɪ/ *adj.* männlich; (brave) mannhaft (geh.)

ˈman-made *adj.* künstlich ‹*See, Blumen, Schlucht*›; vom Menschen geschaffen ‹*Gesetze*›; (synthetic) Kunst‹*faser, -stoff*›

manna /ˈmænə/ *n.* (Bibl.) Manna, *das;* **be ~ [from heaven]** (fig.) ein wahrer Segen sein

manned /mænd/ *adj.* bemannt ‹*Raumschiff usw.*›

mannequin /ˈmænɪkɪn/ *n.* 1) (person) Mannequin, *das* 2) (dummy) Schaufensterpuppe, *die*

manner /ˈmænə(r)/ *n.* 1) (way, fashion) Art, *die;* Weise, *die;* (more emphatic) Art und Weise, *die;* **in this ~:** auf diese Art und Weise; **he did it in a very unorthodox ~:** er machte es auf [eine ganz] unorthodoxe Art; **he acted in such a ~ as to offend her** er benahm sich so, dass sie beleidigt war; **in the French ~:** auf französische Art; **celebrate in the grand ~:** in großem Stil feiern; **[as] to the ~ born** (coll.) wie dafür geschaffen; **in a ~ of speaking** mehr oder weniger; **adverb of ~** (Ling.) Umstandsbestimmung der Art und Weise 2) *no pl.* (bearing) Art, *die;* (towards others) Auftreten, *das* 3) *in pl.* (social behaviour) Manieren *Pl.;* Benehmen, *das;* **teach sb. some ~s** jmdm. Manieren beibringen; **forget one's ~s** seine guten Manieren zu Hause lassen; **where are your ~s?** wo hast du deine Manieren gelassen?; **that's good ~s** das gehört sich so; **that's bad ~s** das gehört sich nicht; das macht man nicht; **mind** *or* **watch your ~s!** benimm dich!; **~s maketh man** (prov.) es kommt vor allem auf gutes Benehmen an; *see also* **mend A 2** 4) *in pl.* (modes of life) Sitten *Pl.* 5) (artistic style) Stil, *der;* **~s** Stilrichtungen 6) (type) **all ~ of** ▸**all A 2**; **no ~ of** keinerlei; **what ~ of man is he?** (arch.) was für ein Mensch ist er?; *see also* **means 3**

mannered /ˈmænəd/ *adj.* 1) (showing mannerism) manieriert 2) *in comb.* **... -~:** mit ... Manieren *nachgestellt;* **be well-~/bad-~:** gute/schlechte Manieren haben; **he's a mild-~ man** er hat ein sanftes Wesen

mannerism /ˈmænərɪzm/ *n.* 1) (addiction to a manner) Manieriertheit, *die* 2) (trick of style) Manierismus, *der* 3) (in behaviour) Eigenart, *die* 4) *no pl., no art.* (Art) Manierismus, *der*

manning /ˈmænɪŋ/ *n.* (of ship, aircraft) Bemannung, *die;* (of factory, industry, etc.) Personalausstattung, *die*

mannish /ˈmænɪʃ/ *adj.* männlich; männlich, maskulin ‹*Kleidung*›; **a ~ woman** ein Mannweib (abwertend)

manoeuvrable /məˈnuːvrəbl/ *adj.* (Brit.) manövrierfähig ‹*Schiff, Flugzeug, Auto*›; **be easily ~:** leicht zu manövrieren *od.* zu lenken sein

manoeuvre /məˈnuːvə(r)/ (Brit.)

A *n.* 1) (Mil., Navy) Manöver, *das;* **be/go on ~s** im Manöver sein/ins Manöver ziehen *od.* rücken 2) (deceptive movement, scheme; also of vehicle, aircraft) Manöver, *das;* **room for ~** (fig.) Spielraum, *der*

B *v.t.* 1) (Mil., Navy) führen; dirigieren 2) (bring by ~s) manövrieren; bugsieren ‹*Sperriges*›; **~ sb./oneself/sth. into a good position** (fig.) jmdn./sich/etw. in eine gute Position manövrieren 3) (manipulate) beeinflussen; **~ sb. into doing sth.** jmdn. dazu bringen, etw. zu tun; **~ sb. away from sth.** jmdn. von etw. abbringen

C *v.i.* 1) (Mil., Navy) [ein] Manöver durchführen 2) (move, scheme) manövrieren; **room to ~:** Platz zum Manövrieren; (fig.) Spielraum, *der;* **~ for power** auf Machtgewinn hinarbeiten

man-of-ˈwar *n., pl.* **men-of-war** Kriegsschiff, *das; see also* **Portuguese man-of-war**

manor /ˈmænə(r)/ *n.* 1) (land) [Land]gut, *das;* **lord/lady of the ~:** Gutsherr, *der*/Gutsherrin, *die* 2) (house) Herrenhaus, *das* 3) (Brit. coll.: police area) Revier, *das*

ˈmanor house ▸**manor 2**

manorial /məˈnɔːrɪəl/ *adj.* Guts‹*hof, -besitz*›; gutsherrschaftlich ‹*System, Rechte*›

ˈmanpower *n.* 1) (available power) Arbeitspotenzial, *das;* (workers) Arbeitskräfte *Pl.; attrib.* Personal‹*mangel, -planung*› 2) (Mil.) Stärke, *die*

ˈman-powered *adj.* **~ flight** Flug mit [menschlicher] Muskelkraft

manqué /ˈmɑ̃keɪ/ *adj. postpos.* verhindert ‹*Poet, Künstler, Intellektueller usw.*›

mansard /ˈmænsɑːd/ *n.* **~ [roof]** (Archit.) Mansard[en]dach, *das*

manse /mæns/ *n.* Pfarrhaus, *das*

ˈmanservant *n., pl.* **ˈmenservants** Diener, *der*

mansion /ˈmænʃn/ *n.* Villa, *die;* (of lord of the manor) Herrenhaus, *das*

man: ~-size, ~-sized *adj.* (suitable for a man) ‹*Mahlzeit, Steak*› für einen [ganzen] Mann; (large) groß; **~slaughter** *n.* (Law) Totschlag, *der*

manta /ˈmæntə/ *n.* (Zool.) Teufelsrochen, *der;* Manta, *der*

mantel /ˈmæntl/ ▸**mantelpiece**

mantel: ~piece *n.* 1) (above fireplace) Kaminsims, *der od. das;* 2) (around fireplace) Kamineinfassung, *die;* **~shelf** ▸**mantelpiece 1**

mantis /ˈmæntɪs/ *n., pl. same* (Zool.) Fang[heu]schrecke, *die;* **praying ~:** Gottesanbeterin, *die*

mantle /ˈmæntl/

A *n.* 1) (cloak) Umhang, *der;* (fig.) Mantel, *der;* **~ of snow** Schneedecke, *die* 2) (Geol.) Mantel, *der*

B *v.t.* (literary: cover) bedecken

ˈman-to-man *adj.* von Mann zu Mann *nachgestellt*

mantra /ˈmæntrə/ *n.* (Relig.) Mantra, *das*

ˈmantrap *n.* Fußangel, *die*

manual /ˈmænjʊəl/

A *adj.* 1) manuell; **~ work/labour** manuelle Tätigkeit *od.* Handarbeit/körperliche Arbeit *od.* Schwerarbeit; **~ worker/labourer** Handarbeiter/Schwerarbeiter, *der* 2) (not automatic) handbetrieben; ‹*Bedienung, Kontrolle, Schaltung*› von Hand; **~ steering/signals** Handsteuerung, *die*/-zeichen

B *n.* 1) (handbook) Handbuch, *das* 2) (Mus.) Manual, *das*

manually /ˈmænjʊəlɪ/ *adv.* manuell; von Hand; mit der Hand; **a ~ operated machine** eine handbetriebene Maschine

manufacture /mænjʊˈfæktʃə(r)/

A *n.* Herstellung, *die;* **cost/country of ~:** Herstellungskosten, *Pl.*/-land, *das;* **articles of home/foreign/British ~:** inländische/ausländische/britische Erzeugnisse

B *v.t.* 1) (Commerc.) herstellen; **~ iron into steel/cloth into garments** Eisen zu Stahl verarbeiten/aus Stoff Kleidungsstücke herstellen; **~d goods** Fertigprodukte *Pl.;* **manufacturing costs/firm/fault** Herstellungskosten *Pl.* /Herstellerfirma, *die*/Produktionsfehler, *der;* **manufacturing town** Industriestadt, *die* 2) (invent) erfinden ‹*Geschichte, Ausrede usw.*›

manufacturer /mænjʊˈfæktʃərə(r)/ *n.* Hersteller, *der;* **'~'s recommended [retail] price'** „unverbindliche Preisempfehlung"

manuˈfacturing fault *n.* Herstellungsfehler, *der;* Produktionsfehler, *der*

manure /məˈnjʊə(r)/

A *n.* (dung) Dung, *der;* (fertilizer) Dünger, *der*

B *v.t.* düngen

maˈnure heap *n.* Misthaufen, *der*

manuscript /ˈmænjʊskrɪpt/

A *n.* 1) Handschrift, *die* 2) (not yet printed) Manuskript, *das;* **the novel is still in ~:** der Roman liegt [erst] im *od.* als Manuskript vor

B *adj.* handschriftlich

ˈman-week *n.* (Work Study) Mannwoche, *die*

Manx /mæŋks/ ▸❶ **p. 1277**

A *adj.* der Insel Man *nachgestellt*

B *n.* (Ling.) Manx, *das*

Manx: ~ ˈcat *n.* Man[x]katze, *die;* **~man** /ˈmæŋksmən/ *n., pl.* **~men** /ˈmæŋksmən/ Bewohner der Insel Man; Manx, *der*

many /ˈmenɪ/

A *adj.* 1) viele; *pred.* zahlreich; **how ~ people/books?** wie viele *od.* wie viel Leute/Bücher?; **as ~ as** so viele wie; **there were as ~ as 50 of them** es waren mindestens *od.* bestimmt 50; **three accidents in as ~ days** drei Unfälle in ebenso vielen *od.* ebenso viel Tagen; **~'s the tale/the time** so manche Geschichte/so manches Mal; **too ~ people/books** zu viele *od.* zu viel Leute/Bücher; **there were too ~ of them** es waren zu viele *od.* zu viel; **two [copies] too ~:** zwei [Exemplare] zu viel; **one is too ~/there is one too ~:** einer/eine/eins ist zu viel; **he/she is one too ~ here** er/sie ist hier überflüssig; **he's had one too ~** (is drunk) er hat einen *od.* ein Glas zu viel getrunken 2) **~ a man** so mancher; manch einer; **~ a time** so manches Mal

B *n.* viele [Leute]; **there weren't ~ of them there** es waren nicht viele da; **~ of us** viele von uns; **a good/great ~ [of them/of the books]** eine Menge/eine ganze Reihe [von ihnen/der Bücher]; **there were a good ~ there** eine Menge war *od.* waren da

ˈmany-coloured *adj.* vielfarbig

ˈman-year *n.* (Work Study) Mannjahr, *das*

ˈmany-sided *adj.* (Geom.; also fig.) vielseitig

Mao /maʊ/ *adj.* ‹*Jacke, Schirmmütze*› im Mao-Look; Mao-‹*Jacke, Mütze*›

Maoism /ˈmaʊɪzm/ *n., no pl.* Maoismus, *der*

Maoist /ˈmaʊɪst/ *n.* Maoist, *der; attrib.* maoistisch

Maori /ˈmaʊrɪ/ ▸❶ **p. 1277**, ▸❶ **p. 1345**

A *n.* 1) (person) Maori, *der* 2) (language) Maori, *das*

B *adj.* maorisch

map /mæp/

A *n.* 1) [Land]karte, *die;* (street plan) Stadtplan, *der* 2) (fig. coll.) **off the ~:** abgelegen; **we're a bit off the ~ up here** wir leben hier ein bisschen hinter dem Mond (ugs.); **wipe off the ~:** ausradieren; **[put sth./sb.] on the ~:** [etw./jmdn.] bekannt [machen]

B *v.t.*, **-pp-** (make ~ of) kartographieren; (make survey of) vermessen

Phrasal verb

• **~ ˈout** *v.t.* im Einzelnen festlegen

maple /ˈmeɪpl/ *n.* Ahorn, *der*

maple: ~ leaf *n.* Ahornblatt, *das;* **~ sugar** *n.* Ahornzucker, *der;* **~ syrup** *n.* Ahornsirup, *der*

map: ~-maker *n.* ▸❶ **p. 1260** Kartograph, *der*/Kartographin, *die;* **~-reader** *n.* Kartenleser, *der*/-leserin, *die;* **~-reading** *n., no pl.* Kartenlesen, *das*

mar /mɑː(r)/ *v.t.*, **-rr-** 1) (spoil, disfigure) verderben; entstellen ‹*Aussehen*›; stören ‹*Veranstaltung*›; **the book was ~red by a number of small mistakes** die Qualität des Buches wurde durch eine Reihe kleiner Fehler beeinträchtigt 2) (ruin) ▸**make A 16**

Mar. *abbr.* **= March** Mrz.

marabou /ˈmærəbuː/ *n.* (Ornith.) 1) (African) Marabu, *der* 2) ▸**adjutant 2**

maraca /məˈrækə/ *n.* Maraca, *die*

maraschino /mærəˈskiːnəʊ/ *n., pl.* **~s** Maraschino, *der;* **~ cherry** Maraschinokirsche, *die*

marathon /ˈmærəθən/ *n.* 1) (race) Marathon[lauf], *der; attrib.* Marathon‹*läufer*› 2) (fig.) Marathon, *das; attrib.* Marathon‹*rede, -spiel, -sitzung*›; **a chess ~:** ein Schachmarathon

maraud /məˈrɔːd/

A *v.i.* plündern; marodieren (Soldatenspr.)

B *v.t.* plündern

marauder /məˈrɔːdə(r)/ *n.* Plünderer, *der;* Marodeur, *der* (Soldatenspr.); (animal) Räuber, *der*

marble /ˈmɑːbl/ *n.* 1) (stone) Marmor, *der* (auch fig.); *attrib.* Marmor-; aus Marmor *nachgestellt;* marmorn (dichter., fig.) 2) *in pl.* (statues) Marmorskulpturen; **the Elgin M~s** die Elgin Marbles (Kunstwiss.) 3) (toy) Murmel, *die;* **[game of] ~s** Murmelspiel, *das;* **play ~s** murmeln; [mit] Murmeln spielen 4) *in pl.* **not have all** *or* **have lost one's ~s** (coll.) nicht alle Tassen im Schrank haben (ugs.)

marbled /ˈmɑːbld/ *adj.* 1 marmoriert ‹*Papier, Seife usw.*› 2 (streaked) durchwachsen ‹*Fleisch*›

march[1]

A *n.* 1 (Mil., Mus.; hike) Marsch, *der;* (gait) Marschschritt, *der;* Marschtritt, *der;* **on the ~:** auf dem Marsch; (fig.) unterwegs; **~ past** Vorbeimarsch, *der;* Defilee, *das;* **a day's/three days' ~:** ein Tagesmarsch/drei Tagesmärsche; **an hour's ~ away** eine Marschstunde *od.* eine Stunde Marsch entfernt; *see also* **forced march**; **line**[1] **A 11**; **steal A 3** 2 (in protest) **[protest] ~:** Protestmarsch, *der* 3 (progress of time, events, etc.) Gang, *der;* **the onward ~ of science** der Vormarsch der Wissenschaft

B *v.i.* (also Mil.) marschieren; (fig.) fortschreiten; **~ away** abmarschieren; **forward/quick ~!** vorwärts/im Eilschritt marsch!; **~ing song** Marschlied, *das;* **~ing order** (Brit.) Marschordnung, *die;* **~ing orders** Marschbefehl, *der;* **give sb. his/her ~ing orders** (fig. coll.) jmdm. den Laufpass geben (ugs.)

C *v.t.* (Mil.) marschieren lassen

Phrasal verbs

• **~ 'off**

A *v.i.* losmarschieren

B *v.t.* ‹*Polizei usw.:*› abführen

• **~ on** *v.t.* (Mil.) marschieren gegen ‹*Feind*›; marschieren auf (+ *Akk.*) ‹*Stadt*›

march[2] *n.* (Hist.: frontier) Mark, *die;* **the Welsh ~es** das Grenzland zwischen Wales und England

March /mɑːtʃ/ *n.* ▸ⓘ **p. 1047** März, *der; see also* **August**; **hare A 1**

marcher /ˈmɑːtʃə(r)/ *n.* **[protest] ~:** Demonstrant, *der*/Demonstrantin, *die;* **~s on a demonstration** Teilnehmer an einem Demonstrationszug

marchioness /mɑːʃəˈnes/ *n.* Marquise, *die*

Mardi Gras /mɑːdiː ˈgrɑː/ *n.* 1 (Shrove Tuesday) Fastnachtsdienstag, *der* 2 (carnival) Karneval, *der*

mare /meə(r)/ *n.* Stute, *die*

Margaret /ˈmɑːgrɪt/ *pr. n.* (Hist., as name of ruler etc.) Margarete (*die*)

margarine /mɑːdʒəˈriːn, mɑːgəˈriːn/, (coll.) **marge** /mɑːdʒ/ *ns.* Margarine, *die*

margin /ˈmɑːdʒɪn/ *n.* 1 (of page) Rand, *der;* **notes [written] in the ~:** Randbemerkungen; Anmerkungen am Rand; **~ release** Randlöser, *der;* Randfreigabe, *die* 2 (extra amount) Spielraum, *der;* **profit ~:** Gewinnspanne, *die;* **win by a narrow/wide ~:** knapp/mit großem Vorsprung gewinnen; **~ of error** Spielraum für mögliche Fehler; **allow for a considerable ~ of error** eine beachtliche Fehlerzahl mit einkalkulieren 3 (edge) Rand, *der;* Saum, *der* (geh.); **[be] on the ~ of sth.** (fig.) am Rande einer Sache (*Gen.*) [sein]

marginal /ˈmɑːdʒɪnl/ *adj.* 1 (barely adequate, slight) geringfügig; unwesentlich; **of ~ importance/use** von geringer Bedeutung/geringem Nutzen 2 (close to limit) marginal; (of profitability) kaum rentabel 3 knapp ‹*Wahlergebnis*›; **~ seat/constituency** (Brit. Polit.) wackeliger (ugs.) *od.* nur mit knapper Mehrheit gehaltener Parlamentssitz/Wahlkreis 4 **~ cost** Grenzkosten *Pl.* 5 (of or written in margin) an den Rand geschrieben; **~ notes/references** Randbemerkungen/-verweise 6 (of or at the edge) Rand‹*gebiet, -bereich, -besitzung, -bepflanzung usw.*›

marginalia /mɑːdʒɪˈneɪlɪə/ *n. pl.* Marginalien *Pl.*

marginalization /mɑːdʒɪnəlaɪˈzeɪʃn/ *n., no pl.* Marginalisierung, *die*

marginalize /ˈmɑːdʒɪnəlaɪz/ *v.t.* marginalisieren

marginally /ˈmɑːdʒɪnəlɪ/ *adv.* geringfügig; unwesentlich; **only ~ profitable** kaum rentabel

marguerite /mɑːgəˈriːt/ *n.* (Bot.) Margerite, *die*

marigold /ˈmærɪgəʊld/ *n.* (Calendula) Studentenblume, *die;* Ringelblume, *die;* (Tagetes) Studentenblume, *die; see also* **corn marigold**; **marsh marigold**

marijuana (**marihuana**) /mærɪˈhwɑːnə/ *n.* Marihuana, *das; attrib.* Marihuana‹*zigarette, -raucher, -süchtiger*›

marimba /məˈrɪmbə/ *n.* (Mus.) 1 (native xylophone) Marimba, *die* 2 (modern instrument) Marimbaphon, *das*

marina /məˈriːnə/ *n.* Marina, *die;* Jachthafen, *der*

marinade /mærɪˈneɪd/

A *n.* 1 (spiced mixture) Marinade, *die* 2 (marinaded meat) **a ~ of beef/pork** mariniertes Rind-/Schweinefleisch; **a ~ of fish** marinierter Fisch; eine Marinade

B *v.t.* marinieren

marinate /ˈmærɪneɪt/ ▸**marinade B**

marine /məˈriːn/

A *adj.* 1 (of the sea) Meeres-; **~ life** Meeresflora und -fauna; **~ mammal** Meeressäuger, *der;* Meeressäugetier, *das* 2 (of shipping) See‹*versicherung, -recht, -schifffahrt*›; **~ biologist** ▸ⓘ **p. 1260** Meeresbiologe, *der*/-biologin, *die;* **~ biology** Meeresbiologie, *die;* **~ engineering** Schiffsmaschinenbau, *der;* **~ engineer** ▸ⓘ **p. 1260** Schiffbauingenieur, *der;* **~ science** Meereskunde, *die;* Ozeanologie, *die;* **~ sciences** Meereswissenschaften *Pl.;* **~ scientist** ▸ⓘ **p. 1260** Meereswissenschaftler, *der*/-wissenschaftlerin, *die;* Ozeanologe, *der*/Ozeanologin, *die* 3 (for use at sea) Schiffs‹*ausrüstung, -chronometer, -kessel, -turbine usw.*›

B *n.* 1 (person) Marineinfanterist, *der;* **the M~s** die Marineinfanterie; die Marinetruppen; **tell that/it to the [horse] ~s** (coll.) das kannst du deiner Großmutter erzählen (ugs.); *see also* **Royal Marine** 2 (shipping) **merchant** *or* **mercantile ~:** Handelsmarine, *die*

mariner /ˈmærɪnə(r)/ *n.* Seemann, *der;* **master ~:** Kapitän eines Handelsschiffes; *see also* **compass A 2**

marionette /mærɪəˈnet/ *n.* Marionette, *die*

marital /ˈmærɪtl/ *adj.* ehelich ‹*Rechte, Pflichten, Harmonie*›; Ehe‹*beratung, -glück, -krach, -krise, -probleme*›; **~ rape** Vergewaltigung in der Ehe; **~ status** Familienstand, *der*

maritime /ˈmærɪtaɪm/ *adj.* 1 (found near the sea) Küsten‹*bewohner, -gebiet, -stadt, -provinz*›; **~ climate** Meeresklima, *das* 2 (connected with the sea) See‹*recht, -versicherung, -volk, -wesen*›

marjoram /ˈmɑːdʒərəm/ *n.* (Bot., Cookery) Majoran, *der*

mark[1]

A *n.* 1 (trace) Spur, *die;* (of finger, foot also) Abdruck, *der;* (stain etc.) Fleck, *der;* (scratch) Kratzer, *der;* **dirty ~:** Schmutzfleck, *der;* **make/leave a ~ on sth.** auf etw. (*Dat. od. Akk.*) einen Fleck/einen Kratzer machen/auf etw. (*Dat.*) einen Fleck/eine Spur/einen Kratzer hinterlassen; **leave one's/its ~ on sth.** (fig.) einer Sache (*Dat.*) seinen Stempel aufdrücken; **leave its ~ on sb.** Spuren bei jmdm. hinterlassen; **make one's/its ~** (fig.) sich (*Dat.*) einen Namen machen (*see also* **2**); **of ~** *postpos.* von Bedeutung *nachgestellt; see also* **birthmark** 2 (affixed sign, indication, symbol) Zeichen, *das;* (in trade names) Typ, *der* (Technik); (made by illiterate) Kreuz, *das;* **distinguishing ~:** Kennzeichen, *das;* **M~ 2 version/model** Version/Modell 2; **make one's ~:** ein Kreuz *od.* drei Kreuze machen (*see also* **1**); **bear the ~ of sth.** (lit. or fig.) den Stempel von etw. tragen; **have all the ~s of sth.** alle Anzeichen von etw. haben; **be a ~ of good taste/breeding** ein Zeichen guten Geschmacks/guter Erziehung sein; **sth. is the ~ of a good writer** an etw. (*Dat.*) erkennt man einen guten Schriftsteller 3 (Sch.: grade) Zensur, *die;* Note, *die;* (Sch., Sport: unit of numerical award) Punkt, *der;* **get good/bad/35 ~s in** *or* **for a subject** gute/schlechte Noten *od.* Zensuren/35 Punkte in einem Fach bekommen; **there are no ~s for guessing that ...** (fig. coll.) es ist ja wohl nicht schwer zu erraten, dass ...; *see also* **black mark**; **full marks**; **pass mark** 4 (line etc. to indicate position) Markierung, *die;* (Naut.) Marke, *die* (*an der Lotleine*); **be up to/below** *or* **not up to the ~** (fig.) den Anforderungen entsprechen/nicht entsprechen; **his work hasn't really been up to the ~ lately** seine Arbeit war in letzter Zeit wirklich nicht sonderlich; **[not] feel up to the ~:** [nicht] auf der Höhe sein 5 (level) Marke, *die;* **reach the 15%/25 million/£300 ~:** die 15%-Marke/25-Millionen-Marke/300-Pfund-Marke erreichen; **around the 300 ~:** ungefähr 300 6 (Sport: starting position) Startlinie, *die;* **on your ~s! [get set! go!]** auf die Plätze! [Fertig! Los!]; **get off the ~ quickly** (fig.) einen guten Start haben; **be quick/slow off the ~:** einen guten/schlechten Start haben; (fig.) fix (ugs.)/langsam sein; **he is usually the quickest/first off the ~:** er ist gewöhnlich der Schnellste/Erste 7 (Rugby) (spot) Marke, *die;* (fair catch) Freifang, *der;* **'~!'** „Marke!" 8 (target, desired object) Ziel, *das;* (coll.: intended victim) Opfer, *das;* **hit/miss the ~** (fig.) ins Schwarze treffen/danebenschießen (ugs.) *od.* -treffen; **be wide of the ~** (lit. or fig.) danebentreffen; **his calculations were wide of the ~:** mit seinen Berechnungen hat er völlig danebengetroffen; **my guess was off the ~:** mit meiner Schätzung lag ich daneben (ugs.); **be close to the ~** (fig.) der Sache nahe kommen; *see also* **overshoot**; **overstep**

B *v.t.* 1 (stain, dirty) Flecke[n] machen auf (+ *Dat.*); schmutzig machen; (scratch) zerkratzen; **be ~ed for life** bleibende Narben zurückbehalten; (fig.) fürs Leben gezeichnet sein 2 (put distinguishing ~ on, signal) kennzeichnen, markieren (**with** mit); **the bottle was ~ed 'poison'** die Flasche trug die Aufschrift „Gift"; **~ sb.'s name on sth.** etw. mit jmds. Namen kennzeichnen; **~ an item with its price** eine Ware auszeichnen *od.* mit einem Preisschild versehen; **~ a route on a map** eine Route auf *od.* in einer *od.* in eine Landkarte einzeichnen; **ceremonies to ~ the tenth anniversary** Feierlichkeiten aus Anlass des 10. Jahrestages 3 (Sch.) (correct) korrigieren; (grade) benoten; zensieren; **~ an answer wrong** eine Antwort als falsch bewerten 4 **~ time** (Mil.; also fig.) auf der Stelle treten 5 (characterize) kennzeichnen; charakterisieren; **be ~ed by sth.** durch etw. gekennzeichnet *od.* charakterisiert sein; **his style is ~ed by a great variety of metaphors** sein Stil zeichnet sich durch eine reiche Metaphorik aus 6 (heed) hören auf (+ *Akk.*) ‹*Person, Wort*›; **~ carefully how it is done** pass genau auf, wie es gemacht wird; **[you] ~ my words** höre auf mich; eins kann ich dir sagen; (as a warning) lass dir das gesagt sein; **~ you, it may not be true** vielleicht stimmt es ja doch gar nicht 7 (manifest) bekunden ‹*Missfallen, Zustimmung usw.*› 8 (record) notieren, aufschreiben ‹*Spielstand*›; **~ a pupil absent** einen Schüler als fehlend eintragen 9 (Brit. Sport: keep close to) markieren (fachspr.), decken ‹*Gegenspieler*› 10 (choose as victim) ▸**mark down 1** 11 (arch./literary: notice) bemerken ‹*Vorfall, Vorgang*›

Phrasal verbs

• **~ 'down** *v.t.* 1 (choose as victim, lit. or fig.) [sich (*Dat.*)] auswählen; ausersehen (geh.) 2 [im Preis] herabsetzen ‹*Ware*›; herabsetzen ‹*Preis*›; *see also* **mark-down**

• **~ 'off** *v.t.* abgrenzen (**from** von, gegen)

• **~ 'out** *v.t.* 1 (trace out boundaries of) markieren ‹*Spielfeld*›; **~ out a tennis court** auf einen Tennisplatz die Spielfeldlinien markieren 2 (plan) festlegen ‹*Strategie, Vorgehen*› 3 (destine) versehen; ‹*Schicksal:*› bestimmen, ausersehen

• **~ 'up** *v.t.* [im Preis] heraufsetzen ‹*Ware*›; heraufsetzen ‹*Preis*›; *see also* **mark-up**

mark[2] *n.* (former monetary unit) Mark, *die*

Mark /mɑːk/ *pr. n.* **St ~:** der hl. Markus

'mark-down *n.* (Econ.) Preissenkung, *die;* **there has been a ~:** der Preis ist/die Preise sind gesenkt worden

marked /mɑːkt/ *adj.* 1 (noticeable) deutlich ‹*Gegensatz, Unterschied, [Ver]besserung, Veränderung*›; ausgeprägt ‹*Akzent, Sprachfehler, Kennzeichen, Merkmal, Fähigkeit, Neigung*› 2 (given distinctive mark) gezinkt ‹*Spielkarte*› 3 **be a ~ man** auf der schwarzen Liste stehen (ugs.)

m

markedly /ˈmɑːkɪdlɪ/ *adv.* eindeutig; deutlich

marker /ˈmɑːkə(r)/ *n.* 1 (to mark place) Markierung, *die* 2 ▸**bookmark** 3 (of examination etc.) Korrektor, *der*/Korrektorin, *die*; **be a fair/severe ~:** gerecht/streng [korrigieren und] benoten 4 (Aeronaut.: flare) Marker, *der* (fachspr.); Sichtzeichen, *das*

ˈ**marker pen** *n.* Markierstift, *der*

market /ˈmɑːkɪt/

A *n.* 1 Markt, *der*; *attrib.* Markt‹*händler, -stand*›; **at the ~:** auf dem Markt; **go to ~:** auf den Markt gehen; **take sth. to ~:** etw. auf den Markt bringen; **there is a ~ every Friday** freitags *od.* jeden Freitag ist Markt 2 (demand) Markt, *der*; **find a [ready] ~:** [guten] Absatz finden; **price oneself/one's goods out of the ~:** sich/seine Waren durch Überteuerung konkurrenzunfähig machen 3 (area of demand) Absatzmarkt, *der*; (persons) Abnehmer *Pl.* 4 (conditions for buying and selling, trade) Markt, *der*; **the corn/coffee** *etc.* **~:** der Getreide-/Kaffeemarkt *usw.*; **be in the ~ for sth.** an etw. (*Dat.*) interessiert sein; **be on/come into** *or* **on to the ~** ‹*Haus:*› zum Verkauf stehen/kommen; ‹*neue Produkte:*› auf dem Markt sein/auf den Markt kommen; **put on the ~:** zum Verkauf anbieten ‹*Haus*›; **bring on to the ~:** auf den Markt bringen ‹*neues Produkt*›; **make a ~** (St. Exch.) [künstlich] Nachfrage erzeugen; **the M~** (Brit. Polit.) der Gemeinsame Markt; *see also* **buyer 3**; **Common Market**; **corner B 2**; **play C 9**; **seller 1**

B *v.t.* vermarkten

marketable /ˈmɑːkɪtəbl/ *adj.* 1 (suitable for the market) marktfähig 2 (wanted by purchasers) marktgängig; **~ securities** börsengängige Effekten

market: ~ day *n.* Markttag, *der*; **~ eˈconomy** *n.* Marktwirtschaft, *die*; **~ ˈforces** *n. pl.* Kräfte des freien Marktes; **~ ˈgarden** *n.* (Brit.) Gartenbaubetrieb, *der*; **~ ˈgardener** *n.* ▸❶ **p. 1260** (Brit.) Gemüseanbauer, *der*/-anbauerin, *die*; **~ ˈgardening** *n.* (Brit.) Gemüseanbau, *der*

marketing /ˈmɑːkɪtɪŋ/ *n., no pl.* (Econ.) Marketing, *das*; *attrib.* Marketing-; **~ manager** ▸❶ **p. 1260** Marketingmanager, *der*/-managerin, *die*; **~ research** Marketingresearch, *das*

market: ~ ˈleader *n.* (company, brand) Marktführer, *der*; (product) meistverkauftes Produkt; **the company is the ~ leader in its field** die Firma ist marktführend auf ihrem Gebiet; **~-maker** *n.* (St. Exch.) *die Preise bestimmender Wertpapierhändler*; **~ peneˈtration** *n., no pl.* 1 (entry into a market) Marktpenetration, *die*; 2 (market share) Marktdurchdringung, *die*; **~ place** *n.* Marktplatz, *der*; (fig.) Markt, *der*; **~ power** *n.* Marktmacht, *die*; **~ ˈprice** *n.* Marktpreis, *der*; **~-ready** *adj.* marktbereit; **~ ˈresearch** *n.* Marktforschung, *die*; **~ share** *n.* Marktanteil, *der*; **~ square** *n.* Marktplatz, *der*; **~ ˈstudy**, **~ ˈsurvey** *ns.* Marktstudie, *die*; Marktuntersuchung, *die*; **~ town** *n.* Marktort, *der*; **~ ˈtrader** *n.* ▸❶ **p. 1260** 1 (on stock market) Börsenmakler, *der*/-maklerin, *die*; 2 (stallholder) Markthändler, *der*/-händlerin, *die*; **~ ˈvalue** *n.* Marktwert, *der*

marking /ˈmɑːkɪŋ/ *n.* 1 (identification symbol) Markierung, *die*; Kennzeichen, *das* 2 (on animal) Zeichnung, *die* 3 (Sch.) (correcting) Korrektur, *die*; (grading) Benotung, *die*; Zensieren, *das*; **I've got some ~ to do** ich muss noch korrigieren

ˈ**marking ink** *n.* Wäschetinte, *die*

marksman /ˈmɑːksmən/ *n., pl.* **marksmen** /ˈmɑːksmən/ Scharfschütze, *der*

marksmanship /ˈmɑːksmənʃɪp/ *n., no pl.* Treffsicherheit, *die*

ˈ**mark-up** *n.* (Econ.) 1 (price increase) Preiserhöhung, *die* 2 (amount added) Handelsspanne, *die* (Kaufmannsspr.)

marl /mɑːl/ *n.* Mergel, *der*

marmalade /ˈmɑːməleɪd/ *n.* **[orange] ~:** Orangenmarmelade, *die*; **tangerine/lime ~:** Mandarinen-/Limonenmarmelade, *die*

marmalade ˈcat *n.* orangefarbene Katze

marmoset /ˈmɑːməzet/ *n.* (Zool.) Marmosette, *die*

marmot /ˈmɑːmət/ *n.* (Zool.) Murmeltier, *das*

maroon¹ /məˈruːn/

A *adj.* kastanienbraun

B *n.* Kastanienbraun, *das*

maroon² *v.t.* 1 (Naut.: put ashore) aussetzen 2 ‹*Flut, Hochwasser:*› von der Außenwelt abschneiden; **she was ~ed at home without transport** ohne Transportmittel saß sie zu Hause fest

marque /mɑːk/ *n.* Marke, *die*; (of cars also) Fabrikat, *das*

marquee /mɑːˈkiː/ *n.* 1 (large tent) großes Zelt; (for public entertainment) Festzelt, *das* 2 (Amer.: canopy) Vordach, *das*

marquess ▸**marquis**

marquetry /ˈmɑːkɪtrɪ/ *n.* Marketerie, *die* (Kunstwiss.); Einlegearbeit, *die*; Intarsie, *die*; *attrib.* Intarsien‹*arbeit, -schrank*›

marquis /ˈmɑːkwɪs/ *n.* Marquis, *der*

marriage /ˈmærɪdʒ/ *n.* 1 Ehe, *die* (**to** mit); **state of ~:** Ehestand, *der*; **proposal** *or* **offer of ~:** Heiratsantrag, *der*; **his son by a former ~:** sein Sohn aus einer früheren Ehe; **related by ~:** verschwägert; **uncle/cousin by ~:** angeheirateter Onkel/Cousin; **take sb. in ~:** jmdn. zum Mann/zur Frau nehmen; *see also* **convenience 1**; **give A 8** 2 (wedding) Hochzeit, *die*; (act of marrying) Heirat, *die*; (ceremony) Trauung, *die*; **~ ceremony** Trauzeremonie, *die*; Eheschließung, *die*; **church ~:** kirchliche Trauung; *see also* **civil marriage** 3 (fig.) Verbindung, *die*

marriageable /ˈmærɪdʒəbl/ *adj.* heiratsfähig; **of ~ age** im heiratsfähigen Alter

marriage: ~ broker *n.* Heiratsvermittler, *der*/-vermittlerin, *die*; **~ bureau** *n.* Eheanbahnungs- *od.* Ehevermittlungsinstitut, *das*; **~ certificate** *n.* Trauschein, *der*; (record of civil marriage also) Heiratsurkunde, *die*; **~ ˈguidance** *n.* Eheberatung, *die*; **~ licence** *n.* Heirats- *od.* Eheerlaubnis, *die*; **~ lines** *n. pl.* (Brit.) ▸**~ certificate**; **~ market** *n.* Heiratsmarkt, *der*; **~ settlement** *n.* (Law) Ehevertrag, *der*; **~ stakes** *n. pl.* (joc.) Heiratsmarkt, *der*; **~ vows** *n. pl.* Ehegelöbnis, *das* (geh.)

married /ˈmærɪd/

A *adj.* 1 verheiratet; **~ couple** Ehepaar, *das* 2 (marital) ehelich ‹*Leben, Liebe*›; Ehe‹*leben, -name, -stand*›; **~ name** Ehename, *der*; **~ quarters** Verheiratetenquartiere

B *n.* Verheiratete, *der/die*; **young/newly ~s** Jungverheiratete

marron glacé /mærɒn ˈglɑːseɪ/ *n.* kandierte Kastanie

marrow /ˈmærəʊ/ *n.* 1 **[vegetable] ~:** Speisekürbis, *der* 2 (Anat.) [Knochen]mark, *das*; **spinal ~:** Rückenmark, *das*; **to the ~** (fig.) durch und durch; **be chilled to the ~** (fig.) völlig durchgefroren sein

marrow: ~bone *n.* Markknochen, *der*; **~fat** *n.* Markerbse, *die*; **~ squash** (Amer.) ▸**marrow 1**

marry /ˈmærɪ/

A *v.t.* 1 (take in marriage) heiraten; **~ money** Geld *od.* (ugs.) reich heiraten; (for financial gain only) jmds. Geld heiraten 2 (join in marriage) trauen; **they were** *or* **got married last summer** sie haben letzten Sommer geheiratet 3 (give in marriage) verheiraten ‹*Kind*› (**to** mit) 4 (fig.: unite intimately) verquicken; eng miteinander verbinden; **~ sth. with** *or* **to sth.** etw. mit etw. verquicken *od.* eng verbinden

B *v.i.* heiraten; **~ for money** wegen des Geldes heiraten; **~ in haste, repent at leisure** (prov.) Heirat in Eile bereut man in Weile (Spr.); **~ into a [rich] family** in eine [reiche] Familie einheiraten

Phrasal verbs

• **~ ˈoff** *v.t.* verheiraten ‹*Tochter*› (**to** mit)

• **~ ˈup**

A *v.i.* 1 (join up) zusammenpassen (**with** mit + *Dat.*) 2 (fig.: match) zusammenpassen

B *v.t.* zusammenfügen

marrying /ˈmærɪɪŋ/ *adj.* **he's not the ~ sort** *or* **kind** *or* **type** er ist nicht der Typ [von Mann], der heiratet

Mars /mɑːz/ *pr. n.* 1 (Astron.) Mars, *der* 2 (Roman Mythol.) Mars (*der*)

Marsala /mɑːˈsɑːlə/ *n.* Marsala[wein], *der*

Marseillaise /mɑːsəˈleɪz, mɑːseɪˈjeɪz/ *n.* Marseillaise, *die*

Marseilles /mɑːˈseɪlz, mɑːˈseɪ/ *pr. n.* ▸❶ **p. 1643** Marseille (*das*)

marsh /mɑːʃ/ *n.* Sumpf, *der*; *attrib.* (Bot., Zool.) Sumpf‹*klee, -kresse, -[kratz]distel, -krokodil, -hirsch*›

marshal /ˈmɑːʃl/

A *n.* 1 (officer of state) [Hof]marschall, *der* 2 (officer in army) Marschall, *der*; *see also* **Field Marshal** 3 (Sport) Ordner, *der* 4 (Amer.) (head of police department) Polizeipräsident, *der*; (head of fire department) Branddirektor, *der*. *See also* **provost marshal**

B *v.t.*, (Brit.) **-ll-** 1 (arrange in order) aufstellen ‹*Truppen*›; sich (*Dat.*) zurechtlegen ‹*Argumente*›; ordnen ‹*Fakten*›; **the teacher ~led the children on to the coach** der Lehrer führte die Kinder zu ihren Plätzen im Bus 2 (Her.) vereinigen, verbinden ‹*Wappen*›

ˈ**marshalling yard** /ˈmɑːʃəlɪŋ jɑːd/ *n.* (Railw.) Rangierbahnhof, *der*

marsh: ~ gas *n.* (Chem.) Sumpfgas, *das*; **~ ˈharrier** *n.* (Ornith.) Rohrweihe, *die*; **~land** *n.* Sumpfland, *das*; **~ mallow** *n.* (Bot.) Eibisch, *der*; süßer Speck; **~ˈmallow** *n.* (sweet) ≈ Mohrenkopf, *der*; **~ ˈmarigold** *n.* Sumpfdotterblume, *die*; **~ tit** *n.* (Ornith.) Nonnenmeise, *die*

marshy /ˈmɑːʃɪ/ *adj.* sumpfig; Sumpf‹*boden, -gebiet, -land*›

marsupial /mɑːˈsjuːpɪəl, mɑːˈsuːpɪəl/ (Zool.)

A *adj.* Beutel‹*tier, -frosch, -mulle*›

B *n.* Beuteltier, *das*

mart /mɑːt/ *n.* 1 (market place) Markt, *der* 2 (auction-room) Auktionsraum, *der*; **sale ~:** Verkaufsraum, *der*

marten /ˈmɑːtɪn/ *n.* (Zool.) Marder, *der*; **stone ~:** Steinmarder, *der*; *see also* **pine marten**

martial /ˈmɑːʃl/ *adj.* kriegerisch; *see also* **court martial**

martial: ~ ˈarts *n. pl.* (Sport) Kampfsportarten; **~ ˈlaw** *n.* Kriegsrecht, *das*; **state of ~ law** Kriegszustand, *der*

Martian /ˈmɑːʃn/

A *adj.* Mars-

B *n.* Marsmensch, *der*

martin /ˈmɑːtɪn/ *n.* (Ornith.) **[house] ~:** Mehlschwalbe, *die*

martinet /mɑːtɪˈnet/ *n.* Zuchtmeister, *der* (veralt., noch scherzh.)

Martini ® /mɑːˈtiːnɪ/ *n.* Martini, *der*; **dry ~:** Martini dry, *der*

martyr /ˈmɑːtə(r)/

A *n.* (Relig.; also fig.) Märtyrer, *der*/Märtyrerin, *die*; **die a ~'s death** den Märtyrertod erleiden *od.* sterben; **a ~ to** *or* **in the cause of sth.** Märtyrer/Märtyrerin einer Sache (*Gen.*); **be a ~ to rheumatism** entsetzlich unter Rheumatismus leiden; **make a ~ of oneself** den Märtyrer/die Märtyrerin spielen; **make sb. a ~, make a ~ of sb.** jmdn. zum Märtyrer/zur Märtyrerin machen

B *v.t.* 1 den Märtyrertod sterben lassen; **be ~ed** den Märtyrertod sterben 2 (fig.: torment) martern (geh.); **a ~ed expression** eine Duldermiene

martyrdom /ˈmɑːtədəm/ *n.* Martyrium, *das*; **suffer ~:** ein Martyrium durchleiden

marvel /ˈmɑːvl/

A *n.* Wunder, *das*; **work ~s** Wunder wirken; **it's a ~ to me how ...:** es ist mir schleierhaft, wie ...; **it will be a ~ if ...:** es wäre ein Wunder, wenn ...; **be a ~ of patience/neatness** eine sagenhafte Geduld haben/sagenhaft ordentlich sein (ugs.)

B *v.i.*, (Brit.) **-ll-** (literary) 1 (be surprised) **~ at sth.** über etw. (*Akk.*) staunen; etw. bestaunen; **~ that ...:** erstaunt sein, dass ... 2 (wonder) sich wundern; sich fragen; **~ how/why** *etc.* sich fragen *od.* (bes. schweiz.) sich wundern, wie/warum *usw.*

marvellous /ˈmɑːvələs/ *adj.*, **marvellously** /ˈmɑːvələslɪ/ *adv.* wunderbar

marvelous, marvelously (Amer.) ▸**marvell-**

Marxian /ˈmɑːksɪən/ ▸**Marxist**

Marxism /ˈmɑːksɪzm/ *n.* Marxismus, *der*

Marxist /ˈmɑːksɪst/

A *n.* Marxist, *der*/Marxistin, *die*

B *adj.* marxistisch

Mary /ˈmeərɪ/ *pr. n.* (Hist., as name of ruler, saint, etc.) Maria *(die)*; *see also* **Bloody Mary**

marzipan /ˈmɑːzɪpæn/ *n.* Marzipan, *das*

mascara /mæˈskɑːrə/ *n.* Mascara, *das*

mascot /ˈmæskɒt/ *n.* Maskottchen, *das*

masculine /ˈmæskjʊlɪn/

A *adj.* **1** (of men) männlich **2** (manly, manlike) maskulin **3** (Ling.) männlich; maskulin (fachspr.)

B *n.* (Ling.) Maskulinum, *das*

masculine ˈrhyme *n.* (Pros.) männlicher *od.* stumpfer Reim

masculinity /mæskjʊˈlɪnɪtɪ/ *n.*, *no pl.* Männlichkeit, *die*

maser /ˈmeɪzə(r)/ *n.* (Phys.) Maser, *der*

mash /mæʃ/

A *n.* **1** (Brewing) Maische, *die* **2** (as fodder) Mischfutter, *das* **3** (pulp) Brei, *der* **4** (Brit. coll.: ~ed potatoes) Kartoffelbrei, *der*

B *v.t.* zerdrücken, zerquetschen, stampfen ‹*Kartoffeln*›; zerdrücken, zerquetschen ‹*Gemüse, Obst*›; **~ed potatoes** Kartoffelbrei, *der*

mask /mɑːsk/

A *n.* (also fig., Phot.) Maske, *die* ; (worn by surgeon) Gesichtsmaske, *die*; Mundschutz, *der*; **throw off the ~** (fig.: abandon pretence) die Maske fallen lassen

B *v.t.* **1** (cover with mask) maskieren **2** (Mil.) tarnen **3** (fig.: disguise, conceal) maskieren; ‹*Wolken, Bäume:*› verdecken; überdecken ‹*Geschmack*› **4** (cover for protection) abdecken

masked ˈball *n.* Maskenball, *der*

ˈmasking tape *n.* Abklebeband, *das*

masochism /ˈmæsəkɪzm/ *n.* Masochismus, *der*

masochist /ˈmæsəkɪst/ *n.* Masochist, *der*/Masochistin, *die*

masochistic /mæsəˈkɪstɪk/ *adj.* masochistisch

mason /ˈmeɪsn/ *n.* **1** (builder) ▸❶ **p. 1260** Baumeister, *der*; Steinmetz, *der* **2** **M~** (Free~) [Frei]maurer, *der*

Masonic /məˈsɒnɪk/ *adj.* [frei]maurerisch; **~ lodge** [Frei]maurerloge, *die*

masonry /ˈmeɪsnrɪ/ *n.* **1** (stonework) Mauerwerk, *das*; (work of a mason) Steinmetzarbeit, *die* **2** **M~** (Free~) [Frei]maurertum, *das*

masque /mɑːsk/ *n.* Maskenspiel, *das*

masquerade /mæskəˈreɪd, mɑːskəˈreɪd/

A *n.* (lit. or fig.) Maskerade, *die*

B *v.i.* **~ as sb./sth.** sich als jmd./etw. ausgeben; vorgeben, jmd./etw. zu sein

mass¹ /mæs/ *n.* (Eccl., Mus.) Messe, *die*; *attrib.* Mess‹*buch, -gewand*›; **say/hear ~:** die Messe lesen/hören; **go to** *or* **attend ~:** zur Messe gehen; **high ~:** Hochamt, *das*; **low ~:** stille Messe; *see also* **black mass**

mass²

A *n.* **1** (solid body of matter) Brocken, *der*; (of dough, rubber) Klumpen, *der*; **a ~ of rock/stone** ein Felsbrocken/Steinblock **2** (dense aggregation of objects) Masse, *die*; **a tangled ~ of threads** ein wirres Knäuel von Fäden; **a ~ of curls** eine Fülle von Locken; **a confused ~ of ideas** ein Wust von Ideen **3** (large number or amount of) **a ~ of ...:** eine Unmenge von ...; **a ~ of people** eine große Menschenmenge; **~es of ...:** massenhaft ... (ugs.); eine Masse ... (ugs.) **4** (unbroken expanse) **a ~ of blossom/colour/red** ein Blütenmeer/Farbenmeer/Meer von Rot; **be a ~ of bruises/mistakes/inhibitions** (coll.) voll blauer Flecken sein/von Fehlern nur so wimmeln/nur aus Hemmungen bestehen **5** (main portion) Masse, *die*; **the [great] ~ of people/voters** die Masse des Volkes/der Wähler; **the ~es** die breite Masse; die Massen; **in the ~:** als Ganzes **6** (Phys.) Masse, *die*; **centre of ~:** Massenmittelpunkt, *der* **7** (bulk) massige Form; **the huge ~ of the pyramid** die riesige Größe der Pyramide **8** *attrib.* (for many people) Massen-

B *v.t.* **1** anhäufen; **~ed bands** mehrere gleichzeitig spielende Kapellen **2** (Mil.) massieren, zusammenziehen ‹*Truppen*›

C *v.i.* sich ansammeln; ‹*Truppen:*› sich massieren, sich zusammenziehen; ‹*Wolken:*› sich zusammenziehen

massacre /ˈmæsəkə(r)/

A *n.* **1** (slaughter) Massaker, *das*; **make a ~ of ...:** ein Massaker anrichten unter (+ *Dat.*) ... **2** (coll.: defeat) völlige Zerstörung

B *v.t.* **1** (slaughter) massakrieren **2** (coll.: defeat heavily) massakrieren (ugs., meist scherzh.)

massage /ˈmæsɑːʒ/

A *n.* Massage, *die*; **give sb./sb.'s back a ~:** jmdn./jmds. Rücken massieren; **~ parlour** (often euphem.) Massagesalon, *der*

B *v.t.* massieren

mass communiˈcations *n. pl.* Massenkommunikation, *die*

masseur /mæˈsɜː(r)/ *n.* ▸❶ **p. 1260** Masseur, *der*

masseuse /mæˈsɜːz/ *n.* ▸❶ **p. 1260** *fem.* Masseurin, *die*; Masseuse, *die* (oft verhüll.)

mass: ~ ˈgrave *n.* Massengrab, *das*; **~ hyˈsteria** *n.* Massenhysterie, *die*

massif /mæˈsiːf/ *n.* (Geog.) Massiv, *das*

massive /ˈmæsɪv/ *adj.* (lit. or fig.) massiv; wuchtig ‹*Statur, Stirn*›; kräftig ‹*Augenbrauen, Gesicht*›; gewaltig ‹*Ausmaße, Aufgabe*›; enorm ‹*Schulden, Vermögen*›; **be [conceived] on a ~ scale** groß angelegt sein; **receive aid on a ~ scale** massive Unterstützung erhalten

massively /ˈmæsɪvlɪ/ *adv.* (lit. or fig.) massiv

mass: ~ ˈmarket *n.* Massenmarkt, *der*; **~-ˈmarket** *attrib. adj.* für den Massenmarkt *nachgestellt*; **~ ˈmedia** *n. pl.* Massenmedien *Pl.*; **~ ˈmeeting** *n.* Massenversammlung, *die*; (Pol.) Massenkundgebung, *die*; (Industry) Belegschaftsversammlung, *die*; **~ ˈmurder** *n.* Massenmord, *der*; **~ ˈmurderer** *n.* Massenmörder, *der*/-mörderin, *die* **~ noun** *n.* nicht zählbares Substantiv; **~-proˈduced** *adj.* in Massenproduktion hergestellt; Massen‹*artikel*›; **~-proˈducer** *n.* Massenproduzent, *der*; **~ proˈduction** *n.* Massenproduktion, *die*

mast¹ /mɑːst/ *n.* (for sail, flag, aerial, etc.) Mast, *der*; **work** *or* **serve** *or* **sail before the ~:** als Matrose dienen; **[mooring] ~:** Ankermast, *der*; *see also* **colour A 10**; **half mast**

mast² *n.* (for fodder) Mast, *die*

mastectomy /mæˈstektəmɪ/ *n.* (Med.) Mastektomie, *die* (fachspr.); Brustamputation, *die*

-masted /mɑːstɪd/ *adj. in comb.* (Naut.) -mastig; **two-~:** zweimastig

master /ˈmɑːstə(r)/

A *n.* **1** Herr, *der*; **be ~ of sth./oneself** Herr über etw. (*Akk.*)/sich selbst sein; **be ~ of the situation/[the] ~ of one's fate** Herr der Lage/seines Schicksals sein; **be one's own ~:** sein eigener Herr sein; **make oneself ~ of sth.** sich zum Herrn über etw. (*Akk.*) machen **2** (of animal, slave) Halter, *der*; (of dog) Herrchen, *das*; (Hunting) Master, *der*; (of ship) Kapitän, *der*; (of college) Rektor, *der*; (of livery company, masonic lodge) Meister, *der*; **~ of the house** Hausherr, *der*; **be ~ in one's own house** Herr im eigenen Hause sein; **~'s certificate** *or* **ticket** (Naut.) Kapitänspatent, *das*; *see also* **mariner** **3** ▸❶ **p. 1260** (Sch.: teacher) Lehrer, *der*; **French ~:** Französischlehrer, *der* **4** **find** *or* **meet [in sb.] one's ~:** [in jmdm.] seinen Meister finden **5** (employer) Herr, *der* **6** *in titles* ‹*Hofkapell-, Schatz-, Ritt-, Waffen- usw.*›meister, *der*; **M~ of Ceremonies** Zeremonienmeister, *der*; (for variety programme etc.) Conférencier, *der*; **M~ of the Rolls** (Brit. Law) Präsident des Berufungsgerichts **7** (original of document, film, etc.) Original, *das* **8** (expert, great artist) Meister, *der* (**at** in + *Dat.*); **be a ~ of sth.** etw. meisterhaft beherrschen; *see also* **grand master**; **old master**; **past master** **9** (skilled workman) **~ craftsman/carpenter** Handwerks-/Tischlermeister, *der* **10** (Univ.: postgraduate degree) ≈ Magister, *der*; **~ of Arts/Science** ≈ Magister Artium/rerum naturalium; **he got his ~'s degree in 1971** ≈ er hat 1971 den *od.* seinen Magister gemacht **11** (boy's title) ≈ junger Herr (veralt.); **M~ Theo/Richard** *etc.* Master Theo/Richard *usw.*

B *adj.* **1** (commanding) **the ~ race** die Herrenrasse; **~ card** Leitkarte, *die* (DV) **2** (principal) Haupt‹*strategie, -liste*›; **~ bedroom** großes Schlafzimmer; ≈ Elternschlafzimmer, *das*; **~ tape/copy** Originalband, *das*/Original, *das*; **~ plan** Gesamtplan, *der*

C *v.t.* **1** (learn) erlernen; **have ~ed a language/subject/instrument** eine Sprache/ein Fach/ein Instrument beherrschen **2** (overcome) meistern ‹*Probleme usw.*›; besiegen ‹*Feind*›; beherrschen ‹*Natur*›; zügeln ‹*Emotionen, Gefühle*›

-master *n. in comb.* (Naut.) -master, *der*; **two-~:** Zweimaster, *der*

ˈmaster class *n.* (Mus. etc.) Meisterklasse, *die*

masterful /ˈmɑːstəfl/ *adj.* **1** (imperious) herrisch ‹*Haltung, Ton, Person*› **2** (masterly) meisterhaft ‹*Beherrschung, Fähigkeit*›

masterfully /ˈmɑːstəfəlɪ/ *adv.* ▸**masterful**: herrisch; meisterhaft

master: ~ hand *n.* (person) Meister, *der* (**at** im + *Dat.*); **~ key** *n.* General- *od.* Hauptschlüssel, *der*; (fig.) Schlüssel, *der*

masterly /ˈmɑːstəlɪ/ *adj.* meisterhaft

master: ~mind **A** *n.* führender Kopf; **B** *v.t.* **~mind the plot/conspiracy** *etc.* der Kopf des Komplotts/der Verschwörung *usw.* sein; **~piece** *n.* (work of art) Meisterwerk, *das*; (production showing masterly skill) Meisterstück, *das*; **a ~piece of tact/irony** ein Meisterstück an Takt/Ironie *od.* des Taktes/der Ironie; **~singer** *n.* (Hist.) Meistersinger, *der*; **~ spy** *n.* Agentenführer, *der*/-führerin, *die*; **~ stroke** *n.* Geniestreich, *der*; **be a ~ stroke** genial sein; **~ switch** *n.* Hauptschalter, *der*; **~work** ▸**~piece**

mastery /ˈmɑːstərɪ/ *n.* **1** (skill) Meisterschaft, *die* **2** (knowledge) Beherrschung, *die* (**of** *Gen.*) **3** (upper hand) Oberhand, *die*; **gain ~ over sb.** die Oberhand über jmdn. gewinnen **4** (control) Herrschaft, *die* (**of** über + *Akk.*)

ˈmasthead *n.* **1** (Naut.) [Mast]topp, *der* **2** (Journ.) Impressum, *das*; (title) Titel, *der*

mastic /ˈmæstɪk/ *n.* **1** (gum, resin, asphalt) Mastix, *der* **2** (cement) Mastik, *der*

masticate /ˈmæstɪkeɪt/ *v.t.* zerkauen

mastication /mæstɪˈkeɪʃn/ *n.* Zerkauen, *das*

mastiff /ˈmæstɪf/ *n.* (Zool.) Mastiff, *der*

mastitis /mæsˈtaɪtɪs/ *n.* ▸❶ **p. 1231** (Med.) Mastitis, *die*

mastodon /ˈmæstədɒn/ *n.* (Zool., Palaeont.) Mastodon, *das*

mastoid /ˈmæstɔɪd/ *n.* (Anat.) Mastoid, *das*

masturbate /ˈmæstəbeɪt/ *v.i. & t.* masturbieren

masturbation /mæstəˈbeɪʃn/ *n.* Masturbation, *die*

mat¹ /mæt/

A *n.* **1** (on floor, Sport) Matte, *die*; **pull the ~ from under sb.'s feet** (fig.) jmdm. den Boden unter den Füßen wegziehen; **be on the ~** (coll.: be in trouble) zusammengestaucht werden (ugs.) **2** (to protect table etc.) Untersetzer, *der*; (as decorative support) Deckchen, *das* **3** (tangled mess) (of hair) Wust, *der* (ugs.); (of weeds, foliage) Gewirr, *das*

B *v.t.*, **-tt-** **1** (furnish with mats) mit Matten belegen ‹*Boden*›; mit Matten auslegen ‹*Zimmer*› **2** *usu. in p.p.* (entangle) verflechten ‹*Äste, Unkraut*›; verfilzen ‹*Haar*›; **~ted** verflochten; verfilzt

C *v.i.*, **-tt-** ‹*Äste, Unkraut usw.:*› sich [ineinander] verflechten; ‹*Haare, Wolle:*› verfilzen

mat² ▸**matt**

matador /ˈmætədɔː(r)/ *n.* Matador, *der*

match¹ /mætʃ/

A *n.* **1** (equal) Ebenbürtige, *der*/*die*; **be a/no ~ for sb.** es mit jmdm. aufnehmen/nicht aufnehmen [können]; sich mit jmdm. messen/nicht messen können; **she is more than a ~**

m

for him sie ist ihm mehr als gewachsen; **find** *or* **meet one's ~:** einen ebenbürtigen Gegner finden; (be defeated) seinen Meister finden [2] (sb./sth. similar or appropriate) **be a [good** *etc.***] ~ for sth.** [gut *usw.*] zu etw. passen; **the colours are a poor ~:** die Farben passen schlecht zueinander *od.* zusammen; **find a ~ for this paint** genau die gleiche Farbe finden [3] (Sport) Spiel, *das;* (Football, Tennis, etc. also) Match, *das;* (Boxing) Kampf, *der;* (Athletics) Wettkampf, *der* [4] (marriage) Heirat, *die;* (marriage partner) Partie, *die;* **make a ~:** sich verheiraten; **make a good ~:** eine gute Partie machen

B *v.t.* [1] (equal) **~ sb. at chess/in shooting/in argument/in originality** es mit jmdm. im Schach/Schießen/Argumentieren/an Originalität (*Dat.*) aufnehmen [können]; **can you ~ that for impudence?** das ist eine Unverschämtheit ohnegleichen!; **~ that if you can!** das mach [mir] erst mal einer nach! [2] (pit) **~ sb. with** *or* **against sb.** jmdn. jmdm. gegenüberstellen; **be ~ed against sb.** gegen jmdn. antreten; **~ one's skill/strength against sb.** sein Können/seine Kräfte mit jmdm. messen [3] **be well ~ed** ‹*Mann u. Frau:*› gut zusammenpassen; ‹*Spieler, Mannschaften:*› sich (*Dat.*) ebenbürtig sein; **they are a well ~ed couple/pair** die beiden passen gut zusammen [4] (harmonize with) passen zu; **a handbag and ~ing shoes** eine Handtasche und [dazu] passende Schuhe; **~ each other exactly** genau zueinander passen; **form a ~ing pair** [als Paar] gut zueinander passen [5] (find matching material etc. for) **~ sth. with sth.** etw. auf etw. abstimmen; **~ people with jobs** geeignete Personen für die Stellen finden

C *v.i.* (correspond) zusammenpassen; **with a scarf** *etc.* **to ~:** mit [dazu] passendem Schal *usw.*

Phrasal verb

• **~ 'up**

A *v.i.* [1] (correspond) zusammenpassen [2] (be equal) **~ up to sth.** einer Sache (*Dat.*) entsprechen; **~ up to the situation** der Situation gewachsen sein

B *v.t.* aufeinander abstimmen ‹*Farben usw.*›; passend zusammenfügen ‹*Teile, Hälften*›; **~ up one colour with another** eine Farbe auf eine andere abstimmen

match² *n.* (for lighting) Streichholz, *das;* Zündholz, *das* (südd., österr.)

match: ~box *n.* Streichholzschachtel, *die;* **~-fit** *adj.* (Sport) spielfähig

matchless /ˈmætʃlɪs/ *adj.* unvergleichlich; beispiellos

match: ~maker *n.* Ehestifter, *der*/Ehestifterin, *die;* **~making** *n.* Ehestiftung, *die;* **~ point** *n.* (Tennis etc.) Matchball, *der;* **~stick** *n.* [1] Streichholz, *das;* Zündholz, *das* (südd., österr.); [2] **~stick man** ▸ **stick figure;** **~wood** *n.* **make ~wood of sth., smash sth. to ~wood** Kleinholz aus etw. machen; **the storm had made ~wood of the boat** der Sturm hatte das Boot zertrümmert

mate¹ /meɪt/

A *n.* [1] Kumpel, *der* (ugs.); (friend also) Kamerad, *der*/Kameradin, *die;* (workmate also) [Arbeits]kollege, *der*/-kollegin, *die* [2] (coll.: as form of address) Kumpel, *der* (ugs.); **look** *or* **listen, ~, ...:** jetzt hör [mir] mal gut zu, Freundchen, ... [3] (Naut.: officer on merchant ship) ≈ Kapitänleutnant, *der;* **chief** *or* **first/second ~:** Erster/Zweiter Offizier [4] (workman's assistant) Gehilfe, *der* [5] (spouse) Lebensgefährte, *der*/-gefährtin, *die* (geh.) [6] (Zool.) (male) Männchen, *das;* (female) Weibchen, *das*

B *v.i.* [1] (for breeding) sich paaren [2] (Mech.: fit well) **~ with sth.** [genau] auf/in etw. (*Akk.*) passen

C *v.t.* paaren ‹*Tiere*›; **~ a mare and** *or* **with a stallion** eine Stute von einem Hengst decken lassen

mate² (Chess) ▸ **checkmate A, C**

material /məˈtɪərɪəl/

A *adj.* [1] (physical, tangible, bodily) materiell [2] (not spiritual) materiell (oft abwertend) ‹*Mensch, Einstellung, Lebensführung*› [3] (relevant, important) wesentlich; **be not ~ to sth.** für etw. nicht relevant sein

B *n.* [1] (matter from which thing is made) Material, *das;* **cost of ~s** Materialkosten *Pl.;* *see also* **raw material** [2] *in sing. or pl.* (elements) Material, *das;* (for novel, sermon also) Stoff, *der* [3] (cloth) Stoff, *der* [4] *in pl.* **building/writing ~s** Bau-/Schreibmaterial, *das;* **cleaning ~s** Reinigungsmaterial, *das;* **reading ~:** Lesestoff, *der* [5] **be leadership/university/officer** *etc.* **~:** das Zeug für einen Führungsposten/zum Hochschulstudium/zum Offizier *usw.* haben

materialise ▸ **materialize**

materialism /məˈtɪərɪəlɪzm/ *n., no pl.* Materialismus, *der*

materialist /məˈtɪərɪəlɪst/ *n.* Materialist, *der*/Materialistin, *die; attrib.* materialistisch ‹*Philosophie*›

materialistic /mətɪərɪəˈlɪstɪk/ *adj.* materialistisch

materialize /məˈtɪərɪəlaɪz/ *v.i.* [1] ‹*Hoffnung:*› sich erfüllen; ‹*Plan, Idee:*› sich verwirklichen; ‹*Treffen, Versammlung:*› zustande kommen; **he promised help/money, but it never ~d** aus seiner versprochenen Hilfe/seinem versprochenen Geld wurde nichts; **this idea will never ~:** aus dieser Idee wird nie etwas; **problems kept materializing** dauernd traten Probleme auf [2] (come into view, appear) [plötzlich] auftauchen; (coll.) ‹*Person:*› sich blicken lassen (ugs.), kommen

materially /məˈtɪərɪəlɪ/ *adv.* [1] (considerably) wesentlich [2] (in respect of material interests) materiell

materiel /mətɪərɪˈel/ *n.* Ausrüstung, *die*

maternal /məˈtɜːnl/ *adj.* [1] (motherly) mütterlich ‹*Liebe, Sorge, Typ*›; Mutter‹*instinkt*› [2] (related) ‹*Großeltern, Onkel, Tante*› mütterlicherseits

maternity /məˈtɜːnɪtɪ/ *n.* (motherhood) Mutterschaft, *die*

maternity: ~ allowance *n.* Mutterschaftshilfe, *die;* **~ benefit** *n.* Mutterschaftsgeld, *das;* **~ dress** *n.* Umstandskleid, *das;* **~ home, ~ hospital** *ns.* Entbindungsheim, *das;* **~ leave** *n.* Mutterschaftsurlaub, *der;* **~ nurse** *n.* Hebamme, *die;* **~ pay** *n.* Mutterschaftsgeld, *das;* **~ unit, ~ ward** *ns.* Entbindungsstation, *die;* **~ wear** *n.* Umstandskleidung, *die*

matey /ˈmeɪtɪ/ (Brit. coll.)

A *adj.*, **matier** /ˈmeɪtɪə(r)/, **matiest** /ˈmeɪtɪɪst/ kameradschaftlich ‹*Typ, Atmosphäre*›; **be/get ~ with sb.** mit jmdm. vertraulich sein/werden

B *n.* Kumpel, *der* (ugs.); **watch it, ~!** pass bloß auf, Freundchen!

math /mæθ/ (Amer. coll.) ▸ **maths**

mathematical /mæθɪˈmætɪkl/ *adj.* [1] mathematisch [2] (precise) mathematisch ‹*Genauigkeit, Exaktheit, Bestimmtheit*›; mathematisch genau ‹*Beweis*›

mathematically /mæθɪˈmætɪkəlɪ/ *adv.* mathematisch; **prove sth. ~:** etw. mathematisch genau beweisen

mathematician /mæθɪməˈtɪʃn/ *n.* ▸ **i** **p. 1260** Mathematiker, *der*/Mathematikerin, *die*

mathematics /mæθɪˈmætɪks/ *n., no pl.* [1] (subject) Mathematik, *die;* **pure/applied ~:** reine/angewandte Mathematik [2] *constr. as pl.* (application) **the ~ of this problem are complicated** diese Aufgabe ist mathematisch kompliziert; **your ~ are good** du bist gut in Mathematik

maths /mæθs/ *n.* (Brit. coll.) Mathe, *die* (Schülerspr.)

matinée (*Amer.:* **matinee**) /ˈmætɪneɪ/ *n.* Matinee, *die;* Frühvorstellung, *die;* (in the afternoon) Nachmittagsvorstellung, *die*

mating /ˈmeɪtɪŋ/: **~ call, ~ cry** *ns.* Paarungsruf, *der;* **~ season** *n.* Paarungszeit, *die*

matins /ˈmætɪnz/ *n., constr. as sing. or pl.* [1] (RC Ch.) Matutin, *die* [2] (Anglican Ch.) Früh- *od.* Morgenandacht, *die*

matriarch /ˈmeɪtrɪɑːk/ *n.* Matriarchin, *die*

matriarchal /meɪtrɪˈɑːkl/ *adj.* matriarchalisch

matriarchy /ˈmeɪtrɪɑːkɪ/ *n.* Matriarchat, *das*

matrices *pl. of* **matrix**

matricide /ˈmætrɪsaɪd/ *n.* [1] (murder) Muttermord, *der* [2] (murderer) Muttermörder, *der*/-mörderin, *die*

matriculate /məˈtrɪkjʊleɪt/ (Univ.)

A *v.t.* immatrikulieren (**in** an + *Dat.*)

B *v.i.* sich immatrikulieren

matriculation /mətrɪkjʊˈleɪʃn/ *n.* (Univ.) Immatrikulation, *die*

matrimonial /mætrɪˈməʊnɪəl/ *adj.* Ehe-

matrimony /ˈmætrɪmənɪ/ *n.* [1] (rite of marriage) Eheschließung, *die;* **sacrament of ~:** Ehesakrament, *das* [2] (married state) Ehestand, *der;* **enter into [holy] ~:** in den [heiligen] Stand der Ehe treten (geh.)

matrix /ˈmeɪtrɪks, ˈmætrɪks/ *n., pl.* **matrices** /ˈmeɪtrɪsiːz, ˈmætrɪsiːz/ *or* **~es** [1] (Geol., Math.) Matrix, *die* [2] (mould) Matrize, *die*

matron /ˈmeɪtrən/ *n.* [1] ▸ **i** **p. 1260** (in school) ≈ Hausmutter, *die;* (in hospital) Oberin, *die;* Oberschwester, *die* [2] (arch./literary: married woman) Matrone, *die;* **~ of honour** (verheiratete) Brautführerin

matronly /ˈmeɪtrənlɪ/ *adj.* matronenhaft (meist abwertend)

matt /mæt/ *adj.* matt; **have a ~ finish** ‹*Fotografie:*› auf mattem Papier abgezogen sein

matter /ˈmætə(r)/

A *n.* [1] (affair) Angelegenheit, *die;* **~s** die Dinge; **business ~s** geschäftliche Angelegenheiten *od.* Dinge; **money ~s** Geldangelegenheiten *od.* -fragen; **~s of state** Staatsangelegenheiten; **raise an important ~:** einen wichtigen Punkt ansprechen; **police investigation into the ~:** polizeiliche Ermittlung in dieser Sache; **it's only a minor** *or* **it's no great ~:** es ist nicht wichtig; **that's another** *or* **a different ~ altogether** *or* **quite another ~:** das ist etwas ganz anderes; **it will only make ~s worse** das macht die Sache nur schlimmer; **and to make ~s worse ...:** und was die Sache noch schlimmer macht/machte, ...

[2] (cause, occasion) **a/no ~ for** *or* **of ...:** ein/kein Grund *od.* Anlass zu ...; **it's a ~ of complete indifference to me** es ist mir völlig gleichgültig

[3] (topic) Thema, *das;* Gegenstand, *der;* **~ on the agenda** Punkt der Tagesordnung; **it's a ~ for the committee [to decide]** das muss der [zuständige] Ausschuss entscheiden

[4] **a ~ of ...** (something that amounts to) eine Frage (+ *Gen.*) ...; eine Sache von ...; **it's a ~ of taste/habit** das ist Geschmacks-/Gewohnheitssache; **it's a ~ of common knowledge** es ist allgemein bekannt; **it's a ~ of policy with us** das ist für uns eine Grundsatzfrage; **a ~ of how fast I can type** eine Frage, wie schnell ich tippen kann; **[only] a ~ of time** [nur noch] eine Frage der Zeit; **it's a ~ of repairing the switch** der Schalter muss repariert werden; **it's just a ~ of working harder** man muss sich ganz einfach [bei der Arbeit] mehr anstrengen; **it's a ~ of a couple of hours** es wird ein paar Stunden dauern; das ist eine Sache von ein paar Stunden; **in a ~ of minutes** in wenigen Minuten; **it's only a ~ of seconds** das ist eine Sache von Sekunden; **a [plain] ~ of fact** eine [schlichte] Tatsache; **That's odd! As a ~ of fact, I was just thinking the same** Das ist komisch! Ich habe nämlich gerade dasselbe gedacht; **Do you know him? — Yes, as a ~ of fact, I do/I know him quite well** Kennst du ihn? — Ja, und ob [ich ihn kenne]/und sogar recht gut; **no, as a ~ of fact, you're wrong** nein, da irrst du dich aber; **~ of fact** (Law) Tatfrage, *die;* **~ of law** Rechtsfrage, *die; see also* **course A 2; form A 8**

[5] **what's the ~?** was ist [los]?; **is something the ~?** stimmt irgendetwas nicht?; ist [irgend-]was (ugs.)?; **there's nothing the ~:** gar nichts ist los; **there must be something the ~:** irgendetwas stimmt da nicht; **What's the ~ with you? — There's nothing the ~ with me** Was hast du *od.* ist [los] mit dir? — Gar nichts [ist los mit mir]; **there's nothing the ~ with him really, he's just pretending** es fehlt ihm eigentlich gar nichts, er tut nur so

[6] **for that ~:** eigentlich; **... and for that ~ so am/do I** ... und ich eigentlich auch

[7] **no ~!** [das] macht nichts!; **no ~ how/who/**

m

ℹ May/might

Possibility

Where *may* simply means *can*, **können** is used in German:

These flowers may be grown in any soil
= Diese Blumen kann man in jeder Art Erde pflanzen

But where *may* in English is used to express degrees of possibility and uncertainty, there are a number of possible translations in German:

She may come (*it's possible*)
= Es kann sein *or* Es ist möglich, dass sie kommt

***She may come* (*and on the other hand she may not*)**
= Vielleicht kommt sie (und vielleicht auch nicht)

She may* or *might come (*a more distant possibility*)
= Sie könnte kommen

She may* (*well*) *come (= *there's a good possibility*)
= Es kann schon sein *or* Es ist schon möglich, dass sie kommt

She may yet come
= Sie kann immerhin noch kommen; Es ist immerhin möglich, dass sie noch kommt

With *may have*, the perfect tense is applied to the verb governed and not to the translation of *may:*

I may have seen him
= Es kann sein *or* Es ist möglich, dass ich ihn gesehen habe

The train may have been late
= Vielleicht hat der Zug Verspätung gehabt

***I might have said it* (*but I don't remember*)**
= Es könnte sein, dass ich es gesagt habe (aber ich weiß es nicht mehr)

She might have come if she had known
= Sie wäre vielleicht gekommen, wenn sie es gewusst hätte

However, where *might* is **könnte,** *might have* is **hätte ... können:**

***It might have been worse* (= *could have been*)**
= Es hätte schlimmer sein können

You might have told me
= Du hättest es mir doch sagen können

Permission

This can always be translated by **dürfen:**

May I have the next dance?
= Darf ich [um den nächsten Tanz] bitten?

You may not smoke
= Sie dürfen nicht rauchen

***Dear Bertie* (*if I may*)**
= Lieber Bertie (wenn ich dich so nennen darf)

---

what/why *etc.* ganz gleich *od.* egal (ugs.), wie/wer/was/warum *usw.*; **no ~ how hard he tried** sosehr er sich auch bemühte
8 **in the ~ of sth.** was etw. (*Akk.*) anbelangt; **in the ~ of A versus B** (Law) in Sachen *od.* in der Sache A gegen B
9 (material, as opposed to mind, spirit, etc.) Materie, *die;* **[in]organic/solid/vegetable ~:** [an]organische/feste/pflanzliche Stoffe; **the triumph of mind over ~:** der Sieg des Geistes über die Materie
10 (Physiol.) Substanz, *die;* (pus) Eiter, *der;* **faecal ~:** Fäzes *Pl.*; *see also* **grey matter**
11 *no pl., no indef. art.* (written or printed material) **reading ~:** Lesestoff, *der;* **advertising ~:** Reklame, *die*
12 (material for thought etc.) Material, *das*
13 (content) Inhalt, *der*
B *v.i.* etwas ausmachen; **what does it ~?** was macht das schon?; was machts? (ugs.); **what ~s is that ...:** worum es geht, ist ...; **not ~ a damn** vollkommen egal sein; **[it] doesn't ~:** [das] macht nichts (ugs.); **it ~s a great deal** es macht eine ganze Menge aus; **it doesn't ~ how/when** *etc.* es ist einerlei, wie/wann *usw.*; **does it ~ to you if ...?** macht es dir etwas aus, wenn ...?; **it doesn't ~ at all to me** es ist mir völlig einerlei; **some things ~ rather more than others** manche Dinge sind eben wichtiger als andere; **that's all that ~s** das ist die Hauptsache; **the things which ~ in life** [das,] worauf es im Leben ankommt; **she knows the people who really ~:** sie kennt die Leute, die wirklich etwas gelten

'matter-of-fact *adj.* sachlich; nüchtern

matter-of-'factly /mætərəv'fæktlɪ/ *adv.* sachlich; nüchtern

Matthew /'mæθjuː/ *pr. n.* **St ~:** der hl. Matthäus *od.* (ökumen.) Mattäus

matting /'mætɪŋ/ *n.* (fabric) **coconut/straw/reed ~:** Kokos-/Stroh-/Schilf- *od.* Rohrgeflecht, *das;* (as floor covering) Kokos-/Stroh-/Schilfmatten *Pl.*; **a piece of ~:** ein Stück Matte

mattock /'mætək/ *n.* (Agric.) Breithacke, *die*

mattress /'mætrɪs/ *n.* Matratze, *die; see also* **spring mattress**

maturation /mætjʊ'reɪʃn/ *n.* 1 (maturing) Reifung, *die* 2 (of fruit) [Heran]reifen, *das*

mature /mə'tjʊə(r)/
A *adj.*, **~r** /mə'tjʊərə(r)/, **~st** /mə'tjʊərɪst/ 1 reif; ausgereift ‹*Plan, Methode, Stil, Käse, Portwein, Sherry*›; durchgegoren ‹*Wein*›; ausgewachsen ‹*Pflanze, Tier*›; voll entwickelt ‹*Zellen*›; **~ student** Spätstudierende, *der/die;* **a man of ~ years** ein Mann im reiferen Alter *od.* in reiferen Jahren 2 (Finance) fällig ‹*Rechnung, Schuldschein usw.*›
B *v.t.* reifen lassen ‹*Frucht, Wein, Käse*›; reifer machen ‹*Personen*›; ausreifen lassen ‹*Plan*›; **port is ~d in oak casks** Portwein reift in Eichenfässern
C *v.i.* 1 ‹*Frucht, Wein, Käse usw.:*› reifen 2 ‹*Person:*› reifen, reifer werden 3 ‹*Rechnung, Police usw.:*› fällig werden

maturity /mə'tjʊərɪtɪ/ *n.* 1 Reife, *die;* **reach ~, come to ~** ‹*Person:*› erwachsen werden; ‹*Tier:*› ausgewachsen sein 2 (Finance) Fälligkeit, *die;* **come to ~:** fällig werden

maty ▸ **matey**

maudlin /'mɔːdlɪn/ *adj.* gefühlsselig

maul /mɔːl/
A *v.t.* 1 ‹*Tiger, Löwe, Bär usw.:*› Pranken-/Tatzenhiebe versetzen (+ *Dat.*); (fig.) malträtieren; verreißen ‹*Theaterstück, Buch*›; ‹*Boxer:*› losgehen auf (+ *Akk.*) ‹*Gegner*›; **he was ~ed by a lion** er wurde von einem Löwen angefallen 2 (fondle roughly) betatschen (ugs.)
B *n.* (Rugby) **[loose] ~:** offenes Gedränge

Maundy /'mɔːndɪ/ *n.* (Brit.) *Verteilung von Almosen am Gründonnerstag*

Maundy: ~ money *n.* (Brit.) *englische silberne Sondermünzen, die am Gründonnerstag als Almosen verteilt werden;* Maundy money, *das;* **~ 'Thursday** *n.* Gründonnerstag, *der*

Mauritania /mɒrɪ'teɪnɪə/ *pr. n.* Mauretanien (*das*)

Mauritian /mə'rɪʃn/ ▸ℹ **p. 1345**
A *adj.* mauritisch; **sb. is ~:** jmd. ist Mauritier/Mauritierin
B *n.* Mauritier, *der*/Mauritierin, *die*

Mauritius /mə'rɪʃəs/ *pr. n.* Mauritius (*das*)

mausoleum /mɔːsə'liːəm/ *n.* Mausoleum, *das*

mauve /məʊv/ *adj.* mauve

maverick /'mævərɪk/
A *n.* Einzelgänger, *der*/Einzelgängerin, *die;* (Amer.: politician) Alleingänger, *der*
B *adj.* einzelgängerisch

maw /mɔː/ *n.* 1 (stomach) Magen, *der;* (of ruminant) Labmagen, *der* 2 (jaws) Rachen, *der*

mawkish /'mɔːkɪʃ/ *adj.* (sentimental) rührselig

max. *abbr.* = **maximum** (*adj.*) max., (*n.*) Max.

maxi /'mæksɪ/ *n.* (coll.) (dress) Maxi, *das* (ugs.); (skirt) Maxi, *der* (ugs.)

maxi- *in comb.* Maxi‹*kleid, -mantel, -rock*›

maxim /'mæksɪm/ *n.* Maxime, *die*

maximal /'mæksɪml/ *adj.*, **maximally** /'mæksɪməlɪ/ *adv.* maximal

maximisation, maximise ▸ **maximiz-**

maximization /mæksɪmaɪ'zeɪʃn/ *n.* Maximierung, *die;* **~ of profit** Profitmaximierung, *die*

maximize /'mæksɪmaɪz/ *v.t.* maximieren

maximum /'mæksɪməm/
A *n., pl.* **maxima** /'mæksɪmə/ Maximum, *das;* **a ~ of happiness** ein Maximum *od.* Höchstmaß an Glück; **production is at a ~:** die Produktion befindet sich auf einem Höchststand
B *adj.* ▸ℹ **p. 1620** maximal; Maximal-; **~ security prison** Hochsicherheitsgefängnis, *das;* **~ temperatures today around 20°** Höchsttemperaturen heute um 20°

'maximum-security *attrib. adj.* Hochsicherheits‹[*gefängnis*]*trakt*›

may *v. aux., only in pres.* **may,** *neg.* (coll.) **mayn't** /meɪnt/, *past* **might** /maɪt/, *neg.* (coll.) **mightn't** /'maɪtnt/ ▸ℹ **p. 1315** 1 *expr. possibility* können; **it ~ be true** das kann stimmen; **it ~ or ~ not be true** vielleicht stimmts, vielleicht auch nicht; **I ~ be wrong** vielleicht irre ich mich; **they ~ be related** es kann sein, dass sie verwandt sind; vielleicht sind sie verwandt; **it ~ not be possible** das wird vielleicht nicht möglich sein; **he ~ have missed his train** vielleicht hat er seinen Zug verpasst; **he ~ have finished already** vielleicht ist er schon fertig; **it ~** *or* **might be true, though I doubt it** das kann schon *od.* könnte stimmen, obwohl ich es bezweifle; **it ~** *or* **might rain** es könnte regnen; **he might come round later** vielleicht kommt er später noch vorbei; **they might decide to stay** womöglich beschließen sie zu bleiben; **he might have been right** vielleicht hat er [ja] Recht gehabt; er könnte Recht gehabt haben; **he might have agreed if ...:** vielleicht hätte er zugestimmt, wenn ...; **it's not so bad as it might have been** es hätte schlimmer kommen können; **that ~ well be** das ist durchaus möglich; das kann durchaus sein; **it ~** *or* **might well be true** das kann *od.* könnte durchaus stimmen; **it ~** *or* **might well turn out to be quite easy** es ist durchaus möglich, dass es sich als recht einfach herausstellt; **you ~ well say so** das kann man wohl sagen; **as well he ~/might** wozu er [auch] allen Grund hat/hatte; **we ~** *or* **might as well go** wir könnten eigentlich ebenso gut [auch] gehen; (we are not achieving anything here) dann können wir ja gehen; **that is as '~ be** das kann *od.* mag schon sein; **be that as it ~:** wie dem auch sei
2 *expr. permission* dürfen; **you ~ go now** du kannst *od.* darfst jetzt gehen; **~ I ask why ...?** darf ich fragen, warum ...?; **if I ~ say so ...:** wenn ich das sagen darf, ...; **~** *or* **might I be permitted to ...?** (formal) gestatten Sie, dass ...?; **we ~ safely assert that ...:** wir dürfen wohl behaupten, dass ...; **~** *or* **might I ask** (iron.) ..., wenn ich [mal] fragen darf?
3 *expr. wish* mögen; **~ you be happy together!** ich hoffe, ihr werdet glücklich miteinander!; **~ the best man win!** auf dass der Beste gewinnt!; **~ God bless you** Gott segne dich
4 *expr. request* **you might help me with this** du könntest mir dabei helfen; **you might offer to help instead of ...:** du solltest lieber helfen, statt ...; **you might at least try [it]** du könntest es wenigstens versuchen; **you might have asked permission** du hättest um Erlaubnis fragen können
5 *used concessively* **he ~ be slow but he's accurate** mag *od.* kann sein, dass er langsam ist, aber dafür ist er auch genau

m

6 *in clauses* **so that I ~/might do sth.** damit ich etw. tun kann; **I hope he ~ succeed** ich hoffe, es gelingt ihm; **I wish it might happen** ich wünschte, es würde geschehen; **you never know what ~ happen** man weiß nie, was passieren kann; **come what ~, whatever ~ happen** geschehe was will; was auch geschieht; **whatever you ~ say ...:** ganz gleich, was du sagst ...
7 **who ~ you be?** wer bist du denn *od.* bist denn du?; **how old might she be?** wie alt mag sie *od.* wird sie wohl sein?

May /meɪ/ *n.* **1** ▸ⓘ **p. 1047** (month) Mai, *der; see also* **August**; **queen 1** **2** **may** (hawthorn) Weißdorn, *der*

maybe /ˈmeɪbiː, ˈmeɪbɪ/ *adv.* vielleicht

ˈMayday *n.* (distress signal) Mayday; **~ signal/call** Maydaysignal, *das*

ˈMay Day *n.* der Erste Mai; **~ celebrations/demonstrations** Maifeiern/-demonstrationen; **the ~ holiday** der Maifeiertag

ˈmayfly *n.* (Zool.) Eintagsfliege, *die*

mayhem /ˈmeɪhem/ *n.* **1** (confusion, chaos) Chaos, *das;* **there was ~:** es gab ein Chaos; **cause** *or* **create ~:** ein Chaos verursachen *od.* hervorrufen **2** (Brit. Hist./Amer.) schwere Körperverletzung

mayn't /meɪnt/ (coll.) = **may not;** ▸**may**

mayo /ˈmeɪəʊ/ *n.* (coll.) Mayo, *die* (ugs.); Majo, *die* (ugs.)

mayonnaise /meɪəˈneɪz/ *n.* Mayonnaise, *die;* **egg/fish ~:** Ei/Fisch in Mayonnaise

mayor /meə(r)/ *n.* ▸ⓘ **p. 1260**, ▸ⓘ **p. 1634** Bürgermeister, *der;* **Lord M~** (Brit.) Lord Mayor, *der;* ≈ Oberbürgermeister, *der;* **Lord Mayor's Show** (Brit.) *Festzug des Lord Mayor durch die City von London*

mayoral /ˈmeərl/ *adj.* des Bürgermeisters *nachgestellt*

mayoralty /ˈmeərltɪ/ *n.* (office) Amt des Bürgermeisters; (period of office) Amtszeit eines Bürgermeisters

mayoress /ˈmeərɪs/ *n.* ▸ⓘ **p. 1260**, ▸ⓘ **p. 1634** (woman mayor) Bürgermeisterin, *die;* (mayor's wife) [Ehe]frau des Bürgermeisters; **Lady M~** (Brit.) Oberbürgermeisterin, *die*/[Ehe]frau des Oberbürgermeisters

ˈmaypole *n.* Maibaum, *der*

ˈMay queen *n.* Maikönigin, *die*

maze /meɪz/ *n.* (lit. or fig.) Labyrinth, *das*

mazurka /məˈzɜːkə/ *n.* (Mus.) Mazurka, *die*

MB *abbr.* **1** (Computing) = **megabyte** MB **2** = **Bachelor of Medicine** ≈ zweites medizinisches Staatsexamen; *see also* **BSc**

MBA *abbr.* = **Master of Business Administration** *Diplom in Betriebswirtschaft; see also* **BSc**

MBE *abbr.* (Brit.) = **Member [of the Order] of the British Empire** Träger des Ordens des British Empire 5. Klasse

ˈm-business *n., no pl.* M-Business, *das;* M-Handel, *der*

Mbyte *abbr.* = **megabyte** Mbyte; MByte

MC *abbr.* **1** = **Master of Ceremonies** **2** (Brit.) = **Military Cross** *militärisches Verdienstkreuz*

MCC /emsɪːˈsɪː/ *n. britischer Kricketverband*

McCoy /məˈkɔɪ/ **the real ~** (coll.) der/die/das Echte; (not a fake or replica) das Original

ˈm-commerce *n., no pl.* ▸**m-business**

MCP *abbr.* (coll.) = **male chauvinist pig**

MD *abbr.* **1** = **Doctor of Medicine** Dr. med.; *see also* **BSc** **2** = **Managing Director** Ltd. Dir.

me¹ /mɪ, *stressed* miː/ *pron.* mich; *as indirect object* mir; **bigger than/as big as me** größer als/so groß wie ich; **silly me** ich Dussel! (salopp); **why me?** warum ich/mich/mir?; **who, me?** wer, ich?; **not me** ich/mich/mir nicht; **it's me** ich bins; **it isn't me** das bin ich nicht; **yes, me** ja, ich/mich/mir; **the real me** mein wahres Ich

me² /miː/ *n.* (Mus.) mi

ME *abbr.* (Med.) = **myalgic encephalomyelitis**

mead¹ /miːd/ *n.* (drink) Met, *der*

mead² *n.* (poet./arch.: meadow) Aue, *die*

meadow /ˈmedəʊ/ *n.* Wiese, *die;* **in the ~:** auf der Wiese

meadow: ~ grass *n.* [Wiesen]rispengras, *das;* **~ pipit** *n.* (Ornith.) Wiesenpieper, *der;* **~ ˈsaffron** *n.* (Bot.) Herbstzeitlose, *die;* **~sweet** *n.* (Brit. Bot.) Mädesüß, *das;* (Amer.) Weidenblättriger Spierstrauch

meager, meagerly, meagerness (Amer.) ▸**meagre** *etc.*

meagre /ˈmiːgə(r)/ *adj.* **1** spärlich; dürftig (auch fig.); mager ‹*Boden*›; **a ~ attendance** eine geringe Teilnehmerzahl **2** mager ‹*Gesicht, Mensch*›; hager ‹*Gestalt*›

meagrely /ˈmiːgəlɪ/ *adv.* spärlich; dürftig ‹*leben, sich ernähren, behandeln*›

meagreness /ˈmiːgənɪs/ *n., no pl.* Spärlichkeit, *die;* Dürftigkeit, *die*

meal¹ /miːl/ *n.* Mahlzeit, *die;* **stay for a ~:** zum Essen bleiben; **go out for a ~:** essen gehen; **have a [hot/cold/light] ~:** [warm/kalt/etwas Leichtes] essen; **enjoy your ~:** guten Appetit!; **did you enjoy your ~?** hat es Ihnen geschmeckt?; **~s on wheels** (Brit.) Essen auf Rädern; **make a ~ of sth.** etw. verzehren *od.* essen; (fig.) eine große Sache aus etw. machen

meal² *n.* **1** (ground grain) Schrot[mehl], *das* **2** (Scot.: oatmeal) Hafermehl, *das* **3** (Amer.: maize flour) Maismehl, *das*

mealies /ˈmiːlɪz/ *n. pl.* (S. Afr.) **1** (maize) Mais, *der* **2** (corn cob) Maiskolben, *der*

meal: ~ ticket *n.* Essenmarke, *die;* (fig. coll.) melkende Kuh (ugs.); **~time** *n.* Essenszeit, *die;* **at ~times** während des Essens; bei Tisch; **my usual ~time is ...:** ich esse gewöhnlich um ...

mealy /ˈmiːlɪ/ *adj.* mehlig ‹*Kartoffeln, Äpfel*›

mealy-mouthed /ˈmiːlɪmaʊðd/ *adj.* (derog.) unaufrichtig

mean¹ *adj.* **1** (niggardly) schäbig (abwertend); **you ~ old thing!** du alter Geizhals! (abwertend) **2** (ignoble) schäbig (abwertend), gemein ‹*Person, Verhalten, Gesinnung*›; (malicious) hinterhältig ‹*Blick*› **3** (unimpressive) schäbig (abwertend) ‹*Haus, Wohngegend*›; armselig ‹*Verhältnisse*›; **be no ~ athlete/feat** kein schlechter Sportler/keine schlechte Leistung sein **4** (coll.: ashamed) **feel ~ [about sth.]** sich [wegen etw.] schäbig vorkommen; **he made me feel ~:** ich kam mir ihm gegenüber richtig schäbig vor **5** (inferior) minder... ‹*Qualität*›; **this is clear to the ~est intelligence** das ist selbst dem Dümmsten klar **6** (Amer.: vicious) bösartig, heimtückisch ‹*Person, Tier*› **7** (Amer. coll.: unwell) **feel ~:** sich mies fühlen (ugs.) **8** (coll.: skilful) spitze (ugs.); klasse (ugs.); **blow a ~ trumpet** spitze *od.* klasse Trompete spielen

mean² *v.t.*, **meant** /ment/ **1** (have as one's purpose) beabsichtigen; **~ well** es gut meinen; **~ sb. well, ~ well by** *or* **to** *or* **towards sb.** es gut mit jmdm. meinen; **I ~t no harm** ich habs nicht böse gemeint; **I ~t him no harm** ich wollte ihm nichts Böses; **what do you ~ by [saying] that?** was willst du damit sagen?; **what do you ~ by entering without first knocking?** was fällt dir ein, einfach, ohne anzuklopfen, hereinzukommen? **I ~t it** *or* **it was ~t as a joke** das sollte ein Scherz sein; **~ to do sth.** etw. tun wollen; **I ~ to do it** ich bin fest dazu entschlossen; **I ~ to be obeyed** ich verlange, dass man mir gehorcht; **if he ~s to come ...:** wenn er [schon] unbedingt kommen will, ...; **I ~t to write, but forgot** ich hatte [fest] vor zu schreiben, aber habe es [dann] vergessen; **I only ~t to be helpful** ich wollte [doch] nur helfen; **I didn't ~ to be rude** ich wollte nicht unhöflich sein; **I never ~t to imply that** das habe ich niemals sagen wollen; **do you ~ to say that ...?** willst du damit sagen, dass ...?; *see also* **business 6** **2** (design, destine) **these plates are ~t to be used** diese Teller sind zum Gebrauch bestimmt *od.* sind da, um benutzt zu werden; **what's this gadget ~t to be?** welche Funktion hat dieses Gerät?; **I ~t it to be a surprise/as a surprise for him** es sollte eine Überraschung für ihn sein; ich wollte ihn damit überraschen; **you were never ~t for a diplomat** du bist eben nicht der geborene Diplomat; **they are ~t for each other** sie sind füreinander bestimmt; **I am ~t for greater things than this** ich bin zu Höherem bestimmt; **is this ~t for me?** soll das für mich sein?; **I ~t you to read the letter** ich wollte, dass du den Brief liest; **be ~t to do sth.** etw. tun sollen; **you are ~t to arrive on time** es wird erwartet, dass Sie pünktlich eintreffen *od.* sind; **you weren't ~t to say that** das hättest du nicht sagen sollen; **I am ~t to be giving a lecture** ich soll einen Vortrag halten; **are we ~t to go this way?** (permitted) dürfen wir hier langgehen?; **the Russians are ~t to be good at chess** die Russen sollen gut im Schach sein **3** (intend to convey, refer to) meinen; **I ~ [to say], ...:** ich meine ...; **if you know** *or* **see what I ~:** du verstehst, was ich meine?; **what do you ~ by that?** was hast du damit gemeint?; **what I ~ is, will you marry me?** ich meine, willst du mich heiraten?; **I really ~ it, I ~ what I say** ich meine das ernst; es ist mir Ernst damit; **I didn't ~ it literally** ich habe das nicht wörtlich gemeint **4** (signify, entail, matter) bedeuten; **the name ~s/the instructions ~ nothing to me** der Name sagt mir nichts/ich kann mit der Anleitung nichts anfangen; **this ~s serious problems for him** das wird ihn in ernste Schwierigkeiten bringen

mean³ /miːn/
A *n.* **1** Mittelweg, *der;* Mitte, *die;* **a happy ~:** der goldene Mittelweg; *see also* **golden mean** **2** (Math.) Mittelwert, *der*
B *adj.* (Math.) mittler...

meander /mɪˈændə(r)/
A *v.i.* **1** ‹*Fluss:*› sich schlängeln *od.* winden; mäandern (Geogr.) **2** ‹*Person:*› schlendern
B *n. in pl.* Windungen; (of river also) Mäander (Geogr.)

meanderings /mɪˈændərɪŋz/ *n. pl.* Windungen; (of stream also) Mäander (Geogr.)

meanie /ˈmiːnɪ/ *n.* (coll.) Geizhals, *der* (abwertend); Geizkragen, *der* (ugs. abwertend)

meaning /ˈmiːnɪŋ/
A *n.* Bedeutung, *die;* (of text etc., life) Sinn, *der;* **this sentence has no ~:** dieser Satz ergibt keinen Sinn; **if you get my ~:** du verstehst, was ich meine?; **I don't get your ~:** ich verstehe dich nicht; ich weiß nicht, was du meinst; **I mistook his ~:** ich habe ihn missverstanden; **what's the ~ of this?** was hat [denn] das zu bedeuten?; **you don't know the ~ of suffering/of the word** du weißt ja gar nicht, was Leiden bedeutet *od.* ist/was das bedeutet; **with ~:** bedeutungsvoll
B *adj.* bedeutungsvoll

meaningful /ˈmiːnɪŋfl/ *adj.* sinntragend ‹*Wort, Einheit*›; (fig.) bedeutungsvoll ‹*Blick, Ergebnis, Folgerung*›; sinnvoll ‹*Leben, Aufgabe, Arbeit, Gespräch*›

meaningfully /ˈmiːnɪŋfəlɪ/ *adv.* sinnvoll; bedeutungsvoll ‹*gucken*›; **this was an issue to which I could ~ contribute** das war ein Punkt, zu dem ich etwas Sinvolles beitragen konnte; **he spoke slowly and ~:** er sprach langsam und mit bedeutungsvoller Stimme

meaningless /ˈmiːnɪŋlɪs/ *adj.* ‹*Wort, Satz, Gespräch*› ohne Sinn; (fig.) sinnlos ‹*Aktivität, Leben, Leiden, Opfer, Verhalten*›

meanly /ˈmiːnlɪ/ *adv.* schäbig (abwertend) gemein ‹*sich verhalten, jmdn. behandeln*›; armselig, dürftig ‹*bekleidet, ausgestattet, ausgerüstet*›; **live ~:** in armseligen Verhältnissen leben

meanness /ˈmiːnnɪs/ *n., no pl.* **1** (stinginess) Schäbigkeit, *die* (abwertend) **2** (baseness) Schäbigkeit, *die* (abwertend); Gemeinheit, *die* **3** (shabbiness) ▸**mean² 3**: Schäbigkeit, *die;* Armseligkeit, *die*

means /miːnz/ *n. pl.* **1** *usu. constr. as sing.* (way, method) Möglichkeit, *die;* [Art und] Weise; **by this ~:** hierdurch; auf diese Weise; **by what ~?** wie? auf welche Weise?; **by some ~ or other** auf die eine oder andere Weise; irgendwie; **a ~ to an end** ein Mittel zum Zweck; **do the ends justify the ~?** heiligt der Zweck die Mittel?; **we have no ~ of doing this** wir haben keine Möglichkeit, dies zu tun; **he used poetry as a ~ of expressing his ideas** er benutzte Dichtung als Mittel, um seine Gedanken auszudrücken; **an easy ~ of escape** eine bequeme Fluchtmöglichkeit; **~ of transport** Transportmittel, *das;* **a ~ of communicating with sb.** eine Möglichkeit *od.* ein Weg, sich

m

mit jmdm. zu verständigen; **how this happened we have no ~ of telling/knowing** wie es passierte *od.* (geh.) geschah, können wir nicht sagen/wissen; *see also* **way A 3** **2** (resources) Mittel *Pl.*; **live within/beyond one's ~:** seinen Verhältnissen entsprechend-/über seine Verhältnisse leben; **he/she is a man/woman of ~:** er/sie ist vermögend **3** **Will you help me? — By all ~:** Hilfst du mir? — Selbstverständlich!; **May I go now? — By all ~:** Darf ich jetzt gehen? — Ja, gern *od.* sicher; **do so by all ~, but ...:** tu das ruhig, aber ...; **by no [manner of] ~, not by any [manner of] ~:** ganz und gar nicht; keineswegs; **by ~ of** durch; mit [Hilfe von]

means: ~ test *n.* Überprüfung der Bedürftigkeit; **~-test** *v.t.* jmds. Bedürftigkeit überprüfen; **~-tested benefits** nach Bedürftigkeit gestaffelte Unterstützungszahlungen

meant ▸ **mean**³

mean: ~time A *n.* **in the ~time** in der Zwischenzeit; inzwischen. **B** *adv.* inzwischen. **~while** *adv.* inzwischen

meany ▸ **meanie**

measles /'mi:zlz/ *n.*, *constr. as pl. or sing.* ▸ **i p. 1231** Masern *Pl.*; *see also* **German measles**

measly /'mi:zlɪ/ *adj.* (coll. derog.) pop[e]lig (ugs. abwertend); **a ~ little portion** eine mickrige Portion (ugs. abwertend)

measurable /'meʒərəbl/ *adj.* messbar ‹*Anzahl, Menge, Größe*›; (fig.) merklich ‹*Besserung, Veränderung, Fortschritte*›; **bring sb. within ~ distance of bankruptcy** jmdn. an den Rand des Bankrotts bringen

measurably /'meʒərəblɪ/ *adv.* merklich ‹*besser, größer*›

measure /'meʒə(r)/

A *n.* **1** ▸ **i p. 911**, ▸ **i p. 1702** Maß, *das*; **~ of length** Längenmaß, *das*; **weights and ~s** Maße und Gewichte; **for good ~:** sicherheitshalber; (as an extra) zusätzlich; **give short/full ~** (in public house) zu wenig/vorschriftsmäßig ausschenken; (in shop) zu wenig/vorschriftsmäßig abwiegen; **made to ~** *pred.* (Brit., lit. or fig.) maßgeschneidert **2** (degree) Menge, *die*; **in some ~:** in gewisser Hinsicht; **in large/full ~:** in hohem/vollem Maße; **a ~ of freedom/responsibility** ein gewisses Maß an Freiheit/Verantwortung (*Dat.*) **3** (instrument or utensil for measuring) Maß, *das*; (for quantity also) Messglas, *das*; Messbecher, *der*; (for size also) Messstab, *der*; Maßstab, *der* (selten); (fig.) Maßstab, *der*; **be a/the ~ of sth.** Maßstab für etw. sein; **it gave us some ~ of the problems** das gab uns eine Vorstellung *od.* einen Begriff von den Problemen; **beyond [all] ~:** grenzenlos; über die *od.* alle Maßen *adv.* **4** (Pros.) Versmaß, *das*; Metrum, *das* **5** (Mus.: time, bar) Takt, *der* **6** (step, law) Maßnahme, *die*; (Law: bill) Gesetzesvorlage, *die*; **take ~s to stop/ensure sth.** Maßnahmen ergreifen *od.* treffen, um etw. zu unterbinden/sicherzustellen; *see also* **half measure 2** **7** (Geol.) ▸ **coal measures**

B *v.t.* **1** messen ‹*Größe, Menge usw.*›; ausmessen ‹*Raum*›; **~ sb. for a suit** [bei] jmdm. Maß *od.* die Maße für einen Anzug nehmen **2** (fig.: estimate) abschätzen; **~ sb. by one's own standards** jmdn. an seinen eigenen Maßstäben messen **3** (mark off) **~ sth. [off]** etw. abmessen **4** (fig.: put in competition) messen (geh.); **~ oneself against sb.** sich mit jmdm. messen (geh.) **5** **~ one's length** (fig.) der Länge nach hinfallen

C *v.i.* **1** (have a given size) messen **2** (take measurement[s]) Maß nehmen

Phrasal verbs

- **~ 'out** *v.t.* abmessen
- **~ 'up to** *v.t.* entsprechen (+ *Dat.*) ‹*Maßstäben, Erwartungen*›; gewachsen sein (+ *Dat.*) ‹*Anforderungen*›

measured /'meʒəd/ *adj.* rhythmisch, gleichmäßig ‹*Geräusch, Bewegung*›; gemessen ‹*Schritt, Worte, Ausdrucksweise*›; **speak in ~ terms** sich gemessen ausdrücken

measureless /'meʒəlɪs/ *adj.* unermesslich

measurement /'meʒəmənt/ *n.* ▸ **i p. 911**, ▸ **i p. 1286** **1** (act, result) Messung, *die* **2** *in pl.* (dimensions) Maße *Pl.*; **take sb.'s ~s** [bei] jmdm. Maß *od.* die Maße nehmen

measuring /'meʒərɪŋ/: **~ jug** *n.* Messbecher, *der*; **~ tape** *n.* Bandmaß, *das*

meat /mi:t/ *n.* **1** Fleisch, *das* **2** **~ and drink** Speis und Trank (geh.); **one man's ~ is another man's poison** (prov.) was dem einen sin Uhl, ist dem andern sin Nachtigall (Spr.); **be ~ and drink to sb.** (fig.) genau das sein, was jmd. braucht **3** (fig.: chief part, essence) Substanz, *die*

meat: ~ axe *n.* Fleischbeil, *das*; Spalter, *der* (fachspr.); **~ball** *n.* Fleischkloß, *der*; Fleischklößchen, *das*; **~-fly** *n.* Fleischfliege, *die*; **~ grinder** (Amer.) ▸ **mincer**

meatless /'mi:tlɪs/ *adj.* fleischlos

meat: ~ loaf *n.* Hackbraten, *der*; **~ 'pie** *n.* Fleischpastete, *die*; **~ safe** *n.* (Brit.) Fliegenschrank, *der*

meaty /'mi:tɪ/ *adj.* **1** (full of meat) fleischig; ‹*Gulasch usw.*› mit reichlich Fleisch; **have a ~ taste** nach Fleisch schmecken **2** (fig.: full of substance) gehaltvoll

Mecca /'mekə/ *n.* ▸ **i p. 1643** Mekka, *das*; **the ~ of golfers** das Mekka für Golfer

mechanic /mɪ'kænɪk/ *n.* ▸ **i p. 1260** Mechaniker, *der*/Mechanikerin, *die*

mechanical /mɪ'kænɪkl/ *adj.* (lit. or fig.) mechanisch; **produced by ~ means** maschinell produziert; maschinell erzeugt ‹*Strom*›; **~ contrivance** Mechanismus, *der*

mechanical: ~ engi'neer *n.* Maschinenbauer, *der*/-bauerin, *die*; (graduate) Maschinenbauingenieur, *der*/-ingenieurin, *die*; **~ engi'neering** *n.* Maschinenbau, *der*

mechanically /mɪ'kænɪkəlɪ/ *adv.* (lit. or fig.) mechanisch; **~ inclined/minded** technisch interessiert/veranlagt

mechanical 'pencil *n.* (Amer.) Drehbleistift, *der*

mechanics /mɪ'kænɪks/ *n.*, *no pl.* **1** Mechanik, *die* **2** *constr. as pl.* (means of construction or operation) Mechanismus, *der*; (of writing, painting, etc.) Technik, *die*; **understand the ~ of sth.** wissen, wie etw. funktioniert

mechanisation, mechanise ▸ **mechaniz-**

mechanism /'mekənɪzm/ *n.* Mechanismus, *der*

mechanization /mekənaɪ'zeɪʃn/ *n.* Mechanisierung, *die*

mechanize /'mekənaɪz/ *v.t.* **1** mechanisieren **2** (Mil.) motorisieren

mechatronics /mekə'trɒnɪks/ *n.*, *no pl.* Mechatronik, *die*

Med /med/ *pr. n.* (coll.) **the ~:** das Mittelmeer

medal /'medl/ *n.* Medaille, *die*; (decoration) Orden, *der*; **~ for bravery/pole-vaulting** Tapferkeitsmedaille, *die*/Medaille im Stabhochsprung; **the reverse of the ~** (fig.) die Kehrseite der Medaille

medalist (Amer.) ▸ **medallist**

medallion /mɪ'dæljən/ *n.* **1** (large medal) [große] Medaille **2** (thing shaped like medal) Medaillon, *das*

medallist /'medəlɪst/ *n.* Medaillengewinner, *der*/-gewinnerin, *die* (Sport); **be a ~:** eine Medaille gewonnen haben

meddle /'medl/ *v.i.* **~ with sth.** sich (*Dat.*) an etw. (*Dat.*) zu schaffen machen; **~ in sth.** sich in etw. (*Akk.*) einmischen; **don't ~:** Finger weg! (ugs.); (stop interfering) misch dich nicht ein!; **she's always meddling** sie muss sich immer in alles einmischen

meddler /'medlə(r)/ *n.* **he's [such] a ~** (with things) er muss immer alles in die Finger nehmen *od.* (ugs.) an allem herumspielen; (in things) er muss sich immer in alles einmischen

meddlesome /'medlsəm/ *adj.* **she is so ~** *or* **such a ~ person** (interferes with things) sie muss sich (*Dat.*) immer an was zu schaffen machen; (interferes in things) sie muss sich in alles einmischen

Mede /mi:d/ *n.* **law of the ~s and Persians** (fig.) unumstößliches Gesetz

media /'mi:dɪə/ ▸ **mass media**; **medium A 1**

'media company *n.* Medienhaus, *das*

mediaeval ▸ **medieval**

'media event *n.* Medienereignis, *das*

medial /'mi:dɪəl/ *adj.* mittler...; ‹*Buchstabe, Zeichen*› mitten im Wort

median /'mi:dɪən/

A *adj.* mittler...; median (Anat.)

B *n.* (Statistics) Median[wert], *der*; Zentralwert, *der*

median strip /mi:dɪən 'strɪp/*n.* (Amer.) Mittelstreifen, *der*

'media studies *n. sing.* Medienwissenschaft, *die*; (school subject) Medienkunde, *die*

mediate /'mi:dɪeɪt/

A *v.i.* vermitteln

B *v.t.* **1** (settle) vermitteln in (+ *Dat.*) **2** (bring about) vermitteln

mediation /mi:dɪ'eɪʃn/ *n.* Vermittlung, *die*

mediator /'mi:dɪeɪtə(r)/ *n.* Vermittler, *der*/Vermittlerin, *die*

medic /'medɪk/ ▸ **medico**

Medicaid /'medɪkeɪd/ *n.* (Amer.)

> **Medicaid**
>
> Staatliche Krankenversicherung in den USA für Versicherungsnehmer unter 65 Jahren mit kleinem Einkommen.

medical /'medɪkl/

A *adj.* medizinisch; ärztlich ‹*Behandlung*›; **~ ward** ≈ medizinische *od.* innere Abteilung

B *n.* (coll.) ▸ **medical examination**

medical: ~ attendant *n.* Leibarzt, *der*/-ärztin, *die*; **~ certificate** *n.* Attest, *das*; **~ exami'nation** *n.* ärztliche Untersuchung; **~ 'history** *n.* **1** Geschichte der Medizin; **make ~ history** auf dem Gebiet der Medizin Geschichte machen; **2** (of person) Krankengeschichte, *die*; **~ insurance** *n.* Krankenversicherung, *die*; **have ~ insurance** krankenversichert sein

medically /'medɪkəlɪ/ *adv.* medizinisch

medical: ~ officer *n.* ▸ **i p. 1260** (Brit.) **1** Amtsarzt, *der*/-ärztin, *die*; **2** (Mil.) Sanitätsoffizier, *der*; **~ prac'titioner** *n.* ▸ **i p. 1260** praktischer Arzt/praktische Ärztin; Arzt/Ärztin für Allgemeinmedizin; **~ report** *n.* medizinisches Gutachten; **~ school** *n.* medizinische Hochschule; (faculty) medizinische Fakultät; **~ 'science** *n.* Medizin, *die*; **~ sciences** Medizinwissenschaften *Pl.*; **~ student** *n.* Medizinstudent, *der*/-studentin, *die*

medicament /mɪ'dɪkəmənt, 'medɪkəmənt/ *n.* Medikament, *das*

Medicare /'medɪkeə(r)/ *n.* (Amer.)

> **Medicare**
>
> Staatliche Gesundheitsversorgung und Krankenversicherung in den USA für Versicherungsnehmer über 65 Jahren.

medicated /'medɪkeɪtɪd/ *adj.* **~ shampoo/soap** medizinisches Haarwaschmittel/medizinische Seife; **~ gauze** imprägnierter Mull

medication /medɪ'keɪʃn/ *n.* **1** (treatment) Behandlung, *die*; Medikation, *die* (Med.) **2** (medicament) Medikament, *das*

medicinal /mɪ'dɪsɪnl/ *adj.* medizinisch; Arznei‹*mittel, -kohle*›; **~ qualities** Heilkräfte

medicinally /mɪ'dɪsɪnəlɪ/ *adv.* medizinisch; **use sth. ~:** etw. zu medizinischen Zwecken *od.* Heilzwecken verwenden

medicine /'medsən, 'medɪsɪn/ *n.* (science) Medizin, *die*; (preparation) Medikament, *das*; Medizin, *die* (veralt.); **give sb. some** *or* **a little** *or* **a dose** *or* **a taste of his/her own ~** (fig.) es jmdm. mit gleicher Münze heimzahlen; **they got a taste of their own ~** (fig.) man zahlte es ihnen mit gleicher Münze heim; **take one's ~** (fig.) die bittere Pille schlucken (ugs.); (bear the consequences) die Suppe auslöffeln (ugs.)

medicine: ~ ball *n.* Medizinball, *der*; **~ box, ~ cabinet** *ns.* Arzneischränkchen, *das*; Hausapotheke, *die*; **~ chest** *n.* Medikamentenschränkchen, *das*; (in home) Hausapotheke, *die*; **~ man** *n.* Medizinmann, *der*

m

medico /ˈmedɪkəʊ/ *n., pl.* **~s** (coll.) **1** (doctor) Doktor, *der* (ugs.) **2** (student) Mediziner, *der*/Medizinerin, *die* (ugs.)

medieval /medɪˈiːvl/ *adj.* (lit. or fig.) mittelalterlich; **the ~ period** das Mittelalter; **~ studies** Mediävistik, *die;* **in ~ times** im Mittelalter; **~ Latin** ▸ **Latin B**

medieval ˈhistory *n.* Geschichte des Mittelalters; (as subject) mittelalterliche Geschichte

medievalist /medɪˈiːvəlɪst/ *n.* Mediävist, *der*/Mediävistin, *die*

mediocre /miːdɪˈəʊkə(r)/ *adj.* mittelmäßig

mediocrity /miːdɪˈɒkrɪtɪ/ *n.* **1** *no pl.* Mittelmäßigkeit, *die* **2** (person) mittelmäßiger Mensch; **he is a ~/they are mediocrities** er ist/sie sind [ausgesprochenes] Mittelmaß

meditate /ˈmedɪteɪt/

A *v.t.* (consider) denken an (+ *Akk.*); erwägen; (design) planen; **~ revenge** auf Rache (*Akk.*) sinnen (geh.)

B *v.i.* nachdenken, (esp. Relig.) meditieren (**[up]on** über + *Akk.*)

meditation /medɪˈteɪʃn/ *n.* **1** (act of meditating) Nachdenken, *das* **2** (Relig.) Meditation, *die*

meditative /ˈmedɪtətɪv/ *adj.*, **meditatively** /ˈmedɪtətɪvlɪ/ *adv.* nachdenklich; (esp. Relig.) meditativ

Mediterranean /medɪtəˈreɪnɪən/

A *pr. n.* **the ~:** das Mittelmeer

B *adj.* mediterran (Geogr.); südländisch; **~ coast/countries** Mittelmeerküste, *die*/Mittelmeerländer

Mediterranean: ~ ˈclimate *n.* (Geog.) mediterranes Klima; **~ ˈSea** *pr. n.* Mittelmeer, *das*

medium /ˈmiːdɪəm/

A *n., pl.* **media** /ˈmiːdɪə/ *or* **~s** **1** (substance) Medium, *das;* (fig.: environment) Umgebung, *die* **2** (intermediate agency) Mittel, *das;* **by** *or* **through the ~ of** durch **3** *pl.* **~s** (Spiritualism) Medium, *das* **4** (means of communication or artistic expression) Medium, *das* **5** *in pl.* (means of mass communication) Medien *Pl.* **6** (middle degree) Mittelweg, *der; see also* **happy 1** **7** (liquid) Bindemittel, *das*

B *adj.* mittler...; medium *nur präd.*, halb durchgebraten ‹*Steak*›; *see also* **-size**

medium: ~-dry *adj.* halbtrocken ‹*Wein, Sherry*›; **~-size[d]** *adj.* mittelgroß; **~-sweet** *adj.* mittelsüß ‹*Wein, Sherry*›; **~ term** ▸ **term A 4**; **~ wave** *n.* (Radio) Mittelwelle, *die*

medlar /ˈmedlə(r)/ *n.* (Bot.) Mispel, *die*

medley /ˈmedlɪ/ *n.* **1** (forming a whole) buntes Gemisch; (collection of items) Sammelsurium, *das* (abwertend); (of colours) Kunterbunt, *das;* **his mind was confused with a ~ of thoughts** die verschiedensten Gedanken schossen durch seinen verwirrten Kopf **2** (Mus.) Potpourri, *das;* Medley, *das* **3** ▸ **medley relay**

medley ˈrelay *n.* (Athletics) Schwellstaffel, *die;* (Swimming) Lagenstaffel, *die*

medulla /mɪˈdʌlə/ *n.* (Anat.) **1** Medulla, *die* (fachspr.); ‹*Knochen-, Rücken-, Haar*›mark, *das* **2** (of brain) ▸ **medulla oblongata**

medulla oblongata /mɪdʌlə ɒblɒŋˈɡɑːtə/ *n.* (Anat.) verlängertes Rückenmark; Medulla oblongata, *die* (fachspr.)

meek /miːk/ *adj.* **1** (humble) sanftmütig **2** (tamely submissive) zu nachgiebig; **be [far] too ~:** sich (*Dat.*) [viel] zu viel gefallen lassen; **[as] ~ as a lamb** fromm wie ein Lamm

meekly /ˈmiːklɪ/ *adv.* **1** (humbly) demütig **2** (submissively) widerstandslos

meekness /ˈmiːknɪs/ *n., no pl.* **1** (humbleness) Sanftmütigkeit, *die* **2** (submissiveness) [zu große] Nachgiebigkeit

meerkat /ˈmɪəkæt/ *n.* Erdmännchen, *das*

meerschaum /ˈmɪəʃəm/ *n.* **1** (Min.) Meerschaum, *der* **2** (pipe) Meerschaumpfeife, *die*

meet¹ /miːt/

A *v.t.,* **met** /met/ **1** (come face to face with or into the company of) treffen; **I have to ~ my boss at 11 a.m.** ich muss um 11 Uhr zum Chef (ugs.) *od.* habe um 11 Uhr einen Termin beim Chef; **arrange to ~ sb.** sich mit jmdm. verabreden **2** (go to place of arrival of) treffen; (collect) abholen; **I'll ~ your train** ich hole dich vom Zug ab; **~ sb. halfway** (fig.) jmdm. [auf halbem Wege] entgegenkommen; **~ trouble halfway** sich (*Dat.*) unnötig Sorgen machen **3** (make the acquaintance of) kennen lernen; **I'd like you to ~ my wife** ich möchte Sie gern meiner Frau vorstellen *od.* mit meiner Frau bekannt machen; **I have never met her** ich kenne sie nicht persönlich; **pleased to ~ you** [sehr] angenehm; sehr erfreut; **Maimie, ~ Charlene. Charlene, ~ Maimie** (Amer.) Maimie, [dies ist] Charlene. Charlene, [dies ist] Maimie **4** (reach point of contact with) treffen auf (+ *Akk.*); **~ the eye/sb.'s eye[s]** sich den/jmds. Blicken darbieten; **~ the ear/sb.'s ears** das/jmds. Ohr treffen; **she met his eye[s], her eyes met his** (fig.) sie sah ihn an, er sah sie an; **he could not ~ his father's eyes** er konnte seinem Vater nicht in die Augen sehen; **there's more to** *or* **in it/him** *etc.* **than ~s the eye** da ist *od.* steckt mehr dahinter, als man zuerst denkt/in ihm *usw.* steckt mehr, als man auf den ersten Blick denkt **5** (oppose) treffen auf (+ *Akk.*) ‹*Feind, Herausforderer usw.*›; (grapple with) begegnen (+ *Dat.*) **6** (experience) stoßen auf (+ *Akk.*) ‹*Widerstand, Problem*›; ernten ‹*Gelächter, Drohungen*›; **~ [one's] death** *or* **one's end/disaster/one's fate** den Tod finden (geh.)/von einer Katastrophe/seinem Schicksal ereilt werden (geh.); **~ one's fate bravely** sich seinem Schicksal tapfer stellen **7** (satisfy) entsprechen (+ *Dat.*) ‹*Forderung, Wunsch, Bedürfnis, Erfordernis*›; einhalten ‹*Termin, Zeitplan*›; Rechnung tragen (+ *Dat.*) ‹*Einwand, Kritik*›; **~ the case** angemessen sein **8** (pay) decken ‹*Kosten, Auslagen*›; bezahlen ‹*Rechnung*›; **~ one's obligations** seinen Verpflichtungen nachkommen

B *v.i.,* **met** **1** (come face to face) (by chance) sich (*Dat.*) begegnen; (by arrangement) sich treffen; **goodbye, until we ~ again** auf Wiedersehen bis zum nächsten Mal; **we've met before** wir kennen uns bereits **2** (assemble) ‹*Komitee, Ausschuss usw.:*› tagen; **~ together** sich versammeln **3** (be in opposition) aufeinander treffen **4** (come together) ‹*Bahnlinien, Straßen usw.:*› aufeinander treffen; ‹*Flüsse:*› zusammenfließen; **their eyes/lips met** ihre Blicke/Lippen begegneten sich; **the tables don't quite ~:** die Tische stehen nicht ganz dicht aneinander; *see also* **end A 8, 14** **5** (be united) **~ in sb.** in jmdm. zusammentreffen; sich in jmdm. vereinen (geh.)

C *n.* (Hunting) Treffen, *das*

Phrasal verbs

- **~ ˈup** *v.i.* sich treffen; **~ up with sb.** (coll.) jmdn. [zufällig] treffen
- **~ with** *v.t.* **1** (encounter) begegnen (+ *Dat.*) **2** (experience) haben ‹*Erfolg, Unfall*›; finden ‹*Zustimmung, Verständnis, Tod*›; stoßen auf (+ *Akk.*) ‹*Widerstand*›; **be met with sth.** etw. hervorrufen; **all her attempts met with failure** alle ihre Bemühungen endeten in einem Misserfolg **3** (Amer.) ▸ **~ A 1**

meet² *adj.* (arch.: proper) **it is ~ to do sth.** es ziemt sich (geh. veralt.), etw. zu tun

meeting /ˈmiːtɪŋ/ *n.* **1** Begegnung, *die* (auch fig.); (by arrangement) Treffen, *das;* (of rivers) Zusammenfluss, *der;* **~ of minds** Verständigung, *die;* Annäherung der Standpunkte **2** (assembly) (of shareholders, club members, etc.; also Relig.) Versammlung, *die;* (of committee, Cabinet, council, etc.) Sitzung, *die;* (social gathering) Treffen, *das;* **call a ~ of the committee** den Ausschuss einberufen **3** (persons assembled) Versammlung, *die* **4** (Sport) Treffen, *das;* (Racing) Rennen, *das*

meeting: ~ place *n.* Treffpunkt, *der;* **~ point** *n.* (of lines, roads) Schnittpunkt, *der;* (of rivers) Zusammenfluss, *der;* **at the ~ point of the roads** wo die Straßen zusammentreffen

meg /meɡ/ *n.* (Computing) Meg, *das*

mega /ˈmeɡə/ (coll.)

A *adj.* **1** (enormous) Mega- (Jugendspr.) **2** (excellent) geil (ugs.)

B *adv.* äußerst; **~ cool** megacool (ugs.); **be ~ rich** super- *od.* megareich (Jugendspr.) sein; **be ~ talented** höchst talentiert sein

mega- /ˈmeɡə/ *pref.* mega-/Mega-

ˈmegabyte *n.* (Computing) Megabyte, *das*

ˈmegacycle *n.* Megahertz, *das*

ˈmegadeath *n.* Megatote *Pl.;* **one ~:** 1 Million Tote

ˈmegahertz *n.* (Phys.) Megahertz, *das*

megalith /ˈmeɡəlɪθ/ *n.* (Archaeol.) Megalith, *der*

megalithic /meɡəˈlɪθɪk/ *adj.* (Archaeol.) megalithisch

megalomania /meɡələˈmeɪnɪə/ *n.* Größenwahn, *der;* Megalomanie, *die* (Psych.)

megalomaniac /meɡələˈmeɪnɪæk/

A *n.* Größenwahnsinnige, *der/die;* Megalomane, *der/die* (Psych.); **he's a ~:** er ist größenwahnsinnig

B *adj.* größenwahnsinnig; megaloman[isch] (Psych.)

ˈmegaphone *n.* Megaphon, *das*

ˈmegapixel *n.* (Computing etc.) Megapixel, *das*

ˈmegastar *n.* Megastar, *der* (ugs.)

ˈmegastore *n.* Großmarkt, *der*

ˈmegaton[ne] *n.* Megatonne, *die*

ˈmegawatt *n.* (Electr.) Megawatt, *das*

meiosis /maɪˈəʊsɪs/ *n., pl.* **meioses** /maɪˈəʊsiːz/ (Biol.) Meiose, *die*

Meissen /ˈmaɪsn/ *pr. n.* **~ [porcelain]** ▸ **porcelain 1**

melamine /ˈmeləmɪn/ *n., no pl.* Melamin, *das*

melancholia /melənˈkəʊlɪə/ *n.* (Med.) Melancholie, *die*

melancholic /melənˈkɒlɪk/ *adj.* melancholisch; schwermütig

melancholy /ˈmelənkəlɪ/

A *n.* Melancholie, *die;* (pensive sadness) Schwermut, *die*

B *adj.* **1** (gloomy, expressing sadness) melancholisch; schwermütig **2** (saddening) deprimierend

Melanesia /meləˈniːʃə/ *pr. n.* Melanesien (*das*)

Melanesian /meləˈniːʃən/ ▸ **ⓘ p. 1277**, ▸ **ⓘ p. 1345**

A *adj.* melanesisch

B *n.* **1** (person) Melanesier, *der*/Melanesierin, *die* **2** (language) Melanesisch, *das*

melanin /ˈmelənɪn/ *n.* Melanin, *das*

melanoma /meləˈnəʊmə/ *n.* (Med.) Melanom, *das*

Melba /ˈmelbə/ ▸ **peach Melba**

Melba ˈtoast *n.: dünner, knuspriger Toast*

meld /meld/

A *v.t.* verschmelzen (**into** zu)

B *v.i.* [miteinander] verschmelzen

mêlée (*Amer.:* **melee**) /ˈmeleɪ/ *n.* **1** (scuffle) Handgemenge, *das* **2** (muddle) Durcheinander, *das;* (of things or people moving to and fro) Gewühl, *das*

mellifluous /meˈlɪfluəs/ *adj.* einschmeichelnd ‹*Stimme, Melodie*›

mellow /ˈmeləʊ/

A *adj.* **1** (softened by age or experience) abgeklärt **2** (ripe, well-matured) reif; ausgereift ‹*Wein*› **3** (genial) freundlich; (slightly drunk) angeheitert; **~ in mood** heiter gestimmt; aufgeräumt **4** (full and soft) weich ‹*Stimme, Ton, Licht, Farben*›

B *v.t.* reifer machen ‹*Person*›; [aus]reifen lassen ‹*Wein*›

C *v.i.* ‹*Person, Obst, Wein:*› reifen; ‹*Licht, Farbe:*› weicher werden

melodeon /mɪˈləʊdɪən/ *n.* Melodion, *das*

melodic /mɪˈlɒdɪk/ *adj.* melodisch; **~ minor** melodisches Moll

melodious /mɪˈləʊdɪəs/ *adj.*, **melodiously** /mɪˈləʊdɪəslɪ/ *adv.* melodisch

melodrama /ˈmelədrɑːmə/ *n.* (lit. or fig.) Melodrama, *das*

melodramatic /melədrəˈmætɪk/ *adj.*, **melodramatically** /melədrəˈmætɪkəlɪ/ *adv.* (lit. or fig.) melodramatisch

melody /ˈmelədɪ/ *n.* **1** (pleasing sound) Gesang, *der* **2** (tune) Melodie, *die* **3** *no pl.* (musical quality) Melodik, *die* **4** (Mus.: part in harmonized music) Melodiestimme, *die*

melon /ˈmelən/ *n.* Melone, *die*

melt /melt/

A *v.i.* **1** schmelzen; (dissolve) sich auflösen; **~ in one's** *or* **the mouth** auf der Zunge zergehen;

m

see also **butter A** 2 (fig.: be softened) dahinschmelzen (geh.) (**at** bei); sich erweichen lassen (**at** durch); **her heart ~ed with pity** ihr Herz schmolz vor Mitleid; **~ into tears** in Tränen zerfließen

B *v.t.* 1 schmelzen ‹*Schnee, Eis, Metall*›; (Cookery) zerlassen ‹*Butter*› 2 (fig.: make tender) erweichen ‹*Person, Herz*›; **he was ~ed by her entreaties** er ließ sich durch ihre Bitten erweichen

Phrasal verbs

- **~ a'way** *v.i.* ‹*Schnee, Eis:*› [weg]schmelzen; (fig.: dwindle away) ‹*Nebel, Dunst, Menschenmenge:*› sich auflösen; ‹*Verdacht, Mehrheit, Furcht:*› dahinschwinden (geh.); ‹*Geld:*› dahinschmelzen
- **~ 'down**

A *v.i.* schmelzen

B *v.t.* einschmelzen ‹*Metall, Glas*›. *See also* **meltdown**

- **~ into** *v.t.* übergehen in (+ *Akk.*)

'meltdown *n.* 1 Schmelzen, *das* 2 (Finance) Einbruch, *der*

melting/'meltɪŋ/: **~ point** *n.* Schmelzpunkt, *der;* **~ pot** *n.* (fig.) Schmelztiegel, *der;* **be in the ~ pot** in rascher Veränderung begriffen sein

member /'membə(r)/ *n.* 1 Mitglied, *das; attrib.* Mitglieds‹*staat, -land*›; **be a ~ of the club** Mitglied des Vereins sein; Vereinsmitglied sein; **~ of the expedition** Expeditionsteilnehmer, *der*/-teilnehmerin, *die;* **be a ~ of an expedition** an einer Expedition teilnehmen; **~ of a/the family** Familienangehörige, *der/die* 2 ▸ℹ **p. 1634 M~ [of Parliament]** (Brit. Polit.) Abgeordnete [des Unterhauses], *der/die;* **M~ of Congress** (Amer. Polit.) Kongressabgeordnete, *der/die* 3 (limb) Gliedmaße, *die;* Glied, *das;* (organ of the body) [Körper]organ, *das*

> **Member of Parliament (MP)**
>
> Ein Abgeordneter des **House of Commons**, der einen der 659 *constituencies* (Wahlkreise) in England, Schottland, Wales und Nordirland repräsentiert.

membership /'membəʃɪp/ *n.* 1 (being a member) Mitgliedschaft, *die* (**of** in + *Dat.*); *attrib.* Mitglieds‹*karte, -ausweis, -beitrag*›; Mitglieder‹*liste, -verzeichnis*›; **he was elected to ~ of the Society** er wurde zum Mitglied der Gesellschaft gewählt 2 (number of members) Mitgliederzahl, *die;* **the club has a ~ of a few hundred** der Verein hat einige hundert Mitglieder 3 (body of members) Mitglieder *Pl.*

membrane /'membreɪn/ *n.* (Biol.) Membran, *die*

membranous /'membrənəs/ *adj.* (Biol.) membranös; **~ bag** Hautsack, *der*

memento /mɪ'mentəʊ/ *n., pl.* **~es** *or* **~s** Andenken, *das* (**of** an + *Akk.*)

memo /'meməʊ/ *n., pl.* **~s** (coll.) ▸**memorandum 1, 2**

memoir /'memwɑː(r)/ *n.* 1 *in pl.* (autobiography) Memoiren *Pl.* 2 (biography) Biografie, *die*

memorabilia /memərə'bɪlɪə/ *n. pl.* Erinnerungsstücke *Pl.*; Memorabilien *Pl.* (veralt.)

memorable /'memərəbl/ *adj.* denkwürdig ‹*Ereignis, Gelegenheit, Tag*›; unvergesslich ‹*Film, Buch, Aufführung*›; **not a very ~ play** kein sehr beeindruckendes Stück

memorably /'memərəblɪ/ *adv.* nachhaltig ‹*beeindrucken*›; auf unvergessliche Weise ‹*spielen*›

memorandum /memə'rændəm/ *n., pl.* **memoranda** /memə'rændə/ *or* **~s** 1 (note) Notiz, *die;* **make a ~ of sth.** sich (*Dat.*) etw. notieren 2 (letter) Mitteilung, *die* 3 (Diplom.) Memorandum, *das* 4 (Law) rechtskräftiges Dokument

memorial /mɪ'mɔːrɪəl/

A *adj.* Gedenk‹*stein, -gottesdienst, -ausstellung*›

B *n.* 1 (monument) Denkmal, *das* (**to** für); (ceremony) Gedenkzeremonie, *die* 2 (statement of facts) Denkschrift, *die* (**to** an + *Akk.*) 3 (Diplom.) Memorandum, *das*

memorial: M~ Day *n.* (Amer.) *Trauertag zum Gedenken an die Gefallenen;* ≈ Volkstrauertag, *der;* **~ park** *n.* (Amer.) Friedhof, *der*

memorize (**memorise**) /'meməraɪz/ *v.t.* sich (*Dat.*) merken *od.* einprägen; (learn by heart) auswendig lernen

memory /'memərɪ/ *n.* 1 (faculty or capacity, recovery of knowledge) Gedächtnis, *das;* **have a good/poor ~ for faces** ein gutes/schlechtes Personengedächtnis haben; **commit sth. to ~** ▸**memorize** 2 (recollection, person or thing remembered, act of remembering) Erinnerung, *die* (**of** an + *Akk.*); **have a vague ~ of sth.** sich nur ungenau *od.* vage an etw. (*Akk.*) erinnern; **to the best of my ~:** soweit ich mich erinnere *od.* erinnern kann; **if my ~ is right** wenn ich mich recht erinnere; **search one's ~:** versuchen, sich zu erinnern; **it slipped** *or* **escaped my ~:** es ist mir entfallen; **from ~:** aus dem Gedächtnis *od.* Kopf; **speaking from ~, ...:** soweit *od.* soviel ich mich erinnere, ...; **in ~ of** zur Erinnerung an (+ *Akk.*); *attrib.* **a trip down ~ lane** eine Reise in die Vergangenheit 3 (remembered time) **a time within the ~ of men still living** eine Zeit, an die sich heute lebende Menschen noch erinnern können; **it is beyond the ~ of anyone alive today** es lebt niemand mehr, der sich daran erinnern könnte; *see also* **living B 1** 4 (posthumous repute) Andenken, *das* (**of** an + *Akk.*); **of happy** *or* **blessed ~:** seligen Angedenkens (veralt.) 5 (Computing) Speicher, *der*

memory: ~ bank *n.* Speicherbank, *die;* **~ board** *n.* (Computing) Speicherplatine, *die;* **~ card** *n.* (Electron.) Speicherkarte, *die;* **~ chip** *n.* (Electron.) Speicherchip, *der;* **~ loss** *n., no pl.* Gedächtnisverlust, *der;* **~ stick** *n.* (Computing) Memorystick, *der;* Speicherstab, *der*

men *pl. of* **man**

menace /'menɪs/

A *v.t.* bedrohen ‹*Person*›; **~ sb. with sth.** jmdm. mit etw. drohen

B *v.i.* drohen

C *n.* 1 Plage, *die;* **an absolute** *or* **a public ~** (fig. coll.) (dangerous person) eine öffentliche Gefahr; (obnoxious person) ein [richtiges] Ekel (ugs.); (child) ein kleiner Teufel 2 (literary: threat) Drohung, *die;* **a sense of ~:** ein Gefühl der Bedrohung; *see also* **demand B 1**

menacing /'menɪsɪŋ/ *adj.* drohend

ménage /meɪ'nɑːʒ/ *n.* Haushalt, *der;* **~ à trois** /meɪnɑːʒ ɑː 'trwɑː/ Menage à trois, *die;* ≈ Dreiecksverhältnis, *das*

menagerie /mɪ'nædʒərɪ/ *n.* Tierschau, *die;* Menagerie, *die* (veralt.); (fig. iron.: collection of persons) Gesellschaft, *die*

mend /mend/

A *v.t.* 1 (repair) reparieren; ausbessern, flicken ‹*Kleidung, Fischernetz*›; kleben, kitten ‹*Glas, Porzellan, Sprung*›; beheben ‹*Schaden*›; beseitigen ‹*Riss*› 2 (improve) **~ one's manners** sich (*Dat.*) bessere Umgangsformen angewöhnen; **~ one's ways** sich bessern; **~ matters** die Sache bereinigen; **it is never too late to ~** (prov.) zum Bessermachen/Verbessern ist es nie zu spät; *see also* **fence A 1; least B**

B *v.i.* gesund werden; genesen (geh.); (knit together) ‹*Knochen, Bein, Finger usw.:*› heilen; **has his leg ~ed yet?** ist sein Bein schon verheilt?

C *n.* (in glass, china, etc.) Kleb[e]stelle, *die;* (in cloth) ausgebesserte Stelle; (repair) Ausbesserung, *die;* **be on the ~** ‹*Person:*› auf dem Wege der Besserung sein; ‹*Verhältnisse, Lage:*› sich bessern

mendacious /men'deɪʃəs/ *adj.* unwahr ‹*Bericht, Behauptung, Darstellung*›; verlogen (abwertend) ‹*Person, Rede, Buch*›

mendacity /men'dæsɪtɪ/ *n.* 1 *no pl.* (*untruthfulness*) ▸**mendacious**: Unwahrheit, *die;* Verlogenheit, *die* (abwertend) 2 (a lie) Lüge, *die*

Mendelian /men'diːlɪən/ *adj.* (Biol.) mendelsch

mender /'mendə(r)/ *n.* Ausbesserer, *der*/Ausbesserin, *die;* (of clocks, watches, machines) Reparateur, *der;* **take one's watch/shoes to the ~'s** seine Uhr zum Uhrmacher *od.* zur Reparatur/seine Schuhe zum Schuster *od.* zur Reparatur bringen

mendicant /'mendɪkənt/

A *adj.* bettelnd; **~ friar** Bettelmönch, *der*

B *n.* 1 (beggar) Bettler, *der*/Bettlerin, *die* 2 (friar) Bettelmönch, *der*

menfolk /'menfəʊk/ *n. pl.* Männer

menhir /'menhɪə(r)/ *n.* (Archaeol.) Menhir, *der*

menial /'miːnɪəl/

A *adj.* niedrig; untergeordnet ‹*Aufgabe*›

B *n.* (derog.) Domestik, *der* (veralt. abwertend)

meningitis /menɪn'dʒaɪtɪs/ *n.* ▸ℹ **p. 1231** (Med.) Meningitis, *die* (fachspr.); Hirnhautentzündung, *die*

meniscus /me'nɪskəs/ *n., pl.* **menisci** /me'nɪskaɪ/ (Phys., Anat., Optics) Meniskus, *der*

menopausal /'menəpɔːzl/ *adj.* (Physiol.) klimakterisch; menopausal

menopause /'menəpɔːz/ *n.* 1 (period of life) Wechseljahre *Pl.*; Klimakterium, *das* (fachspr.); **male ~:** Wechseljahre des Mannes 2 (Physiol.) Menopause, *die*

menses /'mensiːz/ *n. pl.* 1 (discharge) Menstruationsflüssigkeit, *die* 2 (menstruation) Menses *Pl.*

menstrual /'menstrʊəl/ *adj.* (Physiol.) menstrual (fachspr.); Menstruations-

menstruate /'menstrʊeɪt/ *v.i.* (Physiol.) menstruieren

menstruation /menstrʊ'eɪʃn/ *n.* (Physiol.) Menstruation, *die*

menswear /'menzweə(r)/ *n., no pl.* Herrenbekleidung, *die; attrib.* Herrenbekleidungs-; für Herrenbekleidung *od.* -moden *nachgestellt*

mental /'mentl/ *adj.* 1 (of the mind) geistig; seelisch ‹*Belastung, Labilität*›; Geistes‹*zustand, -verfassung, -störung*›; **the previous ~ history of the patient** die Vorgeschichte der seelischen Erkrankungen des Patienten 2 (done by the mind) geistig; gedanklich; **make a quick ~ calculation** es im Kopf schnell überschlagen; **~ process** Denkprozess, -vorgang, *der;* **make a ~ note of sth.** sich (*Dat.*) etw. merken; **make a ~ note to do sth.** versuchen, daran zu denken, etw. zu tun 3 (Brit. coll.: mad) verrückt (salopp); bekloppt (salopp)

mental: ~ age *n.* geistiger Entwicklungsstand; Intelligenzalter, *das* (Psych.); **~ a'rithmetic** *n.* Kopfrechnen, *das;* **~ asylum** *n.* (Hist.) Irrenanstalt, *die* (veralt.); **~ 'block** ▸**block A 12; ~ case** *n.* (coll.) Verrückte, *der/die* (salopp); (mental patient) Geisteskranke, *der/die;* **~ 'cruelty** *n., no pl.* seelische Grausamkeit; **~ de'fective** *n.* (dated/offensive) Schwachsinnige, *der/die;* **~ de'ficiency** *n.* (dated/offensive) Geistesschwäche, *die;* **~ 'handicap** *n.* geistige Behinderung; **people with ~ handicaps** geistig behinderte Menschen; **~ 'health** *n.* seelische Gesundheit; *attrib.* **~ health services** psychiatrische Versorgung; **~ home** *n.* Nervenklinik, *die;* **~ hospital** *n.* (dated) psychiatrische Klinik; Nervenklinik, *die;* **~ 'illness** *n.* Geisteskrankheit, *die*

mentality /men'tælɪtɪ/ *n.* 1 (outlook) Mentalität, *die* 2 (mental capacity) geistige Fähigkeit

mentally /'mentəlɪ/ *adv.* 1 geistig; geistes‹*gestört, -krank*›; **~ deficient** *or* **defective** (dated/offensive) schwachsinnig 2 (inwardly) innerlich *od.* im Geiste ‹*fluchen, sich Vorwürfe machen*›; im Kopf ‹*rechnen*›

mental: ~ patient *n.* Geisteskranke, *der/die;* **~ reser'vation** *n.* geheimer Vorbehalt

menthol /'menθɒl/ *n.* Menthol, *das*

mentholated /'menθəleɪtɪd/ *adj.* mit Menthol *nachgestellt;* Menthol‹*zigarette*›

mention /'menʃn/

A *n.* 1 Erwähnung, *die;* **there is a brief/no ~ of sth.** etw. wird kurz/nicht erwähnt; **the earliest ~ of this is in ...:** das wird zum ersten Mal in ... (*Dat.*) erwähnt; **get a ~:** erwähnt werden; **make [no] ~ of sth.** etw. [nicht] erwähnen 2 (commendation) Belobigung, *die;* **honourable ~:** ehrenvolle Erwähnung

B *v.t.* 1 erwähnen (**to** gegenüber); **~ as the reason for sth.** als Grund für etw. nennen; **now that you [come to] ~ it** jetzt, wo Sie es sagen; **not to ~ ...:** ganz zu schweigen von ...; **not to ~ the fact that ...:** ganz abgesehen davon, dass ...; **Thank you very much. — Don't ~ it** Vielen Dank. — Keine Ursache 2 (commend) **be ~ed** lobend erwähnt werden. *See also* **dispatch B 1**

m

mentor /'mentɔ:(r)/ *n.* Mentor, *der*/Mentorin, *die*

menu /'menju:/ *n.* 1 [Speise]karte, *die;* **ensure a varied ~:** für einen abwechslungsreichen Speiseplan sorgen; **a ~ at 20 euros** ein Menü zu 20 Euro 2 (fig.: diet) Nahrung, *die* 3 (fig.: programme) Angebot, *das* 4 (Computing, Telev.) Menü, *das*

menu: ~ bar *n.* (Computing) Menüleiste, *die;* **~-driven** *adj.* (Computing) menügesteuert; **~ item** *n.* (Computing) Menüpunkt, *der*

MEP *abbr.* = **Member of the European Parliament** MdEP

Mephistopheles /mefɪ'stɒfɪli:z/ *n.* 1 *pr. n.* Mephisto[pheles] (*der*) 2 *n.* (fiendish person) Mephisto, *der*

mercantile /'mɜ:kəntaɪl/ *adj.* 1 (commercial) Handels-; **the ~ system** der Merkantilismus; das Merkantilsystem 2 (trading) Handel treibend ‹*Nation*›; **~ marine** ▸**merchant navy**

Mercator /mɜ:'keɪtə(r)/ *n.* **~'s projection** (Geog.) Mercatorprojektion, *die;* Zylinderprojektion, *die*

mercenary /'mɜ:sɪnərɪ/

A *adj.* 1 gewinnsüchtig 2 (hired) Söldner-

B *n.* Söldner, *der*

merchandise /'mɜ:tʃəndaɪz/

A *n., no pl., no indef. art.* [Handels]ware, *die*

B *v.t.* auf den Markt bringen

merchant /'mɜ:tʃənt/ *n.* 1 (trader) Kaufmann, *der;* **corn/timber ~:** Getreide-/Holzhändler, *der*/-händlerin, *die; see also* **coal merchant; scrap merchant; wine merchant** 2 (Amer., Scot.: retailer) Einzelhändler, *der*/-händlerin, *die* 3 (coll.: person engaged in specified activity) **rip-off ~:** Halsabschneider, *der* (ugs. abwertend); **gloom ~:** Schwarzseher, *der*/-seherin, *die; see also* **speed merchant**

merchant: ~ 'bank *n.* Handelsbank, *die;* **~ 'banker** *n.* ▸ℹ **p. 1260** Leiter einer Handelsbank; ≈ Bankier, *der;* **~ 'fleet** ▸**~ navy; ~man** /'mɜ:tʃəntmən/ *n., pl.* **~men** /'mɜ:tʃəntmən/ ▸**~ ship; ~ ma'rine** (Amer.), **~ 'navy** (Brit.) *ns.* Handelsmarine, *die;* **~ 'prince** *n.* Großkaufmann, *der;* Handelsherr, *der* (veralt.); **~ 'seaman** *n.* Matrose bei der Handelsmarine; **~ service** ▸**~ navy; ~ ship** *n.* Handelsschiff, *das*

merciful /'mɜ:sɪfl/ *adj.* gnädig; **his death must have come as a ~ release from his sufferings** der Tod muss für ihn eine Erlösung gewesen sein; **~ Heavens!** gütiger *od.* barmherziger Himmel!; **God is ~ to sinners** Gott ist den Sündern gnädig

mercifully /'mɜ:sɪfəlɪ/ *adv.* gnädig; *as sentence-modifier* (fortunately) glücklicherweise

merciless /'mɜ:sɪlɪs/ *adj.,* **mercilessly** /'mɜ:sɪlɪslɪ/ *adv.* gnadenlos; unbarmherzig

mercurial /mɜ:'kjʊərɪəl/ *adj.* (quick-witted) quecksilbrig; (changeable) wechselhaft

mercury /'mɜ:kjʊrɪ/ *n.* 1 Quecksilber, *das;* **the ~ is rising/falling** das Barometer steigt/fällt 2 *pr. n.* **M~** (Roman Mythol.) Merkur (*der*) 3 *pr. n.* **M~** (Astron.) Merkur, *der* 4 (Bot.) Bingelkraut, *das*

mercy /'mɜ:sɪ/

A *n.* 1 *no pl., no indef. art.* (compassion; also Theol.) Erbarmen, *das* (**on** mit); **show sb. [no] ~:** mit jmdm. [kein] Erbarmen haben; **beg for ~:** um Gnade bitten *od.* flehen; **act of ~:** Gnadenakt, *der;* **God's great ~:** Gottes große Barmherzigkeit; **be at the ~ of sb./sth.** jmdm./einer Sache [auf Gedeih und Verderb] ausgeliefert sein; **the ship was at the ~ of the waves** das Schiff war den Wellen preisgegeben; **have ~!** Gnade!; **Lord have ~ [up]on us** (Relig.) Herr, erbarme dich [unser]; **~ [me]!, ~ [up]on us!** gütiger Himmel! 2 (instance) glückliche Fügung; **one** *or* **we must be thankful** *or* **grateful for small mercies** (coll.) man darf [ja] nicht zu viel verlangen; **leave sb. to the [tender] mercies of sb.** (iron.) jmdn. jmds. [liebevoller] Fürsorge überlassen; **it is a ~:** es ist ein Glück *od.* Segen; **what a ~ it is that ...:** welch ein Glück *od.* Segen, dass ...

B *attrib. adj.* Hilfs-, Rettungs‹*einsatz, -flug*›; **~ killing** aktive Sterbehilfe; **~ killings** Fälle aktiver Sterbehilfe

mere[1] /mɪə(r)/ *adj.* bloß; rein ‹*Tautologie, Versehen*›; **he is a ~ child** er ist nur ein Kind; **it's a ~ copy** es ist bloß eine Kopie; **~ courage is not enough** Mut allein genügt nicht; **the ~st hint/trace of sth.** die kleinste Andeutung/Spur von etw.; **~ words won't help** Worte allein tun es nicht

mere[2] *n.* (arch./literary) See, *der*

merely /'mɪəlɪ/ *adv.* bloß; lediglich; **not ~ ...:** nicht bloß ...

meretricious /merɪ'trɪʃəs/ *adj.* trügerisch ‹*Argument, Methode*›

merganser /mɜ:'gænzə(r)/ *n.* (Ornith.) Säger, *der*

merge /mɜ:dʒ/

A *v.t.* 1 (combine) zusammenschließen ‹*Firmen, Unternehmen*› (**into** zu); zusammenlegen ‹*Anteile, Abteilungen*›; **~ one firm/department with another** eine Firma mit einer anderen zusammenschließen/eine Abteilung mit einer anderen zusammenlegen 2 (blend gradually) verschmelzen (**with** mit); **his library should not be ~d with another collection** seine Bibliothek sollte nicht einer anderen Sammlung einverleibt werden

B *v.i.* 1 (combine) ‹*Firma, Unternehmen:*› sich zusammenschließen, fusionieren (**with** mit); ‹*Abteilung:*› zusammengelegt werden (**with** mit) 2 (blend gradually) ‹*Straße:*› zusammenlaufen (**with** mit); **~ with sth.** ‹*Kontur, Muster:*› verschmelzen mit etw.; ‹*Unterhaltung:*› untergehen in etw. (*Dat.*); **~ into sth.** ‹*Farbe usw.:*› in etw. (*Akk.*) übergehen

merger /'mɜ:dʒə(r)/ *n.* (of departments, parties) Zusammenschluss, *der;* Vereinigung, *die;* (of companies) Fusion, *die*

meridian /mə'rɪdɪən/ *n.* (Astron., Geog.) Meridian, *der; see also* **prime meridian**

meringue /mə'ræŋ/ *n.* Meringe, *die;* Baiser, *das*

merino /mə'ri:nəʊ/ *n., pl.* **~s** 1 **~ [sheep]** Merinoschaf, *das;* Merino, *der* 2 (material) Merino, *der* 3 (yarn) Merinogarn, *das*

merit /'merɪt/

A *n.* 1 *no pl.* (worth) Verdienst, *das;* **a man of great ~:** ein Mann von hohen Verdiensten (geh.); ein sehr verdienter Mann; **promotion is by ~:** Beförderung richtet sich nach Leistung; **there is no ~ in doing that** es ist nicht [sehr] sinnvoll, das zu tun; **be without ~** ‹*Buch, Film:*› kein Niveau haben 2 (good feature) Vorzug, *der;* **on his/its ~s** nach seinen Vorzügen 3 *in pl.* (rights and wrongs) Für und Wider, *das* 4 (Theol.) Verdienst, *der* 5 **Order of M~** (Brit.) Order of Merit, *der; britischer Verdienstorden*

B *v.t.* verdienen; **sb. ~s reward/punishment** jmd. hat eine Belohnung/Strafe verdient

'merit award, 'merit increase *ns.* Leistungszulage, *die*

meritocracy /merɪ'tɒkrəsɪ/ *n.* Meritokratie, *die;* Verdienstadel, *der* (veralt.)

meritorious /merɪ'tɔ:rɪəs/ *adj.* verdienstvoll ‹*Tat, Verhalten, Person*›; verdient ‹*Person*›

'merit system *n.* (Amer.) Leistungsprinzip im öffentlichen Dienst

mermaid /'mɜ:meɪd/ *n.* Nixe, *die*

merrie England ▸**merry England**

merrily /'merɪlɪ/ *adv.* munter

merriment /'merɪmənt/ *n., no pl.* Fröhlichkeit, *die;* **fall into fits of helpless ~:** sich vor Lachen nicht mehr halten können

merry /'merɪ/ *adj.* 1 ▸ℹ **p. 1189** (full of laughter or gaiety) fröhlich; **the M~ Widow/Wives of Windsor** die lustige Witwe/die lustigen Weiber von Windsor; **a ~ time was had by all** alle haben sich prächtig amüsiert; **make ~:** sich amüsieren; **make ~ over sb./sth.** sich über jmdn./etw. lustig machen; **the more the merrier** je mehr, desto besser; **~ Christmas!** frohe *od.* fröhliche Weihnachten! 2 (coll.: tipsy) beschwipst (ugs.)

merry: ~ 'England *pr. n.* das gute alte England; **~-go-round** *n.* Karussell, *das;* **~ 'hell** ▸**hell 2; ~making** *n.* 1 *no pl., no indef. art.* Feiern, *das;* **the sound of ~making** fröhlicher Festlärm; 2 (occasion) Fest, *das;* **~ 'men** *n. pl.* Getreue; Kumpane (ugs.)

mesa /'meɪsə/ *n.* (Amer. Geog.) Tafelberg, *der*

mescaline /'meskəlɪn/ *n., no pl.* Meskalin, *das*

Mesdames *pl. of* **Madame; Mrs**

mesh /meʃ/

A *n.* 1 Masche, *die* 2 (netting; also fig.: network) Geflecht, *das;* **wire ~ [fence]** Maschendraht[zaun], *der* 3 *in pl.* (fig.: snare) Maschen 4 (fabric) Netzgewebe, *das; attrib.* Netz‹*strumpf, -hemd, -vorhang*› 5 **be in ~** ‹*Zahnräder:*› ineinander greifen, im Eingriff stehen (Technik)

B *v.i.* 1 (Mech. Engin.) ‹*Zahnräder:*› ineinander greifen; **~ with** eingreifen in (*Akk.*) 2 (fig.: be harmonious) harmonisieren (**with** mit)

mesmerism /'mezmərɪzm/ *n., no pl.* 1 Mesmerismus, *der* 2 (dated: influence) hypnotische Kraft; **powers of ~:** hypnotische Fähigkeiten

mesmerize /'mezməraɪz/ *v.t.* faszinieren; erstarren lassen ‹*Tier*›

Mesolithic /mesə'lɪθɪk, mi:ze-/ *adj.* (Archaeol.) mesolithisch; **~ period** Mesolithikum, *das*

Mesopotamia /mesəpə'teɪmɪə/ *pr. n.* Mesopotamien (*das*); Zweistromland, *das*

Mesozoic /mesəʊ'zəʊɪk/ (Geol.)

A *adj.* mesozoisch

B *n.* Mesozoikum, *das*

mess /mes/

A *n.* 1 (dirty/untidy state) **[be] a ~** *or* **in a ~:** schmutzig/unaufgeräumt [sein]; **[be] a complete** *or* **in an awful ~:** in einem fürchterlichen Zustand [sein]; **what a ~!** was für ein Dreck (ugs.)/Durcheinander; **look a ~:** schlimm aussehen; **your hair is a ~:** dein Haar ist ganz durcheinander; **don't make too much ~:** mach nicht zu viel Schmutz/Durcheinander 2 (sth. out of place) **leave a lot of ~ behind one** (dirt) viel Schmutz hinterlassen; (untidiness) eine große Unordnung hinterlassen; **I'm not tidying up your ~:** ich mache deinen Schmutz/räume deinen Kram nicht weg (ugs.); **make a ~ with sth.** mit etw. Schmutz machen 3 (excreta) **dog's/cat's ~es** Hunde-/Katzenkot, *der;* **make/leave a ~ on the carpet** auf den Teppich machen (ugs.) 4 (bad state) **be [in] a ~:** sich in einem schlimmen Zustand befinden; ‹*Person:*› schlimm dran sein; **get into a ~:** in Schwierigkeiten geraten; **clear up the ~:** die Dinge wieder in Ordnung bringen; **what a ~!** (troubled situation) das ist ja eine schöne Bescherung!; (unpleasant sight) das sieht ja schlimm aus!; **make a ~ of** verpfuschen (ugs.) ‹*Arbeit, Leben, Bericht, Vertrag*›; ruinieren ‹*Wirtschaft*›; durcheinander bringen ‹*Pläne*›; **make a ~ of things** alles verpfuschen (ugs.) 5 (food) **give sth. away for a ~ of pottage** (fig. arch.) etw. für ein Linsengericht hergeben (geh.) 6 (derog.: disagreeable concoction) Mischmasch, *der* (ugs.) 7 (eating place) Kantine, *die;* (for officers) Kasino, *das;* (on ship) Messe, *die;* **officers' ~:** Offizierskasino, *das*/Offiziersmesse, *die*

B *v.i.* (Mil., Navy) essen

C *v.t.* ▸**~ up**

Phrasal verbs

• **~ a'bout, ~ a'round**

A *v.i.* 1 (potter) herumwerken; (fool about) herumalbern; **~ about with cars** an Autos herumbasteln (ugs.) 2 (interfere) **~ about** *or* **around with** sich einmischen in (+ *Akk.*) ‹*Angelegenheit*›; herumspielen an (+ *Dat.*) ‹*Mechanismus, Stromkabel usw.*›

B *v.t.* **~ sb. about** *or* **around** mit jmdm. nach Belieben umspringen (abwertend); **he's been ~ed about** *or* **around by the doctors** die Ärzte haben ihn in der Mangel gehabt (ugs.)

• **~ 'up** *v.t.* 1 (make dirty) schmutzig machen; (make untidy) in Unordnung bringen 2 (bungle) verpfuschen 3 (interfere with) durcheinander bringen ‹*Plan*›. *See also* **mess-up**

message /'mesɪdʒ/

A *n.* 1 (communication) Mitteilung, *die;* Nachricht, *die;* **send/take/leave a ~:** eine Nachricht übermitteln/entgegennehmen/hinterlassen; **give sb. a ~:** jmdm. etwas ausrichten; **did you give him my ~?** haben Sie ihm meine Nachricht übermittelt?; **can I take a ~?** kann *od.* soll ich etwas ausrichten?; **send sb. a ~ by**

sb. (orally) jmdm. etwas durch jmdn. ausrichten lassen; (in writing) jmdm. durch jmdn. eine Nachricht zukommen lassen **2** (teaching) Aussage, *die;* (Relig.) Botschaft, *die;* **get the ~** (fig. coll.) verstehen; es schnallen (salopp)
B *v.t.* (by e-mail) anmailen; (by SMS) ansimsen (ugs.); eine SMS schicken (+ *Dat.*)

'message box *n.* (Computing) Meldungsfenster, *das*

messaging /'mesɪdʒɪŋ/ *n., no pl.* (by email) Mailen, *das;* (by SMS) ▸ **text messaging**

messenger /'mesɪndʒə(r)/ *n.* **1** Bote, *der*/Botin, *die* **2** **King's/Queen's M~:** königlicher Kurier

'messenger boy *n.* ▸❶ **p. 1260** Botenjunge, *der*

Messiah /mɪ'saɪə/ *n.* (lit. or fig.) Messias, *der*

Messianic /mesɪ'ænɪk/ *adj.* messianisch

messily /'mesɪlɪ/ *adv.* nachlässig; unordentlich ‹*arbeiten*›; **eat/drink ~:** sich beim Essen/Trinken bekleckern

mess: ~ jacket *n.* (Mil., Navy) Messjackett, *das;* **~mate** *n.* (Mil., Navy) Kamerad, *der;* **he was a ~mate of mine** er und ich waren Kameraden [in der Armee/Marine]

Messrs /'mesəz/ *n. pl.* **1** (in name of firm) ≈ Fa. **2** *pl. of* **Mr;** (in list of names) **~ A, B, and C** die Herren A, B und C

'mess-up *n.* Durcheinander, *das;* **there has been a ~ with your order** bei deiner Bestellung ist etwas durcheinander geraten

messy /'mesɪ/ *adj.* **1** (dirty) schmutzig; (untidy) unordentlich; **be a ~ workman** unordentlich arbeiten; **be a ~ eater** sich beim Essen bekleckern **2** (awkward) vertrackt (ugs.)

met¹ ▸ **meet¹ A, B**

met² /met/ (coll.)
A *adj.* ▸ **meteorological**
B *n.* **the Met 1** (Brit.) **The Metropolitan Police** ▸ **metropolitan A 1 2** (Amer.: Metropolitan Opera) die Met

metabolic /metə'bɒlɪk/ *adj.* (Physiol.) metabolisch (fachspr.); Stoffwechsel‹*krankheit, -typ*›

metabolism /mɪ'tæbəlɪzm/ *n.* (Physiol.) Metabolismus, *der* (fachspr.); Stoffwechsel, *der;* **basal ~:** Grundumsatz, *der*

metabolize /mɪ'tæbəlaɪz/ *v.t.* (Physiol.) umsetzen

metal /'metl/
A *n.* **1** Metall, *das; see also* **gunmetal; white metal 2** *in pl.* (Brit.: rails) Schienen; Gleise; **leave the ~s** entgleisen
B *adj.* Metall-; **be ~:** aus Metall sein
C *v.t.,* (Brit.) **-ll-** (Brit.: surface) schottern ‹*Straße*›

'metal detector *n.* Metallsuchgerät, *das*

metalize (Amer.) ▸ **metallize**

metallic /mɪ'tælɪk/ *adj.* **1** (of metal) metallisch ‹*Element, Substanz*›; Metall‹*salz, -oxid*›; **~ currency** Hart- *od.* Metallgeld, *das* **2** (like metal) metallisch ‹*Härte, Glanz, Farbe, Geräusch, Stimme*›; metallisch glänzend ‹*Glasur, Anstrich*›; **have a ~ taste** nach Metall schmecken

metallize (**metallise**) /'metəlaɪz/ *v.t.* metallisieren

metallurgic /metə'lɜ:dʒɪk/, **metallurgical** /metə'lɜ:dʒɪkl/ *adj.* metallurgisch

metallurgist /mɪ'tælədʒɪst, 'metəlɜ:dʒɪst/ *n.* ▸❶ **p. 1260** Metallurg, *der*/Metallurgin, *die*

metallurgy /mɪ'tælədʒɪ, 'metəlɜ:dʒɪ/ *n., no pl.* Metallurgie, *die*

metal: ~ polish *n.* Metallputzmittel, *das;* **~work** *n., no pl.* **1** (activity) Metallbearbeitung, *die;* **2** (metal products) Metallarbeiten *Pl.;* **a piece of ~work** eine Metallarbeit; **~worker** *n.* Metallarbeiter, *der*/-arbeiterin, *die*

metamorphic /metə'mɔ:fɪk/ *adj.* (Geol.) metamorph ‹*Gestein*›

metamorphose /metə'mɔ:fəʊz/
A *v.t.* verwandeln (**into** in + *Akk.*)
B *v.i.* sich verwandeln (**into** in + *Akk.*)

metamorphosis /metə'mɔ:fəsɪs, metəmɔ:'fəʊsɪs/ *n., pl.* **metamorphoses** /metə'mɔ:fəsi:z, metəmɔ:'fəʊsi:z/ **1** (change of form or character) Metamorphose, *die* (**into** in + *Akk.*); **undergo a [gradual] ~:** sich [allmählich] verändern **2** (Zool.) Metamorphose, *die*

metaphor /'metəfə(r)/ *n.* **1** *no pl., no art.* (stylistic device) **[the use of] ~:** der Gebrauch von Metaphern **2** (instance) Metapher, *die;* **mixed ~:** Bildbruch, *der;* Katachrese, *die* (Literaturw.)

metaphoric /metə'fɒrɪk/, **metaphorical** /metə'fɒrɪkl/ *adj.* metaphorisch

metaphorically /metə'fɒrɪkəlɪ/ *adv.* metaphorisch; **be ~ true** metaphorisch betrachtet zutreffen; **~ speaking** bildlich gesprochen

metaphysical /metə'fɪzɪkl/ *adj.* **1** (Philos.) metaphysisch; **~ language/terminology** Sprache/Terminologie der Metaphysik **2** (in popular use: abstract) theoretisch

metaphysics /metə'fɪzɪks/ *n., no pl.* **1** (Philos.) Metaphysik, *die* **2** (in popular use: abstract talk or theory) abstrakte Theorie

metastasis /me'tæstəsɪs/ *n., pl.* **metastases** /me'tæstəsi:z/ (Med.) Metastasierung, *die*

mete /mi:t/ *v.t.* (literary) **~ out** zuteil werden lassen (geh.) ‹*Belohnung*› (**to** *Dat.*); auferlegen ‹*Strafe*› (**to** *Dat.*); **~ out justice** Recht sprechen

meteor /'mi:tɪə(r)/ *n.* (Astron.) Meteor, *der;* **~ shower** Meteorschauer, *der*

meteoric /mi:tɪ'ɒrɪk/ *adj.* **1** (Astron.) Meteor‹*schweif, -tätigkeit*›; meteorisch **2** (fig.) kometenhaft; meteorhaft

meteorite /'mi:tɪəraɪt/ *n.* (Astron.) Meteorit, *der*

meteoroid /'mi:tɪərɔɪd/ *n.* (Astron.) Meteoroid, *der*

meteorological /mi:tɪərə'lɒdʒɪkl/ *adj.* meteorologisch ‹*Instrument*›; Wetter‹*ballon, -bericht*›; **M~ Office** (Brit.) Meteorologisches Amt; Wetteramt, *das*

meteorologist /mi:tɪə'rɒlədʒɪst/ *n.* ▸❶ **p. 1260** Meteorologe, *der*/Meteorologin, *die*

meteorology /mi:tɪə'rɒlədʒɪ/ *n.* **1** *no pl.* Meteorologie, *die* **2** (weather of region) meteorologische Bedingungen

meter¹ /'mi:tə(r)/
A *n.* **1** (measuring device) Zähler, *der;* (for coins) Münzzähler, *der;* **humidity ~:** Hygrometer, *das; see also* **electricity meter; gas meter; water meter 2** (parking ~) Parkuhr, *die;* **feed the ~** (coll.) Geld [in die Parkuhr] nachwerfen **3** ▸ **taximeter**
B *v.t.* [mit einem Zähler] messen ‹[*Wasser-, Gas-, Strom*]*verbrauch*›

meter² (Amer.) ▸ **metre¹**

meter³ (Amer.) ▸ **metre²**

'meter maid *n.* (coll.) Politesse, *die*

methadone /'meθədəʊn/ *n.* Methadon, *das*

methane /'mi:θeɪn, 'meθeɪn/ *n.* (Chem.) Methan, *das*

methanol /'meθənɒl/ *n., no pl.* (Chem.) Methanol, *das*

methinks /mɪ'θɪŋks/ *v.i. impers., p. t.* **methought** /mɪ'θɔ:t/ (arch.) mich dünkt *od.* deucht (geh. veralt.)

method /'meθəd/ *n.* **1** (procedure) Methode, *die;* **~ of proceeding** *or* **procedure** Vorgehensweise, *die;* **brew by the traditional ~:** nach traditionellem Verfahren brauen; **police ~s** die Arbeitsweise der Polizei **2** *no pl., no art.* (arrangement of ideas, orderliness) System, *das;* Systematik, *die;* **there was a lack of** *or* **was no ~ in the book** das Buch war unmethodisch *od.* unsystematisch aufgebaut; **a man of ~:** ein systematisch denkender Mensch; **use ~:** methodisch *od.* systematisch vorgehen; **there's ~ in his madness** (fig. joc.) der Wahnsinn hat Methode **3** (scheme of classification) System, *das*

methodic /mɪ'θɒdɪk/ *adj.* (Amer.) **1** ▸ **methodical 2** (relating to methodology) methodologisch

methodical /mɪ'θɒdɪkl/ *adj.* methodisch; systematisch; **in a ~ way** methodisch; systematisch; **be ~:** methodisch *od.* systematisch vorgehen

methodically /mɪ'θɒdɪkəlɪ/ *adv.* mit Methode; systematisch

Methodism /'meθədɪzm/ *n., no pl.* (Relig.) Methodismus, *der*

Methodist /'meθədɪst/ *n.* (Relig.) Methodist, *der*/Methodistin, *die; attrib.* Methodisten‹*kapelle, -gottesdienst, -pfarrer*›

methodological /meθədə'lɒdʒɪkl/ *adj.* methodologisch

methodology /meθə'dɒlədʒɪ/ *n.* **1** *no pl., no art.* (science of method) Methodik, *die;* Methodologie, *die* **2** (methods used) Methodik, *die*

methought ▸ **methinks**

meths /meθs/ *n., no pl., no indef. art.* (Brit. coll.) [Brenn]spiritus, *der*

'meths drinker *n.* (Brit. coll.) ≈ Fuseltrinker, *der*/-trinkerin, *die*

Methuselah /mɪ'θju:zələ/ *n.* **1** *pr. n.* (Bibl.) Methusalem (*der*) **2** **[old] ~:** Methusalem, *der* (ugs.)

methyl /'meθɪl, 'mi:θaɪl/ *n.* (Chem.) Methyl, *das*

methyl 'alcohol *n.* (Chem.) Methylalkohol, *der;* Methanol, *das*

methylated spirit[s] /meθɪleɪtɪd 'spɪrɪt(s)/ *n.* [*pl.*] Brennspiritus, *der;* vergällter *od.* denaturierter Alkohol (fachspr.)

meticulous /mɪ'tɪkjʊləs/ *adj.* (scrupulous) sorgfältig; (overscrupulous) übergenau; pedantisch (abwertend); **be ~ about sth.** es peinlich genau mit etw. nehmen; **be a ~ person** es sehr genau nehmen

meticulously /mɪ'tɪkjʊləslɪ/ *adv.* **1** (scrupulously) sorgfältig; (overscrupulously) übergenau; pedantisch (abwertend); **~ clean** peinlich sauber **2** (coll.: carefully) sehr sorgfältig; haargenau (ugs.) ‹*abbilden, wiedergeben*›

métier /'metjeɪ/ *n.* **1** (calling) Metier, *das* **2** (forte) Stärke, *die*

metonymy /mɪ'tɒnɪmɪ/ *n.* (Rhet.) Metonymie, *die*

metre¹ /'mi:tə/ *n.* (Brit.) **1** (poetic rhythm) Metrum, *das* (Verslehre); Versmaß, *das;* **written in an iambic ~:** in Jamben geschrieben **2** (Pros.: metrical group) Metrum, *das*

metre² *n.* ▸❶ **p. 1072**, ▸❶ **p. 1286** (Brit.: unit) Meter, *der od. das;* **sell cloth by the ~:** Stoff meterweise verkaufen; *see also* **cubic 2; square B 2**

metric /'metrɪk/ *adj.* metrisch; **~ system** metrisches System; **go ~:** das metrische System einführen; *see also* **hundredweight; ton 1**

metrical /'metrɪkl/ *adj.,* **metrically** /'metrɪkəlɪ/ *adv.* metrisch

metricate /'metrɪkeɪt/ *v.t. & i.* auf das metrische System umstellen

metrication /metrɪ'keɪʃn/ *n.* Umstellung auf das metrische System

metro /'metrəʊ/ *n., pl.* **~s** U-Bahn, *die;* **the Paris M~:** die [Pariser] Metro

metronome /'metrənəʊm/ *n.* (Mus.) Metronom, *das*

metropolis /mɪ'trɒpəlɪs/ *n.* (capital) Hauptstadt, *die;* (chief city) Metropole, *die;* **the ~** (Brit.) London (*das*)

metropolitan /metrə'pɒlɪtən/
A *adj.* **1** (of a metropolis) **[the] ~ hotels/cinemas** die Hotels/Kinos der Metropole; **~ New York/Tokyo** der Großraum New York/Tokio; **~ London** Großlondon (*das*); **the M~ Police** die Londoner Polizei; **~ borough/district** (Brit. Admin.) Gemeinde/Bezirk im Großraum einer Großstadt; **~ county** (Brit. Admin.) *eines von sechs Ballungsgebieten außerhalb Großlondons* **2** (not colonial) mutterländisch; **~ France** das Mutterland Frankreich
B *n.* ▸ **metropolitan bishop**

metropolitan 'bishop *n.* (Gk. Orthodox Ch., RC Ch.) Metropolit, *der;* (Anglican Ch.) Erzbischof, *der*

mettle /'metl/ *n.* **1** (quality of temperament) Wesensart, *die;* **show one's ~:** zeigen, aus welchem Holz man [geschnitzt] ist **2** (spirit) Mut, *der;* **a man of ~:** ein mutiger Mann; **be on one's ~:** zeigen müssen, was man kann; **put sb./sth. on his/its ~:** jmdn./etw. fordern **3** (animal's vigour) Feuer, *das*

Meuse /mɜ:z/ *pr. n.* (Geog.) Maas (*die*)

mew /mju:/
A v.i. ‹*Katze:*› miauen; ‹*Möwe:*› kreischen
B n. (of cat) Miauen, *das;* (of seagull) Kreischen, *das*

mews /mju:z/ n., pl. *same* (Brit.) Stallungen *Pl.;* (*converted into dwellings/garages*) *zu [eleganten] Wohnhäusern/Garagen umgebaute ehemalige Stallungen [in ruhigen Seitenstraßen]*

Mexican /'meksɪkən/ ▸ **p. 1345**
A adj. mexikanisch; **sb. is ~:** jmd. ist Mexikaner/Mexikanerin; **~ wave** La-Ola[-Welle], *die; see also* **English A**
B n. Mexikaner, *der*/Mexikanerin, *die*

Mexico /'meksɪkəʊ/ *pr. n.* ▸ **p. 1643** Mexiko (*das*); **~ City** Mexiko [City] (*das*)

mezzanine /'metsəni:n, 'mezəni:n/ n. **1** (Archit.) Mezzanin, *das* (fachspr.); Halbgeschoss, *das* **2** (Amer. Theatre) erster Rang

mezzo /'metsəʊ/: **~-soprano** n. Mezzosopranistin, *die;* **~tint** n. (Art) Mezzotinto, *das;* (method) Mezzotinto, *das;* Schabkunst, *die*

mg. *abbr.* ▸ **p. 1702 = milligram[s]** mg

MHz *abbr.* **= megahertz** MHz

mi /mi:/ ▸ **me²**

mi. *abbr.* (Amer.) **= mile[s]** M

MI n. (Brit. Hist./coll.) **MI5** *die britische Spionageabwehr;* **MI6** *der britische Nachrichtendienst*

miaow /mɪ'aʊ/
A v.i. miauen
B n. Miauen, *das*

miasma /mɪ'æzmə, maɪ'æzmə/ n., pl. **~ta** /mɪ'æzmətə, maɪ'æzmətə/ *or* **~s** Miasma, *das;* Gestank, *der*

mica /'maɪkə/ n. (Min.) Glimmer, *der*

mice *pl. of* **mouse**

Michaelmas /'mɪklməs/ n. Michaeli[s] (*das*); Michaelistag, *der*

Michaelmas: ~ 'daisy n. (Bot.) Herbstaster, *die;* **~ term** n. (Brit. Univ.) Herbsttrimester, *das*

mickey /'mɪkɪ/ n. (Brit. coll.) **take the ~ [out of sb./sth.]** jmdn./etw. durch den Kakao ziehen (ugs.)

Mickey 'Mouse *attrib. adj.* (derog.) lächerlich; **croquet is a bit of a ~ sport** Krocket ist doch gar kein richtiger Sport; **this is a ~ job** diese Arbeit ist ein Witz

mickle /'mɪkl/ (arch./Scot.)
A groß
B n. **many a ~ makes a muckle** (prov.) Kleinvieh macht auch Mist (ugs.)

micky ▸ **mickey**

micro /'maɪkrəʊ/ n., pl. **~s** ▸ **microcomputer**

micro- /maɪkrəʊ/ *in comb.* mikro-/Mikro-

microbe /'maɪkrəʊb/ n. (Biol.) Mikrobe, *die*

micro: ~bi'ology n., *no pl.* Mikrobiologie, *die;* **~brewery** n. Mikrobrauerei, *die;* **M~card** ® n. Mikrokarte, *die;* **~chip** n. (Electronics) [Mikro]chip, *der;* **~circuit** n. Mikroschaltkreis, *der;* **~climate** n. Mikroklima, *das;* **~computer** n. (Computing) Mikrocomputer, *der;* **~controller** n. (Electronics) Mikrocontroller, *der*

microcosm /'maɪkrəkɒzm/ n. Mikrokosmos, *der*

micro: ~dot n. Mikrat, *das;* **~eco'nomic** adj. mikroökonomisch; **~economics** n. Mikroökonomie, *die;* **~elec'tronics** n. Mikroelektronik, *die;* **~fibre** n. Mikrofaser, *die;* **~fiche** n., *pl. same or* **~s** Mikrofiche, *das od. der;* **~film A** n. Mikrofilm, *der;* **B** v.t. auf Mikrofilm (*Akk.*) aufnehmen; **~film reader** n. Mikrofilmlesegerät, *das;* **~light ['aircraft]** n. (Aeronaut.) Ultraleichtflugzeug, *das;* **~mesh stockings** n. pl. Mikrofaserstrümpfe *Pl.*

micrometer /maɪ'krɒmɪtə(r)/ n. (Mech. Engin.) [Fein]messschraube, *die*

'microminiaturize v.t. (Electron.) mikrominiaturisieren ‹*elektronische Bauteile etc.*›

micron /'maɪkrɒn/ n. Mikrometer, *der od. das*

Micronesia /maɪkrə'ni:ʃə/ *pr. n.* Mikronesien (*das*)

micro-'organism n. Mikroorganismus, *der;* Kleinstlebewesen, *das*

microphone /'maɪkrəfəʊn/ n. Mikrofon, *das*

micro: ~photograph n. Mikrokopie, *die;* **~physics** n., *no pl.* Mikrophysik, *die;* **~processor** n. (Computing) Mikroprozessor, *der*

microscope /'maɪkrəskəʊp/ n. Mikroskop, *das;* **examine sth. through** *or* **under a ~:** etw. unter dem Mikroskop untersuchen; **put** *or* **have sth. under the ~** (fig.) etw. unter die Lupe nehmen (ugs.); **be under the ~** (fig.) unter die Lupe genommen werden (ugs.); auf den Zahn gefühlt werden (ugs.)

microscopic /maɪkrə'skɒpɪk/ adj. **1** mikroskopisch; sehr stark vergrößernd ‹*Linse*› **2** (fig.: very small) winzig ‹*Portion, Auto*›; mikroskopisch klein ‹*Tier, Portion*›

microscopically /maɪkrə'skɒpɪkəlɪ/ adv. mikroskopisch

microscopy /maɪ'krɒskəpɪ/ n., *no pl., no art.* Mikroskopie, *die;* **by ~:** mikroskopisch; unter dem Mikroskop

micro: ~second n. Mikrosekunde, *die;* **~sleep** n. Sekundenschlaf, *der;* Mikroschlaf, *der* (fachspr.); **~structure** n. Mikrostruktur, *die;* **~surgery** n., *no pl.* (Med.) Mikrochirurgie, *die;* **~technology** n., *no pl.* Mikrotechnik, *die;* **~transmitter** n. Mikrosender, *der;* **~wave A** n. Mikrowelle, *die.* **B** v.t. in der Mikrowelle zubereiten

microwaveable /'maɪkrəʊweɪvəbl/ adj. mikrowellengeeignet

microwave ['oven] n. Mikrowellenherd, *der*

mid- /mɪd/ *in comb.* ▸ **p. 894 1 in ~air/-stream** in der Luft/Strommitte; **~air collision** Zusammenstoß in der Luft; **in ~flight/sentence** mitten im Flug/Satz; **in ~course** mittendrin; **[in] ~afternoon** [mitten] am Nachmittag **2** *forming compound adj. used attrib.* **~afternoon siesta** Nachmittagsschläfchen, *das;* **~morning break** ≈ Frühstückspause, *die;* große Pause (Schulw.); **a ~season game** ein Spiel in der Mitte der Saison; **~term exams** Prüfungen in der Mitte des Trimesters; **~term elections** (Amer.) Kongress- und Kommunalwahlen in der Mitte der Amtszeit des Präsidenten **3** *with months, decades, persons' ages* **~July** Mitte Juli; **the ~60s** die Mitte der Sechzigerjahre; **a man in the** *or* **his ~fifties** ein Mittfünfziger; **be in one's ~thirties** Mitte dreißig sein

Midas touch /'maɪdəs tʌtʃ/ n. **he has the ~:** was er anfasst, wird zu Gold (fig.)

midday /'mɪddeɪ, mɪd'deɪ/ n. ▸ **p. 1001** **1** (noon) zwölf Uhr; **round about ~:** um die Mittagszeit **2** (middle of day) Mittag, *der; attrib.* Mittags-

midden /'mɪdn/ n. **1** (dunghill) Misthaufen, *der* **2** (refuse heap) Abfallhaufen, *der*

middle /'mɪdl/
A *attrib. adj.* **1** mittler…; **the ~ one** der/die/das mittlere; **~ space** Zwischenraum, *der;* **the ~ years of the 19th century** die Jahre in der Mitte des 19. Jahrhunderts; **man/house of ~ height/size** mittelgroßer Mann/-großes Haus **2** (equidistant from extremities) **~ point** Mittelpunkt, *der* **3** (Ling.) Mittel‹*latein, -hochdeutsch*›; *see also* **English B 1**
B n. **1** ▸ **p. 1047** Mitte, *die;* (central part) Mittelteil, *der;* **in the ~ of the room/the table** in der Mitte des Zimmers/des Tisches; (emphatic) mitten im Zimmer/auf dem Tisch; **right in the ~ of Manchester** genau im Zentrum von Manchester; **in the ~ of the forest** mitten im Wald; **the boat sank in the ~ of the Atlantic** das Schiff sank mitten im Atlantik; **grasp the ~ of sth.** etw. in der Mitte festhalten; **fold sth. down the ~:** etw. in der Mitte falten; **in the ~ of the day** mittags; **in the ~ of the morning/afternoon** mitten am Vor-/Nachmittag; **in the ~ of the night/week** mitten in der Nacht/Woche; **happen in the ~ of next week/month** Mitte nächster Woche/nächsten Monats geschehen; **the ~ of the day** die Mitte des Tages; **be in the ~ of doing sth.** (fig.) gerade mitten dabei sein, etw. zu tun; **in the ~ of the operation/washing her hair** (fig.) mitten in der Operation/im Haarewaschen; *see also* **knock A 3; nowhere B 2** (waist) Taille, *die*

middle: ~ 'age n. mittleres [Lebens]alter; **a man in ~ age** ein Mann mittleren Alters; **complaints of ~ age** Beschwerden von Menschen mittleren Alters; **~-aged** /'mɪdleɪdʒd/ adj. mittleren Alters *nachgestellt;* **acquire a ~-aged spread** [in den mittleren Jahren] Speck ansetzen; **M~ 'Ages** n. pl. **the M~ Ages** das Mittelalter; **M~ A'merica** n., *no pl.* **1** (middle class in America) die amerikanische Mittelschicht; **2** (US Midwest) der [amerikanische] Mittlere Westen; **~brow** (coll.) **A** adj. für den [geistigen] Normalverbraucher *nachgestellt* (ugs.); **B** n. [geistiger] Normalverbraucher (ugs.); **~ 'C** n. (Mus.) das eingestrichene C; **~ 'class** n. Mittelstand, *der;* Mittelschicht, *die;* **~-class** adj. bürgerlich ‹*Vorort, Einstellung, Moral, Werte*›; ‹*Moral, Werte*› des Mittelstandes; **~-class people** Mittelständler; **~ 'common room** n. (Brit. Univ.) Gemeinschaftsraum für graduierte Studenten; **~ 'course** n. Mittelweg, *der;* **~ 'distance** ▸ **distance A 4; ~-distance runner** Mittelstreckenläufer, *der*/-läuferin, *die;* **~ 'ear** n. (Anat.) Mittelohr, *das;* **M~ 'East** *pr. n.* **the M~ East** der Nahe [und Mittlere] Osten; **M~ 'Eastern** adj. nahöstlich; des Nahen Ostens *nachgestellt;* ‹*Person*› aus dem Nahen Osten; **~ 'England** n. die konservative englische Mittelklasse *od.* -schicht; **~ finger** n. Mittelfinger, *der;* **~ 'life** n., *no pl.* mittleres Lebensalter; **~man** n. (Commerc.) Zwischenhändler, *der*/-händlerin, *die;* (fig.) Vermittler, *der*/Vermittlerin, *die;* **~ 'management** n. mittleres Management; **~ 'manager** n. **be a ~ manager** im mittleren Management arbeiten; **~ name** n. **1** zweiter Vorname; **2** (fig.: characteristic quality) **carefulness is my ~ name** ich bin die Vorsicht in Person; **modesty is not his ~ name** Bescheidenheit ist nicht seine Stärke; **~-of-the-'road** adj. gemäßigt; moderat; **~-of-the-road politician/politics** Politiker/Politik der Mitte; **~ school** n. (Brit.) **1** (State school) *Schule für 9- bis 13-Jährige;* **2** (third and fourth forms) *dritte und vierte Klasse einer höheren Schule;* **~-size[d]** adj. mittelgroß; **~ 'way** n. **1** ▸ **~ course;** **2** (Buddhism) **the ~ way** der mittlere Weg; **~weight** n. (Boxing etc.) Mittelgewicht, *das;* (person also) Mittelgewichtler, *der;* **M~ 'West** *pr. n.* (Amer.) **the M~ West** der Mittlere Westen; **M~ 'Western** adj. (Amer.) des Mittleren Westens *nachgestellt*

> **middle school**
>
> Eine staatliche Schule in einigen Teilen von England und Wales, die Kinder im Alter von 9 bis 13 Jahren unterrichtet. In den USA geht die *middle school* mit vierjähriger Schulzeit der **high school** voraus.

middling /'mɪdlɪŋ/
A adj. **1** (second-rate) mittelmäßig **2** (moderately good) **[fair to] ~:** ganz ordentlich (ugs.); [ganz] passabel **3** (coll.: in fairly good health) mittelprächtig (ugs. scherzh.); **How are you? — Oh, ~:** Wie geht es dir? — Ach, so einigermaßen **4** (Commerc.) mittler… ‹*Qualität, Ware*›
B adv. recht; (only moderately) ganz

middlingly /'mɪdlɪŋlɪ/ adv. **1** ganz ordentlich *od.* passabel **2** (only moderately well) mäßig

'Mideast (Amer.) ▸ **Middle East**

Mid'eastern (Amer.) ▸ **Middle Eastern**

'midfield n. (Footb.) Mittelfeld, *das;* **play in ~:** im Mittelfeld spielen; *attrib.* **~ player** Mittelfeldspieler, *der*

midge /mɪdʒ/ n. **1** (in popular use) Stechmücke, *die* **2** (Zool.) Zuckmücke, *die*

midget /'mɪdʒɪt/
A n. **1** (person) Liliputaner, *der*/Liliputanerin, *die;* Zwerg, *der*/Zwergin, *die* **2** (thing) Zwerg, *der* (fig.); (animal) Zwergform, *die*
B adj. winzig; (in design) Mini‹*flugzeug, -U-Boot*›

midi /'mɪdɪ/ n. Midi[rock], *der;* (dress) Midikleid, *das;* **~-length coat** Midimantel, *der*

midland /'mɪdlənd/
A n. Binnenland, *das;* **the M~s** (Brit.) Mittelengland
B adj. im Landesinnern *nachgestellt;* **M~[s]** (Brit.)

in den Midlands *nachgestellt;* ‹*Dialekt*› der Midlands

midlander /ˈmɪdləndə(r)/ *n.* Bewohner/Bewohnerin des Binnenlandes; **M~** (Brit.) Bewohner/Bewohnerin der Midlands

midlife crisis /mɪdlaɪf ˈkraɪsɪs/ *n.* Midlife-crisis, *die*

ˈmidline *n.* Mittellinie, *die*

ˈmid-morning

A *n.* [später] Vormittag

B *adj.* Vormittags-

ˈmidnight *n.* ▸❶ **p. 1001** Mitternacht, *die; attrib.* Mitternachts‹*stunde, -messe, -zug*›; mitternächtlich ‹*Festgelage, Feiern*›

midnight: ~ ˈfeast *n.* Mitternachtsessen, *das;* **~ ˈoil** ▸**oil A 1**; **~ ˈsun** *n.* Mitternachtssonne, *die*

mid-ˈoff *n.* (Cricket) Feldspieler links vom Werfer (*bei rechtshändigem Schlagmann*)

mid-ˈon *n.* (Cricket) Feldspieler rechts vom Werfer (*bei rechtshändigem Schlagmann*)

ˈmidpoint *n.* Mitte, *die*

ˈmidrib *n.* (Bot.) [mittlere] Blattrippe

midriff /ˈmɪdrɪf/ *n.* **1** **the bulge below his ~:** die Wölbung seiner Taillengegend; **with bare ~:** nabelfrei; **he landed a blow on his opponent's ~:** er traf seinen Gegner unterhalb des Brustkorbs **2** (diaphragm) Zwerchfell, *das* **3** (Amer.: garment exposing ~) die Taille freilassender Zweiteiler

midshipman /ˈmɪdʃɪpmən/ *n., pl.* **midshipmen** /ˈmɪdʃɪpmən/ (Navy) **1** (Brit.) Midshipman, *der; unterster Seeoffiziersrang* **2** (Amer.) Midshipman, *der;* Seeoffiziersanwärter, *der*

midst /mɪdst/ *n.* **in the ~ of sth.** mitten in einer Sache; **be in the ~ of doing sth.** gerade mitten dabei sein, etw. zu tun; **in our/their/your ~:** in unserer/ihrer/eurer Mitte

midsummer /ˈmɪdsʌmə(r), mɪdˈsʌmə(r)/ *n.* die [Zeit der] Sommersonnenwende; der Mittsommer; **[on] M~['s] Day** [am] Johannistag; **~ madness** [heller] Wahnsinn (ugs.)

ˈmidterm *n.* **1** (Pol.) Mitte der Amtszeit; **resign in ~:** mitten in der Amtszeit zurücktreten; *attrib.* **~ elections** Zwischenwahlen **2** (Educ.) Mitte des Semesters/Trimesters **3** (Amer.: exam) Prüfung zur Halbzeit des Semesters/Trimesters

ˈmidtown *n.* (Amer.) *am Rande des Zentrums gelegener Stadtbezirk; attrib.* am Rande des Zentrums *nachgestellt*

midway /ˈmɪdweɪ, mɪdˈweɪ/ *adv.* auf halbem Weg[e] ‹*sich treffen, sich befinden*›; **~ through sth.** (fig.) mitten in etw. (*Dat.*)

midweek /ˈmɪdwiːk, mɪdˈwiːk/ *n.* **in ~:** in der Wochenmitte; **~ flights** Flüge in der Wochenmitte

ˈMidwest (Amer.) ▸**Middle West**

Midˈwestern (Amer.) ▸**Middle Western**

midwife /ˈmɪdwaɪf/ *n., pl.* **midwives** /ˈmɪdwaɪvz/ ▸❶ **p. 1260** Hebamme, *die*

midwifery /ˈmɪdwɪfrɪ, mɪdˈwɪfərɪ/ *n., no pl., no art.* Geburtshilfe, *die*

midˈwinter *n.* die [Zeit der] Wintersonnenwende; der Mittwinter

mien /miːn/ *n.* (literary) (look) Miene, *die;* (bearing) Gebaren, *das*

miff /mɪf/ (coll.)

A *n.* **1** (huff) **get into a ~:** sich auf den Schlips getreten fühlen (**about** wegen) (ugs.); **be in a ~:** beleidigt *od.* eingeschnappt sein (ugs.) **2** (quarrel) Knies, *der* (ugs.); **have a ~ with sb.** mit jmdm. Ärger *od.* (ugs.) Knies haben

B *v.t.* verärgern; **be ~ed** beleidigt *od.* (ugs.) eingeschnappt sein

might¹ /maɪt/ ▸**may**

might² *n.* **1** (force) Gewalt, *die;* (inner strength) Macht, *die;* **with all one's ~:** mit aller Kraft; **with ~ and main** mit aller Macht **2** (power) Macht, *die;* **~ is right** Macht geht vor Recht

might-have-been /ˈmaɪtəvbiːn/ *n.* **1** nicht verwirklichte Möglichkeit; **the ~s** das, was hätte sein können **2** (person) *jemand, der es zu etwas hätte bringen können;* **he is a ~:** er hat seine Chancen verpasst

mightily /ˈmaɪtɪlɪ/ *adv.* **1** mit aller Kraft **2** (coll.: very) überaus; **be ~ amused** sich köstlich amüsieren

mightn't /ˈmaɪtnt/ (coll.) **= might not;** ▸**may**

mighty /ˈmaɪtɪ/

A *adj.* **1** (powerful) mächtig; gewaltig ‹*Krieger, Anstrengung*› **2** (massive) gewaltig **3** (coll.: great) riesig; stark ‹*Trinker*›. *See also* **high A 5**

B *adv.* (coll.) verdammt (ugs.)

mignonette /mɪnjəˈnet/ *n.* **1** (plant) Reseda, *die;* (Reseda odorata) Gartenresede, *die* **2** (colour) Resedagrün, *das*

migraine /ˈmiːgreɪn, ˈmaɪgreɪn/ *n.* ▸❶ **p. 1231** (Med.) Migräne, *die*

migraine: ~ attack *n.* Migräneanfall, *der;* **~ sufferer** *n.* an Migräne leidender Mensch; **be a ~ sufferer** an Migräne leiden

migrant /ˈmaɪgrənt/

A *adj.* **1** **~ tribe** Nomadenstamm, *der;* **~ worker** Wanderarbeiter, *der*/-arbeiterin, *die;* (in EU) Gastarbeiter, *der*/-arbeiterin, *die* **2** (coming and going with the seasons) **~ bird/fish** Zugvogel, *der*/Wanderfisch, *der;* **~ herds** wandernde Herden

B *n.* **1** Auswanderer, *der*/Auswanderin, *die;* (worker) Wanderarbeiter, *der*/-arbeiterin, *die* **2** (bird) Zugvogel, *der;* (fish) Wanderfisch, *der*

migrate /maɪˈgreɪt/ *v.i.* **1** (from rural area to town) abwandern; (to another country) auswandern; (to another town) übersiedeln (**to** nach); (to another place of work) überwechseln **2** (with the seasons) ‹*Vogel:*› fortziehen; ‹*Fisch:*› wandern; **~ to the south/sea** nach Süden ziehen/zum Meer wandern

migration /maɪˈgreɪʃn/ *n.* **1** ▸**migrate 1**: Abwandern, *das;* Auswandern, *das;* Übersiedeln, *das;* Überwechseln, *das;* **a great ~:** eine große Auswanderungswelle **2** (with the seasons) (of birds) Fortziehen, *das;* (of fish) Wandern, *das;* (instance) (of birds) Zug, *der;* (of fish) Wanderung, *die*

migratory /ˈmaɪgrətərɪ, maɪˈgreɪtərɪ/ *adj.* **1** **~ tribe** Nomadenstamm, *der;* **these workers are ~:** dies sind Wanderarbeiter/(in EEC) Gastarbeiter **2** (moving according to seasons) **~ bird/fish** Zugvogel, *der*/Wanderfisch, *der*

mike *n.* (coll.) Mikro, *das*

Mike /maɪk/ *pr. n.* **for the love of ~** (coll.) um Himmels willen

milady /mɪˈleɪdɪ/ *n.* **1** Lady, *die* **2** (form of address) Mylady; gnädige Frau

Milan /mɪˈlæn/ *pr. n.* ▸❶ **p. 1643** Mailand (*das*)

Milanese /mɪləˈniːz/

A *n.* Mailänder, *der*/Mailänderin, *die*

B *adj.* mailändisch; Mailänder

milch /mɪltʃ/ *attrib. adj.* **~ cow** Milchkuh, *die*

mild /maɪld/

A *adj.* **1** (gentle) sanft ‹*Person*› **2** (not severe) mild ‹*Urteil, Bestrafung, Kritik*›; leicht ‹*Erkrankung, Gefühlsregung*›; gemäßigt ‹*Ausdrucksweise, Sprache, Satire*›; (moderate) leicht ‹*Ermutigung, Aufregung*› **3** (moderately warm) mild ‹*Wetter, Winter*› **4** (having gentle effect) mild, leicht ‹*Arzneimittel, Stimulans*› **5** (not strong in taste) mild; leicht ‹*Bier*› **6** (feeble) zahm (ugs.) ‹*Versuch, Spiel*›. *See also* **draw A 3**

B *n.: schwach gehopfte englische Biersorte;* **~ and bitter** (Brit.) *Mischgetränk aus schwach und stark gehopftem Bier*

mildew /ˈmɪldjuː/

A *n.* **1** (on paper, cloth, wood) Schimmel, *der;* **be spotted with ~:** Stockflecke haben **2** (on plant) Mehltau, *der*

B *v.t.* **be/become ~ed** schimm[e]lig sein/verschimmeln; ‹*Pflanze:*› von Mehltau befallen sein/werden

mildewy /ˈmɪldjuːɪ/ *adj.* schimm[e]lig ‹*Papier, Stoff, Holz*›; von Mehltau befallen ‹*Pflanze*›; muffig, mod[e]rig ‹*Atmosphäre, Luft*›; (spotted with mildew) stock[fleck]ig

mildly /ˈmaɪldlɪ/ *adv.* **1** (gently) mild[e] **2** (slightly) ein bisschen *od.* wenig ‹*enttäuscht, bestürzt, ermutigend, begeistert*› **3** **to put it ~:** gelinde gesagt; **and that's putting it ~:** und das ist noch gelinde ausgedrückt

mild ˈsteel *n.* weicher *od.* kohlenstoffarmer Stahl

mile /maɪl/ *n.* **1** ▸❶ **p. 911**, ▸❶ **p. 1072**, ▸❶ **p. 1566** Meile, *die;* **~ after** *or* **upon ~** *or* **~s and ~s of sand/beaches** meilenweit Sand/Strände; **~s per hour** Meilen pro Stunde; **not a hundred** *or* **thousand** *or* **million ~s from** (joc.) nicht allzu weit von; **someone not a hundred** *etc.* **~s from here** (joc.) einer ganz hier in der Nähe; **go the extra ~** (fig.) [noch] einen Schritt weiter gehen; *see also* **square B 2** **2** **geographical** *or* **nautical** *or* **sea ~** ▸**nautical mile** **3** (fig. coll.: great amount) **win/miss by a ~:** haushoch gewinnen/meilenweit verfehlen; **~s better/too big** tausendmal besser/viel zu groß; **beat sb. by ~s** jmdn. haushoch schlagen; **be ~s ahead of sb.** jmdm. weit voraus sein; **be ~s out [in one's answers]** [mit seinen Antworten] völlig danebenliegen (ugs.); **run a ~** (fig.) das Weite suchen; **you can see it a ~ off** (fig.) das sieht doch ein Blinder [mit dem Krückstock] (ugs.); **sb. is ~s away** (in thought) jmd. ist mit seinen Gedanken ganz woanders; *see also* **stand out 2**; **stick out B 2** **4** (race) Meilenlauf, *der;* **run the ~ in under four minutes** die Meile in weniger als vier Minuten laufen

mileage /ˈmaɪlɪdʒ/ *n.* **1** (number of miles) [Anzahl der] Meilen; **state the exact ~ travelled** die gefahrenen Meilen genau angeben; **a low ~** (on milometer) ein niedriger Meilenstand **2** (number of miles per gallon) [Benzin]verbrauch, *der;* **what ~ do you get with your car?** wie viel verbraucht dein Auto? **3** (fig.: benefit) Nutzen, *der;* **get ~ out of sth.** Nutzen aus etw. ziehen; **there is no ~ in the idea** dieser Vorschlag rentiert sich nicht **4** (expenses) ≈ Kilometergeld, *das*

ˈmileage allowance *n.* Kilometergeld, *das*

mile: ~post *n.* **1** Meilenpfosten, *der;* **2** (Sport) Meilenmarkierung, *die;* **by/at the ~post** eine Meile vor dem Ziel; **~stone** *n.* (lit. or fig.) Meilenstein, *der*

milieu /mɪˈljɜː, ˈmiːljɜː/ *n., pl.* **~x** *or* **~s** /mɪˈljɜːz, ˈmiːljɜːz/ Milieu, *das*

militancy /ˈmɪlɪtənsɪ/ *n., no pl.* Kampfbereitschaft, *die;* Militanz, *die*

militant /ˈmɪlɪtənt/

A *adj.* **1** (aggressively active) kämpferisch; militant; (less aggressive) aktiv **2** (engaged in warfare) Krieg führend

B *n.* Militante, *der/die*

militaria /mɪlɪˈteərɪə/ *n. pl.* Militaria *Pl.*

militarism /ˈmɪlɪtərɪzəm/ *n.* Militarismus, *der*

militaristic /mɪlɪtəˈrɪstɪk/ *adj.* militaristisch

militarize (**militarise**) /ˈmɪlɪtəraɪz/ *v.t.* militarisieren; (equip) militärisch ausrüsten

military /ˈmɪlɪtərɪ/

A *adj.* militärisch; Militär‹*regierung, -akademie, -uniform, -parade*›; **~ man** Soldat, *der;* **~ service** Militärdienst, *der;* Wehrdienst, *der*

B *n., constr. as sing. or pl.* **the ~:** das Militär

military: ~ ˈband *n.* Militärkapelle, *die;* **~ poˈlice** *n.* Militärpolizei, *die*

militate /ˈmɪlɪteɪt/ *v.i.* **~ against/in favour of sth.** [deutlich] gegen/für etw. sprechen; (have effect) sich zuungunsten/zugunsten einer Sache (*Gen.*) auswirken

militia /mɪˈlɪʃə/ *n.* Miliz, *die;* Bürgerwehr, *die* (hist.)

militiaman /mɪˈlɪʃəmən/ *n., pl.* **militiamen** /mɪˈlɪʃəmən/ Milizionär, *der*

milk /mɪlk/

A *n.* Milch, *die;* **it's no use crying over spilt ~** (prov.) [was] passiert ist[, ist] passiert; **be [like] ~ and water** bieder und harmlos sein; **~-and-water** (fig.) nichts sagend ‹*Rede, Predigt, Meinung, Buch*›; halbherzig ‹*Politik*›; **a land of** *or* **flowing with ~ and honey** (fig.) ein Land, darin Milch und Honig fließt (bibl. fig.); **the ~ of human kindness** die Milch der frommen Denkart (dichter.); **M~ of Magnesia** ® Magnesiamilch, *die; see also* **condense A 1**; **dried**; **powder B 2**

B *v.t.* (draw ~ from) melken; (fig.: get money out of) melken (salopp); **be ~ed dry by sb.** von jmdm. ausgenommen werden (ugs.)

milk: ~ bar *n.* Milchbar, *die;* **~ bottle** *n.* Milchflasche, *die;* **~ ˈchocolate** *n.* Milchschokolade, *die;* **~ churn** *n.* Milchkanne, *die;*

m

~ float *n.* (Brit.) Milchwagen, *der*
milking /ˈmɪlkɪŋ/ *n.* Melken, *das*
milking: ~ machine *n.* Melkmaschine, *die;* **~ stool** *n.* Melkschemel, *der*
milk: ~ jug *n.* Milchkrug, *der;* (with tea, coffee, etc.) Milchkännchen, *das;* **~ loaf** *n.* Milchbrot, *das;* **~maid** *n.* ▸ℹ **p. 1260** Melkerin, *die;* **~man** /ˈmɪlkmən/ *n., pl.* **~men** /ˈmɪlkmən/ ▸ℹ **p. 1260** Milchmann, *der;* **~ powder** *n.* Milchpulver, *das;* **~ ˈpudding** *n.* Milchpudding, *der;* **~ round** *n.* (Brit.) [1] (of milkman) Runde, *die* (des Milchmanns); [2] (for recruiting graduates) Rekrutierungstour, *die;* **~ run** *n.* (fig.) [übliche] Tour; **~ shake** *n.* Milkshake, *der;* Milchshake, *der;* **~sop** *n.* Weichling, *der;* **~ tooth** *n.* Milchzahn, *der;* **~ train** *n.* Milkzug, *der;* **take the ~ train into London** (fig.) den ersten Zug nach London nehmen; **~-white** *adj.* milchweiß
milky /ˈmɪlkɪ/ *adj.* milchig; **~ coffee** Milchkaffee, *der*
Milky ˈWay *n.* Milchstraße, *die*
mill /mɪl/
A *n.* [1] Mühle, *die;* **he really went** *or* **was put through the ~** (fig.) er wurde ganz schön in die Mangel genommen (ugs.) [2] (factory) Fabrik, *die;* (machine) Maschine, *die;* **~ town** ≈ Textilstadt, *die*
B *v.t.* [1] mahlen ‹*Getreide*› [2] fräsen ‹*Metallgegenstand*›; rändeln ‹*Münze*›
C *v.i.* ‹*Vieh:*› im Kreis laufen; **crowds of customers were ~ing in the corridors** die Kunden schoben sich in Scharen durch die Gänge
Phrasal verb
• **~ aˈbout** (Brit.), **mill aˈround** *v.i.* durcheinander laufen; **a mass of people ~ing about** *or* **around in the square** eine Menschenmenge, die sich hin und her über den Platz schiebt/schob
milled /mɪld/ *adj.* gemahlen ‹*Korn*›; gerändelt ‹*Münze*›
millennium /mɪˈlenɪəm/ *n., pl.* **~s** *or* **millennia** /mɪˈlenɪə/ [1] Jahrtausend, *das;* Millennium, *das* [2] (Relig.) Tausendjähriges Reich; Millennium, *das* (fachspr.)
milˈlennium bug *n.* (Computing) Jahrtausendvirus, *der od. das*
millepede ▸**millipede**
miller /ˈmɪlə(r)/ *n.* ▸ℹ **p. 1260** Müller, *der*
millet /ˈmɪlɪt/ *n.* (Bot.) Hirse, *die*
milli- /ˈmɪlɪ/ *pref.* milli-/Milli-
milliard /ˈmɪljəd/ *n.* (Brit. dated) Milliarde, *die*
ˈmillibar *n.* (Meteorol.) Millibar, *das*
ˈmilligram *n.* ▸ℹ **p. 1702** Milligramm, *das*
ˈmillilitre (*Brit.;* *Amer.:* **milliliter**) *n.* ▸ℹ **p. 1690** Milliliter, *der od. das*
ˈmillimetre (*Brit.;* *Amer.:* **millimeter**) *n.* ▸ℹ **p. 1208,** ▸ℹ **p. 1286** Millimeter, *der*
milliner /ˈmɪlɪnə(r)/ *n.* ▸ℹ **p. 1260** Putzmacher, *der*/-macherin, *die;* Modist, *der*/Modistin, *die*
millinery /ˈmɪlɪnərɪ/ *n.* [1] *no pl.* (articles) Hüte *Pl.* [2] *no pl.* (business) Hutmacherei, *die* [3] (shop) Hutgeschäft, *das*
million /ˈmɪljən/ ▸ℹ **p. 1358**
A *adj.* [1] **a** *or* **one ~:** eine Million; **two/several ~:** zwei/mehrere Millionen; **a** *or* **one ~ and one** eine Million ein; **half a ~:** eine halbe Million [2] **a ~ [and one]** (fig.: innumerable) tausend; **a ~ books/customers** eine Unmenge Bücher/Kunden; **never in a ~ years** nie im Leben (ugs.); **I've got a ~ [and one] things to do** ich habe tausend Sachen zu erledigen; *see also* **dollar**; **mile 1**
B *n.* [1] Million, *die;* **a** *or* **one/two ~:** eine Million/zwei Millionen; **a ~-to-one chance** eine Chance von einer Million zu eins; **in** *or* **by ~s** millionenweise; **a ~ and one** *etc.* eine Million einer/eine/eins; **the starving ~s** die Millionen [von] Hungerleidenden; **make a ~:** eine Million machen [2] (indefinite amount) **there were ~s of people** eine Unmenge Leute waren da; **thanks a ~:** tausend Dank; **~s of times** tausendmal; x-mal (ugs.); **he is a man/she is one in a ~:** so jemanden wie ihn/sie findet man nicht noch einmal; **the ~[s]** die breite Masse
millionaire /mɪljəˈneə(r)/ *n.* (lit. or fig.) Millionär, *der*/Millionärin, *die*
millionth /ˈmɪljənθ/
A *adj.* ▸ℹ **p. 1358** millionst...; **a ~ part** ein Millionstel
B *n.* (fraction) Millionstel, *das;* **a ~ of a second** eine Millionstelsekunde
millipede /ˈmɪlɪpiːd/ (Zool.) [1] (myriapod) Tausendfüß[l]er, *der* [2] (crustacean) Assel, *die*
ˈmillisecond *n.* Millisekunde, *die*
ˈmillivolt *n.* (Electr., Phys.) Millivolt, *das*
ˈmilliwatt *n.* (Electr., Phys.) Milliwatt, *das*
mill: ~ owner *n.* Textilfabrikant, *der;* **~pond** *n.* Mühlteich, *der;* **the sea was like a ~pond** die See war ruhig wie ein Teich; **~ race** *n.* Mühlbach, *der;* **~stone** *n.* Mühlstein, *der;* **be a ~stone round sb.'s neck** (fig.) jmdm. ein Klotz am Bein sein (ugs.); **~ wheel** *n.* Mühlrad, *das*
milometer /maɪˈlɒmɪtə(r)/ *n.* Meilenzähler, *der*
mime /maɪm/
A *n.* [1] (performance) Pantomime, *die* [2] *no pl., no art.* (art) Pantomimik, *die;* Pantomime, *die* (ugs.) [3] (performer) Pantomime, *der*/Pantomimin, *die*
B *v.i.* pantomimisch agieren
C *v.t.* pantomimisch darstellen
mimeograph /ˈmɪmɪəgrɑːf/
A *n.* (machine) Mimeograph, *der*
B *v.t.* [auf einen Mimeographen] herstellen ‹*Kopien*›/vervielfältigen ‹*Vorlage*›
mimesis /mɪˈmiːsɪs, maɪ-/ *n., no pl.* (Art, Lit.) Mimesis, *die*
mimetic /mɪˈmetɪk, maɪ-/ *adj.* (Art, Lit.) mimetisch
mimic /ˈmɪmɪk/
A *n.* Imitator, *der;* **that child is such a ~!** das Kind macht/plappert alles nach!
B *v.t.,* **-ck-** [1] nachahmen; imitieren; (ridicule by imitating) parodieren [2] (resemble closely) aussehen wie
mimicry /ˈmɪmɪkrɪ/ *n.* [1] *no pl.* Nachahmen, *das;* Nachäffen, *das* (abwertend) [2] (instance of imitation) (of person) Parodie, *die* [3] (Zool.) Mimikry, *die*
mimosa /mɪˈməʊzə/ *n.* Mimose, *die*
min. *abbr.* [1] **= minute[s]** Min [2] **= minimum** (*adj.*) mind., (*n.*) Min.
Min. *abbr.* **= Minister/Ministry** Min.
minaret /ˈmɪnəret/ *n.* Minarett, *das*
mince /mɪns/
A *n.* Hackfleisch, *das;* Gehackte, *das*
B *v.t.* in kleine Stücke schneiden; (chop) klein hacken; **~ beef in a machine** Rindfleisch durch den [Fleisch]wolf drehen; **~d meat** Hackfleisch, *das;* **not ~ matters** die Dinge beim Namen nennen; **there is no point in mincing matters** es hat keinen Sinn, etwas zu beschönigen; **she doesn't ~ her words** sie spricht ganz offen und unverblümt
C *v.i.* trippeln
mince: ~meat *n.* [1] Hackfleisch, *das;* Gehackte, *das;* **make ~meat of sb.** (fig.) Hackfleisch aus jmdm. machen (ugs.); **make ~meat of sb.'s arguments** (fig.) jmds. Argumente zerpflücken; [2] (sweet) *süße Pastetenfüllung aus Obst, Rosinen, Gewürzen, Nierenfett usw.;* **~ ˈpie** *n.: mit süßem „mincemeat" gefüllte Pastete*
mincer /ˈmɪnsə(r)/ *n.* Fleischwolf, *der*
mind /maɪnd/
A *n.* [1] (remembrance) **bear** *or* **keep sth. in ~:** an etw. (*Akk.*) denken; etw. nicht vergessen; **have [it] in ~ to do sth.** vorhaben, etw. zu tun; etw. zu tun gedenken (geh.); **we have in ~ a new project** uns (*Dat.*) schwebt ein neues Projekt vor; **bring sth. to ~:** etw. in Erinnerung rufen; **call sth. to ~:** sich (*Dat.*) an etw. erinnern; **many things came to ~:** vielerlei kam mir/ihm *usw.* in den Sinn; **sth. comes into sb.'s ~:** jmdm. fällt etw. ein; **it went out of my ~:** ich habe es vergessen; es ist mir entfallen; **put sb. in ~ of sb./sth.** jmdn. an jmdn./etw. erinnern; **put sth./sb. out of one's ~:** etw./jmdn. aus seinem Gedächtnis streichen; *see also* **sight A 6**; **time A 2**
[2] (opinion) **in** *or* **to my ~:** meiner Meinung *od.* Ansicht nach; **be of a** *or* **of one** *or* **of the same ~, be in one ~:** einer Meinung sein; **be in two ~s about sth.** [sich (*Dat.*)] unschlüssig über etw. (*Akk.*) sein; **change one's ~:** seine Meinung ändern; **have a ~ of one's own** seinen eigenen Kopf haben; **I have a good ~/a** *or* **half a ~ to do that** ich hätte große Lust/nicht übel Lust, das zu tun; **he doesn't know his own ~:** er weiß nicht, was er will; **make up one's ~, make one's ~ up** sich entscheiden; **make up one's ~ to do sth.** sich entschließen, etw. zu tun; **I've finally made up my ~:** ich bin zu einem Entschluss gekommen; **if your ~ is made up** wenn Sie einen Entschluss gefasst haben; **he made up my ~ for me** er nahm mir die Entscheidung ab; (made my decision easy) er machte mir die Entscheidung leicht; **tell sb. one's ~ frankly** freimütig jmdm. seine Meinung sagen; **give sb. a piece of one's ~:** jmdm. gründlich die Meinung sagen; **read sb.'s ~:** jmds. Gedanken lesen; *see also* **speak B 2**
[3] (direction of thoughts) **his ~ is on other things** er ist mit den Gedanken woanders; **give** *or* **put** *or* **set** *or* **turn one's ~ to** sich konzentrieren auf (+ *Akk.*) ‹*Arbeit, Aufgabe, Angelegenheit*›; **I have had sb./sth. on my ~:** jmd./etw. hat mich beschäftigt; (remembered) ich habe an jmdn./etw. gedacht; (worried) ich habe mir Sorgen wegen jmdm./etw. gemacht; **she has a lot of things on her ~:** sie hat viele Sorgen; **sth. preys** *or* **weighs on sb.'s ~:** etw. macht jmdm. zu schaffen *od.* lässt jmdn. nicht los; **take sb.'s ~ off sth.** jmdn. von etw. ablenken; **keep one's ~ on sth.** sich auf etw. (*Akk.*) konzentrieren; **close one's ~ to sth.** sich einer Sache (*Dat.*) verschließen (geh.); **have a closed ~:** sich entschieden haben; **set one's ~ on sth./on doing sth.** sich (*Dat.*) etw. in den Kopf setzen/sich (*Dat.*) in den Kopf setzen, etw. zu tun; *see also* **absence 3**; **open A 7**; **presence 5**
[4] (way of thinking and feeling) Denkweise, *die;* **frame of ~:** [seelische] Verfassung; **state of ~:** [Geistes]zustand, *der;* **be in a frame of ~ to do sth.** in der Verfassung sein, etw. zu tun; **be in a calm frame of ~:** ruhig sein; **her state of ~ was confused** sie konnte nicht mehr klar denken; **have a logical ~:** logisch denken; **he has the ~ of a child** er hat ein kindliches Gemüt; **the secrets of the human ~:** die Geheimnisse des menschlichen Geistes; **the Victorian/Classical** *etc.* **~:** die Denkweise des viktorianischen Zeitalters/der Klassik *usw.*
[5] (seat of consciousness, thought, volition) Geist, *der;* **a triumph/the power of ~ over matter** ein Triumph/die Macht des Geistes über die Materie; **it was a case of ~ over matter** der Geist hat über die Materie triumphiert; **it's all in the ~:** es ist alles nur Einstellung; **in one's ~:** im Stillen; **in my ~'s eye** vor meinem geistigen Auge; im Geiste; **nothing could be further from my ~ than ...:** nichts läge mir ferner, als ...; **no such thought ever entered his ~:** so etwas kam ihm nie in den Sinn; **his ~ was filled with gloomy forebodings** er war von düsteren Vorahnungen erfüllt
[6] (intellectual powers) Verstand, *der;* Intellekt, *der;* **have a very fine** *or* **good ~:** einen klaren *od.* scharfen Verstand haben; **[not] have a good ~:** [nicht] intelligent sein; **great ~s think alike** (joc.) große Geister denken [eben] gleich
[7] (normal mental faculties) Verstand, *der;* **lose** *or* **go out of one's ~:** den Verstand verlieren; **be out of one's ~:** verrückt sein; den Verstand verloren haben; **in one's right ~:** im Vollbesitz seiner geistigen Kräfte; bei klarem Verstand
[8] (person) Geist, *der;* **a fine ~:** ein großer Geist *od.* (ugs.) kluger Kopf
B *v.t.* [1] (heed) **don't ~ what he says** gib nichts auf sein Gerede *od.* (geh.) seine Worte; **~ what I say** glaub mir; **let's do it, and never ~ the expense** machen wir es doch, egal, was es kostet
[2] (concern oneself about) **he ~s a lot what people think of him** es ist für ihn sehr wichtig, was die Leute von ihm denken; **I can't afford a bicycle, never ~ a car** ich kann mir kein Fahrrad leisten, geschweige denn ein

Auto; **never ~ him/that** (don't be anxious) er/das kann dir doch egal sein (ugs.); **never ~ him — what about me/my predicament?** er interessiert mich nicht — was ist mit mir/mit meinem Dilemma?; **never ~ how/where ...:** es tut nichts zur Sache, wie/wo ...; **never ~ your mistake** lass dir über diesen Fehler *od.* wegen dieses Fehlers keine grauen Haare wachsen (ugs.); **don't ~ me** nimm keine Rücksicht auf mich; (don't let my presence disturb you) lass dich [durch mich] nicht stören; (iron.) nimm bloß keine Rücksicht auf mich; **~ the doors!** Vorsicht an den Türen!; **~ your back[s]!** (coll.) Bahn frei! (ugs.); **~ one's P's and Q's** sich anständig benehmen; (follow the correct procedure) sich nichts zuschulden kommen lassen

3 (apply oneself to) sich kümmern um; *see also* **business 3**

4 *usu. neg. or interrog.* (object to) **did he ~ being woken up?** hat es ihm was ausgemacht, aufgeweckt zu werden?; **would you ~ opening the door?** würdest du bitte die Tür öffnen?; **do you ~ my asking you a personal question?** darf ich Sie etwas Persönliches fragen?; **do you ~ my smoking?** stört es Sie *od.* haben Sie etwas dagegen, wenn ich rauche?; **I don't ~ what he says** es ist mir gleichgültig *od.* egal, was er sagt; **I don't ~ him** ich habe nichts gegen ihn; **I wouldn't ~ a new car/a walk** ich hätte nichts gegen ein neues Auto/einen Spaziergang; **Have a cup of tea. — I don't ~ if I do** Eine Tasse Tee? — Ach ja, warum nicht?; **do you ~ not helping yourself to all the sweets?** (iron.) wie wärs, wenn du ein paar von den Süßigkeiten übrig ließest?

5 (remember and take care) **~ you don't go too near the cliff edge!** pass auf, dass du nicht zu nah an den Felsenrand gehst!; **~ [that] you wash your hands before lunch!** denk daran *od.* vergiss nicht, vor dem Essen die Hände zu waschen!; **~ you don't leave anything behind** denk daran, nichts liegen lassen!; **~ how you go!** pass auf! sei vorsichtig!; (as general farewell) machs gut! (ugs.); **~ you get this work done** sieh zu, dass du mit dieser Arbeit fertig wirst!

6 (have charge of) aufpassen auf (+ *Akk.*); hüten ‹*Schafe*›; **~ the shop** *or* (Amer.) **the store** (fig.) sich um den Laden kümmern (ugs.)

7 (Amer.: be obedient to) gehorchen (+ *Dat.*) ‹*Person*›; befolgen ‹*Befehl*›; **~ what they tell you** tu, was sie sagen!

C *v.i.* **1** **~!** Vorsicht!; Achtung!

2 *usu. in imper.* (take note) **follow the signposts, ~, or ...:** denk daran und halte dich an die Wegweiser, sonst...; **I didn't know that, ~, or ...:** das habe ich allerdings nicht gewusst, sonst ...; wohlgemerkt, das habe ich nicht gewusst, sonst ...; **~ you, I could see he was good** dass er gut war, war mir durchaus klar

3 (care) **do you '~?** (iron.) ich muss doch sehr bitten!; **turn it on; nobody will ~:** mach es an — es wird keinen stören *od.* keiner wird etwas dagegen haben; **he doesn't ~ about your using the car** er hat nichts dagegen, wenn Sie den Wagen benutzen; **do you ~?** (may I?) hätten Sie etwas dagegen?; (please do not) darf ich bitten! (iron.); **if you don't ~:** wenn es Ihnen recht ist; (iron.) wenn ich bitten darf!

4 (give heed) **never [you] ~** (it's not important) macht nichts; ist nicht schlimm; **never ~: I can do it** schon gut — das kann ich machen; **never you ~** (do not be inquisitive) das braucht dich nicht zu interessieren; **Never ~ about that now! This work is more important** Lass das jetzt mal [sein/liegen]! Dies hier ist wichtiger; **never ~ about him — what happened to her?** er interessiert mich nicht — was ist ihr passiert?

Phrasal verb

- **~ 'out** *v.i.* **I told them to ~ out** ich sagte ihnen, sie sollten aufpassen; **~ out for sth.** auf etw. (*Akk.*) aufpassen; **~ out!** Vorsicht!

mind: ~-bending, (coll.) **~-blowing** *adjs.* bewusstseinsverändernd; **the concert was ~-blowing** das Konzert war wahnsinnig (ugs.); **~-boggling** /ˈmaɪndbɒglɪŋ/ *adj.* (coll.) wahnsinnig (ugs.)

minded /ˈmaɪndɪd/ *adj.* **1** (disposed) **be ~ to do sth.** bereit *od.* (geh.) geneigt sein, etw. zu tun; **he could do it if he were so ~:** er könnte es tun, wenn ihm der Sinn danach stünde **2** **mechanically ~:** technisch veranlagt; **he is not in the least politically ~:** er ist vollkommen unpolitisch; **romantically ~:** romantisch veranlagt; **religious-~:** religiös; **be Establishment-~:** sich nach dem Establishment richten

minder /ˈmaɪndə(r)/ *n.* **1** (for child) **we need a ~ for the child** wir brauchen jemanden, der auf das Kind aufpasst *od.* das Kind betreut **2** (for machine) Maschinenwart, *der* **3** (sl.: protector of criminal) Gorilla, *der* (salopp)

mindful /ˈmaɪndfl/ *adj.* **be ~ of sth.** (take into account) etw. bedenken *od.* berücksichtigen; (give attention to) an etw. (*Akk.*) denken

mindless /ˈmaɪndlɪs/ *adj.* geistlos, (ugs.) hirnlos ‹*Person*›; sinnlos ‹*Handlung, Gewalt*›

'mind: ~-reader ▸ **thought-reader**; **~set** *n.* Denkart, *die*

mine[1] /maɪn/

A *n.* **1** (for coal) Bergwerk, *das;* (for metal, diamonds, etc.) Bergwerk, *das;* Mine, *die;* **go** *or* **work down the ~:** unter Tage arbeiten **2** (fig.: abundant source) unerschöpfliche Quelle; **he is a ~ of useful facts/of information** von ihm kann man eine Menge Nützliches/eine Menge erfahren **3** (explosive device) Mine, *die*

B *v.t.* **1** graben ‹*Loch, unterirdischen Gang*› **2** schürfen ‹*Gold*›; abbauen, fördern ‹*Erz, Kohle, Schiefer*› **3** (dig into for ore etc.) **~ an area** in einem Gebiet Bergbau betreiben; **~ an area for ore** *etc.* in einem Gebiet Erz *usw.* abbauen *od.* fördern **4** (Mil.: lay ~s in) verminen

C *v.i.* (dig the earth) Bergbau betreiben; **~ for** ▸ **B 2**

mine[2] *poss. pron.* **1** *pred.* meiner/meine/mein[e]s; der/die/das Meinige (geh.); **you do your best and I'll do ~:** du tust dein Bestes und ich auch; **look at that dog of ~!** sieh dir bloß mal meinen Hund an! (ugs.); **those big feet of ~:** meine großen Quanten (ugs.); **when will you be ~?** wann wirst du die Meine/der Meine sein? (veralt.); **vengeance is ~:** die Rache ist mein (geh., veralt.); *see also* **hers** **2** *attrib.* (arch./poet.) mein

mine: ~-detector *n.* Minensuchgerät, *das;* **~field** *n.* (lit. or fig.) Minenfeld, *das;* **~layer** *n.* Minenleger, *der*

miner /ˈmaɪnə(r)/ *n.* ▸ **ⓘ p. 1260** Bergmann, *der;* Kumpel, *der* (Bergmannsspr.)

mineral /ˈmɪnərl/

A *adj.* mineralisch; Mineral‹*salz, -quelle*›; **~ wealth** Mineralienreichtum, *der;* Reichtum an Bodenschätzen; *see also* **kingdom 4**

B *n.* **1** (**~ substance**) Mineral, *das;* **a country rich in ~s** ein an Bodenschätzen reiches Land **2** *esp. in pl.* (Brit.: soft drink) Erfrischungsgetränk, *das*

mineralize /ˈmɪnərəlaɪz/ *v.t. & i.* mineralisieren

mineralogist /mɪnəˈrælədʒɪst/ *n.* ▸ **ⓘ p. 1260** Mineraloge, *der*/Mineralogin, *die*

mineralogy /mɪnəˈrælədʒɪ/ *n.* Mineralogie, *die*

mineral: ~ oil *n.* Mineralöl, *das;* **~ water** *n.* Mineralwasser, *das*

'mineshaft *n.* [Gruben]schacht, *der*

minestrone /mɪnɪˈstrəʊnɪ/ *n.* (Gastr.) Minestrone, *die*

mine: ~sweeper *n.* Minensuchboot, *das;* **~worker** *n.* ▸ **ⓘ p. 1260** Bergmann, *der;* Kumpel, *der* (Bergmannsspr.)

mingle /ˈmɪŋgl/

A *v.t.* [ver]mischen

B *v.i.* sich [ver]mischen (**with** mit); **~ with** *or* **among the crowds** sich unters Volk mischen; **he ~s with millionaires** er hat Umgang mit Millionären

mingy /ˈmɪndʒɪ/ *adj.* (Brit. coll.) mick[e]rig (ugs.) ‹*Gegenstand*›; knick[e]rig (ugs.) ‹*Person*›; lumpig (ugs.) ‹*Betrag*›

mini /ˈmɪnɪ/ *n.* (coll.) **1** (car) **M~** ® Mini, *der* **2** (skirt) Mini, *der* (ugs.)

mini- /ˈmɪnɪ/ *in comb.* Mini-; Klein‹*bus, -wagen, -taxi*›

miniature /ˈmɪnɪtʃə(r)/

A *n.* **1** (picture) Miniatur, *die* **2** *no pl., no art.* (branch of painting) Miniaturmalerei, *die;* **a portrait in ~:** ein Miniaturportrait **3** (small version) Miniaturausgabe, *die;* **in ~:** im Kleinformat

B *adj.* **1** (small-scale) Miniatur- **2** (smaller than normal) Mini- (ugs.); Kleinst-; **~ poodle** Zwergpudel, *der;* **~ golf** Minigolf, *das;* **~ camera** Miniaturkamera, *die;* **~ railway** Miniaturbahn, *die*

miniaturise ▸ **miniaturize**

miniaturist /ˈmɪnɪtʃərɪst/ *n.* Miniaturmaler, *der*/-malerin, *die*

miniaturize /ˈmɪnɪtʃəraɪz/ *v.t.* verkleinern

mini: ~bar *n.* Minibar, *die;* **~break** *n.* Kurzurlaub, *der;* **~bus** *n.* Kleinbus, *der;* **~cab** *n.* Kleintaxi, *das;* Minicar, *das;* **~computer** *n.* Minicomputer, *der;* **~disc** *n.* Minidisc, *die;* **~dress** *n.* Minikleid, *das;* **~golf** *n., no pl.* Minigolf, *das*

minim /ˈmɪnɪm/ *n.* **1** (Brit. Mus.) halbe Note **2** (fluid measure) Minim, *das* (*ca.* $0{,}06\ cm^3$)

minimal /ˈmɪnɪml/ *adj.* minimal

minimalism /ˈmɪnɪməlɪzm/ *n., no pl.* Minimalismus, *der*

minimalist /ˈmɪnɪməlɪst/

A *adj.* minimalistisch

B *n.* Minimalist, *der*/Minimalistin, *die*

minimalize /ˈmɪnɪməlaɪz/ *v.t.* minimalisieren

minimally /ˈmɪnɪməlɪ/ *adv.* minimal

mini: ~market *n.* Minimarkt, *der;* **~mart** *n.* (Amer.) Minimarkt, *der*

minimisation, minimise ▸ **minimiz-**

minimization /mɪnɪmaɪˈzeɪʃn/ *n.* **1** Minimierung, *die* **2** (understating) Verharmlosung, *die*

minimize /ˈmɪnɪmaɪz/ *v.t.* **1** (reduce) minimieren; auf ein Mindestmaß reduzieren **2** (understate) bagatellisieren; verharmlosen ‹*Gefahr*›; herunterspielen ‹*Bedeutung*›

minimum /ˈmɪnɪməm/

A *n., pl.* **minima** /ˈmɪnɪmə/ Minimum, *das* (**of** an + *Dat.*); **reduce to a ~:** auf ein Minimum reduzieren; **keep sth. to a ~:** etw. so gering/niedrig wie möglich halten; **a ~ of £5** mindestens 5 Pfund; **at the ~:** mindestens

B *attrib. adj.* ▸ **ⓘ p. 1620** Mindest-; **~ temperatures tonight around 5°** nächtliche Tiefsttemperaturen um 5°

minimum: ~ 'lending rate *n.* (Finance) *Mindestausleihsatz [der Bank von England];* ≈ Mindestdiskontsatz, *der;* **~ 'wage** *n.* Mindestlohn, *der*

mining /ˈmaɪnɪŋ/ *n.* Bergbau, *der; attrib.* Bergbau-; **~ area** *or* **district** Bergbaugebiet, *das;* Revier, *das*

mining: ~ engineer *n.* ▸ **ⓘ p. 1260** Berg[bau]ingenieur, *der;* **~ engineering** *n.* Bergbautechnik, *die;* **~ industry** *n.* Montanindustrie, *die;* Bergbau, *der;* **~ town** *n.* Bergbaustadt, *die;* **~ village** *n.* Bergbaudorf, *das*

minion /ˈmɪnjən/ *n.* (derog.) **1** (servile agent) Ergebene, *der/die;* Lakai, *der* (abwertend) **2** (favourite of king etc.) Günstling, *der* (abwertend); Protegé, *der*

'mini roundabout *n.* (Brit.) *sehr kleiner, oft nur aufs Pflaster aufgezeichneter Kreisverkehr*

'miniskirt *n.* Minirock, *der*

minister /ˈmɪnɪstə(r)/

A *n.* ▸ **ⓘ p. 1260** **1** ▸ **ⓘ p. 1634** (Polit.) Minister, *der*/Ministerin, *die;* **M~ of the Crown** (Brit.) Kabinettsminister, *der*/-ministerin, *die;* **M~ of State** (Brit.) ≈ Staatssekretär, *der*/-sekretärin, *die;* *see also* **portfolio 2**; **prime minister** **2** (diplomat) Gesandte, *der*/Gesandtin, *die* **3** (Eccl.) **~ [of religion]** Geistliche, *der/die;* Pfarrer, *der*/Pfarrerin, *die*

B *v.i.* **~ to sb.** sich um jmdn. kümmern; **~ to sb.'s wants/needs** jmds. Wünsche/Bedürfnisse befriedigen; **~ing angel** barmherziger Engel

ministerial /mɪnɪˈstɪərɪəl/ *adj.* **1** (Eccl.) geistlich; **~ candidate** Kandidat [für das Pfarramt]

m

2 (Polit.) Minister-; ministeriell

ministration /mɪnɪˈstreɪʃn/ *n.* 1 (giving aid) Hilfe[leistung], *die;* Fürsorge, *die;* **under the ∼s of sb.** durch jmds. Fürsorge *od.* Pflege 2 (Relig.) Seelsorge, *die;* seelsorgerischer Dienst (**to** an + *Dat.*)

ministry /ˈmɪnɪstrɪ/ *n.* 1 (Government department or building) Ministerium, *das;* **∼ official** Ministerialbeamte, *der*/-beamtin, *die* 2 (Polit.: body of ministers) Kabinett, *das;* Regierung, *die* 3 (Eccl.: body of ministers) Geistlichkeit, *die* 4 (profession of clergyman) geistliches Amt; **go into** *or* **enter the ∼:** Geistlicher werden 5 (Relig:) (office as minister) geistliches Amt; (period of tenure) Amtszeit als Geistlicher; **perform a ∼ among the poor** die Armen seelsorgerisch betreuen 6 (Polit.: period of office) Amtszeit [als Minister]

mink /mɪŋk/ *n.* Nerz, *der; attrib.* **∼ coat** Nerzmantel, *der*

minnow /ˈmɪnəʊ/ *n.* (Zool.) Elritze, *die;* (fig.) kleiner Fisch

minor /ˈmaɪnə(r)/

A *adj.* 1 (lesser) kleiner...; leicht ‹*Operation, Verletzung, Anfall*›; Neben‹*figur, -rolle*›; **∼ piece** (Chess) Leichtfigur, *die* 2 (comparatively unimportant) weniger bedeutend; geringer ‹*Bedeutung*›; **∼ matter** Nebensächlichkeit, *die;* **∼ road** kleine Straße 3 (Brit. Sch.) **Jones ∼:** der jüngere Jones; Jones No. 2 (ugs.) 4 (Mus.) Moll-; **∼ key/scale/chord** Molltonart, *die*/Molltonleiter, *die*/Mollakkord, *der;* **A ∼:** a-Moll; **in a ∼ key** in Moll; **∼ third** *etc.* kleine Terz *usw*

B *n.* 1 (person) Minderjährige, *der/die;* **be a ∼:** minderjährig sein 2 (Amer. Univ.) Nebenfach, *das*

C *v.i.* (Amer.) **∼ in sth.** etw. als Nebenfach haben

minor ˈaxis *n.* (Geom.) kleine Achse

minority /maɪˈnɒrɪtɪ, mɪˈnɒrɪtɪ/ *n.* 1 Minderheit, *die;* Minorität, *die;* **be in a ∼ of one** allein dastehen; **in the ∼:** in der Minderheit 2 *attrib.* Minderheits‹*regierung, -bericht*›; **∼ group** Minderheit, *die;* Minorität, *die;* **∼ rights** Minderheitenrechte; **∼ sport** Randsportart, *die*

minority ˈrule *n.* Herrschaft einer/der Minderheit; **white ∼:** die Herrschaft der weißen Minderheit

minor: ∼ league (Amer.) *n.* untere Liga; *attrib.* Unterliga-; **∼ planet** ▸**planet**; **∼ suit** *n.* (Bridge) niedrige Farbe

minster /ˈmɪnstə(r)/ *n.* Münster, *das;* **York M∼:** die Kathedrale von York

minstrel /ˈmɪnstrl/ *n.* 1 (medieval singer or musician) Spielmann, *der;* fahrender Sänger; **∼s' gallery** Musikantengalerie, *die* 2 (Hist.: entertainer) Minstrel, *der* (hist.)

mint[1] /mɪnt/

A *n.* 1 (place) Münzanstalt, *die;* Münze, *die;* **Royal M∼** (Brit.) Königlich-Britische Münzanstalt 2 (sum of money) **a ∼ [of money]** eine schöne Stange *od.* ein Haufen Geld (ugs.); **have a ∼ [of money]** Geld wie Heu haben (ugs.); im Geld schwimmen (ugs.) 3 (fig.: source) Prägestätte, *die*

B *adj.* funkelnagelneu (ugs.); vorzüglich ‹*Münze*› (fachspr.); ungestempelt ‹*Briefmarke*›; **in ∼ condition** *or* **state** ‹*Auto, Bild usw.*› in tadellosem Zustand

C *v.t.* (lit. or fig.) prägen

mint[2] *n.* 1 (plant) Minze, *die* 2 (peppermint) Pfefferminz, *das; attrib.* Pfefferminz-

mint ˈsauce *n.* Minzsoße, *die*

minty /ˈmɪntɪ/ *adj.* Pfefferminz‹*aroma, -geschmack*›; **be/taste ∼:** nach Pfefferminz schmecken

minuet /mɪnjʊˈet/ *n.* (Mus.) Menuett, *das*

minus /ˈmaɪnəs/

A *prep.* 1 (with the subtraction of) minus; weniger; (without) ohne; abzüglich (+ *Gen.*); 2 (below zero) minus; **a temperature of ∼ 20 degrees** [eine Temperatur von] 20 Grad Kälte *od.* minus 20 Grad 3 (coll.: lacking) ohne

B *adj.* 1 (Math.) negativ ‹*Wert, Menge, Größe*›; Minus‹*zeichen, -betrag*› 2 (Electr.) **∼ pole/terminal** Minuspol, *der*

C *n.* 1 (Math.) (symbol) **∼ [sign]** Minus[zeichen], *das;* (negative quantity) negative Größe 2 (disadvantage) Minus, *das;* Nachteil, *der*

minuscule /ˈmɪnəskjuːl/

A *adj.* winzig

B *n.* (lower-case letter) Minuskel, *die* (Druckw.); Kleinbuchstabe, *der*

minute[1] /ˈmɪnɪt/

A *n.* 1 ▸❶ **p. 1001** Minute, *die;* (moment) Moment, *der;* Augenblick, *der;* **I expect him [at] any ∼ [now]** ich erwarte ihn jeden Augenblick; **for a ∼:** eine Minute/einen Moment [lang]; **I'm not for a ∼ saying you're wrong** ich will keinesfalls sagen, dass du Unrecht hast; **in a ∼** (very soon) gleich; **half a ∼!** einen Augenblick!; **have not a ∼ to spare** keine [Minute] Zeit haben; **have you got a ∼?** hast du mal eine Minute *od.* einen Augenblick Zeit?; **can you just give me a ∼'s peace?** kannst du mich mal eine Minute *od.* einen Augenblick in Frieden lassen?; **come back this ∼!** komm sofort *od.* auf der Stelle zurück!; **at that very ∼:** genau in diesem Augenblick; **at the ∼** (coll.) momentan; im Moment; **to the ∼:** auf die Minute; **up to the ∼:** hochaktuell; **the ∼ [that] I left** in dem Augenblick, als ich wegging; **the ∼ he gets home, he's out in the garden** kaum ist er zu Hause, geht er in den Garten; **just a ∼!, wait a ∼!** (coll.) einen Augenblick!; (objecting) Augenblick mal! (ugs.); **would you mind waiting a ∼?** würden Sie sich einen Moment gedulden?; **live ten ∼s from town** zehn Minuten von der Stadt entfernt wohnen; **be five ∼s' walk [away]** fünf Minuten zu Fuß entfernt sein; *see also* **last minute** 2 (of angle) Minute, *die* 3 (draft) Entwurf, *der;* (note) Notiz, *die;* Vermerk, *der* 4 *in pl.* (brief summary) Protokoll, *das;* **keep** *or* **take** *or* **record the ∼s** das Protokoll führen 5 (official memorandum) Memorandum, *das*

B *v.t.* 1 (record) protokollieren ‹*Vernehmung, Aussage*›; zu Protokoll nehmen ‹*Bemerkung*› 2 (send note to) **∼ sb. [about sth.]** jmdn. schriftlich [von etw.] unterrichten

minute[2] /maɪˈnjuːt/ *adj.*, **∼r** /maɪˈnjuːtə(r)/, **∼st** /maɪˈnjuːtɪst/ 1 (tiny) winzig; **not the ∼st interest** nicht das geringste Interesse 2 (petty) [völlig] unbedeutend 3 (precise) minutiös; exakt; **with ∼ care** mit peinlicher Sorgfalt

minute hand /ˈmɪnɪthænd/ *n.* Minutenzeiger, *der;* großer Zeiger

minutely /maɪˈnjuːtlɪ/ *adv.* (with precision) genauestens; sorgfältigst; **∼ planned** bis ins kleinste Detail geplant; **a ∼ detailed analysis** eine Untersuchung bis ins kleinste Detail

minuteman /ˈmɪnɪtmæn/ *n.* (Amer. Hist.) *auf Abruf bereitstehender Freiwilliger im amerikanischen Unabhängigkeitskrieg;* Minuteman, *der* (fachspr.)

minute steak /ˈmɪnɪt steɪk/ *n.* Minutensteak, *das*

minutiae /maɪˈnjuːʃiː, mɪˈnjuːʃiː/ *n. pl.* Details

minx /mɪŋks/ *n.* kleines Biest (ugs.)

miracle /ˈmɪrəkl/ *n.* Wunder, *das;* **perform** *or* **work ∼s** Wunder tun *od.* vollbringen; ‹*Mittel, Behandlung usw.*:› Wunder wirken; **be nothing short of a ∼:** an ein Wunder *od.* ans Wunderbare grenzen; **the age of ∼s is not past** es geschehen noch Zeichen und Wunder; **economic ∼:** Wirtschaftswunder, *das;* **we'll do our best but we can't promise ∼s!** wir tun unser Bestes, aber wir können nicht hexen *od.* zaubern; **be a ∼ of ingenuity** ein Wunder an Genialität sein

ˈmiracle play *n.* (Hist.) Mirakel[spiel], *das*

miraculous /mɪˈrækjʊləs/ *adj.* 1 wunderbar; wundersam (geh.); (supernatural) übernatürlich ‹*Ereignisse*›; (having ∼ power) wunderkräftig 2 (surprising) erstaunlich; unglaublich

miraculously /mɪˈrækjʊləslɪ/ *adv.* 1 auf wunderbare *od.* (geh.) wundersame Weise; **∼, he escaped injury** wie durch ein Wunder blieb er unverletzt 2 (surprisingly) erstaunlicherweise

mirage /ˈmɪrɑːʒ, mɪˈrɑːʒ/ *n.* 1 (optical illusion) Fata Morgana, *die;* Luftspiegelung, *die* 2 (illusory thing) Illusion, *die;* Trugbild, *das*

mire /maɪə(r)/ *n.* Morast, *der;* **be** *or* **stick** *or* **find oneself in the ∼** (fig.) im Dreck *od.* in der Klemme stecken *od.* sitzen (ugs.); **drag sb.'s name through the ∼** (fig.) jmds. Namen in den Schmutz *od.* (ugs.) Dreck ziehen

mirror /ˈmɪrə(r)/

A *n.* (lit. or fig.) Spiegel, *der;* **hold the ∼ up to sb./sth.** (fig.) jmdm./einer Sache den Spiegel vorhalten; **it's all done with ∼s** (coll.) das Ganze ist nur ein Trick

B *v.t.* (lit. or fig.) [wider]spiegeln; **be ∼ed in sth.** sich in etw. (*Dat.*) [wider]spiegeln

The Mirror

Eine überregionale Tageszeitung. Am Sonntag erscheint ihr Pendant *The Sunday Mirror*. Der *Mirror* ist gemäßigt links und eine **tabloid**-Zeitung, also ein Blatt, das zur Boulevardpresse gezählt wird.

mirror: ∼ ˈimage *n.* Spiegelbild, *das;* **∼ site** *n.* (Computing) Spiegelsite, *die;* **∼ writing** *n.* Spiegelschrift, *die*

mirth /mɜːθ/ *n.* (literary) Frohsinn, *der;* Fröhlichkeit, *die;* (laughter) Heiterkeit, *die*

mirthful /ˈmɜːθfl/ *adj.* (literary) heiter, fröhlich ‹*Lachen*›

misadventure /mɪsədˈventʃə(r)/ *n.* 1 (piece of bad luck) Missgeschick, *das;* **I had a ∼:** mir ist ein Missgeschick passiert 2 (Law) **death by ∼:** Tod durch Unfall

misalliance /mɪsəˈlaɪəns/ *n.* Mesalliance, *die* (geh.); Missheirat, *die*

misanthrope /ˈmɪzənθrəʊp/, **misanthropist** /mɪˈzænθrəpɪst/ *ns.* Misanthrop, *der* (geh.); Menschenfeind, *der*

misanthropic /mɪzənˈθrɒpɪk/ *adj.* misanthropisch (geh.); menschenfeindlich

misanthropy /mɪˈzænθrəpɪ/ *n.* Menschenfeindlichkeit, *die*

misapprehend /mɪsæprɪˈhend/ *v.t.* missverstehen

misapprehension /mɪsæprɪˈhenʃn/ *n.* Missverständnis, *das;* **be under a ∼:** einem Irrtum unterliegen; **have a lot of ∼s about sth.** völlig falsche Vorstellungen von etw. haben

misappropriate /mɪsəˈprəʊprɪeɪt/ *v.t.* unterschlagen, (Rechtsspr.) veruntreuen ‹*Geld usw.*›; stehlen ‹*Idee*›

misappropriation /mɪsəprəʊprɪˈeɪʃn/ *n.* (of money) Unterschlagung, *die;* Veruntreuung, *die* (Rechtsspr.)

misbegotten /mɪsbɪˈgɒtn/ *adj.* 1 (badly conceived) schlecht konzipiert ‹*Plan, Vorhaben, Projekt*› 2 (dated: illigitimate) unehelich ‹*Kind*›

misbehave /mɪsbɪˈheɪv/

A *v.i.* sich schlecht benehmen

B *v. refl.* **∼ oneself** sich schlecht benehmen; sich danebenbenehmen (ugs.); **he and his girlfriend have been misbehaving themselves** (euphem.) er und seine Freundin haben sich miteinander eingelassen

misbehaviour (*Amer.:* **misbehavior**) /mɪsbɪˈheɪvɪə(r)/ *n.* schlechtes Benehmen *od.* Betragen

miscalculate /mɪsˈkælkjʊleɪt/

A *v.t.* falsch berechnen ‹*Menge*›; (misjudge) falsch einschätzen ‹*Folgen, Auswirkungen, Stärke*›; **∼ the distance/the budget** sich bei der Entfernung/beim Budget verkalkulieren *od.* verschätzen

B *v.i.* sich verrechnen

miscalculation /mɪskælkjʊˈleɪʃn/ *n.* (arithmetical error) Rechenfehler, *der;* (misjudgement) Fehleinschätzung, *die;* **make a ∼ about sth.** (misjudge sth.) etw. falsch einschätzen

miscarriage /mɪsˈkærɪdʒ/ *n.* 1 (Med.) Fehlgeburt, *die* 2 (of plans, projects, etc.) Fehlschlagen, *das;* Misslingen, *das;* **∼ of justice** Justizirrtum, *der*

miscarry /mɪsˈkærɪ/ *v.i.* 1 (Med.) eine Fehlgeburt haben 2 ‹*Plan, Vorhaben usw.*:› fehlschlagen 3 (not reach destination) ‹*Brief usw.*:› fehlgeleitet werden

miscast /mɪsˈkɑːst/ *v.t.*, **miscast** falsch *od.* schlecht besetzen ‹*Rolle, Film, Theaterstück*›; fehlbesetzen ‹*Rolle*›

m

miscellaneous /mɪsə'leɪnɪəs/ *adj.* 1 (mixed) [kunter]bunt ‹[*Menschen*]*menge, Sammlung*› 2 *with pl. n.* (of various kinds) verschieden; verschiedenerlei

miscellany /mɪ'selənɪ/ *n.* 1 (mixture) [bunte] Sammlung; [buntes] Gemisch 2 (book) Sammelband, *der*

mischance /mɪs'tʃɑ:ns/ *n.* 1 (piece of bad luck) unglücklicher Zufall; **by a** *or* **some ~:** durch einen unglücklichen Zufall 2 *no pl., no art.* (bad luck) Pech, *das*

mischief /'mɪstʃɪf/ *n.* 1 Unsinn, *der;* Unfug, *der;* (pranks) [dumme] Streiche *Pl.;* (playful malice) Schalk, *der;* **mean ~:** etwas im Schilde führen; **be up to ~ again** wieder etwas im Schilde führen; **be** *or* **get up to [some] ~:** etwas anstellen; **keep out of ~:** keine Dummheiten *od.* keinen Unfug machen; **keep sb. out of ~:** jmdn. vor Dummheiten bewahren; **what ~ have you been up to now?** was hast du denn jetzt schon wieder angestellt?; **sb.'s eyes are full of ~:** jmdm. sieht *od.* schaut der Schalk aus den Augen 2 (harm) Schaden, *der;* **do sb./oneself a ~** (coll.) jmdm./sich etwas antun; **make** *or* **stir up ~:** Ärger machen 3 (person) Schlawiner, *der* (ugs.); (child also) Racker, *der*

'mischief-maker *n.* Böswillige, *der/die*

mischievous /'mɪstʃɪvəs/ *adj.* 1 spitzbübisch, schelmisch ‹*Blick, Gesichtsausdruck, Lächeln*›; schalkhaft (geh.); **~ trick** Schabernack, *der;* [dummer] Streich 2 (malicious) boshaft ‹*Person*›; böse ‹*Absicht*› 3 (harmful) schädlich ‹*Effekt*›; bösartig ‹*Gerücht*›; böse ‹*Zeitungsartikel*›

mischievously /'mɪstʃɪvəslɪ/ *adv.* 1 spitzbübisch; schalkhaft (geh.); **behave ~:** Schabernack treiben; Unfug anstellen 2 (maliciously) aus [reiner] Bosheit

miscible /'mɪsɪbl/ *adj.* mischbar

misconceive /mɪskən'si:v/
A *v.i.* **~ of sth.** eine falsche Vorstellung von etw. haben; etw. verkennen
B *v.t.* **be ~d** ‹*Projekt, Vorschlag, Aktion:*› schlecht konzipiert sein

misconception /mɪskən'sepʃn/ *n.* falsche Vorstellung (**about** von); **be [labouring] under a ~ about sth.** sich (*Dat.*) eine falsche Vorstellung von etw. machen; etw. verkennen; **it is a ~ to think that ...:** es ist ein Irrtum, anzunehmen, dass ...

misconduct
A /mɪs'kɒndʌkt/ *n., no pl.* 1 (improper conduct) unkorrektes Verhalten; (Sport) unsportliches *od.* unfaires Verhalten; **he was accused of gross ~:** er wurde grober Verfehlungen bezichtigt; **professional ~:** standeswidriges Verhalten 2 (bad management) schlechte Verwaltung; **~ of the war** schlechte Kriegsführung
B /mɪskən'dʌkt/ *v. refl.* sich unkorrekt verhalten

misconstrue /mɪskən'stru:/ *v.t.* missdeuten; missverstehen; **~ sb.'s meaning** jmdn. missverstehen; **~ sth. as sth.** etw. irrtümlicherweise für etw. halten

miscount
A /'mɪskaʊnt/ *n.* falsche Zählung; (of votes) falsche Auszählung; **there had been a ~:** bei der Zählung hatte es einen Fehler gegeben
B /mɪs'kaʊnt/ *v.i.* sich verzählen; (when counting votes) falsch [aus]zählen; (when calculating) sich verrechnen
C /'mɪskaʊnt/ *v.t.* falsch zählen; falsch ausrechnen ‹*Zahl*›

miscreant /'mɪskrɪənt/ *n.* Übeltäter, *der/*-täterin, *die*

misdeal /mɪs'di:l/ (Cards)
A *v.i., forms as* **deal[1] A** sich vergeben; falsch geben
B *v.t., forms as* **deal[1] B** vergeben, falsch geben ‹*Karten*›

misdeed /mɪs'di:d/ *n.* 1 (evil deed) Missetat, *die* (geh. veralt.) 2 (crime) Verbrechen, *das;* Untat, *die*

misdemeanour (*Amer.:* **misdemeanor**) /mɪsdɪ'mi:nə(r)/ *n.* 1 (misdeed) Missetat, *die* (veralt., scherzh.) 2 (Law) Vergehen, *das;* Übertretung, *die*

misdiagnosis /mɪsdaɪəg'nəʊsɪs/ *n.* Fehldiagnose, *die*

misdial /mɪs'daɪəl/ (Brit.)
A *v.t.* falsch wählen ‹*Telefonnummer*›
B *v.i.* sich verwählen (ugs.)

misdirect /mɪsdɪ'rekt, mɪsdaɪ'rekt/ *v.t.* 1 (direct wrongly) falsch adressieren ‹*Brief*›; vergeuden, falsch einsetzen ‹*Energien*›; in die falsche Richtung schicken ‹*nach dem Weg Fragenden*› 2 (Law) falsch informieren; falsch belehren ‹*Geschworene*›

miser /'maɪzə(r)/ *n.* Geizhals, *der;* Geizkragen, *der* (ugs.)

miserable /'mɪzərəbl/ *adj.* 1 (unhappy) unglücklich; erbärmlich, elend ‹*Leben*[*sbedingungen*]›; **make sb.'s life ~:** jmdm. das Leben schwer machen; **feel ~:** sich elend fühlen 2 (causing wretchedness) trostlos; trist ‹*Wetter, Urlaub*›; elend, armselig ‹*Wohnviertel, Slums*›; öde ‹*Beschäftigung*›; [sehr] unglücklich ‹*Ehe*› 3 (contemptible, mean) armselig; **a ~ five pounds** klägliche *od.* (ugs. abwertend) miese fünf Pfund

miserably /'mɪzərəblɪ/ *adv.* 1 (uncomfortably, unhappily) unglücklich; elend, jämmerlich ‹*leben, zugrunde gehen*›; elend ‹*kalt, nass*›; **~ poor** bettelarm 2 (meanly) spärlich ‹*beleuchtet, möbliert*›; miserabel, (ugs.) mies ‹*bezahlt*› 3 (to a deplorable extent) kläglich, jämmerlich ‹*versagen*›; völlig, total ‹*verpfuscht, unzureichend*›

miserliness /'maɪzəlɪnɪs/ *n., no pl.* Geiz, *der*

miserly /'maɪzəlɪ/ *adj.* geizig; armselig ‹*Portion, Essen*›; **~ creature** Geizhals, *der;* Geizkragen, *der* (ugs.)

misery /'mɪzərɪ/ *n.* 1 (wretched state) Elend, *das;* **make sb.'s life a ~:** jmdm. das Leben zur Qual *od.* zur Hölle machen; **live in ~, live a life of ~:** ein erbärmliches *od.* jämmerliches Leben führen; **put an animal out of its ~:** ein Tier von seinen Qualen erlösen; **put sb. out of his ~** (fig.) jmdn. nicht länger auf die Folter spannen 2 (thing) **the ~ of it was that ...:** das Unglück dabei war, dass ...; **miseries** Elend, *das;* Nöte 3 (coll.: discontented person) **~ [guts]** Miesepeter, *der* (ugs. abwertend)

misfire /mɪs'faɪə(r)/
A *v.i.* 1 ‹*Motor:*› eine Fehlzündung/Fehlzündungen haben; ‹*Kanone, Gewehr:*› versagen, nicht losgehen 2 ‹*Plan, Versuch:*› fehlschlagen; ‹*Streich, Witz:*› danebengehen
B *n.* 1 (of engine) Fehlzündung, *die;* (of gun) Versager, *der* 2 (of plan, attempt) Fehlschlag, *der* 3 (sth. that fails) Schlag ins Wasser; (book, play) Flop, *der*

misfit /'mɪsfɪt/ *n.* (person) Außenseiter, *der/*Außenseiterin, *die*

misfortune /mɪs'fɔ:tʃən, mɪs'fɔ:tʃu:n/ *n.* 1 *no pl., no art.* (bad luck) Missgeschick, *das;* **suffer ~:** [viel] Unglück haben; **companions in ~:** Leidensgenossen 2 (stroke of fate) Schicksalsschlag, *der;* (unlucky incident) Missgeschick, *das;* **bear one's ~s bravely** sein Schicksal tapfer tragen; **it was his ~** *or* **he had the ~ to ...:** er hatte das Pech, zu ...; **~s rarely come singly** ein Unglück kommt selten allein

misgiving /mɪs'gɪvɪŋ/ *n.* Bedenken *Pl.;* Zweifel, *der;* **have some ~s about sth.** wegen einer Sache Bedenken haben

misgovern /mɪs'gʌvn/ *v.t.* schlecht regieren

misgovernment /mɪs'gʌvnmənt/ *n., no pl.* politische Misswirtschaft

misguided /mɪs'gaɪdɪd/ *adj.* töricht ‹*Mensch*›; unangebracht ‹*Eifer, Freundlichkeit*›; unsinnig ‹*Bemühung, Maßnahme*›

misguidedly /mɪs'gaɪdɪdlɪ/ *adv.* (in error) irrigerweise; (ill-advisedly) törichterweise

mishandle /mɪs'hændl/ *v.t.* 1 (deal with incorrectly) falsch behandeln ‹*Angelegenheit*›; schlecht verwalten ‹*Finanzen*› 2 (handle roughly) misshandeln

mishap /'mɪshæp, mɪs'hæp/ *n.* Missgeschick, *das;* **sb. suffers** *or* **meets with a ~:** jmdm. passiert ein Missgeschick; **without further ~:** ohne weitere Zwischenfälle

mishear /mɪs'hɪə(r)/, **misheard** /mɪs'hɜ:d/
A *v.i.* sich verhören
B *v.t.* falsch verstehen

mishit
A /'mɪshɪt/ *n.* Fehlschlag, *der;* **have** *or* **make a ~:** [den Ball] verschlagen
B /mɪs'hɪt/ *v.t., forms as* **hit A** verschlagen ‹*Ball*›

mishmash /'mɪʃmæʃ/ *n.* Mischmasch, *der* (ugs.) (**of** aus)

misinform /mɪsɪn'fɔ:m/ *v.t.* falsch informieren *od.* unterrichten

misinformation /mɪsɪnfə'meɪʃn/ *n., no pl., no indef. art.* Fehlinformationen *Pl.;* (on radio, in newspaper) Falschmeldungen *Pl.*

misinterpret /mɪsɪn'tɜ:prɪt/ *v.t.* 1 (interpret wrongly) fehlinterpretieren, falsch auslegen ‹*Text, Inschrift, Buch*›; ‹*Übersetzung:*› falsch wiedergeben ‹*Sinn*› 2 (make wrong inference from) falsch deuten; missdeuten; **he ~ed her letter as meaning that ...:** er las fälschlicherweise aus ihrem Brief heraus, dass ...

misinterpretation /mɪsɪntɜ:prɪ'teɪʃn/ *n.* Fehlinterpretation, *die;* **be open to ~:** leicht falsch ausgelegt werden können

misjudge /mɪs'dʒʌdʒ/
A *v.t.* falsch einschätzen; falsch beurteilen ‹*Person*›; **~ the height/distance/length of time** sich in der Höhe/Entfernung/Zeit verschätzen
B *v.i.* sich verschätzen

misjudgement, misjudgment /mɪs'dʒʌdʒmənt/ *n.* Fehleinschätzung, *die;* (of person) falsche Beurteilung; (of distance, length, etc.) falsche Einschätzung

miskick
A /'mɪskɪk/ *n.* Fehlschuss, *der;* missglückter Schuss
B /mɪs'kɪk/ *v.t.* **~ the ball** den Ball nicht richtig treffen
C /mɪs'kɪk/ *v.i.* (fail to kick) danebenschießen (ugs.); (kick badly) schlecht schießen (ugs.); **he completely ~ed** sein Schuss ging voll daneben

mislay /mɪs'leɪ/ *v.t.,* **mislaid** /mɪs'leɪd/ verlegen

mislead /mɪs'li:d/ *v.t.,* **misled** /mɪs'led/ irreführen; täuschen; **~ sb. about sth.** jmdm. ein falsches Bild von etw. vermitteln

misleading /mɪs'li:dɪŋ/ *adj.* irreführend

mismanage /mɪs'mænɪdʒ/ *v.t.* herunterwirtschaften ‹*Firma, Land*›; schlecht führen ‹*Haushalt*›; schlecht handhaben *od.* abwickeln ‹*Angelegenheit, Projekt, Sache*›; schlecht abwickeln ‹*Geschäft*›

mismanagement /mɪs'mænɪdʒmənt/ *n.* Misswirtschaft, *die;* (of finances) schlechte Verwaltung; (of matters or affairs) schlechte Handhabung *od.* Abwicklung

mismatch
A /mɪs'mætʃ/ *v.t.* **~ parts of sth.** Teile von etw. nicht richtig zusammenfügen; **~ colours/fabrics/patterns** Farben/Gewebe/Muster miteinander kombinieren, die nicht zusammenpassen; **a badly ~ed couple** ein Paar, das absolut nicht zusammenpasst
B /'mɪsmætʃ/ *n.* Nichtübereinstimmung, *die;* (Boxing) ungleicher Kampf; **their marriage was a ~:** sie passten als Eheleute nicht zusammen

misnomer /mɪs'nəʊmə(r)/ *n.* 1 (use of wrong name) falsche Bezeichnung *od.* Benennung; **this seems like a slight ~** (iron.) das ist wohl etwas danebengegriffen 2 (wrong name) unzutreffende Bezeichnung

misogynist /mɪ'sɒdʒɪnɪst/ *n.* Frauenhasser, *der;* Misogyn, *der* (geh.)

misogyny /mɪ'sɒdʒɪnɪ/ *n.* Frauenhass, *der;* Misogynie, *die* (geh.)

misplace /mɪs'pleɪs/ *v.t.* 1 (put in wrong place) an die falsche Stelle *od.* den falschen Platz stellen/legen/setzen *usw.* 2 (bestow on wrong object) **~ one's affection/confidence** seine Zuneigung/sein Vertrauen dem Falschen/der Falschen schenken; **have a ~d reliance on sb./sth.** so töricht sein, fest auf jmdn./etw. zu vertrauen 3 **be ~d** (inappropriate) unangebracht *od.* fehl am Platz sein

misplay /mɪs'pleɪ/ *v.t.* verschießen ‹*Elfmeter, Eckball usw.*›; schlecht spielen, verschlagen ‹*Ball, Return*›; **~ one's stroke** den Ball verschlagen

m

misprint
A /ˈmɪsprɪnt/ *n.* Druckfehler, *der*
B /mɪsˈprɪnt/ *v.t.* verdrucken

mispronounce /mɪsprəˈnaʊns/ *v.t.* falsch aussprechen

mispronunciation /mɪsprənʌnsɪˈeɪʃn/ *n.* falsche Aussprache; (mistake) Ausspracheféhler, *der*

misquotation /mɪskwəʊˈteɪʃn/ *n.* falsches Zitat; **he is given to ~:** er zitiert oft falsch

misquote /mɪsˈkwəʊt/ *v.t.* falsch zitieren; **he was ~d as saying that ...:** man unterstellte ihm, gesagt zu haben, dass ...

misread /mɪsˈriːd/ *v.t.*, **misread** /mɪsˈred/ (read wrongly) falsch *od.* nicht richtig lesen ‹*Text, Wort, Schrift*›; (interpret wrongly) falsch verstehen ‹*Anweisungen*›; missdeuten ‹*Text, Absichten*›; **~ an 'a' as a 'b'** ein „a" als „b" lesen

misremember /mɪsrɪˈmembə(r)/ *v.t.* **~ sth.** etw. nicht richtig in Erinnerung haben

misrepresent /mɪsreprɪˈzent/ *v.t.* falsch darstellen; verdrehen ‹*Tatsachen*›; **~ sb.'s character** ein falsches Bild von jmds. Charakter geben

misrepresentation /mɪsreprɪzenˈteɪʃn/ *n.* falsche Darstellung; (of facts) Verdrehung, *die*

misrule /mɪsˈruːl/ *n.*, *no pl.* (bad government) Missregierung, *die*

miss
A *n.* 1 (failure to hit or attain) Fehlschlag, *der;* (shot) Fehlschuss, *der;* (throw) Fehlwurf, *der;* **be a ~:** danebengehen (ugs.); **a ~ is as good as a mile** (prov.) fast getroffen ist auch daneben 2 **give sb./sth. a ~:** sich (*Dat.*) jmdn./etw. schenken; **we'll give the pub a ~ tonight** wir werden heute Abend mal nicht in die Kneipe gehen; *see also* **near C 3**
B *v.t.* 1 (fail to hit, lit. or fig.) verfehlen; **~ed!** nicht getroffen!; **the car just ~ed the tree** das Auto wäre um ein Haar gegen den Baum geprallt; **we just ~ed having an accident** wir hätten um ein Haar einen Unfall gehabt 2 (fail to get) nicht bekommen; (fail to find or meet) verpassen; **they ~ed each other** sie verpassten *od.* verfehlten sich; **~ a catch** einen Ball nicht fangen; **~ the goal** am Tor vorbeischießen; danebenschießen; **he just ~ed being first** er wäre um ein Haar Erster geworden 3 (let slip) verpassen; versäumen; **~ an opportunity** sich (*Dat.*) eine Gelegenheit entgehen lassen; **you don't know what you're ~ing** du weißt ja gar nicht, was dir entgeht; **it is too good to ~** *or* **is not to be ~ed** das darf man sich (*Dat.*) [einfach] nicht entgehen lassen; **an experience he would not have ~ed** eine Erfahrung, die er nicht hätte missen wollen 4 (fail to catch) versäumen, verpassen ‹*Bus, Zug, Flugzeug*›; **~ the boat** *or* **bus** (fig.) den Anschluss verpassen (fig.) 5 (fail to take part in) versäumen; **~ school** in der Schule fehlen 6 (fail to see) übersehen; (fail to hear or understand) nicht mitbekommen; **you can't ~ it** es ist nicht zu übersehen; **he doesn't ~ much** ihm entgeht so schnell nichts 7 (feel the absence of) vermissen; **she ~es him** er fehlt ihr 8 (fail to keep or perform) versäumen ‹*Verabredung, Vorstellung*›; **she ~ed her pill** sie hat vergessen, ihre Pille zu nehmen
C *v.i.* 1 (not hit sth.) nicht treffen; (not catch sth.) danebengreifen 2 ‹*Ball, Schuss usw.:*› danebengehen 3 ‹*Motor:*› aussetzen

Phrasal verb
• **~ 'out**
A *v.t.* weglassen; **his name was ~ed out from the list** sein Name fehlte auf der Liste
B *v.i.* **~ out on sth.** (coll.) sich (*Dat.*) etw. entgehen lassen; **he can't afford to ~ out** er kann es sich nicht leisten, sich das entgehen zu lassen

Miss /mɪs/ *n.* ▸ⓘ **p. 1634** 1 ▸ⓘ **p. 1287** (title of unmarried woman) **~ Brown** Frau Brown; Fräulein Brown (veralt.); (girl) Fräulein Brown; **the ~es Smith[s]** die Damen/Fräulein Smith 2 (title of beauty queen) **~ France** Miss Frankreich; **~ World Contest** Miss-Universum-Wahl, *die* 3 (as form of address to teacher etc.) Frau Schmidt *usw.*; (from servant) gnädiges Fräulein 4 **m~** (derog. or playful: girl) **the young ~es** die jungen Dinger (ugs.); **she is a saucy [little] ~:** sie ist ein freches [junges] Ding (ugs.)

missal /ˈmɪsl/ *n.* 1 (RC Ch.) Missal[e], *das* 2 (book of prayers) [illuminiertes] Gebetbuch

mis-sell /mɪsˈsel/ *v.t.*, **mis-sold** /mɪsˈsəʊld/ unlauter vermarkten; **they have been mis-sold personal pensions** man hat ihnen auf unlautere Art und Weise private Rentenversicherungen verkauft

mis-selling /mɪsˈselɪŋ/ *n.*, *no pl.* unlauteres Verkaufen; **accusations of ~:** Anschuldigungen wegen unlauterer Verkaufsmethoden

missel [thrush] /ˈmɪsl(θrʌʃ)/ *n.* (Ornith.) Misteldrossel, *die*

misshapen /mɪsˈʃeɪpn/ *adj.* missgebildet, missgestaltet ‹*Körper[teil]*›; verwachsen ‹*Baum, Pflanze*›; verbogen ‹*Münze*›

missile /ˈmɪsaɪl/ *n.* 1 (thrown) [Wurf]geschoss, *das* 2 (self-propelled) Missile, *das;* Flugkörper, *der;* **intercontinental ballistic ~:** [ballistische] Interkontinentalrakete

missile: ~ base *n.* [Raketen]abschussbasis, *die;* **~ launcher** *n.* [Raketen]abschussrampe, *die*

missilery /ˈmɪslrɪ/ *n.*, *no pl.* 1 (missiles) Geschosse *Pl.;* (modern) Raketen *Pl.* 2 (science) Raketentechnik, *die*

'missile site ▸**missile base**

missing /ˈmɪsɪŋ/ *adj.* vermisst; fehlend ‹*Seite, Kapitel, Teil, Hinweis, Indiz*›; **be ~** ‹*Kapitel, Wort, Seite:*› fehlen; ‹*Brille, Bleistift usw.:*› verschwunden sein; ‹*Mensch:*› vermisst werden; (not be present) nicht da sein; fehlen; **she went ~ two hours ago** sie wird seit zwei Stunden vermisst; **the jacket has two buttons ~:** an der Jacke fehlen zwei Knöpfe; **I am ~ £10** mir fehlen 10 Pfund; **the dead, wounded, and ~:** die Toten, Verwundeten und Vermissten; **~ person** Vermisste *der/die;* **~ link** (Biol.) Missing Link, *das*

mission /ˈmɪʃn/ *n.* 1 (task) Mission, *die;* Auftrag, *der* 2 (journey) Mission, *die;* **go/come on a ~ to do sth.** mit dem Auftrag reisen/kommen, etw. zu tun 3 (planned operation) Einsatz, *der;* (order) Befehl, *der;* **space ~:** Weltraumflug, *der* 4 (vocation) Mission, *die;* **~ in life** Lebensaufgabe, *die;* **have a ~ to do sth.** dazu berufen sein, etw. zu tun 5 (persons) Mission, *die* 6 (Relig.) Mission, *die;* (missionary post) Mission[sstation], *die;* (religious body) Mission[sgesellschaft], *die;* **foreign/home ~** (campaign) äußere/innere Mission

missionary /ˈmɪʃənərɪ/
A *adj.* missionarisch; Missions‹*station, -arbeit, -schrift*›; **~ box** Opferbüchse [für die Mission]
B *n.* ▸ⓘ **p. 1260** Missionar, *der*/Missionarin, *die*

'mission statement *n.* Unternehmensleitbild, *das*

missis /ˈmɪsɪz, ˈmɪsɪs/ *n.* 1 (uneducated/joc.: wife) **the** *or* **my/his/your ~:** die *od.* meine/seine/deine Alte (salopp); meine/seine/deine bessere Hälfte (ugs. scherzh.) 2 (coll.: as form of address) **well, ~. ...:** na, die Dame, ... (ugs.)

missive /ˈmɪsɪv/ *n.* (formal/joc.) Missiv, *das* (veralt.); Schreiben, *das*

misspell /mɪsˈspel/ *v.t.*, *forms as* **spell¹** falsch schreiben

misspelling /mɪsˈspelɪŋ/ *n.* falsch geschriebenes Wort

misspend /mɪsˈspend/ *v.t.*, *forms as* **spend** verschwenden; vergeuden; **his was a misspent youth** er hat seine Jugend vertan

misstate /mɪsˈsteɪt/ *v.t.* falsch darstellen

misstatement /mɪsˈsteɪtmənt/ *n.* falsche Darstellung

missus /ˈmɪsɪz/ ▸**missis**

mist /mɪst/
A *n.* 1 (fog) Nebel, *der;* (haze) Dunst, *der;* (on windscreen etc.) Beschlag, *der; see also* **Scotch mist** 2 **in the ~s of time** *or* **antiquity** (fig.) im Dunkel *od.* (geh.) Nebel der Vergangenheit 3 (of spray, vapour, etc.) Wolke, *die* 4 (blurring of sight) Schleier, *der*
B *v.t.* beschlagen lassen ‹*Glas*›; ‹*Tränen:*› verschleiern ‹*Blick*›

Phrasal verbs
• **~ 'over**
A *v.i.* ‹*Glas usw.:*› [sich] beschlagen; **his eyes ~ed over** Tränen verschleierten seinen Blick
B *v.t.* beschlagen lassen
• **~ 'up** *v.i.* ‹*Glas, Brille:*› [sich] beschlagen

mistakable /mɪˈsteɪkəbl/ *adj.* verwechselbar (**for** mit)

mistake /mɪˈsteɪk/
A *n.* Fehler, *der;* (misunderstanding) Missverständnis, *das;* **make a ~:** einen Fehler machen; (in thinking) sich irren; **there was a ~ about sth.** man hat sich in etw. (*Dat.*) geirrt; **there's some ~!** da liegt ein Irrtum *od.* Fehler vor!; **we all make ~s** jeder macht mal einen Fehler; (in thinking) jeder kann sich mal irren; **the ~ is mine** der Fehler liegt bei mir; **it is a ~ to assume that ...:** es ist ein Irrtum anzunehmen, dass ...; **by ~:** versehentlich; aus Versehen; **... and no ~:** ..., aber wirklich; **I was properly scared and no ~:** ich habe einen ganz schönen Schrecken gekriegt, kann ich dir sagen; **make no ~ about it, ...:** täusch dich nicht, ...
B *v.t.*, *forms as* **take A** 1 (misunderstand meaning of) falsch verstehen; missverstehen; **~ sth./sb. as meaning that ...:** etw./jmdn. [fälschlicherweise] so verstehen, dass ... 2 (wrongly take one for another) **~ x for y** x mit y verwechseln; x [fälschlich] für y halten; **there is no mistaking what ought to be done** es steht außer Frage *od.* ist ganz klar, was getan werden muss; **there is no mistaking him** man kann ihn gar nicht verwechseln; **~ sb.'s identity** jmdn. [mit jmd. anderem] verwechseln 3 (choose wrongly) verfehlen ‹*Beruf, Weg*›

mistaken /mɪˈsteɪkn/ *adj.* **be ~:** sich täuschen; **you're ~ in believing that** wenn du das glaubst, täuschst du dich; **~ kindness/zeal** unangebrachte Freundlichkeit/unangebrachter Eifer; **or** *or* **unless I'm very much ~:** wenn mich nicht alles täuscht; **a case of ~ identity** eine Verwechslung

mistakenly /mɪˈsteɪknlɪ/ *adv.* irrtümlicherweise

mister /ˈmɪstə(r)/ *n.* 1 (coll./joc.) **hey, ~:** he, Meister *od.* Chef (ugs.) 2 (person without title) **a mere ~:** ein gewöhnlicher Bürger

mistime /mɪsˈtaɪm/ *v.t.* einen ungünstigen Zeitpunkt wählen für; schlecht timen (bes. Sport)

mistletoe /ˈmɪsltəʊ/ *n.* Mistel, *die;* (sprig) Mistelzweig, *der*

mistook ▸**mistake B**

mistral /mɪsˈtrɑːl/ *n.* (Meteorol.) Mistral, *der*

mistranslate /mɪstrænsˈleɪt/ *v.t.* falsch übersetzen

mistranslation /mɪstrænsˈleɪʃn/ *n.* falsche Übersetzung; (error) Übersetzungsfehler, *der*

mistreat /mɪsˈtriːt/ *v.t.* schlecht behandeln; (violently) misshandeln; **~ one's tools** nachlässig mit seinem Werkzeug umgehen

mistreatment /mɪsˈtriːtmənt/ *n.* schlechte Behandlung; (violent) Misshandlung, *die*

mistress /ˈmɪstrɪs/ *n.* 1 (of a household) Hausherrin, *die;* **the ~ of the house** *or* **family** die Frau des Hauses 2 (person in control, employer) Herrin, *die;* **she is ~ of the situation** sie ist Herr der Lage; **she is her own ~:** sie ist ihr eigener Herr; **the dog's ~:** das Frauchen [des Hundes] 3 (Brit. Sch.: teacher) Lehrerin, *die;* **'French ~:** Französischlehrerin, *die* 4 (man's illicit lover) Geliebte, *die;* Mätresse, *die* (veralt. abwertend) 5 (expert) Expertin, *die;* Meisterin, *die* 6 (of college) Rektorin, *die*

mistrial /mɪsˈtraɪəl/ *n.* (Law) 1 (invalid trial) fehlerhaft geführter Prozess; **on the grounds that there had been a ~:** wegen Verfahrensfehlern in der Prozessführung 2 (Amer.: inconclusive trial) ergebnisloser Prozess

mistrust /mɪsˈtrʌst/
A *v.t.* misstrauen (+ *Dat.*); **~ oneself** sich (*Dat.*) selbst misstrauen
B *n.*, *no pl.* Misstrauen, *das* (**of** gegenüber + *Dat.*); **[show] ~ towards sb.** Misstrauen gegen jmdn. [hegen]

mistrustful /mɪsˈtrʌstfl/ *adj.* misstrauisch; **be ~ of sb./sth.** jmdm./einer Sache gegenüber misstrauisch sein

m

misty /ˈmɪstɪ/ *adj.* **1** verschleiert ‹*Augen, Blick*›; neb[e]lig, dunstig ‹*Tag, Morgen*›; in Nebel *od.* Dunst gehüllt ‹*Berg, Hügel*›; nebelverhangen (geh.), dunstig ‹*Tal*›; **~ blue** rauchiges Blau **2** (indistinct in form) unklar; verschwommen

ˈmisty-eyed *adj.* mit verschleiertem Blick *nachgestellt;* **be ~:** einen [tränen]verschleierten Blick haben

misunderstand /mɪsʌndəˈstænd/ *v.t., forms as* **understand** missverstehen; falsch verstehen; **~ the word x as meaning y** das Wort x im Sinne von y verstehen; **don't ~ me** versteh mich nicht falsch

misunderstanding /mɪsʌndəˈstændɪŋ/ *n.* Missverständnis, *das;* **there has been a ~:** da lag ein Missverständnis vor; **I don't want there to be any ~ about it** ich möchte nicht, dass deswegen ein Missverständnis aufkommt

misunderstood /mɪsʌndəˈstʊd/ *adj.* unverstanden; verkannt ‹*Künstler, Genie*›; **be ~:** kein Verständnis finden

misuse

A /mɪsˈjuːz/ *v.t.* missbrauchen; zweckentfremden ‹*Werkzeug, Gelder*›; falsch bedienen ‹*Maschine*›; nichts Rechtes machen aus ‹*Gelegenheit, Talent*›; vergeuden, verschwenden ‹*Reserven, Zeit*›

B /mɪsˈjuːs/ *n.* Missbrauch, *der;* (of funds) Zweckentfremdung, *die;* (of resources, time) Vergeudung, *die;* Verschwendung, *die;* **a ~ of language** eine unangemessene *od.* unangebrachte Ausdrucksweise

mite /maɪt/ *n.* **1** (Zool.) Milbe, *die* **2** (contribution) Scherflein, *das;* **the widow's ~:** das Scherflein der armen Witwe **3** (small object) Dingelchen, *das;* kleines Ding; (small child) Würmchen, *das* (fam.); **poor little ~:** armes Kleines **4** (coll.: somewhat) **a ~ too strong/outˈspoken** ein bisschen *od.* etwas zu stark/geradeheraus

miter, mitered (Amer.) ▸ **mitre, mitred**

mitigate /ˈmɪtɪgeɪt/ *v.t.* **1** (alleviate) lindern **2** (make less severe) mildern; **mitigating circumstances** mildernde Umstände **3** (appease) besänftigen ‹*Zorn, Wut*›

mitigation /mɪtɪˈgeɪʃn/ *n.* ▸ **mitigate**: Linderung, *die;* Milderung, *die;* Besänftigung, *die;* **it must be said, in ~ of his faults, that …:** es muss zu seiner Verteidigung *od.* Entlastung gesagt werden, dass …; **~ of punishment** Strafmilderung, *die*

mitochondrion /maɪtəʊˈkɒndrɪən/ *n.* (Biol.) Mitochondrion, *das*

mitosis /maɪˈtəʊsɪs/ *n., pl.* **maitoses** /maɪˈtəʊsiːz/ (Biol.) Mitose, *die*

mitre /ˈmaɪtə(r)/ *n.* (Brit.) **1** (Eccl.) Mitra, *die* **2** (joint) Gehrung, *die* (bes. Technik)

mitred /ˈmaɪtəd/ *adj.* **1** (Brit. Eccl.) eine Mitra tragend **2** **~ joint** (Carpentry) Gehrungsverbindung, *die*

mitt /mɪt/ *n.* **1** (fingerless glove) fingerloser Handschuh **2** (Baseball) Fanghandschuh, *der* **3** (coll.: hand) Flosse, *die* (ugs.)

mitten /ˈmɪtn/ *n.* Fausthandschuh, *der;* Fäustling, *der;* (not covering fingers) fingerloser Handschuh

Mitty /ˈmɪtɪ/ *n., pl.* **~s [Walter] ~ [figure]** *Mensch, der sich gern Tagträumen von eigenen Großtaten hingibt*

mix /mɪks/

A *v.t.* **1** (combine) [ver]mischen; vermengen; verrühren ‹*Zutaten*›; verbinden ‹*Harmonien, Komponenten, Stilrichtungen*›; **~ one's drinks** alles durcheinander trinken; **~ an egg into the batter** ein Ei in den Teig rühren **2** (prepare by mixing) mischen, mixen ‹*Cocktail*›; anrühren, ansetzen ‹*Lösung, Teig*›; zubereiten ‹*Medikament*› **3** **~ it [with sb.]** (coll.) sich [mit jmdm.] prügeln

B *v.i.* **1** (become ~ed) sich vermischen **2** (be sociable, participate) Umgang mit anderen [Menschen] haben; **~ well** kontaktfreudig *od.* gesellig sein; **you should ~ with other people** du solltest unter Leute gehen; **I don't ~ with that sort of people/in those circles** ich verkehre nicht mit solchen Leuten/in diesen Kreisen **3** (be compatible) zusammenpassen; sich [miteinander] vertragen; ‹*Ideen:*› sich verbinden lassen

C *n.* **1** (coll.: mixture) Mischung, *die* (**of** aus) **2** (proportion) [Mischungs]verhältnis, *das* **3** (ready ingredients) [gebrauchsfertige] Mischung; **[cake] ~:** Backmischung, *die* **4** (Radio, Cinemat., TV) **~[es]** Mischung, *die*

Phrasal verbs

• **~ ˈin**

A *v.i.* **1** (be compatible) zu jmdm./etw. passen **2** (start fighting) aufeinander losgehen

B *v.t.* einrühren

• **~ ˈup** *v.t.* **1** vermischen; verrühren ‹*Zutaten*› **2** (make a muddle of) durcheinander bringen; (confuse one with another) verwechseln; *see also* **mix-up** **3** *in pass.* (involve) **be/get ~ed up in sth.** in etw. (*Akk.*) verwickelt sein/werden; **get ~ed up with a gang** sich mit einer Gang einlassen

mixed /mɪkst/ *adj.* **1** (diverse) unterschiedlich ‹*Reaktionen, Kritiken*›; **a ~ assortment** eine [bunte] Mischung (**of** von); **~ feelings** gemischte Gefühle; **get ~ reviews** sehr unterschiedliche Kritiken bekommen **2** (containing people from various backgrounds etc.) gemischt ‹*Gesellschaft*›; **a ~ bunch** ein bunt gemischter Haufen **3** (for both sexes) gemischt

mixed: ~ ˈbag *n.* bunte Mischung; **a very ~ bag of people** eine bunt gemischte Gruppe [von Leuten]; **~ ˈblessing** *n.* **be a ~ blessing** nicht nur Vorteile haben; **children are a ~ blessing** Kinder sind kein reiner Segen; **~ ˈcompany** *n.* **in ~ company** in Gesellschaft von Damen [und Kindern]; **~ ˈdoubles** ▸ **double C 10**; **~ ˈfarming** *n.* Kombination von Ackerbau und Viehzucht; **~ ˈgrill** *n.* Mixed grill, *der* (Gastr.); gemischte Grillplatte; **~ ˈmarriage** *n.* Mischehe, *die;* **~ ˈmetaphor** ▸ **metaphor 2**; **~-ˈup** *adj.* (fig. coll.) verwirrt, konfus ‹*Person*›; **be/feel very ~-up** völlig durcheinander sein; **[crazy] ~-up kids** Jugendliche ohne [jeden] inneren Halt

mixer /ˈmɪksə(r)/ *n.* **1** (for foods) Mixer, *der;* (for concrete) Mischmaschine, *die* **2** (merging pictures) (apparatus) Mischpult, *das;* (person) Bildmischer, *der* **3** (combining sounds) (apparatus) Mischpult, *das;* Tonmischer, *der;* (person) Tonmischer, *der* **4** (drink) Getränk zum Mischen **5** (in society) **be a good ~:** mit den unterschiedlichsten Leuten gut zurechtkommen

ˈmixer tap *n.* (Brit.) Mischbatterie, *die*

mixture /ˈmɪkstʃə(r)/ *n.* **1** (mixing, being mixed) Mischen, *das;* (of harmonies) Verbinden, *das* **2** (result) Mischung, *die* (**of** aus); **~ of gases** Gasgemisch, *das;* **he is such a ~** (fig.) er ist so unausgeglichen **3** (medicinal preparation) Mixtur, *die;* **the ~ as before** (fig.) die altbekannte Mischung **4** (Motor Veh.: gas or vaporized petrol) Gemisch, *das* **5** (ready ingredients) ▸ **mix C 3** **6** **[mechanical] ~** (act) Vermengen, *das;* (product) Gemenge, *das*

ˈmix-up *n.* Durcheinander, *das;* (misunderstanding) Missverständnis, *das;* **there has been some sort of ~:** da ist irgendetwas schief gelaufen (ugs.); **there's been a ~ about who should be invited** es gab einige Verwirrung darüber, wer eingeladen werden sollte

mizen ▸ **mizzen**

mizzen (mizen) /ˈmɪzn/ *n.* (Naut.) Besan, *der*

mizzen: ~mast *n.* (Naut.) Besanmast, *der;* **~sail** *n.* (Naut.) Besansegel, *das*

Mk. *abbr.* ▸ **mark[1] A 2**

ml. *abbr.* **1** ▸ℹ **p. 1690 = millilitre[s]** ml **2** **= mile[s]** M

MLR *abbr.* **= minimum lending rate**

mm. *abbr.* ▸ℹ **p. 1208**, ▸ℹ **p. 1286 = millimetre[s]** mm

MMR *abbr.* **= measles, mumps, and rubella**; **~ vaccination** MMR-Impfung, *die*

mnemonic /nɪˈmɒnɪk/ *n.* Gedächtnishilfe, *die;* Eselsbrücke, *die* (ugs.)

mo /məʊ/ *n., pl.* **~s** /məʊz/ (coll.) Moment, *der;* **half a ~, wait a ~:** Momentchen!

mo. *abbr.* (Amer.) **= month** Mo.

moa /ˈməʊə/ *n.* (Ornith.) Moa, *der*

moan /məʊn/

A *n.* **1** Stöhnen, *das;* (fig.: of wind) Heulen, *das* **2** (complaint) **have a ~** (complain at length) jammern; (have a grievance) eine Beschwerde haben

B *v.i.* **1** stöhnen (**with** vor + *Dat.*); (fig.) ‹*Wind:*› heulen **2** (complain) jammern (**about** über + *Akk.*); **what is he ~ing [and groaning] about now?** was hat er denn jetzt wieder zu jammern?; **~ at sb.** jmdm. etwas vorjammern

C *v.t.* stöhnen

moat /məʊt/

A *n.* [Wasser]graben, *der;* **[castle] ~:** Burggraben, *der*

B *v.t.* mit einem Wassergraben umgeben

mob /mɒb/

A *n.* **1** (rabble) Mob, *der* (abwertend); Pöbel, *der* (abwertend); **a ~ gathered outside the police station** eine aufgebrachte Menge versammelte sich vor der Polizeiwache **2** (coll.: associated group) **~ [of criminals]** Bande, *die* (abwertend); **Peter and his ~:** Peter und seine ganze Blase (salopp); **~ law/rule** Gesetz/Herrschaft der Straße **3** (derog.: populace) **the ~:** die [breite] Masse

B *v.t.,* **-bb-** **1** (crowd round) belagern (ugs.) ‹*Schauspieler, Star*›; stürmen ‹*Kino*› **2** (attack) herfallen über (+ *Akk.*); sich stürzen auf (+ *Akk.*); **he was ~bed** sie fielen über ihn her

mobile /ˈməʊbaɪl/

A *adj.* **1** (able to move easily) beweglich; (on wheels) fahrbar **2** lebhaft ‹*Gesicht[szüge]*› **3** (Mil.) mobil **4** (accommodated in vehicle) mobil; fahrbar; **~ library** Fahrbücherei, *die;* **~ canteen** Kantine auf Rädern **5** (in social status) mobil (bes. Soziol.); **upwardly ~:** sozial aufsteigend; **be upwardly ~:** sozial aufsteigen; **downwardly ~:** im sozialen Abstieg begriffen; **be downwardly ~:** sich im sozialen Abstieg befinden

B *n.* **1** (**~** phone) Handy, *das* **2** (decorative structure) Mobile, *das*

mobile: ~ communiˈcations *n. pl.* mobile Kommunikation; **~ ˈhome** *n.* transportable Wohneinheit; (caravan) Wohnwagen, *der;* **~ ˈInternet** *n.* mobiles Internet; **~ ˈphone** *n.* Mobiltelefon, *das;* Handy, *das;* **~ teˈlephony** *n., no pl.* Mobiltelefonie, *die;* Mobilfunk, *der*

mobilisation, mobilise ▸ **mobiliz-**

mobility /məˈbɪlɪtɪ/ *n.* **1** (ability to move) (of person) Beweglichkeit, *die;* (on wheels) Fahrbarkeit, *die* **2** (in social status) Mobilität, *die* (bes. Soziol.)

moˈbility allowance *n.* (Brit.) *staatliche Geldleistung, die Gehbehinderten gewährt werden kann*

mobilization /məʊbɪlaɪˈzeɪʃn/ *n.* **1** (act of mobilizing) Mobilisierung, *die* **2** (Mil.) Mobilmachung, *die*

mobilize /ˈməʊbɪlaɪz/ *v.t.* **1** (render movable or effective) mobilisieren **2** (Mil.) mobil machen; *abs.* **make preparations to ~:** die Mobilmachung vorbereiten

mobster /ˈmɒbstə(r)/ *n.* (coll.) Gangster, *der*

moccasin /ˈmɒkəsɪn/ *n.* Mokassin, *der*

mocha /ˈmɒkə/ *n.* Mokka, *der*

mock /mɒk/

A *v.t.* **1** (subject to ridicule) sich lustig machen über (+ *Akk.*); verspotten; **he was ~ed** man machte sich über ihn lustig **2** (ridicule by imitation) **~ sb./sth.** jmdn./etw. nachmachen[, um sich über ihn/darüber lustig zu machen]

B *v.i.* **~ at sb./sth.** sich über jmdn./etw. mokieren *od.* lustig machen

C *attrib. adj.* gespielt ‹*Feierlichkeit, Bescheidenheit, Ernst*›; Schein‹*kampf, -angriff, -ehe*›; **~ Tudor style** Pseudotudorstil, *der;* **~ examination** simulierte Prüfung; *see also* **orange A 2**

D *n.* (thing deserving scorn) **make [a] ~ of sb./sth.** sich über jmdn./etw. lustig machen

mocker /ˈmɒkə(r)/ *n.* **1** Spötter, *der*/Spötterin, *die* **2** **put the ~s on sb./sth.** (coll.) jmdm. alles vermasseln/etw. vermasseln (salopp)

mockery /ˈmɒkərɪ/ *n.* **1** (inadequate form) **be a ~ of justice/the truth** der Gerechtigkeit/Wahrheit (*Dat.*) hohnsprechen (geh.); **he received only the ~ of a trial** sein Verfahren war eine einzige Farce **2** (futile action) **it would be a ~ to …** (be absurd) es wäre grotesk *od.* absurd, zu …; (be impudent) es wäre geschmacklos *od.* unverschämt, zu … **3** *no pl., no indef. art.* (derision) Spott, *der* **4** (person or thing derided)

m

Gespött, *das;* **make a ~ of sth.** etw. zur Farce machen

mock-he'roic *adj.* komisch-heroisch (Literaturw.); **~ poem** komisches Heldengedicht *od.* Epos

mocking /'mɒkɪŋ/
A *adj.* spöttisch
B *n.* Spott, *der*

'mockingbird *n.* Spottdrossel, *die*

'mock turtle soup *n.* Mockturtlesuppe, *die*

'mock-up *n.* Modell [in Originalgröße]; (of book etc.) Layout, *das*

Mod /mɒd/ *n.* (Brit.) *sich modisch kleidender [Motorroller fahrender] Jugendlicher in den Sechzigerjahren;* Mod, *der*

MOD /emәʊ'diː/ *abbr.* **1** (Brit.) **= Ministry of Defence** Verteidigungsministerium, *das* **2** **= movies-on-demand** MOD

modal /'mәʊdl/ *adj.* **1** (of mode, form) formal **2** (Ling.) modal; **~ auxiliary** *or* **verb** Modalverb, *das* **3** (Mus.) modal

modality /mә'dælɪtɪ/ *n.* **the modalities are** *or* **the ~ is as follows** die Modalitäten sind wie folgt

mod cons /mɒd 'kɒnz/ *n. pl.* (Brit. coll.) [moderner] Komfort; **have all ~:** mit allem Komfort *od.* (ugs.) allen Schikanen ausgestattet sein

mode /mәʊd/ *n.* **1** (way in which thing is done) Art [und Weise], *die;* (method of procedure) Methode, *die;* (Computing) Betriebsart, *die;* **~ of behaviour** *or* **conduct/life** Verhaltens-/Lebensweise, *die;* **~ of transport** Transportmittel, *das* **2** (fashion) Mode, *die;* **the ~ for short skirts** die Mode der kurzen Röcke; **~s and fashions** Moden und Modetrends **3** (Mus.) Tonart, *die* **4** (Statistics) Modus, *der* (fachspr.); statistischer Mittelwert

model /'mɒdl/
A *n.* **1** Modell, *das;* **a sports ~:** ein Sportmodell; *see also* **working model** **2** (perfect example) Muster, *das* (**of** an + *Dat.*); (to be imitated) Vorbild, *das;* **be a ~ of industry** ein Muster an Fleiß (*Dat.*) sein; **on the ~ of sth.** nach dem Vorbild einer Sache (*Gen.*); **make sth. on the ~ of sth.** etw. einer Sache (*Dat.*) nachbilden; **take sb. as a ~:** [sich (*Dat.*)] jmdn. zum Vorbild nehmen **3** (person employed to pose) Modell, *das;* (Fashion) Model, *das;* Mannequin, *das;* (male) Dressman, *der;* **photographer's ~:** Fotomodell, *das;* **be a painter's ~:** einem Maler Modell stehen/sitzen
B *adj.* **1** (exemplary) vorbildlich; mustergültig; Muster- (oft iron.); **~ child** Musterkind, *das;* (boy) Musterknabe, *der* (iron.) **2** (miniature) Modell- ‹*stadt, -eisenbahn, -flugzeug*›
C *v.t.*, (Brit.) **-ll- 1** (shape figure of) modellieren; formen; **~ sth. in clay** etw. in Ton modellieren; **delicately ~led features** (fig.) fein geschnittene Gesichtszüge **2** (form in imitation of sth.) **~ sth. after** *or* **[up]on sth.** etw. einer Sache (*Dat.*) nachbilden; **we ~led our system on the European one** wir haben unser System nach europäischem Vorbild aufgebaut; **~ oneself on sb.** sich (*Dat.*) jmdn. zum Vorbild nehmen **3** (Fashion) vorführen ‹*Kleid, Entwurf usw.*›
D *v.i.*, (Brit.) **-ll- 1** (Fashion) als Mannequin *od.* Model arbeiten; ‹*Mann:*› als Dressman arbeiten; (Photog.) als [Foto]modell arbeiten; (Art) Modell stehen/sitzen **2** **~ in clay** *etc.* in Ton *usw.* modellieren

modelling (*Amer.:* **modeling**) /'mɒdәlɪŋ/ *n.* **1** *no art.* (posing) **do ~** (Fashion) als Mannequin *od.* Model arbeiten; ‹*Mann:*› als Dressman arbeiten; (Photog., Art) als Modell arbeiten; **do [some] ~ for sb.** (Fashion) jmds. Kreationen vorführen; (Photog., Art) jmdm. Modell stehen/sitzen **2** *no indef. art.* (sculpturing) Modellieren, *das;* **~ clay** Modellierton, *der*

modem /'mәʊdem/ *n.* (Communications) Modem, *der*

moderate
A /'mɒdәrәt/ *adj.* **1** (avoiding extremes) gemäßigt ‹*Partei, Ansichten*›; mäßig, maßvoll ‹*Person, bes. Trinker, Esser; Forderungen*›; mäßig ‹*Begeisterung, Interesse*›; **be ~ in one's demands** maßvolle Forderungen erheben *od.* stellen **2** (fairly large or good) mittler... ‹*Größe, Menge, Wert*›; nicht allzu groß ‹*Entfernung, Wert*›; **[only] ~:** mäßig ‹*Qualität, Ernte*›; **a ~ amount of coal** eine gewisse Menge Kohle; **the water was of only ~ depth** das Wasser war nicht besonders *od.* nur mäßig tief **3** (reasonable) angemessen, vernünftig ‹*Preis, Summe*› **4** mäßig ‹*Wind*›
B /'mɒdәrәt/*n.* Gemäßigte, *der/die;* **be a ~ in politics** gemäßigte politische Ansichten vertreten
C /'mɒdәreɪt/ *v.t.* mäßigen ‹*Begierde, Ungeduld, Gefühl*›; lindern ‹*Schmerzen, Sorgen*›; dämpfen ‹*Eifer*›; zügeln ‹*Begeisterung*›; senken ‹*Stimme*›; mildern ‹*negativen Effekt*›; **~ one's demands** seine Forderungen einschränken *od.* abschwächen
D /'mɒdәreɪt/*v.i.* nachlassen; ‹*Forderungen:*› gemäßigter *od.* maßvoller werden

moderately /'mɒdәrәtlɪ/ *adv.* einigermaßen; mäßig ‹*begeistert, groß, begabt; rauchen*›; **there was only a ~ large audience** es waren nicht übermäßig viele Zuschauer da; **be only ~ enthusiastic/concerned about sth.** sich nicht allzu sehr *od.* übermäßig für etw. begeistern/sich keine allzu großen Sorgen um etw. machen

moderation /mɒdә'reɪʃn/ *n.* **1** (moderating) Mäßigung, *die;* (of wind, fever) Nachlassen, *das* **2** *no pl.* (moderateness) Mäßigkeit, *die;* (of demands etc.) Angemessenheit, *die;* Vernünftigkeit, *die;* **~ in all things** alles mit Maßen; **in ~:** mit *od.* in Maßen

moderator /'mɒdәreɪtә(r)/ *n.* **1** (arbitrator) Schlichter, *der;* (mediator) Vermittler, *der*/Vermittlerin, *die* **2** (presiding officer) Vorsitzende, *der/die* **3** (Eccl.) Moderator, *der*

modern /'mɒdn/
A *adj.* **1** (of the present) modern; heutig ‹*Zeit[alter], Welt, Mensch*›; **~ jazz** Modern Jazz, *der;* **in ~ times** in der heutigen Zeit; **~ English** modernes Englisch; **~ history** neuere Geschichte; **~ languages** neuere Sprachen; (subject of study) Neuphilologie, *die;* **~ maths** die neue Mathematik; *see also* **Latin B 2** (in current fashion) modern; neumodisch (oft abwertend); **the ~ fashion is to wear a hat** es ist [jetzt] Mode, einen Hut zu tragen
B *n. usu. in pl.* moderner Mensch; (Art) Modernist, *der*/Modernistin, *die;* (person alive at present) Zeitgenosse, *der/-genossin, die*

'modern-day *attrib. adj.* von heute *nachgestellt;* heutig

modernisation, modernise ▸**moderniz-**

modernism /'mɒdәnɪzm/ *n.* Modernismus, *der*

modernist /'mɒdәnɪst/ *n.* Modernist, *der*/Modernistin, *die*

modernistic /mɒdә'nɪstɪk/ *adj.* modernistisch

modernity /mә'dɜːnɪtɪ/ *n.* Modernität, *die*

modernization /mɒdәnaɪ'zeɪʃn/ *n.* **1** (modernizing) Modernisierung, *die* **2** (version) modernisierte Fassung

modernize /'mɒdәnaɪz/
A *v.t.* modernisieren
B *v.i.* sich der modernen Zeit anpassen

modernizer /'mɒdәnaɪzә(r)/ *n.* Modernisierer, *der*/Modernisiererin, *die*

modest /'mɒdɪst/ *adj.* **1** (not conceited) bescheiden; (shy) bescheiden; zurückhaltend; **be ~ about one's achievements** nicht mit seinen Leistungen prahlen **2** (not excessive) bescheiden (auch iron.); genügsam, anspruchslos ‹*Mensch*›; vorsichtig ‹*Schätzung*› **3** (unpretentious in appearance, amount, etc.) bescheiden; einfach, unauffällig ‹*Haus, Kleidung*›; **have a ~ lifestyle** bescheiden *od.* einfach leben; **~ in appearance** unauffällig **4** (decorous, chaste) anständig ‹*Charakter*›; anständig, (veralt.) sittsam ‹*Mensch, Benehmen*›; schicklich ‹*Benehmen, Ausdrucksweise*›; dezent, unauffällig ‹*Kleidung*›

modestly /'mɒdɪstlɪ/ *adv.* **1** (not conceitedly) bescheiden **2** (decently) dezent, unauffällig ‹*sich kleiden*›; schicklich, sittsam (veralt.) ‹*sich benehmen*›

modesty /'mɒdɪstɪ/ *n., no pl.* **1** (freedom from conceit) Bescheidenheit, *die;* **in all ~:** bei aller Bescheidenheit; **the [sheer] ~ of the man!** (iron.) die Bescheidenheit in Person! **2** **the ~ of their demands** ihre maßvollen Forderungen **3** (regard for propriety) ▸**modest 4:** Anständigkeit, *die;* Sittsamkeit, *die* (veralt.); Schicklichkeit, *die;* Unauffälligkeit, *die;* Dezentheit, *die*

modicum /'mɒdɪkәm/ *n.* Minimum, *das;* **a ~ of luck/truth** ein Quäntchen Glück/ein Körnchen Wahrheit

modification /mɒdɪfɪ'keɪʃn/ *n.* [Ab]änderung, *die;* Modifizierung, *die;* **without any sort of ~:** ohne jede Änderung

modifier /'mɒdɪfaɪә(r)/ *n.* (esp. Ling., Biol.) Modifikator, *der*

modify /'mɒdɪfaɪ/ *v.t.* **1** (make changes in) [abver]ändern; modifizieren **2** (tone down) mäßigen; mildern ‹*Klima*›; **~ one's position** in seiner Haltung gemäßigter werden; **you'd better ~ your tone** mäßigen Sie sich mal in Ihrem Ton! **3** (Ling.) (qualify sense of) näher bestimmen ‹*Verb, Adjektiv usw.*›; (change by umlaut) umlauten ‹*Vokal*›

modish /'mәʊdɪʃ/ *adj.* modisch

modular /'mɒdjʊlә(r)/ *adj.* **1** (employing module[s]) aus Elementen [zusammengesetzt]; (in construction) aus Baueinheiten *od.* -elementen [zusammengesetzt]; **~ system** Baukastensystem, *das;* **~ construction/design** Konstruktion/Entwurf nach dem Baukastensystem; **~ unit** [Bau-, Konstruktions]element, *das* **2** (Educ.) **~ course** *aus vielen verschiedenen, beliebig kombinierten Unterrichtseinheiten bestehender Kurs*

modulate /'mɒdjʊleɪt/
A *v.t.* **1** (regulate) abstimmen (**to** auf + *Akk.*); anpassen (**to** *Dat.*, an + *Akk.*) **2** (adjust pitch) modulieren ‹*Stimme, Sprache, Ton*› **3** (Radio) modulieren ‹*Welle, Sender*›
B *v.i.* modulieren; **~ from one key to another** von einer Tonart in die andere übergehen

modulation /mɒdjʊ'leɪʃn/ *n.* Modulation, *die*

modulator /'mɒdjʊleɪtә(r)/ *n.* (Electronics) Modulator, *der*

module /'mɒdjuːl/ *n.* **1** (in construction or system) Bauelement, *das;* (Electronics) Modul, *das* **2** (Educ.) Unterrichtseinheit, *die* **3** (Astronaut.) **command ~:** Kommandoeinheit *od.* -kapsel, *die; see also* **lunar module**

modulus /'mɒdjʊlәs/ *n., pl.* **moduli** /'mɒdjʊlaɪ/ (Math., Phys.) Modul, *der*

modus operandi /mәʊdәs ɒpә'rændiː/ *n.* Modus operandi, *der* (geh.)

modus vivendi /mәʊdәs vɪ'vendiː/ *n.* Modus vivendi, *der* (geh.)

mog /mɒg/, **moggie** /'mɒgɪ/ *ns.* (Brit. coll.) Katze, *die;* Katzenvieh, *das* (abwertend)

Mogul /'mәʊgl, mәʊ'gʌl/
A *n.* **1** (Hist.: Mongolian) Mongole, *der*/Mongolin, *die;* **the Great** *or* **Grand ~:** der Großmogul **2** **m~** (coll.: important person) Mogul, *der* (fig.)
B *adj.* (Hist.) mongolisch; **the ~ empire** das Reich der Moguln

mohair /'mәʊheә(r)/ *n.* Mohair, *der;* (yarn) Mohair- *od.* Angorawolle, *die*

Mohammedan /mә'hæmɪdәn/ ▸**Muhammadan**

Mohican /mәʊ'hiːkәn/ *n.* (hairstyle) Irokesenschnitt, *der*

moist /mɔɪst/ *adj.* feucht (**with** von)

moisten /'mɔɪsn/ *v.t.* anfeuchten; feucht machen; **~ one's lips** sich (*Dat.*) die Lippen [mit der Zunge] befeuchten

moisture /'mɔɪstʃә(r)/ *n.* Feuchtigkeit, *die;* **~ in the air** Luftfeuchtigkeit, *die;* **film of ~:** Feuchtigkeitsfilm, *der*

moisturise, moisturiser, moisturising ▸**moisturiz-**

moisturize /'mɔɪstjʊraɪz, 'mɔɪstʃәraɪz/ *v.t.* befeuchten; **~ the skin** der Haut (*Dat.*) Feuchtigkeit zuführen; ‹*Creme:*› der Haut (*Dat.*) Feuchtigkeit verleihen

moisturizer /'mɔɪstjʊraɪzә(r), 'mɔɪst ʃәraɪzә(r)/, **'moisturizing cream** *ns.* Feuchtigkeitscreme, *die*

moke /mәʊk/ *n.* (Brit. coll.) Esel, *der*

molar /ˈməʊlə(r)/
A *n.* Backenzahn, *der;* Molar[zahn], *der* (Anat.); Mahlzahn, *der* (bes. Zool.)
B *adj.* **~ tooth** ▸**A**

molasses /məˈlæsɪz/ *n.* **1** (syrup drained from raw sugar) Melasse, *die* **2** (Amer.: treacle) Sirup, *der*

mold (Amer.) ▸**mould**[1, 2, 3]

Moldavia /mɒlˈdeɪvɪə/ *pr. n.* Moldau, *die*

molder, molding, moldy (Amer.) ▸**mould-**

mole[1] /məʊl/ *n.* (on skin) Leberfleck, *der;* Pigmentfleck, *der* (Med.); (prominent) Muttermal, *das*

mole[2] *n.* **1** (animal) Maulwurf, *der* **2** (coll.: spy) Maulwurf, *der* (ugs.)

mole[3] *n.* **1** (breakwater) Mole, *die* **2** (artificial harbour) [künstlicher] Hafen

mole[4] *n.* (Chem.) Mol, *das*

molecular /məˈlekjʊlə(r)/ *adj.* (Phys., Chem.) molekular; **~ weight/biology** Molekulargewicht, *das*/-biologie, *die*

molecule /ˈmɒlɪkjuːl, ˈməʊlɪkjuːl/ *n.* **1** (Phys., Chem.) Molekül, *das* **2** (small particle) winziges Teilchen

ˈ**molehill** *n.* Maulwurfshügel, *der;* **make a mountain out of a ~** (fig.) aus einer Mücke einen Elefanten machen (ugs.)

molest /məˈlest/ *v.t.* **1** belästigen; (to rob) überfallen **2** (sexually) [unsittlich] belästigen

molestation /məʊlɪˈsteɪʃn, mɒlɪˈsteɪʃn/ *n.* **1** Belästigung, *die;* (to rob) Überfallen, *das* **2** (sexual) [unsittliche] Belästigung

moll /mɒl/ *n.* (coll.) Gangsterbraut, *die*

mollify /ˈmɒlɪfaɪ/ *v.t.* besänftigen; beschwichtigen; **be finally mollified** sich schließlich beruhigen

mollusc (*Amer.:* **mollusk**) /ˈmɒləsk/ *n.* (Zool.) Molluske, *die* (fachspr.); Weichtier, *das*

mollycoddle /ˈmɒlɪkɒdl/
A *v.t.* [ver]hätscheln (oft abwertend); verzärteln (abwertend)
B *n.* Weichling, *der* (abwertend)

Molotov cocktail /mɒlətɒf ˈkɒkteɪl/ *n.* Molotowcocktail, *der*

molt (Amer.) ▸**moult**

molten /ˈməʊltn/ *adj.* geschmolzen; flüssig ‹*Lava*›

molybdenum /məˈlɪbdɪnəm/ *n.* (Chem.) Molybdän, *das*

mom /mɒm/ (Amer. coll.) ▸**mum**[2]

moment /ˈməʊmənt/ *n.* **1** Moment, *der;* Augenblick, *der;* **barely a ~ had elapsed ...:** es war kaum eine Minute vergangen ...; **help came not a ~ too soon** die Hilfe hätte keinen Moment später kommen dürfen; **for a ~ or two** für einen kurzen Augenblick; **for a few ~s** für ein paar Augenblicke; ein paar Augenblicke lang; **there was never a dull ~:** man langweilte sich keinen Augenblick lang; **at this ~ in time** in diesem Moment *od.* Augenblick; **after a ~'s hesitation** nach kurzem Zögern; **at any ~,** (coll.) **any ~:** jeden Augenblick *od.* Moment; **on the spur of the ~:** ganz spontan; **it was over in just a few ~s** es dauerte nur wenige Augenblicke *od.* war im Nu geschehen; **it is the ~ [for sth.]** es ist der richtige Zeitpunkt [für etw.]; **this is the ~!** dies ist der geeignete Augenblick!; **a few ~s of peace** ein paar Minuten der Ruhe; ein paar ruhige Minuten; **the film had its ~s** der Film hatte einige starke Stellen; **he has his ~s** manchmal ist er gar nicht so übel (ugs.); **at odd ~s** gelegentlich[, wenn ein wenig Zeit ist]; **a ~ to remember** ein denkwürdiger Augenblick; **at the precise ~ she came in ...:** genau in dem Augenblick *od.* gerade, als sie hereintrat, ...; **the ~ I get home** gleich *od.* sofort, wenn ich nach Hause komme; **one** *or* **half a** *or* **just a** *or* **wait a ~!** einen Moment *od.* Augenblick!; Moment[chen] *od.* Augenblick mal!; **in a ~** (instantly) im Nu (ugs.); (very soon) sofort; gleich; **for a ~:** einen Moment [lang]; für einen Moment; **not for a ~:** keinen Moment [lang]; **[at] the [very] ~ it happened** in dem *od.* im selben Augenblick, als es passierte; **the ~ of truth** die Stunde der Wahrheit; **at the ~:** im Augenblick; momentan; **for the ~:** im *od.* für den Augenblick; vorläufig; **I shan't be a ~** (I'll be back very soon) ich bin sofort zurück; (I have very nearly finished) ich bin sofort so weit; **have you got a ~?** hast du mal einen Augenblick Zeit?; **be the man of the ~:** der Mann des Tages sein; **come here this ~!** komm sofort *od.* auf der Stelle her!; **just this ~:** soeben; gerade *od.* eben [erst]; **from ~ to ~:** alle Augenblicke **2** (formal: importance) **of ~:** von Bedeutung; **of little** *or* **small/no ~:** von geringer/ohne Bedeutung **3** (Phys.) Moment, *das;* **~ of inertia** Trägheitsmoment, *das*

momentarily /ˈməʊməntərɪlɪ/ *adv.* **1** (for a moment) einen Augenblick lang; (for a while) vorübergehend **2** (Amer.) (at any moment) jeden Augenblick *od.* Moment; (in a few minutes) in wenigen Minuten

momentary /ˈməʊməntərɪ/ *adj.* **1** (lasting only a moment) kurz; **a ~ forgetfulness/aberration** ein Augenblick geistiger Abwesenheit/der Verwirrung **2** (transitory) vorübergehend

momentous /məˈmentəs/ *adj.* (important) bedeutsam; bedeutungsvoll; (of consequence) folgenschwer; von großer Tragweite *nachgestellt;* **of ~ importance** von entscheidender Bedeutung

momentum /məˈmentəm/ *n., pl.* **momenta** /məˈmentə/ **1** (impetus) Schwung, *der;* **lose ~:** Schwung *od.* Fahrt verlieren; (fig.) [an] Schwung *od.* Fahrt verlieren; **gain** *or* **gather ~:** schneller werden; (fig.) in Schwung kommen; ‹*Idee:*› an Boden gewinnen **2** (Mech.) Impuls, *der; see also* **angular** 3; **conservation 2**

mommy /ˈmɒmɪ/ (Amer. coll.) ▸**mummy**[2]

Mon. *abbr.* ▸ⓘ **p. 1048 = Monday** Mo.

Monaco /ˈmɒnəkəʊ/ *pr. n.* Monaco *(das)*

monarch /ˈmɒnək/ *n.* (king, emperor, etc.) Monarch, *der*/Monarchin, *die;* (supreme ruler) [Allein]herrscher, *der*/-herrscherin, *die*

monarchic /məˈnɑːkɪk/, **monarchical** /məˈnɑːkɪkl/ *adj.* **1** (of government) monarchisch **2** (of monarchy) monarchistisch

monarchism /ˈmɒnəkɪzm/ *n.* (monarchical government) Monarchie, *die;* (attachment to monarchy) Monarchismus, *der*

monarchist /ˈmɒnəkɪst/ *n.* Monarchist, *der*/Monarchistin, *die*

monarchy /ˈmɒnəkɪ/ *n.* Monarchie, *die; see also* **constitutional A 2**

monastery /ˈmɒnəstrɪ/ *n.* [Mönchs]kloster, *das*

monastic /məˈnæstɪk/ *adj.* **1** (of or like monks) mönchisch **2** (of monasteries) klösterlich; Kloster‹*gebäude, -architektur*›

monasticism /məˈnæstɪsɪzm/ *n.* Mönch[s]tum, *das*

Monday /ˈmʌndeɪ, ˈmʌndɪ/ ▸ⓘ **p. 1048**
A *n.* Montag, *der*
B *adv.* (coll.) **she comes ~s** sie kommt montags. *See also* **Friday**

monetarism /ˈmʌnɪtərɪzm/ *n.* (Econ.) Monetarismus, *der*

monetarist /ˈmʌnɪtərɪst/ *n.* (Econ.) Monetarist, *der*/Monetaristin, *die*

monetary /ˈmʌnɪtərɪ/ *adj.* **1** (of the currency in use) monetär; Währungs‹*politik, -system*›; **~ union** Währungsunion, *die* **2** (of money) finanziell; **~ gift** Geldgeschenk, *das*

ˈ**monetary policy** *n.* Geldpolitik, *die*

money /ˈmʌnɪ/ *n.* ▸ⓘ **p. 1332** **1** *no pl.* Geld, *das;* **your ~ or your life!** Geld oder Leben!; **be in the ~** (coll.) (be winning ~ prizes) am Scheffeln sein (ugs.); (have plenty of ~) im Geld schwimmen (ugs.); **there is ~ in sth.** mit etw. kann man [viel] Geld verdienen; **~ for jam** *or* **old rope** (Brit. fig. coll.) leicht *od.* schnell verdientes Geld; **make ~** ‹*Person:*› [viel] Geld verdienen, (ugs.) [das große] Geld machen; ‹*Geschäft:*› etwas einbringen, sich rentieren; **earn good ~:** gut verdienen; **come into ~:** zu Geld kommen; **~ talks** das Geld machts (ugs.); **~ makes the world go round** Geld regiert die Welt; **put ~ into sth.** Geld in etw. (*Akk.*) investieren *od.* (ugs.) hineinstecken; **have ~ to burn** (fig. coll.) Geld wie Heu haben (ugs.); **[not] be made of ~** (fig. coll.) [k]ein Goldesel *od.* Krösus sein; **spend ~ like water** mit dem Geld nur so um sich werfen (ugs.); **good ~** (earned/spent) gutes/teueres Geld; **this would only be to throw** *or* **pour good ~ after bad** das wäre nur rausgeschmissenes *od.* rausgeworfenes Geld (ugs.); **for 'my ~:** wenn man mich fragt; **he/she is the one for my ~:** ich tippe auf ihn/sie; **put one's ~ on sth.** auf etw. (*Akk.*) wetten *od.* setzen; (fig.) [seine Hoffnung] auf etw. (*Akk.*) setzen; **the best that ~ can buy** das Beste, was es für Geld gibt; **~ can't buy happiness!** Geld allein macht nicht glücklich!; **~ supply** Geldmenge, *die* **2** *pl.* **~s** *or* **monies** /ˈmʌnɪz/ (sum of money) Geld, *das;* [Geld]betrag, *der;* **the rent ~:** [das Geld für] die Miete **3** (rich person[s]) **that's not where the real ~ lives** da ist nicht das große Geld zu Hause. *See also* **account C 1; big A 1; conscience money; cost B 1; love A 1; run A 1**

money: ~-back *attrib. adj.* **~-back guarantee** Geld-zurück-Garantie, *die;* **~ bag** *n.* Geldsack, *der;* **~ bags** *n. sing.* (coll.: person) Geldsack, *der* (ugs. abwertend); **~ belt** *n.* Geldgürtel, *der;* **~ box** *n.* Sparbüchse, *die;* (for collection) Sammelbüchse, *die;* **~ changer** *n.* ▸ⓘ **p. 1260** Geldwechsler, *der*

moneyed /ˈmʌnɪd/ *adj.* (rich) vermögend; begütert; **the ~ classes** die besitzenden Klassen

money: ~-grubber *n.* Raffzahn, *der* (ugs.); **~-grubbing A** *adj.* geldgierig (abwertend); **B** *n.* Geldgier, *die* (abwertend); **~lender** *n.* ▸ⓘ **p. 1260** Geldverleiher, *der;* **~maker** *n.* **be a ~maker** ‹*Projekt, Produkt, Film:*› Geld bringen; **~making A** *adj.* Gewinn bringend, einträglich ‹*Geschäft, Beschäftigung*›; **B** *n., no pl.* Geldverdienen, *das;* **~ market** *n.* Geldmarkt, *der;* **~ order** *n.* Zahlungsanweisung, *die;* (issued by Post Office) Postanweisung, *die;* **~-spinner** *n.* (Brit.) Verkaufsschlager, *der;* (business) Goldgrube, *die* (ugs.); **he turned that idea into a ~-spinner** er hat diese Idee versilbert (ugs.); **~'s worth** *n.* **get** *or* **have one's ~'s worth** etwas für sein Geld bekommen

Mongol /ˈmɒŋgl/
A *n.* Mongole, *der*/Mongolin, *die;* (Anthrop.) Mongolide, *der/die*
B *adj.* mongolisch; (Anthrop.) mongolid

Mongolia /mɒŋˈgəʊlɪə/ *pr. n.* Mongolei, *die*

Mongolian /mɒŋˈgəʊlɪən/
A *adj.* **1** ▸ⓘ **p. 1345** mongolisch **2** (Anthrop.) mongolid (fachspr.); mongolisch
B *n.* **1** ▸ⓘ **p. 1345** (person) Mongole, *der*/Mongolin, *die* **2** (Anthrop.) Mongolide, *der/die* **3** (language) Mongolisch, *das;* das Mongolische

mongolism /ˈmɒŋgəlɪzm/ *n.* (Med.) Mongolismus, *der*

mongoose /ˈmɒŋguːs/ *n.* (Zool.) Indischer Mungo

mongrel /ˈmʌŋgrəl, ˈmɒŋgrəl/
A *n.* **1** (Bot., Zool.) Bastard, *der* (fachspr.); Hybride, *der* (fachspr.); Kreuzung, *die;* (often derog.: dog) Promenadenmischung, *die* (scherzh., auch abwertend) **2** (derog.: person) Mischling, *der;* Bastard, *der* (derb abwertend)
B *adj.* (of mixed origin) hybrid (fachspr.) ‹*Pflanze, Tier*›; **~ animal/plant** [tierischer/pflanzlicher] Hybride *od.* Bastard (fachspr.); [Tier-/Pflanzen-]kreuzung, *die*

moni[c]ker /ˈmɒnɪkə(r)/ *n.* (coll.) Name, *der;* (nickname) Spitzname, *der*

monitor /ˈmɒnɪtə(r)/
A *n.* **1** (Sch.) Aufsichtsschüler, *der*/-schülerin, *die;* **pencil/milk/lunch ~:** Bleistift-/Milch-/Essen[s]wart, *der;* **school ~:** Präfekt, *der* **2** (Zool.) **~ [lizard]** Waran, *der* **3** (listener) Mithörer, *der*/Mithörerin, *die* **4** (Mech. Engin., Phys., Med., Telev.) Monitor, *der*
B *v.t.* **1** (maintain surveillance over) kontrollieren ‹*Strahlungsintensität*›; beobachten ‹*Wetter, Flugzeug, Gewohnheit, Bewegung*›; abhören ‹*Sendung, Telefongespräch*› **2** (regulate) kontrollieren ‹*Radio-, Fernsehempfang*›; überwachen ‹*Verteilung, Ein-/Ausfuhr*›

monk /mʌŋk/ *n.* Mönch, *der;* **order of ~s** Mönchsorden, *der; see also* **White Monk**

monkey /ˈmʌŋkɪ/
A *n.* **1** Affe, *der;* **the three wise ~s** (Mythol.) die „Drei Affen"; **make a ~ of sb.** (coll.) jmdn.

m

ℹ Money

Money in the euro zone

90 cents
= 90 cts, 0,90 € = neunzig Cent
one euro
= 1 € = ein Euro
1 euro 90 [cents]
= 1,90 € = ein Euro neunzig, ein Euro und neunzig Cent
50 euros
= 50 € = fünfzig Euro
1,000 euros
= 1 000 € = [ein]tausend Euro
100 cents make one euro
= 100 Cent sind ein Euro
a 20 euro note
= ein Zwanzigeuroschein *or* 20-Euro-Schein
a five euro piece
= ein Fünfeurostück *or* 5-Euro-Stück
a 50 cent coin
= ein Fünfzigcentstück *or* 50-Cent-Stück

Note that there is a comma before the number of cents, also that as with all denominations the plural form is the same as the singular when an amount is being quoted (and on most other occasions).

Swiss money

The Swiss unit of currency is the Swiss franc (**Schweizer Franken,** abbreviation sfr or sFr). The abbreviations precede the number when prices are given in catalogues or advertisements, or are omitted.

Special offer 18 Swiss francs 90 centimes
= Sonderangebot sfr *or* sFr 18,90

British money

one penny
= 1p = ein Penny
five pence
= 5p = fünf Pence
one pound fifty [pence]
= £1.50 = ein Pfund fünfzig [Pence]
eight pounds thirty-four pence
= £8.34 = acht Pfund vierunddreißig Pence
one thousand two hundred and fifty pounds **or** ***twelve hundred and fifty pounds***
= £1 250 = [ein]tausendzweihundertfünfzig Pfund *or* zwölfhundertfünfzig Pfund
a five-pound note
= ein Fünfpfundschein
a pound coin
= ein Pfundstück
a 50 pence piece
= ein Fünfzigpencestück

American money

one cent
= 1c = ein Cent
five cents
= 5c = fünf Cent
one dollar
= $1 *or* $1.00 = ein Dollar
one dollar fifty
= $1.50 = ein Dollar fünfzig [Cent]
a ten dollar bill
= ein Zehndollarschein
a dollar bill
= ein Dollarschein
a dollar coin
= ein Dollarstück
a dime, a ten cent piece
= ein Zehncentstück
a quarter, a twenty-five cent piece
= ein Vierteldollarstück

Other money phrases

What **or** ***How much does it cost?***
= Was *or* Wie viel kostet das?
It costs just under/just over £950
= Es kostet knapp 950/etwas über 950 Pfund
The potatoes are 30p a pound
= Die Kartoffeln kosten 30 Pence das Pfund
$100 in cash
= 100 Dollar in bar
Can I pay by cheque/by credit card?
= Kann ich mit Scheck/mit Kreditkarte zahlen?
a cheque for £50
= ein Scheck über 50 Pfund
a dollar/sterling traveller's cheque **or (Amer.)** ***traveler's check***
= ein Reisescheck in Dollar/Pfund [Sterling]
Can you change **or** ***give me change for a 20 euro note?***
= Können Sie mir einen 2o-Euro-Schein wechseln *or* auf einen 20-Euro-Schein herausgeben?
I want to change euros into dollars
= Ich will Euro in Dollar wechseln
Our pounds are hardly worth anything
= Unsere Pfunde sind kaum etwas wert

Notice again that the plural form of the various currencies is the same as the singular. The one exception is the use of the plural form with an ending in examples such as the last one (here "Pfunde" – one can also talk of "Euros" and "Dollars").

---

zum Gespött machen; **get one's ~ up** (Brit. coll.) auf die Palme gehen (ugs.); **sb.'s ~ is up** (Brit. coll.) jmd. ist auf der Palme; **I'll be a ~'s uncle!** (coll.) ich denk, mich laust der Affe (ugs.) **2** (in playful abuse) Schlingel, *der* (scherzh.); **cheeky ~:** Frechdachs, *der* (fam.) **3** (coll.: £500, $500) halber Riese (salopp)
B *v.i.* **~ about** *or* **around [with]** (coll.) herumalbern [mit] (ugs.) ‹*Person*›; (interfere) herumspielen [mit *od.* an (+ *Dat.*)] ‹*Gegenstand*›

monkey: ~ business *n.* (coll.) (mischief) Schabernack, *der;* (unlawful or unfair activities) krumme Touren *Pl.* (ugs.); **~ jacket** *n.* (Naut., Fashion) Monkijacke, *die;* Affenjäckchen, *das* (Soldatenspr. scherzh.); **~ nut** *n.* (Bot.) Erdnuss, *die;* **~ puzzle** *n.* (Bot.) Chilefichte, *die;* Araukarie, *die* (fachspr.); **~ tricks** *n. pl.* (Brit. coll.) **be up to one's ~ tricks** etwas aushecken; **no ~ tricks!** mach keinen Quatsch (ugs.); **~ wrench** *n.* Rollgabelschlüssel, *der* (fachspr.); Universalschraubenschlüssel, *der*

monkish /ˈmʌŋkɪʃ/ *adj.* **1** mönchisch; Mönchs‹*kleidung*›; Kloster‹*leben, -bibliothek*› **2** (derog.: sanctimonious) pfäffisch (abwertend) **3** (modest) anspruchslos **4** (derog.: unsociable) ungesellig

monkshood /ˈmʌŋkshʊd/ *n.* (Bot.) Blauer Eisenhut

mono /ˈmɒnəʊ/ *adj.* Mono‹*platte[nspieler], -wiedergabe*›

monochrome /ˈmɒnəkrəʊm/
A *n.* **1** (picture) monochromes (fachspr.) *od.* einfarbiges Bild **2** (representation) monochrome (fachspr.) *od.* einfarbige Darstellung; **in ~:** monochrom (fachspr.); einfarbig; Schwarzweiß- (Ferns.)
B *adj.* monochrom (fachspr.); einfarbig; Schwarzweiß- (Ferns.)

monocle /ˈmɒnəkl/ *n.* Monokel, *das;* Einglas, *das* (veralt.)

monocotyledon /mɒnəkɒtɪˈliːdn/ *n.* (Bot.) Monokotyle[done], *die* (fachspr.); einkeimblättrige Pflanze

monoculture /ˈmɒnəkʌltʃə(r)/ *n.* Monokultur, *die*

monocycle /ˈmɒnəsaɪkl/ *n.* Einrad, *das*

monogamous /məˈnɒgəməs/ *adj.* monogam

monogamy /məˈnɒgəmɪ/ *n.* Monogamie, *die;* Einehe, *die*

monogram /ˈmɒnəgræm/ *n.* Monogramm, *das*

monogrammed /ˈmɒnəgræmd/ *adj.* monogrammiert; ‹*Taschentuch usw.:*› mit Monogramm

monograph /ˈmɒnəgrɑːf/ *n.* Monographie, *die;* Einzeldarstellung, *die*

monohull /ˈmɒnəhʌl/ *n.* (Naut.) Einrumpfschiff, *das;* Einkörperschiff, *das*

monolingual /mɒnəˈlɪŋgwəl/ *adj.* einsprachig

monolith /ˈmɒnəlɪθ/ *n.* (Prehist., Building; lit. or fig.) Monolith, *der*

monolithic /mɒnəˈlɪθɪk/ *adj.* (Prehist., Building; lit. or fig.) monolithisch; Monolith‹*denkmal, -säule, -charakter, -beton*›

monologue (*Amer.:* **monolog**) /ˈmɒnəlɒg/ *n.* (lit. or fig.) Monolog, *der*

monomania /mɒnəˈmeɪnɪə/ *n.* **1** (Med., Psych.) Monomanie, *die* **2** (fig.) übertriebene Begeisterung (**for** für); Leidenschaft, *die* (**for** für)

monomaniac /mɒnəˈmeɪnɪæk/ (Med., Psych.)
A *n.* Monomane, *der*/Monomanin, *die*
B *adj.* monoman

monophonic /mɒnəˈfɒnɪk/ *adj.* monophon

monoplane /ˈmɒnəpleɪn/ *n.* (Aeronaut.) Eindecker, *der*

monopolisation, monopolise ▸**monopoliz-**

monopolistic /mənɒpəˈlɪstɪk/ *adj.* (Econ.) monopolistisch ‹*Wettbewerb usw.*›

monopolization /mənɒpəlaɪˈzeɪʃn/ *n.* (Econ.) Monopolisierung, *die*

monopolize /məˈnɒpəlaɪz/ *v.t.* (Econ.) monopolisieren; (fig.) mit Beschlag belegen; **~ the conversation** den/die anderen nicht zu Wort kommen lassen

monopoly /məˈnɒpəlɪ/ *n.* **1** (Econ.) Monopol, *das* (**of** auf + *Akk.*, für) **2** (exclusive possession) alleiniger Besitz; **have a ~ on sth.** ein Monopol auf etw. (*Akk.*) haben; **you can't have a ~ on the car** du kannst das Auto nicht ständig mit Beschlag belegen **3** (thing monopolized) Monopol, *das* **4** **M~, (P)** (game) Monopoly Ⓦⓩ, *das*

monorail /ˈmɒnəreɪl/ *n.* **1** (single rail) Einschienengleis, *das* **2** (vehicle) Einschienenbahn, *die* **3** (overhead) Schwebebahn, *die*

monosodium glutamate /mɒnəsəʊdɪəm ˈgluːtəmeɪt/ *n., no pl.* (Biochem.) [Mono]natriumglutamat, *das*

monosyllabic /mɒnəsɪˈlæbɪk/ *adj.* **1** einsilbig ‹*Antwort, Person*›; aus einsilbigen Wörtern bestehend ‹*Rede, Dichtung, Schrift, Sprache*› **2** (Ling.) monosyllabisch

monosyllable /ˈmɒnəsɪləbl/ *n.* 1 einsilbiges Wort; **speak** *or* **talk/answer in ~s** einsilbig reden/antworten 2 (Ling.) Einsilber, *der*

monotheism /ˈmɒnəθiːɪzm/ *n.* (Relig.) **[doctrine of/belief in] ~:** Monotheismus, *der*

monotheistic /mɒnəθiːˈɪstɪk/ *adj.* (Relig.) monotheistisch

monotone /ˈmɒnətəʊn/

A *n.* 1 gleich bleibender Ton 2 (uniformity) (general) Einerlei, *das;* (of colour) Einfarbigkeit, *die;* (of style) eintöniger *od.* monotoner Stil; **grey ~:** graues Einerlei; **engravings in ~:** einfarbige Stiche

B *adj.* 1 (monotonous) eintönig, monoton ‹*Geräusch, Sprache, Akzent, Rezitation*› 2 (in one colour) einfarbig

monotonous /məˈnɒtənəs/ *adj.* eintönig, monoton ‹*Laut, Leben, Landschaft usw.*›

monotonously /məˈnɒtənəslɪ/ *adv.* eintönig

monotonousness /məˈnɒtənəsnɪs/, **monotony** /məˈnɒtənɪ/ *ns.* Eintönigkeit, *die;* Monotonie, *die*

monoxide /məˈnɒksaɪd/ *n.* (Chem.) Monoxid, *das;* Monoxyd, *das*

Monseigneur /mɔ̃seˈnjɜː(r)/ *n., pl.* **Messeigneurs** /meseˈnjɜː(r)/ Monseigneur, *der*

Monsignor /mɒnˈsiːnjə(r)/ *n., pl.* **~i** /mɒnsiːˈnjɔːriː/ (Eccl.) Monsignore, *der*

monsoon /mɒnˈsuːn/ *n.* (Geog.) 1 (wind) Monsun, *der* 2 (season) Monsunzeit, *die*

monster /ˈmɒnstə(r)/

A *n.* 1 (imaginary or huge creature) Ungeheuer, *das;* Monster, *das;* (huge thing) Ungetüm, *das;* Monstrum, *das;* **a ~ of a fish/car** ein Ungeheuer/ Ungetüm von einem Fisch/Auto; **that's a real ~!, what a ~!** (in surprise or admiration) das ist ja ungeheuer! 2 (inhuman person) Unmensch, *der;* (iron.: naughty child) Monster, *das* (scherzh.)

B *adj.* riesig; monströs; Mammut‹*sitzung, -veranstaltung*›

monstrance /ˈmɒnstrəns/ *n.* (RC Ch.) Monstranz, *die*

monstrosity /mɒnˈstrɒsɪtɪ/ *n.* 1 (physical deformity) Missbildung, *die;* (deviation from the norm, unnatural thing) Abnormität, *die;* Widernatürlichkeit, *die* 2 (outrageous thing) Ungeheuerlichkeit, *die;* (hideous building etc.) Ungetüm, *das* 3 (imaginary or huge creature) Ungeheuer, *das;* Monster, *das*

monstrous /ˈmɒnstrəs/ *adj.* 1 (huge) monströs (geh.); ungeheuer ‹*Lärm, Jubel, Menge*›; riesig ‹*Lkw, Kuchen, Buch*›; unnatürlich groß ‹*Gemüse, Person, Baum, Pflanze*› 2 (outrageous) ungeheuerlich (abwertend) ‹*Vorschlag, Vorstellung, Glaube, Einstellung, Wahl, Entscheidung*› 3 (atrocious) scheußlich; monströs (meist abwertend) 4 (misshapen) missgestaltet

monstrously /ˈmɒnstrəslɪ/ *adv.* 1 (hugely) schrecklich (ugs.), furchtbar (ugs.) ‹*hoch, beschäftigt, kurz, dick*› 2 (outrageously) unmöglich (ugs. meist abwertend) ‹*sich benehmen*›

mons Veneris /mɒnz ˈvenərɪs/ *n.* (Anat.) Venushügel, *der* (fachspr.); weiblicher Schamberg

montage /mɒnˈtɑːʒ/ *n.* (Photog., Art, Radio, Film) Montage, *die;* (Mus.) Collage, *die;* **work in ~:** Montagen herstellen

Montenegro /mɒntɪˈniːgrəʊ/ *pr. n.* Montenegro (*das*)

month /mʌnθ/ *n.* ▸ⓘ **p. 1047** 1 Monat, *der;* **last day of the ~:** Monatsletzte, *der;* Ultimo, *der* (Kaufmannsspr.); **on the last day of the ~:** ultimo; am Monatsletzten; **the ~ of January** der [Monat] Januar; **come every ~:** jeden Monat kommen; **for a ~/several ~s** einen Monat [lang]/mehrere Monate [lang] *od.* monatelang; **for ~s [on end]** monatelang; **I haven't seen him for ~s** ich habe ihn seit Monaten nicht mehr gesehen; **~s ago** vor Monaten; **every six ~s** alle sechs Monate; halbjährlich; **once every** *or* **a ~:** einmal monatlich *od.* im Monat; **in a ~['s time]** in einem Monat; **in two ~s[' time]** in zwei Monaten; **in alternate ~s** alle zwei Monate; **take a ~'s holiday** [sich (*Dat.*)] einen Monat Urlaub nehmen; **£10 a** *or* **per ~:** zehn Pfund im Monat; **from ~ to ~:** Monat um *od.* für Monat; **she is in the third/last ~ of her pregnancy** sie ist im dritten/neunten Monat schwanger; **a ~ from today** heute in einem Monat; **a three-~ period** ein Zeitraum von drei Monaten; **a six-~[s]-old baby/strike** ein sechs Monate altes *od.* sechsmonatiges Baby/ein bereits sechsmonatiger Streik; *see also* **calendar 1**; **next A 2**; **Sunday A 1**; **this A 5** 2 (period of 28 days) vier Wochen; 28 Tage

ˈmonth-long *attrib. adj.* einmonatig

monthly /ˈmʌnθlɪ/

A *adj.* 1 (of or relating to a month) monatlich; Monats‹*umsatz, -einkommen, -gehalt*›; **three-~:** dreimonatlich; vierteljährlich 2 (lasting a month) einmonatig ‹*Abstand*›; Monats‹*zyklus, -karte*›; **three-~ season ticket** Dreimonats- *od.* Vierteljahreskarte, *die* 3 (happening every month) monatlich; (happening once a month) [ein]monatlich; **a woman's ~ period** die Periode *od.* Monatsblutung einer Frau

B *adv.* [ein]monatlich; einmal im Monat

C *n.* (publication) monatlich erscheinende Zeitschrift; Monatsschrift, *die*

monty /ˈmɒntɪ/ *n., no pl.* (Brit. coll.) 1 (everything) alles; das volle Programm (ugs.); **go the full ~:** Nägel mit Köpfen machen (ugs.); **go the full ~ with sth.** etw. voll durchziehen (ugs.) 2 (total nudity) **do the full ~:** sich ganz ausziehen

monument /ˈmɒnjʊmənt/ *n.* 1 Denkmal, *das; see also* **ancient A 2** 2 (on grave) Grabmal, *das* (geh.) 3 **the M~:** *in der Londoner Innenstadt stehende Säule zur Erinnerung an den großen Brand von 1666*

monumental /mɒnjʊˈmentl/ *adj.* 1 (of a monument) Denkmals‹*architekt, -inschrift*› 2 (massive) gewaltig ‹*Auffahrt, Skulptur*›; monumental ‹*Plastik, Gemälde, Gebäude*› 3 (extremely great) kolossal (ugs.)

monumentally /mɒnjʊˈmentəlɪ/ *adv.* enorm ‹*stur, schlau, kreativ*›; **~ boring/stupid** sterbenslangweilig/strohdumm

monumental ˈmason *n.* Steinmetz, *der*

moo /muː/

A *n.* Muhen, *das;* **give** *or* **utter a loud ~:** laut muhen

B *v.i.* muhen

mooch /muːtʃ/ (coll.)

A *v.i.* **~ about** *or* **around/along** herumschleichen (ugs.)/zockeln (ugs.)

B *v.t.* (Amer.) 1 (steal) mopsen (fam.) 2 (beg) schnorren (ugs.)

ˈmoo-cow *n.* (child lang.) Muhkuh, *die* (Kinderspr.)

mood¹ /muːd/ *n.* 1 (state of mind) Stimmung, *die;* **there was a [general] ~ of optimism** es herrschte allgemeiner Optimismus; **be in a very good/good/bad ~:** [bei] bester/guter/ schlechter Laune sein; **be in a cheerful ~:** froh gelaunt *od.* fröhlich gestimmt sein; **be in a militant ~:** in Kampfstimmung sein; **be in a serious/pensive ~:** ernst/nachdenklich gestimmt sein; **be in no ~ for joking/dancing** nicht zum Scherzen/Tanzen aufgelegt sein; **I'm not in the ~:** ich hab keine Lust dazu 2 (fit of melancholy or bad temper) Verstimmung, *die;* schlechte Laune; **have one's ~s** [seine] Launen haben

mood² *n.* (Ling.) Modus, *der* (fachspr.); Aussageweise, *die;* **the subjunctive ~:** der Konjunktiv (fachspr.); die Möglichkeitsform

moodily /ˈmuːdɪlɪ/ *adv.* übel gelaunt; missgestimmt; (in a sullen manner) missmutig; verdrossen

ˈmood music *n.* stimmungsvolle Musik

moody /ˈmuːdɪ/ *adj.* 1 (sullen) missmutig; verdrossen; (gloomy) niedergeschlagen 2 (subject to moods) launenhaft

moon /muːn/

A *n.* 1 Mond, *der;* **light of the ~:** Mondlicht, *das;* Mondschein, *der;* **the ~ is full/waning/ waxing** es ist Vollmond/abnehmender/zunehmender Mond; **there is no ~ tonight** heute Nacht ist der Mond nicht zu sehen; **be over the ~** (fig. coll.) im siebten Himmel sein (ugs.); **offer sb. the ~** (fig.) jmdm. ein Vermögen bieten; **promise sb. the ~** (fig.) jmdm. das Blaue vom Himmel versprechen (ugs.); **ask for the ~:** Unmögliches verlangen; *see also* **blue moon**; **cry C 1**; **full moon**; **half moon**; **man A 2**; **new moon**; **shoot B 4** 2 (poet.: month) Mond, *der* (dichter. veralt.) 3 **that was many ~s ago** das liegt schon lange zurück

B *v.i.* (coll.) **~ about** *or* **around [the house]** trübselig [im Haus] herumschleichen (ugs.)

(Phrasal verb)

• **~ over** *v.t.* in Gedanken an … (*Akk.*) verloren *od.* versunken *od.* vertieft sein

moon: ~beam *n.* Mondstrahl, *der;* **~beams** Mondschein, *der;* Mondlicht, *das;* **~face** *n.* Mondgesicht, *das*

Moonie /ˈmuːnɪ/ *n.* (coll.) Anhänger der Mun-Sekte

moon: ~ landing *n.* Mondlandung, *die;* **~less** *adj.* mondlos ‹*Nacht, Himmel*›; **~light** A *n.* Mondlicht, *das;* Mondschein, *der;* B *attrib. adj.* mondhell (geh.) ‹*Nacht*›; **do a ~light [flit]** (Brit. coll.) bei Nacht und Nebel wegziehen, ohne die Schulden zu bezahlen; C *v.i.* (coll.) nebenberuflich abends arbeiten; (hold two jobs at once) zwei Jobs gleichzeitig haben; **~lit** *adj.* mondbeschienen (geh.); **~shine** *n.* 1 (visionary ideas) Unsinn, *der;* 2 (liquor) schwarz gebrannter Alkohol; **~shine whisky** schwarz gebrannter Whiskey; **~shot** *n.* (Astronaut.) Mondflug, *der;* **~stone** *n.* (Min.) Mondstein, *der;* Adular, *der* (fachspr.)

moor¹ *n.* 1 (Geog.) [Hoch]moor, *das* 2 (for shooting) *im Moor gelegenes Wildhegegebiet*

moor²

A *v.t.* festmachen; vertäuen

B *v.i.* festmachen

Moor /mʊə(r), mɔː(r)/ *n.* Maure, *der*/Maurin, *die*

ˈmoorhen *n.* (Ornith.) [Grünfüßiges] Teichhuhn

mooring /ˈmʊərɪŋ, ˈmɔːrɪŋ/ *n.* 1 *usu. in pl.* (means of attachment) Vertäuung, *die* 2 *usu. in pl.* (place) Anlegestelle, *die;* **set sail from one's ~:** ablegen 3 (action of making fast) Vertäuung, *die*

mooring: ~ line *n.* Festmacher, *der;* **~-mast** ▸**mast¹**; **~ post** *n.* Pfahl, *der;* ≈ Duckdalben, *der;* **~ rope** *n.* Festmachetrosse, *die*

Moorish /ˈmʊərɪʃ, ˈmɔːrɪʃ/ *adj.* maurisch

moorland /ˈmʊələnd, ˈmɔːlənd/ *n.* (Geog.) Moorland, *das*

moose /muːs/ *n., pl. same* (Zool.) Amerikanischer Elch

moot /muːt/

A *adj.* umstritten; offen ‹*Frage*›; strittig ‹*Punkt*›

B *v.t.* (broach, suggest) zur Sprache bringen ‹*Maßnahme, Plan*›; anschneiden ‹*Thema*›; erörtern ‹*Frage, Punkt*›

mop /mɒp/

A *n.* 1 Mopp, *der;* (for washing up) ≈ Spülbürste, *die;* (Naut.) Dweil, *der* 2 **~ [of hair]** Wuschelkopf, *der*

B *v.t.*, **-pp-** 1 (clean with mop) moppen ‹*Fußboden*› 2 (wipe) abwischen ‹*Träne, Schweiß, Stirn*› 3 **~ the floor with sb.** (fig. coll.) jmdn. fertig machen (ugs.)

(Phrasal verb)

• **~ ˈup** *v.t.* 1 (wipe up) aufwischen ‹*Flüssigkeit*›; **here's some bread to ~ up the gravy** hier ist etwas Brot, um die Soße vom Teller zu wischen 2 (Brit. coll.) (drink greedily) wegschlabbern (ugs.) ‹*Getränk*›; (eat greedily) reinstopfen (ugs.) ‹*Essen*› 3 (Mil.) ausheben ‹*Widerstandsnest*›; aufreiben ‹*versprengte Truppen*›; säubern ‹*Gebiet*›

ˈmopboard *n.* (Amer.) Fußleiste, *die*

mope /məʊp/ *v.i.* Trübsal blasen (ugs.); **~ about** *or* **around** trübselig herumschleichen (ugs.)

moped /ˈməʊped/ *n.* Moped, *das*

ˈmophead *n.* 1 (at end of mop) Mopp, *der* 2 (of hair; person) Wuschelkopf, *der* (ugs.)

moppet /ˈmɒpɪt/ *n.* 1 (endearing: baby, little girl) Fratz, *der* (fam.) 2 (coll.: child) Matz, *der* (fam.)

moquette /mɒˈket/ *n.* (Textiles) Mokett, *der* (fachspr.); Möbelplüsch aus Wolle

moraine /məˈreɪn/ *n.* (Geol.) Moräne, *die*

moral /ˈmɒrl/

A *adj.* 1 (of right and wrong) moralisch ‹*Gefühl, Bewusstsein*›; sittlich ‹*Wert*›; Moral‹*begriff, -prinzip, -vorstellung*› 2 (dealing with regulation of conduct) moralisch ‹*Erzählung, Rede*›; Lehr‹*gedicht,*

-stück› 3 (concerned with rules of morality) Moral‹philosoph[ie], -psychologie› 4 (virtuous) moralisch, sittlich, (veralt.) tugendhaft ‹Leben, Person› 5 (founded on ~ law) moralisch, sittlich ‹Verpflichtung, Pflicht›; **be under a ~ obligation** eine moralische *od.* sittliche Pflicht haben 6 (not physical) moralisch ‹Stärke, Zusammenbruch›

B *n.* 1 (lesson) Moral, *die;* **draw the ~ from sth.** die Lehre aus etw. ziehen 2 *in pl.* (habits) Moral, *die;* Moralvorstellungen *Pl.* 3 (maxim) Moral, *die;* Lehre, *die;* **point a ~:** einen moralischen Grundsatz aufstellen

moral: ~ 'certainty *n.* **it is a ~ certainty [that ...]** es ist so gut wie sicher[, dass ...]; **~ 'courage** *n.* Rückgrat, *das;* Zivilcourage, *die;* **~ 'cowardice** *n.* Mangel an Rückgrat *od.* Zivilcourage

morale /məˈrɑːl/ Moral, *die;* **high/low ~:** gute/schlechte Moral

mo'rale-booster *n.* **be a** *or* **work** *or* **act as a ~ for sb.** jds. Moral heben *od.* stärken

moralise ▸**moralize**

moralist /ˈmɒrəlɪst/ *n.* 1 (one who practises morality) moralischer *od.* sittlicher Mensch 2 (philosopher) Moralist, *der*/Moralistin, *die;* Moralphilosoph, *der*/Moralphilosophin, *die*

moralistic /mɒrəˈlɪstɪk/ *adj.* moralistisch

morality /məˈrælɪtɪ/ *n.* 1 (conduct) Moral, *die;* Sittlichkeit, *die;* Moralität, *die* (geh.) 2 (moral science) Moralphilosophie, *die;* Ethik, *die;* Sittenlehre, *die* 3 *in pl.* (moral principles) Moralgesetze *Pl.;* Moralprinzipien *Pl.* 4 (particular system) Ethik, *die* 5 (conformity to moral principles) Sittlichkeit, *die;* Moralität, *die* (geh.) 6 (Hist., Lit.) **~ [play]** Moralität, *die*

moralize /ˈmɒrəlaɪz/ *v.i.* moralisieren (geh.); moralische Betrachtungen anstellen (**[up]on** über + *Akk.*); **do stop moralizing!** hör auf mit deinen Moralpredigten!

moral 'law *n.* Moralgesetz, *das*

morally /ˈmɒrəlɪ/ *adv.* 1 (as regards right and wrong) moralisch ‹verantwortlich› 2 (virtuously) moralisch einwandfrei, integer ‹sich benehmen› 3 (virtually) praktisch, so gut wie ‹sicher› 4 (not physically) moralisch; psychisch

moral: ~ 'majority *n.: vermutete Mehrheit, die für strengere öffentliche Moral eintritt;* **~ phi'losophy** *n.* Moralphilosophie, *die;* **~ 'pressure** *n.* moralischer Druck; **~ 'sense** *n.* moralisches *od.* sittliches Bewusstsein; **~ sup'port** *n.* moralische Unterstützung; **~ the'ology** *n.* Moraltheologie, *die;* **~ 'victory** *n.* moralischer Sieg

morass /məˈræs/ *n.* 1 (bog) Morast, *der* 2 (fig.: entanglement) Wirrnis, *die* (geh.); Labyrinth, *das;* **a ~ of confusion** heillose Verwirrung

moratorium /mɒrəˈtɔːrɪəm/ *n., pl.* **~s** *or* **moratoria** /mɒrəˈtɔːrɪə/ 1 vorläufige Einstellung (**on** *Gen.*); [vorläufiger] Stopp (**on** für); **declare a ~ on sth.** etw. vorläufig einstellen *od.* stoppen 2 (authorized delay) Moratorium, *das*

Moravia /məˈreɪvɪə/ *pr. n.* Mähren (*das*)

morbid /ˈmɔːbɪd/ *adj.* 1 (unwholesome, having such feelings) krankhaft; makaber, (geh.) morbid ‹Freude, Faszination, Fantasie, Neigung› 2 (coll.: melancholy) trübselig; **make sb. feel ~:** jmdn. trübselig machen 3 (Med.) pathologisch (fachspr.) ‹Anatomie›; krankhaft ‹Zustand, Veränderung›; krank ‹Körper›; pathogen (fachspr.) ‹Substanz›

morbidity /mɔːˈbɪdɪtɪ/ *n., no pl.* 1 Krankhaftigkeit, *die* 2 (Med.) (diseased state) Krankheit, *die;* (rate of sickness) Morbidität, *die* (fachspr.)

morbidly /ˈmɔːbɪdlɪ/ *adv.* 1 (Med.) krankhaft 2 (coll.: in melancholy way) trübselig

mordant /ˈmɔːdənt/ *adj.* bissig ‹Bemerkung, Rede›; beißend ‹Humor›; sarkastisch ‹Person›

more /mɔː(r)/

A *adj.* 1 (additional) mehr; **would you like any** *or* **some/a few ~?** (apples, books, etc.) möchten Sie noch welche/ein paar?; **would you like any** *or* **some ~ apples?** möchten Sie noch Äpfel?; **would you like any** *or* **some/a little ~?** (tea, paper, etc.) möchten Sie noch etwas/ein wenig?; **would you like any** *or* **some ~ tea/paper?** möchten Sie noch Tee/Papier?; **I haven't any ~ [apples/tea]** ich habe keine [Äpfel]/keinen [Tee] mehr; **~ and ~:** immer mehr; **offer ~ coffee** noch Kaffee anbieten; **for a few dollars ~:** für ein paar Dollar mehr; **[just] one ~ thing before I go** [nur] noch eins, bevor ich gehe; **one ~ word and ...:** noch ein Wort und ...; **many ~ things** noch viel mehr [Dinge]; **two/twenty ~ things** noch zwei/zwanzig Dinge; **some ~ things** noch einige Dinge; noch einiges 2 (greater in degree) größer; **~'s the pity** leider!; **the ~ fool 'you** du bist vielleicht ein Dummkopf

B *n., no pl., no indef. art.* 1 (greater amount or number or thing) mehr; **he is ~ of a poet than a musician** er ist mehr Dichter als Musiker; **~ and ~:** mehr und mehr; immer mehr; **six or ~:** mindestens sechs; **I hope to see ~ of you** hoffentlich sehen wir uns öfter; **the ~ the merrier** ▸**merry 1** 2 (additional number or amount or thing) mehr; **what is ~ ...:** außerdem ...; **do no ~ than do sth.** nur etw. tun; **~ means worse** ein Mehr an Zahl heißt ein Weniger an Qualität; **and ~:** mindestens *vorangestellt;* oder mehr; **there's plenty ~ where that came from** es ist noch viel mehr da; man braucht keineswegs zu geizen; **there's no need to do/say [any] ~:** da braucht nichts weiter getan/gesagt zu werden; *see also* **say A 1** 3 **~ than** (coll.: exceedingly) über‹satt, -glücklich, -froh›; hoch‹erfreut, -willkommen›; sehr ‹aufgeregt›; tief‹traurig›; **at least you enjoyed yourself, which is ~ than I did** im Gegensatz zu mir *od.* anders als ich hast du dich wenigstens noch amüsiert; **which is ~ than you** *or* **one can say of X** und das kann man nicht von X behaupten; **neither ~ nor less [than ridiculous** *etc.*] [lächerlich *usw.*,] nicht mehr und nicht weniger

C *adv.* 1 mehr ‹mögen, interessieren, gefallen, sich wünschen›; *forming compar.* **a ~ interesting book** ein interessanteres Buch; **this book is ~ interesting** dieses Buch ist interessanter; **~ often** häufiger; **~ than a little tiresome** ziemlich langweilig; **~ than anything [else]** vor allem; **~ than sb. can say** mehr als jmd. sagen kann 2 (nearer, rather) eher; **~ ... than ...:** eher ... als ...; **~ dead than alive** mehr tot als lebendig 3 **you couldn't be ~** (are extremely) **mistaken** *or* **wrong** du irrst dich gewaltig; **I couldn't be ~** (am extremely) **sorry** es tut mir schrecklich leid 4 (again) wieder; **never ~:** nie wieder *od.* mehr; **not any ~:** nicht mehr; **once ~:** noch einmal; **a couple of times ~:** noch ein paarmal 5 **~ and ~ ...:** mehr und mehr *od.* immer mehr ...; *with adj. or adv.* immer ... (+ *Komp.*); **become ~ and ~ absurd** immer absurder werden 6 **~ or less** (fairly) mehr oder weniger; (approximately) annähernd 7 **~ so** noch mehr; **Is she equally attractive? — Rather ~ so, if anything** Ist sie genauso attraktiv? — Ja, wenn nicht noch attraktiver; **the ~ so because ...:** umso mehr, als *od.* weil ... 8 **not any ~ [than]** nicht mehr [als]. *See also* **like¹ A 1; little C 2; no B 1; the B; what F 1**

moreish /ˈmɔːrɪʃ/ *adj.* (coll.) lecker; **this cake is rather ~:** dieser Kuchen schmeckt nach mehr

morel /məˈrel/ *n.* (Bot.: edible fungus) [Speise]morchel, *die*

morello /məˈreləʊ/ *n., pl.* **~s** (Bot.) Schattenmorelle, *die*

moreover /mɔːˈrəʊvə(r)/ *adv.* und außerdem; zudem (geh.)

mores /ˈmɔːriːz, ˈmɔːreɪz/ *n. pl.* Sitten *Pl.;* **sexual ~:** Sexualethik *od.* -moral, *die*

morganatic /mɔːgəˈnætɪk/ *adj.* morganatisch; **~ marriage** morganatische Ehe; Ehe zur linken Hand (hist.)

morgue /mɔːg/ *n.* 1 ▸**mortuary** 2 (Journ.) Archiv, *das*

moribund /ˈmɒrɪbʌnd/ *adj.* (lit. or fig.) moribund (Med.); dem Tode geweiht (geh.); im Sterben liegend ‹Person›; im Aussterben begriffen ‹Spezies›; dem Untergang geweiht ‹Nation, Volk, Brauch›

Mormon /ˈmɔːmən/

A *n.* Mormone, *der*/Mormonin, *die;* **Book of ~:** Buch Mormon

B *adj.* mormonisch

morn /mɔːn/ *n.* 1 (poet.: morning) Morgen, *der;* **from ~ to** *or* **till night** von früh bis spät 2 (poet.: dawn) Morgengrauen, *das*

mornay /ˈmɔːneɪ/ *n.* (Gastr.) Sauce Mornay, *die* (*eine Käsesoße*)

morning /ˈmɔːnɪŋ/ *n.* 1 ▸❶ **p. 1001,** ▸❶ **p. 1048** Morgen, *der;* (as opposed to afternoon) Vormittag, *der;* **this ~:** heute Morgen *od.* früh; **tomorrow ~:** morgen früh; **during the ~:** am Morgen/Vormittag; **[early] in the ~:** am [frühen] Morgen; (regularly) [früh] morgens; **at one** *etc.* **in the ~ = at one a.m.** *etc.* ▸**a.m. A;** **begin next ~:** am anderen Morgen beginnen; **on Wednesday ~s/~:** Mittwoch morgens/[am] Mittwochmorgen *od.* Mittwoch früh; **one ~:** eines Morgens; **the other ~:** neulich morgens *od.* früh; **~, noon, and night** Tag und Nacht; **~ came** es wurde Morgen; **~s, of a ~:** morgens; *see also* **good A 13** 2 **in the ~** (coll.: next ~) morgen früh; **see you in the ~!** bis morgen früh! 3 (spent in a particular way) **a ~ of shopping** ein mit Einkaufen verbrachter Morgen 4 ▸❶ **p. 1189** (coll. greeting) **~, all!** Morgen, zusammen! 5 (fig.) Anfang, *der;* Beginn, *der* 6 *attrib.* morgendlich; Morgen‹kaffee, -spaziergang›

morning: ~ 'after *n.* (coll.: hangover) **~-'after [feeling]** Katzenjammer, *der;* Kater, *der;* **~-'after pill** *n.* Pille [für den Morgen] danach; **~ coat** *n.* Cut[away], *der;* **~ dress** *n.* Stresemann, *der;* **~ 'glory** *n.* (Bot.) Winde, *die;* **~ 'paper** *n.* Morgenzeitung, *die;* **~ 'prayer** *n.* Morgenandacht, *die;* **~ 'service** *n.* (Eccl.) Morgenandacht, *die;* (RC Ch.) Frühmesse, *die;* **~ sickness** *n.* morgendliche Übelkeit; **~ 'star** *n.* Morgenstern, *der*

Moroccan /məˈrɒkən/ ▸❶ **p. 1345**

A *adj.* marokkanisch; **sb. is ~:** jmd. ist Marokkaner/Marokkanerin; *see also* **English A**

B *n.* Marokkaner, *der*/Marokkanerin, *die*

morocco *n., pl.* **~s** Maroquin, *der*

Morocco /məˈrɒkəʊ/ *pr. n.* Marokko (*das*)

moron /ˈmɔːrɒn/ *n.* 1 (coll.) Trottel, *der* (ugs. abwertend); Schwachkopf, *der* (ugs.) 2 (mental defective) Geistesschwache, *der/die;* Schwachsinnige, *der/die*

moronic /məˈrɒnɪk/ *adj.* geistesschwach; schwachsinnig; debil (fachspr.)

morose /məˈrəʊs/ *adj.,* **morosely** /məˈrəʊslɪ/ *adv.* verdrießlich

morph /mɔːf/

A *n.* 1 (Biol.: variant form) Morphe, *die* 2 (Ling.: linguistic form) Morph, *das* 3 (Computing: image) Morphingbild, *das*

B *v.i.* 1 (change shape) sich verändern; (change into something else) sich verwandeln 2 (Computing) morphen

morpheme /ˈmɔːfiːm/ *n.* (Ling.) Morphem, *das*

morphia /ˈmɔːfɪə/, **morphine** /ˈmɔːfiːn/ *ns.* Morphin, *das* (fachspr.); Morphium, *das;* **be a ~ addict** morphiumsüchtig sein

morphing /ˈmɔːfɪŋ/ *n., no pl.* (Cinemat., Computing) Morphing, *das*

morphological /mɔːfəˈlɒdʒɪkl/ *adj.* (Biol., Ling.) morphologisch

morphology /mɔːˈfɒlədʒɪ/ *n.* 1 (Biol.) Morphologie, *die;* Gestaltlehre, *die* 2 (Ling.) Morphologie, *die* (fachspr.); Formen- und Wortbildungslehre, *die*

morris /ˈmɒrɪs/: **~ dance** *n.* Moriskentanz, *der;* **~ dancer** *n.* Moriskentänzer, *der;* **~ dancing** *n.* Moriskentanzen, *das*

morrow /ˈmɒrəʊ/ *n.* (literary) **the ~** (the next day) der folgende *od.* kommende Tag; **on the ~:** tags drauf; am nächsten Tag. *See also* **good A 13**

Morse /mɔːs/ *n.* ▸ℹ **p. 1277** Morseschrift, *die;* Morsezeichen *Pl.;* **can you use ~?** können Sie morsen?

Morse 'code *n.* Morseschrift, *die;* Morsealphabet, *das*

morsel /'mɔːsl/ *n.* **1** (of food) Bissen, *der;* Happen, *der* **2** (fragment) Stückchen, *das;* Bröckchen, *das;* (fig.) Quäntchen, *das*

mortal /'mɔːtl/

A *adj.* **1** (that must die) sterblich **2** (fatal, fought to the death, intense) tödlich (**to** für); **~ combat** ein Kampf auf Leben und Tod; **give ~ offence to sb.** jmdn. tödlich beleidigen; **~ sin** Todsünde, *die* **3** (implacable) tödlich; erbittert; **~ enemy** Todfeind, *der* **4** (coll.: whatsoever) **every ~ thing** alles Menschenmögliche **5** (accompanying death) Todes‹*strudel, -kampf, -angst*› **6** (human, earthly) vergänglich; irdisch ‹*Dasein*›; menschlich ‹*Verlangen, Geist*›

B *n.* Sterbliche, *der/die;* **be a mere ~:** auch nur ein Mensch sein

mortality /mɔː'tælɪtɪ/ *n.* **1** Sterblichkeit, *die* **2** (loss of life) [Dahin]sterben, *das* **3** (number of deaths) Sterblichkeit, *die;* Todesfälle *Pl.;* Mortalität, *die* (Med.) **4** **~ [rate]** Sterblichkeitsrate, *die;* Sterbeziffer, *die;* Mortalität, *die* (Med.)

mortally /'mɔːtəlɪ/ *adv.* **1** **~ wounded** tödlich verletzt **2** (intensely) **~ offended** zutiefst *od.* tödlich beleidigt

mortar /'mɔːtə(r)/ *n.* **1** (substance) Mörtel, *der* **2** (vessel) Mörser, *der* **3** (cannon) Minenwerfer, *der;* Mörser, *der*

'mortarboard *n.* (Univ.) *bei bestimmten Anlässen zum Talar getragene viereckige Kopfbedeckung der Studenten und Lehrer an britischen und amerikanischen Universitäten;* ≈ Barett, *das*

mortgage /'mɔːgɪdʒ/

A *n.* **1** Hypothek, *die* **2** (deed) Pfandverschreibung, *die;* Hypothekenbrief, *der* **3** *attrib.* Hypotheken‹*schuld, -zinssatz, -darlehen, -geld*›; *attrib.* **~ payment** Hypothekenrate, *die;* **~ rate** Hypothekenzins[satz], *der;* **~ repayment** Hypothekenzahlung, *die*

B *v.t.* mit einer Hypothek *od.* hypothekarisch belasten

mortgagee /mɔːgɪ'dʒiː/ *n.* Hypothekar, *der;* Hypothekengläubiger, *der*

mortgager /'mɔːgɪdʒə(r)/, **mortgagor** /mɔːgɪ'dʒɔː(r)/ *n.* Hypothekenschuldner, *der*

mortice ▸ **mortise**

mortician /mɔː'tɪʃn/ *n.* ▸ℹ **p. 1260** (Amer.) Leichenbestatter, *der/*-bestatterin, *die*

mortification /mɔːtɪfɪ'keɪʃn/ *n.* (humiliation) Beschämung, *die;* Kränkung, *die;* **feel great ~ at sth.** etw. als eine große Schmach empfinden; tief beschämt über etw. (*Akk.*) sein

mortify /'mɔːtɪfaɪ/ *v.t.* **1** (humiliate) beschämen; kränken; **he felt mortified** er empfand es als beschämend **2** (subdue desires of) **~ the flesh/oneself** sich kasteien

mortise /'mɔːtɪs/ *n.* **1** (Woodw.) Zapfenloch, *das;* **~ and tenon [joint]** Zapfenverbindung, *die;* Verzapfung, *die* **2** *attrib.* **~ lock** Steckschloss, *das*

mortuary /'mɔːtjʊərɪ/ *n.* (building) Leichenschauhaus, *das;* (room) Leichenkammer, *die*

mosaic /məʊ'zeɪɪk/ *n.* (lit. or fig.) Mosaik, *das; attrib.* Mosaik‹*fußboden, -arbeit, -stein usw.*›

Moscow /'mɒskəʊ/ ▸ℹ **p. 1643**

A *pr. n.* Moskau (*das*)

B *attrib. adj.* Moskauer

Moselle /məʊ'zel/ *pr. n.* **1** ▸ℹ **p. 1491** Mosel, *die* **2** (wine) Mosel[wein], *der*

Moses /'məʊzɪz/ *pr. n.* (Bibl.) Moses (*der*); Mose (*der*) (ökum.)

mosey /'məʊzɪ/ *v.i.* (coll.) schlendern

Moslem /'mɒzləm/ ▸ **Muslim**

mosque /mɒsk/ *n.* Moschee, *die*

mosquito /mɒs'kiːtəʊ/ *n., pl.* **~es** Stechmücke, *die;* (in tropics) Moskito, *der;* **~ bite** Mücken-/Moskitostich, *der*

mos'quito net *n.* Moskitonetz, *das*

moss /mɒs/ *n.* **1** Moos, *das* **2** (Scot., N. Engl.: bog) Moor, *das;* Sumpf, *der*

moss: ~-covered *adj.* bemoost; moosbedeckt; **~-green** *adj.* moosgrün

mossy /'mɒsɪ/ *adj.* moosig; bemoost; moosbewachsen

most /məʊst/

A *adj.* (in greatest number, the majority of) die meisten; (in greatest amount) meist...; größt... ‹*Fähigkeit, Macht, Bedarf, Geduld, Lärm*›; **make the ~ mistakes/noise** die meisten Fehler/den meisten *od.* größten Lärm machen; **~ people** die meisten Leute; die Mehrheit [der Leute]; **he has the ~ need of it** er braucht es am nötigsten; **for the ~ part** größtenteils; zum größten Teil

B *n.* **1** (greatest amount) das meiste; **offer [the] ~ for it** das meiste *od.* am meisten dafür bieten; **pay the ~:** am meisten bezahlen; **want sth. the ~:** sich (*Dat.*) etw. am meisten wünschen; **the ~ one can say** das Beste, was man sagen kann **2** (the greater part) **~ of the girls** die meisten Mädchen; **~ of his friends** die meisten seiner Freunde; **~ of the poem** der größte Teil des Gedichts; **~ of the time** die meiste Zeit; (on ~ occasions) meistens; **lead for ~ of the race** während des größten Teils des Rennens führen; **be more enterprising than ~:** unternehmungslustiger als die meisten anderen sein; **~ of what he said** das meiste von dem, was er sagte **3** **make the ~ of sth., get the ~ out of sth.** etw. voll ausschöpfen; (employ to the best advantage) etw. voll ausnützen; (represent at its best) das Beste aus etw. machen **4** **at [the] ~:** höchstens; **at the very ~:** allerhöchstens

C *adv.* **1** (more than anything else) am meisten ‹*mögen, interessieren, gefallen, sich wünschen, verlangt*›; **~ of all** am allermeisten **2** *forming superl.* **the ~ interesting book** das interessanteste Buch; **this book is the ~ interesting** dieses Buch ist das interessanteste; **~ probably** höchstwahrscheinlich; **~ often** am häufigsten **3** (exceedingly) überaus; äußerst; **~ decidedly** ganz entschieden; ausgesprochen; **~ certainly** ohne jeden Zweifel **4** (Amer. coll.: almost) fast

mostly /'məʊstlɪ/ *adv.* (most of the time) meistens; (mainly) größtenteils; hauptsächlich

MOT /eməʊ'tiː/ ▸ **MOT test**

mote /məʊt/ *n.* **the ~ in sb.'s eye** (fig. dated) die Schwächen anderer

motel /məʊ'tel/ *n.* Motel, *das*

motet /məʊ'tet/ *n.* (Mus.) Motette, *die*

moth /mɒθ/ *n.* Nachtfalter, *der;* (in clothes) Motte, *die;* **[the] ~** (collect.) die [Kleider]motten *Pl.*

moth: ~ball **A** *n.* Mottenkugel, *die;* **in ~balls** (fig.: stored) eingemottet ‹*Kleidung*›; (Mil.) eingelagert, eingemottet ‹*Schiffe, Waffen*›; beiseite geschoben ‹*Plan, Projekt*›; **put sth. in ~balls** etw. einmotten; **B** *v.t.* einmotten ‹*Kleider, alte Sachen, Vorschlag*›; einlagern, einmotten ‹*militärisches Gerät*›; beiseite schieben ‹*Plan, Projekt*›; **~-eaten** *adj.* von Motten zerfressen; vermottet; (fig.: antiquated) verstaubt ‹*Idee, Politik*›; altmodisch ‹*Person, System*›

mother /'mʌðə(r)/

A *n.* **1** Mutter, *die;* **she is a** *or* **the ~ of six [children]** sie ist Mutter von sechs Kindern; **like ~ used to make** ‹*Essen*› wie bei Muttern (ugs.); **every ~'s son [of you]** jeder Einzelne [von euch]; **~ animal** Muttertier, *das;* **~ hen** Glucke, *die; see also* **expectant 2** **2** (Relig.) **M~ Superior** Äbtissin, *die* **3** (fig.: source) Ursprung, *der;* Wurzel, *die;* **necessity is the ~ of invention** (prov.) Not macht erfinderisch (Spr.)

B *v.t.* **1** großziehen ‹*Familie*›; hervorbringen ‹*Idee, Gerücht*› **2** (over-protect) bemuttern

mother: ~board *n.* (Computing) Mutterplatine, *die;* **M~ Church** *n.* **1** /'---/ Mutterkirche, *die;* **2** /--'-/ (authority) Mutter Kirche *o. Art.;* die Kirche; **~ country** *n.* Mutterland, *das;* **~craft** *n., no pl.* Kinderpflege, *die;* **~ 'earth** *n.* Mutter Erde; **~ fixation** *n.* (Psych.) Mutterbindung, *die;* **M~ 'Goose rhyme** *n.* (Amer.) Kinderreim, *der*

motherhood /'mʌðəhʊd/ *n., no pl.* Mutterschaft, *die*

Mothering Sunday /'mʌðərɪŋ sʌndɪ/ (Brit. Eccl.) ▸ **Mother's Day**

mother: ~-in-law *n., pl.* **~s-in-law** Schwiegermutter, *die;* **~-in-law's 'tongue** *n.* (Bot.) Bajonettpflanze, *die;* Frauenzunge, *die;* **~land** *n.* Vaterland, *das;* Heimatland, *das*

motherless /'mʌðəlɪs/ *adj.* mutterlos; **the child was left ~:** das Kind verlor seine Mutter

motherly /'mʌðəlɪ/ *adj.* mütterlich; **~ love** Mutterliebe, *die*

mother: M~ of 'God *n.* Mutter Gottes, *die;* Muttergottes, *die;* **~-of-'pearl** *n.* Perlmutt, *das;* **~'s boy** *or* **darling** *n.* (coll. derog.) Muttersöhnchen, *das* (ugs.); **M~'s Day** *n.* Muttertag, *der;* **~ 'tongue** *n.* Muttersprache, *die;* **~ wit** *n.* Mutterwitz, *der*

moth: ~ hole *n.:* Mottenloch, *das;* **~proof** **A** *adj.* mottenfest; **B** *v.t.* mottenfest machen

motif /məʊ'tiːf/ *n.* **1** Motiv, *das* **2** (on goods) Markenzeichen, *das;* **the BMW ~:** das BMW-Zeichen **3** (Mus.) [Leit]motiv, *das* **4** (on clothing) Applikation, *die* (fachspr.); Aufnäher, *der*

motion /'məʊʃn/

A *n.* **1** (movement) Bewegung, *die;* Gang, *der;* **be in ~:** in Bewegung sein; sich bewegen; ‹*Maschine:*› laufen; ‹*Fahrzeug:*› fahren; **set** *or* **put sth. in ~** (lit. or fig.) etw. in Bewegung *od.* Gang setzen; *see also* **perpetual motion; slow motion** **2** (gesture) Bewegung, *die;* Wink, *der;* **make a ~ to sb. to do sth.** jmdm. ein Zeichen geben, etw. zu tun; **a ~ of the hand** ein Zeichen mit der Hand; eine Handbewegung **3** (formal proposal; also Law) Antrag, *der;* **put forward** *or* **propose a ~:** einen Antrag stellen **4** (of bowels) Stuhlgang, *der;* **have** *or* **make a ~:** Stuhlgang haben **5** *in sing. or pl.* (faeces) Stuhl, *der* **6** (manner of moving) [Körper]haltung, *die* **7** (change of posture) Bewegung, *die;* **make a ~ to leave** Anstalten machen wegzugehen **8** **go through the ~s of doing sth.** (simulate) so tun, als ob man etw. täte; (do superficially) etw. pro forma tun; **go through the ~s** (simulate) nur so tun; (do superficially) es nur pro forma tun

B *v.t.* **~ sb. to do sth.** jmdm. bedeuten (geh.) *od.* winken, etw. zu tun; **~ sb. to[wards]/away from sth.** jmdm. bedeuten (geh.), zu etw. [hin]zugehen/von etw. wegzugehen; **~ sb. aside/to a seat** jmdn. zur Seite winken/jmdm. bedeuten (geh.), Platz zu nehmen

C *v.i.* winken; **~ to sb. to come in** jmdn. hereinwinken; **~ to** *or* **for sb. to do sth.** jmdm. bedeuten (geh.), etw. zu tun

motionless /'məʊʃnlɪs/ *adj.* reg[ungs]los; bewegungslos; unbewegt ‹*See, Teich*›; **be/stay** *or* **remain ~:** sich nicht bewegen

'motion picture *n.* (esp. Amer.) Film, *der; attrib.* Film-

motivate /'məʊtɪveɪt/ *v.t.* **1** (be motive of, stimulate) motivieren **2** (cause to act) **~ sb. to do sth.** jmdn. veranlassen, etw. zu tun

motivation /məʊtɪ'veɪʃn/ *n.* **1** (process) Motivierung, *die;* **give/receive ~:** motivieren/motiviert werden **2** (incentive) Motivation, *die* (**for** zu); Anreiz, *der* **3** (condition) Motiviertheit, *die;* Motivation, *die;* **have good/poor** *or* **little ~:** sehr/wenig motiviert sein

motivational /məʊtɪ'veɪʃənl/ *adj.* motivierend; Motivations‹*rede, -programm*›

motive /'məʊtɪv/

A *n.* **1** Motiv, *das;* Beweggrund, *der;* **the ~ for the crime** das Tatmotiv; **do sth. from ~s of kindness** etw. aus Freundlichkeit tun **2** ▸ **motif 1, 3**

B *adj.* (moving to action) treibend ‹*Geist, Kraft*›; (productive of motion) Antriebs-

motiveless /'məʊtɪvlɪs/ *adj.* unmotiviert

'motive power *n.* Antriebskraft, *die*

mot juste /məʊ 'ʒuːst/ *n., pl.* **mots justes** /məʊ 'ʒuːst/ treffender *od.* passender Ausdruck

motley /'mɒtlɪ/

A *adj.* **1** [bunt] gescheckt; (multicoloured) [kunter]bunt **2** (varied) bunt gemischt; bunt ‹*Auswahl*›; *see also* **crew A 2**

B *n.* (Hist.: jester's dress) Narrenkostüm, *das;* Narrenkleid, *das*

motocross /'məʊtəʊkrɒs/ *n., no pl., no art.* Motocross, *das*

motor /ˈməʊtə(r)/
A *n.* 1 (machine) Motor, *der* 2 (Brit.: ~ car) Auto, *das*
B *adj.* 1 (driven by engine or ~) Motor‹*schlitten, -mäher, -jacht usw.*› 2 (of ~ vehicles) Kraftfahrzeug‹*ersatzteile, -mechaniker, -verkehr, -motor*›
C *v.t.* (Brit.) fahren
D *v.i.* (Brit.) [mit dem Auto] fahren

Motorail /ˈməʊtəreɪl/ *n.* (Brit.) Autoreisezug, *der*

motor: **~bike** (coll.) ▸ **motorcycle**; **~ boat** *n.* Motorboot, *das*

motorcade /ˈməʊtəkeɪd/ *n.* Fahrzeug- *od.* Wagenkolonne, *die*

motor: **~ car** *n.* (Brit.) Kraftfahrzeug, *das;* Automobil, *das* (geh.); **~ caravan** *n.* (Brit.) Caravan, *der;* Wohnmobil, *das;* **~cycle** *n.* Motorrad, *das;* Kraftrad, *das* (Amtsspr.); *attrib.* **~cycle combination** (Brit.) Motorrad mit Beiwagen; **~cyclist** *n.* Motorradfahrer, *der*/-fahrerin, *die;* **~ home** *n.* Reisemobil, *das;* **~ industry** *n.* Kraftfahrzeugindustrie, *die*

motoring /ˈməʊtərɪŋ/ *n.* (Brit.) Autofahren, *das;* **~ correspondent** Motorjournalist, *der*/-journalistin, *die;* **school of ~:** Fahrschule, *die;* **~ offence** Verstoß gegen die [Straßen]verkehrsordnung; **~ organization** Automobilklub, *der*

motorise ▸ **motorize**

motorist /ˈməʊtərɪst/ *n.* Autofahrer, *der*/-fahrerin, *die*

motorize /ˈməʊtəraɪz/ *v.t.* motorisieren

motor: **~man** *n.* Wagenführer, *der;* **~mouth** *n.* (coll.) Quassler, *der*/Quasslerin, *die* (ugs.); Quasselstrippe, *die* (ugs.); **~ nerve** *n.* (Anat.) motorischer Nerv; **~ racing** *n.* Autorennsport, *der;* **~ scooter** ▸ **scooter 2**; **~ show** *n.* Auto[mobil]ausstellung, *die;* **~ trade** *n.* Kraftfahrzeughandel, *der;* **~ vehicle** *n.* Kraftfahrzeug, *das;* **~way** *n.* (Brit.) Autobahn, *die;* **~way ˈmadness** *n., no pl.* (coll.) Autobahnraserei, *die;* **~way ˈservices** *n. pl.* Autobahnraststätte, *die*

> **motorway**
>
> Eine britische Autobahn. In Großbritannien gibt es ein gut ausgebautes Autobahnnetz, die meisten Autobahnen sind dreispurig. Sie sind mit dem Buchstaben 'M' und einer nachfolgenden Nummer gekennzeichnet und haben eine Geschwindigkeitsbegrenzung von 70 mph (112 km/h). Mit einer Ausnahme sind die britischen Autobahnen gebührenfrei. Der erste mautpflichtige Autobahnabschnitt in Großbritannien, die Birminghamer nördliche Entlastungsstraße, wurde im Dezember 2003 eröffnet.

motte /mɒt/ *n.* Motte, *die* (fachspr.); Erdhügelburg, *die*

MOˈT test *n.* (Brit.) ≈ TÜV, *der*

mottle /ˈmɒtl/ *v.t.* sprenkeln

mottled /ˈmɒtld/ *adj.* gesprenkelt

motto /ˈmɒtəʊ/ *n., pl.* **~es** 1 Motto, *das;* **my ~ is 'live and let live'** meine Devise ist „leben und leben lassen" 2 (in cracker) Spruch, *der* 3 (Mus.) Leitmotiv, *das*

moufflon /ˈmuːflən/ *n.* (Zool.) Mufflon, *der*

mould¹ /məʊld/ *n.* 1 (earth) Erde, *die* 2 (upper soil) [Mutter]boden, *der*

mould²
A *n.* 1 (hollow) Form, *die;* (Metallurgy) Kokille, *die;* (Plastics) Pressform, *die;* (Papermaking) Schöpfform, *die;* **break the ~ of sth.** (fig.) neue Wege in etw. (*Dat.*) gehen 2 (Cookery: hollow utensil) [Kuchen-/Back-/Pudding]form, *die* 3 (fig.) Wesensart, *die;* **be cast in heroic/pedantic** *etc.* **~:** von heldischer/pedantischer *usw.* Wesensart sein
B *v.t.* formen (**out of, from** aus); **~ sth. into a certain shape** etw. in bestimmter Weise formen; **~ sb. into a fine character/person** einen feinen Menschen aus jmdm. machen

mould³ *n.* (Bot.) Schimmel, *der;* (in Roquefort, Stilton, etc. cheese) Edelschimmelpilz, *der;* **grow [a]/get ~:** schimmlig werden

moulder /ˈməʊldə(r)/ *v.i.* **~ [away]** (lit. or fig.) [ver]modern

moulding /ˈməʊldɪŋ/ *n.* 1 (process of forming, lit. or fig.) Formen, *das* 2 (object) Formteil, *das* (**of, in** aus); Formling, *der* (fachspr.); (Archit.) Zierleiste, *die* 3 (wooden strip) Leiste, *die*

mouldy /ˈməʊldɪ/ *adj.* (overgrown with mould) schimmlig ‹*Lebensmittel*›; verschimmelnd, [ver-]modernd ‹*Buch, Vorhang, Teppich*›; **a ~ smell** ein Modergeruch; **become** *or* **grow** *or* **get** *or* **go ~:** verschimmeln; schimmlig werden

moult /məʊlt/
A *v.t.* 1 (Ornith.) verlieren ‹*Federn, Gefieder*› 2 (Zool.) verlieren ‹*Haar*›; abstreifen ‹*Haut*›; abwerfen ‹*Horn, Geweih*›
B *v.i.* ‹*Vogel:*› sich mausern; ‹*Hund, Katze:*› sich haaren; ‹*Schlange, Krebs usw.:*› sich häuten
C *n.* (of bird) Mauser, *die;* (of snake, crab, etc.) Häutung, *die*

mound /maʊnd/ *n.* 1 (of earth) Hügel, *der;* (of stones) Steinhaufen, *der;* **defensive ~:** Verteidigungshügel, *der;* **burial** *or* **sepulchral** *or* **grave ~:** Grabhügel, *der* 2 (hillock) Anhöhe, *die* 3 (heap) Haufen, *der* 4 (Baseball) [erhöhtes] Wurfmal

mount /maʊnt/
A *n.* 1 (mountain, hill) Berg, *der;* **M~ Vesuvius/Everest** der Vesuv/der Mount Everest; *see also* **sermon 1** 2 (animal) Reittier, *das;* (horse) Pferd, *das* 3 (of picture, photograph) Passepartout, *das;* (backing) Unterlage, *die* 4 (for gem) Fassung, *die* 5 (Philat.) [Klebe]falz, *der*
B *v.t.* 1 (ascend) hinaufsteigen ‹*Treppe, Leiter, Stufe*›; steigen auf (+ *Akk.*) ‹*Plattform, Berg, Kanzel*›; besteigen ‹*Thron*› 2 (get on) steigen auf (*Akk.*) ‹*Reittier, Fahrzeug*›; *abs.* aufsitzen; **~ the pavement** auf den Bürgersteig fahren 3 (place on support) montieren (**on** auf + *Akk.*) 4 (prepare) aufstellen ‹*Maschine, Apparat*›; präparieren ‹*Exemplar, Haut, Skelett*›; (fasten) in ein Album einkleben ‹*Briefmarke*›; (for microscope) fixieren; (raise into position) in Stellung bringen ‹*Kanone, Geschütz, Mörser*› 5 (Art) aufziehen ‹*Bild usw.*›; [ein]fassen ‹*Edelstein usw.*› 6 (put on stage) inszenieren ‹*Stück, Show, Oper*›; organisieren ‹*Festspiele, Ausstellung*› 7 (carry out) durchführen ‹*Angriff, Operation usw.*›; *see also* **guard A 2, 4** 8 (for copulation) bespringen ‹*Tier*›; besteigen (salopp) ‹*Frau*›
C *v.i.* 1 (move up, rise in rank) aufsteigen 2 **~ [up]** (fig.: increase) steigen (**to** auf + *Akk.*); ‹*Unruhe, Besorgnis, Unwillen:*› wachsen; **it all ~s up** es summiert sich

mountain /ˈmaʊntɪn/ *n.* 1 (lit. or fig.) Berg, *der;* **in the ~s** im Gebirge; **~s high** (fig.) berg[e-]hoch; **~s of books** (fig.) Berge von Büchern; **butter/grain** *etc.* **~** (fig.) Butter-/Getreideberg *usw., der;* **move ~s** (fig.) Berge versetzen; Himmel und Hölle in Bewegung setzen; *see also* **molehill** 2 *attrib.* Gebirgs-; **~ lake** Bergsee, *der*

mountain: **~ ˈash** *n.* (Bot.) Eberesche, *die;* **~ bike** *n.* Mountainbike, *das;* **~ biker** *n.* Mountainbiker, *der*/-bikerin, *die;* **~ chain** *n.* (Geog.) Gebirgskette, *die*

mountaineer /maʊntɪˈnɪə(r)/ *n.* ▸ℹ **p. 1260** Bergsteiger, *der*/Bergsteigerin, *die*

mountaineering /maʊntɪˈnɪərɪŋ/ *n.* Bergsteigen, *das; attrib.* **~ expedition/party** Bergpartie, *die*/Seilschaft, *die; attrib.* **~ experience** bergsteigerische Erfahrung; **~ equipment/club** Bergsteigerausrüstung, *die*/-verein, *der*

mountain ˈgoat *n.* Schneeziege, *die*

mountainous /ˈmaʊntɪnəs/ *adj.* 1 (characterized by mountains) gebirgig 2 (huge) riesig ‹*Gegenstand, Welle*›; riesenhaft ‹*Person*›; groß ‹*Leistung*›

mountain: **~ ˈrailway** *n.* [Schienen]bergbahn, *die;* **~ ˈrange** *n.* Gebirgszug, *der;* **~ ˈrescue** *n.* 1 *no pl.* (action) Rettungseinsatz in den Bergen; 2 (organization) Bergwacht, *die;* Bergrettung, *die; attrib.* Bergrettungs-; Bergwacht-; **~ ˈroad** *n.* Gebirgsstraße, *die;* **~ sickness** *n.* Höhenkrankheit, *die;* **~side** *n.* [Berg]hang, *der;* **~ top** *n.* Berggipfel, *der*

mountebank /ˈmaʊntɪbæŋk/ *n.* 1 (derog.: quack) Quacksalber, *der* (abwertend) 2 (derog.: charlatan) Scharlatan, *der* (abwertend)

mounted /ˈmaʊntɪd/ *adj.* 1 (on animal) beritten 2 (on support) montiert ‹*Gerät*›; aufgezogen ‹*Stich*›; (for display) präpariert ‹*Tier*›

Mountie /ˈmaʊntɪ/ *n.* (coll.) Mountie, *der; berittener kanadischer Polizist*

mounting /ˈmaʊntɪŋ/ *n.* 1 (of performance) Inszenierung, *die;* (of programme) Durchführung, *die* 2 (support) (Art: of drawing) Passepartout, *das;* (backing) Unterlage, *die;* (of engine, axle, etc.) Aufhängung, *die* (Technik)

Mount of ˈOlives *pr. n.* Ölberg, *der*

mourn /mɔːn/
A *v.i.* 1 (feel sorrow or regret) trauern; **~ for** *or* **over** trauern um ‹*Toten*›; nachtrauern (+ *Dat.*) ‹*Jugend, Augenlicht, Haustier*›; betrauern ‹*Verlust, Missgeschick*› 2 (observe conventions of ~ing) trauern; Trauer tragen
B *v.t.* betrauern; nachtrauern ‹*etw. Verlorenem*›

mourner /ˈmɔːnə(r)/ *n.* 1 (one who mourns) Trauernde, *der/die;* Trauergast, *der* 2 (person hired to attend funeral) (man) Klagemann, *der;* (woman) Klageweib, *das*

mournful /ˈmɔːnfl/ *adj.* traurig, bitter ‹*Träne*›; klagend ‹*Stimme, Ton, Schrei, Geheul*›; trauervoll (geh.) ‹*Person*›

mournfully /ˈmɔːnfəlɪ/ *adv.* traurig; klagend ‹*sprechen, tönen*›

mourning /ˈmɔːnɪŋ/ *n.* 1 (clothes) Trauer[kleidung], *die;* **be [dressed] in** *or* **wear/put on** *or* **go into ~:** Trauer tragen/anlegen 2 (sorrowing, lamentation) Trauer, *die;* (period) Trauer[zeit], *die;* **a national day of ~:** eintägige Staatstrauer

mouse /maʊs/
A *n., pl.* **mice** /maɪs/ 1 Maus, *die;* **as quiet as a ~:** ganz leise; mucksmäuschenstill (fam.) ‹*dasitzen*›; (by nature) sehr still; *see also* **cat 1**; **church mouse** 2 (fig.: timid person) Angsthase, *der* (ugs.); **a man or a ~:** ein Mann oder ein Schwächling 3 (Computing) Maus, *die*
B *v.i.* mausen; **go mousing** auf Mäusejagd gehen

mouse: **~ button** *n.* (Computing) Maustaste, *die;* **~ click** *n.* (Computing) Mausklick, *der;* **~-coloured** *adj.* mausfarben; mausgrau; **~-driven** *adj.* (Computing) mausgesteuert; **~ hole** *n.* Mauseloch, *das* **~ mat** *n.* (Computing) Mauspad, *das;* **~ pointer** *n.* (Computing) Mauszeiger, *der*

mouser /ˈmaʊsə(r)/ *n.* Mäusefänger, *der*

ˈmousetrap *n.* 1 Mausefalle, *die* 2 (joc.: cheese) billiger *od.* einfacher Käse

moussaka /muˈsɑːkə/ *n.* (Gastr.) Moussaka, *die*

mousse /muːs/ *n.* Mousse, *die*

moustache /məˈstɑːʃ/ *n.* Schnurrbart, *der*

mousy /ˈmaʊsɪ/ *adj.* 1 (nondescript) mattbraun ‹*Haar*› 2 (timid) scheu ‹*Blick, Wesen, Bewegung*›

mouth
A /maʊθ/ *n., pl.* **~s** /maʊðz/ 1 ▸ℹ **p. 951** (of person) Mund, *der;* (of animal) Maul, *das;* **his ~ quivered/twitched/moved** seine Lippen zitterten/zuckten/bewegten sich; **hit sb. in the ~:** jmdn. auf den Mund schlagen; **with one's ~ open** mit offenem Mund; **keep one's ~ shut** (fig. sl.) die *od.* seine Klappe halten (salopp); **put one's money where one's ~ is** (fig. coll.) seinen Worten Taten folgen lassen; **shut sb.'s ~** (fig. sl.) jmdm. den Mund stopfen (ugs.); **with one's ~ full** mit vollem Mund; **my ~ feels dry** ich habe einen trockenen Mund; **out of sb.'s own ~** (fig.) aus jmds. eigenem Mund; von jmdm. selbst; **hear sb. say sth. out of his own ~:** hören, wie jmd. etw. selbst sagt; **out of the ~s of babes [and sucklings]!** (fig.) Kindermund tut Wahrheit kund (Spr.); **put words into sb.'s ~:** jmdm. etwas in den Mund legen; (misrepresent) jmdm. das Wort im Munde [her-]umdrehen; **have got many ~s to feed** viele hungrige Mäuler zu stopfen haben (ugs.); **take the words out of sb.'s ~:** jmdm. das Wort aus dem Mund *od.* von der Zunge nehmen; **go** *or* **be passed** *or* **be spread from ~ to ~:** von Mund zu Mund gehen 2 (fig.) (entrance to harbour) [Hafen]einfahrt, *die;* (of valley, gorge, mine, burrow, tunnel, cave) Eingang, *der;* (of well) Loch, *das;* (of volcano) Krater, *der;* (of bottle, cannon) Mündung, *die;* (of pocket, womb, pit) Öffnung, *die* 3 ▸ℹ **p. 1491** (of river) Mündung, *die. See also* **down³ A 29**; **open A 1, C 1**; **shoot off A**; **water C 2**; **word A 4**

m

B /maʊð/ *v.t.* **1** (declaim) schwülstig vortragen ‹*Gedicht, Rede, Zitat, Satz*› **2** (express by silent lip-movement) mit Lippenbewegungen sagen; **~ sth. to oneself** etw. unhörbar vor sich (*Akk.*) hin sagen

C /maʊð/ *v.i.* **1** (grimace) den Mund verziehen **2** (move lips silently) lautlos die Lippen bewegen; **~ to oneself** unhörbar vor sich (*Akk.*) hin sprechen

mouthful /ˈmaʊθfʊl/ *n.* **1** (bite) Mundvoll, *der;* (of solid food) Bissen, *der;* (of drink) Schluck, *der;* **a ~ of abuse** ein Schwall Schimpfwörter **2** (small quantity) **a ~:** ein Bisschen **3** (sth. difficult to say) Zungenbrecher, *der* (ugs.) **4** (Amer. coll.: sth. important) etwas Wichtiges

mouth: ~ organ *n.* Mundharmonika, *die;* **~piece** *n.* **1** (Mus., Med.; for cigar[ette], pipe) Mundstück, *das;* (of telephone) Sprechmuschel, *die;* **2** (speaker for others) Sprachrohr, *das;* **act as the ~piece** Sprachrohr sein; **~-to-~ resusciˈtation** *n.* Wiederbelebung durch Mund-zu-Mund-Beatmung; **~wash** *n.* Mundwasser, *das;* **~-watering** *adj.* appetitlich ‹*Essen, Geruch, Anblick*›; lecker ‹*Essen, Geruch, Geschmack*›

movable /ˈmuːvəbl/ *adj.* **1** (capable of being moved) beweglich ‹*Möbel, Teppich, Regal*› **2** (Law) beweglich ‹*Vermögen, Güter*›; (Scot. Law) nicht vererbbar. *See also* **doh; feast A 1**

move /muːv/

A *n.* **1** (change of residence) Umzug, *der;* (change of job) **after three years with the same firm it was time for a ~:** nach drei Jahren bei derselben Firma war es Zeit, sich (*Dat.*) eine neue Stelle zu suchen

2 (action taken) Schritt, *der;* (Footb. etc.) Spielzug, *der*

3 (turn in game) Zug, *der;* (fig.) [Schach]zug, *der;* **make a ~:** ziehen; **it's your ~:** du bist am Zug

4 **be on the ~** (moving about) ‹*Person:*› unterwegs *od.* (ugs.) auf Achse sein; ‹*Tier, Tramp:*› umherziehen; (progressing) ‹*Land usw.:*› sich weiterentwickeln; ‹*Person:*› vorankommen

5 **make a ~** (initiate action) etwas tun *od.* unternehmen; (**~** from motionless position) sich rühren; (rise from table) aufstehen; (coll.: leave, depart) losziehen (ugs.); **make the first ~:** den Anfang machen; **make no ~:** sich nicht rühren; **make no ~ to help sb.** keine Anstalten machen, jmdm. zu helfen

6 **get a ~ on** (coll.) einen Zahn zulegen (ugs.); **get a ~ on!** (coll.) [mach] Tempo! (ugs.)

B *v.t.* **1** (change position of) bewegen; wegräumen ‹*Hindernis, Schutt*›; (transport) befördern; **~ the chair over here** rück den Stuhl hier herüber!; **~ sth. somewhere else** etw. anderswohin tun; **~ sth. from the spot/its place** etw. von der Stelle/seinem Platz wegnehmen; **~ sth. to a new position** etw. an einen neuen Platz bringen; **~ house** umziehen; **~ the furniture about** umräumen; **who has ~d my papers?** wer war an meinen Papieren?; **please ~ your car** bitte fahren Sie Ihr Auto weg; **~ the luggage/equipment into the building** das Gepäck/die Ausrüstung ins Gebäude hineinbringen; **not ~ a muscle** sich nicht rühren; **~ one's/sb.'s bowels** Stuhlgang haben/jmds. Verdauung in Gang bringen; **please ~ your head [to one side]** bitte tun Sie Ihren Kopf zur Seite; **please ~ your legs out of the way** bitte nehmen Sie Ihre Beine aus dem Weg; **~ it!** (coll.) Beeilung! (ugs.); **~ yourself!** (coll.) Beeilung! (ugs.); **~ sb. to another department/job** jmdn. in eine andere Abteilung/Position versetzen; **the residents were ~d out of the area** die Bewohner wurden aus dem Gebiet evakuiert; **~ one's child to a different school** sein Kind in eine andere Schule schicken; **the patient was ~d to a different ward** der Patient wurde in eine andere Abteilung verlegt; **~ police/troops into an area** Polizeikräfte/Truppen in ein Gebiet schicken; **~ sb. into new accommodation** jmdn. in eine neue Unterkunft bringen lassen

2 (in game) ziehen

3 (put or keep in motion) bewegen; in Marsch setzen ‹*Truppe*›; auseinander treiben ‹*Demonstranten*›; in Bewegung setzen ‹*Mechanismus*›

4 (provoke) erregen ‹*Ärger, Eifersucht, Begierde*›; wecken ‹*Ehrgeiz, Hass*›; hervorrufen ‹*Gelächter*›; **~ sb. to laughter** jmdn. zum Lachen bringen; **~ sb. to anger** jmds. Ärger erregen

5 (affect) bewegen; berühren; **~ sb. to tears** jmdn. zu Tränen rühren; **~ sb. to pity/compassion** jmds. Mitleid erregen; **be ~d to pity/compassion** vor Mitleid ergriffen sein; **be ~d by sth.** über etw. (*Akk.*) gerührt sein

6 (prompt) **~ sb. to do sth.** jmdn. dazu bewegen, etw. zu tun; **he was ~d by this** *or* **this ~d him to do it** das bewog ihn dazu, es zu tun; **~ sb. to action** jmdn. aktivieren *od.* mobilisieren; **I shall not be ~d** ich bleibe dabei; **sb. is not to be ~d** jmd. lässt sich nicht erschüttern

7 (propose) beantragen ‹*Beendigung, Danksagung*›; stellen ‹*Antrag*›; **~ that sth. should be done** beantragen, dass etw. getan wird

8 (make formal application to) einen Antrag stellen bei ‹*Gericht usw.*›

9 (Commerc.: sell) absetzen

C *v.i.* **1** (go from place to place) sich bewegen; (by car, bus, train) fahren; (on foot) gehen; (coll.: start, leave) gehen; ‹*Wolken:*› ziehen (**across** über + *Akk.*); **~ with the times** (fig.) mit der Zeit gehen; **it's time we got moving** es ist Zeit aufzubrechen; **get moving!** beeil dich!; **start to ~** ‹*Fahrzeug:*› sich in Bewegung setzen; **nobody ~d** niemand rührte sich von der Stelle; **keep moving!** bewegt euch!; (**~** on) gehen Sie bitte weiter; **Don't ~. You're not in the way** Bleiben Sie sitzen/stehen. Sie stehen nicht im Weg; **he has ~d to another department** er ist jetzt in einer anderen Abteilung; **Don't ~. I'll be back soon** Bleib hier *od.* Geh nicht weg. Ich bin gleich zurück; **in which direction are your thoughts moving?** in welche Richtung gehen Ihre Gedanken?

2 (in games) ziehen; **it's your turn to ~:** du bist am Zug; **White to ~** (Chess) Weiß zieht

3 (fig.: initiate action) handeln; aktiv werden; **~ quickly** *etc.* **to do sth.** schnell *usw.* handeln und etw. tun

4 (be socially active) (in certain circles, part of society, part of town) verkehren; (in certain part of country) sich aufhalten

5 (change residence or accommodation) umziehen (**to** nach); (into flat etc.) einziehen (**into** in + *Akk.*); (out of town) wegziehen (**out of** aus); (out of flat etc.) ausziehen (**out of** aus); **I want to ~ to London** ich will nach London ziehen; **I hate moving** ich hasse Umzüge

6 (change posture or state) sich bewegen; (in order to make oneself comfortable etc.) eine andere Haltung einnehmen; **don't ~ or I'll shoot** keine Bewegung, oder ich schieße; **nobody/nothing ~d** niemand/nichts rührte sich; **~ aside to make room** zur Seite gehen/rücken, um Platz zu machen; **~ back/forward in one's seat** sich auf seinem Sitz zurücklehnen/vorbeugen; **have your bowels ~d?** hatten Sie Stuhlgang?; haben Sie abgeführt?; **lie without moving** regungslos daliegen

7 (operate) ‹*Maschine:*› laufen; ‹*Pendel:*› schwingen

8 (make progress) vorankommen; **get things moving** vorankommen; **things are moving now** jetzt geht es voran; **~ towards** näher kommen (+ *Dat.*) ‹*Einigung, Höhepunkt, Kompromiss*›; **~ away from** abrücken von ‹*Standpunkt*›; **~ in the direction of sth.** sich auf etw. (*Akk.*) zubewegen

9 (Commerc.: be sold) ‹*Waren:*› Absatz finden, sich absetzen lassen

10 (coll.: go fast) **that car can really ~:** der Wagen ist enorm schnell (ugs.); **that's really moving!** das nenn ich Tempo! (ugs.)

Phrasal verbs

• **~ aˈbout**

A *v.i.* zugange sein; (travel) unterwegs sein; **I need more room to ~ about** ich brauche mehr Bewegungsfreiheit *od.* Spielraum

B *v.t.* herumräumen ‹*Möbel, Bücher*›; herumschieben ‹*Teile einer Collage*›

• **~ aˈlong**

A *v.i.* **1** gehen/fahren **2** (make room) Platz machen; **~ along, please!** gehen/fahren Sie bitte weiter!; (on bus etc.) bitte weiter [durchgehen!

B *v.t.* zum Weitergehen/-fahren auffordern

• **~ aˈround** ▸ **~ about**

• **~ ˈin**

A *v.i.* **1** einziehen; (to start work) ‹*Bauarbeiter:*› kommen **2** (come closer) ‹*Truppen, Polizeikräfte:*› anrücken; ‹*Kamera:*› näher herangehen; **~ in on** ‹*Truppen, Polizeikräfte:*› vorrücken gegen; **~ in on a new market** beginnen, sich auf einem neuen Markt zu etablieren

B *v.t.* einrücken lassen ‹*Truppen, Polizeikräfte*›; hineinbringen ‹*Gepäck, Ausrüstung*›

• **~ ˈoff** *v.i.* sich in Bewegung setzen

• **~ ˈon**

A *v.i.* weitergehen/-fahren; (leave job) sich verändern; **~ on to another question** (fig.) zu einer anderen Frage übergehen

B *v.t.* zum Weitergehen/-fahren auffordern

• **~ ˈout** *v.i.* ausziehen (**of** aus); (in car) nach rechts/(im Rechtsverkehr) links ausbiegen

• **~ ˈover** *v.i.* rücken; **~ over!** (said rudely) Platz da!; **would you mind moving over a little?** würden Sie bitte ein Stück [weiter]rücken?

• **~ ˈup**

A *v.i.* **1** (in queue, hierarchy) aufrücken; ‹*Fahrzeug:*› vorfahren; (to new class) versetzt werden; (to new school) wechseln (**to** auf); **she's moving up in the world** sie kommt voran [im Leben] **2** ▸ **~ over**

B *v.t.* versetzen ‹*Schüler*›

movement /ˈmuːvmənt/ *n.* **1** (change of position or posture, or to and fro) Bewegung, *die;* (of people: towards city, country, etc.) [Ab]wanderung, *die;* (of clouds) Zug, *der;* (of air) Regung, *die;* (trend, tendency) Tendenz, *die,* (fashion) Trend, *der* (**towards** zu); **a ~ of the head/arm/leg** eine Kopf-/Arm-/Beinbewegung; **without ~:** bewegungslos **2** *in pl.* Aktivitäten *Pl.;* **keep track of sb.'s ~s** jmdn. überwachen **3** (Mus.) Satz, *der* **4** (group of people with same aims or ideas) Bewegung, *die* **5** *in sing. or pl.* (Mech. esp. in clock, watch) Räderwerk, *das* **6** (Mil.) Manöver, *das;* (shifting) Verlegung, *die;* (advance) Vorstoß, *der* **7** (mental impulse) Regung, *die* **8** (progressive development) (of plot) Fortgang, *der;* (of story, poem, etc.) Handlung, *die* **9** (Commerc.: activity) Geschäft, *das* (**in** mit); Bewegung im Handel (**in** mit) **10** (rise or fall in price) Preisbewegung, *die;* **a downward/an upward ~ in shares** *or* **share prices/[the price of] coffee** ein Rückgang/Anstieg der Aktienkurse/des Kaffeepreises **11** (of bowels) ▸ **motion A 4**

mover /ˈmuːvə(r)/ *n.* **1** (of proposition) Antragsteller, *der*/-stellerin, *die* **2** (Amer.: of furniture) Möbelspediteur, *der;* (employee) Möbelpacker, *der;* **firm** *or* **company of ~s** Möbelspedition, *die* **3** **prime ~** (God) Schöpfer, *der;* (source of motive power) Energiequelle, *die;* (fig.: of plan etc.) Urheber, *der*/Urheberin, *die* **4** **this animal is a slow** *etc.* **~:** die Bewegungen dieses Tieres sind langsam *usw.;* **she is a beautiful ~:** ihre Bewegungen sind anmutig; **be a slow ~** (think slowly) langsam schalten (ugs.); (work slowly) langsam arbeiten; **be a fast ~:** von der schnellen Truppe sein (ugs.)

movie /ˈmuːvɪ/ *n.* (Amer. coll.) Film, *der; attrib.* Film‹*publikum, -projektor, -studio usw.*›; **the ~s** (art form, cinema industry) der Film; (cinema) das Kino; **go to the ~s** ins Kino gehen

movie: ~-goer *n.* (Amer. coll.) Kinogänger, *der*/-gängerin, *die;* **~ house, ~ theater** *ns.* (Amer. coll.) Kino, *das;* **~s-on-deˈmand** *n., no pl.* Movies-on-Demand-System, *das*

moving /ˈmuːvɪŋ/ *adj.* **1** beweglich; **from a ~ car** ‹*sehen, erkennen*› von einem fahrenden Auto aus; ‹*fallen, werfen, schießen*› aus einem fahrenden Auto **2** (affecting) ergreifend; bewegend; rührend

movingly /ˈmuːvɪŋlɪ/ *adv.* in rührender Weise; ergreifend ‹*schreiben, sprechen*›

moving: ~ ˈpavement *n.* (Brit.) Rollbürgersteig, *der;* **~ ˈpicture** *n.* Film, *der;* **~ ˈsidewalk** (Amer.) ▸ **~ pavement**; **~ ˈspirit** *n.* treibende Kraft; **~ ˈstaircase** *n.* (Brit.) ▸ **escalator 1**

mow /məʊ/ *v.t., p.p.* **~n** /məʊn/*or* **~ed** /məʊd/ mähen ‹*Gras, Getreide, Rasen, Feld usw.*›; **newly-~n** frisch gemäht

(Phrasal verb)
- ~ **'down** *v.t.* niedermähen ‹*Soldaten*›; überfahren ‹*Fußgänger*›; (fig.: rout, smash) zerschlagen ‹*Opposition*›

mower /'məʊə(r)/ *n.* [1] (lawn~) Rasenmäher, *der* [2] (Agric.) Mäher, *der*

'mowing machine ▸ **mower 2**

Mozambican /məʊzəm'bi:kn/ ▸ⓘ **p. 1345**
[A] *adj.* mosambikanisch, mosambikisch
[B] *n.* Mosambikaner, *der*/Mosambikanerin, *die*

Mozambique /məʊzəm'bi:k/ *pr. n.* Mosambik (*das*)

mozzie /'mɒzɪ/ *n.* (coll.) Mücke, *die*

MP *abbr.* [1] = **Member of Parliament; committee of MPs** Unterhausausschuss, *der* [2] = **military police** MP [3] = **military policeman/policewoman** Militärpolizist, *der*/-polizistin, *die* [4] = **melting point** Schmp.

MP'3 player *n.* MP3-Spieler, *der*

mpg /empi:'dʒi:/ *abbr.* (Motor Veh.) **miles per gallon; do/get 34 ~** (Brit.) ≈ 8,3 l auf 100 km [ver]brauchen

mph /empi:'eɪtʃ/ *abbr.* ▸ⓘ **p. 1566** = **miles per hour; How many ~ are we doing? — We are travelling at/driving at/doing 30 ~:** Wie schnell fahren wir? — Wir fahren 50 [km/h]

MPhil /em'fɪl/ *abbr.* = **Master of Philosophy;** *see also* **BSc**

MPV *abbr.* = **multi-purpose vehicle**

Mr /'mɪstə(r)/ *n., pl.* **Messrs** /'mesəz/ ▸ⓘ **p. 1287**, ▸ⓘ **p. 1634** (title) Herr; (third person also) Hr.; (in an address) Herrn; **Messrs** Hrn.; (firm) Fa.; **Mr Right** (joc.: destined husband) der Richtige (ugs.); **Mr Big** (coll.) der Boss (ugs.)

MRI *abbr.* = **magnetic resonance imaging** MRI

Mrs /'mɪsɪz/ *n., pl. same or* **Mesdames** /meɪ 'dæm, meɪ'dɑ:m/ [1] ▸ⓘ **p. 1287**, ▸ⓘ **p. 1634** (title) Frau; (third person also) Fr. [2] (coll.: wife) **the** *or* **my/your** *etc.* **~:** meine/deine *usw.* Madam (ugs. scherzh.). *See also* **mop A 1**

Ms /mɪz/ *n., no pl.* ▸ⓘ **p. 1287**, ▸ⓘ **p. 1634** Frau

MS *abbr.* [1] = **manuscript** Ms. [2] ▸ⓘ **p. 1231** (Med.) = **multiple sclerosis** MS

MSc /emes'si:/ *abbr.* = **Master of Science** ≈ Mag. rer. nat. (österr.); *see also* **BSc**

MSS *abbr.* /em'esɪz/ = **manuscripts** Mss.

Mt. *abbr.* = **Mount; ~ Etna/Everest/Sinai** (Geog.) der Ätna/der Mount Everest/der Berg Sinai

mth *abbr.* = **month**

much /mʌtʃ/
[A] *adj.*, **more** /mɔ:(r)/, **most** /məʊst/ [1] viel; groß ‹*Erleichterung, Sorge, Dankbarkeit, Verachtung*›; **with ~ love** voller Liebe; **with ~ love from ...** (familiar ending to letter) herzlichst, ...; **he never eats ~ breakfast/lunch/supper** er isst nicht viel zum Frühstück/zu Mittag/zum Abendbrot; **too ~:** zu viel *indekl.*
[2] **be a bit ~** (coll.) ein bisschen zu viel sein; (fig.) ein bisschen zu weit gehen. *See also* **good C 2; how A; nothing A 1; so A 1; this C; too 1**
[B] *n.; see also* **more B; most B;** vieles; **we don't see ~ of her any more** wir sehen sie kaum noch; **we haven't ~ to go on yet** bis jetzt haben wir noch nicht viel; **that doesn't come** *or* **amount to ~:** es kommt nicht viel dabei heraus; **he/this beer isn't up to ~** (coll.) mit ihm/diesem Bier ist nicht viel los (ugs.); **spend ~ of the day/week/month doing sth.** den Großteil des Tages/der Woche/des Monats damit verbringen, etw. zu tun; **they have done ~ to improve the situation** sie haben viel für die Verbesserung der Situation getan; **not be ~ of a cinema-goer** *etc.* (coll.) kein großer Kinogänger *usw.* sein (ugs.); **not have ~ of a singing voice/head for heights** keine besonders schöne Stimme haben/leicht schwindelig werden; **it isn't ~ of a bicycle/car/house** es ist kein besonders tolles Fahrrad/Auto/Haus (ugs.); **not be ~ to look at** nicht sehr ansehnlich sein; **he/the plan/plant didn't come to ~:** aus ihm/dem Plan/der Pflanze ist nichts Richtiges geworden; **it's as ~ as she can do to get up the stairs** sie kommt gerade noch die Treppe hinauf; **I expected/thought as ~:** das habe ich erwartet/mir gedacht; **he stared at me as ~ as to say ...:** er starrte mich an, als ob er sagen wollte: ...; **you are as ~ to blame as he is** du bist ebenso sehr schuld wie er; **she knows as ~ as we do** sie weiß genauso viel wie wir; **we didn't have so ~ as the bus fare home** wir hatten nicht einmal das Geld für den Bus nach Hause; **without so ~ as saying goodbye/a backward glance** ohne auch nur Auf Wiedersehen zu sagen/einen Blick zurückzuwerfen; *see also* **again 1; as A; in 1; make A 13; so A 1; think A 1; up A 22**
[C] *adv.*, **more, most** [1] *modifying comparatives* viel ‹*besser*›; **~ more lively/happy/attractive** viel lebhafter/glücklicher/attraktiver
[2] *modifying superlatives* mit Abstand ‹*der/die/das Beste, Schlechteste, Klügste usw.*›
[3] *modifying passive participles and predicative adjectives* sehr; **he is ~ improved** (in behaviour) er hat sich sehr gebessert; (in health) es geht ihm viel besser
[4] *modifying verbs* (greatly) sehr ‹*lieben, mögen, genießen*›; (often) oft ‹*sehen, treffen, besuchen*›; (frequently) viel; **she loved him too ~:** sie liebte ihn zu sehr; **I don't ~ like him** *or* **like him ~:** ich mag ihn nicht besonders; **not go ~ on sb./sth.** (coll.) nicht viel von jmdm./etw. halten; **it doesn't matter ~:** es ist nicht so wichtig; **I don't very ~ want to come** ich habe keine sehr große Lust zu kommen; **I would ~ prefer to stay at home** ich würde viel lieber zu Hause bleiben; **~ to my surprise/annoyance, I found that ...:** zu meiner großen Überraschung/Verärgerung stellte ich fest, dass ...; **it's not so ~ a problem of money as of time** es ist nicht so sehr ein finanzielles als ein zeitliches Problem
[5] (approximately) fast; **[pretty** *or* **very] ~ the same** fast [genau] der-/die-/dasselbe; **the old house was ~ as it had always been** das alte Haus hatte sich kaum verändert
[6] (for a large part of time) viel ‹*gärtnern, lesen, spielen*›; (often) oft; häufig
[7] **~ as** *or* **though** (although) sosehr ... auch; **~ as he disliked the idea** sosehr ihm die Idee auch missfiel; **~ as I should like to go** so gern ich auch gehen würde
[8] **not ~** (coll.: certainly not) nicht die Bohne (ugs.); denkste! (ugs.). *See also* **less B; oblige A 4; same A**

muchly /'mʌtʃlɪ/ *adv.* (joc.) sehr ‹*beeindruckt*›; **ta** *or* **thanks ~!** tausend Dank! (ugs.)

muchness /'mʌtʃnɪs/ *n., no pl., no def. art.* **be much of a ~** (coll.) sich (*Dat.*) so ziemlich gleichen (ugs.); **they are much of a ~ when it comes to ...:** wenn es um ... geht, kann der eine es nicht besser als der andere

muck /mʌk/
[A] *n.* [1] (farmyard manure) Mist, *der; see also* **common A 5** [2] (coll.: anything disgusting) Dreck, *der* (ugs.); (liquid) Brühe, *die* (ugs. abwertend); **covered in ~:** verdreckt (ugs.) [3] (coll.: defamatory remarks, nonsense) Mist, *der* (ugs.); Dreck, *der* (ugs.) [4] (coll.: untidy state) Schweinerei, *die* (derb abwertend); **make a ~ of sth.** (coll.) [bei einer Sache] Mist bauen (ugs.)
[B] *v.t.* ▸ **muck up 2**

(Phrasal verbs)
- **~ a'bout, ~ a'round** (Brit. coll.)
  [A] *v.i.* [1] herumalbern (ugs.) [2] (tinker) herumfummeln (**with** an + *Dat.*)
  [B] *v.t.* [1] herumstreifen *od.* umherstreifen in (+ *Dat.*) (ugs.) ‹*Stadt, Straße*› [2] **~ sb. about** *or* **around** jmdn. verarschen (derb); **the bank really ~ed us about** es war ein ewiges Hin und Her mit der Bank (ugs.)
- **~ 'in** *v.i.* (coll.) mit zugreifen *od.* mit anpacken (**with** bei)
- **~ 'out** *v.t.* ausmisten ‹*Stall*›; (fig.) aufräumen ‹*Haus, Garage, Zimmer*›
- **~ 'up** *v.t.* [1] (Brit. coll.: bungle) vermurksen, verbocken (ugs.); **~ it up** Mist bauen (ugs.) [2] (make dirty) voll schmieren, dreckig machen (ugs.); einsauen (derb) [3] (coll.: spoil) vermasseln (salopp). *See also* **muck-up**

muckle /'mʌkl/ ▸ **mickle**

muck: ~raker /'mʌkreɪkə(r)/ *n.* **he's just a ~raker** er ist nur auf Sensationen aus; **~raking** /'mʌkreɪkɪŋ/ [A] *adj.* skandalträchtig ‹*Rede, Brief, Angriff, Politik*›; skandalsüchtig (abwertend) ‹*Person*›; Skandal‹*artikel, -blatt, -journalismus, -presse*› (abwertend); [B] *n.* Skandalhascherei, *die* (abwertend); Sensationsmache, *die* (ugs. abwertend); **~-up** *n.* (Brit. coll.) (confusing or confused situation) Kuddelmuddel, *der od. das* (ugs.); (blunder, mess) Mist, *der* (ugs.); **make a ~-up of sth.** etw. vermasseln (salopp)

mucky /'mʌkɪ/ *adj.* dreckig (ugs.); (with manure) mistig; (fig.) schmierig ‹*Zeitung, Witz, usw.*›

mucous /'mju:kəs/ *adj.* (Med., Bot., Zool.) schleimig; Schleim-; mukös (fachspr.)

mucous 'membrane *n.* Schleimhaut, *die*

mucus /'mju:kəs/ *n.* (Med., Bot., Zool.) Schleim, *der*

mud /mʌd/ *n.* [1] Schlamm, *der;* Morast, *der;* **patch/expanse** *or* **area of ~:** schlammige *od.* morastige Stelle/Fläche; **covered with ~:** schlammbedeckt; **be as clear as ~** (joc. iron.) absolut unklar sein; **[here's] ~ in your eye!** (coll. dated.) Pröstercher! (fam.) [2] (hard ground) Lehm, *der; attrib.* Lehm-; lehmig; **~ hut** Lehmhütte, *die* [3] (fig.) **be dragged through the ~:** in den Schmutz gezogen werden; **his name is ~** (coll.) er ist unten durch (ugs.) (**with** bei); **fling** *or* **sling** *or* **throw ~ at sb.** (fig.) jmdn. mit Dreck (ugs.) *od.* Schmutz bewerfen; *see also* **stick A 5; stick-in-the-mud**

'mudbath *n.* (Med.; also fig.) Schlammbad, *das*

muddle /'mʌdl/
[A] *n.* Durcheinander, *das;* **the room is in a hopeless ~:** in dem Zimmer herrscht ein heilloses Durcheinander *od.* eine heillose Unordnung; **get sth. in a ~:** etw. in Unordnung bringen; etw. durcheinander bringen; **my mind/brain is in a ~:** ich bin ganz durcheinander; ich kann nicht klar denken; **get/get sb. in[to] a ~:** durcheinander kommen (ugs.)/jmdn. durcheinander bringen; **make a ~ of sth.** (bungle) etw. verpfuschen
[B] *v.t.* [1] **~ [up]** durcheinander bringen; **~ up** (mix up) verwechseln (**with** mit); **be ~d up** (out of order) durcheinander geraten sein [2] (mismanage) verderben
[C] *v.i.* wursteln (ugs.) (**with** an + *Dat.*)

(Phrasal verbs)
- **~ a'long, ~ 'on** *v.i.* vor sich (*Akk.*) hin wursteln (ugs.) (**with** bei); **~ on towards sth.** planlos auf etw. (*Akk.*) hinarbeiten
- **~ 'through** *v.i.* sich durchwursteln (ugs.)

muddled /'mʌdld/ *adj.* [1] (confused) benebelt ‹*Person*›; konfus ‹*Verhalten, Denken*› [2] (mixed-up, jumbled) verworren ‹*Situation, Information, Ideen*›

muddle-'headed *adj.* wirr[köpfig]; **a ~ thinker/person** ein Wirrkopf

muddy /'mʌdɪ/
[A] *adj.* [1] schlammig; **get** *or* **grow** *or* **become ~:** verschlammen [2] (turbid, dull) trübe ‹*Flüssigkeit, Licht, Farbe*›; grau ‹*Haut*› [3] (obscure) wirr; **a ~ thinker** ein Wirrkopf
[B] *v.t.* (cover with mud) schmutzig machen; (make turbid) trüben ‹*Flüssigkeit*›; **~ the waters** (fig.) die Dinge [noch] undurchschaubarer *od.* verworrener machen; für zusätzliche Verwirrung sorgen

mud: ~flap *n.* (Motor Veh.) Schmutzfänger, *der;* **~flat[s]** *n.* [*pl.*] (Geog.) Watt, *das;* **~guard** *n.* Schutzblech, *das;* (of car) Kotflügel, *der;* **~pack** *n.* Schlammpackung [für das Gesicht]; Gesichtsmaske aus Schlamm; **~ 'pie** *n.* Kuchen *aus Sand usw.;* **~slide** *n.* Schlammlawine, *die;* **~ vol'cano** *n.* (Geog.) Schlammvulkan, *der;* Salse, *die* (fachspr.)

muesli /'mju:zlɪ/ *n.* Müsli, *das*

muezzin /mʊ'ezɪn/ *n.* Muezzin, *der*

muff[1] /mʌf/ *n.* (for hands) Muff, *der; see also* **earmuffs; footmuff**

muff[2]
[A] *n.* (person) Tölpel, *der* (abwertend)
[B] *v.t.* [1] (bungle) verderben; verpatzen (ugs.); verhauen (ugs.) ‹*Examen*›; **I ~ed everything today** mir ging heute alles daneben (ugs.) [2] (Theatre) verpatzen (ugs.); **~ a line** einen Patzer machen (ugs.)

muffin /'mʌfɪn/ *n.* Muffin, *der*

m

muffle /ˈmʌfl/ *v.t.* 1 (envelop) ~ **[up]** einhüllen; einmumme[l]n (ugs.) 2 (deaden [sound of]) dämpfen ‹*Geräusch*›; [zur Schalldämpfung] umwickeln ‹*Fuß, Schuh, Ruder, Trommel, Glocke*›; ~ **sb.'s cries/screams** ‹*Kopfkissen, Wand:*› jmds. Schreie dämpfen; ‹*Person:*› jmdn. am Schreien hindern 3 (suppress sound of) unterdrücken ‹*Fluch, Bemerkung*›; hinunterschlucken ‹*Fluch*›

muffler /ˈmʌflə(r)/ *n.* 1 (wrap, scarf) Schal, *der* 2 (deadener of sound) Dämpfer, *der* 3 (Amer. Motor Veh.: silencer) Schalldämpfer, *der;* Auspufftopf, *der*

mufti /ˈmʌftɪ/ *n.* 1 (plain clothes) Zivil, *das;* **in** ~: in Zivil 2 (Muslim priest) Mufti, *der*

mug[1] /mʌg/

A *n.* 1 (vessel, contents) Becher, *der* (meist mit Henkel); (for beer etc.) Krug, *der;* **a** ~ **of milk** ein Becher Milch 2 (coll.: face, mouth) Visage, *die* (salopp); Fresse, *die* (derb) 3 (Brit. coll.: simpleton) Schwachkopf, *der* (ugs.) 4 (Brit. coll.: gullible person) Trottel, *der* (ugs. abwertend); Doofi, *der* (ugs.); **make a** ~ **of sb.** jmdn. anschmieren *od.* beschupsen (salopp); **that's a mug's game** das macht kein klar denkender Mensch (ugs.) 5 (Amer. coll.: hoodlum) Ganove, *der* (ugs.)

B *v.t.*, **-gg-** (rob) überfallen und berauben

mug[2] (Brit. coll.: study) *v.t.*, **-gg-:** ~ **up** büffeln (ugs.) ‹*Fach, Zitate, Formeln*›; durchackern (ugs.) ‹*Buch, Notizen*›

mugful /ˈmʌgfʊl/ (contents) ▸ **mug[1] A 1**

mugger /ˈmʌgə(r)/ *n.* Straßenräuber, *der*/Straßenräuberin, *die*

mugginess /ˈmʌgɪnɪs/ *n., no pl.* Schwüle, *die*

mugging /ˈmʌgɪŋ/ *n.* Straßenraub, *der* (**of** an + *Dat.*)

muggins /ˈmʌgɪnz/ *n., pl.* ~**es** *or same* (coll.) 1 (simpleton) Dummkopf, *der* (ugs.); Esel, *der* (ugs.) 2 (myself, stupidly) ich Dummkopf (ugs.)

muggy /ˈmʌgɪ/ *adj.* schwül; drückend ‹*Klima, Zeit, Tag, Luft*›; **a** ~ **place** ein Ort mit schwülem Klima

ˈ**mug shot** *n.* (coll.) 1 **[police]** ~**s of criminals** Verbrecherfotos 2 (passport photo etc.) [Pass]foto, *das*

mugwort /ˈmʌgwɜːt/ *n.* (Bot.) Beifuß, *der*

Muhammadan /məˈhæmədn/ (Relig.)

A *n.* Moslem, *der*

B *adj.* moslemisch

Muhammadanism /məˈhæmədənɪzm/ *n., no pl.* (Relig.) Islam, *der*

mulatto /mjuːˈlætəʊ/ *n., pl.* ~**s** (*Amer.:* ~**es**) Mulatte, *der*/Mulattin, *die*

mulberry /ˈmʌlbərɪ/ *n.* 1 (fruit) Maulbeere, *die; attrib.* Maulbeer- 2 (tree) Maulbeerbaum, *der; attrib.* Maulbeer-

mulch /mʌltʃ/ (Agric., Hort.)

A *n.* Mulch, *der*

B *v.t.* mulchen

mulct /mʌlkt/ *v.t.* 1 (Law: fine) eine Geldstrafe auferlegen (geh.) (+ *Dat.*) 2 (literary: deprive) berauben (geh.) (**of** *Gen.*)

mule[1] /mjuːl/ *n.* 1 (Zool.) Maultier, *das;* **have a kick like a** ~ (fig.) einen umwerfen; *see also* **obstinate; stubborn 1** 2 (coll.) (stupid person) Esel, *der* (ugs.); (obstinate person) Dickkopf, *der* (ugs.) 3 (Textiles) Mule-Maschine, *die*

mule[2] *n.* (slipper) Pantoffel, *der*

muleteer /mjuːlɪˈtɪə(r)/ *n.* Maultiertreiber, *der*/Maultiertreiberin, *die*

mulish /ˈmjuːlɪʃ/ *adj.* (stubborn) stur; ~ **stubbornness/obstinacy** Sturheit, *die*

mull[1] /mʌl/ *v.t.* ~ **over** nachdenken über (+ *Akk.*); (in conversation) diskutieren

mull[2] *v.t.* (prepare) erhitzen und würzen ‹*Wein*›; ~ **wine** Glühwein zubereiten; ~**ed wine** Glühwein, *der*

mull[3] *n.* (Scot.: promontory) Kap, *das*

mullah /ˈmʌlə/ *n.* (Islam) Mullah, *der*

mullet /ˈmʌlɪt/ *n., pl.* ~**s** *or same* (Zool.) **red** ~: Gewöhnliche Meerbarbe; **grey** ~: Meeräsche, *die*

mulligatawny /mʌlɪgəˈtɔːnɪ/ *n.* ~ **[soup]** Mulligatawny-Suppe, *die* (*mit Curry scharf gewürzte indische Geflügelsuppe*)

mullion /ˈmʌljən/ *n.* 1 (Archit.) Längspfosten, *der* 2 *in pl.* (Gothic Archit.) Stabwerk, *das*

mullioned /ˈmʌljənd/ *adj.* längs unterteilt; ~ **windows** Fenster mit Stabwerk

multi- /ˈmʌltɪ/ *pref.* (several) mehr-/Mehr-; (many) viel-/Viel-; multi-/Multi-, poly-/Poly- (bes. mit Fremdwörtern)

multi: ~**channel** *adj.* mehrkanalig; Mehrkanal‹*system, -verstärker, -receiver etc.*›; ~**coloured** (*Brit.; Amer.:* ~**colored**) *adj.* (with several colours) mehrfarbig, (with many colours) vielfarbig ‹*Gegenstand, Tier, Pflanze*›; bunt ‹*Stoff, Kleid*›; ~ˈ**cultural** *adj.* multikulturell; ~ˈ**culturalism** /mʌltɪˈkʌltʃərəlɪzm/ *n., no pl.* Multikulturalismus, *der;* ~**disciˈplinary** *adj.* multidisziplinär

multifarious /mʌltɪˈfeərɪəs/ *adj.* 1 (having great variety) vielgestaltig 2 (many and various) mannigfach; vielfältig

multi: ~ˈ**functional** *adj.* multifunktional; ~ **device** Multifunktionsgerät, *das;* ~**function button** *n.* Multifunktionstaste, *die;* ~**grade** *adj., n.:* ~**grade [oil]** Mehrbereichsöl, *das;* ~**gym** *n.* 1 (equipment) Multifunktionsfitnessgerät, *das;* 2 (room) Fitnessraum, *der;* ~ˈ**lateral** *adj.* mehrseitig; (Polit.) multilateral

multilingual /mʌltɪˈlɪŋgwəl/ *adj.* mehrsprachig

multi: ~**media** *n. sing.* Multimedia, *das; attrib.* Multimedia-; ~**million** *adj.* in Millionenhöhe *nachgestellt;* Millionen‹*investitionen, -absätze*›; ~**millioˈnaire** *n.* Multimillionär, *der*/-millionärin, *die;* ~ˈ**national A** *adj.* multinational. **B** *n.* (Econ.) multinationaler Konzern; Multi, *der* (ugs.); ~**pack** *n.* Multipack, *der*

multiple /ˈmʌltɪpl/

A *adj.* 1 (manifold) mehrfach; ~ **birth** Mehrlingsgeburt, *die;* ~ **crash/pile-up** Massenkarambolage, *die* 2 (many and various) vielerlei; vielfältig; mannigfach 3 (Bot.) multipel; ~ **fruit** Sammelfrucht, *die. See also* **sclerosis 1**

B *n.* 1 (Math.) Vielfache, *das; see also* **common multiple** 2 ▸ **multiple store**

multiple: ~-ˈ**choice** *adj.* Multiple-Choice-‹*Verfahren, Test, Frage*›; ~ ˈ**ownership** *n., no pl.* gemeinschaftliches Eigentum; ~ ˈ**store** *n.* (Brit.) Kettenladen, *der*

multiplex /ˈmʌltɪpleks/

A *adj.* Multiplex- ‹*kino, -filmtheater etc.*›

B *n.* (Cinema) Multiplex[-kino], *das*

multiplication /mʌltɪplɪˈkeɪʃn/ *n.* (increase) Vervielfachung, *die;* (Math.) Multiplikation, *die* (fachspr.); Malnehmen, *das; attrib.* Multiplikations-; **do/use** ~: multiplizieren (fachspr.); malnehmen; ~ **sign** Malzeichen, *das;* ~ **table** Multiplikationstabelle, *die;* **do** *or* **learn/recite** *or* **say/practise one's** ~ **table[s]** das Einmaleins lernen/aufsagen/üben

multiplicity /mʌltɪˈplɪsɪtɪ/ *n.* 1 (manifold variety) Vielfalt, *die* (**of, in** an, von + *Dat. Pl.*); ~ **in size/age** Größen-/Altersvielfalt, *die;* ~ **of habits/beliefs/ideas** vielfältige Gewohnheiten/Überzeugungen/Ideen 2 (great number) Vielzahl, *die* (**of** von, an + *Dat.*)

multiply[1] /ˈmʌltɪplaɪ/

A *v.t.* 1 (Math., also abs.) multiplizieren (fachspr.), malnehmen (**by** mit) 2 (increase) vervielfachen; **be multiplied** sich vervielfachen 3 (Biol.) fortpflanzen; züchten

B *v.i.* (Biol.) sich vermehren; sich fortpflanzen; **be fruitful and** ~ (Bibl.) seid fruchtbar und mehret euch (bibl.)

multiply[2] /ˈmʌltɪplɪ/ *adv.* mehrfach

ˈ**multi-purpose** *adj.* Mehrzweck-

multi-purpose ˈ**vehicle** *n.* Großraumlimousine, *die*

multiˈracial *adj.* mehrrassig; gemischtrassig

multiˈracialism *n., no pl.* Gemischtrassigkeit, *die*

multi: ~**-screen** *n.* Multiplex, *das;* ~**-speed** *adj.* ~**-speed gearbox** Mehrganggetriebe, *das;* **a** ~**-speed Europe** ein Europa der verschiedenen Geschwindigkeiten; ~**-stage** *adj.* mehrstufig; Mehrstufen-; ~**-storey** *adj.* mehrstöckig; mehrgeschossig; ~**-storey car park/block of flats** Parkhaus/Wohnhochhaus, *das;* ~**task A** *v.i.* 1 (perform different tasks) mehrere Dinge gleichzeitig erledigen; 2 (Computing) mehrere Operationem gleichzeitig ausführen; **B** *v.t.* (Computing) gleichzeitig ausführen ‹*mehrere Programme*›; im Multitask-Betriebssystem laufen lassen ‹*mehrere Geräte*›; ~**tasking** /ˈmʌltɪtɑːskɪŋ/ *n., no pl.* (Computing) Multitasking, *das;* ~**tool** *n.* Multifunktionswerkzeug, *das;* ~**track** *adj.* mehrspurig; Mehrspur‹*aufnahme, -ton, -tonbandgerät*›

multitude /ˈmʌltɪtjuːd/ *n.* 1 (crowd) Menge, *die;* (great number) Vielzahl, *die;* **cover a** ~ **of sins** (joc.) ein weites Feld umfassen; (compensate) vieles aufwiegen; **a** ~ **of animals/vehicles/men** eine Vielzahl von Tieren/Fahrzeugen/Männern 2 **the [common]** ~: die [breite] Masse (oft abwertend) 3 (numerousness) Vielheit, *die*

multitudinous /mʌltɪˈtjuːdɪnəs/ *adj.* 1 (comprising many individuals) vielköpfig ‹*Herde, Versammlung*› 2 (very many) zahlreich

ˈ**multi-volume** *adj.* vielbändig

mum[1] /mʌm/ (coll.)

A *int.* pst; ~**'s the word** nicht weitersagen!; (I won't tell anyone else) ich sags nicht weiter

B *adj.* leise; ruhig; still; **keep** ~: den Mund halten (ugs.); **keep** ~ **about sth.** etw. nicht weitersagen

mum[2] *n.* (Brit. coll.: mother) Mama, *die* (fam.)

mumble /ˈmʌmbl/

A *v.i.* nuscheln (ugs.); ~ **[away] about sth.** über etw. (*Akk.*) nuscheln (ugs.)

B *v.t.* 1 (utter indistinctly) nuscheln (ugs.); ~ **one's words/phrases** *etc.* nuscheln (ugs.) 2 (chew) mit zahnlosem Mund kauen

C *n.* Nuscheln, *das*

mumbo-jumbo /mʌmbəʊˈdʒʌmbəʊ/ *n., pl.* ~**s** 1 (meaningless ritual) Brimborium, *das* (ugs.); Theater, *das* (ugs. abwertend) 2 (gibberish) Kauderwelsch, *das* 3 (object of senseless veneration) Idol, *das;* Götze, *der*

mummer /ˈmʌmə(r)/ *n.* (Theatre) Pantomime, *der*/Pantomimin, *die*

mummery /ˈmʌmərɪ/ *n.* (derog.) Mummenschanz, *der* (abwertend)

mummify /ˈmʌmɪfaɪ/ *v.t.* 1 mumifizieren 2 (shrivel) austrocknen

mummy[1] /ˈmʌmɪ/ *n.* Mumie, *die*

mummy[2] *n.* (Brit. coll.: mother) Mutti, *die* (fam.); Mami, *die* (fam.); Mama, *die* (fam.)

mumps /mʌmps/ *n. sing.* ▸ⓘ **p. 1231** (Med.) Mumps, *der*

munch /mʌnʃ/

A *v.t.* ~ **one's food** mampfen (salopp); schmatzend kauen

B *v.i.* mampfen (salopp); ~ **[away] at sth.** an etw. (*Dat.*) kauen

munchkin /ˈmʌntʃkɪn/ *n.* (Amer. coll) Wonneproppen, *der* (ugs. scherzh.)

mundane /mʌnˈdeɪn/ *adj.* 1 (dull) banal; profan (geh.); stumpfsinnig ‹*Entschluss, Routine*› 2 (worldly) weltlich; irdisch

mung bean /ˈmʌŋ biːn/ *n.* Mung[o]bohne, *die*

Munich /ˈmjuːnɪk/ *pr. n.* München (*das*); *attrib.* Münchner

municipal /mjuːˈnɪsɪpl/ *adj.* gemeindlich; kommunal; Kommunal‹*politik, -verwaltung*›; Gemeinde‹*rat, -verwaltung, -beschluss*›; ~ **district** (Can., Austral.) Landgemeinde, *die*

municipality /mjuːnɪsɪˈpælɪtɪ/ *n.* 1 (political unit) Gemeinde, *die* 2 (governing body) Gemeindeverwaltung, *die*

munificence /mjuːˈnɪfɪsəns/ *n.* (formal) Generosität, *die;* Hochherzigkeit, *die* (geh.)

munificent /mjuːˈnɪfɪsənt/ *adj.*, **munificently** /mjuːˈnɪfɪsəntlɪ/ *adv.* (formal) generös (geh.)

munition /mjuːˈnɪʃn/ *n., usu. in pl.* Kriegsmaterial, *das;* ~**s dump** Munitionsdepot, *das;* ~**[s] factory** Rüstungsbetrieb, *der;* ~**[s] worker** Arbeiter in einem Rüstungsbetrieb

muntjac, muntjak /ˈmʌntdʒæk/ *n.* (Zool.) Muntjak, *der*

m

mural /ˈmjʊərl/
A *adj.* (on a wall) Wand-; an Wänden *nachgestellt*
B *n.* Wandbild, *das;* Wandgemälde, *das;* (on ceiling) Deckengemälde, *das*

murder /ˈmɜːdə(r)/
A *n.* 1) (Law) Mord, *der* (**of** an + *Dat.*); *attrib.* ~ **case** Mordfall, *der; attrib.* ~ **charge** Mordanklage, *die;* ~ **hunt** Fahndung nach dem/einem Mörder; ~ **investigation** Ermittlungen *Pl.* in dem/einem Mordfall; ~ **victim** Mordopfer, *das;* **be accused of** ~**:** des Mordes beschuldigt werden; **be arrested on a charge of** ~**:** unter Mordverdacht verhaftet werden; ~ **will out** (prov.: sth. cannot be hidden) die Wahrheit kommt doch an den Tag 2) (fig.) **the exam/journey was** ~**:** die Prüfung/Reise war der glatte *od.* reine Mord (ugs.). *See also* **blue murder**; **get away with 3**; **judicial 1**
B *v.t.* 1) (kill unlawfully) ermorden; ~ **sb. with a gun/knife** jmdn. erschießen/erstechen; **I could** ~ **him/a hamburger/a beer** (fig. coll.) ich könnte ihn umbringen/einen Hamburger vertragen/ein Bier vertragen (ugs.) 2) (coll.: spoil) verhunzen (ugs.) 3) (coll.: defeat) fertig machen (ugs.)

murderer /ˈmɜːdərə(r)/ *n.* Mörder, *der*/Mörderin, *die;* **be accused of being a** ~**:** des Mordes beschuldigt werden

murderess /ˈmɜːdərɪs/ *n.* Mörderin, *die*

murderous /ˈmɜːdərəs/ *adj.* tödlich; Mord‹*absicht, -drohung*›; vernichtend ‹*Blick*›; mörderisch (ugs.) ‹*Fahrweise, Wetter, Kampf, Bedingung*›; ~ **nature/mentality/psychology** Wesen/Mentalität/Psyche eines Mörders

murk /mɜːk/ *n.* Dunkelheit, *die;* Nebelnacht, *die* (geh.)

murky /ˈmɜːkɪ/ *adj.* 1) (dark) düster; trüb ‹*Tag, Wetter*› 2) (dirty) schmutzig-trüb ‹*Wasser*› 3) (thick, opaque) trüb ‹*Luft, Atmosphäre*›; verhangen ‹*Himmel*›; tief ‹*Dunkelheit*›; (fig.: obscure) dunkel; undurchsichtig; unergründlich ‹*Geheimnis, Tiefen*›; ~ **past** dunkle Vergangenheit

murmur /ˈmɜːmə(r)/
A *n.* 1) (subdued sound) Rauschen, *das;* (of brook also) Murmeln, *das* (dichter.); (of bee) Summen, *das* 2) (Med.) **heart** ~**:** Herzgeräusch, *das;* Klappengeräusch, *das* 3) (expression of discontent) Murren, *das;* **raise a few** ~**s** einige unzufriedene Stimmen laut werden lassen; ~ **of disagreement/impatience** ablehnendes/ungeduldiges Murren; **without a** ~**:** ohne Murren; ohne zu murren 4) (soft speech) Murmeln, *das;* ~ **of approval/delight** beifälliges/freudiges Murmeln; **a** ~ **of voices** ein Gemurmel; **say sth. in a** ~**:** etw. murmeln
B *v.t.* murmeln; raunen (geh.), hauchen ‹*Zärtlichkeiten*›
C *v.i.* 1) ‹*Person:*› murmeln; (make soft sound) ‹*Brise:*› rauschen 2) (complain) murren (**against, at** über + *Akk.*)

murphy /ˈmɜːfɪ/ *n.* (coll.) Kartoffel, *die;* Knolle, *die* (ugs.)

muscadel ▸ **muscatel**

muscat /ˈmʌskət/ *n.* (grape) Muskattraube, *die;* (vine) Muskatrebe, *die*

muscatel /mʌskəˈtel/ *n.* 1) (raisin) Muskadinerosine, *die* 2) (wine) Muskateller[wein], *der*

muscle /ˈmʌsl/
A *n.* 1) ▸ⓘ **p. 951** Muskel, *der;* **not move a** ~ (fig.) sich nicht rühren 2) (tissue) Muskeln *Pl.;* **be all** ~**:** nur aus Muskeln bestehen 3) (muscular power) [Muskel-, Körper]kraft, *die;* Muskeln *Pl.;* (fig.: force, power, influence) Stärke, *die;* **have financial** ~**:** finanzkräftig *od.* -stark sein; [finanziell] potent sein; **have industrial** ~**:** eine leistungsfähige Industrie haben
B *v.i.* ~ **ˈin** (coll.) sich hineindrängen (**on** in + *Akk.*); **they're muscling in on our market** sie machen sich auf unserem Markt breit (ugs.); **you're muscling in [on my territory]** (fig.) du kommst mir ins Gehege

muscle: ~**-bound** *adj.* 1) (with powerful muscles) muskelbepackt (ugs.); 2) (with stiff muscles) **be** ~**-bound** Muskelkater haben; (fig.) verknöchert sein; **become** ~**-bound** (fig.) verknöchern; ~**man** *n.* 1) (intimidator) Gorilla, *der* (ugs.); 2) (sb. with powerful physique) Muskelmann, *der* (ugs.); ~ **shirt** *n.* Muskelshirt, *das*

Muscovite /ˈmʌskəvaɪt/
A *n.* Moskauer, *der*/Moskauerin, *die;* Moskowiter, *der*/Moskowiterin, *die* (veralt.)
B *adj.* moskauisch, Moskauer ‹*Winter, Arbeiter*›

muscular /ˈmʌskjʊlə(r)/ *adj.* 1) (Med.) Muskel-; muskulär (fachspr.) 2) (strong) muskulös. *See also* **dystrophy**

muscularity /mʌskjʊˈlærɪtɪ/ *n., no pl.* Muskulosität, *die*

muse[1] /mjuːz/ *n.* 1) **M**~ (Greek and Roman Mythol.) Muse, *die* 2) (Lit.) Genius, *der* (geh.)

muse[2] (literary)
A *v.i.* (ponder) grübeln; [nach]sinnen (geh.), sinnieren (**on, about, over** über + *Akk.*)
B *v.t.* sinnieren

museum /mjuːˈziːəm/ *n.* Museum, *das;* **an art** ~**, a** ~ **of art** ein Kunstmuseum; **a** ~ **of modern art** ein Museum für moderne Kunst

muˈseum piece *n.* 1) (specimen of art) Museumsstück, *das* 2) (joc. derog.) (old-fashioned thing) Museumsstück, *das* (ugs. iron.); (old-fashioned person) Fossil, *das*

mush[1] /mʌʃ/ *n.* 1) (soft pulp) Mus, *das;* Brei, *der;* **boil into a** ~ ‹*Kartoffeln:*› zu Mus kochen *od.* verkochen; ~ **of mud/snow** Matsch, *der* 2) (weak sentimentality) Schmalz, *der* (ugs. abwertend)

mush[2] /mʊʃ/ *n.* (sl.: face, mouth) Schnauze, *die* (derb)

mushroom /ˈmʌʃrʊm, ˈmʌʃruːm/
A *n.* 1) Pilz, *der;* (edible) [Speise]pilz, *der;* (cultivated, esp. Agaricus campestris) Champignon, *der; attrib.* Pilz-; **grow like** ~**s** (fig.) wie Pilze aus dem Boden schießen 2) (fig.) ~ **of smoke** Rauchpilz, *der; see also* **mushroom cloud**
B *v.i.* 1) (spring up) wie Pilze aus dem Boden schießen; (grow rapidly) **demand** ~**ed overnight** die Nachfrage schoss über Nacht in die Höhe 2) (expand and flatten) ‹*Aschenwolke, Rauch:*› sich pilzförmig ausbreiten

mushroom: ~ **cloud** *n.* Rauchpilz, *der;* (after nuclear explosion) Atompilz, *der;* ~**-colour** *n.* blasses Gelbbraun; ~**-coloured** *adj.* blass gelbbraun

mushy /ˈmʌʃɪ/ *adj.* 1) (soft) breiig; matschig ‹*Boden*› 2) (feebly sentimental) schmalzig (abwertend); gefühlsduselig (ugs. abwertend) ‹*Mensch*›; **be full of** ~ **sentiment** vor Schmalz triefen (abwertend)

music /ˈmjuːzɪk/ *n.* 1) Musik, *die;* **make** ~**:** Musik machen; musizieren; **student of** ~**:** Musikstudent, *der*/-studentin, *die;* **piece of** ~**:** Musikstück, *das;* Musik, *die;* **set** *or* **put sth. to** ~**:** etw. vertonen *od.* in Musik setzen; **have a gift for** ~**:** musikalisch begabt *od.* musikbegabt sein; **be** ~ **to sb.'s ears** (fig.) Musik in jmds. Ohren sein (ugs.); *see also* **face B 3**; **set A 19**; **sphere 3** 2) (of waves, wind, brook) Rauschen, *das;* (of birds) Gesang, *der* 3) (score) Noten *Pl.;* (as merchandise also) Musikalien *Pl.;* **sheet of** ~**:** Notenblatt, *das;* **play from** ~**:** nach Noten spielen

musical /ˈmjuːzɪkl/
A *adj.* 1) (of music) musikalisch ‹*Abend, Begabung*›; Musik‹*instrument, -verein, -verständnis, -notation, -abend*› 2) (melodious) musikalisch ‹*Stimme, Klänge*›; melodiös, melodisch ‹*Stück*› 3) (fond of or skilled in music) musikalisch 4) (set to music) musikalisch; Musik‹*film, -theater*›
B *n.* (Mus., Theatre) Musical, *das*

musical: ~ **box** *n.* (Brit.) Spieldose, *die;* ~ **ˈchairs** *n. sing.* Reise nach Jerusalem; ~ **director** *n.* (Theatre) Musikdirektor, *der*/-direktorin, *die;* (conductor) Kapellmeister, *der*/-meisterin, *die*

musicality /mjuːzɪˈkælɪtɪ/ *n., no pl.* Musikalität, *die*

musically /ˈmjuːzɪkəlɪ/ *adv.* (with regard to music) musikalisch; (melodiously) melodisch; melodiös; ~ **gifted** musikalisch [begabt]; musikbegabt

music: ~ **box** (Amer.) ▸ **musical box**; ~ **centre** *n.* Kompaktanlage, *die;* ~ **drama** *n.* Musikdrama, *das;* ~ **hall** *n.* (Brit.) A *n.* Varietee, *das;* B *attrib. adj.* Varietee-

musician /mjuːˈzɪʃn/ *n.* ▸ⓘ **p. 1260** Musiker, *der*/Musikerin, *die;* (minstrel, street ~ etc.) Musikant, *der*/Musikantin, *die*

musicianship /mjuːˈzɪʃnʃɪp/ *n., no pl.* musikalisches Können; **the standard of** ~**:** das musikalische Niveau

ˈmusic lesson *n.* Musikstunde, *die*

musicologist /mjuːzɪˈkɒlədʒɪst/ *n.* ▸ⓘ **p. 1260** Musikwissenschaftler, *der*/-wissenschaftlerin, *die;* Musikologe, *der*/Musikologin, *die* (geh.)

musicology /mjuːzɪˈkɒlədʒɪ/ *n.* Musikwissenschaft, *die;* Musikologie, *die* (geh.)

music: ~ **paper** *n.* Notenpapier, *das;* ~ **rest** *n.* Notenpult, *das;* ~ **room** *n.* Musiksaal, *der;* (for concerts) Konzertsaal, *der;* ~ **stand** *n.* Notenständer, *der;* ~ **stool** *n.* Klavierhocker, *der;* Klavierschemel, *der;* ~ **teacher** *n.* ▸ⓘ **p. 1260** Musiklehrer, *der*/-lehrerin, *die;* ~ **video** *n.* Musikvideo, *das*

musk /mʌsk/ *n.* 1) (substance) Moschus, *der;* ~**-scented** mit Moschus parfümiert 2) (odour) Moschusgeruch, *der* 3) (Bot.) Moschusgauklerblume, *die*

ˈmusk deer *n.* (Zool.) Moschushirsch, *der*

musket /ˈmʌskɪt/ *n.* (Arms Hist.) Muskete, *die*

musketeer /mʌskɪˈtɪə(r)/ *n.* (Hist.) Musketier, *der*

musketry /ˈmʌskɪtrɪ/ *n.* (Hist.) (muskets) Musketen *Pl.;* (musketeers) Musketiere *Pl.*

musk: ~ **melon** *n.* Zuckermelone, *die;* Gartenmelone, *die;* ~ **ox** *n.* (Zool.) Moschusochse, *der;* ~**rat** *n.* 1) (Zool.) Bisamratte, *die;* 2) (fur) Bisam, *der;* ~ **rose** *n.* (Bot.) Moschusrose, *die*

musky /ˈmʌskɪ/ *adj.* moschusartig duftend; moschusartig ‹*Duft, Geruch, Geschmack*›; Moschus‹*duft, -parfüm*›

Muslim /ˈmʊslɪm, ˈmʌzlɪm/
A *adj.* muslimisch (bes. fachspr.); moslemisch; **be** ~ ‹*Person:*› Muslim/Muslime sein, Moslem/Moslime sein
B *n.* Muslim, *der*/Muslime, *die* (bes. fachspr.); Moslem, *der*/Moslime, *die*

muslin /ˈmʌzlɪn/
A *n.* Musselin, *der*
B *adj.* musselinen; Musselin-

musquash /ˈmʌskwɒʃ/ *n.* 1) (Zool.) Bisamratte, *die* 2) (fur) Bisam, *der*

muss /mʌs/ *v.t.* (Amer. coll.) verstrubbeln (ugs.) ‹*Haar, Frisur*›; zerknittern ‹*Stoff*›

Phrasal verb

- ~ **ˈup** *v.t.* durcheinander bringen; verstrubbeln (ugs.) ‹*Haar*›; zerknittern ‹*Kleidung*›

mussel /ˈmʌsl/ *n.* Muschel, *die;* **bed of** ~**s,** ~ **bed** Muschelbank, *die*

must[1] /məst, *stressed* mʌst/, *stressed*
A *v. aux., only in pres. and past* ~**,** *neg.* (coll.) ~**n't** /ˈmʌsnt/ 1) (have to) müssen; *with negative* dürfen; **you** ~ **not/never do that** das darfst du nicht/nie tun; **you** ~ **remember ...:** du darfst nicht vergessen, ...; du musst daran denken, ...; **you** ~ **stop that noise/listen to me!** hör mit dem Lärm auf/hör mir zu!; **you** ~**n't do that again!** tu das [ja] nie wieder!; **I** ~ **get back to the office** ich muss wieder ins Büro; **I** ~ **go to London** ich muss nach London; **I** ~ **leave at 6 o'clock** ich muss um 6 Uhr weg *od.* los; **do it if you** ~**:** wenn es sein muss, tu es eben; tu, was du nicht lassen kannst (ugs.); **I will go if I** ~**:** wenn es sein muss, gehe ich; ~ **I?** muss das sein?; **ˈ**~ **you shout so loudly?** musst du denn so laut schreien?; **I** ~ **away** (arch.) ich muss fort; **I** ~ **have a new dress** ich brauche ein neues Kleid; **why** ~ **it always rain on Saturdays?** warum muss es ausgerechnet sonnabends immer regnen?; **I ˈ**~ **say ...:** ich muss sagen ...; **[that] I ˈ**~ **say** [das] muss ich schon sagen; **if you ˈ**~ **know** wenn du es unbedingt wissen willst 2) (ought to) müssen; *with negative* dürfen; **I** ~ **ask you to leave** ich muss Sie bitten zu gehen; **you** ~ **think about it** du solltest [unbedingt] darüber nachdenken; **I** ~ **not sit here drinking coffee** ich sollte *od.* dürfte eigentlich nicht hier sitzen und Kaffee trinken 3) (be certain to) müssen; **you** ~ **be tired** du musst müde sein; du bist bestimmt müde; **you** ~ **be crazy** du bist wohl

m

wahnsinnig!; **there ~ be a reason** es muss einen Grund geben; **it ~ be about 3 o'clock** es wird wohl *od.* dürfte *od.* müsste etwa 3 Uhr sein; **I ~ have lost it** ich muss es verloren haben; **it ~ have stopped raining by now** es dürfte *od.* müsste inzwischen aufgehört haben zu regnen; **I think they ~ have left** ich denke, sie sind sicher *od.* bestimmt weggegangen; **20 people ~ have visited me** es haben mich bestimmt 20 Leute besucht; **there ~ have been forty of them** (forty) es müssen vierzig gewesen sein; (probably about forty) es dürften etwa vierzig gewesen sein; **you ~ have seen it** (necessarily would have) du hättest es sehen müssen; *expr. indignation or annoyance* **he ~ come just when ...** er muss/musste natürlich *od.* ausgerechnet kommen, wenn/als ...; **what ~ I do but break my leg?** Was musste natürlich kommen? Ich musste mir das Bein brechen; *see also* **joke B**

B *n.* (coll.) Muss, *das;* **be a ~ for sb./sth.** ein Muss für jmdn./unerlässlich für etw. sein

must² *n.* **1** (wine) neuer Wein **2** (grape juice) Most, *der*

must³ ▸**mustiness**

mustache ▸**moustache**

mustachio /mə'stɑːʃəʊ/ *n., pl.* **~s** Schnauzbart, *der*

mustachioed /mə'stɑːʃəʊd/ *adj.* schnauzbärtig

mustang /'mʌstæŋ/ *n.* Mustang, *der*

mustard /'mʌstəd/ *n.* **1** Senf, *der; attrib.* Senf‹*geschmack usw.*›; **~ and cress** (Brit.) Senfkeimlinge und Kresse **2** (colour) Senffarbe, *die; attrib.* senffarben **3** (Amer. coll.: thing that provides zest) Pep, *der* (ugs.); **cut the ~:** es bringen (ugs.); **I can't cut the ~:** ich bringe es nicht (ugs.)

mustard: ~-coloured *adj.* senffarben; **~ gas** *n.* (Chem., Mil.) Senfgas, *das;* **~ plaster** *n.* Senfpflaster, *das;* **~ pot** *n.* Senftopf, *der;* **~-yellow** *adj.* senfgelb

muster /'mʌstə(r)/

A *n.* **1** (Mil.) Appell, *der;* **pass ~** (fig.) akzeptabel sein **2** (assembly) Zusammenkunft, *die*

B *v.t.* **1** (summon) versammeln; (Mil., Naut.) [zum Appell] antreten lassen **2** (collect) zusammenbringen; zusammenziehen ‹*Streitkräfte, Truppen*›; zusammentreiben ‹*Vieh*›; (raise) aufstellen ‹*Armee*›; ausheben ‹*Truppen*› **3** (fig.: summon up) zusammennehmen ‹*Kraft, Mut, Verstand*›; aufbringen ‹*Unterstützung*›; **~ [the] strength to do sth.** all seine Kräfte zusammennehmen, um etw. zu tun; **he couldn't ~ [the] courage to do it** er brachte nicht den Mut auf, es zu tun

C *v.i.* sich [ver]sammeln; ‹*Truppen:*› aufmarschieren; (for parade) antreten

Phrasal verb

• **~ 'up** *v.t.* aufbringen ‹*Unterstützung, Mut, Verständnis*›; **~ up all one's courage** seinen ganzen *od.* all seinen Mut zusammennehmen

must-'have

A *attrib. adj.* **a ~ thing** eine Sache die man unbedingt haben muss; **this is a ~ experience** das muss man unbedingt erlebt haben

B *n.* Muss, *das;* **a list of ~s** eine Liste der Dinge, die man unbedingt haben muss

mustiness /'mʌstɪnɪs/ *n., no pl.* **1** (of smell, taste) Muffigkeit, *die;* Muff, *der* (nordd.) **2** (mouldiness) Stockigkeit, *die*

mustn't /'mʌsnt/ (coll.) = **must not**

must-'see

A *attrib. adj.* **a ~ film** ein Film den man gesehen haben muss

B *n.* Muss, *das;* **this town/film is a ~:** diese Stadt/diesen Film muss man gesehen haben; **other ~s include ...** außerdem sollte man sich unbedingt ... ansehen

musty /'mʌstɪ/ *adj.* **1** (smelling or tasting stale) muffig **2** (mouldy) stockig **3** (fig.: stale, antiquated) verstaubt

mutable /'mjuːtəbl/ *adj.* **1** (formal: liable to change) wandelbar (geh.) **2** (Ling., Biol.) mutabel (fachspr.)

mutagen /'mjuːtədʒən/ *n.* (Biol.) Mutagen, *das*

mutant /'mjuːtənt/ (Biol.)

A *adj.* mutiert ‹*Gen, Zelle, Stamm*›

B *n.* Mutante, *die*

mutate /mjuː'teɪt/ (Biol.)

A *v.t.* zur Mutation anregen; **be ~d** mutieren

B *v.i.* mutieren

mutation /mjuː'teɪʃn/ *n.* **1** (formal: change) Wandel, *der;* Wandlung, *die* **2** (Biol.) Mutation, *die; attrib.* Mutations-

mute /mjuːt/

A *adj.* (dumb, silent; also Ling.) stumm; (silent also) schweigend; (temporarily bereft of speech also) sprachlos; **be ~ with rage/amazement/grief/from shock** vor Zorn/Staunen/Kummer/Entsetzen kein Wort hervorbringen *od.* über die Lippen bringen

B *n.* **1** (dumb person) Stumme, *der/die* **2** (Mus.) Dämpfer, *der*

C *v.t.* dämpfen

'mute button *n.* Stummtaste, *die*

muted /'mjuːtɪd/ *adj.* gedämpft; verhalten ‹*Kritik, Begeisterung*›

mutely /'mjuːtlɪ/ *adv.* stumm; (silently also) schweigend

mute 'swan *n.* Höckerschwan, *der*

mutilate /'mjuːtɪleɪt/ *v.t.* (deprive of limb; fig.: render imperfect) verstümmeln; mutilieren (Med.); (cut off) abtrennen ‹*Gliedmaße*›

mutilation /mjuːtɪ'leɪʃn/ *n.* (deprivation of limb; fig.: rendering imperfect) Verstümmelung, *die;* Mutilation, *die* (Med.)

mutineer /mjuːtɪ'nɪə(r)/ *n.* Meuterer, *der*

mutinous /'mjuːtɪnəs/ *adj.* rebellisch ‹*Geist, Person*›; aufrührerisch ‹*Rede, Gedanke*›; meuternd ‹*Mannschaft eines Schiffs, Truppen*›; **~ acts** Akte der Meuterei; **become ~:** meutern

mutinously /'mjuːtɪnəslɪ/ *adv.* rebellisch, aufrührerisch ‹*sich benehmen*›

mutiny /'mjuːtɪnɪ/

A *n.* Meuterei, *die*

B *v.i.* meutern

mutt /mʌt/ *n.* (coll.) **1** (person) Schafskopf, *der* (ugs.); **poor ~:** armer Irrer (salopp) **2** (derog.: dog) Köter, *der* (abwertend)

mutter /'mʌtə(r)/

A *v.i.* **1** (speak low) murmeln; brummeln; **~ [away] to oneself** vor sich (*Akk.*) hin murmeln *od.* brummeln **2** (grumble) murren (**at, about** über + *Akk.*)

B *v.t.* (utter) murmeln ‹*Beleidigung, Gebet, Drohung*›; **~ sth. under one's breath/to oneself** sich (*Dat.*) etw. in den Bart/etw. vor sich (*Akk.*) hin murmeln

C *n.* Gemurmel, *das;* **~ of voices** Gemurmel [von Stimmen]

muttering /'mʌtərɪŋ/ *n.* **1** *no pl.* (low speech) Gemurmel, *das* **2** **~[s]** (complaints) Gemurre, *das*

mutton /'mʌtn/ *n.* Hammelfleisch, *das;* Hammel, *der;* **[a case of] ~ dressed [up] as lamb** (coll. derog.) eine Alte, die auf jugendlich macht (ugs.); *see also* **dead A 1**

mutton: ~ 'chop *n.* **1** Hammelkotelett, *das;* **2** **~-chop [whiskers]** [Bart]koteletten *Pl.;* **~head** *n.* (coll. derog.) Schafskopf, *der* (ugs.)

mutual /'mjuːtjʊəl/ *adj.* **1** (given and received) gegenseitig; beiderseitig ‹*Einvernehmen, Vorteil, Bemühung*›; wechselseitig ‹*Abhängigkeit*›; **look at each other with ~ suspicion** sich argwöhnisch ansehen; **I can't bear you! — The feeling's ~:** Ich kann dich nicht riechen! — Das beruht auf Gegenseitigkeit; **to our ~ satisfaction/benefit** zu unser beider Zufriedenheit/Nutzen; **~ aid programme** Programm zur gegenseitigen Hilfe; **be ~ well-wishers** es gut miteinander meinen **2** (coll.: shared) gemeinsam ‹*Interesse, Freund, Abneigung usw.*›

mutual: ~ admi'ration society *n.* (joc.) *Kreis von Leuten, die alle eine ungerechtfertigt hohe Meinung voneinander haben;* **~ 'fund** *n.* (Amer. Econ.) Investmentgesellschaft, *die;* **~ in'surance company** *n.* Versicherungsverein auf Gegenseitigkeit

mutuality /mjuːtjʊ'ælɪtɪ/ *n., no pl.* Gegenseitigkeit, *die;* (of interests) Gemeinsamkeit, *die*

mutually /'mjuːtjʊəlɪ/ *adv.* **1** gegenseitig; **be ~ exclusive** einander (geh.) *od.* sich [gegenseitig] ausschließen; **~ beneficial/accepted** für beide Seiten vorteilhaft/von beiden Seiten akzeptiert **2** (in common) gemeinsam

muzak /'mjuːzæk/ *n.* (often derog.) Hintergrundmusik, *die;* Berieselungsmusik, *die* (ugs. abwertend)

muzzle /'mʌzl/

A *n.* **1** (of dog) Schnauze, *die;* (of horse, cattle) Maul, *das* **2** (of gun) Mündung, *die* **3** (put over animal's mouth) Maulkorb, *der*

B *v.t.* **1** einen Maulkorb umbinden *od.* anlegen (+ *Dat.*) ‹*Hund*› **2** (fig.) mundtot machen, einen Maulkorb anlegen (ugs.) (+ *Dat.*) ‹*Presse, Kritiker*›; knebeln ‹*Presse, Redefreiheit*›; unterdrücken ‹*Protest*›

muzzle: ~-loader *n.* Vorderlader, *der;* **~ velocity** *n.* Mündungsgeschwindigkeit, *die*

muzzy /'mʌzɪ/ *adj.* **1** (mentally hazy, blurred) verschwommen; verworren ‹*Verstand*›; **feel ~:** ein dumpfes Gefühl haben **2** (from intoxication) benebelt (**with** von)

MW *abbr.* **1** (Radio) = **medium wave** MW **2** (Electr., Phys.) = **megawatt[s]** MW

my /maɪ/ *poss. pron. attrib.* **1** (belonging to me) mein **2** *in affectionate, jocular, patronizing, etc. use* mein; **my poor fellow** du Ärmster; *see also* **man A 2** **3** *in excl. of surprise* **my[, my]!, [my] oh my!** [ach du] meine Güte! (ugs.); ach du grüne Neune! (ugs.). *see also* **god 2**; **her²**; **word A 3**

myalgia /maɪ'ældʒə/ *n., no pl.* (Med.) Muskelschmerzen *Pl.*; Myalgie, *die* (fachspr.)

myalgic encephalomyelitis /maɪ ældʒɪk ensefələʊmaɪə'laɪtɪs/ *n.* ▸**i** p. 1231 (Med.) myalgische Enzephalomyelitis

mycelium /maɪ'siːlɪəm/ *n., pl.* **mycelia** /maɪ 'siːlɪə/ (Bot.) Myzel[ium], *das*

Mycenaean /maɪsɪ'niːən/ *adj.* (Archaeol.) mykenisch

mycology /maɪ'kɒlədʒɪ/ *n.* Mykologie, *die*

mynah (myna) /'maɪnə/ *n.* (Ornith.) **~ [bird]** Maina, *der;* (talking species) Beo, *der*

myopia /maɪ'əʊpɪə/ *n.* Kurzsichtigkeit, *die* (auch fig.); Myopie, *die* (fachspr.)

myopic /maɪ'əʊpɪk/ *adj.* kurzsichtig (auch fig.); myopisch (fachspr.)

myriad /'mɪrɪəd/ (literary)

A *adj.* unzählig; Myriaden von (geh.) ‹*Insekten, Sternen*›

B *n.* (great number) Unzahl, *die;* Myriade, *die* (geh.); **a ~ of possibilities** Myriaden von Möglichkeiten

myriapod /'mɪrɪəpɒd/ *n.* (Zool.) Myriapode, *der;* Myriopode, *der*

myrrh /mɜː(r)/ *n.* Myrrhe, *die*

myrtle /'mɜːtl/ *n.* (Bot.) **1** **common ~:** Myrte, *die* **2** (Amer.: periwinkle) Immergrün, *das*

myself /maɪ'self/ *pron.* **1** *emphat.* selbst; **I thought so ~:** das habe ich auch gedacht; **I haven't been there, ~:** ich war nicht selbst da; **[even] though/if I say it ~:** wenn ich es auch selbst sage; **I am quite ~ again** mir geht es wieder gut; **I want to be ~:** ich will ich selbst sein **2** **you know more than ~:** du weißt mehr als ich [selbst]; **there were the three of them and ~:** da waren die drei und ich [selbst] **3** *refl.* mich/mir; **I washed ~:** ich wusch mich; **I'm going to get ~ a car** ich werde mir ein Auto zulegen; **I said to ~:** ich sagte mir; **I need to have time to ~:** ich brauche Zeit für mich. *See also* **herself**

mysterious /mɪ'stɪərɪəs/ *adj.* **1** (curious, strange) mysteriös; rätselhaft; geheimnisvoll ‹*Fremder, Orient*›; **~-looking** geheimnisvoll aussehend; **he did it for some ~ reason of his own** er hat es aus irgendeinem unerfindlichen Grunde getan **2** (secretive) geheimnisvoll; **be very ~ about sth.** ein großes Geheimnis aus etw. machen; **why are you being so ~?** warum tust du so geheimnisvoll?

mysteriously /mɪ'stɪərɪəslɪ/ *adv.* auf mysteriöse *od.* rätselhafte Weise; sonderbar ‹*erfreut usw.*›; geheimnisvoll ‹*lächeln usw.*›

mystery /'mɪstərɪ/ *n.* **1** (hidden, inexplicable matter) Rätsel, *das;* **it's a ~ to me why ...:** es ist mir schleierhaft (ugs.) *od.* ein Rätsel, warum ...; **make a ~ [out] of sth.** ein Geheimnis aus etw. machen; **make no ~ of sth.** kein *od.*

keinen Hehl aus etw. machen; **the mysteries of a trade** die Geheimnisse eines Handwerks; **he's a bit of a ~:** er hat etwas Rätselhaftes *od.* Geheimnisvolles **2)** (secrecy) Geheimnis, *das;* **wrapped in** *or* **shrouded in** *or* **surrounded by ~:** geheimnisumwittert *od.* -umwoben (geh.); **there's no ~ about it** das ist überhaupt kein Geheimnis; **~ man, man of ~:** rätselhafter Mann **3)** (making a secret of things) Heimlichtuerei, *die* **4)** (religious truth) Mysterium, *das* (geh.) **5)** ▸ **mystery play; mystery story**

mystery: ~ novel *n.* ≈ Detektiv- *od.* Kriminalroman, *der;* **~ play** *n.* Mysterienspiel, *das;* **~ story** *n.* (detective story) ≈ Detektiv- *od.* Kriminalgeschichte, *die;* (mysterious story) rätselhafte Erzählung; **~ tour, ~ trip** *ns.* Fahrt ins Blaue (ugs.); **~ writer** Kriminalschriftsteller, *der*/-schriftstellerin, *die;* Krimiautor, *der*/-autorin, *die* (ugs.)

mystic /ˈmɪstɪk/
A *adj.* **1)** mystisch **2)** (mysterious) geheimnisvoll
B *n.* Mystiker, *der*/Mystikerin, *die*

mystical /ˈmɪstɪkl/ *adj.* mystisch

mysticism /ˈmɪstɪsɪzm/ *n.* Mystik, *die;* Mystizismus, *der* (geh.)

mystification /mɪstɪfɪˈkeɪʃn/ *n.* Verwirrung, *die;* **add to sb.'s ~:** jmdn. noch mehr verwirren

mystify /ˈmɪstɪfaɪ/ *v.t.* verwirren; **this mystifies me** das ist mir ein Rätsel *od.* rätselhaft; **the police are completely mystified** die Polizei steht vor einem absoluten Rätsel

mystique /mɪˈstiːk/ *n.* geheimnisvoller Nimbus

myth /mɪθ/ *n.* **1)** Mythos, *der* **2)** (fictitious thing or idea) Mythos, *der;* (untrue tale) Legende, *die;* (rumour) Gerücht, *das*

mythical /ˈmɪθɪkl/ *adj.* **1)** (based on myth) mythisch; **~ creatures** Sagengestalten; **the ~ land of Atlantis** das sagenhafte Land Atlantis **2)** (invented) fiktiv

mythological /mɪθəˈlɒdʒɪkl/ *adj.* mythologisch

mythology /mɪˈθɒlədʒɪ/ *n.* Mythologie, *die*

myxomatosis /mɪksəməˈtəʊsɪs/ *n., pl.* **myxomatoses** /mɪksəməˈtəʊsiːz/ (Vet. Med.) Myxomatose, *die*

N¹, n /en/ *n., pl.* **Ns** *or* **N's** **1** (letter) N, n, *das* **2** (Math.) n; **nth** /enθ/: **to the nth [degree]** in der n-ten Potenz; (fig.: to the utmost) in höchster Potenz (ugs.); **for the nth time** zum x-ten Mal (ugs.)

N² *abbr.* **1** ▸ⓘ **p. 1013 = north** N **2** ▸ⓘ **p. 1013 = northern** n. **3** (Chess) **= knight** S **4** **= nuclear; N-weapons** A-Waffen **5** (Phys.) **= newton** N

n. *abbr.* **1** **= note** Anm. **2** **= nano-** n **3** **= neuter** n.

'n, 'n' /ən/ *conj.* (coll.: and) und

n/a *abbr.* **1** **= not available** n. bek. **2** **= not applicable** entf.

NAAFI /'næfɪ/ *abbr.* (Brit.) **= Navy, Army and Air Force Institutes** *Kaufhaus für Angehörige der britischen Truppen*

nab /næb/ *v.t.*, **-bb-** (coll.) **1** (arrest) schnappen (ugs.) **2** (seize) sich (*Dat.*) schnappen; **~ him before he goes** sieh zu, dass du ihn noch erwischst, bevor er geht (ugs.); **all the best seats had been ~bed** die besten Plätze waren alle schon weggeschnappt **3** (steal) klauen (salopp); krallen (salopp)

nacelle /næ'sel/ *n.* Gondel, *die*

nacre /'neɪkə(r)/ ▸**mother-of-pearl**

nadir /'neɪdɪə(r)/ *n.* **1** (lowest point) Tief[st-]punkt, *der;* **at the ~:** auf dem Tiefpunkt; **he was at the ~ of despair** er war zutiefst verzweifelt **2** (Astron.) Nadir, *der*

naff /næf/ (coll.)

A *adj.* ätzend (ugs.)

B *v.i.* **~ off** abhauen (ugs.)

nag¹ /næg/

A *v.i.*, **-gg-** **1** (scold) nörgeln (abwertend); meckern (ugs. abwertend); **~ at sb.** an jmdm. herumnörgeln *od.* -meckern; **~ at sb. to do sth.** jmdm. zusetzen (ugs.), dass er etw. tut **2** (cause distress) **~ at sb.** jmdn. plagen; jmdm. zusetzen (ugs.) *od.* keine Ruhe lassen

B *v.t.*, **-gg-** **1** (scold) herumnörgeln an (+ *Dat.*) (abwertend); herummeckern an (+ *Dat.*) (abwertend); **don't ~ me!** lass mich [mit deinem Genörgel *od.* (ugs.) Gemecker] in Ruhe!; **~ sb. about sth./to do sth.** jmdn. wegen etw. zusetzen (ugs.)/jmdm. zusetzen (ugs.), dass er etw. tut **2** (cause distress) plagen; keine Ruhe lassen (+ *Dat.*)

nag² *n.* **1** (coll.: horse) Gaul, *der* **2** (old or inferior horse) Klepper, *der* (abwertend)

nagging /'nægɪŋ/

A *adj.* **1** (annoying) nörglerisch (abwertend); ständig nörgelnd (abwertend) **2** (persistent) quälend ‹*Durst, Angst, Sorge, Zweifel*›; bohrend ‹*Schmerz*›; **a ~ conscience** [quälende] Gewissensbisse *Pl.*

B *n.* Genörgel, *das* (abwertend); Gemecker, *das* (ugs. abwertend); **stop your ~:** hör auf zu nörgeln *od.* meckern

naiad /'naɪæd/ *n., pl.* **~s** *or* **~es** /'naɪədi:z/ Najade, *die*

naïf /nɑ:'i:f/

A *adj.* ▸**naïve**

B *n.* Naive, *der/die;* Naivling, *der* (ugs. abwertend)

nail /neɪl/

A *n.* **1** ▸ⓘ **p. 951** (on finger, toe) Nagel, *der;* **cut one's ~s** sich (*Dat.*) die Nägel schneiden; **bite one's ~s** an den Nägeln kauen; (fig.) wie auf Kohlen sitzen **2** (metal spike) Nagel, *der;* **be hard as ~s** (fig.) steinhart sein; (fit) topfit sein; (unfeeling, insensitive) knallhart sein (ugs.); **hit the [right] ~ on the head** (fig.) den Nagel auf den Kopf treffen (ugs.); **be a ~ in sb.'s/sth.'s coffin, drive a ~ into sb.'s/sth.'s coffin** (fig.) ein Nagel zu jmds. Sarg/ein Sargnagel für etw. sein (ugs.); **on the ~** (fig. coll.) pünktlich ‹*bezahlen, sein Geld kriegen*› **3** (claw, talon) Kralle, *die. See also* **tooth 1**

B *v.t.* **1** (fasten) nageln (**to** an + *Akk.*); **~ planks over sth.** etw. mit Brettern vernageln; **~ two planks together** zwei Bretter zusammennageln **2** (fig.: expose) **~ sth. [to the counter** *or* **barn door]** etw. anprangern **3** (fig.: fix) **be ~ed to the spot/ground** wie angenagelt sein (ugs.); **~ one's eyes/attention on sth.** seine Augen auf etw. (*Akk.*) heften (geh.)/seine Aufmerksamkeit auf etw. (*Akk.*) konzentrieren **4** (fig.: secure, catch, engage) an Land ziehen (ugs.) ‹*Vertrag, Auftrag*› **5** (coll.: arrest) einkassieren (salopp). *See also* **colour A 10**

Phrasal verbs

- **~ 'down** *v.t.* **1** festnageln; zunageln ‹*Kiste, Fenster*› **2** (fig.) (define) untermauern ‹*Argument*›; festlegen ‹*Strategie*›; (bind) **~ sb. down to sth.** jmdn. auf etw. (*Akk.*) festnageln
- **~ 'up** *v.t.* **1** (close) vernageln **2** (affix with ~) annageln (**against** an + *Akk.*)

nail: ~-biting **A** *n., no pl.* Nägelkauen, *das;* **B** *adj.* (fig.) bang ‹*Minuten, Schweigen, Sorge*›; angstvoll ‹*Spannung*›; spannungsgeladen ‹*Spiel, Film*›; **~ bomb** *n.* Nagelbombe, *die;* **~ brush** *n.* Nagelbürste, *die;* **~ clippers** *n. pl.* **[pair of] ~ clippers** Nagelknipser, *der;* **~ enamel** (Amer.) ▸**~ polish;** **~ file** *n.* Nagelfeile, *die;* **~ polish** *n.* Nagellack, *der; attrib.* **~ polish remover** Nagellackentferner, *der;* **~ scissors** *n. pl.* **[pair of] ~ scissors** Nagelschere, *die;* **~ varnish** (Brit.) ▸**~ polish**

naïve, naive /nɑ:'i:v, naɪ'i:v/ *adj.* naiv; einfältig

naïvely, naively /nɑ:'i:vlɪ, naɪ'i:vlɪ/ *adv.* naiv; *as sentence-modifier* naiverweise

naïvety, naivety /nɑ:'i:vtɪ, naɪ'i:vtɪ/, **(naïveté** /nɑ:'i:vteɪ/) *n.* **1** (state, quality) Naivität, *die;* Einfalt, *die* **2** (action) Naivität, *die*

naked /'neɪkɪd/ *adj.* **1** nackt; **as ~ as the day I was born** wie Gott mich geschaffen hat (scherzh.); **go ~:** nackt herumlaufen; **strip sb. ~:** jmdn. nackt ausziehen; **I feel ~ without my make-up on** ohne mein Make-up fühle ich mich nackt **2** (unshaded) nackt ‹*Glühbirne*›; (unshielded) offen ‹*Licht, Flamme*› **3** (defenceless) wehrlos **4** (without covering) blank ‹*Schwert*›; bloß ‹*Faust*› **5** (plain) nackt ‹*Tatsache, Wahrheit, Aggression, Gier, Ehrgeiz*›

naked: ~ 'eye *n.* **visible to** *or* **with the ~ eye** mit bloßem Auge zu erkennen; **~-eye** *adj.* mit bloßem Auge sichtbar

nakedness /'neɪkɪdnɪs/ *n., no pl.* Nacktheit, *die;* Blöße, *die* (geh.)

namby-pamby /næmbɪ'pæmbɪ/ *adj.* seicht (abwertend) ‹*Literatur usw.*›; verzärtelt (abwertend) ‹*Person*›; lax (oft abwertend) ‹*Handhabung, Normen*›

name /neɪm/

A *n.* **1** Name, *der;* **what's your ~/the ~ of this place?** wie heißt du/dieser Ort?; **my ~ is Jack** ich heiße Jack; mein Name ist Jack; **call sb. by his ~:** jmdn. bei seinem Namen rufen; **no one of** *or* **by that ~:** niemand mit diesem Namen *od.* (geh.) dieses Namens; **last ~:** Zuname, *der,* Nachname, *der;* **know sb./sth. by** *or* **under another ~:** jmdn./etw. unter einem anderen Namen kennen; **the ~ of Edwards** der Name Edwards; **mention no ~s** keine Namen nennen; **fill in one's ~ and address** Name und Adresse eintragen; **she took her mother's ~:** sie nahm den Mädchennamen ihrer Mutter an; **what ~ shall I say?** wen darf ich melden?; **I can't put a ~ to the plant/his face** ich kann die Pflanze nicht benennen/sein Gesicht mit keinem Namen in Verbindung bringen; **a man of** *or* **by the ~ of Miller** ein Mann namens Miller *od.* mit Namen Miller; **go** *or* **be known by** *or* **under the ~ of ...:** unter dem Namen ... bekannt sein; **by ~:** namentlich ‹*erwähnen, aufrufen usw.*›; **refer to sb./sth. by ~:** jmdn./etw. namentlich nennen; **know sb. by ~/by ~ only** jmdn. mit Namen/nur dem Namen nach kennen; **she goes by the ~ of Madame Lola** sie ist unter dem Namen Madame Lola bekannt; **that's the ~ of the game** (coll.) darum geht es; **with us speed is the ~ of the game** (coll.) bei uns heißt die Devise Schnelligkeit; **put one's/sb.'s ~ down for sth.** sich/jmdn. für etw. vormerken lassen; **put one's/sb.'s ~ down on the waiting list** sich auf die Warteliste setzen lassen/jmdn. auf die Warteliste setzen; **take sb.'s ~ off the books** jmdn. ausschließen *od.* von der Mitgliederliste streichen; **without a penny to his ~:** ohne einen Cent in der Tasche; **he hasn't a pair of shoes to his ~:** er kann nicht einmal ein Paar Schuhe sein Eigen nennen (ugs.); **what's in a ~?** Name ist Schall und Rauch; **... or my ~ is not John Smith ...** so wahr ich John Smith heiße; **if this doesn't work, my ~ is not Peter Brown** *etc.* wenn das nicht funktioniert, will ich Emil heißen (ugs.); **that bullet had my ~ [and number] on it** die Kugel war für mich bestimmt; **have/see one's ~ [up] in lights** ganz groß herauskommen (ugs.); *see also* **mud 3**

2 (word denoting object of thought) Bezeichnung, *die;* Name, *der;* **~s cannot hurt me** Beschimpfungen tun mir nicht weh

3 **in ~ [only]** [nur] auf dem Papier; **a Christian/town in ~ only** nur dem Namen nach ein Christ/eine Stadt; **in all but ~:** im Grunde genommen

4 **in the ~ of** im Namen (+ *Gen.*); **in God's ~, in the ~ of God** um Gottes willen; **in Heaven's ~:** um Himmels willen; **in one's own ~:** im eigenen Namen; (independently) von sich aus

5 (reputation) Ruf, *der;* **have a ~ for honesty** für seine Ehrlichkeit bekannt sein; **make a ~ for oneself, win oneself a ~:** sich (*Dat.*) einen Namen machen; **make one's/sb.'s ~:** berühmt werden/jmdn. berühmt machen; **this book made his ~:** mit diesem Buch machte er sich einen Namen; **clear one's/sb.'s ~:** seine/jmds. Unschuld beweisen

6 (famous person) Name, *der;* **many great** *or* **big ~s** viele namhafte Persönlichkeiten; viele Größen; **be a big ~:** einen großen Namen haben

7 *attrib.* **~ brand** Markenartikel, *der;* **~ band** Starband, *die. See also* **assume 3; bad A 1; call B 9; dog A 1; false A 2; proper name; take A 25; use B 1; what E 1**

B *v.t.* **1** (give name to) einen Namen geben (+ *Dat.*); **~ sb. John** jmdn. John nennen; jmdm. den Namen John geben; **~ a ship 'Mary'** ein Schiff [auf den Namen] „Mary" taufen; **~**

sb./sth. after *or* (Amer.) **for sb.** jmdn./etw. nach jmdm. benennen; **be ~d John** John heißen; **a man ~d Smith** ein Mann namens *od.* mit Namen Smith; **~ sb. John after** *or* (Amer.) **for sb.** jmdn. nach jmdm. John nennen 2 (call by right name) benennen; **~ the capital of Zambia** nenne die Hauptstadt von Sambia; **can you ~ the books of the Bible?** kannst du die Bücher der Bibel aufzählen? 3 (nominate) ernennen; **~ sb. [as] sth.** jmdn. zu etw. ernennen; **~ sb. to an office/a post** jmdn. in ein Amt berufen *od.* einsetzen/auf einen Posten berufen; **~ one's successor/heir** seinen Nachfolger/Erben bestimmen; **he has been ~d as the winner** ihm wurde der Sieg zuerkannt; **be ~d actress of the year** zur Schauspielerin des Jahres gewählt werden 4 (mention) nennen; (specify) benennen; **~ sb. as witness** jmdn. als Zeugen benennen; **~ ~s** Namen nennen; **he was ~d as the thief** er wurde als der Dieb genannt; **~ the time and I'll meet you there** sag die Zeit, und dann treffen wir uns dort; **~ the day** (choose wedding day) den Tag der Hochzeit festlegen *od.* -setzen; **to ~ but a few** um nur einige zu nennen; **we were given champagne, oysters, you ~ it** (coll.) wir kriegten Champagner, Austern, und, und, und; **you ~ it, he's got/done** *etc.* **it** (coll.) es gibt nichts, was er nicht hat/noch nicht gemacht hat *usw.*

name: ~-calling *n., no pl.* Beschimpfungen *Pl.*; **the debate degenerated into mere ~-calling** die Debatte artete in bloße gegenseitige Beschimpfungen aus; **~check** A *n.* 1 (check of sb.'s credentials) Personenüberprüfung, *die;* 2 (mention) [öffentliche] ehrenhafte Erwähnung *od.* Nennung. B *v.t.* ehrenhaft erwähnen *od.* nennen; **~ day** *n.* Namenstag, *der;* **~-drop** *v.i.* [scheinbar beiläufig] bekannte Namen fallen lassen; **she is always ~-dropping** sie lässt dauernd einfließen, wen sie alles kennt; **~-dropping** *n., no pl.* Namedropping, *das; Nennung bedeutender Namen, um Eindruck zu machen*

nameless /ˈneɪmlɪs/ *adj.* 1 (having no name, obscure) namenlos; **a ~ grave** das Grab eines Unbekannten *od.* Namenlosen 2 (not mentioned by name) **a person who shall remain ~:** eine Person, die ungenannt bleiben soll 3 (anonymous) namenlos; anonym; **a ~ woman** eine namentlich nicht bekannte Frau; eine Unbekannte 4 (abominable) unaussprechlich; unsäglich (geh.) 5 (inexpressible) unbeschreiblich

namely /ˈneɪmlɪ/ *adv.* nämlich

name: ~ part *n.* Titelrolle, *die;* **~plate** *n.* Namensschild, *das;* **~sake** *n.* Namensvetter, *der*/-schwester, *die;* **~ tag** *n.* Namensschild, *das;* **~ tape** *n.* Namensschildchen, *das;* ≈ Wäschezeichen, *das*

Namibia /nəˈmɪbɪə/ *pr. n.* Namibia *(das)*

Namibian /nəˈmɪbɪən/
A *adj.* namibisch; **he/she is ~:** er ist Namibier/sie ist Namibierin
B *n.* Namibier, *der*/Namibierin, *die*

nan /næn/ *n.* (child lang./coll.) Omi, *die* (Kinderspr.)

nancy /ˈnænsɪ/ (coll.)
A *n.* **~ [boy]** Tunte, *die* (salopp)
B *adj.* tuntig (salopp)

nandrolone /ˈnændrələʊn/ *n., no pl.* (Med.) Nandrolon, *das*

nanny /ˈnænɪ/ *n.* 1 (Brit.: nursemaid) Kindermädchen, *das* 2 (coll.: granny) Großmama, *die* (fam.) 3 ▸ **nanny goat**

nanny: ~ goat *n.* Ziege, *die;* Geiß, *die* (südd., österr., schweiz., westmd.); **~ ˈstate** *n.* (esp. Brit.) (derog.) Bevormundungsstaat, *der*

nanosecond /ˈnænəʊsekənd/ *n.* Nanosekunde, *die*

nanotechnology /ˈnænəʊteknɒlədʒɪ/ *n., no pl.* Nanotechnologie, *die*

nap¹ /næp/
A *n.* Schläfchen, *das* (ugs.); Nickerchen, *das* (fam.); **take** *or* **have a ~:** ein Schläfchen *od.* Nickerchen machen *od.* halten; **have an afternoon ~:** ein [Nach]mittagsschläfchen machen *od.* halten
B *v.i.*, **-pp-** dösen (ugs.); **catch sb. ~ping** (fig.) jmdn. überrumpeln

nap² *n.* (of cloth) Flor, *der*

nap³ *n.* 1 **go ~** (Cards) die höchste Zahl von Stichen ansagen; (fig.: risk everything) alles auf eine Karte setzen 2 (Horseracing etc. coll.: tip) Tipp auf Sieg

napalm /ˈneɪpɑːm/ *n.* Napalm, *das*

nape /neɪp/ *n.* **~ [of the neck]** Nacken, *der;* Genick, *das*

naphtha /ˈnæfθə/ *n.* Naphtha, *das*

naphthalene /ˈnæfθəliːn/ *n.* Naphthalin, *das*

napkin /ˈnæpkɪn/ *n.* 1 Serviette, *die* 2 (Brit.: nappy) Windel, *die* 3 (waiter's) Serviertuch, *das. See also* **sanitary napkin**

ˈnapkin ring *n.* Serviettenring, *der*

Naples /ˈneɪplz/ *pr. n.* ▸ℹ **p. 1643** Neapel *(das)*

Napoleonic /nəpəʊlɪˈɒnɪk/ *adj.* napoleonisch; **the ~ Wars** die Napoleonischen Kriege

nappy /ˈnæpɪ/ *n.* (Brit.) Windel, *die;* **when you were still in nappies** als du noch in den Windeln gelegen hast

narcissism /nɑːˈsɪsɪzm/ *n., no pl.* (Psych.) Narzissmus, *der*

narcissistic /nɑːsɪˈsɪstɪk/ *adj.* (Psych.) narzisstisch

narcissus /nɑːˈsɪsəs/ *n., pl.* **narcissi** /nɑːˈsɪsaɪ/ *or* **~es** (Bot.) Narzisse, *die*

narcosis /nɑːˈkəʊsɪs/ *n., pl.* **narcoses** /nɑːˈkəʊsiːz/ Betäubung, *die;* (Med.: general anaesthesia) Narkose, *die*

narcoterrorism /ˈnɑːkəʊterərɪzm/ *n., no pl.* Drogenterrorismus, *der*

narcotic /nɑːˈkɒtɪk/
A *n.* 1 (drug) Rauschgift, *das;* Betäubungsmittel, *das* (Rechtsw.); **~s squad** Rauschgiftdezernat, *das* 2 (active ingredient) Betäubungsmittel, *das;* Narkotikum, *das* (Med.); (fig.) Narkotikum, *das;* Droge, *die*
B *adj.* 1 narkotisch; **~ drug** Rauschgift, *das;* Betäubungsmittel, *das* (Rechtsw.) 2 (inducing drowsiness, fig.) einschläfernd

narcotourist /ˈnɑːkəʊtʊərɪst/ *n.* Drogentourist, *der*/-touristin, *die*

nark /nɑːk/ (sl.)
A *n.* 1 (Brit.: informer) Spitzel, *der* (abwertend) 2 (Brit.: policeman) Bulle, *der* (salopp)
B *v.t.* (annoy) stinken (+ *Dat.*) (salopp); **be ~ed [about sb./at** *or* **about sth.]** [auf jmdn./über etw. (*Akk.*)] sauer sein (ugs.); **that really got me ~ed** das hat mir echt gestunken (salopp)

narrate /nəˈreɪt/ *v.t.* 1 (give account of) erzählen; schildern ‹*Ereignisse*› 2 kommentieren ‹*Film*›; *abs.* erzählen

narration /nəˈreɪʃn/ *n.* 1 Erzählen, *das;* Erzählung, *die;* (of events) Schilderung, *die;* Schildern, *das* 2 ▸ **narrative A 1**

narrative /ˈnærətɪv/
A *n.* 1 (tale, story) Geschichte, *die;* Erzählung, *die* 2 *no pl.* (kind of composition) **be written in ~:** in der Erzählform geschrieben sein; **writer of ~:** erzählender Autor; Erzähler, *der*
B *adj.* narrativ (Sprachw.); erzählend; erzählerisch ‹*Gabe, Talent*›; Erzähl‹*kunst, -technik*›; **~ writer** Erzähler, *der*/Erzählerin, *die*

narrator /nəˈreɪtə(r)/ *n.* Erzähler, *der*/Erzählerin, *die;* (of film) Kommentator, *der*/Kommentatorin, *die;* **first-/third-person ~:** Ich-/Er-Erzähler, *der*

narrow /ˈnærəʊ/
A *adj.* 1 schmal; schmal geschnitten ‹*Rock, Hose, Ärmel usw.*›; eng ‹*Tal, Gasse*›; **the road became ~:** die Straße verschmälerte sich 2 (limited) eng; begrenzt, schmal ‹*Auswahl*›; **in the ~est sense** im engsten Sinne 3 (with little margin) knapp ‹*Sieg, Führung, Mehrheit*›; **have a ~ escape** mit knapper Not entkommen **(from** *Dat.*); **win by a ~ margin** knapp gewinnen 4 (not tolerant) spießig (abwertend); engstirnig (abwertend); **have a ~ mind** engstirnig *od.* spießig sein; **a ~ existence** ein Spießerdasein 5 (restricted) eng ‹*Grenzen, Toleranzen*›; klein, begrenzt ‹*Freundeskreis*›; beengt ‹*Verhältnisse*›; schmal ‹*Einkommen*› 6 (precise) genau; gründlich, eingehend ‹*Prüfung, Befragung*›
B *n. usu. in pl.* (of sea) Meerenge, *die*
C *v.i.* sich verschmälern; ‹*Augen, Tal:*› sich verengen; (fig.) [zusammen]schrumpfen; **the road ~s to one lane** die Straße wird einspurig
D *v.t.* verschmälern; (fig.) einengen; enger fassen ‹*Definition*›; **~ one's eyes** die Augen zusammenkneifen; **~ the field** (fig.) eine Vorauswahl treffen

Phrasal verb

• **~ ˈdown**
A *v.t.* einengen, beschränken (**to** auf + *Akk.*)
B *v.i.* sich reduzieren (**to** auf + *Akk.*); **the choice ~s down to two possibilities** es bleiben zwei Möglichkeiten [übrig]

narrow: ~ boat *n.* (Brit.) *besonders schmales Binnenschiff;* **~-gauge** *adj.* schmalspurig; Schmalspur-

narrowly /ˈnærəʊlɪ/ *adv.* 1 (with little width) schmal 2 (only just) knapp; mit knapper Not ‹*entkommen*›; **he ~ escaped being run over by a car** er wäre um ein Haar (ugs.) überfahren worden; **~ miss winning [the election/race]** [bei der Wahl/in dem Rennen] knapp unterliegen 3 (closely) genau; eng ‹*auslegen*›

narrow: ~-ˈminded *adj.*, **~-mindedly** /nærəʊˈmaɪndɪdlɪ/ *adv.* engstirnig (abwertend); **~-mindedness** /nærəʊˈmaɪndɪdnɪs/ *n., no pl.* Engstirnigkeit, *die* (abwertend); **~-ˈshouldered** *adj.* schmalschultrig; **~ ˈsqueak** ▸ **squeak A 2**

narwhal /ˈnɑːwəl/ *n.* (Zool.) Narwal, *der*

nary /ˈneərɪ/ *adj.* (coll./dial.) **~ a ...:** kein einziger/keine einzige/kein einziges ...

NASA /ˈnæsə/ *abbr.* (Amer.) **= National Aeronautics and Space Administration** NASA, *die*

nasal /ˈneɪzl/
A *adj.* 1 (Anat.) Nasen- 2 näselnd; **speak in a ~ voice** durch die Nase sprechen; näseln; **have a ~ intonation** näselnd sprechen; näseln 3 (Ling.) nasal; Nasal-
B *n.* (Ling.) Nasal[laut], *der*

nasalize /ˈneɪzəlaɪz/ *v.t.* (Ling.) nasalieren

nasal ˈstrip *n.* Nasenpflaster, *das*

nascent /ˈnæsnt/ *adj.* 1 (literary: coming into existence) werdend; im Entstehen begriffen; aufkommend, (geh.) aufkeimend ‹*Hoffnung, Stolz*› 2 (Chem.) naszierend

nastily /ˈnɑːstɪlɪ/ *adv.* 1 (disagreeably, unpleasantly) scheußlich 2 (ill-naturedly) gemein; gehässig; ärgerlich ‹*etwas sagen*›; **behave ~:** hässlich sein 3 (disgustingly) eklig; widerlich

nasturtium /nəˈstɜːʃəm/ *n.* 1 (in popular use: garden plant) Kapuzinerkresse, *die* 2 (Bot.: cruciferous plant) Brunnenkresse, *die*

nasty /ˈnɑːstɪ/
A *adj.* 1 (disagreeable, unpleasant) scheußlich ‹*Geruch, Geschmack, Arznei, Essen, Wetter*›; gemein ‹*Trick, Verhalten, Äußerung, Mensch*›; hässlich ‹*Angewohnheit*›; **her ~ little ways** ihre kleinen Gemeinheiten; **that was a ~ thing to say/do** das war gemein *od.* eine Gemeinheit; **that's a ~ one** (awkward question) das ist vertrackt; (injury) das ist übel *od.* sieht böse aus; **a ~ bit** *or* **piece of work** (coll.) (man) ein fieser Kerl (ugs. abwertend); (woman) ein fieses Weibsstück (ugs. abwertend); *see also* **cheap A 1** 2 (ill-natured) böse; **be ~ to sb.** hässlich zu jmdm. sein; **he has a ~ temper** er ist jähzornig; **cut up** *or* **turn ~** (coll.) eklig werden (ugs.) 3 (serious) übel; böse ‹*Verletzung, Husten usw.*›; schlimm ‹*Krankheit, Husten, Verletzung, Wende*›; **that's a ~-looking wound** die Wunde sieht übel *od.* böse aus; **she had a ~ fall** sie ist übel *od.* böse gefallen; **He had to have his leg amputated — N~!** Sein Bein musste amputiert werden — Das ist schlimm! 4 (disgusting) eklig; widerlich; **don't touch that, it's ~:** pfui, fass das nicht an! (fam.); nicht anfassen, das ist bä bä (Kinderspr.) 5 (obscene) schweinisch (ugs. abwertend); **call sb. ~ names** jmdn. mit schweinischen Ausdrücken beschimpfen
B *n.* 1 (person) Ekel, *das* (ugs. abwertend); Fiesling, *der* (salopp abwertend) 2 (thing) ekliges Ding; *see also* **video nasty**

Nat. *abbr.* (Polit.) **= Nationalist**

natal /ˈneɪtl/ *adj.* Geburts-

natch /nætʃ/ *adv.* (coll.) versteht sich (ugs.); logisch (ugs.)

nation /ˈneɪʃn/ *n.* Nation, *die;* (people) Volk, *das;* **law of ~s** Völkerrecht, *das;* **throughout the ~:** im ganzen Land. *See also* **League of**

Nationalities

In English, words such as German, French, Italian etc. are both adjectives referring to the language and the people and nouns meaning a language or a person, and are always written with a capital. In German, the words **deutsch, französisch, italienisch** and so on are also used as both adjectives and nouns, with the differences that only the nouns are written with a capital, and the noun meaning a language is only in a few cases the same as the noun meaning a person, and then it has endings while that meaning a language usually does not (for full details of these see ◻ **Languages**).

Adjectives

Translating adjective plus noun combinations is straightforward (remembering the small letter for the adjective):

an Italian car
= ein italienisches Auto
the French government
= die französische Regierung
a German painter
= ein deutscher Maler/eine deutsche Malerin

When referring to a unique national institution, the name of the country in the genitive is often preferred (just as one can also use *of* plus the name of the country in English):

the Indian capital = the capital of India
= die Hauptstadt Indiens

When the adjective is predicative, i.e. standing on its own, and refers to a person or persons, the English nationality adjective will always be translated by the noun in German:

He is Italian
= Er ist Italiener
She is Indian
= Sie ist Inderin
The tourists are French
= Die Touristen sind Franzosen

Referring to a thing, German often prefers to avoid having the adjective standing on its own:

The car is Italian
= Es ist ein italienisches Auto, *rather than* Das Auto ist italienisch

Nouns

As in English, the nouns for people of different nationalities vary in form, but in German there are feminine forms in all cases ending in **-in**. A large number of them have the **-er** ending added to the word for the country for the masculine, and **-erin** for the feminine:

an Englishman/Englishwoman
= ein Engländer/eine Engländerin
an Italian
= ein Italiener/eine Italienerin (*Italy* = Italien)
an Austrian
= ein Österreicher/eine Österreicherin (*Austria* = Österreich)
a Japanese
= ein Japaner/eine Japanerin

A number of these nouns end in **-e**, and this disappears when the feminine ending is added:

a Frenchman/Frenchwoman
= ein Franzose/eine Französin
a Chinese
= ein Chinese/eine Chinesin
a Dane
= ein Däne/eine Dänin
a Russian
= ein Russe/eine Russin

The plural in these cases adds an **-n** (**Franzosen, Chinesen, Dänen, Russen**) to the masculine, and it is this masculine plural form that is used when referring to a group of mixed gender, or the whole nation:

the French
= die Franzosen
the English
= die Engländer

Last but not least, the noun for a German is the adjective as a noun:

a German
= ein Deutscher/eine Deutsche
the Germans
= die Deutschen
He was the only German
= Er war der einzige Deutsche
The prize was awarded to a German
= Der Preis wurde einem Deutschen verliehen

Phrases

She is Spanish by birth
= Sie ist von Geburt Spanierin *or* gebürtige Spanierin
He is of German extraction
= Er ist deutscher Abstammung
I come from the north of England
= Ich stamme *or* komme aus Nordengland
He's a Belgian national or citizen
= Er ist belgischer Staatsbürger
a naturalized Swiss citizen
= ein eingebürgerter *or* naturalisierter Schweizer/eine eingebürgerte *or* naturalisierte Schweizerin

n

Nations; **United Nations**

national /ˈnæʃənl/
A *adj.* national; National‹*flagge, -denkmal, -held, -theater, -tanz, -gericht, -charakter, -kirche, -ökonomie, -einkommen*›; Landes‹*durchschnitt, -sprache*›; Volks‹*wirtschaft, -charakter, -held*›; Staats‹*sicherheit, -religion, -symbol*›; überregional ‹*Rundfunkstation, Zeitung*›; landesweit ‹*Streik*›; **the rose is the ~ flower of England** die Rose ist das Symbol Englands
B *n.* **1** (citizen) Staatsbürger, *der*/-bürgerin, *die*; **foreign ~:** Ausländer, *der*/Ausländerin, *die* **2** (fellow countryman) Landsmann, *der*/-männin, *die* **3** *usu. in pl.* (newspaper) überregionale Zeitung; [großes] überregionales Blatt **4** (Brit.: horse race) **the N~:** das Grand National

national: ~ ˈanthem *n.* Nationalhymne, *die*; **N~ Asˈsembly** *n.* Nationalversammlung, *die*; **N~ Asˈsistance** *n.* (Brit. dated) Sozialhilfe, *die*; **be on N~ Assistance** Sozialhilfe beziehen; **~ ˈbank** *n.* (Amer.) Nationalbank, *die*; **~ call** *n.* (Brit. Teleph.) Inlandsgespräch, *das*; **~ conˈvention** *n.* (Amer.) Nationalkonvent, *der*; ≈ Bundeskongress, *der*; **~ ˈcostume** *n.* Nationaltracht, *die*; Landestracht, *die*; **N~ Curˈriculum** *n.* (Brit.) Nationales Curriculum; **N~ ˈDebt** ▸**debt**; **~ ˈdress** ▸**~ costume**; **~ ˈfootball** *n.* (Austral.) australischer Fußball; **N~ ˈFront** *n.* (Brit.) National Front, *die* (*britische Organisation mit extremen reaktionären Positionen z. B. in Bezug auf die Einwanderungspolitik*); *attrib.* National-Front-‹*Mitglied, Slogan usw.*›; **~ ˈgrid** *n.* (Brit.) **1** (Electr.) nationales Verbundnetz; **~ grid system** nationales Verbundsystem; **2** (Geog.) nationales Gitternetz; **N~ ˈGuard** *n.* (Amer.) Nationalgarde, *die*; **N~ ˈHealth [Service]** *n.* (Brit.) *staatlicher Gesundheitsdienst*; **he had his teeth done on the N~ Health** er hat sich (*Dat.*) seine Zähne auf Kosten des staatlichen Gesundheitsdienstes in Ordnung bringen *od.* (ugs.) machen lassen; *attrib.* **National Health doctor/patient/spectacles** ≈ Kassenarzt, *der*/-patient, *der*/-brille, *die*; **~ ˈholiday** *n.* Nationalfeiertag, *der*; (statutory holiday) gesetzlicher Feiertag; **N~ Inˈsurance** *n.* (Brit.) Sozialversicherung, *die*

National Health Service (NHS)

Das staatliche Gesundheitssystem in Großbritannien, das die ärztliche Versorgung gewährleistet. Es wird größtenteils aus öffentlichen Geldern finanziert. Ein Großteil der medizinischen Versorgung ist kostenlos. Kostenpflichtig sind jedoch Zahnarztbehandlungen und verschriebene Medikamente. Von der Zahlung ausgenommen sind Kinder, Jugendliche unter 18 Jahren und Rentner.

National Insurance (NI)

Obligatorische Sozialabgaben von Arbeitgebern und Arbeitnehmern in Großbritannien werden *National Insurance contributions* genannt. Jeder Erwachsene muss eine *National Insurance number* haben. Mithilfe dieses Systems werden verschiedene staatliche Zuwendungen finanziert, wie z.B. die **jobseeker's allowance**, die Altersrenten sowie der **National Health Service**.

nationalisation, nationalise ▸**nationaliz-**

nationalism /ˈnæʃənəlɪzm/ *n.* Nationalismus, *der*; (patriotism) nationale Gesinnung; **feelings of ~:** nationale Gefühle

nationalist /ˈnæʃənəlɪst/
A *n.* Nationalist, *der*/Nationalistin, *die*
B *adj.* nationalistisch

nationalistic /næʃənəˈlɪstɪk/ *adj.* **1** (patriotic) nationalistisch **2** (national) national

nationality /næʃəˈnælɪtɪ/ *n.* **1** Staatsangehörigkeit, *die*; Nationalität, *die* (geh.); **be of** *or* **have British ~:** britischer Nationalität sein (geh.); die britische Staatsangehörigkeit haben; **what's his ~?** welche Staatsangehörigkeit hat er?; welcher Nationalität ist er? (geh.) **2** (ethnic group) Nationalität, *die*; Volksgruppe, *die* **3** (of ship, aircraft, company) Nationalität, *die*

nationalization /næʃənəlaɪˈzeɪʃn/ *n.* **1** (bringing under state control) Verstaatlichung, *die*; Nationalisierung, *die* **2** (making national) Nationalisierung, *die*

nationalize /ˈnæʃənəlaɪz/ *v.t.* **1** (bring under state control) verstaatlichen, nationalisieren ‹*Betriebe, Industriezweige*› **2** (make national) nationalisieren

National Lottery

Eine Lotterie in Großbritannien, die ihre Einnahmen einer Vielzahl von Projekten in der Kunst, dem Sport, nationalen historischen Stätten und wohltätigen Zwecken zuführt. Die *National Lottery* wurde 1994 von der Regierung eingeführt.

nationally /ˈnæʃənəlɪ/ *adv.* als Nation; (throughout the nation) landesweit

National: ~ ˈmonument *n.* nationales Denkmal; (national park) Nationalpark, *der*; **n~ ˈpark** *n.* Nationalpark, *der*; **~ ˈSavings** *n. pl.* (Brit.) Staatsschuldverschreibungen *Pl.*; *attrib.* **~ Savings certificate** Sparkassengutschein, *der*; öffentlicher Sparbrief; **n~ ˈservice** *n.* (Brit.) Wehrdienst, *der*; **do n~ service** seinen Wehrdienst ableisten; **~ ˈSocialist** *n.* (Hist.) Nationalsozialist, *der*/-sozialistin, *die*; *attrib.* nationalsozialistisch; **~ ˈTrust** *n.* (Brit.) *nationale Einrichtung für Naturschutz und Denkmalpflege*; **~ Voˈcational Qualification** *n.* (Brit.) *staatliches Berufsausbildungsprogramm*

> **National Trust**
>
> Eine Stiftung zur Erhaltung und Pflege von Stätten von historischem Interesse oder besonderer Naturschönheiten. Der *National Trust* finanziert sich aus Stiftungsgeldern und privaten Spenden und ist der größte Privateigner von Land in Großbritannien. Er hat riesige Landflächen, Dörfer und Häuser gekauft oder erhalten, die alle zu bestimmten Zeiten öffentlich zugänglich sind.

nationhood /'neɪʃnhʊd/ *n.* nationale Selbstständigkeit

nation: ~ **'state** *n.* Nationalstaat, *der;* **~wide** **A** /'---/ *adj.* landesweit; national ‹*Bedeutung*›. **B** /--'-/ *adv.* landesweit; im ganzen Land

native /'neɪtɪv/

A *n.* **1** (of specified place) **a ~ of Britain** ein gebürtiger Brite/eine gebürtige Britin; **speak English like a ~:** Englisch wie seine Muttersprache sprechen **2** (indigenous person) Eingeborene, *der/die* **3** (local inhabitant) Einheimische, *der/die;* **the ~s** die Einheimischen; die einheimische Bevölkerung **4** (Zool., Bot.) **be a ~ of a place** in einem Ort beheimatet *od.* heimisch sein **5** (S. Afr.: Black) Schwarze, *der/die*

B *adj.* **1** (indigenous) eingeboren; (local) einheimisch ‹*Pflanze, Tier*›; **be a ~ American** gebürtiger Amerikaner/gebürtige Amerikanerin sein; **the ~ habitat of the zebra** die Heimat des Zebras; **~ inhabitant** Eingeborene/Einheimische, *der/die* **2** (of one's birth) Geburts-, Heimat‹*land, -stadt*›; Vater‹*land, -stadt*› (geh.); Mutter‹*sprache, -sprachler*›; heimatlich ‹*Wälder*›; **one's ~ soil** die Heimaterde; **in his ~ France** in seiner Heimat Frankreich; **~ speaker** Muttersprachler, *der/-sprachlerin, die;* **he's not a ~ speaker of English** Englisch ist nicht seine Muttersprache **3** (innate) angeboren ‹*Qualitäten, Schläue, Humor, Wissen*› **4** (of the ~s) Eingeborenen-; **go ~:** die Lebensweise der Eingeborenen annehmen **5** (Mining) gediegen

> **Native American**
>
> Dies ist die heute akzeptierte Bezeichnung für die Ureinwohner Nordamerikas. Sie wird besonders im offiziellen Kontext dem Ausdruck *American Indian* vorgezogen, da sie akkurater und positiver ist, denn *Indian* rührt daher, dass Kolumbus bei seiner Ankunft in Amerika annahm, in Indien zu sein. *American Indian* wird aber weiterhin viel verwendet und von den betreffenden Völkern nicht als diskriminierend empfunden.

native: ~ **'bear** (Austral., NZ) ▸ **koala bear;** ~ **'rock** *n.* anstehendes Gestein; gewachsener Fels

nativity /nə'tɪvɪtɪ/ *n.* **1** Geburt, *die;* **the N~ [of Christ]** die Geburt Christi **2** (festival) **the N~ of Christ** das Fest der Geburt Christi **3** (picture) Geburt Christi

na'tivity play *n.* Krippenspiel, *das*

NATO, Nato /'neɪtəʊ/ *abbr.* = **North Atlantic Treaty Organization** NATO, *die*

natter /'nætə(r)/ (Brit. coll.)

A *v.i.* quatschen (ugs.); quasseln (ugs.)

B *n.* Schwatz, *der* (fam.); Schwätzchen, *das* (fam.); **have a bit of a ~:** ein bisschen quatschen (ugs.); ein Schwätzchen halten (fam.)

natterjack /'nætədʒæk/ *n.* (Zool.) ~ **[toad]** Kreuzkröte, *die*

nattily /'nætɪlɪ/ *adv.* (coll.) schick; flott (ugs.)

natty /'nætɪ/ *adj.* (coll.) **1** (spruce) schick, (ugs.) flott ‹*Kleidungs[stück]*›; **be a ~ dresser** immer schick *od.* flott angezogen sein **2** (handy) praktisch ‹*Gerät, Werkzeug usw.*›

natural /'nætʃrəl/

A *adj.* **1** (existing in or by nature) natürlich; Natur‹*zustand, -begabung, -talent, -seide, -schwamm, -faser, -gewalt, -erscheinung*›; gediegen ‹*Gold, Mineralien*›; naturgetreu ‹*Wiedergabe, Darstellung*›; **the ~ world** die Natur[welt]; **in its ~ state** im ursprünglichen Zustand *od.* Naturzustand; **be a ~ blonde** naturblondes Haar haben; von Natur aus blond sein **2** (normal) natürlich; **it is ~ for dogs to fight** es ist natürlich, dass Hunde kämpfen; **it is ~ for you to think that** es ist klar, dass du das denkst; **die of** *or* **from ~ causes** eines natürlichen Todes sterben; **have a ~ tendency to ...:** naturgemäß dazu neigen, ... zu ... **3** (unaffected) natürlich ‹*Art, Lächeln, Stil*› **4** (destined) natürlich ‹*Feinde*›; **be a ~ artist** *etc.* der geborene Künstler *usw.* sein **5** (related by nature) leiblich ‹*Eltern, Kind usw.*›; natürlich (Rechtsspr. veralt.) ‹*Kind*› **6** (instinctive) Natur‹*recht*›; auf das Naturrecht gegründet ‹*Gerechtigkeit*›

B *n.* **1** (person naturally expert or endowed) Naturtalent, *das;* **she's a ~ for the part** die Rolle ist ihr auf den Leib geschrieben; **he was a ~ for the job** er war der Mann für die Stelle **2** (arch.: mentally deficient person) Schwachsinnige, *der/die* **3** (Mus.) (symbol) Auflösungszeichen, *das;* (note) Stammton, *der;* (white key on piano) weiße Taste; **he played C sharp instead of C ~:** er hat cis statt c gespielt

natural: ~ **'childbirth** *n.* natürliche Geburt; ~ **'death** *n.* natürlicher Tod; **die a ~ death** eines natürlichen Todes sterben; **let the gossip die a ~ death** warten, bis sich das Gerede von selber legt; ~ **'food** *n.* naturreines Nahrungsmittel; **~ food[s]** Naturkost, *die;* ~ **'gas** ▸ **gas A 1;** ~ **hi'storian** *n.* Naturkundler, *der/-kundlerin, die;* ~ **'history** *n.* **1** (study) Naturkunde, *die; attrib.* Naturkunde-; naturkundlich ‹*Museum*›; **2** (facts) Naturgeschichte, *die*

naturalisation, naturalise ▸ **naturaliz-**

naturalism /'nætʃrəlɪzm/ *n.* Naturalismus, *der*

naturalist /'nætʃrəlɪst/ *n.* **1** Naturforscher, *der/-forscherin, die* **2** (believer in naturalism) Naturalist, *der*/Naturalistin, *die*

naturalistic /nætʃrə'lɪstɪk/ *adj.* naturalistisch

naturalization /nætʃrəlaɪ'zeɪʃn/ *n.* (admission to citizenship) Einbürgerung, *die;* Naturalisierung, *die; attrib.* Einbürgerungs-

naturalize /'nætʃrəlaɪz/

A *v.t.* **1** (admit to citizenship) einbürgern; naturalisieren **2** (adopt) übernehmen ‹*Fremdwort, Sitte*› **3** (introduce) naturalisieren, einbürgern ‹*Tiere, Pflanzen*›; **this plant has become ~d here** diese Pflanze wurde hier heimisch

B *v.i.* eingebürgert werden

natural: ~ **'language** *n.* natürliche Sprache; *attrib.* **~-language processing** (Computing) Verarbeitung natürlichsprachlicher Informationen; **~-language programming** Programmieren in natürlicher Sprache; ~ **'law** *n.* Naturrecht, *das;* (regularity) Naturgesetz, *das;* ~ **'life** *n.* Erdenleben, *das* (meist dichter., geh. od. veralt.); ~ **'logarithm** *n.* natürlicher Logarithmus

naturally /'nætʃrəlɪ/ *adv.* **1** (by nature) von Natur aus ‹*musikalisch, blass, fleißig usw.*›; (in a true-to-life way) naturgetreu; (with ease) natürlich; (in a natural manner) auf natürliche Weise; **a ~ posed photograph** ein natürlich wirkendes Foto; **it comes ~ to her** es fällt ihr leicht; es liegt in ihrer Natur; **leadership comes so ~ to him** die Führungsrolle liegt ihm sehr; **lead ~ to sth.** naturgemäß zu etw. führen **2** (of course) natürlich

naturalness /'nætʃrəlnɪs/ *n.* Natürlichkeit, *die*

natural: ~ **note** *n.* (Mus.) Stammton, *der;* ~ **'number** *n.* (Math.) natürliche Zahl; ~ **'order** *n.* (Biol.) natürliche Kategorie; ~ **phi'losopher** *n.* Naturphilosoph, *der/-philosophin, die;* ~ **phi'losophy** *n.* **1** (physics) Naturphilosophie, *die;* **2** (~ science) die Naturwissenschaften; ~ **re'ligion** *n.* natürliche Religion; ~ **re'sources** *n. pl.* natürliche Ressourcen; Naturschätze *Pl.;* ~ **'scale** *n.* (Mus.) Grundskala, *die;* ~ **'science** *n.* **~ science** die Naturwissenschaften; ~ **se'lection** *n., no pl.* (Biol.) natürliche Auslese; ~ **'wastage** *n., no pl.* (Brit.) natürliche Fluktuation; natürlicher Schwund

nature /'neɪtʃə(r)/ *n.* **1** Natur, *die;* **a gift from N~:** ein Geschenk der Natur; **balance of ~:** Gleichgewicht der Natur; **against** *or* **contrary to ~:** wider die Natur *od.* widernatürlich; **back to ~:** zurück zur Natur; **get back** *or* **return to ~:** zu einer natürlichen Lebensweise zurückkehren; **paint from ~:** nach der Natur malen; **in ~** (actually existing) in der Wirklichkeit; (anywhere) auf Erden; **one of ~'s gentlemen** ein geborener Gentleman; **one of ~'s innocents** die Unschuld selbst; **in a state of ~** (undomesticated, uncultivated) in der Wildform; *see also* **call C 6; course A 1; law 8** **2** (essential qualities) Beschaffenheit, *die;* **in the ~ of things** naturgemäß; **it is in** *or* **by the [very] ~ of the case/of things** es liegt in der Natur der Sache/Dinge **3** (kind, sort) Art, *die;* **things of this ~:** Derartiges; Dinge dieser Art; **or something of that ~:** oder etwas in der Art; **it's in** *or* **of the ~ of a command** es hat Befehlscharakter **4** (character) [Wesens]art, *die;* Wesen, *das;* **have a happy ~:** eine Frohnatur sein; ein glückliches Naturell haben; **be of** *or* **have a placid ~:** eine ruhige Art haben; **have a jealous ~:** eifersüchtig sein; **it is not in her ~ to lie** es ist nicht ihre Art zu lügen; **be proud/friendly** *etc.* **by ~:** ein stolzes/freundliches *usw.* Wesen haben; **[human] ~:** menschliche Natur; **it's only human ~ to ...:** es ist nur menschlich, ... zu ...; *see also* **better A; second nature** **5** (inherent impulses) Natur, *die;* **commit a sin/crime against ~:** sich wider die Natur versündigen (geh.) **6** (person) Natur, *die*

nature: ~ **conservation** *n.* Naturschutz, *der;* ~ **cure** *n.* Naturheilverfahren, *das*

-natured /'neɪtʃəd/ *adj. in comb.* -artig; *see also* **good-natured; ill-natured**

nature: ~ **lover** *n.* Naturfreund, *der/-freundin, die;* ~ **reserve** *n.* Naturschutzgebiet, *das;* ~ **study** *n.* Naturkunde, *die;* ~ **trail** *n.* Naturlehrpfad, *der;* ~ **worshipper** *n.* Naturanbeter, *der/-anbeterin, die*

naturism /'neɪtʃərɪzm/ *n.* (nudism) Naturismus, *der;* Freikörperkultur, *die*

naturist /'neɪtʃərɪst/ *n.* (nudist) Naturist, *der*/Naturistin, *die;* FKK-Anhänger, *der*/FKK-Anhängerin, *die*

naught /nɔːt/ *n.* (arch./dial.) ~ **but** nur; **I care ~ for what they say** ich scher mich keinen Deut darum, was sie sagen; **bring to ~:** zunichte machen; **come to ~:** zunichte werden; **it matters ~:** es ist ohne Belang

naughtily /'nɔːtɪlɪ/ *adv.* ungezogen, unartig ‹*sich benehmen*›; frech ‹*etw. tun, bemerken*›

naughtiness /'nɔːtɪnɪs/ *n.* Ungezogenheit, *die;* Unartigkeit, *die*

naughty /'nɔːtɪ/ *adj.* **1** (disobedient) unartig; ungezogen; **the dog has been ~ on the carpet** (coll. euphem.) der Hund hat auf den Teppich gemacht (ugs.); **you ~ boy/dog** du böser Junge/Hund **2** (indecent) unanständig; **how ~ of him** das war aber frech *od.* kess von ihm; **~, ~!** du bist ja ein ganz Schlimmer!/eine ganz Schlimme!

nausea /'nɔːzɪə, 'nɔːsɪə/ *n.* **1** ▸ **❶ p. 1231** Übelkeit, *die;* **even the idea fills me with ~:** schon beim bloßen Gedanken daran wird mir übel **2** (fig.: disgust) Ekel, *der,* Abscheu, *der* (**with, at** vor + *Dat.*)

nauseate /'nɔːzɪeɪt, 'nɔːsɪeɪt/ *v.t.* **1** ▸ **❶ p. 1231** ~ **sb.** in jmdm. Übelkeit erregen; **the smell ~d him** bei dem Geruch wurde ihm übel **2** (fig.: disgust) anekeln; anwidern

nauseating /'nɔːzɪeɪtɪŋ, 'nɔːsɪeɪtɪŋ/ *adj.* **1** Übelkeit verursachend *od.* erregend **2** (fig.: disgusting) widerlich; Ekel erregend ‹*Anblick, Geruch, Essen*›; ekelhaft ‹*Mensch*›

nauseatingly /'nɔːzɪeɪtɪŋlɪ, 'nɔːsɪeɪtɪŋlɪ/ *adv.* (lit. or fig.) widerlich

nauseous /'nɔːzɪəs, 'nɔːsɪəs/ *adj.* **1** ▸ **❶ p. 1231 sb. is** *or* **feels ~:** jmdm. ist übel **2** (fig.: nasty, disgusting) widerlich

nautical /'nɔːtɪkl/ *adj.* nautisch; seemännisch ‹*Ausdruck, Können*›; ~ **map** Seekarte, *die;* **be interested in ~ matters** sich für die Seefahrt interessieren

nautically /'nɔːtɪkəlɪ/ *adv.* nautisch

nautical 'mile *n.* Seemeile, *die;* nautische Meile

nautilus /ˈnɔːtɪləs/ *n., pl.* **~es** *or* **nautili** /ˈnɔːtɪlaɪ/ (Zool.) Nautilus, *der*

naval /ˈneɪvl/ *adj.* Marine-; Flotten‹*parade, -abkommen*›; See‹*schlacht, -macht, -streitkräfte*›; ‹*Überlegenheit*› zur See; **~ ship** Kriegsschiff, *das*

naval: ~ aˈcademy *n.* Marineakademie, *die;* **~ ˈarchitect** *n.* ▸❶ **p. 1260** Schiffsbauingenieur, *der;* **~ base** *n.* Flottenstützpunkt, *der;* **~ officer** *n.* Marineoffizier, *der;* **~ ˈstores** *n. pl.* Schiffsvorräte *Pl.;* **~ ˈwarfare** *n.* Seekrieg, *der;* Krieg zur See

nave /neɪv/ *n.* (Archit.) [Mittel-, Haupt]schiff, *das*

navel /ˈneɪvl/ *n.* Nabel, *der;* **contemplate one's ~** (fig.) Nabelschau halten (ugs. abwertend)

ˈnavel orange *n.* Navelorange, *die*

navigable /ˈnævɪgəbl/ *adj.* [1] (suitable for ships) schiffbar; befahrbar [2] (seaworthy) seetüchtig ‹*Schiff, Zustand*› [3] (steerable) lenkbar, steuerbar ‹*Ballon, Luftschiff*›

navigate /ˈnævɪgeɪt/

A *v.t.* [1] (sail on) beschiffen (veralt.), befahren ‹*Kanal, Fluss, Gewässer*› [2] (direct course of) navigieren ‹*Schiff, Flugzeug*› [3] (fig.) **~ one's way to the bar** sich (*Dat.*) einen Weg zur Bar bahnen [4] (Computing) **to ~ the Web** im Netz navigieren

B *v.i.* [1] (in ship, aircraft) navigieren [2] (assist driver) den Lotsen spielen (ugs.); franzen (Rallyesport); **you drive, I'll ~:** du fährst, und ich dirigiere *od.* lotse dich

navigation /nævɪˈgeɪʃn/ *n.* [1] (navigating) Navigation, *die;* Navigieren, *das;* (sailing on river etc.) Befahren, *das;* (assisting driver) Dirigieren, *das;* Lotsen, *das;* Franzen, *das* (Rallyesport); **I'm relying on you to do the ~:** ich verlasse mich darauf, dass du mich richtig dirigierst [2] (art, science) Navigation, *die* [3] (voyage) Fahrt, *die;* Reise, *die* [4] (Computing) Navigation, *die; attrib.* Navigations-

navigational /nævɪˈgeɪʃənl/ *adj.* Navigations-

navigation: ~ lights *n. pl.* (Naut.) Lichter; (Aeronaut.) Kennlichter; **~ satellite** *n.* Navigationssatellit, *der;* **~ system** *n.* Navigationssystem, *das*

navigator /ˈnævɪgeɪtə(r)/ *n.* [1] (one skilled in navigation) Navigator, *der*/Navigatorin, *die;* **his co-driver was acting as ~:** sein Beifahrer dirigierte *od.* lotste ihn [2] (sea explorer) Seefahrer, *der*

navvy /ˈnævɪ/ (Brit.)

A *n.* (labourer) Bau-/Straßenarbeiter, *der*

B *v.i.* Bau-/Straßenarbeiter sein

navy /ˈneɪvɪ/ *n.* [1] [Kriegs]marine, *die;* (ships also) [Kriegs]flotte, *die* [2] ▸**navy blue**

navy: ~ ˈblue *n.* Marineblau, *das;* **~-blue** *adj.* marineblau; **N~ Department** *n.* (Amer.) Marineministerium, *das;* **N~ List** *n.* (Brit.) Rangliste der Marine; **~ yard** *n.* (Amer.) Marinewerft, *die*

nay /neɪ/

A *adv.* [1] (literary: or rather) ja [sogar] [2] (arch./dial.: no) nein

B *n.* [1] (negative vote) Neinstimme, *die* [2] (arch./dial.: no) Nein, *das. See also* **yea B**

Nazi /ˈnɑːtsɪ/

A *n.* [1] (party member) Nationalsozialist, *der*/-sozialistin, *die;* Nazi, *der* [2] (fig. derog.) Faschist, *der*/Faschistin, *die* (abwertend); Nazi, *der* (abwertend)

B *adj.* [1] nazistisch; Nazi- [2] (fig. derog.) faschistisch (abwertend); Nazi- (abwertend)

Naziism /ˈnɑːtsɪɪzm/, **Nazism** /ˈnɑːtsɪzm/ *n.* Nazismus, *der*

NB *abbr.* **= nota bene** NB

NBC *abbr.* **= nuclear, biological, chemical;** *attrib.* **~ weapons** ABC-Waffen

> **NBC – National Broadcasting Company**
>
> Die erste Rundfunkgesellschaft in den USA. Sie wurde 1926 gegründet. Das erste *NBC*-Nachrichtenprogramm wurde 1940 ausgestrahlt.

NCO *abbr.* **= non-commissioned officer** Uffz.

NE *abbr.* ▸❶ **p. 1013** [1] /ˈnɔːθiːst/ **= north-east** NO [2] /ˈnɔːθiːstən/ **= north-eastern** nö.

Neanderthal /nɪˈændətɑːl/ *adj.* Neandertaler-; (fig.) neandertalerhaft; **~ man** Neandertaler, *der*

neap /niːp/ ▸**neap tide**

Neapolitan /niːəˈpɒlɪtn/

A *n.* Neapolitaner, *der*/Neapolitanerin, *die*

B *adj.* Neapolitaner; neapolitanisch

ˈneap tide *n.* Nipptide, *die*

near /nɪə(r)/

A *adv.* [1] ▸❶ **p. 1072,** ▸❶ **p. 1699** (at a short distance) nah[e]; **stand/live [quite] ~:** [ganz] in der Nähe stehen/wohnen; **come** *or* **draw ~/~er** ‹*Tag, Zeitpunkt:*› nahen/näher rücken; **take the one ~est to you** nimm das am nächsten Liegende; **get ~er together** näher zusammenrücken; **~ at hand** in Reichweite (*Dat.*); ‹*Ort*› ganz in der Nähe; **be ~ at hand** ‹*Ereignis:*› nahe bevorstehen; **~ by** in der Nähe; **so ~ and yet so far** so nah und doch so fern

[2] (closely) **it is 7.10 or as ~ as makes no difference** *or* **matter** es ist ziemlich genau *od.* fast 7.10 Uhr; **as ~ as I can judge** soweit ich es beurteilen kann; **no, but ~ enough** nein, aber beinah[e] *od.* fast

[3] **~ to = B 1, 2, 3; he came ~ to being the winner/to tears** er hätte fast *od.* beinah[e] gewonnen/war den Tränen nahe; **we were ~ to being drowned** wir wären fast *od.* beinah[e] ertrunken

B *prep.* [1] ▸❶ **p. 1072** (in space) (position) nahe an/bei (+ *Dat.*); (motion) nahe an (+ *Akk.*); (fig.) nahe (geh.) *nachgestellt* (+ *Dat.*); in der Nähe (+ *Gen.*); **go ~ the water's edge** nahe ans Ufer gehen; **keep ~ me** halte dich *od.* bleib in meiner Nähe; **~ where ...:** in der Nähe *od.* unweit der Stelle (*Gen.*), wo ...; **move it ~er her** rücke es näher zu ihr; **I won't go ~ the police** (fig.) ich gehe der Polizei aus dem Weg; **don't stand so ~ the fire** geh nicht so nahe *od.* dicht an das Feuer; **when we got ~er Oxford** als wir in die Nähe von Oxford kamen; **wait till we're ~er home** warte, bis wir nicht mehr so weit von zu Hause weg sind; **don't come ~ me** komm mir nicht zu nahe; **it's ~ here** es ist hier in der Nähe; **the man ~/~est you** der Mann, der bei dir/der dir am nächsten steht

[2] (in quality) **nobody comes anywhere ~ him at swimming** im Schwimmen kommt bei weitem keiner an ihn heran; **we're no ~er solving the problem** wir sind der Lösung des Problems nicht näher gekommen; **be very ~ the original** dem Original sehr nahe kommen; **be ~ completion** kurz vor der Vollendung stehen

[3] (in time) **it's getting ~ the time when I must leave** der Zeitpunkt, wo ich gehen muss, rückt näher; **ask me again ~er the time** frag mich, wenn der Zeitpunkt etwas näher gerückt ist, noch einmal; **the Monday ~est Christmas** der Montag, der dem Weihnachtstag am nächsten liegt; **it's drawing ~ Christmas** es geht auf Weihnachten zu; **come back ~er 8 o'clock/the appointed time** komm kurz vor 8 Uhr/dem verabredeten Zeitpunkt noch einmal zurück; **~ the end/the beginning of sth.** gegen Ende/zu Anfang einer Sache (*Gen.*)

[4] *in comb.* (close in nature) Beinahe‹*unfall, -zusammenstoß, -katastrophe*›; **~-hysterical/-human** fast hysterisch/menschlich; **a state of ~-panic** ein panikähnlicher Zustand; **be in a state of ~-collapse** kurz vor dem Zusammenbruch stehen; **a ~-miracle** fast *od.* beinahe ein Wunder; **~-famine conditions** Zustände schon fast wie bei einer Hungersnot. *See also* **heart A 2; knuckle 3; nowhere A 3; wind¹ A 1**

C *adj.* [1] (in space or time) nahe; **in the ~ future** in nächster Zukunft; **the ~est man** der am nächsten stehende Mann; **the chair is ~er** der Stuhl steht näher; **our ~est neighbours** unsere nächsten Nachbarn

[2] (closely related) nahe ‹*Verwandte, Freunde*›; eng ‹*Freund*›; **~ and dear** lieb und teuer; *abs.* **my/your** *etc.* **~est and dearest** meine/deine *usw.* Lieben

[3] (in nature) fast richtig ‹*Vermutung*›; groß ‹*Ähnlichkeit*›; genau ‹*Übersetzung*›; **£30 or ~/~est offer** 30 Pfund oder nächstbestes Angebot; **this is the ~est equivalent** dies entspricht dem am ehesten; **that's the ~est you'll get to an answer** eine weiter gehende Antwort wirst du nicht bekommen; **~ escape** Entkommen mit knapper Not; **round it up to the ~est penny** runde es auf den nächsthöheren Pennybetrag; **be a ~ miss** ‹*Schuss, Wurf:*› knapp danebengehen; **I had a ~ miss** (accident) ich hätte um Haaresbreite einen Unfall gehabt; **that was a ~ miss** (escape) das war aber knapp!

[4] **the ~ side** (Brit.) (travelling on the left/right) die linke/rechte Seite

[5] (direct) **4 miles by the ~est road** 4 Meilen auf dem kürzesten Wege

D *v.t.* sich nähern (+ *Dat.*); **the building is ~ing completion** das Gebäude geht seiner Vollendung entgegen *od.* steht kurz vor seiner Vollendung; **he's ~ing his end** sein Ende naht

E *v.i.* ‹*Zeitpunkt:*› näher rücken, (geh.) nahen

ˈnearby *adj.* nahe gelegen

near-ˈdeath experience *n.* Nahtoderfahrung, *die*

Near: ~ ˈEast *n.* [1] ▸**Middle East**; [2] (arch.: Turkey and Balkans) Balkan, *der;* **~ ˈEastern** *adj.* nahöstlich

nearly /ˈnɪəlɪ/ *adv.* [1] ▸❶ **p. 894** (almost) fast; **it ~ fell over** es wäre fast umgefallen; **be ~ crying** *or* **in tears** den Tränen nahe sein; **it is ~ six o'clock** es ist kurz vor sechs Uhr; **are you ~ ready?** bist du bald fertig? [2] (closely) nah[e] ‹*verwandt*›; sehr ‹*ähneln*›; weitgehend ‹*sich entsprechen*› [3] (at all) **not ~:** nicht annähernd; bei weitem nicht

nearness /ˈnɪənɪs/ *n., no pl.* [1] (proximity) Nähe, *die;* **their ~ in age** der geringe Altersunterschied zwischen ihnen [2] (similarity) große Ähnlichkeit

near: ~-sighted *adj.* (Amer.) kurzsichtig; **~ ˈthing** *n.* **that was a ~ thing/what a ~ thing [that was]!** das war knapp!/war das aber knapp!

neat /niːt/ *adj.* [1] (tidy, clean) sauber, ordentlich ‹*Handschrift, Arbeit*›; gepflegt ‹*Haar, Person*›; **keep one's desk ~:** auf seinem Schreibtisch Ordnung halten [2] (undiluted) pur ‹*Getränk*›; **she drinks vodka ~:** sie trinkt Wodka pur [3] (smart) gepflegt ‹*Erscheinung, Kleidung*›; elegant, schick ‹*Anzug, Auto, Haus*› [4] (deft) geschickt; raffiniert ‹*Diebstahl, Trick, Plan, Lösung, Gerät*›; **make a ~ job of sth./repairing sth.** etw. sehr geschickt machen/reparieren [5] (brief, clear) prägnant ‹*Beschreibung, Antwort, Formulierung*› [6] (esp. Amer. coll.: excellent) toll; geil (ugs.)

neath /niːθ/ *prep.* (arch./poet.) unter (+ *Dat.*); nid (+ *Dat.*) (schweiz. veralt.)

neatly /ˈniːtlɪ/ *adv.* [1] (tidily) ordentlich; [fein] säuberlich [2] (smartly) gepflegt; **~ groomed** äußerst gepflegt [3] (deftly) geschickt; auf raffinierte [Art und] Weise [4] (briefly, clearly) prägnant; **a ~ turned phrase** eine prägnante Formulierung

neatness /ˈniːtnɪs/ *n., no pl.* ▸**neat 1, 3, 4, 5**: Sauberkeit, *die;* Ordentlichkeit, *die;* Gepflegtheit, *die;* Eleganz, *die;* Geschick, *das;* Geschicktheit, *die;* Raffiniertheit, *die;* Prägnanz, *die*

nebula /ˈnebjʊlə/ *n., pl.* **~e** /ˈnebjʊliː/ *or* **~s** (Astron.) Nebel, *der*

nebular /ˈnebjʊlə(r)/ *adj.* (Astron.) Nebel-

nebulizer /ˈnebjʊlaɪzə(r)/ *n.* Zerstäuber, *der*

nebulous /ˈnebjʊləs/ *adj.* [1] (hazy) nebelhaft, (geh.) nebulös ‹*Vorstellung, Werte*›; verschwommen ‹*Grenze*›; unbestimmt, vage ‹*Angst, Hoffnung*› [2] (cloudlike) wolkenartig ‹*Form*›

necessarily /nesɪˈserɪlɪ/ *adv.* notwendigerweise; zwangsläufig; **it is not ~ true** es muss nicht [unbedingt] stimmen; **Do we have to do it? — Not ~:** Müssen wir es tun? — Nicht unbedingt

necessary /ˈnesɪsərɪ/

A *adj.* [1] (indispensable) nötig; notwendig; unbedingt ‹*Erfordernis*›; **be ~ to life** lebensnotwendig sein; **patience is ~ for a teacher** ein Lehrer muss Geduld haben; **it is not ~ for you to go** es ist nicht nötig *od.* notwendig, dass du gehst; du brauchst nicht zu *od.* musst nicht gehen; **it may be ~ for him to leave** vielleicht

n

muss er gehen; **they made it ~ for him to attend** ihretwegen musste er hingehen; **do no more than is ~:** nur das Nötigste tun; **do everything ~** (that must be done) das Nötige *od.* Notwendige tun [2] (inevitable) zwangsläufig ‹*Ergebnis, Folge*›; zwingend ‹*Schluss*› [3] **a ~ evil** ein notwendiges Übel

B *n.* **the necessaries of life** das Lebensnotwendige; **will he come up with the ~?** (coll.: money) wird er die Kohle auftreiben? (salopp); **will you do the ~?** kümmerst du dich drum?

necessitate /nɪˈsesɪteɪt/ *v.t.* [1] (make necessary) erforderlich machen [2] (Amer.: force) zwingen; nötigen; **be ~d to do sth.** gezwungen *od.* genötigt sein, etw. zu tun

necessitous /nɪˈsesɪtəs/ *adj.* (formal) bedürftig

necessity /nɪˈsesɪtɪ/ *n.* [1] (power of circumstances) Not, *die;* äußerer Zwang; **bow to ~:** der Not gehorchen (geh.); **do sth. out of** *or* **from ~:** etw. notgedrungen *od.* gezwungenermaßen tun; **make a virtue of ~:** aus der Not eine Tugend machen; **of ~:** notwendigerweise [2] (necessary thing) Notwendigkeit, *die;* **the necessities of life** das Lebensnotwendige; **be a ~ of life** lebensnotwendig sein; **be a ~ for sth.** eine notwendige Voraussetzung für etw. sein [3] (indispensability, imperative need) Notwendigkeit, *die;* **there is no ~ for rudeness** es besteht keine Notwendigkeit *od.* es ist nicht notwendig, unhöflich zu sein; **if the ~ arises** wenn es unbedingt nötig ist; **in case of ~:** nötigenfalls; **~ is the mother of invention** (prov.) Not macht erfinderisch (Spr.) [4] (want) Not, *die;* Bedürftigkeit, *die;* **be/live in ~:** Not leiden

neck /nek/

A *n.* [1] ▸ ❶ **p. 951** Hals, *der;* **be breathing down sb.'s ~** (fig.) (be close behind sb.) jmdm. im Nacken sitzen (ugs.); (watch sb. closely) jmdm. ständig auf die Finger sehen; **get it in the ~** (coll.) eins auf den Deckel *od.* das Dach kriegen (ugs.); **be** *or* **come down on sb.'s ~** (coll.) jmdm. eins auf den Deckel *od.* aufs Dach geben (ugs.); **give sb./be a pain in the ~** (coll.) jmdm. auf die Nerven *od.* den Wecker gehen (ugs.); **have sb. round one's ~** (coll.) jmdn. auf dem *od.* am Hals haben (ugs.); **you'll bring the police down on our ~s** wir werden deinetwegen die Polizei auf den Hals kriegen (ugs.); **break one's/sb.'s ~** (fig. coll.) sich/jmdm. den Hals brechen; **risk one's ~:** Kopf und Kragen riskieren; **save one's ~:** seinen Kopf retten; **be up to one's ~ in work** (coll.) bis über den Hals in Arbeit stecken (ugs.); **be [in it] up to one's ~** (coll.) bis über den Hals drinstecken (ugs.); **~ and ~:** Kopf an Kopf; **~ or nothing** alles oder nichts; **it's [a matter of] ~ or nothing** es geht um die Wurst (ugs.); *see also* **dead A 1**; **millstone**; **stick out A 1** [2] (length) Halslänge, *die;* (fig.) Nasenlänge, *die;* **short ~** (Horseracing) kurze Halslänge [3] (cut of meat) Hals, *der;* **~ of lamb/mutton** *etc.* Lammfleisch/Hammelfleisch *usw.* vom Hals [4] (part of garment) Kragen, *der;* **that dress has a high ~:** das Kleid ist hochgeschlossen [5] (narrow part) Hals, *der* [6] (Geog.: isthmus) Landenge, *die;* **~ of land** Landzunge, *die* [7] **~ of the woods** (coll.) Breiten *Pl.*

B *v.i.* (coll.) knutschen (ugs.)

neck: ~band *n.* Halsbündchen, *das;* **~cloth** *n.* (Hist.) Halstuch, *das*

-necked /nekt/ *adj. in comb.* **red/long-~:** rot-/langhalsig; **polo-~:** Rollkragen-

neckerchief /ˈnekətʃɪf/ *n.* Halstuch, *das*

necklace /ˈneklɪs/ *n.* [Hals]kette, *die;* (with jewels) Collier, *das*

neck: ~line *n.* [Hals]ausschnitt, *der;* **~tie** *n.* Krawatte, *die;* Binder, *der*

necromancer /ˈnekrəmænsə(r)/ *n.* Nekromantiker, *der*/Nekromantikerin, *die*

necromancy /ˈnekrəmænsɪ/ *n., no pl.* Nekromantie, *die*

necrophilia /nekrəˈfɪlɪə/ *n., no pl.* Nekrophilie, *die*

necrosis /neˈkrəʊsɪs/ *n., pl.* **necroses** /neˈkrəʊsiːz/ (Med.) Nekrose, *die*

nectar /ˈnektə(r)/ *n.* [1] (Bot., Greek and Roman Mythol.) Nektar, *der* [2] (delicious drink) Göttertrank, *der* (scherzh.); (drink of blended fruit juices) Nektar, *der* (fachspr.)

nectarine /ˈnektərɪn, ˈnektəriːn/ *n.* Nektarine, *die*

nectary /ˈnektərɪ/ *n.* (Bot.) Nektarium, *das* (fachspr.); Honigdrüse, *die*

NEDC *abbr.* (Brit. Hist.) = **National Economic Development Council** Rat für Wirtschaftsentwicklung

neddy /ˈnedɪ/ *n.* (child lang.: donkey) Esel, *der;* Langohr, *das* (scherzh.)

née (*Amer.:* **nee**) /neɪ/ *adj.* geborene

need /niːd/

A *n.* [1] *no pl.* Notwendigkeit, *die* (**for, of** *Gen.*); (demand) Bedarf, *der* (**for, of** an + *Dat.*); **as the ~ arises** nach Bedarf; **if ~ arise/be** nötigenfalls; falls nötig; **the ~ for discussion** die Notwendigkeit zu diskutieren; **there's no ~ for that** (as answer) [das ist] nicht nötig; **there's no ~ to do sth.** es ist nicht nötig *od.* notwendig, etw. zu tun; **there is no ~ to worry/get angry** es besteht kein Grund zur Sorge/sich zu ärgern; **is there any ~ [for us] to hurry?** müssen wir uns beeilen?; **there was a ~ for caution** Vorsicht war geboten; **be in ~ of sth.** etw. brauchen *od.* nötig haben; **there is no ~ for such behaviour** solch ein Verhalten ist unnötig; **is there any ~ for all this hurry?** ist diese Eile nötig *od.* notwendig?; **there's no ~ for you to apologize** du brauchst dich nicht zu entschuldigen; **feel the ~ to do sth.** sich gezwungen *od.* genötigt sehen, etw. zu tun; **feel the ~ to confide in sb.** das Bedürfnis haben, sich jmdm. anzuvertrauen; **have ~ to do sth.** (dated) es nötig haben, etw. zu tun; **be badly in ~ of sth.** etw. dringend nötig haben; etw. nötig brauchen; **be in ~ of a coat of paint** einen Anstrich nötig haben; **be in ~ of repair** reparaturbedürftig sein; **have ~ of sb./sth.** jmdn./etw. brauchen *od.* nötig haben; **your ~ is greater than mine** du hast es nötiger als ich; du brauchst es dringender als ich

[2] *no pl.* (emergency) Not, *die;* **in case of ~:** im Notfall; **in times of ~:** in Notzeiten; *see also* **friend 1**

[3] *no pl.* (destitution) Not, *die;* Bedürftigkeit, *die;* **be in ~:** Not leiden; **those in ~:** die Notleidenden *od.* Bedürftigen

[4] (thing) Bedürfnis, *das;* **my ~s are few** ich brauche nicht viel; **each will receive according to his ~s** jeder bekommt, was er braucht

B *v.t.* [1] (require) brauchen; **sth. that urgently ~s doing** etw., was dringend gemacht werden muss; **much ~ed** dringend notwendig; **that's all I ~ed!** (iron.) auch das noch!; das hat mir gerade noch gefehlt!; **it ~s a coat of paint** es muss gestrichen werden; **it ~s careful consideration** es muss gut überlegt werden; **~ correction** berichtigt werden müssen; **Education? Who ~s it?** (coll.) Bildung? Wozu?

[2] *expr. necessity* müssen; **I ~ to do it** ich muss es tun; **it ~s/doesn't ~ to be done** es muss getan werden/es braucht nicht getan zu werden; **you don't ~ to do that** das brauchst du nicht zu tun; **I don't ~ to be reminded** du brauchst/ihr braucht mich nicht daran zu erinnern; **it ~ed doing** es musste getan werden; **he ~s cheering up** er muss [ein bisschen] aufgeheitert werden; **he doesn't ~ to be told** das braucht man ihm nicht erst zu sagen; **you shouldn't ~ to be told** das solltest *od.* müsstest du eigentlich wissen; **it doesn't ~ me to tell you** das muss ich dir nicht sagen *od.* brauche ich dir nicht zu sagen; **she ~s everything [to be] explained to her** man muss ihr alles erklären; **you ~ only ask** du brauchst nur zu fragen; **don't be away longer than you ~ [be]** bleib nicht länger als nötig weg

[3] *only in pres.* **need,** *neg.* **need not** *or* (coll.) **needn't** /ˈniːdnt/ *expr. desirability* müssen; *with neg.* brauchen zu; **~ anybody be there?** muss jemand dort sein?; **~ I say more?** muss ich noch mehr sagen?; **~ she have come at all?** hätte sie überhaupt kommen müssen?; **N~ you go? — No, I ~n't** Musst du gehen? — Nein; **I ~ hardly** *or* **hardly ~ say that ...:** ich brauche wohl kaum zu sagen, dass ...; **I don't think that ~ be considered** ich glaube, das braucht nicht berücksichtigt zu werden; **no one ~ know this** das braucht niemand zu wissen; **he ~n't be told** (let's keep it secret) das braucht er nicht zu wissen; **we ~n't** *or* **~ not have done it, if ...:** wir hätten es nicht zu tun brauchen, wenn ...; **it ~ not follow that ...:** daraus folgt nicht unbedingt, dass ...; daraus muss nicht [unbedingt] folgen, dass ...; **that ~ not be the case** das muss nicht so sein *od.* der Fall sein

needful /ˈniːdfl/ *adj.* (arch.) nötig; **it is ~ to do it** es ist vonnöten *od.* (geh., veralt.) tut not, dass es getan wird; **everything/the ~:** alles/das Nötige

needle /ˈniːdl/

A *n.* Nadel, *die;* **it is like looking/searching for a ~ in a haystack** es ist, als wollte man eine Stecknadel in einem Heuhaufen finden; **~ and thread** *or* **cotton** Nadel und Faden; **~'s eye** Nadelöhr, *das;* **give sb. the ~** (Brit. coll.) jmdn. ärgern; **get the ~** (Brit. coll.) sich ärgern; *see also* **pin A 1**

B *v.t.* (coll.) ärgern; nerven (ugs.); **what's needling him?** was fuchst ihn [denn so]? (ugs.)

needle: ~cord *n.* (Textiles) Feinkord, *der;* **~craft** *n.* Nadelarbeit, *die;* **~ exchange** *n.* [1] (service) Nadelaustausch, *der;* [2] (place, building) Fixerstube, *die;* **~ felt** *n.* Nadelfilz, *der;* **~ game, ~ match** *ns.* (Brit.) erbitterter Fight (Sportjargon); **~point** *n.* [1] Nadelspitze, *die;* (fig.) springender Punkt; [2] (embroidery) Stickerei, *die*

needless /ˈniːdlɪs/ *adj.* unnötig; (senseless) sinnlos; **~ to say** *or* **add, he didn't do it** überflüssig zu sagen, dass er es nicht getan hat

needlessly /ˈniːdlɪslɪ/ *adv.* unnötigerweise; (senselessly) sinnlos

needle: ~ valve *n.* (Mech. Engin.) Nadelventil, *das;* **~woman** *n.* (seamstress) Näherin, *die;* **be a good/bad ~woman** gut nähen [können]/schlecht nähen *od.* nicht gut nähen können; **~work** *n.* Handarbeit, *die;* Nadelarbeit, *die* (veralt.); (school subject) Handarbeiten, *das;* Nadelarbeit, *die* (veralt.); **do ~work** handarbeiten; **a piece of ~work** eine Handarbeit

needn't /ˈniːdnt/ (coll.) = **need not;** ▸ **need B 3**

needs /niːdz/ *adv.* (dated) **~ must when the devil drives** (prov.) was sein muss, muss sein; **if ~ must** wenn es [unbedingt] sein muss *od.* nötig ist

need-to-ˈknow *attrib. adj.* **information is shared only on a ~ basis** es werden nur so viele Informationen wie unbedingt nötig weitergegeben; **~ policy/principle** restriktive Informationspolitik

needy /ˈniːdɪ/ *adj.* [1] (poor) Not leidend, bedürftig ‹*Person, Familie*›; **the neediest cases** die schlimmsten Fälle von Bedürftigkeit; **the ~:** die Notleidenden *od.* Bedürftigen [2] ärmlich, dürftig ‹*Verhältnisse*›

ne'er /neə(r)/ *adv.* (poet.: never) nimmer (geh. veralt.); nie; **~ a ...:** kein einziger/keine einzige/kein einziges ...

ne'er-do-well /ˈneəduwel/

A *n.* Tunichtgut, *der*

B *adj.* nichtsnutzig (veralt. abwertend); **~ fellow** Tunichtgut, *der*

nefarious /nɪˈfeərɪəs/ *adj.* ruchlos (geh.); frevelhaft (geh.)

negate /nɪˈgeɪt/ *v.t.* [1] (formal: be negation of) widersprechen (+ *Dat.*) [2] (nullify) zunichte machen [3] (Ling.) negieren (fachspr.); verneinen

negation /nɪˈgeɪʃn/ *n.* [1] (refusal to accept) Ablehnung, *die;* (refusal to accept existence of sth.) Verleugnung, *die* [2] (negative statement) negative Aussage; **be the ~ of sth.** im Widerspruch zu etw. stehen [3] (opposite of sth. positive) Negation, *die* [4] (Ling.) Negation, *die* (fachspr.); Verneinung, *die*

negative /ˈnegətɪv/

A *adj.* [1] (also Math.) negativ; **~ vote** Neinstimme, *die* [2] (Ling.) verneint; Negations‹*partikel*› [3] (Electr.) **~ pole/terminal** Minuspol, *der* [4] (Photog.) negativ; Negativ-. *See also* **feedback 2**

B *n.* **1** (Photog.) Negativ, *das* **2** (~ statement) negative Aussage; (answer) Nein, *das;* **two ~s make an affirmative** doppelte Verneinung ergibt Bejahung; **be in the ~** ‹*Antwort:*› negativ *od.* „Nein" sein; ‹*Votum:*› ablehnend ausfallen **3** (~ quality) negative Eigenschaft; fehlende Eigenschaft **4** (Ling.) Negation, *die* (fachspr.); Verneinung, *die*
C *v.t.* **1** (veto) ablehnen **2** (disprove) widerlegen

negative 'equity *n.* Negativwert, *der*

negatively /ˈneɡətɪvlɪ/ *adv.* **1** (in the negative) negativ; **answer ~:** eine negative Antwort geben **2** (unsympathetically) negativ; ablehnend **3** (Electr.) negativ

'negative sign *n.* (Math.) negatives Vorzeichen; (symbol) Minuszeichen, *das*

neglect /nɪˈɡlekt/
A *v.t.* **1** (disregard, leave uncared for) vernachlässigen; nicht hören auf (+ *Akk.*) ‹*Rat*›; versäumen ‹*Gelegenheit*› **2** (leave undone) unerledigt lassen, liegen lassen ‹*Korrespondenz, Arbeit*› **3** (omit) versäumen; **she ~ed to write** sie hat es versäumt zu schreiben; **not ~ doing** *or* **to do sth.** es nicht versäumen, etw. zu tun
B *n.* **1** (neglecting, disregard) Vernachlässigung, *die;* **be in a state of ~** ‹*Gebäude:*› verwahrlost sein; **years of ~:** jahrelange Vernachlässigung; **suffer from ~:** vernachlässigt werden; **~ of duty** Pflichtvergessenheit, *die* **2** (negligence) Nachlässigkeit, *die;* Fahrlässigkeit, *die*

neglectful /nɪˈɡlektfl/ *adj.* (careless) gleichgültig (**of** gegenüber); **be ~ of** sich nicht kümmern um

négligé, negligee /ˈneɡlɪʒeɪ/ *n.* Negligee, *das*

negligence /ˈneɡlɪdʒəns/ *n., no pl.* (carelessness) Nachlässigkeit, *die;* (Law, Insurance, etc.) Fahrlässigkeit, *die; see also* **contributory 1**

negligent /ˈneɡlɪdʒənt/ *adj.* **1** nachlässig; **be ~ about sth.** sich um etw. nicht kümmern; **be ~ of one's duties/sb.** seine Pflichten/jmdn. vernachlässigen **2** (offhand) ungezwungen; zwanglos

negligently /ˈneɡlɪdʒəntlɪ/ *adv.* **1** nachlässig ‹*arbeiten*›; unvorsichtig ‹*fahren*›; *as sentence-modifier* nachlässigerweise/unvorsichtigerweise **2** (in an offhand manner) lässig

negligible /ˈneɡlɪdʒɪbl/ *adj.* unerheblich; unbedeutend ‹*Fehler*›; *see also* **quantity 5**

negotiable /nɪˈɡəʊʃəbl/ *adj.* **1** (open to discussion) verhandlungsfähig ‹*Forderung, Bedingungen*› **2** (that can be got past) zu bewältigend; zu bewältigen *nicht attr.;* passierbar ‹*Straße, Fluss*› **3** (Commerc.) übertragbar ‹*Sicherheit, Scheck usw.*›

negotiate /nɪˈɡəʊʃɪeɪt/
A *v.i.* verhandeln (**for, on, about** über + *Akk.*); **the negotiating table** der Verhandlungstisch
B *v.t.* **1** (arrange) aushandeln **2** (get past) bewältigen; überwinden ‹*Hindernis*›; passieren ‹*Straße, Fluss*›; nehmen ‹*Kurve*›; **~ the stairs** die Treppe schaffen (ugs.) **3** (Commerc.) (convert into cash) einlösen ‹*Scheck*›; (transfer) übertragen ‹*Wechsel, Papiere usw.*›

negotiation /nɪɡəʊʃɪˈeɪʃn, nɪɡəʊsɪˈeɪʃn/ *n.* **1** (discussion) Verhandlung, *die* (**for, about** über + *Akk.*); **by ~:** durch Verhandeln *od.* Verhandlungen; **enter into ~:** in Verhandlungen (*Akk.*) eintreten; **be in ~ with sb.** mit jmdm. verhandeln; **be a matter of ~:** Verhandlungssache sein **2** *in pl.* (talks) Verhandlungen *Pl.* **3** ▸ **negotiate B 2**: Bewältigung, *die;* Überwindung, *die;* Passieren, *das* **4** ▸ **negotiate B 3**: Einlösung, *die;* Übertragung, *die*

negotiator /nɪˈɡəʊʃɪeɪtə(r)/ *n.* Unterhändler, *der*/-händlerin, *die*

Negress /ˈniːɡrɪs/ *n.* (dated/offensive) Negerin, *die* (oft als diskriminierend empfunden)

Negro /ˈniːɡrəʊ/ (dated/offensive)
A *n., pl.* **~es** Neger, *der* (oft als diskriminierend empfunden)
B *adj.* Neger- (oft als diskriminierend empfunden); **~ woman** Negerin, *die;* **~ art/music** Kunst/Musik der Neger; *see also* **spiritual B**

Negroid /ˈniːɡrɔɪd/
A *adj.* negrid; (akin to or resembling Negroes) negroid
B *n.* Negride, *der/die;* (akin to or resembling Negro) Negroide, *der/die*

neigh /neɪ/
A *v.i.* wiehern
B *n.* Wiehern, *das*

neighbor *etc.* (*Amer.*) ▸ **neighbour** *etc.*

neighbour /ˈneɪbə(r)/
A *n.* Nachbar, *der*/Nachbarin, *die;* (at table) [Tisch]nachbar, *der*/[Tisch]nachbarin, *die;* (thing) der/die/das daneben; (building/country) Nachbargebäude/-land, *das;* **we're next-door ~s** wir wohnen Tür an Tür; **my next-door ~s** meine unmittelbaren Nachbarn; meine Nachbarn von nebenan; **we were ~s at dinner** wir haben beim Essen nebeneinander gesessen
B *v.t. & i.* **~ [upon]** grenzen an (+ *Akk.*)

neighbourhood /ˈneɪbəhʊd/ *n.* **1** (district) Gegend, *die;* **sb.'s ~:** jmds. Nachbarschaft; **the children from the ~:** die Kinder aus der Nachbarschaft *od.* Umgebung **2** (nearness) Nähe, *die;* **it was [somewhere] in the ~ of £100** es waren [so] um [die] 100 Pfund **3** (neighbours) Nachbarschaft, *die* **4** *attrib.* an der *od.* um die Ecke *nachgestellt* (ugs.); **small ~ shop/store** [kleiner] Laden um die Ecke; **your friendly ~ bobby/milkman** *etc.* (coll. joc.) der nette Polizist, der bei uns die Runde macht/der nette Milchmann, der uns täglich die Milch bringt

'neighbourhood watch *n.* Bürgerwehr, *die*

neighbouring /ˈneɪbərɪŋ/ *adj.* benachbart; Nachbar-; angrenzend ‹*Felder*›

neighbourliness /ˈneɪbəlɪnɪs/ *n., no pl.* gut- *od.* freundnachbarliche Art

neighbourly /ˈneɪbəlɪ/ *adj.* **1** (characteristic of neighbours) [gut]nachbarlich **2** (friendly) freundlich

neither /ˈnaɪðə(r), niːðə(r)/
A *adj.* keiner/keine/keins der beiden; **in ~ case** in keinem Falle
B *pron.* keiner/keine/keins von *od.* der beiden; **~ of them** keiner von *od.* der beiden; (none) keiner von ihnen; **~ of the accusations** keine der [beiden] Beschuldigungen; **Which will you have? — N~:** Welches nehmen Sie? — Keins [von beiden]; **we ~ of us moved** keiner von uns [beiden] hat sich bewegt
C *adv.* (also not) auch nicht; **I'm not going — N~ am I** *or* (coll.) **Me ~:** Ich gehe nicht — Ich auch nicht; **if you don't go, ~ shall I** wenn du nicht gehst, gehe ich auch nicht; **he didn't go and ~ did I** er ging nicht und ich auch nicht
D *conj.* **1** (not either, not on the one hand) weder; **~ … nor** weder … noch; **he ~ knows nor cares** weder weiß er es, noch will er es wissen; **he ~ ate, drank, nor smoked** er aß nicht, noch trank oder rauchte er; *see also* **here A 1** **2** (arch.: and also not) noch

nelly /ˈnelɪ/ *n.* **not on your ~** (Brit. coll.) nie im Leben (ugs.); im Leben nicht (ugs.)

nelson /ˈnelsn/ *n.* (Wrestling) Nelson, *der*

nem. con. /nem ˈkɒn/ *abbr.* = **nemine contradicente** nem. con.

nemesis /ˈnemɪsɪs/ *n., pl.* **nemeses** /ˈnemɪsiːz/ **1** (formal: justice) Nemesis, *die;* ausgleichende Gerechtigkeit **2** (downfall) gerechte Strafe (**of** für)

neo- /niːəʊ/ *in comb.* neo-/Neo-

neo'classic, neo'classical *adj.* klassizistisch

neo'classicism *n.* Klassizismus, *der*

neocon'servative
A *adj.* neokonservativ
B *n.* Neokonservative, *der/die*

neo-'liberal
A *adj.* neoliberal
B *n.* Neoliberale, *der/die*

Neolithic /niːəˈlɪθɪk/ *adj.* (Archaeol.) neolithisch (fachspr.); jungsteinzeitlich; (fig.) vorsintflutlich; **~ period** Neolithikum, *das;* Jungsteinzeit, *die;* **~ man** Neolithiker, *der*

neologism /nɪˈɒlədʒɪzm/ *n.* Neubildung, *die;* Neologismus, *der* (Sprachw.)

neon /ˈniːɒn/ *n.* (Chem.) Neon, *das*

neo'natal *adj.* Neugeborenen‹*klinik, -station, -alter, -krankheit*›

neo-'Nazi
A *n.* Neonazi, *der.*
B *adj.* neonazistisch; **a ~ group** eine Neonazigruppe

neon: ~ 'lamp *n.* Neonlampe, *die;* **~ 'light** *n.* Neonlicht, *das;* (fitting) Neonlampe, *die;* **~ 'sign** *n.* Neonreklame, *die*

neophyte /ˈniːəfaɪt/ *n.* **1** (Relig.) Neophyt, *der* **2** (beginner) Anfänger, *der*

neoprene /ˈniːəpriːn/ *n.* Neopren(Wz), *das*

Nepal /nɪˈpɔːl/ *pr. n.* Nepal (*das*)

Nepalese /nepəˈliːz/, **Nepali** /nɪˈpɔːlɪ/ ▸ **p. 1277**, ▸ **p. 1345**
A *adj.* nepalesisch
B *n.* **1** *pl.* **Nepalese, Nepalis** (person) Nepalese, *der*/Nepalesin, *die* **2** (language) Nepali, *das*

nephew /ˈnevjuː, ˈnefjuː/ *n.* Neffe, *der*

nephritis /nɪˈfraɪtɪs/ *n.* ▸ **p. 1231** (Med.) Nephritis, *die* (fachspr.); Nierenentzündung, *die*

nepotism /ˈnepətɪzm/ *n.* Nepotismus, *der* (geh.); Vetternwirtschaft, *die* (abwertend)

Neptune /ˈneptjuːn/ *pr. n.* **1** (Roman Mythol.) Neptun (*der*) **2** (Astron.) Neptun, *der*

NERC *abbr.* (Brit.) = **Natural Environment Research Council** ≈ Umweltbundesamt

nerd /nɜːd/ *n.* (coll. derog.) Depp, *der* (abwertend)

nerve /nɜːv/
A *n.* **1** Nerv, *der;* **~ tissue** Nervengewebe, *das* **2** *in pl.* (fig., of mental state) **be suffering from ~s** nervös sein; **bundle of ~s** Nervenbündel, *das* (ugs.); **have a fit of ~s** durchdrehen (ugs.); sehr nervös werden; **get on sb.'s ~s** jmdm. auf die Nerven gehen *od.* fallen (ugs.); **~s of steel** Nerven wie Drahtseile (ugs.) **3** **strain every ~** (fig.) alle Anstrengungen machen **4** (coolness, boldness) Kaltblütigkeit, *die;* Mut, *der;* **not have the ~ for sth.** für *od.* zu etw. nicht die Nerven haben; **lose one's ~:** die Nerven verlieren; **a man with an iron ~:** ein Mann mit eisernen Nerven **5** (coll.: audacity) **of all the ~!** das ist doch die Höhe!; **what [a] ~!** [so eine] Frechheit!; **have the ~ to do sth.** den Nerv haben, etw. zu tun (ugs.); **he's got a ~:** der hat Nerven (ugs.)
B *v.t.* **1** (give strength or courage to) ermutigen; **~ oneself** *or* **one's heart** seinen ganzen Mut zusammennehmen **2** (brace) **~ oneself** *or* **one's mind** sich wappnen (geh.)

nerve: ~ cell *n.* (Anat.) Nervenzelle, *die;* **~ centre** *n.* **1** (Anat.) Nervenzentrum, *das;* **2** (fig.) Schaltzentrale, *die;* **~ ending** *n.* (Anat.) Nervenendigung, *die;* **~ gas** *n.* Nervengas, *das*

nerveless /ˈnɜːvlɪs/ *adj.* **1** (inert) schwach; kraftlos ‹*Arm, Hand*› **2** (flabby) kraftlos ‹*Stil*› **3** (cool, confident) nervenstark

nerve: ~-racking *adj.* nervenaufreibend; **~-shattering** *adj.* nervenzerrüttend

nervous /ˈnɜːvəs/ *adj.* **1** (Anat., Med.) Nerven-; **[central] ~ system** [Zentral]nervensystem, *das;* **~ breakdown** Nervenzusammenbruch, *der* **2** (having delicate nerves) nervös; **be a ~ wreck** mit den Nerven völlig am Ende sein **3** (Brit.: timid) **be ~ of** *or* **about** Angst haben vor (+ *Dat.*); **I'm ~ of offending him** ich habe Angst, ihn zu kränken; **be a ~ person** ängstlich sein

nervously /ˈnɜːvəslɪ/ *adv.* nervös

nervousness /ˈnɜːvəsnɪs/ *n., no pl.* Ängstlichkeit, *die;* (temporary) Angst, *die*

nervure /ˈnɜːvjə(r)/ *n.* **1** (Zool.) [Flügel]ader, *die* **2** (Bot.) [Blatt]ader, *die*

nervy /ˈnɜːvɪ/ *adj.* **1** (jerky, nervous) nervös; unruhig **2** (Amer. coll.) (cool, confident) dreist; (impudent) unverschämt

nest /nest/
A *n.* **1** (of bird, animal, insect) Nest, *das;* **foul one's own ~** (fig.) (denigrate one's own family) das eigene *od.* sein eigenes Nest beschmutzen; (harm one's own interests) sich (*Dat.*) selbst schaden; *see also* **feather B 1** **2** (fig.: retreat, shelter, receptacle) Nest, *das* (fig.); Zufluchtsort, *der;* **leave the ~:** flügge werden **3** (haunt of robbers etc.) Nest, *das;* Schlupfwinkel, *der* **4** (place fostering vice etc.) Brutstätte, *die* **5** (brood or swarm in a ~) Nest, *das;* (of rabbits) Satz, *der* (Jägerspr.); (of wasps, hornets, ants) Schwarm, *der* **6** (group of machine guns) (Mil.) [MG-]Nest, *das* **7** (set) Satz, *der;* **~ of tables** Satz Tische

n

B *v.i.* **1** (make or have ~) nisten **2** (take ~s) Nester entfernen; (take eggs) Nester ausnehmen *od.* ausheben **3** (fit together) ~ **[into one another]** ineinander passen
C *v.t.* **1** (place as in ~) einbetten **2** (pack one inside the other) ineinander setzen ‹*Töpfe usw.*›; (fig.) einbetten

'nest egg *n.* **1** Nestei, *das* **2** (fig.) Notgroschen, *der*

'nesting box *n.* Nistkasten, *der*

nestle /'nesl/
A *v.i.* **1** (settle oneself) sich kuscheln; ~ **down in a sleeping bag** sich in einen Schlafsack kuscheln **2** (press oneself affectionately) sich schmiegen (**to, up against** an + *Akk.*); **they ~d [up] together** sie schmiegten sich aneinander **3** (lie half hidden) eingebettet sein
B *v.t.* **1** (push affectionately or snugly) kuscheln, schmiegen (**against** an + *Akk.*) **2** (hold as in nest) ~ **a baby in one's arms** ein Baby schützend in den Armen halten

nestling /'nestlɪŋ/ *n.* Nestling, *der*

net¹ /net/
A *n.* (lit. or fig.) Netz, *das;* **cast one's ~ wide** (fig.) seine Netze weit spannen; **spread one's ~** (fig.) seine Netze stellen *od.* spannen; **the Net** (Computing) das Netz
B *v.t.,* **-tt- 1** (cover) ~ **[over]** mit einem Netz überziehen ‹*Baum, Busch*›; (catch) [mit einem Netz] fangen ‹*Tier*›; einfangen ‹*Person*›; ~ **sb. sth.** (fig. coll.) jmdm. etw. einbringen **2** (put in net) ins Netz schlagen; (put in goal) ins Tor schießen; ~ **a goal** ein Tor schießen

net²
A *adj.* **1** (free from deduction) netto; Netto‹*einkommen, -[verkaufs]preis usw.*› **2** (not subject to discount); ~ **price** gebundener Preis; ~ **book** preisgebundenes Buch; **N~ 'Book Agreement** Vereinbarung zur Preisbindung bei Büchern **3** ▸ **p. 1702** (excluding weight of container etc.) netto; ~ **weight** Nettogewicht, *das* **4** (effective, ultimate) End‹*ergebnis, -effekt*›
B *v.t.,* **-tt-** (gain) netto einnehmen; (yield) netto einbringen

net: ~ball *n.* Korbball, *der;* ~ **cord** *n.* (Tennis) **1** Spannseil, *das;* **2** (stroke) Netzball, *der;* ~ **'curtain** *n.* Store, *der* [aus Gittertüll]; Tüllgardine, *die;* ~ **generation** *n.* Internetgeneration, *die;* **~head** *n.* (coll.) Internetfreak, *der* (ugs.)

nether /'neðə(r)/ *adj.* (arch./joc.) unter...; Unter‹*lippe, -kiefer*›

Netherlands /'neðələndz/
A *pr. n. sing. or pl.* Niederlande *Pl.*
B *attrib. adj.* niederländisch

nether 'regions, nether 'world *ns.* Unterwelt, *die*

netiquette /'netɪket/ *n.* (Computing) Netiquette, *die;* **breaches of ~:** Verstöße gegen die Netiquette

netizen /'netɪzən/ *n.* (coll.) Netzbürger, *der*/-bürgerin, *die*

net 'profit *n.* Reingewinn, *der*

netrepreneur /'netrəprənɜ:(r)/ *n.* Internetunternehmer, *der*/-unternehmerin, *die*

'netspeak *n.* Internetjargon, *der*

'netsurf *v.i.* im *od.* durch das Internet surfen

netsurfer *n.* Internetsurfer, *der*/-surferin, *die*

'netsurfing *n., no pl.* Internetsurfen, *das; attrib.* Surf-

nett ▸**net²**

netting /'netɪŋ/ *n.* **1** (making net) Knüpfen, *das* **2** ([piece of] net) Netz, *das;* (needlework) Filet- *od.* Netzarbeit, *die;* **cover with ~:** mit Netzen/mit einem Netz bedecken; **wire ~:** Drahtgeflecht, *das;* Maschendraht, *der*

nettle /'netl/
A *n.* Nessel, *die; see also* **grasp B 2**; **stinging nettle**
B *v.t.* reizen; aufbringen

'nettlerash *n.* (Med.) Nesselsucht, *die;* Nesselausschlag, *der*

'network
A *n.* **1** (of intersecting lines, electrical conductors) Netzwerk, *das* **2** (of railways etc., persons, operations) Netz, *das* **3** (of broadcasting stations) [Sender-]netz, *das;* (company) Sender, *der* **4** (Computing) Netzwerk, *das*
B **1** *v.t.* (broadcast) [im ganzen Sendebereich] ausstrahlen **2** (Computing) miteinander verbinden *od.* vernetzen ‹*Computer*›
C *v.i.* sich austauschen; netzwerken (ugs.)

'networkable *adj.* (Computing) netzwerkfähig

'network card *n.* (Computing) Netzwerkkarte, *die*

'networker *n.* **1** (Computing: teleworker) Telearbeiter, *der*/-arbeiterin, *die* **2** (user of contacts) *Person, die Kontakte knüpft und nutzt*

'networking *n., no pl.* **1** (Computing) Arbeiten mit *od.* in Netzwerken; *attrib.* Netzwerk‹*technologie, -aktivitäten etc.*› **2** (using contacts) Kontaktnahme, *die;* Erfahrungsaustausch, *der;* **smart ~ can lead to better pay** geschicktes Nutzen von Kontakten kann zu einer besseren Bezahlung führen

'network provider *n.* (Computing, Teleph.) Netzanbieter, *der*

Neuchâtel /nɜ:ʃæ'tel/ *pr. n.* ▸ **p. 1643** Neuenburg (*das*)

neural /'njʊərl/ *adj.* (Anat.) neural (fachspr.); Nerven-

neuralgia /njʊə'rældʒə/ *n.* ▸ **p. 1231** (Med.) Neuralgie, *die* (fachspr.); Nervenschmerz, *der*

neural 'network *n.* (Computing) neurales Netzwerk

neuritis /njʊə'raɪtɪs/ *n.* ▸ **p. 1231** (Med.) Neuritis, *die* (fachspr.); Nervenentzündung, *die*

neurobiology /njʊərəʊbaɪ'ɒlədʒɪ/ *n., no pl.* Neurobiologie, *die*

neurological /njʊərə'lɒdʒɪkl/ *adj.* neurologisch

neurologist /njʊə'rɒlədʒɪst/ *n.* ▸ **p. 1260** Neurologe, *der*/Neurologin, *die;* Nervenarzt, *der*/Nervenärztin, *die*

neurology /njʊə'rɒlədʒɪ/ *n.* Neurologie, *die*

neuron /'njʊərɒn/, **neurone** /'njʊərəʊn/ *n.* (Anat.) Neuron, *das*

neurosis /njʊə'rəʊsɪs/ *n., pl.* **neuroses** /njʊə'rəʊsi:z/ Neurose, *die*

neurosurgeon /njʊərəʊ'sɜ:dʒn/ *n.* ▸ **p. 1260** Neurochirurg, *der*/-chirurgin, *die*

neurosurgery /njʊərəʊ'sɜ:dʒərɪ/ *n.* Neurochirurgie, *die*

neurotic /njʊə'rɒtɪk/
A *adj.* **1** (suffering from neurosis) nervenkrank **2** (of neurosis) neurotisch; ~ **affection** *or* **ailment** Nervenkrankheit, *die* **3** (coll.: unduly anxious) neurotisch; **don't get ~ about it** lass es nicht zu einer Neurose werden
B *n.* Neurotiker, *der*/Neurotikerin, *die*

neurotically /njʊə'rɒtɪkəlɪ/ *adv.* neurotisch

neurotransmitter /'njʊərəʊtrɑ:nsmɪtə(r)/ *n.* (Physiol.) Neurotransmitter, *der*

neuter /'nju:tə(r)/
A *adj.* **1** (Ling.) sächlich; neutral (fachspr.) **2** (Bot.: asexual) weder männlich noch weiblich; ungeschlechtlich ‹*Blüte*› **3** (Zool.: sterile) unfruchtbar
B *n.* **1** (Ling.) Neutrum, *das* **2** (Zool.) (insect) unfruchtbares Insekt; (ant, bee) Arbeiterin, *die* **3** (castrated animal) kastriertes Tier
C *v.t.* kastrieren

neutral /'nju:trl/
A *adj.* neutral; ~ **gear** Leerlauf, *der; see also* **equilibrium**
B *n.* **1** Neutrale, *der/die;* **be ~s/a ~:** neutral sein **2** (~ gear) Leerlauf, *der;* **in ~:** im Leerlauf

neutralise ▸**neutralize**

neutrality /nju:'trælɪtɪ/ *n.* Neutralität, *die*

neutralize /'nju:trəlaɪz/ *v.t.* **1** (Chem.) neutralisieren **2** (counteract) neutralisieren; entkräften ‹*Argument*›

neutrally /'nju:trəlɪ/ *adv.* neutral

neutrino /nju:'tri:nəʊ/ *n., pl.* **~s** (Phys.) Neutrino, *das*

neutron /'nju:trɒn/ *n.* (Phys.) Neutron, *das*

neutron: ~ bomb *n.* Neutronenbombe, *die;* ~ **star** *n.* Neutronenstern, *der*

never /'nevə(r)/ *adv.* **1** (at no time) nie; **I ~ thought I would see her again** ich hätte nie gedacht, dass ich sie wiedersehen würde; **the rain seemed as if it would ~ stop** der Regen schien gar nicht mehr aufhören zu wollen; **will the rain ~ stop?** hört denn der Regen überhaupt nicht mehr auf?; **he has ~ been abroad** er war [noch] nie im Ausland; **he ~ so much as apologized** er hat sich nicht einmal entschuldigt; **I ~ slept a wink all night** ich habe die ganze Nacht kein Auge zugetan; **~ is a long time** man soll niemals nie sagen; **~, ~:** nie, nie; niemals; (more emphatic) nie im Leben; **~ so** [auch] noch so; **be it ~ so great** wenn es auch noch so groß ist; mag es auch noch so groß sein; **~-to-be-forgotten** unvergesslich; **~-satisfied** unersättlich; **~-ending** endlos; **~-failing** unfehlbar; unerschöpflich ‹*Quelle*› **2** (not ... at any time, not ... at all) nie; **he was ~ one to do sth.** es war nicht seine Art, etw. zu tun; **he is ~ likely to succeed** er wird es nie schaffen; **I ~ remember her winning** ich kann mich nicht erinnern, dass sie je gewonnen hätte; **~ a** (not one) kein Einziger/keine Einzige/kein Einziges **3** (coll.) *expr. surprise* **you ~ believed that, did you?** du hast das doch wohl nicht geglaubt?; **He ate the whole turkey. — N~!** Er hat den ganzen Truthahn aufgegessen. — Nein! (ugs.); **well, I ~ [did]!** [na *od.* nein *od.* also] so was!

never: ~'more *adv.* nie wieder; **~-'~** *n.* (Brit. coll.) Abzahlungskauf, *der;* **on the ~-~ [system]** auf Stottern (ugs.); auf Raten; **~the'less** *adv.* trotzdem; nichtsdestoweniger

new /nju:/
A *adj.* **1** (not existing before) neu; **'~ boy/girl** (lit. or fig.) Neuling, *der;* **a ~ baby** ein neugeborenes Kind; ein Neugeborenes **2** (unfamiliar) neu; **flying was an experience ~ to him** Fliegen war für ihn eine neue Erfahrung; **that's a ~ one on me** (coll.) das ist mir neu; (of joke etc.) den habe ich noch nicht gehört; (of style etc.) das habe ich noch nicht gesehen; **visit ~ places** unbekannte Orte besuchen; **so what else is ~?** (iron.) sonst was Neues? (ugs.); **that is not** *or* **nothing ~ to me** das ist mir nichts Neues **3** (renewed, additional, changed) neu; (in place names) Neu-; **the ~ mathematics** die neue Mathematik; **the ~ poor** die erst vor kurzem Verarmten; **the ~ rich** die Neureichen (abwertend); **the ~ woman** die moderne Frau; die Frau von heute; **be like a ~ man/woman** wie neugeboren sein; *see also* **birth 1**; **broom 1**; **deal¹ C 1**; **leaf A 2** **4** (of recent origin, growth, or manufacture) neu; frisch ‹*Brot, Gemüse*›; neu ‹*Kartoffeln*›; neu, jung ‹*Wein*›; neu, lebend ‹*Sprache*›; **as good as ~:** so gut wie neu; **as ~:** neuwertig
B *adv.* **1** (recently) vor kurzem; frisch ‹*gebacken, gewaschen, geschnitten*›; gerade erst ‹*erblüht*› **2** (afresh) neu

'New Age *n.* Newage, *das; attrib.* Newage-

New Ager /nju: 'eɪdʒə(r)/ *n.* Newager, *der*/Newagerin, *die*

New Age 'Traveller *n.* (Brit.) New-Age-Vagabund, *der*/-Vagabundin, *die*

newbie /'nju:bɪ/ *n.* (coll.) Neuling, *der;* **Net ~:** Internetneuling, *der*

'newborn *adj.* **1** (recently born) neugeboren **2** (regenerated) neu gewonnen ‹*Mut, Kraft usw.*›; neu ‹*Person*›

'newcomer *n.* Newcomer, *der;* (new arrival also) Neuankömmling, *der;* (one having no experience also) Neuling, *der* (**to** in + *Dat.*); (thing also) Neuheit, *die* (**to** für)

New Delhi /nju: 'delɪ/ *pr. n.* ▸ **p. 1643** Neu-Delhi (*das*)

new e'conomy *n.* neue Wirtschaft

newel /'nju:əl/ *n.* **1** (pillar) Spindel, *die* **2** ~ **[post]** (supporting stair handrail) [Treppen]pfosten, *der*

New 'England
A *n.* Neuengland (*das*)
B *attrib. adj.* aus Neuengland; ‹*Stadt usw.*› in Neuengland

New Englander /nju: 'ɪŋgləndə(r)/ *n.* Neuengländer, *der*/Neuengländerin, die

new: ~fangled /nju:ˈfæŋgld/ *adj.* (derog.) neumodisch (abwertend); **~-found** *adj.* neu; (recently discovered) neu [entdeckt]

Newfoundland /nju:ˈfaʊndlənd/
A *n.* **1** *pr. n.* Neufundland *(das)* **2** (dog) Neufundländer, *der*
B *adj.* neufundländisch; **~ dog** Neufundländer, *der*

Newfoundlander /nju:ˈfaʊndləndə(r)/ *n.* Neufundländer, *der*/Neufundländerin, *die*

New ˈGuinea *pr. n.* Neuguinea *(das)*

newish /ˈnju:ɪʃ/ *adj.* ziemlich neu

new: N~ ˈLabour *n.* (Brit. Pol.) New Labour *(das)*; neue Labour-Partei; **~-laid** *adj.* frisch [gelegt]; **New ˈLeft** *n.* neue Linke; **~ ˈlook** *n.* (coll.) neuer Stil; **~-look** *adj.* neu

newly /ˈnju:lɪ/ *adv.* **1** (recently) neu; **~ married** seit kurzem verheiratet **2** (in new way) neu

ˈnewly-wed *n.* Jungverheiratete, *der/die*

new: New ˈMan *n.* der neue Mann; **~ ˈmoon** *n.* Neumond, *der*; **~-mown** *adj.* frisch gemäht

news /nju:z/ *n., no pl.* **1** (new information) Nachricht, *die*; **items** *or* **pieces** *or* **bits of ~**: Neuigkeiten; **be in the** *or* **make ~**: Schlagzeilen machen; **that's ~ to me** (coll.) das ist mir neu; **what's the latest ~?** was gibt es Neues?; **have you heard the/this ~?** hast du schon gehört/das schon gehört?; weißt du schon das Neueste? (ugs.); **have you had any ~ of your brother?** hast du etwas von deinem Bruder gehört?; hast du Nachricht von deinem Bruder?; **I have ~ for you** (also iron.) ich habe eine Neuigkeit für dich; **bad/good ~**: schlechte/gute Nachrichten; **sb./sth. is good ~** (coll.) jmd./etw. ist wirklich toll (ugs.); **he/she/that firm is bad ~** (coll.) er/sie/diese Firma ist mit Vorsicht zu genießen (ugs.); **no ~ is good ~** (prov.) keine Nachricht, gute Nachricht **2** (Radio, Telev.) Nachrichten *Pl.*; **the 10 o'clock ~**: die 10-Uhr-Nachrichten; **listen to/watch the ~**: [die] Nachrichten hören/sehen; **I heard it on the ~**: ich habe es in den Nachrichten gehört; **here is the ~** (Radio) Sie hören Nachrichten; (Telev.) ≈ ich begrüße Sie zu den Nachrichten; **summary of the ~**: Nachrichtenüberblick, *der*; **~ in brief** Kurznachrichten *Pl.*

> **The News of the World**
>
> Eine britische Sonntagszeitung. Schwerpunkte der Berichterstattung sind die Themen Verbrechen und Sport. Das Blatt ist besonders für seine Sensationsberichterstattung über Prominente und die königliche Familie bekannt. Es ist eine **tabloid**-Zeitung, Teil der Boulevardpresse, und in Großbritannien die auflagenstärkste Zeitung.

news: ~ agency *n.* Nachrichtenagentur, *die*; **~agent** *n.* ▸ℹ p. 1260 Zeitungshändler, *der*/-händlerin, *die*; **~boy** *n.* Zeitungsjunge, *der*; **~ bulletin** *n.* Nachrichten *Pl.*; **~cast** *n.* Nachrichtensendung, *die*; **~caster** *n.* ▸ℹ p. 1260 Nachrichtensprecher, *der*/-sprecherin, *die*; **~ conference** *n.* Pressekonferenz, *die*; **~dealer** *n.* ▸ℹ p. 1260 (Amer.) Zeitungshändler, *der*/-händlerin, *die*; **~ desk** *n.* Nachrichtenredaktion, *die*; **this is Joe Smith at the ~ desk** (Radio) hier ist Joe Smith mit den Nachrichten; **~flash** *n.* Kurzmeldung, *die*; **~girl** *n.* (delivering) Zeitungsausträgerin, *die*; **~group** *n.* (Computing) Newsgroup, *die*; **~hawk** ▸**~hound**; **~ ˈheadline** *n.* Schlagzeile, *die*; **~hound** *n.* (Amer.) Zeitungsmann, *der* (ugs.); Journalist, *der*; **~letter** *n.* Rundschreiben, *das*; **~man** *n.* ▸ℹ p. 1260 Reporter, *der*; **~-on-deˈmand** *n., no pl.* News-on-Demand, *das*; Nachrichten auf Abruf; **~paper** *n.* **1** Zeitung, *die*; *attrib.* **~paper boy/girl** Zeitungsausträger, *der*/-austrägerin, *die*; **2** (material) Zeitungspapier, *das*; **~paperman** *n.* ▸ℹ p. 1260 Zeitungsmann, *der* (ugs.); Journalist, *der*

ˈnewspeak *n., no pl.* Newspeak, *der*

news: ~print *n.* Zeitungspapier, *das*; (ink) Druckerschwärze, *die*; **~reader** *n.* ▸ℹ p. 1260 Nachrichtensprecher, *der*/-sprecherin, *die*; **~reel** *n.* Wochenschau, *die*; **~room** *n.* Nachrichtenredaktion, *die*; **~-sheet** *n.* Informationsblatt, *das*; **~stand** *n.* Zeitungskiosk, *der*; Zeitungsstand, *der*; **~ summary** *n.* Kurznachrichten *Pl.*

new ˈstar *n.* (Astron.) Nova, *die*

news: ~ vendor *n.* Zeitungsverkäufer, *der*/-verkäuferin, *die*; **~worthy** *adj.* [für die Medien] interessant ‹*Person, Ereignis*›; berichtenswert ‹*Ereignis*›

> **Newsweek**
>
> Eine 1933 gegründete amerikanische Wochenzeitschrift, die in New York herausgegeben wird. Berichte und Artikel beschäftigen sich mit wissenschaftlichen, politischen und kulturellen Themen. Mit einer Auflage von drei Millionen gehört das New Yorker Nachrichtenmagazin jetzt zum Medienunternehmen der **Washington Post**.

newsy /ˈnju:zɪ/ *adj.* (coll.) **1** (full of news) voller Neuigkeiten *nachgestellt* **2** (newsworthy) interessant

newt /nju:t/ *n.* [Wasser]molch, *der*; *see also* **pissed 1**

New ˈTestament ▸**testament 1**

newton /ˈnju:tn/ *n.* (Phys.) Newton, *das*

new: ~ town *n.*: *mit Unterstützung der Regierung völlig neu entstandene Ansiedlung*; **~ ˈworld** ▸**world 1**; **~ ˈyear** *n.* ▸ℹ p. 1189 Neujahr, *das*; **over the New Year** über Neujahr; **the Jewish New Year** das jüdische Neujahrsfest; **a Happy New Year** ein glückliches *od.* gutes neues Jahr; **New Year honours** (Brit.) Titel- und Ordensverleihungen am Neujahrstag; **bring in the New Year** Silvester feiern; *see also* **resolution 2**; **New ˈYear's** (Amer.), **New Year's ˈDay** *ns.* Neujahrstag, *der*; **New Year's ˈEve** *n.* Silvester, *der od. das*; Neujahrsabend, *der*

New Yorker /nju: ˈjɔ:kə(r)/ *n.* New Yorker, *der*/New Yorkerin, *die*

> **New York Stock Exchange — NYSE**
>
> Die zentrale Wertpapierbörse der USA ist weltweit eine der größten Börsen. Die New Yorker Börse in der Wall Street wurde 1792 von Wertpapierhändlern gegründet und erhielt 1863 ihren heutigen Namen. Nach dem Kurssturz an der New Yorker Börse am 24.10.1929 und der darauf folgenden Weltwirtschaftskrise wurde der Handel 1934 erstmals einer staatlichen Aufsicht unterstellt.

> **New York Times**
>
> Eine amerikanische Tageszeitung mit landesweiter Verbreitung, die zur seriösen Presse zählt. Die in New York verlegte Zeitung kommt auch sonntags heraus und wird wegen der Qualität ihrer kulturellen und sozialen Berichterstattung gelesen. Sie ist in der ganzen Welt erhältlich und hat eine Auflage von über einer Million. Die *New York Times* wurde 1851 gegründet.

New Zealand /nju: ˈzi:lənd/
A *pr. n.* Neuseeland *(das)*
B *attrib. adj.* neuseeländisch

New Zealander /nju: ˈzi:ləndə(r)/ *n.* Neuseeländer, *der*/Neuseeländerin, *die*

next /nekst/
A *adj.* **1** (nearest) nächst...; **[the] ~ thing to sth.** fast *od.* beinahe etw.; **the seat ~ to me** der Platz neben mir; **the ~ room** das Nebenzimmer; **~ friend** (Law) ≈ Beistand, *der*; **the ~ but one** der/die/das Übernächste; **be the one ~ to the door** der/die neben der Tür sein; **~ to** (fig.: almost) fast; nahezu; **get ~ to sb.** (Amer. coll.: friendly) sich an jmdn. ranmachen (ugs.) **2** ▸ℹ p. 1047 (in order) nächst...; **within the ~ few days** in den nächsten Tagen; **~ week/month/year** nächste Woche/nächsten Monat/nächstes Jahr; **on the first of ~ month** am nächsten Ersten; **~ year's results** die Ergebnisse des nächsten Jahres; **during the ~ year** während der nächsten zwölf Monate; **we'll come ~ May** wir kommen im Mai nächsten Jahres; **the ~ largest/larger** der/die/das Nächstkleinere/Nächstgrößere; **[the] ~ time** das nächste Mal; **the ~ best** der/die/das Nächstbeste; **taking one year** *etc.* **with the ~**: im Ganzen gesehen; **am I ~?** komme ich jetzt dran?; **he's as able as the ˈ~ man** er kann es wie jeder andere auch; *see also* **door 1**; **world 1**
B *adv.* (in the next place) als Nächstes; (on the next occasion) das nächste Mal; **when I ~ see him** wenn ich ihn das nächste Mal sehe; **whose name comes ~?** wessen Name kommt als Nächstes *od.* Nächster?; **it is my turn ~**: ich komme als Nächster dran; **what ˈwill they think of ~?** was fällt denen als Nächstes ein?; **sit/stand ~ to sb.** neben jmdm. sitzen/stehen; **place sth. ~ to sb./sth.** etw. neben jmdn./etw. stellen; **come ~ to last** (in race) Zweitletzter/Zweitletzte werden; **come ~ to bottom** (in exam) der/die Zweitschlechteste sein;
C *n.* **1** (letter, issue, etc.) nächster Brief/nächste Ausgabe *usw.* **2** (period of time) **from one day to the ~**: von einem Tag zum andern; **the week after ~**: [die] übernächste Woche **3** (person) **~ of kin** nächster/nächste Angehörige; **~ please!** der Nächste, bitte!

ˈnext-door *adj.* gleich nebenan *nachgestellt*; *see also* **neighbour A**

ˈnext-generation *adj.* **~ product/member of the family** Produkt/Familienangehörige[r] der nächsten Generation

nexus /ˈneksəs/ *n.* Nexus, *der* (fachspr.)

NGO *abbr.* = **non-governmental organization**

NHS *abbr.* (Brit.) = **National Health Service**; *attrib.* **~ Trust** NHS-Trust, *der*

NI *abbr.* (Brit.) = **National Insurance**

Niagara Falls /naɪægərə ˈfɔ:lz/ *pr. n. pl.* Niagarafälle *Pl.*

nib /nɪb/ *n.* Feder, *die*; (tip) Spitze, *die*

nibble /ˈnɪbl/
A *v.t.* knabbern; **~ off** abknabbern
B *v.i.* knabbern (**at, on** an + *Dat.*); **the cheese had been ~d at** der Käse war angeknabbert worden; **they are nibbling at the idea** (fig.) sie beginnen, sich langsam für die Idee zu interessieren
C *n.* **1** (lit. or fig.) Anbeißen, *das*; **he didn't get a single ~**: bei ihm biss nicht einer an **2** *in pl.* (coll.: things to eat) etwas zum Knabbern

nibs /nɪbz/ *n.* (coll./joc.) **his ~**: der hohe Herr (scherzh.)

Nicaragua /nɪkəˈrægjʊə/ *pr. n.* Nicaragua *(das)*

Nicaraguan /nɪkəˈrægjʊən/ ▸ℹ p. 1345
A *adj.* nicaraguanisch; **sb. is ~**: jmd. ist Nicaraguaner/Nicaraguanerin
B *n.* Nicaraguaner, *der*/Nicaraguanerin, *die*

nice /naɪs/ *adj.* **1** (pleasing) nett; angenehm ‹*Stimme*›; schön ‹*Wetter*›; (iron.: disgraceful, difficult) schön; sauber (iron.); **the hotel is ~ enough** das Hotel ist nicht schlecht *od.* ganz ordentlich; **she has a ~ smile** sie lächelt so nett; **a ~ friend you are!** (iron.) du bist mir [ja] ein schöner Freund!; **you're a ~ one, I must say** (iron.) du bist mir vielleicht einer; **be in a ~ mess** (iron.) in einem schönen Schlamassel sitzen (ugs.); **[do a piece of] ~ work** saubere *od.* gute Arbeit [leisten]; **~ to meet you** freut mich, Sie kennen zu lernen; **~ [and] warm/fast/high** schön warm/schnell/hoch; **a ~ long holiday** schöne lange Ferien; **~-looking** gut aussehend; **not very ~** (unpleasant) nicht sehr nett; nicht sehr schön ‹*Wetter*›; **he is not very ~ to his sister** er ist nicht gerade nett zu seiner Schwester; **~ one!** (coll.) nicht schlecht!; **~ one, Cyril!** (Brit. coll.) so ein Schlaumeier!; **~ work if you can get it** (iron.) das ließe ich mir auch gefallen! **2** (fastidious) anspruchsvoll; (punctilious) genau **3** (requiring precision) fein, genau ‹*Unterscheidung*› **4** (subtle) fein ‹*Bedeutungsunterschied*›

Nice /ni:s/ *pr. n.* Nizza *(das)*

nicely /ˈnaɪslɪ/ *adv.* **1** (well) nett; gut ‹*arbeiten, sich benehmen, platziert sein*›; **a ~ behaved child** ein wohlerzogenes Kind **2** (all right) gut; **he's got a new job and is doing very ~**: er hat eine neue Arbeit und kommt prima (ugs.) *od.* sehr gut damit zurecht; **the patient is doing ~**: der Patient macht gute Fortschritte; **that will do ~**: das reicht völlig; *see also* **thank**

nicety /ˈnaɪsɪtɪ/ *n.* **1** *no pl.* (punctiliousness) [peinliche] Genauigkeit **2** *no pl.* (precision, accuracy) Feinheit, *die;* Genauigkeit, *die;* **to a ~:** perfekt ‹*arrangieren*›; sehr genau ‹*schätzen*› **3** *no pl.* (intricate or subtle quality) Feinheit, *die;* **make a point of great ~:** höchst subtil argumentieren **4** *in pl.* (minute distinctions) Feinheiten

niche /nɪtʃ, niːʃ/ *n.* **1** (in wall) Nische, *die* **2** (fig.: suitable place) Platz, *der;* **there he soon carved out a ~ for himself** dort fand er bald den richtigen Platz für sich

niche: ~ market *n.* Nischenmarkt, *der;* **~ product** *n.* Nischenprodukt, *das*

Nicholas /ˈnɪkələs/ *pr. n.* (Hist., as name of ruler etc.) Nikolaus (*der*)

nick
A *n.* **1** (notch) Kerbe, *die* **2** (sl.: prison) Kittchen, *das* (ugs.); Knast, *der* (salopp) **3** (Brit. sl.: police station) Wache, *die;* Revier, *das* **4** **in good/poor ~** (coll.) gut/nicht gut in Schuss (ugs.) **5** **in the ~ of time** gerade noch rechtzeitig
B *v.t.* **1** (make ~ in) einkerben ‹*Holz*›; **~ one's chin** sich am Kinn schneiden **2** (Brit. coll.) (catch) schnappen (ugs.); (arrest) einlochen (salopp) **3** (Brit. coll.: steal) klauen (salopp); mitgehen lassen (ugs.)

Nick /nɪk/ *n.* **Old ~:** der Teufel; der Leibhaftige (verhüll.)

nickel /ˈnɪkl/ *n.* **1** (metal) Nickel, *das* **2** (US coin) Fünfcentstück, *das*

nickel-ˈplate *v.t.* vernickeln

nicker /ˈnɪkə(r)/ *n., pl. same* (Brit. coll.) Pfund, *das;* **it's a hundred ~:** ≈ es sind dreihundert Eier (salopp)

nickname /ˈnɪkneɪm/
A *n.* **1** (name added or substituted) Spitzname, *der* **2** (abbreviation) Spitzname, *der;* (affectionate) Koseform, *die*
B *v.t.* einen Spitznamen geben (+ *Dat.*); **~ sb. ...:** jmdm. den Spitznamen ... geben; jmdn. ... taufen

nicotine /ˈnɪkətiːn/ *n.* Nikotin, *das*

ˈnicotine patch *n.* Nikotinpflaster, *das*

niece /niːs/ *n.* Nichte, *die*

nifty /ˈnɪftɪ/ *adj.* (coll.) **1** (smart, excellent) klasse (ugs.); flott ‹*Kleidung*› **2** (clever) geschickt; clever ‹*Plan, Idee*›

Niger[1] /ˈnaɪdʒə(r)/ *pr. n.* ▸ⓘ **p. 1491** (river) Niger, *der*

Niger[2] /niːˈʒeə(r)/ *pr. n.* (country) Niger (*das od. der*)

Nigeria /naɪˈdʒɪərɪə/ *pr. n.* Nigeria (*das*)

Nigerian /naɪˈdʒɪərɪən/ ▸ⓘ **p. 1345**
A *adj.* nigerianisch; **sb. is ~:** jmd. ist Nigerianer/Nigerianerin
B *n.* Nigerianer, *der*/Nigerianerin, *die*

niggardly /ˈnɪgədlɪ/ *adj.* **1** (miserly) knaus[e]rig (ugs. abwertend) **2** (given in small amounts) armselig, kümmerlich (abwertend) ‹*Portion*›

nigger /ˈnɪgə(r)/ *n.* (derog. offensive: Negro, dark-skinned person) Nigger, *der* (abwertend); **there's a ~ in the woodpile** *or* (Amer.) **in the fence** (fig.) es gibt einen Haken bei *od.* an der Sache; **who's the ~ in the woodpile?** (fig.) wer schießt hier quer?

niggle /ˈnɪgl/
A *v.i.* **1** (spend time on petty details) **~ over** [endlos] herumtüfteln an (+ *Dat.*) ‹*Vertrag, Klausel*›; **~ over every small point** sich mit jeder winzigen Einzelheit aufhalten **2** (find fault pettily) [herum]nörgeln (ugs. abwertend) (**at** an + *Dat.*)
B *v.t.* herumnörgeln an (+ *Dat.*); **be ~d** verärgert sein
C *n.* (criticism) kleiner Einwand; (discomfort) kleine Unpässlichkeit

niggling /ˈnɪglɪŋ/ *adj.* **1** (petty) belanglos **2** (trivial) nichts sagend; oberflächlich ‹*Kritik*›; krittelig ‹*Rezension, Rezensent*› **3** (nagging) nagend ‹*Zweifel*›; quälend ‹*Gefühl*›

niggly /ˈnɪglɪ/ *adj.* **1** (irritable) gereizt **2** ▸**niggling 1**

nigh /naɪ/ (arch./literary/dial.)
A *adv.* nahe; **come** *or* **draw ~:** näher kommen; ‹*Tag, Zeitpunkt:*› nahen; **it's ~ on impossible** es ist nahezu unmöglich; *see also* **well-nigh**
B *prep.* nahe (geh.) *nachgestellt* (+ *Dat.*)

night /naɪt/ *n.* ▸ⓘ **p. 1001**, ▸ⓘ **p. 1048** **1** Nacht, *die;* (evening) Abend, *der;* **~ after ~:** Nacht für Nacht/Abend für Abend; **the following ~:** die Nacht/der Abend darauf; **the previous ~:** die vorausgegangene Nacht/der vorausgegangene Abend; **one ~ he came** eines Nachts/Abends kam er; **two ~s ago** vorgestern Nacht/Abend; **the other ~:** neulich abends/nachts; **far into the ~:** bis spät *od.* tief in die Nacht; **on Sunday ~:** Sonntagnacht-/[am] Sonntagabend; **on Sunday ~s** sonntagabends; **on the ~ of Friday the 13th** am Freitag, dem 13., nachts/abends; **[on] the ~ after/before** die Nacht danach/davor; **[on] the ~ after/before sth.** die Nacht nach/vor etw. (*Dat.*); **for the ~:** über Nacht; **late at ~:** spätabends; **a ~ raid** ein nächtlicher Überfall; ein Nachtangriff (Milit.); **a ~'s rest will make you feel better** wenn du eine Nacht richtig geschlafen hast, wirst du dich wieder besser fühlen; **take all ~** (fig.) den ganzen Abend brauchen; **at ~** (in the evening, at **~fall**) abends; (during the **~**) nachts; bei Nacht; **make a ~ of it** die Nacht durchfeiern; durchmachen (ugs.); **~ and day** Tag und Nacht; **as ~ follows day** so sicher wie das Amen in der Kirche; **a ~ off** eine Nacht/ein Abend frei; **have a ~ out** [abends] ausgehen; **she works one ~ a week** sie arbeitet einen Abend/eine Nacht in der Woche; **spend the ~ with sb.** bei jmdm. übernachten; (implying sexual intimacy) die Nacht mit jmdm. verbringen; **stay the ~** *or* **over ~:** über Nacht bleiben; **work ~s** nachts arbeiten; (be on **~shift**) ‹*Krankenschwester:*› Nachtdienst haben; ‹*Schichtarbeiter:*› Nachtschicht haben; *see also* **good A 13**; **last**[1] **A 2** (darkness, lit. or fig.) Nacht, *die;* **black as ~:** schwarz wie die Nacht; **it went as dark as ~:** es wurde stockdunkel **3** (**~fall**) Einbruch der Dunkelheit; **wait for ~:** darauf warten, dass es Nacht wird; **when ~ comes** wenn es dunkel wird **4** (**~'s** sleep) **have a good/bad ~:** gut/schlecht schlafen; **have a sleepless ~:** eine schlaflose Nacht haben **5** (evening of performance etc.) Abend, *der;* **opening ~:** Premiere, *die; see also* **first night**; **ladies' night** **6** *attrib.* Nacht-/Abend-

night: ~ bell *n.* (Brit.) Nachtglocke, *die;* **~bird** *n.* (person) Nachteule, *die* (ugs. scherzh.); **~ blindness** *n.* Nachtblindheit, *die;* **~cap** *n.* **1** Nachtmütze, *die;* (woman's) Nachthaube, *die;* **2** (drink) Schlaftrunk, *der;* **~clothes** *n. pl.* Nachtwäsche, *die;* **in one's ~clothes** im Nachthemd/Schlafanzug; **~club** *n.* Nachtklub, *der;* Nachtlokal, *das;* **~dress** *n.* Nachthemd, *das;* **~ duty** *n.* Nachtdienst, *der;* **be on ~ duty** Nachtdienst haben; **~fall** *n., no art.* Einbruch der Dunkelheit; **at/after ~fall** bei/nach Einbruch der Dunkelheit; **~ fighter** *n.* (Air Force) Nachtjäger, *der;* **~ flying** *n.* Nachtfliegen, *das;* **~gown** ▸**~dress**

nightie /ˈnaɪtɪ/ *n.* (coll.) Nachthemd, *das*

nightingale /ˈnaɪtɪŋgeɪl/ *n.* Nachtigall, *die*

night: ~jar *n.* (Ornith.) Ziegenmelker, *der;* **~life** *n.* Nachtleben, *das;* **~ light** *n.* Nachtlicht, *das;* **~-long** **A** *adj.* sich über die ganze Nacht hinziehend; **keep a ~-long vigil** die ganze Nacht wachen; **B** *adv.* die ganze Nacht [lang *od.* über]

nightly /ˈnaɪtlɪ/
A *adj.* (happening, done, etc. in the night/evening) nächtlich/abendlich; (happening every night/evening) allnächtlich/allabendlich
B *adv.* (every night) jede Nacht; (every evening) jeden Abend; **twice ~** (Theatre etc.) zweimal pro Abend

night: ~mare *n.* (lit. or fig.) Albtraum, *der;* **~marish** /ˈnaɪtmeərɪʃ/ *adj.* albtraumhaft; **~-ˈ~** *int.* (coll.) [gute] Nacht; **~ nurse** *n.* Nachtschwester, *die;* **~ owl** *n.* **1** (Ornith.) Eule, *die;* Nachteule, *die* (veralt.); **2** (coll.: person) Nachteule, *die* (ugs. scherzh.); Nachtschwärmer, *der* (scherzh.); **~ porter** *n.* Nachtportier, *der;* **~robe** (Amer.) ▸**nightdress**; **~ safe** *n.* Nachttresor, *der;* **~-scented ˈstock** *n.* (Bot.) Abendlevkoje, *die;* **~ school** *n.* Abendschule, *die;* **~shade** *n.* (Bot.) Nachtschatten, *der;* **black ~shade** Schwarzer Nachtschatten; **woody ~shade** Bittersüß, *das;* Bittersüßer Nachtschatten; *see also* **deadly**; **~ shelter** *n.* Nachtasyl, *das;* **~ shift** *n.* Nachtschicht, *die;* **be on ~ shift** Nachtschicht haben *od.* machen; **~shirt** *n.* Nachthemd, *das;* **~ ˈsky** *n.* Nachthimmel, *der;* **~ spot** (coll.) ▸**~club**; **~stick** *n.* (Amer.) Schlagstock, *der;* **~ ˈstorage heater** *n.* Nachtspeicherofen, *der;* **~-time** *n., no indef. art.* Nacht, *die;* **at ~-time** nachts; **wait until ~-time** warten, bis es Nacht *od.* dunkel wird; **in the ~-time** während der Nacht; nachts; **~ ˈwatch** *n.* Nachtwache, *die;* **in the ~ watches** während der Nacht; **~ˈwatchman** *n.* **1** ▸ⓘ **p. 1260** Nachtwächter, *der;* **2** (Cricket) *Auswechselspieler, der am Ende eines Tages eingesetzt wird, damit ein besserer Spieler geschont wird;* **~wear** *n. sing.:* ▸**nightclothes**

nihilism /ˈnaɪɪlɪzm, ˈnɪhɪlɪzm/ *n.* Nihilismus, *der*

nihilist /ˈnaɪɪlɪst, ˈnɪhɪlɪst/ *n.* Nihilist, *der*

nihilistic /naɪɪˈlɪstɪk, nɪhɪˈlɪstɪk/ *adj.* nihilistisch

nil /nɪl/ *n.* **1** nichts; **his chances were ~:** seine Chancen waren gleich null; **our investment has shown a ~ return** unsere Investition hat keinen Gewinn gebracht **2** (Sport) null; **win one ~** *or* **by one goal to ~:** eins zu null gewinnen

Nile /naɪl/ *pr. n.* ▸ⓘ **p. 1491** Nil, *der*

nimble /ˈnɪmbl/ *adj.* **1** (quick in movement) flink; behände **2** (quick in mind) beweglich ‹*Geist*›; lebhaft ‹*Fantasie*›; **his mind remained ~:** er blieb geistig beweglich **3** (dextrous) geschickt

nimbly /ˈnɪmblɪ/ *adv.* flink ‹*arbeiten, sich bewegen*›

nimbus /ˈnɪmbəs/ *n., pl.* **nimbi** /ˈnɪmbaɪ/ *or* **~es** **1** (halo) Nimbus, *der* (bild. Kunst); Heiligenschein, *der* **2** (Meteorol.) Nimbostratus, *der*

Nimby /ˈnɪmbɪ/ *n.* (coll.) *Querulant, der/Querulantin, die gegen neue Bauprojekte vor der eigenen Haustür opponiert;* Sankt-Florians-Jünger, *der*/-Jüngerin, *die* (ugs.)

nincompoop /ˈnɪŋkəmpuːp/ *n.* Trottel, *der* (ugs. abwertend)

nine /naɪn/ ▸ⓘ **p. 894**, ▸ⓘ **p. 1001**, ▸ⓘ **p. 1358**
A *adj.* neun; **~-tenths of the time/inhabitants** (fig.) fast die ganze Zeit/fast *od.* so gut wie alle Einwohner; **~ times out of ten** (fig.: nearly always) in den weitaus meisten Fällen; **a ~ days' wonder** nur eine Eintagsfliege (ugs.); *see also* **eight A**
B *n.* **1** (number, symbol) Neun, *die;* **work from ~ to five** die übliche Arbeitszeit [von 9 bis 17 Uhr] haben; **the ~-to-five world** die Welt des geregelten Achtstundentags; **~-to-five mentality** Angestelltenmentalität, *die* (abwertend) **2** (Amer.: baseball team) Mannschaft, *die;* „Neun", *die* **3** **the N~** (literary: the Muses) die neun Musen **4** **dressed [up] to the ~s** sehr festlich gekleidet; **~-~-~, 999** (Brit.: emergency number) ≈ eins, eins, null. *See also* **eight B 1, 3, 4**

ninefold /ˈnaɪnfəʊld/ *adj., adv.* neunfach; *see also* **eightfold**

ˈninepins *n.* (Brit.) **1** (game) Kegeln, *das;* **play ~:** kegeln **2** *constr. as pl.* (pins) Kegel; **go down like ~** (fig.) reihenweise umfallen (ugs.)

nineteen /naɪnˈtiːn/ ▸ⓘ **p. 894**, ▸ⓘ **p. 1001**, ▸ⓘ **p. 1358**
A *adj.* neunzehn; *see also* **eight A**
B *n.* **1** Neunzehn, *die; see also* **eight B 1**; **eighteen B** **2** **talk ~ to the dozen** (Brit.) wie ein Wasserfall reden (ugs.)

nineteenth /naɪnˈtiːnθ/ ▸ⓘ **p. 1047**
A *adj.* ▸ⓘ **p. 1358** neunzehnt...; **~ hole** (joc.: golf club's bar) neunzehntes Loch (fig. scherzh.); *see also* **eighth A**
B *n.* (fraction) Neunzehntel, *das; see also* **eighth B**

ninetieth /ˈnaɪntɪɪθ/
A *adj.* ▸ⓘ **p. 1358** neunzigst...; *see also* **eighth A**
B *n.* (fraction) Neunzigstel, *das; see also* **eighth B**

ninety /ˈnaɪntɪ/ ▸ⓘ **p. 894**, ▸ⓘ **p. 1358**
A *adj.* neunzig; *see also* **eight A**
B *n.* Neunzig, *die. See also* **eight B 1**; **eighty B**

ninety: ~-ˈfirst *etc. adj.* ▸ⓘ **p. 1358** einundneunzigst... *usw.; see also* **eighth A**; **~-ˈone** *etc.* **A** *adj.* einundneunzig *usw.;* **~-nine times out of a hundred** (fig.: nearly always) so gut wie immer; *see also* **eight A**; **B** *n.* ▸❶ **p. 1358** Einundneunzig *usw., die; see also* **eight B 1**

ninny /ˈnɪnɪ/ *n.* Dummkopf, *der* (ugs.); Dussel, *der* (ugs.)

ninth /naɪnθ/

A *adj.* ▸❶ **p. 1358** neunt…; *see also* **eighth A**

B *n.* **1** (in sequence, rank) Neunte, *der/die/das;* (fraction) Neuntel, *das* **2** (Mus.) None, *die* **3** ▸❶ **p. 1047** (day) **the ~ of May** der neunte Mai; **the ~ [of the month]** der Neunte [des Monats]. *See also* **eighth B**

niobium /naɪˈəʊbɪəm/ *n.* (Chem.) Niobium, *das*

nip¹

A *v.t.*, **-pp-** **1** (pinch, squeeze, bite) zwicken; **~ sb.'s toe/sb. on the leg** jmdn. *od.* jmdm. in den Zeh/jmdn. am Bein zwicken **2** **~ off** abzwicken; (with scissors) abknipsen. *See also* **bud A**

B *v.i.*, **-pp-** (Brit. coll.: step etc. quickly) **~ in** hinein-/hereinflitzen (ugs.); **~ out** hinaus-/herausflitzen (ugs.); **~ up** hochflitzen (ugs.); **~ out to get a paper** kurz rausgehen, um eine Zeitung zu holen (ugs.); **~ across to Mrs Jones and ...:** spring mal zu Frau Jones rüber und …

C *n.* **1** (pinch, squeeze) Kniff, *der;* (bite) Biss, *der;* **give sb.'s cheek a ~, give sb. a ~ on the cheek** jmdn. in die Wange zwicken **2** (coldness of air) Kälte, *die;* **there's a ~ in the air** es ist frisch

nip² *n.* (of spirits etc.) Schlückchen, *das;* **have a ~ of wine** ein Schlückchen Wein nehmen

Nip /nɪp/ *n.* (sl. derog.) Japs, *der* (ugs., oft abwertend)

nip and ˈtuck *n.* **it was ~:** es war ganz knapp

nipper /ˈnɪpə(r)/ *n.* **1** (Brit. coll.: child) Gör, *das* (nordd.); Balg, *das* (ugs.) **2** *in pl.* (pincers) Beißzange, *die;* Kneifzange, *die* **3** (claw) Schere, *die;* Zange, *die*

nipple /ˈnɪpl/ *n.* **1** (on breast) Brustwarze, *die* **2** (of feeding bottle) Sauger, *der* **3** **[grease] ~:** [Schmier]nippel, *der*

Nippon /ˈnɪpɒn/ *pr. n.* Nippon *(das)*

nippy /ˈnɪpɪ/ *adj.* (coll.) **1** (nimble) flink; spritzig ‹*Auto*› **2** (cold) frisch; kühl

nirvana /nɜːˈvɑːnə, nɪəˈvɑːnə/ *n.* Nirwana, *das*

nisi /ˈnaɪsaɪ/ *adj.* (Law) vorläufig; mit Vorbehalt; *see also* **decree A 2**

Nissen hut /ˈnɪsn hʌt/ *n.* Nissenhütte, *die*

nit /nɪt/ *n.* **1** (egg) Nisse, *die* **2** (coll.: stupid person) Dussel, *der* (ugs.); Blödmann, *der* (salopp)

niter (Amer.) ▸**nitre**

ˈnit: ~-pick *v.i.* kritteln (abwertend); **~-picking** (coll.) **A** *n.* Kritteleien *Pl.* (abwertend); **B** *adj.* kleinlich (abwertend)

nitrate /ˈnaɪtreɪt/ *n.* **1** (salt) Nitrat, *das* **2** (fertilizer) Nitratdünger, *der*

nitre /ˈnaɪtə(r)/ *n.* (Brit.) Salpeter, *der*

nitric /ˈnaɪtrɪk/ *adj.* (Chem.: of or containing nitrogen) stickstoffhaltig; Stickstoff-

nitric: ~ ˈacid *n.* (Chem.) Salpetersäure, *die;* **~ ˈoxide** *n.* (Chem.) Stickoxid, *das*

nitride /ˈnaɪtraɪd/ *n.* (Chem.) Nitrid, *das*

nitrite /ˈnaɪtraɪt/ *n.* (Chem.) Nitrit, *das*

nitrogen /ˈnaɪtrədʒən/ *n.* Stickstoff, *der*

nitrogen: ~ cycle *n.* (Bot.) Stickstoffkreislauf, *der;* **~ fixation** *n.* (Bot.) Bindung des freien Stickstoffs

nitrogenous /naɪˈtrɒdʒɪnəs/ *adj.* stickstoffhaltig

nitroglycerine /naɪtrəʊˈglɪsəriːn/ *n.* Nitroglyzerin, *das*

nitrous/ˈnaɪtrəs/: **~ ˈacid** *n.* (Chem.) salpet[e]rige Säure; **~ ˈoxide** *n.* (Chem.) Distickstoff[mon]oxid, *das*

nitty-gritty /nɪtɪˈgrɪtɪ/ *n.* (coll.) **the ~ [of the matter]** der Kern [der Sache]; **the ~ of the situation** das, worum es eigentlich geht; **get down to the ~:** zur Sache kommen

nitwit /ˈnɪtwɪt/ *n.* (coll.) Trottel, *der* (ugs.)

nitwitted /ˈnɪtwɪtɪd/ *adj.* dämlich (ugs.)

nix /nɪks/ *n.* (coll.) **1** (nothing) nix (ugs.) **2** ▸**no B 2**

NNE /nɔːθnɔːθˈiːst/ *abbr.* ▸❶ **p. 1013 = north-north-east** NNO

NNW /nɔːθnɔːθˈwest/ *abbr.* ▸❶ **p. 1013 = north-north-west** NNW

no /nəʊ/

A *adj.* **1** (not any) kein **2** (not a) kein; (quite other than) alles andere als; **she is no beauty** sie ist keine Schönheit *od.* nicht gerade eine Schönheit; **you are no friend** du bist kein [wahrer] Freund; **friend or no friend** Freund oder nicht; Freund hin oder her; *see also* **go¹ C 6** **3** (hardly any) **it's no distance from our house to the shopping centre** von unserem Haus ist es nicht weit bis zum Einkaufszentrum; *see also* **time 2**

B *adv.* **1** (by no amount) nicht; **we went no further than the Post Office** wir gingen nicht weiter als bis zum Postamt; **no fewer than** nicht weniger als; **no less [than]** nicht weniger [als]; **it is no different from before** es hat sich nichts geändert; **it was no less a person than Gladstone** *or* **Gladstone, no less** es war kein Geringerer als Gladstone; **I ask no more of you other than ...:** ich verlange nicht mehr von dir als …; **no more wine?** keinen Wein mehr?; **no more war!** nie wieder Krieg!; **he is no more upper-class than I am** er ist auch nicht mehr *od.* nichts Besseres (ugs.) als ich; **I'm not entirely innocent in this matter — No more am ˈI** Ich bin nicht ganz unschuldig in dieser Sache — Und ich [bins] ebenso wenig; **I saw no more of him** ich habe ihn nicht mehr gesehen; **he is no more** (is dead) er ist nicht mehr (geh.) **2** (equivalent to negative sentence) nein; **say/answer 'no'** Nein sagen/mit Nein antworten; **I won't take 'no' for an answer** ein Nein lasse ich nicht gelten; **I won't say 'no'** da kann ich nicht Nein sagen **3** (not) nicht; **like it or no** ob es mir *usw.* [nun] passt/passte oder nicht; **whether or no anyone else helps** [egal] ob sonst jemand hilft oder nicht **4** **no can do** (coll.) geht nicht (ugs.)

C *n.*, *pl.* **noes** /nəʊz/ Nein, *das;* (vote) Neinstimme, *die;* **the ayes and noes** die Stimmen für und wider; **the noes have it** die Mehrheit ist dagegen

No. *abbr.* **1** **= number** Nr. **2** ▸❶ **p. 1013** (Amer.) **= North** N

ˈno-account *adj.* unbedeutend

Noah's ark /nəʊəz ˈɑːk/ **1** (Bibl.) die Arche Noah **2** (toy) Arche Noah *(als Spielzeug)*

nob¹ /nɒb/ *n.* (coll.: head) Rübe, *die* (salopp)

nob² *n.* (Brit. coll.: wealthy or upper-class person) **the ~s** die besseren Leute

no-ˈball (Cricket)

A *n.* Fehlball, *der*

B *v.t.* **~ sb.** jmds. Wurf für ungültig erklären

nobble /ˈnɒbl/ *v.t.* (Brit. coll.) **1** (tamper with) (durch Spritzen o. Ä.) langsam machen ‹*Rennpferd*› **2** (get the favour of) (durch Bestechung o. Ä.) auf seine Seite ziehen ‹*Person*› **3** (take dishonestly) klauen (salopp) ‹*Geld, Schmuck*› **4** (catch) schnappen (ugs.) ‹*Dieb*›

nobbut /ˈnɒbət/ *adv.* (dial.) bloß (ugs.); nur; **it's ~ Thursday** es ist erst Donnerstag

Nobel Prize /nəʊbel ˈpraɪz/ *n.* Nobelpreis, *der*

nobility /nəˈbɪlɪtɪ/ *n.* **1** *no pl.* (character) hohe Gesinnung; Adel, *der;* **a true ~ of character** ein wahrhaft nobler Charakter; **~ of soul** Seelenadel, *der* (geh.) **2** (class) Adel, *der;* **many of the ~:** viele Adlige; **be born into the ~:** von adliger Geburt sein (geh.)

noble /ˈnəʊbl/

A *adj.* **1** (by rank, title, or birth) ad[e]lig; **be of ~ birth** von adliger *od.* edler Geburt sein (geh.); adlig sein; **the ~ Lord/Earl** der edle Lord/Graf (geh.) **2** (of lofty character) edel ‹*Gedanken, Gefühle*›; **~ ideals** hohe Ideale **3** (showing greatness of character) edel; hochherzig (geh.); **make ~ efforts** sich in hochherziger Weise bemühen (geh.) **4** (splendid) edel (geh.); vortrefflich

B *n.* Adlige, *der/die;* Edelmann, *der*/Edelfrau, *die* (hist.); **the ~s** die Adligen; die Edelleute (hist.)

noble: ˈgas *n.* (Chem.) Edelgas, *das;* **~man** /ˈnəʊblmən/ *n.*, *pl.* **~men** /ˈnəʊblmən/ Adlige, *der;* Edelmann, *der* (hist.); **~ ˈmetal** *n.* (Chem.) Edelmetall, *das;* **~-ˈminded** *adj.* edel gesinnt; edel ‹*Tat*›; **~ ˈsavage** *n.* edler Wilder (Literaturw.)

noblesse /nəˈbles/ *n.*, *no pl.* Noblesse, *die* (veralt.); Adel, *der;* **~ oblige** /nəʊbles əʊˈbliːʒ/ noblesse oblige (geh., oft scherzh.); Adel verpflichtet

ˈnoblewoman *n.* Adlige, *die;* Edelfrau, *die* (hist.); (unmarried) Edelfräulein, *das* (hist.)

nobly /ˈnəʊblɪ/ *adv.* **1** (with noble spirit) edel [gesinnt] **2** (generously) edelmütig (geh.) **3** (splendidly) edel (geh.)

nobody /ˈnəʊbədɪ/ *n.* & *pron.* niemand; keiner; (person of no importance) Niemand, *der; see also* **business 3**; **fool¹ A 1**

no-brainer /nəʊˈbreɪnə(r)/ *n.* (Amer. coll.: simple decision, idea) nahe liegende Sache

no-ˈclaim[s] bonus *n.* (Insurance) Schadenfreiheitsrabatt, *der*

nocturnal /nɒkˈtɜːnl/ *adj.* nächtlich; nachtaktiv ‹*Tier*›; **~ animal/bird** Nachttier, *das*/-vogel, *der*

nocturne /ˈnɒktɜːn/ *n.* **1** (Mus.) Nocturne, *das od. die* **2** (Art) Nachtstück, *das*

nod /nɒd/

A *v.i.*, **-dd-** **1** (as signal) nicken; **~ to sb.** jmdm. zunicken; **have a ~ding acquaintance with sth.** nur über geringe Kenntnisse in etw. *(Dat.)* verfügen; **he's only a ~ding acquaintance** ich kenne ihn nur flüchtig; **he ~ded to him to take charge** er gab ihm durch ein Nicken zu verstehen, dass er das Kommando übernehmen solle; *see also* **goodbye B** **2** (in drowsiness) **she sat ~ding by the fire** sie war neben dem Kamin eingenickt (ugs.); **her head started to ~:** sie begann einzunicken (ugs.) **3** (make a mistake) patzen (ugs.); einen Fehler machen **4** (move up and down) nicken (fig. dichter.)

B *v.t.*, **-dd-** **1** (incline) **~ one's head [in greeting]** [zum Gruß] mit dem Kopf nicken **2** (signify by nod) **~ approval** *or* **agreement** zustimmend nicken; **~ sb. a welcome, ~ a welcome to sb.** jmdm. zum Gruß *od.* zur Begrüßung zunicken

C *n.* **1** (nodding) [Kopf]nicken, *das;* **a ~ is as good as a wink [to a blind man** *or* **horse]** (fig.) es bedarf/bedurfte keiner weiteren Worte; **land of N~:** Land der Träume (geh.); **on the ~** (coll.) (on credit) auf Pump (salopp); (with merely formal assent) ohne große Diskussion **2** (sign of approval) **get the ~ from sb.** von jmdm. grünes Licht bekommen; **give sth. the ~:** grünes Licht für etw. geben

Phrasal verb

• **~ ˈoff** *v.i.* einnicken (ugs.)

NOD *abbr.* **= news-on-demand** NOD

noddle /ˈnɒdl/ *n.* (coll.: head) Birne, *die* (salopp)

noddy /ˈnɒdɪ/ *n.* Dummkopf, *der*

node /nəʊd/ *n.* **1** (Bot., Astron.) Knoten, *der* **2** (Phys.) Schwingungsknoten, *der* **3** (Math.) Knoten[punkt], *der* **4** (Computing, Teleph.) (junction in network) Knoten[punkt], *der;* (networked device) mit einem Netzwerk verbundenes Gerät

nodule /ˈnɒdjuːl/ *n.* **1** Klümpchen, *das* **2** (Bot.) Knötchen, *das*

Noel /nəʊˈel/ *n.* (esp. in carols) Weihnachten, *das od. Pl.;* Weihnacht, *die* (geh.)

ˈno ˈentry' (for people) „Zutritt verboten"; (for vehicles) „Einfahrt verboten"; **a ~ sign** ein Schild mit der Aufschrift „Zutritt/Einfahrt verboten"

ˈno-fault divorce *n.* Scheidung in gegenseitigem Einvernehmen

ˈno-fault insurance *n.* (Amer.) ≈ Vollkaskoversicherung

no-ˈfly zone *n.* Flugverbotszone, *die*

noggin /ˈnɒgɪn/ *n.* **1** (mug) Becher, *der;* (drink) Schlückchen, *das* **2** (coll.: head) Birne, *die* (salopp)

no-ˈgo *adj.* Sperr‹*gebiet, -zone*›

ˈno-good *adj.* (coll.) nichtsnutzig (abwertend)

no-hoper /nəʊˈhəʊpə(r)/ *n.* absoluter Außenseiter; **be a ~:** keine Chance haben; **a team of ~s** eine völlig chancenlose Mannschaft

nohow /ˈnəʊhaʊ/ *adv.* (Amer. coll.) in keiner Weise

noise /nɔɪz/

A *n.* **1** (loud outcry) Lärm, *der;* Krach, *der;* **don't**

make so much ~/such a loud ~: sei nicht so laut/mach nicht solchen Lärm *od.* Krach; **make a ~ about sth.** (fig.: complain) wegen etw. Krach machen *od.* schlagen (ugs.); **make a ~** (fig.: be much talked about) von sich reden machen; Aufsehen erregen; *see also* **hold² A 20** **2** (any sound) Geräusch, *das;* (loud, harsh, unwanted) Lärm, *der;* **~s off** Geräuschkulisse, *die* **3** (Communications: irregular fluctuations of signal) Geräusch, *das;* (hissing) Rauschen, *das* **4** *in pl.* (conventional remarks or sounds) **make friendly** *etc.* **~s [at sb.]** [jmdm. gegenüber] freundliche *usw.* Bemerkungen von sich geben; **make ~s about doing sth.** davon reden, etw. tun zu wollen

B *v.t.* (dated/formal) **~ sth. abroad** *or* **about** etw. verbreiten

'noise abatement *n.* Lärmbekämpfung, *die*

noise: ~less /ˈnɔɪzlɪs/ *adj.*, **noiselessly** /ˈnɔɪzlɪslɪ/ *adv.* **1** (silent[ly]) lautlos; **2** (making no avoidable noise) geräuschlos; **~ level** *n.* Geräuschpegel, *der;* (of unpleasant noise) Lärmpegel, *der*

'noise pollution *n.* Lärmbelästigung, *die*

noisily /ˈnɔɪzɪlɪ/ *adv.* laut; lärmend ‹*spielen*›; geräuschvoll ‹*stolpern, schlürfen*›

noisome /ˈnɔɪsəm/ *adj.* (literary) **1** (harmful, noxious) gefährlich; übel (geh.) ‹*Umgebung*› **2** (evil-smelling) übel riechend **3** (objectionable, offensive) unangenehm

noisy /ˈnɔɪzɪ/ *adj.* laut; lärmend, laut ‹*Menschenmasse, Kinder*›; lautstark ‹*Diskussion, Begrüßung*›; geräuschvoll ‹*Aufbruch, Ankunft*›

nomad /ˈnəʊmæd/

A *n.* **1** Nomade, *der* **2** (wanderer) jmd., der ein Nomadendasein führt

B *adj.* **1** nomadisch **2** (wandering) **~ existence** Nomadendasein, *das*

nomadic /nəʊˈmædɪk/ *adj.* nomadisch; **~ tribe** Nomadenstamm, *der*

'no man's land *n.* Niemandsland, *das*

nom de plume /nɒm də ˈpluːm/ *n.*, *pl.* **noms de plume** /nɒm də ˈpluːm/ Schriftstellername, *der;* Pseudonym, *das*

nomenclature /nəˈmenklətʃə(r), ˈnəʊmənkleɪtʃə(r)/ *n.* **1** (system of names) Vokabular, *das* **2** (terminology, systematic naming, catalogue) Nomenklatur, *die*

nominal /ˈnɒmɪnl/ *adj.* **1** (in name only) nominell **2** (virtually nothing) äußerst gering; äußerst niedrig ‹*Preis, Miete*› **3** (Ling.) nominal; Nominal‹*phrase, -präfix*›

nominalism /ˈnɒmɪnəlɪzm/ *n.* (Philos.) Nominalismus, *der*

nominally /ˈnɒmɪnəlɪ/ *adv.* namentlich

nominal 'value *n.* (Econ.) Nennwert, *der*

nominate /ˈnɒmɪneɪt/ *v.t.* **1** (call by name of) nennen **2** (propose for election) nominieren **3** (appoint to office) ernennen

nomination /nɒmɪˈneɪʃn/ *n.* **1** (appointment to office) Ernennung, *die* **2** (proposal for election) Nominierung, *die*

nominative /ˈnɒmɪnətɪv/ (Ling.)

A *adj.* Nominativ-; nominativisch; **~ case** Nominativ, *der*

B *n.* Nominativ, *der; see also* **absolute 3**

nominee /nɒmɪˈniː/ *n.* **1** (candidate) Kandidat, *der*/Kandidatin, *die* **2** (representative) Stellvertreter, *der*/-vertreterin, *die*

non- /nɒn/ *pref.* nicht-

non-ac'ceptance *n.* (Commerc.) Annahmeverweigerung, *die*

nonagenarian /nəʊnədʒɪˈneərɪən/

A *adj.* neunzigjährig; (more than 90 years old) in den Neunzigern *nachgestellt*

B *n.* Neunziger, *der*/Neunzigerin, *die*

non-ag'gression *n.* Gewaltverzicht, *der;* **~ pact** *or* **treaty** Nichtangriffspakt, *der*

non-alco'holic *adj.* alkoholfrei

non-a'ligned *adj.* blockfrei

non-a'lignment *n., no pl.* Blockfreiheit, *die*

non-bel'ligerent

A *adj.* nicht Krieg führend

B *n.* nicht Krieg führendes Land

nonce /nɒns/ *n.* **for the ~:** einstweilen

'nonce word *n.* Ad-hoc-Bildung, *die*

nonchalance /ˈnɒnʃələns/ *n.* Nonchalance, *die* (geh.); Unbekümmertheit, *die;* (lack of interest) Desinteresse, *das;* Gleichgültigkeit, *die*

nonchalant /ˈnɒnʃələnt/ *adj.*, **nonchalantly** /ˈnɒnʃələntlɪ/ *adv.* nonchalant (geh.); unbekümmert; (without interest) desinteressiert; gleichgültig

non-'combatant

A *n.* Nichtkämpfende, *der/die*

B *adj.* nicht am Kampf beteiligt

non-com'missioned *adj.* ohne Patent *nachgestellt;* **~ officer** Unteroffizier, *der*

non-com'mittal *adj.* unverbindlich

non compos [mentis] /nɒn ˈkɒmpɒs (ˈmentɪs)/ *pred. adj.* nicht im Vollbesitz seiner/ihrer *usw.* geistigen Kräfte

non-con'ducting *adj.* (Phys.) nicht leitend

non-con'ductor *n.* (Phys.) Nichtleiter, *der*

noncon'formism *n.* Nonkonformismus, *der*

noncon'formist *n.* Nonkonformist, *der*/Nonkonformistin, *die*

noncon'formity *n.* **1** Nonkonformismus, *der* **2** (lack of correspondence or agreement) Nonkonformität, *die*

non-con'tributory *adj.* beitragsfrei

non-cooper'ation *n.* Verweigerung der Kooperation

non-denomi'national *adj.* konfessionslos

nondescript /ˈnɒndɪskrɪpt/ *adj.* unscheinbar; undefinierbar ‹*Farbe*›

'non-drip *adj.* nicht tropfend ‹*Farbe*›

non-'driver *n.* Nicht[auto]fahrer, *der*

none /nʌn/

A *pron.* kein…; **I want ~ of your cheek!** sei nicht so frech!; **~ of them** keiner/keine/keines von ihnen; **~ of this money is mine** von diesem Geld gehört mir nichts; **~ of these houses** kein[e]s dieser Häuser; **~ but they/he** keiner *od.* niemand außer ihnen/ihm; nur sie/er; **~ other than …:** kein anderer/keine andere als …; **Is there any bread left? — No, ~ at all** Ist noch Brot da? — Nein, gar keins mehr; **it is ~ of my concern** das geht mich nichts an; **his understanding is ~ of the clearest** seine Auffassungsgabe ist nicht gerade die beste

B *adv.* keineswegs; **I'm ~ the wiser now** jetzt bin ich um nichts klüger; **~ the less** nichtsdestoweniger; *see also* **too 1**

non'entity *n.* (non-existent thing, person or thing of no importance) Nichts, *das*

nonesuch ▸ nonsuch

nonetheless /nʌnðəˈles/ *adv.* nichtdestoweniger; dessen ungeachtet

'non-event *n.* Reinfall, *der* (ugs.); Enttäuschung, *die*

non-ex'istence *n., no pl.* Nichtvorhandensein, *das*

non-ex'istent /nɒnɪgˈzɪstənt/ *adj.* nicht vorhanden

non-'ferrous *adj.* Nichteisen-

non-'fiction *n.* **~ [literature]** Sachliteratur, *die;* **~ novel** Tatsachenroman, *der*

non-'flammable *adj.* nicht entzündbar

non-governmental organi'zation *n.* Nichtregierungsorganisation, *die*

non-inter'ference, non-inter'vention *ns., no pl.* Nichteinmischung, *die*

non-in'vasive *adj.* nichtinvasiv ‹*Diagnostik, Methode usw.*›

non-'iron *adj.* bügelfrei

'non-issue *n.* Bagatelle, *die;* Nebensächlichkeit, *die;* **expense was a ~:** Kosten waren kein Thema

non-'member *n.* Nichtmitglied, *das*

non-'metal *n.* (Chem.) Nichtmetall, *das*

non-me'tallic *adj.* (Chem.) nichtmetallisch

non-'net *adj.* nicht preisgebunden

non-'nuclear *adj.* Nichtnuklear-; **~ club** Gruppe der Nichtnuklearstaaten; **~ weapons** konventionelle Waffen

'no-no *n., pl.* **~es** (coll.) **be a ~:** nicht infrage kommen (ugs.); **that's a ~:** das kannste vergessen (ugs.)

no-'nonsense ▸ nonsense A 3

nonpareil /nɒnpəˈreɪl/ *n.* (person) jemand, der nicht seinesgleichen hat; Ausnahmeerscheinung, *die;* (thing) Nonplusultra, *das*

non-'party *adj.* **1** (not attached to a party) parteilos **2** (not related to a party) überparteilich **3** (nonpartisan) unparteiisch

non-'payment *n.* Nichtzahlung, *die*

non-'perishable

A *adj.* unverderblich ‹*Lebensmittel*›

B *n.* (foodstuff) unverderbliches Lebensmittel

non-'playing *adj.* nicht mitspielend; zuschauend; **~ captain** Mannschaftsführer, *der*

nonplus /nɒnˈplʌs/ *v.t.*, **-ss-** verblüffen; **he was ~sed by sth.** etw. verblüffte ihn

non-'profit[-making] *adj.* nicht auf Gewinn ausgerichtet

non-prolife'ration *n., no pl.* Nichtverbreitung von Atomwaffen; Nonproliferation, *die* (Politik); **~ treaty** Atom[waffen]sperrvertrag, *der*

non-'reader *n.* **1** (person who cannot read) Leseunkundige, *der/die* **2** (person averse to reading) Nichtleser, *der*/-leserin, *die*

non-re'cyclable *adj.* nicht recycelbar

non-re'fillable *adj.* nicht nachfüllbar; Einweg‹*feuerzeug, -patrone usw.*›

non-re'flective *adj.* reflexionsfrei

non-'resident

A *adj.* (residing elsewhere) nicht im Haus wohnend; (outside a country) nicht ansässig; **a ~ landlord** ein Vermieter, der nicht im [selben] Haus wohnt

B *n.* nicht im Haus Wohnende, *der/die;* (outside a country) Nichtansässige, *der/die;* **the bar is open to ~s** die Bar ist auch für Gäste geöffnet, die nicht im Hotel wohnen

non-re'turnable *adj.* Einweg‹*behälter, -flasche, -[ver]packung*›; nicht rückzahlbar ‹*Anzahlung*›

non-'scheduled *adj.* Charter‹*flugzeug, -Airline etc.*›

nonsense /ˈnɒnsəns/

A *n.* **1** *no pl., no art.* (meaningless words, ideas, or behaviour) Unsinn, *der;* **make ~ of sth.** etw. ad absurdum führen; **piece of ~:** Firlefanz, *der* (ugs. abwertend); **talk ~:** Unsinn reden; **it's all a lot of ~:** das ist alles Unsinn **2** (instance) Unsinn, *der;* **~s** Unsinn; **make a ~ of** verpfuschen (ugs.); ‹*Ereignis:*› unsinnig *od.* widersinnig machen; ad absurdum führen ‹*Idee, Ideal*› **3** (sth. one disapproves of) Unsinn, *der;* (trifles) Firlefanz, *der* (ugs. abwertend); **what's all this ~ about …?** was soll das [dumme] Gerede über (+ *Akk.*) …?; **let's have no more ~, stop your ~:** Schluss mit dem Unsinn; **stand no ~:** keinen Unfug dulden; **no-~:** nüchtern; **come along now, and no ~:** kommt jetzt, und mach keinen Unsinn

B *int.* Unsinn!

'nonsense verses *n. pl.* (Lit.) Nonsensdichtung, *die*

nonsensical /nɒnˈsensɪkl/ *adj.* unsinnig

nonsensically /nɒnˈsensɪkəlɪ/ *adv.* unsinnigerweise; ohne Sinn und Verstand ‹*handeln*›

non sequitur /nɒn ˈsekwɪtə(r)/ *n.* unlogische Folgerung

non-'skid *adj.* rutschfest

non-'slip *adj.* rutschfest

non-'smoker *n.* **1** (person) Nichtraucher, *der*/Nichtraucherin, *die* **2** (train compartment) Nichtraucherabteil, *das*

non-'standard *adj.* **1** (not usual) nicht normgerecht; **people working ~ hours** Leute mit ungewöhnlichen Arbeitszeiten **2** (Ling.) Nonstandard-

non-'starter *n.* **1** (Sport) Nichtstartende, *der/die* **2** (fig. coll.) Reinfall, *der* (ugs.); (person) Blindgänger, *der* (fig. salopp)

non-'stick *adj.* **~ frying pan** *etc.* Bratpfanne *usw.* mit Antihaftbeschichtung

non-stop

A /'--/ *adj.* durchgehend ‹*Zug, Busverbindung*›; Nonstop‹*flug, -revue*›

B /-'-/ *adv.* ohne Unterbrechung ‹*tanzen, reden,*

reisen, senden›; nonstop, im Nonstop ‹*fliegen, tanzen, fahren*›
non-'stretch *adj.* unelastisch
nonsuch /'nʌnsʌtʃ/ *n.* 1 Ausnahmeerscheinung, *die* 2 (plant) Hopfenklee, *der*
'non-toxic *adj.* ungiftig; nichttoxisch (fachspr.)
non-U /nɒn'juː/ *adj.* (coll.) nicht vornehm
non-'union *adj.* nicht organisiert; (made by ~ members) von Nichtorganisierten hergestellt ‹*Fabrikat*›
non-'violence *n.*, *no pl.* Gewaltlosigkeit, *die*
non-'violent *adj.* gewaltlos
non-'voter *n.* Nichtwähler, *der*/-wählerin, *die*
non-'white
A *adj.* farbig
B *n.* Farbige, *der/die*
noodle¹ /'nuːdl/ *n.* (pasta) Nudel, *die*
noodle² *n.* (dated coll.: simpleton) Dummkopf, *der* (ugs.); **gape like a ~:** dumm gucken (ugs.)
nook /nʊk/ *n.* Winkel, *der*; Ecke, *die*; **in every ~ and cranny** in allen Ecken und Winkeln
nooky /'nʊkɪ/ *n.* (sl.) Aufhupfer, *der* (ugs.)
noon /nuːn/ *n.* ▸ℹ **p. 1001** Mittag, *der*; zwölf Uhr [mittags]; **at/before ~:** um/vor zwölf [Uhr mittags]
'noonday *n.* Mittag, *der*; *attrib.* Mittags‹*sonne, -hitze*›; **at ~:** mittags
'no one
A *pron.* 1 **~ of them** keiner/keine/keines von ihnen 2 ▸**nobody**
B *adj.* **~ person could do that** einer allein könnte das nicht tun
'noontide (dated/rhet.), **'noontime** (Amer.) *ns.* Mittagszeit, *die*; **at ~:** zur Mittagszeit
noose /nuːs/
A *n.* Schlinge, *die*; **put one's head in a ~** (fig.) den Kopf in die Schlinge stecken
B *v.t.* [mit einer Schlinge] fangen
nope /nəʊp/ *adv.* (coll.) nee (ugs.)
'no place *adv.* (Amer.) ▸**nowhere A**
nor /nə(r), *stressed* nɔː(r)/ *conj.* noch; **neither ... ~ ..., not ... ~ ...:** weder ... noch ...; **he can't do it, ~ can I, ~ can you** er kann es nicht, ich auch nicht und du auch nicht; **~ will I deny that ...:** [und] ich will auch nicht bestreiten, dass ...
Nordic /'nɔːdɪk/
A *adj.* nordisch
B *n.* nordischer Typus; Nordide, *der/die* (Ethnol.)
norm /nɔːm/ *n.* Norm, *die*; **IQ above the ~:** überdurchschnittlicher IQ; **rise above the ~:** über den Normalwert steigen; **behavioural ~:** Verhaltensnorm *od.* -regel, *die*
normal /'nɔːml/
A *adj.* 1 normal; **be back to ~ working hours** wieder normal arbeiten; **recover one's ~ self** sein seelisches Gleichgewicht wieder finden 2 (Geom.) senkrecht (**to** auf + *Dat.*, zu)
B *n.* 1 (normal value) Normalwert, *der* 2 (usual state) normaler Stand; **everything is back to** *or* **has returned to ~:** es hat sich wieder alles normalisiert; **his temperature is above ~:** er hat erhöhte Temperatur 3 (Geom.) Normale, *die*
normalcy /'nɔːmlsɪ/ *n.*, *no pl.* (normality) Normalität, *die*
normalise ▸**normalize**
normality /nɔː'mælɪtɪ/ *n.*, *no pl.* Normalität, *die*; **return to ~ after Christmas** nach Weihnachten wieder zum gewohnten Alltag zurückkehren
normalize /'nɔːməlaɪz/
A *v.t.* normalisieren
B *v.i.* sich normalisieren
normally /'nɔːməlɪ/ *adv.* 1 (in normal way) normal 2 (ordinarily) normalerweise
Norman /'nɔːmn/
A *n.* 1 Normanne, *der*/Normannin, *die* 2 (king) normannischer König 3 (Ling.) Normannisch, *das* 4 (Archit.) normannischer Baustil
B *adj.* normannisch; *see also* **conquest 1**
Normandy /'nɔːməndɪ/ *pr. n.* Normandie, *die*
Norman: ~ 'French *n.* (Ling.) Normannisch, *das*; **~ style** *n.* (Archit.) normannischer Baustil

normative /'nɔːmətɪv/ *adj.* normativ (geh.)
Norse /nɔːs/
A *n.* (Ling.) 1 (Scandinavian language group) nordische Sprachen 2 **[Old] ~:** Altnordisch, *das*
B *adj.* nordisch
Norseman /'nɔːsmən/ *n.*, *pl.* **Norsemen** /'nɔːsmən/ (Hist.) Wikinger, *der*
north /nɔːθ/ ▸ℹ **p. 1013**
A *n.* 1 Norden, *der*; **the ~:** Nord (Met., Seew.); **in/to[wards]/from the ~:** im/nach *od.* (geh.) gen/von Norden; **to the ~ of** nördlich von; nördlich (+ *Gen.*); **magnetic ~:** magnetischer Nordpol 2 *usu.* **N~** (part lying to the ~) Norden, *der*; **from the N~:** aus dem Norden; **the N~** (Brit.: of England) Nordengland (*das*); der Norden; (the Arctic) die Arktis; der Nordpol; (Amer.: the Northern states) die Nordstaaten; der Norden 3 (Cards) Nord
B *adj.* nördlich; Nord‹*wind, -küste, -grenze, -tor*›
C *adv.* nordwärts; nach Norden; **~ of** nördlich von; nördlich (+ *Gen.*); **~ and south** nach Norden und Süden ‹*verlaufen, sich erstrecken*›; *see also* **by¹ A 4**
north: N~ 'Africa *pr. n.* Nordafrika (*das*); **N~ A'merica** *pr. n.* Nordamerika (*das*); **N~ A'merican A** *adj.* nordamerikanisch; **B** *n.* Nordamerikaner, *der*/-amerikanerin, *die*; **N~ At'lantic** *pr. n.* Nordatlantik, *der*; **North Atlantic Treaty Organization** Nordatlantikpakt, *der*; **~bound** *adj.* ▸ℹ **p. 1013** ‹*Zug, Verkehr usw.*› in Richtung Norden; **~ country** *n.* (Brit.) Nordengland (*das*); Norden, *der*; **~-country** *adj.* (Brit.) nordenglisch; **~-'countryman** *n.* (Brit.) Nordengländer, *der*; **~-'east** ▸ℹ **p. 1013 A** *n.* Nordosten, *der*; **in/to[wards]/from the ~-east** im/nach *od.* (geh.) gen/von Nordosten; **to the ~-east of** nordöstlich von; nordöstlich (+ *Gen.*); **B** *adj.* nordöstlich; Nordost‹*wind, -küste*›; **~-east passage** Nordostpassage, *die*; **C** *adv.* nordostwärts; nach Nordosten; **~-east of** nordöstlich von; nordöstlich (+ *Gen.*); *see also* **by¹ A 4**; **~-'easter** Nordostwind, *der*; **~-'easterly** ▸ℹ **p. 1013 A** *adj.* nordöstlich; **B** *adv.* (position) im Nordosten; (direction) nach Nordosten; **~-'eastern** *adj.* ▸ℹ **p. 1013** nordöstlich
northerly /'nɔːðəlɪ/ ▸ℹ **p. 1013**
A *adj.* 1 (in position or direction) nördlich; **in a ~ direction** nach Norden 2 (from the north) ‹*Wind*› aus nördlichen Richtungen; **the wind was ~:** der Wind kam aus nördlichen Richtungen
B *adv.* 1 (in position) nördlich; (in direction) nordwärts 2 (from the north) aus *od.* von Nord[en]
C *n.* Nord[wind], *der*
northern /'nɔːðən/ *adj.* ▸ℹ **p. 1013** nördlich; Nord‹*grenze, -hälfte, -seite, -fenster, -wind*›
northerner /'nɔːðənə(r)/ *n.* (male) Nordengländer/-deutsche *usw.*, *der*; (female) Nordengländerin/-deutsche *usw.*, *die*; (Amer.) Nordstaatler, *der*/-staatlerin, *die*; **he's a ~:** er kommt aus dem Norden
Northern: ~ 'Europe *pr. n.* Nordeuropa (*das*); **~ Euro'pean A** *adj.* nordeuropäisch; **B** *n.* Nordeuropäer, *der*/Nordeuropäerin, *die*; **~ 'Ireland** *pr. n.* Nordirland (*das*); **N~ 'Lights** *n. pl.* Nordlicht, *das*
northernmost /'nɔːðənməʊst/ *adj.* ▸ℹ **p. 1013** nördlichst...
North: ~ 'German A *adj.* norddeutsch; **B** *n.* Norddeutsche, *der/die*; **~ 'Germany** *pr. n.* Norddeutschland (*das*); **~ Ko'rea** *pr. n.* Nordkorea (*das*); **~ Ko'rean A** *adj.* nordkoreanisch; **B** *n.* Nordkoreaner, *der*/-koreanerin, *die*; **'~land** *n.* (poet.) Nordland, *das* (selten); **n~ 'light** *n.* Licht von Norden; **~man** /'nɔːθmən/ *n.*, *pl.* **Northmen** /'nɔːθmən/ ▸**Norseman**; **n~-~-'east** ▸ℹ **p. 1013 A** *n.* Nordnordosten, *der*; **B** *adj.* nordnordöstlich; **C** *adv.* nordnordostwärts; **n~-~-'west** ▸ℹ **p. 1013 A** *n.* Nordnordwesten, *der*; **B** *adj.* nordnordwestlich; **C** *adv.* nordnordwestwärts; **~ of 'England** *pr. n.* Nordengland (*das*); *attrib.* nordenglisch; **~ 'Pole** *pr. n.* Nordpol, *der*; **~ Rhine West'phalia** *pr. n.* Nordrhein-Westfalen (*das*); **~ 'Sea** *pr. n.* Nordsee, *die*; **~ Sea gas/oil** Nordseegas/-öl, *das*; **~ 'star** *n.* Nordstern, *der*

northward /'nɔːθwəd/ ▸ℹ **p. 1013**
A *adj.* nach Norden gerichtet; (situated towards the north) nördlich; **in a ~ direction** nach Norden; [in] Richtung Norden
B *adv.* nordwärts; **they are ~ bound** sie fahren nach *od.* [in] Richtung Norden
C *n.* Norden, *der*
northwards /'nɔːθwədz/ ▸ℹ **p. 1013** ▸**northward B**
north: ~-'west ▸ℹ **p. 1013 A** *n.* Nordwesten, *der*; **in/to[wards]/from the ~-west** im/nach *od.* (geh.) gen/von Nordwesten; **to the ~-west of** nordwestlich von; nordwestlich (+ *Gen.*); **B** *adj.* nordwestlich; Nordwest‹*wind, -küste*›; **~-west passage** Nordwestpassage, *die*; **C** *adv.* nordwestwärts; nach Nordwesten; **~-west of** nordwestlich von; nordwestlich (+ *Gen.*); *see also* **by¹ A 4**; **~-wester** /nɔːθ 'westə(r)/ *n.* Nordwestwind, *der*; **~-'westerly** ▸ℹ **p. 1013 A** *adj.* nordwestlich; **B** *adv.* (position) im Nordwesten; (direction) nach Nordwesten; **~-'western** *adj.* ▸ℹ **p. 1013** nordwestlich
Norway /'nɔːweɪ/ *pr. n.* Norwegen (*das*)
Norwegian /nɔː'wiːdʒn/ ▸ℹ **p. 1277**, ▸ℹ **p. 1345**
A *adj.* norwegisch; *see also* **English A**
B *n.* 1 (person) Norweger, *der*/Norwegerin, *die* 2 (language) Norwegisch, *das*; *see also* **English B 1**
Nos. *abbr.* **= numbers** Nrn.
'no-score draw *n.* torloses Unentschieden
nose /nəʊz/
A *n.* 1 ▸ℹ **p. 951** Nase, *die*; **have one's ~ [stuck] in a book** (coll.) die Nase in ein Buch stecken (ugs.); **it's as plain as the ~ on your face** (coll.) das sieht doch ein Blinder [mit dem Krückstock] (ugs.); **[win] by a ~:** mit einer Nasenlänge [gewinnen]; **follow one's ~** (fig.) (be guided by instinct) seinem Instinkt folgen; (go forward) der Nase nachgehen; **then just follow your ~:** dann einfach immer der Nase nach (ugs.); **get up sb.'s ~** (coll.: annoy sb.) jmdm. auf den Wecker gehen *od.* fallen (salopp); **hold one's ~:** sich (*Dat.*) die Nase zuhalten; **keep one's ~ clean** (fig. coll.) eine saubere Weste behalten (ugs.); **keep your ~ clean!** bleib sauber! (ugs.); **on the ~** (Amer. coll.: on time) pünktlich auf die Minute; **hit it** *or* **be right on the ~** (Amer. coll.) den Nagel auf den Kopf treffen (ugs.); **parson's** *or* **pope's ~** (Gastr.) Bürzel, *der*; **pay through the ~:** tief in die Tasche greifen müssen (ugs.); **poke** *or* **thrust** *etc.* **one's ~ into sth.** (fig.) seine Nase in etw. (*Akk.*) stecken (fig. ugs.); **put sb.'s ~ out of joint** (fig. coll.) jmdn. vor den Kopf stoßen (ugs.); **rub sb.'s ~ in it** (fig.) es jmdm. ständig unter die Nase reiben (ugs.); **see no further than one's ~** (fig.) nicht weiter sehen, als seine Nase reicht (ugs.); **speak through one's ~:** näseln; durch die Nase sprechen; **turn up one's ~ at sth.** (fig. coll.) die Nase über etw. (*Akk.*) rümpfen; **under sb.'s ~** (fig. coll.) vor jmds. Augen (*Dat.*); **keep one's ~ out of sth.** (fig. coll.) sich aus etw. [he]raushalten; **keep your ~ out of this!** halt [du] dich da raus!; **go** *or* **walk about with one's ~ in the air** die Nase hoch tragen; *see also* **blow¹ B 7**; **grindstone**; **lead² A 1**; **spite B**; **thumb B 3** 2 (sense of smell) Nase, *die*; **have a good ~ for sth.** eine gute Nase für etw. haben 3 (of ship, aircraft) Nase, *die*; (of torpedo) Schnauze, *die* (ugs.) 4 (of wine) Blume, *die*
B *v.t.* 1 (detect, smell out) **~ [out]** aufspüren 2 **~ one's way** sich (*Dat.*) vorsichtig seinen Weg bahnen
C *v.i.* sich vorsichtig bewegen; **~ out of sth.** sich vorsichtig aus etw. hinausbewegen

Phrasal verb

- **~ a'bout, ~ a'round** *v.i.* (coll.) herumschnüffeln (ugs.)

nose: ~bag *n.* Futterbeutel, *der*; **~band** *n.* Nasenriemen, *der*; **~bleed** *n.* Nasenbluten, *das*; **~ candy** *n.*, *no pl.* (Amer. coll.) Nasenpulver, *das*; **~ cone** *n.* [Rumpf]spitze, *die*; **~dive A** *n.* 1 Sturzflug, *der*; 2 (fig.) Einbruch, *der*; **take a ~dive** einen Einbruch erleben; **B** *v.i.* im Sturzflug hinuntergehen; ‹*Schiff:*› mit dem Bug wegtauchen; **~ flute** *n.* Nasenflöte, *die*; **~gay** *n.* (literary) [duftendes] Blumensträußchen; **~ ring** *n.* Nasenring, *der*;

n

~ **stud** *n.* Nasenstecker, *der;* ~ **wheel** *n.* (Aeronaut.) Bugrad, *das*

nosey ▸**nosy**

nosh /nɒʃ/ (esp. Brit. coll.)

A *v.t. & i.* (eat) futtern (ugs.); (between meals) naschen

B *n.* (snack) Imbiss, *der;* (food) Futter, *das* (salopp)

no-'show *n.* (for a flight) No-show, *der* (fachspr.); **be a ~ at a dinner/at an event/on a flight /in a hotel** bei einem Abendessen/einer Veranstaltung nicht erscheinen/eine Flug-/Hotelreservierung nicht in Anspruch nehmen

'nosh-up *n.* (Brit. coll.) Essen, *das;* (good meal) Festessen, *das;* **have a ~:** spachteln (ugs.)

no 'side *n.* (Rugby) Spielende, *das*

nostalgia /nɒ'stældʒə/ *n.* Nostalgie, *die;* ~ **for sth.** Sehnsucht nach etw.

nostalgic /nɒ'stældʒɪk/ *adj.* nostalgisch

nostril /'nɒstrɪl/ *n.* ▸ⓘ **p. 951** Nasenloch, *das;* (of horse) Nüster, *die*

nostrum /'nɒstrəm/ *n.* **1** (medicine) Mittelchen, *das* **2** (pet scheme) Patentrezept, *das*

nosy /'nəʊzɪ/ *adj.* (coll.) neugierig

Nosy 'Parker *n.* Schnüffler, *der*/Schnüfflerin, *die* (ugs. abwertend)

not /nɒt/ *adv.* **1** nicht; **he is ~ a doctor** er ist kein Arzt; **isn't she pretty?** ist sie nicht hübsch?; **I do ~ feel like doing it** ich habe keine Lust, es zu tun **2** *in ellipt. phrs.* nicht; **I hope ~:** hoffentlich nicht; **~ so** keineswegs; **~ at all** überhaupt nicht; (in polite reply to thanks) keine Ursache; gern geschehen; **~ that [I know of]** nicht, dass [ich wüsste] **3** *in emphat. phrs.* **~ ... but ...** nicht ..., sondern ...; **it was ~ a small town but a big one** es war keine kleine Stadt, sondern eine große; **lazy he is ~:** faul ist er keineswegs; **~ I/they** *etc.* ich/sie *usw.* [bestimmt] nicht; **~ a moment/grey hair** nicht ein *od.* kein einziger Augenblick/einziges graues Haar; **~ a thing** gar nichts; **come ~ a day too soon** keinen Tag zu früh kommen; **~ a few/everybody** nicht wenige/jeder; **~ a small sacrifice** kein kleines Opfer; **~ once or** *or* **nor twice, but ...:** nicht nur einoder zweimal, sondern ...; **feel ~ so** *or* **too well** sich nicht besonders gut fühlen

notability /nəʊtə'bɪlɪtɪ/ *n.* **1** *no pl.* (being notable) Ansehen, *das;* **a painter of [some] ~:** ein [ziemlich] angesehener Maler **2** (person) ▸**notable B**

notable /'nəʊtəbl/

A *adj.* bemerkenswert; bedeutend, angesehen ‹*Person*›; **be ~ for sth.** für etw. bekannt sein

B *n.* bekannte Persönlichkeit; Notabilität, *die* (geh.)

notably /'nəʊtəblɪ/ *adv.* besonders

notarial /nəʊ'teərɪəl/ *adj.* (Law) **1** (of a notary) Notariats- **2** (prepared by a notary) notariell ‹*Urkunde*›

notary /'nəʊtərɪ/ *n.* ▸ⓘ **p. 1260 ~ ['public]** Notar, *der*/Notarin, *die*

notation /nəʊ'teɪʃn/ *n.* **1** (Math., Mus., Chem.) Notation, *die* (fachspr.); Notierung, *die* **2** (Amer.: annotation) Anmerkung, *die. See also* **scale³ A 6**

notch /nɒtʃ/

A *n.* Kerbe, *die;* (in damaged blade) Scharte, *die;* (in belt) Loch, *das;* **be a ~ above the others** (fig.) eine Klasse besser als die anderen sein; **tighten one's belt another ~** (lit. or fig.) seinen Gürtel ein Loch enger schnallen

B *v.t.* **1** (make ~es in) kerben **2** (score by ~es) mit Kerben notieren; (fig.: score, achieve) erreichen; erzielen ‹*Tor, Eckstoß*›; erringen ‹*Sieg*›

Phrasal verb

• ~ **'up** *v.t.* erreichen; aufstellen ‹*Rekord*›; erringen ‹*Sieg*›

notched /nɒtʃt/ *adj.* kerbig; gekerbt ‹*Blattrand*›

note /nəʊt/

A *n.* **1** (Mus.) (sign) Note, *die;* (key of piano) Taste, *die;* (single sound) Ton, *der;* (bird's song) Gesang, *der;* **strike a false ~:** unangebracht sein; **strike the right ~** ‹*Sprecher, Redner, Brief:*› den richtigen Ton treffen; **hit the wrong ~:** einen falschen Ton anschlagen **2** (tone of expression) [Unter]ton, *der;* **~ of discord** Missklang, *der;* **~ of caution/anger** warnender/ärgerlicher [Unter]ton; **sound a ~ of caution** eine Warnung aussprechen; **on a ~ of optimism, on an optimistic ~:** in optimistischem Ton; **his voice had a peevish ~:** seine Stimme klang gereizt; **a festive ~, a ~ of festivity** eine festliche Note **3** (jotting) Notiz, *die;* **take** *or* **make ~s** sich (*Dat.*) Notizen machen; **take** *or* **make a ~ of sth.** sich (*Dat.*) etw. notieren; **speak without ~s** frei sprechen **4** (annotation, footnote) Anmerkung, *die;* **author's ~:** Anmerkung des Verfassers **5** (short letter) [kurzer] Brief; **write a ~:** ein paar Zeilen schreiben **6** (Diplom.) Note, *die* **7** ▸ⓘ **p. 1332** (Finance) **~ [of hand]** Schuldschein, *der;* **£10 ~:** Zehn-Pfund-Schein, *der* **8** *no pl., no art.* (importance) Bedeutung, *die;* **person/sth. of ~:** bedeutende Persönlichkeit/etw. Bedeutendes; **nothing of ~:** nichts von Bedeutung; **be of ~:** bedeutend sein **9** *no pl., no art.* (attention) Beachtung, *die;* **worthy of ~:** beachtenswert; **take ~ of sth.** (heed) einer Sache (*Dat.*) Beachtung schenken; (notice) etw. zur Kenntnis nehmen

B *v.t.* **1** (register) beobachten **2** (pay attention to) beachten **3** (notice) bemerken **4** (set down) **~ [down]** [sich (*Dat.*)] notieren

note: ~book *n.* **1** Notizbuch, *das;* (for lecture notes) Kollegheft, *das;* **2** **~book [computer]** Notebook, *das;* **~case** *n.* Brieftasche, *die*

noted /'nəʊtɪd/ *adj.* **1** (famous) bekannt, berühmt (**for** für, wegen) **2** (significant) beachtlich

notelet /'nəʊtlɪt/ *n.* Grußkarte, *die*

note: ~pad *n.* **1** (paper) Notizblock, *der;* **2** (Computing) **~ [computer]** Notepad, *das;* **~paper** *n.* Briefpapier, *das;* **~-row** *n.* (Mus.) Tonreihe, *die;* **~worthy** *adj.* bemerkenswert

nothing /'nʌθɪŋ/

A *n.* **1** nichts; **~ interesting** nichts Interessantes; **~ much** nichts Besonderes; **~ more than** nur; **~ more, ~ less** nicht mehr, nicht weniger; **I should like ~ more than sth./to do sth.** ich würde etw. nur zu gern haben/tun; **next to ~:** so gut wie nichts; **~ less than the best treatment** die bestmögliche Behandlung; **~ less than a miracle is needed to save ...:** nur ein Wunder kann ... retten; **it's ~ less than suicidal to do this** es ist reiner *od.* glatter Selbstmord, dies zu tun; **there's ~ so good as ...:** es gibt nichts Besseres als ...; **be ~ [when] compared to sth.** nichts sein im Vergleich zu etw.; **~ else than, ~ [else] but** nur; **do ~ [else] but grumble** nur murren; **there was ~ [else] for it but to do sth.** es blieb nichts anderes übrig, als etw. zu tun; **he is ~ if not active** wenn er eins ist, dann [ist er] aktiv; **be ~ if not conscientious/brutal** überaus gewissenhaft/brutal sein; **there is ~ in it** (in race etc.) es ist noch nichts entschieden; (it is untrue) es ist nichts daran wahr; **there's ~ 'of him** (he is very thin) an ihm ist nichts dran; **there is ~ 'to it** es ist kinderleicht (fam.); **he/she is ~ to me** er/sie interessiert mich nicht; **your problems are ~ compared to his** deine Probleme sind nichts im Vergleich zu seinen; **~ ventured ~ gained, ~ venture ~ win** (prov.) wer nicht wagt, der nicht gewinnt (Spr.); **£300 is ~ to him** 300 Pfund sind ein Klacks für ihn (ugs.); **have [got]** *or* **be ~ to do with sb./sth.** (not concern) nichts zu tun haben mit jmdm./etw.; **have ~ to do with sb./sth.** (avoid) jmdm./einer Sache aus dem Weg gehen; **[not] for ~:** [nicht] umsonst; **count** *or* **go for ~** (be unappreciated) ‹*Person:*› nicht zählen; (be profitless) ‹*Arbeit, Bemühung:*› umsonst *od.* vergebens sein; **have [got] ~ on sb./sth.** (be not better than; iron.: be inferior to) nicht mit jmdm./etw. zu vergleichen sein; nichts sein im Vergleich zu jmdm./etw.; **have [got] ~ on sb.** (know ~ bad about) nichts gegen jmdn. in der Hand haben; **have ~ on** (be naked) nichts anhaben; (have no engagements) nichts vorhaben; **make ~ of sth.** (make light of) keine große Sache aus etw. machen; (not understand) mit etw. nichts anfangen [können]; **it means ~ to me** (is not understood) ich werde nicht klug daraus; (is not loved) es bedeutet mir nichts; **no ~** (coll.) kein gar nichts (ugs.); **to say ~ of** ganz zu schweigen von **2** (zero) **multiply by ~:** mit null multiplizieren; **register ~** ‹*Thermometer:*› null Grad anzeigen **3** (trifling event) Nichtigkeit, *die;* (trifling person) Nichts, *das;* Niemand, *der;* **soft** *or* **sweet ~s** Zärtlichkeiten *Pl. See also* **do¹ A 2, B 10; like¹ A 1; short A 4; stop A 3, B 2; think of 7**

B *adv.* keineswegs; **~ near so bad as ...:** nicht annähernd so schlecht wie ...

nothingness /'nʌθɪŋnɪs/ *n., no pl.* Nichts, *das*

notice /'nəʊtɪs/

A *n.* **1** Anschlag, *der;* Aushang, *der;* (in newspaper) Anzeige, *die;* **no-smoking ~:** Rauchverbotsschild, *das* **2** (warning) **~ of a forthcoming strike** Meldungen über einen bevorstehenden Streik; **give [sb.] [three days'] ~ of one's arrival** [jmdm.] seine Ankunft [drei Tage vorher] mitteilen; **have [no] ~ [of sth.]** [von etw.] [keine] Kenntnis haben; **at short/a moment's/ten minutes' ~:** kurzfristig/von einem Augenblick zum andern/innerhalb von zehn Minuten **3** (formal notification) Ankündigung, *die;* **give ~ of appeal** Berufung einlegen; **until further ~:** bis auf weiteres; **~ is given of sth.** etw. wird angekündigt; *see also* **quit B 2** **4** (ending an agreement) Kündigung, *die;* **give sb. a week's/month's ~:** jmdm. mit einer Frist von einer Woche/einem Monat kündigen; **hand in one's ~** *or* **give ~** (Brit.), **give one's ~** (Amer.) kündigen **5** (attention) Beachtung, *die;* **attract ~:** Beachtung finden; **bring sb./sth. to sb.'s ~:** jmdn. auf jmdn./etw. aufmerksam machen; **worthy of ~:** beachtenswert; **it has come to my ~ that ...:** ich habe bemerkt *od.* mir ist aufgefallen, dass ...; **not take much ~ of sb./sth.** jmdm./einer Sache keine große Beachtung schenken; **take no ~ of sb./sth.** (not observe) jmdn./etw. nicht bemerken; (disregard) keine Notiz von jmdm./etw. nehmen; **take no ~:** sich nicht darum kümmern; **take ~ of** wahrnehmen; hören auf ‹*Rat*›; zur Kenntnis nehmen ‹*Leistung*› **6** (review) Besprechung, *die;* Rezension, *die*

B *v.t.* **1** (perceive, take notice of) bemerken; **~ the details [on this painting]** beachten Sie die Einzelheiten [auf diesem Gemälde]; **he likes to get himself ~d** er drängt sich gern in den Vordergrund; *abs.* **I pretended not to ~:** ich tat so, als ob ich es nicht bemerkte; **but not so you'd ~** (coll.) aber es fällt/fiel nicht auf **2** (remark upon) erwähnen **3** (acknowledge) Notiz nehmen von

noticeable /'nəʊtɪsəbl/ *adj.* **1** (perceptible) wahrnehmbar ‹*Fleck, Schaden, Geruch*›; merklich ‹*Verbesserung*›; spürbar ‹*Mangel*› **2** (worthy of notice) bemerkenswert

noticeably /'nəʊtɪsəblɪ/ *adv.* sichtlich ‹*größer, kleiner*›; merklich ‹*verändern*›; spürbar ‹*kälter*›

'noticeboard *n.* (Brit.) Anschlagbrett, *das;* schwarzes Brett

notifiable /'nəʊtɪfaɪəbl/ *adj.* meldepflichtig ‹*Krankheit*›

notification /nəʊtɪfɪ'keɪʃn/ *n.* Mitteilung, *die* (**of sb.** an jmdn.; **of sth.** über etw. [*Akk.*]); (of disease) Meldung, *die* (**of** über + *Akk.*)

notify /'nəʊtɪfaɪ/ *v.t.* **1** (make known) ankündigen **2** (inform) benachrichtigen (**of** über + *Akk.*)

notion /'nəʊʃn/ *n.* **1** Vorstellung, *die;* **not have the faintest/least ~ of how/what** *etc.* nicht die blasseste/geringste Ahnung haben, wie/was *usw.*; **he has no ~ of time** er hat kein Verhältnis zur Zeit **2** (intention) **have no ~ of doing sth.** nicht beabsichtigen *od.* vorhaben, etw. zu tun **3** (knack, inkling) **have no ~ of sth.** keine Ahnung von etw. haben **4** *in pl.* (Amer.: haberdashery) Kurzwaren *Pl.*

notional /'nəʊʃənl/ *adj.* **1** (imaginary) imaginär **2** (theoretical) theoretisch ‹*Ansatz, Wissen, Gewinn*›; (token) symbolisch; (hypothetical) angenommen **3** (vague, abstract) abstrakt

notionally /'nəʊʃənəlɪ/ *adv.* theoretisch

notoriety /nəʊtə'raɪətɪ/ *n., no pl.* traurige Berühmtheit

notorious /nə'tɔːrɪəs/ *adj.* bekannt; (infamous) berüchtigt; notorisch ‹*Lügner*›; niederträchtig ‹*List*›; **be** *or* **have become ~ for sth.** wegen *od.* für etw. bekannt/berüchtigt sein

notoriously /nə'tɔːrɪəslɪ/ *adv.* notorisch

no 'trump *n.* (Bridge) Sans atout, *das*

notwithstanding /nɒtwɪθˈstændɪŋ, nɒtwɪðˈstændɪŋ/
A *prep.* ungeachtet
B *adv.* dennoch; dessen ungeachtet
C *conj.* **~ that ...** ungeachtet dessen, dass ...

nougat /ˈnuːgɑː/ *n.* Nougat, *das od. der*

nought /nɔːt/ *n.* [1] ▸ⓘ **p. 1358** (zero) Null, *die;* **~s and crosses** (Brit.) *Spiel, bei dem innerhalb eines Feldes von Kästchen Dreierreihen von Kreisen bzw. Kreuzen zu erzielen sind* [2] (poet./arch.: nothing) ▸**naught**

noun /naʊn/ *n.* (Ling.) Substantiv, *das;* Hauptwort, *das;* Nomen, *das* (fachspr.)

nourish /ˈnʌrɪʃ/ *v.t.* [1] ernähren (**on** mit); (fig.) nähren (geh.) [2] (in one's heart) hegen, nähren (geh.) ‹*Gefühl, Hoffnung*›

nourishing /ˈnʌrɪʃɪŋ/ *adj.* nahrhaft

nourishment /ˈnʌrɪʃmənt/ *n.* (food) Nahrung, *die;* (fig.) Förderung, *die*

nous /naʊs/ *n.* (coll.) Grips, *der* (ugs.); **use a bit of ~:** seinen Grips ein bisschen anstrengen

nouveau riche /nuːvəʊ ˈriːʃ/
A *n., pl.* **nouveaux riches** /nuːvəʊ ˈriːʃ/ Neureiche, *der/die*
B *adj.* neureich

Nov. *abbr.* **= November** Nov.

nova /ˈnəʊvə/ *n., pl.* **~e** /ˈnəʊviː/ *or* **~s** (Astron.) Nova, *die*

Nova Scotia /nəʊvə ˈskəʊʃə/ *pr. n.* Neuschottland (*das*)

novel /ˈnɒvl/
A *n.* Roman, *der*
B *adj.* neuartig

novelette /nɒvəˈlet/ *n.* Novelette, *die* (Literaturw.); (Brit. derog.) Groschenroman, *der*

novelist /ˈnɒvəlɪst/ *n.* ▸ⓘ **p. 1260** Romanautor, *der/*-autorin, *die*

novella /nəˈvelə/ *n.* Novelle, *die*

novelty /ˈnɒvltɪ/ *n.* [1] **be a/no ~:** etwas/nichts Neues sein [2] (newness) Neuheit, *die;* Neuartigkeit, *die;* **the ~ will wear off** der Reiz des Neuen wird nachlassen; **have a certain ~ value** den Reiz des Neuen haben [3] (gadget) Überraschung, *die;* **jokes and novelties** Scherzartikel

November /nəˈvembə(r)/ *n.* ▸ⓘ **p. 1047** November, *der; see also* **August**

novice /ˈnɒvɪs/ *n.* [1] (Relig.) Novize, *der/*Novizin, *die* [2] (new convert) Neubekehrte, *der/die* [3] (beginner) Anfänger, *der/*Anfängerin, *die*

noviciate, novitiate /nəˈvɪʃɪət/ *n.* [1] (Relig.: period, quarters) Noviziat, *das;* (fig.: period or state of initiation) Lehrzeit, *die;* Lehre, *die* [2] ▸**novice 1, 3**

now /naʊ/
A *adv.* [1] jetzt; (nowadays) heutzutage; (immediately) [jetzt] sofort; (this time) jetzt [schon wieder]; **it's ten years ago ~ that** *or* **since he died** es ist schon zehn Jahre her, seit er gestorben ist; **just ~** (very recently) gerade eben; (at this particular time) gerade jetzt; **I can't see you just ~:** ich habe im Augenblick leider keine Zeit für Sie; **~ for a cup of tea** jetzt eine Tasse Tee; **[every] ~ and then** *or* **again** hin und wieder; **~ sunshine, ~ showers** bald Sonne, bald Regen; **[it's] ~ or never!** jetzt oder nie! [2] (not referring to time) **well ~:** also; **come ~:** na, komm (ugs.); **~, ~:** na, na; **~, what happened is this ...:** also, passiert ist Folgendes: ...; **~ just listen to me** jetzt hör mir mal gut zu; **~ then** na (ugs.); **quickly ~!** nun aber schnell; **goodbye ~:** also dann, auf Wiedersehen; **He thinks he can stay here for nothing. — Does he, ~!** Er glaubt, er könnte hier umsonst bleiben. — Da hat er sich aber geirrt!
B *conj.* **~ [that] ...** jetzt, wo *od.* da ...
C *n.* **the here and ~:** das Hier und Jetzt; **~ is the time to do sth.** es ist jetzt an der Zeit, etw. zu tun; **before ~:** früher; **up to** *or* **until ~:** bis jetzt; **never before ~:** noch nie; **by ~:** inzwischen; **a week from ~:** [heute] in einer Woche; **you've got from ~ till Friday to do it** du hast bis Freitag Zeit, es zu tun; **between ~ and Friday** bis Freitag; **from ~ on** von jetzt an; **as of ~:** jetzt; **that's all for ~:** das ist im Augenblick alles; **put it aside for ~:** leg es einstweilen zur Seite; **bye** *etc.* **for ~!** (coll.) bis bald!

nowadays /ˈnaʊədeɪz/ *adv.* heutzutage

nowhere /ˈnəʊweə(r)/
A *adv.* [1] (in no place) nirgends; nirgendwo [2] (to no place) nirgendwohin [3] **~ near** (not even nearly) nicht annähernd; **be ~ near prepared** völlig unzureichend vorbereitet sein
B *pron.* **as if from ~:** wie aus dem Nichts; **live in the middle of ~** (coll.) am Ende der Welt *od.* (ugs.) jwd wohnen; **the train stopped in the middle of ~:** der Zug hielt mitten in der Wildnis (ugs.); **start from ~:** bei Null anfangen; **come from ~:** wie aus dem Nichts auftauchen; **come [in]/be ~** (in race etc.) unter „ferner liefen" rangieren (ugs.); **get ~** (make no progress) nicht vorankommen; (have no success) nichts erreichen; **get sb. ~:** [jmdm.] nichts nützen

no-'win *attrib. adj.* Verlierer-

nowt /naʊt/ *n.* (Brit. dial. or coll.) nix (ugs.)

noxious /ˈnɒkʃəs/ *adj.* giftig

nozzle /ˈnɒzl/ *n.* Düse, *die;* (of gun) Mündung, *die;* (of petrol pump) Zapfhahn, *der*

nr. *abbr.* **= near**

NSPCC *abbr.* (Brit.) **= National Society for the Prevention of Cruelty to Children** ≈ Kinderschutzbund, *der*

NT *abbr.* **= New Testament** N.T.

nth /enθ/ ▸**N**[1]**, n 2**

nuance /ˈnjuːɑ̃s/
A *n.* Nuance, *die;* (Mus.) Nuancierung, *die;* **~s of meaning** Bedeutungsnuancen; **~ of colour** Farbnuance, *die;* Farbschattierung, *die*
B *v.t.* nuancieren (geh.)

nub /nʌb/ *n.* [1] (small lump) Stückchen, *das;* (stub) Stummel, *der* [2] (fig.) Kernpunkt, *der*

nubile /ˈnjuːbaɪl/ *adj.* [1] (marriageable) heiratsfähig [2] (sexy) sexy (ugs.); anziehend

nuclear /ˈnjuːklɪə(r)/ *adj.* [1] Kern- [2] (using ~ energy or weapons) Atom-; Kern‹*explosion, -technik*›; atomar ‹*Antrieb, Gefechtskopf, Bedrohung, Gegenschlag, Wettrüsten*›; nuklear ‹*Abschreckungspotenzial, Sprengkörper, Streitkräfte*›; atomgetrieben ‹*Unterseeboot, Schiff*›

nuclear: **~ 'age** *n.* Atomzeitalter, *das;* **~ 'bomb** *n.* Atombombe, *die;* **~ capa'bility** *n.* nukleares Potenzial; **a missile with ~ capability** eine nuklearfähige Rakete; **have ~ capability** nuklearfähig sein; **~ de'terrent** *n.* atomare *od.* nukleare Abschreckung; **~ de'vice** *n.* Atombombe, *die;* **~ dis'armament** *n., no pl.* atomare *od.* nukleare Abrüstung; **~ 'energy** *n., no pl.* Atom- *od.* Kernenergie, *die;* **~ 'family** *n.* (Sociol.) Kernfamilie, *die;* **~ 'fission** *n., no pl.* Kernspaltung, *die;* **~-free** *adj.* atomwaffenfrei ‹*Zone*›; **~ 'fuel** *n.* Kernbrennstoff, *der;* **~ 'fusion** *n., no pl.* Kernfusion, *die;* **~ 'holocaust** *n.* atomarer Holocaust; **~ 'industry** *n.* Atomindustrie, *die;* **~ 'physicist** *n.* ▸ⓘ **p. 1260** Atomphysiker, *der/*-physikerin, *die;* **~ 'physics** *n., no pl.* Kernphysik, *die;* **~ 'power** *n., no pl.* [1] Atom- *od.* Kernkraft, *die;* [2] (country) Atom- *od.* Nuklearmacht, *die;* **~-'powered** *adj.* atomgetrieben; **~ 'power plant, ~ power station** *ns.* Atom- *od.* Kernkraftwerk, *das;* **~ re'actor** ▸**reactor 1**; **~ re'processing plant** *n.* atomare Wiederaufarbeitungsanlage; **~ 'shelter** *n.* Atom[schutz]bunker, *der;* **~ 'testing** *n., no pl.* Atomversuche *Pl.;* **~ 'warfare** *n., no pl.* Atomkrieg, *der;* **~ 'waste** *n.* Atommüll, *der;* **~ 'winter** *n.* nuklearer Winter

nuclei *pl. of* **nucleus**

nucleic acid /njuːkliːɪk ˈæsɪd/ *n.* (Biochem.) Nukleinsäure, *die*

nucleus /ˈnjuːklɪəs/ *n., pl.* **nuclei** /ˈnjuːklɪaɪ/ Kern, *der;* (of collection) Grundstock, *der*

nude /njuːd/
A *adj.* nackt; **~ figure/revue** Akt, *der/*Nacktrevue, *die*
B *n.* [1] (Art) (figure) Akt, *der;* (painting) Aktgemälde, *das* [2] **in the ~:** nackt [3] (person) Nackte, *der/die*

nudge /nʌdʒ/
A *v.t.* [1] (push gently) anstoßen; **~ aside** zur Seite schieben; **~ sth.** (fig.) einer Sache (*Dat.*) einen Schubs geben (ugs.) [2] (touch) stoßen an (+ *Akk.*) ‹*Mauer*›
B *n.* Stoß, *der;* Puff, *der;* **give sb. a ~:** jmdn. anstoßen

nudism /ˈnjuːdɪzm/ *n.* Nudismus, *der;* Freikörperkultur, *die*

nudist /ˈnjuːdɪst/ *n.* Nudist, *der/*Nudistin, *die;* FKK-Anhänger, *der/*-Anhängerin, *die; attrib.* Nudisten-

nudity /ˈnjuːdɪtɪ/ *n.* Nacktheit, *die*

nugatory /ˈnjuːgətərɪ/ *adj.* (literary) belanglos

nugget /ˈnʌgɪt/ *n.* [1] (Mining) Klumpen, *der;* (of gold) Goldklumpen, *der;* Nugget, *das* [2] (fig.) **~s of wisdom** goldene Weisheiten; **~s of information** wertvolle Informationen

nuisance /ˈnjuːsəns/ *n.* [1] Ärgernis, *das;* Plage, *die;* **what a ~!** so etwas Dummes!; **be a bit of a ~:** eine ziemliche Plage sein; **make a ~ of oneself** lästig werden [2] (Law) Belästigung, *die*

nuisance: **~ call** *n.* Terroranruf, *der;* Belästigungsanruf, *der;* **~ caller** *n.* Telefonterrorist, *der/*-terroristin, *die*

nuke /njuːk/ (coll.)
A *n.* (bomb) Atombombe, *die*
B *v.t.* Atombomben/eine Atombombe werfen auf (+ *Akk.*)

null /nʌl/ *adj.* (Law) **declare sth. ~ [and void]** etw. für null und nichtig erklären

nullify /ˈnʌlɪfaɪ/ *v.t.* [1] (cancel) für null und nichtig *od.* rechtsungültig erklären ‹*Vertrag, Testament*› [2] (neutralize) zunichte machen; entkräften ‹*Beweis*›

nullity /ˈnʌlɪtɪ/ *n.* (Law) Ungültigkeit, *die*

numb /nʌm/
A *adj.* (without sensation) gefühllos, taub (**with** vor + *Dat.*); (fig.) (without emotion) benommen; (unable to move) starr; gelähmt; **go ~ with horror** vor Entsetzen (*Dat.*) erstarren
B *v.t.* [1] ‹*Kälte, Schock:*› gefühllos machen; ‹*Narkosemittel:*› betäuben [2] (fig.) **her emotions were ~ed** sie war betäubt *od.* benommen; **be ~ed by horror/with fear** vor Entsetzen/Angst (*Dat.*) erstarren

number /ˈnʌmbə(r)/
A *n.* ▸ⓘ **p. 1358** [1] (in series) Nummer, *die;* **~ 3 West Street** West Street [Nr.] 3; **my ~ came up** (fig.) ich war dran (ugs.) *od.* an der Reihe; **the ~ of sb.'s car** jmds. Autonummer; **you've got the wrong ~** (Teleph.) Sie sind falsch verbunden; **dial a wrong ~:** sich verwählen (ugs.); **what page ~ is it?** welche Seite ist es?; **~ one** (oneself) man selbst; *attrib.* Nummer eins *nachgestellt;* erstklassig ‹*Darstellung*›; Spitzen‹*position, -platz*›; **take care of** *or* **look after ~ one** an sich (*Akk.*) selbst denken; **be sb.'s ~ one priority** bei jmdm. an erster Stelle stehen; **~ two** (in organisation) zweiter Mann; (of sb. else) rechte Hand; **N~ Ten [Downing Street]** (Brit.) *Amtssitz des britischen Premierministers/der britischen Premierministerin;* **paint by ~s** nach einer Vorlage [mit nummerierten Farbfeldern] malen; **have [got] sb.'s ~** (fig. coll.) jmdn. durchschaut haben; **sb.'s ~ is up** (coll.) jmds. Stunde hat geschlagen [2] (esp. Math.: numeral) Zahl, *die;* **memory for ~s** Zahlengedächtnis, *das* [3] (sum, total, quantity) [An]zahl, *die;* **a ~ of people/things** einige Leute/Dinge; **a ~ of times/on a ~ of occasions** mehrfach *od.* -mals; **a small ~:** eine geringe [An]zahl; **large ~s** eine große [An]zahl; **in [large** *or* **great] ~s** in großer Zahl; **in a small ~ of cases** in einigen wenigen Fällen; **a and b in equal ~s** a und b in gleicher Anzahl; **a fair ~:** eine ganze Anzahl *od.* Reihe; **any ~:** beliebig viele; **on any ~ of occasions** oft[mals]; **without** *or* **beyond ~:** ohne Zahl (geh.); **times without ~** unzählige Male; **in ~[s]** zahlenmäßig ‹*überlegen sein, überwiegen*›; **ten in ~:** zehn an der Zahl; **be few in ~:** gering an Zahl sein [4] (person, song, turn, edition) Nummer, *die;* **final/May ~:** Schluss-/Mainummer, *die* [5] (coll.) (outfit) Kluft, *die;* (girl) Mieze, *die* (salopp); (job) Job, *der* (ugs.); **it's not a bad little ~** (job) da kann man eine ruhige Kugel schieben (ugs.) [6] (Bibl.) **[the Book of] Numbers** das vierte Buch Mose [7] (company) [Personen]kreis, *der;* Gruppe, *die;* **he was [one] of our ~:** er war einer von uns

n

Numbers

Cardinal numbers = Kardinalzahlen

0 (*nought, zero*) = null
1 (*one*) = eins, ein...[1]
2 (*two*) = zwei
3 (*three*) = drei
4 (*four*) = vier
5 (*five*) = fünf
6 (*six*) = sechs
7 (*seven*) = sieben
8 (*eight*) = acht
9 (*nine*) = neun
10 (*ten*) = zehn
11 (*eleven*) = elf
12 (*twelve*) = zwölf
13 (*thirteen*) = dreizehn
14 (*fourteen*) = vierzehn
15 (*fifteen*) = fünfzehn
16 (*sixteen*) = sechzehn
17 (*seventeen*) = siebzehn
18 (*eighteen*) = achtzehn
19 (*nineteen*) = neunzehn
20 (*twenty*) = zwanzig
21 (*twenty-one*) = einundzwanzig
22 (*twenty-two*) = zweiundzwanzig
30 (*thirty*) = dreißig
40 (*forty*) = vierzig
50 (*fifty*) = fünfzig
60 (*sixty*) = sechzig
70 (*seventy*) = siebzig
80 (*eighty*) = achtzig
90 (*ninety*) = neunzig
100 (*a* or *one hundred*) = [ein]hundert
101 (*a* or *one hundred and one*) = [ein]hundert[und]ein[s][2]
555 (*five hundred and fifty-five*) = fünfhundert[und]fünfundfünfzig
1,000 (*a* or *one thousand*) = [ein]tausend[3]
1,001 (*a* or *one thousand and one*) = [ein]tausend[und]ein[s][2]
1,200 (*one thousand two hundred* or *twelve hundred*) = [ein]tausendzweihundert *or* zwölfhundert[4]
100,000 (*a* or *one hundred thousand*) = [ein]hunderttausend
1,000,000 (*a* or *one million*) = eine Million
3,536,000 (*three million five hundred and thirty-six thousand*) = drei Millionen fünfhundertsechsunddreißigtausend
1,000,000,000 (*a* or *one billion, a* or *one thousand million*) = eine Milliarde
1,000,000,000,000 (*a* or *one trillion, a* or *one million million*) = eine Billion

[1] The form **eins** is used when the number appears on its own, e.g. when counting (eins, zwei, drei), calculating, giving times or scores (*a quarter to one* = Viertel vor eins, *to win one-nil* = eins zu null gewinnen) or quoting decimals (*O point one* = null Komma eins, *one point five* = eins Komma fünf).

Where the number comes before a noun, it is treated like an indefinite article and declined accordingly.

I would like one large knob and two small ones
= Ich möchte einen großen Knopf und zwei kleine

You mustn't use one new battery and three old ones
= Man darf nicht eine neue Batterie und drei alte verwenden

For other uses see the entry for *one*.

In larger numbers ending in **eins** it is not usually declined before a noun

201 days
= zweihundert[und]eins Tage

But note

A Thousand and one Nights
= Tausendundeine Nacht

[2] The bracketed **und** is usually included in numbers from 101 to 109, but omitted from 110 (hundertzehn) onwards except when counting. The bracketed **ein** may be included for emphasis. For the use of the final **s** see the note on **eins** above.

[3] Where English style usually has a comma for thousands, Continental European usage has a space:

1,000 = 1 000; 5,500 = 5 500; 123,467 = 123 467; 6,327,456 = 6 327 456

[4] Note that in dates the **hundert** should not be omitted:

1895
= ***eighteen ninety-five***
= achtzehnhundertfünfundneunzig

Fractions = Brüche

½	ein halb	1½	ein[und]einhalb
¼	ein viertel	2¾	zwei[und]dreiviertel
⅓	ein drittel	5⅔	fünf[und]zweidrittel
⅛	ein achtel	8⅞	acht[und]siebenachtel

Fractions are formed in German by adding **-tel** to the number, except where the number ends in **t**, **d** or **g**. In these cases an **s** is inserted before the **-tel**:

ein hundertstel ein tausendstel ein zwanzigstel

The fractions are written as above with a small letter in a calculation or with units of measure, but when combined with other nouns they are written with a capital:

two thirds of the distance
= zwei Drittel des Weges

one eighth of the amount
= ein Achtel des Betrages

but:

an eighth of a litre
= ein achtel Liter, ein Achtelliter

Note that with measures, "of a" is not translated and the fraction is often written with the unit to form one word. Also with plural fractions the unit of measure is in the plural:

five eighths of a mile
= fünf achtel Meilen

six hundredths of a second
= sechs hundertstel Sekunden, sechs Hundertstelsekunden

▶

8▸ *in pl.* (arithmetic) Rechnen, *das* **9▸** (Ling.) Numerus, *der* (*fachspr.*). *See also* **eight B 1**; **opposite number**; **round number**

B *v.t.* **1▸** (assign ~ to) beziffern; nummerieren **2▸** (amount to, comprise) zählen; **the nominations ~ed ten in all** es wurden insgesamt zehn Kandidaten nominiert; **a town ~ing x inhabitants** eine Stadt mit x Einwohnern **3▸** (include, regard as) zählen, rechnen (**among, with** zu) **4▸ be ~ed** (be limited) begrenzt sein; **sb.'s days** *or* **years are ~ed** jmds. Tage sind gezählt **5▸** (count) zählen

Phrasal verb

• **~ 'off** *v.i.* abzählen

number: ~ cruncher /ˈnʌmbə krʌntʃə(r)/ *n.* (coll.) **1▸** (computer) Zahlenfresser, *der* (Jargon); **2▸** (often derog.: person) Zahlenjongleur, *der*/-jongleurin, *die*; **~ crunching** /ˈnʌmbə krʌntʃɪŋ/ *n.*, *no pl.* (coll.) Zahlenfresserei, *die* (Jargon)

numbering /ˈnʌmbərɪŋ/ *n.* Nummerierung, *die*

numberless /ˈnʌmbəlɪs/ *adj.* unzählig; zahllos

▸ ℹ Numbers continued

Ordinal numbers = Ordinalzahlen

1st (first) = 1. (erst...)[5]
2nd (second) = 2. (zweit...)
3rd (third) = 3. (dritt...)
4th (fourth) = 4. (viert...)
5th (fifth) = 5. (fünft...)
6th (sixth) = 6. (sechst...)
7th (seventh) = 7. (sieb[en]t...)
8th (eighth) = 8. (acht...)
9th (ninth) = 9. (neunt...)
10th (tenth) = 10. (zehnt...)
11th (eleventh) = 11. (elft...)
12th (twelfth) = 12. (zwölft...)
13th (thirteenth) = 13. (dreizehnt...)
14th (fourteenth) = 14. (vierzehnt...)
15th (fifteenth) = 15. (fünfzehnt...)
16th (sixteenth) = 16. (sechzehnt...)
17th (seventeenth) = 17. (siebzehnt...)
18th (eighteenth) = 18. (achtzehnt...)
19th (nineteenth) = 19. (neunzehnt...)
20th (twentieth) = 20. (zwanzigst...)
21st (twenty-first) = 21. (einundzwanzigst...)
22nd (twenty-second) = 22. (zweiundzwanzigst...)
30th (thirtieth) = 30. (dreißigst...)
40th (fortieth) = 40. (vierzigst...)
50th (fiftieth) = 50. (fünfzigst...)
60th (sixtieth) = 60. (sechzigst...)
70th (seventieth) = 70. (siebzigst...)
80th (eightieth) = 80. (achtzigst...)
90th (ninetieth) = 90. (neunzigst...)
100th ([one] hundredth) = 100. ([ein]hundertst...)
101st ([one] hundred and first) = 101. ([ein]hundert[und]erst...)
555th (five hundred and fifty-fifth) = 555. (fünfhundert[und]fünfundfünfzigst...)
1,000th ([one] thousandth) = 1 000. ([ein]tausendst...)
1,001st (one thousand and first) = 1 001. ([ein]tausend[und]erst...)
1,200th (one thousand two hundredth or twelve hundredth) = 1 200. ([ein]tausendzweihundertst... *or* zwölfhundertst...)
100,000th ([one] hundred thousandth) = 100 000. ([ein]hunderttausendst...)
1,000,000th ([one] millionth) = 1 000 000. (millionst...)
3,536,000th (three million five hundred and thirty-six thousandth) = 3 536 000. (drei Millionen fünfhundertsechsunddreißigtausendst...)
1,000,000,000th ([one] billionth, [one] thousand millionth) = 1 000 000 000. (milliardst...)
1,000,000,000,000th ([one] trillionth, [one] million millionth) = 1 000 000 000 000. (billionst...)

[5] Ordinal numbers are conjugated like adjectives:
the first time
= das erste Mal
her ninetieth birthday
= ihr neunzigster Geburtstag
at the tenth attempt
= beim zehnten Versuch
the end of his fifth symphony
= der Schluss seiner fünften Symphonie
For the use of ordinals in dates, *see* ◻ **Dates**
For order in races, note the following phrases:
He came (in) first
= Er kam als Erster ins Ziel
She finished third
= Sie ging als Dritte durchs Ziel *or* belegte den dritten Platz
I was sixth
= Ich wurde Sechster/Sechste

Decimal numbers = Dezimalzahlen

0.1	= 0,1 (null Komma eins)
0.015	= 0,015 (null Komma null eins fünf)
1.43	= 1,43 (eins Komma vier drei)
11.70	= 11,70 (elf Komma sieben null)
12.333 recurring	= $12,\bar{3}$ (zwölf Komma Periode drei)

Calculations

7 + 3	= 10 (sieben plus drei ist [gleich] zehn)
10 – 3	= 7 (zehn minus drei ist [gleich] sieben)
10 x 3	= 30 (zehn mal *or* multipliziert mit drei ist [gleich] dreißig)
30 ÷ 3	= 10 (dreißig [dividiert *or* geteilt] durch drei ist [gleich] zehn)

Powers = Potenzen

3^2 = ***three squared*** = drei [im *or* zum] Quadrat, drei hoch zwei
3^3 = ***three cubed*** = drei hoch drei
3^{10} = ***three to the power of ten*** = drei hoch zehn
$\sqrt{25}$ = ***the square root of twenty-five*** = die [Quadrat]wurzel aus fünfundzwanzig

See also ◻ **Age, Area, the Clock, Distance, Height and Depth, Length and Width, Money, Temperature, Volume,** and **Weight.**

'number plate *n.* Nummernschild, *das*

numbly /'nʌmlɪ/ *adv.* wie betäubt

numbness /'nʌmnɪs/ *n., no pl.* (caused by cold) Gefühllosigkeit, *die;* Taubheit, *die;* (caused by anaesthetic, sleeping pill) Betäubung, *die;* (fig.: stupor) Benommenheit, *die*

numbskull /'nʌmskʌl/ *n.* Hohlkopf, *der* (abwertend)

numeracy /'nju:mərəsɪ/ *n.* rechnerische Fähigkeiten

'numeracy hour *n.* (Brit. Educ.) Rechenstunde, *die*

numeral /'nju:mərl/ *n.* Ziffer, *die;* (word) Zahlwort, *das;* **cardinal ~:** Kardinal- *od.* Grundzahl, *die*

numerate /'nju:mərət/ *adj.* rechenkundig; **be ~:** rechnen können

numerator /'nju:məreɪtə(r)/ *n.* (Math.) Zähler, *der*

n

numerical /njuːˈmerɪkl/ *adj.* Zahlen‹*wert, -folge*›; numerisch ‹*Reihenfolge, Stärke, Überlegenheit*›; zahlenmäßig ‹*Überlegenheit*›; rechnerisch ‹*Fähigkeiten*›

numerically /njuːˈmerɪkəlɪ/ *adv.* numerisch; **~ speaking, ...:** numerisch *od.* zahlenmäßig ...

numerous /ˈnjuːmərəs/ *adj.* zahlreich

numismatics /njuːmɪzˈmætɪks/ *n., no pl.* Numismatik, *die;* Münzkunde, *die*

numismatist /njuːˈmɪzmətɪst/ *n.* ▸❶ **p. 1260** Numismatiker, *der*/Numismatikerin, *die*

numskull ▸**numbskull**

nun /nʌn/ *n.* Nonne, *die*

nuncio /ˈnʌnʃɪəʊ/ *n., pl.* **~s** (RC Ch.) Nuntius, *der*

nunnery /ˈnʌnərɪ/ *n.* [Nonnen]kloster, *das*

nuptial /ˈnʌpʃl/

A *adj.* ehelich; **~ vow/feast/day** Eheversprechen, *das*/Hochzeitsfest, *das*/Hochzeitstag, *der*

B *n. in pl.* (literary/joc.) Hochzeit, *die*

nurd ▸**nerd**

nurse /nɜːs/

A *n.* ▸❶ **p. 1260** Krankenschwester, *die;* **thank you, ~:** danke, Schwester; **hospital ~:** Krankenhausschwester, *die;* **[male] ~:** Krankenpfleger, *der;* **~s' home/uniform** Schwesternwohnheim, *das*/-tracht, *die*

B *v.t.* **1** (act as ~ to) pflegen ‹*Kranke*›; **take up nursing the handicapped/sick** in der Behinderten-/Krankenpflege tätig werden; **~ sb. through an illness** jmdn. während seiner Krankheit pflegen; **~ sb. back to health** jmdn. gesund pflegen **2** (act as ~maid to) betreuen ‹*Kind*›; (fig.: foster, tend) hegen (geh.) ‹*Projekt*›; fördern ‹*Begabung*› **3** (try to cure) versorgen; auskurieren ‹*Erkältung*› **4** (suckle) die Brust geben (+ *Dat.*), stillen ‹*Säugling*› **5** (manage carefully) hegen, pflegen ‹*Pflanze*› **6** (cradle) vorsichtig halten; wiegen ‹*Baby*› **7** (keep burning) hüten ‹*Feuer*› **8** (treat carefully) **~ gently/carefully** behutsam *od.* schonend umgehen mit **9** (fig.: harbour) hegen (geh.) ‹*Gefühl, Plan, Groll*›

C *v.i.* **1** (act as wet ~) stillen **2** (be a sick ~) Krankenschwester/-pfleger sein. *See also* **wet nurse**

ˈnursemaid *n.* (lit. or fig.) Kindermädchen, *das*

nursery /ˈnɜːsərɪ/ *n.* **1** (room for children) Kinderzimmer, *das* **2** (crèche) Kindertagesstätte, *die* **3** ▸**nursery school** **4** (Agric.) (for plants) Gärtnerei, *die;* (for trees) Baumschule, *die;* (fig.: training ground) Schule, *die*

nursery: ~man /ˈnɜːsərɪmən/ *n., pl.* **~men** /ˈnɜːsərɪmən/ Gärtner, *der;* **~ nurse** *n.* Kindermädchen, *das;* Kinderpflegerin, *die;* **~ rhyme** *n.* Kinderreim, *der;* **~ school** *n.* Kindergarten, *der;* **~-school teacher** *n.* ▸❶ **p. 1260** (female) Kindergärtnerin, *die;* Erzieherin, *die;* (male) Erzieher, *der;* **~ slopes** *n. pl.* (Skiing) Idiotenhügel, *der* (ugs. scherzh.)

nursing /ˈnɜːsɪŋ/ *n., no pl., no art.* ▸❶ **p. 1260** (profession) Krankenpflege, *die; attrib.* Pflege‹*personal, -beruf*›

nursing: ~ auxiliary *n.* ▸❶ **p. 1260** (female) Schwesternhelferin, *die;* (male) Hilfspfleger, *der;* **~ home** *n.* (Brit.) (for the aged, infirm) Pflegeheim, *das;* (for convalescents) Genesungsheim, *das;* (maternity hospital) Entbindungsheim, *das;* **~ ˈmother** *n.* stillende Mutter

nurture /ˈnɜːtʃə(r)/

A *n.* **1** *no pl.* (bringing up) Erziehung, *die* **2** (nourishment, lit. or fig.) Nahrung, *die*

B *v.t.* **1** (rear) aufziehen **2** (fig.: foster) nähren (geh.) **3** (train) erziehen; schulen, bilden ‹*Geist*›

nut /nʌt/ *n.* **1** Nuss, *die;* **she can't sing/spell for ~s** (Brit. coll.) sie kann nicht für fünf Pfennig (ugs.) singen/schreiben; **be a hard** *or* **tough ~ [to crack]** (fig.) eine harte Nuss sein (ugs.); ‹*Person:*› schwierig sein; **~s to you** (coll.) du kannst/ihr könnt mir den Buckel runterrutschen (ugs.) **2** (Mech. Engin.) [Schrauben]mutter, *die;* **~s and bolts** (fig.) praktische Grundlagen **3** (coll.: head) Kürbis, *der* (salopp); **go/be off one's ~:** verrückt (ugs.) werden/sein; **do one's ~:** durchdrehen (ugs.) **4** (crazy person) Verrückte, *der/die* (ugs.); **be a bit of a ~:** ein bisschen spinnen (ugs.) **5** *in pl.* (coarse: testicles) Eier (derb). *See also* **nuts**

nut: ~-brown *adj.* nussbraun; **~ ˈbutter** *n.* [Erd]nussbutter, *die;* **~case** *n.* (coll.) Verrückte, *der/die* (ugs.); **~crackers** *n. pl.* Nussknacker, *der;* **~ cutlet** *n.* Nussschnitzel, *das;* **~hatch** *n.* (Ornith.) Kleiber, *der;* **~house** *n.* (sl.) Klapsmühle, *die* (salopp); **~ meat** *n.* (Amer.) Nusskern, *der*

nutmeg /ˈnʌtmeg/ *n.* Muskatnuss, *die;* Muskat, *der*

nutrient /ˈnjuːtrɪənt/

A *adj.* **1** (serving as nourishment) nahrhaft **2** (providing nourishment) Ernährungs-; Nähr‹*lösung, -salze*›

B *n.* Nährstoff, *der*

nutriment /ˈnjuːtrɪmənt/ *n.* (lit. or fig.) Nahrung, *die*

nutrition /njuːˈtrɪʃn/ *n.* **1** (nourishment, diet) Ernährung, *die* **2** (food, lit. or fig.) Nahrung, *die*

nutritional /njuːˈtrɪʃənl/ *adj.* nahrhaft; **~ value** Nährwert, *der;* **~ deficiency/deficiencies** Nährstoffmangel, *der*

nutritionist /njuːˈtrɪʃənɪst/ *n.* Ernährungswissenschaftler, *der*/-wissenschaftlerin, *die*

nutritious /njuːˈtrɪʃəs/ *adj.* nahrhaft

nutritive /ˈnjuːtrɪtɪv/ *adj.* nahrhaft; **~ value/function** Nährwert, *der*/Ernährungsfunktion, *die*

ˈnut roast *n.* Nussbraten, *der*

nuts /nʌts/ *pred. adj.* (coll.) verrückt (ugs.); **be ~ about** *or* **on sb./sth.** nach jmdm./etw. verrückt sein (ugs.)

nuts-and-ˈbolts *adj.* praktisch[veranlagt] ‹*Mensch*›; konkret ‹*Diskussion, Verhandlung*›

ˈnutshell *n.* **1** Nussschale, *die* **2** (fig.) **in a ~:** in aller Kürze; **to put it** *or* **the matter** *or* **the whole thing in a ~:** kurz [gesagt]

nutter /ˈnʌtə(r)/ *n.* (coll.) Verrückte, *der/die* (ugs.); **be a ~:** verrückt sein (ugs.)

ˈnut tree *n.* Haselnussstrauch, *der;* (walnut) Nussbaum, *der*

nutty /ˈnʌtɪ/ *adj.* **1** (tasting like nuts) nussig **2** (abounding in nuts) voller Nüsse *nachgestellt* **3** (coll.: crazy) verrückt (ugs.); **be ~ about** *or* **on sb./sth.** (coll.) nach jmdm./etw. verrückt sein (ugs.); *see also* **fruit cake**

nuzzle /ˈnʌzl/

A *v.i.* **1** (with nose) **~ in** *or* **into sth.** die Schnauze in etw. (*Akk.*) drücken; **~ against sth.** die Schnauze gegen etw. drücken **2** (nestle) sich kuscheln (**[up] to, at, against** an + *Akk.*)

B *v.t.* schmiegen ‹*Gesicht, Kopf, Schulter*›

NVQ *abbr.* (Brit.) = **National Vocational Qualification**

NVQ — National Vocational Qualification

Eine Qualifikation in Großbritannien, die man durch Ausbildung am Arbeitsplatz oder in bestimmten Colleges und Schulen erhält. Die Fächer sind konkret berufsbezogen und auf verschiedenen Niveaus angesiedelt.

NW *abbr.* ▸❶ **p. 1013** **1** /nɔːθˈwest/ = **north-west** NW **2** /nɔːθˈwestən/ = **north-western** nw.

NY *abbr.* New York

nylon /ˈnaɪlɒn/ *n.* **1** *no pl.* (Textiles) Nylon, *das; attrib.* Nylon- **2** *in pl.* (stockings) Nylonstrümpfe; Nylons (ugs.)

nymph /nɪmf/ *n.* (Mythol., Zool.) Nymphe, *die*

nymphet /ˈnɪmfet, nɪmˈfet/ *n.* Nymphchen, *das*

nympho /ˈnɪmfəʊ/ *n., pl.* **~s** (coll.) Nymphomanin, *die*

nymphomania /nɪmfəˈmeɪnɪə/ *n.* Nymphomanie, *die;* Mannstollheit, *die* (veralt.)

nymphomaniac /nɪmfəˈmeɪnɪæk/

A *n.* Nymphomanin, *die*

B *adj.* nymphoman; mannstoll (veralt.)

NZ *abbr.* = **New Zealand**

Oo

O¹, o /əʊ/ *n., pl.* **Os** *or* **O's** 1 (letter) O, o, *das* 2 (zero) Null, *die*

O² *int.* (arch./poet./rhet.) o; **O God** *etc.* o Herr *usw.*; *see also* **that F 3**

o' /ə/ *prep.* (esp. arch./poet./dial.) 1 **= of** von; **man-o'-war** Kriegsschiff, *das;* **cup o' tea** (coll.) Tasse Tee; *see also* **o'clock** 2 **= on: o' nights/Sundays** nachts/sonntags

oaf /əʊf/ *n., pl.* **~s** *or* **oaves** /əʊvz/ 1 (stupid person) Dummkopf, *der* (ugs.); **great ~:** Riesenrindvieh, *das* (ugs.) 2 (awkward lout) Stoffel, *der* (ugs.); **you clumsy ~!** du Trampeltier! (ugs.)

oafish /ˈəʊfɪʃ/ *adj.* stoffelig (ugs.)

oak /əʊk/ *n.* Eiche, *die; attrib.* Eichen‹*wald, -möbel, -kiste, -blatt*›

ˈoak apple *n.* (Bot.) Gallapfel, *der*

oaken /ˈəʊkn/ *attrib. adj.* eichen

ˈoak tree *n.* Eiche, *die*

OAP *abbr.* (Brit.) **= old-age pensioner** Rentner, *der*/Rentnerin, *die;* **~ [social] club** Seniorenklub, *der*

oar /ɔː(r)/ *n.* 1 Ruder, *das;* Riemen, *der* (Sport, Seemannsspr.); **put in one's ~, put one's ~ in** (fig. coll.) seinen Senf dazugeben (ugs.); sich einmischen; **rest on one's ~s, lie** *or* (Amer.) **lay on one's ~s** die Riemen hochnehmen; (fig.: relax one's efforts) sich ausruhen 2 (rower) Ruderer, *der*/Ruderin, *die*

-oared /ɔːd/ *adj. in comb.* mit … Riemen *nachgestellt;* -ruderig

oarsman /ˈɔːzmən/ *n., pl.* **oarsmen** /ˈɔːzmən/ Ruderer, *der*

oarsmanship /ˈɔːzmənʃɪp/ *n., no pl.* ruderisches Können

oarswoman /ˈɔːzwʊmn/ *n.* Ruderin, *die*

oasis /əʊˈeɪsɪs/ *n., pl.* **oases** /əʊˈeɪsiːz/ (lit. or fig.) Oase, *die*

oast /əʊst/ *n.* (Agric., Brewing) Darre, *die*

ˈoast house *n.* (Agric., Brewing) Hopfendarre, *die*

oat /əʊt/ *n.* 1 **~s** Hafer, *der;* **be off one's ~s** (fig.) keinen Appetit haben; **rolled ~s** Haferflocken *Pl.* 2 (plant) Haferpflanze, *die;* **field of ~s** Haferfeld, *das;* **wild ~:** Flug- *od.* Windhafer, *der;* **sow one's wild ~s** (fig.) sich (*Dat.*) die Hörner abstoßen (ugs.)

ˈoatcake *n.* [flacher] Haferkuchen

oath /əʊθ/ *n., pl.* **~s** /əʊðz/ 1 Eid, *der;* Schwur, *der;* **be bound by ~:** durch einen Eid *od.* Schwur gebunden sein; **take** *or* **swear an ~ [on sth.] that …:** einen Eid [auf etw. (*Akk.*)] schwören, dass … 2 (Law) **swear** *or* **take the ~:** vereidigt werden; **on** *or* **under ~:** unter Eid; **be on** *or* **under ~ to do sth.** geschworen haben, etw. zu tun; **put sb. on** *or* **under ~:** jmdn. vereidigen *od.* unter Eid nehmen; **[I swear] on my ~ I am telling the truth** ich schwöre, dass ich die Wahrheit sage; **~ of office** Amts- *od.* Diensteid, *der;* **~ of allegiance/supremacy** Treu-/Suprematseid, *der* 3 (expletive) Fluch, *der*

ˈoatmeal *n.* 1 Hafermehl, *das* 2 (colour) Graubeige, *das*

OAU *abbr.* (Polit.) **= Organization of African Unity** OAE

oaves *pl. of* **oaf**

obbligato /ɒblɪˈgɑːtəʊ/ (Mus.)
A *adj.* obligat
B *n., pl.* **~s** Obligato, *das*

obduracy /ˈɒbdjʊrəsɪ/ *n., no pl.* (hard-heartedness) Unerbittlichkeit, *die;* (stubbornness) Verstocktheit, *die*

obdurate /ˈɒbdjʊərət/ *adj.* (hardened) unerbittlich ‹*Brutalität*›; verstockt ‹*Herz, Sünder*›; (stubborn) verstockt; hartnäckig ‹*Weigerung, Ablehnung*›

OBE *abbr.* (Brit.) **= Officer [of the Order] of the British Empire**

obedience /əˈbiːdɪəns/ *n.* Gehorsam, *der;* **show ~:** gehorsam sein; **in ~ to** gemäß

obedient /əˈbiːdɪənt/ *adj.* gehorsam; (submissive) fügsam; **teach a dog to be ~:** einem Hund Gehorsam beibringen; **be ~ to sb./sth.** jmdm./einer Sache gehorchen; *see also* **servant 3**

obediently /əˈbiːdɪəntlɪ/ *adv.* gehorsam; (submissively) fügsam

obeisance /əʊˈbeɪsəns/ *n.* 1 (gesture) Verbeugung, *die;* Verneigung, *die* (geh.); (prostration) Fußfall, *der* 2 *no pl.* (homage) Ehrerbietung, *die* (geh.); Reverenz, *die* (geh.); **do** *or* **make** *or* **pay ~ to sb.** jmdm. seine Reverenz bezeigen *od.* erweisen (geh.)

obelisk /ˈɒbəlɪsk, ˈɒbɪlɪsk/ *n.* 1 (pillar) Obelisk, *der* 2 (Printing) Kreuzchen, *das;* **double ~:** Doppelkreuzchen, *das*

obese /əʊˈbiːs/ *adj.* fett (abwertend); fettleibig (bes. Med.)

obesity /əʊˈbiːsɪtɪ/ *n., no pl.* Fettheit, *die* (abwertend); Fettleibigkeit, *die* (bes. Med.); Obesität, *die* (Med.)

obey /əʊˈbeɪ/
A *v.t.* gehorchen (+ *Dat.*); ‹*Kind, Hund:*› folgen (+ *Dat.*), gehorchen (+ *Dat.*); sich halten an (+ *Akk.*) ‹*Vorschrift, Regel*›; befolgen ‹*Befehl*›; folgen (+ *Dat.*) ‹*Aufforderung*›; nachkommen (geh.) (+ *Dat.*), Folge leisten (+ *Dat.*) ‹*Vorladung*›
B *v.i.* gehorchen; ‹*Kind, Hund:*› folgen, gehorchen; **refuse to ~:** den Gehorsam verweigern

obfuscate /ˈɒbfəskeɪt/ *v.t.* (literary) (obscure) vernebeln; (confuse) verwirren

obituary /əˈbɪtjʊərɪ/
A *n.* Nachruf, *der* (**to, of** auf + *Akk.*); (notice of death) Todesanzeige, *die*
B *adj.* **~ notice/memoir** Todesanzeige, *die*/Nachruf, *der;* **the ~ page/column** die Todesanzeigen

object
A /ˈɒbdʒɪkt/ *n.* 1 (thing) Gegenstand, *der;* (Philos.) Objekt, *das;* **he was no longer the ~ of her affections** ihre Zuneigung gehörte ihm nicht mehr 2 (purpose) Ziel, *das;* **~ in life** Lebensziel, *das od.* -zweck, *der;* **with this ~ in mind** *or* **view** mit diesem Ziel [vor Augen]; **with the ~ of doing sth.** in der Absicht, etw. zu tun; **make it one's ~ [in life]** es sich (*Dat.*) zum Ziel setzen; es zu seinem Lebensziel machen; *see also* **defeat A 2**; **exercise A 2** 3 (obstacle, hindrance) **money/time** *etc.* **is no ~:** Geld/Zeit *usw.* spielt keine Rolle 4 (Ling.) Objekt, *das; see also* **direct object**; **indirect object**
B /əbˈdʒekt/ *v.i.* 1 (state objection) Einwände/einen Einwand erheben (**to** gegen); (protest) protestieren (**to** gegen); **I ~, your Honour** (Law) Einspruch, Herr Vorsitzender! 2 (have objection or dislike) etwas dagegen haben; **~ to sb./sth.** etwas gegen jmdn./etw. haben; **if you don't ~:** wenn Sie nichts dagegen haben; **I ~ to your smoking** es stört mich, dass du rauchst; **~ to sb.'s doing sth.** etw. dagegen haben, dass jmd. etw. tut; **I strongly ~ to this tone** ich verbitte mir diesen Ton; **I ~ to being blamed for this error** ich verwahre mich dagegen, für diesen Fehler verantwortlich gemacht zu werden
C *v.t.* einwenden

objectify /əbˈdʒektɪfaɪ/ *v.t.* objektivieren

objection /əbˈdʒekʃn/ *n.* 1 Einwand, *der;* Einspruch, *der* (Amtsspr., Rechtsw.); **raise** *or* **make an ~ [to sth.]** einen Einwand *od.* (Rechtsw.) Einspruch [gegen etw.] erheben; **make no ~ to sth.** nichts gegen etw. einzuwenden haben 2 (feeling of opposition or dislike) Abneigung, *die;* **have an/no ~ to sb./sth.** etw./nichts gegen jmdn./etw. haben; **have an/no ~:** etwas/nichts dagegen haben; **have no ~ to sb.'s doing sth.** nichts dagegen haben, dass jmd. etw. tut

objectionable /əbˈdʒekʃənəbl/ *adj.* unangenehm ‹*Anblick, Geruch*›; anstößig ‹*Bemerkung, Wort, Benehmen*›; unausstehlich ‹*Kind*›

objectionably /əbˈdʒekʃənəblɪ/ *adv.* unerträglich ‹*überheblich, aufdringlich*›; anstößig ‹*sich benehmen*›

objective /əbˈdʒektɪv/
A *adj.* 1 (unbiased) objektiv; sachlich 2 (esp. Philos.: real) objektiv
B *n.* (goal) Ziel, *das;* **establish one's ~:** sich (*Dat.*) ein Ziel setzen

objective: ~ case *n.* (Ling.) **be in the ~ case** Objekt sein; **~ ˈgenitive** *n.* (Ling.) Genitivus obiectivus, *der*

objectively /əbˈdʒektɪvlɪ/ *adv.* 1 objektiv 2 (Ling.) als Objekt ‹*gebrauchen*›

objectiveness /əbˈdʒektɪvnɪs/, **objectivity** /ɒbdʒekˈtɪvɪtɪ/ *ns., no pl.* Objektivität, *die;* **maintain objectivity** objektiv bleiben

ˈobject lesson *n.* (warning) Denkzettel, *der;* (very clear example) Musterbeispiel, *das* (**in, on** für); **it was an ~ to him** es war ihm eine Lehre; **an ~ in** *or* **on how to do sth.** ein Musterbeispiel dafür, wie man etw. macht

objector /əbˈdʒektə(r)/ *n.* Gegner, *der*/Gegnerin, *die* (**to** *Gen.*); *see also* **conscientious**

objet d'art /ɒbʒeɪ ˈdɑː(r)/ *n., pl.* **objets d'art** /ɒbʒeɪ ˈdɑː(r)/ Kunstgegenstand, *der*

obligate /ˈɒblɪgeɪt/ *v.t., usu. in p.p.* verpflichten

obligation /ɒblɪˈgeɪʃn/ *n.* 1 Verpflichtung, *die;* (constraint) Zwang, *der;* **be under** *or* **have an/no ~ to do sth.** verpflichtet/nicht verpflichtet sein, etw. zu tun; **have an/no ~ to[wards] sb.** jmdm. gegenüber eine/keine Verpflichtung haben; **there's no ~ to buy** es besteht kein Kaufzwang; **without ~:** unverbindlich 2 (indebtedness) Dankesschuld, *die* (geh.); **put** *or* **place sb. under an ~:** jmdm. eine Dankespflicht auferlegen; **be under an ~ to sb.** in jmds. Schuld stehen (geh.); jmdm. verpflichtet sein; **be under no ~ to sb.** jmdm. nicht verpflichtet sein

obligatory /əˈblɪgətərɪ/ *adj.* obligatorisch; **make sth. ~ for sb.** etw. für jmdn. vorschreiben; **it has become ~ to do sth.** es ist zur Pflicht geworden, etw. zu tun

oblige /əˈblaɪdʒ/
A *v.t.* 1 (be binding on) **~ sb. to do sth.** jmdm. vorschreiben, etw. zu tun; **one is ~d by law to do sth.** etw. ist gesetzlich vorgeschrieben 2 (constrain, compel) zwingen; nötigen; **be ~d**

O

to do sth. gezwungen *od.* genötigt sein, etw. zu tun; **you are not ~d to answer these questions** Sie sind nicht verpflichtet, diese Fragen zu beantworten; **feel ~d to do sth.** sich verpflichtet fühlen, etw. zu tun **3** (be kind to) **~ sb. by doing sth.** jmdm. den Gefallen tun und etw. tun; **would you please ~ me by doing it?** würden Sie bitte so gut sein und es tun?; **~ sb. with sth.** (help out) jmdm. mit etw. aushelfen; **could you ~ me with a lift?** könnten Sie mich freundlicherweise mitnehmen? **4** **~d** (bound by gratitude) **be much/greatly ~d to sb. [for sth.]** jmdm. [für etw.] sehr verbunden sein; **much ~d** besten Dank!
B *v.i.* **be always ready to ~:** immer sehr gefällig sein; **anything to ~** (as answer) stets zu Diensten; **~ with a song** *etc.* ein Lied *usw.* zum Besten geben

obliging /əˈblaɪdʒɪŋ/ *adj.* entgegenkommend

obligingly /əˈblaɪdʒɪŋlɪ/ *adv.* entgegenkommenderweise

oblique /əˈbliːk/
A *adj.* **1** (slanting) schief ‹*Gerade, Winkel*› **2** (fig.: indirect) indirekt ‹*Bemerkung, Hinweis, Frage*›; versteckt ‹*Hinweis*›
B *n.* Schrägstrich, *der*

obliquely /əˈbliːklɪ/ *adv.* **1** (in a slanting direction) schräg ‹*einfallen, abzweigen*› **2** (fig.: indirectly) indirekt ‹*sich beziehen, antworten*›

obliterate /əˈblɪtəreɪt/ *v.t.* **1** auslöschen; (cancel) entwerten ‹*Briefmarke*› **2** (fig.) verschleiern ‹*Wahrheit*›; auslöschen ‹*Erinnerung*›; zerstreuen ‹*Bedenken*›; vernichtend schlagen ‹*Gegner*›

obliteration /əblɪtəˈreɪʃn/ *n.* ▸**obliterate**: Auslöschung, *die;* Verschleierung, *die;* Zerstreuung, *die*

oblivion /əˈblɪvɪən/ *n., no pl.* **1** (being forgotten) Vergessenheit, *die;* **sink** *or* **fall into ~:** in Vergessenheit geraten; **rescued from ~:** der Vergessenheit (*Dat.*) entrissen **2** (forgetting) Vergessen, *das*

oblivious /əˈblɪvɪəs/ *adj.* **be ~ to** *or* **of sth.** (be unconscious of) sich (*Dat.*) einer Sache (*Gen.*) nicht bewusst sein; (not notice) etw. nicht bemerken *od.* wahrnehmen

oblong /ˈɒblɒŋ/
A *adj.* rechteckig
B *n.* Rechteck, *das*

obloquy /ˈɒbləkwɪ/ *n.* (literary) **1** (abuse) Beschimpfungen *Pl.* **2** (disgrace) Schande, *die*

obnoxious /əbˈnɒkʃəs/ *adj.*, **obnoxiously** /əbˈnɒkʃəslɪ/ *adv.* widerlich (abwertend)

oboe /ˈəʊbəʊ/ *n.* (Mus.) Oboe, *die*

oboist /ˈəʊbəʊɪst/ *n.* ▸**i** **p. 1260** (Mus.) Oboist, *der*/Oboistin, *die*

obscene /əbˈsiːn/ *adj.* obszön; (coll.: offensive) widerlich (abwertend); unanständig ‹*Profit*›

obscenely /əbˈsiːnlɪ/ *adv.* obszön; (coll.: offensively) widerlich (abwertend); unanständig ‹*reich*›

obscenity /əbˈsenɪtɪ/ *n.* Obszönität, *die;* (coll.: offensive nature) Widerlichkeit, *die* (abwertend)

obscurantism /ɒbskjʊəˈræntɪzm/ *n.* Obskurantismus, *der*

obscurantist /ɒbskjʊəˈræntɪst/
A *n.* Obskurant, *der*/Obskurantin, *die* (geh.)
B *adj.* **~ doctrine/argument** Obskurantentum, *das* (geh.)

obscure /əbˈskjʊə(r)/
A *adj.* **1** (unexplained) dunkel; **for some ~ reason** aus irgendeinem unerfindlichen (geh.) *od.* verborgenen Grund **2** (hard to understand) schwer verständlich ‹*Argument, Dichtung, Autor, Stil*›; unklar ‹*Hinweis, Textstelle*› **3** (unknown) unbekannt ‹*Herkunft, Schriftsteller*›; (undistinguished) unbedeutend **4** (indistinct, vague) undeutlich ‹*Spur, Gemurmel*›; vage ‹*Anhaltspunkt*› **5** (remote) abgelegen, entlegen ‹*Ort*› **6** (dark, dim) dunkel
B *v.t.* **1** (make indistinct) verdunkeln; (block) versperren ‹*Aussicht*›; (conceal) ‹*Nebel:*› verhüllen **2** (fig.: make unintelligible) unverständlich machen; **be ~d** unverständlich werden **3** (fig.: outshine) in den Schatten stellen

obscurely /əbˈskjʊəlɪ/ *adv.* **1** (indirectly) vage **2** (in obscurity) im Verborgenen

obscurity /əbˈskjʊərɪtɪ/ *n.* **1** *no pl.* (being unknown or inconspicuous) Unbekanntheit, *die;* **rise out of ~:** bekannt werden; **sink into ~:** in Vergessenheit geraten; **in ~:** unbeachtet, unauffällig ‹*leben*› **2** *no pl.* (being not clearly known or understood) **be lost in [the mists of] ~:** im Dunkeln liegen **3** (unintelligibleness, unintelligible thing) Unverständlichkeit, *die* **4** *no pl.* (darkness) Dunkelheit, *die*

obsequies /ˈɒbsɪkwɪz/ *n. pl.* (funeral rites) Beisetzungsfeierlichkeiten (geh.)

obsequious /əbˈsiːkwɪəs/ *adj.*, **obsequiously** /əbˈsiːkwɪəslɪ/ *adv.* unterwürfig (abwertend)

observable /əbˈzɜːvəbl/ *adj.* erkennbar; spürbar ‹*Mangel, Zunahme, Übergewicht*›

observance /əbˈzɜːvəns/ *n.* **1** *no pl.* (observing, keeping) Einhaltung, *die;* Befolgung, *die;* (of prescribed times) Einhaltung, *die* **2** (esp. Relig.: practice, rite) Regel, *die* **3** (rule) Ordensregel, *die*

observant /əbˈzɜːvənt/ *adj.* **1** aufmerksam; **be ~ of sth.** ein Auge für etw. haben; **how very ~ of you!** sehr scharf beobachtet! **2** (mindful, regardful) **be ~ of** beachten, sich halten an (+ *Akk.*) ‹*Gesetz, Regel*›

observation /ɒbzəˈveɪʃn/ *n.* **1** *no pl.* Beobachtung, *die;* **escape ~:** unbeobachtet bleiben; **powers of ~:** Beobachtungsgabe, *die;* **stay in hospital for ~:** zur Beobachtung im Krankenhaus bleiben; **be [kept] under ~:** beobachtet werden; (by police, detectives) observiert *od.* überwacht werden **2** (remark) Bemerkung, *die* (**on** über + *Akk.*); **make an ~ on sth.** sich zu etw. äußern

observational /ɒbzəˈveɪʃənl/ *adj.* Beobachtungs‹*gabe, -methode*›

observation: ~ car *n.* (Railw.) Aussichtswagen, *der;* **~ post** *n.* (Mil.) Beobachtungsposten, *der*

observatory /əbˈzɜːvətərɪ/ *n.* Observatorium, *das;* (Astron. also) Sternwarte, *die;* (Meteorol. also) Wetterstation, *die*

observe /əbˈzɜːv/ *v.t.* **1** (watch) beobachten; ‹*Polizei, Detektiv:*› observieren, überwachen; *abs.* aufpassen; (perceive) bemerken **2** (abide by, keep) einhalten; feiern ‹*Weihnachten, Jahrestag*›; einlegen ‹*Schweigeminute*›; halten ‹*Gelübde*›; nachkommen (geh.) (+ *Dat.*) ‹*Bitte*› **3** (say) bemerken

observer /əbˈzɜːvə(r)/ *n.* Beobachter, *der*/Beobachterin, *die*

> **The Observer**
>
> Eine britische Sonntagszeitung, die für die Qualität ihres investigativen Journalismus bekannt ist. Ihre politische Position ist links von der Mitte, besonders in sozialen Fragen. Der Observer ist eine **broadsheet**-Zeitung, zählt zur seriösen Presse und gehört jetzt der **Guardian**-Gruppe an.

obsess /əbˈses/ *v.t.* **~ sb.** von jmdm. Besitz ergreifen (fig.); **be/become ~ed with** *or* **by sb./sth.** von jmdm./etw. besessen sein/werden; **don't let yourself become ~ed by her** versuch in deiner Beziehung zu ihr einen kühlen Kopf zu behalten

obsession /əbˈseʃn/ *n.* **1** (persistent idea) Zwangsvorstellung, *die;* **be/become an ~ with sb.** für jmdn. zur Sucht geworden sein/werden; **have an ~ with sb.** von jmdm. besessen sein; **have an ~ with sex** sexbesessen sein; **have an ~ with cleanliness/guns** einen Sauberkeits-/Waffenfimmel haben; **have an ~ with detail** ein Kleinkrämer sein **2** *no pl.* (Psych.: condition) Obsession, *die* (fachspr.); Besessenheit, *die;* **develop an ~ about washing** einen Waschzwang entwickeln

obsessional /əbˈseʃənl/ *adj.* zwanghaft; obsessiv (Psych.)

obsessive /əbˈsesɪv/ *adj.* zwanghaft; obsessiv (Psych.); **be ~ about sth.** von etw. besessen sein; **be an ~ eater/gambler** unter Esszwang leiden/dem Spiel verfallen sein

obsessively /əbˈsesɪvlɪ/ *adv.* zwanghaft

obsolescence /ɒbsəˈlesəns/ *n., no pl.* Veralten, *das;* **fall into ~:** veralten; **built-in** *or* **planned ~:** geplanter Verschleiß

obsolescent /ɒbsəˈlesənt/ *adj.* veraltend; **become/have become** *or* **be ~:** allmählich veralten/nahezu veraltet sein

obsolete /ˈɒbsəliːt/ *adj.* veraltet; obsolet (geh.); **become/have become ~:** veralten/veraltet sein

obstacle /ˈɒbstəkl/ *n.* Hindernis, *das* (**to** für); **put ~s in sb.'s path** (fig.) jmdm. Hindernisse *od.* Steine in den Weg legen; **give rise to ~s** Schwierigkeiten verursachen

obstacle: ~ course *n.* Hindernisparcours, *der;* **~ race** *n.* Hindernisrennen, *das*

obstetric /ɒbˈstetrɪk/, **obstetrical** /ɒbˈstetrɪkl/ *adj.* (Med.) Geburts‹*schock, -kanal*›; **~ ward** Entbindungsstation, *die*

obstetrician /ɒbstəˈtrɪʃn/ *n.* ▸**i** **p. 1260** (Med.) Geburtshelfer, *der*/-helferin, *die*

obstetrics /ɒbˈstetrɪks/ *n., no pl.* (Med.) Obstetrik, *die* (fachspr.); Geburtshilfe, *die*

obstinacy /ˈɒbstɪnəsɪ/ *n., no pl.* ▸**obstinate**: Starrsinn, *der;* Hartnäckigkeit, *die;* Sturheit, *die* (ugs.)

obstinate /ˈɒbstɪnət/ *adj.* starrsinnig; (adhering to particular course of action) hartnäckig; stur (ugs.); **an ~ cold** eine hartnäckige Erkältung; **be as ~ as a mule** ein sturer Bock sein (ugs. abwertend)

obstinately /ˈɒbstɪnətlɪ/ *adv.* ▸**obstinate**: starrsinnig; hartnäckig; stur (ugs.)

obstreperous /əbˈstrepərəs/ *adj.* **1** randalierend; **be/become ~:** randalieren/zu randalieren beginnen **2** (protesting) widerspenstig; **stop being so ~!** mach nicht so ein Geschrei! (ugs.)

obstruct /əbˈstrʌkt/ *v.t.* **1** (block) versperren; blockieren; (Med.) verstopfen; behindern ‹*Verkehr*›; versperren ‹*Sicht*›; **~ sb.'s view** jmdm. die Sicht versperren **2** (fig.: impede; also Sport) behindern **3** (Parl.) obstruieren

obstruction /əbˈstrʌkʃn/ *n.* **1** *no pl.* (blocking) Blockierung, *die;* (Med.) Verstopfung, *die;* Obstruktion, *die* (Med.); (of progress; also Sport) Behinderung, *die;* (to success) Hindernis, *das* (**to** für) **2** (Parl.) Obstruktion, *die* **3** (obstacle) Hindernis, *das;* Hemmnis, *das*

obstructionism /əbˈstrʌkʃənɪzm/ *n., no pl.* (Polit.) **[policy of] ~:** Obstruktionspolitik, *die*

obstructionist /əbˈstrʌkʃənɪst/ *n.* (Polit.) Obstruktionspolitiker, *der*/-politikerin, *die*

obstructive /əbˈstrʌktɪv/ *adj.* hinderlich; obstruktiv ‹*Politik, Taktik*›; **be ~** ‹*Person:*› sich quer legen (ugs.)

obtain /əbˈteɪn/
A *v.t.* bekommen ‹*Ware, Information, Hilfe*›; erreichen, erzielen ‹*Resultat, Wirkung*›; erwerben, erlangen ‹*akademischen Grad*›; **~ a divorce** geschieden werden
B *v.i.* Geltung haben; ‹*Ansicht, Brauch:*› herrschen, verbreitet sein; ‹*Regelung:*› in Kraft sein

obtainable /əbˈteɪnəbl/ *adj.* erhältlich ‹*Ware, Eintrittskarte*›; erzielbar ‹*Wirkung*›

obtrude /əbˈtruːd/
A *v.t.* **~ one's beliefs/opinions on sb.** jmdm. seine Überzeugung/Meinung aufdrängen; **~ oneself [up]on sb./into sth.** sich jmdm. aufdrängen/sich in etw. (*Akk.*) hineindrängen
B *v.i.* sich aufdrängen (**upon** *Dat.*); **~ upon sb.'s grief** jmdn. in seinem Kummer stören

obtrusive /əbˈtruːsɪv/ *adj.* aufdringlich; (conspicuous) auffällig

obtrusively /əbˈtruːsɪvlɪ/ *adv.* in aufdringlicher Weise

obtrusiveness /əbˈtruːsɪvnɪs/ *n., no pl.* Aufdringlichkeit, *die;* (conspicuousness) Auffälligkeit, *die*

obtuse /əbˈtjuːs/ *adj.* **1** (blunt; also Geom.) stumpf ‹*Winkel, Messer*› **2** (stupid) einfältig; **he's being deliberately ~:** er stellt sich dumm

obtusely /əbˈtjuːslɪ/ *adv.* einfältig

obverse /ˈɒbvɜːs/ *n.* **1** (of coin or medal) Vorderseite, *die;* Avers, *der* (Münzk.) **2** (front) Schauseite, *die* **3** (fig.: counterpart) Gegenstück, *das* (**of** zu)

obviate /ˈɒbvɪeɪt/ *v.t.* begegnen (+ *Dat.*) ‹*Gefahr, Risiko, Einwand*›; **~ the necessity of sth.** etw. unnötig machen

obvious /ˈɒbvɪəs/ *adj.* offenkundig; eindeutig ‹*Sieger*›; (easily seen) augenfällig; sichtlich ‹*Empfindung, innerer Zustand*›; plump ‹*Trick, Mittel*›; **she was the ~ choice** es lag nahe, dass die Wahl auf sie fiel; **the answer is ~:** die Antwort liegt auf der Hand; **the ~ thing to do is ...:** das Naheliegende ist ...; **it's not ~ what we should do next** es ist nicht ersichtlich, was wir als Nächstes tun sollten; **with the ~ exception of ...:** natürlich mit Ausnahme von ...; **be ~ [to sb.] that ...:** [jmdm.] klar sein, dass ...; **that's stating the ~:** das ist nichts Neues

obviously /ˈɒbvɪəslɪ/ *adv.* offenkundig; sichtlich ‹*enttäuschen, überraschen usw.*›; **~, we can't expect any help** es ist klar, dass wir keine Hilfe erwarten können

ocarina /ɒkəˈriːnə/ *n.* (Mus.) Okarina, *die*

Occam's razor /ɒkəmz ˈreɪzə(r)/ *n.* (Philos.) Ökonomieprinzip, *das;* Ockham's Razor, *der*

occasion /əˈkeɪʒn/

A *n.* **1** (opportunity) Gelegenheit, *die;* **rise to the ~:** sich der Situation gewachsen zeigen **2** (reason) Grund, *der* (**for** zu); (cause) Anlass, *der;* **should the ~ arise** falls sich die Gelegenheit ergibt; **there is no ~ for alarm** es besteht kein Grund zur Sorge; **be [an] ~ for celebration** ein Grund zum Feiern sein; **have ~ to do sth.** [eine] Gelegenheit haben, etw. zu tun; **I had ~ to be in Rome** ich hatte in Rom zu tun **3** (point in time) Gelegenheit, *die;* **on several ~s** bei mehreren Gelegenheiten; **on that ~:** bei der Gelegenheit; damals; **[up]on ~[s]** gelegentlich **4** (special occurrence) Anlass, *der;* **on state ~s** bei offiziellen Anlässen; **it was quite an ~:** es war ein Ereignis; **on the ~ of** anlässlich (+ *Gen.*)

B *v.t.* verursachen; erregen, Anlass geben zu ‹*Besorgnis*›; geben ‹*Denkanstoß, Anregung*›; **~ sb. to do sth.** jmdn. veranlassen, etw. zu tun

occasional /əˈkeɪʒənl/ *adj.* **1** (happening irregularly) gelegentlich; vereinzelt ‹*Regenschauer*›; **take an** *or* **the ~ break** gelegentlich eine Pause machen **2** (specially written) Gelegenheits‹*musik, -dichtung*›

occasionally /əˈkeɪʒənəlɪ/ *adv.* gelegentlich; **[only] very ~:** gelegentlich einmal

ocˈcasional table *n.* Beistelltisch, *der*

Occident /ˈɒksɪdənt/ *n.* (poet./rhet.) **the ~** (the west, European civilization) der Okzident; das Abendland

occidental /ɒksɪˈdentl/

A *adj.* **1** abendländisch **2** (Polit.) westlich

B **O~** *n.* Abendländer, *der*/Abendländerin, *die*

occlude /əˈkluːd/ *v.t.* **1** (Med.) verschließen **2** (Chem.) okkludieren ‹*Gas*› **3** (Meteorol.) **~d front** Okklusion, *die*

occlusion /əˈkluːʒn/ *n.* **1** (Med.) Okklusion, *die* (fachspr.); Verschluss, *der* **2** (Chem., Meteorol., Dent.) Okklusion, *die*

occult /ɒˈkʌlt, əˈkʌlt/ *adj.* **1** (mystical) okkult ‹*Kunst, Wissenschaft*›; **the ~:** das Okkulte **2** (mysterious) unergründlich, dunkel ‹*Rätsel, Geheimnis*› **3** (secret) verborgen

occultism /ɒˈkʌltɪzm, əˈkʌltɪzm/ *n.* Okkultismus, *der*

occultist /ɒˈkʌltɪst, əˈkʌltɪst/ *n.* Okkultist, *der*/Okkultistin, *die*

occupancy /ˈɒkjʊpənsɪ/ *n.* (residence in a place) Bewohnung, *die;* (moving into property) Einzug, *der*

occupant /ˈɒkjʊpənt/ *n.* **1** (resident) Bewohner, *der*/Bewohnerin, *die;* (of post) Inhaber, *der*/Inhaberin, *die;* (of car, bus, etc.) Insasse, *der*/Insassin, *die;* (of room) [Zimmer]bewohner, *der*/-bewohnerin, *die* **2** (Law) Besitzer, *der*/Besitzerin, *die*

occupation /ɒkjʊˈpeɪʃn/ *n.* **1** (of property) (tenure) Besitz, *der;* (occupancy) Bewohnung, *die;* **take over the ~ of** in Besitz nehmen; einziehen in (+ *Akk.*) ‹*Haus, Wohnung, Zimmer*›; **the owners of the house are [still]/the new tenants are already in ~:** die Hausbesitzer sind noch nicht ausgezogen/die neuen Mieter sind schon eingezogen **2** (Mil.) Okkupation, *die;* Besetzung, *die;* (period) Besatzungszeit, *die;* **army of ~:** Besatzungsarmee, *die* **3** (activity) Beschäftigung, *die;* (pastime) Zeitvertreib, *der* **4** (profession) Beruf, *der;* **his ~ is civil engineering** er ist Bauingenieur [von Beruf]; **what's her ~?** was ist sie von Beruf?

occupational /ɒkjʊˈpeɪʃənl/ *adj.* Berufs‹*beratung, -risiko*›; betrieblich ‹*Altersversorgung*›

occupational: ~ diˈsease *n.* (also joc.) Berufskrankheit, *die;* **~ ˈtherapist** *n.* ▸ **p. 1260** Beschäftigungstherapeut, *der*/-therapeutin, *die;* **~ ˈtherapy** *n.* Beschäftigungstherapie, *die*

occupier /ˈɒkjʊpaɪə(r)/ *n.* (Brit.) Besitzer, *der*/Besitzerin, *die;* (tenant) Bewohner, *der*/Bewohnerin, *die*

occupy /ˈɒkjʊpaɪ/ *v.t.* **1** (Mil.; Polit. as demonstration) besetzen; **the terrorists are ~ing the building** die Terroristen halten das Gebäude besetzt **2** (reside in, be a tenant of) bewohnen; **~ a flat on a one-year lease** eine Wohnung für ein Jahr gemietet haben **3** (take up, fill) einnehmen; liegen in (+ *Dat.*) ‹*Bett*›; besetzen ‹*Sitzplatz, Tisch*›; belegen ‹*Zimmer*›; in Anspruch nehmen ‹*Zeit, Aufmerksamkeit*›; **how did you ~ your time?** wie hast du die Zeit verbracht?; **the hotel occupies an attractive site** das Hotel ist schön gelegen; **~ a special place in sb.'s affections** einen besonderen Platz in jmds. Herzen haben **4** (hold) innehaben ‹*Stellung, Amt*› **5** (busy, employ) beschäftigen; **~ oneself [with doing sth.]** sich [mit etw.] beschäftigen; **be occupied with** *or* **in doing sth.** damit beschäftigt sein, etw. zu tun; **keep sb.['s mind] occupied** jmdn. [geistig] beschäftigen

occur /əˈkɜː(r)/ *v.i.*, **-rr-** **1** (be met with) vorkommen; ‹*Gelegenheit, Schwierigkeit, Problem:*› sich ergeben; ‹*Gelegenheit:*› sich bieten; ‹*Krankheit, Problem, Schwierigkeit:*› auftreten; **if the case should ~ that ...:** sollte der Fall eintreten, dass ... **2** (happen) ‹*Veränderung:*› eintreten; ‹*Unfall, Vorfall, Zwischenfall:*› sich ereignen; ‹*Olympiade:*› stattfinden; ‹*Todesfall:*› auftreten; **how did your injuries ~?** wie kam es zu deinen Verletzungen?; **this must not ~ again** das darf nicht wieder vorkommen **3** **~ to sb.** (be thought of) jmdm. einfallen *od.* in den Sinn kommen; ‹*Idee:*› jmdm. kommen; **it ~red to me that she was looking rather pale** mir fiel auf, dass sie ziemlich blass aussah; **it never ~red to me** auf den Gedanken *od.* darauf bin ich nie gekommen

occurrence /əˈkʌrəns/ *n.* **1** (incident) Ereignis, *das;* Begebenheit, *die* **2** (occurring) Vorkommen, *das;* (of disease) Vorkommen, *das;* Auftreten, *das;* **be of frequent ~:** häufig vorkommen

ocean /ˈəʊʃn/ *n.* **1** Ozean, *der;* Meer, *das;* *attrib.* Meeres‹*strömung, -boden*› **2** *in pl.* (fig. coll.) **~s of time** massenhaft Zeit (ugs.); **he's got ~s of money** er hat Geld wie Heu (ugs.); **weep ~s of tears** Ströme von Tränen vergießen

ˈocean-going *adj.* Übersee‹*handel, -dampfer, -schiff*›

Oceania /əʊʃɪˈɑːnɪə, əʊsɪˈɑːnɪə/ *pr. n.* Ozeanien (*das*)

oceanic /əʊʃɪˈænɪk, əʊsɪˈænɪk/ *adj.* ozeanisch; Meeres‹*tier, -klima, -tiefe, -strömung*›; See‹*vogel, -klima*›; (fig.) gewaltig

oceanographer /əʊʃəˈnɒgrəfə(r)/ *n.* ▸ **p. 1260** Ozeanograf, *der*/Ozeanografin, *die*

oceanography /əʊʃəˈnɒgrəfɪ/ *n.* Ozeanographie, *die;* Meereskunde, *die*

ocelot /ˈɒsɪlɒt/ *n.* (Zool.) Ozelot, *der*

och /ɒx/ *int.* (Scot., Ir.) ach

ochre (*Amer.:* **ocher**) /ˈəʊkə(r)/ *n.* Ocker, *der od. das*

ocker /ˈɒkə(r)/ *n.* (Austral. coll.) *ungehobelter, rüpelhafter Australier*

o'clock /əˈklɒk/ *adv.* **1** ▸ **p. 1001** **it is two/six ~:** es ist zwei/sechs Uhr; **at two/six ~:** um zwei/sechs Uhr; **six ~** *attrib.* Sechs-Uhr‹*Zug, Maschine, Nachrichten*› **2** *indicating direction or position* **see a plane at 3/6/9/12 ~:** ein Flugzeug rechts/genau unter sich (*Dat.*)/links/genau über sich (*Dat.*) sehen; (horizontally) ein Flugzeug rechts/genau hinter sich (*Dat.*)/links/genau vor sich (*Dat.*) sehen

OCR *abbr.* (Computing) **= optical character recognition**

Oct. *abbr.* **= October** Okt.

octagon /ˈɒktəgən/ *n.* (Geom.) Achteck, *das;* Oktogon, *das* (fachspr.)

octagonal /ɒkˈtægənl/ *adj.* (Geom.) achteckig; oktogonal (fachspr.)

octahedron /ɒktəˈhiːdrən/ *n., pl.* **~s** *or* **octahedra** /ɒktəˈhiːdrə/ (Geom.) Oktaeder, *das* (fachspr.); Achtflächner, *der*

octane /ˈɒkteɪn/ *n.* Oktan, *das*

octave /ˈɒktɪv/ *n.* (Mus.) Oktave, *die*

octavo /ɒkˈtɑːvəʊ/ *n., pl.* **~s** **1** (book) Oktavband, *der;* (page) Oktavseite, *die* **2** (size) Oktav[format], *das*

octet, octette /ɒkˈtet/ *n.* (Mus.) Oktett, *das;* **string ~** Streichoktett, *das*

October /ɒkˈtəʊbə(r)/ *n.* ▸ **p. 1047** Oktober, *der;* **the ~ Revolution** (Hist.) die Oktoberrevolution; *see also* **August**

octogenarian /ɒktədʒɪˈneərɪən/

A *adj.* achtzigjährig; (more than 80 years old) in den Achtzigern *nachgestellt*

B *n.* Achtziger, *der*/Achtzigerin, *die*

octopus /ˈɒktəpəs/ *n.* (lit. or fig.) Tintenfisch, *der;* Krake, *der;* Octopus, *der* (Zool.)

ocular /ˈɒkjʊlə(r)/ *adj.* Augen‹*maß, -krankheit, -täuschung*›

oculist /ˈɒkjʊlɪst/ *n.* ▸ **p. 1260** Augenarzt, *der*/Augenärztin, *die*

OD *abbr.* (esp. Amer. coll.)

A **= overdose 1**

B **OD's, OD'd, ODing: = overdose 3**

odd /ɒd/ *adj.* **1** (surplus, spare) übrig ‹*Stück*›; überzählig ‹*Spieler*›; restlich, übrig ‹*Silbergeld*› **2** (additional) **£25 and a few ~ pence** 25 Pfund und ein paar Pence; **1,000 and ~ pounds** etwas über 1000 Pfund **3** (occasional, random) gelegentlich; **use the occasional ~ moment to do sth.** etw. tun, wenn sich die Gelegenheit ergibt; **I like the ~ whisky** gelegentlich trinke ich gern einen Whisky; **the ~ bit of translating** gelegentliche kleine Übersetzungen; **~ job/~-job man** Gelegenheitsarbeit, *die*/-arbeiter, *der;* **do ~ jobs** Gelegenheitsarbeiten verrichten; (about the house) anfallende Arbeiten erledigen **4** (one of pair or group) einzeln; **~ socks/gloves** *etc.* nicht zusammengehörende Socken/Handschuhe *usw.;* **~ numbers/volumes** Einzelnummern/Einzelbände **5** (uneven) ungerade ‹*Zahl, Seite, Hausnummer*› **6** (plus something) **she must be forty ~:** sie muss etwas über vierzig sein; **sixty thousand ~:** etwas über sechzigtausend; **twelve pounds ~:** etwas mehr als zwölf Pfund **7** (extraordinary) merkwürdig; (strange, eccentric) seltsam

odd: ~ball, ~ ˈfish *ns.* (coll.) komischer Kauz (ugs.)

oddity /ˈɒdɪtɪ/ *n.* **1** (strangeness, peculiar trait) Eigentümlichkeit, *die* **2** (odd person) Sonderling, *der* **3** (fantastic object, strange event) Kuriosität, *die*

oddly /ˈɒdlɪ/ *adv.* seltsam; merkwürdig; **~ enough** seltsamer- *od.* merkwürdigerweise

odd ˈman *n.* **be the ~:** die entscheidende Stimme haben; **~ out** Außenseiter, *der*/Außenseiterin, *die;* **be the ~ out** (extra person) überzählig sein; (thing) zu etw. nicht passen; **find the ~ out** das finden, was überzählig ist/nicht passt

oddment /ˈɒdmənt/ *n.* **1** (left over) [Über]rest, *der;* (in sales) Reststück, *das* **2** *in pl.* (odds and ends) Kleinigkeiten; **~s of furniture** einzelne Möbelstücke

oddness /ˈɒdnɪs/ *n., no pl.* Merkwürdigkeit, *die;* (strangeness) Seltsamkeit, *die*

odd: ~-numbered *adj.* ungerade; **~ one** ▸**odd man**

odds /ɒdz/ *n. pl.* **1** (Betting) Odds *pl.;* **the ~ were on Black Bess** Black Bess hatte die besten Chancen; **lay** *or* **give/take ~ of six to one in favour of/against sb./a horse** eine 6 : 1-Wette auf/gegen jmdn./ein Pferd anbieten/annehmen; **I'll lay ~ that ...** (fig.) ich wette, dass ...; **take ~ on sth.** auf etw. (*Akk.*) wetten; **over the ~** (fig.) zu viel; **pay over the ~ for**

sth. einen überhöhten Preis für etw. bezahlen; **be/go over the ~** (more than is reasonable) zu weit gehen; *see also* **long odds**; **short odds** 2) (chances for or against) Möglichkeit, *die;* (chance for) Aussicht, *die;* Chance, *die;* **[the] ~ are that she did it** wahrscheinlich hat sie es getan; **the ~ are against/in favour of sb./sth.** jmds. Aussichten *od.* Chancen/die Aussichten *od.* Chancen für etw. sind gering/gut; **the ~ are against/in favour of sth. happening** es besteht kaum/durchaus die Möglichkeit, dass etw. geschieht; **struggle against considerable/impossible ~:** mit ziemlich geringen Chancen/völlig chancenlos kämpfen; **by all ~:** bei weitem 3) (balance of advantage) **against [all] the ~:** allen Widrigkeiten zum Trotz 4) (difference) Unterschied, *der;* **make no/little ~ [whether ...]** es ist völlig/ziemlich gleichgültig[, ob ...]; **what's the ~?** was macht das schon? 5) (variance) **be at ~ [with sb./sth.]** sich nicht [mit jmdm./etw.] vertragen; **be at ~ with sb. over sth.** mit jmdm. in etw. (*Dat.*) uneinig sein 6) **~ and ends,** (coll.) **~ and bobs** Kleinigkeiten; (of food) Reste; **~ and sods** (coll.) (things) Krempel, *der* (ugs. abwertend); (persons) Figuren (salopp)

'odds-on
A *adj.* gut ‹*Chance, Aussicht*›; hoch, klar ‹*Favorit*›; **be ~ [favourite] to win/for sth.** klarer *od.* hoher Favorit/Favorit für etw. sein
B *adv.* wahrscheinlich; **it's ~ that he is alive** die Chancen stehen gut, dass er am Leben ist

ode /əʊd/ *n.* Ode, *die* (**to** an + *Akk.*)

odious /ˈəʊdɪəs/ *adj.*, **odiously** /ˈəʊdɪəslɪ/ *adv.* widerwärtig

odium /ˈəʊdɪəm/ *n.* (hatred) Hass, *der;* **be held in ~ by sb.** bei jmdm. verhasst sein

odometer /əˈdɒmɪtə(r)/ *n.* Hodometer, *das;* Wegmesser, *der*

odor *etc.* (*Amer.*) ▸**odour** *etc.*

odoriferous /əʊdəˈrɪfərəs/ *adj.* wohlriechend (geh.); duftend

odorous /ˈəʊdərəs/ *adj.* 1) (fragrant) wohlriechend (geh.); duftend 2) (malodorous) übel riechend; übel ‹*Geruch*›

odour /ˈəʊdə(r)/ *n.* 1) (smell) Geruch, *der;* (fragrance) Duft, *der;* **~ of cats** Katzengeruch, *der; see also* **body odour** 2) (fig.) Note, *die;* **be in/fall** *or* **get into good/bad ~ with sb.** bei jmdm. in gutem/schlechtem Geruch stehen/in guten/schlechten Geruch kommen

odourless /ˈəʊdəlɪs/ *adj.* geruchlos

Odysseus /əˈdɪsjuːs/ *pr. n.* Odysseus (*der*)

odyssey /ˈɒdɪsɪ/ *n.* abenteuerliche Reise; Odyssee, *die* (geh.); **the O~** (Myth.) die Odyssee

OECD *abbr.* = **Organization for Economic Cooperation and Development** OECD, *die*

oedema /ɪˈdiːmə/ *n.* (Med.) Ödem, *das;* Gewebewassersucht, *die*

Oedipus complex /ˈiːdɪpəs kɒmpleks/ *n.* (Psych.) Ödipuskomplex, *der*

o'er /ɔː(r)/ (poet.) ▸**over A, B**

oesophagus /iːˈsɒfəgəs/ *n.*, *pl.* **oesophagi** /iːˈsɒfədʒaɪ/ *or* **~es** (Anat.) Ösophagus, *der* (fachspr.)

oestrogen /ˈiːstrədʒən/ *n.* (Biochem.) Östrogen, *das*

oeuvre /ɜːvr/ *n.* Œuvre, *das* (geh.); Werk, *das*

of /əv, *stressed* ɒv/ *prep.* 1) *indicating belonging, connection, possession* **articles of clothing** Kleidungsstücke; **be a thing of the past** der Vergangenheit (*Dat.*) angehören; **topic of conversation** Gesprächsthema, *das;* **the brother of her father** der Bruder ihres Vaters; **a friend of mine/the vicar's** ein Freund von mir/des Pfarrers; **that dog of yours** Ihr Hund da; **it's no business of theirs** es geht sie nichts an; **where's that pencil of mine?** wo ist mein Bleistift?
2) *indicating starting point* von; **within a mile of the centre** nicht weiter als eine Meile vom Zentrum entfernt; **for upwards of 10 years** seit mehr als 10 Jahren
3) *indicating origin, cause, agency* **have a taste of garlic** nach Knoblauch schmecken; **it was clever of you to do that** es war klug von dir, das zu tun; **the approval of sb.** jmds. Zustimmung; **be of a good family** aus guter Familie sein; **the works of Shakespeare** Shakespeares Werke; **R. T. Smith, of Oxford** R. T. Smith, Oxford; **Lord Morrison of Lambeth** Lord Morrison von Lambeth
4) *indicating material, substance* aus; **a dress of cotton** ein Kleid aus Baumwolle; **be made of ...:** aus ... [hergestellt] sein
5) *indicating closer definition, identity, or contents* **a pound of apples** ein Pfund Äpfel; **a glass of wine** ein Glas Wein; **a painting of the queen** ein Gemälde der Königin; **the city of Chicago** die Stadt Chicago; **the Republic of Ireland** die Republik Irland; **Professor of Chemistry** Professor der Chemie; **the Gospel of St Mark** das Markusevangelium; das Evangelium des Markus; **family of eight** achtköpfige Familie; **increase of 10%** Zuwachs/Erhöhung von zehn Prozent; **Battle of Hastings** Schlacht von *od.* bei Hastings; **University of Oxford** Universität [von] Oxford; **President of the Philippines** Präsident/Präsidentin der Philippinen; **the Queen of Spades** die Pikdame; **the love of God** die Liebe Gottes; **the fifth of January** der fünfte Januar; **your letter of 2 January** Ihr Brief vom 2. Januar; **that fool of a personnel manager** dieser Idiot von Personalleiter; **a fool of a woman** eine törichte Frau; **the worst liar of any man I know** der gemeinste Lügner, den ich kenne; **be of value/interest** to von Nutzen/von Interesse *od.* interessant sein für; **the whole of ...:** der/die/das ganze ...; **tales of adventure** Abenteuergeschichten
6) *indicating concern, reference, respect* **do not speak of such things** sprich nicht von solchen Dingen; **inform sb. of sth.** jmdn. über etw. (*Akk.*) informieren; **well, what of it?** (asked as reply) na und?
7) *indicating objective relation* **love of virtue** Tugendliebe, *die;* **his love of his father** seine Liebe zu seinem Vater
8) *indicating description, quality, condition* **a frown of disapproval** ein missbilligendes Stirnrunzeln; **person of extreme views** Mensch mit extremen Ansichten; **work of authority** maßgebendes Werk; **a boy of 14 years** ein vierzehnjähriger *od.* ein 14 Jahre alter Junge; **a city of wide boulevards** eine Stadt mit breiten Alleen
9) *indicating partition, classification, inclusion, selection* von; **of these, three ...:** drei von ihnen ...; (inanimate) drei davon; **the five of us** wir fünf; **the five of us went there** wir sind zu fünft hingegangen; **some/five of us** einige/fünf von uns; **there are five of us waiting to see the doctor** wir sind fünf, die auf den Doktor warten; **the most dangerous of enemies** ein sehr gefährlicher Feind; **be too much of a gentleman to do sth.** zu sehr Gentleman sein, um etw. zu tun; **he of all men** (most unsuitably) ausgerechnet er; (especially) gerade er; **of all the impudence!** das ist doch die Höhe!; **here of all places** ausgerechnet hier; **on this night of nights** in solch einer herrlichen Nacht; **of an evening** abends; des Abends; **of an evening in June** an einem Juniabend
10) (Amer.: before the hour of) **a quarter of two** Viertel vor zwei
11) (arch.: by) von; **beloved of all** von allen geliebt

off /ɒf/
A *adv.* 1) (away, at or to a distance) **be a few miles ~:** wenige Meilen entfernt sein; **the lake is not far ~:** der See ist nicht weit [weg *od.* entfernt]; **Christmas is not far ~:** es ist nicht mehr lang bis Weihnachten; **some way ~:** in einiger Entfernung; **where are you ~ to?** wohin gehst du?; **I must be ~:** ich muss fort *od.* weg *od.* los; **I'm ~ now** ich gehe jetzt; **~ with you!** geh/geht!; los jetzt!; **~ with his head!** schlagt ihm den Kopf ab!; **~ we go!** (we are starting) los *od.* ab gehts!; (let us start) gehen/fahren wir!; **they're ~!** sie sind gestartet!; *see also* **make off**; **put off**; **straight off**
2) (not on or attached or supported) **get the lid ~:** den Deckel abbekommen
3) (not in good condition) mitgenommen; **the meat** *etc.* **is ~:** das Fleisch *usw.* ist schlecht [geworden]; **be a bit ~** (Brit. fig.) ein starkes Stück sein (ugs.)
4) **be ~** (switched or turned ~) ‹*Wasser, Gas, Strom:*› abgestellt sein; **the light/radio** *etc.* **is ~:** das Licht/Radio *usw.* ist aus; **put the light ~:** das Licht ausmachen; **leave the bathroom tap ~:** den Hahn im Badezimmer zulassen; **is the gas tap ~?** ist der Gashahn zu?; **neither the water nor the electricity was ~:** weder Wasser noch Strom waren abgestellt
5) **be ~** (cancelled) abgesagt sein; ‹*Verlobung:*› [auf]gelöst sein; **the strike is ~:** der Streik ist abgeblasen (ugs.); **is Sunday's picnic ~?** fällt das Picknick am Sonntag aus?; **~ and on** immer mal wieder (ugs.)
6) (not at work) frei; **on my day ~:** an meinem freien Tag; **take/get/have a week** *etc.* **~:** eine Woche *usw.* Urlaub nehmen/bekommen/haben; **be given a day ~ from school** einen Tag schulfrei haben; **be ~ sick** wegen Krankheit fehlen
7) (no longer available) **soup** *etc.* **is ~:** es gibt keine Suppe *usw.* mehr
8) (situated as regards money etc.) **he is badly** *etc.* **~:** er ist schlecht *usw.* gestellt; ihm geht es [finanziell] schlecht *usw.*; **we'd be better ~ without him** ohne ihn wären wir besser dran; **there are many people worse ~ than you** vielen geht es schlechter als dir; **he left her comfortably ~:** er hinterließ ihr genug, um gut zu leben; **how are you ~ for food?** wie viel Essbares hast du noch?; **be badly ~ for sth.** mit etw. knapp sein; *see also* **well off**
9) (Theatre) **take place ~:** hinter der Bühne stattfinden; *see also* **noise A 2**
B *prep.* 1) (from) von; **take a little ~ the price** ein bisschen vom Preis nachlassen; **cut a couple of slices ~ the loaf** einige Scheiben Brot abschneiden; **be a few inches ~ the finish** ein paar Zentimeter vom Ziel entfernt sein; **be ~ school/work** in der Schule/am Arbeitsplatz fehlen
2) (diverging from) **get ~ the subject, talk ~ the point** [vom Thema] abschweifen; **be ~ the point** nicht zur Sache gehören
3) (having lost interest in) **be ~ sth.** etw. leid sein *od.* haben (ugs.); **be ~ one's food** keinen Appetit haben; **be quite ~ sth.** von etw. vollkommen abgekommen sein
4) (no longer obliged to use) **be ~ drugs** vom Rauschgift losgekommen sein; clean sein (ugs.); **be ~ one's diet** seine Diät abgesetzt haben; **be ~ the tablets** ohne Tabletten auskommen
5) (leading from, not far from) **just ~ the square** ganz in der Nähe des Platzes; **a street ~ the main road** eine Straße, die von der Hauptstraße abgeht; **take a turning ~ the main road** von der Hauptstraße abbiegen
6) (to seaward of) vor (+ *Dat.*)
7) (Golf) **play ~ three** mit Vorgabe drei spielen. *See also* **offside**
C *adj.* 1) **the ~ side** (Brit.) (when travelling on the left/right) die rechte/linke Seite
2) (Cricket) ‹*Seite, Torstab:*› links vom Werfer, (if batsman is left-handed) rechts vom Werfer; **~ drive** Treibschlag nach rechts; (by left-handed batsman) Treibschlag nach links; **~ side** (Cricket) *Spielfeldhälfte rechts vom rechtshändigen bzw. links vom linkshändigen Schlagmann*
D *n.* (start of race) Start, *der*

offal /ˈɒfl/ *n.*, *no pl.* 1) (parts of animal's carcass) Innereien *Pl.* 2) (carrion) Aas, *das* 3) (refuse) Abfall, *der* 4) (fig.: dregs, scum) Abschaum, *der*

off: ~beat A *n.* (Mus.) unbetonter Taktteil; Off-Beat, *der* (fachspr.); B *adj.* 1) (Mus.) Off-Beat-; 2) (fig.: eccentric) unkonventionell ‹*Mensch, Lebensweise*›; außergewöhnlich ‹*Vorlesung, Kursus*›; **~'centre** A *adj.* nicht zentriert; B *adv.* nicht [genau] in der Mitte; **~ chance** ▸**chance A 3**; **~ 'colour** *adj.* 1) (not in good health) unwohl; **be** *or* **feel ~ colour** sich unwohl *od.* schlecht fühlen; 2) (Amer.: somewhat indecent) schlüpfrig; **~cut** *n.* Rest, *der;* **~ day** *n.* schlechter Tag; **~-duty** *attrib. adj.* Freizeit-; dienstfrei ‹*Zeit*›; ‹*Polizist usw.,*› der dienstfrei hat

off-Broadway

Off-Broadway ist eine Bezeichnung für das nicht kommerzielle amerikanische Theater. Diese experimentelle Gegenrichtung mit kleineren Truppen und Bühnen gewann nach 1952 an Bedeutung. Viele junge Intendanten sind nicht an kommerziellen Aufführungen, wie sie an den Bühnen am New Yorker Broadway gespielt werden, interessiert, und ihre Inszenierungen finden in alten Lagerhäusern - in *lofts* - in SoHo statt, einem Stadtteil von Manhattan, in dem viele Künstler leben.

offence /əˈfens/ *n.* (Brit.) 1 (hurting of sb.'s feelings) Kränkung, *die;* **I meant** *or* **intended no ~:** ich wollte Sie/ihn *usw.* nicht kränken; **your behaviour caused [great] ~:** Ihr Benehmen war [sehr] kränkend *od.* verletzend 2 (annoyance) **give ~:** Missfallen erregen; **take ~:** beleidigt *od.* verärgert sein; **don't take ~, but ...:** nimm es mir nicht übel, aber ...; **no ~** (coll.) nichts für ungut; **no ~ to you, but ...** (coll.) nichts gegen dich, aber ... (ugs.) 3 (transgression) Verstoß, *der;* (crime) Delikt, *das;* Straftat, *die;* **an ~ against good taste** eine Beleidigung des guten Geschmacks; **criminal/petty ~:** strafbare Handlung/geringfügiges Vergehen 4 (attacking) Angriff, *der*

offend /əˈfend/
A *v.i.* verstoßen (**against** gegen)
B *v.t.* **~ sb.** bei jmdm. Anstoß erregen; (hurt feelings of) jmdn. kränken; **she was ~ed with him** sie war ihm böse; **~ the eye** das Auge beleidigen; **her delicacy was ~ed** ihr Zartgefühl war verletzt; *abs.* **a refusal often ~s** eine Ablehnung wird oft als Kränkung empfunden

offender /əˈfendə(r)/ *n.* (against law) Straffällige, *der/die;* Täter, *der*/Täterin, *die;* (against rule) Zuwiderhandelnde, *der/die; see also* **first offender**

offending /əˈfendɪŋ/ *attrib. adj.* 1 (that outrages) anstößig; Anstoß erregend; **he removed the ~ object** er beseitigte den Stein des Anstoßes 2 (that transgresses) zuwiderhandelnd; **there are penalties for ~ persons** Zuwiderhandlungen werden bestraft

offense (Amer.) ▸ **offence**

offensive /əˈfensɪv/
A *adj.* 1 (aggressive) offensiv; Angriffs‹*waffe, -krieg*› 2 (giving offence, insulting) ungehörig; (indecent) anstößig; **~ language** Beschimpfungen *Pl.* 3 (repulsive) widerlich; **be ~ to sb.** jmdm. zuwider sein; auf jmdn. abstoßend wirken
B *n.* 1 (attitude of assailant) offensive Haltung; **take the** *or* **go on the ~:** in die *od.* zur Offensive übergehen; **be on the ~:** aggressiv sein 2 (attack) Offensive, *die;* Angriff, *der* 3 (fig.: forceful action) Offensive, *die*

offensively /əˈfensɪvlɪ/ *adv.* 1 (aggressively) offensiv 2 (insultingly) auf beleidigende Weise; (indecently) unverschämt 3 (repulsively) widerlich; abstoßend

offer /ˈɒfə(r)/
A *v.t.* 1 anbieten; vorbringen ‹*Entschuldigung*›; bieten ‹*Chance*›; aussprechen ‹*Beileid*›; sagen ‹*Meinung*›; unterbreiten, machen ‹*Vorschläge*›; bieten, spenden ‹*Schatten*›; **have something to ~:** etwas zu bieten haben; **the job ~s good prospects** der Arbeitsplatz hat Zukunft 2 (present to deity etc.) **~ [up]** opfern; **~ up a sacrifice** ein Opfer darbringen (geh.); **~ prayers for the dead** für die Toten beten 3 (have for sale) anbieten 4 (show readiness for) **~ resistance** Widerstand leisten; **~ violence** gewalttätig werden; **~ peace** für den Frieden eintreten; **~ to do sth.** anbieten, etw. zu tun; **~ to help** seine Hilfe anbieten 5 (present to sight or notice) bieten 6 (Sch., Univ.) belegen ‹*Fach*›
B *v.i.* ‹*Gelegenheit, Chance:*› sich bieten
C *n.* 1 Angebot, *das;* (in auction) Gebot, *das;* **all ~s of help** alle Hilfeangebote; **[have/be] on ~:** im Angebot [haben/sein] 2 (marriage proposal) Antrag, *der*

offering /ˈɒfərɪŋ/ *n.* 1 *no pl.* (act) Anbieten, *das;* (to deity) Opfern, *das* 2 (thing) Angebot, *das;* (to a deity) Opfer, *das;* **the latest ~ from the publishers** (joc.) was die Verleger als Neuestes anbieten

offertory /ˈɒfətərɪ/ *n.* (Eccl.) 1 (part of Mass) Offertorium, *das* 2 (collection of money) Kollekte, *die*

off: ~'hand A *adv.* 1 (without preparation) auf Anhieb, aus der Hand (ugs.) ‹*sagen, wissen*›; spontan ‹*beschließen, entscheiden*›; 2 (casually) leichthin; **B** *adj.* 1 (without preparation) impulsiv; spontan; 2 (casual) beiläufig; **be ~hand with sb.** zu jmdm. kurz angebunden sein; **he was very ~hand about the whole business** er war, was die ganze Geschichte betrifft, sehr kurz angebunden; **~handed** /ɒfˈhændɪd/ ▸ **~hand B 2**

office /ˈɒfɪs/ *n.* 1 Büro, *das;* **goods ~:** Güterabfertigung, *die* 2 (branch of organization) Zweigstelle, *die;* Geschäftsstelle, *die* 3 (position with duties) Amt, *das;* **be in/out of ~:** im/nicht mehr im Amt sein; ‹*Partei:*› an der/nicht mehr an der Regierung sein; **resign ~:** sein Amt niederlegen; **hold ~:** amtieren 4 (government department) **Home O~** (Brit.) ≈ Innenministerium, *das;* **the Passport O~:** das Passamt 5 **the usual ~s** (Brit.: of house) ≈ Küche, Bad, WC *usw.* 6 (Eccl.) (service) Gottesdienst, *der;* (mass) Messe, *die* (kath. Kirche); **O~ for Baptism** Taufbekenntnis *od.* -versprechen, *das;* **O~ for the Dead** Trauergottesdienst, *der;* Totenmesse, *die* (kath. Kirche) 7 **the Holy O~** (RC Ch.) das Heilige Officium 8 (kindness) **[good] ~s** Hilfe, *die;* Unterstützung, *die;* **use one's good ~s to help sb.** jmdm. mit Rat und Tat zur Seite stehen 9 (Amer.: consulting-room) Büro, *das;* (of lawyer) Kanzlei, *die;* Büro, *das;* (of physician) Sprechzimmer, *das*

office: ~-bearer *n.* Amtsinhaber, *der*/-inhaberin, *die;* **~ block** *n.* Bürogebäude, *das;* **~ boy** *n.* Bürogehilfe, *der;* **~ equipment** *n., no pl.* Bürogeräte *Pl.;* **~ girl** *n.* Bürogehilfin, *die;* **~ hours** *n. pl.* Dienststunden *Pl.;* Dienstzeit, *die;* **after ~ hours** nach Dienstschluss; **~ job** *n.* Bürotätigkeit, *die;* Bürojob, *der* (ugs.); **~ 'junior** *n.* Bürogehilfe, *der*/-gehilfin, *die;* **~ 'manager** *n.* ▸ **p. 1260** Büroleiter, *der*/-leiterin, *die;* **~ 'party** *n.* Bürofeier, *die*

officer /ˈɒfɪsə(r)/ *n.* 1 (Army etc.) Offizier, *der;* **~ of the day** Offizier vom Dienst 2 (holder of office) Beamte, *der*/Beamtin, *die;* **~ of arms** (Her.) Mitglied des Heroldskollegiums 3 (of club etc.) Funktionär, *der*/Funktionärin, *die* 4 ▸ **p. 1634** (constable) Polizeibeamte, *der*/-beamtin, *die;* **yes, ~:** jawohl, Herr Wachtmeister/Frau Wachtmeisterin 5 ▸ **p. 1260** (bailiff) **[sheriff's] ~:** Vollstreckungsbeamte, *der*/-beamtin, *die* 6 (member of honorary Order) **O~ of the Order of the British Empire** Träger des britischen Verdienstordens; **O~ of the Legion of Honour** Ritter der Ehrenlegion

office: ~ space *n., no pl.* Bürofläche, *die;* **~ space is expensive** Büroflächen sind teuer; **~ staff** *n., no pl.* Büropersonal, *das;* **~ supplies** *n. pl.* Büromaterial, *das;* **~ technology** *n., no pl.* Bürotechnik, *die;* **~ worker** *n.* ▸ **p. 1260** Büroangestellte, *der/die*

official /əˈfɪʃl/
A *adj.* 1 Amts‹*pflicht, -robe, -person*› 2 (derived from authority, formal) offiziell; amtlich ‹*Verlautbarung*›; regulär ‹*Streik*›; **he is here on ~ business** er ist dienstlich hier; **~ secret** Staatsgeheimnis, *das;* **O~ Secrets Act** (Brit.) Gesetz über Landesverrat und Gefährdung der äußeren Sicherheit; **is it ~ yet?** (coll.) ist das schon amtlich?
B *n.* Beamte, *der*/Beamtin, *die;* (party, union, or sports ~) Funktionär, *der*/Funktionärin, *die*

officialdom /əˈfɪʃldəm/ *n., no pl., no art.* Beamtentum, *das;* Bürokratie, *die*

officialese /əfɪʃəˈliːz/ *n., no pl.* (derog.) Behördensprache, *die;* (German) Amtsdeutsch, *das*

officially /əˈfɪʃəlɪ/ *adv.* offiziell

officiate /əˈfɪʃɪeɪt/ *v.i.* 1 **~ as ...:** fungieren als ...; **she ~d as hostess** sie übernahm die Rolle der Gastgeberin 2 (perform religious ceremony) **~ at the service** den Gottesdienst abhalten; **~ at a wedding** eine Trauung vornehmen

officious /əˈfɪʃəs/ *adj.*, **officiously** /əˈfɪʃəslɪ/ *adv.* übereifrig

officiousness /əˈfɪʃəsnɪs/ *n., no pl.* Übereifer, *der*

offing /ˈɒfɪŋ/ *n.* **be in the ~** (fig.) bevorstehen; ‹*Gewitter:*› aufziehen

off: ~'key A *adj.* verstimmt; (fig.: incongruous) falsch; **B** *adv.* falsch ‹*singen, spielen*›; **~-licence** *n.* (Brit.) 1 (premises) ≈ Wein- und Spirituosenladen, *der;* 2 (licence) Konzession für den Verkauf alkoholischer Getränke über die Straße; **~line** (Computing) **A** /ˈ-ˈ-/ *adj.* Offline‹*gerät, -betrieb*›; **B** /-ˈ-/ *adv.* offline; **~load** *v.t.* abladen; **~load sth. on to sb.** (fig.: get rid of) etw. bei jmdm. loswerden; **~-'message A** *adj.* von der Parteilinie abweichend ‹*Antwort, Aussage*›; **be ~-message** von der Parteilinie abweichen; **B** *adv.* **go ~-message** von der Parteilinie abweichen; **~-peak** *attrib. adj.* **during ~-peak hours** außerhalb der Spitzenlastzeiten; (of traffic) außerhalb der Stoßzeiten; **at ~-peak times** (Telev.) außerhalb der Haupteinschaltzeit; **~-peak power** *or* **electricity** Nachtstrom, *der;* **~-peak storage heating** Nachtspeicherheizung, *die;* **~-piste A** *adj.* **~-piste skiing/slope** Skilaufen/Hang außerhalb der [präparierten] Pisten; **~-piste skiers** Skiläufer, die außerhalb der [präparierten] Pisten laufen. **B** *adv.* außerhalb der [präparierten] [Ski]pisten; **~print** *n.* Sonderdruck, *der;* **~-putting** /ˈɒfpʊtɪŋ/ *adj.* (Brit.) abstoßend ‹*Gesicht, Äußeres, Weg*›; abschreckend ‹*Umfang*›; deprimierend ‹*Anblick*›; **~-ramp** *n.* (Amer.) Abfahrt, *die;* **~-road** *attrib. adj.* Gelände-, Offroad‹*fahrzeug, -fahrrad, -wagen, -fahrt, -einsatz*›; **~-road driving** Fahren im Gelände; **~-roader** /ɒfˈrəʊdə(r)/ *n.* 1 (driver) Geländewagenfahrer, *der*;/-fahrerin, *die;* 2 (vehicle) Geländewagen, *der;* **~ season** *n.* Nebensaison, *die;* **~set A** *n.* 1 (compensation) Ausgleich, *der;* **act as an ~set to sth., be an ~set for sth.** etw. ausgleichen *od.* aufwiegen; 2 (Printing: unwanted transfer of ink) Schmutzen, *das;* Abliegen, *das;* 3 **~set [process]** (Printing) Offsetdruck, *der;* 4 (Archit.) Vorsprung, *der;* **B** /ˈ--, -ˈ-/ *v.t., forms as* **set** 1 (counterbalance) ausgleichen; 2 (place out of line) versetzen; 3 (Printing) im Offsetverfahren drucken; **~shoot** *n.* 1 (of plant) Spross, *der;* (of mountain range) Ausläufer, *der;* 2 (fig.: descendant) Spross, *der* (geh.); Nachkomme, *der;* 3 (derivative) Ableger, *der* (fig.); (of religion, philosophy, etc.) Nebenströmung, *die;* **~shore** *adj.* 1 (situated at sea) küstennah; offshore (Energiewirtsch.); **~shore island** küstennahe Insel; 2 (made or registered abroad) Auslands-; **~shore order** Offshoreauftrag, *der;* 3 (blowing seawards) ablandig (Seemannsspr.); **~'side** *adj.* (Sport) Abseits-; **be ~side** abseits *od.* im Abseits sein; **~side trap** Abseitsfalle, *die;* **~spring** *n., pl. same* (progeny) (human) Nachkommenschaft, *die;* (of animal) Junge; **~-'stage A** *adj.* in den Kulissen *nachgestellt;* **B** *adv.* in den Kulissen; **go ~-stage** abgehen; **~-street** *adj.* außerhalb des Straßenbereiches *nachgestellt;* **~-street parking** Stellplatz, *der;* (for several cars) Stellplätze; **~-the-cuff** *adj.* (coll.) aus dem Stegreif; Stegreif‹*kommentar, -analyse usw.*›; **~-the-peg** *attrib. adj.* Konfektions-; von der Stange *nachgestellt;* **~-the-shoulder** *attrib. adj.* schulterfrei ‹*Kleid, T-Shirt*›; **~-the-wall** *attrib. adj.* (esp. Amer. coll.) ausgeflippt (ugs.); **~ time** *n.* ruhige Zeit; **~-'white** *adj.* gebrochen weiß; (yellowish) vergilbt; **~ year** *n.* (Amer.) Wahljahr, in dem kein Präsident gewählt wird

Ofgas /ˈɒfgæs/ *abbr.* (Brit.) = **Office of Gas Supply**

OFSTED, Ofsted /ˈɒfsted/ *abbr.* (Brit. Educ.) = **Office for Standards in Education**

oft /ɒft/ *adv.* (arch./literary) oft; **the ~-told tales** die immer wieder erzählten Geschichten; **~-repeated/-recurring** häufig wiederholt/wiederkehrend; **many a time and ~:** oft genug

Oftel /ˈɒftel/ *abbr.* (Brit.) = **Office of Telecommunications**

often /ˈɒfn, ˈɒftn/ *adv.* oft; **more ~:** häufiger; **do sth. as ~ as not** etw. genauso oft tun wie man es nicht tut; **more ~ than not** meistens; **every so ~:** gelegentlich; hin und wieder; **once too ~:** einmal zu viel

O

Ofwat /ˈɒfwɒt/ *abbr.* (Brit.) **= Office of Water Services**

ogee /ˈəʊdʒiː, əʊˈdʒiː/
A *n.* Karnies, *das* (Archit.); (line) S-Kurve, *die*
B *adj.* S-förmig; **~ arch** (Archit.) Eselsrücken, *der*

ogle /ˈəʊgl/
A *v.i.* gaffen (ugs. abwertend); **~ at sb.** jmdn. angaffen (ugs. abwertend)
B *v.t.* **~ sb.** jmdn. angaffen (ugs. abwertend)

ogre /ˈəʊgə(r)/ *n.* **1** (giant) Oger, *der;* [menschenfressender] Riese **2** (terrifying person) Ungeheuer, *das;* (terrifying thing) Schreckbild, *das*

oh[1] /əʊ/ *int.* oh; *expr. pain* au; **ˈoh no [you don't]!** auf keinen Fall!; **oh ˈno!** oh nein!; oje!; **oh ˈwell** na ja (ugs.); tja (ugs.); **ˈoh yes** oh ja; **oh ˈyes?** ach ja?; **oh, ˈhim/ˈthat!** ach, der/das!; *see also* **boy B**

oh[2] *n.* (zero) Null, *die*

ohm /əʊm/ *n.* (Electr.) Ohm, *das;* **Ohm's law** das ohmsche Gesetz

OHMS *abbr.* **= on Her/His Majesty's service ▸service A 13**

oho /əʊˈhəʊ/ *int.* he

OHP *abbr.* **= overhead projector**

ˈoh-so- *pref.* (coll. derog.) ach so ‹*schlau, schick*›

OIEO *abbr.* (Brit.) **= offers in excess of**

oil /ɔɪl/
A *n.* **1** Öl, *das;* **burn the midnight ~** (fig.) bis spät in die Nacht arbeiten; **strike ~** (lit.) auf Öl stoßen; (fig.) das große Los ziehen; *see also* **mineral oil**; **pour A 1 2** *in pl.* (paints) Ölfarben; **paint in ~s** in Öl malen **3** (coll.: picture) Ölbild, *das*
B *v.t.* **1** (apply ~ to) ölen; **~ the wheels** (fig.) den Karren schmieren **2** (supply with ~) [mit Öl] betanken ‹*Schiff usw.*› **3** (impregnate with ~) mit Öl behandeln; **~ed silk** Ölseide, *die* **4** **well ~ed** (fig. coll.: drunk) abgefüllt

oil: ~-burner *n.* **1** (steamship/locomotive) Dampfschiff/Lokomotive mit Ölfeuerung; **2** (device) Ölbrenner, *der;* **~-burning** *adj.* ölbetrieben; ölgeheizt ‹*Ofen*›; ölgefeuert ‹*Lokomotive, Schiff*›; Ölfeuerungs‹*anlage, -kessel*›; Öl‹*ofen, -heizung, -lampe*›; **~cake** *n., no pl.* (Agric.) Ölkuchen, *der;* **~can** *n.* Ölkanne, *die;* **~ change** *n.* (Motor Veh.) Ölwechsel, *der;* **~cloth** *n.* **1** *no pl.* (waterproofed fabric) Öltuch, *das;* **2** (covering for tables or shelves) Wachstuch, *das;* Öltuch, *das;* (covering for floor) ≈ Linoleum, *das;* **~ colour** *n., usu. in pl.* Ölfarbe, *die;* **[painted] in ~ colours** in Öl [gemalt]; **~ drum** *n.* Ölfass, *das;* **~field** *n.* Ölfeld, *das;* **~-fired** *adj.* ölgefeuert; ölbetrieben ‹*Zentralheizung*›; **~ gauge** *n.* (Mech. Engin.) Ölstandsanzeiger, *der;* **~ heater** *n.* Ölofen, *der;* **~ industry** *n.* Mineralölindustrie, *die;* **~ lamp** *n.* Öllampe, *die;* Petroleumlampe, *die;* **~ level** *n.* Ölstand, *der;* **~man** *n.* **1** (seller of ~) Ölhändler, *der*/-händlerin, *die;* **2** (industrialist) Unternehmer in der Ölbranche; (worker) Ölarbeiter, *der;* **~ paint ▸oil colour**; **~ painting** *n.* **1** (activity) Ölmalerei, *die;* **2** (picture) Ölgemälde, *das;* **he/she is no ~ painting** (coll.) er/sie ist keine [strahlende] Schönheit; **~ platform** *n.* Ölplattform, *die;* **~ pollution** *n., no pl.* Ölverschmutzung, *die;* **~ pressure** *n.* Öldruck, *der;* **~-producing** *attrib. adj.* Öl‹*pflanze, -saat, -schiefer, -sand, -schicht*›; [Erd]öl fördernd ‹*Land*›; **~ rag** *n.* Öllappen, *der;* **~ refinery** *n.* [Erd]ölraffinerie, *die;* **~-ˈrich** *adj.* ölreich ‹*Land, Gebiet*›; **~ rig ▸rig**[1] **A 2**; **~ shale** *n.* (Geol.) Ölschiefer, *der;* **~skin** *n.* **1** (material) Öltuch, *das; attrib.* aus Öltuch *nachgestellt;* **~skin jacket** Öljacke, *die;* **2** (garment) **put on ~skins/an ~skin** Ölzeug anziehen; **~ slick ▸slick B**; **~-soluble** *adj.* öllöslich; **~ spill** *n.* Ölaustritt, *der;* Ölunfall, *der;* **~ stove** *n.* Ölofen, *der;* **~ tanker** *n.* Öltanker, *der;* **~ well** *n.* Ölquelle, *die*

oily /ˈɔɪlɪ/ *adj.* **1** ölig ‹*Oberfläche, Hände, Lappen, Flüssigkeit, Geschmack*›; Öl‹*lache, -fleck*›; ölverschmiert ‹*Gesicht, Hände*›; verölt ‹*Motor*›; (containing oil) viel Öl enthaltend ‹*Soße*›; fettig ‹*Haut, Haar*›; **the food is very ~:** das Essen schwimmt in Öl (ugs.) **2** (fig.: unctuous, fawning) schmierig (abwertend) ‹*Kerl, Art*›; ölig ‹*Lächeln, Stimme*›

ointment /ˈɔɪntmənt/ *n.* Salbe, *die; see also* **fly**[1] **1**

OIRO *abbr.* (Brit.) **= offers in the region of** ≈ VHB

OK /əʊˈkeɪ/ (coll.)
A *adj.* in Ordnung; okay (ugs.); **[it's] OK by me** mir ist es recht
B *adv.* gut; **be doing OK** seine Sache gut machen
C *int.* okay (ugs.); **OK?** [ist das] klar?; okay?
D *n.* Zustimmung, *die;* Okay, *das* (ugs.)
E *v.t.* (approve) zustimmen (+ *Dat.*); sein Okay geben (+ *Dat.*) (ugs.); **be OK'd by sb.** von jmdm. das Okay bekommen (ugs.)

okay /əʊˈkeɪ/ **▸OK**

okey-doke /əʊkɪˈdəʊk/ (coll.), **okey-dokey** /əʊkɪˈdəʊkɪ/ (coll.) **▸OK C**

OLAF *abbr.* **= Office Européen de Lutte Anti-Fraud** OLAF

old /əʊld/
A *adj.* **1** **▸❶ p. 894** alt; **[not] be ~ enough to do sth.** [noch nicht] alt genug sein, um etw. zu tun; **he is ~ enough to know better** aus diesem Alter ist er heraus; **he/she is ~ enough to be your father/mother** er/sie könnte dein Vater/deine Mutter sein; **be/get too ~ for doing sth.** *or* **to do sth.** zu alt sein/langsam zu alt sein, um etw. zu tun; **be ~ beyond one's years** seinem Alter voraus sein; **if I live to be that ~:** wenn ich je so alt werde; **grow ~ [gracefully]** [mit Würde] alt werden; **that dress/that new hairstyle makes you look ~:** dieses Kleid/diese neue Frisur macht dich alt; **make/get/be/seem ~ before one's time** frühzeitig altern lassen/altern/gealtert sein/gealtert wirken; **be [more than] 30 years ~:** [über] 30 Jahre alt sein; **at ten years ~:** im Alter von 10 Jahren; mit 10 Jahren; *see also* **buffer**[2]; **fogy**; **fool**[1] **A 1**; **shoulder A 2**
2 (experienced) **be an ~ hand** *or* (Brit.) **stager** ein alter Hase sein (ugs.); **an ~ offender** ein mehrfach Vorbestrafter; *see also* **campaigner 2**; **contemptible**; **lag**[2]; **retainer 1**; **salt A 4**
3 (long in use, matured with keeping, long familiar) alt; **~ iron** Alteisen, *das;* **be still working for one's** *or* **the same ~ firm** noch immer in seiner alten *od.* derselben Firma arbeiten; **you see the same ~ people/faces wherever you go** man sieht immer dieselben Leute/Gesichter, wohin man auch geht; **keep quarrelling over the same ~ thing** immer wieder über dasselbe leidige Thema streiten; **O~ Pals Act** (Brit. joc.) ≈ Vitamin B (ugs. scherzh.); **the ~ firm** (fig. coll.) das altbewährte Team; **of the ~ school** (fig.) der alten Schule; **that's an ˈ~ one!** (joke) der ist [doch] alt!; (excuse) das kennen wir schon!; **[as] ~ as the hills** uralt; **that joke is [as] ~ as the hills** dieser Witz hat so einen Bart (ugs.); **be as ~ as time** seit Urzeiten bestehen; *see also* **brigade 1**; **score A 6**; **story**[1] **1**; **world 4**
4 *in playful or friendly mention* alt (ugs.); **you lucky ~ so-and-so!** du bist vielleicht ein alter Glückspilz!; **I saw ~ George today** ich habe heute unsern Freund George getroffen; **I pulled out the ~ cigarette lighter** ich holte mein Feuerzeug raus; **~ chap/fellow/son** alter Junge (fam.); **~ bean/stick/thing** (coll.) altes Haus (ugs. scherzh.); **[such] a dear ~ thing** [so] ein lieber Mensch; **O~ Bill** (Brit. coll.) (police force) die Polente (salopp); (policeman) Polyp, *der* (salopp); **O~ Harry** *or* **Nick** der Teufel; der Leibhaftige (verhüll.); **good/dear ~ Harry/London** (coll.) der gute alte Harry/das gute alte London; **that car needs a good ~ clean** *or* **wash** (coll.) das Auto muss einmal ordentlich gewaschen werden; **have a fine** *or* **good ~ time** (coll.) sich köstlich amüsieren; **a fair ~ wind** (coll.) ein ganz schöner Wind; **poor ~ Jim/my poor ~ arm** armer Jim/mein armer Arm (ugs.); **there was little ~ me, not knowing what to do** (Amer.) da war ich nun und wusste nicht, was ich tun sollte; **your silly** *or* **stupid ~ camera** deine blöde (ugs.) Kamera; **you silly ~ thing** du dummer Kerl/(woman) dummes Ding (ugs.); **a load of ~ rubbish** (coll.) nichts als blanker Unsinn; **any ~ thing** (coll.) irgendwas (ugs.); irgendetwas; **any ~ how** (coll.) irgendwie; **he just pulls his hat on any ~ how** er setzt sich den Hut auf, wies grad kommt (ugs.); **any ~ place** *or* **where** (coll.) irgendwo; **any ~ place will do for me** mir ist alles *od.* jeder Ort recht; **any ~ time** (coll.) jederzeit; **any ~ piece of paper** (coll.) irgendein Blatt Papier; *see also* **high A 14**
5 (belonging to past times) alt; **in the ~ days** früher; *see also* **bad A 1**; **good A 4, 8**
6 (former) alt ‹*Wohnung, Firma, Arbeit, Name*›; **at ˈmy ~ school** in meiner Schule; **~ school tie** *Krawatte mit den Farben der Public School; (fig.) Begünstigung von Absolventen der Public Schools;* ≈ Vitamin B (ugs. scherzh.); **the ~ year** das alte Jahr; *see also* **flame A 3**
7 (Ling.) alt‹*englisch, -lateinisch*›
B *n.* **1** **the ~** *constr. as pl.* (old people) alte Menschen; *constr. as sing.* (old things) Altes; das Alte; **young and ~, ~ and young** Jung und Alt; Alt und Jung
2 **the customs/knights of ~:** die Sitten/Ritter früherer Zeiten; die alten Sitten/Ritter; **in [the] days of ~:** in [den] alten Zeiten; **of ~** (formerly) einst; (since the old days) seit jeher; **I know him of ~:** ich kenne ihn von früher; **as of ~:** wie eh und je; wie seit jeher; **from of ~:** von alters her (geh.)

old: ~ ˈage *n., no pl.* [fortgeschrittenes] Alter; **it must be the effect of ~ age** das muss das Alter bewirken; **die of ~ age** an Altersschwäche sterben; **in ~ age** im [fortgeschrittenen] Alter; **in my** *etc.* **~ age** auf meine *usw.* alten Tage; **you've become quite sensible in your ~ age** (joc.) du bist ja doch noch ein ganz vernünftiger Mensch geworden; **live to a ripe ~ age/to the ripe ~ age of ...** (coll.) ein hohes Alter/das hohe Alter von ... erreichen; **~-age** *attrib. adj.* Alters‹*rente, -ruhegeld, -versicherung*›; **~-age pensioner** Rentner, *der*/Rentnerin, *die;* **Old ˈBailey ▸bailey**; **~ boy** *n.* **1** ehemaliger Schüler; Ehemalige, *der;* **old boys' reunion** Ehemaligentreffen, *das;* **2** (coll.: elderly man or male animal) alter Knabe (ugs.); **3** *as voc.* alter Junge *od.* Knabe (ugs.); Alter (ugs.); **~ boy network** *n.: Filzokratie (ugs.) der Absolventen britischer Eliteschulen und -universitäten;* **~ ˈclothes** *n. pl.* (worn, shabby clothes) alte Kleidung *od.* (ugs.) Klamotten; (discarded clothes) getragene Kleidung *od.* Kleider; Altkleider *Pl.;* **~ ˈcountry** *n.* **the ~ country** das Heimatland; die Heimat; **~ ˈdear** *n.* (woman) ältere Frau; (iron.) Alte, *die* (ugs.)

olden /ˈəʊldn/ *adj.* (literary) alt; **in [the] ~ days** *or* **times** in alten Zeiten; **people** *etc.* **of ~ times** Menschen *usw.* früherer Zeiten

Old ˈEnglish
A *n.* (Ling.) **▸English B 1**
B *adj.* altenglisch; **~ marmalade** englische Marmelade nach altem Rezept; *see also* **sheepdog**

old-esˈtablished *adj.* alt ‹*Tradition, Brauch*›; alteingesessen ‹*Firma, Geschäft, Familie*›

olde-worlde /əʊldɪˈwɜːldɪ/ *adj.* (coll. joc.) altertümlich

old: ~-fashioned /əʊldˈfæʃnd/ **A** *adj.* altmodisch; ‹*Weihnachtsfest*› nach altem Brauch; **an ~-fashioned look** ein missbilligender Blick; **B** *n.* (Amer.) Old Fashioned, *der;* **~ ˈfolk's home ▸old people's home**; **Old ˈFrench** (Ling.) **A** *n.* Altfranzösisch, *das;* **B** *adj.* altfranzösisch; **~ ˈgirl** *n.* **1** ehemalige Schülerin; Ehemalige, *die;* **2** (coll.: elderly woman or female animal) altes Mädchen (ugs.); alte Dame; **3** **the/one's ~ girl** (coll.) (mother) die/seine Alte Dame (ugs.); (mother, wife) die/seine Alte (ugs.); (car) die/seine alte Kutsche (ugs.); **4** *as voc.* altes Mädchen; **Old ˈGlory** *n., no pl., no art.* (Amer.) das Sternenbanner; **~ ˈgold** **A** *n.* Altgold, *das;* **B** *adj.* altgolden; **~ guard** *n.* alte Garde; **a man** *or* **one of the ~ guard** einer von der alten Garde; **~ ˈhat** *pred. adj.* **▸hat 2**; **Old High ˈGerman** (Ling.) **A** *n.* Althochdeutsch, *das;* **B** *adj.* althochdeutsch; **Old ˈHundredth ▸hundredth B 2**

oldie /ˈəʊldɪ/ *n.* (coll.) (person) Oldie, *der* (ugs.); Oldtimer, *der* (scherzh.); (song, record, etc.) Oldie, *der* (ugs.); (film) alter Streifen (ugs.); (joke) olle *od.* alte Kamelle (ugs.); **golden ~:** guter Oldie

oldish /ˈəʊldɪʃ/ *adj.* älter

O

old: ~ 'lady *n.* **1** alte *od.* ältere Dame; **quite an ~ lady** eine recht alte Dame; **2** **the/one's ~ lady** (coll.) ▸~ **girl 3**; **the Old L~ of Threadneedle Street** (Brit.) die Bank von England; **~-line** *adj.* (Amer.) (established, experienced) alterfahren ‹*Personen*›; alteingeführt ‹*Unternehmen, Institution*›; (conservative) konservativ; (traditional) ‹*Diplomat*› alter Schule; **~ 'maid** *n.* **1** (elderly spinster) alte Jungfer (abwertend); **2** (fig.: precise, fussy, prim person) altjüngferliche Person; **~-maidish** /əʊld'meɪdɪʃ/ *adj.* altjüngferlich; **~ 'man** *n.* **1** (aged man) alter Mann; **2** (coll.: superior) **the ~ man** der Alte (ugs.); **3** (coll.: father, husband) **the/one's ~ man** der Alte/sein Alter (ugs.); **4** *as voc.* alter Junge *od.* Knabe (ugs. oft scherzh.); Alter (ugs.); **~ man's 'beard** *n.* (Bot.) Waldrebe, *die;* **~ 'master** *n.* (Art) alter Meister; **~ 'people's home** *n.* Altenheim, *das;* Altersheim, *das;* **Old Pre'tender** ▸**pretender**; **~ 'soldier** *n.* alt[gedient]er Soldat; (fig.) alter Hase (ugs.); **come the ~ soldier over sb.** (fig.) sich jmdm. gegenüber als der Erfahrenere aufspielen; **~ soldiers never die** ein alter Soldat ist nicht so leicht unterzukriegen (ugs.)

oldster /'əʊldstə(r)/ *n.* alter Mensch; **the/we ~s** die/wir Alten

old: ~-style *attrib. adj.* alten Stils *nachgestellt;* alt ‹*Geldschein, Münze*›; **Old 'Testament** ▸**testament 1**; **~-time** *adj.* früherer Zeiten *nachgestellt;* von anno dazumal *nachgestellt;* **~-time dancing** alte Tänze; **~-'timer** *n.* **1** (person with long experience) alter Hase (ugs.); Oldtimer, *der* (scherzh.); **2** (Amer.) (old person) Alte, *der/die;* (old or antique thing) Oldtimer, *der;* **~ 'wives' tale** *n.* Ammenmärchen, *das;* Altweibermärchen, *das;* **~ 'woman** *n.* **1** alte Frau; (fig.: fussy or timid person) altes Weib (abwertend); **2** (coll.: mother, wife) **the/one's ~ woman** ▸**old girl c**; **~-'womanish** *adj.* altweiberhaft; **~-world** *adj.* (belonging to old times, quaint) altertümlich; altväterisch ‹*Höflichkeit, Benehmen*›

oleaginous /əʊlɪ'ædʒɪnəs/ *adj.* **1** (oily, greasy) ölig **2** (producing oil) ölhaltig

oleander /əʊlɪ'ændə(r)/ *n.* (Bot.) Oleander, *der*

O level /'əʊ levl/ *n.* (Brit. Sch. Hist.) *Abschluss der Mittelstufe* (auch in der Erwachsenenbildung als Qualifikation); **he has five ~s** er hat die 'O'-Level-Prüfung in fünf Fächern bestanden

olfactory /ɒl'fæktərɪ/ *adj.* olfaktorisch (geh.); Geruchs‹*nerv, -sinn*›

oligarch /'ɒlɪgɑːk/ *n.* (Polit.) Oligarch, *der/*Oligarchin, *die*

oligarchic[al] /ɒlɪ'gɑːkɪk(l)/ *adj.* (Polit.) oligarchisch

oligarchy /'ɒlɪgɑːkɪ/ *n.* (Polit.) Oligarchie, *die*

olive /'ɒlɪv/

A *n.* **1** (tree) Ölbaum, *der;* Olivenbaum, *der* **2** (fruit) Olive, *die* **3** (emblem of peace) Ölzweig, *der* **4** **~ [wood]** Olivenholz, *das* **5** (Cookery) **[beef] ~:** [Rinds]roulade, *die* **6** (colour) Olivgrün, *das*

B *adj.* **1** olivgrün **2** (in complexion) oliv[farben]; olivbraun

olive: ~ branch *n.* (fig.) Friedensangebot, *das;* **offer the ~ branch** ein Versöhnungs- *od.* Friedensangebot machen; **~ 'drab** *n.* Olivgrau, *das;* **~-green** **A** /'---/ *adj.* olivgrün; **B** /--'-/ *n.* Olivgrün, *das;* **~ 'oil** *n.* Olivenöl, *das*

Olympiad /ə'lɪmpɪæd/ *n.* Olympiade, *die*

Olympian /ə'lɪmpɪən/

A *adj.* **1** (Greek Mythol.) olympisch; **the ~ gods** die Götter des Olymp **2** (superior) olympisch (geh.) **3** ▸**Olympic**

B *n.* **1** (Greek Mythol.) Olympier, *der/*Olympierin, *die* **2** (competitor in modern Olympics) olympischer [Wett]kämpfer/olympische [Wett]kämpferin; Olympionike, *der/*Olympionikin, *die*

Olympic /ə'lɪmpɪk/ *adj.* olympisch; **~ Games** Olympische Spiele; **~ champion** Olympiasieger, *der/*-siegerin, *die*

Olympics /ə'lɪmpɪks/ *n. pl.* Olympiade, *die;* **Winter ~:** Winterolympiade, *die*

Olympus /ə'lɪmpəs/ (Greek Ant.) Olymp, *der*

OM *abbr.* (Brit.) = **Order of Merit**

ombudsman /'ɒmbʊdzmən/ *n., pl.* **ombudsmen** /'ɒmbʊdzmən/ Ombudsmann, *der*

omega /'əʊmɪgə/ *n.* (letter) Omega, *das; see also* **alpha 1**

omelette (**omelet**) /'ɒmlɪt/ *n.* (Gastr.) Omelett, *das;* **one cannot make an ~ without breaking eggs** wo gehobelt wird, [da] fallen Späne (Spr.)

omen /'əʊmən/ *n.* Omen, *das;* Vorzeichen, *das*

ominous /'ɒmɪnəs/ *adj.* (of evil omen) ominös; (worrying) beunruhigend; **seem ~:** Schlimmes ahnen lassen

ominously /'ɒmɪnəslɪ/ *adv.* bedrohlich; beunruhigend ‹*still*›

omissible /ə'mɪsɪbl/ *adj.* weglassbar; **that is ~:** das kann man weglassen

omission /ə'mɪʃn/ *n.* **1** Auslassung, *die* **2** (non-performance) Unterlassung, *die;* **sins of ~ and commission** Unterlassungs- und Begehungssünden

omit /ə'mɪt/ *v.t.,* **-tt-** **1** (leave out) weglassen **2** (not perform) versäumen; **~ to do sth.** es versäumen, etw. zu tun

omnibus /'ɒmnɪbəs/

A *n.* **1** (arch.) ▸**bus A 1**; **Clapham** **2** (book) Sammelband, *der*

B *adj.* Sammel‹*band, -ausgabe*›

omnidirectional /ɒmnɪdɪ'rekʃənl, ɒmnɪdaɪ'rekʃənl/ *adj.* allseitig empfindlich ‹*Mikrofon*›; allseitig abstrahlend ‹*Lautsprecher*›; **~ aerial** Rundstrahler, *der*

omnipotence /ɒm'nɪpətəns/ *n., no pl.* Allmacht, *die* (geh.); Omnipotenz, *die* (geh.)

omnipotent /ɒm'nɪpətənt/ *adj.* allmächtig; omnipotent (geh.); **be made ~:** unbeschränkte Machtbefugnisse erhalten

omnipresent /ɒmnɪ'presənt/ *adj.* (Rel.; also fig.) allgegenwärtig

omniscience /ɒm'nɪsɪəns, ɒm'nɪʃjəns/ *n., no pl.* Allwissenheit, *die*

omniscient /ɒm'nɪsɪənt, ɒm'nɪʃjənt/ *adj.* allwissend

omnivore /'ɒmnɪvɔː(r)/ *n.* (animal) Allesfresser, *der;* Omnivore, *der* (fachspr.); (person) Allesesser, *der/*-esserin, *die*

omnivorous /ɒm'nɪvərəs/ *adj.* **1** omnivor (Fachspr.); **~ animal** Allesfresser, *der* **2** (fig.) unstillbar ‹*Appetit, Neugier, Wissbegier*›

on /ɒn/

A *prep.* **1** (position) auf (+ *Dat.*); (direction) auf (+ *Akk.*); (attached to) an (+ *Dat./Akk.*); **put sth. on the table** etw. auf den Tisch legen *od.* stellen; **be on the table** auf dem Tisch sein; **put/keep a dog on a lead** den Hund an die Leine nehmen/an der Leine halten; **write sth. on the wall** etw. an die Wand schreiben; **be hanging on the wall** an der Wand hängen; **have sth. on one** etw. bei sich (*Dat.*) haben; **on the mountain [side]** am Berghang; **on the bus/train** im Bus/Zug; (by bus/train) mit dem Bus/Zug; **on the shore** am Ufer; **be on the board/committee** im Vorstand/Ausschuss sein; **be on the team** (Amer.)**/staff** zum Team/zur Belegschaft gehören; **on Oxford 556767** unter der Nummer Oxford 556767

2 (with basis, motive, etc. of) **on the evidence** aufgrund des Beweismaterials; **borrow money on one's house** eine Grundschuld auf sein Haus aufnehmen; **on the assumption/hypothesis that …:** angenommen, …

3 (close to) an ‹*einer Straße*›; (in the direction of) auf ‹*eine Stadt*› zu

4 (coll.: in a position to get) **the player is on a hat-trick** der Spieler steht vor einem Hattrick

5 ▸❶ **p. 1047**, ▸❶ **p. 1048** *in expressions of time* an ‹*einem Abend, Tag usw.*›; **on Sundays** sonntags; **it's just on nine** es ist gerade 9; **on [his] arrival** bei seiner Ankunft; **on entering the room …:** beim Betreten des Zimmers …; **on time** *or* **schedule** pünktlich

6 *expr. state etc.* **be on heroin** heroinabhängig sein; **be on beer** (coll.) Bier trinken; **Armstrong on trumpet** Armstrong, Trompete; **the drinks are on me** (coll.) die Getränke gehen auf mich; **the fire went out on me** (coll.) mir ist das Feuer ausgegangen; **there is a lot of money on that horse** auf das Pferd ist viel gesetzt worden; **be on £20,000 a year** 20 000 Pfund im Jahr kriegen *od.* haben

7 (added to) **failure on failure** Fehlschlag auf Fehlschlag; **trouble on trouble** nichts als Ärger; **loss on loss** anhaltende Verluste

8 (concerning, about) über (+ *Akk.*)

B *adv.* **1** **with/without a hat/coat on** mit/ohne Hut/Mantel; **have a hat on** einen Hut aufhaben; **your hat is on crooked** dein Hut sitzt schief; **boil sth. with/without the lid on** etw. in geschlossenem/offenem Topf kochen; **the potatoes are on** die Kartoffeln sind aufgesetzt

2 (in some direction) **face on** mit dem Gesicht voran; **on and on** immer weiter; **speak/wait/work** *etc.* **on** (in time) weiterreden/-warten/-arbeiten *usw.*; **wait on until …:** so lange warten, bis …

3 (switched or turned on) **the light/radio** *etc.* **is on** das Licht/Radio *usw.* ist an; **put the light on** das Licht anmachen; **leave the bathroom tap on** das Wasser im Badezimmer laufen lassen; **is there a gas tap on?** ist ein Gashahn aufgedreht?; **neither the water nor the electricity was on** es gab weder Wasser noch Strom

4 (arranged) **the strike is still on** der Streik wird [weiterhin] fortgesetzt; **is Sunday's picnic on?** findet das Picknick am Sonntag statt?; **I have nothing of importance on** ich habe nichts Wichtiges vor

5 *ellipt.* (= **go on** *etc.*) weiter; **on with the show!** weitermachen!

6 (being performed) **what's on at the cinema?** was gibt es *od.* läuft im Kino?; **his play is currently on in London** sein Stück wird zurzeit in London aufgeführt *od.* gespielt; **the race is on** (fig.) das Wettrennen hat begonnen

7 **be on** (on the stage) auftreten; (on the playing field) spielen

8 (on duty) **come/be on** seinen Dienst antreten/Dienst haben

9 **sth. is on** (feasible)**/not on** etw. ist möglich/ausgeschlossen; **are you on?** (coll.: will you agree?) machst du mit?; **you're on!** (coll.: I agree) abgemacht!; (making bet) die Wette gilt!; **be on about sb./sth.** (coll.) [dauernd] über jmdn./etw. sprechen; es von jmdm./etw. haben (ugs.); **what is he on about?** was will er [sagen]?; **be on at/keep on and on at sb.** (coll.) jmdm. in den Ohren/dauernd in den Ohren liegen (ugs.); **on to, onto** auf (+ *Akk.*); **be on to sb.** (be aware of sb.'s intentions etc.) jmdn. *od.* jmds. Absichten durchschauen; (nag sb., suspect sb.) jmdn. auf dem Kieker haben (ugs.); **be on to sb. to do sth.** jmdn. bearbeiten, etw. zu tun; **be on to sth.** (have discovered sth.) etw. ausfindig gemacht haben; (realize importance of sth.) etw. [klar] erkennen; **the police/researchers are on to something** die Polizei hat/die Forscher haben eine heiße Spur; **on and off = off and on** ▸**off A 5**. *See also* **right D 4**

C *adj.* (Cricket) rechts vom Werfer; (if batsman is left-handed) links vom Werfer; **on drive** Treibschlag nach links; (by lefthanded batsman) Treibschlag nach rechts; **on side** (Cricket) *Spielfeldhälfte links vom rechtshändigen bzw. rechts vom linkshändigen Schlagmann*

on: ~-air *adj.* in der Sendung gemacht ‹*Scherz*›; in der Sendung abgegeben ‹*Kommentar*›; (live) Live-; **his ~-air language and behaviour** die Art, wie er in der Sendung spricht und sich benimmt; **~-board** *adj.* Bord‹*computer, -service*›

once /wʌns/

A *adv.* **1** einmal; **~ a week/month** einmal die Woche/im Monat; **~ or twice** ein paarmal; einige Mal; **~ again** *or* **more** noch einmal; **~ [and] for all** ein für alle Mal; **[every] ~ in a while** *or* (Brit.) **way** von Zeit zu Zeit; hin und wieder; **for ~ in a way** (Brit.) [wenigstens] dieses eine Mal; ausnahmsweise einmal; **~ an X always an X** X bleibt X; **~ seen never forgotten** jmd./etw. ist unvergesslich; *see also* **for A 15** **2** (multiplied by one) ein mal **3** (even for one or the first time) je[mals]; **never/not ~:** nicht ein einziges Mal **4** (formerly) früher einmal; einst (geh.); **~ upon a time there lived a king** es war einmal ein König **5** **at ~** (immediately) sofort; sogleich; (at the same time) gleichzeitig; **all at ~** (all together) alle auf einmal; (without warning) mit einem Mal; **they were all shouting at ~:** sie schrien alle durcheinander

B *conj.* wenn; (with past tense) als; **~ past the**

O

fence we are safe wenn wir [nur] den Zaun hinter uns bringen, sind wir in Sicherheit; **will you get it, ~ he finds out how valuable it is?** wirst du es auch bekommen, wenn er [einmal] herausfindet, wie wertvoll es ist?

C *n.* **[just** *or* **only] this ~, for [this/that] ~:** [nur] dieses eine Mal; **~ was enough for her** sie hatte nach dem ersten Mal schon genug

'once-over *n.* **give sb./sth. a/the ~:** jmdn./etw. kurz in Augenschein nehmen; **sth. needs a ~ every month** etw. muss einmal im Monat kurz überprüft/(cleaning) gereinigt werden

oncology /ɒŋ'kɒlədʒɪ/ *n., no pl., no art.* (Med.) Onkologie, *die*

'oncoming *adj.* [heran]nahend ‹*Person*›; entgegenkommend ‹*Fahrzeug, Verkehr*›; aufkommend ‹*Sturm*›; **'caution: ~ vehicles'** „Vorsicht! Gegenverkehr"

'oncost *n.* (Brit.) Zusatzkosten *Pl.*

on-'demand *adj.* abrufbar; **~ access** Zugriff bei *od.* je nach Bedarf

one /wʌn/ ▸**i** **p. 894**, ▸**i** **p. 1001**, ▸**i** **p. 1358**

A *adj.* **1** *attrib.* ein; **~ thing I must say/admit** ein[e]s muss ich sagen/zugeben; **~ man, ~ vote** ≈ gleiches Wahlrecht für alle; **~ or two** (fig.: a few) ein paar; **~ more ...:** noch ein ...; **~ more time** noch einmal; **Act O~** (Theatre) erster Akt; **from day ~:** vom ersten Tag an; **it's ~ [o'clock]** es ist eins *od.* ein Uhr; *see also* **eight A**; **half A 1, C 1**; **many A 1**; **quarter A 1**

2 *attrib.* (single, only) einzig; **the ~ thing** das Einzige; **any ~:** irgendein; **in any ~ day/year** an einem Tag/in einem Jahr; **at any ~ time** zu jeder Zeit; **no ~:** kein; **not ~ [little] bit** überhaupt nicht; **not** *or* **never for ~ [single] moment** *or* **minute** nicht einen Augenblick *od.* eine Minute [lang]; *see also* **only A, B 1**; **thing 1, 3, 6, 7**

3 (identical, same) ein; **the writer and his principal character are ~:** der Autor und sein Protagonist sind identisch; **~ and the same person/thing** ein und dieselbe Person/Sache; **it's ~ and the same thing** das ist ein und dasselbe; **at ~ and the same time** gleichzeitig; *see also* **all B 1**

4 *pred.* (united, unified) **be ~:** eine Einheit bilden; **we are ~:** wir sind uns einig; **be ~ as a family/nation** eine einige Familie/Nation sein; **become ~:** sich vereinigen; **be made ~** (married) getraut werden; *see also* **with**

5 *attrib.* (a particular but undefined) **at ~ time** einmal; einst (geh.); **~ morning/evening/night** eines Morgens/Abends/Nachts; **~ day** (on day specified) einmal; (at unspecified future date) eines Tages; **~ day soon** bald einmal; **~ day next week** irgendwann nächste Woche; **~ Sunday/weekend/afternoon** an einem Sonntag/Wochenende/Nachmittag

6 *attrib. contrasted with 'other'/'another'* ein; **for ~ thing** zum einen; **~ book** *etc.* **after another** *or* **the other** ein Buch *usw.* nach dem anderen; **deal with ~ thing after the other** eins nach dem andern machen; **what with ~ thing and another** wie das so ist *od.* geht, wenn viel zusammenkommt; **neither ~ thing nor the other** weder das eine noch das andere; **for ~ reason or another** aus irgendeinem Grund; **at ~ time or another** irgendwann einmal; zu irgendeinem Zeitpunkt; *see also* **hand A 14**; **way A 3, 10**

7 *qualifying implied n.* ein...; (Brit.: one-pound coin or note) Pfundnote, *die;* (Amer.: one-dollar bill) Dollarnote, *die;* **three to ~, three-~** (Sport) drei zu eins; **~-nil** (Sport) eins zu null; **in ~** (coll.: at first attempt) auf Anhieb; **got it in ~!** (coll.) [du hast es] erraten!; *see also* **every 1**; **hole A 5**

B *n.* **1** eins; **~, two, three ...!** eins, zwei, drei ...!

2 (number, symbol) Eins, *die;* **a Roman/arabic ~:** eine römische/arabische Eins; *see also* **eight B 1**

3 (unit) **in ~s** einzeln; **in** *or* **by ~s and twos** (fig.) kleckerweise (ugs.); **two for the price of ~:** zwei zum Preis von einem; *see also* **number A 1**; **ten B 3**

C *pron.* **1** **~ of ...:** ein... (+ *Gen.*); **~ of the boys/books** einer der Jungen/eins der Bücher; **~ of them/us** *etc.* einer von ihnen/uns *usw.;* **any ~ of them** jeder/jede/jedes von ihnen; **every ~ of them** jeder/jede/jedes [Einzelne] von ihnen; **not ~ of them** keiner/keine/keines von ihnen; *see also* **thing 7**

2 *replacing n. implied or mentioned* ein...; **red ~s and yellow ~s, big ~s and little ~s** rote und gelbe, große und kleine; **the jacket is an old ~:** die Jacke ist [schon] alt; **the older/younger ~:** der/die/das Ältere/Jüngere; **the problem is ~ of great complexity/is not ~ that will simply go away** das Problem ist sehr komplex/wird sich nicht von selbst lösen; **not that book — the ~ on the table** nicht das Buch — das auf dem Tisch; **who is that man, the ~ in the blue suit?** wer ist dieser Mann, der im blauen Anzug?; **of the three books, this is the ~ which appealed to me most** von den drei Büchern hat mir dieses am besten gefallen; **this is the ~ I like** den/die/das mag ich; **my husband is the tall ~ over there** mein Mann ist der Große da; **you are** *or* **were the ~ who insisted on going to Scotland** du warst der-/diejenige, der/die unbedingt nach Schottland wollte; **this ~:** dieser/diese/dieses [da]; **that ~:** der/die/das [da]; **these ~s** *or* **those ~s?** (coll.) die [da] oder die [da]?; **these/those blue** *etc.* **~s** diese/die blauen *usw.;* **which ~?** welcher/welche/welches?; **which ~s?** welche?; **not ~:** keiner/keine/keines; *emphatic* nicht einer/eine/eines; **never a ~:** kein Einziger; **many a ~:** viele; **all but ~:** alle außer einem/einer/einem; **the last house but ~:** das vorletzte Haus; **[all] in ~:** in einem; (in a person) in einer Person; **I for ~:** ich für mein[en] Teil; **~ by ~, ~ after another** *or* **the other** einzeln; **love/like/hate ~ another** sich *od.* (geh.) einander lieben/mögen/hassen; **be kind to ~ another** nett zueinander sein; *see also* **all B 1**; **better B 5**; **many A 1**

3 (contrasted with 'other'/'another') **[the] ~ ... the other** der/die/das eine ... der/die/das andere

4 (person or creature of specified kind) **the little ~:** der/die/das Kleine; **dear** *or* **loved ~:** lieber Mensch; **our dear** *or* **loved ~s** unsere Lieben; **my sweet ~:** mein Liebling *od.* Schatz; **young ~** (youngster) Kind, *das;* (young animal) Junge, *das;* **the Holy O~, the O~ above** Gott; der Vater im Himmel; **like ~ dead** wie ein Toter; **as ~ enchanted/bewitched** wie verzaubert/verhext; **~ John Smith** ein John Smith

5 **[not] ~ who does** *or* **to do** *or* **for doing sth.** [nicht] der Typ, der etw. tut; **[not] be ~ for parties** *or* **for going to parties** [k]ein Partytyp sein; **be a great ~ for tennis** ein begeisterter Tennisspieler sein; **be a great ~ for playing practical jokes** gerne anderen einen Streich spielen; ein großer Witzbold sein; **not be much of a ~ for sth./doing sth.** nicht sehr für etw. sein/etw. nicht gern tun; **you 'are a ~** (coll.) du bist [mir] vielleicht einer/eine

6 (representing people in general; also coll.: I, we) man; *as indirect object* einem; *as direct object* einen; **~'s** sein; **lose ~'s job** seinen Arbeitsplatz verlieren; **wash ~'s hands** sich (*Dat.*) die Hände waschen

7 (coll.: joke, story) **a good/naughty ~:** ein guter/unanständiger Witz; **have you heard the ~ about the Irishman who ...?** kennst du den von dem Iren, der ...?; *see also* **good A 8**

8 (coll.: drink) **I'll have just a little ~:** ich trinke nur einen Kleinen (ugs.); **this ~'s on me/the house** der geht auf mich/auf Kosten des Hauses; **have ~ on me** ich geb dir einen aus; **have ~ too many** einen über den Durst trinken (ugs.); *see also* **quick one**; **road 1**

9 (coll.: blow) **give sb. ~ on the head/nose** jmdm. eins über den Kopf/auf die Nase geben (ugs.); **he hit me ~ between the eyes** er verpasste mir einen zwischen die Augen (ugs.)

10 (Knitting, Crochet: stitch) eine Masche; **knit ~, purl ~:** eins rechts, eins links; **make ~** eine Masche zunehmen

one: ~-armed *adj.* einarmig; **~-armed bandit** (coll.) einarmiger Bandit (ugs.); **~-day** *attrib. adj.* eintägig; [für] einen Tag gültig ‹*Karte, Genehmigung*›; **~-eyed** *adj.* einäugig; **in the land of the blind the ~-eyed [man] is king** (prov.) unter [den] Blinden ist der Einäugige König (Spr.); **~-handed** /wʌnhændɪd/ **A** /'--/ *adj.* einhändig; **B** /-'--/ *adv.* mit einer Hand; **~-horse** *attrib. adj.* **1** (drawn by only ~ horse) einspännig; **it's a ~-horse race** (fig.) das Rennen ist schon so gut wie gelaufen; **2** (fig. coll.: second-rate) **~-horse town** [verschlafenes] Nest (ugs.); **~-legged** *adj.* einbeinig; **~-line** *attrib. adj.* einzeilig; **~-'liner** *n.* Einzeiler, *der;* **~-man** *attrib. adj.* Einmann‹*boot, -betrieb usw.*›; **a ~-man fight/war against sth.** ein einsamer Kampf/Krieg gegen etw.; **~-man band** Einmannkapelle, *die;* (fig.: firm etc.) Einmannbetrieb, *der;* **~-man show** (exhibition) Einzelausstellung, *die;* (play etc.) Einmannstück, *das;* (fig.: firm etc.) Einmannbetrieb, *der;* **~-nation** *attrib. adj.* (Brit. Pol.) für eine integrative Gesellschaft eintretend; **a ~-nation society** eine integrative Gesellschaft

oneness /'wʌnnɪs/ *n., no pl.* **1** (singleness) **~ of purpose** Zielstrebigkeit, *die* **2** (unity, harmony) Übereinstimmung, *die;* Einklang, *der* (geh.)

one: ~-night 'stand *n.* (coll.) **1** (single performance) Einzelauftritt, *der;* **2** (sexual) [sexuelles] Abenteuer für eine Nacht; (partner) Bettgenosse/-genossin für eine Nacht; **~-off** (Brit.) **A** *n.* (article) Einzelstück, *das;* Einzelexemplar, *das;* (operation) einmalige Sache; **B** *adj.* einmalig ‹*Zahlung, Angebot, Produktion, Verkauf*›; Einzel‹*stück, -modell, -anfertigung, -auftritt, -arbeit*›; **~-parent family** *n.* Einelternfamilie, *die;* **~-party** *adj.* (Polit.) Einparteien‹*system, -staat*›; **~-piece** *adj.* einteilig; **~-'quarter** *attrib. adj.* Viertel-; ‹*Anteil*› von einem Viertel; ‹*Anstieg*› um ein Viertel; **~-room[ed]** /'wʌnru:m(d)/ *adj.* Einzimmer‹*wohnung, -appartement*›; **a ~-room school/shack** eine aus einem [einzigen] Raum bestehende Schule/Hütte

onerous /'ɒnərəs, 'əʊnərəs/ *adj.* schwer; **find sth. increasingly ~:** etw. zunehmend als Belastung empfinden

onerously /'ɒnərəslɪ, 'əʊnərəslɪ/ *adv.* schwer

one: ~'self *pron.* **1** *emphat.* selbst; **as old/rich as ~self** so alt/reich wie man selbst; **older/richer than ~self** älter/reicher als man selbst; **be ~self** man selbst sein; **2** *refl.* sich; *see also* **herself**; **~-shot** *adj.* (coll.) einmalig; Einzel‹*auftritt, -anfertigung*›; ‹*Medikament, Verfahren*› zur einmaligen Anwendung; **a ~-shot solution to a problem** eine auf Anhieb wirksame Lösung eines Problems; **~-sided** *adj.* einseitig; **~-size-fits-'all** *adj.* **1** (clothing) **~-size-fits-all T-shirt** *etc.* T-Shirt usw. in Einheitsgröße; **2** (pej.: appropriate for all) Nullachtfünfzehn- (ugs. abwertend); **~step** *n.* Onestep, *der;* **~-stop 'shopping** *n., no pl.* Einkaufen in einem Einkaufszentrum [mit Komplettangebot]; **~-storey** *adj.* eingeschossig; **~-'third** *attrib. adj.* Drittel-; ‹*Anteil*› von einem Drittel; ‹*Anstieg*› um ein Drittel; **~-time** *adj.* **1** (former) ehemalig; **2** (used once only) einmalig; **~-to-'~** *adj.* **~-to-~ relation/correspondence** hundertprozentige Parallelität; **~-to-~ translation** Wort-für-Wort-Übersetzung, *die;* **~-to-~ teaching** Einzelunterricht, *der;* **~-touch** *adj.* **~-touch dialling** Zielwahl, *die;* Zielwahlverfahren, *das;* **~-touch cooking** Kochen per Knopfdruck; Kochen mit einem einzigen Knopfdruck; **~-track** *adj.* eingleisig; **have a ~-track mind** (lack flexibility) eingleisig denken; (be obsessed by one subject) [immer] nur eins im Kopf haben; **~-trick 'pony** *n.* (coll.) **be a ~-trick pony** eine Sache können, aber sonst nichts draufhaben (ugs.); **not be a ~-trick pony** noch mehr draufhaben (ugs.); **~-'two** *n.* (coll.) (Boxing) Eins-zwei-Schlag, *der;* (Sport) Doppelpass, *der;* **~-'up** *pred. adj.* (coll.) **be ~-up [on** *or* **over sb.]** (Sport) [vor jmdm.] mit einem Punkt/Tor in Führung liegen; (fig.) [jmdm.] um eine Nasenlänge voraus sein; **it is ~-up for** *or* **to sb.** jmd. ist im Vorteil; **~-up for** *or* **to you** (fig.) eins zu null für dich; **~-upmanship** /wʌn'ʌpmənʃɪp/ *n., no pl., no indef. art.* die Kunst, den anderen immer um eine Nasenlänge voraus zu sein; **~-way** *adj.* **1** in einer Richtung *nachgestellt;* Einbahn‹*straße, -verkehr*›; Einweg‹*spiegel, -scheibe*›; **~-way radio** Funkempfänger, *der;* **~-way switch** (Electr.) einfacher Schalter; **2** (single) einfach ‹*Fahrpreis, Fahrkarte, Flug usw.*›; **3** (fig.: ~-sided) einseitig; **~-woman** *attrib. adj.* Einfrau‹*betrieb,*

O

-*job, -firma*›; **a ~-woman fight/war against sth.** ein einsamer Kampf/Krieg gegen etw.; **~-woman show** (exhibition) Einzelausstellung [einer Künstlerin]; (play etc.) Einfraustück, *das*; (fig.: firm etc.) Einfraubetrieb, *der*

'ongoing *adj.* aktuell ‹*Problem, Aktivitäten, Debatte*›; laufend ‹*Forschung, Projekt*›; andauernd ‹*Situation*›

onion /'ʌnjən/ *n.* Zwiebel, *die*; **know one's ~s** (fig. coll.) sein Geschäft verstehen

onion: ~ dome *n.* (Archit.) Zwiebelkuppel, *die*; **~ skin** *n.* 1) Zwiebelschale, *die*; 2) (paper) Florpost, *die*; **~ 'soup** *n.* Zwiebelsuppe, *die*

oniony /'ʌnjənɪ/ *adj.* Zwiebel‹*geruch, -geschmack*›

online (Computing)
A /'--/ *adj.* Online‹*computer, -betrieb*›
B /-'-/ *adv.* online

online: ~ 'bank *n.* Onlinebank, *die*; **~ 'banking** *n., no pl.* Onlinebanking, *das*; **~ gamer** /ɒnlaɪn 'geɪmə(r)/ *n.* Onlinespieler, *der*/-spielerin, *die*; **~ 'gaming** /ɒnlaɪn 'geɪmɪŋ/ *n., no pl.* Onlinegaming, *das*; **~ 'shop** *n.* Onlineshop, *der*; **~ 'shopping** *n., no pl.* Onlineshopping, *das*

'onlooker *n.* Zuschauer, *der*/Zuschauerin, *die*; (at scene of accident) Schaulustige, *der*/*die*

only /'əʊnlɪ/
A *attrib. adj.* 1) einzig...; **the ~ person** der/die Einzige; **my ~ regret is that ...:** ich bedaure nur, dass ...; **for the first and ~ time** zum ersten und einzigen Mal; **an ~ child** ein Einzelkind; **the ~ one/ones** der/die/das Einzige/die Einzigen; **the ~ thing** das Einzige; **one and ~** (sole) einzig...; (incomparable) einzigartig; *see also* **pebble**; **thing 2, 3** 2) (best by far) **the ~:** der/die/das einzig wahre; **he/she is the ~ one for me** es gibt nur ihn/sie für mich; **the ~ thing** das einzig Wahre
B *adv.* 1) nur; **we had been waiting ~ 5 minutes when ...:** wir hatten erst 5 Minuten gewartet, als ...; **it's ~/~ just 6 o'clock** es ist erst 6 Uhr/gerade erst 6 Uhr vorbei; **the meat is ~ half done** das Fleisch ist erst halb durch; **I ~ wish I had known** wenn ich es doch nur gewusst hätte; **you ~ have** *or* **you have ~ to ask** *etc.* du brauchst nur zu fragen *usw.*; **you may each take one and one ~:** ihr dürft euch jeder einen/eine/eins nehmen, aber [wirklich] nur einen/eine/eins; **you ~ live once** man lebt nur einmal; **you're ~ young once** man ist nur einmal jung; **~ ever** (coll.: never more than) lediglich; **~ if** nur [dann] ..., wenn; **~ if the weather is fine** nur bei gutem Wetter; **he ~ just managed it/made it** er hat es gerade so/gerade noch geschafft; **not ~ ... but also** nicht nur ... sondern auch; *see also* **if A 4** 2) (no longer ago than) erst; **~ the other day/week** erst neulich *od.* kürzlich; **~ the other evening** erst neulich abends; **~ just** gerade erst; **it is ~ now I realize ...:** erst jetzt wird mir klar ... 3) (with no better result than) **~ to find/discover that ...:** nur, um zu entdecken, dass ... 4) **~ too ...** *in context of desirable circumstances* [sogar] ausgesprochen ‹*froh, begierig, bereitwillig*›; *in context of undesirable circumstances* viel zu; **be ~ too aware of sth.** sich (*Dat.*) einer Sache (*Gen.*) voll bewusst sein; **it's ~ too true** es ist nur zu wahr; **~ too well** nur zu gut ‹*wissen, kennen, sich erinnern*›; gerne ‹*mögen*›; nur zu genau ‹*hören, aufpassen auf*›
C *conj.* 1) (but then) nur 2) (were it not for the fact that) **~ [that] I am/he is** *etc.* **...:** ich bin/er ist *usw.* nur ...

only-be'gotten *adj.* (Relig.) **Jesus Christ, the ~ Son of the Father** Jesus Christus, Gottes eingeborener Sohn

on-'message
A *adj.* der Parteilinie entsprechend ‹*Antwort, Aussage*›; **be ~:** mit der Parteilinie übereinstimmen.
B *adv.* **stay ~:** sich an die Parteilinie halten

o.n.o. /əʊ en 'əʊ/ *abbr.* (Brit.) **= or near offer** ≈ VHB

'on-off *adj.* **~ switch** Ein-aus-Schalter, *der*

onomatopoeia /ɒnəmætə'piːə/ *n.* (Ling.) Onomatopöie, *die*

onomatopoeic /ɒnəmætə'piːɪk/ *adj.* (Ling.) onomatopoetisch

'onrush *n.* Ansturm, *der*

on-screen
A *adj.* 1) (Computing, TV) Bildschirm-; **~ editing** redaktionelle Bearbeitung am Bildschirm 2) (Cinemat.) Leinwand-; **~ violence** Gewalt im Fernsehen/im Film; **her ~ daughter** ihre Filmtochter
B *adv.* 1) (Computing, TV) auf dem Bildschirm 2) (Cinemat.) auf der Leinwand; **appear ~ simultaneously** gleichzeitig im Bild sein; **~ they were lovers** im Film waren sie ein Liebespaar

'onset *n.* 1) (attack) [Sturm]angriff, *der* 2) (beginning) (of storm) Einsetzen, *das*; (of winter) Einbruch, *der*; (of disease) Ausbruch, *der*

'onshore *adj.* auflandig (Seemannsspr.)

on'side *adj.* (Footb.) nicht abseits

onslaught /'ɒnslɔːt/ *n.* [heftige] Attacke (fig.)

on-'stage
A *adj.* auf der Bühne *nachgestellt*
B *adv.* auf die Bühne ‹*gehen*›; auf der Bühne ‹*stehen*›

'on-street *adj.* auf der Straße *nachgestellt*

'on-target *attrib. adj.* **~ earnings £50,000** Verdienst bei erfolgreicher Tätigkeit 50 000 Pfund

'on-the-job *attrib. adj.* berufsbegleitend ‹*Unterricht, Fortbildungskurs usw.*›; **~ experience** Berufserfahrung, *die*; **~ training** Ausbildung am Arbeitsplatz

on-the-'spot *adj.* vor Ort *nachgestellt*

onto ▸**on B 9**

ontological /ɒntə'lɒdʒɪkl/ *adj.* (Philos.) ontologisch

ontology /ɒn'tɒlədʒɪ/ *n.* (Philos.) Ontologie, *die*

onus /'əʊnəs/ *n.* Last, *die*; **the ~ [of proof]** die Beweislast; **the ~ is on him to do it** es ist seine Sache, es zu tun

onward /'ɒnwəd/
A *adv.* 1) (in space) vorwärts; **from X ~:** von X an; **they moved ~ into the forest** sie gingen *od.* zogen weiter in den Wald [hinein] 2) (in time) **from that day ~:** von diesem Tag an; **history from the 12th century ~:** Geschichte vom 12. Jahrhundert an
B *adj.* nach vorn *nachgestellt*; **~ movement** Vorwärtsbewegung, *die*; **~ march** Vormarsch, *der*

onwards /'ɒnwədz/ ▸**onward A**

onyx /'ɒnɪks/ *n.* (Min.) Onyx, *der*; **~ marble** Onyxmarmor, *der*

oodles /'uːdlz/ *n. pl., constr. as sing. or pl.* (coll.) **~ of** haufenweise (ugs.); jede Menge (ugs.)

ooh /uː/
A *n.* Oh, *das*; Ah, *das*; **the ~s [and ahs] of the audience** die Ohs und Ahs der Zuschauer
B *int. expr. disapproval or delight* oh; *expr. pain* au

oojah /'uːdʒɑː/ *n.* (coll.) Ding, *das* (ugs.)

oompah /'uːmpɑː/ *n.* Humpta, *das*

oomph /ʊmf/ *n.* (coll.) 1) (attractiveness) Sex-Appeal, *der* 2) (energy) Elan, *der*

oops /uːps/ *int.* (coll.) *expr. surprise* huch; *expr. apology* oh; oje; *expr. apology for a faux pas* oh

ooze /uːz/
A *v.i.* 1) (percolate, exude) sickern (**from** aus); (more thickly) quellen (**from** aus); **the juice ~s out** der Saft trieft heraus 2) (become moistened) triefen (**with** von, vor + *Dat.*)
B *v.t.* 1) **~ [out]** triefen von *od.* vor (+ *Dat.*) 2) (fig.: radiate) ausstrahlen ‹*Charme, Optimismus*›; ausströmen ‹*Sarkasmus*›
C *n.* 1) (mud) Schlick, *der* 2) (sluggish flow) Sickern, *das*; (sluggish stream) Rinnsal, *das* (**of** von + *Dat.*)

op /ɒp/ *n.* (coll.) 1) (Med.) Operation, *die* 2) (Mil., Navy, Air Force) Einsatz, *der* 3) (radio operator) Funker, *der*/Funkerin, *die*; (telegraph operator) Telegrafist, *der*/Telegrafistin, *die*

op. /ɒp/ *abbr.* (Mus.) **= opus** op.

opacity /ə'pæsɪtɪ/ *n., no pl.* 1) (not transmitting light) Opazität, *die* (Optik); Lichtundurchlässigkeit, *die* 2) (obscurity) Undurchsichtigkeit, *die*

opal /'əʊpl/ *n.* (Min.) Opal, *der*

opalescence /əʊpə'lesəns/ *n.* Schillern, *das*; Opaleszenz, *die* (Optik)

opalescent /əʊpə'lesənt/ *adj.* schillernd; opalisierend; opaleszierend (Optik)

'opal glass *n.* Opalglas, *das*

opaque /əʊ'peɪk/ *adj.* 1) (not transmitting light) lichtundurchlässig; opak (fachspr.) 2) (obscure) dunkel; unverständlich

opaqueness /əʊ'peɪknɪs/ ▸**opacity**

'op art *n., no pl., no indef. art.* Op-Art, *die*

op. cit. /ɒp 'sɪt/ *abbr.* **= in the work already quoted** op. cit.

OPEC /'əʊpek/ *abbr.* **= Organization of Petroleum Exporting Countries** OPEC, *die*

open /'əʊpn/
A *adj.* 1) offen; **with the window ~:** bei geöffnetem Fenster; **~ goal** (Sport) leeres Tor; **wear an ~ shirt** sein Hemd offen tragen; **be [wide/half] ~:** [weit/halb] offen stehen; **stand ~:** offen stehen; **swing ~:** aufschwingen; **come ~:** aufgehen; **get sth. ~:** etw. aufbekommen; **hold the door ~ [for sb.]** [jmdm.] die Tür aufhalten; **push/pull/kick the door ~:** die Tür aufstoßen/aufziehen/eintreten; **force sth. ~:** etw. mit Gewalt öffnen; **fling** *or* **throw a door/window [wide] ~:** eine Tür/ein Fenster [weit] aufreißen; **tear** *or* **rip sth. ~:** etw. aufreißen; **with one's mouth ~:** mit offenem Mund; **have one's eyes ~:** die Augen geöffnet haben; **[not] be able to keep one's eyes ~:** [nicht mehr] die Augen offen halten können; **with ~ eyes** (attentive, surprised) mit großen Augen; *see also* **eye[1] 1**
2) (unconfined) offen ‹*Gelände, Feuer*›; frei ‹*Feld, Blick*›; **~ country** (with wide views) weites Land; (without buildings) offenes Land; **on the ~ road** auf freier Strecke; **the ~ road lay before me** vor mir lag die freie Landstraße; **the ~ sea** die offene See; **in the ~ air** im Freien; *see also* **sky A 1**
3) (not blocked or obstructed) frei; offen, eisfrei ‹*Hafen, Fluss, Wasser*›; frostfrei ‹*Winter, Wetter*›
4) (ready for business or use) **be ~** ‹*Laden, Museum, Bank usw.:*› geöffnet sein; **'~'/'~ on Sundays'/'~ 24 hours'** „geöffnet"/„Sonntags geöffnet"/„24 Stunden geöffnet"; **declare a building/an exhibition ~:** ein Gebäude/eine Ausstellung für eröffnet erklären
5) (accessible) offen; öffentlich ‹*Treffen, Rennen*›; (available) frei ‹*Stelle*›; freibleibend ‹*Angebot*›; **it is ~ to you to refuse** es steht dir frei abzulehnen; **lay ~:** offen legen ‹*Plan*›; **be ~ to the public** für die Öffentlichkeit zugänglich sein; **the competition is ~ to children under 16** [nur] Kinder unter 16 Jahren sind zum Wettbewerb zugelassen; **the job/offer is ~ to men over 25 years of age** die Stelle ist für/das Angebot gilt für Männer über 25 Jahren; **the offer remains** *or* **will be kept ~ until the end of the month** das Angebot bleibt bestehen *od.* gilt noch bis Ende des Monats; **keep a position ~ for sb.** jmdm. eine Stelle freihalten; **keep an account ~:** ein Konto [weiterhin] bestehen lassen; **~ champion** Sieger einer offenen Meisterschaft; **~ cheque** (Brit.) Barscheck, *der*; **in ~ court** in öffentlicher Sitzung *od.* Verhandlung; **~ ward** offene Station; *see also* **house A 1**
6) **be ~ to** (exposed to) ausgesetzt sein (+ *Dat.*) ‹*Wind, Sturm*›; (receptive to) offen sein für ‹*Ratschlag, andere Meinung, Vorschlag*›; **~ to infection** infektionsgefährdet *od.* -anfällig; **be ~ to criticism** kritisierbar sein; **~ to attack by dry rot** anfällig für Trockenfäule; **be ~ to attack from the air** aus der Luft angreifbar sein; **sth. may be ~ to misinterpretation** etw. kann [leicht] falsch ausgelegt werden; **be ~ to sb.'s influence** sich leicht von jmdm. beeinflussen lassen; **I hope to sell it for £1,000, but I am ~ to offers** ich möchte es für 1 000 Pfund verkaufen, aber ich lasse mit mir handeln; **lay sb. wide ~** (fig.) jmdn. bloßstellen; **lay oneself [wide] ~ to ridicule/attack/criticism** *etc.* sich der Lächerlichkeit preisgeben/sich Angriffen/der Kritik *usw.* aussetzen; **lay oneself [wide] ~ to blackmail/a charge** sich der Gefahr der Erpressung/einer Anklage aussetzen; **be ~ to question/doubt/argument** fraglich/zweifelhaft/umstritten sein; **I am ~ to correction** ich lasse mich gern korrigieren
7) (undecided) offen; **~ invitation** Einladung,

O

gelegentlich einmal zu Besuch zu kommen; ~ **return ticket** nicht termingebundene Rückfahrkarte; **have an ~ mind about** *or* **on sth.** einer Sache gegenüber aufgeschlossen *od.* unvoreingenommen sein; **with an ~ mind** aufgeschlossen; **have/keep an ~ mind on a question** in einer Sache unvoreingenommen sein/bleiben; **be [wide] ~:** [völlig] offen sein; **leave sth. ~:** etw. offen lassen; *see also* **verdict 1**

8 (undisguised, manifest) unverhohlen ‹*Bewunderung, Hass, Verachtung*›; offen ‹*Verachtung, Empörung, Bruch, Widerstand*›; offensichtlich ‹*Spaltung, Zwiespalt*›; ~ **war/warfare** offener Krieg/Kampf; *see also* **secret B 1**

9 (frank, communicative) offen ‹*Wesen, Streit, Abstimmung, Gesicht, Regierungsstil*›; (not secret) öffentlich ‹*Wahl*›; **be ~ [about sth./with sb.]** [in Bezug auf etw. (*Akk.*)/gegenüber jmdm.] offen sein

10 (not close) grob ‹*Muster, Gewebe, Maserung*›; offen ‹*Anordnung*›; ~ **order** (Mil., Navy) offene Ordnung

11 (expanded, unfolded) offen, geöffnet ‹*Pore, Regenschirm*›; aufgeblüht ‹*Blume, Knospe*›; aufgeschlagen ‹*Zeitung, Landkarte, Stadtplan*›; ~ **book** offenes *od.* aufgeschlagenes Buch; **sb./sth. is an ~ book [to sb.]** (fig.) jmd./etw. ist ein aufgeschlagenes *od.* offenes Buch [für jmdn.]; **an ~ hand** eine aufgehaltene Hand; (fig.) eine milde *od.* offene Hand; **with an ~ hand, with ~ hands** (fig.) mit einer milden *od.* offenen Hand; **with [an] ~ heart** (frankly) offenherzig; (kindly) herzlich; *see also* **arm[1] 1; ~-heart**

12 (Mus.) ~ **string** leere Saite; ~ **pipe** offene Pfeife; ~ **note** Naturton, *der*

13 (Ling.) offen ‹*Vokal, Silbe*›

B *n.* **1** **the ~:** das offene Land; **in the ~** (outdoors) unter freiem Himmel; (in an open space) auf offenem Gelände; (in open water) auf offener *od.* hoher See; **[out] in the ~** (fig.) [öffentlich] bekannt; **come [out] into the ~** (fig.) (become obvious) herauskommen (ugs.); an den Tag kommen; (speak out) offen sprechen; **bring sth. [out] into the ~** (fig.) etw. an die Öffentlichkeit bringen

2 (Sport) offene Meisterschaft; Open, *das* (fachspr.)

C *v.t.* **1** öffnen; aufmachen (ugs.); ~ **sth. with a key** etw. aufschließen; ~ **sth. wide** etw. weit aufmachen (ugs.) *od.* öffnen; **half ~ sth.** etw. halb aufmachen (ugs.) *od.* öffnen; **[not] ~ one's mouth** *or* **lips** (fig.) den Mund [nicht] aufmachen *od.* auftun (ugs.); ~ **one's big mouth [to sb. about sth.]** (fig.) [etw. jmdm. aus]plaudern; ~ **the** *or* **one's bowels** den Darm entleeren; *see also* **eye A 1; floodgate**

2 (allow access to) ~ **sth. [to sb./sth.]** etw. öffnen [für jmdn./etw.]; (fig.) [jmdm./einer Sache] etw. öffnen; ~ **a road to traffic** eine Straße für den Verkehr freigeben; ~ **sth. to the public** etw. der Öffentlichkeit (*Dat.*) zugänglich machen; *see also* **door 2**

3 (establish) eröffnen ‹*Konferenz, Kampagne, Diskussion, Laden*›; aufmachen (ugs.) ‹*Laden*›; beginnen ‹*Verhandlungen, Krieg, Spiel*›; (declare open) eröffnen ‹*Gebäude usw.*›; ~ **the scoring** (Sport) den ersten Treffer erzielen; (Cricket) den ersten Lauf machen; (Rugby) die ersten Punkte machen; ~ **the betting with a £5 stake** das Spiel mit einem Einsatz von 5 Pfund eröffnen; ~ **the bidding** (in auction) das erste Gebot abgeben; (Bridge) eröffnen; ~ **an account** ein Konto eröffnen; ~ **fire [on sb./sth.]** das Feuer [auf jmdn./etw.] eröffnen; *see also* **ball[2]; parliament**

4 (unfold, spread out) aufschlagen ‹*Zeitung, Landkarte, Stadtplan, Buch*›; aufspannen, öffnen ‹*Schirm*›; öffnen ‹*Fallschirm, Poren*›; ~ **one's hand** die *od.* seine Hand öffnen; ~ **one's arms [wide]** die *od.* seine Arme [weit] ausbreiten; ~ **one's legs** die *od.* seine Beine spreizen

5 (reveal, expose) ~ **a view** *or* **prospect of sth. [to sb.]** [jmdm.] den Blick auf etw. freigeben; **sth. ~s new prospects/horizons/a new world to sb.** (fig.) etw. eröffnet jmdm. neue Aussichten/Horizonte/eine neue Welt; ~ **one's heart to sb.** (fig.) sich jmdm. öffnen

6 (make more receptive) ~ **one's mind** aufgeschlossener werden; ~ **one's heart** *or* **mind to sb./sth.** sich jmdm./einer Sache öffnen; ~ **sb.'s mind to sth.** jmdm. etw. nahe bringen

7 (cut) graben ‹*Stollen, Brunnen, Loch, Gang*›; bauen ‹*Straße durch Berge/Wald*›; (break up) bearbeiten ‹*Boden*›; ~ **a hole in the wall** ein Loch in die Wand machen

D *v.i.* **1** sich öffnen; aufgehen; ‹*Spalt, Kluft:*› sich auftun; **'Doors ~ at 7 p.m.'** „Einlass ab 19 Uhr"; **the safe ~s with a special key** der Tresor lässt sich mit einem Spezialschlüssel öffnen; ~ **inwards/outwards** nach innen/außen aufgehen; **the door would not ~:** die Tür ging nicht auf *od.* ließ sich nicht öffnen; **his mouth ~ed in a big yawn** sein Mund öffnete sich zu einem ausgiebigen Gähnen; **his eyes ~ed wide** er riss die Augen weit auf; ~ **into/on to sth.** zu etw. führen; sich zu etw. hin öffnen; **the kitchen ~s into the living room** die Küche hat eine Tür zum Wohnzimmer; **the road ~s into a square** die Straße öffnet sich zu einem Platz; *see also* **heaven 2**

2 (become open to customers) öffnen; aufmachen (ugs.); (start trading etc.) eröffnet werden; **the shop does not ~ on Sundays** der Laden ist sonntags geschlossen

3 (make a start) beginnen; ‹*Ausstellung:*› eröffnet werden; ‹*Theaterstück:*› Premiere haben; **shares ~ed steady** *or* **firm** (St. Exch.) die Aktien eröffneten fest; ~ **for the prosecution** (Law) das Eröffnungsplädoyer [in der Hauptverhandlung] halten

4 (become visible) ~ **before sb./sb.'s eyes** sich jmdm./jmds. Augen bieten; (fig.) sich jmdm. eröffnen

Phrasal verbs

• ~ **'out**

A *v.t.* **1** (unfold) auseinander falten **2** (enlarge, widen) erweitern **3** (develop) erweitern

B *v.i.* **1** (unfold) ‹*Landkarte:*› sich auseinander falten lassen; ‹*Knospe:*› sich öffnen; (fig.) ‹*Person:*› auftauen **2** (widen, expand) ~ **out into sth.** sich zu etw. erweitern *od.* verbreitern **3** (be revealed) ~ **out before sb./sb.'s eyes** vor jmdm./jmds. Augen liegen

• ~ **'up**

A *v.t.* **1** aufmachen (ugs.); öffnen; aufschlagen ‹*Buch*›; aufspannen, öffnen ‹*Schirm*›; ~ **up a room/house** ein Zimmer/ein Haus öffnen *od.* zugänglich machen **2** (form or make by cutting etc.) machen ‹*Loch, Riss*›; ~ **up a path through the jungle** einen Weg durch den Urwald schlagen; **the frost has ~ed up big cracks** durch den Frost sind große Risse entstanden; ~ **up a lead** *or* **gap of ten metres/points** einen Vorsprung von zehn Metern/Punkten gewinnen **3** (establish, make more accessible) eröffnen ‹*Laden, Filiale*›; erschließen ‹*neue Märkte usw.*›; ~ **up a region to trade/tourism** ein Gebiet für den Handel/Tourismus erschließen; ~ **up a new world to sb.** jmdm. eine neue Welt erschließen; ~ **up new opportunities for sb.** jmdm. neue Möglichkeiten eröffnen **4** (make more lively, accelerate) aufdrehen (ugs.)

B *v.i.* **1** (open a door) aufmachen **2** ‹*Blüte, Knospe:*› sich öffnen **3** (be established) ‹*Filiale:*› eröffnet werden; ‹*Firma:*› sich niederlassen **4** (appear, be revealed) entstehen; ‹*Aussichten, Möglichkeiten:*› sich eröffnen; ~ **up before sb.** ‹*Blick, Aussicht:*› sich jmdm. bieten; ‹*neue Welt:*› sich vor jmdm. auftun **5** (talk freely) gesprächig werden; ~ **up to sb.** sich jmdm. anvertrauen; sich jmdm. eröffnen (geh.) **6** (begin shooting) das Feuer eröffnen; (begin sounding) ertönen **7** (become more lively or active) ‹*Spiel, Handel:*› sich beleben; (accelerate) aufdrehen (ugs.)

open: ~ access *n.*, *no pl.* freier Zugang; **~-access** *adj.* frei zugänglich; **~-access library** *n.* Freihandbibliothek, *die;* **~-air** *attrib. adj.* Open-Air-‹*Konzert*›; Freiluft‹*restaurant, -aktivitäten*›; Freilicht‹*kino, -aufführung*›; ‹*Ausstellung, Markt, Versammlung*› im Freien *od.* unter freiem Himmel; **~-air [swimming] pool** Freibad, *das;* **~-and-'shut case** *n.* (coll.) klarer Fall; **~-armed** *adj.* herzlich; **receive** *or* **welcome sb. ~-armed** jmdn. mit offenen Armen aufnehmen *od.* empfangen; **~cast** *adj.* (Brit. Mining) **~cast mining/coal/method** Tagebau, *der*/Kohle aus dem Tagebau/Methode des Tagebaus; **~ day** *n.* Tag der offenen Tür; **~-'door** *attrib. adj.* **~-door policy** Politik der offenen Tür; **~-ended** /əʊpən'endɪd/ *adj.* [am Ende] offen; (fig.: with no predetermined limit) unbefristet ‹*Aufenthalt, Vertrag*›; uneingeschränkt ‹*Verpflichtung*›; unbegrenzt ‹*Unterstützung, Kredit*›; Open-End--‹*Diskussion, Debatte*›; offen ‹*Frage*›; unerschöpflich ‹*Thema*›; **~-ended spanner** Gabelschlüssel, *der*

opener /'əʊpnə(r)/ *n.* **1** Öffner, *der* **2** (opening item or event) (of entertainment) Eröffnungsnummer, *die;* (of a serial) erste Folge; (Sport) Eröffnungsspiel, *das* **3** (Cricket) eröffnender Schlagmann **4** **for ~s** (coll.) zu Beginn; zunächst einmal

open: ~-eyed *adj.* **1** mit offenen Augen *nachgestellt;* **in ~-eyed amazement** mit großen Augen; **gaze/stare ~-eyed at sb./sth.** jmdn./etw. mit großen Augen ansehen/anstarren; **gaze/stare ~-eyed** große Augen machen; **2** (watchful, alert) **do sth. ~eyed** etw. bewusst tun; **~-'field system** *n.* (Agric.) alte Dreifelderwirtschaft; **~-'fronted** *adj.* vorne offen; **~-'handed** *adj.* freigebig; **~-'heart** *attrib. adj.* (Med.) am offenen Herzen *nachgestellt;* **~-'hearted** *adj.* aufrichtig ‹*Person, Mitgefühl*›; herzlich ‹*Empfang*›

opening /'əʊpnɪŋ/

A *n.* **1** Öffnen, *das;* (becoming open) Sichöffnen, *das;* (of crack, gap, etc.) Entstehen, *das;* (of exhibition, new centre) Eröffnen, *das;* (of road to traffic) Freigabe, *die* (**to** für); **hours** *or* **times of ~:** Öffnungszeiten; **it's late ~:** heute haben die Läden länger geöffnet; **'late ~ Thursday'** „donnerstags auch abends geöffnet" **2** (establishment, inauguration, ceremony) Eröffnung, *die;* ~ **of Parliament** Parlamentseröffnung, *die* **3** (first performance) Premiere, *die* **4** (initial part) Anfang, *der;* (Chess) Eröffnung, *die* **5** (gap, aperture) Öffnung, *die* **6** (opportunity) Möglichkeit, *die;* (for goods) Absatzmöglichkeit, *die;* (vacancy) freie *od.* offene Stelle; **wait for an ~:** auf eine günstige Gelegenheit warten; **give sb. an ~:** jmdm. eine Gelegenheit geben; **give sb. an ~ into sth.** ‹*Person:*› jmdm. den Einstieg in etw. (*Akk.*) ermöglichen; ‹*Job:*› für jmdn. ein Einstieg in etw. (*Akk.*) sein **7** (facing pages of book etc.) Seitenpaar, *das*

B *adj.* einleitend; **the ~ lines** (of play, poem, etc.) die ersten Zeilen; **~ night** (Theatre) Premiere, *die;* ~ **speech/address** Eröffnungsrede/-ansprache, *die;* ~ **move** (Chess) Eröffnung, *die;* (fig.) erster Schachzug; ~ **bid** (at auction; also Bridge) erstes Gebot; ~ **batsman** (Cricket) eröffnender Schlagmann

opening: ~ ceremony *n.* feierliche Eröffnung (**for** *Gen.*); **~ hours** *n. pl.* Öffnungszeiten *Pl.;* **~ time** *n.* **1** Öffnungszeit, *die;* **wait for ~ time** darauf warten, dass geöffnet wird; **2** **~ times** ▸ **~ hours**

open 'letter *n.* offener Brief

openly /'əʊpnlɪ/ *adv.* **1** (publicly) in der Öffentlichkeit; öffentlich ‹*zugeben, verurteilen, abstreiten*›; **quite ~:** in aller Öffentlichkeit **2** (frankly) offen

open: ~ 'market *n.* offener *od.* freier Markt; **~-'minded** *adj.* aufgeschlossen (**about** für); **~-mindedness** /əʊpn'maɪndɪdnɪs/ *n.*, *no pl.* Aufgeschlossenheit, *die;* **~-mouthed** /əʊpn'maʊðd/ *adj.* mit offenem Mund; **gape in ~-mouthed amazement** mit offenem Munde staunen; **~-necked** *adj.* ‹*Hemd, Bluse*› mit offenem Kragen; ausgeschnitten ‹*Kleid, Pullover*›

openness /'əʊpnnɪs/ *n.*, *no pl.* **1** (of countryside etc.) Weite, *die* **2** (susceptibility) Empfindlichkeit, *die* (**to** gegen) **3** (receptiveness) Empfänglichkeit, *die;* ~ **of mind** Aufgeschlossenheit, *die* **4** (manifestness) Offenheit, *die;* **I was surprised by the ~ of the people's resistance** ich war überrascht, wie offen die Leute Widerstand leisteten **5** (frankness) Offenheit, *die* **6** (being spread out) Grobheit, *die;* (of arrangement) Offenheit, *die*

open: ~-plan *adj.* mit ineinander übergehenden Räumen *nachgestellt;* offen angelegt ‹*Haus*›; **~-plan office** Großraumbüro, *das;* **~ 'prison** *n.* offene Anstalt; **~ 'sandwich**

n. belegtes Brot; ~ **season** *n.* (Brit.) Jagdzeit, *die;* (for fish) Fangzeit, *die;* **it is [the] ~ season for** *or* **on sth.** (fig.) etw. ist an der Tagesordnung; ~ **'sesame** ▸ **sesame 3**; ~ **'shelf library** (Amer.) ▸ ~ **access library**; ~ **'shelves** *n. pl.* **these books are on ~ shelves** diese Bücher sind in der Freihandzone [aufgestellt]; ~ **'shop** *n.* Open Shop, *der;* nicht gewerkschaftspflichtiger Betrieb; ~ **so'ciety** *n.* (Sociol.) offene Gesellschaft; **~-toe[d]** /əʊpn'təʊ(d)/ *adj.* vorn offen ‹*Schuh, Sandale*›; **~-top** *attrib. adj.* offen; oben offen ‹*Bus*›; **O~ Uni'versity** *pr. n.* (Brit.) **the O~ University** die Open University (*britische Fernuniversität*); *attrib.* ‹*Kurs*› an der Fernuniversität; ‹*akademischer Grad*› der Fernuniversität; ~ **'weave** *n.* (Textiles) loses *od.* grobes Gewebe; *attrib.* locker *od.* grob gewebt ‹*Stoff, Struktur*›; **~work** *n.* durchbrochene Struktur; (Sewing) Durchbrucharbeit, *die; attrib.* durchbrochen

Open University — OU

Eine britische Fernuniversität, die 1969 gegründet wurde und vor allem Berufstätigen im Fernstudium Kurse auf verschiedenem Niveau bietet, insbesondere wissenschaftliche und berufliche Fortbildungsprogramme. Studenten jeder Altersgruppe, selbst solche ohne die sonst erforderlichen Schulabschlüsse, können das Studium nach vier oder fünf Jahren mit dem *Bachelor's degree* und dem *Master's degree* abschließen. Teilnehmer studieren von zu Hause — teilweise mittels audiovisueller Medien — schicken ihre Arbeit ein und erhalten eine Rückantwort von ihrem *tutor* (Dozent). Studenten können auch am Direktunterricht mit wöchentlichen Seminaren in Studienzentren und an Sommerschulen teilnehmen. Nach dem erfolgreichen Vorbild der *Open University* gibt es inzwischen auch in anderen Teilen der Welt ähnliche Fortbildungsprogramme.

opera[1] /'ɒpərə/ *n.* **1** Oper, *die* **2** *no pl.* (branch of art) **[the] ~**: die Oper **3** **light ~**: Operette, *die*

opera[2] *pl. of* **opus**

operable /'ɒpərəbl/ *adj.* (Med.) operabel

opera: ~ **glasses** *n. pl.* Opernglas, *das;* ~ **hat** *n.* Chapeau claque, *der;* ~ **house** *n.* Opernhaus, *das;* ~ **singer** *n.* ▸ **i p. 1260** Opernsänger, *der*/-sängerin, *die*

operate /'ɒpəreɪt/

A *v.i.* **1** (be in action) in Betrieb sein; ‹*Bus, Zug usw.:*› verkehren; (have an effect) sich auswirken; **the system ~s against our interests/in our favour** das System, wie es derzeit funktioniert, bringt uns Nachteile/Vorteile; **the hospital is operating normally again** im Krankenhaus herrscht wieder normaler Betrieb **2** (function) arbeiten; **the torch ~s on batteries** die Taschenlampe arbeitet mit Batterien **3** (perform operation) operieren; arbeiten; **~ on sth.** etw. bearbeiten; **~ [on sb.]** (Med.) [jmdn.] operieren **4** (exercise influence) **~ [up]on sb./sth.** auf jmdn./etw. einwirken **5** (follow course of conduct) agieren; **the gang ~d by posing as workmen** die Methode der Bande bestand darin, dass sie sich als Arbeiter ausgaben **6** (produce effect) wirken **7** (Mil.) operieren

B *v.t.* bedienen ‹*Maschine*›; betätigen ‹*Hebel, Bremse*›; betreiben ‹*Unternehmen*›; unterhalten ‹*Werk, Post, Busverbindung, Telefondienst*›

operatic /ɒpə'rætɪk/ *adj.* **1** Opern‹*sänger, -musik*› **2** (like opera) opernhaft

operating: ~ **room** *n.* (Med.) Operationssaal, *der;* ~ **system** *n.* (Computing) Betriebssystem, *das;* ~ **table** *n.* (Med.) Operationstisch, *der;* ~ **theatre** *n.* (Brit. Med.) Operationssaal, *der*

operation /ɒpə'reɪʃn/ *n.* **1** (causing to work) (of machine) Bedienung, *die;* (of factory, mine, etc.) Betrieb, *der;* (of bus service, telephone service, etc.) Unterhaltung, *die;* **ease of ~**: leichte Bedienbarkeit **2** (way sth. works) Arbeitsweise, *die;* **the engine is noted for its quiet ~** *or* **quietness in ~**: der Motor ist für seinen leisen Lauf bekannt **3** (being operative) **come into ~** ‹*Maschine, Gerät:*› zu arbeiten beginnen; ‹*Gesetz, Gebühr usw.:*› in Kraft treten; **be in ~** ‹*Maschine, Gerät usw.:*› in Betrieb sein; ‹*Service:*› zur Verfügung stehen; ‹*Gesetz:*› in Kraft sein; **be out of ~** ‹*Maschine, Gerät usw.:*› außer Betrieb sein; ‹*Service:*› nicht zur Verfügung stehen **4** (active process) Vorgang, *der;* **drilling ~s** Bohrarbeiten; **~[s] research** ▸ **operational research** **5** (performance) Tätigkeit, *die;* **repeat the ~**: das Ganze [noch einmal] wiederholen **6** ▸ **i p. 1231** (Med.) Operation, *die;* **have an ~ [on one's foot]** [am Fuß] operiert werden; **an ~ for appendicitis** eine Blinddarmoperation **7** (Air Force, Mil., Navy) Einsatz, *der;* Operation, *die;* **night ~s** Nachteinsätze; **~s room** Befehlsstelle, *die; see also* **combined** **8** (financial transaction) [Geschäfts]tätigkeit, *die* **9** (Math., Computing) Operation, *die*

operational /ɒpə'reɪʃənl/ *adj.* **1** (concerned with operations) Einsatz‹*flugzeug, -breite*›; Betriebs‹*wirtschaftlichkeit, -personal*›; (Mil.) Einsatz- **2** (esp. Mil.: ready to function) einsatzbereit

operational re'search *n.* (Brit.) Unternehmensforschung, *die*

operative /'ɒpərətɪv/

A *adj.* **1** (in operation) **the law became ~**: das Gesetz trat in Kraft; **the scheme is fully ~**: das Programm läuft **2** (effective) wirksam **3** (most relevant) **the ~ word is 'quietly'** die Betonung liegt auf „leise" **4** (Med.) operativ

B *n.* [Fach]arbeiter, *der*/-arbeiterin, *die;* **machine ~**: Maschinist, *der*/Maschinistin, *die*

operator /'ɒpəreɪtə(r)/ *n.* **1** ▸ **i p. 1260** (worker) [Maschinen]bediener, *der*/-bedienerin, *die;* Bedienungskraft, *die;* (of crane, excavator, etc.) Führer, *der* **2** ▸ **i p. 1260** (Teleph.) (at exchange) Vermittlung, *die;* (at switchboard) Telefonist, *der*/Telefonistin, *die* **3** (person engaged in business) Unternehmer, *der*/Unternehmerin, *die;* (coll.: shrewd person) Schlitzohr, *das* (ugs.); **a sly ~** (coll.) ein gewiefter Bursche (ugs.) **4** (Math., Computing) Operator, *der*

operetta /ɒpə'retə/ *n.* (Mus.) Operette, *die*

ophthalmic /ɒf'θælmɪk/ *adj.* Augen‹*arterie, -krankheit, -chirurg, -salbe*›

ophthalmic op'tician *n.* ▸ **i p. 1260** (Brit.) Augenoptiker, *der*/-optikerin, *die*

ophthalmologist /ɒfθæl'mɒlədʒɪst/ *n.* ▸ **i p. 1260** Ophthalmologe, *der*/Ophthalmologin, *die;* Augenarzt, *der*/-ärztin, *die*

ophthalmology /ɒfθæl'mɒlədʒɪ/ *n.* Ophthalmologie, *die* (fachspr.); Augenheilkunde, *die*

opiate /'əʊpɪət/ *n.* **1** (Med.) Opiat, *das* **2** (fig.) Betäubungsmittel, *das;* (causing addiction) Droge, *die*

opine /ə'paɪn/ *v.t.* **1** (express as one's opinion) meinen **2** (hold as opinion) denken

opinion /ə'pɪnjən/ *n.* **1** (belief, judgement) Meinung, *die* (**on** über + *Akk.*, zu); Ansicht, *die* (**on** von, zu, über + *Akk.*); **his [political] ~s** seine [politische] Einstellung; **his ~s on the matter/on religion** seine Meinung dazu/seine Einstellung zur Religion; **in my ~**: meiner Meinung nach; **be of [the] ~ that ...**: der Ansicht sein, dass ...; **be a matter of ~**: Ansichtssache sein; *see also* **difference 1** **2** *no pl., no art.* (beliefs etc. of group) Meinung, *die* (**on** über + *Akk.*); **~ is swinging in his favour** es gibt einen Meinungsumschwung zu seinen Gunsten; **public ~**: die öffentliche Meinung **3** (estimate) **have a high/low ~ of sb.** eine hohe/schlechte Meinung von jmdm. haben; **I formed a better ~ of the place** ich bekam einen besseren Eindruck von dem Ort; **have a great ~ of oneself** sehr von sich überzeugt sein; **have no ~ of sth./sb.** von etw./jmdm. nicht sehr überzeugt sein **4** (formal statement of expert) Gutachten, *das;* **[get** *or* **secure a] solicitor's/expert's ~**: [ein] Rechts-/Sachverständigengutachten [einholen]; **another** *or* **a second ~**: die Meinung eines weiteren *od.* zweiten Sachverständigen **5** (Law) (expression of reasons for decision) Urteilsbegründung, *die;* (judgement, decision) Entscheidung, *die;* Urteil, *das*

opinionated /ə'pɪnjəneɪtɪd/ *adj.* **1** (obstinate) rechthaberisch **2** (self-willed) eigensinnig

o'pinion poll *n.* Meinungsumfrage, *die*

opium /'əʊpɪəm/ *n.* Opium, *das*

opium: ~ **den** *n.* Opiumhöhle, *die* (abwertend); ~ **pipe** *n.* Opiumpfeife, *die*

opossum /ə'pɒsəm/ *n.* (Zool.) **1** Opossum, *das* **2** (Austral., NZ) ▸ **possum 3**

oppo /'ɒpəʊ/ *n., pl.* **~s** (Brit. coll.) Kumpel, *der* (salopp)

opponent /ə'pəʊnənt/ *n.* Gegner, *der*/Gegnerin, *die*

opportune /'ɒpətju:n/ *adj.* **1** (favourable) günstig **2** (well-timed) zur rechten Zeit *nachgestellt;* **be ~**: zur rechten Zeit kommen

opportunely /'ɒpətju:nlɪ/ *adv.* ▸ **opportune**: günstig; zur rechten Zeit; **be ~ timed** zeitlich günstig liegen

opportunism /ɒpə'tju:nɪzm/ *n., no pl.* Opportunismus, *der*

opportunist /ɒpə'tju:nɪst/ *n.* Opportunist, *der*/Opportunistin, *die*

opportunistic /ɒpətju:'nɪstɪk/ *adj.* (also Ecol., Med.) opportunistisch

opportunity /ɒpə'tju:nɪtɪ/ *n.* Gelegenheit, *die;* **have plenty of/little ~ for doing** *or* **to do sth.** reichlich/wenig Gelegenheit haben, etw. zu tun; **~ knocks for sb.** eine Gelegenheit bietet sich jmdm.; *see also* **equal opportunity**; **take A 5**

opposable /ə'pəʊzəbl/ *adj.* (Anat., Zool.) opponierbar

oppose /ə'pəʊz/

A *v.t.* **1** (set oneself against) sich wenden gegen; opponieren gegen **2** (place as obstacle) entgegenstellen (**to** *Dat.*) **3** (set as contrast) gegenüberstellen (**to, against** *Dat.*) **4** (Anat., Zool.) opponieren

B *v.i.* ‹*Opposition:*› opponieren; **the opposing team** die gegnerische Mannschaft

opposed /ə'pəʊzd/ *adj.* **1** (contrary, opposite) gegensätzlich; entgegengesetzt; **X and Y are diametrically ~**: X und Y sind einander diametral entgegengesetzt; **as ~ to** im Gegensatz zu **2** (hostile) **be ~** ‹*Personen:*› Gegner sein; **be ~ to sth.** gegen etw. sein

opposite /'ɒpəzɪt/

A *adj.* **1** (on other or farther side) gegenüberliegend ‹*Straßenseite, Ufer*›; entgegengesetzt ‹*Ende*› **2** (contrary) entgegengesetzt ‹*Weg, Richtung*› **3** (very different in character) entgegengesetzt, gegensätzlich ‹*Beschreibungen, Aussagen*›; **be ~ to sth.** das Gegenteil von etw. sein; **be of an ~ kind from ...**: von einer ganz anderen Art sein als ... **4** **the ~ sex** das andere Geschlecht

B *n.* Gegenteil, *das* (**of** von); **be the extreme ~ of sth.** das genaue Gegenteil von etw. sein; **be ~s** einen Gegensatz bilden

C *adv.* gegenüber; **sit ~**: auf der gegenüberliegenden Seite sitzen

D *prep.* gegenüber; **~ each other** einander gegenüber; **play ~ sb.** (Theatre) neben jmdm. spielen

opposite 'number *n.* (fig.) Pendant, *das*

opposition /ɒpə'zɪʃn/ *n.* **1** *no pl.* (antagonism) Opposition, *die;* (resistance) Widerstand, *der* (**to** gegen); **in ~ to** entgegen; **offer ~ to sth.** einer Sache (*Dat.*) Widerstand entgegensetzen; **without ~**: ohne Widerstand **2** (Brit. Polit.) **the O~, Her Majesty's O~**: die Opposition; **Leader of the O~**: Oppositionsführer, *der*/-führerin, *die;* **[be] in ~**: in der Opposition [sein] **3** (body of opponents or competitors) Gegner *Pl.* **4** (contrast, antithesis) Gegensatz, *der* (**to** zu) **5** (placing or being placed opposite) Platzierung an gegenüberliegenden Stellen; **by the ~ of sth. to sth.** indem man etw. gegenüber einer Sache (*Dat.*) platziert **6** (Astron., Astrol.) **be in ~**: in Opposition stehen (**with** zu); *abs.* in Opposition zur Sonne stehen

oppress /ə'pres/ *v.t.* **1** (govern cruelly) unterdrücken **2** (fig.: weigh down) ‹*Gefühl:*› bedrücken; ‹*Hitze:*› schwer zu schaffen machen (+ *Dat.*)

oppression /ə'preʃn/ *n.* Unterdrückung, *die*

oppressive /ə'presɪv/ *adj.* **1** (tyrannical) repressiv **2** (fig.: hard to endure) bedrückend ‹*Ängste, Atmosphäre*› (**to** für) **3** (fig.: hot and close) drückend ‹*Wetter, Klima, Tag*› **4** (fig.: burdensome) drückend ‹*Steuer*›; repressiv ‹*Gesetz, Beschränkung*›

oppressively /əˈpresɪvlɪ/ *adv.* **1** (tyrannically) mit unterdrückerischen Methoden; repressiv ‹*regieren*› **2** (fig.: so as to weigh down) drückend ‹*heiß*›; **weigh ~ on sb.** schwer auf jmdm. lasten

oppressor /əˈpresə(r)/ *n.* Unterdrücker, *der*

opprobrious /əˈprəʊbrɪəs/ *adj.* **1** (abusive) verächtlich **2** (shameful) schändlich

opprobrium /əˈprəʊbrɪəm/ *n.* Schande, *die*

opt /ɒpt/ *v.i.* sich entscheiden (**for** für); **~ to do sth.** sich dafür entscheiden, etw. zu tun; **~ out** (not join in) nicht mitmachen; (cease taking part) nicht länger mitmachen; **~ out of** nicht/nicht länger mitmachen bei; (give up membership of) austreten aus; (not take up invitation to) sich entschließen, doch nicht teilzunehmen an (+ *Dat.*)

optic /ˈɒptɪk/

A *adj.* (Anat.) Seh‹*nerv, -hügel, -bahn*›; (Med.) Sehnerven‹*entzündung, -atrophie*›

B *n.* **1** (in optical instrument) optisches Element **2** (arch./joc.: eye) Auge, *das* **3** *or* **O~** ® (Brit.: for measuring out spirits) Portionierer, *der*

optical /ˈɒptɪkl/ *adj.* optisch ‹*Zielvorrichtung, Täuschung, Gerät, Fernrohr*›; **~ microscope** Lichtmikroskop, *das;* **~ aid** Sehhilfe, *die*

optical: ~ ˈcharacter reader *n.* (Computing) Klarschriftleser, *der;* **~ ˈdisk** *n.* (Computing) optische Platte; **~ ˈfibre** *n.* Lichtleitfaser, *die*

optically /ˈɒptɪkəlɪ/ *adv.* optisch

optician /ɒpˈtɪʃn/ *n.* ▸ⓘ **p. 1260** **1** (maker or seller of spectacles etc.) Optiker, *der*/Optikerin, *die* **2** ▸**ophthalmic optician**

optics /ˈɒptɪks/ *n., no pl.* Optik, *die*

optima *pl. of* **optimum**

optimal /ˈɒptɪml/ ▸**optimum B**

optimise ▸**optimize**

optimism /ˈɒptɪmɪzm/ *n., no pl.* Optimismus, *der*

optimist /ˈɒptɪmɪst/ *n.* Optimist, *der*/Optimistin, *die*

optimistic /ɒptɪˈmɪstɪk/ *adj.* optimistisch

optimistically /ɒptɪˈmɪstɪkəlɪ/ *adv.* optimistisch; **~ speaking, ...:** mit etwas Optimismus kann man sagen, dass ...

optimize /ˈɒptɪmaɪz/ *v.t.* **1** (make optimum) optimieren **2** (make the most of) das Beste machen aus

optimum /ˈɒptɪməm/

A *n., pl.* **optima** /ˈɒptɪmə/ **1** (most favourable conditions) Optimum, *das* **2** (best compromise) goldener Mittelweg

B *adj.* optimal

option /ˈɒpʃn/ *n.* **1** (choice) Wahl, *die;* (thing that may be chosen) Wahlmöglichkeit, *die;* (Brit. Univ., Sch.) Wahlfach, *das;* **I have no ~ but to do sth.** mir bleibt nichts [anderes] übrig, als etw. zu tun; **keep** *or* **leave one's ~s open** sich (*Dat.*) alle Möglichkeiten offen halten; *see also* **soft option** **2** *no pl.* (freedom of choice) Entscheidungsfreiheit, *die;* **she had no ~ about accepting ...:** sie hatte keine andere Wahl, als ... anzunehmen; **that leaves us no ~ [but to ...]** dann bleibt uns keine andere Wahl[, als zu ...] **3** (St. Exch.) Option, *die*

optional /ˈɒpʃənl/ *adj.* nicht zwingend; fakultativ; **~ subject** Wahlfach, *das;* **formal dress is ~:** Gesellschaftskleidung ist nicht vorgeschrieben; **~ extra** Extra, *das;* **take an ~ paper** eine freiwillige Klausur schreiben

optionally /ˈɒpʃənəlɪ/ *adv.* freiwillig

optoelectronic /ɒptəʊɪlekˈtrɒnɪk/ *adj.* optoelektronisch

optoelectronics /ɒptəʊɪlekˈtrɒnɪks/ *n., no pl.* Optoelektronik, *die*

ˈopt-out *n.* **1** (opportunity to withdraw) Opt-out, *das; attrib.* **~ clause** Opt-out-Klausel, *die* **2** (Brit.) (act of opting out) Ausstieg, *der; attrib.* **~ school/hospital** Schule/Krankenhaus in freier Trägerschaft

opulence /ˈɒpjʊləns/ *n., no pl.* Wohlstand, *der*

opulent /ˈɒpjʊlənt/ *adj.* (rich) wohlhabend ‹*Person, Aussehen*›; (luxurious) feudal ‹*Auto, Haus, Hotel usw.*›

opulently /ˈɒpjʊləntlɪ/ *adv.* im Luxus ‹*leben*›; feudal ‹*möbliert, eingerichtet*›

opus /ˈəʊpəs, ˈɒpəs/ *n., pl.* **opera** /ˈɒpərə/ **1** (Mus.) Opus, *das* **2** **magnum ~, ~ [magnum]** (great work) großes Werk; (greatest work) Hauptwerk, *das*

or[1] /ə(r), *stressed* ɔː(r)/ *conj.* **1** oder; **he cannot read or write** er kann weder lesen noch schreiben; **without food or water** ohne Essen und Wasser; **[either] ... or [else] ...:** entweder ... oder [aber] ... **2** *introducing synonym* oder [auch]; *introducing explanation* das heißt; **or rather** beziehungsweise; [oder] genauer gesagt **3** *indicating uncertainty* oder; **15 or 20 minutes** 15 bis 20 Minuten; **in a day or two** in ein, zwei Tagen; **a doctor or something** ein Arzt oder so [was] (ugs.); **he must be ill or something** vielleicht ist er krank oder so (ugs.); **have you gone out of your mind or something?** bist du übergeschnappt, oder was? (ugs.); **he or somebody else** er oder sonst jemand; **in Leeds or somewhere** in Leeds oder irgendwo da; *see also* **so**[1] **B 4** *expr. significant afterthought* oder; **he was obviously lying — or was he?** er hat ganz offensichtlich gelogen — oder [doch nicht]?; **they cannot throw you out — or can they?** sie können dich doch nicht hinauswerfen — oder [etwa doch]?

or[2] /ɔː(r)/ (Her.)

A *n.* Gold, *das*

B *adj.* golden

OR *abbr.* **= operational research** OR

oracle /ˈɒrəkl/ *n.* **1** (infallible guide or indicator) Orakel, *das* (fig.) **2** (very wise person) Koryphäe, *die;* Autorität, *die* **3** (place or response of deity) Orakel, *das* **4** **work the ~** (Brit. fig.) [ein wenig] nachhelfen

oracular /əˈrækjʊlə(r)/ *adj.* **1** (of oracle[s]) Orakel‹*stätte, -priester*› **2** (infallible) über alle Zweifel erhaben ‹*Äußerung, Buch*› **3** (derog.: obscure or ambiguous) orakelhaft

oral /ˈɔːrl/

A *adj.* **1** (spoken) mündlich ‹*Prüfung, Vereinbarung*›; mündlich überliefert ‹*Tradition*›; **the agreement was only ~:** die Vereinbarung war nur mündlich getroffen worden **2** (done or taken by the mouth) oral; **~ sex** Oralsex, *der;* **~ intercourse** Oralverkehr, *der* **3** (Anat.) Mund‹*höhle, -schleimhaut*›

B *n.* (coll.: examination) **the ~[s]** das Mündliche

orally /ˈɔːrəlɪ/ *adv.* **1** (in speech) mündlich **2** (by the mouth) oral; **take ~:** einnehmen

orange /ˈɒrɪndʒ/

A *n.* **1** (fruit) Orange, *die;* Apfelsine, *die* **2** (tree) Orangenbaum, *der;* **mock ~** (Bot.) Falscher Jasmin; Blasser Pfeifenstrauch **3** (colour) **~ [colour]** Orange, *das*

B *adj.* orange[farben]; Orangen‹*geschmack*›; **~ drink** Getränk mit Orangengeschmack

orangeade /ˈɒrɪndʒeɪd/ *n., no pl.* (Brit.) Orangeade, *die*

orange: ~ blossom *n.* Orangenblüte, *die;* **~ box** *n.* Apfelsinenkiste, *die;* **~ juice** *n.* Orangensaft, *der;* **O~man** /ˈɒrɪndʒmən/ *n., pl.* **O~men** /ˈɒrɪndʒmən/ (Polit.) Orangeman, *der;* Mitglied der Orange Society; **~ peel** *n.* Orangenschale, *die*

> **Orangemen**
>
> Mitglieder der nordirischen *Orange Society*, die im Kampf gegen die irische Nationalbewegung hervortrat und die protestantische Herrschaft in Nordirland aufrechterhalten will. Die *Orangemen* marschieren jedes Jahr am 12. Juli durch die Straßen. Die Märsche erinnern an den Sieg des protestantischen Königs Wilhelm III. von Oranien, auch *William of Orange* genannt, über den Katholiken Jakob II. Die jährlichen Umzüge werden von der katholischen Bevölkerung in Nordirland als Provokation empfunden.

orangery /ˈɒrɪndʒərɪ/ *n.* Orangerie, *die*

orange: ~ ˈsquash ▸**squash**[1] **C 1**; **~ stick** *n.* Maniküreстäbchen, *das*

orang-utan /ɔːræŋʊˈtæn/ *n.* (Zool.) Orang-Utan, *der*

orate /əˈreɪt/ *v.i.* (joc.) Reden schwingen (ugs.); (derog.) salbadern (ugs. abwertend)

oration /əˈreɪʃn/ *n.* Rede, *die*

orator /ˈɒrətə(r)/ *n.* Redner, *der*/Rednerin, *die;* (eloquent speaker) Rhetoriker, *der*/Rhetorikerin, *die*

oratorical /ɒrəˈtɒrɪkl/ *adj.* ausdrucksstark

oratorio /ɒrəˈtɔːrɪəʊ/ *n., pl.* **~s** (Mus.) Oratorium, *das*

oratory /ˈɒrətərɪ/ *n.* **1** *no pl.* (art of public speaking) Redekunst, *die;* Rhetorik, *die* **2** *no pl.* (rhetorical language) Rhetorik, *die* **3** (small chapel) Oratorium, *das*

orb /ɔːb/ *n.* **1** (sphere) Kugel, *die* **2** (part of regalia) Reichsapfel, *der*

orbit /ˈɔːbɪt/

A *n.* **1** (Astron.) [Umlauf]bahn, *die* **2** (Astronaut.) Umlaufbahn, *die;* Orbit, *der;* (single circuit) Umkreisung, *die;* **be in/go into ~ [around the moon]** in der [Mond]umlaufbahn sein/in die [Mond]umlaufbahn eintreten; **put/send into ~:** in die Umlaufbahn bringen/schießen **3** (fig.) Sphäre, *die* **4** (Anat.) Augenhöhle, *die;* Orbita, *die* (fachspr.) **5** (Phys.: of electron) Orbital, *das*

B *v.i.* kreisen

C *v.t.* umkreisen

orbital /ˈɔːbɪtl/ *adj.* **1** (Anat.) Orbital- **2** (Astron., Phys.) Bahn- **3** Ring‹*straße, -linie*›; **north ~ route** Nordring, *der*

orbiter /ˈɔːbɪtə(r)/ *n.* (Astronaut.) Orbiter, *der*

Orcadian /ɔːˈkeɪdɪən/

A *adj.* Orkney-; der Orkneyinseln *nachgestellt*

B *n.* Bewohner/Bewohnerin der Orkneyinseln

orchard /ˈɔːtʃəd/ *n.* Obstgarten, *der;* (commercial) Obstplantage, *die;* **cherry ~:** Kirschgarten, *der*

orchestra /ˈɔːkɪstrə/ *n.* **1** (Mus.) Orchester, *das* **2** ▸**orchestra pit**

orchestral /ɔːˈkestrl/ *adj.* Orchester-; (suggestive of orchestra) orchestral

orchestra: ~ pit *n.* Orchestergraben, *der;* **~ stalls** *n. pl.* Parkett, *das;* **seat in the ~ stalls** Sperrsitz, *der*

orchestrate /ˈɔːkɪstreɪt/ *v.t.* (Mus.; also fig.) orchestrieren

orchestration /ɔːkɪˈstreɪʃn/ *n.* **1** (Mus.) Orchesterbearbeitung, *die;* Orchestrierung, *die* **2** (fig.) Orchestrierung, *die*

orchid /ˈɔːkɪd/ *n.* Orchidee, *die*

orchis /ˈɔːkɪs/ *n.* (Bot.) Knabenkraut, *das;* Orchis, *die* (fachspr.)

ordain /ɔːˈdeɪn/ *v.t.* **1** (Eccl.) ordinieren; **be ~ed priest** ordiniert werden **2** (destine) bestimmen; **if fate should so ~ it** wenn es das Schicksal so will *od.* fügt **3** (decree) verfügen

ordeal /ɔːˈdiːl/ *n.* **1** Qual, *die;* (geh.) Tortur, *die* (**by** durch) **2** (Hist.) Ordal, *das* (fachspr.); Gottesurteil, *das;* **~ by fire/water** Feuer-/Wasserprobe, *die*

order /ˈɔːdə(r)/

A *n.* **1** (sequence) Reihenfolge, *die;* **~ of words, word ~:** Wortstellung, *die;* **~ of play** (Tennis etc.) Spielfolge, *die;* **in ~ of importance/size/age** nach Wichtigkeit/Größe/Alter; **be in subject ~** *or* **~ of subject** nach Gebieten geordnet sein; **put sth. in ~:** etw. [in der richtigen Reihenfolge] ordnen; **keep sth. in ~:** etw. in der richtigen Reihenfolge halten; **answer the questions in ~:** die Fragen der Reihe nach beantworten; **out of ~:** nicht in der richtigen Reihenfolge; durcheinander; **the cards get out of ~:** die Karten geraten in Unordnung *od.* durcheinander; **put sth. back out of ~:** etw. nicht an den richtigen Platz zurückstellen/-legen **2** (regular array, normal state) Ordnung, *die;* **put** *or* **set sth./one's affairs in ~:** Ordnung in etw. bringen/seine Angelegenheiten ordnen; **be/not be in ~:** in Ordnung/nicht in Ordnung sein (ugs.); **put sth. in ~** (repair) etw. in Ordnung bringen (ugs.); **be out of/in ~** (not in/in working condition) nicht funktionieren/funktionieren; **'out of ~'** „außer Betrieb"; **the engine is now in running ~:** der Motor läuft jetzt wieder *od.* ist jetzt wieder betriebsbereit; **in good/bad ~:** in gutem/schlechtem Zustand; **in working ~:** betriebsfähig; *see also* **house A 1** **3** *in sing. and pl.* (command) Anweisung, *die;*

Anordnung, *die;* Weisung, *die* (geh.); (Mil.) Befehl, *der;* (Law) Beschluss, *der;* Verfügung, *die;* **my ∼s are to ..., I have ∼s to ...:** ich habe Anweisung zu ...; **while following ∼s** bei Befolgung der Anweisung/bei der Befehlsausführung; **act on ∼s** auf Befehl handeln; **be the one who gives the ∼s** das Sagen haben; **I don't take ∼s from anyone!** ich lasse mir von keinem etwas befehlen!; **∼s are ∼s** Befehl ist Befehl; **court ∼:** Gerichtsbeschluss, *der;* **by ∼ of** auf Anordnung (+ *Gen.*); *see also* **doctor A 1; further A 2; starter 1**

[4] **in ∼ to do sth.** um etw. zu tun; **in ∼ that sb. should do sth.** damit jmd. etw. tut

[5] (Commerc.) Auftrag, *der* (**for** über + *Akk.*); Bestellung, *die* (**for** *Gen.*); Order, *die* (Kaufmannsspr.); (to waiter, ∼ed goods) Bestellung, *die;* **place an ∼ [with sb.]** [jmdm.] einen Auftrag erteilen; **have sth. on ∼:** etw. bestellt haben; **put goods on ∼:** Waren in Bestellung geben; **to ∼:** auf Bestellung; **she could cry to ∼** (fig.) sie konnte auf Befehl weinen; **made to ∼:** nach Maß angefertigt, maßgeschneidert ‹*Kleidung*›; **a suit made to ∼:** ein Maßanzug; **last ∼s please** (Brit.) die letzten Bestellungen (*vor der Sperrstunde*), bitte!; *see also* **tall A 2**

[6] (law-abiding state) [öffentliche] Ordnung; **forces of ∼:** Ordnungsmächte; **keep ∼:** Ordnung [be]wahren; *see also* **law 2**

[7] (Eccl.: fraternity) Orden, *der*

[8] (Eccl.: grade of ministry) Weihestufe, *die;* **holy ∼s** heilige Weihen; **be in [holy] ∼s** dem geistlichen Stand angehören; **take [holy] ∼s** die [heiligen] Weihen empfangen

[9] (social class) [Gesellschafts]schicht, *die;* (clerical ∼, ∼ of baronets, etc.) Stand, *der; see also* **lower² A 2**

[10] (principles of decorum and rules of procedure) [Geschäfts]ordnung, *die;* **O∼! O∼!** zur Ordnung!; Ruhe bitte!; **∼ in court** (Brit.) *or* (Amer.) **the courtroom** Ruhe im Gerichtssaal; **call sb./the meeting to ∼:** jmdn./die Versammlung zur Ordnung rufen; **call a meeting to ∼** (open the proceedings) eine Versammlung für eröffnet erklären; **point of ∼:** Verfahrensfrage, *die;* **[on a] point of ∼, Mr Chairman** Antrag zur Geschäftsordnung, Herr Vorsitzender; **be in ∼:** zulässig sein; (fig.) ‹*Forderung:*› berechtigt sein; ‹*Drink, Erklärung:*› angebracht sein; **the speaker is in ∼:** der Redner hält sich an die Geschäftsordnung; **it is in ∼ for him to do that** es ist in Ordnung, wenn er das tut; **be out of ∼:** gegen die Geschäftsordnung verstoßen; ‹*Verhalten, Handlung:*› unzulässig sein; **that's/you're out of ∼, mate** (coll.) so [gehts] nicht, Kumpel (ugs.); **∼ of the day** (lit. or fig.) Tagesordnung, *die;* **be the ∼ of the day** auf der Tagesordnung stehen; (fig.) an der Tagesordnung sein; **∼ of business** Geschäftsordnung, *die;* (sequence of matters) Tagesordnung, *die; see also* **standing order 2**

[11] (constitution of things) Ordnung, *die;* **a new ∼ of literary criticism** eine neue Art *od.* Gattung von Literaturkritik

[12] (kind, degree) Klasse, *die;* Art, *die;* **intelligence of a high ∼:** hochgradige Intelligenz; **his work is usually of a high ∼:** seine Arbeit ist gewöhnlich erstklassig

[13] (Archit.) Säulenordnung, *die*

[14] (company of distinguished persons, badge or insignia) Orden, *der;* **O∼ of Merit** (Brit.) Verdienstorden, *der;* **Masonic O∼:** Freimaurerloge, *die*

[15] (Finance) Order, *die;* Zahlungsanweisung, *die;* **[banker's] ∼:** [Bank]anweisung, *die;* **'pay to the ∼ of ...'** „zahlbar an ..." (+ *Akk.*); *see also* **money order; standing order 1**

[16] (Mil.) Ordnung, *die;* **marching ∼:** Marschordnung, *die;* **in close ∼:** in geschlossener Formation; **in battle ∼:** in Kampfaufstellung

[17] (Math.) Ordnung, *die;* **∼ [of magnitude]** Größenordnung, *die;* **of** *or* **in the ∼ of ...:** in der Größenordnung von ...; **of the first ∼** ‹*Gleichung*› ersten Grades; **a scoundrel of the first ∼** (fig. coll.) ein Schurke ersten Ranges

[18] (Eccl.: form of service) Ritual, *das*

[19] (Biol.) Ordnung, *die; see also* **natural order**

B *v.t.* [1] (command) befehlen; anordnen; ‹*Gott, Schicksal:*› bestimmen; ‹*Richter:*› verfügen; verordnen ‹*Arznei, Ruhe usw.*›; **∼ sb. to do sth.** jmdn. anweisen/(Milit.) jmdm. befehlen, etw. zu tun; **∼ sth. [to be] done** anordnen, dass etw. getan wird; **the dog was ∼ed to be destroyed** es wurde die Tötung des Hundes verfügt *od.* angeordnet; *see also* **doctor A 1**

[2] (direct the supply of) bestellen (**from** bei); ordern ‹*Kaufmannsspr.*›; **∼ in advance** vorbestellen

[3] (arrange) ordnen; **∼ed** geordnet *od.* geregelt ‹*Leben*›; **∼ arms** (Mil.) Gewehr bei Fuß stehen

[4] (command to go) schicken; (Mil.) beordern; **∼ sb. [to go] to Spain** jmdn. nach Spanien schicken/beordern; **∼ sb. [to come] home** jmdn. befehlen, nach Hause zu kommen; **∼ sb. out of the house** jmdn. aus dem Haus weisen; **∼ back** zurückbeordern

[5] (ordain) bestimmen

Phrasal verbs

- **∼ a'bout, ∼ a'round** *v.t.* herumkommandieren
- **∼ 'off** *v.t.* (Sport) **∼ sb. off [the pitch/field]** jmdn. vom Platz stellen
- **∼ 'out** *v.t.* hinausschicken; ausschicken, einsetzen ‹*Truppen usw.*›

order: ∼ book *n.* [1] (Commerc.) Auftragsbuch, *das;* [2] **O∼ Book** (Brit. Parl.) Buch mit Eintragungen der angemeldeten Anträge; **∼ form** *n.* Bestellformular, *das;* Bestellschein, *der;* **O∼ in 'Council** *n.* (Brit.) Regierungserlass, *der*

orderly /ˈɔːdəlɪ/

A *adj.* [1] friedlich ‹*Demonstration usw.*›; diszipliniert ‹*Menge*›; (conforming to order) ordnungsgemäß; (methodical) methodisch; geordnet ‹*Linie, Leben*›; geregelt ‹*Leben, Gewohnheiten*›; ordentlich ‹*Person*›; (tidy) ordentlich [2] (Mil.) Dienst habend *od.* tuend

B [1] *n.* (Mil.) [Offiziers]bursche, *der* [2] **medical ∼:** ≈ Krankenpflegehelfer, *der*

orderly: ∼ officer *n.* (Brit.) Offizier vom Dienst, *der;* **∼ room** *n.* Schreibstube, *die*

order: ∼ pad *n.* Bestellblock, *der;* **O∼ Paper** *n.* (Brit. Parl.) Tagesordnung, *die*

ordinal /ˈɔːdɪnl/ (Math.) ▸ⓘ **p. 1358**

A *adj.* **∼ number** ▸**B**

B *n.* Ordnungs-, Ordinalzahl, *die*

ordinance /ˈɔːdɪnəns/ *n.* [1] (order, decree) Verordnung, *die;* **divine ∼:** göttliche Bestimmung [2] (enactment by local authority) Verfügung, *die;* Bestimmung, *die* [3] (religious rite) Ritus, *der*

ordinand /ˈɔːdɪnænd/ *n.* (Eccl.) Weihekandidat, *der*

ordinarily /ˈɔːdɪnərɪlɪ/ *adv.* normalerweise; gewöhnlich; in der Regel; (unexceptionally) gewöhnlich

ordinary /ˈɔːdɪnərɪ/ *adj.* [1] (regular, normal) normal ‹*Gebrauch*›; üblich ‹*Verfahren*›; (not exceptional) gewöhnlich; (average) durchschnittlich; **very ∼** (derog.) ziemlich mittelmäßig; **in the ∼ way** (usually) normalerweise; **better/worse than ∼:** besser/schlechter als sonst; **∼ tap water** normales *od.* gewöhnliches Leitungswasser; **in ∼ life** im Alltagsleben; **be no ∼ thing** kein gewöhnliches Ding sein; **∼ people** *or* **folk** einfache Leute; *see also* **course A 1** [2] (Brit. St. Exch.) **∼ share** Stammaktie, *die;* **∼ stock** Stammaktien [3] **above the ∼:** über dem Durchschnitt; überdurchschnittlich ‹*Intelligenz usw.*›; **out of the ∼:** außergewöhnlich; ungewöhnlich; **something/nothing out of the ∼:** etwas/nichts Außergewöhnliches

ordinary: ∼ level ▸**O level; ∼ 'seaman** *n.* Leichtmatrose, *der*

ordination /ɔːdɪˈneɪʃn/ *n.* [1] (Eccl.) Ordination, *die;* Ordinierung, *die* [2] (decreeing) Bestimmung, *die;* **God's ∼:** Gottes Wille

ordnance /ˈɔːdnəns/ *n.* [1] (guns) Artillerie, *die;* Geschütze *Pl.;* **∼ factory** Waffenfabrik, *die;* **piece of ∼:** Geschütz, *das* [2] (service) Feldzeugwesen, *das;* Feldzeugmeisterei, *die; attrib.* Feldzeug-; **O∼ Corps** Technische Truppe

Ordnance 'Survey *n.* (Brit.) amtliche Landesvermessung; **∼ survey map** amtliche topographische Karte

ore /ɔː(r)/ *n.* Erz, *das*

oregano /ɒrɪˈgɑːnəʊ, əˈregənəʊ/ *n., no pl.* (Cookery) Oregano, *der;* Origano, *der*

organ /ˈɔːgən/ *n.* [1] (Mus.) Orgel, *die;* (harmonium) Harmonium, *das; see also* **American organ** [2] (Biol.) Organ, *das;* **speech ∼s** Sprechwerkzeuge; **the male ∼** (euphem.) das männliche Glied [3] (medium of communication) Sprachrohr, *das;* (of political party etc.) Organ, *das*

'organ bank *n.* Organbank, *die*

organdie (*Amer.:* **organdy**) /ˈɔːgəndɪ, ɔːˈgændɪ/ *n.* (Textiles) Organdy, *der*

organ: ∼ donor *n.* Organspender, *der*/Organspenderin, *die; attrib.* **∼ donor card** Organspende[r]ausweis, *der;* **∼-grinder** *n.* Drehorgelspieler, *der*/-spielerin, *die;* Leierkastenmann, *der*

organic /ɔːˈgænɪk/ *adj.* [1] (also Chem. Physiol.) organisch [2] (constitutional, inherent, structural) konstitutionell; (fundamental, vital) konstitutiv (geh.) ‹*Teile*› [3] (without chemicals) biologisch, biodynamisch ‹*Nahrungsmittel*›; biologisch-dynamisch ‹*Ackerbau usw.*›; **∼ farmer** Biobauer, *der*/-bäuerin, *die;* **∼ waste** Biomüll, *der* [4] (Med.) organisch, körperlich ‹*Leiden*›

organically /ɔːˈgænɪkəlɪ/ *adv.* [1] (also Med.) organisch [2] (without chemicals) biologisch; biodynamisch

organic 'chemist *n.* ▸ⓘ **p. 1260** Organiker, *der*/Organikerin, *die*

organisation, organise, organised, organiser ▸**organiz-**

organism /ˈɔːgənɪzm/ *n.* [1] (organized body) Organismus, *der* [2] (Biol.) Organismus, *der;* (structure) Aufbau, *der*

organist /ˈɔːgənɪst/ *n.* ▸ⓘ **p. 1260** Organist, *der*/Organistin, *die*

organization /ɔːgənaɪˈzeɪʃn/ *n.* [1] (organizing, systematic arrangement) Organisation, *die;* (of material) Ordnung, *die;* (of library) Anordnung, *die;* **∼ of time/work** Zeit-/Arbeitseinteilung, *die* [2] (organized body, system) Organisation, *die;* **O∼ for Economic Cooperation and Development** Organisation für wirtschaftliche Zusammenarbeit und Entwicklung

organizational /ɔːgənaɪˈzeɪʃənl/ *adj.* organisatorisch

organi'zation man *n.:* *Mensch, der die Belange der Organisation, der er dient, über alles stellt*

organize /ˈɔːgənaɪz/ *v.t.* [1] (give orderly structure to) ordnen; planen ‹*Leben*›; einteilen ‹*Arbeit, Zeit*›; (frame, establish) veranstalten ‹*Konferenz, Festival*›; organisieren ‹*Verein, Partei, Firma, Institution*›; **organizing ability** Organisationstalent, *das;* **I must get ∼d** (get ready) ich muss fertig werden; **∼ sb.** jmdn. an die Hand nehmen (fig.); **as soon as I've got myself ∼d** sobald ich so weit bin [2] (arrange) organisieren; **can you ∼ the catering?** kümmerst du dich um die Verpflegung? [3] **∼ into groups/teams** in Gruppen/Mannschaften einteilen

organized /ˈɔːgənaɪzd/ *adj.* (systematic, structured) organisiert; geregelt ‹*Leben*›; **be well ∼ for a trip** für eine Reise gut vorbereitet sein; **∼ crime** das organisierte Verbrechen; die organisierte Kriminalität

organizer /ˈɔːgənaɪzə(r)/ *n.* [1] Organisator, *der*/Organisatorin, *die;* (of event, festival) Veranstalter, *der*/Veranstalterin, *die* [2] (bag) Aktentasche, *die*

organ: ∼ loft *n.* Orgelempore, *die;* **∼ music** *n.* Orgelmusik, *die;* **∼ pipe** *n.* (Mus.) Orgelpfeife, *die;* **∼ stop** *n.* (Mus.) Orgelregister, *das;* (handle) Registerzug, *der*

'organ transplant *n.* Organverpflanzung, *die;* Organtransplantation, *die* (fachspr.)

orgasm /ˈɔːgæzəm/ *n.* Orgasmus, *der;* Höhepunkt, *der* (auch fig.)

orgasmic /ɔːˈgæzmɪk/ *adj.* [1] orgastisch; Orgasmus‹*störung, -reaktion*› [2] (coll.: very enjoyable) geil (ugs.)

orgiastic /ɔːdʒɪˈæstɪk/ *adj.* orgiastisch

orgy /ˈɔːdʒɪ/ *n.* Orgie, *die;* **drunken ∼:** Orgie unter Alkoholeinfluss; **an ∼ of spending** eine Kauforgie; Kaufexzesse *Pl.;* **an ∼ of killing** eine Orgie des Tötens; ein Blutrausch

oriel /ˈɔːrɪəl/ *n.* Erkerfenster, *das*

orient

A /ˈɔːrɪənt/ *n.* **the O∼:** der Orient; (East Asia) der Ferne Osten

B /ˈɔːrɪent, ˈɒrɪent/ *v.t.* [1] (set or determine position

O

of) ausrichten (**towards** nach) 2 (fig.) einweisen (**in** in + *Akk.*); ausrichten, abstellen (**towards** auf + *Akk.*) ‹*Programm*›; **~ oneself** sich orientieren *od.* zurechtfinden; **-~ed** -orientiert; **money-~ed** materiell orientiert; **career-~ed** berufsbezogen; praxisorientiert

oriental /ɔːrɪˈentl, ɒrɪˈentl/
A *adj.* orientalisch; Orient‹*teppich*›; asiatisch ‹*Unergründlichkeit*›; **the O~ Church** die Ostkirche; die orientalische Kirche; **O~ studies** Orientalistik, *die;* **~ trade/travel** Orienthandel, *der*/Orientreisen
B *n.* Asiat, *der*/Asiatin, *die*

orientalist /ɔːrɪˈentəlɪst, ɒrɪˈentəlɪst/ *n.* Orientalist, *der*/Orientalistin, *die*

orientate /ˈɒrɪənteɪt, ˈɔːrɪənteɪt/ ▸**orient B**

orientation /ɒrɪənˈteɪʃn, ɔːrɪənˈteɪʃn/ *n.* 1 (orienting) Orientierung, *die;* (of new employees etc.) Einweisung, *die;* **sense of ~:** Orientierungssinn, *der* 2 (relative position) Ausrichtung, *die;* (fig.) Orientierung, *die;* **what is the ~ of ...?** wie ist ... ausgerichtet?; **my ~ was always towards ...:** ich war immer auf ... ausgerichtet

orienˈtation course *n.* Einführungsveranstaltung, *die*

orienteering /ɔːrɪənˈtɪərɪŋ, ɒrɪənˈtɪərɪŋ/ *n.* (Brit.) Orientierungslauf, *der*

orifice /ˈɒrɪfɪs/ *n.* Öffnung, *die;* (of tube) Mündung, *die;* **nasal ~:** Nasenloch, *das*

origami /ɒrɪˈɡɑːmɪ/ *n.* Origami, *das*

origin /ˈɒrɪdʒɪn/ *n.* (derivation) Abstammung, *die;* Herkunft, *die;* (beginnings) Anfänge *Pl.;* (of world etc.) Entstehung, *die;* (source) Ursprung, *der;* (of belief, rumour) Quelle, *die;* **be of humble ~, have humble ~s** bescheidener Herkunft sein; **be Irish by ~:** irischer Herkunft sein; **the ~ of species** die Entstehung der Arten; **country of ~:** Herkunftsland, *das;* **words which are of French ~** *or* **are French in ~:** Wörter französischen Ursprungs; **have its ~ in sth.** seinen Ursprung in etw. (*Dat.*) haben; einer Sache (*Dat.*) seinen Ursprung verdanken

original /əˈrɪdʒɪnl/
A *adj.* 1 (first, earliest) ursprünglich; **~ edition** Originalausgabe, *die;* **the ~ inhabitants** die Ureinwohner; **~ sin** (Theol.) Erbsünde, *die* 2 (primary) original; Original-; Ur‹*text, -fassung*›; eigenständig ‹*Forschung*›; (inventive) originell; (creative) schöpferisch; **an ~ painting** ein Original; **from the ~ German** aus der deutschen Urfassung
B *n.* 1 Original, *das* 2 (eccentric person) Original, *das* (ugs.)

original ˈgravity *n.* Stammwürze, *die*

originality /ərɪdʒɪˈnælɪtɪ/ *n.* Originalität, *die*

originally /əˈrɪdʒɪnəlɪ/ *adv.* 1 ursprünglich; **be ~ from ...:** [ursprünglich] aus ... stammen 2 (in an original way) originell ‹*schreiben usw.*›; **think ~:** originelle Gedanken haben

originate /əˈrɪdʒɪneɪt/
A *v.i.* **~ from** entstehen aus; **~ in** seinen Ursprung haben in (+ *Dat.*); **~ with sb.** von jmdm. stammen
B *v.t.* schaffen; hervorbringen; kreieren ‹*neue Mode*›; (discover) erfinden; **who ~d the idea?** von wem stammt die Idee?

origination /ərɪdʒɪˈneɪʃn/ *n.* Entstehung, *die*

originator /əˈrɪdʒɪneɪtə(r)/ *n.* Urheber, *der*/Urheberin, *die;* (inventor) Erfinder, *der*/Erfinderin, *die;* **who was the ~ of that idea?** von wem stammt diese Idee?

Orkney [Islands] /ˈɔːknɪ (aɪləndz)/ *pr. n.* [*pl.*], **Orkneys** /ˈɔːknɪz/ *pr. n. pl.* Orkneyinseln *Pl.;* Orkneys *Pl.*

ornament
A /ˈɔːnəmənt/ *n.* 1 (decorative object) Schmuck-, Ziergegenstand, *der;* (on pillar etc.) Ornament, *das;* (person) Zierde, *die* 2 *no pl.* (decorating) Verzierungen *Pl.;* Zierrat, *der* (geh.); **for** *or* **by way of ~:** zum Schmuck *od.* zur Zierde; **an altar rich in ~:** ein reich verzierter Altar 3 *usu. in pl.* (Eccl.) Kirchengerät, *das;* liturgisches Gerät 4 *in pl.* (Mus.) Verzierungen *Pl.;* Ornamente *Pl.*
B /ˈɔːnəment/ *v.t.* verzieren

ornamental /ɔːnəˈmentl/
A *adj.* dekorativ; ornamental (bes. Kunst); Zier‹*pflanze, -naht usw.*›; **purely ~:** nur zum Schmuck *od.* zur Zierde; rein dekorativ; **an ~ lake** ein Zierteich
B *n.* (plant) Zierpflanze, *die*

ornamentally /ɔːnəˈmentəlɪ/ *adv.* dekorativ

ornamentation /ɔːnəmenˈteɪʃn/ *n., no pl.* 1 (ornamenting) Ausschmückung, *die* 2 (embellishment[s]) Verzierung, *die*

ornate /ɔːˈneɪt/ *adj.* 1 (elaborately adorned) reich verziert; prunkvoll ‹*Dekoration*›; **heavily ~:** überladen 2 (style) blumig (abwertend); reich ausgeschmückt ‹*Prosa*›

ornery /ˈɔːnərɪ/ *adj.* (Amer. coll.) 1 (of poor quality) primitiv (abwertend) 2 (cantankerous) aggressiv; streitlustig

ornithological /ɔːnɪθəˈlɒdʒɪkl/ *adj.* ornithologisch; vogelkundlich

ornithologist /ɔːnɪˈθɒlədʒɪst/ *n.*. Ornithologe, *der*/Ornithologin, *die;* Vogelkundler, *der*/Vogelkundlerin, *die*

ornithology /ɔːnɪˈθɒlədʒɪ/ *n.* Ornithologie, *die;* Vogelkunde, *die*

orphan /ˈɔːfn/
A *n.* Waise, *die;* Waisenkind, *das;* **be left an ~:** [zur] Waise werden
B *attrib. adj.* Waisen-
C *v.t.* zur Waise machen; **be ~ed** [zur] Waise werden

orphanage /ˈɔːfənɪdʒ/ *n.* Waisenhaus, *das*

orthodontics /ɔːθəˈdɒntɪks/ *n., no pl.* Kieferorthopädie, *die*

orthodontist /ɔːθəˈdɒntɪst/ *n.* ▸❶ **p. 1260** Kieferorthopäde, *der*/Kieferorthopädin, *die*

orthodox /ˈɔːθədɒks/ *adj.* orthodox; (conservative) konventionell

Orthodox ˈChurch *n.* orthodoxe Kirche

orthodoxy /ˈɔːθədɒksɪ/ *n.* Orthodoxie, *die*

orthographic[al] /ɔːθəˈɡræfɪk(l)/ *adj.* orthographisch

orthography /ɔːˈθɒɡrəfɪ/ *n.* Orthographie, *die;* Rechtschreibung, *die*

orthopaedic /ɔːθəˈpiːdɪk/ *adj.* orthopädisch

orthopaedics /ɔːθəˈpiːdɪks/ *n., no pl.* (Med.) Orthopädie, *die*

orthopaedist /ɔːθəˈpiːdɪst/ *n.* ▸❶ **p. 1260** (Med.) Orthopäde, *der*/Orthopädin, *die*

orthopedic, orthopedics, orthopedist (Amer.) ▸**orthopaed-**

Orwellian /ɔːˈwelɪən/ *adj.* orwellsch

OS *abbr.* 1 (Brit.) = **Ordnance Survey** 2 = **outsize** übergr.

Oscar /ˈɒskə(r)/ *n.* (Cinemat.) Oscar, *der*

> **Oscar**
>
> Eine Bezeichnung für den amerikanischen *Academy Award*. Dieser Filmpreis, eine vergoldete Statuette, wird jährlich von der amerikanischen Filmakademie (*Academy of Motion Picture Arts and Sciences*) verliehen. Die Kategorien für den Preis sind: bester Film, beste Regie, bester Hauptdarsteller, bester Nebendarsteller, bestes Drehbuch, beste Kamera, bester Schnitt, beste Musik, beste Ausstattung, beste Maske, bestes Kostüm, bester nicht englischsprachiger Film. *Oscars*, gleichzeitig eine Bezeichnung für die feierliche Verleihung, wurden 1929 zum ersten Mal vergeben.

oscillate /ˈɒsɪleɪt/ *v.i.* 1 (swing like a pendulum) schwingen; oszillieren (fachspr.) 2 (move to and fro between points) pendeln 3 (fig.) schwanken; (vary between extremes of condition or action) hin und her gerissen sein 4 (Radio) schwingen

oscillation /ɒsɪˈleɪʃn/ *n.* 1 (action) ▸**oscillate**: Schwingen, *das;* Oszillieren, *das;* Pendeln, *das;* Schwanken, *das;* Hin-und-her-gerissen-Sein, *das;* Schwingung, *die* 2 (single ~) Schwingung, *die;* (of pendulum) Pendelausschlag, *der*

oscillator /ˈɒsɪleɪtə(r)/ *n.* (Electr.) Oszillator, *der*

oscillograph /əˈsɪləɡrɑːf/ *n.* (Electr.) Oszillograph, *der*

oscilloscope /əˈsɪləskəʊp/ *n.* (Electr.) Oszilloskop, *das*

osier /ˈəʊzɪə(r)/ *n.* 1 (Bot.) Korbweide, *die* 2 *attrib.* Weiden‹*korb, -rute*›; Korb‹*sessel, -möbel*›

osmosis /ɒzˈməʊsɪs/ *n., pl.* **osmoses** /ɒzˈməʊsiːz/ Osmose, *die*

osmotic /ɒzˈmɒtɪk/ *adj.* osmotisch

osprey /ˈɒspreɪ/ *n.* (Ornith.) Fischadler, *der*

Ossie ▸**Aussie**

ossify /ˈɒsɪfaɪ/
A *v.i.* ossifizieren (fachspr.); verknöchern (auch fig.)
B *v.t.* (turn into bone) ossifizieren (fachspr.) *od.* verknöchern lassen

Ostend /ɒˈstend/ *pr. n.* ▸❶ **p. 1643** Ostende (*das*)

ostensible /ɒˈstensɪbl/ *adj.* vorgeschoben; Schein-; **~ excuse/reason** Ausrede, *die* (abwertend)/Vorwand, *der*

ostensibly /ɒˈstensɪblɪ/ *adv.* vorgeblich

ostentation /ɒstenˈteɪʃn/ *n.* Ostentation, *die* (geh.); Prahlerei, *die* (abwertend); (showiness) Prunk, *der*

ostentatious /ɒstenˈteɪʃəs/ *adj.* prunkhaft ‹*Kleidung, Schmuck*›; prahlerisch ‹*Art*›; auffällig großzügig ‹*Spende*›; **be ~ about sth.** mit etw. prunken *od.* (ugs.) protzen

ostentatiously /ɒstenˈteɪʃəslɪ/ *adv.* ostentativ (geh.), demonstrativ ‹*fehlen, schweigen*›; prunkhaft ‹*leben*›; prahlerisch ‹*bemerken*›; auffällig ‹*sich kleiden, sich benehmen*›

osteopath /ˈɒstɪəpæθ/ *n.* ▸❶ **p. 1260** (Med.) Osteopath, *der*/Osteopathin, *die*

osteopathy /ɒstɪˈɒpəθɪ/ *n., no pl.* Osteopathie, *die*

osteoporosis /ɒstɪəʊpəˈrəʊsɪs/ *n., no pl.* ▸❶ **p. 1231** (Med.) Osteoporose, *die*

ostler /ˈɒslə(r)/ *n.* (Brit. Hist.) Pferdeknecht, *der* (veralt.); Reitknecht, *der* (früher)

ostracise ▸**ostracize**

ostracism /ˈɒstrəsɪzm/ *n.* Ächtung, *die*

ostracize /ˈɒstrəsaɪz/ *v.t.* ächten; **~ from sth.** ausschließen von etw.

ostrich /ˈɒstrɪtʃ/ *n.* 1 Strauß, *der* 2 *attrib.* Straußen‹*ei*›; **~ attitude** Vogel-Strauß-Einstellung, *die*

ostrich: ~ feather *n.* Straußenfeder, *die;* **~-like** *adj.* Vogel-Strauß-‹*Reaktion, Einstellung*›; **~ plume** *n.* Straußenfedern *Pl.*

Ostrogoth /ˈɒstrəɡɒθ/ *n.* (Hist.) Ostgote, *der*/Ostgotin, *die*

OT *abbr.* = **Old Testament** A.T.

OTE *abbr.* = **on-target earnings**

other /ˈʌðə(r)/
A *adj.* 1 (not the same) ander...; **the ~ two/three** *etc.* (the remaining) die beiden/drei *usw.* anderen; **the ~ way round** *or* **about** gerade umgekehrt; **~ people's property** fremdes Eigentum; **the ~ one** der/die/das andere; **the ~ thing** (coll.) das Gegenteil; **there is no ~ way** es geht nicht anders; **I know of no ~ way of doing it** ich weiß nicht, wie ich es sonst machen soll; **some ~ time** ein andermal 2 (further) **two ~ people/questions** noch zwei [andere *od.* weitere] Leute/Fragen; **one ~ thing** noch eins; **there's just one ~ thing I need to do** ich muss nur noch eines tun; **have you any ~ news/questions?** hast du noch weitere *od.* sonst noch Neuigkeiten/Fragen?; **some/six ~ people** noch ein paar/noch sechs [andere *od.* weitere] Leute; **no ~ questions** keine weiteren Fragen; **do you know of any ~ person who ...?** weißt du noch jemand anderen *od.* sonst noch jemanden, der ...? 3 **~ than** (different from) anders als; (except) außer; **never ~ than charming** immer charmant; **any person ~ than yourself** jeder außer dir 4 **some writer/charity or ~:** irgendein Schriftsteller/Wohltätigkeitsverein; **some time/way or ~:** irgendwann/-wie; **something/somehow/somewhere/somebody or ~:** irgendetwas/-wie/-wo/-wer. *See also* **another A 4**; **every 3**; **half A 1**; **none A**; **place B 2**; **side A 7**; **this B 3**; **woman 1**; **world 1** 5 **the ~ day/evening** neulich/neulich abends
B *n.* 1 (**~** person or thing) anderer/andere/anderes; **there are six ~s** es sind noch sechs andere da; **are there any ~s who ...?** ist noch

jemand da, der …?; **tell one from the ~:** sie auseinander halten; **one or ~ of you/them** irgendwer *od.* -einer/-eine von euch/ihnen; **any ~:** irgendein anderer/-eine andere/-ein anderes; **not any ~:** kein anderer/keine andere/kein anderes; **one after the ~:** einer/eine/eins nach dem/der/dem anderen; **a bit of the ~** (sl.) Sex, *der;* **have a bit of the ~** (sl.) es treiben (ugs.); **all he ever wants is a bit of the ~** (sl.) er will immer nur das eine; *see also* **each B 2** [2] (arch.) **no ~** (person) kein anderer/keine andere; **he could do no ~ than come** er konnte nichts anderes tun als kommen
C *adv.* anders; **I've never seen her ~ than with him** ich habe sie immer nur mit ihm zusammen gesehen; **~ than that, no real news** abgesehen davon, keine echten Neuigkeiten

otherwise /'ʌðəwaɪz/
A *adv.* [1] (in a different way) anders; **think ~:** anders darüber denken; anderer Meinung sein; **it cannot be ~:** es kann nicht anders sein; **be ~ engaged** anderweitige Verpflichtungen haben; **except where ~ stated** sofern nicht anders angegeben; **…, ~ [known as] Barbarossa** …, auch als Rotbart bekannt [2] (or else) sonst; anderenfalls; **he would have let me know ~:** sonst *od.* anderenfalls hätte er mich benachrichtigt [3] (in other respects) ansonsten (ugs.); im Übrigen; **the merits, or ~, of his paintings** die Vorzüge oder Mängel seiner Gemälde; **the probability or ~ of sth.** die Wahrscheinlichkeit oder Unwahrscheinlichkeit einer Sache; **workers enjoyed (or ~) an enforced holiday** die Arbeiter genossen einen erzwungenen Urlaub (oder auch nicht)
B *pred. adj.* anders

otiose /'əʊtɪəʊs/ *adj.* (literary: not required) überflüssig

OTT *abbr.* (Brit. coll.) **= over the top** übertrieben

otter /'ɒtə(r)/ *n.* [Fisch]otter, *der;* (fur) [Fisch]otterpelz, *der*

otter: ~ dog, ~ hound *ns.* (Zool., Hunting) Otterhund, *der*

ottoman *n.* [1] (seat) Ottomane, *die* [2] (footstool) Polsterschemel, *der*

Ottoman /'ɒtəmən/ *adj.* osmanisch ‹*Reich*›

OU *abbr.* (Brit.) **= Open University**

oubliette /u:blɪ'et/ *n.* (Hist.) Oubliette, *die;* Burgverlies, *das*

ouch /aʊtʃ/ *int.* autsch

ought[1] /ɔ:t/ *v. aux. only in pres. and past* **ought**, *neg.* (coll.) **oughtn't** /'ɔ:tnt/ [1] **I ~ to do/have done it** *expr. moral duty* ich müsste es tun/hätte es tun müssen; *expr. desirability* ich sollte es tun/hätte es tun sollen; **he tries to tell me what I ~ to think** er will mir vorschreiben, was ich zu denken habe; **behave as one ~:** sich richtig verhalten *od.* korrekt benehmen; **you ~ to see that film** diesen Film solltest du sehen; **she ~ to have been a teacher** sie hätte Lehrerin werden sollen; **~ not** *or* **~n't you to have left by now?** müsstest du nicht schon weg sein?; hättest du nicht schon gehen müssen?; **one ~ not to do it** man sollte es nicht tun; **he ~ to be hanged/in hospital** er gehört an den Galgen/ins Krankenhaus [2] *expr. probability* **that ~ to be enough** das dürfte reichen; **there ~ to be a signpost soon** jetzt müsste bald ein Wegweiser kommen; **he ~ to win** er müsste [eigentlich] gewinnen; **he ~ to have reached Paris by now** er müsste *od.* dürfte inzwischen in Paris [angekommen] sein

ought[2] *n.* (coll.) Null, *die*

oughtn't /'ɔ:tnt/ (coll.) **= ought not;** ▸**ought**

Ouija [board] ®, **ouija [board]** /'wi:dʒə (bɔ:d)/ *n.: Tafel mit Buchstaben und anderen Zeichen für spiritistische Sitzungen;* Oui-ja-board, *das* (Parapsych.)

ounce /aʊns/ *n.* [1] ▸❶ **p. 1690**, ▸❶ **p. 1702** (measure) Unze, *die;* **fluid ~** (Brit.) ≈ 0,0284 l; (Amer.) ≈ 0,0296 l [2] (fig.) **not an ~ of common sense** kein Fünkchen Verstand; **there is not an ~ of truth in it** daran ist kein Körnchen Wahrheit; **not have an ~ of sympathy** nicht für fünf Pfennig Mitgefühl haben (ugs.)

our /'aʊə(r)/ *poss. pron. attrib.* [1] unser; **we bumped ~ heads** wir stießen uns (*Dat.*) den Kopf *od.* die Köpfe an; **as soon as we've made ~ minds up** sobald wir uns (*Akk.*) entschieden haben; **we have done ~ share** wir haben unseren Teil *od.* (geh.) das Unsere getan; **~ Joe** *etc.* (coll.) unser *od.* (ugs.) uns Joe *usw.* [2] (of all people) unser; *see also* **father A 5**; **lady 5**; **lord A 2**; **saviour 2**. *See also* **her**[2]

ours /'aʊəz/ *poss. pron. pred.* unserer/unsere/unseres; **that car is ~:** das ist unser Wagen; **~ is a different system** wir haben ein anderes System; unser System ist anders; **in this country of ~:** hierzulande [bei uns]; in diesem unserem Lande (geh.); *see also* **hers**

ourselves /aʊə'selvz/ *pron.* [1] *emphat.* selbst [2] *refl.* uns. *See also* **between A 2**; **herself**

oust /aʊst/ *v.t.* [1] (expel, force out) **~ sb. from his job** jmdn. von seinem Arbeitsplatz vertreiben; **~ sb. from office/his position** jmdn. aus dem Amt/seiner Stellung vertreiben; **~ the president/king/government from power** den Präsidenten/den König /die Regierung entmachten *od.* stürzen [2] (force out and take place of) verdrängen; ablösen ‹*Regierung*› [3] (Law: deprive) berauben (**of, from** *Gen.*)

ouster /'aʊstə(r)/ *n.* (Amer.: dismissal) Entlassung, *die*

out /aʊt/
A *adv.* [1] (away from place) **~ here/there** hier/da draußen; **'Out'** „Ausfahrt"/„Ausgang" *od.* „Aus"; **that book is ~** (from library) das Buch ist ausgeliehen; **~ from under sth.** unter etw. (*Dat.*) hervor; **~ with him!** raus (ugs.) *od.* hinaus mit ihm!; **please keep the dog ~:** lassen Sie bitte den Hund nicht herein; **put the cat ~:** die Katze hinauslassen; **be ~ in the garden** draußen im Garten sein; **what's it like ~?** wie ist es draußen?; **shut the door to keep the wind ~:** die Tür schließen, damit es nicht zieht; **go ~ shopping** *etc.* einkaufen *usw.* gehen; **be ~** (not at home, not in one's office, etc.) nicht da sein; **go ~ in the evenings** abends aus- *od.* weggehen; **she was/stayed ~ all night** sie war/blieb eine/die ganze Nacht weg; **have a day ~ in London/at the beach** einen Tag in London/am Strand verbringen; **would you come ~ with me?** würdest du mit mir ausgehen?; **row ~ to …:** hinaus-/herausrudern zu …; **ten miles ~ from the harbour** 10 Meilen vom Hafen entfernt; **be ~ at sea** auf See sein; **anchor some way ~:** weit draußen ankern; **the journey ~:** die Hinfahrt; **the goods were damaged on the journey ~:** die Waren wurden auf dem Transport beschädigt; **missionaries were going ~ to India** Missionare gingen nach Indien; **he is ~ in Africa** er ist in Afrika; **~ in the fields** [draußen] auf dem Feld; **how long have you been living ~ here in Australia?** wie lange lebst du schon hier in Australien?; **the Socialist Party is ~:** die Sozialisten sind nicht mehr an der Regierung *od.* (ugs.) am Ruder; **that idea/proposal is ~:** die Idee/der Vorschlag ist indiskutabel; **Tell him that you're married — No, that's ~:** Sag ihm, dass du verheiratet bist. — Nein, das kommt nicht in Frage
[2] (Sport, Games) **be ~** ‹*Ball:*› aus *od.* im Aus sein; ‹*Mitspieler:*› ausscheiden; ‹*Schlagmann:*› aus[geschlagen] sein; **not ~:** nicht aus; **give sb. ~** ‹*Schiedsrichter:*› jmdn. für „Aus" erklären
[3] **be ~** (asleep) weg sein (ugs.); (drunk) hinüber sein (ugs.); (unconscious) bewusstlos sein; (Boxing) aus sein; **~ on one's feet** (Boxing) stehend k. o.; (fig.) total erschlagen; *see also* **count**[1] **A 4**
[4] (no longer burning) aus[gegangen]
[5] (no longer visible) **rub** *etc.* **~:** ausradieren *usw.*
[6] (in error) **be 3% ~ in one's calculations** sich um 3% verrechnet *od.* vertan haben; **his reckoning was ~:** seine Berechnung war falsch; **you're a long way ~:** du hast dich gewaltig geirrt; **this is £5 ~:** das stimmt um 5 Pfund nicht *od.* ist um 5 Pfund verkehrt; **my watch is 5 minutes ~:** meine Uhr geht 5 Minuten falsch *od.* verkehrt; *see also* **far A 4**
[7] (not in fashion) passé (ugs.); out (ugs.)
[8] (so as to be seen or heard) heraus; raus (ugs.); **there is a warrant ~ for his arrest** es liegt ein Haftbefehl gegen ihn vor; **say it ~ loud** es laut sagen; **tell sb. sth. right ~:** jmdm. etw. geradeheraus *od.* ohne Umschweife sagen; **with the waterproof side ~:** mit der wasserdichten Seite nach außen; **[come] ~ with it!** heraus *od.* (ugs.) raus damit *od.* mit der Sprache; **their secret is ~:** ihr Geheimnis ist herausgekommen *od.* bekannt geworden; **[the] truth will ~:** die Wahrheit wird herauskommen *od.* an den Tag kommen; **just ~ — the third volume** soeben erschienen — der dritte Band; **is the evening paper ~ yet?** ist die Abendausgabe schon erschienen?; **the roses are just ~:** die Rosen fangen gerade an zu blühen; **the apple blossom is ~:** die Apfelbäume stehen in Blüte; **the sun/moon is ~:** die Sonne/der Mond scheint
[9] (known to exist) **that is the best car ~:** das ist das beste Auto auf dem Markt
[10] **be ~ for sth./to do sth.** auf etw. (*Akk.*) aus sein/darauf aus sein, etw. zu tun; **be ~ for all one can get** alles haben wollen, was man bekommen kann; **be ~ for trouble** Streit suchen; **he's ~ for your money** er hat es auf dein Geld abgesehen; **be ~ to pass the exam/capture the market** entschlossen sein, die Prüfung zu bestehen/den Markt zu erobern; **she's ~ to get him/find a husband** sie ist hinter ihm her/sucht einen Mann; **they're just ~ to make money** sie sind nur aufs Geld aus; ihnen geht es nur ums Geld
[11] (to or at an end) **he had it finished before the day/month was ~:** er war noch am selben Tag/vor Ende des Monats damit fertig; **please hear me ~:** lass mich bitte ausreden; **Eggs? I'm afraid we're ~:** Eier? Die sind leider ausgegangen *od.* (ugs.) alle; **school is ~** (Amer.) die Schule ist aus
[12] (to a solution or result) **work ~:** ausrechnen; ausarbeiten ‹*Plan, Strategie*›
[13] (in finished form) **type ~ a thesis** eine Dissertation [ins Reine] tippen; **do it ~ in rough first** sich (*Dat.*) erst ein Konzept machen
[14] (in radio communication) Ende
[15] **~ and away** mit Abstand; bei weitem; **a scoundrel ~ and ~, an ~ and ~ scoundrel** ein Schurke durch und durch; **an ~ and ~ disgrace** eine ungeheure *od.* (ugs.) bodenlose Schande. *See also* **about A 4**; **luck 2**; **out of**; **tide A 1**
B *prep.* aus; **go ~ the door** zur Tür hinausgehen; **throw sth. ~ the window** etw. aus dem Fenster werfen
C *n.* (way of escape) Ausweg, *der* (fig.); (excuse) Alibi, *das*
D *v.t.* (coll.: expose) outen (ugs.)

out'act *v.t.* an die Wand spielen

outage /'aʊtɪdʒ/ *n.* Ausfall, *der;* **power ~:** Stromausfall, *der*

out: ~back *n.* (esp. Austral.) Hinterland, *das;* **an ~back farm** eine Farm im Hinterland; **~'bid** *v.t.*, **~'bid** [1] überbieten; **~bid sb. for sth.** für etw. mehr bieten *od.* ein besseres Angebot machen als jmd.; [2] (surpass) übertrumpfen; **~board** (Naut., Aeronaut., Motor Veh.) **A** *adj.* [1] Außenbord-; **~board motor** Außenbordmotor, *der;* Außenborder, *der* (ugs.); **~board motor boat** Boot mit Außenbordmotor; [2] (on outside) sich außenbords befindend; Außenbord-; **B** *n.* Außenborder, *der* (ugs.); **~bound** /'aʊtbaʊnd/ *adj.* [1] abgehend ‹*Flug*›; ausgehend ‹*Gespräch, Kommunikation*›; abfliegend ‹*Fluggast*›; [2] (as opposed to return) Hin‹*flug, -fahrt, -reise*›; **~-box** *n.* (Computing) Entwürfeordner, *der;* **~break** *n.* Ausbruch, *der;* **a recent ~break of fire caused …:** ein Brand verursachte kürzlich …; **at the ~break of war** bei Kriegsausbruch *od.* Ausbruch des Krieges; **an ~break of flu/smallpox** eine Grippe-/Pockenepidemie; **there will be ~breaks of rain during the afternoon** am Nachmittag wird es zu Regenfällen kommen; **~building** *n.* Nebengebäude, *das;* **~burst** *n.* Ausbruch, *der;* **an ~burst of weeping/laughter** ein Weinkrampf/Lachanfall *od.* -krampf; **an ~burst of anger/temper** ein Zornesausbruch (geh.) *od.* Wutanfall; **apologize for one's ~burst** sich für seinen Gefühlsausbruch entschuldigen; **there was an ~burst of applause** Beifall brach los; **~bursts of flame**

Auflodern von Flammen; **an ~burst of energy** ein Anfall von Energie; **his ~bursts of violence** seine Anfälle von Gewalttätigkeit; **~cast** A *n.* Ausgestoßene, *der/die;* **a social ~cast, an ~cast of society** ein Geächteter/eine Geächtete; ein Outcast (Soziol.); B *adj.* ausgestoßen; verstoßen ‹*Familienmitglied*›; **~'class** *v.t.* 1 (belong to higher class than) überlegen sein (+ *Dat.*); 2 (defeat easily) in den Schatten stellen; **he was ~classed in that race** er wurde in diesem Rennen deklassiert; **~come** *n.* Ergebnis, *das;* Resultat, *das;* **what was the ~come of your meeting?** was ist bei eurer Versammlung herausgekommen?; **~crop** A *n.* 1 (Geol.: stratum) Ausgehende, *das;* Ausstreichende, *das;* **a rock ~crop** ausstreichendes Gestein; 2 (fig.) Auftreten, *das;* B *v.i.* 1 (Geol.) ausstreichen (fachspr.); 2 (fig.) auftauchen; **~cry** *n.* 1 *no pl.* (clamour) [Aufschrei der] Empörung; [Sturm der] Entrüstung; **a public/general ~cry about/against sth.** allgemeine Empörung *od.* Entrüstung über etw. (*Akk.*); **the ~cry in the press** die heftigen Proteste in der Presse; **raise an ~cry about sth.** lautstarken Protest gegen etw. erheben; 2 (crying ~) Aufschrei, *der;* **~'dated** *adj.* veraltet; überholt; antiquiert (abwertend) ‹*Ausdrucksweise*›; altmodisch ‹*Vorstellung, Kleidung*›; **~'distance** *v.t.* [weit] hinter sich (*Dat.*) lassen; überflügeln; **John was ~distanced by his brother in the race** John fiel in dem Rennen [weit] hinter seinem Bruder zurück; **~'do** *v.t.*, **~'doing** /aʊt'du:ɪŋ/, **~'did** /aʊt'dɪd/, **~done** /aʊt'dʌn/ übertreffen, überbieten (**in** an + *Dat.*); **not to be ~done [by sb.]** um nicht zurückzustehen [hinter jmdm.]; **~door** *adj.* **~door shoes/things** Straßenschuhe/-kleidung, *die;* **be an ~door type** gern und oft im Freien sein; **lead an ~door life** viel im Freien sein; **~door games/pursuits** Spiele/Beschäftigungen im Freien; **~door shots** (Photog.) Außenaufnahmen; **~door swimming pool** Freibad, *das;* **~door ice rink** nicht überdachte Eisbahn; **~'doors** A *adv.* draußen; **sleep ~doors** draußen *od.* im Freien schlafen; **go ~doors** nach draußen gehen; B *n.* **the [great] ~doors** die freie Natur

outer /'aʊtə(r)/ *adj.* 1 äußer...; Außen‹*fläche, -seite, -wand, -tür, -hafen*›; **sb.'s ~ appearance** jmds. äußere Erscheinung; jmds. Äußeres; **~ garments** Oberbekleidung, *die* 2 (objective, physical) äußerlich; **the ~ world** die Außenwelt. *See also* **bar¹ A 9**

outermost /'aʊtəməʊst/ *adj.* äußerst...

outer 'space *n.* Weltraum, *der;* All, *das;* **come from ~** (fig. coll.) von einem anderen Stern sein

out: ~'face *v.t.* [durch Blicke] einschüchtern; zum Schweigen bringen ‹*Kritiker*›; **~fall** *n.* Ausfluss, *der;* (in river engineering) Vorfluter, *der;* **~fall pipe** Abflussrohr, *das;* **~field** *n.* (Cricket, Baseball) Außenfeld, *das;* **~fit** *n.* 1 (person's clothes) Kleider *Pl.;* (for fancy-dress party) Kostüm, *das;* **wear the same ~fit** dasselbe tragen *od.* anhaben; **I do like your ~fit!** du bist sehr gut angezogen; 2 (complete equipment) Ausrüstung, *die;* Ausstattung, *die;* 3 (coll.: group of persons) Haufen, *der* (ugs.); Clique, *die* (abwertend); (Mil.) Haufen, *der* (Soldatenspr.); Trupp, *der;* (jazz band) Ensemble, *das;* 4 (coll.: organization) Laden, *der* (ugs.); **a publishing/manufacturing ~fit** ein Verlag/ein Produktionsbetrieb; **~fitter** *n.* ▸ **O p. 1260** Ausrüster, *der*/Ausrüsterin, *die;* Ausstatter, *der*/Ausstatterin, *die;* **camping/sports ~fitter** Camping-/Sportgeschäft, *das;* **a gents' ~fitter's** ein Herrenausstatter; **~'flank** *v.t.* 1 (Mil.: ~manoeuvre; also fig.) überlisten; ausmanövrieren; 2 (Mil.: extend beyond flank of) umgehen, umfassen ‹*Armee*›; **~flanking movement** Umfassungsbewegung, *die;* **~flow** *n.* 1 (~ward flow) Austritt, *der;* (fig.: of gold, capital, etc.) Abfluss, *der;* 2 (amount) Ausfluss, *der;* Abflussmenge, *die;* 3 **~flow [pipe** *or* **channel]** Abfluss, *der;* **~'fox** *v.t.* (coll.) austricksen (ugs.); **~going** A *adj.* 1 (retiring from office) [aus dem Amt] scheidend ‹*Regierung, Präsident, Ausschuss*›; 2 (friendly) kontaktfreudig ‹*Person*›; **you should be more ~going** du solltest mehr aus dir herausgehen; 3 (going ~) abgehend ‹*Zug, Schiff*›; ausziehend ‹*Mieter*›; **~going flights will be delayed** bei den Abflügen wird es zu Verzögerungen kommen; **the ~going post** *or* **mail** die ausgehende Post; der Postausgang (Bürow.); B *n. in pl.* (expenditure) Ausgaben *Pl.;* **~'grow** *v.t., forms as* **grow** 1 (leave behind) entwachsen (+ *Dat.*); hinauswachsen über (+ *Akk.*); ablegen ‹*Interesse, Schüchternheit, Vorliebe*›; überwinden ‹*Ansicht, Schüchternheit*›; **we've ~grown all that** das alles haben wir hinter uns; 2 (become taller than) größer werden als; über den Kopf wachsen (+ *Dat.*) ‹*älterem Bruder usw.*›; (grow too big for) herauswachsen aus ‹*Kleidung*›; **~growth** *n.* Auswuchs, *der;* **~'guess** *v.t.* gedanklich voraus sein (+ *Dat.*); ausrechnen (Sportjargon); **~'gun** *v.t.* (fig.) **be ~gunned** an Feuerkraft unterlegen sein; **~house** *n.* 1 (building) Nebengebäude, *das;* 2 (Amer.: privy) Außentoilette, *die*

outing /'aʊtɪŋ/ *n.* 1 (pleasure trip) Ausflug, *der;* **school/day's ~:** Schul-/Tagesausflug, *der;* **firm's/works ~:** Betriebsausflug, *der;* **go on an ~:** einen Ausflug machen; **go for an ~ in the car** eine Spazierfahrt machen 2 (appearance) (in athletic contest) Wettkampf, *der;* (in race) Rennen, *das;* (in game) Spiel, *das* 3 (of homosexual) Outing, *das*

out: ~landish /aʊt'lændɪʃ/ *adj.* 1 (looking or sounding foreign) fremdländisch; 2 (bizarre) ausgefallen; seltsam, sonderbar ‹*Benehmen*›; verschroben ‹*Ansichten*›; **~'last** *v.t.* überdauern; überleben ‹*Person, Jahrhundert*›; **~law** A *n.* 1 (lawless violent person) Bandit, *der*/Banditin, *die;* 2 (person deprived of protection of law) Geächtete, *der/die* (hist.); B *v.t.* 1 (deprive of the protection of law) ächten (hist.); für vogelfrei erklären (hist.); 2 (make illegal) verbieten ‹*Zeitung, Handlung*›; **~lay** *n.* **an ~lay** Ausgaben *Pl.* (**on** für); **initial ~lay** Anschaffungskosten *Pl.;* **~lay of capital** Kapitalaufwand, *der;* **recover the ~lay** seine Auslagen zurückbekommen; **~let** /'aʊtlet, 'aʊtlɪt/ 1 (means of exit) Ablauf, -fluss, *der;* Auslauf, -lass, *der;* (of lake) Abfluss, *der;* **~let valve** Ablassventil, *das;* 2 (fig.: vent) Ventil, *das;* 3 (Commerc.) (market) Absatzmarkt, *der;* (shop) Verkaufsstelle, *die;* 4 (Electr.) Steckdose, *die;* (connection) Stromanschluss, *der;* **~line** A *n.* 1 *in sing. or pl.* (line[s]) Umriss, *der;* Kontur, *die;* Silhouette, *die;* **the ~lines of the trees/drawing** die Umrisse der Bäume/Zeichnung; **visible only in ~line** nur in Umrissen sichtbar; 2 (short account) Grundriss, *der;* Grundzüge *Pl.;* (of topic) Übersicht, die (**of** über + *Akk.*); (rough draft for essay, book, play, etc.) Entwurf, *der* (**of, for** *Gen. od.* zu); Konzept, *das* (**of, for** *Gen.*); **trace the development in ~line** die Entwicklung im Grundriss *od.* in ihren Grundzügen verfolgen; *attrib.* **~ agreement** Rahmenvertrag, *der;* **~line plan** Übersichtsplan, *der;* 3 *in pl.* (main features) Grundzüge *Pl.;* 4 (sketch) Skizze, *die;* **sketch/draw sth. in ~line** etw. in Umrissen skizzieren/zeichnen; **~line map** Umrisskarte, *die;* B *v.t.* 1 (draw ~line of) **~line sth.** die Umrisse *od.* Konturen einer Sache zeichnen; 2 (define ~line of) **~line sth.** die Umrisse *od.* Konturen einer Sache hervorheben; **the mountain was ~lined against the sky** die Silhouette/Umrisse *od.* Konturen des Berges zeichnete/zeichneten sich gegen den Himmel ab; 3 (trace or ascertain ~line of) **~line the limits/boundaries of sth.** den Verlauf der Grenzen von etw. ermitteln; 4 (describe in general terms) skizzieren, umreißen ‹*Programm, Plan, Projekt*›; **~live** /aʊt'lɪv/ *v.t.* überleben; **it's ~lived its usefulness** es ist unbrauchbar geworden; es hat ausgedient; **~look** *n.* 1 (prospect) Aussicht, *die* (**over** über + *Akk.*, **on to** auf + *Akk.*); (fig., Meteorol.) Aussichten *Pl.;* **the house has a wonderful ~look over ...:** vom Haus aus hat man eine herrliche Aussicht über ... (*Akk.*); **what's the ~look?** wie sind die Aussichten?; **business ~look** Geschäftsaussichten *Pl.;* 2 (mental attitude) Haltung, *die* (**on** gegenüber); Einstellung, *die* (**on** zu); Auffassung, *die* (**on** von); **~look on life** Lebensauffassung, *die;* **his whole ~look** seine ganze Einstellung; **adopt a narrow ~look on things** in seinen Anschauungen beschränkt sein; die Dinge zu eng sehen; 3 (looking out) Hinaussehen, *das;* **~lying** *adj.* abgelegen, entlegen ‹*Gegend, Vorort, Dorf*›; **the ~lying suburbs of Tokyo** die Außenbezirke von Tokio; **~ma'noeuvre** *v.t.* überlisten ‹*Truppen*›; ausstechen, ausmanövrieren ‹*Rivalen*›; **~moded** /aʊt'məʊdɪd/ *adj.* 1 (no longer in fashion) altmodisch; 2 (obsolete) antiquiert (abwertend) ‹*Ausdrucksweise*›; **~'number** *v.t.* zahlenmäßig überlegen sein (+ *Dat.*); **they were ~numbered five to one** die anderen waren fünfmal so viele wie sie; **be [vastly] ~numbered [by sb.]** [jmdm.] zahlenmäßig [weit] unterlegen sein

'out of *prep.* 1 (from within) aus; **go ~ the door** zur Tür hinausgehen; **fall ~ sth.** aus etw. [heraus]fallen 2 (not within) **be ~ the country** im Ausland sein; außer Landes sein (geh.); **be ~ town/the room** nicht in der Stadt/im Zimmer sein; **feel ~ it** *or* **things** sich ausgeschlossen *od.* nicht dazugehörig fühlen; **I'm glad to be ~ it** ich bin froh, dass ich die Sache hinter mir habe 3 (outside the limits of) **marry ~ one's faith** einen Anhänger/eine Anhängerin eines anderen Glaubens heiraten; **born ~ wedlock** unehelich geboren; **be ~ the tournament** aus dem Turnier ausgeschieden sein; *see also* **order A 1, 2** 4 (from among) **one ~ every three smokers** jeder dritte Raucher; **58 ~ every 100** 58 von hundert; **pick one ~ the pile** einen/eine/eins aus dem Stapel herausgreifen; **eighth ~ ten** als Achter von zehn Teilnehmern *usw.;* **choose ~ what is there** unter dem auswählen, was vorhanden ist; **only one instance ~ several** nur einer von mehreren Fällen 5 (beyond range of) außer ‹*Reich-/Hörweite, Sicht, Kontrolle*› 6 (from) aus; **get money ~ sb.** Geld aus jmdm. herausholen; **do well ~ sb./sth.** von jmdm./etw. profitieren 7 (owing to) aus ‹*Mitleid, Trotz, Furcht, Verehrung, Neugier usw.*› 8 (no longer in) **~ danger** außer Gefahr 9 (without) **be ~ luck** kein Glück haben; **~ money** ohne Geld; **~ work** ohne Arbeit; arbeitslos; **we're ~ tea** der Tee ist uns ausgegangen; wir haben keinen Tee mehr; **be ~ a suit** (Cards) keine Karten einer Farbe haben; *see also* **out-of-work** 10 (by use of) aus; **make a profit ~ sth.** mit etw. ein Geschäft machen; **made ~ silver** aus Silber; **what did you make it ~?** woraus hast du es gemacht? 11 (away from) von ... entfernt; **three days ~ port** drei Tage nach dem Auslaufen aus dem Hafen; **ten miles ~ London** 10 Meilen außerhalb von London 12 (beyond) ▸ **depth 4; ordinary 3**

out: ~-of-court settlement *n.* (Law) (agreement) außergerichtlicher Vergleich; außergerichtliche Einigung; (payment) Vergleichssumme, *die;* **~-of-date** *attrib. adj.* (old, not relevant) veraltet; (old-fashioned) altmodisch; unmodern; antiquiert (abwertend) ‹*Ausdrucksweise*›; (expired) ungültig, verfallen ‹*Karte*›; **~-of-'pocket** *attrib. adj.* Bar‹*auslagen*›; **~-of-print** *attrib. adj.* vergriffen; **~-of-the-way** *attrib. adj.* (remote) abgelegen; entlegen; (unusual, seldom met with) ausgefallen; entlegen; **~-of-town** *attrib. adj.* außerhalb der Stadt gelegen ‹*Einkaufszentrum*›; (fig.: unsophisticated) Provinz- (abwertend); **~-of-work** *attrib. adj.* arbeitslos; **~'pace** *v.t.* ausstechen ‹*Konkurrenten*›; (Sport) besiegen ‹*Läufer*›; **be ~paced** ‹*Sportler*:› überholt werden; **~patient** *n.* ambulanter *od.* poliklinischer Patient/ambulante *od.* poliklinische Patientin; **~patients[' department]** Poliklinik, *die;* **have sth. done as an ~patient** etw. ambulant *od.* in der Ambulanz machen lassen; **be an ~patient** ambulant behandelt werden; **~per'form** *v.t.* überbieten; **~'play** *v.t.* (Sport) besser spielen als; **we can ~play them** wir sind ihnen spielerisch überlegen; **be ~played [by sb.]** [jmdm.] unterlegen sein; **~placement** /'aʊtpleɪsmənt/ *n., no pl.* (Commerc.) Outplacement, *das* (fachspr.); **~'point** *v.t.* (Sport, esp. Boxing) auspunkten; **~post** *n.* Außenposten, *der;* (of civilization etc.; also Mil.) Vorposten, *der;* **~pouring** *n., usu. in pl.* (expression of emotion) Gefühlsäußerung, *die;* (impetuous, passionate) Erguss, *der* (geh. abwertend); **~put** A *n.* 1 (amount) Output, *der* (fachspr.); Produktion, *die;* (of liquid, electricity, etc.) Leistung, *die;* (of coal mine etc.) Förderung, *die;* Fördermenge, *die;* **total/daily/average/literary ~put** Gesamt- / Tages- / Durchschnitts- / literarische

Produktion; **the factory has a daily ~put of 200 pairs** in der Fabrik werden pro Tag 200 Paar hergestellt; **2** (Computing) Ausgabe, *die;* Output, *der* (fachspr.); **~ device** Ausgabegerät, das; **~put capacity/terminal** Ausgabekapazität, *die*/-terminal, *das;* **3** (Electr.) (energy) [Ausgangs]leistung, *die;* Output, *der* (fachspr.); (signal) Ausgangssignal, *das;* **~put circuit/current** Ausgangsschaltung, *die*/-strom, *der;* **4** (place) Ausgang, *der;* (recording or printing device) Ausgabegerät, *das;* **B** *v.t.*, **-tt-**, **~put** *or* **~putted** /ˈaʊtpʊtɪd/ (Computing) ausgeben ‹*Information*›

outrage

A /ˈaʊtreɪdʒ/ *n.* **1** (deed of violence, violation of rights) Verbrechen, *das;* (during war) Gräueltat, *die;* (against good taste or decency) grober *od.* krasser Verstoß; (upon dignity) krasse *od.* grobe Verletzung (**upon** *Gen.*); **be an ~ against good taste/decency/upon dignity** den guten Geschmack/Anstand/die Würde in grober *od.* krasser Weise verletzen; **an ~ against humanity** ein Verbrechen gegen die Menschheit; **an ~ upon decency/justice** eine Verhöhnung des Anstands/der Gerechtigkeit; **a bomb ~:** ein verbrecherischer Bombenanschlag **2** (strong resentment) Empörung, *die* (**at** *gegen*); **react with a sense of ~:** empört sein **B** /ˈaʊtreɪdʒ, aʊtˈreɪdʒ/ *v.t.* **1** (cause to feel resentment, insult) empören; **be ~d at** *or* **by sth.** über etw. (*Akk.*) empört sein **2** (infringe) in grober *od.* krasser Weise verstoßen gegen ‹*Anstand, Moral*›

outrageous /aʊtˈreɪdʒəs/ *adj.* **1** (immoderate) unverschämt (ugs.) ‹*Forderung*›; unverschämt hoch ‹*Preis, Summe*›; grell, schreiend ‹*Farbe*›; zu auffällig ‹*Kleidung*›; maßlos ‹*Übertreibung*›; **it's ~!** das ist unverschämt *od.* eine Unverschämtheit! **2** (grossly cruel, offensive) ungeheuer ‹*Grausamkeit*›; haarsträubend, (ugs.) katastrophal ‹*Behandlung, Bedienung*›; unverschämt ‹*Lüge, Benehmen, Unterstellung*›; wüst ‹*Schmähung*›; geschmacklos ‹*Witz*›; ungeheuerlich ‹*Anklage*›; unerhört ‹*Frechheit, Unhöflichkeit, Skandal*›; unflätig ‹*Sprache*› **3** (violent) grausam ‹*Rache*›; **~ deeds** Untaten; Grausamkeiten

outrageously /aʊtˈreɪdʒəslɪ/ *adv.* **1** (to an immoderate degree) zu auffällig, aufdringlich ‹*sich kleiden, schminken*›; maßlos ‹*übertreiben*›; **an ~ low neckline** ein herausfordernd tiefer Ausschnitt **2** (atrociously, flagrantly) unverschämt, schamlos ‹*lügen, sich benehmen*›; fürchterlich ‹*fluchen*›; **~ bad service** haarsträubend schlechte Bedienung; **he suggested quite ~ that ...:** er war so unverschämt vorzuschlagen, dass ...

outˈrank *v.t.* (Mil.) einen höheren Rang einnehmen als; rangmäßig stehen über (+ *Dat.*); **be ~ed by sb.** einen niedrigeren Rang als jmd. haben; rangmäßig unter jmdm. stehen

outré /ˈuːtreɪ/ *adj.* outriert (geh. veralt.); überspannt ‹*Vorstellung, Geschmack*›; absurd ‹*Kleidung*›

out: ~reach *n., no pl.* **1** (extent of influence) Präsenz, *die;* **2** (in social work) aufsuchende Sozialarbeit; *attrib.* **~reach worker** ≈ Streetworker, *der*/-workerin, *die;* **~reach program** Outreachprogramm, *das;* **~rider** *n.* **1** (mounted attendant) berittener Begleiter/berittene Begleiterin; **2** (motorcyclist) **[motorcycle] ~rider** Kradbegleiter, *der*/-begleiterin, *die;* **3** (Amer.: herdsman) berittener Viehhirte; **~rigger** *n.* (Naut.) (beam, spar, framework) Maststütze, *die;* (log fixed to canoe) Schwimmbalken, *der;* Ausleger, *der;* (iron bracket) Ausleger, *der;* (boat) Auslegerboot, *das;* **~right A** /ˈ-ˈ-/ *adv.* **1** (altogether, entirely) ganz, komplett ‹*kaufen, verkaufen*›; (instantaneously, on the spot) auf der Stelle; **pay for/purchase/buy sth. ~right** sofort den ganzen Preis für etw. bezahlen; **2** (openly) geradeheraus (ugs.), freiheraus, rundheraus ‹*erzählen, sagen, lachen*›; **B** /ˈ--/ *adj.* ausgemacht ‹*Unsinn, Schlechtigkeit, Unehrlichkeit*›; offen, direkt ‹*Wesensart*›; rein, pur (ugs.) ‹*Arroganz, Unverschämtheit, Irrtum, Egoismus, Unsinn*›; glatt (ugs.) ‹*Ablehnung, Absage, Lüge*›; klar ‹*Sieg, Niederlage, Sieger*›; **~right sale** Verkauf in Bausch und Bogen; **~ˈrun** *v.t., forms as* **run C 1** (run faster than) schneller laufen *od.* sein als; **2** (escape) entkommen (+ *Dat.*); **~ˈsell** *v.t., forms as* **sell A 1** (be sold in greater quantities than) sich besser verkaufen als; **be ~sold by ...:** sich schlechter verkaufen als ...; **2** (sell more than) mehr verkaufen als; **~sell sb. by two to one** zweimal so viel wie jmd. verkaufen; **~set** *n.* Anfang, *der;* Beginn, *der;* **at the ~set** zu Beginn *od.* Anfang; am Anfang; **from the ~set** von Anfang an; **~ˈshine** *v.t.*, **~shone** /aʊtˈʃɒn/ **1** (shine brighter than) heller leuchten als; **2** (fig.) in den Schatten stellen

outside

A /ˈ-ˈ-, ˈ--/ *n.* **1** (external side) Außenseite, *die;* **the ~ of the car is red** das Auto ist außen rot; **on the ~:** außen; **on the ~ of the door** außen an der Tür; **overtake sb. on the ~** (in driving) jmdn. außen überholen; **~ lane** Überholspur, *die* **2** (position on outer side) **to/from the ~:** nach/von außen; **see a problem from the ~:** ein Problem als Außenstehender/Außenstehende sehen; **be kept on the ~:** ausgeschlossen bleiben **3** (external appearance) Äußere, *das;* äußere Erscheinung **4** (of path etc.) Rand, *der* **5** **at the [very] ~:** äußerstenfalls; höchstens **B** /ˈ--/ *adj.* **1** (of, on, nearer the ~) äußer...; Außen‹*wand, -mauer, -antenne, -reparatur, -belag, -kajüte, -toilette, -ansicht, -durchmesser*› **2** (remote) **have only an ~ chance** nur eine sehr geringe Chance *od.* eine Außenseiterchance haben **3** (not coming from or belonging within) fremd ‹*Hilfe*›; äußer... ‹*Einfluss*›; Freizeit‹*aktivitäten, -interessen*›; **~ pressure** Druck von außen; **some ~ help** (extra workers) zusätzliche Arbeitskräfte; **~ investment** Investitionen von außen; **an ~ opinion** die Meinung eines Außenstehenden; **the ex-convict had to adjust to the ~ world** der ehemalige Sträfling musste sich an das Leben draußen gewöhnen **4** (greatest possible) maximal, höchst... ‹*Schätzung*›; **at an ~ estimate** maximal *od.* höchstens *od.* im Höchstfall **C** /-ˈ-/ *adv.* **1** (on the ~) draußen; (to the ~) nach draußen; **the world ~:** die Außenwelt; **come from ~:** von draußen kommen; **seen from ~ it looks ...:** von [dr]außen sieht es ... aus; **come** *or* **step ~** (as challenge to fight) komm mal mit nach draußen *od.* vor die Tür; **who's that ~?** wer ist das da draußen? **2** **~ of** ▸ **D** **3** (sl.: not in prison) draußen (ugs.) **D** /-ˈ-/ *prep.* **1** (on outer side of) außerhalb (+ *Gen.*); **~ the door** vor der Tür; draußen; **prowl about/park ~ the house** ums Haus herumstreichen/vor dem Haus parken **2** (beyond) außerhalb (+ *Gen.*) ‹*Reichweite, Festival, Familie*›; **it's ~ the terms of the agreement** es gehört nicht zu den Bedingungen der Abmachung; **this falls ~ the scope of ...:** das geht über den Rahmen von ... hinaus **3** (to the ~ of) aus ... hinaus; **go ~ the house** nach draußen gehen

outside: ~ ˈbroadcast *n.* (Brit.) Außenübertragung, *die;* **~ ˈedge** *n.* (Skating, Cricket) Außenkante, *die;* **~ examiner** *n.* (Sch., Univ.) externer Prüfer/externe Prüferin, *die;* **~ ˈforward** *n.* (Footb., Hockey) Außenstürmer, *der;* **~ ˈhalf** *n.* (Rugby) Flügelhalbspieler, *der;* **~ ˈleft** *n.* (Footb., Hockey) Linksaußen, *der*

outsider /aʊtˈsaɪdə(r)/ *n.* **1** (non-member, person without special knowledge) Außenstehende, *der/die* **2** (Sport; also fig.) Außenseiter, *der;* Outsider, *der*

outside: ~ ˈright *n.* (Footb., Hockey) Rechtsaußen, *der;* **~ seat** *n.* Platz am Rand; **~ ˈtrack** *n.* (Racing) Außenbahn, *die*

out: ~size *adj.* überdimensional; **~size person/clothes** Person mit/Kleidung in Übergröße; **~size shop/department** Geschäft/Abteilung für Übergrößen; **~skirts** *n. pl.* Stadtrand, *der;* **on the ~skirts [of Paris]** am Stadtrand [von Paris]; **the ~skirts of the city** die Außenbezirke der Stadt; **~ˈsmart** *v.t.* (coll.) überlisten; **~source A** *v.t.* extern vergeben ‹*Arbeit, Aufträge*›; **B** *v.i.* Arbeiten/Aufträge extern vergeben; **~sourcing** /ˈaʊtsɔːsɪŋ/ *n., no pl.* Outsourcing, *das* (fachspr.); Fremdbezug, *der* (fachspr.); **~ˈspoken** *adj.* freimütig ‹*Person, Kritik, Bemerkung, Kommentar*›; **be ~spoken about sth.** sich freimütig über etw. äußern; **the book was ~spoken on the subject** in dem Buch wurde das Thema freimütig *od.* offenherzig *od.* (ugs.) unverblümt behandelt; **~spread** *adj.* /ˈ--, *pred.* -ˈ-/ ausgebreitet; **he stood there, [with] arms ~spread** er stand mit ausgebreiteten Armen da; **~ˈstanding** *adj.* **1** (conspicuous) hervorstechend ‹*Merkmal*›; **2** (exceptional) hervorragend ‹*Leistung, Redner, Künstler, Dienst*›; überragend ‹*Bedeutung*›; außergewöhnlich ‹*Person, Mut, Fähigkeit, Geschick*›; **not be ~standing** nicht überragend sein; **~standing in courage and skill** außergewöhnlich mutig und geschickt; **of ~standing ability/skill** außergewöhnlich fähig/geschickt; **be ~standing at skating** hervorragend Schlittschuh laufen können; **work of ~standing excellence** ganz hervorragende Arbeit; **3** (not yet settled) ausstehend ‹*Schuld, Verbindlichkeit, Geldsumme*›; offen, unbezahlt ‹*Rechnung*›; unerledigt ‹*Arbeit*›; ungelöst ‹*Problem*›; **there's £5 still ~standing** es stehen noch 5 Pfund aus; **have work still ~standing** noch etwas zu erledigen haben; **~standingly** /aʊtˈstændɪŋlɪ/ *adv.* außergewöhnlich ‹*intelligent, gut, begabt*›; **not ~standingly** nicht besonders; **be ~standingly good at tennis/Latin** hervorragend Tennis spielen/Latein können; **~station** *n.* Außenposten, *der;* **~ˈstay** *v.t.* **1** (stay beyond) überziehen ‹*Urlaub*›; **2** (stay longer than) länger bleiben als; (surpass in staying power, endurance) mehr Stehvermögen haben als; *see also* **welcome B 1**; **~ˈstep** *v.t.* hinausgehen über (+ *Akk.*); **~stretched** *adj.* ausgestreckt; (spread out) ausgebreitet; **~ˈstrip** *v.t.* **1** (pass in running) überholen; **2** (surpass in competition) überflügeln; übersteigen ‹*Einsicht, Ressourcen, Ersparnisse*›; **~-take** *n.* (Cinemat. etc.) Outtake, *der od. das;* **~tray** *n.* Ablage für Ausgänge; **~ˈvote** *v.t.* überstimmen

outward /ˈaʊtwəd/

A *adj.* **1** (external, apparent) [rein] äußerlich; äußere ‹*Erscheinung, Bedingung*›; **sb.'s ~ self** jmds. äußere Erscheinung; **with an ~ show of confidence** mit einem Anstrich von Selbstsicherheit; **an ~ display of fear** eine Demonstration der Angst; **~ form** Erscheinungsform, *die;* äußere Form **2** (directed towards outside) nach außen gerichtet ‹*Neigung, Bewegung*›; (going out) Hin‹*reise, -fracht*›; **~ flow of money/traffic** Kapitalabfluss, *der*/abfließender Verkehr; **the ~ half of a return ticket** der Hinfahrtabschnitt einer Fahrkarte **B** *adv.* nach außen ‹*aufgehen, richten*›; **be ~ bound [for New York]** ‹*Schiff:*› [mit Kurs auf New York (*Akk.*)] auslaufen; ‹*Person:*› [in Richtung New York] abreisen

outward-ˈbound *attrib. adj.* auslaufend (**for** nach) ‹*Schiff*›; abreisend ‹*Passagier*›

outwardly /ˈaʊtwədlɪ/ *adv.* nach außen hin ‹*Gefühle zeigen*›; öffentlich ‹*Loyalität erklären*›

outwards ▸ **outward B**

out: ~ˈweigh *v.t.* schwerer wiegen als; überwiegen ‹*Nachteile*›; [mehr als] wettmachen ‹*Verluste*›; **~ˈwit** *v.t.*, **-tt-** überlisten; **~work** *n.* **1** (part of fortification) **~work[s]** Vorfestung, *die;* Vorwerk, *das;* Außenbefestigung, *die;* **2** (work) Arbeit außerhalb des Betriebs; Heimarbeit, *die;* **~worker** *n.: jmd., der außerhalb des Betriebs arbeitet;* Heimarbeiter, *der*/-arbeiterin, *die;* **~ˈworn** *adj.* (obsolete) veraltet ‹*Brauch, Ansicht, Lehre, Theorie*›

ouzo /ˈuːzəʊ/ *n., no pl.* Ouzo, *der*

ova *pl. of* **ovum**

oval /ˈəʊvl/

A *adj.* **1** oval; länglich rund ‹*Form*›; eiförmig ‹*Ball*› **2** (having outline of egg) oval; **O~ Office** *Büro des US-Präsidenten im Weißen Haus* **B** *n.* Oval, *das*

ovarian /əʊˈveərɪən/ *adj.* (Anat., Med.) Eierstock-; ovarial (fachspr.)

ovary /ˈəʊvərɪ/ *n.* (Anat.) Ovarium, *das;* Eierstock, *der;* (Bot.) Ovarium, *das;* Fruchtknoten, *der*

ovation /əʊˈveɪʃn/ *n.* Ovation, *die;* begeisterter Beifall; **get an ~ for sth.** Ovationen *od.* begeisterten Beifall für etw. bekommen; **a standing ~:** stehende Ovationen

oven /ˈʌvn/ *n.* [Back]ofen, *der;* **put sth. in the ~ for 40 minutes** etw. 40 Minuten backen; **cook in a hot/moderate/slow ~:** bei starker/mäßiger/schwacher Hitze backen/braten/schmoren; **it's like an ~ in here** hier ist es warm wie in einem Backofen; **have a bun in the ~** (coll.) ein Kind kriegen (ugs.)

oven: ~ chip *n.* Backofenfritte, *die;* **~ cleaner** *n.* Backofenreiniger, *der;* **~ cloth** *n.* Topflappen, *der;* **~-fresh** *adj.* ofenfrisch; **~ glove** *n.* Topfhandschuh, *der;* **~proof** *adj.* feuerfest; **~-ready** *adj.* backfertig ‹*Pommes frites, Pastete*›; bratfertig ‹*Geflügel*›; **~-to-table** *adj.* feuerfest ‹*Geschirr*›; **~ware** *n., no pl.* feuerfestes Geschirr

over /ˈəʊvə(r)/

A *adv.* 1) (outward and downward) hinüber; **kick ~:** umstoßen

2) (so as to cover surface) **draw/board/cover ~:** zuziehen/-nageln/-decken; **paint ~:** [an]streichen ‹*Raum, Wand*›; überstreichen ‹*Inschrift*›

3) (with motion above sth.) **climb/look/jump ~:** hinüber- *od.* (ugs.) rüberklettern/-sehen/-springen; **boil ~:** überkochen; **this goes under and that goes ~:** dies kommt darunter und das darüber

4) (so as to reverse position etc.) herum; **change ~:** umschalten ‹*Programm, Sender*›; austauschen ‹*Bilder, Format*›; **switch ~:** umschalten ‹*Programm, Sender*›; **it rolled ~ and ~:** es rollte und rollte

5) (across a space) hinüber; (towards speaker) herüber; **row ~ to a place** an einen Ort hinüberrudern; **he swam ~ to us/the other side** er schwamm zu uns herüber/hinüber zur anderen Seite; **fly ~:** vorüberfliegen; **drive sb. ~ to the other side of town** jmdn. ans andere Ende der Stadt fahren; **be ~** (have arrived) drüben [angekommen] sein; **~ here/there** (direction) hier herüber/dort hinüber; (location) hier/dort; **they are ~ [here] for the day** sie sind einen Tag hier; **ask sb. ~ [for dinner]** jmdn. [zum Essen] einladen; **~ against** (opposite) gegenüber; (in contrast to) im Gegensatz zu

6) (with change from one to another) **[come in, please,] ~** (Radio) übernehmen Sie bitte; **~ and out** (Radio) Ende; **and now, ~ to ...** (Radio) wir schalten jetzt um nach ...; **and it's ~ to you** jetzt bist du dran; (Radio) ich übergebe an Sie

7) ▸ ❶ p. 894 (in excess etc.) **children of 12 and ~:** Kinder im Alter von zwölf Jahren und darüber; **there are two cakes each and one ~:** es sind zwei Kuchen für jeden da und einer übrig; **be [left] ~:** übrig [geblieben] sein; **have ~:** übrig haben ‹*Geld*›; zu viel haben ‹*Spielkarte*›; **9 into 28 goes 3 and 1 ~:** 28 geteilt durch neun ist gleich 3, Rest 1; **it's a bit ~** (in weight) es ist ein bisschen mehr; **do you want it ~ or under?** darf es mehr oder soll es weniger sein?; **run three minutes ~:** drei Minuten über die Zeit laufen; **£50 ~ and above** obendrein noch *od.* überdies noch 50 Pfund

8) (from beginning to end) von Anfang bis Ende; **say sth. twice ~:** etw. wiederholen *od.* zweimal sagen; **[all] ~ again,** (Amer.) **~:** noch einmal [ganz von vorn]; **~ and ~ [again]** immer wieder; wieder und wieder (geh.); **several times ~:** mehrmals

9) (at an end) vorbei; vorüber; **be ~:** vorbei sein; ‹*Aufführung:*› zu Ende sein; **the rain is ~:** der Regen hat aufgehört; **get sth. ~ with** etw. hinter sich (*Akk.*) bringen; **be ~ and done with** erledigt sein

10) **all ~** (completely finished) aus [und vorbei]; (in or on one's whole body etc.) überall; (in characteristic attitude) typisch; **it is all ~ with him** es ist aus mit ihm (ugs.); **I ache all ~:** mir tut alles weh; **be shaking all ~:** am ganzen Körper zittern; **be wet all ~:** völlig nass sein; **the dog licked her all ~:** der Hund leckte sie von oben bis unten ab; **I feel stiff all ~:** ich bin ganz steif; **embroidered all ~ with flowers** ganz mit Blumen bestickt; **it happens all ~** (Amer.: everywhere) das kommt überall vor; **that is him/sth. all ~:** das ist typisch für ihn/etw.

11) (overleaf) umseitig; rückseitig; auf der Rückseite; **see ~:** siehe Rückseite

B *prep.* 1) (above) (indicating position) über (+ *Dat.*); (indicating motion) über (+ *Akk.*); **bent ~ his books** über seine Bücher gebeugt; **his crime will hang ~ him until he dies** sein Verbrechen wird ihn bis zu seinem Tode verfolgen

2) (on) (indicating position) über (+ *Dat.*); (indicating motion) über (+ *Akk.*); **hit sb. ~ the head** jmdm. auf den Kopf schlagen; **carry a coat ~ one's arm** einen Mantel über dem Arm tragen; **tie a piece of paper ~ a jar** ein Stück Papier auf einem Glas befestigen; **~ the page** auf der nächsten Seite

3) (in or across every part of) [überall] in (+ *Dat.*); (to and fro upon) über (+ *Akk.*); (all through) durch; **all ~** (in or on all parts of) überall in (+ *Dat.*); **sell sth./travel all ~ the country** etw. im ganzen Land verkaufen/das ganze Land bereisen; **all ~ Spain** überall in Spanien; in ganz Spanien; **all ~ everything** überall; **you've got jam all ~ your face** du hast überall im Gesicht Marmelade *od.* dein Gesicht ist ganz voller Marmelade; **she spilt wine all ~ her skirt** sie hat sich (*Dat.*) Wein über den ganzen Rock geschüttet; **all ~ the world** in der ganzen Welt; **be all ~ sb.** (coll.: be very attentive to) sich an jmdn. ranschmeißen (salopp); **show sb. ~ the house** jmdm. das Haus zeigen; **~ all** ▸ **overall C**

4) (round about) (indicating position) über (+ *Dat.*); (indicating motion) über (+ *Akk.*); **a sense of gloom hung ~ him** ihn umgab eine gedrückte Stimmung; **doubt hangs ~ the authenticity of the diaries** es besteht *od.* bestehen Zweifel an der Echtheit der Tagebücher

5) (on account of) wegen; **laugh ~ sth.** über etw. (*Akk.*) lachen

6) (engaged with) bei; **take trouble ~ sth.** sich (*Dat.*) mit etw. Mühe geben; **be a long time ~ sth.** lange für etw. brauchen; **fall asleep ~ one's work** bei der Arbeit einschlafen; **~ work/dinner/a cup of tea/a bottle** bei der Arbeit/beim Essen/bei einer Tasse Tee/einer guten Flasche; **~ the telephone** am Telefon

7) (superior to, in charge of) über (+ *Akk.*); **have command/authority ~ sb.** Befehlsgewalt über jmdn./Weisungsbefugnis gegenüber jmdm. haben; **be ~ sb.** (in rank) über jmdm. stehen

8) (beyond, more than) über (+ *Akk.*); **an increase ~ last year's total** eine Zunahme gegenüber der letztjährigen Gesamtmenge; **it's been ~ a month since ...:** es ist über einen Monat her, dass ...; **~ and above** zusätzlich zu

9) (in comparison with) **a decrease ~ last year** eine Abnahme gegenüber dem letzten Jahr

10) (out and down from etc.) über (+ *Akk.*); **look ~ a wall** über eine Mauer sehen; **the window looks ~ the street** das Fenster geht zur Straße hinaus *od.* liegt zur Straße; **fall ~ a cliff** von einem Felsen stürzen; **jump ~ a precipice** in einen Abgrund springen

11) (across) über (+ *Akk.*); **the pub ~ the road** die Wirtschaft auf der anderen Straßenseite *od.* gegenüber; **~ sea and land/hill and dale** über Meer und Land/Berg und Tal; **climb ~ the wall** über die Mauer steigen *od.* klettern; **be safely ~ an obstacle** sicher über ein Hindernis gekommen sein; **be ~ the worst** das Schlimmste hinter sich (*Dat.*) *od.* überstanden haben; **come from ~ the wall** ‹*Lärm:*› von der anderen Seite der Mauer kommen; **be ~ an illness** eine Krankheit überstanden haben

12) (throughout, during) über (+ *Akk.*); **stay ~ Christmas/the weekend/Wednesday** über Weihnachten/das Wochenende/bis Donnerstag bleiben; **~ the summer** den Sommer über; **~ the past years** in den letzten Jahren; **mellow ~ the years** ‹*Person:*› mit den Jahren abgeklärter werden

13) (Math.: divided by) [geteilt] durch

C *n.* (Cricket) Over, *das;* [Anzahl von] 6/(esp. in Australia) 8 Würfe[n]; *see also* **maiden over**

over: ~aˈbundant *adj.* überreichlich; **~aˈchieve** *v.i.* (Psych.) einen Leistungsüberschuss haben; **~ˈact A** *v.t.* übertrieben spielen ‹*Rolle, Theaterstück*›; chargieren ‹*Nebenrolle*›; **B** *v.i.* übertreiben; **~ˈactive** *adj.* hyperaktiv; **have an ~active thyroid** an Schilddrüsenüberfunktion leiden; **~-ˈage** *adj.* zu alt; **~all A** *n.* 1) (Brit.: garment) Arbeitsmantel, *der;* Arbeitskittel, *der;* 2) *in pl.* **[pair of] ~alls** Overall, *der;* (with a bib and strap top) Latzhose, *die;* **B** *adj.* 1) (from end to end; total) Gesamt‹*breite, -einsparung, -klassement, -abmessung*›; **have an ~all majority** die absolute Mehrheit haben; 2) (general) allgemein ‹*Verbesserung, Wirkung*›; **C** /ˈ---, --ˈ-/ *adv.* 1) (in all parts) insgesamt; **a ship dressed ~all** ein über die Toppen geflaggtes Schiff; 2) (taken as a whole) im Großen und Ganzen; **come fourth ~all** (Sport) Vierter/Vierte der Gesamtwertung werden; **~amˈbitious** *adj.* allzu ehrgeizig ‹*Projekt, Plan*›; **~anˈxiety** *n.* Überängstlichkeit, *die;* übergroße Sorge (**about** um); **~ˈanxious** *adj.* **be ~anxious to do sth.** sich übereifrig bemühen, etw. zu tun; **be ~anxious about making mistakes** übermäßig besorgt sein, Fehler zu machen; **~arm A** *adj.* 1) (Cricket) **~arm bowling** Werfen mit über die Schulter erhobenem Arm; 2) (Swimming) **~arm stroke** Zug, bei dem ein Arm/beide Arme aus dem Wasser gehoben wird/werden; 3) (Tennis) **~arm service** Aufschlag von oben; **B** *adv.* mit über die Schulter erhobenem Arm ‹*werfen, aufschlagen*›; **~ˈawe** *v.t.* Ehrfurcht einflößen (+ *Dat.*); ‹*Waffe, Anzahl:*› einschüchtern; **they were ~awed by the splendour** die Pracht flößte ihnen Ehrfurcht ein; **~ˈbalance A** *v.i.* 1) ‹*Person:*› das Gleichgewicht verlieren, aus dem Gleichgewicht kommen; 2) (capsize) ‹*Gegenstand:*› umkippen; ‹*Boot:*› kentern; **B** *v.t.* 1) aus dem Gleichgewicht bringen ‹*Person*›; 2) (capsize) umkippen ‹*Gegenstand*›; zum Kentern bringen ‹*Boot*›; **~ˈbearing** *adj.,* **~bearingly** /əʊvəˈbeərɪŋlɪ/ *adv.* herrisch; **~bid A** /--ˈ-/ *v.t., forms as* **bid A 2** überbieten ‹*Händler, Gegner, Gebot*›; **B** /--ˈ-/ *v.i., forms as* **bid B** (Bridge) überrufen; **C** /ˈ---/ *n.* höheres Angebot; Übergebot, *das;* (higher than justified) überhöhtes Angebot; **~blouse** *n.* Überziehbluse, *die;* **~ˈblown** *adj.* 1) (past its prime, lit. or fig.) verblühend; **be ~blown** [fast] verblüht sein; 2) (inflated or pretentious) geschraubt, gestelzt, gespreizt ‹*Stil, Prosa*›; **~board** *adv.* über Bord; **fall ~board** über Bord gehen; **go ~board** (fig. coll.) ausflippen (ugs.) (**about** wegen); **~ˈbook** *v.t.* überbuchen; **~boot** *n.* Überschuh, *der;* **~ˈburden** *v.t.* (fig.) überlasten ‹*System, Person*› (**by** mit); **I don't want to ~burden you** ich möchte Sie nicht überbeanspruchen; **be ~burdened with care/grief** zu viele Sorgen/zu viel Kummer haben; **~call** (Bridge) **A** /--ˈ-/ *v.t.* überbieten ‹*Gegner, Gebot*›; **B** /--ˈ-/ *v.i.* (Brit.) überrufen; ein Übergebot *od.* höheres Gebot machen *od.* abgeben; **C** /ˈ---/ *n.* Übergebot, *das;* höheres Gebot; **~ˈcareful** *adj.* übervorsichtig; **~cast** *adj.* 1) trübe ‹*Wetter, Himmel, Tag*›; bewölkt ‹*Himmel, Nacht*›; bedeckt, bezogen ‹*Himmel*›; 2) (Sewing) überwendlich ‹*Naht*›; **~ˈcautious** *adj.* übervorsichtig; **~ˈcharge A** *v.t.* 1) (charge beyond reasonable price) zu viel abnehmen *od.* abverlangen (+ *Dat.*); **we were ~charged for the eggs** wir haben für die Eier zu viel *od.* einen überhöhten Preis bezahlt; 2) (charge beyond right price) zu viel berechnen (+ *Dat.*); **~charge sb. by 25p** jmdm. 25 Pence zu viel berechnen; 3) (put too much charge into) überladen ‹*Batterie*›; über[be]lasten ‹*Elektrogerät*›; **B** *v.i.* zu viel berechnen; **~coat** *n.* 1) (coat) Mantel, *der;* 2) (of paint) Anstrich, *der;* **~ˈcome A** *v.t., forms as* **come A** 1) (prevail ~) überwinden; bezwingen ‹*Feind*›; ablegen ‹*Angewohnheit*›; widerstehen (+ *Dat.*) ‹*Versuchung*›; ‹*Schlaf:*› überkommen, übermannen; ‹*Dämpfe:*› betäuben; 2) *in p.p.* (exhausted, affected) **he was ~come by grief/with emotion** Kummer/Rührung übermannte *od.* überwältigte ihn; **she was ~come by fear/shyness** Angst/Schüchternheit überkam *od.* überwältigte sie; **they were too ~come with fatigue** sie waren zu müde; **~come with loneliness** von Einsamkeit übermannt; **they were ~come with remorse** Reue befiel sie; **I'm quite ~come** ich bin ganz überwältigt; **B** *v.i., forms as* **come A** siegen; siegreich sein; **~ˈcompensate** *v.i.* überkompensieren; **~compensate for sth.** etw. überkompensieren; **~compenˈsation** *n.* Überkompensation, *die;* **~ˈconfidence** *n.* übersteigertes Selbstvertrauen; **~ˈconfident** *adj.* übertrieben zuversichtlich; **be ~confident of success** sich (*Dat.*) des Erfolges allzu sicher sein; **~ˈconfidently** *adv.* übertrieben zuversichtlich; **~ˈcooked** *adj.* verkocht; **~ˈcritical** *adj.* zu kritisch; überkritisch; **be ~critical of sth.** etw. zu sehr kritisieren; **~ˈcrowded** *adj.* überfüllt ‹*Zug,*

O

Bus, Raum›; übervölkert ‹*Stadt*›; **~'crowding** *n.* (of room, bus, train) Überfüllung, *die;* (of city) Übervölkerung, *die;* **~de'velop** *v.t.* (Photog.) überentwickeln; **~de'veloped** *adj.* überentwickelt; frühreif ‹*Kind, Jugendliche*›; **~'do** *v.t.*, **~doing** /əʊvəˈduːɪŋ/, **~'did** /əʊvəˈdɪd/, **~done** /əʊvəˈdʌn/ **[1]** (carry to excess) übertreiben; überladen ‹*Geschichte*›; übertrieben spielen ‹*Rolle, Szene*›; **~do one's gratitude/the sympathy** es mit der Dankbarkeit/dem Mitleid übertreiben; **~do the salt** zu großzügig mit dem Salz umgehen; **[2]** **~do it** *or* **things** (work too hard) sich übernehmen; (exaggerate) es übertreiben; **~'done** *adj.* **[1]** (exaggerated) übertrieben; **[2]** (cooked too much) verkocht; verbraten ‹*Fleisch*›; **~dose** **[A]** /ˈ---/ *n.* Überdosis, *die;* **[B]** /--ˈ-/ *v.t.* eine Überdosis geben (+ *Dat.*); **[C]** *v.i.* eine Überdosis nehmen; **~dose on heroin/amphetamines** eine Überdosis Heroin/Amphetamine nehmen; **~draft** *n.* Kontoüberziehung, *die;* **have an ~draft of £50 at the bank** sein Konto um 50 Pfund überzogen haben; **get/pay off an ~draft** einen Überziehungskredit erhalten/abbezahlen; **~'draw** *v.t., forms as* **draw A** (Banking) überziehen ‹*Konto*›; **~'drawn** *adj.* überzogen ‹*Konto*›; **I am ~drawn [at the bank]** mein Konto ist überzogen; **~'dress** *v.i.* sich zu fein anziehen; **~'dressed** *adj.* zu fein angezogen; overdressed (geh.); **~drive** *n.* (Motor Veh.) Overdrive, *der;* Schongang, *der;* **~'due** *adj.* überfällig; **the train is 15 minutes ~due** der Zug hat schon 15 Minuten Verspätung; **your rent is ~due** Ihre Miete steht noch aus; **~'eager** *adj.* übereifrig; **be ~eager to do sth.** sich übereifrig bemühen, etw. zu tun; **we weren't ~eager to go back** wir waren nicht gerade wild darauf zurückzukehren (ugs.); **~'easy** *adj.* beidseitig kurz gebraten ‹*Ei*›; **~'eat** *v.i., forms as* **eat** zu viel essen; **~eating** übermäßiges Essen; **~egg** *v.t.* **~egg the pudding** übertreiben; **~-e'laborate** *adj.* allzu *od.* übertrieben kunstvoll ‹*Konstruktion, Frisur, Stil*›; allzu ausgefeilt ‹*Plan*›; allzu ausgeklügelt ‹*Plan, Entschuldigung*›; **~'emphasis** *n.* Überbetonung, *die;* **~'emphasize** *v.t.* überbetonen; **one cannot ~emphasize the importance of this** man kann nicht genug betonen, wie wichtig das ist; **~-enthusi'astic** *adj.* übertrieben begeistert (**at, about** von); **~estimate** **[A]** /əʊvərˈestɪmeɪt/ *v.t.* überschätzen; **~estimate one's own importance** sich zu wichtig nehmen (ugs.); **[B]** /əʊvərˈestɪmət/ *n.* zu hohe Schätzung; **~ex'cite** *v.t.* zu sehr aufregen ‹*Patient*›; **~excited** überreizt ‹*Zustand, Gemüt*›; **become ~excited** ganz aufgeregt werden; **~ex'citement** *n.* Überreizung, *die;* **~ex'ert** *v. refl.* sich überanstrengen; **~ex'pose** *v.t.* **[1]** (Photog.) überbelichten; **[2]** **be ~exposed to sth.** einer Sache (*Dat.*) im Übermaß ausgesetzt sein; **he is becoming ~exposed** (on TV) man sieht sich (*Dat.*) ihn über (ugs.); **~ex'posure** *n.* **[1]** (Photog.) Überbelichtung, *die;* **[2]** (to radiation) übermäßige Belastung (**to** durch); (by the media) zu häufige Präsentation (**by** durch); **~'feed** *v.t., forms as* **feed A** überfüttern ‹*Tier,* (*fam.*) *Kind*›; **~'fill** *v.t.* zu voll machen; **~'fish** *v.t.* überfischen; **~fishing** Überfischung, *die;* **~flight** *n.* Überflug, *der;* **~flow** **[A]** /--ˈ-/ *v.t.* **[1]** (flow ~) laufen über (+ *Akk.*) ‹*Rand*›; **[2]** (flow ~ brim of) überlaufen aus ‹*Tank*›; **a river ~flowing its banks** ein Fluss, der über die Ufer tritt; **[3]** (extend beyond limits of) ‹*Menge, Personen:*› nicht genug Platz finden in (+ *Dat.*); **[4]** (flood) überschwemmen ‹*Feld*›; **[B]** *v.i.* **[1]** (flow ~ edge or limit) überlaufen; **be filled/full to ~flowing** ‹*Raum:*› überfüllt sein; ‹*Flüssigkeitsbehälter:*› zum Überlaufen voll sein; ‹*Schublade:*› fast überquellen; **~flow into the street** ‹*Menge:*› bis auf die Straße stehen; **[2]** (fig.) ‹*Herz, Person:*› überfließen (geh.), überströmen (**with** vor + *Dat.*); **[C]** /ˈ---/ *n.* **[1]** (what flows ~, lit. or fig.) **the ~flow** das Übergelaufene; **the ~flow from the cities** die Menschen, für die in den Städten kein Platz ist; **~flow of population** Bevölkerungsüberschuss, *der;* **[2]** (outlet) **~flow [pipe]** Überlauf, *der;* **~flow 'car park** *n.* Ausweichparkplatz, *der;* **~flow meeting** *n.* Parallelversammlung, *die;* **~'fly** *v.t., forms as* **fly² B** **[1]** (fly ~) überfliegen; **[2]** (fly beyond) hinausschießen über (+ *Akk.*) ‹*Landebahn*›; **~'fond** *adj.* **be/not be ~fond of sb./sth.** jmdn./etw. nur zu gern/nicht sonderlich mögen; **be/not be ~fond of doing sth.** etw. nur zu gern/nicht sonderlich gern tun; **~'fondness** *n., no pl.* übertriebene Vorliebe (**for** für); **~ful'fil** (*Amer.:* **~ful'fill**) *v.t.* übererfüllen ‹[*Plan*]*soll, Plan*›; **~ful'filment** (*Amer.:* **~ful'fillment**) *n.* Überfüllung, *die;* **~'full** *adj.* zu voll; übervoll; **~'generous** *adj.* zu *od.* übertrieben großzügig ‹*Person*›; reichlich groß ‹*Portion*›; **you weren't ~generous with the butter** mit der Butter bist du ja nicht gerade verschwenderisch umgegangen; **~graze** *v.t.* überweiden; **~grazing** *n., no pl.* Überweidung, *die;* **~ground** *adj.* oberirdisch ‹*Krypta, Pflanzenteil*›; oberirdisch verkehrend ‹*Bahn*›; **~'grow** *v.t., forms as* **grow B** überwachsen, überwuchern ‹*Beet*›; **~grown** *adj.* **[1]** überwachsen, überwuchert ‹*Beet*› (**with** von); **[2]** **he acts like an ~grown schoolboy** er führt sich auf wie ein großes Kind; **~hand knot** *n.* einfacher Knoten; **~hang** **[A]** /--ˈ-/ *v.t.*, **~hung** /əʊvəˈhʌŋ/ ‹*Felsen, Stockwerk:*› hinausragen über (+ *Akk.*); **[B]** /--ˈ-/ *v.i.*, **~hung** ‹*Fels, Klippe:*› überhängen; **[C]** /ˈ---/ *n.* Überhang, *der;* **rock ~hang** Felsvorsprung, *der;* Überhang, *der;* **~'hanging** *adj.* überhängend; **~'hasty** *adj.* vorschnell, übereilt ‹*Urteil, Verurteilung, Entschluss, Schluss, Antwort*›; **be ~hasty in doing sth.** etw. vorschnell *od.* übereilt tun; **~haul** **[A]** /--ˈ-/ *v.t.* **[1]** (examine and adjust) überholen ‹*Auto, Schiff, Maschine, Motor*›; überprüfen ‹*System*›; **[2]** (~take) überholen ‹*Fahrzeug, Person*›; **[B]** /ˈ---/ *n.* Überholung, *die;* **need an ~haul** ‹*Maschine:*› überholt werden müssen; ‹*System:*› überarbeitet werden müssen; **give sth. an ~haul** etw. überholen; **~head** **[A]** /--ˈ-/ *adv.* über mir/ihm/uns *usw.*; **the sky ~head** der Himmel darüber; (above me/him/us etc.) der Himmel über mir/ihm/uns *usw.*; **the clouds ~head** die Wolken am Himmel; **hear a sound ~head** ein Geräusch über sich (*Dat.*) hören; **[B]** /ˈ---/ *adj.* **[1]** **~head wires** Hochleitung, *die;* **~head cable** Luftkabel, *das;* Freileitung, *die;* **~head railway** Hochbahn, *die;* **~head lighting** Deckenbeleuchtung, *die;* **~head locker** Gepäckfach über dem Sitz; **~head projector** Overheadprojektor, *der;* **[2]** **~head expenses/charges/costs** (Commerc.) Gemeinkosten *Pl.*; **[C]** /ˈ---/ *n.* **[1]** **~heads,** (Amer.) **~head** (Commerc.) Gemeinkosten *Pl.*; **[2]** (Sport) Überkopfball, *der;* **~'hear** *v.t., forms as* **hear A** (accidentally) zufällig [mit]hören, mitbekommen ‹*Unterhaltung, Bemerkung*›; (intentionally) belauschen ‹*Gespräch, Personen*›; **speak quietly, so that we can't be ~heard** sprich leise, damit niemand etwas mitbekommt; *abs.* **not want sb. to ~hear** nicht wollen, dass jmd. mithört; **~'heat** **[A]** *v.t.* überhitzen ‹*Motor, Metall usw.*›; **~heated imagination** überdrehte Fantasie; **~heated economy** überhitzte Konjunktur; **[B]** *v.i.* zu heiß werden; ‹*Maschine, Lager:*› heißlaufen; (fig.) ‹*Konjunktur:*› sich überhitzen; **~-in'dulge** **[A]** *v.t.* zu sehr frönen (geh.) (+ *Dat.*) ‹*Appetit*›; **~-indulge a child** einem Kind gegenüber zu nachgiebig sein; **~-indulge oneself** sich allzu sehr gehen lassen; **[B]** *v.i.* es übertreiben; **~-indulge in food and drink** sich an Essen und Trinken mehr als gütlich tun; **~in'dulgence** *n.* übermäßiger Genuss (**in** von); (towards a person) zu große Nachgiebigkeit; **~indulgence in drink/drugs/sex** übermäßiges Trinken/übermäßiger Drogengenuss/zu viel Sex; **~in'dulgent** *adj.* unmäßig; (towards a person) zu nachgiebig; **~in'sured** *adj.* zu hoch versichert; **~in'terpret** *v.t.* überinterpretieren

overjoyed /əʊvəˈdʒɔɪd/ *adj.* überglücklich (**at** über + *Akk.*)

over: ~kill *n.* (Mil.) Overkill, *das od. der;* **be ~kill** (fig.) zu viel des Guten sein; **~land** **[A]** /--ˈ-/ *adv.* auf dem Landweg; **[B]** /ˈ---/ *adj.* **by the ~land route** auf dem Landweg; **~land transport/journey** Beförderung/Reise auf dem Landweg; **~lap** **[A]** /--ˈ-/ *v.t.* überlappen ‹*Fläche, Dachziegel*›; teilweise überdecken ‹*Farbe*›; sich überschneiden mit ‹*Aufgabe, Datum*›; **[B]** /--ˈ-/ *v.i.* ‹*Flächen, Dachziegel:*› sich überlappen; ‹*Aufgaben, Daten, Zuständigkeitsbereiche:*› sich überschneiden; ‹*Farben:*› sich teilweise überdecken; ‹*Bretter:*› teilweise übereinander liegen; **[C]** /ˈ---/ *n.* **[1]** Überlappung, *die;* (of colours) teilweise Überdeckung; (of dates or tasks; between subjects, periods, etc.) Überschneidung, *die;* **have an ~lap of 4 cm** ‹*Bretter usw.:*› sich auf einer Breite von 4 cm überdecken; **[2]** (~lapping part) Überlappung, *die;* (between map-sheets) sich überschneidende Teile; **~'large** *adj.* übergroß; **~-large for sth.** zu groß für etw.; **~lay** **[A]** /--ˈ-/ *v.t., forms as* **lay² A** **[1]** (cover) bedecken; (with film, veneer) überziehen; **[2]** ▸ **~lie**; **[B]** /ˈ---/ *n.* **[1]** (cover) Überzug, *der;* **[2]** (transparent sheet) Auflegefolie, *die;* **~'leaf** *adv.* auf der Rückseite; **see diagram ~leaf** siehe das umseitige Diagramm; **see ~leaf for details** Details siehe Rückseite; **~'lie** *v.t., forms as* **lie² B** überlagern; **~load** **[A]** /--ˈ-/ *v.t.* überladen (auch fig.), überlasten ‹*Stromkreis, Lautsprecher usw.*›; überbelasten ‹*Maschine, Motor, Mechanismus usw.*›; **[B]** *v.i.* überbelastet werden; **[C]** /ˈ---/ *n.* (Electr.) Überlastung, *die;* **~'long** *adj.* überlang; **~'look** *v.t.* **[1]** (have view of) ‹*Hotel, Zimmer, Haus:*› Aussicht haben *od.* bieten auf (+ *Akk.*); **house ~looking the lake** Haus mit Blick auf den See; **[2]** (be higher than) überragen; **[3]** (not see, ignore) übersehen; (allow to go unpunished) hinwegsehen über (+ *Akk.*) ‹*Vergehen, Beleidigung*›; **~lord** *n.* Oberherr, *der*

overly /ˈəʊvəlɪ/ *adv.* allzu

over: ~'man *v.t.* überbesetzen; **~manning** *n.* [personelle] Überbesetzung; **~mantel** *n.* Kaminaufsatz, *der;* **~'modest** *adj.* zu bescheiden; **~'much** **[A]** *adj.* allzu viel; **[B]** *adv.* allzu sehr

overnight

[A] /--ˈ-/ *adv.* (also fig.: suddenly) über Nacht; **stay ~ in a hotel** in einem Hotel übernachten;

[B] /ˈ---/ *adj.* **[1]** **~ train/bus** Nachtzug, *der*/Nachtbus, *der;* **~ stay** Übernachtung, *die;* **make an ~ stay** übernachten **[2]** (fig.: sudden) **be an ~ success** über Nacht Erfolg haben

overnight: ~ bag *n.* [kleine] Reisetasche; **~ case** *n.* Handköfferchen, *das*

over: ~pass ▸ **flyover**; **~'pay** *v.t., forms as* **pay B** überbezahlen; **~'payment** *n.* Überbezahlung, *die;* **receive an ~payment of £20** 20 Pfund zu viel bekommen; **~'play** *v.t.* **[1]** (overact) übertrieben spielen ‹*Rolle*›; **[2]** (exaggerate) hochspielen ‹*Faktor, Bedeutung*›; **~play one's hand** (Cards) sich überreizen; (fig.) den Bogen überspannen; **~'populated** *adj.* überbevölkert; **~popu'lation** *n.* Übervölkerung, *die;* **~'power** *v.t.* **[1]** (subdue, overwhelm) überwältigen; (wrestling) bezwingen; **[2]** (render imperceptible) überdecken (fig.); **~'powered** *adj.* (Motor Veh.) übermotorisiert; **~powering** /əʊvəˈpaʊərɪŋ/ *adj.* überwältigend; durchdringend ‹*Geruch*›; **the heat was ~powering** die Hitze war unerträglich; **I find him a bit ~powering** seine Art ist mir manchmal zu viel; **~'praise** *v.t.* zu sehr loben; **~priced** /əʊvəˈpraɪst/ *adj.* zu teuer; **~print** **[A]** *v.t.* **[1]** /--ˈ-/ (print too many/extra copies of) **~print sth. by 100 copies** 100 Exemplare zu viel/mehr von etw. drucken; **[2]** /ˈ---/ (print further matter on, print over) überdrucken (**with** mit); **[B]** /ˈ---/ *n.* [zusätzlicher] Aufdruck; (on stamp also) Überdruck, *der;* **~pro'duce** *v.t.* **~produce milk/steel** *etc.* zu viel Milch/Stahl *usw.* produzieren; **~pro'duction** *n., no pl., no indef. art.* Überproduktion, *die;* **~pro'tective** *adj.* überfürsorglich (**towards** gegenüber); **~'qualified** *adj.* überqualifiziert; **~'rate** *v.t.* überschätzen; **be ~rated** überschätzt werden; ‹*Buch, Film:*› überbewertet werden; **~'reach** *v. refl.* sich übernehmen; **~re'act** *v.i.* unangemessen heftig reagieren (**to** auf + *Akk.*); **~re'action** *n.* Überreaktion, *die* (**to** auf + *Akk.*); **~-'regulate** *v.t.* überregulieren; **~regu'lation** *n., no pl.* Überregulierung, *die;* **~ride** **[A]** /--ˈ-/ *v.t., forms as* **ride C** sich hinwegsetzen über (+ *Akk.*); **be ~ridden** missachtet werden; **[B]** /ˈ---/ *n.* (control) **[manual] ~ride** Automatikabschaltung, *die;* **~'riding** *adj.* vorrangig; **be of ~riding importance** wichtiger als alles

O

andere sein; **~ripe** *adj.* überreif; **~'rule** *v.t.* 1) (set aside) aufheben ‹*Entscheidung*›; zurückweisen ‹*Einwand, Appell, Forderung, Argument*›; 2) (reject proposal of) **~rule sb.** jmds. Vorschlag ablehnen; **be ~ruled by the majority** von der Mehrheit überstimmt werden; **objection ~ruled!** Einspruch abgelehnt!; **~'run** *v.t., forms as* **run C 1)** **be ~run with** überlaufen sein von ‹*Touristen*›; überwuchert sein von ‹*Unkraut*›; wimmeln von ‹*Mäusen, Schädlingen*›; 2) (Mil.) einfallen in (+ *Akk.*) ‹*Land*›; überrennen ‹*Stellungen*›; 3) (exceed) **~run its allotted time** ‹*Programm, Treffen, Diskussion:*› länger als vorgesehen dauern; **~run [one's time]** ‹*Dozent, Redner:*› überziehen; *abs.* **the programme ~ran by five minutes** die vorgesehene Sendezeit wurde um fünf Minuten überzogen; **~'scrupulous** *adj.* übertrieben gewissenhaft; **he is not ~scrupulous about that** damit nimmt er es nicht allzu genau; **~seas** A /--'-/ *adv.* in Übersee ‹*leben, sein, sich niederlassen*›; nach Übersee ‹*gehen*›; **colonies ~seas** überseeische Kolonien; Überseekolonien; B /'---/ *adj.* 1) (across the sea) Übersee‹*postgebühren, -handel, -telefonat*›; **~seas broadcasting** Sendungen für Hörer in Übersee; 2) (foreign) Auslands‹*hilfe, -zulage, -ausgabe, -nachrichten*›; ausländisch ‹*Student*›; **~seas visitors/ambassadors** Besucher/Botschafter aus dem Ausland; **~'see** *v.t., forms as* **see^1 A** überwachen; (manage) leiten ‹*Abteilung*›; **~seer** ▸ **supervisor**; **~'sell** *v.t.* 1) (overpraise) zu sehr anpreisen; 2) (sell too much of) **~sell one's goods** mehr Waren verkaufen, als man liefern kann; **~'sensitive** *adj.* überempfindlich; übersensibel; **~sew** *v.t., forms as* **sew A** überwendlich nähen; **~-sexed** /əʊvə'sekst/ *adj.* sexbesessen; **~'shadow** *v.t.* (lit. or fig.) überschatten; (fig.: make seem minor) in den Schatten stellen ‹*Leistung, Person*›; **~shoe** *n.* Überschuh, *der;* **~'shoot** *v.t., forms as* **shoot B** hinausschießen über (+ *Akk.*); vorbeifahren an (+ *Akk.*) ‹*Abzweigung*›; **~shoot the mark** (fig.) über das Ziel hinausschießen; **~shoot [the runway]** ‹*Pilot, Flugzeug:*› zu weit kommen; **~sight** *n.* 1) Versehen, *das;* **by** *or* **through an ~sight** versehentlich; aus Versehen; 2) ▸ **supervision**; **~simplifi'cation** *n.* zu starke Vereinfachung; **~'simplify** *v.t.* zu stark vereinfachen; **~size, ~sized** ▸ **outsize**; **~'sleep** *v.i., forms as* **sleep B** verschlafen; **~sleep by half an hour** eine halbe Stunde zu lange schlafen; **~-so'licitous** *adj.* übermäßig *od.* allzu besorgt; **~'specialize** *v.i.* sich überspezialisieren; **~specialized** überspezialisiert; **~'spend** A *v.i., forms as* **spend** zu viel [Geld] ausgeben; **~spending** zu hohe Ausgaben; **~spend by £100** 100 Pfund zu viel ausgeben; B *v.t.* überschreiten, überziehen ‹*Etat, Budget, Einkommen*›; **~spill** *n.* 1) (surplus population) Bevölkerungsüberschuss, *der; attrib.* Satelliten‹*stadt, -siedlung*›; 2) (overflow) **the ~spill** [das,] was übergelaufen ist/überläuft; **~'staff** *v.t.* überbesetzen; **~'staffing** *n.* Überbesetzung, *die;* **~'state** *v.t.* übertrieben darstellen; überbetonen ‹*Argument*›; **~'statement** *n.* Übertreibung, *die;* (of case, problem) übertriebene Darstellung; **~'stay** *v.t.* überziehen ‹*Urlaub*›; **~stay one's time [by three days]** [drei Tage] länger als vorgesehen bleiben; *see also* **welcome B 1**; **~steer** (Motor Veh.) A /--'-/ *v.i.* übersteuern; B /'---/ *n.* Übersteuern, *das;* **~'step** *v.t.* überschreiten; **~step the mark** (fig.) zu weit gehen; **~'stock** *v.t.* überbestücken ‹*Lager*›; zu stark besetzen (Fischereiw.) ‹*Teich*›; **~'strain** A *n.* Überforderung, die; B *v.t.* überfordern; **~'stretch** *v.t.* überdehnen; (fig.) überfordern; **~strung** *adj.* kreuzsaitig ‹*Klavier*›; (fig.) überreizt; **~sub'scribed** *adj.* (Finance) überzeichnet

overt /'əʊvət, əʊ'vɜːt/ *adj.* unverhohlen; **their actions were ~:** sie haben mit offenen Karten gespielt *od.* nichts verborgen

over: ~'take *v.t.* 1) *also abs.* (esp. Brit.: pass) überholen; **'no ~taking'** (Brit.) „Überholen verboten"; 2) (catch up) einholen; 3) (fig.) **be ~taken by events** ‹*Plan:*› von den Ereignissen überholt werden; 4) (exceed) **supply will ~take demand** das Angebot wird die Nachfrage übersteigen; 5) (befall) hereinbrechen über (+ *Akk.*); ‹*Schicksal:*› ereilen (geh.); **~'tax** *v.t.* 1) (demand too much tax from) überbesteuern; 2) (~strain) überstrapazieren, überfordern ‹*Verstand, Geduld*›; überanstrengen ‹*Verstand*›; **~tax one's strength** sich übernehmen; **don't ~tax my patience!** stell meine Geduld nicht auf die Probe!; **~-the-top** *adj.* überzogen; **~throw** A /--'-/ *v.t., forms as* **throw A** 1) stürzen ‹*Regierung, Regime usw.*›; aus dem Weg räumen ‹*Gegner*›; (defeat) schlagen, besiegen ‹*Feind*›; 2) (subvert) umstoßen, (ugs.) über den Haufen werfen ‹*Verfassung, Theorie, Überzeugung*›; B /'---/ *n.* 1) (removal from power) Sturz, *der;* 2) (subversion) Umsturz, *der;* (of ideas) Umwälzung, *die;* **~time** A *n.* Überstunden *Pl.;* **work ten hours'/put in a lot of ~time** zehn/eine Menge Überstunden machen; **be on ~time** Überstunden machen; **~time ban/payment** Überstundenstopp, *der*/-zuschlag, *der;* B *adv.* **work ~time** Überstunden machen; (fig. coll.) ‹*Apparat:*› auf Hochtouren laufen; **his brain/imagination was working ~time** er dachte fieberhaft nach/er hatte eine überspannte Fantasie; **~'tire** *v.t.* übermüden; **~tire oneself** sich übernehmen *od.* überanstrengen

overtly /'əʊvətlɪ, əʊ'vɜːtlɪ/ *adv.* unverhohlen

over: ~tone *n.* 1) (fig.: implication) Unterton, *der;* **the crime had political ~tones** das Verbrechen hatte auch politische Implikationen; 2) (Mus.) Oberton, *der;* **~'train** (Sport) A *v.t.* übertrainieren; B *v.i.* zu viel trainieren; **~trick** *n.* (Bridge) Überstich, *der;* **~'trump** *v.t.* (Cards) übertrumpfen

overture /'əʊvətjʊə(r)/ *n.* 1) (Mus.) Ouvertüre, *die* 2) (formal proposal or offer) Angebot, *das;* **~s of peace** Friedensangebot, *das;* **make ~s [to sb.]** [jmdm.] ein Angebot machen; (to woman) [bei jmdm.] Annäherungsversuche machen

over: ~'turn A *v.t.* 1) (upset) umstoßen; 2) (overthrow) umstürzen ‹*bestehende Ordnung, Vorstellung, Prinzip*›; stürzen ‹*Regierung*›; beseitigen ‹*Institution*›; (reverse) aufheben ‹*Urteil, Entscheid[ung]*›; B *v.i.* ‹*Auto, Boot, Kutsche:*› umkippen; ‹*Boot:*› kentern; ‹*Auto:*› sich überschlagen; **~use** A /əʊvə'juːz/ *v.t.* zu oft verwenden; B /əʊvə'juːs/ *n.* zu häufiger Gebrauch; **~'value** *v.t.* überbewerten ‹*Währung*›; **his contribution cannot be ~valued** sein Beitrag kann gar nicht hoch genug bewertet werden; **~view** *n.* Überblick, *der* (**of** über + *Akk.*)

overweening /əʊvə'wiːnɪŋ/ *adj.* maßlos ‹*Ehrgeiz, Gier, Stolz*›

'overweight

A *adj.* 1) (obese) übergewichtig ‹*Person*›; **be [12 pounds] ~:** [12 Pfund] Übergewicht haben 2) (weighing in excess) zu schwer; (very heavy) bleischwer

B *n.* Übergewicht, *das*

overwhelm /əʊvə'welm/ *v.t.* 1) (overpower, lit. or fig.) überwältigen; **be ~ed with work** die Arbeit kaum bewältigen können 2) (crush, destroy) **be ~ed by the enemy** vom übermächtigen Feind völlig aufgerieben werden 3) (bury) verschütten; ‹*Wasser:*› überschwemmen, überfluten

overwhelming /əʊvə'welmɪŋ/ *adj.* überwältigend; unbändig ‹*Wut, Kraft, Verlangen, Zorn*›; unermesslich ‹*Leid, Kummer*›; **against ~ odds** entgegen aller Wahrscheinlichkeit

over: ~wind /əʊvə'waɪnd/ *v.t., forms as* **wind^2 A, B** überdrehen; **~winter** *v.i. & t.* überwintern; **~'work** A *v.t.* 1) (make work too hard) mit Arbeit überlasten; **~work oneself** sich überarbeiten; 2) (fig.) überstrapazieren ‹*Metapher, Wort usw.*›; B *v.i.* sich überarbeiten; C *n.* [Arbeits]überlastung, *die;* **become ill from ~work** sich krank arbeiten; **~'write** *v.t.* (Computing) überschreiben; **~'wrought** *adj.* überreizt; **~'zealous** *adj.* übereifrig

oviduct /'əʊvɪdʌkt/ *n.* (Anat., Zool.) Ovidukt, *der* (fachspr.); Eileiter, *der*

oviparous /əʊ'vɪpərəs/ *adj.* (Zool.) ovipar

ovo-lacto-vegetarian /əʊvəʊlæktəʊvedʒɪ'teərɪən/

A *n.* Ovolaktovegetarier, *der*/Ovolaktovegetarierin, *die*

B *adj.* ovolaktovegetarisch

ovulate /'ɒvjʊleɪt, 'əʊvjʊleɪt/ *v.i.* (Physiol.) ovulieren (fachspr.); reife *od.* befruchtungsfähige Eizellen abstoßen

ovulation /ɒvjʊ'leɪʃn, əʊvjʊ'leɪʃn/ *n.* Ovulation, *die* (fachspr.); Eisprung, *der*

ovum /'əʊvəm/ *n., pl.* **ova** /'əʊvə/ Ovum, *das* (fachspr.); (Biol.) Ei, *das*

ow /aʊ/ *int.* au

owe /əʊ/ *v.t.,* **owing** /'əʊɪŋ/ 1) schulden; **~ sb. sth., ~ sth. to sb.** jmdm. etw. schulden; **~ it to sb. to do sth.** es jmdm. schuldig sein, etw. zu tun; **I ~ you an explanation** ich bin dir eine Erklärung schuldig; **you ~ it to yourself to take a break** du musst dir einfach eine Pause gönnen; **can I ~ you the rest?** kann ich dir den Rest schuldig bleiben?; **money was ~d to them** sie hatten Außenstände; **I hate owing money** ich hasse es, Schulden zu haben; **~ [sb.] for sth.** [jmdm.] etw. bezahlen müssen; **I [still] ~ you for the ticket** du kriegst von mir noch das Geld für die Karte (ugs.) 2) (feel gratitude for, be indebted for) verdanken; **~ sth. to sb.** jmdm. etw. verdanken *od.* zu verdanken haben

owing /'əʊɪŋ/ *pred. adj.* ausstehend; **be ~:** ausstehen; **money is ~ to them** sie haben noch Außenstände; **£10 is ~ on the furniture** für die Möbel müssen noch 10 Pfund bezahlt werden

'owing to *prep.* wegen; **~ his foresight** dank seinem Weitblick; **~ unfortunate circumstances** auf Grund unglücklicher Umstände

owl /aʊl/ *n.* 1) Eule, *die* 2) (fig. person) **he's a wise ~:** er ist weise wie eine Eule

owlet /'aʊlɪt/ *n.* Eulenjunge, *das*

owlish /'aʊlɪʃ/ *adj.* eulenhaft

own /əʊn/

A *adj.* eigen; **with one's ~ eyes** mit eigenen Augen; **be sb.'s ~ [property]** jmds. Eigentum sein; jmdm. selbst gehören; **look after one's ~ affairs** sich selbst um seine Angelegenheiten kümmern; **this is your ~ responsibility** dafür bist du selbst verantwortlich; **speak from one's ~ experience** aus eigener Erfahrung sprechen; **this is all my ~ work** das habe ich alles selbst *od.* ganz allein gemacht; **reserve sth. for one's ~ use** etw. für sich selbst reservieren; **have one's ~ room** [s]ein eigenes Zimmer haben; **one's ~ brother** der eigene Bruder; **sb.'s ~ country** jmds. Heimatland; **do one's ~ cooking/housework** selbst kochen/die Hausarbeit selbst machen; **make one's ~ clothes** seine Kleidung selbst schneidern; **virtue is its ~ reward** die Tugend trägt ihren Lohn in sich selbst; **have a charm all [of] its ~:** einen ganz eigenen Reiz haben; **a house/ideas** *etc.* **of one's ~:** ein eigenes Haus/eigene Ideen *usw.;* **have nothing of one's ~:** kein persönliches Eigentum haben; **have enough problems of one's ~:** selbst genug Probleme haben; **have [got] one of one's ~:** selbst einen/eine/eins haben; **for reasons of his ~ ...:** aus nur ihm selbst bekannten Gründen ...; **come into one's ~** (Law.: inherit property) sein Erbe antreten; **that's where he/it comes into his/its ~** (fig.) da kommt er/es voll zur Geltung; **on one's/its ~** (alone) allein; **drink whisky on its ~:** Whisky pur trinken; **get better on its ~:** von selbst besser werden; **start up on one's ~:** sich selbstständig machen; **he's on his ~** *or* **in a class of his ~** (fig.) er ist eine Klasse für sich; **be on one's ~** (without outside help) auf sich (*Akk.*) selbst gestellt sein; *see also* **business 3**; **call B 10**; **flesh A 1**; **get back B 2**; **hold^2 A 11**; **man A 2**; **master A 1**; **right C 1**

B *v.t.* 1) (possess) besitzen; **be ~ed by sb.** jmdm. gehören; **who ~s that house?** wem gehört das Haus?; **be privately ~ed** sich in Privatbesitz befinden; **they behaved as if they ~ed the place** sie benahmen sich, als ob der Laden ihnen gehörte (ugs.) 2) (acknowledge) anerkennen 3) ▸ **admit A 3**

C *v.i.* **~ to** eingestehen; **~ to doing sth./to being ashamed** [ein]gestehen *od.* zugeben, dass man etw. tut/dass man sich schämt

(Phrasal verb)

- ~ **'up** *v.i.* ‹*Schuldiger, Täter:*› gestehen; ~ **up to sth.** etw. [ein]gestehen *od.* zugeben; ~ **up to having done sth.** [ein]gestehen *od.* zugeben, dass man etw. getan hat; **Come on, ~ up! Who did it?** Na los, raus mit der Sprache! Wer ist es gewesen?

'own-brand
A *attrib. adj.* Eigenmarken-
B *n.* Hausmarke, *die*

owned /əʊnd/ *adj.* **publicly ~:** gemeinde-/staatseigen; **company-~:** firmeneigen; **privately ~:** in Privatbesitz *nachgestellt;* **English-/American-~:** in englischem/amerikanischem Besitz befindlich ‹*Firma, Bank*›

owner /'əʊnə(r)/ *n.* Besitzer, *der*/Besitzerin, *die;* Eigentümer, *der*/Eigentümerin, *die;* (of shop, hotel, firm, etc.) Inhaber, *der*/Inhaberin, *die;* **at ~'s risk** auf eigene Gefahr; **dog/property ~s** Hunde-/Grundbesitzer

owner-'driver *n.* (Brit.) *Halter/Halterin eines Autos, der/die das Auto selbst fährt*

ownerless /'əʊnəlɪs/ *adj.* herrenlos

owner-'occupier *n.* (Brit.) Eigenheimbesitzer, *der*/-besitzerin, *die*

ownership /'əʊnəʃɪp/ *n., no pl.* Besitz, *der;* ~ **is disputed** die Besitzverhältnisse sind umstritten; **the ~ of the land was disputed** es war umstritten, wem das Land gehörte; **be under new ~** ‹*Firma, Laden, Restaurant:*› einen neuen Inhaber/eine neue Inhaberin haben

own 'goal *n.* (lit. or fig.) Eigentor, *das*

'own-label ▸ **own brand**

ox /ɒks/ *n., pl.* **oxen** /'ɒksn/ Ochse, *der; see also* **strong A 2**

oxalic acid /ɒksælɪk 'æsɪd/ *n.* (Chem.) Oxalsäure, *die* (fachspr.); Kleesäure, *die*

'oxbow *n.* **1** (of yoke) Brustholz, *das* **2** (Geog.: river bend) Flussschleife, *die;* (one of several) Mäander, *der*

ox-bow 'lake *n.* (Geog.) Altwasser, *das*

Oxbridge /'ɒksbrɪdʒ/ *n.* (Brit.) die Universitäten Oxford und Cambridge; *attrib.* ~ **graduate/education** Absolvent[in] der/Ausbildung an der Universität Oxford oder Cambridge

> **Oxbridge**
>
> Eine Wortbildung aus den Namen Oxford und Cambridge. Diese Zusammensetzung wird als Sammelbegriff für die zwei Eliteuniversitäten in England verwendet, um sie von anderen Hochschulen zu unterscheiden. Oxford und Cambridge sind die ältesten britischen Universitäten mit dem besten Ruf. Die beiden Universitäten wetteifern miteinander auf akademischer und sportlicher Ebene, z. B. im **Boat Race**. *Oxbridge*-Absolventen werden häufig von Arbeitgebern bevorzugt und sind im öffentlichen Dienst hoch geschätzt.

Oxfam /'ɒksfæm/ *pr. n.* Oxforder Hungerhilfekomitee

Oxford /'ɒksfəd/ ▸ **Oxford shoe**

Oxford: ~ **'accent** *n.* Oxford-Akzent, *der;* ~ **'blue** *n.* Dunkelblau, *das;* ~ **shoe** *n.* Schnürhalbschuh, *der*

'oxhide *n.* (skin) Rindshaut, *die;* (leather) Rindsleder, *das*

oxidant /'ɒksɪdənt/ *n.* (Chem.) Oxidationsmittel, *das*

oxidation /ɒksɪ'deɪʃn/ *n.* (Chem.) Oxidation, *die*

oxide /'ɒksaɪd/ *n.* (Chem.) Oxid, *das*

oxidize (oxidise) /'ɒksɪdaɪz/ *v.t. & i.* (Chem.) oxidieren

oxlip *n.* Primel, *die;* Schlüsselblume, *die*

Oxon. /'ɒksn/ *abbr.* **1** = **Oxfordshire** **2** = **of Oxford University**

Oxonian /ɒk'səʊnɪən/
A *adj.* der Universität Oxford *nachgestellt*
B *n.* Mitglied der Universität Oxford

'oxtail *n.* Ochsenschwanz, *der*

oxtail 'soup *n.* (Gastr.) Ochsenschwanzsuppe, *die*

'ox-tongue *n.* (Gastr.) Ochsenzunge, *die*

oxyacetylene /ɒksɪə'setɪli:n/ *adj.* ~ **welding** Autogenschweißen, *das;* ~ **torch** *or* **blowpipe** *or* **burner** Schweißbrenner, *der*

oxygen /'ɒksɪdʒən/ *n.* (Chem.) Sauerstoff, *der*

oxygenate /'ɒksɪdʒəneɪt/ *v.t.* (Chem., Physiol.) oxygenieren (fachspr.)

oxygenation /ɒksɪdʒə'neɪʃn/ *n.* (Chem., Physiol.) Oxygenation, *die* (fachspr.)

oxygenator /'ɒksɪdʒəneɪtə(r)/ **1** (Med.) Oxygenator, *der* **2** (aquatic plant) Sauerstoffpflanze, *die*

oxygen: ~ **bar** *n.* Sauerstoffbar, *die;* ~ **bottle,** ~ **cylinder** *ns.* Sauerstoffflasche, *die;* ~ **mask** *n.* Sauerstoffmaske, *die;* ~ **tent** *n.* (Med.) Sauerstoffzelt, *das*

oxymoron /ɒksɪ'mɔ:rɒn/ *n.* (Rhet.) Oxymoron, *das*

oyez (oyes) /əʊ'jez, əʊ'jes/ *int.* Achtung (Ruf eines Ausrufers)

oyster /'ɔɪstə(r)/ *n.* Auster, *die;* **the world's his ~** (fig.) ihm liegt die Welt zu Füßen

oyster: ~ **bed** *n.* Austernbank, *die;* **~catcher** *n.* (Ornith.) Austernfischer, *der;* ~ **farm** *n.* Austernpark, *der;* ~ **knife** *n.* Austernmesser, *das*

oz. *abbr.* ▸ **i** **p. 1702 = ounce[s]**

Oz /ɒz/ *n.* (coll.) Australien (*das*)

ozone /'əʊzəʊn, əʊ'zəʊn/ *n.* Ozon, *das*

ozone: ~-depleting *adj.* ozonabbauend; ~ **depletion** *n., no pl* Ozonabbau, *der;* **~-friendly** *adj.* ozonsicher; (not using CFCs) FCKW-frei; ~ **hole** *n.* Ozonloch, *das* (ugs.); ~ **killer** *n.* Ozonkiller, *der* (ugs.); ~ **layer** *n.* Ozonschicht, *die;* **the hole in the ~ layer** das Ozonloch (ugs.); ~ **value** *n.* Ozonwert, *der*

Pp

P¹, p /piː/ *n., pl.* **Ps** *or* **P's** P, p, *das; see also* **mind B 2**

P² *abbr.* (Chess) **= pawn** B

p. *abbr.* **1** **= page** S. **2** /piː/ ▸ⓘ **p. 1332** (Brit.) **= penny/pence** p **3** (Mus.) **= piano** p **4** (Phys.) **= pico-** p

pa /pɑː/ *n.* (coll.) Papa, *der* (fam.)

p.a. *abbr.* **= per annum** p.a.

Pa *abbr.* (Phys.) **= Pascal** Pa

PA *abbr.* **1** ▸ⓘ **p. 1260 = personal assistant** pers. Ass. **2** **= public address: ~ [system]** LS-Anlage, *die*

pabulum /ˈpæbjʊləm/ *n.* (lit. or fig.) Nahrung, *die*

pace¹ /peɪs/

A *n.* **1** (step, distance) Schritt, *der* **2** (speed) Tempo, *das;* **slacken/quicken one's ~** (walking) seinen Schritt verlangsamen/beschleunigen; **at a steady/good ~:** in gleichmäßigem/zügigem Tempo; **at a snail's ~:** im Schneckentempo (ugs.); **set the ~:** das Tempo angeben *od.* bestimmen; (act as pacemaker) Schrittmacher sein; **keep ~ [with sb./sth.]** [mit jmdm./etw.] Schritt halten; **stay** *or* **stand the ~, stay** *or* **keep with the ~** (Sport) das Tempo durchhalten; **be off the ~** (Sport) zurückliegen; **he couldn't stand the ~ of life** (fig.) ihm war das Leben zu hektisch **3** (of horse) Passgang, *der;* **put sb./a horse through his/its ~s** (fig.) jmdn./ein Pferd zeigen lassen, was er/es kann; **show one's ~s** zeigen, was man kann

B *v.i.* **1** schreiten (geh.); [gemessenen Schrittes] gehen; **~ up and down [the platform/room]** [auf dem Bahnsteig/im Zimmer] auf und ab gehen *od.* marschieren **2** (amble) ‹*Pferd:*› im Pass[gang] gehen

C *v.t.* **1** auf und ab gehen in (+ *Dat.*) **2** (set the ~ for) Schrittmacher sein für

(Phrasal verb)

• **~ ˈout** *v.t.* abschreiten ‹*Entfernung, Weg*›

pace² /ˈpeɪsɪ, ˈpɑːtʃeɪ/ *prep.* (formal) **~ Mr Smith ...:** ohne Mr. Smith (*Dat.*) zu nahe treten zu wollen ...

pace ˈbowler ▸**fast bowler**

-paced /peɪst/ *adj. in comb.* **a well-~ performance** eine [rhythmisch] ausgewogene Aufführung; **be even-~:** ein gleichförmiges Tempo haben

ˈpacemaker *n.* **1** (Sport) Schrittmacher, *der*/-macherin, *die* **2** (Med.) [Herz]schrittmacher, *der*

ˈpacesetter *n.* Schrittmacher, *der*/-macherin, *die*

pachyderm /ˈpækɪdɜːm/ *n.* (Zool.) Dickhäuter, *der*

pacific /pəˈsɪfɪk/

A *adj.* **1** (conciliatory, peaceable) versöhnlich **2** (tranquil) friedlich **3** (Geog.) Pazifik‹*küste, -insel*›; **P~ Ocean** Pazifischer *od.* Stiller Ozean

B *n.* **the P~:** der Pazifik

pacification /pæsɪfɪˈkeɪʃn/ *n., no pl.* Befriedung, *die*

pacifier /ˈpæsɪfaɪə(r)/ *n.* **1** (person) Friedensstifter, *der*/-stifterin, *die* **2** (Amer.: baby's dummy) Schnuller, *der*

pacifism /ˈpæsɪfɪzm/ *n., no pl., no art.* Pazifismus, *der*

pacifist /ˈpæsɪfɪst/

A *n.* Pazifist, *der*/Pazifistin, *die*

B *adj.* pazifistisch

pacify /ˈpæsɪfaɪ/ *v.t.* **1** besänftigen; beruhigen ‹*weinendes Kind*› **2** (bring peace to) befrieden ‹*Land, Provinz*›

pack /pæk/

A *n.* **1** (bundle) Bündel, *das;* (Mil.) Tornister, *der;* (rucksack) Rucksack, *der* **2** (derog.: lot) (people) Bande, *die;* **a ~ of lies/nonsense** ein Sack voll Lügen/eine Menge Unsinn; **what a ~ of lies!** alles erlogen! **3** (Brit.) **~ [of cards]** [Karten-]spiel, *das* **4** (wolves, wild dogs) Rudel, *das;* (grouse) Schwarm, *der;* (hounds, beagles) Meute, *die* **5** (Cub Scouts, Brownies) Gruppe, *die* **6** (packet, set) Schachtel, *die;* Packung, *die;* **~ of ten** Zehnerpackung, *die;* Zehnerpack, *der;* **disc ~** (Computing) [Magnet]plattenstapel, *der* **7** ▸**ice pack 3** **8** (Med.) Packung, *die;* Kompresse, *die;* (compress) Tampon, *der;* Kompresse, *die; see also* **ice pack 1** **9** (cosmetic) Packung, *die;* (for face) [Gesichts]maske, *die* **10** (Rugby) *die Stürmer einer Mannschaft, die die eine Hälfte des Gedränges bilden;* (scrum) Gedränge, *das* **11** (Sport: runners) Feld, *das*

B *v.t.* **1** (put into container) einpacken; **~ sth. into sth.** etw. in etw. (*Akk.*) packen **2** (fill) packen; **~ one's bags** seine Koffer packen **3** (cram) voll stopfen (ugs.); (fill with a crowd) füllen ‹*Raum, Stadion usw.*›; **he ~ed the jury** er sorgte dafür, dass als Geschworene nur ihm genehme Leute berufen wurden **4** (wrap) verpacken (**in** + *Dat. od. Akk.*); **~ed in** verpackt in (+ *Dat.*) **5** (Med.) tamponieren **6** (coll.: carry) tragen, dabeihaben ‹*Waffe*› **7** **~ [quite] a punch** (coll.) ganz schön zuschlagen können (ugs.); ‹*Getränk:*› ganz schön reinhauen (salopp)

C *v.i.* packen; **send sb. ~ing** (fig.) jmdn. rausschmeißen (ugs.)

(Phrasal verbs)

• **~ aˈway** *v.t.* wegpacken

• **~ ˈin** *v.t.* **1** (coll.: give up) aufstecken (ugs.); aufhören mit ‹*Arbeit, Spiel*›; **~ it in!** hör [doch] auf damit! **2** (Theatre. coll.) in Scharen anziehen ‹*Publikum*›; **the new play is ~ing them in** das neue Stück ist ein Zuschauer- *od.* Publikumsmagnet **3** (find time for) hineinpacken

• **~ into** *v.t.* sich drängen in (+ *Akk.*); **we all ~ed into the car** wir quetschten uns alle in das Auto (ugs.)

• **~ ˈoff** *v.t.* (send away) fortschicken

• **~ ˈup**

A *v.t.* **1** (package) zusammenpacken ‹*Sachen, Werkzeug*›; packen ‹*Paket*›; **~ up one's luggage** packen **2** (coll.: stop) aufhören *od.* (ugs.) Schluss machen mit; **~ up work** Feierabend machen; (permanently) aufhören zu arbeiten; **~ it up!** (coll.) hör [doch] auf damit!

B *v.i.* (coll.) **1** (give up) aufhören; Schluss machen (ugs.) **2** (break down) den Geist aufgeben (ugs.); **the car ~ed up on me** das Auto ist mir verreckt (ugs.)

package /ˈpækɪdʒ/ *n.*

A **1** (bundle; fig. coll.: transaction) Paket, *das* **2** (container) Verpackung, *die* **3** (~ deal) Package, *das* (Werbespr.)

B *v.t.* (lit. or fig.) verpacken; **~d into 1 lb. bags** in 1-Pfund-Tüten abgepackt

package: ~ ˈdeal *n.* Paket, *das;* **~ ˈholiday, ~ ˈtour** *ns.* Pauschalreise, *die;* **~ ˈtourist** *n.* Pauschaltourist, *der*/-touristin, *die*

packaging /ˈpækɪdʒɪŋ/ *n., no pl.* **1** (material) Verpackung, *die* **2** (action) Verpacken, *das*

ˈpack drill *n.* (Mil.) Strafexerzieren in voller Marschausrüstung

packed /pækt/ *adj.* **1** gepackt ‹*Kiste, Koffer*›; **~ meal/lunch** Espaket, *das*/Lunchpaket, *das* **2** (crowded) [über]voll ‹*Theater, Kino, Halle*›; **~ to overflowing** völlig überfüllt (**with** von); **~ out** (coll.) gerammelt voll (ugs.)

packer /ˈpækə(r)/ *n.* Packer, *der*/Packerin, *die;* (in factory) Abpacker, *der*/Abpackerin, *die*

packet /ˈpækɪt/ *n.* **1** (package) Päckchen, *das;* (box) Schachtel, *die;* **a ~ of cigarettes** eine Schachtel/ein Päckchen Zigaretten; *see also* **pay packet** **2** (coll.: large sum of money) Haufen Geld (ugs.); **cost/earn a ~:** ein Heidengeld kosten (ugs.)/Schweinegeld verdienen (ugs.) **3** (Naut.) **[steam] ~:** ▸**packet steamer**

packet: ~ ˈsoup *n.* Instantsuppe, *die;* Tütensuppe, *die* (ugs.); **~ steamer** *n.* (dated) Postschiff, *das;* **~ switching** *n., no pl.* (Computing, Teleph.) Paketvermittlung, *die*

pack: ~horse *n.* Packpferd, *das;* **~ ice** *n.* Packeis, *das*

packing /ˈpækɪŋ/ *n., no pl.* **1** (packaging) (material) Verpackungsmaterial, *das;* (action) Verpacken, *das;* **including postage and ~:** einschließlich Porto und Verpackung **2** (to seal joint) Dichtungsmaterial, *das* **3** **do one's ~:** packen

packing: ~ case *n.* [Pack]kiste, *die;* **~ slip** *n.* Packzettel, *der*

ˈpacksack *n.* (Amer.) Rucksack, *der*

pact /pækt/ *n.* Pakt, *der;* **make a ~ with sb.** einen Pakt mit jmdm. schließen

pacy /ˈpeɪsɪ/ *adj.* schnell; mitreißend, packend ‹*Film, Thriller*›; turbulent ‹*Handlung*›

pad¹ /pæd/

A *n.* **1** (cushioning material) Polster, *das;* (to protect wound) Kompresse, *die;* (Sport) (on leg) Beinschützer, *der;* (on shoulder) Schulterschützer, *der;* (on knee) Knieschützer, *der* **2** (block of paper) Block, *der;* **a ~ of notepaper, a [writing] ~:** ein Schreibblock **3** (launching surface) Abschussrampe, *die;* **[helicopter] ~:** [Hubschrauber-]Start-und-Lande-Platz, *der* **4** (coll.: house, flat) Bude, *die* (ugs.) **5** (Zool.) (sole) Ballen, *der;* (paw) Pfote, *die* **6** (of brake) Belag, *der*

B *v.t.,* **-dd-** **1** polstern ‹*Jacke, Schulter, Stuhl*› **2** (fig.: lengthen unnecessarily) auswalzen (ugs.) ‹*Brief, Aufsatz usw.*› (**with** durch)

(Phrasal verb)

• **~ ˈout** ▸**pad¹ B**

pad² *v.t. & i.,* **-dd-** (walk softly) (in socks, slippers, etc.) tappen; (along path etc.) trotten

padded /ˈpædɪd/ *adj.* gepolstert

padded: ~ ˈcell *n.* Gummizelle, *die;* **~ ˈenvelope** *n.* wattierter Umschlag

padding /ˈpædɪŋ/ *n., no pl.* **1** Polsterung, *die;* **be filled/covered with ~:** gepolstert sein **2** (fig. superfluous matter) Füllsel, *das*

paddle¹ /ˈpædl/

A *n.* **1** (oar) [Stech]paddel, *das* **2** (paddling) (in canoe) Fahrt im Paddelboot; (in rowing boat) Ruderpartie, *die;* **go for a ~:** paddeln/rudern gehen **3** (stirring implement) Paddel, *das* **4** (wheel) Schaufelrad, *das;* (blade) Schaufel, *die* **5** (on lock gate) Schütz, *das* **6** (Zool.: fin) Flosse, *die*

B *v.t. & i.* (in canoe) paddeln; (in rowing boat) gemächlich rudern; ~ **one's own canoe** (fig. coll.) auf eigenen Beinen stehen

paddle²
A *v.i.* (with feet) planschen
B *n.* **have a/go for a ~:** ein bisschen planschen/ planschen gehen

paddle: ~ boat, ~ steamer *ns.* [Schaufel-]raddampfer, *der;* ~ **wheel** *n.* Schaufelrad, *das*

paddling pool /ˈpædlɪŋpuːl/ *n.* Planschbecken, *das*

paddock /ˈpædək/ *n.* **1** Koppel, *die* **2** (Horse-racing) Sattelplatz, *der;* (Motor racing) Fahrerlager, *das*

paddy¹ *n.* (Brit. coll.: bad temper) Koller, *der* (ugs.); **be in a ~:** einen Koller haben

paddy², 'paddy field *ns.* Reisfeld, *das*

Paddy /ˈpædɪ/ *n.* (coll.) Ire, *der;* Paddy, *der*

'padlock
A *n.* Vorhängeschloss, *das*
B *v.t.* [mit einem Vorhängeschloss] verschließen

padre /ˈpɑːdrɪ, ˈpɑːdreɪ/ *n.* Feldgeistliche, *der; as voc.* Herr Pfarrer

paean /ˈpiːən/ *n.* ~ **[of praise]** Preislied, *das;* (fig.) Lobeshymne, *die*

paediatric /piːdɪˈætrɪk/ *adj.* (Med.) pädiatrisch; Kinder‹*schwester, -station*›

paediatrician /piːdɪəˈtrɪʃn/ *n.* ▸ⓘ **p. 1260** (Med.) Kinderarzt, *der/-ärztin, die*

paediatrics /piːdɪˈætrɪks/ *n., no pl.* (Med.) Pädiatrie, *die* (fachspr.); Kinderheilkunde, *die*

paedophile /ˈpiːdəfaɪl/
A *n.* Pädophile, *der*
B *adj.* pädophil

paedophilia /piːdəˈfɪlɪə/ *n., no pl.* Pädophilie, *die*

paella /pɑːˈelə/ *n.* (Gastr.) Paella, *die*

pagan /ˈpeɪgən/
A *n.* **1** (heathen) Heide, *der*/Heidin, *die* **2** (fig.: irreligious person) Ungläubige, *der/die;* gottloser Mensch
B *adj.* **1** (heathen) heidnisch; ungläubig ‹*Person*› **2** (fig.: irreligious) gottlos

paganism /ˈpeɪgənɪzm/ *n.* Heidentum, *das;* Paganismus, *der*

page¹ /peɪdʒ/
A *n.* Page, *der*
B *v.t. & i.* ~ **[for] sb.** (over loudspeaker) jmdn. ausrufen; (by paging device) jmdn. anpiepen (ugs.); **paging Mr Miller** Herr Miller, bitte!

page²
A *n.* **1** Seite, *die;* (leaf, sheet of paper) Blatt, *das;* **front/sports/fashion ~:** erste Seite/Sport-/ Modeseite, *die;* ~ **three girl** Pin-up-Girl, *das;* **write on one side of the ~ only** beschreiben Sie das Blatt nur auf einer Seite; **turn to the next ~:** umblättern; *attrib.* **three-/double-~:** drei-/doppelseitig ‹*Artikel, Brief*› **2** (fig.: episode) Kapitel, *das;* **go down in the ~s of history** in die Annalen der Geschichte eingehen
B *v.t.* ▸**paginate**

pageant /ˈpædʒənt/ *n.* **1** (spectacle) Schauspiel, *das* **2** (procession) [Fest]umzug, *der;* (play) **historical ~:** Historienspiel, *das*

pageantry /ˈpædʒəntrɪ/ *n., no pl.* Prachtentfaltung, *die;* Prunk, *der;* **empty ~:** eitler Pomp

'pageboy *n.* **1** ▸**page¹ A 2** (hairstyle) Pagenkopf, der

page: ~ break *n.* (Computing) Seitenbruch, *der;* ~ **number** *n.* Seitenzahl, *die*

'page proof *n.* (Printing) Umbruch, *der*

pager /ˈpeɪdʒə(r)/ *n.* Piepser, *der* (ugs.)

'page set-up *n.* (Computing) Seiteneinrichtung, *die; attrib.* ~ **button** Knopf „Seite einrichten"

paginate /ˈpædʒɪmeɪt/ *v.t.* paginieren

pagination /pædʒɪˈneɪʃn/ *n.* Paginierung, *die*

'paging device ▸**pager**

pagoda /pəˈgəʊdə/ *n.* Pagode, *die*

pah /pɑː/ *int. expr. disgust* bah; *expr. contempt* pa

paid /peɪd/
A ▸**pay B, C**
B *adj.* bezahlt ‹*Urlaub, Arbeit*›; **put ~ to** (Brit. fig. coll.) (terminate) zunichte machen ‹*Hoffnung, Plan, Aussichten*›; (deal with) kurzen Prozess machen mit (ugs.) ‹*Person*›

'paid-up *adj.* bezahlt; **[fully] ~ member** Mitglied, das alle Beträge bezahlt hat; (fig.) überzeugtes Mitglied

pail /peɪl/ *n.* Eimer, *der*

pailful /ˈpeɪlfʊl/ *n.* Eimer, *der;* **a ~ of water** ein Eimer [voll] Wasser

pain /peɪn/
A *n.* **1** *no indef. art.* Schmerzen *Pl.;* (mental ~) Qualen *Pl.;* **feel [some] ~, be in ~:** Schmerzen haben; **cause sb. ~** (lit. or fig.) jmdm. wehtun **2** ▸ⓘ **p. 1231** (instance) Schmerz, *der;* **I have a ~ in my shoulder/knee/stomach** meine Schulter/mein Knie/Magen tut weh; ich habe Schmerzen in der Schulter/im Knie/habe Magenschmerzen; (fig.) **be a ~ in the arse** (coarse) einem auf die Eier gehen (derb); **be a ~ in the neck** ▸**neck A 1** **3** (coll.: nuisance) Plage, *die;* (sb./sth. getting on one's nerves) Nervensäge, *die* (ugs.); **this job/he is a real ~:** diese Arbeit/er kann einem wirklich auf die Nerven *od.* (ugs.) den Wecker gehen **4** *in pl.* (trouble taken) Mühe, *die;* Anstrengung, *die;* **spare no ~s** keine Mühe *od.* Anstrengung scheuen; **take ~s** sich (*Dat.*) Mühe geben (**over** mit, bei); **be at ~s to do sth.** sich sehr bemühen *od.* sich (*Dat.*) große Mühe geben, etw. zu tun; **he got nothing for all his ~s** seine ganze Mühe war umsonst **5** (Law) **on** *or* **under ~ of death/imprisonment** bei Todesstrafe/unter Androhung (*Dat.*) einer Gefängnisstrafe
B *v.t.* schmerzen

pain: ~ barrier *n.* Schmerzgrenze, *die;* **go/push through the ~ barrier** die Schmerzgrenze überwinden; ~ **clinic** *n.* Schmerzklinik, *die*

pained /peɪnd/ *adj.* gequält

painful /ˈpeɪnfl/ *adj.* **1** (causing pain) schmerzhaft ‹*Krankheit, Operation, Wunde*›; **be/become ~** ‹*Körperteil:*› wehtun *od.* schmerzen/anfangen, wehzutun; **the glare was ~ to the eyes** das grelle Licht tat in den Augen weh; **suffer from a ~ shoulder** Schmerzen in der Schulter haben **2** (distressing) schmerzlich ‹*Gedanke, Erinnerung*›; traurig ‹*Pflicht*›; **it was ~ to watch him** es tat weh, ihm zuzusehen **3** (troublesome) schwierig ‹*Problem*›; (laborious) beschwerlich ‹*Aufstieg*›; **make only ~ progress** nur mühsam weiterkommen

painfully /ˈpeɪnfəlɪ/ *adv.* **1** (with great pain) unter großen Schmerzen; **my shoes are ~ tight** meine Schuhe drücken fürchterlich (ugs.) **2** (fig.) (excessively) über die Maßen (geh.); (laboriously) quälend ‹*langsam*›; ~ **obvious** nur zu offensichtlich

'painkiller *n.* schmerzstillendes Mittel; Schmerzmittel, *das* (ugs.)

painless /ˈpeɪnlɪs/ *adj.* **1** (not causing pain) schmerzlos **2** (fig.: free of trouble, not causing problems) unproblematisch

painlessly /ˈpeɪnlɪslɪ/ *adv.* **1** schmerzlos ‹*behandeln*› **2** (fig.) mühelos ‹*Problem lösen*›; problemlos ‹*verlaufen*›

'pain relief *n., no pl.* Schmerzlinderung, *die;* **provide/give ~ [to sb.]** [jds.] Schmerzen lindern

painstaking /ˈpeɪnzteɪkɪŋ/ *adj.* gewissenhaft; **it is ~ work** es ist eine mühsame Arbeit; **with ~ care** mit äußerster Sorgfalt

paint /peɪnt/
A *n.* **1** Farbe, *die;* (on car) Lack, *der;* **'wet ~'** „Frisch gestrichen!"; **as clever** *or* **smart as ~:** äußerst intelligent; *see also* **fresh A 1; luminous 1; wet A 3** **2** (joc.: cosmetic) Schminke, *die;* **put one's ~ on** sich anmalen (ugs.)
B *v.t.* **1** (cover, colour) [an]streichen; ~ **one's body** seinen Körper bemalen; ~ **the town red** (fig. coll.) auf die Pauke hauen (ugs.); ~ **oneself into a corner** (fig. coll.) sich selbst in die Bredouille bringen (ugs.); *see also* **black A 6** **2** (make picture of, make by ~ing) malen; *abs.* ~ **for a living** Maler/Malerin sein; **the picture was ~ed by R.** das Bild ist von R. **3** (adorn with ~ing) bemalen ‹*Wand, Vase, Decke*› **4** (fig.: describe) zeichnen ‹*Bild*›; ~ **sth. in glowing/gloomy colours, ~ a glowing/gloomy picture of sth.** etw. in leuchtenden/düsteren Farben malen *od.* schildern **5** (apply cosmetic to) schminken ‹*Augen, Gesicht, Lippen*›; lackieren ‹*Nägel*› **6** (Med.) pinseln ‹*Hals*›; bepinseln ‹*Verletzung*›

Phrasal verbs
- ~ **'in** *v.t.* hineinmalen
- ~ **'on** *v.t.* aufmalen
- ~ **'out** *v.t.* übermalen; ~ **sb. out of a picture** jmdn. auf einem Bild übermalen

paint: ~ball *n.* **1** (paint capsule) Paintball, *der;* **2** *no pl.* (war game) Paintball, *das; attrib.* **~ball gun** Paintballmarkierer, *der;* **~box** *n.* Malkasten, *der;* Farb[en]kasten, *der;* **~brush** *n.* Pinsel, *der*

painted/ˈpeɪntɪd/: ~ **'lady** *n.* (Zool.) Distelfalter, *der;* ~ **'woman** *n.* Dirne, *die*

painter¹ /ˈpeɪntə(r)/ *n.* ▸ⓘ **p. 1260** **1** (artist) Maler, *der*/Malerin, *die* **2** **[house] ~:** Maler, *der*/Malerin, *die;* Anstreicher, *der*/Anstreicherin, *die*

painter² *n.* (Naut.: rope) Fangleine, *die*

pain: ~ therapy *n.* Schmerztherapie, *die;* ~ **threshold** *n.* Schmerzschwelle, *die*

painting /ˈpeɪntɪŋ/ *n.* **1** *no pl., no indef. art.* (art) Malerei, *die* **2** (picture) Gemälde, *das;* Bild, *das*

'painting book *n.* Malbuch, *das*

paint: ~pot *n.* Farbtopf, *der;* ~ **remover** *n.* Farbentferner, *der;* (for old doors, furniture) Abbeizmittel, *das;* Abbeizer, *der;* ~ **roller** *n.* Farbrolle, *die;* Farbroller, *der;* ~ **shop** *n.* **1** (shop selling paint) Farbengeschäft, *das;* **2** (in factory) Lackiererei, *die;* Lackierwerkstatt, *die;* ~ **stripper** *n.* Abbeizer, *der;* Abbeizmittel, *das;* **hot-air ~ stripper** Heißluftpistole [zum Entfernen alter Farbe]; **~work** *n., no pl.* (on walls etc.) Anstrich, *der;* (of car) Lack, *der*

pair /peə(r)/
A *n.* **1** (set of two) Paar, *das;* **a ~ of gloves/ socks/shoes** *etc.* ein Paar Handschuhe/ Socken/Schuhe *usw.;* **a** *or* **one ~ of hands/eyes** zwei Hände/Augen; **in ~s** paarweise; **the ~ of them** die beiden; **fine ~ [of rascals]** (iron.) feines [Gauner]pärchen *od.* [Gauner]gespann **2** (single article) **a ~ of pyjamas/ scissors** *etc.* ein Schlafanzug/eine Schere *usw.;* **a ~ of trousers/jeans** eine Hose/Jeans; ein Paar Hosen/Jeans **3** (married couple) [Ehe]paar, *das;* (mated animals) Paar, *das;* Pärchen, *das* **4** (Cards) Pärchen, *das;* **a ~ of tens** zwei Zehnen **5** ~ **[of horses]** Zweiergespann [Pferde], *das;* **carriage** *or* **coach and ~:** Zweispänner, *der* **6** (Parl.) *zwei Abgeordnete gegnerischer Parteien, die vereinbaren, sich bei einer Abstimmung zu enthalten* **7** (Rowing) (crew) Zweiermannschaft, *die;* **~s** (race) Zweierrennen, *das*
B *v.t.* **1** (arrange in couples) paaren; [paarweise] zusammenstellen **2** (marry) verheiraten (**with** an + *Akk.*, mit)
C *v.i.* ‹*Tiere:*› sich paaren

Phrasal verbs
- ~ **'off**
A *v.t.* zu Paaren *od.* paarweise zusammenstellen; **she was ~ed off with Alan** sie bekam Alan als Partner
B *v.i.* Zweiergruppen bilden
- ~ **'up** ▸~ **off B**
- ~ **with** *v.t.* (Parl.) ~ **with sb.** ‹*Abgeordneter:*› *mit jmdm. von der gegnerischen Fraktion vereinbaren, sich bei einer Abstimmung zu enthalten*

pairing /ˈpeərɪŋ/ *n.* (Parl.) ~ **[arrangement]** *Absprache zwischen Abgeordneten gegnerischer Parteien, sich bei einer Abstimmung zu enthalten*

Paisley /ˈpeɪzlɪ/ *adj.* (Textiles) Paisley‹*schal, -kleid, -samt usw.*›; ~ **pattern** Paisleymuster, *das*

pajamas /pəˈdʒɑːməz/ (Amer.) ▸**pyjamas**

Pak /pæk/, **Paki** /ˈpækɪ/ *n.* (Brit. sl. derog.: Pakistani) Pakistaner, *der*/Pakistanerin, *die;* **Paki-bashing** Zusammenschlagen von Pakistanern

Pakistan /pɑːkɪˈstɑːn/ *pr. n.* Pakistan (*das*)

Pakistani /pɑːkɪˈstɑːnɪ/ ▸ⓘ **p. 1345**
A *adj.* pakistanisch; **sb. is ~:** jmd. ist Pakistani; *see also* **English A**
B *n.* Pakistani, *der/die;* Pakistaner, *der/* Pakistanerin, *die*

pal /pæl/ (coll.)
A *n.* Kumpel, *der* (ugs.); (derog.) Kumpan, *der* (ugs.

P

abwertend); **be a ~ and ...:** sei so nett und ...; *see also* **old A 3**

B *v.i.*, **-ll-:** **~ up with sb.** sich mit jmdm. anfreunden

palace /ˈpælɪs/ *n.* Palast, *der;* (of bishop or aristocrat also) Palais, *das;* (stately mansion) Schloss, *das; attrib.* Schloss‹*garten, -park*›; Palast‹*wache, -truppe usw.*›

palace revoˈlution *n.* (lit. or fig.) Palastrevolution, *die*

paladin /ˈpælədɪn/ *n.* **1** (Hist.: knight errant) fahrender Ritter **2** (knightly hero) Recke, *der*

Palaeocene /ˈpælɪəsiːn, ˈpeɪlɪəsiːn/ (Geol.)

A *adj.* paläozän

B *n.* Paläozän, *das*

palaeography /pælɪˈɒgrəfɪ, peɪlɪˈɒgrəfɪ/ *n.* Paläographie, *die*

Palaeolithic /pælɪəˈlɪθɪk, peɪlɪəˈlɪθɪk/ *adj.* (Archaeol.) paläolithisch (fachspr.); altsteinzeitlich; **~ man** Paläolithiker, *der*

palaeontologist /pælɪɒnˈtɒlədʒɪst, peɪlɪɒnˈtɒlədʒɪst/ *n.* ▸ℹ **p. 1260** Paläontologe, *der*/Paläontologin, *die*

palaeontology /pælɪɒnˈtɒlədʒɪ, peɪlɪɒnˈtɒlədʒɪ/ *n.* Paläontologie, *die*

Palaeozoic /pælɪəˈzəʊɪk, peɪlɪəˈzəʊɪk/ (Geol.)

A *adj.* paläozoisch

B *n.* Paläozoikum, *das*

palatable /ˈpælətəbl/ *adj.* **1** (acceptable in taste) genießbar; trinkbar ‹*Wein*›; (pleasant) wohlschmeckend ‹*Speise*› **2** (fig.) annehmbar, akzeptabel ‹*Gesetz, Erhöhung, Aufführung*›; **make sth. ~ to sb.** jmdm. etw. schmackhaft machen (ugs.); **not be ~ to sb.** jmdm. nicht schmecken (ugs.)

palatal /ˈpælətəl/

A *adj.* **1** (Anat.) Gaumen- **2** (Phonet.) palatal

B *n.* (Phonet.) Palatal, *der*

palate /ˈpælət/ *n.* **1** (Anat.) Gaumen, *der;* **hard/soft ~:** harter/weicher Gaumen; *see also* **cleft² B 2** (taste) Gaumen, *der* (geh.); **be sharp on the ~** ‹*Wein:*› sauer schmecken; **not be to sb.'s ~** (fig.) nicht [nach] jmds. Geschmack sein

palatial /pəˈleɪʃl/ *adj.* palastartig; **built in ~ style** wie ein Palast gebaut

Palatinate /pəˈlætɪnət/ *pr. n.* **the ~** (in Germany) die Pfalz

Palatine /ˈpælətaɪn/ *adj.* palatinisch

palaver /pəˈlɑːvə(r)/ *n.* **1** (coll.: fuss) Umstand, *der;* Theater, *das* (ugs.) **2** (conference; derog.: idle talk) Palaver, *das*

pale¹ /peɪl/ *n.* **1** **be beyond the ~** ‹*Verhalten, Benehmen:*› unmöglich sein; **regard sb. as beyond the ~:** jmdn. indiskutabel finden **2** (stake) Pfahl, *der;* (slat) [Zaun]latte, *die*

pale² /peɪl/

A *adj.* **1** blass, (esp. in illness) fahl, (nearly white) bleich ‹*Gesichtsfarbe, Haut, Gesicht, Aussehen*›; **go ~:** blass/bleich werden; **his face was ~:** er war blass/bleich **2** (light in colour) von blasser Farbe *nachgestellt;* blass ‹*Farbe*›; hell ‹*Sherry*›; **a ~ blue/red dress** ein blassblaues/-rotes Kleid; **~ ale** Pale Ale, *das* **3** (faint) fahl ‹*Licht*› **4** (fig.: poor) **~ imitation/reflection** schlechte Nachahmung/schwacher Abglanz

B *v.i.* bleich *od.* blass werden (**at** bei); **his face ~d** er wurde bleich *od.* blass; **~ into insignificance** völlig bedeutungslos werden; **~ in comparison with sth.** neben etw. (*Dat.*) verblassen

ˈpaleface *n.* Bleichgesicht, *das*

ˈpale-faced *adj.* blass

palely /ˈpeɪllɪ/ *adv.* fahl, bleich ‹*scheinen*›; matt, schwach ‹*erleuchten*›

paleness /ˈpeɪlnɪs/ *n., no pl.* (of person) Blässe, *die*

paleo- (Amer.) ▸ **palaeo-**

Palestine /ˈpælɪstaɪn/ *pr. n.* Palästina (*das*)

Palestinian /pælɪˈstɪnɪən/ ▸ℹ **p. 1345**

A *adj.* palästinensisch; **sb. is ~:** jmd. ist Palästinenser/Palästinenserin

B *n.* Palästinenser, *der*/Palästinenserin, *die*

palette /ˈpælɪt/ *n.* Palette, *die*

ˈpalette knife *n.* (Art) Palettenmesser, *das*

palfrey /ˈpɔːlfrɪ/ *n.* (Hist.) Zelter, *der*

palimpsest /ˈpælɪmpsest/ *n.* Palimpsest, *der od. das*

palindrome /ˈpælɪndrəʊm/ *n.* Palindrom, *das*

paling /ˈpeɪlɪŋ/ *n.* **1** (stake) [Zaun]pfahl, *der;* (slat) [Zaun]latte, *die* **2** (fence) Lattenzaun, *der*

palisade /pælɪˈseɪd/ *n.* **1** (fence) Palisade, *die;* Palisadenzaun, *der* **2** *in pl.* (*Amer.: cliffs*) *steile, bes. säulenähnliche Formationen aufweisende Felswand*

palish /ˈpeɪlɪʃ/ *adj.* blässlich

pall¹ /pɔːl/ *n.* **1** (over coffin) Sargtuch, *das* **2** (fig.) Schleier, *der;* **cast a ~ of gloom over sb.** jmdn. in gedrückte Stimmung versetzen

pall² *v.i.* **~ [on sb.]** [jmdm.] langweilig werden

Palladian /pəˈleɪdɪən/ *adj.* (Archit.) palladianisch

ˈpall-bearer *n.* Sargträger, *der*/-trägerin, *die*

pallet¹ /ˈpælɪt/ *n.* **1** (bed) Pritsche, *die* **2** (mattress) Strohsack, *der*

pallet² *n.* (platform) Palette, *die*

palliasse /ˈpælɪæs, pælɪˈæs/ *n.* Strohsack, *der*

palliate /ˈpælɪeɪt/ *v.t.* **1** (alleviate) lindern, erträglicher machen ‹*Krankheit*› **2** (excuse) entschuldigen; (gloss over) beschönigen

palliative /ˈpælɪətɪv/ (Med.)

A *adj.* palliativ (fachspr.); lindernd; **~ drug** Palliativ[um], *das* (fachspr.); Linderungsmittel, *das*

B *n.* Palliativ[um], *das* (fachspr.); Linderungsmittel, *das*

pallid /ˈpælɪd/ *adj.* **1** ▸ **pale² A 1** **2** matt, blass ‹*Farbe*›

pallor /ˈpælə(r)/ *n.* Blässe, *die;* Fahlheit, *die*

pally /ˈpælɪ/ *adj.* (coll.) **they are very ~ [with each other]** sie sind dicke Freunde (ugs.); **be ~** *or* **on ~ terms with sb.** mit jmdm. dick befreundet sein (ugs.); **his ~ manner** seine kumpelhafte Art

palm¹ /pɑːm/ *n.* **1** (tree) Palme, *die; attrib.* **~ leaf/oil/kernel/frond** Palmblatt, *das*/-öl, *das*/-kern, *der*/-wedel, *der;* **~ [branch]** (also Eccl.) Palmzweig, *der* **2** (symbol of victory) Siegespalme, *die;* (Bibl.) Palme, *die;* **bear** *or* **take the ~** (fig.) die Siegespalme davontragen (geh.)

palm²

A *n.* **1** ▸ℹ **p. 951** (of hand) Handteller, *der;* Handfläche, *die;* **hold/weigh sth. in one's ~** *or* **the ~ of one's hand** etw. in der Hand halten/wiegen; **have sth. in the ~ of one's hand** (fig.) etw. in der Hand haben; **on the ~s of one's hands** auf den Handtellern *od.* -flächen; **the ~ of one's right hand** der rechte Handteller; die rechte Handfläche; *see also* **cross B 1; grease B 2** (of glove) Innenfläche, *die*

B *v.t.* in der [hohlen] Hand verschwinden lassen

Phrasal verb

• **~ ˈoff** *v.t.* **~ sth. off on sb., ~ sb. off with sth.** jmdm. etw. andrehen (ugs.); **~ sb. off on sb. else** jmdn. zu jmd. anderem abschieben (ugs.); **~ sth. off as sth.** etw. als etw. verkaufen; **~ sb. off with promises** jmdn. mit Versprechungen abspeisen (ugs.)

ˈpalmcorder /ˈpɑːmkɔːdə(r)/ *n.* Palmcorder, *der*

palm ˈcourt *adj.* **~ music/orchestra** ≈ Kaffeehausmusik, *die*/-orchester, *das*

palmist /ˈpɑːmɪst/ *n.* Handleser, *der*/-leserin, *die;* Handliniendeuter, *der*/-deuterin, *die*

palmistry /ˈpɑːmɪstrɪ/ *n., no pl.* Handlesekunst, *die;* Handliniendeutung, *die*

palm: P~ ˈSunday *n.* (Eccl.) Palmsonntag, *der;* **~top** *n.* **~top [computer]** Palmtop, *der;* **~ tree** *n.* Palme, *die*

palomino /pæləˈmiːnəʊ/ *n., pl.* **~s** (Zool.) Isabelle, *die*

palpable /ˈpælpəbl/ *adj.* **1** (tangible) fühlbar; tastbar **2** (perceptible) spürbar ‹*Unterschied*›; eindeutig ‹*Zeichen*›; (obvious) offenkundig ‹*Lüge, Unwissenheit, Absurdität*›

palpably /ˈpælpəblɪ/ *adv.* offenkundig

palpate /pælˈpeɪt/ *v.t.* (Med.) betasten; palpieren (fachspr.)

palpitate /ˈpælpɪteɪt/ *v.i.* **1** (pulsate) ‹*Herz:*› palpitieren (fachspr.), pochen, hämmern **2** (throb) beben; zucken; (tremble) zittern (**with** vor + *Dat.*)

palpitation /pælpɪˈteɪʃn/ *n.* **1** (throbbing) Beben, *das;* Zucken, *das;* (trembling) Zittern, *das* **2** *in pl.* (Med.: of heart) Palpitation, *die* (fachspr.); Herzklopfen, *das;* **suffer from ~s** Herzklopfen haben

palsy /ˈpɔːlzɪ, ˈpɒlzɪ/ *n.* (Med. dated) Lähmung, *die;* Paralyse, *die* (*fachspr.*); *see also* **cerebral palsy**

paltry /ˈpɔːltrɪ, ˈpɒltrɪ/ *adj.* schäbig; armselig ‹*Auswahl*›; (trivial) belanglos; **~ matters** Belanglosigkeiten; **a ~ £5** schäbige 5 Pfund

pampas /ˈpæmpəz, ˈpæmpəs/ *n. pl.* (Geog.) Pampas *Pl.*

ˈpampas grass *n.* Pampasgras, *das*

pamper /ˈpæmpə(r)/ *v.t.* verhätscheln; **~ oneself** sich verwöhnen

pamphlet /ˈpæmflɪt/ *n.* (leaflet) Prospekt, *der;* (esp. Polit.) Flugblatt, *das;* (booklet) Broschüre, *die;* (Polit., Relig.: tract) Streitschrift, *die*

pamphleteer /pæmflɪˈtɪə(r)/ *n.* Verfasser/Verfasserin des Flugblatts/der Streitschrift/der Flugblätter/der Streitschriften

pan¹ /pæn/

A *n.* **1** [Koch]topf, *der;* (for frying) Pfanne, *die;* **pots and ~s** Kochtöpfe; **a ~ of milk** ein Topf Milch; *see also* **saucepan** **2** (of scales) Schale, *die* **3** (Brit.: of WC) **[lavatory] ~:** Toilettenschüssel, *die* **4** (Amer. coll.: face) Visage, *die* (*ugs. abwertend*). *See also* **flash A 1**

B *v.t.*, **-nn-** (coll.) verreißen ‹*Theaterstück, Buch, Film usw.*›; harte Kritik üben an (+ *Dat.*) ‹*Person*›

Phrasal verb

• **~ ˈout** *v.i.* (progress) sich entwickeln

pan²

A *v.t.*, **-nn-** (Cinemat., Telev.) schwenken; (Photog.) mitziehen

B *v.i.*, **-nn-** (Cinemat., Telev.) schwenken (**to** auf + *Akk.*); (Photog.) [die Kamera] mitziehen; **~ning shot** [Kamera]schwenk, *der*

C *n.* (Cinemat., Telev.) Schwenk, *der*

pan- /pæn/ *in comb.* pan‹*amerikanisch, -slawistisch, -islamisch, -germanisch usw.*›; Pan‹*afrikanismus, -slawist usw.*›

panacea /pænəˈsiːə/ *n.* Allheilmittel, *das*

panache /pəˈnæʃ/ *n.* Schwung, *der;* Elan, *der*

Panama /pænəˈmɑː/

A *pr. n.* Panama (*das*)

B *n.* **p~ [hat]** Panamahut, *der*

Panama Caˈnal *pr. n.* Panamakanal, *der*

Panamanian /pænəˈmeɪnɪən/ ▸ℹ **p. 1345**

A *adj.* panamaisch; **sb. is ~:** jmd. ist Panamaer/Panamaerin

B *n.* Panamaer, *der*/Panamaerin, *die*

panatella /pænəˈtelə/ *n.* Panatela, *die*

pancake /ˈpænkeɪk/ *n.* Pfannkuchen, *der;* **be flat as a ~:** platt wie ein Pfannkuchen sein; ‹*Gelände:*› topfeben sein; (squashed) platt wie eine Briefmarke sein; ‹*Reifen:*› völlig platt sein

pancake: P~ Day *n.* (Brit.) Fastnachtsdienstag, *der;* **~ ˈlanding** *n.* (Aeronaut.) Bauchlandung, *die;* **~ roll** *n.* gerollter Pfannkuchen mit Füllung

panchromatic /pænkrəˈmætɪk/ *adj.* (Photog.) panchromatisch

pancreas /ˈpæŋkrɪəs/ *n.* (Anat.) Bauchspeicheldrüse, *die;* Pankreas, *das* (fachspr.)

pancreatic /pæŋkrɪˈætɪk/ *adj.* (Anat., Physiol.) Pankreas-; **~ duct** Ausführungsgang des Pankreas

panda /ˈpændə/ *n.* (Zool.) Panda, *der*

ˈpanda car *n.* (Brit. Police) Streifenwagen, *der*

pandemic /pænˈdemɪk/ (Med.)

A *adj.* pandemisch

B *n.* Pandemie, *die*

pandemonium /pændɪˈməʊnɪəm/ *n.* Chaos, *das;* (uproar) Tumult, *der;* **there was ~ in the stadium** das Stadion war ein Hexenkessel; **~ reigned** es herrschte ein einziges Chaos

pander /ˈpændə(r)/

A *n.* (go-between) Kuppler, *der*/Kupplerin, *die;* (procurer) Zuhälter, *der*

B *v.i.* **~ to** allzu sehr entgegenkommen (+ *Dat.*) ‹*Person, Geschmack, Instinkt*›; frönen (+ *Dat.*) ‹*Laster*›

P

Pandora's box /pændɔːrəz 'bɒks/ *n.* (Mythol.; also fig.) Büchse der Pandora

p. & p. *abbr.* (Brit.) **= postage and packing** Porto und Verpackung

pane /peɪn/ *n.* (glass) Scheibe, *die;* **window ~/~ of glass** Fenster-/Glasscheibe, *die*

panegyric /pænɪ'dʒɪrɪk/
A *n.* Lobrede, *die* (**on** auf + *Akk.*)
B *adj.* panegyrisch (geh.)

panel /'pænl/
A *n.* **1** (of door, wall, etc.) Paneel, *das;* (of fence) Bretterzaunelement, *das;* (of screen, triptych) Flügel, *der* **2** (esp. Telev., Radio, etc.) (quiz team) Rateteam, *das;* (in public discussion) Podium, *das;* **~ discussion** Podiumsdiskussion, *die* **3** (advisory body) Gremium, *das;* Kommission, *die;* **~ of experts** Expertengremium, *das* **4** (Dressmaking) Einsatz, *der. See also* **control panel**; **instrument panel**
B *v.t.*, (Brit.) **-ll-** paneelieren ‹*Tür, Zimmer, Wand*›; täfeln ‹*Zimmer, Wand*›

panel: ~ beater *n.* Autospengler, *der*/-spenglerin, *die;* **~ game** *n.* Ratespiel, *das;* Quiz, *das;* (Telev., Radio) Rate-, Quizsendung, *die*

paneling, panelist (Amer.) ▸ **panell-**

panelling /'pænəlɪŋ/ *n.* Täfelung, *die*

panellist /'pænəlɪst/ *n.* (Telev., Radio) (on quiz programme) Mitglied des Rateteams; (on discussion panel) Diskussionsteilnehmer, *der*/-teilnehmerin, *die*

panel: ~ pin *n.* Tapeziernagel, *der;* **~ truck** *n.* Lieferwagen, *der*

'pan-fry *v.t.* [in der Pfanne] braten

panful /'pænfʊl/ *n.* Topf, *der;* **a ~ of water** ein Topf [voll] Wasser

pang /pæŋ/ *n.* **1** (of pain) Stich, *der; see also* **hunger A 2** (of distress) **feel ~s of conscience/guilt** Gewissensbisse haben; **feel ~s of remorse** bittere Reue empfinden

'panhandle
A *n.* **1** Topfstiel, *der;* (of frying pan) Pfannenstiel, *der* **2** (of land) schmaler Landstreifen; (in US) Panhandle, *der*
B *v.t.* (coll.) anschnorren (ugs.) (**for** um)
C *v.i.* (coll.) schnorren (ugs.)

panic /'pænɪk/
A *n.* Panik, *die;* **be in a [state of] ~ [over** *or* **at having done sth.]** von Panik erfasst *od.* ergriffen sein[, weil man etw. getan hat]; **there was ~ on the stock market** es kam zu einer Börsenpanik
B *v.i.*, **-ck-** in Panik (*Akk.*) geraten; **don't ~!** nur keine Panik!
C *v.t.*, **-ck-** in Panik versetzen; **~ sb. into doing sth.** jmdn. so in Panik versetzen, dass er etw. tut
D *attrib. adj.* (overhasty) übereilt, überstürzt ‹*Maßnahmen*›; wild, atemlos ‹*Hast*›; **~ buying** Hamsterkäufe *Pl.;* **~ selling** Panikverkäufe *Pl.*

panic: ~ attack *n.* Angstanfall, *der;* Anfall von Panik; **she suffers from ~ attacks** sie leidet an Angstzuständen **~ bolt** *n.* Panikverschluss, *der;* **~ button** *n.* Alarmknopf, *der;* **hit the ~ button** (fig. coll.) Alarm schlagen; (go into a ~) durchdrehen (ugs.); die Panik kriegen (ugs.); **~ buying** *n., no pl.* Panikkäufe *Pl.*

panicky /'pænɪkɪ/ *adj.* von Panik bestimmt ‹*Verhalten, Handeln, Rede*›; **be ~:** in Panik sein

panicle /'pænɪkl/ *n.* (Bot.) Rispe, *die*

panic: ~monger *n.* Panikmacher, *der*/-macherin, *die;* **~ stations** *n. pl.* (fig. coll.) **be at ~ stations** am Rotieren sein (ugs.) (**about** wegen); **it was ~ stations** alles war am Rotieren (ugs.); **~-stricken**, **~-struck** *adjs.* von Panik erfasst *od.* ergriffen

panjandrum /pæn'dʒændrəm/ *n.* Zampano, *der*

pannier /'pænɪə(r)/ *n.* **1** (basket) Lastkorb, *der* **2** (bag) Packtasche, *die*

panoply /'pænəplɪ/ *n.* Palette, *die* (fig.); **the full ~ of a state burial** ein Staatsbegräbnis mit allem, was dazugehört; **a wonderful ~ of colours** eine herrliche Farbenpracht

panorama /pænə'rɑːmə/ *n.* Panorama, *das;* (fig.: survey) Überblick, *der* (**of** über + *Akk.*); **aerial ~:** Luftaufnahme, *die*

panoramic /pænə'ræmɪk/ *adj.* Panorama-; **~ survey** (fig.) umfassender Überblick (**of** über + *Akk.*)

'pan pipes *n. pl.* (Mus.) Panflöte, *die*

pansy /'pænzɪ/ *n.* **1** (Bot.) Stiefmütterchen, *das* **2** (coll.: effeminate man) Schwuchtel, *die* (ugs.); Tunte, *die* (ugs.)

pant /pænt/
A *v.i.* keuchen; ‹*Hund:*› hecheln
B *v.t.* **~ [out]** keuchend hervorstoßen ‹*Nachricht, Worte*›

Phrasal verb
• **~ for** *v.t.* ringen nach ‹*Luft, Atem*›; schnappen nach ‹*Luft*›; lechzen nach ‹*Getränk*›

pantaloons /pæntə'luːnz/ *n. pl.* **1** (baggy trousers) Pluderhose, *die* **2** (hist.) Pantalons *Pl.*

pantechnicon /pæn'teknɪkən/ *n.* **~ [van]** (Brit.) Möbelwagen, *der*

pantheism /'pænθɪɪzm/ *n., no art.* (Relig.) Pantheismus, *der*

pantheist /'pænθɪɪst/ *n.* (Relig.) Pantheist, *der*/Pantheistin, *die*

pantheistic /pænθɪ'ɪstɪk/, **pantheistical** /pænθɪ'ɪstɪkl/ *adj.* (Relig.) pantheistisch

pantheon /'pænθɪən, pæn'θiːən/ *n.* Pantheon, *das*

panther /'pænθə(r)/ *n.* (Zool.) **1** Panther, *der* **2** (Amer.: puma) Puma, *der;* Berglöwe, *der*

pantie-girdle /'pæntɪgɜːdl/ *n.* (coll.) Miederhose, *die*

panties /'pæntɪz/ *n. pl.* (coll.) **[pair of] ~:** Schlüpfer, *der*

pantihose /'pæntɪhəʊz/ ▸ **tight C 1**

pantile /'pæntaɪl/ *n.* (Building) Hohlpfanne, *die*

panto /'pæntəʊ/ *n., pl.* **~s** (Brit. coll.) ▸ **pantomime 1**

pantograph /'pæntəgrɑːf/ *n.* **1** (for copying) Pantograph, *der;* Storchschnabel, *der* **2** (Electr.) Scherenstromabnehmer, *der*

pantomime /'pæntəmaɪm/ *n.* **1** (Brit.) *Märchenspiel im Varieteestil, das um Weihnachten aufgeführt wird* **2** (gestures) Pantomime, *die*

> **pantomime**
>
> Eine Form der Theateraufführung, die traditionell in den Wochen vor und nach Weihnachten auf Bühnen in ganz Großbritannien hauptsächlich für Kinder gezeigt wird. Die Handlung ist oft die komische Adaption eines Märchens oder einer Volkssage und bezieht die Zuschauer stark mit ein. Gemäß der Tradition wird die Rolle des *principal boy* oder Helden von einer Frau gespielt und die Rolle der *dame*, einer grotesken Frauenfigur, von einem Mann.

pantry /'pæntrɪ/ *n.* Speisekammer, *die;* **[butler's] ~:** Anrichtezimmer, *das*

pants /pænts/ *n. pl.* **1** (esp. Amer.: trousers) **[pair of] ~:** Hose, *die;* **bore/scare the ~ off sb.** (fig. coll.) jmdn. zu Tode langweilen/erschrecken; **talk the ~ off sb.** (fig. coll.) jmdn. voll labern *od.* voll quatschen (ugs.); **catch sb. with his ~ down** (fig. coll.) jmdn. unvorbereitet treffen; *see also* **kick A 1** **2** (Brit.: underpants) Unterhose, *die* **3** (Brit. sl.: rubbish) Scheiße, *die* (derb abwertend)

'pant suit *n.* Hosenanzug, *der*

panty: ~-girdle ▸ **pantie-girdle**; **~hose** /'pæntɪhəʊz/ ▸ **tights C 1**

panzer /'pæntsə(r)/ *adj.* (Mil.) Panzer-

pap /pæp/ *n.* (food) Brei, *der;* (fig. derog.) Schmarren, *der* (ugs. abwertend)

papa /pə'pɑː/ *n.* (arch. child lang.) Papa, *der* (fam.)

papacy /'peɪpəsɪ/ *n.* **1** *no pl.* (office) Papat, *der;* **be elected to the ~:** zum Papst gewählt werden **2** (tenure) Amtszeit als Papst **3** *no pl.* (papal system) Papsttum, *das*

papal /'peɪpl/ *adj.* päpstlich; *see also* **infallibility**

paparazzo /pæpæ'rɑːtsəʊ/ *n., pl.* **paparazzi** /pæpæ'rɑːtsiː/ Paparazzo, *der*

papaw /pə'pɔː/, **papaya** /pə'paɪə/ *n.* (Bot.) **1** (tree) **~ [tree]** Papaya- *od.* Melonenbaum, *der* **2** (fruit) Papaya[frucht], *die*

paper /'peɪpə(r)/
A *n.* **1** (material) Papier, *das;* **put sth. down on ~:** etw. schriftlich festhalten *od.* niederlegen; **it looks all right on ~** (in theory) auf dem Papier sieht es ganz gut aus; **put pen to ~:** zur Feder greifen; **the treaty** *etc.* **isn't worth the ~ it's written on** (coll.) der Vertrag *usw.* ist nicht das Papier wert, auf dem er geschrieben steht **2** *in pl.* (documents) Dokumente *Pl.;* Unterlagen *Pl.;* (to prove identity etc.) Papiere *Pl.* **3** (in examination) (Univ.) Klausur, *die;* (Sch.) Arbeit, *die* **4** (newspaper) Zeitung, *die;* **daily/weekly ~:** Tages-/Wochenzeitung, *die* **5** (wallpaper) Tapete, *die* **6** (wrapper) Stück Papier; **don't scatter the ~s all over the floor** wirf das Papier nicht überall auf den Boden **7** (learned article) Referat, *das;* (shorter) Paper, *das* **8** *no pl., no indef. art.* (Commerc.: bills of exchange etc.) [Wert]papiere *Pl.*
B *adj.* **1** (made of ~) aus Papier *nachgestellt;* Papier‹*mütze, -taschentuch*› **2** (theoretical) nominell ‹*zahlenmäßige Stärke, Profit*›
C *v.t.* tapezieren

Phrasal verb
• **~ 'over** *v.t.* [mit Tapete] überkleben; **~ over the cracks** (fig.: cover up mistakes/differences) die Fehler/Differenzen übertünchen

paper: ~back **A** *n.* Paperback, *das;* (pocket-size) Taschenbuch, *das;* **available in ~back** als Paperback/Taschenbuch erhältlich; **B** *adj.* **~back edition** Paperback-/Taschenbuchausgabe, *die;* **~back book** Paperback, *das*/Taschenbuch, *das;* **~ 'bag** *n.* Papiertüte, *die;* **~ boy** *n.* Zeitungsjunge, *der;* **~ chain** *n.* Papiergirlande, *die;* **~chase** *n.* Schnitzeljagd, *die;* **~ clip** *n.* Büroklammer, *die;* (larger) Aktenklammer, *die;* **~ 'cup** *n.* Pappbecher, *der;* **~ currency** ▸ **~ money**; **~ 'dart** Papierflieger, *der;* **~ girl** ▸ **newsgirl**; **~ 'handkerchief** *n.* Papiertaschentuch, *das;* **~hanger** *n.* Tapezierer, *der*/Tapeziererin, *die;* **~hanging** *n., no pl.* Tapezieren, *das;* **~ 'hanky** *n.* (coll.) Papiertaschentuch, *das;* **~ jam** *n.* Papierstau, *der;* **~knife** *n.* Brieföffner, *der;* **~less** /'peɪpəlɪs/ *adj.* papierlos ‹*Transaktion, System*›; **the ~less office** das papierlose Büro; **~making** *n., no pl.* Papierherstellung, *die;* **~ mill** *n.* Papierfabrik *od.* -mühle, *die;* **~ money** *n.* Papiergeld, *das;* **~ 'napkin** *n.* Papierserviette, *die;* **~ 'plate** *n.* Pappteller, *der;* **~ qualification** *n.* Zeugnis, *das;* **~ round** *n.* Zeitungsaustragen, *das;* **on one's ~ round** beim Zeitungsaustragen; **have/do a ~ round** Zeitungen austragen; **~ servi'ette** ▸ **~ napkin**; **~ shop** *n.* Zeitungsgeschäft, *das;* **~-thin** *adj.* (lit. or fig.) hauchdünn; **~ 'tiger** ▸ **tiger 1**; **~ 'towel** *n.* Papierhandtuch, *das;* **~weight** *n.* Briefbeschwerer, *der;* **~work** *n., no pl.* **1** Schreibarbeit, *die;* Papierkram, *der* (abwertend); **2** (documents) Unterlagen *Pl.*

papery /'peɪpərɪ/ *adj.* papierartig; **be ~:** wie Papier sein

papier mâché /pæpjeɪ 'mæʃeɪ, pæpjeɪ 'mɑːʃeɪ/ *n.* Papiermaschee, *das;* Pappmaschee, *das*

papist /'peɪpɪst/ *n.* (Relig. derog.) Papist, *der*/Papistin, *die* (abwertend)

papoose /pə'puːs/ *n.* Kleinkind, *das* (*bei den nordamerikanischen Indianern*)

paprika /'pæprɪkə, pə'priːkə/ *n.* **1** ▸ **pepper A 2** **2** (Cookery: condiment) Paprika, *der*

Papua New Guinea /pɑːpʊə njuː 'gɪnɪ/ *pr. n.* Papua-Neuguinea (*das*)

papyrus /pə'paɪrəs/ *n., pl.* **papyri** /pə'paɪraɪ/ Papyrus, *der*

par /pɑː(r)/ *n.* **1** (average) **above/below ~:** über/unter dem Durchschnitt; **the work is [well] below ~:** die Arbeit liegt [weit] unter dem üblichen Niveau; **feel rather below ~, not feel up to ~** (fig.) nicht ganz auf dem Posten *od.* Damm sein (ugs.) **2** (equality) **be on a ~:** vergleichbar sein; **be on a ~ with sb./sth.** jmdm./einer Sache gleichkommen **3** (Golf) Par, *das;* **that's about ~ for the course** (fig. coll.) das ist so das Übliche **4** (Commerc.: nominal value) **~ [of exchange]** Wechselkurs, *der;* **be at/above/below ~** ‹*Aktie, Wert:*› al/über/unter pari stehen

para /'pærə/ *n.* (coll.) **1** (paratrooper) Para, *der* **2** (paragraph) Absatz, der

P

para. *abbr.* **= paragraph** Abs.; (in contract or law) Paragr.

parable /ˈpærəbl/ *n.* Gleichnis, *das;* Parabel, *die* (bes. Literaturw.)

parabola /pəˈræbələ/ *n.* (Geom.) Parabel, *die*

parabolic /pærəˈbɒlɪk/ *adj.* (Geom.) parabolisch; **~ antenna** Parabolantenne, *die;* **~ mirror** Parabolspiegel, *der*

paracetamol /pærəˈsetəmɒl/ *n.* (Brit. Med.) Parazetamol, *das;* (tablet) Parazetamoltablette, *die*

parachute /ˈpærəʃuːt/

A *n.* **1** Fallschirm, *der* **2** (to brake aircraft etc.) Bremsfallschirm, *der*

B *v.t.* [mit dem Fallschirm] absetzen ‹*Person*› (**into** über + *Dat.*); mit dem Fallschirm abwerfen ‹*Vorräte*›

C *v.i.* ‹*Truppen:*› [mit dem Fallschirm] abspringen (**into** über + *Dat.*)

D *adj.* Fallschirm‹*absprung, -abwurf*›; (Mil.) Fallschirmjäger‹*truppen, -regiment*›

ˈparachute drop *n.* (delivery of supplies) Fallschirmabwurf, *der;* (parachute jump) Fallschirmspringen, *das*

parachutist /ˈpærəʃuːtɪst/ *n.* **1** **[sports] ~:** Fallschirmspringer, *der*/-springerin, *die* **2** (Mil.) Fallschirmjäger, *der*

parade /pəˈreɪd/

A *n.* **1** (display) Zurschaustellung, *die;* **make a ~ of** zur Schau stellen ‹*Tugend, Eigenschaft*›; **make a ~ of one's knowledge** mit seinem Wissen paradieren (geh.) **2** (Mil.: muster) Appell, *der;* **on ~:** beim Appell **3** (procession) Umzug, *der;* (of troops) Parade, *die* **4** (succession) Reihe, *die* **5** (promenade, street) Promenade, *die;* **a ~ of shops** eine Reihe Läden

B *v.t.* **1** (display) zur Schau stellen; vorzeigen ‹*Person*› (**before** bei) **2** (march through) **~ the streets** durch die Straßen marschieren **3** (Mil.: muster) antreten lassen

C *v.i.* paradieren; ‹*Demonstranten:*› marschieren; **the national teams ~d round the stadium** die Nationalmannschaften marschierten durch das Stadion

paˈrade ground *n.* Exerzierplatz, *der*

paradigm /ˈpærədaɪm/ *n.* (esp. Ling.) Paradigma, *das; attrib.* **~ shift** Paradigmawechsel, *der*

paradise /ˈpærədaɪs/ *n.* Paradies, *das;* **children's/gourmet's ~:** Paradies für Kinder/Gourmets; **an earthly ~:** ein Paradies auf Erden; **this is ~!** himmlisch! *See also* **bird of paradise**; **fool's paradise**

paradox /ˈpærədɒks/ *n.* **1** Paradox[on], *das* **2** *no pl., no indef. art.* (quality) Paradoxie, *die;* Widersprüchlichkeit, *die*

paradoxical /pærəˈdɒksɪkl/ *adj.* paradox

paradoxically /pærəˈdɒksɪkəlɪ/ *adv.* paradox; *as sentence-modifier* paradoxerweise

paraffin /ˈpærəfɪn/ *n.* **1** (Chem.) Paraffin, *das* **2** (Brit.: fuel) Petroleum, *das; attrib.* Petroleum‹*lampe, -kocher*› **3** **liquid ~** (Brit.: laxative) Paraffinöl, *das*

paraffin: ~ ˈoil (Brit.) ▸ **paraffin 2**; **~ ˈstove** *n.* Petroleumkocher, *der;* (for heating) Petroleumofen, *der;* **~ ˈwax** *n.* Paraffin[wachs], *das*

paragliding /ˈpærəglaɪdɪŋ/ *n., no pl.* Paragliding, *das;* Gleitschirmfliegen, *das*

paragon /ˈpærəgən/ Muster, *das* (**of** an + *Dat.*); **a ~ of beauty** der Inbegriff der Schönheit; **~ of virtue** Tugendheld, *der*/-heldin, *die*

paragraph /ˈpærəgrɑːf/ *n.* **1** (section of text) Absatz, *der* **2** (subsection of law etc.) Paragraph, *der* **3** (Journ.: news item) Notiz, *die* **4** (symbol) Absatzzeichen, *das*

Paraguay /ˈpærəgwaɪ/ *pr. n.* Paraguay (*das*)

Paraguayan /pærəˈgwaɪən/ ▸ **i p. 1345**

A *adj.* paraguayisch; **sb. is ~:** jmd. ist Paraguayer/Paraguayerin

B *n.* Paraguayer, *der*/Paraguayerin, *die*

parakeet /ˈpærəkiːt/ *n.* (Ornith.) Sittich, *der*

parallax /ˈpærəlæks/ *n.* (Astron., Phys.) Parallaxe, *die*

parallel /ˈpærəlel/

A *adj.* **1** parallel; **line A is ~ to line B** (Geom.) Gerade A ist der Geraden B parallel; **the railway ran ~ to the river** die Bahnlinie verlief parallel zum Fluss; **~ bars** (Gymnastics) Barren, *der* **2** (fig.: similar) vergleichbar; **be ~:** sich (*Dat.*) [genau] entsprechen; (share common features) Parallelen aufweisen; **there is nothing ~ to this in history** dazu gibt es in der Geschichte keine Parallele

B *n.* **1** Parallele, *die;* **this has no ~** *or* **is without ~:** dazu gibt es keine Parallele; **there is a ~ between x and y** es gibt eine Parallelität zwischen x und y; **the two societies are ~s** die beiden Gesellschaften gleichen sich **2** (Electr.) **in ~:** parallel; **be connected in ~:** parallel geschaltet sein **3** (Geog.) **~ [of latitude]** Breitenkreis, *der;* **the 42nd ~:** der 42. Breitengrad **4** (Astron.) Deklinationskreis, *der*

C *v.t.* **1** (match) gleichkommen (+ *Dat.*); **his arrogance cannot be ~ed** seine Arroganz ist beispiellos **2** (find sth. similar to) **this behaviour may be ~ed in human life** eine Parallele zu diesem Verhalten lässt sich beim Menschen feststellen **3** (compare) vergleichen

parallelism /ˈpærəlelɪzm/ *n.* (lit. or fig.) Parallelität, *die* (**in** *Gen.*); Übereinstimmung, *die* (**in** *Gen.*)

parallelogram /pærəˈleləgræm/ *n.* (Geom.) Parallelogramm, *das*

parallel: ~ port *n.* (Computing) Parallelanschluss, *der;* **~ ˈprocessing** *n., no pl.* (Computing) Parallelverarbeitung, *die*

Paralympics /pærəˈlɪmpɪks/ *n. pl.* Paralympics *Pl.*

paralyse /ˈpærəlaɪz/ *v.t.* **1** lähmen; paralysieren (Med.); **he is ~d in both legs** seine beiden Beine sind gelähmt **2** (fig.) lahm legen ‹*Verkehr, Industrie*›; zum Erliegen bringen ‹*Verkehr*›; **be ~d with fright** vor Schreck wie gelähmt sein; **be ~d** ‹*Verkehr:*› zum Erliegen gekommen sein

paralysis /pəˈrælɪsɪs/ *n., pl.* **paralyses** /pəˈrælɪsiːz/ Lähmung, *die;* Paralyse, *die* (Med.); (fig., of industry, traffic) Lahmlegung, *die*

paralytic /pærəˈlɪtɪk/

A *adj.* **1** gelähmt; paralytisch (Med.) **2** (Brit. coll.: very drunk) stockvoll, sternhagelvoll (salopp)

B *n.* Gelähmte, *der/die;* Paralytiker, *der*/Paralytikerin, *die* (Med.)

paralyze (Amer.) ▸ **paralyse**

paramedic /pærəˈmedɪk/ *n.* ▸ **i p. 1260** medizinische Hilfskraft; (ambulance worker) Sanitäter, *der*/Sanitäterin, *die*

paramedical /pærəˈmedɪkl/ *adj.* **~ personnel/staff** medizinisches Hilfspersonal; (in hospital) nichtärztliches Personal; **~ training** Ausbildung zur medizinischen Hilfskraft

parameter /pəˈræmɪtə(r)/ *n.* **1** (defining feature) Faktor, *der* **2** (Math.) Parameter, *der*

paramilitary /pærəˈmɪlɪtərɪ/ *adj.* paramilitärisch; halbmilitärisch

paramount /ˈpærəmaʊnt/ *adj.* **1** (supreme) höchst... ‹*Macht, Autorität*›; oberst... ‹*Herrscher, Souverän*› **2** (pre-eminent) größt..., höchst... ‹*Wichtigkeit*›; Haupt‹*gesichtspunkt, -überlegung*›; **be ~** ‹*Wunsch:*› Vorrang haben

paramour /ˈpærəmʊə(r)/ *n.* (arch./rhet.) Buhle, *der/die* (dichter. veralt.)

paranoia /pærəˈnɔɪə/ *n.* **1** (disorder) Paranoia, *die* (Med.) **2** (tendency) **[feeling of] ~:** krankhaftes Misstrauen; Verfolgungswahn, *der*

paranoiac /pærəˈnɔɪæk/, **paranoic** /pærəˈnəʊɪk/

A *n.* (Med.) Paranoiker, *der*/Paranoikerin, *die;* **be a ~** (fig.) an Verfolgungswahn leiden

B *adj.* (Med.) paranoisch; (fig.) krankhaft [gesteigert] ‹*Misstrauen*›

paranoid /ˈpærənɔɪd/

A *adj.* (Med.) paranoid (fachspr.); (fig.) wahnhaft; krankhaft [gesteigert] ‹*Misstrauen, Abneigung, Angst*›; **be ~:** an Verfolgungswahn leiden; **he's ~ about his boss** er bildet sich ein, dass sein Chef ihn schikanieren will

B *n.* (Med.) Paranoiker, *der*/Paranoikerin, *die;* **be a ~:** paranoid sein; an Verfolgungswahn leiden

paranormal /pærəˈnɔːml/ *adj.* paranormal; übersinnlich

parapet /ˈpærəpɪt, ˈpærəpet/ *n.* **1** (low wall or barrier) Brüstung, *die* **2** (Mil.) Parapett, *das* (hist.); Brustwehr, *die*

paraphernalia /pærəfəˈneɪlɪə/ *n. sing.* **1** (personal belongings) Utensilien *Pl.* **2** (equipment) (of justice, power) Instrumentarium, *das* (geh.); Apparat, *der;* (of war) Material, *das;* **equestrian/sporting/photographic ~:** Reit-/Sport-/Fotoausrüstung, *die;* **the whole ~** (coll.) alles, was so dazugehört (ugs.)

paraphrase /ˈpærəfreɪz/

A *n.* Umschreibung, *die;* Paraphrase, *die* (fachspr.)

B *v.t.* umschreiben; paraphrasieren (fachspr.)

paraplegia /pærəˈpliːdʒɪə/ *n.* (Med.) Paraplegie, *die* (fachspr.); ≈ Querschnittslähmung, *die*

paraplegic /pærəˈpliːdʒɪk/ (Med.)

A *adj.* doppelseitig gelähmt; paraplegisch (fachspr.)

B *n.* doppelseitig Gelähmter/Gelähmte; Paraplegiker, *der*/Paraplegikerin, *die* (fachspr.)

parapsychology /pærəsaɪˈkɒlədʒɪ/ *n.* Parapsychologie, *die*

paraquat /ˈpærəkwɒt/ *n.* (Agric.) Paraquat, *das* (*ein Kontaktherbizid*)

parasail /ˈpærəseɪl/ *v.i.* Fallschirm segeln

parasailing /ˈpærəseɪlɪŋ/ *n., no pl.* Parasailing, *das*

parascending /ˈpærəsendɪŋ/ *n., no pl.* **1** ▸ **parasailing** **2** ▸ **paragliding**

parasite /ˈpærəsaɪt/ *n.* **1** (Biol.) Schmarotzer, *der;* Parasit, *der* (fachspr.) **2** (fig. derog.: person) Schmarotzer, *der;* Parasit, *der;* **be a total ~:** nur schmarotzen

parasitic /pærəˈsɪtɪk/ *adj.* **1** (Biol.) parasitisch; parasitär ‹*Pilz*›; **be ~ on** schmarotzen in (+ *Dat.*); ‹*Pflanze:*› schmarotzen auf *od.* an (+ *Dat.*) **2** (fig.) schmarotzerisch; schmarotzerhaft; **be ~ on** als Schmarotzer leben von

parasitism /ˈpærəsaɪtɪzm/ *n., no pl.* **1** (Biol.) Parasitismus, *der* **2** (fig.) Schmarotzertum, *das*

parasol /ˈpærəsɒl/ *n.* Sonnenschirm, *der;* Parasol, *der od. das* (veralt.)

parasympathetic /pærəsɪmpəˈθetɪk/ *adj.* (Anat.) parasympathisch; **~ nerve** Parasympathikus, *der*

paratrooper /ˈpærətruːpə(r)/ *n.* ▸ **i p. 1260** (Mil.) Fallschirmjäger, *der*

paratroops /ˈpærətruːps/ *n. pl.* (Mil.) Fallschirmjägertruppe, *die;* Fallschirmjäger *Pl.*

paratyphoid /pærəˈtaɪfɔɪd/ *n.* ▸ **i p. 1231** (Med.) Paratyphus, *der*

parboil /ˈpɑːbɔɪl/ *v.t.* (Cookery) ankochen

parcel /ˈpɑːsl/

A *n.* **1** (package) Paket, *das;* **send/receive sth. by ~ post** etw. mit der Paketpost *od.* als Postpaket schicken/bekommen **2** **a ~ of land** ein Stück Land; *see also* **part A 1**

B *v.t.,* (Brit.) **-ll-** [zu Paketen] verpacken

Phrasal verbs

- **~ ˈout** *v.t.* aufteilen ‹*Land*›
- **~ ˈup** *v.t.* einwickeln

ˈparcel: ~ bomb *n.* Paketbombe, *die;* **~ service** *n.* Paketdienst, *der*

parch /pɑːtʃ/

A *v.t.* **1** (dry out) ausdörren, austrocknen ‹*Land, Boden*› **2** (toast) rösten ‹*Kerne*›

B *v.i.* ‹*Haut:*› austrocknen

parched /pɑːtʃt/ *adj.* ausgedörrt ‹*Kehle, Land, Boden*›; trocken ‹*Lippen*›; **I am [absolutely] ~ [with thirst]** meine Kehle ist wie ausgetrocknet

parchment /ˈpɑːtʃmənt/ *n.* **1** (skin) Pergament, *das* **2** (manuscript) Pergament, *das;* (document) Urkunde, *die*

pardon /ˈpɑːdn/

A *n.* **1** (forgiveness) Vergebung, *die* (geh.); Verzeihung, *die;* **ask sb.'s ~ for sth.** jmdn. wegen etw. um Verzeihung bitten; **no ~ will be given** es gibt kein Pardon; Pardon wird nicht gegeben **2** **beg sb.'s ~:** jmdn. um Entschuldigung *od.* (geh.) Verzeihung bitten; **I beg your ~:** entschuldigen *od.* verzeihen Sie bitte; (please repeat) wie bitte? (auch iron.); **I do beg your ~:** entschuldigen Sie bitte vielmals; **beg ~** (coll.) Entschuldigung; Verzeihung; **~?** bitte?; **~!** Entschuldigung! **3** (Law) **[free] ~:** Begnadigung, *die;* **grant sb. a ~:** jmdn. begnadigen

P

B *v.t.* **1** (forgive) ~ **sb.'s infidelity** jmdm. seine Untreue verzeihen; ~ **sb. [for] sth.** jmdm. etw. verzeihen **2** (excuse) entschuldigen; ~ **my saying so, but ...:** entschuldigen Sie bitte, dass ich es so ausdrücke, aber...; **one could be ~ed for thinking ...** es wäre zu entschuldigen, wenn man dächte, ...; ~ **'me!** Entschuldigung! **3** (Law) begnadigen

pardonable /ˈpɑːdənəbl/ *adj.* verzeihlich; entschuldbar; verständlich ‹*Sorge*›

pardonably /ˈpɑːdənəblɪ/ *adv.* verständlicherweise

pare /peə(r)/ *v.t.* **1** (trim) schneiden ‹*Finger-, Zehennägel*›; zurichten, beschneiden ‹*Hufe*› **2** (peel) schälen ‹*Apfel, Kartoffel*›

Phrasal verbs

• ~ **a'way** *v.t.* abschälen ‹*Rinde*›; (fig.) beschneiden, schmälern ‹*Privileg, Profit usw.*›

• ~ **'down** *v.t.* (fig.: reduce) reduzieren, kürzen ‹*Ausgaben, Kosten, Zuschuss*›

parent /ˈpeərənt/ *n.* **1** Elternteil, *der;* **~s** Eltern *Pl.;* **duties as a ~:** elterliche Pflichten **2** (Bot., Zool.) Elter, *der od. das* (fachspr.); (Bot. also) Mutterpflanze, *die;* (Zool. also) Elterntier, *das* **3** (fig.: source) Quelle, *die* **4** *attrib.* Mutter‹*pflanze, -baum, -zelle, -gesellschaft*›; Stamm‹*firma, -organisation, -organismus*›; ~ **ship** (Naut.) Mutterschiff, *das*

parentage /ˈpeərəntɪdʒ/ *n.* (lit. or fig.) Herkunft, *die;* (fig. also) Ursprung, *der*

parental /pəˈrentl/ *adj.* elterlich ‹*Gewalt*›; Eltern‹*pflicht, -haus, -liebe*›; ‹*Abweisung*› durch die Eltern; ~ **approval/discipline** Zustimmung/disziplinierende Maßnahmen der Eltern

parental 'guidance *n., no pl.* Parental Guidance, *die;* **film in the ~ category** nur bedingt jugendfreier Film (*erfordert die Begleitung eines Elternteils*)

'parentcraft *n., no pl.* Erziehungskunst, *die*

parent 'governor *n.* (Brit. Educ.) ≈ Elternsprecher, *der*/-sprecherin, *die* [*im Schulelternbeirat*]

parenthesis /pəˈrenθɪsɪs/ *n., pl.* **parentheses** /pəˈrenθɪsiːz/ **1** (bracket) runde Klammer; Parenthese, *die* (fachspr.) **2** (word, clause, sentence) Parenthese, *die* (geh.); Einschub, *der;* **in ~:** als Parenthese *od.* Einschub; (fig.) nebenbei; am Rande

parenthetic /pærənˈθetɪk/, **parenthetical** /pærənˈθetɪkl/ *adj.* eingeschoben; parenthetisch (fachspr.)

parenthetically /pærənˈθetɪkəlɪ/ *adv.* parenthetisch; in Parenthese (geh.); (fig.) nebenbei, am Rande ‹*hinzufügen, erwähnen, sagen*›

parenthood /ˈpeərənthʊd/ *n., no pl.* Elternschaft, *die;* **joys of ~:** Elternfreuden *Pl.*

'parents' evening *n.* Elternabend, *der*

parent-'teacher association *n.* Eltern-Lehrer-Vertretung, *die*

parer /ˈpeərə(r)/ *n.* Küchenmesser, *das;* **potato ~:** Kartoffelschälmesser, *das*

par excellence /pɑːr ˈeksəlɑ̃s/ *adv.* par excellence (geh.); schlechthin

pariah /pəˈraɪə/ **[social] ~:** Paria, *der* (geh.); Ausgestoßene, *der/die*

parietal /pəˈraɪətl/ *adj.* (Anat.) parietal (fachspr.); seitlich; ~ **bone** Scheitelbein, *das*

paring /ˈpeərɪŋ/ *n.* **1** (action) (of fruit, vegetables) Schälen, *das;* (of nails) Schneiden, *das;* (of hoofs) Zurichten, *das;* Beschneiden, *das* **2** *usu. in pl.* (peel, shaving, etc.) Schalen, *die;* **nail ~s** abgeschnittene Nägel

'paring knife ▸ **parer**

Paris /ˈpærɪs/ *pr. n.* ▸ℹ **p. 1643** Paris (*das*)

parish /ˈpærɪʃ/ *n.* Gemeinde, *die*

parish: ~ **'church** *n.* Pfarrkirche, *die;* ~ **'council** *n.* (Brit.) Gemeinderat, *der;* ~ **'councillor** *n.* (Brit.) Gemeinderat, *der*/Gemeinderätin, *die*

parishioner /pəˈrɪʃənə(r)/ *n.* Gemeinde[mit]glied, *das;* **the ~s** die Gemeinde

parish: ~ **'priest** *n.* Gemeindepfarrer, *der;* **~-'pump** *adj.* (Brit.) krähwinklig (abwertend), provinziell (abwertend) ‹*Angelegenheit*›; **~-pump politics** Kirchturmpolitik, *die;* ~ **'register** *n.* Kirchenbuch, *das*

Parisian /pəˈrɪzɪən/ ▸ℹ **p. 1643**

A *n.* Pariser, *der*/Pariserin, *die*

B *adj.* Pariser ‹*Mode*›; **be ~** ‹*Person:*› Pariser/Pariserin sein

parity /ˈpærɪtɪ/ *n.* **1** (equality) Parität, *die* (geh.); Gleichheit, *die;* **have ~ in voting rights** das gleiche Stimmrecht haben; ~ **of pay** gleiche Bezahlung **2** (Commerc.) Parität, *die;* **the ~ of sterling against the dollar** die Pfund-Dollar-Parität

park /pɑːk/

A *n.* **1** Park, *der;* (land kept in natural state) Natur[schutz]park, *der* **2** (sports ground) Sportplatz, *der;* (stadium) Stadion, *das;* (Baseball, Footb.) Spielfeld, *das* **3** **amusement ~:** Vergnügungspark, *der;* **business ~:** Betriebsgelände, *das. See also* **industrial park; science park; theme park**

B *v.i.* parken; **find somewhere to ~:** einen Parkplatz finden; **there's nowhere to ~:** da kann man nicht parken; (all spaces are occupied) da ist kein Parkplatz frei

C *v.t.* **1** (place, leave) abstellen; parken ‹*Kfz*›; **the car was ~ed right in front of the house** das Auto parkte genau vor dem Haus; **a ~ed car** ein geparktes *od.* parkendes Auto **2** (coll.: leave, put) deponieren (*scherzh.*); ~ **oneself [down]** (coll.) sich [hin]pflanzen (ugs.); ~ **oneself on sb.** (coll.) sich bei jmdm. häuslich niederlassen (ugs.)

parka /ˈpɑːkə/ *n.* Parka, *der*

park-and-'ride *n.* Park-and-ride-System, *das;* (place) Park-and-ride-Parkplatz, *der*

parking /ˈpɑːkɪŋ/ *n., no pl., no indef. art.* Parken, *das;* **'no ~'** „Parken verboten"; **there is no ~ in the main street** auf der Hauptstraße ist Parkverbot; **'P~ for 500 cars'** „500 Parkplätze"

parking: ~ **attendant** *n.* ▸ℹ **p. 1260** Parkplatzwächter, *der*/-wächterin, *die;* ~ **bay** *n.* Parkbucht, *die;* (allocated parking space) Stellplatz, *der;* ~ **brake** *n.* Feststellbremse, *die;* ~ **disc** *n.* Parkscheibe, *die;* ~ **fine** *n.* Geldbuße für falsches Parken; ~ **light** *n.* Parklicht, *das;* Parkleuchte, *die;* ~ **lot** *n.* (Amer.) Parkplatz, *der;* ~ **meter** *n.* Parkuhr, *die;* Parkometer, *das od. der;* ~ **offence** *n.* Verstoß gegen das Parkverbot; ~ **permit** *n.* Parkerlaubnis, *die;* ~ **space** *n.* **1** *no pl.* Parkraum, *der;* **2** (single space) Platz zum Parken; Parkplatz, *der;* (between other vehicles) Parklücke, *die;* ~ **ticket** *n.* Strafzettel [für falsches Parken]; ~ **violation** *n.* Parkverstoß, *der*

Parkinson's /ˈpɑːkɪnsənz/: ~ **disease** *n.* ▸ℹ **p. 1231** (Med.) Parkinson-Krankheit, *die;* ~ **law** *n.* (joc.) das parkinsonsche Gesetz

park: **~-keeper** *n.* ▸ℹ **p. 1260** Parkwächter, *der*/-wächterin, *die;* **~land** *n.* Parklandschaft, *die;* ~ **'ranger** *n.* ▸ℹ **p. 1260** Nationalparkwächter, *der*/-wächterin, *die;* Parkranger, *der*/-rangerin, *die;* **~way** *n.* (Amer.) [*für Lkw gesperrte*] Allee

parky /ˈpɑːkɪ/ *adj.* (Brit. coll.) frisch (ugs.); kühl

parlance /ˈpɑːləns/ *n.* Ausdrucksweise, *die;* Sprache, *die;* **in common/legal/modern ~:** im allgemeinen/juristischen/modernen Sprachgebrauch

parley /ˈpɑːlɪ/

A *n.* Verhandlungen *Pl.*

B *v.i.* verhandeln; **meet to ~:** sich zu Verhandlungen treffen

parliament /ˈpɑːləmənt/ *n.* Parlament, *das;* **[Houses of] P~** (Brit.) Parlament, *das;* **in P~:** im Parlament; **be before P~** ‹*Antrag:*› im Parlament beraten werden; **open P~:** das parlamentarische Sitzungsjahr eröffnen; *see also* **member 2**

> **Parliament**
>
> Das britische Parlament ist die höchste gesetzgebende Gewalt in Großbritannien und besteht aus dem Souverän (dem König oder der Königin), dem **House of Lords** (Oberhaus) und dem **House of Commons** (Unterhaus). Der Name *Parliament* bürgerte sich im 13. Jahrhundert unter Heinrich III. ein und beschrieb die Versammlungen zwischen dem König und dem Adel. Die hohen Lehnsherren im *Great Council* (Rat) und Vertreter des niederen Adels und der Städte mussten Abgaben an den König leisten, um seine Kriege zu finanzieren. Im Laufe der Zeit wurde aus den Lehnsherren im *Great Council* das *House of Lords*, und die Vertreter des niederen Adels, der *counties* und *towns*, bildeten das *House of Commons*. Die Trennung des Unterhauses vom Oberhaus entwickelte sich im 14. Jahrhundert, und seit dem 15. Jahrhundert wirkt das Unterhaus an der Gesetzgebung mit. Die Rechte des Souveräns und des Oberhauses wurden im Laufe der Zeit zugunsten des Unterhauses zurückgedrängt. Seit dem 19. Jahrhundert bildet die Partei mit der Mehrheit im Unterhaus die Regierung.

parliamentarian /pɑːləmənˈteərɪən/ *n.* Parlamentarier, *der*/Parlamentarierin, *die*

parliamentary /pɑːləˈmentərɪ/ *adj.* parlamentarisch; Parlaments‹*geschäfte, -wahlen, -reform*›; **P~ approval** Zustimmung des Parlaments; *see also* **privilege A 1; secretary 2**

'parlor car *n.* (Amer. Railw.) Salonwagen, *der*

parlour (*Brit.; Amer.:* **parlor**) /ˈpɑːlə(r)/ *n.* **1** (dated: sitting room) Wohnzimmer, *das;* gute Stube (veralt.) **2** (in mansion, convent, inn) Salon, *der* **3** **ice cream ~:** Eisdiele, *die;* **beauty/massage ~:** Schönheits-/Massagesalon, *der*

parlour: ~ **game** *n.* Gesellschaftsspiel, *das;* **~maid** *n.* (Hist.) Hausangestellte *od.* -gehilfin, *die;* ~ **tricks** *n. pl.* gesellschaftliche Spielchen

parlous /ˈpɑːləs/ *adj.* (arch./joc.) kritisch, bedenklich, Besorgnis erregend ‹*Zustand*›; kritisch ‹*Zeit*›

Parmesan /ˈpɑːmɪzæn, pɑːmɪˈzæn/ *adj., n.* ~ **[cheese]** Parmesan[käse], *der*

parochial /pəˈrəʊkɪəl/ *adj.* **1** (narrow) krähwinklig (abwertend); eng ‹*Horizont*›; **be ~ in one's outlook** einen engen Horizont haben **2** (Eccl.) Gemeinde-; parochial (fachspr.)

parochialism /pəˈrəʊkɪəlɪzm/ *n.* Provinzialismus, *der* (abwertend); Engstirnigkeit, *die* (abwertend)

parodist /ˈpærədɪst/ *n.* Parodist, *der*/Parodistin, *die;* **be a ~ of sth.** etw. parodieren

parody /ˈpærədɪ/

A *n.* **1** (humorous imitation) Parodie, *die,* (geh.) Persiflage, *die* (**of** auf + *Akk.*) **2** (feeble imitation) Abklatsch, *der* (abwertend); (of justice) Verhöhnung, *die*

B *v.t.* parodieren; persiflieren (geh.)

parole /pəˈrəʊl/

A *n.* (conditional release) bedingter Straferlass (Rechtsw.); (word of honour) Ehrenwort, *das;* **he was released** *or* **let out on ~/he is on ~:** er wurde auf Bewährung entlassen; **he's on three months' ~:** er hat drei Monate Bewährung

B *v.t.* (Law) ~ **sb.** jmdm. seine Strafe bedingt erlassen

paroxysm /ˈpærəksɪzm/ *n.* Krampf, *der;* (fit, convulsion) Anfall, *der* (**of** von); Paroxysmus, *der* (Med., Geol.); ~ **of rage/laughter** Wut-/Lachanfall, *der;* **burst into ~s of laughter** einen Lachkrampf bekommen; **in a ~ of grief** außer sich vor Trauer

parquet /ˈpɑːkɪ, ˈpɑːkeɪ/ *n.* ~ **[flooring]** Parkett, *das;* ~ **floor** Parkettfußboden, *der*

parricide /ˈpærɪsaɪd/ ▸ **patricide**

parrot /ˈpærət/

A *n.* **1** Papagei, *der;* **I was as sick as a ~** (coll.) mir war zum Kotzen zumute (salopp) **2** (fig.: person) Nachplapperer, *der*/-plapperin, *die* (abwertend)

B *v.t.* nachplappern (abwertend); ~ **sb.** jmdm. alles nachplappern

'parrot-fashion *adv.* papageienhaft, wie ein Papagei ‹*wiederholen*›; stur, mechanisch ‹*lernen*›; **repeat things ~:** [papageienhaft *od.* wie ein Papagei] nachplappern *od.* nachschwatzen

parry /'pærɪ/
A *v.t.* (Boxing) abwehren ‹*Faustschlag*›; (Fencing; also fig.) parieren ‹*Fechthieb, Frage*›
B *n.* (Boxing) Abwehr, *die;* (Fencing) Parade, *die;* **make a ~** (Boxing) abwehren; (Fencing) parieren

parse /pɑːz/ *v.t.* [1] (Ling.) grammatisch beschreiben ‹*Wort*›; grammatisch analysieren ‹*Satz*› [2] (Computing) parsen

parsec /'pɑːsek/ *n.* (Astron.) Parsec, *das*

parser /'pɑːzə(r)/ *n.* (Computing) Parser, *der*

parsimonious /pɑːsɪ'məʊnɪəs/ *adj.* sparsam; (niggardly) geizig; (sparing) sparsam; **be ~ with sth.** mit etw. geizen

parsimony /'pɑːsɪmənɪ/ *n.* (meanness) Geiz, *der;* (carefulness) Sparsamkeit, *die*

parsley /'pɑːslɪ/ *n., no pl., no indef. art.* Petersilie, *die*

parsley: ~ butter *n.* Petersilienbutter, *die;* **~ 'sauce** *n.* Petersiliensauce, *die*

parsnip /'pɑːsnɪp/ *n.* Gemeiner Pastinak, *der;* Pastinake, *die; see also* **butter B**

parson /'pɑːsn/ *n.* (vicar, rector) Pfarrer, *der;* (coll.: any clergyman) Geistliche, *der;* Pfaffe, *der* (*abwertend*); *see also* **nose A 1**

parsonage /'pɑːsənɪdʒ/ *n.* Pfarrhaus, *das*

part /pɑːt/
A *n.* [1] Teil, *der;* (element of history, family, character) Bestandteil, *der;* **~ of the cake/newspaper** *etc.* ein Teil des Kuchens/der Zeitung *usw.;* **the greater ~:** der größte Teil; der Großteil; **four-~:** vierteilig ‹*Serie*›; **the hottest ~ of the day** die heißesten Stunden des Tages; **accept ~ of the blame** einen Teil der Schuld auf sich (Akk.) nehmen; **he deserves no small ~ of the credit for this achievement** an diesem Erfolg hat er keinen geringen Anteil; **for the most ~:** größtenteils; zum größten Teil; **in ~:** teilweise; **in large ~:** groß[en]teils; **in ~s** zum Teil; **~ and parcel** wesentlicher Bestandteil; **the funny ~ of it was that he ...:** das Komische daran war, dass er ...; **it's [all] ~ of the fun/job** *etc.* das gehört [mit] dazu; **be** *or* **form ~ of sth.** zu etw. gehören; **be very much a ~ of sth.** wesentlicher Bestandteil von etw. sein; **the affected ~:** die befallene Partie; *see also* **better A**
[2] (of machine or other apparatus) [Einzel]teil, *das;* **spare/machine ~:** Ersatz-/Maschinenteil, *das*
[3] (share) Anteil, *der;* **I want no ~ in this** ich möchte damit nichts zu tun haben; **what's your ~ in all this?** was hast du mit all dem zu tun?
[4] (duty) Aufgabe, *die;* **do one's ~:** seinen Teil *od.* seine Pflicht *od.* das Seine tun
[5] (Theatre: character, words) Rolle, *die;* Part, *der* (geh.); (copy) Rollentext, *der;* (fig.) **dress the ~:** die angemessene Kleidung tragen; **play a noble ~:** nobel handeln; **play a [great/considerable] ~** (contribute) eine [wichtige] Rolle spielen; **play a ~** (act deceitfully) schauspielern (abwertend); sich verstellen; *see also* **act B 2; look A 5**
[6] (Mus.) Part, *der;* Partie, *die;* Stimme, *die;* **six-~:** sechsstimmig ‹*Fuge, Harmonie*›
[7] *usu. in pl.* (region) Gegend, *die;* (of continent, world) Teil, *der;* **be in foreign ~s** im Ausland sein; **I am a stranger in these ~s** ich kenne mich hier nicht aus; **in this** *or* **our/your ~ of the world** hierzulande/bei Ihnen
[8] (side) Partei, *die;* **take sb.'s ~:** jmds. *od.* für jmdn. Partei ergreifen; **for my ~:** für mein[en] Teil; **on the ~ of** seitens (+ *Gen.*) (Papierdt.); vonseiten (+ *Gen.*); **on my/your** *etc.* **~:** meiner-/deinerseits *usw.*
[9] *pl.* (abilities) **a man of [many] ~s** ein [vielseitig] begabter *od.* befähigter Mann
[10] (Ling.) **~ of speech** Wortart *od.* -klasse, *die; see also* **principal parts**
[11] **take [no] ~ [in sth.]** sich [an etw. (*Dat.*)] [nicht] beteiligen; [bei etw.] [nicht] mitmachen; **those taking ~ were ...:** teilgenommen haben ...
[12] **take sth. in good ~:** etw. nicht übel nehmen
[13] (Amer.) ▸ **parting A 2**
B *adv.* teils; **an alloy which is ~ copper, ~ zinc** eine Legierung aus Kupfer und Zink; **~ ... [and] ~ ...:** teils ..., teils ...
C *v.t.* [1] (divide into parts) teilen; scheiteln ‹*Haar*› [2] (separate) trennen; **a fool and his money are soon ~ed** (prov.) wer nicht aufpasst, dem rinnt das Geld durch die Finger; **till death us do ~** (in marriage vow) bis dass der Tod uns scheidet; *see also* **company 1**
D *v.i.* [1] (divide into parts) ‹*Menge:*› eine Gasse bilden; ‹*Wolken:*› sich teilen; ‹*Vorhang:*› sich öffnen; (become divided or broken) ‹*Seil, Tau, Kette:*› reißen; ‹*Lippen:*› sich öffnen
[2] (separate) ‹*Wege, Personen:*› sich trennen; **~ from sb./sth.** sich von jmdm./etw. trennen; **let us ~ friends** wir wollen als Freunde auseinander gehen; **~ with** sich trennen von ‹*Besitz, Geld*›; verzichten auf ‹*Kontrolle*›

partake /pɑː'teɪk/ *v.i., forms as* **take B** (formal) [1] **~ of** (eat) zu sich nehmen, einnehmen (geh.) ‹*Kost, Mahlzeit*›; (joc.) sich einverleiben (scherzh.) [2] (share) **~ in** sich (*Dat.*) teilen ‹*Beute*›; teilhaben an (+ *Dat.*), teilen ‹*jmds. Schicksal, Freuden*›

partaken ▸ **partake**

parterre /pɑː'teə(r)/ *n.* [1] (Hort.) Parterreanlage, *die* [2] (Amer. Theatre) Parterre, *das*

part ex'change
A *n.* **accept sth. in ~ for sth.** etw. für etw. in Zahlung nehmen; **sell sth. in ~:** etw. in Zahlung geben
B *v.t.* in Zahlung geben

parthenogenesis /pɑːθɪnə'dʒenɪsɪs/ *n., no pl.* (Biol.) Parthenogenese, *die* (fachspr.); Jungfernzeugung, *die*

Parthian shot /pɑːθɪən 'ʃɒt/ *n.* (remark) spitze Schlussbemerkung; (action) Abschiedsgeste, *die*

partial /'pɑːʃl/ *adj.* [1] (biased, unfair) voreingenommen; parteiisch ‹*Urteil*› [2] **be/not be ~ to sb./sth.** (like/dislike) eine Schwäche/keine besondere Vorliebe für jmdn./etw. haben [3] (incomplete) partiell ‹*Lähmung, Sonnen-, Mondfinsternis*›; teilweise ‹*Verlust, Misserfolg*›; Mit‹*verantwortung, -eigentümer usw.*›; **a ~ success** ein Teilerfolg

partiality /pɑːʃɪ'ælɪtɪ/ *n.* [1] (fondness) Vorliebe, *die;* (for alcohol etc.) Schwäche, *die* [2] (bias) Voreingenommenheit, *die;* Parteilichkeit, *die;* **show ~:** parteiisch *od.* voreingenommen sein

partially /'pɑːʃəlɪ/ *adv.* zum Teil; teilweise

participant /pɑː'tɪsɪpənt/ *n.* (actively involved) Beteiligte, *der/die* (**in** an + *Dat.*); (in arranged event) Teilnehmer, *der*/Teilnehmerin, *die* (**in** an + *Dat.*)

participate /pɑː'tɪsɪpeɪt/ *v.i.* (be actively involved) sich beteiligen (**in** an + *Dat.*); (in arranged event) teilnehmen (**in** an + *Dat.*); (have part or share) partizipieren (geh.), teilhaben (**in** an + *Dat.*)

participation /pɑːtɪsɪ'peɪʃn/ *n.* (active involvement) Beteiligung, *die* (**in** an + *Dat.*); (in arranged event) Teilnahme, *die* (**in** bei, an + *Dat.*); **worker ~:** industrielle Mitbestimmung; **audience ~:** Publikumsbeteiligung, *die*

participator /pɑː'tɪsɪpeɪtə(r)/ *n.* Beteiligte, *der/die;* **be a ~ in sth.** sich an etw. (*Dat.*) beteiligen

participatory /pɑː'tɪsɪpeɪtərɪ/ *adj.* ‹*Fernsehsendung, Theaterstück*› mit Zuschauerbeteiligung; ‹*Radiosendung*› mit Hörerbeteiligung; (Polit.) mit Bürgerbeteiligung *nachgestellt*

participial /pɑːtɪ'sɪpɪəl/ *adj.* (Ling.) partizipial; Partizipial-

participle /'pɑːtɪsɪpl/ *n.* (Ling.) Partizip, *das;* Mittelwort, *das;* **present/past ~:** Partizip Präsens/Perfekt; Mittelwort der Gegenwart/Vergangenheit

particle /'pɑːtɪkl/ *n.* [1] (tiny portion; also Phys.) Teilchen, *das;* (of sand) Körnchen, *das* [2] (fig.) Quäntchen, *das* (geh.); (of sense, truth) Fünkchen, *das;* (of truth also) Körnchen, *das* [3] (Ling.) Partikel, *die*

particle 'physics *n., no pl.* Teilchenphysik, *die*

particoloured (Brit.; Amer.: **particolored**) /pɑːtɪ'kʌləd/ *adj.* bunt

particular /pə'tɪkjʊlə(r)/
A *adj.* [1] (special; more than ordinary) besonder...; **which ~ place do you have in mind?** an welchen Ort denkst du speziell?; **here in ~:** besonders hier; **nothing/anything [in] ~:** nichts/irgendetwas Besonderes; **what in ~ made you so angry?** was genau hat dich so geärgert? [2] (individual) **each ~ hair** jedes [einzelne] Haar; **in his ~ case** in seinem [besonderen] Fall; **one ~ example of each type** ein Beispiel für jede Sorte [3] (fussy, fastidious) genau; eigen (landsch.); **I am not ~:** es ist mir gleich; **be ~ about sth.** es mit etw. genau nehmen; in etw. (*Dat.*) eigen sein (landsch.); **be ~ in one's habits** in allem genau *od.* (landsch.) eigen sein; **be ~ about what one eats** wählerisch im Essen sein [4] (detailed) detailliert, ausführlich ‹*Bericht*›; eingehend, genau, gründlich ‹*Kenntnis*›
B *n.* [1] *in pl.* (details) Einzelheiten; Details; (of person) Personalien *Pl.;* (of incident) nähere Umstände [2] (detail) Einzelheit, *die;* Detail, *das;* **describe sth. in every ~:** etw. in allen Einzelheiten beschreiben

particularize (**particularise**) /pə'tɪkjʊləraɪz/
A *v.t.* spezifizieren
B *v.i.* ins Detail gehen

particularly /pə'tɪkjʊləlɪ/ *adv.* [1] (especially) besonders [2] (specifically) speziell; insbesondere

parting /'pɑːtɪŋ/
A *n.* [1] (leave-taking) **[final] ~:** Trennung, *die;* Abschied, *der* [2] (Brit.: in hair) Scheitel, *der;* **side ~:** Seitenscheitel, *der* [3] **~ of the ways** (of road) Gabelung, *die;* (fig.: critical point) Scheideweg, *der;* **we came to a ~ of the ways** (fig.) unsere Wege trennten sich
B *attrib. adj.* Abschieds-; **~ shot** Schlussbemerkung, *die;* **~ glance/advice** Blick/Ratschlag zum Abschied

partisan /pɑːtɪ'zæn, 'pɑːtɪzæn/
A *n.* [1] (adherent) Anhänger, *der*/Anhängerin, *die;* (of party also) Parteigänger, *der*/-gängerin, *die* (oft abwertend); (of cause also) Befürworter, *der*/Befürworterin, *die* [2] (Mil.) Partisan, *der*/Partisanin, *die*
B *adj.* [1] (often derog.: biased) voreingenommen, parteiisch ‹*Ansatz, Urteil, Versuch*›; Partei‹*politik, -geist*› [2] (Mil.) Partisanen‹*gruppe, -krieg, -aktivität*›

partisanship /pɑːtɪ'zænʃɪp, 'pɑːtɪzænʃɪp/ *n., no pl.* Parteinahme, *die;* Parteilichkeit, *die;* Voreingenommenheit, *die*

partita /pɑː'tiːtə/ *n.* (Mus.) Partita, *die;* Suite, *die*

partition /pɑː'tɪʃn/
A *n.* [1] (division) (of text etc.) Unterteilung, *die* (**into** in + *Akk.*); (between subjects) Trennung, *die* [2] (Polit.) Teilung, *die* [3] (room divider) Trennwand, *die* [4] (section of hall or library) Abteilung, *die;* Bereich, *der* [5] (Law: of estate etc.) Aufteilung, *die*
B *v.t.* [1] (divide) aufteilen ‹*Land, Zimmer*›; [unter-]teilen ‹*Zimmer*› [2] (Polit.) teilen ‹*Land*›

Phrasal verb
• **~ 'off** *v.t.* abteilen ‹*Teil, Raum*›

partitive /'pɑːtɪtɪv/ (Ling.) *adj.* partitiv ‹*Wort, Nomen*›

partly /'pɑːtlɪ/ *adv.* zum Teil; teilweise; **he was ~ responsible for the accident** er war mitschuldig an dem Unglück; **~ ... [and] ~ ...:** teils ..., teils ...

partner /'pɑːtnə(r)/
A *n.* Partner, *der*/Partnerin, *die;* **~ in crime** Komplize, *der*/Komplizin, *die* (abwertend); **business ~:** Geschäftspartner, *der*/-partnerin, *die;* **be a ~ in a firm** Teilhaber/-haberin einer Firma sein; **junior/senior ~:** Junior, *der*/Senior, *der;* **[dancing] ~:** Tanzpartner, *der*/-partnerin, *die;* **take your ~s** bitte Aufstellung nehmen; **tennis/croquet ~:** Tennis-/Krocketpartner, *der*/-partnerin, *die;* **~ [in marriage]** Ehepartner, *der*/-partnerin, *die; see also* **sleeping partner**
B *v.t.* [1] (make a ~) **~ sb. with sb.** jmdn. mit jmdm. zusammenbringen; **be ~ed with sb.** jmds. Partner/Partnerin sein [2] (be ~ of) **~ sb.** jmds. Partner/Partnerin sein; **~ sb. at**

p

tennis/in the dance mit jmdm. Tennis spielen/tanzen

partnership /ˈpɑːtnəʃɪp/ *n.* **1** (association) Partnerschaft, *die;* **they were a marvellous ~:** sie waren großartige Partner **2** (Commerc.) **business ~:** [Personen]gesellschaft, *die;* **go** *or* **enter into ~ with sb.** mit jmdm. eine [Personen]gesellschaft gründen; **leave the ~:** aus der Gesellschaft ausscheiden

partook ▸**partake**

part: ~-owner *n.* Mitbesitzer, *der*/-besitzerin, *die;* **~ ˈpayment** *n.* **1** ▸**part exchange A; 2** (sum) Anzahlung, *die*

partridge /ˈpɑːtrɪdʒ/ *n., pl. same or* **~s** Rebhuhn, *das*

part: ~-song *n.* mehrstimmiges Lied; **~ ˈtime** *n.* **some employees were put on ~ time** einige Beschäftigte mussten kurzarbeiten; **~-time A** /ˈ--/ *adj.* Teilzeit⟨*arbeit, -arbeiter*⟩; **be engaged on a ~-time basis to teach French** als Teilzeitlehrer/-lehrerin für Französisch eingestellt sein; **he is only ~-time** er ist nur eine Teilzeitkraft; **B** /-ˈ-/ *adv.* stundenweise, halbtags ⟨*arbeiten, studieren*⟩; **work ~-time** als Teilzeitkraft beschäftigt sein; **~-ˈtimer** *n.* Teilzeitkraft, *die;* **study as a ~-timer** halbtags *od.* stundenweise studieren

parturition /pɑːtjʊˈrɪʃn/ *n.* (Physiol.) Partus, *der* (fachspr.); Geburt, *die*

part: ~-way *adv.* **~-way down the slope he slipped** nachdem er ein Stück des Hangs bewältigt hatte, rutschte er aus; **we were ~-way through the tunnel** wir hatten ein Stück des Tunnels hinter uns; **go ~-way towards meeting sb.'s demands** jmds. Forderungen (*Dat.*) teilweise *od.* halbwegs entsprechen; **~-way through her speech** mitten in ihrer Rede; **~-work** *n.* (Publishing) Lieferungswerk, *das;* Partwork, *das*

party /ˈpɑːtɪ/ *n.* **1** (group united in a cause etc.; Polit., Law) Partei, *die; attrib.* Partei⟨*apparat, -versammlung, -mitglied, -politik, -politiker usw.*⟩; **opposing ~:** Gegenpartei, *die;* gegnerische Partei; **the P~:** die Partei; **~ loyalty** Treue zur Partei **2** (group) Gruppe, *die;* **a ~ of tourists** eine Touristengruppe; **hunting ~:** Jagdgesellschaft, *die;* **tennis ~:** Gruppe von Tennisspielern **3** (social gathering) Party, *die;* Fete, *die* (ugs.); (more formal) Gesellschaft, *die;* **office ~:** Betriebsfest, *das; see also* **birthday**; **dinner party**; **tea party** **4** (participator) Beteiligte, *der/die;* **be [a] ~ in** *or* **to sth.** sich an etw. (*Dat.*) beteiligen; **parties to an agreement/a dispute** Parteien bei einem Abkommen/streitende Parteien; **the guilty ~:** der/die Schuldige; *see also* **third party** **5** (coll.: person) Figur, *die* (salopp); **he's a funny old ~:** er ist ein komischer Kauz (ugs.)

party: ~ ˈanimal *n.* Partymensch, *der;* **~ game** *n.* Gesellschaftsspiel, *das;* **~ line** *n.* **1** /ˈ---/ (Teleph.) Gemeinschafts-, Sammelanschluss, *der;* **2** /-ˈ-ˈ-/ (Polit.) Parteilinie, *die;* **what is the ~ line on this problem?** welche Linie verfolgt die Partei bei diesem Problem?; **~-ˈliner** *n.* (Polit.) linientreues Parteimitglied; **~ piece** *n.* **this song was my ~ piece** dieses Lied gab ich auf jeder Gesellschaft zum Besten; **~ poˈlitical** *adj.* parteipolitisch ⟨*Propaganda, Sendung, Ziele, Fragen etc.*⟩; **~ political broadcast** parteipolitische Sendung; **a Labour ~ political broadcast** eine Sendung der Labour Party; **~ ˈpolitics** *n.* Parteipolitik, *die;* **~ pooper** /ˈpɑːtɪ puːpə(r)/ *n.* (Amer. coll.) Partymuffel, *der;* **~ popper** *n.* Partyknaller, *der;* **~ spirit** *n.* (festive atmosphere) Partystimmung, *die;* **get the ~ spirit going** die Party in Schwung *od.* Schwung in die Party bringen (ugs.); **~ trick** *n.* Trick, der auf Partys Stimmung erzeugt; **~ ˈwall** *n.* Mauer zum Nachbargrundstück/-gebäude; Kommunmauer, *die* (Rechtsspr.)

parvenu /ˈpɑːvənuː/
A *n.* Parvenü, *der* (geh.); Emporkömmling, *der*
B *adj.* arriviert; neureich; parvenühaft ⟨*Dreistigkeit*⟩

pascal /ˈpæskl/ *n.* (Phys.) Pascal, *das*

paschal /ˈpæskl/ *adj.* **1** (of Jewish Passover) Passah-; **~ lamb** Passah[lamm], *das;* (fig.) Lamm Gottes; Agnus Dei (fachspr.) **2** (of Easter) Oster-

pash /pæʃ/ *n.* (dated. coll.) Schulmädchenschwärmerei, *die;* (person) Schwarm, *der* (ugs.); **have a ~ for sb.** für jmdn. schwärmen

pasha /ˈpɑːʃə/ *n.* (Hist.) Pascha, *der*

pashmina /pæʃˈmiːnə/ *n.* Paschminaschal, *der*

paso doble /pɑːsəʊ ˈdəʊbleɪ/ *n.* (Dancing) Paso doble, *der*

pasque flower *n.* Kuhschelle, *die*

pass /pɑːs/
A *n.* **1** (passing of an examination) bestandene Prüfung; **be awarded a ~ with distinction** ein Examen mit Auszeichnung bestehen; **get a ~ in maths** die Mathematikprüfung bestehen; **'~'** (mark or grade) Ausreichend, *das;* [Note] Vier, *die*
2 (written permission) Ausweis, *der;* Erlaubnisschein, *der;* (for going into or out of a place also) Passierschein, *der;* (Mil.: for leave) Urlaubsschein, *der;* (for free transportation) Freifahrschein, *der;* (for free admission) Freikarte, *die*
3 (critical position) Notlage, *die;* kritische Lage; **things have come to a pretty ~ [when ...]** es muss schon weit gekommen sein[, wenn ...]
4 (Football) Pass, *der* (fachspr.); Ballabgabe, *die;* (Tennis) ▸**passing shot**; (Fencing) Ausfall, *der;* **make a ~ to a player** [den Ball] zu einem Spieler passen (fachspr.) *od.* abgeben; **make a ~ over** (Aeronaut.) überfliegen
5 (by conjuror, hypnotist) **~ [of the hands]** Handbewegung, *die*
6 **make a ~ at sb.** (fig. coll.: amorously) jmdm. gegenüber Annäherungsversuche machen; jmdn. anmachen (ugs.)
7 (in mountains) Pass, *der*
8 (strategic entrance into a country) strategisch wichtiger Zugang; Schlüsselstellung, *die*
9 (Cards) Passen, *das*
B *v.i.* **1** (move onward) ⟨*Prozession:*⟩ ziehen; ⟨*Wasser:*⟩ fließen; ⟨*Gas:*⟩ strömen; (fig.) ⟨*Redner:*⟩ übergehen (**to** zu); **~ further along** *or* **down the bus, please!** bitte weiter durchgehen!
2 (go) passieren; **~ through** ⟨*Blut:*⟩ fließen durch ⟨*Organ*⟩; ⟨*Zug, Reisender:*⟩ fahren durch ⟨*Land*⟩; ⟨*Faden:*⟩ gehen durch ⟨*Nadelöhr*⟩; **~ over** (in plane) überfliegen ⟨*Ort*⟩; **a cloud ~ed over the sun** eine Wolke schob sich vor die Sonne; **let sb. ~:** jmdn. durchlassen *od.* passieren lassen
3 (be transported, lit. or fig.) kommen; **~ into history/oblivion** in die Geschichte eingehen/in Vergessenheit geraten; **messages ~ed between them** Nachrichten wurden zwischen ihnen ausgetauscht; **the title/property ~es to sb.** der Titel/Besitz geht auf jmdn. über
4 (change) wechseln; **~ from one state/stage to another** von einem Zustand in einen anderen/von einem Stadium in ein anderes übergehen
5 (go by) ⟨*Fußgänger:*⟩ vorbeigehen; ⟨*Fahrer, Fahrzeug:*⟩ vorbeifahren; ⟨*Prozession:*⟩ vorbeiziehen; ⟨*Zeit, Sekunde:*⟩ vergehen; (by chance) ⟨*Person, Fahrzeug:*⟩ vorbeikommen; **let sb./a car ~:** jmdn./ein Auto vorbeilassen (ugs.); **make it impossible for sb./sth. to ~:** jmdm./einer Sache den Weg versperren; **he said hello as he ~ed** er grüßte im Vorbeigehen; **~ unheeded** ⟨*Bemerkung:*⟩ keine Beachtung finden; **she would not let this ~ without comment** das wollte sie nicht unkommentiert [im Raum stehen] lassen
6 (be accepted as adequate) durchgehen; hingehen; **let that/it/the matter ~:** das/es/die Sache durch- *od.* hingehen lassen
7 (come to an end) vorbeigehen; ⟨*Fieber:*⟩ zurückgehen, [ab]sinken; ⟨*Ärger, Zorn, Sturm:*⟩ sich legen; ⟨*Gewitter, Unwetter:*⟩ vorüberziehen; ⟨*Königreich, Volk:*⟩ untergehen
8 (formal/arch. euphem.: die) ableben (veralt. geh.); **~ out of this world** aus dieser Welt gehen *od.* scheiden (geh. verhüll.)
9 (happen) passieren; (between persons) vorfallen; **bring/come to ~** (arch.) bewirken/sich zutragen *od.* begeben (geh.)
10 (be known) **~ by** *or* **under the name of White** unter dem Namen White bekannt sein
11 (be accepted) durchgehen (**as** als, **for** für); **~ as currency** als Währung akzeptiert werden
12 (be sanctioned) ⟨*Gesetzentwurf:*⟩ angenommen werden, durchgehen
13 (satisfy examiner) bestehen; **let ~** ⟨*Zensor:*⟩ freigeben ⟨*Film, Buch, Theaterstück*⟩
14 (circulate, be current) im Umlauf sein
15 (Chess) **~ed pawn** Freibauer, *der*
16 (Cards) passen; **[I] ~!** [ich] passe! *See also* **crowd A 1**; **ship A 1**
C *v.t.* **1** (move past) ⟨*Fußgänger:*⟩ vorbeigehen an (+ *Dat.*); ⟨*Fahrer, Fahrzeug:*⟩ vorbeifahren an (+ *Dat.*); ⟨*Prozession:*⟩ vorbeiziehen an (+ *Dat.*); (by chance) ⟨*Person, Fahrzeug:*⟩ vorbeikommen an (+ *Dat.*)
2 (overtake) vorbeifahren an (+ *Dat.*) ⟨*Fahrzeug, Person*⟩
3 (cross) überschreiten ⟨*Schwelle, feindliche Linien, Grenze, Marke*⟩; nehmen, überwinden ⟨*Hindernis*⟩
4 (be approved by) ⟨*Film:*⟩ passieren ⟨*Zensur*⟩; ⟨*Gesetzentwurf:*⟩ verabschiedet werden von ⟨*Parlament*⟩; (reach standard in) bestehen ⟨*Prüfung*⟩; (satisfy requirements of) kommen durch ⟨*Kontrolle*⟩
5 (approve) verabschieden ⟨*Gesetzentwurf*⟩; annehmen ⟨*Vorschlag*⟩; ⟨*Zoll:*⟩ abfertigen ⟨*Gepäck*⟩; ⟨*Zensor:*⟩ freigeben ⟨*Film, Buch, Theaterstück*⟩; bestehen lassen ⟨*Prüfungskandidaten*⟩; **~ sb. as fit** ⟨*Arzt:*⟩ jmdn. für gesund erklären
6 (be too great for) überschreiten, übersteigen ⟨*Auffassungsgabe, Verständnis*⟩
7 (move) bringen; **~ one's hand across one's face** sich mit der Hand über das Gesicht streichen; **~ a rope/thread through a ring/the eye of a needle** ein Seil/einen Faden durch einen Ring/ein Nadelöhr ziehen *od.* führen; **~ a duster over the furniture** mit einem Staubtuch über die Möbel wischen; **~ meat through a mincer/tomatoes through a sieve** Fleisch durch einen Fleischwolf drehen/Tomaten durch ein Sieb streichen; **~ one's eye over a letter** *etc.* einen Brief *usw.* überfliegen
8 (Footb. etc.) passen (fachspr.) (**to** zu); abgeben (**to** an + *Akk.*); zuspielen (**to** *Dat.*)
9 (spend) verbringen ⟨*Leben, Zeit, Tag*⟩
10 (hand) **~ sb. sth.** jmdm. etw. reichen *od.* geben; **would you ~ the salt, please?** gibst *od.* reichst du mir bitte das Salz?; **~ sth. to another department** etw. an eine andere Abteilung weitergeben; *see also* **around A 2**
11 (cause to circulate) in Umlauf bringen ⟨*Geld*⟩
12 (Mil.) **~ in review** defilieren *od.* vorbeimarschieren lassen ⟨*Truppen*⟩; (fig.) Revue passieren lassen
13 (utter) fällen, verkünden ⟨*Urteil*⟩; machen ⟨*Bemerkung*⟩; **~ censure on sth.** etw. tadeln
14 (discharge) lassen ⟨*Wasser*⟩; **~ blood** (from the bowels) Blut im Stuhl haben; (by spitting) Blut spucken; (by coughing) Blut husten; (in urine) Blut im Urin haben. *See also* **buck²**; **hat 2**; **muster A 1**; **time A 2**

Phrasal verbs

- **~ aˈway**

A *v.i.* **1** (cease to exist) ⟨*Reich:*⟩ untergehen **2** (euphem.: die) verscheiden (geh.); **~ away in one's sleep** im Schlaf dahingehen (geh. verhüll.)
B *v.t.* verbringen ⟨*Zeit[raum], Abend*⟩

- **~ by**

A /ˈ--/ *v.t.* **1** (go past) ⟨*Fußgänger:*⟩ vorbeigehen an (+ *Dat.*); ⟨*Fahrer, Fahrzeug:*⟩ vorbeifahren an (+ *Dat.*); ⟨*Prozession:*⟩ vorbeiziehen an (+ *Dat.*); (by chance) ⟨*Person, Fahrzeug:*⟩ vorbeikommen an (+ *Dat.*) **2** (omit, disregard) übergehen
B /-ˈ-/ *v.i.* ⟨*Fußgänger:*⟩ vorbeigehen; ⟨*Fahrer, Fahrzeug:*⟩ vorbeifahren; ⟨*Prozession:*⟩ vorbeiziehen; (by chance) ⟨*Person, Fahrzeug:*⟩ vorbeikommen; *see also* **side A 5**

- **~ ˈdown** ▸**hand down 1, 3**
- **~ for** *v.t.* durchgehen für; gehalten werden für
- **~ ˈoff**

A *v.t.* **1** (represent falsely) ausgeben (**as, for** als); als echt ausgeben ⟨*Fälschung*⟩ **2** (turn attention away from) hinweggehen über (+ *Akk.*)
B *v.i.* **1** (disappear gradually) ⟨*Schock, Schmerz, Hochstimmung:*⟩ abklingen, sich legen **2** (take place, be carried through) verlaufen

- **~ ˈon**

A *v.i.* **1** (proceed) fortfahren; weitermachen; **~ on to sth.** zu etw. übergehen **2** (euphem.: die) die Augen schließen *od.* zumachen (verhüll.)

P

B *v.t.* weitergeben (**to** an + *Akk.*); vererben ‹*Besitz, Krankheit*›
- **~ out**

A /'-'-/ *v.i.* **1** (faint) ohnmächtig werden (**with** vor + *Dat.*) **2** (complete military training) seine militärische Ausbildung abschließen
B /'--/ *v.t.* bekannt geben, bekannt machen ‹*Informationen*›
- **~ 'over**

A *v.t.* übergehen; überschreiten ‹*Grenze, Schwelle*›; **~ sth. over in silence** etw. stillschweigend übergehen; *see also* **~ B 2**
B *v.i.* (euphem.: die) die Augen schließen *od.* zumachen (verhüll.)
- **~ through**

A /'--/ *v.t.* durchmachen ‹*schwierige Zeit, Krankheit*›; durchleben ‹*Augenblick*›; ‹*Buch:*› gehen durch ‹*Hände*›; **it ~ed through my mind** es ging mir durch den Sinn; *see also* **~ B 2**
B /-'-/ *v.i.* durchreisen; **be just ~ing through** nur auf der Durchreise sein
- **~ 'up** *v.t.* sich (*Dat.*) entgehen lassen, ungenutzt vorübergehen lassen ‹*Gelegenheit*›; ablehnen, ausschlagen ‹*Angebot, Einladung*›

passable /'pɑːsəbl/ *adj.* **1** (acceptable) passabel, annehmbar ‹*Versuch, Arbeit, Essen, Porträt*› **2** (in condition to be crossed, traversed) passierbar, befahrbar ‹*Straße*›

passably /'pɑːsəblɪ/ *adv.* passabel; annehmbar; einigermaßen ‹*höflich, angenehm, gut aussehend*›

passage /'pæsɪdʒ/ *n.* **1** (going by, through, etc.) (of river) Überquerung, *die;* (of time) [Ab-, Ver]lauf, *der;* Verstreichen, *das;* (of seasons) Wechsel, *der;* **erased by the ~ of time** ausgelöscht vom Strom der Zeit; **their ~ was halted by an obstruction** ein Hindernis hemmte ihren Weg **2** (transition) Übergang, *der* **3** (voyage) Überfahrt, *die* **4** (way) Gang, *der;* (corridor) Korridor, *der;* (between houses) Durchgang, *der;* (in shopping precinct) Passage, *die;* (for ship, boat, car) Durchfahrt, *die* **5** *no art., no pl.* (liberty or right to pass through) Durchreise, *die;* **guarantee sb. rights of ~ through a territory** jmdm. die Durchreise durch ein Gebiet genehmigen **6** (right to travel) Passage, *die;* **work one's ~:** seine Überfahrt abarbeiten **7** (part of book etc.) Passage, *die;* Textstelle, *die* **8** (Mus.) Passage, *die;* Stelle, *die* **9** (of a bill into law) parlamentarische Behandlung; (final) Annahme, *die;* Verabschiedung, *die* **10** (duct) **urinary ~:** Harntrakt, *der;* **ear ~:** Gehörgang, *der;* **air ~s** Luft- *od.* Atemwege. *See also* **back passage**; **bird of passage**; **front passage**; **purple passage**; **rite**

'passageway *n.* Gang, *der;* (between houses) Durchgang, *der*

pass: ~book *n.* **1** (bank book) Bankbuch, *das;* Kontobuch, *das;* **2** (S. Afr.) *Ausweispapier für Farbige;* **~ degree** *n.* (Brit. Univ.) **get a ~ degree** ein Examen ohne Prädikat bestehen

passé *adj. masc.*, **passée** *adj. fem.* /'pæseɪ/ **1** (past prime) angekratzt (salopp); verblüht ‹*Frau*› **2** (outmoded) überholt; passee *nicht attr.*

passel /'pæsl/ *n.* (Amer. coll.) Schar, *die*

passenger /'pæsɪndʒə(r)/ *n.* **1** (traveller) (on ship) Passagier, *der;* (on plane) Passagier, *der;* Fluggast, *der;* (on train) Reisende, *der/die;* (on bus, in taxi) Fahrgast, *der;* (in car, on motorcycle) Mitfahrer, *der*/Mitfahrerin, *die;* (in front seat of car) Beifahrer, *der*/Beifahrerin, *die* **2** (coll.: ineffective member) *Mensch, der/Tier, das von den anderen mit durchgeschleppt wird* (ugs.); **feel like a mere ~ in an enterprise** sich bei einem Unternehmen wie das fünfte Rad am Wagen fühlen; **we cannot afford to have ~s in our team** Leute, die nichts leisten, können wir in unserem Team nicht gebrauchen

passenger: ~ aircraft *n.* Passagierflugzeug, *das;* **~ door** *n.* Beifahrertür, *die;* **~ elevator** (Amer.), **~ lift** (Brit.) *ns.* Personenaufzug, *der;* **~ ferry** *n.* Personenfähre, *die;* **~ list** *n.* Passagierliste, *die;* **~ lounge** *n.* Warteraum, *der;* **~ mile** *n.* Personenmeile, *die;* Passagiermeile, *die* (Flugw.); **~ plane** *n.* Passagierflugzeug, *das;* **~ seat** *n.* Beifahrersitz, *der;* **~ service** *n.* (train) Personenzugverbindung, *die;* (ferry) Personenfährverbindung, *die;* **all ~ services out of London Victoria Station** alle Personenzüge ab London Victoria Station; **~ train** *n.* Zug im Personenverkehr

passer-by /pɑːsə'baɪ/ *n.* Passant, *der*/Passantin, *die*

passim /'pæsɪm/ *adv.* (literary) passim

passing /'pɑːsɪŋ/

A *n.* **1** (going by) (of time, years) Lauf, *der;* (of winter) Vorübergehen, *das;* (of old year) Ausklang, *der;* (death) Ende, *das;* Hinscheiden, *das* (geh. verhüll.); **in ~:** beiläufig ‹*bemerken usw.*›; flüchtig ‹*begrüßen*› **2** ▸ **passage 9**
B *adj.* **1** (going past) vorbeifahrend ‹*Zug, Auto*›; vorbeikommend ‹*Person*›; vorbeiziehend ‹*Schatten*›; **they depend on the ~ trade** sie sind von der Laufkundschaft abhängig; **with every ~ moment** von Minute zu Minute **2** (fleeting) flüchtig ‹*Blick*›; vorübergehend ‹*Mode, Laune, Interesse*› **3** (superficial) flüchtig ‹*Bekanntschaft*›; oberflächlich ‹*Kenntnisse*›; (cursory) beiläufig ‹*Bemerkung*›; schnell vorübergehend ‹*Empfindung*›
C *adv.* (arch.) überaus

passing: ~ note *n.* (Mus.) Durchgangston, *der;* Durchgangsdissonanz, *die;* **~-'out [ceremony]** *n.* (Mil. etc.) Abschlussfeier, *die;* **~ place** *n.* Ausweichstelle, *die;* **~ shot** *n.* (Tennis) Passierschlag, *der;* Passierschuss, *der;* **~ tone** (Amer.) ▸ **~ note**

passion /'pæʃn/ *n.* **1** (emotion) Leidenschaft, *die;* Leidenschaftlichkeit, *die* **2** (outburst) Gefühlsausbruch, *der;* (of anger) Wutanfall, *der;* **fly into a ~:** einen Wutanfall bekommen **3** (sexual love) Leidenschaft, *die;* (lust) Begierde, *die;* (desire) Verlangen, *das* **4** (enthusiasm) leidenschaftliche Begeisterung; (object arousing enthusiasm) Leidenschaft, *die;* **he has a ~ for steam engines** Dampfloks sind seine Leidenschaft; er hat eine Passion für Dampfloks; **have a ~ for lobster/interfering in people's lives** leidenschaftlich gern Hummer essen/sich mit Begeisterung in anderer Leute Angelegenheiten einmischen; **sth. is sb.'s ~/sb.'s ~ is doing sth.** etw./etw. tun ist jmds. Leidenschaft *od.* ist bei jmdm. eine Leidenschaft **5** **P~** (Relig., Mus.) Passion, *die;* Leiden Christi *Pl.;* (narrative) Leidens- *od.* Passionsgeschichte, *die;* **Bach's 'St Matthew P~'** die Matthäuspassion von Bach

passionate /'pæʃənət/ *adj.* **1** (quick-tempered) hitzig; leidenschaftlich; heftig; **a ~ young man** ein Hitzkopf **2** (ardent) leidenschaftlich ‹*Person*›; heftig ‹*Verlangen*›; **have a ~ faith in sb.** mit glühender Begeisterung an jmdn. glauben; **have a ~ belief in sth.** mit unbeirrbarem Eifer von etw. überzeugt sein **3** (expressing violent or intense feeling) leidenschaftlich ‹*Rede*›; (unrestrained) leidenschaftlich; hemmungslos; **make a ~ plea for mercy** inständig um Gnade bitten *od.* flehen

passionately /'pæʃənətlɪ/ *adv.* leidenschaftlich; mit Leidenschaft; hemmungslos ‹*weinen*›; inständig ‹*bitten*›; **be ~ fond of lobster/cricket** leidenschaftlich gerne Hummer essen/Cricket mögen

passion: ~ flower *n.* (Bot.) Passionsblume, *die;* **~ fruit** *n.* Passionsfrucht, *die;* Maracuja, *die;* **~ play** *n.* Passionsspiel, *das;* **P~ 'Sunday** *n.* Passionssonntag, *der;* **P~ Week** *n.* **1** (before Palm Sunday) die Woche nach dem ersten Passionssonntag; **2** (after Palm Sunday) die Karwoche

passive /'pæsɪv/

A *adj.* **1** (suffering action, acted upon) passiv **2** (without opposition) passiv; teilnahmslos; widerstandslos; widerspruchslos ‹*Hinnahme, Annahme*›; **remain ~:** unbeteiligt bleiben; **~ resistance** passiver Widerstand; **~ smoker** Passivraucher, *der*/-raucherin, *die;* **~ smoking** passives Rauchen **3** (inert) regungslos ‹*Gestalt, Körper, Wasserfläche*›; unbewegt ‹*Wasserfläche*›; passiv ‹*Rolle*›; **your son is too ~:** Ihr Sohn ist zu passiv *od.* hat zu wenig Initiative **4** (not expressed) unausgesprochen **5** (Metallurgy: unreactive) passiv **6** (Ling.) Passiv-; passivisch; **~ voice** Passiv, *das;* **~ vocabulary** passiver Wortschatz
B *n.* (Ling.) Passiv, *das*

passive 'house *n.* (Archit.) Passivhaus, *das*

passively /'pæsɪvlɪ/ *adv.* teilnahmslos, unbeteiligt ‹*dasitzen, lächeln, hinnehmen*›; tatenlos ‹*zusehen*›; **be ~ involved in sth.** bei etw. eine passive Rolle spielen

passiveness /'pæsɪvnɪs/, **passivity** /pæ'sɪvɪtɪ/ *ns., no pl.* Passivität, *die;* Teilnahmslosigkeit, *die*

pass: ~ key *n.* **1** (master key) Hauptschlüssel, *der;* **2** (private key) Hausschlüssel, *der;* **~ mark** *n.* Mindestpunktzahl, *die;* **the ~ mark was 40%** zum Bestehen [der Klausur *etc.*] mussten mindestens 40% der Punkte erreicht werden; **P~over** *n.* Passah, *das;* **the feast of P~over** das Passahfest; **~port** *n.* **1** [Reise]pass, *der; attrib.* Pass-; **2** (fig.) Schlüssel, *der* (**to** zu); **~word** *n.* **1** Parole, *die;* Losung, *die;* **2** (Computing) Passwort, *das;* **~word-pro'tected** *adj.* passwortgeschützt

past /pɑːst/

A *adj.* **1** *pred.* (over) vorbei; vorüber **2** *attrib.* (previous) früher; vergangen; verflossen (geh.) ‹*Jahre*›; früher, ehemalig ‹*Präsident, Vorsitzende usw.*›; **~ history** Vorleben, *das;* **she has a ~ history of violence** sie hat ein gewalttätiges Vorleben; **this is all ~ history** das ist alles Vergangenheit; **her ~ behaviour** *or* **conduct** ihr Verhalten in der Vergangenheit; **in centuries ~:** in vergangenen *od.* früheren Jahrhunderten **3** (just gone by) letzt...; vergangen; **for weeks ~:** während der letzten Wochen; **in the ~ few days** während der letzten Tage; **the ~ hour/decade** die letzte *od.* vergangene Stunde/das letzte *od.* vorige Jahrzehnt **4** (Ling.) **~ tense** Vergangenheit, *die;* Präteritum, *das;* **~ definite, ~ historic** historisches Perfekt; **~ perfect** ▸ **pluperfect**; *see also* **participle**
B *n.* **1** Vergangenheit, *die;* (that which happened in the **~**) Vergangene, *das;* Gewesene, *das;* **in the ~:** früher; in der Vergangenheit ‹*leben*›; **be a thing of the ~:** der Vergangenheit (*Dat.*) angehören **2** (previous history) Vergangenheit, *die;* **a woman with a ~:** eine Frau mit Vergangenheit **3** (Ling.) Vergangenheit, *die;* **be/put in the ~:** in der Vergangenheit stehen/in die Vergangenheit setzen
C *prep.* ▸ **❶ p. 1001** **1** (beyond in time) nach; (beyond in place) hinter (+ *Dat.*); **half ~ three** halb vier; **five [minutes] ~ two** fünf [Minuten] nach zwei; **it's ~ midnight** es ist schon nach Mitternacht *od.* Mitternacht vorbei; **it's ~ the time he said he'd arrive** um diese Zeit wollte er eigentlich schon hier sein; **he is ~ sixty** er ist über sechzig; **she's ~ the age for having children** sie ist schon zu alt, um Kinder zu bekommen; **gaze/walk ~ sb./sth.** an jmdm./etw. vorbeiblicken/vorüber- *od.* vorbeigehen **2** (not capable of) **~ repair/all comprehension** nicht mehr zu reparieren/völlig unverständlich; **he is ~ help/caring** ihm ist nicht mehr zu helfen/es kümmert ihn nicht mehr; **be/be getting ~ it** (coll.) [ein bisschen] zu alt sein/allmählich zu alt werden; **I wouldn't put it ~ her to do that** ich würde es ihr schon zutrauen, dass sie das tut; **I wouldn't put anything ~ him** ihm ist alles zuzutrauen
D *adv.* vorbei; vorüber; **hurry ~:** vorüber- *od.* vorbeieilen

pasta /'pæstə, 'pɑːstə/ *n.* Nudeln *Pl.;* Teigwaren *Pl.*

paste /peɪst/

A *n.* **1** Brei, *der;* (for cakes) Teig, *der;* **mix into a smooth/thick ~:** zu einem lockeren/dicken Brei anrühren; zu einem glatten/festen Teig anrühren ‹*Backmischung*› **2** (glue) Kleister, *der* **3** (of meat, fish, etc.) Paste, *die;* (sweet doughy confection) Masse, *die;* **anchovy ~:** Sardellenpaste, *die;* **almond ~:** Marzipanmasse, *die* **4** *no pl., no indef. art.* (imitation gems) Strass, *der;* Similisteine *Pl.* **5** (Pottery) Brei, *der*
B *v.t.* **1** (fasten with glue) kleben; **~ sth. down/into sth.** etw. ankleben/in etw. (*Akk.*) einkleben **2** (coll.: beat, thrash, bomb) in die Pfanne hauen (ugs.) **3** (Computing) einfügen (**into** in + *Akk.*); *see also* **cut**

Phrasal verbs

- **~ 'over** *v.t.* überkleben
- **~ 'up** *v.t.* ankleben (**on** an + *Akk.*); *see also* **paste-up**

P

'pasteboard
A n. Pappe, *die;* Karton, *der;*
B *adj.* Papp-; (fig.) hohl ‹*Glanz*›; billig ‹*Konstruktion*›

pastel /'pæstl/
A *n.* **1** (crayon) Pastellstift, *der;* Pastellkreide, *die* **2** (drawing) Pastellzeichnung, *die* **3** (art) Pastellmalerei, *die;* Pastell, *das*
B *adj.* pastellen; pastellfarben; Pastell‹*farben, -töne, -zeichnung, -bild*›; **~ green** Pastellgrün, *das*

'paste-up *n.* Klebeumbruch, *der;* Montage, *die*

pasteurisation, pasteurise ▸ **pasteuriz-**

pasteurization /pæstʃəraɪ'zeɪʃn, pɑːstʃəraɪ'zeɪʃn/ *n.* Pasteurisation, *die;* Pasteurisierung, *die*

pasteurize /'pæstʃəraɪz, 'pɑːstʃəraɪz/ *v.t.* pasteurisieren

pastiche /pæ'stiːʃ/
A *n.* Pastiche, *das*
B *adj.* pasticheartig

pastie ▸ **pasty**[1]

pastille /'pæstɪl/ *n.* Pastille, *die*

pastime /'pɑːstaɪm/ *n.* Zeitvertreib, *der;* (person's specific ~) Hobby, *das;* **my ~s are tennis and cricket** in meiner Freizeit spiele ich Tennis und Cricket; **amuse oneself/while away the time with various ~s** sich (*Dat.*) die Zeit mit verschiedenen Beschäftigungen vertreiben; **national ~:** Nationalsport, *der* (auch iron.); **favourite ~:** Lieblingsbeschäftigung, *die*

pasting /'peɪstɪŋ/ *n.* (coll.) **give sb. a ~:** jmdm. eins überbraten (salopp); **take a ~:** eins übergebraten kriegen (salopp); (from critics) verrissen werden (ugs.)

past 'master *n.* (fig.) Meister, *der*

pastor /'pɑːstə(r)/ *n.* ▸❶ **p. 1260** Pfarrer, *der*/Pfarrerin, *die;* Pastor, *der*/Pastorin, *die*

pastoral /'pɑːstərl/
A *adj.* **1** Weide-; ländlich ‹*Reiz, Idylle, Umgebung*› **2** (Lit., Art, Mus.) pastoral; **~ poetry** Hirten-, Schäferdichtung, *die;* (ancient) Bukolik, *die;* **~ drama** Schäferspiel, *das;* **~ theme** ländliches Motiv **3** (Eccl.) pastoral; des Pfarrers *nachgestellt;* Hirten‹*amt, -brief*›; seelsorgerisch ‹*Pflicht, Aufgabe, Leitung, Aktivitäten*›; **~ care** Seelsorge, *die* **4** (relating to shepherds) **~ economy** Weidewirtschaft, *die;* **a ~ people** ein Hirtenvolk
B *n.* (Lit., Art, Mus.) Pastorale, *das od. die*

pastorale /pæstə'rɑːl/ ▸ **pastoral B**

pastrami /pæ'strɑːmɪ/ *n., no pl. geräuchertes, stark gewürztes Rindfleisch (vom Schulterstück)*

pastry /'peɪstrɪ/ *n.* **1** (flour paste) Teig, *der* **2** (article of food) Gebäckstück, *das* **3** **pastries** *collect.* [Fein]gebäck, *das*

pastry: ~ board *n.* Backbrett, *das;* **~ cook** *n.* Konditor, *der*/Konditorin, *die;* **~ cutter** *n.* Ausstechform, *die;* **~ wheel** *n.* Kuchenrad, *das*

pasturage /'pɑːstʃərɪdʒ, 'pɑːstjʊərɪdʒ/ *n.* **1** (grazing) Weide, *die;* **rights of ~:** Weiderecht, *das* **2** (grass) Futter, *das;* Gras, *das* **3** (land) Weideland, *das*

pasture /'pɑːstʃə(r)/
A *n.* **1** (grass) Futter, *das;* Gras, *das;* **~ for cattle** Viehfutter, *das* **2** (land) Weideland, *das;* (piece of land) Weide, *die* **3** (fig.) **home ~s** heimatliche Gefilde *Pl.* (scherzh.); **in search of ~s new** auf der Suche nach etwas Neuem
B *v.t.* (lead or put to pasture) weiden [lassen]
C *v.i.* weiden; grasen

'pastureland *n.* Weideland, *das*

pasty[1] /'pæstɪ/ *n.* Pastete, *die*

pasty[2] /'peɪstɪ/ *adj.* **1** teigig; zähflüssig **2** ▸ **pasty-faced**

pasty-faced /'peɪstɪfeɪst/ *adj.* mit teigigem Gesicht *nachgestellt;* **be ~:** ein teigiges Gesicht haben

pat[1] /pæt/
A *n.* **1** (stroke, tap) Klaps, *der;* leichter Schlag; **give sb./a dog a ~:** jmdn./einen Hund tätscheln; (once) jmdm./einem Hund einen Klaps geben; **give sb./a dog a ~ on the head** jmdm./einem Hund den Kopf tätscheln; **give sb. a ~ on the shoulder** jmdm. auf die Schulter klopfen; **a ~ on the back** (fig.) eine Anerkennung; **she deserves a ~ on the back** (fig.) sie verdient Anerkennung *od.* ein Lob; **give oneself/sb. a ~ on the back** (fig.) sich (*Dat.*) [selbst] auf die Schulter klopfen/jmdm. einige anerkennende Worte sagen **2** (of butter) Stückchen, *das;* (of mud, clay) Klümpchen, *das; see also* **cowpat**
B *v.t.*, **-tt-** **1** (strike gently) leicht klopfen auf (+ *Akk.*); tätscheln, (once) einen Klaps geben (+ *Dat.*) ‹*Person, Hund, Pferd*›; **~ sb. on the arm/head/cheek** jmdm. den Arm/Kopf/die Wange tätscheln; **~ oneself/sb. on the back** (fig.) sich (*Dat.*) [selbst]/jmdm. auf die Schulter klopfen; **~ one's face dry** sein Gesicht trockentupfen **2** (flatten) festklopfen ‹*Sand*›; andrücken ‹*Haare*›; **~ flat** flach klopfen; **~ one's hair into place** sich (*Dat.*) das Haar zurechtlegen

pat[2]
A *adv.* (ready, prepared) **have sth. off ~:** etw. parat haben; **know sth. off ~:** etw. aus dem Effeff können *od.* beherrschen (ugs.); etw. in- und auswendig können; **come ~** ‹*Antwort:*› wie aus der Pistole geschossen kommen; (opportunely) ‹*Geschichte:*› wie gerufen kommen; **stand ~** (fig.) keinen Zollbreit nachgeben; unbeirrbar sein
B *adj.* (ready) allzu schlagfertig ‹*Antwort*›; (opportune) passend; treffend; **he has some ~ phrases for every occasion** er hat für jede Gelegenheit einen Spruch parat (ugs.)

patch /pætʃ/
A *n.* **1** Stelle, *die;* **inflamed ~es of skin** entzündete [Haut]stellen; **a ~ of blue sky** ein Stückchen blauer Himmel; **there were still ~es of snow** es lag vereinzelt *od.* hier und da noch Schnee; **the dog had a black ~ on its ear** der Hund hatte einen schwarzen Fleck am Ohr; **there were ~es of black ice on the roads** auf den Straßen war stellenweise Glatteis; **there were ~es of sunshine** auf einige Stellen schien die Sonne; **~es of rain** (during period of time) ab und zu Regen; (in several places) stellenweise Regen; **fog ~es** Nebelfelder; **we went through one or two rough ~es on our crossing** während der Überfahrt hatten wir ein- oder zweimal raue See; **in ~es** stellenweise; **go through** *or* **strike a bad/good ~** (Brit.) eine Pech-/Glückssträhne haben; **a sticky ~ in her life** eine schwierige Phase in ihrem Leben **2** (on worn garment) Flicken, *der;* **be not a ~ on sth.** (fig. coll.) nichts gegen etw. sein; nicht an etw. (*Akk.*) heranreichen **3** (on eye) Augenklappe, *die;* **wear a ~ on one eye** eine Augenklappe tragen **4** (piece of ground) Stück Land, *das;* **every ~ of ground** jeder Zentimeter Boden; **potato ~:** Kartoffelacker, *der;* (in garden) Kartoffelbeet, *das* **5** (area patrolled by police; also fig.) Revier, *das;* **keep off our ~** (fig.) komm uns ja nicht ins Gehege **6** (Mil.: badge) Schulterklappe, *die;* Schulterstück, *das* **7** (Hist.: beauty spot) Schönheitspflästerchen, *das;* Mouche, *die* (geh.)
B *v.t.* (apply ~ to) flicken

Phrasal verbs

- **~ to'gether** *v.t.* zusammenstücke[l]n; (fig.) zusammenflicken, zusammenstoppeln (ugs. abwertend) ‹*Buch, Artikel*›; zusammenschustern (ugs. abwertend) ‹*Grundsatzprogramm, Vereinbarung*›
- **~ 'up** *v.t.* reparieren; zusammenflicken ‹*Segel, Buch*›; notdürftig verbinden ‹*Wunde*›; zusammenflicken (scherzh.) ‹*Verletzten*›; (fig.) beilegen ‹*Streit, Differenzen*›; kitten ‹*Ehe, Freundschaft*›; **try to ~ the matter up** versuchen, die Sache wieder ins Lot zu bringen

patch: ~ pocket *n.* aufgesetzte Tasche; **~work** *n.* Patchwork, *das;* **a ~work quilt** eine Patchworkdecke; (fig.) **a ~work of fields** ein bunter Teppich von Feldern

patchy /'pætʃɪ/ *adj.* uneinheitlich ‹*Qualität*›; ungleichmäßig, unterschiedlich ‹*Arbeit, Aufführung, Ausstoß*›; unausgewogen ‹*Darbietung*›; fleckig ‹*Anstrich*›; stellenweise spärlich ‹*Ernte*›; sehr lückenhaft ‹*Wissen*›; in der Qualität unterschiedlich ‹*Film, Buch, Theaterstück*›

pate /peɪt/ *n.* (arch.) Haupt, *das* (geh.); (coll.) Birne, *die* (salopp); Rübe, *die* (salopp); **bald ~:** Glatze, *die*

pâté /'pæteɪ/ *n.* Pastete, *die;* **~ de foie gras** /'pæteɪ/'pɑːteɪ də fwɑ 'grɑː/ Gänseleberpastete, *die*

patella /pə'telə/ *n., pl.* **~e** /pə'teliː/ (Anat.) Kniescheibe, *die;* Patella, *die* (fachspr.)

paten /'pætn/ *n.* (Eccl.) Patene, *die;* Hostienteller, *der*

patent /'peɪtənt, 'pætənt/
A *adj.* **1** patentiert; patentrechtlich geschützt; gesetzlich geschützt; (fig.: characteristic) ureigen; **~ medicine** Markenmedizin, *die;* patentrechtlich geschütztes Arzneimittel; **~ article** Markenartikel, *der;* **~ remedy** Spezial- *od.* Patentrezept, *das;* Patentlösung, *die* **2** (obvious) offenkundig; offensichtlich
B *n.* **1** (licence) Patent, *das;* **~ applied for** *or* **pending** Patent angemeldet; **take out a ~ for** *or* **on sth.** sich (*Dat.*) etw. patentieren lassen **2** (invention or process) Patent, *das* **3** (fig.: exclusive property or claim) Patent, *das* (**on** auf + *Akk.*)
C *v.t.* patentieren lassen; **sth. has been ~ed** etw. ist patentrechtlich geschützt

patentable /'peɪtəntəbl, 'pætəntəbl/ *adj.* patentfähig

patent: ~ agent (Brit.), **~ attorney** (Amer.) *ns.* ▸❶ **p. 1260** Patentanwalt, *der*/-anwältin, *die*

patentee /peɪtən'tiː, pætən'tiː/ *n.* Patentinhaber, *der*/-inhaberin, *die*

patent 'leather *n.* Lackleder, *das;* **~ shoes** Lackschuhe

patently /'peɪtəntlɪ, 'pætəntlɪ/ *adv.* offenkundig; offensichtlich; **~ obvious** ganz offenkundig *od.* offensichtlich

patent: ~ office *n.* Patentamt, *das;* **~ rights** *n. pl.* Erfinderrecht, *das*

paterfamilias /peɪtəfə'mɪlɪæs, pætəfə'mɪlɪæs/ *n.* (often joc.) Familienoberhaupt, *das;* Paterfamilias, *der* (geh. scherzh.)

paternal /pə'tɜːnl/ *adj.* **1** (fatherly) väterlich **2** (related) ‹*Großeltern, Onkel, Tante*› väterlicherseits

paternalism /pə'tɜːnəlɪzm/ *n.* Bevormundung, *die*

paternalistic /pətɜːnə'lɪstɪk/ *adj.* patriarchalisch; paternalistisch

paternally /pə'tɜːnəlɪ/ *adv.* väterlich

paternity /pə'tɜːnɪtɪ/ *n.* **1** (fatherhood) Vaterschaft, *die;* **deny ~ of a child** die Vaterschaft an einem Kind bestreiten *od.* leugnen **2** (origin) Abstammung väterlicherseits, *die*

paternity: ~ leave *n.* Vaterschaftsurlaub, *der;* **~ suit** *n.* Vaterschaftsklage, *die;* Vaterschaftsprozess, *der;* **~ test** *n.* Vaterschaftsuntersuchung, *die*

paternoster /pætə'nɒstə(r)/ *n.* **1** (prayer) Vaterunser, *das;* Paternoster, *das* **2** (lift) Paternoster, *der*

path /pɑːθ/ *n., pl.* **~s** /pɑːðz/ **1** (way) Weg, *der;* Pfad, *der;* (merely made by walking) Trampelpfad, *der;* **keep to the ~:** auf dem Weg bleiben **2** (line of motion) Bahn, *die;* (of tornado, caravan, etc.) Weg, *der;* **his ~ led across fields and meadows** sein Weg führte ihn über Felder und Wiesen; **into the ~ of a moving vehicle** vor ein Fahrzeug; *see also* **flight path** **3** (fig.: course of action) Weg, *der;* **the middle ~:** der Mittelweg; **our ~s crossed/diverged** unsere Wege kreuzten/trennten sich; **the ~ to salvation/of virtue** der Weg des Heils/der Pfad der Tugend

pathetic /pə'θetɪk/ *adj.* **1** (pitiful) Mitleid erregend; herzergreifend; **be a ~ sight** ein Bild des Jammers bieten **2** (full of pathos) pathetisch **3** (contemptible) armselig ‹*Entschuldigung*›; erbärmlich ‹*Darbietung, Rede, Person, Leistung*›; **you're/it's ~:** du bist ein hoffnungsloser Fall/es ist wirklich ein schwaches Bild (ugs.); **are these ~ scribbles meant to be art?** soll dieses jämmerliche Gekritzel vielleicht Kunst sein? **4** **~ fallacy** Vermenschlichung der Natur, *die*

pathetically /pə'θetɪkəlɪ/ *adv.* **1** (pitifully) Mitleid erregend ‹*stöhnen*›; herzergreifend ‹*flehen*› **2** (contemptibly) erbärmlich; erschreckend

P

‹wenig›; ~ **bad** miserabel

'pathfinder n. 1 (person) jmd., der jmdm. den Weg findet/zeigt; (fig.) Wegbereiter, der/-bereiterin, die; Bahnbrecher, der/Bahnbrecherin, die 2 (aircraft) Pfadfinder, der (Milit.)

pathless /'pɑːθlɪs/ adj. weglos

'pathname n. (Computing) Pfad[name], der

pathogen /'pæθədʒən/ n. (Med.) [Krankheits]erreger, der

pathogenic /pæθə'dʒenɪk/ adj. (Med.) pathogen (fachspr.); krankheitserregend

pathological /pæθə'lɒdʒɪkl/ adj. 1 pathologisch; Pathologie- 2 (morbid) pathologisch; krankhaft 3 (fig.: obsessive) krankhaft; pathologisch

pathologically /pæθə'lɒdʒɪkəlɪ/ adv. pathologisch; (fig.: obsessively) krankhaft

pathologist /pə'θɒlədʒɪst/ n. ▸ℹ **p. 1260** Pathologe, der/Pathologin, die

pathology /pə'θɒlədʒɪ/ n. 1 (science) Pathologie, die 2 (symptoms) Symptomatik, die; **the ~ of a disease** das Krankheitsbild

pathos /'peɪθɒs/ n. Pathos, das

'pathway n. 1 ▸**path 1** 2 (Physiol.) Bahn, die; Leitung, die; **optical ~:** Sehbahn, die

patience /'peɪʃəns/ n. 1 no pl., no art. Geduld, die; (perseverance) Ausdauer, die; Beharrlichkeit, die; (forbearance) Langmut, die; **with ~:** geduldig; **have endless ~:** eine Engelsgeduld haben; **my ~ is finally exhausted** meine Geduld ist jetzt am Ende od. erschöpft; **lose [one's] ~ [with sth./sb.]** [mit etw./jmdm.] die Geduld verlieren; **I lost my ~:** mir riss der Geduldsfaden (ugs.) od. die Geduld; **~ is a virtue** (prov.) Geduld ist eine Tugend; **it is enough to try the ~ of a saint** das ist eine harte Geduldsprobe; **have the ~ of a saint** eine Engelsgeduld haben 2 (Brit. Cards) Patience, die. See also **Job**

patient /'peɪʃənt/

A adj. geduldig; (forbearing) langmütig; (persevering) beharrlich; **please be ~:** bitte hab Geduld; gedulde dich bitte; **remain ~:** sich in Geduld fassen

B n. ▸ℹ **p. 1231** Patient, der/Patientin, die

patient 'care n., no pl. Patientenversorgung, die

patiently /'peɪʃəntlɪ/ adv. (with composure) geduldig; mit Geduld; (with forbearance) geduldig; nachsichtig; (with calm) geduldig; (with perseverance) beharrlich; ausdauernd

patina /'pætɪnə/ n. (on bronze) Patina, die; (on woodwork) Altersglanz, der; (fig.) Patina, die

patio /'pætɪəʊ/ n., pl. **~s** 1 (paved area) Veranda, die; Terrasse, die 2 (inner court) Innenhof, der; Patio, der

patio 'door n. große Glasschiebetür (zum Garten)

patisserie /pə'tɪsərɪ/ n. 1 (shop) Konditorei, die 2 (cakes and pastries) Feingebäck, das

Patna rice /'pætnə raɪs/ n. Patnareis, der

patois /'pætwɑː/ n., pl. same 1 (dialect) Mundart, die; Dialekt, der 2 (jargon) Jargon, der

patriarch /'peɪtrɪɑːk/ n. 1 (of family) Familienoberhaupt, das; Patriarch, der; (of tribe) Stammesoberhaupt, das; Häuptling, der 2 (Relig.) (in early and Orthodox Church) Patriarch, der; (RC Ch.) Bischof von Rom, der 3 (founder) Begründer, der 4 (old man) ehrwürdiger Greis

patriarchal /peɪtrɪ'ɑːkl/ adj. 1 patriarchalisch 2 (old, venerable) [alt]ehrwürdig

patriarchy /'peɪtrɪɑːkɪ/ n. Patriarchat, das

patrician /pə'trɪʃn/

A n. (Hist.) Patrizier, der/Patrizierin, die

B adj. 1 (noble) vornehm; edel 2 (Hist.) patrizisch; Patrizier-; **~ family** Patrizierfamilie, die; Patriziergeschlecht, das

patricide /'pætrɪsaɪd/ n. 1 (murder) Vatermord, der 2 (murderer) Vatermörder, der/Vatermörderin, die

patrimony /'pætrɪmənɪ/ n. Patrimonium, das; väterliches Erbe; (fig.) Erbe, das; (endowment) Vermögen, das

patriot /'pætrɪət, 'peɪtrɪət/ n. Patriot, der/Patriotin, die

patriotic /pætrɪ'ɒtɪk, peɪtrɪ'ɒtɪk/ adj. patriotisch

patriotism /'pætrɪətɪzm, 'peɪtrɪətɪzm/ n. Patriotismus, der; vaterländische Gesinnung

patrol /pə'trəʊl/

A n. 1 (of police) Streife, die; (of watchman) Runde, die; Rundgang, der; (of aircraft, ship) Patrouille, die; (Mil.) Patrouille, die; **put sb. on ~:** jmdn. auf Streife od. (Milit.) Patrouille schicken; **policeman on ~:** Streifenpolizist, der; **be on** or **keep ~** ‹Soldat, Wächter:› patrouillieren 2 (person, group) (Police) Streife, die; (Mil.) Patrouille, die; **coast ~:** Küstenwache, die; Küstenwacht, die; **police ~:** Polizeistreife, die; **army ~:** Militärpatrouille, die; Militärstreife, die; **fire ~:** Brandwache, die 3 (troops) Spähtrupp, der; Spähpatrouille, die 4 (unit) (of Scouts) Fähnlein, das; (of Guides) Gilde, die

B v.i., **-ll-** patrouillieren; ‹Polizei:› Streife laufen/fahren; ‹Wachmann:› seine Runde[n] machen; ‹Flugzeug:› Patrouille fliegen

C v.t., **-ll-** patrouillieren durch (+ Akk.); abpatrouillieren ‹Straßen, Mauer, Gegend, Lager›; patrouillieren vor (+ Dat.) ‹Küste, Grenze›; ‹Polizei:› Streife laufen/fahren in (+ Dat.) ‹Straßen, Stadtteil›; ‹Wachmann:› seine Runde[n] machen in (+ Dat.)

patrol: ~ boat n. Patrouillenboot, das; **~ car** n. Streifenwagen, der; **~man** /pə'trəʊlmən/ n., pl. **~men** /pə'trəʊlmən/ ▸ℹ **p. 1260** (Amer.) [Streifen]polizist, der; **~ wagon** n. (Amer.) Gefangenenwagen, der

patron /'peɪtrən/ n. 1 (supporter) Gönner, der/Gönnerin, die; (of institution, campaign) Schirmherr, der/Schirmherrin, die; **~ of the arts** Kunstmäzen, der 2 (customer) (of shop) Kunde, der/Kundin, die; (of restaurant, hotel) Gast, der; (of theatre, cinema) Besucher, der/Besucherin, die; **'~s only'** „nur für Kunden/Gäste" 3 **~ [saint]** Schutzheilige, der/die; Schutzpatron, der/Schutzpatronin, die 4 (Brit. Eccl.) Pfründner, der/Pfründnerin, die

patronage /'pætrənɪdʒ/ n. 1 (support) Gönnerschaft, die; Unterstützung, die; (for campaign, institution) Schirmherrschaft, die 2 (customer's support) Kundschaft, die; **we thank our customers for their ~:** wir danken unseren Kunden für ihr od. das in uns gesetzte Vertrauen; **withdraw one's ~:** ein Geschäft usw. nicht mehr betreten 3 (dated: condescension) Gönnerhaftigkeit, die; **with an air of ~:** mit Gönnermiene od. gönnerhafter Miene 4 (Polit.) Recht der Ämterbesetzung

patroness /'peɪtrənes/ n. 1 (supporter) Gönnerin, die; (of campaign, institution) Schirmherrin, die 2 (saint) Schutzheilige, die; Schutzpatronin, die

patronise, patronising, patronisingly ▸**patroniz-**

patronize /'pætrənaɪz/ v.t. 1 (frequent) besuchen; **we hope you will continue to ~ our services** bitte beehren Sie uns bald wieder; bitte schenken Sie uns auch weiterhin Ihr Vertrauen 2 (support) fördern; unterstützen 3 (condescend to) **~ sb.** jmdn. gönnerhaft od. von oben herab od. herablassend behandeln

patronizing /'pætrənaɪzɪŋ/ adj., **patronizingly** /'pætrənaɪzɪŋlɪ/ adv. gönnerhaft; herablassend

patronymic /pætrə'nɪmɪk/

A n. Patronymikon, das; Vater[s]name, der

B adj. patronymisch

patsy /'pætsɪ/ n. (Amer. coll.) Einfaltspinsel, der (ugs.)

patter /'pætə(r)/

A n. 1 (of rain) Prasseln, das; (of feet, footsteps) Trappeln, das; Getrappel, das; **the ~ of tiny feet** (fig.) fröhliches Kindertreiben 2 (language of salesman or comedian) Sprüche Pl.; **sales ~:** Vertretersprüche Pl.; **keep up a ~:** ohne Unterbrechung reden 3 (jargon) Fachjargon, der

B v.i. 1 (make tapping sounds) ‹Regen, Hagel:› prasseln; ‹Schritte:› trappeln 2 (run) trippeln

pattern /'pætən/

A n. 1 (design) Muster, das; (on carpet, wallpaper, cloth, etc. also) Dessin, das; **frost ~s** Eisblumen; **a ~ of footprints** Fußspuren Pl. 2 (form, order) Muster, das; Schema, das; **follow a ~:** einem regelmäßigen Muster od. Schema folgen; **behaviour ~:** Verhaltensmuster, das; **~ of development** Entwicklungsschema, das; **~ of thought** Denkmuster, das; Denkschema, das; **~ of life** Lebensweise, die; **~ of events** Ereignisfolge, die 3 (model) Vorlage, die; (for sewing) Schnittmuster, das; Schnitt, der; (for knitting) Strickanleitung, die; Strickmuster, das; **follow a ~:** nach einer Vorlage arbeiten; (knitting) nach einem Strickmuster stricken; **a democracy on the British ~:** eine Demokratie nach britischem Muster 4 (sample) Muster, das 5 (on target) [Treffer]bild, das

B v.t. 1 (model) gestalten; **~ sth. after/on sth.** etw. einer Sache (Dat.) nachbilden; **she ~ed her behaviour on her father's** sie richtete sich in ihrem Verhalten nach dem Vorbild ihres Vaters 2 (decorate) mustern; **~ sth. with intricate designs** etw. mit verschlungenen Mustern verzieren

'pattern book n. Musterbuch, das

patty /'pætɪ/ n. 1 (pie, pastry) Pastetchen, das 2 (Amer.: of meat) Frikadelle, die

paucity /'pɔːsɪtɪ/ n. (formal) Mangel, der (**of** an + Dat.); **~ of support** geringe od. mangelnde Unterstützung; **a growing ~ of ...:** immer weniger ...

Paul /pɔːl/ pr. n. (Hist., as name) (of ruler etc.) Paul; (of saint) Paulus

Pauline /'pɔːlaɪn/ adj. (Bibl.) paulinisch

paunch /pɔːntʃ/ n. Bauch, der; Wanst, der (salopp abwertend); **develop a ~:** einen Bauch ansetzen

paunchy /'pɔːntʃɪ/ adj. dickbäuchig; **become ~:** einen Bauch ansetzen

pauper /'pɔːpə(r)/ n. 1 Arme, der/die; **they were ~s** sie waren arm; **live like ~s** leben wie arme Leute 2 (Hist.) Unterstützungsempfänger, der/-empfängerin, die; **~'s grave** Armengrab, das

pauperism /'pɔːpərɪzm/ n., no pl. Armut, die; **be reduced to ~:** völlig verarmen

pauperize /'pɔːpəraɪz/ v.t. arm machen; **be ~d** verarmt sein

pause /pɔːz/

A n. 1 Pause, die; **without [a] ~:** ohne Pause; **an anxious ~:** ängstliches Schweigen; **a ~ in the fighting** eine Kampfpause; **give sb. ~:** jmdm. zu denken geben 2 (Mus.) Fermate, die

B v.i. 1 (wait) eine Pause machen; eine Pause einlegen; ‹Redner:› innehalten; (hesitate) zögern; **~ for reflection/thought** in Ruhe überlegen; **he ~d to consider his next move** er hielt ein und überlegte, wie er weiter vorgehen solle; **~ for a rest** eine Erholungspause od. Ruhepause einlegen 2 (linger) verweilen (**upon, over** bei)

'pause button n. Pausetaste, die

pavan /'pævən/, **pavane** /pə'vɑːn/ n. (Hist./Mus.) Pavane, die

pave /peɪv/ v.t. 1 (cover, lit. or fig.) befestigen; (with stones) pflastern 2 (fig.: prepare) **~ the way for** or **to sth.** einer Sache (Dat.) den Weg ebnen; für etw. den Weg ebnen

pavement /'peɪvmənt/ n. 1 (Brit.: footway) Bürgersteig, der; Gehsteig, der 2 (paved surface) Belag, der; Pflaster, das 3 (Amer.: roadway) Fahrbahn, die

pavement: ~ artist n. Pflastermaler, der/-malerin, die; **~ café** n. Straßencafé, das

pavilion /pə'vɪljən/ n. 1 (tent) Festzelt, das; Pavillon, der 2 (ornamental building) Pavillon, der 3 (Brit. Sport) Klubhaus, das 4 (stand at exhibition) [Messe]pavillon, der

paving /'peɪvɪŋ/ n. 1 (action) Pflastern, das 2 (paced surface) Pflaster, das

'paving stone n. Platte, die; Pflasterstein, der

paw /pɔː/

A n. 1 Pfote, die; (of bear, lion, tiger) Pranke, die 2 (coll. derog.: hand) Pfote, die (ugs. abwertend); **keep your ~s off [me]/off my car!** Pfoten weg!/Pfoten weg von meinem Auto!

B v.t. 1 ‹Hund, Wolf:› mit der Pfote/den Pfoten berühren; ‹Bär, Löwe, Tiger:› mit der Pranke/

den Pranken berühren; (playfully) tätscheln; **~ the ground** scharren **2)** (coll. derog.: fondle) befummeln (ugs.)

C *v.i.* **1)** scharren; **~ at** mit der Pfote/den Pfoten *usw.* berühren **2)** **~ at sb./sth.** (coll. derog.) jmdn./etw. befummeln (ugs.)

pawl /pɔ:l/ *n.* (Mech. Engin.) Sperre, *die;* Sperrklinke, *die*

pawn¹ /pɔ:n/ *n.* **1)** (Chess) Bauer, *der* **2)** (fig.) Schachfigur, *die;* **a ~ in the hands of Fate** ein Spielball des Schicksals

pawn²
A *n.* Pfand, *das;* **in ~:** verpfändet; versetzt; **put sth. in ~:** etw. verpfänden *od.* versetzen; **take sth. out of ~:** etw. einlösen
B *v.t.* **1)** verpfänden; versetzen **2)** (fig.) verpfänden ‹*Leben, Ehre, Wort, Seele*›

pawn: ~broker *n.* ▸ ⓘ **p. 1260** Pfandleiher, *der*/-leiherin, *die;* **~broking** *n., no art.* Pfandleihgeschäft, *das;* **~shop** *n.* Leihhaus, *das;* Pfandleihe, *die*

pawpaw /pɔ:'pɔ:/ ▸ **papaw**

pay /peɪ/
A *n., no pl., no indef. art.* (wages) Lohn, *der;* (salary) Gehalt, *das;* (of soldier) Sold, *der;* **the ~ is good** die Bezahlung ist gut; **be in the ~ of sb./sth.** für jmdn./etw. arbeiten; in jmds. Sold/im Sold einer Sache stehen (abwertend); *see also* **equal A 1**
B *v.t.*, **paid** /peɪd/ **1)** (give money to) bezahlen; (fig.) belohnen; **I paid him for the tickets** ich habe ihm das Geld für die Karten gegeben; **~ sb. to do sth.** jmdn. dafür bezahlen, dass er etw. tut; *see also* **coin A**
2) (hand over) zahlen; (so as to discharge an obligation) bezahlen; (**~** back) zurückbezahlen; (in instalments) abbezahlen; **I paid what I owed him** ich habe meine Schulden bei ihm bezahlt; **~ the bill** die Rechnung bezahlen; **~ sb.'s expenses** (reimburse) jmds. Auslagen erstatten; **~ sb. £10** jmdm. 10 Pfund zahlen; **~ £10 for sth.** 10 Pfund für etw. [be]zahlen; **you ~s your money and you takes your choice** (Brit. fig. coll.) die Wahl steht bei Ihnen; **~ sth. into a bank account** etw. auf ein Konto ein[be]zahlen
3) (bestow) **~ sb. a visit** jmdm. einen Besuch abstatten (geh.); *see also* **attention A 1; compliment A 1; heed B; regard B 1; respect A 2, 5; tribute 1**
4) (yield) einbringen, abwerfen ‹*Dividende usw.*›; **this job ~s very little** diese Arbeit bringt sehr wenig ein
5) (be profitable to) **it ~s him to live overseas** er steht sich finanziell besser (ugs.), seit er im Ausland lebt; **it would ~ her to do that** (fig.) es würde ihr nichts schaden *od.* es würde sich für sie bezahlt machen, das zu tun
6) **~ the price** den Preis zahlen; **it's too high a price to ~:** das ist ein zu hoher Preis. *See also* **court A 6; devil A 3; piper 1**
C *v.i.*, **paid** **1)** zahlen; **~ for sth./sb.** etw./für jmdn. bezahlen; **I'll ~ for you as well** ich bezahle für dich mit; **sth. ~s for itself** etw. macht sich bezahlt; **has this been paid for?** ist das schon bezahlt?; **I'd like to know what I'm ~ing for** ich wüsste gern, wofür ich eigentlich mein Geld ausgebe
2) (yield) sich lohnen; sich auszahlen; ‹*Geschäft:*› rentabel sein; **it ~s to be careful** es lohnt sich, vorsichtig zu sein
3) (fig.: suffer) büßen müssen; **if you do this you'll have to ~ for it later** wenn du das tust, wirst du später dafür büßen müssen. *See also* **crime 2; nose A 1; paid**

Phrasal verbs
- **~ a'way** ▸ **~out A 2**
- **~ 'back** *v.t.* **1)** zurückzahlen; **I'll ~ you back later** ich gebe dir das Geld später zurück **2)** (fig.) erwidern ‹*Kompliment*›; sich revanchieren für ‹*Beleidigung, Untreue*›; **I'll ~ him back** ich werde es ihm heimzahlen; **I'll ~ him back with interest** ich werde es ihm mit Zins und Zinseszins zurückzahlen
- **~ 'in** *v.t. & i.* einzahlen
- **~ 'off**

A *v.t.* **1)** auszahlen ‹*Arbeiter*›; abmustern ‹*Schiffsbesatzung*›; abbezahlen ‹*Schulden*›; ablösen ‹*Hypothek*›; befriedigen ‹*Gläubiger*›; (fig.) abgelten ‹*Verpflichtung*› **2)** (coll.: bribe) schmieren (salopp abwertend); (pay hush-money to) Schweigegeld zahlen (+ *Dat.*)
B *v.i.* **1)** (coll.) sich auszahlen; sich bezahlt machen **2)** (Naut.) leewärts steuern. *See also* **pay-off**
- **~ 'out**

A *v.t.* **1)** auszahlen; (spend) ausgeben; **we've already paid out a fortune to these people** wir haben schon ein Vermögen an diese Leute bezahlt *od.* für diese Leute ausgegeben; **~ out large sums on sth.** hohe Beträge für etw. ausgeben **2)** (Naut.) ablaufen lassen ‹*Seil, Tau*› **3)** (coll.: punish) **~ sb. out** es jmdm. heimzahlen; **~ sb. out for sth.** jmdm. etw. heimzahlen. *See also* **pay-out**
B *v.i.* bezahlen
- **~ 'up**

A *v.t.* zurückzahlen ‹*Schulden*›
B *v.i.* zahlen. *See also* **paid-up**

payable /'peɪəbl/ *adj.* **1)** (due) zahlbar; **be ~ to sb.** jmdm. *od.* an jmdn. zu zahlen sein **2)** (that may be paid) zahlbar; **make a cheque ~ to the Post Office/to sb.** einen Scheck auf die Post/auf jmds. Namen ausstellen

pay and dis'play *n.* (Brit.) Parken mit Parkschein; **park in the ~:** auf dem [gebührenpflichtigen] Parkplatz mit Parkscheinautomat parken; *attrib.* Parkschein-; **~ car park** parkscheinpflichtiger Parkplatz; **~ ticket** Parkschein, *der*

pay: ~-as-you-'earn *attrib. adj.* (Brit.) **~-as-you-earn system/method** Quellenabzugsverfahren, *das;* **~-as-you-earn tax system** *Steuersystem, bei dem die Lohnsteuer direkt einbehalten wird;* **~-as-you-'enter** *attrib. adj.* ‹*Bus*› *in dem man das Fahrgeld beim Einsteigen bezahlt;* **~-as-you-'go** **A** *adj* Pay-as-you-go-‹*Internetservice, Vertrag, Angebot, usw.*›; **B** *n., no pl.* Pay-as-you-go, *das;* **~-as-you-'talk** **A** *adj.* Pay-as-you-talk-‹*Service, Handy usw.*›. **B** *n., no pl.* Pay-as-you-talk, *das;* **~ award** *n.* Gehaltserhöhung, *die;* **~ bed** *n.* Privatbett, *das;* **~ channel** *n.* (Telev.) Abonnentensender, *der;* **~ cheque** *n.* Lohn-/Gehaltsscheck, *der;* **~ claim** *n.* Lohn-/Gehaltsforderung, *die;* **~ day** *n.* Zahltag, *der;* **~ desk** *n.* Kasse, *die;* **~ dirt** *n.* (Amer.) abbauwürdiges Erzlager; **hit ~ dirt** (fig.) einen Volltreffer landen (fig. ugs.)

PAYE *abbr.* (Brit.) = **pay-as-you-earn**

payee /peɪ'i:/ *n.* Zahlungsempfänger, *der*/-empfängerin, *die*

pay envelope (Amer.) ▸ **pay packet**

payer /'peɪə(r)/ *n.* Zahler, *der*/Zahlerin, *die;* **bad ~:** unzuverlässiger Zahler

'pay increase ▸ **pay rise**

paying/'peɪɪŋ/: **~ 'guest** *n.* zahlender Gast; **~-'in book** *n.* (Brit. Banking) *Heft mit Einzahlungsscheinen;* **~-'in slip** *n.* (Brit. Banking) Einzahlungsschein, *der;* **~ patient** *n.* Privatpatient, *der*/-patientin, *die*

pay: ~load *n.* Nutzlast, *die;* **~master** *n.* Zahlmeister, *der;* (fig.) Geldgeber, *der;* **P~master 'General** *n.* (Brit. Admin.) Generalzahlmeister des englischen Schatzamts

payment /'peɪmənt/ *n.* **1)** (of sum, bill, debt, fine) Bezahlung, *die;* (of interest, instalment, tax, fee) Zahlung, *die;* (paying back) Rückzahlung, *die;* (in instalments) Abzahlung, *die;* **in ~ [for sth.]** als Bezahlung [für etw.]; **~ on account** Akontozahlung, *die;* **stop ~** ‹*Bank:*› die Zahlungen einstellen; **stop ~ on a cheque** einen Scheck sperren; **on ~ of ...:** gegen Zahlung von ... **2)** (amount) Zahlung, *die;* **make a ~:** eine Zahlung leisten; **by monthly ~s** auf Monatsraten **3)** (fig.) Belohnung, *die;* Lohn, *der;* **be fitting ~ for sth.** der gerechte Lohn für etw. sein

pay: ~ negotiations *n. pl.* Tarifverhandlungen; **~-off** *n.* (coll.) (return) Lohn, *der;* (punishment) Quittung, *die;* (climax) Clou, *der* (ugs.); (bribe) Bestechungsgeld, *das;* Schmiergeld, *das* (ugs. abwertend)

payola /peɪ'əʊlə/ *n.* (bribery) Bestechung, *die;* (bribe) Bestechungsgeld, *das;* Schmiergeld, *das* (ugs. abwertend)

pay: ~out *n.* Auszahlung, *die;* **~ packet** *n.* (Brit.) Lohntüte, *die;* **~-per-view** *n.* Pay-per-View, *das;* **~phone** *n.* Münzfernsprecher, *der;* **~ rise** *n.* Lohn-/Gehaltserhöhung, *die;* **~roll** *n.* Lohnliste, *die;* **have 200 workers/people on the ~roll** 200 Arbeiter beschäftigen/Beschäftigte haben; **be on sb.'s ~roll** für jmdn. *od.* bei jmdm. arbeiten; **a ~roll of about a hundred** etwa hundert Arbeitsplätze; **reduce the ~roll** die Lohn- und Gehaltssumme senken; **~ round** *n.* Tarifrunde, *die;* **~ scale** *n.* [Gehalts]tarif, *der;* **~slip** *n.* Lohnstreifen, *der*/Gehaltszettel, *der;* **~ station** (Amer.) ▸ **~phone;** **~ talks** *n. pl.* Tarifverhandlungen; **~ television** *n.* Münzfernsehen, *das;* **~ TV** *n., no pl.* Pay-TV, *das;* Bezahlfernsehen, *das*

> **PBS — Public Broadcasting Service**
>
> Ein staatlich geförderter Rundfunkdienst in den USA, bekannt für seine hohe Programmqualität. Er übermittelt sein Programm an eine Gruppe von lokalen Sendern, die keinen Gewinn anstreben und keine Werbung ausstrahlen.

p.c. *abbr.* = **per cent** v. H.

PC *abbr.* **1)** ▸ ⓘ **p. 1634** (Brit.) = **police constable** Wachtm. **2)** ▸ ⓘ **p. 1634** (Brit.) = **Privy Counsellor** Geh. R.; Geh. Rat **3)** = **personal computer** PC **4)** = **politically correct** politisch korrekt

pct. *abbr.* (Amer.) = **per cent** v. H.

pd. *abbr.* = **paid** bez.

PDA *n.* (Computing) PDA, *der*

PDF *abbr.* = **Portable Document Format** PDF; *attrib.* **~ file** PDF-Datei, *die*

p.d.q. /pi:di:'kju:/ *abbr.* (coll.) = **pretty damn quick** verdammt schnell (ugs.)

PE *abbr.* = **physical education**

pea /pi:/ *n.* Erbse, *die;* (plant) Erbse[npflanze], *die;* **they are as like as two ~s [in a pod]** sie gleichen sich (*Dat.*) *od.* einander wie ein Ei dem anderen; *see also* **chickpea; split pea; sweet pea**

peace /pi:s/ *n.* **1)** (freedom from war) Frieden, *der;* Friede, *der* (geh.); (treaty) Frieden, *der;* Friedensschluss, *der;* **these countries are now at ~:** zwischen diesen Ländern herrscht jetzt Frieden; **maintain/restore ~:** den Frieden bewahren/wieder herstellen; **~ talks/treaty** Friedensgespräche *Pl.*/Friedensvertrag, *der;* **make ~ [with sb.]** [mit jmdm.] Frieden schließen; **the P~ of Utrecht** (Hist.) der Friede von Utrecht **2)** (freedom from civil disorder) Ruhe und Ordnung; öffentliche Ordnung; (absence of discord) Frieden, *der;* **in ~ [and harmony]** in [Frieden und] Eintracht; **restore ~:** Ruhe und Ordnung wieder herstellen; **the [King's/Queen's] ~:** die öffentliche Ordnung; **bind sb. over to keep the ~:** jmdn. verwarnen *od.* rechtlich verpflichten, die öffentliche Ordnung zu wahren; **be at ~ [with sb./sth.]** mit jmdm./etw. in Frieden leben; **be at ~ with oneself** mit sich selbst im Reinen sein; **make [one's] ~ [with sb.]** sich [mit jmdm.] aussöhnen *od.* versöhnen; **make one's ~ with God/the world** seinen Frieden mit Gott/der Welt machen; **hold one's ~:** schweigen; ruhig sein **3)** (tranquillity) Ruhe, *die;* (stillness) Stille, *die;* Ruhe, *die;* **in ~:** in Ruhe; **leave sb. in ~:** jmdn. in Frieden *od.* in Ruhe lassen; **I get no ~:** ich habe keine ruhige Minute; **give sb. no ~:** jmdm. keine Ruhe lassen; **~ and quiet** Ruhe und Frieden; **the ~ and quiet of the countryside** die friedvolle Ruhe der Landschaft **4)** (mental state) Ruhe, *die;* **find ~:** Frieden finden; **~ of mind** Seelenfrieden, *der;* innere Ruhe; **I shall have no ~ of mind until I know it** ich werde keine ruhige Minute haben, bis ich es weiß **5)** (in or following biblical use) **~ be with** *or* **unto you** Friede sei mit dir/euch; **go in ~:** gehe/gehet hin in Frieden; **may his soul rest in ~:** er ruhe in Frieden; **he is at ~** (literary: is dead) er ruht in Frieden (geh.). *See also* **breach A 1; justice 3**

peaceable /'pi:səbl/ *adj.* **1)** (not quarrelsome) friedfertig; friedliebend ‹*Volk*›; (calm) friedlich **2)** (quiet, undisturbed) friedlich

P

peaceably /ˈpiːsəblɪ/ *adv.* **1** (amicably) friedlich **2** (quietly, in peace) friedlich; **go ~ about one's business** in Ruhe seinen Geschäften nachgehen

peace: **~ campaigner** *n.* Friedensaktivist, *der*/-aktivistin, *die;* **~ conference** *n.* Friedenskonferenz, *die;* **P~ Corps** *n.* (Amer.) Friedenskorps, *das;* **~ dividend** *n.* Friedensdividende, *die;* **~ envoy** *n.* Friedensgesandte, *der/die*

peaceful /ˈpiːsfl/ *adj.* friedlich; friedfertig ‹*Person, Volk*›; ruhig ‹*Augenblick*›; *see also* **coexistence**

peacefully /ˈpiːsfəlɪ/ *adv.* friedlich; **die ~:** sanft entschlafen

peace: **~keeper** *n.* Friedenswächter, *der;* **~keeping** **A** *adj.* ‹*Maßnahmen, Operationen*› zur Friedenssicherung; **~keeping force** Friedenstruppe, *die;* **B** *n., no pl.* Friedenssicherung, *die;* **~-loving** *adj.* friedliebend; **~maker** *n.* Friedensstifter, *der*/-stifterin, *die;* **blessed are the ~makers** (Bibl.) selig sind die Friedfertigen; **~ movement** *n.* Friedensbewegung, *die;* **~ offer** *n.* Friedensangebot, *das;* **~ offering** *n.* Friedensangebot, *das;* (fig.) Versöhnungsgeschenk, *das;* **~ pipe** *n.* Friedenspfeife, *die;* **~ plan** *n.* Friedensplan, *der;* **~ process** *n.* Friedensprozess, *der;* **~ settlement** *n.* Friedensabkommen, *das;* **~time** *n.* Friedenszeiten *Pl.; attrib.* Friedens‹*produktion, -wirtschaft, -stärke*›; in Friedenszeiten *nachgestellt;* **in ~time** in Friedenszeiten; **~ treaty** *n.* Friedensvertrag, *der*

peach /piːtʃ/ *n.* **1** Pfirsich, *der;* **~es-and-cream complexion** Pfirsichhaut, *die* **2** ▸ **peach tree** **3** (coll.) **sb./sth. is a ~:** jmd./etw. ist spitze *od.* klasse (ugs.); **a ~ of a woman/man/house** eine klasse Frau/ein klasse Kerl *od.* Typ/ein klasse Haus (ugs.) **4** (colour) Pfirsichton, *der*

peach: **~ blossom** *n.* Pfirsichblüte, *die;* **~ 'brandy** *n.* Pfirsichbrandy, *der;* Pfirsichlikör, *der;* **~-coloured** *adj.* pfirsichfarben

'peachick *n.* Pfauküken, *das*

peach: **~ 'Melba** *n.* Pfirsich Melba, *der;* **~ tree** *n.* Pfirsichbaum, *der*

peachy-keen /ˈpiːtʃɪkiːn/ *adj.* (Amer. coll.) [super]toll (ugs.)

'peacock *n.* Pfau, *der;* Pfauhahn, *der;* **strut like a ~:** wie ein Pfau einherstolzieren; **proud/vain as a ~:** stolz/eitel wie ein Pfau; **be proud as a ~ of sth.** vor Stolz auf etw. (*Akk.*) fast bersten

peacock: **~ 'blue** **A** *adj.* pfauenblau; **B** *n.* Pfauenblau, *das;* **~ butterfly** *n.* Tagpfauenauge, *das*

pea: **~fowl** *n.* Pfau, *der;* **~-green** *adj.* erbsengrün; maigrün; **~hen** *n.* Pfauhenne, *die;* **~ jacket** *n.* Kolani, *der;* Pijacke, *die* (Seew. veralt.)

peak /piːk/
A *n.* **1** (of cap) Schirm, *der;* Schild, *der* **2** (of mountain) Gipfel, *der;* (of waves) Kamm, *der;* Krone, *die* **3** (highest point) Höhepunkt, *der;* **reach/be at/be past its ~:** seinen Höhepunkt erreichen/den Höhepunkt erreicht haben/den Höhepunkt überschritten haben; **his career was at its ~:** er stand auf dem Höhepunkt seiner Laufbahn **4** (Naut.) Piek, *die*
B *attrib. adj.* Höchst-, Spitzen‹*preise, -werte*›; **~ listening/viewing audience** höchste Einschaltquote; **~ listening/viewing period** Hauptsendezeit, *die*
C *v.i.* seinen Höhepunkt erreichen; **~ too soon** (Sport) vorzeitig in Höchstform sein

peaked¹ /piːkt/ *adj.* **~ cap** Schirmmütze, *die*

peaked² *adj.* (pinched) spitz ‹*Gesicht*›; abgehärmt, verhärmt ‹*Person, Gesicht, Aussehen*›

peak: **~-hour** *attrib. adj.* **~-hour travel** Fahren während der Hauptverkehrszeit; **~-hour traffic** Stoßverkehr, *der;* **~-hour listening period** Hauptsendezeit, *die;* **~ load** *n.* Spitzenlast, *die;* **the ~ load of traffic** der Stoßverkehr; **~ season** *n.* Hochsaison, *die*

peaky /ˈpiːkɪ/ *adj.* kränklich; **look ~:** nicht gut aussehen; angeschlagen aussehen

peal /piːl/
A *n.* **1** (ringing) Geläut[e], *das;* Läuten, *das;* **~ of bells** Glockengeläut[e], *das;* Glockenläuten, *das* **2** (set of bells) Glockenspiel, *das* **3** (loud sound) **a ~ of laughter** schallendes Gelächter; **a ~ of thunder** ein Donnerschlag
B *v.i.* ‹*Glocken:*› läuten; ‹*Donner:*› rollen; ‹*Trompete:*› schmettern
C *v.t.* **1** erschallen lassen **2** (ring) läuten ‹*Glocken*›

Phrasal verb
• **~ 'out** *v.i.* tönen

peanut /ˈpiːnʌt/ *n.* Erdnuss, *die;* **~ butter** Erdnussbutter, *die;* **~s** (coll.) (trivial thing) ein Klacks (ugs.); kleine Fische *Pl.;* (money) ein paar Kröten (salopp); **this is ~s compared to ...:** das ist ein Klacks gegen ...; **work for ~s** für ein Butterbrot arbeiten (ugs.); **sell sth. for ~s** etw. für ein Butterbrot *od.* für einen Apfel und ein Ei verkaufen (ugs.); **this costs ~s compared to ...:** das ist [fast] geschenkt im Vergleich zu ... (ugs.); **be worth ~s** kaum etw. wert sein

pear /peə(r)/ *n.* **1** (fruit) Birne, *die* **2** ▸ **pear tree**. *See also* **anchovy pear**; **avocado**; **prickly pear**

'pear drop *n.: hartes Bonbon in Birnenform [mit Birnengeschmack]*

pearl /pɜːl/ *n.* **1** Perle, *die;* **[string of] ~s** (necklace) Perlenkette, *die* **2** (fig.) Juwel, *das;* Kleinod, *das;* Perle, *die;* **be a ~ of architecture** ein Juwel der Baukunst sein; **~ of wisdom** (often iron.) Weisheit, *die;* **cast ~s before swine** (fig.) Perlen vor die Säue werfen (salopp) **3** (**~**-like thing) Perle, *die;* **~s of dew** Tautropfen. *See also* **mother-of-pearl**; **seed pearl**

pearl: **~ 'barley** *n.* Perlengraupen *Pl.;* **~ 'bulb** *n.* matte Glühbirne; **~ 'button** *n.* Perlmutt[er]knopf, *der;* **~ diver** *n.* Perlentaucher, *der*/-taucherin, *die;* **~ fisher** *n.* Perlenfischer, *der*/-fischerin, *die;* **~-grey** *adj.* perlgrau; **~ oyster** *n.* Perlmuschel, *die*

pearly /ˈpɜːlɪ/ *adj.* **1** perlmuttern, perlenähnlich, (geh.) perlengleich ‹*Glanz, Schimmer*›; perl[en]förmig ‹*Regen-, Tautropfen*› **2** (set with pearls) perlenbesetzt; **P~ Gates** Himmelstür, *die;* **~ king/queen** (Brit.) *Straßenverkäufer/-verkäuferin in London mit perlenbestickter Kleidung*

pear: **~-shaped** *adj.* birnenförmig; **go ~-shaped** (Brit. coll.) schief laufen *od.* gehen; **everything went ~-shaped:** alles ging daneben (ugs.); **~ tree** *n.* Birnbaum, *der;* Birne, *die*

peasant /ˈpezənt/ *n.* **1** [armer] Bauer, *der;* Landarbeiter, *der;* **~ farmer** Bauer, *der;* **~ uprising** Bauernaufstand, *der;* **~ economy** Agrarwirtschaft, *die;* **~ woman** Bauersfrau, *die* **2** (coll. derog.) (ignorant or stupid person) Bauer, *der* (ugs. abwertend); (lower-class person) Plebejer, *der* (abwertend)

peasantry /ˈpezəntrɪ/ *n.* Bauernschaft, *die*

pease pudding /piːzˈpʊdɪŋ/ *n.* Erbsenpudding, *der*

pea: **~-shooter** *n.* Pusterohr, *das;* **~ 'soup** *n.* Erbsensuppe, *die;* **~-stick** *n.* Bohnenstange, *die*

peat /piːt/ *n.* **1** (substance) Torf, *der* **2** (piece) Torfstück, *das;* Torfsode, *die;* **cut ~:** Torf stechen

peat: **~bog**, (Brit.) **~moor** *ns.* Torfmoor, *das*

peaty /ˈpiːtɪ/ *adj.* torfig

pebble /ˈpebl/ *n.* Kiesel[stein], *der;* **he is/you are not the only ~ on the beach** es gibt noch andere

pebble: **~dash** *n.* Kieselrauputz, *der; attrib.* mit Kieselrauputz *nachgestellt;* **~ glasses** *n. pl.* [dicke] Brille; **~ lens** *n.* [dickes] Brillenglas

pebbly /ˈpeblɪ/ *adj.* steinig

pecan /prˈkæn/ *n.* **1** (nut) Pekannuss, *die* **2** (tree) Pekannussbaum, *der*

peccadillo /pekəˈdɪləʊ/ *n., pl.* **~es** *or* **~s** (small sin) leichte Verfehlung; (small fault) kleiner Fehler

peccary /ˈpekərɪ/ *n.* (Zool.) Pekari, *das;* Nabelschwein, *das*

peck¹ /pek/
A *v.t.* **1** hacken; picken ‹*Körner*›; **the bird ~ed my finger/was ~ing the bark** der Vogel pickte mir *od.* mich in den Finger/pickte an der Rinde **2** (kiss) flüchtig küssen
B *v.i.* picken (**at** nach); **~ at one's food** im Essen herumstochern
C *n.* **1** **the hen gave its chick a ~:** die Henne pickte *od.* hackte nach ihrem Küken **2** (kiss) flüchtiger Kuss; Küsschen, *das*

Phrasal verbs
• **~ 'out** *v.t.* aushacken; auspicken
• **~ 'up** *v.t.* aufpicken

peck² *n.* (measure) Viertelscheffel, *der;* **a ~ of trouble/dirt** (fig.) ein gerütteltes Maß an Sorgen/eine Menge Schmutz

pecker /ˈpekə(r)/ *n.* **1** (Amer. sl.: penis) Schwanz, *der* (salopp) **2** **keep your ~ up** (Brit. coll.) halt die Ohren steif (ugs.)

pecking order /ˈpekɪŋ ɔːdə(r)/ *n.* Hackordnung, *die*

peckish /ˈpekɪʃ/ *adj.* **1** (coll.: hungry) hungrig; **feel/get ~:** Hunger haben/bekommen **2** (Amer. coll.: irritable) gereizt

pectin /ˈpektɪn/ *n.* (Chem.) Pektin, *das*

pectoral /ˈpektərl/
A *n.* **1** (Med.) Hustenmittel, *das* **2** *in pl.* (often joc.) Brustmuskeln
B *adj.* (Anat.) pektoral (fachspr.); Brust‹*höhle, -atmung*›

pectoral: **~ 'cross** *n.* (Eccl.) Pektorale, *das;* **~ fin** *n.* (Zool.) Brustflosse, *die;* **~ muscle** *n.* (Anat.) Brustmuskel, *der*

peculiar /prˈkjuːlɪə(r)/ *adj.* **1** (strange) seltsam; eigenartig; sonderbar; **what a ~ person he is!** was ist er doch für ein komischer Kauz! (ugs.); **I feel [slightly] ~:** mir ist [etwas] komisch; **a ~ incident occurred** es passierte etwas Seltsames **2** (especial) besonder...; **be of ~ interest [to sb.]** [für jmdn.] von besonderem Interesse sein **3** (belonging exclusively) eigentümlich (**to** *Dat.*); **this bird is ~ to South Africa** dieser Vogel kommt nur in Südafrika vor; **she has a ~ style of acting, all her own** sie hat einen ganz eigenen Stil zu spielen

peculiarity /prkjuːlɪˈærɪtɪ/ *n.* **1** *no pl., no indef. art.* (unusualness) Ausgefallenheit, *die;* (of behaviour, speech) Sonderbarkeit, *die;* Merkwürdigkeit, *die* **2** (odd trait) Eigentümlichkeit, *die;* **behavioural peculiarities** seltsame Verhaltensweisen **3** (distinguishing characteristic) [charakteristisches] Merkmal; Kennzeichen, *das;* (special characteristic) Besonderheit, *die*

peculiarly /prˈkjuːlɪəlɪ/ *adv.* **1** (strangely) seltsam; eigenartig; sonderbar **2** (especially) besonders **3** (in a way that is one's own) **be something ~ British** etwas rein Britisches sein; **a treatment ~ his own** eine ganz eigene Behandlung

pecuniary /prˈkjuːnɪərɪ/ *adj.* (of money) finanziell, (geh.) pekuniär ‹*Hilfe, Überlegungen*›; **~ award** Geldpreis, *der*

pedagog (Amer.) ▸ **pedagogue**

pedagogic[al] /pedəˈgɒgɪk(l), pedəˈgɒdʒɪk(l)/ *adj.* **1** (arch./derog.: of a pedagogue) belehrend; schulmeisterlich (abwertend) **2** (of pedagogy) pädagogisch

pedagogue /ˈpedəgɒg/ *n.* **1** (arch.: teacher) Pädagoge, *der*/Pädagogin, *die* **2** (derog.: pedantic teacher) Schulmeister, *der* (abwertend)

pedagogy /ˈpedəgɒdʒɪ/ *n., no pl.* Pädagogik, *die*

pedal /ˈpedl/
A *n.* **1** (Mus.) (organ key, on piano) Pedal, *das;* (organ stop control) Fußtritt, *der;* Fußhebel, *der;* **loud ~:** rechtes Pedal; Fortepedal, *das;* **soft ~:** linkes Pedal; Pianopedal, *das* **2** (of bicycle, **~** bin; Mech. Engin., Motor Veh.) Pedal, *das*
B *v.i.,* (Brit.) **-ll-** **1** (work bicycle **~s**) **~ [away]** in die Pedale treten; strampeln (ugs.) **2** (ride) [mit dem Fahrrad] fahren; radeln (ugs.); **~ by/off** vorbeiradeln/losradeln (ugs.) **3** (Mus.) (on organ) das Pedal spielen; (on piano) die Pedale benutzen
C *v.t.,* (Brit.) **-ll-** (propel) fahren mit ‹*Fahrrad, Dreirad*›; **~ one's bike** Rad fahren; radeln (ugs.)

pedal: **~ bin** *n.* Treteimer, *der;* **~ car** *n.* Tretauto, *das*

pedalo /ˈpedələʊ/ *n., pl.* **~s** Tretboot, *das*

'pedal pushers *n. pl.: dreiviertellange Damen-/Mädchenhose*

P

pedant /ˈpedənt/ *n.* 1 (one who overrates learning) Stubengelehrte, *der/die* 2 (stickler for formal detail) Pedant, *der*/Pedantin, *die* (abwertend); Kleinigkeitskrämer, *der*/-krämerin, *die* (abwertend)

pedantic /pɪˈdæntɪk/ *adj.* 1 (ostentatiously learned) schulmeisterlich (abwertend) 2 (unduly concerned with formal detail) pedantisch (abwertend)

pedantry /ˈpedəntrɪ/ *n.* Pedanterie, *die;* Kleinlichkeit, *die* (abwertend)

peddle /ˈpedl/ *v.t.* 1 auf der Straße verkaufen; (from door to door) hausieren mit; handeln mit, (ugs.) dealen mit ‹*Drogen, Rauschgift*› 2 (fig.: disseminate) hausieren [gehen] mit ‹*Theorie, Vorschlag*›; verbreiten ‹*Neuigkeiten, Klatsch, Gerücht*›

peddler /ˈpedlə(r)/ ▸**pedlar**

pederast /ˈpedəræst/ *n.* Päderast, *der*

pederasty /ˈpedəræstɪ/ *n., no pl.* Päderastie, *die*

pedestal /ˈpedɪstl/ *n.* Sockel, *der;* **knock sb. off his ~** (fig.) jmdn. von seinem Sockel stoßen; **put** *or* **set sb./sth. on a ~** (fig.) jmdn./etw. in den Himmel heben (ugs.)

pedestrian /pɪˈdestrɪən/

A *adj.* (uninspired) trocken; langweilig

B *n.* Fußgänger, *der*/-gängerin, *die;* **~-controlled** *or* **~-operated lights** Bedarfsampel, *die*

pedestrian ˈcrossing *n.* Fußgängerüberweg, *der*

pedestrianism /pɪˈdestrɪənɪzm/ *n., no pl.* (of style) Trockenheit, *die;* Langweiligkeit, *die*

pedestrianize (pedestrianise) /pɪˈdestrɪənaɪz/ *v.t.* zur Fußgängerzone machen

pedestrian ˈprecinct ▸**precinct 1**

pediatri- (Amer.) ▸**paediatri-**

pedicel /ˈpedɪsl/, **pedicle** /ˈpedɪkl/ *n.* (Biol.) Stiel, *der;* (of flower) [Blüten]stängel, *der*

pedicure /ˈpedɪkjʊə(r)/ *n. no pl., no art.* Pediküre, *die;* Fußpflege, *die;* **give sb. a ~:** jmdn. pediküren

pedigree /ˈpedɪgriː/

A *n.* 1 (genealogical table) Stammbaum, *der;* Ahnentafel, *die* (geh.) 2 (ancestral line) Stammbaum, *der;* Ahnenreihe, *die;* (of animal) Stammbaum, *der* 3 (derivation) Herkunft, *die* 4 *no pl., no art.* (ancient descent) **have ~, be a man/woman of ~:** von berühmten Ahnen abstammen

B *adj.* (with recorded line of descent) mit Stammbaum *nachgestellt*

pedigreed /ˈpedɪgriːd/ ▸**pedigree B**

pediment /ˈpedɪmənt/ *n.* (Archit.) (in Grecian style) Giebeldreieck, *das;* (in Roman or Renaissance style) Ziergiebel, *der*

pedlar /ˈpedlə(r)/ *n.* 1 Straßenhändler, *der*/-händlerin, *die;* (from door to door) Hausierer, *der*/Hausiererin, *die;* (selling drugs) Rauschgifthändler, *der*/-händlerin, *die;* Dealer, *der*/Dealerin, *die* (ugs.) 2 (fig.: disseminator) **be a ~ of gossip/scandal** *etc.* Klatsch/Skandalgeschichten *usw.* verbreiten

pedo- (Amer.) ▸**paedo-**

pedometer /pɪˈdɒmɪtə(r)/ *n.* Pedometer, *das* (fachspr.); Schrittzähler, *der*

peduncle /pɪˈdʌŋkl/ *n.* (Bot., Zool.) Stiel, *der*

pee /piː/ (coll.)

A *v.i.* pinkeln (salopp); Pipi machen (Kinderspr.)

B *n.* 1 (urination) **need/have a ~:** pinkeln müssen/pinkeln (salopp); **I must go for a ~:** ich muss mal eben pinkeln (salopp) 2 (urine) Pipi, *das* (Kinderspr.)

peek /piːk/

A *v.i.* gucken (ugs.); **no ~ing!** nicht gucken!; **~ at sb./sth.** zu jmdm./etw. hingucken; **~ in at sb.** zu jmdm. hereingucken

B *n.* (quick) kurzer Blick; (sly) verstohlener Blick; **take a quick ~ round** sich schnell umgucken; **have a ~ through the keyhole** durch das Schlüsselloch gucken (ugs.); **take a quick ~ at sb.** kurz zu jmdm. hingucken; **give sb. a ~ at sth.** jmdm. einen Blick auf etw. (*Akk.*) werfen lassen

peekaboo /piːkəbuː/

A *n.* (Amer.) ▸**peep-bo**

B *adj.* durchsichtig; (with pattern of small holes) mit Lochmuster *nachgestellt;* **~ design** Lochmuster, *das*

peel /piːl/

A *v.t.* schälen; **~ the shell off an egg/the skin off a banana** ein Ei/eine Banane schälen; *see also* **eye A 1**

B *v.i.* 1 ‹*Person, Haut:*› sich schälen *od.* (bes. nordd.) pellen; ‹*Rinde, Borke:*› sich lösen; ‹*Farbe:*› abblättern 2 (coll.: undress) sich ausziehen

C *n.* Schale, *die; see also* **candy B**

Phrasal verbs

• **~ aˈway**

A *v.t.* abschälen

B *v.i.* 1 ‹*Haut:*› sich schälen *od.* (bes. nordd.) pellen; ‹*Rinde, Borke:*› sich lösen; ‹*Farbe:*› abblättern 2 (veer away) ausscheren

• **~ ˈback** *v.t.* halb abziehen ‹*Kabelmantel, Bananenschale*›; zurückziehen ‹*Bettdecke*›; umschlagen ‹*Stoffmuster*›

• **~ ˈoff**

A *v.t.* abschälen; abstreifen, ausziehen ‹*Kleider*›

B *v.i.* 1 ▸**~ away B 1** 2 (veer away) ausscheren 3 ▸**peel B 2**

peeler /ˈpiːlə(r)/ *n.* Schäler, *der;* Schälmesser, *das*

peeling /ˈpiːlɪŋ/ *n.* Stück Schale; **~s** Schalen

peep¹ /piːp/

A *v.i.* ‹*Maus, Vogel:*› piep[s]en; (squeal) quieken

B *n.* (shrill sound) Piepsen, *das;* (coll.: slight utterance) Piep[s], *der* (ugs.); **one ~ out of you and ...:** ein Pieps [von dir], und …

peep²

A *v.i.* 1 (look through narrow aperture) gucken (ugs.); spähen (geh., veralt., noch landsch.) 2 (look furtively) verstohlen gucken; linsen (ugs.); **~ round** sich umgucken; **no ~ing!** nicht gucken! 3 (come into view) **~ out** [he]rausgucken; hervorgucken; (fig.: show itself) zum Vorschein kommen; durchscheinen

B *n.* kurzer Blick; **steal a ~ at sb.** verstohlen zu jmdm. hingucken; **take a ~ through the curtain** durch die Gardine spähen *od.* (ugs.) linsen

peep-bo /ˈpiːpbəʊ/

A *n.* Guck-guck-Spiel, *das*

B *int.* guck, guck; kuckuck

ˈpeephole *n.* Guckloch, *das*

peeping Tom /piːpɪŋ ˈtɒm/ *n.* Spanner, *der* (ugs.); Voyeur, *der; attrib.* voyeuristisch

ˈpeep show *n.* 1 (exhibition of small pictures in box) Guckkastenschau, *die* 2 (erotic spectacle) Peepshow, *die*

peep-toe[d] /ˈpiːptəʊ(d)/ *adj.* vorn offen ‹*Schuh*›; zehenfrei ‹*Sandale*›; **the shoes had a ~ design** die Schuhe waren vorn offen

peer¹ /pɪə(r)/ *n.* 1 (Brit.: member of nobility) **~ [of the realm]** Peer, *der; see also* **life peer** 2 (noble of any country) hoher Adliger; **the ~s of France** der Hochadel Frankreichs 3 (equal in standing) Gleichgestellte, *der/die;* **be judged by a jury of one's ~s** von seinesgleichen gerichtet werden; **among her social ~s** unter ihresgleichen 4 (equal in attainment) Ebenbürtige, *der/die;* **find sb.'s ~:** jemanden finden, der jmdm. ebenbürtig ist

peer² *v.i.* (look searchingly) forschend schauen; (look with difficulty) angestrengt schauen; **~ at sth./sb.** (searchingly) [sich (*Dat.*)] etw. genau ansehen/jmdn. forschend *od.* prüfend ansehen; (with difficulty) [sich (*Dat.*)] etw. angestrengt ansehen/jmdn. angestrengt ansehen; **~ into a cave/the distance** in eine Höhle/die Ferne spähen; **~ down at sb.** zu jmdm. hinunter-/herunterspähen

peerage /ˈpɪərɪdʒ/ *n.* 1 *no pl.* (Brit.: body of peers) **the ~:** die Peers; **be raised to the ~:** in den Adelsstand erhoben werden 2 (Brit.: rank of peer) Peerswürde, *die; see also* **life peerage** 3 (nobility of any country) Adel, *der* 4 (book) Peerskalender, *der; britisches Adelsverzeichnis*

peeress /ˈpɪəres/ *n.* Peeress, *die*

ˈpeer group *n.* Peergroup, *die* (Psych., Soziol.)

peerless /ˈpɪəlɪs/ *adj.* beispiellos

peer: ~ ˈpressure *n.* Gruppenzwang, *der;* **~ reˈview** *n.* Peer- Review, *das*

peeve /piːv/ (coll.)

A *n.* 1 (cause of annoyance) **it was a bit of a ~:** es war ganz schön ärgerlich; **it was one of his ~s that ...:** es wurmte ihn, dass … (ugs.); *see also* **pet¹ B 3** 2 (mood) **be in a [real] ~:** [stock]sauer sein (ugs.)

B *v.t.* (irritate) nerven (salopp); **it ~d me that ...:** es wurmte *od.* fuchste mich, dass … (ugs.)

peeved /piːvd/ *adj.* (coll.) sauer (ugs.); **be/get ~ with sb.** auf jmdn. sauer sein/werden; **be ~ at/get ~ about sth.** über etw. (*Akk.*) sauer sein/wegen etw. sauer werden

peevish /ˈpiːvɪʃ/ *adj.* (querulous) nörgelig (abwertend); quengelig (ugs.) ‹*Kind*›; (showing vexation) gereizt

peevishly /ˈpiːvɪʃlɪ/ *adv.* missmutig; (in vexation) **do sth. ~:** etw. gereizt tun

peewit /ˈpiːwɪt/ *n.* 1 (Ornith.) Kiebitz, *der* 2 (cry) Kiwitt, *das*

peg /peg/

A *n.* (pin, bolt) (for holding together parts of framework) Stift, *der;* (for tying things to) Pflock, *der;* (for hanging things on) Haken, *der;* (clothes ~) Wäscheklammer, *die;* (for holding tent ropes) Hering, *der;* (for marking cribbage scores etc.) Stift, *der;* (Mus.: for adjusting strings) Wirbel, *der;* **off the ~** (Brit.: ready-made) von der Stange (ugs.); **take sb. down a ~ [or two]** (fig.) jmdm. einen Dämpfer aufsetzen *od.* geben; **be taken down a ~ or two** (fig.) einen Dämpfer bekommen; **a ~ to hang sth. on** (fig.) ein Aufhänger für etw.; *see also* **hole A 1**

B *v.t.,* **-gg-** 1 (fix with ~) mit Stiften/Pflöcken befestigen 2 (Econ.: stabilize) stabilisieren; (support) stützen; (freeze) einfrieren; **~ wages/prices/exchange rates** Löhne/Preise/Wechselkurse stabil halten 3 (Cribbage) durch eingesteckte Holzstifte anzeigen ‹*Spielstand*›; **~ two holes** den Holzstift zwei Löcher weiter einstecken; **they are level ~ging at school** (fig.) sie sind gleich gut in der Schule

C *v.i.,* **-gg-: keep ~ging along** bei der Stange bleiben; **she's still ~ging at her writing** sie schreibt immer noch unverdrossen weiter

Phrasal verbs

• **~ aˈway** *v.i.* schuften (ugs.); **~ away for four hours** vier Stunden lang ununterbrochen schuften; **[keep] ~[ging] away with sth.** nicht lockerlassen mit etw. (ugs.)

• **~ ˈdown** *v.t.* 1 (secure with ~s) festpflocken 2 ▸**pin down 1**

• **~ ˈout**

A *v.t.* 1 (spread out and secure) ausspannen ‹*Felle etc.*›; (Brit.: attach to line) [draußen] aufhängen ‹*Wäsche*› 2 (mark) abstecken ‹*Gebiet, Fläche*›

B *v.i.* 1 (coll.) (faint) zusammenklappen (ugs.); (die) den Löffel abgeben (salopp); (cease to function) den Geist aufgeben (ugs.) 2 (Croquet) den Zielpflock treffen 3 (Cribbage) gewinnen

peg: ~board *n.* 1 (for games) Lochbrett, *das;* 2 (board holding hooks) gelochte Platte; **~ leg** *n.* 1 (artificial leg) Holzbein, *das;* 2 (person) Stelzfuß, *der* (ugs.)

peignoir /ˈpeɪnwɑː(r)/ *n.* Negligé, *das*

pejorative /pɪˈdʒɒrətɪv/

A *adj.* pejorativ (Sprachw.); abwertend; **~ word** Pejorativum, *das* (Sprachw.)

B *n.* Pejorativum, *das* (Sprachw.)

pejoratively /pɪˈdʒɒrətɪvlɪ/ *adv.* abwertend

pekan /ˈpekən/ *n.* (Zool.) Fischermarder, *der*

peke /piːk/ (coll.) ▸**Pekingese A 1**

Pekingese /piːkɪŋˈiːz/ (**Pekinese** /piːkɪˈniːz/)

A *n., pl. same* 1 **Pekinese [dog]** Pekinese, *der* 2 (person) Pekinger, *der*/Pekingerin, *die*

B *attrib. adj.* Pekinger; **~ man/woman** Pekinger, *der*/Pekingerin, *die*

pelican /ˈpelɪkən/ *n.* (Ornith.) Pelikan, *der*

ˈpelican crossing *n.* (Brit.) Ampelübergang, *der*

pellagra /pɪˈlægrə, pɪˈleɪgrə/ *n.* ▸ℹ **p. 1231** (Med.) Pellagra, *das*

pellet /ˈpelɪt/ *n.* 1 (small ball) Kügelchen, *das;* (mass of food) Pellet, *das* (fachspr.) 2 (pill) Pille, *die* 3 (regurgitated mass) Gewölle, *das* (Zool., Jägerspr.); (excreted mass) Kötel, *der* (nordd.) 4 (small shot) Schrot, *der od. das;* **peppered with shotgun ~s** mit Schrot[kugeln] gespickt

pell-mell /pelˈmel/

A *adv.* 1 (in disorder) durcheinander; (without discrimination) wahllos; **everything was heaped together ~:** alles wurde durcheinander auf einen Haufen geworfen 2 (headlong) Hals über Kopf

B *adj.* [kunter]bunt; chaotisch

pellucid /pɪˈluːsɪd, pɪˈljuːsɪd/ *adj.* 1 (transparent) durchsichtig; [glas]klar ‹*Wasser*› 2 (clear in style) klar; in einem klaren Stil gehalten ‹*Schriften*› 3 (mentally clear) klar ‹*Verstand, Kopf*›

pelmet /ˈpelmɪt/ *n.* (of wood) Blende, *die;* (of fabric) Schabracke, *die*

Peloponnese /ˈpeləpəniːs/ *pr. n.* **the ~:** der *od.* die Peloponnes

pelota /pɪˈləʊtə/ *n.* (Sport) Pelota, *die;* Pelotaspiel, *das*

pelt¹ /pelt/ *n.* 1 (of sheep or goat) Fell, *das;* (of furbearing animal) [Roh]fell, *das;* **sheep's ~:** Schaffell, *das* 2 (Tanning: raw skin) enthaartes Fell

pelt²

A *v.t.* 1 (assail with missiles, lit. or fig.) **~ sb. with sth.** jmdn. mit etw. bewerfen *od.* (ugs.) bombardieren; **~ sb. with questions** jmdn. mit Fragen überschütten *od.* (ugs.) bombardieren 2 (throw a stream of) **~ sth. at sb.** jmdn. mit etw. bewerfen *od.* (ugs.) bombardieren; **they ~ed abuse at each other** (fig.) sie warfen sich [gegenseitig] Beschimpfungen an den Kopf

B *v.i.* 1 ‹*Regen:*› prasseln; **it was ~ing down [with rain]** es goss wie aus Kübeln (ugs.) 2 (run fast) rasen (ugs.); pesen (ugs.); **he set off as fast as he could ~:** so schnell er konnte, raste *od.* peste er los (ugs.)

C *n., no pl., no indef. art.* **[at] full ~:** mit Karacho (ugs.); volle Pulle (salopp)

pelvic /ˈpelvɪk/ *adj.* (Anat.) Becken-

pelvis /ˈpelvɪs/ *n., pl.* **pelves** /ˈpelviːz/ *or* **~es** ▸ **i p. 951** (Anat.) Becken, *das;* **renal ~:** Nierenbecken, *das*

pen¹ /pen/

A *n.* 1 (enclosure) Pferch, *der* 2 (Navy) Bunker, *der*

B *v.t.,* **-nn-** 1 (shut up in ~) einpferchen 2 (confine) **~ sb. in a corner** jmdn. in eine Ecke drängen

(Phrasal verbs)

• **~ ˈin** *v.t.* 1 einpferchen 2 (fig.: restrict) einengen; **feel ~ned in by one's life** sein Leben sehr beengend finden

• **~ ˈup** *v.t.* ▸ **~ in 2**

pen²

A *n.* 1 (for writing) Federhalter, *der;* (fountain ~) Füller, *der;* (ball ~) Kugelschreiber, *der;* Kuli, *der* (ugs.); (felt-tip ~) Filzstift, *der;* (ball ~ or felt-tip ~) Stift, *der;* **make one's living by the ~:** vom Schreiben leben; **the ~ is mightier than the sword** (prov.) die Feder ist mächtiger als das Schwert; *see also* **paper A 1** 2 (quill feather) Feder, *die; see also* **quill pen**

B *v.t.,* **-nn-** niederschreiben; **~ a letter to/a note for sb.** jmdm. einen Brief/ein paar Worte schreiben

pen³ *n.* (female swan) weiblicher Schwan

pen⁴ *n.* (Amer. coll.: penitentiary) Knast, *der* (ugs.); **do eight years in the ~:** acht Jahre [Knast] abreißen (salopp) *od.* (ugs.) absitzen

penal /ˈpiːnl/ *adj.* 1 (of punishment) Straf‹*vollzug, -gesetzbuch*›; (concerned with inflicting punishment) strafrechtlich ‹*Bestimmungen, Klauseln*›; Straf‹*gesetze, -gesetzgebung, -maßnahme*›; **~ reform** Strafvollzugsreform, *die* 2 (punishable) strafbar ‹*Handlung, Tat*›; **~ offence** Straftat, *die* 3 **~ colony** *or* **settlement** Strafkolonie, *die*

penalize (**penalise**) /ˈpiːnəlaɪz/ *v.t.* 1 (subject to penalty) bestrafen; pönalisieren (geh.); (Sport) eine Strafe verhängen gegen 2 unter Strafe stellen ‹*Handlung, Tat*›

penal ˈservitude *n., no pl., no indef. art.* (Brit. Law. Hist.) Zwangsarbeit, *die*

penalty /ˈpenltɪ/ *n.* 1 (punishment) Strafe, *die;* **the ~ for this offence is imprisonment/a fine** auf dieses Delikt steht Gefängnis/eine Geldstrafe; **pay/have paid the ~/the ~ for** *or* **of sth.** (lit. or fig.) dafür/für etw. büßen [müssen]/gebüßt haben; **his ~ was a £50 fine** er erhielt eine [Geld]strafe von 50 Pfund; **on** *or* **under ~ of £200/of instant dismissal** bei einer Geldstrafe von 200 Pfund/unter Androhung (*Dat.*) der sofortigen Entlassung 2 (disadvantage) Preis, *der* 3 (Sport: disadvantage imposed) (Horseracing) Pönalität, *die;* (Golf) **~ [stroke]** Strafschlag, *der;* (*Footb., Rugby*) ▸ **penalty kick**; (Hockey) ▸ **penalty bully**; **penalty corner**; **penalty shot** 4 (Bridge) Strafpunkte *Pl.*

penalty: ~ area *n.* (Footb.) Strafraum, *der;* **~ box** *n.* (Footb.) Strafraum, *der;* (Ice Hockey) Strafbank, *die;* **~ bully** *n.* (Hockey) Siebenmeterball, *der;* **~ clause** *n.* Strafklausel, *die;* **~ corner** *n.* (Hockey) Strafecke, *die;* **~ goal** *n.* (Hockey) Siebenmetertor, *das;* (Rugby) durch einen Straftritt erzieltes Tor; **~ kick** *n.* (Footb.) Strafstoß, *der;* Elfmeter, *der;* (Rugby) Straftritt, *der;* **~ ˈshoot-out** *n.* (Footb.) Elfmeterschießen, *das;* **~ shot** *n.* (Hockey) Strafschlag, *der;* **~ spot** *n.* (Footb.) Strafstoßmarke, *die;* Elfmeterpunkt, *der;* (Hockey) Siebenmeterpunkt, *der*

penance /ˈpenəns/ *n., no pl., no art.* Buße, *die;* **act of ~:** Bußübung, *die;* Bußwerk, *das;* **undergo/do ~:** büßen/Buße tun

ˈpen-and-ink *adj.* Feder‹*zeichnung, -skizze*›

pence ▸ **penny**

penchant /ˈpɑ̃ʃɑ̃/ *n.* Schwäche, *die;* Vorliebe, *die* (**for** für); **have a ~ for doing sth.** dazu neigen, etw. zu tun

pencil /ˈpensɪl/

A *n.* 1 Bleistift, *der;* **red/coloured ~:** Rot-/Buntod. Farbstift, *der;* **write in ~:** mit Bleistift schreiben; **a ~ drawing, a drawing in ~:** eine Bleistiftzeichnung; *see also* **lead pencil** 2 (cosmetic) Stift, *der;* **eyebrow ~:** Augenbrauenstift, *der*

B *v.t.,* (Brit.) **-ll-** 1 (mark) mit Bleistift/Farbstift markieren 2 (sketch) mit Bleistift zeichnen *od.* skizzieren 3 (write with ~) mit einem Bleistift/Farbstift schreiben 4 (write tentatively) entwerfen; skizzieren; *see also* **~ in 2**

(Phrasal verb)

• **~ ˈin** *v.t.* 1 (shade with ~) mit Bleistift [aus]schraffieren 2 (note or arrange provisionally) vorläufig notieren

ˈpencil case *n.* Griffelkasten, *der;* (made of a soft material) Federmäppchen, *das;* Schreibmäppchen, *das*

pencilled (*Amer.:* **penciled**) /ˈpensɪld/ *adj.* mit Bleistift geschrieben; nachgezogen ‹*Augenbrauen*›

ˈpencil sharpener *n.* Bleistiftspitzer, *der*

pendant /ˈpendənt/

A *n.* 1 (hanging ornament) Anhänger, *der;* (light) Hängelampe, *die* 2 (companion) Pendant, *das* (geh.) 3 ▸ **pennant 1**

B *adj.* ▸ **pendent**

pendent /ˈpendənt/ *adj.* 1 (hanging) herabhängend 2 (overhanging) überhängend

pending /ˈpendɪŋ/

A *adj.* 1 (undecided) unentschieden ‹*Angelegenheit, Sache*›; anhängig (Rechtsspr.), schwebend ‹*Verfahren*›; laufend ‹*Verhandlungen*›; **be ~** ‹*Verfahren:*› noch anhängig sein (Rechtsspr.), noch schweben; ‹*Sache, Angelegenheit:*› noch unentschieden sein *od.* in der Schwebe sein; ‹*Entscheidung, Probleme:*› noch anstehen; ‹*Debatte, Verhandlungen:*› noch im Gang sein; **a treaty was ~:** es wurde über einen Vertrag verhandelt 2 (about to come into existence) bevorstehend ‹*Krieg*›; **patent ~:** Patent angemeldet

B *prep.* (until) **~ his return** bis zu seiner Rückkehr; **~ the final settlement** bis zur endgültigen Regelung; **~ full discussion of the matter** bis die Angelegenheit ausdiskutiert ist

ˈpending tray *n.* Ablage für noch Unerledigtes

pendulous /ˈpendjʊləs/ *adj.* 1 (suspended, hanging down) herabhängend; Hänge‹*backen, -brüste, -ohren*› 2 (oscillating) pendelnd

pendulum /ˈpendjʊləm/ *n.* Pendel, *das;* **the swing of the ~** (fig.) der Umschwung; **according to the swing of the ~:** je nachdem, nach welcher Seite das Pendel ausschlägt (fig.)

penetrable /ˈpenɪtrəbl/ *adj.* 1 (capable of being entered) durchdringlich; **scarcely ~:** fast undurchdringlich 2 (fig.: capable of being found out) ergründbar; **be ~:** sich ergründen lassen 3 (permeable) durchlässig

penetrate /ˈpenɪtreɪt/

A *v.t.* 1 (find access into) eindringen in (+ *Akk.*); vordringen in (+ *Akk.*) ‹*unbekannte Regionen*›; aufbrechen ‹*Safe*›; (pass through) durchdringen; **get sth. to ~ sb.'s mind** etw. in jmds. Kopf reinkriegen (ugs.); **~ sb.'s disguise** (fig.) hinter jmds. Maske (*Akk.*) schauen 2 (fig.: find out) ergründen ‹*Geheimnis*›; durchschauen ‹*Plan, Absicht, Gedanken*›; herausfinden ‹*Wahrheit*› 3 (permeate) dringen in (+ *Akk.*); (fig.) durchdringen; (infiltrate) infiltrieren; unterwandern; ‹*Spion:*› sich einschleusen in (+ *Akk.*) 4 (see into) ‹*Augen:*› durchdringen ‹*Dunkelheit, Nebel*› 5 (sexually) eindringen in (+ *Akk.*); penetrieren (geh.)

B *v.i.* 1 (make a way) **~ into/to sth.** in etw. (*Akk.*) eindringen/zu etw. vordringen; **~ through sth.** durch etw. hindurchdringen; **the cold ~d through the whole house** die Kälte durchdrang das ganze Haus 2 (be understood or realized) **my hint did not ~:** mein Wink wurde nicht verstanden; **something's finally ~d!** der Groschen ist endlich gefallen (ugs.)

penetrating /ˈpenɪtreɪtɪŋ/ *adj.* 1 (easily heard) durchdringend 2 (gifted with insight) scharf ‹*Verstand*›; (showing insight) scharfsinnig ‹*Bemerkung, Kommentar, Studie*›; scharf ‹*Beobachtung*›; verstehend ‹*Blick*›

penetration /penɪˈtreɪʃn/ *n.* 1 (finding of access into) Eindringen, *das* (**of** in + *Akk.*); (of safe) Aufbrechen, *das;* (act of passing through) Durchdringen, *das;* (passage through) Durchdringung, *die* 2 *no pl.* (fig.: discernment) Scharfsinn, *der;* Scharfsinnigkeit, *die* 3 (act of permeating) Durchdringen, *das;* Durchdringung, *die;* (infiltration) Infiltration, *die;* Unterwanderung, *die* 4 (seeing into sth.) Durchdringen, *das* 5 (sexual) Eindringen des Gliedes [in die Scheide]; Penetration, *die* (geh.)

penetrative /ˈpenɪtrətɪv/ *adj.* 1 **~ sex** penetrierender Sex 2 (permeating) eindringend 3 (acute) scharf ‹*Verstand, Beobachtung*›

ˈpenfriend *n.* Brieffreund, *der*/-freundin, *die*

penguin /ˈpeŋgwɪn/ *n.* Pinguin, *der*

ˈpenholder *n.* Federhalter, *der*

penicillin /penɪˈsɪlɪn/ *n.* (Med.) Penizillin, *das*

peninsula /pɪˈnɪnsjʊlə/ *n.* Halbinsel, *die;* **the Lleyn ~:** die Halbinsel Lleyn

peninsular /pɪˈnɪnsjʊlə(r)/ *adj.* 1 (of a peninsula) peninsular[isch]; Halbinsel-; (like a peninsula) halbinselartig 2 (Hist.: of Spain and Portugal) **the P~ War** der Spanische Unabhängigkeitskrieg

penis /ˈpiːnɪs/ *n., pl.* **~es** *or* **penes** /ˈpiːniːz/ ▸ **i p. 951** (Anat.) Penis, *der;* männliches Glied

ˈpenis envy *n.* (Psych.) Penisneid, *der*

penitence /ˈpenɪtəns/ *n., no pl.* Reue, *die*

penitent /ˈpenɪtənt/

A *adj.* reuevoll (geh.); reuig (geh.) ‹*Sünder*›; **be ~:** bereuen; **feel [sincerely] ~:** [echte] Reue empfinden; **be deeply ~ about sth.** tiefe Reue über etw. (*Akk.*) empfinden

B *n.* (repentant sinner) reuiger Sünder/reuige Sünderin; (person doing penance) Büßer, *der*/Büßerin, *die* (Rel.)

penitential /penɪˈtenʃl/ *adj.* reuevoll; reuig (geh.); Buß‹*tag, -gebet*›; **the ~ psalms** (Relig.) die Bußpsalmen

penitentiary /penɪˈtenʃərɪ/

A *n.* (Amer.) Straf[vollzugs]anstalt, *die;* [Justiz]vollzugsanstalt, *die*

B *adj.* 1 (of penance) **~ pilgrimage** Bußpilgerfahrt, *die* 2 (of reformatory treatment) **~ system** Strafvollzug, *der*

penitently /ˈpenɪtəntlɪ/ *adv.* reuevoll (geh.); reumütig (öfter scherzh.) ‹*zurückkehren*›; **behave ~:** Reue zeigen

pen: ~knife *n.* Taschenmesser, *das;* **~ light** *n.* [Mini]stablampe, *die*

penmanship /ˈpenmənʃɪp/ *n., no pl.* 1 (skill in handwriting) Schönschreiben, *das;* **a piece of good/bad ~:** ein schön/schlecht geschriebener Text 2 (style of writing) Schrift, *die*

ˈpen name *n.* Schriftstellername, *der*

pennant /ˈpenənt/ *n.* 1 (Naut.: tapering flag) Stander, *der;* **broad ~:** Doppelstander, *der*

2 (Amer.: flag symbolizing championship) Meisterschaftswimpel, *der* 3 ▸ **pennon**

penniless /ˈpenɪlɪs/ *adj.* (having no money) **be ~:** keinen Cent Geld haben; (fig.: be poor) mittellos sein; **be left ~:** völlig mittellos *od.* ohne einen Cent Geld dastehen

pennon /ˈpenən/ *n.* 1 Wimpel, *der* 2 (Mil.: long narrow flag) Fähnchen, *das;* Fähnlein, *das*

penn'orth /ˈpenəθ/ ▸ **pennyworth**

Pennsylvania Dutch /pensɪlveɪnɪə ˈdʌtʃ/ *n.* 1 *no pl., no indef. art.* (dialect) Pennsylvaniadeutsch, *das;* Pennsilfaanisch, *das* 2 *constr. as pl.* **the ~:** die Pennsylvaniendeutschen

penny /ˈpenɪ/ *n., pl. usu.* **pennies** /ˈpenɪz/ (for separate coins), **pence** /pens/ (for sum of money) 1 ▸❶ **p. 1332** (British coin, monetary unit) Penny, *der;* **fifty pence** fünfzig Pence; **two/five/ten/twenty/fifty pence [piece]** Zwei-/Fünf-/Zehn-/Zwanzig-/Fünfzigpencestück, *das od.* -münze, *die; see also* **halfpenny** 2 ▸❶ **p. 1332** (Amer. coll.: one-cent coin) Cent, *der;* Centstück, *das* 3 **keep turning up like a bad ~:** immer wieder auftauchen; **the ~ has dropped** (fig. coll.) der Groschen ist gefallen (ugs.); **pennies from heaven** ein warmer Regen (fig. ugs.); **in for a ~, in for a pound** (prov.) wennschon, dennschon (ugs.); **a pretty ~:** eine hübsche *od.* schöne Stange Geld (ugs.); ein hübsches Sümmchen (ugs.); **I was not a ~ the worse** (fig.) es hat mich nichts gekostet (fig.); **take care of the pence** *or* **pennies** im Kleinen sparen; **take care of the pence** *or* **pennies, and the pounds will look after themselves** spare im Kleinen, dann hast du im Großen; **not have two pennies to rub together** keinen roten Heller haben; **look twice at every ~:** jeden Cent dreimal umdrehen; **a ~ for your thoughts** woran denkst du [gerade]?; **sth. is two** *or* **ten a ~:** etw. gibt es wie Sand am Meer (ugs.); **be ~ wise** im Kleinen sparsam sein; **be ~ wise and pound foolish** im Kleinen sparsam und im Großen verschwenderisch sein; am falschen Ende sparen. *See also* **count¹ B 1; honest 5; name A 1; spend 1**

penny: ~ **ˈdreadful** *n.* (Brit.) (cheap story book) Groschenheft, *das* (abwertend); (cheap novel) Groschenroman, *der* (abwertend); **~-ˈfarthing [bicycle]** *n.* (Brit. coll) Hochrad, *das;* **~-pincher** /ˈpenɪpɪnʃə(r)/ *n.* Pfennigfuchser, *der*/-fuchserin, *die* (ugs.); **~-pinching** /ˈpenɪpɪnʃɪŋ/ A *n., no pl., no indef. art.* Pfennigfuchserei, *die* (ugs.); Knauserei, *die* (ugs. abwertend); B *adj.* knaus[e]rig (ugs. abwertend); **~weight** *n.* Pennyweight, *das;* ~ **ˈwhistle** ▸ **whistle C 2**

pennyworth /ˈpen(ɪw)əθ/ *n.* 1 *pl. same* **a ~ of bread/six ~ of sweets** für einen Penny Brot/für sechs Pence Bonbons; **not a ~ [of]** (fig.: not even a small amount) nicht für fünf Pfennig (ugs.) 2 (bargain) **a good/bad ~:** ein guter/schlechter Kauf

penology /piːˈnɒlədʒɪ/ *n.* Pönologie, *die*

pen: ~ **pal** (coll.) ▸ **penfriend**; ~ **portrait** *n.* Charakterbild, *das;* **~-pusher** *n.* (coll.) Büromensch, *der;* (male) Bürohengst, *der* (ugs. abwertend); **~-pushing** *n., no pl., no indef. art.* (coll.) Schreibkram, *der* (ugs. abwertend)

pension /ˈpenʃn/

A *n.* 1 (given by employer) Rente, *die;* (payment to retired civil servant also) Pension, *die;* Ruhegehalt, *das* (Amtsspr.); **retire on a ~:** in *od.* auf Rente gehen (ugs.); ⟨*Beamter:*⟩ in Pension gehen; **be on a ~ [from one's company]** eine Rente [von seiner Firma] beziehen; *attrib.* ~ **contributions** Rentenbeiträge *Pl.;* **make ~ contributions** Rentenbeiträge zahlen; ~ **fund** Rentenfonds, *der;* Pensionsfonds, *der;* ~ **rights** Renten- *od.* Pensionsansprüche; ~ **scheme** Rentenversicherung, *die;* **the company has** *or* **operates a ~ fund/scheme for its employees** die Firma hat eine Pensionskasse/betriebliche Altersversorgung für ihre Beschäftigten 2 (given by State) Rente, *die;* **disability** *or* **disablement ~:** Erwerbsunfähigkeitsrente, *die;* Invalidenrente, *die* (ugs.); **widow's ~:** Witwenrente, *die;* **war ~:** Kriegsopferrente, *die;* ~ **book** ≈ Rentenausweis, *der;* ~ **day** Rentenzahltag, *der; see also* **old-age** 3 /ˈpɒ̃sjɒ̃/ (European boarding house) Pension, *die*

B *v.t.* eine Rente zahlen (+ *Dat.*); **be ~ed** eine Rente bekommen

Phrasal verb

• ~ **ˈoff** *v.t.* 1 (discharge) berenten (Amtsspr.); auf Rente setzen (ugs.); pensionieren ⟨*Lehrer, Beamten*⟩ 2 (fig.: cease to use) ausmustern; ausrangieren (ugs.)

pensionable /ˈpenʃənəbl/ *adj.* 1 (entitled to a pension) rentenberechtigt; pensionsberechtigt ⟨*Beamter*⟩ 2 (entitling to a pension) zu einer Rente berechtigend; **reach ~ age** das Rentenalter erreichen; (as civil servant) das Pensionsalter erreichen; ~ **salary/earnings** rentenfähiges Gehalt/rentenfähiger Verdienst

pensioned-off /penʃndˈɒf/ *adj.* (fig.) ausrangiert (ugs.)

pensioner /ˈpenʃənə(r)/ *n.* Rentner, *der*/Rentnerin, *die;* (retired civil servant) Pensionär, *der*/Pensionärin, *die;* Ruhegehaltsempfänger, *der*/-empfängerin, *die*

pensive /ˈpensɪv/ *adj.* 1 (plunged in thought) nachdenklich 2 (sorrowfully thoughtful) schwermütig

pensively /ˈpensɪvlɪ/ *adv.* ▸ **pensive**: nachdenklich; schwermütig

pent /pent/ *adj.* 1 (literary) eingedämmt; unterdrückt ⟨*Atem*⟩ 2 ~ **in** *or* **up** eingedämmt ⟨*Fluss*⟩; angestaut ⟨*Wut, Ärger*⟩; *see also* **pent-up**

pentagon /ˈpentəgən/ *n.* 1 (Geom.) Fünfeck, *das;* Pentagon, *das* (fachspr.) 2 **the P~** (Amer. Polit.) das Pentagon

The Pentagon

Das fünfeckige Gebäude in Arlington, Virginia, in dem die Verwaltung des Verteidigungsministeriums untergebracht ist. Mit *The Pentagon* bezeichnen Journalisten oft die militärische Führung in den USA.

pentagonal /penˈtægənl/ *adj.* (Geom.) fünfeckig; pentagonal (fachspr.); fünfseitig ⟨*Pyramide, Prisma*⟩

pentagram /ˈpentəgræm/ *n.* Pentagramm, *das;* Drudenfuß, *der*

pentameter /penˈtæmɪtə(r)/ *n.* (Pros.) Pentameter, *der*

pentane /ˈpenteɪn/ *n.* (Chem.) Pentan, *das*

pentaprism /ˈpentəprɪzm/ *n.* Penta[dachkant-]prisma, *das;* ~ **viewfinder** (Photog.) Prismensucher, *der*

Pentateuch /ˈpentətjuːk/ *n.* (Bibl.) **the ~:** die fünf Bücher Mose; der Pentateuch (fachspr.)

pentathlete /penˈtæθliːt/ *n.* Fünfkämpfer, *der*/-kämpferin, *die*

pentathlon /penˈtæθlən/ *n.* (Sport) Fünfkampf, *der*

pentaˈtonic *adj.* (Mus.) pentatonisch; Fünfton-; ~ **scale** fünfstufige Tonleiter

Pentecost /ˈpentɪkɒst/ *n.* (Relig.) Pfingsten, *das;* Pfingstfest, *das;* (Jewish harvest festival) Ernte[dank]fest, *das*

Pentecostal /pentɪˈkɒstl/ *attrib. adj.* (Relig.) pfingstlich; Pfingst⟨*gottesdienst, -hymne, -bewegung*⟩

Pentecostal ˈChurch *n.* (Relig.) Pfingstkirche, *die*

pent: ~**house** *n.* 1 (house, flat) Penthaus, *das;* Penthouse, *das;* 2 (sloping roof) Schleppdach, *das;* **~-up** *attrib. adj.* angestaut ⟨*Ärger, Wut*⟩; verhalten ⟨*Freude*⟩; unterdrückt ⟨*Sehnsucht, Gefühle*⟩

penultimate /peˈnʌltɪmət/ *adj.* vorletzt...

penumbra /pɪˈnʌmbrə/ *n., pl.* **~e** /pɪˈnʌmbriː/ *or* **~s** 1 Halbschatten, *der* 2 (Astron.: of sunspot) Penumbra, *die*

penurious /pɪˈnjʊərɪəs/ *adj.* 1 (poor) arm ⟨*Person*⟩; entbehrungsreich ⟨*Zeit*⟩; armselig, kümmerlich ⟨*Verhältnisse*⟩ 2 (stingy) geizig; knauserig (ugs. abwertend)

penury /ˈpenjʊərɪ/ *n., no pl.* Armut, *die;* Not, *die*

peon /ˈpiːən, pjuːn/ *n.* 1 (in Latin America: day labourer) Tagelöhner, *der;* Peon, *der;* ~ **labour** Peonenarbeit, *die* 2 (in India and Pakistan: messenger, attendant) Bote, *der;* Laufbursche, *der*

peony /ˈpiːənɪ/ *n.* (Bot.) Pfingstrose, *die;* Päonie, *die;* ~ **red** päonienrot; tiefrot

people /ˈpiːpl/

A *n.* 1 (persons composing nation, community, etc.) Volk, *das* 2 *constr. as pl.* (persons forming class etc.) Leute *Pl.;* Menschen; **city/country ~** (inhabitants) Stadt-/Landbewohner; (who prefer the city/the country) Stadt-/Landmenschen; **village ~:** Dorfbewohner; **local ~:** Einheimische; **working ~:** arbeitende Menschen; Werktätige; **coloured/white ~:** Farbige/Weiße; ~ **of wealth** reiche *od.* begüterte Leute *Pl.;* **her [own] sort/kind of ~:** ihresgleichen; *see also* **choose A 1** 3 *constr. as pl.* (subjects of ruler) Volk, *das;* (congregation) Gemeinde, *die* 4 *constr. as pl.* (persons not of nobility) **the ~:** das [gemeine] Volk 5 *constr. as sing. or pl.* (voters) Volk, *das;* **will of the ~:** Volkswille, *der* (Polit.); **go to the ~:** Wahlen ausschreiben 6 *constr. as pl.* (persons in general) Menschen; Leute *Pl.;* (as opposed to animals) Menschen; ~ **say he's very rich** die Leute sagen *od.* man sagt *od.* es heißt, dass er sehr reich sei; er soll sehr reich sein; **that is quite enough to alarm ~:** das reicht zur Genüge, um einen in Alarm zu versetzen; **a crowd of ~:** eine Menschenmenge; **don't tell ~ about this** erzähle niemandem davon; ~ **are like that** so sind die Menschen; **I don't understand ~ any more** ich verstehe die Welt nicht mehr; **'some ~** (certain persons, usu. with whom the speaker disagrees) gewisse Leute; (you) manche Leute; **some '~!** Leute gibt es!; **honestly, some '~!** also wirklich!; **listen, you ~!** hört mal [zu]!; **what do you ~ think?** was denkt ihr [denn]?; **you of 'all ~ ought ...:** gerade du solltest ...; **who do you think I saw at the party? 'Bill, of all ~!** wen, glaubst du, habe ich auf der Party getroffen? Ausgerechnet Bill!; **no sign of any ~:** keine Menschenseele 7 *constr. as pl.* (relatives) Familie, *die*

B *v.t.* 1 (fill with ~ or animals) bevölkern 2 (inhabit) bevölkern; (become inhabitant of) besiedeln

'people carrier *n.* Großraumlimousine, *die;* [Mini]van, *der*

peopled /ˈpiːpld/ *adj.* bevölkert

people: ~ **management** *n., no pl.* Menschenführung, *die; attrib.* ~ **management skills** Führungsqualitäten *Pl.;* ~ **mover** *n.* (vehicle for transporting large numbers of people) Personentransporter, *der;* (multi-purpose vehicle) Van, *der;* Großraumlimousine, *die; attrib.* ~ **mover system** Personenbeförderungssystem, *das;* ~ **power** *n., no pl.* Volksgewalt, *die*

People's Reˈpublic *n.* (Polit.) Volksrepublik, *die;* **the ~ of China** die Volksrepublik China

pep /pep/ (coll.)

A *n., no pl., no indef. art.* Schwung, *der;* Pep, *der* (salopp); **be full of ~:** viel Schwung *od.* (salopp) Pep haben

B *v.t.*, **-pp-:** ~ **[up]** aufpeppen (ugs.)

PEP /pep/ *abbr.* (Brit.) **= personal equity plan**

peplum /ˈpepləm/ *n.* (Fashion) Schößchen, *das*

pepper /ˈpepə(r)/

A *n.* 1 Pfeffer, *der;* **black/white ~:** schwarzer/weißer Pfeffer 2 (capsicum plant) Paprika, *der;* (fruit) Paprikaschote, *die;* **red/yellow/green ~:** roter/gelber/grüner Paprika; **sweet ~:** Gemüsepaprika, *der. See also* **cayenne**

B *v.t.* 1 (sprinkle with ~) pfeffern 2 (besprinkle) übersäen 3 (pelt with missiles) bombardieren (ugs., auch fig.); ~ **the target with shot** das Ziel mit Schrot spicken

pepper: **~-and-ˈsalt** *n.* (Textiles) Pfeffer und Salz; *attrib.* pfeffer- und salzfarben; **~corn** *n.* Pfefferkorn, *das; attrib.* **~corn rent** symbolischer Pachtzins; ~ **mill** *n.* Pfeffermühle, *die;* **~mint** *n.* 1 (plant) Pfefferminze, *die;* 2 (sweet) Pfefferminz, *das; attrib.* Pfefferminz⟨*bonbon, -drops, -pastille*⟩; 3 (oil) Pfefferminzöl, *das;* ~ **pot** *n.* Pfefferstreuer, *der;* ~ **spray** *n.* Pfefferspray, *das*

peppery /ˈpepərɪ/ *adj.* pfeff[e]rig; (spicy) scharf; (fig.: pungent) scharf; (fig.: hot-tempered) jähzornig; **the soup is rather ~:** die Suppe schmeckt ziemlich stark nach Pfeffer/die Suppe ist ziemlich scharf

'pep pill *n.* (coll.) Peppille, *die* (ugs.); Aufputschtablette, *die*

P

peppy /ˈpepɪ/ *adj.* (coll.) lebhaft, quirlig (ugs.); schwungvoll ‹*Tanz*›

pepsin /ˈpepsɪn/ *n.* (Chem.) Pepsin, *das*

ˈpep talk *n.* (coll.) Aufmunterung, *die;* **give sb. a ~:** jmdm. ein paar aufmunternde Worte sagen

peptic /ˈpeptɪk/ *adj.* (Physiol.) peptisch (fachspr.); Verdauungs-

peptic ˈulcer *n.* ▸ⓘ **p. 1231** (Med.) peptisches Ulkus (fachspr.); Magengeschwür, *das*

peptide /ˈpeptaɪd/ *n.* (Chem.) Peptid, *das*

per /pə(r), *stressed* pɜː(r)/ *prep.* **1** (by means of) per ‹*Post, Bahn, Schiff, Bote*›; durch ‹*Spediteur, Herrn X.*› **2** (according to) **[as] ~ sth.** wie in etw. (*Dat.*) angegeben; laut ‹*Anweisung, Preisliste*›; **as ~ usual** (joc.) wie üblich **3** ▸ⓘ **p. 1566** (for each) pro; **£50 ~ week** 50 Pfund in der Woche *od.* pro Woche; **fifty kilometres ~ hour** fünfzig Kilometer in der *od.* pro Stunde; **get 11 francs ~ pound** 11 Francs für ein Pfund bekommen

peradventure /pərədˈventʃə(r), perədˈventʃə(r)/ (arch.) *adv.* vielleicht; **lest ~ ...:** für den Fall, dass ...; **if ~:** im Fall[e], dass ...

perambulator /pəˈræmbjʊleɪtə(r)/ (Brit. formal) ▸ **pram**

per annum /pər ˈænəm/ *adv.* im Jahr; pro Jahr (bes. Kaufmannsspr., ugs.)

per capita /pə ˈkæpɪtə/
A *adv.* pro Kopf; pro Person; **earnings ~:** Pro-Kopf-Einkommen, *das*
B *adj.* Pro-Kopf-‹*Einkommen, Verbrauch usw.*›; **~ tax** Kopfsteuer, *die*

perceivable /pəˈsiːvəbl/ ▸ **perceptible**

perceive /pəˈsiːv/ *v.t.* **1** (with the mind) spüren; bemerken; ‹*menschlicher Geist:*› wahrnehmen; **~ sb.'s thoughts** jmds. Gedanken erraten **2** (through the senses) wahrnehmen; **we ~d a figure in the distance** wir erblickten in der Ferne eine Gestalt **3** (regard mentally in a certain way) wahrnehmen; **~d** vermeintlich ‹*Bedrohung, Gefahr, Wert*›

per cent (*Brit.*; *Amer.:* **percent**) /pəˈsent/
A *adv.* **ninety ~ effective** zu 90 Prozent wirksam; *see also* **hundred A 3**
B *adj.* **a 5 ~ increase** ein Zuwachs von 5 Prozent; ein fünfprozentiger Zuwachs
C *n.* **1** ▸ **percentage 2** (hundredth) Prozent, *das*

percentage /pəˈsentɪdʒ/ *n.* **1** (rate or proportion per cent) Prozentsatz, *der;* **a high ~ of alcohol** ein hoher Alkoholgehalt; **what ~ of 48 is 11?** wie viel Prozent von 48 sind 11?; **~ lead/improvement** prozentualer Vorsprung/prozentuale Verbesserung **2** (proportion) [prozentualer] Anteil

perˈcentage sign *n.* Prozentzeichen, *das*

perceptible /pəˈseptɪbl/ *adj.* wahrnehmbar; **be quite ~:** ganz offensichtlich sein

perceptibly /pəˈseptɪblɪ/ *adv.* sichtlich; sichtbar, merklich ‹*schrumpfen, welken*›

perception /pəˈsepʃn/ *n.* **1** (act) Wahrnehmung, *die;* (result) Erkenntnis, *die;* **have keen ~s** ein stark ausgeprägtes Wahrnehmungsvermögen haben **2** *no pl.* (faculty) Wahrnehmungsvermögen, *das;* **colour ~:** Farbensinn, *der;* **depth ~:** Tiefensehen, *das* (Med.); **~ of sounds** Gehör, *das;* **~ of objects** gegenständliche Wahrnehmung **3** (intuitive recognition) Gespür, *das* (**of** für); (instance) Erfassen, *das;* **the direct ~ of truth** das unmittelbare Erfassen der Wahrheit; **have no clear ~ of sth.** keine klare Vorstellung von etw. haben

perceptive /pəˈseptɪv/ *adj.* **1** (discerning) scharf ‹*Auge*›; fein ‹*Gehör, Nase, Geruchssinn*›; scharfsinnig ‹*Person*› **2** (having intuitive recognition or insight) einfühlsam ‹*Person, Zeitungsartikel, Bemerkung*›

perceptively /pəˈseptɪvlɪ/ *adv.* **1** (discerningly) mit scharfer Wahrnehmung **2** (with intuitive recognition or insight) einfühlsam

perceptiveness /pəˈseptɪvnɪs/, **perceptivity** /pɜːsepˈtɪvɪtɪ/ *ns., no pl.* **1** (discernment) **~ of the senses** scharfes Wahrnehmungsvermögen **2** (intuitive recognition, insight) Einfühlsamkeit, *die*

perch¹ /pɜːtʃ/ *n., pl. same or* **~es** (Zool.) Flussbarsch, *der*

perch²
A *n.* **1** (horizontal bar) Sitzstange, *die;* (for hens) Hühnerstange, *die* **2** (place to sit) Sitzplatz, *der* **3** (fig.: elevated or secure position) guter Posten; **knock sb. off his ~:** jmdn. von seinem hohen Ross herunterholen; **come off one's ~:** von seinem hohen Ross herunterkommen *od.* steigen **4** (Brit.: measure) (of length) Perch, *das;* $5\frac{1}{2}$ Yards; (of area) **[square] ~** (Brit.) Quadratperch, *das*
B *v.i.* **1** sich niederlassen **2** (be supported) sitzen
C *v.t.* setzen/stellen/legen

perchance /pəˈtʃɑːns/ *adv.* (arch.) **1** (possibly) möglicherweise; vielleicht **2** ▸ **peradventure**

perched /pɜːtʃt/ *adj.* **be ~** ‹*Vogel:*› sitzen; **stand ~ on a cliff** hoch auf einer Klippe stehen; **a village ~ on a hill** ein hoch oben auf einem Berg gelegenes Dorf; **with his hat ~ on the back of his head** mit hinten auf dem Kopf sitzendem Hut

percipient /pəˈsɪpɪənt/ *adj.* **1** (conscious) wahrnehmend; **be ~ of sth.** in der Lage sein, etw. zu erkennen **2** (discerning) scharf ‹*Augen*›; fein ‹*Gehör*›; scharfsichtig ‹*Kritiker*›

percolate /ˈpɜːkəleɪt/
A *v.i.* **1** (ooze) **~ through sth.** durch etw. [durch-]sickern **2** (fig.: spread gradually) vordringen **3** (be brewed in percolator) ‹*Kaffee:*› durchlaufen
B *v.t.* **1** (permeate) sickern durch ‹*Gestein*› **2** (fig.: penetrate) dringen in (+ *Akk.*) ‹*Bewusstsein*› **3** (brew in percolator) [mit der Kaffeemaschine] machen ‹*Kaffee*›

percolation /pɜːkəˈleɪʃn/ *n.* **1** (passage of liquid through filter) [Durch]sickern, *das* **2** (fig.: diffusion by spreading) Vordringen, *das* **3** (of coffee) Filtern, *das*

percolator /ˈpɜːkəleɪtə(r)/ *n.* Kaffeemaschine, *die*

percussion /pəˈkʌʃn/ *n.* **1** (Mus.) (playing by striking) Anschlag, *der;* (group of instruments) Schlagzeug, *das; attrib.* Schlagzeug‹*gruppe, -band, -begleitung*›; **~ instrument** Schlaginstrument, *das;* **~ section** Schlagzeug, *das* **2** (forcible striking) **explode by ~:** bei Erschütterung explodieren **3** (Med.) Perkussion, *die;* (massage) Klopfmassage, *die*

perˈcussion cap *n.* (Arms) Zündhütchen, *das;* (in toy) Zündblättchen, *das*

percussionist /pəˈkʌʃənɪst/ *n.* (Mus.) Schlagzeuger, *der*/-zeugerin, *die*

percussive /pəˈkʌsɪv/ *adj.* (Mus.) perkussiv

per diem /pɜː ˈdiːem/
A *adv.* pro Tag; täglich
B *adj.* täglich; **on a ~ basis** tageweise
C *n.* (allowance) Tagegeld, *das;* (payment) Entgelt, *das*

perdition /pəˈdɪʃn/ *n., no pl., no art.* (literary: eternal death) Verdammnis, *die;* **escape ~:** der [ewigen] Verdammnis entkommen; **damn you to ~!** sei auf ewig verdammt!

peregrination /perɪgrɪˈneɪʃn/ *n.* (arch./joc.) **1** *no pl.* (travelling) Reise, *die;* (joc.) Umherreisen, *das* **2** *in pl.* (travels) Reisen; **during your ~s** (joc.) auf deinen Streifzügen

peregrine /ˈperɪgrɪn/ *n.* **~ [falcon]** (Ornith.) Wanderfalke, *der*

peremptorily /pəˈremptərɪlɪ, ˈperɪmptərɪlɪ/ *adv.* **1** (so as to admit no contradiction) kategorisch; (imperiously) herrisch; gebieterisch (geh.) **2** (dogmatically) beharrlich, hartnäckig ‹*leugnen*›; **speak ~ on sth.** sich dogmatisch zu etw. äußern

peremptory /pəˈremptərɪ, ˈperɪmptərɪ/ *adj.* **1** (admitting no contradiction) kategorisch; (imperious) herrisch; gebieterisch (geh.) **2** (essential) unbedingt; unerlässlich ‹*Vorschrift*› **3** (dogmatic) beharrlich; hartnäckig **4** (Law) **~ writ** gerichtliche Verfügung; **~ challenge** Ablehnung [eines Geschworenen] ohne Angabe der Gründe

perennial /pəˈrenjəl/
A *adj.* **1** (lasting all year) ganzjährig; perennierend (fachspr.) ‹*Quelle, Brunnen, Bach*› **2** (lasting indefinitely) immer während; ewig ‹*Jugend, Mythos, Suche*›; immer wieder auftretend ‹*Problem*› **3** (Bot.) ausdauernd; perennierend (fachspr.)
B *n.* (Bot.) ausdauernde *od.* (fachspr.) perennierende Pflanze

perennially /pəˈrenjəlɪ/ *adv.* **1** (throughout the year) **flow ~** ‹*Fluss:*› das ganze Jahr Wasser führen **2** (perpetually) ständig; ewig ‹*ungelöst*›

perestroika /perɪˈstrɔɪkə/ *n.* Perestroika, *die*

perfect
A /ˈpɜːfɪkt/ *adj.* **1** (complete) vollkommen; umfassend ‹*Kenntnisse, Wissen*› **2** (faultless) vollkommen; perfekt ‹*Englisch, Technik, Timing*›; tadellos ‹*Zustand*›; [absolut] gelungen ‹*Aufführung*›; lupenrein ‹*Diamant*›; (conforming to an abstract concept) perfekt; **get a technique ~:** eine Technik vollkommen *od.* absolut beherrschen lernen; **~ gas** (Phys.) ideales Gas **3** (trained, skilled) **be ~ in the performance of one's duties** seine Aufgaben tadellos erfüllen; **practice makes ~:** Übung macht den Meister **4** (very satisfactory) herrlich; wunderbar **5** (exact) perfekt; getreu ‹*Ebenbild, Abbild*›; (fully what the name implies) perfekt ‹*Gentleman, Dame, Ehemann, Gastgeberin*›; *see also* **square A 7** **6** (absolute) **a ~ stranger** ein völlig Fremder; ein Wildfremder (ugs.); **he is a ~ stranger to me** er ist mir völlig unbekannt; **he is a ~ scream** (coll.)/**angel** (coll.)/**charmer** er ist wirklich zum Schreien [komisch]/ein Engel/charmant; **she looks a ~ little angel** sie sieht wie ein richtiger kleiner Engel aus; **I have a ~ right to stay** ich habe eindeutig *od.* durchaus das Recht zu bleiben; **have ~ freedom to make one's own decision** völlig frei entscheiden können **7** (coll.: unmitigated) absolut; **look a ~ fright/mess** wirklich zum Weglaufen/absolut verboten aussehen (ugs.); **a ~ tantrum** ein regelrechter Wutanfall **8** (Ling.) Perfekt-; **the ~ tense** das Perfekt; **future ~ tense** Futur II, *das;* vollendetes Futur; **past ~** ▸ **pluperfect B**; **present perfect** ▸ **present¹ A 4** **9** (Mus.) **~ interval** reines Intervall
B *n.* (Ling.) Perfekt, *das*
C /pəˈfekt/ *v.t.* vervollkommnen; perfektionieren

perfection /pəˈfekʃn/ *n.* **1** *no pl.* (making perfect) Vervollkommnung, *die;* Perfektionierung, *die* **2** *no pl.* (faultlessness) Vollkommenheit, *die;* Perfektion, *die;* **~ of detail** Vollkommenheit *od.* Perfektion im Detail; **~ of technique** technische Perfektion; **to ~:** perfekt; **it/he succeeded to ~:** es war ein voller Erfolg/er war absolut erfolgreich; **you cook to ~:** du bist eine perfekte Köchin/ein perfekter Koch **3** *no pl.* (perfect person or thing) **be ~:** perfekt sein **4** *no pl., no indef. art.* (most perfect degree) Inbegriff, *der;* **sth. has reached its ~:** etw. hat seine höchste Vollkommenheit erreicht

perfectionism /pəˈfekʃənɪzm/ *n., no pl.* Perfektionismus, *der*

perfectionist /pəˈfekʃənɪst/ *n.* Perfektionist, *der*/Perfektionistin, *die*

perfectly /ˈpɜːfɪktlɪ/ *adv.* **1** (completely) vollkommen; völlig; **I understand that ~:** ich verstehe das vollkommen *od.* völlig; **be ~ entitled to do sth.** durchaus berechtigt sein, etw. zu tun **2** (faultlessly) perfekt; tadellos ‹*sich verhalten*›; fehlerlos ‹*singen*› **3** (exactly) vollkommen; exakt, genau ‹*vorhersagbar*› **4** (coll.: to an unmitigated extent) furchtbar (ugs.) ‹*schrecklich, schlimm, ekelhaft*›

perfect ˈpitch *n.* (Mus.) absolutes Gehör

perfidious /pəˈfɪdɪəs/ *adj.* perfid (geh.); *see also* **Albion**

perfidy /ˈpɜːfɪdɪ/ *n.* Perfidie, *die* (geh.)

perforate /ˈpɜːfəreɪt/ *v.t.* **1** (make hole[s] through) perforieren; **suffer from a ~d eardrum/ulcer** ein Loch im Trommelfell/ein durchgebrochenes Magengeschwür haben **2** (make an opening into) durchlöchern

perforation /pɜːfəˈreɪʃn/ *n.* **1** (action of perforating) Perforierung, *die* **2** (hole) Loch, *das;* **~s** (line of holes esp. in paper) Perforation, *die;* (in sheets of stamps) Zähnung, *die;* Perforation, *die*

perforator /ˈpɜːfəreɪtə(r)/ *n.* Perforiermaschine, *die;* (rock drill) Bohrer, *der;* (used in stripping wallpaper) Tapetenperforator, *der*

p

perforce /pəˈfɔːs/ *adv.* (arch./formal) notgedrungen

perform /pəˈfɔːm/

A *v.t.* [1] (fulfil) ausführen ‹*Befehl, Arbeit, Operation*›; erfüllen ‹*Bitte, Wunsch, Pflicht, Vertrag, Versprechen, Bedingung, Aufgabe*›; nachkommen (+ *Dat.*) ‹*Verpflichtung*›; vollbringen ‹*[Helden]tat, Leistung*›; durchführen ‹*Operation*›; einhalten ‹*Versprechen, Vertrag*› [2] (carry out) ausfüllen ‹*Funktion*›; vollbringen ‹*Wunder*›; anstellen ‹*Berechnungen*›; durchführen ‹*Experiment, Sektion*›; vornehmen ‹*Sektion*›; vorführen, zeigen ‹*Trick*›; (in formal manner or according to prescribed ritual) vollziehen ‹*Trauung, Taufe, Riten, Rituale, Opfer*›; [ab]halten ‹*Gottesdienst*›; (render) aufführen ‹*Theaterstück, Scharade*›; vortragen, vorsingen ‹*Lied*›; vorspielen, vortragen ‹*Sonate usw.*›

B *v.i.* [1] eine Vorführung geben; (sing) singen; (play) spielen; ‹*Jongleur:*› Kunststücke zeigen *od.* vorführen; ‹*Zauberer:*› Zaubertricks ausführen *od.* vorführen; **he ~ed very well** seine Darbietung war sehr gut; **she ~s as soloist** sie ist Solistin; (occasionally) sie tritt als Solistin auf; **she ~ed skilfully on the flute/piano** sie spielte mit großer Könnerschaft Flöte/Klavier [2] (Theatre) auftreten; **he ~ed very well** sein Auftritt war sehr gut [3] (execute tricks) ‹*Tier:*› Kunststücke zeigen *od.* vorführen; **train an animal to ~:** einem Tier Kunststücke beibringen [4] (work, function) ‹*Auto:*› laufen, fahren; **he ~ed all right/well [in the exam]** er machte seine Sache [in der Prüfung] ordentlich/gut [5] (coll. euphem.) (accomplish sexual intercourse) es machen (ugs. verhüll.); (excrete, urinate) ‹*Kind, Haustier:*› machen (ugs. verhüll.)

performance /pəˈfɔːməns/ *n.* [1] (fulfilment) (of promise, duty, task) Erfüllung, *die;* (of command) Ausführung, *die* [2] (carrying out) Durchführung, *die* [3] (notable feat) Leistung, *die;* **put up a good ~:** eine gute Leistung zeigen; seine Sache gut machen [4] (performing of play etc.) Vorstellung, *die;* **the ~s of the gymnasts** die Turnveranstaltungen; **her ~ in the play** ihre [schauspielerische] Leistung in dem Theaterstück; **her ~ as Desdemona** ihre Darstellung *od.* Interpretation der Desdemona; **the ~ of a play/opera** die Aufführung eines Theaterstücks/einer Oper; **give a ~ of a symphony/play** eine Sinfonie/ein Stück spielen *od.* aufführen [5] (achievement under test) Leistung, *die;* **the car has good ~:** der Wagen bringt viel Leistung; **give an engine more ~:** die Leistung eines Motors erhöhen; **are you satisfied with the ~ of your new car?** sind Sie mit Ihrem neuen Auto zufrieden?; **the ~ of the equipment, in tests, was somewhat variable** die Anlage hat in Tests nicht immer gleich abgeschnitten [6] (coll.: display of anger etc.) Auftritt, *der* [7] (coll.: difficult procedure) Theater, *das* (ugs., abwertend); Umstand, *der;* **it was a hell of a ~ getting my passport** das war vielleicht ein Umstand *od.* Theater, bis ich meinen Pass hatte

performance: ~ appraisal *n.* Leistungsbeurteilung, *die;* **~ art** *n., no pl.* Performancekunst, *die;* **~ artist** *n.* ▸ⓘ **p. 1260** Performancekünstler, *der*/-künstlerin, *die* **~-enhancing** *adj.* **~-enhancing drug/substance** leistungsfördernde *od.* -steigernde Droge/Substanz; **~-related** *adj.* leistungsbezogen ‹*Bezahlung*›

performer /pəˈfɔːmə(r)/ *n.* Künstler, *der*/Künstlerin, *die;* **as a ~ of tricks he was unsurpassed** im Vorführen von Tricks war er unübertroffen

performing /pəˈfɔːmɪŋ/ *adj.* [1] (acting, singing, etc.) auftretend ‹*Künstler*›; **~ arts** darstellende Künste; **~ rights** Aufführungsrechte *Pl.* [2] (executing tricks) dressiert ‹*Tier*›

performing ˈarts *n. pl.* darstellende Künste

perfume

A /ˈpɜːfjuːm/ *n.* [1] (sweet smell) Duft, *der* [2] (fluid) Parfüm, *das;* **~ atomizer** *or* **spray** Parfümzerstäuber, *der*

B /pəˈfjuːm, ˈpɜːfjuːm/ *v.t.* (impart sweet scent to) mit Wohlgeruch erfüllen; (impregnate with sweet smell) parfümieren

perfumer /pəˈfjuːmə(r)/ *n.* (maker of perfume) Parfümeur, *der*/Parfümeuse, *die;* (seller of perfume) Parfümhändler, *der*/Parfümhändlerin, *die*

perfumery /pəˈfjuːmərɪ/ *n.* [1] *no pl.* (preparation of perfumes) Parfümherstellung, *die* [2] (perfumes) Parfümeriewaren *Pl.;* *attrib.* Parfümerie- [3] (shop) Parfümerie, *die*

perfunctorily /pəˈfʌŋktərɪlɪ/ *adv.* pflichtschuldig; oberflächlich, mechanisch ‹*arbeiten*›

perfunctory /pəˈfʌŋktərɪ/ *adj.* (done for duty's sake only) pflichtschuldig; flüchtig ‹*Erkundigung, Bemerkung*›; (superficial) oberflächlich ‹*Arbeit, Überprüfung*›; **his tidying of his bedroom had been very ~:** er hatte sein Zimmer nur sehr oberflächlich aufgeräumt; **put in a ~ appearance** sich, um seiner Pflicht zu genügen, kurz zeigen

pergola /ˈpɜːgələ/ *n.* (Hort.) Pergola, *die;* Laubengang, *der*

perhaps /pəˈhæps, præps/ *adv.* vielleicht; **I'll go out, ~:** ich gehe vielleicht aus; **~ so** [das] mag [ja] sein; **~ not** (maybe this is or will not be the case) vielleicht auch nicht; (it might be best not to do this) vielleicht lieber nicht

perianth /ˈperɪænθ/ *n.* (Bot.) Perianth[ium], *das* (fachspr.); Blütenhülle, *die*

pericardium /perɪˈkɑːdɪəm/ *n., pl.* **pericardia** /perɪˈkɑːdɪə/ (Anat.) Perikard[ium], *das* (fachspr.); Herzbeutel, *der*

pericarp /ˈperɪkɑːp/ *n.* (Bot.) Perikarp, *das* (fachspr.); Fruchtwand, *die*

perigee /ˈperɪdʒiː/ *n.* (Astron.) Perigäum, *das* (fachspr.); Erdnähe, *die*

perihelion /perɪˈhiːlɪən/ *n., pl.* **perihelia** /perɪˈhiːlɪə/ (Astron.) Perihel, *das;* **at ~:** im Perihel

peril /ˈperəl/ *n.* Gefahr, *die;* **they were in constant ~ from their enemies** sie waren ständig von ihren Feinden bedroht; **be in deadly ~, be in ~ of death** *or* **one's life** in Lebensgefahr sein *od.* schweben; **be in ~ of doing sth.** Gefahr laufen, etw. zu tun; **do sth. at one's ~** (accepting risk of injury) etw. auf eigene Gefahr tun

perilous /ˈperələs/ *adj.* [1] (full of danger) gefahrvoll; **be ~:** gefährlich sein [2] (exposed to imminent risk) gefährdet; anfällig ‹*Beziehung*›; **a ~ pile of chairs** ein gefährlich hoher Turm aus Stühlen

perilously /ˈperələslɪ/ *adv.* gefährlich; **~ ill** todkrank

perimeter /pəˈrɪmɪtə(r)/ *n.* [1] (outer boundary) [äußere] Begrenzung; Grenze, *die;* **troops were stationed all around the ~ to guard the camp** Truppen waren rundherum postiert, um das Lager zu bewachen; **at the ~ of the racetrack** am Rande der Rennbahn; *attrib.* **~ fence** Umfassungszaun, *der* [2] (outline of figure) Umriss, *der;* (length of outline) Umfang, *der*

perinatal /perɪˈneɪtl/ *adj.* (Med.) perinatal

perineum /perɪˈniːəm/ *n., pl.* **~s** *or* **perinea** /perɪˈniːə/ (Anat.) Damm, *der*

period /ˈpɪərɪəd/

A *n.* [1] (distinct portion of history or life) Periode, *die;* Zeit, *die;* **~s of history** geschichtliche Perioden; **the modern ~:** die Moderne; das Zeitalter der Moderne; **the Reformation/Tudor/Victorian ~:** die Reformationszeit/die Tudorzeit/die viktorianische Zeit; **during the ~ of his youth** in seiner Jugend[zeit]; **at a later ~ of her life** zu einem späteren Zeitpunkt ihres Lebens *od.* in ihrem Leben; **a ~ of literature/art** eine literarische/kunstgeschichtliche Epoche; **the Classical/Romantic/Renaissance ~:** die Klassik/Romantik/Renaissance; **of the ~** (of the time under discussion) der damaligen Zeit [2] (any portion of time) Zeitraum, *der;* Zeitspanne, *die;* **over a ~ [of time]** über einen längeren Zeitraum; **within the agreed ~:** innerhalb der vereinbarten Frist; **showers and bright ~s** (Meteorol.) Schauer und Aufheiterungen; **over a longer ~ I changed my mind** im Laufe der Zeit änderte ich meine Meinung; **I've had ~s of anxiety** es gab Zeiten der Angst für mich [3] (Sch.: time allocated for lesson) Stunde, *die;* **teaching/lesson ~:** Unterrichtsstunde, *die;* **geography/chemistry/English ~:** Geographie-/Chemie-/Englischstunde, *die;* **have five ~s a week for French** fünf Stunden Französisch[unterricht] in der Woche haben; **have two chemistry ~s** zwei Stunden Chemie haben; **a detention ~, a ~ of detention** eine Stunde Arrest; **a free ~:** eine Freistunde [4] (occurrence of menstruation) Periode, *die;* Regel[blutung], *die;* **have her/a ~:** ihre Periode *od.* Regel *od.* (ugs. verhüll.) Tage haben; **miss one's ~:** ihre Periode nicht bekommen; **~ pains** Menstruationsschmerzen [5] (punctuation mark) Punkt, *der* [6] (pause in speech) Pause, *die;* (fig.) Stillstand, *der* [7] (appended to statement) [und damit] basta! (ugs.); **we can't pay higher wages, ~:** wir können keine höheren Löhne zahlen, da ist nichts zu machen [8] (time taken by recurring process) Periode, *die;* (Astron.: time of revolution) Umlaufzeit, *die* [9] (Geol.) Periode, *die* [10] (complete sentence) Satz, *der;* Satzgefüge, *das* (Sprachw.) [11] (Math.) (set of figures) [Ziffern]gruppe, *die;* (set of recurring figures) Periode, *die* [12] (Chem.) Periode, *die*

B *adj.* zeitgenössisch ‹*Tracht, Kostüm*›; Zeit‹*roman, -stück*›; antik ‹*Möbel*›; ‹*Zimmer*› im Zeitstil; **~ piece** (play) Zeitstück, *das;* (novel) Zeitroman, *der;* **this Georgian cabinet is a true ~ piece** dieser georgianische Schrank ist ein für die Zeit ausgesprochen typisches Stück

periodic /pɪərɪˈɒdɪk/ *adj.* [1] (recurring at regular intervals) periodisch *od.* regelmäßig [auftretend *od.* wiederkehrend]; (intermittent) gelegentlich [auftretend]; vereinzelt ‹*Regenschauer*›; **make ~ good resolutions** von Zeit zu Zeit *od.* immer mal wieder gute Vorsätze fassen [2] (Astron.) periodisch; **the ~ time of a planet** die Umlaufzeit eines Planeten

periodical /pɪərɪˈɒdɪkl/

A *adj.* [1] ▸**periodic** [2] (published at regular intervals) regelmäßig erscheinend; **~ journal/magazine** Zeitschrift, *die*

B *n.* Zeitschrift, *die;* *attrib.* Zeitschriften-; **weekly/monthly/quarterly ~:** Wochenzeitschrift/Monatsschrift/Vierteljahresschrift, *die*

periodically /pɪərɪˈɒdɪkəlɪ/ *adv.* (at regular intervals) regelmäßig; (intermittently) gelegentlich

periodic ˈtable *n.* (Chem.) Periodensystem, *das*

peripatetic /perɪpəˈtetɪk/ *adj.* **~ teacher** Lehrer, der/Lehrerin, die an mehreren Schulen unterrichtet; **~ teaching** Unterricht durch Lehrer, die an mehreren Schulen arbeiten; **~ lifestyle** Wanderleben, *das*

peripheral /pəˈrɪfərl/

A *adj.* [1] (of the periphery) ‹*Parkraum*› in Randlage; **~ road** Ringstraße, *die;* **~ speed** Umfangsgeschwindigkeit, *die* [2] (of minor importance) peripher (geh.); marginal (geh.); Rand‹*problem, -kultur, -erscheinung, -figur, -gebiet, -bemerkung, -lage*›; **be merely ~** *or* **of merely ~ importance to sth.** für etw. von nur marginaler (geh.) *od.* untergeordneter Bedeutung sein [3] (Anat.) peripher [4] (Computing) peripher

B *n.* (Computing) Peripheriegerät, *das*

peripherally /pəˈrɪfərəlɪ/ *adv.* [1] (at the periphery) außen [2] (marginally) am Rande; peripher (geh.); marginal (geh.)

periphery /pəˈrɪfərɪ/ *n.* [1] (external boundary) Begrenzung, *die;* (of surface) Außenfläche, *die* [2] (outer region) Peripherie, *die* (geh.); Rand, *der*

periphrasis /pəˈrɪfrəsɪs/ *n., pl.* **periphrases** /pəˈrɪfrəsiːz/ [1] *no pl.* (roundabout way of speaking) periphrastischer (Rhet.) *od.* umschreibender Stil [2] (roundabout phrase) Periphrase, *die* (Rhet.); Umschreibung, *die*

periphrastic /perɪˈfræstɪk/ *adj.* periphrastisch (Rhet.); umschreibend

periscope /ˈperɪskəʊp/ *n.* Periskop, *das*

periscopic /perɪˈskɒpɪk/ *adj.* periskopisch

perish /ˈperɪʃ/

A *v.i.* [1] (suffer destruction) umkommen; ‹*Volk, Rasse, Kultur:*› untergehen; ‹*Kraft, Energie:*› versiegen; ‹*Pflanze:*› eingehen; **his name will never ~:** sein Name wird für alle Zeiten fortleben; **~ by the sword/at the hand of the enemy** durch das Schwert/durch Feindes Hand umkommen; **he ~ed from the cold** er erfror; **… or ~ in the attempt** (joc.) …, koste es, was es wolle; **~ the thought!** Gott behüte *od.* bewahre! [2] (rot) verderben; ‹*Fresken, Gemälde:*› verblassen; ‹*Gummi:*› altern

B *v.t.* [1] (reduce to distress) **we were ~ed [with**

cold] wir waren ganz durchgefroren **2** (cause to rot) [schneller] altern lassen ‹*Gummi*›; angreifen ‹*Reifen*›

perishable /ˈperɪʃəbl/
A *adj.* (liable to perish) vergänglich; (subject to speedy decay) [leicht] verderblich
B *n. in pl.* leicht verderbliche Güter *od.* Waren

perisher /ˈperɪʃə(r)/ *n.* (Brit. coll.) (annoying person) Ekel, *das* (ugs.); Miststück, *das* (salopp); (unfortunate person) **poor ~:** armer Hund (ugs.); armes Schwein (ugs.)

perishing /ˈperɪʃɪŋ/ (coll.)
A *adj.* **1** mörderisch ‹*Wind, Kälte*›; (very cold) eiskalt; **it's/I'm ~:** es ist bitterkalt/ich komme um vor Kälte (ugs.) **2** (Brit.: confounded) elend; **that child is a ~ nuisance** das Kind kann einem den Nerv töten (ugs.)
B *adv.* **1** mörderisch ‹*kalt*› **2** (Brit.: confoundedly) fürchterlich (ugs.)

peristaltic /perɪˈstæltɪk/ *adj.* (Physiol.) peristaltisch

peritoneum /perɪtəˈniːəm/ *n., pl.* **~s** *or* **peritonea** /perɪtəˈniːə/ (Anat.) Bauchfell, *das*

peritonitis /perɪtəˈnaɪtɪs/ *n.* ▸**❶ p. 1231** (Med.) Peritonitis, *die* (fachspr.); Bauchfellentzündung, *die*

periwig /ˈperɪwɪg/ *n.* (Hist.) Perücke, *die*

periwinkle¹ /ˈperɪwɪŋkl/ *n.* **1** (Bot.) Immergrün, *das* **2** (colour) **~ [blue]** Veilchenblau, *das*

periwinkle² ▸**winkle A**

perjure /ˈpɜːdʒə(r)/ *v. refl.* (swear to false statement) einen Meineid leisten; (Law: give false evidence under oath) [unter Eid] falsch aussagen

perjured /ˈpɜːdʒəd/ *adj.* **~ testimony** falsche Aussage unter Eid; **be ~:** [unter Eid] falsch ausgesagt haben; meineidig sein

perjurer /ˈpɜːdʒərə(r)/ *n.* Meineidige, *der/die*

perjury /ˈpɜːdʒərɪ/ *n.* **1** (swearing to false statement) Meineid, *der;* (Law: giving false evidence while under oath) eidliche Falschaussage; **commit ~:** einen Meineid leisten/sich der eidlichen Falschaussage schuldig machen **2** (breach of oath) Eidesverletzung, *die;* Eidbruch, *der*

perk¹ /pɜːk/ (coll.)
A *v.i.* **~ up** munter werden; ‹*Wirtschaft:*› in Gang kommen (ugs.); (cheer up) aufleben; **life had ~ed up again** das Leben machte wieder Spaß
B *v.t.* **1** **~ up** (restore liveliness of) aufmuntern; **I need a drink to ~ me up** ich muss jetzt erst mal zur Aufmunterung was trinken (ugs.); **~ up sb.'s spirits** jmdn. aufmuntern; **take pills to ~ oneself up** sich mit Pillen aufputschen **2** **~ up** (raise briskly) aufstellen ‹*Schwanz, Ohren*›; heben ‹*Kopf*› **3** (smarten) **~ oneself/sth. up** sich fein machen/etw. verschönern

perk² *n.* (Brit. coll.: benefit) [Sonder]vergünstigung, *die*

perk³ (coll.)
A *v.i.* ‹*Kaffee:*› durchlaufen; ‹*Kaffeemaschine:*› in Gang sein
B *v.t.* machen ‹*Kaffee*›

perkily /ˈpɜːkɪlɪ/ *adv.* ▸**perky**: lebhaft; munter; keck; selbstbewusst

perky /ˈpɜːkɪ/ *adj.* **1** (lively) lebhaft; munter **2** (self-assertive) keck; selbstbewusst

perlite /ˈpɜːlaɪt/ *n.* Perlit, *der*

perm¹ /pɜːm/
A *n.* (permanent wave) Dauerwelle, *die*
B *v.t.* **~ sb.'s hair** jmdm. eine Dauerwelle machen; **have one's hair ~ed** sich (*Dat.*) eine Dauerwelle machen lassen; **have ~ed hair** eine Dauerwelle haben

perm² (Brit.)
A *n.* (permutation) Tippreihe, *die*
B *v.t.* als Tippreihe ankreuzen

permafrost /ˈpɜːməfrɒst/ *n.* (Geog.) Permafrost, *der;* Dauerfrostboden, *der*

permanence /ˈpɜːmənəns/ *n., no pl.* Dauerhaftigkeit, *die;* **the place had an air of ~:** die Stätte umgab eine Aura von Unvergänglichkeit

permanency /ˈpɜːmənənsɪ/ *n.* **1** *no pl.* ▸**permanence** **2** (condition) Dauerzustand, *der;* (job) Dauerstellung, *die*

permanent /ˈpɜːmənənt/ *adj.* fest ‹*Sitz, Bestandteil, Mitglied*›; beständig, ewig ‹*Werte*›; treu ‹*Freund*›; ständig ‹*Plage, Meckern, Wohnsitz, Adresse, Kampf*›; Dauer‹*gast, -stellung, -visum*›; bleibend ‹*Folge, Zahn, Gebiss, Schaden*›; **be in ~ residence here** ständig hier wohnen; **of ~ value** von bleibendem Wert; **this time it's ~:** diesmal ist es für immer; **sb./sth. is a ~ fixture** jmd./etw. gehört zum Inventar; **be employed on a ~ basis** fest zum Personal gehören *[sic?]*

permanently /ˈpɜːmənəntlɪ/ *adv.* dauernd; auf Dauer ‹*verhindern, bleiben*›; fest ‹*anstellen, einstellen*›; (repeatedly) ständig; dauernd; **they live in France ~ now** sie leben jetzt ganz (ugs.) *od.* ständig in Frankreich; **she was ~ disabled in the accident** sie hat bei dem Unfall eine bleibende Behinderung davongetragen; **she was ~ affected by the shock** der Schock hatte für sie bleibende Folgen

permanent: **~ 'wave** *n.* Dauerwelle, *die;* **~ 'way** *n.* (Brit. Railw.) Oberbau, *der*

permeable /ˈpɜːmɪəbl/ *adj.* durchlässig; **~ by water** wasserdurchlässig; **be ~ to sth.** etw. durchlassen

permeate /ˈpɜːmɪeɪt/
A *v.t.* (get into) dringen in (+ *Akk.*); (pass through) dringen durch; (saturate) erfüllen; **~ sb.'s consciousness** jmdm. ins Bewusstsein dringen; **be ~d with** *or* **by sth.** (fig.) von etw. durchdrungen sein
B *v.i.* **~ through sth.** etw. durchdringen; **~ through to sb.** zu jmdm. durchdringen

permissible /pəˈmɪsɪbl/ *adj.* zulässig; **be ~ to** *or* **for sb.** jmdm. erlaubt sein; **~ under the law** nicht gesetzeswidrig; **~ dose** (Med.) zulässige Dosis; (of radiation) zulässige Belastung

permission /pəˈmɪʃn/ *n., no indef. art.* Erlaubnis, *die;* (given by official body) Genehmigung, *die;* **ask [sb.'s] ~:** [jmdn.] um Erlaubnis bitten; **who gave you ~ to do this?** wer hat dir erlaubt, das zu tun?; **by whose ~?** mit wessen Erlaubnis?; **with your ~:** wenn Sie gestatten; mit Ihrer Erlaubnis; **written ~:** eine schriftliche Genehmigung

permissive /pəˈmɪsɪv/ *adj.* **1** (giving permission) **~ legislation** permissive Gesetzgebung **2** (tolerant) tolerant; großzügig; (in relation to moral matters) freizügig; permissiv (geh.); **the ~ society** die permissive Gesellschaft

permissiveness /pəˈmɪsɪvnɪs/ *n., no pl.* Freizügigkeit, *die;* Toleranz, *die*

permit
A /pəˈmɪt/ *v.t.*, **-tt-** zulassen ‹*Berufung, Einspruch usw.*›; **~ sb. sth.** jmdm. etw. erlauben *od.* (geh.) gestatten; **~ me to offer my congratulations** (formal) gestatten Sie mir, Ihnen meine Glückwünsche auszusprechen (geh.); **sb. is ~ted to do sth.** es ist jmdm. erlaubt *od.* (geh.) gestattet, etw. zu tun
B *v.i.*, **-tt-** **1** (give opportunity) es zulassen; **weather ~ting** bei entsprechendem Wetter; wenn das Wetter mitspielt (ugs.) **2** (admit) **~ of sth.** etw. erlauben *od.* gestatten; **not ~ of sth.** etw. verbieten
C /ˈpɜːmɪt/ *n.* (written order) Genehmigung, *die;* (for entering premises) Passierschein, *der;* (for using car park) Parkausweis, *der;* **fishing ~:** Fischereischein, *der;* Angelschein, *der;* **be a ~-holder** einen Passierschein/Parkausweis/Angelschein *usw.* haben

permutation /pɜːmjʊˈteɪʃn/ *n.* **1** (varying of order) Umstellung, *die* **2** (result of variation of order) Anordnung, *die;* (of series of items) Reihenfolge, *die;* Permutation, *die* (Math.) **3** (selection of items) Auswahl, *die;* (Brit.: in football pools) Tippreihe, *die;* **make a ~:** eine Auswahl treffen/eine Tippreihe ankreuzen

permute /pəˈmjuːt/ *v.t.* umstellen; (Math.) permutieren

pernicious /pəˈnɪʃəs/ *adj.* ▸**❶ p. 1231** verderblich; bösartig ‹*Krankheit, Person*›; schlimm, übel ‹*Angewohnheit*›; (fatal) fatal; **be a ~ influence on sb.** einen schlimmen *od.* üblen Einfluss auf jmdn. ausüben; **be ~ to sb./sth.** jmdm./einer Sache abträglich sein (geh.) *od.* schaden; **~ anaemia** (Med.) perniziöse Anämie

pernickety /pəˈnɪkɪtɪ/ *adj.* (coll.) **1** (fastidious, meticulous) pingelig (ugs.) (**about** in Bezug auf + *Akk.*) **2** (tricky) heikel ‹*Frage, Thema*›; kitzelig ‹*Aufgabe, Job*›; fummelig (ugs.) ‹*Arbeitsvorgang*›

peroration /perəˈreɪʃn/ *n.* Schlusswort, *das*

peroxide /pəˈrɒksaɪd/
A *n.* **1** (Chem.) Peroxid, *das* **2** **[hydrogen] ~:** Wasserstoffperoxid, *das;* **~ blonde** Wasserstoffblondine, *die*
B *v.t.* [mit Wasserstoffperoxid] bleichen

perpendicular /pɜːpənˈdɪkjʊlə(r)/
A *adj.* **1** senkrecht; lotrecht **2** (very steep) [fast] senkrecht ‹*Aufstieg, Abstieg*›; senkrecht abfallend/aufragend ‹*Kliff, Felswand usw.*›; **~ drop/slope/rock face** Steilabfall, *der*/-hang, *der*/-wand, *die* **3** (erect, upright) aufrecht; (joc.: standing) stehend; **be/remain ~** (joc.) stehen/stehen bleiben **4** (Geom.) senkrecht (**to** zu); **two ~ planes/lines** zwei zueinander senkrechte Ebenen/Linien **5** (Archit.) ‹*Bauwerk, Fenster*› im Perpendikularstil; **P~ style** Perpendikularstil, *der*
B *n.* **1** (line) Senkrechte, *die* (**to** zu); Lot, *das* (**to** auf + *Dat.*) **2** (position) **the ~:** die Senkrechte; das Lot; **be [slightly] out of [the] ~:** [etwas] aus dem Lot sein; nicht [ganz] senkrecht sein **3** (instrument) Lot, *das*

perpendicularly /pɜːpənˈdɪkjʊləlɪ/ *adv.* **1** (vertically) senkrecht; lotrecht **2** (steeply) [beinahe] senkrecht **3** (Geom.) senkrecht

perpetrate /ˈpɜːpɪtreɪt/ *v.t.* begehen; anrichten ‹*Blutbad, Schaden*›; verüben ‹*Gemetzel, Gräuel*›; ausführen ‹*Streich*›; (joc.) zum Besten geben (ugs.) ‹*Witz, Lied*›

perpetration /pɜːpɪˈtreɪʃn/ *n.* (of crime, blunder) Begehen, *das;* (of atrocity, outrage) Verübung, *die*

perpetrator /ˈpɜːpɪtreɪtə(r)/ *n.* [Übel]täter, *der*/-täterin, *die;* **be the ~ of a crime/fraud/atrocity/massacre** ein Verbrechen/einen Betrug begangen haben/eine Gräueltat verübt haben/ein Blutbad angerichtet haben

perpetual /pəˈpetjʊəl/ *adj.* **1** (eternal) ewig **2** (continuous) ständig **3** (repeated) ständig; [an]dauernd; **she has ~ crises** sie hat [an]dauernd *od.* ständig Krisen **4** (applicable or valid for ever) immer während; ewig

perpetual 'calendar *n.* **1** (table) ewiger *od.* immer währender Kalender **2** (device) Dauerkalender, *der*

perpetually /pəˈpetjʊəlɪ/ *adv.* **1** (eternally) ewig **2** (continuously) ständig **3** (repeatedly) ständig; [an]dauernd

perpetual: **~ 'motion** *n., no pl., no art.* ewige Bewegung; **~-'motion machine** *n.* Perpetuum mobile, *das*

perpetuate /pəˈpetjʊeɪt/ *v.t.* **1** (preserve from oblivion) lebendig erhalten ‹*Andenken*›; unsterblich machen ‹*Namen*›; aufrechterhalten ‹*Tradition*› **2** (make perpetual) aufrechterhalten; erhalten ‹*Art, Macht*›

perpetuation /pəpetjʊˈeɪʃn/ *n.* **1** (preservation from oblivion) **~ of sb.'s memory** Bewahrung jmds. Andenkens; **in ~ of sb.'s memory** zu jmds. Gedächtnis **2** (action of making perpetual) Aufrechterhaltung, *die;* (of species, power) Erhaltung, *die*

perpetuity /pɜːpɪˈtjuːɪtɪ/ *n., no pl., no indef. art.* ewiger Bestand; **in** *or* **to** *or* **for ~:** für alle Ewigkeit *od.* alle Zeiten

perplex /pəˈpleks/ *v.t.* **1** (bewilder) verwirren; **~ sb.'s mind** jmdn. verwirren; **such questions have ~ed men since time began** solche Fragen haben die Menschheit seit Anbeginn (geh.) beunruhigt **2** (make [more] complicated) [noch] verwickelter machen; komplizieren

perplexed /pəˈplekst/ *adj.* **1** (bewildered) verwirrt; (puzzled) ratlos **2** (complicated) kompliziert

perplexedly /pəˈpleksɪdlɪ/ *adv.* ▸**perplexed 1**: verwirrt; ratlos

perplexity /pəˈpleksɪtɪ/ *n., no pl.* (bewilderment) Verwirrung, *die;* (puzzlement) Ratlosigkeit, *die;* **look at sb. in ~:** jmdn. voller Verwirrung ansehen; **cause sb. ~:** jmdn. verwirren

perquisite /ˈpɜːkwɪzɪt/ *n.* **1** (incidental benefit) Vergünstigung, *die* **2** (customary gratuity) Trinkgeld, *das* **3** (fig.: thing to which person has sole right)

Vorrecht, *das;* Privileg, *das*

Perrier ® /ˈperɪeɪ/ *n.* ~ **[water]** Perrier[wasser], *das*

perry /ˈperɪ/ *n.* (Brit.) Birnenmost, *der*

per se /pɜː ˈseɪ/ *adv.* an sich; per se (geh.); **considered** ~: für sich genommen

persecute /ˈpɜːsɪkjuːt/ *v.t.* [1] verfolgen [2] (harass, worry) plagen; zusetzen (+ *Dat.*); ~ **sb. with sth.** jmdm. mit etw. zusetzen; **stop persecuting me** lass mich in Ruhe

persecution /pɜːsɪˈkjuːʃn/ *n.* [1] Verfolgung, *die;* **suffer** ~: verfolgt werden [2] (harassment) Plagerei, *die*

persecution: ~ **complex**, ~ **mania** *ns.* (Psych.) Verfolgungswahn, *der*

persecutor /ˈpɜːsɪkjuːtə(r)/ *n.* [1] Verfolger, *der*/Verfolgerin, *die* [2] (who harasses) Peiniger, *der*/Peinigerin, *die*

perseverance /pɜːsɪˈvɪərəns/ *n.* Beharrlichkeit, *die;* Ausdauer, *die*

persevere /pɜːsɪˈvɪə(r)/ *v.i.* ausharren; ~ **with** *or* **at** *or* **in sth.** bei etw. dabeibleiben; ~ **in doing sth.** darauf beharren, etw. zu tun

Persia /ˈpɜːʃə/ *pr. n.* (Hist.) Persien (*das*)

Persian /ˈpɜːʃn/ ▸ⓘ **p. 1277**, ▸ⓘ **p. 1345**

A *adj.* persisch; *see also* **English A**

B *n.* [1] (person) Perser, *der*/Perserin, *die* [2] (language) Persisch, *das; see also* **English B 1** [3] ▸**Persian cat**

Persian: ~ **ˈcarpet** *n.* Perser[teppich], *der;* ~ **ˈcat** *n.* Perserkatze, *die;* ~ **ˈlamb** *n.* Persianer, *der;* ~ **lamb coat** Persianermantel, *der*

persiflage /ˈpɜːsɪflɑːʒ/ *n.* **[piece of]** ~: Spöttelei, *die;* Persiflage, *die*

persimmon /pəˈsɪmən/ *n.* Persimone, *die*

persist /pəˈsɪst/ *v.i.* [1] (continue firmly) beharrlich sein Ziel verfolgen; nicht nachgeben; ~ **in sth.** an etw. (*Dat.*) [beharrlich] festhalten; ~ **in doing sth.** etw. weiterhin [beharrlich] tun; ~ **in one's efforts to do sth.** in seinen Anstrengungen, etw. zu tun, nicht nachlassen [2] (continue in existence) anhalten

persistence /pəˈsɪstəns/ *n., no pl.* [1] (continuance in particular course) Hartnäckigkeit, *die;* Beharrlichkeit, *die;* ~ **in a habit/a course of action** hartnäckiges *od.* beharrliches Festhalten an einer Gewohnheit/Vorgehensweise [2] (quality of perseverance) Ausdauer, *die;* Zähigkeit, *die* [3] (continued existence) Fortbestehen, *das*

persistency /pəˈsɪstənsɪ/ ▸**persistence**

persistent /pəˈsɪstənt/ *adj.* [1] (continuing firmly or obstinately) hartnäckig; **be** ~ **in one's beliefs** hartnäckig an seinen Überzeugungen festhalten; **be** ~ **in continuing to do sth.** etw. hartnäckig weiterhin tun; **she was** ~ **in her efforts to ...:** sie gab ihre Versuche, ... zu ..., nicht auf [2] (constantly repeated) dauernd; hartnäckig ‹*Gerüchte*›; nicht nachlassend ‹*Anstrengung, Bemühung*›; ~ **showers** anhaltende Schauertätigkeit; **suffer** ~ **attacks of nausea** dauernd *od.* immer wieder Anfälle von Übelkeit haben [3] (enduring) anhaltend

persistently /pəˈsɪstəntlɪ/ *adv.* [1] (so as to continue firmly or obstinately) hartnäckig; beharrlich [2] (repeatedly) hartnäckig ‹*sich weigern*› [3] (enduringly) ständig; **she has** ~ **made a nuisance of herself** sie hat die ganze Zeit Ärger gemacht

persistent ˈvegetative state *n.* Wachkoma, *das*

persnickety /pəˈsnɪkɪtɪ/ (Amer. coll.) ▸**pernickety**

person /ˈpɜːsn/ *n.* [1] Mensch, *der;* Person, *die* (oft abwertend); **a rich/sick/unemployed** ~: ein Reicher/Kranker/Arbeitsloser/eine Reiche *usw.;* **the first** ~ **to leave was ...:** der/die Erste, der/die wegging, war ...; **if any** ~ **...:** wenn jemand ...; **what sort of** ~ **do you think I am?** wofür halten Sie mich eigentlich?; **in the** ~ **of sb.** in jmdm. *od.* jmds. Person; **in** ~ (personally) persönlich; selbst [2] (living body) Körper, *der;* (appearance) [äußere] Erscheinung; Äußere, *das* [3] (euphem.: genitals) **expose one's** ~: sich entblößen [4] (Ling.) Person, *die;* **first/second/third** ~: erste/zweite/dritte Person [5] (Law) Person, *die;* **natural/artificial** ~: natürliche/juristische Person

persona /pəˈsəʊnə/ *n., pl.* ~**e** /pəˈsəʊniː/ [1] (character assumed by author) Person, *die* [2] (aspect of personality shown to others) Rolle, *die*

personable /ˈpɜːsənəbl/ *adj.* sympathisch

personage /ˈpɜːsənɪdʒ/ *n.* [1] (person of rank) Persönlichkeit, *die* [2] (person not known to speaker) Person, *die*

persona grata /pəsəʊnə ˈgrɑːtə/ *n., pl.* **personae gratae** /pəsəʊniː ˈgrɑːtiː/ Persona grata, *die*

personal /ˈpɜːsənl/ *adj.* [1] (one's own) persönlich; Privat‹*angelegenheit, -leben*›; **be** ~ **to sb.** an jmds. Person gebunden sein; ‹*Sache:*› jmdm. persönlich gehören; *see also* **touch C 6** [2] (of the body) persönlich; ~ **appearance** äußere Erscheinung; ~ **hygiene** Körperpflege, *die;* ~ **contact** (Sport) Körperkontakt, *der;* ~ **foul** (Sport) persönliches Foul [3] (done in person) persönlich; ~ **audience** Privataudienz, *die;* **he gave us a** ~ **tour of his estate** er zeigte uns persönlich seinen Besitz [4] (directed or referring to the individual) persönlich; ~ **call** Privatgespräch, *das;* **pay sb. a** ~ **call** jmdn. privat aufsuchen; **a letter marked 'P~'** ein Brief mit der Aufschrift „Persönlich"; **do you have to make** ~ **remarks?** musst du unbedingt persönlich *od.* anzüglich werden?; **it's nothing** ~**, but ...:** nimm es bitte nicht persönlich, aber ... [5] (given to or making ~ remarks) persönlich; anzüglich [6] (of a person as opposed to an abstraction) persönlich; menschlich; (existing as a person) persönlich; personal [7] (Ling.) persönlich; Personal‹*endung, -pronomen*›

personal: ~ **ˈaccident insurance** *n., no pl.* Unfallversicherung, *die;* ~ **ad** *n.* Privatanzeige, *die;* (seeking friendship, romance) Kontaktanzeige, *die;* ~ **alˈlowance** *n.* [1] (expenses) Unterhaltszuschuss, *der;* Zuschuss für persönliche Ausgaben; [2] (tax allowance) [persönlicher] [Steuer]freibetrag; ~ **asˈsistant** *n.* ▸ⓘ **p. 1260** persönlicher Referent/persönliche Referentin; ~ **ˈbest** *n.* (Sport) persönliche Bestleistung; ~ **column** *n.* Rubrik für private [Klein]anzeigen; ~ **comˈputer** *n.* Personalcomputer, *der;* PC, *der;* ~ **digital asˈsistant** *n.* (Computing) persönlicher digitaler Assistent; ~ **ˈequity plan** *n.* (Brit.) *persönlicher Vermögensplan auf Aktienbasis;* ~ **esˈtate** *n.* (Law) bewegliches Vermögen; ~ **identifiˈcation number** *n.* persönliche Identifikationsnummer; Geheimnummer, *die;* ~ **ˈinjury** *n., no pl.* Körperverletzung, *die;* **risk of** ~ **injury** Verletzungsgefahr, *die;*

personalise ▸**personalize**

personality /pɜːsəˈnælɪtɪ/ *n.* [1] (distinctive personal character) Persönlichkeit, *die;* Wesen, *das;* (of inanimate objects) spezifischer Charakter; **have a strong** ~, (coll.) **have lots of** ~: eine starke Persönlichkeit sein *od.* haben; **be lacking in** ~: keine [starke] Persönlichkeit sein; **there was a [strong]** ~ **clash between them** sie passten [absolut] nicht zusammen [2] (noted person) Persönlichkeit, *die;* **she's quite a** ~ **in the theatre world** sie ist jemand *od.* hat einen Namen in der Welt des Theaters [3] *usu. in pl.* (personal remark) persönlicher Angriff; Anzüglichkeit, *die. See also* **split personality**

personality: ~ **cult** *n.* Personenkult, *der;* Persönlichkeitskult, *der;* ~ **disorder** *n.* (Psych.) Persönlichkeitsstörung, *die*

personalize /ˈpɜːsənəlaɪz/ *v.t.* [1] (make personal) persönlich gestalten; eine persönliche Note geben (+ *Dat.*); (mark with owner's name etc.) als persönliches Eigentum kennzeichnen; ~**d writing paper** persönliches Briefpapier [2] (personify) personifizieren

ˈpersonal loan *n.* Personal- *od.* Privatdarlehen, *das;* Personal- *od.* Privatkredit, *der*

personally /ˈpɜːsənəlɪ/ *adv.* persönlich; ~**, I see no objection** ich persönlich sehe keine Einwände

personal: ~ **ˈorganizer** *n.* Terminplaner, *der;* ~ **ˈpension plan** *n.* persönlicher Renten[vorsorge]plan; persönliche Rentenvorsorge; ~ **ˈproperty** *n.* [1] persönliches Eigentum; **abolish** ~ **property** das Privateigentum abschaffen; [2] ▸**personal estate;** ~ **ˈservice** *n.* individueller Service; **get** ~ **service** individuell *od.* persönlich bedient werden ~ **ˈshopper** *n.* [1] (representative) Einkäufer, *der*/Einkäuferin, *die;* (adviser) Einkaufsberater, *der*/-beraterin, *die;* [2] (purchaser in person) Ladenkunde, *der*/-kundin, *die;* ~ **ˈstereo** *n.* Walkman, *der;* ~ **ˈtrainer** *n.* Privattrainer, *der*/-trainerin, *die*

personalty /ˈpɜːsənltɪ/ *n.* (Law) bewegliches Vermögen

persona non grata /pəsəʊnə nɒn ˈgrɑːtə/ *n., pl.* **personae non gratae** /pəsəʊniː nɒn ˈgrɑːtiː/ Persona non grata, *die;* unerwünschte Person

ˈperson-day *n.* Personentag, *der*

personification /pəsɒnɪfɪˈkeɪʃn/ *n.* Verkörperung, *die;* **be the [very]** ~ **of kindness** die Freundlichkeit selbst *od.* in Person sein

personify /pəˈsɒnɪfaɪ/ *v.t.* **be kindness personified,** ~ **kindness** die Freundlichkeit in Person sein

personnel /pɜːsəˈnel/ *n.* [1] *constr. as sing. or pl.* Belegschaft, *die;* (of shop, restaurant, etc.) Personal, *das;* **military** ~: Militärangehörige; *attrib.* Personal-; ~ **carrier** (Mil.) Schützenpanzer, *der;* ~ **management** Personalverwaltung, *die;* Personalmanagement, *das;* ~ **manager** ▸ⓘ **p. 1260** Personalchef, *der*/-chefin, *die;* ~ **office** Personalbüro, *das;* ~ **officer** ▸ⓘ **p. 1260** Personalsachbearbeiter, *der*/-sachbearbeiterin, *die* [2] *no pl., no art.* (department of firm) Personalabteilung, *die*

person-to-ˈperson *adj.* (Amer. Teleph.) ~ **call** Anruf mit Voranmeldung

ˈperson-year *n.* Personenjahr, *das*

perspective /pəˈspektɪv/

A *n.* [1] Perspektive, *die;* (picture drawn) perspektivische Zeichnung; **in** ~: perspektivisch richtig; **[do] keep things in** ~: das darfst du nicht so eng sehen; (don't get too excited) bleib mal auf dem Teppich [2] (fig.) Blickwinkel, *der;* **throw sth. into** ~: etw. ins rechte Licht rücken; **put a different** ~ **on events** ein neues Licht auf die Ereignisse werfen; **in/out of** ~**, in the** *or* **its right/wrong** ~: unter dem/nicht unter dem richtigen Blickwinkel [3] (view) Aussicht, *die;* (fig.: mental view) Ausblick, *der*

B *adj.* perspektivisch

Perspex ® /ˈpɜːspeks/ *n.* Plexiglas (Wz), *das*

perspicacious /pɜːspɪˈkeɪʃəs/ *adj.* scharfsinnig

perspicacity /pɜːspɪˈkæsɪtɪ/ *n., no pl.* Scharfsinnigkeit, *die*

perspicuity /pɜːspɪˈkjuːɪtɪ/ *n., no pl.* Klarheit, *die;* Verständlichkeit, *die*

perspicuous /pəˈspɪkjʊəs/ *adj.* [1] (easily understood) [klar] verständlich; leicht zu verstehen [2] (expressing things clearly) sich klar ausdrückend; **be** ~: sich klar ausdrücken

perspiration /pɜːspɪˈreɪʃn/ *n.* [1] Schweiß, *der* [2] (action of perspiring) Schwitzen, *das;* Transpiration, *die* (geh.)

perspire /pəˈspaɪə(r)/ *v.i.* schwitzen; transpirieren (geh.)

persuadable /pəˈsweɪdəbl/ *adj.* leicht zu überreden; **be easily** ~: sich leicht überreden lassen; **he might be** ~: vielleicht lässt er sich überreden

persuade /pəˈsweɪd/ *v.t.* [1] (cause to have belief) überzeugen (**of** von); ~ **oneself of sth.** sich (*Dat.*) etw. einreden; ~ **oneself [that] ...:** sich (*Dat.*) einreden, dass ...; ~ **sb. into believing otherwise** jmdm. etwas anderes einreden *od.* (ugs.) weismachen [2] (induce) überreden; ~ **sb. into/out of doing sth.** jmdn. [dazu] überreden, etw. zu tun/nicht zu tun

persuaded /pəˈsweɪdɪd/ *adj.* überzeugt (**of** von)

persuader /pəˈsweɪdə(r)/ *n.* (coll.: gun) Kanone, *die* (salopp)

persuasible /pəˈsweɪzɪbl/ ▸**persuadable**

persuasion /pəˈsweɪʒn/ *n.* [1] (action of persuading) Überzeugung, *die;* (persuasiveness) Überzeugungskraft, *die;* **it didn't take much** ~: es brauchte nicht viel Überredungskunst; **he**

p

didn't need much ~ [to have another drink] man brauchte ihn nicht lange dazu überreden[, noch etwas zu trinken]; **convince sb. by ~:** jmdn. überzeugen; **have considerable powers of ~, be good at ~:** große Überzeugungskraft haben **2** (belief) Überzeugung, *die* **3** (religious belief) Glaubensrichtung, *die;* Glaube, *der;* (sect) Glaubensgemeinschaft, *die*

persuasive /pəˈsweɪsɪv/ *adj.,* **persuasively** /pəˈsweɪsɪvlɪ/ *adv.* überzeugend

persuasiveness /pəˈsweɪsɪvnɪs/ *n., no pl.* Überzeugungskraft, *die*

pert /pɜːt/ *adj.* **1** (saucy, impudent) unverschämt; frech **2** (neat, jaunty) keck ‹*Hut, Anzug usw.*›; hübsch ‹*Körper, Nase, Hinterteil*› **3** (Amer.) ▸**peart**

pertain /pəˈteɪn/ *v.i.* **1** (belong as part) **~ to** [dazu]gehören zu; verbunden sein mit, einhergehen mit ‹*Ereignis, Katastrophe*› **2** (be relevant) ‹*Kriterien usw.:*› gelten; **~ to** von Bedeutung sein für; ‹*Verhalten:*› anstehen (geh.) (+ *Dat.*); ‹*Begeisterung:*› typisch sein für **3** (have reference) **~ to sth.** etw. betreffen; mit etw. zu tun haben

pertinacious /pɜːtɪˈneɪʃəs/ *adj.* (resolute) unbeirrbar; (stubbornly inflexible) starrsinnig ‹*Person*›; starr ‹*Ansichten*›; hartnäckig ‹*Weigerung, Beharren*›; unüberwindlich ‹*Abneigung*›

pertinacity /pɜːtɪˈnæsɪtɪ/ *n., no pl.* ▸**pertinacious**: Starrsinnigkeit, *die;* Hartnäckigkeit, *die*

pertinence /ˈpɜːtɪnəns/ *n., no pl.* Relevanz, *die;* **of/of no** *or* **without ~:** von/ohne Bedeutung *od.* Belang

pertinent /ˈpɜːtɪnənt/ *adj.* relevant (**to** für); **there are some ~ notes in the appendix** im Anhang stehen einige diesbezügliche Bemerkungen *od.* Bemerkungen hierzu

pertinently /ˈpɜːtɪnəntlɪ/ *adv.* (relevantly) zum passenden Zeitpunkt; (so as to be to the point) sachbezogen

pertly /ˈpɜːtlɪ/ *adv.* **1** (saucily, impudently) unverschämt; frech; herausfordernd ‹*gehen, blicken*› **2** (neatly) keck

perturb /pəˈtɜːb/ *v.t.* **1** (throw into confusion) stören; durchkreuzen ‹*Plan*› **2** (disturb mentally) beunruhigen; **get ~ed** unruhig werden **3** (Astron., Phys.) stören

perturbation /pɜːtəˈbeɪʃn/ *n.* **1** (throwing into confusion) Störung, *die;* (of plans) Durchkreuzung, *die* **2** (agitation) Beunruhigung, *die* **3** (Astron., Phys.) Störung, *die;* Perturbation, *die* (fachspr.)

Peru /pəˈruː/ *pr. n.* Peru (*das*)

perusal /pəˈruːzl/ *n.* Lektüre, *die;* (of documents) sorgfältiges Studium; (fig.: action of examining) (of documents) sorgfältige Durchsicht; **give sth. a careful ~:** etw. genau durchlesen *od.* studieren

peruse /pəˈruːz/ *v.t.* genau durchlesen; (fig.: examine) untersuchen; unter die Lupe nehmen (ugs.)

Peruvian /pəˈruːvɪən/ ▸**i p. 1345**
A *adj.* peruanisch; **sb. is ~:** jmd. ist Peruaner/Peruanerin
B *n.* Peruaner, *der*/Peruanerin, *die*

pervade /pəˈveɪd/ *v.t.* **1** (spread throughout) durchdringen; ‹*Licht:*› durchfluten; **be ~d with** *or* **by** durchdrungen sein von **2** (be rife among) ‹*Seuche:*› wüten in (+ *Dat.*); ‹*Ansicht:*› weit verbreitet sein in (+ *Dat.*)

pervasion /pəˈveɪʒn/ *n.* (action of spreading throughout sth.) Durchdringung, *die*

pervasive /pəˈveɪsɪv/ *adj.* (pervading) durchdringend ‹*Geruch, Feuchtigkeit, Kälte*›; weit verbreitet ‹*Ansicht*›; sich ausbreitend ‹*Gefühl*›; (able to pervade) alles durchdringend

pervasively /pəˈveɪsɪvlɪ/ *adv.* alles durchdringend; **spread ~:** um sich greifen

perverse /pəˈvɜːs/ *adj.* **1** (persistent in error) uneinsichtig, verstockt ‹*Person*›; borniert ‹*Person, Argument*› **2** (unreasonable) verrückt **3** (peevish) grimmig; bockig ‹*Kind*› **4** (perverted, wicked) schlecht, verdorben **5** (Law: contrary to evidence or judge's direction) abweichend

perversely /pəˈvɜːslɪ/ *adv.* **1** (with persistence in error) uneinsichtig; verstockt **2** (contrary to what is reasonable) verrückt **3** (peevishly) grimmig; (of child's behaviour) bockig

perverseness /pəˈvɜːsnɪs/ ▸**perversity**

perversion /pəˈvɜːʃn/ *n.* **1** (turning aside from proper use) Missbrauch, *der;* (misconstruction) Pervertierung, *die;* (of words, statement) Verdrehung, *die;* (leading astray) Verführung, *die;* **~ of justice** Rechtsbeugung, *die* **2** (perverted form of sth.) Pervertierung, *die* **3** (sexual) Perversion, *die*

perversity /pəˈvɜːsɪtɪ/ *n.* **1** (persistence in error) Uneinsichtigkeit, *die;* Verstocktheit, *die* **2** (difference from what is reasonable) Verrücktheit, *die*

pervert
A /pəˈvɜːt/ *v.t.* **1** (turn aside from proper use or nature) pervertieren (geh.); beugen ‹*Recht*›; untergraben ‹*Staatsform, Demokratie*›; vereiteln ‹*Absicht*›; **~ [the course of] justice** die Justiz behindern **2** (misconstrue) verfälschen **3** (lead astray) verderben
B /ˈpɜːvɜːt/ *n.* **1** (sexual) Perverse, *der/die;* perverser Mensch; **he must be a ~:** er muss pervers sein **2** (apostate) Renegat, *der*/Renegatin, *die*

perverted /pəˈvɜːtɪd/ *adj.* **1** (turned aside from proper use) pervertiert (geh.) **2** (misconstrued) verdreht **3** (led astray) schlecht; verdorben **4** (sexually) pervers

peseta /pəˈseɪtə/ *n.* Peseta, *die*

pesky /ˈpeskɪ/ *adj.* (Amer. coll.) verdammt (ugs.)

peso /ˈpeɪsəʊ/ *n., pl.* **~s** ▸**i p. 1332** Peso, *der*

pessary /ˈpesərɪ/ *n.* (Med.) **1** Pessar, *das* **2** (vaginal suppository) Vaginalzäpfchen, *das;* Vaginatorium, *das* (fachspr.)

pessimism /ˈpesɪmɪzm/ *n., no pl.* Pessimismus, *der*

pessimist /ˈpesɪmɪst/ *n.* Pessimist, *der*/Pessimistin, *die*

pessimistic /pesɪˈmɪstɪk/ *adj.,* **pessimistically** /pesɪˈmɪstɪkəlɪ/ *adv.* pessimistisch

pest /pest/ *n.* **1** (troublesome thing) Ärgernis, *das;* Plage, *die;* (troublesome person) Nervensäge, *die* (ugs.); (destructive or annoying animal) Schädling, *der;* **~s** (insects) Schädlinge; Ungeziefer, *das;* **I know it's a ~, but …** (a nuisance) ich weiß, es ist lästig, aber …; **he's a real ~:** er ist einfach unausstehlich; **~ officer** Schädlingsbekämpfer, *der;* Kammerjäger, *der* (veralt.); **~ control** Schädlingsbekämpfung, *die* **2** (arch.) (disease) Seuche, *die;* (plague) Pest, *die*

pester /ˈpestə(r)/ *v.t.* belästigen; nerven (ugs.); **~ sb. for sth.** jmdm. wegen etw. in den Ohren liegen; **~ sb. to do sth.** jmdm. in den Ohren liegen, etw. zu tun; **~ sb. for money** jmdn. [um Geld] anbetteln; **~ sb. for an interview** jmdn. wegen eines Interviews bedrängen *od.* (ugs.) nerven

pesticide /ˈpestɪsaɪd/ *n.* Pestizid, *das*

pestilence /ˈpestɪləns/ *n.* Pestilenz, *die;* Seuche, *die;* (bubonic plague) Pest, *die*

pestilent /ˈpestɪlənt/ *adj.* **1** tödlich; todbringend **2** (fig. coll.: troublesome) unausstehlich; lästig ‹*Ansinnen*› **3** (pernicious) verderblich; zersetzend ‹*Lehre*›

pestilential /pestɪˈlenʃl/ *adj.* **1** pestilenzartig **2** (fig. coll.: troublesome) unausstehlich; **he's a ~ nuisance** er ist unausstehlich; **these ~ flies** diese elenden Fliegen **3** (pernicious) verderblich; zersetzend ‹*Lehre*›

pestle /ˈpesl/ *n.* Stößel, *der;* Pistill, *das* (fachspr.)

pesto /ˈpestəʊ/ *n., no pl.* Pesto, *das od. der*

pet¹ /pet/
A *n.* **1** (tame animal) Haustier, *das* **2** (darling, favourite) Liebling, *der;* (sweet person; also as term of endearment) Schatz, *der;* **make a ~ of sb.** jmdn. verhätscheln; **mother's** *or* **mummy's ~** (derog.) Mamas Liebling; (male) Muttersöhnchen, *das* (abwertend); **teacher's ~** (derog.) Liebling des Lehrers/der Lehrerin; **you have been a ~:** du bist ein Schatz; **[do] be a ~ and do sth.** sei so lieb und tue etw
B *adj.* **1** (kept as ~) zahm **2** (of or for ~ animals) Haustier-; **~ accessories** Zoobedarf, *der* **3** (favourite) Lieblings-; **sth./sb. is sb.'s ~ aversion** *or* **hate** jmd. kann etw./jmdn. auf den Tod nicht ausstehen (ugs.); **be sb.'s ~ peeve** jmdm. ein Dorn im Auge sein **4** (expressing fondness) Kose‹*form, -name*›
C *v.t.,* **-tt-** **1** (treat as favourite) bevorzugen; verwöhnen; (indulge) verhätscheln **2** (fondle) streicheln; liebkosen
D *v.i.,* **-tt-** knutschen (ugs.); zärtlich sein (verhüll.)

pet² *n.* (bad temper) **in a ~:** verstimmt; beleidigt; eingeschnappt (ugs.); **she is in one of her ~s** sie hat mal wieder schlechte Laune

PET *abbr.* **= polyethylene terephthalate** PET

petal /ˈpetl/ *n.* Blütenblatt, *das*

-petal[l]ed /ˈpetld/ *adj. in comb.* -blättrig ‹*Blüte*›

petard /pɪˈtɑːd/ *n.* (Hist.) Petarde, *die; see also* **hoist C**

ˈpet door *n.* (Amer.) Katzentür, *die;* Katzenklappe, *die*

Pete /piːt/ *n.* **for ~'s sake** ≈ **for Heaven's sake** ▸**sake¹**

peter *v.i.* **~ out** [allmählich] zu Ende gehen; ‹*Wasserlauf:*› versickern; ‹*Weg:*› sich verlieren; ‹*Briefwechsel:*› versanden; ‹*Angriff:*› sich totlaufen

Peter /ˈpiːtə(r)/ *pr. n.* Peter; Petrus (hist., im MA. u. früher); **Saint ~:** Sankt Petrus *od.* Peter; **rob ~ to pay Paul** ein Loch mit etwas stopfen, was dann woanders fehlt (fig.); *see also* **Blue Peter**

Peter ˈPan *n.* Peter Pan; **be a ~:** ein Kindskopf sein; **~ collar** Bubikragen, *der*

petersham /ˈpiːtəʃəm/ *n.* Gurtband, *das*

ˈpet food *n.* Tierfutter, *das*

petiole /ˈpetɪəʊl/ *n.* (Bot.) Blattstängel, *der*

petit /ˈpetɪ/ (Law) ▸**petty 4**

petit bourgeois /pətiː ˈbʊəʒwɑː/ *n., pl.* **petits bourgeois** /pətiː ˈbʊəʒwɑː/ (usu. derog.) Kleinbürger, *der; attrib.* Kleinbürger-; kleinbürgerlich

petite /pəˈtiːt/ *adj. fem.* zierlich

petite bourgeoisie /pətiːt bʊəʒwɑːˈziː/ *n., no pl., no indef. art.* Kleinbürgertum, *das*

petit four /pətiː ˈfʊə(r)/ *n., pl.* **petits fours** /pətiː ˈfʊə(r)/ Petit Four, *das*

petition /pəˈtɪʃn/
A *n.* **1** (formal written supplication) Petition, *die;* Eingabe, *die;* **get together** *or* **up a ~ for/against sth.** Unterschriften für/gegen etw. sammeln **2** (Law: application for writ etc.) [förmlicher] Antrag; (for divorce) Klage, *die*
B *v.t.* eine Eingabe richten an (+ *Akk.*); eine Eingabe machen bei; **~ sb. for sth.** jmdn. um etw. ersuchen
C *v.i.* **~ for** ersuchen um (geh.); nachsuchen um (geh.); (present ~ for) eine Unterschriftenliste einreichen für; einkommen um (geh.); **~ for divorce** die Scheidung einreichen; **~ against** eine Eingabe machen gegen

petitioner /pəˈtɪʃənə(r)/ *n.* Antragsteller, *der*/Antragstellerin, *die;* (for divorce) Kläger, *der*/Klägerin, *die*

petit point /pətiː ˈpwæ̃/ *n.* **1** (embroidery) Petit Point, *das* **2** (stitch) Perlstich, *der*

petits pois /pətiː ˈpwɑ/ *n. pl.* feine Erbsen

ˈpet owner *n.* Tierhalter, *der*/-halterin, *die*

Petrarch /ˈpetrɑːk/ *pr. n.* Petrarca (*der*)

petrel /ˈpetrl/ *n.* (Ornith.) Sturmvogel, *der*

Petri dish /ˈpetrɪ dɪʃ/ *n.* Petrischale, *die*

petrifaction /petrɪˈfækʃn/ *n.* Versteinerung, *die*

petrify /ˈpetrɪfaɪ/
A *v.t.* **1** (change into stone) petrifizieren (geh.); versteinern lassen; **become petrified** versteinern; petrifizieren (geh.) **2** (fig.: cause to become inert) erstarren lassen; **be petrified with fear/shock** starr vor Angst/Schrecken sein; vor Angst/Schrecken [wie] versteinert sein (geh.); **be petrified by sb./sth.** vor jmdm./etw. erstarren; sich vor jmdm. panisch fürchten; **she looked quite petrified** sie schien entsetzliche Angst zu haben
B *v.i.* (turn to stone) versteinern; (fig.: become inert) erstarren

petrochemical /petrəʊˈkemɪkl/
A *n.* Petrochemikalie, *die*
B *adj.* **1** (of chemistry of rocks) petrochemisch **2** (of chemistry of petroleum) petro[l]chemisch

petrochemistry /petrəʊˈkemɪstrɪ/ *n.* **1** (chemistry of rocks) Petrochemie, *die* **2** (chemistry of petroleum) Petro[l]chemie, *die*

petrodollar /ˈpetrəʊdɒlə(r)/ *n.* Petrodollar, *der*

petrol /ˈpetrl/ *n.* (Brit.) Benzin, *das;* **fill up with ~:** tanken

petrolatum /petrəˈleɪtəm/ *n.* (Amer.) ▸**petroleum jelly**

petrol: ~ bomb *n.* Benzinbombe, *die;* **~ can** *n.* (Brit.) Benzinkanister, *der;* **~ cap** *n.* (Brit.) Tankverschluss, *der;* **~ engine** *n.* Benzinmotor, *der*

petroleum /pɪˈtrəʊlɪəm/ *n.* Erdöl, *das*

petroleum 'jelly *n.* Vaseline, *die*

'petrol gauge *n.* (Brit.) Benzinuhr, *die;* Kraftstoffanzeiger, *der* (Technik)

petrology /pɪˈtrɒlədʒɪ/ *n.* Petrologie, *die*

petrol: ~ pump *n.* (Brit.) 1 (in ~ station) Zapfsäule, *die;* Tanksäule, *die;* **~ pump attendant** Tankwart, *der*/Tankwartin, *die;* 2 (in car, aircraft, etc.) Benzin- *od.* Kraftstoffpumpe, *die;* **~ station** *n.* (Brit.) Tankstelle, *die;* **~ tank** *n.* (Brit.) (in car, aircraft, etc.) Benzintank, *der;* **~ tanker** *n.* (Brit.) Benzintankwagen, *der*

pet: ~ shop *n.* Tierhandlung, *die;* Zoohandlung, *die;* **~ store** *n.* (Amer.) Zoohandlung, *die*

petticoat /ˈpetɪkəʊt/

A *n.* Unterrock, *der*

B *adj.* weiblich; Frauen-; **~ government** Frauenherrschaft, *die;* Weiberregiment, *das* (abwertend)

pettifogging /ˈpetɪfɒgɪŋ/ *adj.* kleinkariert, kleinlich ‹*Person*›; belanglos ‹*Detail*›; kleinlich ‹*Einwand*›; **his ~ mind** seine Kleinkariertheit

petting /ˈpetɪŋ/ *n., no pl.* Petting, *das*

pettish /ˈpetɪʃ/ *adj.,* **pettishly** /ˈpetɪʃlɪ/ *adv.* übellaunig; grantig (ugs.)

petty /ˈpetɪ/ *adj.* 1 (trivial) belanglos ‹*Detail, Sorgen*›; kleinlich ‹*Einwand, Vorschrift*› 2 (minor) Klein‹*staat, -unternehmer, -landwirt*›; klein ‹*Geschäftsmann*›; Duodez‹*fürst, -fürstentum, -staat*›; **~ criminal** Kleinkriminelle, *der/die;* **~ theft** Bagatelldiebstahl, *der;* **~ thief** kleiner Dieb/kleine Diebin 3 (small-minded) kleinlich; kleinkariert 4 (Law) geringfügig; Bagatell-; *see also* **session 7**

petty: ~ 'cash *n.* kleine Kasse; Portokasse, *die;* **~-minded** ▸**small-minded**; **~ 'officer** *n.* (Navy) ≈ [Ober]maat, *der*

petulance /ˈpetjʊləns/ *n., no pl.* Bockigkeit, *die*

petulant /ˈpetjʊlənt/ *adj.,* **petulantly** /ˈpetjʊləntlɪ/ *adv.* bockig

petunia /pɪˈtjuːnɪə/ *n.* (Bot.) Petunie, *die*

pew /pjuː/ *n.* 1 (Eccl.) Kirchenbank, *die* 2 (coll.: seat) [Sitz]platz, *der;* **have** *or* **take a ~:** sich platzen (ugs. scherzh.)

pewit ▸**peewit**

pewter /ˈpjuːtə(r)/

A *n., no pl., no indef. art.* (substance, vessels) Pewter, *der;* [Hart]zinn, *das*

B *attrib. adj.* Zinn‹*becher, -geschirr*›

PFI *abbr.* (Brit.) = **Private Finance Initiative**

PG *abbr.* (Brit. Cinemat.) = **Parental Guidance** ≈ bedingt jugendfrei

PGCE *abbr.* (Brit.) = **Postgraduate Certificate in Education**

pH /piːˈeɪtʃ/ *n.* (Chem.) pH-Wert, *der*

phalanx /ˈfælæŋks/ *n., pl.* **~es** *or* **phalanges** /fæˈlændʒiːz/ 1 (of troops, police, etc.) Phalanx, *die* 2 (Anat.) Phalanx, *die;* (of finger) Fingerglied, *das;* (of toe) Zehenglied, *das*

phallic /ˈfælɪk/ *adj.* phallisch; **~ symbol** Phallussymbol, *das*

phallus /ˈfæləs/ *n., pl.* **~es** *or* **phalli** /ˈfælaɪ/ Phallus, *der*

phantasmagoria /fæntæzməˈgɔːrɪə/ *n.* Trugbild, *das;* Phantasmagorie, *die* (geh.)

phantasy ▸**fantasy 1, 2**

phantom /ˈfæntəm/

A *n.* 1 (spectre) Phantom, *das;* (image) Phantom, *das;* Trugbild, *das* 2 (mental illusion) Fantasiegebilde, *das*

B *adj.* Phantom-

phantom: ~ 'limb *n.* (Med.) Phantomglied, *das;* **~ 'pregnancy** *n.* (Med.) Scheinschwangerschaft, *die*

Pharaoh /ˈfeərəʊ/ *n.* Pharao, *der*

Pharisaic[al] /færɪˈseɪk(l)/ *adj.* pharisäerhaft

Pharisee /ˈfærɪsiː/ *n.* 1 Pharisäer, *der* 2 **p~** (self-righteous person) Pharisäer, *der*

pharm /fɑːm/ *n.* (coll.) Genfarm, *die*

pharmaceutical /fɑːməˈsjuːtɪkl/

A *adj.* pharmazeutisch; Arzneimittel-, Pharma‹*industrie, -konzern, -hersteller*›; **~ chemist** Arzneimittelchemiker, *der/*-chemikerin, *die*

B *n. in pl.* Pharmaka

pharmacist /ˈfɑːməsɪst/ *n.* ▸❶ **p. 1260** Apotheker, *der*/Apothekerin, *die;* (in research) Pharmazeut, *der*/Pharmazeutin, *die*

pharmacological /fɑːməkəˈlɒdʒɪkl/ *adj.* pharmakologisch

pharmacologist /fɑːməˈkɒlədʒɪst/ *n.* Pharmakologe, *der*/Pharmakologin, *die*

pharmacology /fɑːməˈkɒlədʒɪ/ *n.* Pharmakologie, *die*

pharmacopoeia /fɑːməkəˈpiːə/ *n.* Pharmakopöe, *die;* amtliches Arzneibuch

pharmacy /ˈfɑːməsɪ/ *n.* 1 *no pl., no art.* (preparation of drugs) Pharmazie, *die;* Arzneimittelkunde, *die* 2 (dispensary) Apotheke, *die*

'pharm animal *n.* (coll.) Gentier, *das*

pharming /ˈfɑːmɪŋ/ *n., no pl.* Genfarming, *das*

pharyngeal /færɪnˈdʒɪəl/ *adj.* (Anat., Med.) Rachen‹*katarrh, -entzündung, -mandel, -höhle usw.*›; Schlund‹*tasche, -krampf*›

pharyngitis /færɪnˈdʒaɪtɪs/ *n.* ▸❶ **p. 1231** (Med.) Rachenkatarrh, *der;* Pharyngitis, *die* (fachspr.)

pharynx /ˈfærɪŋks/ *n., pl.* **pharynges** /fəˈrɪndʒiːz/ (Anat.) Schlund, *der;* Rachen, *der;* Pharynx, *der* (fachspr.)

phase /feɪz/

A *n.* 1 Phase, *die;* (of project, construction, history also) Abschnitt, *der;* (of illness, development also) Stadium, *das;* **it's only** *or* **just a ~ [he's/she's going through]** das gibt sich [mit der Zeit] wieder (ugs.) 2 (Phys., Astron., Chem.) Phase, *die;* **in ~:** phasengleich; in [gleicher] Phase; **out of ~:** phasenverschoben; **have got out of ~** (fig.) nicht mehr koordiniert sein

B *v.t.* stufenweise durchführen

Phrasal verbs

- **~ 'in** *v.t.* stufenweise einführen
- **~ 'out** *v.t.* 1 (eliminate gradually) nach und nach auflösen ‹*Abteilung*›; allmählich abschaffen ‹*Verfahrensweise, Methode*› 2 (discontinue production of) [langsam] auslaufen lassen

PhD /piːeɪtʃˈdiː/ *abbr.* = **Doctor of Philosophy** Dr. phil.; **he/she is studying for a ~:** er ist Doktorand/sie ist Doktorandin; er/sie promoviert; **John Clarke ~:** Dr. phil. John Clarke; **do one's ~:** seinen Doktor machen; **~ thesis** Doktorarbeit, *die;* Dissertation, *die*

pheasant /ˈfezənt/ *n.* Fasan, *der*

phenobarbitone /fiːnəʊˈbɑːbɪtəʊn/ (*Brit.; Amer.:* **phenobarbital** /fiːnəʊˈbɑːbɪtl/) *n.* (Med.) Phenobarbital, *das*

phenol /ˈfiːnɒl/ *n.* (Chem.) Phenol, *das;* Karbolsäure, *die*

phenomenal /fɪˈnɒmɪnl/ *adj.* 1 (remarkable) phänomenal; sagenhaft (ugs.); unwahrscheinlich (ugs.) ‹*Spektakel, Radau*› 2 (Philos.) phänomenal; wahrnehmbar

phenomenalism /fɪˈnɒmɪnəlɪzm/ *n.* (Philos.) Phänomenalismus, *der*

phenomenally /fɪˈnɒmɪnəlɪ/ *adj.* phänomenal; unglaublich; unwahrscheinlich (ugs.) ‹*schlecht, langweilig, laut*›

phenomenon /fɪˈnɒmɪnən/ *n., pl.* **phenomena** /fɪˈnɒmɪnə/ Phänomen, *das*

phenotype /ˈfiːnətaɪp/ *n.* (Biol.) Phänotyp, *der;* Phänotypus, *der*

pheromone /ˈferəməʊn/ *n.* (Biol.) Pheromon, *das*

phew /fjuː/ *int.* puh

phial /ˈfaɪəl/ *n.* [Medizin]fläschchen, *das;* Phiole, *die*

philander /fɪˈlændə(r)/ *v.i.* (flirt) schäkern; flirten; (with heavier sexual overtones) nachstellen (**with** *Dat.*)

philanderer /fɪˈlændərə(r)/ *n.* Schürzenjäger, *der* (spött.)

philanthropic /fɪlənˈθrɒpɪk/ *adj.* philanthropisch (geh.); menschenfreundlich; Wohltätigkeits‹*organisation, -verein usw.*›

philanthropically /fɪlənˈθrɒpɪkəlɪ/ *adv.* philanthropisch (geh.)

philanthropist /fɪˈlænθrəpɪst/ *n.* Philanthrop, *der*/Philanthropin, *die* (geh.); Menschenfreund, *der*/Menschenfreundin, *die*

philanthropy /fɪˈlænθrəpɪ/ *n.* Philanthropie, *die* (geh.); (love of mankind also) Menschenliebe, *die;* Menschenfreundlichkeit, *die*

philatelic /fɪləˈtelɪk/ *adv.* philatelistisch

philatelist /fɪˈlætəlɪst/ *n.* Philatelist, *der*/Philatelistin, *die;* (collector also) Briefmarkensammler, *der/*-sammlerin, *die*

philately /fɪˈlætəlɪ/ *n.* Philatelie, *die;* Briefmarkenkunde, *die*

philharmonic /fɪlhɑːˈmɒnɪk, fɪlɑːˈmɒnɪk/

A *adj.* philharmonisch

B *n.* Philharmonie, *die*

Philip /ˈfɪlɪp/ *pr. n.* Philipp; (Bibl.) Philippus

philippic /fɪˈlɪpɪk/ *n.* Philippika, *die* (geh.)

Philippine /ˈfɪlɪpiːn/ *adj.* 1 (Geog.) philippinisch 2 ▸**Filipino**

Philippines /ˈfɪlɪpiːnz/ *pr. n. pl.* Philippinen *Pl.*

philistine /ˈfɪlɪstaɪn/

A *n.* 1 (uncultured person) [Kultur]banause, *der/*-banausin, *die* 2 **P~** (native of ancient Philistia) Philister, *der*

B *adj.* banausisch; kulturlos

philistinism /ˈfɪlɪstɪnɪzm/ *n., no pl.* Banausentum, *das;* (bourgeois narrow-mindedness) Philistertum, *das* (geh.)

Phillips /ˈfɪlɪps/ *n.* **~ screw** ® Kreuz[schlitz]schraube, *die;* **~ screwdriver** ® Kreuz[schlitz]schraubenzieher, *der*

philological /fɪləˈlɒdʒɪkl/ *adj.* philologisch

philologist /fɪˈlɒlədʒɪst/ *n.* Philologe, *der*/Philologin, *die*

philology /fɪˈlɒlədʒɪ/ *n.* 1 (science of language) [historische] Sprachwissenschaft 2 (Amer.: study of literature) Philologie, *die;* Literaturwissenschaft, *die*

philosopher /fɪˈlɒsəfə(r)/ *n.* ▸❶ **p. 1260** Philosoph, *der*/Philosophin, *die*

philosopher: ~'s stone, ~s' stone *n.* Stein der Weisen

philosophic /fɪləˈsɒfɪk/, **philosophical** /fɪləˈsɒfɪkl/ *adj.* 1 philosophisch; philosophisch gebildet *od.* geschult ‹*Person*› 2 (resigned, calm) abgeklärt; gelassen

philosophically /fɪləˈsɒfɪkəlɪ/ *adv.* 1 **~ [speaking]** philosophisch betrachtet; vom philosophischen Standpunkt gesehen 2 (calmly) gelassen

philosophize (philosophise) /fɪˈlɒsəfaɪz/ *v.i.* philosophieren (**about, on** über + *Akk.*)

philosophy /fɪˈlɒsəfɪ/ *n.* Philosophie, *die;* **~ of life** Lebensphilosophie, *die;* **~ of education** Erziehungsphilosophie, *die*

phishing /ˈfɪʃɪŋ/ *n., no pl.* Phishing, *das*

phlebitis /flɪˈbaɪtɪs/ *n.* ▸❶ **p. 1231** (Med.) Venenentzündung, *die;* Phlebitis, *die* (fachspr.)

phlegm /flem/ *n., no pl., no indef. art.* 1 (Physiol.) Schleim, *der;* Mucus, *der* (Med.) 2 (coolness) stoische Ruhe; Gleichmut, *der* 3 (stolidness) Phlegma, *das*

phlegmatic /flegˈmætɪk/ *adj.* 1 (cool) gleichmütig 2 (stolid) phlegmatisch

phlegmatically /flegˈmætɪkəlɪ/ *adv.* ▸**phlegmatic**: gleichmütig; phlegmatisch

phloem /ˈfləʊem/ *n.* (Bot.) Phloem, *das*

phlox /flɒks/ *n.* (Bot.) Phlox, *der;* Flammenblume, *die*

phobia /ˈfəʊbɪə/ *n.* Phobie, *die* (Psychol.); [krankhafte] Angst

-phobia /ˈfəʊbɪə/ *n. in comb.* -phobie, *die*

phobic /ˈfəʊbɪk/ *adj.* phobisch; **be ~ about sth.** krankhafte Angst *od.* (*bildungsspr.*) eine Phobie vor etw. haben

-phobic /ˈfəʊbɪk/ *adj. in comb.* -phob

Phoenician /fəˈniːʃn/

A *adj.* phönizisch; phönikisch

B *n.* Phönizier, *der*/Phönizierin, *die;* Phöniker, *der*/Phönikerin, *die*

phoenix /ˈfiːnɪks/ *n.* (Mythol.) Phönix, *der;* **~-like** wie ein Phönix

phone /fəʊn/

A *n.* Telefon, *das;* **pick up/put down the ~:** [den Hörer] abnehmen/auflegen; **by ~:** telefonisch; **speak to sb. by ~** *or* **on the ~:** mit jmdm. telefonieren; **be on the ~ for hours** stundenlang telefonieren; **I'm not on the ~:** ich habe kein Telefon

B *v.i.* anrufen; **can we ~ from here?** können wir von hier aus telefonieren?

C *v.t.* anrufen; **~ the office/home** im Büro/zu Hause anrufen; **~ a message through to sb.** jmdm. eine Nachricht telefonisch übermitteln *od.* durchgeben. *See also* **telephone**

Phrasal verbs

• **~ aˈround**

A *v.i.* herumtelefonieren

B *v.t.* [nacheinander] anrufen

• **~ ˈback** *v.t. & i.* (make a return ~ call [to]) zurückrufen; (make a further ~ call [to]) wieder *od.* nochmals anrufen

• **~ ˈin**

A *v.i.* anrufen

B *v.t.* telefonisch mitteilen *od.* durchgeben. *See also* **phone-in**

• **~ ˈup** *v.t. & i.* anrufen

phone: ~ bill *n.* Telefonrechnung, *die;* **~ book** *n.* Telefonbuch, *das;* **~ booth, ~ box** *ns.* Telefonzelle, *die;* **~ call** *n.* Anruf, *der; see also* **telephone call**; **~card** *n.* Telefonkarte, *die;* **~ company** *n.* Telefongesellschaft, *die;* **~-in** *n.* **~-in [programme]** (Radio) Hörersendung, *die;* (Telev.) Phone-in-Sendung, *die* (Jargon); Sendung mit Zuschaueranrufen; **~ line** *n.* Telefonleitung, *die*

phoneme /ˈfəʊniːm/ *n.* (Phonet.) Phonem, *das*

phone: ~ number *n.* Telefonnummer, *die;* **~ pest** *n.* Telefonterrorist, *der*/Telefonterroristin, *die;* **~ sex** *n., no pl.* Telefonsex, *der;* **~-tapping** *n., no pl.* Anzapfen von Telefonleitungen

phonetic /fəˈnetɪk/ *adj.* phonetisch; *see also* **alphabet**

phonetically /fəˈnetɪkəlɪ/ *adv.* phonetisch

phonetician /fəʊnɪˈtɪʃn/ *n.* ▸❶ **p. 1260** Phonetiker, *der*/Phonetikerin, *die*

phonetics /fəˈnetɪks/ *n.* **1** *no pl.* Phonetik, *die* **2** *no pl.* (phonetic script) phonetische Umschrift **3** *constr. as pl.* (phonetic transcription) phonetische Angaben

phoney /ˈfəʊnɪ/ (coll.)

A *adj.*, **phonier** /ˈfəʊnɪə(r)/, **phoniest** /ˈfəʊnɪɪst/ **1** (sham) falsch; gefälscht ‹*Brief, Dokument*›; **there's something a bit ~ about the whole thing** irgendetwas an der ganzen Sache ist faul (ugs.) **2** (fictitious) falsch ‹*Name*›; erfunden ‹*Geschichte*› **3** (fraudulent) Schein‹*firma, -geschäft, -krieg*›; falsch, scheinbar ‹*Doktor, Diplomat, Geschäftsmann*›

B *n.* **1** (person) Blender, *der*/Blenderin, *die;* **this doctor is just a ~:** dieser Arzt ist ein Scharlatan **2** (sham) Fälschung, *die*

phonograph /ˈfəʊnəgrɑːf/ *n.* (Amer.) ▸**record player**

phonology /fəˈnɒlədʒɪ/ *n.* Phonologie, *die*

phony ▸**phoney**

phooey /ˈfuːɪ/ *int.* pah

phosphate /ˈfɒsfeɪt/ *n.* (Chem.) Phosphat, *das*

phosphor /ˈfɒsfə(r)/ *n.* Phosphor, *der*

phosphorescence /fɒsfəˈresəns/ *n.* Phosphoreszenz, *die*

phosphorescent /fɒsfəˈresənt/ *adj.* phosphoreszierend

phosphorus /ˈfɒsfərəs/ *n.* (Chem.) Phosphor, *der*

photo /ˈfəʊtəʊ/ *n., pl.* **~s** Foto, *das; see also* **photograph A**

photo- /fəʊtəʊ/ *in comb.* **1** (light) photo-/Photo- **2** (photography) foto-/Foto-

photo: ~ album *n.* Fotoalbum, *das;* **~call** *n.* Fototermin, *der;* **~cell** *n.* Fotozelle, *die;* **~ˈchemical** *adj.* Fotochemisch; **~ˈchemistry** *n., no pl.* Fotochemie, *die;* **~composition** ▸**filmsetting**; **~copiable** /ˈfəʊtəʊkɒpɪəbl/ *adj.* fotokopierbar; **~copier** *n.* Fotokopiergerät, *das;* **~copy A** *n.* Fotokopie, *die;* **B** *v.t.* fotokopieren; **~electric** *adj.* fotoelektrisch; **~electric cell** fotozelle, *die;* **~ finish** *n.* Fotofinish, *das;* (fig.) Kopf-an-Kopf-Rennen, *das;* **~fit** *n.* Phantombild, *das;* Phantomfoto, *das;* **~genic** /fəʊtəˈdʒenɪk, fəʊtəˈdʒiːnɪk/ *adj.* fotogen

photograph /ˈfəʊtəgrɑːf/

A *n.* Fotografie, *die;* Foto, *das;* **take a ~ [of sb./sth.]** [jmdn./etw.] fotografieren; ein Foto [von jmdm./etw.] machen

B *v.t. & i.* fotografieren; **he ~s well/badly** (as subject) er lässt sich gut/schlecht fotografieren

ˈphotograph album *n.* Fotoalbum, *das*

photographer /fəˈtɒgrəfə(r)/ *n.* ▸❶ **p. 1260** Fotograf, *der*/Fotografin, *die*

photographic /fəʊtəˈgræfɪk/ *adj.* fotografisch; Foto‹*ausrüstung, -club, -papier, -apparat, -ausstellung, -zeitschrift*›; **~ memory** (fig.) fotografisches Gedächtnis

photographically /fəʊtəˈgræfɪkəlɪ/ *adv.* fotografisch

photography /fəˈtɒgrəfɪ/ *n., no pl., no indef. art.* Fotografie, *die*

photogravure /fəʊtəgrəˈvjʊə(r)/ *n.* Photogravüre, *die*

ˈphotojournalism *n., no pl.* Fotojournalismus, *der*

ˈphoto lab *n.* Fotolabor, *das*

photometer /fəʊˈtɒmɪtə(r)/ *n.* Photometer, *der*

photomonˈtage *n.* Fotomontage, *die*

photon /ˈfəʊtɒn/ *n.* (Phys.) Photon, *das*

photo: ~ opportunity *n.* **1** ▸**~call**; **2** (Brit.: opportunity for a good photograph) [Foto]motiv, *das;* **~ˈsensitive** *adj.* lichtempfindlich; **~sensiˈtivity** *n.* Lichtempfindlichkeit, *die;* **~ session, ~ shoot** *ns.* [Foto]shooting, *das;* **~setting** ▸**filmsetting**; **~ shoot** *n.* [Foto]shooting, *das;* Fotosession, *die;* **~sphere** *n.* (Astron.) Fotosphäre, *die;* **P~stat ®** /ˈfəʊtəstæt/ (Brit.) **A** *n.* ▸**photocopy A**; **B** *v.t.*, **-tt-** ▸**photocopy B**; **~ˈsynthesis** *n.* (Bot.) Fotosynthese, *die;* **~ˈsynthesize** *v.t. & i.* fotosynthetisieren; **~voltaic** *adj.* (Phys.) photovoltaisch

phrasal ˈverb *n.* (Ling.) mehrgliedriges Verb

phrase /freɪz/

A *n.* **1** (Ling.) Phrase, *die* (fachspr.); (idiomatic expression) idiomatische Wendung; [Rede]wendung, *die;* **set ~:** feste [Rede]wendung; **noun/verb ~:** Nominal-/Verbalphrase, *die* **2** (brief expression) kurze Formel; **be good at turning a ~:** ausgezeichnet formulieren können; **hackneyed ~:** abgegriffene *od.* (ugs.) abgedroschene Phrase; *see also* **turn A 10** **3** (Mus.) Phrase, *die*

B *v.t.* **1** (express in words) formulieren; **~ one's idea** seinen Gedanken in Worte fassen **2** (Mus.) phrasieren

ˈphrase book *n.* Sprachführer, *der*

phraseology /freɪzɪˈɒlədʒɪ/ *n.* Ausdrucksweise, *die;* (technical terms) Terminologie, *die*

phrasing /ˈfreɪzɪŋ/ *n.* **1** (style of expression) Ausdrucksweise, *die* **2** (Mus.) Phrasierung, *die*

phrenetic ▸**frenetic**

phrenology /frɪˈnɒlədʒɪ/ *n., no pl.* Phrenologie, *die*

phut /fʌt/

A *adv.* (coll.) **go ~:** kaputtgehen (ugs.); (fig.) ‹*Plan, Projekt:*› in die Binsen gehen (ugs.); ‹*Geschäft, Firma:*› kaputtgehen (ugs.)

B *n.* Knall, *der;* **~!** peng!

phylloxera /fɪˈlɒksərə/ *n.* (Zool.) Reblaus, *die*

phylogenetic /faɪləʊdʒɪˈnetɪk/ *adj.* (Biol.) phylogenetisch

phylogeny /faɪˈlɒdʒənɪ/ *n.* (Biol.) Phylogenie, *die*

phylum /ˈfaɪləm/ *n., pl.* **phyla** /ˈfaɪlə/ (Biol.) [Tier-/Pflanzen]stamm, *der;* Phylum, *das* (fachspr.)

physic /ˈfɪzɪk/ (arch.)

A *n.* **1** (art of healing) Heilkunde, *die* **2** (medicine) Arznei, *die* (veralt.); Heilmittel, *das*

B *v.t.*, **-ck-** mit Arzneimitteln behandeln

physical /ˈfɪzɪkl/

A *adj.* **1** (material) physisch ‹*Gewalt*›; stofflich, dinglich ‹*Welt, Universum*› **2** (of physics) physikalisch; **it's a ~ impossibility** (fig.) es ist absolut unmöglich **3** (bodily) körperlich; physisch; **you need to take more ~ exercise** du brauchst mehr Bewegung; **~ check-up** *or* **examination** ärztliche Untersuchung; **get/be ~** (coll.) rabiat werden/sein **4** (carnal, sensual) körperlich ‹*Liebe*›; sinnlich ‹*Person, Ausstrahlung*›

B *n.* ärztliche [Vorsorge]untersuchung; (for joining the army) Musterung, *die*

physical: ~ ˈchemistry *n.* physikalische Chemie; Physikochemie, *die;* **~ eduˈcation** *n.* Sportunterricht, *der;* (school subject) Sport, *der;* **~ geˈography** *n.* physische Geographie; **~ ˈjerks** *n. pl.* (coll.) Gymnastikübungen

physically /ˈfɪzɪkəlɪ/ *adv.* **1** (in accordance with physical laws) physikalisch; **~ impossible** (fig.) absolut unmöglich **2** (relating to the body) körperlich; physisch; **they had to be ~ removed** sie mussten mit [physischer] Gewalt entfernt werden; **be ~ sick** einen physischen Ekel empfinden; **~ disabled** körperbehindert

physical: ~ ˈscience *n.* exakte Naturwissenschaften; **~ ˈtraining** *n.* Sport, *der;* (in school) Sport[unterricht], *der*

ˈphysic garden *n.* (arch.) [Heil]kräutergarten, *der*

physician /fɪˈzɪʃn/ *n.* ▸❶ **p. 1260** Arzt, *der*/Ärztin, *die*

physicist /ˈfɪzɪsɪst/ *n.* ▸❶ **p. 1260** Physiker, *der*/Physikerin, *die*

physics /ˈfɪzɪks/ *n., no pl.* Physik, *die*

physio /ˈfɪzɪəʊ/ *n., pl.* **~s** ▸❶ **p. 1260** (coll.) Physiotherapeut, *der*/Physiotherapeutin, *die*

physiognomy /fɪzɪˈɒnəmɪ/ *n.* Physiognomie, *die;* Gesichtszüge; (study) Physiognomik, *die;* (fig.: of mountain, country, city, etc.) Physiognomie, *die* (geh.); Gestalt, *die*

physiological /fɪzɪəˈlɒdʒɪkl/ *adj.* physiologisch

physiologist /fɪzɪˈɒlədʒɪst/ *n.* ▸❶ **p. 1260** Physiologe, *der*/Physiologin, *die*

physiology /fɪzɪˈɒlədʒɪ/ *n.* Physiologie, *die*

physiotherapist /fɪzɪəʊˈθerəpɪst/ *n.* ▸❶ **p. 1260** Physiotherapeut, *der*/-therapeutin, *die*

physiotherapy /fɪzɪəʊˈθerəpɪ/ *n.* Physiotherapie, *die*

physique /fɪˈziːk/ *n.* Körperbau, *der;* **be small in ~:** von geringer Körpergröße *od.* kleinem Wuchs sein

pi /paɪ/ *n.* (Math., Greek letter) Pi, *das*

pianissimo /pɪəˈnɪsɪməʊ/ (Mus.)

A *adj.* pianissimo *nicht attr.;* Pianissimo-

B *adv.* pianissimo

C *n., pl.* **~s** *or* **pianissimi** /pɪəˈnɪsɪmiː/ Pianissimo, *das*

pianist /ˈpiːənɪst/ *n.* ▸❶ **p. 1260** Klavierspieler, *der*/Klavierspielerin, *die;* (professional) Pianist, *der*/Pianistin, *die*

piano¹ /pɪˈænəʊ/ *n., pl.* **~s** (Mus.) (upright) Klavier, *das;* (grand) Flügel, *der; attrib.* Klavier-; **play the ~:** Klavier spielen; *see also* **grand piano**; **player-piano**; **upright A 1**

piano² /pɪˈɑːnəʊ/ (Mus.)

A *adj.* piano *nicht attr.;* piano gespielt/gesungen; Piano-

B *adv.* piano

C *n., pl.* **~s** *or* **piani** /pɪˈɑːniː/ (passage) Piano, *das*

piano acˈcordion *n.* Akkordeon, *das*

pianoforte /pɪænəˈfɔːtɪ/ *n.* (Mus. formal/arch.) Pianoforte, *das* (veralt.)

Pianola ® /piːəˈnəʊlə/ *n.* Pianola, *das*

p

piano/pɪˈænəʊ/: ~ **music** *n.* Klaviermusik, *die;* (score) Klaviernoten *Pl.;* ~ **player** *n.* Klavierspieler, *der*/-spielerin, *die;* ~ **stool** *n.* Klavierschemel, *der;* ~ **tuner** *n.* ▸❶ **p. 1260** Klavierstimmer, *der*/-stimmerin, *die*

piazza /pɪˈætsə/ *n.* Piazza, *die*

picador /ˈpɪkədɔː(r)/ *n.* Picador, *der;* Lanzenreiter, *der*

picaresque /pɪkəˈresk/ *adj.* pikaresk; pikarisch; ~ **novel** Schelmenroman, *der*

picayune /pɪkəˈjuːn/ *adj.* (Amer. coll.) [1] (petty) kleinlich [2] (paltry) unbedeutend; unerheblich

piccalilli /pɪkəˈlɪlɪ/ *n.* Piccalilli, *das; scharf gewürztes eingelegtes Senfgemüse*

piccaninny /ˈpɪkənɪnɪ/ *n.* (Brit. offensive) [kleines] Negerkind (oft als diskriminierend empfunden)

piccolo /ˈpɪkələʊ/ *n., pl.* ~**s** (Mus.) Pikkoloflöte, *die;* Pikkolo, *das*

pick¹ /pɪk/ *n.* [1] (for breaking up hard ground, rocks, etc.) Spitzhacke, *die;* (for breaking up ice) [Eis]pickel, *der* [2] ▸**toothpick** [3] (Mus.) Plektrum, *das*

pick²

A *n.* [1] (choice) Wahl, *die;* **take your ~:** du hast die Wahl; **you can take your ~ of the rooms** du kannst dir ein Zimmer aussuchen; **she had the ~ of several jobs** sie konnte zwischen mehreren Jobs [aus]wählen; **have [the] first ~ of sth.** als Erster aus etw. auswählen dürfen [2] (best part) Elite, *die;* **the ~ of the herd/fruit** *etc.* die besten Tiere aus der Herde/die besten Früchte *usw.; see also* **bunch A 2**

B *v.t.* [1] pflücken ‹*Blumen*›; [ab]ernten, [ab]pflücken ‹*Äpfel, Trauben usw.*›; **'~ your own strawberries'** „Erdbeeren zum Selbstpflücken" [2] (select) auswählen; aufstellen ‹*Mannschaft*›; **~ the** *or* **a winner/the winning horse** auf den Sieger/das richtige *od.* siegreiche Pferd setzen; **~ a winner** (fig.) eine gute Wahl treffen; das große Los ziehen; **~ one's words** seine Worte mit Bedacht wählen; **~ one's way** *or* **steps** sich (*Dat.*) vorsichtig [s]einen Weg suchen; **~ one's way through the rules and regulations** sich (*Dat.*) seinen Weg durch das Dickicht der Vorschriften und Bestimmungen suchen; **~ and choose** sich (*Dat.*) aussuchen; **you can't ~ and choose which laws to obey** du kannst dir nicht aussuchen, welche Gesetze du befolgen willst [und welche nicht]; **~ one's time [for sth.]** den Zeitpunkt [für etw.] festlegen; **you certainly ~ your times!** (iron.) du suchst dir aber auch immer die unmöglichsten Zeiten aus!; **~ sides [for the game]** abwechselnd einen Spieler/eine Spielerin [für das Spiel] auswählen
[3] (clear of flesh) **~ the bones [clean]** ‹*Hund:*› die Knochen [sauber] abnagen; **~ the carcass** ‹*Geier, Hyäne usw.:*› den Kadaver abfressen
[4] **~ sb.'s brains [about sth.]** jmdn. [über etw. (*Akk.*)] ausfragen *od.* (ugs.) ausquetschen
[5] **~ one's nose/teeth** in der Nase bohren/in den Zähnen [herum]stochern
[6] **~ sb.'s pocket** jmdn. bestehlen; **he had his pocket ~ed** er wurde von einem Taschendieb bestohlen
[7] **~ a lock** ein Schloss knacken (salopp)
[8] **~ to pieces** (fig.: criticize) kein gutes Haar lassen an (+ *Dat.*) (ugs.)
[9] (Amer. Mus.) zupfen ‹*Saiten*›; **~ a banjo/guitar** Banjo/Gitarre spielen. *See also* **bone A 4; hole A 1; quarrel A 1**

C *v.i.* **~ and choose [too much]** [zu] wählerisch sein

Phrasal verbs

• **~ at** *v.t.* [1] (eat without interest) herumstochern in (+ *Dat.*) ‹*Essen*› [2] (criticize) herumhacken auf (+ *Dat.*) (ugs.) [3] herumspielen an, (landsch.) knaupeln an (+ *Dat.*) ‹*Pickel*›

• **~ off** *v.t.* [1] /ˈ--/ (pluck off) abrupfen ‹*Blüten, Blumen*›; abzupfen, ablesen ‹*Haare, Fusseln*›; **the helicopter ~ed him off his boat** der Hubschrauber holte ihn aus seinem Boot heraus [2] /-ˈ-/ (shoot one by one) [einzeln] abschießen *od.* (ugs.) abknallen

• **~ on** *v.t.* [1] (victimize) es abgesehen haben auf (+ *Akk.*); **he's constantly being ~ed on to do the dirty jobs** ihm wird immer die Dreckarbeit aufgehalst; **why ~ on me every time?** warum immer gerade *od.* ausgerechnet ich?; **~ on someone your own size!** leg dich doch wenigstens mit einem Gleichstarken an! (ugs.) [2] (select) sich (*Dat.*) aussuchen

• **~ ˈout** *v.t.* [1] (choose) auswählen; (for oneself) sich (*Dat.*) aussuchen ‹*Kleid, Blume*›; heraussuchen, [her]aussortieren ‹*rote Kugeln, kleine Bälle, defekte Ware, [un]reife Früchte*›; (from text) herausgreifen ‹*Beispiel, Passage*› [2] (distinguish) ausmachen, entdecken ‹*Detail, jmds. Gesicht in der Menge*›; **the spotlight ~ed out a child in the audience** der Scheinwerfer erfasste ein Kind im Publikum; **~ out sth. from sth.** etw. von etw. unterscheiden [3] (highlight) hervorheben ‹*Buchstaben, Inschrift*› [4] (play by ear etc.) sich (*Dat.*) zusammensuchen ‹*Melodie*›

• **~ ˈover** *v.t.* durchstöbern; **the tomatoes have been well ~ed over** die besten Tomaten sind schon herausgesucht worden

• **~ up**

A /ˈ--/ *v.t.* [1] (take up) [in die Hand] nehmen ‹*Brief, Buch usw.*›; hochnehmen ‹*Baby*›; [wieder] aufnehmen ‹*Handarbeit*›; aufnehmen ‹*Masche*›; auffinden ‹*Fehler*›; (after dropping) aufheben; **~ sth. up from the table** etw. vom Tisch nehmen; **~ a child up in one's arms** ein Kind auf den Arm nehmen; **~ up the telephone** den [Telefon]hörer abnehmen; **~ up the pieces** (lit. or fig.) die Scherben aufsammeln; **~ up your feet** heb die Füße hoch; *see also* **thread A 2** [2] (collect) mitnehmen; (by arrangement) abholen (**at, from** von); (obtain) holen; **~ up sth. on the way home** etw. auf dem Nachhauseweg abholen [3] (become infected by) sich (*Dat.*) einfangen *od.* holen (ugs.) ‹*Virus, Grippe*› [4] (take on board) ‹*Bus, Autofahrer:*› mitnehmen; **~ sb. up at** *or* **from the station** jmdn. vom Bahnhof abholen [5] (rescue from the sea) [aus Seenot] bergen [6] (coll.: earn) einstreichen (ugs.) [7] (coll.: make acquaintance of) aufreißen (ugs.) [8] (find and arrest) festnehmen [9] (receive) empfangen ‹*Signal, Funkspruch usw.*› [10] (hear) aufschnappen (ugs.); **he'd ~ed up some tale that ...:** er hatte davon läuten gehört, dass ... [11] (obtain casually) sich (*Dat.*) aneignen; bekommen ‹*Sache*›; **things we ~ed up on our holidays/journeys** Dinge, die wir aus dem Urlaub/von unseren Reisen mitgebracht haben; **~ up languages easily** mühelos Sprachen lernen; **~ up odd habits** seltsame Gewohnheiten annehmen; **where do you ~ up such expressions?** wo hast du denn diese Ausdrücke her? [12] (obtain) auftreiben (ugs.) [13] (resume) wieder aufnehmen ‹*Erzählung, Gespräch*› [14] (succeed in seeing) ausmachen [15] (regain) wieder finden ‹*Spur, Fährte*›; wieder aufnehmen ‹*Witterung*›; **you cross the field and ~ up the path on the other side** du überquerst das Feld und stößt *od.* kommst auf der anderen Seite wieder auf den Weg [16] (pay) **~ up the bill** *etc.* **for sth.** die Kosten *od.* die Rechnung *usw.* für etw. übernehmen. *See also* **pick-me-up; pickup; speed A 1**

B /-ˈ-/ *v.i.* [1] (improve, recover) ‹*Gesundheitszustand, Befinden, Stimmung, Laune, Wetter:*› sich bessern; ‹*Person:*› sich erholen, wieder auf die Beine kommen; ‹*Markt, Geschäft:*› sich erholen *od.* beleben; ‹*Gewinne:*› steigen, zunehmen [2] (gain speed) beschleunigen; ‹*Wind:*› auffrischen

C *v. refl.* **~ oneself up** wieder aufstehen; (with difficulty) sich wieder aufrappeln (ugs.); (fig.) sich aufrappeln (ugs.)

• **~ ˈup with** *v.t.* (coll.: make the acquaintance of) kennen lernen

pick-a-back /ˈpɪkəbæk/ ▸**piggyback**

ˈpick-and-mix *adj.* **~ holidays** Urlaub nach Maß; **~ selection** individuelle Mischung

pickaninny (Amer.) ▸**piccaninny**

ˈpickaxe (*Amer.:* **ˈpickax**) ▸**pick¹ 1**

picker /ˈpɪkə(r)/ *n.* (of fruit, hops, cotton, etc.) Pflücker, *der*/Pflückerin, *die*

picket /ˈpɪkɪt/

A *n.* [1] (Industry) Streikposten, *der;* **mount a ~ [at** *or* **on a gate]** [an einem Tor] Streikposten aufstellen; *see also* **flying picket** [2] (pointed stake) Pfahl, *der* [3] (Mil.: small body of troops) Feldposten, *der;* **advanced ~:** vorgeschobener Posten; Vorposten, *der* [4] (Mil.: camp policeman) Feldjäger, *der*

B *v.t.* Streikposten aufstellen vor (+ *Dat.*) ‹*Fabrik, Büro usw.*›

C *v.i.* Streikposten stehen

ˈpicket duty *n.* **be on/do ~:** Streikposten stehen

picketer /ˈpɪkɪtə(r)/ *n.* Streikposten, *der*

ˈpicket fence *n.* Palisadenzaun, *der*

picketing /ˈpɪkɪtɪŋ/ *n.* Aufstellen von Streikposten; **secondary ~:** *Streikpostenstehen bei einem Betrieb, dem man selbst nicht angehört*

ˈpicket line *n.* Streikpostenkette, *die;* **be on the ~:** Streikposten stehen; in der Streikpostenkette stehen

picking /ˈpɪkɪŋ/ *n.* [1] Ernten, *das;* (of fruit, hops, cotton also) Pflücken, *das;* (of grapes also) Lesen, *das* [2] (fruit picked) Ernte, *die;* [Ernte]ertrag, *der;* **a large ~ of apples** eine reiche Apfelernte [3] *in pl.* (gleanings) Reste *Pl.;* (things stolen) [Aus]beute, *die;* (things allowed) zusätzliche Vergünstigungen; (yield) Ausbeute, *die;* **it's easy ~s** das ist ein einträgliches Geschäft; *see also* **slim A 2**

pickle /ˈpɪkl/

A *n.* [1] (preservative) *Konservierungsmittel enthaltende Flüssigkeit;* (brine) Salzlake, *die;* (vinegar solution) Marinade, *die* [2] *usu. in pl.* (food) [Mixed] Pickles *Pl.;* Essiggemüse, *das* [3] (coll.: predicament) **be in a ~:** in der Klemme sitzen (ugs.); **get into a ~:** in die Klemme geraten (ugs.); **be in a sorry** *or* (iron.) **nice** *etc.* **~:** ganz schön in der Klemme sitzen (ugs.) [4] (acid solution) Beize, *die*

B *v.t.* [1] (preserve) [in Essig *od.* sauer] einlegen ‹*Gurken, Zwiebeln, Eier*›; marinieren ‹*Hering*› [2] (treat) beizen ‹*Leder, Metall*›

pickled /ˈpɪkld/ *adj.* [1] (coll.: drunk) betrunken; besoffen (derb); **get [thoroughly] ~:** sich [richtig] voll laufen lassen (ugs.) [2] (preserved) eingelegt ‹*Eier usw.*›; mariniert ‹*Hering*›; (in brine) gepökelt ‹*Fleisch*›; **~ onions/gherkins** eingelegte Zwiebeln/saure Gurken

pick: **~lock** *n.* [1] (person) Einbrecher, *der*/Einbrecherin, *die;* [2] (tool) Dietrich, *der;* **~-me-up** *n.* Stärkungsmittel, *das;* **the holiday/hearing that good news was a real ~-me-up** der Urlaub/diese gute Nachricht hat mir richtig gut getan; **~pocket** *n.* Taschendieb, *der*/-diebin, *die;* **~up** *n.* [1] (of goods) Laden, *das;* [2] (improvement) Anstieg, *der;* **a ~up in sales/quality** ein Anstieg der Verkaufszahlen/eine Verbesserung der Qualität; [3] (coll.: person) Zufallsbekanntschaft, *die;* **is that his latest ~up?** ist das seine neueste Errungenschaft? (ugs.); [4] (truck) **~up [truck/van]** Kleinlastwagen, *der;* [5] (of record player, guitar) Tonabnehmer, *der;* Pick-up, *der;* **~up point** *n.* [1] (for person) Zusteigepunkt, *der;* [2] (for goods) Warenausgabe, *die*

pick 'n' mix /pɪkənˈmɪks/ *adj.* ▸ **pick-and-mix**

picky /ˈpɪkɪ/ *adj.* (coll.) pingelig (ugs.)

pick-your-ˈown

A *adj.* ‹*Obst, Blumen*› zum Selberpflücken

B *n.* Selbstpflückbetrieb, *der*

picnic /ˈpɪknɪk/

A *n.* [1] Picknick, *das;* **go for** *or* **on a ~:** ein Picknick machen; picknicken gehen; **have a ~:** ein Picknick machen; picknicken [2] (coll.: easy task, pleasant experience) Kinderspiel, *das;* **be no ~:** kein Zuckerlecken *od.* Honig[sch]lecken sein; **the Korean War was a ~ in comparison** der Koreakrieg war dagegen ein Spaziergang

B *v.i.*, **-ck-** picknicken; Picknick machen

picnic: **~ area** *n.* Picknickgelände, *das;* (small area beside a road) Rastplatz, *der;* **~ basket** *n.* Picknickkorb, *der*

picnicker /ˈpɪknɪkə(r)/ *n.* **there were a lot of ~s on the beach** viele Menschen machten Picknick am Strand; **the ~s cleared up their litter** die Ausflügler räumten nach dem Picknick ihre Abfälle weg

picnic: **~ ˈlunch** *n.* [1] Picknick, *das* (*als Mittagessen*); [2] (packed up) Lunchpaket, *das;* **~ site** *n.* Picknickplatz, *der*

Pict /pɪkt/ *n.* (Hist.) Pikte, *der*/Piktin, *die*

pictogram /ˈpɪktəgræm/, **pictograph** /ˈpɪktəgrɑːf/ *ns.* Piktogramm, *das*

P

pictorial /pɪkˈtɔːrɪəl/
A *adj.* illustriert ‹*Bericht, Zeitschrift, Wochenmagazin*›; bildlich ‹*Darstellung*›; Bild‹*journalismus, -band, -bericht*›; **give a ~ record of sth.** etw. im Bild festhalten
B *n.* (magazine, newspaper, etc.) Illustrierte, *die*

pictorially /pɪkˈtɔːrɪəlɪ/ *adv.* in illustrierter Form; bildhaft ‹*darstellen*›

picture /ˈpɪktʃə(r)/
A *n.* **1** Bild, *das; see also* **pretty A 1**; **tell A 2** **2** (portrait) Porträt, *das;* (photograph) Porträtfoto, *das;* **have one's ~ painted** sich malen *od.* porträtieren lassen **3** (mental image) Vorstellung, *die;* Bild, *das;* **get a ~ of sth.** sich (*Dat.*) von etw. ein Bild machen; von etw. eine Vorstellung bekommen; **give a ~ of sth.** von etw. einen Eindruck vermitteln; **the employment ~** (fig.) das Bild der Arbeitsmarktlage; **present a sorry ~** (fig.) ein trauriges *od.* jämmerliches Bild abgeben; **look the [very] ~ of health/misery/innocence** wie das blühende Leben aussehen/ein Bild des Jammers sein/wie die Unschuld in Person aussehen; **be the ~ of delight** die Freude in Person sein; **get the ~** (coll.) verstehen[, worum es geht]; **I'm beginning to get the ~:** langsam *od.* allmählich verstehe *od.* (ugs.) kapiere ich; **[do you] get the ~?** verstehst du?; **get the whole ~:** den Gesamtzusammenhang erkennen; **put sb. in the ~:** jmdn. ins Bild setzen; **be in the ~** (be aware) im Bilde sein; **keep out of the ~:** sich raushalten; **keep sb. in the ~:** jmdn. auf dem Laufenden halten; **come** *or* **enter into the ~:** [dabei] eine Rolle spielen **4** (film) Film, *der* **5** *in pl.* (Brit.: cinema) Kino, *das;* **go to the ~s** ins Kino gehen; **what's on at the ~s?** was gibts *od.* läuft im Kino?; **is there anything on at the ~s?** läuft etwas [Interessantes] im Kino? **6** (delightful object) **be a ~:** wunderschön *od.* (ugs.) ein Gedicht sein; **her face was a ~:** ihr Gesicht sprach Bände; **she looked a ~:** sie sah bildschön aus
B *v.t.* **1** (represent) abbilden **2** (imagine) **~ [to oneself]** sich (*Dat.*) vorstellen **3** (describe graphically) anschaulich schildern

picture: ~ book **A** *n.* Bilderbuch, *das;* **B** *adj.* Bilderbuch-; **~ card** *n.* Figurenkarte, *die;* Bild, *das;* **~ frame** *n.* Bilderrahmen, *der;* **~-framer** ▸ ❶ **p. 1260** ▸ **framer**; **~ gallery** *n.* Gemäldegalerie, *die;* **~ hook** *n.* Bilderhaken, *der;* **~ palace** *n.* (dated) Filmpalast, *der* (veralt.); **~ 'postcard** *n.* Ansichtskarte, *die;* **~ rail** *n.* Bilderleiste, *die*

picturesque /pɪktʃəˈresk/ *adj.* malerisch; pittoresk (geh.); (vivid) anschaulich, bildhaft ‹*Beschreibung, Erzählung*›

picturesquely /pɪktʃəˈresklɪ/ *adv.* malerisch; (graphically) anschaulich

picture: ~ window *n.* Panoramafenster, *das;* **~-writing** *n.* Bilderschrift, *die*

piddle /ˈpɪdl/ (coll.)
A *v.i.* **1** (act in trifling way) **~ about** *or* **around** herummachen (ugs.) **2** (urinate) Pipi machen (Kinderspr.); pinkeln (ugs.)
B *n.* **1** **have a/do one's ~:** Pipi machen (Kinderspr.); pinkeln (ugs.); **he needs to have a ~:** er muss mal (ugs.) **2** (urine) Pipi, *das* (Kinderspr.)

piddling /ˈpɪdlɪŋ/ *adj.* (coll.) lächerlich (abwertend)

pidgin /ˈpɪdʒɪn/ *n.* Pidgin, *das*

pidgin 'English *n.* Pidginenglisch, *das*

pie /paɪ/ *n.* (of meat, fish, etc.) Pastete, *die;* (of fruit etc.) ≈ Obstkuchen, *der;* **as sweet/nice** *etc.* **as ~** (coll.) superfreundlich (ugs.); scheißfreundlich (salopp); **as easy as ~** (coll.) kinderleicht (ugs.); **have a finger in every ~** (coll.) überall die Finger drin haben (ugs.); **that's all just ~ in the sky** (coll.) das sind alles nur Luftschlösser; das ist alles völlig unrealistisch

piebald /ˈpaɪbɔːld/
A *adj.* gescheckt, scheckig ‹*Pferd, Kuh, Pony*›
B *n.* Schecke, *die/der*

piece /piːs/
A *n.* **1** Stück, *das;* (of broken glass or pottery) Scherbe, *die;* (of jigsaw puzzle, crashed aircraft, etc.) Teil, *der;* (Amer.: distance) [kleines] Stück; **a ~ of meat** ein Stück Fleisch; **[all] in one ~:** unbeschädigt; (fig.) heil; wohlbehalten; **in ~s** (broken) kaputt (ugs.); zerbrochen; (taken apart) [in Einzelteile] zerlegt; **break into ~s, fall to ~s** zerbrechen; kaputtgehen (ugs.); **break sth. to ~s** etw. zerbrechen *od.* (ugs.) kaputtmachen; **go [all] to ~s** (fig.) [völlig] die Fassung verlieren; **[all] of a ~:** aus einem Guss; **be [all] of a ~ with sth.** [ganz] genau zu etw. passen; **say one's ~** (fig.) sagen, was man zu sagen hat **2** (part of set) **~ of furniture/clothing/luggage** Möbel-/Kleidungs-/Gepäckstück, *das;* **a 21-~ teaset** ein 21teiliges Teeservice; **a five-~ band** eine fünfköpfige Band *od.* Kapelle; **a three-/four-~ suite** eine drei-/vierteilige Sitzgarnitur; **a three-~ suit** ein dreiteiliger Anzug **3** (enclosed area) **a ~ of land/property** ein Stück Land/Grundstück; **a ~ of water** ein kleines Gewässer **4** (example) **a ~ of impudence [like that]** eine [solche] Unverschämtheit; **~ of luck** Glücksfall, *der;* **by a ~ of good luck** durch eine glückliche Fügung; **a fine ~ of pottery/Victorian literature** eine sehr schöne Töpferarbeit/ein hervorragendes Werk der viktorianischen Literatur; **fine ~ of work** hervorragende Arbeit; **he's an unpleasant ~ of work** (fig.) er ist ein unangenehmer Vertreter (ugs.); *see also* **nasty A 1** **5** (item) **~ of news/gossip/information** Nachricht, *die*/Klatsch, *der*/Information, *die;* **be paid by the ~** ‹*Arbeiter:*› Akkord- *od.* Stücklohn erhalten; **the work is paid by the ~:** für die Arbeit wird Akkord- *od.* Stücklohn gezahlt; *see also* **advice 1** **6** (Chess) Figur, *die;* (Draughts, Backgammon, etc.) Stein, *der* **7** ▸ ❶ **p. 1332** (coin) **gold ~:** Goldstück, *das;* **~ of silver** Silbermünze, *die;* **a 10p ~:** ein 10-Pence-Stück; eine 10-Pence-Münze; **~ of eight** mexikanischer *od.* spanischer Dollar; Achterstück, *das* (veralt.) **8** (article in newspaper, magazine, etc.) Beitrag, *der* **9** (literary or musical composition) Stück, *das;* **~ of music** Musikstück, *das; see also* **villain 2** **10** (coll.: woman) Mieze, *die* (ugs.) **11** (Mil.: weapon) (firearm) Schusswaffe, *die;* (of artillery) Geschütz, *das* **12** (picture) Stück, *das;* Werk, *das*
B *v.t.* **~ together** (lit. or fig.) zusammenfügen (**from** aus); **~ together what happened** rekonstruieren, was passiert ist

pièce de résistance /piːeɪs də reɪzɪˈstɑ̃s/ *n., pl.* **pièces de résistance** /piːeɪs də reɪzɪˈstɑ̃s/ **1** (dish) Hauptgericht, *das;* Pièce de résistance, *das* (veralt.) **2** (item) Krönung, *die;* **and now for my ~!** und nun die Krönung!

'piecemeal *adv., adj.* stückweise

piece: ~ rate *n.* Akkordsatz, *der;* **be paid at** *or* **be on ~ rates** ‹*Arbeiter:*› Akkord- *od.* Stücklohn erhalten; **the work is paid at ~ rates** für die Arbeit wird Akkord- *od.* Stücklohn gezahlt; **~work** *n., no pl.* Akkordarbeit, *die;* **put sb. on ~work** jmdn. im Akkord beschäftigen; **be on ~work** im Akkord arbeiten; **~work system** Akkordlohnsystem, *das;* **~worker** *n.* Akkordarbeiter, *der*/-arbeiterin, *die*

pie: ~ chart *n.* Kreisdiagramm, *das;* **~crust** *n.* Teigmantel, *der*

pied /paɪd/ *adj.* gescheckt ‹*Pferd, Kuh usw.*›; [bunt] gefleckt ‹*Schmetterling, Vogel*›

pied-à-terre /pjeɪdɑːˈteə(r)/ *n., pl.* **pieds-à-terre** /pjeɪdɑːˈteə(r)/ Zweitwohnung, *die*

'pie dish *n.* Pastetenform, *die*

Pied 'Piper *n.* Rattenfänger, *der;* **the ~ of Hamelin** der Rattenfänger von Hameln

pie: ~-eyed *adj.* (coll.) sternhagelvoll (ugs.); **~man** /ˈpaɪmən/ *n., pl.* **~men** /ˈpaɪmən/ (arch.) Pastetenverkäufer, *der*

pier /pɪə(r)/ *n.* **1** (for landing place, as promenade) Pier, *der od.* (*Seemannsspr.*) *die* **2** (to protect or form harbour) [Hafen]mole, *die;* Hafendamm, *der* **3** (support of bridge) Pfeiler, *der* **4** (Archit.) Trumeau, *der*

pierce /pɪəs/ *v.t.* **1** (prick) durchbohren, durchstechen ‹*Hülle, Verkleidung, Ohrläppchen*›; (penetrate) sich bohren in, [ein]dringen in (+ *Akk.*) ‹*Körper, Fleisch, Herz*›; **~ a hole in sth.** ein Loch in etw. (*Akk.*) stechen; **have one's ears ~d** sich (*Dat.*) Löcher in die Ohrläppchen machen *od.* stechen lassen **2** (fig.) **the cold ~d him to the bone** die Kälte drang ihm bis ins Mark; **a scream ~d the night/silence** ein Schrei gellte durch die Nacht/zerriss die Stille **3** (force one's way through) durchbrechen ‹*feindliche Linien*›; (fig.) erschüttern ‹*Gleichgültigkeit*›

piercing /ˈpɪəsɪŋ/ *adj.* durchdringend ‹*Stimme, Schrei, Blick*›; schneidend ‹*Sarkasmus, Kälte*›

pierrot /ˈpɪərəʊ/ *n.* Pierrot, *der*

pietà /pjerˈtɑː/ *n.* (Art) Pieta, *die*

piety /ˈpaɪətɪ/ *n.* **1** *no pl.* (quality) Frömmigkeit, *die* **2** (act) fromme Handlung

piffle /ˈpɪfl/ (coll.) *n.* **1** (nonsense) Quatsch, *der* (ugs.) **2** (empty talk) Geschwafel, *das* (ugs.); Blabla, *das* (ugs.)

piffling /ˈpɪflɪŋ/ *adj.* (coll.) lächerlich

pig /pɪɡ/
A *n.* **1** Schwein, *das;* **the sow is in ~:** die Sau ist trächtig; **bleed like a [stuck] ~:** wie ein Schwein bluten (derb); heftig bluten; **~s might fly** (iron.) da müsste schon ein Wunder geschehen; **buy a ~ in a poke** (fig.) die Katze im Sack kaufen **2** (coll.) (greedy person) Vielfraß, *der* (ugs.); Fresssack, *der* (salopp); (obstinate person) Dickschädel, *der* (ugs.); (dirty person) Ferkel, *das* (ugs.); [Dreck]schwein, *das* (derb); (unpleasant thing) Scheißding, *das* (salopp); (unpleasant person) Ekel, *das* (ugs.); Schwein, *das* (derb); **make a ~ of oneself** (overeat) sich (*Dat.*) den Bauch *od.* Wanst voll schlagen (salopp); **live like ~s** hausen wie die Schweine (ugs.) **3** (sl. derog.: policeman) Bulle, *der* (salopp abwertend) **4** (metal) Massel, *die* (Metall.) **5** (Amer.: young swine) Ferkel, *das. See also* **chauvinist**
B *v.t.*, **-gg-: ~ it** (coll.) hausen (ugs.)

pigeon[1] /ˈpɪdʒɪn/ *n.* Taube, *die;* **cock ~:** Tauber, *der;* Täuber[ich], *der*

pigeon[2] *n.* **1** ▸ **pidgin** **2** (coll.: business) **be sb.'s ~:** jmdn. angehen; **that's not my ~:** das ist nicht mein Bier (ugs.)

pigeon: ~ fancier *n.* Taubenfreund, *der*/-freundin, *die;* **~hole** **A** *n.* **1** (in cabinet etc.) [Ablage]fach, *das;* (for letters) Postfach, *das;* **put people in ~holes** (fig.) Menschen in Schubladen einordnen *od.* stecken; **2** (for pigeon) [Tauben]flugloch, *das;* **B** *v.t.* **1** (deposit) [in die Fächer] sortieren; **2** (put aside) auf Eis legen; **get ~holed** in die Schublade wandern; auf Eis gelegt werden; **3** (categorize) einordnen; in eine Schublade/in Schubladen stecken; **~ loft** *n.* Taubenschlag, *der;* **~-toed** **A** *adj.* **a ~-toed man** ein Mann, der mit einwärts gerichteten Füßen geht; **be ~-toed** mit einwärts gerichteten Füßen *od.* (ugs.) über den großen Onkel gehen; **B** *adv.* mit einwärts gerichteten Füßen; über den großen Onkel (ugs.)

piggery /ˈpɪɡərɪ/ *n.* **1** (pig-breeding establishment) Schweinezucht, *die* **2** ▸ **pigsty** **3** (coll.: gluttony) Gefräßigkeit, *die* (ugs.)

piggish /ˈpɪɡɪʃ/ *adj.* (coll.) **1** (gluttonous) gefräßig (ugs.); verfressen (salopp) **2** (dirty) schmuddelig (ugs.); dreckig (ugs.) **3** (stubborn) dickschädelig; stur

piggy /ˈpɪɡɪ/ (coll.)
A *n.* Schweinchen, *das;* Ferkel, *das*
B *adj.* **~ face** Schweinchengesicht, *das;* **~ eyes** Schweinsäuglein *Pl.*

piggy: ~back **A** *n.* **give sb. a ~back** jmdn. huckepack nehmen *od.* tragen; **ask for a ~back** huckepack getragen werden wollen; **B** *adv.* huckepack; **C** *adj.* **give a child a ~back ride** ein Kind huckepack tragen; **~ bank** *n.* Sparschwein[chen], *das;* **~ in the middle** *n.* **1** (game) Schweinchen in der Mitte; **2** (fig.: person) **I don't want to be** *or* **play ~ in the middle** ich möchte nicht zwischen die Fronten geraten

pig: ~'headed *adj.* dickschädelig (ugs.); stur; **~'headedness** /pɪɡˈhedɪdnɪs/ *n., no pl.* Dickschädeligkeit, *die* (ugs.); Sturheit, *die;* **~ iron** *n.* Roheisen, *das;* Masseleisen, *das* (Metall.)

piglet /ˈpɪɡlɪt/ *n.* Ferkel, *das*

'pig meat *n.* Schweinefleisch, *das*

pigment /ˈpɪɡmənt/
A *n.* Pigment, *das*
B *v.t.* pigmentieren

pigmentation /pɪɡmənˈteɪʃn/ *n.* Pigmentierung, *die;* Pigmentation, *die*

pigmy ▸**pygmy**

pig: ~pen (Amer.) ▸**pigsty; ~'s 'ear** *n.* (Brit. coll.) **make a ~'s ear of sth.** etw. verpfuschen *od.* (ugs.) vermurksen; **~skin** *n.* [1] Schweinehaut, *die;* [2] (leather) Schweinsleder, *das; attrib.* schweinsledern; Schweinsleder-; [3] (Amer. coll.: football) Leder, *das* (ugs.); **~sty** *n.* (lit. or fig.) Schweinestall, *der;* **~swill** *n.* Schweinefutter, *das;* (fig. coll.) (food) Schweinefraß, *der* (derb); (drink, soup, etc.) Spülwasser, *das* (salopp); **~tail** *n.* (plaited) Zopf, *der;* **~tails** (worn loose, at either side of head) Rattenschwänzchen *Pl.* (ugs.)

pike[1] /paɪk/ *n., pl. same* (Zool.) Hecht, *der*

pike[2] *n.* (Arms Hist.) Pike, *die;* Spieß, *der*

pike[3] *n.* (Brit. Hist., Amer.) [1] (toll bar) Zahlstelle, *die;* Mautstelle, *die* (bes. südd. u. österr.) [2] (road) gebührenpflichtige Straße; Mautstraße, *die* (bes. südd. u. österr.)

pike: ~perch *n.* (Zool.) Zander, *der;* **~staff** *n.* **plain as a ~staff** sonnenklar (ugs.)

pilaff /pɪ'læf/ *n.* Pilaw, *der* (Kochk.)

pilaster /pɪ'læstə(r)/ *n.* (Archit.) Pilaster, *der*

pilchard /'pɪltʃəd/ *n.* Sardine, *die*

pile[1] /paɪl/

A *n.* [1] (heap) (of dishes, plates) Stapel, *der;* (of paper, books, letters) Stoß, *der;* (of clothes) Haufen, *der* [2] (coll.: large quantity) Masse, *die* (ugs.); Haufen, *der* (ugs.); **a ~ of troubles/letters/people** eine *od.* (ugs.) jede Menge Sorgen/Briefe/Leute; **a great ~ of work/problems** eine Unmenge Arbeit/Probleme; **a ~ of difficult problems awaited her** eine Menge schwierige Probleme erwartete sie [3] (coll.: fortune) **make a** *or* **one's ~:** ein Vermögen machen; **he's made his ~:** er hat sein Schäfchen im Trockenen (ugs.) [4] (large building) Bauwerk, *das* [5] (Electr.) voltasche Säule

B *v.t.* [1] (load) [voll] beladen; **~ a table with dishes** einen Tisch mit [Stapeln von] Geschirr vollstellen [2] (heap up) aufstapeln ‹*Holz, Steine*›; aufhäufen ‹*Abfall, Schnee*› [3] **~ furniture into a van/lorry** *etc.* Möbel in einen Liefer-/Lastwagen *usw.* laden

Phrasal verbs

• **~ 'in**

A *v.i.* [1] (get in) (seen from outside) hineindrängen; (seen from inside) hereindrängen; **~ in!** [kommt] nur *od.* immer herein!; quetscht euch rein! (ugs.) [2] (coll.: begin) (to eat) reinhauen (ugs.); zulangen (ugs.); (to work) mit anpacken; (to fight) mitmischen (ugs.); mit von der Partie sein (ugs.)

B *v.t.* hineinquetschen (ugs.)

• **~ into** *v.t.* drängen in (+ *Akk.*) ‹*Stadion, Halle*›; drängen auf (+ *Akk.*) ‹*Platz, Wiese*›; sich zwängen in (+ *Akk.*) ‹*Auto, Zimmer, Zugabteil, Telefonzelle*›

• **~ off** (coll.)

A /-'-/ *v.i.* (seen from inside) hinausdrängen; (seen from outside) herausdrängen

B /'--/ *v.t.* drängen *od.* strömen aus ‹*Bus usw.*›

• **~ 'on**

A *v.i.* ▸**pile in 1**

B *v.t.* (fig.) **~ on the work/praise** massiv mit Arbeit/Lob kommen; **~ on the pressure** Druck machen; **~ on the agony, ~ it on** (coll.) dick auftragen (ugs.)

• **~ on to** *v.t.* [1] (heap on to) **~ logs on to the fire** Holzscheite auf das Feuer legen; **he ~d food on to my plate** er häufte mir Essen auf den Teller; **~ work on to sb.** (fig.) jmdm. Arbeit aufbürden *od.* aufladen [2] (enter) drängen in (+ *Akk.*) ‹*Bus usw.*›

• **~ 'out** *v.i.* nach draußen strömen *od.* drängen

• **~ 'out of** *v.t.* strömen *od.* drängen aus

• **~ 'up**

A *v.i.* [1] (accumulate) ‹*Waren, Post, Aufträge, Arbeit, Schnee:*› sich auftürmen; ‹*Verkehr:*› sich stauen; ‹*Schulden:*› sich vermehren; ‹*Verdacht, Eindruck, Beweise:*› sich verdichten [2] (crash) aufeinander auffahren

B *v.t.* aufstapeln ‹*Steine, Bücher usw.*›; auftürmen ‹*Haar, Frisur*›; aufhäufen ‹*Abfall, Schnee*›; (fig.) zusammentragen ‹*Beweise usw.*›; **~ up debts** sich immer mehr verschulden. *See also* **pile-up**

pile[2] *n.* [1] (soft surface) Flor, *der* [2] (soft hair, down) Flaum, *der*

pile[3] *n.* (stake) Pfahl, *der*

pile: ~driver *n.* [Pfahl]ramme, *die;* **~ dwelling** *n.* Pfahlbau, *der*

piles /paɪlz/ *n. pl.* (Med.) Hämorrhoiden *Pl.*

'pile-up *n.* Massenkarambolage, *die*

pilfer /'pɪlfə(r)/ *v.t.* stehlen; klauen (ugs.)

pilferage /'pɪlfərɪdʒ/ *n.* Diebstahl, *der*

pilferer /'pɪlfərə(r)/ *n.* Dieb, *der*/Diebin, *die;* Langfinger, *der* (oft scherzh.)

'pilfer-proof *adj.* einbruch-/diebstahlsicher

pilgrim /'pɪlgrɪm/ *n.* Pilger, *der*/Pilgerin, *die;* Wallfahrer, *der*/Wallfahrerin, *die*

pilgrimage /'pɪlgrɪmɪdʒ/ *n.* Pilgerfahrt, *die;* Wallfahrt, *die*

Pilgrim 'Fathers *n. pl.* (Hist.) Pilgerväter *Pl.*

> **Pilgrim Fathers**
>
> Die Pilgerväter waren die 102 Engländer, die 1620 auf der *Mayflower* den Atlantik überquerten und sich in Neuengland ansiedelten. Unter ihnen waren 35 Puritaner, die eine religiöse Kolonie in der Neuen Welt gründen wollten. Die Pilgerväter landeten im heutigen Massachusetts und gründeten die erste britische Kolonie, Plymouth.

pill /pɪl/ *n.* [1] Tablette, *die;* Pille, *die* (ugs.); **be on ~s** Tabletten einnehmen müssen [2] (coll.: contraceptive) **the ~** *or* **P~:** die Pille (ugs.); **be on the ~:** die Pille nehmen (ugs.); **come off the ~:** die Pille absetzen *od.* nicht mehr nehmen (ugs.); **go on the ~:** mit der Pille anfangen (ugs.) [3] (fig.: unpleasant thing) **swallow the ~:** die [bittere] Pille schlucken (ugs.); **sweeten the ~:** die bittere Pille versüßen (ugs.); **be a bitter ~ [to swallow]** eine bittere Pille *od.* bitter sein [4] (coll./joc.: ball) Pille, *die* (salopp)

pillage /'pɪlɪdʒ/

A *n.* Plünderung, *die*

B *v.t.* [aus]plündern; **the abbey was ~d of its treasures** die Schätze der Abtei wurden geraubt

C *v.i.* plündern

pillar /'pɪlə(r)/ *n.* [1] (vertical support) Säule, *die;* (with angular cross section) Pfeiler, *der;* (of bed, door) Pfosten, *der;* **a ~ of strength** (fig.) eine Stütze; **from ~ to post** (fig.) hin und her [2] (fig.: supporter) (of church, family, party, society, etc.) Stütze, *die;* (of science, alliance, faith, etc.) Säule, *die* [3] (upright mass) **~ of dust/cloud/water** Staub-/Wolken-/Wassersäule, *die* [4] (Mining) [Abbau]pfeiler, *der*

'pillar box *n.* (Brit.) Briefkasten, *der; attrib.* **~ red** knallrot (ugs.)

'pillbox *n.* [1] Pillenschachtel, *die* [2] **~ [hat]** Pillbox, *die; flacher runder Hut ohne Krempe;* (of bell boy) Pagenkappe, *die* [3] (Mil.) MG-Unterstand, *der*

pillion /'pɪljən/ *n.* Soziussitz, *der;* Beifahrersitz, *der;* **ride ~:** als Beifahrer/Beifahrerin *od.* auf dem Soziussitz mitfahren

pillock /'pɪlək/ *n.* (sl.) Schwachkopf, *der* (ugs.)

pillory /'pɪlərɪ/

A *v.t.* (lit. or fig.) an den Pranger stellen

B *n.* (Hist.) Pranger, *der*

pillow /'pɪləʊ/

A *n.* [Kopf]kissen, *das*

B *v.t.* **her arm ~ed the sleeping child** das schlafende Kind lag in ihren Arm gebettet; **he was like a baby, ~ed in her arms** wie ein Baby lag er in ihren Armen

pillow: ~case *n.* [Kopf]kissenbezug, *der;* **~ fight** *n.* Kissenschlacht, *die;* **~ lava** *n.* (Geol.) Kissenlava, *die;* Pillowlava, *die;* **~slip** ▸**~case; ~ talk** *n.* Bettgeflüster, *das*

'pill-popping *n.* (coll.) Pillenschluckerei, *die* (ugs.)

pilot /'paɪlət/

A *n.* ▸**❶ p. 1260** [1] (Aeronaut.) Pilot, *der*/Pilotin, *die;* Flugzeugführer, *der*/-führerin, *die;* **~'s licence** Flug- *od.* Pilotenschein, *der* [2] (Naut.; also fig.: guide) Lotse, *der*

B *adj.* Pilot‹*programm, -studie, -projekt, -phase usw.*›

C *v.t.* [1] (*Aeronaut.*) fliegen [2] (Naut.) lotsen; **~ sb. into/out of the harbour** jmdn. einlotsen *od.* in den Hafen lotsen/auslotsen *od.* aus dem Hafen lotsen [3] (fig.: guide) lotsen; **~ a bill through the House** (Parl.) einen Gesetzentwurf durch das Parlament bringen

pilot: ~ boat *n.* Lotsenboot, *das;* **~fish** *n.* Lotsenfisch, *der;* Pilotfisch, *der*

pilotless /'paɪlətlɪs/ *adj.* unbemannt; führerlos

pilot: ~ light *n.* [1] (gas burner) Zündflamme, *die;* [2] (electric light) Kontrolllampe, *die od.* -lämpchen, *das;* **~ officer** *n.* (Brit. Air Force) ≈ [Flieger]leutnant, *der;* **~ programme** *n.* (Telev., Radio) Pilotsendung, *die;* **~ study** *n.* Pilotstudie, *die*

pimento /pɪ'mentəʊ/ *n., pl.* **~s** (berry) Piment, *der od. das;* Nelkenpfeffer, *der;* (tree) Pimentbaum, *der;* Nelkenpfefferbaum, *der*

pimp /pɪmp/

A *n.* Zuhälter, *der*

B *v.i.* Zuhälterei betreiben; **~ for sb.** jmds. Zuhälter sein

pimpernel /'pɪmpənel/ *n.* (Bot.) **[scarlet] ~:** Ackergauchheil, *der;* Roter Gauchheil

pimple /'pɪmpl/ *n.* [1] (spot) Pickel, *der;* Pustel, *die;* **he/his face had come out in ~s** er hat Pickel/Pickel im Gesicht bekommen [2] (slight swelling) Erhebung, *die;* (on table tennis bat) Noppe, *die*

pimpled /'pɪmpld/ *adj.* pick[e]lig; genoppt ‹*Tischtennisschläger*›

pimply /'pɪmplɪ/ *adj.* pick[e]lig

pin

A *n.* [1] Stecknadel, *die;* **you could have heard a ~ drop** man hätte eine Stecknadel fallen hören können; **as clean as a new ~:** blitzblank (ugs.); **~s and needles** (fig.) Kribbeln, *das;* **I had ~s and needles in my legs** (fig.) meine Beine kribbelten *od.* waren eingeschlafen [2] (peg) Stift, *der;* **split ~:** Splint, *der* [3] (Electr.) Kontaktstift, *der;* **a two-/three-~ plug** ein zwei-/dreipoliger Stecker [4] **I don't give** *or* **care a ~:** es ist mir völlig egal; **for two ~s I'd resign** es fehlt nicht mehr viel, dann kündige ich [5] (Golf) Flaggenstock, *der* [6] (Mus.: for string of instrument) Wirbel, *der* [7] (half-firkin cask) ≈ Zwanzigliterfass, *das* [8] (in grenade) Zündring, *der* [9] *in pl.* (coll.: legs) Stelzen (salopp) [10] (skittle) Kegel, *der;* (scoring point) Punkt, *der;* Pin, *der* (Kegelsport) [11] (Amer.: brooch) Anstecknadel, *die;* **[lapel] ~** (of society, club, etc.) Abzeichen, *das* [12] (Med.) Stift, *der;* Pin, *der* (fachspr.)

B *v.t.,* **-nn-** [1] nageln ‹*Knochen, Bein, Hüfte*›; **~ a badge to one's lapel** sich (*Dat.*) ein Abzeichen ans Revers heften *od.* stecken; **~ a notice on the board** einen Zettel ans schwarze Brett hängen *od.* (ugs.) pinnen; **~ together** mit einer Stecknadel zusammenhalten; (Dressm.) zusammenstecken [2] (fig.) **~ one's ears back** die Ohren spitzen (ugs.); **~ one's hopes on sb./sth.** seine [ganze] Hoffnung auf jmdn./etw. setzen; **~ the blame/responsibility for sth. on sb.** jmdm. die Schuld an etw. (*Dat.*)/die Verantwortung für etw. zuschieben; **you won't ~ it on him** das wirst du ihm nicht unterschieben *od.* (ugs.) anhängen können; *see also* **faith 1** [3] (seize and hold fast) **~ sb. against the wall** jmdn. an *od.* gegen die Wand drängen *od.* drücken; **~ sb.'s arms to his sides** jmdm. die Arme an den Körper pressen; **~ sb. to the ground** jmdn. auf den Boden drücken; **~ sb.'s arm behind his back** jmdm. den Arm auf den Rücken drehen

Phrasal verbs

• **~ 'down** *v.t.* [1] (fig.: bind) festlegen, festnageln (**to** *or* **on** auf + *Akk.*); **he's a difficult man to ~ down** man kann ihn nur schwer dazu bringen, sich [auf etwas] festzulegen; **he's difficult to ~ down on policies** es ist schwer, ihn auf eine konkrete Politik festzulegen [2] (trap) festhalten; **~ sb. down [to the ground]** jmdn. auf den Boden drücken [3] (define exactly) **~ sth. down in words** etw. in Worte fassen; **I can't quite ~ it down** ich kann es nicht richtig benennen; **~ the fault down to the carburettor** feststellen, dass der Fehler im Vergaser liegt; **~ down the exact meaning of a word** die Bedeutung eines Wortes genau bestimmen

• **~ 'up** *v.t.* aufhängen ‹*Bild, Foto*›; anschlagen

P

‹*Bekanntmachung, Hinweis, Liste*›: aufstecken, hochstecken ‹*Haar, Frisur*›; abstecken ‹*Saum*›; *see also* **pin-up**

PIN /pɪn/ *abbr.* = **PIN [number]** PIN

pinafore /ˈpɪnəfɔː(r)/ *n.* [Träger]schürze, *die*

ˈpinafore dress *n.* Trägerrock, *der;* Trägerkleid, *das*

ˈpinball *n.* Flippern, *das; attrib.* Flipper‹*spiel, -automat*›; **play ~:** flippern; **have a game of ~:** [eine Runde] flippern

pince-nez /ˈpænsneɪ/ *n., pl. same* Kneifer, *der;* Pincenez, *das* (veralt.)

ˈpincer movement /ˈpɪnsə muːvmənt/ *n.* (Mil.) Zangenbewegung, *die*

pincers /ˈpɪnsəz/ *n. pl.* **1** **[pair of] ~:** Beiß- *od.* Kneifzange, *die* **2** (of crab etc.) Schere, *die;* Zange, *die* (ugs.)

pinch /pɪnʃ/

A *n.* **1** (squeezing) Kniff, *der;* **give sb. a ~:** jmdn. kneifen *od.* (bes. südd., österr.) zwicken; **give sb. a ~ on the arm/cheek** *etc.* jmdn. *od.* jmdm. in den Arm/die Backe (*usw.*) kneifen *od.* (bes. südd., österr.) zwicken **2** (fig.) **feel the ~:** knapp bei Kasse sein (ugs.); **the firm is feeling the ~:** der Firma geht es finanziell nicht gut; **at a ~:** zur Not; wenn es [unbedingt] sein muss; **if it comes to a** *or* **the ~:** wenn es zum Äußersten *od.* Schlimmsten kommt **3** (small amount) Prise, *die; see also* **salt A 1**

B *v.t.* **1** (grip tightly) kneifen; zwicken (bes. südd., österr.); **~ sb.'s cheek/bottom** jmdn. in die Wange/den Hintern (ugs.) kneifen; **I had to ~ myself** ich musste mich erst mal in den Arm kneifen (ugs.); **~ed with cold** (fig.) [völlig] durchgefroren; starr vor Kälte **2** (coll.: steal) klauen (salopp) **3** (coll.: arrest) sich (*Dat.*) schnappen (ugs.); **get ~ed** geschnappt werden (ugs.) **4** (Hort.) **~ back** *or* **down** *or* **out** abzwicken; abknipsen (ugs.)

C *v.i.* **1** ‹*Schuh:*› drücken; **that's where the shoe ~es** (fig.) da liegt der Hase im Pfeffer *od.* der Hund begraben (ugs.) **2** (be niggardly) knapsen (ugs.), knausern (ugs. abwertend) (**on** mit)

pinchbeck /ˈpɪntʃbek/

A *n.* Tombak, *der*

B *adj.* **1** aus Tombak *nachgestellt* **2** (fig.: counterfeit) **be ~:** Talmi sein

ˈpinch-hitter *n.* (Baseball) Ersatzspieler, *der/*-spielerin, *die*

ˈpincushion *n.* Nadelkissen, *das*

pine¹ /paɪn/ *n.* **1** (tree) Kiefer, *die; attrib.* Kiefern- **2** (wood) Kiefernholz, *das;* Kiefer, *die; attrib.* Kiefer[nholz]-; **a kitchen in ~:** eine Küche aus Kiefer[nholz]

pine² *v.i.* **1** (languish) (**over, about** wegen) sich [vor Kummer] verzehren (geh.) **2** (long eagerly) **~ for sb./sth.** sich nach jmdm./etw. sehnen *od.* (geh.) verzehren

Phrasal verb

• **~ aˈway** *v.i.* dahinkümmern

pineal /ˈpɪnɪəl/ *adj.* (Anat.) **~ body** *or* **gland** Zirbeldrüse, *die;* Epiphyse, *die*

pineapple /ˈpaɪnæpl/ *n.* Ananas, *die; attrib.* **~ juice** Ananassaft, *der;* **~ rings/chunks** Ananasringe *od.* -scheiben/-stücke

pine: ~ cone *n.* Kiefernzapfen, *der;* **~ marten** *n.* (Zool.) (American) Fichtenmarder, *der;* (European) Edelmarder, *der;* **~ needle** *n.* Kiefernnadel, *die;* **~ nut** *n.* Pinienkern, *der;* **~ tree** *n.* Kiefer, *die*

pinetum /paɪˈniːtəm/ *n., pl.* **pineta** /paɪˈniːtə/ Kiefernarboretum, *das*

ˈpine wood *n.* **1** (material) Kiefernholz, *das* **2** (forest) Kiefernwald, *der*

ping /pɪŋ/

A *n.* (of bullet) Pfeifen, *das;* (of bell) Klingeln, *das;* **the stone made a ~ as it hit the glass** es machte klick, als der Stein gegen das Glas flog

B *v.i.* ‹*Kugel:*› pfeifen, peitschen; ‹*Glocke, Schreibmaschine:*› klingeln

pinger /ˈpɪŋə(r)/ *n.* Kurzzeitwecker, *der;* (in kitchen) Küchenwecker, *der*

ping-pong (*Amer.:* **Ping-Pong ®**) /ˈpɪŋpɒŋ/ *n.* Tischtennis, *das;* Pingpong, *das* (ugs. veralt.)

ping-pong: ~-pong ball *n.* Tischtennisball, *der;* Pingpongball, *der* (ugs. veralt.); **~-pong table** *n.* Tischtennisplatte, *die*

pin: ~head *n.* **1** Stecknadelkopf, *der; attrib.* (fig.) winzig; stecknadelkopfgroß; **2** (coll.: fool) Dummkopf, *der;* Strohkopf, *der* (ugs.); **~-headed** *adj.* blöd (ugs.); dämlich (ugs.); **~-ˈhigh** *adj.* (Golf) auf Flaggenstockhöhe *nachgestellt;* **~hole** *n.* [nadelfeines] Loch; **~hole camera** *n.* (Photog.) Lochkamera, *die;* Camera obscura, *die*

pinion¹ /ˈpɪnjən/ *n.* (cogwheel) Ritzel, *das* (Technik); kleines Zahnrad

pinion²

A *v.t.* **~ sb., ~ sb.'s arms** jmdm. die Arme [an den Körper] fesseln *od.* binden; **~ sb. to sth.** jmdn. an etw. (*Dat.*) festbinden

B *n.* **1** (Ornith.) (terminal segment of wing) Hand[schwinge], *die;* (flight feather) Schwungfeder, *die* **2** (poet.: wing) Schwinge, *die* (geh.); Fittich, *der* (dichter.)

pink¹ /pɪŋk/

A *n.* **1** Rosa, *das* **2** **in the ~ of condition** in hervorragendem Zustand; **be in the ~** (coll.) kerngesund sein **3** (Bot.) [Garten]nelke, *die* **4** ▸**hunting pink**

B *adj.* **1** rosa ‹*Kleid, Wand*›; rosig, rosarot ‹*Himmel, Gesicht, Haut, Wangen*› **2** (Polit. coll.) rosa[rot]; rot angehaucht. *See also* **elephant**; **gin¹**; **rose-pink**; **salmon pink**; **tickle A 2**

pink² *v.i.* (Motor Veh.) klingeln

pink³ *v.t.* **1** (pierce slightly) piksen **2** (Sewing) auszacken

pinkie /ˈpɪŋkɪ/ *n.* (Amer., Scot.) kleiner Finger

pinking /ˈpɪŋkɪŋ/: **~ scissors, ~ shears** *ns. pl.* **[pair of] ~ scissors** *or* **shears** Zackenschere, *die*

pinko /ˈpɪŋkəʊ/ *n., pl.* **~s** (Polit. coll.) Rosarote, *der/die*

ˈpin money *n.* (for private expenditure) Taschengeld, *das;* (for dress expenses) Nadelgeld, *das* (veralt.); (coll.: small sum) Taschen- *od.* Trinkgeld, *das* (ugs.)

pinnace /ˈpɪnəs/ *n.* (Naut.) Pinasse, *die;* Beiboot, *das*

pinnacle /ˈpɪnəkl/ *n.* **1** (Archit.) Fiale, *die* **2** (natural peak) Gipfel, *der* **3** (fig.: climax) Höhepunkt, *der;* Gipfel, *der;* **at the ~ of his fame** auf dem Gipfel *od.* Höhepunkt seines Ruhmes

pinnate /ˈpɪnət/ *adj.* (Bot.) gefiedert

pinny /ˈpɪnɪ/ *n.* (child lang./coll.) Schürze, *die*

pin: ~point **A** *v.t.* (locate, define) genau bestimmen; (determine) genau festlegen; **B** *n.* [Steck]nadelspitze, *die;* **~points of light** winzige Lichter; **C** *adj.* **~point accuracy** höchste Genauigkeit; **~prick** *n.* Nadelstich, *der;* (fig.) [harmlose] Stichelei; **~stripe** *n.* Nadelstreifen, *der;* (suit) Nadelstreifenanzug, *der; attrib.* Nadelstreifen‹*anzug, -kostüm*›

pint /paɪnt/ *n.* **1** ▸**i p. 1690** (one-eighth of a gallon) Pint, *das;* ≈ halber Liter **2** (Brit.: quantity of liquid) Pint, *das;* **a ~ of milk/beer** ≈ ein halber Liter Milch/Bier; **have a ~:** ≈ ein großes Bier trinken; **go to the pub for a couple of ~s** auf ein paar Bier[chen] in die Kneipe gehen; **he likes his ~:** er trinkt gern ein Bier[chen]

pinta /ˈpaɪntə/ *n.* (Brit. coll.) ≈ halber Liter [Milch/Bier *usw.*]; **drink one's daily ~:** täglich seine Milch/sein Bier *usw.* trinken

pin: ~-table *n.* Flipper[automat], *der;* **~tail** *n.* (Ornith.) Spießente, *die*

pint ˈmug *n.* ≈ Halbliterglas, *das od.* -humpen, *der*

pinto /ˈpɪntəʊ/ *adj., n., pl.* **~s** (Amer.) ▸**piebald**

pint: ~ pot *n.* ≈ Halbliterhumpen, *der; see also* **quart 1**; **~-size[d]** *adj.* (fig. coll.) winzig; mick[e]rig (ugs.) ‹*Person*›

pin: ~-tuck *n.* (Sewing) Biese, *die;* **~-up** **A** *n.* **1** (picture) (of beautiful girl) Pin-up[-Foto], *das;* (of famous person) Prominentenfoto, *das;* (esp. of sports, film or pop star) Starfoto, *das;* **2** (beautiful girl) Schönheit, *die;* (in photograph) Pin-up-Girl, *das;* **B** *adj.* Pin-up-‹*Foto, Girl*›; **~-up-girl/~-up-man** Fotomodell, *das;* **~wheel** *n.* **1** (firework) Feuerrad, *das;* **2** (Amer.: toy) Windrädchen, *das*

pioneer /paɪəˈnɪə(r)/

A *n.* Pionier, *der;* (fig. also) Wegbereiter, *der/*Wegbereiterin, *die*

B *v.i.* Pionierarbeit leisten; bahnbrechend sein; **~ing settlers/studies/work** Pioniere *od.* erste Siedler/bahnbrechende Untersuchungen/Pionierarbeit, *die*

C *v.t.* **1** (originate) Pionierarbeit leisten für ‹*Entwicklung, Technologie, Nutzung*› **2** (open up as ~) erkunden

pious /ˈpaɪəs/ *adj.* **1** (devout) fromm; **a ~ hope** (lit. or fig.) ein frommer Wunsch **2** (hypocritically virtuous) heuchlerisch; scheinheilig **3** (dutiful) ehrfurchtsvoll; heilig ‹*Pflicht*›. *See also* **fraud 2**

piously /ˈpaɪəslɪ/ *adv.* **1** (devoutly) **kneel ~:** in frommer Andacht knien **2** (marked by sham) scheinheilig **3** (dutifully) ehrfurchtsvoll

pip¹ /pɪp/

A *n.* (seed) Kern, *der*

B *v.t.*, **-pp-** entkernen

pip² *n.* **1** (on cards, dominoes, etc.) Auge, *das;* Punkt, *der* **2** (Brit. Mil.) Stern, *der* **3** (on radar screen) Echosignal, *das;* (spot of light also) Leuchtpunkt, *der;* Echosignal, *das*

pip³ *n.* (Brit.: sound) [kurzer] Piepston; (time signal also) Zeitzeichen, *das;* **when the ~s go** (during telephone call) wenn die Piepstöne anzeigen, dass eine neue Münze eingeworfen werden muss

pip⁴ *n.* (coll.) **give sb. the ~:** jmdm. auf den Wecker gehen (ugs.); **sb. has [got] the ~:** jmd. ist sauer (ugs.)

pip⁵ *v.t.*, **-pp-** (Brit.) (defeat) knapp besiegen *od.* schlagen; **~ sb. at the post** (coll.) jmdn. im Ziel abfangen; (fig.) jmdn. im letzten Moment ausbooten (ugs.)

pipe /paɪp/

A *n.* **1** (tube) Rohr, *das* **2** (Mus.) Pfeife, *die;* (flute) Flöte, *die;* (in organ) [Orgel]pfeife, *die* **3** *in pl.* (bagpipes) Dudelsack, *der* **4** **[tobacco] ~:** [Tabaks]pfeife, *die;* **light/smoke a ~:** eine Pfeife anzünden/rauchen; **put that in your ~ and smoke it** (fig. coll.) lass dir das gesagt sein; schreib dir das hinter die Ohren (ugs.); *see also* **clay pipe**; **peace pipe** **5** (cask) Pipe, *das od. die;* 105-Gallonen-Fass, *das* **6** (Geol.) Schlot, *der*

B *v.t.* **1** (convey by ~) [durch ein Rohr/durch Rohre] leiten; **be ~d** ‹*Öl, Wasser:*› [durch eine Rohrleitung] fließen; ‹*Gas:*› [durch eine Rohrleitung] strömen **2** (transmit by wire etc.) leiten ‹*Strom*›; übertragen ‹*Sendung*›; [ab]spielen ‹[*Tonband-, Schallplatten*]*musik*›; **~d music** Hintergrundmusik, *die;* Musikberieselung, *die* **3** (Mus.) [auf der Flöte/dem Dudelsack] spielen ‹*Melodie, Lied*›; mit Pfeifenklang geleiten *od.* führen ‹*Soldaten*› **4** (utter shrilly) ‹*Vogel:*› piepsen, pfeifen; ‹*Kind:*› piepsen **5** (Sewing) paspel[iere]n **6** (Cookery) spritzen **7** (Naut.) **~ sb. aboard** jmdn. mit Pfeifenklängen an Bord empfangen

C *v.i.* **1** (whistle) pfeifen **2** ‹*Stimme:*› hell klingen, schrillen; ‹*Person:*› piepsen, mit heller *od.* schriller Stimme sprechen; ‹*Vogel:*› pfeifen, piepsen; ‹*kleiner, junger Vogel:*› piepsen **3** (Mus.) [Flöte/Pfeife] spielen

Phrasal verbs

• **~ ˈdown** *v.i.* (coll.: be less noisy) ruhig sein; **~ down, will you!** sei/seid doch mal ruhig!

• **~ ˈup** *v.i.* (begin to speak) etwas sagen; **~ up with the answer** die Antwort geben

pipe: ~ band *n.* Pfeifer; **~clay** *n.* Pfeifenton, *der;* **~-cleaner** *n.* Pfeifenreiniger, *der;* **~ dream** *n.* Wunschtraum, *der;* Hirngespinst, *das* (abwertend); **~line** *n.* Pipeline, *die;* **in the ~line** (fig.) in Vorbereitung; **pay rises are in the ~line** (fig.) Gehaltserhöhungen stehen bevor; **have some ideas in the ~line** (fig.) ein paar Ideen auf Lager haben (ugs.); **~ organ** *n.* (Mus.) [Pfeifen]orgel, *die*

piper /ˈpaɪpə(r)/ *n.* **1** Pfeifer, *der/*Pfeiferin, *die;* (flautist) Flötenspieler, *der/*-spielerin, *die;* **pay the ~** (fig.) die Kosten tragen; **he who pays the ~ calls the tune** (prov.) wer die Musik bezahlt, sagt *od.* bestimmt, was gespielt wird (Spr.) **2** (bagpiper) Dudelsackspieler, *der/*-spielerin, *die*

pipe: ~ rack *n.* Pfeifenständer, *der;* **~ smoker** *n.* Pfeifenraucher, *der/*-raucherin, *die;* **~ tobacco** *n.* Pfeifentabak, *der*

pipette /pɪˈpet/ *n.* (Chem.) Pipette, *die*

piping /ˈpaɪpɪŋ/
A *n.* **1** (system of pipes) Rohrleitungssystem, *das* **2** (quantity of pipes) Rohrmaterial, *das* **3** (Sewing) Paspel, *die;* (on furniture) Kordel, *die* **4** (Cookery) Spritzgussverzierung, *die* **5** (Mus.) Pfeifen, *das;* (of flute) Flöten, *das* **6** (shrill sound) Pfeifen, *das*
B *adj.* piepsend

piping ˈhot *adj.* kochend heiß

pipistrelle /pɪpɪˈstrel/ *n.* (Zool.) Zwergfledermaus, *die*

pipit /ˈpɪpɪt/ *n.* (Ornith.) Pieper, *der*

pippin /ˈpɪpɪn/ *n.* Tafelapfel, *der*

ˈpipsqueak *n.* (coll. derog.) Würstchen, *das* (ugs.)

piquancy /ˈpiːkənsɪ/ *n.* **1** (sharpness) Würze, *die;* pikanter Geschmack **2** (fig.) Pikanterie, *die* (geh.)

piquant /ˈpiːkənt, ˈpiːkɑːnt/ *adj.*, **piquantly** /ˈpiːkəntlɪ, ˈpiːkɑːntlɪ/ *adv.* (lit. or fig.) pikant

pique /piːk/
A *v.t.* **1** (irritate) verärgern; **be ~d at sb./sth.** über jmdn./etw. verärgert sein **2** (wound the pride of) kränken; **be ~d at sth.** wegen etw. gekränkt sein
B *n.* **in a [fit of] ~:** verstimmt; eingeschnappt (ugs.)

piqué /ˈpiːkeɪ/ *n.* (Textiles) Pikee, *der*

piracy /ˈpaɪrəsɪ/ *n.* Seeräuberei, *die;* Piraterie, *die;* (fig.) Piraterie, *die;* **the ~ of books/records/video tapes** der illegale Nachdruck von Büchern/die illegale Pressung von Schallplatten/die illegale Vervielfältigung von Videobändern

piranha /pɪˈrɑːnə, pɪˈrɑːnjə/ *n.* (Zool.) Piranha, *der*

pirate /ˈpaɪrət/
A *n.* **1** Pirat, *der;* Seeräuber, *der;* (fig.) Schwindler, *der;* (of book etc.) Raubdrucker, *der*/-druckerin, *die;* (of record) Raubpresser, *der*/Raubpresserin, *die;* Hersteller/Herstellerin von Raubpressungen; (of video) Hersteller/Herstellerin von unerlaubten Kopien **2** (Radio) [Rundfunk]pirat, *der; attrib.* **~ radio station** Piratensender, *der;* **~ broadcast[ing]** Piratensendung, *die* **3** (ship) Piratenschiff, *das;* Seeräuberschiff, *das*
B *v.t.* ausplündern ‹*Schiff*›; rauben ‹*Waren usw.*›; (fig.) illegal nachdrucken ‹*Buch*›; illegal pressen ‹*Schallplatte*›; illegal vervielfältigen ‹*Videoband*›; **~d edition** Raubdruck, *der*

piratical /paɪˈrætɪkl/ *adj.* Piraten-; Seeräuber-; seeräuberisch ‹*Praktiken, Umtriebe*›

pirouette /pɪrʊˈet/
A *n.* Pirouette, *die*
B *v.i.* pirouettieren; Pirouetten/eine Pirouette ausführen *od.* drehen

Piscean /ˈpaɪsɪən/ (Astrol.) *n.* Fisch, *der;* Fischemann, *der*/-frau, *die*

Pisces /ˈpaɪsiːz, ˈpaɪskiːz/ *n., pl. same* (Astrol., Astron.) Fische *Pl.;* Pisces *Pl.; see also* **Aries**

piss /pɪs/ (coarse)
A *n.* **1** (urine) Pisse, *die* (derb) **2** (act) Pissen, *das* (derb); **need a ~:** pissen müssen (derb); **have a/go for a ~:** pissen/pissen gehen (derb) **3** **take the ~ out of sb.** jmdn. verarschen (salopp); **stop taking the ~!** lass die Verarscherei! (salopp)
B *v.i.* **1** (urinate) pissen (derb) **2** ▸**piss down**
C *v.t.* pissen (derb); **~ oneself** in die Hose pissen (derb)

Phrasal verbs
- **~ aˈbout, ~ aˈround** (sl.)
A *v.i.* **1** (spend time lazily) rumhängen (ugs.) **2** (behave in foolish way) rummachen (ugs.) **3** (work in disorganized way) sich (*Dat.*) einen abbrechen (salopp); **~ around with sth.** mit etw. rummachen (ugs.)
B *v.t.* **~ sb. about** *or* **around** jmdn. wie [den letzten] Dreck behandeln (salopp)
- **~ down** *v.i.* (sl.) **~ down [with rain]** schiffen (salopp)
- **~ ˈoff** (Brit. sl.)
A *v.i.* sich verpissen (salopp)
B *v.t.* ankotzen (derb); *see also* **pissed off**

ˈpiss artist *n.* (sl.) Suffkopp, *der* (salopp)

pissed /pɪst/ *adj.* (sl.) **1** (drunk) voll (salopp); besoffen (derb); **~ as a lord** *or* **newt** voll wie eine Strandhaubitze (ugs.); **~ out of one's mind** *or* **head** *or* **brain** sturzbesoffen (derb); hackevoll (salopp) **2** (Amer.: angry) [stock]sauer (**with** auf + *Akk.*) (salopp)

pissed ˈoff *adj.* (sl.) stocksauer (**with** auf + *Akk.*) (salopp); **get ~ [with sb./sth.]** langsam die Schnauze voll haben [von jmdm./etw.] (salopp)

piss: ~head *n.* (sl.) Saufkopp, *der* (ugs.); **~-poor** *adj.* (sl.) saumäßig (salopp); saudumm, -blöde (salopp abwertend) ‹*Ausrede*›; **the recording is ~-poor** die Aufnahme ist unter aller Sau (derb abwertend); **~-take** *n.* (sl.) Verarschung, *die* (salopp); Verhohnepipelung, *die* (ugs.); **~-up** *n.* (sl.) Sauferei, *die* (salopp)

pistachio /pɪˈstɑːʃɪəʊ/ *n., pl.* **~s** **1** Pistazie, *die* **2** (colour) Pistaziengrün, *das*

piste /piːst/ *n.* Piste, *die*

pistil /ˈpɪstɪl/ *n.* (Bot.) Stempel, *der*

pistol /ˈpɪstl/ *n.* (small firearm) Pistole, *die;* **hold a ~ to sb.'s head** jmdm. die Pistole an die Schläfe *od.* den Kopf setzen; (fig.) jmdm. die Pistole auf die Brust setzen

pistol: ~ grip *n.* Pistolengriff, *der;* **~ shot** *n.* Pistolenschuss, *der;* **~-whip** *v.t.* mit der Pistole schlagen

piston /ˈpɪstən/ *n.* Kolben, *der*

piston: ~ engine *n.* Kolbenmotor, *der;* **~ ring** *n.* Kolbenring, *der;* **~ rod** *n.* Kolbenstange, *die;* Pleuelstange, *die*

pit¹ /pɪt/
A *n.* **1** (hole, mine) Grube, *die;* (natural) Vertiefung, *die;* (as trap) Fallgrube, *die;* (for cockfighting) Kampfplatz, *der;* **[work] down the ~:** unter Tage [arbeiten] (Bergmannsspr.); **dig a ~ for sb.** (fig.) jmdm. eine Falle stellen; **this really is the ~s** (coll.) das ist wirklich das Letzte (ugs.) **2** **~ of the stomach** Magengrube, *die* **3** (scar) [vertiefte] Narbe; (after smallpox) Pockennarbe, *die* **4** (Brit. Theatre) (for audience) Parkett, *das;* (for orchestra) Orchestergraben, *der* **5** (in garage) Grube, *die;* (Motor racing) Box, *die* **6** (Amer. St. Exch.) Maklerstand, *der*
B *v.t.*, **-tt-** **1** (set to fight) kämpfen lassen **2** (fig.: match) **~ sth. against sth.** etw. gegen etw. einsetzen; **~ one's wits/skill** *etc.* **against sth.** seinen Verstand/sein Können *usw.* an etw. (*Dat.*) messen **3** **be ~ted** (have ~s) voller Vertiefungen sein; **the ~ted surface of the moon** die mit Kratern bedeckte Mondoberfläche

pit² (Amer.)
A *n.* (stone in fruit) Kern, *der*
B *v.t.*, **-tt-** (remove ~s from) entkernen

pit-a-pat /ˈpɪtəpæt/
A *adv.* **go ~** ‹*Herz:*› schneller schlagen; ‹*Regen:*› [sanft] klopfen
B *n.* (of heart) Pochen, *das;* (of hoofs, feet) Getrappel, *das;* (of rain etc.) Klopfen, *das*

ˈpit babe *n.* (coll.) Boxenluder, *das*

ˈpit bull terrier *n.* Pitbullterrier, *der*

pitch¹ /pɪtʃ/
A *n.* **1** (Brit.: usual place) [Stand]platz, *der;* (stand) Stand, *der;* (Sport: playing area) Feld, *das;* Platz, *der;* **artificial ~:** Spielfeld mit künstlichem Rasen; *see also* **queer C** **2** (Mus.) Tonhöhe, *die;* (of voice) Stimmlage, *die;* (of instrument) Tonlage, *die;* **have perfect ~:** absolutes Gehör haben; *see also* **concert pitch** **3** (slope) Neigung, *die;* **the ~ of the roof** die Dachneigung **4** (fig.: degree, intensity) **the children were at a high ~ of excitement** die Kinder waren wahnsinnig aufgedreht (ugs.); **reach such a ~ that ...:** sich so zuspitzen, dass...; *see also* **fever pitch** **5** ▸**pitching** **6** (Baseball: delivery) Pitch, *der;* Wurf, *der;* (*Golf*) ▸**pitch shot** **7** (Mech.: distance) (between cogwheel teeth or screw ridges) Teilung, *die;* (in one turn of propeller) Steigung, *die* **8** (Mountaineering) Seillänge, *die* **9** (sales talk) Verkaufsargumentation, *die;* **make one's ~** (lit. or fig.) seine Vorstellung geben; **get one's ~ in early** (fig.) seine Sache frühzeitig vorbringen
B *v.t.* **1** (erect) aufschlagen; **~ camp** ein/das Lager aufschlagen **2** (throw) werfen; **the horse ~ed its rider over its head** das Pferd warf den Reiter vornüber; **the car overturned and the driver was ~ed out** der Wagen überschlug sich, und der Fahrer wurde herausgeschleudert; **~ sb. out of sth.** jmdn. aus etw. hinauswerfen **3** (Mus.) anstimmen ‹*Melodie*›; stimmen ‹*Instrument*›; **~ one's voice too high/at the right level** eine zu hohe/die richtige Stimmlage wählen **4** (fig.) **~ a programme at a particular level** ein Programm auf ein bestimmtes Niveau abstimmen; **our expectations were ~ed too high** unsere Erwartungen waren zu hoch gesteckt **5** **~ed battle** offene [Feld]schlacht; **the debate became a ~ed battle** (fig.) aus der Debatte wurde eine Redeschlacht
C *v.i.* (fall) [kopfüber] stürzen; ‹*Schiff, Fahrzeug, Flugzeug:*› mit einem Ruck nach vorn kippen; (Cricket) ‹*Ball:*› aufschlagen; (repeatedly) ‹*Schiff:*› stampfen; ‹*Fahrzeug, Flugzeug:*› ruckartig schwingen; **~ forward** vornüberstürzen; ‹*Fahrzeug:*› ruckartig anfahren

Phrasal verbs
- **~ ˈin** *v.i.* (coll.) loslegen (ugs.); (begin) sich daranmachen (ugs.); **~ in [and** *or* **to help]** zupacken (ugs.) [und helfen]; mit anpacken
- **~ into** *v.t.* (coll.) herfallen über (+ *Akk.*); sich hermachen über (+ *Akk.*) (ugs.) ‹*Essen*›

pitch² *n.* (substance) Pech, *das;* **as black as ~:** pechschwarz

pitch: ~-ˈblack *adj.* pechschwarz; stockdunkel (ugs.), pechfinster ‹*Nacht, Raum*›; **~blende** /ˈpɪtʃblend/ *n.* (Min.) Pechblende, *die;* **~-ˈdark** *adj.* stockdunkel (ugs.); pechfinster; **~-ˈdarkness** *n.* tiefste Finsternis

pitched ˈroof *n.* schräges Dach

pitcher¹ /ˈpɪtʃə(r)/ *n.* **1** (vessel) [Henkel]krug, *der;* (in bedroom etc.) Wasserkanne, *die* **2** (Bot.) Kanne, *die*

pitcher² *n.* (Baseball) Werfer, *der;* Pitcher, *der*

ˈpitcher plant *n.* (Bot.) Kannenpflanze, *die*

ˈpitchfork
A *n.* (for hay) Heugabel, *die;* (for manure) Mistgabel, *die*
B *v.t.* gabeln; **~ sb. into sth.** (fig.) jmdn. in etw. ‹*Akk.*› katapultieren

pitching /ˈpɪtʃɪŋ/ *n.* (of ship) Stampfen, *das;* (of vehicle, aircraft) ruckartiges Schwingen

pitch: ~ pine *n.* Pechkiefer, *die;* (wood) Pitchpine, *das;* Pechkiefernholz, *das;* **~-pipe** *n.* (Mus.) Stimmpfeife, *die;* **~ shot** *n.* (Golf) kurzer Annäherungsschlag; Pitchshot, *der*

piteous /ˈpɪtɪəs/ *adj.* erbärmlich; (causing pity) Mitleid erregend; kläglich ‹*Schrei*›

piteously /ˈpɪtɪəslɪ/ *adv.* erbärmlich

ˈpitfall *n.* **1** Fallstrick, *der;* (risk) Gefahr, *die;* **avoid all ~s** alle Klippen umgehen **2** (animal trap) Fallgrube, *die*

pith /pɪθ/ *n.* **1** (in plant) Mark, *das;* (of orange etc.) weiße Haut; Albedo, *die* (Bot.) **2** (fig.: essential part) Kern, *der* **3** (fig.) (strength) Kraft, *die;* (force of words etc.) Überzeugungskraft, *die;* **men of ~:** starke Männer; **of ~ and moment** gewichtig

ˈpithead *n.* ≈ Zechengelände, *das;* **at the ~:** am Schachteingang; **~ baths** Waschkauen (Bergmannsspr.); **~ ballot** Abstimmung der Bergleute auf der Zeche

ˈpith helmet *n.* Tropenhelm, *der*

pithily /ˈpɪθɪlɪ/ *adv.* prägnant

pithy /ˈpɪθɪ/ *adj.* **1** markhaltig; reich an Mark *nicht attr.;* ‹*Orange usw.*› mit dicker weißer Haut **2** (fig.) (full of meaning) prägnant; (vigorous) markig

pitiable /ˈpɪtɪəbl/ ▸**pitiful**

pitiably /ˈpɪtɪəblɪ/ *adv.* jämmerlich

pitiful /ˈpɪtɪfl/ *adj.* **1** Mitleid erregend; (with strong emotional appeal) erbärmlich; jämmerlich; kläglich ‹*Versuch*› **2** (contemptible) jämmerlich (abwertend)

pitifully /ˈpɪtɪfəlɪ/ *adv.* erbärmlich; jämmerlich

pitiless /ˈpɪtɪlɪs/ *adj.*, **pitilessly** /ˈpɪtɪlɪslɪ/ *adv.* unbarmherzig (auch fig.); erbarmungslos

pitman /ˈpɪtmən/ *n.* **1** *pl.* **pitmen** /ˈpɪtmən/ (miner) Bergmann, *der* **2** *pl.* **~s** (Amer.: connecting rod) Pleuelstange, *die*

piton /ˈpiːtɒn/ *n.* (for rock) Felshaken, *der;* (for ice) Eishaken, *der*

P

pit: ~ pony *n.* (Brit.) Grubenpferd, *das;* **~ prop** *n.* [Gruben]stempel, *der;* (of wood also) Grubenholz, *das;* **~ saw** *n.* Schrot- *od.* Zugsäge, *die;* **~ stop** *n.* (Motor racing) Boxenstopp, *der*

pitta /ˈpɪtə/ *n.* **~ [bread]** Pittabrot, *das;* Fladenbrot, *das*

pittance /ˈpɪtəns/ *n.* 1 Hungerlohn, *der* (abwertend); (small allowance) [magere] Beihilfe 2 (small amount of money) **a ~:** ein paar Cents

pitter-patter /pɪtəˈpætə(r)/ ▸**pit-a-pat**

pituitary /pɪˈtjuːɪtərɪ/ *n.* **~ [body** *or* **gland]** (Anat., Zool.) Hirnanhangdrüse, *die;* Hypophyse, *die* (fachspr.)

ˈ**pit viper** *n.* Grubenotter, *die*

pity /ˈpɪtɪ/

A *n.* 1 (sorrow) Mitleid, *das;* Mitgefühl, *das;* **feel ~ for sb.** Mitgefühl für jmdn. *od.* mit jmdm. empfinden; **have you no ~?** hast du [denn] kein Mitleid?; **be moved to ~:** Mitleid empfinden; **have/take ~ on sb./an animal** Erbarmen mit jmdm./einem Tier haben; **for ~'s sake!** um Gottes *od.* Himmels willen! 2 (cause for regret) **[what a] ~!** [wie] schade!; **it's a ~ about sb./sth.** es ist ein Jammer mit jmdm./etw. (ugs.); **it's a [great] ~/a thousand pities [that] ...:** es ist [sehr *od.* zu] schade/jammerschade (ugs.) *od.* ein Jammer (ugs.), dass ...; **the ~ of it is [that] ...:** das Traurige daran ist, dass ...; **more's the ~** leider!

B *v.t.* bedauern; bemitleiden; **I ~ you** (also contemptuously) du tust mir Leid

pitying /ˈpɪtɪɪŋ/ *adj.*, **pityingly** /ˈpɪtɪɪŋlɪ/ *adv.* mitleidig

pivot /ˈpɪvət/

A *n.* 1 [Dreh]zapfen, *der;* (of a hinge) Angelzapfen, *der* 2 (fig.) [Dreh- und] Angelpunkt, *der;* (crucial point) springender Punkt

B *v.t.* (provide with ~[s]) mit Zapfen/mit einem Zapfen versehen; (mount on ~[s]) drehbar lagern

C *v.i.* sich drehen; **the guns ~ easily** die Geschütze lassen sich leicht schwenken; **~ on sth.** (fig.) von etw. abhängen

pivotal /ˈpɪvətl/ *adj.* (fig.: crucial) zentral; **~ figure/position** Schlüsselfigur, *die*/Schlüsselstellung, *die*

pix /pɪks/ *n. pl.* (coll.) Bilder

pixel /ˈpɪksel/ *n.* (Computing etc.) Bildpunkt, *der;* Pixel, *das*

pixie /ˈpɪksɪ/ *n.* Kobold, *der*

pixie: ~ hat, ~ hood *ns.: spitz zulaufendes Käppchen*

pixilate /ˈpɪksɪleɪt/ *v.t.* pixeln

pixy ▸**pixie**

pizza /ˈpiːtsə/ *n.* Pizza, *die*

pizzazz /pɪˈzæz/ *n.* Klasse, *die;* (showiness) Glamour, *der*

pizzeria /piːtsəˈriːə/ *n.* Pizzeria, *die*

pizzicato /pɪtsɪˈkɑːtəʊ/ (Mus.)

A *adj.* **~ accompaniment** Pizzikatobegleitung; **a series of ~ notes** eine pizzicato gespielte Tonfolge

B *adv.* pizzicato

C *n., pl.* **~s** *or* **pizzicati** /pɪtsɪˈkɑːtiː/ Pizzicato, *das*

pl. *abbr.* 1 **= plate 1 g** 2 **= plural** Pl.

placard /ˈplækɑːd/

A *n.* Plakat, *das;* **a ~ announcing the date of the next meeting** ein Anschlag *od.* Aushang mit dem nächsten Sitzungstermin

B *v.t.* 1 (post up ~s on) mit Plakaten bekleben ‹*Wand usw.*›; **the town is ~ed with posters** überall in der Stadt kleben Plakate 2 (advertise) plakatieren

placate /pləˈkeɪt/ *v.t.* beschwichtigen, besänftigen ‹*Person*›

placatory /pləˈkeɪtərɪ/ *adj.* beschwichtigend; besänftigend; Versöhnungs‹*opfer, -gabe*›

place /pleɪs/

A *n.* 1 Ort, *der;* (spot) Stelle, *die;* Platz, *der;* **put it in a ~ where you can find it** tun Sie es an einen Platz, wo Sie es wieder finden; **I left it in a safe ~:** ich habe es an einem sicheren Ort gelassen; **it was still in the same ~:** es war noch an derselben Stelle *od.* am selben Platz; **the [exact] ~ where ...:** die [genaue] Stelle, wo *od.* an der ...; **this was the ˈlast ~ I expected to find you** hier hätte ich dich am allerwenigsten erwartet; **a ~ in the queue** ein Platz in der Schlange; **all over the ~:** überall; (coll.: in a mess) ganz durcheinander (ugs.); **I can't be in two ~s at once** ich kann nicht an zwei Orten gleichzeitig sein *od.* (ugs.) alles auf einmal machen; **from ~ to ~:** von Ort zu Ort; **in ~s** hier und da; (in parts) stellenweise; **the animal does still exist in ~s** das Tier kommt noch vereinzelt vor; **find a ~ in sth.** (be included) in etw. (*Akk.*) eingehen; *see also* **take A 4**

2 (fig.: rank, position) Stellung, *die;* **as a critic, his ~ is in the front rank** als Kritiker rangiert er ganz vorn; **keep/put sb. in his/her ~:** jmdn. immer wieder/jmdn. in seine/ihre Schranken weisen; jmdm. immer wieder/jmdm. einen Dämpfer aufsetzen (ugs.); **know one's ~:** wissen, was sich für einen gehört; **it's not my ~ to do that** es kommt mir nicht zu, das zu tun

3 (building or area for specific purpose) **a [good] ~ to park/to stop** ein [guter] Platz zum Parken/eine [gute] Stelle zum Halten; **do you know a good/cheap ~ to eat?** weißt du, wo man gut/billig essen kann?; **We couldn't get into the café. The ~ was full** Wir kamen gar nicht erst in das Café. Es war alles voll *od.* besetzt; **~ of residence** *or* **domicile** Wohnort, *der;* **~ of work** Arbeitsplatz, *der;* Arbeitsstätte, *die;* **~ of worship** Andachtsort, *der;* **~ of amusement** Vergnügungsstätte, *die; see also* **another B 3**

4 (country, town) Ort, *der;* **the best hotel in the ~:** das beste Hotel am Platz; **Paris/Italy is a great ~:** Paris ist eine tolle Stadt/Italien ist ein tolles Land (ugs.); **~ of birth** Geburtsort, *der;* **know the ~:** sich [hier/dort] auskennen; ˈ**go ~s** (coll.) herumkommen (ugs.); (fig.) es [im Leben] zu was bringen (ugs.)

5 (coll.: premises) Bude, *die* (ugs.); (hotel, restaurant, etc.) Laden, *der* (ugs.); **liven the ~ up** Leben in die Bude bringen (ugs.); **she is at his/John's ~:** sie ist bei ihm/John; **[shall we go to] your ~ or mine?** [gehen wir] zu dir oder zu mir?; **I called at your ~:** ich bin bei dir [zu Hause] vorbeigegangen; **a ~ in the country** ein Haus auf dem Lande

6 (seat etc.) [Sitz]platz, *der;* **change ~s [with sb.]** [mit jmdm.] die Plätze tauschen; (fig.) [mit jmdm.] tauschen; **lay a/another ~:** ein/noch ein Gedeck auflegen; **take one's ~ at table** am Tisch Platz nehmen; **is this anyone's ~?** ist dieser Platz noch frei?

7 (particular spot on surface) Stelle, *die*

8 (in book etc.) Stelle, *die;* **lose one's ~:** die Seite verschlagen *od.* verblättern; (on page) nicht mehr wissen, an welcher Stelle man ist; **keep one's ~:** die Stelle markieren, an der man ist/war; **find one's ~:** die Stelle wieder finden

9 (step, stage) **in the first ~:** zuerst; **why didn't you say so in the first ~?** warum hast du das nicht gleich gesagt?; **they should never have got married in the first ~:** sie hätten von vornherein nicht heiraten sollen; **I objected to it in the first ~:** ich war von Anfang an dagegen; **in the first/second/third** *etc.* **~:** erstens/zweitens/drittens *usw.*

10 (proper ~) Platz, *der;* **everything fell into ~** (fig.) alles wurde klar; **take your ~s for the next dance** stellen Sie sich zum nächsten Tanz auf; **he likes to have everything in [its] ~:** bei ihm muss alles an seinem Platz sein; **a woman's ~ is in the home** eine Frau gehört ins Haus; **this is no ~ for a child** das ist kein Ort für ein Kind; **give ~ to sb./sth.** jmdm./einer Sache Platz machen; **winter gave ~ to spring** der Winter räumte dem Frühling das Feld; **the clamp is properly in ~:** die Klammer sitzt richtig; **her hat was held in ~ by a hatpin** ihr Hut wurde von einer Hutnadel festgehalten; **into ~:** fest‹*nageln, -schrauben, -kleben*›; **out of ~:** nicht am richtigen Platz; (several things) in Unordnung; (fig.) fehl am Platz; **your suggestion is rather out of ~** (fig.) dein Vorschlag ist nicht ganz angebracht *od.* passend; **with not a hair out of ~:** makellos frisiert; **in ~ of** anstelle *od.* an Stelle (+ *Gen.*); **I'll go in ~ of you/in your ~:** ich werde an deiner Stelle gehen; **take the ~ of sb./sth.** jmds. Platz *od.* den Platz von jmdm./den Platz von etw. einnehmen; *see also* **sun A**

11 (position in competition) Platz, *der;* **drop/go up two ~s in the charts** [um] zwei Plätze in der Hitparade fallen/steigen; **first ~ went to ...:** der erste Platz ging an ... (+ *Akk.*); **take first/second** *etc.* **~:** den ersten/zweiten *usw.* Platz belegen; (fig.: have priority) an erster/zweiter *usw.* Stelle kommen; **in second ~:** auf dem zweiten Platz; **beat sb. into second ~:** jmdn. auf den zweiten Platz verweisen; **get a ~** (Racing) eine Platzierung erreichen; (Amer.: second ~) den zweiten Platz belegen

12 (Math.: position of figure in series) Stelle, *die; see also* **decimal place**

13 (job, position, etc.) Stelle, *die;* (as pupil; in team, crew) Platz, *der;* **university ~:** Studienplatz, *der*

14 (personal situation) **what would you do in my ~?** was würden Sie an meiner Stelle tun?; **put yourself in my ~:** versetzen Sie sich in meine Lage

B *v.t.* 1 (put) (vertically) stellen; (horizontally) legen; **he ~d himself where ...:** er stellte sich dahin, wo ...; **~ a foot on a chair** einen Fuß auf einen Stuhl setzen; **~ the ball on the penalty spot** den Ball auf den Elfmeterpunkt legen; **~ in position** richtig hinstellen/hinlegen; **~ an announcement/advertisement in a paper** eine Anzeige/ein Inserat in eine Zeitung setzen; **~ a bet/~ money on a horse** auf ein Pferd wetten/Geld auf ein Pferd setzen

2 (fig.) **~ one's trust in sb./sth.** sein Vertrauen auf *od.* in jmdn./etw. setzen; **he ~s happiness above all other things** Glück steht für ihn an erster Stelle; *see also* **emphasis 1, 3**

3 *in p.p.* (situated) gelegen; **a badly ~d window** ein Fenster an einer ungünstigen Stelle; **be well ~d to watch sth.** einen guten Platz *od.* Standort haben, um bei etw. zuzusehen; **he was not well ~d to return the shot** (Tennis) er stand ungünstig zum Ball; **we are well ~d for buses/shops** *etc.* wir haben es nicht weit zur Bushaltestelle/zum Einkaufen *usw.*; **how are you ~d for time/money?** (coll.) wie stehts mit deiner Zeit/deinem Geld?; **how are you ~d [for lending me a fiver]?** (coll.) wie siehts bei dir aus[, kannst du mir einen Fünfer leihen]? (ugs.); **be well ~d financially** sich [finanziell] gut stehen (ugs.)

4 (find situation or home for) unterbringen (**with** bei); **~ sb. in command of a company** jmdm. das Kommando über eine Kompanie erteilen; **~ sb. under sb.'s care** jmdn. in jmds. Obhut geben

5 (invest) anlegen ‹*Geld*›; (Commerc.) absetzen ‹*Waren*›; **~ an order with a firm** einer Firma (*Dat.*) einen Auftrag erteilen

6 (class, identify) einordnen; einstufen; **~ sb. among the greatest statesmen** jmdn. zu den größten Staatsmännern zählen; **~ an artefact in the Neolithic period** ein Artefakt der Jungsteinzeit zuordnen; **I've seen him before but I can't ~ him** ich habe ihn schon einmal gesehen, aber ich weiß nicht, wo ich ihn einordnen *od.* (ugs.) hinstecken soll

7 (Sports etc.) **be ~d** sich platzieren; (Brit.: in first three) unter den ersten drei sein; (Amer.: second) Zweiter sein; **be ~d second in the race/charts** im Rennen/in der Hitliste den zweiten Platz belegen

ˈ**place bet** *n.* Platzwette, *die*

placebo /pləˈsiːbəʊ/ *n., pl.* **~s** (Med.) Placebo, *das; attrib.* **~ effect** Placeboeffekt, *der*

place: ~ card *n.* Tischkarte, *die;* **~holder** *n.* (Computing, Ling.) Platzhalter, *der;* **~ kick** *n.* (Footb.) Platztritt, *der;* **~ mat** *n.* Set, *der od. das*

placement /ˈpleɪsmənt/ *n.* Platzierung, *die*

ˈ**place name** *n.* Ortsname, *der*

placenta /pləˈsentə/ *n., pl.* **~e** /pləˈsentiː/ *or* **~s** (Anat., Zool.) Plazenta, *die* (fachspr.); Mutterkuchen, *der*

placer /ˈpleɪsə(r), ˈplæsə(r)/ *n.* (Geol.) Seife, *die;* (place) [Seifen]lagerstätte, *die*

ˈ**place setting** *n.* Gedeck, *das*

P

placid /ˈplæsɪd/ *adj.* ruhig, gelassen ‹*Person*›; ruhig ‹*Wasser, Wesensart*›; (peaceable) friedlich, friedfertig ‹*Person*›

placidity /pləˈsɪdɪtɪ/ *n., no pl.* ▸**placid**: Ruhe, *die;* Gelassenheit, *die;* Friedfertigkeit, *die*

placidly /ˈplæsɪdlɪ/ *adv.* ▸**placid**: ruhig; gelassen; friedlich

placket /ˈplækɪt/ *n.* (Dressm.) Schlitz, *der*

plagiarism /ˈpleɪdʒərɪzm/ *n.* Plagiat, *das*

plagiarist /ˈpleɪdʒərɪst/ *n.* Plagiator, *der*

plagiarize (**plagiarise**) /ˈpleɪdʒəraɪz/ *v.t.* plagiieren

plague /pleɪg/

A *n.* **1** (esp. Hist.: epidemic) Seuche, *die;* **the ~** (bubonic) die Pest; **spread like the ~:** sich wie eine Seuche ausbreiten; **avoid/hate sb./sth. like the ~:** jmdn./etw. wie die Pest meiden/hassen; **a ~ on it/you!** (arch.) hols/hol dich die Pest!; **a ~ on both your houses!** (fig. arch.) hol euch beide die Pest! **2** (esp. Bibl.: punishment; coll.: nuisance) Plage, *die* **3** (infestation) **~ of rats/insects** Ratten-/Insektenplage, *die*

B *v.t.* **1** (afflict) plagen; quälen; **~d with** *or* **by sth.** von etw. geplagt; **a disease that ~s mankind** eine Krankheit, die die Menschheit heimsucht **2** (bother) **~ sb. [with sth.]** jmdm. [mit etw.] auf die Nerven gehen (ugs.); **be ~d with sth.** von etw. geplagt werden; **be ~d by bad weather** unter schlechtem Wetter zu leiden haben

plaice /pleɪs/ *n., pl. same* **1** Scholle, *die* **2** (Amer.: summer flounder) Sommerflunder, *die*

plaid /plæd/

A *n.* Plaid, *das od. der*

B *adj.* [bunt] kariert; **~ blanket** Plaid, *das od. der*

> **Plaid Cymru**
>
> Die nationalistische politische Partei in Wales. Ihr wesentliches Ziel ist die völlige Unabhängigkeit vom Vereinigten Königreich. Im Rahmen dieses Ziels sind Anstrengungen unternommen worden, **Welsh** (das Walisische) weiter zu beleben und die walisische Kultur zu pflegen.

plain /pleɪn/

A *adj.* **1** (clear) klar; (obvious) offensichtlich; **He didn't like us. That was ~ enough** Er mochte uns nicht. Das war ganz klar *od.* offenkundig; **make sth. ~ [to sb.]** [jmdm.] etw. klarmachen; **make it ~ that ...:** klarstellen, dass ...; **make oneself/one's meaning ~:** sich verständlich machen; sich klar ausdrücken; **make one's views/intentions ~:** seine Ansichten/Absichten klar zum Ausdruck bringen; **do I make myself ~?** ist das klar?; habe ich mich klar ausgedrückt?; **the reason is ~ [to see]** der Grund liegt auf der Hand; **the consequences of the act were not ~ at the time** die Folgen dieses Schrittes waren zu dieser Zeit nicht absehbar *od.* klar zu erkennen; *see also* **English B 1**; **pikestaff 2** (frank, straightforward) ehrlich; offen; schlicht ‹*Wahrheit*›; **be ~ with sb.** mit jmdm. *od.* jmdm. gegenüber offen sein; **there was some ~ speaking** es fielen einige offene Worte; **be [all] ~ sailing** (fig.) [ganz] einfach sein; **~ dealing** Redlichkeit, *die* **3** (unsophisticated) einfach; schlicht ‹*Kleidung, Frisur*›; klar ‹*Wasser*›; einfach, bescheiden ‹*Lebensstil*›; (not lined) unliniert ‹*Papier*›; (not patterned) ‹*Stoff*› ohne Muster; **she is a ~ cook** sie kocht einfach; **~ cooking** gutbürgerliche Küche; **~ stitch** rechte Masche; **~ text** (without notes) [unkommentierter] Originaltext; (decoded) Klartext, *der; see also* **cover A 3**; **plain clothes 4** (unattractive) wenig attraktiv ‹*Mädchen*›; **she's rather a ~ Jane** (coll.) sie ist nicht gerade eine Schönheit **5** (sheer) rein; **that's ~ bad manners** das ist einfach schlechtes Benehmen; **that's just ~ common sense** das sagt einem doch der gesunde Menschenverstand

B *adv.* **1** (clearly) deutlich **2** (simply) einfach; **I'm just ~ tired** ich bin einfach nur müde

C *n.* **1** Ebene, *die;* **the P~s** (of North America) die Prärie **2** (Knitting) rechte Masche; **two ~, two purl** zwei rechts, zwei links

plain: **~chant** ▸**plainsong**; **~ 'chocolate** *n.* halbbittere Schokolade; (without any sweetness) bittere Schokolade; **~ 'clothes** *n. pl.* **in ~ clothes** in Zivil; *attrib.* **~-clothes detective** *etc.* Kriminalbeamter *usw.* in Zivil; **~ 'flour** *n., no pl.* (Brit.) einfaches *od.* normales Mehl

plainly /ˈpleɪnlɪ/ *adv.* **1** (clearly) deutlich; verständlich ‹*erklären*› **2** (obviously) offensichtlich; (undoubtedly) eindeutig **3** (frankly) offen **4** (simply, unpretentiously) einfach; schlicht; bescheiden ‹*leben*›

plainness /ˈpleɪnnɪs/ *n., no pl.* **1** (clearness) Klarheit, *die* **2** (frankness) Offenheit, *die;* **his ~ of speech** seine Offenheit **3** (simplicity) Schlichtheit, *die* **4** (ugliness) Unattraktivität, *die;* Unansehnlichkeit, *die*

plainsman /ˈpleɪnzmən/ *n., pl.* **plainsmen** /ˈpleɪnzmən/ Flachländer, *der;* (in North America) Präriebewohner, *der*

plain: **~song** *n.* (Mus., Eccl.) Cantus planus, *der* (fachspr.); gregorianischer Gesang; **~-'spoken** *adj.* freimütig

plaint /pleɪnt/ *n.* **1** (literary: lamentation) [Weh]klage, *die* **2** (Brit. Law) Klage, *die*

plaintiff /ˈpleɪntɪf/ *n.* (Law) Kläger, *der*/Klägerin, *die*

plaintive /ˈpleɪntɪv/ *adj.* klagend; traurig, leidend ‹*Blick*›

plaintively /ˈpleɪntɪvlɪ/ *adv.* klagend; in klagendem Ton ‹*sprechen usw.*›; traurig, leidend ‹*blicken*›

plain: **~ weave** *n.* Leinwandbindung, *die;* **~ weaving** *n.* Gewebe in Leinwandbindung

plait /plæt/

A *n.* (of hair) Zopf, *der;* Flechte, *die* (geh.); (of straw, ribbon, etc.) geflochtenes Band

B *v.t.* flechten

plan /plæn/

A *n.* Plan, *der;* (for story etc.) Konzept, *das;* Entwurf, *der;* (intention) Absicht, *die;* **~ of action** Aktionsprogramm, *das;* **what is your ~ of action?** wie willst du vorgehen?; **have great ~s for sb.** große Pläne mit jmdm. haben; **~ of campaign** Strategie, *die;* **make ~s for sth.** Pläne für etw. machen *od.* schmieden; **what are your ~s for tomorrow?** was hast du morgen vor?; **your best ~ is to stay on at school** am besten bleibst du auf der Schule; **[go] according to ~:** nach Plan [gehen]; planmäßig [verlaufen *od.* laufen]; *see also* **five-year plan**

B *v.t.,* **-nn-** **1** planen; (design) entwerfen ‹*Gebäude, Maschine*›; **~ to do sth.** planen *od.* vorhaben, etw. zu tun; **as ~ned** plangemäß; wie geplant; *see also* **obsolescence 2** (make plan of) **~ sth.** einen [Lage]plan einer Sache (*Gen.*) *od.* von etw. anfertigen

C *v.i.,* **-nn-** planen; **~ [weeks] ahead** [Wochen] im Voraus planen *od.* vorausplanen; **~ for sth.** Pläne für etw. machen; **we hadn't ~ned on that** damit hatten wir nicht gerechnet; **~ on doing sth.** (coll.) vorhaben, etw. zu tun; **what do you ~ on doing today?** was hast du heute vor?

planchette /plænˈʃet/ *n.* Planchette, *die*

plane[1] /pleɪn/ *n.* **~ [tree]** Platane, *die*

plane[2]

A *n.* (tool) Hobel, *der*

B *v.t.* hobeln

plane[3]

A *n.* **1** (Geom.) Ebene, *die;* (flat surface) Fläche, *die; see also* **inclined plane 2** (fig.) Ebene, *die;* (moral, intellectual) Niveau, *das;* **~ of thought/attainment/knowledge** Denk-/Leistungs-/Wissensniveau, *das* **3** (aircraft) Flugzeug, *das;* Maschine, *die* (ugs.); (Aeronaut.: supporting surface) Tragfläche, *die*

B *v.i.* gleiten

'planeload *n.* Flugzeugladung, *die*

planet /ˈplænɪt/ *n.* Planet, *der;* **major ~:** Riesenplanet, *der;* **minor ~:** kleiner Planet

planetarium /plænɪˈteərɪəm/ *n., pl.* **~s** *or* **planetaria** /plænɪˈteərɪə/ Planetarium, *das*

planetary /ˈplænɪtərɪ/ *adj.* planetarisch; Planeten‹*forscher, -system, -bewegung*›

planetoid /ˈplænətɔɪd/ *n.* (Astron.) Planetoid, *der*

plangent /ˈplændʒənt/ *adj.* **1** (resounding) klangvoll **2** (plaintive) schwermütig und ergreifend; getragen ‹*Melodie usw.*›

planish /ˈplænɪʃ/ *v.t.* glätten; glatt hämmern ‹*Blech*›

plank /plæŋk/

A *n.* **1** (piece of timber) Brett, *das;* (thicker) Bohle, *die;* (on ship) Planke, *die;* **be as thick as two [short] ~s** (coll.) dumm wie Bohnenstroh sein (ugs.); **be made to walk the ~** (Hist.) über die Planke laufen müssen (fig.) **2** (fig.: item of political programme) Programmpunkt, *der*

B *v.t.* **1** mit Brettern/Bohlen/Planken versehen; beplanken ‹*Schiff*›; **~ sth. over** etw. mit Brettern abdecken **2** (coll.: put down) knallen (ugs.) **3** (Amer.) *auf einem Holzbrett garen und servieren;* **~ed steak** Steak auf dem Holzbrett

planking /ˈplæŋkɪŋ/ *n.* (planks) ▸**plank A 1**: Bretter *Pl.;* Bohlen *Pl.;* Planken *Pl.;* (of ship) Beplankung, *die*

plankton /ˈplæŋktn/ *n.* (Biol.) Plankton, *das*

planned: **~ e'conomy** *n.* (Econ.) Planwirtschaft, *die;* **~ obso'lescence** *n., no pl.* geplante Obsoleszenz

planner /ˈplænə(r)/ *n.* Planer, *der*/Planerin, *die*

planning /ˈplænɪŋ/ *n.* Planen, *das;* Planung, *die;* **at the ~ stage** im Planungsstadium; **~ permission** Baugenehmigung, *die*

'planning blight *n., no pl.* Planungsschäden *Pl.;* **cases of ~:** Planungsschäden *Pl.*

plant /plɑːnt/

A *n.* **1** (Bot.) Pflanze, *die* **2** (machinery) *no indef. art.* Maschinen *Pl.;* (single complex) Anlage, *die;* **earth-moving ~** *no indef. art.* Maschinen für Erdarbeiten; **generating ~** *no indef. art.* Generatoren *Pl.;* **a generating ~:** eine Generatorenanlage **3** (factory) Fabrik, *die;* Werk, *das* **4** (coll.: undercover agent) Spitzel, *der* **5** (coll.: thing concealed) Untergeschobene, *das;* **he said the heroin was a ~:** er sagte, das Heroin sei ihm untergeschoben worden

B *v.t.* **1** (put in ground) pflanzen; aussäen ‹*Samen*›; anlegen ‹*Garten usw.*›; anpflanzen ‹*Beet*›; bepflanzen ‹*Land*›; **~ a field with barley** auf einem Feld Gerste anpflanzen **2** (fix) setzen; **~ stakes [in the ground]** Pfähle setzen; **he ~ed his feet wide apart** er stellte seine Füße weit auseinander; **~ oneself** sich hinstellen *od.* (ugs.) aufpflanzen **3** (in mind) **~ an idea** *etc.* **in sb.'s mind/in sb.** jmdm. eine Idee *usw.* einimpfen (ugs.) *od.* (geh.) einpflanzen **4** (deliver etc.) **~ a blow** *etc.* **on sb.'s nose** *etc.* jmdm. einen Schlag *usw.* auf die Nase *usw.* verpassen; **~ a kiss on sb.'s forehead** *etc.* jmdm. einen Kuss auf die Stirn *usw.* drücken **5** (coll.: conceal) schmuggeln (ugs.); anbringen ‹*Wanze*›; legen ‹*Bombe*›; **~ sth. on sb.** jmdm. etw. unterschieben **6** (station as spy etc.) einschmuggeln

Phrasal verb

- **~ 'out** *v.t.* auspflanzen ‹*Setzlinge*›

Plantagenet /plænˈtædʒɪnɪt/ (Brit. Hist.)

A *n.* Plantagenet, *der/die*

B *attrib. adj.* Plantagenet-

plantain[1] /ˈplæntɪn/ *n.* (Bot.: in temperate regions, Plantago) Wegerich, *der*

plantain[2] (Bot.: in tropics, Musa) Kochbanane, *die;* Mehlbanane *die;* Plante, *die* (fachspr.)

plantain 'lily *n.* (Bot.) Funkie, *die*

plantation /plænˈteɪʃn, plɑːnˈteɪʃn/ *n.* **1** (estate) Pflanzung, *die;* Plantage, *die* **2** (group of plants) Anpflanzung, *die*

'plant breeding *n.* Pflanzenzucht, *die*

planter /ˈplɑːntə(r)/ *n.* **1** Pflanzer, *der*/Pflanzerin, *die* **2** (machine) Pflanzmaschine, *die;* (for seeds) Sämaschine, *die* **3** (container) Pflanzgefäß, *das*

plant: **~ food** *n.* Pflanzennahrung, *die;* (naturally occurring) Nährstoffe *Pl.;* **~ hire** *n.* Baumaschinenverleih, *der;* **~ kingdom** *n.* Pflanzenreich, *das;* **~-louse** *n.* (Zool.) Pflanzenlaus, *die*

plaque /plɑːk, plæk/ *n.* **1** (ornamental tablet) [Schmuck]platte, *die;* (commemorating sb.) [Gedenk]tafel, *die;* Plakette, *die* (Kunstwiss.) **2** (Dent.) Plaque, *die* (fachspr.); [weißer] Zahnbelag

plasma /ˈplæzmə/ *n.* **1** (Anat., Zool., Phys.) Plasma, *das* **2** (Biol.) ▸**protoplasm**

ˈplasma screen *n.* Plasmabildschirm, *der*

plaster /ˈplɑːstə(r)/
A *n.* **1** (for walls etc.) [Ver]putz, *der* **2** ~ **[of Paris]** Gips, *der;* **have one's leg in ~:** ein Gipsbein *od.* sein Bein in Gips haben; **put sb.'s leg in ~:** jmds. Bein in Gips legen **3** ▸**sticking plaster**
B *v.t.* **1** verputzen ‹*Wand*›; vergipsen, zugipsen ‹*Loch, Riß*› **2** (daub) **~ sth. on sth.** etw. dick auf etw. (*Akk.*) auftragen; **~ make-up on one's face, ~ one's face with make-up** sich (*Dat.*) Make-up ins Gesicht kleistern (ugs.); **~ed with mud** mit Schlamm bedeckt **3** (stick on) kleistern (ugs.) ‹*Plakate, Briefmarken*› (**on** auf + *Akk.*); **~ posters all over the wall/the wall with posters** die Wand mit Plakaten zukleistern (salopp) **4** (coll.: shell, bomb) bepflastern (Soldatenspr.)
(Phrasal verbs)
• **~ ˈdown** *v.t.* **~ sb.'s/one's hair down** jmdm./sich das Haar anklatschen
• **~ ˈover** *v.t.* vergipsen ‹*Loch, Riss*›

plaster: ~board *n.* Gipsplatte, *die;* **~ cast** *n.* **1** (model in plaster) Gipsabguss *od.* -abdruck, *der;* **2** (Med.) Gipsverband, *der*

plastered /ˈplɑːstəd/ *pred. adj.* (sl.: drunk) voll (salopp); **get ~:** sich voll laufen lassen (salopp)

plasterer /ˈplɑːstərə(r)/ *n.* ▸**i** **p. 1260** Gipser, *der*

plaster ˈsaint *n.* Heiligenfigur aus Gips; (fig., usu. iron.) Heilige, *der/die* (ugs.)

plastic /ˈplæstɪk/
A *n.* **1** Plastik, *das;* Kunststoff, *der; in pl., attrib.* Plastik-; Kunststoff- **2** (coll.: credit cards etc.) Plastikgeld, *das*
B *adj.* **1** (made of plastic) Plastik-; Kunststoff-; aus Plastik/Kunststoff/Plast *nachgestellt;* (coll. derog.: synthetic) Plastik-; **~ bag** Plastiktüte, *die;* **~ money** (joc.) Kreditkarten *Pl.;* Plastikgeld, *das* **2** (produced by moulding) plastisch; **~ figure** Plastik, *die* **3** (malleable, lit. or fig.) formbar; bildbar; **the ~ qualities of wax** die plastischen Eigenschaften von Wachs **4** **the ~ arts** die Plastik; (including painting etc.) die bildende Kunst

plastic: ~ ˈbullet *n.* Plastikgeschoss, *das;* **~ exˈplosive** *n.* Plastiksprengstoff, *der*

Plasticine ® /ˈplæstɪsiːn/ *n.* Plastilin, *das*

plasticise ▸**plasticize**

plasticity /plæˈstɪsɪtɪ/ *n., no pl.* (lit. or fig.) Formbarkeit, *die;* Plastizität, *die*

plasticize /ˈplæstɪsaɪz/ *v.t.* geschmeidig machen; plasti[fi]zieren (fachspr.)

plasticizer /ˈplæstɪsaɪzə(r)/ *n.* Weichmacher, *der;* Plasti[fi]kator, *der* (Chemie)

plasticky /ˈplæstɪkɪ/ *adj.* (coll. derog.) plastikartig; **be very ~:** billiges Plastikzeug sein

plastic: ~ ˈsurgeon *n.* ▸**i** **p. 1260** Facharzt für plastische Chirurgie; **~ ˈsurgery** *n., no pl.* plastische Chirurgie; **undergo** *or* **have ~ surgery** sich einer plastischen *od.* kosmetischen Operation unterziehen; **~ ˈwood** *n., no pl.* plastisches Holz; Holzkitt, *der;* **~ ˈwrap** *n., no pl.* (Amer.) Frischhaltefolie, *die*

plastinate /ˈplæstɪneɪt/ *v.t.* plastinieren

plastination /plæstɪˈneɪʃn/ *n., no pl.* Plastination, *die*

plate /pleɪt/
A *n.* **1** (for food) Teller, *der;* (large ~ for serving food) Platte, *die;* (Amer.: main course on one ~) Tellergericht, *das;* (Amer.: food for one person) Gedeck, *das;* **a ~ of soup/sandwiches** ein Teller Suppe/belegte Brote *od.* mit belegten Broten; **have sth. handed to one on a ~** (fig. coll.) etw. auf silbernem Tablett serviert bekommen (fig.); **have a lot** *etc.* **on one's ~** (fig. coll.) viel *usw.* am Hals *od.* um die Ohren haben (ugs.) **2** (for collection in church) Teller für die Kollekte **3** (sheet of metal etc.) Platte, *die* **4** (metal ~ with name etc.) Schild, *das;* **[number] ~:** Nummernschild, *das;* **put up one's ~** (fig.) seine eigene Praxis eröffnen **5** (Photog.) [fotografische] Platte **6** *no pl., no indef. art.* (Brit.: tableware) [Tafel]silber, *das;* (gold) Gold[geschirr], *das;* (pewter) Zinn, *das;* Silber-/Gold-/Zinnsachen *Pl.;* (plated) **[made of] real silver, not ~:** aus echtem Silber, nicht nur versilbert **7** (for engraving, printing) Platte, *die;* (impression) Stich, *der;* (illustration) [Bild]tafel, *die* (Druckw.); **printing ~:** Druckplatte, *die* **8** (Sport) (trophy) Pokal, *der;* (race) Pokal[wettbewerb], *der* **9** (Dent.) Gaumenplatte, *die;* (coll.: denture) [Zahn]prothese, *die;* Gebiss, *das* **10** (Amer. Electronics) Anode, *die* **11** (Geol.) Platte, *die* **12** (Baseball) Wurfmal, *das;* **home ~:** Schlagmal, *das. See also* **tracery 1**
B *v.t.* **1** (coat) plattieren; **~ sth. [with gold/silver/chromium]** etw. vergolden/versilbern/verchromen **2** panzern ‹*Schiff*›

plateau /ˈplætəʊ/ *n., pl.* **~x** /ˈplætəʊz/ *or* **~s** **1** Hochebene, *die;* Plateau, *das* **2** (fig.) **a price ~:** eine Stabilisierung der Preise; **reach/be on a ~** ‹*Preise, Produktion usw.:*› sich einpendeln/sich eingependelt haben

plated /ˈpleɪtɪd/ *adj.* plattiert; **[gold-]~:** dubliert; vergoldet; **[silver-/chromium-/nickel-]~:** versilbert/verchromt/vernickelt

plateful /ˈpleɪtfʊl/ *n.* Teller, *der;* **a ~ of rice** ein Teller [voll] Reis; **I've already had two ~s** ich habe schon zwei Teller voll gegessen; **I've had a ~** (fig. coll.) ich habe die Nase voll davon (ugs.)

plate: ~ ˈglass *n.* Flachglas, *das;* **~-holder** *n.* (Photogr.) [Platten]kassette, *die;* **~layer** *n.* (Brit. Railw.) Streckenarbeiter, *der*

platelet /ˈpleɪtlət/ *n.* (Physiol.) Blutplättchen, *das*

platen /ˈplætn/ *n.* (Printing) Drucktiegel, *der;* (on typewriter) [Schreib]walze, *die*

plate: ~ rack *n.* (Brit.) Abtropfständer, *der;* Geschirrablage, *die;* **~-warmer** *n.* Tellerwärmer, *der*

platform /ˈplætfɔːm/ *n.* **1** (Brit. Railw.) Bahnsteig, *der;* **the train leaves from/will arrive at ~ 4** der Zug fährt von Gleis 4 ab/in Gleis 4 ein; **edge of the ~:** Bahnsteigkante, *die* **2** (stage) Podium, *das* **3** (Polit.) Wahlplattform, *die* **4** (Geol.) Strandterrasse, *die* **5** (in bus etc.) Plattform, *die* **6** (of shoe) Plateausohle, *die; attrib.* Plateau‹*schuh, -sohle*› **7** (Computing) Plattform, *die*

platform: ~ shoe *n.* Plateauschuh, *der;* **~ ticket** *n.* (Brit.) Bahnsteigkarte, *die*

plating /ˈpleɪtɪŋ/ *n.* (process) Plattierung, *die;* (coat) Plattierung, *die;* Auflage, *die;* **gold/silver/chromium ~:** Vergoldung/Versilberung/Verchromung, *die*

platinum /ˈplætɪnəm/ *n.* Platin, *das*

platinum ˈblonde
A *n.* Platinblonde, *die*
B *adj.* platinblond

platitude /ˈplætɪtjuːd/ *n.* **1** (trite remark) Plattitüde, *die* (geh.); Gemeinplatz, *der* **2** *no pl.* (triteness) Banalität, *die*

platitudinous /plætɪˈtjuːdɪnəs/ *adj.* banal; platt (abwertend)

Plato /ˈpleɪtəʊ/ *pr. n.* Plato[n] (*der*)

Platonic /pləˈtɒnɪk/ *adj.* **1** (of Plato) platonisch **2** **p~** (not sexual) platonisch ‹*Liebe, Freundschaft*›

platonically /pləˈtɒnɪkəlɪ/ *adv.* platonisch

Platonist /ˈpleɪtənɪst/ *n.* Platoniker, *der*

platoon /pləˈtuːn/ *n.* (Mil.) Zug, *der*

platter /ˈplætə(r)/ *n.* (Amer./arch.) Platte, *die;* (arch.: plate) Teller, *der;* **have sth. handed to one on a ~** (fig. coll.) etw. auf silbernem Tablett serviert bekommen (fig.)

platypus /ˈplætɪpəs/ *n.* (Zool.) Schnabeltier, *das*

plaudits /ˈplɔːdɪts/ *n. pl.* Beifall, *der*

plausibility /plɔːzɪˈbɪlɪtɪ/ *n., no pl.* Plausibilität, *die;* Glaubwürdigkeit, *die;* (of person) Glaubwürdigkeit, *die;* **this version has more ~:** diese Version ist glaubwürdiger *od.* plausibler

plausible /ˈplɔːzɪbl/ *adj.* plausibel; einleuchtend; glaubwürdig ‹*Person*›; **a ~ liar** ein guter Lügner; **be a ~ liar** gut lügen können

plausibly /ˈplɔːzɪblɪ/ *adv.* plausibel; einleuchtend; **as long as she ~ could** so lange es sich vertreten ließ

play /pleɪ/
A *n.* **1** (Theatre) [Theater]stück, *das;* **television ~:** Fernsehspiel, *das;* **put on a ~:** ein Stück aufführen; **go to [see] a ~:** ins Theater gehen; **a ~ within a ~:** ein Spiel im Spiel; **it was as good as a ~:** dafür hätte man Eintrittsgeld verlangen können
2 (recreation) Spielen, *das;* Spiel, *das;* **time for ~:** Zeit zum Spielen; **at ~:** beim Spielen; **say/do sth. in ~:** etw. aus *od.* im *od.* zum Spaß sagen/tun; **~ [up]on words** Wortspiel, *das*
3 (Sport) Spiel, *das;* (Amer.: manoeuvre) Spielzug, *der;* **abandon ~:** das Spiel abbrechen; **~ is impossible because of the weather** wegen des Wetters kann nicht gespielt werden; **start/close of ~:** Spielbeginn, *der/*-ende, *das;* **in the last minute of ~:** in der letzten Spielminute; **forward ~:** Angriffsspiel, *das;* **a good piece of ~:** ein guter Spielzug; **be in/out of ~** ‹*Ball:*› im Spiel/aus [dem Spiel] sein; **keep the ball in ~:** den Ball im Spiel halten; **make a ~ for sb./sth.** (fig. coll.) hinter jmdm./etw. her sein (ugs.); es auf jmdn./etw. abgesehen haben; *see also* **child's play**; **fair[2] A 1**; **foul A 5**
4 (gambling) Spiel, *das*
5 **sb.'s imagination is brought** *or* **called into ~:** jmds. Fantasie wird angeregt; **come into ~, be brought** *or* **called into ~:** ins Spiel kommen; **put into ~:** ins Spiel bringen; **make great ~ of sth.** etw. demonstrativ zur Schau stellen; **make [great] ~ with sth.** viel Wesen um etw. machen
6 (freedom of movement) Spiel, *das* (Technik); (fig.) Spielraum, *der;* **some/2 mm of/too much ~:** etwas/2 mm/zu viel Spiel; **the knot has too much ~:** der Knoten ist zu locker; **give the rope more ~:** das Seil lockern; **give full ~ to one's emotions/imagination** *etc.*, **allow one's emotions/imagination** *etc.* **full ~** (fig.) seinen Gefühlen/seiner Fantasie *usw.* freien Lauf lassen
7 (rapid movement) **the ~ of light on water** das Spiel des Lichts auf Wasser
8 (turn, move) **it's your ~:** du bist dran *od.* an der Reihe (ugs.); (in board game) du bist am Zug
B *v.i.* **1** spielen; **~ for money** um Geld spielen; **~ with sb./sth.** (lit. or fig.) mit jmdm./etw. spielen; **have no one to ~ with** niemanden zum Spielen haben; **he won't ~** (coll.: won't do what sb. wants) er will nicht mitspielen; **~ with oneself** (euphem.: sexually) an sich (*Dat.*) herumspielen (ugs. verhüll.); **~ [up]on words** Wortspiele/ein Wortspiel machen; **~ fair [with sb.]** fair [gegen jmdn.] spielen; (fig.) [jmdm. gegenüber] fair sein; sich [jmdm. gegenüber] fair verhalten; **not have much time** *etc.* **to ~ with** (coll.) zeitlich *usw.* nicht viel Spielraum haben; **~ into sb.'s hands** (fig.) jmdm. in die Hand *od.* Hände arbeiten; **~ safe** sichergehen; auf Nummer Sicher gehen (ugs.); **~ing safe, she took an umbrella** sicherheits- *od.* vorsichtshalber nahm sie einen Schirm mit; **~ for time** Zeit gewinnen wollen; [ver]suchen, Zeit zu gewinnen; *see also* **fire A 2**
2 (be suitable for ~) **the pitch is ~ing well/badly** auf dem Platz spielt es sich gut/schlecht
3 (Mus.) spielen (**on** auf + *Dat.*); **~ by ear** nach dem Gehör spielen
4 (Theatre) spielen; **what is ~ing at the theatre?** was wird im Theater gespielt *od.* gegeben?; *see also* **gallery 2**
5 (move about) spielen; **a smile ~ed on/about her lips** ein Lächeln spielte um ihre Lippen
6 ‹*Springbrunnen:*› in Betrieb sein
7 (fiddle about) spielen; herumspielen (ugs.) (**with** mit, an + *Dat.*)
C *v.t.* **1** (Mus.: perform on) spielen; **~ the violin** *etc.* Geige *usw.* spielen; **~ sth. on the piano** *etc.* etw. auf dem Klavier *usw.* spielen; **~ sb. in/out** jmdn. musikalisch begrüßen/verabschieden; **~ sth. by ear** etw. nach dem Gehör spielen; **~ it by ear** (fig.) es dem Augenblick/der Situation überlassen
2 spielen ‹*Grammophon, Tonbandgerät*›; abspielen ‹*Schallplatte, Tonband*›; spielen lassen ‹*Radio*›; **~ sb. a record** jmdm. eine [Schall]platte vorspielen
3 (Theatre; also fig.) spielen; **~ a town** in einer Stadt spielen; **~ a theatre** an einem Theater spielen; **~ the fool/innocent** den Clown/Unschuldigen spielen; *see also* **man A 2**
4 (execute, practise) **~ a trick/joke on sb.**

jmdn. hereinlegen (ugs.)/jmdm. einen Streich spielen
[5] (Sport, Cards) spielen ‹*Fußball, Karten, Schach usw.*›; spielen *od.* antreten gegen ‹*Mannschaft, Gegner*›; (include in team) einsetzen, aufstellen ‹*Stürmer, Verteidiger*›; ~ **a match** einen Wettkampf bestreiten; (in team games) ein Spiel machen; **he ~ed me at chess/squash** er war im Schach/Squash mein Gegner; ~ **it cool** (fig. coll.) auf cool machen (salopp); ~ **it right/safe/straight** es geschickt anstellen/auf Nummer Sicher gehen/es sachlich behandeln; ~ **oneself in** (esp. Cricket) sich einspielen; (fig.) sich einarbeiten; *see also* **ball¹ A 2**; **duck¹ A 1**; **fast² A 1**; **game¹ A 1, 2, 4**; **hand A 16**; **hell 2**; **hookey**
[6] (Sport: execute) ausführen ‹*Schlag*›; (Cricket etc.) schlagen ‹*Ball*›
[7] (Chess etc.: move) ziehen; (Cards) spielen; ~ **one's last card** (fig.) alle seine Karten ausspielen; **have ~ed all one's cards** (fig.) seinen letzten Trumpf ausgespielt haben; ~ **one's cards right** (fig.) es richtig anfassen (fig.); *see also* **trump¹ A**
[8] (Angling) drillen
[9] (gamble on) ~ **the market** spekulieren (**in** mit *od. Wirtsch.* in + *Dat.*); ~ **the stock market** an der Börse spekulieren

(Phrasal verbs)

- ~ **a'bout** ▸ ~ **around**
- ~ **a'long** *v.i.* mitspielen; ~ **along with sb./sth.** sich mit jmdm./etw. arrangieren
- ~ **a'round** *v.i.* (coll.) spielen; ~ **around with sb./sb.'s affections/sth.** mit jmdm./jmds. Zuneigung spielen/mit etw. herumspielen (ugs.); **stop ~ing around!** hör [doch] auf mit dem Blödsinn!
- ~ **at** *v.t.* spielen; **what do you think you're ~ing at?** was soll denn das?; ~ **at being sb.** jmdn. spielen
- ~ **'back** *v.t.* abspielen ‹*Tonband, Aufnahme*›; **he ~ed part of the discussion back to them** er spielte ihnen einen Teil der Diskussion vor; *see also* **playback**
- ~ **'down** *v.t.* herunterspielen
- ~ **'off**

[A] *v.i.* zum Entscheidungsspiel antreten; *see also* **play-off**
[B] *v.t.* ausspielen; ~ **one person/firm** *etc.* **off against another** eine Person/Firma *usw.* gegen eine andere ausspielen

- ~ **on**

[A] /'--/ *v.t.* ▸ ~ **upon**
[B] /-'-/ *v.i.* (Cricket) auf das eigene Mal schlagen

- ~ **'up**

[A] *v.i.* [1] (play vigorously) ~ **up!** los, vorwärts! [2] (coll.) ‹*Kinder:*› nichts als Ärger machen; ‹*Auto:*› verrückt spielen; ‹*Rücken, Bein usw.:*› Schwierigkeiten *od.* Ärger machen
[B] *v.t.* [1] (coll.: annoy, torment) ärgern; ‹*Krankheit:*› zu schaffen machen (+ *Dat.*) [2] (exploit) hochspielen; Wesen machen von (ugs.) ‹*Krankheit*›; hervor-, herauskehren ‹*Eigenschaft usw.*›

- ~ **upon** *v.t.* sich (*Dat.*) zunutze machen ‹*Gefühle, Ängste usw.*›; ~ **upon sb.'s sympathies** auf jmds. Mitgefühl (*Akk.*) spekulieren (ugs.)
- ~ **'up to** *v.t.* [1] (Theatre coll.) gut in Szene setzen ‹*Schauspieler*› [2] (fig.: flatter) ~ **up to sb.** sich bei jmdm. beliebt machen

playable /'pleɪəbl/ *adj.* [1] (able to be played) spielbar [2] (Sport: able to be played on) bespielbar ‹*Spielfeld*›

play: ~-acting *n., no pl.* Schauspielkunst, *die;* Schauspielerei, *die* (ugs.); (fig.) Theater, *das* (ugs.); **~-actor** *n.* (fig., usu. derog.) **he's just a ~-actor** er spielt immer nur Theater (ugs.); **~ area** *n.* Spielplatz, *der;* **~back** *n.* Wiedergabe, *die;* **listen to the ~back** die Aufnahme anhören; **~bill** *n.* [1] (poster) Theaterplakat, *das;* [2] (Amer.: theatre programme) Theaterprogramm, *das;* **~book** *n.* (Amer.) Spielbuch, *das;* **~boy** *n.* Playboy, *der*

played 'out *adj.* verbraucht; erschöpft ‹*Person, Tier*›; **this idea is ~:** diese Idee hat sich überlebt

player /'pleɪə(r)/ *n.* [1] Spieler, *der*/Spielerin, *die;* **amateur/professional ~:** Amateur, *der*/Profi[spieler], *der* [2] (Mus.) Musiker, *der*/Musikerin, *die;* Spieler, *der*/Spielerin, *die;* **orchestral ~:** Orchestermusiker, *der*/-musikerin, *die;* **organ-~:** Orgelspieler, *der*/-spielerin, *die* [3] (actor) Schauspieler, *der*/Schauspielerin, *die* [4] ▸ **record player**

player-'manager *n.* Spielertrainer, *der*/-[in]trainerin, *die*

'player-piano *n.* automatisches Klavier; Pianola, *das*

'playfellow *n.* Spielkamerad, *der*/Spielkameradin, *die*

playful /'pleɪfl/ *adj.* [1] (fond of playing) spielerisch; (frolicsome) verspielt [2] (teasing) neckisch; (joking) scherzhaft

playfully /'pleɪfəlɪ/ *adv.* [1] (gaily) spielerisch; ausgelassen [2] (teasingly) neckisch; (jokingly) aus *od.* im *od.* zum Scherz

play: ~goer *n.* Theaterbesucher, *der*/-besucherin, *die;* **be a regular ~goer** regelmäßig ins Theater gehen; **~ground** *n.* Spielplatz, *der;* (Sch.) Schulhof, *der;* **the ~ground of the rich** (fig.) der Tummelplatz der Reichen; **~group** *n.* Spielgruppe, *die;* **~house** *n.* [1] (theatre) Schauspielhaus, *das;* [2] (toy house) Spielhaus, *das*

playing /'pleɪɪŋ/ *n.* Spiel, *das*

playing: ~ area *n.* (Sport) Spielfeld, *das;* **~ card** *n.* Spielkarte, *die;* **~ field** *n.* Sportplatz, *der;* **they are not competing on a level ~ field** (fig.) zwischen ihnen besteht keine Chancengleichheit; **~ time** *n.* Spieldauer, *die;* Spielzeit, *die*

playlet /'pleɪlɪt/ *n.* Dramolett, *das*

play: ~list *n.* Senderepertoire, *das;* **ban a singer from the ~list** einen Sänger nicht mehr spielen; **~maker** *n.* Spielmacher, *der*/-macherin, *die;* **~mate** *n.* Spielkamerad, *der*/Spielkameradin, *die;* **~-off** *n.* Entscheidungsspiel, *das;* **~pen** *n.* Laufgitter, *das;* Laufstall, *der;* **~school** *n.* Kindergarten, *der;* **~suit** *n.* Spielanzug, *der;* **~thing** *n.* (lit. or fig.) Spielzeug, *das;* **~things** Spielzeug, *das;* Spielsachen *Pl.;* **~time** *n.* Zeit zum Spielen; **during ~time** (Sch.) in der [großen] Pause; **~wright** /'pleɪraɪt/ *n.* ▸❶ **p. 1260** Dramatiker, *der*/Dramatikerin, *die;* Stückeschreiber, *der*/-schreiberin, *die*

plaza /'plɑːzə/ *n.* Piazza, *die*

PLC, plc *abbr.* (Brit.) = **public limited company** ≈ GmbH

plea /pliː/ *n.* [1] (entreaty) Bitte, *die;* (public appeal) Appell, *der* (**for** zu); **make a ~ for sth.** zu etw. aufrufen [2] (pleading) Begründung, *die;* (excuse) Entschuldigung, *die;* **excuse oneself on the ~ of sth.** sich mit etw. entschuldigen [3] (Law) Verteidigungsrede, *die;* **special ~:** besondere Einrede; *attrib.* **~ bargain** Deal [zwischen Anklage und Verteidigung]; **~ bargaining** *Praktik, bei der Verteidigung und Anklage übereinkommen, dass der Angeklagte ein [Teil]geständnis ablegt und dafür bestimmte Zusicherungen (milderes Strafmaß o. Ä.) erhält*

plead /pliːd/
[A] *v.i.,* **~ed** *or* (esp. Amer., Scot., dial.) **pled** /pled/ [1] (make appeal) inständig bitten (**for** um); (imploringly) flehen (**for** um); **~ with sb. for sth./to do sth.** jmdn. inständig um etw. bitten/jmdn. inständig [darum] bitten, etw. zu tun; (imploringly) jmdn. um etw. anflehen/jmdn. anflehen, etw. zu tun [2] (Law: put forward plea; also fig.) plädieren; **I'd get a lawyer to ~ for me** ich würde mich von einem Anwalt vertreten lassen [3] (Law) **how do you ~?** bekennen Sie sich schuldig?
[B] *v.t.,* **~ed** *or* (esp. Amer., Scot., dial.) **pled** [1] (beg) inständig bitten; (imploringly) flehen [2] (Law: offer in mitigation) sich berufen auf (+ *Akk.*); geltend machen; (as excuse) sich entschuldigen mit; **he ~ed insanity** er plädierte auf Unzurechnungsfähigkeit; **~ guilty/not guilty** (lit. or fig.) sich schuldig/nicht schuldig bekennen; **~ guilty to [having committed] the crime** sich des Verbrechens schuldig bekennen [3] (present in court) **~ sb.'s case** *or* **~ the case for sb.** jmds. Sache vor Gericht vertreten

pleading /'pliːdɪŋ/
[A] *adj.* flehend
[B] *n.* [1] Bitten, *das;* (imploring) Flehen, *das* [2] *usu. in pl.* (Law) Plädoyer, *das;* Vortrag, *der;* (written) Schriftsatz, *der; see also* **special pleading**

pleadingly /'pliːdɪŋlɪ/ *adv.* flehentlich

pleasant /'plezənt/ *adj.,* **~er** /'plezəntə(r)/, **~est** /'plezəntɪst/ (agreeable) angenehm; schön ‹*Tag, Zeit*›; nett ‹*Gesicht, Lächeln*›; **be ~ with** *or* **to sb.** nett zu jmdm. sein

pleasantly /'plezəntlɪ/ *adv.* angenehm; schön ‹*singen*›; freundlich ‹*sprechen, lächeln usw.*›

pleasantry /'plezəntrɪ/ *n.* [1] (agreeable remark) Nettigkeit, *die;* (humorous remark) Scherz, *der* [2] (jocularity) Humor, *der*

please /pliːz/
[A] *v.t.* [1] (give pleasure to) gefallen (+ *Dat.*); Freude machen (+ *Dat.*); **there's no pleasing her** man kann ihr nichts *od.* es ihr nicht recht machen; **she's easy to ~** *or* **easily ~d/hard to ~:** sie ist leicht/nicht leicht zufrieden zu stellen; **[just] to ~ you** [nur] dir zu Gefallen; **one can't ~ everybody** man kann es nicht allen recht machen; **~ the eye** das Auge erfreuen; **~ oneself** tun, was man will; **~ yourself** ganz wie du willst [2] ([may it] be the will of) gefallen; **~ God** das gebe Gott; so Gott will; **may it ~ your Honour** (to a judge) mit Ihrer Erlaubnis, Hohes Gericht
[B] *v.i.* [1] (think fit) **what he ~s** was ihm gefällt; was er will; **they come and go as they ~:** sie kommen und gehen, wie es ihnen gefällt; **do as one ~s** tun, was man will; **take as much as you ~:** nimm, so viel[, wie] du willst *od.* möchtest [2] (give pleasure) gefallen; **anxious** *or* **eager to ~:** bemüht, gefällig zu sein; **the poem is sure to ~:** das Gedicht kommt garantiert gut an (ugs.) *od.* wird bestimmt gefallen [3] *in requests* bitte; **may I have the bill, ~?** kann ich bitte zahlen?; **~ do!** aber bitte *od.* gern!; **~ don't** bitte nicht [4] **if you ~:** bitte schön; (iron.: believe it or not) stell dir vor

pleased /pliːzd/ *adj.* (satisfied) zufrieden (**by** mit); (glad, happy) erfreut (**by** über + *Akk.*); **he'll be ~ when he sees that** (iron.) er wird seine Freude haben, wenn er das sieht; **be ~ at** *or* **about sth.** sich über etw. (*Akk.*) freuen; **be ~ with sth./sb.** mit etw./jmdm. zufrieden sein; **~ with oneself** mit sich selbst zufrieden; **don't look so ~ with yourself** guck nicht so selbstzufrieden *od.* selbstgefällig (ugs.); **be ~ to do sth.** sich freuen, etw. zu tun; (formal/iron.: with condescension) belieben, etw. zu tun (geh./iron.); **I am [only too] ~ to be of assistance** es ist mir [wirklich] eine Freude, Ihnen zu helfen; **I shall be ~ to [come]** [ich komme] gerne; *see also* **meet¹ A 3**

pleasing /'pliːzɪŋ/ *adj.* gefällig; ansprechend; nett ‹*Person, Ausblick*›; **it is ~ to see how well ...:** es ist eine Freude zu sehen, wie gut ...; **be ~ to the eye/ear** *etc.* das Auge/Ohr *usw.* erfreuen

pleasurable /'pleʒərəbl/ *adj.,* **pleasurably** /'pleʒərəblɪ/ *adv.* angenehm

pleasure /'pleʒə(r)/
[A] *n.* [1] (feeling of joy) Freude, *die;* (usu. derog.: sensuous enjoyment) Vergnügen, *das;* **sth. gives sb. ~:** etw. macht jmdm. Freude; **for ~:** zum Vergnügen; **it's no ~ to do sth.** es macht keinen Spaß, etw. zu tun; **get a lot of ~ from** *or* **out of sb./sth.** viel Freude *od.* Spaß an jmdm./etw. haben [2] (gratification) **have the ~ of doing sth.** das Vergnügen haben, etw. zu tun; **it's a ~ to talk to him** es ist ein Vergnügen, mit ihm zu reden; **may I have the ~ [of the next dance]?** darf ich [Sie um den nächsten Tanz] bitten?; **do me the ~ of dining with me** machen Sie mir das Vergnügen *od.* die Freude, mit mir zu speisen; **he had the ~ of knowing that he was always welcome** er war in der glücklichen Lage zu wissen, dass er immer willkommen war; **I don't think I've had the ~:** wir kennen uns noch nicht; **take [a] ~ in** Vergnügen finden *od.* Spaß haben an (+ *Dat.*); **he takes ~ in teasing me** es macht ihm Spaß *od.* bereitet ihm Vergnügen, mich zu necken; **my ~, it's a ~:** gern geschehen; es war mir ein Vergnügen; **the ~ is all mine** das Vergnügen ist ganz meinerseits *od.* auf meiner Seite; **it gives me great ~ to inform you that ..., I have much ~ in informing you that ...** (formal) ich freue mich, Ihnen mitteilen zu können,

p

dass ...; **Mrs P. requests the ~ of your company** (formal) Frau P. gibt sich (*Dat.*) die Ehre, Sie einzuladen; **Mr F. has great ~ in accepting the invitation** (formal) Herr F. nimmt die Einladung mit dem größten Vergnügen an; **with ~:** mit Vergnügen; gern[e]; **with the greatest of ~:** mit dem größten Vergnügen **3** (will, desire) **what is your ~?** (formal) Sie wünschen?; **at ~:** nach Wunsch *od.* Belieben; **come and go at one's ~:** kommen und gehen, wie es einem beliebt (geh.) *od.* wann immer man will; **consult sb.'s ~** (formal) fragen, was jmdm. genehm ist (geh.); **we await your ~** (formal) wir warten auf Ihren Bescheid; **be detained during Her Majesty's ~:** eine Haftstrafe auf unbestimmte Zeit verbüßen

B *v.t.* (give ~ to) erfreuen; (sexually) beglücken (scherzh.)

pleasure: ~ boat *n.* Vergnügungsboot, *das;* **~ craft** *n., pl. same* Vergnügungsboot, *das;* **~ cruise** *n.* Vergnügungsfahrt, *die;* **~ ground** *n.* Vergnügungspark, *der;* **~-loving** *adj.* lebenslustig; (~-seeking) vergnügungssüchtig; **~ principle** *n.* (Psych.) Lustprinzip, *das;* **~-seeking A** *adj.* vergnügungssüchtig; **B** *n.* Vergnügungssucht, *die*

pleat /pliːt/

A *n.* Falte, *die;* **inverted ~:** Kellerfalte, *die; see also* **box-pleat**; **knife pleat**

B *v.t.* in Falten legen; fälteln

pleated /ˈpliːtɪd/ *adj.* gefältelt; Falten‹*rock*›

pleb /pleb/ *n.* (coll.) Prolet, *der* (ugs.)

plebby /ˈplebɪ/ *adj.* (coll.) primitiv (abwertend)

plebeian /plɪˈbiːən/

A *adj.* **1** proletarisch **2** (coarse) plebejisch; gewöhnlich

B *n.* **1** (in ancient Rome) Plebejer, *der*/Plebejerin, *die* **2** (commoner) Bürgerliche, *der/die;* **the ~s** das [einfache] Volk

plebiscite /ˈplebɪsɪt, ˈplebɪsaɪt/ *n.* Plebiszit, *das*

plectrum /ˈplektrəm/ *n., pl.* **plectra** /ˈplektrə/ *or* **~s** (Mus.) Plektrum, *das*

pled ▸ **plead**

pledge /pledʒ/

A *n.* **1** (promise, vow) Versprechen, *das;* Gelöbnis, *das* (geh.); **under the ~ of secrecy** unter dem Siegel der Geheimhaltung; **take** *or* **sign the ~:** sich zur Abstinenz verpflichten; dem Alkohol abschwören **2** (as security) Pfand, *das;* Sicherheit, *die* **3** (token) [Unter]pfand, *das* (geh.) **4** (state of being ~d) Verpfändung, *die;* **put sth. in ~:** etw. verpfänden; **take sth. out of ~:** etw. auslösen

B *v.t.* **1** (promise solemnly) versprechen; geloben ‹*Treue*›; **~ one's word/honour** sein Wort/seine Ehre verpfänden (geh.); **~ one's service[s]** seine Dienste zusichern **2** (bind by promise) verpflichten **3** (deposit, pawn) verpfänden (**to** *Dat.*) **4** (drink to health of) einen Trinkspruch *od.* Toast ausbringen auf (+ *Akk.*); **they ~d each other** sie tranken auf ihr gegenseitiges Wohl

Pleiades /ˈplaɪədiːz/ *n. pl.* (Astron.) Plejaden *Pl.*

plein-air /plenˈeə(r)/ *adj.* (Art) Pleinair-

Pleistocene /ˈplaɪstəsiːn/ (Geol.)

A *adj.* pleistozän; Pleistozän-

B *n.* Pleistozän, *das*

plenary /ˈpliːnərɪ/ *adj.* **1** (entire, absolute) uneingeschränkt; **~ powers** uneingeschränkte Vollmacht **2** (of all members) Plenar‹*sitzung*›; Voll‹*versammlung*›

plenipotentiary /plenɪpəˈtenʃərɪ/

A *adj.* **1** (invested with full power) [general]bevollmächtigt ‹*Gesandte*›; absolut ‹*Herrscher*›; allmächtig ‹*Parlament*› **2** (absolute) uneingeschränkt

B *n.* [General]bevollmächtigte, *der*

plenitude /ˈplenɪtjuːd/ *n., no pl.* (abundance) Fülle, *die* (**of** von)

plenteous /ˈplentɪəs/ *adj.* (rhet.) reichlich; reich ‹*Ernte*›

plentiful /ˈplentɪfl/ *adj.* **1** (abundant, copious) reichlich; häufig ‹*Element, Rohstoff*›; **be ~** *or* **in ~ supply** reichlich vorhanden sein; **there was a ~ supply of food** es gab reichlich zu essen **2** (yielding abundance) fruchtbar ‹*Land*›; ertragreich ‹*Jahr*›

plentifully /ˈplentɪfəlɪ/ *adv.* reichlich

plenty /ˈplentɪ/

A *n., no pl.* **~ of** viel; eine Menge; (coll.: enough) genug; **have you all got ~ of meat?** habt ihr alle reichlich Fleisch?; **take ~ of exercise** sich viel bewegen; **time[s] of ~:** Zeit[en] des Überflusses; **that's ~** (coll.) das ist genug *od.* reichlich; das reicht; **take ~!** nimm dir reichlich *od.* (ugs.) ordentlich!; **we gave him ~ of warning** wir haben ihn früh genug gewarnt; *see also* **horn A 6**

B *adj.* (coll.) reichlich vorhanden

C *adv.* (coll.) **it's ~ large enough** es ist groß genug; **there's ~ more where this/those** *etc.* **came from** es ist noch genug da (ugs.)

pleonasm /ˈpliːənæzm/ *n.* (Ling.) Pleonasmus, *der*

pleonastic /pliːəˈnæstɪk/ *adj.* (Ling.) pleonastisch

plethora /ˈpleθərə/ *n.* **1** (fig.: excess) Unmenge, *die* (**of** von) **2** (Med.) Plethora, *die* (fachspr.); Blutandrang, *der*

plethoric /plɪˈθɒrɪk/ *adj.* (Med.) vollblütig; plethorisch (fachspr.)

pleura /ˈplʊərə/ *n., pl.* **~e** /ˈplʊəriː/ (Anat.) Pleura, *die* (fachspr.); Brustfell, *das*

pleural /ˈplʊərl/ *adj.* (Anat.) pleural; **~ cavity** Brusthöhle, *die;* **~ inflammation** Brustfellentzündung, *die*

pleurisy /ˈplʊərɪsɪ/ *n.* ▸ **p. 1231** (Med.) Pleuritis, *die* (fachspr.); Brustfellentzündung, *die*

Plexiglas ® /ˈpleksɪglɑːs/ *n.* (esp. Amer.) Plexiglas, *das* (Wz)

plexus /ˈpleksəs/ *n.* (Anat.) Plexus, *der; see also* **solar plexus**

pliability /plaɪəˈbɪlɪtɪ/ *n., no pl.* Biegsamkeit, *die;* (of leather etc.) Geschmeidigkeit, *die;* (fig.: of person, disposition) Fügsamkeit, *die;* Nachgiebigkeit, *die*

pliable /ˈplaɪəbl/ *adj.* (flexible, yielding) biegsam; geschmeidig ‹*Ton, Leder*›; (fig.) nachgiebig ‹*Charakter*›; **be ~ to sb.'s wishes** jmds. Wünschen nachgeben

pliant /ˈplaɪənt/ *adj.* biegsam ‹*Ast, Körper*›; geschmeidig ‹*Körper*›; (fig.) formbar

pliers /ˈplaɪəz/ *n. pl.* **[pair of] ~:** Zange, *die*

plight¹ /plaɪt/ *n.* Notlage, *die;* **hopeless/miserable ~:** trostloser/jämmerlicher Zustand; **what a ~ to find yourself in!** was für eine verzweifelte Lage!

plight² *v.t., esp. in p.p.* (arch.) geloben (geh.) ‹*Treue*›; schwören ‹*Eid*›; **~ one's word [that ...]** sein Wort [dafür] verpfänden[, dass ...]; *see also* **troth 2**

plimsoll /ˈplɪmsl/ *n.* (Brit.) Turnschuh, *der*

Plimsoll: ~ line, ~ mark *ns.* (Naut.) Freibordmarke, *die;* Plimsollmarke, *die*

plinth /plɪnθ/ *n.* **1** (for vase, statue, etc.; of wall) Sockel, *der* **2** (of column) Plinthe, *die* (fachspr.)

Pliocene /ˈplaɪəsiːn/ (Geol.)

A *adj.* pliozän; Pliozän-

B *n.* Pliozän, *das*

PLO *abbr.* = **Palestine Liberation Organization** PLO, *die*

plod /plɒd/

A *v.i.*, **-dd-** trotten; **~ along** dahintrotten; **~ [on] through the snow** [weiter] durch den Schnee stapfen; **~ through a book/one's work** (fig.) sich durch ein Buch kämpfen/sich mit seiner Arbeit abplagen

B *v.t.*, **-dd-** entlangtrotten; **~ one's way home** nach Hause trotten

C *n.* (laborious walk) Stapfen, *das;* (laborious work) Plackerei, *die* (ugs.)

Phrasal verbs

- **~ aˈway** *v.i.* (fig.) sich abmühen; **~ away at sth.** sich mit etw. abmühen
- **~ ˈon** *v.i.* (fig.) sich weiterkämpfen; **~ on with sth.** sich weiter durch etw. kämpfen

plodder /ˈplɒdə(r)/ *n.* (worker) Arbeitstier, *das;* (walker) Fußlahme, *der/die* (ugs.); **he is a ~:** er arbeitet schwerfällig/hat einen schwerfälligen Gang; (Sch.) er ist ein bisschen langsam

plonk¹ /plɒŋk/ *v.t.* (coll.) **~ sth. [down]** etw. hinknallen (ugs.) *od.* hinwerfen; **~ sth. down in a corner** etw. in eine Ecke knallen (ugs.); **~ oneself [down] in an armchair** sich in einen Sessel knallen *od.* hauen (ugs.)

plonk² *n.* (coll.: wine) [billiger] Wein

plop /plɒp/

A *v.i.*, **-pp-** plumpsen (ugs.); ‹*Regen:*› klatschen, platschen

B *v.t.*, **-pp-** plumpsen lassen (ugs.)

C *n.* Plumpsen, *das;* **with a ~:** mit einem Plumps

D *adv.* plumps

plosive /ˈpləʊsɪv/ (Ling.)

A *adj.* plosiv; Verschluss-

B *n.* Plosiv, *der;* Verschlusslaut, *der*

plot /plɒt/

A *n.* **1** (conspiracy) Komplott, *das;* Verschwörung, *die* **2** (of play, film, novel) Handlung, *die;* Fabel, *die;* Plot, *der* (Literaturw.) **3** (of ground) Stück Land; **vegetable ~:** Gemüsebeet, *das;* **building ~:** Baugrundstück, *das;* Bauplatz, *der* **4** (curve etc.) Diagramm, *das* **5** (Amer.: ground plan) Plan, *der*

B *v.t.*, **-tt-** **1** (plan secretly) [heimlich] planen; **~ treason** auf Verrat sinnen (geh.); **~ to do sth.** [heimlich] planen, etw. zu tun **2** (make plan or map of) kartieren, kartographieren ‹*Gebiet usw.*›; einen Plan zeichnen (+ *Gen.*) ‹*Gebäude usw.*›; (make by ~ing) zeichnen ‹*Karte, Plan*›; (fig.) entwerfen ‹*Roman*› **3** (mark on map, diagram) **~ [down]** eintragen; einzeichnen

C *v.i.*, **-tt-:** **~ against sb.** sich gegen jmdn. verschwören; ein Komplott gegen jmdn. schmieden

plotter /ˈplɒtə(r)/ *n.* **1** (conspirator) Verschwörer, *der*/Verschwörerin, *die* **2** (instrument) Plotter, *der;* Planzeichner, *der*

plough /plaʊ/

A *n.* (Agric.) Pflug, *der;* **put one's hand to the ~** (fig.) eine Sache in Angriff nehmen; **the P~** (Astron.) der Große Wagen *od.* Bär

B *v.t.* **1** pflügen; **~ the sand[s]** (fig.) Wasser mit einem Sieb schöpfen **2** (cut furrows in) zerpflügen **3** **~ furrows** Furchen ziehen *od.* pflügen; **~ a lonely furrow** (fig.) allein auf weiter Flur sein *od.* stehen (geh.) **4** (fig.) ‹*Schiff:*› [durch]pflügen ‹*Wasserfläche*› **5** (Brit. coll.: reject in examination) durchrasseln lassen (salopp)

C *v.i.* (Brit. coll.: fail in examination) durchrasseln (salopp)

Phrasal verbs

- **~ ˈback** *v.t.* **1** unterpflügen **2** (Finance) reinvestieren; **~ profits** *etc.* **back into the business** *etc.* Gewinne *usw.* wieder in die Firma *usw.* stecken
- **~ ˈin** *v.t.* unterpflügen
- **~ ˈinto** *v.t.* (move violently) rasen *od.* (salopp) rasseln in (+ *Akk.*)
- **~ ˈthrough** *v.t.* (advance laboriously in) sich kämpfen durch; ‹*Schiff:*› sich pflügen durch; (move violently through) rasen durch
- **~ ˈup** *v.t.* auspflügen ‹*Kartoffeln, Rüben usw.*›; zerpflügen ‹*Boden*›

plough: ~man /ˈplaʊmən/ *n., pl.* **~men** /ˈplaʊmən/ Pflüger, *der;* **~man's [lunch]** (Brit.) *Imbiss aus Käse, Brot und Mixedpickles;* **~share** *n.* Pflugschar, *die*

plover /ˈplʌvə(r)/ *n.* (Ornith.) Regenpfeifer, *der*

plow (Amer./arch.) ▸ **plough A, B 1, 2, 3, 4**

ploy /plɔɪ/ *n.* Trick, *der;* (tactical approach) Taktik, *die;* (gambit) Manöver, *das;* (method) Masche, *die* (ugs.)

PLR *abbr.* (Brit.) = **Public Lending Right**

pluck /plʌk/

A *v.t.* **1** (pull off, pick) pflücken ‹*Blumen, Obst*›; **~ [out]** auszupfen ‹*Federn, Haare*› **2** (pull at, twitch) zupfen an (+ *Dat.*); zupfen ‹*Saite, Gitarre*›; **he ~ed his mother's skirt** er zupfte seine Mutter am Rock **3** (strip of feathers) rupfen

B *v.i.* **~ at sth.** an etw. (*Dat.*) zupfen; **he ~ed at his mother's skirt** er zupfte seine Mutter am Rock

C *n.* **1** (courage) Mut, *der;* Schneid, *der* (ugs.) **2** (heart, liver, lungs of animal as food) Innereien *Pl.*

Phrasal verb

- **~ ˈup** *v.t.* **~ up [one's] courage** all seinen Mut zusammennehmen; **~ up courage to do sth.** den Mut finden, etw. zu tun; **he ~ed up**

[enough] courage to ask her out er fasste sich (*Dat.*) ein Herz und bat sie, mit ihm auszugehen

pluckily /ˈplʌkɪlɪ/ *adv.*, **plucky** /ˈplʌkɪ/ *adj.* tapfer

plug /plʌg/

A *n.* 1 (filling hole) Pfropfen, *der;* (in cask) Spund, *der;* Zapfen, *der;* (stopper for basin, vessel, etc.) Stöpsel, *der;* (of wax etc.) Pfropf, *der* 2 (Electr.) Stecker, *der;* (coll.: socket) Stecker, *der* (ugs.); **pull the ~ on sb./sth.** (coll.) jmdn./einer Sache den Hahn zudrehen (ugs.); *see also* **sparking plug** 3 (coll.: of water closet) Stöpsel, *der;* **pull the ~:** [ab]ziehen 4 (of tobacco) Plug, *der* (fachspr.); (piece of chewing tobacco) Priem, *der* 5 (coll.: piece of good publicity) **give sth. a ~:** Werbung für etw. machen; **give sb. a ~:** jmdm. [etwas] Publicity verschaffen

B *v.t.*, **-gg-** 1 **~ [up]** zustopfen, verstopfen ‹*Loch usw.*› 2 (coll.: advertise) Schleichwerbung machen für; (by presenting sth. repeatedly) pushen (ugs.)

Phrasal verbs

- **~ aˈway** *v.i.* (coll.) vor sich hin schuften (ugs.); **~ away at sth.** sich mit etw. abschuften (ugs.)
- **~ ˈin** *v.t.* anschließen; **is it ~ged in?** ist der Stecker in der Steckdose *od.* (ugs.) drin?; *see also* **plug-in**

plug: ~-and-play (Computing) **A** *adj.* Plug-and-play ‹*Software, Zugang etc.*› **B** *n.* Plug and play, *das;* **~ hat** *n.* (Amer. coll.) Angströhre, *die* (ugs. scherzh.); **~hole** *n.* Abfluss, *der;* **go down the ~hole** (fig. coll.) im Eimer sein (salopp); **~-in** *adj.* anschließbar; **~-in module** Steckmodul, *das;* **~-ˈugly** *adj.* (Amer. coll.) potthässlich (ugs.)

plum /plʌm/ *n.* 1 (tree) Pflaumenbaum, *der;* Pflaume, *die;* (fruit) Pflaume, *die;* **speak with a ~ in one's mouth** (Brit. coll.) affektiert sprechen 2 (fig.) Leckerbissen, *der;* **a ~ job/position** ein Traumjob (ugs.); **his job is a real ~:** sein Job ist einfach traumhaft 3 (colour) Pflaumenblau, *das*

plumage /ˈpluːmɪdʒ/ *n.* Gefieder, *das*

plumb¹ /plʌm/

A *v.t.* (sound, measure) [aus]loten; (fig.) ergründen ‹*Geheimnis*›; **~ the depths of loneliness/sorrow** die tiefsten Tiefen der Einsamkeit/Trauer erleben

B *adv.* 1 (vertically) senkrecht; lotrecht 2 (fig.: exactly) genau 3 (Amer. coll.: utterly) total (ugs.); **you get ~ out of here!** raus hier, aber 'n bisschen plötzlich! (ugs.)

C *adj.* 1 (vertical) senkrecht; lotrecht 2 (fig.: downright, sheer) völlig; absolut

D *n.* Lot, *das;* Senkblei, *das;* **off** *or* **out of ~:** außer *od.* nicht im Lot

plumb² *v.t.* **~ in** (connect) fest anschließen

plumbago /plʌmˈbeɪgəʊ/ *n.*, *pl.* **~s** 1 (Min.) Graphit, *der* 2 (Bot.) Bleiwurz, *die*

plumber /ˈplʌmə(r)/ *n.* Klempner, *der;* Installateur, *der*

plumbing /ˈplʌmɪŋ/ *n.* 1 (plumber's work) Klempnerarbeiten *Pl.;* Installationsarbeiten *Pl.* 2 (water pipes) Wasserrohre *Pl.;* Wasserleitungen *Pl.;* **a cottage without ~:** ein Häuschen ohne Wasseranschluss 3 (coll.: lavatory) Klo, *das* (ugs.); **go and inspect the ~:** die Örtlichkeit aufsuchen

ˈplumb line *n.* 1 (for measuring) Lot, *das* 2 (fig.) Maßstab, *der*

ˈplum cake *n.* Rosinenkuchen, *der*

plume /pluːm/

A *n.* 1 (feather) Feder, *die;* (ornamental bunch) Federbusch, *der;* **~ of white feathers** weißer Federbusch; **borrowed ~s** (fig.) fremde Federn 2 **~ of smoke/steam/snow** Rauchwolke *od.* -fahne/Dampfwolke/Schneefahne, *die*

B *v.t.* mit Federn schmücken; befiedern ‹*Pfeil*›

plummet /ˈplʌmɪt/

A *v.i.* stürzen

B *n.* 1 (weight) Lotblei, *das;* (plumb line) Lot, *das* 2 (sounding lead) Lot, *das;* Senkblei, *das* 3 (Angling) Bleigewicht, *das;* Blei, *das*

plummy /ˈplʌmɪ/ *adj.* 1 (coll.) sonor ‹*Stimme*›; (derog.: affected) affektiert 2 (coll.: desirable, good) bombig (ugs.); Bomben‹*stelle, -job*› (ugs.)

plump¹ /plʌmp/ *adj.* mollig; rundlich; stämmig ‹*Arme, Beine*›; fleischig ‹*Brathuhn usw.*›; **~ cheeks** Pausbacken *Pl.* (fam.); runde *od.* volle Backen

Phrasal verbs

- **~ ˈout**

A *v.i.* sich runden; rund werden

B *v.t.* runden; rund werden lassen

- **~ ˈup**

A *v.t.* aufschütteln ‹*Kissen*›; (fatten up) mästen

B *v.i.* Fett ansetzen

plump²

A *v.t.* **~ sb./oneself/sth. down** jmdn./sich/etw. fallen lassen; **he ~ed the cases in the hall** er setzte die Koffer schwungvoll in der Halle ab

B *v.i.* 1 (drop) fallen 2 (Amer.: move abruptly) stürmen; stürzen

Phrasal verb

- **~ for** *v.t.* 1 (Brit.: vote for) stimmen für 2 (choose) sich entscheiden für

plumpness /ˈplʌmpnɪs/ *n.*, *no pl.* ▸ **plump¹**: Molligkeit, *die;* Rundlichkeit, *die;* Stämmigkeit, *die;* Fleischigkeit, *die*

plum: ~ ˈpudding *n.* Plumpudding, *der;* (*suet pudding*) *mit Nierenfett zubereiteter Pudding mit Rosinen;* ≈ Rosinenpudding, *der;* **~ tree** *n.* Pflaumenbaum, *der*

plunder /ˈplʌndə(r)/

A *v.t.* [aus]plündern ‹*Gebäude, Gebiet*›; ausplündern ‹*Person*›; rauben ‹*Sache*›; **the church was ~ed of its holy relics** die heiligen Reliquien wurden aus der Kirche geraubt

B *n.* 1 (action) Plünderung, *die;* (spoil, booty) Beute, *die* 2 (coll.: profit) Profit, *der*

plunderer /ˈplʌndərə(r)/ *n.* Plünd[e]rer, *der*

plunge /plʌndʒ/

A *v.t.* 1 (thrust violently) stecken; (into liquid) tauchen; **~ a knife into sb.'s back** jmdm. ein Messer in den Rücken stoßen 2 (fig.) **~d in thought** in Gedanken versunken; **be ~d into sth.** in etw. (*Akk.*) gestürzt werden; **~ oneself into sth.** sich in etw. (*Akk.*) stürzen; **be ~d into darkness** in Dunkelheit getaucht sein (geh.)

B *v.i.* 1 **~ into sth.** (lit. or fig.) in etw. (*Akk.*) stürzen; **he ~d into the crowd** er tauchte in die Menge ein; **~ in** sich hineinstürzen; **they ~d into a political discussion** sie stürzten sich in eine politische Diskussion 2 (descend suddenly) ‹*Straße usw.*:› steil abfallen; **plunging neckline** tiefer Ausschnitt; [tiefes] Dekolleté; **~ down the stairs** die Treppe hinunterstürzen 3 (enter impetuously) stürzen 4 (start violently forward) ‹*Pferd:*› durchgehen; (pitch) ‹*Schiff:*› eintauchen 5 (coll.: gamble) spielen

C *n.* Sprung, *der;* **take the ~** (fig. coll.) den Sprung wagen; **they have decided to take the ~ and do it** sie haben sich dazu durchgerungen, es zu tun

plunger /ˈplʌndʒə(r)/ *n.* 1 (part of mechanism) [Tauch]kolben, *der;* Plunger[kolben], *der* 2 (rubber suction cup) Stampfer, *der*

plunk /plʌŋk/ ▸ **plonk¹**

pluperfect /pluːˈpɜːfɪkt/ (Ling.)

A *n.* Plusquamperfekt, *das*

B *adj.* **~ tense** Plusquamperfekt, *das*

plural /ˈplʊərl/ (Ling.)

A *adj.* pluralisch; Plural-; **~ noun** Substantiv im Plural; **~ form** Pluralform, *die;* **third person ~:** dritte Person Plural

B *n.* Mehrzahl, *die;* Plural, *der*

pluralise ▸ **pluralize**

pluralism /ˈplʊərəlɪzm/ *n.* 1 (holding of more than one office) Ämterhäufung, *die* 2 (Polit., Sociol.) Pluralismus, *der*

pluralist /ˈplʊərəlɪst/ *n.* 1 (holder of more than one office) Inhaber mehrerer [Kirchen]ämter 2 (Polit., Sociol.) Pluralist, *der*

pluralistic /plʊərəˈlɪstɪk/ *adj.* pluralistisch

plurality /plʊəˈrælɪtɪ/ *n.* 1 (being plural) Pluralität, *die* 2 (large number) Vielzahl, *die* 3 (majority) Majorität, *die;* Mehrheit, *die;* **~ of sth.** Mehrheit einer Sache (*Gen.*) 4 (Amer. Polit.) [Stimmen]vorsprung, *der* (**over** vor + *Dat.*)

pluralize /ˈplʊərəlaɪz/ *v.t.* pluralisieren (Sprachw.); in den Plural setzen

plural: ~ ˈnumber ▸ **plural B**; **~ soˈciety** *n.* plurale Gesellschaft; **~ ˈvote** *n.* Mehrstimmenrecht, *das;* **~ ˈvoting** *n.* Pluralwahlrecht, *das*

plus /plʌs/

A *prep.* 1 (with the addition of) plus (+ *Dat.*); (and also) und [zusätzlich] 2 (above zero) plus; **~ ten degrees** plus zehn Grad; zehn Grad plus 3 (coll.); **he returned from America ~ a wife and child** er kam aus Amerika zurück — mit Frau und Kind; **a ~ one** *etc.* **player** (Golf) ein Spieler mit einer Vorgabe von eins *usw.*

B *adj.* 1 (additional, extra) zusätzlich 2 (at least) **fifteen** *etc.* **~:** über fünfzehn *usw.;* **alpha** *etc.* **~:** Eins *usw.* plus 3 (Math.: positive) positiv ‹*Wert, Menge, Größe*› 4 (Electr.) **~ pole/terminal** Pluspol, *der*

C *n.* 1 (symbol) **~ [sign]** Plus[zeichen], *das* 2 (additional quantity) Plus, *das* 3 (advantage) Pluspunkt, *der*

D *conj.* (coll.) und außerdem

plus-ˈfours *n. pl.* Überfallhose, *die*

plush /plʌʃ/

A *n.* Plüsch, *der*

B *adj.* 1 (made of plush) Plüsch-; plüschen 2 (covered in plush) mit Plüsch bezogen 3 (coll.: luxurious) feudal (ugs.)

plushy /ˈplʌʃɪ/ *adj.* 1 (of, like plush) plüschig 2 ▸ **plush B 3**

ˈplus-size *adj.* (Amer.) ‹*Kleidungsstück*› in großer Größe, in Übergröße; stark ‹*Frau*›

Pluto /ˈpluːtəʊ/ *pr. n.* 1 (Astron.) Pluto, *der* 2 (Roman Mythol.) Pluto (*der*)

plutocracy /pluːˈtɒkrəsɪ/ *n.* 1 (rule by the rich; state) Plutokratie, *die* 2 (rich ruling class) Plutokraten *Pl.*

plutocrat /ˈpluːtəkræt/ *n.* Plutokrat, *der*

plutocratic /pluːtəˈkrætɪk/ *adj.* plutokratisch

plutonic /pluːˈtɒnɪk/ *adj.* (Geol.) plutonisch; **~ theory** Plutonismus, *der*

plutonium /pluːˈtəʊnɪəm/ *n.* (Chem.) Plutonium, *das*

pluvial /ˈpluːvɪəl/ *adj.* Regen-

ply¹ /plaɪ/

A *v.t.* 1 (use, wield) gebrauchen; führen; **they plied their oars** sie legten sich in die Ruder 2 (work at) nachgehen (+ *Dat.*) ‹*Handwerk, Arbeit*› 3 (sell) verkaufen 4 (supply) **~ sb. with sth.** jmdn. mit etw. versorgen 5 (assail) überhäufen; **~ sb. with questions** jmdn. mit Fragen überschütten 6 (sail over) befahren

B *v.i.* 1 (go to and fro) **~ between** zwischen ‹*Orten*› [hin- und her]pendeln; (operate on regular services) zwischen ‹*Orten*› verkehren 2 (attend regularly for custom) seine Dienste anbieten; **~ for customers** auf Kunden *od.* Kundschaft warten; **a taxi ~ing for hire** ein auf Kundschaft wartendes Taxi

ply² *n.* 1 (of yarn, wool, etc.) [Einzel]faden, *der;* (of rope, cord, etc.) Strang, *der;* (of plywood, cloth, etc.) Lage, *die;* Schicht, *die; see also* **three-ply**; **two-ply** 2 ▸ **plywood**

ˈplywood *n.* Sperrholz, *das*

p.m. /piːˈem/ ▸ ℹ **p. 1001**

A *adv.* nachmittags; **one ~:** ein Uhr mittags; **two/five ~:** zwei/fünf Uhr nachmittags; **six/eleven ~:** sechs/elf Uhr abends

B *n.* Nachmittag, *der;* **Monday/this ~:** Montag/heute Nachmittag

PM *abbr.* 1 **= post-mortem** 2 **= Prime Minister**

PMT *abbr.* **= premenstrual tension** PMS

pneumatic /njuːˈmætɪk/ *adj.* pneumatisch; mit Druckluft betrieben *od.* arbeitend ‹*Maschine*›; Druckluft‹*werkzeug, -hammer*›

pneumatically /njuːˈmætɪkəlɪ/ *adv.* pneumatisch; mit Druckluft *nachgestellt*

pneumatic: ~ ˈblonde *n.* (joc.) üppige Blondine; **~ ˈdrill** *n.* Pressluftbohrer, *der;* **~ ˈtyre** *n.* Luftreifen, *der;* Pneumatik, *der*

pneumoconiosis /njuːməʊkɒnɪˈəʊsɪs/ *n.*, *no pl.* ▸ ℹ **p. 1231** (Med.) Pneumokoniose, *die* (fachspr.); Staublunge, *die*

pneumonia /njuːˈməʊnɪə/ *n.* ▸ ℹ **p. 1231** (Med.) Lungenentzündung, *die;* Pneumonie, *die* (Med.); **double/single ~:** doppelseitige/einseitige Lungenentzündung

po /pəʊ/ *n.*, *pl.* **pos** (coll.) [Nacht]topf, *der;* Pott, *der* (ugs., bes. nordd.)

PO *abbr.* 1 **= postal order** PA 2 **= Post Office** PA 3 (Brit. Navy) **= Petty Officer**

P

4 (Brit. Air Force) = **Pilot Officer** LT

poach[1] /ˈpəʊtʃ/

A *v.t.* **1** (catch illegally) wildern; illegal fangen ‹*Fische*›; ~ **pupils away from other teachers** anderen Lehrern die Schüler abspenstig machen **2** (obtain unfairly) stehlen, (ugs.) klauen ‹*Idee*›; sich (*Dat.*) erschleichen ‹*Vorteil*›

B *v.i.* **1** (catch animals illegally) wildern **2** (encroach) ~ **[on sb.'s territory]** jmdm. ins Handwerk pfuschen; (Sport) dazwischengehen

poach[2] *v.t.* (Cookery) pochieren ‹*Ei*›; dünsten, pochieren ‹*Fisch, Fleisch, Gemüse*›; **~ed eggs** pochierte *od.* verlorene Eier

poacher[1] /ˈpəʊtʃə(r)/ *n.* Wilderer, *der;* Wilddieb, *der;* **the ~ turns gamekeeper** aus einem Saulus wird ein Paulus

poacher[2] *n.* (Cookery) Dünster, *der;* **[egg] ~:** Eierkocher für pochierte Eier

PO box ▸ **post office box**

pochard /ˈpəʊtʃəd/ *n.* (Ornith.) Tafelente, *die*

pock /pɒk/ *n.* Pickel, *der;* Pustel, *die* (Med.); (of smallpox) Pocke, *die*

pocked /pɒkt/ *adj.* durchlöchert (**with** von)

pocket /ˈpɒkɪt/

A *n.* **1** Tasche, *die;* (in suitcase etc.) Seitentasche, *die;* (in handbag) [Seiten]fach, *das;* (on rucksack etc.) [Außen]tasche, *die;* (Billiards etc.) Loch, *das;* Tasche, *die;* **be in sb.'s ~** (fig.) von jmdm. abhängig sein; **the business is virtually in his ~:** in der Firma ist er praktisch der Boss (ugs.); **have [got] sb. in one's ~:** jmdn. in der Tasche haben (ugs.); **make a hole in sb.'s ~** (fig.) ein Loch in jmds. Geldbeutel (*Akk.*) reißen **2** (fig.: financial resources) **with an empty ~, with empty ~s** mit leeren Taschen; **pay for sth. out of one's own ~:** etw. aus eigener *od.* der eigenen Tasche bezahlen; **it is beyond my ~:** es übersteigt meine finanziellen Möglichkeiten; **put one's hand in one's ~:** in die Tasche greifen (ugs.); **be in ~:** Geld verdient haben; **be £100 in ~:** 100 Pfund gutgemacht haben; **be out of ~** (have lost money) draufgelegt haben (ugs.); zugesetzt haben; **I don't want you to be out of ~ because of me** ich möchte nicht, dass du meinetwegen drauflegst (ugs.) *od.* zusetzt; *see also* **out-of-pocket 3** (Mil.) (area) Kessel, *der;* **enemy ~:** [versprengte] feindliche Einheit; **~ of resistance** Widerstandsnest, *das* **4** (isolated group) ≈ Schwerpunkt, *der;* **~ of unemployment** schwerpunktmäßiges Auftreten von Arbeitslosigkeit **5** (Mining, Geol.) Nest, *das. See also* **line**[2]

B *adj.* Taschen‹*rechner, -uhr, -ausgabe*›

C *v.t.* **1** (put in one's pocket) einstecken **2** (steal) in die eigene Tasche stecken (ugs.) **3** (fig.: submit to) wegstecken; einstecken **4** (fig.: conceal) verbergen, hinunterschlucken (ugs.) ‹*Zorn, Gefühlsregung*› **5** (Billiards etc.) einlochen

ˈ**pocketbook** *n.* **1** (wallet) Brieftasche, *die* **2** (notebook) Notizbuch, *das* **3** (Amer.: paperback) Taschenbuch, *das;* **in ~:** als Taschenbuch **4** (Amer.: handbag) Handtasche, *die*

pocketful /ˈpɒkɪtfʊl/ *n.* **a ~ of loose change** eine Tasche voll Kleingeld

pocket: ~ ˈhandkerchief *n.* **1** Taschentuch, *das;* **2** (fig.: very small area) **a ~ handkerchief of a garden** ein winziger Garten; **~ knife** *n.* Taschenmesser, *das;* **~ money** *n.* Taschengeld, *das;* **~-size[d]** *adj.* **1** im Taschenformat *nachgestellt;* **~-sized edition** Taschenausgabe, *die;* **2** (fig.: small scale) Westentaschen- (ugs. scherzh.); im [Westen]taschenformat *nachgestellt* (ugs. scherzh.); **~ ˈveto** *n.* (Amer. Polit.) *durch Nichtunterzeichnung einer Gesetzesvorlage ausgeübtes Veto*

pock: ~mark *n.* **1** (Med.) Pockennarbe, *die;* **2** Delle, *die;* (from bullet) Einschuss, *der;* **~marked** *adj.* **1** pockennarbig ‹*Gesicht, Haut*›; **2 a wall ~marked with bullets** eine mit Einschüssen übersäte Wand

pod /pɒd/

A *n.* **1** (seed case) Hülse, *die;* (of pea) Schote, *die;* Hülse, *die* **2** (in aircraft etc.) (for engine) Gondel, *die;* (for fuel) Außentank, *der;* (for missile etc.) Behälter, *der;* Pod, *der;* (radome) Radom, *das*

B *v.t.*, **-dd-** aus- *od.* enthülsen

C *v.i.*, **-dd-** (form pods) [Früchte] ansetzen; (bear pods) [Früchte] tragen

podge /pɒdʒ/ *n.* (coll.) Pummel, *der* (ugs.)

podgy /ˈpɒdʒɪ/ *adj.* dicklich; pummelig (ugs.), rundlich (fam.), mollig ‹*Frau*›; pausbäckig, (fam.) rundlich ‹*Gesicht*›; **~ cheek** Pausbacke, *die* (fam.); **~ fingers** Wurstfinger (ugs.)

podium /ˈpəʊdɪəm/ *n.*, *pl.* **podia** /ˈpəʊdɪə/ *or* **-s** Podium, *das*

podzol /ˈpɒdzɒl/ *n.* (Soil Sci.) Podsol, *der*

poem /ˈpəʊɪm/ *n.* Gedicht, *das;* **symphonic ~** (Mus.) sinfonische Dichtung

poesy /ˈpəʊɪsɪ, ˈpəʊɪzɪ/ *n.* (arch./poet.) (poetry) Poesie, *die;* (art) Dichtkunst, *die;* (poems collectively) Dichtung, *die*

poet /ˈpəʊɪt/ *n.* ▸ℹ **p. 1260** (writer of poems) Dichter, *der;* Poet, *der* (geh.); (sb. with great creativity) Künstler, *der;* **P~s' Corner** die Dichterecke *od.* der Dichterwinkel (in der Westminsterabtei); *see also* **laureate**

poetaster /pəʊɪˈtæstə(r)/ *n.* (dated derog.) Dichterling, *der* (abwertend); Poetaster, *der* (geh. abwertend)

poetess /ˈpəʊɪtes/ *n.* ▸ℹ **p. 1260** Dichterin, *die;* Poetin, *die* (geh.)

poetic /pəʊˈetɪk/ *adj.* dichterisch; poetisch (geh.); anmutig ‹*Bewegung*›; ‹*Bild, Anblick*› voller Poesie; **in ~ form** in Versen; *see also* **justice 1**; **licence A 4**

poetical /pəʊˈetɪkl/ *adj.* **1** ▸ **poetic 2** (written in verse) in Gedichtform *nachgestellt;* **~ drama** Versdrama, *das;* **his ~ works** seine Gedichte

poetically /pəʊˈetɪkəlɪ/ *adv.* dichterisch; poetisch (geh.)

Poet Laureate

In Großbritannien der Titel für den offiziell erwählten Hofdichter, dessen Amt mit bestimmten Verpflichtungen verbunden ist. Als solcher verfasst er Gedichte zu feierlichen Anlässen, wie königlichen Hochzeiten, Geburten und Beerdigungen. 1616 wurde Ben Jonson (1572-1637) als erster *Poet Laureate* ernannt. Andere Hofdichter waren: Dryden (1631-1700), Wordsworth (1770-1850), Tennyson (1809-92) und in letzter Zeit Day-Lewis (1904-72), Betjeman (1906-84) und Ted Hughes (1930-98). Seit 1999 hat Andrew Motion das Amt inne. In den Vereinigten Staaten werden *Poets Laureate* seit 1986 auf eine Dauer von zwei Jahren ernannt. Robert Penn Warren (1905-89) war der erste amerikanische *Poet Laureate*.

poetry /ˈpəʊɪtrɪ/ *n.* [Vers]dichtung, *die;* Lyrik, *die;* (fig.) Poesie, *die* (geh.); **prose ~:** Prosadichtung, *die;* **~ reading** ≈ Dichterlesung, *die*

ˈ**po-faced** /ˈpəʊfeɪst/ *adj.* mit unbewegter Miene *nachgestellt;* (smug, priggish) blasiert (abwertend); (narrow-minded) borniert; **sound ~:** abweisend klingen

pogo /ˈpəʊgəʊ/ *n.*, *pl.* **~s 1 ~ [stick]** Springstab, *der* **2** (dance) Pogo, *der*

pogrom /ˈpɒgrəm/ *n.* Pogrom, *das od. der*

poignancy /ˈpɔɪnjənsɪ/ *n.*, *no pl.* [schmerzliche] Intensität; (of words, wit, etc.) Schärfe, *die*

poignant /ˈpɔɪnjənt/ *adj.* tief ‹*Bedauern, Trauer, Schmerz, Verzweiflung*›; überwältigend ‹*Schönheit*›; quälend ‹*Hunger*›; (causing sympathy) ergreifend, herzzerreißend ‹*Anblick, Geschichte*›

poignantly /ˈpɔɪnjəntlɪ/ *adv.* (touchingly) ergreifend; in bewegenden Worten ‹*sprechen, schreiben*›; (regretfully) wehmütig; (pungently) beißend

poinsettia /pɔɪnˈsetɪə/ *n.* (Bot.) Weihnachtsstern, *der*

point /pɔɪnt/

A *n.* **1** (tiny mark, dot) Punkt, *der;* **nought ~ two** null Komma zwei; *see also* **decimal point**; **full point**

2 (sharp end of tool, weapon, pencil, etc.) Spitze, *die;* **come to a [sharp] ~:** spitz zulaufen; **at gun~/knife~:** mit vorgehaltener [Schuss]waffe/vorgehaltenem Messer; **hold sb. at gun~/knife~:** jmdn. mit vorgehaltener Pistole/vorgehaltenem Messer bedrohen; **not to put too fine a ~ on it** (fig.) um nichts zu beschönigen

3 (single item) Punkt, *der;* **the ~ under dispute** der strittige Punkt; die strittige Frage; **~ of conscience** Gewissensfrage, *die;* **agree on a ~:** in einem Punkt *od.* einer Frage übereinstimmen; **Are you an experienced cook? — No, in ~ of fact I've never cooked a meal before** Sind Sie ein erfahrener Koch? — Nein, ganz im Gegenteil. Ich habe [bisher] noch nie gekocht; **You haven't met him, have you? — Yes, in ~ of fact, I have** Du kennst ihn nicht, oder? — Doch, wir kennen uns; **be a ~ of honour with sb.** für jmdn. [eine] Ehrensache sein; **possession is nine ~s of the law** das Gesetz ist meistens auf der Seite des Besitzers; *see also* **law 1**; **order A 10**; **stretch A 4**

4 (unit of scoring) Punkt, *der;* **win by 100 ~s** mit 100 Punkten Vorsprung gewinnen; **give ~s to sb.** jmdm. eine Vorgabe geben; **score ~s off sb.** (fig.) jmdn. an die Wand spielen; **win on ~s** (Boxing; also fig.) nach Punkten gewinnen; **a win on ~s** ein Sieg nach Punkten; ein Punktsieg

5 (stage, degree) **things have reached a ~ where** *or* **come to such a ~ that …:** die Sache ist dahin *od.* so weit gediehen, dass …; (negatively) es ist so weit gekommen, dass …; **the shares reached their highest ~:** die Aktien erreichten ihren höchsten Stand *od.* Höchststand; **up to a ~:** bis zu einem gewissen Grad; **beyond a certain ~:** über einen bestimmten Punkt hinaus; **he gave up at this ~:** an diesem Punkt gab er auf; **she was abrupt to the ~ of rudeness** sie war in einer Weise barsch, die schon an Unverschämtheit grenzte; *see also* **boiling point**; **freezing point**; **melting point**

6 (moment) Zeitpunkt, *der;* **when it comes/came to the ~:** wenn es so weit ist/als es so weit war; wenn es ernst wird/als es ernst wurde; **be at/on the ~ of sth.** kurz vor etw. (*Dat.*) sein; einer Sache (*Dat.*) nahe sein; **be at the ~ of death** im Sterben liegen; **be on the ~ of doing sth.** im Begriff sein, etw. zu tun; etw. gerade tun wollen

7 (distinctive trait) Seite, *die;* (feature in animal) [Rassen]merkmal, *das;* **best/strong ~:** starke Seite; Stärke, *die;* **good/bad ~:** gute/schlechte Seite; **getting up early has its ~s** frühes Aufstehen hat auch seine Vorzüge; **the ~** (essential thing) das Entscheidende; **the ~ is, what am I to do if I can't get a job?** fragt sich nur: was mache ich, wenn ich keinen Job finde?; (thing to be discussed) **that is just the ~** *or* **the whole ~:** das ist genau der springende Punkt; **come to** *or* **get to the ~:** zur Sache *od.* zum Thema kommen; **keep** *or* **stick to the ~:** beim Thema bleiben; **keep sb. to the ~:** verhindern, dass jmd. [vom Thema] abschweift; **be beside the ~:** unerheblich sein; keine Rolle spielen; **that's beside the ~:** darum geht es nicht; **~ taken** habe verstanden; **carry** *or* **make one's ~:** sich durchsetzen; sein Ziel erreichen; **right, I agree with you, you've made your ~:** also gut, ich gebe dir Recht, ich habe verstanden; **in ~:** relevant (geh.); **not in ~:** irrelevant (geh.); **a case in ~:** ein typisches Beispiel; **that's not in ~:** das gehört nicht zur Sache *od.* hierher; **make a ~ of doing sth.** [großen] Wert darauf legen, etw. zu tun; **… and I shall make a ~ of telling him so** … und ich werde ihm das jetzt auch mal sagen; **make a ~ of it** Wert darauf legen; **make** *or* **prove a ~:** etw. beweisen; **make** *or* **prove a ~ against sth.** ein Argument gegen etw. anführen *od.* (geh.) ins Feld führen; **be always making** *or* **proving a ~ of some kind** ständig etwas beweisen wollen; **to the ~:** sachbezogen; **more to the ~:** wichtiger; **a topic that is not strictly to the ~:** ein Punkt, der nicht direkt zum Thema gehört; **he was very brief and to the ~:** seine Ausführungen waren sehr knapp und sachbezogen; **you have a ~ there** da hast du Recht; da ist [et]was dran (ugs.); *see also* **take A 20**

8 (tip) Spitze, *die;* (Boxing) Kinnspitze, *die;* Kinn, *das;* (Ballet) Spitze, *die;* *in pl.* (of horse, dog, etc.) (extremities) Extremitäten *Pl.;* (area of contrasting colour in an animal's fur) Abzeichen *Pl.;* **the ~ of his jaw** seine Kinnspitze; **the ~s of his ears** seine Ohrläppchen; **dance on the ~s of one's toes** auf den Zehen- *od.* Fußspitzen tanzen; **on ~, on one's ~s, on the ~s** (Ballet) auf Spitzen; **a ~ [of land]** eine Landspitze *od.* -zunge

9 (of story, joke, remark) Pointe, *die;* (pungency, effect) (of literary work) Eindringlichkeit, *die;* (of remark) Durchschlagskraft, *die;* Überzeugungskraft, *die;* **see** *or* **get/miss the ~:** die Pointe verstehen/nicht verstehen; **miss the ~ of a joke** die Pointe eines Witzes nicht verstehen *od.* (ugs.) mitkriegen
10 (purpose, value) Zweck, *der;* Sinn, *der;* **what's the ~ of worrying?** was für einen Sinn *od.* Zweck hat es, sich (*Dat.*) Sorgen zu machen?; wozu sich (*Dat.*) Sorgen machen? (ugs.); **there's no ~ in protesting** es hat keinen Sinn *od.* Zweck zu protestieren; es ist sinnlos *od.* zwecklos zu protestieren
11 (precise place, spot) Punkt, *der;* Stelle, *die;* (Geom.) Punkt, *der;* **fire broke out at several ~s** an mehreren Punkten *od.* Stellen brach Feuer aus; **Bombay and ~s east** Bombay und Orte östlich davon; **~ of contact** Berührungspunkt, *der;* **~ of no return** Punkt, an dem es kein Zurück mehr gibt; **~ of view** (fig.) Standpunkt, *der;* **from my/a money/an atheistic ~ of view** (fig.) aus meiner/finanzieller/atheistischer Sicht; von meinem/von einem finanziellen/atheistischen Standpunkt aus; *see also* **departure 4**
12 (Brit.) **[power** *or* **electric] ~:** Steckdose, *die*
13 (Brit. Railw.) *usu in pl.* Weiche, *die*
14 (sharp-pointed tool) spitzes Werkzeug; (in engraving, etching, etc.) Grabstichel, *der;* (in masonry) Grabmeißel, *der;* Punktiereisen, *das*
15 (of deer) Ende, *das* (Jägerspr.); Sprosse, *die* (Jägerspr.)
16 *usu in pl.* (Motor Veh.: contact device) Kontakt, *der;* **contact breaker ~:** Unterbrecherkontakt, *der*
17 (unit in Bridge, competition, rationing, stocks, shares, etc.) Punkt, *der;* (unit of weight for precious stones) ein Hundertstel Karat; 0,01 Karat; **prices/the cost of living went up three ~s** die Preise/Lebenshaltungskosten sind um drei [Prozent]punkte gestiegen
18 (on compass) Strich, *der; see also* **cardinal points**
19 (Printing) Punkt, *der;* **eight-~:** Achtpunkt, *der*
20 (Cricket) *Feldspieler, der einige Meter seitlich vom Torwächter steht;* (Lacrosse) *dem Torwart am nächsten stehender Verteidiger*

B *v.i.* 1 zeigen, weisen, ‹*Person auch:*› deuten (**to, at** auf + *Akk.*); **it's rude to ~:** es gehört sich nicht, mit dem Finger auf jemanden zu zeigen; **she ~ed through the window** sie zeigte aus dem Fenster; **the compass needle ~ed to the north** die Kompassnadel zeigte *od.* wies nach Norden
2 **~ towards** *or* **to** (fig.) [hin]deuten *od.* hinweisen auf (+ *Akk.*)

C *v.t.* 1 (direct) richten ‹*Waffe, Kamera*› (**at** auf + *Akk.*); **~ one's finger at sth./sb.** mit dem Finger auf etw./jmdn. deuten *od.* zeigen *od.* weisen; **~ me in the right direction** zeige mir den richtigen Weg
2 (Building) aus-, verfugen ‹*Mauer, Steine*›; ausfüllen ‹*Fugen*›
3 (give force to) Nachdruck verleihen (+ *Dat.*), unterstreichen ‹*Bemerkung*›; würzen ‹*Erzählung, Rede*›; verstärken ‹*Gefühl*›
4 (sharpen) [an]spitzen ‹*Bleistift*›
5 (show presence of) ‹*Hund:*› vorstehen (Jägerspr.)
6 (punctuate) mit Satzzeichen versehen; mit Deklamationszeichen versehen ‹*Psalm usw.*›; (in Hebrew etc.) mit diakritischen Zeichen versehen

Phrasal verbs

- **~ 'out** *v.t.* hinweisen auf (+ *Akk.*); **~ sth./sb. out to sb.** jmdn. auf etw./jmdn. hinweisen *od.* aufmerksam machen; **I ~ed him out to the others** ich zeigte ihn den anderen; **he ~ed out the house** er zeigte das Haus; **he ~ed out my mistake** er zeigte meinen Fehler auf
- **~ 'up** *v.t.* (emphasize) herausstellen; (make clear) verdeutlichen

point-and-'click *adj.* (Computing) Point-and-click‹*-Benutzeroberfläche, -Software*›; **~ access** Zugriff per Mausklick

point-'blank
A *adj.* (direct, flat) direkt; (fig.) direkt ‹*Frage, Art*›; glatt ‹*Weigerung*›; **~ shot** Schuss aus kürzester Entfernung; Kern- *od.* Fleckschuss, *der* (Jägerspr.); **~ distance** *or* **range** kürzeste Entfernung; Kernschussweite, *die* (Jägerspr.); **give a ~ denial** alles leugnen
B *adv.* 1 (at very close range) aus kürzester Entfernung ‹*schießen*› 2 (in direct line) direkt; (fig.: directly) rundheraus, (ugs.) geradeheraus ‹*fragen, sagen*›; **tell sb. ~ that ...:** jmdm. direkt ins Gesicht *od.* unverblümt *od.* (ugs.) geradeheraus sagen, dass ...

'point-by-point *adj.* Punkt für Punkt *nachgestellt*

'point duty *n.* (Brit.) *Einsatz zur Verkehrsregelung;* **policeman on ~:** Verkehrspolizist, *der*

pointed /'pɔɪntɪd/ *adj.* 1 spitz; **~ arch** Spitzbogen, *der* 2 (fig.: sharply expressed) unmissverständlich; deutlich 3 (emphasized) ostentativ (geh.); betont ‹*Interesse, Aufmerksamkeit*›

pointedly /'pɔɪntɪdlɪ/ *adv.* (explicitly, significantly) demonstrativ; ostentativ (geh.)

pointer /'pɔɪntə(r)/ *n.* 1 (indicator) Zeiger, *der;* (rod) Zeigestock, *der* 2 **~ [dog]** Pointer, *der;* englischer Vorstehhund 3 (coll.) (hint) Fingerzeig, *der;* Tipp, *der* (ugs.); (indication) Hinweis, *der* (**to** auf + *Akk.*) 4 *in pl.* (*Astron.*) (*in Great Bear*) *die vorderen Kastensterne* (*des Großen Wagens*); (*in Southern Cross*) *die beiden die Längsachse des Kreuzes markierenden Sterne* (*im Kreuz des Südens*)

pointillism /'pwæntɪlɪzm/ *n., no pl.* (Art) Pointillismus, *der*

pointing /'pɔɪntɪŋ/ *n.* (of brickwork) Fugung, *die;* (action) Ausfugen, *das;* Verfugen, *das;* (material) [Fugen]mörtel, *der*

pointless /'pɔɪntlɪs/ *adj.* (without purpose or meaning, useless) sinnlos; (without force, meaningless) belanglos ‹*Bemerkung, Geschichte*›

pointlessly /'pɔɪntlɪslɪ/ *adv.* sinnlos; unnötig ‹*sich Sorgen machen*›; unmotiviert ‹*lachen*›; ohne Zweck und Ziel ‹*herumlungern*›

point: ~ of 'sale *n.* Verkaufsstelle *die;* **~-of-sale** *adj.* an der Verkaufsstelle *nachgestellt;* POS-; **~-of-sale advertising** POS-Werbung, *die;* **~-of-sale terminal** Kassenterminal, *das;* POS-Terminal, *das* (fachspr.); **~-to-'point [race]** *n.* (Horseracing) Kirchturmrennen, *das*

'pointy-headed *n. adj.* (coll.) abgehoben; intellektuell

poise /pɔɪz/
A *n.* 1 (composure) Haltung, *die;* (self-confidence) Selbstsicherheit, *die;* Selbstvertrauen, *das;* **have ~:** beherrscht sein/selbstsicher sein; **keep one's ~:** Haltung/Selbstsicherheit behalten; **lose one's ~:** die Haltung *od.* Beherrschung *od.* Fassung/sein Selbstvertrauen verlieren 2 (good carriage) Haltung, *die;* (of body) Körperhaltung, *die*
B *v.t.* 1 *in p.p.* (in readiness) **sit ~d on the edge of one's chair** auf der Stuhlkante balancieren; **be ~d for action** einsatzbereit sein; **hang ~d** ‹*Vogel, Insekt:*› schweben; *see also* **poised** 2 (balance) balancieren 3 (hold suspended, carry in a particular way) **~ the spear ready to hurl it** den Speer wurfbereit in der Hand halten; **~ oneself on one's toes** auf den Zehen stehen

poised /pɔɪzd/ *adj.* selbstsicher; *see also* **poise B 1**

poison /'pɔɪzn/
A *n.* (harmful substance; lit. or fig.) Gift, *das;* **slow ~:** langsam wirkendes Gift; **hate sb./sth. like ~:** jmdn./etw. wie die Pest hassen; **what's your ~?** (coll.) was trinkst du?
B *v.t.* 1 vergiften; (cause disease in) infizieren; (contaminate) verseuchen ‹*Boden, Luft, Wasser*›; verpesten (abwertend) ‹*Luft*›; (smear with poison) vergiften ‹*Pfeil*›; **die of ~ing** an einer Vergiftung sterben; **~ed hand** infizierte Hand; **~ed arrow** Giftpfeil, *der* 2 (fig.) (corrupt) vergiften ‹*Gedanken, Seele*›; (injure, destroy) zerstören, ruinieren ‹*Ehe, Leben*›; vergällen ‹*Freude*›; verderben ‹*Speisen, Feldfrüchte usw.*›; **~ sb.'s mind** jmdn. verderben *od.* (geh.) korrumpieren; **she ~ed his mind** *or* **caused his thoughts to be ~ed against me** sie hat ihn gegen mich aufgebracht

poisoner /'pɔɪzənə(r)/ *n.* Giftmörder, *der*/Giftmörderin, *die*

poison 'gas *n.* Giftgas, *das*

poisoning /'pɔɪzənɪŋ/ *n.* Vergiftung, *die;* (contamination) Verseuchung, *die*

poison 'ivy *n.* Giftefeu, *der;* Kletternder Giftsumach (Bot.)

poisonous /'pɔɪzənəs/ *adj.* 1 giftig; tödlich ‹*Dosis*›; **~ snake/mushroom/substance** Giftschlange, *die*/-pilz, *der*/-stoff, *der* 2 (fig.) verderblich ‹*Lehre, Wirkung*›; giftig ‹*Blick, Zunge*›

poke[1] /pəʊk/ *n.* (dial.: bag) Beutel, *der;* Sack, *der; see also* **pig A 1**

poke[2]
A *v.t.* 1 **~ sth. [with sth.]** [mit etw.] gegen etw. stoßen; **she ~d the hedgehog to see if it was dead** sie stieß den Igel an, um zu sehen, ob er tot war; **~ sth. into sth.** etw. in etw. (*Akk.*) stoßen; **~ one's finger up one's nose** den Finger in die Nase stecken; **~ the fire** das Feuer schüren; **he accidentally ~d me in the eye** er stieß mir versehentlich ins Auge; **~ sb. in the ribs** jmdm. einen Rippenstoß geben *od.* versetzen; *see also* **fun A 2** (thrust forward) stecken ‹*Kopf*›; **~ one's head in through the window** den Kopf zum Fenster hin-/hereinstecken; **~ one's head round the corner/door** um die Ecke gucken (ugs.)/den Kopf in die Türöffnung stecken; **~ one's head in** reingucken (ugs.); **~ one's finger at sb.** mit dem Finger nach jmdm. stoßen 3 (pierce) bohren 4 (coarse: have sexual intercourse with) stoßen (derb)
B *v.i.* 1 (in pond, at food, among rubbish) [herum]stochern (**at, in, among** in + *Dat.*); **~ at sth. with a stick** *etc.* mit einem Stock *usw.* nach etw. stoßen 2 (thrust itself) sich schieben; **his elbows were poking through the sleeves** seine Ärmel hatten Löcher, aus denen die Ellbogen hervorguckten 3 (pry) schnüffeln (ugs. abwertend); **~ into things that don't concern one** seine Nase in Dinge stecken, die einen nichts angehen (ugs.)
C *n.* 1 (thrust) Stoß, *der;* **give sb. a ~ [in the ribs]** jmdm. einen [Rippen]stoß versetzen *od.* geben; **give sb. a ~ in the eye** jmdn. ins Auge stoßen; **give the fire a ~:** das Feuer [an]schüren; **better than a ~ in the eye [with a pointed stick]** (coll.) besser als gar nichts *od.* (derb) als in die hohle Hand geschissen 2 **have a ~ around a shop** *etc.* in einem Laden *usw.* herumstöbern; **have a ~ around in sb.'s writing desk** in jmds. Schreibtisch herumstöbern *od.* -wühlen 3 (coarse: sexual intercourse) Fick, *der* (vulg.); **have a ~:** stoßen (derb)

Phrasal verbs

- **~ a'bout, ~ a'round** *v.i.* 1 herumschnüffeln (ugs. abwertend) 2 (rummage) herumsuchen (ugs.); herumkramen (ugs.); **~ about in sth. for sth.** etw. nach etw. durchwühlen
- **~ 'out**
A *v.t.* rausstrecken; **you nearly ~d my eye out** du hast mir fast das Auge ausgestochen; **~ the dirt out of sth.** den Schmutz aus etw. kratzen; **~ one's head out** rausgucken (ugs.)
B *v.i.* rausgucken (ugs.)

'poke bonnet *n.* Schutenhut, *der*

poker[1] /'pəʊkə(r)/ *n.* (for fire) Schürstange, *die;* Schüreisen, *das;* **as stiff as a ~:** stocksteif (ugs.)

poker[2] *n.* (Cards) Poker, *das od. der;* **have a game of ~:** eine Runde pokern

poker: ~ dice *n. pl.: Würfel mit Spielkartensymbolen;* ≈ Skatwürfel; **~ face** *n.* Pokerface, *das;* Pokergesicht, *das;* **~-faced** *adj.* mit unbewegter Miene *nachgestellt;* **remain ~-faced** keine Miene verziehen

poky /'pəʊkɪ/ *adj.* winzig; **~ little** winzig klein; **it's so ~ in here** es ist so eng hier drinnen

Poland /'pəʊlənd/ *pr. n.* Polen (*das*)

polar /'pəʊlə(r)/ *adj.* 1 (of pole) polar ‹*Kaltluft, Kälte, Fauna, Klima, Gewässer*›; Polar‹*eis, -gebiet, -luft, -meer, -nacht, -fuchs, -hase*› 2 (Magn.) polar 3 (fig.: central) zentral 4 (directly opposite) [diametral] entgegengesetzt; polar (geh.); äußerst ‹*Extrem*›; grundlegend ‹*Unterschied*›

polar: ~ bear *n.* Eisbär, *der;* **~ 'cap** *n.* (Geog.) Polkappe, *die;* **~ 'circles** *n. pl.* (Geog.) Polarkreise; **~ 'front** *n.* (Meteorol.) Polarfront, *die*

P

Polaris /pə'lɑ:rɪs/ *pr. n.* 1 (missile) Polaris, *die* 2 (Astron.) Polaris (*die*)

polarisation, polarise ▸**polariz-**

polarity /pə'lærɪtɪ/ *n.* 1 (Magn.) Polung, *die;* Polarität, *die* 2 (direction of axis; having two poles) Polarität, *die* 3 (fig.: contrary qualities) Gegensatz, *der;* Polarität, *die* (geh.) 4 (Electr.) Polung, *die;* **change of ∼:** Polwechsel, *der*

polarization /pəʊləraɪ'zeɪʃn/ *n.* (Phys.) Polarisation, *die;* (fig.) Polarisierung, *die;* Polarisation, *die*

polarize /'pəʊləraɪz/

A *v.t.* 1 (Phys.) polarisieren 2 (fig.: divide) spalten; polarisieren (geh.); **∼ political life** eine Polarisierung des politischen Lebens bewirken

B *v.i.* sich [auf]spalten; sich polarisieren (geh.)

Polaroid ® /'pəʊlərɔɪd/ *n.* 1 (material) Polaroidfolie, *die* (Wz) 2 **∼s** (sunglasses) Polaroidbrille, *die* (Wz) 3 **∼ [camera]** Polaroidkamera, *die* (Wz)

polar 'star ▸**pole star**

polder /'pəʊldə(r)/ *n.* Polder, *der*

pole¹ *n.* 1 (support) Stange, *die;* (for ∼ vaulter) Stab, *der;* (for large tent, house in lake) Pfahl, *der;* **be up the ∼** (Brit. coll.) (in difficulty) in der Klemme sitzen (ugs.); (crazy) nicht ganz dicht sein (ugs. abwertend); **drive sb. up the ∼** (Brit. coll.) jmdn. zum Wahnsinn treiben (ugs.); **climb the greasy ∼** (fig.) sich hocharbeiten 2 (for propelling boat) Stake, *die* (nordd.) 3 (of horse-drawn vehicle) Deichsel, *die;* **∼s** [Gabel]deichsel, *die* 4 (measure) Rute, *die*

pole² *n.* 1 (Astron., Geog., Magn., Electr., Geom., Biol.) Pol, *der;* **positive/negative ∼:** positiver/negativer Pol; Plus-/Minuspol, *der;* **they are ∼s apart** zwischen ihnen liegen Welten; *see also* **magnetic pole**; **North Pole**; **South Pole** 2 (fig.) Pol, *der;* **be at opposite ∼s** sich (*Dat.*) als Pol und Gegenpol gegenüberstehen; einander entgegengesetzte Pole bilden

Pole /pəʊl/ *n.* ▸ⓘ **p. 1345** Pole, *der*/Polin, *die*

pole-axed /'pəʊlækst/ *adj.* **as if ∼:** wie vor den Kopf geschlagen

'polecat *n.* (Zool.) 1 (Brit.) Iltis, *der* 2 (Amer.) ▸**skunk 1**

polemic /pə'lemɪk/

A *adj.* polemisch

B *n.* 1 (discussion) Polemik, *die;* (written also) Streitschrift, *die* 2 *in pl.* (practice) Polemik, *die*

polemical /pə'lemɪkl/ *adj.*, **polemically** /pə'lemɪkəlɪ/ *adv.* polemisch

pole: ∼ position *n.* (Motor racing) Poleposition, *die;* **∼ star** *n.* (Astron.) Polarstern, *der;* **∼ vault** *n.* Stabhochsprung, *der;* **∼ vaulter** *n.* Stabhochspringer, *der*/-springerin, *die;* **∼-vaulting** *n.* Stabhochsprung, *der;* Stabhochspringen, *das*

police /pə'li:s/

A *n. pl.* 1 Polizei, *die;* **be in the ∼:** bei der Polizei sein; **river ∼:** Wasserschutzpolizei, *die; attrib.* Polizei‹*wagen, -hund, -schutz, -eskorte, -staat*› 2 (members) Polizisten *Pl.;* Polizeibeamte *Pl.; attrib.* Polizei-; **whole squads of ∼:** ein gewaltiges Polizeiaufgebot; **the ∼ are on his trail** die Polizei ist ihm auf der Spur; **extra ∼ were called in** zusätzliche Polizeikräfte wurden hinzugezogen; **help the ∼ with their enquiries** von der Polizei vernommen werden

B *v.t.* 1 [polizeilich] überwachen ‹*Gebiet, Verkehr, Fußballspiel*›; kontrollieren ‹*Gebiet, Grenze, Gewässer*› 2 (fig.: check on) überwachen; kontrollieren 3 (provide with ∼) Polizeibeamte einsetzen in (+ *Dat.*) ‹*Gebiet, Stadt usw.*›; **the inadequate policing of the district** die unzureichende Polizeipräsenz in dem Bezirk

police: ∼ academy *n.* (esp. Amer.) Polizeiakademie, *die;* **∼ chief** *n.* Polizeichef, *der*/-chefin, *die;* **∼ college** *n.* Polizeischule, *die;* **∼ constable** *n.* ▸ⓘ **p. 1260** Polizist, *der*/Polizistin, *die;* (rank) Polizeihauptwachtmeister, *der;* **∼ force** *n.* Polizeitruppe, *die;* **the ∼ force** die Polizei; **∼ informer** *n.* Polizeispitzel, *der;* **∼man** /pə'li:smən/ *n., pl.* **-men** /pə'li:smən/ ▸ⓘ **p. 1260** Polizist, *der;* Polizeibeamte, *der; see also* **sleeping policeman**; **∼ notice** *n.* polizeilicher Hinweis; **'P∼ Notice: No Parking'** „Parken polizeilich verboten"; **∼ officer** *n.* ▸ⓘ **p. 1260** Polizeibeamte, *der*/-beamtin, *die;* **∼ record** ▸**record C 5**; **∼ state** *n.* Polizeistaat, *der;* **∼ station** *n.* Polizeiwache, *die;* Polizeirevier, *das;* **∼woman** *n.* ▸ⓘ **p. 1260** Polizistin, *die;* Polizeibeamtin, *die*

policy¹ /'pɒlɪsɪ/ *n.* 1 (method) Handlungsweise, *die;* Vorgehensweise, *die;* (overall plan) Politik, *die;* **it is company ∼ to ...:** es ist Firmenpolitik, ... zu ...; **adopt** *or* **pursue a wise/cautious/foolish ∼:** klug/vorsichtig/töricht vorgehen; **it is the store's ∼ to prosecute shoplifters** der Laden erstattet grundsätzlich Anzeige gegen Ladendiebe; **it is not our ∼ to do that, our ∼ is not to do that** wir machen das grundsätzlich nicht; **government ∼:** Regierungspolitik, *die;* **∼ on immigration** Einwanderungspolitik, *die;* **party ∼:** Parteikurs, *der;* **the firm's policies** die Politik der Firma; **∼ decision/document** Grundsatzentscheidung, *die*/-papier, *das;* **∼ statement** programmatische Erklärung; Grundsatzerklärung, *die;* **it's bad ∼ to ...:** es ist [taktisch] unklug, ... zu ...; *see also* **honesty 2** 2 *no pl., no art.* (prudent conduct) **∼ demands occasional compromise** manchmal sind Kompromisse das einzig Vernünftige

policy² *n.* (Insurance) Police, *die;* Versicherungsschein, *der;* **take out a ∼ on sth.** eine Versicherung für etw. abschließen; **the ∼ on my car** meine Autoversicherung

'policy: ∼ holder *n.* Versicherte, *der/die;* Versicherungsnehmer, *der*/-nehmerin, *die* (fachspr.); **∼-making** *attrib. adj.* richtungsweisend; **∼ statement** *n.* Grundsatzerklärung, *die*

polio /'pəʊlɪəʊ/ *n., no pl., no art.* ▸ⓘ **p. 1231** (Med.) Polio, *die;* [spinale] Kinderlähmung; *attrib.* Polio-; **∼ vaccine** Polioimpfstoff, *der*

poliomyelitis /pəʊlɪəʊmaɪ'laɪtɪs/ *n.* ▸ⓘ **p. 1231** (Med.) Poliomyelitis, *die;* [spinale] Kinderlähmung

polish /'pɒlɪʃ/

A *v.t.* 1 (make smooth) polieren; bohnern ‹*Fußboden*›; putzen ‹*Schuhe*›; **highly ∼ed** auf Hochglanz poliert 2 (fig.) ausfeilen ‹*Text, Theorie, Technik, Stil*›; polieren ‹*Text*›; Schliff beibringen (+ *Dat.*) ‹*Person*›; **∼ed** geschliffen ‹*Stil, Manieren, Sprache, Auftreten, Weltmann*›; ausgefeilt ‹*Technik, Taktik, Plan, Satz*›; **a highly ∼ed piece of prose** ein bis ins Kleinste ausgefeiltes Stück Prosa

B *n.* 1 (smoothness) Glanz, *der;* **put a ∼ on** polieren; **a table with a high ∼:** ein auf Hochglanz polierter Tisch; **take off** *or* **spoil the ∼** ‹*Person:*› die Politur beschädigen; ‹*Substanz:*› die Politur angreifen 2 (substance) Poliermittel, *das;* Politur, *die* 3 (fig.) Geschliffenheit, *die;* Schliff, *der* 4 (action) **my shoes could do with a ∼:** meine Schuhe müssten mal geputzt werden; **give sth. a ∼:** etw. polieren; **give the floor a ∼:** den Fußboden bohnern; **give the shoes a ∼:** die Schuhe putzen; *see also* **spit¹ C 2**

Phrasal verbs

- **∼ 'off** *v.t.* (coll.) 1 (consume) verdrücken (ugs.); wegputzen (ugs.) ‹*Essen*›; aussüffeln (ugs.) ‹*Getränk*› 2 (complete quickly) durchziehen (ugs.) 3 (defeat) erledigen; abservieren (salopp, bes. Sport)
- **∼ 'up** *v.t.* 1 (make shiny) polieren 2 (improve) ausfeilen ‹*Stil, Technik*›; aufpolieren ‹[*Sprach*]*kenntnisse*›

Polish /'pəʊlɪʃ/ ▸ⓘ **p. 1277**, ▸ⓘ **p. 1345**

A *adj.* polnisch; **sb. is ∼:** jmd. ist Pole/Polin; *see also* **English A**

B *n.* Polnisch, *das; see also* **English B 1**

polisher /'pɒlɪʃə(r)/ *n.* 1 (person) ▸ⓘ **p. 1260** Polierer, *der*/Poliererin, *die* 2 (tool) Poliergerät, *das;* (for floors) Bohnerklotz, *der;* (machine) Poliermaschine, *die;* (for floors) Bohnermaschine, *die;* (cloth) Poliertuch, *das*

politburo /'pɒlɪtbjʊərəʊ/ *n., pl.* **∼s** Politbüro, *das*

polite /pə'laɪt/ *adj.*, **∼r** /pə'laɪtə(r)/, **∼st** /pə'laɪtɪst/ 1 (courteous) höflich; **the ∼ form of address** die höfliche Anredeform; **be ∼ about her dress** mach ihr ein paar Komplimente zu ihrem Kleid; **he was just being ∼:** er wollte nur höflich sein 2 (cultured) kultiviert 3 (well-mannered) schicklich (geh.) ‹*Verhalten*›; wohlerzogen, artig ‹*Kind*›; **it's not [considered] ∼:** es gehört sich *od.* (geh.) schickt sich nicht; **in some circles it is considered ∼ to ...** in manchen Kreisen gehört es zum guten Ton, zu ...

politely /pə'laɪtlɪ/ *adv.* höflich

politeness /pə'laɪtnɪs/ *n., no pl.* Höflichkeit, *die*

politic /'pɒlɪtɪk/

A *adj.* 1 (prudent) klug ‹*Person, Handlung*›; opportun (geh.) ‹*Handlung*›; **it would be ∼ to make some changes** es wäre klug *od.* (geh.) opportun, einiges zu ändern; **it's not ∼ to do sth.** es ist unklug *od.* nicht ratsam, etw. zu tun 2 **body ∼** (State) das Staatswesen

B *v.i.*, **-ck-** sich politisch betätigen *od.* engagieren

political /pə'lɪtɪkl/ *adj.* politisch; **∼ animal** politischer *od.* politisch engagierter Mensch

political: ∼ a'sylum ▸**asylum**; **∼ cor'rectness** *n., no pl.* Political Correctness, *die;* **∼ economy** *n., no pl.* politische Ökonomie; **∼ ge'ography** *n., no pl.* politische Geographie; **a map of the ∼ geography of Britain** eine politische Karte von Großbritannien

politically /pə'lɪtɪkəlɪ/ *adv.* politisch; **be ∼ aware** *or* **conscious** politisches Bewusstsein haben; **∼ correct** politisch korrekt; *von „richtigem" politischem Bewusstsein zeugend;* **∼ incorrect** politisch inkorrekt; politisch nicht korrekt; **∼ speaking** politisch gesehen; vom politischen Standpunkt betrachtet

> **politically correct - PC**
>
> Von richtigem politischen Bewusstsein zeugend ist das Bestreben, nichts zu sagen oder zu tun, was als kränkend oder negativ empfunden werden könnte - besonders wenn es sich um Minderheiten oder in irgendeiner Weise Benachteiligte handelt. Der Begriff *political correctness* gewann sich in den 1980er und 90er-Jahren in Amerika und später in Großbritannien zunehmend an Bedeutung. Hauptanliegen der *political correctness* ist es, rassistische und sexistische Äußerungen zu vermeiden.

political: ∼ 'prisoner *n.* politischer Gefangener/politische Gefangene; **∼ 'science** *n.* Politologie, *die*

politician /pɒlɪ'tɪʃn/ *n.* 1 ▸ⓘ **p. 1260** Politiker, *der*/Politikerin, *die* 2 (Amer. derog.: one seeking gain) Politiker/Politikerin aus Eigennutz

politicize (politicise) /pə'lɪtɪsaɪz/ *v.t.* politisieren

politicking /'pɒlɪtɪkɪŋ/ *n.* (derog.) politischer Aktionismus (abwertend)

politico /pə'lɪtɪkəʊ/ *n., pl.* **∼s** (coll.) Politiker, *der*/Politikerin, *die*

politics /'pɒlɪtɪks/ *n., no pl.* 1 *no art.* (political administration) Politik, *die;* (Univ.: subject) Politik[wissenschaft], *die;* Politologie, *die* 2 *no art., constr. as sing. or pl.* (political affairs) Politik, *die;* **∼ is a dirty business** die Politik ist ein schmutziges Geschäft; **interested/involved in ∼:** politisch interessiert/engagiert; **enter ∼:** in die Politik gehen 3 *as pl.* (political principles) Politik, *die;* (of individual) politische Einstellung; **world ∼ are complex** die Weltpolitik ist eine komplizierte Angelegenheit; **what are his ∼?** wo steht er politisch?; **the ∼ of the decision** der politische Hintergrund der Entscheidung; **it is not good ∼ to do sth.** es ist politisch unklug, etw. zu tun; **practical ∼:** Realpolitik, *die*

polity /'pɒlɪtɪ/ *n.* 1 (form of government) politisches System; politische Ordnung 2 (formal/arch.: State) Staat, *der;* Gemeinwesen, *das*

polka /'pɒlkə, 'pəʊlkə/ *n.* Polka, *die*

'polka dot *n.* [großer] Tupfen; **the blouse is patterned with ∼s** die Bluse hat ein Muster aus großen Tupfen; **a polka-dot scarf** ein Halstuch mit großen Tupfen

poll /pəʊl/

A *n.* 1 (voting) Abstimmung, *die;* (to elect sb.) Wahl, *die;* (result of vote) Abstimmungsergebnis, *das*/Wahlergebnis, *das;* (number of votes) Wahlbeteiligung, *die;* **take a ~:** abstimmen lassen; eine Abstimmung durchführen; **day of the ~:** Wahltag, *der;* **at the ~[s]** bei den Wahlen; **the result of the ~:** das Abstimmungsergebnis/Wahlergebnis; **a defeat at the ~s** eine Wahlniederlage; **go to the ~:** seine Stimme abgeben; zur Wahl gehen; wählen [gehen]; **Britain goes to the ~s** Großbritannien wählt; in Großbritannien wird gewählt; **be at the head of the ~:** die meisten Stimmen erhalten [haben]; **the declaration of the ~:** die Bekanntgabe des Wahlergebnisses; **a heavy/light** *or* **low ~:** eine starke/geringe *od.* niedrige Wahlbeteiligung **2** (survey of opinion) Umfrage, *die;* **~ findings** Umfrageergebnis, *das* **3** (human head) Kopf, *der;* Schädel, *der;* (part of head) [Hinter]kopf, *der*

B *v.t.* **1** (take vote[s] of) abstimmen/wählen lassen; **be ~ed** seine Stimme abgeben **2** (take opinion of) befragen; (take survey of) [demoskopisch] erforschen; **those ~ed** die Befragten **3** (obtain in poll) erhalten ‹*Stimmen*› **4** (cut off top of) kappen ‹*Baum, Baumkrone*›

C *v.i.* wählen; seine Stimme abgeben

pollack /ˈpɒlək/ *n.* (Zool.) Köhler, *der;* (Commerc.) Seelachs, *der*

pollard /ˈpɒləd/

A *n.* (Bot.) gekappter Baum

B *v.t.* (Bot.) kappen

pollen /ˈpɒlən/ *n.* (Bot.) Pollen, *der;* Blütenstaub, *der*

pollen: ~ analysis *n.* Pollenanalyse, *die;* **~ count** *n.* Pollenmenge, *die;* **~ sac** *n.* Pollensack, *der*

pollinate /ˈpɒlɪneɪt/ *v.t.* (Bot.) bestäuben

pollination /pɒlɪˈneɪʃn/ *n.* (Bot.) Bestäubung, *die;* Pollination, *die* (fachspr.)

polling /ˈpəʊlɪŋ/: **~ booth** *n.* Wahlkabine, *die;* **~ card** *n.* Wahlausweis, *der;* **~ day** *n.* Wahltag, *der;* **~ district** *n.* Wahlbezirk, *der;* **~ station** *n.* (Brit.) Wahllokal, *das*

pollock ▸ **pollack**

pollster /ˈpəʊlstə(r)/ *n.* Meinungsforscher, *der*/Meinungsforscherin, *die;* Demoskop, *der*/Demoskopin, *die*

ˈpoll tax *n.* Kopfsteuer, *die*

pollutant /pəˈluːtənt/

A *n.* (substance) [Umwelt]schadstoff, *der*

B *adj.* [umwelt]schädlich; **~ substance** [Umwelt]schadstoff, *der*

pollute /pəˈluːt/ *v.t.* **1** (contaminate) verschmutzen, verunreinigen ‹*Luft, Boden, Wasser*›; verpesten (abwertend) ‹*Luft*›; **the most ~d cities** die am stärksten mit [Umwelt]schadstoffen belasteten Städte **2** (make foul) verseuchen **3** (fig.) verderben ‹*Jugend, Menschen, Charakter*›

polluter /pəˈluːtə(r)/ *n.* [Umwelt]verschmutzer, *der*/-verschmutzerin, *die*

pollution /pəˈluːʃn/ *n.* **1** (contamination) [Umwelt]verschmutzung, *die;* **atmospheric ~:** atmosphärische Verschmutzung; Verschmutzung der Atmosphäre; **water ~:** Gewässerverschmutzung, *die;* **noise ~:** Lärmbelästigung, *die* **2** (polluting substance[s]) Verunreinigungen *Pl.;* Schadstoffe *Pl.* **3** (fig.) Verderben, *das*

Pollyanna /pɒlɪˈænə/ *n.* unverbesserlicher Optimist/unverbesserliche Optimistin; *attrib.* [übertrieben *od.* grundlos] optimistisch

polo /ˈpəʊləʊ/ *n., no pl.* Polo, *das*

polonaise /pɒləˈneɪz/ *n.* (dance, music) Polonaise, *die;* Polonäse, *die*

ˈpolo neck *n.* Rollkragen, *der;* **~[ed]** *attrib.* Rollkragen-; **~ [jumper]** Rollkragenpulli, *der* (ugs.); Rolli, *der* (Mode Jargon)

polo: ~ shirt *n.* Polohemd, *das;* **~ stick** *n.* Polostock, *der*

poltergeist /ˈpɒltəgaɪst/ *n.* Klopfgeist, *der;* Poltergeist, *der*

poltroon /pɒlˈtruːn/ *n.* (derog.) Angsthase, *der* (ugs. abwertend)

poly /ˈpɒlɪ/ *n., pl.* **~s** (coll.) Polytechnikum, *das;* ≈ TH, *die*

polyanthus /pɒlɪˈænθəs/ *n.* (Bot.) [Garten]primel, *die*

polychromatic /pɒlɪkrəˈmætɪk/ *adj.* **1** (many-coloured) vielfarbig; polychrom (fachspr.) **2** (Phys.) polychromatisch

polyclinic /ˈpɒlɪklɪnɪk/ *n.* Poliklinik, *die*

polyester /pɒlɪˈestə(r)/ *n.* Polyester, *der*

polyethylene /pɒlɪˈeθɪliːn/ (Amer.) ▸ **polythene**

polygamist /pəˈlɪgəmɪst/ *n.* Polygamist, *der* (geh.); **be a ~:** polygam leben (geh.); (in disposition) polygam sein (geh.)

polygamous /pəˈlɪgəməs/ *adj.* polygam (geh., fachspr.)

polygamy /pəˈlɪgəmɪ/ *n.* Polygamie, *die* (geh., fachspr.); Mehrehe, *die;* Vielehe, *die*

polyglot /ˈpɒlɪglɒt/

A *adj.* **1** polyglott (geh., fachspr.); mehrsprachig **2** (speaking several languages) polyglott (geh.)

B *n.* Polyglotte, *der/die* (geh.)

polygon /ˈpɒlɪgən/ *n.* (Geom.) Vieleck, *das;* Polygon, *das* (fachspr.)

polygraph /ˈpɒlɪgrɑːf/ *n.* (lie detector) Lügendetektor, *der;* Polygraph, *der* (fachspr.)

polyhedron /pɒlɪˈhiːdrən/ *n., pl.* **~s** *or* **polyhedra** /pɒlɪˈhiːdrə/ (Geom.) Polyeder, *das* (fachspr.); Vielflächner, *der*

polymath /ˈpɒlɪmæθ/ *n.* universell Gebildeter/Gebildete

polymer /ˈpɒlɪmə(r)/ *n.* (Chem.) Polymer[e], *das*

polymeric /pɒlɪˈmerɪk/ *adj.* (Chem.) polymer

polymerisation, polymerise ▸ **polymeriz-**

polymerization /pɒlɪməraɪˈzeɪʃn/ *n.* (Chem.) Polymerisation, *die*

polymerize /ˈpɒlɪməraɪz/ *v.t. & i.* (Chem.) polymerisieren

Polynesia /pɒlɪˈniːʒə/ *pr. n.* Polynesien (*das*)

Polynesian /pɒlɪˈniːʒən/ ▸ⓘ **p. 1345**

A *adj.* polynesisch

B *n.* Polynesier, *der*/Polynesierin, *die*

polynomial /pɒlɪˈnəʊmɪəl/ *n.* (Math.) Polynom, *das*

polyp /ˈpɒlɪp/ *n.* (Zool., Med.) Polyp, *der*

polyphonic /pɒlɪˈfɒnɪk/, **polyphonous** /pəˈlɪfənəs/ *adjs.* (Mus.) polyphon

polyphony /pəˈlɪfənɪ/ *n.* (Mus.) Polyphonie, *die*

polystyrene /pɒlɪˈstaɪriːn/ *n.* Polystyrol, *das;* **~ foam** Styropor (Wz), *das*

polysyllabic /pɒlɪsɪˈlæbɪk/ *adj.* vielsilbig

polytechnic /pɒlɪˈteknɪk/ *n.* (Brit.) ≈ technische Hochschule *od.* Universität; **~ student/teacher/term** Student/Lehrer/Semester am Polytechnikum

polytheism /ˈpɒlɪθiːɪzm/ *n.* Polytheismus, *der*

polythene /ˈpɒlɪθiːn/ *n.* Polyäthylen, *das;* Polyethylen, *das* (fachspr.); (coll.: plastic) Plastik, *das;* **~ bag/sheet** Plastikbeutel, *der*/-folie, *die*

polyunsaturated /pɒlɪʌnˈsætʃəreɪtɪd/ *adj.* mehrfach ungesättigt

polyunsaturates /pɒlɪʌnˈsætjʊrəts/ *pl. n.* mehrfach ungesättigte Fettsäuren

polyurethane /pɒlɪˈjʊərɪθeɪn/ *n.* Polyurethan, *das*

polyvinyl chloride /pɒlɪvaɪnɪl ˈklɔːraɪd/ *n.* Polyvinylchlorid, *das*

pom /pɒm/ *n.* **1** (dog) Spitz, *der* **2** (Austral. and NZ coll.: Briton) Brite, *der*/Britin, *die*

pomade /pəˈmɑːd/ *n.* Pomade, *die*

pomaded /pəˈmeɪdɪd/ *adj.* pomadig ‹*Haar*›

pomander /pəˈmændə(r)/ *n.* Duftkugel, *die*

pome /pəʊm/ *n.* (Bot.) Sammelbalgfrucht, *die*

pomegranate /ˈpɒmɪgrænɪt/ *n.* **1** (fruit) Granatapfel, *der* **2** (tree) Granatapfel[baum], *der;* Granatbaum, *der*

Pomerania /pɒməˈreɪnɪə/ *pr. n.* Pommern (*das*)

Pomeranian /pɒməˈreɪnɪən/ *n.* (dog) Spitz, *der*

pommel /ˈpʌml, ˈpɒml/

A *n.* **1** (on sword) [Schwert]knauf, *der* **2** (on saddle) Sattelknopf, *der* **3** (Gymnastics) Pausche, *die*

B *v.t.,* (Brit.) **-ll-** ▸ **pummel**

ˈpommel horse *n.* Seitpferd, *das*

pommy (**pommie**) /ˈpɒmɪ/ *n.* (Austral. and NZ sl. derog.) Brite, *der*/Britin, *die;* **~ bastard** Scheißbrite, *der*/-britin, *die* (salopp abwertend)

pomp /pɒmp/ *n.* Pomp, *der* (abwertend); Prunk, *der;* Gepränge, *das* (geh.); **~ and circumstance** festliches Gepränge (geh.)

Pompeii /pɒmˈpeɪiː/ *pr. n.* ▸ⓘ **p. 1643** Pompeji (*das*)

pompom /ˈpɒmpɒm/, **pompon** /ˈpɒmpɒn/ *n.* **1** (tuft) Pompon, *der;* Troddel, *die;* **~ hat** Pudelmütze, *die* **2** (Bot.) **~ [dahlia]** Pompondahlie, *die*

pom-pom /ˈpɒmpɒm/ *n.* (Arms) Maschinenkanone, *die*

pomposity /pɒmˈpɒsɪtɪ/ *n., no pl.* Großspurigkeit, *die;* Aufgeblasenheit, *die;* **~ of language** geschwollene *od.* gespreizte Sprache

pompous /ˈpɒmpəs/ *adj.* (self-important) großspurig; aufgeblasen; geschwollen (abwertend); gespreizt (abwertend) ‹*Sprache*›; **don't be so ~!** blas dich nicht so auf!

pompously /ˈpɒmpəslɪ/ *adv.* großspurig, aufgeblasen ‹*auftreten, sich benehmen*›; geschwollen (abwertend), gespreizt (abwertend) ‹*schreiben, reden*›

ˈpon /pɒn/ (poet./arch.) ▸ **upon**

ponce /pɒns/ (Brit. sl.)

A *n.* **1** (pimp) Zuhälter, *der* **2** (derog.: homosexual) Schwule, *der* (ugs.); Homo, *der* (ugs.); **be a ~:** schwul sein

B *v.i.* Zuhälterei betreiben; **~ for sb.** jmds. Zuhälter sein

Phrasal verbs

- **~ aˈbout, ~ aˈround** *v.i.* (derog.) herumtänzeln (ugs.)
- **~ ˈup** *v.t.* (derog.) [tuntenhaft] auftakeln (ugs. abwertend); **what are you all ~d up for?** wozu hast du dich denn so aufgedonnert? (salopp)

poncho /ˈpɒntʃəʊ/ *n., pl.* **~s** Poncho, *der;* Umhang, *der*

pond /pɒnd/ *n.* Teich, *der;* **the [big] ~** (joc.: Atlantic) der große Teich (ugs. scherzh.); **a big fish in a small ~** (fig.) eine Lokalgröße; ein Lokalmatador (ugs.)

ponder /ˈpɒndə(r)/

A *v.t.* nachdenken über (+ *Akk.*) ‹*Frage, Problem, Ereignis*›; bedenken ‹*Folgen*›; abwägen ‹*Vorteile, Worte*›; **~ whether/how to do sth.** sich (*Dat.*) überlegen, ob man etw. tun soll/wie man etw. tun kann

B *v.i.* nachdenken (**over, on** über + *Akk.*); **careful ~ing** sorgfältige Überlegung; sorgfältiges Nachdenken

ponderous /ˈpɒndərəs/ *adj.* **1** (heavy) schwer **2** (unwieldy, laborious) schwerfällig; umständlich ‹*Ausdrucksweise*› **3** (dull) ermüdend

ponderously /ˈpɒndərəslɪ/ *adv.* schwerfällig; umständlich ‹*sich ausdrücken*›

pond: ~ life *n.* (Zool.) Teichfauna, *die;* **~ skater** *n.* (Zool.) Wasserläufer, *der;* **~weed** *n.* (Bot.) Laichkraut, *das*

pong /pɒŋ/ (Brit. coll.)

A *n.* Gestank, *der* (abwertend); Mief, *der* (ugs. abwertend)

B *v.i.* stinken (abwertend); miefen (ugs. abwertend)

pongy /ˈpɒŋɪ/ *adj.* (Brit. coll.) miefig (ugs. abwertend;) **be ~:** miefen (ugs. abwertend)

pontiff /ˈpɒntɪf/ *n.* Papst, *der*

pontifical /pɒnˈtɪfɪkl/ *adj.* **1** (of pontiff) päpstlich **2** (fig.: dogmatic) pastoral

pontificate /pɒnˈtɪfɪkeɪt/ *v.i.* dozieren; in dozierendem Ton sprechen

pontoon¹ /pɒnˈtuːn/ *n.* **1** (boat) Ponton, *der;* Prahm, *der* **2** (support) Ponton, *der*

pontoon² *n.* (Brit. Cards) Siebzehnundvier, *das*

pontoon ˈbridge *n.* Pontonbrücke, *die*

pony /ˈpəʊnɪ/

A *n.* **1** Pony, *das; see also* **shank 1** **2** (Amer. coll.: small glass) kleines Glas; (of beer) Kleine, *das* **3** (Amer. coll.: dancer) kleine Tänzerin **4** (Amer. coll.: crib) Klatsche, *die* (Schülerspr. landsch.); Schmierer, *der* (österr.) **5** (Brit. coll.: £25) 25 Pfund

B *v.t.* (Amer. coll.) **~ up** löhnen (salopp); blechen (ugs.)

pony: ~ exˈpress *n.* Ponyexpress, *der;* **~tail** *n.* Pferdeschwanz, *der;* **wear one's hair in a ~tail** einen Pferdeschwanz tragen *od.*

P

haben; **~-trekking** /ˈpəʊnɪtrekɪŋ/ *n.* (Brit.) Ponyreiten, *das*

pooch /puːtʃ/ *n.* (Amer. coll.) Köter, *der* (abwertend)

poodle /ˈpuːdl/ *n.* Pudel, *der;* **be sb.'s ~** (fig.) immer nach jmds. Pfeife tanzen

poof /pʊf/ *n.* (Brit. coll. derog.), **poofter** /ˈpʊftə(r)/ *n.* (Austral. coll. derog.) Schwule, *der* (ugs.); Schwuchtel, *die* (salopp abwertend); Tunte, *die* (salopp abwertend)

poofy /ˈpʊfɪ/ *adj.* (Brit. coll. derog.) tuntig (salopp abwertend)

pooh /puː/ *int.* **1** *expr. disgust* bah; bäh; pfui [Teufel] **2** *expr. disdain* pah

pooh-ˈpooh *v.t.* [als läppisch] abtun

pool[1] /puːl/ *n.* **1** (permanent) Tümpel, *der;* Wasserloch, *das* **2** (temporary) Pfütze, *die;* Lache, *die;* **~ of blood** Blutlache, *die;* **~ of sunlight/shade** (fig.) sonnige/schattige Stelle **3** (swimming ~) Schwimmbecken, *das;* (public swimming ~) Schwimmbad, *das;* (in house or garden) [Swimming]pool, *der;* **sit at the edge of the ~:** am Beckenrand sitzen; **go to the ~:** ins Schwimmbad gehen **4** (in river) tiefe Stelle (in einem Fluss od. Bach); Kolk, *der* (fachspr.); **the P~ [of London]** (Brit.) *Themseabschnitt unterhalb der London Bridge*

pool[2]

A *n.* **1** (Gambling) [gemeinsame Spiel]kasse; **the ~s** (Brit.) das Toto; **do the ~s** Toto spielen; **win the ~s** im Toto gewinnen; **have a big win on the ~s** einen großen Gewinn im Toto haben **2** (common supply) Fonds, *der;* Topf, *der;* **that goes into the common ~:** das kommt in den großen Topf (ugs.); **a [great] ~ of experience** ein [großer] Fundus von *od.* an Erfahrung; ein [umfangreicher] Erfahrungsschatz **3** (group of people) Reservoir, *das;* Potenzial, *das;* **typing** *or* **typists' ~:** Schreibzentrale, *die* **4** (Commerc.) Kartell, *das* **5** (game) Pool[billard], *das*

B *v.t.* zusammenlegen ‹*Geld, Ersparnisse, Mittel, Besitz*›; bündeln ‹*Anstrengungen*›; **they ~ed their experience** sie nutzten ihre Erfahrung gemeinsam

pool: ~hall, ~room *ns.* Billardzimmer, *das;* **~side** *n.* [Schwimm]beckenrand, *der; attrib.* ‹*Bar, Tisch*› am [Schwimm]beckenrand; **~ table** *n.* Pool[billard]tisch, *der*

poop[1] /puːp/ *n.* (Naut.) **1** (stern) Heck, *das;* Hinterschiff, *das* **2** **~ [deck]** Poop, *die* (fachspr.); Hütte, *die* (fachspr.)

poop[2] (coll.)

A *v.t.* schlauchen (ugs.)

B *v.i.* **~ out** schlappmachen (ugs.); ‹*Maschine usw.:*› streiken (ugs.)

poor /pʊə(r)/

A *adj.* **1** arm; **I am the ~er by £10** *or* **£10 the ~er** ich bin um 10 Pfund ärmer; *see also* **church mouse** **2** (inadequate) schlecht; schwach ‹*Rede, Spiel, Gedächtnis, Beteiligung, Besuch, Leistung, Witz, Gesundheit*›; dürftig ‹*Essen, Kleidung, Unterkunft, Ausrede, Entschuldigung*›; **of ~ quality** minderer Qualität; **he's a ~ speller** er ist schlecht in Rechtschreibung; **I'm a ~ traveller** ich vertrage das Reisen nicht gut; **be ~ at maths** *etc.* schlecht *od.* schwach in Mathematik *usw.* sein; **sb. is ~ at games** Ballspiele liegen jmdm. nicht; **have a ~ sense of responsibility** zu wenig Verantwortungsgefühl haben; **have a ~ grasp of sth.** etw. nur unzureichend beherrschen; **I only came a ~ second** bei mir hat es nur für einen schlechten zweiten Platz gereicht; **compared with Joe he comes a ~ second** gegen Joe hat er absolut nichts drin (ugs.) **3** (paltry) schwach ‹*Trost*›; schlecht ‹*Aussichten, Situation*›; (disgusting) mies (ugs. abwertend); **it's very ~ of them not to have replied** es ist sehr schäbig von ihnen *od.* (ugs.) es ist ein schwaches Bild, dass sie nicht geantwortet haben; **have** *or* **stand a ~ chance of success** kaum Aussicht auf Erfolg haben; **that's pretty ~!** das ist reichlich dürftig *od.* (ugs.) ganz schön schwach; *see also* **show A 5** **4** (unfortunate) arm (auch iron.); **~ you!** du Armer/Arme!; du Ärmster/Ärmste!; **~ thing/creature!** armes Ding!; das arme Ding!; **~ things!** die Armen *od.* Ärmsten!; **she's all alone, ~ woman** die Ärmste ist ganz allein; sie ist ganz allein, die arme Frau; **~ old Joe** der arme Joe; **~ Joe** (dead) der gute Joe **5** (infertile) karg, schlecht ‹*Boden, Land*› **6** (spiritless, pathetic) arm ‹*Teufel, Dummkopf*›; armselig, (abwertend) elend ‹*Kreatur, Stümper*›; **cut a ~ figure** eine schlechte *od.* klägliche Figur abgeben **7** (iron./joc.: humble) **in my ~ opinion** nach meiner unmaßgeblichen Meinung; **my ~ self** meine Wenigkeit (scherzh.) **8** (deficient) arm (**in** an + *Dat.*); **~ in content/ideas/vitamins** inhalts-/ideen-/vitaminarm; **~ in minerals** ‹*Land*› arm an Bodenschätzen **9** **take a ~ view of** nicht [sehr] viel halten von; für gering halten ‹*Aussichten, Chancen*›; **have a ~ opinion of** eine schlechte *od.* keine [sehr] hohe Meinung haben von ‹*Person*›; gering einschätzen ‹*jmds. Fähigkeit*›

B *n. pl.* **the ~:** die Armen; **respected by both rich and ~:** geachtet von *od.* bei Arm und Reich

poor: ~ box *n.* Almosenbüchse, *die;* **~house** *n.* (Hist.) Armenhaus, *das;* **~ law** *n.* (Hist.) Armengesetz, *das*

poorly /ˈpʊəlɪ/

A *adv.* **1** (scantily) schlecht; unzureichend; **they're ~ off** es geht ihnen [finanziell] schlecht; **sb. is ~ off for sth.** es fehlt *od.* mangelt jmdm. an etw. (*Dat.*) **2** (badly) schlecht; unbeholfen ‹*schreiben, sprechen*›; **he did ~ in his exams** er war in seinen Prüfungen schlecht; **the team is doing ~:** die Mannschaft spielt schlecht; **exports are doing ~:** das Exportgeschäft geht schlecht **3** (meanly) schlecht ‹*leben*›

B *pred. adj.* schlecht ‹*aussehen, sich fühlen*›; **he has been ~ lately** ihm geht es in letzter Zeit schlecht

ˈpoor: ~ man's *adj.* (coll.) des kleinen Mannes *nachgestellt;* **a kind of ~ man's Marlon Brando** ein Marlon-Brando-Verschnitt; ein Westentaschen-Marlon-Brando; **~ reˈlation** *n.* arme Verwandte, *der/die;* (fig.) Stiefkind, *das;* **be the ~ relation** (fig.) im Vergleich schlecht abschneiden; **feel like a ~ relation** sich (*Dat.*) wie ein Stiefkind vorkommen; **~-relief** *n.* (Hist.) Armenpflege, *die;* **~ ˈwhite** *n.* (Amer. Black derog.) armer Weißer/arme Weiße; **~ white trash** weißer Pöbel (abwertend); weißes Gesindel (abwertend)

poove /puːv/ ▸ **poof**

pop[1] /pɒp/

A *v.i.*, **-pp-** **1** (make sound) ‹*Korken:*› knallen; ‹*Schote, Samenkapsel:*› aufplatzen, aufspringen; **a faint ~ping sound** ein leises Knacken; **his buttons ~ped open** seine Knöpfe sprangen auf; (fig.) **his eyes ~ped with amazement** er guckte wie ein Auto (ugs.); **prices that would make your eyes ~:** Preise, bei denen Sie staunen würden **2** (coll.: move, go quickly) **let's ~ round to Fred's** komm, wir gehen mal eben *od.* schnell *od.* kurz bei Fred vorbei (ugs.); **I'll just ~ upstairs and see granny** ich gehe *od.* (ugs.) springe nur mal eben hoch zu Oma; **~ down to London** mal eben *od.* schnell nach London fahren; **you must ~ round and see us** du musst mal vorbeikommen und uns besuchen *od.* musst mal bei uns reingucken (ugs.); **she ~ped back for her book** sie lief *od.* (ugs.) flitzte noch mal zurück, um ihr Buch zu holen **3** (fire gun) ballern (ugs.) (**at** auf + *Akk.*)

B *v.t.*, **-pp-** **1** (coll.: put) **~ the meat in the fridge** das Fleisch in den Kühlschrank tun; **~ a cake into the oven** einen Kuchen in den Ofen schieben; **~ a peanut into one's mouth** [sich (*Dat.*)] eine Erdnuss in den Mund stecken; **~ one's head in at the door** den Kopf zur Tür reinstecken; mal eben hereinschauen; **~ one's head out [of the window]** den Kopf [zum Fenster] rausstrecken; **~ the kettle on** den Kessel aufsetzen; **~ a letter in the post** einen Brief einwerfen; einen Brief in den Briefkasten werfen; **~ sth. into a bag** etw. in eine Tasche tun *od.* stecken **2** (cause to burst) enthülsen ‹*Erbsen, Bohnen*›; platzen *od.* (ugs.) knallen lassen ‹*Luftballon*›; zerknallen ‹*Papiertüte*› **3** (sl.: take as drug) nehmen; schlucken, (Jargon) schmeißen ‹*Pillen, Trips*›; (by injection) schießen (Jargon); drücken (Jargon) **4** (cause to burst) puffen; **~ corn** Popcorn machen **5** **~ the question [to sb.]** (coll.) jmdm. einen [Heirats]antrag machen

C *n.* **1** (sound) Knall, *der;* Knallen, *das* **2** (coll.: drink) Sprudel, *der;* (flavoured) Brause, *die* (ugs.); **soda ~:** Selter[s], *das*

D *adv.* **go ~:** knallen; peng machen (ugs.)

Phrasal verbs

- **~ ˈoff** *v.i.* **1** (coll.: die) abnibbeln (ugs., bes. nordd.); den Löffel weglegen *od.* abgeben (salopp) **2** (move or go away) ‹*Person:*› verschwinden, (ugs.) abdampfen
- **~ ˈout** *v.i.* hervorschießen aus; **~ one's head out of the window** den Kopf zum Fenster herausstrecken; **~ out from behind a bush** hinter einem Busch hervorspringen; **~ out for a newspaper/to the shops** schnell *od.* eben mal eine Zeitung holen gehen/einkaufen gehen (ugs.); **~ out for a beer** eben mal ein Bier[chen] trinken gehen (ugs.); **he's just ~ped out for a moment** er ist nur mal kurz weggegangen (ugs.)
- **~ ˈout of** *v.t.* hervorschieben aus; **~ one's head out of the window** den Kopf zum Fenster herausstrecken; **sb.'s eyes nearly** *or* **almost ~ out of his head** *or* **skull** (coll.) (with surprise) jmdm. fallen fast die Augen aus dem Kopf; (with excitement) jmd. (bes. Kind) macht große Augen
- **~ ˈup** *v.i.* **1** (fig.: appear) auftauchen; **sb./sth. keeps ~ping up** (fig.) jmd./etw. begegnet einem immer wieder (fig.) **2** (rise up) sich aufstellen; (spring up) hochspringen; *see also* **pop-up**

pop[2] (coll.)

A *n.* (popular music) Popmusik, *die;* Pop, *der;* **be top of the ~s** an der Spitze der Charts *od.* Hitlisten stehen

B *adj.* Pop- ‹*star, -musik usw.*›

pop[3] *n.* (Amer. coll.: father) Pa[pa], *der* (fam.)

pop. *abbr.* **= population** Einw.

pop: ~ art *n., no pl., no indef. art.* Pop-Art, *die; attrib.* Pop-Art-; **~ concert** *n.* Popkonzert, *das;* **~corn** *n.* Popcorn, *das*

pope /pəʊp/ *n.* **1** (RC Ch.; also fig.) Papst, *der*/Päpstin, *die* **2** (Coptic Ch.) Patriarch, *der* **3** (Orthodox Ch.) Pope, *der. See also* **nose A 1**

popery /ˈpəʊpərɪ/ *n., no pl., no art.* (derog.) Pfaffentum, *das* (abwertend); Papismus, *der* (abwertend)

pop: ~-eyed /ˈpɒpaɪd/ *adj.* (coll.) **1** (wide-eyed) großäugig; **they were ~-eyed with amazement** sie staunten Bauklötze (salopp); **2** (having bulging eyes) glotzäugig; glupschäugig (nordd.); **~ festival** *n.* Popfestival, *das;* **~ group** *n.* Popgruppe, *die;* **~gun** *n.* Spielzeuggewehr, *das*/Spielzeugpistole, *die*

popish /ˈpəʊpɪʃ/ *adj.* (arch./derog.) papistisch (abwertend); **the ~ religion** der Papismus (abwertend)

poplar /ˈpɒplə(r)/ *n.* Pappel, *die*

poplin /ˈpɒplɪn/ *n.* (Textiles) Popelin, *der;* Popeline, *der od. die*

pop: ~ music *n.* Popmusik, *die;* **~over** *n.* (Amer.) **1** *stark aufgehendes Backwerk aus Eiern, Milch, Mehl und Butter;* **2** (garment) weites Kleidungsstück (das über den Kopf gezogen wird)

poppadom, poppadum /ˈpɒpədəm/ *n.* Papadam, *der;* indischer Linsenfladen

popper /ˈpɒpə(r)/ *n.* (Brit. coll.) Druckknopf, *der*

poppet /ˈpɒpɪt/ *n.* (Brit. coll.) Schätzchen, *das;* Schatz, *der*

poppy /ˈpɒpɪ/ *n.* **1** (Bot.) Mohn, *der;* **a field of poppies** ein Mohnfeld; **Californian ~:** Goldmohn, *der;* **opium ~:** Schlafmohn, *der;* **Welsh ~:** Scheinmohn, *der* **2** (Brit.: emblem) [künstliche] Mohnblume (*als Zeichen des Gedenkens am 'Poppy Day'*)

poppycock /ˈpɒpɪkɒk/ *n., no pl., no art.* (coll.) Mumpitz, *der* (ugs. abwertend)

poppy: P~ Day (Brit.) ▸ **Remembrance Sunday**; **~ head** *n.* Mohnkapsel, *die;* **~ seed** *n.* Mohnsamen, *der;* **~ seeds** (Cookery) Mohn, *der*

Popsicle ® /ˈpɒpsɪkl/ *n.* (Amer.) [Wasser]eis am Stiel

pop: ~ singer *n.* Popsänger, *der*/-sängerin, *die;* Schlagersänger, *der*/-sängerin, *die;* **~ song** *n.* Popsong, *der;* Schlager, *der;* **~ star** *n.* Popstar, *der;* Schlagerstar, *der*

popsy (**popsie**) /ˈpɒpsɪ/ *n.* (coll.) (young woman) Mieze, *die* (salopp); (young girl) Maus, *die;* (as form of address) Schätzchen, *das*

ˈpop-top *n.* (Amer.) Ring-Pull-Verschluss, *der; attrib.* **~ beer can** Ring-Pull-Bierdose, *die*

populace /ˈpɒpjʊləs/ *n., no pl.* **1** (common people) [breite] Masse; Volk, *das;* **the Roman ~:** das Volk von Rom **2** (derog.: rabble) Pöbel, *der* (abwertend)

popular /ˈpɒpjʊlə(r)/ *adj.* **1** (well liked) beliebt; populär ‹*Entscheidung, Maßnahme*›; **I know I shan't be ~ if I suggest that** ich weiß, dass ich mich mit diesem Vorschlag nicht gerade beliebt mache; **he was a very ~ choice** mit ihm hatte man sich für einen sehr beliebten *od.* populären Mann entschieden; **be ~ with sb.** bei jmdm. beliebt sein; **he's ~ with the girls** die Mädchen mögen ihn; **I'm not very ~ in the office just now** im Büro ist man zurzeit nicht gut auf mich zu sprechen; **prove ~:** gut ankommen **2** (suited to the public) volkstümlich; populär (geh.); **at ~ prices** zu günstigen Preisen; **~ edition** Volksausgabe, *die;* **~ journal/newspaper** Massenblatt, *das;* **a ~ romance** ein Liebesroman; **~ science** die Populärwissenschaft **3** (prevalent) landläufig; allgemein ‹*Unzufriedenheit*›; **~ etymology** Volksetymologie, *die* **4** (of the people) Volks-; verbreitet ‹*Aberglaube, Irrtum, Meinung*›; allgemein ‹*Wahl, Zustimmung, Unterstützung*›; **~ remedy** Hausmittel, *das;* **by ~ request** auf allgemeinen Wunsch

popular: ~ ˈart *n.* Volkskunst, *die;* **~ ˈfront** *n.* (Polit.) Volksfront, *die*

popularise ▸ **popularize**

popularity /pɒpjʊˈlærɪtɪ/ *n., no pl.* Popularität, *die;* Beliebtheit, *die;* (of decision, measure) Popularität, *die;* **that won her ~ with her classmates** das machte sie bei ihren Klassenkameradinnen beliebt

popuˈlarity rating *n.* Beliebtheitsquote, *die*

popularize /ˈpɒpjʊləraɪz/ *v.t.* **1** (make popular) populär machen; **~ sth.** einer Sache (*Dat.*) Popularität verschaffen **2** (make known) bekannt machen **3** (make understandable) breiteren Kreisen zugänglich machen; popularisieren (geh.)

popularly /ˈpɒpjʊləlɪ/ *adv.* **1** (generally) allgemein; landläufig; **it is ~ believed that ...:** es ist ein im Volk verbreiteter Glaube, dass ... **2** (for the people) volkstümlich; allgemein verständlich

popular ˈmusic *n.* Unterhaltungsmusik, *die;* Populärmusik, *die* (fachspr.)

populate /ˈpɒpjʊleɪt/ *v.t.* bevölkern ‹*Land, Gebiet*›; bewohnen ‹*Insel, Gebiet*›; **the characters that ~ his novel** die Charaktere, die seinen Roman bevölkern; **thickly** *or* **heavily** *or* **densely/sparsely ~d** dicht/dünn besiedelt ‹*Land, Gebiet usw.*›; dicht/dünn bevölkert ‹*Stadt*›

population /pɒpjʊˈleɪʃn/ *n.* **1** Bevölkerung, *die;* **Britain has a ~ of 56 million** Großbritannien hat 56 Millionen Einwohner; *attrib.* **~ density** Bevölkerungsdichte, *die;* **the growing immigrant ~ of London** der wachsende Einwandereranteil an der Londoner Bevölkerung; **the seal ~ of Greenland** der Seehundbestand *od.* (fachspr.) die Seehundpopulation Grönlands **2** (Statistics) Grundgesamtheit, *die*

popuˈlation explosion *n.* Bevölkerungsexplosion, *die*

populism /ˈpɒpjʊlɪzm/ *n., no pl.* Populismus, *der*

populist /ˈpɒpjʊlɪst/
A *n.* Populist, *der*/Populistin, *die*
B *adj.* populistisch

populous /ˈpɒpjʊləs/ *adj.* dicht bevölkert

ˈpop-up *adj.* Stehauf‹*buch, -illustration*›; **~ toaster** Toaster mit Auswerfmechanismus; **~ menu** (Computing) Pop-up-Menü, *das;* **~ window** (Computing) Pop-up-Fenster, *das*

porcelain /ˈpɔːslɪn/ *n.* **1** Porzellan, *das; attrib.* Porzellan-; **Meissen ~:** Meißner Porzellan **2** (article) Porzellangegenstand, *der;* **~s** Porzellan, *das*

porch /pɔːtʃ/ *n.* **1** (Archit.) Vordach, *das;* (with side walls) Vorbau, *der;* (enclosed) Windfang, *der;* (of church etc.) Vorhalle, *die* **2** (Amer.: veranda) [offene] Veranda

porcine /ˈpɔːsaɪn/ *adj.* Schweine-; (fig.) schweineähnlich; wie ein Schwein *nachgestellt*

porcupine /ˈpɔːkjʊpaɪn/ *n.* (Zool.) **1** (Brit.: Hystricidae) Stachelschwein, *das* **2** (Amer.: Erethizontidae) Baumstachler, *der*

pore[1] /pɔː(r)/ *n.* Pore, *die*

pore[2] *v.i.* **~ over sth.** etw. [genau] studieren; (think deeply) **~ over** *or* **on sth.** über etw. (*Akk.*) [gründlich] nachdenken

pork /pɔːk/ *n.* Schweinefleisch, *das; attrib.* Schweine-; Schweins- (bes. südd.); **a leg of ~:** eine Schweinekeule

pork: ~ barrel *n.* (Amer. coll.) *aus politischen Gründen bewilligte staatliche Zuschüsse;* **~ butcher** *n.* Schweinemetzger, *der* (bes. südd.); Schweineschlachter, *der* (bes. nordd.); **~ ˈchop** *n.* Schweinekotelett, *das*

porker /ˈpɔːkə(r)/ *n.* Mastschwein, *das;* (young pig) Mastferkel, *das*

pork: ~ ˈpie *n.* Schweinepastete, *die;* **~-pie ˈhat** *n.* flacher [Herren]hut; **~ ˈsausage** *n.* Schweinswürstchen, *das*

porn /pɔːn/ *n., no pl.* (coll.) Pornographie, *die;* Pornos, *Pl.* (ugs.); **write ~:** Pornos schreiben (ugs.); *attrib.* **~ film** Pornofilm, *der* (ugs.); **~ shop** (coll.) Pornoladen, *der* (ugs.)

porno /ˈpɔːnəʊ/ (coll.)
A *n., no pl.* ▸ **porn**
B *adj.* Porno- (ugs.)

pornographer /pɔːˈnɒgrəfə(r)/ *n.* Pornograf, *der*/Pornografin, *die*

pornographic /pɔːnəˈgræfɪk/ *adj.* pornographisch; Porno- (ugs.)

pornography /pɔːˈnɒgrəfɪ/ *n., no pl.* Pornographie, *die*

porosity /pɔːˈrɒsɪtɪ/ *n., no pl.* Porosität, *die*

porous /ˈpɔːrəs/ *adj.* porös ‹*Fels, Gestein, Stoff*›; porenreich ‹*Haut, Holz*›

porpoise /ˈpɔːpəs/ *n.* (Zool.) Schweinswal, *der*

porridge /ˈpɒrɪdʒ/ *n., no pl.* **1** (food) Porridge, *der;* Haferbrei, *der* **2** (sl.: imprisonment) Knast, *der* (ugs.); **do ~:** Knast schieben (salopp); im Knast sitzen (ugs.)

porridge ˈoats *n. pl.* Haferflocken *Pl.*

port[1] /pɔːt/
A *n.* **1** (harbour) Hafen, *der;* **come** *or* **put into ~:** [in den Hafen] einlaufen; **leave ~:** [aus dem Hafen] auslaufen; **reach ~:** den Hafen erreichen; ankommen; **out of ~:** auf See; **naval ~:** Kriegshafen, *der;* **any ~ in a storm** (fig. coll.) manchmal kann man sichs eben nicht aussuchen (ugs.); ≈ in der Not frisst der Teufel Fliegen (ugs.); **~ of call** Anlaufhafen, *der;* (fig.) Ziel, *das;* **where's your next ~ of call?** (fig.) wo willst du als Nächstes hin?; **~ of entry** Zoll[abfertigungs]hafen, *der;* (for goods) Einfuhrhafen, *der;* (for persons) Einreisehafen, *der; see also* **free port** **2** (town) Hafenstadt, *die;* Hafen, *der* **3** (Naut., Aeronaut.: left side) Backbord, *das;* **land to ~!** Land an Backbord!; **turn** *or* **put the helm to ~:** nach Backbord drehen
B *adj.* (Naut., Aeronaut.: left) Backbord-; backbordseitig; **on the ~ bow/quarter** Backbord voraus/Backbord achteraus; *see also* **beam A 5**; **tack**[1] **A 3**; **watch A 3**

port[2] *n.* **1** (Naut.: opening) Pforte, *die* **2** (Naut.: porthole) Seitenfenster, *das;* (circular) Bullauge, *das* **3** (aperture) Öffnung, *die* **4** (gun aperture) Schießscharte, *die;* (on ship) Geschützpforte, *die* **5** (Computing) Port, *der;* Anschluss, *der*

port[3] *n.* (wine) Portwein, *der;* Port, *der* (ugs.)

portable /ˈpɔːtəbl/
A *adj.* tragbar; portabel (Werbespr.)
B *n.* (television) Portable, *der;* (radio) Portable, *der;* Koffergerät, *das;* (typewriter) Portable, *die;* Koffermaschine, *die*

portage /ˈpɔːtɪdʒ/ *n.* **1** (carrying) Transport über Land **2** (place) Portage, *die*

Portakabin ® /ˈpɔːtəkæbɪn/ *n.* Container, *der;* (as temporary office etc.) Bürocontainer, *der;* (as temporary living accommodation) Wohncontainer, *der*

portal /ˈpɔːtl/ *n.* **1** Eingang, *der;* Pforte, *die* (geh.); (of church, palace, etc.) Portal, *das;* **pass through the ~s of a place** (fig.) einen Ort besuchen; **the ~s of heaven** die Pforten des Himmels *od.* Himmelspforten (dichter.) **2** (Computing) Portal, *das*

port auˈthority *n.* Hafenbehörde, *die*

portcullis /pɔːtˈkʌlɪs/ *n.* (Archit.) Fallgitter, *das;* Fallgatter, *das*

portend /pɔːˈtend/ *v.t.* hindeuten auf (+ *Akk.*); **what does this ~?** was hat das zu bedeuten?

portent /ˈpɔːtent/ *n.* (literary) Vorzeichen, *das;* Omen, *das;* **a ~ of doom** ein schlimmes [Vor-]zeichen; ein böses Omen; **~s of war** Vorzeichen *od.* Vorboten des Krieges; **a ~ of the project's success** ein gutes Omen für den Erfolg des Vorhabens

portentous /pɔːˈtentəs/ *adj.* bedeutungsvoll; schicksalhaft ‹*Bedeutung*›; (ominous) unheilvoll

porter[1] /ˈpɔːtə(r)/ *n.* ▸**❶ p. 1260** (Brit.: doorman) Pförtner, *der;* (of hotel etc.) Portier, *der*

porter[2] *n.* **1** ▸**❶ p. 1260** (luggage handler) [Gepäck]träger, *der*/-trägerin, *die;* (in hotel) Hausdiener, *der* **2** (beer) Porter, *der od. das* **3** (Amer. Railw.) Schlafwagenschaffner, *der*/-schaffnerin, *die*

porterage /ˈpɔːtərɪdʒ/ *n.* (charge) Trägerlohn, *der*

porterhouse ˈsteak *n.* Porterhousesteak, *das*

porter's ˈlodge ▸ **lodge A 2**

portfolio /pɔːtˈfəʊlɪəʊ/ *n., pl.* **~s** **1** (list) Portefeuille, *das* **2** (Polit.) Geschäftsbereich, *der;* Portefeuille, *das* (geh.) **3** (case, contents) Mappe, *die*

portfolio: ~ caˈreer *n.* (Brit.) Portfoliokarriere, *die;* **~ manager** *n.* Portfoliomanager, *der*/-managerin, *die*

ˈporthole ▸ **port**[2] **2**

portico /ˈpɔːtɪkəʊ/ *n., pl.* **~es** *or* **~s** (Archit.) Säulenvorbau, *der;* Portikus, *der* (fachspr.)

portière /pɔːˈtjeə(r)/ *n.* [schwerer] Türvorhang; Portiere, *die*

portion /ˈpɔːʃn/
A *n.* **1** (part) Teil, *der;* (of ticket) Abschnitt, *der;* (of inheritance) Anteil, *der* **2** (amount of food) Portion, *die* **3** (arch./literary: destiny) Los, *das;* Schicksal, *das* **4** (quantity) gewisses Maß (**of** an + *Dat.*)
B *v.t.* aufteilen (**among** unter + *Akk.*, **into** in + *Akk.*)

Phrasal verb
- **~ ˈout** *v.t.* aufteilen (**among, between** unter + *Akk.*); **she ~ed out the food** sie verteilte das Essen

Portland /ˈpɔːtlənd/: **~ ceˈment** *n.* Portlandzement, *der;* **~ ˈstone** *n.* Portland[kalk-]stein, *der*

portly /ˈpɔːtlɪ/ *adj.* beleibt; korpulent; **have a ~ frame** beleibt *od.* korpulent sein

portmanteau /pɔːtˈmæntəʊ/ *n., pl.* **~s** *or* **~x** /pɔːtˈmæntəʊz/ Reisekoffer, *der*

portˈmanteau word *n.* Port[e]manteauform, *die* (fachspr.); (fig.: generalized term) weiter Begriff

portrait /ˈpɔːtrɪt/ *n.* **1** (picture) Porträt, *das;* Bildnis, *das* (*geh.*); *attrib.* Porträt-; **sit for one's ~ [to sb.]** [jmdm.] Porträt sitzen; sich [von jmdm.] porträtieren lassen; **have one's ~ painted** sich porträtieren lassen; **full-length ~:** Ganzporträt, *das;* **~ photographer** Porträtfotograf, *der*/-fotografin, *die* **2** (description) Porträt, *das;* Bild, *das;* **give/convey an unflattering ~ of sb./sth.** ein wenig schmeichelhaftes Bild von jmdm./etw. zeichnen

ˈportrait format *n.* (also Computing) Hochformat, *das*

portraitist /ˈpɔːtrɪtɪst/ *n.* ▸**❶ p. 1260** Porträtist, *der*/Porträtistin, *die;* (painter also) Porträtmaler, *der*/-malerin, *die;* (photographer also) Porträtfotograf, *der*/-fotografin, *die*

portraiture /ˈpɔːtrɪtʃə(r)/ *n.* Porträtieren, *das;* (painting also) Porträtmalerei, *die;* (photographing also) Porträtfotografie, *die;* **he is known for his ~:** er ist für *od.* durch seine Porträts bekannt

portray /pɔːˈtreɪ/ *v.t.* **1** (describe) darstellen; schildern **2** (make likeness of) porträtieren ‹*Person*›; darstellen, wiedergeben ‹*Atmosphäre usw.*›; ‹*Schauspieler:*› darstellen ‹*Rolle, Person*›

P

portrayal /pɔːˈtreɪəl/ *n.* **1** (description) Darstellung, *die;* Schilderung, *die;* (esp. of person) Porträt, *das* **2** (acting) Darstellung, *die* **3** (portrait) Darstellung, *die;* Porträt, *das*

Portugal /ˈpɔːtjʊgl/ *pr. n.* Portugal *(das)*

Portuguese /pɔːtjʊˈgiːz/ ▸ⓘ **p. 1277**, ▸ⓘ **p. 1345**

A *adj.* portugiesisch; **sb. is ~:** jmd. ist Portugiese/Portugiesin; *see also* **English A**

B *n., pl. same* **1** (person) Portugiese, *der*/Portugiesin, *die* **2** (language) Portugiesisch, *das; see also* **English B 1**

Portuguese man-of-ˈwar *n.* (Zool.) Portugiesische Galeere

POS *abbr.* = **point-of-sale**

pose /pəʊz/

A *v.t.* **1** (be cause of) aufwerfen ‹*Frage, Problem*›; darstellen ‹*Bedrohung, Problem*›; bedeuten ‹*Bedrohung*›; mit sich bringen ‹*Schwierigkeiten*› **2** (propound) vorbringen; aufstellen ‹*Theorie*› **3** (place) Aufstellung nehmen lassen, sich aufstellen lassen ‹*Gruppe, Kinder, Mannschaft, Gesellschaft*›; Positur einnehmen lassen, posieren lassen ‹*Modell*›

B *v.i.* **1** (assume attitude) posieren; (fig.) sich geziert benehmen *od.* geben (abwertend); **~ [in the] nude** für einen Akt posieren **2** **~ as** sich geben als; **he likes to ~ as an expert** er spielt gern den Experten

C *n.* Haltung, *die;* Pose, *die;* (fig.) Pose, *die;* Gehabe, *das* (abwertend); **strike a ~:** eine Pose einnehmen; **she's always striking ~s** (fig.) sie benimmt sich immer so geziert; **hold a ~:** eine Pose beibehalten; in einer Haltung verharren (geh.); **hold that ~!** bleib so!; **it's just a [big] ~** (fig.) es ist reine Pose

poser /ˈpəʊzə(r)/ *n.* (question) knifflige Frage; (problem) schwieriges Problem; **that's a real ~:** das ist eine harte Nuss (ugs.); **set some ~s for sb.** jmdm. manche harte Nuss zu knacken geben (ugs.)

poseur /pəʊˈzɜː(r)/ *n.* Blender, *der* (abwertend); Poseur, *der* (geh. abwertend)

poseuse /pəʊˈzɜːz/ *n. fem.* Blenderin, *die* (abwertend)

posh /pɒʃ/

A *adj.* (coll.) vornehm; nobel (spött.); stinkvornehm (salopp); **~ hotel/newspaper** Nobelhotel, *das*/Nobelgazette, *die* (spött.); **the ~ people** die Schickeria (ugs.)

B *adv.* **talk ~:** hochgestochen reden/mit vornehmem Akzent sprechen

C *v.t.* **~ up** aufmotzen (ugs.)

posit /ˈpɒzɪt/ *v.t.* postulieren (geh.)

position /pəˈzɪʃn/

A *n.* **1** (place occupied) Platz, *der;* (of player in team or line-up, of actor, of plane, ship, etc.) Position, *die;* (of hands of clock, words, stars) Stellung, *die;* (of building etc., of organ in body) Lage, *die;* (of river) [Ver]lauf, *der;* **find one's ~ on a map** seinen Standort auf einer Karte finden; **take [up] one's ~:** seinen Platz einnehmen; **they took their ~ at the end of the queue** sie stellten sich ans Ende der Schlange; **after the second lap he was in fourth ~:** nach der zweiten Runde lag er an vierter Stelle; **he finished in second ~:** er belegte den zweiten Platz; **what ~ do you play [in]?** (Sport) in welcher Position spielst du?; **in the starting ~:** auf Startposition **2** (proper place) **be in/out of ~:** an seinem Platz/nicht an seinem Platz sein; **put sth. into ~:** etw. an seinen Platz stellen **3** (Mil.) Stellung, *die* **4** (Chess) Position, *die;* Stellung, *die;* **~ play** Positionsspiel, *das;* Stellungsspiel, *das;* **leave the pieces in ~:** die Figuren aufgestellt *od.* stehen lassen **5** (fig.: mental attitude) Standpunkt, *der;* Haltung, *die;* **take up a ~ on sth.** einen Standpunkt *od.* eine Haltung zu etw. einnehmen; **take the ~ that ...:** auf dem Standpunkt stehen *od.* sich auf den Standpunkt stellen, dass ... **6** (fig.: situation) **be in a good ~ [financially]** [finanziell] gut gestellt sein *od.* dastehen; **be in a ~ of strength** eine starke Position haben; **negotiate from a ~ of strength** aus einer Position der Stärke heraus verhandeln; **what's the ~?** wie stehen *od.* liegen die Dinge?; **what would you do if you were in my ~?** was würdest du in meiner Lage tun?; **put yourself in my ~!** versetz dich [einmal] in meine Lage!; **be in a/no ~ to do sth.** in der Lage/nicht in der Lage sein, etw. zu tun; **he's in no ~ to criticize us** es steht ihm nicht zu, uns zu kritisieren; *see also* **jockey B** **7** (rank) Stellung, *die;* Position, *die;* **a person of ~:** eine hoch gestellte Persönlichkeit; **a high ~ in society** eine hohe gesellschaftliche Stellung; **a pupil's ~ in class** die Stellung eines Schülers innerhalb der Klasse; **social ~:** gesellschaftliche *od.* soziale Stellung **8** (employment) [Arbeits]stelle, *die;* Stellung, *die;* **the ~ of ambassador in Bogotá** die Position des Botschafters in Bogotá; **permanent ~:** Dauerstellung, *die;* **the ~ of assistant manager** die Stelle *od.* Position des stellvertretenden Geschäftsführers; **rise to a ~ of responsibility** in eine verantwortliche Stellung aufsteigen; **~ of trust** Vertrauensstellung, *die;* Vertrauensposten, *der* **9** (posture) Haltung, *die;* (during sexual intercourse) Stellung, *die;* Position, *die;* (ballet) Position, *die;* (yoga) Stellung, *die;* **in a reclining ~:** zurückgelehnt; **in a sitting ~:** in sitzender Position *od.* Stellung; sitzend; **in an uncomfortable ~:** in unbequemer Stellung *od.* Haltung

B *v.t.* **1** platzieren; positionieren ‹*Lautsprecherboxen, Leuchten usw.*›; aufstellen, postieren ‹*Polizisten, Wachen*›; **~ oneself near the exit** sich in die Nähe des Ausgangs stellen/setzen; ‹*Wache, Posten usw.:*› sich in der Nähe des Ausgangs aufstellen **2** (Mil.: station) stationieren

positional /pəˈzɪʃənl/ *adj.* **1** (Ling.) isolierend ‹*Sprache*› **2** (Sport) positionell (fachspr.); **~ play** Stellungsspiel, *das* **3** (Mil.) **~ war** Stellungskrieg, *der*

positive /ˈpɒzɪtɪv/

A *adj.* **1** (definite) eindeutig; entschieden ‹*Weigerung*›; positiv ‹*Recht*›; **in a ~ tone of voice** in bestimmtem *od.* entschiedenem Ton; **to my ~ knowledge ...:** wie ich ganz sicher weiß, ... **2** (convinced) sicher; **Are you sure? — P~!** Bist du sicher? — Absolut [sicher]!; **he is ~ that he is right** er ist sich *(Dat.)* völlig sicher, dass er Recht hat; **I'm ~ of it** ich bin [mir] [dessen] ganz sicher **3** (affirmative) positiv **4** (optimistic) positiv; **regard sth. in a ~ light** etw. in positivem Licht sehen **5** (showing presence of sth.) positiv ‹*Ergebnis, Befund, Test*› **6** (constructive) konstruktiv ‹*Kritik, Vorschlag, Anregung, Rat, Hilfe*›; positiv ‹*Philosophie, Erfahrung, Denken*›; **she's the most ~ of the group** sie hat von allen in der Gruppe die positivste Einstellung **7** (Math.) positiv **8** (Ling.) ungesteigert **9** (Electr.) positiv ‹*Elektrode, Platte, Ladung, Ion*›; Plus‹*platte, -leiter*›; *see also* **feedback 2** **10** *as intensifier* (coll.) echt; **it would be a ~ miracle** es wäre ein echtes Wunder *od.* (ugs.) echt ein Wunder **11** (Photog.) positiv; Positiv-

B *n.* **1** (Ling.) Positiv, *der;* Grundstufe [des Adjektivs], *die* **2** (Photog.) Positiv, *das;* Positivbild, *das*

positive discrimiˈnation *n.* positive Diskriminierung (fachspr.); Bevorzugung, *die*

positively /ˈpɒzɪtɪvlɪ/ *adv.* **1** (constructively) konstruktiv ‹*kritisieren*›; positiv ‹*denken*› **2** (Electr.) positiv **3** (definitely) eindeutig, entschieden ‹*sich weigern*› **4** *as intensifier* (coll.) echt (ugs.); **it's ~ marvellous that ...:** es ist echt Spitze, dass ...

ˈpositive: ~ sign *n.* (Math.) positives Vorzeichen; (symbol) Pluszeichen, *das;* **~ vetting** *n., no indef. art.* (Brit.) Sicherheitsüberprüfung, *die*

positivism /ˈpɒzɪtɪvɪzm/ *n.* (Philos., Relig.) Positivismus, *der; see also* **logical positivism**

positivist /ˈpɒzɪtɪvɪst/

A *n.* Positivist, *der*/Positivistin, *die*

B *adj.* positivistisch

positron /ˈpɒzɪtrɒn/ *n.* (Phys.) Positron, *das*

posse /ˈpɒsɪ/ *n.* **1** (Amer.: force with legal authority) [Polizei]trupp, *der;* [Polizei]aufgebot, *das* **2** (crowd) Schar, *die;* **~ of advisers** Beraterstab, *der*

possess /pəˈzes/ *v.t.* **1** (own) besitzen; verfügen über (+ *Akk.*) (geh.); **be ~ed of** gesegnet sein mit (geh.); **~ed of money/wealth** bemittelt/begütert; **~ed of reason** vernunftbegabt **2** (have as faculty or quality) haben; **~ great passion** sehr leidenschaftlich sein **3** (dominate) ‹*Furcht usw.:*› ergreifen, Besitz nehmen von ‹*Person*›; **what ~ed you/him?** was ist in dich/ihn gefahren?; was für ein Teufel hat dich/ihn geritten? (ugs.) **4** (dated: copulate with) besitzen (geh. verhüll.) **5** (arch./formal) **~ oneself of sth.** sich einer Sache *(Gen.)* bemächtigen; sich *(Dat.)* etw. aneignen

possessed /pəˈzest/ *adj.* (dominated) besessen; **he's a man ~:** er ist ein Besessener; **~ by the devil/by** *or* **with an idea** vom Teufel/von einer Idee besessen; **be ~ by** *or* **with fear/horror** von Angst/Schrecken ergriffen sein; **be ~ by** *or* **with greed/ambition** von Gier/Ehrgeiz besessen sein; **be ~ by** *or* **with envy** von Neid erfüllt sein; **like one ~:** wie ein Besessener/eine Besessene

possession /pəˈzeʃn/ *n.* **1** (thing possessed) Besitz, *der;* **some of my ~s** einige meiner Sachen **2** *in pl.* (property) Besitz, *der;* (territory) Besitzungen; **worldly ~s** irdische Güter; **all his ~s** sein ganzer Besitz; all seine Habe **3** (controlling) **take ~ of** (Mil.) einnehmen ‹*Festung, Stadt usw.*›; besetzen ‹*Gebiet*›; **the enemy's ~ of the town** die feindliche Herrschaft *od.* Herrschaft des Feindes über die Stadt; **~ by the devil** Besessensein vom Teufel **4** (possessing) Besitz, *der;* **~ of land/firearms** Landbesitz, *der*/Waffenbesitz, *der;* **be in ~ of sth.** im Besitz einer Sache *(Gen.)* sein; **come into** *or* **get ~ of sth.** in den Besitz einer Sache *(Gen.)* gelangen; **regain** *or* **resume ~ of sth.** wieder in den Besitz einer Sache *(Gen.)* gelangen; **be in ~ of a high income** über ein hohes Einkommen verfügen; **put sb. in ~ of sth./of the facts** jmdn. in den Besitz einer Sache *(Gen.)* bringen/jmdn. ins Bild setzen; **in full ~ of one's senses** im Vollbesitz seiner geistigen Kräfte; **be in full ~ of the facts** voll im Bilde sein; **the information in my ~:** die mir vorliegenden Informationen; **have sth. in one's ~:** im Besitz einer Sache *(Gen.)* sein; **take ~ of** in Besitz nehmen; beziehen ‹*Haus, Wohnung*› **5** (Sport) **win ~ of the ball** in Ballbesitz gelangen; **lose ~:** den Ball verlieren; **in ~:** im Ballbesitz **6** (Law) Besitz, *der;* **enter into ~ of sth.** etw. in Besitz nehmen; *see also* **point A 3; vacant 1**

possessive /pəˈzesɪv/

A *adj.* **1** (jealously retaining possession) besitzergreifend; **be ~ about sth.** etw. eifersüchtig hüten; **be ~ about** *or* **towards sb.** an jmdn. Besitzansprüche stellen **2** (Ling.) possessiv; **~ adjective** Possessivadjektiv, *das; see also* **pronoun**

B *n.* (Ling.) Possessivum, *das*

posˈsessive case *n.* Possessiv[us], *der*

possessively /pəˈzesɪvlɪ/ *adv.* besitzergreifend

possessor /pəˈzesə(r)/ *n.* Besitzer, *der*/Besitzerin, *die;* **be the ~ of a fine singing voice** eine schöne Singstimme besitzen

posset /ˈpɒsɪt/ *n.* (Hist.) *heiße Milch mit Bier od. Wein und Gewürzen*

possibility /pɒsɪˈbɪlɪtɪ/ *n.* **1** Möglichkeit, *die;* **be within the range** *or* **bounds of ~:** im Bereich des Möglichen liegen; **there's no ~ of his coming/agreeing** es ist ausgeschlossen, dass er kommt/zustimmt; **there's not much ~ of success** die Erfolgschancen sind nicht groß; **the constant ~ of failure** die ständige Gefahr des Scheiterns; **if by any ~ ...:** falls tatsächlich ...; (if without taking any trouble) falls zufällig ...; **is there any ~ of our being able to do it?** gibt es für uns irgendeine Möglichkeit, es zu tun?; **it's a distinct ~ that ...:** es ist gut möglich, dass ...; **accept that sth. is a ~:** es akzeptieren, dass etw. möglich ist *od.* nicht auszuschließen ist; **he is a ~ for the job** er ist ein möglicher Anwärter auf die Stelle; er kommt für die Stelle in Betracht; **what are the possibilities?** welche Möglichkeiten gibt es? **2** *in pl.* (potential) Möglichkeiten *Pl.;* **the house/subject has possibilities** aus dem Haus/Thema lässt sich etwas machen; **the scheme has possibilities** in dem Plan stecken Möglichkeiten

p

possible /ˈpɒsɪbl/
A *adj.* **1)** möglich; **if ~:** wenn *od.* falls möglich; wenn es geht; **as ... as ~:** so ... wie möglich; möglichst ...; **the greatest ~ assistance** die größtmögliche Unterstützung; **all the assistance ~:** alle denkbare Unterstützung; **anything is ~:** alles ist möglich; es ist alles möglich; **at the earliest ~ time** so früh wie möglich; (formal) zum frühestmöglichen Termin/Zeitpunkt; **they made it ~ for me to be here** sie haben es mir ermöglicht, hier zu sein; **the worst ~ solution** die denkbar schlechteste Lösung; die schlechteste der möglichen Lösungen; **if it's at all ~:** wenn es irgend geht *od.* möglich ist; **would it be ~ for me to ...?** könnte ich vielleicht ...?; **it is not ~ to do more** mehr kann man unmöglich tun; **for ~ emergencies** für eventuelle Notfälle; **all ~ risks** alle denkbaren Risiken; **I'll do everything ~ to help you** ich werde mein Möglichstes *od.* alles nur Erdenkliche tun, um dir zu helfen; **be as kind to her as ~:** sei so nett zu ihr, wie [nur irgend] möglich; **we will help as far as ~:** wir werden helfen, so weit wir können **2)** (likely) [durchaus *od.* gut] möglich; **few thought his election was ~:** nur wenige glaubten an seine Wahl **3)** (acceptable) möglich; **there's no ~ excuse for it** dafür gibt es keine Entschuldigung; **the only ~ man for the position** der einzige Mann, der für die Stellung infrage kommt
B *n.* Anwärter, *der*/Anwärterin, *die;* Kandidat, *der*/Kandidatin, *die;* **presidential ~:** Präsidentschaftsanwärter, *der*

possibly /ˈpɒsɪblɪ/ *adv.* **1)** (by possible means) **I cannot ~ commit myself** ich kann mich unmöglich festlegen; **how can I ~?** wie könnte ich?; **how could I ~ have come?** wie hätte ich denn kommen können?; **can that ~ be true?** kann das überhaupt wahr sein *od.* stimmen?; **they did all they ~ could** sie haben alles Menschenmögliche *od.* alles in ihrer Macht Stehende getan; **if I ~ can** wenn es mir irgendwie möglich ist; **as often as I ~ can** sooft ich irgend kann; **I'll come as soon as I ~ can** ich komme so früh, wie es nur irgend geht; **can you ~ lend me £10?** kannst du mir vielleicht *od.* wohl 10 Pfund leihen? **2)** (perhaps) möglicherweise; vielleicht; **he might ~ be related to them** er ist vielleicht *od.* möglicherweise mit ihnen verwandt; **Do you think ...? — P~:** Glaubst du ...? — Möglich[erweise] *od.* Vielleicht

possum /ˈpɒsəm/ *n.* (coll.) **1)** ▸ **opossum 1 2) play ~** (pretend to be asleep) sich schlafend stellen; (pretend to be dead) sich tot stellen **3)** (Austral., NZ) Fuchskusu, *der*

post¹ /pəʊst/
A *n.* **1)** (as support) Pfosten, *der* **2)** (stake) Pfahl, *der;* **deaf as a ~** (coll.) stocktaub (ugs.); *see also* **pillar 1 3)** (Racing) (starting/finishing ~) Start-/Zielpfosten, *der;* **be left at the ~:** [hoffnungslos] abgehängt werden (ugs.); weit zurückbleiben; (fig.) von Anfang an keine Chancen haben; **be first past the ~:** als Erster durchs Ziel gehen; **the 'first past the ~' system** das Mehrheitswahlsystem; **be beaten at the ~** (lit. or fig.) im letzten Moment noch geschlagen werden; *see also* **pip⁵ 4)** (Sport: of goal) Pfosten, *der*
B *v.t.* **1)** (stick up) anschlagen, ankleben ‹*Plakat, Aufruf, Notiz, Zettel*›; **~ something on the noticeboard** einen Anschlag am schwarzen Brett machen; **'~ no bills'** „Plakate ankleben verboten" **2)** (make known) [öffentlich] anschlagen *od.* bekannt geben; ausschreiben ‹*Belohnung*›; ausweisen ‹*Ansteigen, Gewinn, Verlust*›; öffentlich ankündigen, bekannt machen ‹*Veranstaltung*›; **~ [as] missing** als vermisst melden **3)** (Amer.: achieve) erreichen; schaffen; erringen ‹*Sieg*›

(Phrasal verb)
• **~ 'up** *v.t.* anschlagen; ankleben; **~ up a notice** einen Anschlag machen

post²
A *n.* **1)** (Brit.: one dispatch of letters) Postausgang, *der;* **by the same ~:** mit gleicher Post; **by return of ~:** postwendend; **sort the ~:** die Postausgänge sortieren **2)** (Brit.: one collection of letters) [Briefkasten]leerung, *die* **3)** (Brit.: one delivery of letters) Post[zustellung], *die;* **in the ~:** bei der Post (*see also* **4**); **the ~ has come** die Post ist da *od.* ist schon gekommen; **the arrival of the ~:** das Eintreffen der Briefpost; **sort the ~:** die Posteingänge sortieren; **is there a second ~ in this area?** gibt es hier eine zweite Postzustellung?; **there is no ~ on Sundays** sonntags kommt keine Post; **there has been no ~ today** heute ist keine Post gekommen; **is there any ~ for me?** habe ich Post?; **have a heavy ~:** viel Post bekommen; **the morning's ~:** die Morgenpost; **you'll get it in tomorrow's ~:** du bekommst es mit der morgigen Post **4)** *no pl., no indef. art.* (Brit.: official conveying) Post, *die;* **by ~:** mit der Post; per Post; **in the ~:** in der Post (*see also* **3**) **5)** (~ office) Post, *die;* (~box) Briefkasten, *der;* **take sth. to the ~:** etw. zur Post bringen/(to ~box) etw. einwerfen *od.* in den Briefkasten werfen; **drop sth. in the ~:** etw. einwerfen *od.* in den Briefkasten werfen
B *v.t.* **1)** (dispatch) abschicken; (take to ~ office) zur Post bringen; (put in ~box) einwerfen; **~ sb. sth.** jmdm. etw. schicken; **~ sth. off** etw. abschicken **2)** (Bookk.) übertragen; **~ up** auf den letzten Stand bringen ‹*Bücher*›; verbuchen ‹*Verkäufe, Abschlüsse*› **3)** (fig. coll.) **keep sb. ~ed [about** *or* **on sth.]** jmdn. [über etw. (*Akk.*)] auf dem Laufenden halten

post³
A *n.* **1)** (job) Stelle, *die;* Posten, *der;* **in ~:** im Amt; **a teaching ~:** eine Stelle als Lehrer *od.* Lehrerstelle; **a ~ as director** ein Posten als Direktor *od.* Direktorenposten; **the ~ of driver** die Stelle des Fahrers; **a diplomatic ~:** ein diplomatischer Posten **2)** (Mil.: place of duty) Posten, *der;* (fig.) Platz, *der;* Posten, *der;* **the sentries are at/took up their ~s** die Wachen sind auf ihren/bezogen ihre Posten; **take up one's ~** (fig.) seinen Platz einnehmen; **all workers must be at their ~s by 8.30** alle Arbeiter müssen um 8.30 Uhr an ihren Arbeitsplätzen sein; **last/first ~** (Brit. Mil.) letzter/erster Zapfenstreich **3)** (Mil.: position of unit) Garnison, *die;* Standort, *der* **4)** (Mil.: fort) Fort, *das* **5)** (trading-~) Niederlassung, *die*
B *v.t.* **1)** (place) postieren; aufstellen **2)** (appoint) einsetzen; **~ sb. overseas/to Abu Dhabi/to a ship** jmdn. in Übersee/in Abu Dhabi/auf einem Schiff einsetzen; **be ~ed to an embassy** an eine Botschaft versetzt werden; **~ an officer to a unit** einen Offizier einer Einheit (*Dat.*) zuweisen; **be ~ed away** versetzt *od.* (Mil.) abkommandiert werden; **where's he being ~ed to?** wo wird er eingesetzt?; (to new place) wohin wird er versetzt?

post- /pəʊst/ *pref.* nach-/Nach-; post-/Post- (*mit Fremdwörtern*)

postage /ˈpəʊstɪdʒ/ *n.* Porto, *das*

postage: ~ 'due *n.* Nachgebühr, *die; attrib.* **~-due stamp** Portomarke, *die;* **~ meter** *n.* (Amer.) Frankiermaschine, *die;* [Post]freistempler, *der;* **~ paid** *adj.* freigemacht; frankiert; Frei‹*umschlag*›; **the price, ~ paid, is £20** es kostet 20 Pfund, einschließlich Porto; **~ stamp** *n.* Briefmarke, *die;* Postwertzeichen, *das* (Postw.)

postal /ˈpəʊstl/ *adj.* **1)** (of the post) Post-; postalisch ‹*Aufgabe, Einrichtung*› **2)** (by post) per Post *nachgestellt;* **~ tuition** Fernunterricht, *der*

postal: ~ card (Amer.) ▸ **postcard; ~ code** ▸ **postcode; ~ district** *n.* Zustellbezirk, *der;* **~ meter** *n.* (Amer.) ▸ **postage meter; ~ order** *n.* ≈ Postanweisung, *die;* **~ rate** *n.* Postgebühr, *die;* **P~ Union** *n.* Postverein, *der;* **~ vote** *n.* Briefwahl, *die*

post: ~bag (Brit.) ▸ **mailbag; ~box** *n.* (Brit.) Briefkasten, *der;* **~card** *n.* Postkarte, *die;* **~-chaise** *n.* (Hist.) Postchaise, *die*

post-'classic[al] *adj.* nachklassisch

'postcode *n.* (Brit.) Postleitzahl, *die*

post'date *v.t.* **1)** (give later date to) vordatieren **2)** (belong to later date than) späteren *od.* jüngeren Datums sein als (+ *Nom.*); von einem späteren Zeitpunkt/aus einer späteren Zeit datieren als (+ *Nom.*)

post-'doctoral *adj.* **~ thesis/grant** Habilitationsschrift, *die*/-stipendium, *das;* **~ research** *Forschungen im Anschluss an die Promotion*

poster /ˈpəʊstə(r)/ *n.* **1)** (placard) Plakat, *das;* (notice) Anschlag, *der* **2)** (printed picture) Plakat, *das;* Poster, *das*

'poster colour ▸ **poster paint**

poste restante /pəʊst reˈstɑ̃t/ *n.* Abteilung/Schalter für postlagernde Sendungen; **write to sb. [at the] ~ in Rome** jmdm. postlagernd nach Rom schreiben

posterior /pɒˈstɪərɪə(r)/
A *adj.* **1)** (formal: later) später; **~ to** nach **2)** (placed behind) hinter...
B *n.* (joc.) Hinterteil, *das* (ugs.)

posterity /pɒˈsterɪtɪ/ *n., no pl., no art.* (future generations) die Nachwelt; **go down to ~ [as sth.]** [als etw.] in die Geschichte eingehen

'poster paint *n.* Plakatfarbe, *die*

post: ~ exchange *n.* (Amer. Mil.) PX, *das; Kaufhaus für Angehörige der amerikanischen Truppen;* **~-'free** (Brit.) **A** *adj.* **1)** (free of charge) portofrei; **2)** (with postage prepaid) freigemacht; frankiert; **B** *adv.* portofrei

postgrad /pəʊstˈgræd/ (coll.), **post'graduate**
A *adj.* Graduierten-; ‹*College, Studiengang*› für Graduierte; postgraduell (fachspr.); **postgraduate study** ≈ Aufbaustudium, *das;* ≈ *weiterführendes Studium;* **postgraduate student** Graduierte, *der/die;* **postgraduate degree** höherer akademischer Grad
B *n.* Graduierte, *der/die*

post: ~'haste *adv.* schnellstens; **~ horn** *n.* (Hist.) Posthorn, *das;* **~ horse** *n.* (Hist.) Postpferd, *das;* **~ house** *n.* (Hist.) Poststation, *die*

posthumous /ˈpɒstjʊməs/ *adj.* **1)** nachgelassen, (geh.) postum ‹*Buch usw.*› **2)** (occurring after death) nachträglich; post[h]um (geh.); **~ fame** Nachruhm, *der* **3)** nach dem Tode des Vaters geboren, post[h]um (geh.) ‹*Kind*›

posthumously /ˈpɒstjʊməslɪ/ *adv.* postum (geh.), nach dem Tode ‹*veröffentlicht werden*›; postum (geh.), nachträglich ‹*rehabilitieren, verleihen*›; nach dem Tode des Vaters ‹*geboren*›

postil[l]ion /pəˈstɪljən/ *n.* (Hist.) Postillion, *der*

post-im'pressionism *n.* Postimpressionismus, *der*

post-im'pressionist *n.* Postimpressionist, *der*/Postimpressionistin, *die*

post-impression'istic *adj.* postimpressionistisch

post-in'dustrial *adj.* postindustriell

posting /ˈpəʊstɪŋ/ *n.* (appointment) Versetzung, *die;* (post) Stelle, *die;* Posten, *der;* **he's got a new ~:** er ist versetzt worden

'Post-it ® *n.* Klebezettel, *der*

post: ~man /ˈpəʊstmən/, *pl.* **~men** /ˈpəʊstmən/ *n.* ▸ ❶ **p. 1260** Briefträger, *der;* Postbote, *der* (ugs.); **~man's 'knock** *n.* (Brit.) *Gesellschaftsspiel, bei dem der 'Postbote' Briefe gegen einen Kuss aushändigt;* **~mark A** *n.* Poststempel, *der;* **'date as ~mark'** „Datum des Poststempels"; **B** *v.t.* abstempeln; **the letter was ~marked 'Brighton'** der Brief war in Brighton abgestempelt; **~master** *n.* ▸ ❶ **p. 1260** Postamtvorsteher, *der;* Postmeister, *der* (veralt.); **P~master 'General** *n., pl.* **P~masters General** (Hist.) Postminister, *der*/-ministerin, *die;* **~ mill** *n.* Bockmühle, *die;* **~mistress** *n.* ▸ ❶ **p. 1260** Postamtvorsteherin, *die;* Postmeisterin, *die* (veralt.); **~'modern** ▸ **~modernist A**; **~'modernism** *n.* Postmodernismus, *der;* Postmoderne, *die;* **~'modernist A** *adj.* postmodernistisch; postmodern; **B** *n.* Postmodernist, *der*/Postmodernistin, *die;* Vertreter, *der*/Vertreterin, *die* der Postmoderne

post-mortem /pəʊstˈmɔːtəm/
A *adv.* nach dem Tode; post mortem (fachspr.)
B *adj.* **1)** (after death) nach dem Tode eintretend, (fachspr., geh.) postmortal ‹*Veränderung*›; **~ examination** Leichenschau, *die;* (with dissection) Obduktion, *die* **2)** (fig.: after an event) nachträglich
C *n.* **1)** (examination) Obduktion, *die* **2)** (fig.) nachträgliche Bewertung *od.* Analyse; Manöverkritik, *die* (fig.); **hold** *or* **have a ~ on sth.** etw. einer nachträglichen Bewertung *od.* Analyse unterziehen; **hold a ~ on the election** eine Wahlanalyse durchführen; das Wahlergebnis einer Analyse (*Dat.*) unterziehen

P

post'natal *adj.* nach der Geburt *nachgestellt;* nachgeburtlich (fachspr.); postnatal (fachspr.)

post: ~ **office** *n.* 1 (organization) **the P~ Office** die Post; *attrib.* **P~ Office** Post-; **work for the P~ Office** bei der Post arbeiten; 2 (place) Postamt, *das;* Post, *die;* 3 (Amer.) ▸**postman's knock**; ~ **office box** *n.* ▸ p. 1287 Postfach, *das;* ~**paid** A /'--/ *adj.* frankiert; freigemacht; ~**paid envelope** Freiumschlag, *der;* B /-'-/ *adv.* portofrei; franko (fachspr. veralt.); **£6.50 ~paid** 6,50 Pfund einschließlich Porto; **reply ~paid** mit vorfrankiertem Umschlag/mit vorfrankierter Postkarte antworten

postpone /pəʊst'pəʊn, pə'spəʊn/ *v.t.* verschieben; (for an indefinite period) aufschieben; ~ **sth. until next week** etw. auf nächste Woche verschieben; ~ **sth. for a year** etw. um ein Jahr verschieben; ~ **further discussion of a matter** die weitere Diskussion einer Angelegenheit zurückstellen

postponement /pəʊst'pəʊnmənt, pə'spəʊnmənt/ *n.* Verschiebung, *die;* (for an indefinite period) Aufschub, *der;* **a 30-day ~:** eine Verschiebung um 30 Tage

postpositive /pəʊst'pɒzɪtɪv/ *adj.* (Ling.) nachgestellt; postpositiv (fachspr.)

postprandial /pəʊst'prændɪəl/ *adj.* (formal/joc.) Verdauungs‹*schläfchen, -spaziergang, -schnaps*› (ugs.); ‹*Rede, Gespräch, Schwatz*› nach dem Essen, nach Tisch

'post room *n.* Poststelle, *die*

postscript /'pəʊstskrɪpt, 'pəʊskrɪpt/ *n.* Nachschrift, *die;* Postskript, *das;* (fig.) Nachtrag, *der;* **the ~ was that ...** (fig.) das Ende vom Lied war, dass ... (ugs.); **add a ~** (fig.) einen Nachtrag machen, etwas nachtragen (**to** zu)

post-'tax *adj.* nach Abzug der Steuern (nachgestellt)

'post town *n.* Postort, *der*

'post-traumatic stress disorder *n.* (Med.) posttraumatische Belastungsstörung

postulate
A /'pɒstjʊleɪt/ *v.t.* (claim as true, existent, necessary) postulieren; ausgehen von; (depend on) voraussetzen; (put forward) aufstellen ‹*Theorie*›
B /'pɒstjʊlət/ *n.* (fundamental condition) Postulat, *das* (geh.); (prerequisite) Voraussetzung, *die;* Postulat, *das* (geh.); (Math.) Axiom, *das*

posture /'pɒstʃə(r)/
A *n.* (relative position) [Körper]haltung, *die;* (fig.: mental, political, military) Haltung, *die;* **have poor/good ~:** eine schlechte/gute Haltung haben; **put the country in a ~ of defence** das Land in Verteidigungsbereitschaft versetzen
B *v.i.* posieren; (strike a pose) sich in Positur werfen (ugs., leicht spött.)

'post-war *adj.* Nachkriegs-; der Nachkriegszeit *nachgestellt;* ~ **credits** Kriegsanleihen

'postwoman *n.* ▸ p. 1260 Briefträgerin, *die;* Postbotin, *die* (ugs.)

posy /'pəʊzɪ/ *n.* Sträußchen, *das*

pot¹ /pɒt/
A *n.* 1 (cooking vessel) [Koch]topf, *der;* **it's [a case of] the ~ calling the kettle black** (coll.) ein Esel schimpft *od.* (geh.) schilt den andern Langohr; der soll/die soll/die sollen sich an die eigene Nase fassen (ugs.); **go to ~** (coll.) den Bach runtergehen (ugs.); **let oneself go to ~** (coll.) sich hängen lassen [und den Bach runtergehen] (ugs.); *see also* **boil¹ A 1**; **pan¹ A 1** 2 (container, contents) Topf, *der;* (tea~, coffee ~) Kanne, *die;* **a ~ of tea** eine Kanne Tee; (in café etc.) ein Kännchen Tee; *see also* **gold A 2** 3 (drinking vessel) Becher, *der;* (with handle) Krug, *der* 4 (coll.: as prize) Pott, *der* (ugs.) 5 (coll.: prize) Preis, *der* 6 (coll.: ~belly) Schmerbauch, *der* (ugs.); Wampe, *die* (ugs. abwertend) 7 (coll.: large sum) **a ~ of/~s of** massenweise; jede Menge 8 (amount bet) [Gesamt]einsatz, *der;* Pot, *der;* **contribute to the ~:** [ein]setzen
B *v.t.*, **-tt-** 1 (put in container[s]) in einen Topf/in Töpfe füllen 2 (put in plant ~) ~ **[up]** eintopfen; ~ **out** austopfen 3 (kill) abschießen; abknallen (ugs. abwertend) 4 (Brit. Billiards, Snooker) einlochen. *See also* **potted**
C *v.i.*, **-tt-** ballern (ugs.) (**at** auf + *Akk.*)

pot² *n.* (sl.: marijuana) Pot, *das* (Jargon)

potable /'pəʊtəbl/ *adj.* (formal) trinkbar

potash /'pɒtæʃ/ *n.* Kaliumkarbonat, *das;* Pottasche, *die* (veralt.); ~ **fertilizer** Kalidünger, *der*

potassium /pə'tæsɪəm/ *n.* (Chem.) Kalium, *das*

potato /pə'teɪtəʊ/ *n., pl.* ~**es** 1 Kartoffel, *die;* **a hot ~** (fig. coll.) ein heißes Eisen (ugs.); **drop sb./sth. like a hot ~** (coll.) jmdn./etw. fallen lassen wie eine heiße Kartoffel; *see also* **bake A 1**; **boil B 1**; **chip B 2**; **crisp B 1**; **fry¹ B**; **mash A 4, B** 2 (plant) Kartoffel[pflanze], *die*

potato 'salad *n.* Kartoffelsalat, *der*

pot: ~ **belly** *n.* (bulging belly) Schmerbauch, *der* (ugs.); Wampe, *die* (ugs. abwertend); (from malnutrition) Blähbauch, *der;* ~**boiler** *n.* (derog.) (novel etc.) Fließbandprodukt, *das* (abwertend); (film, theatre production) Fließbandproduktion, *die* (abwertend)

poteen /pɒ'ti:n/ *n., no pl.* (esp. Irish) schwarz gebrannter Schnaps

potency /'pəʊtənsɪ/ *n.* 1 (of drug) Wirksamkeit, *die;* (of alcoholic drink) Stärke, *die;* (Mil.) Schlagkraft, *die;* (of reason, argument) Gewichtigkeit, *die;* (influence) Einfluss, *der;* Potenz, *die* (geh.); **the ~ to do sth.** die Fähigkeit, etw. zu tun 2 (of male) **[sexual] ~:** [sexuelle] Potenz

potent /'pəʊtənt/ *adj.* 1 [hoch]wirksam ‹*Droge, Medizin*›; stark ‹*Schnaps, Kaffee, Tee usw.*›; schlagkräftig ‹*Mannschaft, Truppe, Waffe*›; gewichtig, schwerwiegend ‹*Grund, Argument*›; wichtig, entscheidend ‹*Faktor*›; stark ‹*Motiv*›; (influential) einflussreich; potent (geh.) 2 (sexually) potent ‹*Mann*›

potentate /'pəʊtənteɪt/ *n.* Herrscher, *der*/Herrscherin, *die;* Potentat, *der*/Potentatin, *die* (geh. abwertend)

potential /pə'tenʃl/
A *adj.* potenziell (geh.); möglich; ~ **energy** potenzielle Energie
B *n.* 1 (possibility) Potenzial, *das* (geh.); Möglichkeiten *Pl.;* ~ **for growth/development** Wachstums-/Entwicklungspotenzial, *das;* **acting ~:** schauspielerisches Talent; **leadership ~:** Führungsqualitäten; **realize/reach one's ~:** seine Möglichkeiten ausschöpfen; **develop one's ~:** seine Fähigkeiten [weiter]entwickeln 2 (Phys.) Potenzial, *das*

potentiality /pətenʃɪ'ælɪtɪ/ *n.* 1 (capacity) Möglichkeiten *Pl.;* **have great growth ~:** ein großes Wachstumspotenzial haben 2 (possibility) Möglichkeit, *die*

potentially /pə'tenʃəlɪ/ *adv.* potenziell (geh.); **he's ~ dangerous** er kann gefährlich werden; **a ~ useful invention** eine Erfindung mit Anwendungsmöglichkeiten; **he's ~ capable of it** er wäre dazu fähig; **a ~ rich country** ein Land, das reich sein könnte

potentilla /pəʊtən'tɪlə/ *n.* (Bot.) Fingerkraut, *das*

pot: ~**head** *n.* (sl.) Kiffer, *der*/Kifferin, *die* (ugs.); ~ **herb** *n.* Küchenkraut, *das;* ~**hole** A *n.* 1 (in road) Schlagloch, *das;* 2 (deep cave) [tiefe] Höhle; B *v.i.* Höhlen erkunden; ~**holed** /'pɒthəʊld/ *adj.* löchrig ‹*Straße, Piste, Asphalt*›; ~**holer** /'pɒthəʊlə(r)/ *n.* [Hobby]höhlenforscher, *der*/-forscherin, *die;* ~**holing** /'pɒthəʊlɪŋ/ *n., no pl.* Erkundung von Höhlen; **go ~holing** Höhlen erkunden gehen; Höhlenfahrten/eine Höhlenfahrt machen (fachspr.); ~**-hunter** *n.* 1 (hunter) Jäger, der alles abschießt[, was ihm vor die Flinte kommt] (abwertend); 2 (athlete) Pokalsammler, *der*/-sammlerin, *die*

potion /'pəʊʃn/ *n.* Trank, *der*

pot: ~ **'luck** *n.* **take ~ luck [with sb.]** sich überraschen lassen; **there are so many to choose from; I'll just take ~ luck** die Auswahl ist so groß; ich greife einfach mal aufs Geratewohl *od.* blind einen/eine/eins raus; ~ **plant** *n.* Topfpflanze, *die*

potpourri /pəʊpʊə'ri:, pəʊ'pʊərɪ/ *n.* 1 Duftmischung, *die* 2 (fig.) (of music) Potpourri, *das;* (of literary writings) Sammlung, *die;* Anthologie, *die* (Literaturw.); (mixture) Sammelsurium, *das;* buntes Allerlei

pot: ~ **roast** A *n.* Schmorbraten, *der;* B *v.t.* schmoren; ~**sherd** /'pɒtʃɜ:d/ *n.* (Archaeol.) [Ton]scherbe, *die;* ~**shot** *n.* 1 (random shot) Schuss aufs Geratewohl; **take a ~shot [at sb./sth.]** aufs Geratewohl [auf jmdn./etw.] schießen; 2 (fig.: critical remark) Attacke, *die;* **take a ~shot at sth.** etw. attackieren; 3 (fig.: random attempt) Versuch auf gut Glück; Schuss ins Blaue [hinein]

pottage /'pɒtɪdʒ/ ▸**mess A 5**

potted /'pɒtɪd/ *adj.* 1 (preserved) eingemacht; ~ **meat/fish** Fleisch-/Fischkonserven 2 (planted) Topf- 3 kurz [gefasst]; (derog.: easily assimilated) für schlichtere Gemüter *nachgestellt;* **a ~ biography/history of England** eine Kurzbiografie/ein Abriss der Geschichte Englands

potter¹ /'pɒtə(r)/ *n.* ▸ p. 1260 Töpfer, *der*/Töpferin, *die*

potter² *v.i.* [he]rumwerkeln (ugs.); ~ **round the shops** durch die Geschäfte bummeln; ~ **along the road** ‹*Autofahrer:*› gemütlich die Straße entlangzuckeln; ~ **[about] in the garden** sich (*Dat.*) im Garten zu schaffen machen

Phrasal verb

• ~ **a'bout**, ~ **a'round** *v.i.* herumwerkeln (ugs.) (**with** an + *Dat.*); ~ **about in a canoe** in einem Kanu herumpaddeln; ~ **about in the garden** ▸~²

potter's 'wheel *n.* Töpferscheibe, *die*

pottery /'pɒtərɪ/ *n.* 1 *no pl., no indef. art.* (vessels) Töpferware, *die;* Keramik, *die; attrib.* Ton-; Keramik- 2 (workshop) Töpferei, *die* 3 *no pl., no indef. art.* (craft) Töpferei, *die*

'potting compost *n.* Blumenerde, *die*

potting-shed /'pɒtɪŋʃed/ *n.* (Brit.) Gewächshaus [zum Vorziehen von Pflanzen]

potty¹ /'pɒtɪ/ *adj.* (Brit. coll.: crazy) verrückt (ugs.) (**about, on** nach); **he's driving me ~:** er macht mich wahnsinnig (ugs.); **they've gone ~:** sie sind [völlig] übergeschnappt (ugs.)

potty² *n.* (Brit. coll.) Töpfchen, *das;* **be ~-trained** aufs Töpfchen gehen

'potty-train *v.t.* ~ **a baby** ein Baby an den Topf *od.* ans Töpfchen gewöhnen; **the baby is ~ed** das Baby ist sauber *od.* geht aufs Töpfchen

pouch /paʊtʃ/ *n.* 1 (small bag) Tasche, *die;* Täschchen, *das;* (worn on belt) Gürteltasche, *die;* (drawstring bag) Beutel, *der* 2 (under eye) [Tränen]sack, *der* 3 (ammunition bag) [Patronen]tasche, *die* 4 (mailbag) Postsack, *der;* Postbeutel, *der;* (diplomatic bag) Kuriertasche, *die* 5 (Zool.) (of marsupial) Beutel, *der;* (of pelican) Kehlsack, *der*

pouffe /pu:f/ *n.* (cushion) Sitzpolster, *das;* Puff, *der*

poulterer /'pəʊltərə(r)/ *n.* Geflügelhändler, *der*/-händlerin, *die; see also* **baker**

poultice /'pəʊltɪs/
A *n.* Breiumschlag, *der;* Breipackung, *die*
B *v.t.* einen Breiumschlag auflegen auf (+ *Akk.*)

poultry /'pəʊltrɪ/ *n.* 1 *constr. as pl.* (birds) Geflügel, *das* 2 *no pl., no indef. art.* (as food) Geflügel, *das. See also* **farm A 1**; **farmer**

pounce /paʊns/
A *v.i.* 1 sich auf sein Opfer stürzen; ~ **[up]on** sich stürzen auf (+ *Akk.*); ‹*Raubvogel:*› herabstoßen auf (+ *Akk.*); **be ~d upon by sb.** von jmdm. angefallen werden 2 (fig.) ~ **[up]on/at** sich stürzen auf (+ *Akk.*); **then we'll ~!** dann schlagen wir zu!
B *n.* Sprung, *der;* Satz, *der;* **make a ~ on sb.** sich auf jmdn. stürzen

pound¹ /paʊnd/ *n.* 1 ▸ p. 1702 (unit of weight) [britisches] Pfund (*453,6 Gramm*); **two ~s of apples** 2 Pfund Äpfel; **by the ~:** pfundweise; **it's 20 pence a ~:** es kostet 20 Pence das Pfund; **two-~:** Zwei-Pfund-‹*Dose, Brot, Packung*›; zweipfündig, zwei Pfund schwer ‹*Kugel, Kohlkopf*›; **exact** *or* **demand one's ~ of flesh** (fig.) sein Recht rücksichtslos verlangen 2 ▸ p. 1332 (unit of currency) Pfund, *das;* **five-~ note** Fünfpfundnote, *die;* Fünfpfundschein, *der;* **it must have cost ~s** das muss eine schöne Stange Geld gekostet haben (ugs.); **[it's] a ~ to a penny** (fig. coll.) es ist so gut wie sicher; ich wette hundert zu eins

pound² *n.* (enclosure) Pferch, *der;* (for stray dogs) Zwinger, *der* [für eingefangene Hunde]; (for cars) Abstellplatz, *der* [für polizeilich abgeschleppte Fahrzeuge]

p

pound³
A *v.t.* **1** (crush) zerstoßen; zerdrücken ‹*Tomaten*› **2** (thump) einschlagen auf (+ *Akk.*) ‹*Person*›; herumhämmern auf (+ *Dat.*) (ugs.) ‹*Klavier, Tisch, Schreibmaschine*›; klopfen ‹*Fleisch*›; ‹*Sturm:*› heimsuchen ‹*Gebiet, Insel*›; ‹*Wellen:*› klatschen auf (+ *Akk.*) ‹*Strand, Ufer,*› gegen *od.* an (+ *Akk.*) ‹*Felsen, Schiff*›; ‹*Geschütz:*› unter Beschuss (*Akk.*) nehmen ‹*Ziel*›; ‹*Bombenflugzeug:*› bombardieren ‹*Ziel*›; **~ sb./sth. with one's fists** jmdn./etw. mit den Fäusten bearbeiten *od.* traktieren; **the ship was ~ed by the waves** die Wellen klatschten gegen das Schiff; **~ the beat** (coll.) ‹*Polizist:*› zu Fuß seine Runde machen **3** (knock) **~ to pieces** ‹*Wellen:*› zertrümmern, zerschmettern ‹*Schiff*›; ‹*Geschütz, Bomben:*› in Trümmer legen ‹*Stadt, Mauern*› **4** (compress) **~ [down]** feststampfen ‹*Erde, Boden*›; (by treading) festtreten
B *v.i.* **1** (make one's way heavily) stampfen **2** (beat rapidly) ‹*Herz:*› heftig schlagen *od.* klopfen *od.* (geh.) pochen **3** (strike) ‹*See, Brandung:*› donnern; **~ away** ‹*Artillerie:*› donnern; **~ at/on** herumhämmern auf (+ *Dat.*) (ugs.) ‹*Klavier, Tisch, Schreibmaschine*›

(Phrasal verbs)
- **~ a'way at** *v.t.* unter schweren [ständigen] Beschuss nehmen ‹*Feind, Stadt*›; (fig.) herumhämmern auf (+ *Dat.*) (ugs.) ‹*Klavier, Schreibmaschine usw.*›; (work at) ackern an (+ *Dat.*) (ugs.)
- **~ 'out** *v.t.* (on typewriter) herunterhämmern (ugs.) ‹*Brief, Aufsatz*›; (on piano) hämmern (ugs.) ‹*Lied, Stück*›; **~ out sth. on the typewriter** etw. in die [Schreib]maschine hämmern

poundage /'paʊndɪdʒ/ *n.* **1** (per pound of weight) Gebühr [pro Pfund] **2** (per pound sterling) (charge, fee) Gebühr, *die;* (commission) Provision [pro Pfund]

-pounder /'paʊndə(r)/ *n. in comb.* -pfünder, *der*

pounding /'paʊndɪŋ/ *n.* **1** (striking) (of hammer etc.) Schlagen, *das;* Klopfen, *das;* (of artillery) [schwerer] Beschuss; (of waves) Klatschen, *das;* **the ship took a ~ from the waves** das Schiff wurde von den Wellen kräftig durchgeschüttelt; **our team took a ~:** unsere Mannschaft musste eine Schlappe einstecken (ugs.); **his play took a ~ from the critics** sein Stück wurde von den Kritikern verrissen **2** (of hooves, footsteps) Stampfen, *das;* (of train) Rumpeln, *das* **3** (beating) (of heart) Klopfen, *das;* Pochen, *das* (geh.); (of music, drums) Dröhnen, *das*

pound 'note *n.* (Hist.) Pfundnote, *die;* Pfundschein, *der*

'pound[s] sign *n.* Pfundzeichen, *das*

pour /pɔː(r)/
A *v.t.* **1** gießen, schütten ‹*Flüssigkeit*›; schütten ‹*Sand, Kies, Getreide usw.*›; (into drinking vessel) einschenken; eingießen; **~ a bucket of water over sb.'s head** jmdm. einen Eimer Wasser über den Kopf gießen *od.* schütten; **~ water over the flowers** die Blumen wässern *od.* [mit Wasser] gießen; **they ~ed beer all over him** sie übergossen ihn mit Bier; **~ scorn** *or* **ridicule on sb./sth.** jmdn. mit Spott übergießen *od.* überschütten/über etw. (*Akk.*) spotten; **~ oil on the flames** (fig.) Öl ins Feuer gießen; **~ oil on troubled waters** *or* **the water** (fig.) Öl auf die Wogen gießen; *see also* **water A 1** **2** (discharge) ‹*Fluss:*› ergießen (geh.) ‹*Wasser*›; (fig.) pumpen ‹*Geld, Geschosse*›
B *v.i.* **1** (flow) strömen; ‹*Rauch:*› hervorquellen (**from** aus); **sweat was ~ing off the runners** den Läufern lief der Schweiß in Strömen herunter; **~ [with rain]** in Strömen regnen; [in Strömen] gießen (ugs.); **it never rains but it ~s** (fig.) da kommt aber auch alles zusammen **2** (fig.) strömen; **~ in** herein-/hineinströmen; **~ out** heraus-/hinausströmen; **tourists/refugees ~ into the city** Touristen/Flüchtlinge strömen in Scharen in die Stadt; **~ out of** strömen aus; (fig.) ‹*Menge, Personen:*› strömen aus ‹*Gebäude, Halle*›; ‹*Musik:*› schallen aus ‹*Musikbox*›; ‹*Propaganda:*› tönen aus ‹*Lautsprecher*›; **the crowd ~ed out of the doors** die Menge strömte durch die Türen hinaus; **cars ~ed along the road** ein [endloser] Strom von Autos flutete über die Straße; **letters/protests ~ed in** eine Flut von Briefen/Protesten brach herein

(Phrasal verbs)
- **~ 'down** *v.i.* **it's ~ing down** es gießt [in Strömen] (ugs.); **the rain ~ed down** es regnete in Strömen
- **~ 'forth**
A *v.t.* von sich geben; erklingen lassen ‹*Lied*›; ausschütten ‹*Kummer*›; erzählen ‹*Geschichte*›
B *v.i.* ‹*Gesang, Musik usw.:*› ertönen, erklingen; ‹*Menge, Personen:*› herausströmen
- **~ 'off** *v.t.* abgießen
- **~ 'out**
A *v.t.* eingießen, einschenken ‹*Getränk*›; ‹*Fabrik:*› ausstoßen ‹*Produkte*›; ‹*Sender:*› in den Äther schicken ‹*Musik usw.*›; **the chimney was ~ing out smoke** aus dem Schornstein quoll Rauch; **~ out one's thanks** sich überschwänglich bedanken; **~ out a torrent of words** eine Flut von Worten von sich geben *od.* hervorsprudeln lassen; **~ out one's woes** *or* **troubles/heart to sb.** jmdm. seinen Kummer/sein Herz ausschütten; **~ out one's feelings** seinen Gefühlen Luft machen *od.* Ausdruck geben; **~ out one's story to sb.** [jmdm.] seine Geschichte erzählen
B *v.i.* ▸ **~ B 2**

pouring /'pɔːrɪŋ/ *adj.* **1** strömend ‹*Regen*›; **a ~ wet day** ein völlig verregneter Tag **2** (for dispensing) Gieß-; (for being poured) flüssig

pout /paʊt/
A *v.i.* **1** einen Schmollmund machen *od.* ziehen; **~ing lips** Schmolllippen *Pl.;* **his mouth ~ed** er zog einen Schmollmund **2** (sulk) schmollen
B *v.t.* **1** (protrude) aufwerfen, schürzen ‹*Lippen*› **2** (say) schmollend sagen; schmollen
C *n.* Schmollmund, *der;* **have the** *or* **be in the ~s** schmollen; im Schmollwinkel sitzen (ugs.)

poverty /'pɒvətɪ/ *n.* **1** Armut, *die;* **plead ~:** behaupten, kein Geld zu haben; **fall into ~:** in Armut (*Akk.*) geraten; **be reduced to ~:** verarmt sein **2** (Relig.) Armut, *die* **3** (fig.: deficiency) Armut, *die* (**in** an + *Dat.*); **~ of ideas** Ideenarmut, *die;* gedankliche Armut; **~ of the soil/the region** Kargheit des Bodens/der Gegend; **spiritual ~:** seelische Verelendung **4** (inferiority) (of language, vocabulary) Armut, *die;* **~ of imagination/intellect** Fantasielosigkeit, *die*/geistige Unzulänglichkeit

poverty: ~ line *n.* Armutsgrenze, *die;* **be on the ~ line** an der Armutsgrenze liegen; **~-stricken** *adj.* Not leidend; verarmt; (fig.) armselig; kümmerlich; **~ trap** *n.: soziale Situation, die dadurch gekennzeichnet ist, dass die Aufnahme einer Erwerbstätigkeit für den Betroffenen zu einer Verschlechterung seiner wirtschaftlichen Lage führen kann, weil er durch sie seinen Anspruch auf staatliche Sozialhilfe verlieren würde*

pow /paʊ/ *int.* peng

POW *abbr.* **= prisoner of war**

powder /'paʊdə(r)/
A *n.* **1** Pulver, *das* **2** (cosmetic) Puder, *der;* **put ~ on one's face** sich (*Dat.*) das Gesicht pudern **3** (medicine) Pulver, *das;* **take a ~** (Amer. fig. coll.) die Flatter machen (salopp) **4** (gun~) Pulver, *das;* **keep one's ~ dry** (fig.) sein Pulver trocken halten; **he/it is not worth ~ and shot** (fig.) er ist keinen Schuss Pulver wert (ugs.)/es ist die Mühe nicht wert
B *v.t.* **1** pudern; **I'll just go and ~ my nose** (euphem.) ich muss [nur] mal verschwinden (ugs. verhüll.) **2** (reduce to ~) pulverisieren; zu Pulver verarbeiten ‹*Milch, Eier*›; **~ed milk** Milchpulver, *das;* Trockenmilch, *die;* **~ed eggs** Eipulver, *das;* Trockenei, *das;* **~ed sugar** Puderzucker, *der*

powder: ~ 'blue *n.* **1** (for laundry) Waschblau, *das;* **2** (colour) Himmelblau, *das;* **~ compact** ▸ **compact² 1**

powdering /'paʊdərɪŋ/ *n.* **1** (act) [Ein]pudern, *das* **2** **a ~ of snow** eine dünne Schicht Schnee

powder: ~ keg *n.* (lit. or fig.) Pulverfass, *das;* **~ magazine** *n.* Pulvermagazin, *das;* **~ puff** *n.* Puderquaste, *die;* **~ room** *n.* [Damen]toilette, *die;* **~ snow** *n.* Pulverschnee, *der*

powdery /'paʊdərɪ/ *adj.* **1** (like powder) pulv[e]rig; (in powder form) pulverförmig; (finer) pud[e]rig/puderförmig **2** (crumbly) bröckelig; bröselig

power /paʊə(r)/
A *n.* **1** (ability) Kraft, *die;* **if they had the ~:** wenn sie könnten *od.* die Möglichkeit hätten; **do all in one's ~ to help sb.** alles in seiner Macht *od.* seinen Kräften Stehende tun, um jmdm. zu helfen; **be beyond** *or* **outside** *or* **not be within sb.'s ~:** nicht in jmds. Macht (*Dat.*) liegen
2 (faculty) Fähigkeit, *die;* Vermögen, *das* (geh.); (talent) Begabung, *die;* Talent, *das;* **~ of smell** Riechvermögen, *das;* Geruchssinn, *der;* **tax sb.'s ~s to the utmost** ‹*Arbeit, Aufgabe:*› jmdn. bis an die Grenzen seiner Leistungsfähigkeit beanspruchen; **psychic ~s** übersinnliche Kräfte; **~s of observation** Beobachtungsgabe, *die;* **~s of persuasion** Überredungskünste
3 (vigour, intensity) (of sun's rays) Kraft, *die;* (of sermon, performance) Eindringlichkeit, *die;* (solidity, physical strength) Kraft, *die;* (of a blow) Wucht, *die;* **more ~ to you** *or* **your elbow!** viel Erfolg!; **have no ~** ‹*Schuss, Schlag:*› schwach *od.* kraftlos sein
4 (authority) Macht, *die,* Herrschaft, *die* (**over** über + *Akk.*); **have sth. in one's ~** ‹*Diktator:*› etw. in seiner Gewalt haben; die Herrschaft über etw. (*Akk.*) haben; **she was in his ~:** sie war in seiner Gewalt; er hatte sie in seiner Gewalt; **~ corrupts** Macht korrumpiert
5 (personal ascendancy) **[exercise/get] ~:** Einfluss [ausüben/gewinnen] (**over** auf + *Akk.*)
6 (political or social ascendancy) Macht, *die;* **student/worker ~:** ≈ Mitbestimmung der Studenten/Arbeiter; **hold ~:** an der Macht sein; **fall from ~:** die Macht verlieren; ‹*Präsident:*› gestürzt werden; **come into ~:** an die Macht kommen; **the party in ~:** die herrschende Partei; die Partei an der Macht; **~ politics** Machtpolitik, *die;* **balance of ~:** Kräftegleichgewicht, *das;* **hold the balance of ~:** das Zünglein an der Waage sein
7 (authorization) Vollmacht, *die;* Befugnis, *die;* **~ to negotiate** Verhandlungsvollmacht, *die;* **exceed one's ~s** seine Kompetenzen *od.* Befugnisse überschreiten; *see also* **attorney 1**
8 (influential person) Autorität, *die;* (influential thing) Machtfaktor, *der;* **be a real ~ in these circles** in diesen Kreisen großen Einfluss haben; **a ~ in the land** eine einflussreiche Macht; **be the ~ behind the throne** (Polit.) die graue Eminenz sein; **the ~s that be** die maßgeblichen Stellen; die da oben (ugs.)
9 (State) Macht, *die;* **four-~ conference** Viermächtekonferenz, *die;* **a sea/world ~:** eine See-/Weltmacht; *see also* **Great Power**
10 (coll.: large amount) Menge, *die* (ugs.); **do sb. a ~ of good** jmdm. außerordentlich gut tun
11 ▸ **i** **p. 1358** (Math.) Potenz, *die;* **3 to the ~ of 4** 3 hoch 4
12 (mechanical, electrical) Kraft, *die;* (electric current) Strom, *der;* (of loudspeaker, transmitter) Leistung, *die;* **under one's/its own ~:** mit eigener Kraft; **steam ~:** Dampfkraft, *die;* **turn off the ~:** den Strom ausschalten *od.* abstellen
13 (capacity for force) Leistung, *die; see also* **horsepower**
14 (Optics) **[magnifying] ~:** Vergrößerungskraft, *die;* [Brenn]stärke, *die*
15 (deity) Macht, *die;* **the ~s of darkness** die Mächte der Finsternis
16 (of drug) Wirkung, *die*
B *v.t.* ‹*Treibstoff, Dampf, Strom, Gas:*› antreiben; ‹*Person:*› betreiben ‹*Maschine*›; ‹*Batterie:*› mit Energie versehen *od.* versorgen; **he ~ed the ball past the goalkeeper** (fig.) er hämmerte den Ball ins Netz
C *v.i.* (coll.) rasen

power: ~-assisted *adj.* **~-assisted steering/brakes** Servolenkung, *die*/-bremsen *Pl.;* **~ base** *n.* **the unions are the party's ~ base** die Gewerkschaften sind die Stützen der Partei; **have one's ~ base in the Middle West** seine treueste Anhängerschaft im Mittelwesten haben; **~ boat** *n.* Motorboot, *das;* **~ brakes** *n. pl.* Servobremsen *Pl.;* **~ cable** *n.* Hochspannungsleitung, *die;* **~ cut** *n.* Stromsperre, *die;* Stromabschaltung, *die;* (failure)

Stromausfall, *der;* ~ **dive** **A** *n.* Sturzflug mit Vollgas, *der;* **B** *v.i.* einen Sturzflug machen, ohne den Motor zu drosseln; ~ **dressing** *n.: das Tragen betont streng wirkender Kleidung;* ~ **drill** *n.* elektrische Bohrmaschine; ~**-driven** *adj.* motorbetrieben; ~ **failure** *n.* Stromausfall, *der*

powerful /ˈpaʊəfl/ *adj.* **1** (strong) stark; kräftig ‹*Tritt, Schlag, Tier, Geruch, Körperbau, Statur*›; heftig ‹*Gefühl, Empfindung*›; hell, strahlend ‹*Licht*›; scharf ‹*Verstand, Geist*›; überzeugend ‹*Redner, Schauspieler*›; eindringlich ‹*Buch, Rede*›; beeindruckend ‹*Film, Darstellung*› **2** (influential); mächtig ‹*Clique, Person, Stadt, Herrscher*›; wesentlich ‹*Faktor*›

powerfully /ˈpaʊəfəlɪ/ *adv.* kräftig ‹*gebaut*›; eindringlich ‹*predigen*›; **he was** ~ **attracted to her** sie übte eine starke Anziehungskraft auf ihn aus

powerhouse /ˈpaʊəhaʊs/ *n.* **1** ▸**power station** **2** (fig.) treibende Kraft; **be an intellectual** ~: intellektuell stets produktiv sein; **be a** ~ **of ideas and energy** ‹*Person:*› ein einfallsreiches Energiebündel sein

powerless /ˈpaʊəlɪs/ *adj.* **1** (wholly unable) machtlos; **be** ~ **to do sth.** nicht die Macht haben, etw. zu tun; **be** ~ **to help** nicht helfen können **2** (without power) machtlos; ~ **in the hands of the enemy** hilflos in den Händen des Feindes; **leave sb.** ~ **against sth.** ‹*Gesetz:*› jmdn. machtlos gegen etw. machen; **leave sb.** ~ **to do sth.** ‹*Gesetz:*› jmdn. daran hindern *od.* es jmdm. unmöglich machen, etw. zu tun

powerlessly /ˈpaʊəlɪslɪ/ *adv.* machtlos ‹*zusehen, den Kopf schütteln*›

power: ~ **line** *n.* Stromleitung, *die;* **overhead** ~ **line** Freileitung, *die;* ~ **pack** *n.* Netzteil, *das;* Netzgerät, *das;* (for camera flash) Generatorteil, *das od. der;* ~ **plant** *n.* **1** ▸~ **station**; **2** (engine) Triebwerk, *das;* ~ **point** *n.* (Brit.) Steckdose, *die;* ~ **saw** *n.* Motorsäge, *die;* ~**-sharing** *n., no pl.* Machtaufteilung, *die;* ~ **station** *n.* Kraftwerk, *das;* Elektrizitätswerk, *das;* ~ **steering** *n., no pl.* Servolenkung, *die;* ~ **stroke** *n.* Arbeitstakt, *der;* Arbeitshub, *der;* ~ **structure** *n.* Machtstruktur, *die;* ~ **supply** *n.* Energieversorgung, *die* (**to** *Gen.*); ~ **tool** *n.* Elektrowerkzeug, *das;* ~**-training** *n., no pl.* Krafttraining, *das;* ~ **user** *n.* **1** /ˈ- -/ (consumer of energy) Energieverbraucher, *der*/-verbraucherin, *die;* **2** /-ˈ-/ (Computing) versierter Nutzer/versierte Nutzerin; ausgefuchster Nutzer/ausgefuchste Nutzerin (ugs.)

powwow /ˈpaʊwaʊ/

A *n.* Pow-Wow, *das* (Völkerk.); (fig.) Besprechung, *die*

B *v.i.* (fig.) sich beraten

pox /pɒks/ *n.* ▸**i** **p. 1231** **1** (disease with pocks) Pocken *Pl.;* Blattern *Pl.* (veralt.); **a** ~ **on him!** (arch.) dass ihn die Pest hole! (veralt.) **2** (coll.: syphilis) Syphilis, *die;* Syph, *die od. der* (salopp)

poxy /ˈpɒksɪ/ *adj.* (esp. Brit. coll. derog.) beschissen (salopp abwertend)

pp *abbr.* **= pianissimo** pp

pp. *abbr.* **= pages**

p.p. /piːˈpiː/ *abbr.* **= by proxy** pp[a].

PPI *abbr.* **= producer price index**

p.p.m. *abbr.* **= parts per million** (by volume) mm³/l; (by weight) mg/kg

PPP *n.* **= personal pension plan**

PPS *abbr.* **= second postscript** PPS

PPV *abbr.* (Telev.) **= pay-per-view**

pr. *abbr.* **= pair** P.

PR *abbr.* **1** **= proportional representation** **2** **= public relations** PR; Public Relations; **PR man** Werbefachmann, *der;* PR-Mann, *der*

practicable /ˈpræktɪkəbl/ *adj.* **1** (feasible) durchführbar ‹*Projekt, Idee, Plan*›; praktikabel ‹*Lösung, Vorschlag, Plan, Methode*› **2** (usable) befahrbar, passierbar ‹*Straße, Gelände*›

practical /ˈpræktɪkl/

A *adj.* **1** praktisch; **for all** ~ **purposes** praktisch; **be true for all** ~ **purposes** in der Praxis Gültigkeit haben **2** (inclined to action) praktisch veranlagt ‹*Person*›; praktisch ‹*Denkweise, Veranlagung, Einstellung*›; ~ **man** Praktiker, *der;* **have a** ~ **approach/mind** praktisch an die Dinge herangehen **3** (virtual) tatsächlich ‹*Freiheit, Organisator*› **4** (feasible) möglich ‹*Alternative*›; praktikabel ‹*Alternative, Möglichkeit*›; *see also* **politics 3**

B *n.* praktische Prüfung

practicality /præktɪˈkælɪtɪ/ *n.* **1** *no pl.* (of plan) Durchführbarkeit, *die;* (of person) praktische Veranlagung **2** *in pl.* (practical details) **the practicalities of the situation are that ...:** die Situation sieht praktisch so aus, dass ...; **deal in practicalities** sich mit praktischen Dingen befassen

practical: ~ **ˈjoke** *n.* Streich, *der;* **play** ~ **jokes on sb.** jmdm. Streiche spielen; ~ **ˈjoker** *n.* Witzbold, *der*

practically /ˈpræktɪkəlɪ/ *adv.* **1** (almost) praktisch (ugs.); so gut wie; beinahe **2** (in a practical manner) praktisch; ~ **orientated course** praxisbezogener Kurs; ~ **speaking, I see no way out** ich sehe praktisch keinen Ausweg

ˈpractical nurse *n.* (Amer.) praktisch ausgebildete, nicht examinierte Krankenschwester; Hilfsschwester, *die*

practice¹ /ˈpræktɪs/ *n.* **1** (repeated exercise) Praxis, *die;* Übung, *die;* **years of** ~: Jahre der Praxis; jahrelange Übung; **put in** *or* **do some/a lot of** ~: üben/viel üben; **after all the** ~ **he has had, he should ...:** nach so viel Übung sollte er ...; **it's all good** ~ (means of improving) es ist alles Übung; ~ **makes perfect** (prov.) Übung macht den Meister; **be out of** ~, **not be in** ~: außer Übung sein; **be in** ~: in der Übung sein **2** (spell) Übungen *Pl.;* **piano** ~: Klavierüben, *das;* **do one's piano** ~: Klavier üben **3** (work or business of doctor, lawyer, etc.) Praxis, *die; see also* **general practice** **4** (habitual action) übliche Praxis; Gewohnheit, *die;* ~ **shows that ...:** die Erfahrung zeigt *od.* lehrt, dass ...; **make a** ~ **of doing sth.** es sich (*Dat.*) zur [An]gewohnheit machen, etw. zu tun; **good** ~ (satisfactory procedure) gutes Vorgehen; gute Vorgehensweise **5** (action) Praxis, *die;* **the** ~ **tends to be different** in der Praxis sieht es gewöhnlich *od.* die Praxis sieht gewöhnlich anders aus; **actual** ~: Praxis, *die;* **in** ~: in der Praxis; in Wirklichkeit; **be quite useless in** ~: in der Praxis nutzlos sein; praktisch nutzlos sein; **put sth. into** ~: etw. in die Praxis umsetzen **6** (custom) Gewohnheit, *die;* **don't make a** ~ **of it** lass es nicht zur Gewohnheit werden; **regular** ~: Brauch, *der;* **it is the regular** ~ **to do sth.** es ist Brauch *od.* üblich, etw. zu tun **7** (legal procedures) **[legal]** ~: Gerichtspraxis, *die. See also* **sharp A 6**

practice², **practiced, practicing** (Amer.) ▸**practis-**

practise /ˈpræktɪs/

A *v.t.* **1** (apply) anwenden; praktizieren **2** (be engaged in) ausüben ‹*Beruf, Tätigkeit, Religion*›; ~ **medicine** [als Arzt] praktizieren **3** (exercise oneself in) trainieren in (+ *Dat.*) ‹*Sportart*›; ~ **gymnastics** Gymnastik treiben; ~ **the bicycle kick** den Fallrückzieher trainieren; ~ **the piano/flute** Klavier/Flöte üben

B *v.i.* üben

practised /ˈpræktɪst/ *adj.* geübt ‹*Person, Auge, Blick*›; erfahren, versiert, routiniert ‹*Person*›; **with [a]** ~ **eye** mit geübtem Blick; **with** ~ **skill** routiniert

practising /ˈpræktɪsɪŋ/ *adj.* praktizierend ‹*Arzt, Katholik, Anglikaner usw.*›; ~ **homosexual** aktiv Homosexueller; ~ **barrister** niedergelassener Anwalt

practitioner /prækˈtɪʃənə(r)/ *n.* Fachmann, *der;* Praktiker, *der*/Praktikerin, *die;* ~ **of the law, legal** ~: Anwalt, *der*/Anwältin, *die; see also* **general practitioner**; **medical practitioner**

praesidium /praɪˈsɪdɪəm/ ▸**presidium**

pragmatic /prægˈmætɪk/ *adj.* pragmatisch

pragmatically /prægˈmætɪkəlɪ/ *adv.* pragmatisch; *as sentence-modifier* pragmatisch betrachtet

pragmatism /ˈprægmətɪzm/ *n.* Pragmatismus, *der*

pragmatist /ˈprægmətɪst/ *n.* Pragmatiker, *der*/Pragmatikerin, *die*

Prague /prɑːg/ *pr. n.* ▸**i** **p. 1643** Prag (*das*)

prairie /ˈpreərɪ/ *n.* Grasland, *das;* Grassteppe, *die;* (in North America) Prärie, *die;* **animal of the** ~**s** Steppentier, *das;* **out on the** ~: in der Grassteppe

prairie: ~ **ˈchicken** *n.* Präriehuhn, *das;* ~ **dog** *n.* Präriehund, *der;* ~ **fire** *n.* (fig.) Lauffeuer, *das;* ~ **ˈhen** ▸ ~ **chicken**; ~ **ˈoyster** *n.* Prärieauster, *die;* ~ **ˈschooner** *n.* (Amer. Hist.) Planwagen, *der;* ~ **ˈwolf** *n.* Kojote, *der;* Präriewolf, *der*

praise /preɪz/

A *v.t.* **1** (commend) loben; (more strongly) rühmen; ~ **sb. for sth.** jmdn. für *od.* wegen etw. loben; (more strongly) jmdn. wegen etw. rühmen; ~ **sb. for doing sth.** jmdn. dafür loben, dass er etw. tut/getan hat **2** (glorify) preisen (geh.), (dichter.) lobpreisen ‹*Gott*›

B *n.* **1** (approval) Lob, *das;* **win high** ~: großes *od.* hohes Lob erhalten *od.* ernten; **be loud in one's** ~**s of sth.** des Lobes voll sein über etw. (geh.); **a speech in** ~ **of sb.** eine Lobrede auf jmdn.; **sing one's own/sb.'s** ~**s** ein Loblied auf sich/jmdn. singen **2** (worship) Lobpreisung, *die* (dichter.); **offer** ~ **to God for sth.** Gott für etw. preisen (geh.) *od.* (dichter.) lobpreisen; ~ **be!** Gott dem Herrn sei Lob und Preis! *See also* **damn A 1**

praiseworthy /ˈpreɪzwɜːðɪ/ *adj.* lobenswert; löblich (oft iron.)

praline /ˈprɑːliːn/ *n.* gebrannte Nuss; gebrannte Mandel

pram /præm/ *n.* (Brit.) Kinderwagen, *der;* (for dolls) Puppenwagen, *der*

prance /prɑːns/ *v.i.* **1** ‹*Pferd:*› tänzeln **2** (fig.) stolzieren; ‹*Tänzer:*› tänzeln; ~ **about** *or* **around** ‹*Kind, Tänzer:*› herumhüpfen

prang /præŋ/ (Brit. coll.)

A *v.t.* **1** (bomb) bombardieren; bepflastern (Soldatenspr.) **2** (crash) zu Bruch fahren ‹*Fahrzeug*›; bruchlanden mit ‹*Flugzeug*›; kaputtfahren (ugs.) ‹*Auto*› **3** (damage) ramponieren (ugs.)

B *n.* (of aircraft) Absturz, *der;* (of vehicle) Unfall, *der;* **have a** ~: Bruch machen (Fliegerspr.); einen Unfall bauen (ugs.)

prank /præŋk/ *n.* Streich, *der;* Schabernack, *der;* **play a** ~ **on sb.** jmdm. einen Streich *od.* Schabernack spielen

prankster /ˈpræŋkstə(r)/ *n.* Witzbold, *der* (ugs. abwertend)

prat /præt/ *n.* (coll.) Trottel, *der* (ugs. abwertend)

prate /preɪt/ *v.i.* **1** (chatter) daherreden (abwertend); sabbeln (salopp abwertend); ~ **about sth.** sich lang und breit über etw. (*Akk.*) auslassen **2** (talk foolishly) dumm daherreden; schwafeln (ugs. abwertend); labern (ugs. abwertend)

pratfall /ˈprætfɔːl/ *n.* (coll.) **1** (fall) **do** *or* **take a** ~: auf den Hintern fallen **2** (embarrassing mistake) Panne, *die*

prating /ˈpreɪtɪŋ/ *adj.* geschwätzig (abwertend); schwatzhaft (abwertend)

prattle /ˈprætl/

A *v.i.* schwafeln (ugs. abwertend); ‹*Kleinkind:*› plappern (ugs.); ~ **on about sth.** ohne Pause über etw. (*Akk.*) plappern; ~ **away to sb.** zu jmdm. drauflosplappern

B *n.* Geplapper, *das* (ugs. abwertend); Geschwafel, *das* (ugs. abwertend)

prawn /prɔːn/ *n.* Garnele, *die*

prawn: ~ **ˈcocktail** *n.* Krabbencocktail, *der;* ~ **ˈcracker** *n.* Krabbencracker, *der*

pray /preɪ/

A *v.i.* beten (**for** um); **let us** ~: lasset uns beten; ~ **[to God] for sb.** für jmdn. beten; ~ **to God for help** Gott um Hilfe anflehen; ~ **to God to do sth.** zu Gott beten, dass er etw. tue; **he is past** ~**ing for** ihm ist nicht mehr zu helfen

B *v.t.* **1** (beseech) anflehen, flehen zu ‹*Gott, Heiligen, Jungfrau Maria*› (**for** um); ~ **God for sth.** etw. von Gott erflehen **2** (~ to) beten zu; ~ **God she is safe** bitte, lieber Gott, lass sie in Sicherheit sein **3** (arch./formal: I ask) bitte; ~ **consider what ...:** überlegen Sie doch bitte, was ...; **what is the use of that,** ~**?** wozu, bitte [schön], soll das gut sein? *See also* **mantis**

prayer /preə(r)/ *n.* **1** Gebet, *das;* **make/offer up a** ~ **for sb.** für jmdn. beten; ein Gebet für jmdn. sprechen; **offer** ~**s for** beten für; **offer**

up a quick ~: schnell ein Gebet sprechen; **say one's ~s** beten; **say your ~s!** (iron.) jetzt hast du Grund zum Beten (iron.); **lead the ~s** die Gebete vorsprechen; *see also* **lord A 2** 2) *no pl., no art.* (praying) Beten, *das;* **gather in ~:** sich zum Gebet versammeln; **what's the use of ~?** was nützt es zu beten? 3) (service) Andacht, *die;* **family ~s** Familienandacht, *die* 4) (entreaty) inständige *od.* eindringliche Bitte 5) (coll.: slight chance of success) Hauch einer Chance; **without a ~ of doing sth.** ohne die geringste Chance *od.* Aussicht, etw. erfolgreich zu tun

prayer: ~ book *n.* 1) Gebetbuch, *das;* 2) **the ~ book = the Book of Common Prayer** ▸**Common Prayer**; **~ mat** *n.* Gebetsteppich, *der;* **~ meeting** *n.* Gebetsversammlung, *die;* **~ wheel** *n.* Gebetsmühle, *die*

preach /priːtʃ/

A *v.i.* 1) (deliver sermon) predigen (**to** zu, vor + *Dat.;* **on** über + *Akk.*); **~ to the converted** (fig.) offene Türen einrennen (ugs.) 2) (fig.: give moral advice) eine Predigt halten (ugs.); (abwertend) Moralpredigten halten (**at, to** *Dat.*)

B *v.t.* 1) (deliver) halten ‹*Predigt, Ansprache*› 2) (proclaim) predigen ‹*Evangelium, Botschaft*›; verkündigen ‹*Glauben, Lehre, Evangelium, Botschaft*› 3) (advocate) predigen (ugs.); **practise what one ~es** (fig.) was man [anderen] predigt, selbst auch tun

preacher /ˈpriːtʃə(r)/ *n.* 1) Prediger, *der*/Predigerin, *die* 2) (fig.) **be a ~ of privatization** die Privatisierung predigen (ugs.)

preachify /ˈpriːtʃɪfaɪ/ *v.i.* predigen

preachy /ˈpriˈtʃɪ/ *adj.* (coll.) predigerhaft

preadolescent /priːædəˈlesənt/

A *adj.* vorpubertär

B *n.* Kind im vorpubertären Alter

preamble /priːˈæmbl/ *n.* 1) (preliminary statement) Vorbemerkung, *die;* Einleitung, *die;* (to a book) Geleitwort, *das* 2) (Law) Präambel, *die*

pre-arrange /priːəˈreɪndʒ/ *v.t.* vorher absprechen; vorher ausmachen *od.* verabreden ‹*Treffpunkt, Zeichen*›

pre-arrangement /priːəˈreɪndʒmənt/ *n.* vorherige Absprache; **by ~:** nach vorheriger Absprache

prebend /ˈprebənd/ *n.* Pfründe, *die*

prebendary /ˈprebəndərɪ/ *n.* 1) (honorary canon) ehrenamtlicher Pfründner/ehrenamtliche Pfründnerin 2) (holder of prebend) Pfründner, *der*/Pfründnerin, *die*

precancerous /priːˈkænsərəs/ *adj.* (Med.) präkanzerös

precarious /prɪˈkeərɪəs/ *adj.* 1) (uncertain) labil, prekär ‹*Gleichgewicht, Situation*›; gefährdet ‹*Friede, Ernte*›; **make a ~ living** eine unsichere Existenz haben 2) (insecure) gefährlich ‹*Weg, Pfad*›; riskant, gefährlich ‹*Politik, Leben, Balanceakt*›; instabil (geh.) ‹*Bauwerk*›; kritisch, bedenklich ‹*Gesundheitszustand*›; unsicher ‹*Koalition*›

precariously /prɪˈkeərɪəslɪ/ *adv.* **live ~:** eine unsichere Existenz haben; **be perched ~ on the edge of a steep slope** ‹*Haus:*› gefährlich nahe am Rand eines Steilhangs stehen

pre-cast /ˈpriːkɑːst/

A *v.t.,* **pre-cast** vorfabrizieren, vorfertigen ‹*Beton*›

B *adj.* vorgefertigt; vorfabriziert

precaution /prɪˈkɔːʃn/ *n.* 1) (action) Vorsichts-, Schutzmaßnahme, *die;* **take ~s against sth.** Vorsichts- *od.* Schutzmaßnahmen gegen etw. treffen; **do sth. as a ~:** vorsichts- *od.* sicherheitshalber etw. tun; **do you take ~s?** (euphem.) nimmst du Verhütungsmittel? 2) *no pl.* (foresight) Vorsicht, *die*

precautionary /prɪˈkɔːʃənərɪ/ *adj.* vorsorglich; vorbeugend; prophylaktisch (geh., Med.); präventiv (geh.); **~ measure** Vorsichts- *od.* Schutzmaßnahme, *die;* **as a ~ measure** vorsichts- *od.* sicherheitshalber

precede /prɪˈsiːd/ *v.t.* 1) (in rank) rangieren vor (+ *Dat.*); (in importance) wichtiger sein als; Vorrang haben vor (+ *Dat.*); **be ~d by sth.** hinter etw. (*Dat.*) rangieren 2) (in order or time) vorangehen (+ *Dat.*); (in vehicle) voranfahren (+ *Dat.*); (in time also) vorausgehen (+ *Dat.*); **the words that ~ [this paragraph]** die [diesem Absatz] vorangehenden Worte 3) (preface, introduce) **~ X with Y** X (*Dat.*) Y vorausschicken *od.* voranstellen; **~ an address with a welcome** einer Ansprache einen Willkommensgruß vorausschicken *od.* voranstellen

precedence /ˈpresɪdəns/, **precedency** /ˈpresɪdənsɪ/ *n., no pl.* 1) (in rank) Priorität, *die* (geh.) (**over** vor + *Dat.*, gegenüber); Vorrang, *der* (**over** vor + *Dat.*) 2) (in time) Priorität, *die* (geh.) (**over** vor + *Dat.*, gegenüber); zeitliches Vorhergehen; **have [the] ~ over all the others** Priorität vor *od.* gegenüber allen anderen haben 3) (in ceremonies) Rangordnung, *die*

precedent

A /ˈpresɪdənt/ *n.* 1) (example) Präzedenzfall, *der;* [vorangegangenes] exemplarisches Beispiel; **there is no ~ for this** so ein Fall ist noch nicht vorgekommen; **it is without ~ [that ...]** es ist noch nie da gewesen[, dass ...]; **set** *or* **create** *or* **establish a ~:** einen Präzedenzfall schaffen 2) (Law) Präzedenzfall, *der;* Präjudiz, *das* (fachspr.)

B /prɪˈsiːdənt/ *adj.* 1) (in order) vorangestellt; vorangehend 2) (in time) voran-, vorausgehend; vorhergehend

precept /ˈpriːsept/ *n.* 1) (command) Grundsatz, *der;* Prinzip, *das* 2) (moral instruction) moralischer Grundsatz; Moralprinzip, -gesetz, *das*

precession /prɪˈseʃn/ *n.* (Phys.) Präzession, *die;* **~ of the equinoxes** (Astron.) Präzession, *die*

prechilled /priːˈtʃɪld/ *adj.* vorgekühlt

pre-Christian /priːˈkrɪstjən/ *adj.* vorchristlich

precinct /ˈpriːsɪŋkt/ *n.* 1) (traffic-free area) **[pedestrian] ~:** Fußgängerzone, *die;* **[shopping] ~:** für den Verkehr weitgehend gesperrtes Einkaufsviertel 2) (enclosed area) Areal, *das;* Bereich, *der;* Bezirk, *der;* **temple/cathedral ~:** Tempel-/Dombereich, *der;* **in the hospital ~s** auf dem Krankenhausgelände 3) (boundary) Grenze, *die;* **within the ~s of the school** auf dem Schulgelände 4) (Amer.: police or electoral district) Bezirk, *der*

preciosity /preʃɪˈɒsɪtɪ/ *n., no pl.* Affektiertheit, *die*

precious /ˈpreʃəs/

A *adj.* 1) (costly) wertvoll, kostbar ‹*Schmuckstück*›; Edel‹*metall, -stein*› 2) (highly valued) wertvoll, kostbar ‹*Zeit, Eigenschaft, Trostwort, Privileg*›; **be ~ to sb.** jmdm. lieb und wert sein 3) (beloved) teuer (geh.), lieb ‹*Freund*›; **my ~ one!** mein Schatz 4) (affected) affektiert 5) (coll.: considerable) beträchtlich; erheblich; **do a ~ sight more work/cost a ~ sight more than ...:** beträchtlich *od.* erheblich mehr tun/kosten als ...

B *adv.* (coll.) herzlich ‹*wenig*›; **~ few of them** herzlich wenige von ihnen

precipice /ˈpresɪpɪs/ *n.* Abgrund, *der;* **we are on the edge of a ~** (fig.) wir stehen am Rande einer Katastrophe

precipitant /prɪˈsɪpɪtənt/ ▸**precipitate A**

precipitate

A /prɪˈsɪpɪtət/ *adj.* 1) (hurried) eilig ‹*Flucht, Entbindung*›; hastig ‹*Abreise*›; **make a ~ exit** hastig *od.* eilig hinausgehen 2) (rash) übereilt, überstürzt ‹*Tat, Entschluss, Maßnahme*›; groß, fliegend ‹*Eile*›; **be ~ in doing sth.** etw. übereilt tun; **do nothing ~:** nichts übereilt tun

B /prɪˈsɪpɪteɪt/ *v.t.* 1) (throw down) hinunterschleudern; **be ~d into a chasm** in eine Spalte stürzen; **~ a nation into war** ‹*Nachricht, Aggression:*› ein Volk in einen Krieg stürzen 2) (hasten) beschleunigen; (trigger) auslösen 3) (Chem.) ‹*Säure:*› ausfällen 4) (Phys.) kondensieren

C /prɪˈsɪpɪtət/ *n.* 1) (Chem.) Niederschlag, *der* 2) (Phys.) Niederschlag, *der;* Kondensat, *das*

precipitately /prɪˈsɪpɪtətlɪ/ *adv.* übereilt, überstürzt ‹*fliehen, flüchten*›; unüberlegt, voreilig ‹*handeln, sich in etw. stürzen*›; hastig ‹*hetzen, eilen, stürzen*›

precipitation /prɪsɪpɪˈteɪʃn/ *n.* 1) (Meteorol.) Niederschlag, *der* 2) Voreiligkeit, *die;* Unüberlegtheit, *die*

precipitous /prɪˈsɪpɪtəs/ *adj.* 1) (very steep) sehr steil ‹*Schlucht, Abhang, Treppe, Weg*›; schroff ‹*Abhang, Felswand*›; abschüssig ‹*Straße*›; steilwandig ‹*Cañon*›; **~ slope/drop** Steilhang, *der*/[steiler] Absturz 2) ▸**precipitate A**

precipitously /prɪˈsɪpɪtəslɪ/ *adv.* 1) sehr steil ‹[*an*]*steigen sich erheben, abfallen*›; schroff ‹*ansteigen, abfallen*›; jäh (geh.) ‹*abfallen*› 2) ▸**precipitately**

précis /ˈpreɪsiː/

A *n., pl. same* /preɪsiːz/ Inhaltsangabe, *die;* Zusammenfassung, *die;* Précis, *der* (fachspr.); **~ of German history** Abriss der deutschen Geschichte; **do** *or* **make a ~ of sth.** eine Inhaltsangabe einer Sache (*Gen.*) anfertigen

B *v.t.* zusammenfassen

precise /prɪˈsaɪs/ *adj.* genau; präzise; fein ‹*Instrument*›; groß ‹*Genauigkeit*›; förmlich ‹*Art*›; **be very ~ about sth.** es mit etw. sehr genau nehmen; **put sth. in more ~ terms** etw. präziser *od.* präziser ausdrücken; **be [more] ~:** sich präzise[r] ausdrücken; **what are your ~ intentions?** was genau hast du vor?; **..., to be ~** ..., um genau zu sein; ..., genauer gesagt; **be the ~ opposite of sth.** genau das Gegenteil von etw. sein; **this is the ~ design/colour/shade that ...:** das ist genau das Muster/die Farbe/der Ton, das/die/der ...; **the ~ moment at which ...:** genau der Augenblick, in dem ...; **at that ~ moment** genau in dem Augenblick

precisely /prɪˈsaɪslɪ/ *adv.* genau; präzise ‹*antworten*›; **speak ~:** sich präzise ausdrücken; **the date is not ~ known** das genaue Datum ist nicht bekannt; **that is ~ what/why ...:** genau das/deswegen ...; **what ~ do you want/mean?** was willst/meinst du eigentlich genau?; **do ~ the opposite** genau das Gegenteil tun; **it is ~ because ...:** gerade weil ...; **it will be 5.21 ~:** es wird genau 5 Uhr 21; **at ~ 1.30, at 1.30 ~:** Punkt 1 Uhr 30; genau um 1 Uhr 30

precision /prɪˈsɪʒn/ *n., no pl.* Genauigkeit, *die;* **with[out] a great deal of ~:** [nicht] sehr präzise ‹*sich ausdrücken*›; *attrib.* **a ~ landing** eine Präzisionslandung

precision: ~ ˈbombing *n., no pl.* (Mil.) Punktzielbombardement, *das;* **~ engiˈneering** *n., no pl.* Feinwerktechnik, *die;* Präzisionstechnik, *die;* **~ ˈinstrument** *n.* Präzisions[mess]gerät, *das;* Feinmessgerät, *das;* **~ ˈtool** *n.* Präzisionswerkzeug, *das*

pre-classical /priːˈklæsɪkl/ *adj.* vorklassisch

preclude /prɪˈkluːd/ *v.t.* ausschließen ‹*Zweifel*›; **~ sb. from a duty/taking part** jmdn. von einer Pflicht/der Teilnahme entbinden; **so as to ~ all doubt** um jeden Zweifel auszuschließen

precocious /prɪˈkəʊʃəs/ *adj.* frühreif ‹*Kind, Jugendlicher, Genie*›; altklug ‹*Äußerung*›; verfrüht ‹*Wachstum, Erfolg*›; **at the ~ age of 25** schon mit 25 Jahren; **a ~ interest in sth.** frühzeitiges Interesse an etw. (*Dat.*)

precociously /prɪˈkəʊʃəslɪ/ *adv.* frühreif ‹*sich benehmen*›; altklug ‹*reden*›

precognition /priːkɒgˈnɪʃn/ *n.* vorherige Kenntnis (**of** von); (Parapsych.) Präkognition, *die*

preconceived /priːkənˈsiːvd/ *adj.* vorgefasst ‹*Ansicht, Vorstellung*›

preconception /priːkənˈsepʃn/ *n.* vorgefasste Meinung (**of** über + *Akk.*); **with too many ~s** allzu voreingenommen

precondition /priːkənˈdɪʃn/ *n.* Vorbedingung, *die* (**of** für)

pre-cook /priːˈkʊk/ *v.t.* vorkochen

pre-cooked /priːˈkʊkt/ *adj.* vorgekocht

precursor /priːˈkɜːsə(r)/ *n.* 1) (of revolution, movement, etc.) Wegbereiter, *der*/-bereiterin, *die;* (of illness) Vorbote, *der*/Vorbotin, *die* 2) (predecessor) Vorgänger, *der*/-gängerin, *die*

pre-date /priːˈdeɪt/ *v.t.* 1) (precede in date) **~ sth.** ‹*Ereignis:*› einer Sache (*Dat.*) vorausgehen; ‹*Sache:*› aus der Zeit vor etw. (*Dat.*) stammen 2) (give earlier date to) zurückdatieren ‹*Brief, Scheck*›

pre-dated /priːˈdeɪtɪd/ *adj.* zurückdatiert ‹*Brief, Scheck*›

P

predator /ˈpredətə(r)/ *n.* Raubtier, *das;* (fish) Raubfisch, *der*

predatory /ˈpredətərɪ/ *adj.* 1 (plundering, robbing) räuberisch; Raub‹*instinkte, -krieg*›; beutegierig ‹*Gesellschaftsschicht, Charakter*› 2 (preying upon others) räuberisch; **~ animal** Raubtier, *das*

predatory 'pricing *n., no pl.* Preisschleuderei, *die*

predecease /priːdɪˈsiːs/ *v.t.* **~ sb.** vor jmdm. sterben

predecessor /ˈpriːdɪsesə(r)/ *n.* 1 (former holder of position) Vorgänger, *der*/-gängerin, *die;* **~ in office/title** Amts-/Rechtsvorgänger, *der* 2 (preceding thing) Vorläufer, *der;* **his second novel is better than its ~:** sein zweiter Roman ist besser als sein erster 3 (ancestor) Vorfahr[e], *der*/-fahrin, *die;* Ahn, *der* (geh.)/ Ahne, *die* (geh.)

predestination /prɪdestɪˈneɪʃn/ *n., no pl.* Vorherbestimmung, *die;* Prädestination, *die* (geh.)

predestine /prɪˈdestɪn/ *v.t.* von vornherein bestimmen (**to** zu); prädestinieren (**to** zu) (geh.)

predetermination /priːdɪtɜːmɪˈneɪʃn/ *n., no pl.* 1 (predestination) Vorherbestimmung, *die;* Prädestination, *die* (geh.) 2 (intention) Vorsatz, *der;* Absicht, *die;* **with a ~ to do sth.** mit dem Vorsatz *od.* in der Absicht, etw. zu tun

predetermine /priːdɪˈtɜːmɪn/ *v.t.* 1 im Voraus *od.* von vornherein bestimmen; ‹*Gott, Schicksal:*› vorherbestimmen 2 (impel) zwingen (**to** zu)

predicament /prɪˈdɪkəmənt/ *n.* Dilemma, *das;* Zwangslage, *die;* **he found himself in a ~:** er befand sich in einem Dilemma

predicate

A /ˈpredɪkət/ *n.* 1 (Ling.) Prädikat, *das* 2 (Logic) Prädikat, *das;* Prädikator, *der*

B /ˈpredɪkeɪt/ *v.t.* 1 (affirm) **~ sth. of sb./sth.** jmdm./einer Sache etw. zuschreiben; **~ of sb./sth. that ...:** von jmdm./etw. behaupten *od.* sagen, dass ... 2 (found, base) gründen (**on** auf + *Dat.*); **be ~d on** basieren (geh.) *od.* sich gründen auf (+ *Dat.*) 3 (Logic) zusprechen (**of** *Dat.*)

predicative /prɪˈdɪkətɪv/ *adj.* 1 (making a predication) eine Aussage beinhaltend (**of, about** über + *Akk.*) 2 (Ling.) prädikativ

predicatively /prɪˈdɪkətɪvlɪ/ *adv.* (Ling.) prädikativ

predict /prɪˈdɪkt/ *v.t.* voraus-, vorhersagen; prophezeien; voraus-, vorhersehen ‹*Folgen*›; **what do you ~ will be the result?** wie glaubst du, wird das Ergebnis aussehen?

predictable /prɪˈdɪktəbl/ *adj.* voraus-, vorhersagbar; voraus-, vorhersehbar ‹*Folgen, Reaktion, Ereignis*›; berechenbar ‹*Person*›

predictably /prɪˈdɪktəblɪ/ *adv.* wie voraus- *od.* vorherzusehen war; **he was ~ annoyed** wie voraus- *od.* vorherzusehen [war], war er verärgert

prediction /prɪˈdɪkʃn/ *n.* Voraus-, Vorhersage, *die*

predictive /prɪˈdɪktɪv/ *adj.* **~ text messaging** Texteingabe mit automatischer Worterkennung

predigest /priːdɪˈdʒest, priːdaɪˈdʒest/ *v.t.* vorverdauen

predilection /priːdɪˈlekʃn/ *n.* Vorliebe, *die*

predispose /priːdɪˈspəʊz/ *v.t.* **~ sb. to do sth.** jmdn. etw. tun lassen; **be ~d to do sth.** (be willing to do sth.) geneigt sein, etw. zu tun; (tend to do sth.) dazu neigen, etw. zu tun; **~ sb. to sth.** jmdn. zu etw. neigen lassen; **~ sb. to an illness** jmdn. für eine Krankheit anfällig machen; **~ sb. in favour of sb./sth.** jmdn. für jmdn./etw. einnehmen

predisposition /priːdɪspəˈzɪʃn/ *n.* Neigung, *die* (**to** zu); (Med.) Anfälligkeit, *die* (**to** für); Prädisposition, *die* (fachspr.)

predominance /prɪˈdɒmɪnəns/ *n.* 1 (control) (of country) Vorherrschaft, *die* (**over** über + *Akk.*); Vorrangstellung, *die* (**over** gegenüber); (of person) Überlegenheit, *die* (**over** gegenüber) 2 (majority) Überzahl, *die* (**of** von); **there is a ~ of newcomers** die Neulinge sind in der Überzahl

predominant /prɪˈdɒmɪnənt/ *adj.* 1 (having more power) dominierend ‹*Interesse, Partei, Macht, Persönlichkeit*› 2 (prevailing) vorherrschend; **the ~ desire expressed by them** der von ihnen über- *od.* vorwiegend zum Ausdruck gebrachte Wunsch

predominantly /prɪˈdɒmɪnəntlɪ/ *adv.* überwiegend

predominate /prɪˈdɒmɪneɪt/ *v.i.* (be more powerful) dominierend sein; (be more important) vorherrschen; überwiegen; (be more numerous) in der Überzahl sein

pre-eminence /priːˈemɪnəns/ *n., no pl.* Vorrangstellung, *die;* **achieve ~:** eine herausragende Stellung erlangen; **her ~ in this field** ihre herausragende Stellung auf diesem Gebiet

pre-eminent /priːˈemɪnənt/ *adj.* herausragend; **be ~:** eine herausragende Stellung einnehmen

pre-eminently /priːˈemɪnəntlɪ/ *adv.* herausragend; überaus ‹*gelehrt*›; (mainly) vor allem; in erster Linie; **figure ~:** an herausragender Stelle stehen

pre-empt /priːˈempt/ *v.t.* (forestall) zuvorkommen (+ *Dat.*) (**on** bei); **she had been ~ed** man war ihr zuvorgekommen

pre-emptive /priːˈemptɪv/ *adj.* 1 Vorkaufs‹*preis, -recht*›; **~ right** (of shareholder) Bezugsrecht, *das;* **he made a ~ bid to gain power** er machte im Vorfeld seine Machtansprüche geltend 2 (Mil.) Präventiv‹*krieg, -maßnahme, -schlag*› 3 (Bridge) **~ bid** Sperrgebot, *das*

preen /priːn/

A *v.t.* ‹*Vogel:*› putzen ‹*Federn, Gefieder*›

B *v. refl.* ‹*Vogel:*› sich putzen; ‹*Person:*› sich herausputzen; **~ oneself on sth.** sich (*Dat.*) etwas auf etw. (*Akk.*) einbilden; **he is always ~ing himself on ...:** er brüstet sich dauernd mit ...

prefab /ˈpriːfæb/ *n.* (coll.) (house) Fertighaus, *das;* (building) Gebäude aus Fertigteilen; Fertigbau, *der*

prefabricate /priːˈfæbrɪkeɪt/ *v.t.* vorfertigen ‹*Produkt, Teil, Gebäude usw.*›

prefabricated *adj.* /priːˈfæbrɪkeɪtɪd/ vorgefertigt; **~ house/building** Fertighaus, *das*/Fertigbau, *der;* **a ~ garage** eine in Fertigbauweise errichtete Garage; **a ~ system/scheme** (fig.) ein vorfabriziertes System/Schema

prefabrication /priːfæbrɪˈkeɪʃn/ *n.* Vorfabrikation, *die;* Vorfertigung, *die*

preface /ˈprefəs/

A *n.* 1 (of book) Vorwort, *das* (**to** *Gen.*); Vorbemerkung, *die* (**to** zu) 2 (of speech) Vorrede, *die;* Einleitung, *die*

B *v.t.* 1 (introduce) einleiten 2 (furnish with a ~) mit einem Vorwort *od.* einer Vorbemerkung versehen

prefatory /ˈprefətərɪ/ *adj.* einleitend ‹*Hinweise, Worte*›; **be ~ to sth.** etw. einleiten

prefect /ˈpriːfekt/ *n.* (Sch.) *die Aufsicht führender älterer Schüler/führende ältere Schülerin;* **form ~** *Schüler/Schülerin einer Klasse, der/die die Aufsicht führt*

prefer /prɪˈfɜː(r)/ *v.t.*, **-rr-** 1 (like better) vorziehen; **~ to do sth.** etw. lieber tun; es vorziehen, etw. zu tun; **~ sth. to sth.** etw. einer Sache (*Dat.*) vorziehen; **I ~ skiing to skating** ich fahre lieber Ski als Schlittschuh; **I ~ not to talk about it** darüber möchte ich lieber nicht sprechen; **I should ~ to wait** ich würde lieber warten; **I'd ~ it if ...:** mir wäre es lieb, wenn ...; **~ to go to prison rather than pay** eher *od.* lieber ins Gefängnis gehen als zu bezahlen; **I ~ that we should wait rather than act now** ich meine, wir sollten lieber warten, als jetzt handeln; **this plant ~s cool conditions** diese Pflanze bevorzugt einen kühlen Standort; **they ~ blondes** sie bevorzugen Blondinen; **I ~ water to wine** ich trinke lieber Wasser als Wein; **which of them do you ~, John or Peter?** wer ist dir lieber, John oder Peter?; **there is tea or coffee, which do you ~?** es gibt Tee oder Kaffee, was ist Ihnen lieber?; **I should ~ something more elegant** ich hätte gerne etwas Eleganteres 2 (submit) erheben ‹*Anklage, Anschuldigungen*› (**against** gegen, **for** wegen); vorbringen ‹*Beschwerde*› 3 (promote) befördern; **be ~red to a post** auf einen Posten berufen werden; **he was ~red to the See of Chichester** er wurde zum Bischof von Chichester ernannt

preferable /ˈprefərəbl/ *adj.* vorzuziehen *präd.*; vorzuziehend *attr.*; besser (**to** als); **which do you think ~, x or y?** was ist Ihrer Meinung nach vorzuziehen, x oder y?; **he felt it ~ to be silent** er fand, dass es besser war zu schweigen; **the cold was ~ to the smoke** die Kälte war noch erträglicher als der Rauch

preferably /ˈprefərəblɪ/ *adv.* am besten; (as best liked) am liebsten; **a piano, ~ not too expensive** ein möglichst nicht zu teures Klavier; **Wine or beer? — Wine, ~!** Wein oder Bier? — Lieber Wein!

preference /ˈprefərəns/ *n.* 1 (greater liking) Vorliebe, *die;* **for ~** ▸**preferably**; **have a ~ for sth. [over sth.]** etw. [einer Sache (*Dat.*)] vorziehen; **he has a ~ for tea over coffee** er mag *od.* trinkt lieber Tee als Kaffee; **do sth. in ~ to sth. else** etw. lieber als etw. anderes tun 2 (thing preferred) **of the three skirts the blue one is my ~:** von den drei Röcken gefällt mir der blaue am besten; **his ~ is a holiday abroad** ein Urlaub im Ausland ist ihm am liebsten; **what are your ~s?** was wäre dir am liebsten?; **I have no ~:** mir ist alles gleich recht; **have you any ~ among his novels?** magst du einen seiner Romane besonders? 3 (prior right) Vorrecht, *das* (**for** auf + *Akk.*); **give a creditor ~ over sb.** einen Gläubiger gegenüber jmdm. begünstigen 4 (favouring of one person or country) Präferenzbehandlung, *die;* (Econ.) Präferenz, *die;* **give [one's] ~ to sb.** jmdn. bevorzugen; **give sb. ~ over others** jmdn. vor anderen bevorzugen 5 *attrib.* (Brit. Finance) Vorzugs-, Prioritäts‹*obligation, -aktie*›

preferential /prefəˈrenʃl/ *adj.* bevorzugt ‹*Behandlung*›; bevorrechtigt ‹*Ansprache, Stellung*›; **[a] ~ status** eine Vorzugsstellung; **give sb. ~ treatment** jmdn. bevorzugt behandeln; **~ customs duties** Präferenz- *od.* Vorzugszölle

preferentially /prefəˈrenʃəlɪ/ *adv.* 1 bevorzugt ‹*behandeln*› 2 (to a greater extent) vorwiegend

preferment /prɪˈfɜːmənt/ *n.* 1 (promotion) Beförderung, *die;* (advancement) Voran-, Vorwärtskommen, *das;* **receive ~:** befördert werden 2 (post) höhere *od.* gehobene Stellung; (Eccl.) höheres Amt 3 (Law) **~ of charges** Anklageerhebung, *die*

preferred /prɪˈfɜːd/ *adj.* 1 bevorzugt; **my ~ conclusion/solution** *etc.* die Schlussfolgerung/Lösung *usw.*, der ich den Vorzug gebe 2 **~ share** *etc.* **= preference share** *etc.* ▸**preference 5**

prefigure /priːˈfɪgə(r)/ *v.t.* 1 (represent beforehand) ankünd[ig]en; hindeuten auf (+ *Akk.*) 2 (picture to oneself) sich (*Dat.*) [vorher] vorstellen; sich (*Dat.*) ausmalen

prefix

A /ˈpriːfɪks, prɪˈfɪks/ *v.t.* 1 (add) voranstellen (**to** *Dat.*); **~ a title to a name** einen Titel vor einen Namen setzen 2 (Ling.) als Präfix setzen (**to** vor + *Akk.*); **~ the definite article to sth.** den bestimmten Artikel vor etw. (*Akk.*) setzen

B /ˈpriːfɪks/ *n.* 1 (Ling.) Präfix, *das;* Vorsilbe, *die* 2 (title) [Namens]zusatz, *der;* **the ~ 'Mr' before a name** der Zusatz „Mr." vor einem Namen

preflight /ˈpriːflaɪt/ *attrib. adj.* ‹*Informationen, Kontrollen*› vor dem Flug

preform /priːˈfɔːm/ *v.t.* vorbilden; **~ed ideas** vorgeformte Ideen

preggers /ˈpregəz/ (Brit.), **preggy** /ˈpregɪ/ *adj.* (coll.) dick (derb); schwanger

pregnancy /ˈpregnənsɪ/ *n.* 1 (of woman) Schwangerschaft, *die;* (of animal) Trächtigkeit, *die;* **her advanced state of ~:** ihre fortgeschrittene Schwangerschaft; **in the fourth week of ~:** in der vierten Woche der Schwangerschaft *od.* Schwangerschaftswoche 2 (fig.:

of speech, words) Bedeutungsgehalt, *der;* Bedeutungsschwere, *die* (geh.)

'pregnancy test *n.* Schwangerschaftstest, *der*

pregnant /'pregnənt/ *adj.* **1** schwanger ‹*Frau*›; trächtig ‹*Tier*›; **be six months ~:** im siebten Monat schwanger sein; **she is ~ with her second child** sie erwartet ihr zweites Kind; **heavily** *or* (coll.) **very ~:** hoch schwanger **2** (fig.: full of meaning) bedeutungsvoll; bedeutungsschwer (geh.); **~ with consequences/meaning** folgenschwer/bedeutungsschwanger

preheat /pri:'hi:t/ *v.t.* vorheizen ‹*Backofen*›; vorwärmen ‹*Geschirr, Essen*›; vorher erwärmen ‹*Gas, Werkzeug*›

prehensile /prɪ'hensaɪl/ *adj.* (Zool.) Greif‹*vermögen, -fuß, -schwanz*›

prehistoric /pri:hɪ'stɒrɪk/ *adj.* **1** vorgeschichtlich; prähistorisch; **tools dating from ~ times** vorgeschichtliche *od.* prähistorische Werkzeuge **2** (coll.) (ancient) uralt (ugs.); (out of date) vorsintflutlich (ugs.)

prehistory /pri:'hɪstərɪ/ *n.* **1** Vorgeschichte, *die;* Prähistorie, *die* **2** (of a situation etc.) Vorgeschichte, *die*

pre-ignition /pri:ɪg'nɪʃn/ *n.* (Motor Veh.) Frühzündung, *die*

pre-industrial /pri:ɪn'dʌstrɪəl/ *adj.* vorindustriell

prejudge /pri:'dʒʌdʒ/ *v.t.* **1** (form premature opinion about) vorschnell *od.* voreilig urteilen über (+ *Akk.*) **2** (judge before trial) im Voraus beurteilen, vorverurteilen ‹*Person*›; im Voraus entscheiden ‹*Fall*›

prejudg[e]ment /pri:'dʒʌdʒmənt/ *n.* vorschnelles Urteil (**of** über + *Akk.*); **we must avoid any ~ of the case/accused** wir dürfen den Fall nicht im Voraus entscheiden/den Angeklagten nicht vorverurteilen

prejudice /'predʒʊdɪs/

A *n.* **1** (bias) Vorurteil, *das;* **colour ~:** Vorurteil aufgrund der Hautfarbe; **overcome ~:** Vorurteile ablegen; **this is mere ~!** das sind bloße Vorurteile! **2** (injury) Schaden, *der;* Nachteil, *der;* **to sb.'s ~:** zu jmds. Nachteil *od.* Schaden; **without ~ [to court action]** (Law) ohne Schaden für die eigenen Rechte [bei gerichtlichem Vorgehen]; **without ~ to sth.** unbeschadet einer Sache (*Gen.*); **be without ~ to sth.** etw. unberührt lassen

B *v.t.* **1** (bias) beeinflussen; **~ sb.** *or* **sb.'s mind in sb.'s favour/against sb.** jmdn. für/gegen jmdn. einnehmen; jmdn. zu jmds. Gunsten/Ungunsten beeinflussen **2** (injure) beeinträchtigen

prejudiced /'predʒʊdɪst/ *adj.* voreingenommen (**about** gegenüber, **against** gegen); **the most ~ passages in this book** die einseitigsten Passagen dieses Buches; **~ opinion** Vorurteil, *das;* **be racially ~:** Rassenvorurteile haben; **be totally ~ against women** Frauen gegenüber völlig voreingenommen *od.* voller Vorurteile sein

prejudicial /predʒʊ'dɪʃl/ *adj.* abträglich (geh.) (**to** *Dat.*); nachteilig (**to** für); **be ~ to** beeinträchtigen ‹*Anspruch, Chance, Recht*›; schaden (+ *Dat.*) ‹*Interesse*›

prejudicially /predʒʊ'dɪʃəlɪ/ *adv.* nachteilig; **affect ~:** beeinträchtigen ‹*Anspruch, Recht*›; schaden (+ *Dat.*) ‹*Interesse*›

prelate /'prelət/ *n.* Prälat, *der*

prelim /'pri:lɪm/ *n.* **1** (coll.: exam) Vorprüfung, *die* **2** *in pl.* (Printing) Titelei, *die*

preliminarily /prɪ'lɪmɪnərɪlɪ/ *adv.* vorher

preliminary /prɪ'lɪmɪnərɪ/

A *adj.* Vor-; vorbereitend ‹*Forschung, Schritt, Maßnahme*›; einleitend ‹*Kapitel, Vertragsbestimmungen*›; **~ inquiry/request/search** erste Nachforschung/Bitte/Suche; **~ draft** Rohentwurf, *der*

B *n., usu. in pl.* **preliminaries** Präliminarien *Pl.;* (Sports) Ausscheidungskämpfe; **as a ~ to sth.** (as a preparation) als Vorbereitung auf etw. (*Akk.*); **just a ~:** nur ein Vorspiel (**to** zu); **we have now completed the preliminaries** wir haben die Vorbereitungen jetzt abgeschlossen; **dispense with the preliminaries** ohne Umschweife *od.* direkt zur Sache kommen; in medias res gehen (geh.); **without any further preliminaries** ohne [weitere] Umschweife

C *adv.* ▸**preparatory B**

prelude /'prelju:d/

A *n.* **1** (introduction) Auftakt, *der* (**to** zu) **2** (of play) Vorspiel, *das* (**to** zu); (of poem) Einleitung, *die* (**to** zu *od. Gen.*) **3** (Mus.) Präludium, *das;* Vorspiel, *das*

B *v.t.* **1** (foreshadow) ankündigen **2** (start) **~ sth. by** *or* **with sth.** etw. mit etw. einleiten

premarital /pri:'mærɪtl/ *adj.* vorehelich; **~ sex** Geschlechtsverkehr vor der Ehe; vorehelicher Geschlechtsverkehr

premature /'premətjʊə(r)/ *adj.* **1** (hasty) voreilig, übereilt ‹*Entscheidung, Handeln*› **2** (early) früh-, vorzeitig ‹*Altern, Ankunft, Haarausfall*›; verfrüht ‹*Bericht, Eile, Furcht*›; **~ baby** Frühgeburt, *die;* **the baby was five weeks ~:** das Baby wurde fünf Wochen zu früh geboren

prematurely /'premətjʊəlɪ/ *adv.* (early) vorzeitig; zu früh ‹*geboren werden*›; (hastily) voreilig, übereilt ‹*entscheiden, handeln*›

premedical /prɪ:'medɪkl/ *adj.* (Amer.) auf das Medizinstudium vorbereitend

premedication /pri:medɪ'keɪʃn/ *n.* (Med.) Prämedikation, *die*

premeditated /pri:'medɪteɪtɪd/ *adj.* vorsätzlich

premeditation /pri:medɪ'teɪʃn/ *n.* Vorsatz, *der;* **with ~:** nach vorheriger Planung; vorsätzlich ‹*ermorden, ein Verbrechen begehen*›

premenstrual /pri:'menstrʊəl/ *adj.* (Med.) prämenstruell; **~ tension** prämenstruelles Syndrom

premier /'premɪə(r)/

A *adj.* (first) erst…; (best) best… ‹*Qualität*›; (most important) bedeutendst…, wichtigst… ‹*Position, Stellung*›

B *n.* Premier[minister], *der*/Premierministerin, *die*

premiere /'premjeə(r)/

A *n.* (of production) Premiere, *die;* Erstaufführung, *die;* (of work) Uraufführung, *die*

B *v.t.* erst-/uraufführen

premiership /'premɪəʃɪp/ *n.* **1** Amtsperiode als Premierminister/-ministerin; (office) Amt des Premier[minister]s/der Premierministerin **2** (Sport) Erstliga, *die*

premise /'premɪs/ *n.* **1** *in pl.* (building) Gebäude, *das;* (buildings and land of factory or school) Gelände, *das;* (rooms) Räumlichkeiten *Pl.;* **on the ~s** hier/dort; (of public house, restaurant, etc.) im Lokal; **all repairs are done on the ~s** alle Reparaturen werden an Ort und Stelle erledigt **2** ▸**premiss**

premiss /'premɪs/ *n.* (Logic) Prämisse, *die*

premium /'pri:mɪəm/ *n.* **1** (Insurance) Prämie, *die* **2** (reward) Preis, *der;* Prämie, *die;* **put a ~ on sth.** (make advantageous) etw. belohnen; (attach special value to) etw. [hoch ein]schätzen; großen Wert auf etw. (*Akk.*) legen **3** (bonus) Zusatzzahlung, *die;* (additional to fixed price/wage) Aufgeld, *das*/Prämie, *die* **4** (Amer.: charge for loan) Kreditgebühr, *die* **5** (St. Exch.) Agio, *das;* Aufgeld, *das;* **be at a ~:** über pari stehen; (fig.: be highly valued) sehr gefragt sein; hoch im Kurs stehen; **those shares are on offer at a ~:** diese Aktien werden über pari *od.* mit einem Agio angeboten

'Premium [Savings] Bond *n.* (Brit.) Prämienanleihe, *die;* Losanleihe, *die*

premolar /pri:'məʊlə(r)/ *n.* (Anat.) vorderer Backenzahn; Prämolar, *der* (fachspr.)

premonition /pri:mə'nɪʃn/ *n.* **1** (forewarning) Vorwarnung, *die;* **falling leaves gave a ~ of coming winter** fallendes Laub gemahnte an den kommenden Winter **2** (presentiment) Vorahnung, *die;* **feel/have a ~ of sth.** eine Vorahnung von etw. haben

premonitory /prɪ'mɒnɪtərɪ/ *adj.* warnend ‹*An-, Vorzeichen*›; ungut ‹*Gefühl*›

pre-natal /pri:'neɪtl/ *adj.* (Med.) pränatal (fachspr.); vor der Geburt *nachgestellt;* **~ care** Schwangerschaftsfürsorge, *die*

prenuptial a'greement /pri:nʌpʃəl ə'gri:mənt/ *n.* Ehevertrag, *der*

preoccupation /prɪɒkjʊ'peɪʃn/ *n.* Sorge, *die* (**with** um); **his ~ with his work left little time for his family** er war so sehr mit seiner Arbeit beschäftigt, dass wenig Zeit für die Familie blieb; **first** *or* **greatest** *or* **main ~:** Hauptanliegen, *das;* Hauptsorge, *die*

preoccupied /prɪ'ɒkjʊpaɪd/ *adj.* (lost in thought) gedankenverloren; (concerned) besorgt (**with** um); (absorbed) beschäftigt (**with** mit)

preoccupy /prɪ'ɒkjʊpaɪ/ *v.t.* beschäftigen; **my mind is preoccupied** meine Gedanken sind beschäftigt

pre-op /'pri:ɒp/ (coll.)

A *adj.* präoperativ; ‹*Behandlung usw.*› vor der Operation; **~ patients** Patienten, die eine Operation vor sich haben

B *n.* Operationsvorbereitung, *die;* (injection) Beruhigungsspritze, *die*

preoperative /pri:'ɒpərətɪv/ *adj.* präoperativ; ‹*Behandlung usw.*› vor der Operation

pre-ordain /pri:ɔ:'deɪn/ *v.t.* vorherbestimmen

pre-owned /'pri:əʊnd/ *adj.* gebraucht

prep /prep/ *n.* (Brit. Sch. coll.) **1** (homework) [Haus-, Schul]aufgaben *Pl.;* Schularbeiten *Pl.* **2** (homework period) Hausaufgabenvorbereitung, *die*

pre-packaged /pri:'pækɪdʒd/, **pre-packed** /pri:'pækt/ *adjs.* abgepackt; (fig.) vorgefertigt ‹*Ideen, Meinung*›

prepaid ▸**prepay**

preparation /prepə'reɪʃn/ *n.* **1** Vorbereitung, *die;* **be in a state of ~ for combat** kampfbereit sein; **be in ~** ‹*Publikation:*› in Vorbereitung sein; **be in ~ for sth.** der Vorbereitung einer Sache (*Gen.*) dienen; **in ~ for the new baby/term** als Vorbereitung auf das neue Baby/Semester **2** *in pl.* (things done to get ready) Vorbereitungen *Pl.* (**for** für); **~s for war/the funeral/the voyage/the wedding** Kriegs-/Begräbnis-/Reise-/Hochzeitsvorbereitungen; **make ~s for sth.** Vorbereitungen für etw. treffen **3** (Chem., Med., Pharm.) Präparat, *das;* **herbal ~:** Kräuterpräparat, *das;* (Cookery) Kräutermischung, *die* **4** (Brit. Sch.) [Haus-, Schul]aufgaben *Pl.;* Schularbeiten *Pl.*

preparative /prɪ'pærətɪv/ ▸**preparatory A 1**

preparatory /prɪ'pærətərɪ/

A *adj.* **1** (introductory) vorbereitend, einleitend ‹*Maßnahme, Schritt*›; einleitend ‹*Ermittlung, Geste, Untersuchung*›; Vor‹*ermittlung, -untersuchung*›; **~ work** Vorarbeiten *Pl.* **2** (Sch., Univ.) für die Aufnahme an einer Public School/einem College vorbereitend; ‹*Ausbildung, Stunden, Unterricht*› an einer privaten Vorbereitungsschule

B *adv.* **~ to sth.** vor etw. (*Dat.*); **~ to doing sth.** bevor man etw. tut; **I am packing ~ to departure** *or* **departing** ich packe vor meiner Abreise

pre'paratory school *n.* **1** (Brit. Sch.) *für die Aufnahme an einer Public School vorbereitende Privatschule* **2** (Amer. Univ.) *meist private, für die Aufnahme an einem College vorbereitende Schule*

preparatory school

Eine Privatschule in Großbritannien, auch *prep school* genannt, für Schüler im Alter von sieben bis dreizehn Jahren. Einige sind Tagesschulen, einige Internate und viele eine Mischung aus beidem. Eine *preparatory school* ist normalerweise entweder für Jungen oder für Mädchen, hat also keine gemischten Klassen. Die Eltern zahlen für die Ausbildung ihrer Kinder und andere Angebote innerhalb der Schule Schulgeld. Die meisten Schüler gehen anschließend auf eine **public school** (Privatschule). *Preparatory schools* und *public schools* nennen sich heute oft **independent schools.**

prepare /prɪ'peə(r)/

A *v.t.* **1** (make ready) vorbereiten; entwerfen, ausarbeiten ‹*Plan, Rede*›; herrichten (ugs.), fertig machen ‹*Gästezimmer*›; (make mentally ready, equip with necessary knowledge) vorbereiten ‹*Person*› (**for** auf + *Akk.*); **~ the ground** *or* **way for sb./sth.** (fig.) für jmdn./etw. die nötige Vorarbeit leisten; jmdm. die Steine aus dem Weg räumen; **~ oneself for a shock/the worst** sich auf

P

einen Schock/das Schlimmste gefasst machen; **be ~d for anything** auf alles gefasst sein; **be ~d to do sth.** (be willing) bereit sein, etw. zu tun [2] (make) herstellen ‹*Chemikalie, Metall usw.*›; zubereiten ‹*Essen*›
B *v.i.* sich vorbereiten (**for** auf + *Akk.*); **~ for battle/war** ‹*Land:*› zum Kampf/Krieg rüsten; **~ to do sth.** sich bereit machen *od.* (geh.) anschicken, etw. zu tun; **~ to advance/retreat** sich zum Vorstoß/Rückzug bereit machen

preparedness /prɪˈpeərɪdnɪs/ *n., no pl.* (willingness) Bereitschaft, *die* (**for** zu); **[state of] ~** (readiness) Vorbereitetsein, *das* (**for** für, auf + *Akk.*); **be in a state of ~ for action** sich in Alarmbereitschaft befinden

prepay /priːˈpeɪ/ *v.t.*, **prepaid** /priːˈpeɪd/ im Voraus [be]zahlen; (pay postage of) frankieren, freimachen ‹*Brief, Paket usw.*›; **send a parcel carriage prepaid** ein Paket frachtfrei versenden; **prepaid envelope** frankierter Umschlag; Freiumschlag, *der*

prepayment /prɪːˈpeɪmənt/ *n.* [Be]zahlung im Voraus; Voraus[be]zahlung, *die;* (of letters, parcels, etc.) Frankierung, *die;* Freimachung, *die*

preponderance /prɪˈpɒndərəns/ *n.* Überlegenheit, *die* (**over** über + *Akk.*, gegenüber); Übergewicht, *das;* **[numerical] ~, ~ in numbers** zahlenmäßige Überlegenheit; zahlenmäßiges Übergewicht

preponderant /prɪˈpɒndərənt/ *adj.* überlegen; **~ in numbers** zahlenmäßig überlegen

preponderantly /prɪˈpɒndərəntlɪ/ *adv.* überwiegend

preponderate /prɪˈpɒndəreɪt/ *v.i.* überwiegen (**over** gegenüber)

preposition /prepəˈzɪʃn/ *n.* (Ling.) Präposition, *die;* Verhältniswort, *das*

prepositional /prepəˈzɪʃənl/ *adj.* (Ling.) präpositional; Präpositional‹*attribut, -fall, -objekt*›

prepossess /priːpəˈzes/ *v.t.* [1] (preoccupy mentally) erfüllen; beherrschen [2] (prejudice) beeinflussen; **~ sb. in sb.'s favour/against sb.** jmdn. zu jmds. Gunsten/Ungunsten beeinflussen

prepossessing /priːpəˈzesɪŋ/ *adj.* einnehmend, anziehend ‹*Äußeres, Erscheinung, Person, Lächeln usw.*›

preposterous /prɪˈpɒstərəs/ *adj.* absurd; grotesk ‹*Äußeres, Kleidung*›

preposterously /prɪˈpɒstərəslɪ/ *adv.* absurd; absurderweise ‹*etw. tun*›; **suggest, quite ~, that ...:** absurderweise vorschlagen, dass ...

preppy /ˈprepɪ/ (Amer.)
A *n.: Schüler/Schülerin einer „preparatory school", der/die sich teuer und gepflegt kleidet, aus wohlhabendem Elternhaus stammt, eher konservativ eingestellt ist*
B *adj.* für einen „Preppy" typisch ‹*Kleidung, Meinung usw.*›

preprandial /priːˈprændɪəl/ *adj.* (formal/joc.) ‹*Drink usw.*› vor dem Essen, vor Tisch

preprint /ˈpriːprɪnt/ *n.* Vorabdruck, *der*

ˈpre-program *v.t.*, **-mm-** [vor]programmieren

ˈprep school (coll.) ▸ **preparatory school**

prepubescent /priːpjuːˈbesənt/ *adj.* vorpubertär

prepuce /ˈpriːpjuːs/ *n.* (Anat.) Vorhaut, *die*

prequel /ˈpriːkwəl/ *n.* Vorgeschichte, *die*

Pre-Raphaelite /priːˈræfəlaɪt/ (Art)
A *n.* Präraffaelit, *der*/-raffaelitin, *die*
B *adj.* präraffaelitisch

pre-record /priːrɪˈkɔːd/ *v.t.* vorher aufnehmen; **~ed tape** bespieltes Band

prerequisite /priːˈrekwɪzɪt/
A *n.* [Grund]voraussetzung, *die*
B *adj.* unbedingt erforderlich

prerogative /prɪˈrɒgətɪv/ *n.* [1] Privileg, *das;* Vorrecht, *das;* **the ~ of mercy** das Begnadigungsrecht [2] (of sovereign) **[royal] ~:** [königliche] Prärogative

Pres. *abbr.* = **President** Präs.

presage
A /ˈpresɪdʒ/ *n.* [1] (omen) Vorzeichen, *das;* **a ~ of worse to come** ein schlechtes Omen [2] (foreboding) Vorahnung, *die*
B /ˈpresɪdʒ, prɪˈseɪdʒ/ *v.t.* (foreshadow) ankündigen; (give warning of) ankünden

Presbyterian /prezbɪˈtɪərɪən, presbɪˈtɪərɪən/
A *adj.* presbyterianisch
B *n.* Presbyterianer, *der*/Presbyterianerin, *die*

Presbyterianism /prezbɪˈtɪərɪənɪzm, presbɪˈtɪərɪənɪzm/ *n.* Presbyterianismus, *der*

presbytery /ˈprezbɪtərɪ, ˈpresbɪtərɪ/ *n.* Presbyterium, *das*

preschool /ˈpriːskuːl/ *adj.* Vorschul-; **~ years** Vorschulalter, *das*

prescience /ˈpresɪəns/ *n.* Vorausschau, *die*

prescient /ˈpresɪənt/ *adj.* weitblickend

pre-scientific /priːsaɪənˈtɪfɪk/ *adj.* vorwissenschaftlich

prescribe /prɪˈskraɪb/
A *v.t.* [1] (impose) vorschreiben; **~d book** ▸ **set D 2** [2] (Med.; also fig.) verschreiben; verordnen
B *v.i.* Vorschriften machen

prescript /ˈpriːskrɪpt/ *n.* Vorschrift, *die*

prescription /prɪˈskrɪpʃn/ *n.* [1] (prescribing) Anordnung, *die;* Vorschreiben, *das* [2] (Med.) Rezept, *das;* Verschreibung, *die;* (medicine) [verordnete *od.* verschriebene] Medizin; Verordnung, *die* (fachspr.); **be available only on ~:** nur auf Rezept *od.* Verschreibung erhältlich sein; rezept- *od.* verschreibungspflichtig sein

preˈscription charge *n.* Rezeptgebühr, *die*

prescriptive /prɪˈskrɪptɪv/ *adj.* (Ling.) präskriptiv

pre-select /priːsɪˈlekt/ *v.t.* vorwählen

presence /ˈprezəns/ *n.* [1] (being present) (of person) Gegenwart, *die;* Anwesenheit, *die;* (of things) Vorhandensein, *das;* **in the ~ of his friends** in Gegenwart *od.* Anwesenheit seiner Freunde; **in the ~ of danger** angesichts von Gefahren; **make one's ~ felt** sich bemerkbar machen; **be admitted to/be banished from the King's ~:** zum König vorgelassen werden/aus der Umgebung des Königs verbannt werden [2] (appearance) Äußere, *das;* (bearing) Auftreten, *das;* **[stage] ~:** Ausstrahlung [auf der Bühne]; **she has ~:** sie stellt etwas dar *od.* strahlt etwas aus [3] (being represented) Präsenz, *die;* **police ~:** Polizeipräsenz, *die;* **the British ~ east of Suez** die britische Präsenz östlich von Suez [4] (person or thing) Erscheinung, *die;* **feel an invisible ~ in the room** die Anwesenheit von etwas Unsichtbarem im Zimmer spüren [5] **~ of mind** Geistesgegenwart, *die*

present[1] /ˈprezənt/
A *adj.* [1] anwesend, (geh.) zugegen (**at** bei); **be ~ in the air/water/in large amounts** in der Luft/im Wasser/in großen Mengen vorhanden sein; **all ~ and correct** (joc.) alle sind da; **all those ~:** alle Anwesenden; **~ company excepted** Anwesende ausgenommen; **be ~ to sb.** *or* **sb.'s mind** jmdm. gegenwärtig sein [2] (being dealt with) betreffend; **it's not relevant to the ~ matter** es ist für diese Angelegenheit nicht von Bedeutung; **in the ~ connection** in diesem Zusammenhang; **in the ~ case** im vorliegenden Fall [3] (existing now) gegenwärtig; jetzig, derzeitig ‹*Dekan, Bischof, Chef usw.*›; **during the ~ month** im laufenden Monat; **the ~ writer/author** der Autor des vorliegenden Textes [4] (Ling.) **~ tense** Präsens, *das;* Gegenwart, *die;* **~ perfect** Perfekt, *das;* vollendete Gegenwart; *see also* **participle** [5] **a very ~ help in trouble** (arch.) eine allgegenwärtige Hilfe in der Not
B *n.* [1] **the ~:** die Gegenwart; **up to the ~:** bis jetzt; bisher; **at ~:** zur Zeit; **I can't help you/say more at ~:** im Augenblick kann ich dir nicht helfen/kann ich nicht mehr sagen; **for the ~:** vorläufig; **[there is] no time like the ~:** die Gelegenheit ist günstig; jetzt ist der beste Augenblick [2] (Ling.) Präsens, *das;* Gegenwart, *die*

present[2]
A /ˈprezənt/ *n.* (gift) Geschenk, *das;* Präsent, *das* (geh.); **parting ~:** Abschiedsgeschenk, *das;* **make a ~ of sth. to sb., make sb. a ~ of sth.** jmdm. etw. zum Geschenk machen; *see also* **give A 2**
B /prɪˈzent/ *v.t.* [1] schenken; überreichen ‹*Preis, Medaille, Geschenk*›; **~ sth. to sb.** *or* **sb. with sth.** jmdm. etw. schenken/überreichen; **~ sb. with gifts** jmdm. Geschenke machen; **~ sb. with difficulties/a problem** jmdn. vor Schwierigkeiten/ein Problem stellen; **he was ~ed with an opportunity that ...:** ihm bot sich eine Gelegenheit, die ... [2] (express) **~ one's compliments to sb.** sich jmdm. empfehlen; **~ one's regards to sb.** jmdm. Grüße bestellen *od.* ausrichten; jmdm. seine Grüße entbieten (geh.) [3] (deliver) überreichen ‹*Gesuch*› (**to** bei); vorlegen ‹*Scheck, Bericht, Rechnung*› (**to** *Dat.*); **~ one's case** seinen Fall darlegen [4] (exhibit) zeigen; bereiten ‹*Schwierigkeit*›; aufweisen ‹*Aspekt*›; **~ a bold front** *or* **brave face to the world** sich nach außen hin unerschrocken geben [5] (introduce) vorstellen (**to** *Dat.*) [6] (to the public) geben, aufführen ‹*Theaterstück*›; zeigen ‹*Film*›; moderieren ‹*Sendung*›; bringen ‹*Fernsehserie, Schauspieler in einer Rolle*›; vorstellen ‹*Produkt usw.*›; vorlegen ‹*Abhandlung*›; darlegen ‹*Theorie usw.*› [7] (Parl.) vorlegen ‹*Gesetzentwurf*› [8] **~ arms!** (Mil.) präsentiert das Gewehr! [9] (aim, hold horizontally) anlegen ‹*Gewehr usw.*›; **he ~ed his weapon** er legte an
C *v. refl.* ‹*Problem:*› auftreten; ‹*Möglichkeit:*› sich ergeben; **~ itself to sb.** ‹*Möglichkeit:*› jmdm. vor Augen stehen; ‹*Erinnerung usw.:*› sich bei jmdm. einstellen; ‹*Gedanke:*› jmdm. kommen; **~ oneself to sb.** sich jmdm. vorstellen; **~ oneself for interview/an examination** zu einem Gespräch/einer Prüfung erscheinen

presentable /prɪˈzentəbl/ *adj.* ansehnlich; **she is quite a ~ young lady** man kann sie gut vorzeigen *od.* sich gut mit ihr sehen lassen; **the flat is not very ~ at the moment** die Wohnung ist im Augenblick nicht besonders präsentabel; **I'm not ~:** ich kann mich nicht so zeigen; **make oneself/sth. ~:** sich/etw. zurechtmachen; **his most ~ jacket** sein bestes Jackett

presentably /prɪˈzentəblɪ/ *adv.* ansehnlich; angemessen ‹*sich kleiden*›; ganz ordentlich ‹*Klavier spielen, malen usw.*›

presentation /prezənˈteɪʃn/ *n.* [1] (giving) Schenkung, *die;* (of prize, medal, gift) Überreichung, *die;* **make sb. a ~ of sth.** jmdm. etw. schenken/überreichen [2] (ceremony) Verleihung, *die;* **~ of the awards/medals** Preis-/Ordensverleihung, *die* [3] (delivering) (of petition) Überreichung, *die;* (of cheque, report, account) Vorlage, *die;* (of case, position, thesis) Darlegung, *die;* (manner of putting forward, presenting) Präsentation, *die* (geh.); Darbietung, *die;* **on ~ of** gegen Vorlage (+ *Gen.*) [4] (exhibition) Darstellung, *die* [5] (Theatre, Radio, Telev.) Darbietung, *die;* (Theatre also) Inszenierung, *die;* (Radio, Telev. also) Moderation, *die* [6] (introduction) Vorstellung, *die* [7] (Med.) Lage, *die;* **head/breech ~:** Kopf-/Steißlage, *die*

presenˈtation: ~ copy *n.* Dedikationsexemplar, *das;* **~ skills** *n. pl.* Presentationsfähigheiten *Pl.*

present-ˈday *adj.* heutig; zeitgemäß ‹*Einstellungen, Ansichten*›; **by ~ standards** nach heutigen *od.* gegenwärtigen Maßstäben

presenter /prɪˈzentə(r)/ *n.* [1] (of cheque) Überbringer, *der*/Überbringerin, *die;* **be the ~ of a petition/report** eine Petition überreichen/einen Bericht vorlegen [2] ▸ **p. 1260** (Radio, Telev.) Moderator, *der*/Moderatorin, *die*

presentiment /prɪˈzentɪmənt/ *n.* Vorahnung, *die;* **I have a ~ about the opening night** ich habe das Gefühl, dass bei der Premiere irgendetwas passiert; **have a ~ that ...:** vorausahnen, dass ...

presently /ˈprezəntlɪ/ *adv.* [1] (soon) bald; **see you ~:** bis gleich [2] (Amer., Scot.: now) zurzeit; derzeit

present: ~ ˈvalue, ~ ˈworth *ns.* (Econ.) jetziger Wert; Tageswert, *der*

preservation /prezəˈveɪʃn/ *n., no pl.* [1] (action) Erhaltung, *die;* (of leather, wood, etc.)

Konservierung, *die;* **the ~ of peace** die Erhaltung des Friedens [2] (state) Erhaltungszustand, *der;* **be in an excellent state of ~:** außerordentlich gut erhalten sein; ‹*Person:*› sich außerordentlich gut gehalten haben

preser'vation order *n.: Verordnung, die etw. unter Denkmalschutz stellt;* **put a ~ on sth.** etw. unter Denkmalschutz stellen

preservative /prɪˈzɜːvətɪv/
A *n.* Konservierungsmittel, *das*
B *adj.* konservierend; Konservierungs-; konservativ ‹*Lösung*›

preserve /prɪˈzɜːv/
A *n.* [1] *in sing. or pl.* (fruit) Eingemachte, *das;* **strawberry/quince ~s** eingemachte Erdbeeren/Quitten [2] (jam) Konfitüre, *die* [3] (fig.: special sphere) Domäne, *die* (geh.); (of political power) Einflussbereich, *der* [4] (for wildlife) [Natur]schutzgebiet, *das;* Reservat, *das;* (water) [Fisch]gehege, *das;* **wildlife/game ~:** Tierschutzgebiet, *das*/Wildpark *der*
B *v.t.* [1] (keep safe) schützen (**from** vor + *Dat.*); **~ sth. from destruction** etw. vor der Zerstörung bewahren [2] (maintain) aufrechterhalten ‹*Disziplin*›; bewahren ‹*Sehfähigkeit, Brauch, Würde*›; behalten ‹*Stellung*›; wahren ‹*Anschein, Reputation*›; **~ the peace** den Frieden bewahren *od.* erhalten [3] (retain) speichern ‹*Hitze*›; bewahren ‹*Haltung, Distanz, Humor*› [4] (prepare, keep from decay) konservieren; (bottle) einmachen ‹*Obst, Gemüse*›; präparieren; ‹*Leiche, Kadaver*› [5] (keep alive) erhalten; (fig.) bewahren ‹*Erinnerung, Andenken*›; **Heaven ~ us!** [Gott] bewahre! [6] (care for and protect) hegen ‹*Tierart, Wald*›; unter Schutz stellen ‹*Gewässer, Gebiet*›

preset /priːˈset/ *v.t., forms as* **set A:** vorher einstellen

pre-shrink /priːˈʃrɪŋk/ *v.t., forms as* **shrink B** (Textiles) vorschrumpfen; vorwaschen ‹*Jeans*›

pre-shrunk /priːˈʃrʌŋk/ *adj.* (Textiles) vorgeschrumpft, vorgewaschen ‹*Jeans*›

preside /prɪˈzaɪd/ *v.i.* [1] (at meeting etc.) den Vorsitz haben (**at** bei); präsidieren, vorsitzen (**over** *Dat.*) [2] (at meal) den Vorsitz haben; **~ at dinner** bei Tisch vorsitzen [3] (exercise control) **~ over** leiten ‹*Abteilung, Organisation, Programm*›; lenken ‹*Geschick*›; vorstehen (+ *Dat.*) ‹*Familie*›; bestimmen ‹*Bildung, Gründung*›

presidency /ˈprezɪdənsɪ/ *n.* [1] (also EU) Präsidentschaft, *die* [2] (of legislative body) Vorsitz, *der* [3] (Univ., esp. Amer.) Präsidentschaft, *die;* Rektorat, *das* [4] (of society etc.) Vorsitz, *der;* Präsidentschaft, *die* [5] (of council, board, etc.) Vorsitz, *der* [6] (Amer.: of bank or company) Vorstandsvorsitz, *der*

president /ˈprezɪdənt/ *n.* ▸ℹ **p. 1260**, ▸ℹ **p. 1634** [1] Präsident, *der*/Präsidentin, *die;* **P~ of the European Commission** Präsident/Präsidentin der Europäischen Kommission [2] (of legislative body) Vorsitzende, *der/die* [3] (Univ., esp. Amer.) Präsident, *der*/Präsidentin, *die;* Rektor, *der*/Rektorin, *die* [4] (of society etc.) Vorsitzende, *der/die;* Präsident, *der*/Präsidentin, *die* [5] (of council, board, etc.) Vorstand, *der;* Vorsitzende, *der/die;* **Lord P~ of the Council** (Brit.) *Titel des dem Privy Council präsidierenden Kabinettsmitglieds* [6] (Amer.: of bank or company) Vorstandvorsitzende, *der/die;* Generaldirektor, *der*/-direktorin, *die*

> **President**
>
> Der Präsident der Vereinigten Staaten ist das Staatsoberhaupt, trägt außenpolitische Verantwortung und hat den Oberbefehl über die Streitkräfte. Er kann mit Zustimmung des Senats Bundesrichter und leitende Minister ernennen und wird vom **Congress** gebeten, neue Gesetze zu bewilligen. Er selbst hat kein Recht auf Gesetzesinitiative, aber er kann dem Kongress Maßnahmen zur Beratung empfehlen. Außerdem hat er ein Vetorecht gegenüber Beschlüssen des Kongresses. Ein Präsident kann maximal für zwei *terms* (Legislaturperioden), also für 8 Jahre regieren. Er kann nur auf dem Wege der Anklage wegen Amtsmissbrauchs – *Impeachment* – abgesetzt werden.

> **Presidents' Day**
>
> Der dritte Montag im Februar, Feiertag in den USA zu Ehren der Präsidenten George Washington und Abraham Lincoln. In einigen Staaten werden die zwei Geburtstage als Washingtons Geburtstag und Lincolns Geburtstag einzeln gefeiert.

presidential /prezɪˈdenʃl/ *adj.* Präsidenten-; **~ campaign** Präsidentschaftswahlkampf, *der;* **~ address** Ansprache des Präsidenten; **~ ambitions** Streben nach der Präsidentschaft; **~ election** Präsidentschaftswahl, *die*

presidium /prɪˈsɪdɪəm, prɪˈzɪdɪəm/ *n.* Präsidium, *das*

press¹ /pres/
A *n.* [1] (newspapers etc.) Presse, *die; attrib.* Presse-; der Presse *nachgestellt;* **get/have a good/bad ~** (fig.) eine gute/schlechte Presse bekommen/haben; *see also* **freedom 1** [2] ▸**printing press** [3] (printing house) Druckerei, *die;* **at** *or* **in [the] ~:** im Druck; **send to [the] ~:** in Druck geben; **go to [the] ~:** in Druck gehen: [4] (publishing firm) Verlag, *der* [5] (for flattening, compressing, etc.) Presse, *die;* (for sports racket) Spanner, *der* [6] (crowding) Gedränge, *das* [7] (crowd) Menge, *die;* **a ~ of people** eine Menschenmenge, *die* [8] (in battle) Getümmel, *das;* Gewühl, *das* [9] (~ing) Druck, *der;* **give sth. a ~:** etw. drücken; **your trousers could do with a ~:** deine Hosen sollten wieder einmal gebügelt werden; **with a ~ of the button** mit einem Knopfdruck *od.* Druck auf den Knopf [10] (Weightlifting) Drücken, *das*
B *v.t.* [1] drücken; pressen; drücken auf (+ *Akk.*) ‹*Klingel, Knopf*›; treten auf (+ *Akk.*) ‹*Gas-, Brems-, Kupplungspedal usw.*›; **~ the trigger** abdrücken; den Abzug betätigen [2] (urge) drängen ‹*Person*›; (force) aufdrängen (**[up]on** *Dat.*); (insist on) nachdrücklich vorbringen ‹*Forderung, Argument, Vorschlag*›; verfechten ‹*Standpunkt*›; **~ sb. for an answer** jmdn. zu einer Antwort drängen; **he did not ~ the point** er ließ die Sache auf sich beruhen; **~ the analogy too far** die Analogie zu weit treiben [3] (exert force on) drücken; pressen [4] (squeeze) drücken; **~ sb.'s hand** jmdm. die Hand drücken; **~ the flesh** (coll.) Hände drücken [5] (compress) pressen; auspressen ‹*Orangen, Saft*›; keltern ‹*Trauben, Äpfel*› [6] (iron) bügeln [7] (bear heavily on) bedrängen; **be hard ~ed** (by enemy) hart bedrängt werden; (experience great difficulty) unter großem Druck stehen [8] **be ~ed for space/time/money** (have barely enough) zu wenig Platz/Zeit/Geld haben [9] (Weightlifting) drücken [10] (make) pressen ‹*Schallplatte*›
C *v.i.* [1] (exert pressure) drücken; **the child ~ed against the railings** das Kind drückte sich gegen das Geländer [2] (weigh) **~ [up]on sb.'s mind/heart** jmdn. bedrücken [3] (be urgent) drängen; **time/sth. ~es** die Zeit drängt/etw. eilt *od.* ist dringend [4] (make demand) **~ for sth.** auf etw. (*Akk.*) drängen [5] (crowd) [sich] drängen; **~ up** sich herandrängen; **~ in upon sb.** ‹*Gedanken:*› auf jmdn. eindringen

Phrasal verbs

- **~ a'head, ~ 'forward, ~ 'on** *v.i.* (continue activity) [zügig] weitermachen; (continue travelling) [zügig] weitergehen/-fahren; **~ on with one's work** sich mit der Arbeit ranhalten (ugs.)
- **~ 'out** *v.t.* auspressen; (out of cardboard) herausdrücken

press² *v.t.* **~ into service/use** in Dienst nehmen; einsetzen

press: ~ agent *n.* ▸ℹ **p. 1260** Presseagent, *der*/-agentin, *die;* **~ attaché** ▸**attaché;** **~ box** *n.* Pressekabine, *die;* **~-button** ▸**push-button;** **~ campaign** *n.* Pressefeldzug, *der;* Pressekampagne, *die;* **~ card** *n.* Presseausweis, *der;* **~ clipping** (Amer.) ▸**~ cutting;** **~ conference** *n.* Pressekonferenz, *die;* **~ coverage** *n.* Berichterstattung in der Presse; **~ cutting** *n.* (Brit.) Zeitungsausschnitt, *der;* **~ gallery** *n.* Pressetribüne, *die;* **~ gang A** *n.* (Hist.) Pressgang, *der* (veralt.); **B** *v.t.* (Hist.) pressen; zwangsrekrutieren; (fig.) zwingen, pressen (**into** zu)

pressing /ˈpresɪŋ/
A *adj.* [1] (urgent) dringend; **the danger was ~:** Gefahr war im Verzug [2] (persistent) dringlich; nachdrücklich
B *n.* [1] (exertion of pressure) Drücken, *das;* (of apples, grapes) Keltern, *das;* (of cheese, olives) Pressen, *das;* (of clothes) Bügeln, *das* [2] (product, esp. record) Pressung, *die*

pressingly /ˈpresɪŋlɪ/ *adv.* dringend

press: ~man *n.* ▸ℹ **p. 1260** (Brit.: journalist) Journalist, *der;* Pressemann, *der* (ugs.); **~ office** *n.* Pressebüro, *das;* **~ officer** *n.* ▸ℹ **p. 1260** Pressereferent, *der*/-referentin, *die;* Pressesprecher, *der*/-sprecherin, *die;* **~ pack** *n.* Pressemappe, *die;* **~ pass** *n.* Presseausweis, *der;* **~ photographer** *n.* ▸ℹ **p. 1260** Pressefotograf, *der*/-fotografin, *die;* **~ release** *n.* Presseinformation, *die;* **~ report** *n.* Pressebericht, *der;* **~room** *n.* [1] (Printing) Druckerei, *die;* [2] (Journ.) Presseraum, *der;* **~ stud** *n.* (Brit.) Druckknopf, *der;* **~-up** *n.* Liegestütz, *der*

pressure /ˈpreʃə(r)/
A *n.* [1] (exertion of force, amount) Druck, *der;* **apply firm ~ to the joint** die Verbindung fest zusammendrücken; **atmospheric ~:** Luftdruck, *der* [2] (oppression) Last, *die;* Belastung, *die;* **mental ~:** psychische Belastung [3] (trouble) Druck, *der;* **under financial ~:** finanziell unter Druck; **~s at [one's] work** berufliche Belastungen; **the finances of the company were under ~:** die Firma stand [finanziell] unter Druck [4] (urgency) Druck, *der;* (of affairs) Dringlichkeit, *die;* **the ~ was on him** er stand unter Zeitdruck; **he [positively] thrives under ~:** er braucht den Druck [geradezu] [5] (constraint) Druck, *der;* Zwang, *der;* **put ~ on sb.** jmdn. unter Druck setzen; **be under a lot of ~ to do sth.** stark unter Druck gesetzt werden, etw. zu tun; **put the ~ on** die Daumenschrauben anlegen *od.* -setzen. *See also* **high pressure; low pressure**
B *v.t.* [1] (coerce) **~ sb. into doing sth.** jmdn. [dazu] drängen, etw. zu tun [2] (fig.: apply ~ to) unter Druck setzen

pressure: ~ cooker *n.* Schnellkochtopf, *der;* **~ gauge** *n.* (Motor Veh.) Druckluftmesser, *der;* Manometer, *das;* (Railw.) Druckanzeige, *die;* **~ group** *n.* Pressuregroup, *die;* **~ point** *n.* (Med.) [1] (where sore may develop) Druckstelle, *die;* [2] (where bleeding can be stopped) Druckpunkt, *der;* **~ sore** *n.* (Med.) Druckwunde, *die;* **~ suit** *n.* (Astronaut.) Druckanzug, *der;* **~ vessel** *n.* (of boiler in nuclear reactor) Druckbehälter, *der*

pressurize (pressurise) /ˈpreʃəraɪz/ *v.t.* [1] ▸**pressure B 1** [2] (raise to high pressure) unter Druck setzen [3] (maintain normal pressure in) druckfest machen, auf Normaldruck halten ‹*Flugzeugkabine*›; **~d cabin/suit** Druckkabine, *die*/-anzug, *der*

prestige /preˈstiːʒ/
A *n.* Prestige, *das;* Renommee, *das*
B *adj.* renommiert; Nobel‹*hotel, -gegend*›; **~ value** Prestigewert, *der*

prestigious /preˈstɪdʒəs/ *adj.* angesehen

presto /ˈprestəʊ/ ▸**hey**

pre-stressed /priːˈstrest/ *adj.* (Building) vorgespannt; **~ concrete** Spannbeton, *der*

presumable /prɪˈzjuːməbl/ *adj.* mutmaßlich

presumably /prɪˈzjuːməblɪ/ *adv.* vermutlich; **~ he knows what he is doing** er wird schon wissen, was er tut; **~ something must have delayed them** etwas muss sie aufgehalten haben

presume /prɪˈzjuːm/
A *v.t.* [1] (venture) **~ to do sth.** sich (*Dat.*) anmaßen, etw. zu tun; (take the liberty) sich (*Dat.*) erlauben, etw. zu tun [2] (suppose) annehmen; **be ~d innocent** als unschuldig gelten *od.* angesehen werden; **missing ~d dead** vermisst, wahrscheinlich *od.* mutmaßlich tot
B *v.i.* sich (*Dat.*) anmaßen; **~ [up]on sth.** etw. ausnützen

presumption /prɪˈzʌmpʃn/ *n.* [1] (arrogance) Anmaßung, *die;* Vermessenheit, *die;* **have the ~ to do sth.** die Vermessenheit besitzen, etw. zu tun; sich (*Dat.*) anmaßen, etw. zu tun

P

2 (assumption) Annahme, *die;* Vermutung, *die;* **the ~ is that he lost it** vermutlich hat er es verloren; es ist zu vermuten, dass er es verloren hat; **we are working on the ~ that ...:** wir gehen von der Annahme aus, dass ...; **the ~ of innocence** die Unschuldsvermutung **3** (ground for belief) **there is a strong ~ against its truth** es besteht hinreichend Grund zu der Annahme, dass es nicht stimmt

presumptive /prɪˈzʌmptɪv/ *adj.* **~ evidence** Indizienbeweis, *der;* **heir ~:** mutmaßlicher Erbe/mutmaßliche Erbin

presumptuous /prɪˈzʌmptjʊəs/ *adj.* anmaßend; überheblich; (impertinent) aufdringlich

presumptuously /prɪˈzʌmptjʊəslɪ/ *adv.* überheblich; (impertinently) aufdringlich

presuppose /priːsəˈpəʊz/ *v.t.* **1** (assume) voraussetzen **2** (imply) voraussetzen; zur Voraussetzung haben

presupposition /priːsʌpəˈzɪʃn/ *n.* **1** (presupposing) Annahme, *die;* Voraussetzung, *die* **2** (thing assumed) Prämisse, *die* (bes. Philos., Rechtsw.); Voraussetzung, *die;* **work on a ~:** von einer Prämisse/Voraussetzung ausgehen

pre-tax /ˈpriːtæks/ *adj.* vor Steuern *nachgestellt;* **~ profits** Gewinn vor Steuern

pre-teen /ˈpriːtiːn/ *adj.* ≈ zehn- bis zwölfjährig

pretence /prɪˈtens/ *n.* (Brit.) **1** (pretext) Vorwand, *der;* **under [the] ~ of helping** unter dem Vorwand zu helfen; *see also* **false pretences** **2** *no art.* (make-believe, insincere behaviour) Verstellung, *die* **3** (piece of insincere behaviour) **it is all** *or* **just a ~:** das ist alles nicht echt **4** (affectation) Affektiertheit, *die* (abwertend); Unnatürlichkeit, *die* **5** (claim) Anspruch, *der;* **make the/no ~ of** *or* **to sth.** Anspruch/keinen Anspruch auf etw. (*Akk.*) erheben

pretend /prɪˈtend/

A *v.t.* **1** vorgeben; **she ~ed to be asleep** sie tat, als ob sie schlief[e] **2** (imagine in play) **~ to be sth.** so tun, als ob man etw. sei; **let's ~ that we are king and queen** lass uns König und Königin spielen **3** (profess falsely) vortäuschen; simulieren, vorschützen ‹*Krankheit*›; (say falsely) vorgeben, fälschlich beteuern (**to** gegenüber); **~ illness** krank spielen (ugs.) **4** (claim) **not ~ to do sth.** nicht behaupten wollen, etw. zu tun

B *v.i.* **1** sich verstellen; **she's only ~ing** sie tut nur so; **~ to sb.** jmdm. etwas vormachen **2** (presume) sich unterfangen (geh.); wagen **3** **~ to** (claim) für sich in Anspruch nehmen; Anspruch erheben auf (+ *Akk.*) (Titel, Amt)

pretender /prɪˈtendə(r)/ *n.* Prätendent, *der* (geh.)/Prätendentin, *die* (geh.) (**to** auf + *Akk.*); **~ to the throne** Thronanwärter *od.* -prätendent, *der*/Thronanwärterin *od.* -prätendentin, *die;* **Old/Young P~:** *Sohn/Enkel von Jakob II. als britischer Thronanwärter*

pretense (Amer.) ▸ **pretence**

pretension /prɪˈtenʃn/ *n.* **1** (claim) Anspruch, *der;* **have/make ~s to great wisdom** vorgeben *od.* den Anspruch erheben, sehr klug zu sein **2** (justifiable claim) Anspruch, *der* (**to** auf + *Akk.*); **a country estate of some ~s** ein Landsitz, der sich sehen lassen kann; **people with ~s to taste and culture** Menschen, die Geschmack und Kultur für sich in Anspruch nehmen können **3** (pretentiousness) Überheblichkeit, *die;* Anmaßung, *die;* (of things: ostentation) Protzigkeit, *die*

pretentious /prɪˈtenʃəs/ *adj.* **1** prätentiös (geh.); hochgestochen; wichtigtuerisch ‹*Person*› **2** (ostentatious) protzig (abwertend); großspurig (abwertend) ‹*Person, Verhalten, Art*›

pretentiously /prɪˈtenʃəslɪ/ *adv.* **1** prätentiös (geh.); hochgestochen; **speak ~:** wichtigtuerische Reden führen **2** (ostentatiously) protzig (abwertend); großspurig (abwertend) ‹*sich benehmen*›

preterite (*Amer.:* **preterit**) /ˈpretərɪt/ (Ling.)

A *adj.* Präteritums-; **~ tense** Präteritum, *das*

B *n.* Präteritum, *das*

preternatural /priːtəˈnætʃərl/ *adj.* **1** (non-natural) außergewöhnlich **2** (supernatural) übernatürlich; übersinnlich

pretext /ˈpriːtekst/ *n.* Vorwand, *der;* Ausrede, *die;* **make illness the ~ for staying at home** Krankheit vorschützen, um zu Hause zu bleiben; **[up]on** *or* **under the ~ of doing sth./being ill** unter dem Vorwand *od.* mit der Entschuldigung, etw. tun zu wollen/krank zu sein; **on the slightest ~:** mit *od.* unter dem fadenscheinigsten Vorwand

pretrial /ˈpriːtraɪəl/ *attrib. adj.* **1** (before trial) ‹*Befragung usw.*› vor der Verhandlung; **~ detention** Untersuchungshaft, *die;* **~ publicity** Publicity im Vorfeld der Verhandlung **2** (Amer.: relating to a preliminary hearing) vorgerichtlich

prettify /ˈprɪtɪfaɪ/ *v.t.* verschönern; (in an insipid way) verkitschen

prettily /ˈprɪtɪlɪ/ *adv.* hübsch; sehr schön ‹*singen, tanzen*›; **curtsy ~:** einen graziösen Knicks machen; **thank sb. ~:** sich [bei jmdm.] sehr nett bedanken

pretty /ˈprɪtɪ/

A *adj.* **1** (attractive) hübsch; nett ‹*Art*›; niedlich ‹*Geschichte, Liedchen*›; **she's not just a ~ face!** sie ist nicht nur hübsch[, sie kann auch was]!; **as ~ as a picture** bildhübsch; **not a ~ sight** (iron.) kein schöner Anblick **2** (iron.) hübsch, schön (ugs. iron.); **a ~ state of affairs** eine schöne Geschichte; **a ~ mess** eine schöne Bescherung

B *adv.* ziemlich; **I am ~ well** es geht mir ganz gut; **~ much** *or* **well as ...:** so ziemlich wie ...; **we have ~ nearly finished** wir sind so gut wie fertig; **be ~ well over/exhausted** so gut wie vorbei/erschöpft sein; **~ much the same** ziemlich unverändert; **~ much the same thing** so ziemlich *od.* fast das Gleiche; **be sitting ~** (coll.) sein Schäfchen im Trockenen haben (ugs.); ausgesorgt haben; **~-~** (coll.) kitschig (abwertend)

pretzel /ˈpretsl/ *n.* Brezel, *die*

prevail /prɪˈveɪl/ *v.i.* **1** (gain mastery) siegen, die Oberhand gewinnen (**against, over** über + *Akk.*); **~ [up]on sb.** auf jmdn. einwirken; jmdn. überreden; **~ [up]on sb. to do sth.** jmdn. dazu bewegen *od.* überreden, etw. zu tun; **be ~ed [up]on to do sth.** sich bewegen *od.* überreden lassen, etw. zu tun **2** (predominate) ‹*Zustand, Bedingung:*› vorherrschen **3** (be current) herrschen; **this type of approach ~ed for many years** dieser Ansatz war jahrelang gängig *od.* üblich

prevailing /prɪˈveɪlɪŋ/ *adj.* **1** (common) [vor]herrschend; aktuell ‹*Mode*› **2** (most frequent) **the ~ wind is from the West** der Wind kommt vorwiegend von Westen

prevalence /ˈprevələns/ *n., no pl.* Vorherrschen, *das;* (of crime, corruption, etc.) Überhandnehmen, *das;* (of disease, malnutrition, etc.) weite Verbreitung; **gain ~** ‹*Standpunkt:*› sich durchsetzen

prevalent /ˈprevələnt/ *adj.* **1** (existing) herrschend; gängig, geläufig ‹*Schreibweise*›; weit verbreitet ‹*Krankheit*›; aktuell ‹*Trend*› **2** (predominant) vorherrschend; **be/become ~:** vorherrschen/sich durchsetzen

prevaricate /prɪˈværɪkeɪt/ *v.i.* Ausflüchte machen (**over** wegen)

prevarication /prɪværɪˈkeɪʃn/ *n.* **1** (prevaricating) Ausflüchte *Pl.* **2** (statement) Ausflucht, *die*

prevent /prɪˈvent/ *v.t.* (hinder) verhindern; verhüten; (forestall) vorbeugen; verhüten; **~ sb. from doing sth., ~ sb.'s doing sth.,** (coll.) **~ sb. doing sth.** jmdn. daran hindern *od.* davon abhalten, etw. zu tun; **there is nothing to ~ me** nichts hindert mich daran; **~ sb. from coming** jmdn. am Kommen hindern; **catch sb.'s arm to ~ him [from] falling** jmdn. am Arm fassen, damit er nicht fällt; **do everything to ~ it from happening** *or* **~ its happening** alles tun, um es zu verhindern *od.* damit es nicht geschieht

preventable /prɪˈventəbl/ *adj.* vermeidbar

preventative /prɪˈventətɪv/ ▸ **preventive**

prevention /prɪˈvenʃn/ *n.* Verhinderung, *die;* Verhütung, *die;* (forestalling) Vorbeugung, *die;* Verhütung, *die;* **~ of crime** Verbrechensverhütung, *die;* **society for the ~ of cruelty to children/animals** Kinderschutzbund/Tierschutzverein, *der;* **~ is better than cure** (prov.) Vorbeugen ist besser als Heilen (Spr.)

preventive /prɪˈventɪv/

A *adj.* vorbeugend; präventiv (geh.); Präventiv‹*maßnahme, -krieg*›; **~ treatment** (Med.) Präventivbehandlung, *die*

B *n.* Vorbeugungsmaßnahme, *die;* Präventivmittel, *das* (Med.); **as a ~:** zur/als Vorbeugung

preventive: ~ deˈtention *n.* (Brit. Law) Sicherungsverwahrung, *die;* **~ ˈmedicine** *n.* Präventivmedizin, *die*

preview /ˈpriːvjuː/

A *n.* **1** (of film, play) Voraufführung, *die;* (of exhibition) Vernissage, *die* (geh.); (of book) Vorbesprechung, *die;* **give a ~:** eine Voraufführung geben/Vernissage veranstalten/Vorbesprechung geben **2** (Amer.: trailer of film) Vorschau, *die*

B *v.t.* eine Vorschau sehen von ‹*Film*›

previous /ˈpriːvɪəs/

A *adj.* **1** (coming before) früher ‹*Anstellung, Gelegenheit*›; ‹*Tag, Morgen, Abend, Nacht*› vorher; vorherig ‹*Abend*›; vorig ‹*Besitzer, Wohnsitz*›; **the ~ page** die Seite davor; **no ~ experience necessary** keine Berufserfahrung nötig; **no ~ convictions** keine Vorstrafen **2** (prior) **~ to** vor (+ *Dat.*) **3** (hasty) verfrüht; voreilig

B *adv.* **~ to** vor (+ *Dat.*); **~ to being a nurse, she was ...:** bevor sie Krankenschwester wurde, war sie ...

previously /ˈpriːvɪəslɪ/ *adv.* vorher; **two years ~:** zwei Jahre zuvor

pre-war /ˈpriːwɔː(r)/ *adj.* Vorkriegs-; **these houses are all ~:** diese Häuser stammen alle aus der Zeit vor dem Krieg

prey /preɪ/

A *n., pl. same* **1** (animal[s]) Beute, *die;* Beutetier, *das;* **beast/bird of ~:** Raubtier, *das*/-vogel, *der;* **easy ~** (lit. or fig.) leichte Beute **2** (victim) Beute, *die* (geh.); Opfer, *das;* **fall [a] ~ to sth.** einer Sache (*Dat.*) zum Opfer fallen; **be a ~ to sth.** eine Beute *od.* ein Opfer von etw. werden

B *v.i.* **~ [up]on** ‹*Raubtier, Raubvogel:*› schlagen; (take as ~) erbeuten; (plunder) ausplündern ‹*Person*›; (exploit) ausnutzen; **~ [up]on sb.'s mind** jmdm. keine Ruhe lassen; ‹*Krankheit:*› jmdm. sehr zusetzen; ‹*Kummer, Angst:*› an jmdm. nagen

prezzie /ˈprezɪ/ *n.* (coll.) Geschenk, *das*

price /praɪs/

A *n.* **1** ▸ **p. 1332** (money etc.) Preis, *der;* **the ~ of wheat/a pint** der Weizenpreis/der Preis für ein Bier; **what is the ~ of this?** was kostet das?; **at a ~ of** zum Preis von; **for the ~ of a few drinks** für ein paar Drinks; **~s and incomes policy** Preis- und Einkommenspolitik, *die;* Lohn-Preis-Politik, *die;* **sth. goes up/down in ~:** der Preis von etw. steigt/fällt; etw. steigt/fällt im Preis; **what sort of ~ do they charge for a meal?** was verlangen *od.* berechnen sie für eine Mahlzeit?; **at a ~:** zum entsprechenden Preis; **set a ~ on sth.** einen Preis für etw. festsetzen; **set a ~ on sb.'s head** *or* **life** einen Preis *od.* eine Belohnung auf jmds. Kopf (*Akk.*) aussetzen **2** (betting odds) Eventualquote, *die* **3** (value) **be without/beyond ~:** [mit Geld] nicht zu bezahlen sein **4** (fig.) Preis, *der;* **be achieved at a ~:** seinen Preis haben; **he succeeded, but at a great ~:** er hatte Erfolg, musste aber einen hohen Preis dafür bezahlen; **every man has his ~:** jeder Mensch hat seinen Preis *od.* ist käuflich; **at/not at any ~:** um jeden/keinen Preis; **at the ~ of ruining his marriage/health** auf Kosten seiner Ehe/Gesundheit; **what ~ ...?** (Brit. coll.) (what is the chance of ...) wie wärs mit ...?; (... has failed) wie stehts jetzt mit ...? *See also* **pay B 6**

B *v.t.* (fix ~ of) kalkulieren ‹*Ware*›; (label with ~) auszeichnen; **modestly ~d** zu niedrigem Preis *nachgestellt;* **favourably ~d** preisgünstig

Phrasal verbs

- **price down**

A *v.t.* [im Preis] herab- *od.* heruntersetzen

B *v.i.* die Preise herunter- *od.* herabsetzen; mit den Preisen heruntergehen;

- **price up**

A *v.t.* [im Preis] heraufsetzen; verteuern

B *v.i.* die Preise heraufsetzen; mit den Preisen hochgehen

price: ~ **bracket** ▸**price range**; ~ **control** *n.* Preiskontrolle, *die;* ~ **cut** *n.* Preissenkung, *die;* ~**-cutting** *n., no pl.* Preisschleuderei, *die;* ~ **difference** *n.* Preisunterschied, *der;* ~ **discrimination** *n., no pl.* Preisdiskriminierung, *die;* ~**-fixing** *n., no pl.* Preisabsprache, *die;* ~ **freeze** *n.* Preisstopp, *der*

priceless /ˈpraɪslɪs/ *adj.* **1** (invaluable) unbezahlbar; unschätzbar ‹*Gut*› **2** (coll.: amusing) köstlich

price: ~ **limit** *n.* Preisgrenze, *die;* ~ **list** *n.* Preisliste, *die;* ~ **rally** *n.* (St. Exch.) Kursrallye, *die od. schweiz. das;* ~ **range** *n.* Preisspanne, *die;* **it's within/outside my** ~ **range** das kann ich mir leisten/nicht leisten; ~**-rigging** *n., no pl.* Preismanipulation, *die;* ~ **ring** *n.* (Econ.) Preiskartell, *das;* ~ **rise** *n.* Preisanstieg, *der* (**on** bei); **constant** ~ **rises** ständig steigende Preise; ständige Preiserhöhungen; ~**-sensitive** *adj.* **1** (influenced by price) preisempfindlich; **2** (affecting share prices) kursempfindlich; ~ **tag** *n.* Preisschild, *das;* (fig.) Kosten *Pl.;* ~ **war** *n.* Preiskrieg, *der*

pricey /ˈpraɪsɪ/ *adj.,* **pricier** /ˈpraɪsɪə(r)/, **priciest** /ˈpraɪsɪɪst/ (Brit. coll.) teuer

prick /prɪk/

A *v.t.* **1** (pierce) stechen; stechen in ‹*Ballon*›; aufstechen ‹*Blase*›; **he** ~**ed his finger with the needle** er stach sich (*Dat.*) mit der Nadel in den Finger; ~ **the bubble** (fig.) die Illusion zerstören; ~ **out** auspflanzen ‹*Setzlinge*› **2** (fig.) quälen; plagen; **my conscience** ~**ed me** ich hatte Gewissensbisse **3** (mark) ~ **[off** *or* **out]** vorstechen ‹*Stickmuster, Linie usw.*› **4** (mark off) markieren

B *v.i.* **1** (hurt) stechen **2** (thrust) stechen; ~ **at sb.'s conscience** jmdm. Gewissensbisse verursachen

C *n.* **1** **I felt a little** ~: ich fühlte einen leichten Stich; **give sb.'s finger a** ~ **with the needle** jmdn. mit der Nadel in den Finger stechen; ~**s of conscience** Gewissensbisse *Pl.* **2** (mark) Punkt, *der* **3** (coarse: penis) Pimmel, *der* (fam.); Schwanz, *der* (derb) **4** (coarse derog.: man) Wichser, *der* (derb) **5** (arch.: goad) Stachel, *der;* **kick against the** ~**s** (fig.) wider den Stachel löcken (geh.)

Phrasal verb

• ~ **up**

A *v.t.* aufrichten ‹*Ohren*›; ~ **up one's/its ears** (listen) die Ohren spitzen

B *v.i.* ‹*Ohren:*› sich aufrichten

prickle /ˈprɪkl/

A *n.* **1** (thorn) Dorn, *der* **2** (Zool., Bot.) Stachel, *der*

B *v.t.* stechen; ‹*Wolle:*› kratzen auf (+ *Dat.*), ‹*Hitze, Wind:*› prickeln auf (+ *Dat.*) ‹*Haut*›

C *v.i.* kratzen

prickly /ˈprɪklɪ/ *adj.* **1** (with prickles) ▸**prickle A**: dornig; stachelig; **be** ~ ‹*Pflanze:*› Stacheln/Dornen haben **2** (fig.) empfindlich **3** (tingling) kratzig; **a** ~ **sensation in the limbs** ein Kribbeln *od.* Prickeln in den Gliedern

prickly: ~ **'heat** *n.* (Med.) rote Frieseln; ~ **'pear** *n.* **1** (cactus) Feigenkaktus, *der;* **2** (fruit) Kaktusfeige, *die*

pricy ▸**pricey**

pride /praɪd/

A *n.* **1** Stolz, *der;* (arrogance) Hochmut, *der* (abwertend); ~ **goes before a fall** (prov.) Hochmut kommt vor dem Fall (Spr.); **take** *or* **have** ~ **of place** die Spitzenstellung einnehmen *od.* innehaben; (in collection etc.) das Glanzstück sein; **proper** ~: gesunder Stolz; **a proper** ~ **in oneself** ein gesundes Selbstwertgefühl; **she has a lot of** ~: sie ist sehr stolz; **his own** ~ **prevented him from doing that** sein Ehrgefühl verbot ihm, das zu tun; **false** ~: falscher Stolz; **take [a]** ~ **in sb./sth.** auf jmdn./etw. stolz sein **2** (object, best one) Stolz, *der;* **sb.'s** ~ **and joy** jmds. ganzer Stolz; **give sth.** ~ **of place** einer Sache einen Ehrenplatz einräumen **3** (of lions) Rudel, *das*

B *v. refl.* ~ **oneself [up]on sth.** (congratulate oneself) auf etw. (*Akk.*) stolz sein; (plume oneself) sich mit etw. brüsten (abwertend)

priest /priːst/ *n.* Priester, *der; see also* **high priest**

priestess /ˈpriːstɪs/ *n.* Priesterin, *die*

priesthood /ˈpriːsthʊd/ *n.* (office) geistliches Amt; (order of priests; priests) Geistlichkeit, *die;* **go into the** ~: Priester werden

priestlike /ˈpriːstlaɪk/ *adv.* priesterlich

priestly /ˈpriːstlɪ/ *adj.* priesterlich; Priester‹*kaste, -rolle*›

prig /prɪg/ *n.* (didactic) Besserwisser, *der*/-wisserin, *die* (abwertend); (smug) selbstgefälliger Mensch; (self-righteous) Tugendbold, *der* (ugs., iron.)

priggish /ˈprɪgɪʃ/ *adj.* (didactic) besserwisserisch (abwertend); (smug) selbstgefällig (abwertend); (self-righteous) übertrieben tugendhaft

prim /prɪm/ *adj.* **1** spröde, steif ‹*Person*›; streng ‹*Kleidung*›; ~ **and proper** etepetete (ugs.) **2** (prudish) zimperlich; prüde

prima ballerina /priːmə bæləˈriːnə/ *n.* Primaballerina, *die*

primacy /ˈpraɪməsɪ/ *n.* **1** (pre-eminence) Vorrang, *der;* Primat, *der od. das* (geh.); **position of** ~: Vorrangstellung, *die* **2** (Eccl.: office) Primat, *der od. das*

prima donna /priːmə ˈdɒnə/ *n.* (Theatre; also fig.) Primadonna, *die*

primaeval ▸**primeval**

prima facie /praɪmə ˈfeɪʃiː/

A *adv.* auf den ersten Blick

B *adj.* glaubhaft klingend; ~ **evidence** (Law) Anscheinsbeweis, *der;* **I don't see a** ~ **reason for it** ich sehe keinen einleuchtenden Grund dafür

primal /ˈpraɪml/ *adj.* ursprünglich; primitiv; ~ **forces** Urkräfte *Pl.*

primarily /ˈpraɪmərɪlɪ/ *adv.* in erster Linie

primary /ˈpraɪmərɪ/

A *adj.* **1** (first in sequence) primär (geh.); grundlegend; **the** ~ **meaning of a word** die Grundbedeutung eines Wortes; ~ **source** Primärquelle, *die* (geh.) **2** (chief) Haupt‹*rolle, -sorge, -ziel, -zweck*›; **of** ~ **importance** von höchster Bedeutung

B *n.* (Amer.: election) Vorwahl, *die*

primary: ~ **'battery** *n.* (Electr.) Primärbatterie, *die;* ~ **care** *n., no pl.* Erstversorgung, *die;* ~ **'cell** *n.* (Electr.) Primärelement, *das;* ~ **'coil** *n.* (Electr.) Primärspule, *die;* ~ **'colour** ▸**colour A 1**; ~ **edu'cation** *n., no pl.* Grundschulerziehung, *die;* ~ **e'lection** *n.* (Amer.) Vorwahl, *die;* ~ **'feather** *n.* (Ornith.) Schwungfeder, *die;* ~ **'planet** *n.* (Astron.) Hauptplanet, *der;* ~ **school** *n.* Grundschule, *die; attrib.* ~**-school teacher** ▸ⓘ **p. 1260** Grundschullehrer, *der*/-lehrerin, *die;* ~ **stress** *n.* (Ling.) Hauptakzent, *der*

> **primary school**
>
> Eine Grundschule in Großbritannien, an der Kinder von fünf bis elf unterrichtet werden.

primate /ˈpraɪmeɪt/ *n.* **1** (Eccl.) Primas, *der;* **P**~ **of England** Primas von England; *Titel des Erzbischofs von York;* **P**~ **of all England** Primas von ganz England; *Titel des Erzbischofs von Canterbury* **2** (Zool.) Primat, *der*

prime[1] /praɪm/

A *n.* **1** (perfection) Höhepunkt, *der;* Krönung, *die;* **in the** ~ **of life/youth/manhood** in der Blüte seiner/ihrer Jahre/der Jugend (geh.)/im besten Mannesalter; **be in/past one's** ~: in den besten Jahren sein/die besten Jahre überschritten haben **2** (best part) Beste, *das* **3** (Math.) Primzahl, *die*

B *adj.* **1** (chief) Haupt-; hauptsächlich; ~ **motive** Hauptmotiv, *das;* **be of** ~ **importance** von höchster Wichtigkeit sein **2** (excellent) erstklassig; vortrefflich ‹*Beispiel*›; ~ **ham/lamb/pork** Schinken/Lamm/Schweinefleisch erster Güteklasse; **in** ~ **condition** ‹*Sportler, Tier*› in bester Verfassung; voll ausgereift ‹*Obst*›

prime[2] *v.t.* **1** (equip) vorbereiten; ~ **sb. with sth.** jmdn. mit etw. vertraut machen; ~ **sb. with information/advice** jmdn. instruieren/jmdm. Ratschläge erteilen; **well** ~**d** gut vorbereitet **2** (ply with liquor) betrunken machen; abfüllen (ugs.); **be well** ~**d** voll sein (salopp) **3** grundieren ‹*Wand, Decke*› **4** füllen ‹*Pumpe*› **5** (inject petrol into) Anlasskraftstoff einspritzen in (+ *Akk.*) ‹*Motor, Zylinder*› **6** schärfen ‹*Sprengkörper*›

prime: ~ **'cost** *n.* (Econ.) Selbstkosten *Pl.;* ~ **me'ridian** *n.* (Geog.) Nullmeridian, *der;* ~ **'minister** *n.* ▸ⓘ **p. 1260**, ▸ⓘ **p. 1634** Premierminister, *der*/-ministerin, *die;* ~ **'number** *n.* (Math.) Primzahl, *die*

> **Prime Minister**
>
> Der Premierminister ist der Regierungschef in Großbritannien. Als Vorsitzender der Partei mit den meisten Abgeordneten (**Members of Parliament** im **House of Commons**) wird er automatisch Premierminister. Der Premierminister beruft die Minister.

primer[1] /ˈpraɪmə(r)/ *n.* (book) Fibel, *die*

primer[2] *n.* **1** (explosive) Zündvorrichtung, *die* **2** (paint etc.) Grundierlack, *der*

prime: ~ **rate** *n.* (Econ.) Prime rate, *die;* ~ **'ribs** *n. pl.* Hochrippen *Pl.;* ~ **time** *n.* Hauptsendezeit, *die;* ~**-time TV** Hauptsendezeit im Fernsehen

primeval /praɪˈmiːvl/ *adj.* urzeitlich; ~ **times/forests** Urzeiten/Urwälder

priming /ˈpraɪmɪŋ/ *n.* (paint) Grundanstrich, *der;* Grundierung, *die*

primitive /ˈprɪmɪtɪv/

A *adj.* **1** primitiv; (original) ursprünglich; (prehistoric) urzeitlich ‹*Mensch*›; frühzeitlich ‹*Ackerbau, Technik*› **2** (Ling.) ~ **word** Stammwort, *das;* Primitivum, *das* (fachspr.)

B *n.* (painter) *Maler der Zeit vor der Renaissance;* (in modern art) Primitive, *der/die*

primitively /ˈprɪmɪtɪvlɪ/ *adv.* primitiv

primly /ˈprɪmlɪ/ *adv.* steif; streng ‹*sich kleiden*›

primness /ˈprɪmnɪs/ *n., no pl.* Steifheit, *die;* (of dress) Strenge, *die*

primogeniture /praɪməˈdʒenɪtʃə(r)/ *n.* (Law) **[right of]** ~: Primogenitur, *die;* **rights of** ~: Erstgeburtsrechte *Pl.*

primordial /praɪˈmɔːdɪəl/ *adj.* ursprünglich; Ur‹*masse, -zustand, -zeiten*›; primordial (bes. Philos.); ~ **soup** Urschleim, *der*

primp /prɪmp/ *v.t.* zurechtstreichen, zurechtzupfen ‹*Haar, Kleid*›; ~ **oneself** sich zurecht- *od.* schönmachen (ugs.)

primrose /ˈprɪmrəʊz/ *n.* **1** (plant, flower) gelbe Schlüsselblume; Himmelsschlüsselchen, *das;* **the** ~ **path** (fig.) der Pfad des Vergnügens; (path of least resistance) der Weg des geringsten Widerstandes; *see also* **evening primrose** **2** (colour) schlüsselblumengelb

primula /ˈprɪmjʊlə/ *n.* (Bot.) Primel, *die*

Primus ® /ˈpraɪməs/ *n.* ~ **[stove]** Primuskocher, *der*

prince /prɪns/ *n.* ▸ⓘ **p. 1634** **1** (ruler) Fürst, *der* **2** (member of royal family) ~ **[of the blood]** Prinz [von Geblüt]; **P**~ **of Wales** Prinz von Wales **3** (rhet.: sovereign ruler) Fürst, *der;* **the P**~ **of Peace** der Friedensfürst; **the P**~ **of Darkness** der Fürst der Finsternis *od.* der Hölle **4** (fig.: greatest one) König, *der* (**of** unter + *Dat.*); **a** ~ **among men** ein Fürst unter den Sterblichen (geh.)

Prince: ~ **Albert** /prɪns ˈælbət/ *n.* (Amer. coll.) Gehrock, *der;* Bratenrock, *der* (veralt., scherzh.); ~ **'Charming** *n.* (fig.) Märchenprinz, *der;* **p**~ **'consort** *n.* Prinzgemahl, *der*

princely /ˈprɪnslɪ/ *adj.* (lit. or fig.) fürstlich; ~ **houses** Fürstenhäuser

Prince 'Regent *n.* Prinzregent, *der*

princess /ˈprɪnses, prɪnˈses/ *n.* ▸ⓘ **p. 1634** **1** Prinzessin, *die;* ~ **[of the blood]** Prinzessin [von Geblüt] **2** (wife of prince) Fürstin, *die*

princess: ~ **dress** *n.* Prinzesskleid, *das;* ~ **line** *n.* Prinzessform, *die;* ~ **'royal** *n.* [*Titel für*] *älteste Tochter eines Monarchen*

principal /ˈprɪnsɪpl/

A *adj.* **1** Haupt-; (most important) wichtigst...; bedeutendst...; **the** ~ **cause of lung cancer** die häufigste Ursache für Lungenkrebs **2** (Mus.) ~ **horn/bassoon** *etc.* erstes Horn/Fagott *usw*

B *n.* **1** ▸ⓘ **p. 1634** (head of school or college) Rektor, *der*/Rektorin, *die* **2** (performer) Haupt-

P

darsteller, *der/-darstellerin, die* (Theater, Film) 3 (leader) Vorsitzende, *der/die* 4 (employer of agent) Auftraggeber, *der/-geberin, die* 5 (in duel) Duellant, *der* 6 (Finance) (invested) Kapitalbetrag, *der;* (lent) Kreditsumme, *die* 7 (Law) (for whom another is surety) Hauptschuldner, *der/-schuldnerin, die;* (directly responsible for crime) Hauptschuldige, *der/die*

principal: ~ 'boy *n.* (Brit. Theatre) [*gewöhnlich von einer Frau gespielte*] *männliche Hauptrolle im britischen Weihnachtsmärchen;* **~ clause** *n.* (Ling.) Hauptsatz, *der;* **~ 'girl** *n.* (Brit. Theatre) *weibliche Hauptrolle im britischen Weihnachtsmärchen*

principality /prɪnsɪ'pælɪtɪ/ *n.* Fürstentum, *das;* **the P~** (Brit.) Wales

principally /'prɪnsɪpəlɪ/ *adv.* in erster Linie

principal 'parts *n. pl.* (Ling.) Stammformen

principle /'prɪnsɪpl/ *n.* 1 Prinzip, *das;* **on the ~ that ...:** nach dem Grundsatz, dass ...; **be based on the ~ that ...:** auf dem Grundsatz basieren, dass ...; **basic ~:** Grundprinzip, *das;* **go back to first ~s** zu den Grundlagen zurückgehen; **in ~:** im Prinzip; **it's the ~ [of the thing]** es geht [dabei] ums Prinzip; **make it a ~ to do sth.** es sich (*Dat.*) zum Prinzip machen, etw. zu tun; **a man of high ~** *or* **strong ~s** ein Mann von *od.* mit hohen Prinzipien; **a matter of ~:** eine Prinzipfrage; **do sth. on ~** *or* **as a matter of ~:** etw. prinzipiell *od.* aus Prinzip tun; **operate by** *or* **work on the same ~:** nach demselben Prinzip funktionieren; **work on the ~ of 'first come, first served'** nach dem Prinzip „wer zuerst kommt, mahlt zuerst" vorgehen 2 (Phys.) Lehrsatz, *der* 3 (Chem.) Komponente, *die*

principled /'prɪnsɪpld/ *adj.* von Prinzipien geleitet

prink /prɪŋk/ *v.t.* zurechtmachen (ugs.) ‹*Person, Haar*›; schmücken ‹*Kleid, Haus*›; **~ oneself [up]** sich herausputzen; sich zurechtmachen (ugs.)

print /prɪnt/

A *n.* 1 (impression) Abdruck, *der;* (finger~) Fingerabdruck, *der;* (foot~) Fußabdruck, *der* 2 (~ed lettering) Gedruckte, *das;* (typeface) Druck, *der;* **clear/large ~:** deutlicher/großer Druck; **this ~ is too small** das ist zu klein gedruckt; **editions in large ~:** Großdruckbücher; *see also* **small print** 3 (handwriting) **write [sth.] in ~:** [etw.] in Druckschrift schreiben 4 (published or ~ed state) **be in/out of ~** ‹*Buch:*› erhältlich/vergriffen sein; **appear in/get into ~:** gedruckt werden; *see also* **rush into** 5 (~ed picture or design) Druck, *der* 6 (Photog.) Abzug, *der;* (Cinemat.) Kopie, *die;* **black and white/colour ~:** Schwarzweiß-/Farbabdruck, *der/-kopie, die* 7 (Textiles) (cloth with design) bedruckter Stoff; (design) Druckmuster, *das* 8 (~ed publication) Publikation, *die;* **~s** (Amer. Post) Druckschriften; **the ~s** (Amer. Journ.) die Presse

B *v.t.* 1 drucken ‹*Buch, Zeitschrift, Geldschein usw.*› 2 (write) in Druckschrift schreiben 3 (cause to be published) veröffentlichen ‹*Artikel, Roman, Ansichten usw.*› 4 (Photog.) abziehen; (Cinemat.) kopieren 5 (Textiles) bedrucken ‹*Stoff*› 6 (impress) eindrücken; **~ sth. with sth.** etw. mit etw. bedrucken; **~ sth. on** etw. drücken in (+ *Akk.*) ‹*Haut*›; etw. aufdrucken auf (+ *Akk.*) ‹*Papier, Holz*›

C *v.i.* 1 (Printing) drucken 2 (write) in Druckschrift schreiben

Phrasal verbs

- **~ off** *v.t.* [ab]drucken; abziehen; (on a computer) ausdrucken
- **~ 'out** *v.t.* (Computing) ausdrucken; *see also* **printout**

printable /'prɪntəbl/ *adj.* druckbar; **be ~** (Photog.) einen guten Abzug ermöglichen; **what he replied is not ~** (fig.) was er geantwortet hat, kann man [hier] nicht wiederholen

printed /'prɪntɪd/ *adj.* 1 (Printing) gedruckt; **~ characters** *or* **letters** Druckbuchstaben; **on the ~ page** gedruckt 2 (written like print) in Druckschrift 3 (published) veröffentlicht ‹*Artikel, Roman, Ansichten usw.*› 4 (Textiles) bedruckt ‹*Stoff*›; **~ design** Druckmuster, *das*

printed: ~ 'circuit *n.* (Electronics) gedruckte Schaltung; **~ matter** *n., no pl., no indef. art.* Gedruckte, *das;* (Post) Drucksachen *Pl.;* **[item of] ~ matter** Drucksache, *die;* **~ 'papers** (Brit. Post) ▸ **~ matter**

printer /'prɪntə(r)/ *n.* 1 (Printing) (worker) Drucker, *der/Druckerin, die;* **firm of ~s** Druckerei, *die;* **send sth. off to the ~'s** etw. in die Druckerei schicken; **at the ~'s** in der Druckerei 2 (Computing) Drucker, *der*

printer: ~'s 'devil *n.* (Hist.) Setzerjunge, *der;* **~'s 'error** *n.* Druckfehler, *der;* **~'s 'ink** *n.* Druckfarbe, *die*

printing /'prɪntɪŋ/ *n.* 1 Drucken, *das;* **[the] ~ [trade]** das Druckgewerbe 2 (writing like print) Druckschrift, *die* 3 (edition) Auflage, *die* 4 (Photog.) Abziehen, *das* 5 (Textiles) Bedrucken, *das*

printing: ~ error *n.* Druckfehler, *der;* **~ house** *n.* Druckerei, *die;* **~ ink** *n.* Druckfarbe, *die;* **~ machine** *n.* (Brit.) Druckmaschine, *die;* **~ press** *n.* Druckerpresse, *die*

print: ~maker *n.* ▸❶ **p. 1260** (Graph. Arts) Grafiker, *der/Grafikerin, die;* **~out** *n.* (Computing) Ausdruck, *der;* **~ 'preview** *n.* (Computing) Druckvorschau, *die;* **~ queue** *n.* (Computing) Druckerwarteschlange, *die;* **~ run** *n.* (Publishing) Auflage, die; **what is the ~ run?** wie hoch ist die Auflage?; **~ seller** *n.* ▸❶ **p. 1260** Grafikhändler, *der/-händlerin, die;* **~shop** *n.* 1 (shop) Grafikhandlung, *die;* 2 (~ing establishment) [kleinere] Druckerei

'prion /'pri:ɒn/ *n.* (Biol.) Prion, *das*

prior /'praɪə(r)/

A *adj.* vorherig ‹*Warnung, Zustimmung, Vereinbarung usw.*›; früher ‹*Verabredung, Ehe*›; vorrangig ‹*Bedeutung, Interesse*›; Vor‹*geschichte, -kenntnis, -warnung*›; **give a matter ~ consideration** eine Angelegenheit vorher überdenken *od.* überprüfen; **have a** *or* **the ~ claim to sth.** ältere Rechte an etw. (*Dat.*) *od.* auf etw. (*Akk.*) haben

B *adv.* **~ to** vor (+ *Dat.*); **~ to doing sth.** bevor man etw. tut/tat; **~ to that** vorher

C *n.* (Eccl.) Prior, *der*

prioritisation, prioritise ▸ **prioritiz-**

prioritization /praɪɒrɪtaɪ'zeɪʃn/ *n., no pl.* Priorisierung, *die*

prioritize /praɪ'ɒrɪtaɪz/ *v.t.* nach Vordringlichkeit ordnen

priority /praɪ'ɒrɪtɪ/ *n.* 1 (precedence) Vorrang, *der; attrib.* vorrangig; **have** *or* **take ~:** Vorrang haben (**over** vor + *Dat.*); (on road) Vorfahrt haben; **give ~ to sb./sth.** jmdm./einer Sache den Vorrang geben; **give top ~ to sth.** einer Sache (*Dat.*) höchste Priorität einräumen; **what is the order of ~ for those jobs?** in welcher Reihenfolge sollen die Arbeiten erledigt werden?; **be listed in order of ~:** der Vorrangigkeit nach aufgeführt sein; **according to ~:** der Vorrangigkeit nach 2 (matter) vordringliche Angelegenheit; **our first ~ is to ...:** zuallererst müssen wir ...; **be high/low on the list of priorities** oben/unten auf der Prioritätenliste stehen; **get one's priorities right/wrong** seine Prioritäten richtig/falsch setzen; **it depends on one's** *or* **your priorities** es kommt darauf an, was einem wichtig ist

priory /'praɪərɪ/ *n.* (Eccl.) Priorat, *das*

prise *v.t.* (force) **~ [open]** aufstemmen; **~ up** abheben ‹*Diele*›; **~ the lid off a crate** eine Kiste aufstemmen; **~ sth. out of sth.** etw. aus etw. herausbekommen; **~ information/a secret out of sb.** Informationen/ein Geheimnis aus jmdm. herauspressen

Phrasal verbs

- **~ a'part** *v.t.* auseinander stemmen
- **~ 'out** *v.t.* herausbrechen

prism /'prɪzm/ *n.* (Optics, Geom.) Prisma, *das*

prismatic /prɪz'mætɪk/ *adj.* 1 (in shape) prismenförmig 2 **~ colours** Spektralfarben

prismatic: ~ bi'noculars *n. pl.* Prismenglas, *das;* **~ 'compass** *n.* (Surv.) Patentbussole, *die*

prison /'prɪzn/ *n.* 1 (lit. or fig.) Gefängnis, *das; attrib.* Gefängnis-; **~ without bars** offene [Vollzugs]anstalt; **stone walls do not a ~ make [nor iron bars a cage]** (prov.) ≈ die Gedanken sind frei 2 *no pl., no art.* (custody) Haft, *die;* **10 years' ~:** eine zehnjährige Gefängnisstrafe; **in ~:** im Gefängnis; **go to ~:** ins Gefängnis gehen *od.* (ugs.) wandern; **send sb. to ~:** jmdn. ins Gefängnis schicken; **escape/be released from ~:** aus dem Gefängnis ausbrechen/entlassen werden; **put sb. in ~:** jmdn. verhaften *od.* (ugs.) einsperren; **let sb. out of ~:** jmdn. aus der Haft entlassen

'prison camp *n.* Gefangenenlager, *das*

prisoner /'prɪznə(r)/ *n.* (lit. or fig.) Gefangene, *der/die;* **~ [at the bar]** (accused person) Angeklagte, *der/die;* **~ of conscience** *aus politischen od. religiösen Gründen Inhaftierter/Inhaftierte;* **a ~ of circumstance** (fig.) ein Opfer der Umstände; **hold** *or* **keep sb. ~** (lit. or fig.) jmdn. gefangen halten; **take sb. ~:** jmdn. gefangen nehmen

prisoner of 'war *n.* Kriegsgefangene, *der/die;* **prisoner-of-war camp** [Kriegs]gefangenenlager, *das*

prison: ~ 'guard *n.* ▸❶ **p. 1260** Gefängniswärter, *der/-wärterin, die;* **~ life** *n., no art.* Gefängnisleben, *das;* **~ 'riot** *n.* Gefängnisrevolte, *die;* **~ sentence** *n.* Gefängnisstrafe, *die;* **~ service** *n.* Strafvollzugsbehörde, *die;* **~ term** *n.* Gefängnisstrafe, *die;* Freiheitsstrafe, *die;* **~ van** *n.* Gefangenentransporter, *der;* **~ 'visitor** *n.* ≈ Gefangenenfürsorger, *der/-fürsorgerin, die*

prissy /'prɪsɪ/ *adj.* (coll.) zickig (ugs.); piepsig (ugs.) ‹*Stimme*›

pristine /'prɪsti:n, 'prɪstaɪn/ *adj.* unberührt; ursprünglich ‹*Glanz, Weiße, Schönheit*›; **in ~ condition** in tadellosem Zustand

privacy /'prɪvəsɪ, 'praɪvəsɪ/ *n.* 1 Privatsphäre, *die;* (being undisturbed) Ungestörtheit, *die;* **guard one's ~:** seine Privatsphäre abschirmen; **in the ~ of one's [own] home/living room** in den eigenen vier Wänden (ugs.); **invasion of ~/sb.'s ~:** Eindringen in die/jmds. Privatsphäre; **I have** *or* **get no ~ in this house** ich habe keine Ruhe in diesem Haus; **allow sb. no ~:** jmdm. kein Privatleben erlauben 2 (confidentiality) **in the strictest ~:** unter strengster Geheimhaltung

'privacy policy *n.* Datenschutzpolitik, *die*

private /'praɪvət/

A *adj.* 1 (outside State system) privat; Privat‹*unterricht, -schule, -industrie, -klinik, -patient, -station usw.*›; **a doctor working in ~ medicine** ein Arzt, der Privatpatienten hat; **have a ~ education** auf eine Privatschule gehen 2 (belonging to individual, not public, not business) persönlich ‹*Dinge*›; nicht öffentlich ‹*Versammlung, Sitzung*›; privat ‹*Telefongespräch, Schriftverkehr*›; Privat‹*flugzeug, -strand, -parkplatz, -leben, -konto*›; '~' (on door) „Privat"; (in public building) „kein Zutritt"; (on ~ land) „Betreten verboten"; **for [one's own] ~ use** für den persönlichen Gebrauch; **do some ~ studying in the holidays** in den Ferien allein lernen; **the funeral was ~:** die Beisetzung hat in aller Stille stattgefunden; **they were married in a ~ ceremony** ihre Hochzeit wurde im engen Familien- und Freundeskreis gefeiert; **in a ~ capacity** als Privatperson 3 (personal, affecting individual) persönlich ‹*Meinung, Interesse, Überzeugung, Rache*›; privat ‹*Vereinbarung, Zweck*›; **~ joke** Witz, den nur Eingeweihte verstehen; **~ war** Privatkrieg, *der* 4 (not for public disclosure) geheim ‹*Verhandlung, Geschäft, Tränen*›; still ‹*Gebet, Nachdenken, Grübeln*›; persönlich ‹*Gründe*›; (confidential) vertraulich; **have a ~ word with sb.** jmdn. unter vier Augen sprechen 5 (secluded) still ‹*Ort*›; (undisturbed) ungestört; **we can be ~ here** hier sind wir ungestört 6 (not in public office) nicht beamtet (Amtsspr.); **~ citizen** *or* **individual** Privatperson, *die*

B *n.* 1 (Brit. Mil.) einfacher Soldat; (Amer. Mil.) Gefreite, *der;* **~ first 'class** (Amer.) Obergefreite, *der;* **P~ X** Soldat/Gefreiter X 2 **in ~:** privat; in kleinem Kreis ‹*feiern*›; (confidentially) ganz im Vertrauen; **speak to sb. in ~:** jmdn. unter vier Augen sprechen; **make a deal in ~:** ein privates Geschäft abschließen; **you should**

P

do it in ~: du solltest das nicht in der Öffentlichkeit tun 3 *in pl.* (coll.: genitals) Geschlechtsteile *Pl.*

private: ~ 'army *n.* Privatarmee, *die;* **~ 'bed** *n.* Bett für Privatpatienten; **~ 'car** *n.* Privatwagen, *der;* **~ 'company** *n.* (Brit. Commerc.) Privatgesellschaft, *die;* **~ de'tective** *n.* ▸ **p. 1260** [Privat]detektiv, *der*/-detektivin, *die;* **~ 'enterprise** *n.* (Commerc.) das freie *od.* private Unternehmertum; **[spirit of] ~ enterprise** (fig.) Unternehmungsgeist, *der*

privateer /praɪvə'tɪə(r)/ *n.* 1 Kaperschiff, *das* 2 (person) Kaper, *der*

private: ~ 'eye *n.* (coll.) [Privat]detektiv, *der*/-detektivin, *die;* **P~ 'Finance Initiative** *n.* (Brit.) Privatfinanzierungsinitiative, *die;* **~ 'health care** *n., no pl.* private Gesundheitsfürsorge; **~ 'health insurance** *n., no pl.* private Krankenversicherung; **~ ho'tel** *n.* Pension, *die;* **~ 'income** *n.* private Einkünfte; **~ investigator** *n.* Privatdetektiv, *der*/-detektivin, *die;* **~ key** *n.* (Computing) privater *od.* geheimer Schlüssel

privately /'praɪvətlɪ/ *adv.* privat ‹*erziehen, zugeben, korrespondieren*›; vertraulich ‹*jmdn. sprechen*›; insgeheim ‹*denken, glauben, verhandeln*›; **study ~:** private Studien betreiben; **~ owned** in Privatbesitz; **~ held opinion** persönliche Meinung

private: ~ 'means *n. pl.* ▸ **private income; ~ 'member** *n.* (Brit. Parl.) *nicht der Regierung angehörende Abgeordneter/angehörende Abgeordnete;* **~ 'member's bill** *n.* (Brit. Parl.) *Gesetzesvorlage eines/einer nicht der Regierung angehörenden Abgeordneten;* **~ 'parts** *n. pl.* Geschlechtsteile *Pl.;* **~ 'pension plan** *n.* private Altersvorsorge; **~ 'pension scheme** *n.* private Altersvorsorge; **~ 'practice** *n.* 1 (Med.) Privatpraxis, *die;* (patients) Stamm von Privatpatienten; **he is now in ~ practice** er hat jetzt eine Privatpraxis; 2 (of architect/lawyer) eigenes Büro/eigene Kanzlei; **be in ~ practice** ein eigenes Büro/eine eigene Kanzlei haben; **~ 'press** *n.* Privatdruckerei, *die;* **~ 'property** *n.* Privateigentum, *das;* **~ 'secretary** *n.* Privatsekretär, *der*/-sekretärin, *die;* **~ sector** *n.* **the ~ sector [of industry]** die Privatwirtschaft; **~ 'soldier** *n.* 1 (Brit. Mil.) einfacher Soldat; 2 (Amer. Mil.) Gefreite, *der;* **~ 'treaty** *n.* privater Vertrag; **sold by ~ treaty** auf privater Basis verkauft; **~ 'view[ing]** *n.* (Art) Vernissage, *die;* (Cinemat.) *Aufführung eines Films für geladene Zuschauer vor der öffentlichen Erstaufführung*

privation /praɪ'veɪʃn/ *n.* (lack of comforts) Not, *die;* **suffer many ~s** viele Entbehrungen erleiden

privatisation, privatise ▸ **privatiz-**

privatization /praɪvətaɪ'zeɪʃn/ *n.* Privatisierung, *die*

privatize /'praɪvətaɪz/ *v.t.* privatisieren

privet /'prɪvɪt/ *n.* (Bot.) Liguster, *der*

privilege /'prɪvɪlɪdʒ/

A *n.* 1 (right, immunity) Privileg, *das; collect.* Privilegien *Pl.;* **tax ~s** Steuervorteile *Pl.;* **that's a lady's ~:** das ist das Vorrecht einer Dame; **Parliamentary ~:** Immunität des Abgeordneten 2 (special benefit) Sonderrecht, *das;* (honour) Ehre, *die;* **it was a ~ to listen to him** es war ein besonderes Vergnügen, ihm zuzuhören; **we were expected to pay for the ~** (iron.) wir hatten auch noch die Ehre, dafür bezahlen zu dürfen 3 (monopoly) Vorrecht, *das;* (sole right of selling sth.) Alleinverkaufsrecht, *das* 4 (Amer. St. Exch.) Termingeschäft, *das;* **buy ~s** Optionsrechte erwerben

B *v.t.* **~ sb. to do sth.** jmdm. das Recht einräumen, etw. zu tun

privileged /'prɪvɪlɪdʒd/ *adj.* privilegiert; **the ~ classes** die privilegierten Schichten; **a/the ~ few** einige wenige Privilegierte/die kleine Gruppe von Privilegierten; **sb. is ~ to do sth.** jmd. hat die Ehre, etw. zu tun; **I am [greatly] ~ to introduce sb./sth.** es ist mir eine [große] Ehre, Ihnen jmdn./etw. vorstellen zu können; **have a** *or* **be in a ~ position** eine bevorzugte Position innehaben

privy /'prɪvɪ/

A *adj.* **be ~ to sth.** in etw. (*Akk.*) eingeweiht sein

B *n.* (arch./Amer.) Abtritt, *der* (veralt.); Häuschen, *das* (ugs.)

privy: P~ 'Council *n.* (Brit.) Geheimer [Staats]rat; **~ 'counsellor** (**~ 'councillor**) *n.* (Brit.: member of Privy Council) Geheimer Rat; **~ 'seal** *n.* (Brit.) Geheimsiegel, *das;* Kleines Siegel; **Lord P~ Seal** Lordsiegelbewahrer, *der*

prize[1] /praɪz/

A *n.* 1 (reward, money) Preis, *der;* **win** *or* **take first/second/third ~:** den ersten/zweiten/dritten Preis gewinnen; **for sheer impudence he takes the ~!** (fig.) für seine Frechheit müsste er einen Preis bekommen (iron.); **there are no ~s for doing sth.** (iron.) es ist kinderleicht, etw. zu tun; **cash** *or* **money ~:** Geldpreis, *der* 2 (in lottery) Gewinn, *der;* (got by buying goods) Werbegeschenk, *das;* **win sth. as a ~:** etw. gewinnen; **I won a ~ of £1,000** ich habe 1000 Pfund gewonnen 3 (fig.: something worth striving for) Lohn, *der;* **glittering ~s** verlockender Lohn

B *v.t.* (value) **~ sth. [highly]** etw. hoch schätzen; **gold is one of the most ~d [of] metals** Gold ist eines der begehrtesten Metalle; **we ~ liberty more than life** wir lieben die Freiheit mehr als das Leben; **sb.'s most ~d possessions** jmds. wertvollster Besitz

C *attrib. adj.* 1 (~winning) preisgekrönt 2 (awarded as ~) **~ medal/trophy** Siegesmedaille, *die*/Siegestrophäe, *die* 3 (iron.) **~ idiot** Vollidiot, *der*/-idiotin, *die* (ugs.); **~ muddle** Durcheinander erster Güte; **~ example** Musterbeispiel, *das* (iron.)

prize[2] (Amer.) ▸ **prise**

prize[3] *n.* 1 (captured ship) Prise, *die* 2 (chance find) [zufälliger] Fund; **this is a rare ~!** das ist ein seltener Fund!

prize: ~ day *n.* (Sch.) Tag der Preisverleihung; **~-day speech** Rede zur Preisverleihung; **~fight** *n.* (Boxing) Preisboxkampf, *der;* **enter a ~fight** an einem Preisboxen teilnehmen; **~fighter** *n.* (Boxing) Preisboxer, *der;* **~fighting** *n.* (Boxing) Preisboxen, *das;* **~-giving** *n.* (Sch.) Preisverleihung, *die;* **~ money** *n.* Geldpreis, *der;* (Sport) Preisgeld, *das;* **offer £5,000 in ~ money** Geldpreise in Höhe von insgesamt 5 000 Pfund anbieten; **~winner** *n.* Preisträger, *der*/-trägerin, *die;* (in lottery) Gewinner, *der*/Gewinnerin, *die;* **~winning** *adj.* preisgekrönt; (in lottery) Gewinner-

pro[1] /prəʊ/

A *n. in pl.* **the ~s and cons** das Pro und Kontra; **there are more ~s than cons** die Sache hat mehr Vorteile als Nachteile

B *adv.* **~ and con** pro und kontra

C *prep.* für; **~ and con** für und gegen

pro[2]

A *n.* (coll.) 1 (Sport, Theatre) Profi, *der* 2 (prostitute) Nutte, *die* (derb)

B *adj.* Profi-

pro-[3] *pref.* pro-; **~Communist** prokommunistisch; **be ~hanging** für die Todesstrafe [durch den Strang] sein

PRO *abbr.* 1 **= public relations officer** PR-Manager, *der*/-Managerin, *die* 2 **= public relations office** PR-Abteilung, *die*

'pro-abortion *adj.* Pro-Abtreibungs-; **be ~:** für [die] Abtreibung sein *od.* eintreten

pro-a'bortionist *n.* Abtreibungsbefürworter, *der*/-befürworterin, *die*

proactive /prəʊ'æktɪv/ *adj.* aktiv ‹*Haltung, Rolle*›; **be ~** ‹*Person:*› [selbst] die Initiative ergreifen; Eigeninitiative zeigen

pro-am /prəʊ'æm/ *adj.* (Sport) **~ competition** Wettbewerb für Profis und Amateure

probability /prɒbə'bɪlɪtɪ/ *n.* 1 (likelihood; also Math.) Wahrscheinlichkeit, *die;* **exceed the bounds of ~:** die Grenzen des Wahrscheinlichen übersteigen; **against all ~:** entgegen aller Wahrscheinlichkeit; **in all ~:** aller Wahrscheinlichkeit nach; **there is little/a strong ~ that ...:** die Wahrscheinlichkeit, dass ..., ist gering/groß; **there's every ~ of a victory** höchstwahrscheinlich wird es zu einem Sieg kommen 2 (likely event) **the ~ is that ...:** es ist zu erwarten, dass ...; **war is becoming a ~:** der Ausbruch eines Krieges wird immer wahrscheinlicher; **it is more than a possibility, it is a ~:** es ist nicht nur möglich, es ist wahrscheinlich

probable /'prɒbəbl/

A *adj.* wahrscheinlich; **highly ~:** höchstwahrscheinlich; **his explanation did not sound very ~:** seine Erklärung klang nicht sehr glaubhaft; **another wet summer looks ~:** es sieht ganz nach einem weiteren verregneten Sommer aus; **he seems the most ~ winner** er scheint die besten Aussichten auf einen Sieg zu haben

B *n.* (participant) wahrscheinlicher Teilnehmer/wahrscheinliche Teilnehmerin (**for** an + *Dat.*); (candidate) wahrscheinlicher Kandidat/wahrscheinliche Kandidatin (**for** für)

probably /'prɒbəblɪ/ *adv.* wahrscheinlich

probate /'prəʊbeɪt/ *n.* (Law) 1 gerichtliche Testamentsbestätigung 2 (copy) beglaubigte Testamentsabschrift

probation /prə'beɪʃn/ *n.* 1 Probezeit, *die;* **a year's ~:** eine einjährige Probezeit; **[be put] on ~:** auf Probe [eingestellt werden]; **be on ~:** Probezeit haben; **while on ~:** während der Probezeit 2 (Law) Bewährung, *die;* **give sb. [two years'] ~, put sb. on ~ [for two years]** jmdm. [zwei Jahre] Bewährung geben; **be on ~:** auf Bewährung sein

probationary /prə'beɪʃənərɪ/ *adj.* Probe-; **~ period** Probezeit, *die;* **~ appointment** Einstellung auf Probe

probationer /prə'beɪʃənə(r)/ *n.* 1 (employee) Angestellter/Angestellte auf Probe; (nurse) Lernschwester, *die*/-pfleger, *der;* (candidate) Probekandidat, *der*/-kandidatin, *die* 2 (Law: offender) auf Bewährung Freigelassener/Freigelassene

pro'bation officer *n.* ▸ **p. 1260** Bewährungshelfer, *der*/-helferin, *die*

probe /prəʊb/

A *n.* 1 (investigation) Untersuchung, *die* (**into** *Gen.*); **a ~ is being conducted** Nachforschungen werden angestellt 2 (Med., Electronics, Astron.) Sonde, *die* 3 (pointed instrument) Tastgerät, *das*

B *v.t.* 1 (investigate) erforschen; untersuchen 2 (with pointed instrument) stechen in (+ *Akk.*); sondieren (Med.) 3 (reach deeply into) gründlich untersuchen ‹*Tasche usw.*›; gründlich erforschen ‹*Kontinent, Weltall*›

C *v.i.* 1 (make investigation) forschen; **he kept probing** er bohrte weiter (ugs.); **~ into a matter** einer Angelegenheit (*Dat.*) auf den Grund gehen 2 (with pointed instrument) herumstochern; (Med.) sondieren 3 (reach deeply) vordringen (**into** in + *Akk.*)

probing /'prəʊbɪŋ/ *adj.* (penetrating) gründlich; durchdringend ‹*Blick*›; **~ question** Testfrage, *die*

probity /'prəʊbɪtɪ/ *n., no pl.* Rechtschaffenheit, *die*

problem /'prɒbləm/ *n.* 1 (difficult matter) Problem, *das; attrib.* Problem‹*gebiet, -fall, -familie, -stück*›; **~ child** Problemkind, *das;* (fig.: cause of difficulties) Sorgenkind, *das;* **I find it a ~ to start** *or* **have a ~ [in] starting the car** ich habe Probleme, das Auto anzulassen; **[I see] no ~** (coll.) kein Problem; **what's the ~?** (coll.) wo fehlts denn?; **the ~ about** *or* **with sb./sth.** das Problem mit jmdm./bei etw.; **the ~ of how to do sth.** das Problem *od.* die Frage, wie man etw. tun soll; **the Northern Ireland ~:** die Nordirlandfrage; **he has a drink ~:** er hat ein Alkoholproblem; **that presents a ~:** das ist ein Problem; **the least of her ~s** ihre geringste Sorge; **you think 'you've got ~s!** (coll. iron.) deine Sorgen möchte ich haben! (ugs. iron.) 2 (puzzle) Rätsel, *das* 3 (Chess, Bridge, Math., Phys., Geom.) Problem, *das*

problematic /prɒblə'mætɪk/, **problematical** /prɒblə'mætɪkl/ *adj.* problematisch; (doubtful) fragwürdig

problematically /prɒblə'mætɪkəlɪ/ *adv.* auf problematische Weise

problem: ~ 'drinker *n.* Gewohnheitstrinker, *der*/-trinkerin, *die;* **be a ~ drinker** ein

P

Alkoholproblem haben; ~ '**drinking** *n., no pl.* gewohnheitsmäßiges Trinken

proboscis /prə'bɒsɪs/ *n., pl.* ~**es** *or* **proboscides** /prə'bɒsɪdi:z/ (Zool.) Rüssel, *der;* (of monkey) Nase, *die*

procedural /prə'si:djʊrl/ *adj.* verfahrensmäßig; (Law) verfahrensrechtlich

procedure /prə'si:djə(r)/ *n.* 1 (particular course of action) Verfahren, das; Prozedur, *die* (meist abwertend); ~**s are under way** es sind Maßnahmen im Gange 2 (way of doing sth.) Verfahrensweise, *die;* (Parl.) [parlamentarisches] Verfahren; (Law) Verfahrensordnung, *die;* **according to democratic** ~**s** gemäß den Spielregeln der Demokratie; **what is the normal** ~**?** wie wird das normalerweise gehandhabt?

proceed /prə'si:d/ *v.i.* (formal) 1 (go) (on foot) gehen; (as or by vehicle) fahren; (on horseback) reiten; (after interruption) weitergehen/-fahren/-reiten; ~ **somewhere** sich irgendwohin begeben; ~ **on one's way** seinen Weg fortsetzen; **as the evening** ~**ed** im [weiteren] Verlauf des Abends; ~ **to business** sich geschäftlichen Dingen zuwenden; ~ **to the next item on the agenda** zum nächsten Punkt der Tagesordnung übergehen; ~ **[from Rome] to Venice** (continue) [von Rom] nach Venedig weiterreisen 2 (begin and carry on) beginnen; (after interruption) fortfahren; ~ **to talk/eat** *etc.* (begin and carry on) beginnen, zu sprechen/essen *usw.;* (after interruption) weitersprechen/-essen *usw.;* ~ **in** *or* **with sth.** (begin) [mit] etw. beginnen; (continue) etw. fortsetzen 3 (adopt course) vorgehen; **we must** ~ **carefully in this case** wir müssen in diesem Fall umsichtig vorgehen; ~ **harshly** *etc.* **with sb.** hart *usw.* mit jmdm. umgehen; ~ **discreetly with sth.** etw. diskret behandeln 4 (be carried on) ‹*Rennen:*› verlaufen; (be under way) ‹*Verfahren:*› laufen; (be continued after interruption) fortgesetzt werden; **how is the project** ~**ing?** wie geht das Projekt voran? 5 (go on to say) fortfahren 6 (originate) ~ **from** (issue from) kommen von; (be caused by) herrühren von

(Phrasal verb)

• ~ **against** *v.t.* (Law) gerichtlich vorgehen gegen

proceeding /prə'si:dɪŋ/ *n.* 1 (action) Vorgehensweise, *die* 2 *in pl.* (events) Vorgänge; **lose control of the** ~**s** nicht mehr Herr der Lage sein; **I'll go along to watch the** ~**s** ich geh mal gucken, was da läuft; **be involved in questionable** ~**s** in eine fragwürdige Sache verwickelt sein 3 *in pl.* (Law) Verfahren, *das;* **court** ~**s** Gerichtsverhandlung, *die;* **court** ~**s can be lengthy** eine Gerichtsverhandlung kann sich in die Länge ziehen; **legal** ~**s** Gerichtsverfahren, *das;* **start/take [legal]** ~**s [against sb.]** gerichtlich [gegen jmdn.] vorgehen; **civil/criminal** ~**s** Zivil-/Strafprozess, *der;* **take criminal/divorce** ~**s against sb.** ein Strafverfahren gegen jmdn. einleiten/einen Scheidungsprozess gegen jmdn. anstrengen 4 *in pl.* (report) Tätigkeitsbericht, *der;* (of single meeting) Protokoll, *das*

proceeds /'prəʊsi:dz/ *n. pl.* Erlös, *der* (**from** aus)

pro-ce'lebrity *adj.* (Sport) Schau‹*wettkampf, -turnier*› (*mit Prominenten und Profis*)

process¹ /'prəʊses/

A *n.* 1 (of time or history) Lauf, *der;* **he learnt a lot in the** ~**:** er lernte eine Menge dabei; **in the** ~ **of the operation** *or* **being operated on** im Verlauf der Operation; **in the** ~ **of teaching his children** bei der Erziehung seiner Kinder; **be in the** ~ **of doing sth.** gerade etw. tun; **be in** ~**:** in Gang sein; **sth. is in** ~ **of formation** etw. wird gerade gebildet 2 (proceeding) Vorgang, *der;* Prozedur, *die;* **undergo** *or* **be subjected to a** ~ **of interrogation** mehrfach verhört werden; **by due** ~ **of law** nach rechtsmäßigem Verfahren; **the democratic** ~**:** das demokratische Verfahren 3 (method) Verfahren, *das;* ~**es of communication** Kommunikationsprozesse; **by a** ~ **of elimination** durch Eliminierung 4 (natural operation) Prozess, *der;* Vorgang, *der;* ~ **of evolution/natural selection** Evolutionsprozess, *der*/natürliche Auslese 5 (Anat., Bot., Zool.: protuberance) Fortsatz, *der*

B *v.t.* verarbeiten ‹*Rohstoff, Signal, Daten*›; bearbeiten ‹*Antrag, Akte, Darlehen*›; aufbereiten ‹*Abwasser, Abfall*›; (for conservation) behandeln ‹*Leder, Lebensmittel*›; (Photog.) entwickeln ‹*Film*›

process² /prə'ses/ *v.i.* ziehen

'**process cheese** (Amer.), '**processed cheese** *ns.* Schmelzkäse, *der*

processer ▸ **processor**

procession /prə'seʃn/ *n.* 1 Zug, *der;* (religious) Prozession, *die;* (festive) Umzug, *der;* **go/march/move** *etc.* **in** ~**:** ziehen; **funeral** ~**:** Trauerzug, *der* 2 (fig.: series) Reihe, *die;* **his life was an endless** ~ **of parties** sein Leben war eine endlose Folge von Partys; **there has been a** ~ **of people in and out of my office all day** heute war in meinem Büro ein ständiges Kommen und Gehen

processional /prə'seʃənl/

A *adj.* Prozessions-; **at a** ~ **pace** im Schritttempo

B *n.* (hymn) Prozessionshymne, *die*

processor /'prəʊsesə(r)/ *n.* (machine) Prozessor, *der;* **central** ~ (Computing) Zentralprozessor, *der*

pro-'choice *adj.* **be** ~**:** für die Freigabe der Abtreibung sein; ~ **voters** Wähler, die für die Freigabe der Abtreibung sind

proclaim /prə'kleɪm/ *v.t.* 1 erklären ‹*Absicht*›; bekannt geben ‹*Fakten, Einzelheiten*›; beteuern ‹*Unschuld*›; geltend machen ‹*Recht, Anspruch*›; (declare officially) verkünden ‹*Amnestie*›; ausrufen ‹*Republik*›; ~ **sb./oneself King/Queen** jmdn./sich zum König/zur Königin ausrufen; ~ **a country [to be] a republic** in einem Land die Republik ausrufen; ~ **1 January a public holiday** den 1. Januar zum Feiertag erklären; ~ **sb./oneself heir to the throne** jmdn./sich zum Thronfolger ernennen 2 (reveal) verraten; ~ **sb./sth. [to be] sth.** verraten, dass jmd./etw. etw. ist

proclamation /prɒklə'meɪʃn/ *n.* 1 (act of proclaiming) Verkündung, *die;* Proklamation, *die* (geh.); **the** ~ **of a new sovereign** die Ausrufung *od.* Proklamation eines neuen Herrschers; **by** ~**:** durch Bekanntmachung 2 (notice) Bekanntmachung, *die;* (edict, decree) Erlass, *der;* **issue** *or* **make a** ~**:** eine Bekanntmachung/einen Erlass herausgeben

proclivity /prə'klɪvɪtɪ/ *n.* Neigung, *die;* **have/show a** ~ *or* **proclivities for** *or* **towards sth.** einen Hang zu etw. haben/zeigen

procrastinate /prə'kræstɪneɪt/ *v.i.* zaudern (geh.); ~ **in doing sth.** es hinauszögern, etw. zu tun; **I ought to start but I keep procrastinating** ich müsste anfangen, aber ich schiebe es immer vor mir her

procrastination /prəkræstɪ'neɪʃn/ *n.* Saumseligkeit, *die* (geh.); **there is no time for** ~**:** die Sache duldet keinen Aufschub; ~ **is the thief of time** (prov.) ≈ was du heute kannst besorgen, das verschiebe nicht auf morgen (Spr.)

procreate /'prəʊkrɪeɪt/

A *v.t.* 1 ~ **children** Kinder bekommen 2 (fig.: produce) hervorbringen

B *v.i.* sich fortpflanzen

procreation /prəʊkrɪ'eɪʃn/ *n.* Fortpflanzung, *die;* (fig.: production) Erzeugung, *die*

Procrustean /prə'krʌstɪən/ *adj.* starr ‹*Gesetze, Regeln, Prinzipien, Einstellung*›; unnachgiebig ‹*Strenge, Entschlossenheit*›

proctor /'prɒktə(r)/ *n.* 1 (Brit. Univ.) *Aufsichtsbeamter der Universität* 2 (Amer. Univ.) ▸ **invigilator**

procurator /'prɒkjʊəreɪtə(r)/ *n.* Stellvertreter, *der*/Stellvertreterin, *die;* Bevollmächtigte, *der/die*

procurator 'fiscal *n.* (Scot. Law) Staatsanwalt, *der*

procure /prə'kjʊə(r)/

A *v.t.* 1 (obtain) beschaffen; ~ **for sb./oneself** jmdm./sich verschaffen ‹*Arbeit, Unterkunft, Respekt, Reichtum*›; jmdm./sich beschaffen ‹*Arbeit, Ware*› 2 (bring about) herbeiführen ‹*Ergebnis, Wechsel, Frieden*›; bewirken ‹*Freilassung*› 3 (for sexual gratification) beschaffen

B *v.i.* Kuppelei betreiben; **procuring** Kuppelei, *die;* ~ **for a prostitute** einer Prostituierten (*Dat.*) Kunden beschaffen

procurement /prə'kjʊəmənt/ *n.* ▸ **procure A**: Beschaffung, *die;* Herbeiführung, *die;* Bewirkung, *die*

procurer /prə'kjʊərə(r)/ *n.* (for sexual purposes) Kuppler, *der;* **act as a** ~ **of girls/boys for sb.** jmdm. Mädchen/Jungen besorgen

procuress /prə'kjʊrɪs/ *n.* Kupplerin, *die*

prod /prɒd/

A *v.t.,* **-dd-** 1 (poke) stupsen (ugs.); stoßen mit ‹*Stock, Finger usw.*›; **he** ~**ded the map with his finger** er stieß mit dem Finger auf die Karte; ~ **sb. gently** jmdn. anstupsen *od.* leicht anstoßen; ~ **the fire/pile of leaves** im Feuer stochern/im Blätterhaufen herumstochern; ~ **sb. in the ribs** jmdm. einen Rippenstoß versetzen; jmdn. in die Rippen stoßen 2 (fig.: rouse) antreiben; nachhelfen (+ *Dat.*) ‹*Gedächtnis*›; **he needs** ~**ding before he will do anything** man muss ihn zu allem erst antreiben; ~ **sb. to do sth.** *or* **into doing sth.** jmdn. drängen, etw. zu tun

B *v.i.,* **-dd-** stochern

C *n.* Stupser, *der;* **a** ~ **in the/my** *etc.* **ribs** ein Rippenstoß; **give sb. a** ~**:** jmdm. einen Stupser geben; (fig.) jmdn. auf Touren bringen; **this sight gave my memory a** ~ (fig.) dieser Anblick half meinem Gedächtnis auf die Sprünge

(Phrasal verbs)

• ~ **a'bout,** ~ **a'round** *v.i.* (lit. or fig.) herumstochern

• ~ **at** *v.t.* anstupsen

Prod /prɒd/ *n.* (Ir. coll.) Protestant, *der*/Protestantin, *die;* Evangele, *der* (ugs.)

prodigal /'prɒdɪgl/

A *adj.* verschwenderisch; **be** ~ **with sth.** verschwenderisch mit etw. umgehen; **be** ~ **of sth.** (literary) freigebig mit etw. sein

B *n.* Verschwender, *der*/Verschwenderin, *die*

prodigality /prɒdɪ'gælɪtɪ/ *n., no pl.* 1 (extravagance) Verschwendungssucht, *die* 2 (liberality) Großzügigkeit, *die*

prodigal 'son *n.* (Bibl.; also fig. iron.) verlorener Sohn; **the return of the** ~**:** die Heimkehr des verlorenen Sohnes

prodigious /prə'dɪdʒəs/ *adj.* ungeheuer; unglaublich ‹*Lügner, Dummkopf*›; wunderbar ‹*Ereignis, Anblick, Taten*›; außerordentlich ‹*Begabung, Können*›; gewaltig ‹*Fortschritt, Kraft, Energie*›; **to a** ~ **degree** über alle Maßen

prodigiously /prə'dɪdʒəslɪ/ *adv.* ungeheuer; außerordentlich ‹*begabt, dumm*›

prodigy /'prɒdɪdʒɪ/ *n.* 1 (gifted person) [außergewöhnliches] Talent; **musical** ~**:** musikalisches Wunderkind; *see also* **child prodigy; infant prodigy** 2 (marvel) Wunder, *das* 3 **be a** ~ **of sth.** ein Wunder/(derog.) ein Ausbund an etw. (*Dat.*) sein

produce

A /'prɒdju:s/ *n.* 1 (things produced) Produkte *Pl.;* Erzeugnisse *Pl.;* '~ **of Spain'** „spanisches Erzeugnis" 2 (yield) Ertrag, *der;* (Mining) Ausbeute, *die*

B /prə'dju:s/ *v.t.* 1 (bring forward) erbringen ‹*Beweis*›; vorlegen ‹*Beweismaterial*›; beibringen ‹*Zeugen*›; angeben ‹*Grund*›; geben ‹*Erklärung*›; vorzeigen ‹*Pass, Fahrkarte, Papiere*›; herausholen ‹*Brieftasche, Portemonnaie, Pistole*›; ~ **sth. from one's pocket** etw. aus der Tasche ziehen; **he** ~**d a splendid shot** ihm gelang ein großartiger Schuss; ~ **a rabbit out of a hat** ein Kaninchen aus einem Zylinder hervorzaubern; **he** ~**d a few coins from his pocket** er holte einige Münzen aus seiner Tasche 2 produzieren ‹*Show, Film*›; inszenieren ‹*Theaterstück, Hörspiel, Fernsehspiel*›; herausgeben ‹*Schallplatte, Buch*›; **well-**~**d** gut gemacht ‹*Film, Theaterstück, Programm*› 3 (manufacture) herstellen; zubereiten ‹*Mahlzeit*›; (in nature; Agric.) produzieren 4 (create) schreiben ‹*Roman, Gedichte, Artikel, Aufsatz, Symphonie*›; schaffen ‹*Gemälde, Skulptur, Meisterwerk*›; aufstellen ‹*Theorie*› 5 (cause) hervorrufen; bewirken ‹*Änderung*›; herbeiführen ‹*Reformen*› 6 (bring into being) erzeugen; führen zu ‹*Situation, Lage, Zustände*›; **chemical reactions producing poisonous gases** chemische Reaktionen, bei denen giftige Gase entstehen 7 (yield) erzeugen ‹*Ware, Produkt*›; geben

‹*Milch*›; tragen ‹*Wolle*›; legen ‹*Eier*›; liefern ‹*Ernte*›; fördern ‹*Metall, Kohle*›; abwerfen ‹*Ertrag, Gewinn*›; hervorbringen ‹*Dichter, Denker, Künstler*›; führen zu ‹*Resultat*› **8** (bear) gebären; ‹*Säugetier:*› werfen; ‹*Vogel, Reptil:*› legen ‹*Eier*›; ‹*Fisch, Insekt:*› ablegen ‹*Eier*›; ‹*Bäume, Blumen:*› tragen ‹*Früchte, Blüten*›; entwickeln ‹*Triebe*›; bilden ‹*Keime*›; **~ offspring** Nachwuchs bekommen (fam.)

C *v.i.* **1** (manufacture goods) produzieren; **producing nation** Erzeugerland, *das* **2** (Brit. Theatre/Radio/Telev.) Stücke/Hörspiele/Fernsehspiele inszenieren; (Cinemat.) Filme produzieren **3** (yield) Ertrag bringen; **the mine has stopped producing** das Bergwerk fördert nicht mehr *od.* hat die Förderung eingestellt **4** (joc.: bear offspring) ein Kind/Kinder kriegen (ugs.)

producer /prəˈdjuːsə(r)/ *n.* **1** ▸❶ **p. 1260** (Cinemat., Theatre, Radio, Telev.) Produzent, *der*/Produzentin, *die* **2** ▸❶ **p. 1260** (Brit. Theatre/Radio/Telev.) Regisseur, *der*/Regisseurin, *die* **3** (Econ.) Produzent, *der*/Produzentin, *die*

producer 'price index *n.* Produzentenpreisindex, *der*

product /ˈprɒdʌkt/ *n.* **1** (thing produced) Produkt, *das;* (of industrial process) Erzeugnis, *das;* (of art or intellect) Werk, *das;* **beauty ~s** Kosmetika; **food ~:** Nahrungsmittelprodukt, *das;* **what is your company's ~?** was stellt Ihre Firma her?; **the ~ of a fertile imagination** das Produkt einer lebhaften Fantasie; **carbon dioxide is a ~ of respiration** Kohlendioxid entsteht bei der Atmung **2** (result) Folge, *die;* **be the ~ of one's age** ein Kind seiner Zeit sein **3** (Math.) Produkt, *das* (**of** aus) **4** (total produced) Produktion, *die;* **the national ~:** das Sozialprodukt; *see also* **gross**[1] **A 4**

product de'velopment *n., no pl.* Produktentwicklung, *die*

production /prəˈdʌkʃn/ *n.* **1** (bringing forward) (of evidence) Erbringung, *die;* (in physical form) Vorlage, *die;* (of witness) Beibringung, *die;* (of reason) Angabe, *die;* (of explanation) Abgabe, *die;* (of passport etc.) Vorzeigen, *das;* **on ~ of your passport** gegen Vorlage Ihres Passes **2** (public presentation) (Cinemat.) Produktion, *die;* (Theatre) Inszenierung, *die;* (of record, book) Herausgabe, *die* **3** (action of making) Produktion, *die;* (manufacturing) Herstellung, *die;* (thing produced) Produkt, *das;* **cease ~:** die Produktion einstellen; **be in/go into ~:** in Produktion sein/gehen; **be** *or* **have gone out of ~:** nicht mehr hergestellt werden; **have a play in ~** ‹*Theater:*› ein Stück inszenieren; *see also* **mass production** **4** (thing created) Werk, *das;* (Brit. Theatre: show produced) Inszenierung, *die* **5** (causing) Hervorrufen, *das* **6** (bringing into being) Hervorbringung, *die;* **the ~ of crystals/toxic gases** die Kristallbildung/die Bildung giftiger Gase **7** (process of yielding) Produktion, *die;* (Mining) Förderung, *die;* **the mine has ceased ~:** das Bergwerk hat die Förderung eingestellt **8** (yield) Ertrag, *der;* **~ of eggs, egg ~:** Legeleistung, *die;* **[the] annual/total ~ from the mine** die jährliche/gesamte Förderleistung des Bergwerks

production: ~ company *n.* Produktionsfirma, *die;* **~ control** *n.* Produktionssteuerung, *die;* **~ cost** *n.* Herstellungskosten *Pl.;* **~ engineer** *n.* ▸❶ **p. 1260** Betriebsingenieur, *der*/-ingenieurin, *die;* **~ line** *n.* Fertigungsstraße, *die;* **~ manager** *n.* ▸❶ **p. 1260** Produktionsleiter, *der*/-leiterin, *die*

productive /prəˈdʌktɪv/ *adj.* **1** (producing) **be ~** ‹*Fabrik:*› produzieren; **the writer's ~ period** die produktive *od.* schöpferische Periode des Schriftstellers; **be ~ of** produzieren ‹*Ware, Getreide*›; hervorbringen ‹*Ideen, Kunstwerke*›; zutage bringen ‹*Ergebnis, Information*› **2** (producing abundantly) ertragreich ‹*Land, Boden, Obstbaum, Mine*›; leistungsfähig ‹*Betrieb, Bauernhof*›; produktiv ‹*Künstler, Komponist, Schriftsteller, Geist*› **3** (yielding favourable results) fruchtbar ‹*Gespräch, Verhandlungen, Forschungsarbeit*›; ergiebig ‹*Nachforschungen*›; **it's not very ~ arguing about it** es bringt nichts, darüber zu streiten

productivity /prɒdʌkˈtɪvɪtɪ/ *n.* Produktivität, *die;* **~ agreement** *or* **deal** Produktivitätsvereinbarung, *die;* **~ bonus** Leistungszulage, *die*

product: ~ manager *n.* ▸❶ **p. 1260** Produktmanager, *der*/-managerin, *die;* **~ placement** *n., no pl.* Produktplacement, *das;* **~ range** *n.* Produktpalette, *die;* **~ 'recall** *n.* Rückrufaktion, *die*

pro-Euro'pean

A *adj.* proeuropäisch

B *n.* EU-Anhänger, *der*/EU-Anhängerin, *die*

prof *n.* (coll.) Prof, *der* (ugs.)

Prof. /prɒf/ *abbr.* ▸❶ **p. 1634 = Professor** Prof.

pro-'family *adj.* (Amer.) familienfreundlich; **~ movement** Pro-Familie-Bewegung, *die*

profanation /prɒfəˈneɪʃn/ *n.* **1** (desecration) Entweihung, *die;* Profanierung, *die* (geh.) **2** (disrespectful treatment) Verunglimpfung, *die* (geh.)

profane /prəˈfeɪn/

A *adj.* **1** (irreligious) gotteslästerlich **2** (irreverent) respektlos ‹*Bemerkung, Person*›; profan ‹*Humor, Sprache*› **3** (secular) weltlich; profan

B *v.t.* entweihen

profanity /prəˈfænɪtɪ/ *n.* **1** (irreligiousness, irreligious act) Gotteslästerung, *die* **2** (irreverent behaviour, act, or utterance) Respektlosigkeit, *die* **3** (indecent remark) Fluch, *der*

profess /prəˈfes/ *v.t.* **1** (declare openly) bekunden ‹*Vorliebe, Abneigung, Interesse*›; **~ to be/do sth.** erklären, etw. zu sein/tun; **~ oneself satisfied** sich zufrieden erklären **2** (claim) vorgeben; geltend machen ‹*Recht, Anspruch*›; **~ to be/do sth.** behaupten, etw. zu sein/tun; **he ~ed regret that ...:** er behauptete, es tue ihm leid, dass … **3** (affirm faith in) sich bekennen zu

professed /prəˈfest/ *adj.* **1** (self-acknowledged) erklärt ‹*Marxist, Bewunderer, Absicht*›; ausdrücklich ‹*Zweck*›; **be a ~ Christian** ein bekennender Christ sein **2** (alleged) angeblich **3** (Relig.) **be ~:** die [Ordens]gelübde *od.* (fachspr.) die Profess abgelegt haben; **~ monk/nun** Mönch, der/Nonne, die die [Ordens]gelübde abgelegt hat

professedly /prəˈfesɪdlɪ/ *adv.* **1** (avowedly) erklärtermaßen **2** (allegedly) angeblich

profession /prəˈfeʃn/ *n.* **1** Beruf, *der;* **what is your ~?** was sind Sie von Beruf?; **medicine/teaching/the law is a ~ requiring great dedication** der Beruf des Mediziners/Lehrers/Juristen erfordert große Hingabe; **he is training** *or* **studying for the ~ of doctor/banker** er wird Arzt/geht ins Bankfach; **take up/go into** *or* **enter a ~:** einen Beruf ergreifen/in einen Beruf gehen; **be in a ~:** einen Beruf ausüben; **she is in the legal ~:** sie ist Juristin; **be a pilot by ~:** von Beruf Pilot sein; **the teaching/medical ~:** der Lehr-/Arztberuf; **the idea has been rejected by the medical ~:** die Idee ist von der Ärzteschaft abgelehnt worden; **his career in the teaching ~:** seine Karriere als Lehrer; **the [learned] ~s** Theologie, Jura und Medizin; **the oldest ~** (joc. euphem.) das älteste Gewerbe der Welt (verhüll. scherzh.) **2** (body of people) Berufsstand, *der;* **the ~** (Theatre coll.) die Bühne **3** (declaration) **~ of faith/love/loyalty** Glaubensbekenntnis, *das*/Liebeserklärung, *die*/Treuegelöbnis, *das;* **~ of friendship/sympathy** Freundschafts-/Sympathiebekundung, *die;* **make a ~ of, make ~s of** erklären ‹*Liebe*›; geloben ‹*Treue*› **4** (Relig.: affirmation of faith) Bekenntnis, *das* (**of** zu); (faith affirmed) Glaube, *der;* **make ~ of a faith** sich zu einem Glauben bekennen **5** (Relig.) (vow) [Ordens]gelübde, *das;* (entrance into order) Profess, *die* (fachspr.); **make one's ~:** die Gelübde ablegen

professional /prəˈfeʃənl/

A *adj.* **1** (of profession) Berufs‹*ausbildung, -leben*›; beruflich ‹*Qualifikation, Laufbahn, Tätigkeit, Stolz, Ansehen*›; **~ body** Berufsorganisation, *die;* **on ~ business/for ~ reasons/on a ~ matter** geschäftlich; **~ advice** fachmännischer Rat; **~ jealousy** Konkurrenzneid, *der* **2** (worthy of profession) (in technical expertise) fachmännisch; (in attitude) professionell; (in experience) routiniert; **make a ~ job of sth.** etw. fachmännisch erledigen **3** (engaged in profession) **~ people** Angehörige hoch qualifizierter Berufe; **'apartment to let to ~ woman'** „Wohnung an berufstätige Dame zu vermieten"; **the ~ class[es]** die gehobenen Berufe **4** (by profession) gelernt; mit abgeschlossener Berufsausbildung *nachgestellt;* (not amateur) Berufs‹*musiker, -sportler, -soldat, -fotograf*›; Profi‹*sportler*›; (fig.) notorisch ‹*Unruhestifter, Schnorrer*›; **a ~ killer/spy** (derog.) ein professioneller Killer/Agent **5** (paid) Profi‹*sport, -boxen, -fußball, -tennis*›; **go** *or* **turn ~:** Profi werden; **be in the ~ army** Berufssoldat sein; **be in the ~ theatre/on the ~ stage** beruflich am Theater/als Schauspieler arbeiten; **make a career in ~ dancing** Berufstänzer werden

B *n.* (trained person, lit. or fig.) Fachmann, *der*/Fachfrau, *die;* (paid worker) Berufstätige, *der/die;* (non-amateur; also Sport, Theatre) Profi, *der;* **better leave it to a ~/the ~s** überlass das lieber einem Fachmann/den Fachleuten

professional 'foul *n.* (Footb.) absichtliches Foul

professionalism /prəˈfeʃənəlɪzm/ *n., no pl.* **1** (of work) fachmännische Ausführung; (of person) fachliche Qualifikation; (in artistic field) technisches Können; (attitude) professionelle Einstellung; (ethical quality) Berufsethos, *das* **2** (paid participation) Professionalismus, *der;* Profitum, *das;* **~ in one's attitude to the game** eine profihafte Einstellung zum Spiel

professionally /prəˈfeʃənəlɪ/ *adv.* **1** (in professional capacity) geschäftlich ‹*beraten, besuchen, konsultieren*›; beruflich ‹*erfolgreich*›; (in manner worthy of profession) professionell; (ethically) dem Berufsethos entsprechend; **I'm here ~:** ich bin geschäftlich hier; **be ~ trained/qualified** eine Berufsausbildung/abgeschlossene Berufsausbildung haben **2** (as paid work) berufsmäßig; **she plays tennis/the piano ~:** sie ist Tennisprofi/von Beruf Pianistin; **she acts ~:** sie ist Berufsschauspielerin **3** (by professional) fachmännisch ‹*leiten, betreiben*›; von einem Fachmann/von Fachleuten ‹*erledigen lassen*›; **the play was performed ~:** das Stück wurde an einem professionellen Theater aufgeführt

professor /prəˈfesə(r)/ *n.* **1** ▸❶ **p. 1260,** ▸❶ **p. 1634** (Univ.: holder of chair) Professor, *der*/Professorin, *die;* **the mathematics ~:** der Professor/die Professorin für Mathematik; **~ of ...** (title) Professor/Professorin für …; **P~ Smith** Herr/Frau Professor Smith; **how do you do, P~?** guten Tag, Herr/Frau Professor! **2** ▸❶ **p. 1260,** ▸❶ **p. 1634** (Amer.: teacher at university) Dozent, *der*/Dozentin, *die* **3** (one who professes a religion) Bekenner, *der*/Bekennerin, *die;* **be a ~ of sth.** sich zu etw. bekennen

professorial /prɒfɪˈsɔːrɪəl/ *adj.* **1** (Univ.) professoral; **his ~ duties** seine Pflichten als Professor; **~ chair** Professur, *die* **2** (characteristic of professor) ‹*Wissen, Autorität, Art*› eines Professors; (pedagogic, dogmatic) professoral (abwertend) ‹*Stil, Ton*›; (fig.) professorhaft ‹*Aussehen*›

professorship /prəˈfesəʃɪp/ *n.* Professur, *die;* **she has been appointed to a ~:** sie ist auf einen Lehrstuhl berufen worden; **hold the P~ of History** den Lehrstuhl für Geschichte innehaben

proffer /ˈprɒfə(r)/ *v.t.* (literary) darbieten ‹*Hand, Krone, Geschenk*›; anbieten ‹*Frieden, Hilfe, Dienstleistung, Arm, Freundschaft*›; aussprechen ‹*Dank*›; vorbringen ‹*Vorschlag*›

proficiency /prəˈfɪʃənsɪ/ *n.* Können, *das;* **degree** *or* **standard of ~:** Fertigkeit, *die;* **his ~ in mathematics/horsemanship** seine Mathematikkenntnisse/sein reiterliches Können; **achieve great ~ in sth.** große Fertigkeiten in etw. (*Dat.*) erlangen

proficiency: ~ certificate *n.* Leistungsnachweis, *der;* **~ test** *n.* Leistungstest, *der*

proficient /prəˈfɪʃənt/ *adj.* fähig; gut ‹*Pianist, Reiter, Skiläufer usw.*›; geschickt ‹*Radfahrer, Handwerker, Lügner*›; (in field of knowledge) bewandert (**at, in** in + *Dat.*); **be ~ at** *or* **in cooking/maths/French** gut kochen können/viel von Mathematik verstehen/gute Französischkenntnisse haben; **he soon became ~:** er beherrschte die Sache bald

P

profile /ˈprəʊfaɪl/
A n. **1** (side aspect) Profil, *das;* **in ~:** im Profil; **a drawing in ~:** eine Profilzeichnung **2** (representation) Profilbild, *das;* (outline) Umriss, *der* **3** (biographical sketch) Porträt, *das* (**of, on** *Gen.*) **4** (personal record) [Personal]akte, *die;* **interest ~:** Interessenprofil, *das* **5** (vertical cross section) Längsschnitt, *der;* (Archit., Geol., Palaeont.) Profil, *das;* (Archaeol.) Schnitt, *der* **6** (graph, curve) Kurve, *die* **7** (fig.) **low ~ [attitude]** Zurückhaltung, *die;* **keep** *or* **maintain a low ~:** sich zurückhalten; **adopt a low ~ approach [to sth.]** sich [in einer Sache] zurückhalten; **high ~ [tactics]** starkes Engagement
B v.t. **1** (represent from side) im Profil darstellen **2** (outline) im Umriss abbilden **3** (sketch biographically) porträtieren

profit /ˈprɒfɪt/
A n. **1** (Commerc.) Gewinn, *der;* Profit, *der;* **at a ~:** mit Gewinn ‹*verkaufen*›; **at a 10% ~:** mit einem Gewinn von 10%; **run sth. at a ~:** mit etw. Gewinne erzielen; **run at a ~** ‹*Geschäft:*› Gewinn abwerfen; **make a ~ from** *or* **out of sth.** mit etw. Geld verdienen; **make [a few pence] ~ on sth.** [ein paar Pence] an etw. (*Dat.*) verdienen; **show a ~:** einen Gewinn verzeichnen; **yield a ~:** Gewinn abwerfen; **~ and loss** Gewinn und Verlust; **~-and-loss account** Gewinn-und-Verlust-Rechnung, *die* **2** (advantage) Nutzen, *der;* **there is no ~ in sth.** etw. ist zwecklos; **be to sb.'s ~:** von Nutzen für jmdn. sein; **find ~ in sth./doing sth.** von etw. profitieren/davon profitieren, dass man etw. tut
B v.t. **~ sb.** für jmdn. von Nutzen sein; **it ~s me nothing to do that** es nützt mir nichts, das zu tun; **it did not ~ them in the end** es hat ihnen letzten Endes gar nichts gebracht
C v.i. (derive benefit) profitieren

Phrasal verbs
- **~ by** v.t. profitieren von; Nutzen ziehen aus ‹*Fehler, Erfahrung*›; ausnützen ‹*Verwirrung*›
- **~ from** v.t. profitieren von ‹*Reise, Studium, Ratschlag*›; nutzen ‹*Gelegenheit*›

profitability /prɒfɪtəˈbɪlɪtɪ/ n., *no pl.* Rentabilität, *die*

profitable /ˈprɒfɪtəbl/ adj. **1** (lucrative) rentabel; einträglich **2** (beneficial) lohnend ‹*Unternehmung, Zeitvertreib, Kauf*›; nützlich ‹*Studium, Diskussion, Verhandlung, Nachforschungen*›

profitably /ˈprɒfɪtəblɪ/ adv. **1** (lucratively) Gewinn bringend; **run ~** ‹*Geschäft:*› Gewinn abwerfen **2** (beneficially) nutzbringend

ˈ**profit centre** n. (Brit.) Profitcenter, *das*

profiteer /prɒfɪˈtɪə(r)/
A n. Profitmacher, *der*/-macherin, *die*
B v.i. sich bereichern

profiteering /prɒfɪˈtɪərɪŋ/ n., *no pl,* Wucher, *der*

profiterole /prəˈfɪtərəʊl/ n. (Gastr.) Profiterole, *die* (Kochk.)

ˈ**profit forecast** n. Gewinnprognose, *die*

profitless /ˈprɒfɪtlɪs/ adj. **1** (useless) nutzlos **2** (yielding no profit) unrentabel

profit: ~-making adj. gewinnorientiert; **it was intended to be ~-making** es sollte Gewinn bringen; **~ margin** n. Gewinnspanne, *die;* **~-sharing** n., *no pl.* Gewinnbeteiligung, *die; attrib.* Gewinnbeteiligungs-; **~-sharing scheme** Gewinnbeteiligungsplan, *der;* **~-taking** n., *no pl.* (St. Exch.) Gewinnmitnahme, *die;* **~ warning** n. Gewinnwarnung, *die*

profligacy /ˈprɒflɪgəsɪ/ n., *no pl.* **1** (extravagance) Verschwendung, *die* (**with** von) **2** (dissipation) Sittenlosigkeit, *die;* **a life of ~:** ein ausschweifendes Leben

profligate /ˈprɒflɪgət/
A adj. **1** (extravagant) verschwenderisch; **be ~ in spending money** das Geld mit vollen Händen ausgeben; **be ~ of** *or* **with sth.** verschwenderisch umgehen mit etw.; **~ squandering of sth.** allzu bereitwillige Vergeudung von etw. **2** (dissipated) hemmungslos ‹*Lust, Trunkenheit, Gier*›; ausschweifend ‹*Person*›
B n. **1** (spendthrift) Verschwender, *der*/Verschwenderin, *die* **2** (rake) Wüstling, *der* (abwertend)

pro forma /prəʊ ˈfɔːmə/
A adv. pro forma
B adj. **1** (as formality) Pro-Forma- **2** (Commerc.) Muster-
C n. ▸**pro forma invoice**

pro forma ˈinvoice n. (Commerc.) Pro-Forma-Rechnung, *die*

profound /prəˈfaʊnd/ adj., **~er** /prəˈfaʊndə(r)/, **~est** /prəˈfaʊndɪst/ **1** (extreme) tief; heftig ‹*Erregung, Verlangen*›; nachhaltig ‹*Wirkung, Einfluss, Eindruck*›; tief greifend ‹*Wandel, Veränderung*›; lebhaft ‹*Interesse*›; tief empfunden ‹*Beileid, Mitgefühl*›; tief sitzend ‹*Angst, Misstrauen*›; völlig ‹*Unwissenheit*›; gespannt ‹*Aufmerksamkeit*›; verborgen ‹*Geheimnis, Tiefe*›; tödlich ‹*Langeweile*›; hochgradig ‹*Schwerhörigkeit*›; **it is a matter of ~ indifference to me** es ist mir völlig gleichgültig **2** (penetrating) tief; profund (geh.) ‹*Wissen, Erkenntnis, Werk, Kenner*›; tiefgründig ‹*Untersuchung, Abhandlung, Betrachtung*›; tief schürfend ‹*Essay, Vortrag, Analyse, Forscher*›; tiefsinnig ‹*Gedicht, Buch, Schriftsteller*›; scharfsinnig ‹*Politiker, Denker, Forscher*›; **that's a very ~ remark** (also iron.) das ist sehr tiefsinnig **3** (demanding thought) tief ‹*Geheimnis, Bedeutung, Sinn*›; unergründlich ‹*Rätsel, Geheimnis*›; schwierig ‹*Lektüre, Problem, Theorie*›; inhaltsschwer ‹*Symbolik, Worte*› **4** (rhet./fig.: deep) tief

profoundly /prəˈfaʊndlɪ/ adv. **1** (extremely) zutiefst; tief ‹*schlafen*›; stark ‹*interessiert, beeinflusst, mitgenommen*›; überaus ‹*friedlich, verschlossen, geheimnisvoll*›; völlig ‹*unbedarft, gleichgültig, versunken, rätselhaft*›; hochgradig ‹*schwerhörig*›; **I am ~ indifferent about it** es ist mir völlig gleichgültig **2** (penetratingly) ungemein ‹*scharfsinnig, beschlagen, feinfühlig*›; hoch‹*intelligent, -gelehrt, -gebildet*›; **a ~ wise man** ein Mann von tiefer Weisheit; **..., she said ~:** ..., sagte sie tiefsinnig

profundity /prəˈfʌndɪtɪ/ n. **1** *no pl.* (extremeness) (of feelings, silence, sleep, respect) Tiefe, *die;* (of joy, sorrow, concern, change) [großes] Ausmaß **2** *no pl.* (depth of intellect) Tiefsinnigkeit, *die;* (of analysis, book) Tiefe, *die* **3** (depth of meaning) Tiefgründigkeit, *die; in pl.* tiefgründige Gedanken

profuse /prəˈfjuːs/ adj. **1** (giving freely) überschwänglich; großzügig ‹*Schenkender, Gebender*›; **be ~ in one's thanks/praise** überschwänglich danken/loben; **be ~ in one's apologies** sich wieder und wieder entschuldigen **2** (abundant) verschwenderisch ‹*Fülle, Üppigkeit, Vielfalt*›; reichlich ‹*Beifall*›; reich ‹*Ernte*›; massenhaft ‹*Wachstum, Vorkommen*›; groß ‹*Dankbarkeit*›; überschwänglich ‹*Entschuldigung, Lob*›; **~ bleeding** starke Blutung

profusely /prəˈfjuːslɪ/ adv. **1** (liberally) großzügig ‹*spenden, schenken*›; übermäßig ‹*loben*› **2** (abundantly) massenhaft ‹*wachsen, vorkommen*›; heftig ‹*bluten, erröten, schwitzen*›; überaus ‹*dankbar*›; üppig ‹*beladen, gedeihen*›; überschwänglich ‹*sich entschuldigen*›

profusion /prəˈfjuːʒn/ n. **1** (abundance) ungeheure *od.* überwältigende Menge; **a ~ of choice** *or* **in the choice offered** eine überreiche Auswahl; **in ~:** in Hülle und Fülle; **in gay/chaotic ~:** in bunter/chaotischer Vielfalt **2** (large amount) [Über]fülle, *die;* **a ~ of flowers/debts** eine verschwenderische Fülle von Blumen/große Menge Schulden

progenitor /prəˈdʒenɪtə(r)/ n. **1** (ancestor) Vorfahr[e], *der*/Vorfahrin, *die* **2** (fig.: predecessor) Vorläufer, *der*/Vorläuferin, *die;* (intellectual ancestor) geistiger Vater

progeny /ˈprɒdʒənɪ/ n., *no pl.* Nachkommenschaft, *die;* **they are the ~ of transported convicts** sie sind die Nachkommen deportierter Sträflinge

progesterone /prəˈdʒestərəʊn/ n. (Physiol., Pharm.) Gelbkörperhormon, *das;* Progesteron, *das* (fachspr.)

prognosis /prɒgˈnəʊsɪs/ n., *pl.* **prognoses** /prɒgˈnəʊsiːz/ **1** (Med.) (forecast) Prognose, *die;* **what is the doctor's ~?** welche Prognose stellt der Arzt?; **make a ~ of sth.** eine Prognose über etw. (*Akk.*) stellen **2** (prediction) Vorhersage, *die;* Prognose, *die;* **give** *or* **make a ~ of sth.** einen Ausblick auf etw. (*Akk.*) geben

prognostic /prɒgˈnɒstɪk/ adj. (also Med.) prognostisch

prognosticate /prɒgˈnɒstɪkeɪt/
A v.t. **1** (foretell; also Med.) prognostizieren **2** (indicate) deuten auf (+ *Akk.*)
B v.i. eine Prognose stellen

prognostication /prɒgnɒstɪˈkeɪʃn/ n. **1** (predicting, forecast) Prognose, *die;* **make a ~ [about sth.]** [über etw. (*Akk.*)] eine Prognose stellen **2** (indication) Vorzeichen, *das* (**of** für)

program /ˈprəʊgræm/
A n. **1** (Amer.) ▸**programme A** **2** (Computing, Electronics) Programm, *das; attrib.* **~ file** Programmdatei, *die*
B v.t., **-mm-** **1** (Amer.) ▸**programme B** **2** (Computing, Electronics) programmieren; **~ a computer to do sth.** einen Computer so programmieren, dass er etw. tut; **~ming language** Programmiersprache, *die*

programer (Amer.) ▸**programmer**

programmable /ˈprəʊgræməbl/ adj. programmierbar

programmatic /prəʊgrəˈmætɪk/ adj. **1** programmatisch ‹*Politik, Ansatz, Werk, Autor*›; klar umrissen ‹*Plan, System, Stufen, Projekt*›; genau festgelegt ‹*Zeitplan*› **2** (Mus.) programmatisch ‹*Komposition, Trend*›

programme /ˈprəʊgræm/
A n. **1** ([notice of] events) Programm, *das;* **the evening's ~:** das Abendprogramm; **a ~ of Schubert songs** ein Programm mit *od.* aus Schubertliedern; eine Darbietung von Schubertliedern; **what is the ~ for today?** was steht heute auf dem Programm?; **my ~ for today** mein [heutiges] Tagesprogramm **2** (Radio, Telev.) (presentation) Sendung, *die;* (Radio: service) Sender, *der;* Programm, *das;* **the ~ is on at 6 o'clock** die Sendung läuft um 6 Uhr **3** (plan, instructions for machine) Programm, *das;* **a five-year ~:** ein Fünfjahresprogramm; **a ~ of study** ein Studienprogramm
B v.t. **1** (make ~ for) ein Programm zusammenstellen für **2** (plan) festlegen ‹*Soll*›; planen, vorbereiten ‹*Maßnahmen*›; durchplanen ‹*Leben, Tagesablauf*›; **the tumble-drier can be ~d to operate for between 10 and 60 minutes** der Trockner kann auf 10-60 Minuten Betriebszeit eingestellt werden **3** (print in ~) **be ~d** auf dem Programm stehen; **an event not officially ~d** ein Ereignis, das nicht offiziell angekündigt war/ist **4** (fig.) **~ sb. to do sth.** jmdn. darauf drillen, etw. zu tun (ugs.)

programme: ~ maker n. ▸ⓘ p. 1260 (Telev., Radio) Programmmacher, *der*/-macherin, *die;* **~ music** n. (Mus.) Programmmusik, *die;* **~ note** n. Erläuterung zum Programm

programmer /ˈprəʊgræmə(r)/ n. (Computing, Electronics) **1** ▸ⓘ p. 1260 (operator) Programmierer, *der*/Programmiererin, *die* **2** (component) Programmiergerät, *das;* Programmspeicher, *der*

ˈ**programming language** n. (Computing) Programmiersprache, *die*

progress
A /ˈprəʊgres/ n. **1** *no pl., no indef. art.* (onward movement) [Vorwärts]bewegung, *die;* **our ~ has been slow** wir sind nur langsam vorangekommen; **he continued his ~ across the fields** er setzte seinen Weg durch die Felder fort; **make ~:** vorankommen; **I saw how much ~ I had made** ich sah, wie weit ich vorangekommen war; **in ~:** im Gange **2** *no pl., no indef. art.* (advance) Fortschritt, *der;* **~ of science/civilization** wissenschaftlicher/kultureller Fortschritt; **there has been some ~ towards peace** man ist dem Frieden etwas näher gekommen; **make ~:** vorankommen; ‹*Student, Patient:*› Fortschritte machen; **make good ~ [towards recovery]** ‹*Patient:*› sich gut erholen; **some ~ was made** es wurden einige Fortschritte erzielt; **that's ~ [for you]** (iron.) [und] das nennt man nun Fortschritt!; **you can't stand in the way of ~:** man kann den Fortschritt nicht aufhalten **3** (Brit. Hist.) (royal journey) Rundreise, *die;* (state procession) prunkvolle Prozession
B /prəˈgres/ v.i. **1** (move forward) vorankommen; **the concert had not ~ed very far** das Konzert war noch nicht weit fortgeschritten; **~ to**

P

the next point of discussion zum nächsten Diskussionspunkt übergehen 2 (be carried on, develop) Fortschritte machen; ‹*Krankheit:*› fortschreiten; **my novel is ~ing nicely** ich komme mit meinem Roman gut voran; **~ towards sth.** einer Sache (*Dat.*) näher kommen
C /prəˈgres/ *v.t.* vorantreiben

progress /ˈprəʊgres/: **~ chart** *n.* Arbeitsdiagramm, *das;* **~ chaser** *n.* ≈ Kontrolleur, *der*/Kontrolleurin, *die* (verantwortlich für die Einhaltung von Produktionszeitplänen)

progression /prəˈgreʃn/ *n.* 1 (progressing) Fortbewegung, *die;* (of career) Verlauf, *der;* **his ~ through life** sein Lebensweg; **his ~ from office clerk to head of department** sein Aufstieg vom Büroangestellten zum Abteilungsleiter 2 (development) Fortschritt, *der* (**in** bei) 3 (succession) Folge, *die* 4 (Mus.) Fortschreitung, *die;* Progression, *die* 5 (Math.) Reihe, *die; see also* **arithmetical**; **geometrical**

progressive /prəˈgresɪv/
A *adj.* 1 (moving forward) fortschreitend; **~ motion** *or* **movement** Vorwärtsbewegung, *die* 2 (gradual) fortschreitend ‹*Verbesserung, Verschlechterung*›; schrittweise ‹*Reform*›; aufeinander folgend ‹*Ereignisse*›; allmählich ‹*Veränderung, Herannahen, Fortschreiten, Prozess, Besserung*›; **in ~ stages** Schritt für Schritt 3 (improving) sich [weiter] entwickelnd 4 (worsening) schlimmer werdend; (Med.) progressiv 5 (favouring reform; in culture) fortschrittlich; progressiv; **~ music** progressive Musik 6 (informal; also Educ.) progressiv 7 (Taxation) gestaffelt; progressiv (fachspr.); **~ tax** Progressivsteuer, *die* 8 (Ling.) **~ tense** Verlaufsform, *die*
B *n.* Progressive, *der/die;* **the ~s** die fortschrittlichen Kräfte

progressively /prəˈgresɪvlɪ/ *adv.* 1 (continuously) immer ‹*weiter, schlechter*›; (gradually) stetig; Schritt für Schritt ‹*reformieren*›; (successively) [chronologisch] fortschreitend; **move ~ towards sth.** sich immer weiter auf etw. zubewegen; **~ approach bankruptcy** sich Schritt für Schritt auf den Bankrott zubewegen 2 (with progressive views, informally; also Educ., Taxation) progressiv

ˈprogress report *n.* Tätigkeitsbericht, *der;* (fig.: news) Lagebericht, *der*

prohibit /prəˈhɪbɪt/ *v.t.* 1 (forbid) verbieten; **~ sb.'s doing sth., ~ sb. from doing sth.** jmdm. verbieten, etw. zu tun; **it is ~ed to do sth.** es ist verboten, etw. zu tun 2 (prevent) verhindern; **~ sb.'s doing sth., ~ sb. from doing sth.** jmdn. daran hindern, etw. zu tun

prohibition /prəʊhɪˈbɪʃn, prəʊɪˈbɪʃn/ *n.* 1 (forbidding) Verbot, *das* 2 (edict) [gesetzliches] Verbot (**against** *Gen.*) 3 *no pl., no art.* (Amer. Hist.) [gesetzliches] Alkoholverbot; **P~** (1920-33) die Prohibition; *attrib.* Prohibitions-

Prohibition

Das staatliche Verbot der Herstellung, des Verkaufs, und des Genusses von Alkohol in den USA von 1919 bis 1933. Die Prohibition konnte nur begrenzt durchgesetzt werden und führte zu Schwarzbrennerei, Schmuggel und illegalem Ausschank. Sie förderte bundesweite Korruption, da Kriminelle wie Al Capone ihren eigenen Alkohol herstellten und verkauften. Obwohl die Prohibtion schließlich aus fiskalen Gründen aufgehoben wurde, hielten sich einige Staaten weiterhin an das Gesetz, und in bestimmten Bundestaaten bestehen noch heute Verkaufsbeschränkungen.

prohibitionist /prəʊhɪˈbɪʃənɪst, prəʊɪˈbɪʃənɪst/ *n.* (Amer. Hist.: person supporting prohibition) (19th century) Mitglied der Prohibitionspartei; (20th century) **P~:** Prohibitionist, *der*/Prohibitionistin, *die*

prohibitive /prəˈhɪbɪtɪv/ *adj.* 1 (prohibiting) prohibitiv (geh.); Verbots‹*zeichen, -gesetz*› 2 (too high) unerschwinglich ‹*Preis, Miete*›; untragbar ‹*Kosten*›

prohibitively /prəˈhɪbɪtɪvlɪ/ *adv.* (excessively) unerschwinglich ‹*hoch, teuer*›

prohibitory /prəˈhɪbɪtərɪ/ ▸**prohibitive**

project
A /prəˈdʒekt/ *v.t.* 1 (throw) schleudern; abfeuern ‹*Kugel, Geschoss*›; abschießen ‹*Rakete*›; **~ one's voice to the very back of the auditorium** seine Stimme so erheben, dass sie auch ganz hinten im Zuschauerraum zu hören ist 2 werfen ‹*Schatten, Schein, Licht*›; senden ‹*Strahl*›; (Cinemat.) projizieren; **~ against** *or* **on to sth.** gegen *od.* auf etw. (*Akk.*) projizieren ‹*Schatten, Umriss*› 3 (make known) vermitteln; **~ the product more favourably** ein positiveres Bild des Produkts vermitteln; **~ one's own personality** seine eigene Person in den Vordergrund stellen 4 (plan) planen 5 (extrapolate) übertragen (**to** auf + *Akk.*) 6 (Psych.) projizieren; **~ sth. [on] to** *or* **on sb./sth.** etw. auf jmdn./etw. projizieren 7 (Geom., Cartography) projizieren
B *v.i.* 1 (jut out) ‹*Felsen:*› vorspringen; ‹*Zähne, Brauen:*› vorstehen; **~ into the sea** ‹*Felsen:*› ins Meer hinausragen; **~ over the street** ‹*Balkon:*› über die Straße ragen 2 (Theatre) laut und deutlich sprechen
C *v. refl.* (transport oneself) **~ oneself into sth.** sich in etw. (*Akk.*) [hinein]versetzen; **~ oneself back in time** sich in eine frühere Zeit/in frühere Zeiten zurückversetzen
D /ˈprɒdʒekt/ *n.* 1 (plan) Plan, *der* 2 (enterprise) Projekt, *das;* **~ manager** Projektmanager, *der*/-managerin, *die;* Projektleiter, *der*/-leiterin, *die*

projectile /prəˈdʒektaɪl/ *n.* Geschoss, *das;* Projektil, *das* (Waffent.)

projection /prəˈdʒekʃn/ *n.* 1 (throwing) Schleudern, *das;* (of missile) Abschuss, *der;* (of bullet, shell) Abfeuern, *das* 2 (protruding) Vorstehen, *das;* (protruding thing) Vorsprung, *der* 3 (making of visible image) Projektion, *die;* (of film) Vorführung, *die* 4 (making known) (of image or character) Darstellung, *die;* (of product or invention) Präsentation, *die;* **the ~ of his own personality** seine Selbstdarstellung 5 (planning) Planung, *die;* (thing planned) Plan, *der;* **make a ~ [for sth.]** einen Plan [für etw.] machen *od.* aufstellen 6 (extrapolation) Übertragung, *die;* Hochrechnung, *die* (Statistik); (estimate of future possibilities) Voraussage, *die* (**of** über + *Akk.*) 7 (Psych.) Projektion, *die;* **~ of sth. on [to] sb./sth.** Projektion einer Sache (*Gen.*) auf jmdn./etw. 8 (Geom.) Projektion, *die* 9 (Cartography) [Karten]projektion, *die;* **conical ~:** Kegelprojektion, *die;* **cylindrical ~:** Zylinderprojektion, *die; see also* **Mercator**

projectionist /prəˈdʒekʃənɪst/ *n.* ▸❶ p. 1260 (Cinemat.) Filmvorführer, *der*/-vorführerin, *die*

proˈjection room *n.* (Cinemat.) Vorführraum, *der*

projector /prəˈdʒektə(r)/ *n.* Projektor, *der;* (for slides) Diaprojektor, *der*

prolapse (Med.)
A /prəʊˈlæps/ *v.i.* prolabieren (fachspr.); vorfallen
B /ˈprəʊlæps/ *n.* Prolaps[us], *der* (fachspr.); Vorfall, *der*

prole /prəʊl/ (Brit. coll. derog.) *n.* Prolet, *der*/Proletin, *die* (abwertend)

proletarian /prəʊlɪˈteərɪən/
A *adj.* proletarisch
B *n.* Proletarier, *der*/Proletarierin, *die*

proletarianism /prəʊlɪˈteərɪənɪzm/ *n., no pl.* Proletariertum, *das*

proletariat, proletariate /prəʊlɪˈteərɪət/ *n.* 1 (Roman Hist.) Proletariat, *das* 2 (derog.: lowest class) Proleten *Pl.* (abwertend) 3 (Econ., Polit.) Proletariat, *das*

ˈpro-life *adj.* Lebensschutz-; **a ~ movement/position** eine Pro-Leben-Bewegung; **a ~ activist** ein aktiver Befürworter des Rechts auf Leben

ˈpro-lifer *n.* Verfechter, *der*/Verfechterin, *die* des Rechts auf Leben

proliferate /prəˈlɪfəreɪt/ *v.i.* 1 (Biol.) sich stark vermehren; (Med.) proliferieren (fachspr.); wuchern 2 (increase, lit. or fig.) sich ausbreiten

proliferation /prəlɪfəˈreɪʃn/ *n.* 1 (Biol.) starke Vermehrung; (Med.) Proliferation, *die* (fachspr.); Wucherung, *die* 2 (increase, lit. or fig.) starke Zunahme; (of nuclear weapons) Proliferation, *die;* (abundance, lit. or fig.) Unmenge, *die*

prolific /prəˈlɪfɪk/ *adj.* 1 (fertile) fruchtbar 2 (productive) produktiv; **be ~ in sth.** reich an etw. (*Dat.*) sein; **be ~ of sth.** etw. in großen Mengen hervorbringen 3 (abundant) reich

prolifically /prəˈlɪfɪkəlɪ/ *adv.* 1 (productively) reichlich 2 (abundantly) in Hülle und Fülle

prolix /ˈprəʊlɪks, prəˈlɪks/ *adj.* weitschweifig

prolixity /prəˈlɪksɪtɪ/ *n., no pl.* Weitschweifigkeit, *die*

prologue (*Amer.:* **prolog**) /ˈprəʊlɒg/ *n.* 1 (introduction) Prolog, *der* (**to** zu) 2 (fig.) Vorspiel, *das* (**to** zu)

prolong /prəˈlɒŋ/ *v.t.* 1 (extend in duration or length) verlängern; **~ the agony** (fig. coll.) die Qual [unnötig] in die Länge ziehen; **don't ~ the agony!** (fig. coll.) mach es nicht so spannend! (ugs.) 2 (Phonet.) dehnen

prolongation /prəʊlɒŋˈgeɪʃn/ *n.* 1 Verlängerung, *die;* (fig.) Weiterführung, *die* 2 (Phonet.) Dehnung, *die* 3 (Mus.) Aushalten, *das*

prolonged /prəˈlɒŋd/ *adj.* lang; lang anhaltend ‹*Beifall*›; lang gezogen ‹*Schrei*›

prom /prɒm/ *n.* (coll.) 1 (Brit.: seaside walkway) [Strand]promenade, *die* 2 (Brit.: concert) Promenadenkonzert, *das;* **the P~s** *Konzerte, die alljährlich im Sommer in der Royal Albert Hall in London stattfinden* 3 (Amer.: dance) **school/college ~:** Schul-/Studentenball, *der*

promenade /prɒməˈnɑːd/
A *n.* 1 (walkway) Promenade, *die;* (Brit.: at seaside) [Strand]promenade, *die* 2 (leisured walk) Spaziergang, *der;* Promenade, *die* (veralt.); **go for** *or* **make** *or* **take a ~:** einen Spaziergang machen 3 (Amer.: dance) ▸**prom 3**
B *v.i.* promenieren (geh.)
C *v.t.* (lead) führen

promenade: ~ concert *n.* Promenadenkonzert, *das;* **~ deck** *n.* (Naut.) Promenadendeck, *das*

promenader /prɒməˈnɑːdə(r)/ *n.* 1 (one who promenades) Spaziergänger, *der*/Spaziergängerin, *die* 2 (Brit.: concert-goer) Konzertbesucher, *der*/-besucherin, *die* (*auf Stehplätzen bei einem Promenadenkonzert*)

Promethean /prəˈmiːθɪən/ *adj.* prometheisch (geh.)

prominence /ˈprɒmɪnəns/ *n.* 1 (conspicuousness) Auffälligkeit, *die;* **the continual ~ of his name in the newspapers** das ständige [auffällige] Auftauchen seines Namens in den Zeitungen 2 (distinction) Bekanntheit, *die;* **come into** *or* **rise to ~:** bekannt werden; **fade from ~:** in Vergessenheit geraten; **give ~ to sth.** etw. in den Vordergrund stellen 3 (projecting part) Vorsprung, *der*

prominent /ˈprɒmɪnənt/ *adj.* 1 (conspicuous) auffallend 2 (foremost) herausragend; **become very ~ as a singer** als Sänger/Sängerin sehr bekannt werden; **he was ~ in politics** er war ein prominenter Politiker; **a ~ topic of discussion** ein viel diskutiertes Thema 3 (projecting) vorspringend; vorstehend ‹*Backenknochen, Brauen*›

prominently /ˈprɒmɪnəntlɪ/ *adv.* 1 (conspicuously) auffallend 2 (in forefront) in einer führenden Rolle; **he figured ~ in the case** er spielte in dem Fall eine wichtige Rolle

promiscuity /prɒmɪˈskjuːɪtɪ/ *n., no pl.* 1 (in sexual relations) Promiskuität, *die* (geh.) 2 (indiscriminate action) Wahllosigkeit, *die*

promiscuous /prəˈmɪskjʊəs/ *adj.* 1 (in sexual relations) promiskuitiv (geh.); promisk; **be ~:** ‹*Person:*› den [Sexual]partner/die [Sexual]partnerin häufig wechseln; **a ~ man** ein Mann, der häufig die Partnerin wechselt; **~ behaviour** häufige Partnerwechsel 2 (mixed) bunt gemischt 3 (indiscriminate) wahllos 4 (coll.: casual) nachlässig

promiscuously /prəˈmɪskjʊəslɪ/ *adv.* 1 (in sexual relations) promiskuitiv (geh.); promisk 2 (indiscriminately) wahllos

promise /ˈprɒmɪs/
A *n.* 1 (assurance) Versprechen, *das;* **sb.'s ~s** jmds. Versprechungen; **give** *or* **make a ~ [to sb.]** [jmdm.] ein Versprechen geben; **give** *or* **make a ~ [to sb.] to do sth.** [jmdm.] versprechen, etw. zu tun; **I'm not making any ~s** ich

kann nichts versprechen; **give** *or* **make a ~ [to sb.] that sth. will happen** [jmdm.] versprechen, dass etw. geschehen wird; **you have my ~:** ich verspreche es dir; **give** *or* **make a ~ of sth. [to sb.]** [jmdm.] etw. versprechen; **~s of love/reform** Liebes-/Reformversprechungen; **it's a ~:** ganz bestimmt; **~s, ~s!** (coll. iron.) Versprechungen, nichts als Versprechungen!; **is that a threat or a ~?** (coll. iron.) soll das eine Drohung oder ein Versprechen sein? **2** (guarantee) Zusicherung, *die;* **they gave me a ~ that the work would be ready on time** sie sicherten mir zu, dass die Arbeit rechtzeitig fertig sein werde **3** (fig.: reason for expectation) Hoffnung, *die;* **he never fulfilled his early ~:** er enttäuschte die Erwartungen, die man zunächst in ihn gesetzt hatte; **land of ~:** Land der Verheißung (geh.); **a painter of** *or* **with ~:** ein viel versprechender Maler; **~ of sth.** Aussicht auf etw. (*Akk.*); **show [great] ~:** zu großen Hoffnungen berechtigen. *See also* **breach A 1**

B *v.t.* **1** (give assurance of) versprechen; **~ sth. to sb., ~ sb. sth.** jmdm. etw. versprechen; **~ revenge** Rache schwören **2** (fig.: give reason for expectation of) verheißen (geh.); **~ sb. sth.** jmdm. etw. in Aussicht stellen; **~ to do/be sth.** versprechen, etw. zu tun/zu sein **3** **~ oneself sth./that one will do sth.** sich (*Dat.*) etw. vornehmen/sich vornehmen, etw. zu tun **4** (coll.: assure) **I ~ you** das sage ich dir; **I ~** *or* **let me ~ you this/that** das verspreche ich dir

C *v.i.* **1** **~ well** *or* **favourably [for the future]** viel versprechend [für die Zukunft] sein; **he ~s well as a teacher** er ist ein viel versprechender Lehrer **2** (give assurances) Versprechungen machen; **I can't ~:** ich kann es nicht versprechen

promised land /prɒmɪst 'lænd/ *n.* **1** **the ~** (Bibl.) das Gelobte Land **2** (fig.: ideal state) Paradies, *das*

promising /'prɒmɪsɪŋ/ *adj.*, **promisingly** /'prɒmɪsɪŋlɪ/ *adv.* viel versprechend

'promissory note *n.* (Finance) Schuldschein, *der*

promontory /'prɒməntərɪ/ *n.* Vorgebirge, *das*

promote /prə'məʊt/ *v.t.* **1** (advance) befördern **2** (encourage) fördern; **a lifestyle which does not ~ health** ein Lebensstil, der der Gesundheit nicht förderlich ist; **~ the success of the firm** der Firma zu mehr Erfolg verhelfen **3** (publicize) Werbung machen für **4** (initiate) in Angriff nehmen ‹*Projekt*›; gründen ‹*Tochtergesellschaft*›; **~ a bill** (Parl.) einen Gesetzentwurf einbringen **5** (Chess) umwandeln **6** (Footb.) **be ~d** aufsteigen

promoter /prə'məʊtə(r)/ *n.* **1** (who organizes and finances event) Veranstalter, *der*/Veranstalterin, *die;* (of ballet tour, pop festival, boxing match, cycle race also) Promoter, *der*/Promoterin, *die* **2** (furtherer) Förderer, *der*/Förderin, *die* **3** (publicizer) Promoter, *der*/Promoterin, *die* **4** (initiator) Begründer, *der*/Begründerin, *die;* (*Parl.*) *jmd., der einen Gesetzentwurf einbringt und unterstützt;* **[company] ~:** Firmengründer, *der*/-gründerin, *die*

promotion /prə'məʊʃn/ *n.* **1** (advancement) Beförderung, *die;* **win** *or* **gain ~:** befördert werden; **he is due for ~:** er dürfte bald befördert werden; **~ to [the rank of] sergeant** *etc.* Beförderung zum Unteroffizier *usw.* **2** (furtherance) Förderung, *die* **3** (Sport, Theatre: event) Veranstaltung, *die* **4** (publicization) Werbung, *die;* (instance) Werbekampagne, *die;* **sales ~:** Werbung, *die* **5** (initiation) Begründung, *die;* (Parl.: of bill) Einbringung, *die* **6** (of a company) Gründung, *die* **7** (Chess) Umwandlung, *die* **8** (Footb.) Aufstieg, *der;* **be sure of ~:** mit Sicherheit aufsteigen

promotional /prə'məʊʃənl/ *adj.* **1** (of advancement) Beförderungs‹*aussichten, -möglichkeiten*› **2** (of publicity) Werbe‹*kampagne, -broschüre, -strategie usw.*›

prompt /prɒmpt/

A *adj.* **1** (ready to act) bereitwillig; **be a ~ helper/volunteer** bereitwillig helfen/sich bereitwillig zur Verfügung stellen; **be ~ in doing sth.** *or* **to do sth.** etw. unverzüglich tun; **he was ~ in his reply** er antwortete prompt **2** (done readily) sofortig; **her ~ answer/reaction** ihre prompte Antwort/Reaktion; **take ~ action** sofort handeln; **make a ~ decision** sich sofort entschließen **3** (punctual) pünktlich

B *adv.* pünktlich; **at 6 o'clock ~:** Punkt 6 Uhr

C *v.t.* **1** (incite) veranlassen; **~ sb. to sth./to do sth.** jmdn. zu etw. veranlassen/dazu veranlassen, etw. zu tun **2** (supply with words; also Theatre) soufflieren (+ *Dat.*); (supply with answers) vorsagen (+ *Dat.*); (give suggestion to) weiterhelfen (+ *Dat.*); **~ sb. with sth.** jmdm. etw. soufflieren/vorsagen/jmdm. mit etw. weiterhelfen; **he had to be ~ed** man musste ihm soufflieren/vorsagen/weiterhelfen **3** (inspire) hervorrufen ‹*Kritik, Eifersucht usw.*›; provozieren ‹*Antwort*›; **this ~s the question ...:** hierbei drängt sich die Frage auf: ...

D *v.i.* soufflieren

E *n.* **1** Soufflieren, *das;* **give a ~:** soufflieren; **I'll give you a ~ if you need one** (a suggestion) wenn nötig, werde ich dir weiterhelfen **2** (Computing) Bereitschaftsmeldung, *die;* Prompt, *der* (fachspr.)

prompt: ~ box *n.* (Theatre) Souffleurkasten, *der;* **~ copy** *n.* (Theatre) Rollenheft, *das*

prompter /'prɒmptə(r)/ *n.* (Theatre) Souffleur, *der*/Souffleuse, *die*

prompting /'prɒmptɪŋ/ *n.* **1** **the ~s of his heart/conscience** die Stimme seines Herzens/Gewissens **2** **he never needs ~:** man muss ihn nicht zweimal bitten **3** (Theatre) Soufflieren, *das*

promptitude /'prɒmptɪtju:d/ ▸ **promptness**

promptly /'prɒmptlɪ/ *adv.* **1** (quickly) prompt; **he ~ went and did the opposite** (iron.) er hat natürlich prompt [genau] das Gegenteil getan **2** (punctually) pünktlich; **at 8 o'clock ~, ~ at 8 o'clock** Punkt 8 Uhr; pünktlich um 8 Uhr

promptness /'prɒmptnɪs/ *n., no pl.* Promptheit, *die;* **be carried out with ~:** prompt durchgeführt werden; **the public's ~ in responding to the appeal** die Geschwindigkeit, mit der die Öffentlichkeit auf den Aufruf reagierte

'prompt side *n.* (Brit. Theatre) *Bühnenseite links vom Schauspieler;* (*Amer. Theatre*) *Bühnenseite rechts vom Schauspieler*

promulgate /'prɒməlgeɪt/ *v.t.* **1** (disseminate) verbreiten **2** (announce officially) verkünden

promulgation /prɒməl'geɪʃn/ *n.* ▸ **promulgate**: Verbreitung, *die;* Verkündung, *die*

prone /prəʊn/ *adj.* **1** (liable) **be ~ to** anfällig sein für ‹*Krankheiten, Depressionen*›; neigen zu ‹*Faulheit, Meditation*›; **be ~ to do sth.** dazu neigen, etw. zu tun; *in comb.* **strike-~:** streikanfällig; **a disaster-~ country** ein Land, in dem es häufig zu Katastrophen kommt; *see also* **accident-prone** **2** (down-facing) **assume a ~ position on the floor** sich in Bauchlage auf den Boden legen; **fall/throw oneself ~ to** *or* **on the ground** sich flach auf den Boden fallen lassen/werfen; **slumped ~ over her typewriter** vornüber über ihre Schreibmaschine gesunken **3** (prostrate) lang gestreckt

prong /prɒŋ/

A *n.* **1** (of fork) Zinke, *die* **2** (of antler) Ende, *das*

B *v.t.* aufspießen

-pronged /prɒŋd/ *adj. in comb.* -zinkig; **three-~ attack** (Mil.; also fig.) Angriff von drei Seiten

pronominal /prə'nɒmɪnl/ *adj.* (Ling.) pronominal; Pronominal‹*adjektiv, -adverb*›

pronoun /'prəʊnaʊn/ *n.* (Ling.) (word replacing noun) Pronomen, *das;* Fürwort, *das;* (pronominal adjective) Pronominaladjektiv, *das;* **demonstrative ~:** Demonstrativpronomen, *das;* **distributive ~:** Distributivum, *das;* **impersonal** *or* **indefinite ~:** Indefinitpronomen, *das;* **possessive ~:** Possessivpronomen, *das;* besitzanzeigendes Fürwort; **reflexive ~:** Reflexivpronomen, *das*

pronounce /prə'naʊns/

A *v.t.* **1** (declare formally) verkünden; **~ a curse [up]on sb.** jmdn. verfluchen; **~ excommunication [up]on sb.** die Exkommunikation über jmdn. verhängen; **~ judgement** das Urteil verkünden; **~ judgement on sb./sth.** über jmdn./etw. das Urteil sprechen; **~ sb./sth. [to be] sth.** jmdn./etw. für etw. erklären; **he was ~d [to be] a traitor** er wurde zum Verräter erklärt; **~ sb. fit for work** jmdn. für arbeitsfähig erklären **2** (declare as opinion) erklären für; **he has been ~d an excellent actor** es heißt, er sei ein ausgezeichneter Schauspieler; **he ~d himself [to be]** *or* **~d that he was disgusted with it** er erklärte, er sei empört darüber **3** (speak) aussprechen ‹*Wort, Buchstaben usw.*›

B *v.i.* **~ on sth.** zu etw. Stellung nehmen; **~ for** *or* **in favour of/against sth.** sich für/gegen etw. aussprechen

pronounceable /prə'naʊnsəbl/ *adj.* aussprechbar

pronounced /prə'naʊnst/ *adj.* **1** (declared) erklärt; ausgesprochen ‹*Gegner, Autorität*› **2** (spoken) ausgesprochen; **the h is not ~:** das h wird nicht gesprochen **3** (marked) ausgeprägt; **walk with a ~ limp** stark hinken

pronouncement /prə'naʊnsmənt/ *n.* Erklärung, *die;* **make a ~ [about sth.]** eine Erklärung [zu etw.] abgeben; **make the ~ that ...:** erklären, dass ...

pro'nouncing dictionary *n.* Aussprachewörterbuch, *das*

pronto /'prɒntəʊ/ *adv.* (coll.) dalli (ugs.); **and [do it] ~!** aber fix! (ugs.); aber [ein bisschen] dalli! (ugs.)

pronunciation /prənʌnsɪ'eɪʃn/ *n.* Aussprache, *die;* **error of ~:** Aussprachefehler, *der;* **what is the ~ of this word?** wie wird dieses Wort ausgesprochen?; **this word has two ~s** dieses Wort kann auf zwei Arten ausgesprochen werden

proof /pru:f/

A *n.* **1** (fact, evidence) Beweis, *der;* **very good ~:** sehr gute Beweise; **~ positive** eindeutige Beweise; **~ of purchase** Kaufbeleg, *der; see also* **burden A 1** **2** *no pl., no indef. art.* (Law) Beweismaterial, *das* **3** *no pl.* (proving) **in ~ of** zum Beweis (+ *Gen.*); **be capable of experimental ~:** sich experimentell beweisen lassen **4** *no pl.* (test, trial) Beweis, *der;* **put a theory to the ~:** eine Theorie unter Beweis stellen; **the ~ of the pudding is in the eating** (prov.) Probieren geht über Studieren (Spr.) **5** *no pl., no art.* (standard of strength) Proof *o. Art.;* **100 ~** (Brit.), **128 ~** (Amer.) 64 Vol.-% Alkohol; **above/below ~:** über/unter 57,27 Vol.-% Alkohol **6** (Printing) [Korrektur]abzug, *der;* **first ~:** Erstsatz, *der; see also* **galley 3**; **page proof**; **read A 1** **7** (Photog., Art) [Probe]abzug, *der*

B *adj.* **1** (impervious) **be ~ against sth.** unempfindlich gegen etw. sein; (fig.) gegen etw. immun sein; **~ against wind/bullets/the weather** windundurchlässig/kugelsicher/wetterfest **2** *in comb.* (resistant to) ‹*kugel-, bruch-, einbruch-, diebes-, idioten*›sicher; ‹*schall-, wasser*›dicht **3** hochprozentig ‹*Alkohol*›; **this liqueur is 67.4°** (Brit.) or (Amer.) **76.8° ~:** dieser Likör hat 38,4 Vol.-% Alkohol

C *v.t.* **1** (Printing) (take ~ of) andrucken; (proof-read) Korrektur lesen **2** (Photog., Art) einen [Probe]abzug herstellen von **3** (make resistant) **~ [against sth.]** [gegen etw.] imprägnieren ‹*Stoff, Gewebe*›; [gegen etw.] abdichten ‹*Wand*›; *in comb.* **sound/water-~:** schall-/wasserdicht machen; **flame-~ sth.** etw. nicht brennbar machen **4** (in baking) gehen lassen

proof: ~-read *v.t.* (Printing) Korrektur lesen; **~-reader** *n.* ▸ **i** **p. 1260** (Printing) Korrektor, *der*/Korrektorin, *die;* **~-reading** *n.* (Printing) Korrekturlesen, *das;* **~ sheet** *n.* (Printing) Korrekturfahne, *die;* **~ 'spirit** *n.*: *Alkohol-Wasser-Gemisch mit einem bestimmten Alkoholanteil;* Proofspirit, *der*

prop[1] /prɒp/

A *n.* **1** (support, lit. or fig.) Stütze, *die;* (Mining) Strebe, *die* **2** (Rugby) *Spieler außen in der vorderen Reihe des Gedränges*

B *v.t.*, **-pp-** **1** (support) stützen; **the ladder was ~ped against the house** die Leiter war gegen das Haus gelehnt; **the door was ~ped open with a brick** die Tür wurde von einem Ziegelstein offen gehalten **2** (fig.) ▸ **~ up 2**

(Phrasal verb)
• ~ **'up** *v.t.* **1** (support) stützen; ~ **oneself up on one's elbows** sich auf die Ellbogen stützen; **sit ~ped up against the wall** [mit dem Rücken] an die Wand gelehnt sitzen; ~ **up the bar** (joc./iron.) an der Theke rumhängen (ugs.) **2** (fig.) aufrichten ‹*Person*›; vor dem Konkurs bewahren ‹*Firma*›; stützen ‹*Regierung, Währung*›

prop² *n.* (coll.) **1** (Theatre, Cinemat.: also fig.) Requisit, *das* **2** *in pl.* ▸**property man**

prop³ *n.* (Aeronaut. coll.) Propeller, *der*

propaganda /prɒpə'gændə/ *n., no pl., no indef. art.* Propaganda, *die*

propagandist /prɒpə'gændɪst/
A *n.* Propagandist, *der*/Propagandistin, *die* (**of, for** *Gen.*)
B *adj.* propagandistisch; Propaganda‹*schrift, -blatt*›

propagate /'prɒpəgeɪt/
A *v.t.* **1** (Hort., Bacteriol.) vermehren (**from, by** durch); (Breeding, Zool.) züchten **2** (hand down) vererben ‹*Eigenschaft, Merkmal*› (**to** auf + *Akk.*) **3** (spread) verbreiten **4** (Phys.) **be ~d** sich fortpflanzen
B *v.i.* **1** (Bot., Zool., Bacteriol.) sich vermehren **2** (spread, extend, travel) sich ausbreiten
C *v. refl.* (Bot., Zool., Bacteriol.) sich vermehren

propagation /prɒpə'geɪʃn/ *n.* **1** (Hort., Breeding, Bacteriol.: causing to propagate) Züchtung, *die* **2** (Bot., Zool., Bacteriol.: reproduction) Vermehrung, *die* **3** (handing down) Vererbung, *die* (**to** auf + *Akk.*) **4** (spreading) Verbreitung, *die* **5** (Phys.) Fortpflanzung, *die*

propagative /'prɒpəgeɪtɪv/ *adj.* **1** (Hort.) Vermehrungs- **2** (reproductive) Fortpflanzungs-

propagator /'prɒpəgeɪtə(r)/ *n.* **1** (Hort.) (person) Züchter, *der*/Züchterin, *die*; (device) [beheizbare] Saatkiste **2** (disseminator) Propagator, *der*/Propagatorin, *die* (geh.)

propane /'prəʊpeɪn/ *n.* (Chem.) Propan, *das*

propel /prə'pel/ *v.t.*, **-ll-** (lit. or fig.) antreiben; **the boat was ~led through the water by the oarsmen** die Ruderer trieben das Boot durchs Wasser; **the rider was ~led over the horse's head** der Reiter wurde über den Kopf des Pferdes geschleudert

propellant /prə'pelənt/ *n.* **1** Treibstoff, *der* **2** (of aerosol spray) Treibgas, *das* **3** (explosive charge) Treibladung, *die*

-propelled /prə'peld/ *adj. in comb.* -getrieben

propellent /prə'pelənt/ *adj.* Antriebs‹*kraft, -energie, -leistung, -mittel, -system*›

propeller /prə'pelə(r)/ *n.* Propeller, *der*

propeller: ~-head *n.* (coll.) Technikfreak, *der* (ugs.); (computer expert) Computerfreak, *der* (ugs.); **~ shaft** *n.* (Aeronaut.) Propellerwelle, *die*; (Motor Veh.) Kardanwelle, *die*; **~ turbine** *n.* (Aeronaut.) Propellerturbine, *die*

propelling 'pencil *n.* (Brit.) Drehbleistift, *der*

propensity /prə'pensɪtɪ/ *n.* Neigung, *die*; **[have] a ~ to** *or* **towards sth.** einen Hang zu etw. [haben]; **have a ~ to do sth.** *or* **for doing sth.** dazu neigen, etw. zu tun

proper /'prɒpə(r)/
A *adj.* **1** (accurate) richtig; wahrheitsgetreu ‹*Bericht*›; zutreffend ‹*Beschreibung*›; eigentlich ‹*Wortbedeutung*›; ursprünglich ‹*Fassung*›; **in the ~ sense** im wahrsten Sinne des Wortes **2** *postpos.* (strictly so called) im engeren Sinn *nachgestellt*; **within the sphere of architecture ~:** auf dem Gebiet der Architektur an sich; **in London ~:** in London selbst **3** (genuine) echt; richtig ‹*Wirbelsturm, Schauspieler*› **4** (satisfactory) richtig; zufrieden stellend ‹*Antwort*›; hinreichend ‹*Grund*› **5** (suitable) angemessen; (morally fitting) gebührend; **do sth. the ~ way** etw. richtig machen; **we must do the ~ thing by him** wir müssen ihn fair behandeln; **he did not know which was the ~ knife to use** er wusste nicht, welches Messer er benutzen sollte; **do as you think ~:** tu, was du für richtig hältst; **that's not a ~ attitude to take towards ...:** so verhält man sich nicht gegenüber ... **6** (conventionally acceptable) gehörig; **have no notion of what is ~:** nicht wissen, was sich gehört; **language not ~ for a lady's ears** eine Ausdrucksweise, die nicht für die Ohren einer Dame bestimmt ist; **it would not be ~ for me to ...:** es gehört sich nicht, dass ich ...; **the conduct ~ to a gentleman** das Benehmen, das sich für einen Gentleman gehört **7** (conventional, prim) förmlich **8** *attrib.* (coll.: thorough) richtig; **she gave him a ~ hiding** sie gab ihm eine ordentliche Tracht Prügel; **you gave me a ~ turn** du hast mir einen ganz schönen Schrecken eingejagt
B *adv.* (coll.) **good and ~:** gehörig; nach Strich und Faden (ugs.)

proper 'fraction *n.* (Math.) echter Bruch

properly /'prɒpəlɪ/ *adv.* **1** richtig; (rightly) zu Recht; (with decency) anständig; **~ speaking** genau genommen; **he is ~ considered to be a great artist** er wird mit Recht als ein großer Künstler angesehen; **he is not ~ a captain at all** er ist eigentlich gar kein Kapitän; **I'm not ~ authorized to do it** ich bin eigentlich nicht dazu berechtigt; **he very ~ went to see the doctor** er tat das einzig Richtige und ging zum Arzt **2** (primly) förmlich **3** (coll.: thoroughly) total (ugs.)

proper: ~ 'motion *n.* (Astron.) Eigenbewegung, *die*; **~ 'name, ~ 'noun** *ns.* (Ling.) Eigenname, *der*

propertied /'prɒpətɪd/ *adj.* begütert; **the ~ class[es]** die besitzende[n] Klasse[n]

property /'prɒpətɪ/ *n.* **1** (possession[s], ownership) Eigentum, *das*; **the ~-owning classes** die besitzenden Klassen; **~ speculator/dealer** Immobilienspekulant, *der*/-händler, *der*; **make sth. sb.'s ~:** jmdm. etw. übereignen; **lost ~:** Fundsachen *Pl.*; **lost ~ [department** *or* **office]** Fundbüro, *das*; **man of ~:** begüterter Mann; **common ~:** Gemeingut, *das*; (*fig.*) ▸**common knowledge** **2** (estate) Besitz, *der*; Immobilie, *die* (fachspr.); **~ in London is expensive** die Immobilienpreise in London sind hoch; *see also* **personal property 1**; **real property** **3** (attribute) Eigenschaft, *die*; (effect, special power) Wirkung, *die* **4** (Cinemat., Theatre) Requisit, *das*

property: ~ developer *n.* ≈ Bauunternehmer, *der*/-unternehmerin, *die*; **~ man** *n.* (Cinemat., Theatre) Requisiteur, *der*; **~ market** *n.* Immobilienmarkt, *der*; **~ master** ▸ **~ man**; **~ owner** *n.* Grundbesitzer, *der*/-besitzerin, *die*; **~ qualification** *n.*: *Eigentumsnachweis als Voraussetzung für ein Amt od. Recht*; **~ tax** *n.* Vermögenssteuer, *die*

prop 'forward ▸**prop¹ A 2**

prophecy /'prɒfɪsɪ/ *n.* **1** (prediction) Vorhersage, *die*; **make the ~ that ...:** vorhersagen, dass ... **2** (prophetic utterance) Prophezeiung, *die* **3** (prophetic faculty) **[the power** *or* **gift of] ~:** die Gabe der Prophetie (geh.)

prophesy /'prɒfɪsaɪ/
A *v.t.* (predict) vorhersagen; (fig.) prophezeien ‹*Unglück*›; (as fortune-teller) weissagen; **what do you ~ will happen?** was wird deiner Vorhersage nach geschehen?
B *v.i.* **1** (foretell future) Vorhersagen machen; **~ of sth.** (lit. or fig.) etw. ankündigen **2** (speak as prophet) Prophezeiungen machen

prophet /'prɒfɪt/ *n.* **1** (lit. or fig.) Prophet, *der*; **be the ~ of sth.** etw. prophezeien; **~ of doom** Schwarzseher, *der* **2** (advocate) Vorkämpfer, *der*

prophetess /'prɒfɪtɪs/ *n.* **1** Prophetin, *die* **2** (advocate) Vorkämpferin, *die*

prophetic /prə'fetɪk/ *adj.* prophetisch; **be ~ of sth.** ein Vorzeichen für etw. sein

prophetically /prə'fetɪkəlɪ/ *adv.* prophetisch

prophylactic /prɒfɪ'læktɪk/
A *adj.* prophylaktisch (Med., geh.); vorbeugend
B *n.* **1** Prophylaxe, *die* (Med.); Vorbeugung, *die*; (preventive measure) Vorbeugungsmaßnahme, *die* **2** (contraceptive) Verhütungsmittel, *das*

prophylaxis /prɒfɪ'læksɪs/ *n., pl.* **prophylaxes** /prɒfɪ'læksiːz/ (Med.) Prophylaxe, *die*

propinquity /prə'pɪŋkwɪtɪ/ *n., no pl.* (formal) **1** (nearness) Nähe, *die* (**to** zu); **in close ~ [to each other]** nah beieinander **2** (kinship) [nahe] Verwandtschaft (**to** mit, **between** zwischen)

propitiate /prə'pɪʃɪeɪt/ *v.t.* (formal) (appease) besänftigen; (make favourably inclined) günstig stimmen

propitiation /prəpɪʃɪ'eɪʃn/ *n.* (formal) Besänftigung, *die*

propitiatory /prə'pɪʃɪətərɪ/ *adj.* (formal) (of propitiation) Besänftigungs-; besänftigend ‹*Wort, Lächeln, Geste*›

propitious /prə'pɪʃəs/ *adj.* **1** (auspicious) verheißungsvoll **2** (favouring, benevolent) günstig; **~ for** *or* **to sth.** günstig für etw.; **~ for** *or* **to doing sth.** dafür geeignet, etw. zu tun; **be hardly ~ to sth.** einer Sache (*Dat.*) kaum förderlich sein

propitiously /prə'pɪʃəslɪ/ *adv.* (auspiciously, favourably) günstig

'prop jet *n.* (Aeronaut.) (aircraft) Turbo-Prop-Flugzeug, *das*; (engine) Turbo-Prop-Triebwerk, *das*

proponent /prə'pəʊnənt/ *n.* Befürworter, *der*/Befürworterin, *die*

proportion /prə'pɔːʃn/
A *n.* **1** (portion) Teil, *der*; (in recipe) Menge, *die*; **the ~ of deaths is high** der Anteil der Todesfälle ist hoch; **what ~ of candidates pass the exam?** wie groß ist der Anteil der erfolgreichen Prüfungskandidaten? **2** (ratio) Verhältnis, *das*; **the ~ of sth. to sth.** das Verhältnis von etw. zu etw.; **the high ~ of imports to exports** der hohe Anteil der Importe im Vergleich zu den Exporten; **in ~ [to sth.]** [einer Sache (*Dat.*)] entsprechend; **our excitement grew in ~ as the ship came closer** je näher das Schiff kam, desto aufgeregter wurden wir **3** (correct relation) Proportion, *die*; (fig.) Ausgewogenheit, *die*; **the design lacks ~:** der Entwurf ist schlecht proportioniert; **sense of ~:** Sinn für Proportionen; **be in ~ [to** *or* **with sth.]** (lit. or fig.) im richtigen Verhältnis [zu *od.* mit etw.] stehen; **try to keep things in ~** (fig.) versuchen Sie, die Dinge im richtigen Licht zu sehen; **be out of ~/all** *or* **any ~ [to** *or* **with sth.]** (lit. or fig.) in keinem/keinerlei Verhältnis zu etw. stehen; **get things out of ~** (fig.) die Dinge zu wichtig nehmen; (worry unnecessarily) sich (*Dat.*) zu viele Sorgen machen **4** *in pl.* (size) Dimensionen *Pl.*; **the ~s of each room were modest** die Räume waren von bescheidener Größe; **of mountainous ~s** riesenhaften Ausmaßes **5** (Math.) **[geometric] ~:** Proportion, *die*; **in direct/inverse ~:** direkt/umgekehrt proportional; **rule of ~ = rule of three** ▸**rule A 1**. *See also* **direct proportion**; **inverse proportion**
B *v.t.* (make proportionate) proportionieren; (harmonize) aufeinander abstimmen; **~ sth. to sth.** etw. einer Sache (*Dat.*) anpassen; **the architect has ~ed the whole building** der Architekt hat das ganze Gebäude ausgewogen gestaltet; *see also* **proportioned**

proportional /prə'pɔːʃənl/ *adj.* **1** (in proportion) entsprechend; **be ~ to sth.** einer Sache (*Dat.*) entsprechen **2** (in correct relation) ausgewogen; **be ~ to sth.** (lit. or fig.) einer Sache (*Dat.*) entsprechen **3** (Math.) **~ [to sth.]** proportional [zu etw.]; **be directly/indirectly ~ to sth.** einer Sache (*Dat.*) direkt/umgekehrt proportional sein **4** (of proportions) proportional

proportionality /prəpɔːʃə'nælɪtɪ/ *n., no pl.* **1** (being in proportion) Verhältnismäßigkeit, *die*; **there is a ~ between A and B** A und B verhalten sich proportional zueinander **2** (harmony) Ausgewogenheit, *die*; **~ to sth.** ausgewogenes Verhältnis zu etw.

proportionally /prə'pɔːʃənəlɪ/ *adv.* **1** (in proportion) [dem]entsprechend **2** (in correct relation) proportional gesehen; **correspond/not correspond ~ to sth.** im richtigen/in keinem Verhältnis zu etw. stehen

proportional: ~ represen'tation *n.* (Polit.) Verhältniswahlsystem, *das*; **~ tax** *n.* Proportionalsteuer, *die*

proportionate /prə'pɔːʃənət/ *adj.* **1** (in proportion) entsprechend; **~ to sth.** proportional zu etw. **2** (in correct relation) ausgewogen; **~ to sth.** einer Sache (*Dat.*) entsprechend; **the length of the room is not ~ to its breadth** die Länge des Zimmers steht in keinem Verhältnis zu seiner Breite

P

proportionately /prəˈpɔːʃənətlɪ/ *adv.* 1 (in proportion) entsprechend 2 (in correct relation) angemessen

proportioned /prəˈpɔːʃnd/ *adj.* proportioniert; **well-/ill-~:** wohlproportioniert/schlecht proportioniert

proposal /prəˈpəʊzl/ *n.* 1 (thing proposed) Vorschlag, *der;* (offer) Angebot, *das;* **make ~s for peace** Friedensvorschläge unterbreiten; **make a ~ for doing sth.** *or* **to do sth.** einen Vorschlag machen, etw. zu tun; **his ~ for improving the system** sein Vorschlag zur Verbesserung des Systems; **draw up ~s/a ~:** Pläne/einen Plan aufstellen 2 **~ [of marriage]** [Heirats]antrag, *der* 3 (act of proposing) Unterbreitung, *die;* **he was interrupted in the middle of his ~ to her/the committee** er wurde unterbrochen, während er ihr einen Heiratsantrag machte/dem Ausschuss seinen Vorschlag unterbreitete

propose /prəˈpəʊz/
A *v.t.* 1 (put forward for consideration) vorschlagen; **~ sth. to sb.** jmdm. etw. vorschlagen; **~ marriage [to sb.]** [jmdm.] einen Heiratsantrag machen; **~ a truce** einen Waffenstillstand anbieten *od.* vorschlagen 2 (nominate) **~ sb. as/for sth.** jmdn. als/für etw. vorschlagen 3 (for drinking of toast) **~ a toast to sb./sth.** einen Trinkspruch auf jmdn./etw. ausbringen; **~ sb.'s health** sein Glas erheben, um auf jmds. Gesundheit zu trinken; **I [should like to] ~: 'The bride and groom!'** trinken wir auf das Brautpaar! 4 (intend) **~ doing** *or* **to do sth.** beabsichtigen, etw. zu tun 5 (set up as aim) planen; **~ sth. to oneself** sich (*Dat.*) etw. vornehmen; **he ~s their destruction** sein Ziel ist ihre Vernichtung
B *v.i.* 1 (offer marriage) **~ [to sb.]** jmdm. einen Heiratsantrag machen 2 ▸ **dispose B**

proposer /prəˈpəʊzə(r)/ *n.* (of motion) Antragsteller, *der*/-stellerin, *die;* (of candidate) Vorschlagende, *der/die*

proposition /prɒpəˈzɪʃn/
A *n.* 1 (proposal) Vorschlag, *der;* **make** *or* **put a ~ to sb.** jmdm. einen Vorschlag machen 2 (statement) Aussage, *die;* **Galileo's ~ that the Earth revolves around the Sun** Galileis These, dass die Erde sich um die Sonne dreht 3 (coll.: undertaking, problem) Sache, *die* (ugs.); **paying ~:** lohnendes Geschäft; **it's not a ~:** das kommt nicht infrage; **the project is no longer a practical/viable ~:** das Projekt ist nicht mehr durchführbar/rentabel; **he looks a tough/nasty ~:** er scheint ein zäher/widerlicher Typ zu sein (ugs.) 4 (Logic) Satz, *der;* Proposition, *die* (fachspr.) 5 (Math.) Satz, *der*
B *v.t.* (coll.) jmdn. anmachen (ugs.)

propositional /prɒpəˈzɪʃənl/ *adj.* 1 (Logic) propositional 2 (Math.) lehrsatzartig

propound /prəˈpaʊnd/ *v.t.* darlegen; **~ a question** eine Frage aufwerfen; **~ sth. to sb.** jmdm. etw. vortragen

proprietary /prəˈpraɪətərɪ/ *adj.* 1 (belonging to private owner) Eigentums-; ‹*Pflichten*› als Eigentümer; **~ rights/claims** Eigentumsrechte/-ansprüche 2 (characteristic of a proprietor) **have a ~ attitude to sb.** jmdn. als seinen Besitz betrachten 3 (holding property) Eigentümer-; **~ owner** Eigenbesitzer, *der*/-besitzerin, *die* (Wirtsch.) 4 (privately owned) privat 5 (under trade name) Marken-; **~ brand** *or* **make of washing powder** Markenwaschmittel, *das*

proprietary: ~ 'brand *n.* Markenprodukt, *das;* Markenfabrikat, *das;* **~ 'company** *n.* (Brit.) Privatfirma, *die;* **~ 'medicine** *n.* Markenmedikament, *das;* **~ 'name, ~ 'term** *ns.* Markenname, *der*

proprietor /prəˈpraɪətə(r)/ *n.* Inhaber, *der*/Inhaberin, *die;* (of newspaper) Besitzer, *der*/Besitzerin, *die*

proprietorial /prəpraɪəˈtɔːrɪəl/ *adj.* 1 (of proprietor) Inhaber-; ‹*Pflichten*› als Inhaber 2 (characteristic of proprietor) **have a ~ attitude to sb.** jmdn. als seinen Besitz betrachten; **~ pride** Besitzerstolz, *der*

proprietorship /prəˈpraɪətəʃɪp/ *n.* (ownership) Eigentum, *das;* (of newspaper) Besitz, *der;* **under sb.'s ~:** während jmd. Inhaber ist/war

proprietress /prəˈpraɪətrɪs/ *n.* Inhaberin, *die;* (of newspaper) Besitzerin, *die*

propriety /prəˈpraɪətɪ/ *n.* 1 *no pl.* (decency) Anstand, *der;* **with ~:** anständig; **breach of ~:** Verstoß gegen die guten Sitten 2 *in pl.* **the proprieties** die Regeln des Anstands; **observe the proprieties** Anstand und Sitte bewahren 3 *no pl.* (fitness) Angemessenheit, *die* 4 *no pl.* (accuracy) Richtigkeit, *die;* **with perfect ~:** völlig zu Recht

propulsion /prəˈpʌlʃn/ *n.* Antrieb, *der;* (driving force, lit. or fig.) Antriebskraft, *die; see also* **jet propulsion**

propulsive /prəˈpʌlsɪv/ *adj.* Antriebs-; (fig.) mobilisierend

pro rata /prəʊ ˈrɑːtə/
A *adv.* anteilmäßig
B *adj.* anteilmäßig; **be paid on a ~ basis** anteilmäßig bezahlt werden

prorogation /prəʊrəˈgeɪʃn/ *n.* Vertagung, *die* (**to** auf + *Akk.*); (Parl.: interval between sessions) Parlamentsferien *Pl.*

prorogue /prəˈrəʊg/
A *v.t.* (also Parl.) vertagen
B *v.i.* (also Parl.) sich vertagen

prosaic /prəˈzeɪɪk, prəʊˈzeɪɪk/ *adj.*, **prosaically** /prəˈzeɪɪkəlɪ, prəʊˈzeɪɪkəlɪ/ *adv.* prosaisch (geh.); nüchtern

proscenium /prəˈsiːnɪəm/ *n., pl.* **~s** *or* **proscenia** /prəˈsiːnɪə/ (Theatre) (front of stage) Proszenium, *das;* (framework) Bühnenrahmen, *der*

proscenium 'arch *n.* (Theatre) Bühnenrahmen, *der*

proscribe /prəˈskraɪb/ *v.t.* 1 (Hist.: outlaw) für vogelfrei erklären 2 (exile) verbannen; (fig.) ächten 3 (prohibit) verbieten

proscription /prəˈskrɪpʃn/ *n.* 1 (Hist.: outlawing) Ächtung, *die* 2 (exile) Verbannung, *die;* **issue a ~ against sb.** jmdn. in die Verbannung schicken 3 (prohibition) Verbot, *das*

prose /prəʊz/ *n.* 1 (form of language) Prosa, *die; attrib.* Prosa‹*werk, -stil*› 2 (Sch., Univ.) **~ [translation]** Übersetzung in die Fremdsprache; **a ~ passage for translation** ein Text zur Übersetzung in die Fremdsprache. *See also* **idyll 1; poetry**

prosecute /ˈprɒsɪkjuːt/
A *v.t.* 1 (Law) strafrechtlich verfolgen; **~ sb. for sth./doing sth.** jmdn. wegen etw. strafrechtlich verfolgen/jmdn. strafrechtlich verfolgen, weil er etw. tut/getan hat 2 (pursue) verfolgen 3 (carry on) ausüben
B *v.i.* Anzeige erstatten; **as a barrister, he preferred defending to prosecuting** als Rechtsanwalt zog er die Verteidigung der Anklage vor

prosecuting/ˈprɒsɪkjuːtɪŋ/: **~ at'torney** *n.* (Amer. Law), **~ 'counsel** *n.* (Brit. Law) Staatsanwalt, *der*/-anwältin, *die*

prosecution /prɒsɪˈkjuːʃn/ *n.* 1 (Law) (bringing to trial) [strafrechtliche] Verfolgung; (court procedure) Anklage, *die;* **start a ~ against sb.** Anklage gegen jmdn. erheben 2 (Law: prosecuting party) Anklage[vertretung], *die;* **the [case for the] ~:** die Anklage; **witness for the ~, ~ witness** Zeuge/Zeugin der Anklage; **~ lawyer** Staatsanwalt, *der*/-anwältin, *die* 3 (pursuing) Verfolgung, *die* 4 (carrying on) Ausübung, *die*

prosecutor /ˈprɒsɪkjuːtə(r)/ *n.* (Law) Ankläger, *der*/Anklägerin, *die;* **public ~:** ≈ Generalstaatsanwalt, *der*/-anwältin, *die*

proselyte /ˈprɒsɪlaɪt/ *n.* (convert; also Jewish Relig.) Proselyt, *der*/Proselytin, *die*

proselytize (**proselytise**) /ˈprɒsɪlɪtaɪz/ *v.i.* missionieren

prose: ~ writer *n.* Prosaschriftsteller, *der*/-schriftstellerin, *die;* **~ writing** *n.* Prosa, *die*

prosodic /prəˈsɒdɪk/ *adj.* prosodisch

prosodist /ˈprɒsədɪst/ *n.* Prosodiker, *der*/Prosodikerin, *die*

prosody /ˈprɒsədɪ/ *n.* 1 Verslehre, *die* 2 (Ling.) Prosodie, *die*

prospect
A /ˈprɒspekt/ *n.* 1 (extensive view) Aussicht, *die* (**of** auf + *Akk.*); (spectacle) Anblick, *der;* (mental view) Einsicht, *die* (**of** in + *Akk.*); **open [up] new ~s to sb.'s mind** jmds. geistigen Horizont erweitern 2 (expectation) Erwartung, *die* (**of** hinsichtlich); **[at the] ~ of sth./doing sth.** (mental picture, likelihood) [bei der] Aussicht auf etw. (*Akk.*)/[darauf], etw. zu tun; **what are the ~s of your coming?** wie sind die Aussichten, dass du kommst?; **have the ~ of sth., have sth. in ~:** etw. in Aussicht haben 3 *in pl.* (hope of success) Zukunftsaussichten; **a man with [good] ~s** ein Mann mit Zukunft; **a job with no ~s** eine Stelle ohne Zukunft; **sb.'s ~s of sth./doing sth.** jmds. Chancen auf etw. (*Akk.*)/darauf, etw. zu tun; **what are his ~s of being accepted?** wie stehen seine Chancen, angenommen zu werden?; **~s of survival** Überlebenschancen; **the ~s for sb./sth.** die Aussichten für jmdn./etw. 4 (possible customer) [möglicher] Kunde/[mögliche] Kundin; (possible candidate) Anwärter, *der*/Anwärterin, *die;* (possible winner) Kandidat, *der*/Kandidatin, *die;* **be a good ~ for a race/the job** bei einem Rennen gute Chancen haben/ein aussichtsreicher Kandidat für den Job sein
B /prəˈspekt/ *v.i.* (explore for mineral) prospektieren (Bergw.); nach Bodenschätzen suchen; (fig.) Ausschau halten (**for** nach); **~ for gold** nach Gold suchen
C /prəˈspekt/ *v.t.* 1 (Mining) erkunden; prospektieren (fachspr.); **~ sth. for sth.** in etw. (*Dat.*) nach etw. suchen 2 (investigate) untersuchen

prospective /prəˈspektɪv/ *adj.* 1 (expected) voraussichtlich; zukünftig ‹*Erbe, Braut*›; potenziell ‹*Käufer, Kandidat*› 2 (referring to the future) zukünftig; **make ~ enquiries** sich vorab informieren; **take a ~ view of sth.** etw. vorausschauend betrachten

prospectively /prəˈspektɪvlɪ/ *adv.* 1 (with foresight) vorsorglich 2 (with future effectiveness) in der Zukunft

prospector /prəˈspektə(r)/ *n.* Prospektor, *der* (Bergw.); (for gold) Goldsucher, *der*

prospectus /prəˈspektəs/ *n.* 1 (of enterprise) Prospekt, *der* (Wirtsch.) 2 (of book) Prospekt, *der* 3 (Brit. Sch.) Lehrprogramm, *das;* (Brit. Univ.) Studienführer, *der*

prosper /ˈprɒspə(r)/ *v.i.* gedeihen; ‹*Geschäft:*› florieren; ‹*Kunst usw.:*› eine Blütezeit erleben; ‹*Berufstätiger:*› Erfolg haben; **how is he ~ing in that business of his/in his career?** läuft sein Geschäft gut?/was macht seine Karriere?; **cheats never ~:** ≈ unrecht Gut gedeihet nicht (Spr.)

prosperity /prɒˈsperɪtɪ/ *n., no pl.* Wohlstand, *der*

prosperous /ˈprɒspərəs/ *adj.* 1 (flourishing) wohlhabend; gut gehend, florierend ‹*Unternehmen*›; (blessed with good fortune) erfolgreich; **~ years/time** Jahre/Zeit des Wohlstands 2 (auspicious) günstig

prostate /ˈprɒsteɪt/ *n.* **~ [gland]** (Anat., Zool.) Prostata, *die;* Vorsteherdrüse, *die;* **~ cancer** Prostatakrebs, *der*

prosthesis /prɒsˈθiːsɪs/ *n., pl.* **prostheses** /prɒsˈθiːsiːz/ 1 (Med.) (artificial part) Prothese, *die;* (branch of surgery) Prothetik, *die* 2 (Ling., Pros.) Prothese, *die*

prosthetic /prɒsˈθetɪk/ *adj.* (Med., Ling., Pros.) prothetisch; **~ leg** Beinprothese, *die;* **~ surgery** Prothetik, *die*

prosthetics /prɒsˈθetɪks/ *n., no pl.* (Med.) Prothetik, *die*

prostitute /ˈprɒstɪtjuːt/
A *n.* 1 (woman) Prostituierte, *die* 2 (man) Strichjunge, *der* (salopp)
B *v.t.* zur Prostitution anbieten; (fig.) prostituieren ‹*Talent, Integrität*›; **~ oneself** (lit. or fig.) sich prostituieren

prostitution /prɒstɪˈtjuːʃn/ *n.* (lit. or fig.) Prostitution, *die*

prostrate
A /ˈprɒstreɪt/ *adj.* 1 [auf dem Bauch] ausgestreckt; **she lay ~ before him** sie lag ihm zu Füßen; **~ with grief/shame** von Schmerz/Trauer übermannt 2 (exhausted) erschöpft; **be ~ with fever** vom Fieber geschwächt sein 3 (Bot.) kriechend
B /prɒˈstreɪt, prəˈstreɪt/ *v.t.* 1 (lay flat) zu Boden

P

werfen ‹*Person*› **2** (make submissive, lay low) zermürben; (overcome emotionally) übermannen **3** (exhaust) erschöpfen; **be ~d by exhaustion** vor Erschöpfung ganz kraftlos sein

C *v. refl.* (throw oneself down) **~ oneself [at sth./before sb.]** sich [vor etw./jmdm.] niederwerfen; **~ oneself at sb.'s feet** sich jmdm. zu Füßen werfen; **~ oneself [before sb.]** (humble oneself) sich [vor jmdm.] demütigen

prostration /prɒˈstreɪʃn, prəˈstreɪʃn/ *n.* **1** (prostrating oneself) Fußfall, *der;* **in ~:** [demütig] ausgestreckt **2** (submission) Unterwürfigkeit, *die;* (subjugation) Unterdrückung, *die* **3** (being emotionally overcome) Erschütterung, *die* **4** (reduction to powerlessness) (of country or party) Entmachtung, *die;* (of business) Ruin, *der;* **reduce a country to economic ~:** ein Land wirtschaftlich ruinieren **5** (exhaustion) Erschöpfung, *die*

prosy /ˈprəʊzɪ/ *adj.* langatmig

Prot /prɒt/ ▸ **Prod**

protagonist /prəʊˈtægənɪst/ *n.* **1** (advocate) Vorkämpfer, *der*/Vorkämpferin, *die;* (spokesperson) Wortführer, *der*/-führerin, *die* **2** (Lit./Theatre: chief character) Protagonist, *der*/Protagonistin, *die;* (fig.) Hauptakteur, *der*/-akteurin, *die*

protean /ˈprəʊtɪən, prəʊˈti:ən/ *adj.* proteisch (geh.)

protect /prəˈtekt/ *v.t.* **1** (defend) schützen (**from** vor + *Dat.*, **against** gegen); **~ed by law** gesetzlich geschützt; **they led happy ~ed lives** sie führten ein glückliches, behütetes Leben; **~ sb. against** *or* **from himself/herself** jmdn. vor sich (*Dat.*) selbst schützen; **~ one's/sb.'s interests** seine/jmds. Interessen wahren; **~ the peace** den Frieden sichern **2** (preserve) unter [Natur]schutz stellen ‹*Pflanze, Tier, Gebiet*›; **~ed plants/animals** geschützte Pflanzen/Tiere; **the golden eagle is a ~ed bird** der Steinadler steht unter Naturschutz **3** (give legal immunity to) schützen; **the law ~s foreign diplomats** ausländische Diplomaten genießen den Schutz der Immunität; **be a ~ed tenant** mietrechtlich geschützt sein **4** (Econ.) durch Protektionismus schützen **5** (render safe) sichern ‹*Gerät, Leitung*›

protected /prəˈtektɪd/: **~ ˈspecies** *n.* geschützte Art; **~ ˈstate** *n.* (Polit.) Schutzstaat, *der*

protection /prəˈtekʃn/ *n.* **1** (defence) Schutz, *der* (**from** vor + *Dat.*, **against** gegen); **under the ~ of sb./sth.** unter jmds. Schutz/dem Schutz einer Sache (*Gen.*); **[under] police ~:** [unter] Polizeischutz **2** (immunity from molestation) Schutz, *der;* (money paid) Schutzgeld, *das* **3** (of wildlife etc.) Schutz, *der* **4** (legal immunity) Immunität, *die* **5** (Econ.) Schutz, *der;* (system) Protektionismus, *der* **6** (protective agent) Schutz, *der;* **as a ~ against** zum *od.* als Schutz gegen

proˈtection factor *n.* [Licht]schutzfaktor, *der*

protectionism /prəˈtekʃənɪzm/ *n., no pl.* (Econ.) Protektionismus, *der*

protectionist /prəˈtekʃənɪst/ (Econ.)

A *n.* Protektionist, *der*/Protektionistin, *die*

B *adj.* protektionistisch

protection: ~ money *n.* Schutzgeld, *das;* **~ racket** *n.* Erpresserorganisation, *die;* **run a ~ racket** die Erpressung von Schutzgeldern organisieren

protective /prəˈtektɪv/ *adj.* **1** (protecting) schützend; Schutz‹*hülle, -anstrich, -vorrichtung, -maske*›; **be ~ towards sb.** fürsorglich gegenüber jmdm. sein; **~ instinct** Beschützerinstinkt, *der;* **be ~ against sth.** vor etw. (*Dat.*) schützen; **butterflies/tigers have ~ camouflage/colouring** Schmetterlinge/Tiger haben eine Tarntracht/Tarn- *od.* Schutzfärbung; **the soldiers wore ~ camouflage** die Soldaten trugen Tarnanzüge; **~ clothing** Schutzkleidung, *die* **2** (Econ.) protektionistisch; Schutz‹*zoll*›

protective: ~ arˈrest, **~ ˈcustody** *ns.* Schutzgewahrsam, *der* (Amtsspr.); Schutzhaft, *die*

protectively /prəˈtektɪvlɪ/ *adv.* schützend; **she brought up her children too ~:** sie hat ihre Kinder zu behütet aufgezogen; **these insects are ~ coloured** diese Insekten haben eine Schutz- *od.* Tarnfärbung; **a vaccine acts** *or* **works ~:** ein Impfstoff hat eine Schutzwirkung

protector /prəˈtektə(r)/ *n.* **1** (person) Beschützer, *der*/Beschützerin, *die* **2** (thing) Schutz, *der; in comb.* -schutz, *der* **3** (regent) Regent, *der;* **P~ of the Realm** (Brit. Hist.) Regent des Königreiches

protectorate /prəˈtektərət/ *n.* (Int. Law, Brit. Hist.) Protektorat, *das*

protégé /ˈprɒteʒeɪ/ *n.* Protegé, *der* (geh.); Schützling, *der*

protégée /ˈprɒteʒeɪ/ *n.* Schützling, *der*

protein /ˈprəʊti:n/ *n.* (Chem.) Protein, *das* (fachspr.); Eiweiß, *das;* **a high-~ diet** eine eiweißreiche Kost

ˈprotein-rich *adj.* eiweißreich; proteinreich (fachspr.)

pro tem /prəʊ ˈtem/ (coll.)

A *adj.* befristet; ‹*Vorsitzender*› auf Zeit

B *adv.* vorübergehend

pro tempore /prəʊ ˈtempərɪ/

A *adj.* befristet; (temporary) vorübergehend

B *adv.* vorübergehend

protest

A /ˈprəʊtest/ *n.* **1** (remonstrance) Beschwerde, *die;* (Sport) Protest, *der;* **make** *or* **lodge a ~ [against sb./sth.]** eine Beschwerde [gegen jmdn./etw.] einreichen **2** (show of unwillingness, gesture of disapproval) **~[s]** Protest, *der;* **under ~:** unter Protest; **in ~ [against sth.]** aus Protest [gegen etw.] **3** *no pl., no art.* (dissent) Protest, *der;* **the right of ~:** das Recht zu protestieren; **literature/song of ~:** Protestliteratur, *die*/Protestsong, *der* **4** (Brit. Commerc.: written declaration) Protest, *der*

B /prəˈtest/ *v.t.* **1** (affirm) beteuern; **I ~, I have never seen you before** ich versichere, dass ich Sie noch niemals zuvor gesehen habe **2** (Amer.: object to) protestieren gegen **3** (Commerc.) protestieren; zu Protest gehen lassen; **be ~ed** zu Protest gehen

C /prəˈtest/ *v.i.* protestieren; (make written or formal ~) Protest einlegen (**to** bei); **~ about sb./sth.** gegen jmdn./etw. protestieren; **~ against being/doing sth.** dagegen protestieren, dass man etw. ist/tut

Protestant /ˈprɒtɪstənt/ (Relig.)

A *n.* Protestant, *der*/Protestantin, *die;* Evangelische, *der/die*

B *adj.* protestantisch; evangelisch

Protestantism /ˈprɒtɪstəntɪzm/ *n., no pl., no art.* (Relig.) Protestantismus, *der*

protestation /prɒtɪˈsteɪʃn/ *n.* **1** (affirmation) Beteuerung, *die;* **a formal ~ that ...:** eine formelle Erklärung, dass ...; **~s of innocence** Unschuldsbeteuerungen *Pl.* **2** (protest) Protest, *der*

protester /prəˈtestə(r)/ *n.* (dissenter) Protestierende, *der/die;* (at demonstration) Demonstrant, *der*/Demonstrantin, *die*

protest /ˈprəʊtest/: **~ march** *n.* Protestmarsch, *der;* **~ marcher** ▸ **marcher;** **~ song** *n.* Protestsong, *der;* **~ vote** *n.* Proteststimme, *die*

proto- /prəʊtə/ *in comb.* proto-/Proto-; **~Germanic** urgermanisch

protocol /ˈprəʊtəkɒl/ *n.* Protokoll, *das;* **observe/defy ~:** das Protokoll befolgen/sich über das Protokoll hinwegsetzen

proton /ˈprəʊtɒn/ *n.* (Phys.) Proton, *das*

protoplasm /ˈprəʊtəplæzəm/ *n.* (Biol.) Protoplasma, *das*

prototype /ˈprəʊtətaɪp/ *n.* Prototyp, *der;* **a ~ aeroplane/machine** der Prototyp eines Flugzeugs/einer Maschine

protozoa /prəʊtəˈzəʊə/ *n. pl.* (Zool.) Protozoen *Pl.*

protozoan /prəʊtəˈzəʊən/ (Zool.)

A *adj.* protozoisch

B *n.* Protozoon, *das*

protract /prəˈtrækt/ *v.t.* verlängern; **a ~ed argument/visit/illness/period of idleness** ein langwieriger Streit/ein längerer Besuch/eine längere Krankheit/eine längere Untätigkeit; **delays became more and more ~ed** die Verzögerungen wurden immer gravierender

protraction /prəˈtrækʃn/ *n.* Verlängerung, *die*

protractor /prəˈtræktə(r)/ *n.* (Geom.) Winkelmesser, *der*

protrude /prəˈtru:d/

A *v.i.* herausragen (**from** aus); ‹*Zähne:*› vorstehen; **~ above/beneath/from behind sth.** etw. überragen/unter/hinter etw. (*Dat.*) hervorragen; **~ beyond sth.** über etw. (*Akk.*) hinausragen

B *v.t.* ausstrecken ‹*Fühler*›; vorstülpen ‹*Lippen*›

protrusion /prəˈtru:ʒn/ *n.* **1** (projection) (of jaw or teeth) Vorstehen, *das* **2** (projecting thing) Vorsprung, *der*

protuberance /prəˈtju:bərəns/ *n.* **1** (state) Vorstehen, *das* **2** (thing) Auswuchs, *der*

protuberant /prəˈtju:bərənt/ *adj.* vorstehend; hervortretend ‹*Augen*›

proud /praʊd/

A *adj.* **1** stolz; **it made me [feel] really ~:** es erfüllte mich mit Stolz; **I'm ~ to say I'm never late** ich kann mit Stolz behaupten, nie zu spät zu kommen; **~ to do sth.** *or* **to be doing sth.** stolz darauf, etw. zu tun; **~ of sb./sth./doing sth.** stolz auf jmdn./etw./darauf, etw. zu tun; **he is far too ~ of himself/his house** er bildet sich (*Dat.*) zu viel ein/zu viel auf sein Haus ein; **she answered his offer with a ~ refusal** sie lehnte sein Angebot stolz ab **2** (arrogant) hochmütig; stolz ‹*Tier*›; **I'm not too ~ to scrub floors** ich bin mir nicht zu gut zum Fußbodenschrubben **3** (Brit.: projecting) herausstehend; **stand** *or* **be ~ of sth.** (vertically) über etw. (*Akk.*) herausragen; **stand out too ~:** zu weit herausragen **4** **~ flesh** (Med.) wildes Fleisch

B *adv.* (Brit. coll.) **do sb. ~** (treat generously) jmdn. verwöhnen; (honour greatly) jmdm. eine Ehrung bereiten; **do oneself ~:** sich (*Dat.*) etwas Gutes tun

proud-hearted /praʊdˈhɑ:tɪd/ *adj.* stolz

proudly /ˈpraʊdlɪ/ *adv.* **1** stolz; **remain ~ silent/loyal** stolz schweigen/seine Loyalität bewahren **2** (arrogantly) hochmütig

provable /ˈpru:vəbl/ *adj.* beweisbar; nachweisbar

prove /pru:v/

A *v.t., p.p.* **~d** *or* **~n** /ˈpru:vn/ **1** beweisen; nachweisen ‹*Identität*›; **~ one's ability** sein Können unter Beweis stellen; **an expert of ~n ability** ein ausgewiesener Fachmann; **his guilt/innocence was ~d, he was ~d [to be] guilty/innocent** er wurde überführt/seine Unschuld wurde bewiesen; **~ sb. right/wrong** ‹*Ereignis:*› jmdm. Recht/Unrecht geben; **be ~d wrong** *or* **to be false** ‹*Theorie, System:*› widerlegt werden; **~ sth. to be true** beweisen, dass etw. wahr ist; **~ one's/sb.'s case** *or* **point** beweisen, dass man Recht hat/jmdm. Recht geben; **it was ~d that ...:** es stellte sich heraus *od.* erwies *od.* zeigte sich, dass ...; **not ~n** (Scot. Law) Schuldbeweis nicht erbracht; *see also* **exception 1; point A 7** **2** (establish validity of) beglaubigen ‹*Testament*› **3** (Cookery: cause to rise) ‹*Hefe:*› gehen lassen ‹*Teig*›

B *v. refl., p.p.* **~d** *or* **~n: ~ oneself** sich bewähren; **~ oneself intelligent/a good player** sich als intelligent/als [ein] guter Spieler erweisen

C *v.i., p.p.* **~d** *or* **~n** **1** (be found to be) sich erweisen als; **~ [to be] unnecessary/interesting/a failure** sich als unnötig/interessant/[ein] Fehlschlag erweisen **2** (Cookery: rise) [auf]gehen

proven /ˈpru:vn/ ▸ **prove**

provenance /ˈprɒvɪnəns/ *n.* Herkunft, *die*

Provençal /prɒvɑ̃ˈsɑ:l/

A *adj.* provenzalisch; *see also* **English A**

B *n.* **1** (language) Provenzalisch, *das* **2** (person) Provenzale, *der*/Provenzalin, *die. See also* **English B 1**

Provence /prɒˈvɑ̃s/ *pr. n.* die Provence

provender /ˈprɒvɪndə(r)/ *n.* Futter, *das;* (joc.: food for humans) Futter, *das* (salopp)

proverb /ˈprɒvɜ:b/ *n.* Sprichwort, *das;* **be a ~** (fig.) ‹*Eigenschaft:*› sprichwörtlich sein; **[Book**

of] **P~s** *sing.* (Bibl.) [Buch der] Sprüche; Sprüche Salomos

proverbial /prəˈvɜːbɪəl/ *adj.*, **proverbially** /prəˈvɜːbɪəlɪ/ *adv.* sprichwörtlich

provide /prəˈvaɪd/ *v.t.* **1** (supply) besorgen; sorgen für; liefern ‹*Beweis*›; bereitstellen ‹*Dienst, Geld*›; **instructions are ~d with every machine** mit jeder Maschine wird eine Anleitung mitgeliefert; **~ homes/materials/a car for sb.** jmdm. Unterkünfte/Materialien/ein Auto [zur Verfügung] stellen; **~ shade for sb.** ‹*Baum usw.:*› jmdm. Schatten spenden; **~ sb. with money** jmdn. unterhalten; (for journey etc.) jmdm. Geld zur Verfügung stellen; **be [well] ~d with sth.** mit etw. [wohl] versorgt *od.* [wohl] versehen sein; **~ oneself with sth.** sich (*Dat.*) etw. besorgen **2** (stipulate) ‹*Vertrag, Gesetz:*› vorsehen **3** **providing that** ▸**provided**

(Phrasal verbs)

- **~ against** *v.t.* sich wappnen gegen; **have ~d against sth.** gegen etw. gewappnet sein
- **~ for** *v.t.* **1** (make provision for) vorsorgen für; Vorsorge treffen für; ‹*Plan, Gesetz:*› vorsehen ‹*Maßnahmen, Steuern*›; ‹*Schätzung:*› berücksichtigen ‹*Inflation*›; **has everybody been ~d for?** sind alle versorgt? **2** (maintain) sorgen für, versorgen ‹*Familie, Kind*›

provided /prəˈvaɪdɪd/ *conj.* **~ [that] ...** vorausgesetzt, [dass] ...

providence /ˈprɒvɪdəns/ *n.* **1** (care of God etc.) Vorsehung, *die;* **[divine] ~:** die [göttliche] Vorsehung; **a special ~:** eine besondere Fügung [des Schicksals] **2** **P~** (God) der Himmel **3** (foresight) Weitblick, *der;* **have the ~ to do sth.** so vorausschauend sein, etw. zu tun **4** (thrift) Sparsamkeit, *die*

provident /ˈprɒvɪdənt/ *adj.* **1** (having foresight) weitblickend; vorausschauend **2** (thrifty) sparsam; haushälterisch; **P~ Society** (Brit.) ▸**Friendly Society**

providential /prɒvɪˈdenʃl/ *adj.* **1** (opportune) **it was ~ that ...:** es war ein Glück, dass ...; **your arrival was quite ~:** es war wirklich ein Glück, dass du [dazu] kamst **2** (of divine providence) durch die [göttliche] Vorsehung bewirkt ‹*Befreiung, Rettung*›

providentially /prɒvɪˈdenʃəlɪ/ *adv.* **1** (opportunely) durch einen glücklichen Zufall; **help came quite ~:** die Hilfe kam wie eine glückliche Fügung; **work out ~:** sich glücklich fügen **2** (by divine providence) durch die [göttliche] Vorsehung

providently /ˈprɒvɪdəntlɪ/ *adv.* **1** (with foresight) vorausschauend ‹*handeln*›; **he had ~ equipped himself with ...:** er hatte sich vorsorglich mit ... ausgestattet **2** (thriftily) sparsam, haushälterisch ‹*mit etw. umgehen*›

provider /prəˈvaɪdə(r)/ *n.* **1** **he was the chief ~ of money/work** er war der Hauptgeldgeber/der größte Arbeitgeber; **the principal ~ of subsidies** der Hauptsubventionsträger **2** (breadwinner) Ernährer, *der*/Ernährerin, *die;* Versorger, *der*/Versorgerin, *die;* **be the ~ for sb.** jmdn. ernähren *od.* versorgen

province /ˈprɒvɪns/ *n.* **1** (administrative area) Provinz, *die* **2** **the ~s** (regions outside capital) die Provinz (oft abwertend) **3** (sphere of action) [Arbeits-, Tätigkeits-, Wirkungs]bereich, *der;* [Arbeits-, Tätigkeits]gebiet, *das;* (area of responsibility) Zuständigkeitsbereich, *der;* **that is not my ~:** da kenne ich mich nicht aus; (not my responsibility) dafür bin ich nicht zuständig

provincial /prəˈvɪnʃl/

A *adj.* Provinz-; (of the provinces) Provinz-; (typical of the provinces) provinziell

B *n.* Provinzbewohner, *der*/-bewohnerin, *die* (oft abwertend); (of the provinces also) Provinzler, *der*/Provinzlerin, *die* (abwertend)

provincialism /prəˈvɪnʃəlɪzm/ *n.* **1** (mode of thought) Provinzialismus, *der* (abwertend) **2** (Ling.) Provinzialismus, *der*

provincially /prəˈvɪnʃəlɪ/ *adv.* provinziell; **~ narrow-minded** provinziell und engstirnig

proving ground /ˈpruːvɪŋgraʊnd/ *n.* Versuchsgelände, *das*

provision /prəˈvɪʒn/ *n.* **1** (providing) Bereitstellung, *die;* **as a** *or* **by way of ~ against ...:** zum Schutz gegen ...; **~ of medical care** medizinische Versorgung; **make ~ for** vorsorgen *od.* Vorsorge treffen für ‹*Notfall*›; berücksichtigen ‹*Inflation*›; **make ~ for sb. in one's will** jmdn. in seinem Testament bedenken; **make ~ against sth.** Vorkehrungen zum Schutz gegen etw. treffen **2** (amount available) Vorrat, *der* **3** *in pl.* (food) Lebensmittel; (for expedition also) Proviant, *der;* **stock up with ~s** Lebensmittelvorräte anlegen **4** (legal statement) Verordnung, *die;* (clause) Bestimmung, *die*

provisional /prəˈvɪʒənl/

A *adj.* vorläufig; provisorisch; **~ government** provisorische Regierung; **~ arrangement** Provisorium, *das*

B *n. in pl.* **the P~s** die provisorische IRA

provisional: P~ IR'A *n.* provisorische IRA; **~ licence** *n.* vorläufige Fahrerlaubnis

provisionally /prəˈvɪʒənəlɪ/ *adv.* vorläufig; provisorisch

proviso /prəˈvaɪzəʊ/ *n., pl.* **~s** Vorbehalt, *der*

provisory /prəˈvaɪzərɪ/ *adj.* **1** (conditional) vorbehaltlich; **~ clause** Vorbehaltsklausel, *die* **2** (provisional) vorläufig; provisorisch

provocation /prɒvəˈkeɪʃn/ *n.* Provokation, *die;* Herausforderung, *die;* **be under severe ~:** stark provoziert werden; **he hit him without ~:** er hat ihn ohne jeden Anlass geschlagen; **he loses his temper at** *or* **on the slightest** *or* **smallest ~:** er verliert die Beherrschung beim geringsten Anlass

provocative /prəˈvɒkətɪv/ *adj.* provozierend; herausfordernd; (sexually) aufreizend; **his actions were felt to be ~:** seine Aktionen wurden als Provokation empfunden; **be ~ of** hervorrufen; provozieren; **be ~** (be intentionally annoying) provozieren

provoke /prəˈvəʊk/ *v.t.* **1** (annoy, incite) provozieren ‹*Person*›; reizen ‹*Person, Tier*›; (sexually) aufreizen; **be easily ~d** leicht reizbar sein; sich leicht provozieren lassen; **~ sb. to anger/fury** jmdn. in Wut (*Akk.*)/zur Raserei bringen; **~ sb. into doing sth.** jmdn. so sehr provozieren *od.* reizen, dass er etw. tut; **he was finally ~d into taking action** er ließ sich schließlich dazu hinreißen *od.* provozieren, etwas zu unternehmen **2** (give rise to) hervorrufen; erregen ‹*Ärger, Neugier, Zorn*›; auslösen ‹*Kontroverse, Krise*›; herausfordern ‹*Widerstand*›; verursachen ‹*Zwischenfall*›; Anlass geben zu ‹*Klagen, Kritik*›; **what ~d the incident?** wie kam es zu dem Zwischenfall?

provoking /prəˈvəʊkɪŋ/ *adj.* provozierend; herausfordernd; **his behaviour/refusal was [very] ~:** sein Benehmen/seine Weigerung war eine [große] Provokation

provost /ˈprɒvəst/ *n.* **1** (Scot.: mayor) Bürgermeister, *der*/-meisterin, *die;* **Lord P~:** Oberbürgermeister, *der* **2** (Eccl.) Propst, *der*/Pröpstin, *die* **3** (Univ.) Provost, *der* **4** /prəˈvəʊ/ ▸**provost marshal**

provost /prəˈvəʊ/: **~ guard** *n.* (Amer. Mil.) *Sondertrupp der Militärpolizei;* **~ 'marshal** *n.* (Mil.) *Kommandeur der Militärpolizei*

prow /praʊ/ *n.* (Naut.) Bug, *der*

prowess /ˈpraʊɪs/ *n.* **1** (valour) Tapferkeit, *die* **2** (skill) Fähigkeiten *Pl.;* Können, *das;* **~ at sports** [große] Sportlichkeit; **sexual ~:** sexuelle Leistungsfähigkeit

prowl /praʊl/

A *v.i.* streifen; **~ about/around sth.** etw. durchstreifen; **~ about** *or* **around** herumschleichen (ugs.)

B *v.t.* durchstreifen

C *n.* Streifzug, *der;* **be on the ~:** auf einem Streifzug sein; (fig. in search of sexual contact) was zum Vernaschen suchen (salopp)

'prowl car *n.* (Amer.) Streifenwagen, *der*

prowler /ˈpraʊlə(r)/ *n.* **the police have warned of ~s in the area** die Polizei warnt vor verdächtigen Personen, die in der Gegend herumstreifen; **see a ~ in the back yard** sehen, wie jmd. im Hinterhof herumschleicht (ugs.)

prox. /prɒks/ *abbr.* = **proximo** n. M.

proximate /ˈprɒksɪmət/ *adj.* unmittelbar ‹*Ursache, Zukunft*›; nächst... ‹*Zukunft*›

proximity /prɒkˈsɪmɪtɪ/ *n., no pl.* Nähe, *die* (**to** zu); **a house with equal ~ to the shops and to the beach** ein Haus, das gleichermaßen nah zu den Geschäften und zum Strand liegt

prox'imity fuse *n.* (Mil.) [An]näherungszünder, *der*

proximo /ˈprɒksɪməʊ/ *adj.* (Commerc.) [des] nächsten Monats

proxy /ˈprɒksɪ/ *n.* **1** (agency, document) Vollmacht, *die;* Bevollmächtigung, *die;* **by ~:** durch einen Bevollmächtigten/eine Bevollmächtigte; **give one's ~ to sb.** jmdn. bevollmächtigen; **marriage by ~:** ≈ Ferntrauung, *die; see also* **stand A 7** **2** (person) Bevollmächtigte, *der/die;* (vote) durch einen Bevollmächtigten/eine Bevollmächtigte abgegebene Stimme; **make sb. one's ~:** jmdn. bevollmächtigen

prude /pruːd/ *n.* prüder Mensch

prudence /ˈpruːdəns/ *n., no pl.* Besonnenheit, *die;* Überlegtheit, *die;* **act with ~:** besonnen *od.* überlegt handeln

prudent /ˈpruːdənt/ *adj.* **1** (careful) besonnen ‹*Person*›; besonnen, überlegt ‹*Verhalten*› **2** (circumspect) vorsichtig; **think it more ~ to do sth.** es für klüger halten, etw. zu tun

prudently /ˈpruːdəntlɪ/ *adv.* **1** (in a prudent manner) besonnen, überlegt ‹*handeln, sich verhalten*›; **they ~ waited for more information before acting** sie warteten klugerweise ab, bis sie mehr wussten, ehe sie handelten **2** (circumspectly) vorsichtig

prudery /ˈpruːdərɪ/ *n., no pl.* Prüderie, *die*

prudish /ˈpruːdɪʃ/ *adj.* prüde

prune[1] /pruːn/ *n.* **1** (fruit) **[dried] ~:** Back- *od.* Dörrpflaume, *die* **2** (coll.: simpleton) Trottel, *der* (ugs. abwertend)

prune[2] *v.t.* **1** (trim) [be]schneiden; **~ back** zurückschneiden **2** (lop off) **~ [away/off]** ab- *od.* wegschneiden; **~ [out]** herausschneiden **3** (fig.: reduce) reduzieren; **~ back** Abstriche machen an (+ *Dat.*) ‹*Projekt*›

pruning shears /ˈpruːnɪŋ ʃɪəz/ *n. pl.* Gartenschere, *die;* Rosenschere, *die*

prurience /ˈprʊərɪəns/ *n., no pl.* Lüsternheit, *die*

prurient /ˈprʊərɪənt/ *adj.* lüstern

pruritus /prʊəˈraɪtəs/ *n.* (Med.) Pruritus, *der* (fachspr.); Hautjucken, *das*

Prussia /ˈprʌʃə/ *pr. n.* (Hist.) Preußen (*das*)

Prussian /ˈprʌʃən/

A *adj.* preußisch

B *n.* **1** (person) Preuße, *der*/Preußin, *die* **2** (language) **Old ~:** Altpreußisch, *das*

Prussian 'blue

A *n.* Preußischblau, *das*

B *adj.* preußischblau

prussic /ˈprʌsɪk/ *adj.* (Chem.) **~ acid** Blausäure, *die*

pry[1] /praɪ/ *v.i.* neugierig sein

(Phrasal verbs)

- **~ a'bout** *v.i.* herumschnüffeln (ugs. abwertend) *od.* -spionieren
- **~ into** *v.t.* seine Nase stecken in (+ *Akk.*) (ugs.) ‹*Angelegenheit*›; herumschnüffeln in (+ *Dat.*) (ugs. abwertend) ‹*Buch, Brief*›

pry[2] *v.t.* (Amer.) **1** (get with effort) **~ sth. open** etw. aufbrechen; **~ a secret** *etc.* **out of sb.** jmdm. ein Geheimnis *usw.* abringen **2** ▸**prise**

prying /ˈpraɪɪŋ/ *adj.* neugierig

PS *abbr.* = **postscript** PS

psalm /sɑːm/ *n.* (Eccl.) Psalm, *der;* **the Book of P~s** (Bibl.) das Buch der Psalmen; **the P~s** (Bibl.) die Psalmen

'psalm book *n.* (Eccl.) Psalter, *der*

psalter /ˈsɔːltə(r), ˈsɒltə(r)/ *n.* Psalter, *der*

psaltery /ˈsɔːltərɪ, ˈsɒltərɪ/ *n.* (Mus.) Psalterium, *das*

PSBR *abbr.* (Brit.) = **public sector borrowing requirement** ▸**public sector**

psephologist /seˈfɒlədʒɪst/ *n.* Psephologe, *der*/Psephologin, *die* (fachspr.); Wahlanalytiker, *der*/-analytikerin, *die*

psephology /seˈfɒlədʒɪ/ *n, no pl., no art.* (Polit.) Psephologie, *die* (fachspr.); Wahlanalytik, *die*

pseud /sju:d/ (coll.)
A *adj.* **1▸** (pretentious) pseudointellektuell **2▸** ▸**pseudo A 1**
B *n.* ▸**pseudo B**

pseudo /'sju:dəʊ/
A *adj.* **1▸** (sham, spurious) unecht; **intellectuals, real or ~:** Intellektuelle, seien es richtige oder solche, die gern welche wären **2▸** (insincere) verlogen
B *n., pl.* **~s** **1▸** (pretentious person) Möchtegern, *der* (ugs. spött.) **2▸** (insincere person) Heuchler, *der*/Heuchlerin, *die*

pseudo- /sju:dəʊ/ *in comb.* pseudo-/Pseudo- (fachspr., geh.)

pseudonym /'sju:dənɪm/ *n.* Pseudonym, *das*

pshaw /pʃɔ:, ʃɔ:/ *int.* (arch.) *expr. contempt* pah; *expr. impatience* heieiei

psoriasis /sə'raɪəsɪs/ *n., pl.* **psoriases** /sə'raɪəsi:z/ ▸**❶ p. 1231** (Med.) Psoriasis, *die* (fachspr.); Schuppenflechte, *die*

psst, pst /pst/ *int.:* st

PST *abbr.* **= Pacific Standard Time** pazifische Standardzeit

psych /saɪk/ *v.t.* (coll.) **~ sb. out** jmdn. durchschauen; **~ sb./oneself up** jmdn./sich einstimmen

psyche /'saɪkɪ/ *n.* Psyche, *die*

psychedelic /saɪkɪ'delɪk/
A *adj.* psychedelisch
B *n.* Psychedelikum, *das;* psychedelische Substanz

psychiatric /saɪkɪ'ætrɪk/ *adj.* psychiatrisch

psychiatrist /saɪ'kaɪətrɪst/ *n.* ▸**❶ p. 1260** Psychiater, *der*/Psychiaterin, *die; see also* **couch[1] A 2**

psychiatry /saɪ'kaɪətrɪ/ *n.* Psychiatrie, *die*

psychic /'saɪkɪk/
A *adj.* **1▸** ▸**psychical 1** **2▸** ▸**psychical 2** **3▸** (having occult powers) **be ~:** übernatürliche Fähigkeiten haben; **you must be ~** (fig.) du kannst wohl Gedanken lesen
B *n.* (medium) Medium, *das;* (clairvoyant) Hellseher, *der*/-seherin, *die*

psychical /'saɪkɪkl/ *adj.* **1▸** (of the soul) psychisch; seelisch; **~ life** Seelenleben, *das* **2▸** (of paranormal phenomena) parapsychisch; **~ research** Parapsychologie, *die*

psycho /'saɪkəʊ/ (coll.)
A *adj.* verrückt (ugs.)
B *n., pl.* **~s** Verrückte, *der/die* (ugs.)

psycho'analyse *v.t.* psychoanalysieren (fachspr.); psychoanalytisch behandeln

psychoa'nalysis *n.* Psychoanalyse, *die*

psycho'analyst *n.* ▸**❶ p. 1260** Psychoanalytiker, *der*/-analytikerin, *die*

psychoana'lytic, psychoana'lytical *adj.* psychoanalytisch

psychological /saɪkə'lɒdʒɪkl/ *adj.* **1▸** (of the mind) psychisch ‹*Problem*›; psychologisch ‹*Wirkung, Druck*›; *see also* **block A 12** **2▸** (of psychology) psychologisch

psychologically /saɪkə'lɒdʒɪkəlɪ/ *adv.* **1▸** (mentally) psychisch **2▸** (in relation to psychology) psychologisch

psychological: ~ 'profile *n.* psychologisches Profil; **~ 'warfare** *n., no pl.* psychologische Kriegführung

psychologist /saɪ'kɒlədʒɪst/ *n.* ▸**❶ p. 1260** (also fig.) Psychologe, *der*/Psychologin, *die*

psychology /saɪ'kɒlədʒɪ/ *n.* **1▸** Psychologie, *die* **2▸** (characteristics) Psychologie, *die* (ugs.); **I can't make out his ~:** ich werde aus ihm nicht schlau (ugs.)

psychometric /saɪkə'metrɪk/ *adj.* psychometrisch

psychopath /'saɪkəpæθ/ *n.* Psychopath, *der*/Psychopathin, *die*

psychopathic /saɪkə'pæθɪk/ *adj.* psychopathisch

psychopathology /saɪkəʊpə'θɒlədʒɪ/ *n., no pl.* Psychopathologie, *die*

psychosis /saɪ'kəʊsɪs/ *n., pl.* **psychoses** /saɪ'kəʊsi:z/ Psychose, *die*

psychosomatic /saɪkəʊsə'mætɪk/ *adj.* (Med.) psychosomatisch

psychotherapist /saɪkəʊ'θerəpɪst/ *n.* ▸**❶ p. 1260** Psychotherapeut, *der*/-therapeutin, *die*

psycho'therapy *n., no pl.* (Med.) Psychotherapie, *die;* **treat sth. by ~:** etw. psychotherapeutisch behandeln

psychotic /saɪ'kɒtɪk/
A *adj.* psychotisch; **~ illness** Psychose, *die*
B *n.* Psychotiker, *der*/Psychotikerin, *die*

pt. *abbr.* **1▸ = part** T. **2▸ = pint** pt. **3▸ = point** Pkt.; **pts.** Pkte.

PT *abbr.* **= physical training**

PTA *abbr.* **= parent-teacher association**

ptarmigan /'tɑ:mɪgən/ *n.* (Ornith.) Schneehuhn, *das*

Pte. *abbr.* (Mil.) **= Private**

pterodactyl /terə'dæktɪl/ *n.* (Palaeont.) Pterodaktylus, *der;* Flugfinger, *der*

PTO *abbr.* **= please turn over** b. w.

pub /pʌb/ *n.* (Brit.) Kneipe, *die* (ugs.); (esp. in British Isles) Pub, *das; attrib.* Kneipen-; **go to the ~:** in die Kneipe gehen

'pub crawl *n.* (Brit. coll.) Zechtour, *die;* Bierreise, *die* (ugs. scherzh.); Zug durch die Gemeinde (ugs. scherzh.)

puberty /'pju:bətɪ/ *n., no pl., no art.* Pubertät, *die;* **at ~:** in *od.* während der Pubertät; **age of ~:** Pubertätsalter, *das*

pubescent /pju:'besənt/ *adj.* heranreifend

pub food, pub grub *ns., no pl.* Kneipenessen, *das*

pubic /'pju:bɪk/ *adj.* (Anat.) Scham-

pubis /'pju:bɪs/ *n., pl.* **pubes** /'pju:bi:z/ (Anat.) Schambein, *das*

public /'pʌblɪk/
A *adj.* öffentlich; **~ assembly** Volksversammlung, *die;* **~ confidence** das Vertrauen der Öffentlichkeit; **a ~ danger/service** eine Gefahr für die/ein Dienst an der Allgemeinheit; **the ~ good** das allgemeine Wohl; **be a matter of ~ knowledge** allgemein bekannt sein; **in the ~ eye** im Blickpunkt der Öffentlichkeit; **make a ~ announcement of sth.** etw. öffentlich bekannt geben *od.* machen; **make a ~ protest** öffentlich protestieren; **make sth. ~:** etw. publik (geh.) od. bekannt machen; **go ~** (Econ.) in eine Aktiengesellschaft umgewandelt werden; (fig.) an die Öffentlichkeit treten; *see also* **image 6**
B *n., no pl.; constr. as sing. or pl.* **1▸** (the people) Öffentlichkeit, *die;* Allgemeinheit, *die;* **the general ~:** die Allgemeinheit; die breite Öffentlichkeit; **member of the ~:** Bürger, *der*/Bürgerin, *die;* **be open to the ~:** für den Publikumsverkehr geöffnet sein **2▸** (section of community) Publikum, *das;* (author's readers also) Leserschaft, *die;* **the reading ~:** das Lesepublikum **3▸ in ~** (publicly) öffentlich; (openly) offen; **behave oneself in ~:** sich in der Öffentlichkeit benehmen; **make a fool of oneself in ~:** sich in aller Öffentlichkeit lächerlich machen

public access 'television *n., no pl.* (Amer.) offenes Fernsehen

public-ad'dress system *n.* Lautsprecheranlage, *die*

publican /'pʌblɪkən/ *n.* **1▸** (Brit.) ▸**❶ p. 1260** [Gast]wirt, *der*/-wirtin, *die* **2▸** (Roman Hist., Bibl.) Zöllner, *der*/Zöllnerin, *die*

public as'sistance *n.* (Amer.) staatliche Fürsorge

publication /pʌblɪ'keɪʃn/ *n.* **1▸** (making known) Bekanntmachung, *die;* Bekanntgabe, *die* **2▸** (issuing of book etc.; book etc. issued) Veröffentlichung, *die;* Publikation, *die;* **the magazine ceased ~:** das Magazin hat sein Erscheinen eingestellt; **the magazine is a weekly ~:** die Zeitschrift erscheint wöchentlich

public: ~ 'bar *n.* (Brit.) ≈ Ausschank, *der;* **~ 'building** *n.* öffentliches Gebäude; **~ 'company** *n.* (Brit. Econ.) Aktiengesellschaft, *die;* **~ convenience** ▸**convenience 5**; **~ do'main** *n.* **in the ~ domain** gemeinfrei ‹*Werk*›; **be in the ~ domain** Allgemeingut sein; frei sein; (not protected by patent/copyright) patentrechtlich/urheberrechtlich nicht [mehr] geschützt sein; **~ 'enemy** *n.* Staatsfeind, *der;* **~ 'figure** *n.* Persönlichkeit des öffentlichen Lebens; **~ 'footpath** *n.* öffentlicher Fußweg; **~ 'health** *n., no pl., no art.* [öffentliches] Gesundheitswesen; **~ 'holiday** *n.* gesetzlicher Feiertag; **~ 'house** *n.* (Brit.) Gastwirtschaft, *die;* Gaststätte, *die;* **the 'Lion' ~ house** die Gaststätte „The Lion"; **~ in'quiry** *n.* öffentliche Untersuchung; **~ 'interest** *n.* Interesse der Allgemeinheit

publicise ▸**publicize**

publicist /'pʌblɪsɪst/ *n.* **1▸** (writer) Publizist, *der*/Publizistin, *die* **2▸** (publicity agent) Publicity-Manager, *der*/-Managerin, *die*

publicity /pʌb'lɪsɪtɪ/ *n., no pl., no indef. art.* **1▸** Publicity, *die;* (advertising) Werbung, *die;* **~ campaign** Werbekampagne, *die;* **~ material** Werbematerial, *das;* **get ~ for sth.** [es] erreichen, dass etw. in der Öffentlichkeit bekannt wird **2▸** (being public) Öffentlichkeit, *die* **3▸** (attention) Publicity, *die;* Publizität, *die* (geh.); **in the full glare of ~:** im grellen Licht der Öffentlichkeit; **attract ~** ‹*Vorfall:*› Aufsehen erregen

publicity: ~ agent *n.* ▸**❶ p. 1260** Publicity-manager, *der*/-managerin, *die;* **~ campaign, ~ drive** *ns.* Publicitykampagne, *die;* **~ machine** *n.* Publicitymaschine, *die;* **~ photograph** *n.* Werbefoto, *das;* **~-seeking** *adj.* publicitysüchtig ‹*Mensch*›; **~ stunt** *n.* Werbegag, *der*

publicize /'pʌblɪsaɪz/ *v.t.* publik machen ‹*Ungerechtigkeit*›; werben für, Reklame machen für ‹*Produkt, Veranstaltung*›; **well-~d** ausreichend publik gemacht

public: ~ key *n.* (Computing) öffentlicher Schlüssel; **~ 'law** *n., no pl.* (branch of law) öffentliches Recht; **~ 'lending right** *n.* Anspruch (der Autoren u. Verleger) auf eine Bibliotheksabgabe; **~ 'libel** ▸**libel A 1**; **~ 'library** *n.* öffentliche Bücherei; **~ limited 'company** *n.* (Brit.) ≈ Aktiengesellschaft, *die*

publicly /'pʌblɪklɪ/ *adv.* **1▸** (in public) öffentlich **2▸** (by the public) mit öffentlichen Geldern ‹*finanzieren, subventionieren*›; **~ owned** staatseigen; staatlich

public: ~ 'nuisance *n.* **1▸** (Law) Störung der öffentlichen [Sicherheit und] Ordnung; **2▸** (coll.) **make a ~ nuisance of oneself** sich danebenbenehmen (ugs.); **be a ~ nuisance** ein allgemeines Ärgernis sein; **~ o'pinion** ▸**opinion 2**; **~ 'order offence** *n.* Störung der öffentlichen Sicherheit und Ordnung; **~ 'ownership** *n., no pl.* Staatseigentum, *das* (**of** an + *Dat.*); Gemeineigentum, *das* (**of** an + *Dat.*); **be taken into ~ ownership** verstaatlicht werden; **~ property** *n.* Staatsbesitz, *der;* **sth. is ~ property** (fig.) etw. ist allgemein bekannt; **~ 'prosecutor** *n.* ▸**❶ p. 1260** (Law) Staatsanwalt, *der*/-anwältin, *die;* **~ 'purse** ▸**purse A 1**; **P~ 'Record Office** *n.* ≈ Bundesarchiv, *das* (Bundesrepublik Deutschland); ≈ Deutsches Zentralarchiv (DDR); **~ re'lations** *n. pl., constr. as sing. or pl.* Public Relations *Pl.;* Öffentlichkeitsarbeit, *die; attrib.* Public-Relations-‹*Abteilung, Berater*›; **~ relations officer** Öffentlichkeitsreferent, *der*/-referentin, *die;* **~ school** *n.* **1▸** (Brit.) Privatschule, *die; attrib.* Privatschul-; **2▸** (Scot., Amer.: school run by public authorities) staatliche *od.* öffentliche Schule; **~ 'sector** *n.* **the ~ sector** der öffentliche *od.* staatliche Sektor; *attrib.* **~ sector borrowing requirement** Kreditbedarf der öffentlichen Hand; **~ 'servant** *n.* Inhaber/Inhaberin eines öffentlichen Amtes; **~ service 'broadcasting** *n., no pl.* öffentlicher Rundfunk; **~ 'service industry** *n.* öffentlicher Dienstleistungsbetrieb; **~ 'service vehicle** *n.* öffentliches Verkehrsmittel; **~ 'speaking** *n., no pl.* Sprechen vor Publikum; **take lessons in ~ speaking** Rhetorikunterricht nehmen; **~ 'spirit** *n.* Gemeinsinn, *der;* **~-'spirited** *adj.* von Gemeinsinn zeugend ‹*Verhalten*›; **be a ~-spirited person**

P

Gemeinsinn haben; **it was ~-spirited of him to ...:** es zeugt von Gemeinsinn, dass er ...; **~ 'television** *n., no pl.* (Amer.) öffentliches Fernsehen; **~ 'transport** *n., no pl.* öffentlicher Personenverkehr; **travel by ~ transport** mit öffentlichen Verkehrsmitteln fahren; **~ u'tility** *n.* öffentlicher Versorgungsbetrieb; **~ 'works** *n. pl.* staatliche Bauvorhaben *od.* -projekte

public school

Eine Privatschule in England und Wales für Schüler im Alter von dreizehn bis achtzehn Jahren, die vorher meist eine **preparatory school** besucht haben. Die meisten *public schools* sind Internate, normalerweise entweder für Jungen oder Mädchen. Die Eltern zahlen für die Ausbildung ihrer Kinder und andere Angebote innerhalb der Schule Schulgeld. In Schottland und den USA ist eine *public school* eine staatliche Schule.

publish /'pʌblɪʃ/ *v.t.* **1** (issue) ‹*Verleger, Verlag:*› verlegen ‹*Buch, Zeitschrift, Musik usw.*›; ‹*Autor:*› publizieren, veröffentlichen ‹*Text*›; **we will ~ his novel** wir werden seinen Roman verlegen *od.* herausbringen; **be ~ed** erscheinen; **the book has been ~ed by a British company** das Buch ist in *od.* bei einem britischen Verlag erschienen; **he has had a novel ~ed** von ihm ist ein Roman erschienen **2** (announce publicly) verkünden; (read out) verlesen ‹*Aufgebot*› **3** (make generally known) publik machen ‹*Ergebnisse, Einzelheiten*›

publishable /'pʌblɪʃəbl/ *adj.* zur Veröffentlichung geeignet

publisher /'pʌblɪʃə(r)/ *n.* ▸ **p. 1260** Verleger, *der*/Verlegerin, *die;* **~[s]** (company) Verlag, *der;* **who are the ~s of this book?** in welchem Verlag ist dieses Buch erschienen?; **~s of children's books** Kinderbuchverlag, *der;* **music/scientific/magazine ~s** Musikverlag, *der*/wissenschaftlicher Verlag/Zeitschriftenverlag, *der*

publishing /'pʌblɪʃɪŋ/ *n., no pl., no art.* Verlagswesen, *das; attrib.* Verlags-; **be in ~:** im Verlagswesen [tätig] sein; **~ firm/company** Verlag, *der;* **the ~ business** das Verlagswesen

'publishing house *n.* Verlag, *der*

pub 'lunch *n.* Kneipen[mittag]essen, *das*

puce /pju:s/
A *n.* Flohbraun, *das*
B *adj.* flohbraun; **go ~ in the face** puterrot werden

puck /pʌk/ *n.* (Ice Hockey) Puck, *der*

pucker /'pʌkə(r)/
A *v.t.* **~ [up]** runzeln ‹*Brauen, Stirn*›; krausen, kraus ziehen ‹*Stirn*›; kräuseln ‹*Lippen*›; (sewing) kräuseln ‹*Stoff*›; **~ed** runzlig, faltig ‹*Haut*›
B *v.i.* **~ [up]** ‹*Gesicht:*› sich in Falten legen; ‹*Stoff:*› sich kräuseln
C *n.* Knitter, *der;* (in face) Falte, *die*

puckish /'pʌkɪʃ/ *adj.* koboldhaft

pud /pʊd/ (coll.) ▸ **pudding 1, 2**

pudding /'pʊdɪŋ/ *n.* **1** Pudding, *der* **2** (dessert) süße Nachspeise **3** (person or thing like ~) Kloß, *der* (ugs.)

pudding: ~ basin, ~ bowl *ns.* Puddingform, *die;* **~ club** *n.* (coll.) **be in the ~ club** 'n dicken Bauch haben (ugs.); **~ face** *n.* [Voll]mondgesicht, *das* (ugs.); **~-head** *n.* Gipskopf, *der* (ugs. abwertend)

puddle /'pʌdl/ *n.* Pfütze, *die*

pudendum /pju:'dendəm/ *n., pl.* **pudenda** /pju:'dendə/ *in sing. or pl.* (Anat.) Scham, *die*

pudge /pʌdʒ/ ▸ **podge**

pudgy /'pʌdʒɪ/ ▸ **podgy**

puerile /'pjʊəraɪl/ *adj.* kindisch (abwertend); infantil (abwertend)

puerility /pjʊə'rɪlɪtɪ/ *n., no pl.* Infantilität, *die* (abwertend)

puerperal /pju:'ɜ:pərl/ *adj.* (Med.) puerperal (fachspr.); **~ fever** Kindbettfieber, *das*

Puerto Rican /pwɜ:təʊ 'ri:kən/ ▸ **p. 1345**
A *adj.* puerto-ricanisch; **sb. is ~:** jmd. ist Puerto-Ricaner/Puerto-Ricanerin
B *n.* Puerto-Ricaner, *der*/Puerto-Ricanerin, *die*

Puerto Rico /pwɜ:təʊ 'ri:kəʊ/ *pr. n.* Puerto Rico (*das*)

puff /pʌf/
A *n.* **1** Stoß, *der;* **~ of breath/wind** Atem-/Windstoß, *der* **2** (sound of escaping vapour) Zischen, *das* **3** (quantity) **~ of smoke** Rauchstoß, *der;* **~ of steam** Dampfwolke, *die* **4** (in dress etc.) Bausch, *der;* Puff, *der* (veralt.) **5** (pastry) Blätterteigteilchen, *das; see also* **cream puff** **6** (advertisement) Reklame, *die;* **give sth. a ~:** Reklame für etw. machen **7** ▸ **powder puff** **8** **sb. runs out of ~** (lit. or fig. coll.) jmdm. geht die Puste aus (ugs.)
B *v.i.* **1** ‹*Blasebalg:*› blasen; **~ [and blow]** pusten (ugs.) *od.* schnaufen [und keuchen] **2** (~ cigarette smoke etc.) paffen (ugs.) (**at** an + *Dat.*) **3** (move with ~ing) ‹*Person:*› keuchen; ‹*Zug, Lokomotive, Dampfer:*› schnaufend fahren **4** (be emitted) ‹*Dampf, Luft, Rauch:*› stoßweise entweichen, (ugs.) puffen **5** (swell) **~ up** ‹*Frosch:*› sich aufblähen; **~ out** ‹*Finger:*› [an]schwellen
C *v.t.* **1** (blow) pusten (ugs.), blasen ‹*Rauch*›; stäuben ‹*Puder*› **2** (smoke in ~s) paffen (ugs.) **3** (put out of breath) ▸ **~ out A 2** **4** (utter pantingly) keuchen **5** (advertise) hochjubeln (ugs.) **6** **~ed sleeve** ▸ **puff sleeve**

(Phrasal verbs)

- **~ 'out**

A *v.t.* **1** (inflate) ‹*Wind:*› blähen, bauschen ‹*Segel*›; **he ~ed out his chest** er blähte seine Brust **2** (put out of breath) außer Puste (salopp) *od.* Atem bringen ‹*Person*›; **be ~ed out** außer Puste (salopp) *od.* Atem sein **3** (utter pantingly) heraus-, hervorstoßen **4** (extinguish) ausblasen; auspusten (ugs.)
B *v.i.* ‹*Segel, Fahne:*› sich bauschen, sich [auf]blähen

- **~ 'up**

A *v.t.* **1** (inflate) aufblasen; aufpusten (ugs.) **2** **be ~ed up** (proud) aufgeblasen sein (**by** infolge)
B *v.i.* sich [auf]blähen

puff: ~ adder *n.* (Zool.) Puffotter, *die;* **~ball** *n.* (Bot.) Bovist, *der*

'puffer [train] ▸ **puff-puff**

puffin /'pʌfɪn/ *n.* (Ornith.) Papageientaucher, *der*

'puffin crossing *n.* (Brit.) *Fußgängerüberweg mit elektronisch gesteuerter Ampel*

puff: ~ 'pastry *n.* (Cookery) Blätterteig, *der;* **~-~** *n.* (Brit. child. lang.) Puffzug, *der* (Kinderspr.); **~ 'sleeve** *n.* Puffärmel, *der*

puffy /'pʌfɪ/ *adj.* verschwollen

pug /pʌg/ *n.* **~ [dog]** Mops, *der*

pugilism /'pju:dʒɪlɪzm/ *n., no pl., no art.* (formal) Pugilismus, *der* (veralt.); Faustkampf, *der* (geh.)

pugilist /'pju:dʒɪlɪst/ *n.* (formal) Pugilist, *der* (veralt.); Faustkämpfer, *der* (geh.)

pugilistic /pju:dʒɪ'lɪstɪk/ *adj.* (formal) pugilistisch (veralt.)

pugnacious /pʌg'neɪʃəs/ *adj.* (literary) kampflustig

pugnaciously /pʌg'neɪʃəslɪ/ *adv.* (literary) mit großem Einsatz ‹*kämpfen*›

pugnacity /pʌg'næsɪtɪ/ *n., no pl.* Kampflust, *die*

pug: ~ nose *n.* Stumpfnase, *die;* **~-nosed** *adj.* stumpfnasig

puissance /'pju:ɪsəns, pwɪsəns/ *n.* (Showjumping) Mächtigkeitsspringen, *das*

puke /pju:k/ (coarse)
A *v.i.* kotzen (salopp); **the smell nearly made me ~:** von dem Geruch musste ich beinahe kotzen
B *v.t.* **~ up** auskotzen (salopp); ausspucken (ugs.); **~ one's guts up** kotzen wie ein Reiher (derb)
C *n.* Kotze, *die* (salopp); Ausgespuckte, *das* (ugs.)

pukka /'pʌkə/ *adj.* **1** (genuine) richtig; **it's ~ information** es ist Tatsache **2** (Brit. coll.: excellent) klasse (ugs.)

pulchritude /'pʌlkrɪtju:d/ *n.* (literary) Lieblichkeit, *die* (geh.)

Pulitzer Prize

Ein amerikanischer Preis, der seit 1917 für hervorragende Leistungen auf dem Gebiet des Journalismus, der Literatur und der Musik verliehen wird - an die 30 Preise werden jeden Mai vergeben. Der Preis wurde von Joseph Pulitzer (1847-1911), dem Besitzer der *New York World*, gestiftet. Der amerikanische Verleger, der 1864 aus Ungarn in die USA kam, gilt als Schöpfer der modernen amerikanischen Tagespresse. Er stiftete die *School of Journalism* an der Columbia University in New York, die mit der Verleihung der Preise beauftragt ist.

pull /pʊl/
A *v.t.* **1** (draw, tug) ziehen an (+ *Dat.*); ziehen ‹*Hebel*›; **~ aside** beiseite ziehen; **~ sb.'s** *or* **sb. by the hair/ears/sleeve** jmdn. an den Haaren/Ohren/am Ärmel ziehen; **~ shut** zuziehen ‹*Tür*›; **~ sth. over one's ears/head** sich (*Dat.*) etw. über die Ohren/den Kopf ziehen; **~ the other one** *or* **leg[, it's got bells on]** (fig. coll.) das kannst du einem anderen erzählen; **~ sth. out of the fire** (fig.) etw. [doch] noch retten; **~ to pieces** in Stücke reißen; (fig.: criticize severely) zerpflücken ‹*Argument, Artikel*›
2 (extract) [her]ausziehen; [heraus]ziehen ‹*Zahn*›; zapfen ‹*Bier*›
3 (coll.: accomplish) bringen (ugs.); **~ a stunt** *or* **trick** etwas Wahnsinniges tun; **~ a dirty trick** ein linkes Ding drehen (ugs.); *see also* **fast² A 4**
4 (strain) sich (*Dat.*) zerren ‹*Muskel, Sehne, Band*›
5 **~ a long/wry** *etc.* **face** ein langes/ironisches *usw.* Gesicht machen; *see also* **face A 1**
6 (draw from sheath etc.) ziehen ‹*Waffe*›; **~ a knife/gun on sb.** ein Messer/eine Pistole ziehen und jmdn. damit bedrohen
7 (Rowing) pullen (Seemannsspr.); rudern; **~ one's weight** (do one's fair share) sich voll einsetzen
8 (hold back) parieren, verhalten ‹*Pferd*›; **~ one's punches** ‹*Boxer:*› verhalten schlagen; (fig.: be gentle or lenient) sich zurückhalten; **not ~ one's punches** (fig.) nicht zimperlich sein
9 (coll: succeed in attracting sexually) aufreißen (salopp)
10 (Printing) machen ‹*Abzug*›
B *v.i.* **1** ziehen; **'Pull'** „Ziehen"
2 **~ [to the left/right]** ‹*Auto, Boot:*› [nach links/rechts] ziehen
3 (move with effort) sich schleppen
4 (pluck) **~ at** ziehen an (+ *Dat.*); **~ at sb.'s sleeve** jmdn. am Ärmel ziehen
5 (draw) **~ at** ziehen an (+ *Dat.*) ‹*Pfeife*›
C *n.* **1** Zug, *der;* Ziehen, *das;* (of the moon, sun, etc.) Anziehungskraft, *die;* (of tide) Sog, *der;* (of conflicting emotions) Widerstreit, *der;* **give a ~ at sth.** an etw. (*Dat.*) ziehen; **feel a ~ on** *or* **at sth.** ein Ziehen an etw. (*Dat.*) spüren
2 *no pl.* (influence) Einfluss, *der* (**with** auf + *Akk.*, bei)
3 ▸ **bell pull**
4 (drink) Zug, *der* (**at** aus)
5 (Rowing) Ruderfahrt, *die*
6 (Printing) Abzug, *der*

(Phrasal verbs)

- **~ a'bout** *v.t.* (treat roughly) zurichten
- **~ a'head** *v.i.* in Führung gehen; sich an die Spitze setzen; **~ ahead of** sich setzen vor (+ *Akk.*); **~ ahead by a few metres** mit einigen Metern Vorsprung in Führung gehen; **the firm is beginning to ~ ahead of its competitors** die Firma überholt die Konkurrenz allmählich
- **~ a'part** *v.t.* **1** (take to pieces) auseinander nehmen; zerlegen **2** (fig.: criticize severely) zerpflücken ‹*Interpretation, Argumentation usw.*›; verreißen ‹*Buch, [literarisches] Werk*›
- **~ a'way**

A *v.t.* wegziehen
B *v.i.* anfahren; (with effort) anziehen; **~ away from the kerb/platform** anfahren

- **~ 'back**

A *v.i.* **1** (retreat) zurücktreten; ‹*Truppen:*› sich

P

zurückziehen 2 (Sport) [wieder] aufholen (**to** bis auf + *Akk.*)
B *v.t.* 1 zurückziehen 2 (Sport) aufholen. *See also* **pull-back**
• ~ **'down** *v.t.* 1 herunterziehen 2 (demolish) abreißen 3 (make less) drücken ‹*Preis*›; (weaken) mitnehmen ‹*Person*› 4 (in exam) ~ **sb. down** jmds. [Gesamt]note drücken
• ~ **'in**
A *v.t.* 1 hereinziehen; zurückziehen ‹*Beine*› 2 (earn) kriegen (ugs.) 3 (attract) anziehen 4 (coll.: detain in custody) einkassieren (salopp): kassieren (ugs.)
B *v.i.* 1 ‹*Zug:*› einfahren 2 (move to side of road) an die Seite fahren; (stop) anhalten; ~ **in to the side of the road** an den Straßenrand fahren; **a good place to ~ in** eine gute Stelle zum [An]halten 3 ~ **in to the bank** ‹*Boot:*› ans Ufer fahren. *See also* **pull-in**
• ~ **into** *v.t.* 1 ‹*Zug:*› einfahren in (+ *Akk.*) 2 (move off road into) fahren in (+ *Akk.*)
• ~ **'off** *v.t.* 1 (remove) abziehen; (violently) abreißen; ausziehen ‹*Kleidungsstück*›; ausziehen, abstreifen ‹*Handschuhe*› 2 (accomplish) an Land ziehen (ugs.) ‹*Geschäft, Knüller*›; einfahren (ugs.) ‹*Sieg*›; abziehen (salopp) ‹*Raubüberfall*›
• ~ **'on** *v.t.* [sich (*Dat.*)] an- *od.* überziehen; (in a hurry) sich werfen in (+ *Akk.*)
• ~ **'out**
A *v.t.* 1 (extract) herausziehen; [heraus]ziehen ‹*Zahn*› 2 (take out of pocket etc.) aus der Tasche ziehen; herausziehen ‹*Messer, Pistole*›; [heraus-]ziehen, (scherzh.) zücken ‹*Brieftasche*› 3 (detach) heraustrennen ‹*Zeitungsbeilage, Foto*› 4 (withdraw) abziehen ‹*Truppen*›; herausnehmen ‹*Spieler, Mannschaft*›. *See also* **stop C 5**
B *v.i.* 1 (depart) ‹*Zug:*› abfahren; ~ **out of the station** aus dem Bahnhof ausfahren 2 (away from roadside) ausscheren 3 (withdraw) ‹*Truppen:*› abziehen (**of** aus); (from deal, project, competition, etc.) aussteigen (ugs.) (**of** aus); **the first country to ~ out of the negotiations** das erste Land, das seine Teilnahme an den Verhandlungen eingestellt hat 4 ~ **out of a dive** ‹*Flugzeug:*› aus dem Sturzflug abgefangen werden; ‹*Pilot:*› die Maschine aus dem Sturzflug abfangen. *See also* **pull-out**
• ~ **'over**
A *v.i.* ▸~ **in B 2**
B *v.t.* ~ **one's car over to the side of the road** seinen Wagen an den Straßenrand *od.* an die Seite fahren
• ~ **'round**
A *v.i.* (regain health) wieder auf die Beine kommen; (regain former success) wieder Tritt fassen
B *v.t.* wieder auf die Beine bringen ‹*Patienten*›; (fig.: put into a better condition) herausreißen (ugs.)
• ~ **'through**
A *v.t.* durchziehen; ~ **sb. through** (cause to recover or succeed) jmdn. durchbringen; ~ **through sth.** etw. überstehen
B *v.i.* ‹*Patient:*› durchkommen; ‹*Firma:*› überleben
• ~ **to'gether**
A *v.i.* an einem *od.* am selben Strang ziehen
B *v.t.* näher zusammenziehen; zusammenschweißen ‹*Partei, Allianz*›; in Schuss bringen (ugs.) ‹*Firma*›; ~ **sb. together** jmdm. auf die Beine helfen
C *v. refl.* sich zusammennehmen
• ~ **'up**
A *v.t.* 1 hochziehen 2 ~ **up a chair** einen Stuhl heranziehen 3 [he]rausziehen ‹*Unkraut, Pflanze usw.*›; (violently) [he]rausreißen 4 (stop) anhalten, zum Stehen bringen ‹*Auto*› 5 (reprimand) zurechtweisen; rügen
B *v.i.* 1 (stop) anhalten 2 (improve) sich verbessern *od.* vorarbeiten
C *v. refl.* sich hocharbeiten. *See also* **bootstraps**; **pull-up**; **sock¹ 1**

'pull: ~-back *n.* (withdrawal) Abzug, *der;* **~-down menu** *n.* (Computing) Pull-down-Menü, *das* (fachspr.)

pullet /'pʊlɪt/ *n.* Junghenne, *die*

pulley /'pʊlɪ/ *n.* Rolle, *die;* (for drive belt) Riemenscheibe, *die;* **set of ~s** (tackle) Flaschenzug, *der*

'pull-in *n.* 1 (place at the side of the road for vehicles) Haltebucht, *die* 2 (Brit.: transport café) Fernfahrerlokal, *das*

'pulling power *n.*, *no pl.* (also fig.) Zugkraft, *die*

Pullman /'pʊlmən/ *n.* ~ **[car** *or* **coach]** Pullman[wagen], *der*

pull: ~-out *n.* 1 (folding portion of book etc.) ausfaltbarer Teil; (map) Faltkarte, *die;* (detachable section) heraustrennbarer Teil; 2 (withdrawal) Abzug, *der;* **~-out of troops** Truppenabzug, *der;* **~over** /'pʊləʊvə(r)/ *n.* Pullover, *der;* Pulli, *der* (ugs.); ~ **tab** *n.* (Amer.) 1 (ring pull) Ring-Pull-Verschluss, *der;* 2 (gambling card) Glückslos, *das;* **~-up** *n.* 1 (stopping place) Platz zum Haltmachen; 2 (Gymnastics) Klimmzug, *der*

pulmonary /'pʌlmənərɪ/ *adj.* (Anat., Physiol.) Lungen-

pulp /pʌlp/
A *n.* 1 (of fruit) Fruchtfleisch, *das* 2 (soft mass) Brei, *der;* **beat sb. to a ~:** jmdn. zu Brei schlagen (salopp) 3 (Anat., Zool.: fleshy or soft part) Mark, *das* 4 (ore) Trübe, *die*
B *v.t.* zerdrücken, zerstampfen ‹*Rübe*›; einstampfen ‹*Druckerzeugnis*›

'pulp fiction *n.*, *no pl.* Schundliteratur, *die*

pulpit /'pʊlpɪt/ *n.* (Eccl.) Kanzel, *die*

pulp: ~ magazine *n.* Groschenheft, *das;* ~ **novel** *n.* Schundroman, *der;* **~wood** *n.* (Papermaking etc.) Industrieholz, *das*

pulpy /'pʌlpɪ/ *adj.* 1 (soft and moist) fleischig ‹*Frucht*› 2 (consisting of a soft mass) breiig

pulsar /'pʌlsɑ:(r)/ *n.* (Astron.) Pulsar, *der*

pulsate /pʌl'seɪt, 'pʌlseɪt/ *v.i.* 1 (beat, throb) pulsieren; ‹*Herz:*› schlagen; (fig. literary) pulsieren 2 (fig.: vibrate) schwingen; ‹*Land:*› pulsieren

pulsation /pʌl'seɪʃn/ *n.* 1 (beating, throbbing) Schlagen, *das;* (of artery; also fig.) Pulsieren, *das* 2 (fig.: vibration) Schwingen, *das*

pulse¹ /pʌls/
A *n.* 1 (lit. or fig.) Puls, *der;* (single beat) Pulsschlag, *der;* **have/keep one's finger on the ~ of sth.** die Hand am Puls einer Sache (*Gen.*) haben/auf dem Laufenden über etw. (*Akk.*) bleiben; *see also* **feel A 1** 2 (rhythmical recurrence) Rhythmus, *der* 3 (single vibration) Schwingung, *die;* (Mus.) Betonung, *die;* (Electronics) Impuls, *der*
B *v.i.* ▸**pulsate 1, 2**

pulse² *n.* 1 *no pl.*, *constr. as sing. or pl.* (seeds) Hülsenfrüchte *Pl.* 2 (variety of edible seed) Hülsenfrucht, *die*

pulse: ~ dialling *n.*, *no pl.* Impulswahl, *die;* ~ **rate** *n.* Pulsfrequenz, *die;* **push up sb's ~ rate** jmds. Puls hochtreiben

pulverize (**pulverise**) /'pʌlvəraɪz/ *v.t.* 1 (to powder or dust) pulverisieren 2 (into spray) zerstäuben 3 (fig.: crush) aufreiben ‹*Truppen*›; abservieren (Sport) ‹*Gegner*›; **I'll ~ you!** ich schlag dich zu Brei! (derb)

puma /'pju:mə/ *n.* (Zool.) Puma, *der*

pumice /'pʌmɪs/
A *n.* (Min.) ~ **[stone]** Bimsstein, *der*
B *v.t.* bimsen; mit Bimsstein abreiben

pummel /'pʌml/ *v.t.*, (Brit.) **-ll-** einschlagen auf (+ *Akk.*)

pump¹ /pʌmp/
A *n.* (machine; also fig.) Pumpe, *die*
B *v.i.* pumpen
C *v.t.* 1 pumpen; ~ **sb. full of lead** jmdn. mit Blei voll pumpen (salopp); ~ **bullets into sth.** Kugeln in etw. (*Akk.*) jagen (ugs.); ~ **information into sb.** jmdn. mit Wissen voll stopfen (ugs.) 2 ~ **sth. dry** etw. leer pumpen *od.* auspumpen *od.* (Seemannsspr.) lenzen; ~ **sb. for information** Auskünfte aus jmdm. herausholen 3 ~ **up** (inflate) aufpumpen ‹*Reifen, Fahrrad*›

pump² *n.* 1 (shoe) Turn-, Sportschuh, *der;* **[dancing]** ~: Tanzschuh, *der* 2 (Amer.: court shoe) Pumps, *der*

pump: ~-action *adj.* **~-action shotgun** Pumpgun, *das;* **~-action spray** Pumpspray, *das od. der;* ~ **attendant** *n.* Tankwart, *der/-wartin, die*

pumped 'up *adj.* (coll.) aufgedreht

pumpernickel /'pʌmpənɪkl, 'pʊmpənɪkl/ *n.* Pumpernickel, *der*

pumping station /'pʌmpɪŋsteɪʃn/ *n.* Pumpwerk, *das*

pumpkin /'pʌmpkɪn/ *n.* (Bot.) Kürbis, *der; attrib.* Kürbis-

'pump room *n.* Pumpenhaus, *das;* (in spa) Brunnenhaus, *das*

pun /pʌn/
A *n.* Wortspiel, *das;* **the sentence is a ~ on the words 'bread' and 'bred'** in dem Satz wird mit den Worten „bread" und „bred" gespielt
B *v.i.*, **-nn-** ein Wortspiel/Wortspiele *Pl.* machen (**on** mit)

punch¹ /pʌntʃ/
A *v.t.* 1 (strike with fist) boxen; mit der Faust schlagen; **the boxer ~ed his opponent with his left fist** der Boxer traf seinen Gegner mit der Linken 2 (pierce, open up) lochen; ~ **a hole** ein Loch stanzen; ~ **a hole/holes in sth.** etw. lochen 3 (prod) stoßen 4 (Amer.: drive) vorwärts treiben ‹*Vieh*›
B *n.* 1 (blow) Faustschlag, *der;* **a ~ on the head/chin/chest** ein Faustschlag an den Kopf/an das Kinn/vor die Brust; **give sb. a ~ on the jaw/in the ribs** jmdm. einen Kinnhaken/Rippenstoß versetzen; **a ~ with the left fist** ein Schlag mit der linken Faust 2 *no pl.* (ability to deliver blow) Punch, *der* (Boxen); Schlagkraft, *die;* **have a good/strong ~** ‹*Boxer:*› einen guten/harten Schlag haben 3 (coll.: vigour) Pep, *der* (ugs.); **have [a] ~:** Pep haben; **put ~ into sth.** einer Sache (*Dat.*) Pep geben 4 (device for making holes) (in leather, tickets) Lochzange, *die;* (in paper) Locher, *der;* (in leather) Locheisen, *das;* (Printing) Stempel, *der. See also* **pack B 7**; **pull A 8**

punch² *n.* (drink) Punsch, *der*

Punch /pʌntʃ/ *n.* Punch, *der;* Hanswurst, *der;* ~ **and Judy show** Kasperletheater, *das;* **be as proud/pleased as ~:** stolz wie ein Pfau *od.* Spanier sein/(ugs.) sich freuen wie ein Schneekönig

punch: ~bag *n.* Sandsack, *der;* **~ball** *n.* (Brit.) (ball) Punchingball, *der;* (bag) Sandsack, *der;* **~bowl** *n.* Bowlengefäß, *das;* Bowle, *die;* ~ **card** *n.* Lochkarte, *die;* **~-drunk** *adj.* 1 an einem Boxersyndrom leidend; **be ~-drunk** ein Boxersyndrom haben; punchdrunk sein (Boxen); 2 (fig.) benommen; **the troops were ~-drunk** die Truppen waren schwer angeschlagen

punched /pʌntʃt/: ~ **card** ▸**punch card**; ~ **tape** ▸**punch tape**

punching bag /'pʌntʃɪŋ bæg/ (Amer.) ▸**punchbag**

punch: ~line *n.* Pointe, *die;* ~ **tape** *n.* Lochstreifen, *der;* **~-up** *n.* (Brit. coll.) (fist fight, brawl) Prügelei, *die*

punchy /'pʌntʃɪ/ *adj.* (forceful) ausdrucksstark ‹*Sprache*›; zündend ‹*Rede*›; schwungvoll ‹*Handlung*›

punctilious /pʌŋk'tɪlɪəs/ *adj.* [peinlich] korrekt; peinlich ‹*Genauigkeit*›

punctiliously /pʌŋk'tɪlɪəslɪ/ *adv.* [peinlich] korrekt ‹*arbeiten*›; peinlich ‹*genau*›

punctual /'pʌŋktʃʊəl/ *adj.* pünktlich

punctuality /pʌŋktʃʊ'ælɪtɪ/ *n.*, *no pl.* Pünktlichkeit, *die*

punctually /'pʌŋktʃʊəlɪ/ *adv.* pünktlich

punctuate /'pʌŋktʃʊeɪt/ *v.t.* interpunktieren (fachspr.); mit Satzzeichen versehen; (fig.: interrupt) unterbrechen (**with** durch)

punctuation /pʌŋktʃʊ'eɪʃn/ *n.*, *no pl.* Interpunktion, *die* (fachspr.); Zeichensetzung, *die*

punctu'ation mark *n.* Satzzeichen, *das*

puncture /'pʌŋktʃə(r)/
A *n.* 1 (flat tyre) Reifenpanne, *die;* Platte, *der* (ugs.) 2 (hole) Loch, *das;* (in skin) Einstich, *der;* ~ **[repair] kit** Flickzeug, *das;* Pannenset, *das; see also* **lumbar**
B *v.t.* durchstechen; (fig.) verletzen ‹*Würde*›; kratzen an (+ *Dat.*) ‹*Mythos*›; lädieren ‹*Ruf*›; **be ~d** ‹*Reifen:*› ein Loch haben, platt sein; ‹*Haut:*› einen Einstich aufweisen
C *v.i.* ‹*Reifen:*› ein Loch bekommen, platt werden

pundit /'pʌndɪt/ *n.* 1 (expert) Experte, *der*/Expertin, *die;* (iron.) Augur, *der* 2 (learned Hindu) Pandit, *der*

P

punditry /ˈpʌndɪtrɪ/ *n.* Expertentum, *das*

pungency /ˈpʌndʒənsɪ/ *n., no pl.* (lit. or fig.) [beißende od. ätzende] Schärfe

pungent /ˈpʌndʒənt/ *adj.* **1** beißend, ätzend ‹*Rauch, Dämpfe*›; scharf ‹*Soße, Gewürz usw.*›; stechend riechend ‹*Gas*› **2** (fig.: biting) beißend; ätzend

punish /ˈpʌnɪʃ/ *v.t.* **1** bestrafen ‹*Person, Tat*›; strafen (geh.) ‹*Person*›; **he has been ~ed enough** (fig.) er ist gestraft genug **2** (Boxing coll.: inflict severe blows on) schwer zusetzen (+ *Dat.*) **3** (Sport coll.: take advantage of) kein Pardon kennen bei ‹*schwachen Würfen, Schlägen des Gegners*›; **the bowlers were ~ed by the batsmen** die Werfer bekamen ihre Quittung von den Schlagmännern **4** (coll.: tax) auf eine harte Probe stellen **5** (coll.: put under stress) strapazieren ‹*Nerven, Bauwerk*›

punishable /ˈpʌnɪʃəbl/ *adj.* strafbar; **it is a ~ offence to ...:** es ist strafbar, ... zu ...; **be ~ by sth.** mit etw. bestraft werden

punishing /ˈpʌnɪʃɪŋ/ *adj.* **1** (Boxing coll.) mörderisch ‹*Haken*› **2** (Sport coll.) tödlich (Sportjargon) ‹*Schuss, Schlag, Volley*›; **he is a ~ hitter** wenn der Gegner ihm eine Blöße bietet, schlägt er gnadenlos zu **3** (taxing) mörderisch (ugs.) ‹*Rennen, Zeitplan, Kurs*›; aufreibend ‹*Wahlkampf*›

punishment /ˈpʌnɪʃmənt/ *n.* **1** *no pl.* (punishing) Bestrafung, *die;* **inflict ~ on sb.** jmdn. bestrafen; **undergo ~:** bestraft werden; eine Strafe erhalten; **deserve ~:** [eine] Strafe verdient haben; **crime and ~:** Verbrechen und Strafe **2** (penalty) Strafe, *die;* **the ~ for cheating is disqualification** Betrug wird mit Disqualifikation bestraft; **make the ~ fit the crime** (lit. or fig.) Gleiches mit Gleichem vergelten; **as a ~ for sth.** zur Strafe für etw. **3** (coll.: rough treatment) **take a lot of ~:** ganz schön getriezt *od.* gezwiebelt werden (ugs.). *See also* **take A 23**

punitive /ˈpjuːnɪtɪv/ *adj.* **1** (penal) Straf- **2** (severe) [allzu] rigoros ‹*finanzielle Maßnahmen, Besteuerung*›; unzumutbar ‹*Steuersatz*› **3** (Law) **~ damages** verschärfter Schadenersatz

Punjab /pʌnˈdʒɑːb/ *pr. n.* **the ~:** das Pandschab

punk /pʌŋk/

A *n.* **1** (Amer. sl.: worthless person) Dreckskerl, der (salopp) **2** (Amer. coll.: young ruffian) Rabauke, *der* (ugs.) **3** (admirer of ~ rock) Punk, *der;* (performer of ~ rock) Punk[rock]er, *der*/-rockerin, *die* **4** (music) ►**punk rock**

B *adj.* **1** (coll.: worthless) mies (abwertend) **2** (of or playing ~ rock) Punk-

punk ˈrock *n.* Punkrock, *der*

punnet /ˈpʌnɪt/ *n.* (Brit.) Körbchen, *das*

punt¹ /pʌnt/

A *n.* Stechkahn, *der*

B *v.t.* **1** (propel) staken ‹*Boot*› **2** (convey) in einem Stechkahn fahren ‹*Person*›

C *v.i.* staken

punt² (Footb.)

A *v.t.* aus der Hand schießen; ‹*Torwart:*› abschlagen

B *n.* Schuss aus der Hand; (by goalkeeper) Abschlag, *der*

punt³ *v.i.* (Brit. coll.: bet) wetten; (speculate) spekulieren

punt⁴ /pʊnt/ *n.* (Finance) Irisches Pfund

punter¹ /ˈpʌntə(r)/ *n.* (coll.) **1** (gambler) Zocker, *der*/Zockerin, *die* (salopp) **2** (client of prostitute) Freier, *der* (verhüll.) **3** **the ~s** (customers) die Leutchen (ugs.)

punter² *n.* (in punt¹) Stechkahnfahrer, *der*/-fahrerin, *die*

puny /ˈpjuːnɪ/ *adj.* **1** (undersized) zu klein ‹*Baby, Junge*› **2** (feeble) gering ‹*Kraft*›; schwach ‹*Waffe, Person*› **3** (petty) belanglos, unerheblich ‹*Leistung, Einwand*›

pup /pʌp/

A *n.* **1** (young dog or wolf) Welpe, *der;* **be in ~** ‹*Hündin:*› trächtig sein **2** (young animal) Junge, *das* **3** (objectionable young man) Schnösel, *der* (ugs. abwertend)

B *v.i.*, **-pp-** ‹*Hündin:*› werfen

pupa /ˈpjuːpə/ *n., pl.* **~e** /ˈpjuːpiː/ (Zool.) Puppe, *die*

pupal /ˈpjuːpl/ *adj.* (Zool.) Puppen-

pupate /pjuːˈpeɪt/ *v.i.* (Zool.) sich verpuppen

pupil /ˈpjuːpɪl/ *n.* **1** (schoolchild, disciple) Schüler, *der*/Schülerin, *die* **2** (Anat.) Pupille, die

pupil-ˈteacher ratio *n.* (Educ.) Schüler-Lehrer-Relation, *die*

puppet /ˈpʌpɪt/ *n.* **1** Puppe, *die;* (marionette) Marionette, *die; see also* **glove puppet** **2** (person) Marionette, *die; attrib.* Marionetten‹*regime, -regierung*›

puppeteer /pʌpɪˈtɪə(r)/ *n.* Puppenspieler, *der*/-spielerin, *die*

puppetry /ˈpʌpɪtrɪ/ *n., no pl., no art.* (making of puppets) Puppenmachen, *das;* (production of puppet shows) Puppenspiel, *das*

ˈpuppet show *n.* Puppenspiel, *das;* (with marionettes) Marionettenspiel, *das*

puppy /ˈpʌpɪ/ *n.* Hundejunge, *das;* Welpe, *der;* **the dog is still only a ~:** der Hund ist noch ganz jung

ˈpuppy dog *n.* (child lang.) Hündchen, *das;* kleiner Hund

puppy: ~ fat *n., no pl.* (Brit.) Babyspeck, *der;* **~ love** *n.* Jugendschwärmerei, *die*

purblind /ˈpɜːblaɪnd/ *adj.* (literary) halb blind; (fig.) kurzsichtig

purchasable /ˈpɜːtʃəsəbl/ *adj.* käuflich; (available on the market) [im Handel] erhältlich

purchase /ˈpɜːtʃəs/

A *n.* **1** (buying) Kauf, *der;* **make several ~s/a ~:** Verschiedenes/etwas kaufen **2** (thing bought) Kauf, *der;* **carry one's ~s home** seine Einkäufe nach Hause tragen *od.* bringen **3** *no pl.* (hold) Halt, *der;* (leverage) Hebelwirkung, *die;* Hebelkraft, *die;* **get a ~:** guten *od.* festen Halt finden

B *v.t.* **1** kaufen; erwerben (geh.); **purchasing power** Kaufkraft, *die* **2** (acquire) erkaufen

ˈpurchase price *n.* Kaufpreis, *der*

purchaser /ˈpɜːtʃəsə(r)/ *n.* Käufer, *der*/Käuferin, *die*

ˈpurchase tax *n.* (Brit. Hist.) ≈ Verbrauchssteuer, *die*

ˈpurchasing power *n.* Kaufkraft, *die*

purdah /ˈpɜːdə/ *n.* (seclusion of women) Absonderung der Frauen; **they were kept in ~:** sie durften nicht in Erscheinung treten; (fig.) sie wurden kaltgestellt (ugs.)

pure /pjʊə(r)/

A *adj.* **1** (unmixed) rein; rein, pur ‹*Gold, Silber*›; (not discordant) rein ‹*Ton, Note*› **2** (of unmixed descent) reinblütig ‹*Mensch*›; rein ‹*Blut*› **3** (mere) pur; rein; **it is madness ~ and simple** es ist schlicht *od.* ganz einfach Wahnsinn **4** (Phonet.) einfach ‹*Vokal*› **5** (not corrupt) rein; **blessed are the ~ in heart** (Bibl.) selig sind, die reinen Herzens sind **6** (chaste) rein. *See also* **mathematics 1; science 1**

B *adv.* **a ~ blue sky** ein klarer blauer Himmel

pure: ~-blooded *adj.* reinblütig; **~-bred** *adj.* reinrassig

purée /ˈpjʊəreɪ/

A *n.* Püree, *das;* **tomato ~:** Tomatenmark, *das*

B *v.t.* pürieren

purely /ˈpjʊəlɪ/ *adv.* **1** (solely) rein **2** (merely) lediglich

pureness /ˈpjʊənɪs/ ►**purity**

purgative /ˈpɜːgətɪv/

A *adj.* **1** (laxative) [stark] abführend; Abführ‹*mittel, -tablette*›; purgativ (fachspr.) **2** (purifying) läuternd (geh.)

B *n.* (medicine) [starkes] Abführmittel; Purgativum, *das* (fachspr.)

purgatory /ˈpɜːgətərɪ/ *n.* (Relig.) Fegefeuer, *das;* Purgatorium, das (fachspr.); **undergo ~:** durchs Fegefeuer gehen; **it was ~** (fig.) es war eine Strafe *od.* die Hölle

purge /pɜːdʒ/

A *v.t.* **1** (cleanse) reinigen (**of** von); **~ me from my sin** (Relig.) reinige mich von meiner Sünde **2** (remove) entfernen; **~ away** *or* **out** beseitigen **3** (rid) säubern ‹*Partei*› (**of** von); (remove) entfernen ‹*Person*› **4** (Med.) abführen lassen ‹*Patienten*›; **use sth. to ~ the bowels** etw. zum Abführen verwenden **5** (Law: atone for) sühnen [für]

B *n.* **1** (clearance) Säuberung[saktion], *die;* (Polit.) Säuberung, *die;* **a ~ of writers** eine gegen Schriftsteller gerichtete Säuberung[saktion] **2** (Med.) [starkes] Abführmittel

purification /pjʊərɪfɪˈkeɪʃn/ *n.* **1** Reinigung, *die* **2** (spiritual cleansing) Läuterung, *die* **3** (ceremonial cleansing) Reinigung, *die;* **the P~ [of Our Lady** *or* **the Virgin Mary]** (Relig.) Mariä Reinigung; (feast) [Mariä] Lichtmess; Mariä Reinigung

purifier /ˈpjʊərɪfaɪə(r)/ *n.* Reiniger, *der;* Reinigungsmittel, *das;* (machine) Reinigungsapparat, *der;* Reinigungsanlage, *die*

purify /ˈpjʊərɪfaɪ/ *v.t.* **1** (make pure or clear) reinigen **2** (spiritually) reinigen; läutern **3** (ceremonially) reinigen

purism /ˈpjʊərɪzm/ *n., no pl.* Purismus, *der*

purist /ˈpjʊərɪst/ *n.* Purist, *der*/Puristin, *die*

puritan /ˈpjʊərɪtn/

A *n.* **1** Puritaner, *der*/Puritanerin, *die* **2** **P~** (Hist.) Puritaner, *der*/Puritanerin, *die*

B *adj.* **1** puritanisch **2** **P~** (Hist.) puritanisch

puritanic /pjʊərɪˈtænɪk/, **puritanical** /pjʊərɪˈtænɪkl/ *adj.* puritanisch; moralinsauer (abwertend)

puritanism /ˈpjʊərɪtənɪzm/ *n., no pl.* **1** Puritanismus, *der;* puritanische Einstellung **2** **P~** (Hist.) Puritanismus, *der*

purity /ˈpjʊərɪtɪ/ *n., no pl.* **1** Reinheit, *die* **2** (chastity) Keuschheit, *die*

purl /pɜːl/

A *n.* linke Masche

B *v.t.* links stricken; **~ three stitches** drei linke Maschen stricken

purler /ˈpɜːlə(r)/ *n.* (Brit. coll.) **come** *or* **take a ~:** längelang hinknallen (ugs.)

purlieus /ˈpɜːljuːz/ *n. pl.* Außenbezirke *Pl.;* Weichbild, *das;* **within the ~ of A** innerhalb des Stadtgebietes *od.* Weichbildes von A

purlin /ˈpɜːlɪn/ *n.* (Building) Pfette, *die*

purloin /pəˈlɔɪn/ *v.t.* (literary) entwenden (geh.)

purple /ˈpɜːpl/

A *adj.* lila; violett; (crimson) purpurn; (fig.) überfrachtet, überladen ‹*Prosa*›; **his face went ~ with rage** vor Zorn bekam er ein hochrotes Gesicht

B *n.* **1** Lila, *das;* Violett, *das;* (crimson) Purpur, *das* **2** (dress of cardinal) Purpur, *der;* **the ~** (fig.) das Kardinalskollegium

C *v.i.* ‹*Gesicht:*› dunkelrot anlaufen

purple: ~ ˈheart *n.* (Brit.) Purple Heart, *das* (Drogenjargon); **P~ ˈHeart** *n.* (Amer. Mil.) *US-amerikanisches Verwundetenabzeichen;* **~ passage, ~ patch** *ns.* [über]reich ausgeschmückte Passage

purplish /ˈpɜːplɪʃ/ *adj.* ins Violette spielend; **be ~:** ins Violette spielen

purport

A /pəˈpɔːt/ *v.t.* **1** **~ to do sth.** (profess) [von sich] behaupten, etw. zu tun; (be intended to seem) den Anschein erwecken sollen, etw. zu tun; **the ~ed intention/object** die angebliche Absicht/der angebliche Zweck; **a letter ~ing to be written by the president** ein angeblich vom Präsidenten geschriebener Brief; **the document ~s to be official** die Urkunde soll angeblich amtlich sein; **the law ~s to protect morality** das Gesetz soll angeblich die Moral schützen **2** (convey) beinhalten; **~ that ...:** besagen, dass ...

B /ˈpɜːpɔːt/ *n.* Inhalt, *der*

purportedly /pəˈpɔːtɪdlɪ/ *adv.* angeblich

purpose /ˈpɜːpəs/

A *n.* **1** (object) Zweck, *der;* (intention) Absicht, *die;* **what is the ~ of doing that?** was hat es für einen Zweck, das zu tun?; **he never did anything without a ~:** er tat nie etwas ohne eine bestimmte Absicht; **you must have had some ~ in mind** du musst irgendetwas damit bezweckt haben; **wander around with no particular ~:** ziellos *od.* ohne Ziel umherwandern; **answer** *or* **suit sb.'s ~:** jmds. Zwecken dienen *od.* entsprechen; **for a ~:** zu einem bestimmten Zweck; **I did it for a ~:** ich habe damit einen bestimmten Zweck verfolgt; **for**

the ~ of discussing sth. um etw. zu besprechen; **on ~:** mit Absicht; absichtlich; **for ~s of** zum Zwecke (+ *Gen.*); *see also* **cross purposes**; **serve A 3** 2▸ (effect) **to no ~:** ohne Erfolg; **to some/little/good ~:** mit einigem/wenig/gutem Erfolg 3▸ (determination) Entschlossenheit, *die;* **have a ~ in life** in seinem Leben einen Sinn sehen; **give sb. a ~ in life** jmds. Leben (*Dat.*) einen Sinn geben 4▸ (intention to act) Absicht, *die*

B *v.t.* beabsichtigen

'purpose-built *adj.* [eigens] zu diesem Zweck errichtet ‹*Gebäude*›; [eigens] zu diesem Zweck hergestellt, speziell angefertigt ‹*Gerät, Bauteil*›

purposeful /'pɜ:pəsfl/ *adj.* 1▸ zielstrebig; (with specific aim) entschlossen 2▸ (with intention) absichtsvoll

purposefully /'pɜ:pəsfəlɪ/ *adv.* 1▸ entschlossen 2▸ (intentionally) absichtsvoll

purposeless /'pɜ:pəslɪs/ *adj.* sinnlos

purposely /'pɜ:pəslɪ/ *adv.* absichtlich; mit Absicht

'purpose-made *adj.* spezialgefertigt; eigens angelegt ‹*Straße*›

purposive /'pɜ:pəsɪv/ *adj.* ▸**purposeful 1**

purr /pɜ:(r)/

A *v.i.* schnurren; (fig.: be in satisfied mood) strahlen

B *v.t.* durch Schnurren zum Ausdruck bringen; (fig.) säuseln; **the cat ~ed her contentment** die Katze schnurrte zufrieden

C *n.* Schnurren, *das*

purse /pɜ:s/

A *n.* 1▸ (lit. or fig.) Portemonnaie, *das;* Geldbeutel, *der* (bes. südd.); **the public ~:** die Staatskasse; **light ~** (fig.) kleiner Geldbeutel (fig.); *see also* **silk B** 2▸ (prize) Geldpreis *der;* Börse, *die* (Boxen) 3▸ (Amer.: handbag) Handtasche, *die*

B *v.t.* kräuseln, schürzen ‹*Lippen*›

purser /'pɜ:sə(r)/ *n.* ▸❶ **p. 1260** Zahlmeister, *der*/-meisterin, *die*

'purse strings *n. pl.* **hold the ~** (fig.) über das Geld bestimmen; **tighten/loosen the ~** (fig.) sparen/mehr ausgeben

pursuance /pə'sju:əns/ *n., no pl.* **in ~ of [one's] duties/instructions** pflichtgemäß/auftragsgemäß; **in [the] ~ of his ends** bei der Verfolgung seiner Ziele; **in ~ of the act/decree** gemäß dem Gesetz/der Verfügung

pursuant /pə'sju:ənt/ *adv.* **~ to sth.** gemäß einer Sache

pursue /pə'sju:/ *v.t.* 1▸ (literary: chase, lit. or fig.) verfolgen; **bad luck ~d him** er war vom Pech verfolgt 2▸ (seek after) streben nach; suchen nach; verfolgen ‹*Ziel*› 3▸ (look into) nachgehen (+ *Dat.*) 4▸ (engage in) betreiben; **~ a career as an accountant** als Buchhalter tätig sein; **~ one's studies** seinem Studium nachgehen 5▸ (carry out) durchführen ‹*Plan*›

pursuer /pə'sju:ə(r)/ *n.* Verfolger, *der*/Verfolgerin, *die*

pursuit /pə'sju:t, pə'su:t/ *n.* 1▸ (pursuing) (of person, animal, aim) Verfolgung, *die;* (of knowledge, truth, etc.) Streben, *das* (**of** nach); (of pleasure) Jagd, *die* (**of** nach); **the ~ of his studies** die Beschäftigung mit seinen Studien; **in ~ of** auf der Jagd nach ‹*Wild, Dieb usw.*›; in Ausführung (+ *Gen.*) ‹*Beschäftigung, Tätigkeit, Hobby*›; **with the police in [full] ~:** mit der Polizei [dicht] auf den Fersen; *see also* **hot A 10** 2▸ (pastime) Beschäftigung, *die;* Betätigung, *die*

pursuit: ~ plane (Amer.) ▸**fighter 2**; **~ race** *n.* (Cycling) Verfolgungsrennen, *das*

purulent /'pjʊərʊlənt/ *adj.* (Med.) (consisting of pus, full of pus) eitrig; (discharging pus) eiternd; **be ~:** eitern

purvey /pə'veɪ/ *v.t.* (lit. or fig.) liefern

purveyor /pə'veɪə(r)/ *n.* Lieferant, *der*/Lieferantin, *die;* **a ~ of [wild] rumours** ein Kolporteur [wilder Gerüchte]

purview /'pɜ:vju:/ *n.* (of act, document) Geltungsbereich, *der;* (of scheme, book, occupation) Rahmen, *der;* **fall within sb.'s ~:** in jmds. Aufgaben- *od.* Zuständigkeitsbereich fallen

pus /pʌs/ *n., no indef. art.* (Med.) Eiter, *der*

push /pʊʃ/

A *v.t.* 1▸ schieben; (make fall) stoßen; schubsen (ugs.); **don't ~ me like that!** schieb *od.* drängel [doch] nicht so!; **~ a car** (to start the engine) ein Auto anschieben; **~ the door to/open** die Tür zu-/aufstoßen; **she ~ed the door instead of pulling** sie drückte gegen die Tür, statt zu ziehen; **did he/you** *etc.* **fall** *or* **jump or was he/were you** *etc.* **~ed?** (fig.) freiwillig oder unfreiwillig?; **~ sb. about in a wheelchair** jmdn. im Rollstuhl herumfahren; **~ one's hair back** sich (*Dat.*) das Haar zurückstreichen; **the policemen ~ed the crowd back** die Polizisten drängten die Menge zurück; **~ sth. between sth.** etw. zwischen etw. (*Akk.*) schieben; (to pass right through) etw. zwischen etw. (*Dat.*) hindurchschieben; **~ sth. under the bottom of the door** etw. unter der Tür [hin]durchschieben; **~ sth. up the hill** etw. den Berg hinaufschieben; **~ one's way through/into/on to** *etc.* **sth.** sich (*Dat.*) einen Weg durch/in/auf *usw.* etw. (*Akk.*) bahnen 2▸ (fig.: impel) drängen; **~ sb. into doing sth.** jmdn. dahin bringen, dass er etw. tut 3▸ (tax) **~ sb. [hard]** jmdn. [stark] fordern; **~ sb. too hard/too far** jmdn. überfordern; **he ~es himself very hard** er verlangt sich (*Dat.*) sehr viel ab; **be ~ed for sth.** (coll.: find it difficult to provide sth.) mit etw. knapp sein; **be ~ed for money** *or* **cash** knapp bei Kasse sein (ugs.); **be ~ed to do sth.** (coll.) Mühe haben, etw. zu tun; **~ one's luck** (coll.) übermütig werden; **~ one's luck with sth.** sich mit etw. auf ein gefährliches Spiel einlassen 4▸ (press for sale of) die Werbetrommel rühren für; pushen (Werbejargon) 5▸ (sell illegally, esp. drugs) dealen; pushen (Drogenjargon) 6▸ (advance) **~ sth. a step/stage further** etw. einen Schritt vorantreiben; **not ~ the point** die Sache auf sich beruhen lassen; **~ sth. too far** mit etw. zu weit gehen; es mit etw. zu weit treiben; **~ things to extremes** die Dinge *od.* es zum Äußersten *od.* auf die Spitze treiben; **~ one's claims** auf seine Ansprüche pochen

B *v.i.* 1▸ schieben; (in queue) drängeln; (at door) drücken; **'Push'** (on door etc.) „Drücken"; **~ and shove** schubsen und drängeln; **~ at sth.** gegen etw. drücken 2▸ (make demands) **~ for sth.** etw. fordern 3▸ (make one's way) **he ~ed between us** er drängte sich zwischen uns; **~ through the crowd** sich durch die Menge drängeln; **~ past** *or* **by sb.** sich an jmdm. vorbeidrängeln *od.* -drücken; **~ by** (not stop) weiterrennen (ugs.) 4▸ (assert oneself for one's advancement) sich in den Vordergrund spielen

C *n.* 1▸ Stoß, *der;* Schubs, *der* (ugs.); **give sth. a ~:** etw. schieben *od.* stoßen; **give sb. a ~:** jmdm. einen Schubs geben (ugs.); jmdm. einen Stoß versetzen; **My car won't start; can you give me a ~?** Mein Auto springt nicht an. Kannst du mich anschieben?; **give sth. a gentle ~:** etw. leicht anstoßen; **we gave a great ~:** wir haben gewaltig gedrückt 2▸ (effort) Anstrengungen *Pl.;* (Mil.: attack) Vorstoß, *der;* Offensive, *die;* **a ~ forward** (Mil.) ein Vorstoß; **make a ~:** sich ins Zeug legen (ugs.); (Mil.) einen Vorstoß unternehmen; eine Offensive durchführen 3▸ (determination) Tatkraft, *die;* Initiative, *die* 4▸ (crisis) **when it comes/came to the ~,** (coll.) **when ~ comes/came to shove** wenn es ernst wird/als es ernst wurde; **at a ~:** wenn es sein muss 5▸ (Brit. coll.: dismissal) **get the ~:** rausfliegen (ugs.); **give sb. the ~:** jmdn. rausschmeißen (ugs.) 6▸ (influence) Förderung, *die;* Protektion, *die* 7▸ ▸**push-button**

Phrasal verbs

- **~ a'bout** *v.t.* herumschieben; (bully) herumkommandieren
- **~ a'head** *v.i.* (*Armee:*) [weiter] vorstoßen *od.* -rücken; (with [regard to] plans etc.) weitermachen; **~ ahead with sth.** etw. vorantreiben
- **~ a'long**

A *v.t.* [vor sich (*Dat.*) her]schieben

B *v.i.* (coll.) sich [wieder] auf den Weg machen

- **~ a'round** ▸**~ about**
- **~ a'side** *v.t.* (lit. or fig.) beiseite schieben
- **~ a'way** *v.t.* wegschieben
- **~ 'forward**

A *v.i.* ▸**~ ahead**

B *v.t.* vorschieben; (Mil.) vorstoßen; **~ oneself forward** sich in den Vordergrund schieben

- **~ 'in**

A /-'-/ *v.t.* eindrücken; (make fall into the water) hineinstoßen *od* (ugs.) -schubsen

B /'--/ *v.i.* sich hineindrängen

- **~ 'off**

A *v.i.* 1▸ (Boating) abstoßen 2▸ (coll.: leave) abhauen (salopp); abschieben (salopp)

B *v.t.* 1▸ abdrücken ‹*Deckel, Verschluss usw.*› 2▸ (Boating) abstoßen

- **~ 'on**

A ▸**~ ahead**

B *v.t.* draufdrücken ‹*Deckel, Verschluss usw.*›

- **~ 'out**

A *v.t.* hinausschieben; ‹*Pflanzen:*› [aus]treiben ‹*Wurzeln*›; *see also* **boat A 1**

B *v.i.* hinausragen

- **~ 'out of** *v.t.* (force to leave) hinausdrängen aus
- **~ 'over** *v.t.* (make fall) umstoßen; *see also* **pushover**
- **~ 'through** *v.t.* (fig.) durchpeitschen (ugs.) ‹*Gesetzesvorlage*›; durchdrücken (ugs.) ‹*Vorschlag*›; **we ~ed it through successfully** wir haben es durchgekriegt (ugs.)
- **~ 'up** *v.t.* hochschieben; (fig.) hochtreiben; *see also* **daisy**; **push-up**

push: ~-ball *n.* (game, ball) Pushball, *der;* **~bike** *n.* (Brit. coll.) Fahrrad, *das;* **~-button** **A** *adj.* Drucktasten‹*telefon, -radio*›; **~-button warfare** Krieg per Knopfdruck; automatisierte Kriegführung; **B** *n.* [Druck]knopf, *der;* Drucktaste, *die;* **~cart** *n.* 1▸ ▸**handcart**; 2▸ (Amer.: trolley) Einkaufswagen, *der;* **~chair** *n.* (Brit.) Sportwagen, *der*

pusher /'pʊʃə(r)/ *n.* 1▸ (seller of drugs) Dealer, *der* (Drogenjargon); Pusher, *der* (Drogenjargon) 2▸ (pushy person) Streber, *der*/Streberin, *die* (abwertend); Ehrgeizling, *der* (ugs. abwertend)

'push-fit *adj.* zusammensteckbar; **~ joint/fitting/connection** Steckverbindung, *die*

pushing /'pʊʃɪŋ/ *adj.* 1▸ [übermäßig] ehrgeizig 2▸ (coll.) **be ~ sixty** auf die Sechzig zugehen

push: ~over *n.* (coll.) Kinderspiel, *das;* **he'll be a ~over for her** sie steckt ihn [glatt] in die Tasche (ugs.); **the match should be a ~over for Leeds** das Spiel dürfte für Leeds ein Spaziergang werden (Sportjargon); **~-start** **A** *n.* Schubstart, *der;* **give sb. a ~-start** jmdn. *od.* jmds. Auto anschieben; **B** *v.t.* anschieben; **~ technology** *n.* (Computing) Pushtechnologie, *die;* **~-up** (Amer.) ▸**press-up**

pushy /'pʊʃɪ/ *adj.* (coll.) [übermäßig] ehrgeizig ‹*Person*›

pusillanimity /pju:sɪlə'nɪmɪtɪ/ *n., no pl.* Ängstlichkeit, *die;* Zaghaftigkeit, *die;* (lack of courage) Feigheit, *die*

pusillanimous /pju:sɪ'lænɪməs/ *adj.*, **pusillanimously** /pju:sɪ'lænɪməslɪ/ *adv.* ängstlich; zaghaft; (without courage) feige

puss /pʊs/ *n.* (coll.) Mieze, *die* (fam.); **~, ~, ~!** Miez, Miez, Miez!; **P~ in Boots** der Gestiefelte Kater

pussy /'pʊsɪ/ *n.* 1▸ (child lang.: cat) Miezekatze, *die* (fam.); Muschi, *die* (Kinderspr.) 2▸ (coarse) (vulva) Kätzchen, *das* (salopp); Muschi, *die* (vulg.); (sexual intercourse) Sex, *der*

pussy: ~ cat ▸**pussy 1**; **~foot** *v.i.* [herum]schleichen; (act cautiously) überängstlich sein; **stop ~footing!** hör auf, wie die Katze um den heißen Brei zu schleichen!; **~ willow** *n.* Salweide, *die;* Palmweide, *die*

pustule /'pʌstju:l/ *n.* (Med.) (pimple) Pustel, *die*

put[1] /pʊt/

A *v.t.*, **-tt-, put** 1▸ (place) tun; (vertically) stellen; (horizontally) legen; (through or into narrow opening) stecken; **~ plates on the table** Teller auf den Tisch stellen; **~ books on the shelf/on top of the pile** Bücher ins Regal stellen/auf den Stapel legen; **~ clean sheets on the bed** das Bett frisch beziehen; **don't ~ your elbows on the table** lass deine Ellbogen vom Tisch; **I ~ my hand on his shoulder** ich legte meine Hand auf seine Schulter; **~ a stamp on the letter** eine Briefmarke auf den Brief kleben; **~ salt on one's food** Salz auf sein Essen tun *od.*

P

streuen; ~ **some more coal on the fire** Kohle nachlegen; ~ **antiseptic on one's finger** sich (*Dat.*) Antiseptikum auf den Finger tun; ~ **the letter in an envelope/the letter box** den Brief in einen Umschlag/in den Briefkasten stecken; ~ **sth. in one's pocket** etw. in die Tasche stecken; etw. einstecken; ~ **the shopping in the car** die Einkäufe ins Auto tun *od.* legen; ~ **one's hands in one's pockets** die Hände in die Taschen stecken; ~ **sugar in one's tea** sich (*Dat.*) Zucker in den Tee tun; ~ **petrol in the tank** Benzin in den Tank tun *od.* füllen; ~ **the car in[to] the garage** das Auto in die Garage stellen; ~ **rubbish in the waste-paper basket** Abfall in den Papierkorb tun *od.* werfen; ~ **the cork in the bottle** den Korken in die Flasche stecken; ~ **the plug in the socket** den Stecker in die Steckdose stecken; ~ **paper in the typewriter** Papier in die Schreibmaschine tun *od.* einspannen; ~ **tobacco in the pipe** Tabak in die Pfeife tun; die Pfeife stopfen; ~ **a new pane of glass in the window** eine neue Glasscheibe in das Fenster [ein]setzen; ~ **a new engine in the car** einen neuen Motor in das Auto einbauen; ~ **the letters in the file** die Briefe in den Ordner tun *od.* [ein]heften; ~ **documents in the safe** Urkunden in den Safe tun *od.* legen; ~ **fish into a pond** Fische in einen Teich setzen; ~ **the cat into a basket** die Katze in einen Korb setzen *od.* stecken; ~ **the ball into the net/over the bar** den Ball ins Netz befördern *od.* setzen/über die Latte befördern; ~ **one's arm round sb.'s waist** den Arm um jmds. Taille legen; ~ **a bandage round one's wrist** sich (*Dat.*) einen Verband ums Handgelenk legen; ~ **one's hands over one's eyes** sich (*Dat.*) die Hände auf die Augen legen; ~ **one's finger to one's lips** den *od.* seinen Finger auf die Lippen legen; ~ **one's foot through the rotten floorboards/on a chair** den Fuß durch die morschen Dielen stecken/auf einen Stuhl setzen; ~ **the letter at the bottom of the pile** den Brief unter den Stapel legen; ~ **the boxes one on top of the other** die Kisten übereinander stellen; ~ **the jacket on its hanger** die Jacke auf den Bügel tun *od.* hängen; **where shall I ~ it?** wohin soll ich es tun (ugs.)/stellen/legen *usw.?*; wo soll ich es hintun (ugs.)/-stellen/-legen *usw.?*; ~ **sb. into a taxi** jmdn. in ein Taxi setzen; ~ **a child on a swing** ein Kind auf eine Schaukel setzen; **we ~ our guest in Peter's room** wir haben unseren Gast in Peters Zimmer (*Dat.*) untergebracht; ~ **the baby in the pram** das Baby in den Kinderwagen legen *od.* (ugs.) stecken; **not know where to ~ oneself** (fig.) sehr verlegen sein/werden; ~ **it there!** (coll.) lass mich deine Hand schütteln!

2 (cause to enter) stoßen; ~ **a knife into sb.** jmdm. ein Messer in den Leib stoßen; ~ **a satellite into orbit** einen Satelliten in eine Umlaufbahn bringen; ~ **a bullet** *etc.* **through sb./sth.** (coll.) jmdm. eine Kugel verpassen/etw. zerballern (ugs.)

3 (bring into specified state) setzen; ~ **through Parliament** im Parlament durchbringen ‹*Gesetzentwurf usw.*›; ~ **one's proposals through the committee** seine Vorschläge im Ausschuss durchbringen; ~ **sb. in a difficult** *etc.* **position** jmdn. in eine schwierige *usw.* Lage bringen; **be ~ in a difficult** *etc.* **position** in eine schwierige *usw.* Lage geraten; **be ~ in a position of trust** eine Vertrauensstellung erhalten; ~ **sb. in[to] a job** jmdm. eine Arbeit[sstellung] *od.* (ugs.) einen Job geben; **be ~ into power** an die Macht kommen; ~ **sb. on the committee** jmdn. in den Ausschuss schicken; ~ **sth. above** *or* **before sth.** (fig.) einer Sache (*Dat.*) den Vorrang vor etw. (*Dat.*) geben; ~ **sth. out of order** etw. kaputtmachen (ugs.); etw. funktionsuntüchtig machen; **be ~ out of order** kaputtgehen (ugs.); defekt werden; ~ **sb. on to sth.** (fig.) jmdn. auf etw. (*Akk.*) hinweisen *od.* aufmerksam machen; jmdm. etw. zeigen; ~ **sb. on to a job** (assign) jmdm. eine Arbeit zuweisen

4 (impose) ~ **a limit/an interpretation on sth.** etw. begrenzen *od.* beschränken/interpretieren; *see also* **end A 1**; **stop C 1**; **veto A 2**

5 (submit) unterbreiten (**to** *Dat.*) ‹*Vorschlag, Plan usw.*›; ~ **the situation to sb.** jmdm. die Situation darstellen; ~ **sth. to the vote** über etw. (*Akk.*) abstimmen lassen; etw. zur Abstimmung bringen (Papierdt.); **I ~ it to you that you never saw him** ich behaupte *od.* sage, dass Sie ihn nie gesehen haben

6 (cause to go or do) ~ **sb. to work** jmdn. arbeiten lassen; ~ **sb. on the job** jmdn. damit *od.* mit der Arbeit beauftragen; ~ **sb. out of contention for sth.** jmdn. aus dem Rennen um etw. werfen; jmdm. sämtliche Chancen auf etw. nehmen; **be ~ out of the game by an injury** wegen einer Verletzung nicht mehr spielen können; ~ **sb. out of the championship** jmdm. den Titel abnehmen; **they were ~ out of the cup by Liverpool** sie scheiterten an Liverpool und mussten aus dem Cupwettbewerb ausscheiden; ~ **the troops on full alert** die Streitkräfte in volle Alarm- *od.* Gefechtsbereitschaft versetzen; ~ **sb. on antibiotics** jmdn. auf Antibiotika setzen; ~ **sb. on the stage** jmdn. zur Bühne schicken; *see also* **pace[1] A 3**

7 (impose) ~ **taxes** *etc.* **upon sth.** etw. mit Steuern *usw.* belegen; Steuern *usw.* für etw. erheben

8 (express) ausdrücken; **let's ~ it like this: ...:** sagen wir so: ...; **that's one way of ~ting it** (also iron.) so kann man es [natürlich] auch ausdrücken; **I don't quite know how to ~ this, but ...:** ich weiß nicht recht, wie ich es sagen soll, aber ...

9 (render) ~ **sth. into English** *etc.* etw. ins Englische *usw.* übertragen *od.* übersetzen; ~ **sth. into words** etw. in Worte fassen; ~ **sth. into one's own words** etw. mit seinen eigenen Worten sagen

10 (write) schreiben; ~ **one's name on the list** seinen Namen auf die Liste setzen; ~ **a tick in the box** ein Häkchen in das Kästchen machen; ~ **a cross against sth.** etw. ankreuzen; ~ **one's signature to sth.** seine Unterschrift unter etw. setzen; ~ **a black mark against a name** einen Namen schwarz markieren *od.* anstreichen; ~ **sth. on the bill** etw. auf die Rechnung setzen; ~ **sth. on the list** (fig.) sich (*Dat.*) etw. [fest] vornehmen; etw. vormerken

11 (imagine) ~ **oneself in sb.'s place** *or* **situation** sich in jmdn. *od.* in jmds. Lage versetzen

12 (substitute) setzen

13 (invest) ~ **money** *etc.* **into sth.** Geld *usw.* in etw. (*Akk.*) stecken; ~ **work/time/effort into sth.** Arbeit/Zeit/Energie in etw. (*Akk.*) stecken *od.* auf etw. (*Akk.*) verwenden

14 (stake) setzen (**on** auf + *Akk.*); ~ **money on a horse/on sth. happening** auf ein Pferd setzen/darauf wetten, dass etw. passiert

15 (estimate) ~ **sb./sth. at** jmdn./etw. schätzen auf (+ *Akk.*); **to ~ it no higher** um das Wenigste zu sagen; *see also* **past C 2**

16 (subject) ~ **sb. to** jmdm. ‹*Unkosten, Mühe, Umstände*› verursachen *od.* machen; *see also* **shame A 2**; **test A 1**

17 (drive) ~ **sb. to sth.** jmdn. zu etw. treiben *od.* zwingen; *see also* **flight[2] 1**; **hard B 4**; **rout[1] A 1**

18 (harness) ~ **to sth.** vor etw. (*Akk.*) spannen

19 (Athletics: throw) stoßen ‹*Kugel*›; ~ **the shot** kugelstoßen

B *v.i.*, **-tt-**, ~ (Naut.) ~ **[out] to sea** in See stechen; auslaufen; ~ **into port** [in den Hafen] einlaufen; ~ **across/over to** übersetzen nach; ~ **out from England** von England aus in See stechen; England verlassen; ~ **off** ablegen; **they had to ~ in at Valetta** sie mussten Valetta anlaufen

C *n.* (Sport) Stoß, *der*

(Phrasal verbs)

• ~ **a'bout**

A *v.t.* **1** (circulate) verbreiten; in Umlauf bringen; **it was ~ about that ...:** man munkelte (ugs.) *od.* es hieß, dass ... **2** (Naut.) ~ **the ship** *etc.* **about** den Kurs [des Schiffes *usw.*] ändern; (cause to change tack) [das Schiff *usw.*] wenden **3** (cause to turn about) wenden ‹*Pferd usw.*› **4** (Scot., N. Engl.) (disconcert) beunruhigen; (upset) verärgern; **don't ~ yourself about** (inconvenience) mach keine Umstände

B *v.i.* (Naut.) den Kurs ändern

• ~ **a'cross** *v.t.* **1** (communicate) vermitteln (**to** *Dat.*) **2** (make acceptable) ankommen mit; (make effective) durchsetzen; ~ **sth. across to sb.** mit etw. bei jmdm. ankommen/etw. bei jmdm. durchsetzen **3** (Amer.) **sb. ~s across a fraud** jmdm. gelingt ein Betrug; **he ~ that tale across them** sie haben ihm diese Geschichte abgenommen **4** ~ **one across sb.** (coll.) (get the better of) es jmdm. zeigen; (deceive) jmdn. reinlegen (ugs.) *od.* (salopp) linken. *See also* ~ **B**

• ~ **a'side** *v.t.* **1** (disregard) absehen von; ~**ting aside the fact that ...:** wenn man von der Tatsache *od.* davon absieht, dass ...; von der Tatsache *od.* davon abgesehen, dass ... **2** (save) beiseite *od.* auf die Seite legen

• ~ **a'sunder** *v.t.* (arch.) scheiden

• ~ **a'way** *v.t.* **1** wegräumen; reinstellen ‹*Auto*›; (in file) wegheften; abheften **2** (abandon) ablegen, aufgeben ‹*Gewohnheiten, Vorurteile*› **3** (save) beiseite *od.* auf die Seite legen **4** (coll.) (eat) verdrücken (ugs.); (drink) runterkippen (ugs.) **5** (confine) einsperren (ugs.); in eine Anstalt stecken (ugs.) **6** (coll.: kill) einschläfern ‹*Tier*›; um die Ecke bringen (ugs.) ‹*Person*›

• ~ **'back** *v.t.* **1** ~ **the book back** das Buch zurücktun; ~ **the book back on the shelf** das Buch wieder ins Regal stellen *od.* ins Regal zurückstellen **2** ~ **the clock back [one hour]** die Uhr [eine Stunde] zurückstellen; *see also* **clock A 1** **3** (delay) zurückwerfen; verzögern ‹*Ernte, Lieferung*› **4** (postpone) verschieben

• ~ **'by** *v.t.* beiseite *od.* auf die Seite legen; **I've got a few hundred pounds ~ by** ich habe ein paar hundert Pfund auf der hohen Kante (ugs.)

• ~ **'down**

A *v.t.* **1** (set down) (vertically) hinstellen; (horizontally) hinlegen; auflegen ‹*Hörer*›; ~ **sth. down on sth.** etw. auf etw. (*Akk.*) stellen/legen; ~ **down a deposit** eine Anzahlung machen **2** (suppress) niederwerfen, -schlagen ‹*Revolte, Rebellion, Aufruhr*› **3** (humiliate) herabsetzen; (snub) eine Abfuhr erteilen (+ *Dat.*); abfahren lassen (salopp); *see also* **put-down** **4** (kill painlessly) töten **5** (write) notieren; aufschreiben; ~ **sth. down in writing** etw. schriftlich niederlegen; **he ~ it all down on paper** er schrieb alles auf; ~ **sb.'s name down on a list** jmdn. *od.* jmds. Namen auf eine Liste setzen; ~ **sb. down for** für jmdn. reservieren ‹*Lose*›; jmdn. notieren für ‹*Dienst, Arbeit*›; jmdn. anmelden bei ‹*Schule, Verein usw.*›; **I ~ him down for a £5 subscription** ich habe ihn mit einem Beitrag von 5 Pfund notiert **6** (Parl.) einbringen; stellen ‹*Antrag*› **7** (allow to alight) aussteigen lassen; absetzen **8** ~ **sb. down as ...:** jmdn. eintragen als ...; ~ **sth. down as ...:** etw. angeben als ...; **he ~ himself down as 'unemployed'** er gab als Beschäftigung „arbeitslos" an; (fig.: classify) ~ **sb./sth. down as ...:** jmdn./etw. halten für *od.* einschätzen als ... **9** (attribute) ~ **sth. down to sth.** etw. auf etw. (*Akk.*) zurückführen **10** (store) einlagern; (in cellar) einkellern **11** (to bed) hinlegen ‹*Baby*› **12** (cease to read) weglegen, aus der Hand legen ‹*Buch*› **13** (land) aufsetzen. *See also* **down[3] A 6**

B *v.i.* (land) niedergehen; **look for a place to ~ down** nach einem geeigneten Landeplatz suchen

• ~ **'forth** *v.t.* (sprout) hervorbringen ‹*neue Triebe, Knospen*›; treiben ‹*Knospen*›

• ~ **'forward** *v.t.* **1** (propose) aufwarten mit; **the explanation ~ forward by him** die Erklärung, mit der er aufwartete; **several theories have been ~ forward to account for this** darüber gibt es verschiedene Theorien **2** (nominate) vorschlagen **3** ~ **the clock forward [one hour]** die Uhr [eine Stunde] vorstellen

• ~ **'in**

A *v.t.* **1** (install) einbauen; einstellen ‹*Arbeiter, Hausmeister, Leiter usw.*› **2** (elect) an die Regierung *od.* Macht bringen; **be ~ in** an die Regierung *od.* Macht kommen **3** (enter) melden ‹*Person*› **4** (submit) stellen ‹*Forderung, Antrag*›; einreichen ‹*Bewerbung, Antrag*›; ~ **in a claim for damages** eine Schadensersatzforderung stellen; ~ **in a plea of not guilty** sich nicht schuldig bekennen **5** (devote) aufwenden

‹*Mühe, Kraft*›; (perform) einlegen ‹*Sonderschicht, Überstunden*›; (spend) einschieben ‹*eine Stunde usw.*› **6** (interpose) einwerfen ‹*Bemerkung*›; **I ~ in a word of warning** ich mischte mich ein und warnte sie/ihn *usw.*; **~ in a blow** zuschlagen **7** (plant) einpflanzen ‹*Setzlinge, Stecklinge*›; setzen ‹*Salat, Tomaten, Saatpflanzen*›; stecken ‹*Bohnen, Kartoffeln, Zwiebeln*›; [ein]säen ‹*Samen*› **8** (Cricket) schlagen lassen ‹*gegnerische Mannschaft*›; spielen lassen, einsetzen ‹*eigenen Spieler*›; **they ~ us in [to bat]** sie ließen uns schlagen. *See also* **~ B**

B *v.i.* **~ in for** sich bewerben um ‹*Stellung, Posten, Vorsitz*›; beantragen ‹*Urlaub, Versetzung*›

- **~ in'side** *v.t.* (sl.: imprison) einlochen (salopp)
- **~ 'off** *v.t.* **1** (postpone) verschieben (**until** auf + *Akk.*); (postpone engagement with) vertrösten (**until** auf + *Akk.*); **can't you ~ her off?** kannst du ihr nicht [erst einmal] absagen? **2** (switch off) ausmachen **3** (repel) abstoßen; **don't be ~ off by his rudeness** lass dich von seiner Grobheit nicht abschrecken; **~ sb. off sth.** jmdm. etw. verleiden **4** (distract) stören; **the noise ~ him off his game** bei dem Lärm konnte er sich nicht mehr auf sein Spiel konzentrieren **5** (fob off) abspeisen **6** (dissuade) **~ sb. off doing sth.** jmdn. davon abbringen *od.* jmdm. ausreden, etw. zu tun **7** (remove) ausziehen, ablegen ‹*Kleidungsstücke*›. *See also* **~ B**
- **~ 'on** *v.t.* **1** anziehen ‹*Kleidung, Hose usw.*›; aufsetzen ‹*Hut, Brille*›; draufsetzen, (ugs.) draufmachen ‹*Deckel, Verschluss usw.*›; (fig.: assume) aufsetzen ‹*Miene, Lächeln, Gesicht*›; **~ on a disguise** sich verkleiden; **~ sb.'s clothes on [for him]** jmdn. anziehen; **~ sb.'s shoes on [for him]** jmdm. die Schuhe anziehen; **~ it on** (coll.) [nur] Schau machen (ugs.); **he does ~ it on, doesn't he?** er übertreibt doch, oder?; **his modesty is all ~ on** seine Bescheidenheit ist nur gespielt *od.* (ugs.) ist reine Schau; **the town had ~ on a holiday look** die Stadt gab sich festlich **2** (switch or turn on) anmachen ‹*Radio, Motor, Heizung, Licht usw.*›; aufmachen ‹*Hahn*›; (cause to heat up) aufsetzen ‹*Wasser, Essen, Kessel, Topf*›; (fig.: apply) ausüben ‹*Druck*›; *see also* **screw A 1** **3** (gain) **~ on weight/two pounds** zunehmen/zwei Pfund zunehmen; **~ it on** (coll.: gain weight) Speck ansetzen (ugs.) **4** (add) **~ on speed** beschleunigen; **~ 8p on [to] the price** den Preis um 8 Pence erhöhen; 8 Pence auf den Preis aufschlagen **5** (stage) spielen ‹*Stück*›; zeigen ‹*Show, Film*›; veranstalten ‹*Ausstellung*›; *see also* **act A 5** **6** (arrange) einsetzen ‹*Sonderzug, -bus*› **7** ▸**~ forward 3** **8** (coll.: tease) veräppeln (ugs.); verarschen (salopp); *see also* **put-on** **9** (Cricket) die Punktzahl erhöhen um ‹*Läufe*›; [als Werfer] einsetzen ‹*Spieler*›; **be ~ on [to bowl]** als Werfer eingesetzt werden. *See also* **~ A 1**
- **~ 'out** *v.t.* **1** rausbringen; auslegen ‹*Futter*›; **~ one's hand out** die Hand ausstrecken; *see also* **tongue 1** **2** (extinguish) ausmachen ‹*Licht, Lampe*›; löschen ‹*Feuer, Brand*› **3** (issue) [he]rausgeben ‹*Buch, Zeitschrift, Broschüre, Anweisung, Erlass*›; abgeben ‹*Stellungnahme, Erklärung*›; (broadcast) senden; bringen **4** (produce) produzieren; ausstoßen ‹*Warenmenge*› **5** (annoy) verärgern; **be ~ out** verärgert *od.* entrüstet sein **6** (inconvenience) in Verlegenheit bringen; **~ oneself out to do sth.** die Mühe auf sich nehmen, etw. zu tun **7** (make inaccurate) verfälschen ‹*Ergebnis, Berechnung*› **8** (dislocate) verrenken; ausrenken ‹*Schulter*›; **~ one's thumb/ankle out** sich (*Dat.*) den Daumen/Knöchel verrenken **9** (give to outside worker) außer Haus geben; **~ sth. out to sb.** jmdn. mit etw. beauftragen **10** (sprout) hervorbringen; [aus]treiben **11** ausstechen ‹*Augen*›. *See also* **~ B**
- **~ 'over** ▸**~ across**
- **~ 'through** *v.t.* **1** (carry out) durchführen ‹*Plan, Programm, Kampagne, Sanierung*›; durchbringen ‹*Gesetz, Vorschlag*›; (complete) zum Abschluss bringen, abschließen ‹*Geschäft usw.*› **2** (Teleph.) verbinden (**to** mit); durchstellen ‹*Gespräch*› (**to** zu); **~ a call through to New York** nach New York telefonieren. *See also* **~ A 3**
- **~ to'gether** *v.t.* zusammensetzen ‹*Bauteile, Scherben, Steine, Einzelteile, Maschine usw.*›; ordnen ‹*Gedanken*›; erstellen, ausarbeiten ‹*Begründung, Argumentation, Beweisführung*›; *see also* **head A 1**; **two B**
- **~ 'under** *v.t.* (make unconscious) betäuben
- **~ 'up**

A *v.t.* **1** heben ‹*Hand*›; (erect) errichten ‹*Gebäude, Denkmal, Gerüst, Zaun usw.*›; bauen ‹*Haus*›; aufstellen ‹*Denkmal, Gerüst, Verkehrsschilder, Leinwand, Zelt*›; aufbauen ‹*Zelt, Verteidigungsanlagen*›; anbringen ‹*Schild, Notiz usw.*› (**on** an + *Dat.*); ‹*Igel:*› aufstellen ‹*Stacheln*›; (fig.) aufbauen ‹*Fassade*›; abziehen ‹*Schau*›; *see also* **put-up** **2** (display) anschlagen; aushängen **3** (offer as defence) hochnehmen ‹*Fäuste*›; leisten ‹*Widerstand, Gegenwehr*›; **~ up a struggle** sich wehren *od.* zur Wehr setzen; **~ up a bold front** sich tapfer wehren; tapfer Widerstand leisten; **~ up a defence** sich verteidigen **4** (present for consideration) einreichen ‹*Petition, Gesuch, Vorschlag*›; sprechen ‹*Gebet*›; (propose) vorschlagen; (nominate) aufstellen; **~ sb. up for election** jmdn. als Kandidaten aufstellen; **~ sb. up for secretary** jmdn. für das Amt des Sekretärs vorschlagen **5** (incite) **~ sb. up to sth.** jmdn. zu etw. anstiften **6** (accommodate) unterbringen **7** (increase) [he]raufsetzen, anheben ‹*Preis, Miete, Steuer, Zins*› **8** (provide) zur Verfügung stellen; *abs.* **~ up or shut up** (coll.) steh zu deinem Wort, oder halt gefälligst den Mund! **9** **~ sth. up for sale** etw. zum Verkauf anbieten; **~ sth. up for auction** etw. versteigern lassen; **~ sth. up for competition** etw. [öffentlich] ausschreiben **10** (Hunting) aufscheuchen; auftun (fachspr.) **11** (arch.: sheathe) in die Scheide stecken. *See also* **back A 1**; **fight C 1**

B *v.i.* **1** (be candidate) kandidieren; sich aufstellen lassen **2** (lodge) übernachten; sich einquartieren

- **~ upon** *v.t.* ausnutzen; **let oneself be ~ upon by sb.** sich von jmdm. ausnutzen lassen
- **~ 'up with** *v.t.* sich (*Dat.*) gefallen *od.* bieten lassen ‹*Beleidigung, Benehmen, Unhöflichkeit*›; sich abfinden mit ‹*Lärm, Elend, Ärger, Bedingungen*›; sich abgeben mit ‹*Person*›

put² ▸**putt**

putative /ˈpjuːtətɪv/ *adj.* mutmaßlich; (erroneously) vermeintlich

put: ~-down *n.* Herabsetzung, *die;* (snub) Abfuhr, *die;* **~-on** *n.* (coll.) Veräppelung, *die* (ugs.); Verarschung, *die* (salopp)

put-put /ˈpʌtpʌt/
A *n.* Tuckern, *das*
B *v.i.*, **-tt-** tuckern

putrefaction /pjuːtrɪˈfækʃn/ *n.*, *no pl.*, *no indef. art.* Zersetzung, *die*

putrefy /ˈpjuːtrɪfaɪ/ *v.i.* sich zersetzen

putrid /ˈpjuːtrɪd/ *adj.* **1** (rotten) faul; **become ~:** sich zersetzen **2** (of putrefaction) faulig; **~ smell** Fäulnisgeruch, *der* **3** (fig.: corrupt) verdorben; verworfen (geh.) **4** (coll.) (dreadful) scheußlich; (stupid) blödsinnig ‹*Ansichten*›

putsch /pʊtʃ/ *n.* Putsch, *der;* **army ~:** Militärputsch, *der*

putt /pʌt/ (Golf)
A *v.i. & t.* putten
B *n.* Putt, *der*

puttee /ˈpʌtɪ/ *n.* **1** Wickelgamasche, *die* **2** (Amer.: leather legging) Ledergamasche, *die*

putter /ˈpʌtə(r)/ (Golf) Putter, *der*

putting green /ˈpʌtɪŋ ɡriːn/ *n.* (Golf) **1** Grün, *das* **2** (miniature golf course) *kleiner Golfplatz nur zum Putten*

putty /ˈpʌtɪ/
A *n.* **1** Kitt, *der;* **glaziers' ~:** Fensterkitt, *der;* Glaserkitt, *der* **2** **[jewellers'] ~:** Zinnasche, *die;* Polierasche, *die*
B *v.t.* **1** (fix with glaziers' ~) einkitten ‹*Fensterscheibe*›; (fill with ~) auskitten ‹*Risse*› **2** (cover with plasterers' ~) verputzen ‹*Wand*›; ausgipsen ‹*Fugen*›

'putty knife *n.* Kittmesser, *das*

'put-up *adj.* **a ~ thing/job** eine abgekartete Sache/ein abgekartetes Spiel

puzzle /ˈpʌzl/
A *n.* **1** (problem) Rätsel, *das;* (brainteaser) Denksportaufgabe, *die;* (toy) Geduldsspiel, *das* **2** (enigma) Rätsel, *das;* **be a ~ to sb.** jmdm. ein Rätsel sein; **be a ~:** rätselhaft sein
B *v.t.* rätselhaft *od.* ein Rätsel sein (+ *Dat.*); vor ein Rätsel stellen; **he would have been ~d to explain it** er hätte nicht gewusst, wie er es hätte erklären sollen; **he was ~d what to do** er wusste nicht, was er tun sollte
C *v.i.* **~ over** *or* **about sth.** sich (*Dat.*) über etw. den Kopf zerbrechen; über etw. rätseln; **we ~d over what had happened** wir rätselten, was wohl passiert war

(Phrasal verb)

- **~ 'out** *v.t.* herausfinden; **~ out an answer to a question** eine Antwort auf eine Frage finden

puzzled /ˈpʌzld/ *adj.* ratlos

puzzlement /ˈpʌzlmənt/ *n.*, *no pl.* Verwirrung, *die*

puzzling /ˈpʌzlɪŋ/ *adj.* rätselhaft

PVC *abbr.* **= polyvinyl chloride** PVC, *das*

PX *abbr.* (Amer.) **= Post Exchange**

pygmy /ˈpɪɡmɪ/
A *n.* **1** Pygmäe, *der* **2** (dwarf; also fig.) Zwerg, *der*/Zwergin, *die*
B *attrib. adj.* **1** pygmäisch; **the ~ people** die Pygmäen **2** (dwarf) Zwerg-

pyjama /pɪˈdʒɑːmə/ *adj.* Pyjama-; Schlafanzug-; **~ suit** Pyjama, *der;* Schlafanzug, *der*

pyjamas /pɪˈdʒɑːməz/ *n. pl.* **[pair of] ~:** Schlafanzug, *der;* Pyjama, *der*

pylon /ˈpaɪlən/ *n.* Mast, *der*

pyramid /ˈpɪrəmɪd/ *n.* Pyramide, *die*

pyramidal /pɪˈræmɪdl/ *adj.* pyramidenförmig

'pyramid selling *n.*, *no pl.*, *no indef. art.:* *Verkauf von Vertriebsrechten nach dem Schneeballsystem*

pyre /paɪə(r)/ *n.* Scheiterhaufen, *der*

Pyrenean /pɪrəˈniːən/ *adj.* pyrenäisch; **~ mountain dog** Pyrenäenhund, *der*

Pyrenees /pɪrəˈniːz/ *pr. n. pl.* **the ~:** die Pyrenäen

pyrethrum /paɪˈriːθrəm/ *n.* **1** (flower) Chrysantheme, *die;* Pyrethrum, *das* (veralt.) **2** (insecticide) Pyrethrum, *das*

Pyrex ® /ˈpaɪreks/ *n.* ≈ Jenaer Glas, *das* (Wz); *attrib.* **~ dish** feuerfeste Glasschüssel

pyrites /paɪˈraɪtiːz/ *n.*, *no pl.* (Min.) **[iron] ~:** Pyrit, *der;* Eisenkies, *der*

pyrolysis /ˈpaɪˈrɒlɪsɪs/ *n.*, *no pl.* (Chem.) Pyrolise, *die*

pyromania /paɪrəˈmeɪnɪə/ *n.*, *no pl.* Pyromanie, *die*

pyromaniac /paɪrəˈmeɪnɪæk/ *n.* Pyromane, *der*/Pyromanin, *die*

pyrotechnic /paɪrəʊˈteknɪk/*adj.* pyrotechnisch; Feuerwerks-; (fig.: brilliant) brillant

pyrotechnics /paɪərəʊˈteknɪks/ *n. pl.* Feuerwerk, *das;* (fig.) Brillanz, *die*

Pyrrhic /ˈpɪrɪk/ *adj.* **~ victory** Pyrrhussieg, *der*

Pythagoras /paɪˈθæɡərəs/ *pr. n.* Pythagoras, *der;* **~' theorem** (Geom.) der Satz des Pythagoras

python /ˈpaɪθən/ *n.* Python, *der;* Pythonschlange, *die*

P

Qq

Q[1], q /kju:/ *n., pl.* **Qs** *or* **Q's** Q, q, *das; see also* **mind B 2**

Q[2] *abbr.* = **question** F

Q. *abbr.* **1** = **Queen** Kgn. **2** = **Queen's** kgl. **3** (Chess) = **queen** D

QC *abbr.* (Brit.) = **Queen's Counsel**

QED *abbr.* = **quod erat demonstrandum** q. e. d.; w. z. b. w.

QMV *abbr.* (EU) **qualified majority voting**

qr. *abbr.* = **quarter[s]** qr.

qt. *abbr.* = **quart[s]** qt

qua /kweɪ, kwɑ:/ *conj.* (literary) qua (geh.)

quack[1] /kwæk/
A *v.i.* ‹*Ente:*› quaken
B *n.* Quaken, *das*

quack[2] (derog.)
A *n.* Quacksalber, *der* (abwertend)
B *attrib. adj.* **1** ~ **doctor** Quacksalber, *der* **2** Quacksalber‹*kur, -tropfen, -pillen*› (abwertend); ~ **remedy** Mittelchen, *das* (ugs. abwertend)

'quack-quack *n.* (child lang.) Quakente, *die* (Kinderspr.)

quad /kwɒd/ *n.* **1** (coll.: quadrangle) Innenhof, *der* **2** (quadraphonic) ~ **[sound system]** Quadroanlage, *die* **3** (coll.: quadruplet) Vierling, *der* **4** (Print.: quadrat) **[em]** ~**/en** ~**:** Geviert/Halbgeviert, *das*

'quad bike *n.* Quad, *das*

quadrangle /'kwɒdræŋgl/ *n.* **1** (enclosed court) viereckiger Innenhof; (with buildings) Block, *der;* Karree, *das* **2** (Geom.) Viereck, *das*

quadrant /'kwɒdrənt/ *n.* **1** (Geom., Astron., Naut.) Quadrant, *der;* (of sphere) Viertelkugel, *die* **2** (object shaped like quarter-circle) viertelkreisförmiger Gegenstand

quadraphonic /kwɒdrə'fɒnɪk/ *adj.* quadrophon; Quadro‹*anlage, -sound usw.*›

quadratic /kwə'drætɪk/ *adj.* (Math.) quadratisch; zweiten Grades *nachgestellt*

quadrilateral /kwɒdrɪ'lætərl/ *n.* (Geom.) Viereck, *das*

quadrille /kwə'drɪl/ *n.* Quadrille, *die*

quadriplegia /kwɒdrɪ'pli:dʒɪə/ *n.* (Med.) Quadri-, Tetraplegie, *die* (fachspr.); gleichzeitige Lähmung aller vier Gliedmaßen

quadriplegic /kwɒdrɪ'pli:dʒɪk/ (Med.)
A *n.* Quadri-, Tetraplegiker, *der*/-plegikerin, *die*
B *adj.* quadri-, tetraplegisch; **be** ~**:** an allen vier Gliedmaßen gelähmt sein

quadruped /'kwɒdrʊped/ *n.* Vierfüßler, *der*

quadruple /'kwɒdrʊpl/
A *adj.* **1** vierfach **2** (four times) viermal; **be** ~ **today's value** viermal so hoch sein wie der heutige Wert; ~ **the amount** die vierfache Menge **3** (Mus.) ~ **time** Viertertakt, *der*
B *v.t.* mit vier malnehmen ‹*Zahl*›; vervierfachen ‹*Einkommen, Produktion, Profit*›
C *v.i.* sich vervierfachen

quadruplet /'kwɒdrʊplɪt, kwɒ'dru:plɪt/ *n.* Vierling, *der*

quadruplicate /kwɒ'dru:plɪkət/ *n.* vierfache Ausfertigung; **in** ~**:** in vierfacher Ausfertigung *nachgestellt*

quaff /kwɑ:f, kwɒf/ (literary)
A *v.i.* zechen (veralt., scherzh.); pokulieren (veralt., scherzh.)
B *v.t.* [mit langen, kräftigen Schlucken] leeren *od.* austrinken ‹*Glas*›; [mit langen, kräftigen Schlucken] trinken ‹*Getränk*›

quag /kwæg, kwɒg/ *n.* (marshy spot) sumpfige *od.* morastige Stelle; (quaking bog) Schwingmoor, *das*

quagmire /'kwægmaɪə(r), kwɒgmaɪə(r)/ *n.* Sumpf, *der;* Morast, *der;* (quaking bog) Schwingmoor, *das;* (fig.: complex or difficult situation) Sumpf, *der;* **be in a** ~ (lit. or fig.) in einem Sumpf stecken; **a** ~ **of details/problems** ein Wust von Einzelheiten/Problemen

quail[1] /kweɪl/ *n., pl. same or* ~**s** (Ornith.) Wachtel, *die*

quail[2] *v.i.* ‹*Person:*› [ver]zagen, den Mut sinken lassen; ‹*Blick, Mut, Hoffnung, Vertrauen:*› sinken; **make sb.'s courage/spirit** ~**:** jmdn. entmutigen; ~ **at the prospect of sth.** bei der Aussicht auf etw. (*Akk.*) verzagen

quaint /kweɪnt/ *adj.* drollig; putzig (ugs.) ‹*Häuschen, Einrichtung*›; malerisch, pittoresk ‹*Ort*›; (odd, strange) kurios, seltsam ‹*Bräuche, Anblick, Begebenheit*›; schnurrig ‹*alter Kauz*›

quaintly /'kweɪntlɪ/ *adv.* putzig (ugs.); drollig ‹*bemerken*›

quake /kweɪk/
A *n.* (coll.) [Erd]beben, *das*
B *v.i.* beben; ‹*Sumpfboden:*› schwingen; ~ **with fear/fright** vor Angst/Schreck zittern *od.* beben

Quaker /'kweɪkə(r)/ *n.* Quäker, *der*/Quäkerin, *die*

> **Quaker**
>
> Ein Mitglied der religiösen Gesellschaft der Freunde, einer im 17. Jahrhundert entstandenen christlichen Gemeinschaft. Die Gesellschaft wurde von George Fox (1624-91) gegründet, der nach einem visionären Erlebnis einen Kreis von Anhängern um sich sammelte, die sich ursprünglich 'Kinder des Lichts' und nach 1652 *Society of Friends* nannte. Der Name *Quaker* leitet sich von *quake* (zittern) ab, weil die Quäker vor religiöser Erregung zitterten. Ihr Glaube beruht auf der Erfahrung des inneren Lichts, das von Christus kommt und die Menschen zum Heil führt. Sie sind gegen zeremoniellen Gottesdienst, ihre Treffen sind von stillen Gebeten geprägt. Die Quäker lehnen jegliche Diskriminierung und Gewaltanwendung ab und haben sich durch Sozialarbeit und Friedensdienste ausgezeichnet. Da sie die englische Staatskirche und den Kriegsdienst ablehnten, waren die Quäker bis 1689 Verfolgungen ausgesetzt, und viele wanderten nach Amerika aus. Der Quäkerführer William Penn (1644-1718) gründete die nach seinem Vater benannte Quäkerkolonie Pennsylvania und 1683 die Stadt Philadelphia.

quaking /'kweɪkɪŋ/: ~ **bog** *n.* Schwingmoor, *das;* ~ **grass** *n.* (Bot.) Zittergras, *das*

qualification /kwɒlɪfɪ'keɪʃn/ *n.* **1** (ability) Qualifikation, *die;* (condition to be fulfilled) Voraussetzung, *die;* **secretarial** ~**s** Ausbildung als Sekretärin **2** (on paper) Zeugnis, *das* **3** (limitation) Vorbehalt, *der;* **without** ~**:** vorbehaltlos; ohne Vorbehalt; **the offer was subject to one** ~**:** das Angebot hatte eine Einschränkung

qualified /'kwɒlɪfaɪd/ *adj.* **1** qualifiziert; (by training) ausgebildet; (entitled, having right to) berechtigt; **be** ~ **for a job/to vote** die Qualifikation für eine Stelle besitzen/wahlberechtigt sein; **you are better** ~ **to judge that** du kannst das besser beurteilen; **I am not** ~ **to speak on that** ich kann darüber nichts sagen; **be** ~ **to vote** wahlberechtigt sein **2** (restricted) nicht uneingeschränkt; **a** ~ **success** kein voller Erfolg; ~ **approval/reply** Zustimmung/Antwort unter Vorbehalt; ~ **acceptance** bedingte Annahme

qualified majority 'voting *n., no pl.* (EU) Abstimmung mit qualifizierter Mehrheit

qualifier /'kwɒlɪfaɪə(r)/ *n.* **1** (restriction) Einschränkung, *die* (**of, on** *Gen.*) **2** (person) **be among the** ~**s** zu denen gehören, die sich qualifiziert haben **3** (Sport: match) Qualifikationsspiel, *das*

qualify /'kwɒlɪfaɪ/
A *v.t.* **1** (make competent, make officially entitled) berechtigen (**for** zu) **2** (modify) einschränken; modifizieren ‹*Meinung, Feststellung*› **3** (describe) bewerten; bezeichnen **4** (moderate) abschwächen; ~ **justice with mercy** Gnade vor Recht ergehen lassen **5** (Ling.) näher bestimmen
B *v.i.* **1** ~ **in law/medicine/education/chemistry** seinen [Studien]abschluss in Jura/Medizin/Pädagogik/Chemie machen; ~ **as a doctor/lawyer/teacher/chemist** sein Examen als Arzt/Anwalt/Lehrer/Chemiker machen **2** (fulfil a condition) infrage kommen (**for** für); ~ **for the vote/a pension** wahl-/rentenberechtigt sein; ~ **for admission to a university/club** die Aufnahmebedingungen einer Universität/eines Vereins erfüllen; ~ **for a post** für eine Stelle qualifiziert sein; ~ **for membership** die Bedingungen für die Mitgliedschaft erfüllen **3** (Sport) sich qualifizieren

qualifying /'kwɒlɪfaɪɪŋ/ *adj.* **1** ~ **statement** einschränkende Aussage **2** (Sport) ~ **match** Qualifikationsspiel, *das;* ~ **round/heat** Ausscheidungs- *od.* Qualifikationsrunde, *die* **3** ~ **examination** Zulassungsprüfung, *die*

qualitative /'kwɒlɪtətɪv/ *adj.*, **qualitatively** /'kwɒlɪtətɪvlɪ/ *adv.* qualitativ

quality /'kwɒlɪtɪ/
A *n.* **1** Qualität, *die;* **of good/poor** *etc.* ~**:** von guter/schlechter *usw.* Qualität; **of the best** ~**:** bester Qualität; ~ **rather than quantity** Qualität, nicht Quantität; **clothes of** ~**:** Qualitätskleidung, *die;* **the** ~ **of her writing/craftsmanship** ihre schriftstellerischen Leistungen/handwerklichen Fähigkeiten **2** (characteristic) Eigenschaft, *die;* **the melodious** ~ **of her voice** die Melodie ihrer Stimme; **possess the qualities of a ruler/leader** eine Führernatur sein; **have the** ~ **of inspiring others with confidence** die Gabe haben, andere mit Zuversicht zu erfüllen; *see also* **defect A 2** **3** (of sound, voice) Klang, *der* **4** (arch.: rank) Rang, *der;* **people of** ~**:** Leute von Rang [und Namen]
B *adj.* **1** (excellent) Qualitäts- **2** (maintaining ~) Qualitäts‹*prüfung, -kontrolle*›; (denoting ~) Güte‹*grad, -klasse, -zeichen*›

quality: ~ **control** *n.* Qualitätskontrolle, *die;* ~ **controller** *n.* ▶ **p. 1260** Qualitätsprüfer, *der;* ~ **time** *n.: ganz dem Miteinander gewidmete Zeit;* **spend** ~ **time with sb.** einen Teil seiner Zeit ganz jmdm. widmen

qualm /kwɑ:m, kwɔ:m/ *n.* **1** (sudden misgiving) ungutes Gefühl **2** (scruple) Bedenken, *das* (*meist Pl.*) (**over, about** gegen); **he had no** ~**s about borrowing money** er hatte keine Bedenken, sich (*Dat.*) Geld zu leihen **3** (sick feeling) Übelkeit, *die*

q

quandary /ˈkwɒndərɪ/ *n.* Dilemma, *das;* **this demand put him in a ~:** diese Forderung brachte ihn in eine verzwickte Lage; **he was in a ~ about what to do next** er wusste nicht, was er als Nächstes tun sollte

quango /ˈkwæŋgəʊ/ *n., pl.* **~s** (Brit.) *halböffentliche Verwaltungseinrichtung*

quango

In Großbritannien eine halböffentliche Verwaltungseinrichtung, die im Auftrag der Regierung bestimmte Bereiche des kulturellen, gesellschaftlichen oder wissenschaftlichen Lebens subventioniert und leitet. Der britische **Arts Council** wird beispielsweise so verwaltet. Das Wort quango setzt sich aus den Anfangsbuchstaben von *quasi-autonomous non-governmental organization* zusammen.

quanta *pl. of* **quantum**

quantifiable /ˈkwɒntɪfaɪəbl/ *adj.* quantifizierbar

quantify /ˈkwɒntɪfaɪ/ *v.t.* quantifizieren

quantitative /ˈkwɒntɪtətɪv/ *adj.*, **quantitatively** /ˈkwɒntɪtətɪvlɪ/ *adv.* quantitativ

quantity /ˈkwɒntɪtɪ/ *n.* 1 Quantität, *die* 2 (amount, sum) Menge, *die;* **what ~ of flour do you need for this recipe?** wie viel Mehl braucht man für dieses Rezept?; **~ of heat** Wärmemenge, *die* 3 (large amount) [Un]menge, *die;* **coal/gold in quantities** Kohle/Gold in Unmengen *od.* (ugs.) rauen Mengen; **buy in quantities** in großen Mengen einkaufen; *see also* **bill³ A 8** 4 (Math.) Größe, *die* 5 (fig.) **negligible ~:** Quantité négligeable, *die* (geh.); **he is a negligible ~:** er ist völlig unwichtig; **an unknown ~:** eine unbekannte Größe 6 (Phonet., Pros.) Quantität, *die*

quantity: **~ mark** *n.* (Pros.) Quantitätszeichen, *das;* **~ surveyor** *n.* ▸ⓘ **p. 1260** Baukostenkalkulator, *der*/-kalkulatorin, *die*

quantum /ˈkwɒntəm/ *n., pl.* **quanta** /ˈkwɒntə/ 1 (literary) (amount) Menge, *die;* (share, portion) Anteil, *der;* (required, desired, or allowed amount) Quantum, *das* 2 (Phys.) Quant, *das*

quantum: **~ jump, ~ leap** *ns.* (Phys.; also fig.) Quantensprung, *der;* **~ meˈchanics** *n.* (Phys.) Quantenmechanik, *die;* **~ theory** *n.* (Phys.) Quantentheorie, *die*

quarantine /ˈkwɒrəntiːn/

A *n.* Quarantäne, *die; attrib.* Quarantäne‹*bestimmungen, -zeit, -flagge*›; **put under ~:** unter Quarantäne stellen; **be in ~:** unter Quarantäne stehen

B *v.t.* unter Quarantäne stellen

quark /kwɑːk, kwɔːk/ *n.* (Phys.) Quark, *das*

quarrel /ˈkwɒrl/

A *n.* 1 Streit, *der;* **have a ~ with sb. [about/over sth.]** sich mit jmdm. [über etw. (*Akk.*) *od.* wegen etw./um etw.] streiten; **let's not have a ~ about it** wir wollen uns nicht darüber streiten; **I don't want to have a ~ with you** ich will mich mit dir nicht streiten *od.* will keinen Streit mit dir; **pick a ~ [with sb. over sth.]** [mit jmdm. wegen etw.] Streit anfangen 2 (cause of complaint) Einwand, *der* (**with** gegen); **I have no ~ with you** ich habe nichts gegen dich

B *v.i.*, (Brit.) **-ll-** 1 [sich] streiten (**over** um, **about** über + *Akk.*, wegen); **~ with each other** [sich] [miteinander] streiten; (fall out, dispute) sich [zer]streiten (**over** um, **about** über + *Akk.*, wegen) 2 (find fault) etwas auszusetzen haben (**with** an + *Dat.*); **I really can't ~ with that** daran habe ich wirklich nichts auszusetzen

quarrelsome /ˈkwɒrlsəm/ *adj.* streitsüchtig; **his ~ nature** seine Streitsucht

quarry¹ /ˈkwɒrɪ/

A *n.* Steinbruch, *der;* **marble/slate ~:** Marmor-/Schieferbruch, *der;* (fig.) Fundgrube, *die* (**of** für); **~ of information** Informationsquelle, *die*

B *v.t.* brechen ‹*Steine, Marmor*›; (fig.) zutage fördern

C *v.i.* (fig.) herumstöbern

quarry² *n.* (prey) Beute, *die;* (fig.) Opfer, *das*

quarry: **~man** /ˈkwɒrɪmən/ *n., pl.* **~men** /ˈkwɒrɪmən/ ▸ⓘ **p. 1260** Steinbrucharbeiter, *der;* **~ tile** *n.* unglasierte Steinfliese

quart /kwɔːt/ *n.* 1 ▸ⓘ **p. 1690** Quart, *das;* **try to put a ~ into a pint pot** (fig.) mehr in etwas unterbringen wollen als hineinpasst 2 (vessel) Quartgefäß, *das*

ˈ**quart bottle** *n.* Quartflasche, *die*

quarter /ˈkwɔːtə(r)/

A *n.* 1 ▸ⓘ **p. 1358**, ▸ⓘ **p. 1702** Viertel, *das;* **a** *or* **one ~ of** ein Viertel (+ *Gen.*); **a ~ [of] the price** ein Viertel des Preises; **divide/cut sth. into ~s** etw. in vier Teile teilen/schneiden; etw. vierteln; **six and a ~:** sechseinviertel; **an hour and a ~:** eineinviertel Stunden; **a ~ [of a pound] of cheese** ein Viertel[pfund] Käse; **~ of lamb/beef** Lamm-/Rinderviertel, *das;* **a ~ of a mile/an hour/a century** eine Viertelmeile/-stunde/ein Vierteljahrhundert; **three ~s of an hour** eine Dreiviertelstunde 2 (of year) Quartal, *das;* Vierteljahr, *das* 3 ▸ⓘ **p. 1001** (point of time) **[a] ~ to/past six** Viertel vor/nach sechs; drei Viertel sechs/viertel sieben (landsch.); **there are buses at ~ to and ~ past [the hour]** es fahren Busse um Viertel vor und Viertel nach jeder vollen Stunde *od.* (ugs.) eine Viertelstunde vor und nach voll 4 (direction) Richtung, *die;* **blow from all ~s** ‹*Wind:*› aus allen Richtungen wehen; **flock in from all ~s** aus allen Himmelsrichtungen zusammenströmen; **from every ~ of the globe** von überall her 5 (source of supply or help) Seite, *die;* **from this ~:** von dieser Stelle; **secret information from a high ~:** Geheiminformationen von höchster Stelle; **turn for support to other ~s** sich woanders *od.* anderweitig um Unterstützung bemühen 6 (area of town) [Stadt]viertel, *das;* Quartier, *das;* **in some ~s** (fig.) in gewissen Kreisen 7 *in pl.* (lodgings) Quartier, *das* (bes. Milit.); Unterkunft, *die;* **take up [one's] ~s** Quartier beziehen; *see also* **close A 1** 8 (Brit.: measure) (of volume) Quarter, *der;* (of weight) ≈ Viertelzentner, *der* 9 (Amer.) (school term) Viertelschuljahr, *das;* (university term) halbes Semester 10 (Astron.) Viertel, *das;* **the moon is in its last ~:** der Mond steht im letzten Viertel 11 (mercy) Schonung, *die;* **give/receive ~:** Schonung *od.* (veralt.) Pardon gewähren/gewährt bekommen; **give no ~ to sb.** jmdm. keinen Pardon (veralt.) gewähren *od.* geben 12 ▸ⓘ **p. 1332** (Amer., Can.: amount, coin) Vierteldollar, *der;* 25-Cent-Stück, *das;* **the bus fare was a ~:** die Busfahrt hat 25 Cent *od.* einen Vierteldollar gekostet 13 (Naut.) Achterschiff, *das;* Hinterschiff, *das* 14 (in shoemaking) Seitenteil, *das;* Quartier, *das* (fachspr.)

B *v.t.* 1 (divide) vierteln ‹*Apfel, Tomate usw.*›; in vier Teile teilen ‹*Stück Fleisch*›; durch vier teilen ‹*Zahl, Summe*› 2 (lodge) einquartieren ‹*Soldaten*› 3 (Hist.) vierteilen ‹*Verbrecher*›

quarter: **~back** *n.* (Amer. Football) Quarterback, *der;* **~ binding** *n.* (Bookbinding) Halbfranz, *das;* **~ day** *n.* Quartalsende, *das;* **~deck** *n.* (Naut.) 1 (of ship) Quarterdeck, *das;* 2 (officers) Marineoffiziere *Pl.;* **~-ˈfinal** *n.* Viertelfinale, *das;* **in the ~-finals** im Viertelfinale; **~-ˈfinalist** *n.* Viertelfinalist, *der*/-finalistin, *die;* **~-ˈhour** *n.* 1 Viertelstunde, *die;* 2 **on the ~-hour** (fifteen minutes before) um Viertel vor; (fifteen minutes after) um Viertel nach

quartering /ˈkwɔːtərɪŋ/ *n.* 1 (dividing) Vierteln, *das* 2 (lodging) Einquartierung, *die*

ˈ**quarter-light** *n.* (Brit. Motor Veh.) (bes. ausstellbares) Teil des Fond-/Türfensters

quarterly /ˈkwɔːtəlɪ/

A *adj.* vierteljährlich

B *n.* Vierteljahr[e]sschrift, *die*

C *adv.* vierteljährlich; alle Vierteljahre

quarter: **~master** *n.* 1 (Naut.) Quartermeister, *der;* 2 (Mil.) Quartiermeister, *der* (veralt.); **~ ˈmile** *n.* Viertelmeile, *die;* **~ note** *n.* (Amer. Mus.) ▸**crotchet**; **~-pounder** *n.* Viertelpfünder, *der;* **~ ˈsessions** *n. pl.* (Brit. Hist.) *vierteljährliche Gerichtssitzungen*

quartet, quartette /kwɔːˈtet/ *n.* (also Mus.) Quartett, *das;* **piano/string ~:** Klavier-/Streichquartett, *das*

quarto /ˈkwɔːtəʊ/ *n., pl.* **~s** 1 (book) Quartband, *der* 2 (size) Quart[format], *das;* **~ paper** Papier im Quartformat

quartz /kwɔːts/ *n.* Quarz, *der*

quartz: **~ clock** *n.* Quarzuhr, *die;* **~ lamp** *n.* Quarzlampe, *die;* **~ watch** *n.* Quarzuhr, *die*

quasar /ˈkweɪsɑː(r), ˈkweɪzɑː(r)/ *n.* (Astron.) Quasar, *der*

quash /kwɒʃ/ *v.t.* 1 (annul, make void) aufheben ‹*Urteil, Entscheidung*›; zurückweisen ‹*Einspruch, Klage*› 2 (suppress, crush) unterdrücken ‹*Opposition*›; niederschlagen ‹*Aufstand, Generalstreik*›

quasi /ˈkweɪzaɪ, ˈkwɑːzɪ/ *adv.* quasi

quasi- *pref.* 1 (not real, seeming) Schein- 2 (half-) Quasi-; quasi; **~official** halbamtlich

Quaternary /kwəˈtɜːnərɪ/ (Geol.)

A *adj.* quartär

B *n.* Quartär, *das*

quatrain /ˈkwɒtreɪn/ *n.* (Pros.) Vierzeiler, *der;* Quatrain, *das od. der* (fachspr.)

quatrefoil /ˈkætrəfɔɪl/ *n.* (Archit.) Vierpass, *der*

quaver /ˈkweɪvə(r)/

A *n.* 1 (Brit. Mus.) Achtelnote, *die* 2 (Mus.: trill) Tremolo, *das* 3 (in speech) Zittern, *das;* Beben, *das* (geh.); **admit with a ~ [in one's voice] that ...:** mit zitternder Stimme zugeben, dass ...

B *v.i.* (vibrate, tremble) zittern; beben (geh.)

quavering /ˈkweɪvərɪŋ/, **quavery** /ˈkweɪvərɪ/ *adjs.* zitternd, bebend ‹*Stimme*›

quay /kiː/, ˈ**quayside** *ns.* Kai, *der;* Kaje, *die* (nordd.)

queasiness /ˈkwiːzɪnɪs/ *n., no pl.* Übelkeit, *die*

queasy /ˈkwiːzɪ/ *adj.* unwohl; (uneasy) mulmig (ugs.); **a ~ feeling** ein Gefühl der Übelkeit; **just the thought of it makes me [feel] ~:** schon beim Gedanken daran wird mir ganz schlecht *od.* übel; **my stomach is in such a ~ state** mir ist so komisch im Magen

queen /kwiːn/ *n.* 1 ▸ⓘ **p. 1634** Königin, *die;* **Q~ of [the] May** Maikönigin, *die* 2 (bee, ant, wasp) Königin, *die* 3 (personified best example of sth.) Juwel, *das;* Perle, *die* 4 (Chess, Cards) Dame, *die;* **~'s bishop/knight/pawn/rook** Damenläufer/-springer/-bauer/-turm, *der;* **~ of hearts** Herzdame, *die* 5 (sl.: male homosexual) Tunte, *die* (salopp). *See also* **bench 4; colour A 10; counsel A 3; English B 1; evidence A 2; guide A 5; highway 1; messenger 2; peace 2; save A 3; scout A 1; shilling**

queen: **~ bee** *n.* Bienenkönigin, *die;* **~ ˈconsort** *n.* Königin, *die;* Gemahlin des Königs

queenly /ˈkwiːnlɪ/ *adj.* königlich; (majestic) majestätisch

queen ˈmother *n.* Königinmutter, *die*

Queen's Speech

Die Verlesung der jährlichen Thronrede, die die Königin zur Parlamentseröffnung im Herbst im **House of Lords** hält. Die Rede, die in Rundfunk und Fernsehen übertragen wird, ist vom Premierminister und Mitgliedern des Kabinetts verfasst und enthält das Regierungsprogramm für das kommende Jahr. Wenn ein König das Staatsoberhaupt ist, dann bezeichnet man die Thronrede als *King's Speech*.

queer /kwɪə(r)/

A *adj.* 1 (strange) sonderbar; seltsam; (eccentric) komisch; verschroben; **a ~ feeling** ein komisches Gefühl; *see also* **fish A 3** 2 (shady, suspect) merkwürdig; seltsam; **there's something ~ about this whole business** die ganze Sache ist nicht ganz hasenrein 3 (Brit. coll. dated: out of sorts, faint) unwohl; **I feel ~:** mir ist komisch *od.* (ugs.) flau; **you are looking a bit ~:** du siehst ein bisschen angegriffen aus 4 (coll.: mad, insane) verrückt (salopp); **~ in the head** plemplem (salopp) 5 (sl. derog.: homosexual) schwul (ugs.)

B *n.* (sl. derog.: homosexual) Schwule, *der* (ugs.)

C *v.t.* (Brit.: spoil) vermasseln (salopp); **~ the pitch for sb., ~ sb.'s pitch** jmdm. einen Strich durch die Rechnung machen

ˈ**queer-bashing** *n., no pl.* (coll.) Zusammenschlagen von Schwulen (ugs.)

queerly /ˈkwɪəlɪ/ *adv.* sonderbar; seltsam

ˈ**Queer Street** *n.* **be in ~** (in difficulties, trouble, debt) in der Tinte sitzen (ugs.); in Schwulitäten sein (ugs.)

q

quell /kwel/ *v.t.* niederschlagen ‹*Aufstand, Rebellion*›; bezwingen; zügeln ‹*Leidenschaft, Furcht*›; überwinden ‹*Ängste, Befürchtungen*›

quench /kwentʃ/ *v.t.* **1** (extinguish) löschen; (fig.) auslöschen (geh.) **2** (satisfy) **~ one's thirst** seinen Durst löschen *od.* stillen **3** (cool) löschen ‹*Koks*›; abschrecken ‹*Metall*› **4** (stifle, suppress) unterdrücken; dämpfen ‹*Begeisterung*›

quern /kwɜːn/ *n.* Handmühle, *die*

querulous /ˈkwerʊləs/ *adj.* gereizt; (by nature) reizbar

querulously /ˈkwerʊləslɪ/ *adv.* gereizt; **discuss sth. ~:** in gereiztem Ton über etw. (*Akk.*) diskutieren

query /ˈkwɪərɪ/

A *n.* **1** (question) Frage, *die;* **put/raise a ~:** eine Frage stellen/aufwerfen; **that raises the ~ whether we ...:** das wirft die Frage auf *od.* damit stellt sich die Frage, ob wir ... **2** (question mark) Fragezeichen, *das*

B *v.t.* **1** (call in question) infrage stellen ‹*Anweisung, Glaubwürdigkeit, Ergebnis usw.*›; beanstanden ‹*Rechnung, Kontoauszug*› **2** (ask, inquire) **~ whether/if ...:** fragen, ob ...

query: ~ language *n.* (Computing) Abfragesprache, *die;* **~ window** *n.* (Computing) **1** (dialogue box) Dialogfenster, *das;* **2** (for database search) Suchfenster, *das*

quest /kwest/ *n.* Suche, *die* (**for** nach); (for happiness, riches, knowledge, etc.) Streben, *das* (**for** nach); **in ~ of sth.** auf der Suche nach etw.; **man's ~ for happiness** das menschliche Glücksstreben

question /ˈkwestʃn/

A *n.* **1** Frage, *die;* **ask sb. a ~:** jmdm. eine Frage stellen; **put a ~ to sb.** an jmdn. eine Frage richten; **don't ask so many ~s!** frag nicht so viel!; **ask ~s** Fragen stellen; **ask me no ~s and I'll tell you no lies** wenn du nicht willst, dass ich lüge, stell mir keine Fragen; **ask a silly ~ and you get a silly answer** (prov.) wie die Frage, so die Antwort (Spr.); **and no ~s asked** ohne dass groß gefragt wird/worden ist (ugs.); **[that's a] good ~!** [das ist eine] gute Frage!; *see also* **leading question**; **pop¹ B 5** **2** (doubt, objection) Zweifel, *der* (**about** an + *Dat.*); **there is no ~ about sth.** es besteht kein Zweifel an (*Dat.*) etw.; **there is no ~ [but] that ...:** es besteht kein Zweifel, dass ...; **accept/follow sth. without ~:** etwas kritiklos akzeptieren/befolgen; **not be in ~:** außer [allem] Zweifel stehen; außer Frage sein *od.* stehen; **your honesty is/is not in ~:** man zweifelt/niemand zweifelt an deiner Ehrlichkeit; **beyond all** *or* **without ~:** zweifellos; ohne Frage *od.* Zweifel; **be beyond all** *or* **be without ~:** außer allem Zweifel stehen; außer Frage sein *od.* stehen; *see also* **call A 3** **3** (problem, concern, subject) Frage, *die;* **sth./it is only a ~ of time** etw./es ist [nur] eine Frage der Zeit; **it is [only] a ~ of doing sth.** es geht [nur] darum, etw. zu tun; **a ~ of money** eine Geldfrage; **there is no/some ~ of his doing that** es kann keine Rede davon sein/es ist die Rede davon, dass er das tut; **the ~ of sth. arises** es erhebt sich die Frage von etw.; **the person/thing in ~:** die fragliche *od.* betreffende Person/Sache; **sth./it is out of the ~:** etw./es ist ausgeschlossen; etw./es kommt nicht in Frage (ugs.); **the ~ is whether ...:** es geht darum, ob ...; **that is not the ~:** darum geht es nicht; **beside the ~:** belanglos; **put the ~:** zur Abstimmung aufrufen (**to** *Akk.*); **come into ~:** infrage kommen; *see also* **beg A 4**; **hour 5**; **open A 6, 7**

B *v.t.* **1** befragen; ‹*Polizei, Gericht usw.*:› vernehmen; **he started ~ing me about where I had been** er fing an, mich danach auszufragen, wo ich gewesen war **2** (throw doubt upon, raise objections to) bezweifeln; **her goodwill cannot be ~ed** an ihrem guten Willen kann nicht gezweifelt werden

questionable /ˈkwestʃənəbl/ *adj.* fragwürdig

questionably /ˈkwestʃənəblɪ/ *adv.* fragwürdig ‹*sich benehmen*›; auf fragwürdige Weise ‹*erwerben*›

questioner /ˈkwestʃənə(r)/ *n.* Fragesteller, *der*/Fragestellerin, *die*

questioning /ˈkwestʃənɪŋ/

A *adj.* fragend; forschend ‹*Geist*›

B *n.* Fragen, *das;* (at examination) Befragung, *die;* (by police etc.) Vernehmung, *die;* **brought in for ~:** ins Verhör genommen

questioningly /ˈkwestʃənɪŋlɪ/ *adv.* fragend

question: ~ mark *n.* (lit. or fig.) Fragezeichen, *das;* **a ~ mark hangs over sth.** etw. muss mit einem [großen] Fragezeichen versehen werden; **~ master** *n.* Quizmaster, *der*

questionnaire /kwestʃəˈneə(r)/ *n.* Fragebogen, *der*

ˈ**question time** *n.* Diskussionszeit, *die;* (Parl.) Fragestunde, *die;* **at ~ time** während der Diskussionszeit/Fragestunde

queue /kjuː/

A *n.* **1** (line) Schlange, *die;* **a ~ of people/cars** eine Menschen-/Autoschlange; **a long ~ of people** eine lange Schlange; **stand** *or* **wait in a ~:** Schlange stehen; anstehen; **join the ~:** sich anstellen; **take one's place in a ~:** sich in eine Schlange einreihen; *see also* **jump C 7** **2** (of hair) Zopf, *der*

B *v.i.* **~ [up]** Schlange stehen; anstehen; (join ~) sich anstellen; **~ to buy admission tickets** nach Eintrittskarten anstehen; **~ for a bus** an der Bushaltestelle Schlange stehen; **~ for vegetables** nach Gemüse anstehen

queue: ~-jumper *n.* (Brit.) *jmd., der sich vordrängt;* **~-jumping** *n.* (Brit.) Vordrängen, *das;* Vordrängeln, *das* (ugs.)

quibble /ˈkwɪbl/

A *n.* **1** (argument) spitzfindiges Argument **2** (petty objection) Spitzfindigkeit, *die*

B *v.i.* streiten; **~ over** *or* **about sth.** über etw. (*Akk.*) streiten; **~ about the quality of sb.'s work** die Qualität von jmds. Arbeit bekritteln

quibbler /ˈkwɪblə(r)/ *n.* Kritt[e]ler, *der;* Nörgler, *der*

quibbling /ˈkwɪblɪŋ/ *adj.* spitzfindig

quiche /kiːʃ/ *n.* Quiche, *die;* **bacon ~:** Speckkuchen, *der*

quick /kwɪk/

A *adj.* **1** schnell; kurz ‹*Rede, Zusammenfassung, Pause*›; flüchtig ‹*Kuss, Blick usw.*›; **it's ~er by train** mit dem Zug geht es schneller; ˈ**that was/**ˈ**you were ~!** das ging aber schnell!; **could I have a ~ word with you?** kann ich Sie kurz einmal sprechen?; **he had a ~ bite to eat** er hat schnell etwas gegessen; **how about a ~ drink?** wollen wir kurz einen trinken gehen? (ugs.); **write sb. a ~ note** jmdm. schnell ein paar Zeilen schreiben; **be ~!** mach schnell! (ugs.); beeil[e] dich!; **be ~ about it!** mach ein bisschen dalli! (ugs.); **please try to be ~ [about it]** (in discussion, on telephone) bitte fassen Sie sich kurz **2** (ready, sensitive, prompt to act or understand) schnell ‹*Person*›; wach ‹*Verstand*›; aufgeweckt ‹*Kind*›; **he is very ~:** er ist sehr schnell von Begriff (ugs.); **be ~ to do sth.** etw. schnell tun; **be ~ to take offence** schnell *od.* leicht beleidigt sein; **she is ~ to criticise** mit Kritik ist sie schnell bei der Hand; **be ~ at figures/repartee** schnell rechnen können/schlagfertig sein; **he's too ~ for me** mit ihm komme ich nicht mit; **have a ~ ear/eye** ein feines Ohr/scharfes Auge haben; **he has a ~ eye/ear for ...:** er hat ein Auge/Ohr für ...; **[have] a ~ temper** ein aufbrausendes Wesen [haben]; **have ~ wits** Köpfchen haben (ugs.) **3** (arch.: living, alive) lebendig; **the ~ and the dead** die Lebenden und die Toten

B *adv.* schnell; **~!** [mach] schnell!

C *n.* empfindliches Fleisch; **bite one's nails to the ~:** die Nägel bis zum Fleisch abkauen; **be cut** *or* **hurt** *or* **stung** *etc.* **to the ~** (fig.) tief getroffen *od.* verletzt sein

quick: ~-acting *attrib. adj.* schnell wirkend; **~-change** *attrib. adj.* (Theatre) Verwandlungs‹*künstler, -nummer*›

quicken /ˈkwɪkn/

A *v.t.* **1** (make quicker) beschleunigen **2** (animate) lebendig machen; erwecken **3** (stimulate, rouse, inspire) beflügeln ‹*Fantasie, Begeisterung*›

B *v.i.* **1** (become quicker) sich beschleunigen; schneller werden; ‹*Herz*:› schneller schlagen; **her breath/steps ~ed** sie atmete/ging schneller **2** (be stimulated, roused) ‹*Hoffnung*:› sich regen (geh.)

quick: ~ fire *n.* (Mil.) Schnellfeuer, *das;* **~-fire questions** (fig.) Fragen wie aus dem Maschinengewehr; **~-firing** *adj.* (Mil.) Schnellfeuer-; **~-freeze** *v.t.* schnell gefrieren

quickie /ˈkwɪkɪ/ *n.* (coll.) im Schnellverfahren hergestellte Sache; (drink) Schluck auf die Schnelle (ugs.); (sexual intercourse) eine Nummer auf die Schnelle (salopp); **be a ~:** im Schnellverfahren hergestellt sein

ˈ**quicklime** *n.* ungelöschter Kalk

quickly /ˈkwɪklɪ/ *adv.* schnell

ˈ**quick march** *n.* (Mil.) Eilmarsch, *der*

quickness /ˈkwɪknɪs/ *n., no pl.* **1** (speed) Schnelligkeit, *die;* **the ~ of the hand deceives the eye** die Geschicklichkeit der Hand täuscht das Auge; **~ of action** schnelles Handeln **2** (acuteness of perception) Schärfe, *die;* **~ of the mind** schnelle Auffassungsgabe **3** (hastiness) **~ of temper** Hitzigkeit, *die;* aufbrausendes Wesen

quick: ~ one *n.* (coll.) Schluck auf die Schnelle (ugs.); **have a ~ one** schnell einen trinken [gehen]; (sexually) eine schnelle Nummer machen (salopp); **~-release** *adj.* **~-release buckle** Schnellverschluss, *der;* **~-release hub** Schnellspannnabe, *die;* **~-release front wheel** Vorderrad, *das* mit Schnellspannnabe; **~sand** *n.* Treibsand, *der;* Mahlsand, *der* (Seemannsspr.); **~set** *n.* Heckenpflanze, *die;* (hedge) Hecke, *die;* **~-setting** *adj.* schnell trocknend ‹*Klebstoff*›; schnell bindend ‹*Zement*›; schnell gelierend ‹*Konfitüre usw.*›; **~silver** *n.* **1** Quecksilber, *das;* **2** *attrib.* (fig.) lebhaft; quecksilbrig; **have a ~silver temperament** Quecksilber im Leib haben (ugs.); **~step** *n.* **1** (Mil.) Eilschritt, *der;* **2** (Dancing) Quickstep, *der;* **~-tempered** *adj.* hitzig; **be ~-tempered** leicht aufbrausen; **~thorn** *n.* (Bot.) Weißdorn, *der;* **~-witted** *adj.* geistesgegenwärtig; schlagfertig ‹*Antwort*›; **~-wittedness** /kwɪkˈwɪtɪdnɪs/ *n., no pl.* Geistesgegenwart, *die;* (of answer) Schlagfertigkeit, *die*

quid¹ /kwɪd/ *n.* (Brit. coll.) **1** *pl. same* (one pound) Pfund, *das;* **a few ~:** ein paar Möpse *od.* Flöhe (salopp); **fifty ~:** fünfzig Kugeln (salopp) **2** **be ~s in** auf sein Geld kommen (ugs.)

quid² *n.* (tobacco) Priem, *der*

quid pro quo /kwɪd prəʊ ˈkwəʊ/ *n.* Gegenleistung, *die;* Quidproquo, *das* (geh.)

quiescence /kwɪˈesəns/ *n.* Ruhe, *die*

quiescent /kwɪˈesənt/ *adj.* still; untätig ‹*Vulkan*›

quiet /ˈkwaɪət/

A *adj.*, **~er** /ˈkwaɪətə(r)/, **~est** /ˈkwaɪətɪst/ **1** (silent) still; (not loud) leise ‹*Schritte, Musik, Stimme, Motor, Fahrzeug*›; **be ~!** (coll.) sei still *od.* ruhig!; **~!** Ruhe!; **keep ~:** still sein; **keep sth. ~, keep ~ about sth.** (fig.) etw. geheim halten; **I want the matter to be kept ~:** ich möchte, dass darüber Stillschweigen bewahrt wird; **keep sb./a child ~:** dafür sorgen, dass jmd. schweigt/ein Kind ruhig ist; **go ~:** still werden **2** (peaceful, not busy) ruhig; **a ~ evening at home** ein geruhsamer Abend zu Hause; **let's go for a ~ drink** gehen wir in aller Ruhe einen trinken; **have a ~ mind** beruhigt sein; **all was ~ on the border** an der Grenze herrschte Ruhe *od.* war alles ruhig **3** (gentle) sanft; ruhig ‹*Kind, Person*› **4** (not overt, disguised) versteckt; heimlich ‹*Groll*›; **have a ~ word with sb.** mit jmdm. unter vier Augen reden; **have a ~ laugh about sth.** im Stillen über etw. (*Akk.*) lachen; **on the ~:** still und heimlich **5** (not formal) zwanglos; klein ‹*Feier*› **6** (not showy) dezent ‹*Farben, Muster*›; schlicht ‹*Eleganz, Stil*›

B *n.* Ruhe, *die;* (silence, stillness) Stille, *die;* **in the ~ of the night** in der Stille der Nacht; *see also* **peace 3**

C *v.t.* ▸ **quieten A**

quieten /ˈkwaɪətn/ (Brit.)

A *v.t.* **1** beruhigen; zur Ruhe bringen ‹*Kind, Schulklasse*› **2** zerstreuen ‹*Bedenken, Angst, Verdacht*›

B *v.i.* sich beruhigen

(Phrasal verb)

• **~ 'down**

A *v.t.* ▸ **~ A 1**

B *v.i.* sich beruhigen; **since her marriage she has ~ed down** seit sie geheiratet hat, ist sie viel ruhiger geworden

quietism /'kwaɪətɪzm/ *n.* Quietismus, *der*

quietly /'kwaɪətlɪ/ *adv.* **1▸** (silently) still; (not loudly) leise; **die ~:** eines sanften Todes sterben (geh.) **2▸** (peacefully, tranquilly) ruhig; **be ~ drinking one's tea** in [aller] Ruhe seinen Tee trinken; **I'll come ~** (said by person being arrested) ich werde ohne Widerstand mitkommen **3▸** (gently) sanft; **be ~ spoken** eine ruhige Art zu sprechen haben **4▸** (not overtly) insgeheim; **they settled the affair ~:** sie haben die Angelegenheit unter sich (*Dat.*) ausgemacht **5▸** (not formally) zwanglos; **get married ~:** im kleinen Rahmen heiraten **6▸** (not showily) dezent; schlicht

quietness /'kwaɪətnɪs/ *n., no pl.* **1▸** (absence of noise or motion) Stille, *die;* (of reply) Ruhe, *die;* (of car, engine) Geräuscharmut, *die;* (of footsteps) Geräusch-, Lautlosigkeit, *die* **2▸** (peacefulness, gentleness) Ruhe, *die*

quietude /'kwaɪətju:d/ *n.* (literary) Stille, *die;* Frieden, *der* (geh.)

quiff /kwɪf/ *n.* (Brit.) **1▸** (curl) Stirnlocke, *die;* Schmachtlocke, *die* (ugs.) **2▸** (tuft of hair) [Haar-]tolle, *die* (ugs.)

quill /kwɪl/ *n.* **1▸** ▸**quill feather 2▸** ▸**quill pen 3▸** (stem of feather) [Feder]kiel, *der* **4▸** (of porcupine) Stachel, *der*

quill: ~ feather *n.* Kielfeder, *die;* **~ pen** *n.* [Feder]kiel, *der*

quilt /kwɪlt/

A *n.* **1▸** (padded bed coverlet) Schlafdecke, *die;* **continental ~:** Steppdecke, *die* **2▸** (bedspread) Tagesdecke, *die; see also* **crazy 4; patchwork**

B *v.t.* **1▸** (cover or line with padded material) wattieren **2▸** (make or join like ~) steppen

quilting /'kwɪltɪŋ/ *n.* **1▸** (process) Steppen, *das* **2▸** (material) gesteppter Stoff

quin /kwɪn/ *n.* (coll.) Fünfling, *der*

quince /kwɪns/ *n.* **1▸** (fruit) Quitte, *die* **2▸** (tree) Quittenbaum, *der; see also* **Japanese quince**

quince 'jelly *n.* Quittengelee, *das*

quinine /'kwɪni:n, kwɪ'ni:n/ *n.* Chinin, *das*

quinquennial /kwɪŋ'kwenɪəl/ *adj.* (lasting five years) fünfjährig; (once every five years) fünfjährlich

quinquennium /kwɪŋ'kwenɪəm/ *n., pl.* **~s** *or* **quinquennia** /kwɪŋ'kwenɪə/ Jahrfünft, *das*

quinsy /'kwɪnzɪ/ *n.* (Med.) Mandelentzündung, *die*

quintessence /kwɪn'tesəns/ *n.* **1▸** (most perfect form) Quintessenz, *die;* (embodiment) Inbegriff, *der* **2▸** (essence, extract of substance) Extrakt, *der*

quintessential /kwɪntɪ'senʃl/ *adj.* typisch; wesentlich

quintessentially /kwɪntɪ'senʃəlɪ/ *adv.* typisch

quintet, quintette /kwɪn'tet/ *n.* (also Mus.) Quintett, *das;* **piano/clarinet ~:** Klavier-/Klarinettenquintett, *das*

quintuple /'kwɪntjʊpl/

A *adj.* fünffach

B *n.* Fünffache, *das*

C *v.t.* verfünffachen

D *v.i.* sich verfünffachen

quintuplet /'kwɪntjʊplɪt, kwɪn'tju:plɪt/ *n.* Fünfling, *der*

quip /kwɪp/

A *n.* **1▸** (clever saying) Witzelei, *die;* Geistreichelei, *die* (scherzh. abwertend) **2▸** (sarcastic remark) Bissigkeit, *die*

B *v.i.*, **-pp-** (make quips) witzeln (**at** über + *Akk.*); geistreicheln (scherzh. abwertend)

quire /kwaɪə(r)/ *n.* (Bookbinding: collection of sheets) Lage, *die;* (24/25 sheets) 24/25 Bögen Papier; (4 sheets) *4 zu 8 Blättern gefaltete Bögen;* **in ~s** ungebunden

quirk /kw3:k/ *n.* Marotte, *die;* Schrulle, *die* (ugs.); **[by a] ~ of nature/fate/history** *etc.* [durch eine] Laune der Natur/des Schicksals/der Geschichte *usw.*

quirky /'kw3:kɪ/ *adj.* schrullig (ugs.)

quisling /'kwɪzlɪŋ/ *n.* Quisling, *der* (abwertend)

quit /kwɪt/

A *v.t.*, **-tt-, quit 1▸** (give up) aufgeben; (cease, stop) aufhören mit; **~ doing sth.** aufhören, etw. zu tun **2▸** (depart from) verlassen; (leave occupied premises) ausziehen aus; *abs.* ausziehen; **they were given** *or* **had notice to ~ [the flat** *etc.***]** ihnen wurde [die Wohnung *usw.*] gekündigt; **~ hold of sth.** etw. loslassen **3▸** *also abs.* (Computing) beenden **4▸** *also abs.* (from job) kündigen; (Computing) [das Programm] beenden

B *pred. adj.* **be ~ of sb./sth.** jmds./einer Sache ledig sein (geh.).

quitch [grass] /'kwɪtʃ (gra:s)/ ▸**couch²**

quite /kwaɪt/ *adv.* **1▸** (entirely) ganz; völlig; vollkommen; gänzlich ‹*unnötig*›; fest ‹*entschlossen*›; **not ~** (almost) nicht ganz; (noticeably not) nicht gerade; **I'm sorry — That's ~ all right** Entschuldigung — Schon gut *od.* in Ordnung; **not ~ five o'clock** noch nicht ganz 5 Uhr; **I don't need any help; I'm ~ all right, thank you** danke, es geht schon, ich komme allein zurecht; **I've had ~ enough of it** jetzt habe ich aber genug davon; **how can you be ~ so sure?** wie kannst du so sicher sein?; **I've never known anyone who was ~ so stubborn** ich kenne niemanden, der so stur wie er/sie ist; **I ~ agree/understand** ganz meine Meinung/ich verstehe schon; **~ [so]!** [ja,] genau *od.* richtig!; **be ~ a hero** wirklich ein Idol sein; **that is ~ a different matter** das ist etwas ganz anderes *od.* schon etwas anderes; **we drove at ~ a speed** wir sind vielleicht schnell gefahren (ugs.); **they had ~ a party** sie haben vielleicht gefeiert (ugs.); **be ~ other than sth.** ‹*Wahrheit, Ansicht:*› sich deutlich von etw. unterscheiden; **~ another story/case** eine ganz andere Geschichte/ein ganz anderer Fall **2▸** (somewhat, to some extent) ziemlich; recht; ganz ‹*gern*›; **it was ~ an effort** es war ziemlich *od.* recht anstrengend; **that is ~ a shock/surprise** das ist ein ziemlicher Schock/eine ziemliche Überraschung; **I'd ~ like to talk to him** ich würde ganz gern mit ihm sprechen; **~ a few** ziemlich viele *od.* eine ganze Menge ‹*Bücher, Preise, Urteile*›; **they had ~ a lot of applicants/a run of success** sie hatten eine ziemlich große Anzahl von Kandidaten/sie waren ziemlich lange [Zeit] erfolgreich

quits /kwɪts/ *pred. adj.* **be ~ [with sb.]** [mit jmdm.] quitt sein (ugs.); **call it ~** ‹*Einzelperson:*› zustimmen *od.* Ruhe geben; ‹*mehrere Personen:*› sich vertragen; **let's call it ~!** wollen wir die Sache auf sich beruhen lassen!; (nothing owed) sagen wir, wir sind quitt; *see also* **double C 3**

quitter /'kwɪtə(r)/ *n.* Drückeberger, *der*/ Drückebergerin, *die* (ugs. abwertend)

quiver¹ /'kwɪvə(r)/

A *v.i.* zittern (**with** vor + *Dat.*); ‹*Stimme, Lippen:*› beben (geh.); ‹*Lid:*› zucken; ‹*Stimme:*› vibrieren; **her legs ~ed** ihr zitterten die Beine; ihre Beine zitterten

B *n.* Zittern, *das;* (of lips, voice also) Beben, *das* (geh.); (of eyelid) Zucken, *das;* **there was a ~ in her voice** ihre Stimme zitterte *od.* (geh.) bebte; **be all in a ~:** am ganzen Körper zittern

quiver² *n.* (for arrows) Köcher, *der*

qui vive /ki: 'vi:v/ *n.* **be on the ~:** auf dem Quivive sein (ugs.); wachsam sein

quixotic /kwɪk'sɒtɪk/ *adj.* lebensfremd ‹*Person, Ideal*›; idealistisch ‹*Verhalten*›; **a ~ act** eine Donquichotterie; **a ~ person** ein Don Quichotte *od.* Quixote *od.* Quijote

quiz /kwɪz/

A *n., pl.* **~zes 1▸** (Radio, Telev., etc.) Quiz, *das;* Ratespiel, *das;* **contestants in/guests on the ~:** Quizteilnehmer *Pl.* **2▸** (interrogation, questionnaire, test) Prüfung, *die;* (for pupils) Aufgabe, *die*

B *v.t.*, **-zz-** ausfragen (**about sth.** nach etw., **about sb.** über jmdn.), fragen (**about** nach); ‹*Polizei:*› verhören, vernehmen ‹*Verdächtige*›

quiz: ~master *n.* ▸**❶ p. 1260** (Radio, Telev.) Quizmaster, *der;* Spielleiter, *der;* **~ night** *n.* Quizabend, *der;* **~ programme** *n.* (Radio, Telev.) Quizsendung, *die;* **~ show** *n.* (Radio, Telev.) Quizshow, *die*

quizzical /'kwɪzɪkl/ *adj.* fragend ‹*Blick, Miene*›; (mocking) spöttisch ‹*Lächeln*›

quizzically /'kwɪzɪkəlɪ/ *adv.* fragend ‹*blicken*›; (mocking) spöttisch ‹*lächeln*›

quoin /kɔɪn/ *n.* **1▸** (angle) Ecke, *die* **2▸** (cornerstone) Eckstein, *der*

quoit /kɔɪt/ *n.* (Games) [Gummi]ring, *der*

quoits /kɔɪts/ *n., no pl.* (Games) Ringtennis, *das*

quorate /'kwɔ:reɪt/ *adj.* beschlussfähig

Quorn ® /kwɔ:n/ *n., no pl.: Fleischersatz auf Speisepilzbasis*

quorum /'kwɔ:rəm/ *n.* Quorum, *das*

quota /'kwəʊtə/ *n.* **1▸** (share) Anteil, *der* **2▸** (maximum quantity) Höchstquote, *die;* (of goods to be produced/imported) maximale Produktions-/Einfuhrquote; (quantity of goods to be produced) Produktionsmindestquote, *die;* (of work) [Arbeits]pensum, *das* **3▸** (maximum number) Höchstquote, *die;* (of immigrants/students permitted) maximale Einwanderungs-/Zulassungsquote

quotable /'kwəʊtəbl/ *adj.* zitierbar

quotation /kwəʊ'teɪʃn/ *n.* **1▸** Zitieren, *das;* Zitate *Pl.;* (passage) Zitat, *das;* **dictionary of ~s** Zitatenlexikon, *das* **2▸** (amount stated as current price) [Börsen]kurs, *der;* Quotation, *die* (fachspr.); [Börsen-, Kurs]notierung, *die* **3▸** (contractor's estimate) Kosten[vor]anschlag, *der;* Kalkulation, *die*

quo'tation marks *n. pl.* Anführungszeichen *Pl.*

quote /kwəʊt/

A *v.t.* **1▸** *also abs.* zitieren (**from** aus); zitieren aus ‹*Buch, Text, Klassiker, Übersetzung*›; (appeal to) sich berufen auf (+ *Akk.*) ‹*Person, Buch, Text, Quelle*›; (mention) anführen ‹*Vorkommnis, Beispiel*›; **he is ~d as saying that ...:** er soll gesagt haben, dass ...; **don't ~ me on it** sagen Sie nicht, dass Sie das von mir haben; **~ an earlier case to sb.** jmdm. einen früheren Fall nennen; **~ sth. as the reason/an example** etw. als Grund/ Beispiel anführen; **..., and I ~, ...:** ..., ich zitiere, ... **2▸** (state price of) angeben, nennen ‹*Preis*›; quotieren (fachspr.); **wheat/the £ is ~d at ...:** der Weizenpreis/Pfundkurs wird mit ... angegeben; **~ sb. a price** jmdm. einen Preis nennen **3▸** (St. Exch.) notieren ‹*Aktie*›; **be ~d at a lower price** niedriger notiert werden **4▸** (enclose in quotation marks) in Anführungszeichen (*Akk.*) setzen; **..., ~, ...:** ..., Zitat, ...

B *n.* (coll.) **1▸** (passage) Zitat, *das* **2▸** (commercial quotation) Kosten[vor]anschlag, *der;* Kalkulation, *die* **3▸** *usu. in pl.* (quotation mark) Anführungszeichen, *das;* Gänsefüßchen, *das* (ugs.)

quoth /kwəʊθ/ *v.t. 1st & 3rd pers. p. t.* (*arch.*) *in sing./pl.* sprach/sprachen (geh.)

quotient /'kwəʊʃnt/ *n.* (Math.) Quotient, *der; see also* **intelligence quotient**

q.v. /kju:'vi:/ *abbr.* **= quod vide** s. d.

Rr

R, r /ɑ:(r)/ *n., pl.* **Rs** *or* **R's** 1 (letter) R, r, *das* 2 **the three Rs** Lesen, Schreiben und Rechnen 3 **the R months** die Monate mit r

r. *abbr.* **= right** re.

R. *abbr.* 1 ▸ ❶ **p. 1491 = River** Fl.; **R. Thames** die Themse 2 **= Regina/Rex** Königin, *die*/König, *der*; **in the case R. v. Smith** in der Sache der Königin/des Königs gegen Smith 3 **® = registered trademark** (Wz) 4 (Amer.) **= Republican** 5 (Chess) **= rook** T

RA *abbr.* 1 **= Royal Academician** Mitglied der „Royal Academy" 2 **= Royal Academy** ▸ **academy 1** 3 **= Royal Artillery** Königl. Art.

rabbet /ˈræbɪt/ *n.* (groove) Falz, *der*; (to receive edge of door or window) Anschlag, *der*

rabbi /ˈræbaɪ/ *n.* Rabbi[ner], *der*; (as title) Rabbi, *der*; **Chief R~:** Oberrabbiner, *der*

rabbit /ˈræbɪt/

A *n.* 1 Kaninchen, *das* 2 (Brit. coll.: poor player) Flasche, *die* (ugs.); Niete, *die* (ugs.) 3 (Amer.: hare) Hase, *der*. *See also* **breed B 1**; **Welsh rabbit**

B *v.i.* (Brit. coll.: talk) **~ [on]** sülzen (salopp); quatschen (salopp)

rabbit: ~ burrow *n.* Kaninchenbau, *der*; Kaninchenhöhle, *die*; **~ food** *n.* Kaninchenfutter, *das*; (fig. joc.) Grünzeug, *das*; Kaninchenfutter, *das* (scherzh.); **~ fur** *n.* Kaninchenfell, *das*; Kanin, *das* (fachspr.); (coat) Kaninmantel, *der*; **~ hole** ▸ **~ burrow**; **~ hutch** *n.* (lit. or fig. joc.) Kaninchenstall, *der*; **~ punch** *n.* Rabbitpunch, *der* (Boxen); Genickschlag, *der*; **~ warren** *n.* Kaninchenbau, *der* (*mit vielen Gängen*); **this building is a ~ warren** dieses Gebäude ist das reinste Labyrinth

rabble /ˈræbl/ *n.* Mob, *der* (abwertend); Pöbel, *der* (abwertend)

rabble: ~-rouser /ˈræblraʊzə(r)/ *n.* Aufwiegler, *der*/Aufwieglerin, *die*; [Auf]hetzer, *der*/[Auf]hetzerin, *die*; **~-rousing** A *adj.* aufwieglerisch, [auf]hetzerisch ‹*Rede, Wort*›; B *n.* [Auf]hetzerei, *die*; Aufwiegelei, *die*

Rabelaisian /ræbəˈleɪzjən/ *adj.* rabelaissch ‹*Stil, Sprachreichtum*›

rabid /ˈræbɪd/ *adj.* 1 ([Vet.] Med.) tollwütig ‹*Tier, Person*›; Tollwut‹*symptom, -erreger, -virus*› 2 (furious, violent) wild ‹*Hass, Wut*›; (unreasoning, extreme) fanatisch ‹*Demokrat, Reformer, Anhänger, Befürworter, Antisemitismus*›

rabies /ˈreɪbi:z/ *n.* ([Vet.] Med.) Tollwut, *die*; Rabies, *die* (fachspr.)

RAC *abbr.* (Brit.) **= Royal Automobile Club** Königlicher Britischer Automobilklub

raccoon ▸ **racoon**

race¹ /reɪs/

A *n.* 1 Rennen, *das*; **have a ~ [with** *or* **against sb.]** mit jmdm. um die Wette laufen/schwimmen/reiten *usw.*; **100 metres ~:** 100-m-Rennen/-Schwimmen, *das*; **be in the ~** (lit. or fig.) gut im Rennen liegen; **be out of the ~** ‹*Läufer, Schwimmer, Reiter usw.*:› ausgeschieden sein; (fig.) ‹*Bewerber*:› nicht mehr im Rennen sein 2 *in pl.* (series) (for horses) Pferderennen, *das*; (for dogs) Hunderennen, *das*; **go to the ~s** zum Rennen gehen; **a day at the ~s** ein Tag auf der Rennbahn 3 (fig.) **a ~ against time** ein Wettlauf mit der Zeit; **sb.'s** *or* **the ~ is [nearly] run** (after pursuit) jmd. ist verloren; (after severe illness, euphem.) jmds. Zeit ist gekommen (geh. verhüll.); **the ~ for governor/nomination** das Rennen um den Gouverneursposten/die Nominierung; **it will be a mad ~ to get the work finished in time** es wird eine wahnsinnige Hetze werden, die Arbeit rechtzeitig fertig zu bekommen 4 (channel of stream) Gerinne, *das* (*veralt.*); *see also* **mill race** 5 (Mech. Engin.: of ball bearing) Ring, *der*

B *v.i.* 1 (in swimming, running, walking, sailing, etc.) um die Wette schwimmen/laufen/gehen/segeln *usw.* **(with, against** mit); **~ against time** ‹*Läufer*:› gegen die Uhr laufen; (fig.) gegen die Uhr *od.* Zeit arbeiten 2 (indulge in horseracing) dem Pferderennsport frönen; (Sports: in car) Autorennen fahren; **~ at a meeting** (own or train horses for it) bei einem Rennen Pferde laufen lassen 3 (go at full or excessive speed) ‹*Motor*:› durchdrehen; ‹*Puls*:› jagen, rasen 4 (rush) sich sehr beeilen; hetzen; ‹*Wolken*:› jagen; (on foot also) rennen; jagen; **~ after sb.** jmdm. hinterherhetzen; **~ [a]round** *or* **about** herumhetzen; hin und her hetzen; **~ to finish sth.** sich beeilen, um etw. fertig zu kriegen (ugs.); **~ ahead with sth.** (hurry) etw. im Eiltempo vorantreiben (ugs.); (make rapid progress) bei etw. mit Riesenschritten vorankommen (ugs.)

C *v.t.* 1 (have ~ with) (in swimming, riding, walking, running, etc.) um die Wette schwimmen/reiten/gehen/laufen *usw.* mit; **I'll ~ you** ich mache mit dir einen Wettlauf 2 (cause to ~) ‹*Fahrer*:› rasen mit (ugs.) ‹*Auto, Kajak usw.*›; ‹*Steuermann*:› sehr schnell fahren mit ‹*Schiff*› 3 hochjagen (salopp) ‹*Motor*›; **~ sb. along** jmdn. vorwärts hetzen (ugs.)

race² *n.* 1 (Anthrop., Biol.) Rasse, *die*; **be of mixed ~:** gemischtrassig *od.* -rassisch sein 2 (class of persons) Klasse, *die*; (esp. Relig.) Kaste, *die* 3 (group with common descent) Geschlecht, *das*; Sippe, *die*; (nation) Volk, *das*; (tribe) Volk, *das*; Stamm, *der*; **the human ~:** die Menschheit; die Menschen; **be of noble ~:** vornehmer Abkunft (geh.) *od.* Abstammung sein

race: ~ car *n.* (Amer.) Rennwagen, *der*; **~card** *n.* Rennprogramm, *das*; **~course** *n.* Rennbahn, *die*; **~ discrimiˈnation** *n., no pl.* Rassendiskriminierung, *die*; **~-goer** *n.* Rennbesucher, *der*/-besucherin, *die*; **~ hatred** *n.* Rassenhass, *der*; **~horse** *n.* Rennpferd, *das*

raceme /rəˈsi:m/ *n.* (Bot.) Blütentraube, *die*

ˈrace meeting *n.* (Sport) Renntag, *der*; (on successive days) Renntage *Pl.*

racer /ˈreɪsə(r)/ *n.* (person) Läufer, *der*/Läuferin, *die*; (horse) Rennpferd, *das*; Renner, *der*; (yacht) Rennjacht, *die*; (bicycle) Rennrad, *das*; Rennmaschine, *die*; (car) Rennwagen, *der*; (plane) Sportflugzeug, *das*

race: ~ relations *n. pl.* Beziehung zwischen den Rassen; **R~ Relations Act** (Brit.) Gesetz gegen Rassendiskriminierung; **~ riot** *n.* Rassenkrawall, *der*; **~track** *n.* Rennbahn, *die*; **~way** *n.* (Amer.) Trabrennbahn, *die*

rachitic /rəˈkɪtɪk/ *adj.* (Med.) rachitisch

rachitis /rəˈkaɪtɪs/ *n.* (Med.) Rachitis, *die*

racial /ˈreɪʃl/ *adj.* Rassen‹*diskriminierung, -konflikt, -gleichheit, -vorurteil, -unruhen, -stolz*›; rassisch ‹*Gruppe, Minderheit*›; **~ attack/assault** rassistischer Angriff/Überfall; **~ equality** Rassengleichheit, *die*; **~ harmony** Eintracht unter den Rassen; **~ harassment** rassistische Belästigung; **incidents of ~ harassment** rassistische Übergriffe; **Commission for R~ Equality** (Brit.) Kommission für Rassengleichheit

racialism /ˈreɪʃəlɪzm/ *n., no pl.* Rassismus, *der*

racialist /ˈreɪʃəlɪst/

A *n.* Rassist, *der*/Rassistin, *die*

B *adj.* rassistisch

racially /ˈreɪʃəlɪ/ *adv.* rassisch; **be ~ prejudiced** Rassenvorurteile haben

racily /ˈreɪsɪlɪ/ *adv.* 1 flott ‹*erzählen, schreiben*›; pikant ‹*gewürzt*›; kraftvoll ‹*gestaltet*› 2 (in a risqué manner) gewagt ‹*erzählen, sich kleiden*›

racing /ˈreɪsɪŋ/ *n., no pl., no indef. art.* 1 (profession, sport) Rennsport, *der*; (with horses) Pferdesport, *der* 2 (races) Rennen *Pl.*; **go ~** (attend horse/motor races) zum Rennen gehen; **it is a ~ certainty that he will ...:** mit größter Wahrscheinlichkeit wird er ...

racing: ~ bicycle *n.* Rennrad, *das*; Rennmaschine, *die*; **~ car** *n.* Rennwagen, *der*; **~ colours** *n. pl.* Rennfarben *Pl.*; **~ driver** *n.* Rennfahrer, *der*/-fahrerin, *die*; **~ track** *n.* Rennbahn, *die*

racism /ˈreɪsɪzm/ *n.* Rassismus, *der*

racist /ˈreɪsɪst/

A *n.* Rassist, *der*/Rassistin, *die*

B *adj.* rassistisch

rack¹ /ræk/

A *n.* 1 (for luggage in bus, train, etc.) Ablage, *die*; (for pipes, hats, spectacles, toast, plates) Ständer, *der*; (for tools) Regal, *das*; (on bicycle, motorcycle) Gepäckträger, *der*; (on car) Dachgepäckträger, *der* 2 (for fodder) Raufe, *die* 3 (instrument of torture) Folter[bank], *die*; **put sb. on the ~:** jmdn. auf die Folter legen; (fig.) ‹*Problem, Ungewissheit*:› jmdn. quälen; **be on the ~** (lit. or fig.) Folterqualen leiden 4 (Mech. Engin.) Zahnstange, *die*; **~ and pinion** Zahntrieb, *der*

B *v.t.* 1 (lit. or fig.: torture) quälen, plagen; **be ~ed by** *or* **with pain** *etc.* von Schmerzen *usw.* gequält und geplagt werden 2 (shake violently) ‹*Husten, Vibration*:› erschüttern, heftig schütteln ‹*Körper*› 3 **~ one's brain[s]** (fig.) sich (*Dat.*) den Kopf zerbrechen *od.* das Hirn zermartern (ugs.) (**for** über + *Akk.*)

Phrasal verb

• **~ ˈup** *v.t.* (coll.: achieve) machen (ugs.), erzielen ‹*Punkte*›; kriegen (ugs.) ‹*Preis*›

rack² *n.* (joint of lamb etc.) vorderes Rippenstück [vom Lamm *usw.*]

rack³ ▸ **ruin A 1**

rack⁴ *v.t.* **~ [off]** abziehen ‹*Wein, Bier*› (**into** auf + *Akk.*)

racket¹ /ˈrækɪt/ *n.* 1 (Sport) Schläger, *der*; (Tennis also) Racket, *das* 2 *in pl., usu. constr. as sing.* (ball game) Racquets, *das*; Racquetball, *der*

racket² *n.* 1 (disturbance, uproar) Lärm, *der*; Krach, *der*; **make a ~:** Krach *od.* Lärm machen; **they kicked up no end of a ~** (coll.) sie machten einen Höllenlärm (ugs.) 2 (dishonest scheme) Schwindelgeschäft, *das* (ugs.); **a narcotics** *or* **drug ~:** krimineller Drogenhandel 3 (coll.: line of business) Job, *der* (ugs.); **I'm in the insurance ~:** ich mache in Versicherungen (salopp)

racketeer /rækɪˈtɪə(r)/ *n.* Ganove, *der*; (profiteer) Wucherer, *der*; **drug ~:** Drogenhändler, *der*/-händlerin, *die*; Dealer, *der*/Dealerin, *die* (ugs.)

racketeering /rækɪˈtɪərɪŋ/ *n.* kriminelle Geschäfte *Pl.*; Schwindel, *der*; (profiteering) Wucher, *der*

ˈracket press *n.* (Sport) Spanner, *der*

r

racking /ˈrækɪŋ/ *attrib. adj.* quälend
rack: ~ **railway** *n.* Zahnrad-, Zahnstangenbahn, *die;* ~ **rent** *n.* (excessive rent) überhöhte Miete; Wuchermiete, *die* (abwertend)
raconteur /rækɒnˈtɜː(r)/ *n.* Geschichten-, Anekdotenerzähler, *der*/-erzählerin, *die*
racoon /rəˈkuːn/ *n.* (Zool.) Waschbär, *der*
racquet ▸**racket¹**
racy /ˈreɪsɪ/ *adj.* **1** flott (ugs.), schwungvoll ‹*Erzählweise, Stil, Sprache*›; schwungvoll ‹*Rede*›; pikant ‹*Aroma*›; saftig (ugs.) ‹*Humor*›; rassig ‹*Traubensorte, Wein*› **2** (risqué) gewagt, pikant ‹*Geschichte, Anekdote*›
rad /ræd/ *n.* (Phys.) Rad, *das*
RADA /ɑːreɪdiːˈeɪ, (coll.) ˈrɑːdə/ *abbr.* (Brit.) = **Royal Academy of Dramatic Art** RADA; Königliche Schauspielakademie
radar /ˈreɪdɑː(r)/ *n.* Radar, *das od. der*
radar: ~ **operator** *n.* ▸❶ **p. 1260** Radartechniker, *der*/-technikerin, *die;* ~ **scanner** *n.* Radarantenne, *die;* ~ **screen** *n.* Radarschirm, *der;* ~ **trap** *n.* Radarfalle, *die* (ugs.)
radial /ˈreɪdɪəl/
A *adj.* **1** (arranged like rays or radii) strahlenförmig angeordnet; radiär (fachspr.); strahlig, strahlenförmig ‹*Muster*› **2** (acting or moving from centre) radial ‹*Durchfluss, Dispersion, Bahn*›; Radial‹*bohrmaschine, -beschleunigung*› **3** (having spokes or radiating lines) strahlenförmig ‹*Bauform*›; ~ **wheel** Radialrad, *das* **4** (Anat.) Speichen‹*nerv, -vene*›; ~ **artery** Speichenarterie, *die;* Puls[schlag]ader, *die* (volkst.)
B *n.* Radial-, Gürtelreifen, *der*
ˈ**radial engine** *n.* Sternmotor, *der*
radially /ˈreɪdɪəlɪ/ *adv.* strahlenförmig; radial (fachspr.)
radial[-ply] tyre *n.* Radial-, Gürtelreifen, *der*
radian /ˈreɪdɪən/ *n.* (Geom.) Radiant, *der*
radiance /ˈreɪdɪəns/, **radiancy** /ˈreɪdɪənsɪ/ *n.* **1** (emission of light rays etc.) Leuchten, *das;* (of sun, stars, lamp also) Strahlen, *das* **2** (joyful, hopeful, etc. appearance) Strahlen, *das;* ~ **of joy/hope** freudiges/hoffnungsvolles Strahlen
radiant /ˈreɪdɪənt/
A *adj.* **1** strahlend, leuchtend ‹*Himmelskörper, Dämmerung*›; leuchtend ‹*Lichtstrahl*›; ~ **colours** leuchtende Farben **2** (fig.) strahlend; fröhlich ‹*Stimmung*›; **be** ~ ‹*Person, Augen:*› strahlen (**with** vor + *Dat.*)
B *n.* **1** (on electric or gas heater) Heizfläche, *die* **2** (Astron.) Radiant, *der*
radiant: ~ **heat** *n.* Strahlungswärme, *die;* ~ **heater** *n.* Heizstrahler, *der*
radiantly /ˈreɪdɪəntlɪ/ *adv.* **1** leuchtend; strahlend; **shine** ~ ‹*Sonne, Sterne:*› leuchten; ‹*Lichtquelle:*› strahlen **2** (fig.) strahlend; **be** ~ **beautiful** von strahlender Schönheit sein
radiate /ˈreɪdɪeɪt/
A *v.i.* **1** ‹*Sonne, Sterne:*› scheinen, strahlen; ‹*Glas, Metall:*› leuchten, glänzen; ‹*Kerze:*› scheinen; ‹*Hitze, Wärme:*› ausstrahlen, sich verbreiten; ‹*Schein, Radiowellen:*› ausgesendet werden, ausgehen (**from** von); ‹*Lichtstrahl:*› leuchten **2** (diverge or spread from central point) strahlenförmig ausgehen (**from** von)
B *v.t.* **1** verbreiten, ausstrahlen ‹*Licht, Wärme, Klang*›; aussenden ‹*Strahlen, Wellen*› **2** ausstrahlen ‹*Glück, Liebe, Hoffnung, Gesundheit, Fröhlichkeit*›; (spread as from centre) verbreiten ‹*Liebe, Heiterkeit usw.*› (**around** um … herum)
radiation /reɪdɪˈeɪʃn/ *n.* **1** (emission of energy) Emission, *die;* (of signals) Ausstrahlung, *die* **2** (energy transmitted) Strahlung, *die;* Strahlenemission, *die;* **solar** ~: Sonneneinstrahlung, *die;* ~ **from a coal fire** Wärmestrahlung eines Kohleofens; **contaminated by** ~: strahlenverseucht **3** *attrib.* Strahlen‹*-therapie, -krankheit, -belastung, -dosis, -verseuchung, -zählrohr, -chemie*›; Strahlungs‹*intensität, -leistung, -messgerät, -energie, -verbrennung, -niveau*›; ~ **leak[age]** Leckstrahlung, *die;* ~ **treatment** (Med.) Strahlenbehandlung, *die;* Bestrahlung, *die*
radiator /ˈreɪdɪeɪtə(r)/ *n.* **1** (for heating a room) [Rippen]heizkörper, *der;* Radiator, *der;* (portable) Heizgerät, *das;* Heizstrahler, *der* **2** (for cooling engine) Kühler, *der*

radiator: ~ **cap** *n.* Kühlverschraubung, *die;* Kühlerverschlussdeckel, *der;* ~ **grille** *n.* Kühlergrill, *der;* Kühlerschutzgitter, *das;* ~ **mascot** *n.* Kühlerfigur, *die*
radical /ˈrædɪkl/
A *adj.* **1** (thorough, drastic; also Polit.) radikal; drastisch, radikal ‹*Maßnahme*›; umwälzend ‹*Auswirkungen*›; durchgreifend ‹*Umstrukturierung, Veränderung usw.*›; (Brit. Hist.) radikal; extrem liberal; (Amer. Hist.) radikal [republikanisch]; **a** ~ **cure** eine Radikalkur **2** (progressive, unorthodox) radikal; revolutionär ‹*Stil, Design, Sprachgebrauch*› **3** (inherent, fundamental) grundlegend ‹*Fehler, Unterschied*› **4** (Med.) ~ **surgery** Radikaloperation, *die* **5** (Bot., Ling., Math.) Wurzel-
B *n.* **1** (Polit.) Radikale, *der/die* **2** (Math.) (quantity) Wurzelausdruck, *der;* Radikal, *das* (fachspr.); (~ sign) Wurzelzeichen, *das* **3** (Chem.) Radikal, *das*
radical ˈ**chic** *n.* linke Schickeria
radicalism /ˈrædɪkəlɪzm/ *n.*, *no pl.* (Polit.) Radikalismus, *der*
radicalize /ˈrædɪkəlaɪz/ *v.t.* **1** (Polit., Soziol.) radikalisieren **2** (change fundamentally) radikal verändern
radically /ˈrædɪkəlɪ/ *adv.* **1** (thoroughly, drastically) radikal; von Grund auf **2** (Polit.) radikal **3** (originally, basically) prinzipiell **4** (inherently, fundamentally) von Grund auf
ˈ**radical sign** *n.* (Math.) Wurzelzeichen, *das*
radicchio /rəˈdɪkjəʊ/ *n.*, *no pl.* Radicchio, *der*
radicle /ˈrædɪkl/ *n.* (Bot.) (part of embryo) Keimwurzel, *die;* Radicula, *die* (fachspr.); (rootlet) Würzelchen, *das*
radio /ˈreɪdɪəʊ/
A *n.*, *pl.* ~**s** **1** *no pl.*, *no indef. art.* Funk, *der;* (for private communication) Sprechfunk, *der;* **over the/by** ~: über/per Funk **2** *no pl.*, *no indef. art.* (Broadcasting) Rundfunk, *der;* Hörfunk, *der;* **listen to the** ~: Radio hören; **on the** ~: im Radio *od.* Rundfunk; **commercial** ~: Werbefunk, *der;* **work in** ~: beim Rundfunk arbeiten **3** (apparatus) Radio, *das;* ~ **[equipment]** Funk[sprech]gerät, *das* **4** (broadcasting station) Rundfunk- *od.* Radiosender, *der;* **R**~ **Luxembourg** Radio Luxemburg; **R**~ **One** Erstes [Rundfunk]programm
B *attrib. adj.* **1** (Broadcasting) Rundfunk‹*antenne, -gerät, -empfänger, -sender, -sendung, -sprecher, -interview, -programm, -übertragung, -techniker, -technik*›; Radio‹*gerät, -sendung, -programm, -welle*›; Sende‹*antenne, -mast, -erlaubnis*›; Funk‹*mast, -turm, -frequenz, -verbindung, -verkehr, -netz, -taxi, -gerät, -wagen*›; ~ **beam** Leitfunkstrahl, *der;* Richtstrahl, *der;* ~ **frequency** Hochfrequenz, *die;* ~ **drama** *or* **play** Hörspiel, *das* **2** (Astron.) Radio‹*astronomie, -galaxis, -teleskop*›. *See also* **fix D 2; ham A 3**
C *v.t.* funken ‹*Meldung, Nachricht*›; durch *od.* per Funk übermitteln; ~ **sb. for sth.** von jmdm. über Funk etw. anfordern
D *v.i.* funken; eine Funkmeldung *od.* einen Funkspruch übermitteln *od.* durchgeben; **the ship** ~**ed for help** das Schiff bat über Funk um Hilfe
radio: ~ˈ**active** *adj.* radioaktiv; ~**acˈtivity** *n.*, *no pl.* Radioaktivität, *die;* ~ **aˈlarm clock** *n.* Radiowecker, *der;* ~ **beacon** *n.* Funkfeuer, *das;* ~**biˈology** *n.*, *no pl.* Strahlenbiologie, *die;* Radiobiologie, *die;* ~ **button** *n.* (Computing) Radiobutton, *der;* Radioknopf, *der;* ~ **cab** *n.* Funktaxi, *das;* ~ **car** *n.* Funkwagen, *der;* ~ˈ**carbon** *n.* Radiokohlenstoff, *der;* Karbon-14, *das;* ~**carbon** ˈ**dating** *n.*, *no pl.* Radiokarbondatierung, *die;* ~ **casˈsette player** *n.* Kassettenradio, *das;* Radio mit Kassettenteil; ~ˈ**chemistry** *n.*, *no pl.* Radiochemie, *die;* Strahlenchemie, *die;* ~ **control** *n.* Funk[fern]steuerung, *die;* ~**-controlled** *adj.* funkgesteuert; ferngesteuert; ~ **frequency** *n.* Hochfrequenz, *die; attrib.* ~**-frequency** Hochfrequenz-
radiogram /ˈreɪdɪəʊgræm/ *n.* **1** (Brit. dated) ≈ Musiktruhe, *die* **2** ▸**radiograph A**
radiograph /ˈreɪdɪəgrɑːf/
A *n.* Röntgenaufnahme, *die;* Radiogramm, *das* (fachspr.)
B *v.t.* eine Röntgenaufnahme/ein Radiogramm machen von

radiographer /reɪdɪˈɒgrəfə(r)/ *n.* ▸❶ **p. 1260** Röntgenologe, *der*/Röntgenologin, *die;* (instrument-operator) Röntgenassistent, *der*/-assistentin, *die*
radiographic /reɪdɪəˈgræfɪk/ *adj.* röntgenographisch; radiographisch
radiography /reɪdɪˈɒgrəfɪ/ *n.*, *no pl.* Radiographie, *die;* Röntgenographie, *die*
radio: ~ **ham** *n.* Funkamateur, *der;* ~ **interview** *n.* Radiointerview, *das;* ~ˈ**isotope** *n.* Radioisotop, *das;* radioaktives Isotop; ~ **link** *n.* Funkverbindung, *die;* ~ **loˈcation** *n.*, *no pl.* Funkortung, *die;* Radar, *der od. das*
radiological /reɪdɪəˈlɒdʒɪkl/ *adj.* radiologisch; röntgenologisch
radiologist /reɪdɪˈɒlədʒɪst/ *n.* ▸❶ **p. 1260** Radiologe, *der*/Radiologin, *die;* Röntgenologe, *der*/Röntgenologin, *die*
radiology /reɪdɪˈɒlədʒɪ/ *n.*, *no pl.* Radiologie, *die;* Röntgenologie, *die*
ˈ**radio mast** *n.* Funkmast, *der*
radiometer /reɪdɪˈɒmɪtə(r)/ *n.* Radiometer, *das;* Strahlungsmesser, *der*
radio: ~ **microphone** *n.* Funkmikrofon, *das;* ~ **play** *n.* **1** (play broadcast on radio) Hörspiel, *das;* **2** *no pl.* (airplay) Radiopräsenz, *die;* ~ **presenter** *n.* Radiomoderator, *der*/-moderatorin, *die;* ~ **silence** *n.*, *no pl.* Funkstille, *die;* ~ **source** *n.* (Astron.) Radioquelle, *die;* ~ **star** *n.* (Astron.) [punktförmige] Radioquelle; ~ **station** *n.* Rundfunkstation, *die;* Rundfunk- *od.* Radiosender, *der;* ~ **taxi** *n.* Funktaxi, *das* ~**-telegram** *n.* Funktelegramm, *das;* Radiotelegramm, *das;* ~**-teˈlegraphy** *n.*, *no pl.* Funktelegrafie, *die;* ~**-ˈtelephone** *n.* Funktelefon, *das;* ~ ˈ**telescope** *n.* Radioteleskop, *das;* ~ˈ**therapist** *n.* ▸❶ **p. 1260** Strahlentherapeut, *der*/-therapeutin, *die;* Radiotherapeut, *der*/-therapeutin, *die;* ~ˈ**therapy** *n.*, *no pl.* Strahlentherapie, *die;* Radiotherapie, *die* (fachspr.)
radish /ˈrædɪʃ/ *n.* Rettich, *der;* (small, red) Radieschen, *das*
radium /ˈreɪdɪəm/ *n.* (Chem.) Radium, *das*
radius /ˈreɪdɪəs/ *n.*, *pl.* **radii** /ˈreɪdɪaɪ/ *or* ~**es** **1** (Math.) Radius, *der;* Halbmesser, *der;* ~ **of action** [Aktions]radius, *der;* Wirkungsbereich, *der;* (of missile) Reichweite, *die;* (fig.) Umkreis, *der;* **within a** ~ **of 20 miles** im Umkreis von 20 Meilen **2** (Anat.) Speiche, *die* **3** (line from centre) Strahl, *der;* (spoke of wheel) Speiche, *die* **4** (Bot.) [Blüten-, Dolden]strahl, *der*
radome /ˈreɪdəʊm/ *n.* Radom, *das*
radon /ˈreɪdɒn/ *n.* (Chem.) Radon, *das*
RAF /ɑːreɪˈef, (coll.) ræf/ *abbr.* = **Royal Air Force**
raffia /ˈræfɪə/ *n.* **1** (fibre) Raphia-, Raffiabast, *der;* ~ **mat** Bastmatte, *die* **2** (tree) Raphia[palme], *die*
raffish /ˈræfɪʃ/ *adj.* **1** liederlich; verkommen **2** (unconventional) flott
raffle /ˈræfl/
A *n.* Tombola, *die;* ~ **ticket** Los, *das*
B *v.t.* ~ **[off]** verlosen
raft /rɑːft/
A *n.* **1** Floß, *das* **2** (floating trees, ice, etc.) Drift, *die*
B *v.t.* (transport) flößen; mit dem Floß befördern
rafter /ˈrɑːftə(r)/ *n.* (Building) Sparren, *der*
rag¹ /ræg/ *n.* **1** [Stoff]fetzen, *der;* [Stoff]lappen, *der;* **[all] in** ~**s** [ganz] zerrissen; **feel like a wet** ~ (coll.) wie ausgelaugt sein; **sb. loses his** ~ (coll.) jmdm. reißt die Geduld **2** *in pl.* (old and torn clothes) Lumpen *Pl.;* **[dressed] in** ~**s [and tatters]** abgerissen; in Lumpen *nachgestellt;* **go from** ~**s to riches** vom armen Schlucker zum Millionär/zur Millionärin werden; *see also* **chew A; glad rags** **3** (derog.: newspaper) Käseblatt, *das* (salopp abwertend) **4** (material for paper) Lumpen, *der;* Hader, *der* (fachspr.); ~ **paper/fibres** Hadernpapier, *das*/Haderstoff, *der* (fachspr.)
rag²
A *v.t.*, **-gg-** (tease, play jokes on) aufziehen; necken
B *v.i.*, **-gg-** **1** (Brit.: engage in rough play) herumtoben **2** (be noisy and riotous) Radau *od.* Rabatz machen (ugs.)

r

C *n.* **1** (Brit. Univ.) spaßige studentische [Wohltätigkeits]veranstaltung; **the university's Rag Week** *die alljährliche Wohltätigkeitswoche der Universität [mit komischen Darbietungen]* **2** (prank) Ulk, *der;* Streich, *der; in pl.* Ulkerei, *die*

rag³ *n.* (Mus.) Rag, *der*

ragamuffin /ˈrægəmʌfɪn/ *n.* [zerlumptes] Gassenkind; **look a proper ~:** ziemlich abgerissen aussehen

rag: ~-and-ˈbone man *n.* (Brit.) Lumpensammler, *der;* **~bag** *n.* **1** Lumpen-, Flickensack, *der;* **2** (fig.: collection) Sammelsurium, *das* (abwertend); **3** (fig. coll.: sloppily-dressed woman) Schlampe, *die* (ugs. abwertend); **~ book** *n.* Kinderbuch aus unzerreißbarem Material; **~ doll** *n.* Stoffpuppe, *die*

rage /reɪdʒ/

A *n.* **1** (violent anger) Wut, *die;* (fit of anger) Wutausbruch, *der;* **be in/fly into a ~:** in Wut *od.* (ugs.) Rage sein/geraten; **in a fit of ~:** in einem Anfall von Wut; in einem plötzlichen Wutausbruch **2** (vehement desire or passion) Besessenheit, *die;* **sth. is [all] the ~:** etw. ist [ganz] groß in Mode *od.* (ugs.) ist der letzte Schrei

B *v.i.* **1** (rave) toben; **~ at** *or* **against sth./sb.** gegen etw./jmdn. wüten *od.* (ugs.) wettern **2** (be violent, operate unchecked) toben; ‹*Krankheit:*› wüten; ‹*Fieber:*› rasen

ragged /ˈrægɪd/ *adj.* **1** zerrissen; kaputt (ugs.); ausgefranst ‹*Saum, Manschetten, Wundränder*› **2** (rough, shaggy) zottig ‹*Pferd, Schaf, Haar, Bart*› **3** (jagged) zerklüftet ‹*Felsen, Küste, Klippe, Landschaft*›; zerzaust ‹*Baum, Strauch*›; (in tattered clothes) abgerissen; zerlumpt **4** (imperfect, lacking finish) stümperhaft (abwertend) ‹*Arbeit, Ausführung*›; holprig ‹*Reim, Rhythmus*› **5** (tired) ermattet; ausgelaugt; **they were run ~:** sie waren völlig erledigt (ugs.) *od.* total groggy (salopp)

raggedly /ˈrægɪdlɪ/ *adv.* **1** abgerissen ‹*gekleidet*› **2** (shaggily) zottig ‹*wachsen*› **3** (jaggedly) zerklüftet ‹*verlaufen*› **4** (imperfectly) stümperhaft (abwertend) ‹*musizieren, arbeiten*›

ragged ˈrobin *n.* (Bot.) Kuckuckslichtnelke, *die*

raglan sleeve /ræglən ˈsliːv/ *n.* Raglanärmel, *der*

ragout /ræˈguː/ *n.* (Gastr.) Ragout, *das*

rag: ~ paper *n.* Hadernpapier, *das* (fachspr.); **~-roll** *v.t.* mit einem Wickelroller auftragen ‹*Farbe*›; **~-roll the wall** mit einem Wickelroller über die Wand rollen; **~-rolling** *n., no pl.* Wandanstrich mit einem Wickelroller; **~stone** *n.* [Kalk-, Kiesel]sandstein, *der;* **~tag [and bobtail]** *n.* Pöbel, *der* (abwertend); Plebs, *der* (abwertend); **~time** *n.* Ragtime, *der; attrib.* Ragtime‹*band, -musik, -sänger*›; **~ trade** *n.* (coll.) Modebranche, *die* (ugs.); **~weed** *n.* (Bot.) **1** ▸**ragwort**; **2** (Amer.: Ambrosia) Ambrosienkraut, *das;* **~wort** *n.* (Bot.) Greiskraut, *das;* Kreuzkraut, *das*

raid /reɪd/

A *n.* **1** Einfall, *der;* Überfall, *der;* (Mil.) Überraschungsangriff *der;* **~ on a bank** Banküberfall, *der;* **make a ~ on sb.'s orchard/the larder** (joc.) jmds. Obstgarten heimsuchen/die Speisekammer plündern (scherzh.); *see also* **air raid** **2** (by police) Razzia, *die* (**on** in + *Dat.*) **3** (St. Exch.) ≈ aggressive Unternehmensaufkäufe

B *v.t.* ‹*Polizei:*› eine Razzia machen auf (+ *Akk.*); ‹*Bande/Räuber/Soldaten:*› überfallen ‹*Bank/Viehherde/Land*›; ‹*Trupp, Kommando:*› stürmen ‹*feindliche Stellung*›; ‹*Kinder:*› heimsuchen, plündern (scherzh.) ‹*Obstgarten*›; **~ the larder** (joc.) die Speisekammer plündern (scherzh.)

raider /ˈreɪdə(r)/ *n.* (on bank, farm) Räuber, *der*/Räuberin, *die;* (looter) Plünderer, *der*/Plünderin, *die;* (burglar) Einbrecher, *der*/Einbrecherin, *die*

rail¹ /reɪl/

A *n.* **1** ‹*Kleider-, Gardinen*›stange, *die;* (as part of fence) (wooden) Latte, *die;* (metal) Stange, *die;* (on ship) Reling, *die;* (as protection against contact) Barriere, *die;* **the ~s** (Horseracing) die Innenumzäunung; die Bande **2** (Railw.: of track) Schiene, *die;* **go off the ~s** (lit.) entgleisen; (fig.) (depart from what is accepted) auf die schiefe Bahn geraten; (go mad) durchdrehen (ugs.); (get out of control or order) aus dem Ruder laufen **3** (~way) [Eisen]bahn, *die; attrib.* Bahn-; **by ~:** mit der Bahn; mit dem Zug; **~ union** Eisenbahnergewerkschaft, *die;*

B *v.t.* **~ in** einzäunen ‹*Grundstück, Gebäudeteil*›; mit einem Geländer *od.* einer Absperrung umgeben ‹*Altar, Denkmal*›; **~ off** abzäunen; mit einem [Schutz]geländer versehen

rail² *n.* (Ornith.) Ralle, *die*

rail³ *v.i.* **~ at/against sb./sth.** auf/über jmdn./etw. schimpfen; **~ at fate** mit dem Schicksal hadern

rail: ~ accident *n.* Zugunglück, *das;* Zugunfall, *der;* **~car** *n.* Triebwagen, *der;* Schienenbus, *der;* **~ card** *n.* Bahnkarte *die;* (for senior citizens) ≈ Seniorenpass, *der;* **~ fence** *n.* (Amer.) (wooden) Lattenzaun, *der;* (metal) Stangenzaun, *der;* **~head** *n.* **1** (farthest point during construction) Ende einer im Bau befindlichen Bahnstrecke; Baustellenende, *das;* **2** (terminal) Ausladebahnhof, *der;* Verladebahnhof, *der*

railing /ˈreɪlɪŋ/ *n.* (round garden, park) Zaun, *der;* (on sides of staircase) Geländer, *das*

ˈrail journey *n.* Bahnreise, *die;* Bahnfahrt, *die;* **Oxford to Aberdeen is a long ~:** von Oxford nach Aberdeen fährt man lange mit der Bahn

raillery /ˈreɪlərɪ/ *n.* Neckerei, *die;* Spöttelei, *die*

rail: ~ link *n.* Bahn[strecke], *die;* **~road** **A** *n.* (Amer.) ▸**railway**; **B** *v.t.* **1** (send or push through in haste) **~road sb. into doing sth.** jmdn. dazu antreiben, etw. zu tun; **~road a bill through parliament** einen Gesetzentwurf im Parlament durchpeitschen (ugs.); **2** (send to prison by fraud) unrechtmäßig einsperren (ugs.); **~ strike** *n.* Eisenbahnerstreik, *der;* **~ terminus** *n.* Endbahnhof, *der;* **R~track** *n., no pl., no art.* (Brit.) *Betreibergesellschaft des britischen Schienennetzes;* **~ traffic** *n., no pl.* Schienenverkehr, *der*

railway /ˈreɪlweɪ/ *n.* **1** (track) Bahnlinie, *die;* Bahnstrecke, *die* **2** (system) [Eisen]bahn, *die;* **work on the ~:** bei der Bahn arbeiten; **what a way to run a ~!** (fig.) komisches Verfahren!; *see also* **cable railway**

railway: ~ carriage *n.* Eisenbahnwagen, *der;* Reisezugwagen, *der* (fachspr.); **~ crossing** *n.* Bahnübergang, *der;* **~ engine** *n.* Lokomotive, *die;* **~ engineer** *n.* ▸**i** p. 1260 Eisenbahningenieur, *der;* **~ guide** *n.* Fahrplan, *der;* (book) Kursbuch, *das;* **~ line** *n.* [Eisen]bahnlinie, *die;* [Eisen]bahnstrecke, *die;* **~man** /ˈreɪlweɪmən/ *n., pl.* **~men** /ˈreɪlweɪmən/ ▸**i** p. 1260 Eisenbahner, *der;* **~ network** *n.* [Eisen]bahnnetz, *das;* **~ station** *n.* Bahnhof, *der;* (smaller) [Eisen]bahnstation, *die;* **~ worker** *n.* ▸**i** p. 1260 Bahnarbeiter, *der;* **~ yard** *n.* Abstellbahnhof, *der;* Rangierbahnhof, *der*

ˈrail worker *n.* (Brit.) Bahnbedienstete, *der/die;* Bahnler, *der*/Bahnlerin, *die* (ugs.)

raiment /ˈreɪmənt/ *n.* (arch./literary) Gewand, *das* (geh.)

rain /reɪn/

A *n.* **1** Regen, *der;* **it looks like ~:** es sieht nach Regen aus; **out in the ~:** draußen im Regen ‹*sein, lassen*›; hinaus in den Regen ‹*gehen*›; **come ~ or shine** bei jedem Wetter; (fig.) unter allen Umständen; *see also* **right A 4** **2** (fig.: of arrows, blows, etc.) Hagel, *der* **3** *in pl.* (falls of ~) **the ~s** die Regenzeit

B *v.i.* **1** *impers.* **it ~s** *or* **is ~ing** es regnet; **it starts ~ing** *or* **to ~:** es fängt an zu regnen; *see also* **cat 1**; **pour B 1** **2** ‹*Tränen:*› strömen; ‹*Konfetti, Reis:*› regnen, niedergehen (**on** auf + *Akk.*); ‹*Schläge:*› niederprasseln (**on** auf + *Akk.*); **bombs ~ed on many cities** auf viele Städte regnete es Bomben

C *v.t.* prasseln *od.* hageln lassen ‹*Schläge, Hiebe*›; regnen lassen ‹*Reis, Konfetti*›; **~ abuse on sb.** eine Schimpfkanonade gegen jmdn. loslassen (ugs.)

Phrasal verbs

• **~ ˈdown** *v.i.* ‹*Schläge, Steine, Flüche usw.:*› niederprasseln; ‹*Schüsse, Kugeln usw.:*› niederhageln

• **~ ˈoff**, (Amer.) **~ ˈout** *v.t.* **be ~ed off** *or* **out** (be terminated) wegen Regen abgebrochen werden; (be cancelled) wegen Regen ausfallen; ins Wasser fallen (ugs. scherzh.)

rainbow /ˈreɪnbəʊ/

A *n.* Regenbogen, *der;* **secondary ~:** Nebenregenbogen, *der;* **all the colours of the ~:** alle Regenbogenfarben; *see also* **gold A 2**

B *adj.* Regenbogen‹*farben, -streifen*›; regenbogenfarbig, -farben ‹*Kleid, Blumen, Federkleid*›

ˈrainbow coalition *n.* Regenbogenkoalition, *die*

rainbow ˈtrout *n.* Regenbogenforelle, *die*

rain: ~ check *n.* (Amer.) Eintrittskarte für Ersatzveranstaltung; **take a ~ check on sth.** (fig.) auf etw. (*Akk.*) später wieder zurückkommen; **~ cloud** *n.* Regenwolke, *die;* **~coat** *n.* Regenmantel, *der;* **~drop** *n.* Regentropfen, *der;* **~fall** *n.* (shower) [Regen]schauer, *der;* (quantity) Niederschlag, *der;* **~forest** *n.* Regenwald, *der;* **~ gauge** *n.* Regenmesser, *der;* **~making** *n.* Erzeugung von künstlichem Regen *od.* Niederschlag; künstliche Niederschlagsauslösung; **~proof** **A** *adj.* regendicht; wasserdicht; **B** *v.t.* appretieren; **~ shower** *n.* Regenschauer, *der;* **~storm** *n.* stürmisches Regenwetter; heftiger Regenguss; **~water** *n.* Regenwasser, *das;* **~wear** *n.* Regenkleidung, *die*

rainy /ˈreɪnɪ/ *adj.* regnerisch ‹*Tag, Wetter*›; regenreich ‹*Klima, Gebiet, Sommer, Winter*›; regenverhangen ‹*Himmel*›; **~ season** Regenzeit, *die;* **keep sth. for a ~ day** (fig.) sich (*Dat.*) etw. für schlechte Zeiten aufheben

raise /reɪz/

A *v.t.* **1** (lift up) heben; erhöhen ‹*Note, Pulsfrequenz, Temperatur, Steuern, Miete, Lohn, Gehalt, Kosten*›; hochziehen ‹*Rollladen, Fahne, Schultern*›; aufziehen ‹*Vorhang*›; hochheben ‹*Koffer, Arm, Hand*›; hochschieben ‹*Schiebefenster*›; höher machen, aufhöhen (fachspr.) ‹*Mauer usw.*› (**by** um); (Cookery) gehen lassen ‹*Brot, Teig*›; **~ one's eyes** den Blick *od.* die Augen heben; hinaufblicken (**to** zu); aufblicken (**from** von); **~ one's eyes to heaven** die Augen zum Himmel erheben (geh.); **~ one's glass to sb.** das Glas auf jmdn. erheben; auf jmdn. anstoßen; **~ one's hand/fist to sb.** die Hand/Faust gegen jmdn. erheben; **~ one's voice** die Stimme heben; **they ~d their voices** (in anger) sie *od.* ihre Stimmen wurden lauter; **don't you ~ your voice at me** schrei mich nicht an!; **war ~d its [ugly] head** der Krieg erhob sein [hässliches] Haupt; **be ~d to the peerage/priesthood** in den Stand eines Peers/in den Priesterstand erhoben werden; *see also* **finger A 1**; **hat 1**; **roof A 1** **2** (set upright, cause to stand up) aufrichten; erheben ‹*Banner*›; aufstellen ‹*Fahnenstange, Zaun, Gerüst*›; **~ the people to revolt** das Volk zum Aufstand mobilisieren; **~ the country against an invader** den Widerstand der Bevölkerung gegen einen Eindringling mobilisieren; **be ~d from the dead** von den Toten [auf]erweckt werden; **~ the dust** (fig.: cause turmoil) Ärger machen; **~ sb.'s spirits** jmds. Stimmung heben **3** (build up, construct) errichten ‹*Gebäude, Statue*›; verursachen ‹*Blutblase usw.*›; (create, start) auslösen ‹*Kontroverse*›; schaffen ‹*Probleme*›; erheben ‹*Forderungen, Einwände, Ansprüche, Bedenken, Protest*›; entstehen lassen ‹*Vorurteile*›; (introduce) aufwerfen ‹*Frage*›; zur Sprache bringen, anschneiden ‹*Angelegenheit, Thema, Problem*›; (utter) erschallen lassen ‹*Ruf, Schrei, Beifallgeschrei, Jubel*› **4** (grow, produce, breed, rear) anbauen ‹*Gemüse, Getreide*›; aufziehen ‹*Vieh, [Haus]tiere*›; großziehen ‹*Familie, Kinder*›; **[be born and] ~d in** ... (Amer.) [geboren und] aufgewachsen [sein] in ... (*Dat.*) **5** (bring together, procure) aufbringen ‹*Geld, Betrag, Summe*›; aufstellen ‹*Armee, Flotte, Truppen*›; aufnehmen ‹*Hypothek, Kredit, Darlehen*› **6** (end, cause to end) aufheben, beenden ‹*Belagerung, Blockade*›; (remove) aufheben ‹*Aufnahme-, Einstellungsstopp, Embargo, Verfügung, Anordnung, Verbot*› **7** (cause to appear) [herbei]rufen, beschwören ‹*Geist, Verstorbenen, Teufel*›; **~ [merry] hell** (coll.) Krach schlagen (ugs.) (**over** wegen) **8** (Math.) **~ to the fourth power** in die 4. Potenz erheben; mit 4 potenzieren **9** (Cards) erhöhen (**to** auf); **~ sb.** jmdn. überbieten; **~ [one's] partner** seinen Mitspieler mit derselben Farbe überbieten *od.* überrufen

10 (coll.: find) ~ **sb.** jmdn. aufstöbern *od.* (ugs.) auftreiben
B *n.* **1** (Cards) Erhöhen, *das* **2** (Amer.) (in wages) Lohnerhöhung, *die;* (in salary) Gehaltserhöhung, *die*
Phrasal verb
• ~ **'up** **1** (cause to stand up) aufstellen **2** (build up) errichten ‹*Mauer, Gebäude*›; aufstapeln ‹*Haufen*›; aufbauen, gestalten ‹*Struktur*›
raised /reɪzd/ *adj.* **1** erhoben ‹*Arm, Augen, Blick, Stimme*› **2** (Amer. Cookery) aufgegangen ‹*Teig, Brot, Kuchen*› **3** [auf]geraut ‹*Gewebe, Stoff*› **4** (having pattern or design in relief) erhaben
raisin /'reɪzn/ *n.* Rosine, *die*
raison d'être /reɪzɔ̃ 'detr/ *n., pl.* **raisons d'être** /reɪzɔ̃ 'detr/ Existenzberechtigung, *die;* **his happiness was her** ~: sie lebte nur für sein Wohlergehen
raj /rɑːdʒ/ *n.* (Ind. Hist.) Herrschaft, *die;* **the British** ~: die britische Oberherrschaft (in Indien vor 1947)
raja[h] /'rɑːdʒə/ *n.* (Hist.) Radscha, *der*
rake¹ /reɪk/
A *n.* **1** (Hort.) Rechen, *der* (bes. südd. u. md.); Harke, *die* (bes. nordd.) **2** (Agric.: wheeled implement) Rechwender, *der* **3** (croupier's) Rateau, *das;* Geldharke, *die. See also* **thin A 2**
B *v.t.* **1** harken ‹*Laub, Erde, Fußboden, Kies, Oberfläche*›; ~ **together** (fig.) zusammentragen ‹*Beweise, Hinweise, Anklagepunkte*› **2** ~ **the fire** die Asche entfernen **3** (sweep) (with eyes) bestreichen; (with shots) bestreichen; beharken (Soldatenspr.)
C *v.i.* ~ **among** *or* **into** *or* **[around] in** herumstöbern in (+ *Dat.*)
Phrasal verbs
• ~ **'in** *v.t.* (coll.) scheffeln (ugs.) ‹*Geld*›; ~ **in the money,** ~ **it in** Geld scheffeln (ugs.)
• ~ **over** *v.t.* **1** harken **2** (fig.) wieder ausgraben; ~ **over old ashes** (fig.) alte Geschichten wieder ausgraben
• ~ **'up** *v.t.* **1** zusammenharken **2** (fig.) wieder ausgraben ‹*Vergangenes*›
rake² *n.* **1** (sloping position, [amount of] slope) Neigung, *die* **2** (in theatre) Schräge, *die;* **there is a** ~ **on this stage** diese Bühne hat eine Schräge
rake³ *n.* (person) Lebemann, *der*
raked /reɪkt/ *adj.* ‹*Bühne, Zuschauerraum:*› mit einer Schräge
'rake-off *n.* (coll.) [Gewinn]anteil, *der*
rakish¹ /'reɪkɪʃ/ *adj.* **1** (dissolute) ausschweifend **2** (jaunty) flott; kess; **wear one's hat at a** ~ **angle** seinen Hut frech *od.* keck aufgesetzt haben
rakish² *adj.* (smartly designed) schnittig
rakishly /'reɪkɪʃlɪ/ *adv.* **1** (dissolutely) wie ein Lebemann **2** (jauntily) kess; keck
rally¹ /'rælɪ/
A *v.i.* **1** (come together) sich versammeln; ~ **to the support of** *or* **the defence of,** ~ **behind** *or* **to sb.** (fig.) sich hinter jmdn. stellen; **the banks rallied to the support of the pound** die Banken versuchten gemeinsam, das Pfund zu stützen; ~ **round** sich zusammentun **2** (regain health) sich wieder [ein wenig] erholen **3** (reassemble) sich [wieder] sammeln **4** (increase in value after fall) ‹*Aktie, Kurs:*› wieder anziehen, sich wieder erholen
B *v.t.* **1** (reassemble) wieder zusammenrufen **2** (bring together) einigen ‹*Partei, Kräfte*›; sammeln ‹*Anhänger*› **3** (rouse) aufmuntern; (revive) ~ **one's strength** seine [ganze] Kraft zusammennehmen; ~ **support for sb./sth.** um Unterstützung für jmdn./etw. werben
C *n.* **1** (mass meeting) Versammlung, *die;* **Scout** ~: [großes] Pfadfindertreffen; **peace** ~: Friedenskundgebung, *die* **2** (competition) **[motor]** ~: Rallye, *die;* **Monte Carlo R~/Isle of Man TT R~:** Rallye Monte Carlo/Tourist Trophy, *die* **3** (Tennis) Ballwechsel, *der* **4** **a** ~ **in prices/shares** ein Anziehen der Preise/Aktienkurse
rally² *v.t.* (tease) aufziehen (ugs.); necken
'rallycross *n.* (Sport) Rallyecross, *das*
ram /ræm/
A *n.* **1** (Zool.) Schafbock, *der;* Widder, *der* **2** **the Ram** (Astrol.) der Widder; *see also* **archer 2** **3** ▸**battering ram** **4** (Naut.: projecting beak) Rammsporn, *der* **5** (hydraulic lifting-machine) hydraulischer Widder **6** (weight) Rammklotz, *der;* Bär, *der* **7** (tool) Stampfer, *der* **8** (piston) Plunger, *der*
B *v.t.,* **-mm-** **1** (force) stopfen; ~ **a post into the ground** einen Pfosten in die Erde rammen; ~ **in** in etw. (*Akk.*) rammen; **he** ~**med his hat down on his head** er knallte sich (*Dat.*) seinen Hut auf den Kopf (ugs.); ~ **sth. into sb.** *or* **sb.'s head** (fig.) jmdm. etw. einhämmern; ~ **sth. home to sb.** jmdm. etw. deutlich vor Augen führen; *see also* **throat 1** **2** (collide with) rammen ‹*Fahrzeug, Pfosten*› **3** ~ **[down]** (beat down) feststampfen ‹*Erde, Ton, Kies*›
RAM /ræm/ *abbr.* (Computing) = **random access memory** RAM, *das; attrib.* ~ **chip** RAM-Chip, *der*
Ramadan /ræmə'dɑːn/ *n.* (Muslim Relig.) **[month of]** ~: Ramadan, *der*
ramble /'ræmbl/
A *n.* **[nature]** ~: Wanderung, *die*
B *v.i.* **1** (walk) umherstreifen (**through, in** in + *Dat.*) **2** (wander in discourse) zusammenhangloses Zeug reden (abwertend); **keep rambling on about sth.** sich endlos über etw. (*Akk.*) auslassen
rambler /'ræmblə(r)/ *n.* **1** Wanderer, *der*/Wanderin, *die* **2** (Bot.) Kletterrose, *die*
rambling /'ræmblɪŋ/
A *n.* Wandern, *das;* ~ **club** Wanderverein, *der*
B *adj.* **1** (irregularly arranged) verschachtelt; verwinkelt ‹*Straßen*› **2** (incoherent) unzusammenhängend ‹*Erklärung, Brief*›; zerstreut ‹*Professor*› **3** (Bot.) ~ **rose** Kletterrose, *die*
rambunctious /ræm'bʌŋkʃəs/ *adj.* (Amer. coll.) nicht zu bändigend; **be** ~: nicht zu bändigen sein
ramekin /'ræmɪkɪn/ **1** (Gastr.) Käsewindbeutel, *der;* Ramequin, *der* (fachspr.) **2** ▸~ **case**
ramekin: ~ **case,** ~ **dish** *ns.* kleine Auflaufform
ramification /ræmɪfɪ'keɪʃn/ *n.* **1** (of river, railway, business; Bot., Anat.) Verzweigung, *die* **2** *usu. in pl.* (consequence) Auswirkungen; **what would be the** ~**s of this?** wie würde sich das auswirken?
ramify /'ræmɪfaɪ/ *v.i.* sich verzweigen; ~**ing network** verzweigtes Netz
'ramjet *n.* (Aeronaut.) ~ **[engine]** Staustrahltriebwerk, *das*
rammer /'ræmə(r)/ *n.* Stampfer, *der*
ramp /ræmp/
A *n.* **1** (slope) Rampe, *die;* **'beware** *or* **caution,** ~**!'** „Vorsicht, unebene Fahrbahn!" **2** (Aeronaut.) Gangway, *die*
B *v.t.* mit einer Rampe versehen
rampage
A /'ræmpeɪdʒ, ræm'peɪdʒ/ *n.* Randale, *die* (ugs.); **be/go on the** ~ ‹*Rowdys:*› randalieren; ‹*verärgerte Person:*› toben
B /ræm'peɪdʒ/ *v.i.* ‹*Rowdys:*› randalieren; ~ **about** ‹*verärgerte Person:*› toben
rampant /'ræmpənt/ *adj.* **1** (unchecked) zügellos ‹*Gewalt, Rassismus, Randalieren*›; schreiend ‹*soziale Ungerechtigkeit*›; steil ansteigend ‹*Verbrechensrate, Inflation*›; üppig ‹*Wachstum*›; **cholera was** ~: die Cholera grassierte **2** *postpos.* (Her.) zum Grimmen geschickt ‹*Löwe*› **3** (rank) **make too** ~, **cause the** ~ **growth of** wuchern lassen ‹*Pflanzen*›
rampart /'ræmpɑːt/ *n.* **1** (walk) Wehrgang, *der* **2** (protective barrier) Wall, *der;* (fig.) Schutzschild, *der*
rampion /'ræmpɪən/ *n.* (Bot.) Rapunzelglockenblume, *die*
ram: ~ **raid** **A** *v.t.* [durch Rammen mit einem Fahrzeug] einbrechen in (+ *Akk.*); **B** *n.* [durch Rammen eines Gebäudes verübter] Einbruch; ~**-raider** *n.: Einbrecher, der sich durch Einrammen bes. eines Schaufensters mit einem Fahrzeug Zutritt verschafft*
'ramrod *n.* Ladestock, *der;* **[with one's back] as straight** *or* **stiff as a** ~ (fig.) so steif, als ob man einen Besenstiel verschluckt hätte; stocksteif
'ramshackle *adj.* klapprig ‹*Auto*›; verkommen ‹*Gebäude*›
ran ▸**run B, C**
ranch /rɑːntʃ/
A *n.* Ranch, *die;* **[mink/poultry]** ~: [Nerz-/Geflügel]farm, *die;* **livestock** ~: Viehbetrieb, *der;* **meanwhile, back at the** ~ (joc. coll.) inzwischen … zu Hause; *see also* **dude ranch**
B *v.i.* Viehwirtschaft treiben
rancher /'rɑːntʃə(r)/ *n.* (owner, operator) Rancher, *der*/Rancherin, *die;* (employee) Farmarbeiter, *der*/-arbeiterin, *die;* **be a** ~: eine Ranch haben/auf einer Ranch arbeiten
ranch: ~ **hand** *n.* Farmarbeiter, *der*/-arbeiterin, *die;* ~ **house** *n.* Wohnhaus auf einer/der Ranch
rancid /'rænsɪd/ *adj.* ranzig
rancor (Amer.) ▸**rancour**
rancorous /'ræŋkərəs/ *adj.* bitter; **feel** ~ **towards sb.** über jmdn. verbittert sein
rancour /'ræŋkə(r)/ *n.* (Brit.) [tiefe] Verbitterung; **she bore him no** ~: sie hegte keinen Groll gegen ihn (geh.)
rand /rænd, rɑːnt/ *n.* ▸**❶ p. 1332** (S. Afr. monetary unit) Rand, *der*
R&B *abbr.* = **rhythm and blues** R&B
R&D *abbr.* = **research and development** F&E
randiness /'rændɪnɪs/ *n., no pl.* Lüsternheit, *die* (geh.); Geilheit, *die*
random /'rændəm/
A *n.* **at** ~: wahllos; willkürlich; (aimlessly) ziellos; **speak/choose at** ~: ins Blaue hinein reden/aufs Geratewohl wählen
B *adj.* **1** (unsystematic) willkürlich ‹*Auswahl*›; **make a** ~ **guess** raten aufs Geratewohl **2** (Statistics) Zufalls-
random: ~ **'access memory** *n.* (Computing) Schreib-Lese-Speicher, *der;* ~ **distribution** *n.* (Statistics) Zufallsverteilung, *die*
randomize (randomise) /'rændəmaɪz/ *v.t.* randomisieren (fachspr.); willkürlich anordnen
random: ~ **'sample** *n.* (Statistics) [Zufalls]stichprobe, *die;* ~ **'variable** *n.* (Statistics) Zufallsvariable, *die*
randy /'rændɪ/ *adj.* geil; scharf (ugs.); **feel** ~: geil sein
rang ▸**ring² B, C**
range /reɪndʒ/
A *n.* **1** (row) ~ **of mountains/cliffs** Berg-/Felsenkette, *die* **2** (of subjects, interests, topics) Palette, *die;* (of musical instrument) Tonumfang, *der;* (of knowledge, voice) Umfang, *der;* (of income, department, possibility) Bereich, *der;* ~ **of influence** Einflussbereich, *der;* **a** ~ **of options** verschiedene Möglichkeiten; **the annual** ~ **of temperature** die Temperaturunterschiede im Verlauf des Jahres; **be outside the** ~ **of a department** nicht in ein Ressort gehören; **sth. is out of** *or* **beyond sb's** ~ (lit. or fig.) etw. ist außerhalb jmds. Reichweite **3** (Bot., Zool.: area of distribution) Verbreitungsgebiet, *das* **4** (of telescope, missile, aircraft, etc.) Reichweite, *die;* (distance between gun and target) Schussweite, *die;* **flying** ~: Flugbereich, *der;* **at a** ~ **of 200 metres** auf eine Entfernung von 200 Metern; **up to a** ~ **of 5 miles** bis zu einem Umkreis von 5 Meilen; **shoot at close** *or* **short/long** ~: aus kurzer/großer Entfernung schießen; **[with]in/out of** *or* **beyond [firing]** ~: in/außer Schussweite; **within** ~ **of a sound** in Hörweite eines Geräuschs; **experience sth. at close** ~: etw. in unmittelbarer Nähe erleben **5** (series, selection) Kollektion, *die* **6** **[shooting]** ~: Schießstand, *der;* (at funfair) Schießbude, *die* **7** (testing site) Versuchsgelände, *das* **8** (grazing ground) Weide[fläche], *die;* **cattle** ~: Viehweide, *die* **9** **give free** ~ **to** (freedom to roam) frei herumlaufen lassen ‹*Tier*›; umherschweifen lassen ‹*Gedanken*› **10** (direction) Verlauf, *der* **11** (cooking stove) Herd, *der*
B *v.i.* **1** (vary within limits) ‹*Preise, Temperaturen:*› schwanken, sich bewegen (**from … to** zwischen [+ *Dat.*] … und); **they** ~ **in age from 3 to 12** sie sind zwischen 3 und 12 Jahre alt **2** (extend) ‹*Klippen, Gipfel, Häuser:*› sich hinziehen; **her hobbies** ~ **from x to y** die Palette ihrer Hobbys reicht von x bis y **3** (Bot., Zool.: occur over wide area) **the plant/animal** ~**s from**

r

... to ...: das Verbreitungsgebiet der Pflanze/des Tieres erstreckt sich von ... bis ... 4) (roam) umherziehen (**around, about** in + *Dat.*); (fig.) ‹*Gedanken:*› umherschweifen; **the discussion ~d over ...:** die Diskussion erstreckte sich auf (+ *Akk.*) ...; **the speaker ~d far and wide** der Redner sprach viele verschiedene Themen an

C *v.t.* 1) (arrange) aufreihen ‹*Bücher, Tische*›; antreten lassen ‹*Soldaten*›; **they ~d themselves in lines** sie stellten sich in Reih und Glied auf; **several enemy platoons were ~d against us** wir standen einer Reihe feindlicher Züge gegenüber; **~ oneself with sb.** (fig.) sich auf jmds. Seite schlagen; **~ oneself against sb./sth.** (fig.) sich gegen jmdn./etw. zusammenschließen; **~ oneself behind sth.** (fig.) sich hinter etw. (*Akk.*) stellen 2) richten ‹*Teleskop, Geschütz*› (**on** auf + *Akk.*) 3) (roam) umherstreifen in (+ *Dat.*); durchstreifen ‹*Landschaft, Berge, Wälder*›; befahren ‹*Meere*›

'rangefinder *n.* Entfernungsmesser, *der*

ranger /'reɪndʒə(r)/ *n.* 1) (keeper) Aufseher, *der*/Aufseherin, *die;* (of forest) Förster, *der*/Försterin, *die* 2) (Amer.: law officer) Ranger, *der; Angehöriger der berittenen Polizeitruppe* 3) (Brit.: Girl Guide) Pfadfinderin (*zwischen 14 und 18 Jahren*) 4) (Amer. Mil.) Ranger, *der*

ranging /'reɪndʒɪŋ/: **~ pole, ~ rod** *ns.* (Surv.) Bake, *die*

rangy /'reɪndʒɪ/ *adj.* langgliedrig

rank¹ /ræŋk/

A *n.* 1) (position in hierarchy) Rang, *der;* (Mil. also) Dienstgrad, *der;* **be above/below sb. in ~:** einen höheren/niedrigeren Rang/Dienstgrad haben als jmd.; **pull ~:** den Vorgesetzten herauskehren (**on** gegenüber); **of high ~:** hochrangig; **be in the front** *or* **top ~ of performers** ein Künstler der Spitzenklasse sein; **of the first ~:** erstklassig 2) (social position) [soziale] Stellung; **people of all ~s** Menschen aus allen [Gesellschafts]schichten; **persons of ~:** hoch gestellte Persönlichkeiten; **belong to a high ~ of society** zur oberen Gesellschaftsschicht gehören 3) (row) Reihe, *die* 4) (Brit.: taxi stand) [Taxen]stand, *der* 5) (line of soldiers) Reihe, *die;* **step forward from the ~:** vortreten; **the ~s** (enlisted men) die Mannschaften und Unteroffiziere; **the ~ and file** die Mannschaften und Unteroffiziere; (fig.) die breite Masse; **close [our/their] ~s** die Reihen schließen; (fig.) sich zusammenschließen; **other ~s** Mannschaften und Unteroffiziere; **rise from the ~s** sich [aus dem Mannschaftsstand] zum Offizier hochdienen; (fig.) sich hocharbeiten 6) (order) **keep/break ~[s]** in Reih und Glied stehen/aus dem Glied treten

B *v.t.* 1) (classify) **~ among** *or* **with** zählen *od.* rechnen zu; **his achievement was ~ed with hers** seine Leistung wurde mit ihrer auf eine Stufe gestellt; **be ~ed second in the world** an zweiter Stelle in der Welt stehen; **~ sth. highly** etw. hoch einstufen 2) (arrange) aufstellen ‹*Schachfiguren*›; in Reih und Glied antreten lassen ‹*Kompanie*› 3) (Amer.: take precedence of) rangmäßig stehen über (+ *Dat.*); **who ~s whom?** wie ist die Rangordnung?

C *v.i.* 1) (have position) **~ among** *or* **with** gehören *od.* zählen zu; **~ above/next to sb.** rangmäßig über/direkt unter jmdm. stehen; **~ high/low** eine hohe/niedere Stellung einnehmen; viel/nicht viel gelten; **it ~s as his best book** es gilt als sein bestes Buch 2) (Amer.: have senior position) **~ing executive** übergeordneter Manager

rank² *adj.* 1) (complete) blank ‹*Unsinn, Frechheit*›; krass ‹*Außenseiter, Illoyalität*› 2) (foul-smelling) stinkend; **~ odour** Gestank, *der;* **smell ~:** stinken 3) (vile) ordinär; unflätig 4) (rampant) überwuchert ‹*Garten*›; **~ weeds** [wild] wucherndes Unkraut

'rank-and-file *adj.* einfach ‹*Mitglied, Mann usw.*›

ranker /'ræŋkə(r)/ *n.* (Mil.) 1) (commissioned officer) aus dem Mannschaftsstand aufgestiegener Offizier 2) (soldier) einfacher *od.* gemeiner Soldat

rankings /'ræŋkɪŋz/ *n. pl.* (Sport) Rangliste, *die;* **the team has fallen in the ~:** die Mannschaft ist in der Tabelle nach unten gerutscht

rankle /'ræŋkl/

A *v.i.* **it/sb.'s success** *etc.* **~s [with sb.]** es/jmds. Erfolg *usw.* wurmt jmdn. (ugs.)

B *v.t.* wurmen (ugs.)

ransack /'rænsæk/ *v.t.* 1) (search) durchsuchen (**for** nach); (fig.) kramen in (+ *Dat.*) (ugs.) ‹*Erinnerung, Gedächtnis*›; erforschen ‹*Gewissen*› 2) (pillage) plündern

ransom /'rænsəm/

A *n.* **~ [money]** Lösegeld, *das;* **hold to ~:** als Geisel festhalten; (fig.) erpressen, unter Druck (*Akk.*) setzen ‹*Regierung*›; *attrib.* **~ demand** Lösegeldforderung, *die;* **~ note** Erpresserbrief, *der;* **jewels worth a king's ~:** Juwelen, die ein Vermögen wert sind

B *v.t.* 1) (redeem) Lösegeld bezahlen für; auslösen 2) (hold to ransom) als Geisel festhalten

rant /rænt/

A *v.i.* wettern (ugs.); **~ at** anschnauzen (ugs.); **~ on about** herumzetern wegen (ugs.); **~ and rave about sth.** über etw. (*Akk.*) wettern (ugs.)

B *n.* 1) (tirade) Tirade, *die* (abwertend); Redeschwall, *der* 2) *no pl.* (empty talk) Schwulst, *der;* leeres Geschwätz (ugs.)

ranunculus /rə'nʌŋkjʊləs/ *n., pl.* **~es** *or* **ranunculi** /rə'nʌŋkjʊlaɪ/ (Bot.) Hahnenfußgewächs, *das*

rap¹ /ræp/

A *n.* 1) (sharp knock) [energisches] Klopfen; **there was a ~ on** *or* **at the door** es klopfte [laut]; **I heard a ~ on** *or* **at the door** ich hörte es [laut] klopfen; **give sb. a ~ on** *or* **over the knuckles** jmdm. auf die Finger schlagen; (fig.) jmdm. auf die Finger klopfen; **get a ~ on** *or* **over the knuckles** (lit. or fig.) eins auf die Finger bekommen 2) (coll.: blame) **take the ~ [for sth.]** [für etw.] den Kopf hinhalten (ugs.); **leave sb. behind to take the ~:** jmdn. die Suppe auslöffeln lassen (ugs.) 3) (Amer. coll.: prison sentence) Kittchen, *das* (ugs.); Knast, *der* (ugs.) 4) (Amer. coll.: criminal charge) Anklage, *die* 5) (Amer. coll.) (conversation) Unterhaltung, *die;* (discussion) Palaver, *das* (ugs.) 6) (in pop music) rhythmischer Sprechgesang; Rap, *der; attrib.* **~ music** Rapmusik, *die*

B *v.t.,* **-pp-** 1) (strike smartly) klopfen; **~ sb. on the knuckles** jmdm. auf die Finger klopfen; **~ sth. on sth.** mit etw. gegen etw. klopfen 2) (criticize) attackieren

C *v.i.,* **-pp-** 1) (make sound) klopfen (**on** an + *Akk.*); **~ on the table** auf den Tisch klopfen 2) (Amer. coll.: talk) quatschen (ugs.)

Phrasal verb

- **~ 'out** *v.t.* ausstoßen ‹*Befehl, Fluch*›; **~ out a message** melden

rap² *n.* **I don't care** *or* **give a ~:** es ist mir völlig egal (ugs.)

rapacious /rə'peɪʃəs/ *adj.* (greedy) habgierig; (predatory) räuberisch

rapaciously /rə'peɪʃəslɪ/ *adv.* (greedily) habgierig; (in predatory manner) raublustig

rapacity /rə'pæsɪtɪ/ *n., no pl.* Habgier, *die;* (being predatory) Raublust, *die*

rape¹ /reɪp/

A *n.* Vergewaltigung, *die* (auch fig.); Notzucht, *die* (Rechtsspr.); **statutory ~** (Amer.) Geschlechtsverkehr mit einer Minderjährigen; **homosexual ~:** Vergewaltigung einer gleichgeschlechtlichen Person

B *v.t.* vergewaltigen; notzüchtigen (Rechtsspr.); (fig.: despoil) vergewaltigen ‹*Landschaft*›

rape² *n.* (Bot., Agric.) Raps, *der*

rape: ~ alarm *n.* Personenalarm, *der;* **~ cake** *n.* Rapskuchen, *der;* **~ counselling** *n., no pl.* Beratung für Vergewaltigungsopfer; **~ crisis centre** *n.* Beratungsstelle für vergewaltigte Frauen und Mädchen; **~ oil** ▸ **~seed oil; ~seed** *n.* Rapssamen, *der;* **~seed oil** *n.* Rapsöl, *das;* **~ victim** *n.* Vergewaltigungsopfer, *das*

Raphael /'ræfeɪəl/ *pr. n.* 1) (archangel) Raphael (*der*) 2) (artist) Raffael (*der*)

rapid /'ræpɪd/

A *adj.* schnell ‹*Bewegung, Wachstum, Puls*›; rasch ‹*Folge, Bewegung, Fortschritt, Ausbreitung, Änderung*›; rapide ‹*Niedergang*›; steil ‹*Abstieg*›; reißend ‹*Gewässer, Strömung*›; stark ‹*Gefälle, Strömung*›; **give ~ results** schnell Ergebnisse bringen; **there has been a ~ decline** es ging rapide abwärts

B *n. in pl.* Stromschnellen

rapid-'fire *adj.* Schnellfeuer‹*waffe, -schießen*›; (fig.) schnell aufeinander folgend ‹*Wiederholung*›; Schnellfeuer‹*witze, -fragen*›

rapidity /rə'pɪdɪtɪ/ *n., no pl.* Schnelligkeit, *die*

rapidly /'ræpɪdlɪ/ *adv.* schnell; **descend ~** ‹*Hang:*› steil abfallen

rapid 'transit (Amer.) *n.* Schnellverkehr, *der*

rapier /'reɪpɪə(r)/ *n.* (Fencing) Rapier, *das*

rapine /'ræpaɪn, 'ræpɪn/ *n.* (poet./literary) Plünderung, *die*

rapist /'reɪpɪst/ *n.* Vergewaltiger, *der*

rapper /'ræpə(r)/ *n.* Rapper, *der*/Rapperin, *die*

rapport /ræ'pɔː(r)/ *n.* [harmonisches] Verhältnis; **have a great ~ with sb.** ein ausgezeichnetes Verhältnis zu jmdm. haben; **establish a ~ with sb.** eine Beziehung zu jmdm. aufbauen; **lack of ~:** fehlende Übereinstimmung

rapprochement /ræ'prɒʃmɑ̃/ *n.* (Polit., Diplom.) Rapprochement, *das* (fachspr.); Wiederannäherung, *die*

rapscallion /ræp'skæljən/ *n.* (joc.) Spitzbube, *der* (scherzh.); Schlingel, *der* (scherzh.)

rapt /ræpt/ *adj.* gespannt ‹*Aufmerksamkeit, Miene*›; **in ~ contemplation** in Betrachtungen versunken

raptly /'ræptlɪ/ *adv.* gespannt ‹*zuhören*›

rapture /'ræptʃə(r)/ *n.* 1) (ecstatic delight) **[state of] ~:** Verzückung, *die* 2) *in pl.* (enthusiasm) **be in ~s** entzückt sein (**over, about** über + *Akk.*); **go into ~s** [überschwänglich] schwärmen (**over, about** von); **be sent into ~s by sth.** über etw. (*Akk.*) in Verzückung geraten

rapturous /'ræptʃərəs/ *adj.* begeistert ‹*Applaus, Menge, Willkommen*›; verzückt ‹*Miene*›

rare¹ /reə(r)/ *adj.* 1) (uncommon) selten; **~ occurrence** Seltenheit, *die;* **it's ~ for him to do that** es kommt selten vor, dass er so etwas tut 2) (thin) dünn ‹*Luft, Atmosphäre*› 3) (extreme) **have ~ fun with sb.** mit jmdm. einen Heidenspaß haben; **have a ~ old time** sich köstlich amüsieren

rare² *adj.* (Cookery) englisch gebraten; nur schwach gebraten; **medium ~:** halb durchgebraten

rarebit /'reəbɪt/ ▸ **Welsh rarebit**

rare: ~ 'book *n.* Rarität, *die;* Rarum, *das* (Buchw.); **~ 'earth** (Chem.) *n.* seltene Erde

rarefaction /reərɪ'fækʃn/ *n.* Verdünnung, *die*

rarefied /'reərɪfaɪd/ *adj.* dünn ‹*Luft*›; (fig.) exklusiv

rarefy /'reərɪfaɪ/ *v.t.* 1) verdünnen ‹*Feuchtigkeit, Luft*› 2) (make subtle) verfeinern

rare 'gas ▸ **noble gas**

rarely /'reəlɪ/ *adv.* 1) selten 2) (to an unusual degree) außergewöhnlich

raring /'reərɪŋ/ *adj.* (coll.) **be ~ to go** kaum abwarten können, bis es losgeht

rarity /'reərɪtɪ/ *n.* 1) Seltenheit, *die;* Rarität, *die;* **a collection of rarities** eine Sammlung von Raritäten; **be an object of great ~:** eine große Seltenheit sein; **such people are a ~:** solche Leute sind rar 2) **the ~ of the atmosphere** die dünne Luft

'rarity value *n.* Seltenheitswert, *der*

rascal /'rɑːskl/ *n.* 1) (dishonest person) Halunke, *der;* Schuft, *der* 2) (joc.: mischievous person) Schlingel, *der* (scherzh.); Spitzbube, *der* (scherzh.)

rascally /'rɑːskəlɪ/ *adj.* 1) (dishonest) schurkisch 2) (joc.: mischievous) schlimm ‹*Junge, Streich*›

rase ▸ **raze**

rash¹ /ræʃ/ *n.* (Med.) [Haut]ausschlag, *der;* **develop a** *or* **break out** *or* **come out in a ~:** einen Ausschlag bekommen; **bring sb. out in a ~:** einen Ausschlag bei jmdm. hervorrufen; **a ~ of burglaries/strikes** (fig.) eine Serie von Einbrüchen/Streiks

rash² *adj.* voreilig ‹*Urteil, Entscheidung, Entschluss*›; überstürzt ‹*Versprechungen, Handlung, Erklärung*›; (impetuous) ungestüm ‹*Person*›

rasher /ˈræʃə(r)/ *n.* ~ **[of bacon]** Speckscheibe, *die;* **bacon sliced into ~s** in [dünne] Scheiben geschnittener Speck

rashly /ˈræʃlɪ/ *adv.* voreilig ‹*handeln, etw. versprechen, zustimmen*›

rashness /ˈræʃnɪs/ *n., no pl.* Voreiligkeit, *die;* **regret one's ~ in doing sth.** bedauern, dass man etw. voreilig getan hat

rasp /rɑːsp/
A *n.* 1 (tool) Raspel, *die* 2 (sound) (of metal on wood) schneidendes Geräusch; (of a cricket) Zirpen, *das;* (of breathing) Rasseln, *das*
B *v.i.* kratzen
C *v.t.* 1 (scrape with ~) raspeln ‹*Blech, Kante*› 2 (say gratingly) schnarren

raspberry /ˈrɑːzbərɪ/ *n.* 1 Himbeere, *die;* (plant also) Himbeerstrauch, *der; attrib.* Himbeer‹*marmelade, -torte, -rosa, -eis*› 2 (coll.: rude noise) **blow a ~:** verächtlich prusten

ˈ**raspberry cane** *n.* Himbeerrute, *die;* Himbeerstrauch, *der*

rasping /ˈrɑːspɪŋ/ *adj.* krächzend ‹*Husten, Stimme*›; rasselnd ‹*Geräusch*›

Rasta /ˈræstə/ *n.* Rasta, *der;* **the ~ people** die Rastas

Rastafarian /ræstəˈfeərɪən/ (Relig.)
A *n.* Rastafari, *der*
B *adj.* Rasta-

raster /ˈræstə(r)/ *n.* (Telev.) Raster, *das*

rat /ræt/
A *n.* 1 Ratte, *die;* **brown** *or* **sewer ~:** Wanderratte, *die;* **look like a drowned ~** (coll.) wie eine gebadete Maus aussehen (ugs.); **~s!** (coll.) (drat it!) verflixt! (ugs.); verdammt! (salopp); (nonsense!) Quatsch! (ugs.); **smell a ~** (fig. coll.) Lunte *od.* den Braten riechen (ugs.); **~s leaving** *or* **deserting the [sinking] ship** (fig.) Ratten, die das sinkende Schiff verlassen; *see also* **muskrat; water rat** 2 (coll. derog.: unpleasant person) Ratte, *die* (derb) 3 (Polit.) Abtrünnige, *der/die*
B *v.i.*, **-tt-** Ratten jagen; **be out ~ting** auf Rattenfang sein

(Phrasal verb)
• ~ **on** *v.t.* (coll.) 1 (inform on) verpfeifen (ugs.) 2 (go back on) nicht halten ‹*Versprechen*›; Verrat üben an (+ *Dat.*) ‹*Politik*›; sitzen lassen (ugs.) ‹*Person*›

ˈ**rat-arsed** /ˈrætɑːst/ *adj.* (Brit. sl.) stock- *od.* stinkbesoffen (derb)

ratatouille /rætəˈtuːɪ/ *n.* (Gastr.) Ratatouille, *die*

rat: ~**bag** *n.* (coll.) Knallkopf, *der*/[dumme] Kuh (ugs.); ~**-catcher** *n.* Rattenfänger, *der/*-fängerin, *die*

ratchet /ˈrætʃɪt/ *n.* (Mech. Engin.) 1 (set of teeth) Zahnkranz, *der* 2 ~ **[wheel]** Klinkenrad, *das*

ˈ**ratchet screwdriver** *n.* Drillschraubenzieher, *der*

rate[1] /reɪt/
A *n.* 1 (proportion) Rate, *die;* **increase at a ~ of 50 a week** [um] 50 pro Woche anwachsen; **lose at the ~ of two minutes a day** ‹*Uhr:*› zwei Minuten pro Tag nachgehen; **~ of inflation/absentee ~:** Inflations-/Abwesenheitsrate, *die* 2 (tariff) Satz, *der;* **interest/taxation ~, ~ of interest/taxation** Zins-/Steuersatz, *der;* **lending/premium ~s** Lombardsatz, *der*/Prämientarif, *der; see also* **bank rate; exchange C 4; water rate** 3 (amount of money) Gebühr, *die;* ~ **[of pay]** Lohnsatz, *der;* **the ~ for the job** die festgelegte Vergütung für diese Arbeit; **letter/parcel ~:** Briefporto, *das*/Paketgebühr, *die;* **at reduced ~:** gebührenermäßigt ‹*Drucksache*› 4 (speed) Geschwindigkeit, *die;* Tempo, *das;* **at a** *or* **the ~ of 50 mph** mit [einer Geschwindigkeit von] 80 km/h; **at a good/fast/moderate/dangerous ~:** zügig/mit hoher/mäßiger Geschwindigkeit/gefährlich schnell 5 (Brit.: local authority levy) Gemeindeabgabe, *die;* Realsteuer, *die;* **county/district ~:** Grafschafts-/Bezirksabgabe, *die;* **[local** *or* **council] ~s** Gemeindeabgaben 6 (coll.) **at any ~** (at least) zumindest; wenigstens; (whatever happens) auf jeden Fall; **at this ~ we won't get any work done** so kommen wir zu nichts; **at the ~ you're going, ...** (fig.) wenn du so weitermachst, ...; **we can't afford to spend money at this ~:** wir können es uns (*Dat.*) nicht leisten, so mit unserem Geld umzugehen; **you'll always be hard up at that ~:** so wirst du immer knapp bei Kasse sein. *See also* **knot A 6**
B *v.t.* 1 (estimate worth of) schätzen ‹*Vermögen*›; einschätzen ‹*Intelligenz, Leistung, Fähigkeit*›; ~ **sb./sth. highly** jmdn./etw. hoch einschätzen 2 (consider) betrachten; rechnen (**among** zu); **be ~d the top tennis player in Europe** als der beste Tennisspieler Europas gelten 3 (assign value to) beurteilen, bewerten ‹*schulische Leistung, Lesefertigkeit*›; angeben ‹*Lebensdauer, Schubkraft*› (**at** mit) 4 (Brit.: subject to payment of local authority levy) Gemeindeabgaben auferlegen (+ *Dat.*) 5 (Brit.: value) **the house is ~d at £800 a year** die Grundlage für die Berechnung der Gemeindeabgaben für das Haus beträgt 800 Pfund pro Jahr 6 (merit) verdienen ‹*Auszeichnung, Erwähnung*›; **does his work ~ a pass?** soll man ihn mit dieser Arbeit bestehen lassen?; **he didn't ~ an invitation** (coll.) er war nicht wichtig genug, [um] eingeladen zu werden 7 (coll.: think much of) viel halten von ‹*Person*›; **~/not ~ one's chances** sich (*Dat.*) große/keine großen Chancen ausrechnen
C *v.i.* zählen (**among** zu); ~ **as** gelten als; ~ **high in a team/low on a test** in einer Mannschaft viel gelten/bei einem Test schlecht abschneiden

rate[2] *v.t.* (scold) beschimpfen

rateable /ˈreɪtəbl/ *adj.* (Brit.) [real]steuerpflichtig ‹*Eigentum, Gebäude*›; ~ **value** steuerbarer Wert

rate: ~**-capping** /ˈreɪtkæpɪŋ/ *n., no pl.* (Brit.) *gesetzliches Recht der Regierung, durch Entzug den Etat einer Kommunalverwaltung zu kürzen, wenn diese zu hohe Abgaben erhebt oder im vorangegangenen Haushaltsjahr zu viel Geld ausgegeben hat;* ~**payer** *n.* (Brit.) Realsteuerpflichtige, *der/die;* ≈ Steuerzahler, *der*/-zahlerin, *die;* ~ **tart** *n.* (coll.) *jmd. der häufig von einer Bank usw. zu einer anderen überwechselt, um günstigere Zinssätze auszunutzen*

rather /ˈrɑːðə(r)/ *adv.* 1 (by preference) lieber; **he wanted to appear witty ~ than brainy** er wollte lieber geistreich als klug erscheinen; **~ than accept bribes, he decided to resign** ehe er sich bestechen ließ, trat er lieber zurück; **I had ~ die than ...:** ich würde lieber sterben, als ...; **no, thanks, I'd ~ not** nein danke, lieber nicht; **I would ~ you ...:** es wäre mir lieber, wenn du ... 2 (somewhat) ziemlich ‹*gut, gelangweilt, unvorsichtig, nett, warm*›; **I ~ think that ...:** ich bin ziemlich sicher, dass ...; **be a ~ good one** ziemlich gut sein; **be ~ better/more complicated than expected** um einiges besser/komplizierter sein als erwartet; **fall ~ flat** ein ziemlicher Reinfall sein; **be ~ a nice person** ziemlich nett sein; **it is ~ too early** ich fürchte, es ist zu früh; **it looks ~ like a banana** es sieht ungefähr wie eine Banane aus; **I ~ like beans/him** ich esse Bohnen ganz gern/ich mag ihn recht gern 3 (more truly) vielmehr; **or ~:** beziehungsweise; [oder] genauer gesagt; **he was careless ~ than wicked** er war eher nachlässig als böswillig 4 (Brit. dated coll.: certainly) aber gewiss doch; na klar (ugs.)

rathskeller /ˈrɑːtskelə(r)/ *n.* (Amer.) Kellerlokal, *das*

ratification /rætɪfɪˈkeɪʃn/ *n.* ▸ **ratify**: Ratifizierung, *die;* Bestätigung, *die;* Sanktionierung, *die*

ratify /ˈrætɪfaɪ/ *v.t.* ratifizieren ‹*völkerrechtlichen Vertrag*›; bestätigen ‹*Ernennung*›; sanktionieren ‹*Vertrag, Gesetzentwurf*›

rating[1] /ˈreɪtɪŋ/ *n.* 1 (estimated standing) Einschätzung, *die;* **security ~:** Geheimhaltungsstufe, *die;* **have a high/low ~:** hoch/niedrig eingeschätzt werden 2 (Radio, Telev) **[popularity] ~:** Einschaltquote, *die;* **be high/low in the ~s** eine hohe/niedrige Einschaltquote haben 3 (Navy: rank) Dienstgrad, *der* 4 (Brit. Navy: sailor) **[naval] ~:** Mannschaftsdienstgrad, *der;* **deck ~s** Angehörige der Decksmannschaften 5 (of racing yacht) Rennwert, *der*

rating[2] *n.* (scolding) Schimpfe, *die* (ugs.); **get a ~:** Schimpfe bekommen (ugs.); ausgeschimpft werden; **give sb. a ~:** jmdn. ausschimpfen

ratio /ˈreɪʃɪəʊ/ *n., pl.* **~s** Verhältnis, *das;* **in a** *or* **the ~ of 1 to 5** im Verhältnis 1 : 5; **in direct ~ to** *or* **with** im gleichen Verhältnis wie; **the teacher-student ~:** das Verhältnis von Lehrern zu Schülern; **what is the ~ of men to women?** wie hoch ist der Männeranteil im Vergleich zu dem der Frauen?

ratiocination /rætɪɒsɪˈneɪʃn, ræʃɪɒsɪˈneɪʃn/ *n.* Reflexion, *die* (**on** über + *Akk.*)

ration /ˈræʃn/
A *n.* 1 (daily food allowance) [Tages]ration, *die;* **put sb. on short ~s** jmdn. auf halbe Ration setzen (ugs.) 2 (fixed allowance of food etc. for civilians) **~[s]** Ration, *die* (**of** an + *Dat.*); **sugar/petrol/meat/sweet ~:** Zucker-/Benzin-/Fleisch-/Süßigkeitenration, *die* 3 (single portion) Ration, *die;* **be given [out] with the ~s** (fig. coll.) automatisch vergeben werden (ugs.)
B *v.t.* rationieren ‹*Benzin, Autos*›; Rationen zuteilen (+ *Dat.*) ‹*Person*›; (allocate systematically) einteilen ‹*Zeit*›; **be ~ed to one glass of spirits per day** nur ein Glas Alkohol pro Tag trinken dürfen; ~ **oneself to ten cigarettes a day** sich (*Dat.*) nur zehn Zigaretten pro Tag erlauben

(Phrasal verb)
• ~ ˈ**out** *v.t.* zuteilen (**to** *Dat.*); in Rationen austeilen (**to** an + *Akk.*)

rational /ˈræʃənl/ *adj.* 1 (having reason) rational, vernunftbegabt ‹*Wesen*›; (sensible) vernünftig ‹*Person, Art, Politik usw.*› 2 (based on reason; also Math.) rational ‹*Erklärung, Analyse, Zahl*›

rationale /ræʃəˈnɑːl/ *n.* 1 (statement of reasons) rationale Erklärung (**of** für) 2 (fundamental reason) logische Grundlage

rationalisation, rationalise ▸ **rationaliz-**

rationalism /ˈræʃənəlɪzm/ *n., no pl.* (Theol., Philos.) Rationalismus, *der*

rationalist /ˈræʃənəlɪst/ *n.* (Theol., Philos.) Rationalist, *der*/Rationalistin, *die*

rationalistic /ræʃənəˈlɪstɪk/ *adj.* rationalistisch

rationality /ræʃəˈnælɪtɪ/ *n., no pl.* 1 ▸ **rational 1**: Rationalität, *die;* Vernunftbegabtheit, *die;* Vernünftigkeit, *die;* Vernunft, *die* 2 (of explanation, analysis, etc.) Rationalität, *die*

rationalization /ræʃənəlaɪˈzeɪʃn/ *n.* (Econ., Psych.) Rationalisierung, *die*

rationalize /ˈræʃənəlaɪz/
A *v.t.* 1 (Econ., Psych.) rationalisieren 2 (explain by rationalism) ~ **away** rationalistisch erklären
B *v.i.* 1 Scheinbegründungen finden 2 (be a rationalist) rational denken/handeln

rationally /ˈræʃənəlɪ/ *adv.* rational; (sensibly) vernünftig

ration: ~ **book** *n.* Bezugsscheinheft, *das;* ~ **card**, ~ **coupon** *ns.* Bezugsschein, *der*

rationing /ˈræʃənɪŋ/ *n.* Rationierung, *die*

ratline (ratlin) /ˈrætlɪn/, **ratling** /ˈrætlɪŋ/ *n.* (Naut.) Webeleine, *die*

rat: ~ **pack** *n.* (coll.) Journalistenpack, *das;* ~ **poison** *n.* Rattengift, *das;* ~ **race** *n.* Rattenrennen, *das;* ~ **run** *n.* (Brit. coll.) Schleichweg, *der;* ~**'s-tail** *n.* Rattenschwanz, *der*

rattan /rəˈtæn/ *n.* 1 (cane) Peddigrohr, *das;* Rattan, *das; attrib.* Rattan‹*möbel, -matte, -tau*› 2 (Bot.) Rotangpalme, *die*

rat-tat /rætˈtæt/, **rat-tat-tat** /rætəˈtæt/ *ns.* Klopfen, *das*

ˈ**ratted** /ˈrætɪd/ *adj.* ▸ **rat-arsed**

ratter /ˈrætə(r)/ *n.* Rattenjäger, *der*

rattle /ˈrætl/
A *v.i.* 1 (clatter) ‹*Fenster, Maschinenteil, Schlüssel:*› klappern; ‹*Hagel:*› prasseln; ‹*Flaschen:*› klirren; ‹*Kette:*› rasseln; ‹*Münzen:*› klingen; ~ **at the door** an der Tür rütteln 2 (move) ‹*Zug, Bus:*› rattern; ‹*Kutsche:*› rumpeln
B *v.t.* 1 (make ~) klappern mit ‹*Würfel, Geschirr, Dose, Münzen, Schlüsselbund*›; klirren lassen ‹*Fenster[scheiben]*›; rasseln mit ‹*Kette*› 2 (coll.: disconcert) ~ **sb., get sb. ~d** jmdn. durcheinander bringen; **don't get ~d!** reg dich nicht auf!; **they tried to ~ the performer** sie versuchten, den Künstler aus dem Konzept zu bringen. *See also* **sabre**

C *n.* **1** (of baby, musician) Rassel, *die;* (of sports fan) Ratsche, *die;* Klapper, *die* **2** (sound) Klappern, *das;* (of hail) Prasseln, *das;* (of drums) Schnarren, *das;* (of machine gun) Rattern, *das;* (of chains) Rasseln, *das;* (of bottles) Klirren, *das* **3** (of ~snake) Rassel, *die;* Klapper, *die*

Phrasal verbs
- ~ **a'way** *v.i.* (coll.) (talk) schnattern (ugs.); (on typewriter) klappern (ugs.); ~ **away at** *or* **on** klappern auf (+ *Dat.*) ‹*Schreibmaschine*›
- ~ **'off** *v.t.* (coll.) herunterrasseln (ugs.); ~ **sth. off like a machine gun** etw. herunterrattern wie ein Maschinengewehr
- ~ **'on** *v.i.* (coll.) plappern (ugs.)
- ~ **through** *v.t.* (fig.) herunterrasseln

rattler /'rætlə(r)/ *n.* (Amer. coll.) Klapperschlange, *die*

rattle: ~**snake** *n.* Klapperschlange, *die;* ~**trap** *n.* (coll.) Klapperkasten, *der* (ugs.)

rattling /'rætlɪŋ/
A *adj.* flott ‹*Tempo*›
B *adv.* (coll.) verdammt (ugs.) ‹*gut*›

'rat trap *n.* Rattenfalle, *die*

ratty /'rætɪ/ *adj.* (coll.: irritable) gereizt; **don't get ~ with me!** lass deinen Ärger nicht an mir aus!

raucous /'rɔːkəs/ *adj.* **1** rau ‹*Stimme, Lachen*› **2** (boisterous, disorderly) wild ‹*Benehmen*›; wüst ‹*Gesänge*›; roh ‹*Zuruf*›

raucously /'rɔːkəslɪ/ *adv.* **1** mit rauer Stimme **2** (boisterously) **they sang/laughed/shouted ~:** sie sangen wüste Gesänge/lachten roh/stießen wilde Rufe aus

raunchy /'rɔːntʃɪ/ *adj.* (lewd) vulgär; (suggestive) scharf (salopp)

ravage /'rævɪdʒ/
A *v.t.* heimsuchen ‹*Gebiet, Stadt*›; so gut wie vernichten ‹*Ernte*›; schwer zeichnen ‹*Gesichtszüge*›
B *n. in pl.* verheerende Wirkung; **the ~s of time/war** die Zeichen der Zeit/die Wunden des Krieges; **be marked by the ~s of famine** vom Hunger schwer gezeichnet sein

rave /reɪv/
A *v.i.* **1** (talk wildly) irrereden; **he's just raving** er redet nur irres Zeug (ugs.); ~ **at** [wüst] beschimpfen; *see also* **rant A 2** (speak with admiration) schwärmen (**about, over** von) **3** (howl) ‹*Wind, Sturm, Meer:*› brausen
B *adj.* (coll.) [hellauf] begeistert ‹*Kritik*›
C *n.* **1** (Brit. coll.: fad, fashion) **the latest ~:** der letzte Schrei; **it's all the ~:** es ist der letzte Schrei **2** *n.* (coll.: dancing party) Rave, *der od. das*

ravel /'rævl/
A *v.t.,* (Brit.) **-ll- 1** (entangle) verheddern ‹*Wollstrang*›; ~ **into knots** verwickeln und verknoten **2** ▸**unravel A**
B *v.i.,* (Brit.) **-ll- 1** (become entangled) sich verwickeln **2** ▸**unravel B**

Phrasal verb
- ~ **'out** ▸**unravel A**

raven /'reɪvn/
A *n.* Rabe, *der;* Kolkrabe, *der* (Zool.)
B *adj.* ~**-black** [kohl]rabenschwarz ‹*Haar*›; ~**-haired** mit kohlrabenschwarzem Haar *nachgestellt*

ravening /'rævənɪŋ/ *adj.* beutegierig

ravenous /'rævənəs/ *adj.* **1** ausgehungert; **I'm ~:** ich habe einen Bärenhunger (ugs.); **have a ~ hunger/appetite** einen richtigen Heißhunger haben **2** (greedy) räuberisch

ravenously /'rævənəslɪ/ *adv.* heißhungrig; **be ~ hungry** einen Riesenhunger haben (ugs.); ausgehungert sein

raver /'reɪvə(r)/ *n.* **1** (uninhibited person) Lebemensch, *der;* (man also) Lebemann, *der* **2** (person who goes to raves) Raver, *der*/Raverin, *die*

'rave-up *n.* (Brit. coll.) [wilde] Fete (ugs.)

ravine /rə'viːn/ *n.* Schlucht, *die;* (produced by river also) Klamm, *die*

raving /'reɪvɪŋ/
A *n. in pl.* irres Gerede
B *adj.* **1** (talking madly) irre redend ‹*Wahnsinniger, Idiot*› **2** (outstanding) fantastisch (ugs.) ‹*Erfolg*›; **be a ~ beauty** hinreißend schön sein
C *adv.* **be ~ mad** (insane) hochgradig schwachsinnig sein; (stupid) völlig verrückt sein (ugs.)

ravioli /rævɪ'əʊlɪ/ *n.* (Gastr.) Ravioli *Pl.*

ravish /'rævɪʃ/ *v.t.* **1** (charm) entzücken; bezaubern; **be ~ed** hingerissen *od.* bezaubert sein (**by, with** von) **2** (rape) schänden (veralt.); Gewalt antun (geh. + Dat.)

ravishing /'rævɪʃɪŋ/ *adj.* bildschön ‹*Anblick, Person*›; hinreißend ‹*Schönheit*›; ~ **sight** Augenweide, *die*

raw /rɔː/
A *adj.* **1** (uncooked) roh **2** (inexperienced) unerfahren; frisch gebacken ‹*Akademiker*›; blutig ‹*Anfänger*›; *see also* **recruit A 1, 4 3** (unbound) ungesäumt ‹*Kante, Stoff*› **4** (stripped of skin) blutig ‹*Fleisch*›; offen ‹*Wunde*›; (sore) wund ‹*Füße*›; **touch** *or* **hit a ~ nerve** einen wunden Punkt *od.* eine empfindliche Stelle treffen **5** (chilly) nasskalt **6** (untreated) Roh‹*haut, -holz, -seide, -zucker, -erz, -leder*›; (undiluted) rein ‹*Alkohol*› **7** (fig.: unpolished) grob **8** (Statistics) unaufbereitet. *See also* **deal[1] C 1; sienna; umber**
B *n.* **nature in the ~:** unverfälschte Natur; **life in the ~:** das Leben, wie es wirklich ist; **in the ~** (fig.) unbekleidet ‹*schlafen*›; **touch sb. on the ~** (Brit.) jmdn. an [s]einer verwundbaren Stelle treffen

raw: ~**-boned** /'rɔːbəʊnd/ *adj.* knochig; ~**hide** *n.* **1** (leather) Rohleder, *das;* **2** (whip) Peitsche aus Rohleder

Rawlplug ® /'rɔːlplʌg/ *n.* Dübel, *der*

raw ma'terial *n.* Rohstoff, *der*

ray[1] /reɪ/ *n.* **1** (lit. or fig.) Strahl, *der;* ~ **of sunshine/light** Sonnen-/Lichtstrahl, *der;* ~ **of sunshine** (fig.) Sonnenschein, *der;* ~ **of hope** Hoffnungsstrahl, *der;* **give sb. a ~ of hope** jmdm. Hoffnung machen; **provide a ~ of comfort** etwas Trost spenden **2** *in pl.* (radiation) Strahlen; Strahlung, *die; see also* **cosmic; gamma rays; X-ray A 3** (Zool.) (of fish's fin) Flossenstrahl, *der;* Radius, *der* (fachspr.); (of starfish) Arm, *der*

ray[2] *n.* (fish) Rochen, *der*

ray[3] *n.* (Mus.) re

'ray gun *n.* (Science Fiction) Strahlenpistole, *die*

rayon /'reɪɒn/ *n.* (Textiles) Reyon, *das od. der; attrib.* Reyon‹*kleid, -hemd*›

raze /reɪz/ *v.t.* (completely destroy) völlig zerstören; (pull down) abreißen; ~ **to the ground** dem Erdboden gleichmachen

razor /'reɪzə(r)/ *n.* Rasiermesser, *das;* **[electric] ~:** [elektrischer] Rasierapparat; [Elektro- *od.* Trocken]rasierer, *der* (ugs.); *see also* **safety razor**

razor: ~**bill** *n.* (Ornith.) Tordalk, *der;* ~ **blade** *n.* Rasierklinge, *die;* ~ **edge** *n.* Rasierschneide, *die;* **sharpen to a ~ edge** rasiermesserscharf machen; **be** *or* **stand on a ~ edge** *or* **~'s edge** (fig.) sich auf einer Gratwanderung befinden; ~**fish** *n.* (Zool.) Scheidenmuschel, *die;* ~**-sharp** *adj.* sehr scharf ‹*Messer*›; (fig.) messerscharf ‹*Verstand, Intellekt*›; scharfsinnig ‹*Person*›; ~ **shell** ▸~**fish**; ~ **wire** *n.: wie Stacheldraht verwendeter, dünner, scharfkantiger Draht*

razzamatazz /'ræzəmətæz/ ▸**razzmatazz**

razzle /'ræzl/ *n.* (coll.) **be/go on the ~:** einen draufmachen (ugs.)

razzmatazz/'ræzmətæz/ (**razzle-dazzle** /'ræzldæzl/) *ns.* (coll.) **1** (excitement) Trubel, *der;* **add ~ to sth.** etwas aufmotzen (salopp) **2** (extravagant show) Rummel, *der* (ugs.)

RC *abbr.* = **Roman Catholic** r.-k.; röm.-kath.

Rd. *abbr.* = **Road** Str.

RDA *abbr.* = **recommended daily** *or* **dietary allowance** *empfohlene Tagesmenge od. Tageszufuhr*

re[1] ▸**ray[3]**

re[2] /riː/ *prep.* **1** (coll.) über (+ *Akk.*) **2** (Law) in Sachen **3** (Commerc.) betreffs

're /ə(r)/ = **are;** ▸**be**

RE *abbr.* (Brit.) **1** = **Royal Engineers** Pionierkorps der britischen Armee **2** = **Religious Education** Religionslehre, *die*

reach /riːtʃ/
A *v.t.* **1** (arrive at) erreichen; ankommen *od.* eintreffen in (+ *Dat.*) ‹*Stadt, Land*›; ankommen an (+ *Dat.*) ‹*Reiseziel*›; erzielen ‹*Übereinstimmung, Übereinkunft*›; kommen zu ‹*Entscheidung, Entschluss, Ausgang, Eingang*›; **be easily ~ed** leicht erreichbar *od.* zu erreichen sein (**by** mit); **not a sound ~ed our ears** kein Laut drang an unsere Ohren; **your letter ~ed me today** dein Brief hat mich heute erreicht; **have you ~ed page 45 yet?** bist du schon auf Seite 45 [angelangt]?; **you can ~ her at this number/by radio** du kannst sie unter dieser Nummer-/über Funk erreichen **2** (extend to) ‹*Straße:*› führen bis zu; ‹*Leiter, Haar:*› reichen bis zu **3** (pass) ~ **me that book** reich mir das Buch herüber
B *v.i.* **1** (stretch out hand) ~ **for sth.** nach etw. greifen; ~ **across the table/through the window** über den Tisch/durchs Fenster langen; **how high can you ~?** wie hoch kannst du langen? **2** (be long/tall enough) **sth. will/won't ~:** etw. ist/ist nicht lang genug; **will it ~ as far as ...?** wird es bis zu ... reichen? **I can't ~:** ich komme nicht daran; **he can't ~ up to the top shelf** er kann das oberste Regal nicht [mit der Hand] erreichen; **can you ~?** kannst *od.* kommst du dran? (ugs.) **3** (go as far as) ‹*Wasser, Gebäude, Besitz:*› reichen (**[up] to** bis [hinauf] zu); ‹*Betrag:*› erreichen (**to** *Akk.*); ‹*Stimme:*› zu hören sein (**to** bis); **his influence ~es beyond the limits of the town** sein Einfluss reicht über die Stadtgrenzen hinaus
C *n.* **1** (extent of ~ing) Reichweite, *die;* **be within easy ~** ‹*Ort:*› leicht erreichbar sein; **live within ~ of sb.** in jmds. Nähe leben; **be out of ~** ‹*Ort:*› nicht erreichbar sein; ‹*Gegenstand*› außer Reichweite sein; **be above sb.'s ~:** zu hoch für jmdn. sein; **keep sth. out of ~ of sb.** etw. unerreichbar für jmdn. aufbewahren; **keep sth. within easy ~:** etw. in greifbarer Nähe aufbewahren; **move sth. beyond sb.'s ~:** etw. aus jmds. Reichweite entfernen; **be within/beyond the ~ of sb.** in/außer jmds. Reichweite sein; (fig.) für jmdn. im/nicht im Bereich des Möglichen liegen; (financially) für jmdn. erschwinglich/unerschwinglich sein **2** (act of stretching out hand) **make a ~ for sth.** nach etw. greifen; **it was a long ~ from the bed to the light switch** der Lichtschalter war vom Bett aus schwer zu erreichen **3** (expanse) Abschnitt, *der;* **a ~ of woodland** ein Waldgebiet; **the upper/lower ~es [of the river]** die oberen/unteren [Fluss]abschnitte **4** (Naut.) Segelstrecke zwischen zwei Wendungen; **be on a ~:** raumen Kurs segeln

Phrasal verbs
- ~ **a'cross** *v.i.* die Hand ausstrecken
- ~ **'back** *v.i.* zurückreichen (**over** *Akk.;* **to** bis in + *Akk.*)
- ~ **'down**
A *v.i.* den Arm nach unten ausstrecken; ~ **down to sth.** (be long enough) bis zu etw. [hinunter-]reichen
B *v.t.* hinunterholen; (to receiving speaker) herunterreichen
- ~ **'out**
A *v.t.* (stretch out) ausstrecken ‹*Fuß, Bein, Hand, Arm*› (**for** nach)
B *v.i.* die Hand ausstrecken (**for** nach); ~ **out for,** ~ **out to grasp** ‹*Person, Hand:*› greifen nach; ~ **out to sb.** (fig.) jmdn. zu erreichen versuchen
- ~ **'over** *v.i.* die Hand ausstrecken

reachable /'riːtʃəbl/ *adj.* erreichbar

'reach-me-down (Brit.) ▸**hand-me-down A 2**

react /rɪ'ækt/
A *v.i.* **1** (respond) reagieren (**to** auf + *Akk.*); **be quick to ~ to sth.** auf etw. schnell reagieren **2** (act in opposition) sich widersetzen (**against** *Dat.*) **3** (produce reciprocal effect) zurückwirken (**upon** auf + *Akk.*); seine Wirkung haben (**upon** auf + *Akk.*) **4** (Chem., Phys.) reagieren
B *v.t.* (Chem.) reagieren lassen

reaction /rɪ'ækʃn/ *n.* **1** Reaktion, *die* (**to** auf + *Akk.*); ~ **against sth.** Widerstand gegen etw.; **action and ~:** Wirkung und Gegenwirkung; **what was his ~?** wie hat er reagiert?; **there was a favourable ~ to the proposal** der Vorschlag ist positiv aufgenommen worden; **chemical/nuclear ~:** chemische Reaktion/

Kernreaktion, *die;* **I had a bad ~ after the injection** mein Körper hat die Injektion schlecht vertragen **2** (opposite physical action) Gegenreaktion, *die* **3** (Polit.) Reaktion, *die;* **forces of ~:** reaktionäre Kräfte

reactionary /rɪˈækʃənərɪ/ (Polit.)
A *adj.* reaktionär
B *n.* Reaktionär, *der*/Reaktionärin, *die*

reactivate /rɪˈæktɪveɪt/ *v.t.* reaktivieren; wieder in Gang bringen ‹*Motor, Generator*›; wieder einrichten ‹*Stützpunkt*›

reactive /rɪˈæktɪv/ *adj.* **1** (showing reaction) auf eine Reaktion hindeutend ‹*Symptom*›; **~ response** Gegenreaktion, *die* **2** (Chem., Phys.) reaktiv

reactivity /rɪækˈtɪvɪtɪ/ *n.* (Chem., Phys.) Reaktionsfähigkeit, *die*

reactor /rɪˈæktə(r)/ *n.* **1** **[nuclear] ~:** Kernreaktor, *der;* **pressurized-water ~:** Druckwasserreaktor, *der* **2** (Chem.) Reaktor, *der;* Reaktionsapparat, *der*

reactor: ~ disaster *n.* Reaktorkatastrophe, *die;* **~ safety** *n., no pl.* Reaktorsicherheit, *die*

read /riːd/
A *v.t.,* **read** /red/ **1** lesen; **~ sb. sth., ~ sth. to sb.** jmdm. etwas vorlesen; **~ a Bill for the first/second/third time** (Parl.) einen Gesetzentwurf in erster/zweiter/dritter Lesung beraten; **for 'white' ~ 'black'** statt „weiß“ muss es „schwarz“ heißen; **~ proof[s]** (Print.) Korrektur[en] lesen; **~ the electricity/gas meter** den Strom/das Gas ablesen; **~ all about it!** lesen Sie selbst! **2** (show a ~ing of) anzeigen **3** (interpret) deuten; **~ terror in sb.'s eyes** Schrecken an jmds. Augen (*Dat.*) ablesen können; **~ sb. like a book** (fig.) in jmdm. lesen können wie in einem Buch; **~ the cards/ sb.'s hand** Karten lesen/jmdm. aus der Hand lesen; **~ sb.'s mind** *or* **thoughts** jmds. Gedanken lesen; **~ sth. into sth.** etw. in etw. (*Akk.*) hineinlesen; **~ between the lines** zwischen den Zeilen lesen **4** (understand) hören; **do you ~ me?** können Sie mich hören? **5** (Brit. Univ.: study) studieren **6** (Computing) abtasten ‹*Lochkarte*›; lesen ‹*Band, Information*›; **~ into** einlesen in (+ *Akk.*); **~ out of** entnehmen aus. *See also* **take A 21**
B *v.i.,* **read** **1** lesen; **~ to sb.** jmdm. vorlesen; **~ [a]round a subject** Hintergrundmaterial zu einem Thema lesen **2** (convey meaning) lauten; **the contract ~s as follows** der Vertrag hat folgenden Wortlaut; **Arabic ~s from right to left** die arabische Schrift wird von rechts nach links gelesen **3** (affect ~er) sich lesen; **the play ~s better than it acts** das Stück wirkt besser beim Lesen als auf der Bühne
C *n.* **1** (time spent in ~ing) **have a quiet ~:** in Ruhe lesen; **have a ~ of sth.** (coll.) mal in etw. (*Akk.*) gucken (ugs.) **2** (Brit. coll.: ~ing matter) **be a good ~:** sich gut lesen
D [red] *adj.* **widely** *or* **deeply ~:** sehr belesen ‹*Person*›; **a widely ~/little-~ book/author** ein viel/wenig gelesenes Buch/gelesener Autor; **the most widely ~ book/author** das meistgelesene Buch/der meistgelesene Autor

Phrasal verbs
- **~ 'back** *v.t.* wiederholen; noch einmal vorlesen
- **~ 'in** *v.t.* (Computing) einlesen; *see also* **read-in**
- **~ 'off** *v.t.* durchlesen; (from meter, board) ablesen ‹*Zahl, Stand*›
- **~ 'out** *v.t.* **1** (aloud) laut vorlesen **2** (Computing) ausgeben; *see also* **read-out** **3** (Amer.: expel) ausschließen (**of** aus)
- **~ 'over, ~ 'through** *v.t.* durchlesen
- **~ 'up** *v.t.* sich informieren (**on** über + *Akk.*)

readability /riːdəˈbɪlɪtɪ/ *n., no pl.* Lesbarkeit, *die;* **improve the ~ of sth.** etw. lesbarer machen

readable /ˈriːdəbl/ *adj.* **1** (pleasant to read) lesenswert **2** (legible) leserlich

readdress /riːəˈdres/ *v.t.* umadressieren

reader /ˈriːdə(r)/ *n.* **1** Leser, *der*/Leserin, *die;* **be a slow/good/great ~ [of sth.]** [etw.] langsam/gut/gern lesen **2** (who reads aloud) Vorlesende, *der/die* **3** (Publishing) **[publisher's] ~:** [Verlags]lektor, *der*/-lektorin, *die* **4** (textbook) Lehrbuch, *das;* (to learn to read, containing original texts) Lesebuch, *das;* **Latin/poetry ~:** Latein[lehr]buch, *das*/Gedichtbuch, *das* **5** (Printing) ▸ **proof-reader** **6** (Brit. Univ.) ≈ Assistenzprofessor, *der*/-professorin, *die* (**in** für) **7** (machine) Lesegerät, *das*

readership /ˈriːdəʃɪp/ *n.* **1** (number or type of readers) Leserschaft, *die;* Leserkreis, *der;* **what is the ~ of the paper?** wie groß ist die Leserschaft der Zeitung? **2** (Brit. Univ.) ≈ Assistenzprofessur, *die* (**in** für)

readies /ˈredɪz/ *n. pl.* (coll.) Knete, *die* (ugs.); **short of the ~:** knapp bei Kasse (ugs.)

readily /ˈredɪlɪ/ *adv.* **1** (willingly) bereitwillig **2** (without difficulty) ohne weiteres

read-in /ˈriːdɪn/ *n.* (Computing) Eingabe, *die; attrib.* Eingabe-

readiness /ˈredɪnɪs/ *n., no pl.* **1** Bereitschaft, *die;* **show [a] ~ to do sth.** Bereitschaft zeigen, etw. zu tun; **~ to learn** Lernbereitschaft, *die;* **have/be in ~ [for sth.]** [für etw.] bereithalten/bereit sein **2** (quickness) Schnelligkeit, *die;* **~ of wit** Schlagfertigkeit, *die*

reading /ˈriːdɪŋ/ *n.* **1** Lesen, *das;* **help sb. with his ~:** jmdm. beim Lesen helfen; **do some ~:** [ein wenig] lesen; **on [a] second ~:** beim zweiten Lesen; **a man of vast** *or* **wide/little ~:** ein sehr/wenig belesener Mann **2** (matter to be read) Lektüre, *die;* **plenty of ~:** viel zu lesen; **make interesting/be good/dull ~:** interessant/gut/langweilig zu lesen sein; **a book of ~s from the Bible** ein Buch mit ausgewählten Bibeltexten *od.* Auszügen aus der Bibel **3** (figure shown) Anzeige, *die;* **the temperature ~s for last month** die Temperaturwerte des letzten Monats **4** (recital) Lesung, *die* (**from** aus); **give a poetry ~:** Gedichte vorlesen; **give a ~ from** lesen aus **5** (interpretation) [Aus]deutung, *die;* **my ~ of the sentence was ...:** ich habe den Satz so verstanden: ...; **our ~ of the law is that ...:** wir legen das Recht so aus, dass ... **6** (particular form) Version, *die;* Fassung, *die* **7** (Parl.) **[first/second/third] ~:** [erste/zweite/dritte] Lesung; **have its first ~:** in erster Lesung beraten werden; **be thrown out on the second ~** in zweiter Lesung verworfen werden; **give the bill its second ~** den Gesetzentwurf in zweiter Lesung beraten

reading: ~ age *n.* **a child with a ~ age of 10** ein Kind mit der Lesefertigkeit eines Zehnjährigen; **have a ~ age of 10** wie ein zehnjähriges Kind lesen können; **~ desk** *n.* Lesepult, *das;* **~ glasses** *n. pl.* Lesebrille, *die;* **~ knowledge** *n.* **have a ~ knowledge of a language** Texte in einer Sprache lesen können; **~ lamp, ~ light** *ns.* Leselampe, *die;* **~ list** *n.* Literaturliste, *die;* **~ matter** *n., no pl., no indef. art.* Lesestoff, *der;* Lektüre, *die;* **~ room** *n.* Lesesaal, *der*

readjust /riːəˈdʒʌst/
A *v.t.* neu einstellen; neu anpassen ‹*Gehalt, Zinssatz*›
B *v. refl. & i.* **~ [oneself] to** sich wieder gewöhnen an (+ *Akk.*) ‹*Leben*›

readjustment /riːəˈdʒʌstmənt/ *n.* Änderung, *die;* **period of ~:** Zeit der Neuorientierung

readmission /riːædˈmɪʃn/ *n.* (of student) Wiederzulassung, *die;* (of patient to hospital) Wiederaufnahme, *die;* (of state) Wiedereingliederung, *die;* (of concert-goer) Wiedereinlass, *der*

readmit /riːædˈmɪt/ *v.t.* wieder zulassen ‹*Studenten*›; wieder aufnehmen ‹*Patienten*›; wieder [her/hin]einlassen ‹*Konzertbesucher*›; wieder aufnehmen ‹*Staat*›

readmittance /riːədˈmɪtəns/ *n., no pl.* (of student) Wiederzulassung, *die;* (of concert-goer) Wiedereinlass, *der*

read /riːd/: **~-'only memory** *n.* (Computing) Fest[wert]speicher, *der;* **~-out** *n.* (Computing) Ausgabe, *die;* **~-write** *n. attrib.* (Computing) Schreib-Lese-; **~-write head** Schreib-Lese-Kopf, *der*

re-advertise /riːˈædvətaɪz/ *v.t.* nochmals ausschreiben ‹*Stelle*›

readvertisement /riːədˈvɜːtɪsmənt/ *n.* Wiederholungsanzeige, *die*

read-'write head *n.* (Computing) Schreib-Lese-Kopf, *der*

ready /ˈredɪ/
A *adj.* **1** (prepared) fertig; **be ~ for the fight** *or* **to fight** kampfbereit sein; **be ~ to do sth.** bereit sein, etw. zu tun; **the troops are ~ to march/for battle** die Truppen sind marsch-/gefechtsbereit; **be ~ for work/school** zur Arbeit/für die Schule bereit sein; (about to leave) für die Arbeit/Schule fertig sein; **be ~ to leave** aufbruchsbereit sein; **be ~ for sb.** bereit sein, sich jmdm. zu stellen; **be ~ for anything** auf alles vorbereitet sein; **make ~:** Vorbereitungen treffen (**for** für); **make ~ to go** sich zum Aufbruch bereitmachen **2** (willing) bereit; **I'm ~ to believe it** ich glaube es gerne **3** (prompt) schnell; **have ~, be ~ with** parat haben, nicht verlegen sein um ‹*Antwort, Ausrede, Vorschlag*›; **be too ~ to suspect others** allzu schnell bereit sein, andere zu verdächtigen **4** (likely) im Begriff; **be ~ to burst** ‹*Knospe:*› kurz vor dem Aufbrechen sein; **be ~ to cry** den Tränen nahe sein **5** (within reach) griffbereit ‹*Waffe, Fahrkarte, Taschenlampe*›; **have your tickets ~!** halten Sie Ihre Fahrkarten bitte bereit!; **a ~ source of supplies** eine sofort zugängliche Bezugsquelle **6** (not reluctant) bereitwillig ‹*Zustimmung, Anerkennung*›; willig ‹*Arbeiter*› **7** (easy) leicht ‹*Löslichkeit, Zugänglichkeit*›; **she has a ~ smile** sie lächelt gern
B *adv.* fertig; **~ cooked** vorgekocht
C *n.* **1** **at the ~:** schussbereit, im Anschlag ‹*Schusswaffe*› **2** ▸ **readies**

ready: ~ 'cash ▸ **~ money**; **~-cooked** *adj.* vorgekocht; **~-cooked meal** Fertiggericht, *das;* Fertigmahlzeit, *die;* **~-made** *adj.* **1** Konfektions‹*anzug, -kleidung*›; **~-made curtains** Fertiggardinen; **2** (fig.) vorgefertigt; **~ meal** *n.* Fertiggericht, *das;* **~ 'money** *n.* **1** (cash) Bargeld, *das;* **2** (immediate payment) **for ~ money** gegen bar; **~ 'reckoner** *n.* Berechnungstabelle, *die;* (for conversion) Umrechnungstabelle, *die;* **~, set** *or* **steady, 'go!** *int.* Achtung, fertig, los!; **~-to-eat** *adj.* Fertig‹*mahlzeit, -dessert*›; **~-to-serve** *adj.* tischfertig; **~-to-wear** *adj.* Konfektions‹*anzug, -kleidung*›

reaffirm /riːəˈfɜːm/ *v.t.* [erneut] bekräftigen

reaffirmation /riːæfəˈmeɪʃn/ *n.* [erneute] Bekräftigung

reafforest /riːəˈfɒrɪst/ (Brit.) ▸ **reforest**

reafforestation /riːəfɒrɪˈsteɪʃn/ *n.* Wiederaufforstung, *die*

reagent /riːˈeɪdʒənt/ *n.* (Chem.) Reagens, *das;* Reagenz, *das*

real /rɪəl/
A *adj.* **1** (actually existing) real ‹*Gestalt, Ereignis, Lebewesen*›; wirklich ‹*Macht*› **2** (genuine) echt ‹*Interesse, Gold, Seide*›; **very ~** (coll.) wirklich groß ‹*Vergnügen, Ehre*› **3** (complete) total (ugs.) ‹*Desaster, Bauernfängerei, Wucher, Enttäuschung*› **4** (true) wahr ‹*Grund, Freund, Name, Glück*›; echt ‹*Mitleid, Vergnügen, Sieg*›; **the ~ thing** (genuine article) der/die/das Echte; (fig.: true love) [die] wahre Liebe; **look like the ~ thing** wie echt aussehen; **be [not] the ~ thing** [un]echt sein; **have experienced the ~ thing** das Echte kennen; **feel a ~ fool** sich (*Dat.*) wie ein richtiger Idiot vorkommen **5** (Econ.) real; Real-; **in ~ terms** real ‹*sinken, steigen*›; **salaries decreased in ~ terms** die Realgehälter sind gesunken **6** **be for ~** (coll.) echt sein; ‹*Angebot, Drohung:*› ernst gemeint sein; ‹*Person:*› aufrichtig sein; **fight for ~:** richtig kämpfen **7** (Philos.) real **8** (Math., Optics) reell ‹*Zahl, Bild, Analyse*›. *See also* **tennis**
B *adv.* (Scot. and Amer. coll. as intensifier) echt (ugs.) ‹*gut, schön, usw.*›; recht ‹*bald*›

real: ~ 'ale *n.* (Brit.) echtes Ale; **~ 'coffee** *n.* Bohnenkaffee, *der;* **~ estate** *n.* (Law) Immobilien *Pl.;* **be in ~ estate** Immobilienhandel betreiben; **~-estate** *adj.* Immobilien‹*büro, -makler*›

realign /riːəˈlaɪn/ *v.t.* neu ordnen ‹*Text, Daten*›; neu aufeinander abstimmen ‹*Währungen*›

realignment /riːəˈlaɪnmənt/ *n.* Neuordnung, *die;* (of currency) Realignment, *das* (Finanzw.)

realisable, realisation, realise ▸ **realiz-**

realism /ˈrɪəlɪzm/ *n.* Realismus, *der;* **[sense of] ~:** Wirklichkeitssinn, *der*

r

realist /ˈrɪəlɪst/ *n.* Realist, *der*/Realistin, *die*

realistic /rɪəˈlɪstɪk/ *adj.* realistisch; **be ~ about sth.** etw. realistisch sehen

realistically /rɪəˈlɪstɪkəlɪ/ *adv.* realistisch

reality /rɪˈælɪtɪ/ *n.* **1** *no pl.* Realität, *die;* **appearance and ~:** Schein und Sein; **bring sb. back to ~:** jmdn. in die Realität zurückholen; **in ~:** in Wirklichkeit **2** *no pl.* (resemblance to original) Naturtreue, *die;* **with [startling] ~:** [erstaunlich] naturgetreu **3** (real fact) Gegebenheit, *die;* **the realities of the situation** die tatsächliche Situation

reality: ~-based *adj.* **1** (realistic) realistisch ‹*Mensch, Einschätzung*›; **2** (Telev.: non-fictional) dokumentarisch; **~-based television show** Dokushow, *die;* **~ check** *n.* (esp. Amer. coll.) Realitätscheck, *der;* **~ ˈtelevision, reality TˈV** *ns.* Reality-TV, *das*

realizable /ˈrɪəlaɪzəbl/ *adj.* realisierbar

realization /rɪəlaɪˈzeɪʃn/ *n.* **1** (understanding) Erkenntnis, *die* **2** (becoming real) Verwirklichung, *die* **3** (Finance: act of selling) Realisierung, *die*

realize /ˈrɪəlaɪz/ *v.t.* **1** (be aware of) bemerken; realisieren; erkennen ‹*Fehler*›; **they've ~d the importance of tact** sie merkten, wie wichtig Taktgefühl ist; **I never ~d how much I depend on him** erst jetzt wird mir bewusst, wie sehr ich auf ihn angewiesen bin; **~ [that] ...:** merken, dass ...; **I hardly ~d what was happening** ich habe kaum mitbekommen, was da vor sich ging; **I didn't ~** (abs.) ich habe es nicht gewusst/(had not noticed) bemerkt **2** (make happen) verwirklichen; **be ~d** wahr werden **3** (Finance: sell for cash) realisieren (fachspr.); in Geld (*Akk.*) umsetzen **4** (fetch as price or profit) erbringen ‹*Summe, Gewinn, Preis*› **5** (gain) erwerben ‹*Vermögen*›; machen ‹*Gewinn*›

real: ~ ˈlife *n.* das wirkliche Leben; die Realität; **~-life** *attrib. adj.* real

really /ˈrɪəlɪ/ *adv.* wirklich; **it's a ~ good film** es ist ein wirklich guter Film; **I don't ~/~ don't know what to do now** ich weiß eigentlich/wirklich nicht, was ich jetzt tun soll; **I ~ think you ought to apologize** ich finde wirklich, dass du dich entschuldigen solltest; **not ~:** eigentlich nicht; **that's not ~ a problem** das ist eigentlich kein Problem; **he didn't ~ mean it** er hat es nicht so gemeint; **I ~ don't know** ich weiß es wirklich nicht; **[well,] ~!** [also] so was!; **~, I would never have expected that of you** also wirklich, das hätte ich nie von dir erwartet; **~?** wirklich?; tatsächlich?; **~ and truly** wirklich

realm /relm/ *n.* [König]reich, *das;* **be in the ~[s] of fancy** ins Reich der Fantasie gehören; **be within/beyond the ~s of possibility** *or* **the possible** im/nicht im Bereich des Möglichen liegen

real: ~ ˈman *n.* richtiger Mann; **~ ˈmoney** *n.* Bargeld, *das;* **pay in ~ money** bar bezahlen; **~ ˈproperty** *n.* (Law) Grundvermögen, *das;* **~ time** *n.* (Computing) Realzeit, *die;* Echtzeit, *die*

realtor /ˈriːəltə(r)/ (Amer.) ▸ **estate agent 1**

real ˈworld *n.* (beyond school) Arbeitswelt, *die;* (as opposed to film etc.) Realität, *die;* **the ~ outside** die [reale] Außenwelt

ream /riːm/ *n.* **1** (quantity) 500 Blatt; halbes [Neu]ries; **three ~s** 1500 Blatt; anderthalb [Neu]ries **2** *in pl.* (fig.) ein ganzer Roman; **write ~s [and ~s] of poetry** ganze Bände von Gedichten schreiben

reanimate /rɪˈænɪmeɪt/ *v.t.* wieder beleben

reap /riːp/ *v.t.* **1** (cut) schneiden ‹*Getreide*› **2** (gather in) einfahren ‹*Getreide, Ernte*› **3** (harvest) abernten ‹*Feld*› **4** (fig.) ernten ‹*Ruhm, Lob*›; erhalten ‹*Belohnung*›; erzielen ‹*Gewinn*›; **~ what one has sown** ernten, was man gesät hat; **~ the benefits of sth.** die Früchte einer Sache ernten; *see also* **whirlwind 1**

reaper /ˈriːpə(r)/ *n.* **1** ▸ **harvester 2** **the [Grim] R~** (fig.) der Sensenmann (verhüll.); der Schnitter [Tod]

reaping/ˈriːpɪŋ/: **~ hook** *n.* Sichel, *die;* **~ machine** ▸ **harvester 1**

reappear /riːəˈpɪə(r)/ *v.i.* wieder auftauchen; (come back) [wieder] zurückkommen; ‹*Sonne:*› wieder zum Vorschein kommen

reappearance /riːəˈpɪərəns/ *n.* Wiederauftauchen, *das*

reapply /riːəˈplaɪ/

A *v.i.* sich erneut bewerben (**for** um)

B *v.t.* noch einmal auftragen ‹*Kleister*›

reappoint /riːəˈpɔɪnt/ *v.t.* wieder einstellen

reappointment /riːəˈpɔɪntmənt/ *n.* Wiedereinstellung, *die*

reappraisal /riːəˈpreɪzl/ *n.* Neubewertung, *die*

reappraise /riːəˈpreɪz/ *v.t.* neu bewerten

rear[1] /rɪə(r)/

A *n.* **1** (back part) hinterer Teil; **at** *or* (Amer.) **in the ~ of** im hinteren Teil (+ *Gen.*); **please move to the ~:** bitte nach hinten durchgehen **2** (back) Rückseite, *die;* **bring up the ~, be in the ~:** den Schluss bilden; **to the ~ of the house there is ...:** hinter dem Haus ist ...; **go round to the ~ of the house** hinter das Haus gehen; **in the ~ of the procession** am Schluss der Prozession; **the spectators at the ~:** die hinten sitzenden/stehenden Zuschauer **3** (Mil.) Rücken, *der;* rückwärtiger Teil; **attack in the ~:** von hinten angreifen **4** (coll.: buttocks) Hintern, *der* (ugs.)

B *adj.* hinter ... ‹*Eingang, Tür, Blinklicht*›; **~ axle** Hinterachse, *die*

rear[2]

A *v.t.* **1** (bring up) großziehen ‹*Kind, Familie*›; halten ‹*Vieh*›; hegen ‹*Wild*› **2** (lift up) heben ‹*Kopf*›; aufrichten ‹*Leiter*›; **~ its ugly head** (fig.) seine hässliche Fratze zeigen

B *v.i.* **1** (raise itself on hind legs) **~ [up]** ‹*Pferd:*› sich aufbäumen **2** (extend to great height) ‹*Gebäude, Berg:*› sich erheben (**over, above** über + *Akk.*)

rear: ~ ˈadmiral *n.* (Navy) Konteradmiral, *der;* **~ ˈdoor** *n.* (Motor Veh.) Fondtür, *die;* Hintertür, *die;* (to boot) Hecktür, *die;* **~ ˈend** *n.* (coll.: buttocks) Hinterteil, *das* (ugs.); **~-engined** *adj.* (Motor Veh.) mit Heckantrieb *nachgestellt;* **be ~-engined** Heckantrieb haben; **~guard** *n.* (Mil.) Nachhut, *die;* **~guard action** *n.* (Mil.) Nachhutgefecht, *das;* (fig.) Rückzugsgefecht, *das;* **~ lamp, ~ light** *ns.* Rücklicht, *das*

rearm /riːˈɑːm/

A *v.i.* wieder aufrüsten

B *v.t.* wieder aufrüsten ‹*Land*›; wieder bewaffnen ‹*Truppen*›; (give more modern arms to) neu bewaffnen *od.* ausrüsten ‹*Truppen*›; **~ sb./oneself** jmdn./sich wieder bewaffnen

rearmament /riːˈɑːməmənt/ *n.* Wiederbewaffnung, *die;* (of country also) Wiederaufrüstung, *die*

rearmost /ˈrɪəməʊst/ *adj.* hinterst ...

rearrange /riːəˈreɪndʒ/ *v.t.* (alter plan of) umräumen ‹*Möbel, Zimmer*›; verlegen ‹*Treffen, Spiel*› (**for** auf + *Akk.*); ändern ‹*Anordnung, Programm*›

rearrangement /riːəˈreɪndʒmənt/ *n.* ▸ **rearrange:** Umräumen, *das;* Verlegung, *die;* Änderung, *die*

rear: ~-view ˈmirror *n.* Rückspiegel, *der;* **~ward** /ˈrɪəwəd/ **A** *n.* **be to ~ward of the troops** sich im Rücken der Truppen befinden; **B** *adj.* hinter ... ‹*Teil*›; nach hinten gerichtet ‹*Bewegung*›; **in a ~ward direction** nach hinten; **C** *adv.* nach hinten; **~-wheel drive A** *n.* Hinterradantrieb, *der;* Heckantrieb, *der;* **B** *adj.* **a ~-wheel drive vehicle** ein Fahrzeug mit Hinterrad- *od.* Heckantrieb; **the car is ~-wheel drive** das Auto hat Hinterrad- *od.* Heckantrieb

reason /ˈriːzn/

A *n.* **1** (cause) Grund, *der;* **what is your ~ for doing that?** aus welchem Grund tust du das/hast du das getan?; **there is [no/every] ~ to assume** *or* **believe that ...:** es besteht [kein/ein guter] Grund zu der Annahme, dass ...; **have every ~ to suppose that ...:** allen Grund zu der Annahme haben, dass ...; **have no ~ to complain** *or* **for complaint** sich nicht beklagen können; **for that [very] ~:** aus [eben] diesem Grund; **for no ~:** grundlos; **no particular ~** (as answer) einfach so; **see ~ to do sth.** es für gerechtfertigt halten, etw. zu tun; **all the more ~ for doing sth.** ein Grund mehr, etw. zu tun; **for ~s best known to himself** aus Gründen, die er allein kennt; **for some ~, for one ~ or another** aus irgendeinem Grund; **for ~s of health** aus gesundheitlichen Gründen; **for obvious ~s** aus gutem Grund; **for no obvious ~:** aus keinem ersichtlichen Grund; **for the [simple] ~ that ...:** [einfach,] weil ...; **by ~ of** wegen; aufgrund; **with ~:** aus gutem Grund **2** *no pl., no art.* (power to understand; sense; Philos.) Vernunft, *die;* (sanity) gesunder Verstand; **lose one's ~:** den Verstand verlieren; **regain one's ~:** wieder normal werden; (fig.) wieder zur Vernunft kommen; **contrary to ~:** unsinnig; absurd; **be out of all ~:** völlig unsinnig sein; **be** *or* **go beyond all ~:** völlig überzogen sein; **I can't see the ~ of it** ich sehe keinen Sinn darin; **in** *or* **within ~:** innerhalb eines vernünftigen Rahmens; **you can have anything within ~:** du kannst alles haben, solange es im Rahmen bleibt; **stand to ~:** unzweifelhaft sein; **not listen to ~:** sich (*Dat.*) nichts sagen lassen; **see ~:** zur Einsicht kommen; **make sb. see ~, bring sb. to ~:** jmdn. zur Einsicht bringen; **Age of R~** (Hist.) Zeitalter der Aufklärung *od.* Vernunft; **for ~s of State** aus Gründen der Staatsräson

B *v.i.* **1** schlussfolgern (**from** aus); **ability to ~:** logisches Denkvermögen; **he can ~ clearly** er hat einen klaren Verstand **2** **~ with** diskutieren mit (**about, on** über + *Akk.*); **you can't ~ with her** mit ihr kann man nicht vernünftig reden

C *v.t.* **1** (conclude) schlussfolgern **2** (persuade) **~ sb. into doing sth.** jmdn. dazu überreden, etw. zu tun; **~ sb. out of sth.** jmdm. etw. ausreden **3** (question) **ours not to ~ why** es ist nicht unsere Sache, nach dem Warum zu fragen

Phrasal verb

- **~ ˈout** *v.t.* sich (*Dat.*) überlegen; **he could ~ out the result** (knew in advance) er konnte sich (*Dat.*) das Ergebnis schon denken; **it's easy to ~ out what ...:** man kann sich leicht denken, was ...

reasonable /ˈriːzənəbl/ *adj.* **1** vernünftig; angemessen, vernünftig ‹*Forderung*›; **be ~!** sei [doch] vernünftig!; **not be ~ in one's demands** überzogene Forderungen stellen; **beyond ~ doubt** unzweifelhaft **2** (inexpensive) günstig; **it's a ~ price** das ist ein vernünftiger Preis **3** (fair) passabel ‹*Leistung, Wein*›; **with a ~ amount of luck** mit ein bisschen Glück **4** (within limits) realistisch ‹*Chancen, Angebot*›

reasonably /ˈriːzənəblɪ/ *adv.* **1** (within reason) vernünftig; **no one could ~ believe that ...:** niemand kann ernsthaft glauben, dass ... **2** (moderately) **~ priced** preisgünstig **3** (fairly) ganz ‹*gut*›; ziemlich ‹*gesund*›

reasoned /ˈriːznd/ *adj.* durchdacht

reasoner /ˈriːzənə(r)/ *n.* **skilful** *or* **clever ~:** kluger *od.* heller Kopf

reasoning /ˈriːzənɪŋ/ *n.* logisches Denken; (argumentation) Argumentation, *die;* **a brilliant piece of ~:** eine brillante Argumentation; **power of ~:** logisches Denkvermögen; **there's no ~ with her** mit ihr kann man nicht vernünftig reden

reassemble /riːəˈsembl/

A *v.i.* sich wieder versammeln; ‹*Streitkräfte, Truppen:*› sich wieder sammeln

B *v.t.* **1** (bring together again) wieder versammeln ‹*Anhänger*›; [wieder] sammeln ‹*Truppen*› **2** (put together again) wieder zusammenbauen

reassert /riːəˈsɜːt/ *v.t.* [erneut] bekräftigen

reassertion /riːəˈsɜːʃn/ *n.* [erneute] Bekräftigung

reassess /riːəˈses/ *v.t.* neu bewerten ‹*Situation*›; überdenken ‹*Vorschlag*›; überprüfen ‹*Argument, Beweis, Anspruch*›; (for taxation) neu veranlagen ‹*Besitz*›

reassessment /riːəˈsesmənt/ *n.* (of evidence, argument, claim) Überprüfung, *die;* (of proposal) Überdenken, *das;* (of situation) Neubewertung, *die;* (for taxation) Neuveranlagung, *die*

reassign /riːəˈsaɪn/ *v.t.* neu zuweisen

reassignment /riːəˈsaɪnmənt/ *n.* (of personnel) Versetzung, *die;* (of resources, money) Übertragung, *die*

reassurance /riːəˈʃʊərəns/ *n.* **1** (calming) **give sb. ~:** jmdn. beruhigen **2** (confirmation in opinion) Bestätigung, *die; in pl.* [wiederholte] Versicherungen

reassure /riːəˈʃʊə(r)/ *v.t.* **1** (calm fears of) beruhigen **2** (confirm in opinion) bestätigen; **he needs to be constantly ~d that ...:** man muss ihm dauernd aufs Neue bestätigen *od.* versichern, dass ...; **~ sb. about his health** jmdm. versichern, dass er gesund ist

reassuring /riːəˈʃʊərɪŋ/ *adj.*, **reassuringly** /riːəˈʃʊərɪŋlɪ/ *adv.* beruhigend

reawaken /riːəˈweɪkn/

A *v.t.* (lit. or fig.) wieder erwecken

B *v.i.* (lit. or fig.) wieder erwachen

reawakening /riːəˈweɪknɪŋ/ *n.* (fig.) Wiedererwachen, *das*

rebate¹ /ˈriːbeɪt/ *n.* **1** (refund) Rückzahlung, *die;* **~ on tax** Steuerrückzahlung, *die;* **get a ~ on the gas bill** Geld von den Gaswerken zurückbekommen **2** (discount) Preisnachlass, *der* (**on** auf + *Akk.*); Rabatt, *der* (**on** auf + *Akk.*); **rate ~** (Brit.) Ermäßigung der Gemeindeabgaben

rebate² /ˈræbɪt/ ▸ **rabbet**

rebel

A /ˈrebl/ *n.* Rebell, *der*/Rebellin, *die*

B *attrib. adj.* **1** (of rebels) Rebellen- **2** (refusing obedience to ruler) rebellisch; aufständisch

C /rɪˈbel/ *v.i.*, **-ll-** rebellieren

rebellion /rɪˈbeljən/ *n.* Rebellion, *die;* **rise [up] in ~:** sich erheben; rebellieren

rebellious /rɪˈbeljəs/ *adj.* **1** (defiant) rebellisch; aufsässig **2** (in rebellion) rebellierend ‹*Sklave, Untertan*›

rebind /riːˈbaɪnd/ *v.t.*, **rebound** /riːˈbaʊnd/ neu [ein]binden

rebirth /riːˈbɜːθ/ *n.* **1** Wiedergeburt, *die* **2** (revival) Wiederaufleben, *das*

reboot /riːˈbuːt/ (Computing)

A *v.t. & i* neu booten

B *n.* Neubooten, *das;* Reboot, *das*

reborn /riːˈbɔːn/ *adj.* wieder geboren; **feel ~:** sich wie neugeboren fühlen; **be ~:** wieder geboren werden

rebound¹

A /rɪˈbaʊnd/ *v.i.* **1** (spring back) abprallen (**from** von) **2** (have reactive effect) zurückfallen (**upon** auf + *Akk.*); **the plan ~ed on her** *or* **on her head** der Plan schadete ihr nur selbst

B /ˈriːbaʊnd/ *n.* **1** (recoil) Abprall, *der;* Rebound, *der* (Basketball); **catch the ball on the ~:** den Abpraller *od.* (Basketball) Rebound fangen **2** (fig.: emotional reaction) **marry/turn to sb. on the ~:** in seiner Enttäuschung jmdn. heiraten/sich jmdm. zuwenden

rebound² ▸ **rebind**

ˈrebrand /riːˈbrænd/ *v.t.* **1** (Marketing: apply new brand name) umfirmieren ‹*Firma*› **2** (present differently) umbenennen (**as** in + *Akk.*)

rebroadcast /riːˈbrɔːdkɑːst/

A *n.* Wiederholung, *die*

B *v.t., forms as* **broadcast B** wiederholen

rebuff /rɪˈbʌf/

A *n.* [schroffe] Abweisung; **be met with a ~:** auf Ablehnung stoßen; **suffer a ~:** abgelehnt werden

B *v.t.* [schroff] zurückweisen

rebuild /riːˈbɪld/ *v.t.*, **rebuilt** /riːˈbɪlt/ (lit. or fig.) wieder aufbauen; (make extensive changes to) umbauen

rebuke /rɪˈbjuːk/

A *v.t.* tadeln, rügen (**for** wegen); **~ sb. for doing sth.** jmdn. zurechtweisen, weil er etwas tut/getan hat

B *n.* Rüge, *die;* Zurechtweisung, *die*

rebus /ˈriːbəs/ *n.* Bilderrätsel, *das*

rebut /rɪˈbʌt/ *v.t.*, **-tt-** (formal) widerlegen

rebuttal /rɪˈbʌtl/ *n.* (Law) Widerlegung, *die;* **call evidence in ~ of it** den Gegenbeweis dafür antreten

recalcitrance /rɪˈkælsɪtrəns/ *n., no pl.* ▸ **recalcitrant:** Aufsässigkeit, *die;* Schwergängigkeit, *die*

recalcitrant /rɪˈkælsɪtrənt/

A *adj.* aufsässig ‹*Person*›; schwergängig ‹*Hebel, Mechanismus*›

B *n.* Unruhestifter, *der*/-stifterin, *die*

recall

A /rɪˈkɔːl/ *v.t.* **1** (remember) sich erinnern an (+ *Akk.*); **~ what/how ...:** sich daran erinnern, was/wie ... **2** (serve as reminder of) erinnern an (+ *Akk.*); **~ sth. to sb.** jmdn. an etw. (*Akk.*) erinnern **3** (summon back) zurückrufen ‹*Soldat, fehlerhaftes Produkt*›; zurückfordern ‹*Buch*›; **~ Parliament** das Parlament zurückrufen; **the noise ~ed her to the present** der Lärm brachte sie in die Wirklichkeit zurück **4** (suspend appointment of) abberufen ‹*Botschafter, Delegation*› (**from** aus)

B /rɪˈkɔːl, ˈriːkɔːl/ *n.* **1** (ability to remember) **[powers of] ~:** Erinnerungsvermögen, *das;* Gedächtnis, *das; see also* **total recall 2** (possibility of annulling) **beyond** *or* **past ~:** unwiderruflich **3** (summons back) Rückruf, *der;* (to active duty) Wiedereinberufung, *die* **4** (suspension of appointment abroad) Abberufung, *die*

recant /rɪˈkænt/

A *v.i.* [öffentlich] widerrufen

B *v.t.* widerrufen

recantation /riːkænˈteɪʃn/ *n.* Widerruf, *der;* **make a ~ of sth.** etw. widerrufen

recap¹ /riːˈkæp/ *v.t.*, **-pp-** (Amer.) **1** (replace cap on) wieder verschließen ‹*Flasche*› **2** (retread) runderneuern ‹*Reifen*›

recap² /ˈriːkæp/ (coll.)

A *v.t. & i.*, **-pp-** rekapitulieren; kurz zusammenfassen

B *n.* Zusammenfassung, *die;* **let's just have a quick ~:** fassen wir kurz zusammen

recapitulate /riːkəˈpɪtjʊleɪt/ *v.t. & i.* rekapitulieren; kurz zusammenfassen

recapitulation /riːkəpɪtjʊˈleɪʃn/ *n.* **1** (summing up) Zusammenfassung, *die;* Rekapitulation, *die* **2** (Mus.) Reprise, *die*

recapture /riːˈkæptʃə(r)/

A *v.t.* **1** (capture again) wieder ergreifen ‹*Gefangenen*›; wieder einfangen ‹*Tier*›; zurückerobern ‹*Stadt*› **2** (recreate) wieder lebendig werden lassen ‹*Atmosphäre*›; (experience again) noch einmal durchleben ‹*Aufregung, Vergangenheit, Jugend, Glück*›

B *n.* (retaking) Rückeroberung, *die*

recast /riːˈkɑːst/ *v.t.*, **recast 1** (remould) neu gießen **2** (refashion) revidieren ‹*Vorstellung, Einstellung*› **3** (rewrite) umschreiben

recce /ˈrekɪ/ (Brit. coll.) *n.* Erkundung, *die;* **make a ~:** die Lage peilen (ugs.)

recede /rɪˈsiːd/ *v.i.* **1** ‹*Hochwasser, Flut:*› zurückgehen; ‹*Küste:*› zurückweichen; **his hair is beginning to ~:** er bekommt eine Stirnglatze **2** (be left at increasing distance) **~ [into the distance]** in der Ferne verschwinden **3** (decline) ‹*Preis:*› fallen; **~ in importance** an Bedeutung verlieren

receding /rɪˈsiːdɪŋ/ *adj.* fliehend ‹*Kinn, Stirn*›; zurückweichend ‹*Küste*›; zurückgehend ‹*Flut, Hochwasser*›; *see also* **hairline 1**

receipt /rɪˈsiːt/

A *n.* **1** Empfang, *der;* **please acknowledge ~ of this letter/order** bestätigen Sie bitte den Empfang dieses Briefes/dieser Bestellung; **be in ~ of** (formal) erhalten haben ‹*Brief*›; **those in ~ of a pension** Rentenempfänger; **[up]on ~ of the news/your remittance** (formal) nach Eingang der Nachricht/Ihrer Überweisung **2** (written acknowledgement) Empfangsbestätigung, *die;* Quittung, *die;* **~ for payment** Quittung, *die* **3** *in pl.* (amount received) Einnahmen (**from** aus)

B *v.t.* quittieren

receivable /rɪˈsiːvəbl/ *adj.* (Commerc.) offen; ausstehend

receive /rɪˈsiːv/ *v.t.* **1** (get) erhalten; beziehen ‹*Gehalt, Rente*›; verliehen bekommen ‹*akademischen Grad*›; **~ a cordial welcome** herzlich begrüßt werden; **~ one's education at a private school** eine Privatschule besuchen; **she ~d a lot of attention/sympathy [from him]** es wurde ihr [von ihm] viel Aufmerksamkeit/Verständnis entgegengebracht; **~ [fatal] injuries** [tödlich] verletzt werden; **'payment ~d with thanks'** „Betrag dankend erhalten"; **your letter will ~ our immediate attention** wir werden Ihren Brief umgehend bearbeiten; **~ insults/praise** beschimpft/gelobt werden; **~ much unfavourable comment** stark kritisiert werden; **~ 30 days [imprisonment]** 30 Tage Gefängnis bekommen; **~ the sacraments/holy communion** (Relig.) das Abendmahl/die heilige Kommunion empfangen **2** (accept) entgegennehmen ‹*Bukett, Lieferung*›; (submit to) über sich (*Akk.*) ergehen lassen; **be convicted for receiving [stolen goods]** (Law) der Hehlerei überführt werden **3** (serve as receptacle for) aufnehmen **4** (greet) reagieren auf (*Akk.*), aufnehmen ‹*Angebot, Nachricht, Theaterstück, Roman*›; empfangen ‹*Person*› **5** (entertain) empfangen ‹*Botschafter, Delegation, Nachbarn, Gast*› **6** (consent to hear) abnehmen ‹*Beichte, Eid*›; entgegennehmen ‹*Gesuch*› (**from** *Gen.*); **~ sb.'s confession/oath** jmdm. die Beichte/den Eid abnehmen **7** (Radio,Telev.) empfangen ‹*Sender, Signal*›; **are you receiving me?** können Sie mich hören? **8** tragen ‹*Last, Gewicht*› **9** (accept as true) anerkennen ‹*Theorie, Lehre*› **10** (Tennis) **~ the serve** den Aufschlag nehmen; **Hingis to ~:** Hingis nimmt den Aufschlag. *See also* **end A 4**

Phrasal verb

• **~ into** *v.t.* aufnehmen in (+ *Akk.*)

received /rɪˈsiːvd/ *adj.* landläufig ‹*Vorstellung, Weisheit, Meinung*›; gültig ‹*Version, Text*›

received pronunciˈation (*Amer.:* **Received ˈStandard**) *ns.* (Ling.) englische Standardaussprache

receiver /rɪˈsiːvə(r)/ *n.* **1** Empfänger, *der*/Empfängerin, *die* **2** ([Table]Tennis) Rückschläger, *der*/-schlägerin, *die* **3** (Teleph.) [Telefon]hörer, *der* **4** (Radio, Telev.) Empfänger, *der;* Receiver, *der* (Technik) **5** **[official] ~** (Law) (for property of bankrupt) [gerichtlich bestellter/bestellte] Konkursverwalter/-verwalterin; (for insane person) Pfleger, *der*/Pflegerin, *die* **6** (who receives stolen goods) Hehler, *der*/Hehlerin, *die* **7** (Chem.: vessel) Vorlage, *die*

receivership /rɪˈsiːvəʃɪp/ *n.* (Law: being in hands of receiver) Konkursverwaltung, *die;* **put sth. in** *or* **into ~:** etw. unter Konkursverwaltung stellen

recension /rɪˈsenʃn/ *n.* Überarbeitung, *die;* Rezension, *die* (fachspr.)

recent /ˈriːsənt/ *adj.* **1** (not long past) jüngst ‹*Ereignisse, Wahlen, Vergangenheit usw.*›; **the ~ closure of the factory** die kürzlich erfolgte Schließung der Fabrik; **at our ~ meeting** als wir uns kürzlich *od.* vor kurzem trafen; **a ~/more ~ survey** eine neuere Untersuchung; **the most ~ survey** die neueste Untersuchung; **at our most ~ meeting** bei unserer letzten Begegnung **2** (not long established) Neu‹*auflage, -anschaffung, -erscheinung*›; **~ additions to the library's holdings** Neuerwerbungen der Bibliothek **3** **R~** (Geol.) Holozän, *das*

recently /ˈriːsəntlɪ/ *adv.* (a short time ago) neulich; kürzlich; vor kurzem; (in the recent past) in der letzten Zeit; **until ~/until quite ~:** bis vor kurzem/bis vor ganz kurzer Zeit; **~ we've been following a different policy** seit kurzem verfolgen wir eine andere Politik; **as ~ as last year** (last year still) noch letztes Jahr; **as ~ as this morning** (not until this morning) [gerade] erst heute Morgen; **one morning ~:** neulich morgens; **I haven't seen him ~:** ich habe ihn in letzter Zeit nicht gesehen

receptacle /rɪˈseptəkl/ *n.* **1** (container) Behälter, *der;* Gefäß, *das* **2** (Bot.) Blütenboden, *der;* Receptaculum, *das* (fachspr.)

reception /rɪˈsepʃn/ *n.* **1** (welcome) (of person) Empfang, *der;* Aufnahme, *die;* (of play, speech) Aufnahme, *die;* **meet with a cool ~:** kühl aufgenommen werden; **give sb. a warm ~:** jmdn. herzlich empfangen; **give a favourable ~ to** positiv aufnehmen ‹*Theaterstück, Rede*› **2** (formal party, welcome) Empfang, *der;* **hold** *or* **give a ~:** einen Empfang geben **3** *no art.* (Brit.: foyer) die Rezeption **4** *no art.* (Radio, Telev.) der Empfang; **get good ~:** guten Empfang haben

r

reception: ~ class *n.* (Brit.) Vorschul- *od.* Anfängerklasse, *die;* **~ committee** *n.* Empfangskomitee, *das*

re'ception desk *n.* Rezeption, *die*

receptionist /rɪ'sepʃənɪst/ *n.* ▸ⓘ **p. 1260** (in hotel) Empfangschef, *der*/-dame, *die;* (at doctor's, dentist's) Sprechstundenhilfe, *die;* (*at hairdresser's, solarium, etc.*) *Angestellter, der/Angestellte, die die Kunden empfängt und mit ihnen die Termine vereinbart;* (with firm) Empfangssekretärin, *die*

reception: ~ office (Amer.) ▸**reception 3**; **~ room** *n.* 1) Empfangsraum, *der;* 2) (esp. Brit.: in private house) Wohnzimmer, *das*

receptive /rɪ'septɪv/ *adj.* 1) aufgeschlossen, empfänglich (**to** für); paarungsbereit ‹*Tier*›; **have a ~ mind** aufgeschlossen sein 2) (Biol.) Rezeptor-; rezeptorisch

receptively /rɪ'septɪvlɪ/ *adv.* rezeptiv

receptor /rɪ'septə(r)/ *n.* (Biol.) Rezeptor, *der;* **~ organ** Rezeptionsorgan, *das*

recess /rɪ'ses, 'ri:ses/
A *n.* 1) (alcove) Nische, *die* 2) (Brit. Parl.; Amer.: short vacation) Ferien *Pl.;* (Amer. Sch.: between classes) Pause, *die;* **be in ~** ‹*Parlament:*› in den Ferien sein; **adjourn for summer ~** (Amer.) sich bis nach der Sommerpause vertagen 3) (lit. or fig.: remote place) Winkel, *der*
B *v.t.* 1) (set back) [in die Wand] einlassen ‹*Schrank, Fenster*› 2) (provide with ~) eine Nische aussparen in (+ *Dat.*) ‹*Wand, Mauer*› 3) (Amer.: end sitting of) unterbrechen ‹*Verhandlung, Sitzung*›
C *v.i.* (Amer.: end a sitting) sich vertagen

recession /rɪ'seʃn/ *n.* 1) (Econ.: decline) Rezession, *die* (fachspr.); Konjunkturrückgang, *der;* **period of ~:** Rezession[sphase], *die* 2) (receding) Zurückgehen, *das*

recessional /rɪ'seʃənl/ (Eccl.)
A *adj.* Schluss‹*hymne, -musik*›
B *n.* [*während des Auszugs der Geistlichen und des Chors gesungene*] Schlusshymne, *die*

recessive /rɪ'sesɪv/ *adj.* (Genetics, Phonet.) rezessiv

recharge
A /ri:'tʃɑ:dʒ/ *v.t.* aufladen ‹*Batterie*›; nachladen ‹*Waffe*›; **~ one's batteries** (fig.) neue Kräfte auftanken
B /'ri:tʃɑ:dʒ/ *n.* Nachfüllen, *das;* **the battery needs a ~:** die Batterie muss aufgeladen werden

rechargeable /ri:'tʃɑ:dʒəbl/ *adj.* wieder aufladbar

recherché /rə'ʃeəʃeɪ/ *adj.* ausgefallen ‹*Vorstellungen, Ansichten*›; gesucht ‹*Ausdruck, Formulierung*›

rechristen /ri:'krɪsn/ *v.t.* 1) (christen again) noch einmal taufen 2) ▸**rename**

recidivism /rɪ'sɪdɪvɪzm/ *n.* Rückfälligkeit, *die*

recidivist /rɪ'sɪdɪvɪst/
A *n.* Rückfällige, *der/die;* (habitual criminal) Rückfalltäter, *der*/-täterin, *die*
B *adj.* rückfällig

recipe /'resɪpɪ/ *n.* (lit. or fig.) Rezept, *das;* **~ for success** Erfolgsrezept, *das;* **it's a ~ for disaster** damit ist die Katastrophe vorprogrammiert

recipient /rɪ'sɪpɪənt/ *n.* Empfänger, *der*/Empfängerin, *die;* **she was the unwilling ~ of his attention** sie war das unfreiwillige Opfer seiner Aufmerksamkeit

reciprocal /rɪ'sɪprəkl/
A *adj.* 1) gegenseitig ‹*Abkommen, Zuneigung, Hilfe*› 2) (Ling.) reziprok ‹*Pronomen*›
B *n.* (Math.) Kehrwert, *der*

reciprocally /rɪ'sɪprəkəlɪ/ *adv.* gegenseitig

reciprocate /rɪ'sɪprəkeɪt/
A *v.t.* 1) austauschen ‹*Versprechen*›; erwidern ‹*Gruß, Lächeln, Abneigung, Annäherungsversuch*›; sich revanchieren für ‹*Hilfe*› 2) (Mech. Engin.) hin- und herbewegen
B *v.i.* 1) (respond) sich revanchieren 2) (Mech. Engin.) sich hin- und herbewegen; **reciprocating engine/saw** Kolbenmaschine, *die*/Gattersäge, *die;* **reciprocating motion** Hin- und Herbewegung, *die*

reciprocity /resɪ'prɒsɪtɪ/ *n.* 1) (mutual action) **there is deep ~ of feeling** es besteht eine innige wechselseitige Gefühlsbindung; **~ of influence** gegen- *od.* wechselseitige Beeinflussung 2) (interchange of privileges) Wechselseitigkeit, *die;* Reziprozität, *die* (fachspr.); **~ in trade** Handelsreziprozität, *die*

recital /rɪ'saɪtl/ *n.* 1) (performance) [Solisten]konzert, *das;* (of literature also) Rezitation, *die;* **piano/poetry ~:** Klavierkonzert, *das*/Gedichtrezitation, *die;* **give one's first solo ~:** seinen ersten Soloauftritt haben 2) (detailed account) Schilderung, *die;* **give a ~ of sth.** etw. eingehend schildern

recitation /resɪ'teɪʃn/ *n.* Rezitation, *die;* **give ~s from Shakespeare** Shakespeare rezitieren; **a ~ of her grievances/my faults** eine detaillierte Aufzählung ihrer Probleme/meiner Fehler

recitative /resɪtə'ti:v/ *n.* (Mus.) Rezitativ, *das*

recite /rɪ'saɪt/
A *v.t.* 1) (speak from memory) rezitieren ‹*Passage, Gedicht*› 2) (give list of) aufzählen
B *v.i.* rezitieren

reckless /'reklɪs/ *adj.* unbesonnen; rücksichtslos ‹*Fahrweise*›; tollkühn ‹*Fluchtversuch*›; **~ of the dangers/consequences** ungeachtet der Gefahren/Folgen

recklessly /'reklɪslɪ/ *adv.* unbesonnen; (without concern for others) rücksichtslos

recklessness /'reklɪsnɪs/ *n., no pl.* ▸**reckless**: Unbesonnenheit, *die;* Rücksichtslosigkeit, *die;* Tollkühnheit, *die*

reckon /'rekn/
A *v.t.* 1) (work out) ausrechnen ‹*Kosten, Lohn, Ausgaben*›; bestimmen ‹*Position*› 2) (conclude) schätzen; **what do you ~ are his chances?** wie beurteilst du seine Chancen?; **I ~ you're lucky to be alive** ich glaube, du kannst von Glück sagen, dass du noch lebst!; **I ~ to arrive** *or* **I shall arrive there by 8.30** ich nehme an, dass ich [spätestens] halb neun dort bin; **I usually ~ to arrive there by 8.30** in der Regel bin ich [spätestens] halb neun dort 3) (consider) halten (**as** für); **be ~ed as** *or* **to be sth.** als etw. gelten; **~ sb./sth. [to be] among the best** jmdn./etw. zu den Besten zählen *od.* rechnen; **be ~ed among sth.** zu etw. zählen 4) (arrive at as total) kommen auf (+ *Akk.*); **I ~ 53 of them** ich komme auf 53
B *v.i.* rechnen; **~ from 1 April** vom 1. April an rechnen

Phrasal verbs

- **~ 'in** *v.t.* [mit] einrechnen
- **~ on** ▸**~ upon**
- **~ 'up**
A *v.t.* zusammenzählen; **~ up the bill** die Rechnungsposten zusammenzählen
B *v.i.* **~ up with sb.** mit jmdm. abrechnen
- **~ upon** *v.t.* 1) (rely on) zählen auf (+ *Akk.*); **I was ~ing upon doing that this morning** ich hatte gedacht, ich könnte das heute früh tun 2) (expect) rechnen mit
- **~ with** *v.i.* 1) (take into account) rechnen mit ‹*Hindernis, Möglichkeit*›; **he is a man to be ~ed with** er ist ein Mann, den man nicht unterschätzen sollte 2) (deal with) abrechnen mit; **you'll have me/the police to ~ with** du bekommst es mit mir/der Polizei zu tun
- **~ without** *v.i.* nicht rechnen mit; **we had ~ed without the weather** das Wetter hat uns einen Strich durch die Rechnung gemacht

reckoner /'rekənə(r)/ ▸**ready reckoner**

reckoning /'reknɪŋ/ *n.* 1) (calculation) Berechnung, *die;* **by my ~:** nach meiner Rechnung; **day of ~** (fig.) Tag der Abrechnung; (moment of truth) Stunde der Wahrheit; **be [wildly] out in one's ~:** sich [gehörig] verrechnet haben 2) (bill) Rechnung, *die. See also* **dead**

reclaim /rɪ'kleɪm/
A *v.t.* 1) urbar machen ‹*Land, Wüste*›; **~ land from the sea** dem Meer Land abgewinnen 2) (recover possession of) zurückbekommen ‹*Steuern*›; zurückerlangen ‹*Recht*› 3) (for reuse) zur Wiederverwertung sammeln; wieder verwenden ‹*Rohstoff*›; regenerieren (Technik)
B *n.* **be past** *or* **beyond ~:** unwiederbringlich verloren sein; *see also* **baggage reclaim**

reclamation /reklə'meɪʃn/ *n.* Urbarmachung, *die;* **land ~:** Landgewinnung, *die*

recline /rɪ'klaɪn/
A *v.i.* 1) (lean back) sich zurücklehnen; **the chair ~s** die Rückenlehne des Sessels lässt sich [nach hinten] verstellen; **reclining seat** (in car) Liegesitz, *der* 2) (be lying down) liegen
B *v.t.* [nach hinten] lehnen; **~ the seat** die Rückenlehne des Sitzes nach hinten verstellen

recliner /rɪ'klaɪnə(r)/ *n.* Lehnsessel, *der;* **~ seat** Liegesitz, *der*

recluse /rɪ'klu:s/ *n.* Einsiedler, *der*/Einsiedlerin, *die*

reclusive /rɪ'klu:sɪv/ *adj.* einsiedlerisch

recognisability, recognisable, recognisably, recognisance, recognise ▸**recogniz-**

recognition /rekəg'nɪʃn/ *n.* 1) *no pl., no art.* Wiedererkennen, *das;* **he's changed beyond all ~:** er ist nicht mehr wieder zu erkennen; **escape ~:** unerkannt bleiben 2) (acceptance, acknowledgement) Anerkennung, *die;* **achieve/receive ~:** Anerkennung finden; **in ~ of** als Anerkennung für

recognizability /rekəgnaɪzə'bɪlɪtɪ/ *n., no pl.* Erkennbarkeit, *die*

recognizable /'rekəgnaɪzəbl/ *adj.* erkennbar; deutlich ‹*Unterschied*›; **be ~:** wieder zu erkennen sein

recognizably /'rekəgnaɪzəblɪ/ *adv.* erkennbar; **be not ~ different from sth.** sich kaum von etw. unterscheiden

recognizance /rɪ'kɒgnɪzəns/ *n.* 1) (bond) Verpflichtung, *die;* **enter into ~s to do sth.** (Law) sich vor Gericht dazu verpflichten, etw. zu tun 2) (sum) Kaution, *die*

recognize /'rekəgnaɪz/ *v.t.* 1) (know again) wieder erkennen (**by** an + *Dat.*, **from** durch) 2) (acknowledge) erkennen; anerkennen ‹*Gültigkeit, Land, Methode, Leistung, Bedeutung, Dienst*›; **be ~d as** angesehen werden *od.* gelten als 3) (admit) zugeben; **~ sth. as valid** etw. als gültig anerkennen; **~ sb. as heir** jmdn. als Erben anerkennen; **~ sb. to be cleverer** *or* **that sb. is cleverer** zugeben, dass jmd. klüger ist 4) (identify nature of) erkennen; **~ sb. to be a fraud** erkennen, dass jmd. ein Betrüger ist 5) (allow to speak) das Wort erteilen (+ *Dat.*)

recoil
A /rɪ'kɔɪl/ *v.i.* 1) (shrink back) zurückfahren; **he ~ed visibly** er zuckte sichtbar zurück; **~ from an idea** vor einem Gedanken zurückschrecken 2) ‹*Waffe:*› einen Rückstoß haben
B /'ri:kɔɪl, rɪ'kɔɪl/ *n.* (of gun) Rückstoß, *der* (**from** *Gen.*)

Phrasal verb

- **~ [up]on** *v.i.* zurückfallen auf (+ *Akk.*); **~ upon sb.'s [own] head** *or* **upon sb.** auf jmdn. [selbst] zurückfallen

recollect /rekə'lekt/
A *v.t.* 1) sich erinnern an (+ *Akk.*); **~ meeting sb.** sich daran erinnern, jmdn. getroffen zu haben 2) **~ oneself** wieder zu sich selbst finden
B *v.i.* sich erinnern

recollection /rekə'lekʃn/ *n.* Erinnerung, *die;* **to the best of my ~ ...:** soweit ich mich erinnern kann, ...; **have a/no ~ of sth.** sich an etw. (*Akk.*) erinnern/nicht erinnern können

recombinant /ri:'kɒmbɪnənt/ *adj.* (Genetics) rekombinant

recombination /ri:kɒmbɪ'neɪʃn/ *n.* (Phys., Genetics) Rekombination, *die*

recombine /ri:kəm'baɪn/
A *v.t.* neu kombinieren
B *v.i.* sich neu kombinieren

recommence /ri:kə'mens/
A *v.i.* wieder beginnen
B *v.t.* wieder beginnen mit

recommencement /ri:kə'mensmənt/ *n.* Wiederbeginn, *der*

recommend /rekə'mend/ *v.t.* 1) empfehlen; **~ sb. to do sth.** jmdm. empfehlen, etw. zu tun 2) (make acceptable) sprechen für; **the plan has little/nothing to ~ it** es spricht wenig/nichts für den Plan

recommendable /rekəˈmendəbl/ *adj.* empfehlenswert; **it is [not] ~ to do sth.** es empfiehlt sich [nicht], etw. zu tun

recommendation /rekəmenˈdeɪʃn/ *n.* (also EU) Empfehlung, *die;* **speak in ~ of sth./sb.** etw./jmdn. empfehlen; **on sb.'s ~:** auf jmds. Empfehlung (*Akk.*); **letter of ~:** Empfehlungsschreiben, *das;* **make ~s to sb.** jmdn. beraten; **be a ~ for sth.** für etw. sprechen

recompense /ˈrekəmpens/ (formal)
A *v.t.* **1** (reward) belohnen **2** (make amends to) entschädigen
B *n., no art., no pl.* **1** (reward) Lohn, *der;* Anerkennung, *die;* **in ~ for** als Dank für; **work without ~:** unentgeltlich arbeiten **2** (compensation) Entschädigung, *die*

reconcilable /ˈrekənsaɪləbl/ *adj.* versöhnbar ‹*Personen*›; überbrückbar ‹*Differenzen*›; miteinander vereinbar ‹*Unterschiede, Standpunkte*›

reconcile /ˈrekənsaɪl/ *v.t.* **1** (restore to friendship) versöhnen; **become ~d** sich versöhnen **2** (resign oneself) **~ oneself** *or* **become/be ~d to sth.** sich mit etw. versöhnen **3** (make compatible) in Einklang bringen ‹*Vorstellungen, Überzeugungen*›; (show to be compatible) miteinander vereinen; **one cannot ~ dictatorship and freedom of speech** Diktatur und Redefreiheit sind miteinander unvereinbar **4** (settle) beilegen ‹*Meinungsverschiedenheit*›

reconciliation /rekənsɪlɪˈeɪʃn/ *n.* **1** (restoring to friendship) Versöhnung, *die;* **bring about a ~ between persons** Personen miteinander versöhnen; **try for a ~:** einen Versöhnungsversuch unternehmen **2** (making compatible) Harmonisierung, *die*

recondite /ˈrekəndaɪt, rɪˈkɒndaɪt/ *adj.* (formal) abstrus

recondition /riːkənˈdɪʃn/ *v.t.* [general]überholen; **~ed engine** Austauschmotor, *der*

reconnaissance /rɪˈkɒnɪsəns/ *n., no pl., no def. art.* (Mil.) Aufklärung, *die;* (of area) Erkundung, *die;* **after ~:** nach Erkundung der Lage; **the plane was on ~:** das Flugzeug war auf einem Aufklärungsflug; **make a ~ [of the area]** (lit. or fig.) das Terrain sondieren; *attrib.* **~ aircraft** Aufklärungsflugzeug, *das;* **~ party** Spähtrupp, *der*

reconnoitre (*Brit.; Amer.:* **reconnoiter**) /rekəˈnɔɪtə(r)/
A *v.t.* (esp. Mil.) auskundschaften; erkunden ‹*Gelände*›; (fig.) erkunden; in Augenschein nehmen ‹*Hotel, Restaurant*›
B *v.i.* (esp. Mil.) auf Erkundung [aus]gehen; (fig.) sich umsehen

reconquer /riːˈkɒŋkə(r)/ *v.t.* zurückerobern

reconsider /riːkənˈsɪdə(r)/ *v.t.* [noch einmal] überdenken; **~ a case** einen Fall von neuem aufrollen; *abs.* **there is still time to ~:** du kannst es dir/wir können es uns *usw.* immer noch überlegen

reconsideration /riːkənsɪdəˈreɪʃn/ *n.* Überdenken, *das;* **put a case before the court for ~:** einen Fall zur neuerlichen Beratung vor ein Gericht bringen

reconstitute /riːˈkɒnstɪtjuːt/ *v.t.* **1** (build up again) wieder aufbauen; rekonstruieren **2** (restore to natural state) **~ [with water]** [mit Wasser] anrühren; [in Wasser] einweichen ‹*Trockenobst*› **3** (piece together) rekonstruieren ‹*Ereignisse*› **4** (reorganize) umbauen ‹*Anlage*›; umbilden ‹*Komitee, Kabinett*› **5** (bring back into existence) wieder einrichten

reconstitution /riːkɒnstɪˈtjuːʃn/ *n.* **1** (building up again) Rekonstruktion, *die* **2** (restoration to natural state) Anrühren, *das;* (of dried fruit) Einweichen, *das* **3** (reorganization) Umbildung, *die* **4** (bringing back into existence) Wiedereinrichtung, *die*

reconstruct /riːkənˈstrʌkt/ *v.t.* **1** (build again) wieder aufbauen ‹*Stadt, Gebäude*›; neu errichten ‹*Gerüst*›; rekonstruieren ‹*Anlage*›; (fig.) rekonstruieren **2** (reorganize) umstrukturieren

reconstruction /riːkənˈstrʌkʃn/ *n.* **1** (process) Wiederaufbau, *der;* (reorganization) Umstrukturierung, *die* **2** (thing reconstructed) Rekonstruktion, *die*

reconvene /riːkənˈviːn/
A *v.t.* wieder einberufen ‹*Gremium*›
B *v.i.* ‹*Personen:*› wieder zusammenkommen; ‹*Gremium, Parlament:*› wieder zusammentreten

record
A /rɪˈkɔːd/ *v.t.* **1** aufzeichnen; **~ a new CD** eine neue CD aufnehmen; **~ sth. in a book/painting** etw. in einem Buch/auf einem Gemälde festhalten; **be ~ed for ever in sb.'s memory** auf ewig in jmds. Gedächtnis eingegraben sein; **history ~s that ...:** es ist geschichtlich belegt, dass ... **2** (register officially) dokumentieren; protokollieren ‹*Verhandlung*›; **~ one's vote** seine Stimme abgeben; **count and ~ the votes** die Stimmen auszählen [und das Ergebnis schriftlich festhalten]
B *v.i.* aufzeichnen; (on tape) Tonbandaufnahmen/eine Tonbandaufnahme machen; **the tape recorder isn't ~ing properly** das Tonbandgerät nimmt nicht richtig auf
C /ˈrekɔːd/ *n.* **1** **be on ~** ‹*Prozess, Verhandlung, Besprechung:*› protokolliert sein; **there is no such case on ~:** ein solcher Fall ist nicht dokumentiert; **it is on ~ that ...:** es ist dokumentiert, dass ...; **have sth. on ~:** etw. dokumentiert haben; **there is nothing on ~ to prove that ...:** es gibt keine Aufzeichnungen, die beweisen, dass ...; **put sth. on ~:** etw. schriftlich festhalten; **I am quite happy to go on ~ as having said that** man kann ruhig festhalten, dass ich das gesagt habe; **it is a matter of ~ that ...:** es ist eine verbürgte Tatsache, dass ... **2** (report) Protokoll, *das;* (Law: official report) [Gerichts]akte, *die* **3** (document) Dokument, *das;* (piece of evidence) Zeugnis, *das;* Beleg, *der;* **medical ~s** medizinische Unterlagen; **criminal ~s** Strafregister, *das;* **~ of attendance** Anwesenheitsliste, *die;* **keep a ~ of sth.** über etw. (*Akk.*) Buch führen; (listing persons) eine Liste von etw. führen; **for the ~:** für das Protokoll; **just for the ~:** der Vollständigkeit halber; (iron.) nur der Ordnung halber; **[strictly] off the ~:** [ganz] inoffiziell; **I would like to put** *or* **set the ~ straight** ich möchte das richtig stellen **4** (disc for ~ player) [Schall]platte, *die;* **make a ~:** eine Platte machen (ugs.) **5** (facts of sb.'s/sth.'s past) Ruf, *der;* **have a good ~ [of achievements]** gute Leistungen vorweisen können; **the aircraft has an excellent ~ for reliability/a good safety ~:** das Flugzeug hat sich als höchst zuverlässig/sehr sicher erwiesen; **have a [criminal/police] ~:** vorbestraft sein; **keep a clean ~:** sich (*Dat.*) nichts zuschulden kommen lassen **6** (best performance) Rekord, *der;* **set a ~:** einen Rekord aufstellen; **break** *or* **beat the ~:** den Rekord brechen
D *attrib. adj.* Rekord-

record /ˈrekɔːd/: **~ album** *n.* [Schall]plattenalbum, *das;* **~-breaking** *adj.* Rekord-; **~ deck** *n.* Plattenspieler, *der*

recorded /rɪˈkɔːdɪd/ *adj.* aufgezeichnet ‹*Film, Konzert, Rede*›; überliefert ‹*Ereignis, Geschichte*›; bespielt ‹*Band*›; **~ music** Musikaufnahmen

recorded deˈlivery *n.* (Brit. Post) eingeschriebene Sendung (*ohne Versicherung*); **send sth. by ~:** etw. per Einschreiben schicken

recorder /rɪˈkɔːdə(r)/ *n.* **1** (instrument/apparatus) Aufzeichnungsgerät, *das;* **earthquake ~:** Seismograph, *der* **2** ▸**tape recorder** **3** (Mus.) Blockflöte, *die* **4** (Brit. Law) nebenamtlicher Richter (*beim Crown Court usw.*)

ˈrecord holder *n.* (Sport) Rekordhalter, *der*/-halterin, *die*

recording /rɪˈkɔːdɪŋ/ *n.* **1** (process) Aufzeichnung, *die* **2** (what is recorded) Aufnahme, *die;* (to be heard or seen later) Aufzeichnung, *die*

recording: ~ ˈangel *n.* (Theol.) Engel der Gerechtigkeit; **~ head** *n.* Aufnahmekopf, *der;* **~ session** *n.* Aufnahme, *die;* **~ studio** *n.* Tonstudio, *das;* **~ van** *n.* Aufnahmewagen, *der*

recordist /rɪˈkɔːdɪst/ *n.* **[sound] ~:** Tonmeister, *der*/-meisterin, *die*

record /ˈrekɔːd/: **~ label** *n.* Plattenlabel, *das;* **~ library** *n.* Phonothek, *die;* **R~ Office** ▸**Public R~ Office**; **~ player** *n.* Plattenspieler, *der;* **~ shop** *n.* [Schall]plattengeschäft, *das;* **~ sleeve** *n.* Plattenhülle, *die;* Plattencover, *das;* **~ token** *n.* [Schall]plattengutschein, *der*

recount /rɪˈkaʊnt/ *v.t.* (tell) erzählen

re-count
A /riːˈkaʊnt/ *v.t.* (count again) [noch einmal] nachzählen
B /ˈriːkaʊnt/ *n.* Nachzählung, *die;* **have a ~:** nachzählen

recoup /rɪˈkuːp/ *v.t.* **1** (regain) ausgleichen ‹*Verlust*›; [wieder] hereinbekommen ‹[*Geld*]*einsatz*›; wiedergewinnen ‹*Stärke, Gesundheit*› **2** (reimburse) wieder einbringen ‹*Auslagen*›; **~ oneself** seine Ausgaben ausgleichen

recourse /rɪˈkɔːs/ *n.* **1** (resort) Zufluchtnahme, *die;* **have ~ to sb./sth.** bei jmdm./zu etw. Zuflucht nehmen **2** (person or thing resorted to) Zuflucht, *die;* **your only ~ is legal action** das Einzige, was dir bleibt, ist vor Gericht zu gehen **3** (Finance) Regress, *der;* Rückgriff, *der*

recover /rɪˈkʌvə(r)/
A *v.t.* **1** (regain) zurückerobern **2** (find again) wieder finden ‹*Verlorenes, Fährte, Spur*› **3** (retrieve) zurückbekommen; bergen ‹*Wrack*› **4** (make up for) aufholen ‹*verlorene Zeit*› **5** (acquire again) wiedergewinnen ‹*Vertrauen*›; wieder finden ‹*Gleichgewicht, innere Ruhe usw.*›; **have ~ed one's lost appetite/normal colour** wieder Appetit/Farbe haben; **~ consciousness** das Bewusstsein wiedererlangen; **~ one's senses** (lit. or fig.) wieder zur Besinnung kommen; **~ the use of one's hands/feet** seine Hände/Füße wieder gebrauchen können; **~ one's sight** sein Sehvermögen wiedergewinnen; **~ one's voice** seine Stimme wieder finden; **~ one's breath** wieder zu Atem kommen; **~ oneself** sich fangen **6** (reclaim) **~ land from the sea** dem Meer Land abgewinnen; **~ metal from scrap** Metall aus Schrott gewinnen **7** (Law) erheben ‹*Steuer, Abgabe*›; erhalten ‹*Schadenersatz, Schmerzensgeld*›; *abs.* Schadenersatz erhalten
B *v.i.* ▸❶ **p. 1231** **~ from sth.** sich von etw. [wieder] erholen; **how long will it take him to ~?** wann wird er wieder gesund sein?; **be [completely** *or* **totally** *or* **fully** *or* **quite] ~ed** [völlig] wiederhergestellt sein

re-cover /riːˈkʌvə(r)/ *v.t.* neu beziehen ‹*Sessel, Schirm usw.*›

recoverable /rɪˈkʌvərəbl/ *adj.* **1** (capable of being regained) erstattungsfähig ‹*Unkosten*›; ersetzbar ‹*Schaden, Verlust*›; rückzahlbar ‹*Kaution, Geldeinlage*›; **the cost was ~ through his insurance policy** die Kosten konnten durch seine Versicherung ersetzt werden **2** (capable of being restored) wieder herstellbar; wieder gewinnbar ‹*Brauchwasser*› **3** (Law) eintreibbar ‹*Geldstrafe, Schulden usw.*› **4** (extractable) abbaufähig; abbaubar; förderbar ‹*Öl-, Gasreserven*›

recovery /rɪˈkʌvərɪ/ *n.* **1** ▸❶ **p. 1231** (restoration) Erholung, *die;* **be on the road to ~:** auf dem Wege der Besserung sein; **make a quick/good ~:** sich schnell/gut erholen; **he is past ~:** für ihn gibt es keine Hoffnung mehr **2** (regaining of sth. lost) Wiederfinden, *das;* Fund, *der* **3** (Law) (of debts) Eintreibung, *die;* **~ of damages** Erfüllung des Anspruchs auf Schadenersatz **4** (Swimming, Rowing) Rückkehr in die Grundstellung **5** (extraction, reclamation) Rückgewinnung, *die*

recovery: ~ position *n.* (Med.) stabile Seitenlage; **~ room** *n.* (Med.) Aufwachraum, *der;* **~ vehicle** *n.* Bergungsfahrzeug, *das*

recreant /ˈrekrɪənt/ (literary)
A *adj.* **1** (cowardly) kleinmütig (geh.); verzagt (geh.) **2** (treacherous) verräterisch; (apostate) abtrünnig
B *n.* **1** (coward) Feigling, *der* **2** (betrayer) Verräter, *der*/Verräterin, *die;* (apostate) Abtrünnige, *der/die*

recreate /riːkrɪˈeɪt/ *v.t.* **1** (create over again) [wieder] neu [er]schaffen; wieder aufleben lassen ‹*Industrie*› **2** (simulate, re-enact) nachempfinden, nachbilden ‹*Kunstwerk, Gegenstand*›; reproduzieren (geh.) ‹*Atmosphäre, Klänge*›; nachstellen ‹*Szene*›

recreation /rekrɪˈeɪʃn/ *n.* **1** (act of relaxing) Ausruhen, *das* **2** (means of entertainment) Freizeitbeschäftigung, *die;* Hobby, *das;* **for** *or* **as a ~:** zur Freizeitbeschäftigung *od.* Entspannung;

r

he enjoys driving as a ~: Fahren bedeutet für ihn Entspannung

recreational /rekrɪ'eɪʃənl/ *adj.* Freizeit⟨*wert, -möglichkeiten, -gelände*⟩; Erholungs⟨*gebiet*⟩; **~ drug** Freizeitdroge, *die;* Droge zum Entspannen; **~ vehicle** (Amer.) Wohnmobil, *das*

recreation: ~ centre *n.* Freizeitzentrum, *das;* **~ ground** *n.* Freizeitgelände, *das;* (for children) Spielplatz, *der;* **~ period** *n.* Pause, *die;* **~ room** *n.* **1** (playroom) Spielzimmer, *das;* (hobbyroom) Hobbyraum, *der;* **2** (public room) Aufenthaltsraum, *der;* **~ time** *n.* Freizeit, *die;* (in school) Pause, *die*

recriminate /rɪ'krɪmɪneɪt/ *v.i.* Gegenbeschuldigungen erheben

recrimination /rɪkrɪmɪ'neɪʃn/ *n.* Gegenbeschuldigung, *die;* (counter-accusation) **[mutual] ~s** [gegenseitige] Beschuldigungen

recrudescence /ri:kru:'desəns/ *n.* (of symptoms, disease) erneutes Auftreten; (of epidemic, aggression, violence) Wiederaufflackern, *das*

recruit /rɪ'kru:t/

A *n.* **1** (Mil.) Rekrut, *der;* **a raw ~:** ein frisch Eingezogener **2** (Amer.) (soldier of lowest rank) einfacher Soldat; (sailor of lowest rank) Matrose, *der* **3** (new member) neues Mitglied **4** **[raw] ~** (fig.: novice) blutiger Anfänger

B *v.t.* **1** (Mil.: enlist) anwerben; (into society, party, etc.) werben ⟨*Mitglied*⟩ **2** (select for appointment) einstellen; **staff were ~ed once a year** einmal im Jahr wurden neue Mitarbeiter eingestellt

C *v.i.* **1** (Mil.: enlist) Rekruten anwerben; ⟨*Partei, Klub:*⟩ neue Mitglieder finden **2** (select for appointment) Neueinstellungen vornehmen; **~ for staff** neue Mitarbeiter einstellen; **~ from one's own staff** freie Stellen aus den eigenen Reihen besetzen

recruitment /ri'kru:tmənt/ *n.* **1** (Mil.) Anwerbung, *die;* (for membership) **~ of members** Mitgliederwerbung, *die;* **~ has been good this year** die Mitgliederwerbung war dieses Jahr sehr erfolgreich; **~ for evening classes** Werbung für Abendkurse **2** (process of selecting for appointment) Neueinstellung, *die*

recta *pl. of* **rectum**

rectal /'rektl/ *adj.* (Anat.) rektal

rectangle /'rektæŋgl/ *n.* Rechteck, *das*

rectangular /rek'tæŋgjʊlə(r)/ *adj.* **1** **~[-shaped]** rechteckig **2** (placed at right angles) rechtwinklig

rectifiable /'rektɪfaɪəbl/ *adj.* korrigierbar ⟨*Fehler*⟩; **do you think the situation is ~?** glauben Sie, dass noch etwas zu machen ist?

rectification /rektɪfɪ'keɪʃn/ *n.* **1** (correction of error) Berichtigung, *die;* Korrektur, *die* **2** (Electr.) Gleichrichtung, *die*

rectifier /'rektɪfaɪə(r)/ *n.* (Electr.) Gleichrichter, *der*

rectify /'rektɪfaɪ/ *v.t.* **1** korrigieren ⟨*Fehler, Berechnung, Kurs*⟩; richtig stellen ⟨*Bemerkung, Sachverhalt*⟩; Abhilfe schaffen (+ *Dat.*) ⟨*Mangel, Missstand*⟩; **~ the situation** die Sache wieder ins Lot bringen **2** (Electr.) gleichrichten

rectilineal /rektɪ'lɪnɪəl/, **rectilinear** /rektɪ'lɪnɪə(r)/ *adj.* geradlinig ⟨*Bewegung, Strecke, Anordnung*⟩; aus Geraden gebildet ⟨*Winkel*⟩; geradlinig begrenzt ⟨*Figur, Garten*⟩

rectitude /'rektɪtju:d/ *n.* **1** (with regard to morality) Rechtschaffenheit, *die;* **a life of ~:** ein rechtschaffenes Leben **2** (with regard to correctness) Richtigkeit, *die*

recto /'rektəʊ/ *n., pl.* **~s** (Printing, Bibliog.) **1** (right-hand page) rechte Seite **2** (front of leaf) Rekto, *das* (fachspr.); Vorderseite, *die*

rector /'rektə(r)/ *n.* **1** Pfarrer, *der* **2** (Univ.) Rektor, *der*/Rektorin, *die*

rectory /'rektərɪ/ *n.* Pfarrhaus, *das*

rectum /'rektəm/ *n., pl.* **~s** *or* **recta** /'rektə/ (Anat.) Mastdarm, *der;* Rektum, *das* (fachspr.)

recumbent /rɪ'kʌmbənt/ *adj.* ruhend; liegend ⟨*Skulptur*⟩; **be [lying] ~:** ruhen

recuperate /rɪ'kju:pəreɪt/

A *v.i.* sich erholen

B *v.t.* wieder herstellen ⟨*Gesundheit*⟩; **~ one's strength/health** wieder zu Kräften kommen/gesund werden

recuperation /rɪkju:pə'reɪʃn/ *n.* Erholung, *die;* **in rest and ~:** in Ruhe und Entspannung

recuperative /rɪ'kju:pərətɪv/ *adj.* stärkend; **~ remedies/powers** Heilmittel/-kräfte

recur /rɪ'kɜ:(r)/ *v.i.,* **-rr-** **1** sich wiederholen; ⟨*Beschwerden, Krankheit usw.:*⟩ wiederkehren; ⟨*Problem, Symptom:*⟩ wieder auftreten **2** (return to one's mind) ⟨*Gedanke, Furcht, Gefühl:*⟩ wiederkehren **3** (Math.) **~ring decimal** periodischer Dezimalbruch; **2.3 ~ring** 2 Komma 3 Periode

recurrence /rɪ'kʌrəns/ *n.* **1** Wiederholung, *die;* (of illness, complaint) Wiederkehr, *die;* (of problem, symptom) Wiederauftreten, *das;* **there's to be no ~ of this type of behaviour** dieses Verhalten darf sich nicht wiederholen **2** (to mind) Wiederkehr, *die*

recurrent /rɪ'kʌrənt/ *adj.* immer wiederkehrend; wiederholt ⟨*Hinweis, Bezugnahme*⟩; **have ~ problems with sth.** häufig Probleme mit etw. haben

recyclable /ri:'saɪkləbl/ *adj.* recycelbar

recycle /ri:'saɪkl/ *v.t.* (reuse) wieder verwerten ⟨*Papier, Glas, Abfall*⟩; (convert) wieder aufbereiten ⟨*Metall, Brauchwasser, Abfall*⟩; **~d paper** Recyclingpapier, *das*

recycling /ri:'saɪklɪŋ/ *n.* Recycling, *das;* Wiederaufbereitung, *die; attrib.* **~ plant** Recyclingwerk, *das*

red /red/

A *adj.* **1** rot; Rot⟨*wild, -buche*⟩; rot glühend ⟨*Feuer, Lava usw.*⟩; **the ~ colour of the setting sun** das Rot der untergehenden Sonne; **go ~ with shame** rot vor Scham werden; **go ~ in the face** rot werden; **as ~ as a beetroot** puterrot; rot wie eine Tomate (ugs. scherzh.); **her eyes were ~ with crying** sie hatte rot geweinte Augen; *see also* **paint B 1**; **see¹ B 1** **2** (anarchistic) rot **3** **R~** (Hist.: Soviet Russian) rot, kommunistisch ⟨*Soldat, Propaganda*⟩; **the R~ Army** die Rote Armee; **better R~ than dead** lieber rot als tot

B *n.* **1** (colour) Rot, *das;* (in roulette) Rouge, *das;* (redness) Röte, *die;* **the ~s** die Rottöne; **underline sth. in ~:** etw. rot unterstreichen **2** (debt) **get out of the ~:** aus den roten Zahlen kommen; **[be] in the ~:** in den roten Zahlen [sein] **3** **R~** (communist) Rote, *der/die;* **Reds under the bed scare** Angst vor kommunistischer Unterwanderung **4** (ball) rote Kugel **5** (red clothes) **dressed in ~:** rot gekleidet **6** (traffic light) Rot, *das;* **the traffic light is at ~:** die Ampel steht auf Rot; **we drove straight through on ~:** wir fuhren bei Rot durch (ugs.)

red: ~ admiral ▸**admiral 2**; **~ alert** *n.* [höchste] Alarmbereitschaft; **be on ~ alert** sich in Alarmzustand befinden; **~-blooded** /'redblʌdɪd/ *adj.* heißblütig; **~breast** *n.* (Ornith.) Rotkehlchen, *das;* **~brick** *adj.* (Brit.) weniger traditionsreich ⟨*Universität*⟩; **~cap** *n.* **1** (Brit.: military policeman) Militärpolizist, *der;* **2** (Amer.: railway porter) Gepäckträger, *der;* **~ 'card** *n.* (Footb.) rote Karte; **he was shown the ~ card** er bekam die rote Karte; **~ 'carpet** *n.* (lit. or fig.) roter Teppich; **~-carpet** *adj.* **give sb. the ~-carpet treatment** *or* **a ~-carpet reception** jmdn. mit großem Bahnhof (ugs.) *od.* mit allen Ehren empfangen; **~ cell** *n.* (Anat., Zool.) rotes Blutkörperchen; **~ 'cent** *n.* (Amer.) roter Heller; **~-cheeked** *adj.* rotwangig (geh.); **Red 'China** *n.* Rotchina, *das;* **~coat** *n.* (Brit. Hist.) Rotrock, *der;* *britischer Soldat;* **~ corpuscle** ▸**red cell**; **Red 'Crescent** *n.* Roter Halbmond; **Red 'Cross** *n.* Rotes Kreuz; **~'currant** *n.* [rote] Johannisbeere

redden /'redn/

A *v.i.* ⟨*Gesicht, Himmel:*⟩ sich röten; ⟨*Person:*⟩ rot werden, erröten; ⟨*Blätter, Wasser:*⟩ sich rot färben; **his face ~ed [with shame** *etc.*] er lief rot an *od.* bekam einen roten Kopf [vor Scham *usw.*]

B *v.t.* rot färben; röten (geh.)

reddish /'redɪʃ/ *adj.* rötlich; **~ brown** rotbraun

redecorate /ri:'dekəreɪt/ *v.t.* renovieren; (with wallpaper) neu tapezieren; (with paint) neu streichen

redecoration /ri:dekə'reɪʃn/ *n.* Renovierung, *die;* (with wallpaper) Neutapezieren, *das;* (with paint) Neuanstrich, *der*

redeem /rɪ'di:m/ *v.t.* **1** (regain) wieder herstellen ⟨*Ehre, Gesundheit*⟩; wiedergewinnen ⟨*Position*⟩ **2** (buy back) tilgen ⟨*Hypothek*⟩; [wieder] einlösen ⟨*Pfand*⟩; abzahlen ⟨*Grundstück*⟩ **3** (convert) einlösen ⟨*Gutschein, Coupon*⟩ **4** (make amends for) ausgleichen, wettmachen ⟨*Fehler, Schuld usw.*⟩; **he has one ~ing feature** man muss ihm eins zugute halten **5** (repay) abzahlen ⟨*Schuld, Kredit*⟩; **~ one's obligation to sb.** seine Schuld jmdm. gegenüber begleichen **6** (fulfil) einlösen, halten ⟨*Versprechen*⟩ **7** (save) retten; **~ sb. from his sins/from hell** jmdn. von seinen Sünden/aus der Hölle erlösen **8** (make less bad) retten ⟨*Situation, Beziehung, Party usw.*⟩; **~ oneself** sich freikaufen; **he ~ed himself in their eyes by apologizing** er fand Gnade vor ihren Augen, indem er sich entschuldigte

redeemable /rɪ'di:məbl/ *adj.* einlösbar ⟨*Gutschein, Pfand, Aktien usw.*⟩; tilgbar ⟨*Schuld*⟩; kündbar ⟨*Obligation*⟩

redeemer /rɪ'di:mə(r)/ *n.* **1** Retter, *der* **2** **R~** (Relig.) Erlöser, *der;* Heiland, *der*

redefine /ri:dɪ'faɪn/ *v.t.* neu bestimmen *od.* festlegen ⟨*Aufgaben, Bedingungen*⟩; neu formulieren ⟨*These, Vertrag[spunkte]*⟩

redemption /rɪ'dempʃn/ *n.* **1** (of pawned goods) Einlösen, *das;* Rückkauf, *der* **2** (of tokens, trading stamps, stocks, etc.) Einlösen, *das* **3** (of mortgage, debt) Tilgung, *die;* (of land) Abzahlung, *die* **4** (of promise, pledge) Erfüllung, *die* **5** (of person, country) Befreiung, *die;* **he's past** *or* **beyond ~:** für ihn gibt es keine Rettung mehr; **the situation is beyond ~:** die Lage ist hoffnungslos verfahren *od.* völlig ausweglos **6** (deliverance from sin) Erlösung, *die* **7** (thing that redeems) Rettung, *die*

redeploy /ri:dɪ'plɔɪ/ *v.t.* umstationieren ⟨*Truppen, Raketen*⟩; woanders einsetzen ⟨*Arbeitskräfte*⟩; **~ from ... to ...:** von ... nach ... verlegen

redeployment /ri:dɪ'plɔɪmənt/ *n.* (of troops, missiles) Umstationierung, *die;* (of labour force, workers, staff) Einsatz an anderer Stelle; **~ from ... to ...:** Verlegung von ... nach ...

redesign /ri:dɪ'zaɪn/ *v.t.* umgestalten ⟨*Raum, Mechanismus, Verpackung, Modell*⟩; überarbeiten ⟨*Plan, Design*⟩

redevelop /ri:dɪ'veləp/ *v.t.* **1** (redesign) umgestalten; neu entwickeln ⟨*Theorie*⟩ **2** (reconstruct) umbauen, sanieren ⟨*Gebäude*⟩; sanieren ⟨*Stadtteil*⟩; neu bebauen ⟨*Gelände*⟩

red: ~-eyed *adj.* **be ~-eyed** rote Augen haben; **~-faced** *adj.* rotgesichtig; **be ~-faced** (with rage/embarrassment) ein [hoch]rotes Gesicht haben/vor Verlegenheit rot werden; **go ~-faced with rage** vor Wut rot anlaufen; **~ 'flag** ▸**flag¹ A**; **Red 'Guard** *n.* Rote Garde; (member) Rotgardist, *der*/-gardistin, *die;* **~-haired** *adj.* rothaarig; **~-handed** /red 'hændɪd/ *adj.* **catch sb. ~-handed** jmdn. auf frischer Tat ertappen; **~head** *n.* Rotschopf, *der* (ugs.); Rothaarige, *der/die;* **~-headed** /'redhedɪd/ *adj.* rothaarig; **be ~-headed** rote Haare haben; **~ heat** *n.* Rotglut, *die;* (fig.) Glut, *die;* **bring to a ~ heat** auf Rotglut erhitzen; **~ 'herring** *n.* **1** (fish) Räucherhering, *der;* **2** (fig.) Ablenkungsmanöver, *das;* (in thriller, historical research) falsche Fährte; **~-hot** *adj.* **1** [rot] glühend; **2** (fig.) glühend ⟨*Anhänger, Gläubiger, Liebhaber, Zorn*⟩; heiß ⟨*Blondine, Thema, Musik*⟩; brandaktuell ⟨*Nachricht*⟩; **this new film is ~-hot stuff** dieser neue Film ist heiß

redial

A /ri:'daɪəl/ *v.t.* noch einmal wählen ⟨*Telefonnummer*⟩; *abs.* noch einmal wählen; **to ~, just press the button** zur Wahlwiederholung einfach diese Taste drücken

B /'ri:daɪəl/ *n.* Wahlwiederholung, *die;* **last number ~:** Wahlwiederholung, *die;* **~ button** Wahlwiederholungstaste, *die*

redid ▸**redo**

Red 'Indian (Brit. dated)

A *n.* Indianer, *der*/Indianerin, *die*

B *adj.* Indianer-

r

redirect /riːdaɪˈrekt, riːdɪˈrekt/ *v.t.* nachsenden ‹*Post, Brief usw.*›; umleiten ‹*Verkehr*›; weiterleiten (**to** an + *Akk.*) ‹*Anfrage*›; richten (**to** auf + *Akk.*) ‹*Aufmerksamkeit*›

redirection /riːdaɪˈrekʃn, riːdɪˈrekʃn/ *n.* (of mail) Nachsendung, *die;* (of traffic) Umleitung, *die;* (of question) Weiterleitung, *die* (**to** an + *Akk.*)

rediscover /riːdɪˈskʌvə(r)/ *v.t.* wieder entdecken

rediscovery /riːdɪˈskʌvərɪ/ *n.* Wiederentdeckung, *die*

redistribute /riːdɪˈstrɪbjuːt/ *v.t.* umverteilen ‹*Besitz, Einkommen*›; versetzen ‹*Arbeitskräfte*›; (reorganize) neu aufteilen

redistribution /riːdɪstrɪˈbjuːʃn/ *n.* (of land, wealth) Umverteilung, *die;* (of labour etc.) Versetzung, *die,* (reorganization) Neuaufteilung, *die*

red: ~ lead /red ˈled/ *n.* Mennige, *die;* **~-ˈletter day** *n.* **1** (memorable day) im Kalender rot anzustreichender Tag; großer Tag; **2** (Relig.) Feiertag, *der;* **~ ˈlight** *n.* **1** [rotes] Warnlicht; (of traffic lights) rote [Verkehrs]ampel; **drive straight through the ~ light** bei Rot über die Ampel fahren; **2** (fig.) Warnzeichen, *das;* **they saw the** *or* **a ~ light** bei ihnen leuchtete ein [rotes] Warnsignal auf; **~-ˈlight district** *n.* Rotlichtviertel, *das;* Rotlichtbezirk, *der;* **~ meat** *n.* dunkles Fleisch (*z. B. vom Rind*); **~neck** *n.* (Amer.) armer weißer Landbewohner aus den Südstaaten; (derog.) weißer Rassist *od.* Reaktionär

redness /ˈrednɪs/ *n., no pl.* (of face, skin, eyes, sky) Röte, *die;* (of blood, fire, rose, dress, light) rote Farbe

redo /riːˈduː/ *v.t.,* **redoes** /riːˈdʌz/, **redoing** /riːˈduːɪŋ/, **redid** /riːˈdɪd/, **redone** /riːˈdʌn/ **1** (do again) wiederholen ‹*Prüfung, Spiel, Test*›; neu frisieren ‹*Haare*›; erneuern ‹*Make-up, Lidschatten*›; noch einmal machen ‹*Bett, Hausaufgabe*›; überarbeiten ‹*Aufsatz, Übersetzung, Komposition*›; **~ one's face** sein Make-up erneuern **2** (redecorate) [gründlich] renovieren; (repaper) neu tapezieren; (repaint) neu streichen

redolent /ˈredələnt/ *adj.* **1** duftend; **~ odours** Düfte *Pl.;* **~ of** *or* **with sth.** nach etw. duftend **2** (fig.) **be ~ of sth.** stark an etw. (*Akk.*) erinnern

redone ▸ **redo**

redouble /riːˈdʌbl/
A *v.t.* **1** verdoppeln **2** (Bridge) rekontrieren
B *v.i.* sich verdoppeln
C *n.* (Bridge) Rekontra, *das*

redoubt /rɪˈdaʊt/ *n.* (Mil.) Redoute, *die*

redoubtable /rɪˈdaʊtəbl/ *adj.* Ehrfurcht gebietend ‹*Person*›; gewaltig, enorm ‹*Aufgabe, Pflicht usw.*›; gefürchtet ‹*Gegner, Krieger*›; glänzend ‹*Anwalt*›

redound /rɪˈdaʊnd/ *v.i.* **~ to sb.'s advantage/disadvantage/honour** *or* **credit/fame** jmdm. Vorteile/Nachteile/Ehre/Ruhm einbringen; **~ to sb.'s reputation/good name** zu jmds. Ruf/gutem Namen beitragen

red ˈpepper *n.* **1** ▸ **cayenne** **2** (vegetable) rote Paprika[schote]

redraft /riːˈdrɑːft/ *v.t.* neu entwerfen; neu aufsetzen ‹*Vertrag*›; neu abfassen ‹*Schriftstück*›

red ˈrag *n.* (fig.) rotes Tuch (**to** für); **be like a ~ to a bull [to sb.]** wie ein rotes Tuch [auf jmdn.] wirken

redraw /riːˈdrɔː/ *v.t., forms as* **draw** neu zeichnen

redress /rɪˈdres/
A *n.* (reparation, correction) Entschädigung, *die;* **seek ~ for sth.** eine Entschädigung für etw. verlangen; **seek [legal] ~:** auf Schadenersatz klagen; **have no ~:** keine Entschädigung erhalten; (Law) keinen Rechtsanspruch auf Entschädigung haben
B *v.t.* **1** (adjust again) ins Gleichgewicht bringen; **~ the balance** das Gleichgewicht wieder herstellen **2** (set right, rectify) wieder gutmachen ‹*Unrecht*›; ausgleichen ‹*Ungerechtigkeiten*›; beseitigen ‹*Missstand, Übel, Despotie*›; abhelfen (+ *Dat.*) ‹*Beschwerden, Missbrauch*›

Red: ~ ˈRiding Hood *pr. n.* Rotkäppchen, *das;* **~ ˈSea** *pr. n.* Rote Meer, *das*

red: ~shank *n.* (Ornith.) Rotschenkel, *der;* **~ shift** *n.* (Astron.) Rotverschiebung, *die;* **~skin** (dated/derog.) ▸ **Red Indian A**; **~ ˈsquirrel** *n.* Eichhörnchen, *das;* **Red ˈStar** *n.* Roter Stern; **~start** *n.* (Ornith.) Rotschwanz, *der;* **~ ˈtape** *n.* (fig.) [unnötige] Bürokratie; **cut through the ~ tape** die Bürokratie umgehen; **Red ˈTerror** ▸ **terror 1**

reduce /rɪˈdjuːs/
A *v.t.* **1** (diminish) senken ‹*Preis, Gebühr, Fieber, Aufwendungen, Blutdruck usw.*›; verbilligen ‹*Ware*›; reduzieren ‹*Geschwindigkeit, Gewicht, Anzahl, Menge, Preis*›; **at ~d prices** zu herabgesetzten Preisen; **~ one's weight** abnehmen; **~ waste** Müll vermeiden **2** **~ to order/despair/silence/tears/submission** auf Vordermann bringen (ugs.)/in Verzweiflung stürzen/verstummen lassen/zum Weinen bringen/ zum Aufgeben zwingen; **~ sb. to begging** jmdn. an den Bettelstab bringen; **be ~d to starvation** hungern müssen; **be ~d to borrowing money/pawning sth.** sich (*Dat.*) Geld leihen müssen/etw. versetzen müssen; **live in ~d circumstances** in verarmten Verhältnissen leben; **~ sb. to the ranks** jmdn. in den Mannschaftsstand degradieren **3** (convert to other form) **~ wood to pulp** Holz zu einem Brei verarbeiten; **~ yards to inches** Yards in Inches umwandeln **4** (Photog.) abschwächen **5** (Med.) einrenken ‹*Gliedmaße, Gelenk*›; einrichten ‹*Bruch*› **6** (Chem.) reduzieren
B *v.i.* abnehmen

reducer /rɪˈdjuːsə(r)/ *n.* **1** (Photog.) Abschwächer, *der* **2** (Chem.) Reduktionsmittel, *das*

reducible /rɪˈdjuːsɪbl/ *adj.* **1** reduzierbar (**to** auf + *Akk.*); **be ~:** reduziert werden können (**to** auf + *Akk.*) **2** (Chem.) reduzierbar

reducing/rɪˈdjuːsɪŋ/: **~ agent** *n.* (Chem.) Reduktionsmittel, *das;* **~ diet** *n.* Schlankheitskur, *die*

reductio ad absurdum /rɪdʌktɪəʊ æd əbˈsɜːdəm/ *n., no pl.* Reductio ad absurdum, *die* (geh.)

reduction /rɪˈdʌkʃn/ *n.* **1** (amount, process) (in price, costs, wages, rates, speed, etc.) Senkung, *die* (**in** *Gen.*); (in numbers, output, etc.) Verringerung, *die* (**in** *Gen.*); **~ in prices/wages/weight** Preis-/Lohnsenkung, *die*/Gewichtsabnahme, *die;* **there is a ~ on all furniture** alle Möbel sind im Preis heruntergesetzt; **a ~ of £10** ein Preisnachlass von 10 Pfund **2** (smaller copy) Verkleinerung, *die* **3** (conversion to other form) Verarbeitung, *die;* **~ of yards to metres** Umwandlung von Yards in Meter **4** (Photog.) Abschwächung, *die* **5** (Chem.) Reduktion, *die*

reductionism /rɪˈdʌkʃənɪzm/ *n.* (Philos.) Reduktionismus, *der*

reductive /rɪˈdʌktɪv/ *adj.* (Philos.) reduktiv

redundancy /rɪˈdʌndənsɪ/ *n.* **1** (Brit.) Arbeitslosigkeit, *die;* **redundancies** Entlassungen; **take** *or* **accept voluntary ~:** seiner betriebsbedingten Kündigung zustimmen **2** (being more than needed) Überfluss, *der;* (of materials, capital) Überschuss, *der;* (being more than suitable) Redundanz, *die;* (of style) Überladenheit, *die*

reˈdundancy payment *n.* Abfindung, *die*

redundant /rɪˈdʌndənt/ *adj.* **1** (Brit.: now unemployed) arbeitslos; **be made** *or* **become ~:** den Arbeitsplatz verlieren; **make ~:** entlassen **2** (more than needed) überflüssig; überschüssig ‹*Kapital, Material*›; (more than suitable) redundant; überflüssig ‹*Absatz, Kapitel, Wort*›; überladen ‹*Stil*›

reduplicate /rɪˈdjuːplɪkeɪt/
A *v.t.* **1** verdoppeln; (repeat) wiederholen **2** (Ling.) verdoppeln
B *v.i.* (Ling.) redupliziеren

reduplication /rɪdjuːplɪˈkeɪʃn/ *n.* **1** (act of doubling) Verdopplung, *die;* (repetition) Wiederholung, *die* **2** (Ling.) Reduplikation, *die*

red: ~ ˈwine *n.* Rotwein, *der;* **~wood** *n.* (Bot.) Mammutbaum, *der*

re-echo /riːˈekəʊ/ *v.i.* **1** widerhallen (**with** von); **the cry echoed and ~ed round the cave** der Ruf wurde in dem Gewölbe wieder und wieder zurückgeworfen **2** (fig.) **these words ~ through the book** an diese Worte wird man in dem Buch immer wieder erinnert

reed /riːd/ *n.* **1** (Bot.) Schilf[rohr], *das;* Ried, *das;* **the tall ~s by the river's edge** das hohe Schilf *od.* Ried am Flussufer; **prove to be a broken ~** (fig.) sich als unzuverlässig erweisen **2** (Mus.) (part of instrument) Rohrblatt, *das;* (instrument) Rohrblattinstrument, *das*

reed: ~ bunting *n.* (Ornith.) Rohrammer, *die;* **~ instrument** *n.* (Mus.) Rohrblattinstrument, *das;* **~ mace** *n.* (Bot.) Breitblättriger Rohrkolben; **~ organ** *n.* (Mus.) Harmonium, *das*

re-educate /riːˈedjʊkeɪt/ *v.t.* umerziehen

re-education /riːedjʊˈkeɪʃn/ *n., no pl.* Umerziehung, *die*

reed warbler, reed wren *ns.* (Ornith.) Teichrohrsänger, *der*

reedy /ˈriːdɪ/ *adj.* **1** schnarrend ‹*Musik, Singen*›; dünn ‹*Stimme*› **2** (full of reeds) schilfig

reef[1] /riːf/ (Naut.)
A *n.* (on sail) Reff, *das* (Seemannsspr.); **take in a ~:** die Segel reffen
B *v.t.* reffen (Seemannsspr.)

reef[2] *n.* **1** (ridge) Riff, *das;* **~ of sand/rocks/coral** Sand-/Fels-/Korallenriff, *das* **2** (fig.) Klippe, *die* **3** (lode) Erzgang, *der*

reefer /ˈriːfə(r)/ *n.* (sl.: marijuana cigarette) Joint, *der* (Drogenjargon)

ˈreefer jacket *n.* Kolani, *der*

ˈreef knot *n.* Kreuzknoten, *der*

reek /riːk/
A *n.* Geruch, *der;* Gestank, *der* (abwertend)
B *v.i.* **1** riechen, (abwertend) stinken (**of** nach) **2** (fig.) riechen (ugs.) (**of, with** nach)

reel /riːl/
A *n.* **1** (roller, cylinder) ‹*Papier-, Schlauch-, Garn-, Angel*›rolle, *die;* ‹*Film-, Tonband-, Garn*›spule, *die* **2** (quantity) Rolle, *die;* **steel rope in ~s of 1800 feet** Stahlseil auf Rollen zu 1800 Fuß; **~ of film** Filmrolle, *die* **3** (dance, music) Reel, *der*
B *v.t.* **~ [up]** (wind on) aufspulen
C *v.i.* **1** (be in a whirl) sich drehen; **his head was ~ing** in seinem Kopf drehte sich alles; **her mind ~ed with all the facts** ihr schwirrte der Kopf von all den Daten **2** (sway) torkeln; (fig.: be shaken) taumeln; **begin to ~:** ins Wanken geraten; **his mind ~ed when he heard the news** als er die Nachricht hörte, drehte sich ihm alles

Phrasal verbs
- **~ ˈin** *v.t.* an Land ziehen ‹*Fisch*›
- **~ ˈoff** *v.t.* **1** (say rapidly) herunterleiern (ugs. abwertend), hersagen ‹*Geschichte*›; (without apparent effort) abspulen (ugs.) ‹*Gedicht, Namen, Einzelheiten*› **2** (take off) abwickeln

re-elect /riːɪˈlekt/ *v.t.* wieder wählen

re-election /riːɪˈlekʃn/ *n.* Wiederwahl, *die*

re-eligible /riːˈelɪdʒɪbl/ *adj.* wieder wählbar; **be ~:** wieder gewählt werden können

re-embark /riːɪmˈbɑːk/
A *v.t.* wieder einschiffen ‹*Ladung, Passagiere*›
B *v.i.* sich wieder einschiffen (**for** nach); **~ on sth.** (fig.) bei etw. wieder einsteigen

re-emerge /riːɪˈmɜːdʒ/ *v.i.* **1** (out of liquid) wieder auftauchen **2** (into view; crop up) wieder auftauchen; ‹*Mond, Sonne usw.:*› wieder hervorkommen **3** (return) zurückkehren (**in** nach, **from** aus)

re-emergent /riːɪˈmɜːdʒənt/ *adj.* wieder auftauchend ‹*Frage, Idee*›; wiederkehrend ‹*Glaube*›; wieder erstehend (geh.) ‹*Nation*›

re-enact /riːɪˈnækt/ *v.t.* **1** wieder in Kraft setzen ‹*Gesetz, Erlass usw.*› **2** (perform) wiederholen ‹*Tatsachen, Einzelheiten*›; nachstellen ‹*Szene, Schlacht*›; **~ a role** noch einmal in einer Rolle auftreten; **~ a crime** den Hergang eines Verbrechens nachspielen

re-enlist (Mil.)
A *v.i.* wieder [in die Armee/Marine] eintreten
B *v.t.* wieder anwerben

re-enter /riːˈentə(r)/
A *v.i.* **1** wieder eintreten; (come on stage) die Bühne [wieder] betreten; (as stage direction) ~

Hamlet from left Auftritt Hamlet von links **2** (for race, exam, etc.) wieder antreten **3** (penetrate) wieder eindringen
B *v.t.* wieder betreten ‹*Raum, Gebäude*›; wieder eintreffen in (+ *Dat.*) ‹*Ortschaft*›; wieder einreisen in (+ *Akk.*) ‹*Land*›; wieder eintreten in (+ *Akk.*) ‹*Erdatmosphäre*›

re-entry /riːˈentrɪ/ *n.* **1** Wiedereintreten, *das;* (into country) Wiedereinreise, *die;* (for exam) Wiederantreten, *das;* nochmaliges Antreten (**for** zu); (of spacecraft) **[atmospheric] ~:** Wiedereintritt [in die Erdatmosphäre] **2** (Law: taking possession again) Wiederinbesitznahme, *die*

re-erect /riːɪˈrekt/ *v.t.* wieder aufbauen

re-establish /riːɪˈstæblɪʃ/ *v.t.* wieder herstellen ‹*Kontakt, Demokratie, Beziehungen, Frieden, Ordnung*›; wieder beleben ‹*Brauch, Mode*›; wieder aufbauen ‹*Organisation, Stützpunkt*›; wieder einsetzen ‹*Regierung*›; beweisen ‹*Unschuld usw.*›; **~ sb. as ruler** jmdn. als Herrscher wieder einsetzen; **~ oneself as sth./in a position** sich erneut als etw./in einer Position etablieren

reeve¹ /riːv/ *n.* **1** (Hist.) (magistrate) Vogt, *der;* (manorial supervisor) Aufseher, *der* **2** (minor official) Gemeindebeamte, *der/-beamtin, die*

reeve² *v.t.*, **rove** /rəʊv/ *or* **~d** (Naut.) scheren ‹*Tau*›; (fasten) festzurren

re-examination /riːɪgzæmɪˈneɪʃn/ *n.* **1** (Law) erneute [Zeugen]vernehmung **2** (investigation) erneute Untersuchung **3** (act of testing knowledge or ability) Wiederholungsprüfung, *die* **4** (act of scrutinizing again) nochmalige [Über]prüfung

re-examine /riːɪgˈzæmɪn/ *v.t.* **1** (Law) erneut vernehmen **2** (investigate) [erneut] untersuchen **3** (test knowledge or ability of) von neuem *od.* wieder prüfen **4** (scrutinize) erneut überprüfen

re-export /riːɪkˈspɔːt/ *v.t.* reexportieren; wieder ausführen

ref /ref/ *n.* (Sport coll.) Schiri, *der* (Sportjargon); (Boxing) Ringrichter, *der*

ref. *abbr.* **= reference** Verw.; **with ref. to** mit Bz. *od.* unter Bezugn. auf (+ *Akk.*); **your/our ref.** Ihr/unser Zeichen

reface /riːˈfeɪs/ *v.t.* **~ sth.** die Fassade einer Sache (*Gen.*) restaurieren

refashion /riːˈfæʃn/ *v.t.* umgestalten

refectory /rɪˈfektərɪ/ *n.* (in college, university) Mensa, *die;* (in convent, monastery) Refektorium, *das*

refer /rɪˈfɜː(r)/
A *v.i.*, **-rr- 1** **~ to** (allude to) sich beziehen auf (+ *Akk.*) ‹*Buch, Person usw.*›; (speak of) sprechen von ‹*Person, Problem, Ereignis usw.*› **2** **~ to** (apply to, relate to) betreffen; ‹*Beschreibung:*› sich beziehen auf (+ *Akk.*); **does that remark ~ to me?** gilt diese Bemerkung mir? **3** **~ to** (consult, cite as proof) konsultieren (geh.); nachsehen in (+ *Dat.*); **~ to sb./a case** sich auf jmdn./einen Fall berufen
B *v.t.*, **-rr- 1** (send on to) **~ sb./sth. to sb./sth.** jmdn./etw. an jmdn./auf etw. (*Akk.*) verweisen; **~ a patient to a specialist** einen Patienten an einen Facharzt überweisen; **the dispute was ~red to the UN** der Streitfall wurde vor die UNO gebracht; **~ sb. to a paragraph/an article** jmdn. auf einen Absatz/Artikel aufmerksam machen; **~ to drawer** (Banking) zurück an Aussteller **2** **~ to** (assign to) zurückführen auf (+ *Akk.*); **~ sth. to sb.** jmdm. etw. zuschreiben; **~red pain** (Med.) ausstrahlender Schmerz **3** (after examination) zurückstellen ‹*Prüfling*›; [zur Überarbeitung] zurückgeben ‹*Dissertation*›
(Phrasal verb)
• **~ 'back**
A *v.t.* **~ back to** zurückverweisen an (+ *Akk.*)
B *v.i.* **1** (to past event) **~ back to** sich beziehen auf (+ *Akk.*) **2** (to source of information) **~ back to sb./sth.** Rücksprache halten mit jmdm./auf etw. (*Akk.*) zurückgreifen

referee /refəˈriː/
A *n.* **1** (Sport: umpire) Schiedsrichter, *der/-richterin, die;* (Boxing) Ringrichter, *der;* (Wrestling) Kampfrichter, *der* **2** (Brit.: person willing to testify) Referenz, *die* **3** (arbitrator) Schlichter, *der* **4** (person who assesses) Gutachter, *der/Gutachterin, die*
B *v.t.* **1** (Sport: umpire) als Schiedsrichter/-richterin leiten; **~ a football match** ein Fußballspiel pfeifen *od.* leiten **2** (arbitrate) schlichten **3** (assess, evaluate) begutachten
C *v.i.* **1** (Sport: umpire) Schiedsrichter/-richterin sein **2** (arbitrate) schlichten; Schlichter sein **3** (assess or evaluate work) als Gutachter/Gutachterin tätig sein

reference /ˈrefrəns/ *n.* **1** (allusion) Hinweis, *der* (**to** auf + *Akk.*); **make [several] ~[s] to sth.** sich [mehrfach] auf etw. (*Akk.*) beziehen; **make no ~ to sth.** etw. nicht ansprechen; **omit all ~ to sth.** etw. völlig verschweigen; **put a ~ to sth. in the introduction of the book** in der Einleitung des Buches auf etw. (*Akk.*) hinweisen **2** (note directing reader) Verweis, *der* (**to** auf + *Akk.*) **3** (cited book, passage) Quellenangabe, *die* **4** (testimonial) Zeugnis, *das;* Referenz, *die;* **character ~:** persönliche Referenzen; **give sb. a good ~:** jmdm. ein gutes Zeugnis ausstellen **5** (person willing to testify) Referenz, *die;* **quote sb. as one's ~:** jmdn. als Referenz angeben **6** (act of referring) Konsultation, *die* (**to** *Gen.*) (geh.); **~ to a dictionary/map** Nachschlagen in einem Wörterbuch/Nachsehen auf einer Karte; **work of ~:** Nachschlagewerk, *das;* **without ~ to sb.** ohne jmdn. zu fragen; **speak without ~ to one's notes** sprechen, ohne seine Aufzeichnungen zu Hilfe zu nehmen **7** (relation, correspondence) **have ~ to sth.** in Beziehung zu etw. stehen; **in** *or* **with ~ to sth.** mit Bezug auf etw. (*Akk.*); unter Bezugnahme auf etw. (*Akk.*); **with ~ to your suggestion** was deinen Vorschlag anbetrifft. *See also* **cross reference; library 1; term A 2**

reference: ~ book *n.* Nachschlagewerk, *das;* **~ mark** *n.* Verweiszeichen, *das;* **~ number** *n.* [Kenn]nummer, *die;* **~ point** *n.* Bezugspunkt, *der*

referendum /refəˈrendəm/ *n., pl.* **~s** *or* **referenda** /refəˈrendə/ Volksentscheid, *der;* Referendum, *das;* **EU ~:** EU-Referendum, *das*

referral /rɪˈfɜːrl/ *n.* **1** (for advice) Überweisung, *die* (**to** an + *Akk.*) **2** (for action) Weiterleitung, *die* (**to** an + *Akk.*)

refill
A /riːˈfɪl/ *v.t.* nachfüllen ‹*Glas, Feuerzeug*›; neu füllen ‹*Kissen*›; mit einer neuen Füllung versehen ‹*Zahn*›; **~ the glasses** nachschenken; **~ a pen with ink** einen Füller mit Tinte füllen
B /ˈriːfɪl/ *n.* **1** (cartridge) [Nachfüll]patrone, *die;* (for ball pen) Ersatzmine, *die;* (pad of paper) Nachfüllpackung, *die* **2** (with drink) Nachgießen, *das;* **can I have a ~?** (coll.) gießt du mir noch einmal nach?

refillable /riːˈfɪləbl/ *adj.* nachfüllbar; Mehrweg‹*flasche, -verpackung*›

refine /rɪˈfaɪn/
A *v.t.* **1** (purify) raffinieren **2** (make cultured) kultivieren; verfeinern ‹*Stil, Ausdrucksweise*›; stilistisch verbessern ‹*Rede, Aufsatz*› **3** (improve) verbessern; verfeinern ‹*Stil, Technik*›
B *v.i.* **1** (become pure) rein werden **2** (become more cultured) sich verfeinern
(Phrasal verb)
• **~ [up]on** *v.t.* [weiter] verfeinern; weiterentwickeln

refined /rɪˈfaɪnd/ *adj.* **1** (purified) raffiniert; Fein‹*kupfer, -silber usw.*›; **~ sugar** [Zucker]raffinade, *die* **2** (cultured) kultiviert **3** (precise) scharfsinnig, differenziert ‹*Argumentation*›; ausgeklügelt ‹*Technik, Maschine[rie]*›; kompliziert ‹*Rechnung*›

refinement /rɪˈfaɪnmənt/ *n.* **1** (purifying) Raffination, *die* **2** (fineness of feeling, elegance) Kultiviertheit, *die;* **person of ~:** kultivierter Mensch; **~ of feeling** verfeinertes Gefühl **3** (subtle manifestation) Verfeinerung, *die* **4** (improvement) Verbesserung, *die;* Weiterentwicklung, *die* (**[up]on** *Gen.*); **introduce ~s into a machine** eine Maschine weiterentwickeln **5** (piece of reasoning) Spitzfindigkeit, *die* (abwertend)

refinery /rɪˈfaɪnərɪ/ *n.* Raffinerie, *die*

refit
A /riːˈfɪt/ *v.t.*, **-tt-** überholen; reparieren; (equip with new things) neu ausstatten
B *v.i.*, **-tt-** überholt werden; repariert werden; (renew supplies or equipment) sich neu ausrüsten
C /ˈriːfɪt/ *n.* Überholung, *die;* (with supplies or equipment) Neuausstattung, *die*

refitment /riːˈfɪtmənt/ ▸ **refit C**

reflate /riːˈfleɪt/ *v.t.* (Econ.) ankurbeln ‹*Wirtschaft, Konjunktur*›

reflation /riːˈfleɪʃn/ *n.* (Econ.) Reflation, *die*

reflationary /riːˈfleɪʃənərɪ/ *adj.* (Econ.) reflationär

reflect /rɪˈflekt/
A *v.t.* **1** (throw back) reflektieren; **bask in sb.'s ~ed glory** sich in jmds. Ruhm sonnen **2** (reproduce) spiegeln; (fig.) widerspiegeln ‹*Ansichten, Gefühle, Werte*›; **be ~ed** sich spiegeln **3** (contemplate) nachdenken über (+ *Akk.*); **~ what/how ...:** überlegen, was/wie ...
B *v.i.* (meditate) nachdenken
(Phrasal verb)
• **~ [up]on** *v.t.* **1** (consider, contemplate) nachdenken über (+ *Akk.*); abwägen ‹*Konsequenzen*› **2** **~ credit/discredit [up]on sb./sth.** ein gutes/schlechtes Licht auf jmdn./etw. werfen **3** (bring discredit on) diskreditieren; **~ [up]on sb.'s sincerity** an jmds. Aufrichtigkeit (*Dat.*) zweifeln lassen; **~ badly [up]on sb./sth.** auf jmdn./etw. ein schlechtes Licht werfen **4** (bring credit on) **~ well [up]on sb./sth.** jmdn./etw. in einem guten Licht erscheinen lassen **5** (cast doubt or reproach on) in Zweifel ziehen

re'flecting telescope ▸ **reflector 2**

reflection /rɪˈflekʃn/ *n.* **1** (of light etc.) Reflexion, *die;* (by surface of water etc.) Spiegelung, *die;* **angle of ~:** Reflexionswinkel, *der* **2** (reflected light, heat, or colour) Reflexion, *die;* (image; lit. or fig.) Spiegelbild, *das* **3** (meditation, consideration) Nachdenken, *das* (**upon** über + *Akk.*); **be lost in ~:** in Gedanken versunken sein; **on ~:** bei weiterem Nachdenken; **on ~, I think ...:** wenn ich mir das recht überlege, [so] glaube ich ... **4** (censure) **~ on** Kritik an (+ *Dat.*); **be a ~ [up]on sb./sth.** an jmdm./etw. zweifeln lassen; **cast ~s on sth.** etw. in Zweifel ziehen **5** (idea) Vorstellung, *die* **6** (remark) Reflexion, *die* (geh.), Betrachtung, *die* (**on** über + *Akk.*) **7** (Philos.) Nachdenken, *das;* Reflexion, *die* (fachspr.)

reflective /rɪˈflektɪv/ *adj.* **1** reflektierend; **be ~:** reflektieren; **~ power** Reflexionsvermögen, *das* **2** (thoughtful) nachdenklich **3** (reflected) reflektiert **4** (concerned in reflection) gedanklich ‹*Fähigkeiten, Kraft*›

reflectively /rɪˈflektɪvlɪ/ *adv.* nachdenklich

reflector /rɪˈflektə(r)/ *n.* **1** Rückstrahler, *der* **2** (telescope) Reflektor, *der*

reflex /ˈriːfleks/
A *n.* (Physiol.) Reflex, *der;* **conditioned ~:** bedingter Reflex
B *adj.* (by reflection) Reflex-

reflex: ~ action *n.* (Physiol.) Reflexhandlung, *die;* **~ angle** *n.* überstumpfer Winkel; **~ camera** *n.* (Photog.) Spiegelreflexkamera, *die*

reflexion (Brit.) ▸ **reflection**

reflexive /rɪˈfleksɪv/ (Ling.) *adj.* reflexiv; *see also* **pronoun**

reflexively /rɪˈfleksɪvlɪ/ *adv.* (Ling.) reflexiv

reflexology /riːfleksˈɒlədʒɪ/ *n., no pl.* **1** (system of massage) Reflexzonenmassage, *die;* **use ~:** die Reflexzonentherapie anwenden **2** (Psych.) Reflexologie, *die*

reflex re'action *n.* (Physiol.; also fig.) Reflexreaktion, *die*

refloat /riːˈfləʊt/ *v.t.* [wieder] flottmachen ‹*Schiff*›; (fig.) wieder flüssig machen (ugs.)

reflux /ˈriːflʌks/ *n.* **1** Rückfluss, *der* **2** (Chem.) Rückfluss, *der*

reforest /riːˈfɒrɪst/ *v.t.* wieder aufforsten

reforestation /riːfɒrɪˈsteɪʃn/ *n., no pl.* Wiederaufforstung, *die*

reform /rɪˈfɔːm/
A *v.t.* **1** (make better) reformieren ‹*Institution*›; bessern ‹*Person*› **2** (abolish) **~ sth.** mit etw. aufräumen
B *v.i.* sich bessern
C *n.* **1** (of person) Besserung, *die;* (in a system)

Reform, *die* (**in** *Gen.*) 2 (removal) Beseitigung, *die* ; **R~ Bill** (Hist.) Reformgesetz, *das*

re-form /riːˈfɔːm/
A *v.t.* 1 neu gründen ‹*Gesellschaft usw.*› 2 (Mil.) neu formieren
B *v.i.* 1 sich neu bilden; ‹*Band, Gesellschaft:*› neu gegründet werden 2 (Mil.) sich neu formieren

reformation /refəˈmeɪʃn/ *n.* (of attitude) Änderung, *die* (**in** *Gen.*); (of society, procedure, practice) Neugestaltung, *die* (**in** *Gen.*); (of person, character) Wandlung, *die* (**in** *Gen.*); **the R~** (Hist.) die Reformation

re-formation /riːfɔːˈmeɪʃn/ *n.* 1 Wiederaufbau, *der* 2 (Mil.) Neuformierung, *die*

reformatory /rɪˈfɔːmətərɪ/
A *adj.* reformatorisch; **~ measures** Reformmaßnahmen
B *n.* (Hist./Amer.) Besserungsanstalt, *die* (veralt.)

reformed /rɪˈfɔːmd/ *adj.* gewandelt; **he's a ~ character** *or* **man** er hat sich positiv verändert; **R~ Church** Reformierte Kirche

reformer /rɪˈfɔːmə(r)/ *n.* **[political] ~:** Reformpolitiker, *der*/-politikerin, *die*

reformism /rɪˈfɔːmɪzm/ *n.* Reformismus, *der*

reformist /rɪˈfɔːmɪst/
A *n.* Reformist, *der*/Reformistin, *die*
B *adj.* reformistisch

reˈform school *n.* Fürsorge[erziehungs]heim, *das*

refract /rɪˈfrækt/ *v.t.* (Phys.) brechen

reˈfracting telescope *n.* Linsenfernrohr, *das;* Refraktor, *der* (fachspr.)

refraction /rɪˈfrækʃn/ *n.* (Phys.) Brechung, *die;* Refraktion, *die* (fachspr.); **angle of ~:** Brechungswinkel, *der*

refractive /rɪˈfræktɪv/ *adj.* (Phys.) brechend; *see also* **index A 2**

refractor /rɪˈfræktə(r)/ *n.* (telescope) Refraktor, *der*

refractory /rɪˈfræktərɪ/
A *adj.* 1 (stubborn) störrisch; widerspenstig 2 (Med.) hartnäckig 3 (heat-resistant) hitzebeständig; schwer schmelzbar ‹*Metalle usw.*›
B *n.* hitzebeständiges Material

refrain[1] /rɪˈfreɪn/ *n.* Refrain, *der*

refrain[2] *v.i.* **~ from doing sth.** es unterlassen, etw. zu tun; **could you kindly ~?** würden Sie das bitte unterlassen?; **I think I'd better ~:** ich glaube, ich lasse das besser [sein]; **'please ~ from smoking'** „bitte nicht rauchen"; **he ~ed from comment** er enthielt sich jeden Kommentars (geh.)

refresh /rɪˈfreʃ/
A *v.t.* 1 (reanimate) erquicken (geh.); erfrischen; (with food and/or drink) stärken; **~ oneself** (with rest) sich ausruhen; (with food and/or drink) sich stärken 2 (freshen up) auffrischen ‹*Wissen*›; **let me ~ your memory** lassen Sie mich Ihrem Gedächtnis nachhelfen 3 (Computing) auffrischen
B *v.i.* (Computing) sich auffrischen

refresher /rɪˈfreʃə(r)/ *n.* 1 (Brit. Law) Sonderhonorar, *das* 2 Erfrischung, *die;* **have a ~:** etwas trinken

reˈfresher course *n.* Auffrischungskurs, *der*

refreshing /rɪˈfreʃɪŋ/ *adj.* 1 wohltuend ‹*Ruhe*›; erfrischend ‹*Brise, Getränk, Schlaf*› 2 (interesting) erfrischend

refreshment /rɪˈfreʃmənt/ *n.* Erfrischung, *die*

refreshment: ~ room *n.* Imbissstube, *die;* **~ stall** *n.* Erfrischungsstand, *der*

refrigerant /riːˈfrɪdʒərənt/ *n.* Kühlmittel, *das*

refrigerate /rɪˈfrɪdʒəreɪt/ *v.t.* 1 kühl lagern ‹*Lebensmittel*› 2 (chill) kühlen; (freeze) einfrieren 3 (make cool) abkühlen ‹*Luft*›

refrigeration /rɪfrɪdʒəˈreɪʃn/ *n.* kühle Lagerung; (chilling) Kühlung, *die;* (freezing) Einfrieren, *das*

refrigerator /rɪˈfrɪdʒəreɪtə(r)/ *n.* Kühlschrank, *der*

refuel /riːˈfjuːəl/, (Brit.) **-ll-**
A *v.t.* auftanken
B *v.i.* [auf]tanken

refuge /ˈrefjuːdʒ/ *n.* 1 Zuflucht, *die;* **find [a] ~ from the storm** Schutz vor dem Sturm finden; **take ~ in** Schutz *od.* Zuflucht suchen in (+ *Dat.*) (**from** vor + *Dat.*); (fig.) Zuflucht nehmen zu ‹*Alkohol, Religion, Lüge*›; **be a ~ to sb.** jmds. Zuflucht sein; **women's ~:** Frauenhaus, *das* 2 (traffic island) Verkehrsinsel, *die*

refugee /refjʊˈdʒiː/ *n.* Flüchtling, *der;* **~s from the earthquake** Menschen, die Schutz vor dem Erdbeben suchen; **economic ~:** Wirtschaftsflüchtling, *der*

refuˈgee camp *n.* Flüchtlingslager, *das*

refulgent /rɪˈfʌldʒənt/ *adj.* (literary) strahlend ‹*Licht, Tag*›; leuchtend ‹*Farbe, Sonnenuntergang*›

refund
A /riːˈfʌnd/ *v.t.* 1 (pay back) zurückzahlen ‹*Geld, Schulden*›; erstatten ‹*Kosten*›; *abs.* die Schulden zurückzahlen; **your satisfaction guaranteed or your money ~ed** bei Nichtgefallen [bekommen Sie Ihr] Geld zurück 2 (reimburse) das Geld zurückzahlen (+ *Dat.*); **~ sb. for** jmdm. [zurück]erstatten ‹*Kosten*›; jmdm. ersetzen ‹*Verlust, Schaden*›
B /ˈriːfʌnd/ *n.* Rückzahlung, *die;* (of expenses) [Rück]erstattung, *die;* **get a ~ of ten pence on a bottle** zehn Pence [Pfand] für eine Flasche zurückbekommen; **obtain a ~ of sth.** etw. zurückbekommen

refundable /riːˈfʌndəbl/ *adj.* **be ~:** zurückerstattet werden

refurbish /riːˈfɜːbɪʃ/ *v.t.* renovieren ‹*Gebäude, Haus*›; aufarbeiten ‹*Kleidung*›; aufpolieren ‹*Möbel*›

refurbishment /riːˈfɜːbɪʃmənt/ *n., no pl.* (of building) Renovierung, *die;* (of furniture) Aufpolierung, *die*

refurnish /riːˈfɜːnɪʃ/ *v.t.* neu einrichten

refusal /rɪˈfjuːzl/ *n.* Ablehnung, *die;* (after a period of time) Absage, *die;* (of admittance, entry, permission) Verweigerung, *die;* **~ to do sth.** Weigerung, etw. zu tun; **her ~ of food** ihre Weigerung, etwas zu essen; **have/get [the] first ~ on sth.** das Vorkaufsrecht für etw. haben/eingeräumt bekommen; **give sb. [the] first ~:** jmdm. das Vorkaufsrecht einräumen

refuse[1] /rɪˈfjuːz/
A *v.t.* 1 ablehnen; abweisen ‹*Heiratsantrag*›; verweigern ‹*Nahrung, Befehl, Bewilligung, Zutritt, Einreise, Erlaubnis*›; **~ sb. admittance/entry/permission** jmdm. den Zutritt/die Einreise/die Erlaubnis verweigern; **~ to do sth.** sich weigern, etw. zu tun 2 (not oblige) abweisen ‹*Person*› 3 ‹*Pferd:*› verweigern ‹*Hindernis*›
B *v.i.* 1 ablehnen; (after request) sich weigern 2 ‹*Pferd:*› verweigern

refuse[2] /ˈrefjuːs/
A *n.* Abfall, *der;* Müll, *der;* **the ~ is collected once a week** einmal in der Woche ist Müllabfuhr
B *adj.* **~ chemicals/water** Chemieabfälle/Abwasser, *das*

refuse/ˈrefjuːs/: **~ collection** *n.* Müllabfuhr, *die;* **~ collector** *n.* ▸ℹ p. 1260 Müllwerker, *der;* **~ disposal** *n.* Abfallbeseitigung, *die;* **~ heap** *n.* Müllhaufen, *der*

refusenik /rɪˈfjuːznɪk/ *n.* (Hist.) *sowjetischer Jude, dem die Ausreise* [*nach Israel*] *verweigert wurde*

refuse skip /ˈrefjuːs skɪp/ *n.* Müllbehälter, *der;* Abfallbehälter, *der*

refutation /refjʊˈteɪʃn/ *n.* Widerlegung, *die;* **the book was a ~ of the theory** in dem Buch wurde die Theorie widerlegt

refute /rɪˈfjuːt/ *v.t.* widerlegen

regain /rɪˈgeɪn/ *v.t.* 1 (recover possession of) zurückgewinnen ‹*Zuversicht, Vertrauen, Achtung, Augenlicht*›; zurückerobern ‹*Gebiet*›; **~ one's health/strength** wieder gesund werden/zu Kräften kommen; **~ control of sth.** etw. wieder unter Kontrolle bringen; *see also* **consciousness 1** 2 (reach) wieder erreichen ‹*Küste, Land*›; wieder bekommen ‹*Platz*›; **~ firm ground again** wieder festen Boden unter den Füßen haben 3 (recover) **~ one's balance/footing** das Gleichgewicht/den Halt wiedergewinnen; **~ one's feet** wieder auf die Beine kommen

regal /ˈriːgl/ *adj.* 1 (magnificent, stately) majestätisch ‹*Person, Baum, Art, Tier, Würde*›; prachtvoll ‹*Villa, Zustand*›; groß ‹*Luxus*› 2 (royal) königlich; **~ office/power** Amt/Macht des Königs/der Königin

regale /rɪˈgeɪl/ *v.t.* 1 verwöhnen (**with, on** mit); **~ sb. with stories** jmdn. mit Geschichten unterhalten 2 (give delight to) erfreuen ‹*Auge, Ohr, Sinne, Person*›; **be ~d** ‹*Auge, Ohr, Sinne:*› sich laben (geh.); ‹*Person:*› sich erquicken (geh.) (**by** an + *Dat.*)

regalia /rɪˈgeɪlɪə/ *n. pl.* 1 (of royalty) Krönungsinsignien 2 (of order) Ordensinsignien

regally /ˈriːgəlɪ/ *adv.* wie ein König/eine Königin

regard /rɪˈgɑːd/
A *v.t.* 1 (gaze upon) betrachten; **~ sb. fixedly** jmdn. anstarren 2 (give heed to) beachten ‹*jmds. Worte, Rat*›; Rücksicht nehmen auf (+ *Akk.*) ‹*Wunsch, Gesundheit, jmds. Recht*› 3 (fig.: look upon, contemplate) betrachten; **~ sb. kindly/warmly** jmdn. freundlich gesinnt/herzlich zugetan sein; **~ sb. unfavourably** jmdm. ablehnend gegenüberstehen; **~ sth. with suspicion/horror** misstrauisch gegen/entsetzt über etw. (*Akk.*) sein; **~ sb. with envy/scorn** neidisch auf jmdn. sein/jmdn. verachten; **~ sb. with respect/dislike** Respekt vor jmdm./eine Abneigung gegen jmdn. haben; **~ sb. as a friend/fool/genius** jmdn. als Freund betrachten/für einen Dummkopf/ein Genie halten; **be ~ed as** gelten als; **~ sth. as wrong** etw. für falsch halten 4 (concern, have relation to) betreffen; berücksichtigen ‹*Tatsachen*›; **as ~s sb./sth., ~ing sb./sth.** was jmdn./etw. angeht *od.* betrifft
B *n.* 1 (attention) Beachtung, *die;* **pay ~ to/have ~ to** *or* **for sb./sth.** jmdm./etw. Beachtung schenken; **pay due ~ to sb.** jmdm. die nötige Beachtung erweisen; **having ~ to these facts ...:** unter Berücksichtigung dieser Tatsachen ...; **without ~ to** ohne Rücksicht auf (+ *Akk.*) 2 (esteem, kindly feeling) Achtung, *die;* **hold sb./sth. in high/low ~, have** *or* **show a high/low ~ for sb./sth.** jmdn./etw. sehr schätzen/gering schätzen; **show one's high ~ for sth.** seine Wertschätzung für etw. zum Ausdruck bringen 3 ▸ℹ **p. 1287** *in pl.* Grüße; **send one's ~s** grüßen lassen; **give her my ~s** grüße sie von mir; **with kind[est] ~s** mit herzlich[st]en Grüßen 4 (relation, respect) Beziehung, *die;* **in this ~:** in dieser Beziehung *od.* Hinsicht; **in** *or* **with ~ to sb./sth.** in Bezug auf jmdn./etw. 5 (gaze) Blick, *der*

regardful /rɪˈgɑːdfl/ *adj.* aufmerksam; **be ~ of** im Auge behalten ‹*Gefahr, Schwierigkeit*›; Beachtung schenken (+ *Dat.*) ‹*Interesse, Problem, Gefühl*›

regarding /rɪˈgɑːdɪŋ/ ▸ **regard A 4**

regardless /rɪˈgɑːdlɪs/
A *adj.* **~ of sth.** ungeachtet *od.* trotz einer Sache (*Gen.*); **~ of the consequences/cost** ohne Rücksicht auf die Folgen/Kosten
B *adv.* trotzdem; **carry on ~:** trotzdem weitermachen

regatta /rɪˈgætə/ *n.* Regatta, *die;* **sailing ~:** Segelregatta, *die*

regd. *abbr.* **= registered** (Law) ges. gesch.

regency /ˈriːdʒənsɪ/ *n.* 1 Regentschaft, *die* (**of** über + *Akk.*) 2 (commission) Regentschaftsrat, *der;* (fig.) [stellvertretendes] Führungsgremium 3 **the R~** (in England) die Regentschaft Georgs IV (1810-20); **R~** *attrib.* Regency‹*möbel, -stil*›

regenerate
A /rɪˈdʒenəreɪt/ *v.t.* 1 (generate again, recreate) regenerieren (bes. Chemie, Biol.); neu beleben ‹*Hass, Angst, Liebe*› 2 (improve, reform) erneuern ‹*Kirche, Gesellschaft*›; **~ sb.** aus jmdm. einen neuen Menschen machen; **feel ~d** sich wie neugeboren fühlen 3 (Biol.: form afresh) regenerieren (fachspr.), neu bilden ‹*Gewebe, verlorenen Körperteil*›
B /rɪˈdʒenərət/ *adj.* 1 (Relig.: reborn) wieder geboren 2 (improved) gewandelt ‹*Person*›; (reformed) umgestaltet ‹*Gesellschaft, Institution*›

regeneration /rɪdʒenəˈreɪʃn/ *n.* 1 (recreation, re-formation) Neuentstehung, *die;* (fig.: revival, renaissance) Wiederbelebung, *die;* (of church, society) Erneuerung, *die* 2 (Relig.: spiritual rebirth)

r

Wiedergeburt, *die* **3** (Biol.: regrowth) Regeneration, *die* (fachspr.); Neubildung, *die*

regenerative /rɪˈdʒenərətɪv/ *adj.* regenerativ

regent /ˈriːdʒənt/

A *n.* **1** Regent, *der*/Regentin, *die* **2** (Amer. Univ.) Mitglied des Verwaltungsrates; **the R~s** der Verwaltungsrat

B *adj.* **Prince R~:** Prinzregent, *der*

reggae /ˈreɡeɪ/ *n.* (Mus.) Reggae, *der*

regicide /ˈredʒɪsaɪd/ *n.* **1** (murder) Königsmord, *der* **2** (murderer) Königsmörder, *der*/-mörderin, *die*

regime, régime /reɪˈʒiːm/ *n.* **1** (system) [Regierungs]system, *das;* (derog.) Regime, *das;* (fig.) bestehende Ordnung; *see also* **ancien régime** **2** (process) Methode, *die;* **working ~** Funktionsweise, *die* **3** (Med.) ▸**regimen**

reˈgime change *n., no pl.* Regimewechsel, *der*

regimen /ˈredʒɪmən/ *n.* (Med.) Heilprogramm, *das;* (diet) Diätplan, *der*

regiment

A /ˈredʒɪmənt, ˈredʒmənt/ *n.* **1** (Mil.: organizational unit) Regiment, *das;* **parachute/Highland ~:** Luftlande-/Hochlandregiment, *das* **2** (Mil.: operational unit) Abteilung, *die;* **artillery/tank ~:** Artillerie-/Panzerabteilung, *die;* **Royal R~ [of Artillery]** (Brit.) Königliche Artillerie **3** (fig.: large number) (of persons, animals) Heer, *das;* (of books etc.) Masse, *die*

B /ˈredʒɪmənt, ˈredʒɪment/ *v.t.* (organize) reglementieren

regimental /redʒɪˈmentl/ (Mil.)

A *adj.* Regiments‹*kleidung, -vorräte*›; **the ~ officers** die Offiziere des Regiments; *see also* **colour A 10**

B *n. in pl.* [Militär]uniform, *die;* (of particular regiment) Regimentsuniform, *die*

regimentation /redʒɪmənˈteɪʃn, redʒɪmenˈteɪʃn/ *n.* Reglementierung, *die*

Regina /rɪˈdʒaɪnə/ *n.* (Law) **~ v. Jones** die Königin gegen Jones

region /ˈriːdʒn/ *n.* **1** (area) Gebiet, *das;* **the north-western ~:** der Nordwesten **2** (administrative division) Bezirk, *der;* (Brit. Radio) Sendegebiet, *das;* **administrative ~:** Verwaltungsbezirk, *der;* **Strathclyde/North-West R~:** Bezirk Strathclyde/Nordwest **3** (fig.: sphere) Bereich, *der;* Gebiet, *das;* **in the ~ of two tons** ungefähr zwei Tonnen **4** (layer) Schicht, *die;* Region, *die* **5** (Anat.) Region, *die;* **~ of the eyes/mouth** Augen-/Mundpartie, *die; see also* **lower regions**

> **region**
>
> Die größte Verwaltungseinheit in Schottland. Es gibt davon neun, jede mit einem eigenen council.

regional /ˈriːdʒənl/ *adj.* regional ‹*System, Akzent, Förderung*›; Regional‹*planung, -fernsehen, -programm, -ausschuss*›; **~ aid** Regionalförderung, *die;* (EU) Regionalbeihilfe, *die;* **~ dialect** Regiolekt, *der* (Sprachw.); regionaler Dialekt; **~ wines of France** Weine aus französischen Anbaugebieten

regionalism /ˈriːdʒənəlɪzm/ *n.* (Polit., Ling.) Regionalismus, *der*

regionalization /riːdʒənəlaɪˈzeɪʃn/ *n., no pl.* Regionalisierung, *die*

regionalize /ˈriːdʒənəlaɪz/ *v.t.* regionalisieren

register /ˈredʒɪstə(r)/

A *n.* **1** (book, list) Register, *das;* (at school) Klassenbuch, *das;* **parish/hotel/marriage ~:** Kirchen-/Fremden-/Heiratsbuch, *das;* **~ of births, deaths and marriages** Personenstandsbuch, *das;* **medical ~:** Ärzteregister, *das;* **electoral** *or* **parliamentary ~, ~ of voters** Wählerliste, *die;* Wählerverzeichnis, *das;* **~ of members/patients** Mitgliederverzeichnis, *das*/Patientenkartei, *die;* **civil service ~:** Verzeichnis der Beamten; **call** *or* **mark the ~** (at school) die Anwesenheit der Schüler überprüfen **2** (Mus.) (in organ) Registerzug, *der;* (in harpsichord) Rechen, *der;* (set of pipes) Register, *das* **3** (Mus.: range of tones) Tonumfang, *der;* (part of voice-compass) Register, *das* (fachspr.); Tonlage, *die;* **middle ~:** Mittellage, *die;* **head/chest ~:** Kopf-/Brustregister, *das* **4** (Mech.) Klappe, *die;* Schieber, *der* **5** (recording device) Zählwerk, *das; see also* **cash register** **6** (Printing) Register, *das;* **be in ~:** Register halten **7** (Photog.) Register, *das;* Passer, *der* **8** (Ling.) Register, *das*

B *v.t.* **1** (set down) schriftlich festhalten ‹*Name, Zahl, Experiment, Detail*›; (on file; fig.: make mental note of) registrieren (**on** in + *Dat.*) ‹*Name, Faktum, Rat*› **2** (enter) registrieren ‹*Geburt, Heirat, Todesfall, Patent*›; (cause to be entered) registrieren lassen; eintragen ‹*Warenzeichen, Firma, Verein*›; anmelden ‹*Auto, Patent*›; (at airport) einchecken ‹*Gepäck*›; *abs.* (at hotel) sich ins Fremdenbuch eintragen; **~ [oneself] with the police** sich polizeilich anmelden **3** (enrol) anmelden; (Univ.) einschreiben, immatrikulieren; (as voter) eintragen (**on** in + *Akk.*) ‹*Person*›; *abs.* (as student) sich einschreiben *od.* immatrikulieren; (in list of voters) sich ins Wählerverzeichnis eintragen lassen; **~ as unemployed** sich arbeitslos melden; **~ [oneself] with a doctor** sich bei einem praktischen Arzt eintragen lassen **4** (record) anzeigen, registrieren ‹*Temperatur*› **5** (Post) eingeschrieben versenden; **have sth. ~ed** etw. einschreiben lassen **6** (express) zeigen ‹*Gefühlsregung, Freude*›; widerspiegeln ‹*Angst*›; zum Ausdruck bringen ‹*Entsetzen, Überraschung*›; **~ a protest** Protest anmelden

C *v.i.* (make impression) einen Eindruck machen (**on, with** auf + *Akk.*); **it didn't ~ with him** er hat das nicht registriert

registered /ˈredʒɪstəd/ *adj.* [ins Standesregister] eingetragen ‹*Taufe, Heirat*›; [ins Handelsregister] eingetragen ‹*Firma*›; eingeschrieben, immatrikuliert ‹*Student*›; schriftlich festgehalten ‹*Fakten, Zahlen*›; eingeschrieben ‹*Brief, Post, Päckchen*›; **~ disabled** ≈ Behinderter/Behinderte mit Schwerbehindertenausweis; **State R~ Nurse** (Brit.) staatlich geprüfte Krankenschwester/staatlich geprüfter Krankenpfleger; **~ trademark** eingetragenes Warenzeichen; **by ~ post** per Einschreiben

ˈregister office *n.* (Brit.) Standesamt, *das*

registrar /ˈredʒɪstrɑː(r), redʒɪˈstrɑː(r)/ *n.* ▸**ⓘ p. 1260** **1** (official recorder) (at university) ≈ Kanzler, *der*/Kanzlerin, *die;* (local official) Standesbeamte, *der*/-beamtin, *die* **2** (Brit.: in court of law) ≈ Rechtspfleger, *der*/-pflegerin, *die* **3** (Med.) *Arzt/Ärztin in der klinischen Fachausbildung*

Registrar ˈGeneral *n.: Leiter/Leiterin des Amtes für Bevölkerungsstatistik*

registration /redʒɪˈstreɪʃn/ *n.* **1** (act of registering) Registrierung, *die;* (enrolment) Anmeldung, *die;* (of students) Einschreibung, *die;* Immatrikulation, *die;* (of voters) Eintragung ins Wählerverzeichnis; (Post) Einschreiben, *das;* **cost of ~** (of letter, parcel) Einschreibegebühr, *die* **2** (entry) [Register]eintrag, *der;* **make a ~ of** registrieren; **~ fee** Anmeldegebühr, *die;* (for educational course) Kursgebühr, *die*

registration: ~ document *n.* (Brit.) Kraftfahrzeugbrief, *der;* **~ form** *n.* Anmeldeformular, *das;* **~ mark, ~ number** *ns.* (Motor Veh.) amtliches *od.* polizeiliches Kennzeichen; **~ plate** *n.* (Motor Veh.) Nummernschild, *das;* **~ tag** *n.* (Amer.) Nummernschild, *das*

registry /ˈredʒɪstrɪ/ *n.* **1** ▸ **~ [office]** Standesamt, *das; attrib.* standesamtlich ‹*Trauung*›; **be married in a ~ [office]** sich standesamtlich trauen lassen **2** (place for registers) Registratur, *die* **3** (registration) Registrierung, *die;* Eintragung, *die;* (of students) Einschreibung, *die;* Immatrikulation, *die*

Regius /ˈriːdʒɪəs/ *adj.* **~ professor** (Brit. Univ.) *Inhaber/Inhaberin eines von einem Monarchen errichteten od. durch Berufung der Krone besetzten Lehrstuhls*

regress /rɪˈɡres/ *v.i.* **1** (in development) sich zurückentwickeln; (in career) Rückschritte machen; **a sign of society ~ing** ein Zeichen gesellschaftlichen Rückschritts **2** (Psych.) regredieren (**to** in + *Akk.*)

regression /rɪˈɡreʃn/ *n.* **1** (return to previous state) rückläufige Entwicklung; **a ~ to less civilized standards** ein Rückfall in weniger zivilisierte Normen **2** (Psych.) Regression, *die* **3** (Med.: decline) Rückbildung, *die* **4** (backward movement) Rückkehr, *die*

reˈgression curve *n.* (Statistics) Regressionskurve, *die*

regressive /rɪˈɡresɪv/ *adj.* **1** (Psych., Med., Logic) regressiv **2** (tending to go back in development) rückschrittlich

regret /rɪˈɡret/

A *v.t.*, **-tt-** **1** (feel sorrow for loss of) nachtrauern (+ *Dat.*) **2** ▸**ⓘ p. 908** (be sorry for) bedauern; **~ having done sth.** es bedauern, dass man etw. getan hat; **~ being unable to do sth.** *or* **that one cannot do sth.** es bedauern, dass man etw. nicht tun kann; **it is to be ~ted that …:** es ist bedauerlich, dass …; **I ~ to say that …:** ich muss leider sagen, dass …; **we ~ to hear that …:** wir hören mit Bedauern, dass …

B *n.* Bedauern, *das;* **feel ~ at sb.'s doing sth.** bedauern, dass jmd. etw. tut; **feel ~ for having done sth.** es bedauern, dass man etw. getan hat; **there's no point in having ~s** es hat keinen Sinn, sich jetzt noch darüber Gedanken zu machen; **much to my ~:** zu meinem großen Bedauern; **have no ~s** nichts bereuen; **send one's ~s** (polite refusal) sich entschuldigen lassen; **please accept my ~s at having to refuse** seien Sie mir bitte nicht böse, aber ich muss leider ablehnen

regretful /rɪˈɡretfl/ *adj.* bedauernd ‹*Blick*›; **be ~ that one has done sth.** bedauern, dass man etw. getan hat

regretfully /rɪˈɡretfəlɪ/ *adv.* mit Bedauern

regrettable /rɪˈɡretəbl/ *adj.* bedauerlich

regrettably /rɪˈɡretəblɪ/ *adv.* bedauerlicherweise; bedauerlich ‹*teuer*›

regroup /riːˈɡruːp/

A *v.t.* **1** umgruppieren; (into classes) neu einteilen (**into** in + *Akk.*) **2** (Mil.: reorganize) neu formieren ‹*Truppen*›

B *v.i.* **1** (form a new group) sich neu gruppieren; (meet again) wieder zusammenkommen **2** (Mil.) sich neu formieren

regular /ˈreɡjʊlə(r)/

A *adj.* **1** (recurring uniformly, habitual, orderly) regelmäßig; geregelt ‹*Arbeit*›; fest ‹*Anstellung, Reihenfolge*›; **~ customer** Stammkunde, *der*/-kundin, *die;* **~ staff** Stammpersonal, *das;* **~ doctor** Hausarzt, *der;* **our ~ postman** unser [gewohnter] Briefträger; **get ~ work** ‹*Freiberufler:*› regelmäßig Aufträge bekommen; **my bowels are ~, I am ~:** ich habe regelmäßig Stuhlgang; **what's the ~ procedure for opening a deposit account?** wie richtet man normalerweise ein Sparkonto ein?; **her periods are always ~:** sie bekommt ihre Periode immer regelmäßig; **have** *or* **lead a ~ life** ein geregeltes Leben führen; *see also* **hour 3** **2** (evenly arranged, symmetrical) regelmäßig **3** (correct) angemessen ‹*Verhalten, Verfahren*› **4** (properly qualified) ausgebildet; **~ army** reguläre Armee; **~ soldiers** Berufssoldaten **5** (Ling.) regelmäßig **6** (coll.: thorough) richtig (ugs.) **7** (Geom.) regelmäßig; regulär (fachspr.) **8** (Eccl.) Regular‹*kleriker, -geistlicher*›

B *n.* **1** (coll.: ~ customer, visitor, etc.) Stammkunde, *der*/-kundin, *die;* (in pub) Stammgast, *der* **2** (coll.: permanently employed person) Festangestellte, *der/die* **3** (soldier) Berufssoldat, *der* **4** (esp. Amer.: gasoline) Normal, *das* (ugs.) **5** (Eccl.) Regularkleriker, *der*

regularise ▸**regularize**

regularity /reɡjʊˈlærɪtɪ/ *n.* **1** Regelmäßigkeit, *die* **2** (Ling.) regelmäßige Flexion

regularize /ˈreɡjʊləraɪz/ *v.t.* **1** (make regular) regeln; (by law) gesetzlich regeln *od.* festlegen; **~ the proceedings** vorschriftsmäßig verfahren **2** (make steady) stabilisieren ‹*Atmung, Puls, Spannung*›

regularly /ˈreɡjʊləlɪ/ *adv.* **1** (at fixed times) regelmäßig; (constantly) ständig **2** (steadily) gleichmäßig **3** (symmetrically) regelmäßig ‹*bauen, anlegen*› **4** (in an orderly manner) korrekt

regulate /ˈreɡjʊleɪt/ *v.t.* **1** (control) regeln; (subject to restriction) begrenzen **2** (adjust) regulieren; einstellen ‹*Apparat, Maschine, Zeit*›; [richtig ein]stellen ‹*Uhr*›; **she ~s her hours to fit in with his** sie passt sich ihm in ihrer Zeiteinteilung an **3** (moderate) senken ‹*Ausgaben*›; (adapt)

r

anpassen ‹*Lebensstil, Verhalten, Gewohnheit*›; ~ **one's lifestyle to fit in with sth.** seinen Lebensstil an etw. (*Akk.*) anpassen

regulation /regjʊˈleɪʃn/ *n.* **1** (regulating) Regelung, *die;* (of quantity, speed) Regulierung, *die;* (of machine) Einstellen, *das;* (of lifestyle, conduct, habit, mind) Anpassung, *die;* (of expenses) Senkung, *die* **2** (rule) Vorschrift, *die;* **be against ~s** vorschriftswidrig sein; **school/safety/fire ~s** Schulordnung, *die*/Sicherheits-/Brandschutzvorschriften **3** *attrib.* (according to rule) vorgeschrieben ‹*Geschwindigkeit*›; vorschriftsmäßig ‹*Kleidung*›; (usual) üblich ‹*Größe, Kleidung, Frisur*›

regulative /ˈregjʊlətɪv/ *adj.* regulativ; ~ **mechanism** Regelmechanismus, *der*

regulator /ˈregjʊleɪtə(r)/ *n.* **1** (device) Regler, *der;* (of clock, watch) Gangregler, *der* **2** (clock) Normaluhr, *die;* Regulator, *der* (veralt.)

regulatory /ˈregjʊlətərɪ/ *adj.* regulativ (geh.); ~ **body** Aufsichtsgremium, *das;* ~ **authority** Regulierungsbehörde, *die;* Aufsichtsbehörde, *die*

regurgitate /riːˈgɜːdʒɪteɪt/ *v.t.* **1** ‹*Person:*› erbrechen ‹*Essen*›; ‹*Tier:*› herauswürgen ‹*Beute*›; (Med.) zurückpumpen ‹*Blut*› **2** (fig.) ausspucken

rehab /ˈriːhæb/ *n., no pl.* (coll.) (treatment) Reha, *die;* (programme) Rehaprogramm, *das* **be in ~:** in Reha sein ; **go into ~:** in Reha gehen; *attrib.* ~ **clinic/centre** Rehaklinik, *die*/-zentrum, *das*

rehabilitate /riːhəˈbɪlɪteɪt/ *v.t.* rehabilitieren; renovieren, wieder herrichten ‹*altes Gebäude*›; ~ **[back into society]** wieder [in die Gesellschaft] eingliedern

rehabilitation /riːhəbɪlɪˈteɪʃn/ *n.* Rehabilitation, *die;* (of building) Renovierung, *die;* Instandsetzung, *die;* ~ **[in society]** Wiedereingliederung [in die Gesellschaft]

rehash

A /riːˈhæʃ/ *v.t.* aufwärmen; **just ~ a text** einen Text ein bisschen aufpolieren (ugs.)

B /ˈriːhæʃ/ *n.* **1** (restatement) Aufguss, *der* (abwertend) **2** (act or process of restating) (of old arguments) Aufwärmen, *das;* **do a ~ of the text** den Text ein bisschen aufpolieren (ugs.)

rehearsal /rɪˈhɜːsl/ *n.* **1** (Theatre, Mus., etc.) Probe, *die;* **have a ~/~s** proben (**of** *Akk.*); **the play is now in ~:** das Stück wird jetzt geprobt; *see also* **dress rehearsal** **2** (recounting) Aufzählung, *die;* (recital) Vortrag, *der;* **give a ~ of** aufzählen ‹*Ereignisse*›

rehearse /rɪˈhɜːs/ *v.t.* **1** (Theatre, Mus., etc.) proben **2** (recite) sprechen ‹*Gebet*›; rezitieren ‹*Gedicht, Stück*›; (repeat) wiederholen; ~ **sth. again to sb.** jmdm. etw. noch einmal erzählen **3** (enumerate) aufzählen **4** (train) proben mit ‹*Schauspieler, Musiker*›; **be ~d in the correct use of sth.** in den korrekten Gebrauch von etw. eingeübt werden

reheat /riːˈhiːt/ *v.t.* wieder erwärmen; aufwärmen ‹*Essen*›

rehouse /riːˈhaʊz/ *v.t.* umquartieren

rehousing /riːˈhaʊzɪŋ/ *n.* Umquartierung, *die*

Reich /raɪk, raɪx/ *n.* (Hist.) [Deutsches] Reich; **the First/Second ~:** das Heilige Römische/Deutsche Reich; **the Third ~:** das Dritte Reich

reign /reɪn/

A *n.* Herrschaft, *die;* (of monarch also) Regentschaft, *die;* **in the ~ of King Charles** während der Regentschaft König Karls; *see also* **terror 1**

B *v.i.* **1** (hold office) herrschen (**over** über + *Akk.*); **~ing champion** amtierender Meister/amtierende Meisterin; *see also* **supreme A 2** **2** (prevail) herrschen; **silence ~s** es herrscht Ruhe

reignite /riːɪgˈnaɪt/

A *v.t.* wieder anzünden; wieder entzünden ‹*Gas*›

B *v.i.* sich wieder entzünden

Reilly ▸ **Riley**

reimburse /riːɪmˈbɜːs/ *v.t.* [zurück]erstatten ‹*[Un]kosten, Spesen*›; entschädigen ‹*Person*›; ~ **sb. for** jmdm. [zurück]erstatten ‹*[Un]kosten, Spesen*›; jmdm. ersetzen ‹*Verlust*›

reimbursement /riːɪmˈbɜːsmənt/ *n.* Rückzahlung, *die;* (of expenses) Erstattung, *die*

reimport /riːɪmˈpɔːt/ *v.t.* reimportieren (**into** nach)

reimpose /riːɪmˈpəʊz/ *v.t.* erneuern; wieder erheben ‹*Zoll, Steuer*›; erneut verhängen ‹*Kriegsrecht, Sanktionen*›; wieder anordnen ‹*Rationierung*›

rein /reɪn/

A *n.* **1** Zügel, *der;* **keep a child on ~s** ein Kind am Laufgurt führen; **draw ~:** die Zügel anziehen; **give one's horse the ~[s]** [seinem Pferd] die Zügel schießen lassen **2** (fig.) Zügel, *der;* **hold the ~s** die Zügel in der Hand haben; **give [full] ~ to sth.** einer Sache (*Dat.*) die Zügel schießen lassen; **keep a tight ~ on** an der Kandare halten ‹*Person*›; im Zaum halten ‹*Gefühle*›; in Schranken halten ‹*Ausgaben*›; **assume/drop the ~s of government/power** die Amtsgeschäfte/Macht übernehmen/abgeben; *see also* **free A 3**

B *v.t.* **1** (check, guide) lenken ‹*Pferd*›; ~ **to a halt** zum Stehen bringen ‹*Pferd*› **2** (restrain) im Zaum halten ‹*Zunge*›

Phrasal verbs

- **~ 'back**

A *v.t.* zügeln ‹*Pferd*›

B *v.i.* die Zügel anziehen

- **~ 'in**

A *v.t.* (check, lit. or fig.) zügeln

B *v.i.* Halt machen

- **~ 'up**

A *v.t.* zügeln ‹*Pferd*›

B *v.i.* die Zügel anziehen

reincarnate /riːɪnˈkɑːneɪt/ *v.t.* (Relig.) reinkarnieren; **be ~d** wieder geboren werden

reincarnation /riːɪnkɑːˈneɪʃn/ *n.* (Relig.) Reinkarnation, *die;* Wiedergeburt, *die*

reindeer /ˈreɪndɪə(r)/ *n., pl. same* Ren[tier], *das*

'reindeer moss *n.* (Bot.) Rentierflechte, *die*

reinforce /riːɪnˈfɔːs/ *v.t.* verstärken ‹*Truppen, Mauer, Festung, Stoff*›; aufstocken ‹*Vorräte*›; stärken ‹*Partei, Gesundheit*›; erhöhen ‹*Anzahl*›; untermauern ‹*Argument*›; bestätigen ‹*Behauptung*›; ~ **sb.'s opinion/determination** jmdn. in seiner Meinung/Entschlossenheit bestärken; **~d concrete** Stahlbeton, *der;* ~ **the message** was man zu verstehen geben wollte, unterstreichen *od.* bekräftigen

reinforcement /riːɪnˈfɔːsmənt/ *n.* **1** (of bridge etc.) Verstärkung, *die;* (of provisions) Aufstockung, *die;* (of numbers) Zunahme, *die;* (of argument) Untermauerung, *die;* (of determination) Bestärkung, *die* **2** **~[s]** (additional men etc.) Verstärkung, *die* **3** (on punch holes) Verstärkungsring, *der;* (for elbow of garment) Schoner, *der;* (for buckled girder) Armierung, *die*

reinsert /riːɪnˈsɜːt/ *v.t.* noch einmal einwerfen ‹*Münze*›; ‹*Arzt:*› noch einmal einstechen ‹*Nadel*›; noch einmal setzen ‹*Inserat*›

reinstate /riːɪnˈsteɪt/ *v.t.* wieder herstellen ‹*Recht und Ordnung*›; wieder einstellen ‹*Arbeiter*›; (in position) wieder einsetzen; **be ~d in sb.'s favour** jmds. Gunst wiedergewonnen haben; **be ~d on the throne** wieder auf den Thron gehoben werden

reinstatement /riːɪnˈsteɪtmənt/ *n.* (of law and order) Wiederherstellung, *die;* **his ~ in the job** seine Wiedereinstellung

reinsurance /riːɪnˈʃʊərəns/ *n.* Rückversicherung, *die;* (extension) Verlängerung der Versicherung

reinsure /riːɪnˈʃʊə(r)/ *v.t.* rückversichern; (extend) die Versicherung verlängern für

reintegrate /riːˈɪntɪgreɪt/

A *v.t.* wieder eingliedern (**into** in + *Akk.*).

B *v. refl.* sich wieder eingliedern (**into** in + *Akk.*)

reintegration /riːɪntɪˈgreɪʃn/ *n.* Wiedereingliederung, *die* (**into** in + *Akk.*)

reinter /riːɪnˈtɜː(r)/ *v.t.*, **-rr-** wieder begraben

reinterpret /riːɪnˈtɜːprɪt/ *v.t.* (interpret afresh) noch einmal interpretieren; (give different interpretation) neu interpretieren

reintroduce /riːɪntrəˈdjuːs/ *v.t.* **1** (bring back) wieder einführen; erneut einbringen ‹*Gesetzesvorlage*› **2** (return to former habitat) wieder einbürgen ‹*Tier-, Pflanzenart*›

reinvent /riːɪnˈvent/ *v.t.* ▸ **wheel A 1**

reinvest /riːɪnˈvest/ *v.t.* reinvestieren (fachspr.); wieder anlegen ‹*Kapital*›

reinvestment /riːɪnˈvestmənt/ *n.* (fresh investment) Reinvestition, *die* (fachspr.); Wiederanlage, *die*

reinvigorate /riːɪnˈvɪgəreɪt/ *v.t.* neu beleben; **feel ~d** sich gestärkt fühlen

reissue /riːˈɪʃuː, riːˈɪsjuː/

A *v.t.* neu herausbringen

B *n.* Neuauflage, *die;* (of film) Wiederveröffentlichung, *die*

reiterate /riːˈɪtəreɪt/ *v.t.* wiederholen

reiteration /riːɪtəˈreɪʃn/ *n.* Wiederholung, *die*

reject

A /rɪˈdʒekt/ *v.t.* **1** ablehnen; abweisen ‹*Freier*›; verweigern ‹*Nahrung*›; zurückweisen ‹*Bitte, Annäherungsversuch*› **2** (Med.) nicht vertragen ‹*Bluttransfusion, Nahrung, Medizin*›; abstoßen ‹*Transplantat*›

B /ˈriːdʒekt/ *n.* (person) Ausgestoßene, *der/die;* (Mil.) Untaugliche, *der/die;* (thing) Ausschuss, *der*

rejection /rɪˈdʒekʃn/ *n.* **1** ▸ **reject A 1**: Ablehnung, *die;* Abweisung, *die;* Verweigerung, *die;* Zurückweisung, *die;* **parental ~:** Ablehnung durch die Eltern **2** (Med.) Abstoßung, *die;* ~ **of food indicates that …:** dass der Körper Nahrung nicht verträgt, lässt erkennen, dass …

rejectionist /rɪˈdʒekʃənɪst/ *n.* Gegner, *der*/Gegnerin, *die;* (opponent of peace settlement) Friedensgegner, *der*/-gegnerin, *die;* *attrib.* ablehnend; (rejecting peace settlement) friedensfeindlich

re'jection slip *n.* Absage, *die*

rejig /riːˈdʒɪg/ *v.t.*, **-gg-** umrüsten (**with** auf + *Akk.*); (coll.: rearrange) ummodeln

rejoice /rɪˈdʒɔɪs/ *v.i.* **1** (feel great joy) sich freuen (**over, at** über + *Akk.*); ~ **in the Lord!** freut euch im Herrn! **2** (make merry) feiern

Phrasal verb

- ~ **in** *v.i.* **1** (joc.: be called by) ~ **in a name/title** sich mit einem Namen/Titel schmücken (scherzh.) **2** (joc.: have) sich erfreuen (+ *Gen.*); gesegnet sein mit (oft spött.)

rejoicing /rɪˈdʒɔɪsɪŋ/ *n.* **1** **[sounds of] ~:** Jubel, *der* **2** *in pl.* (celebrations) Feier, *die*

rejoin[1] /rɪˈdʒɔɪn/ *v.t.* (reply) erwidern (**to** auf + *Akk.*)

rejoin[2] /riːˈdʒɔɪn/

A *v.t.* **1** (join again) wieder stoßen zu ‹*Regiment*›; wieder eintreten in (+ *Akk.*) ‹*Partei, Verein*›; ~ **each other** sich wieder treffen; ~ **one's ship** wieder an Bord gehen **2** (reunite) wieder zusammenfügen ‹*Bruchstücke*›; ‹*Verkehrsteilnehmer:*› wieder kommen auf (+ *Akk.*) ‹*Straße, Autobahn*›; ‹*Straße:*› wieder [ein]münden in (+ *Akk.*) ‹*Straße, Autobahn*›

B *v.i.* ‹*Personen:*› sich wieder treffen; ‹*Straßen:*› wieder zusammentreffen

rejoinder /rɪˈdʒɔɪndə(r)/ *n.* Erwiderung, *die* (**to** auf + *Akk.*)

rejuvenate /rɪˈdʒuːvəneɪt/ *v.t.* verjüngen ‹*Person, Haut*›; neu beleben ‹*Institution, wirtschaftliches/gesellschaftliches Leben*›

rejuvenation /rɪdʒuːvəˈneɪʃn/ *n.* Verjüngung, *die;* (of institutions, economic life, social life) Neubelebung, *die*

rekey /riːˈkiː/ *v.t.* neu eingeben; neu erfassen

rekindle /riːˈkɪndl/

A *v.t.* **1** (relight) wieder anfachen **2** (fig.: reawaken) wieder entfachen ‹*Liebe, Leidenschaft*›; wieder aufleben lassen ‹*Sehnsucht, Verlangen, Hoffnung*›

B *v.i.* sich wieder entzünden; (fig.) wieder aufflammen

relabel /riːˈleɪbl/ *v.t.* **1** (label again) neu etikettieren, umetikettieren ‹*Waren*› **2** (rename) umbenennen; ~ **sth. [as] sth.** etw. als etw. bezeichnen

relapse /rɪˈlæps/

A *v.i.* ‹*Kranker:*› einen Rückfall bekommen; ~ **into** zurückfallen in (+ *Akk.*) ‹*Götzendienst, Barbarei*›; ~ **into drug-taking/shoplifting** rückfällig werden [und wieder Drogen nehmen/Ladendiebstähle begehen]; ~ **into**

r

silence/lethargy wieder in Schweigen/Lethargie verfallen
B *n.* (*also* /ˈriːlæps/) Rückfall, *der* (**into** in + *Akk.*)

relate /rɪˈleɪt/
A *v.t.* **1** (tell) erzählen ‹*Geschichte*›; erzählen von ‹*Abenteuer*› **2** (bring into relation) in Zusammenhang bringen (**to, with** mit); **~ two things** eine Verbindung zwischen zwei Dingen herstellen **3** (establish relation or connection between) einen Zusammenhang herstellen zwischen
B *v.i.* **1** **~ to** (have reference) ‹*Vorlesung:*› handeln von; ‹*Behauptung, Frage, Angelegenheit:*› in Zusammenhang stehen mit; betreffen ‹*Person*› **2** **~ to** (feel involved or connected with) eine Beziehung haben zu

related /rɪˈleɪtɪd/ *adj.* **1** (by kinship or marriage) verwandt (**to** mit); **~ by marriage** verschwägert; **they are all ~ [to one another]** sie sind alle miteinander verwandt **2** (connected) miteinander in Zusammenhang stehend; verwandt ‹*Sprache, Begriff, Art, Spezies, Fach*›

relation /rɪˈleɪʃn/ *n.* **1** (connection) Beziehung, *die* (**of** … **and** zwischen … und); Zusammenhang, *der* (**of** … **and** zwischen … und); **be out of all ~ to** in keinem Verhältnis stehen zu ‹*Kosten, geleisteter Arbeit*›; **have some ~ to** in einem gewissen Zusammenhang stehen zu; **bear some/little ~ to sth.** einen gewissen/wenig Bezug zu etw. haben; **in** *or* **with ~ to** in Bezug auf (+ *Akk.*); **the ~s expressed by prepositions** die durch Präpositionen ausgedrückten Bezüge **2** *in pl.* (dealings) (with parents, police) Verhältnis, *das* (**with** zu); (with country) Beziehungen (**with** zu, mit); (sexual intercourse) intime Beziehungen (**with** zu); **trading ~s** Handelsbeziehungen **3** (kin, relative) Verwandte, *der/die;* **what ~ is he to you?** wie ist er mit dir verwandt?; **is she any ~ [to you]?** ist sie mit dir verwandt? **4** (narrative, account) Erzählung, *die;* (of details) Aufzählung, *die* **5** (Law) Anzeige, *die;* **at the** *or* **by ~ of** auf Anzeige (*Akk.*) von

relational database /riːleɪʃənl ˈdeɪtəbeɪs/ *n.* (Computing) relationale Datenbank

relationship /rɪˈleɪʃnʃɪp/ *n.* **1** (mutual tie) Beziehung, *die* (**with** zu); **have a good/bad ~ with sb.** zu jmdm. ein gutes/schlechtes Verhältnis haben; **doctor-patient ~:** Verhältnis zwischen Arzt und Patient **2** (kinship) Verwandtschaftsverhältnis, *das;* **what is your ~ to him?** in welchem Verwandtschaftsverhältnis stehst du zu ihm? **3** (connection) Beziehung, *die;* (between cause and effect) Zusammenhang, *der* **4** (sexual) Verhältnis, *das*

relative /ˈrelətɪv/
A *n.* **1** (family connection) Verwandte, *der/die;* **have many ~s** eine große Verwandtschaft haben **2** (related species) Verwandte, *der/die* **3** (Ling.) Relativ[um], *das*
B *adj.* **1** (corresponding) relativ; **the ~ value of British and German currency is …:** das Wertverhältnis von der englischen zur deutschen Währung beträgt … **2** (comparative) jeweilig; **the ~ costs of a and b** die Kostenrelation zwischen a und b; **with ~ calmness** relativ gelassen **3** (defined in relation to sth. else) relativ ‹*Dichte, Feuchtigkeit*›; **~ positions of troops** Truppenkonstellation, *die;* **~ densities/heights** Dichte-/Höhenrelation, *die;* **~ majority** (Brit. Polit.) relative Mehrheit **4** (proportioned to sth. else) **be ~ to sth.** sich nach etw. richten; **a large population ~ to the town's size** eine im Verhältnis zur Größe der Stadt beachtliche Einwohnerzahl **5** (implying comparison with sth. else) relativ ‹*Begriff*› **6** (conditioned by relation to sth. else) abhängig (**to** von); **be ~ to sth./sb.** ‹*Geschmack, Größe:*› durch etw./jmdn. relativiert werden **7** (correlative) sich gegenseitig bedingend; **'parents' and 'children' are ~ terms** die Begriffe „Eltern" und „Kinder" bedingen sich gegenseitig **8** (having reference to sth.) **~ to** in Zusammenhang mit; **give me the grid references ~ to your location** geben Sie mir die Koordinaten Ihres Standorts **9** (Mus.) parallel ‹*Dur-, Molltonart*›

relative: ~ ˈadjective *n.* (Ling.) Relativadjektiv, *das;* **~ ˈadverb** *n.* (Ling.) Relativadverb, *das;* **~ ˈclause** *n.* (Ling.) Relativsatz, *der*

relatively /ˈrelətɪvlɪ/ *adv.* relativ; verhältnismäßig

relative ˈpronoun *n.* Relativpronomen, *das*

relativise ▸**relativize**

relativism /ˈrelətɪvɪzm/ *n.* (Philos.) Relativismus, *der*

relativist /ˈrelətɪvɪst/ *n.* (Philos.) Relativist, *der*/Relativistin, *die*

relativistic /relətɪˈvɪstɪk/ *adj.* **1** relativistisch **2** (Phys.) Relativitäts‹*theorie, -korrektion*›

relativity /reləˈtɪvɪtɪ/ *n.* **1** (fact of being relative) Abhängigkeit, *die* (**to** von) **2** (Phys.) Relativität, *die;* **~ theory, the theory of ~:** die Relativitätstheorie **3** (Econ.) (of posts) Stellenstaffelung, *die;* (of salaries) Gehaltsstaffelung, *die;* **campaign for ~ in pay with men** ‹*Frauen:*› sich für die tarifliche Gleichstellung mit den Männern einsetzen

relativize /ˈrelətɪvaɪz/ *v.t.* relativieren

relax /rɪˈlæks/
A *v.t.* **1** (make less tense) entspannen ‹*Muskel, Körper[teil]*›; lockern ‹*Muskel, Feder, Griff*›; (fig.) lockern; **winter ~ed its grip on the landscape** (fig.) der Winter ließ die Landschaft aus seiner Umklammerung **2** (make less strict) lockern ‹*Gesetz, Vorschrift, Disziplin*› **3** (slacken) nachlassen in (+ *Dat.*) ‹*Bemühungen, Aufmerksamkeit*›; verlangsamen ‹*Tempo*›; **he began to ~ his attention** seine Aufmerksamkeit ließ allmählich nach
B *v.i.* **1** (become less tense) sich entspannen; **his face** *or* **features ~ed into a smile** sein Gesicht entspannte sich zu einem Lächeln **2** (slacken) nachlassen (**in** in + *Dat.*) **3** (become less stern) sich mäßigen (**in** in + *Dat.*) **4** (cease effort) sich entspannen; ausspannen; (stop worrying, calm down) sich beruhigen; **let's just ~!** (stop worrying!) nur ruhig Blut!

relaxant /riːˈlæksənt/ *n.* (Med.) Relaxans, *das*

relaxation /riːlækˈseɪʃn/ *n.* **1** (recreation) Entspannung, *die;* **play tennis as a** *or* **for ~:** zur Entspannung Tennis spielen **2** (cessation of effort) Erholung, *die* (**from** von); **find time for ~:** Zeit für Muße finden **3** (of law, rule, discipline) Lockerung, *die* **4** (Phys.) Relaxation, *die*

relaxed /rɪˈlækst/ *adj.* **1** (informal, not anxious) entspannt, gelöst ‹*Atmosphäre, Lächeln, Gefühl, Person*›; **she's a very ~ person** sie ist ein sehr gelassener Mensch *od.* die Gelassenheit in Person; **at a ~ pace** gemächlich **2** (not strict or exact) gelockert ‹*Regel, Beschränkung*›; locker ‹*Moral*›

relaxing /rɪˈlæksɪŋ/ *adj.* entspannend; erholsam; **have a ~ bath** zur Entspannung ein Bad nehmen

relay
A /ˈriːleɪ/ *n.* **1** (gang) Schicht, *die;* **work in ~s** schichtweise arbeiten **2** (race) Staffel, *die* **3** (vehicles) **~ [of cars]** [Fahrzeug]stafette, *die* **4** (driving operation) Fahrzeugstafette, *die* **5** (Electr.) Relais, *das;* **protective ~:** Schutzrelais, *das* **6** (Radio, Telev.) **radio ~:** Richtfunkverbindung, *die;* **~ station** Relaisstation, *die* **7** (transmission) Übertragung, *die;* **direct ~:** Direktübertragung, *die*
B /ˈriːleɪ, ˈriːleɪ/ *v.t.* **1** (pass on) weiterleiten; **~ a message to sb. that …:** jmdm. ausrichten *od.* mitteilen, dass … **2** (Radio, Telev., Teleph.) übertragen **3** (transport) [in einer Stafette] befördern; **form a chain to ~ water to the scene of the fire** eine Kette bilden, um Wasser zur Brandstelle durchzureichen

re-lay /riːˈleɪ/ *v.t.*, **re-laid** /riːˈleɪd/ wieder verlegen ‹*Teppich, Fliesen*›; neu belegen ‹*Fußboden, Straße*›; (after damage) neu [ver]legen ‹*Rohr, Leitung*›

ˈrelay race *n.* (Running, Hurdling) Staffellauf, *der;* (Swimming) Staffelschwimmen, *das;* **the 4×100 metres ~:** die 4×100-Meter-Staffel; **hurdles ~:** Hürdenstaffel, *die*

release /rɪˈliːs/
A *v.t.* **1** (free) freilassen ‹*Tier, Häftling, Sklaven*›; (from imprisonment, jail) entlassen (**from** aus); (from bondage, trap) befreien (**from** aus); (from pain) erlösen (**from** von); (from promise, obligation, vow) entbinden (**from** von); (from work) freistellen (**from** von) **2** (let go, let fall) loslassen; lösen ‹*Handbremse, Sprungfeder*›; ausklinken ‹*Bombe*›; **~ one's hold** *or* **grip on sth.** etw. loslassen; **~ the shutter** (Photog.) den Verschluss auslösen; **~ the pressure** den Druck verringern **3** (make known) veröffentlichen ‹*Erklärung, Nachricht*›; (issue) herausbringen ‹*Film, Schallplatte, Produkt*› **4** (emit) ablassen ‹*Dampf*›; freisetzen ‹*Energie, Strahlung*›
B *n.* **1** (act of freeing) ▸**A 1**: Freilassung, *die;* Entlassung, *die;* Befreiung, *die;* Erlösung, *die;* Entbindung, *die;* Freistellung, *die* **2** (of published item) Veröffentlichung, *die;* **when does the film go out on general ~?** wann kommt der Film in die Kinos?; **the film/album is scheduled for ~ in the autumn** der Film/das Album soll im Herbst herausgebracht werden *od.* herauskommen; **a new ~ by Bob Dylan** eine neue Platte *od.* eine Neuveröffentlichung von Bob Dylan; **the film is a recent ~:** der Film ist erst vor kurzem herausgekommen **3** (handle, lever, button) Auslöser, *der;* **carriage ~:** Wagenrücklauf, *der* **4** (of steam) Ablassen, *das;* (of pressure) Verringerung, *die;* (of energy, radiation) Freisetzung, *die*

relegate /ˈrelɪgeɪt/ *v.t.* **1** (dismiss, consign) **~ sb. to the position** *or* **status of …:** jmdn. zu … degradieren; **~ sth. to the rubbish bin** etw. in den Mülleimer wandern lassen **2** (Sport) absteigen lassen; **be ~d** absteigen (**to** in + *Akk.*) **3** (hand over) weiterleiten (**to** an + *Akk.*) **4** (banish) verbannen

relegation /relɪˈgeɪʃn/ *n.* **1** (action of dismissing, consigning) Degradierung, *die;* **her ~ to the position of …:** ihre Degradierung zu … **2** (Sport) Abstieg, *der* **3** (action or state of banishment) Verbannung, *die*

relent /rɪˈlent/ *v.i.* nachgeben; (yield to compassion) Mitleid zeigen; ‹*Wetter:*› besser werden

relentless /rɪˈlentlɪs/ *adj.* unerbittlich; erbarmungslos ‹*Necken*›; schonungslos ‹*Kritik, Heftigkeit*›

relentlessly /rɪˈlentlɪslɪ/ *adv.* unerbittlich; erbarmungslos ‹*necken*›; schonungslos ‹*kritisieren*›

relevance /ˈrelɪvəns/, **relevancy** /ˈrelɪvənsɪ/ *n.* Relevanz, die (**to** für); **what ~ does it have to this?** inwiefern ist es dafür relevant?; **be of ~ to sth.** für etw. relevant sein

relevant /ˈrelɪvənt/ *adj.* relevant (**to** für); wichtig ‹*Information, Dokument*›; entsprechend ‹*Formular*›; zuständig ‹*Person*›; **~ to the case** sachdienlich (Amtsspr.); **is this question ~ to the argument?** tut diese Frage etwas zur Sache?

reliability /rɪlaɪəˈbɪlɪtɪ/ *n.*, *no pl.* Zuverlässigkeit, *die*

reliable /rɪˈlaɪəbl/ *adj.* zuverlässig

reliableness /rɪˈlaɪəblnɪs/ ▸**reliability**

reliably /rɪˈlaɪəblɪ/ *adv.* zuverlässig; **I am ~ informed that …:** ich habe aus zuverlässiger Quelle erfahren, dass …

reliance /rɪˈlaɪəns/ *n.* (trust, confidence) Vertrauen, *das* (**in** zu, **on** auf + *Akk.*); (dependence) Abhängigkeit, *die* (**on** von); **she resented her ~ on his money** es ärgerte sie, dass sie auf sein Geld angewiesen war; **have ~ on** *or* **in sb./sth.** zu jmdm./etw. Vertrauen haben; **place much ~ [up]on sb.** großes Vertrauen in jmdn. setzen; **there is little ~ to be placed on sth./sb.** auf etw./jmdn. ist kaum Verlass

reliant /rɪˈlaɪənt/ *adj.* (dependent) **be ~ on sb./sth.** von jmdm./etw. abhängig sein; (for help also) auf jmdn./etw. angewiesen sein

relic /ˈrelɪk/ *n.* **1** (Relig.) Reliquie, *die* **2** (surviving trace or memorial) Überbleibsel, *das* (ugs.); Relikt, *das* **3** (remains, residue) Überrest, *der* **4** (derog./joc.: old or oldfashioned person or thing) Fossil, *das* (fig.); **he is a ~ from the Sixties** er ist noch aus den Sechzigerjahren übrig geblieben

relict /ˈrelɪkt/ *n.* **1** (arch.: widow) Witib, *die* (veralt.) **2** (Biol., Geog., Geol.) Relikt, *das*

relief[1] /rɪˈliːf/ *n.* **1** (alleviation, deliverance) Erleichterung, *die;* **give** *or* **bring [sb.] ~ [from pain]** [jmdm.] [Schmerz]linderung verschaffen *od.* bringen; **it was with great ~ that I heard the news of …:** mit großer Erleichterung habe ich die Nachricht vom … vernommen;

r

breathe *or* **heave a sigh of ~:** erleichtert aufatmen; **it was a ~ to take off his tight shoes/to bump into somebody he knew** es war eine Wohltat für ihn, die engen Schuhe auszuziehen/dass ihm ein Bekannter über den Weg lief; **what a ~!, that's a ~!** da bin ich aber erleichtert! 2 (that which makes a change from monotony) Abwechslung, *die; see also* **comic** **A 3; light² A 1** 3 (assistance) Hilfe, *die;* (financial state assistance) Sozialhilfe, *die; attrib.* Hilfs‹*fond, -organisation, -komitee*›; **~ party** *or* **team** Rettungsmannschaft, *die;* **~ worker** Rettungshelfer, *der*/-helferin, *die;* (in disaster) Katastrophenhelfer, *der*/-helferin, *die;* **go/live on ~:** Fürsorge beantragen/von der Fürsorge leben; **go** *or* **come to sb.'s ~:** jmdm. zu Hilfe eilen *od.* kommen 4 (Brit. Hist.: assistance) Fürsorge, *die* 5 (replacement of person) Ablösung, *die; attrib.* **~ watchman/driver/troops** ablösender Wachmann/Fahrer/ablösende Truppen; **~ sentry** Wachablösung, *die* 6 (Mil.) (reinforcement) Verstärkung, *die;* (raising of siege) Entsatz, *der* 7 (Law: redress) Entschädigung, *die*

relief² *n.* 1 (Art) **works in ~:** Reliefarbeiten; **high/low ~:** Hoch-/Flachrelief, *das* 2 (piece of sculpture) Relief, *das* 3 (appearance of being done in ~) reliefartiges Aussehen; **stand out in strong ~ against sth.** sich scharf gegen etw. abheben; (fig.) in krassem Gegensatz zu etw. stehen; **bring out in [full] ~** (lit. or fig.) deutlich herausarbeiten

relief: ~ agency *n.* Hilfsorganisation, *die;* Hilfswerk, *das;* **~ bus, ~ coach** *ns.* (additional) Entlastungsbus, *der;* (as replacement) Ersatzbus, *der;* **~ effort** *n.* Hilfsmaßnahme, *die;* **~ map** *n.* Reliefkarte, *die;* **~ organization** *n.* Hilfsorganisation, *die;* **~ road** *n.* Entlastungsstraße, *die;* **~ supplies** *n. pl.* Hilfsgüter *Pl.;* **~ worker** *n.* Helfer, *der*/Helferin, *die*

relieve /rɪˈliːv/ *v.t.* 1 (lessen, mitigate) lindern; helfen (+ *Dat.*) ‹*Notleidenden*›; verringern ‹*Dampfdruck, Anspannung*›; unterbrechen ‹*Eintönigkeit*›; erleichtern ‹*Gewissen*›; (remove) abbauen ‹*Anspannung*›; stillen ‹*Schmerzen*›; (remove or lessen monotony of) auflockern; **I am** *or* **feel ~d to hear that ...:** es erleichtert mich zu hören, dass ... 2 (release from duty) ablösen ‹*Wache, Truppen*› 3 **~ sb.** (of task, duty) jmdn. entbinden (**of** von); (of responsibility, load) jmdm. abnehmen (**of** *Akk.*); (from debt) jmdm. erlassen (**from** *Akk.*); (of burden, duty, from sorrow, worry) jmdn. befreien (**of, from** von); **~ sb.'s mind of doubt** jmdm. die Zweifel nehmen 4 **~ sb. of sth.** (joc.: steal from) jmdn. um etw. erleichtern (scherzh.) 5 **~ one's feelings** seinen Gefühlen Luft machen 6 **~ oneself** (empty the bladder or bowels) sich erleichtern (verhüll.) 7 (release from a post) entbinden (**of, from** von); (dismiss) entheben (geh.) (**of, from** *Gen.*); **~ sb. from duty** *or* **of his post** *or* **office** *or* **duties** jmdn. ablösen 8 (Mil.: free from siege) entsetzen (bes. Mil.); befreien

religion /rɪˈlɪdʒn/ *n.* 1 Religion, *die;* **freedom of ~:** Glaubensfreiheit, *die;* **what is your ~?** welcher Religion gehörst du an?; **that's against my ~:** das verstößt gegen meinen Glauben; **no thanks, I won't have a cigarette; it's against my ~** (joc.) nein danke, ich möchte keine Zigarette, ich bin überzeugter Nichtraucher; *see also* **established 3** 2 (recognition of God) Glaube, *der;* **get ~** (coll./joc.) fromm werden 3 (object of devotion or obligation) **he makes a ~ of snooker** Snooker ist ihm heilig; **she makes a ~ of keeping her house clean** es ist ihr eine heilige Pflicht, ihr Haus sauber zu halten (iron.)

religious /rɪˈlɪdʒəs/

A *adj.* 1 (pious) religiös; fromm 2 (concerned with religion) Glaubens‹*freiheit, -eifer*›; Religions‹*freiheit, -unterricht, -kenntnisse*›; religiös ‹*Überzeugung, Zentrum*› 3 (of monastic order) religiös ‹*Orden*›; **~ community** Ordensgemeinschaft, *die;* **~ house** Kloster, *das* 4 (scrupulous) peinlich ‹*Sorgfalt, Genauigkeit, Ordnung*›; **with ~ care** *or* **exactitude** sehr gewissenhaft ‹*arbeiten*›; **pay ~ attention to details** peinlich genau auf Details achten

B *n., pl. same* Ordensmitglied, *das*

religiously /rɪˈlɪdʒəslɪ/ *adv.* 1 (piously, reverently) inbrünstig ‹*beten*›; ehrfürchtig ‹*verehren, niederknien*› 2 (conscientiously, scrupulously) gewissenhaft ‹*beachten, durchsehen, verbessern*›; peinlich genau ‹*sauber machen, verbessern*›

reline /riːˈlaɪn/ *v.t.* neu [aus]füttern ‹*Kleidungsstück*›; neu belegen ‹*Bremse*›; doublieren ‹*Gemälde*›; **~ a hat with a silk lining** einen Hut mit Seide neu ausfüttern

relinquish /rɪˈlɪŋkwɪʃ/ *v.t.* 1 (give up, abandon) aufgeben; ablassen von ‹*Gewohnheit, Glaube*›; zurückziehen ‹*Klage*›; verzichten auf (+ *Akk.*) ‹*Recht, Anspruch, Macht*›; aufgeben ‹*Anspruch, Stelle, Arbeit, Besitz*›; **~ the right/one's claim to sth.** auf sein Recht/seinen Anspruch auf etw. verzichten; **~ sth. to sb.** etw. an jmdn. abtreten; zugunsten von jmdm. auf etw. (*Akk.*) verzichten 2 **~ one's hold** *or* **grip on sb./sth.** jmdn./etw. loslassen 3 (fig.) **~ one's hold on reality** den Bezug zur Realität verlieren; **he has ~ed his hold over** *or* **on her** er hat aufgehört, sie zu bevormunden

relinquishment /rɪˈlɪŋkwɪʃmənt/ *n.* Aufgabe, *die;* (of belief) Ablassen, *das* (**of** von); (of right, power, claim, territory) Verzicht, *der* (**of** auf + *Akk.*)

reliquary /ˈrelɪkwərɪ/ *n.* Reliquiar, *das*

relish /ˈrelɪʃ/

A *n.* 1 (liking) Vorliebe, *die;* **show a real ~ for doing sth.** etw. mit Vorliebe tun; **have a great/no ~ for sth.** viel/nichts für eine Sache übrig haben; **do sth. with [great] ~:** etw. mit [großem] Genuss tun; **he takes [great] ~ in doing sth.** es bereitet ihm [große] Freude, etw. zu tun 2 (condiment) Relish, *das* (Kochk.) 3 (attractive quality) Reiz, *der;* **have no/great ~:** reizlos/sehr verlockend sein; **meat has no ~ when one is ill** man hat keine Lust auf Fleisch, wenn man krank ist

B *v.t.* genießen; reizvoll finden ‹*Gedanke, Vorstellung*›; **I should ~ a lobster and a bottle of wine** was ich jetzt gern hätte, wäre ein Hummer und eine Flasche Wein

relive /riːˈlɪv/ *n.* noch einmal durchleben; **~ one's life** noch einmal leben

reload /riːˈləʊd/ *v.t.* nachladen ‹*Schusswaffe*›; wieder beladen ‹*Lastwagen*›; wieder aufladen ‹*Waren*›; **~ the camera** einen neuen Film einlegen

relocate /riːləˈkeɪt/

A *v.t.* 1 (move to another place) verlegen ‹*Fabrik, Büro*›; versetzen ‹*Angestellten, Fenster, Ventil*› 2 (find again) wieder ausfindig machen ‹*Aufenthaltsort*›; wieder finden ‹*Eingang, Gleise*›

B *v.i.* (settle) sich niederlassen

relocation /riːləˈkeɪʃn/ *n.* (of factory, office) Verlegung, *die;* (of employee) Versetzung, *die;* **~ expenses** Umzugskosten *Pl.*

reluctance /rɪˈlʌktəns/ *n., no pl.* Widerwille, *der;* Abneigung, *die;* **have a [great] ~ to do sth.** etw. nur mit Widerwillen tun; **show some ~ at doing sth.** etw. nur ungern tun

reluctant /rɪˈlʌktənt/ *adj.* unwillig; **be ~ to do sth.** etw. nur ungern *od.* widerstrebend tun; **give sb. ~ assistance** jmdm. nur widerstrebend helfen

reluctantly /rɪˈlʌktəntlɪ/ *adv.* nur ungern; widerstrebend

rely /rɪˈlaɪ/ *v.i.* 1 (have trust) sich verlassen (**[up]on** auf + *Akk.*); **you can always ~ on him to turn up too early** (iron.) du kannst dich darauf verlassen, dass er immer zu früh kommt 2 (be dependent) angewiesen sein (**[up]on** auf + *Akk.*); **[have to] ~ on sb. to help** darauf angewiesen sein, dass jmd. hilft

remade ▸ **remake A**

remain /rɪˈmeɪn/ *v.i.* 1 (be left over) übrig bleiben; **all that ~ed for me to do was to ...:** ich musste *od.* brauchte nur noch ...; **nothing ~s but to thank you all** es bleibt mir nur, Ihnen allen zu danken; **only one match still ~s to be played** es muss nur noch ein Spiel ausgetragen werden; **the few pleasures that ~ to an old man** die wenigen Freuden, die einem alten Mann [noch] bleiben 2 (stay) bleiben; **~ behind** noch dableiben; **~ in sb.'s memory** jmdm. im Gedächtnis bleiben 3 (continue to be) bleiben; **~ true to sb.'s memory** jmdm. ein treues Andenken bewahren; **that** *or* **it ~s to be seen** das bleibt abzuwarten *od.* wird sich zeigen; **the fact ~s that ...:** das ändert nichts an der Tatsache *od.* daran, dass ...; **I ~, yours faithfully, J. Smith** ich verbleibe mit freundlichen Grüßen Ihr J. Smith

remainder /rɪˈmeɪndə(r)/

A *n.* 1 (sb. or sth. left over; also Math.) Rest, *der;* **the ~ of the guests** die übrigen Gäste 2 (remaining stock) Restposten, *der;* **[publisher's] ~:** Restauflage, *die* 3 (Law) Anwartschaft auf die Nacherbschaft 4 (right to succeed to a title or position) Anwartschaft auf die Nachfolge

B *v.t.* (Publishing) [als Restauflage] zu herabgesetztem Preis verkaufen

remaining /rɪˈmeɪnɪŋ/ *adj.* restlich; übrig; **spend one's ~ years ...:** seinen Lebensabend ... verbringen

remains /rɪˈmeɪnz/ *n. pl.* 1 (left-over part) Reste 2 (corpse) sterbliche [Über]reste (verhüll.) 3 (relics) Relikte; Reste; **Roman ~:** Relikte aus der Römerzeit

remake

A /riːˈmeɪk/ *v.t.,* **remade** /riːˈmeɪd/ wieder machen ‹*Bett*›; neu vereinbaren ‹*Verabredung*›; wieder herrichten ‹*Kleidung*›; **~ the booking** neu buchen

B /ˈriːmeɪk/ *n.* (Cinemat.) Remake, *das* (fachspr.); Neuverfilmung, *die;* **do a ~ of sth.** etw. neu verfilmen

remand /rɪˈmɑːnd/

A *v.t.* **~ sb. [in** *or* **into custody]** jmdn. in Untersuchungshaft behalten; **be ~ed in custody/on bail** in Untersuchungshaft bleiben müssen/gegen Kaution aus der Untersuchungshaft entlassen werden

B *n.* **[period of] ~:** Untersuchungshaft, *die;* **place sb. on ~:** jmdn. in Untersuchungshaft nehmen; **be on ~:** in Untersuchungshaft sein; **be held on ~:** in Untersuchungshaft bleiben müssen; *attrib.* **~ prisoner** Untersuchungsgefangene, *der/die*

remand: ~ centre *n.* (Brit.) *Untersuchungsgefängnis für jugendliche Straftäter zwischen 14 und 21 Jahren;* **~ home** *n.* (Brit. Hist.) *Untersuchungsgefängnis für jugendliche Straftäter unter 17 Jahren*

remark /rɪˈmɑːk/

A *v.t.* 1 (say) bemerken (**to** gegenüber) 2 (arch.: observe) gewahr werden

B *v.i.* eine Bemerkung machen (**[up]on** zu, über + *Akk.*)

C *n.* 1 (comment) Bemerkung, *die* (**on** über + *Akk.*); **make a ~:** eine Bemerkung machen (**about, at** über + *Akk.*); **I have a few ~s to make about that** ich habe dazu einiges zu sagen 2 *no art.* (commenting) Kommentar, *der;* **without ~:** kommentarlos; **be worthy of special ~** (formal) besondere Beachtung verdienen; **nothing worthy of ~** (formal) nichts Bemerkenswertes

remarkable /rɪˈmɑːkəbl/ *adj.* 1 (notable) bemerkenswert 2 (extraordinary) außergewöhnlich; **a boy who is ~ for his stupidity** ein Junge von ganz außergewöhnlicher Dummheit

remarkably /rɪˈmɑːkəblɪ/ *adv.* 1 (notably) bemerkenswert 2 (exceptionally) außergewöhnlich

remarriage /riːˈmærɪdʒ/ *n.* Wiederverheiratung, *die*

remarry /riːˈmærɪ/ *v.i. & t.* wieder heiraten

rematch /ˈriːmætʃ/ *n.* Rückkampf, *der*

remediable /rɪˈmiːdɪəbl/ *adj.* behebbar; **be ~:** beseitigt werden können; **is the situation ~?** gibt es einen Ausweg aus der Situation?

remedial /rɪˈmiːdɪəl/ *adj.* 1 (affording a remedy) Heil‹*behandlung, -wirkung*›; (intended to remedy deficiency etc.) rehabilitierend ‹*Maßnahme*›; **take ~ action** Hilfsmaßnahmen ergreifen; **be ~ rather than preventive** eher therapeutischer als vorbeugender Natur sein 2 (Educ.) Förder-; **classes in ~ reading** Förderunterricht im Lesen; **~ education** Förderunterricht, *der*

remedy /ˈremɪdɪ/

A *n.* 1 (cure) [Heil]mittel, *das* (**for** gegen); **cough/herbal ~:** Husten-/Kräutermittel, *das;* **cold/flu ~:** Mittel gegen Erkältung/Grippe; **be past** *or*

beyond ~: unheilbar sein **2** (means of counteracting) [Gegen]mittel, *das* (**for** gegen) **3** (Law: redress) (through civil proceedings) Rechtsbehelf, *der;* (through self-help) Entschädigung, *die*
B *v.t.* beheben ‹*Sprachfehler, Problem*›; ausgleichen ‹*Kurzsichtigkeit*›; retten ‹*Situation*›; **the problem/situation cannot be remedied** das Problem kann nicht behoben werden/die Situation ist nicht zu retten

remember /rɪ'membə(r)/ *v.t.* **1** (keep in memory) denken an (+ *Akk.*); (bring to mind) sich erinnern an (+ *Akk.*); **I've just ~ed what I wanted to tell you** mir ist gerade [wieder] eingefallen, was ich dir sagen wollte; **don't you ~ me?** erinnern Sie sich nicht an mich?; **~ who/where you are!** vergiss nicht, wer/wo du bist; **I can't ~ the word I want** das Wort, das ich brauche, fällt mir gerade nicht ein; **she gave him something to ~ her by** sie gab ihm etwas, das ihn an sie erinnern sollte; (fig.) sie gab ihm einen Denkzettel; **I ~ed to bring the book** ich habe daran gedacht, das Buch mitzubringen; **I can't ~ how to put it back together** ich weiß nicht mehr, wie es wieder zusammengesetzt wird; **do you ~ when the bus leaves?** weißt du noch, wann der Bus abfährt?; **I can never ~ her name** ich kann mir ihren Namen einfach nicht merken; **I distinctly ~ posting the letter** ich erinnere mich genau, dass ich den Brief eingeworfen habe; **if I ~ correctly** (abs.) wenn ich mich recht erinnere; **an evening to ~:** ein unvergesslicher Abend **2** (convey greetings from) grüßen; **~ me to them** grüße sie von mir; **she asked to be ~ed to you** sie lässt dich grüßen **3** **~ oneself** sich zusammennehmen **4** **~ sb. in one's will/prayers** jmdn. in seinem Testament bedenken/in sein Gebet einschließen

remembrance /rɪ'membrəns/ *n.* Gedenken, *das;* **in ~ of sb.** zu jmds. Gedächtnis; zum Gedenken an jmdn.

Remembrance: ~ Day *n.* (Brit.) **1** (Hist.: 11 Nov.) Gedenktag für die Gefallenen der beiden Weltkriege; **2** ▸ **~ Sunday**; **~ Sunday** *n.* (Brit.) ≈ Volkstrauertag, *der*

remind /rɪ'maɪnd/ *v.t.* erinnern (**of** an + *Akk.*); **~ sb. to do sth.** jmdn. daran erinnern, etw. zu tun; **can you ~ me how to do it?** kannst du mal meinem Gedächtnis nachhelfen, wie man das macht?; **that ~s me, ...:** dabei fällt mir ein, ...; **you are ~ed that ...:** beachten Sie bitte, dass ...; **travellers are ~ed that ...:** Reisende werden darauf hingewiesen, dass ...

reminder /rɪ'maɪndə(r)/ *n.* Erinnerung, *die* (**of** an + *Akk.*); (mnemonic) Gedächtnishilfe *od.* -stütze, *die;* (photo etc.) Andenken, *das* (**of** an + *Akk.*); **give sb. a ~ that ...:** jmdn. daran erinnern, dass ...; **serve as/be a ~ of sth.** an etw. (*Akk.*) erinnern; **~ [letter]** Mahnung, *die;* Mahnbrief, *der;* **a gentle ~:** ein zarter Wink

reminisce /remɪ'nɪs/ *v.i.* sich in Erinnerungen (*Dat.*) ergehen (**about** an + *Akk.*)

reminiscence /remɪ'nɪsəns/ *n.* **1** Erinnerung, *die* (**of** an + *Akk.*) **2** *in pl.* (memoirs) [Lebens]erinnerungen *Pl.;* Memoiren *Pl.*

reminiscent /remɪ'nɪsənt/ *adj.* **1** **~ of sth.** an etw. (*Akk.*) erinnernd; **be ~ of sth.** an etw. (*Akk.*) erinnern **2** (nostalgic) **~ mood** nostalgische Stimmung

remiss /rɪ'mɪs/ *adj.* nachlässig (**of** von)

remission /rɪ'mɪʃn/ *n.* **1** (of sins) Vergebung, *die* **2** (of debt, punishment) Erlass, *der* **3** (prison sentence) Straferlass, *der;* **he gained one year's ~:** ihm ist ein Jahr erlassen worden **4** (Med.) Remission, *die;* **go into ~:** remittieren

remit
A /rɪ'mɪt/ *v.t.*, **-tt-** **1** (pardon) vergeben ‹*Sünde, Beleidigung usw.*› **2** (cancel) erlassen ‹*Steuer, Gebühr usw.*›; **~ sb.'s punishment** jmdm. seine Strafe erlassen **3** (refer) weiterleiten ‹*Frage, Angelegenheit*› (**to** an + *Akk.*); (Law) zurückverweisen ‹*Fall, Bericht*› **4** (postpone) verschieben, vertagen (**until** bis, **to** auf + *Akk.*) **5** (send) überweisen ‹*Geld*›
B /'riːmɪt, rɪ'mɪt/ *n.* Aufgabe, *die;* Auftrag, *der*

remittance /rɪ'mɪtəns/ *n.* Überweisung, *die*

remnant /'remnənt/ *n.* **1** Rest, *der;* **only a ~ of the family survives** nur noch wenige Mitglieder der Familie leben; **~s of carpet/wood** Teppich-/Holzreste *Pl.;* **sale of ~s** Restverkauf, *der* **2** (trace) Überrest, *der;* **salvage the ~s of sth.** retten, was von etw. übrig geblieben ist

remodel /riː'mɒdl/ *v.t.*, (Brit.) **-ll-** (lit. or fig.) umgestalten

remold (Amer.) ▸ **remould**

remonstrance /rɪ'mɒnstrəns/ *n.* Protest, *der* (**with, against** gegen)

remonstrate /'remənstreɪt, rɪ'mɒnstreɪt/ *v.i.* protestieren (**against** gegen); **~ with sb.** jmdm. Vorhaltungen machen (**on** wegen)

remonstration ▸ **remonstrance**

remonstrative /'remənstreɪtɪv, rɪ'mɒnstrətɪv/ *adv.* protestierend; Protest‹*brief usw.*›

remorse /rɪ'mɔːs/ *n.* Reue, *die* (**for, about** über + *Akk.*); **without ~:** erbarmungslos

remorseful /rɪ'mɔːsfl/ *adj.* reuig, reuevoll (geh.); reumütig (öfter scherzh.); Reue‹*gefühl*›; **feel ~:** Reue empfinden

remorseless /rɪ'mɔːslɪs/ *adj.* **1** (merciless) erbarmungslos ‹*Grausamkeit, Barbarei*› **2** (relentless) unerbittlich ‹*Schicksal, Logik*›

remorselessly /rɪ'mɔːslɪslɪ/ *adv.* ▸ **remorseless**: erbarmungslos; unerbittlich

remortgage /riː'mɔːgɪdʒ/ *v.t.* nochmals mit einer Hypothek belasten

remote /rɪ'məʊt/ *adj.*, **~r** /rɪ'məʊtə(r)/, **~st** /rɪ'məʊtɪst/ **1** (far apart) entfernt; **be very ~ from each other** sehr weit voneinander entfernt sein; **nations as ~ in culture as X and Y** Völker mit so verschiedenen *od.* unterschiedlichen Kulturen wie X und Y **2** (far off) fern ‹*Vergangenheit, Zukunft, Zeit*›; früh ‹*Altertum*›; abgelegen, (geh.) entlegen ‹*Ort, Gebiet*›; **~ from** (lit. or fig.) weit entfernt von; **~ from the road** weitab von der Straße **3** (not closely related) entfernt, weitläufig ‹*Vorfahr, Nachkomme, Verwandte*› **4** (aloof) unnahbar, distanziert ‹*Person, Art*› **5** (slight) gering ‹*Auswirkung, Chance, Möglichkeit, Vorstellung*›; **I don't have the ~st idea what you're talking about** ich habe nicht die geringste *od.* leiseste Ahnung, wovon du sprichst

remote: ~ con'trol *n.* (of vehicle) Fernlenkung, *die;* Fernsteuerung, *die;* (of apparatus) Fernbedienung, *die;* **~-con'trol[led]** *adj.* ferngesteuert; ferngelenkt; fernbedient ‹*Anlage*›; **~ 'learning** *n.*, *no pl.* (Educ.) Fernstudium, *das;* Fernunterricht, *der*

remotely /rɪ'məʊtlɪ/ *adv.* **1** (distantly) entfernt, weitläufig ‹*verwandt*›; **~ controlled** ▸ **remote-control[led]** **2** (aloofly) distanziert, unnahbar ‹*lächeln, antworten*› **3** (slightly) **they are not [even] ~ alike** sie haben [aber auch] nicht die entfernteste Ähnlichkeit [miteinander]; **it is not [even] ~ possible that ...:** es besteht [aber auch] nicht die geringste Möglichkeit, dass ...; **it is ~ conceivable that ...:** es ist nicht völlig auszuschließen, dass ...

remoteness /rɪ'məʊtnɪs/ *n.*, *no pl.* **1** (seclusion) Abgeschiedenheit, *die;* Abgelegenheit, *die;* (distance) große Entfernung (**from** von) **2** (of relationship) Weitläufigkeit, *die* **3** (separateness) fehlender Zusammenhang (**of ... from** zwischen ... und); **~ from everyday life** Lebensfremdheit, *die*

remould
A /riː'məʊld/ *v.t.* (refashion) ummodeln, umgestalten (**into** zu); (Motor Veh.) runderneuern ‹*Reifen*›
B /'riːməʊld/ *n.* (Motor Veh.) runderneuerter Reifen

remount /riː'maʊnt/
A *v.t.* **1** (ascend again) wieder hinaufsteigen ‹*Leiter*›; **~ one's horse/bicycle** wieder aufs Pferd/Fahrrad steigen **2** (put in fresh mount) wieder aufziehen ‹*Bild*›
B *v.i.* (on horse) wieder aufsitzen; (on bicycle) wieder aufs Fahrrad steigen

removable /rɪ'muːvəbl/ *adj.* abnehmbar; entfernbar ‹*Fleck, Trennwand*›; herausnehmbar ‹*Futter*›; **be ~:** sich entfernen lassen

removal /rɪ'muːvl/ *n.* **1** (taking away) Entfernung, *die;* (of passage from book) Streichung, *die* (**from** aus); (of traces) Beseitigung, *die;* (taking off) **the ~ of the valve from the tyre proved difficult** es war schwierig, das Ventil aus dem Reifen herauszunehmen **2** (dismissal) Entlassung, *die;* **the minister's ~ from office** die Entfernung des Ministers aus dem Amt **3** ▸ **remove A 3**: Beseitigung, *die;* Vertreibung, *die;* Zerstreuung, *die* **4** (transfer) **his ~ to another school** seine Umschulung; **the ~ of the books to the next room** die Umräumung *od.* das Umräumen der Bücher in das andere Zimmer; **his ~ to another department** seine Versetzung in eine andere Abteilung; **his ~ to hospital** seine Einlieferung ins Krankenhaus **5** (transfer of furniture) Umzug, *der;* **'Smith & Co., R~s'** „Smith & Co., Spedition"; **office/factory ~:** Büro-/Werksverlegung, *die*

removal: ~ expenses *n. pl.* Umzugskosten *Pl.;* **~ firm** *n.* Spedition, *die;* **~ man** *n.* Möbelpacker, *der;* **~ van** *n.* Möbelwagen, *der*

remove /rɪ'muːv/
A *v.t.* **1** (take away) entfernen; streichen ‹*Buchpassage*›; wegnehmen, wegräumen ‹*Papiere, Ordner usw.*›; abräumen ‹*Geschirr*›; beseitigen ‹*Spur*›; (take off) abnehmen; ausziehen ‹*Kleidungsstück*›; **she ~d her/the child's coat** sie legte ihren Mantel ab/sie zog dem Kind den Mantel aus; **~ a book from the shelf/the valve from a tyre** ein Buch vom Regal nehmen/das Ventil aus einem Reifen [heraus]nehmen; **~ one's make-up** sich abschminken; **~ the papers/dishes from the table** die Papiere/das Geschirr vom Tisch räumen; **the parents ~d the child from the school** die Eltern nahmen das Kind von der Schule **2** (dismiss) entlassen; **~ sb. from office/his post** jmdn. aus dem Amt/von seinem Posten entfernen **3** (eradicate) beseitigen ‹*Gefahr, Hindernis, Problem, Zweifel*›; vertreiben ‹*Angst*›; zerstreuen ‹*Verdacht, Befürchtungen*› **4** (transfer) **~ a pupil to another school** einen Schüler auf eine andere Schule schicken; **we ~d the books to another room** wir haben die Bücher in ein anderes Zimmer umgeräumt; **~ an employee to another department** einen Angestellten in eine andere Abteilung versetzen **5** (euphem.: kill) beseitigen (verhüll.) **6** *in p.p.* ▸ **cousin** **7** *in p.p.* (remote) **be entirely ~d from politics/everyday life** gar nichts mit Politik zu tun haben/völlig lebensfremd sein
B *v.i.* [um]ziehen; **~ to the country** aufs Land ziehen; **they ~d from here** sie sind [von hier] weggezogen
C *n.* **1** (degree) Schritt, *der;* **be only a few ~s/but one ~ from** nicht mehr weit/nur noch einen Schritt entfernt sein von; **at one ~:** auf Distanz (**from** gegenüber) **2** (distance) Abstand, *der* (**from** zu); **be a far ~ from sth.** weit entfernt von etw. sein

remover /rɪ'muːvə(r)/ *n.* **1** (of paint/varnish/hair/rust) Farb-/Lack-/Haar-/Rostentferner, *der* **2** (removal man) Möbelpacker, *der;* **[firm of] ~s** Spedition[sfirma], *die*

'REM sleep *n.*, *no pl.* REM-Schlaf, *der*

remunerate /rɪ'mjuːnəreɪt/ *v.t.* bezahlen; entlohnen; (recompense) belohnen

remuneration /rɪmjuːnə'reɪʃn/ *n.* Bezahlung, *die;* Entlohnung, *die;* (reward) Belohnung, *die*

remunerative /rɪ'mjuːnərətɪv/ *adj.* lohnend; einträglich

Renaissance /rə'neɪsəns, rə'neɪsɑ̃s, rɪ'neɪsəns/ *n.* **1** *no pl.* (Hist.) Renaissance, *die;* **~ man** der Renaissancemensch **2** **r~** (rebirth) Renaissance, *die;* Wiedergeburt, *die* (geh.)

renal /'riːnl/ *adj.* (Anat., Med.) Nieren-

rename /riː'neɪm/ *v.t.* umbenennen; umtaufen ‹*Schiff*›

renascence ▸ **Renaissance 2**

rend /rend/ **rent** /rent/ *v.t.* (literary) **1** (tear) reißen (**from** aus) **2** (split) spalten ‹*Baum, Gruppe, Land*›; ‹*Schrei:*› zerreißen ‹*Stille*›

render /'rendə(r)/ *v.t.* **1** (make) machen; **the tone ~ed the statement an insult** der Ton machte die Feststellung zu einer Beleidigung **2** (show, give) leisten ‹*Gehorsam, Hilfe*›; erweisen ‹*Ehre, Achtung, Respekt, Dienst*›; bieten, gewähren ‹Schutz›; ~ **a service to sb.,** ~ **sb. a service** jmdm. einen Dienst erweisen; ~ **thanks [un]to God** Gott Dank sagen; ~ **[un]to Caesar the things that are Caesar's** (Bibl.) gebet dem Kaiser, was des Kaisers ist **3** (pay) entrichten ‹*Tribut, Steuern, Abgaben*› **4** (represent, reproduce) wiedergeben, spielen ‹*Musik, Szene, Rolle*›; (translate) übersetzen (**by** mit); ~ **a text into another language** einen Text in eine andere Sprache übertragen **5** (present) ~ **a report to sb.** jmdm. Bericht erstatten; ~ **an annual account [to sb.]** [jmdm.] einen Jahresbericht vorlegen; **account ~ed** (Commerc.) ausgestellte Rechnung **6** (Building: plaster) berappen (fachspr.), verputzen ‹*Mauer*› **7** ~ **[down]** auslassen ‹*Fett*›

(Phrasal verb)

• ~ **'up** *v.t.* (formal) übergeben (**to** *Dat.*) ‹*Festung, Fort, Stadt*›

rendering /'rendərɪŋ/ *n.* **1** Wiedergabe, *die;* (translation) Übersetzung, *die* (**into** in + *Akk.*); (of play also) Aufführung, *die;* (of musical piece, poem also) Vortrag, *der;* (of historical events also) Darstellung, *die;* **give a [superb] ~ of sth.** etw. [meisterhaft] wiedergeben / aufführen / vortragen / darstellen **2** (Building: plastering) Berapp, *der* (fachspr.); Putz, *der*

rendezvous /'rɒndɪvuː, 'rɒndeɪvuː/

A *n., pl. same* /'rɒndɪvuːz, 'rɒndeɪvuːz/ **1** (meeting place) Treffpunkt, *der* **2** (meeting) Rendezvous, *das* (veralt., meist noch scherzh.); Verabredung, *die* **3** (Astronaut.) Rendezvous, *das*

B *v.i., pres.* **~es** /'rɒndɪvuːz, 'rɒndeɪvuːz/, *p.t. & p.p.* **~ed** /'rɒndɪvuːd, 'rɒndeɪvuːd/, *pres. p.* **~ing** /'rɒndɪvuːɪŋ, 'rɒndeɪvuːɪŋ/ sich treffen

rendition /ren'dɪʃn/ ▸**rendering 1**

renegade /'renɪgeɪd/

A *n.* Abtrünnige, *der/die;* Renegat, *der*/Renegatin, *die* (abwertend)

B *adj.* abtrünnig

renege, renegue /rɪ'niːg, rɪ'neɪg/ *v.i.* **1** (Amer. Cards) nicht bedienen **2** ~ **[on an agreement/a promise]** [eine Vereinbarung/ein Versprechen] nicht einhalten

renegotiate /riːnɪ'gəʊʃɪeɪt/ *v.t.* neu aushandeln; erneut verhandeln über (+ *Akk.*)

renew /rɪ'njuː/ *v.t.* **1** (restore, regenerate, recover) erneuern; wieder wecken *od.* wachrufen ‹*Gefühle*›; wiederherstellen ‹*Kraft*›; ~ **sb.'s energy** jmdm. neue Energie geben; **feel spiritually ~ed** sich wie neugeboren fühlen **2** (replace) erneuern; auffüllen ‹*Vorrat*›; ausbessern ‹*Kleidungsstück*› **3** (begin again) erneuern ‹*Bekanntschaft*›; wieder aufnehmen ‹*Kampf, Korrespondenz*›; fortsetzen ‹*Angriff, Bemühungen*›; **~ed exhortations/outbreaks of rioting** erneute Ermahnungen/Krawalle **4** (repeat) wiederholen ‹*Aussage, Beschuldigung*› **5** (extend) erneuern, verlängern ‹*Vertrag, Genehmigung, Ausweis etc.*›; ~ **a library book** ‹*Bibliothekar/Benutzer:*› ein Buch [aus der Bücherei] verlängern/verlängern lassen

renewable /rɪ'njuːəbl/ *adj.* regenerationsfähig ‹*Energiequelle*›; verlängerbar ‹*Vertrag, Genehmigung, Ausweis, Visum*›

renewal /rɪ'njuːəl/ *n.* **1** Erneuerung, *die;* (of contract, passport, etc. also) Verlängerung, *die;* (of attack) Wiederaufnahme, *die;* (of library book) Verlängerung der Leihfrist **2** **[urban]** ~: [Stadt-]sanierung, *die*

rennet /'renɪt/ *n.* Lab, *das*

renounce /rɪ'naʊns/

A *v.t.* **1** (abandon) verzichten auf (+ *Akk.*) **2** (refuse to recognize) aufkündigen ‹*Vertrag, Freundschaft*›; aufgeben ‹*Grundsatz, Plan, Versuch*›; leugnen ‹*jmds. Autorität*›; verstoßen ‹*Person*›; ~ **the world** der Welt (*Dat.*) entsagen (geh.); ~ **the devil/one's faith** dem Teufel/seinem Glauben abschwören

B *v.i.* **1** (Law) offiziell seinen Verzicht erklären **2** (Cards) nicht bedienen

renouncement /rɪ'naʊnsmənt/ ▸**renunciation 1**

renovate /'renəveɪt/ *v.t.* renovieren ‹*Gebäude*›; restaurieren ‹*Möbel, Gemälde*›

renovation /renə'veɪʃn/ *n.* Renovierung, *die;* (of furniture etc.) Restaurierung, *die*

renown /rɪ'naʊn/ Renommee, *das;* Ansehen, *das;* **of [great]** ~: von hohem Ansehen; sehr berühmt ‹*Stadt*›

renowned /rɪ'naʊnd/ *adj.* berühmt (**for** wegen, für); **he is ~ as a portrait painter** er hat als Porträtmaler einen großen Namen

rent¹ ▸**rend**

rent² /rent/ *n.* (tear, cleft) Riss, *der* (auch fig.); (cleft also) Spalte, *die;* ~ **in the clouds** Wolkenspalt, *der*

rent³ /rent/

A *n.* (for house, flat, etc.) Miete, *die;* (for land) Pacht, *die;* **have a house free of ~**: ein Haus mietfrei bewohnen; **for** ~ (Amer.) ‹*Haus, Wohnung etc.*› zu vermieten; ‹*Land*› zu verpachten; ‹*Kostüme*› zu verleihen

B *v.t.* **1** (use) mieten ‹*Haus, Wohnung usw.*›; pachten ‹*Land*›; mieten ‹*Auto, Gerät*› **2** (let) vermieten ‹*Haus, Wohnung, Auto etc.*› (**to** *Dat.*, an + *Akk.*); verpachten ‹*Land*› (**to** *Dat.*, an + *Akk.*)

C *v.i.* ‹*Haus, Wohnung, Auto usw.:*› vermietet werden; ‹*Land:*› verpachtet werden

(Phrasal verb)

• ~ **'out** *v.t.* ▸**rent³ B 2**

rentable /'rentəbl/ *adj.* ▸**rent³ B**: zu [ver]mieten/[ver]pachten *präd.;* zu [ver]mietend/[ver]pachtend *attr.*

rent: **~-a-car** *attrib. adj.* **~-a-car business/company/service** Autoverleih, *der;* **~-a-crowd** *n.* bestellter Haufen; (claque) Claque, *die*

rental /'rentl/ *n.* **1** (from houses etc.) Miete, *die;* (from land) Pacht, *die* **2** ▸**rent³ B**: Mietung, *die;* Pachtung, *die;* (letting) Vermietung, *die;* Verpachtung, *die;* **car ~**: Autoverleih, *der;* **the property is on ~**: der Besitz ist verpachtet *od.* in Pacht **3** (Amer.: thing rented) Mietgegenstand, *der;* Mietsache, *die* (Rechtsw.)

'rental library *n.* (Amer.) (kommerzielle) Leihbücherei

rent: **~-a-mob** *n.* bestellter Haufen von Randalierern; **~-a-van** *attrib. adj.* **~-a-van business/company/service** Transportervermietung, *die;* ~ **boy** *n.* (coll.) Strichjunge, *der* (salopp); ~ **collector** *n.: jmd., der für den Hausbesitzer die Miete kassiert;* ~ **control** *n.* ≈ Mietpreisbindung, *die;* **~-controlled** *adj.* mietpreisgebunden; **~-free** *adj.* mietfrei; ~ **officer** *n.: Beamter/Beamtin der kommunalen Beratungsstelle für mietrechtliche Fragen;* ~ **rebate** *n.* Mietermäßigung, *die;* ~ **tribunal** *n.* Mietgericht, *das*

renumber /riː'nʌmbə(r)/ *v.t.* umnummerieren; neu beziffern *od.* benummern

renunciation /rɪnʌnsɪ'eɪʃn/ *n.* **1** ▸**renounce A 1, 2**: Verzicht, *der;* Aufkündigung, *die;* Aufgabe, *die;* Leugnung, *die;* Verstoßung, *die* **2** (self-denial) Selbstverleugnung, *die*

reoccupation /riːɒkjʊ'peɪʃn/ *n.* Wiederbesetzung, *die;* (of house etc.) Wiederübernahme, *die*

reoccupy /riː'ɒkjʊpaɪ/ *v.t.* wieder besetzen (Milit.) ‹*Ort, Stellung*›; wieder übernehmen ‹*Haus, Wohnung*›

reopen /riː'əʊpn/

A *v.t.* **1** (open again) wieder öffnen; wieder aufmachen; wieder eröffnen ‹*Geschäft, Lokal usw.*› **2** (return to) wieder aufnehmen ‹*Diskussion, Verhandlung, Feindseligkeiten*›; wieder aufnehmen, wieder aufrollen ‹*Fall*›; zurückkommen auf (+ *Akk.*) ‹*Angelegenheit*›

B *v.i.* ‹*Geschäft, Lokal usw.:*› wieder öffnen; wieder eröffnet werden; ‹*Verhandlungen, Unterricht:*› wieder beginnen

reorder /riː'ɔːdə(r)/

A *v.t.* **1** (Commerc.: order again) nachbestellen ‹*Ware*›; (after theft, loss) neu bestellen **2** (rearrange) umordnen; neu ordnen; (on list) umstellen ‹*Namen*›; neu festlegen ‹*Reihenfolge*›

B *n.* (Commerc.) Nachbestellung, *die*

reorganisation, reorganise ▸**reorganiz-**

reorganization /riːɔːgənaɪ'zeɪʃn/ *n.* Umorganisation, *die;* (of text) Neugliederung, *die;* (of time, work) Neueinteilung, *die*

reorganize /riː'ɔːgənaɪz/ *v.t.* umorganisieren; neu einteilen ‹*Zeit, Arbeit*›; neu gliedern ‹*Aufsatz, Referat*›

reorient /riː'ɔːrɪent, riː'ɒrɪent/, **reorientate** /riː'ɒrɪənteɪt, riː'ɔːrɪənteɪt/ *v.t.* neu ausrichten ‹*Programm, Politik, Denken, Handeln*›; ~ *or* **reorientate a person** einem Menschen eine neue Orientierung geben

reorientation /riːɒrɪən'teɪʃn, riːɔːrɪən'teɪʃn/ *n.* Neuorientierung, *die*

rep¹ /rep/ *n.* (Textiles) Rips, *der*

rep² *n.* ▸ⓘ **p. 1260** (coll.: representative) Vertreter, *der*/Vertreterin, *die*

rep³ *n.* (Theatre coll.) Repertoiretheater, *das;* **be in ~**: an einem Repertoiretheater spielen

Rep. *abbr.* (Amer.) **1** = **Representative** Abg. **2** = **Republican** Rep.

repaginate /riː'pædʒɪneɪt/ *v.t.* neu paginieren

repaid ▸**repay**

repaint

A /riː'peɪnt/ *v.t.* neu streichen ‹*Gebäude, Wand, Tür usw.*›; neu lackieren ‹*Auto*›

B /'riːpeɪnt/ *n.* **the door needs a ~**: die Tür braucht einen neuen Anstrich; **give sth. a ~**: etw. neu streichen/lackieren

repair¹ /rɪ'peə(r)/

A *v.t.* **1** (restore, mend) reparieren; ausbessern ‹*Kleidung, Straße*› **2** (remedy) wieder gutmachen ‹*Schaden, Fehler*›; beheben ‹*Schaden, Mangel*›

B *n.* **1** (restoring, renovation) Reparatur, *die;* **be beyond ~**: sich nicht mehr reparieren lassen; **be in need of ~**: reparaturbedürftig sein; ‹*Schuhe:*› repariert werden müssen; **be under ~** ‹*Maschine, Gerät, Fahrzeug:*› in Reparatur sein; **the road is under ~**: an der Straße werden gerade Bauarbeiten ausgeführt; **closed for ~s** wegen Reparaturarbeiten geschlossen; **'~s [done] while you wait'** „Reparaturschnelldienst" **2** *no pl., no art.* (condition) **be in good/bad ~** *or* **in a good/bad state of ~**: in gutem/schlechtem Zustand sein

repair² *v.i.* (formal: go) sich begeben (**to** nach/zu/in + *Akk.*) (Papierdt.)

repairable /rɪ'peərəbl/ *adj.* reparabel; **be ~** *or* **in a ~ state** zu reparieren sein

repairer /rɪ'peərə(r)/ *n.* (of watches/shoes) Uhr-/Schuhmacher, *der;* **take sth. to the ~'s** etw. zur Reparatur bringen

repair: **~man** *n.* (of mechanism) Mechaniker, *der;* (in house) Handwerker, *der;* ~ **shop** *n.* Reparaturwerkstatt, *die*

repaper /riː'peɪpə(r)/ *v.t.* neu tapezieren

reparation /repə'reɪʃn/ *n.* **1** (making amends) Wiedergutmachung, *die* **2** (compensation) Entschädigung, *die;* **~s** (for war damage) Reparationen; **make ~ [for sth.]** [für etw.] Ersatz leisten

repartee /repɑː'tiː/ *n.* **1** (skill in making retorts) Schlagfertigkeit, *die* **2** (conversation) von [Geist und] Schlagfertigkeit sprühende Unterhaltung

repast /rɪ'pɑːst/ *n.* (formal) Mahl, *das* (geh.)

repatriate /riː'pætrɪeɪt/ *v.t.* repatriieren

repatriation /riːpætrɪ'eɪʃn/ *n.* Repatriierung, *die*

repay /riː'peɪ/

A *v.t.,* **repaid** /riː'peɪd/ **1** (pay back) zurückzahlen ‹*Schulden usw.*›; erstatten ‹*Spesen*›; **if you'll lend me £1, I'll ~ you next week** wenn du mir ein Pfund leihst, zahle *od.* gebe ich es dir nächste Woche zurück **2** (return) erwidern ‹*Besuch, Gruß, Freundlichkeit*› **3** (give in recompense) ~ **sb. for sth.** jmdm. etw. vergelten **4** (requite) ~ **efforts** *etc.* für Bemühungen *usw.* entschädigen

B *v.i.,* **repaid** Rückzahlungen leisten

repayable /riː'peɪəbl/ *adj.* rückzahlbar; **be ~ at the end of the year** zum Jahresende zurückgezahlt werden müssen

repayment /riː'peɪmənt/ *n.* **1** (paying back) Rückzahlung, *die;* **she's having trouble with the ~s** sie hat Schwierigkeiten mit der Rückzahlung **2** (reward) Lohn, *der* (**for** für)

re'payment mortgage *n.* Tilgungshypothek, *die*

repeal /rɪ'pi:l/
A *v.t.* aufheben ‹*Gesetz, Erlass usw.*›
B *n.* Aufhebung, *die*

repeat /rɪ'pi:t/
A *n.* **1** Wiederholung, *die;* (Radio, TV also) Wiederholungssendung, *die;* **do a ~ of sth.** etw. wiederholen; **there will be a ~ of this programme** diese Sendung wird wiederholt **2** (Commerc.) Nachbestellung, *die* **3** (Mus.) (passage) Wiederholung, *die;* (sign) Wiederholungszeichen, *das* **4** (repeated pattern) Rapport, *der* (bes. Kunstwiss.)
B *v.t.* **1** (say, do, broadcast again) wiederholen; **'not, ~ 'not** auf [gar] keinen Fall; unter [gar] keinen Umständen; **'nobody, [I] ~ 'nobody** niemand, ich betone, niemand; (Radio) niemand, ich wiederhole, niemand; **please ~ after me: …:** sprich/sprecht/sprechen Sie mir bitte nach: … **2** (recite) aufsagen ‹*Gedicht, Strophe, Text*› **3** (report) weitererzählen (**to** *Dat.*); **do you want me to ~ the conversation?** soll ich dir das Gespräch wiedergeben?
C *v.i.* **1** (Math.: recur) ‹*Zahl:*› periodisch sein **2** (Amer.: vote more than once) seine Stimme mehrmals abgeben
D *v. refl.* **~ oneself/itself** sich wiederholen

repeated /rɪ'pi:tɪd/ *adj.* wiederholt; (several) mehrere; **make ~ efforts to…:** wiederholt *od.* mehrfach versuchen, zu…

repeatedly /rɪ'pi:tɪdlɪ/ *adv.* mehrmals

repeater /rɪ'pi:tə(r)/ *n.* **1** (Horol.) Repetieruhr, *die* **2** (Arms) Repetiergewehr, *das;* Mehrlader, *der*

repeating 'decimal *n.* (Math.) periodische Dezimalzahl

repeat: ~ of'fender *n.* Wiederholungstäter, *der*/-täterin, *die;* **~ 'order** *n.* (Commerc.) Nachbestellung, *die;* **~ per'formance** *n.* Wiederholungsvorstellung, *die* (Theater); (of music) Wiederholungskonzert, *das;* **~ pre'scription** *n.* (Brit.) Folgerezept, *das*

repêchage /'repəʃɑ:ʒ/ *n.* (esp. Rowing) Hoffnungslauf, *der;* (Fencing) Trostrunde, *die*

repel /rɪ'pel/ *v.t.*, **-ll-** **1** (drive back) abwehren ‹*Feind, Angriff, Annäherungsversuch, Schlag usw.*›; widerstehen (+ *Dat.*) ‹*Versuchung*›; abstoßen ‹*Feuchtigkeit, elektrische Ladung, Magnetpol*› **2** (be repulsive to) abstoßen

repellent /rɪ'pelənt/
A *adj.* **1** (repugnant) abstoßend **2** (repelling) **water-~:** Wasser abstoßend *od.* (seltener) abweisend; **mosquito ~:** Mückenschutz‹*mittel usw.*›
B *n.* **[insect] ~:** Insektenschutzmittel, *das*

repent /rɪ'pent/
A *v.i.* bereuen (**of** *Akk.*)
B *v.t.* bereuen

repentance /rɪ'pentəns/ *n.* Reue, *die*

repentant /rɪ'pentənt/ *adj.* reuig, reuevoll (geh.); reumütig (öfter scherzh.); **a ~ sinner** ein reuiger Sünder

repercussion /ri:pə'kʌʃn/ *n. usu. in pl.* Auswirkung, *die* (**[up]on** auf + *Akk.*)

repertoire /'repətwɑ:(r)/ *n.* **1** (Mus., Theatre) Repertoire, *das* (**of** an + *Dat.*, von) **2** (complete list) Spektrum, *das*

repertory /'repətərɪ/ *n.* **1** ▸**repertoire** **2** (Theatre) Repertoiretheater, *das;* **play/be in ~:** an einem Repertoiretheater spielen

'repertory company *n.* Repertoiretheater, *das*

répétiteur /repetɪ'tɜ:(r)/ *n.* (Mus., Theatre) [Kor]repetitor, *der*

repetition /repɪ'tɪʃn/ *n.* Wiederholung, *die*

repetitious /repɪ'tɪʃəs/ *adj.* sich immer wiederholend *attr.;* **his style is ~:** er wiederholt sich immer

repetitive /rɪ'petɪtɪv/ *adj.* eintönig; **sth. is ~:** etw. bietet keine Abwechslung

repetitive 'strain injury *n.* chronisches Überlastungssyndrom

rephrase /ri:'freɪz/ *v.t.* umformulieren; **I'll ~ that** ich will es anders ausdrücken

repine /rɪ'paɪn/ *v.i.* (literary) hadern (geh.) (**at** mit)

replace /rɪ'pleɪs/ *v.t.* **1** (put back in place) (vertically) zurückstellen; wieder einordnen ‹*Karteikarte*›; (horizontally) zurücklegen; [wieder] auflegen ‹*Telefonhörer*›; **I ~d the key in the lock** ich steckte den Schlüssel wieder ins Schloss; **he ~d the fish in the tank** er setzte den Fisch wieder in den Tank **2** (take place of, provide substitute for) ersetzen; **~ A with** *or* **by B** A durch B ersetzen **3** (renew) ersetzen ‹*Gestohlenes usw.*›; austauschen, auswechseln ‹*Maschinen[teile] usw.*›; auswechseln ‹*Glühbirne*›; auffüllen ‹*Vorrat*›

replaceable /rɪ'pleɪsəbl/ *adj.* ersetzbar ‹*Person, Verlorenes usw.*›; austauschbar, auswechselbar ‹*Maschinenteil usw.*›

replacement /rɪ'pleɪsmənt/ *n.* **1** (putting back) ▸**replace 1**: Zurückstellen, *das;* Zurücklegen, *das;* Wiedereinordnen, *das;* Auflegen, *das* **2** (provision of substitute for) Ersatz, *der;* Ersetzen, *das; attrib.* Ersatz-; **the ~ of the blood loss** der Ausgleich des Blutverlusts **3** (substitute) Ersatz, *der;* **~ [part]** Ersatzteil, *das;* **~s** (staff, troops) Ersatz, *der;* **my ~:** mein Nachfolger/meine Nachfolgerin

replant /ri:'plɑ:nt/ *v.t.* **1** (plant again) umpflanzen **2** (provide with new plants) neu bepflanzen; **~ a forest** einen Wald wieder aufforsten

replay
A /ri:'pleɪ/ *v.t.* wiederholen ‹*Spiel*›; nochmals abspielen ‹*Tonband usw.*›
B /'ri:pleɪ/ *n.* Wiederholung, *die;* (match) Wiederholungsspiel, *das*

replenish /rɪ'plenɪʃ/ *v.t.* [wieder] auffüllen

replenishment /rɪ'plenɪʃmənt/ *n.* **1** (renewing) (of supplies) Auffüllung, *die;* Wiederauffüllen, *das;* (of stocks) Ergänzung, *die* **2** (fresh supply) **~s** Nachschub, *der*

replete /rɪ'pli:t/ *adj.* **1** (filled) reich (**with** an + *Dat.*); **a story ~ with drama** eine Geschichte voller Dramatik **2** (gorged) satt

repleteness /rɪ'pli:tnɪs/ *n., no pl.* Sattheit, *die;* **feeling of ~:** Völlegefühl, *das*

repletion /rɪ'pli:ʃn/ *n.* Sättigung, *die;* **eat to ~:** sich satt essen

replica /'replɪkə/ *n.* Nachbildung, *die;* (of work of art) Kopie, *die;* (by original artist) Replik, *die;* (esp. on smaller scale) Modell, *das;* **he is a ~ of his brother** er ist das Ebenbild (geh.) seines Bruders

replicate /'replɪkeɪt/
A *v.t.* nachbilden; replizieren (Kunstwiss.); (Biol.) replizieren
B *v.i.* (Biol.) sich reproduzieren

replication /replɪ'keɪʃn/ *n.* **1** Nachbildung, *die* **2** (Biol.) Replikation, *die*

reply /rɪ'plaɪ/
A *v.i.* **~ [to sb./sth.]** [jmdm./auf etw. (*Akk.*)] antworten; **~ [to the gunfire]** das Feuer erwidern
B *v.t.* **~ that …** antworten, dass …
C *n.* **1** Antwort, *die* (**to** auf + *Akk.*); **my ~ to him** die Antwort, die ich ihm gegeben habe/geben werde *usw.;* **in/by way of ~:** als Antwort; **in ~ to your letter** in Beantwortung Ihres Schreibens (Amtsspr.); **what did he say in ~?** was hat er darauf geantwortet?; **make [a] ~** (formal) [eine] Antwort geben **2** (Law) Replik, *die*

reply: ~ card *n.* Antwortkarte, *die;* **~ coupon** *n.* (Post) internationaler Antwortschein; **~-paid** *adj.* **~-paid telegram** RP-Telegramm, *das;* **~-paid envelope** Freiumschlag, *der*

repoint /ri:'pɔɪnt/ *v.t.* (Building) neu ausfugen *od.* verfugen

repopulate /ri:'pɒpjʊleɪt/ *v.t.* neu besiedeln

report /rɪ'pɔ:t/
A *v.t.* **1** (relate) berichten/(in writing) einen Bericht schreiben über (+ *Akk.*) ‹*Ereignis usw.*›; (state formally also) melden; **sb. is/was ~ed to be …:** jmd. soll … sein/gewesen sein; **she ~ed all the details to me** sie berichtete mir [über] alle Einzelheiten; **it is ~ed from Buckingham Palace that …:** aus dem Buckingham-Palast wird gemeldet *od.* berichtet, dass …; **nothing to ~:** keine besonderen Vorkommnisse; **~ sb. missing** jmdn. als vermisst melden; **the papers ~ed him [as] dead** laut Zeitungsberichten war er tot; **~ progress on** (Brit.) einen Tätigkeitsbericht abgeben über (+ *Akk.*) **2** (repeat) übermitteln (**to** *Dat.*) ‹*Botschaft*›; wiedergeben (**to** *Dat.*) ‹*Worte, Sinn*›; **he is ~ed as having said that …:** er soll gesagt haben, dass … **3** (name or notify to authorities) melden (**to** *Dat.*); (for prosecution) anzeigen (**to** bei) **4** (present) **~ oneself [to sb.]** sich [bei jmdm.] melden; **~ oneself present** (Mil.) sich zur Stelle melden
B *v.i.* **1** Bericht erstatten (**on** über + *Akk.*); berichten (**on** über + *Akk.*); **he ~s on financial affairs for the 'Guardian'** er schreibt für den Wirtschaftsteil des „Guardian" **2** (present oneself) sich melden (**to** bei); **~ for duty** sich zum Dienst melden; **~ sick** sich krankmelden **3** (be responsible) **~ to sb.** jmdm. unterstehen **4** (give report) **~ well/badly of sb./sth.** Gutes/Schlechtes *od.* nichts Gutes über jmdn./etw. berichten; (Radio/Telev.) **Mark Tally ~ing [from Delhi]** Mark Tally berichtet [aus Delhi]
C *n.* **1** (account) Bericht, *der* (**on, about** über + *Akk.*); (in newspaper etc. also) Reportage, *die* (**on** über + *Akk.*); **make a ~:** einen Bericht abfassen; **an official ~ on price trends** ein Gutachten über die Preisentwicklung **2** (Sch.) Zeugnis, *das* **3** (sound) Knall, *der* **4** (rumour) Gerücht, *das;* **the ~ goes that …:** man sagt, dass …; **know sth. only by ~:** etw. nur vom Hörensagen kennen/wissen

Phrasal verb
- **~ 'back** *v.i.* **1** (present oneself again) sich zurückmelden (**for** zu) **2** (give a report) Bericht erstatten (**to** *Dat.*)

reportage /repɔ:'tɑ:ʒ/ *n.* Reportage, *die*

re'port card *n.* (Amer.) Zeugnis, *das*

reportedly /rɪ'pɔ:tɪdlɪ/ *adv.* wie verlautet; **they have ~ made huge profits** sie sollen sehr große Gewinne gemacht haben

reported 'speech *n.* (Ling.) indirekte Rede

reporter /rɪ'pɔ:tə(r)/ *n.* ▸**i** **p. 1260** (Radio, Telev., Journ.) Reporter, *der*/Reporterin, *die;* Berichterstatter, *der*/-erstatterin, *die*

re'port stage *n.* (Brit. Parl.) *Unterhausdebatte über Gesetzentwurf nach dessen Beratung im Ausschuss*

repose /rɪ'pəʊz/ (literary)
A *n.* **1** (rest, respite) Ruhe, *die;* **in ~:** ruhend **2** (composure) Gelassenheit, *die*
B *v.i.* **1** (lie) ruhen; (joc.: be situated) liegen; sich befinden **2** (be supported) beruhen (**[up]on** auf + *Dat.*)
C *v.t.* (rest) ausruhen

reposition /ri:pə'zɪʃn/ *v.t.* umstellen; verstellen ‹*Teil*›

repository /rɪ'pɒzɪtərɪ/ *n.* **1** (receptacle) Behälter, *der* **2** (store) Lager, *das;* (fig.) (book etc.) Fundgrube, *die* (**of** für); (person) Quelle, *die* (**of** für)

repossess /ri:pə'zes/ *v.t.* wiedergewinnen ‹*Gebiet usw.*›; wieder in Besitz nehmen ‹*Waren*›; ‹*Bausparkasse:*› beschlagnahmen lassen ‹*Haus*›

repossession /ri:pə'zeʃn/ *n.* (of territories etc.) Wiedergewinnung, *die;* (of goods) Wiederinbesitznahme, *die;* (of house) Erwirkung der Beschlagnahme

repot /ri:'pɒt/ *v.t.*, **-tt-** umtopfen

repp ▸**rep**[1]

reprehend /reprɪ'hend/ *v.t.* tadeln; rügen

reprehensible /reprɪ'hensɪbl/ *adj.* tadelnswert; sträflich; **be morally ~:** moralisch zu verurteilen sein

reprehensibly /reprɪ'hensɪblɪ/ *adv.* tadelnswert; sträflich

represent /reprɪ'zent/ *v.t.* **1** (symbolize) verkörpern **2** (denote, depict, present) darstellen (**as** als); (Theatre also) spielen; **the symbol x ~s guttural sounds** das Zeichen x steht für Gutturallaute; **I am not what you ~ me as** *or* **to be** ich bin nicht so, wie du mich hinstellst **3** (correspond to) entsprechen (+ *Dat.*) **4** (be specimen of, act for) vertreten

re-present /ri:prɪ'zent/ *v.t.* erneut vorlegen

representation /reprɪzen'teɪʃn/ *n.* **1** (depicting, image) Darstellung, *die* **2** (acting for sb.) Vertretung, *die* **3** (protest) Protest, *der;* **make ~s to sb.** bei jmdm. Protest einlegen

representational /reprɪzen'teɪʃənl/ *adj.* 1 gegenständlich ‹*Kunst*› 2 ▸**representative B 3**

representative /reprɪ'zentətɪv/

A *n.* 1 ▸ⓘ **p. 1260** (member, successor, agent, deputy) Vertreter, *der*/Vertreterin, *die;* (firm's agent, deputy also) Repräsentant, *der*/Repräsentantin, *die;* **there were no ~s of the family at the funeral** die Familie war bei der Beerdigung nicht vertreten; **High R~ of the CFSP** (EU) Hoher Vertreter/Hohe Vertreterin für die GASP 2 **R~** (Amer. Polit.) Abgeordneter/Abgeordnete im Repräsentantenhaus; **House of R~s** Repräsentantenhaus, *das*

B *adj.* 1 (typical) repräsentativ (**of** für); **a ~ modern building** ein typisches modernes Gebäude; **Charles II was fully ~ of his age** Charles II war ein typischer Vertreter seiner Zeit 2 (consisting of deputies) Abgeordneten‹*versammlung, -kammer usw.*› 3 (Polit.: based on representation) repräsentativ; Repräsentativ‹*system, -verfassung*›; **~ government/institutions** parlamentarische Regierung/Institution 4 **be ~ of** (portray) darstellen; (symbolize) symbolisieren; ‹*Person:*› verkörpern 5 (that presents sth. to the mind) **~ faculty/power** Vorstellungsvermögen, *das*/-kraft, *die*

> **House of Representatives**
>
> Das Unterhaus des amerikanischen **Congress.** Es gibt 435 **Representatives** (Abgeordnete), die alle zwei Jahre gewählt werden. Proportional zu seiner Bevölkerung hat jeder Staat eine bestimmte Anzahl von Abgeordneten. Das *House of Representatives* bringt Gesetzesvorlagen ein und verabschiedet alle neuen Gesetze.

> **Representative**
>
> Ein Mitglied des amerikanischen **House of Representatives.**

representatively /reprɪ'zentətɪvlɪ/ *adv.* repräsentativ

representativeness /reprɪ'zentətɪvnɪs/ *n., no pl.* Repräsentanz, *die*

repress /rɪ'pres/ *v.t.* 1 unterdrücken ‹*Aufruhr, Gefühle, Lachen usw.*› 2 (Psych.) verdrängen ‹*Gefühle*› (**from** aus)

repressed /rɪ'prest/ *adj.* unterdrückt; (Psych.) verdrängt

repression /rɪ'preʃn/ *n.* Unterdrückung, *die;* (Psych.) Verdrängung, *die*

repressive /rɪ'presɪv/ *adj.* repressiv; **~ measures** Repressivmaßnahmen

reprieve /rɪ'pri:v/

A *v.t.* **~ sb.** (postpone execution) jmdm. Strafaufschub gewähren; (remit execution) jmdn. begnadigen; (fig.) verschonen

B *n.* Strafaufschub, *der* (**of** für); Begnadigung, *die;* (fig.) Gnadenfrist, *die*

reprimand /'reprɪmɑ:nd/

A *n.* Tadel, *der;* Verweis, *der*

B *v.t.* tadeln; einen Verweis erteilen (+ *Dat.*)

reprint

A /ri:'prɪnt/ *v.t.* 1 (print again) wieder abdrucken 2 (make reprint of) nachdrucken

B /'ri:prɪnt/ *n.* 1 (book reprinted) Nachdruck, *der* 2 **how big was the ~?** wie viel Exemplare wurden nachgedruckt?; **it has had ten ~s** es ist zehnmal nachgedruckt worden 3 (article printed separately) Sonderdruck, *der*

reprisal /rɪ'praɪzl/ *n.* Vergeltungsakt, *der* (**for** gegen)

reprise /rə'pri:z/ *n.* (Mus.) Reprise, *die*

repro /'ri:prəʊ/

A *n.* (Printing) Repro, *das;* **~ [proof]** Reproabzug, *der*

B *adj.* **it's only ~:** es ist nur eine Reproduktion

reproach /rɪ'prəʊtʃ/

A *v.t.* **~ sb.** jmdm. Vorwürfe machen; **~ sb. with** *or* **for sth.** jmdm. etw. vorwerfen *od.* zum Vorwurf machen; **~ sb. bitterly for having done sth.** jmdm. bittere Vorwürfe machen, dass er etw. getan hat; **have nothing to ~ oneself for** *or* **with** sich (*Dat.*) nichts vorzuwerfen haben

B *n.* 1 (rebuke) Vorwurf, *der;* **be above** *or* **beyond ~:** über jeden Vorwurf erhaben sein; **be used as a term of ~:** abwertend gebraucht werden; **look of ~:** vorwurfsvoller Blick 2 (disgrace) Schande, *die* (**to** für)

reproachful /rɪ'prəʊtʃfl/ *adj.*, **reproachfully** /rɪ'prəʊtʃfəlɪ/ *adv.* vorwurfsvoll

reprobate /'reprəbeɪt/

A *n.* Halunke, *der*

B *adj.* verkommen

reprocess /ri:'prəʊses/ *v.t.* wieder aufbereiten; **~ing plant** Wiederaufbereitungsanlage, *die*

reproduce /ri:prə'dju:s/

A *v.t.* 1 wiedergeben; reproduzieren (Druckw.) ‹*Bilder usw.*› 2 **~ oneself** sich fortpflanzen; sich vermehren 3 (Biol.: form afresh) neu bilden ‹*Organe, Gliedmaßen usw.*›

B *v.i.* 1 (multiply) sich fortpflanzen; sich vermehren 2 (give copy) sich reproduzieren lassen

reproducible /ri:prə'dju:sɪbl/ *adj.* reproduzierbar; **be ~:** sich reproduzieren lassen

reproduction /ri:prə'dʌkʃn/ *n.* 1 Wiedergabe, *die;* Reproduktion, *die* (Druckw.); **~ of sound** Tonwiedergabe, *die* 2 (producing offspring) Fortpflanzung, *die* 3 (copy) Reproduktion, *die;* **printed ~:** Druck, *der; attrib.* **~ furniture** Stilmöbel *Pl.;* **a ~ Chippendale chair** ein Stuhl im Chippendalestil 4 (Biol.: forming afresh) Regeneration, *die*

reproductive /ri:prə'dʌktɪv/ *adj.* Fortpflanzungs-

reprographic /ri:prə'græfɪk/ *adj.* reprographisch (Druckw.)

reproof /rɪ'pru:f/ *n.* Tadel, *der;* **a glance/word of ~:** ein tadelnder Blick/ein tadelndes Wort; **deserving of ~:** tadelnswert

reprove /rɪ'pru:v/ *v.t.* tadeln ‹*Verhalten usw.*›; tadeln, zurechtweisen ‹*Person*›

reproving /rɪ'pru:vɪŋ/ *adj.* tadelnd

reprovingly /rɪ'pru:vɪŋlɪ/ *adv.* tadelnd

reptile /'reptaɪl/ *n.* Reptil, *das;* Kriechtier, *das;* (fig. derog.) Ekel, *das* (ugs. abwertend)

reptilian /rep'tɪljən/

A *adj.* reptilartig; (of the Reptilia) Reptilien‹*knochen, -schädel*›

B *n.* Reptil, *das;* Kriechtier, *das*

republic /rɪ'pʌblɪk/ *n.* Republik, *die*

republican /rɪ'pʌblɪkən/

A *adj.* 1 republikanisch 2 (Amer. Polit.) **R~ Party** Republikanische Partei

B *n.* **R~** (Amer. Polit.) Republikaner, *der*/Republikanerin, *die*

> **Republican Party**
>
> Neben der **Democratic Party** eine der zwei großen politischen Parteien in den USA. Sie wird als die konservativere der beiden Parteien eingestuft.

republicanism /rɪ'pʌblɪkənɪzm/ *n.* Republikanismus, *der*

republication /ri:pʌblɪ'keɪʃn/ *n.* Wiederveröffentlichung, *die*

republish /ri:'pʌblɪʃ/ *v.t.* wieder veröffentlichen

repudiate /rɪ'pju:dɪeɪt/ *v.t.* 1 (deny) zurückweisen ‹*Anschuldigung usw.*›; (reject) nicht anerkennen ‹*Autorität, Vertrag usw.*› 2 (disown) verstoßen ‹*Person*›

repudiation /rɪpju:dɪ'eɪʃn/ *n.* ▸**repudiate**: Zurückweisung, *die;* Nichtanerkennung, *die;* Verstoßung, *die*

repugnance /rɪ'pʌgnəns/ *n.* (strong dislike) [starke] Abneigung (**to[wards]** gegen); Abscheu, *der* (**to[wards]** vor + *Dat.*)

repugnant /rɪ'pʌgnənt/ *adj.* (distasteful) widerlich; abstoßend; **be ~ to sb.** jmdm. widerlich sein

repulse /rɪ'pʌls/

A *v.t.* abwehren (auch fig.); zurückweisen ‹*Unterstellung*›

B *n.* Abwehr, *die;* **suffer a ~:** eine Niederlage erleiden

repulsion /rɪ'pʌlʃn/ *n.* 1 (disgust) Widerwille, *der* (**towards** gegen) 2 (Phys.) Repulsion, *die*

repulsive /rɪ'pʌlsɪv/ *adj.* 1 (disgusting) abstoßend; widerwärtig 2 (Phys.) repulsiv

repulsively /rɪ'pʌlsɪvlɪ/ *adv.* abstoßend

repurchase /ri:'pɜ:tʃɪs/

A *v.t.* zurückkaufen

B *n.* Rückkauf, *der*

reputable /'repjʊtəbl/ *adj.* angesehen ‹*Person, Familie, Beruf, Zeitung usw.*›; anständig ‹*Verhalten*›; seriös ‹*Firma*›

reputably /'repjʊtəblɪ/ *adv.* anständig

reputation /repjʊ'teɪʃn/ *n.* 1 Ruf, *der;* **have a ~ for** *or* **of doing/being sth.** in dem Ruf stehen, etw. zu tun/sein; **he has a ~ for integrity/stealing** er gilt als integer/man sagt, dass er stiehlt; **what sort of ~ do they have?** wie ist ihr Ruf? 2 (good name) Name, *der;* Renommee, *das;* **men with a ~ as scientists** Männer, die sich als Wissenschaftler einen Namen gemacht haben; **make one's** *or* **gain a ~:** sich (*Dat.*) einen Namen machen (**as** als) 3 (bad name) schlechter Ruf; **get oneself** *or* **acquire quite a ~:** sich in Verruf bringen

repute /rɪ'pju:t/

A *v.t. in pass.* **be ~d [to be] sth.** als etw. gelten; **she is ~d to have/make ...:** man sagt, dass sie ... hat/macht; **be very highly ~d [as a doctor]** einen sehr guten Ruf [als Arzt] haben

B *n.* Ruf, *der;* Ansehen, *das;* **hold sb./sth. in high ~:** von jmdm./etw. eine hohe Meinung haben; jmdn./etw. hoch schätzen (geh.); **of ill ~:** von schlechtem Ruf; **know sb. by ~:** von jmdm. schon viel gehört haben; **a philosopher of ~:** ein angesehener Philosoph; *see also* **house A 5**

reputed /rɪ'pju:tɪd/ *adj.* angeblich; **the ~ father** der mutmaßliche Vater

reputedly /rɪ'pju:tɪdlɪ/ *adv.* angeblich; vermeintlich

request /rɪ'kwest/

A *v.t.* bitten; **~ sth. of** *or* **from sb.** jmdn. um etw. bitten; **~ sb.'s presence** um jmds. Anwesenheit bitten; **~ silence** um Ruhe bitten; **~ a record** einen Plattenwunsch äußern; **~ that ...:** darum bitten, dass ...; **~ sb. to do sth.** jmdn. [darum] bitten, etw. zu tun; **the essay I am ~ed to write** der Essay, den ich schreiben soll; **'You are ~ed not to smoke'** „Bitte nicht rauchen"

B *n.* Bitte, *die* (**for** um); **at sb.'s ~:** auf jmds. Bitte *od.* Wunsch (*Akk.*) [hin]; **make a ~ for sth.** um etw. bitten; **I have one ~ to make of** *or* **to you** ich habe eine Bitte an Sie; **by** *or* **on ~:** auf Wunsch; **have one's ~:** seine Bitte *od.* seinen Wunsch erfüllt bekommen; **record ~s** (Radio) Plattenwünsche *Pl.;* **we do not receive many ~s for it** dafür haben wir keine große Nachfrage; *no art., no pl.* (demand) **be much in ~:** sehr gefragt sein

request: ~ programme *n.* (Radio) Wunschkonzert, *das;* **~ stop** *n.* (Brit.) Bedarfshaltestelle, *die*

requiem /'rekwɪem/ *n.* Requiem, *das*

requiem 'mass *n.* (Eccl.) Requiem, *das* (kath. Kirche); Totenmesse, *die*

require /rɪ'kwaɪə(r)/ *v.t.* 1 (need, wish to have) brauchen; benötigen; erfordern ‹*Tun, Verhalten*›; **a catalogue/guide is available if ~d** bei Bedarf ist ein Katalog erhältlich/auf Wunsch steht ein Führer zur Verfügung; **is there anything else you ~?** brauchen/(want) wünschen Sie außerdem noch etwas?; **I have all I ~:** ich habe alles, was ich brauche; **it ~d all his authority ...:** es bedurfte seiner ganzen Autorität ... (geh.) 2 (order, demand) verlangen (**of** von); **~ sb. to do sth., ~ of sb. that he does sth.** von jmdm. verlangen, dass er etw. tut; **be ~d to do sth.** etw. tun müssen *od.* sollen; **~d reading** Pflichtlektüre, *die*

requirement /rɪ'kwaɪəmənt/ *n.* 1 (need) Bedarf, *der;* **meet the ~s** den Bedarf decken; **meet sb.'s ~s** jmds. Wünschen entsprechen; **what are your ~s?** was brauchen Sie?; **borrowing ~:** Kreditbedarf, *der* 2 (condition) Erfordernis, *das;* (for a job) Voraussetzung, *die;* **fulfil sb.'s ~s** jmds. Anforderungen (*Dat.*) genügen; **there are certain language ~s for this job** diese Stelle setzt [bestimmte] Sprachkenntnisse voraus

requisite /'rekwɪzɪt/

A *adj.* notwendig (**to, for** für); erforderlich ‹*Voraussetzung, Kenntnisse*›

r

B *n.* Erfordernis, *das* (**for** für); **be a ~ for sth.** für etw. erforderlich sein; **toilet/travel ~s** Toiletten-/Reiseartikel *Pl.*

requisition /rekwɪˈzɪʃn/

A *n.* **1** (esp. Law: demand) Aufforderung, *die* **2** (order for sth.) Anforderung, *die* (**for** *Gen.*); (by force if necessary) Beschlagnahmung, *die* (**for** *Gen.*); **make a ~ on sb. for sth.** etw. bei jmdm. anfordern; **be put under ~:** beschlagnahmt werden

B *v.t.* anfordern; (by force if necessary) beschlagnahmen

requital /rɪˈkwaɪtl/ *n.* Vergeltung, *die*

requite /rɪˈkwaɪt/ *v.t.* vergelten; **~ sb. for sth.** jmdm. etw. vergelten; (avenge) jmdm. etw. heimzahlen

reran ▸ **rerun A**

reread /riːˈriːd/ *v.t.*, **reread** /riːˈred/ wieder *od.* nochmals lesen; **~ sth. several times** etw. mehrmals *od.* wiederholt lesen

reredos /ˈrɪədɒs/ *n.* (Eccl.) Altaraufsatz, *der;* Retabel, *das*

re-route /riːˈruːt/ *v.t.*, **~ing** umleiten

rerun

A /riːˈrʌn/ *v.t.*, *forms as* **run** wiederholen ‹*Rennen*›; wieder auf- *od.* vorführen ‹*Film*›; wieder abspielen ‹*Tonband*›

B /ˈriːrʌn/ *n.* ▸ **A**: Wiederholung, *die;* Wiederaufführung, *die;* Wiederabspielen, *das*

resale /riːˈseɪl/ *n.* Weiterverkauf, *der* (Wirtsch.) (**to** an + *Akk.*); **'not for ~'** „nicht zum Wiederverkauf bestimmt"; (on free samples) „unverkäufliches Muster"; **~ price maintenance** Preisbindung, *die*

resat ▸ **resit A, B**

reschedule /riːˈʃedjuːl/ *v.t.* **1** zeitlich neu festlegen ‹*Veranstaltung, Flug, Programm usw.*›; **the flight will be ~d for 5 o'clock** der Flug wird auf 5 Uhr verlegt **2** (Fin.) umschulden, refinanzieren ‹*Kredit, Darlehen*›; refinanzieren ‹*Schulden*›

rescind /rɪˈsɪnd/ *v.t.* für ungültig erklären

rescue /ˈreskjuː/

A *v.t.* retten (**from** aus); (set free) befreien (**from** aus); **~ sb. from drowning** jmdn. vorm Ertrinken retten

B *n.* ▸ **A**: Rettung, *die;* Befreiung, *die; attrib.* Rettungs‹*dienst, -versuch, -mannschaft, -aktion*›; **go/come to the/sb.'s ~:** jmdm. zu Hilfe kommen; **once again it was Margaret to the ~:** es war wieder mal Margaret, die die Situation gerettet hat

rescue: ~ bid *n.* Rettungsversuch, *der;* **~ package** *n.* Rettungspaket, *das*

rescuer /ˈreskjuːə(r)/ *n.* Retter, *der*/Retterin, *die*

'rescue worker *n.* [Einsatz]helfer, *der*/-helferin, *die*

research /rɪˈsɜːtʃ, ˈriːsɜːtʃ/

A *n.* **1** (scientific study) Forschung, *die* (**into, on** über + *Akk.*); **do ~ in biochemistry** auf dem Gebiet der Biochemie forschen; **carry out/be engaged in ~ into sth.** wissenschaftliche Untersuchungen über etw. (*Akk.*) durchführen/sich in seiner Forschungsarbeit mit etw. befassen; **piece of ~:** Forschungsarbeit, *die;* (investigation) Untersuchung, *die* **2** (inquiry) Nachforschung, *die* (**into** über + *Akk.*)

B *v.i.* forschen; **~ into sth.** etw. erforschen *od.* untersuchen; (esp. Univ.) über etw. (*Akk.*) forschen

C *v.t.* erforschen; untersuchen; recherchieren (*Buch usw.*)

research assistant /-ˈ- ---, ˈ- ---/ *n.* ▸ **i p. 1260** wissenschaftlicher Assistent/wissenschaftliche Assistentin

researcher /rɪˈsɜːtʃə(r), ˈriːsɜːtʃə(r)/ *n.* ▸ **i p. 1260** Forscher, *der*/Forscherin, *die*

research: ~ fellow *n.* Forschungsstipendiat, *der*/-stipendiatin, *die;* **~ fellowship** *n.* Forschungsstipendium, *das;* **~ grant** *n.* Forschungsstipendium, *das;* **~ laboratory** *n.* Forschungslabor, *das;* **~ student** *n.* ≈ Doktorand, *der*/Doktorandin, *die;* **~ work** *n.* Recherchen *Pl.;* (medical, scientific) Forschungsarbeit, *die;* **~ worker** *n.* ▸ **i p. 1260** ≈ Rechercheur, *der*/Rechercheurin, *die;* (medical, scientific) Forscher, *der*/Forscherin, *die*

resection /rɪˈsekʃn/ *n.* (Med.) Resektion, *die*

reselect /riːsɪˈlekt/ *v.t.* (Parl.) wieder aufstellen ‹*Abgeordneten*›

reselection /riːsɪˈlekʃn/ *n.* (Parl.) Wiederaufstellung, *die*

resell /riːˈsel/ *v.t.*, **resold** /riːˈsəʊld/ weiterverkaufen (**to** an + *Akk.*)

resemblance /rɪˈzembləns/ *n.* Ähnlichkeit, *die* (**to** mit, **between** zwischen + *Dat.*); **bear a faint/strong/no ~ to ...:** eine geringe/starke/keine Ähnlichkeit mit ... haben

resemble /rɪˈzembl/ *v.t.* ähneln, gleichen (+ *Dat.*); **they ~ each other** sie ähneln *od.* gleichen sich (*Dat.*) *od.* einander

resent /rɪˈzent/ *v.t.* übel nehmen; **she ~ed his familiarity/success** sie nahm ihm seine Vertraulichkeit übel/missgönnte ihm seinen Erfolg; **I ~ the way you take my help for granted** es gefällt mir nicht, wie du meine Hilfe als selbstverständlich hinnimmst; **she ~ed his having won** sie ärgerte sich darüber, dass er gewonnen hatte

resentful /rɪˈzentfl/ *adj.* übelnehmerisch, nachtragend ‹*Person, Art, Verhalten*›; grollend (geh.) ‹*Blick*›; **be ~ of** *or* **feel ~ about sth.** etw. übel nehmen; **be ~ of sb.'s criticism/success** jmdm. seine Kritik übel nehmen/seinen Erfolg missgönnen

resentfully /rɪˈzentfəlɪ/ *adv.* grollend (geh.); voller Groll *nachgestellt* (geh.)

resentment /rɪˈzentmənt/ *n.*, *no pl.* Groll, *der* (geh.); **feel ~ towards** *or* **against sb.** einen Groll auf jmdn. haben

reservation /rezəˈveɪʃn/ *n.* **1** Reservierung, *die;* **[seat] ~:** [Platz]reservierung, *die;* **have a ~ [for a room]** ein Zimmer reserviert haben **2** (doubt, objection) Vorbehalt, *der* (**about** gegen); Bedenken (**about** bezüglich + *Gen.*); **without ~:** ohne Vorbehalt; vorbehaltlos; **with ~s** mit [gewissen] Vorbehalten; *see also* **mental reservation** **3** **central ~** (Brit. Road Constr.) Mittelstreifen, *der* **4** (Amer.: land reserved for Indians) Reservat, *das;* Reservation, *die*

reserve /rɪˈzɜːv/

A *v.t.* **1** (secure) reservieren lassen ‹*Zimmer, Tisch, Platz*›; (set aside) reservieren; **~ the right to do sth.** sich (*Dat.*) [das Recht] vorbehalten, etw. zu tun; **all seats ~d** Plätze nur auf Vorbestellung; **all rights ~d** alle Rechte vorbehalten **2** *in pass.* (be kept) **be ~d for sb.** ‹*Funktion, Tätigkeit:*› jmdm. vorbehalten sein **3** (postpone) aufheben ‹*Überraschung, Neuigkeit*›; **~ judgement** sein Urteil aufschieben; **~ oneself for sth.** sich für etw. schonen; **~ one's strength** seine Kräfte schonen

B *n.* **1** (extra amount) Reserve, *die* (**of** an + *Dat.*) (Banking also) Rücklage, *die;* **~s of energy/strength** Energie-/Kraftreserven; **hidden ~:** stille Reserve; **have/hold** *or* **keep sth. in ~:** etw. in Reserve haben/halten **2** *in sing. or pl.* (Mil.) (troops) Reserve, *die;* **the ~s** die Reservetruppen *od.* -einheiten **3** ▸ **reservist** **4** (Sport) Reservespieler, *der*/-spielerin, *die;* **the Reserves** die Reserve **5** (place set apart) Reservat, *das* **6** (restriction) Vorbehalt, *der;* **without ~:** ohne Vorbehalt; vorbehaltlos **7** ▸ **~ price** **8** (self-restraint, reticence) Reserve, *die;* Zurückhaltung, *die*

reserve 'currency *n.* Reservewährung, *die*

reserved /rɪˈzɜːvd/ *adj.* **1** (reticent) reserviert; zurückhaltend **2** (booked) reserviert

reserve: ~ list *n.* (Mil.) **be on the ~ list** Reservist sein; **~ player** *n.* Reservespieler, *der*/-spielerin, *die;* **~ price** *n.* Mindestgebot, *das*

reservist /rɪˈzɜːvɪst/ *n.* (Mil.) Reservist, *der*

reservoir /ˈrezəvwɑː(r)/ *n.* **1** ([artificial] lake) Reservoir, *das* **2** (container) Behälter, *der;* Speicher, *der;* (of fountain pen) Tintenraum, *der* **3** (reserve supply) Vorrat, *der* (**of** an + *Dat.*); (fig.) Reservoir, *das*

reset /riːˈset/ *v.t.*, **-tt-**, **reset** **1** neu [ein]fassen ‹*Schmuck-, Edelstein*›; neu stellen ‹*Uhr, Timer*›; umstellen ‹*Uhr*› (**for, to** auf + *Akk.*) **2** (Med.) wieder einrichten ‹*Gliedmaße, Knochen*›; wieder einrenken ‹*ausgerenktes Gelenk*› **3** (Printing) neu setzen

resettle /riːˈsetl/ *v.t.* **1** umsiedeln ‹*Flüchtlinge usw.*› (**in** in + *Akk.*) **2** (repopulate) wieder besiedeln ‹*Gebiet*›

resettlement /riːˈsetlmənt/ *n.* **1** (of refugees) Umsiedlung, *die* **2** (repopulating) Neubesiedlung, *die*

reshape /riːˈʃeɪp/ *v.t.* **1** (give new form to) umgestalten; umstellen ‹*Politik*› **2** (remould) umformen

reshuffle /riːˈʃʌfl/

A *v.t.* **1** (reorganize) umbilden ‹*Kabinett usw.*› **2** (Cards) neu mischen

B *n.* Umbildung, *die;* **Cabinet ~:** Kabinettsumbildung, *die*

reside /rɪˈzaɪd/ *v.i.* (formal) **1** (dwell) wohnen; wohnhaft sein (Amtsspr.); ‹*Monarch, Präsident usw.:*› residieren **2** (be vested, present, inherent) liegen (**in** bei)

residence /ˈrezɪdəns/ *n.* **1** (abode) Wohnsitz, *der;* (house) Wohnhaus, *das;* (mansion) Villa, *die;* (of a head of state or church, an ambassador) Residenz, *die;* **the President's official ~:** der offizielle Wohnsitz des Präsidenten; **have one's ~ in London/in Victoria Street** seinen Wohnsitz in London haben/seine Privatwohnung in der Victoria Street haben **2** (residing) Aufenthalt, *der;* **take up [one's] ~ in Rome** seinen Wohnsitz in Rom nehmen; **be in ~** ‹*König, Präsident usw.:*› [an seinem offiziellen Wohnsitz] anwesend sein; ‹*Student:*› im College sein; **we have a doctor in ~:** wir haben einen Arzt im Hause; **writer** *etc.* **in ~:** *von einer Gemeinde od. einer Institution geförderter, am Ort lebender Schriftsteller usw.*

'residence permit *n.* Aufenthaltsgenehmigung, *die*

residency /ˈrezɪdənsɪ/ *n.* (Amer. Med.) Zeit als Assistenzarzt/-ärztin im Krankenhaus

resident /ˈrezɪdənt/

A *adj.* **1** (residing) wohnhaft; **~ population** [orts]ansässige Bevölkerung; **he is ~ in England** er hat seinen Wohnsitz in England **2** (living in) im Haus wohnend ‹*Haushälterin*›; Anstalts‹*arzt, -geistlicher*›; **~ tutor** Hauslehrer, *der*

B *n.* **1** (inhabitant) Bewohner, *der*/Bewohnerin, *die;* (in a town etc. also) Einwohner, *der*/Einwohnerin, *die;* (at hotel) Hotelgast, *der;* **'access/parking for ~s only'** „Anlieger frei"/„Parken nur für Anlieger"; **local ~:** Anwohner, *der*/Anwohnerin, *die;* **~s association** *Interessengemeinschaft von [benachbarten] Anwohnern eines bestimmten Gebiets* **2** (Amer. Med.) ≈ Assistenzarzt, *der*/-ärztin, *die*

residential /rezɪˈdenʃl/ *adj.* **1** Wohn‹*gebiet, -siedlung, -straße*›; **for ~ purposes** zu Wohnzwecken; **~ hotel** Hotel für Dauergäste **2** **~ course** *Kurs, dessen Teilnehmer am Ort wohnen;* **the ~ qualification for voters** *Nachweis des Wohnsitzes als Voraussetzung zur Ausübung des Wahlrechts*

residential 'care *n.* stationäre Pflege

resident's 'parking *n.* Parken nur für Anlieger

residual /rɪˈzɪdjʊəl/ *adj.* zurückgeblieben; noch vorhanden; ungeklärt ‹*Problem, Frage*›

residue /ˈrezɪdjuː/ *n.* **1** (remainder) Rest, *der* **2** (Law) restlicher Nachlass *(nach Abzug aller Nachlassverbindlichkeiten)* **3** (Chem.) Rückstand, *der*

'residue-free *adj.* rückstandslos

residuum /rɪˈzɪdjʊəm/ *n.*, *pl.* **residua** /rɪˈzɪdjʊə/ (Chem.) Rückstand, *der*

resign /rɪˈzaɪn/

A *v.t.* (hand over) zurücktreten von ‹*Amt*›; verzichten auf (+ *Akk.*) ‹*Recht, Anspruch*›; **~ the leadership to sb.** jmdm. die Führung überlassen *od.* -geben; **~ one's commission** (Mil.) seinen Abschied nehmen; **~ one's job/post** seine Stelle/Stellung kündigen

B *v. refl.* **~ oneself to sth./to doing sth.** sich mit etw. abfinden/sich damit abfinden, etw. zu tun

C *v.i.* **1** ‹*Arbeitnehmer:*› kündigen; ‹*Regierungsbeamter:*› zurücktreten (**from** von); ‹*Geistlicher, Richter:*› sein Amt niederlegen; ‹*Vorsitzender:*› zurücktreten, sein Amt niederlegen; **~ from one's post** ‹*Beamter:*› seine Stellung kündigen **2** (Chess) aufgeben

resignation /rezɪg'neɪʃn/ *n.* **1** ▸**resign C 1**: Kündigung, *die;* Verzicht, *der* (**of** auf + *Akk.*); Rücktritt, *der;* Amtsniederlegung, *die;* **give** *or* **send in** *or* **tender one's ~**: seinen Rücktritt/seine Kündigung einreichen/sein Amt niederlegen **2** (being resigned) Resignation, *die;* **with ~**: resigniert

resigned /rɪ'zaɪnd/ *adj.* resigniert; **become/be ~ to sth.** sich mit etw. abfinden/abgefunden haben

resignedly /rɪ'zaɪnɪdlɪ/ *adv.* resigniert

resilience /rɪ'zɪlɪəns/, **resiliency** /rɪ'zɪlɪənsɪ/ *n., no pl.* **1** (elasticity) Elastizität, *die* **2** (fig.) Unverwüstlichkeit, *die*

resilient /rɪ'zɪlɪənt/ *adj.* **1** (elastic) elastisch **2** (fig.) unverwüstlich; **be ~**: sich nicht [so leicht] unterkriegen lassen

resin /'rezɪn/ *n.* **1** (Bot.) Harz, *das* **2** **[synthetic] ~**: Kunstharz, *das*

resinous /'rezɪnəs/ *adj.* (like resin) harzartig; (containing resin) harzig; harzhaltig

resist /rɪ'zɪst/

A *v.t.* **1** (withstand action of) standhalten (+ *Dat.*) ‹*Frost, Hitze, Feuchtigkeit usw.*›; **be unable to ~ an infection/a disease** keine Abwehrkräfte gegen eine Infektion/Krankheit haben **2** (oppose, repel) sich widersetzen (+ *Dat.*) ‹*Maßnahme, Festnahme, Plan usw.*›; widerstehen (+ *Dat.*) ‹*Versuchung, jmds. Charme*›; Widerstand leisten gegen ‹*Angriff, Feind*›; sich wehren gegen ‹*Veränderung, Einfluss*›

B *v.i.* ▸**A 2**: sich widersetzen; widerstehen; Widerstand leisten; sich wehren

resistance /rɪ'zɪstəns/ *n.* **1** (resisting, opposing force; also Phys., Electr.) Widerstand, *der* (**to** gegen); **make** *or* **offer no ~ [to sb./sth.]** [jmdm./einer Sache] keinen Widerstand leisten; **take the line of least ~** (fig.) den Weg des geringsten Widerstandes gehen; *see also* **passive A 2** **2** (power of resisting) Widerstandsfähigkeit, *die* (**to** gegen); **~ to wear and tear** Strapazierfähigkeit, *die;* **~ to heat/cold** Hitze-/Kältebeständigkeit, *die* **3** (Biol., Med.) Widerstandskraft, *die* (**to** gegen) **4** (against occupation) Widerstand, *der;* **the French R~**: die Résistance

resistance: ~ fighter *n.* Widerstandskämpfer, *der*/-kämpferin, *die;* **~ movement** *n.* Widerstandsbewegung, *die*

resistant /rɪ'zɪstənt/ *adj.* **1** (opposed) **be ~ to** sich widersetzen (+ *Dat.*); sich entgegenstellen (+ *Dat.*) **2** (having power to resist) widerstandsfähig (**to** gegen); **highly ~ to wear and tear** sehr strapazierfähig; **heat-/water-/rust-~**: hitze-/wasser-/rostbeständig **3** (Med., Biol.) resistent (**to** gegen)

resistor /rɪ'zɪstə(r)/ *n.* (Electr.) Widerstand, *der*

resit

A /ri:'sɪt/ *v.t.*, **-tt-**, **resat** /ri:'sæt/ wiederholen ‹*Prüfung*›

B *v.i.*, **-tt-**, **resat** die Prüfung wiederholen

C /'ri:sɪt/ *n.* Wiederholungsprüfung, *die*

reskill /ri:'skɪl/ *v.t.* fort- *od.* weiterbilden; umschulen ‹*Arbeitslose*›

reskilling /ri:'skɪlɪŋ/ *n., no pl.* Weiterbildung, *die;* Fortbildung, *die;* (of an unemployed person) Umschulung, *die*

resold ▸**resell**

resole /ri:'səʊl/ *v.t.* neu besohlen

resolute /'rezəlu:t/ *adj.* resolut, energisch ‹*Person*›; entschlossen ‹*Tat*›; entschieden ‹*Antwort, Weigerung*›

resolutely /'rezəlu:tlɪ/ *adv.* entschlossen

resolution /rezə'lu:ʃn/ *n.* **1** (decision) Entschließung, *die;* (Polit. also) Resolution, *die;* **a ~ of sympathy/solidarity** eine Sympathie-/Solidaritätserklärung **2** (resolve) Vorsatz, *der;* **make a ~**: einen Vorsatz fassen; **make a ~ to do sth.** den Vorsatz fassen, etw. zu tun; **break one's ~**: seinem Vorsatz untreu werden; **good ~s** gute Vorsätze; **New Year['s] ~s** gute Vorsätze fürs neue Jahr **3** *no pl.* (firmness) Entschlossenheit, *die* **4** *no pl.* (*solving*) ▸**resolve A 1, 2**: Beseitigung, *die;* Ausräumung, *die;* Lösung, *die* **5** (separation; also Phys., Mus.) Auflösung, *die*

resolve /rɪ'zɒlv/

A *v.t.* **1** (dispel) beseitigen, ausräumen ‹*Schwierigkeit, Zweifel, Unklarheit*› **2** (explain) lösen ‹*Problem, Rätsel*› **3** (decide) beschließen; **they ~d that they must part** sie beschlossen, sich zu trennen; **this discovery made me ~ to leave** diese Entdeckung hat mich zu dem Entschluss gebracht, fortzugehen **4** (settle) beilegen ‹*Streit*›; klären ‹*Streitpunkt*›; regeln ‹*Angelegenheit*› **5** (separate; also Phys., Mus.) auflösen (**into** in + *Akk.*) **6** (analyse, divide; also Mech.) zerlegen (**into** in + *Akk.*)

B *v.i.* **1** (decide) **~ [up]on sth./doing sth.** sich zu etw. entschließen/sich [dazu] entschließen, etw. zu tun **2** (dissolve) sich auflösen (**into** in + *Akk.*)

C *n.* **1** Vorsatz, *der;* **make a/keep one's ~**: einen Vorsatz fassen/bei seinem Vorsatz bleiben; **make a ~ to do sth.** den Vorsatz fassen, etw. zu tun **2** (Amer.) ▸**resolution 1** **3** (resoluteness) Entschlossenheit, *die*

resolved /rɪ'zɒlvd/ *pred. adj.* **~ [to do sth.]** entschlossen[, etw. zu tun]; **he was ~ that ...**: es stand für ihn fest, dass ...

re'solving power *n.* (Phys.) Auflösungsvermögen, *das*

resonance /'rezənəns/ *n.* Resonanz, *die;* (of voice) voller Klang; (fig.) Widerhall, *der*

resonant /'rezənənt/ *adj.* **1** (resounding) hallend ‹*Echo, Ton, Klang*›; volltönend ‹*Stimme*› **2** (tending to reinforce sounds) ‹*Raum, Körper:*› mit viel Resonanz

resonate /'rezəneɪt/ *v.i.* mitschwingen; resonieren (Physik, Musik)

resonator /'rezəneɪtə(r)/ *n.* (Phys., Mus.) Resonator, *der*

resorption /rɪ'sɔ:pʃn/ *n.* (Biol., Med.) Resorption, *die*

resort /rɪ'zɔ:t/

A *n.* **1** (resource, recourse) Ausweg, *der;* **have ~ to force** Gewalt anwenden; **without ~ to force** ohne Gewaltanwendung; **you were my last ~**: du warst meine letzte Rettung (ugs.); **as a** *or* **in the last ~**: als letzter Ausweg; **in the last ~** (in the end) letzten Endes **2** (place frequented) Aufenthalt[sort], *der;* **[holiday] ~**: Urlaubsort, *der;* Ferienort, *der;* **ski/health ~**: Skiurlaubs-/Kurort, *der;* **mountain/coastal ~**: Ferienort im Gebirge/an der Küste; **seaside ~**: Seebad, *das* **3** (frequenting) häufiger Besuch

B *v.i.* **~ to sth./sb.** zu etw. greifen/sich an jmdn. wenden (**for** um); **~ to violence** *or* **force** Gewalt anwenden; **~ to stealing/shouting** *etc.* sich aufs Stehlen/Schreien *usw.* verlegen; **~ to crime** kriminell werden

resound /rɪ'zaʊnd/ *v.i.* **1** (ring) widerhallen (**with** von) **2** (produce echo) hallen; **his fame ~ed through Greece** (fig.) sein Ruhm hallte durch [ganz] Griechenland

resounding /rɪ'zaʊndɪŋ/ *adj.* hallend ‹*Lärm, Schreie, Schritte*›; schallend ‹*Gelächter, Stimme*›; überwältigend ‹*Mehrheit, Sieg, Erfolg*›; gewaltig ‹*Niederlage, Misserfolg*›

resoundingly /rɪ'zaʊndɪŋlɪ/ *adv.* schallend ‹*ertönen, erklingen*›; **be ~ successful** ein durchschlagender Erfolg sein

resource /rɪ'sɔ:s, rɪ'zɔ:s/ *n.* **1** *usu. in pl.* (stock) Mittel *Pl.;* Ressource, *die;* **have no inner ~s** keine inneren Reserven haben; **financial/mineral ~s** Geldmittel *Pl.*/Bodenschätze *Pl.;* **~s in** *or* **of men and money** Reserven an Menschen und Geldmitteln **2** *usu. pl.* (Amer.: asset) Aktivposten, *der* **3** (expedient) Ausweg, *der;* **be at the end of one's ~s** am Ende seiner Möglichkeiten sein; **be left to one's own ~s** sich (*Dat.*) selbst überlassen sein; **as a last ~**: als letzter Ausweg **4** *no art., no pl.* (ingenuity) Findigkeit, *die;* **be full of ~**: sich (*Dat.*) immer zu helfen wissen

resourceful /rɪ'sɔ:sfl, rɪ'zɔ:sfl/ *adj.* findig ‹*Person*›; einfallsreich ‹*Plan*›

resourcefully /rɪ'sɔ:sfəlɪ, rɪ'zɔ:sfəlɪ/ *adv.* findig

resourcefulness /rɪ'sɔ:sflnɪs, rɪ'zɔ:sflnɪs/ *n., no pl.* (of person) Findigkeit, *die;* (of plan etc.) Einfallsreichtum, *der*

respect /rɪ'spekt/

A *n.* **1** (esteem) Respekt, *der* (**for** vor + *Dat.*); Achtung, *die* (**for** vor + *Dat.*); **show ~ for sb./sth.** Respekt vor jmdm./etw. zeigen; **hold sb. in [high** *or* **great] ~**: jmdn. [sehr] achten; **command ~**: Respekt einflößen; **treat sb./sth. with ~**: jmdm./etw. mit Respekt *od.* Achtung begegnen/etw. mit Vorsicht behandeln; **with [all due] ~, ...**: bei allem Respekt, ...; mit Verlaub, ... (geh.) **2** (consideration) Rücksicht, *die* (**for** auf + *Akk.*); **have** *or* **pay [no] ~ to sth.** etw. [nicht] berücksichtigen **3** (aspect) Beziehung, *die;* Hinsicht, *die;* **in ~ of style** hinsichtlich des Stils; in stilistischer Hinsicht; **in all/many/some ~s** in jeder/vieler/mancher Beziehung *od.* Hinsicht **4** (reference) Bezug, *der;* **with ~ to ...**: in Bezug auf ... (*Akk.*); was ... [an]betrifft; **have ~ to sth.** etw. betreffen; sich auf etw. (*Akk.*) beziehen **5** *in pl.* **give him my ~s** grüße ihn von mir; **pay one's ~s to sb.** (formal) jmdm. seine Aufwartung machen (veralt.); **pay one's last ~s** jmdm. die letzte Ehre erweisen (geh.)

B *v.t.* respektieren; achten; **he doesn't ~ his teachers much** er hat nicht viel Respekt vor seinen Lehrern; **much ~ed** sehr angesehen ‹*Politiker, Firma*›; **~ sb.'s feelings** auf jmds. Gefühle Rücksicht nehmen; **~ the rules of the road** die Verkehrsregeln beachten

respectability /rɪspektə'bɪlɪtɪ/ *n., no pl.* ▸**respectable 1**: Ansehen, *das;* Ehrbarkeit, *die* (geh.); **I do not doubt the ~ of his motives** ich zweifle nicht daran, dass seine Motive ehrenwert sind

respectable /rɪ'spektəbl/ *adj.* **1** (of good character) angesehen ‹*Bürger usw.*›; ehrenwert ‹*Motive*›; (decent) ehrbar (geh.) ‹*Leute, Kaufmann, Hausfrau*› **2** (presentable) anständig, respektabel ‹*Beschäftigung usw.*›; vornehm, gut ‹*Adresse*›; ordentlich, (that one can be seen in) vorzeigbar (ugs.) ‹*Kleidung*›; **are you ~?** (joc.) hast du was an? (ugs.) **3** (considerable) beachtlich ‹*Summe*› **4** (passable) passabel

respectably /rɪ'spektəblɪ/ *adv.* **1** anständig ‹*sich benehmen*›; ordentlich ‹*gekleidet*›; **be ~ employed** eine anständige Beschäftigung haben **2** (passably) passabel

respecter /rɪ'spektə(r)/ *n.* **be no ~ of persons** alle ohne Ansehen der Person gleich behandeln

respectful /rɪ'spektfl/ *adj.* respektvoll (**to[wards]** gegenüber)

respectfully /rɪ'spektfəlɪ/ *adv.* respektvoll; **~ yours, X** (formal) Ihr sehr ergebener X

respecting /rɪ'spektɪŋ/ *prep.* bezüglich; hinsichtlich

respective /rɪ'spektɪv/ *adj.* jeweilig; **you must go to your ~ places** jeder von euch muss auf seinen Platz gehen; **he and I contributed ~ amounts of £10 and £1** er und ich steuerten Beträge von 10 bzw. 1 Pfund bei

respectively /rɪ'spektɪvlɪ/ *adv.* beziehungsweise; **the two cars were red and white ~**: die beiden Autos waren rot bzw. weiß; **he and I contributed £10 and £1 ~**: er und ich steuerten 10 bzw. 1 Pfund bei

respell /ri:'spel/ *v.t.*, **respelt** (Brit.) /ri:'spelt/ *or* **respelled** noch einmal buchstabieren

respiration /respɪ'reɪʃn/ *n.* (one breath) Atemzug, *der;* (breathing) Atmung, *die;* **she was finding ~ difficult** das Atmen fiel ihr schwer

respirator /'respɪreɪtə(r)/ *n.* **1** (protecting device) Atemschutzgerät, *das* **2** (Med.) Respirator, *der*

respiratory /'respərətərɪ, rɪ'spɪrətərɪ/ *adj.* Atem‹*geräusch, -wege*›; Atmungs‹*system, -organ, -funktion*›; **~ disease** Atemwegserkrankung, *die;* **~ infection** Infektion der Atemwege

respire /rɪ'spaɪə(r)/ *v.t. & i.* atmen

respite /'respaɪt/ *n.* **1** (delay) Aufschub, *der* **2** (interval of relief) Ruhepause, *die;* **~ from sth.** Erholung von etw.; **without ~**: ohne Pause *od.* Unterbrechung

resplendent /rɪ'splendənt/ *adj.* prächtig; **~ in his uniform** in der vollen Pracht seiner Uniform

resplendently /rɪ'splendəntlɪ/ *adv.* prächtig

respond /rɪ'spɒnd/

A *v.i.* **1** (answer) antworten (**to** auf + *Akk.*); **~ to sb.'s greeting** jmds. Gruß erwidern **2** (react)

r

reagieren (**to** auf + *Akk.*); ‹*Patient, Bremsen, Lenkung usw.:*› ansprechen (**to** auf + *Akk.*); **[not] ~ to kindness** [nicht] empfänglich für Freundlichkeit sein; **they ~ed very generously to this appeal** der Aufruf fand bei ihnen ein großes Echo; **the illness ~s to treatment** die Krankheit lässt sich behandeln
B *v.t.* antworten; erwidern
C *n.* (Archit.) Wandpfeiler, *der;* Pilaster, *der* (fachspr.)

respondent /rɪˈspɒndənt/ *n.* (Law) Beklagte, *der/die;* (in divorce case) Scheidungsbeklagte, *der/die*

response /rɪˈspɒns/ *n.* **1** (answer) Antwort, *die* (**to** auf + *Akk.*); **in ~ [to]** als Antwort [auf (+ *Akk.*)]; **in ~ to your letter** in Beantwortung Ihres Schreibens (Papierdt.); **make no ~:** nicht antworten **2** (reaction) Reaktion, *die;* **make no ~ to sth.** auf etw. (*Akk.*) nicht reagieren; **his ~ was to resign** er reagierte mit seinem Rücktritt; **meet with no/a large ~:** kein Echo/großes Echo finden; **£20,000 was raised in ~ to the appeal** der Aufruf brachte Spenden in Höhe von 20 000 Pfund ein **3** (Eccl.) Responsorium, *das*

responsibility /rɪspɒnsɪˈbɪlɪtɪ/ *n.* **1** *no pl., no indef. art.* (being responsible) Verantwortung, *die;* **take** *or* **bear** *or* **accept** *or* **assume/claim [full] ~ [for sth.]** die [volle] Verantwortung [für etw.] übernehmen; **'the management accepts no ~ for garments left here'** „die Geschäftsleitung übernimmt keine Haftung für die Garderobe"; **lay** *or* **put** *or* **place the ~ for sth. on sb.['s shoulders]** jmdn. für etw. verantwortlich machen; **claim ~ for a bombing** sich zu einem Bombenanschlag bekennen; **do sth. on one's own ~:** etw. in eigener Verantwortung tun; (at one's own risk) etw. auf eigene Verantwortung tun **2** (duty) Verpflichtung, *die;* **the responsibilities of office** die Dienstpflicht; **that's 'your ~:** dafür bist du verantwortlich

responsible /rɪˈspɒnsɪbl/ *adj.* **1** verantwortlich (**for** für); **hold sb. ~ for sth.** jmdn. für etw. verantwortlich machen; **be ~ to sb. [for sth.]** jmdm. gegenüber [für etw.] verantwortlich sein; **be ~ for sth.** ‹*Person:*› für etw. verantwortlich sein; ‹*Sache:*› die Ursache für etw. sein; **what's ~ for the breakdown?** woran liegt die Betriebsstörung?; **I've made you ~ for the travel arrangements** ich habe dir die Verantwortung für die Reisevorbereitungen übertragen **2** verantwortlich, verantwortungsvoll ‹*Stellung, Tätigkeit, Aufgabe*› **3** (trustworthy) verantwortungsvoll, verantwortungsbewusst ‹*Person*›

responsibly /rɪˈspɒnsɪblɪ/ *adv.* verantwortungsbewusst ‹*handeln, sich verhalten*›

responsive /rɪˈspɒnsɪv/ *adj.* (reacting positively) aufgeschlossen ‹*Person*›; gut ansprechend ‹*Bremsen, Motor usw.*›; **the audience was very ~, it was a very ~ audience** das Publikum ging sehr gut mit; **be ~ to sth.** auf etw. (*Akk.*) reagieren *od.* eingehen

respray
A /riːˈspreɪ/ *v.t.* neu spritzen ‹*Auto*›
B /ˈriːspreɪ/ *n.* neue Lackierung; **give the car a ~:** den Wagen neu spritzen

rest[1] /rest/
A *v.i.* **1** (lie, lit. or fig.) ruhen; **~ on** ruhen auf (+ *Dat.*); ‹*Schatten, Licht:*› liegen auf (+ *Dat.*); (fig.) ‹*Argumentation:*› sich stützen auf (+ *Akk.*); ‹*Ruf:*› beruhen auf (+ *Dat.*); **~ against sth.** an etw. (*Dat.*) lehnen; **sit with one's back ~ing against sth.** mit dem Rücken an etw. (*Akk.*) gelehnt sitzen; **her head is ~ing against his shoulder** ihr Kopf liegt an seiner Schulter **2** (take repose) ruhen; sich ausruhen (**from** von); (pause) eine Pause machen *od.* einlegen; **never let one's enemy ~:** seinem Feind keine Ruhepause gönnen; **she never ~s** ihre Hände ruhen nie; **I won't ~ until ...:** ich werde nicht ruhen noch rasten, bis ...; **tell sb. to ~** ‹*Arzt:*› jmdm. Ruhe verordnen; **be ~ing** (Brit. Theatre) ‹*Schauspieler:*› ohne Engagement sein **3** (euphem.: lie in death) ruhen (geh.); **let her/may she ~ in peace** lass sie/möge sie in Frieden ruhen **4** (be left) **let the matter ~:** die Sache ruhen lassen; **... and there the matter ~ed** ... und dabei blieb es; **~ assured that ...:** seien Sie versichert, dass ... **5** **~ with sb.** ‹*Verantwortung, Entscheidung, Schuld:*› bei jmdm. liegen **6** (Agric.: lie fallow) ruhen; brachliegen **7** (Amer. Law) ‹*Verteidigung:*› die Beweiserhebung abschließen. *See also* **laurel 1**; **oar 1**
B *v.t.* **1** (place for support) **~ sth. against sth.** etw. an etw. (*Akk.*) lehnen; **~ sth. on sth.** (lit. or fig.) etw. auf etw. (*Akk.*) stützen; **she was ~ing all her hopes on her son** sie setzte ihre ganze Hoffnung auf ihren Sohn; **he ~ed the load on the ground [for a moment]** er setzte die Last [für einen Augenblick] ab **2** (give relief to) ausruhen lassen ‹*Pferd, Person*›; ausruhen ‹*Augen*›; schonen ‹*Stimme, Körperteil*›; **~ oneself** sich ausruhen **3** (Agric.: allow to lie fallow) brachliegen (fachspr.); ruhen lassen **4** (Law) **~ one's case** sein Plädoyer beschließen **5** **[may] God ~ his soul!** Gott hab ihn selig!
C *n.* **1** (repose) Ruhe, *die;* **need nine hours' ~:** neun Stunden Schlaf brauchen; **go** *or* **retire to ~:** sich zur Ruhe legen *od.* begeben (geh.); **get a good night's ~:** sich ordentlich ausschlafen; **be at ~** (euphem.: be dead) ruhen (geh.); **go to one's ~** (euphem.: die) zur ewigen Ruhe eingehen (geh. verhüll.); **lay to ~** (euphem.: bury) zur letzten Ruhe betten (geh. verhüll.) **2** (freedom from exertion) Ruhe[pause], *die;* Erholung, *die* (**from** von); **take a ~:** sich ausruhen (**from** von); **tell sb. to take a ~** ‹*Arzt:*› jmdm. Ruhe verordnen; **set sb.'s mind at ~:** jmdn. beruhigen (**about** hinsichtlich) **3** (pause) **~ period** [Ruhe]pause, *die;* **have** *or* **take a ~:** [eine] Pause machen; **give sb./sth. a ~:** ausruhen lassen ‹*Person, Nutztier*›; ruhen lassen ‹*Maschine*›; (fig.) ruhen lassen ‹*Thema, Angelegenheit*›; **give it a ~!** (coll.) hör jetzt mal auf damit! **4** (stationary position) **at ~:** in Ruhe; **come to ~:** zum Stehen kommen; (have final position) landen; **bring to ~:** zum Stehen bringen **5** (support) (for telephone receiver) Gabel, *die;* (for billiard cue, telescope, firearm) Auflage, *die;* (for neck) Stütze, *die* **6** (Mus.) Pause, *die*

Phrasal verb
• **~ 'up** *v.i.* sich ausruhen

rest[2] *n.* (remainder) **the ~:** der Rest; **we'll do the ~:** alles Übrige erledigen wir; **the ~ of her clothes** ihre übrigen Kleider; **the ~ of the butter** die restliche *od.* übrige Butter; **she's no different from the ~:** sie ist nicht besser als die anderen; **and [all] the ~ of it** und so weiter; **for the ~:** im Übrigen; sonst

restart
A /riːˈstɑːt/ *v.t.* **1** (start again) wieder anstellen ‹*Maschine*›; wieder anlassen ‹*Auto, Motor*› **2** (resume) wieder aufnehmen ‹*Verhandlungen, Berufstätigkeit*›; fortsetzen ‹*Spiel*›; neu starten ‹*Rennen*›; **~ work** wieder anfangen zu arbeiten **3** neu starten ‹*Computer*›
B /riːˈstɑːt/ *v.i.* **1** ‹*Motor:*› wieder anspringen **2** (resume) wieder anfangen; ‹*Verhandlungen:*› wieder aufgenommen werden
C /ˈriːstɑːt/ *n.* ▸**A 2**: Wiederaufnahme, *die;* Fortsetzung, *die*

restate /riːˈsteɪt/ *v.t.* (express again) noch einmal darlegen; (express differently) anders darlegen; (Mus.: repeat) wieder aufnehmen ‹*Thema*›

restatement /riːˈsteɪtmənt/ *n.* (repetition) nochmalige Darlegung; nochmalige Feststellung; (reformulation) Neuformulierung, *die;* (Mus.) Wiederaufnahme, *die*

restaurant /ˈrestərɔ̃, ˈrestərɒnt/ *n.* Restaurant, *das*

'restaurant car *n.* (Brit. Railw.) Speisewagen, *der*

restaurateur /restərəˈtɜː(r)/ *n.* ▸ⓘ **p. 1260** Gastwirt, *der*

rest: **~ cure** *n.* (Med.) Erholungskur, *die;* **~ day** *n.* Ruhetag, *der*

rested /ˈrestɪd/ *adj.* ausgeruht

restful /ˈrestfl/ *adj.* **1** (free from disturbance) ruhig ‹*Tag, Woche, Ort*› **2** (conducive to rest) beruhigend; **be a ~ person to be with** Ruhe ausstrahlen

restfully /ˈrestfəlɪ/ *adv.* ruhig ‹*schlafen*›; geruhsam ‹*Zeit verbringen*›

restfulness /ˈrestflnɪs/ *n., no pl.* Entspanntheit, *die;* Gelöstheit, *die*

rest home *n.* Pflegeheim, *das*

'resting place *n.* Rastplatz, *der;* **last ~** (euphem.) letzte Ruhestätte (geh.)

restitution /restɪˈtjuːʃn/ *n.* Rückgabe, *die;* (of sth. lost) Erstattung, *die;* Ersatz, *der;* **make ~:** Ersatz leisten; **make ~ of sth. to sb.** jmdm. etw. zurückgeben/erstatten

restive /ˈrestɪv/ *adj.* **1** (stubborn) störrisch ‹*Pferd, Person*›; **become ~** ‹*Pferd:*› bocken **2** (unmanageable) aufsässig ‹*Einwohner, Bevölkerung*› **3** (restless) unruhig

restively /ˈrestɪvlɪ/ *adv.* **1** (stubbornly) störrisch **2** (in fidgety manner) unruhig

restless /ˈrestlɪs/ *adj.* **1** (affording no rest) unruhig ‹*Nacht, Schlaf, Bewegung*› **2** (uneasy) ruhelos ‹*Person, Sehnsucht*› **3** (taking no rest) rastlos ‹*Person, Lebensstil*›

restlessly /ˈrestlɪslɪ/ *adv.* ▸**restless 1, 2**: unruhig; ruhelos

restlessness /ˈrestlɪsnɪs/ *n., no pl.* ▸**restless 2, 3**: Ruhelosigkeit, *die;* Rastlosigkeit, *die*

restock /riːˈstɒk/
A *v.t.* **1** **~ a shop** das Lager eines Geschäfts wieder auffüllen **2** wieder besetzen ‹*Fluss, Teich*›; wieder aufforsten ‹*Wald*›; **~ a farm** einen [landwirtschaftlichen] Betrieb wieder mit Vieh besetzen
B *v.i.* (Commerc.) das Lager auffüllen

restoration /restəˈreɪʃn/ *n.* **1** (restoring) (of peace, health) Wiederherstellung, *die;* (of a work of art, building, etc.) Restaurierung, *die;* Restauration, *die* (fachspr.); **her ~ to health** ihre [gesundheitliche] Wiederherstellung **2** (giving back) Rückgabe, *die* **3** (re-establishment) Wiedereinführung, *die;* **the R~** (Brit. Hist.) die Restauration

restorative /rɪˈstɒrətɪv, rɪˈstɔːrətɪv/
A *adj.* stärkend; aufbauend; Stärkungs-, Aufbau‹*mittel*›; Aufbau-, Kräftigungs‹*kost*›
B *n.* Stärkungs- *od.* Aufbaumittel, *das*

restore /rɪˈstɔː(r)/ *v.t.* **1** (give back) zurückgeben **2** (bring to original state) restaurieren ‹*Bauwerk, Kunstwerk usw.*›; konjizieren ‹*Text, Satz*› (Literaturw.); **~ sb. to health, ~ sb.'s health** jmds. Gesundheit *od.* jmdn. wieder herstellen; **his strength was ~d** er kam wieder zu Kräften; **~ sb. to better spirits** jmdn. aufheitern **3** (reinstate) wieder einsetzen (**to** in + *Akk.*); **~ sb. to the throne/to power** jmdn. als König/Königin wieder einsetzen/jmdn. wieder an die Macht bringen; **her success ~d her to her place as leading actress** der Erfolg hat sie wieder zur führenden Schauspielerin gemacht **4** (re-establish) wiederherstellen ‹*Ordnung, Ruhe, Vertrauen*› **5** (put back) **~ the book to its place [on the shelf]** das Buch wieder an seinen Platz [im Regal] zurückstellen

restorer /rɪˈstɔːrə(r)/ *n.* **1** (Art, Archit.: person) Restaurator, *der*/Restauratorin, *die* **2** (agent) ≈ Pflegemittel, *das; see also* **hair-restorer**

restrain /rɪˈstreɪn/ *v.t.* zurückhalten ‹*Gefühl, Lachen, Drang, Person*›; bändigen ‹*unartiges Kind, Tier*›; **~ sb./oneself from doing sth.** jmdn. davon abhalten/sich zurückhalten, etw. zu tun; **~ yourself!** beherrsch dich!

restrained /rɪˈstreɪnd/ *adj.* zurückhaltend ‹*Wesen, Kritik*›; verhalten ‹*Blick, Geste, Gefühl*›; beherrscht ‹*Reaktion, Worte*›; unaufdringlich ‹*Stil*›

restraint /rɪˈstreɪnt/ *n.* **1** (restriction) Einschränkung, *die;* **without ~:** ungehindert **2** (reserve) Zurückhaltung, *die* **3** (moderation) Unaufdringlichkeit, *die;* (self-control) Selbstbeherrschung, *die;* **with ~:** unaufdringlich; **without ~:** ungehemmt; **his style shows a lack of ~:** er hat einen aufdringlichen Stil

restrict /rɪˈstrɪkt/ *v.t.* beschränken (**to** auf + *Akk.*); ‹*Kleidung:*› be-, einengen; **the trees ~ed our view** die Bäume nahmen uns die freie Sicht

restricted /rɪˈstrɪktɪd/ *adj.* **1** (limited) beschränkt; begrenzt; **~ diet** Diät, *die;* **I feel ~ in these clothes** ich fühle mich in dieser Kleidung beengt *od.* eingeengt **2** (subject to restriction) Sperr‹*gebiet*›; begrenzt ‹*Zulassung, Aufnahme, Anwendbarkeit*›; **be ~ to 30 mph** nicht schneller als 30 Meilen in der Stunde fahren dürfen; **be ~ to doing sth.** sich darauf beschränken müssen, etw. zu tun; **be ~ within narrow limits** ‹*Freiheit:*› stark eingeschränkt sein **3** (not for disclosure) geheim ‹*Dokument, Information*›

restricted 'area *n.* **1** Sperrgebiet, *das* **2** (Brit.: with speed limit) *Gebiet mit Geschwindigkeitsbeschränkung*

restriction /rɪ'strɪkʃn/ *n.* Be-, Einschränkung, *die* (**on** *Gen.*); (of persons) Einengung, *die;* **without ~:** ohne Einschränkung; uneingeschränkt; **put** *or* **place** *or* **impose ~s on sth.** etw. einschränken *od.* Einschränkungen (*Dat.*) unterwerfen; **speed/weight/price ~:** Geschwindigkeits-/ Gewichts-/ Preisbeschränkung, *die*

restrictive /rɪ'strɪktɪv/ *adj.* restriktiv; einschränkend; beengend ‹*Kleidung*›

restrictively /rɪ'strɪktɪvlɪ/ *adv.* restriktiv; einschränkend

restrictive 'practice *n.* (Commerc.) wettbewerbsbeschränkende Geschäftspraktik

'restroom *n.* (esp. Amer.) Toilette, *die*

restructure /riː'strʌktʃə(r)/ *v.t.* umstrukturieren

'rest stop *n.* (Amer.) Raststätte, *die*

restyle /riː'staɪl/ *v.t.* neu stylen; **~ sb.'s hair** jmdm. eine neue Frisur machen

result /rɪ'zʌlt/

A *v.i.* **1** (follow) **~ from sth.** die Folge einer Sache (*Gen.*) sein; von etw. herrühren; (future) aus etw. resultieren **2** (end) **~ in sth.** in etw. (*Dat.*) resultieren; zu etw. führen; **the game ~ed in a draw** das Spiel endete mit einem Unentschieden; **~ in sb.'s doing sth.** zur Folge haben, dass jmd. etw. tut

B *n.* Ergebnis, *das;* Resultat, *das;* **be the ~ of sth.** die Folge einer Sache (*Gen.*) sein; **as a ~ [of this]** infolgedessen; **he knows how to get ~s** er weiß, wie man Ergebnisse *od.* Erfolg erzielt; **without ~:** ergebnislos; **What was the ~? — Leeds won 3-2** Wie ist es ausgegangen? — Leeds hat 3 : 2 gewonnen; **when you add up the figures, what is the ~?** was kommt heraus, wenn du die Zahlen zusammenzählst?

resultant /rɪ'zʌltənt/

A *adj.* daraus resultierend; sich daraus ergebend

B *n.* (Phys.) Resultante, *die;* Resultierende, *die*

resume /rɪ'zjuːm/

A *v.t.* **1** (begin again) wieder aufnehmen; fortsetzen ‹*Reise*›; wieder annehmen ‹*Gewohnheit*› **2** (get back) wieder-, zurückgewinnen; wieder übernehmen ‹*Kommando*›; **~ possession of sth.** etw. wieder in Besitz nehmen; *see also* **seat A 2**

B *v.i.* weitermachen; ‹*Parlament:*› die Sitzung fortsetzen; ‹*Unterricht:*› wieder beginnen

résumé /'rezʊmeɪ/ *n.* **1** (summary) Zusammenfassung, *die* **2** (Amer.: curriculum vitae) Lebenslauf, *der*

resumption /rɪ'zʌmpʃn/ *n.* **1** ▸**resume A 1**: Wiederaufnahme, *die;* Fortsetzung, *die;* Wiederannahme, *die* **2** ▸**resume A 2**: Wieder-, Zurückgewinnung, *die;* Wiederübernahme, *die;* Wiedereinnahme, *die*

resurface /riː'sɜːfɪs/

A *v.t.* **~ a road** den Belag einer Straße erneuern

B *v.i.* (lit. or fig.) wieder auftauchen

resurgence /rɪ'sɜːdʒəns/ *n.* Wiederaufleben, *das*

resurgent /rɪ'sɜːdʒənt/ *adj.* wieder auflebend; wieder erwachend ‹*Leben*›; **be ~:** wieder aufleben

resurrect /rezə'rekt/ *v.t.* **1** (raise from the dead) wieder zum Leben erwecken **2** (revive) wieder beleben; wieder aufleben lassen ‹*Vorstellungen, Bräuche*›; (coll.: dig out) wieder ausgraben ‹*alte Kleider usw.*›

resurrection /rezə'rekʃn/ *n.* **1** (Relig.) Auferstehung, *die;* **the R~:** die Auferstehung Christi **2** (revival) Wiederbelebung, *die;* Wiederaufleben, *das*

resuscitate /rɪ'sʌsɪteɪt/ *v.t.* (lit. or fig.) wieder beleben

resuscitation /rɪsʌsɪ'teɪʃn/ *n.* (lit. or fig.) Wiederbelebung, *die*

ret. *abbr.* = **retired** a. D.; i. R.

retail

A /'riːteɪl/ *n.* Einzelhandel, *der*

B *adj.* Einzel‹*handel*›; Einzelhandels‹*geschäft, -preis*›; [End]verkaufs‹*preis*›

C *adv.* **buy/sell ~:** en détail kaufen/verkaufen (Kaufmannsspr.)

D *v.t.* **1** /'riːteɪl, rɪ'teɪl/ (sell) [im Einzelhandel] verkaufen **2** /rɪ'teɪl/ (relate) weitererzählen ‹*Klatsch*›; **~ a conversation to sb.** jmdm. ein Gespräch wiedererzählen

E /'riːteɪl, rɪ'teɪl/ *v.i.* im Einzelhandel verkauft werden (**at, for** für)

retailer /'riːteɪlə(r), rɪ'teɪlə(r)/ *n.* Einzelhändler, *der*/-händlerin, *die*

retailing /'riːteɪlɪŋ/ *n., no pl., no art.* Einzelhandel, *der; attrib.* Einzelhandels-

retail: ~ park *n.* Einkaufszentrum auf der grünen Wiese; **~ 'price index** *n.* (Brit.) Preisindex des Einzelhandels; **~ sales** *n. pl.* Einzelhandelsumsatz, *der;* **~ trade** *n.* Einzelhandel, *der*

retain /rɪ'teɪn/ *v.t.* **1** (keep) behalten; sich (*Dat.*) bewahren ‹*Witz, Einfallsreichtum, Fähigkeit*›; ein-, zurückbehalten ‹*Gelder*›; gespeichert lassen ‹*Information*›; **~ power** ‹*Partei:*› an der Macht bleiben; **~ possession of sth.** etw. im Besitz behalten; **~ control [of sth.]** die Kontrolle [über etw. (*Akk.*)] behalten **2** (continue to practise) festhalten an (*Dat.*), beibehalten ‹*Gewohnheit, Tradition, Brauch*› **3** (keep in place) ‹*Damm:*› stauen/‹*Deich:*› zurückhalten/‹*Boden:*› speichern/‹*Gefäß:*› halten ‹*Wasser*›; **~ sth. in position** etw. in der richtigen Position halten **4** (secure services of) beauftragen ‹*Anwalt*› **5** (not forget) behalten, sich (*Dat.*) merken ‹*Gedanke, Tatsache*›

retainer /rɪ'teɪnə(r)/ *n.* **1** (Hist.: follower) Trabant, *der;* **old ~** (joc.) altes Faktotum **2** (fee) Honorarvorschuss, *der*

retaining: ~ fee *n.* Honorarvorschuss, *der;* **~ wall** *n.* Böschungsmauer, *die*

retake

A /riː'teɪk/ *v.t., forms as* **take A, B** **1** (recapture) wieder einnehmen ‹*Stadt, Festung*› **2** (take again) wiederholen ‹*Prüfung, Strafstoß*› **3** (Cinemat.) nachdrehen ‹*Szene*›

B /'riːteɪk/ *n.* **1** (of exam) Wiederholung, *die* **2** (Cinemat.) Retake, *das;* Neuaufnahme, *die*

retaliate /rɪ'tælɪeɪt/ *v.i.* Vergeltung üben (**against** an + *Dat.*); sich revanchieren (ugs.); ‹*Truppen:*› zurückschlagen; kontern (**against** *Akk.*) ‹*Maßnahme, Kritik*›; **~ by doing sth.** sich revanchieren, indem man etw. tut

retaliation /rɪtælɪ'eɪʃn/ *n.* (in war, fight) Vergeltung, *die;* Gegenschlag, *der;* (in argument etc.) Konter, *der* (ugs.); Konterschlag, *der;* **in ~ for** als Vergeltung für; **she did that in ~ for his cruelty** sie revanchierte sich damit für seine Grausamkeit

retaliatory /rɪ'tæljətərɪ/ *adj.* Vergeltungs‹*maßnahme, -angriff*›

retard /rɪ'tɑːd/ *v.t.* verzögern; retardieren (bes. Physiol., Psych.)

retardant /rɪ'tɑːdənt/

A *adj.* hemmend; **flame-/rust-~:** feuer-/rosthemmend

B *n.* Hemmstoff, *der*

retardation /riːtɑː'deɪʃn/ *n.* Verzögerung, *die;* Retardation, *die* (bes. Physiol., Psych.); (braking) Bremswirkung, *die*

retarded /rɪ'tɑːdɪd/ *adj.* **1** (Psychol.) **[mentally] ~:** [geistig] zurückgeblieben **2** (Motor Veh.) **~ ignition** Spätzündung, *die*

retarder /rɪ'tɑːdə(r)/ *n.* (Motor Veh.) Dauerbremse, *die*

retch /retʃ, riːtʃ/

A *v.i.* würgen

B *n.* Würgen, *das*

retd. *abbr.* = **retired** a. D.; i. R.

retell /riː'tel/ *v.t.*, **retold** /riː'təʊld/ nacherzählen; (tell again) noch einmal erzählen

retention /rɪ'tenʃn/ *n.* **1** (keeping) (of power) Erhaltung, *die;* (of money) Einbehaltung, *die* **2** ▸**retain 2**: Festhalten, *das* (**of** an + *Dat.*); Beibehaltung, *die* **3** **~ of water** (by soil, plant) Speicherung von Wasser **4** ▸**retain 4**: Beauftragung, *die* **5** (Med.) Retention, *die;* (of urine) Verhaltung, *die* **6** **powers of ~:** Merkfähigkeit, *die*

retentive /rɪ'tentɪv/ *adj.* **1** gut ‹*Gedächtnis*›; **a memory ~ of details** ein gutes Gedächtnis für Details **2** (holding moisture) Feuchtigkeit speichernd ‹*Boden*›; **soil ~ of moisture** Boden, der Feuchtigkeit speichert

rethink /riː'θɪŋk/

A *v.t.*, **rethought** /riː'θɔːt/ noch einmal überdenken

B *n.* **have a ~ about sth.** etw. noch einmal überdenken

reticence /'retɪsəns/ *n., no pl.* Zurückhaltung, *die* (**on** in Bezug auf + *Akk.*)

reticent /'retɪsənt/ *adj.* **1** (reserved) zurückhaltend (**on, about** in Bezug auf + *Akk.*) **2** (restrained) schlicht ‹*Stil*›

retina /'retɪnə/ *n., pl.* **~s** *or* **~e** /'retɪniː/ (Anat.) Retina, *die* (fachspr.); Netzhaut, *die*

retinitis /retɪ'naɪtɪs/ *n.* (Med.) Netzhautentzündung, *die;* Retinitis, *die* (fachspr.)

retinue /'retɪnjuː/ *n.* Gefolge, *das*

retiracy /rɪ'taɪərəsɪ/ *n., no pl.* (Amer.) Abgeschiedenheit, *die*

retiral /rɪ'taɪərl/ *n.* (Scot.) Rücktritt, *der* (**from** von); Ausscheiden, *das* (**from** aus)

retire /rɪ'taɪə(r)/

A *v.i.* **1** (give up work or position) ausscheiden (**from** aus); aufhören [zu arbeiten]; ‹*Angestellter, Arbeiter:*› in Rente (*Akk.*) gehen; ‹*Beamter, Militär:*› in Pension *od.* den Ruhestand gehen; ‹*Selbstständiger:*› sich zur Ruhe setzen; **~ on a pension** ‹*Angestellter, Arbeiter:*› auf *od.* in Rente (*Akk.*) gehen; ‹*Beamter, Militär:*› in Pension (*Akk.*) gehen **2** (withdraw) sich zurückziehen (**to** in + *Akk.*); (Sport) aufgeben; **~ [to bed]** sich [zum Schlafen] zurückziehen; **~ from the world/into oneself** sich von der Welt/in sich (*Akk.*) selbst zurückziehen

B *v.t.* (compel to leave) aus Altersgründen entlassen; pensionieren, in den Ruhestand versetzen ‹*Beamten, Militär*›; **be ~d early** in den vorzeitigen Ruhestand versetzt werden

retired /rɪ'taɪəd/ *adj.* **1** (no longer working) aus dem Berufsleben ausgeschieden ‹*Angestellter, Arbeiter, Selbstständiger*›; ‹*Beamter, Soldat*› im Ruhestand, pensioniert; **be ~:** nicht mehr arbeiten; ‹*Angestellter, Arbeiter:*› Rentner/Rentnerin *od.* in Rente (*Akk.*) sein; ‹*Beamter, Soldat:*› im Ruhestand *od.* pensioniert sein **2** (withdrawn) zurückgezogen ‹*Leben*›

retired list *n.* (Mil.) Liste der aus dem aktiven Dienst Ausgeschiedenen

retiree /rɪtaɪə'riː/ *n.* (Amer.) Ruheständler, *der*/-ständlerin, *die;* (ex-employee also) Rentner, *der*/Rentnerin, *die;* (ex-civil servant/serviceman also) Pensionär, *der*/Pensionärin, *die*

retirement /rɪ'taɪəmənt/ *n.* **1** (leaving work) Ausscheiden aus dem Arbeitsleben **2** *no art.* (period) Ruhestand, *der;* **go into ~** ‹*Selbstständiger:*› sich zur Ruhe setzen; ‹*Angestellter, Arbeiter:*› in Rente (*Akk.*) gehen; ‹*Beamter, Militär:*› in Pension *od.* den Ruhestand gehen; **take early ~** ‹*Selbstständiger:*› sich vorzeitig zur Ruhe setzen; ‹*Angestellter, Arbeiter:*› vorzeitig in Rente (*Akk.*) gehen; ‹*Beamter, Militär:*› sich vorzeitig pensionieren lassen; **how will you spend your ~?** was machen Sie, wenn Sie einmal nicht mehr arbeiten/in Rente/im Ruhestand sind? **3** (withdrawing) Rückzug, *der* (**to, into** in + *Akk.*) **4** (seclusion) Zurückgezogenheit, *die;* **live in ~:** zurückgezogen leben

retirement: ~ age *n.* Altersgrenze, *die;* (of employees also) Rentenalter, *das;* (of civil servants, servicemen also) Pensionsalter, *das;* **~ home** *n.* **1** (house, flat) Alters- *od.* Ruhesitz, *der;* **2** (institution) Alters- *od.* Altenheim, *das;* **~ pay, ~ pension** *ns.* (for employees) [Alters]rente, *die;* (for civil servants, servicemen) Pension, *die*

retiring /rɪ'taɪərɪŋ/ *adj.* (shy) zurückhaltend

retiring: ~ age ▸**retirement age**; **~ collection** *n.* (at church service) Kollekte, *die;* (at concert) Spendensammlung, *die*

retold ▸**retell**

retook ▸**retake A**

retool /riː'tuːl/ *v.t.* umrüsten (**for** auf + *Akk.*)

r

retort¹ /rɪ'tɔːt/
A *n.* Entgegnung, *die,* Erwiderung, *die* (**to** auf + *Akk.*)
B *v.t.* entgegnen
C *v.i.* scharf antworten

retort² *n.* (Chem., Industry) Retorte, *die*

retouch /riː'tʌtʃ/ *v.t.* (Art, Photog., Printing) retuschieren

retrace /rɪ'treɪs/ *v.t.* [1] (trace back) zurückverfolgen [2] (trace again) nachvollziehen ‹*Entwicklung*› [3] (go back over) zurückgehen; **~ one's steps/path** denselben Weg noch einmal zurückgehen

retract /rɪ'trækt/
A *v.t.* [1] (withdraw) zurücknehmen; *abs.* **he refused to ~:** er weigerte sich, es zurückzunehmen [2] (Aeronaut.) einziehen, einfahren ‹*Fahrgestell*› [3] (draw back) zurückziehen; einziehen ‹*Fühler, Krallen*›
B *v.i.* [1] (Aeronaut.) ‹*Fahrgestell:*› einziehbar *od.* einfahrbar sein [2] (be drawn back) ‹*Fühler, Krallen:*› eingezogen werden

retractable /rɪ'træktəbl/ *adj.* (Aeronaut.) einziehbar, einfahrbar ‹*Fahrgestell*›

retraction /rɪ'trækʃn/ *n.* [1] (withdrawing) Zurücknahme, *die;* **make a ~ of sth.** etw. zurücknehmen [2] (drawing-back of undercarriage, claws, etc.) Einziehen, *das*

retrain /riː'treɪn/
A *v.i.* [sich] umschulen [lassen]
B *v.t.* umschulen ‹*Person*›

retraining /riː'treɪnɪŋ/ *n.* Umschulung, *die; attrib.* Umschulungs‹*programm*›

retranslate /riːtræns'leɪt/ *v.t.* [zu]rückübersetzen

retranslation /riːtræns'leɪʃn/ *n.* Rückübersetzung, *die*

retransmit /riːtræns'mɪt/ *v.t.*, **-tt-** [1] (transmit again) noch einmal übermitteln ‹*Nachricht*›; noch einmal senden ‹*Signal*› [2] (transmit further) weiterübermitteln ‹*Nachricht*›; weitersenden ‹*Signal*›

retread (Motor Veh.)
A /'riːtred/ *n.* runderneuerter Reifen
B /riː'tred/ *v.t.* runderneuern ‹*Reifen*›

retreat /rɪ'triːt/
A *n.* [1] (withdrawal; also Mil. or fig.) Rückzug, *der;* **their ~ from the territory/position** ihr Rückzug aus dem Gebiet/von der Stellung; **beat a ~:** den Rückzug antreten; (fig.) das Feld räumen; **make good one's ~:** sich in Sicherheit (*Akk.*) bringen; (fig.) sich aus dem Staub machen (ugs.); *see also* **hasty** [2] (place of seclusion) Zuflucht, *die;* Zufluchtsort, *der;* (hiding place also) Unterschlupf, *der;* **country ~:** Refugium auf dem Lande [3] (Relig.: for prayer) Exerzitien *Pl.* [4] (Mil.: bugle-call) (for return to barracks) Zapfenstreich, *der;* (for withdrawal) **sound/give the ~:** zum Rückzug blasen
B *v.i.* [1] (withdraw; also Mil. or fig.) sich zurückziehen; (in fear) zurückweichen; **~ within oneself** sich in sich (*Akk.*) selbst zurückziehen; **~ from a territory/position** sich aus einem Gebiet/von einer Stellung zurückziehen; **~ from an aggressive stance** eine aggressive Haltung aufgeben [2] (recede) ‹*Überschwemmung, Gletscher usw.:*› zurückgehen

retrench /rɪ'trenʃ/
A *v.t.* senken ‹*Ausgaben, Lohn*›
B *v.i.* sich einschränken

retrenchment /rɪ'trenʃmənt/ *n.* Senkung, *die;* **policy of ~:** Sparpolitik, *die*

retrial /riː'traɪəl/ *n.* (Law) Wiederaufnahmeverfahren, *das;* **he asked for a ~:** er verlangte eine Wiederaufnahme des Verfahrens

retribution /retrɪ'bjuːʃn/ *n.* Vergeltung, *die;* **in ~ for** zur Vergeltung für

retributive /rɪ'trɪbjʊtɪv/ *adj.* vergeltend; ausgleichend ‹*Gerechtigkeit*›

retrievable /rɪ'triːvəbl/ *adj.* [1] (able to be set right) noch nicht ausweglos *od.* völlig verfahren ‹*Situation*›; wieder gutzumachend ‹*Fehler*›; **be ~** ‹*Situation:*› zu retten sein; ‹*Fehler:*› wieder gutzumachen sein [2] (able to be rescued) zu rettend/(from wreckage) zu bergend; **be ~:** zu retten/bergen sein [3] (able to be recovered) **the ball/money is ~:** den Ball/das Geld kann man wiederholen/-bekommen [4] (Computing) wieder auffindbar ‹*Informationen*›

retrieval /rɪ'triːvl/ *n.* [1] (setting right) (of situation) Rettung, *die;* (of mistake) Wiedergutmachung, *die;* **beyond** *or* **past ~:** hoffnungslos [2] (rescue) Rettung, *die;* (from wreckage) Bergung, *die* (**from** aus) [3] (recovery) ▸ **retrieve A 3:** Zurückholen, *das;* Wiederholen, *das;* Wiedergewinnung, *die;* **the ~ of the money was difficult** es war schwierig, das Geld wiederzubekommen; **the money/chance was lost beyond ~:** das Geld/die Gelegenheit war unwiederbringlich verloren [4] (Computing) Wiederauffinden, *das*

retrieve /rɪ'triːv/ *v.t.* [1] (set right) wieder gutmachen ‹*Fehler*›; retten ‹*Situation*› [2] (rescue) retten (**from** aus); (from wreckage) bergen (**from** aus); **timber ~d from the beach** als Strandgut aufgelesenes Holz [3] (recover) zurückholen ‹*Brief*›; wiederholen ‹*Ball*›; wiedergewinnen ‹*Ansehen, Würde*›; wiederbekommen ‹*Geld*›; **~ sth. from the depths of one's subconscious** etw. aus den Tiefen seines Unterbewusstseins hervorholen [4] (Computing) wieder auffinden ‹*Information*› [5] (fetch) ‹*Hund:*› apportieren

retriever /rɪ'triːvə(r)/ *n.* Apportierhund, *der;* (breed) Retriever, *der*

retro /'retrəʊ/ *adj.* retro; **~ look** Retrolook, *der*

retroactive /retrəʊ'æktɪv/ *adj.* rückwirkend; **~ effect** Rückwirkung, *die*

retrochoir /'retrəʊkwaɪə(r)/ *n.* (Eccl. Archit.) Retrochor, *der*

retrograde /'retrəgreɪd/ *adj.* [1] (retreating) **~ motion** Rückwärtsbewegung, *die;* **~ step** (fig.) Rückschritt, *der* [2] (reverting to the past) rückschrittlich ‹*Idee, Politik, Maßnahme*› [3] (inverse) umgekehrt ‹*Reihenfolge*›

retrogress /retrə'gres/ *v.i.* [1] sich zurückbewegen [2] (fig.: deteriorate) ‹*Gesundheitszustand:*› sich verschlechtern

retrogression /retrə'greʃn/ *n.* [1] Rückwärtsbewegung, *die* [2] (Biol.) Rückentwicklung, *die*

retrogressive /retrə'gresɪv/ *adj.* [1] ▸ **retrograde 1, 2** [2] (Biol.) rückläufig ‹*Entwicklung*›

retro-rocket /'retrəʊrɒkɪt/ *n.* (Astronaut.) Bremsrakete, *die*

retrospect /'retrəspekt/ *n.* **in ~:** im Nachhinein; **in ~, I think ...:** rückblickend *od.* im Nachhinein glaube ich, ...

retrospection /retrə'spekʃn/ *n.* Rückschau, *die*

retrospective /retrə'spektɪv/
A *adj.* [1] retrospektiv (geh.); **~ exhibition** Retrospektive, *die* (geh.); **take a ~ look at sth.** Rückschau auf etw. (*Akk.*) halten (geh.) [2] (applying to the past) rückwirkend ‹*Lohnerhöhung, Gesetz, Vertragsänderung*›; **be ~:** Rückwirkung haben
B *n.* (Art) Retrospektive, *die* (geh.)

retrospectively /retrə'spektɪvlɪ/ *adv.* [1] (by retrospection) im Nachhinein, rückblickend ‹*betrachten*› [2] (so as to apply to the past) rückwirkend; **a law operating ~:** ein rückwirkendes Gesetz; ein Gesetz mit Rückwirkung

retroussé /rə'truːseɪ/ *adj.* **~ nose** Stupsnase, *die*

retrovirus /'retrəʊvaɪrəs/ *n.* (Biol.) Retrovirus, *das od. der*

retry /riː'traɪ/ *v.t.* (Law) neu verhandeln ‹*Fall*›; neu verhandeln gegen ‹*Person*›

retsina /re'tsiːnə/ *n.* Retsina, *der*

retune /riː'tjuːn/ *v.t.* [1] neu stimmen ‹*Musikinstrument*› [2] neu einstellen ‹*Radio*›

returf /riː'tɜːf/ *v.t.* neuen Rasen verlegen auf (+ *Dat.*) ‹*Platz, Spielfeld usw.*›

return /rɪ'tɜːn/
A *v.i.* [1] (come back) zurückkommen; zurückkehren (geh.); ‹*Jahreszeit:*› wiederkehren; (go back) zurückgehen; zurückkehren (geh.); (go back by vehicle) zurückfahren; zurückkehren (geh.); **~ home** wieder nach Hause kommen/gehen/fahren/zurückkehren; **~ to work** (after holiday or strike) die Arbeit wieder aufnehmen; **she had gone never to ~:** sie war für immer gegangen; **~ to health** wieder gesund werden; **his good spirits quickly ~ed** seine gute Laune stellte sich rasch wieder ein
[2] (revert) **~ to a subject/one's old habits** auf ein Thema zurückkommen/in seine alten Gewohnheiten zurückfallen; **unto dust thou shalt ~** (Relig.) zu Staub sollst du wieder werden
B *v.t.* [1] (bring back) zurückbringen; zurückgeben ‹*geliehenen/gestohlenen Gegenstand, gekaufte Ware*›; [wieder] zurückschicken ‹*unzustellbaren Brief*›; (to original position) zurückstellen ‹*Hebel*›; (hand back, refuse) zurückweisen ‹*Scheck*›; (put back) (vertically) [wieder] zurückstellen ‹*Buch, Ordner*›; (horizontally) [wieder] zurücklegen ‹*Geld, Buch, Ordner*›; (to file) wieder einheften ‹*Brief*›; **~ed with thanks** mit Dank zurück; **'~ to sender'** (on letter) „zurück an Absender"; **he ~ed his purse to his pocket** er steckte sein Portemonnaie wieder ein; **he ~ed the fish to the water** er setzte den Fisch wieder ins Wasser
[2] (restore) **~ sth. to its original state** *or* **condition** etw. wieder in seinen ursprünglichen Zustand versetzen
[3] (yield) abwerfen ‹*Gewinn*›
[4] (give back sth. similar) erwidern ‹*Besuch, Gruß, Liebe, Gewehrfeuer*›; sich revanchieren für (ugs.) ‹*Freundlichkeit, Gefallen*›; zurückgeben ‹*Schlag*›
[5] (elect) wählen ‹*Kandidaten*›; **~ sb. to Parliament** jmdn. ins Parlament wählen
[6] (Sport) zurückschlagen ‹*Ball*›; (throw back) zurückwerfen
[7] (answer) erwidern; entgegnen
[8] (declare) **~ a verdict of guilty/not guilty** ‹*Geschworene:*› auf „schuldig"/„nicht schuldig" erkennen; **~ sb. guilty** jmdn. schuldig sprechen
C *n.* [1] ▸ ❶ **p. 1189** (coming back) Rückkehr, *die;* (to home) Heimkehr, *die;* (of illness) Wiederauftreten, *das;* **his ~ to work/school had to be delayed** er musste die Wiederaufnahme seiner *od.* der Arbeit verschieben/er konnte erst später [als vorgesehen] wieder zur Schule gehen; **point of no ~** ▸ **point A 11; ~ to health** Genesung, *die* (geh.); **many happy ~s [of the day]!** herzlichen Glückwunsch [zum Geburtstag]!; **wish sb. many happy ~s [of the day]** jmdm. [zum Geburtstag] alles Gute wünschen
[2] **by ~ [of post]** postwendend
[3] (ticket) Rückfahrkarte, *die;* (for flight) Rückflugschein, *der;* **single or ~?** einfach oder hin und zurück?
[4] (proceeds) **~[s]** Ertrag, Gewinn, *der* (**on, from** aus); **~ on capital** Kapitalgewinn, *der; see also* **diminishing**
[5] (bringing back) Zurückbringen, *das;* (of property, goods, book) Rückgabe, *die* (**to** an + *Akk.*); (of cheque) Zurückweisung, *die;* (of loan) Rückzahlung, *die*
[6] (giving back of sth. similar) Erwiderung, *die;* **receive/get sth. in ~ [for sth.]** etw. [für etw.] bekommen
[7] (Sport: striking back) Rückschlag, *der;* (throw back) Rückwurf, *der;* **pick up the ~** (Footb. etc.) den zurückgespielten Ball annehmen
[8] (report) Bericht, *der;* (set of statistics) statistischer Bericht; Statistik, *die;* **income-tax ~:** Einkommenssteuererklärung, *die;* **election ~s** Wahlergebnisse
[9] (Brit. Parl.: electing) Wahl, *die*
[10] *attrib.* (Archit.) Flügel‹*mauer, -wand*›
[11] (Computing) **press ~:** Return *od.* die Returntaste drücken; **~ key** Returntaste, *die*

returnable /rɪ'tɜːnəbl/ *adj.* Mehrweg‹*behälter, -flasche usw.*›; rückzahlbar ‹*Gebühr, Kaution*›; **~ bottle** Pfandflasche, *die;* **~ deposit** Pfand, *der*

re'turn channel *n.* (Teleph., Telev.) Rückkanal, *der*

returned /rɪ'tɜːnd/ *adj.* heimgekehrt; **~ emigrant** Rückwanderer, *der*

returnee /rɪtɜː'niː/ *n.* Rückkehrer, *der*/Rückkehrerin, *die*

return: ~ envelope *n.* Rückumschlag, *der;* **~ 'fare** *n.* Preis für eine Rückfahrkarte/(for flight) einen Rückflugschein; **what is the ~ fare?** wie viel kostet eine Rückfahrkarte/ein Rückflugschein?; **~ 'flight** *n.* Rückflug, *der;* (both ways) Hin- und Rückflug, *der;* **~ 'game** *n.* Rückspiel, *das*

re'turning officer *n.* (Brit. Parl.) Wahlleiter, *der*/-leiterin, *die*

r

return: ~ 'journey *n.* Rückreise, *die;* Rückfahrt, *die;* (both ways) Hin- und Rückfahrt, *die;* **~ 'match** *n.* Rückspiel, *das;* **~ 'ticket** *n.* (Brit.) Rückfahrkarte, *die;* (for flight) Rückflugschein, *der;* **~ 'trip** *n.* **1** (trip back) Rückweg, *der;* Rückfahrt, *die;* **2** (trip out and back) Hin- und Rückfahrt, *die;* Hin- und Rückreise, *die;* (by plane) Hin- und Rückflug, *der;* **~ 'visit** *n.* **1** (further visit) nochmaliger Besuch; **make a ~ visit to a place** einen Ort noch einmal besuchen; **2** (visit in reciprocation) Gegenbesuch, *der*

retype /riːˈtaɪp/ *v.t.* neu tippen

reunification /riːjuːnɪfɪˈkeɪʃn/ *n.* Wiedervereinigung, *die*

reunify /riːˈjuːnɪfaɪ/ *v.t.* wieder vereinigen

reunion /riːˈjuːnjən/ *n.* **1** (gathering) Treffen, *das* **2** (reuniting) Wiedersehen, *das* **3** (reunited state) Wiedervereinigung, *die*

reunite /riːjʊˈnaɪt/

A *v.t.* wieder zusammenführen; **a ~d Germany** ein wieder vereinigtes Deutschland

B *v.i.* sich wieder zusammenschließen; ‹*Kirchen:*› sich wieder vereinigen

reusable /riːˈjuːzəbl/ *adj.* wieder verwendbar

reuse

A /riːˈjuːz/ *v.t.* wieder verwenden

B /riːˈjuːs/ *n.* Wiederverwendung, *die*

rev /rev/ (coll.)

A *n., usu. in pl.* Umdrehung, *die;* Tour, *die* (Technikjargon); **~ counter** (Brit.) Tourenzähler, *der* (ugs.)

B *v.i.,* **-vv-** mit hoher Drehzahl *od.* hochtourig laufen

C *v.t.,* **-vv-** hochdrehen (Technikjargon); (noisily) aufheulen lassen ‹*Motor*›

Phrasal verb

• **~ 'up**

A *v.i.* ‹*Motor:*› hochgejagt werden (Technikjargon); **I heard [the sound of] a car ~ving up** ich hörte den Motor eines Autos aufheulen

B *v.t.* hochjagen (Technikjargon); aufheulen lassen ‹*Motor[rad]*›

Rev. /ˈrevərənd, (coll.) rev/ *abbr.* ▸ℹ p. 1634 **= Reverend** Rev.

revaluation /riːvæljʊˈeɪʃn/ *n.* **1** (of object) Neubewertung, *die* **2** (Econ.: of currency) Aufwertung, *die*

revalue /riːˈvæljuː/ *v.t.* **1** neu bewerten **2** (Econ.) aufwerten ‹*Währung*›

revamp /riːˈvæmp/ *v.t.* renovieren ‹*Zimmer, Gebäude*›; [wieder] aufmöbeln *od.* aufpolieren ‹*Schrank, Auto usw.*›; neu bearbeiten ‹*Stück, Musical usw.*›; auf Vordermann bringen (ugs.) ‹*Firma*›

Revd. /ˈrevərənd, (coll.) rev/ *abbr.* ▸ℹ p. 1634 **= Reverend** Rev.

reveal /rɪˈviːl/

A *v.t.* enthüllen (geh.); verraten; offenbaren (geh., Theol.), [offen] zeigen ‹*Gefühle*›; **be ~ed** ‹*Wahrheit:*› ans Licht kommen; **all will be ~ed** (joc.) es kommt alles ans Licht (scherzh.); **~ one's identity** seine Identität preisgeben (geh.); **~ oneself/itself to be** *or* **as being sth.** sich als etw. erweisen; **~ sb. to be sth.** jmdn. als etw. enthüllen (geh.); **the rising curtain ~ed a street scene** der sich hebende Vorhang gab den Blick auf eine Straßenszene frei; **there was not much that the dress did not ~:** das Kleid verhüllte nur wenig

B *n.* (Archit.) Laibung, *die*

revealed religion /rɪviːld rɪˈlɪdʒn/ *n.* Offenbarungsreligion, *die*

revealing /rɪˈviːlɪŋ/ *adj.* aufschlussreich ‹*Darstellung, Dokument*›; verräterisch ‹*Bemerkung, Versprecher*›; offenherzig (scherzh.) ‹*Kleid, Bluse usw.*›; **be ~ about sth.** etwas *od.* einiges über etw. (*Akk.*) verraten

reveille /rɪˈvælɪ, rɪˈvelɪ/ *n.* (Mil.) Reveille, *die* (fachspr. veralt.); Wecksignal, *das;* **sound [the] ~:** das Wecksignal geben; **~ was at 6 a.m.** Wecken war um sechs Uhr morgens

revel /ˈrevl/

A *v.i.,* (Brit.) **-ll- 1** (take delight) genießen (**in** *Akk.*); **~ in doing sth.** es [richtig] genießen, etw. zu tun **2** (carouse) feiern; **~ the night away, ~ till dawn** die Nacht durchfeiern (ugs.)

B *n. usu pl.* Feiern, *das;* Feierei, *die* (ugs.)

revelation /revəˈleɪʃn/ *n.* **1** Enthüllung, *die* (geh.); **be a ~:** einem die Augen öffnen; **the dessert/concert was a ~:** das Dessert/Konzert war eine Offenbarung (scherzh.); **what a ~!** unglaublich!; **be a ~ to sb.** jmdm. die Augen öffnen **2** (Relig.) Offenbarung, *die;* **[the** *or* **the Book of] R~[s]** die Offenbarung [des Johannes]; **R~[s] 3:14** Offenbarung 3,14

reveller /ˈrevələ(r)/ *n.* Feiernde, *der/die*

revelry /ˈrevəlrɪ/ *n.* Feiern, *das;* Feierei, *die* (ugs.); **spend the whole night in ~:** die ganze Nacht durchfeiern (ugs.); **hear sounds of ~:** hören, wie gefeiert wird

revenge /rɪˈvendʒ/

A *v.t.* rächen ‹*Person, Tat*›; sich rächen für ‹*Tat*›; **~ oneself** *or* **be ~d [on sb.] [for sth.]** sich [für etw.] [an jmdm.] rächen

B *n.* **1** (action) Rache, *die;* **[desire for] ~:** Rachsucht, *die* (geh.); **take ~** *or* **have** *or* (literary) **exact one's ~ [on sb.] [for sth.]** Rache [an jmdm.] [für etw.] nehmen *od.* (geh.) üben; **~ is sweet** Rache ist süß; **in ~ for sth.** als Rache für etw. **2** (Sport, Games) Revanche, *die;* **give sb. his ~:** jmdm. Revanche geben

revengeful /rɪˈvendʒfl/ *adj.* rachsüchtig (geh.); **~ act** Racheakt, *der*

revenue /ˈrevənjuː/ *n.* **1** (State's income) **[national/state] ~:** Staatseinnahmen; öffentliche Einnahmen **2** **~[s]** (income) Einnahmen; Einkünfte *Pl.;* **source of ~:** Einnahmequelle, *die* **3** **R~** (department) *oberste Finanzbehörde*

revenue: ~ officer *n.* ≈ Zollbeamter, *der/*-beamtin, *die;* **~ stamp** *n.* Steuerzeichen, *das;* (paper strip on cigarette packet etc.); [Steuer]banderole, *die*

reverberate /rɪˈvɜːbəreɪt/

A *v.i.* ‹*Geräusch, Musik:*› widerhallen

B *v.t.* zurückwerfen; reflektieren

reverberation /rɪvɜːbəˈreɪʃn/ *n.* **~[s]** Widerhall, *der;* **~ of sound** Schallreflexion, *die;* **the ~s of that episode** (fig.) der Nachhall dieser Begebenheit

revere /rɪˈvɪə(r)/ *v.t.* verehren

reverence /ˈrevərəns/ *n.* **1** (revering) Verehrung, *die;* Ehrfurcht, *die;* **hold sb. in** *or* **regard sb. with ~:** jmdn. verehren; **hold sth. in ~:** etw. heilig halten; **pay ~ to sb.** jmdm. Verehrung entgegenbringen; **have/show ~ for sth./sb.** vor etw./jmdm. Ehrfurcht haben/zeigen **2** **Your/His R~** (arch./Ir./joc.) Euer/Seine Hochwürden

reverend /ˈrevərənd/ ▸ℹ p. 1634

A *adj.* ehrwürdig; **the R~ John Wilson, the R~ Mr Wilson** Hochwürden [John] Wilson; **the Very/Right R~ Donald Todd** Hochwürden [Donald] Todd; **the Most R~ Archbishop of York** Seine Exzellenz der Hochwürdigste Erzbischof von York; **the R~ Father [O'Higgins]** Hochwürden [O'Higgins]; **the ~ gentleman** Hochwürden; **R~ Mother** Ehrwürdige Schwester Oberin *od.* Frau Oberin

B *n.* (coll.) Pfarrer, *der;* (form of address) Hochwürden

reverent /ˈrevərənt/ *adj.* ehrfürchtig; **have a ~ attitude to sb., be ~ towards sb.** Ehrfurcht vor jmdm. haben; **in hushed and ~ tones** mit ehrfurchtsvoll gedämpfter Stimme

reverential /revəˈrenʃl/ *adj.* ehrfürchtig

reverently /ˈrevərəntlɪ/ *adv.* ehrfürchtig; ehrerbietig ‹*sich verneigen*›

reverie /ˈrevərɪ/ *n.* Träumerei, *die;* **be deep** *or* **lost** *or* **sunk in [a] ~:** in Träumereien (*Akk.*) versunken sein; **fall into a ~:** in Träumereien (*Akk.*) versinken

reversal /rɪˈvɜːsl/ *n.* **1** Umkehrung, *die;* **~ [colour] film** Umkehrfilm, *der* **2** (Law) Aufhebung, *die*

reverse /rɪˈvɜːs/

A *adj.* entgegengesetzt ‹*Richtung*›; Rück‹*seite*›; umgekehrt ‹*Reihenfolge*›; **the ~ side of the coin** (fig.) die Kehrseite der Medaille

B *n.* **1** (contrary) Gegenteil, *das;* **quite the ~!** ganz im Gegenteil!; **in ~:** rückwärts ‹*schreiben, drucken*› **2** (Motor Veh.) Rückwärtsgang, *der;* **in ~:** im Rückwärtsgang; **put the car into ~, go into ~:** den Rückwärtsgang einlegen **3** (defeat) Rückschlag, *der;* **~s of fortune** Schicksalsschläge *Pl.* **4** (back side of coin etc.) Rückseite, *die;* Revers, *der* (Münzk.); (design) Rückseitenbild, *das* **5** (back of page) Rückseite, *die;* Verso, *das* (Buchw.)

C *v.t.* **1** (turn around) umkehren ‹*Reihenfolge, Wortstellung, Bewegung, Richtung*›; grundlegend revidieren ‹*Politik*›; **~ the charge[s]** (Brit.) ein R-Gespräch anmelden; **make a ~d-charge call** (Brit.) ein R-Gespräch führen; **~ arms** (Mil.) die Gewehre mit dem Kolben nach oben halten **2** (cause to move backwards) zurücksetzen; **~ a car into sth.** ein Auto rückwärts in etw. (*Akk.*) fahren **3** (revoke) aufheben ‹*Urteil, Anordnung*›; kassieren (Rechtsspr.) ‹*Urteil*›; rückgängig machen ‹*Maßnahme*›

D *v.i.* zurücksetzen; rückwärts fahren; **~ into sth.** rückwärts in etw. (*Akk.*) fahren

reverse: ~-charge *adj.* (Brit.) **make a ~-charge call** ein R-Gespräch führen; **~ dis'crimi'nation** *n., no pl.* umgekehrte Diskriminierung; **~-engi'neer** *v.t.* **1** (examine) analysieren; **2** (make) nachbauen ‹*Produkt*›; **~ engi'neering** *n., no pl.* Reverse-Engineering, *das* (fachspr.); **~ 'gear** *n.* (Motor Veh.) Rückwärtsgang, *der; see also* **gear A 1**

reversible /rɪˈvɜːsɪbl/ *adj.* **1** umkehrbar, (fachspr.) reversibel ‹*Vorgang*›; (capable of being revoked) aufhebbar ‹*Entscheidung, Anordnung*› **2** (having two usable sides) beidseitig verwendbar, (Textilw.) beidrecht ‹*Stoff*›; beidseitig tragbar ‹*Kleidungsstück*›; Wende‹*mantel, -jacke*›

re'versing light *n.* Rückfahrscheinwerfer, *der*

reversion /rɪˈvɜːʃn/ *n.* **1** (return) Rückkehr, *die* (**to** zu); **~ to type** (Biol.) Rückschlag auf eine frühere Ahnenform; (fig.) atavistischer Rückfall **2** (Law: return of estate) Rückfall, *der;* Heimfall, *der* (Rechtsspr.)

revert /rɪˈvɜːt/ *v.i.* **1** (recur, return) zurückkommen (**to** auf + *Akk.*), wieder aufgreifen (**to** *Akk.*) ‹*Thema, Angelegenheit, Frage*›; ‹*Gedanken:*› zurückkehren (geh.) (**to** zu); **to ~ to ...:** um wieder auf ... (*Akk.*) zurückzukommen; **she has ~ed to using her maiden name** sie hat wieder ihren Mädchennamen angenommen; **~ to type** (Biol.) auf eine frühere Ahnenform zurückschlagen; **he has ~ed to type** (fig.) er geht jetzt wieder seinen alten Gewohnheiten nach; **~ to its natural state** in den Naturzustand zurückkehren; **~ to savagery** ‹*Menschen:*› in den Zustand der Wildheit zurückfallen; **~ to desert** *etc.* ‹*Land:*› wieder verwüsten *usw.* **2** (Law) ‹*Eigentum:*› zurückfallen, (Rechtsspr.) heimfallen (**to** an + *Akk.*)

revetment /rɪˈvetmənt/ *n.* Futtermauer, *die* (Archit.)

review /rɪˈvjuː/

A *n.* **1** (survey) Übersicht, *die* (**of** über + *Akk.*); Überblick, *der* (**of** über + *Akk.*); (of past events) Rückschau, *die* (**of** auf + *Akk.*); **be a ~ of sth.** einen Überblick *od.* eine Übersicht über etw. (*Akk.*) geben **2** (re-examination) [nochmalige] Überprüfung; nochmalige Prüfung; (of salary) Revision, *die;* **be under ~** ‹*Vereinbarung, Lage:*› nochmals geprüft werden **3** (account) Besprechung, *die;* Kritik, *die;* Rezension, *die;* **~ copy** (Publishing) Rezensionsexemplar, *das* **4** (periodical) Zeitschrift, *die* **5** (Mil.) Inspektion, *die;* (march) Parade, *die;* **naval ~:** Flottenparade, *die;* **pass in ~:** [vorbei]defilieren; **pass sth. in ~** (fig.) etw. Revue passieren lassen

B *v.t.* **1** (survey) untersuchen; prüfen **2** (re-examine) überprüfen **3** (Mil.) inspizieren; mustern **4** (write a criticism of) besprechen; rezensieren **5** (Law) überprüfen

reviewer /rɪˈvjuːə(r)/ *n.* Rezensent, *der/* Rezensentin, *die;* Kritiker, *der/*Kritikerin, *die*

revile /rɪˈvaɪl/ *v.t.* schmähen (geh.)

revise /rɪˈvaɪz/

A *v.t.* **1** (amend) revidieren ‹*Urteil, Gesetz, Vorschlag*›; **R~d Version** (Brit.) *revidierte Fassung der „Authorized Version" der Bibel (im 19. Jh.)* **2** (check over) durchsehen ‹*Manuskript, Text, Notizen*› **3** (reread) noch einmal durchlesen ‹*Notizen*›; *abs.* lernen; **~ one's maths** Mathe (ugs.) wiederholen

B *n.* (Printing) Revisionsbogen, *der*

r

reviser /rɪˈvaɪzə(r)/ *n.* Bearbeiter, *der*/Bearbeiterin, *die;* (of printer's proof) Korrektor, *der*/Korrektorin, *die*

revision /rɪˈvɪʒn/ *n.* 1 (amending) Revision, *die;* **in need of ~:** revisionsbedürftig 2 (checking over) Durchsicht, *die* 3 (amended version) [Neu]bearbeitung, *die;* überarbeitete *od.* revidierte Fassung 4 (rereading) Wiederholung, *die;* **~ exercises** Wiederholungsübungen

revisionism /ˈrɪˈvɪʒənɪzm/ *n.* Revisionismus, *der*

revisionist /rɪˈvɪʒənɪst/
A *n.* Revisionist, *der*/Revisionistin, *die*
B *adj.* revisionistisch

revisit /riːˈvɪzɪt/ *v.t.* wieder besuchen

revitalize (**revitalise**) /riːˈvaɪtəlaɪz/ *v.t.* neu beleben

revival /rɪˈvaɪvl/ *n.* 1 (making active again, bringing back into use) Wieder- *od.* Neubelebung, *die;* **~ of learning/letters** neue geistige/literarische Blüte 2 (Theatre) Wiederaufführung, *die;* Revival, *das* 3 (Relig.: awakening) Erweckung, *die;* **~ meeting** Erweckungsversammlung, *die* 4 (restoration) Wiederherstellung, *die;* Regenerierung, *die* (geh.); (to consciousness or life; also fig.) Wiederbelebung, *die*

revivalism /rɪˈvaɪvəlɪzm/ *n.* Erweckungsglaube, *der;* Revivalism, *der*

revivalist /rɪˈvaɪvəlɪst/ *n.* Erwecker, *der*/Erweckerin, *die;* (evangelist) Erweckungsprediger, *der*

revive /rɪˈvaɪv/
A *v.i.* 1 (come back to consciousness) wieder zu sich kommen 2 (be reinvigorated) wieder aufleben; zu neuem Leben erwachen; ‹*Geschäft:*› sich wieder beleben; **his spirits/hopes ~d** er lebte wieder auf/schöpfte neue Hoffnung
B *v.t.* 1 (restore to consciousness) wieder beleben 2 (restore to healthy state) wieder auf die Beine bringen ‹*Person*›; wieder aufleben lassen ‹*Blume*›; (reinvigorate) wieder zu Kräften kommen lassen 3 (strengthen, reawaken) wieder wecken ‹*Lebensgeister, Ehrgeiz, Interesse, Wunsch*›; **~ sb.'s hopes** jmdn. neue Hoffnung schöpfen lassen 4 (make active again, bring back into use) wieder aufleben lassen; **the mini-skirt was ~d** der Minirock kam wieder in Mode (*Akk.*) 5 (Theatre) wieder auf die Bühne bringen 6 (renew memory of) wieder lebendig werden lassen

revocable /ˈrevəkəbl/ *adj.* widerrufbar

revocation /revəˈkeɪʃn/ *n.* ▸**revoke A**: Aufhebung, *die;* Widerrufung, *die;* Zurückziehen, *das;* Zurücknahme, *die*

revoke /rɪˈvəʊk/
A *v.t.* 1 (cancel) aufheben ‹*Erlass, Privileg, Entscheidung*›; widerrufen ‹*Befehl*›; zurückziehen ‹*Auftrag*› 2 (withdraw) widerrufen ‹*Erlaubnis, Genehmigung*›; zurücknehmen ‹*Versprechen*›
B *v.i.* (Cards) [unzulässigerweise] nicht bedienen
C *n.* (Cards) Revoke, *die*

revolt /rɪˈvəʊlt/
A *v.i.* 1 (rebel) revoltieren, aufbegehren (geh.) (**against** gegen) 2 (feel revulsion) sich sträuben (**at, against, from** gegen); ‹*Magen:*› revoltieren, rebellieren (**from** bei)
B *v.t.* mit Abscheu erfüllen; **she was ~ed by their brutality** ihre Brutalität erfüllte sie mit Abscheu
C *n.* (rebelling) Aufruhr, *der;* Rebellion, *die;* (rising) Revolte, *die* (auch fig.); Aufstand, *der;* **a spirit of ~:** eine rebellische Stimmung; **be** *or* **rise in ~:** revoltieren; aufbegehren (geh.)

revolting /rɪˈvəʊltɪŋ/ *adj.* (repulsive) abscheulich; scheußlich ‹*Gedanke, Wetter*›; widerlich ‹*Person*›; **be ~ to sb.'s sense of decency** jmds. Anstandsgefühl verletzen

revoltingly /rɪˈvəʊltɪŋlɪ/ *adv.* abstoßend ‹*hässlich, grausam*›

revolution /revəˈluːʃn/ *n.* 1 (lit. or fig.) Revolution, *die;* **the American R~:** die Amerikanische Revolution; der Nordamerikanische Unabhängigkeitskrieg 2 (single turn) Umdrehung, *die;* **number of ~s** Drehzahl, *die* 3 (Astron.: movement in orbit) Umlauf, *der*

revolutionary /revəˈluːʃənərɪ/
A *adj.* 1 (Polit.) revolutionär 2 (involving great changes) revolutionär; umwälzend; (pioneering) bahnbrechend 3 **R~** (Amer. Hist.) des Nordamerikanischen Unabhängigkeitskrieges *nachgestellt;* der Amerikanischen Revolution *nachgestellt*
B *n.* Revolutionär, *der*/Revolutionärin, *die*

revoˈlution counter *n.* Drehzahlmesser, *der*

revolutionize (**revolutionise**) /revəˈluːʃənaɪz/ *v.t.* grundlegend verändern; revolutionieren ‹*Gesellschaft, Technik*›

revolve /rɪˈvɒlv/
A *v.t.* 1 (turn round) drehen 2 **~ sth. in one's mind** (ponder) etw. erwägen
B *v.i.* sich drehen (**round, about, on** um); **everything ~s around her** sie ist der Mittelpunkt[, um den sich alles dreht]

revolver /rɪˈvɒlvə(r)/ *n.* [Trommel]revolver, *der*

revolving /rɪˈvɒlvɪŋ/ *attrib. adj.* drehbar; Dreh‹*stuhl, -tür, -bühne*›; **~ credit** (Finance) Revolvingkredit, *der*

revue /rɪˈvjuː/ *n.* Kabarett, *das;* (musical show) Revue, *die*

revulsion /rɪˈvʌlʃn/ *n.* 1 (feeling) Abscheu, *der* (**at** vor + *Dat.*, gegen); **have a sense of ~ about sth.** von etw. angewidert sein 2 (recoiling) Distanzierung, *die* (**from** von)

reward /rɪˈwɔːd/
A *n.* Belohnung, *die;* (for kindness) Dank, *der;* Lohn, *der;* (recognition of merit etc.) Auszeichnung, *die;* **get very little ~:** kaum belohnt werden; **offer a ~ of £100** 100 Pfund Belohnung aussetzen
B *v.t.* belohnen; **is that how you ~ me for my help?** ist das der Dank für meine Hilfe?

rewarding /rɪˈwɔːdɪŋ/ *adj.* lohnend ‹*Zeitvertreib, Beschäftigung*›; **be ~/financially ~:** sich lohnen/einträglich sein; **bringing up a child can be very ~:** das Großziehen eines Kindes kann einem sehr viel geben

rewind /riːˈwaɪnd/ *v.t.*, **rewound** /riːˈwaʊnd/ 1 (wind again) wieder aufziehen ‹*Uhr*› 2 (wind back) zurückspulen ‹*Film, Band*›

ˈrewind button *n.* (on camera) Rückspulknopf, *der;* (on tape recorder etc.) Rücklauftaste, *die*

rewire /riːˈwaɪə(r)/ *v.t.* mit neuen Leitungen versehen; **~ a house/car** in einem Haus/Auto die Leitungen erneuern

reword /riːˈwɜːd/ *v.t.* umformulieren; neu formulieren

rework /riːˈwɜːk/ *v.t.* neu bearbeiten ‹*Theaterstück, Szene usw.*›; neu formulieren ‹*Satz, Absatz, Text*›

rewound ▸**rewind**

rewritable /ˈriːraɪtəbl/ *adj.* (Computing) wiederbeschreibbar

rewrite
A /riːˈraɪt/ *v.t.*, **rewrote** /riːˈrəʊt/, **rewritten** /riːˈrɪtn/ (write again) noch einmal [neu] schreiben; (write differently) umschreiben
B /ˈriːraɪt/ *n.* Neufassung, *die;* **a complete ~:** eine völlig neue Fassung

ˈrewrite man *n.* (Amer.) Rewriter, *der* (fachspr.); Bearbeiter, *der*

Reynard /ˈrenəd, ˈreɪnəd/ **~[, the fox]** Reineke [Fuchs]

r. h. *abbr.* = **right hand** r.

rhapsodic /ræpˈsɒdɪk/ *adj.* 1 (Mus.) rhapsodisch 2 (fig.: ecstatic) ekstatisch

rhapsodize (**rhapsodise**) /ˈræpsədaɪz/ *v.i.* schwärmen (**about, on** von; **over** über + *Akk.*)

rhapsody /ˈræpsədɪ/ *n.* 1 (Mus.) Rhapsodie, *die* 2 (ecstatic utterance) Schwärmerei, *die;* **go into rhapsodies over sth.** über etw. (*Akk.*) in Ekstase geraten

rhea /ˈriːə/ *n.* (Ornith.) Nandu, *der*

Rhenish /ˈriːnɪʃ, ˈrenɪʃ/ (arch.) *adj.* rheinisch; **~ wine** Rheinwein, *der;* **~ Confederation** (Hist.) Rheinbund, *der*

rheostat /ˈriːəstæt/ *n.* (Electr.) Rheostat, *der*

rhesus/ˈriːsəs/: **~ baby** *n.* (Med.) Rh-geschädigtes Baby; **~ factor** *n.* (Med.) Rhesusfaktor, *der;* **~ monkey** *n.* Rhesusaffe, *der;* **~ ˈnegative** *n.* (Med.) Rhesusfaktor negativ; **~ ˈpositive** *n.* (Med.) Rhesusfaktor positiv

rhetoric /ˈretərɪk/ *n.* 1 (art of discourse) **[art of] ~:** Redekunst, *die;* Rhetorik, *die* 2 (derog.) Phrasen (abwertend) *Pl.*

rhetorical /rɪˈtɒrɪkl/ *adj.* 1 rhetorisch ‹*Frage, Diskurs*› 2 (derog.: designed to impress) phrasenhaft (abwertend)

rheumatic /ruːˈmætɪk/
A *adj.* rheumatisch
B *n.* 1 *in pl.* (coll.) Rheuma, *das* (ugs.) 2 (person) Rheumatiker, *der*/Rheumatikerin, *die;* Rheumakranke, *der*/*die*

rheumatism /ˈruːmətɪzm/ *n.* ▸**i p. 1231** (Med.) Rheumatismus, *der;* Rheuma, *das* (ugs.)

rheumatoid /ˈruːmətɔɪd/ *adj.* (Med.) rheumatisch

rheumatoid arthritis /ruːmətɔɪd ɑːˈθraɪtɪs/ *n.* ▸**i p. 1231** (Med.) chronischer Gelenkrheumatismus

Rhine /raɪn/ *pr. n.* ▸**i p. 1491** Rhein, *der*

ˈRhineland *pr. n.* Rheinland, *das*

Rhineland-Paˈlatinate /raɪnlænd pəˈlætɪnət/ *pr. n.* Rheinland-Pfalz (*das*)

ˈrhinestone *n.* Strass, *der*

Rhine ˈwine *n.* Rheinwein, *der*

rhino /ˈraɪnəʊ/ *n.*, *pl. same or* **~s** (coll.), **rhinoceros** /raɪˈnɒsərəs/ *n.*, *pl. same or* **~ceroses** Nashorn, *das;* Rhinozeros, *das*

rhizome /ˈraɪzəʊm/ *n.* (Bot.) Rhizom, *das* (fachspr.); Wurzelstock, *der*

Rhodes /rəʊdz/ *pr. n.* Rhodos (*das*)

Rhodesia /rəʊˈdiːʒə/ *pr. n.* (Hist.) Rhodesien (*das*)

Rhodesian /rəʊˈdiːʒən/ ▸**i p. 1345** (Hist.)
A *adj.* rhodesisch
B *n.* Rhodesier, *der*/Rhodesierin, *die*

rhododendron /rəʊdəˈdendrən/ *n.* (Bot.) Rhododendron, *der;* Alpenrose, *die*

rhombic /ˈrɒmbɪk/ *adj.* rhombisch

rhomboid /ˈrɒmbɔɪd/
A *adj.* rautenförmig; rhombisch
B *n.* Raute, *die;* Rhomboid, *das*

rhombus /ˈrɒmbəs/ *n.*, *pl.* **~es** *or* **rhombi** /ˈrɒmbaɪ/ (Geom.) Rhombus, *der;* Raute, *die*

rhubarb /ˈruːbɑːb/ *n.* 1 Rhabarber, *der;* (root, purgative) Rhabarberwurzel, *die* 2 (Theatre coll.) **~, ~, ~ ...:** Rhabarber, Rhabarber, Rhabarber ...

rhyme /raɪm/
A *n.* 1 Reim, *der;* **find no ~ or reason in sth.** sich (*Dat.*) auf etw. (*Akk.*) keinen Reim machen können; **without ~ or reason** ohne Sinn und Verstand 2 (short poem) Reim, *der;* (rhyming verse) gereimte Verse; **put sth. into ~:** etw. in Reime setzen 3 (rhyming word) Reimwort, *das;* **'honey' is a ~ for** *or* **to 'money'** „honey" reimt sich auf „money"
B *v.i.* 1 sich reimen (**with** auf + *Akk.*) 2 (versify) reimen
C *v.t.* reimen

ˈrhyme scheme *n.* (Pros.) Reimschema, *das*

rhyming/ˈraɪmɪŋ/: **~ ˈcouplet** *n.* (Pros.) Reimpaar, *das;* **~ dictionary** *n.* Reimwörterbuch, *das;* **~ slang** *n.* Rhyming Slang, *der;* *Slang, bei dem das eigentliche Wort durch eine sich darauf reimende Phrase oder einen Teil einer solchen ersetzt wird*

rhythm /rɪðm/ *n.* Rhythmus, *der;* **~ and blues** (Mus.) Rhythm and Blues, *der*

rhythmic /ˈrɪðmɪk/, **rhythmical** /ˈrɪðmɪkl/ *adj.* rhythmisch; gleichmäßig

rhythmically /ˈrɪðmɪklɪ/ *adv.* rhythmisch; gleichmäßig

rhythmic gymˈnastics *n.* rhythmische Sportgymnastik

rhythm: ~ method *n.* Knaus-Ogino-Methode, *die;* **~ section** *n.* Rhythmusgruppe, *die*

RI *abbr.* (Sch.) = **religious instruction**

rib /rɪb/
A *n.* 1 ▸**i p. 951** (Anat.) Rippe, *die;* **bruised ~s** Rippenprellung, *die;* **dig in the ~s** Rippenstoß, *der* 2 **~[s]** (joint of meat) Rippenstück, *das* 3 (supporting piece) (of insect's wing) Ader, *die;* (of feather) Kiel, *der;* Schaft, *der;* (of boat, ship) Spant, *das;* (of bridge, leaf, ceiling, in knitting, fabric) Rippe, *die;* (of umbrella) Speiche, *die* 4 (Amer. coll.: joke)

Witz, *der;* Flachs, *der* (ugs.)
B *v.t.*, **-bb-** (coll.) aufziehen (ugs.)

ribald /ˈrɪbəld/ *adj.* zotig; schmutzig ‹*Lachen*›; unanständig ‹*Ausdrücke*›; (irreverent) anzüglich; rüde ‹*Gesellschaft*›

ribaldry /ˈrɪbəldrɪ/ *n.* Derbheit, *die;* Zotigkeit, *die;* (irreverence) Anzüglichkeit, *die*

riband /ˈrɪbənd/ ▸**ribbon 1**

ribbed /rɪbd/ *adj.* gerippt

ribbon /ˈrɪbn/ *n.* **1** (band for hair, dress, etc.) Band, *das;* (on typewriter) [Farb]band, *das;* (on medal) [Ordens]band, *das;* **campaign/service ~:** Kriegs-/Dienstauszeichnung, *die; see also* **blue ribbon** **2** (fig.: strip) Streifen, *der;* **~ of light** Lichtstreifen, *der* **3** *in pl.* (ragged strips) Fetzen *Pl.;* **tear to ~s** zerfetzen; (fig.: condemn) fertig machen (ugs.); in der Luft zerreißen ‹*Buch, Stück usw.*›

ribbon: ~ building, ~ development *ns., no pl.* Bandbebauung, *die*

ˈribcage *n.* (Anat.) Brustkorb, *der*

ribonucleic acid /raɪbənju:kli:ɪk ˈæsɪd/ *n.* (Biol.) Ribonukleinsäure, *die*

ribosome /ˈraɪbəzəʊm/ *n.* (Biochem.) Ribosom, *der*

rice /raɪs/ *n.* Reis, *der*

rice: ~ field *n.* Reisfeld, *das;* **~ paper** *n.* Reispapier, *das;* **~ ˈpudding** *n.* Milchreis, *der*

ricer /ˈraɪsə(r)/ *n.* (Amer.) ≈ Kartoffelpresse, *die*

ˈrice wine *n.* Reiswein, *der*

rich /rɪtʃ/
A *adj.* **1** reich; *see also* **get-~-quick** **2** (having great resources) reich (**in** an + *Dat.*); (fertile) fruchtbar ‹*Land, Boden*›; **oil-~:** ölreich; **~ in vitamins/lime/forests** vitamin-/kalk-/waldreich; **a play ~ in new ideas** ein Stück voll neuer Ideen; **strike it ~:** das große Geld machen **3** (splendid) prachtvoll; prächtig; reich ‹*Ausstattung*› **4** (containing much fat, oil, eggs, etc.) gehaltvoll; (indigestible) schwer ‹*Essen*› **5** (deep, full) voll[tönend] ‹*Stimme*›; voll ‹*Ton*›; satt ‹*Farbe, Farbton*›; schwer ‹*Geruch*›; voll ‹*Geschmack*› **6** (ample) reichlich **7** (valuable) wertvoll; reich (geh.) ‹*Geschenke, Opfergaben*› **8** (amusing) köstlich; **that's ~!** köstlich!; (iron.) das ist stark! (ugs.) **9** (Motor Veh.) fett ‹*Gemisch*›
B *n. pl.* **the ~:** die Reichen; **~ and poor** Arm und Reich

riches /ˈrɪtʃɪz/ *n. pl.* Reichtum, *der*

richly /ˈrɪtʃlɪ/ *adv.* **1** (splendidly) reich; üppig ‹*ausgestattet*›; prächtig ‹*gekleidet*›; **~ ornamented** reich verziert; reich geschmückt; **~ coloured** farbenprächtig; **~ endowed** reichlich ausgestattet **2** (fully) voll und ganz; **~ deserved** wohlverdient

richness /ˈrɪtʃnɪs/ *n., no pl.* **1** (elaborateness) Pracht, *die;* Prächtigkeit, *die;* **the ~ of ornamentation** der Reichtum der Ornamentik; die reiche Ornamentik **2** (of food) Reichhaltigkeit, *die;* (indigestibility) Schwere, *die* **3** (fullness) (of voice) voller Klang; Vollheit, *die;* (of colour) Sattheit, *die* **4** (great resources) Reichtum, *der* (**in** an + *Dat.*); (of soil) Fruchtbarkeit, *die*

Richter scale /ˈrɪktə skeɪl/ *n.* (Geol.) Richterskala, *die*

rick[1] /rɪk/ *n.* (stack of hay) Dieme, *die* (bes. nordd.); Schober, *der* (bes. südd., österr.)

rick[2] (Brit.)
A *n.* (slight sprain or strain) Verrenkung, *die;* **have a ~ in one's neck** einen verrenkten Hals haben
B *v.t.* verrenken; **~ one's neck** sich (*Dat.*) den Hals verrenken

rickets /ˈrɪkɪts/ *n. constr. as sing. or pl.* ▸**ⓘ p. 1231** (Med.) Rachitis, *die*

rickety /ˈrɪkɪtɪ/ *adj.* **1** wack[e]lig ‹*Tisch, Stuhl usw.*›; klapp[e]rig ‹*Auto*› **2** (feeble) hinfällig, gebrechlich, (ugs.) wack[e]lig ‹*alter Mensch*›

rickshaw /ˈrɪkʃɔ:/ *n.* Rikscha, *die*

ricochet /ˈrɪkəʃeɪ/
A *n.* **1** Abprallen, *das* **2** (hit) Abpraller, *der*
B *v.i.*, **~[t]ing** /ˈrɪkəʃeɪɪŋ/, **~[t]ed** /ˈrɪkəʃeɪd/ abprallen (**off** von)

rictus /ˈrɪktəs/ *n.* **1** (Anat., Zool.) Mund-/Maul-/Schnabelöffnung, *die* **2** (fig.) weit aufgerissener Mund

rid /rɪd/ *v.t.*, **-dd-, rid: ~ sth. of sth.** etw. von etw. befreien; **~ oneself of sb./sth.** sich von jmdm./etw. befreien; sich jmds./einer Sache entledigen (geh.); **be ~ of sb./sth.** jmdn./etw. los sein (ugs.); **get ~ of sb./sth.** jmdn./etw. loswerden; **we are well ~ of him** wir sind froh, dass wir ihn los sind (ugs.)

riddance /ˈrɪdəns/ *n.* **good ~ [to bad rubbish]** zum Glück *od.* Gott sei Dank ist er/es *usw.* weg!; **he's left at last — and good ~ to him!** er ist endlich gegangen — Gott sei Dank!

ridden ▸**ride B, C**

riddle[1] /ˈrɪdl/ *n.* Rätsel, *das;* **talk** *or* **speak in ~s** in Rätseln sprechen; **tell sb. a ~:** jmdm. ein Rätsel aufgeben

riddle[2]
A *n.* (sieve) [Schüttel]sieb, *das*
B *v.t.* **1** (fill with holes) durchlöchern; **~d with bullets** von Kugeln durchsiebt *od.* durchlöchert; **~d with corruption/mistakes** (fig.) von Korruption durchsetzt/mit *od.* von Fehlern übersät **2** (sift) sieben

ride /raɪd/
A *n.* **1** (journey) (on horseback) [Aus]ritt, *der;* (in vehicle, at fair) Fahrt, die; **~ in a train/coach** Zug-/Busfahrt, *die;* **go for a ~:** ausreiten; **go for a [bi]cycle ~:** Rad fahren; (longer distance) eine Radtour machen; **go for a ~ [in the car]** [mit dem Auto] wegfahren; **have a ~ in a train/taxi/on the merry-go-round** mit dem Zug/Taxi/Karussell fahren; **can I have a ~ on your bike/pony?** darf ich mal mit deinem Rad fahren/auf deinem Pony reiten?; **give sb. a ~:** jmdn. mitnehmen; **give sb. a ~ on one's back** jmdn. auf seinen Schultern reiten lassen; **be/come along for the ~** (coll.) nur so (ugs.) *od.* nur aus Interesse dabei sein/mitkommen; **take sb. for a ~:** jmdn. spazieren fahren; (fig. coll.: deceive) jmdn. reinlegen (ugs.) **2** (quality of ~) Fahrkomfort, *der;* **the car gives [you] a bumpy/smooth** *etc.* **~:** das Auto fährt holprig/sanft *usw.;* **give sb. a rough/an easy ~** (fig.) es jmdm. schwer/leicht machen; **have a rough/an easy ~:** es schwer/leicht haben **3** (path) Reitweg, *der*
B *v.i.*, **rode** /rəʊd/, **ridden** /ˈrɪdn/ **1** (travel) (on horse) reiten; (on bicycle, in vehicle; Amer.: in elevator) fahren; **~ to town on one's bike/in one's car/on the train** mit dem Rad/Auto/Zug in die Stadt fahren **2** (float) **~ at anchor** vor Anker liegen *od.* (Seemannsspr.) reiten; **~ high [in the sky]** (fig.) ‹*Mond:*› hoch am Himmel schweben **3** (be carried) reiten; rittlings sitzen; **'X ~s again'** (fig.) „X ist wieder da"; **be riding on sth.** (fig.) von etw. abhängen; **be riding for a fall** halsbrecherisch reiten; (fig.) in sein Unglück rennen (ugs.); **be riding high** (fig.) Oberwasser haben (ugs.); **let sth. ~** (fig.) etw. auf sich beruhen lassen; *see also* **forth 3**; **hound A 1**; **roughshod**
C *v.t.*, **rode, ridden** **1** (**~ on**) reiten ‹*Pferd usw.*›; fahren mit ‹*Fahrrad*›; **learn to ~ a bicycle** Rad fahren lernen; **~ the waves** sich auf den Wellen wiegen **2** (oppress) plagen; **ridden by fears/guilt** von Ängsten/von Schuldgefühlen geplagt *od.* heimgesucht **3** (traverse) (on horseback) reiten; (on cycle) fahren **4** (yield to) reiten (Boxsport), ausweichen (+ *Dat.*) ‹*Schlag*› **5** (Amer. coll.: harass) fertig machen (ugs.); **I guess I've been riding you pretty hard** ich hab dir wohl ziemlich zugesetzt

Phrasal verbs
- **~ aˈway** *v.i.* wegreiten/wegfahren
- **~ ˈdown** *v.t.* umreiten
- **~ ˈoff** ▸**~ away**
- **~ ˈout** *v.t.* abreiten (Seemannsspr.) ‹*Sturm*›; (fig.) überstehen
- **~ ˈup** *v.i.* **1** **~ up [to sth.]** ‹*Reiter:*› an etw. (*Akk.*) heranreiten; ‹*Fahrer:*› an etw. (*Akk.*) heranfahren **2** **the skirt rode up over her knees** (fig.) der Rock rutschte über ihr Knie

rider /ˈraɪdə(r)/ *n.* **1** Reiter, *der*/Reiterin, *die;* (of cycle) Fahrer, *der*/Fahrerin, *die* **2** (addition) Zusatz, *der;* **add a ~:** einen Zusatz machen; (Brit. Law) eine zusätzliche Erklärung *od.* Feststellung abgeben

riderless /ˈraɪdəlɪs/ *adj.* reiterlos

ridge /rɪdʒ/
A *n.* **1** (of roof) First, *der;* (of nose) Rücken, *der* **2** (long hilltop) Grat, *der;* Kamm, *der;* **~ of hills** Höhenrücken, *der;* **~ of mountains** Gebirgskamm, *der* **3** (Agric.) Kamm, *der;* Rücken, *der* **4** (Meteorol.) **~ [of high pressure]** lang gestrecktes Hoch; (connecting two highs) Hochdruckbrücke, *die*
B *v.t.* häufeln

ridge: ~ piece *n.* Firstbalken, *der;* **~ pole** *n.* Firststange, *die;* **~ tent** *n.* Hauszelt, *das;* **~ tile** *n.* Firstziegel, *der;* **~way** *n.* Gratweg, *der*

ridicule /ˈrɪdɪkju:l/
A *n.* Spott, *der;* **object of ~:** Zielscheibe des Spotts; Gespött, *das;* **hold sb./sth. up to ~:** jmdn./etw. der Lächerlichkeit preisgeben; **lay oneself open to ~:** sich dem Gespött aussetzen
B *v.t.* verspotten; spotten über (+ *Akk.*)

ridiculous /rɪˈdɪkjʊləs/ *adj.* lächerlich; **don't be ~!** sei nicht albern!; **make oneself [look] ~:** sich lächerlich machen

ridiculously /rɪˈdɪkjʊləslɪ/ *adv.* lächerlich

riding /ˈraɪdɪŋ/ *n.* Reiten, *das*

riding: ~ breeches *n. pl.* Reithose, *die;* **~ crop** *n.* Reitgerte, *die;* **~ habit** *n.* Reitkleid, *das;* **~ lamp** *n.* (Naut.) Ankerlaterne, *die;* **~ lesson** *n.* Reitstunde, *die;* **~ light** ▸**~ lamp**; **~ school** *n.* Reitschule, *die*

Riesling /ˈri:zlɪŋ, ˈri:slɪŋ/ *n.* Riesling, *der*

rife /raɪf/ *pred. adj.* **1** (widespread) weit verbreitet; **rumours were ~:** es gingen Gerüchte um **2** **~ with** (full of) voller; voll von; **the country was ~ with rumours of war** im ganzen Land gab es Kriegsgerüchte

riff /rɪf/ *n.* (Mus.) Riff, *der*

riff-raff /ˈrɪfræf/ *n.* Gesindel, *das*

rifle /ˈraɪfl/
A *n.* (firearm) Gewehr, *das;* (hunting **~**) Büchse, *die*
B *v.t.* **1** (ransack) durchwühlen; (pillage) plündern; **~ sth. of its contents** etw. ausplündern **2** (make grooves in) ziehen (fachspr.) ‹*Gewehrlauf*›
C *v.i.* **~ through sth.** etw. durchwühlen

rifle: ~ barrel *n.* Gewehrlauf, *der;* (of hunting **~**) Büchsenlauf, *der;* **~ butt** *n.* Gewehrkolben, *der;* **~man** /ˈraɪflmən/ *n., pl.* **~men** /ˈraɪflmən/ Schütze, *der;* **~ range** *n.* Schießstand, *der;* Schießplatz, *der;* **~ shot** *n.* Gewehrschuss, *der*

rift /rɪft/ *n.* **1** (dispute) Unstimmigkeit, *die* **2** (cleft) Spalte, *die;* (in cloud) Riss, *der*

ˈrift valley *n.* (Geog.) Graben[bruch], *der*

rig[1] /rɪg/
A *n.* **1** (Naut.) Takelung, *die* **2** (for oil well) [Öl]förderturm, *der;* (off shore) Förderinsel, *die;* **drilling ~:** Bohrturm, *der;* (off shore) Bohrinsel, *die* **3** (outfit) Kluft, *die;* **in full ~** in Schale (ugs.); **in full climbing ~:** in voller Klettermontur (ugs.)
B *v.t.*, **-gg-** **1** (Naut.) auftakeln **2** (Aeronaut.) (assemble) montieren; (fit out) ausrüsten ‹*Flugzeug*›

Phrasal verbs
- **~ ˈout** *v.t.* ausstaffieren
- **~ ˈup** *v.t.* aufbauen

rig[2] *v.t.*, **-gg-** (falsify) fälschen ‹*Wahl*›; verfälschen, (geh.) manipulieren ‹[*Wahl*]*ergebnis*›; **~ the market** die Preise/(St. Exch.) die Kurse manipulieren (geh.) *od.* künstlich beeinflussen; **the whole thing was ~ged** das war alles Schiebung (ugs.)

rigger /ˈrɪgə(r)/ *n.* ▸**ⓘ p. 1260** **1** (Naut.) Takler, *der*/Taklerin, *die* **2** (Aeronaut.) [Rüst]mechaniker, *der*/[Rüst]mechanikerin, *die*

rigging[1] /ˈrɪgɪŋ/ *n.* **1** (Naut.) Takelung, *die;* (ropes and chains also) Gut, *das;* Takelage, *die* **2** (Aeronaut.) Ausrüstung, *die*

rigging[2] *n.* (illicit manipulation) Manipulation, *die* (geh.); Schiebung, *die* (ugs.)

right /raɪt/
A *adj.* **1** (just, morally good) richtig; **it's not ~ for sb. to do sth.** es ist nicht richtig *od.* recht von jmdm., dass er etw. tut; **it is only ~ [and proper] to do sth./that sb. should do sth.** es ist nur recht und billig, etw. zu tun/dass jmd. etw. tut; **do the ~ thing by sb.** sich jmdm. gegenüber anständig verhalten

r

2 (correct, true) richtig; **~ enough** völlig richtig; **~ enough!** in Ordnung!; okay! (ugs.); **you're [quite] ~:** du hast [völlig] Recht; **too ~** (coll.) allerdings!; **how ~ you are!** wie Recht du hast!; **you are ~ to do** *or* **in doing it** du tust recht daran, es zu tun; **be ~ in sth.** Recht mit etw. haben; **let's get it ~ this time!** machen wir es diesmal besser!; **let's get this ~!** das wollen wir doch mal klarstellen!; **is that clock ~?** geht die Uhr da richtig?; **have you got the ~ fare?** haben Sie das Fahrgeld passend?; **put** *or* **set ~:** richtig stellen ‹*Irrtum, Behauptung*›; wieder gutmachen ‹*Unrecht*›; berichtigen ‹*Fehler*›; bereinigen ‹*Missverständnis, Angelegenheit*›; beheben ‹*Missstand, Mangel*›; wieder in Ordnung bringen ‹*Situation, Angelegenheit, Maschine, Gerät*›; richtig stellen ‹*Uhr*›; **put** *or* **set sb. ~:** jmdn. berichtigen *od.* korrigieren; **~ [you are]!,** (Brit.) **~ oh!** (coll.) ja, gut!; okay! (ugs.); **that's ~:** ja [wohl]; so ist es; **that's ~, smash the place up!** (iron.) recht so, hau nur immer auf den Putz (ugs. iron.); **is that ~?** stimmt das?; (indeed?) aha!; **[am I] ~?** nicht [wahr]?; oder [nicht]? (ugs.); *see also* **all C**; **road 2**; **track A 1**

3 (preferable, most suitable) richtig; recht; **the ~ man for the job** der richtige Mann [dafür]; **do sth. the ~ way** etw. richtig machen; **say/do the ~ thing** das Richtige sagen/tun; **know how to say the ~ thing** die richtigen *od.* passenden Worte finden; **I did the ~ thing when I ...:** es war richtig, dass ich ...; *see also* **Mr**; **whale 1**

4 (sound, sane) richtig; **all's ~ with the world** die Welt *od.* alles ist in Ordnung; **not be quite ~ in the head** nicht ganz bei Verstand sein; nicht ganz richtig [im Kopf] sein; **as ~ as rain** (coll.) (in health) gesund wie ein Fisch im Wasser; (satisfactory) in bester Ordnung; **put** *or* **set sb. ~** (restore to health) jmdn. [wieder] in Ordnung *od.* auf die Beine bringen; **she'll be ~** (Austral. coll.) das geht [schon] in Ordnung (ugs.); **I'll/we'll** *etc.* **see you ~:** es soll dein Schaden nicht sein; *see also* **mind A 7**

5 (coll./arch.: real, properly so called) richtig; recht (veralt.); **you're a ~ one!** du bist mir der/die Richtige!; **your room's in a ~ mess** in deinem Zimmer sieht es wüst aus; **he made a ~ mess of that job/of it** er hat die Sache/es total vermurkst (ugs.)

6 ▸**❶ p. 1699** (opposite of left) recht...; *see also* **turn A 3**; **be sb.'s ~ arm** (fig.) jmds. rechte Hand sein

7 **R~** (Polit.) recht... *See also* **right side**

B *v.t.* **1** (avenge) aus der Welt schaffen ‹*Unrecht*› **2** (correct) berichtigen; richtig stellen **3** (restore to upright position) [wieder] aufrichten; ‹*Boot usw.*:› **~ itself** sich [von selbst] [wieder] aufrichten; (fig.: come to proper state) ‹*Mangel*:› sich [von selbst] geben; ‹*Körper, Organismus*:› (ugs.) von selbst in Ordnung kommen

C *n.* **1** (fair claim, authority) Recht, *das;* Anrecht, *das;* **have a/no ~ to sth.** ein/kein Anrecht *od.* Recht auf etw. (*Akk.*) haben; **have a** *or* **the/no ~ to do sth.** das/kein Recht haben, etw. zu tun; **as of ~:** kraft Gesetzes; **by ~ of** aufgrund (+ *Gen.*); **belong to sb. as of** *or* **by ~:** jmds. rechtmäßiges Eigentum sein; **what ~ has he [got] to do that?** mit welchem Recht tut er das?; **in one's own ~:** aus eigenem Recht; **an authoress in her own ~:** eine eigenständige Autorin; **the ~ to work** das Recht auf Arbeit; **~-to-work** *attrib.* (Amer.) gegen Gewerkschaftszwang gerichtet ‹*Gesetz, Politik*›; **~-to-work state** Staat ohne Gewerkschaftszwang; **the ~ to life** das Recht auf Leben (*des ungeborenen Kindes*); **film ~s** Filmrechte *Pl.;* **grazing ~s** Weiderechte *Pl.;* **~ of way** (~ to pass across) Wegerecht, *das;* (path) öffentlicher Weg; (precedence) Vorfahrtsrecht, *das;* **who has the ~ of way?** wer hat Vorfahrt?; **Bill of R~s** Bill of Rights, *die;* **Black R~s** Rechte der Schwarzen; **be within one's ~s to do sth.** etw. mit [Fug und] Recht tun können; *see also* **right-to-life**

2 (what is just) Recht, *das;* **~ is on our side** das Recht ist auf unserer Seite; **understand the ~s and wrongs of a situation** beurteilen können, was [bei einer Sache] richtig und was falsch ist; **by ~[s]** von Rechts wegen; **do ~ by sb.** jmdn. anständig behandeln; **do ~:** sich richtig verhalten; richtig handeln; **do ~ to do sth.** recht daran tun, etw. zu tun; **in the ~:** im Recht

3 ▸**❶ p. 1699** (~-hand side) rechte Seite; **move to the ~:** nach rechts rücken; **on** *or* **to the ~ [of the door]** rechts [von der Tür]; **on** *or* **to my ~, to the ~ of me** rechts von mir; zu meiner Rechten; **from ~ and left** von rechts und links; **drive on the ~:** rechts fahren

4 (Polit.) **the R~:** die Rechte; (radicals) die Rechten; **be on the R~ of the party** dem rechten Flügel der Partei angehören

5 *in pl.* (proper state) **set** *or* **put sth. to ~s** etw. in Ordnung bringen; **set** *or* **put the world to ~s** die Welt verbessern

6 (Boxing) Rechte, *die*

7 **get sb. bang to ~s** (Brit. coll.) *or* (Amer. coll.) **dead to ~s** jmdn. auf frischer Tat ertappen

8 (Theatre [stage] right:) linke Bühnenseite

9 (in marching) ▸**left² C 5**

D *adv.* **1** (properly, correctly, justly) richtig ‹*machen, raten, halten*›; **go ~** (succeed) klappen (ugs.); **nothing is going ~ for** *or* **with me today** bei mir klappt heute nichts (ugs.); **if I remember ~:** wenn ich mich recht *od.* richtig erinnere

2 ▸**❶ p. 1699** (to the side opposite left) nach rechts; **~ of the road** rechts von der Straße; **~, left, and centre, left, ~, and centre** (fig. coll.) überall; (repeatedly) immer wieder

3 (all the way) bis ganz; (completely) ganz; völlig; **windows coming ~ down to the floor** Fenster, die bis ganz auf den Fußboden herunterreichen; **~ through the summer** den ganzen Sommer hindurch; **turn ~ round** sich ganz umdrehen; ‹*Zeiger*:› eine ganze Umdrehung machen; **~ round the house** ums ganze Haus [herum]; **rotten ~ through** durch und durch verfault

4 (exactly) genau; **~ in the middle of sth.** mitten in etw. (*Dat./Akk.*); **~ now** im Moment; jetzt sofort, gleich ‹*handeln*›; **~ on the chin** direkt *od.* genau am/ans Kinn; **he was '~ next to me** (coll.) er war direkt *od.* genau neben mir; **~ at the beginning** gleich am Anfang; **~ on!** (coll.) (approving) recht so!; so ists recht!; (agreeing) genau!; ganz recht!

5 (straight) direkt; genau; **go ~ on [the way one is going]** [weiter] geradeaus gehen *od.* fahren; **I'm going ~ home now** ich gehe jetzt direkt nach Hause

6 (coll.: immediately) **~ [away/off]** sofort; gleich; **I'll be ~ 'with you** ich bin gleich [wieder] da; **things went wrong ~ at** *or* **from the beginning** es ging schon am Anfang *od.* von Anfang an schief

7 (very) sehr; **~ royal** [wahrhaft] fürstlich ‹*Mahl, Empfang*›; **a ~ royal dressing down** eine Standpauke, die sich gewaschen hat (ugs.); *see also* **honourable 4**; **reverend A**

right: ~ a'bout ['turn *or* (Amer.) **'face]** *n.* (Mil.) Rechtsummachen, *das;* Kehrtwendung nach rechts; (as command) rechtsum!; (fig.) Kehrtwendung, *die;* **~ angle** *n.* rechter Winkel; **at ~ angles to ...:** rechtwinklig zu ...; im rechten Winkel zu ...; **~-angled** *adj.* rechtwinklig; **~ 'back** *n.* (Footb.) rechter Verteidiger/rechte Verteidigerin

righteous /'raɪtʃəs/

A *adj.* **1** (upright) rechtschaffen, (bibl.) gerecht ‹*Person*›; gerecht ‹*Gott, Staat, Herr*› **2** (morally justifiable) gerecht ‹*Zorn, Sache*›; gerechtfertigt ‹*Maßnahme, Tat*›

B *n. pl.* **the ~:** die Gerechten

'right-footed *adj.* mit dem rechten Fuß geschickter; rechtsfüßig ‹*Fußballspieler*›

rightful /'raɪtfl/ *adj.* **1** (fair) gerecht ‹*Sache, Strafe*›; berechtigt ‹*Forderung, Anspruch*› **2** (entitled) rechtmäßig ‹*Besitzer, Eigentümer, Herrscher, Erbe, Anteil*›

rightfully /'raɪtfəlɪ/ *adv.* **1** (fairly) rechtmäßig **2** (correctly) mit *od.* zu Recht

right: ~ 'hand *n.* **1** rechte Hand; Rechte, *die;* **2** (~ side) **on** *or* **at sb.'s ~ hand** zu jmds. Rechten; rechts von jmdm.; **3** (fig.: chief assistant) rechte Hand; **~-hand** *adj.* recht...; rechtsgängig, rechtsdrehend ‹*Schraube, Gewinde*›; **~-hand bend** Rechtskurve, *die;* **on the/your ~-hand side you see ...:** rechts *od.* auf der rechten Seite sehen Sie ...; *see also* **drive A 9**; **~-handed** /raɪt'hændɪd/ **A** *adj.* **1** rechtshändig; ‹*Schlag*› mit der Rechten; ‹*Werkzeug*› für Rechtshänder; **be ~-handed** Rechtshänder/Rechtshänderin sein; **2** (turning to ~) rechts angeschlagen ‹*Tür*›; Rechts‹*gewinde, -drehung*›; rechtsgängig, rechtsdrehend ‹*Schraube, Gewinde*›; **B** *adv.* rechtshändig; mit der rechten Hand; **~-handedness** /raɪt 'hændɪdnɪs/ *n.* Rechtshändigkeit, *die;* **~-hander** /raɪt'hændə(r)/ *n.* **1** (person) Rechtshänder, *der*/-händerin, *die;* **2** (blow) Schlag mit der Rechten; (Boxing) Rechte, *die;* **~-hand 'man** *n.* (chief assistant) rechte Hand

rightism /'raɪtɪzm/ *n., no pl.* (Polit.) Konservativismus, *der*

rightist /'raɪtɪst/ (Polit.)

A *adj.* rechtsorientiert

B *n.* Rechte, *der/die*

rightly /'raɪtlɪ/ *adv.* **1** (fairly, correctly) richtig; **do ~:** richtig handeln; **..., and ~ so** ..., und zwar zu Recht; **~ or wrongly, ...:** ob es nun richtig ist/war oder nicht, ... **2** (fitly) zu Recht

right-'minded *adj.* gerecht denkend

rightness /'raɪtnɪs/ *n., no pl.* Richtigkeit, *die*

righto /'raɪtəʊ, raɪ'təʊ/ *int.* (Brit.) okay (ugs.); alles klar (ugs.)

'right side *n.* **1** (of fabric) Oberseite, *die* **2** **be on the ~ of fifty** noch keine fünfzig sein; **[the] ~ out/up** richtig herum; **get on the ~ of sb.** (fig.) sich mit jmdm. gut stellen

'rights issue *n.* (Finance) Bezugsangebot, *das*

'right-thinking *adj.* billig denkend

right-to-'life *attrib. adj.* Recht-auf-Leben-; **~ advocate** Befürworter des Rechts auf Leben

rightward /'raɪtwəd/

A *adv.* [nach] rechts ‹*abbiegen*›; nach rechts ‹*blicken, sich wenden*›; **lie ~ of sth.** rechts von etw. liegen

B *adj.* rechter Hand *nachgestellt*

rightwards /'raɪtwədz/ ▸**rightward A**

right: ~-wing *adj.* **1** (Sport) Rechtsaußen‹*spieler, -position*›; **2** (Polit.) recht...; rechtsgerichtet; Rechts‹*intellektueller, -extremist, -radikalismus*›; **~-winger** *n.* **1** (Sport) Rechtsaußen, *der;* **2** (Polit.) Rechte, *der/die;* **extreme ~-winger** Rechtsaußen, *der/die* (Jargon); Rechtsradikale, *der/die*

rigid /'rɪdʒɪd/ *adj.* **1** starr; (stiff) steif; (hard) hart; (firm) fest; **~ airship** Starrluftschiff, *das* **2** (fig.: harsh, inflexible) streng ‹*Person*›; unbeugsam ‹*Haltung, System*›

rigidity /rɪ'dʒɪdɪtɪ/ *n., no pl.* ▸**rigid: 1** Starrheit, *die;* Steifheit, *die;* Härte, *die;* Festigkeit, *die* **2** Strenge, *die*

rigidly /'rɪdʒɪdlɪ/ *adv.* **1** starr **2** (harshly, inflexibly) [allzu] streng; peinlich ‹*korrekt*›; rigoros ‹*vernichten, beschränken*›

rigmarole /'rɪgmərəʊl/ *n.* (derog.) **1** (long story) langatmiges Geschwafel (ugs. abwertend) **2** (complex procedure) Zirkus, *der* (ugs. abwertend)

rigor /'rɪgə(r)/ (Amer.) ▸**rigour**

rigor mortis /rɪgə 'mɔːtɪs/ *n.* (Med.) Totenstarre, *die;* Rigor mortis, *der* (fachspr.)

rigorous /'rɪgərəs/ *adj.* **1** (strict) streng; rigoros ‹*Methode, Maßnahme, Beschränkung, Strenge*›; **~ tests** strenge Prüfungen **2** (marked by extremes) hart ‹*Leben, Bedingungen, Winter*›; extrem ‹*Klima*› **3** (precise) peinlich ‹*Genauigkeit, Beachtung*›; exakt ‹*Analyse*›; streng ‹*Beurteilung, Maßstab*›; scharf ‹*Auge*›; genau ‹*Arbeit*›; schlüssig ‹*Argumentation*›

rigorously /'rɪgərəslɪ/ *adv.* **1** (strictly) streng; rigoros ‹*durchführen, ausschließen*› **2** (precisely) exakt ‹*berechnen*›

rigour /'rɪgə(r)/ *n.* (Brit.) **1** (strictness) Strenge, *die* **2** (extremeness) Härte, *die;* Strenge, *die;* **the ~s of sth.** (geh.) die Unbilden (geh.) einer Sache (*Gen.*) **3** (precision) Stringenz, *die* (geh.); (of argument) Schlüssigkeit, *die*

rile /raɪl/ *v.t.* (coll.) ärgern; **get/feel ~d** sich ärgern; **it ~s me when ...:** es fuchst mich, wenn ... (ugs.)

Riley /'raɪlɪ/ *n.* **live** *or* **lead the life of ~** (coll.) wie die Made im Speck leben (ugs.)

rill /rɪl/ *n.* Bächlein, *das*

rim /rɪm/ *n.* Rand, *der;* (of wheel) Felge, *die*

rime /raɪm/ *n.* (frost) [Rau]reif, *der*

rimless /ˈrɪmlɪs/ *adj.* randlos

-rimmed /rɪmd/ *adj. in comb.* -randig

rind /raɪnd/ *n.* (of fruit) Schale, *die;* (of cheese) Rinde, *die;* (of bacon) Schwarte, *die*

ring¹ /rɪŋ/

A *n.* 1 Ring, *der* 2 (Horseracing, Boxing) Ring, *der;* (bull~) Arena, *die;* (in circus) Manege, *die;* **the ~** (bookmakers) der Ring; die Buchmacher 3 (group) Ring, *der;* (gang) Bande, *die;* (controlling prices) Kartell, *das* 4 (circle) Kreis, *der;* **make** *or* **run ~s [a]round sb.** (fig.) jmdn. in die Tasche stecken (ugs.) 5 (halo round moon) Hof, *der* 6 (Chem.) Ring, *der*

B *v.t.* 1 (surround) umringen; einkreisen ‹*Wort, Buchstaben usw.*› 2 (Brit.: put ~ on leg of) beringen ‹*Vogel*›

ring²

A *n.* 1 (act of sounding bell) Läuten, *das;* Klingeln, *das;* **there's a ~ at the door** es hat geklingelt; **give two ~s** zweimal läuten *od.* klingeln 2 (Brit. coll.: telephone call) Anruf, *der;* **give sb. a ~:** jmdn. anrufen 3 (resonance; fig.: impression) Klang, *der;* (fig.) **have the ~ of plausibility/truth** einleuchtend/glaubhaft klingen; (fig.) **a ~ of insistence in her tone** ein nachdrücklicher Ton in ihrer Stimme

B *v.i.*, **rang** /ræŋ/, **rung** /rʌŋ/ 1 (sound clearly) [er]schallen; ‹*Hammer:*› [er]dröhnen; **oaths rang across the yard** Flüche hallten über den Hof 2 (be sounded) ‹*Glocke, Klingel, Telefon:*› läuten; ‹*Wecker, Telefon, Kasse:*› klingeln; **the doorbell rang** die Türklingel ging; es klingelte 3 (~ bell) läuten (**for** nach); **please ~ for attention** bitte läuten 4 (Brit.: make telephone call) anrufen 5 (resound) ‹*Wald, Raum, Halle:*› [wider]hallen (**with** von); **~ in sb.'s ears** jmdm. in den Ohren klingen; **~ true/false** ‹*Münze:*› echt/falsch klingen; (fig.) glaubhaft/unglaubhaft klingen 6 (hum) summen; (loudly) dröhnen; **my ears are ~ing** mir dröhnen die Ohren

C *v.t.*, **rang, rung** 1 läuten ‹*Glocke*›; **~ the [door]bell** läuten; klingeln; **~ a peal** die Glocken läuten; **it ~s a bell** (fig. coll.) es kommt mir [irgendwie] bekannt vor; **~ the bell [with sb.]** (fig.) [bei jmdm.] ankommen (ugs.); *see also* **change A 8; knell 2** 2 (Brit.: telephone) anrufen

Phrasal verbs

- **~ ˈback** *v.t. & i.* (Brit.) 1 (again) wieder anrufen 2 (in return) zurückrufen
- **~ down** *v.t.* (Theatre) fallen lassen, herunterlassen ‹*Vorhang*›; **~ the curtain down on a project/a love affair** (fig.) unter ein Vorhaben/Liebesverhältnis einen Schlussstrich ziehen
- **~ ˈin**
  A *v.i.* (Brit.) anrufen
  B *v.t.* einläuten
- **~ ˈoff** *v.i.* (Brit.) auflegen; abhängen
- **~ ˈout**
  A *v.i.* ertönen
  B *v.t.* ausläuten
- **~ round** (Brit.)
  A /-ˈ-/ *v.i.* herumtelefonieren
  B /ˈ--/ *v.t.* herumtelefonieren bei
- **~ ˈup** *v.t.* 1 (Brit.: telephone) anrufen 2 (record on cash register) [ein]tippen; bongen (ugs.) 3 (Theatre) **~ up the curtain** den Vorhang hochziehen

ring: ~-a-~-o'-ˈroses *n.* Ringelreihen, *der;* **~ binder** *n.* Ringbuch, *das;* **~ circuit** *n.* (Electr.) Ringschaltung, *die;* **~dove** *n.* Ringeltaube, *die*

ringed /rɪŋd/ *adj.* beringt; **the ~ planet** der Ringplanet

ringer /ˈrɪŋə(r)/ *n.* 1 (bell-~) [Glocken]läuter, *der* 2 **be a [dead] ~ for sb./sth.** (coll.: very similar) für jmdn. durchgehen [können]/einer Sache (*Dat.*) [aufs Haar] gleichen

ring: ~ fence *n.* Umzäunung, *die;* **~-fence** *v.t.* [ab]sichern ‹*Gelder*›; **~ finger** *n.* Ringfinger, *der*

ringing /ˈrɪŋɪŋ/

A *adj.* 1 (clear and full) schallend ‹*Stimme, Gelächter*›; (sonorous) klangvoll, volltönend ‹*Stimme, Lachen, Lied*›; (resounding) dröhnend ‹*Schlag*› 2 (decisive) eindringlich ‹*Appell*›

B *n.* 1 (sounding, sound) Läuten, *das* 2 (Brit. Teleph.) **~ tone** Freiton, *der* 3 (sensation) **~ in the** *or* **one's ears** Ohrensausen, *das*

ˈringleader *n.* Rädelsführer, *der* (abwertend); Anführer, *der*/Anführerin, *die*

ringlet /ˈrɪŋlɪt/ *n.* [Ringel]löckchen, *das*

ring: ~ main *n.* (Electr.) Ringnetz, *das;* **~master** *n.* Dresseur, *der;* **~ pull** *n.* (Brit.) Pullring, *der;* **~-pull** *adj.* **~-pull can** Aufreißdose, *die;* Ring-Pull-Dose, *die;* **~ road** *n.* Ringstraße, *die;* **~side** **A** *n.* **at (the) ~side** [direkt] am Ring; **B** *adj.* **~side seat** (Boxing) Ringplatz, *der;* (in circus) Manegenplatz, *der;* Logenplatz, *der* (auch fig.); **~sider** /ˈrɪŋsaɪdə(r)/ *n.* Zuschauer mit Ring-/Manegenplatz; **~tone** *n.* Klingelton, *der;* **~ vaccination** *n.* Ringimpfung, *die;* **~way** *n.* Ringstraße, *die;* **~worm** *n.* (Med.) Kopfgrind, *der;* Flechtengrind, *der*

rink /rɪŋk/ *n.* (for ice skating) Eisbahn, *die;* (for curling) Eisschießbahn, *die;* (for roller skating) Rollschuhbahn, *die;* (bowling green) Bowlingfläche, *die*

rinse /rɪns/

A *v.t.* 1 (wash out) ausspülen ‹*Mund, Gefäß usw.*›; *abs.* **please ~** (said by dentist) bitte mal [aus]spülen 2 (wash lightly) durchspülen ‹*Wäsche*› 3 (put through water) [aus]spülen ‹*Wäsche usw.*›; abspülen ‹*Hände, Geschirr*›

B *n.* 1 (rinsing) Spülen, *das;* Spülung, *die;* **give sth. a [good/quick] ~:** etw. [gut/schnell] abspülen/ausspülen/spülen; **after several ~s** nach mehrmaligem Spülen; **have a ~** (said by dentist) bitte [aus]spülen 2 (solution) [Haar]tönung, *die;* [Haar]töner, *der*

Phrasal verbs

- **~ aˈway** *v.t.* wegspülen
- **~ ˈout** *v.t.* 1 (wash with clean water) ausspülen ‹*Wäsche, Mund, Behälter*› 2 (remove by washing) [her]ausspülen

ˈrinse aid *n.* Klarspülmittel, *das*

ˈrinsing agent *n.* Klarspüler, *der*

riot /ˈraɪət/

A *n.* 1 (violent disturbance) Aufruhr, *der;* **~s** Unruhen *Pl.;* Aufstand, *der;* **there'll be a ~** (fig.) es wird Ärger *od.* einen Aufstand geben (ugs.) 2 (noisy or uncontrolled behaviour) Krawall, *der;* Tumult, *der;* **run ~:** randalieren; (in protest) auf die Barrikaden gehen (ugs.); **run ~ [all over sth.]** ‹*Pflanze:*› [etw. völlig über]wuchern; **let one's imagination run ~:** seiner Fantasie freien Lauf lassen 3 (unrestrained indulgence) Orgie, *die* 4 (coll.: amusing thing or person) **be a ~:** zum Piepen sein (ugs.)

B *v.i.* randalieren; **the mob had been ~ing all night** der Mob hatte während der ganzen Nacht gewütet; **the ~ing** der Aufruhr; die Unruhen

ˈRiot Act *n.* (Hist.) Aufruhrgesetz, *das;* **read sb. the ~** (fig. coll.) jmdm. die Leviten lesen

ˈriot control *n., no pl.* Aufstandsbekämpfung, *die*

rioter /ˈraɪətə(r)/ *n.* Randalierer, *der*

ˈriot gear *n.* (*bei Krawallen von Polizeibeamten getragene*) Schutzkleidung *od.* -ausrüstung

riotous /ˈraɪətəs/ *adj.* 1 (violent) gewalttätig; tumultartig ‹*Vorgang*› 2 (dissolute) ausschweifend 3 (unrestrained) wild; schallend ‹*Gelächter*›; **a ~ display of colour** eine reiche Farbenpracht

riotously /ˈraɪətəslɪ/ *adv.* 1 (dissolutely) ausschweifend 2 **~ funny** (coll.) urkomisch; zum Schreien *präd.* (ugs.)

riot: ~ police *n.* Bereitschaftspolizei, *die;* **~ shield** *n.* Schutzschild, *der;* **~ squad** *n.* Einsatzkommando, *das od.* -truppe, *die* (*der Bereitschaftspolizei*)

rip¹ /rɪp/

A *n.* 1 (tear) Riss, *der* 2 (act of ripping) Reißen, *das*

B *v.t.*, **-pp-** 1 (make tear in) zerreißen; **~ open** aufreißen; (with knife) aufschlitzen; **~ one's skirt on sth.** sich (*Dat.*) an etw. (*Dat.*) das Kleid einreißen *od.* zerreißen; **~ sth. down the middle/to pieces** etw. in der Mitte *od.* mitten durchreißen/in Stücke zerreißen 2 (make by tearing) reißen ‹*Loch*›

C *v.i.*, **-pp-** 1 (split) [ein]reißen 2 (coll.) **let ~:** loslegen (ugs.); **he let ~ down the motorway** er bretterte volles Rohr über die Autobahn (ugs.); **let ~ at sb.** jmdn. zur Minna machen (ugs.)

Phrasal verbs

- **~ aˈpart** *v.t.* (tear apart) auseinander reißen; zerreißen; (destroy) demolieren
- **~ aˈway** *v.t.* abreißen; **~ sth. away from sth.** etw. von etw. reißen
- **~ ˈdown** *v.t.* abreißen; herunterreißen
- **~ into** *v.t.* **~ into sb.** (attack) über jmdn. herfallen; (fig.: attack verbally) jmdm. ins Gesicht springen (ugs.)
- **~ ˈoff** *v.t.* 1 (remove from) reißen von; (remove) abreißen; herunterreißen ‹*Maske, Kleidungsstück*› 2 (coll.: defraud) übers Ohr hauen (ugs.); bescheißen (derb) 3 (coll.: steal) klauen (salopp). *See also* **rip-off**
- **~ ˈout** *v.t.* herausreißen (**of** aus)
- **~ ˈup** *v.t.* zerreißen; kaputtreißen (ugs.); **~ up an agreement** (fig.) aus einer Vereinbarung einfach wieder aussteigen (ugs.)

rip² *n.* 1 (roué) Windhund, *der* (abwertend) 2 (rascal) Halunke, *der* (scherzh.)

RIP *abbr.* **= rest in peace** R.I.P.

ˈripcord *n.* Reißleine, *die*

ripe /raɪp/ *adj.* reif (**for** zu); ausgereift ‹*Käse, Wein, Plan*›; vollkommen, vollendet ‹*Gelehrsamkeit*›; reich ‹*Erfahrung*›; groß ‹*Verständnis*›; **the time is ~ for doing sth.** es ist an der Zeit, etw. zu tun; **be ~ for development** ‹*Land:*› entwicklungsreif sein; **~ old age** hohes Alter

ripen /ˈraɪpn/

A *v.t.* zur Reife bringen; (fig.) reifen lassen (geh.)

B *v.i.* (lit. or fig.) reifen; **~ into sth.** (fig.) zu etw. reifen (geh.)

ripeness /ˈraɪpnɪs/ *n., no pl.* (lit. or fig.) Reife, *die*

rip-off *n.* (coll.) Nepp, *der* (ugs. abwertend); **that place is a ~:** das ist ein Neppladen (ugs. abwertend)

riposte /rɪˈpɒst/

A *n.* 1 (retort) [rasche] Entgegnung *od.* (geh.) Replik 2 (Fencing) Riposte, *die*

B *v.i.* 1 (retort) [rasch] antworten 2 (Fencing) ripostieren

ripper /ˈrɪpə(r)/ *n.* Lustmörder, *der;* **the Yorkshire R~:** der Ripper von Yorkshire

ripping /ˈrɪpɪŋ/ *adj.* (Brit. dated coll.) famos (ugs. veralt.)

ripple /ˈrɪpl/

A *n.* 1 (small wave) kleine Welle; **the breeze sent ~s along the surface** die Brise kräuselte die Oberfläche 2 (sound) **a ~ of applause/laughter** kurzer Beifall/ein perlendes Lachen 3 (Electr.) leichte [Strom]schwankung

B *v.i.* 1 (form ~s) ‹*See:*› sich kräuseln; ‹*Muskeln:*› spielen 2 (flow) ‹*Welle:*› plätschern; ‹*Bach:*› in kleinen Wellen fließen 3 (sound) erklingen

C *v.t.* kräuseln

ˈripple mark *n.* Rippelmarke, *die*

rip: ~-roaring *adj.* wahnsinnig (ugs.); Wahnsinns- (ugs.); **~saw** *n.* Längsschnittsäge, *die;* **~snorter** /ˈrɪpsnɔːtə(r)/ *n.* (coll.) (person) Teufelskerl, *der* (ugs.); (thing) **a ~snorter of a storm/match** *etc.* ein mordsmäßiger Sturm/mordsmäßiges Spiel *usw.;* **~ tide** *n.* (turbulence) Kabbelung, *die;* (current) Brandungsrückströmung, *die*

rise /raɪz/

A *n.* 1 (going up) (of sun etc.) Aufgang, *der;* (Theatre: of curtain) Aufgehen, *das;* (advancement) Aufstieg, *der;* **~ and ~** (joc.) unaufhaltsamer Aufstieg 2 (emergence) Aufkommen, *das* 3 (increase) (in value, price, cost) Steigerung, *die;* (St. Exch.: in shares) Hausse, *die;* (in population, temperature) Zunahme, *die;* **be on the ~:** steigen; zunehmen 4 (Brit.) **[pay] ~** (in wages) Lohnerhöhung, *die;* (in salary) Gehaltserhöhung, *die* 5 (hill) Anhöhe, *die;* Erhebung, *die;* **a ~ in the road** eine Steigung 6 (origin) Ursprung, *der;* **give ~ to** führen zu; ‹*Ereignis:*› Anlass geben zu ‹*Spekulation*›; **what has given ~ to this bizarre idea?** woher kommt denn diese seltsame Idee? 7 (Angling) Steigen, *das;* (fish) steigender Fisch 8 **get** *or* **take a ~ out of sb.** (fig.) (make fun of)

r

sich über jmdn. lustig machen; (annoy, provoke) jmdn. reizen
9 (height of step) [Stufen]höhe, *die*
B *v.i.*, **rose** /rəʊz/, **risen** /ˈrɪzn/ 1 (go up) aufsteigen; **~ [up] into the air** ‹*Rauch:*› aufsteigen, in die Höhe steigen; ‹*Ballon, Vogel, Flugzeug:*› sich in die Luft erheben
2 (come up) ‹*Sonne, Mond:*› aufgehen; ‹*Blase:*› aufsteigen; **indignation rose in him** Unmut stieg in ihm hoch
3 (reach higher level) steigen; ‹*Stimme:*› höher werden; **her pleading rose to heights of passionate eloquence** ihr inständiges Bitten steigerte sich zu leidenschaftlicher Beredtheit
4 (extend upward) aufragen; sich erheben; ‹*Weg, Straße:*› ansteigen; **~ to 2,000 metres** ‹*Berg:*› 2 000 m hoch aufragen; **~ [a storey] higher than sth.** etw. [um ein Stockwerk] überragen
5 (advance) ‹*Person:*› aufsteigen, aufrücken; **~ to a rank/to be the director** in einen Rang/zum Direktor aufsteigen; **~ in one's profession** in seinem Beruf voran- *od.* vorwärts- *od.* weiterkommen; **~ in the world** voran- *od.* weiterkommen; *see also* **fame**; **rank**[1] **A 5**
6 (increase) steigen; ‹*Interesse:*› wachsen; ‹*Stimme:*› lauter werden; (blow more strongly) ‹*Wind, Sturm:*› auffrischen, stärker werden; **~ to a gale** zum Sturm werden
7 (Cookery) ‹*Teig, Kuchen:*› aufgehen
8 (become more cheerful) ‹*Stimmung, Moral:*› steigen
9 (come to surface) ‹*Fisch:*› steigen; **~ to the bait** (fig.) sich ködern lassen (ugs.); **~ to sb.'s taunts** sich von jmdm. herausfordern lassen
10 (Theatre) ‹*Vorhang:*› aufgehen, sich heben; **~ on a scene** *or* **to reveal a scene** [aufgehen *od.* sich heben und] den Blick auf eine Szene freigeben
11 (rebel, cease to be quiet) ‹*Person:*› aufbegehren (geh.), sich erheben; **~ as one man** wie ein Mann aufstehen; **~ in arms** einen bewaffneten Aufstand machen; **my whole soul ~s against it** mein ganzes Inneres sträubt sich dagegen; *see also* **gorge A 2**
12 (get up) **~ [to one's feet]** aufstehen; (from sitting or lying also; after accolade) sich erheben; **he fell, never to ~ again** er stürzte und kam nicht wieder auf die Beine; **~ on its hind legs** ‹*Pferd:*› steigen; **~ and shine!** (coll.) aufstehen!; raus aus den Federn! (ugs.); *see also* **sun A**
13 (adjourn) ‹*Parlament:*› in die Ferien gehen, die Sitzungsperiode beenden; (end a session) die Sitzung beenden
14 (come to life again) auferstehen; **Christ is ~n** Christus ist auferstanden *od.* (geh.) erstanden; **~ from the ashes** (fig.) ‹*Industrie:*› aus den Trümmern wiedererstehen; **look as though one had ~n from the grave** wie eine lebende Leiche aussehen (salopp)
15 (have origin) ‹*Fluss:*› entspringen

(Phrasal verbs)

- **~ above** *v.t.* überragen; (fig.) hinauskommen über (+ *Akk.*) ‹*Niveau*›; (morally) erhaben sein über (+ *Akk.*)
- **~ to** *v.t.* ▸ **challenge A 2**; **occasion A 1**
- **~ ˈup** *v.i.* 1 (get up) aufstehen; sich erheben 2 (advance) aufsteigen; (in level) ansteigen 3 (rebel) **~ up [in revolt]** aufbegehren (geh.); sich erheben 4 (extend upward) ‹*Berg:*› aufragen; **~ up to 2,000 metres** 2 000 m hoch aufragen

risen ▸ **rise B**

riser /ˈraɪzə(r)/ *n.* 1 (one who gets up) **early ~:** Frühaufsteher, *der*/Frühaufsteherin, *die*; **late ~:** Spätaufsteher, *der*/Spätaufsteherin, *die* 2 (of stair, step) Setzstufe, *die* 3 (vertical pipe) Steigrohr, *das;* Steigleitung, *die*

risible /ˈrɪzɪbl/ *adj.* (literary) lächerlich

rising /ˈraɪzɪŋ/
A *n.* 1 (appearance above the horizon) Aufgang, *der* 2 (increase in height) Steigen, *das;* **he waited for the ~ of the tide** er wartete auf die Flut 3 (getting up) Aufstehen, *das* 4 (revolt) Aufstand, *der* 5 (resurrection) Auferstehung, *die*
B *adj.* 1 (appearing above the horizon) aufgehend 2 (increasing) steigend ‹*Kosten, Temperatur*›; (fig.) wachsend ‹*Entrüstung, Wut, Ärger, Bedeutung*› 3 (mounting) steigend ‹*Wasser, Flut*›; hochgehend ‹*Welle*› 4 **the ~ generation** die heranwachsende Generation 5 (advancing in standing) aufstrebend 6 (sloping upwards) ansteigend 7 (approaching the age of) **be ~ forty** auf die Vierzig zugehen; **be ~ sixteen** sechzehn werden; **the ~ fives** die fast fünfjährigen Kinder

rising: ~ butt ▸ **~ hinge**; **~ ˈdamp** *n.* aufsteigende Feuchtigkeit; **~ hinge** *n.* Hebescharnier, *das*

risk /rɪsk/
A *n.* 1 (hazard) Gefahr, *die;* (chance taken) Risiko, *das;* **~ of infection/loss** Ansteckungsgefahr, *die*/Verlustrisiko, *das;* **there is a/no ~ of sb.'s doing sth.** *or* **that sb. will do sth.** es besteht die/keine Gefahr, dass jmd. etw. tut; **at the ~ of one's life** unter Lebensgefahr; **be at ~** ‹*Zukunft, Plan:*› in Gefahr sein, gefährdet sein; **at one's own ~:** auf eigene Gefahr *od.* eigenes Risiko; **at owner's ~:** auf Gefahr *od.* Risiko des Eigentümers; **'coats/luggage** *etc.* **left at owner's ~'** „keine Haftung für Garderobe/Gepäck *usw.*"; **put at ~:** gefährden; in Gefahr bringen; **run** *or* **take a ~:** ein Risiko *od.* Wagnis eingehen *od.* auf sich (*Akk.*) nehmen; **run** *or* **take ~s/a lot of ~s** etwas/viel riskieren; **take ~s with one's life** sein Leben in Gefahr bringen *od.* riskieren; **run the ~ of doing sth.** Gefahr laufen, etw. zu tun; (knowingly) es riskieren, etw. zu tun; **take the ~ of doing sth.** es riskieren, etw. zu tun; das Risiko eingehen *od.* in Kauf nehmen, etw. zu tun 2 (Insurance) **he is a poor/good ~:** bei ihm ist das Risiko groß/gering
B *v.t.* riskieren; wagen ‹*Sprung, Kampf*›; **you'll ~ losing your job** du riskierst es, deinen Job zu verlieren; **I'll ~ it!** ich lasse es drauf ankommen; ich riskiere es; **~ one's life/neck** sein Leben/seinen Hals riskieren; (thoughtlessly) sein Leben aufs Spiel setzen

riskily /ˈrɪskɪlɪ/ *adv.* riskant; gewagt

ˈrisk-money *n.* Fehlgeld, *das*

risky /ˈrɪskɪ/ *adj.* gefährlich; riskant, gewagt ‹*Experiment, Unternehmen, Projekt*›

risotto /rɪˈzɒtəʊ/ *n.*, *pl.* **~s** (Cookery) Risotto, *der od. das*

risqué /ˈrɪskeɪ/ *adj.* gewagt; nicht ganz salonfähig

rissole /ˈrɪsəʊl/ *n.* (Cookery) Frikadelle, *die*

rite /raɪt/ *n.* Ritus, *der;* **~ of passage** Rite de passage (Völkerk.); Übergangsritus, *der*

ritual /ˈrɪtʃʊəl/
A *adj.* (of ~) rituell; Ritual‹*mord, -tötung*›; (done as ~) ritualisiert; **~ object** Kultgegenstand, *der*
B *n.* 1 (act) Ritual, *das* 2 *no pl.* (prescribed procedure) Ritus, *der;* Ritual, *das;* **he likes ~:** er mag Rituale

ritual aˈbuse *n.*, *no pl.* ritueller Missbrauch

ritualistic /rɪtʃʊəˈlɪstɪk/ *adj.* ritualistisch

ritually /ˈrɪtʃʊəlɪ/ *adv.* rituell; in einem rituellen Akt ‹*töten*›

ritzy /ˈrɪtsɪ/ *adj.* (coll.) 1 (high-class) feudal, nobel ‹*Hotel, Restaurant, Wohnung usw.*›; smart ‹*Mann, Kleidung*› 2 (derog.: ostentatiously smart) stinkfein ‹*Vorort, Schule*›; (pretentious-looking) protzig (ugs. abwertend)

rival /ˈraɪvl/
A *n.* 1 (competitor) Rivale, *der*/Rivalin, *die;* **they were ~s for her affection** sie rivalisierten um ihre Zuneigung; **~s in love** Nebenbuhler; **business ~s** Konkurrenten 2 (equal) **have no ~/~s** seines-/ihresgleichen suchen; **without ~s** konkurrenzlos
B *v.t.*, (Brit.) **-ll-** gleichkommen (+ *Dat.*); nicht nachstehen (+ *Dat.*); **he can't ~ that** da kann er nicht mithalten; **I cannot ~ him for speed** an Geschwindigkeit kann ich es nicht mit ihm aufnehmen
C *adj.* rivalisierend ‹*Gruppen*›; konkurrierend ‹*Forderungen*›; Konkurrenz‹*unternehmen usw.*›; **~ applicant** Mitbewerber, *der*/-bewerberin, *die*

rivalry /ˈraɪvlrɪ/ *n.* Rivalität, *die* (geh.); **business ~:** Wettbewerb, *der;* **friendly ~:** freundschaftlicher Wettstreit

riven /ˈrɪvn/ *adj.* (dated, literary) zerrissen; **~ by grief** vom Gram zerfressen

river /ˈrɪvə(r)/
A *n.* 1 ▸ ❶ **p. 1491** Fluss, *der;* (large) Strom, *der;* **the ~ Thames** (Brit.), **the Thames ~** (Amer.) die Themse; **sell sb. down the ~** (fig. coll.) jmdn. verschaukeln (ugs.); **go up the ~** (Amer. fig. coll.) ins Kittchen wandern (ugs.) 2 (fig.) Strom, *der;* **~ of lava** Lavastrom, *der;* **~s of tears/blood** Ströme von Tränen/Blut
B *attrib. adj.* 1 (Biol.) Fluss‹*delphin, -aal, -krebs*› 2 (of ~) Fluss‹*tal, -ufer, -gott usw.*›

river: ~ bank *n.* Flussufer, *das;* **~ basin** *n.* Stromgebiet, *das;* Einzugsgebiet [eines Flusses]; **~ bed** *n.* Flussbett, *das;* **~ bottom** *n.* (Amer.) Flussebene, *die;* **~ head** *n.* Flussquelle, *die;* **~ police** *n. pl.* Wasser[schutz]polizei, *die;* **~side** A *n.* Flussufer, *das;* **on** *or* **by the ~side** am Fluss; B *attrib. adj.* am Fluss gelegen; am Fluss *nachgestellt;* **~ valley** *n.* Flusstal, *das*

rivet /ˈrɪvɪt/
A *n.* Niete, *die;* Niet, *der od. das* (Technik)
B *v.t.* 1 [ver]nieten; **~ sth. down/together** etw. annieten *od.* festnieten/zusammennieten 2 (fig.: hold firmly) fesseln ‹*Person, Aufmerksamkeit, Blick*›; **be ~ed to the spot** wie angenagelt [da]stehen (ugs.); **be ~ed on sth.** ‹*Aufmerksamkeit:*› durch etw. gefesselt werden; **his eyes were ~ed on** *or* **to the screen** seine Augen waren auf den Bildschirm geheftet (geh.)

riveter /ˈrɪvɪtə(r)/ *n.* Nieter, *der*/Nieterin, *die;* (machine) Nietmaschine, *die*

riveting /ˈrɪvɪtɪŋ/ *adj.* fesselnd

Riviera /rɪvɪˈeərə/ *n.* Riviera, *die*

rivulet /ˈrɪvjʊlɪt/ *n.* (lit. or fig.) Bach, *der*

rly. *abbr.* **= railway** Eisenb.

rm. *abbr.* **= room** Zi.

RM *abbr.* (Brit.) 1 **= Royal Mail** 2 **= Royal Marines**

RN *abbr.* (Brit.) **= Royal Navy** Königl. Mar.

RNA *abbr.* **= ribonucleic acid** RNS

RNIB *abbr.* (Brit.) **= Royal National Institute for the Blind** *Königliches Blindeninstitut*

RNLI *abbr.* (Brit.) **= Royal National Lifeboat Institution** *Königliches Institut für Rettungsboote*

RNR, RNVR *abbrs.* (Brit. Hist.) **Royal Navy [Volunteer] Reserve** *[Freiwillige] Reserve der Königlichen Marine*

roach[1] /rəʊtʃ/ *n.*, *pl. same* (fish) Plötze, *die;* Rotauge, *das*

roach[2] (Amer.) ▸ **cockroach**

road /rəʊd/ *n.* 1 Straße, *die;* **the Birmingham/London ~:** die Straße nach Birmingham/London; (name of ~/street) **London/Shelley R~:** Londoner Straße/Shelleystraße; **'~ up'** „Straßenarbeiten"; **'~ narrows'** „Fahrbahnverengung"; **across** *or* **over the ~ [from us]** [bei uns *od.* (geh.) uns (*Dat.*)] gegenüber; **by ~** (by car/bus) per Auto/Bus; (by lorry/truck) per LKW; **off the ~** (on the verge etc.) neben der Straße *od.* Fahrbahn; (across country) im Gelände ‹*ein Fahrzeug benutzen*›; durchs Gelände ‹*fahren*›; (being repaired) in der Werkstatt; in Reparatur; **take a vehicle off the ~** (no longer use it) ein Fahrzeug stilllegen; **one for the ~** (coll.) ein Glas zum Abschied; **be a danger on the ~:** eine Gefahr für den Straßenverkehr sein; **be on the ~:** auf Reisen *od.* unterwegs sein; ‹*Theaterensemble usw.:*› auf Tournee *od.* (ugs.) Tour (*Dat.*) sein; **put a vehicle on the ~:** ein Fahrzeug in Betrieb nehmen; **take the ~:** sich auf den Weg machen; aufbrechen; (become tramp) ein Tramp werden; **the rule of the ~:** die Verkehrsregeln 2 (means of access) Weg, *der;* **set sb. on the ~ to ruin** jmdn. ins Verderben führen; **be on the right ~:** auf dem richtigen Weg sein; **be on the ~ to success/ruin** auf dem Weg zum Erfolg sein/in sein Verderben rennen; **change one's mind somewhere along the ~** (fig.) es sich (*Dat.*) irgendwo unterwegs anders überlegen; **end of the ~** (destination) Ziel, *das;* (limit) Ende, *das;* **it's the end of the ~ for us** (fig.) mit uns ist es jetzt vorbei 3 (one's way) Weg, *der;* **get in sb.'s ~** (coll.) jmdm. in die Quere kommen (ugs.); **get out of my ~!** (coll.) geh mir aus dem Weg! 4 (Amer.) ▸ **railway** 5 (Mining) Strecke, *die* 6 *usu. in pl.* (Naut.) Reede, *die;* **lie in the ~s** auf der Reede liegen

ℹ Rivers

German has two words for *river.* The usual one is **der Fluss,** which applies to any river, while **der Strom** is only used for a really large river such as the Rhine (**der Rhein**), the Danube (**die Donau**), the Volga (**die Wolga**), the Zambezi (**der Sambesi**), the Amazon (**der Amazonas**), and so on. Most rivers are masculine, but there are quite a number of exceptions (including of course the two already mentioned). All French rivers are feminine for a start, since they are feminine in French. The following German and most Austrian rivers are also feminine:

die Weser, die Elbe, die Saar, die Mosel, die Ruhr, die Isar, die Spree, die Havel, die Oder, die Neisse; (and in Austria) die Salzach, die Enns, die Etsch, die Drau and many others.

In addition there are a couple of rivers in neighbouring countries:

die Maas, die Amstel in Holland;

die Moldau (the Vltava) in the Czech Republic;

die Weichsel (the Vistula) in Poland.

Virtually all rivers in the rest of the world are masculine, with the one exception of the Thames (die Themse).

German does not insert a word for river before the name as does English:

the river Main
= der Main

the river Seine
= die Seine

When rivers occur in place names, the preposition used is **an.** Such mentions often distinguish between places with the same name:

Frankfurt am Main ↔ Frankfurt an der Oder

Linz am Rhein ↔ Linz an der Donau

am can be abbreviated as **a.** and **an der** as **a.d.**, and the names of the rivers can be reduced to the initial letter where these are familiar, giving e.g.

Frankfurt a.M. ↔ Frankfurt a.d.O.

Bruck a.d. Mur

Some river phrases

to go upstream/downstream or ***up/down the river***
= flussaufwärts/flussabwärts fahren

to go up/down the Rhine
= rheinaufwärts/rheinabwärts fahren

Similar adverbs can be formed with the name of any river (**donauaufwärts, themseabwärts** etc.).

a house by or ***on the river***
= ein Haus am Fluss

on the right bank of the Weser
= am rechten Weserufer

He was carried along by the current
= Er wurde von der Strömung mitgerissen

The river is in flood or ***in full spate***
= Der Fluss führt Hochwasser

The river is very low
= Der Fluss führt sehr wenig Wasser

The Rhine rises in Switzerland and flows into the North Sea
= Der Rhein entspringt in der Schweiz und mündet in die Nordsee

The ship sank in the mouth of the Elbe or ***the Elbe estuary***
= Das Schiff ist in der Elbmündung gesunken

---

road: ~ accident *n.* Verkehrsunfall, *der; attrib.* **~ accident victims** Verkehrsopfer; **~ atlas** *n.* Autoatlas, *der;* **~bed** *n.* **1** (foundation of ~, railway) Unterbau, *der;* **2** (Amer.: part of ~ on which vehicles travel) Fahrbahn, *die;* **~block** *n.* Straßensperre, *die;* **~ book** *n.* Autoreiseführer, *der;* **~ bridge** *n.* Straßenbrücke, *die;* **~ fund licence** *n.* (Brit.) Kfz-Steuerbeleg, *der;* **~ haulage** *n.* Gütertransport auf der Straße; **~ hog** *n.* Verkehrsrowdy, *der* (abwertend); **~holding** *n., no pl.* (Brit. Motor Veh.) Straßenlage, *die;* **~ house** *n.* Rasthaus, *das;* **~ hump** ▸**speed hump**

roadie /ˈrəʊdɪ/ *n.* (coll.) Roadie, *der*

road: ~ junction *n.* [Straßen]kreuzung, *die;* (T-junction) [Straßen]einmündung, *die;* **~kill** *n.* **1** (killing of an animal) **die from/as ~:** totgefahren werden; **2** (animals killed) überfahrene Tiere; **live on a diet of ~s** sich von totgefahrenen Tieren ernähren; **~ manager** *n.* ▸ℹ **p. 1260** Roadmanager, *der;* **~ map** *n.* **1** Straßenkarte, *die;* **2** (fig.: plan of action) [Aktions]plan, *der;* **a ~ map for peace** ein Friedensplan; **~mender** *n.* ▸ℹ **p. 1260** Straßen[bau]arbeiter, *der/-arbeiterin, die;* **~ metal** *n., no pl.* Schotter, *der;* (smaller pieces) Splitt, *der;* **~ noise** *n., no pl.* Abrollgeräusche *Pl.;* **~ rage** *n.: häufig zu gewalttätigen Ausbrüchen führende Wut eines Autofahrers;* **~ roller** *n.* Straßenwalze, *die;* **~runner** *n.* (Ornith.) (Geococcyx californianus) Erdkuckuck, *der;* (G. velox) Rennkuckuck, *der;* **~ safety** *n., no pl.* Verkehrssicherheit, *die;* **~ sense** *n.* Gespür für Verkehrssituationen; **~ show** *n.* (promotional) [Werbe]tour, *die;* Roadshow, *die;* (political) [Wahlkampf]tour, *die;* **'Radio One R~show'** 'Radio One unterwegs *od.* vor Ort'; **~side** **A** *n.* Straßenrand, *der;* **at** *or* **by/along the ~side** am Straßenrand; an/entlang der Straße; **B** *adj.* ‹*Gasthaus usw.*› am Straßenrand, an der Straße; **~side inn** Rasthaus, *das;* **~ sign** *n.* Straßenschild, *das* (ugs.); Verkehrszeichen, *das*

roadster /ˈrəʊdstə(r)/ *n.* **1** (open car) Roadster, *der;* Sportkabrio[lett], *das* **2** (bicycle) Tourenrad, *das*

road: ~ sweeper *n.* **1** ▸ℹ **p. 1260** (person) Straßenkehrer, *der/-kehrerin, die* (bes. südd.); Straßenfeger, *der/-fegerin, die* (bes. nordd.); **2** (machine) [Straßen]kehrmaschine, *die;* **~ tax** *n.* (Brit.) Kraftfahrzeugsteuer, *die;* Kfz-Steuer, *die;* **~ test** *n.* Fahrtest, *der;* **~-test** *v.t.* einem Fahrtest unterziehen; **~ transport** *n., no pl.* **1** **form of ~ transport** Verkehrsmittel der Straße; **2** (process) Personen- und Güterbeförderung auf der Straße; **~ user** *n.* Verkehrsteilnehmer, *der/-teilnehmerin, die;* **~way** *n.* **1** (road) Straße, *die;* **2** (central part of road) Fahrbahn, *die;* **~works** *n. pl.* Straßenbauarbeiten *Pl.;* **'~works'** „Baustelle"; **~worthy** *adj.* fahrtüchtig ‹*Fahrzeug*›

roam /rəʊm/
A *v.i.* umherstreifen; herumstreifen (ugs.); ‹*Nomade:*› wandern; (stray) ‹*Tier:*› streunen; **~ through the town** durch die Stadt streifen; **be free to ~** ‹*Tier:*› frei herumlaufen dürfen; **tendency to ~:** Hang zum Streunen
B *v.t.* streifen durch; durchstreifen (geh.)
C *n.* Streifzug, *der*

Phrasal verb
• **~ a'bout, ~ a'round**
A *v.i.* herumstreifen (ugs.); umherstreifen; **he ~s about all over the place** er zieht überall in der Gegend herum (ugs.)
B *v.t.* herumstreifen in (+ *Dat.*) (ugs.); durchstreifen (geh.)

roamer /ˈrəʊmə(r)/ *n.* (person) Herumtreiber, *der* (ugs.); (animal) streunendes Tier

roaming /ˈrəʊmɪŋ/
A *adj.* wandernd ‹*Herde*›; (fig.) schweifend, wandernd ‹*Gedanke*›.
B *n., no pl.* (Teleph.) Roaming, *das*

roan¹ /rəʊn/
A *adj.* stichelhaarig ‹*Fell, Tier*›
B *n.* (horse) stichelhaariges Pferd; (cow) stichelhaarige Kuh; **be a ~:** stichelhaarig sein

roan² *n.* (Bookbinding) Schafleder, *das*

roar /rɔː(r)/
A *n.* (of wild beast) Brüllen, *das;* Gebrüll, *das;* (of water) Tosen, *das;* Getose, *das;* (of avalanche, guns) Donner, *der;* (of applause) Tosen, *das;* (of machine, traffic) Dröhnen, *das;* Getöse, *das;* **a ~ of applause** tosender Beifall; **~s/a ~ [of laughter]** dröhnendes *od.* brüllendes Gelächter
B *v.i.* **1** (cry loudly) brüllen (**with** vor + *Dat.*); **~ [with laughter]** [vor Lachen] brüllen **2** (make loud noise) ‹*Motor:*› dröhnen; ‹*Artillerie:*› donnern; (blaze up) ‹*Feuer:*› bullern (ugs.) **3** (travel fast) ‹*Fahrzeug:*› donnern
C *v.t.* brüllen; **~ [one's] approval [of sth.]** [einer Sache (*Dat.*)] lautstark zustimmen

roaring /ˈrɔːrɪŋ/
A *adj.* **1** (making loud noise) dröhnend ‹*Motor, Donner*›; tosend ‹*Meer*›; brüllend ‹*Löwe*› **2** (blazing loudly) bullernd (ugs.) ‹*Feuer*›; **a ~ inferno** ein tosendes Inferno **3** (riotous) **a ~ success** ein Bombenerfolg (ugs.); **the ~ twenties** die wilden Zwanzigerjahre; die Roaring Twenties **4** (brisk) **do a ~ business** *or* **trade** ein Bombengeschäft machen; *see also* **forty B**
B *adv.* **~ drunk** sternhagelvoll (salopp)

roast /rəʊst/
A *v.t.* **1** (cook by radiant heat) braten; (prepare by heating) rösten ‹*Kaffeebohnen, Erdnüsse, Mandeln, Kastanien*› **2** (expose to heat) **~ oneself in front of the fire/in the sun** sich am Feuer rösten lassen/in der Sonne braten lassen (scherzh.) **3** (Metallurgy) rösten ‹*Erz*› **4** (coll.) (tell off) zusammenstauchen (ugs.) ‹*Person*›; (esp. Amer.: criticize) abqualifizieren; heruntermachen (salopp); geißeln, anprangern ‹*Vorgehensweise*›; verreißen ‹*Buch usw.*›
B *attrib. adj.* gebraten ‹*Fleisch, Ente usw.*›; Brat‹*hähnchen, -kartoffeln*›; Röst‹*kastanien*›; **eat ~ duck/pork/beef** Enten-/Schweine-/Rinderbraten essen; **~ [sirloin of] beef** Roastbeef, *das*
C *n.* **1** (~ meat, meat for ~ing) Braten, *der* **2** ▸**A 1:** Braten, *das;* Rösten, *das;* **give sth. a ~:** etw. braten/rösten **3** (social gathering) Grillparty, *die;* Grillfest, *das*
D *v.i.* **1** ‹*Fleisch:*› braten **2** (bask in warmth of sun/fire) sich braten/rösten lassen (scherzh.)

roaster /ˈrəʊstə(r)/ *n.* **1** (oven) Bratofen, *der;* (dish) Bratentopf, *der;* (for coffee) Röstmaschine, *die* **2** (chicken) Brathähnchen, *das* **3** (Metallurgy: furnace) Röstofen, *der* **4** (coll.: hot day) knallheißer Tag (ugs.)

roasting /ˈrəʊstɪŋ/
A *n.* **1** (cooking) Braten, *das;* (of coffee, ore) Rösten, *das; attrib.* ‹*Fleisch, Huhn*› zum Braten; Brat‹*spieß, -zeit*›; Braten‹*wender, -gabel*› **2** (severe criticism) (by parent, boss, etc.) Standpauke, *die* (ugs.); (by critic) Verriss, *der* (ugs.); **get a ~:** eins auf den Deckel kriegen (ugs.); **give sb. a ~:** jmdn. zusammenstauchen (ugs.); **give sth. a ~** ‹*Kritiker:*› etw. verreißen (ugs.)
B *adj.* (coll.: hot) knallheiß (ugs.); **I am ~:** ich komme um vor Hitze

rob /rɒb/ *v.t.,* **-bb-** ausrauben ‹*Bank, Safe, Kasse*›; berauben ‹*Person*›; *abs.* rauben; **~ sth. of sth.** einer Sache (*Dat.*) etw. nehmen; **~ sb. of sth.** jmdm. etw. rauben *od.* stehlen; (deprive of what is due) jmdn. um etw. bringen *od.* betrügen; (withhold sth. from) jmdm. etw. vorenthalten; **~ a bird of its eggs** einem Vogel die Eier wegnehmen; **be ~bed** bestohlen werden; (by force) beraubt werden; **we wuz ~bed** (Sport coll.) das war Schiebung! (ugs.); *see also* **Peter**

robber /ˈrɒbə(r)/ *n.* Räuber, *der/*Räuberin, *die;* **band of ~s** Räuberbande, *die*

robbery /ˈrɒbərɪ/ *n.* Raub, *der;* **robberies** Raubüberfälle; **it's sheer ~!** das ist ja die reinste Halsabschneiderei (ugs. abwertend)

robe /rəʊb/
A *n.* **1** (ceremonial garment) Gewand, *das* (geh.); (of

judge, vicar) Talar, *der;* **coronation ~s** Krönungsornat, *der;* **~ of office** Amtstracht, *die* 2) (long garment) [langes Über]gewand 3) (dressing gown) Morgenrock, *der;* **beach ~:** Bademantel, *der* 4) **christening ~:** Taufkleid, *das* 5) (Amer.: blanket) [Reise]decke, *die* 6) (Amer.: wardrobe) [Kleider]schrank, *der*
B *v.t.* (formal) **~ sb. in sth.** jmdn. in etw. (*Akk.*) kleiden; jmdm. etw. anlegen (geh.); **the vicar/judge ~d himself** der Pfarrer/Richter legte (geh.) *od.* zog einen/seinen/den Talar an
C *v.i.* (formal) sich ankleiden (geh.)

robin /ˈrɒbɪn/ *n.* (Ornith.) 1) **~ [redbreast]** Rotkehlchen, *das* 2) (Amer.: thrush) Wanderdrossel, *die*

robing room /ˈrəʊbɪŋ ruːm, ˈrəʊbɪŋ rʊm/ *n.* Ankleideraum, *der*

Robin ˈHood *n.* Robin Hood (*der*)

robinia /rəˈbɪnɪə/ *n.* (Bot.) Robinie, *die;* falsche Akazie

robot /ˈrəʊbɒt/ *n.* Roboter, *der*

robotic /rə(ʊ)ˈbɒtɪk/ *adj.* 1) (that uses robotics) Roboter‹*technik, -arm, -sensor*›; robotisiert ‹*Fertigungsstraße*›; **~ device/machine** Roboter, *der* 2) (fig.: monotonous, unemotional) roboterhaft

robotics /rəʊˈbɒtɪks/ *n., no pl.* Robotertechnik, *die;* Robotik, *die*

robust /rəʊˈbʌst/ *adj.* 1) (strong) robust ‹*Person, Gesundheit, Nervenkostüm*›; kräftig ‹*Person, Wein*›; (not delicate) unempfindlich, widerstandsfähig ‹*Pflanze*› 2) (strongly built) kräftig ‹*Gestalt, Körperbau*›; robust ‹*Fahrzeug, Maschine, Konstruktion, Möbel*›; stabil ‹*Haus*› 3) (fig.: straightforward) unerschütterlich ‹*Skepsis*›; nüchtern ‹*Verstand*›; fest ‹*Glaube*›

robustly /rəʊˈbʌstlɪ/ *adv.* stabil, solide ‹*bauen*›; energisch ‹*sich entgegenstellen*›

rock¹ /rɒk/ *n.* 1) (piece of ~) Fels, *der;* **come to grief on the ~s** ‹*Schiff:*› auf Felsen *od.* Klippen auflaufen; **be as solid as a ~** (fig.) absolut zuverlässig sein; **be as steady as a ~:** bombenfest sein; (fig.) durch nichts zu erschüttern sein 2) (large ~, hill) Felsen, *der;* Fels, *der* (geh.); **the R~ [of Gibraltar]** [der Felsen von] Gibraltar 3) (substance) Fels, *der;* (esp. Geol.) Gestein, *das;* **mass of ~:** Felsmasse, *die* 4) (boulder) Felsbrocken, *der;* (Amer.: stone) Stein, *der;* Steinbrocken, *der;* **'danger, falling ~s'** „Achtung *od.* Vorsicht, Steinschlag!"; „Steinschlaggefahr!"; **be caught between a ~ and a hard place** (fig.) in einer Zwickmühle stizen (ugs.) 5) *no pl., no indef. art.* (hard sweet) **stick of ~:** Zuckerstange, *die;* **sell ~:** Zuckerstangen verkaufen 6) (fig.: support) Stütze, *die;* Rückhalt, *der;* (of society) Fundament, *das* 7) (fig.: source of danger or destruction) **a ~ on which others have foundered** eine Klippe, an der schon andere gescheitert sind; **be heading for the ~s** ‹*Ehe:*› zu scheitern drohen; **be on the ~s** (fig. coll.) (be short of/without money) knapp bei Kasse/pleite sein (ugs.); (have failed) ‹*Ehe, Firma:*› kaputt sein (ugs.) 8) **on the ~s** (with ice cubes) mit Eis *od.* on the rocks 9) *in pl.* (Amer. coll.: money) Kies, *der* (salopp) 10) (coll.: gem) Klunker, *der* (ugs.)

rock²
A *v.t.* 1) (move to and fro) wiegen; (in cradle) schaukeln; wiegen; **~ oneself** (in chair) schaukeln; sich wiegen 2) (shake) erschüttern; (fig.) erschüttern ‹*Person*›; **~ sth. to its foundations** (fig.) etw. in seinen Grundfesten erschüttern; **~ the boat** (fig. coll.) Trouble machen (ugs.)
B *v.i.* 1) (move to and fro) sich wiegen; schaukeln 2) (sway) schwanken; wanken; **~ with laughter** sich vor Lachen (*Dat.*) schütteln 3) (dance) rocken; Rock tanzen; **~ and roll** Rock and Roll tanzen
C *n.* 1) (~ing motion, spell of ~ing) Schaukeln, *das;* **give the cradle a ~:** die Wiege schaukeln 2) (music or dance) Rock, *der; attrib.* Rock-; **~ and** *or* **'n' roll [music]** Rock and Roll, *der;* Rock 'n' Roll, *der;*

rock: ~-bottom (coll.) **A** *adj.* **~-bottom prices** Schleuderpreise (ugs.); **at a ~-bottom price/rent** spottbillig (ugs.); **B** *n.* **reach** *or* **hit** *or* **touch ~-bottom** ‹*Handel, Währung, Nachfrage, Preis usw.:*› in den Keller fallen *od.* sinken (ugs.); **her spirits reached ~-bottom** ihre Stimmung war auf dem Tiefpunkt [angelangt]; **~ cake** *n.:* *Rosinengebäck mit rauher Oberfläche;* **~ climber** *n.* Kletterer, *der*/Kletterin, *die;* **~ climbing** *n., no pl.* [Fels]klettern, *das;* **~ concert** *n.* Rockkonzert, *das*

rocker /ˈrɒkə(r)/ *n.* 1) (Brit.: gang member) Rocker, *der* 2) (curved bar of chair, cradle, etc.) Kufe, *die;* **be/go off one's ~** (fig. coll.) übergeschnappt *od.* durchgedreht sein (ugs.)/überschnappen (ugs.) *od.* durchdrehen (ugs.) 3) (rocking chair) Schaukelstuhl, *der* 4) (Electr.) **~ [switch]** Wippschalter, *der* 5) (Mech. Engin.) Kipphebel, *der*

rockery /ˈrɒkərɪ/ *n.* Steingarten, *der*

rocket¹ /ˈrɒkɪt/
A *n.* 1) Rakete, *die;* **~ range** (place) Raketenversuchsgelände, *das* 2) (Brit. coll.: reprimand) **give sb. a ~:** jmdm. eine Zigarre verpassen (ugs.); **get a ~:** eine Zigarre bekommen (ugs.)
B *v.i.* 1) ‹*Preise:*› in die Höhe schnellen 2) **~ into the air** wie eine Rakete in die Luft schießen

rocket² *n.* (Bot.) 1) **[sweet] ~:** Nachtviole, *die* 2) (used in salad) [Öl]rauke, *die*

rocket: ~ base *n.* (Mil.) Raketen[abschuss]basis, *die;* **~ bomb** *n.* 1) (air-to-ground) [Flieger-]rakete, *die;* Luft-Boden-Rakete, *die;* 2) (ground-to-ground) [Artillerie]rakete, *die;* Boden-Boden-Rakete, *die;* **~ engine** *n.* Raketentriebwerk, *das;* **~-firing** *adj.* mit Raketen bewaffnet *nachgestellt;* **~ flight** *n.* Raketenflug, *der;* **~ launcher** *n.* Raketenwerfer, *der;* **~ plane** *n.* Raketenflugzeug, *das;* **~-powered, ~-propelled** *adjs.* raketengetrieben; **~ propulsion** *n., no pl.* Raketenantrieb, *der;* **~ range** *n.* Raketenversuchsgelände, *das*

rocketry /ˈrɒkɪtrɪ/ *n., no pl.* Raketentechnik, *die*

rocket: ~ science *n., no pl.* Raketentechnik, *die;* **it's not ~ science** (coll.) dafür muss man nicht studiert haben; **~ scientist** *n.* Raketentechniker, *der*/-technikerin, *die;* **you don't have to be a ~ scientist to know that ...** (coll.) man muss kein Albert Einstein sein, um zu wissen, dass ...

rock: ~ face *n.* Felswand, *die;* **~fall** *n.* Steinschlag, *der;* **~ festival** *n.* Rockfestival, *das;* **~ formation** *n.* Gesteinsformation, *die;* **~ garden** *n.* Steingarten, *der;* **~-hard** *adj.* steinhart

Rockies /ˈrɒkɪz/ *pr. n. pl.* **the ~:** die Rocky Mountains

rocking/ˈrɒkɪŋ/: **~ chair** *n.* Schaukelstuhl, *der;* **~ horse** *n.* Schaukelpferd, *das*

rock: ~like *adj.* felsartig; felsenfest ‹*Glaube usw.*›; **~ music** *n.* Rockmusik, *die;* **~ plant** *n.* Felsenpflanze, *die;* (Hort.) Steingartengewächs, *das;* **~ pool** *n.* Felsbecken, *das;* **~ salmon** *n.* 1) (Brit.: dogfish) Katzenhai, *der;* 2) (Amer.: Seriola) Gelbschwanzmakrele, *die;* **~ salt** *n.* Steinsalz, *das;* **~-solid** *adj.* 1) (unwavering, certain) unerschütterlich; 2) (fail-safe) bombensicher; absolut zuverlässig; 3) (of good quality) grundsolide

rocky /ˈrɒkɪ/ *adj.* 1) (coll.: unsteady) wackelig (ugs.) 2) (full or consisting of rocks) felsig 3) **the R~ Mountains** ▸ **Rockies**

rococo /rəˈkəʊkəʊ/
A *adj.* Rokoko-; (florid) schwülstig
B *n., pl.* **~s** Rokoko, *das*

rod /rɒd/ *n.* 1) Stange, *die;* **ride the ~s** (Amer. coll.) [im Gestänge unter Eisenbahnwaggons] schwarzfahren 2) (shorter) Stab, *der;* **~ of office** Amtsstab, *der* 3) (for punishing) Stock, *der;* Rute, *die;* **the ~** (punishment) die Prügelstrafe; **make a ~ for one's own back** (fig.) sich (*Dat.*) selbst eine Rute aufbinden (veralt.); **a ~ to beat sb. with** (fig.) Sanktionen gegen jmdn.; **rule with a ~ of iron** (fig.) mit eiserner Faust *od.* Rute regieren; **spare the ~ and spoil the child** wer die Rute schont, verdirbt das Kind 4) (for fishing) [Angel]rute, *die* 5) (measure) Rute, *die* (veralt.) 6) (Amer. coll.: gun) Schießeisen, *das* (ugs.) 7) (Anat.) Stäbchen, *das*

rode ▸ **ride B, C**

rodent /ˈrəʊdənt/ *n.* Nagetier, *das*

ˈrodent officer *n.* (Brit.) Rattenfänger, *der*

rodeo /ˈrəʊdɪəʊ, rəʊˈdeɪəʊ/ *n., pl.* **~s** Rodeo, *der od. das*

roe¹ /rəʊ/ *n.* (of fish) **[hard] ~:** Rogen, *der;* **[soft] ~:** Milch, *die*

roe² *n.* (deer) Reh, *das*

roe: ~buck *n.* Rehbock, *der;* **~ deer** *n.* Reh, *das*

roentgen /ˈrʌntjən/ *n.* (Phys.) Röntgen, *das*

rogation /rəˈgeɪʃn/ *n.* (Eccl.) Bittlitanei, *die;* **R~ Days** Bitttage *Pl.;* **R~ Sunday** [der Sonntag] Rogate; **R~ Week** Bittwoche, *die*

roger /ˈrɒdʒə(r)/ *int.* 1) (message received) verstanden 2) (coll.: I agree) okay (ugs.)

rogue /rəʊg/
A *n.* 1) Gauner, *der* (abwertend); **~s' gallery** (Police) Verbrecheralbum, *das* 2) (joc.: mischievous child) Spitzbube, *der* (scherzh.) 3) (dangerous animal) **~ [buffalo/elephant** *etc.*] bösartiger Einzelgänger
B *attrib. adj.* defekt; fehlerhaft; **~ car** Montagsauto, *das;* **~ result** Ausreißer, *der;* **~ firms** schwarze Schafe unter den Firmen

roguery /ˈrəʊgərɪ/ *n., no pl., no indef. art.* Gaunerei, *die;* (mischief) Spitzbüberei, *die*

ˈrogue state *n.* Schurkenstaat, *der*

roguish /ˈrəʊgɪʃ/ *adj.* 1) gaunerhaft 2) (mischievous) spitzbübisch

roguishly /ˈrəʊgɪʃlɪ/ *adv.* ▸ **roguish:** gaunerhaft; spitzbübisch

roisterer /ˈrɔɪstərə(r)/ *n.* Krakeeler, *der* (ugs. abwertend)

role, rôle /rəʊl/ *n.* Rolle, *die*

role: ~ model *n.* Leitbild, *das;* **~ play, ~ playing** *ns.* Rollenspiel, *das;* Rollenverhalten, *das;* **~ reversal** *n.* Rollentausch, *der*

roll¹ /rəʊl/ *n.* 1) Rolle, *die;* (of cloth, tobacco, etc.) Ballen, *der;* (of fat on body) Wulst, *der;* **~ of film** Rolle Film 2) (of bread etc.) **[bread] ~:** Brötchen, *das;* **egg/ham ~:** Eier-/Schinkenbrötchen, *das;* **jam ~:** [Biskuit]rolle mit Marmelade 3) (document) [Schrift]rolle, *die* 4) (register, catalogue) Liste, *die;* Verzeichnis, *das;* **~ of honour** Gedenktafel [für die Gefallenen] 5) (Brit.: list of solicitors) Anwaltsliste, *die;* **strike sb. off the ~s** jmdm. die Zulassung entziehen 6) (Mil., Sch.: list of names) Liste, *die;* **schools with falling ~s** Schulen mit sinkenden Schülerzahlen; **call the ~:** die Anwesenheit feststellen 7) (Amer.: of paper money) Geldbündel, *das* 8) **be on a ~** (coll.) eine Glückssträhne haben

roll²
A *n.* 1) (of drum) Wirbel, *der;* (of thunder) Rollen, *das*
2) (motion) Rollen, *das*
3) (single movement) Rolle, *die;* (of dice) Wurf, *der*
4) (gait) wiegender Gang
B *v.t.* 1) (move, send) rollen; (between surfaces) drehen
2) (shape by ~ing) rollen; **~ a cigarette** eine Zigarette rollen *od.* drehen; **~ one's own** [selbst] drehen; **~ snow/wool into a ball** einen Schneeball formen/Wolle zu einem Knäuel aufwickeln; **[all] ~ed into one** (fig.) in einem; **~ oneself/itself into a ball** sich zusammenrollen; **~ed in blankets** in Decken eingewickelt
3) (flatten) walzen ‹*Rasen, Metall usw.*›; ausrollen ‹*Teig*›
4) **~ one's eyes** die Augen rollen; **~ one's eyes at sb.** (amorously) jmdm. schöne Augen machen; **~ one's shoulders/head** die Schultern/den Kopf kreisen
5) **~ one's r's** das r rollen
6) (Amer.) **~ dice** würfeln
7) (Amer. coll.: rob) ausrauben
C *v.i.* 1) (move by turning over) rollen; **heads will ~** (fig.) es werden Köpfe rollen
2) (operate) ‹*Maschine:*› laufen; ‹*Presse:*› sich drehen; rotieren; (on wheels) rollen; **let it ~** (start the machine etc.) lass laufen; **be ready to ~** ‹*Kamera:*› aufnahmebereit sein; **get sth. ~ing** (fig.) etw. ins Rollen bringen; **keep things ~ing** (fig.) die Dinge am Laufen halten; *see also* **aisle; ball¹ A 1, 2**
3) (wallow, sway, walk) sich wälzen; (walk also)

r

schwanken; **the way he ~s along** sein wiegender Gang
4 (Naut.) ‹*Schiff:*› rollen, schlingern
5 (revolve) ‹*Augen:*› sich [ver]drehen
6 (flow, go forward) sich wälzen (fig.); ‹*Wolken:*› ziehen; ‹*Tränen:*› rollen; **~ off** *or* **from sb.'s tongue** (fig.) ‹*Worte:*› jmdm. von den Lippen fließen
7 (make deep sound) ‹*Donner:*› rollen; ‹*Trommel:*› dröhnen

Phrasal verbs

• **~ a'bout** *v.i.* herumrollen; ‹*Schiff:*› schlingern, rollen; ‹*Kind, Hund usw.:*› sich wälzen; **be ~ing about with laughter** sich vor Lachen wälzen

• **~ a'long**
A *v.i.* 1 [dahin]rollen; ‹*Fahrzeug:*› [dahin]rollen, [dahin]fahren; **things are ~ing along nicely** (fig.) die Dinge laufen gut 2 (coll.: turn up) eintrudeln (ugs.); aufkreuzen (salopp)
B *v.t.* entlangrollen

• **~ a'way**
A *v.i.* ‹*Ball:*› wegrollen; ‹*Nebel, Wolken:*› sich verziehen
B *v.t.* wegrollen

• **~ 'back**
A *v.t.* 1 zurückrollen 2 (cause to retreat) zurückschlagen ‹*Feinde, Truppen*› 3 **~ back the years/centuries** das Rad der Zeit [um Jahre/Jahrhunderte] zurückdrehen
B *v.i.* ‹*Wagen, Wellen:*› zurückrollen

• **~ 'by** *v.i.* vorbeirollen; ‹*Zeit:*› vergehen; **the years ~ed by** die Jahre zogen ins Land

• **~ 'in**
A *v.i.* (coll.) ‹*Briefe, Geschenke, Geldbeträge:*› eingehen; ‹*Personen, Kunden:*› hereinströmen; **~ in an hour late** mit einer Stunde Verspätung aufkreuzen (salopp)
B *v.t.* herein-/hineinrollen

• **~ 'off** *v.i.* 1 (fall off) herunterrollen 2 (start) sich in Bewegung setzen

• **~ 'on**
A *v.t.* mit einer Rolle auftragen ‹*Farbe*›
B *v.i.* 1 (pass by) ‹*Jahre:*› vergehen 2 (Brit. coll.) **~ on Saturday!** wenn doch schon Samstag wäre! *See also* **roll-on**

• **~ 'out**
A *v.t.* 1 (make flat and smooth) auswalzen ‹*Metall*›; ausrollen ‹*Teig, Teppich*› 2 (bring out) herausbringen; **~ out the barrel** (fig. coll.) ein paar Flaschen den Hals brechen (ugs.)
B *v.i.* heraus-/hinausrollen

• **~ 'over**
A *v.i.* ‹*Person:*› sich umdrehen, (to make room) sich zur Seite rollen; **~ over [and over]** ‹*Auto:*› sich [immer wieder] überschlagen; **the dog ~ed over on to its back** der Hund rollte sich auf den Rücken
B *v.t.* herumdrehen; (with effort) herumwälzen

• **~ 'past** ▸ **~ by**

• **~ 'up**
A *v.t.* 1 aufrollen ‹*Teppich, Maßband*›; zusammenrollen ‹*Regenschirm, Landkarte, Dokument usw.*›; hochkrempeln ‹*Hose*›; *see also* **sleeve 1** 2 (Mil.) aufrollen ‹*feindliche Stellung*›
B *v.i.* 1 (curl up) sich zusammenrollen 2 (arrive) aufkreuzen (salopp); **~ up! ~ up!** hereinspaziert!; **they ~ed up in their new car** sie fuhren in ihrem neuen Auto vor

roll: ~away [bed] *n.* Raumsparbett auf Rollen; **~ bar** *n.* (Motor Veh.) Überrollbügel, *der;* **~-call** *n.* Aufrufen aller Namen; (Mil.) Zählappell, *der*

rolled /rəʊld/: **~ 'gold** *n.* Goldauflage, *die;* **~ 'oats** *n. pl.* Haferflocken *Pl.*

roller /'rəʊlə(r)/ *n.* 1 (heavy, for pressing, smoothing road, lawn, etc.) Walze, *die;* (smaller, for towel, painting, pastry) Rolle, *die* 2 (Med.) **~ [bandage]** Binde, *die* 3 (for hair) Lockenwickler, *der;* **put one's hair in ~s** sich (*Dat.*) die Haare aufdrehen 4 (wave) Roller, *der* (Meeresk.)

roller: ~ bearing *n.* Rollenlager, *das* (Technik); **R~blade** ® *n.* Rollerblade, *der;* **[a pair of] R~blades** [ein Paar] Rollerblades; **~blade** *v.i.* Rollerblades fahren; **~ blind** *n.* Rouleau, *das;* Rollo, *das;* **~ coaster** *n.* Achterbahn, *die;* **~ rink** *n.* Rollschuhbahn, *die;* **~ skate** *n.* Rollschuh, *der;* **~-skate** *v.i.* Rollschuh laufen; **~ skater** *n.* Rollschuhläufer, *der*/-läuferin, *die;* **~ skating** *n., no pl.* Rollschuhlaufen, *das; attrib.* **~-skating rink** Rollschuhbahn, *die;* **~ towel** *n.: auf einer Rolle hängendes endloses Handtuch*

'roll film *n.* Rollfilm, *der*

rollick /'rɒlɪk/ *v.i.* ausgelassen spielen; **~ [about]** [herum]tollen

rollicking /'rɒlɪkɪŋ/
A *adj.* (unrestrained) ausgelassen
B *n.* **give sb. a ~** (coll.) jmdm. den Marsch blasen (salopp)

rolling /'rəʊlɪŋ/ *adj.* 1 (moving from side to side) rollend ‹*Augen*›; schwankend ‹*Gang*›; schlingernd ‹*Schiff*› 2 (undulating) wogend ‹*See*›; wellig ‹*Gelände*›; **~ hills** sanfte Hügel 3 (resounding) rollend ‹*Donner*›; hochtrabend (abwertend) ‹*Phrasen*› 4 (coll.: rich) **be ~ [in it** *or* **in money]** im Geld schwimmen (ugs.)

rolling: ~ mill *n.* Walzwerk, *das;* **~ 'news** *n., no pl.* Nonstopnachrichten *Pl.;* (service) Nachrichtenservice, *der; attrib.* **~ news channel** Nachrichtensender, *der;* **~ pin** *n.* (Cookery) Teigrolle, *die;* Nudelholz, *das;* **~ stock** *n.* 1 (Brit. Railw.) Fahrzeugbestand, *der;* rollendes Material (fachspr.); 2 (Amer.: road vehicles) Fahrzeugpark, *der;* **~ 'stone** *n.* (fig.) unsteter Mensch; **a ~ stone gathers no moss** (prov.) wer ein unstetes Leben führt, bringt es zu nichts

roll: ~mop[s] *n.* (Gastr.) Rollmops, *der;* **~-neck** **A** *n.* Rollkragen, *der;* **B** *adj.* Rollkragen-; **~-on** *n.* 1 (corset) elastischer Hüfthalter; 2 (deodorant) Deoroller, *der;* **~-on ~-off** *adj.* **~-on ~-off ship/ferry** Roll-on-roll-off-Schiff, *das*/-Fähre, *die;* **~-out, out** *ns., no pl.* (launch, unveiling) Rollout, *das;* **~over** *n.* (*von Auslosung zu Auslosung*) aufgestockter Jackpot; **~-over 'credit** *n.* Roll-over-Kredit, *der;* **~-top** *n.* Rollverschluss, *der;* **~-top desk** *n.: Schreibtisch mit Rollverschluss;* **~-up** (Brit. coll.), **~-your-own** (esp. Amer. coll.) *ns.* Selbstgedrehte, *die*

roly-poly /rəʊlɪ'pəʊlɪ/
A *n.* 1 **~ [pudding]** ≈ Strudel, *der* 2 (Amer.: toy) Stehaufmännchen, *das*
B *adj.* (coll.) kugelrund

ROM /rɒm/ *abbr.* (Computing) = **read-only memory** ROM, *das*

Roman /'rəʊmən/
A *n.* 1 ▸ⓘ **p. 1643** Römer, *der*/Römerin, *die* 2 **r~** (Printing) Antiqua, *die*
B *adj.* 1 römisch; **~ road** Römerstraße, *die* 2 ▸ **Roman Catholic A**. *See also* **snail**

roman à clef /rəʊmɑːn ɑː 'kleɪ/ *n.* (Lit.) Schlüsselroman, *der*

Roman: ~ 'alphabet *n.* lateinisches Alphabet; **~ 'candle** *n.* ≈ Goldregen, *der;* **~ 'Catholic** **A** *adj.* römisch-katholisch; **B** *n.* Katholik, *der*/Katholikin, *die;* **sb. is a ~ Catholic** jmd. ist römisch-katholisch; **~ Ca'tholicism** *n., no pl.* Katholizismus, *der*

romance /rə'mæns/
A *n.* 1 (love affair) Romanze, *die* 2 (love story) [romantische] Liebesgeschichte 3 (romantic quality) Romantik, *die;* **there was an air of ~ about the place** der Ort hatte etwas Romantisches 4 (Lit.) (medieval tale) Romanze, *die;* (improbable tale) fantastische Geschichte 5 (make-believe) Fantasterei, *die* 6 (Mus.) Romanze, *die* 7 **R~** (Ling.) Romanisch, *das*
B *adj.* **R~** (Ling.) romanisch; **R~ languages and literature** (subject) Romanistik, *die*
C *v.i.* fantasieren

romancer /rəʊ'mænsə(r)/ *n.* Fantast, *der* (abwertend)

Roman 'Empire *n.* (Hist.) Römisches Reich; **Holy ~:** Heiliges Römisches Reich [Deutscher Nation]

Romanesque /rəʊmə'nesk/ *n.* (Art, Archit.) Romanik, *die*

Romania /rəʊ'meɪnɪə/ *pr. n.* Rumänien (*das*)

Romanian /rəʊ'meɪnɪən/ ▸ⓘ **p. 1277**, ▸ⓘ **p. 1345**
A *adj.* rumänisch; **sb. is ~:** jmd. ist Rumäne/Rumänin; *see also* **English A**
B *n.* 1 (person) Rumäne, *der*/Rumänin, *die* 2 (language) Rumänisch, *das; see also* **English B 1**

romanize (**romanise**) /'rəʊmənaɪz/ *v.t.* 1 (Hist.) romanisieren (veralt.) 2 (Relig.) katholisieren

Roman: ~ law *n.* römisches Recht; **~ 'nose** *n.* Römernase, *die;* **~ 'numeral** *n.* römische Ziffer

Romansh /rə'mænʃ, rə'mɑːnʃ/
A *n.* Romantsch, *das*
B *adj.* Romantsch-

romantic /rəʊ'mæntɪk/
A *adj.* 1 (emotional, fantastic) romantisch; **~ fiction** (love stories) Liebesromane 2 **R~** (Lit., Art) romantisch; der Romantik *nachgestellt*
B *n.* **R~** (Lit., Art, Mus.) Romantiker, *der*/Romantikerin, *die*

romantically /rəʊ'mæntɪkəlɪ/ *adv.* romantisch

Romanticism /rəʊ'mæntɪsɪzm/ *n.* (Lit., Art, Mus.) Romantik, *die*

Romanticist /rəʊ'mæntɪsɪst/ *n.* (Lit., Art, Mus.) Romantiker, *der*

romanticize /rəʊ'mæntɪsaɪz/ *v.t.* romantisieren

'roman type *n.* (Printing) Antiquaschrift, *die*

Romany /'rəʊmənɪ/
A *n.* 1 (gypsy) Rom, *der;* **the Romanies** die Roma 2 ▸ⓘ **p. 1277** (language) Romani, *das*
B *adj.* 1 Roma- 2 (Ling.) Romani-

Rome /rəʊm/ *pr. n.* ▸ⓘ **p. 1643** Rom (*das*); **all roads lead to ~** (prov.) alle Wege führen nach Rom (Spr.); **~ was not built in a day** (prov.) Rom ist nicht an einem Tag erbaut worden (Spr.); **when in ~ do as the Romans [do]** man muss sich den örtlichen Gegebenheiten anpassen

Romeo /'rəʊmɪəʊ/ *n., pl.* **~s** Casanova, *der*

romp /rɒmp/
A *v.i.* 1 [herum]tollen 2 (coll.: win, succeed, etc. easily) **~ home** *or* **in** spielend gewinnen; **~ through sth.** etw. spielend schaffen; **~ along** dahinflitzen (ugs.)
B *n.* Tollerei, *die;* **have a ~** ▸ **A 1**

rompers /'rɒmpəz/ *n. pl.* Spielhöschen, *das*

'romper suit *n.* Spielanzug, *der*

rondo /'rɒndəʊ/ *n., pl.* **~s** (Mus.) Rondo, *das*

roo /ruː/ *n.* (Austral. coll.) Känguru, *das*

rood /ruːd/ *n.* (crucifix) Kruzifix, *das*

rood: ~ loft *n.* Empore des Lettners; **~ screen** *n.* Lettner, *der*

roof /ruːf/
A *n.* 1 Dach, *das;* **under one ~:** unter einem Dach; **live under the same ~ [as sb.]** [mit jmdm.] unter einem Dach wohnen (ugs.); **have a ~ over one's head** ein Dach über dem Kopf haben; **go through the ~** ‹*Preise:*› krass in die Höhe steigen; **sb. goes through** *or* **hits the ~** (fig. coll.) jmd. geht an die Decke (ugs.); **raise the ~** (fig. coll.: make much noise) die Wände zum Beben bringen 2 (Anat.) **~ of the mouth** Gaumen, *der*
B *v.t.* bedachen; **~ in** *or* **over** überdachen

'roof garden *n.* Dachgarten, *der*

roofing /'ruːfɪŋ/ *n.* 1 (action) Bedachung, *die* 2 (material for roof) Deckung, *die*

'roofing felt *n.* Dachpappe, *die*

roofless /'ruːflɪs/ *adj.* dachlos

roof: ~ rack *n.* Dachgepäckträger, *der;* **~ timbers** *n. pl.* Dachstuhl, *der;* **~top** *n.* Dach, *das;* **shout sth. from the ~tops** (fig.) etw. in die Welt hinausrufen

rook¹ /rʊk/
A *n.* (Ornith.) Saatkrähe, *die*
B *v.t.* 1 (charge extortionately) neppen (ugs. abwertend) 2 (in gambling) ausnehmen; **~ sb. of £10** jmdm. 10 Pfund abnehmen

rook² *n.* (Chess) Turm, *der*

rookery /'rʊkərɪ/ *n.* 1 Saatkrähenkolonie, *die* 2 (of penguins or seals) Kolonie, *die*

rookie /'rʊkɪ/ *n.* 1 (Mil. coll.) Rekrut, *der* 2 (esp. Amer.: new member etc.) Neuling, *der*

room /ruːm, rʊm/
A *n.* 1 (in building) Zimmer, *das;* (esp. without furniture) Raum, *der;* (large ~, for function) Saal, *der;* **leave the ~** (coll.: go to lavatory) austreten (ugs.) 2 *no pl., no indef. art.* (space) Platz, *der;* **we have no ~ for idlers** für Müßiggänger ist bei

uns kein Platz; **give sb. ~:** jmdm. Platz machen; **give sb. ~ to do sth.** (fig.) jmdm. die Freiheit lassen, etw. zu tun; **~ and to spare** Platz genug; **make ~ [for sb./sth.]** [jmdm./einer Sache] Platz machen **3** (scope) **there is no ~ for dispute/doubt about that** darüber kann es keine Diskussion/keinen Zweifel geben; **there is still ~ for improvement in his work** seine Arbeit ist noch verbesserungsfähig; **this did not leave us much ~ for manoeuvre** das ließ uns wenig Spielraum **4** *in pl.* (apartments, lodgings) Wohnung, *die;* **'~s to let'** „Zimmer zu vermieten" **5** (persons in a ~) Raum, *der;* Zimmer, *das. See also* **cat 1**

B *v.i.* (Amer.: lodge) wohnen; **~ with sb.** (be tenant of) bei jmdm. wohnen; (share with) mit jmdm. zusammenwohnen

'room divider *n.* Raumteiler, *der*

-roomed /ru:md, rʊmd/ *adj. in comb.* **a three-~ flat** eine Dreizimmerwohnung; **a one-~/four-~ building** ein Haus mit einem Zimmer/vier Zimmern

roomette /ru:'met, rʊ'met/ *n.* (Amer. Railw.) Schlafwagenkabine, *die*

roomful /'ru:mfʊl, 'rʊmfʊl/ *n.* **a ~ of people** *etc.* ein Zimmer voll[er] Leute *usw.*

rooming house /'ru:mɪŋhaʊs/ *n.* Pension, *die*

room: ~-mate *n.* Zimmergenosse, *der*/-genossin, *die;* Stubenkamerad, *der* (Milit.); **~ service** *n.* Zimmerservice, *der;* **~ temperature** *n.* Zimmertemperatur, *die*

roomy /'ru:mɪ/ *adj.* geräumig

roost /ru:st/

A *n.* Schlafplatz, *der;* (perch) [Sitz]stange, *die;* **come home to ~** (fig.) jmdm. heimgezahlt werden; *see also* **rule B 2**

B *v.i.* sich [zum Schlafen] niederlassen

rooster /'ru:stə(r)/ *n.* (Amer.) Hahn, *der*

root¹ /ru:t/

A *n.* **1** Wurzel, *die;* **pull sth. up by the ~/~s** etw. mit der Wurzel/den Wurzeln ausreißen; (fig.) etw. mit der Wurzel ausrotten; **put down ~s/strike** *or* **take ~** (lit. or fig.) Wurzeln schlagen; (fig.) **strike at the ~[s] of sth.** etw. in seinem Lebensnerv treffen; **have ~s** verwurzelt sein; **without ~s** wurzellos **2** (source) Wurzel, *die;* (basis) Grundlage, *die;* **have its ~s in sth.** einer Sache (*Dat.*) entspringen; **get at** *or* **to the ~[s] of things** den Dingen auf den Grund kommen; **be at the ~ of the matter** der Kern der Sache sein; **the ~ cause** der wirkliche Grund **3** (Ling.) Wurzel, *die* **4** (Mus.) Grundton, *der* **5** (Math.: square ~) [Quadrat]wurzel, *die* (**of** aus)

B *v.t.* **~ a plant firmly** eine Pflanze fest einpflanzen; **have ~ed itself in sth.** (fig.) in etw. (*Dat.*) verwurzelt sein; **stand ~ed to the spot** wie angewurzelt dastehen

C *v.i.* ‹*Pflanze:*› wurzeln, anwachsen

Phrasal verbs

- **~ 'out** *v.t.* ausrotten; ausmerzen
- **~ 'up** *v.t.* mit den Wurzeln ausreißen; ausroden ‹*Baum[stumpf], Busch*›

root² *v.i.* **1** (turn up ground) wühlen (**for** nach) **2** (coll.) **~ for** (cheer) anfeuern; (wish for success of) Stimmung machen für

Phrasal verbs

- **~ a'bout, ~ a'round** *v.i.* herumwühlen
- **~ 'out** *v.t.* (find by search) zu Tage fördern

root: ~ and 'branch **A** *adj.* radikal; ‹*Reform*› an Haupt und Gliedern; **B** *adv.* radikal; an Haupt und Gliedern ‹*reformieren*›; **~ beer** *n.* (Amer.) Rootbeer, *das* (*schäumendes Getränk aus Wurzeln und Kräutern*); **~ crop[s]** *n.* [*pl.*] Hackfrüchte *Pl.;* **~ di'rectory** *n.* (Computing) Hauptverzeichnis, *das;* Wurzelverzeichnis, *das*

rooted /'ru:tɪd/ *adj.* eingewurzelt

rootless /'ru:tlɪs/ *adj.* wurzellos

root: ~ mean 'square *n.* (Math.) quadratisches Mittel; **~ sign** ▸**radical sign**; **~stock** *n.* **1** (rhizome) Wurzelstock, *der;* **2** (for grafting) Unterlage, *die;* **~ vegetable** *n.* Wurzelgemüse, *das;* **~ word** *n.* (Ling.) Wurzelwort, *das*

rope /rəʊp/

A *n.* **1** (cord) Seil, *das;* Tau, *das;* **~'s end** (short piece) Tauende, *das* **2** (Amer.: lasso) Lasso, *das* **3** (for hanging sb.) **the ~:** der Strang; (fig.: death penalty) die Todesstrafe **4** *in pl.* (Boxing) **the ~s** die Seile; **be on the ~s** (lit., or fig.: near defeat) in den Seilen hängen **5** *in pl.* **learn the ~s** lernen, sich zurechtzufinden; (at work) sich einarbeiten; **know the ~s** sich auskennen; **show sb. the ~s** jmdn. mit allem vertraut machen **6** **give sb. some ~** (fig.) jmdm. eine gewisse Freiheit lassen; **give him enough ~ and he'll hang himself** (fig.) lass ihn alleine machen, dann schaufelt er sich sein eigenes Grab **7** (Mount.) **on the ~:** am Seil

B *v.t.* **1** festbinden; **~ sb. to a tree** jmdn. an einen Baum binden **2** (Mount.) anseilen

Phrasal verbs

- **~ 'in** *v.t.* **1** mit einem Seil/mit Seilen absperren ‹*Gebiet*› **2** (fig.) einspannen (ugs.); (for membership) anheuern (ugs.); **how did you get ~d in to that?** warum hast du dich dazu breitschlagen lassen? (ugs.)
- **~ 'off** *v.t.* [mit einem Seil/mit Seilen] absperren
- **~ to'gether** *v.t.* (Mount.) aneinander seilen

rope: ~-dancer *n.* Seiltänzer, *der*/-tänzerin, *die;* **~ 'ladder** *n.* Strickleiter, *die;* **~ 'sole** *n.* Kordelsohle, *die;* **~-walker** *n.* Seilakrobat, *der*/-akrobatin, *die;* **~way** *n.* Seilbahn, *die*

ropy /'rəʊpɪ/ *adj.* (coll.) (poor) schäbig; (in a bad state) mitgenommen; **be a bit ~:** nicht viel taugen; **you look a bit ~:** du siehst ziemlich kaputt aus

Roquefort /'rɒkfɔ:(r)/ *n.* Roquefort, *der*

ro-ro /'rəʊrəʊ/ *adj.* Ro-Ro-‹*Schiff, Fähre*›

rorqual /'rɔ:kwəl/ *n.* (Zool.) Finnwal, *der*

Rorschach test /'rɔ:ʃɑ:k test/ *n.* (Psych.) Rorschachtest, *der*

rosary /'rəʊzərɪ/ *n.* (Relig.) Rosenkranz, *der*

rose¹ /rəʊz/

A *n.* **1** (plant, flower) Rose, *die;* **~ of Jericho/Sharon** Jerichorose, *die*/Johanniskraut, *das;* **no bed of ~s** (fig.) kein Honigschlecken; **~s[, ~s,] all the way** (fig.) der Himmel auf Erden; **it's not all ~s** es ist nicht alles [so] rosig; **everything's [coming up] ~s** alles ist bestens; **[there's] no ~ without a thorn** (prov.) keine Rose ohne Dornen (Spr.); **Wars of the R~s** (Brit. Hist.) Rosenkriege *Pl.;* **~s in one's cheeks** rosige Wangen **2** (colour) Rosa, *das* **3** (nozzle) Brause, *die*

B *adj.* rosa[farben]

rose² ▸**rise B**

rosé /rəʊ'zeɪ, 'rəʊzeɪ/ *n.* Rosé, *der*

roseate /'rəʊzɪət/ *adj.* rosenrot

rose: ~ bed *n.* Rosenbeet, *das;* **~bud** *n.* Rosenknospe, *die;* **~bud mouth** Kirschenmund, *der* (dichter.); **~ bush** *n.* Rosenstrauch, *der;* **~-coloured** *adj.* (lit. or fig.) rosarot; **see things through ~-coloured spectacles** die Dinge durch eine rosarote Brille sehen; **~fish** *n.* Rotbarsch, *der;* **~ garden** *n.* Rosengarten, *der;* **~ hip** *n.* (Bot.) Hagebutte, *die;* **~ hip tea** Hagebuttentee, *der;* **~ leaf** *n.* Rosenblatt, *das*

rosemary /'rəʊzmərɪ/ *n.* (Bot.) Rosmarin, *der*

rose: ~ petal *n.* Rosen[blüten]blatt, *das;* **~-pink** **A** *adj.* rosarot; **B** *n.* Rosarot, *das;* **~-red** **A** *adj.* rosenrot; **B** *n.* Rosenrot, *das;* **~-tinted** ▸**rose-coloured**; **~ tree** *n.* Rosenstock, *der*

rosette /rəʊ'zet/ *n.* Rosette, *die*

rose: ~ water *n.* Rosenwasser, *das;* **~ window** *n.* (Archit.) Fensterrose, *die;* **~wood** *n.* Rosenholz, *das*

Rosicrucian /rəʊzɪ'kru:ʃn/

A *n.* Rosenkreuzer, *der*/-kreuzerin, *die*

B *adj.* Rosenkreuzer-

rosin /'rɒzɪn/ *n.* Harz, *das;* (for violin bow) Kolophonium, *das*

RoSPA /'rɒspə/ *abbr.* (Brit.) **= Royal Society for the Prevention of Accidents**

roster /'rɒstə(r)/

A *n.* Dienstplan, *der*

B *v.t.* einteilen ‹*Arbeitskraft*›; **call for flexible ~ing** flexible Dienstpläne fordern

rostrum /'rɒstrəm/ *n., pl.* **rostra** /'rɒstrə/ *or* **~s** (platform) Podium, *das;* (desk) Rednerpult, *das*

rosy /'rəʊzɪ/ *adj.* **1** rosig **2** (fig.) rosig ‹*Zukunft, Aussichten*›; **paint a ~ picture of sth.** etw. in den rosigsten Farben schildern

rot /rɒt/

A *n.* **1** ▸**B 1**: Verrottung, *die;* Fäulnis, *die;* Verwesung, *die;* Vermoderung, *die;* (rust) Rost, *der;* (fig.: deterioration) Verfall, *der;* **stop the ~** (fig.) dem Verfall Einhalt gebieten; **the ~ has set in** (fig.) der Verfall hat eingesetzt; *see also* **dry rot** **2** (coll.: nonsense) Quark, *der* (salopp); **~!** Blödsinn! (ugs.)

B *v.i.*, **-tt-** **1** (decay) verrotten; ‹*Fleisch, Gemüse, Obst:*› verfaulen; ‹*Leiche:*› verwesen; ‹*Metall:*› verrosten; ‹*Laub:*› vermodern, verrotten; ‹*Holz:*› faulen; ‹*Zähne:*› schlecht werden **2** (fig.: go to ruin) verrotten; **leave sb. to ~:** jmdn. verrotten lassen (ugs.)

C *v.t.*, **-tt-** **1** (make rotten) verrotten lassen; verfaulen lassen ‹*Fleisch, Gemüse, Obst*›; vermodern *od.* verrotten lassen ‹*Laub*›; faulen lassen ‹*Holz*›; verwesen lassen ‹*Leiche*›; zerstören ‹*Zähne*›; **that stuff will ~ your guts** (coll.) das Zeug bringt dich um (ugs.) **2** (Brit. coll.: tease) aufziehen (ugs.)

Phrasal verb

- **~ a'way** *v.i.* verfaulen; ‹*Leiche:*› verwesen; ‹*Holz:*› faulen; (moulder away) vermodern

rota /'rəʊtə/ *n.* (Brit.) **1** (order of rotation) Turnus, *der;* **draw up the cleaning ~:** den Putzplan aufstellen; **she has a regular ~ of visitors** sie bekommt in regelmäßigem Turnus Besuch **2** (list of persons) [Arbeits]plan, *der*

Rotarian /rəʊ'teərɪən/

A *n.* Rotarier, *der*

B *adj.* rotarisch; Rotarier-

rotary /'rəʊtərɪ/

A *adj.* **1** (acting by rotation) rotierend; Rotations-; **~ engine** Drehkolbenmotor, *der;* **~ press** (Printing) Rotationsmaschine, *die;* **~ pump** Kreiselpumpe, *die;* **~ mower** Rasenmäher mit rotierenden Messern **2** **R~:** Rotarier-; **R~ Club** Rotary-Club, *der*

B *n.* **1** **The R~, R~ International** der Rotary-Club; Rotary International **2** (Amer.: roundabout) Verkehrskreisel, *der*

rotate /rəʊ'teɪt/

A *v.i.* **1** (revolve) rotieren; sich drehen; **~ on an axis** sich um eine Achse drehen **2** (alternate) **these posts ~ regularly** diese Stellen werden in einem regelmäßigen Turnus neu besetzt; **rotating presidency** (EU) rotierende Präsidentschaft

B *v.t.* **1** (cause to revolve) in Rotation versetzen **2** (alternate) abwechselnd erledigen ‹*Aufgaben*›; abwechselnd erfüllen ‹*Pflichten*›; **~ [the] crops** Fruchtwechselwirtschaft betreiben; **change the way one ~s the crops** die Fruchtfolge ändern

rotation /rəʊ'teɪʃn/ *n.* **1** Rotation, *die,* Drehung, *die* (**about** um) **2** (succession) turnusmäßiger Wechsel; (in political office) Rotation, *die;* **~ of crops** Fruchtfolge, *die;* **the ~ of the seasons** der Wechsel der Jahreszeiten; **by ~:** im Turnus; **~ in office** turnusmäßiger Amtswechsel; **take office in** *or* **by ~:** ein Amt nach dem Rotationsprinzip ausüben

rotatory /'rəʊtətərɪ/ *adj.* Dreh-; drehend

rotavate /'rəʊtəveɪt/ *v.t.* mit der Fräse bearbeiten ‹*Boden*›

Rotavator ® /'rəʊtəveɪtə(r)/ *n.* [Boden]fräse, *die*

rote /rəʊt/ *n.* **by ~:** auswendig ‹*lernen, aufsagen*›; **teach sth. by ~:** etw. durch Auswendiglernen einüben

'rote-learning *n.* Auswendiglernen, *das*

'rotgut (coll.)

A *n.* Fusel, *der* (ugs., abwertend)

B *adj.* fuselig

rotisserie /rəʊ'tɪsərɪ/ *n.* **1** (restaurant) Rotisserie, *die* **2** (appliance) Grill, *der*

rotor /'rəʊtə(r)/ *n.* Rotor, *der* (Technik)

rotten /'rɒtn/

A *adj.*, **~er** /'rɒtənə(r)/, **~est** /'rɒtənɪst/ **1** (decayed) verrottet; verwest ‹*Leiche*›; vermodert, verrottet ‹*Laub, Holz*›; verfault ‹*Obst,*

Gemüse, Fleisch›; faul ‹*Ei, Zähne*›; (rusted) verrostet; **~ to the core** (fig.) verdorben bis ins Mark; völlig verrottet ‹*System, Gesellschaft*› [2] (corrupt) verdorben; verkommen [3] (coll.: bad) mies (ugs.); **feel ~** (ill) sich mies fühlen (ugs.); (have a bad conscience) ein schlechtes Gewissen haben; **it's a ~ shame** so ein Mist (ugs.); **~ luck** saumäßiges Pech (salopp)

B *adv.* (coll.) saumäßig (salopp); **hurt/stink something ~:** saumäßig wehtun/stinken (salopp); **spoilt ~:** ganz schön verwöhnt (ugs.)

rottenly /ˈrɒtnlɪ/ *adv.* (coll.) saumäßig (salopp)

rotter /ˈrɒtə(r)/ *n.* (coll.) mieser Typ (salopp abwertend); Halunke, *der*

rotund /rəʊˈtʌnd/ *adj.* [1] (round) rund [2] (plump) rundlich

rotunda /rəˈtʌndə/ *n.* Rotunde, *die* (Archit.)

rotundity /rəʊˈtʌndɪtɪ/ *n., no pl.* [1] (roundness) Rundheit, *die* [2] (plumpness) Rundlichkeit, *die*

rouble /ˈru:bl/ *n.* ▸ **p. 1332** Rubel, *der*

roué /ˈru:eɪ/ *n.* Roué, *der* (veralt.)

rouge /ru:ʒ/

A *n.* [1] (cosmetic powder) Rouge, *das* [2] (polishing agent) Englischrot, *das; see also* **jeweller**

B *v.t.* **~ one's cheeks** *or* **face** Rouge auflegen

rough /rʌf/

A *adj.* [1] (coarse, uneven) rau; holp[e]rig ‹*Straße usw.*›; uneben ‹*Gelände*›; aufgewühlt ‹*Wasser*›; unruhig ‹*Überfahrt*›; (shaggy) haarig ‹*Lebewesen*›; stopp[e]lig ‹*Bart*› [2] (violent) rau, roh, grob (abwertend) ‹*Person, Worte, Behandlung, Benehmen*›; rau ‹*Gegend*›; **the ~ element [of the population]** die Rowdys [unter der Bevölkerung]; **the remedy was ~ but effective** die Behandlung war eine Rosskur, aber sie hat gewirkt [3] (harsh to the senses) rau; kratzig ‹*Geschmack, Getränk*›; sauer ‹*Apfelwein*› [4] (trying) hart; **this is ~ on him** das ist hart für ihn; **sth. is ~ going** etw. ist nicht einfach; **have a ~ time** es schwer haben; **give sb. a ~ time** es jmdm. schwer machen; **have a ~ tongue** einen rauen Ton am Leibe haben (ugs.); *see also* **edge A 1** [5] (fig.: lacking finish, polish) derb; rau ‹*Empfang*›; unbeholfen ‹*Stil*›; ungeschliffen ‹*Benehmen, Sprache*› [6] (rudimentary) primitiv ‹*Unterkunft, Leben*›; (approximate) grob ‹*Skizze, Schätzung, Einteilung, Übersetzung*›; vag ‹*Vorstellung*›; **~ notes** stichwortartige Notizen; **~ attempt** erster Versuch; **~ draft** Rohentwurf, *der;* **in a somewhat ~ state** in einem einigermaßen unfertigen Zustand; **a ~ circle** ein ungefährer Kreis; **~ paper/notebook** Konzeptpapier, *das*/Kladde, *die* [7] (coll.: ill) angeschlagen (ugs.). *See also* **deal¹ C 1**

B *n.* [1] (hooligan) Schläger, *der* (abwertend); Rowdy, *der* (abwertend) [2] (Golf) Rough, *das* [3] **take the ~ with the smooth** die Dinge nehmen, wie sie kommen [4] (unfinished state) **[be] in ~:** [sich] im Rohzustand [befinden]

C *adv.* rau ‹*spielen*›; scharf ‹*reiten*›; **sleep ~:** im Freien schlafen

D *v.t.* **~ it** primitiv leben; **he had to ~ it for a while** er musste eine Zeit lang auf den gewohnten Komfort verzichten

(Phrasal verbs)

- **~ ˈin** *v.t.* skizzenhaft einzeichnen; [mit wenigen Strichen] andeuten
- **~ ˈout** *v.t.* [grob] entwerfen
- **~ ˈup** *v.t.* [1] (coll.: deal roughly with) zusammenschlagen [2] (ruffle) gegen den Strich streichen ‹*Haare*›

roughage /ˈrʌfɪdʒ/ *n.* [1] (for people) Ballaststoffe *Pl.* (Med.) [2] (for animals) Raufutter, *das* (Landw.)

rough: ~-and-ready *adj.* [1] (not elaborate) provisorisch; skizzenhaft ‹*Beschreibung*›; behelfsmäßig ‹*Hütte, Methode*›; grob ‹*Schätzung*›; **a ~-and-ready method for calculating sth.** eine Faustformel für die Berechnung von etw.; [2] (not refined) raubeinig (ugs.) ‹*Person*›; **~ and ˈtumble A** *adj.* wild; turbulent ‹*Atmosphäre*›; **B** *n.* [wildes] Handgemenge; [wilde] Rauferei; (fig.: turbulent life) Catch-as-catch-can, *das* (ugs. abwertend); **~cast** (Building) **A** *adj.* mit Grobmörtel verputzt; **B** *n.* Grobmörtel, *der;* **C** *v.t.* mit Grobmörtel verputzen; **~ ˈcopy** *n.* [1] (original draft) [erster] Entwurf; Konzept, *das;* [2] (simplified copy) grobe Skizze; **~ ˈdiamond** *n.* (fig.) ungehobelter, aber guter Mensch; **he's a ~ diamond** er ist rau, aber herzlich; **~-dry** *v.t.* [nur] trocknen ‹*Wäsche*›; **~ ˈedges** *n. pl.* (in book) unbeschnittene Kanten; **he has a few ~ edges** (fig.) er ist ein wenig ungeschliffen

roughen /ˈrʌfn/

A *v.t.* aufrauhen ‹*Oberfläche*›; rau machen ‹*Hände*›

B *v.i.* rau werden

rough: ~ ˈgrazing *n.* (Brit.) natürliche Weide; **~ house** *n.* (coll.) Keilerei, *die* (ugs.); **~ ˈjustice** *n.* ziemlich willkürliche Urteile; **~ ˈluck** *n.* Pech, *das*

roughly /ˈrʌflɪ/ *adv.* [1] (violently) roh; grob [2] (crudely) leidlich; grob ‹*skizzieren, bearbeiten, bauen*› [3] (approximately) ungefähr; grob ‹*geschätzt*›; *see also* **speaking B**

ˈroughneck *n.* (coll.) [1] (Amer.: rowdy) Raufbold, *der* (abwertend) [2] (driller on oil rig) Bohrarbeiter, *der*

roughness /ˈrʌfnɪs/ *n.* [1] *no pl.* Rauheit, *die;* (unevenness) Unebenheit, *die* [2] *no pl.* (sharpness) (of wine, fruit juice) Säure, *die;* (of voice) Rauheit, *die* [3] *no pl.* (violence) Rohheit, *die;* **the ~ of the area** die Häufigkeit von Gewalttaten in der Gegend [4] (rough place or part) unausgefeilte Stelle

rough: ~ ˈpassage *n.* [1] (Naut.) raue [Über]fahrt; [2] (fig.) **get a ~ passage** ‹*Gesetzentwurf:*› nur mit Mühe durchkommen; **the interview board gave him a ~ passage** die Prüfungskommission hat es ihm nicht leicht gemacht; **~ ˈride** ▸ **ride A 2**; **~-rider** *n.* [1] (horsebreaker) Zureiter, *der;* [2] (Mil.) irregulärer Kavallerist; **~shod** *adj.* **ride ~shod over sb./sth.** jmdn./etw. mit Füßen treten; **~ stuff** *n.* (coll.) Zoff, *der* (salopp); **~ ˈwork** *n.* [1] (needing force) Knochenarbeit, *die* (ugs.); [2] (preliminary) Vorbereitungsarbeit, *die*

roulette /ru:ˈlet/ *n.* Roulette, *das*

Roumania /ruˈmeɪnɪə/ ▸ **Romania**

Roumanian /ruˈmeɪnɪən/ ▸ **Romanian**

round /raʊnd/

A *adj.* [1] rund; rundlich ‹*Arme*›; **~ cheeks** Pausbacken *Pl.* (fam.); **in ~ figures, it will cost £1,000** rund gerechnet wird es 1000 Pfund kosten; **a ~ dozen** ein volles *od.* ganzes Dutzend

[2] (plain) **in the ~est manner, in ~ terms** ohne Umschweife; rundheraus

[3] (considerable) stattlich ‹*Summe, Preis*›; **a good ~ sum** eine hübsche Summe

[4] (semicircular) **~ arch** Rundbogen, *der*

[5] (Phonet.) gerundet

[6] (full-toned and mellow) voll ‹*Ton*›; volltönend ‹*Stimme*›

B *n.* [1] (recurring series) Serie, *die;* **~ of talks/negotiations** Gesprächs-/Verhandlungsrunde, *die;* **the daily ~:** der Alltag; **the daily ~ of chores** die täglichen Pflichten

[2] (charge of ammunition) Ladung, *die;* **50 ~s [of ammunition]** 50 Schuss Munition; **put five ~s in a magazine** fünf Kugeln in ein Magazin stecken; **fire five ~s** fünf Schüsse abfeuern

[3] (division of game or contest) Runde, *die*

[4] (burst) **~ of applause** Beifallssturm, *der;* **~s of cheers** Hochrufe

[5] **~ [of drinks]** Runde, *die*

[6] (regular calls) Runde, *die;* Tour, *die;* **be on sb.'s ~:** auf jmds. Tour liegen; **the doctor is on her ~ at present** Frau Doktor macht gerade Hausbesuche; **go [on]** *or* **make one's ~s** ‹*Posten, Wächter usw.:*› seine Runde machen *od.* gehen; ‹*Krankenhausarzt:*› Visite machen; **make the ~ of the wards** Visite machen; **do** *or* **go the ~s** ‹*Person, Gerücht usw.:*› die Runde machen (ugs.); **do the ~s of all the second-hand shops/one's relatives** alle Gebrauchtwarenläden/seine Verwandtschaft abklappern (ugs.); **she is certainly doing the ~s** (is promiscuous) sie macht bei den Männern die Runde (ugs.)

[7] (Golf) Runde, *die;* **a ~ of golf** eine Runde Golf

[8] (Mus.) Round, *der* (fachspr.); einfacher Zirkelkanon

[9] (slice) **a ~ of bread/toast** eine Scheibe Brot/Toast; **a ~ of cucumber sandwiches** ein Gurkensandwich (in 2 od. 4 Stücke geschnitten)

[10] **in the ~** *postpos.* (Art) als Vollplastik; vollplastisch; (fig.: as a whole) ganzheitlich; **theatre in the ~:** Arenabühne, *die;* Rundtheater, *das*

[11] (Archery) Runde, *die*

C *adv.* [1] **all the year ~:** das ganze Jahr hindurch; **the third time ~:** beim dritten Mal; **have a wall all ~:** von einer Mauer eingeschlossen sein; **have a look ~:** sich umsehen

[2] (in girth) **be [all of] ten feet ~:** einen Umfang von [mindestens] zehn Fuß haben

[3] (from one point, place, person, etc. to another) **tea was handed ~:** es wurde Tee herumgereicht; **he asked ~ among his friends** er fragte seine Freunde; **the room was hung ~ with portraits** in dem Zimmer hingen ringsum Porträts; **for a mile ~:** im Umkreis einer Meile

[4] (by indirect way) herum; **walk ~:** außen herum gehen; **go a/the long way ~:** einen weiten Umweg machen

[5] (here) hier; (there) dort; **I'll go ~ tomorrow** ich gehe morgen hin; **call ~ any time!** kommen Sie doch jederzeit vorbei!; **ask sb. ~ [for a drink]** jmdn. [zu einem Gläschen zu sich] einladen; **order a car** *etc.* **~:** nach einem Wagen *usw.* schicken; **send a car ~:** einen Wagen vorbeischicken; *see also* **clock A 1**

D *prep.* [1] um [... herum]; **a tour ~ the world** eine Weltreise; **travel ~ England** durch England reisen; **she had a blanket ~ her** sie hatte eine Decke um sich geschlungen; **the box had a band ~ it** war um die Schachtel war ein Band gebunden; **right ~ the lake** um den ganzen See herum; **be ~ the back of the house** hinter dem Haus sein; **run ~ the back of the house** hinten ums Haus rennen; (to position there) hinter das Haus rennen; **run ~ the streets** durch die Straßen rennen; **walk** *etc.* **~ and ~ sth.** immer wieder um etw. herumgehen *usw.*; **she ran ~ and ~ the park** sie lief Runde um Runde durch den Park

[2] (with successive visits to) **he hawks them ~ the cafés** er hausiert mit ihnen in den Cafés; **he sings ~ the pubs** er singt in den Kneipen; **we looked ~ the shops** wir sahen uns in den Geschäften um

[3] (in various directions from) um [... herum]; rund um ‹*einen Ort*›; **look ~ one** um sich schauen; **in Chelsea and ~ it** in und um Chelsea; **do you live ~ here?** wohnst du [hier] in der Nähe?; **if you're ever ~ this way** wenn du hier in der Nähe bist

[4] **argue ~ and ~ a matter/problem** *etc.* um eine Sache/ein Problem *usw.* herumreden (ugs.)

E *v.t.* [1] (give ~ shape to) rund machen; runden ‹*Lippen, Rücken*›

[2] (state as ~ number) runden (**to** auf + *Akk.*)

[3] (go ~) umfahren/umgehen *usw.*; **~ a turn/bend** um eine Kurve fahren/gehen/kommen *usw.*; **~ a cape** um ein Kap fahren

[4] (Phonet.) mit Rundung der Lippen sprechen; labialisieren (Sprachw.)

(Phrasal verbs)

- **~ ˈdown** *v.t.* abrunden ‹*Zahl*› (**to** auf + *Akk.*)
- **~ ˈoff** *v.t.* (also fig.: complete) abrunden
- **~ on** *v.t.* anfahren
- **~ ˈout** *v.t.* vervollständigen
- **~ ˈup** *v.t.* [1] (gather, collect together) verhaften ‹*Verdächtige*›; zusammentreiben ‹*Vieh*›; beschaffen, (ugs.) auftreiben ‹*Geld*›; *see also* **round-up** [2] (to ~ figure) aufrunden (**to** auf + *Akk.*)

round: ~ aˈbout A *adv.* [1] (on all sides) ringsum; **the villages ~ about** die umliegenden Dörfer; [2] (indirectly) auf Umwegen; [3] (approximately) rund; **~ about 2,500 people** um die *od.* rund 2 500 Leute; **B** *prep.* rund um; **~about A** *n.* [1] (Brit.: road junction) Verkehrskreisel, *der;* [2] (Brit.: merry-go-round) Karussell, *das;* **what you lose on the swings you gain on the ~abouts** (prov.) was man auf der einen Seite verliert, gewinnt man auf der anderen; **it is swings and ~abouts** es gleicht sich aus; **B** *adj.* [1] (meandering) **a [very] ~about way** *or* **road** *or* **route** *etc.* ein [sehr] umständlicher Weg; **~about journey** Reise mit Umwegen; **the taxi took us/went a ~about way** das Taxi brachte uns auf einem Umweg zum Ziel/machte einen Umweg; [2] (fig.: indirect) umständlich; **a more**

r

~about method eine weniger direkte Methode; **~ 'brackets** *n. pl.* runde Klammern; **~ dance** *n.* Rundtanz, *der*

rounded /'raʊndɪd/ *adj.* 1) rund; abgerundet ‹*Kante*› 2) (perfected) abgerundet; harmonisch ‹*Person*› 3) (fig.: polished) ausgefeilt 4) (sonorous) voll

roundel /'raʊndl/ *n.* 1) (disc) [kleine runde] Scheibe 2) (mark) Kreiszeichen, *das*

roundelay /'raʊndɪleɪ/ *n.* (Mus.) einfaches Liedchen mit Refrain

rounders /'raʊndəz/ *n. sing.* (Brit.) Rounders, *das;* Rundball, *das;* ≈ Schlagball, *der*

round: ~-eyed *adj.* mit großen Augen *nachgestellt;* **be ~-eyed with amazement** große Augen machen; **~-faced** *adj.* pausbäckig (fam.); **~ game** *n.: Spiel für beliebig viele Mitspieler, bei dem jeder gegen jeden spielt;* **R~head** *n.* (Brit. Hist.) Rundkopf, *der*

roundly /'raʊndlɪ/ *adv.* entschieden

'round-neck *adj.* ‹*Pullover, Bluse usw.*› mit rundem Halsausschnitt

roundness /'raʊndnɪs/ *n., no pl.* Rundheit, *die;* (of figure) Rundlichkeit, *die*

round: ~ 'number *n.* runde Zahl; **~ 'robin** *n.* 1) (petition) Petition, *die* (*mit kreisförmig angeordneten Unterschriften*); 2) (Amer.: tournament) Round-Robin-Turnier, *das* (Sport); **~-'shouldered** *adj.* ‹*Person*› mit einem Rundrücken; **be ~-shouldered** einen Rundrücken haben

roundsman /'raʊndzmən/ *n., pl.* **roundsmen** /'raʊndzmən/ 1) (Brit.) Austräger, *der;* **milk ~:** Milchmann, *der* (ugs.) 2) (Amer.: police officer) ≈ Polizeimeister, *der*

round: R~ 'Table *n.* runde Tafel des Königs Artus; **[King Arthur and the] Knights of the R~ Table** [König Artus und die] Ritter der Tafelrunde; **~-table 'conference** *n.* Roundtablekonferenz, *die;* **~-the-'clock** *adj.* rund um die Uhr *nachgestellt; see also* **clock A 1**; **~-the-world** *attrib. adj.* **~-the-world flight/cruise** *etc.* Flug/Kreuzfahrt *usw.* um die [ganze] Welt; **~-the-world voyage/trip** Weltreise, *die;* **~-the-world yachtsman/yachtswoman** Weltumsegler, *der*/Weltumseglerin, *die;* **~ 'trip** *n.* 1) Rundreise, *die;* 2) (Amer.: return trip) Hin- und Rückfahrt, *die;* **the ~ trip to the island** die Fahrt zu der Insel und zurück; *attrib.* **~-trip ticket** Rückfahrkarte, *die;* **~-up** *n.* 1) (gathering-in) (of persons) Einfangen, *das;* (arrest) Verhaftung, *die;* (of animals) Zusammentreiben, *das;* 2) (summary) Zusammenfassung, *die;* **~worm** *n.* (Zool., Med.) Spulwurm, *der*

rouse /raʊz/

A *v.t.* 1) (awaken, lit. or fig.) wecken (**from** aus); **~ oneself** aufwachen; (overcome indolence) sich aufraffen; **~ sb./oneself to action** jmdn. zur Tat anstacheln/sich zur Tat aufraffen 2) (provoke) reizen; **he is terrible when ~d** er ist furchtbar, wenn man ihn reizt; **~ sb. to anger** jmdn. in Wut bringen 3) (cause) wecken; hervorrufen, auslösen ‹*Empörung, Beschuldigungen*› 4) (startle from cover) aufscheuchen

B *v.i.* **~ [up]** aufwachen

rousing /'raʊzɪŋ/ *adj.* mitreißend ‹*Lied*›; leidenschaftlich ‹*Rede*›; stürmisch ‹*Beifall*›

roustabout /'raʊstəbaʊt/ *n.* 1) (Amer.: labourer) Hilfsarbeiter, *der;* Handlanger, *der;* (dockhand) Schauermann, *der* 2) (labourer on oil rig) Bohrarbeiter, *der*

rout¹ /raʊt/

A *n.* (disorderly retreat) [wilde] Flucht; (disastrous defeat) verheerende Niederlage; **put to ~:** in die Flucht schlagen; (arch., Law: mob) Horde, *die*

B *v.t.* aufreiben ‹*Feind, Truppen*›; vernichtend schlagen ‹*Gegner*›

rout² *v.i.* (root) wühlen

Phrasal verb

• **~ 'out** *v.t.* herausjagen; **~ sb. out of sth.** jmdn. aus etw. jagen

route /ru:t, *Mil. also:* raʊt/

A *n.* 1) (course) Route, *die;* Weg, *der;* **a [very] circuitous ~** (lit. or fig.) ein [großer] Umweg; **shipping ~:** Schifffahrtsstraße, *die;* **bus/air ~:** Bus-/Fluglinie, *die* 2) (Amer.: delivery round) Bezirk, *der*

B *v.t.,* **~ing** fahren lassen ‹*Fahrzeug*›; führen ‹*Linie*›; **the train is ~d through** *or* **via Crewe** der Zug fährt über Crewe

route: ~man /'ru:tmən/ *n., pl.* **~men** /'ru:tmən/ (Amer.) (delivery man) Austräger, *der;* (salesman) Vertreter, *der;* **~ map** *n.* Streckenkarte, *die;* **~ march** *n.* (Mil.) Übungsmarsch, *der;* **~ planner** *n.* Routenplanner, *der*

router¹ /'raʊtə(r)/ *n.* (tool) Nuthobel, *der*

router² /'ru:tə(r)/ *n.* (Computing) Router, *der*

routine /ru:'ti:n/

A *n.* 1) (regular procedure) Routine, *die;* **strict ~s must be kept to** ein genau festgelegter Ablauf muss eingehalten werden; **creature of ~:** Gewohnheitsmensch, *der;* **establish a new ~ after retirement** nach der Pensionierung einen neuen Lebensrhythmus finden 2) (coll.) (set speech) Platte, *die* (ugs.); (formula) Spruch, *der* 3) (Theatre) Nummer, *die;* (Dancing, Skating) Figur, *die;* (Gymnastics) Übung, *die* 4) (Computing) Routine, *die*

B *adj.* routinemäßig; Routine‹*arbeit, -untersuchung usw.*›; **the investigation was purely ~:** die Untersuchung verlief absolut routinemäßig

routinely /ru:'ti:nlɪ/ *adv.* routinemäßig

roux /ru:/ *n., pl. same* (Cookery) Mehlschwitze, *die*

rove¹ /rəʊv/

A *v.i.* ziehen; ‹*Blick:*› schweifen (geh.); **~ [about]** herumziehen

B *v.t.* streifen durch; durchstreifen (geh.); ‹*Blick:*› durchschweifen ‹*Raum*›

rove² ▸ **reeve**

rover¹ /'rəʊvə(r)/ *n.* (wanderer) Vagabund, *der* (veralt.); **R~ Scout** (Hist.) Rover, *der*

rover² *n.* (pirate) Pirat, *der*

roving/'rəʊvɪŋ/: **~ com'mission** *n.* (Brit.) Reiseauftrag, *der;* **have a ~ commission** einen Aufgabenbereich haben, bei dem man viel herumkommt; **~ 'eye** *n.* **have a ~ eye** den Frauen/Männern schöne Augen machen

row¹ /raʊ/ (coll.)

A *n.* 1) (noise) Krach, *der;* **make a ~:** Krach machen; (protest) Rabatz machen (ugs.) 2) (quarrel) Krach, *der* (ugs.); **have/start a ~:** Krach haben/anfangen (ugs.); **they're always having** *or* **they keep having ~s** sie streiten dauernd; sie haben ständig Krach (ugs.) 3) **get into a ~ over sth.** (be reprimanded) wegen etw. Ärger kriegen (ugs.)

B *v.i.* sich streiten

row² /rəʊ/ *n.* 1) Reihe, *die;* **in a ~:** in einer Reihe; (coll.: in succession) nacheinander; hintereinander 2) (line of numbers etc.) Zeile, *die* 3) (terrace) **~ [of houses]** [Häuser]zeile, *die;* [Häuser]reihe, *die*

row³ /rəʊ/

A *v.i.* (move boat with oars etc.) rudern; **~ out/back** hinaus-/zurückrudern

B *v.t.* rudern; **~ sb. across** jmdn. hinüberrudern

C *n.* **go for a ~:** rudern gehen; **after a long ~:** nach langem Rudern

rowan /'rəʊən, 'raʊən/ *n.* ▸ **rowan tree**

rowan: ~ berry *n.* Vogelbeere, *die;* **~ tree** *n.* 1) (Scot., N.Engl.) Eberesche, *die;* 2) (Amer.) amerikanische Eberesche

rowboat /'rəʊbəʊt/ *n.* Ruderboot, *das*

rowdiness /'raʊdɪnɪs/ *n., no pl.* Rabaukenhaftigkeit, *die;* (behaviour) rabaukenhaftes Benehmen

rowdy /'raʊdɪ/

A *adj.* rowdyhaft (abwertend); **~ adolescents** jugendliche Rowdys (abwertend); **the ~ element in the audience** die Rüpel (abwertend) unter den Zuhörern; **~ scenes** tumultartige Szenen; **the party was ~:** auf der Party ging es laut zu

B *n.* Krawallmacher, *der;* Rabauke, *der*

rowdyism /'raʊdɪɪzm/ *n., no pl.* Rabaukentum, *das* (abwertend)

rower /'rəʊə(r)/ *n.* Ruderer, *der*/Ruderin, *die;* **be a ~:** rudern

row house /'rəʊhaʊs/ *n.* (Amer.) Reihenhaus, *das*

rowing /'rəʊɪŋ/ *n., no pl.* Rudern, *das;* **do a lot of/like ~:** viel/gern rudern

rowing: ~ boat *n.* (Brit.) Ruderboot, *das;* **~ club** *n.* Ruderklub, *der;* **~ machine** *n.* Rudergerät, *das*

rowlock /'rɒlək/ *n.* (Brit.) Dolle, *die*

royal /'rɔɪəl/

A *adj.* königlich; **the ~ plural** der Pluralis majestatis; *see also* **academy 1**; **assent B**; **blood A 3**; **commission A 4**; **duke 1**; **Highness**; **regiment A 2**; **right D 7**; **tennis**; **we**

B *n.* (coll.) Mitglied der Königsfamilie; **the ~s** die Königsfamilie

royal: R~ 'Air Force *n.* (Brit.) Königliche Luftwaffe; **~ 'blue** *n.* (Brit.) Königsblau, *das;* **~ 'burgh** *n.* (in Schottland) grafschaftsfreie Stadt; **R~ Engi'neers** *n. pl.: Pioniertruppe der britischen Armee;* **~ 'family** *n.* königliche Familie; **~ 'icing** *n.* (Cookery) Zuckerguss, *der*

royalism /'rɔɪəlɪzm/ *n.* Royalismus, *der*

royalist /'rɔɪəlɪst/ *n.* Royalist, *der*/Royalistin, *die; attrib.* Royalisten-; royalistisch

royal 'jelly *n.* Gelée royale, *das*

royally /'rɔɪəlɪ/ *adv.* königlich

royal: R~ Ma'rine *n.* (Brit.) *britischer Marineinfanterist;* **R~ 'Navy** *n.* (Brit.) Königliche Kriegsmarine; **~ 'oak** *n.: Eichenzweig, der zum Gedenken der Wiedereinsetzung Charles II. als König getragen wird;* **~ stag** *n.* (Hunting) Kapitalhirsch, *der;* **~ 'standard** *n.* königliche Standarte

royalty /'rɔɪəltɪ/ *n.* 1) (payment) Tantieme, *die* (**on** für) 2) *collect.* (royal persons) Mitglieder des Königshauses 3) *no pl., no art.* (member of royal family) ein Mitglied der königlichen Familie; **she's ~:** sie gehört zur königlichen Familie

royal 'warrant *n.: Recht, den königlichen Hof zu beliefern*

rozzer /'rɒzə(r)/ *n.* (Brit. sl.) Polyp, *der* (salopp)

RPI *abbr.* (Brit.) **= retail price index**

r.p.m. /ɑ:pi:'em/ *abbr.* 1) **= resale price maintenance** 2) **= revolutions per minute** U.p.M.

RSI *abbr.* **= repetitive strain injury**

RSPCA *abbr.* (Brit.) **= Royal Society for the Prevention of Cruelty to Animals** *britischer Tierschutzverein*

RSVP *abbr.* **= répondez s'il vous plaît** R.S.V.P.; U.A.w.g.

rt. *abbr.* **= right**

Rt. Hon. *abbr.* ▸ ❶ **p. 1634** (Brit.) **= Right Honourable**

Rt. Rev[d]. *abbr.* ▸ ❶ **p. 1634 = Right Reverend; the Rt. Rev[d].** S./Sr. E[xz].

rub /rʌb/

A *v.t.,* **-bb-** 1) reiben (**on, against** an + *Dat.*); (with ointment etc.) einreiben; (to remove dirt etc.) abreiben; (to dry) trockenreiben; (with sandpaper) [ab]schmirgeln; **~ sth. off sth.** etw. von etw. reiben; **~ sth. dry** etw. trockenreiben; **~ one's hands** sich (*Dat.*) die Hände reiben; **~ noses** die Nasen aneinander reiben; **~ shoulders** *or* **elbows with sb.** (fig.) Tuchfühlung mit jmdm. haben; **~ a hole in sth.** ein Loch in etw. (*Akk.*) scheuern; **~ one's feet on sth.** sich (*Dat.*) die Füße an etw. (*Dat.*) reiben; **~ two things together** zwei Dinge aneinander reiben; **~ sth. through a sieve** etw. durch ein Sieb streichen; **he ~bed liniment over his chest** er rieb sich (*Dat.*) die Brust mit einem Einreibemittel ein; *see also* **nose A 1**; **penny 3** 2) (reproduce by ~bing) *kopieren, indem man auf ein Relief Papier legt und mit Malkreide, Bleistift o. ä. darüber reibt*

B *v.i.,* **-bb-** 1) (exercise friction) reiben (**[up]on, against** an + *Dat.*) 2) (get frayed) sich abreiben; **~ bare** sich blank reiben *od.* scheuern

C *n.* Reiben, *das;* **give it a quick ~:** reib es kurz ab; **there's the ~** (fig.) da liegt der Haken [dabei] (ugs.)

Phrasal verbs

• **~ a'long** *v.i.* 1) **~ along [together]** [gut] miteinander auskommen 2) (financially) auskommen

• **~ a'way** *v.t.* abreiben ‹*Farbe, Schmutz*›; wegmassieren ‹*Schmerzen*›

• **~ 'down** *v.t.* 1) (prepare) abschmirgeln 2) (dry) abreiben. *See also* **rub-down**

• **~ 'in** *v.t.* einreiben; **there's no need to** *or*

don't ~ it in (fig.) reib es mir nicht [dauernd] unter die Nase (ugs.)

• **~ 'off**

A *v.t.* wegreiben; wegwischen

B *v.i.* (lit. or fig.) abfärben (**on** auf + *Akk.*); **a lot of dirt/oil ~bed off on my hands** ich bekam sehr schmutzige/ölige Hände

• **~ 'out**

A *v.t.* ausreiben; (from paper) ausradieren

B *v.i.* sich ausreiben/(from paper) sich ausradieren lassen

• **~ 'up** *v.t.* **1** (polish) blank reiben; wienern (ugs.) **2** (revise) auffrischen; aufpolieren (ugs.) **3** **~ sb. up the right/wrong way** (fig.) jmdm. um den Bart gehen (ugs.)/auf den Schlips treten (ugs.)

rubber¹ /ˈrʌbə(r)/ *n.* **1** Gummi, *das od. der; attrib.* Gummi- **2** (eraser) Radiergummi, *der* **3** (sl.: condom) Gummi, *der* (salopp) **4** *in pl.* (Amer.: galoshes) Galoschen *Pl.*

rubber² *n.* (Cards) Robber, *der*

rubber: ~ 'band *n.* Gummiband, *das;* **~ 'bullet** *n.* Gummigeschoss, *das;* **~ 'cheque** *n.* (coll.) ungedeckter Scheck; **~ 'glove** *n.* Gummihandschuh, *der;* **~ goods** *n. pl.* Gummiwaren *Pl.;* (condoms) Gummis *Pl.* (ugs.)

rubberize /ˈrʌbəraɪz/ *v.t.* gummieren

rubber: ~neck (Amer.) **A** *n.* Gaffer, *der*/Gafferin, *die* (abwertend); **B** *v.i.* gaffen (abwertend); **~ plant** *n.* (Bot.) Gummibaum, *der;* **~ solution** *n.* Gummilösung, *die;* **~ 'stamp** *n.* **1** Gummistempel, *der;* **2** (fig.: one who endorses uncritically) Jasager, *der*/Jasagerin, *die* (abwertend); **the council is a ~ stamp body** die Ratsversammlung sagt zu allem Ja und Amen (ugs.); **~-'stamp** *v.t.* (fig.: approve) absegnen (ugs. scherzh.)

rubbery /ˈrʌbərɪ/ *adj.* gummiartig; (tough) zäh; **be tough and ~:** zäh wie Gummi sein

rubbing /ˈrʌbɪŋ/ *n.: Kopie, die entsteht, wenn man auf ein Relief Papier legt und mit Malkreide, Bleistift o. ä. darüber reibt*

rubbish /ˈrʌbɪʃ/

A *n., no pl., no indef. art.* **1** (refuse) Abfall, *der;* Abfälle; (to be collected and dumped) Müll, *der* **2** (worthless material) Plunder, *der* (ugs. abwertend); **be ~:** nichts taugen **3** (nonsense) Quatsch, *der* (ugs.); Blödsinn, *der* (ugs.); **talk a lot of ~:** eine Menge Blödsinn reden; **what ~!** was für ein Quatsch *od.* Schmarren!

B *int.* Quatsch (ugs. abwertend)

C *v.t.* verreißen

rubbish: ~ bin *n.* Abfall-/Mülleimer, *der;* (in factory) Abfall-/Mülltonne, *die;* **~ chute** *n.* Müllschlucker, *der;* **~ collection** *n.* Müllabfuhr, *die;* **~ dump** *n.* Müllkippe, *die;* **~ heap** *n.* Müllhaufen, *der;* (in garden) Abfallhaufen, *der;* **~ tip** *n.* Müllabladeplatz, *der*

rubbishy /ˈrʌbɪʃɪ/ *adj.* mies (ugs.); **~ newspaper** Käseblatt, *das* (salopp abwertend)

rubble /ˈrʌbl/ *n.* **1** (from damaged building) Trümmer *Pl.;* (Geol. also) Schutt, *der;* **reduce sth. to ~:** etw. in Schutt und Asche legen **2** (water-worn stones) Geröll, *das*

'rub-down *n.* **give sb./sth. a [quick] ~:** jmdn./etw. [kurz *od.* schnell] abreiben

rube /ruːb/ *n.* (Amer. coll.) Bauer, *der* (ugs.)

rubella /rʊˈbelə/ *n.* ▸ **p. 1231** (Med.) Röteln *Pl.*

Rubicon /ˈruːbɪkən/ *n.* **cross the ~** (fig.) den Rubikon überschreiten (geh.)

rubicund /ˈruːbɪkʌnd/ *adj.* (literary) rosig; rotgesichtig ‹*Person*›

Rubik's cube /ruːbɪk ˈkjuːb/ *n.* Zauberwürfel, *der;* Rubik-Würfel, *der*

rubric /ˈruːbrɪk/ *n.* **1** Rubrik, *die* **2** (commentary) Glosse, *die*

ruby /ˈruːbɪ/

A *n.* **1** (precious stone) Rubin, *der;* (Horol.) Stein, *der* **2** (colour) Rubinrot, *das*

B *adj.* **1** (red) rubinfarben; rubinrot **2** (containing stone) Rubin‹*ring, -brosche usw.*›

ruby: ~-red *adj.* rubinrot; **~ 'wedding** *n.* Rubinhochzeit, *die*

RUC *abbr.* **= Royal Ulster Constabulary** nordirische Polizei

ruche /ruːʃ/ *n.* Rüsche, *die*

ruched /ruːʃt/ *adj.* Rüschen-

ruck¹ /rʌk/ *n.* **1** (Sport: main body of competitors) Feld, *das* **2** (fig.: crowd, mass) Masse, *die* **3** (Rugby) offenes Gedränge

ruck², (Brit.) **ruckle** /ˈrʌkl/

A *n.* (crease) Falte, *die*

B *v.i.* **~ up** hochrutschen

rucksack /ˈrʌksæk, ˈrʊksæk/ *n.* Rucksack, *der*

ruckus /ˈrʌkəs/ *n.,* (coll.) **ructions** /ˈrʌkʃnz/ *n. pl.* Rabatz, *der* (ugs.)

rudder /ˈrʌdə(r)/ *n.* [Steuer]ruder, *das*

rudderless /ˈrʌdəlɪs/ *adj.* ruderlos; ohne Ruder *nachgestellt;* (fig.) richtungslos

ruddy /ˈrʌdɪ/ *adj.* **1** (reddish) rötlich **2** (rosy) rosig **3** (Brit. coll. euphem.: bloody) verdammt (salopp)

rude /ruːd/ *adj.* **1** (impolite) unhöflich; (stronger) rüde; **say ~ things** *or* **be ~ about sb.** in ungehöriger Weise von jmdm. sprechen; **be ~ to sb.** zu jmdm. grob unhöflich sein; jmdn. rüde behandeln; **be ~ to a teacher** zu einem Lehrer frech *od.* unverschämt sein **2** (abrupt) unsanft; **~ awakening** böses *od.* (geh.) jähes Erwachen **3** (hearty) **in ~ health** (dated) kerngesund **4** (simple) primitiv **5** (obscene) unanständig

rudely /ˈruːdlɪ/ *adv.* **1** (impolitely) unhöflich; rüde **2** (abruptly) jäh (geh.); **be ~ reminded of sth.** unsanft an etw. (*Akk.*) erinnert werden **3** (roughly) primitiv; **a ~ constructed hut** eine grob gezimmerte Hütte **4** (obscenely) unanständig; **gesture ~ at sb.** jmdm. eine unanständige Geste zeigen

rudeness /ˈruːdnɪs/ *n., no pl.* (bad manners) ungehöriges *od.* rüdes Benehmen

rudiment /ˈruːdɪmənt/ *n.* **1** *in pl.* (first principles) Grundzüge *Pl.;* Grundlagen *Pl.;* **know the ~s of law** über juristische Grundkenntnisse verfügen **2** *in pl.* (imperfect beginning) [erster] Ansatz

rudimentary /ruːdɪˈmentərɪ/ *adj.* **1** (elementary) elementar; primitiv ‹*Gebäude*›; **~ knowledge** Grundkenntnisse *Pl.* **2** (Anat., Zool.) rudimentär

rue /ruː/ *v.t.,* **~ing** *or* **ruing** /ˈruːɪŋ/ (literary: repent of) bereuen; **you'll live to ~ it** es wird dich noch gereuen (geh., veralt.); **~ the day/hour when ...:** den Tag/die Stunde verwünschen, da ...

rueful /ˈruːfl/ *adj.,* **ruefully** /ˈruːfəlɪ/ *adv.* reumütig; reuig

ruff¹ /rʌf/ *n.* Halskrause, *die*

ruff² *n.* (sandpiper) Kampfläufer, *der*

ruff³ (Cards)

A *n.* Trumpfen, *das*

B *v.i.* trumpfen

C *v.t.* mit einem Trumpf stechen

ruffian /ˈrʌfɪən/ *n.* Rohling, *der* (abwertend); **gang of ~s** Schlägerbande, *die;* **the little ~** (joc.) der kleine Strolch

ruffianly /ˈrʌfɪənlɪ/ *adj.* roh; rau ‹*Bursche*›

ruffle /ˈrʌfl/

A *v.t.* **1** (disturb smoothness of) kräuseln; **~ sb.'s hair** jmdm. durch die Haare fahren; *see also* **feather A 1** **2** (upset) aus der Fassung bringen; **her composure was not ~d** sie verlor ihre Fassung nicht; **be easily ~d** leicht aus der Fassung geraten **3** (gather) kräuseln

B *n.* (frill) Rüsche, *die*

Phrasal verb

• **~ 'up** *v.t.* sträuben ‹*Gefieder*›

rug /rʌg/ *n.* **1** (for floor) [kleiner, dicker] Teppich; **Persian ~:** Perserbrücke, *die;* **pull the ~ [out] from under sb.** (fig.) jmdm. den Boden unter den Füßen wegziehen **2** (wrap, blanket) [dicke] Wolldecke

rugby /ˈrʌgbɪ/ *n.* Rugby, *das; see also* **fives**

rugby: ~ ball *n.* Rugbyball, *der;* **~ 'football** *n.* **1** (game) ▸ **rugby; 2** (ball) ▸ **rugby ball; ~ 'footballer** *n.* Rugbyspieler, *der;* **R~ 'League** *n.* (Brit.) *Rugby mit 13 Spielern pro Mannschaft;* **~ player** ▸ **~ footballer; ~ tackle** *n.* tiefes Fassen (Rugby); **the policeman brought him down with a ~ tackle** der Polizist warf sich auf ihn und riss ihn zu Boden; **R~ 'Union** *n.* (Brit.) *Rugby mit 15 Spielern pro Mannschaft*

rugged /ˈrʌgɪd/ *adj.* **1** (sturdy) robust **2** (involving hardship) hart ‹*Test*› **3** (unpolished) rau; unverfälscht ‹*Ehrlichkeit, Freundlichkeit usw.*›; **with ~ good looks** gut aussehend mit markanten Gesichtszügen **4** (uneven) zerklüftet; unwegsam ‹*Land, Anstieg*›; zerfurcht ‹*Gesicht*›

ruggedize /ˈrʌgɪdaɪz/ *v.t.* (Amer.) armieren

ruggedly /ˈrʌgɪdlɪ/ *adv.* **~ constructed** robust gebaut; **~ handsome** gut aussehend mit markanten Gesichtszügen

rugger /ˈrʌgə(r)/ *n.* (Brit. coll.) Rugby, *das*

Ruhr /rʊə(r)/ *pr. n.* **the ~:** das Ruhrgebiet

ruin /ˈruːɪn/

A *n.* **1** *no pl., no indef. art.* (decay) Verfall, *der;* **bring about one's own ~:** sich selbst ruinieren; **be reduced to a state of ~:** völlig verfallen sein; **the ~ of his hopes** das Ende seiner Hoffnungen; **go to** *or* **fall into rack and ~** ‹*Gebäude:*› völlig verfallen; ‹*Garten:*› völlig verwahrlosen; ‹*Pläne:*› zunichte werden **2** *no pl., no indef. art.* (downfall) Ruin, *der;* **his business was facing ~:** sein Geschäft stand am Rande des Ruins; **~ stared her in the face** sie stand vor dem Ruin **3** *in sing. or pl.* (remains) Ruine, *die;* **in ~s** in Trümmern; **he is a ~** (fig.) er ist eine Ruine (ugs.) *od.* ein Wrack; **rise from the ~s of sth.** aus den Trümmern einer Sache entstehen **4** (cause of ~) Ruin, *der;* Untergang, *der;* **you'll be the ~ of me** du ruinierst mich [noch]

B *v.t.* ruinieren; verderben ‹*Urlaub, Abend*›; zunichte machen ‹*Aussichten, Möglichkeiten usw.*›

ruination /ruːɪˈneɪʃn/ *n., no pl.* ▸ **ruin A 4**

ruined /ˈruːɪnd/ *adj.* **1** (reduced to ruins) verfallen; **~ town** Ruinenstadt, *die;* **a ~ castle/palace/church** eine Burg-/Palast-/Kirchenruine **2** (brought to ruin) ruiniert; **his speculations left him a ~ man** seine Spekulationen ruinierten ihn **3** (spoilt) verdorben

ruinous /ˈruːɪnəs/ *adj.* **1** (in ruins) verfallen **2** (disastrous) ruinös; katastrophal ‹*Wirkung*›; **be ~ to sb./sth.** jmdn./etw. ruinieren

ruinously /ˈruːɪnəslɪ/ *adv.* ruinös; katastrophal ‹*teuer, hoch usw.*›

rule /ruːl/

A *n.* **1** (principle) Regel, *die;* **~ of conduct/decorum/cricket/life** Verhaltens-/Anstands-/Kricket-/Lebensregel, *die;* **the ~s of the game** (lit. or fig.) die Spielregeln; **stick to** *or* **play by the ~s** (lit. or fig.) sich an die Spielregeln halten; **~s and regulations** Regeln und Vorschriften; **[always] make it a ~ to do sth.** (fig.) es sich (*Dat.*) zur Regel machen, etw. zu tun; **be against the ~s** regelwidrig sein; (fig.) gegen die Spielregeln verstoßen; **bend** *or* **stretch the ~s** (fig.) ein Auge zudrücken (ugs.); **R~s** (Austral. Footb.) *Fußball nach den australischen Regeln;* **as a ~:** in der Regel; **~ of three** (Math.) Dreisatz, *der;* **~ of thumb** Faustregel, *die;* **the usual ~ of thumb is ...:** als Faustregel gilt ...; **~ of thumb estimate** grobe Schätzung **2** (custom) Regel, *die;* **the ~ of the house is that ...:** in diesem Haus ist es üblich, dass ...; **suits are the ~ on such an occasion** bei einem solchen Anlass trägt man normalerweise einen Anzug **3** *no pl.* (government) Herrschaft, *die* (**over** über + *Akk.*); **the ~ of law** die Autorität des Gesetzes **4** (Eccl.: code) [Ordens]regel, *die* **5** (graduated measure) Maß, *das;* (tape) Bandmaß, *das;* (folding) Zollstock, *der* **6** (Printing) Linie, *die. See also* **road 1; work B 1**

B *v.t.* **1** (control) beherrschen **2** (be the ruler of) regieren; ‹*Monarch, Diktator usw.:*› herrschen über (+ *Akk.*); **~ the roost [in the house]** Herr im Hause sein; *see also* **rod 3** **3** (give as decision) entscheiden; **he ~d the ball out** er entschied, dass der Ball aus war; **~ a motion out of order** einen Antrag nicht zulassen; **~ sb. out of order** jmdm. [unter Hinweis auf die Geschäftsordnung] das Wort entziehen **4** (draw) ziehen ‹*Linie*›; (draw lines on) linieren ‹*Papier*›

C *v.i.* **1** (govern) herrschen; **~ by fear** eine Schreckensherrschaft führen; **X ~s** (coll.) X ist der/die Größte **2** (decide, declare formally)

r

entscheiden (**against** gegen; **in favour of** für); **~ on a matter** in einer Sache entscheiden

Phrasal verbs

- **~ 'off**

A *v.t.* mit einem Strich abtrennen; **~ off a margin** am Rand einen Strich ziehen

B *v.i.* einen Schlussstrich ziehen

- **~ 'out** *v.t.* **1** (exclude, eliminate) ausschließen **2** (prevent) unmöglich machen

'rule book *n.* (lit. or fig.) Regeln; Regelbuch, *das*

ruled /ru:ld/ *adj.* liniert ‹*Papier*›

ruler /'ru:lə(r)/ *n.* **1** (person) Herrscher, *der*/Herrscherin, *die* **2** (for drawing or measuring) Lineal, *das*

ruling /'ru:lɪŋ/

A *n.* **1** (decision) Entscheidung, *die* **2** (using a ruler) Linierung, *die*

B *adj.* **1** (predominating) herrschend ‹*Meinung*›; vorherrschend ‹*Charakterzug*›; **sb.'s ~ ambition/passion** jmds. größter Ehrgeiz/größte Leidenschaft **2** (current) **[the] ~ prices** die geltenden Preise **3** (governing, reigning) herrschend ‹*Klasse*›; regierend ‹*Partei*›; amtierend ‹*Regierung*›

rum^1 /rʌm/ *n.* Rum, *der*

rum^2 *adj.* (Brit. coll.) (odd) seltsam

Rumania /ru:'meɪnɪə/ ▸**Romania**

Rumanian /ru:'meɪnɪən/ ▸**Romanian**

rumba /'rʌmbə/

A *n.* Rumba, *die,* (österr.) *der;* **dance the ~:** Rumba tanzen

B *v.i.,* **~ed** *or* **~'d** /'rʌmbəd/ Rumba tanzen

rumble^1 /'rʌmbl/

A *n.* **1** (sound) Grollen, *das;* (of heavy vehicle) Rumpeln, *das* (ugs.) **2** (Amer. coll.: street fight) Straßenschlacht, *die;* Schlacht, *die* (fig.) **3** (Amer. coll.: rumour) Gerücht, *das;* **the ~ is that ...:** man munkelt, dass ...

B *v.i.* **1** (make low, heavy sound) grollen; ‹*Magen:*› knurren **2** (go with rumbling noise) rumpeln (ugs.)

rumble^2 *v.t.* (coll.: understand) spitzkriegen (ugs.) ‹*Sache*›; auf die Schliche kommen (+ *Dat.*) ‹*Person*›

'rumble: ~ seat *n.* (Amer. dated) Notsitz, *der;* **~ strip** *n.* Signalschwelle, *die;* akustische Schwelle

rumbustious /rʌm'bʌstʃəs/ *adj.* (coll.) wild

ruminant /'ru:mɪnənt/ (Zool.)

A *n.* Wiederkäuer, *der*

B *adj.* wiederkäuend

ruminate /'ru:mɪneɪt/ *v.i.* **1** **~ over** *or* **about** *or* **on sth.** über etw. (*Akk.*) nachsinnen (geh.) *od.* grübeln; **she sat ruminating for a moment** sie saß einen Augenblick nachdenklich da **2** (Zool.) wiederkäuen

rumination /ru:mɪ'neɪʃn/ *n.* **1** Nachsinnen, *das* (geh.); Grübeln, *das;* **his ~s were interrupted** seine Gedanken wurden unterbrochen **2** (Zool.) Wiederkäuen, *das*

ruminative /'ru:mɪnətɪv/ *adj.* beschaulich ‹*Stimmung*›; grüblerisch ‹*Person*›

rummage /'rʌmɪdʒ/

A *v.i.* wühlen (ugs.); kramen (ugs.); **~ among old clothes** in alten Kleidungsstücken herumwühlen *od.* -stöbern; **~ through sth.** etw. durchwühlen (ugs.); **~ about** *or* **around** herumkramen (ugs.)

B *n.* **have a ~ through sth.** etw. durchwühlen *od.* durchstöbern; **enjoy a good ~ around bookshops** gern in Buchhandlungen herumstöbern (ugs.)

Phrasal verb

- **~ 'out** *v.t.* hervorkramen (ugs.)

'rummage sale (esp. Amer.) ▸**jumble sale**

rummy /'rʌmɪ/ *n.* (Cards) Rommé, *das*

rumour (*Brit.; Amer.:* **rumor**) /'ru:mə(r)/

A *n.* **1** (unverified story) Gerücht, *das;* **there is a ~ that ...:** es geht das Gerücht, dass ...; **there is a persistent ~ that ...:** das Gerücht hält sich hartnäckig, dass ... **2** *no pl., no art.* (common talk) Gerücht, *das;* **~ puts the number of casualties at around 5,000** Gerüchten zufolge liegt die Zahl der Opfer bei 5 000; **~ has it that ...:** es geht das Gerücht, dass ...

B *v.t.* **sb. is ~ed to have done sth., it is ~ed that sb. has done sth.** man munkelt (ugs.) *od.* es geht das Gerücht, dass jmd. etw. getan hat; **the ~ed earthquake** das Erdbeben, das sich [Gerüchten zufolge] ereignet haben soll

'rumour mill *n.* (coll.) Gerüchteküche, *die* (ugs. abwertend)

rump /rʌmp/ *n.* **1** (buttocks) Hinterteil, *das* (ugs.); **meat from the ~:** Fleisch aus der Keule **2** (remnant) Rest, *der;* **sth. is only a ~:** von etw. ist nur noch der Rumpf übrig; **the R~** (Brit. Hist.) das Rumpfparlament

rumple /'rʌmpl/ *v.t.* **1** (crease) zerknittern **2** (tousle) zerzausen

'rump steak *n.* Rumpsteak, *das*

rumpus /'rʌmpəs/ *n., no pl.* (coll.) Krach, *der* (ugs.); Spektakel, *der* (ugs.); **kick up** *or* **make a ~:** einen Spektakel veranstalten (ugs.)

'rumpus room *n.* (Amer.) Spielzimmer, *das*

run /rʌn/

A *n.* **1** Lauf, *der;* **let the dogs out for a ~:** die Hunde hinauslassen, damit sie Auslauf haben; **go for a ~ before breakfast** vor dem Frühstück einen Lauf machen; **make a late ~** (Sport or fig.) zum Endspurt ansetzen; **come towards sb./take a hurdle/start off at a ~:** jmdm. entgegenlaufen/eine Hürde im Lauf nehmen/losrennen; **I've had a good ~ for my money** ich bin auf meine Kosten gekommen; **we'll give our opponents a good ~ for their money** wir werden es unseren Gegnern nicht leicht machen; **on the ~:** auf der Flucht; **keep the enemy on the ~:** den Feind nicht zur Ruhe kommen lassen **2** (trip in vehicle) Fahrt, *die;* (for pleasure) Ausflug, *der;* **on the ~ down to Cornwall** auf der Fahrt nach Cornwall; **a two-hour/a day's ~:** eine Fahrt von zwei Stunden/eine Tagesreise; **go for a ~ [in the car]** einen [Auto]ausflug machen **3** (continuous stretch) Länge, *die;* **a 500 ft. ~ of pipe** eine Rohrleitung von 500 Fuß Länge **4** (spell) **have a ~ of fine weather** eine Schönwetterperiode haben; **she has had a long ~ of success** sie war lange [Zeit] erfolgreich; **have a long ~** ‹*Stück, Show:*› viele Aufführungen erleben; **a successful [West End] ~:** eine erfolgreiche Spielzeit [im Westend] **5** (succession) Serie, *die;* (Cards) Sequenz, *die;* **a ~ of victories** eine Siegesserie **6** (tendency) Ablauf, *der;* **~ of [the] play** (Sport) Spielverlauf, *der;* **the general ~ of things/events** der Lauf der Dinge/der Gang der Ereignisse **7** (regular route) Strecke, *die;* **do a regular ~ between London and Edinburgh** regelmäßig die Strecke London-Edinburgh fahren; **he is on** *or* **he does the Glasgow ~:** er fährt die Glasgower Strecke **8** (Cricket, Baseball) Lauf, *der;* Run, *der* **9** ▸**ladder A 2** **10** (Mus.) Lauf, *der* **11** (quantity produced) (of book) Auflage, *die;* **production ~:** Ausstoß, *der* (Wirtsch.) **12** (demand) Run, *der* (**on** auf + *Akk.*) **13** (general type) **the common** *or* **general ~ of people** der Durchschnittsmensch; **he's not like the usual ~ of disc jockeys** er ist anders als die üblichen Diskjockeys **14** **the ~s** (coll.: diarrhoea) Durchmarsch, *der* (salopp) **15** (unrestricted use) **give sb. the ~ of sth.** jmdm. etw. zu seiner freien Verfügung überlassen; **have the ~ of sth.** etw. zu seiner freien Verfügung haben **16** (animal enclosure) Auslauf, *der;* (regular track of animals) Wildwechsel, *der. See also* **long A 3**; **short A 1**; **ski run**

B *v.i.,* **-nn-, ran** /ræn/, **run** **1** laufen; (fast also) rennen; **~ for all one is worth** rennen so schnell man kann; **~ for the bus** laufen *od.* rennen, um den Bus zu kriegen (ugs.); **~ to help sb.** jmdm. zu Hilfe eilen; **~ at sb.** auf jmdn. losstürzen; **the horse ran at the fence** das Pferd lief auf den Zaun zu **2** (compete) laufen; **he ran sixth/a poor third** er wurde sechster/erreichte einen mäßigen dritten Platz **3** (hurry) laufen; **don't ~ to me when things go wrong** komm mir nicht angelaufen, wenn etwas schief geht (ugs.); **~ to meet sb.** jmdm. entgegenlaufen; **he ran to meet her at the gate** er lief ihr bis ans Tor entgegen **4** (roll) laufen; ‹*Ball, Kugel:*› rollen, laufen; **the wheels ran into a rut** die Räder gerieten in eine Furche **5** (slide) laufen; ‹*Schlitten, [Schiebe]tür:*› gleiten **6** (revolve) ‹*Rad, Maschine:*› laufen **7** (Naut.) **~ for Plymouth** Plymouth anlaufen; **~ into port** in den Hafen einlaufen; **~ aground** auf Grund laufen; *see also* **foul A 6** **8** (flee) davonlaufen; **~ for it** sich aus dem Staub machen (ugs.); **~ for cover** schnell in Deckung gehen; *see also* **life 1** **9** (travel) **~ over** *or* **across** hinüberfahren; **~ down/up [to London]** [nach London] runter-/rauffahren (ugs.); **~ into town** in die Stadt fahren **10** (operate on a schedule) fahren; **~ between two places** ‹*Zug, Bus:*› zwischen zwei Orten verkehren; **the train is ~ning late** der Zug hat Verspätung; **we're ~ning late** (fig.) wir sind spät dran (ugs.); **~ on time** pünktlich sein; keine Verspätung haben; **the train doesn't ~ on Sundays** der Zug verkehrt nicht an Sonntagen **11** (pass cursorily) **~ through** überfliegen ‹*Text*›; **~ through one's head** *or* **mind** ‹*Gedanken, Ideen:*› einem durch den Kopf gehen; **~ through the various possibilities** die verschiedenen Möglichkeiten durchspielen; **his eyes ran over the article/photo** er ließ die Augen über den Artikel/das Foto wandern; **her fingers ran over the keys** ihre Finger liefen über die Tasten; **the tune is ~ning in my head** die Melodie geht mir im Kopf herum **12** (flow) laufen; ‹*Fluss:*› fließen; ‹*Augen:*› tränen; **your bath is ~ning** dein Bad läuft ein; **till the blood ran** bis es blutete; **the child's nose was ~ning** dem Kind lief die Nase; **the walls are ~ning with moisture** die Wände triefen vor Nässe (*Dat.*); **~ dry** ‹*Fluss:*› austrocknen; ‹*Quelle:*› versiegen; **the taps had ~ dry** es lief kein Wasser mehr aus der Leitung; **~ low** *or* **short** knapp werden; ausgehen; **we ran short of** *or* **low on fruit** unsere Obstvorräte wurden knapp *od.* gingen aus **13** (flow rapidly) **a heavy sea was ~ning** es herrschte starker Seegang; **the tide ran strong/out** die Flutwellen schlugen hoch/die Flut ging zurück **14** (be current) ‹*Vertrag, Theaterstück:*› laufen **15** (be present) **~ through sth.** sich durch etw. ziehen; **~ in the family** ‹*Eigenschaft, Begabung:*› in der Familie liegen **16** (function) laufen; **keep/leave the engine ~ning** den Motor laufen lassen/nicht abstellen; **the machine ~s on batteries/oil** *etc.* die Maschine läuft mit Batterien/Öl *usw.*; **things aren't ~ning too smoothly in their marriage** (fig.) in ihrer Ehe läuft es [zur Zeit] nicht besonders gut (ugs.) **17** (have a course) ‹*Straße, Bahnlinie:*› verlaufen **18** (have wording) lauten; ‹*Geschichte:*› gehen (fig.) **19** (have tendency) **my inclination does not ~ that way** meine Neigung geht nicht in diese Richtung **20** (have certain level) **inflation is ~ning at 5%** die Inflationsrate beläuft sich auf *od.* beträgt 5%; **interest rates are ~ning at record levels** die Zinsen bewegen sich auf Rekordhöhe **21** (seek election) kandidieren; **~ for mayor** für das Amt des Bürgermeisters kandidieren **22** (spread quickly) **a cheer ran down** *or* **along the lines of soldiers** ein Hurra ging durch die Reihen der Soldaten; **a shiver ran down my spine** ein Schau[d]er (geh.) lief mir den Rücken hinunter **23** (spread undesirably) ‹*Butter, Eis:*› zerlaufen; ‹*Farben:*› (in washing) auslaufen; (on painting etc.) ineinander laufen **24** (Cricket) einen Lauf *od.* Run machen **25** (ladder) Laufmaschen bekommen; **stockings guaranteed not to ~:** garantiert laufmaschensichere Strümpfe. *See also* **also**; **blood A 1**; **cut B 5**; **feeling A 3**; **riot A 2**; **wild A 3**; **writ**^{1} **1**

C *v.t.,* **-nn-, ran, run** **1** (cause to move) laufen lassen; (drive) fahren; **~ the ship aground** das

Schiff auf Grund laufen lassen *od.* (Seemannsspr.) auflaufen lassen; **~ the boat into the water** das Boot zu Wasser lassen; **~ the car into the garage** das Auto in die Garage fahren; **~ one's hand/fingers through/along** *or* **down** *or* **over sth.** mit der Hand/den Fingern durch etw. fahren/über etw. (*Akk.*) streichen; **~ an** *or* **one's eye along** *or* **down** *or* **over sth.** (fig.) etw. überfliegen; **~ one's finger down a list** mit dem Finger eine Liste entlangfahren; **~ a rope through sth.** ein Seil durch etw. führen **2** (cause to flow) [ein]laufen lassen; **~ a bath** ein Bad einlaufen lassen **3** (organize, manage) führen, leiten ‹*Geschäft usw.*›; durchführen ‹*Experiment*›; veranstalten ‹*Wettbewerb*›; führen ‹*Leben*›; **the people who ~ things [in this city]** die maßgeblichen Leute [dieser Stadt]; **~ the show** (fig. coll.) das Sagen haben (ugs.) **4** (operate) bedienen ‹*Maschine*›; verkehren lassen ‹*Verkehrsmittel*›; einsetzen ‹*Sonderbus, -zug*›; laufen lassen ‹*Motor*›; abspielen ‹*Tonband*›; **~ a train service** eine Schienenverbindung unterhalten; **~ a taxi** Taxi fahren; **~ forward/back** vorwärts-/zurückspulen ‹*Film, Tonband*› **5** (own and use) sich (*Dat.*) halten ‹*Auto*›; **a Jaguar is expensive to ~:** ein Jaguar ist im Unterhalt sehr teuer; **~ning a freezer saves money** mit einer Tiefkühltruhe spart man Geld; **~ a car with defective brakes** ein Auto mit defekten Bremsen fahren **6** (take for journey) fahren; **I'll ~ you into town** ich fahre *od.* bringe dich in die Stadt **7** (pursue) jagen; ‹*Tier*›; (fig.) aufspüren; **~ sb. hard** *or* **close** jmdm. auf den Fersen sein *od.* sitzen (ugs.); **be ~ off one's feet** alle Hände voll zu tun haben (ugs.); (in business) Hochbetrieb haben (ugs.); *see also* **earth A 5** **8** (complete) laufen ‹*Rennen, Marathon, Strecke*›; **~ messages/errands** Botengänge machen; **the race will be ~ tomorrow** das Rennen wird morgen gelaufen/gefahren **9** (smuggle) schmuggeln ‹*Waffen, Drogen, Personen*›; schleusen ‹*Personen*› **10** (enter for race or election) laufen lassen ‹*Pferd*›; aufstellen ‹*Kandidaten*› **11** (publish) bringen (ugs.) ‹*Bericht, Artikel usw.*›; in die Zeitung setzen ‹*Anzeige*› **12** **~ a fever/a temperature** Fieber/erhöhte Temperatur haben. *See also* **course A 1**; **fine² A 7**; **gauntlet²**; **ground A 2**; **ragged 5**; **risk A 1**

Phrasal verbs

- **~ a'bout** *v.i.* **1** (bustle) hin- und herlaufen **2** (play without restraint) herumtollen; herumspringen (ugs.). *See also* **runabout**
- **~ a'cross** *v.t.* **~ across sb.** jmdn. treffen; jmdm. über den Weg laufen; **~ across sth.** auf etw. (*Akk.*) stoßen
- **~ after** *v.t.* **1** (~ to catch, follow persistently) hinterherlaufen (+ *Dat.*) **2** nachlaufen (+ *Dat.*) ‹*Mode usw.*›
- **~ a'long** *v.i.* (coll.: depart) sich trollen (ugs.)
- **~ a'round**

A *v.i.* **1** **~ around with sb.** sich mit jmdm. herumtreiben **2** ▸**~ about 1** **3** ▸**~ about 2**
B *v.t.* herumfahren

- **~ a'way** *v.i.* **1** (flee) weglaufen; fortlaufen **2** (abscond) **~ away [from home/from the children's home]** [von zu Hause/aus dem Kinderheim] weglaufen **3** (elope) **~ away with sb./together** mit jmdm./zusammen durchbrennen (ugs.) **4** (bolt) ‹*Pferd:*› durchgehen **5** ‹*Wasser:*› ablaufen **6** (get ahead) **~ away from the rest of the field** dem übrigen Feld davonlaufen. *See also* **runaway**
- **~ a'way with** *v.t.* **1** (coll.: steal) abhauen mit (salopp) **2** (fig.: win) **~ away with the top prize/all the trophies** den 1. Preis/alle Trophäen erringen **3** (fig.: be misled by) **~ away with the idea** *or* **notion that ...:** irrtümlich annehmen, dass ...; **don't ~ away with the idea that ...:** glaub bloß nicht, dass ...; **he let his imagination/enthusiasm ~ away with him** seine Fantasie/Begeisterung ist mit ihm durchgegangen **4** (fig.: consume) verbrauchen; verschlingen ‹*Geld*›; fressen (ugs.) ‹*Benzin*›. *See also* **~ away 3**
- **~ 'back over** *v.t.* sich (*Dat.*) in Erinnerung rufen; **her thoughts ran back over the past** sie dachte an die vergangenen Zeiten
- **~ 'down**

A *v.t.* **1** (collide with) überfahren **2** (find after search) aufspüren **3** (criticize) heruntermachen (ugs.); herabsetzen; **don't ~ yourself down all the time** mach dich nicht immer selbst so schlecht **4** (cause to diminish) abbauen; verringern ‹*Produktion*› **5** (cause to lose power) leer machen ‹*Batterie*›
B *v.i.* **1** hin-/herunterlaufen/-rennen/-fahren **2** (decline) sich verringern; ‹*Schienennetz:*› schrumpfen **3** (lose power) ausgehen; ‹*Batterie:*› leer werden; ‹*Uhr, Spielzeug:*› ablaufen. *See also* **rundown**

- **~ 'in**

A *v.t.* **1** (prepare for use) einfahren ‹*Auto*›; sich einlaufen lassen ‹*Maschine*› **2** (coll.: arrest) hoppnehmen (salopp)
B *v.i.* hin-/hereinlaufen/-rennen

- **~ into** *v.t.* **1** **~ into a telegraph pole/tree** gegen einen Telegrafenmast/Baum fahren; **~ into a sandbank** auf eine Sandbank geraten *od.* (Seemannsspr.) auflaufen **2** (cause to collide with) **~ one's car into a tree** seinen Wagen gegen einen Baum fahren **3** (cause to incur) **~ the family into debt** die Familie in Schulden stürzen **4** (fig.: meet) **~ into sb.** jmdm. in die Arme laufen (ugs.) **5** (be faced with) stoßen auf (+ *Akk.*) ‹*Schwierigkeiten, Widerstand, Probleme usw.*› **6** (enter) geraten in (+ *Akk.*) ‹*Sturm, schlechtes Wetter, Schulden*›; **his debts ~ into thousands** seine Schulden gehen in die Tausende **7** (merge with) **~ into one another** ‹*Seen, Tage:*› ineinander übergehen
- **~ 'off**

A *v.i.* ▸**~ away 1, 3**
B *v.t.* **1** (compose rapidly) hinwerfen ‹*ein paar Zeilen, Verse, Notizen*›; zu Papier bringen ‹*Brief*› **2** (produce on machine) abziehen ‹*Kopien, Handzettel usw.*› **3** (cause to drain away) ablaufen lassen **4** (recite fluently) ▸**rattle off** **5** (decide by run-off) durch Stechen entscheiden; *see also* **run-off**

- **~ 'off with** *v.t.* (coll.: steal) abhauen mit (salopp); *see also* **~ away 3**; **~ away with 2**
- **~ 'on**

A *v.i.* **1** (continue without a break) weitergehen; ‹*Krankheit:*› fortschreiten; ‹*Redner:*› weiterreden **2** (Printing: continue on same line) **'~ on'** „ohne Absatz" **3** (elapse) ‹*Zeit:*› verstreichen **4** (join up) **let the letters ~ on** (beim Schreiben) die Buchstaben miteinander verbinden **5** (talk incessantly) reden wie ein Wasserfall (ugs.); **her tongue ~s on** ihr Mundwerk steht nicht still (ugs.)
B *v.t.* **1** (Printing) als fortlaufenden Text setzen **2** /'--/ (be concerned with) sich befassen mit; **his mind was ~ning on this subject** seine Gedanken kreisten um dieses Thema

- **~ 'out**

A *v.i.* **1** hin-/herauslaufen/-rennen; **he ran out a deserved winner** er ging als verdienter Sieger aus dem Kampf hervor; *see also* **run B 13** **2** (become exhausted) ‹*Vorräte, Bestände:*› zu Ende gehen; ‹*Geduld:*› sich erschöpfen; **we have ~ out** wir haben keinen/keine/keines mehr; (sold everything) wir sind ausverkauft **3** (expire) ‹*Vertrag:*› ablaufen; **time is ~ning out** die Zeit wird knapp **4** (jut out) ‹*Land:*› vorspringen; ‹*Pier:*› ins Meer hinausreichen. *See also* **sand A 3**
B *v.t.* (Cricket) **~ a batsman out** *einen Schlagmann zum Ausscheiden bringen, indem man mit dem Ball das Tor zerstört, bevor er die Schlagmallinie erreicht*

- **~ 'out of** *v.t.* **1** (exhaust stock of) **sb. ~s out of sth.** jmdm. geht etw. aus; **I'm ~ning out of patience** meine Geduld geht zu Ende; **we're ~ning out of time** uns wird die Zeit [allmählich] knapp **2** (flow out of) auslaufen aus
- **~ 'out on** *v.t.* (desert) im Stich lassen
- **~ over**

A /'--/ *v.t.* **1** ▸**go over B 1** **2** (knock down) überfahren. *See also* **~ B 11**
B /-'--/ *v.i.* **1** (overflow) überlaufen **2** (exceed limit) [die Zeit] überziehen

- **~ through** *v.t.* **1** ▸**get through B 8** **2** abspielen ‹*Tonband, Film*› **3** (rehearse) durchspielen ‹*Theaterstück*› **4** /-'-/ (pierce right through) **~ sb. through with sth.** jmdn. mit etw. durchbohren. *See also* **~ B 11, 15**; **run-through**
- **~ to** *v.t.* **1** (amount to) umfassen; ‹*Geldsumme, Kosten:*› sich belaufen auf (+ *Akk.*) **2** (be sufficient for) **sth. will ~ to sth.** etw. reicht für etw. **3** (afford) **sb. can ~ to sth.** jmd. kann sich (*Dat.*) etw. leisten **4** (show inclination towards) **~ to fat** [zu] dick werden; **his style ~s too easily to sentiment** sein Stil gleitet allzu leicht ins Sentimentale ab; *see also* **seed A 2**
- **~ 'up**

A *v.i.* **1** hinlaufen; (Sport) Anlauf nehmen; **he ran up to where they were standing** er lief *od.* rannte zu ihnen hin; **come ~ning along** herangelaufen kommen **2** (amount to) **~ up to** sich belaufen auf (+ *Akk.*)
B *v.t.* **1** (hoist) hissen ‹*Fahne*› **2** (make quickly) rasch nähen ‹*Kleidungsstück*›; zusammenzimmern ‹*Schuppen*›; hochziehen (ugs.) ‹*Gebäude*› **3** (allow to accumulate) **~ up debts/a [big] bill** Schulden/eine hohe Rechnung zusammenkommen lassen. *See also* **run-up**

- **~ 'up against** *v.t.* stoßen auf (+ *Akk.*) ‹*Probleme, Widerstand usw.*›

run: ~about *n.* (coll.) **[little] ~about** Kleinwagen, *der;* **~around** *n.* (coll.) **give sb. the ~around** jmdn. an der Nase herumführen (ugs.); **~away** **A** *n.* Ausreißer, *der*/Ausreißerin, *die* (ugs.); **B** *attrib. adj.* **1** (fleeing) flüchtig; **she was a ~away schoolgirl** sie war aus der Schule weggelaufen; **have a ~away wedding** weglaufen und heiraten; **2** (out of control) durchgegangen ‹*Pferd*›; außer Kontrolle geraten ‹*Fahrzeug, Preise*›; (fig.) galoppierend ‹*Inflation*›; **3** (outstanding) überwältigend ‹*Erfolg*›; triumphal ‹*Sieg*›; **~down** *n.* **1** (coll.: briefing) Übersicht, *die* (**on** über + *Akk.*); **2** (reduction) Abbau, *der;* **~-down** *adj.* **1** (tired) mitgenommen; **in a completely ~-down condition** völlig erschöpft; **2** (neglected) heruntergekommen (ugs.) ‹*Gegend, Stadt, Gewerbe*›

rune /ru:n/ *n.* Rune, *die*

rung¹ /rʌŋ/ *n.* **1** (of ladder) Sprosse, *die* **2** (fig.) **start on the bottom** *or* **lowest/reach the top** *or* **highest ~:** auf der ersten Sprosse beginnen/die oberste Sprosse erreichen

rung² ▸**ring² B, C**

runic /'ru:nɪk/ *adj.* Runen-; runisch

'run-in *n.* **1** (coll.: confrontation) Zusammenstoß, *der;* Auseinandersetzung, *die;* **have a ~ with sb.** mit jmdm. Stunk haben (ugs.) **2** (collision) Zusammenstoß, *der*

runnel /'rʌnl/ *n.* **1** (brook) Wasserlauf, *der;* Rinnsal, *das* (geh.) **2** (gutter) Rinne, *die*

runner /'rʌnə(r)/ *n.* **1** Läufer, *der*/Läuferin, *die* **2** (horse in race) **eight ~s were in the race** acht Pferde liefen beim Rennen **3** (messenger) Bote, *der;* Laufbursche, *der* **4** (Bot.: creeping stem) Ausläufer, *der* **5** (twining plant) Kletterpflanze, *die* **6** **curtain ~:** Gardinenröllchen, *das* **7** (part on which sth. slides) Kufe, *die;* (for curtains) Gardinenleiste, *die;* (groove) Laufschiene, *die* **8** (cloth) Tischläufer, *der;* (carpet) Läufer, *der* **9** (who handles illegal goods) Schieber, *der* (ugs.); **[drug] ~:** [Drogen]kurier, *der* (ugs.) **10** (who runs a blockade) Blockadebrecher, *der* **11** (car) **'good ~'** „fährt *od.* läuft einwandfrei" **12** **do a ~** (Brit. coll.) abhauen (salopp); türmen (salopp)

runner: ~ bean *n.* (Brit.) Stangenbohne, *die;* **~-'up** *n.* Zweite, *der/die;* **the ~s-up** die Platzierten; **they were joint ~s-up** sie teilten sich den zweiten Platz

running /'rʌnɪŋ/

A *n.* **1** (management) Leitung, *die* **2** (action) Laufen, *das;* (jogging) Jogging, *das;* **make the ~** (in competition) an der Spitze liegen; (fig.: have the initiative) den Ton angeben; **take up the ~:** sich an die Spitze setzen; **in/out of the ~:** im/aus dem Rennen; **be out of the ~ for the Presidency** keine Aussichten [mehr] auf die Präsidentschaft haben **3** (ability to run) **have a lot of ~ left** noch gute Laufkondition haben **4** (Horseracing: condition of surface) **the ~ is good/soft** es lässt sich gut laufen/die Laufbahn ist weich **5** (of engine, machine) Laufen, *das*
B *adj.* **1** (continuous) ständig; fortlaufend ‹*Erklä-*

r

rungen›; **have** *or* **fight a ~ battle** (fig.) ständig im Streit liegen; *see also* **fire A 7** 2▸ (in succession) hintereinander; **win for the third year ~:** schon drei Jahre hintereinander gewinnen 3▸ (Motor Veh.) **in ~ order** in fahrbereitem Zustand

running: ~-board *n.* Trittbrett, *das;* ~ **'commentary** *n.* (Broadcasting; also fig.) Livekommentar, *der;* ~ **costs** *n. pl.* Betriebskosten *Pl.;* ~ **dog** *n.* (Polit. derog.) Kettenhund, *der* (abwertend); ~ **'head[line]** *n.* (Printing) Kolumnentitel, *der;* ~ **'jump** *n.* **you can [go and] take a ~ jump [at yourself]** (fig. coll.) du kannst mir den Buckel runterrutschen (ugs.); ~ **knot** *n.* Knoten einer Schlinge; ~ **mate** *n.* (Amer.) 1▸ Mitkandidat, *der*/Mitkandidatin, *die* [*als Vizepräsidentschaftskandidat*]; 2▸ (horse as pacesetter) Pacemacher, *der;* ~ **re'pairs** *n. pl.* laufende Reparaturen; ~ **shoe** *n.* Rennschuh, *der;* ~ **shorts** *n. pl.* Sporthose, *die;* ~ **'sore** *n.* nässende Wunde; (fig.) schwärende Wunde; ~ **stitch** *n.* (Needlework) Vorstich, *der;* ~ **'title** ▸~ **head**; ~ **'total** *n.* fortlaufende Summe; ~ **track** *n.* Aschenbahn, *die;* ~ **'water** *n.* 1▸ (in stream) fließendes Gewässer; 2▸ (available through pipe) fließendes Wasser; **hot and cold ~ water** fließend warm und kalt Wasser

runny /'rʌnɪ/ *adj.* 1▸ (secreting mucus) laufend ‹Nase› 2▸ (excessively liquid) zerlaufend; zu dünn ‹Farbe, Marmelade›

'run-off *n.* 1▸ (election) Stichwahl, *die;* (race) Entscheidungslauf, *der;* Stechen, *das* 2▸ *no pl.* (draining away) Abfluss, *der* 3▸ *no pl.* (liquid) Abflusswasser, *das*

run-of-the-'mill *adj.* ganz gewöhnlich

runt /rʌnt/ *n.* 1▸ (weakling pig) Kümmerer, *der* (Landw.) 2▸ (fig. derog.) Kümmerling, *der* (abwertend)

run: ~-through *n.* 1▸ (cursory reading) **give a text a [quick] ~-through, have a [brief] ~-through of a text** einen Text [kurz] überfliegen; 2▸ (rapid summary) Überblick, *der* (**of** über + *Akk.*); 3▸ (rehearsal) Durchlaufprobe, *die;* **~-up** *n.* 1▸ (approach to an event) **during** *or* **in the ~-up to an event** im Vorfeld (fig.) eines Ereignisses; 2▸ (Sport) Anlauf, *der;* **take a ~-up** Anlauf nehmen

runway /'rʌnweɪ/ *n.* (for take-off) Startbahn, *die;* (for landing) Landebahn, *die*

rupee /ru:'pi:/ *n.* ▸ℹ **p. 1332** Rupie, *die*

rupture /'rʌptʃə(r)/

A *n.* 1▸ (lit. or fig.) Bruch, *der* 2▸ (Med.) Ruptur, *die*

B *v.t.* 1▸ (burst) aufreißen; **a ~d appendix/spleen** ein geplatzter Blinddarm/eine gerissene Milz 2▸ **~ oneself** sich (*Dat.*) einen Bruch zuziehen *od.* heben 3▸ (sever) auseinander brechen lassen ‹Beziehungen, Einheit›

C *v.i.* reißen; ‹*Blutgefäß, Blinddarm:*› platzen

rural /'rʊərl/ *adj.* ländlich; **~ life** Landleben, *das*

rural: ~ 'dean *n.* (Eccl.) ≈ Dekan, *der;* ~ **'district** *n.* (Brit. Admin. Hist.) ≈ Landkreis, *der*

Ruritania /rʊərɪ'teɪnɪə/ *n.: fiktionales mitteleuropäisches Königreich;* Ruritanien (*das*); ≈ Operettenstaat, *der*

ruse /ru:z/ *n.* List, *die*

rush¹ /rʌʃ/ *n.* (Bot.) Binse, *die*

rush²

A *n.* 1▸ (rapid moving forward) **be swept away by the ~ of the current** von der Gewalt der Strömung mitgerissen werden; **make a ~ for sth.** sich auf etw. (*Akk.*) stürzen; **the ~ to the coast** der Ansturm auf die Küste; **the holiday ~:** der [hektische] Urlaubsverkehr

2▸ (hurry) Eile, *die;* **what's all the ~?** wozu diese Hast?; **be in a [great] ~:** in [großer] Eile sein; es [sehr] eilig haben; **everything happened in such a ~:** es ging alles so schnell; **have a ~ to get somewhere** sich abhetzen, um irgendwohin zu kommen

3▸ (surging) Anwandlung, *die* (**of** von); **a ~ of blood [to the head]** (fig. coll.) eine [plötzliche] Anwandlung

4▸ (period of great activity) Hochbetrieb, *der;* (~ hour) Stoßzeit, *die;* **there is a ~ on** es herrscht Hochbetrieb (ugs.); **a ~ of new orders** eine Flut von neuen Aufträgen

5▸ *in pl.* (Cinemat.) [Bild]muster; Musterkopien

6▸ (heavy demand) Ansturm, *der* (**for, on** auf + *Akk.*)

7▸ (Footb.) Sturmangriff, *der*

8▸ (Amer. Footb.) Durchbruch, *der*

B *v.t.* 1▸ (convey rapidly) **~ sb./sth. somewhere** jmdn./etw. auf schnellstem Wege irgendwohin bringen; **~ sb. supplies** jmdn. schnell mit Vorräten versorgen; **~ sb. round the sights** jmdn. von einer Sehenswürdigkeit zur anderen hetzen; **~ through Parliament** im Parlament durchpeitschen (ugs. abwertend) ‹*Gesetz*›; **~ a regiment to the front** ein Regiment an die Front werfen; **be ~ed** (have to hurry) in Eile sein

2▸ (cause to act hastily) **~ sb. into doing sth.** jmdn. dazu drängen, etw. zu tun; **~ sb. into danger/trouble/marriage** jmdn. in Gefahr/Schwierigkeiten bringen/zur Heirat drängen; **she hates to be ~ed** sie kann es nicht ausstehen, wenn sie sich [ab]hetzen muss

3▸ (perform quickly) auf die Schnelle erledigen; (perform too quickly) **~ it** zu schnell machen

4▸ (Mil. or fig.: charge) stürmen; überrumpeln ‹*feindliche Gruppe*›; **~ one's fences** (fig.) überstürzt handeln

5▸ (coll.: swindle) **~ sb.** jmdn. neppen (ugs. abwertend); **how much did they ~ you for that sherry?** wie viel haben sie dir für den Sherry abgeknöpft? (salopp)

6▸ (Amer.) (entertain) keilen (ugs.); umwerben; (date) umwerben. *See also* **foot A 1**

C *v.i.* 1▸ (move quickly) eilen; ‹*Hund, Pferd:*› laufen; **she ~ed into the room** sie stürzte ins Zimmer; **~ through Customs/the exit** durch den Zoll/Ausgang stürmen; **~ to help sb.** jmdm. zu Hilfe eilen

2▸ (hurry unduly) sich zu sehr beeilen; **don't ~!** nur keine Eile!; **don't be tempted to ~!** lass dir Zeit [dabei]!; **there is no need to ~:** es gibt keinen Grund zur Eile

3▸ (flow rapidly) stürzen; **~ past** vorbeistürzen; **~ down** hinunterstürzen

4▸ (surge up rapidly) **the blood ~ed to his face** das Blut schoss ihm ins Gesicht

Phrasal verbs

- **~ a'bout, ~ a'round** *v.i.* herumhetzen
- **~ at** *v.t.* sich stürzen auf (+ *Akk.*); (Mil.: charge) anstürmen gegen ‹*Stellung usw.*›
- **~ 'in** *v.i.* hin-/hereinstürzen; (fig.) **~ in with new solutions** vorschnell neue Lösungen präsentieren; **fools ~ in [where angels fear to tread]** (prov.) blinder Eifer schadet nur (Spr.)
- **~ into** *v.t.* **~ into sth.** in etw. (*Akk.*) hin-/hereinstürzen; (fig.) sich in etw. (*Akk.*) stürzen/etw. überstürzt tun; **~ into print with sth.** etw. schnellstens veröffentlichen; **you shouldn't ~ into it** das sollte man nicht übereilen
- **~ 'up** *v.i.* angestürzt kommen; **~ up to sb.** zu jmdm. stürzen

rush: ~ hour *n.* Stoßzeit, *die;* Hauptverkehrszeit, *die;* **~-hour traffic** Berufsverkehr, *der;* ~ **job** *n.* eilige Arbeit; ~ **mat** *n.* Binsenmatte, *die;* ~ **order** *n.* Eilauftrag, *der;* dringende Bestellung

rusk /rʌsk/ *n.* Zwieback, *der*

russet /'rʌsɪt/

A *n.* 1▸ (reddish-brown) Rotbraun, *das* 2▸ (apple) *Apfel mit rot- od. gelbbrauner od. braun gesprenkelter rauer Schale*

B *adj.* rotbraun

Russia /'rʌʃə/ *pr. n.* Russland (*das*)

Russian /'rʌʃn/ ▸ℹ **p. 1277,** ▸ℹ **p. 1345**

A *adj.* russisch; **sb. is ~:** jmd. ist Russe/Russin; *see also* **English A**

B *n.* 1▸ (person) Russe, *der*/Russin, *die* 2▸ (language) Russisch, *das;* **Little ~:** Ukrainisch, *das; see also* **English B 1**

Russian: ~ 'boot *n.* Russenstiefel, *der;* ~ **Fede'ration** *pr. n.* Russische Föderation; ~ **'mafia** *n.* Russenmafia, *die;* ~ **rou'lette** *n.* russisches Roulett[e]; ~ **'salad** *n.* russischer Salat

Russki /'rʌskɪ/ *n., pl.* **~s** *or* **~es** (joc./derog.) Russki, *der* (salopp)

Russo- /rʌsəʊ/ *in comb.* russisch-/Russisch-

rust /rʌst/

A *n., no pl., no indef. art.* 1▸ Rost, *der;* **protection against ~:** Rostschutz, *der* 2▸ (Bot.) Rost, *der*

B *v.i.* 1▸ rosten 2▸ (fig.: become impaired) ‹*Fähigkeiten, Gedächtnis:*› einrosten (fig.)

C *v.t.* [ver]rosten lassen; **badly ~ed** stark verrostet; **~ed up** festgerostet

Phrasal verb

- **~ 'through** *v.i.* durchrosten

'Rust Belt *n.* Rostgürtel, *der;* **a ~ town** eine Stadt im Rostgürtel

'rust-coloured *adj.* rostfarben

rustic /'rʌstɪk/

A *adj.* 1▸ (of the country) ländlich; **~ life** Landleben, *das* 2▸ (unrefined) bäurisch (abwertend) 3▸ (roughly built) rustikal ‹*Mobiliar*›; grob gezimmert ‹*Bank, Brücke usw.*›

B *n.* Bauer, *der*/Bäuerin, *die* (abwertend)

rustically /'rʌstɪkəlɪ/ *adv.* rustikal

rusticate /'rʌstɪkeɪt/ *v.t.* zeitweilig von der Universität relegieren

rusticity /rʌ'stɪsɪtɪ/ *n.* Ländlichkeit, *die*

'rustic-work *n.* (Archit.) Rustika, *die*

rustle /'rʌsl/

A *n.* Rascheln, *das*

B *v.i.* rascheln

C *v.t.* 1▸ rascheln lassen; rascheln mit ‹*Papieren*› 2▸ (steal) stehlen 3▸ (Amer. coll.) ▸**~ up**

Phrasal verb

- **~ 'up** *v.t.* (coll.: produce) auftreiben (ugs.); zusammenzaubern (fig.) ‹*Mahlzeit*›

rustler /'rʌslə(r)/ *n.* Viehdieb, *der;* **sheep ~:** Schafdieb, *der*

rustless /'rʌstlɪs/ *adj.* rostfrei

'rustproof

A *adj.* rostfrei

B *v.t.* rostfrei *od.* rostbeständig machen

rusty /'rʌstɪ/ *adj.* 1▸ (rusted) rostig 2▸ (fig.: impaired by neglect) eingerostet; **I am a bit ~:** ich bin ein bisschen aus der Übung 3▸ (rust-coloured) rostfarben; rostfarbig; rost‹*braun, -rot*›

rut¹ /rʌt/

A *n.* 1▸ (track) Spurrille, *die* 2▸ (fig.: established procedure) **get into a ~:** in einen gewissen Trott verfallen; **be in a ~:** aus dem [Alltags]trott nicht mehr herauskommen

B *v.t.*, **-tt-** durchfurchen

rut²

A *n.* (sexual excitement) Brunst, *die;* (of roe-deer, stag, etc.) Brunft, *die* (Jägersprache)

B *v.i.*, **-tt-** in der Brunst sein; ‹*Schalenwild:*› brunften (Jägerspr.)

rutabaga /ru:tə'beɪgə/ ▸**swede**

ruthless /'ru:θlɪs/ *adj.*, **ruthlessly** /'ru:θlɪslɪ/ *adv.* rücksichtslos

ruthlessness /'ru:θlɪsnɪs/ *n., no pl.* Rücksichtslosigkeit, *die*

rutted /'rʌtɪd/, **rutty** /'rʌtɪ/ *adjs.* zerfurcht

RV *abbr.* (Amer.) **= recreational vehicle**

Rwanda /rʊ'ændə/ *pr. n.* Ruanda (*das*)

rye /raɪ/ *n.* 1▸ (cereal) Roggen, *der* 2▸ **~ [whisky]** Roggenwhisky, *der;* Rye, *der* 3▸ (Amer.) ▸**rye bread**

rye: ~ bread *n.* Roggenbrot, *das;* **~grass** *n.* Raigras, *das*

Ss

S[1], **s**/es/ *n.*, *pl.* **Ss** *or* **S's** /'esɪs/ [1] (letter) S, s, *das* [2] (curve) **S bend** S-Biegung, *die*

S[2] *abbr.* [1] ▶ⓘ **p. 1013 = south** S [2] ▶ⓘ **p. 1013 = southern** s. [3] **= Saint** St.

s. *abbr.* [1] **= second[s]** Sek. [2] **= singular** Sg. [3] **= son** S.

's (coll.) **= is, has, does; let's** /lets/ **= let us**

SA *abbr.* [1] **= South America** [2] **= South Africa**

Saar /zɑː(r)/ *pr. n.* Saar, *die*

Saarland /'zɑːlænd/ *pr. n.* Saarland, *das*

Saarlander /'zɑːlændə(r)/ *n.* Saarländer, *der*/-länderin, *die*

sabbath /'sæbəθ/ *n.* [1] (Jewish) Sabbat, *der* [2] (Christian) Sonntag, *der* [3] **witches' ∼:** Hexensabbat, *der*

sabbatical /sə'bætɪkl/

A *adj.* [1] (Jewish Relig.) **∼ year** Sabbatjahr, *das:* [2] **∼ term/year** Forschungssemester/-jahr, *das*

B *n.* Forschungsurlaub, *der*

saber (Amer.) ▶ **sabre**

sable /'seɪbl/

A *n.* [1] (Zool., also fur) Zobel, *der* [2] **[American] ∼:** Fichtenmarder, *der* (Zool.); Amerikanischer Zobel

B *adj.* (Literary/Her.) schwarz; **the ∼ blackness of her hair** das Tiefschwarz ihrer Haare

sabotage /'sæbətɑːʒ/

A *n.* (lit. or fig.) Sabotage, *die;* **act of ∼:** Sabotageakt, *der;* **industrial ∼:** Wirtschaftssabotage, *die*

B *v.t.* einen Sabotageakt verüben auf (+ *Akk.*); (fig.) sabotieren ‹*Pläne usw.*›; **vehicles were ∼d** es wurden Sabotageakte auf Fahrzeuge verübt

saboteur /sæbə'tɜː(r)/ *n.* Saboteur, *der*

sabre /'seɪbə(r)/ *n.* (Brit.) Säbel, *der;* **rattle the ∼** (fig.) mit dem Säbel rasseln (abwertend)

sabre: ∼ cut *n.* [1] (blow) Säbelhieb, *der;* [2] (wound) Säbelverletzung, *die;* **∼-rattling A** *n., no pl.* Säbelrasseln, *das* (abwertend); **B** *adj.* säbelrasselnd (abwertend); **∼-toothed tiger** *n.* Säbelzahntiger, *der*

sac /sæk/ *n.* (Biol.) **air ∼:** Luftsack, *der* (Zool.); **fetal ∼:** Fruchtblase, *die* (Med.)

saccharin /'sækərɪn/ *n.* Saccharin, *das*

saccharine /'sækəriːn/ *adj.* (lit. or fig.) süßlich

sacerdotal /sæsə'dəʊtl/ *adj.* (priestly) priesterlich; Priester‹*gewand, -amt*›

sachet /'sæʃeɪ/ *n.* [1] (small packet) (for shampoo etc.) Beutel, *der;* (cushion-shaped) Kissen, *das;* **a ∼ of shampoo** ein Beutel/Kissen Shampoo [2] (bag for scenting clothes) Duftkissen, *das*

sack[1] /sæk/

A *n.* [1] Sack, *der;* **buy sth. by the ∼:** etw. sackweise kaufen; **a ∼ of potatoes** ein Sack Kartoffeln; **three ∼s of mail** drei Säcke mit Post [2] (coll.: dismissal) Rausschmiss, *der* (ugs.); **threaten sb. with the ∼:** jmdm. mit Entlassung drohen; **get the ∼:** rausgeschmissen werden (ugs.); **give sb. the ∼:** jmdn. rausschmeißen (ugs.) [3] **hit the ∼** (coll.) sich in die Falle hauen (salopp)

B *v.t.* [1] (coll.: dismiss) rausschmeißen (ugs.) (**for** wegen) [2] (put into ∼[s]) einsacken

sack[2]

A *v.t.* (loot) plündern

B *n.* Plünderung, *die*

sackable /'sækəbl/ *adj.* (Brit.) **∼ offence** *Vergehen, das eine Entlassung rechtfertigt;* **this is a ∼ offence** das ist ein Kündigungsgrund

'sackcloth *n.* Sackleinen, *das;* (mourning) Trauergewand, *das;* (penitential) Büßergewand, *das;* **in ∼ and ashes** in Sack und Asche (geh.)

sackful /'sækfʊl/ *n.* Sack, *der;* **three ∼s of potatoes/cement** drei Sack Kartoffeln/Zement; **by the ∼:** sackweise

sacking[1] /'sækɪŋ/ *n.* [1] (coll.: dismissal) Rausschmiss, *der* (ugs.) [2] (coarse fabric) Sackleinen, *das*

sacking[2] ▶ **sack**[2] **B**

'sack race *n.* Sackhüpfen, *das*

sacral /'seɪkrl/ *adj.* [1] (Anat.) Sakral-; **the ∼ vertebrae** die Kreuzbeinwirbel; Vertebrae sacrales (Med.) [2] (Anthrop.) sakral

sacrament /'sækrəmənt/ *n.* Sakrament, *das;* **the last ∼s** die Sterbesakramente; **the ∼ [of the altar], the Blessed** *or* **Holy S∼:** das Altarsakrament; **administer/receive the ∼** (the Eucharist) das Sakrament austeilen/empfangen; **the Holy S∼** (the Host) das Allerheiligste

sacramental /sækrə'mentl/ *adj.* sakramental; **∼ doctrine** Lehre von den Sakramenten

sacred /'seɪkrɪd/ *adj.* heilig; geheiligt ‹*Tradition*›; geistlich ‹*Musik, Dichtung*›; **nothing is ∼ to him, he holds nothing ∼** (lit. or fig.) ihm ist nichts heilig; **is nothing ∼?** (iron.) scheut man denn vor nichts mehr zurück?

sacred: ∼ 'cow *n.* (lit. or fig.) heilige Kuh; **S∼ 'Heart** *n.* **the S∼ Heart [of Jesus]** das Herz Jesu

sacredness /'seɪkrɪdnɪs/ *n., no pl.* Heiligkeit, *die*

sacrifice /'sækrɪfaɪs/

A *n.* [1] (giving up valued thing) Opferung, *die;* (of principles) Preisgabe, *die;* (of pride, possessions) Aufgabe, *die;* **make ∼s** Opfer bringen [2] (offering to deity) Opfer, *das;* **∼s to the gods** den Göttern dargebrachte Opfer; (fig.) **fall [a] ∼ to sth.** einer Sache (*Dat.*) zum Opfer fallen [3] (Games: deliberate incurring of loss) Opfern, *das;* (*Baseball*) *Schlag ins Aus, wobei der Läufer weiterkommt;* (Bridge) Opfer, *das* (**against** für)

B *v.t.* [1] (give up, offer as ∼) opfern; **∼ oneself/sth. to sth.** sich/etw. einer Sache (*Dat.*) opfern [2] (sell at a loss) zu einem Schleuderpreis verkaufen (ugs.)

C *v.i.* opfern

sacrificial /sækrɪ'fɪʃl/ *adj.* Opfer-; **∼ victim** Opfer, *das;* **∼ price** (fig.) Schleuderpreis, *der*

sacrilege /'sækrɪlɪdʒ/ *n., no pl.* **[act of] ∼:** Sakrileg, *das;* **be little short of ∼:** an ein Sakrileg grenzen

sacrilegious /sækrɪ'lɪdʒəs/ *adj.* sakrilegisch; (fig.) frevelhaft

sacristan /'sækrɪstən/ *n.* (Eccl.) Küster, *der;* Kirchendiener, *der* (bes. ev. Kirche); Sakristan, *der* (bes. kath. Kirche)

sacristy /'sækrɪstɪ/ *n.* (Eccl.) Sakristei, *die*

sacrosanct /'sækrəsæŋkt/ *adj.* (lit. or fig.) sakrosankt

sacrum /'seɪkrəm/ *n.* (Anat.) Kreuzbein, *das;* Sakrum, *das* (fachspr.)

sad /sæd/ *adj.* [1] (sorrowful) traurig (**at, about** über + *Akk.*); **he was ∼ at** *or* **about not getting the job** er war traurig, weil er die Stelle nicht bekam; **feel ∼, be in a ∼ mood** traurig sein; **it left him a ∼der and a wiser man** er hat dabei viel Lehrgeld zahlen müssen; durch Schaden ist er klug geworden [2] (causing grief) traurig; schmerzlich ‹*Tod, Verlust*›; **it's ∼ about Jim** es ist schade um Jim; **∼ to say, ...:** bedauerlicherweise ...; **I am ∼ to say that ...:** leider *od.* zu meinem Bedauern muss ich sagen, dass ...; leider ... [3] (derog./joc.: deplorably bad) traurig

SAD *abbr.* **= seasonal affective disorder** SAD

sadden /'sædn/ *v.t.* traurig stimmen; **be deeply ∼ed** tieftraurig sein; **his old age was ∼ed by ...:** sein Alter war überschattet von ...; **I was ∼ed to see that ...:** es betrübte mich zu sehen, dass ...

saddle /'sædl/

A *n.* [1] (seat for rider) Sattel, *der;* **be in the ∼** (fig.) das Heft in der Hand haben (geh.) [2] (ridge between summits) [Berg]sattel, *der* [3] (support for cable) Kabelsattel, *der* [4] (Gastr.) Rücken, *der;* Rückenstück, *das;* **∼ of lamb/mutton** Lamm-/Hammelrücken, *der*

B *v.t.* [1] satteln ‹*Pferd usw.*› [2] (fig.) **∼ sb. with sth.** jmdm. etw. aufbürden (geh.); **∼ debts/responsibility [up]on sb.** Schulden/Verantwortung auf jmdn. abwälzen

(Phrasal verb)

• **∼ 'up** *v.t. & i* aufsatteln

saddle: ∼back *n.* [1] (Archit.) Satteldach, *das;* [2] (hill) Hügel mit sattelförmigem Rücken; [3] (pig) Sattelschwein, *das;* **∼backed** *adj.* sattelförmig; **∼bag** *n.* Satteltasche, *die;* **∼ blanket** *n.* Satteldecke, *die;* Woilach, *der;* **∼-bow** /'sædlbəʊ/ *n.* Zwiesel, *der;* **∼cloth** ▶ **∼ blanket**

saddler /'sædlə(r)/ *n.* ▶ⓘ **p. 1260** Sattler, *der*

saddlery /'sædlərɪ/ *n.* [1] (work, place) Sattlerei, *die* [2] (saddles etc.) Sattlerwaren *Pl.*

saddle: ∼ soap *n.* Sattelseife, *die;* **∼ sore** *n.* Sattelwunde, *die;* **∼-sore** *adj.* **be ∼-sore** wund vom Reiten/Radfahren sein; **∼ stitch** *n.* [1] (Bookbinding) Heftstich, *der;* [2] (Needlework) Vorstich, *der*

saddo /'sædəʊ/ *n.* (Brit. coll.) Assi, *der/die* (Jugendspr.)

sadism /'seɪdɪzm/ *n.* Sadismus, *der*

sadist /'seɪdɪst/ *n.* Sadist, *der*/Sadistin, *die*

sadistic /sə'dɪstɪk/ *adj.*, **sadistically** /sə'dɪstɪkəlɪ/ *adv.* sadistisch

sadly /'sædlɪ/ *adv.* [1] (with sorrow) traurig [2] (unfortunately) leider [3] (deplorably) erbärmlich (abwertend); **they are ∼ lacking in common sense** sie haben erbärmlich wenig [gesunden Menschen]verstand

sadness /'sædnɪs/ *n., no pl.* Traurigkeit, *die* (**at, about** über + *Akk.*)

sadomasochism /seɪdəʊ'mæsəkɪzm/ *n.* Sadomasochismus, *der*

sadomasochist /seɪdəʊ'mæsəkɪst/ *n.* Sadomasochist, *der*/Sadomasochistin, *die*

sadomasochistic /seɪdəʊmæsə'kɪstɪk/ *adj.* sadomasochistisch

'sad sack *n.* (Amer. coll.) trübe Tasse (ugs. abwertend)

s.a.e. /eseɪ'iː/ *abbr.* **= stamped addressed envelope** adressierter Freiumschlag

safari /sə'fɑːrɪ/ *n.* Safari, *die;* **be/go on ∼:** auf Safari sein/gehen

sa'fari park *n.* Safaripark, *der*

safe /seɪf/

A *n.* [1] Safe, *der;* Geldschrank, *der* [2] (Amer. coll.:

contraceptive) Präser, *der* (salopp) 3 ▸**meat safe**
B *adj.* 1 (out of danger) sicher (**from** vor + *Dat.*); **he's** ~: er ist in Sicherheit; **the bullfighter was** ~: der Stierkämpfer war nicht in Gefahr; **make sth.** ~ **from sth.** etw. gegen etw. sichern; ~ **and sound** sicher und wohlbehalten 2 (free from danger) ungefährlich; sicher ‹*Ort, Hafen*›; **she's a** ~ **driver** sie fährt sicher; **better** ~ **than sorry** Vorsicht ist besser als Nachsicht (ugs.); **is the water** ~ **to drink?** kann man das Wasser ohne Risiko trinken?; **wish sb. a** ~ **journey** jmdm. eine gute Reise wünschen; **is the car** ~ **to drive?** ist der Wagen verkehrssicher?; **the maximum** ~ **load** das zulässige Ladegewicht; **a** ~ **margin** eine Sicherheitsmarge; **the beach is** ~ **for bathing** es ist ungefährlich, am Strand zu baden; **to be on the** ~ **side** zur Sicherheit; **we had better be on the** ~ **side** wir sollten lieber sichergehen 3 (unlikely to produce controversy) sicher; bewährt (iron.) ‹*Klischee*›; **it is** ~ **to say [that ...]** man kann mit Sicherheit sagen[, dass ...]; **it is not** ~ **to generalize in such a matter** in einer solchen Frage kann man nicht einfach verallgemeinern 4 (reliable) sicher ‹*Methode, Investition, Stelle*›; nahe liegend ‹*Vermutung*›; **in** ~ **hands** in guten Händen; **a** ~ **Conservative seat** (Polit.) eine Hochburg der Konservativen Partei 5 (secure) **be** ~ **in prison, be in** ~ **custody** in sicherem Gewahrsam sein; **your secrets will be** ~ **with me** deine Geheimnisse sind bei mir gut aufgehoben

safe: ~ **'bet** *n.* **it is a** ~ **bet he will be there** man kann darauf wetten, dass er dort ist; **he is a** ~ **bet to win/for Prime Minister** man kann darauf wetten, dass er gewinnt/dass er der nächste Premierminister wird; **~-breaker** *n.* Geldschrankknacker, *der* (ugs.); ~ **'conduct** *n.* 1 (privilege) freies *od.* sicheres Geleit; 2 (document) Schutzbrief, *der* (Politik, Dipl.); **~-cracker** ▸**~-breaker**; ~ **de'posit** *n.* Tresor, *der*; *attrib.* **~-deposit box** (at the bank) Banksafe, *der*; **~guard** A *n.* Schutz, *der*; **as a ~guard against infection** zum Schutz gegen Infektionen; B *v.t.* schützen; **~guard sb.'s future/interests** jmds. Zukunft sichern/Interessen wahren; ~ **'haven** *n.* 1 (safe place) Zuflucht, *die*; Zufluchtsort, *der*; 2 (Polit.: protected zone) Schutzzone, *die*; ~ **house** *n.* geheimer Unterschlupf (*von Terroristen, Agenten usw.*); ~ **'keeping** *n.* sichere Obhut (geh.); (of thing) [sichere] Aufbewahrung

safely /'seɪflɪ/ *adv.* 1 (without harm) sicher; **did the parcel arrive** ~? ist das Paket heil angekommen? 2 (securely) sicher; **the children are** ~ **tucked up in bed** die Kinder liegen friedlich im Bett; **be** ~ **behind bars** [in sicherem Gewahrsam] hinter Schloss und Riegel sein 3 (with certainty) **one can** ~ **say [that] she will come** man kann mit Sicherheit sagen, dass sie kommt

safe: ~ **period** *n.* unfruchtbare Tage; ~ **'seat** *n.* (Polit.) Hochburg, *die*; ≈ sicherer Wahlkreis; ~ **'sex** *n.* Safer Sex, *der*; geschützter Sex

safety /'seɪftɪ/ *n.* 1 (being out of danger) Sicherheit, *die*; **cross the river in** ~: sicher über den Fluss fahren 2 (lack of danger) Ungefährlichkeit, *die*; (of a machine) Betriebssicherheit, *die*; **do sth. with** ~: etw. tun, ohne sich einer Gefahr (*Dat.*) auszusetzen; **there is** ~ **in numbers** zu mehreren ist man sicherer; **a** ~ **first policy** eine Politik der Vorsicht; **one can say with** ~ **that ...:** man kann mit Sicherheit behaupten, dass ... 3 *attrib.* Sicherheits‹*netz, -kette, -faktor, -maßnahmen, -vorrichtungen*›

safety: ~ **belt** *n.* Sicherheitsgurt, *der*; ~ **catch** *n.* (of door) Sicherheitsverriegelung, *die*; (of gun) Sicherungshebel, *der*; ~ **chain** *n.* Sicherheitskette, *die*; ~ **curtain** *n.* (Theatre) eiserner Vorhang; ~ **fuse** *n.* (Electr.) Sicherung, *die*; ~ **glass** *n.* Sicherheitsglas, *das*; ~ **helmet** *n.* Schutzhelm, *der*; ~ **margin** *n.* Spielraum, *der*; ~ **match** *n.* Sicherheitszündholz, *das*; ~ **pin** *n.* Sicherheitsnadel, *die*; ~ **play** *n.* (Bridge) Auf-sicher-Spielen, *das*; *Spiel, bei dem geringe Verluste hingenommen werden, um größere zu vermeiden*; ~ **razor** *n.* Rasierapparat, *der*; ~ **valve** *n.* Sicherheitsventil, *das* (Technik); (fig.) Ventil, *das* (fig.); ~ **zone** *n.* (Amer.: traffic island) Verkehrsinsel, *die*

'safe zone *n.* (Polit.) Schutzzone, *die*

saffron /'sæfrən/
A *n.* Safran, *der*; *see also* **meadow saffron**
B *adj.* safrangelb

sag /sæg/
A *v.i.*, **-gg-** 1 (have downward bulge) durchhängen 2 (sink) sich senken; absacken (ugs.); ‹*Gebäude:*› [in sich (*Akk.*)] zusammensacken (ugs.); ‹*Schultern:*› herabhängen; ‹*Brüste:*› hängen; (fig.: decline) ‹*Mut, Stimmung:*› sinken; **the interest/storyline ~s halfway through the book** die Spannung/Geschichte lässt in der Mitte des Buches [spürbar] nach; **~ging breasts** Hängebusen, *der* (ugs.) 3 (hang lopsidedly) **the gate ~ged half off its hinges** das Tor hing schief in den Angeln; **the bridge ~s on one side** die Brücke ist auf einer Seite abgesackt (ugs.)
B *n.* 1 (amount that rope etc. ~s) Durchhang, *der* 2 (sinking) **there was a** ~ **in the seat/mattress** der Sitz war durchgesessen/die Matratze war durchgelegen

saga /'sɑːgə/ *n.* 1 (story of adventure) Heldenepos, *das* (fig.); (medieval narrative) Saga, *die* (Literaturw.); **knightly** ~: ≈ Ritterroman, *der*; **the** ~ **of a family** die Geschichte einer Familie 2 (long involved story) [ganzer] Roman (fig.); **the** ~ **of our holiday in Spain** die Geschichte unseres Spanienurlaubs

sagacious /sə'geɪʃəs/ *adj.* klug; ~ **mind** scharfer Verstand

sagaciously /sə'geɪʃəslɪ/ *adv.* klug

sagacity /sə'gæsɪtɪ/ *n.*, *no pl.* Klugheit, *die*

sage[1] /seɪdʒ/ *n.* (Bot.) Salbei, *der od. die*; **~-and-onion stuffing** Salbei-und-Zwiebel-Füllung, *die*

sage[2]
A *n.* Weise, *der*
B *adj.* weise

sage: **~brush** *n.* (Bot.) Beifuß, *der* (in nordamerikanischen Steppen); ~ **'cheese**, ~ **'Derby** *ns.* Käse mit Salbeigewürz; **~-'green** A *adj.* salbeigrün; B *n.* Salbeigrün, *das*

sagely /'seɪdʒlɪ/ *adv.* weise

sage 'tea *n.* Salbeitee, *der*

Sagittarian /sædʒɪ'teərɪən/ *n.* (Astrol.) Schütze, *der*

Sagittarius /sædʒɪ'teərɪəs/ *n.* (Astrol., Astron.) der Schütze; der Sagittarius; *see also* **Aries**

sago /'seɪgəʊ/ *n.*, *pl.* **~s** Sago, *der*

Sahara /sə'hɑːrə/ *pr. n.* **the** ~ **[Desert]** die [Wüste] Sahara

Saharan /sə'hɑːrən/ *adj.* Sahara-

sahib /sɑːb, 'sɑːɪb/ *n.* 1 (arch.: title) Sahib, *der* 2 (gentleman) Herr, *der*

said ▸**say A, B**

sail /seɪl/
A *n.* 1 (voyage in ~ing vessel) Segelfahrt, *die*; **go for a** ~: eine Segelfahrt machen; **the island is ten days'** ~ **from Plymouth** von Plymouth aus erreicht man die Insel [mit dem Segelschiff] in zehn Tagen 2 (piece of canvas) Segel, *das*; **in** *or* **under full** ~: mit vollen Segeln; **under** ~: unter Segel (Seemannsspr.) 3 *pl. same* (ship) Segelschiff, *das* 4 (of windmill) [Windmühlen]flügel, *der*. *See also* **make A 19**; **set A 12**; **shorten B 2**; **strike B 20**; **wind**[1] **A 1**
B *v.i.* 1 (travel on water) fahren; (in sailing boat) segeln; **a lovely boat to** ~ **in** ein schönes Boot zum Segeln 2 (start voyage) auslaufen (**for** nach); in See stechen 3 (glide in air) segeln 4 (fig.: be thrown) segeln (ugs.); **the bottle which ~ed past his ear** die Flasche, die an seinem Ohr vorbeisegelte (ugs.) 5 (walk in stately manner) segeln (ugs.); ~ **by** vorübersegeln (salopp) 6 (move smoothly) gleiten; ~ **through** hindurchgleiten 7 (fig. coll.: pass easily) ~ **through an examination** eine Prüfung spielend schaffen. *See also* **colour A 10**; **wind**[1] **A 1**
C *v.t.* 1 steuern ‹*Boot, Schiff*›; segeln mit ‹*Segeljacht, -schiff*› 2 (travel across) durchfahren, befahren ‹*Meer*›; ‹*Segelschiff:*› durchsegeln

Phrasal verbs
- ~ **'in** *v.i.* (coll.: enter) hereinsegeln (ugs.)
- ~ **into** *v.t.* (coll.) 1 ~ **into a room** in ein Zimmer hereingesegelt kommen (ugs.) 2 (attack) ~ **into sb.** über jmdn. herfallen

sail: **~board** *n.* Surfbrett, *das* (*zum Windsurfen*); **~boarding** ▸**windsurfing**; **~boat** *n.* (Amer.) Segelboot, *das*; **~cloth** *n.* Segeltuch, *das*

sailing /'seɪlɪŋ/ *n.* 1 (handling a boat) Segeln, *das*; **weather for** ~: Segelwetter, *das* 2 (departure from a port) Abfahrt, *die*; **there are regular ~s from here across to the island** von hier fahren regelmäßig Schiffe hinüber zur Insel

sailing: ~ **boat** *n.* Segelboot, *das*; ~ **orders** *n. pl.* Order zum Auslaufen; ~ **ship**, ~ **vessel** *ns.* Segelschiff, *das*

'sailmaker *n.* ▸ⓘ **p. 1260** Segelmacher, *der*

sailor /'seɪlə(r)/ *n.* Seemann, *der*; (in navy) Matrose, *der*; **be a good/bad** ~ (not get seasick/get seasick) seefest/nicht seefest sein

'sailor suit *n.* Matrosenanzug, *der*

sainfoin /'sænfɔɪn, 'seɪnfɔɪn/ *n.* (Bot.) Esparsette, *die*

saint
A /sənt/ *adj.* **S~ Michael/Helena** der heilige Michael/die heilige Helena; Sankt Michael/Helena; *as voc.* heiliger Michael/heilige Helena; ~ **Michael's [Church]** die Michaelskirche; ~ **Andrew's/George's cross** Andreas-/Georgskreuz, *das*
B /seɪnt/ *n.* Heilige, *der/die*; **make** *or* **declare sb. a** ~ (RC Ch.) jmdn. heilig sprechen; **be as patient as a** ~: eine Engelsgeduld haben; *see also* **aunt**; **patron 3**

Saint Bernard /sənt 'bɜːnəd/ *n.* ~ **[dog]** Bernhardiner, *der*

sainthood /'seɪnthʊd/ *n.* Heiligkeit, *die*

Saint: ~ **James** /sənt 'dʒeɪmz/ *n.* **Court of** ~ **James** *der britische Hof*; ~ **John's wort** /sənt 'dʒɒnz wɜːt/ *n.* (Bot.) Johanniskraut, *das*; ~ **Lawrence** /sənt 'lɒrəns/ *n.* (Geog.) Sankt-Lorenz-Strom, *der*

saintly /'seɪntlɪ/ *adj.* heilig; ~ **patience** Engelsgeduld, *die*

Saint: ~ **Peter's** /sənt 'piːtəz/ *pr. n.* (in Rome) die Peterskirche; **s~'s day** *n.* Tag eines/einer Heiligen; *see also* **all A 2**; ~ **Swithin's day** /sənt 'swɪðɪnz deɪ/ *n.*: *15. Juli, der nach britischem Volksglauben wetterbestimmend für die folgenden vierzig Tage ist*; ≈ Siebenschläfer, *der*; ~ **Vitus's dance** /sənt vaɪtəsɪz 'dɑːns/ ▸**dance C 4**

sake[1] /seɪk/ *n.* **for the** ~ **of** um ... (*Gen.*) willen; **for my** *etc.* ~: um meinetwillen *usw.*; mir *usw.* zuliebe; **for all our ~s** uns allen zuliebe; **for your/its own** ~: um deiner/seiner selbst willen; **art for art's** ~: Kunst um ihrer selbst willen; **for the** ~ **of a few pounds** wegen ein paar Pfund; **for Christ's** *or* **God's** *or* **goodness'** *or* **Heaven's** *or* (coll.) **Pete's** *etc.* ~: um Gottes *od.* Himmels willen; **for old times'** ~: um der schönen Erinnerung willen; *see also* **appearance 2**; **argument 2**; **convenience 2**

sake[2] /'sɑːkɪ/ *n.* (drink) Sake, *der*

salaam /sə'lɑːm/ *n.* Salam [alaikum] (veralt., noch scherzh.); *in pl.* (respects) Komplimente (veralt.)

salable ▸**saleable**

salacious /sə'leɪʃəs/ *adj.* 1 (lustful) lüstern 2 (inciting sexual desire) pornographisch

salaciously /sə'leɪʃəslɪ/ *adv.* lüstern

salad /'sæləd/ *n.* Salat, *der*; **ham/tomato** ~: Schinken-/Tomatensalat, *der*

salad: ~ **bar** *n.* Salatbar, *die*; Salatbuffet, *das*; ~ **cream** *n.* ≈ Mayonnaise, *die*; ~ **days** *n. pl.* **in my** ~ **days** als ich noch nicht trocken hinter den Ohren war (ugs.); ~ **dressing** *n.* Dressing, *das*; Salatsoße, *die*; ~ **oil** *n.* Salatöl, *das*; ~ **servers** *n. pl.* Salatbesteck, *das*; ~ **shaker** *n.* 1 (mixed salad and dressing) Salatshaker, *der*; 2 (utensil) *Utensil zum Trockenschütteln von Salat*

salamander /'sæləmændə(r)/ *n.* 1 (Zool.) Salamander, *der* 2 (Amer.) ▸**gopher 1**

salami /sə'lɑːmɪ/ *n.* Salami, *die*

S

sal ammoniac /sæl əˈməʊnɪæk/ *n.* Salmiak, *der od. das*

salaried /ˈsælərɪd/ *adj.* **1** (receiving salary) Gehalt beziehend; **~ employee** Angestellte, *der/die;* **the ~ class** die Gehaltsempfänger **2** (having salary attached to it) **~ post** Stelle mit festem Gehalt

salary /ˈsælərɪ/ *n.* Gehalt, *das;* (Amer.: weekly) Lohn, *der;* **~ increase** Gehaltserhöhung, *die;* **what is your ~?** wie hoch ist dein Gehalt?; **draw a ~:** ein Gehalt beziehen

salary: ~ scale *n.* Gehaltsskala, *die;* **~ structure** *n.* Gehaltsstruktur, *die*

sale /seɪl/ *n.* **1** (selling) Verkauf, *der;* **[up] for ~:** zu verkaufen; **put up** *or* **offer for ~:** zum Verkauf anbieten; **on ~:** im Handel; **on ~ at your chemist's** in Ihrer Apotheke erhältlich; **go on ~:** in den Handel kommen; **offer** *etc.* **sth. on a ~ or return basis** etw. auf Kommissionsbasis anbieten *usw.* **2** (instance of selling) Verkauf, *der;* **make a ~:** einen Verkauf tätigen (Kaufmannsspr.); **find a ready ~ for sth.** etw. gut verkaufen; **sth. finds a ready ~:** etw. verkauft sich gut **3** *in pl., no art.* (amount sold) Verkaufszahlen *Pl.* (**of** für); Absatz, *der* **4** **[jumble** *or* **rummage] ~:** [Wohltätigkeits]basar, *der;* **~ of work** Wohltätigkeitsbasar mit eigenen Bastel-, Handarbeiten **5** (disposal at reduced prices) Ausverkauf, *der;* **clearance/end-of-season/summer ~:** Räumungs-/Schluss-/Sommerschlussverkauf, *der;* **at the ~s** im Ausverkauf **6** (public auction) [Verkauf durch] Versteigerung; **put sth. up for ~ [by auction]** etw. zur Versteigerung anbieten

saleable /ˈseɪləbl/ *adj.* verkäuflich; **be [highly] ~:** sich [gut] verkaufen lassen

sale: ~ price *n.* **1** (retail price) Verkaufspreis, *der;* **2** (price in sale) Ausverkaufspreis, *der;* **~ ring** *n.* Käuferring bei einer Auktion; **~room** *n.* (Brit.) Auktionsraum, *der*

sales: ~ assistant (Brit.), **~ clerk** (Amer.) *ns.* ▸ⓘ **p. 1260** Verkäufer, *der*/Verkäuferin, *die;* **~ conference** *n.* Verkaufskonferenz, *die;* Vertriebskonferenz, *die;* **~ department** *n.* Verkaufsabteilung, *die;* **~ desk** ▸**desk 2**; **~ force** *n.* Vertreterstab, *der;* **~girl**, **~lady** *ns.* ▸ⓘ **p. 1260** Verkäuferin, *die;* **~man** /ˈseɪlzmən/ *n., pl.* **~men** /ˈseɪlzmən/ ▸ⓘ **p. 1260** Verkäufer, *der;* **~ manager** *n.* ▸ⓘ **p. 1260** Verkaufsleiter, *der*/-leiterin, *die;* Salesmanager, *der*

salesmanship /ˈseɪlzmənʃɪp/ *n., no pl., no indef. art.* Kunst des Verkaufens

sales: ~ patter, **~ pitch** *ns.* Verkaufsargumentation, *die;* **~ rep** (coll.), **~ representative** *ns.* ▸ⓘ **p. 1260** [Handels]vertreter, *der*/-vertreterin, *die;* **~ resistance** *n., no pl.* Kaufunlust, *die;* **~ talk** ▸**~ patter**; **~ target** *n.* (of a company) Absatzziel, *das;* (of a salesman/-woman) Verkaufsziel, *das;* **~ tax** *n.* Umsatzsteuer, *die;* **~woman** *n.* ▸ⓘ **p. 1260** Verkäuferin, *die*

salient /ˈseɪlɪənt/
A *adj.* **1** (striking) auffallend; ins Auge springend; hervorstechend ‹*Charakterzug*›; **the ~ points of a speech** die herausragenden Punkte einer Rede **2** (pointing outwards) vorspringend
B *n.* (Mil.) vorgeschobene Stellung

saline /ˈseɪlaɪn/ *adj.* salzig; Salz‹*ablagerung*›; **~ solution** Salzlösung, *die;* (Med.) [physiologische] Kochsalzlösung; **~ drip** (Med.) Tropfinfusion, *die*

salinity /səˈlɪnɪtɪ/ *n.* Salzgehalt, *der;* **be high in ~:** stark salzhaltig sein

saliva /səˈlaɪvə/ *n.* Speichel, *der*

salivary /ˈsælɪvərɪ, səˈlaɪvərɪ/ *adj.* (Anat.) **~ gland** Speicheldrüse, *die*

salivate /ˈsælɪveɪt/ *v.i.* speicheln

saˈliva test *n.* Speicheltest, *der* (bes. Med.)

sallow¹ /ˈsæləʊ/ *adj.* blassgelb

sallow² *n.* (Bot.) Salweide, *die*

sallowness /ˈsæləʊnɪs/ *n., no pl.* gelbliche Blässe

sally
A *n.* **1** (Mil.: sortie) Ausfall, *der* **2** (excursion) Ausflug, *der* **3** (verbal attack) **his sallies against the authorities** seine Ausfälle gegen die Obrigkeit **4** (witty remark) Geistesblitz, *der* (ugs.)
B *v.i.* **1** **~ out** (Mil.: make sortie/sorties) einen Ausfall/Ausfälle machen **2** **~ forth** aufbrechen, sich aufmachen (**for** zu)

Sally /ˈsælɪ/ ▸**aunt**

salmon /ˈsæmən/
A *n., pl. same* Lachs, *der*
B *adj.* (colour) lachsfarben; lachsrosa ‹*Farbton*›

ˈsalmon-coloured *adj.* lachsfarben

salmonella /sælməˈnelə/ *n.* ▸ⓘ **p. 1231** Salmonelle, *die;* **~ poisoning** Salmonellenvergiftung, *die*

salmon: ~ farm *n.* Lachsfarm, *die;* **~ ladder**, **~ leap** *ns.* Lachstreppe, *die;* **~ pink** **A** *n.* lachsrosa Farbton; **B** *adj.* lachsfarben; **~ ˈtrout** *n.* Lachsforelle, *die*

salon /ˈsælɔ̃/ *n.* Salon, *der*

ˈsalon music *n.* Salonmusik, *die*

saloon /səˈluːn/ *n.* **1** (public room in ship, hotel, etc.) Salon, *der;* **dining ~:** Speisesaal, *der;* **billiard ~** (Brit.) Billardraum, *der* **2** (Brit.: motor car) Limousine, *die* **3** (Amer.: bar) Saloon, *der*

saloon: ~ ˈbar *n.* (Brit.) *separater Teil eines Pubs mit mehr Komfort;* **~ ˈcar** ▸**saloon 2**; **~ deck** *n.* Salondeck, *das*

salopettes /sæləˈpets/ *n. pl.* Skihose, *die* (*mit Trägern*)

salsa /ˈsælsə/ *n., no pl.* Salsa, *der*

salsify /ˈsælsɪfɪ/ *n.* (Bot.) Haferwurz, *die*

salt /sɔːlt, sɒlt/
A *n.* **1** (for food etc.; also Chem.) **[common] ~:** [Koch]salz, *das;* **above/below the ~** (Hist.) oben/unten an der Tafel; **rub ~ in[to] the wound** (fig.) Salz in die Wunde streuen; **take sth. with a grain** *or* **pinch of ~** (fig.) etw. cum grano salis (geh.) *od.* nicht ganz wörtlich nehmen; **be the ~ of the earth** (fig.) anständig und rechtschaffen sein; das Salz der Erde sein (bibl.); **be worth one's ~:** etwas taugen; (worth the money one is paid) sein Geld wert sein **2** *in pl.* (medicine) Salz, *das;* **like a dose of ~s** (coll.) in null Komma nichts (ugs.); **he went through the department like a dose of ~s** (fig.) er kehrte in der Abteilung mit eisernem Besen [aus] **3** (fig.: zest) Salz, *das* (fig.); Würze, *die* (fig.) **4** **[old] ~** (sailor) [alter] Seebär (ugs. scherzh.)
B *adj.* **1** (containing or tasting of ~) salzig; (preserved with ~) gepökelt ‹*Fleisch*›; gesalzen ‹*Butter*› **2** (bitter) salzig ‹*Tränen*› **3** (biting) scharf, ätzend ‹*Witz*›
C *v.t.* **1** (add ~ to) salzen; (fig.) würzen **2** (preserve with ~ or brine) [ein]pökeln; **~ed beef/pork** gepökeltes Rind-/Schweinefleisch **3** (spread ~ on) **~ the roads** Salz auf die Straßen streuen

Phrasal verb

• **~ aˈway**, **~ ˈdown** *v.t.* (coll.) auf die hohe Kante legen (ugs.)

SALT /sɔːlt, sɒlt/ *abbr.* **= Strategic Arms Limitation Talks/Treaty** SALT

salt: ~ cellar *n.* (open) Salzfässchen, *das;* (sprinkler) Salzstreuer, *der;* **~-ˈfree** *adj.* salzfrei ‹*Essen usw.*›; **~ ˈlake** *n.* Salzsee, *der;* **~ lick** *n.* Salzlecke, *die* (Jägerspr.); **~ marsh** *n.* Salzwiesengebiet, *das;* (formed by evaporation) Salzsumpf, *der;* **~ mine** *n.* Salzbergwerk, *das;* **~ pan** *n.* Salzpfanne, *die*

saltpetre (*Amer.:* **saltpeter**) /ˈsɔːltpiːtə(r), ˈsɒltpiːtə(r)/ *n.* Salpeter, *der*

salt: ~ shaker *n.* (Amer.) Salzstreuer, *der;* **~ spoon** *n.* Salzlöffelchen, *das;* **~ sprinkler** *n.* Salzstreuer, *der;* **~ tablet** *n.* [Koch]salztablette, *die;* **~ ˈwater** *n.* Salzwasser, *das;* **~water** *adj.* Salzwasser-; **~ works** *n. sing., pl. same* Saline, *die*

salty /ˈsɔːltɪ, ˈsɒltɪ/ *adj.* salzig; (fig.) scharf ‹*Witz*›

salubrious /səˈluːbrɪəs/ *adj.* gesund; **not a very ~ area** (fig.) ein etwas zweifelhaftes Viertel

saluki /səˈluːkɪ/ *n.* Saluki, *der;* Persischer Windhund

salutary /ˈsæljʊtərɪ/ *adj.* heilsam ‹*Wirkung, Einfluss, Schock*›; heilkräftig ‹*Medizin*›

salutation /sæljʊˈteɪʃn/ *n.* (formal) Gruß, *der;* Begrüßung, *die;* **form of ~:** Begrüßungsformel, *die;* **raise one's hat [to sb.] in ~:** [vor jmdm.] zum Gruß den Hut ziehen

salute /səˈluːt/
A *v.t.* **1** (Mil., Navy) **~ sb.** jmdn. [militärisch] grüßen; (fig.: pay tribute to) sich vor jmdm. verneigen **2** (greet) grüßen
B *v.i.* (Mil., Navy) [militärisch] grüßen
C *n.* **1** (Mil., Navy) Salut, *der;* militärischer Gruß; **fire a seven-gun ~:** sieben Schuss Salut abfeuern; **give a ~:** militärisch grüßen; **take the ~** ‹*Vorgesetzter:*› den militärischen Gruß entgegennehmen; ‹*Staatsoberhaupt usw.:*› die Parade abnehmen **2** (gesture of greeting) Gruß, *der* **3** (Fencing) [Fecht]gruß, *der*

Salvadorean /sælvəˈdɔːrɪən/ ▸ⓘ **p. 1345**
A *n.* Salvadorianer, *der*/Salvadorianerin, *die*
B *adj.* salvadorianisch

salvage /ˈsælvɪdʒ/
A *n.* **1** (rescue of property) Bergung, *die; attrib.* Bergungs‹*arbeiten, -aktion*› **2** (payment) Bergelohn, *der* (Seew.) **3** (rescued property) Bergegut, *das;* (for recycling) Sammelgut, *das;* **collect bottles for ~:** Flaschen zur Wiedergewinnung von Glas sammeln
B *v.t.* **1** (rescue) bergen; retten (auch fig.) (**from** von); **~ one's valuables from the flames** seine Wertsachen aus den Flammen retten **2** (save for recycling) für die Wiederverwendung sammeln

ˈsalvage operation *n.* Bergungsaktion, *die*

salvation /sælˈveɪʃn/ *n.* **1** *no art.* (Relig.) Erlösung, *die;* **doctrine of ~:** Heilslehre, *die;* **find ~:** zum Heil gelangen; **work out one's own ~** (fig.) auf eigene Weise ans Ziel gelangen **2** (means of preservation) Rettung, *die;* **those biscuits were my ~** (joc.) diese Kekse haben mir das Leben gerettet (scherzh.)

Salvation ˈArmy *n.* Heilsarmee, *die*

Salvationist /sælˈveɪʃənɪst/ *n.* (member of Salvation Army) Heilsarmist, *der*/-armistin, *die*

salve¹ /sælv/
A *n.* Balsam, *der* (geh.) (**to** für); **his apology was merely a ~ for his conscience** mit der Entschuldigung wollte er nur sein Gewissen beruhigen
B *v.t.* (soothe) besänftigen; beruhigen ‹*Gewissen*›

salve² /sælv/ *v.t.* ▸**salvage B 1**

salver /ˈsælvə(r)/ *n.* Tablett, *das*

salvo /ˈsælvəʊ/ *n., pl.* **~es** *or* **~s** **1** (of guns) Salve, *die* **2** **~ of applause/laughter** Beifalls-/Lachsalve, *die*

sal volatile /sæl vɒˈlætɪlɪ/ *n.* Riechsalz, *das*

Samaritan /səˈmærɪtən/ *n.* **good ~:** [barmherziger] Samariter; **I decided to be a good ~:** ich beschloss, ein gutes Werk zu tun; **the ~s** (organization) ≈ die Telefonseelsorge

samba /ˈsæmbə/ *n.* Samba, *der*

Sam Browne /sæm ˈbraʊn/ *n.* **1** **~ [belt]** (*von brit. Offizieren getragenes*) Koppel mit Schulterriemen **2** (cyclist's) Leuchtgurt, *der*

same /seɪm/
A *adj.* **the ~:** der/die/das gleiche; **the ~ [thing]** (identical) der-/die-/dasselbe; **the ~ afternoon/evening** (of ~ day) schon am Nachmittag/Abend; **she seemed just the ~ [as ever] to me** sie schien mir unverändert *od.* immer noch die Alte; **my parents are much the ~** (not much changed) meine Eltern haben sich kaum geändert; **he was no longer the ~ man** er war nicht mehr derselbe; **one and the ~ person/man** ein und dieselbe Person/ein und derselbe Mann; **the very ~:** genau der/die/das; ebenderselbe/-dieselbe/-dasselbe; **much the ~ as** fast genauso wie; **this/that/these** *or* **those ~:** ebender-/ebendie-/ebendasselbe/ebendieselben; genau der-/die-/dasselbe/dieselben; *see also* **token A 4**
B *pron.* **the ~,** (coll.) **~** (the ~ thing) der-/die-/dasselbe; **he ran up big bills but was not strong at paying ~** (coll.) er machte große Schulden, machte aber keine Anstalten, sie zu bezahlen; **an actual banana or a photo of the ~:** eine echte Banane oder ein Foto davon; **things haven't been the ~ since you left** seit du nicht mehr da bist, haben sich die Dinge geändert; **they look [exactly] the ~:** sie sehen

gleich aus; **more of the ~:** noch mehr davon; **and the ~ to you!** (also iron.) danke gleichfalls; **[the] ~ again** das Gleiche noch einmal; **I feel bored — S~ here** (coll.) Ich langweile mich — dito

C *adv.* **[the] ~ as you do** genau wie du; **the ~ as before** genau wie vorher; **be pronounced the ~:** gleich ausgesprochen werden; **all** *or* **just the ~:** trotzdem; nichtsdestotrotz (ugs., oft scherzh.); **think the ~ of/feel the ~ towards** dasselbe halten von/empfinden für

'same-day *adj.* ‹*Dienst*› noch am gleichen Tag

sameness /ˈseɪmnɪs/ *n., no pl.* Gleichheit, *die*

'same-sex *adj.* gleichgeschlechtlich

Samoa /səˈməʊə/ *pr. n.* Samoa *(das)*

Samoan /səˈməʊən/ ▸**i** **p. 1277**, ▸**i** **p. 1345**

A *adj.* samoanisch

B *n.* Samoaner, *der*/Samoanerin, *die*

samosa /səˈməʊsə/ *n.* Samosa, *die*

samovar /ˈsæməvɑː(r)/ *n.* Samowar, *der*

sampan /ˈsæmpæn/ *n.* Sampan, *der*

sample /ˈsɑːmpl/

A *n.* 1 (representative portion) Auswahl, *die;* (in opinion research, statistics) Querschnitt, *der;* Sample, *das* 2 (example) [Muster]beispiel, *das;* (specimen) Probe, *die;* **[commercial] ~:** Muster, *das; attrib.* Probe ‹*exemplar, -seite*›; **~ letter** Musterbrief, *der;* **~ of air/blood** Luft-/Blutprobe, *die* 3 (Mus.) Sample, *das*

B *v.t.* 1 probieren; **~ the pleasures of country life** die Freuden des Landlebens kosten (geh.) 2 (Mus.) sampeln

sampler /ˈsɑːmplə(r)/ *n.* 1 (piece of needlework) Stickarbeit, *die;* Stickerei, *die* 2 (trial pack) Probe[packung], *die* 3 (Mus.) Sampler, *der*

sampling /ˈsɑːmplɪŋ/ *n., no pl.* (Mus.) Sampling, *das*

Samson /ˈsæmsn/ *pr. n.* Samson, *der;* (fig.: strong man) Herkules, *der*

samurai /ˈsæmʊəraɪ/ *n., pl. same or* **~s** (Hist.) Samurai, *der*

sanatarium /sænəˈteərɪəm/ (Amer.) ▸**sanatorium**

sanatorium /sænəˈtɔːrɪəm/ *n., pl.* **~s** *or* **sanatoria** /sænəˈtɔːrɪə/ 1 (clinic) Sanatorium, *das* 2 (sickbay) Krankenzimmer, *das*

sanctification /sæŋktɪfɪˈkeɪʃn/ *n.* Heiligung, *die* (geh.)

sanctify /ˈsæŋktɪfaɪ/ *v.t.* 1 heiligen 2 (consecrate) weihen; heiligen (bes. bibl.)

sanctimonious /sæŋktɪˈməʊnɪəs/ *adj.*, **sanctimoniously** /sæŋktɪˈməʊnɪəslɪ/ *adv.* scheinheilig

sanction /ˈsæŋkʃn/

A *n.* 1 (official approval) Sanktion, *die;* **give one's ~ to sth.** seine Erlaubnis für etw. geben 2 (Polit.: penalty; Law: punishment) Sanktion, *die*

B *v.t.* sanktionieren

'sanctions-busting *n., no pl.* Sanktionsbruch, *der*

sanctity /ˈsæŋktɪtɪ/ *n., no pl.* Heiligkeit, *die*

sanctuary /ˈsæŋktʃʊərɪ/ *n.* 1 (holy place) Heiligtum, *das* 2 (part of church) Altarraum, *der;* Sanktuarium, *das* (kath. Kirche) 3 (place of refuge) Zufluchtsort, *der;* (Hist.: guaranteeing safety) Freistatt, *die* 4 (for animals or plants) Naturschutzgebiet, *das;* **bird/animal ~:** Vogel-/Tierschutzgebiet, *das* 5 (asylum) Asyl, *das;* Freiung, *die* (hist.); **take ~:** Zuflucht suchen

sanctum /ˈsæŋktəm/ *n.* (joc.: private retreat) **[inner] ~:** Allerheiligste, *das* (fig.)

sanctus /ˈsæŋktəs/ *n.* Sanctus, *das* (kath. Kirche)

'sanctus bell *n.* Sakristeiglocke, *die*

sand /sænd/

A *n.* 1 Sand, *der;* **the beach has four miles of ~:** der Sandstrand ist 4 Meilen lang; **built on ~** (fig.) auf Sand gebaut; **have** *or* **keep** *or* **bury one's head in the ~** (fig.) den Kopf in den Sand stecken 2 *in pl.* (expanse) Sandbank, *die;* (beach) Sandstrand, *der* 3 *in pl.* **the ~s [of time] are running out** (fig.) die Zeit läuft ab 4 (Amer. coll.: determination) **have not got ~ enough to do sth.** nicht den Mumm (ugs.) haben, etw zu tun; **he loses his ~:** ihm rutscht das Herz in die Hose (ugs., oft scherzh.). *See also* **plough B 1**

B *v.t.* 1 (sprinkle) **~ the road** die Straße mit Sand streuen 2 (bury) **be ~ed up** *or* **over** versandet sein 3 (polish) **~ sth. down** etw. [ab]schmirgeln

sandal /ˈsændl/ *n.* Sandale, *die*

sandal: ~-tree *n.* Sandelbaum, *der;* **~wood** *n.* **[red] ~wood** Sandelholz, *das;* **~wood oil** Sandel[holz]öl, *das*

sand: ~bag **A** *n.* Sandsack, *der;* **B** *v.t.* 1 (barricade) mit Sandsäcken schützen; 2 (Amer.: coerce) **~bag sb. into sth.** jmdn. zu etw. zwingen; **~bag sb. into doing sth.** jmdn. so lange bearbeiten, bis er etw. tut; **~bank** *n.* Sandbank, *die;* **~ bar** *n.* Sandbank, *die* (an *Flussmündungen, Häfen*); **~ bath** *n.* (Chem.) Sandbad, *das;* **~blast** *v.t.* sandstrahlen (Technik); **~box** *n.* (Amer.) Sandkasten, *der;* **~boy** *n.* **be happy as a ~boy** glücklich und zufrieden sein; **~castle** *n.* Sandburg, *die;* **~ dollar** *n.* (Amer.: Zool.) Sanddollar, *der;* **~ dune** *n.* Düne, *die*

sander /ˈsændə(r)/ *n.* Sandpapierschleifmaschine, *die*

sand: ~glass *n.* Sanduhr, *die;* **~hill** *n.* Düne, *die;* **~lot** *n.* (Amer.) Spielplatz, *der;* (for older children) Bolzplatz, *der* (ugs.); **~man** /ˈsændmæn/ *n.* Sandmann, *der;* **~ martin** *n.* (Brit. Ornith.) Uferschwalbe, *die;* **~paper** **A** *n.* Sandpapier, *das;* **B** *v.t.* [mit Sandpapier] [ab]schmirgeln; **~piper** *n.* (Ornith.) Wasserläufer, *der;* **~pit** *n.* Sandkasten, *der;* **~stone** *n.* Sandstein, *der;* **~storm** *n.* Sandsturm, *der;* **~ trap** *n.* (Amer. Golf) Bunker, *der*

S & M *abbr.*

A *n.* **= sadomasochism** SM

B *adj.* **= sadomasochistic;** SM-

sandwich /ˈsænwɪdʒ, ˈsænwɪtʃ/

A *n.* 1 Sandwich, *der od. das;* ≈ [zusammengeklapptes] belegtes Brot; **cheese ~:** Käsebrot, *das;* **open ~:** belegtes Brot 2 ▸**sandwich cake**

B *v.t.* einschieben (**between** zwischen + *Akk.;* **into** in + *Akk.*); **be ~ed between other people/cars** zwischen andere Personen gequetscht werden/Autos eingeklemmt sein

sandwich: ~ bar *n.* Sandwichbar, *die;* **~ board** *n.: von einem Sandwichmann getragenes Reklameplakat;* **~ box** *n.* Sandwichbox, *die;* **~ cake** *n.: ein- od. mehrschichtig gefüllter Kuchen;* **~ course** *n.: Ausbildung mit abwechselnd theoretischem und praktischem Unterricht;* **~ man** *n.* Sandwichmann, *der;* **~ tin** *n.* Brotbüchse, *die*

sandy /ˈsændɪ/ *adj.* 1 (consisting of sand) sandig; Sand‹*boden, -strand*› 2 (yellowish-red) rotblond ‹*Haar*›

'sand yacht *n.* Strandsegler, *der*

sane /seɪn/ *adj.* 1 geistig gesund; **they do not think him entirely ~:** sie halten ihn nicht für ganz normal; **not ~:** geistesgestört 2 (sensible) vernünftig

sanely /ˈseɪnlɪ/ *adv.* 1 normal 2 (sensibly) vernünftig

sang ▸**sing A, B**

sang-froid /sɑ̃ˈfrwɑː/ *n.* Kaltblütigkeit, *die;* Sang-froid, *das* (veralt.)

sangria /sæŋˈgriːə/ *n.* Sangria, *die*

sanguinary /ˈsæŋgwɪnərɪ/ *adj.* 1 (delighting in bloodshed) blutrünstig 2 (bloody) blutig

sanguine /ˈsæŋgwɪn/ *adj.* 1 (confident) zuversichtlich (**about** was … betrifft); heiter ‹*Temperament*› 2 (florid) blühend ‹*Gesichtsfarbe*›

sanguinely /ˈsæŋgwɪnlɪ/ *adv.* zuversichtlich

sanitarium /sænɪˈteərɪəm/ (Amer.) ▸**sanatorium**

sanitary /ˈsænɪtərɪ/ *adj.* sanitär ‹*Verhältnisse, Anlagen*›; gesundheitlich ‹*Gesichtspunkt, Problem*›; Gesundheits‹*behörde*›; hygienisch ‹*Küche, Krankenhaus, Gewohnheit*›; Sanitär‹*fliesen, -abflussrohr*›

sanitary: ~ engi'neer *n.* Sanitärtechniker, *der*/-technikerin, *die;* **~ engi'neering** *n.* Sanitärtechnik, *die;* **~ inspector** *n.* Gesundheitsinspektor, *der*/-inspektorin, *die;* **~ napkin** (Amer.), **~ towel** (Brit.) *ns.* Damenbinde, *die;* **~ ware** *n., no pl.* Sanitärkeramik, *die*

sanitation /sænɪˈteɪʃn/ *n., no pl.* 1 (drainage, refuse disposal) Kanalisation und Abfallbeseitigung 2 (hygiene) Hygiene, *die*

sani'tation department *n.* (Amer.) Entsorgungsbehörde, *die*

sanitize (sanitise) /ˈsænɪtaɪz/ *v.t.* keimfrei machen ‹*Luft, Toilettensitz, Besteck*›; (fig.) entschärfen ‹*Dokument, Protokoll, Film*›

sanity /ˈsænɪtɪ/ *n.* 1 (mental health) geistige Gesundheit; **lose one's ~:** den Verstand verlieren; **cause sb. to lose his ~:** jmdn. um den Verstand bringen; **fear for/doubt sb.'s ~:** um jmds. Zurechnungsfähigkeit fürchten/an jmds. Verstand (*Dat.*) zweifeln 2 (good sense) Vernünftigkeit, *die;* **restore ~ to the proceedings** die Veranstaltung wieder in vernünftige Bahnen lenken

sank ▸**sink B, C**

sans /sænz/ *prep.* (arch./joc.) ohne

sanserif /sænˈserɪf/ (Printing)

A *n.* Grotesk[schrift], *die*

B *adj.* serifenlos; Grotesk‹*buchstabe, -ziffer*›

Sanskrit /ˈsænskrɪt/ ▸**i** **p. 1277**

A *adj.* sanskritisch; Sanskrit‹*text, -inschrift, -literatur*›; ‹*Grammatik*› des Sanskrits; *see also* **English A**

B *n.* Sanskrit, *das; see also* **English B 1**

Santa /ˈsæntə/ (coll.), **Santa Claus** /ˈsæntə klɔːz/ *n.* der Weihnachtsmann

sap[1] /sæp/

A *n.* 1 (Bot.) Saft, *der;* (fig.: vital spirit) belebende Kraft; **in the spring the ~ rises** im Frühling steigen die Säfte 2 (Amer. coll.: club) Knüppel, *der*

B *v.t.*, **-pp-** 1 (drain) den Saft entziehen (+ *Dat.*) ‹*Holz*›; (for sugar, rubber) anzapfen (**for** zur Gewinnung von) 2 (fig.: exhaust vigour of) zehren an (+ *Dat.*); **~ sb. of [all] his/her strength** jmdn. [völlig] entkräften; **her strength had been ~ped by disease/hunger** Krankheit/Hunger hatte an ihren Kräften gezehrt 3 (Amer. coll.: hit) mit einem Knüppel/mit Knüppeln schlagen

sap[2]

A *v.t.*, **-pp-** unterhöhlen ‹*Fundament, Mauer*›

B *n.* (Mil.) (trench) Sappe, *die;* (under enemy's fortification) Tunnel, *der*

sap[3] *n.* (coll.: fool) Trottel, *der* (ugs. abwertend); **find some ~ to do sth.** einen Dummen finden, der etw. tut

sapele /səˈpiːlɪ/ *n.* 1 (tree) Sapelli[baum], *der* 2 (wood) Sapelli[holz], *das*

'sap-green

A *n.* Saftgrün, *das*

B *adj.* saftgrün

sapling /ˈsæplɪŋ/ *n.* junger Baum

sapper /ˈsæpə(r)/ *n.* (Brit. Mil.) Pionier, *der*

Sapphic /ˈsæfɪk/ (Pros.)

A *adj.* sapphisch

B *n.* sapphischer Vers

sapphire /ˈsæfaɪə(r)/ *n.* Saphir, *der; attrib.* **~ blue** saphirblau; **~ ring** Saphirring, *der;* **~ wedding** 45. Hochzeitstag

sappy /ˈsæpɪ/ *adj.* saftig ‹*Gras*›; (fig.: full of vitality) voll Saft und Kraft *nachgestellt*

'sapwood *n.* (Bot.) Splintholz, *das*

saraband[e] /ˈsærəbænd/ *n.* (Mus., Dancing) Sarabande, *die*

Saracen /ˈsærəsn/ (Hist., Ethnol.)

A *n.* Sarazene, *der*/Sarazenin, *die* (veralt.)

B *adj.* sarazenisch; Sarazenen‹*führer, -frau*›

sarcasm /ˈsɑːkæzəm/ *n.* Sarkasmus, *der;* (remark) sarkastische Bemerkung; **with heavy ~:** mit beißendem Sarkasmus

sarcastic /sɑːˈkæstɪk/ *adj.*, **sarcastically** /sɑːˈkæstɪkəlɪ/ *adv.* sarkastisch

sarcoma /sɑːˈkəʊmə/ *n., pl.* **~ta** /sɑːˈkəʊmətə/ (Med.) Sarkom, *das*

sarcophagus /sɑːˈkɒfəgəs/ *n., pl.* **sarcophagi** /sɑːˈkɒfəgaɪ/ Sarkophag, *der*

sardine /sɑːˈdiːn/ *n.* (Zool.) Sardine, *die;* (Gastr.) [Öl]sardine, *die;* **like ~s** (fig.) wie die Ölsardinen

Sardinia /sɑːˈdɪnɪə/ *pr. n.* Sardinien *(das)*

Sardinian /sɑːˈdɪnɪən/ ▸**i** **p. 1277**, ▸**i** **p. 1345**

A *n.* 1 (person) Sarde, *der*/Sardin, *die;* Sardinier,

S

der/Sardinierin, *die* 2 (language) Sardisch, *das*
B *adj.* sardisch
sardonic /sɑːˈdɒnɪk/ *adj.* höhnisch ‹*Bemerkung*›; sardonisch ‹*Lachen, Lächeln*›; **he can be very ~:** er kann sehr bissig sein
sardonically /sɑːˈdɒnɪkəlɪ/ *adv.* höhnisch ‹*bemerken*›; sardonisch ‹*lächeln, lachen*›
sarge /sɑːdʒ/ *n.* (coll.) Sergeant, *der;* (Mil.) ≈ Hauptfeld, *der* (Militärjargon)
sari /ˈsɑːrɪ/ *n.* Sari, *der*
sarky /ˈsɑːkɪ/ *adj.* (Brit. coll.) ätzend (ugs.)
sarnie /ˈsɑːnɪ/ *n.* (Brit. coll.) ▸**sandwich A 1**
sarong /səˈrɒŋ/ *n.* Sarong, *der*
SARS /sɑːz/ *n.* SARS, *das*
sartorial /sɑːˈtɔːrɪəl/ *adj.* **he has high ~ standards** er stellt hohe Ansprüche, was seine Kleidung betrifft; **~ fashion** Herrenmode, *die;* **he was the height of ~ elegance** er war der Inbegriff des elegant gekleideten Herrn
SAS *abbr.* (Brit. Mil.) = **Special Air Service** *auf Geheimoperationen spezialisiertes Regiment der britischen Armee*
sash¹ /sæʃ/ *n.* Schärpe, *die*
sash² *n.* 1 (of window) Fensterrahmen, *der* 2 (window) Schiebefenster, *das*
sashay /ˈsæʃeɪ/ *v.i.* (Amer.) 1 (walk casually) schlendern 2 (ostentatiously) stolzieren 3 (diagonally) **~ through a crowd** sich durch eine Menschenmenge schlängeln
sash: ~ cord, ~ line *ns.* Gewichtsschnur, *die;* **~ ˈwindow** *n.* Schiebefenster, *das*
sass /sæs/ (Amer. coll.)
A *n.* Frechheit, *die*
B *v.t.* frech sein zu
Sassenach /ˈsæsənæx, ˈsæsənæk/ (Scot., Ir.; usu. derog.)
A *n.* Engländer, *der*/Engländerin, *die*
B *adj.* englisch
sassy /ˈsæsɪ/ *adj.* (Amer. coll.) 1 (cheeky) frech 2 (stylish) schick
sat ▸**sit**
Sat. *abbr.* ▸ⓘ **p. 1048** = **Saturday** Sa.
SAT /sæt/ *abbr.* 1 (Amer. Educ.) = **Scholastic Aptitude Test** ® 2 (Brit. Educ.) = **standard assessment task**

> **SAT**
>
> 1 – *Scholastic Aptitude Test.* Eine standardisierte Eignungsprüfung in den USA, die normalerweise im letzten Schuljahr der **high school** abgelegt wird und die für die meisten Colleges und Universitäten als Zulassungsvoraussetzung gilt. 2 – *standard assessment task.* Ein Test für Schüler im Alter von 7, 11 und 14 Jahren in allen Schulen in England und Wales zur Kontrolle ihres Wissensstandes.

Satan /ˈseɪtən/ *pr. n.* Satan, *der*
satanic /səˈtænɪk/ *adj.* satanisch; teuflisch
satanism /ˈseɪtənɪzm/ *n., no pl., no art.* Satanismus, *der;* Satanskult, *der*
satanist /ˈseɪtənɪst/ *n.* Satanist, *der*/Satanistin, *die*
satchel /ˈsætʃl/ *n.* [Schul]ranzen, *der*
sate /seɪt/ *v.t.* (literary) 1 (gratify) stillen ‹*Hunger, Durst, Verlangen, Zorn*›; zufrieden stellen ‹*Person*›; **feel pleasantly ~d** ein angenehmes Sättigungsgefühl empfinden; **~ oneself on sth.** sich an etw. (*Dat.*) sättigen (geh.) 2 (cloy) übersättigen ‹*Lust, Verlangen*›; **become ~d with/be ~d by sth.** einer Sache (*Gen.*) überdrüssig werden/sein
sateen /səˈtiːn/ *n.* (Textiles) Baumwollsatin, *der*
satellite /ˈsætəlaɪt/
A *n.* 1 (Astronaut., Astron.; also country) Satellit, *der;* **by ~:** über Satellit 2 (fig.) (object associated with another) Ableger, *der* (fig.); (follower) Trabant, *der* (fig.)
B *attrib. adj.* Satelliten‹*film, -bild, -fernsehen, -regierung*›; **~ industries** Zulieferindustrie, *die*
satellite: ~ ˈbroadcasting *n., no pl.* Satellitenfunk, *der;* **~ channel** *n.* Satellitensender, *der;* Satellitenkanal, *der;* **~ dish** *n.* Satellitenschüssel, *die;* **~ film** *n.* Satellitenfilm, *der;* **~ link** *n.* Satellitenverbindung, *die;* **~ naviˈgation** *n., no pl.* Satellitennavigation, *die;* **~ operator** *n.* Satellitenbetreiber, *der;* **~ photograph** *n.* Satellitenaufnahme, *die;* **~ receiver** *n.* Satellitenempfänger, *der;* Satellitenreceiver, *der* (fachspr.); **~ state** *n.* Satellitenstaat, *der;* **~ techˈnology** *n., no pl.* Satellitentechnik, *die;* **~ ˈtelephone** *n.* Satellitentelefon, *das;* **~ ˈtelevision** *n.* Satellitenfernsehen, *das;* **~ town** *n.* Satelliten- *od.* Trabantenstadt, *die*
satiate /ˈseɪʃɪeɪt/ ▸**sate**
satiation /seɪʃɪˈeɪʃn/ *n.* 1 (gratification) Sättigung, *die* 2 (cloying) Übersättigung, *die*
satiety /səˈtaɪətɪ/ *n.* Übersättigung, *die;* **to [the point of] ~:** bis zum Überdruss
satin /ˈsætɪn/
A *n.* Satin, *der*
B *attrib. adj.* 1 (made of ~) Satin- 2 (like ~) seidig
ˈsatinwood *n.* (tree) [ostindischer] Satinholzbaum; (wood) [ostindisches] Satinholz
satiny /ˈsætɪnɪ/ *adj.* seidig
satire /ˈsætaɪə(r)/ *n.* Satire, *die* (**on** auf + *Akk.*); **element/tone of ~:** satirisches Element/satirischer Ton; **gift** *or* **talent for ~:** satirische Begabung
satirical /səˈtɪrɪkl/ *adj.*, **satirically** /səˈtɪrɪkəlɪ/ *adv.* satirisch
satirise ▸**satirize**
satirist /ˈsætɪrɪst/ *n.* Satiriker, *der*/Satirikerin, *die;* **be a ~ of sb./sth.** jmdn./etw. mit satirischen Mitteln angreifen
satirize /ˈsætəraɪz/ *v.t.* 1 (write satire on) satirisch darstellen 2 (describe satirically) ‹*Buch, Film usw.:*› eine Satire sein auf (+ *Akk.*); **be brutally ~d** ‹*Person:*› das Opfer gnadenloser Satire werden
satisfaction /sætɪsˈfækʃn/ *n.* 1 *no pl.* (act) Befriedigung, *die;* **we strive for the ~ of our clients** wir bemühen uns, unsere Kunden zufrieden zu stellen 2 *no pl.* (feeling of gratification) Befriedigung, *die* (**at, with** über + *Akk.*); Genugtuung, *die* (**at, with** über + *Akk.*); **job ~:** Befriedigung in der Arbeit; **it is with [great] ~ that I .../it gives me [great] ~ to ...:** es erfüllt mich mit [großer] Befriedigung, zu ...; **get ~ out of one's work** in seiner Arbeit Befriedigung finden; **there's a lot of ~ [to be had] in doing sth.** es ist sehr befriedigend, etw. zu tun; **what ~ can it give you?** was befriedigt dich daran?; **I can't get any ~ from him** er stellt mich nicht zufrieden 3 *no pl.* (gratified state) **meet with sb.'s** *or* **give sb. [complete] ~:** jmdn. [in jeder Weise] zufrieden stellen; **~ guaranteed** Sie werden garantiert zufrieden sein; **fail to give ~** ‹*Arbeit:*› nicht zufrieden stellend ausfallen; ‹*Angestellte:*› nicht zufrieden stellend arbeiten; **to sb.'s ~, to the ~ of sb.** zu jmds. Zufriedenheit 4 (instance of gratification) Befriedigung, *die;* **it is a great ~ to me that ...:** es erfüllt mich mit großer Befriedigung, dass ...; **give every ~:** in jeder Hinsicht befriedigend sein; **have the ~ of doing sth.** das Vergnügen haben, etw. zu tun; **one of the ~s of the job** eine der Befriedigungen, die die Arbeit gewährt 5 (Hist.: revenge in duel) Satisfaktion, *die*
satisfactorily /sætɪsˈfæktərɪlɪ/ *adv.* zufrieden stellend; richtig ‹*passen*›; **progress ~:** befriedigende Fortschritte machen
satisfactory /sætɪsˈfæktərɪ/ *adj.* zufrieden stellend; angemessen ‹*Bezahlung*›; **'~'** (as school mark) „ausreichend"
satisfied /ˈsætɪsfaɪd/ *adj.* 1 (contented) zufrieden; (replete) satt; **be ~ with doing sth.** sich damit begnügen, etw. zu tun; **be ~ to do sth.** damit zufrieden sein, etw. zu tun 2 (convinced) überzeugt (**of** von); **be ~ that ...:** [davon] überzeugt sein, dass ...
satisfy /ˈsætɪsfaɪ/
A *v.t.* 1 (content) befriedigen; zufrieden stellen ‹*Kunden, Publikum*›; entsprechen (+ *Dat.*) ‹*Vorliebe, Empfinden, Meinung, Zeitgeist*›; erfüllen ‹*Hoffnung, Erwartung*›; **~/fail to ~ the examiners** die Prüfung bestehen/nicht bestehen 2 (rid of want) befriedigen; (put an end to) stillen ‹*Hunger, Durst*›; (make replete) sättigen; **that meal wouldn't ~ a sparrow** davon würde nicht einmal ein Spatz satt 3 (convince) **~ sb. [of sth.]** jmdn. [von etw.] überzeugen; **~ sb. that ...:** jmdn. [davon] überzeugen, dass ...; **~ oneself of** *or* **as to** sich überzeugen von ‹*Wahrheit, Ehrlichkeit*›; sich (*Dat.*) Gewissheit verschaffen über (+ *Akk.*) ‹*Motiv*›; **~ oneself as to what happened** sich (*Dat.*) Klarheit *od.* Gewissheit darüber verschaffen, was geschehen ist 4 (adequately deal with) ausräumen ‹*Einwand, Zweifel*›; erfüllen ‹*Bitte, Forderung, Bedingung*› 5 (pay) begleichen ‹*Schulden*›; befriedigen ‹*Gläubiger, Forderung*› 6 (fulfil) erfüllen ‹*Vertrag, Verpflichtung, Forderung*› 7 (Math.) erfüllen ‹*Gleichung*›
B *v.i.* 1 (make replete) sättigen 2 (be convincing) ‹*Argument:*› überzeugen
satisfying /ˈsætɪsfaɪɪŋ/ *adj.* befriedigend; sättigend ‹*Gericht, Speise*›; zufrieden stellend ‹*Antwort, Lösung, Leistung*›
satphone /ˈsætfəʊn/ *n.* Satellitentelefon, *das*
satsuma /sætˈsuːmə/ *n.* Satsuma, *die*
saturate /ˈsætʃəreɪt, ˈsætjʊreɪt/ *v.t.* 1 (soak) durchnässen; [mit Feuchtigkeit durch]tränken ‹*Boden, Erde*›; **cake ~d in** *or* **with liqueur** mit Likör getränkter Kuchen 2 (fill to capacity) auslasten; sättigen ‹*Markt*› 3 (Mil.: bomb intensively) mit einem Bombenteppich belegen 4 (Phys., Chem.) sättigen
saturated /ˈsætʃəreɪtɪd, ˈsætjʊreɪtɪd/ *adj.* 1 (soaked) durchnässt; völlig nass ‹*Boden*› 2 (imbued) durchdrungen (**with, in** von); **be ~ with** durchdrungen sein von; ganz erfüllt sein von ‹*Duft*›; **be ~ in history/tradition** sehr geschichtsträchtig/traditionsreich sein 3 (filled to capacity) ausgelastet; gesättigt ‹*Markt*› 4 (Phys., Chem.) gesättigt ‹*Lösung, Verbindung, Fett*› 5 (Art) satt ‹*Farbe, Farbton*›
saturation /sætʃəˈreɪʃn, sætjʊˈreɪʃn/ *n.* 1 (soaking, being soaked) Durchnässung, *die* 2 (filling to capacity) Auslastung, *die* (**by, with** mit); (of market) Sättigung, *die* 3 (Mil.) **~ [bombing]** Flächenbombardierung, *die* 4 (Phys., Chem.) Sättigung, *die* 5 (colour intensity) Sattheit, *die*
satuˈration point *n.* 1 (limit of capacity) [Ober]grenze, *die;* (of market) Sättigungspunkt, *der;* (limit of response) Grenze der Aufnahmefähigkeit; (of harmful effect) Grenze der Belastbarkeit 2 (Phys.) Sättigungspunkt, *der*
Saturday /ˈsætədeɪ, ˈsætədɪ/ ▸ⓘ **p. 1048**
A *n.* Sonnabend, *der;* Samstag, *der*
B *adv.* (coll.) **he comes ~s** er kommt sonnabends *od.* samstags. *See also* **Friday**
ˈSaturday job *n.* Samstagsjob, *der*
Saturn /ˈsætən/ *pr. n.* 1 (Astron.) Saturn, *der* 2 (Roman Mythol.) Saturn (*der*)
Saturnalia /sætəˈneɪlɪə/ *n. pl.* (Roman Ant.) Saturnalien *Pl.*
saturnine /ˈsætənaɪn/ *adj.* melancholisch; düster ‹*Einstellung*›; (sinister) finster
satyr /ˈsætə(r)/ *n.* (Mythol.) Satyr, *der*
sauce /sɔːs/
A *n.* 1 Soße, *die;* **be served with the same ~** (fig.) es mit *od.* in gleicher Münze heimgezahlt bekommen; *see also* **gander 1** 2 (fig.: sth. that adds piquancy) Würze, *die* 3 (Amer.: stewed fruit) Kompott, *das* 4 (Amer. coll.) **the ~:** Alkohol; **in the ~:** alkoholisiert 5 (Amer.: vegetables) Beilage, *die* 6 (impudence) Frechheit, *die;* **he's got a lot of ~!** der ist ganz schön frech!; **don't give me any of your ~!** sei nicht so frech!
B *v.t.* (coll.) frech sein zu
sauce: ~ boat *n.* Sauciere, *die;* **~box** *n.* (coll.) Frechdachs, *der* (fam.); **~pan** /ˈsɔːspən/ *n.* Kochtopf, *der;* (with straight handle) [Stiel]kasserolle, *die*
saucer /ˈsɔːsə(r)/ *n.* Untertasse, *die;* **their eyes were like ~s** (fig.) sie machten große Augen (ugs.); **with eyes like ~s** (fig.) mit großen Augen; *see also* **flying saucer**
saucerful /ˈsɔːsəfʊl/ *n.* **a ~ [of milk]** eine Untertasse [Milch *od.* voll Milch]
saucily /ˈsɔːsɪlɪ/ *adv.* 1 (rudely) frech 2 (pertly) keck
sauciness /ˈsɔːsɪnɪs/ *n., no pl.* 1 (rudeness) Frechheit, *die* 2 (pertness, jauntiness) Keckheit, *die*

S

saucy /ˈsɔːsɪ/ *adj.* 1 (rude) frech 2 (pert, jaunty) keck

Saudi /ˈsaʊdɪ/
A *adj.* 1 ▸**Saudi-Arabian A** 2 (of dynasty) saudisch ‹*Prinz, Palast*›
B *n.* 1 ▸**Saudi-Arabian B** 2 (member of dynasty) Saudi, *der*

Saudi Arabia /saʊdɪ əˈreɪbɪə/ *pr. n.* Saudi-Arabien (*das*)

Saudi-Arabian /saʊdɪəˈreɪbɪən/ ▸❶ **p. 1345**
A *adj.* saudi-arabisch
B *n.* Saudi[-Araber], *der*/-Araberin, *die*

sauerkraut /ˈsaʊəkraʊt/ *n.* (Gastr.) Sauerkraut, *das*

sauna /ˈsɔːnə, ˈsaʊnə/ *n.* Sauna, *die;* **have** *or* **take a ~:** saunieren; ein Saunabad nehmen

saunter /ˈsɔːntə(r)/
A *v.i.* schlendern; **I think I will ~ [down/over/up] to the village** ich werde wohl ins Dorf runter-/rüber-/raufschlendern (ugs.)
B *n.* (stroll) Bummel, *der* (ugs.); (leisurely pace) Schlenderschritt, *der;* **at a ~:** im Schlenderschritt; **go for a** *or* **have a ~:** schlendern

saurian /ˈsɔːrɪən/
A *n.* (Zool.) Echse, *die;* (Palaeont.) Saurier, *der*
B *adj.* (Zool.: of the Sauria) der Echsen *nachgestellt;* (lizard-like) echsenartig; **~ reptile** Echse, *die*

sausage /ˈsɒsɪdʒ/ *n.* Wurst, *die;* (smaller) Würstchen, *das;* **not a ~** (fig. coll.) gar nix (ugs.)

sausage: ~ dog *n.* (Brit. coll.) Dackel, *der;* **~ machine** *n.* Wurstfüllmaschine, *die;* (Educ. fig.) Bildungsfabrik, *die* (abwertend); **~ meat** *n.* Wurstmasse, *die;* **~ ˈroll** *n.:* *Blätterteig mit Wurstfüllung*

sauté /ˈsəʊteɪ/ (Cookery)
A *adj.* sautiert (fachspr.); kurz [an]gebraten; **~ potatoes** ≈ Bratkartoffeln
B *n.* Sauté, *das*
C *v.t.*, **~d** *or* **~ed** /ˈsəʊteɪd/ sautieren (fachspr.); kurz [an]braten

Sauterne[s] /səʊˈtɜːn/ *n.* Sauternes[wein], *der*

savage /ˈsævɪdʒ/
A *adj.* 1 (uncivilized) primitiv; wild ‹*Volksstamm*›; unzivilisiert ‹*Land*› 2 (fierce) brutal; wild ‹*Tier*›; scharf ‹*Hund*›; jähzornig ‹*Temperament*›; schonungslos ‹*Kritiker, Satiriker*›; **have a wild, ~ look in one's eye** wild und brutal aussehen; **make a ~ attack on sb.** brutal über jmdn. herfallen; (fig.) jmdn. schonungslos angreifen
B *n.* 1 (uncivilized person) Wilde, *der/die* (veralt.); **behave like ~s** sich wie die Wilden aufführen (abwertend) 2 (barbarous or uncultivated person) Barbar, *der*/Barbarin, *die* (abwertend)
C *v.t.* 1 ‹*Hund:*› anfallen ‹*Kind usw.*›; (lacerate) zerfleischen 2 (fig.) ‹*Kritiker, Journalist:*› herfallen über (+ *Akk.*) ‹*Politiker usw.*›; ‹*Kritiker, Zeitung:*› schonungslos verreißen ‹*Theaterstück usw.*›

savagely /ˈsævɪdʒlɪ/ *adv.* (fiercely) brutal; wild ‹*brüllen*›; wüst ‹*beschimpfen*›; schonungslos ‹*kritisieren*›

savagery /ˈsævɪdʒrɪ/ *n., no pl.* 1 (uncivilized condition) Unzivilisiertheit, *die* 2 (ferocity) Brutalität, *die*

savannah (savanna) /səˈvænə/ *n.* (Geog.) Savanne, *die*

save /seɪv/
A *v.t.* 1 (rescue) retten (**from** vor + *Dat.*); **please, ~ me!** bitte helfen Sie mir!; **~ sb. from the clutches of the enemy/from making a mistake** jmdn. aus den Klauen des Feindes retten/davor bewahren, dass er einen Fehler macht; **alcoholics must be ~d from themselves** Alkoholiker müssen vor sich (*Dat.*) selbst geschützt werden; **he ~d my reputation** er rettete meinen guten Ruf; **~ oneself from falling** sich [beim Hinfallen] fangen; **be ~d by the bell** (fig. coll.) gerade noch mal davonkommen (ugs.); **~ the day** die Situation retten; **sb. can't do sth. to ~ his/her life** (coll.) jmd. kann etw. [ganz] einfach nicht tun; *see also* **bacon; face A 1; life 1; skin A 1** 2 (keep undamaged) schonen ‹*Kleidung, Möbelstück*› 3 **God ~ the King/Queen** *etc.* Gott behüte *od.* beschütze den König/die Königin *usw.;* **[God] ~ sb. from sb./sth.** Gott bewahre jmdn. vor jmdm./etw. 4 (Theol.) retten ‹*Sünder, Seele, Menschen*›; **be past saving** nicht mehr zu retten sein; **~ oneself** ‹*Sünder:*› seine Seele retten; **Jesus ~s!** Jesus ist der Retter! 5 (put aside) aufheben; sparen ‹*Geld*›; sammeln ‹*Rabattmarken, Briefmarken*›; (conserve) sparsam umgehen mit ‹*Geldmitteln, Kräften, Wasser*›; **~ money for a rainy day** (fig.) einen Notgroschen zurücklegen; **~ water for the drought** Wasser für die Trockenzeit sammeln; **~ oneself** sich schonen; seine Kräfte sparen; **~ one's breath** sich (*Dat.*) seine Worte sparen; **you can ~ your pains** *or* **trouble/apologies** die Mühe/deine Entschuldigungen kannst du dir sparen; **~ a seat for sb.** jmdm. einen Platz freihalten 6 (make unnecessary) sparen ‹*Geld, Zeit, Energie*›; **~ sb./oneself sth.** jmdm./sich etw. ersparen; **~ oneself money/half the cost** Geld/die Hälfte des Preises [ein]sparen; **~ sb./oneself doing sth.** *or* **having to do sth.** es jmdm./sich ersparen, etw. tun zu müssen; *see also* **save A 6** 7 (avoid losing) nicht verlieren ‹*Satz, Karte, Stich*›; (prevent from making a score) abwehren ‹*Schuss, Ball*›; verhindern ‹*Tor*›; (Cricket) ‹*Fänger:*› verhindern ‹*Lauf*›; **his goal ~d the match for his team** sein Tor rettete seine Mannschaft vor der Niederlage 8 (Computing) speichern; sichern; **~ sth. on [to a] disk** etw. auf Diskette abspeichern
B *v.i.* 1 (put money by) sparen; **~ with a building society** bei einer Bausparkasse sparen 2 (avoid waste) sparen (**on** *Akk.*); **~ on food** am Essen sparen 3 (Sport) ‹*Torwart:*› halten
C *n.* (Sport) Abwehr, *die;* Parade, *die* (fachspr.); **make a ~** ‹*Torwart:*› halten
D *prep.* (arch./poet./rhet.) mit Ausnahme (+ *Gen.*)
E *conj.* (arch.) außer; **~ for sth.** von etw. abgesehen

Phrasal verb
• **~ ˈup**
A *v.t.* sparen; sammeln, sparen ‹*Marken, Gutscheine usw.*›
B *v.i.* sparen (**for** für, auf + *Akk.*)

save-as-you-ˈearn *n.* (Brit.) *Sparen durch regelmäßige Abbuchung eines bestimmten Betrages vom Lohn-/Gehaltskonto*

saveloy /ˈsævəlɔɪ/ *n.* Zervelatwurst, *die*

saver /ˈseɪvə(r)/ *n.* 1 (of money) Sparer, *der*/Sparerin, *die* 2 *in comb.* (device) **sth. is a time-~/labour-~/money-~:** etw. spart Zeit/Arbeit/Geld 3 **~ of souls** Seelenretter, *der*/-retterin, *die*

saving /ˈseɪvɪŋ/
A *n.* 1 *in pl.* (money saved) Ersparnisse *Pl.;* **have money put by in ~s** Geld zurückgelegt haben; **how much have you got in your ~s?** wie viel Geld hast du [an]gespart? 2 (rescue; also Theol.) Rettung, *die* 3 (instance of economy) Ersparnis, *die;* **~ in** *or* **of** *or* **on time/money/fuel/effort** Zeit-/Geld-/Brennstoff-/Arbeitsersparnis, *die;* **make a ~ in** *or* **of money/on equipment/in** *or* **of time** Geld/Ausrüstung/Zeit [ein]sparen; **there's no ~ at all** es wird überhaupt nichts eingespart; **there are ~s to be made on clothes** man kann beim Kleiderkauf einiges sparen
B *adj.* 1 *in comb.* ‹*Kosten, Benzin*› sparend 2 (redeeming) **the only ~ feature of the play** das einzig Versöhnliche an dem Stück
C *prep.* (except) bis auf (+ *Akk.*)

saving: ~ clause *n.* einschränkende Klausel; Vorbehaltsklausel, *die;* **~ ˈgrace** *n.* versöhnender Zug; **her only ~ grace was her honesty** das Einzige, was einen mit ihr versöhnte, war ihre Ehrlichkeit

savings: ~ account *n.* Sparkonto, *das;* **~ account and loan association** (Amer.) ▸**building society;** **~ bank** *n.* Sparkasse, *die;* **~ certificate** *n.* (Brit.) Staatspapier, *das*

saviour (*Amer.:* **savior**) /ˈseɪvjə(r)/ *n.* 1 Retter, *der*/Retterin, *die;* (thing) Rettung, *die* 2 (Relig.) **our/the S~:** unser/der Heiland

savoir-faire /sævwɑːˈfeə(r)/ *n.* Gewandtheit, *die*

savor (Amer.) ▸**savour**

savory[1] (Amer.) ▸**savoury**

savory[2] /ˈseɪvərɪ/ *n.* (Bot.) Bohnenkraut, *das*

savour /ˈseɪvə(r)/ (Brit.)
A *n.* 1 (flavour) Geschmack, *der;* (fig.) Charakter, *der* 2 (trace) **a ~ of sth.** ein Hauch *od.* Anflug von etw. 3 (enjoyable quality) Reiz, *der*
B *v.t.* (lit. or fig., literary) genießen; **that is a dish/perfume I particularly ~:** das Gericht/Parfüm ist ein ganz besonderer Genuss für mich
C *v.i.* **sth. ~s of sth.** (fig.) etw. schmeckt nach etw. (fig.)

savoury /ˈseɪvərɪ/ (Brit.)
A *adj.* 1 (not sweet) pikant; (having salt flavour) salzig 2 (appetizing) appetitanregend
B *n.* [pikantes] Häppchen

savoy /səˈvɔɪ/ *n.* **~ [cabbage]** Wirsing[kohl], *der*

Savoy *pr. n.* Savoyen (*das*)

savvy /ˈsævɪ/ (coll.)
A *v.t.* kapieren (ugs.); **I don't ~ French** Französisch hab ich nicht drauf (salopp)
B *v.i.* **…, ~?** …, kapiert? (ugs.); **no ~** (I don't know) keine Ahnung (ugs.); (I don't understand) nix capito (salopp)
C *n.* Durchblick, *der* (ugs.)
D *adj.* ausgebufft (salopp)

saw[1] /sɔː/
A *n.* Säge, *die;* **musical ~:** singende Säge
B *v.t., p.p.* **sawn** /sɔːn/ *or* **sawed** [zer]sägen; (make with ~) sägen; **~ across** *or* **through** durchsägen; **~ in half** in der Mitte durchsägen; **~ the air [with one's hands/arms]** [mit den Händen/Armen] in der Luft herumfuchteln (ugs.)
C *v.i., p.p.* **sawn** *or* **sawed** 1 sägen; **~ through sth.** etw. durchsägen 2 (fig.) **~ away [at the violin]** [auf der Geige] drauflossägen (ugs.)

Phrasal verbs
• **~ ˈdown** *v.t.* umsägen ‹*Baum*›
• **~ ˈoff** *v.t.* absägen
• **~ ˈup** *v.t.* zersägen (**into** in + *Akk.*)

saw[2] *n.* (saying) Sprichwort, *das*

saw[3] ▸**see**[1]

saw: ~dust *n.* Sägemehl, *das;* **~-edged** *adj.* gezähnt ‹*Klinge*›; **a ~-edged knife** ein Sägemesser; **~fish** *n.* Sägerochen, *der;* Sägefisch, *der;* **~mill** *n.* Sägemühle, *die*

sawn ▸**saw**[1] **B, C**

ˈsawn-off *adj.* (Brit.) 1 abgesägt; ‹*Gewehr*› mit abgesägtem Lauf 2 (coll.: undersized) mickrig (ugs. abwertend)

saw: ~-pit *n.* Sägegrube, *die;* **~tooth[ed]** /ˈsɔːtuːθ(t)/ *adj.* 1 gezackt ‹*Berge*›; Säge‹*dach*›; 2 (Electr.) Sägezahn‹*generator, -schwingung, -spannung*›

sawyer /ˈsɔːjə(r)/ *n.* Säger, *der;* Sägemüller, *der*

sax /sæks/ *n.* (Mus. coll.) Saxophon, *das*

saxe /sæks/ *n.* **~ [blue]** Sächsischblau, *das*

saxifrage /ˈsæksɪfrɪdʒ, ˈsæksɪfreɪdʒ/ *n.* (Bot.) Steinbrech, *der*

Saxon /ˈsæksn/
A *n.* 1 Sachse, *der*/Sächsin, *die* 2 (Ling.) Sächsisch, *das;* **[Old] ~:** Westsächsisch, *das*
B *adj.* 1 sächsisch 2 (Ling.) sächsisch; (of Old ~) westsächsisch

Saxony /ˈsæksənɪ/ *pr. n.* Sachsen (*das*)

saxophone /ˈsæksəfəʊn/ *n.* (Mus.) Saxophon, *das*

saxophonist /sækˈsɒfənɪst, ˈsæksəfəʊnɪst/ *n.* ▸❶ **p. 1260** Saxophonist, *der*/Saxophonistin, *die*

say /seɪ/
A *v.t., pres. t.* **he says** /sez/, *p.t. & p.p.* **said** /sed/ 1 sagen; **~ sth. out loud** etw. aussprechen *od.* laut sagen; **~ sth. to oneself** sich (*Dat.*) etw. sagen; **he said something about going out** er hat etwas von Ausgehen gesagt; **please ~ something** bitte sag doch etwas; (make a short speech) sage bitte ein paar Worte; **all I can ~ is …:** ich kann nur sagen …; **what more can I ~?** was soll ich da noch [groß] sagen?; **I don't know ˈwhat to ~:** ich weiß nicht, was ich [dazu] sagen soll; **I wouldn't [go so far as to] ~ that, but …:** das würde ich nicht [unbedingt] sagen, aber …; **…, not to ~ …:** …, um nicht zu sagen …; **it ~s a lot** *or* **much** *or* **something for sb./sth. that …:** es spricht sehr für jmdn./etw., dass …; **have a lot/not much to ~**

S

for oneself viel reden/nicht viel von sich geben; **~ no 'more!** (I understand) schon gut; **we'll** *or* **let's ~ no more about it** reden wir nicht mehr davon; **there is no** *or* **nothing more to be said** es erübrigt sich jedes weitere Wort (**on** zu); **to ~ nothing of** (quite apart from) ganz zu schweigen von; mal ganz abgesehen von; **that is to ~:** das heißt; **as much as to ~:** als wollte er/sie *usw.* sagen …; **as you might ~:** wie man sagen könnte; **having said that, that said** (nevertheless) abgesehen davon; **when all is said and done** letzten Endes; **~ what you 'like** du kannst sagen, was du willst; **though I ~ it myself …:** wenn ich es mal selbst so sagen darf; **you can ~ 'that again, you 'said it** (coll.) das kannst du laut sagen (ugs.); **you don't '~ [so]** (coll.) was du nicht sagst (ugs.); **~s** *or* **said he** *etc.*/**said I** *or* (coll.) **~s I** sagt er/(ugs.) sag ich; **~s you** (coll.) wers glaubt, wird selig (ugs. scherzh.); **~s who?** (coll.) wer sagt das?; **I'll ~ [it is]!** (coll.: it certainly is) und wie!; **don't let** *or* **never let it be said [that] …:** niemand soll sagen können, [dass] …; **they** *or* **people ~** *or* **it is said [that] …:** man sagt, [dass] …; **…, they ~:** …, sagt man *od.* heißt es; **I can't ~ [that] I like cats/the idea** ich kann nicht gerade sagen *od.* behaupten, dass ich Katzen mag/die Idee gut finde; **what I [always] ~ is …:** also, ich sage immer, …; **[well,] I 'must ~:** also, ich muss schon sagen; **I should ~ so/not** ich glaube schon/nicht; (emphatic) bestimmt/bestimmt nicht; **Is it true that …? — So she ~s** Stimmt es, dass …? — Das sagt sie [jedenfalls]; **what have you got to ~ for yourself?** was haben Sie zu Ihren Gunsten zu sagen?; **there's a lot to be said for** *or* **in favour of/against sth.** es spricht viel für/gegen etw.; **there's something to be said on both sides/either side** man kann für beide Seiten/jede Seite Argumente anführen; **who can** *or* **who is to ~?** (rhet.) wer weiß das schon *od.* kann das schon sagen?; **I cannot** *or* **could not ~:** das kann ich nicht sagen; **I can't ~ fairer than that** ein besseres Angebot kann ich nicht machen; **he didn't ~:** er hat dazu *od.* darüber nichts gesagt; **I'd rather not ~:** ich möchte es lieber nicht sagen; **and so ~ all of us** der Meinung sind wir auch; **what do** *or* **would you ~ to sb./sth.?** (think about) was hältst du von jmdm./etw.?; was würdest du zu jmdm./etw. sagen?; **how ~ you?** (Law) wie lautet Ihr Urteil?; **[let us** *or* **shall we] ~:** sagen wir mal; **~ it were true, what then?** angenommen es stimmt, was dann?; *see also* **dare A 1; hearsay; no B 2; so¹ B; when A 1; word A 2; yes A**

2 (recite, repeat, speak words of) sprechen ‹*Gebet, Text*›; aufsagen ‹*Einmaleins, Gedicht*›; lesen ‹*Messe*›

3 (have specified wording or reading) sagen; ‹*Zeitung:*› schreiben; ‹*Uhr:*› zeigen ‹*Uhrzeit*›; **the Bible ~s** *or* **it ~s in the Bible [that] …:** in der Bibel heißt es, dass …; die Bibel sagt, dass …; **a sign ~ing …:** ein Schild mit der Aufschrift …; **what does it ~ here?** was steht hier?

4 (express, convey information) sagen; **~ things well/eloquently** sich gut/gewandt ausdrücken; **what I'm trying to ~ is this** was ich sagen will, ist Folgendes; **his expression said it all** sein Gesichtsausdruck sagte alles; **a novel that really ~s something** ein Roman, der wirklich eine Aussage hat; **~ nothing to sb.** (fig.) ‹*Musik, Kunst:*› jmdm. nichts bedeuten; **which/that is not ~ing much** *or* **a lot** was nicht viel heißen will/das will nicht viel heißen; *see also* **soon 2**

5 (order) sagen; **do as** *or* **what I ~:** tun Sie, was ich sage; **he said [to us] to be ready at ten** er hat gesagt, wir sollten um zehn fertig sein

6 *in pass.* **she is said to be clever/have done it** man sagt, sie sei klug/habe es getan; **a horse is said to be a pony when …:** man bezeichnet ein Pferd als Pony, wenn …; **the said Mr Smith** (Law/joc.) besagter Mr. Smith (Papierdt., scherzh.)

7 **215, ~ two hundred and fifteen** 215, in Worten: zweihundert[und]fünfzehn

B *v.i., forms as* **A** **1** (speak) sagen; **I ~!** (Brit.) (seeking attention) Entschuldigung!; (admiring) Donnerwetter!; (dismayed) ich fürchte; (reproachful) ich muss schon sagen!

2 *in imper.* (poet.: tell) sag an! (veralt.)

3 *in imper.* (Amer.) Mensch!

C *n.* **1** (share in decision) **have a** *or* **some ~:** ein Mitspracherecht haben (**in** bei); **have no ~:** nichts zu sagen haben

2 (power of decision) **the [final] ~:** das letzte Wort (**in** bei)

3 (what one has to say) **have one's ~:** seine Meinung sagen; (chance to speak) **get one's** *or* **have a ~:** zu Wort kommen

SAYE *abbr.* (Brit.) **= save-as-you-earn**

saying /'seɪɪŋ/ *n.* **1** (maxim) Redensart, *die;* **there is a ~ that …:** wie es [im Sprichwort/in der Maxime] heißt, …; **as the ~ goes** wie es so schön heißt **2** (remark) Ausspruch, *der;* **the ~s of Chairman Mao** die Worte des Vorsitzenden Mao **3** **there is no ~ what/why …:** man kann nicht sagen, was/warum …; **go without ~:** sich von selbst verstehen

'say-so *n.* **1** (power of decision) **on/without sb.'s ~:** auf/ohne jmds. Anweisung (*Akk.*); **the final ~:** das letzte Wort **2** (assertion) **I won't believe it just on your ~:** das glaube ich dir nicht einfach so

sc. /'saɪlɪset/ *abbr.* **= scilicet** sc.; d.h.

scab /skæb/ *n.* **1** (over wound, sore) [Wund-]schorf, *der;* **form a ~:** verschorfen; **be covered in ~s** mit Schorf bedeckt sein **2** *no pl.* (skin disease) Räude, *die;* (plant disease) Schorf, *der* **3** (derog.: strike-breaker) Streikbrecher, *der*/-brecherin, *die;* **use ~ labour** Streikbrecher einsetzen

scabbard /'skæbəd/ *n.* Scheide, *die*

scabby /'skæbɪ/ *adj.* **1** (covered in scabs) voller Krusten *nachgestellt* **2** (esp. Scottish & Irish coll.: despicable, shabby) schäbig

scabies /'skeɪbi:z/ *n.* ▸ **p. 1231** (Med.) Krätze, *die;* Skabies, *die* (fachspr.)

scabious /'skeɪbɪəs/ *n.* (Bot.) Krätz[en]kraut, *das;* Skabiose, *die* (fachspr.)

scabrous /'skeɪbrəs/ *adj.* **1** (requiring tact) heikel ‹*Thema*› **2** (indecent) geschmacklos **3** (Bot., Physiol., Zool.) rau

scads /skædz/ *n. pl.* (Amer. coll.) **~ of money** *etc.* haufenweise Geld *usw.* (ugs.)

scaffold /'skæfəld/ *n.* **1** (for execution) Schafott, *das;* **go to the ~:** auf das Schafott kommen **2** (for building) Gerüst, *das*

scaffolding /'skæfəldɪŋ/ *n., no pl.* Gerüst, *das;* (materials) Gerüstmaterial, *das;* **be surrounded by ~:** eingerüstet sein (Bauw.); **erect [a] ~ around** einrüsten (Bauw.)

'scaffolding pole *n.* Gerüststange, *die*

scalable /'skeɪləbl/ *adj.* scalierbar

scalar /'skeɪlə(r)/ (Math.)

A *n.* Skalar, *der*

B *adj.* skalar; Skalar-

scald /skɔ:ld, skɒld/

A *n.* Verbrühung, *die*

B *v.t.* **1** verbrühen; **~ oneself** *or* **one's skin** sich verbrühen; **be ~ed to death** tödliche Verbrühungen erleiden; **cry ~ing tears** heiße Tränen weinen; **~ing hot** brühheiß; **like a ~ed cat** wie von der Tarantel gestochen **2** (Cookery) erhitzen ‹*Milch*› **3** (clean with boiling water) auskochen **4** (remove hair or feathers from) [ab]brühen ‹*Schwein, Geflügel*›; (remove skin from) überbrühen ‹*Gemüse, Obst*›

scale¹ /skeɪl/

A *n.* **1** Schuppe, *die;* (of rust) Flocke, *die;* **the ~s fall from sb.'s eyes** (fig.) es fällt jmdm. wie Schuppen von den Augen **2** *no pl.* (deposit in kettles, boilers, etc.) Kesselstein, *der;* (on teeth) Zahnstein, *der*

B *v.t.* **1** (remove scales from) [ab]schuppen ‹*Fisch*› **2** (remove deposit from) von Kesselstein befreien ‹*Kessel, Boiler*›; von Zahnstein befreien ‹*Zähne*›

scale²

A *n.* **1** *in sing. or pl.* (weighing instrument) **~[s]** Waage, *die;* **a pair** *or* **set of ~s** eine Waage; **bathroom/kitchen/letter ~[s]** Personen-/Küchen-/Briefwaage, *die;* **the ~s are evenly balanced** (fig.) die Chancen sind ausgewogen **2** (dish of balance) Waagschale, *die;* **tip** *or* **turn the ~[s]** (fig.) den Ausschlag geben; **tip** *or* **turn the ~[s] at 65 kilos** 65 Kilo wiegen *od.* auf die Waage bringen **3** (Astrol.) **the S~s** die Waage; *see also* **archer 2**

B *v.t.* wiegen

scale³

A *n.* **1** (series of degrees) Skala, *die;* **the social ~:** die gesellschaftliche Stufenleiter **2** (Mus.) Tonleiter, *die* **3** (dimensions) Ausmaß, *das;* (standard) Richtschnur, *die;* **be on a small ~:** bescheidenen Umfang haben; **on a grand ~:** im großen Stil; **on a commercial ~:** gewerbsmäßig; **plan on a large ~:** in großem Rahmen planen; **on an international ~:** auf internationaler Ebene; ‹*Katastrophe*› von internationalem Ausmaß; **economies of ~:** Einsparungen durch Produktionserweiterung **4** (ratio of reduction) Maßstab, *der; attrib.* maßstab[s]gerecht ‹*Modell, Zeichnung*›; **what is the ~ of the map?** welchen Maßstab hat diese Karte?; **a map with a ~ of 1 : 250,000** eine Karte im Maßstab 1 : 250 000; **on a large/small ~:** in großem/kleinem Maßstab; **to ~:** maßstab[s-]gerecht; **be drawn on** *or* **to a ~ of 1 : 2** im Maßstab 1 : 2 gezeichnet sein; **be in ~:** maßstab[s]getreu sein; **be in ~ with sth.** im Maßstab zu etw. passen; **be out of ~:** im Maßstab nicht passen (**with** zu) **5** (indication) (on map, plan) Maßstab, *der;* (on thermometer, ruler, exposure meter) [Anzeige]skala, *die;* (instrument) Messstab, *der;* **what ~ are these temperatures measured in?** nach welcher [Einheiten]skala werden diese Temperaturen gemessen?; **a ruler marked off in the metric ~:** ein Lineal mit Zentimeterskala **6** (Math.) **~ [of notation]** Positionssystem, *das;* **decimal ~:** Dezimalsystem, *das;* **binary ~:** Dualsystem, *das;* Binärsystem, *das*

B *v.t.* **1** (climb, clamber up) ersteigen ‹*Festung, Mauer, Leiter, Gipfel*›; erklettern ‹*Felswand, Leiter, Gipfel*› **2** (represent in proportion) [ab]stufen, staffeln ‹*Fahrpreise*›; maßstab[s]gerecht anfertigen ‹*Zeichnung*›; **~ production/prices to demand** die Produktion/Preise an die Nachfrage anpassen **3** (Computing) skalieren

Phrasal verbs

- **~ 'back** *v.t.* zurückschrauben ‹*Kapazität, Produktion*›; einschränken ‹*Aktivitäten, Aspekte*›; nach unten korrigieren ‹*Prognose*›
- **~ 'down** *v.t.* [entsprechend] drosseln ‹*Produktion*›; [entsprechende] Abstriche machen an (+ *Dat.*) ‹*Ideen*›; **we ~d down our plans** wir haben bei unseren Planungen Abstriche gemacht; **a ~d down version** eine kleinere Version
- **~ 'up** *v.t.* [entsprechend] vergrößern ‹*Umfang, Ausmaß*›; **we ~d up our plans** wir haben im größeren Maßstab neu geplant; **a ~d up version** eine größere Version

scalene /'skeɪli:n/ *adj.* (Geom.) ungleichseitig ‹*Dreieck*›

'scale pan *n.* Waagschale, *die*

scaling ladder /'skeɪlɪŋlædə(r)/ *n.* Sturmleiter, *die;* (of fire engine) Feuer[wehr]leiter, *die*

scallion /'skæljən/ *n.* (Bot.) **1** ▸ **shallot** **2** (spring onion) Frühlingszwiebel, *die*

scallop /'skæləp, 'skɒləp/

A *n.* **1** *in pl.* (ornamental edging) Feston, *das;* Bogenkante, *die* **2** (Zool.) Kammmuschel, *die;* (Gastr.) Jakobsmuschel, *die* **3** (Cookery: pan) muschelförmige Schale

B *v.t.* festonieren

scallop-'edge *n.* Bogenkante, *die*

scalloping /'skæləpɪŋ, 'skɒləpɪŋ/ *n.* Feston, *das;* **be decorated with ~:** festoniert sein

'scallop shell *n.* Kammmuschel[schale], *die*

scallywag /'skælɪwæg/ *n.* Schlingel, *der* (scherzh.); Tunichtgut, *der*

scalp /skælp/

A *n.* **1** ▸ **p. 951** Kopfhaut, *die* **2** (war trophy) Skalp, *der;* (fig.) Trophäe, *die;* **be after sb.'s ~** (fig.) jmdm. an den Kragen wollen; **the newspapers call for ~s** (fig.) die Zeitungen wollen Köpfe rollen sehen

B *v.t.* **1** skalpieren **2** (criticize) kein gutes Haar lassen an (+ *Dat.*) (ugs.) ‹*Person, Buch*› **3** (Amer.) (defeat) vernichtend schlagen, fertig machen (ugs.) ‹*Partei, Gegner*› **4** (Amer. coll.: sell) mit

S

hohem Gewinn weiterverkaufen ‹*Aktien, Eintrittskarte*›; **get ~ed tickets** Karten auf dem Schwarzmarkt bekommen

scalpel /'skælpl/ *n.* (Med.) Skalpell, *das*

scalper /'skælpə(r)/ *n.* (Amer. coll.) kleiner Spekulant/kleine Spekulantin; (ticket tout) [Karten]schwarzhändler, *der*/-händlerin, *die*

scaly /'skeɪlɪ/ *adj.* **1▸** schuppig; abblätternd ‹*Farbe, Rost*›; **be ~** ‹*Schlange*:› eine schuppige Haut haben **2▸** (covered in deposit) mit Kesselstein überzogen; (covered in tartar) mit Zahnstein überzogen **3▸** (forming deposit) **~ substance** *or* **incrustation** Kesselstein, *der*; Wasserstein, *der*

scam /skæm/ *n.* (coll.) Masche, *die* (ugs.)

scamp /skæmp/

A *n.* (coll.) Spitzbube, *der* (fam.)

B *v.t.* ▸**skimp A**

scamper /'skæmpə(r)/

A *v.i.* ‹*Person*:› flitzen; ‹*Tier*:› huschen; (hop) hoppeln; **the mice ~ed to and fro** die Mäuse huschten hin und her; **~ down the stairs** die Treppe hinunterflitzen; (romp) **~ through the woods/park** durch die Wälder/den Park tollen

B *n.* **have a ~** (romp) herumtollen

scampi /'skæmpɪ/ *n. pl.* Scampi *Pl.*

scan /skæn/

A *v.t.*, **-nn-** **1▸** (examine intensely) [genau] studieren; (search thoroughly, lit. or fig.) absuchen (**for** nach) **2▸** (look over cursorily) flüchtig ansehen; überfliegen ‹*Zeitung, Liste usw.*› (**for** auf der Suche nach) **3▸** (Computing) scannen; **~ in** einscannen **4▸** (examine for radioactivity) auf Radioaktivität (*Akk.*) untersuchen **5▸** (examine with beam) durchleuchten ‹*Gepäck*›; ‹*Radar*:› [mittels Strahlen] abtasten ‹*Luftraum*›; ‹*Flugsicherung*:› [mittels Radar] überwachen ‹*Luftraum*› **6▸** (Med.) szintigraphisch untersuchen ‹*Körper, Organ*› **7▸** (Pros.) das Metrum bestimmen von ‹*Vers[zeile]*› **8▸** (Telev.) abtasten ‹*Ziel, Bild*›

B *v.i.*, **-nn-** ‹*Vers[zeile]*:› das richtige Versmaß haben; **make sth. ~:** etw. in das richtige Versmaß bringen

C *n.* **1▸** (thorough search) Absuchen, *das* **2▸** (quick look) **[cursory] ~:** flüchtiger Blick; **do a quick ~ of** *or* **through** überfliegen, flüchtig durchblättern ‹*Zeitung*› **3▸** (examination for radioactivity) Untersuchung auf Radioaktivität (*Akk.*) **4▸** (examination by beam) Durchleuchtung, *die*; **check the radar ~ for sth.** den Radarschirm nach etw. absuchen **5▸** (Med.) szintigraphische Untersuchung; (image) Szintigramm, *das*; **body/brain ~:** Ganzkörper-/Gehirnscan, *der*; **have a ~:** sich szintigraphisch untersuchen lassen

scandal /'skændl/ *n.* **1▸** Skandal, *der* (**about/of** um); (story) Skandalgeschichte, *die*; **cause** *or* **create a ~:** einen Skandal verursachen **2▸** (outrage) Empörung, *die*; **arouse a feeling** *or* **sense of ~ in sb.** jmdn. mit Empörung erfüllen **3▸** *no art.* (damage to reputation) Schande, *die*; **be untouched by ~:** einen makellosen Ruf haben; **be ruined by ~:** durch einen Skandal ruiniert werden **4▸** (malicious gossip) Klatsch, *der* (ugs.); (in newspapers etc.) Skandalgeschichten *Pl.*

scandalize (**scandalise**) /'skændəlaɪz/ *v.t.* schockieren

scandalmonger /'skændlmʌŋgə(r)/ *n.* Klatschmaul, *das* (salopp abwertend); (in the press) Schreiber/Schreiberin von Skandalgeschichten

scandalmongering /'skændlmʌŋgərɪŋ/ *n.* Verbreitung von Skandalgeschichten

scandalous /'skændələs/ *adj.* skandalös; schockierend ‹*Bemerkung*›; Skandal‹*blatt, -presse, -geschichte, -bericht*›; **how ~!** unerhört!; **this is ~:** das ist ein Skandal

'scandal sheet *n.* (derog.) Skandalblatt, *das* (abwertend); Klatschblatt, *das* (ugs. abwertend)

Scandinavia /skændɪ'neɪvɪə/ *pr. n.* Skandinavien (*das*)

Scandinavian /skændɪ'neɪvɪən/

A *adj.* skandinavisch; **sb. is ~:** jmd. ist Skandinavier/Skandinavierin

B *n.* **1▸** (person) Skandinavier, *der*/Skandinavierin, *die* **2▸** (Ling.) skandinavische Sprachen

scanner /'skænə(r)/ *n.* **1▸** (to detect radioactivity) Geigerzähler, *der* **2▸** (radar aerial) Radarantenne, *die* **3▸** (Computing, Med.) Scanner, *der* **4▸** (Telev.) Bildabtaster, *der*

scansion /'skænʃn/ *n.* (Pros.) metrische Gliederung; (rhythm analysis) Bestimmung des Versmaßes

scant /skænt/ *adj.* (arch./literary) karg (geh.) ‹*Lob, Lohn*›; wenig ‹*Rücksicht*›; **pay sb./sth. ~ attention** jmdn./etw. kaum beachten; **a ~ two hours** knappe zwei Stunden

scantily /'skæntɪlɪ/ *adv.* kärglich; spärlich ‹*bekleidet*›

scanty /'skæntɪ/ *adj.* spärlich; knapp ‹*Bikini*›; nur wenig ‹*Vergnügen, Spaß*›

scapegoat /'skeɪpgəʊt/ *n.* Sündenbock, *der*; **make sb. a ~:** jmdn. zum Sündenbock machen; **act as** *or* **be a ~ for sth.** als Sündenbock für etw. herhalten müssen

scapegrace /'skeɪpgreɪs/ *n.* Taugenichts, *der*

scapula /'skæpjʊlə/ *n.*, *pl.* **~e** /'skæpjʊliː/ (Anat.) Schulterblatt, *das*

scar /skɑː(r)/

A *n.* (lit. or fig.) Narbe, *die*; **duelling ~:** Schmiss, *der*; **battle ~:** Kriegsnarbe, *die*; **bear the ~s of sth.** (fig.) von etw. gezeichnet sein; **be a ~ on the landscape** (fig.) ein Schandfleck in der Landschaft sein

B *v.t.*, **-rr-:** **~ sb./sb.'s face** bei jmdm./in jmds. Gesicht (*Dat.*) Narben hinterlassen; **~ sb. for life** (fig.) jmdn. für sein ganzes Leben zeichnen; **leave sb. [badly] ~red** (lit. or fig.) [schlimme] Narben bei jmdm. hinterlassen

C *v.i.* **~ over** vernarben

scarab /'skærəb/ *n.* (Zool., gem) Skarabäus, *der*

scarce /skeəs/

A *adj.* **1▸** (insufficient) knapp **2▸** (rare) selten; **make oneself ~** (coll.) sich aus dem Staub machen (ugs.)

B *adv.* (arch./literary) kaum

scarcely /'skeəslɪ/ *adv.* kaum; **there was ~ a drop of wine left** es war fast kein Tropfen Wein mehr da; **~ [ever]** kaum [jemals]; **it is ~ likely** es ist wenig wahrscheinlich; **she will ~ be pleased** (iron.: by no means) sie wird sich nicht gerade freuen

scarceness /'skeəsnɪs/ *n.*, *no pl.* Knappheit, *die* (**of** an + *Dat.*)

scarcity /'skeəsɪtɪ/ *n.* **1▸** (short supply) Knappheit, *die* (**of** an + *Dat.*); **there is a ~ of sugar** es herrscht Zuckerknappheit; **~ of teachers** Lehrermangel, *der*; **food ~:** Lebensmittelknappheit, *die* **2▸** *no pl.* (rareness) Seltenheit, *die*; **have [a] ~ value** Seltenheitswert haben

scare /skeə(r)/

A *n.* **1▸** (sensation of fear) Schreck[en], *der*; **give sb. a ~:** jmdm. einen Schreck[en] einjagen; **I had/it gave me a [nasty] ~:** ich bekam einen [bösen] Schrecken **2▸** (general alarm; panic) [allgemeine] Hysterie; **bomb ~:** Bombendrohung, *die*; **food poisoning ~:** Alarm wegen Lebensmittelvergiftung; *attrib.* **~ story** Schauergeschichte, *die*

B *v.t.* **1▸** (frighten) Angst machen (+ *Dat.*); (startle) erschrecken; **he/hard work/your threat doesn't ~ me** ich habe keine Angst vor ihm/harter Arbeit/deiner Drohung; **~ sb. into doing sth.** jmdn. dazu bringen, etw. [aus Angst] zu tun; **~ sb. out of his mind** *or* **skin** *or* **wits** (fig.), **~ sb. rigid** *or* **silly** *or* **stiff** (fig.), **~ the wits** *or* (coarse) **the shit out of sb.** (fig.) jmdm. eine wahnsinnige Angst einjagen (ugs.); (startle) jmdn. zu Tode erschrecken; **horror films ~ the pants off me** (coll.) bei Horrorfilmen habe ich immer eine wahnsinnige Angst (ugs.) **2▸** (drive away) verscheuchen ‹*Vögel*›

C *v.i.* erschrecken (**at** bei); ‹*Pferd*:› scheuen (**at** vor + *Dat.*); **~ easily** sich leicht erschrecken lassen

Phrasal verbs

- **~ a'way** *v.t.* verscheuchen
- **~ 'off** *v.t.* verscheuchen
- **~ 'out, ~ 'up** *v.t.* (Amer.: Hunting, fig.) aufstöbern ‹*Wild, Gegenstand*›; auftreiben (ugs.) ‹*etw. zu essen, Informationen*›

scare: ~ buying *n.*, *no pl.* (Amer.) Hamsterkäufe *Pl.*; **~ campaign** *n.* Angstkampagne, *die*; **~crow** *n.* (lit. or fig.) Vogelscheuche, *die*

scared /skeəd/ *adj.* verängstigt ‹*Gesicht, Stimme*›; **be/feel [very] ~:** [große] Angst haben; **be ~ of sb./sth.** vor jmdm./etw. Angst haben; **be ~ of doing/to do sth.** sich nicht [ge]trauen, etw. zu tun; **be ~ [that] sth. might happen** befürchten, dass etw. passieren könnte

scaremonger /'skeəmʌŋgə(r)/ *n.* Panikmacher, *der*/-macherin, *die* (abwertend)

scaremongering /'skeəmʌŋgərɪŋ/ *n.*, *no pl.* Panikmache, *die*

'scare tactics *n. pl.* ≈ Panikmache, *die* (ugs.)

scarf /skɑːf/ *n.*, *pl.* **~s** *or* **scarves** /skɑːvz/ Schal, *der*; (triangular/square piece of fine material) Halstuch, *das*; (worn over hair) Kopftuch, *das*; (worn over shoulders) Schultertuch, *das*

scarf: ~ pin *n.* (Brit.) Vorstecknadel, *die*; Halstuchnadel, *die*; **~ ring** *n.* (Brit.) Halstuchring, *der*

scarify[1] /'skærɪfaɪ, 'skeərɪfaɪ/ *v.t.* **1▸** (Med.) skarifizieren (fachspr.); anritzen **2▸** (fig.: by criticism) geißeln **3▸** (Agric.) auflockern ‹*Boden*›; (Constr.) aufreißen ‹*Straße*›

scarify[2] /'skeərɪfaɪ/ *v.t.* (coll.: frighten) Angst machen (+ *Dat.*); **~ing** beängstigend

scarlatina /skɑːlə'tiːnə/ ▸**i** **p. 1231** ▸**scarlet fever**

scarlet /'skɑːlɪt/

A *n.* Scharlach, *der*; Scharlachrot, *das*

B *adj.* scharlachrot; **I turned ~:** ich wurde puterrot; *see also* **pimpernel**

scarlet: ~ 'fever *n.* ▸**i** **p. 1231** (Med.) Scharlach, *der*; **~ 'runner** *n.* (Bot.) Feuerbohne, *die*

scarp /skɑːp/ *n.* Steilhang, *der*

scarper /'skɑːpə(r)/ *v.i.* (Brit. coll.) abhauen (salopp); sich aus dem Staub machen (ugs.)

'SCART connector, 'scart connector /skɑːt/ *n.* (Electron.) Scartverbinder, *der*

'scar tissue *n.* (Med.) Narbengewebe, *das*

scarves *pl. of* **scarf**

scary /'skeərɪ/ *adj.* (coll.) **1▸** (frightening) Furcht erregend ‹*Anblick*›; schaurig ‹*Film, Geschichte*›; Angst einflößend ‹*Person, Gesicht*›; **a ~ moment** eine Schrecksekunde; **it was ~ to listen to** beim Zuhören konnte man richtig Angst kriegen (ugs.) **2▸** (easily frightened) schreckhaft ‹*Kind, Tier*›; (timid) ängstlich

scat /skæt/ *v.i.* (Mus.) scatten

scathing /'skeɪðɪŋ/ *adj.* beißend ‹*Spott, Kritik*›; scharf ‹*Angriff*›; bissig ‹*Person, Humor, Bemerkung*›; **be ~ about sth.** etw. bissig herabsetzen *od.* (ugs.) heruntermachen

scathingly /'skeɪðɪŋlɪ/ *adv.* scharf ‹*kritisieren*›; bissig ‹*sagen, bemerken*›

scatological /skætə'lɒdʒɪkl/ *adj.* **1▸** (obscene) obszön; **~ language** Fäkalsprache, *die* **2▸** (Med., Palaeont.) skatologisch

scatter /'skætə(r)/

A *v.t.* **1▸** vertreiben; zerstreuen, auseinander treiben ‹*Menge*›; zunichte machen ‹*Hoffnungen*›; **he slammed his fist on the table, ~ing china everywhere** er schlug mit der Faust auf den Tisch, dass das Porzellan in alle Richtungen flog **2▸** (distribute irregularly) verstreuen; ausstreuen ‹*Samen*›; **ice cream with nuts ~ed on top** mit Nüssen bestreutes Eis **3▸** (partly cover) [be]streuen ‹*Straße*›; **~ a field with seeds** Samen auf einem Feld ausstreuen

B *v.i.* sich auflösen; ‹*Menge*:› sich zerstreuen; (in fear) auseinander stieben

C *n.* **1▸** ▸**~ing 1** **2▸** (Arms) Streuung, *die*

scatter: ~brain *n.* zerstreuter Mensch; Schussel, *der* (ugs.); **~brained** *adj.* zerstreut; schusselig (ugs.); **~ cushion** *n.* Sofakissen, *das*

scattered /'skætəd/ *adj.* verstreut; vereinzelt ‹*Fälle, Anzeichen, Regenschauer*›; **thinly ~ population** verstreut lebende Bevölkerung

scattering /'skætərɪŋ/ *n.* **1▸** (small amount) **a ~ of people/customers/letters** ein paar vereinzelte Leute/Kunden/Briefe; **add a ~ of nuts to sth.** Nüsse auf etw. (*Akk.*) streuen; **a thin ~ of snow** eine dünne Schneedecke **2▸** (Phys.) Streuung, *die*

scatter: ~ rug *n.* Brücke, *die*; **~shot** (Amer.) **A** *n.* Streupatrone, *die*; **B** *adj.* willkürlich

scatty /ˈskætɪ/ *adj.* (Brit. coll.) dusslig (salopp); **drive sb. ~:** jmdn. verrückt machen (ugs.)

scavenge /ˈskævɪndʒ/

A *v.t.* **1** sich (*Dat.*) holen; **~ sth. from a jumble sale** etw. auf einem Trödelmarkt ergattern **2** (search) durchstöbern (**for** nach); absuchen ‹*Strand*›; fleddern ‹*Leiche*›

B *v.i.* **~ for sth.** nach etw. suchen; **live by scavenging** ‹*Geier:*› Aasfresser sein; **~ through** durchstöbern (ugs.) ‹*Abfallhaufen*›

scavenger /ˈskævɪndʒə(r)/ *n.* (animal) Aasfresser, *der;* (fig. derog.: person) Aasgeier, *der* (ugs. abwertend)

ˈscavenger cell *n.* (Biol.) Fresszelle, *die*

scenario /sɪˈnɑːrɪəʊ, sɪˈneərɪəʊ/ *n., pl.* **~s** (Theatre, Cinemat.; also fig.) Szenario, *das*

scene /siːn/ *n.* **1** (place of event) Schauplatz, *der;* (in novel, play, etc.) Ort der Handlung; **the ~ of the novel is set in Venice** der Roman spielt in Venedig; **~ of the crime** Ort des Verbrechens; Tatort, *der* **2** (portion of play, film, or book) Szene, *die;* (division of act) Auftritt, *der;* **love/trial ~:** Liebes-/Gerichtsszene, *die;* **steal the ~** ‹*Schauspieler:*› die Szene beherrschen; (fig.) sich in den Vordergrund spielen **3** (display of passion, anger, jealousy) Szene, *die;* **create** *or* **make a ~:** eine Szene machen; **there were ~s of rejoicing** es spielten sich Freudenszenen ab; **end in violent ~s** mit Gewalttätigkeiten enden **4** (view) Anblick, *der;* (as depicted) Aussicht, *die;* **present a ~ of horror** ein Bild des Schreckens bieten (geh.); **change of ~:** Tapetenwechsel, *der* (ugs.) **5** (place of action) Ort des Geschehens; **arrive** *or* **come on the ~:** auftauchen; **a new political party has appeared on the ~:** eine neue Partei ist auf den Plan getreten; **he got into a bad ~** (coll.) er ist ins Schleudern gekommen (salopp); **leave** *or* **quit the ~:** abtreten **6** (field of action) **the political/drug/artistic ~:** die politische/Drogen-/Kunstszene; **the fashion/sporting ~:** die Modewelt/die Welt des Sports; **the social ~:** das gesellschaftliche Leben **7** (coll.: area of interest) **what's your ~?** worauf stehst du? (ugs.); worauf fährst du ab? (salopp); **that's not my ~:** das ist nicht mein Fall (ugs.) **8** (Theatre: set) Bühnenbild, *das;* **change the ~:** die Kulissen auswechseln; **behind the ~s** (lit. or fig.) hinter den Kulissen; **behind-the-~s investigation** (fig.) geheime Untersuchung; **give a behind-the-~s glimpse [of sth.]** einen Blick hinter die Kulissen [einer Sache (*Gen.*)] gewähren; **set the ~ [for sb.]** (fig.) [jmdm.] die Ausgangssituation darlegen

ˈscene: ~ change *n.* (Theatre) Kulissenwechsel, *der;* **~-of-ˈcrime** *adj.* (Brit.) Spurensicherungs-; **~-of-ˈcrime photograph** Tatortfoto, *das;* **~-painter** *n.* ▸ⓘ **p. 1260** Kulissenmaler, *der/*-malerin, *die*

scenery /ˈsiːnərɪ/ *n., no pl.* **1** (Theatre) Bühnenbild, *das* **2** (landscape) Landschaft, *die;* (picturesque) [malerische] Landschaft; **mountain ~:** Gebirgslandschaft, *die;* **some beautiful ~:** einige schöne Landstriche; **change of ~:** Tapetenwechsel, *der* (ugs.)

scene: ~-shifter *n.* ▸ⓘ **p. 1260** (Theatre) Bühnenarbeiter, *der/*-arbeiterin, *die;* **~-shifting** *n.* (Theatre) Kulissenwechsel, *der*

scenic /ˈsiːnɪk/ *adj.* **1** (with fine natural scenery) landschaftlich schön; **a ~ drive** eine Fahrt durch schöne Landschaft; **~ beauty** *or* **qualities** landschaftliche Schönheit; **~ railway** Berg-und-Tal-Bahn, *die* **2** (Theatre) Bühnen-; **be a ~ designer** Bühnenbildner/-bildnerin sein **3** (Art: in painting etc.) szenisch

scent /sent/

A *n.* **1** (smell) Duft, *der;* (fig.) [Vor]ahnung, *die;* **catch the ~ of sth.** den Duft von etw. in die Nase bekommen **2** (Hunting; also fig.: trail) Fährte, *die;* **get/be on the [right] ~** (lit. or fig.) die richtige Fährte finden/auf der richtigen Fährte sein; **be on the ~ of sb./sth.** (fig.) jmdm./einer Sache auf der Spur sein; **[lay** *or* **set] a false ~** (lit. or fig.) eine falsche Fährte [legen]; **put the hounds on/off the ~:** die Hunde auf die Fährte setzen/von der Fährte abbringen; **put** *or* **throw sb. off the ~** (fig.) jmdn. auf eine falsche Fährte bringen; **put sb. on the ~ of sb./sth.** (fig.) jmdn. auf jmds. Spur bringen/einer Sache (*Dat.*) auf die Spur bringen; *see also* **cold A 11; hot A 9** **3** (Brit.: perfume) Parfüm, *das* **4** (sense of smell) Geruchssinn, *der;* (fig.: power to detect) Spürsinn, *der*

B *v.t.* **1** (lit. or fig.) wittern; spüren ‹*Heuchelei*›; ‹*Tier:*› beriechen (ugs.), beschnuppern ‹*Boden*› **2** (apply perfume to) parfümieren

Phrasal verb

• **~ ˈout** *v.t.* (lit. or fig.) aufspüren

ˈscent bottle *n.* (Brit.) Parfümfläschchen, *das*

scented /ˈsentɪd/ *adj.* **1** (having smell) duftend; **be ~** ‹*Blume:*› duften; **~ air** von Düften erfüllte Luft; **~ candle** Duftkerze, *die* **2** (perfumed) parfümiert

ˈscent gland *n.* (Zool.) Duftdrüse, *die*

scentless /ˈsentlɪs/ *adj.* geruchlos; ‹*Blume*› ohne Duft; **be ~:** nicht duften

scepsis /ˈskepsɪs/ *n., no pl.* (Philos.) Skepsis, *die*

scepter (Amer.) ▸**sceptre**

sceptic /ˈskeptɪk/ *n.* Skeptiker, *der/*Skeptikerin, *die;* (with religious doubts) [Glaubens]zweifler, *der/*-zweiflerin, *die*

sceptical /ˈskeptɪkl/ *adj.* skeptisch; **be ~ about** *or* **of sb./sth.** jmdm./einer Sache skeptisch gegenüberstehen

sceptically /ˈskeptɪkəlɪ/ *adv.* skeptisch

scepticism /ˈskeptɪsɪzm/ *n.* Skepsis, *die;* (Philos.) Skeptizismus, *der;* (religious doubt) Glaubenszweifel *Pl.*

sceptre /ˈseptə(r)/ *n.* (Brit.; lit. or fig.) Zepter, *das*

schedule /ˈʃedjuːl/

A *n.* **1** (list) Tabelle, *die;* (for event, festival) Programm, *das* **2** (plan of procedure) Zeitplan, *der;* **filming ~:** Drehplan, *der;* **we are working to a tight ~:** unsere Termine sind sehr eng; **go** *or* **happen [according] to ~:** nach Plan laufen **3** (set of tasks) Terminplan, *der;* Programm, *das;* **work/study ~:** Arbeits-/Studienplan, *der;* **a heavy work ~:** ein umfangreiches Arbeitspensum **4** (tabulated statement) Aufstellung, *die;* (appendix) tabellarischer Anhang; (blank form) Formblatt, *das;* **[tax] ~:** Steuertabelle, *die* **5** (timetable) Fahrplan, *der* **6** (time stated in plan) **on ~:** programmgemäß; **arrive on ~:** pünktlich ankommen; **flight ~s** Ankunfts- und Abflugzeiten; **bus/train ~s** Ankunfts- und Abfahrtszeiten der Busse/Züge; *see also* **ahead 3; behind B 5**

B *v.t.* **1** (make plan of) zeitlich planen; (appoint to be done) anberaumen ‹*Sitzung*›; **be ~d for Thursday** für Donnerstag geplant sein; **we are ~d to start next week** laut Plan sollen wir nächste Woche anfangen; **they have ~d the building for demolition** nach ihren Plänen soll das Gebäude abgerissen werden **2** (make timetable of) einen Fahrplan aufstellen für; (include in timetable) in den Fahrplan aufnehmen; **trains which are ~d to run at a given time** Züge, die zu einer bestimmten Zeit fahren sollen **3** (make list of) auflisten; (include in list) aufführen (**in** in + *Dat.*); (Brit.: to be preserved) unter Denkmalschutz stellen ‹*Gebäude*›

scheduled /ˈʃedjuːld/ *adj.* **1** (according to timetable) [fahr]planmäßig ‹*Zug, Halt*›; flugplanmäßig ‹*Zwischenlandung*›; Linien‹*flugzeug, -dienst, -maschine*›; **~ flight** Linienflug, *der;* **make a ~ stop** ‹*Flugzeug:*› planmäßig zwischenlanden **2** (Brit.: in list of protected buildings) unter Denkmalschutz stehend

schematic /skɪˈmætɪk, skiːˈmætɪk/ *adj.*, **schematically** /skɪˈmætɪkəlɪ, skiːˈmætɪkəlɪ/ *adv.* schematisch

schematize (**schematise**) /ˈskiːmətaɪz/ *v.t.* schematisieren (**into** zu)

scheme /skiːm/

A *n.* **1** (arrangement) Anordnung, *die;* **general ~ of things** allgemeine Gegebenheiten; *see also* **colour scheme** **2** (table of classification, outline) Schema, *das;* **~ [of study]** (syllabus) Studienprogramm, *das* **3** (plan) Programm, *das;* (project) Projekt, *das;* **pension ~:** Altersversorgung, *die* **4** (dishonest plan) Intrige, *die;* **~ of revenge** Racheplan, *der;* **what ~ are you plotting?** was führst du im Schilde?

B *v.i.* Pläne schmieden; **~ for sb.'s downfall/to assassinate sb.** jmds. Sturz/ein Attentat auf jmdn. planen

C *v.t.* im Schilde führen

schemer /ˈskiːmə(r)/ *n.* Intrigant, *der/*Intrigantin, *die;* **your sister is a real little ~:** deine Schwester ist ein raffiniertes kleines Biest (ugs.)

scheming /ˈskiːmɪŋ/

A *n., no pl., no indef. art.* Winkelzüge *Pl.;* Machenschaften *Pl.;* **be given to ~:** gern intrigieren

B *adj.* intrigant; **be a ~ person, have a ~ nature** gern intrigieren

scherzo /ˈskeətsəʊ/ *n., pl.* **~s** (Mus.) Scherzo, *das*

schilling /ˈʃɪlɪŋ/ *n.* ▸ⓘ **p. 1332** Schilling, *der*

schism /ˈsɪzm, ˈskɪzm/ *n.* **1** (Eccl.) Schisma, *das* **2** (in any group) Spaltung, *die*

schismatic /sɪzˈmætɪk, skɪzˈmætɪk/ *adj.* (Eccl.) schismatisch

schist /ʃɪst/ *n.* (Geol.) Schiefer, *der*

schizo /ˈskɪtsəʊ/ (coll.)

A *n., pl.* **~s** Schizophrene, *der/die*

B *adj.* schizophren

schizoid /ˈskɪtsɔɪd/ (Psych.)

A *adj.* schizoid

B *n.* Schizoide, *der/die;* **be a ~:** schizoid sein

schizophrenia /skɪtsəˈfriːnɪə/ *n.* (Psych.) Schizophrenie, *die*

schizophrenic /skɪtsəˈfrenɪk, skɪtsəˈfriːnɪk/ (Psych.; also fig. coll.)

A *adj.* schizophren; ‹*Symptom*› der Schizophrenie

B *n.* Schizophrene, *der/die*

schlock /ʃlɒk/ *n.* (coll.) Mist, *der* (fig.)

schmaltz /ʃmɔːlts/ *n.* (coll.) Schmalz, *der* (ugs. abwertend)

schmaltzy /ˈʃmɔːltsɪ/ *adj.* (coll.) schmalzig (abwertend)

schmuck /ʃmʌk/ *n.* (esp. Amer. coll.) Schwachkopf, *der* (abwertend)

schnapps /ʃnæps/ *n.* Schnaps, *der*

schnauzer /ˈʃnaʊtsə(r)/ *n.* Schnauzer, *der*

schnitzel /ˈʃnɪtsl/ *n.* (Gastr.) [Kalbs]schnitzel, *das*

schnorkel /ˈʃnɔːkl/ ▸**snorkel**

scholar /ˈskɒlə(r)/ *n.* **1** (learned person) Gelehrte, *der/die;* **literary/linguistic/musical ~:** Literatur-/Sprach-/Musikwissenschaftler *der/*-wissenschaftlerin, *die;* **Shakespeare[an] ~:** Shakespeare-Forscher, *der/*-Forscherin, *die;* **be a ~ in one's field** Experte/Expertin auf seinem/ihrem Gebiet sein **2** (one who learns) Schüler, *der/*Schülerin, *die;* **be no ~:** kein guter Schüler/keine gute Schülerin sein **3** (holder of scholarship) Stipendiat, *der/*Stipendiatin, *die*

scholarly /ˈskɒləlɪ/ *adj.* wissenschaftlich; gelehrt ‹*Person*›; **a ~ life** ein Gelehrtenleben; **he has a ~ appearance** er hat das Aussehen eines Gelehrten

scholarship /ˈskɒləʃɪp/ *n.* **1** (payment for education) Stipendium, *das;* **closed ~:** *Stipendium, das nur bestimmten Bewerbern gewährt wird;* **open ~:** *Stipendium, um das sich jeder bewerben kann* **2** *no pl.* (scholarly work) Gelehrsamkeit, *die* (geh.); (methods) Wissenschaftlichkeit, *die;* **a work full of ~:** ein hochwissenschaftliches Werk **3** *no pl.* (body of learning) **literary/linguistic/historical ~:** Literatur-/Sprach-/Geschichtswissenschaft, *die;* **contribute to Shakespearean/Romance ~:** einen Beitrag zur Shakespeareforschung/Romanistik leisten

scholastic /skəˈlæstɪk/ *adj.* **1** akademisch; Akademiker‹*familie, -milieu*›; wissenschaftlich ‹*Buchhandlung, Leistung, Standard*› **2** (Philos., Theol.) scholastisch

Scholastic ˈAptitude Test *n.* (Amer. Educ.) *amerikanischer Universitäts- und College-Aufnahmetest*

scholasticism /skəˈlæstɪsɪzm/ *n.* **1** Scholastizismus, *der* **2** (Philos., Theol.) Scholastik, *die*

school[1] /skuːl/

A *n.* **1** Schule, *die;* (Amer.: university, college) Hochschule, *die; attrib.* Schul-; **what do they teach them in ~s?** was lernen sie in der Schule?; **be at** *or* **in ~:** in der Schule sein; (attend ~) zur Schule gehen; **be kept in ~ [late]** nachsitzen müssen; **to/from ~:** zur/von *od.* aus der

S

Schule; **go to ~:** zur Schule gehen; **leave ~:** die Schule verlassen; **have ~:** Schule *od.* Unterricht haben; **have time off ~:** schulfrei haben; **be absent from ~:** in der Schule fehlen; **one hour before/after ~:** eine Stunde vor Unterrichtsbeginn/nach Schulschluss; **there will be no ~ today** heute ist keine Schule; **the ~ of life** (fig.) die Schule des Lebens; **~ is fun/boring** Schule macht Spaß/ist langweilig; **my first day of ~, the day I started ~:** mein erster Schultag [2] *attrib.* Schul‹*arzt, -aufsatz, -bus, -bibliothek, -gebäude, -jahr, -orchester, -system*›; **~ holidays** Schulferien *Pl.*; **~ exchange** Schüleraustausch, *der;* **the ~ term** die Schulzeit; **take ~ meals** in der Schule [zu Mittag] essen; **the ~ caretaker** der Hausmeister der Schule; **my rusty ~ French** mein eingerostetes Schulfranzösisch [3] (disciples) Schule, *die;* **~ of thought** Lehrmeinung, *die; see also* **old A 3, 6** [4] (Brit.: group of gamblers) Runde, *die* [5] (Univ.: department) Institut, *das;* **~ of history** Institut für Zeitgeschichte; **law/medical ~:** juristische/medizinische Fakultät

B *v.t.* [1] (send to ~) einschulen [2] (train) erziehen; dressieren ‹*Pferd*›; **~ sb. in sth.** jmdn. in etw. (*Akk.*) unterweisen (geh.)

school² *n.* (of fish) Schwarm, *der;* Schule, *die* (Zool.)

school: ~ age *n.* Schulalter, *das;* **children of ~ age** Kinder im schulpflichtigen Alter; **~bag** *n.* Schultasche, *die;* **~ board** *n.* (Amer./Hist.) [örtliche] Schulbehörde; **~ book** *n.* Schulbuch, *das;* **~boy** *n.* Schüler, *der;* (with reference to behaviour) Schuljunge, *der;* **every ~boy knows that** das weiß jeder Schuljunge; **~boyish** *adj.* schuljungenhaft; **~child** *n.* Schulkind, *das;* **~ day** *n.* Schultag, *der;* **Monday is a ~ day** [am] Montag ist Schule; **~days** *n. pl.* Schulzeit, *die;* **~ 'dinner** *n.* Schulessen, *das;* **eat ~ dinner** [mittags] in der Schule essen

schooled /skuːld/ *adj.* geschult ‹*Pferd*›; **be [highly] ~ in sth.** [ausgezeichnet] Bescheid wissen über etw. (*Akk.*)

school: ~ fees *n. pl.* Schulgeld, *das;* **~fellow** *n.* Mitschüler, *der*/-schülerin, *die;* Schulkamerad, *der*/-kameradin, *die;* **~ friend** *n.* Schulfreund, *der*/-freundin, *die;* **~girl** *n.* Schülerin, *die;* (with reference to behaviour) Schulmädchen, *das;* **~girlish** *adj.* schulmädchenhaft; **~ 'holidays** *n. pl.* Schulferien *Pl.*; **~ hours** *n. pl.* Unterrichtszeit, *die;* **~house** *n.* Schulhaus, *das*

schooling /ˈskuːlɪŋ/ *n.* [1] Schulbildung, *die;* **he has had little ~:** er hat keine richtige Schulbildung gehabt; **have one's ~:** zur Schule gehen; **I received my ~ at his hands** er war mein Lehrmeister [2] (Horse riding) Ausbildung, *die*

school: ~kid *n.* (coll.) Schulkind, *das;* **~ leaver** *n.* (Brit.) Schulabgänger, *der*/-abgängerin, *die;* **~-'leaving age** *n.* (Brit.) Schulabgangsalter, *das;* **~ 'life** *n., no pl.* Schulleben, *das;* **her first week of ~ life** ihre erste Schulwoche; **~ 'lunch** *n.* Schulessen, *das;* **eat ~ lunch** mittags in der Schule essen; **~ma'am** *n.* (coll.) ▸**~marm; ~man** /ˈskuːlmən/ *n., pl.* **~men** /ˈskuːlmən/ [1] (medieval teacher) Magister, *der;* (Philos., Theol.) Scholastiker, *der;* [2] (Amer.: teacher) Lehrer, *der;* **~marm** /ˈskuːlmɑːm/ *n.* (coll.) Gouvernante, *die* (ugs.); **~marmish** /ˈskuːlmɑːmɪʃ/ *adj.* (coll.) gouvernantenhaft; altjüngferlich; **~master** *n.* ▶❶ **p. 1260** Lehrer, *der;* **~mastering** /ˈskuːlmɑːstərɪŋ/ *n., no pl.* Schuldienst, *der;* **~mate** ▸**schoolfellow; ~mistress** *n.* ▶❶ **p. 1260** Lehrerin, *die;* **~ 'outing** *n.* Schulausflug, *der;* **the class is going on a ~ outing** die Klasse macht einen Ausflug; **~ 'playground** *n.* (Brit.) Pausenhof, *der;* **~room** *n.* Schulzimmer, *das;* **~ 'rule** *n.* Schulvorschrift, *die;* Schulregel, *die;* **it is a ~ rule that ...:** an der Schule ist es Vorschrift, dass ...; **~teacher** *n.* ▶❶ **p. 1260** Lehrer, *der*/Lehrerin, *die;* **~ time** *n.* [1] (lesson-time) Schule, *die;* Unterricht, *der;* **in** *or* **during ~ time** während des Unterrichts; [2] (~days) Schulzeit, *die;* **~ 'trip** *n.* Schulausflug, *der;* (lasting more than a day) Schulfahrt, *die;* **~ 'uniform** *n.* Schuluniform, *die;* **~ work** *n., no pl.* Schularbeiten *Pl.*; **~ 'year** *n.* Schuljahr, *das*

schooner /ˈskuːnə(r)/ *n.* [1] (Naut.) Schoner, *der* [2] (Brit.: sherry glass) [hohes] Sherryglas [3] (Amer.: beer glass) [großes] Bierglas

schottische /ʃɒˈtiːʃ/ *n.* (Mus.) Schottisch, *der*

schuss /ʃʊs/ (Skiing)

A *n.* (downhill run) Schuss, *der;* (course) Schusspiste, *die*

B *v.i.* Schuss fahren

C *v.t.* in Schussfahrt (*Dat.*) hinunterfahren

schwa /ʃwɑː/ *n.* (Phonet.) Schwa, *das*

sciatic /saɪˈætɪk/ *adj.* (Med.) ischiadisch; Ischias‹*schmerzen, -symptom*›; **have a ~ hip** Ischiasbeschwerden in der Hüfte haben

sciatica /saɪˈætɪkə/ *n.* ▶❶ **p. 1231** (Med.) Ischias, *die* (fachspr. der od. das)

sciatic nerve /saɪætɪk ˈnɜːv/ *n.* (Anat.) Ischiadikus, *der* (fachspr.); Ischiasnerv, *der*

science /ˈsaɪəns/ *n.* [1] *no pl., no art.* Wissenschaft, *die;* **applied/pure ~:** angewandte/reine Wissenschaft; **the ~ of medicine, medical ~:** Medizin, *die* [2] (branch of knowledge) Wissenschaft, *die;* **moral ~:** Sittenlehre, *die* [3] **[natural] ~:** Naturwissenschaften; *attrib.* naturwissenschaftlich ‹*Buch, Labor*› [4] (technique, expert's skill) Kunst, *die*

science: ~ 'fiction *n.* Sciencefiction, *die;* **~ park** *n.* Technologiepark, *der*

scientific /saɪənˈtɪfɪk/ *adj.* [1] wissenschaftlich; (of natural science) naturwissenschaftlich [2] (using technical skill) technisch gut ‹*Boxer, Schauspieler, Tennis*›

scientifically /saɪənˈtɪfɪkəlɪ/ *adv.* [1] wissenschaftlich; (with relation to natural science) naturwissenschaftlich; nach wissenschaftlichen Methoden ‹*Vieh züchten*› [2] (using technical skill) technisch gut ‹*boxen*›

scientist /ˈsaɪəntɪst/ *n.* ▶❶ **p. 1260** Wissenschaftler, *der*/Wissenschaftlerin, *die;* (in physical or natural science) Naturwissenschaftler, *der*/-wissenschaftlerin, *die;* (student of a science) Student/Studentin der Naturwissenschaften; **biological/social/computer ~s** Biologen/Soziologen/Informatiker

Scientologist /saɪənˈtɒlədʒɪst/ *n.* Anhänger/Anhängerin der Scientology [Kirche]

Scientology /saɪənˈtɒlədʒɪ/ *n.* Scientology, *die*

sci-fi /ˈsaɪfaɪ/ *n.* (coll.) Sciencefiction, *die*

scilla /ˈsɪlə/ *n.* (Bot.) Szilla, *die;* Blaustern, *der*

Scillies /ˈsɪlɪz/, **Scilly Isles** /ˈsɪlɪ aɪlz/ *pr. n. pl.* Scillyinseln *Pl.*

scimitar /ˈsɪmɪtə(r)/ *n.* Krummsäbel, *der*

scintillate /ˈsɪntɪleɪt/ *v.i.* (fig.) vor Geist sprühen

scintillating /ˈsɪntɪleɪtɪŋ/ *adj.* (fig.) geistsprühend

scintillation /sɪntɪˈleɪʃn/ *n.* [1] *no pl.* (sparkling) Funkeln, *das* [2] (spark) Funke, *der* [3] (Astron., Phys.) Szintillation, *die*

scion /ˈsaɪən/ *n.* [1] (Hort.) Schössling, *der;* (for grafting) Edelreis, *das* [2] (descendant) Spross, *der*

scissors /ˈsɪzəz/ *n. pl.* **[pair of] ~:** Schere, *die;* **any/some ~:** eine Schere; **be a ~-and-paste job** [aus anderen Werken] zusammengeschrieben sein

'scissors kick *n.* (Swimming) Scherenschlag, *der*

sclerosis /skləˈrəʊsɪs/ *n., pl.* **scleroses** /skləˈrəʊsiːz/ [1] ▶❶ **p. 1231** (Med.) Sklerose, *die;* **disseminated** *or* **multiple ~:** multiple Sklerose [2] (Bot.) Verholzung, *die*

sclerotic /skləˈrɒtɪk/ *adj.* [1] (Med.) sklerotisch; **be a ~ patient** an Sklerose leiden [2] (Bot.) verholzt [3] (Anat.) skleral (fachspr.)

scoff¹ /skɒf/ *v.i.* (mock) spotten; **~ing remarks** spöttische Bemerkungen; **~ at sb./sth.** sich über jmdn./etw. lustig machen; **he ~ed at danger** er spottete der Gefahr (geh.)

scoff² (coll.)

A *v.t.* (eat greedily) verschlingen

B *v.i.* sich [(*Dat.*) den Bauch] voll schlagen (salopp)

scoffer /ˈskɒfə(r)/ *n.* Spötter, *der*/Spötterin, *die*

scold /skəʊld/

A *v.t.* schelten (geh.); ausschimpfen (**for** wegen); **she ~ed him for coming late** sie schimpfte ihn aus *od.* schalt ihn, weil er zu spät kam

B *v.i.* schimpfen; **~ing wife** zänkische Ehefrau

C *n.* Xanthippe, *die* (abwertend)

scolding /ˈskəʊldɪŋ/ *n.* Schimpfen, *das;* (instance) Schelte, *die* (geh.); Schimpfe, *die* (ugs.); **give sb. a ~ [for sth.]** jmdn. [wegen etw.] schelten *od.* ausschimpfen; **get a ~:** ausgeschimpft werden

scollop /ˈskɒləp/ ▸**scallop**

sconce /skɒns/ *n.* [1] (flat candlestick) flacher Kerzenständer; (candlestick fixed to wall) Wandleuchter, *der* [2] (socket) [Kerzen]halterung, *die*

scone /skɒn, skəʊn/ *n.: weicher, oft zum Tee gegessener kleiner Kuchen*

scoop /skuːp/

A *n.* [1] (shovel) Schaufel, *die;* **a ~ of coal** eine Schaufel Kohlen [2] (ladle; ladleful) Schöpflöffel, *der;* [Schöpf]kelle, *die* [3] (for ice cream, mashed potatoes) Portionierer, *der;* (quantity taken by ~) Portion, *die;* (of ice cream) Kugel, *die* [4] **apple ~:** Apfelausschneider, *der;* **cheese ~:** Käsestecher, *der* [5] (large profit) Fischzug, *der* (fig.); **make a [considerable] ~:** einen beachtlichen Schnitt machen (ugs.) [6] (Journ.) Knüller, *der* (ugs.); Scoop, *der* (fachspr.)

B *v.t.* [1] (lift) schaufeln ‹*Kohlen, Zucker*›; (with ladle) schöpfen ‹*Flüssigkeit, Schaum*›; (out of fruit, cheese) ausstechen ‹*Kerngehäuse, Probe*› [2] (secure) erzielen ‹*Gewinn*›; hereinholen (ugs.) ‹*Auftrag*›; (in a lottery, bet) gewinnen ‹*Vermögen*›; **~ the pool** den ganzen Einsatz gewinnen [3] (Journ.) ausstechen

(Phrasal verbs)

- **~ 'out** *v.t.* [1] (hollow out) aushöhlen; schaufeln ‹*Loch, Graben*› [2] (remove) [her]ausschöpfen ‹*Flüssigkeit*›; auslöffeln ‹*Fruchtfleisch*›; schöpfen ‹*Mousse, Brei*›; (with a knife) herausschneiden ‹*Fruchtfleisch, Gehäuse*›; (excavate) ausbaggern ‹*Erde*›
- **~ 'up** *v.t.* schöpfen ‹*Wasser, Suppe*›; schaufeln ‹*Erde*›; aufschaufeln ‹*Kohlen, Kies*›; **he ~ed the child up in his arms** er hob das Kind in seine Arme

'scoop neck *n.* U-Ausschnitt, *der;* **a ~ dress** ein Kleid mit U-Ausschnitt

scoot /skuːt/ *v.i.* (coll.) rasen; (to escape) die Kurve kratzen (ugs.); **off you go, ~!** verschwinde/verschwindet!

scooter /ˈskuːtə(r)/ *n.* [1] (toy) Roller, *der* [2] **[motor] ~:** [Motor]roller, *der*

scope¹ /skəʊp/ *n., no indef. art.* [1] Bereich, *der;* (of person's activities) Betätigungsfeld, *das;* (of person's job) Aufgabenbereich, *der;* (of law) Geltungsbereich, *der;* (of department etc.) Zuständigkeitsbereich, *der;* Zuständigkeit, *die;* (of discussion, meeting, negotiations, investigations, etc.) Rahmen, *der;* **that is a subject within my ~:** davon verstehe ich etwas; **that is a subject beyond my ~:** das fällt nicht in meine Sparte; (beyond my grasp) das ist mir zu hoch; **that is beyond the ~ of my essay** das sprengt den Rahmen meines Aufsatzes [2] (opportunity) Entfaltungsmöglichkeiten *Pl.*; **give ample ~ for new ideas** weiten Raum für neue Ideen bieten

scope² *n.* (coll.) (telescope) Fernrohr, *das;* (microscope) Mikroskop, *das*

'scope creep *n., no pl.* schleichende Umfangserweiterung; Scope Creep, *das* (fachspr.)

scorch /skɔːtʃ/

A *v.t.* verbrennen; versengen

B *v.i.* [1] (become damaged by heat) versengt werden; verbrennen [2] (coll.: run or travel quickly) flitzen

C *n.* versengte Stelle; Brandfleck, *der*

scorched earth policy /skɔːtʃt ˈɜːθ pɒlɪsɪ/ *n.* (Mil.) Politik der verbrannten Erde

scorcher /ˈskɔːtʃə(r)/ *n.* (Brit. coll.) **today's a [real] ~:** heute ist [wirklich] eine Affenhitze (salopp); **what a ~!** ist das eine Affenhitze heute!

scorching /ˈskɔːtʃɪŋ/

A *adj.* [1] glühend heiß; sengend, glühend ‹*Hitze*› [2] (coll.) affenartig (ugs.) ‹*Geschwindigkeit*›

B *adv.* ~ **hot** glühend heiß ‹*Tag, Wetter*›

score /skɔ:(r)/

A *n.* **1** (points) [Spiel]stand, *der;* (made by one player) Punktzahl, *die;* (Golf) Score, *der;* **What's the ~?** — **The ~ was 4-1 at half-time** Wie steht es? — Der Halbzeitstand war 4 : 1; **final ~:** Endstand, *der;* **keep [the] ~:** zählen; (in written form) aufschreiben; anschreiben; **know the ~** (fig. coll.) wissen, was Sache ist *od.* was läuft (salopp) **2** (Mus.) Partitur, *die;* (Film) [Film]musik, *die;* **in ~:** in Partitur **3** *pl.* ~ *or* **~s** (group of 20) zwanzig; **a ~ of people** [ungefähr] zwanzig Leute; **three ~ years and ten** siebzig Jahre **4** *in pl.* (great numbers) **~s [and ~s] of** zig (ugs.); Dutzende [von]; **~s of times** zigmal (ugs.) **5** (notch) Kerbe, *die;* (scratch) Kratzer, *der;* Schramme, *die;* (weal) Striemen, *der;* (crack in skin) Schrunde, *die;* **make a ~ on the cardboard** die Pappe [ein]ritzen **6** (dated: running account) Rechnung, *die;* (in bar, restaurant also) Zeche, *die;* **pay off** *or* **settle an old ~** (fig.) eine alte Rechnung begleichen **7** (reason) Grund, *der;* **on one/this ~:** aus einem/diesem Grund; **on the ~ of** wegen; **on that ~:** was das betrifft *od.* angeht; diesbezüglich

B *v.t.* **1** (win) erzielen ‹*Erfolg, Punkt, Treffer usw.*›; **~ a direct hit on sth.** ‹*Person:*› einen Volltreffer landen; ‹*Bombe:*› etw. voll treffen; **the play ~d a success** das Stück war *od.* wurde ein Erfolg; **they ~d a success** sie hatten Erfolg *od.* konnten einen Erfolg [für sich] verbuchen; **you've ~d a success there** das ist ein Erfolg für dich; **~ a goal** ein Tor schießen/werfen; **we ~d 13** wir haben 13 Punkte gemacht/Tore geschossen/Tore geworfen; **~ points off** (coll.) ▸ **score off** **2** (make notch/notches in) einkerben; (carve in) [ein]ritzen; **~ grooves in sth.** Rillen in etw. (*Akk.*) kratzen; **the wood was deeply ~d** (with notches/grooves) in dem Holz waren tiefe Kerben/Rillen **3** (be worth) zählen; **the ace ~s ten [points]** das Ass zählt zehn [Punkte] **4** (allot ~ to) ‹*Punktrichter, Juror:*› Punkte geben (+ *Dat.*) **5** (dated: mark up) ankreiden (**to** *or* **against** *Dat.*) (veralt.); **~ sth. against** *or* **to sb.** (fig.) jmdm. etw. negativ anrechnen **6** (Mus.) setzen; (orchestrate) orchestrieren ‹*Musikstück*›; (compose music for) die Musik komponieren *od.* schreiben für ‹*Film, Theaterstück*› **7** (make record of) aufschreiben ‹*Punkte*› **8** (Amer.: criticize severely) heftig angreifen; schwere Vorwürfe erheben gegen

C *v.i.* **1** (make ~) Punkte/einen Punkt erzielen *od.* (ugs.) machen; punkten (bes. Boxen); (**~ goal/goals**) ein Tor/Tore schießen/werfen; **~ high** *or* **well** (in test etc.) eine hohe Punktzahl erreichen *od.* erzielen; **do you know how to ~?** weißt du, wie gezählt wird? **2** (keep ~) aufschreiben; anschreiben **3** (secure advantage) die besseren Karten haben (**over** gegenüber, im Vergleich zu); (be a hit) ‹*Schauspieler:*› gut ankommen (ugs.) **4** (sl.: obtain drugs) Stoff auftreiben (ugs.) **5** (sl.: have sex) zum Schuss kommen (salopp) (**with** bei); **I'd like to ~ with her** ich würde sie gerne [mal] aufs Kreuz legen *od.* vernaschen (salopp)

Phrasal verbs

- **~ off** *v.t.* (coll.) als dumm hinstellen
- **~ 'out, ~ 'through** *v.t.* durchstreichen; ausstreichen
- **~ 'up** *v.t.* anschreiben; verbuchen ‹*Erfolg, Sieg usw.*›; **~ up the amount I owe you for these goods** setzen Sie den Betrag für die Waren auf mein Konto

score: ~board *n.* Anzeigetafel, *die;* **~book** *n.* (Sport) Anschreibebögen; **~card** *n.* (Sport) Anschreibekarte, *die;* (Golf) Scorekarte, *die;* **~draw** *n.* Unentschieden mit Toren

scorer /'skɔ:rə(r)/ *n.* **1** (recorder of score) Anschreiber, *der*/Anschreiberin, *die* **2** (Footb.) Torschütze, *der*/-schützin, *die;* **he was the top** *or* **highest ~:** er hat die meisten Tore/Punkte/Treffer *usw.* erzielt

'scoresheet *n.* Anschreibebogen, *der*

scoring /'skɔ:rɪŋ/ *n.* **1** (Mus.) Instrumentierung, *die;* (for orchestra) Orchestrierung, *die* **2** (keeping score) Aufschreiben, *das;* Anschreiben, *das*

scorn /skɔ:n/

A *n., no pl., no indef. art.* Verachtung, *die;* **with ~:** mit *od.* voll[er] Verachtung; verachtungsvoll; **be the ~ of sb.** von jmdm. verachtet werden; *see also* **pour A 1**

B *v.t.* **1** (hold in contempt) verachten **2** (refuse) in den Wind schlagen ‹*Rat*›; ausschlagen ‹*Angebot*›; verschmähen (geh.); **~ doing** *or* **to do sth.** es für unter seiner Würde halten, etw. zu tun

scornful /'skɔ:nfl/ *adj.* verächtlich ‹*Lächeln, Blick*›; **with ~ disdain** voll[er] Verachtung; verachtungsvoll; **be ~ of sth.** für etw. nur Verachtung haben

scornfully /'skɔ:nfəlɪ/ *adv.* verächtlich; voll[er] Verachtung

Scorpian /'skɔ:pɪən/ *n.* (Astrol.) Skorpion, *der*

Scorpio /'skɔ:pɪəʊ/ *n.* (Astrol., Astron.) der Skorpion; der Scorpius; *see also* **Aries**

scorpion /'skɔ:pɪən/ *n.* **1** (Zool.) Skorpion, *der* **2** (Astrol.) **the S~:** der Skorpion; *see also* **archer 2**

Scot /skɒt/ *n.* ▸ⓘ **p. 1345** Schotte, *der*/Schottin, *die*

scotch *v.t.* **1** (frustrate) zunichte machen ‹*Plan*› **2** (put an end to) den Boden entziehen (+ *Dat.*) ‹*Gerücht, Darstellung*›

Scotch /skɒtʃ/

A *adj.* **1** (of Scotland) ▸ **Scottish** **2** (Ling.) ▸ **Scots A 2**

B *n.* **1** (whisky) Scotch, *der;* schottischer Whisky **2** (Ling.) ▸ **Scots B** **3** *constr. as pl.* **the ~:** die Schotten

Scotch: ~ 'broth *n.* (Gastr.) *Hammelfleisch- od. Rindfleischsuppe mit Gemüse und Perlgraupen;* **~ 'egg** *n.* (Gastr.) *hart gekochtes Ei in Wurstbrät;* **~ 'fir** *n.* [Gemeine] Kiefer; Waldkiefer, *die;* **~man** /'skɒtʃmən/ ▸ **Scotsman;** **~ 'mist** *n.* dichter Nieselregen; **~ 'pine** ▸ **~ fir;** **~ tape** ® *n.* (Amer.) ≈ Tesafilm, *der* Ⓦᴢ; **~ 'terrier** *n.* Scotch[terrier], *der;* **~ 'whisky** *n.* schottischer Whisky; **~woman** ▸ **Scotswoman**

scot-'free *pred. adj.* ungeschoren; **get off/go/escape ~:** ungeschoren davonkommen *od.* bleiben

Scotland /'skɒtlənd/ *pr. n.* Schottland (*das*)

Scotland 'Yard *n.* (Brit.) Scotland Yard (*der*)

Scots /skɒts/ ▸ⓘ **p. 1277**

A *adj.* **1** (esp. Scot.) ▸ **Scottish** **2** (Ling.) schottisch

B *n.* (dialect) Schottisch, *das*

Scots: ~man /'skɒtsmən/ *n., pl.* **~men** /'skɒtsmən/ Schotte, *der;* **~woman** *n.* Schottin, *die*

Scottie /'skɒtɪ/ *n.* (coll.) **1** ▸ **Scotch terrier** **2** (man) Schotte, *der*

Scottish /'skɒtɪʃ/ *adj.* ▸ⓘ **p. 1345** schottisch; **he/she is ~:** er ist Schotte/sie ist Schottin

> **Scottish Certificate of Education**
>
> Der verbreitetste Schulabschluss in Schottland, das sein eigenes Ausbildungssystem hat. Die erste Prüfung wird mit 16 abgelegt und ist das Äquivalent zu den GCSE-Prüfungen in England, während die zweite Prüfung mit 17 abgelegt wird und das Äquivalent zu den A levels darstellt.

> **Scottish National Party (SNP)**
>
> Eine schottische Partei, deren Ziel es ist, eine vollkommen unabhängige schottische Regierung zu erwirken.

> **Scottish Parliament**
>
> Das schottische Parlament wurde 1999 nach den schottischen Wahlen in Edinburgh eröffnet und verleiht Schottland eine größere Autonomie gegenüber dem britischen Parlament in London.

Scottish: ~ 'Nationalism *n., no pl.* schottischer Nationalismus; **~ 'Nationalist** **A** *adj.* schottisch-nationalistisch. **B** *n.* schottischer Nationalist/schottische Nationalistin; **~ 'National Party, SN'P** *n.* Schottische Nationalpartei; SNP, *die;* **~ 'Parliament** *n.* schottisches Parlament; **~ Secretary** *n.* (Brit. Polit.) Schottlandminister, *der*/-ministerin, *die*

scoundrel /'skaʊndrl/ *n.* Schuft, *der* (abwertend); (villain) Schurke, *der* (abwertend)

scoundrelly /'skaʊndrəlɪ/ *adj.* schurkisch (abwertend); schuftig (abwertend)

scour[1] /skaʊə(r)/ *v.t.* **1** (cleanse by friction) scheuern ‹*Topf, Metall*›; **~ out** ausscheuern ‹*Topf*› **2** (clear out) **~ [out]** durchspülen ‹*Rohr*› **3** (remove by rubbing) [ab]scheuern; **~ away/off** ab-/wegscheuern

scour[2] *v.t.* (search) durchkämmen (**for** nach)

scourer /'skaʊərə(r)/ *n.* Topfreiniger, *der;* Topfkratzer, *der*

scourge /skɜ:dʒ/

A *n.* (lit. or fig.) Geißel, *die;* **they were the ~ of the English coast** sie suchten die englische Küste immer wieder heim

B *v.t.* **1** (whip) geißeln **2** (afflict) heimsuchen

scouse /skaʊs/ (Brit. coll.)

A *n.* **1** (dialect) Liverpooler Dialekt **2** (person) Liverpooler, *der*/Liverpoolerin, *die*

B *adj.* Liverpooler

scout[1] /skaʊt/

A *n.* **1** **[Boy] S~:** Pfadfinder, *der;* **King's/Queen's S~** (im Britischen Commonwealth) *Pfadfinder der höchsten Rangstufe; see also* **girl scout** **2** (Mil. etc.: sent to get information) Späher, *der*/Späherin, *die;* Kundschafter, *der*/Kundschafterin, *die;* (aircraft) Aufklärer, *der* **3** (Brit. Univ.: college servant) Collegediener, *der* **4** (coll.: helpful person) **be a good ~:** immer bereit sein zu helfen **5** (act of looking) Erkundung, *die;* (Mil.) Aufklärung, *die;* **take a ~ around** sich umsehen

B *v.i.* auf Erkundung gehen; **~ for sb./sth.** nach jmdm./etw. Ausschau halten; **be ~ing for talent** auf Talentsuche sein

Phrasal verbs

- **~ a'bout, ~ a'round** *v.i.* sich umsehen (**for** nach); Ausschau halten (**for** nach)
- **~ 'out** *v.t.* auskundschaften; erkunden

scout[2] *v.t.* (reject) ablehnen; zurückweisen; aus der Welt schaffen ‹*Gerücht*›

'scout car *n.* (Mil.) Panzerspähwagen, *der*

scouting /'skaʊtɪŋ/ *n.* **1** (reconnaissance) Erkundung, *die;* Aufklärung, *die* (Milit.) **2** **S~:** Pfadfindertum, *das;* Pfadfinderei, *die* (ugs.); (Scout movement) Pfadfinderbewegung, *die*

scout: ~ leader, (Hist.) **~master** *ns.* Pfadfinderführer, *der;* **S~ movement** *n.* Pfadfinderbewegung, *die*

scowl /skaʊl/

A *v.i.* ein mürrisches *od.* verdrießliches Gesicht machen; **~ at sb.** jmdn. mürrisch *od.* verdrießlich ansehen

B *n.* mürrischer *od.* verdrießlicher [Gesichts]ausdruck

SCR *abbr.* (Brit. Univ.) **1** = **Senior Common Room** **2** = **Senior Combination Room**

scrabble /skræbl/

A *v.i.* (scratch) ‹*Maus, Hund:*› scharren, kratzen; **~ about** ‹*Maus:*› herumkratzen *od.* -scharren; (for missing object) ‹*Person:*› wühlen (**for** nach); **the child was scrabbling in the sand** das Kind buddelte (ugs.) im Sand

B *n.* **S~** ® Scrabble, *das*

scrag[-end] /skræg('end)/ *n.* (Gastr.) Hals, *der;* Halsstück, *das*

scraggy /'skrægɪ/ *adj.* (derog.) mager ‹*Person, Tier*›; dürr ‹*Arme, Beine*›; hager ‹*Hals*›

scram /skræm/ *v.i.,* **-mm-** (coll.) abhauen (salopp); verschwinden (ugs.)

scramble /'skræmbl/

A *v.i.* **1** (clamber) klettern; kraxeln (ugs.); **~ through a hedge** sich durch eine Hecke zwängen **2** (move hastily) hasten (geh.); rennen (ugs.); **~ for sth.** um etw. rangeln; ‹*Kinder:*› sich um etw. balgen **3** (Air Force) [im Alarmfalle] aufsteigen

B *v.t.* **1** (Cookery) **~ some eggs** Rührei[er] machen; **would you like your eggs ~d?** möchtest du deine Eier als Rührei?; *see also*

S

scrambled egg 2 (Teleph., Radio) verschlüsseln ‹*Botschaft, Nachricht*›; an ein Verschlüsselungsgerät anschließen ‹*Telefon*› 3 (mix together) [ver]mischen 4 (deal with hastily) **~ a bill through Parliament** einen Gesetzentwurf durchs Parlament peitschen (ugs.); **~ the ball away** (Footb.) den Ball [irgendwie] wegschlagen

C *n.* 1 (struggle) Gerangel, *das* (**for** um); (on roads) [Verkehrs]gewühl, *das;* [Verkehrs]chaos, *das* 2 (climb) Kletterpartie, *die* (ugs.)

scrambled egg /skræmbld 'eg/ *n.* (Gastr.) Rührei, *das*

scrambler /'skræmblə(r)/ *n.* (Teleph., Radio) [elektronisches] Verschlüsselungsgerät

scrap[1] /skræp/

A *n.* 1 (fragment) (of paper, conversation) Fetzen, *der;* (of food) Bissen, *der;* **~ of paper** Stück Papier; (small, torn) Papierfetzen, *der* 2 (odds and ends) (of food) Reste *Pl.;* (of language) Brocken *Pl.;* **a few ~s of information/news** ein paar bruchstückhafte Informationen/Nachrichten; **a few ~s of French** ein paar Brocken Französisch 3 (smallest amount) **not a ~ of** kein bisschen; (of sympathy, truth also) nicht ein Fünkchen; (of truth also) nicht ein Körnchen; **not a ~ of evidence** nicht die Spur eines Beweises 4 *no pl., no indef. art.* (waste metal) Schrott, *der;* Altmetall, *das;* **~ iron** Eisenschrott, *der;* Alteisen, *das* 5 *no pl., no indef. art.* (rubbish) Abfall, *der;* **they are ~:** das ist Abfall *od.* sind Abfälle

B *v.t.*, **-pp-** wegwerfen; wegschmeißen (ugs.); (send for ~) verschrotten; (fig.) aufgeben ‹*Plan, Projekt usw.*›; **you can ~ that idea right away** die Idee kannst du gleich vergessen (ugs.)

scrap[2] (coll.)

A *n.* (fight) Rauferei, *die;* Klopperei, *die* (ugs.); (verbal) Kabbelei, *die* (ugs.); **get into a ~ with sb.** sich mit jmdm. in die Wolle kriegen (ugs.); **have a ~:** sich in der Wolle haben (ugs.)

B *v.i.*, **-pp-** sich raufen (**with** mit); (verbally) sich kabbeln

'scrapbook *n.* [Sammel]album, *das*

scrape /skreɪp/

A *v.t.* 1 (make smooth) schaben ‹*Häute, Möhren, Kartoffeln usw.*›; abziehen ‹*Holz*›; (damage) verkratzen, verschrammen ‹*Fußboden, Auto*›; schürfen ‹*Körperteil*›; **~ one's knee/the skin off one's knee** sich (*Dat.*) das Knie schürfen/sich (*Dat.*) am Knie die Haut abschürfen 2 (remove) [ab]schaben, [ab]kratzen (**off, from** von) ‹*Farbe, Schmutz, Rost*› 3 (draw along) schleifen; **~ the bow across the fiddle** mit dem Bogen über die Geige kratzen 4 (remove dirt from) abstreifen ‹*Schuhe, Stiefel*› 5 (draw back) straff kämmen ‹*Haar*› 6 (excavate) scharren ‹*Loch*› 7 (accumulate by care with money) **~ together/up** (raise) zusammenkratzen (ugs.); (save up) zusammensparen 8 **~ together/up** (amass by scraping) zusammenscharren ‹*Sand, Kies*›; (rake together) zusammenharken ‹*Laub usw.*›; (amass with difficulty) zusammenkriegen (ugs.) ‹*Geld*›; **~ [an] acquaintance with sb.** sich bei jmdm. anbiedern (abwertend) 9 (leave no food on or in) abkratzen ‹*Teller*›; auskratzen ‹*Schüssel*› 10 (Naut.) von Bewuchs befreien *od.* reinigen ‹*Schiff*›. *See also* **barrel 1**

B *v.i.* 1 (pass along with sound) schleifen; **the chalk ~d along the blackboard** die Kreide kratzte über die Tafel 2 (emit scraping noise) ein schabendes Geräusch machen 3 (rub) streifen (**against, over** *Akk.*) 4 (very nearly graze or be grazed) **~ over sth.** ‹*Flugzeug:*› haarscharf über etw. (*Akk.*) hinwegfliegen; **~ past each other** ‹*Autos:*› haarscharf aneinander vorbeifahren; **~ into second place** (fig.) mit Hängen und Würgen (ugs.) auf den zweiten Platz kommen 5 **bow and ~:** katzbuckeln (abwertend) 6 (be careful with money) sein Geld zusammenhalten; *see also* **scrimp**

C *n.* 1 (act, sound) Kratzen, *das* (**against** an + *Dat.*); Schaben, *das* (**against** an + *Dat.*); **give the potatoes a ~:** die Kartoffeln schaben 2 (predicament) Schwulitäten *Pl.* (ugs.); **be in a/get into a ~:** in Schwulitäten sein/kommen; **get sb. out of a ~:** jmdm. aus der Bredouille *od.* Patsche helfen (ugs.) 3 (~d place) Kratzer, *der* (ugs.); Schramme, *die*

Phrasal verbs

- **~ a'long** *v.i.* (fig.) sich über Wasser halten (**on** mit)
- **~ a'way** *v.t.* abkratzen, abschaben
- **~ 'by** ▸ **~ along**
- **~ 'out** *v.t.* 1 (excavate) buddeln (ugs.); scharren 2 (clean) auskratzen, -schaben
- **~ through**

A /'--/ *v.t.* 1 sich zwängen durch 2 (fig.: just succeed in passing) mit Hängen und Würgen kommen durch ‹*Prüfung*›

B /-'-/ *v.i.* 1 sich durchzwängen 2 (fig.: just succeed in passing examination) mit Hängen und Würgen durchkommen

scraper /'skreɪpə(r)/ *n.* 1 (for shoes) Kratzeisen, *das;* (grid) Abtreter, *der;* Abstreifer, *der* 2 (hand tool, kitchen utensil) Schaber, *der;* (for clearing snow) Schneescharre, *die;* Schneeschieber, *der;* (for clearing mud or dung) [Schmutz]kratzer, *der;* (decorator's) Spachtel, *der;* (for removing ice from car windows) [Eis]kratzer, *der*

'scraperboard *n.* (Art) Schabpapier, *das*

'scrap heap *n.* Schutthaufen, *der;* Müllhaufen, *der;* (for scrap metal) Schrotthaufen, *der;* **the scheme has been thrown/is on the ~** (fig.) der Plan ist zu Makulatur gemacht worden/ist Makulatur; **sb. is on the ~:** jmd. wird nicht mehr gebraucht; (because of age) jmd. gehört zum alten Eisen (fig. ugs.)

scrapie /'skreɪpɪ/ *n., no pl.* Scrapie, *die* (fachspr.); Traberkrankheit, *die*

scrapings /'skreɪpɪŋz/ *n. pl.* Schabsel; Geschabsel, *das*

scrap: ~ merchant *n.* ▸ ❶ **p. 1260** Schrotthändler, *der*/-händlerin, *die;* **~ metal** *n., no pl.* Schrott, *der;* Altmetall, *das;* **~ 'paper** *n.* Schmierpapier, *das*

scrappily /'skræpɪlɪ/ *adv.* unzulänglich; (without unity) uneinheitlich; (unsystematically) unsystematisch

scrappy /'skræpɪ/ *adj.* 1 (not complete) lückenhaft ‹*Bericht, Bildung usw.*›; (not unified) uneinheitlich 2 (lacking consistency) inkonsistent (geh.), unausgewogen ‹*Aufsatz, Bericht*› 3 (made up of bits or scraps) zusammengestoppelt (abwertend); **a ~ meal, consisting of leftovers** ein aus Resten zusammengestoppeltes Essen

'scrapyard *n.* Schrottplatz, *der;* **be sent to the ~:** verschrottet werden

scratch /skrætʃ/

A *v.t.* 1 (score surface of) zerkratzen; verkratzen; (score skin of) kratzen; **~ the surface [of sth.]** ‹*Geschoss usw.:*› [etw.] streifen; **he has only ~ed the surface [of the problem]** er hat das Problem nur oberflächlich gestreift; **~ an A and find a B** (fig.) in jedem A steckt ein B 2 (get ~[es] on) **~ oneself/one's hands** *etc.* sich schrammen/sich (*Dat.*) die Hände *usw.* zerkratzen *od.* [zer]schrammen *od.* ritzen 3 (scrape without marking) kratzen; kratzen an (+ *Dat.*) ‹*Insektenstich usw.*›; **~ oneself/one's arm** *etc.* sich kratzen/sich (*Dat.*) den Arm *usw. od.* am Arm *usw.* kratzen; *abs.* ‹*Person:*› sich kratzen; **~ one's head** sich am Kopf kratzen; **~ one's head [over sth.]** (fig.) sich (*Dat.*) den Kopf über etw. (*Akk.*) zerbrechen; **you ~ my back and I'll ~ yours** (fig. coll.) eine Hand wäscht die andere (Spr.) 4 (form) kratzen, ritzen ‹*Buchstaben etc.*›; (excavate in ground) kratzen, scharren ‹*Loch*› (**in** in + *Akk.*); (scribble) kritzeln ‹*Zeilen*›; **~ a living** sich schlecht und recht ernähren (**from** von) 5 (erase from list) streichen (**from** aus); (withdraw from competition) von der Starter- *od.* Teilnehmerliste streichen ‹*Rennpferd, Athleten*›; (Amer. Polit.) [von der Kandidatenliste] streichen ‹*Kandidat*›; *abs.* ‹*Rennfahrer:*› [seine Meldung *od.* Nennung] zurückziehen

B *v.i.* 1 (make wounds, cause itching, make grating sound) kratzen 2 (scrape) ‹*Huhn:*› kratzen, scharren

C *n.* 1 (mark, wound; coll.: trifling wound) Kratzer, *der* (ugs.); Schramme, *die;* **be covered in ~es** zer- *od.* verkratzt sein; zer- *od.* verschrammt sein; **without a ~:** ohne eine Schramme 2 (sound) Kratzen, *das* (**at** an + *Dat.*); Kratzgeräusch, *das;* **there was a ~ at the door** es kratzte an der Tür 3 (spell of scratching) **have a [good] ~:** sich [ordentlich] kratzen 4 (Sport) *hinterste Startlinie* (*bei Handicaprennen*); **on ~:** ohne Vorgabe 5 **start from ~** (fig.) bei null anfangen (ugs.); **be up to ~** ‹*Arbeit, Leistung:*› nichts zu wünschen übrig lassen; ‹*Person:*› in Form *od.* (ugs.) auf Zack sein; **not be up to ~:** [einiges] zu wünschen übrig lassen; ‹*Mensch:*› nicht in Form *od.* (ugs.) auf Zack sein; **bring sth. up to ~:** etw. auf Vordermann (scherzh.) *od.* (ugs.) auf Zack bringen; **bring sb.'s performance up to ~:** jmdn. in Form *od.* (ugs.) auf Zack bringen 6 *no pl., no indef. art.* (sl.: money) Kohle, *die* (salopp); Knete, *die* (salopp)

D *adj.* 1 (Sport) ohne Vorgabe *nachgestellt;* **~ player** (Golf) Scratchspieler, *der* 2 (collected haphazardly) bunt zusammengewürfelt; improvisiert ‹*Mahlzeit*›

Phrasal verbs

- **~ a'bout, ~ a'round** *v.i.* scharren; (fig.: search) suchen (**for** nach)
- **~ 'off** *v.t.* abkratzen; (delete) streichen ‹*Person, Name*›
- **~ 'out** *v.t.* 1 (score out) aus-, durchstreichen ‹*Name, Wort*› 2 (gouge out) auskratzen ‹*Auge*›
- **~ 'through** ▸ **~ out 1**
- **~ to'gether, ~ 'up** *v.t.* zusammenstoppeln (ugs.) ‹*Mahlzeit*›; zusammenkratzen (ugs.) ‹*Geld*›

'scratch: ~board ▸ **scraperboard; ~ card** *n.* Rubbellos, *das;* **~ card game** Rubbellos-Gewinnspiel, *das*

scratchily /'skrætʃɪlɪ/ *adv.* kratzend

scratch: ~ mark *n.* Kratzer, *der;* Kratzspur, *die;* **there are ~ marks all over the table** der Tisch ist ganz zer- *od.* verkratzt; **~ pad** *n.* 1 (Amer.: notepad) Notizblock, *der;* 2 (Computing) Notizblock, *der; attrib.* **~ pad memory** Notizblockspeicher, *der*

scratchy /'skrætʃɪ/ *adj.* 1 (making sound of scratching) kratzig [klingend] ‹*Schallplatte*›; **this is a ~ nib** diese Feder kratzt 2 (causing itching) kratzig ‹*Wolle, Kleidungsstück*› 3 (careless) kritzlig (ugs.) ‹*Handschrift, Zeichnung*› 4 (irritable) kratzbürstig; kratzig (ugs.)

scrawl /skrɔːl/

A *v.t.* hinkritzeln; **~ sth. on sth.** etw. auf etw. (*Akk.*) kritzeln

B *v.i.* kritzeln

C *n.* 1 (piece of writing) Gekritzel, *das;* (handwriting) Klaue, *die* (salopp abwertend) 2 (note) hingekritzelte Zeilen

Phrasal verbs

- **~ 'out** *v.t.* wegstreichen ‹*Wort*›
- **~ 'over** *v.t.* voll kritzeln, voll schmieren ‹*Seite, Buch*›

scrawny /'skrɔːnɪ/ *adj.* (derog.) hager, dürr ‹*Hals, Person*›; mager ‹*Vieh*›

scream /skriːm/

A *v.i.* 1 (utter cry) schreien (**with** vor + *Dat.*); **~ at sb.** jmdn. anschreien 2 (give shrill cry) ‹*Vogel, Affe:*› schreien 3 (whistle or hoot shrilly) ‹*Sirene, Triebwerk:*› heulen; ‹*Reifen:*› quietschen; ‹*Säge:*› kreischen; **the car ~ed past** das Auto kam mit heulendem Motor vorbeigerast 4 (laugh) schreien (**with** vor + *Dat.*) 5 (speak or write excitedly) **~ about sth.** um etw. ein großes Geschrei machen (ugs.); **the shipyards are ~ing for work** die Werften schreien nach Aufträgen (geh.) 6 (be blatantly obvious) ‹*Schlagzeile:*› in die Augen springen, einem entgegenspringen

B *v.t.* schreien; **~ sth. at sb.** jmdm. etw. ins Gesicht schreien

C *n.* 1 (cry) Schrei, *der;* (of siren or jet engine) Heulen, *das;* **~s of pain/laughter** Schmerzensschreie/gellendes Gelächter 2 (coll.: comical person or thing) **be a ~:** zum Schreien sein (ugs.)

screaming /'skriːmɪŋ/ *adj.* 1 schreiend; quietschend ‹*Reifen*›; heulend ‹*Sirene, Wind, Triebwerk*› 2 (funny) urkomisch

screamingly /skriːmɪŋlɪ/ *adv.* **~ funny** urkomisch

scree /skriː/ *n.* **~[s]** 1 (stones) Schutt, *der;* Geröll, *das;* Schotter, *der* 2 (mountain slope) Schutthalde, *die*

screech /skriːtʃ/

A *v.i.* (utter cry) ‹*Kind, Eule:*› kreischen, schreien; (make sound like cry) ‹*Bremsen:*› quietschen, kreischen; **~ to a halt, come to a ~ing halt**

‹*Auto*:› quietschend *od.* kreischend zum Stehen kommen
B *v.t.* kreischen
C *n.* (cry) Schrei, *der;* Kreischen, *das;* (sound like cry) Quietschen, *das;* Kreischen, *das;* **give a ~ of laughter** gellend auflachen

'screech owl *n.* **1** (Brit.: barn owl) Schleiereule, *die* **2** (Amer.: of genus Otus) Zwergohreule, *die;* (Otus asio) Kreischeule, *die*

screed /skri:d/ *n.* **1** (lengthy writing) Roman, *der* (ugs.) **2** (harangue) Strafpredigt, *die* **3** (Building) Estrich, *der*

screen /skri:n/
A *n.* **1** (partition) Trennwand, *die;* (piece of furniture) Wandschirm, *der;* (fire ~) [Ofen]schirm, *der; see also* **rood screen** **2** (sth. that conceals from view) Sichtschutz, *der;* (Hunting) [Jagd]schirm, *der;* (of trees, persons, fog) Wand, *die;* (of persons) Mauer, *die;* (expression of face or measure adopted for concealment) Maske, *die;* (of indifference, secrecy also) Wand, *die;* Mauer, *die* **3** (surface on which pictures are projected) Leinwand, *die;* Projektionswand, *die;* (in cathode-ray tube) Schirm, *der;* **[TV] ~:** [Fernseh]schirm, *der;* Bildschirm, *der;* **the ~** (Cinemat.) die Leinwand; **stage and ~:** Bühne und Leinwand; **the small ~:** der Bildschirm **4** (vertical display surface) (for exhibits) Stellwand, *die;* (for notices) Pinnwand, *die;* Anschlagtafel, *die* **5** (Phys.) [Schutz]schirm, *der;* (Electr.) Abschirmung, *die* **6** (Motor Veh.) ▸**windscreen** **7** (Amer.: netting to exclude insects) Fliegendraht, *der;* Fliegengitter, *das* **8** (sieve) [Wurf]sieb, *das;* Durchwurf, *der* **9** (Cricket) ▸**sight screen** **10** (Photog.) Mattscheibe, *die* **11** (Printing) [Bild]raster, *der*
B *v.t.* **1** (shelter) schützen (**from** vor + *Dat.*); (conceal) verdecken; **~ one's eyes from the sun** seine Augen vor der Sonne schützen *od.* (geh.) gegen die Sonne beschirmen; **be ~ed from view** vor Einblicken geschützt sein; **~ sth. from sb.** etw. jmds. Blicken entziehen **2** (show) vorführen, zeigen ‹*Dias, Film*› **3** (test) durchleuchten (**for** auf … [*Akk.*] hin) **4** (fig.: protect) decken ‹*Straftäter*›; (from blame) in Schutz nehmen (**from** gegen); (from justice) bewahren (**from** vor + *Dat.*) **5** (sieve) [durch]sieben **6** (Electr. Phys., Nucl. Engin.) abschirmen

Phrasal verb
- **~ 'off** *v.t.* abteilen ‹*Teil eines Raums*›; [mit einem Wandschirm] abtrennen ‹*Bett*›

screen: ~ capture *n.* (Computing) Bildschirmerfassung, *die;* (snapshot of screen) Screenshot, *der; attrib.* **~ capture program** Screen-Capture-Programm, *das* (fachspr.); **~ dump** *n.* (Computing) Bildschirmausdruck, *der;* **~ editor** *n.* (Computing) Bildschirmeditor, *der*

screening /'skri:nɪŋ/ *n.* **1** (in cinema) Vorführung, *die;* (on TV) Sendung, *die;* Ausstrahlung, *die* **2** (Med.) Untersuchung, *die;* **mass ~:** Reihenuntersuchung, *die*

screen: ~play *n.* (Cinemat.) Drehbuch, *das;* **~ printing** *n., no pl.* (Textiles) Gewebefilmdruck, *der;* **~ saver** *n.* (Computing) Bildschirmschoner, *der;* **~shot** *n.* (Computing) Screenshot, *der;* **~ test** *n.* (Cinemat.) Probeaufnahmen *Pl.;* **~wash** *n., no pl.* Scheibenreiniger, *der;* **~writer** *n.* ▸**❶ p. 1260** (Cinemat.) Filmautor, *der*/-autorin, *die*

screw /skru:/
A *n.* **1** Schraube, *die;* **he has a ~ loose** (coll. joc.) bei ihm ist eine Schraube locker *od.* lose (salopp); **put the ~[s] on sb.** (fig. coll.) jmdm. [die] Daumenschrauben anlegen (ugs.) **2** (turn of ~) [Um]drehung, *die;* **give the bolt another ~:** dreh die Schraube noch eine Umdrehung weiter **3** (Naut., Aeronaut.) Schraube, *die* **4** (sl.: prison warder) Wachtel, *die* (salopp); Schien, *der* (Gaunerspr. veralt.) **5** (coarse) (copulation) Fick, *der* (vulg.); Nummer, *die* (derb); (partner in copulation) Ficker, *der*/Fickerin, *die* (vulg.); **have a ~:** ficken (vulg.); vögeln (vulg.); **be a good ~:** gut ficken *od.* vögeln (vulg.) **6** (Brit. sl.: wages) **they're/he's** *etc.* **paid a good ~:** die Kohlen stimmen [bei ihnen/ihm] (ugs.)
B *v.t.* **1** (fasten) schrauben (**to** an + *Akk.*); **~ together** zusammenschrauben; verschrauben; **~ down** festschrauben; **have one's head ~ed on [straight** *or* **the right way** *or* **properly]** (coll.) ein vernünftiger Mensch sein **2** (turn) schrauben ‹*Schraubverschluss usw.*›; **~ one's head round** den Kopf verdrehen; **~ a piece of paper into a ball** ein Stück Papier zu einer Kugel zusammendrehen **3** (sl.: extort) [raus]quetschen (salopp) ‹*Geld, Geständnis*› (**out of** aus); **can't you ~ a bit more money out of your parents?** kannst du deinen Eltern nicht noch ein bisschen mehr Geld aus dem Kreuz leiern? (salopp); **~ sb. for a loan/for repayment** ein Darlehen/die Rückzahlung aus jmdm. rausquetschen (salopp) **4** (coarse: copulate with) ‹*Mann*:› ficken (vulg.), vögeln (vulg.); ‹*Frau*:› ficken mit (vulg.), vögeln mit (vulg.); **~ you!** (coarse) leck mich am Arsch! (salopp); **~ you and your …!** (coarse) leck mich am Arsch mit deinem/deiner/deinen …! **5** (sl.: burgle) knacken (salopp) ‹*Tresor*›; einen Bruch machen bei (salopp) ‹*Bank usw.*›
C *v.i.* **1** (revolve) sich schrauben lassen; sich drehen lassen; **~ to the right** ein Rechtsgewinde haben; **~ out/together** sich herausschrauben/zusammenschrauben lassen **2** (coarse: copulate) ficken (vulg.); vögeln (vulg.)

Phrasal verbs
- **~ to'gether**
A *v.t.* zusammenschrauben
B *v.i.* sich zusammenschrauben lassen
- **~ 'up** *v.t.* **1** (make tenser) spannen ‹*Saite*›; **~ up one's courage** sich (*Dat.*) ein Herz fassen **2** (crumple up) zusammenknüllen ‹*Blatt Papier*› **3** (make grimace with) verziehen ‹*Gesicht*›; (contract the outer parts of) zusammenkneifen ‹*Augen, Mund*› **4** (sl.: bungle) vermurksen (ugs.); vermasseln (salopp); **~ it/things up** Mist bauen (salopp)

screw: ~ball (Amer. coll.) **A** *n.* Spinner, *der*/Spinnerin, *die* (ugs. abwertend); **be a ~ball** spinnen; **B** *adj.* spleenig; **~ cap** *n.* Schraubdeckel, *der;* Schraubverschluss, *der;* **~ coupling** *n.* (Mech. Engin.) Gewindemuffe, *die;* **~driver** *n.* **1** Schraubenzieher, *der;* Schraubendreher, *der* (fachspr.); **2** (cocktail) Wodka-Orange, *der;* Screwdriver, *der*

screwed /skru:d/ *adj.* (sl.: drunk) besoffen (salopp)

'screwed-up *adj.* (fig. coll.) neurotisch; **get [all] ~ about sth.** wegen etw. ausflippen (ugs.)

screw: ~-in *adj.* einschraubbar; zum Einschrauben *nachgestellt;* **~-on** *adj.* anschraubbar; Schraub‹*deckel, -verschluss usw.*›; **~ thread** *n.* [Schraub]gewinde, *das;* **~ top** ▸ **~ cap**

screwy /'skru:ɪ/ *adj.* (coll.: eccentric) spinnig (ugs. abwertend); spleenig; (crazy) verrückt ‹*Humor, Idee, Plan*›

scribble /'skrɪbl/
A *v.t.* **1** (write hastily) hinkritzeln ‹*Zeilen, Nachricht*› **2** (draw carelessly or meaninglessly) kritzeln ‹*Skizze, Muster*› **3** (joc. derog.: write) absondern (salopp abwertend) ‹*Gedicht, Artikel*›
B *v.i.* **1** (write hurriedly, draw carelessly) kritzeln **2** (joc. derog.: be journalist etc.) schreiben; **are you still scribbling?** machst du [immer] noch auf Schreiberling? (ugs. abwertend)
C *n.* Gekritzel, *das* (abwertend); (handwriting) Klaue, *die* (salopp abwertend)

Phrasal verb
- **~ 'out, ~ 'over** *v.t.* aus-, durchstreichen; überkritzeln

scribbler /'skrɪblə(r)/ *n.* (joc. derog.) Schreiberling, *der* (abwertend); (of poems also) Dichterling, *der* (abwertend)

scribbling/'skrɪblɪŋ/: **~ pad** *n.* (Brit.) Notizblock, *der;* **~ paper** *n.* (Brit.) Schmierpapier, *das* (ugs.)

scribe /skraɪb/ *n.* **1** (producer of manuscripts) Schreiber, *der;* Skriptor, *der;* (copyist) Abschreiber, *der;* Kopist, *der* **2** (Bibl.: theologian) Schriftgelehrte, *der*

scrimmage /'skrɪmɪdʒ/
A *n.* Gerangel, *das*
B *v.i.* rangeln; ‹*spielende Kinder*:› sich balgen

scrimp /skrɪmp/ *v.i.* knausern (ugs.); knapsen (ugs.); **~ and save** *or* **scrape** knapsen und knausern (ugs.); **~ on sth.** mit etw. knausern

scrip /skrɪp/ *n.* (Finance) **1** (certificate) Scrip, *der;* Zwischenschein, *der* **2** (extra share[s]) Gratisaktie, *die*/Gratisaktien *Pl.*

script /skrɪpt/
A *n.* **1** (handwriting) Handschrift, *die;* **in ~:** handgeschrieben; handschriftlich **2** (of play) Regiebuch, *das;* (of film) [Dreh]buch, *das;* Skript, *das* (fachspr.) **3** (for broadcaster) Skript, *das;* Manuskript, *das* **4** (system of writing) Schrift, *die* **5** (Printing) Schreibschrift, *die* **6** (Brit. Educ.) [Prüfungs]arbeit, *die*
B *v.t.* schriftlich ausarbeiten ‹*Rede*›; das [Dreh]buch schreiben zu ‹*Film, Fernsehspot usw.*›; das Storyboard machen zu ‹*Fernsehspot*›

'script girl *n.* ▸**❶ p. 1260** Skriptgirl, *das*

scriptorium /skrɪp'tɔ:rɪəm/ *n., pl.* **scriptoria** /skrɪp'tɔ:rɪə/ *or* **~s** Skriptorium, *das;* [Kloster]schreibstube, *die*

scriptural /'skrɪptʃərl, 'skrɪptʃʊrl/ *adj.* **1** (of the Bible) biblisch ‹*Geschichte*›; Bibel‹*kenntnis*›; Schrift‹*lesung*› **2** (founded on doctrines of the Bible) schriftgemäß

scripture /'skrɪptʃə(r)/ *n.* **1** (Relig.: sacred book) heilige Schrift; **[Holy] S~, the [Holy] S~s** (Christian Relig.) die [Heilige] Schrift; *attrib.* Bibel‹*text, -stunde*› **2** (Christian Relig.: Bible text) Bibeltext, *der* **3** *no pl., no art.* (Sch.) Religion, *die*

'scriptwriter *n.* ▸**❶ p. 1260** (of film) Drehbuchautor, *der*/-autorin, *die;* (for radio) Hörspielautor, *der*/-autorin, *die*

scrofula /'skrɒfjʊlə/ *n.* ▸**❶ p. 1231** (Med.) Skrofulose, *die;* Skrofeln *Pl.*

scroll /skrəʊl/
A *n.* **1** (roll) Rolle, *die* **2** (design) (Archit.) Volute, *die;* Schnecke, *die;* (Mus.: on violin) Schnecke, *die;* (flourish in writing) Schnörkel, *der*
B *v.t.* (Computing) verschieben; scrollen (fachspr.); **~ a few pages** ein paar Seiten durchlaufen lassen

Phrasal verbs
- **~ 'down** *v.i.* (Computing) runterscrollen
- **~ 'up** *v.i.* (Computing) hochscrollen

scrollable /'skrəʊləbl/ *adj.* (Computing) scrollbar

scroll: ~ bar *n.* Rollbalken, *der;* **~ box** (Computing) *n.* Schieberegler, *der*

'scrolling *n., no pl.* (Computing) Scrollen, *das*

scroll: ~ key *n.* (Computing) Scrolltaste, *die;* **~work** *n., no pl.* (Art) Schneckenverzierung, *die*

Scrooge /skru:dʒ/ *n.* (coll.: derog.) Geizkragen, *der* (ugs. abwertend); **don't be such a ~:** sei nicht so geizig

scrotum /skrəʊtəm/ *n., pl.* **scrota** /'skrəʊtə/ *or* **~s** (Anat.) Hodensack, *der;* Skrotum, *das* (fachspr.)

scrounge /skraʊndʒ/ (coll.)
A *v.t.* **1** (cadge) schnorren (ugs.) (**off, from** von); **~ things** schnorren **2** (take illicitly) mitgehen lassen (ugs.); sich (*Dat.*) unter den Nagel reißen (salopp)
B *v.i.* **1** (cadge things) schnorren (ugs.) (**from** bei) **2** (take things illicitly) klauen (salopp) **3** **~ [around]** herumsuchen; herumstöbern (ugs.); **~ for sth.** nach etw. suchen
C *n.* **be on the ~ [for sth.]** [etw.] schnorren wollen (ugs.)

scrounger /'skraʊndʒə(r)/ *n.* (coll.) (cadger) Schnorrer, *der*/Schnorrerin, *die* (ugs. abwertend)

scrub[1] /skrʌb/
A *v.t.*, **-bb- 1** (rub) schrubben (ugs.); scheuern **2** (coll.: cancel, scrap) zurücknehmen ‹*Befehl*›; sausen lassen, schießen lassen (salopp) ‹*Plan, Projekt*›; wegschmeißen (ugs.) ‹*Brief*›; **the project had to be ~bed** das Projekt musste abgeblasen werden (ugs.)
B *v.i.*, **-bb- 1** (use brush) schrubben (ugs.); scheuern **2** ▸ **~ up**
C *n.* **give sth. a ~:** etw. schrubben (ugs.) *od.* scheuern

Phrasal verbs
- **~ 'out** *v.t.* **1** (clean thoroughly) schrubben (ugs.), [aus]scheuern ‹*Pfanne*›; schrubben (ugs.), scheuern ‹*Zimmer*› **2** (remove) ausbürsten ‹*Fleck*› **3** ▸ **~ A 2**
- **~ 'up** *v.i.* (Med.) sich (*Dat.*) die Hände [und Unterarme] desinfizieren

S

scrub² *n.* **1** (brushwood) Buschwerk, *das;* Strauchwerk, *das;* Gesträuch, *das;* (area of brushwood) Buschland, *das* **2** (stunted person, animal, or plant) Kümmerling, *der*

scrubber /ˈskrʌbə(r)/ *n.* **1** (sl.: immoral woman) Flittchen, *das* (ugs. abwertend); Nutte, *die* (abwertend); (sluttish woman) Schlampe, *die* (ugs. abwertend) **2** (Chem.) Wascher, *der*

ˈscrub brush (Amer.), **ˈscrubbing-brush** *ns.* Scheuerbürste, *die*

scrubby /ˈskrʌbɪ/ *adj.* **1** (bristly) stoppelig ‹*Kinn*›; stachelig, borstig ‹*Bart*› **2** (with stunted bushes) mit [niedrigem] Busch- *od.* Strauchwerk bewachsen ‹*Gebiet*› **3** (stunted) krüppelhaft ‹*Büsche, Sträucher*›

scruff¹ /skrʌf/ *n.* **by the ~ of the neck** beim *od.* am Genick

scruff² *n.* (Brit. coll.) (scruffy man) vergammelter Typ (ugs.); (scruffy woman, girl) Schlampe, *die* (abwertend)

scruffily /ˈskrʌfɪlɪ/ *adv.* (coll.) gammelig (ugs. abwertend) ‹*angezogen*›

scruffy /ˈskrʌfɪ/ *adj.* vergammelt (ugs. abwertend); heruntergekommen ‹*Haus, Restaurant, Gegend*›; ungepflegt ‹*Haar*›

scrum /skrʌm/ *n.* **1** (Rugby) Gedränge, *das* **2** (coll.: milling crowd) Gedränge, *das;* Gewimmel, *das;* **a ~ of press photographers** ein Schwarm von Pressefotografen

scrum ˈhalf *n.* (Rugby) Gedrängehalb[spieler], *der*

scrummage /ˈskrʌmɪdʒ/ ▸ **scrum 1**

scrump /skrʌmp/ *v.t. & i.* stehlen

scrumptious /ˈskrʌmʃəs/ *adj.* (coll.) lecker ‹*Essen*›; **she's/she looks ~:** sie ist zum Anbeißen/sie sieht zum Anbeißen aus (ugs.)

scrumpy /ˈskrʌmpɪ/ *n.* (esp. dial.) ≈ saurer Apfelmost (bes. südd.)

scrunch /skrʌntʃ/ ▸ **crunch**

scrunchie, scrunchy /ˈskrʌntʃɪ/ *n.* Haargummi, *das*

scruple /ˈskruːpl/

A *n.* **1** *in sing. or pl.* Skrupel, *der;* Bedenken, *das;* **be [totally] without ~:** keine[rlei] Bedenken *od.* Skrupel haben; **a person with no ~s** ein gewissen- *od.* skrupelloser Mensch; **have no ~s about doing sth.** keine Bedenken *od.* Skrupel haben, etw. zu tun **2** (Brit. Hist.: unit of weight) Skrupel, *das*

B *v.i.* Bedenken *od.* Skrupel haben; **[not] ~ to do sth./about doing sth.** [keine] Bedenken *od.* Skrupel haben, etw. zu tun

scrupulous /ˈskruːpjʊləs/ *adj.* **1** (conscientious) gewissenhaft ‹*Person*›; unbedingt ‹*Ehrlichkeit*›; peinlich ‹*Sorgfalt*›; **pay ~ attention to sth.** peinlich auf etw. (*Akk.*) achten **2** (overattentive to detail) penibel (geh.); pingelig (ugs.); [übermäßig] streng ‹*Eltern*›; **be ~ about sth./in sth.** es mit etw. übertrieben genau nehmen

scrupulously /ˈskruːpjʊləslɪ/ *adv.* **1** (conscientiously) peinlich ‹*sauber, genau*›; **~ honest** auf unbedingte Ehrlichkeit bedacht **2** (with undue attention to detail) penibel (geh.); pingelig (ugs.)

scrutineer /skruːtɪˈnɪə(r)/ *n.* (Brit. Admin.) ≈ Wahlvorstand, *der*

scrutinize (**scrutinise**) /ˈskruːtɪnaɪz/ *v.t.* [genau] untersuchen ‹*Gegenstand, Forschungsgegenstand*›; [über]prüfen ‹*Rechnung, Pass, Fahrkarte*›; mustern ‹*Miene, Person*›

scrutiny /ˈskruːtɪnɪ/ *n., no pl.* **1** (critical gaze) musternder Blick; prüfender Blick; (close examination) (of recruit) Musterung, *die;* (of bill, passport, ticket) [Über]prüfung, *die;* **bear ~:** einer [genauen] Prüfung standhalten **2** (Brit.: examination of votes) Stimmenauszählung, *die*

scuba /ˈskjuːbə, ˈskuːbə/ *n.* (Sport) Regenerationstauchgerät, *das; attrib.* Geräte‹*tauchen*›; [Geräte]tauch‹*ausrüstung*›

scud /skʌd/ *v.i.*, **-dd-** **1** (skim along) ‹*Wolke:*› jagen **2** (Naut.) **~ before the wind** vor dem Wind laufen *od.* (fachspr.) lenzen

scuff /skʌf/

A *v.t.* **1** (graze) streifen; **~ one's shoe against sth.** etw. mit dem Schuh streifen **2** (mark by grazing) verkratzen, verschrammen ‹*Schuhe, Fußboden*›

B *n.* **1** Kratzer, *der;* Kratzspur, *die;* Schramme, *die* **2** (slipper) Pantoffel, *der*

scuffle /ˈskʌfl/

A *n.* Handgreiflichkeiten *Pl.;* Tätlichkeiten *Pl.;* **a ~ broke out** es kam zu Handgreiflichkeiten *od.* Tätlichkeiten

B *v.i.* **1** handgreiflich *od.* tätlich werden (**with** gegen) **2** (shuffle) schlurfen; (scurry) ‹*Mäuse:*› rascheln

scull /skʌl/

A *n.* **1** (oar) Skull, *das* **2** (boat) Skullboot, *das*

B *v.t.* skullen; rudern

C *v.i.* skullen

scullery /ˈskʌlərɪ/ *n.* Spülküche, *die*

sculpt /skʌlpt/

A *v.t.* bildhauern (ugs)

B *v.i.* (coll.) bildhauern (ugs.); **make a living from ~ing** vom Bildhauern leben

sculptor /ˈskʌlptə(r)/ *n.* ▸ **i** **p. 1260** Bildhauer, *der*/-hauerin, *die*

sculptress /ˈskʌlptrɪs/ *n.* ▸ **i** **p. 1260** Bildhauerin, *die*

sculptural /ˈskʌlptʃərl/ *adj.* **1** plastisch **2** (resembling sculpture) skulptural (geh.) ‹*Gesichtszüge, Form*›; plastisch

sculpture /ˈskʌlptʃə(r)/

A *n.* **1** (art) Bildhauerei, *die* **2** (piece of work) Skulptur, *die;* Plastik, *die;* (pieces collectively) Skulpturen; Plastiken

B *v.t.* **1** (represent) skulpt[ur]ieren (geh.); bildhauerisch darstellen; **~d in marble/stone/bronze** in Marmor/Stein gehauen/in Bronze gegossen **2** (shape) formen (**into** zu); **a finely ~d nose** eine schön *od.* fein modellierte Nase

C *v.i.* bildhauern (ugs.); skulpt[ur]ieren (geh.); (in plastic material) modellieren

scum /skʌm/ *n.* **1** Schmutzschicht, *die;* (film) Schmutzfilm, *der;* (on soup etc.) oben schwimmende Schicht; (greasy) Fettschicht, *die;* **a ring of ~ around the bath** ein Schmutzrand in der Badewanne **2** *no pl., no indef. art.* (fig. derog.) Abschaum, *der* (abwertend); Auswurf, *der* (abwertend); **the ~ of the earth/of humanity** der Abschaum der Menschheit

ˈscumbag *n.* (sl. derog.) Schwein, *das* (salopp)

scupper¹ /ˈskʌpə(r)/ *n.* (Naut.) Speigatt, *das*

scupper² *v.t.* (Brit. coll.) **1** (defeat) über den Haufen werfen (ugs.) ‹*Plan*›; **we're ~ed if the police arrive** wenn die Polizei kommt, sind wir erledigt **2** (sink) versenken ‹*Schiff, Mannschaft*›; **be ~ed** ‹*Mannschaft:*› absaufen (salopp)

scurf /skɜːf/ *n.* Schuppen *Pl.*

scurfy /ˈskɜːfɪ/ *adj.* schuppig ‹*Haar, Fell*›

scurrilous /ˈskʌrɪləs/ *adj.* **1** (abusive) niederträchtig **2** (gross, obscene) unflätig

scurrilously /ˈskʌrɪləslɪ/ *adv.* **1** (abusively) in niederträchtiger Weise **2** (grossly, obscenely) in unflätiger Weise

scurry /ˈskʌrɪ/

A *v.i.* huschen; flitzen (ugs.)

B *n.* **1** (bustle) Geschäftigkeit, *die* **2** (act) Hetze, *die;* **a ~ for the best seats** ein Sturm auf die besten Plätze **3** (sound) (of feet) Getrappel, *das*

scurvy /ˈskɜːvɪ/

A *n.* (Med.) Skorbut, *der*

B *adj.* (arch.) niederträchtig

ˈscuse /skjuːz/ *v.t.* (coll.) **~ me** ˈtschuldigung; **~ fingers** ˈtschuldigung, dass *od.* wenn ich die Finger nehme

scut /skʌt/ *n.* (of deer) Wedel, *der* (Jägerspr.); (of rabbit, hare) Blume, *die* (Jägerspr.)

scuttle¹ /ˈskʌtl/ *n.* **1** (coal box) Kohlenfüller, *der* **2** (Brit. Motor Veh.) *Teil der Karosserie zwischen Motorhaube und unterem Rand der Windschutzscheibe*

scuttle² (Naut.)

A *v.t.* versenken

B *n.* Luke, *die*

scuttle³ *v.i.* (scurry) rennen; flitzen (ugs.); ‹*Maus, Krabbe:*› huschen; **she ~d off** sie huschte davon

scuzz /skʌz/ *n.* (Amer. coll.) **1** *no pl.* (vileness) Widerwärtigkeit, *die;* Abscheulichkeit, *die* **2** (person) Ekel, *das;* **they are ~es** sie sind Gesindel (abwertend) *od.* Gesocks (derb abwertend)

ˈscuzzbag, ˈscuzzball *ns.* (Amer. coll.) Ekel, *das*

scuzzy /ˈskʌzɪ/ *adj.* **1** (dirty, murky) versifft (ugs.) **2** (despicable, sleazy) schmierig; **a ~ magazine** ein Schmierblatt

Scylla and Charybdis /sɪlə ənd kəˈrɪbdɪs/ *n., no pl.* **between ~:** zwischen Szylla und Charybdis

scythe /saɪð/

A *n.* Sense, *die*

B *v.t.* [mit der Sense] mähen ‹*Wiese, Gras, usw.*›; [mit der Sense] abmähen ‹*Gras usw.*›

SDI *abbr.* **= strategic defence initiative** SDI

SDLP *abbr.* **= Social Democratic and Labour Party** sozialistische Partei Nordirlands

SDP *abbr.* (Brit. Polit.) **= Social Democratic Party**

SDR *abbr.* (Econ.) **special drawing right** SZR

SE *abbr.* ▸ **i** **p. 1013** **1** /saʊθˈiːst/ **= south-east** SO **2** /saʊθˈiːstən/ **= south-eastern** sö.

sea /siː/ *n.* **1** Meer, *das;* **the ~:** das Meer; die See; **by ~:** mit dem Schiff; **by the ~:** am Meer; an der See; **at ~:** auf See (*Dat.*); **be all at ~** (fig.) nicht mehr weiter wissen; **when it comes to maths I'm all at ~:** von Mathe hab ich nicht die geringste Ahnung; **worse things happen at ~** (joc.) davon geht die Welt nicht unter (ugs.); **beyond [the] ~[s]** (literary) ▸ **overseas 1**; **go to ~:** in See stechen; (become sailor) zur See gehen (ugs.); **on the ~** (in ship) auf See (*Dat.*); (on coast) am Meer; an der See; **put [out] to ~:** in See (*Akk.*) gehen *od.* stechen; auslaufen; *see also* **high seas**; **inland sea** **2** (specific tract of water) Meer, *das;* **the seven ~s** (literary/poet.) die sieben [Welt]meere **3** (freshwater lake) See, *der;* **the S~ of Galilee** der See Genezareth **4** *in sing. or pl.* (state of ~) See, *die;* (wave) Welle, *die;* Woge, *die;* (swell) See, *die* (Seemannsspr.); **there was a heavy ~:** es herrschte schwere See (Seemannsspr.); **run into heavy ~s** in schwere See kommen (Seemannsspr.); *see also* **half-seas-over**; **ship B 4** **5** (fig.: vast quantity) Meer, *das;* (of drink) Strom, *der* **6** *attrib.* (of or on the ~) See‹*klima, -wind, -wasser, -schlacht, -karte, -weg*›; Meer‹*gott, -ungeheuer, -wasser, -salz usw.*›; Meeres‹*grund, -küste, -niveau, -spiegel usw.*›; (in names of marine fauna or flora) See‹*maus, -gurke, -anemone, -löwe, -schildkröte usw.*›; Meer‹*brasse, -neunauge, -gurke usw.*›

sea: ~ ˈair *n.* Seeluft, *die;* **~ aˈnemone** *n.* (Zool.) Seeanemone, *die;* Seerose, *die;* **~ bass** *n.* (Zool.) [Schwarzer] Sägebarsch; **~bed** *n.* Meeresboden *der;* Meeresgrund, *der;* **~bird** *n.* Seevogel, *der;* **~board** *n.* Küste, *die;* **~boot** *n.* Seestiefel, *der;* **~ breeze** *n.* (Meteorol.) Seewind, *der;* Seebrise, *die;* **~ ˈcaptain** *n.* [Schiffs]kapitän, *der;* **~ change** *n.* (esp. literary: unexpected or notable transformation) erstaunliche Metamorphose (geh.); **~ chest** *n.* (Naut.) Seekiste, *die;* **~ coast** *n.* Meeresküste, *die;* **~ ˈcucumber** *n.* (Zool.) Seegurke, *die;* Meergurke, *die;* **~ defences** *n. pl.* Küstenschutzanlagen *Pl.;* **~ dog** *n.* **1** (Zool.) Seehund, *der;* **2** (literary/joc.: experienced sailor) Seebär, *der* (ugs. scherzh.); **~ eagle** *n.* Seeadler, *der;* **~farer** /ˈsiːfeərə(r)/ *n.* (formal) Matrose, *der;* **~faring** /ˈsiːfeərɪŋ/ **A** *adj.* **~faring man** Seemann, *der;* **~faring nation** Seefahrernation, *die;* seefahrende Nation; **his ~faring days** die Zeit, als er zur See fuhr; **B** *n., no pl., no indef. art.* Seefahrt, *die;* **~ fish** *n.* Seefisch, *der;* **~ fog** *n.* Seenebel, *der;* **~food** *n.* Meeresfrüchte *Pl.; attrib.* Fisch‹*restaurant*›; **~food cocktail** Cocktail aus Meeresfrüchten; **~ fowl** ▸ **seabird**; **~front** *n.: unmittelbar am Meer gelegene Straße[n] einer Seestadt;* **a walk along the ~front** ein Spaziergang am Wasser *od.* auf der Uferpromenade; **the hotels on the ~front** die Hotels direkt am Wasser *od.* an der Uferpromenade; **~ god** *n.* Meergott, *der;* **~going** *adj.* (for crossing sea) seegehend; **~going yacht** Hochseejacht, *die;* **~ green** **A** /ˈ-ˈ-/ *n.* Seegrün, *das;* Meergrün, *das;* **B** /ˈ--/ *adj.* seegrün; meergrün; **~gull** *n.* [See]möwe, *die;* **~ horse** *n.* (Zool.) Seepferdchen, *das;* **~kale** *n.* (Bot.) Meerkohl, *der;* Seekohl, *der;* Englischer Kohl

ℹ Seasons

In German, the seasons are always written with an article, whether there is one in English or not:

in spring, in the spring
= im Frühling *or* Frühjahr

in summer, in the summer
= im Sommer

***in autumn, in the autumn* (esp. Brit.)/*in the fall* (Amer.)**
= im Herbst

in winter, in the winter
= im Winter

All four words for the seasons in German are masculine, with the exception of the alternative term for *spring*, **das Frühjahr**. Generally this refers simply to the time of year, whereas **der Frühling** has all the connotations of rebirth etc. associated with spring, while also being the term used in astronomical contexts (there is even a third term, **der Lenz**, which occurs only in poetry).

Spring came early
= Der Frühling ist früh eingetroffen

in early/late spring
= zu Anfang/Ende des Frühjahrs

It's going to be a hard winter
= Der Winter wird hart werden

He is staying [for] the whole summer
= Er bleibt den ganzen Sommer

It lasted all summer* or *throughout the summer
= Es dauerte den ganzen Sommer

She was here last winter
= Sie war letzten Winter hier

They are coming this/next autumn
= Sie kommen diesen/nächsten Herbst

Seasonal adjectives

The four adjectives in German derived from the names of the seasons are **frühlingshaft**, **sommerlich, herbstlich** and **winterlich.** They have the sense "typical or appropriate for the season", like the English *springlike, summery, autumnal* and *wintry* respectively, although they will also equate to some attributive uses of the noun:

winter clothing
= (*worn in winter*) Winterkleidung; (*warm and thus suitable for winter*) winterliche Kleidung

summer clothing
= (*worn in summer*) Sommerkleidung; (*light and thus suitable for summer*) sommerliche Kleidung

winter/summer temperatures
= winterliche/sommerliche Temperaturen

a winter landscape
= (*seen in winter*) eine Winterlandschaft; (*typical of winter, wintry*) eine winterliche Landschaft

seal[1] /siːl/ *n.* **1** (Zool.) Robbe, *die;* **[common] ~:** [Gemeiner] Seehund **2** ▸**sealskin**

seal[2]

A *n.* **1** (piece of wax, lead, etc., stamp, impression) Siegel, *das;* (lead ~ also) Plombe, *die;* (stamp also) Siegelstempel, *der;* Petschaft, *das;* (impression also) Siegelabdruck, *der;* **fix a ~ on** versiegeln; (using lead) verplomben; plombieren; **put [lead] ~s on** verplomben, plombieren ‹*Tür*›; **~s of office** (Brit.) Dienstsiegel; Amtssiegel **2** (adhesive stamp) Julmarke, *die* (Philat.) **3** **set the ~ on** (fig.) zementieren (+ *Akk.*); **set one's ~ to sth.** (fig.) grünes Licht für etw. geben; etw. absegnen (ugs.) **4** (guarantee) **gain the ~ of respectability** sich (*Dat.*) großes Ansehen erwerben; **have the ~ of official approval** offiziell gebilligt werden **5** (to close aperture) Abdichtung, *die;* (odour trap) Geruchsverschluss, *der. See also* **privy seal**

B *v.t.* **1** (stamp with ~, affix ~ to) siegeln ‹*Dokument*›; (fasten with ~) verplomben, plombieren ‹*Tür, Stromzähler*› **2** (close securely) abdichten ‹*Behälter, Rohr usw.*›; zukleben ‹*Umschlag, Paket*›; [zum Verschließen der Poren] kurz anbraten ‹*Fleisch*›; **my lips are ~ed** (fig.) meine Lippen sind versiegelt; **be a ~ed book to sb.** (fig.) ein Buch mit sieben Siegeln für jmdn. sein; **~ed orders** versiegelte Order **3** (stop up) verschließen; abdichten ‹*Leck*›; verschmieren ‹*Riss*› **4** (decide) besiegeln ‹*Geschäft, Abmachung, jmds. Schicksal*› **5** (provide with water ~) mit einem Geruchsverschluss versehen ‹*Rohr*› **6** (Road Constr.) befestigen; mit einer [Fahrbahn]decke versehen

Phrasal verbs

- **~ 'in** *v.t.* bewahren ‹*Geschmack*›; am Austreten hindern ‹*Fleischsaft*›
- **~ 'off** *v.t.* abriegeln
- **~ 'up** ▸**~ B 2, 3**

'sea lane *n.* (Naut.) See[schifffahrts]straße, *die*

sealant /ˈsiːlənt/ *n.* Dichtungsmaterial, *das*

sea: ~ legs *n. pl.* Seebeine *Pl.* (Seemannsspr.); **get** *or* **find one's ~ legs** sich (*Dat.*) Seebeine wachsen lassen (Seemannsspr.); **~ level** *n.* Meeresspiegel, *der* (fachspr.); **200 feet above/below ~ level** 200 Fuß über/unter dem Meeresspiegel *od.* über/unter Meereshöhe *od.* (fachspr.) Normalnull; **at ~ level** auf Meereshöhe (*Dat.*)

sealing wax /ˈsiːlɪŋwæks/ *n.* Siegellack, *der;* Siegelwachs, *das*

'sea lion *n.* (Zool.) Seelöwe, *der*

'Sea Lord *n.* (Brit.) Seelord, *der*

'sealskin *n.* Robbenfell, *das;* (garment) Robbenfelljacke, *die*/Robbenfellmantel, *der usw.*

Sealyham [terrier] /ˈsiːlɪəm (terɪə[r])/ *n.* Sealyhamterrier, *der*

seam /siːm/ *n.* **1** (line of joining) Naht, *die;* (Carpentry) Verbindung, *die;* **come apart at the ~s** aus den Nähten gehen; (fig. coll.: fail) zusammenbrechen; **burst at the ~s** (fig.) aus den *od.* allen Nähten platzen (ugs.); *see also* **fall B 20** **2** (fissure) Spalt, *der;* Spalte, *die;* (in ship) Naht, die (fachspr.) **3** (Mining) Flöz, *das;* (Geol.) (stratum) Schicht, *die;* (line between strata) [Schicht]fuge, *die* **4** (wrinkle) Runzel, *die;* Falte, *die*

seaman /ˈsiːmən/ *n., pl.* **seamen** /ˈsiːmən/ ▸ℹ **p. 1260** **1** (sailor) Matrose, *der; see also* **able seaman; ordinary seaman** **2** (expert in navigation etc.) Seemann, *der*

seamanlike /ˈsiːmənlaɪk/ *adj.* seemännisch

seamanship /ˈsiːmənʃɪp/ *n., no pl.* seemännisches Geschick; Seemannschaft, *die* (fachspr.)

'seamark *n.* (Naut.) Seezeichen, *das*

seamed /siːmd/ *adj.* **1** (having seam) **~ stockings** Strümpfe mit Naht **2** (wrinkled) faltig; runzlig; zerfurcht **3** (Geol.: having seams) geschiefert

sea: ~mew *n.* [See]möwe, *die;* **~ mile** ▸**nautical mile**; **~ mist** *n.* Küstennebel, *der*

seamless /ˈsiːmlɪs/ *adj.* nahtlos

seamlessly /ˈsiːmlɪslɪ/ *adv.* nahtlos; **the houses blend ~ into the landscape** die Häuser fügen sich bruchlos in die Landschaft ein

sea: ~ monster *n.* (Mythol.) Seeungeheuer, *das;* Meerungeheuer, *das;* **~mount** *n.* (Geog.) Tiefseeberg, *der*

seamstress /ˈsemstrɪs/ *n.* ▸ℹ **p. 1260** Näherin, *die*

seamy /ˈsiːmɪ/ *adj.* **1** (having wrinkles) faltig, runzlig **2** (run down) heruntergekommen ‹*Stadtteil*›; **the ~ side [of life** *etc.***]** (fig.) die Schattenseite[n] [des Lebens *usw.*]

seance /ˈseɪɒns/, **séance** /ˈseɪɑ̃s/ *n.* Séance, *die* (fachspr.); spiritistische Sitzung

sea: ~ pink *n.* (Bot.) Grasnelke, *die;* Strandnelke, *die;* **~plane** *n.* Wasserflugzeug, *das;* **~port** *n.* Seehafen, *der;* **~ power** *n.* Seemacht, *die;* **~quake** *n.* Seebeben, *das*

sear /sɪə(r)/ *v.t.* verbrennen, versengen; (Med.: cauterize) ausbrennen ‹*Wunde*›

search /sɜːtʃ/

A *v.t.* durchsuchen (**for** nach); absuchen ‹*Gebiet, Fläche*› (**for** nach); prüfen *od.* musternd blicken in (+ *Akk.*) ‹*Gesicht*›; (fig.: probe) erforschen ‹*Herz, Gewissen*›; suchen in (+ *Dat.*), durchstöbern (ugs.) ‹*Gedächtnis*› (**for** nach); **~ me** (coll.) keine Ahnung!

B *v.i.* suchen; **~ after sth.** etw. *od.* nach etw. suchen; **~ and replace** (Computing) suchen und ersetzen

C *n.* Suche, *die* (**for** nach); (of building, room, etc.) Durchsuchung, *die;* **make a ~ for** suchen nach ‹*Waffen, Drogen, Diebesgut*›; **in ~ of sb./sth.** auf der Suche nach jmdm./etw.; **go off in ~ of sth.** sich auf die Suche nach etw. machen; **right of ~:** Durchsuchungsrecht, *das*

Phrasal verbs

- **~ for** *v.t.* suchen [nach]
- **~ 'out** *v.t.* heraussuchen; aufspüren ‹*Person mit unbekanntem Aufenthalt*›
- **~ through** *v.t.* durchsuchen; durchsehen ‹*Buch*›

searchable /ˈsɜːtʃəbl/ *adj.* durchsuchbar

search and re'place *n.* (Computing) Suchen und Ersetzen; **~ function** "Suchen und Ersetzen"-Funktion, *die*

'search engine *n.* (Computing) Suchmaschine, *die;* Suchroboter, *der*

searcher /ˈsɜːtʃə(r)/ *n.* Sucher, *der*/Sucherin, *die;* Suchende, *der/die;* **the ~s returned with the missing child** die Suchmannschaft kehrte mit dem vermissten Kind zurück

'search function *n.* (Computing) Suchfunktion, *die*

searching /ˈsɜːtʃɪŋ/ *adj.* prüfend, forschend ‹*Blick*›; bohrend ‹*Frage*›; (thorough) eingehend ‹*Untersuchung*›

searchingly /ˈsɜːtʃɪŋlɪ/ *adv.* prüfend, forschend ‹*jmdn. ansehen*›; eingehend ‹*befragen*›

search: ~light *n.* **1** (lamp) Suchscheinwerfer, *der;* **2** (beam of light) Scheinwerferlicht, *das* (auch fig.); (fig.) Rampenlicht, *das;* **the ~light is on him** (fig.) er steht im Scheinwerfer- *od.* Rampenlicht; **~ party** *n.* Suchtrupp, *der;* Suchmannschaft, *die;* **~ warrant** *n.* (Law) Durchsuchungsbefehl, *der*

searing /ˈsɪərɪŋ/ *adj.* sengend ‹*Hitze*›; brennend ‹*Schmerz*›; (fig.: intense) bohrend, stechend ‹*Blick*›

sea: ~ salt *n.* Meersalz, *das;* Seesalz, das; **~scape** /ˈsiːskeɪp/ *n.* **1** (Art: picture) Seestück, *das;* Marine, *die;* **2** (view) Meerespanorama, *das;* **S~ Scout** *n.* (Brit.) Seepfadfinder, *der*/-pfadfinderin, *die;* **~ serpent** *n.* Seeschlange, *die;* **~ shanty** ▸**shanty**[2]; **~shell** *n.* Muschel[schale], *die;* **~shore** *n.* (land near ~) [Meeres]küste, *die;* (beach) Strand, *der;* **walk along the ~shore** am Meer/Strand entlanggehen; **~sick** *adj.* seekrank; **~sick medicine/tablet** Mittel *od.* Medikament/Tablette gegen Seekrankheit; **~sickness** *n., no pl.* Seekrankheit, *die;* **~side** *n., no pl.* [Meeres]küste, *die;* **by/to/at the ~side** am/ans/am Meer; an der/an die/an der See; *attrib.* **~side town** Seestadt, *die;* **the usual ~side attractions** die Vergnügungen, die die Küste gemeinhin bietet

season /ˈsiːzn/

A *n.* **1** ▸ℹ **p. 1515** (time of the year) Jahreszeit, *die;* **dry/rainy ~:** Trocken-/Regenzeit, *die* **2** (time of breeding) (for mammals) Tragezeit, *die;* (for birds) Brutzeit, *die;* (time of flourishing) Blütezeit], *die;* (time when animal is hunted) Jagdzeit, *die;* **blackberry ~:** Brombeerzeit, *die;* **nesting ~:** Nistzeit, *die;* Brut[zeit], *die; see also* **close season; open season** **3** (time devoted to specified, social activity) Saison, *die;* **harvest/opera ~:** Erntezeit, die/Opernsaison, *die;* **football ~:** Fußballsaison, *die;* **holiday** *or* (Amer.) **vacation ~:** Urlaubszeit, *die;* Ferienzeit, *die;* **tourist ~:**

S

Touristensaison, *die;* Reisezeit, *die;* **the ~ of goodwill** (Christmas) die Zeit der Nächstenliebe; **'compliments of the ~'** (formal), **'the ~'s greetings'** „ein frohes Weihnachtsfest und ein glückliches neues Jahr" **4** **raspberries are in/out of** *or* **not in ~:** jetzt ist die/nicht die Saison *od.* Zeit für Himbeeren; **be in ~** (on heat) brünstig sein; **a word in ~** (literary) ein Rat[schlag] zur rechten Zeit; **in and out of ~:** zu jeder passenden oder unpassenden Zeit; (again and again) immer wieder **5** (ticket) ▸**season ticket** **6** (period of time) Zeit, *die;* (Theatre, Cinemat.) Spielzeit, *die;* **for a ~** (dated) eine Zeit lang; **they are doing a ~ in Oxford** sie gastieren [zurzeit] in Oxford; **put on a Shakespeare/Russian ~:** ≈ Shakespeare-/russische Wochen veranstalten. *See also* **high season; low season; off season; silly A 1**

B *v.t.* **1** (make palatable, lit. or fig.) würzen ‹*Fleisch, Rede*› **2** (mature) ablagern lassen ‹*Holz*›; **~ed** erfahren ‹*Wahlkämpfer, Soldat, Reisender*› **3** (temper) mäßigen (geh.) ‹*Impulsivität*›

C *v.i.* ‹*Holz:*› ablagern; ‹*Whisky:*› lagern, reifen

seasonable /ˈsiːzənəbl/ *adj.* **1** (suitable to the time of the year) der Jahreszeit gemäß **2** (opportune) willkommen ‹*Angebot*›; (meeting needs of occasion) geboten ‹*Vorsicht*›; passend ‹*Worte*›

seasonably /ˈsiːzənəblɪ/ *adv.* **1** (in a way typical of the season) der Jahreszeit entsprechend **2** (so as to be opportune) zur rechten Zeit

seasonal /ˈsiːzənl/ *adj.* Saison‹*arbeit, -geschäft*›; saisonabhängig ‹*Preise*›

seasonal af'fective disorder *n., no pl.* saisonabhängige Depression

seasonally /ˈsiːzənəlɪ/ *adv.* saisonal, saisonbedingt ‹*schwanken*›; **~ adjusted** (Statistics) saisonbereinigt ‹*Arbeitslosenzahlen*›

seasoning /ˈsiːzənɪŋ/ *n.* **1** (Cookery) Gewürze *Pl.;* Würze, *die* **2** (fig.) Würze, *die;* **have a ~ of wit** ‹*Unterhaltung:*› witzig *od.* geistreich *od.* mit Witz gewürzt sein

'season ticket *n.* Dauerkarte, *die;* (for one year/month) Jahres-/Monatskarte, *die*

seat /siːt/

A *n.* **1** (thing for sitting on) Sitzgelegenheit, *die;* (in vehicle, cinema, etc.) Sitz, *der;* (of toilet) [Klosett]brille, *die* (ugs.); **use sth. for a ~:** sich auf etw. (*Akk.*) setzen; (be sitting) auf etw. (*Dat.*) sitzen **2** (place) Platz, *der;* (in vehicle) [Sitz]platz, *der;* **have** *or* **take a ~:** sich [hin]setzen; Platz nehmen (geh.); **take one's ~ at table** sich zu Tisch setzen; **keep one's ~:** sitzen bleiben; ‹*Reiter:*› im Sattel bleiben, sich im Sattel halten; **resume one's ~:** sich wieder [hin]setzen; (after the interval etc.) seinen Platz wieder einnehmen; wieder Platz nehmen (geh.); *see also* **back seat** **3** (part of chair) Sitzfläche, *die* **4** (buttocks) Gesäß, *das;* (part of clothing) Gesäßpartie, *die;* (of trousers) Sitz, *der;* Hosenboden, *der;* **by the ~ of one's pants** (coll. fig.) nach Gefühl **5** (site) Sitz, *der;* (of disease also) Herd, *der* (Med.); (of learning) Stätte, *die* (geh.); (of trouble) Quelle, *die;* **~ of the fire** Brandherd, *der* **6** (right to sit in Parliament etc.) Sitz, *der;* Mandat, *das;* **be elected to a ~ in Parliament** ins Parlament gewählt werden; **be appointed to a ~ on a committee** in einen Ausschuss berufen werden **7** **[country] ~** (mansion) Landsitz, *der* **8** (on horseback) Sitz, *der;* [Sitz]haltung, *die* **9** (Mech. Engin.) Sitz, *der;* **valve ~:** Ventilsitz, *der*

B *v.t.* **1** (cause to sit) setzen; (accommodate at table etc.) unterbringen; (ask to sit) ‹*Platzanweiser:*› einen Platz anweisen (+ *Dat.*); **~ oneself** sich setzen **2** (have ~s for) Sitzplätze bieten (+ *Dat.*); **~ 500 people** 500 Sitzplätze haben; **the car ~s five comfortably** in dem Auto haben fünf Personen bequem Platz **3** (fit with seats) bestuhlen ‹*Saal usw.*› **4** (Mech. Engin.) in [die richtige] Position bringen

'seat belt *n.* (Motor Veh., Aeronaut.) Sicherheitsgurt, *der;* **fasten one's ~:** sich anschnallen; den Gurt anlegen; **wear a ~:** angeschnallt sein; (during journey) angeschnallt fahren

'seat-belt tensioner /ˈtenʃnə(r)/*n.* Gurtstraffer, *der*

seated /ˈsiːtɪd/ *adj.* sitzend; **remain ~:** sitzen bleiben; **take 50 ~ passengers** 50 Sitzplätze haben; **be ~** (formal) Platz nehmen (geh.)

-seater /ˈsiːtə(r)/ *adj. in comb.* -sitzig; **two-~ [car]** Zweisitzer, *der*

seating /ˈsiːtɪŋ/ *n., no pl., no indef. art.* **1** (seats) Sitzplätze; Sitzgelegenheiten **2** (act) Platzierung, *die;* Versorgung mit Sitzplätzen **3** *attrib.* Sitz‹*ordnung, -plan*›; **~ accommodation** Sitzgelegenheiten; Sitzplätze; **the ~ arrangements** die Sitzordnung

SEATO /ˈsiːtəʊ/ *abbr.* **= South-East-Asia Treaty Organisation** SEATO, *die*

sea: ~ urchin *n.* (Zool.) Seeigel, *der;* **~ view** *n.* Meerblick, *der;* **~ wall** *n.* Strandmauer, *die;* (dyke) Deich, *der*

seaward /ˈsiːwəd/

A *adj.* seewärtig ‹*Kurs, Wind*›; **the ~ side** die Seeseite; **the ~ view** die Aussicht aufs Meer *od.* auf die See

B *adv.* seewärts; nach See zu

C *n.* **to [the] ~:** zur Seeseite hin

seawards /ˈsiːwədz/ ▸**seaward B**

sea: ~ water *n.* Meerwasser, *das;* Seewasser, *das;* **~weed** *n.* [See]tang, *der;* **~worthy** *adj.* seetüchtig

sebaceous /sɪˈbeɪʃəs/ *adj.* talgig; **~ duct/gland** (Anat.) Talgdrüsenausführungsgang, *der*/Talgdrüse, *die*

seborrhoea (*Amer.:* **seborrhea**) /sebəˈriːə/ *n.* (Med.) Seborrhö[e], *die* (fachspr.); Talgfluss, *der*

sec /sek/ (coll.) ▸**second B 2**

sec. *abbr.* **= second[s]** Sek.

Sec. *abbr.* **= Secretary** Sekr.

secant /ˈsiːkənt, ˈsekənt/ *n.* (Math.) Sekante, *die;* (of angle) Sekans, *der*

secateurs /sekəˈtɜːz, ˈsekətɜːz/ *n. pl.* (Brit. Hort.) Gartenschere, *die;* Rosenschere, *die*

secede /sɪˈsiːd/ *v.i.* (Polit./Eccl./formal) sich abspalten (**from** von); ‹*Mitglied:*› austreten (**from** aus)

secession /sɪˈseʃn/ *n.* (Polit./Eccl./formal) Abspaltung, *die;* (of member) Austritt, *der;* **the ~ of some southern states** die Sezession einiger Südstaaten

seclude /sɪˈkluːd/ *v.t.* absondern; **~ oneself** (from society) sich abkapseln *od.* absondern; (into a room) sich zurückziehen (**into** in + *Akk.*)

secluded /sɪˈkluːdɪd/ *adj.* **1** (hidden from view) versteckt; (somewhat isolated) abgelegen **2** (solitary) zurückgezogen ‹*Leben*›

seclusion /sɪˈkluːʒn/ *n.* **1** (keeping from company) Absonderung, *die;* (being kept from company) Abgesondertheit, *die;* **in ~ from** abgesondert von **2** (privacy) (of life) Zurückgezogenheit, *die;* (of room) Abgeschiedenheit, *die;* **in ~:** zurückgezogen ‹*leben*› **3** *no pl.* (remoteness) Abgelegenheit, *die*

second /ˈsekənd/

A *adj.* ▸**ⓘ p. 1358** zweit...; zweitwichtigst... ‹*Stadt, Hafen usw.*›; **~ largest/highest** *etc.* zweitgrößt.../-höchst... *usw.;* **come in/be ~:** Zweiter/Zweite werden/sein; **every ~ week** jede zweite Woche; **~ to none** unübertroffen

B *n.* **1** ▸**ⓘ p. 1001** (unit of time or angle) Sekunde, *die* **2** (coll.: moment) Sekunde, *die* (ugs.); **wait a few ~s** einen Moment warten; **in a ~** (immediately) sofort (ugs.); (very quickly) im Nu (ugs.); **just a ~!** (coll.) einen Moment! **3** (additional person or thing) **a ~:** noch einer/eine/eins **4** **the ~** (in sequence, rank) der/die/das Zweite; **be the ~ to arrive** als Zweiter/Zweite ankommen; **be a good ~:** einen guten zweiten Platz belegen **5** (in duel, boxing) Sekundant, *der*/Sekundantin, *die;* **~s out [of the ring]** (Boxing) Ring frei! **6** *in pl.* (helping of food) zweite Portion; (~ course) zweiter Gang; **are there any ~s?** kann man eine zweite Portion bekommen? **7** ▸**ⓘ p. 1047** (day) **the ~ of May** der zweite Mai; **the ~ [of the month]** der Zweite [des Monats] **8** (~ form) zweite [Schul]klasse; Zweite, *die* (Schuljargon) **9** *in pl.* (goods of ~ quality) Waren zweiter Wahl; **be ~s** zweite Wahl sein **10** (Motor Veh.) zweiter Gang; **in ~:** im zweiten [Gang]; **change into ~:** in den zweiten [Gang] schalten **11** (Brit. Univ.) ≈ Gut, *das;* ≈ Zwei, *die;* **she got a ~ in mathematics** sie hat in Mathematik mit [einem] Gut *od.* [einer] Zwei abgeschlossen **12** (Mus.) Sekunde, *die*

C *v.t.* **1** (support in debate) unterstützen ‹*Antrag, Nominierung*›; sekundieren (geh.); **I'll ~ that!** (coll.) dem schließe ich mich an! **2** /sɪˈkɒnd/ (transfer) vorübergehend versetzen **3** /ˈsekənd/ (support) unterstützen **4** /sɪˈkɒnd/ (Brit. Mil.) abstellen

secondarily /ˈsekəndərɪlɪ/ *adv.* **1** in zweiter Linie; an zweiter Stelle **2** (indirectly) mittelbar; indirekt

secondary /ˈsekəndərɪ/ *adj.* **1** (of less importance) zweitrangig; sekundär (geh.); Neben‹*akzent, -sache*›; (derived from sth. primary) weiterverarbeitend ‹*Industrie*›; **~ literature** Sekundärliteratur, *die;* **be ~ to sth.** einer Sache (*Dat.*) untergeordnet sein **2** (indirectly caused) sekundär (geh., Med., Biol.); *see also* **picketing** **3** (supplementary) zusätzlich **4** **S~** (Geol.) ▸**Mesozoic A**

secondary: ~ coil *n.* (Electr.) Sekundärspule, *die;* **~ colour** ▸**colour A 1;** **~ education** *n., no pl.* höhere Schule; (result) höhere Schulbildung; **~ 'health care** *n., no pl.* medizinische Sekundärversorgung; **~ in'fection** *n.* (Med.) Sekundärinfektion, *die;* **~ 'modern [school]** *n.* (Brit. Hist.) ≈ Mittelschule, *die* (veralt.); Realschule, *die;* **~ 'picketing** *n., no pl.* (Brit.) *Aufstellen von Streikposten bei nicht betroffenen Firmen;* **~ school** *n.* höhere *od.* weiterführende Schule

second: ~ 'base ▸**base¹ A 3;** **~-best**

A /ˈ---/ *adj.* zweitbest...; **B** /-ˈ-/ *adv.* **come off ~-best** den Kürzeren ziehen (ugs.); **C** /--ˈ-/ *n., no pl.* Zweitbeste, *der/die/das;* **don't settle for [the] ~-best!** gib dich nicht mit halben Sachen zufrieden; **~ 'chamber** *n.* (Parl.) zweite Kammer; **~ 'childhood** ▸**childhood;** **~ 'class** *n.* **1** (set ranking after others) zweite Kategorie; **2** (Transport, Post) zweite Klasse; **travel in the ~ class** zweiter Klasse reisen; **3** (Brit. Univ.) ▸**second B 11;** **~-class** **A** /ˈ---/ *adj.* **1** (of lower class) zweiter Klasse *nachgestellt;* Zweite[r]-Klasse-‹*Post, Passagier, Fahrkarte usw.*›; **~-class stamp** *Briefmarke für langsamere Postzustellung;* **get a ~-class degree** (Brit. Univ.) mit der Note Zwei *od.* Gut abschließen; **2** (of inferior class) zweitklassig (abwertend); **~-class citizen** Bürger zweiter Klasse; **B** /-ˈ-/ *adv.* zweiter Klasse ‹*reisen, fahren*›; **send a letter ~-class** einen Brief mit Zweiter-Klasse-Post schicken; **~ 'coming** *n., no pl.* (Relig.) zweite Ankunft; Wiederkunft, *die;* [zweite] Parusie (fachspr.); **~ 'cousin** ▸**cousin**

seconder /ˈsekəndə(r)/ *n.* Befürworter, *der*/-worterin, *die;* Sekundant, *der*/Sekundantin, *die* (geh.)

second: ~ 'fiddle ▸**fiddle A 1;** **~ 'floor** ▸**floor A 2;** **~ form** ▸**form A 4;** **~ 'gear** *n., no pl.* (Motor Veh.) zweiter Gang; *see also* **gear A 1;** **~-generation** *adj.* der zweiten Generation *nachgestellt;* **~-guess** *v.t.* (Amer.) **1** im Nachhinein kritisieren; **2** (anticipate) voraussehen; **~-guess sb.** voraussehen, was jmd. tun wird; **~ hand** *n.* (Horol.) Sekundenzeiger, *der;* **~-hand** **A** /ˈ---/ *adj.* **1** (used) gebraucht ‹*Kleidung, Auto usw.*›; antiquarisch ‹*Buch*›; Secondhand‹*buch, -schallplatte, -kleidung usw.*›; **~-hand car** Gebrauchtwagen, *der;* **2** (selling used goods) Gebrauchtwaren-; Secondhand‹*laden, -shop*›; **3** (taken on another's authority) ‹*Nachrichten, Bericht*› aus zweiter Hand; **B** /-ˈ-/ *adv.* aus zweiter Hand (auch fig.); gebraucht; **get a book ~-hand** ein Buch antiquarisch kaufen; **~ 'home** *n.* Zweitwohnung, *die;* (holiday house) Ferienhaus, *das;* **~ in com'mand** *n.* (Mil.) stellvertretender Kommandeur; (of ship) stellvertretender Kommandant; (fig. coll.) stellvertretender Leiter; **~ job** *n.* Zweitjob, *der;* **~ lieu'tenant** *n.* (Mil.) ≈ Leutnant, *der*

secondly /ˈsekəndlɪ/ *adv.* zweitens

secondment /sɪˈkɒndmənt/ *n.* (Brit.) **1** (of official) vorübergehende Versetzung; **be on [a] ~:** vorübergehend versetzt sein **2** (Mil.) Abstellung, *die*

second: ~ name *n.* Nachname, *der;* Zuname, *der;* **~ 'nature** *n., no pl., no art.* (coll.) zweite Natur; **become/be ~ nature to sb.** jmdm. zur zweiten Natur werden/geworden sein; jmdm. in Fleisch und Blut (*Akk.*)

übergehen/übergegangen sein; ~ '**officer** *n.* (Naut.) zweiter Offizier; ~ '**person** ▸**person 4**; ~-'**rate** *adj.* zweitklassig; **very/rather ~-rate** sehr/ziemlich mittelmäßig; **~-'rater** *n.* (coll.) **be a ~-rater** zweitklassig sein; ~ '**reading** ▸**reading 7**; **~s hand** ▸**second hand**; ~ **sight** ▸**sight A 1**; ~ '**string** ▸**string A 2**; ~ '**thoughts** *n. pl.* **have ~ thoughts** es sich (*Dat.*) anders überlegen (**about** mit); **we've had ~ thoughts about buying the house** wir wollen das Haus nun doch nicht kaufen; **we've had ~ thoughts about the house** wir haben uns das mit dem Haus doch noch einmal überlegt; **there's no time for ~ thoughts** es ist zu spät, es sich noch einmal anders zu überlegen; **but on ~ thoughts I think I will** wenn ich mirs [noch mal] überlege, werde ich es doch tun; ~ **wind** ▸**wind**[1] **A 6**

secrecy /'si:krɪsɪ/ *n.* 1 (keeping of secret) Geheimhaltung, *die;* **with great ~:** in aller Heimlichkeit *od.* ganz im Geheimen 2 (secretiveness) Heimlichtuerei, *die* (abwertend) 3 (unrevealed state) Heimlichkeit, *die;* **be shrouded in ~:** geheim gehalten werden; **in ~:** im Geheimen

secret /'si:krɪt/
A *adj.* 1 (kept private, not to be made known) geheim; Geheim‹fach, -tür, -abkommen, -kode›; **keep sth. ~:** etw. geheim halten (**from** vor + *Dat.*) 2 (acting in ~) heimlich ‹*Trinker, Liebhaber, Bewunderer*›
B *n.* 1 Geheimnis, *das;* **make no ~ of sth.** kein Geheimnis aus etw. machen; (not conceal feelings, opinion) kein[en] Hehl aus etw. machen; **keep the ~:** es für sich behalten; **keep ~s/a ~:** schweigen (fig.); den Mund halten (ugs.); **can you keep a ~?** kannst du schweigen?; **make sth. a ~:** etw. geheim halten; **keep ~s from sb.** Geheimnisse vor jmdm. haben; **let sb. in on a ~:** jmdn. in ein Geheimnis einweihen; **be in the ~:** eingeweiht sein; **open ~:** offenes Geheimnis; **the ~ of health/success** *etc.* das Geheimnis der Gesundheit/des Erfolgs *usw.*; der Schlüssel zur Gesundheit/zum Erfolg *usw.* 2 **in ~:** im Geheimen; heimlich

secret 'agent *n.* Geheimagent, *der*/-agentin, *die*

secretaire /sekrɪ'teə(r)/ ▸**escritoire**

secretarial /sekrə'teərɪəl/ *adj.* Sekretariats‹*personal*›; Sekretärinnen‹*kursus, -tätigkeit*›; ‹*Arbeit*› als Sekretärin; ~ **skills** Steno- und Schreibmaschinenkenntnisse

secretariat /sekrə'teərɪət/ *n.* Sekretariat, *das*

secretary /'sekrətərɪ/ *n.* ▸ⓘ **p. 1260** 1 (official of organization) Sekretär, *der*/Sekretärin, *die;* (of company) Schriftführer, *der*/-führerin, *die;* **honorary ~:** ehrenamtlicher Sekretär 2 (personal assistant) Sekretär, *der*/Sekretärin, *die;* **Parliamentary [Private] S~** (Brit. Parl.) ≈ parlamentarischer Staatssekretär/parlamentarische Staatssekretärin; **Permanent S~** (Brit. Admin.) ≈ Staatssekretär, *der*/-sekretärin, *die; see also* **private secretary**

secretary: ~ **bird** *n.* Sekretär, *der;* **S~ 'General** *n., pl.* **Secretaries General** Generalsekretär, *der*/-sekretärin, *die;* **S~ of 'State** *n.* 1 (Brit. Polit.) Minister, *der*/Ministerin, *die;* **S~ of State for Defence** Verteidigungsminister, *der*/-ministerin, *die;* 2 (Amer. Polit.) Außenminister, *der*/-ministerin, *die;* 3 (Amer. Admin.: head of records department) *Leiter/Leiterin des Archivs eines Bundesstaates*

secretaryship /'sekrətərɪʃɪp/ *n.* 1 (office) Amt des Sekretärs/der Sekretärin 2 (tenure) Amtszeit als Sekretär/Sekretärin

secret 'ballot *n.* geheime Abstimmung

secrete /sɪ'kri:t/ *v.t.* 1 (Physiol.) absondern; sezernieren (fachspr.) 2 (formal/literary: hide) verbergen; ~ **oneself** sich verbergen

secretion /sɪ'kri:ʃn/ *n.* 1 (Physiol.) Absonderung, *die;* (process also) Sekretion, *die* (fachspr.); (substance also) Sekret, *das* (fachspr.) 2 (formal/literary: concealing) Verbergen, *das*

secretive /'si:krɪtɪv/ *adj.* verschlossen ‹*Person*›; geheimnisvoll ‹*Lächeln*›; **be ~:** heimlich tun (abwertend) *od.* geheimnisvoll tun (**about** mit); **she was being very ~ about something** sie versuchte, irgendetwas zu verheimlichen

secretively /'si:krɪtɪvlɪ, sɪ'kri:tɪvlɪ/ *adv.* geheimnisvoll ‹*lächeln*›; **behave ~:** geheimnisvoll *od.* (abwertend) heimlich tun

secretly /'si:krɪtlɪ/ *adv.* heimlich; insgeheim ‹*etw. glauben*›

secretory /sɪ'kri:tərɪ/ *adj.* (Physiol.) sekretorisch

Secret: ~ **Police** *n.* Geheimpolizei, *die;* ~ **'Service** *n.* Geheimdienst, *der;* **s~ so'ciety** *n.* Geheimbund, *der*

sect /sekt/ *n.* 1 Sekte, *die* 2 (religious denomination) Religionsgemeinschaft, *die* 3 (followers of school of thought) Schule, *die*

sectarian /sek'teərɪən/
A *adj.* konfessionell; konfessionell motiviert ‹*Handlungen*›; konfessionell ausgerichtet ‹*Erziehung*›; Konfessions‹*krieg, -streit*›
B *n.* Sektenanhänger *der*/-anhängerin, *die;* Sektierer, *der*/Sektiererin, *die*

sectarianism /sek'teərɪənɪzm/ *n., no pl.* Sektierertum, *das*

section /'sekʃn/ *n.* 1 (part cut off) Abschnitt, *der;* Stück, *das;* (part of divided whole) Teil, *der;* (of railway track) [Strecken]abschnitt, *der;* Teilstück, *das* 2 (of firm) Abteilung, *die;* (of organization etc.) Sektion, *die;* (of orchestra or band) Gruppe, *die;* **accounts ~** (Econ.) Buchhaltung, *die;* **business ~** (in newspaper) Wirtschaftsteil, *der* 3 (component part) [Einzel]teil, *das;* [Bau]element, *das;* (of ship, bridge, etc. also) Sektion, *die* (Technik) 4 (of chapter, book) Abschnitt, *der;* (of statute, act) Paragraph, *der* 5 (part of community) Gruppe, *die* 6 (Amer.: area of country) [Landes-]teil, *der;* Gebiet, *das* 7 (representation) Schnitt, *der;* **vertical/horizontal/longitudinal/ oblique ~:** Vertikal-/Horizontal-/Längs-/Schrägschnitt, *der* 8 (Amer.: square mile) Sektion, *die* 9 (Geom.) (cutting of solid) Schnitt, *der;* ([area of] figure) Schnitt, *der;* Schnittfläche, *die;* (shape or area of cross-section) Querschnitt, *der; see also* **conic** 10 (Amer.: district) Bezirk, *der;* **the business/residential ~:** die City/die Wohngebiete 11 (Med.) Schnitt, *der;* **abdominal ~:** Bauchdeckenschnitt, *der*

sectional /'sekʃənl/ *adj.* 1 (pertaining to a representation) Schnitt- 2 (pertaining to part of community) Gruppen‹*interessen*›; partikular ‹*Interessen*›; ‹*Auseinandersetzung*› zwischen den Bevölkerungsgruppen 3 (made in parts) zum Zusammenbauen *nachgestellt*

sectionalism /'sekʃənəlɪzm/ *n.* Partikularismus, *der* (meist abwertend)

sector /'sektə(r)/ *n.* 1 (of activity) Sektor, *der;* Bereich, *der;* **the leisure/industrial ~:** der Freizeitsektor/der Bereich der Industrie; *see also* **private sector**; **public sector** 2 (Geom.) Sektor, *der;* (of circle also) Kreisausschnitt, *der* 3 (Mil.) (area) Kampfabschnitt, *der;* Gefechtsabschnitt, *der*

secular /'sekjʊlə(r)/ *adj.* (not sacred) säkular (geh.); weltlich ‹*Angelegenheit, Schule, Musik, Gericht*›; profan (geh.) ‹*Musik*›; ~ **buildings** Profanbauten (fachspr.)

secular 'clergy *n. pl.* (Eccl.) Weltgeistlichkeit, *die;* Weltklerus, *der*

secularism /'sekjʊlərɪzm/ *n.* Säkularismus, *der*

secularize (secularise) /'sekjʊləraɪz/ *v.t.* säkularisieren; verweltlichen; **become ~d** verweltlichen

secure /sɪ'kjʊə(r)/
A *adj.* 1 (safe) sicher; ~ **against burglars/fire** gegen Einbruch/Feuer geschützt; einbruch-/feuersicher; **make sth. ~ from attack/enemies** etw. gegen Angriffe/Feinde sichern 2 (firmly fastened) fest; **be ~** ‹*Ladung:*› gesichert sein; ‹*Riegel, Tür:*› fest zu sein; ‹*Tür:*› verriegelt sein; ‹*Schraube:*› fest sein *od.* sitzen; **make sth. ~:** etw. sichern 3 (untroubled) sicher, gesichert ‹*Existenz*›; **feel ~:** sich sicher *od.* geborgen fühlen; ~ **in the knowledge that ...:** in dem sicheren Bewusstsein, dass ...; **emotionally ~:** emotional stabil
B *v.t.* 1 (obtain) sichern (**for** *Dat.*); beschaffen ‹*Auftrag*› (**for** *Dat.*); (for oneself) sich (*Dat.*) sichern 2 (confine) fesseln ‹*Gefangenen*›; (in container) einschließen ‹*Wertsachen*›; (fasten firmly) sichern, fest zumachen ‹*Fenster, Tür*›; festmachen ‹*Boot*› (**to** an + *Dat.*) 3 (guarantee) absichern ‹*Darlehen*›; ~ **oneself [against sth.]** sich [gegen etw.] absichern 4 (fortify) sichern

securely /sɪ'kjʊəlɪ/ *adv.* 1 (firmly) fest ‹*verriegeln, zumachen*›; sicher ‹*befestigen*› 2 (safely) sicher ‹*untergebracht sein*›; ~ **locked up** unter sicherem Verschluss

se'cure unit *n.* (Brit.) 1 (prison) geschlossene Einrichtung 2 (in psychiatric hospital) geschlossene Abteilung

securitize /sɪ'kjʊərɪtaɪz/ *v.t.* (Finance) verbriefen

security /sɪ'kjʊərɪtɪ/ *n.* 1 (safety) Sicherheit, *die;* (of knot) sicherer Halt 2 (safety of State or organization) Sicherheit, *die;* ~ **[measures]** Sicherheitsmaßnahmen; Sicherheitsvorkehrungen; ~ **reasons** Sicherheitsgründe; **national ~:** nationale Sicherheit; Staatssicherheit, *die* 3 (thing that guarantees) Sicherheit, *die;* Gewähr, *die;* Garantie, *die;* (object of value) Pfand, *das;* **as** *or* **in ~ for sth.** als Sicherheit/Pfand für etw.; **obtain a loan on [the] ~ of sth.** auf etw. (*Akk.*) ein Darlehen bekommen 4 *usu. in pl.* (Finance) Wertpapier, *das;* **securities** Wertpapiere; Effekten *Pl.* 5 **emotional ~:** emotionale Sicherheit; **he needs the ~ of a good home** er braucht die Geborgenheit eines guten Zuhauses 6 (assured freedom from want) Sicherheit, *die*

security: ~ **alarm** *n.* Alarmanlage, *die;* ~ **blanket** *n.* 1 (object affording reassurance) mentaler Schutzschild; (blanket for a child) Schmusedecke, *die;* Kuscheldecke, *die;* 2 (Brit.: security measures) Sicherheitsmaßnahmen *Pl.;* ~ **check** *n.* Sicherheitskontrolle, *die;* ~ **clearance** *n.: Berechtigung, geheime Informationen einzusehen;* **get/be given/have ~ clearance** Zugang zu geheimen Informationen erhalten/haben; **S~ Council** *n.* (Polit.) Sicherheitsrat, *der;* ~ **forces** *n. pl.* Sicherheitskräfte *Pl.;* ~ **guard** *n.* ▸ⓘ **p. 1260** Wächter, *der*/Wächterin, *die;* ~ **man** *n.* ▸ⓘ **p. 1260** Wachmann, *der;* ~ **measures** *n. pl.* Sicherheitsmaßnahmen *Pl.;* ~ **officer** *n.* ▸ⓘ **p. 1260** Sicherheitsbeauftragte, *der/die;* ~ **police** *n., no pl.* Sicherheitspolizei, *die;* ~ **precautions** *n. pl.* Sicherheitsvorkehrungen *Pl.;* ~ **risk** *n.* Sicherheitsrisiko, *das;* ~ **van** *n.* gepanzerter Transporter; (for transporting money) Geldtransporter, *der*

sedan /sɪ'dæn/ *n.* 1 (Hist.: chair) Sänfte, *die* 2 (Amer. Motor Veh.) Limousine, *die*

se'dan chair ▸**sedan 1**

sedate /sɪ'deɪt/
A *adj.* 1 bedächtig; gesetzt ‹*alte Dame*›; ruhig ‹*Kind*›; gemächlich ‹*Tempo, Leben, Auto*›; **in a ~ manner** in aller Ruhe 2 (fig.) schlicht; gemächlich ‹*altes Pferd*›
B *v.t.* (Med.) sedieren (fachspr.); ruhig stellen

sedately /sɪ'deɪtlɪ/ *adv.* bedächtig; gemächlich ‹*fahren*›

sedation /sɪ'deɪʃn/ *n.* (Med.) Sedation, *die* (fachspr.); Ruhigstellung, *die;* **be under ~:** sediert sein (fachspr.); ruhig gestellt sein

sedative /'sedətɪv/
A *n.* (Med.) Sedativum, *das* (fachspr.); Beruhigungsmittel, *das*
B *adj.* 1 (Med.) sedativ (fachspr.); ~ **agent** ▸**A** 2 (fig.: calming) beruhigend ‹*Wirkung*›

sedentary /'sedəntərɪ/ *adj.* sitzend ‹*Haltung, Lebensweise, Tätigkeit*›; **lead a ~ life** eine sitzende Lebensweise haben; viel sitzen

sedge /sedʒ/ *n.* (Bot.) 1 (plant) Segge, *die* 2 *no pl.* (bed) Seggenried, *das*

'sedge warbler, 'sedge wren *ns.* (Ornith.) Schilfrohrsänger, *der*

sediment /'sedɪmənt/ *n.* 1 (matter) Ablagerung, *die;* Ablagerungen *Pl.* 2 (lees) Bodensatz, *der;* (of wine also) Depot, *das* (fachspr.) 3 (Geol.) Sediment, *das*

sedimentary /sedɪ'mentərɪ/ *adj.* (Geol.) sedimentär; Sediment‹*gestein*›

sedimentation /sedɪmən'teɪʃn/ *n.* Sedimentation, *die* (fachspr.); Bildung von Ablagerungen

sedition /sɪˈdɪʃn/ *n.* Aufruhr, *der;* **[incitement to] ~:** Anstiftung zum Aufruhr

seditious /sɪˈdɪʃəs/ *adj.* aufrührerisch; staatsgefährdend ‹*Delikt*›

seduce /sɪˈdjuːs/ *v.t.* **1** (sexually) verführen **2** (lead astray) verführen; (distract) ablenken (**away from** von); **~ sb. into doing sth.** jmdn. dazu verführen *od.* verleiten, etw. zu tun

seducer /sɪˈdjuːsə(r)/ *n.* Verführer, *der*

seduction /sɪˈdʌkʃn/ *n.* **1** (sexual) Verführung, *die* **2** (leading astray) Verführung, *die* (**into** zu); Verleitung, *die* (**into** zu) **3** (thing that tempts) Verlockung, *die;* Versuchung, *die*

seductive /sɪˈdʌktɪv/ *adj.* verführerisch; verlockend ‹*Angebot*›

seductively /sɪˈdʌktɪvlɪ/ *adv.* verführerisch

sedulous /ˈsedʒʊləs/ *adj.* (formal) unermüdlich; eifrig ‹*Sammler*›; (painstaking) akkurat (geh.) ‹*Sorgfalt, Arbeiter*›

sedulously /ˈsedʒʊləslɪ/ *adv.* (formal) unermüdlich; (painstakingly) akkurat; geflissentlich ‹*etw. vermeiden, überhören*›

see[1] /siː/

A *v.t.*, **saw** /sɔː/, **seen** /siːn/ **1** sehen; **let sb. ~ sth.** (show) jmdm. etw. zeigen; **let me ~:** lass mich mal sehen; **I saw her fall** *or* **falling** ich habe sie fallen sehen; **he was ~n to fall down the stairs** man hat gesehen, wie er die Treppe hinunterfiel; **he was ~n to leave** *or* **~n leaving the building** er ist beim Verlassen des Gebäudes gesehen worden; **I'll believe it when I ~ it** das will ich erst mal sehen; **they saw it happen** sie haben gesehen, wie es passiert ist; sie haben es gesehen; **can you ~ that house over there?** siehst du das Haus da drüben?; **for all [the world] to ~:** für jedermann sichtbar; (fig.: in public) in aller Öffentlichkeit; vor aller Welt; **be worth ~ing** sehenswert sein; sich lohnen (ugs.); **~ the light** (fig.: undergo conversion) das Licht schauen (geh.); **I saw the light** (I realized my error etc.) mir ging ein Licht auf (ugs.); **he'll ~ the light eventually** (he'll realize the truth) ihm werden die Augen noch aufgehen; **~ the light [of day]** (be born) das Licht der Welt erblicken (geh.); (fig.: be published or produced) herauskommen; **'~ things** Halluzinationen haben; **I must be ~ing things** (joc.) ich glaub, ich seh nicht richtig; **~ stars** Sterne sehen (ugs.); **~ the sights/town** sich (*Dat.*) die Sehenswürdigkeiten/Stadt ansehen; **~ visions** Visionen *od.* Gesichte haben; **~ one's way [clear] to do** *or* **to doing sth.** es einrichten, etw. zu tun; **we cannot ~ our way [clear] to do it** es ist uns [zurzeit] nicht möglich, es zu tun; *see also* **back A 1**; **something 3, 7**; **world 1**

2 (watch) sehen; **let's ~ a film** sehen wir uns (*Dat.*) einen Film an!

3 (meet [with]) sehen; treffen; (meet socially) zusammenkommen mit; sich treffen mit; **I'll ~ you there/at 5** wir sehen uns dort/um 5; **~ you!** (coll.), **[I'll] be ~ing you!** (coll.) bis bald (ugs.); **~ you on Saturday/soon** bis Samstag/bald; *see also* **long**[1] **A 3**

4 (speak to) sprechen ‹*Person*› (**about** wegen); (pay visit to) gehen zu, (geh.) aufsuchen ‹*Arzt, Anwalt usw.*›; (receive) empfangen; **the doctor will ~ you now** Herr Doktor lässt bitten; **whom would you like to ~?** wen möchten Sie sprechen?; zu wem möchten Sie?

5 (discern mentally) sehen; **I ~ it all!** jetzt ist mir alles klar; **I can ~ it's difficult for you** ich verstehe, dass es nicht leicht für dich ist; **I ~ what you mean** ich verstehe [was du meinst]; **~ what I mean?** siehst du?; **I saw that it was a mistake** mir war klar, dass es ein Fehler war; **I don't ~ the point of it** ich sehe keinen Sinn darin; **I can't ~ the good/advantage of doing it** ich kann keinen Sinn/Vorteil darin sehen, es zu tun; **he didn't ~ the joke** er fand es [gar] nicht lustig; (did not understand) er hat den Witz nicht verstanden; **I can't think what she ~s in him** ich weiß nicht, was sie an ihm findet; **I saw myself [being] obliged to …:** ich sah mich gezwungen, zu…

6 (consider) sehen; **let me ~ what I can do** [ich will] mal sehen, was ich tun kann

7 (foresee) sehen; **I can ~ I'm going to be busy** ich sehe [es] schon [kommen], dass ich beschäftigt sein werde; **I can ~ it won't be easy** ich sehe schon *od.* weiß jetzt schon, dass es nicht einfach sein wird

8 (find out) feststellen; (by looking) nachsehen; **that remains to be ~n** das wird man sehen; **~ if you can read this** guck mal, ob du das hier lesen kannst (ugs.)

9 (take view of) sehen; betrachten; **~ things as sb. does** jmds. Ansichten teilen; **try to ~ it my way** versuche es doch mal aus meiner Sicht zu sehen; **as I ~ it** meines Erachtens; meiner Ansicht *od.* Meinung nach; *see also* **eye A 1**; **fit**[2] **A 3**

10 (learn) sehen; **I ~ from your letter that …:** ich entnehme Ihrem Brief, dass …; **as we have ~n** wie wir schon gesehen haben

11 (make sure) **~ [that] …:** zusehen *od.* darauf achten, dass …

12 *usu. in imper.* (look at) einsehen ‹*Buch*›; **~ below/p. 15** siehe unten/S. 15

13 (experience) erleben; **live to ~ sth.** etw. miterleben; **1936 saw him in India/a revolution in that country** 1936 hielt er sich in Indien auf/kam es in dem Land zu einer Revolution; **I've ~n it all** mir ist nichts unbekannt; **I've ~n it all before** das kenne ich; **now I've ~n everything!** (iron.) hat man so etwas schon erlebt *od.* gesehen!

14 (be witness of) erleben; (be the scene of) Schauplatz (+ *Gen.*) sein; **we shall ~:** wir werden [ja/schon] sehen; **~/have ~n life** das Leben kennen lernen/kennen; **he will not** *or* **never ~ 50 again** er ist [bestimmt] über 50; *see also* **day 3**; **service A 1, 16**

15 (imagine) sich (*Dat.*) vorstellen; **~ sb./oneself doing sth.** sich vorstellen, dass jmd./man etw. tut; **~ oneself as a star** sich schon als Star sehen; **I can ~ it now —…:** ich sehe es schon bildhaft vor mir — …

16 (contemplate) mit ansehen; zusehen bei; **[stand by and] ~ sb. doing sth.** [tatenlos] zusehen *od.* es [tatenlos] mit ansehen, wie jmd. etw. tut; **I'll ~ him damned** *or* **dead** *or* **hanged** *or* **in hell [first]** das wäre das Letzte[, was ich täte]!; nie im Leben!

17 (escort) begleiten, bringen (**to** [bis] zu)

18 (supervise) **~ the doors locked/the book through the press** das Abschließen der Türen/den Druck des Buches überwachen; **I'll stay and ~ you on the bus** ich bleibe noch, bis du im Bus sitzt

19 (consent willingly to) einsehen; **not ~ oneself doing sth.** es nicht einsehen, dass man etw. tut; **he couldn't ~ it** er konnte sich nicht damit anfreunden

20 (Gambling) mithalten mit

B *v.i.*, **saw, seen** **1** (discern objects) sehen; **~ for yourself!** sieh doch selbst!; **~ red** rotsehen (ugs.); **sth. makes sb. ~ red** jmd. sieht bei etw. rot (ugs.); etw. bringt jmdn. zur Weißglut

2 (make sure) nachsehen

3 (reflect) überlegen; **let me ~:** lass mich überlegen; warte mal ['n Moment] (ugs.)

4 **I ~:** ich verstehe; aha (ugs.); ach so (ugs.); **you ~:** weißt du/wisst ihr/wissen Sie; **there you are, you ~!** Siehst du? Ich habs doch gesagt!; **well, you ~, …** (in apologies) es tut mir Leid, aber …; **she used to be a nurse, you ~:** sie war nämlich mal Krankenschwester; **~?** (coll.) verstanden? (salopp); klar? (salopp); **as far as I can ~:** soweit ich das *od.* es beurteilen kann; **~ here!** na hör/hören Sie mal!

Phrasal verbs

- **~ about** *v.t.* sich kümmern um; **I'll ~ about getting the car repaired** ich werde mich darum kümmern, dass das Auto repariert wird; **I've come to ~ about the room/cooker** ich komme wegen des Zimmers/des Herdes; **I'll ~ about it** (consider it) [ich will] mal sehen (ugs.); **we'll ~ about that!** (you may well be wrong) das werden wir ja sehen!
- **~ into** *v.t.* **1** (gain view into) [hinein]sehen in (+ *Akk.*); [rein]gucken (ugs.) in (+ *Akk.*); **~ into it** hineinsehen; reingucken (ugs.) **2** (fig.: investigate) nachgehen, auf den Grund gehen (+ *Dat.*) ‹*Angelegenheit, Klage*›
- **~ 'off** *v.t.* **1** (say farewell to) verabschieden **2** (chase away) vertreiben; **~ him off, Rover!** mach ihm Beine, Rover! (ugs.) **3** (defeat) erledigen; abservieren (Sportjargon)
- **~ 'out**

  A *v.i.* hinaussehen; rausgucken (ugs.)

  B *v.t.* **1** (remain till end of) ‹*Zuschauer:*› sich (*Dat.*) zu Ende ansehen ‹*Spiel*›; ableisten ‹*Amtsperiode*›; ‹*Patient:*› überleben ‹*Zeitraum*›; **enough fuel to ~ the winter out** genug Heizmaterial, um über den Winter zu kommen; **~ sb. out** (be present at sb.'s death) bei jmds. Tod bei ihm/ihr sein; (live or last until sb.'s death) ‹*Person, Gegenstand:*› jmdn. überleben **2** (escort from premises) hinausbegleiten (**of** aus); hinausbringen (**of** aus); **~ oneself out** allein hinausfinden **3** ▸ **~ through 3**
- **~ over, ~ round** *v.t.* besichtigen
- **~ through** *v.t.* **1** /'--/ (penetrate with vision) hindurchsehen durch; durchgucken (ugs.) durch; *see also* **see-through** **2** /'--/ (fig.: penetrate nature of) durchschauen **3** /-'-/ (not abandon) zu Ende *od.* zum Abschluss bringen; **~ things through** bei der Stange bleiben **4** /-'-/ (be sufficient for) **~ sb. through** jmdm. reichen; **we have enough food to ~ us through the weekend** wir haben für das Wochenende genug zu essen **5** **~ sb. through his difficulties** jmdm. über seine Schwierigkeiten hinweghelfen
- **~ to** *v.t.* sich kümmern um; **I'll ~ to that** dafür werde ich sorgen; **~ to it that …:** dafür sorgen, dass …; **well, ~ to it you do!** gut, dann sieh mal zu!

see[2] *n.* (Eccl.) [erz]bischöflicher Stuhl; **the Holy See** *or* **See of Rome** (RC Ch.) der Heilige *od.* Apostolische Stuhl

seed /siːd/

A *n.* **1** (grain) Samen, *der;* Samenkorn, *das;* (of grape etc.) Kern, *der;* (for birds) Korn, *das* **2** *no pl., no indef. art.* (**~s** collectively) Samen[körner] *Pl.;* (as collected for sowing) Saatgut, *das;* Saat, *die;* (of various plants also) Sämereien *Pl.;* **grass ~:** Grassamen *Pl.;* **go** *or* **run to ~:** Samen bilden; ‹*Salat:*› [in Samen] schießen; (fig.) herunterkommen (ugs.) **3** (fig.: beginning) Saat, *die;* Samen, *der* (geh.); **sow [the] ~s of doubt/a conflict/discord** für Zweifel/Konflikt sorgen/Zwietracht säen **4** (Sport coll.) gesetzter Spieler/gesetzte Spielerin; **fourth ~/number one ~:** als Nummer vier/eins gesetzter Spieler/gesetzte Spielerin **5** *no pl.* (arch.) (semen) Samen, *der* **6** *no pl.* (Bibl.: descendants) Same, *der*

B *v.t.* **1** (place **~s** in) besäen **2** (Sport) setzen ‹*Spieler*›; **be ~ed number one** als Nummer eins gesetzt werden/sein **3** (lit. or fig.: sprinkle [as] with **~**) besäen **4** (place crystal[s] in) impfen ‹*Wolken, chemische Lösung*›

C *v.i.* **1** (produce **~s**) Samen bilden **2** (go to **~**) [in Samen] schießen **3** (sow **~s**) säen

seed: ~bed *n.* **1** (Hort.) [Saat]beet, *das;* **2** (fig.: place of development) Grundlage, *die;* (of evil) Brutstätte, *die;* **prepare the ~bed of sth.** einer Sache (*Dat.*) den Boden bereiten; **~ cake** *n.* Kümmelkuchen, *der;* **~corn** *n.* Saatgetreide, *das;* Saatkorn, *das;* **~ crystal** *n.* (Chem.) [Kristallisations]keim, *der;* Impfkristall, *der*

seedless /ˈsiːdlɪs/ *adj.* kernlos ‹*Trauben, Rosinen*›

seedling /ˈsiːdlɪŋ/ *n.* Sämling, *der*

seed: ~ money *n.* Anfangs-, Startkapital, *das;* **~ packet** *n.* Samentüte, *die;* **~ pearl** *n.* Samenperle, *die;* Saatperle, *die;* **~ potato** *n.* (Hort.) Saatkartoffel, *die;* **~sman** /ˈsiːdzmən/ *n., pl.* **~smen** /ˈsiːdzmən/ Samenhändler, *der;* **~time** *n.* [Aus]saatzeit, *die;* **~ tray** *n.* Pflanzschale, *die;* Anzuchtschale, *die*

seedy /ˈsiːdɪ/ *adj.* **1** (coll.: unwell) **feel ~:** sich [leicht] angeschlagen fühlen **2** (shabby) schäbig, (ugs. abwertend) vergammelt ‹*Aussehen, Kleidung*›; heruntergekommen ‹*Stadtteil*› **3** (disreputable) zweifelhaft ‹*Person*›

seeing /ˈsiːɪŋ/

A *conj.* **~ [that] …** da …; wo … (ugs.)

B *n., no pl., no indef. art.* (faculty or power of sight) Sehvermögen, *das;* **~ is believing** so was glaubt man erst, wenn man es gesehen hat

seeing 'eye *n.* (dog) Blindenhund, *der*

seek /siːk/ *v.t.*, **sought** /sɔːt/ **1** suchen; anstreben ‹*Posten, Amt*›; sich bemühen um ‹*Anerkennung, Freundschaft, Interview, Einstellung*›;

(try to reach) aufsuchen; **~ shelter/help/one's fortune/sb.'s advice** Schutz/Hilfe/sein Glück/jmds. Rat suchen; **scientists are ~ing the solution** Wissenschaftler suchen nach der Lösung **2** (literary/formal: attempt) suchen (geh.); versuchen; **~ to do sth.** suchen, etw. zu tun (geh.); **I'm only ~ing to establish a fact** es ist mir nur darum zu tun, eine Tatsache festzustellen (geh.); *see also* **level A 1**

Phrasal verbs
- **~ after** *v.t.* suchen nach; **be much sought after** sehr gesucht sein
- **~ for** *v.t.* suchen nach; **~ing for information** auf der Suche nach Informationen
- **~ 'out** *v.t.* ausfindig machen ‹*Sache, Ort*›; aufsuchen, kommen zu ‹*Personen*›

seeker /'si:kə(r)/ *n.* Sucher, *der*/Sucherin, *die*; **~ after the Truth** Wahrheitssucher, *der*/-sucherin, *die* (geh.); **bargain-~s** Leute, die Jagd auf günstige Angebote machen/machten *usw.*

seem /si:m/ *v.i.* **1** (appear [to be]) scheinen; **you ~ tired** du wirkst müde; **she ~s nice** sie scheint nett zu sein; **it's not quite what it ~s** es ist nicht ganz das, was es [zunächst] zu sein scheint; **it ~s like only yesterday** es ist, als wäre es erst gestern gewesen; **he ~s certain to win** es sieht ganz so aus, als würde er gewinnen; **she ~s younger than 45** sie wirkt jünger als 45; **what ~s to be the trouble?** wo fehlts denn? (ugs.); wo drückt denn der Schuh? (ugs.); **it ~s a pity** es ist doch schade; **I ~ to recall having seen him before** ich glaube mich zu erinnern, ihn schon einmal gesehen zu haben; **it just ~s as if it were** es scheint nur so *od.* kommt einem nur so vor; **doing such a thing just doesn't ~ right somehow** es ist doch irgendwie nicht richtig, so etwas zu tun; **it ~s [that] ...:** anscheinend ...; **it ~s to me that it's silly to do that** ich finde es töricht *od.* es kommt mir töricht vor, das zu tun; **it ~s that we had better decide quickly** wir sollten uns wohl besser schnell entscheiden; **it ~s you were lying** du hast ja wohl gelogen; **it ~s [as if] there will be war** es sieht nach Krieg aus; es sieht so aus, als ob es Krieg geben wird; **it would** *or* (arch.) **should ~ to be ...:** es scheint ja wohl ... zu sein; **you know everything, it would ~:** du scheinst ja wohl alles zu wissen; **it would ~ that he is ...:** er scheint ja wohl ... zu sein; **so it ~s** *or* **would ~:** so will es scheinen; **Dead? — So it would ~:** Tot? — Allem Anschein nach; **so it ~s!** (iron.) was Sie nicht sagen! (iron.) **2** **sb. can't ~ to do sth.** (coll.) jmd. scheint etw. nicht tun zu können; **I just can't ~ to do it** (coll.) ich kann es einfach irgendwie nicht [tun] (ugs.); **she doesn't ~ to notice such things** (coll.) so was merkt sie irgendwie nicht (ugs.); **~ good to sb.** jmdm. das Beste [zu sein] scheinen

seeming /'si:mɪŋ/ *adj.* scheinbar

seemingly /'si:mɪŋlɪ/ *adv.* **1** (evidently) offensichtlich **2** (to outward appearance) scheinbar

seemly /'si:mlɪ/ *adj.* anständig; **it isn't ~ to praise oneself** es gehört sich nicht, sich selbst zu loben

seen ▸ **see**[1]

seep /si:p/ *v.i.* **~ [away]** [ab]sickern; **~ in through** durch etw. hineinsickern; **~ out of sth.** aus etw. heraussickern; **[gradually] ~ through to sb.'s consciousness** (fig.) jmdm. [langsam] dämmern (ugs.) *od.* bewusst werden

seepage /'si:pɪdʒ/ *n.* **1** Versickern, *das;* (into sth.) Hineinsickern, *das* **2** (quantity) Lache, *die;* (of oil) Ölausbiss, *der* (Geol.); (of gas) Austritt, *der*

seer /sɪə(r)/ *n.* (prophet) Seher, *der*/Seherin, *die*

seersucker /'sɪəsʌkə(r)/ *n.* (Textiles) Seersucker, *der; Baumwoll- od. Leinengewebe mit Kreppstreifen; attrib.* ‹*Kleid, Tagesdecke*› aus Seersucker

'see-saw
A *n.* **1** (plank) Wippe, *die* **2** *no art.* (game) Wippen, *das;* **let's have a game of ~:** komm, wir gehen auf die Wippe *od.* wippen **3** (fig.: contest) Auf und Ab, *das*
B *v.i.* **1** (move up and down) ‹*Weg, Straße:*› auf und ab führen; ‹*Deck:*› [auf und ab] schaukeln **2** (vacillate) schwanken **3** (play on ~) wippen

seethe /si:ð/ *v.i.* **1** (surge) ‹*Wellen, Meer:*› branden; ‹*Straßen usw.:*› wimmeln (**with** von); (bubble or foam as if boiling) schäumen **2** (fig.: be agitated) schäumen; **~ [with anger/inwardly]** vor Wut/innerlich schäumen

'see-through *adj.* durchsichtig

segment
A /'segmənt/ *n.* **1** (of orange, pineapple) Scheibe, *die;* Schnitz, *der* (bes. südd.); (of cake, pear) Stück, *das;* (of worm, skull, limb) Segment, *das;* (of bowel) Abschnitt, *der;* Segment, *das* (Med.); (of economy, market) Bereich, *der* **2** (Ling., Geom., Sociol.) Segment, *das;* **~ of a circle** Kreissegment, *das*
B /seg'ment, 'segmənt/ *v.t.* untergliedern; [in Gruppen] aufteilen ‹*Menschen*›
C *v.i.* (Biol.) sich teilen

segmentation /segmən'teɪʃn/ *n.* Untergliederung, *die;* (Biol.) Zellteilung, *die*

segregate /'segrɪgeɪt/ *v.t.* **1** trennen; isolieren ‹*Kranke*›; aussondern ‹*Forschungsgebiet*› **2** (racially) segregieren (geh.); absondern

segregation /segrɪ'geɪʃn/ *n., no pl.* **1** Trennung, *die* **2** **[racial] ~:** Rassentrennung, *die*

segregationist /segrɪ'geɪʃənɪst/ *n.* Befürworter/Befürworterin der Rassentrennung

seine /seɪn/ *n.* (Fishing) **~ [net]** Treibnetz, *das*

seismic /'saɪzmɪk/ *adj.* seismisch; **~ area** *or* **region** Erdbebengebiet, *das;* **of ~ proportions** (fig.) von verheerenden Ausmaßen

seismically /'saɪzmɪkəlɪ/ *adv.* seismisch

seismograph /'saɪzməgrɑ:f/ *n.* Seismograph, *der;* Seismometer, *das*

seismographic /saɪzmə'græfɪk/ *adj.* seismographisch

seismologist /saɪz'mɒlədʒɪst/ *n.* ▸❶ **p. 1260** Seismologe, *der*/Seismologin, *die*

seismology /saɪz'mɒlədʒɪ/ *n., no pl.* Seismologie, *die*

seize /si:z/
A *v.t.* **1** ergreifen; **~ power** die Macht ergreifen; **~ sb. by the arm/collar/shoulder** jmdn. am Arm/Kragen/an der Schulter packen; **~ the opportunity** *or* **occasion/moment [to do sth.]** die Gelegenheit ergreifen/den günstigen Augenblick nutzen [und etw. tun]; **~ any/a** *or* **the chance [to do sth.]** jede/die Gelegenheit nutzen[, um etw. zu tun]; **be ~d with remorse/panic** von Gewissensbissen geplagt/von Panik ergriffen werden; **she ~d it with both hands** (fig.) sie griff mit beiden Händen zu (fig.) **2** (capture) gefangen nehmen ‹*Person*›; kapern ‹*Schiff*›; mit Gewalt übernehmen ‹*Flugzeug, Gebäude*›; einnehmen ‹*Festung, Brücke*› **3** (understand) erfassen **4** (confiscate) beschlagnahmen
B *v.i.* ▸ **~ up**

Phrasal verbs
- **~ on** *v.t.* sich (*Dat.*) vornehmen ‹*Einzelheit, Aspekt, Schwachpunkt*›; aufgreifen ‹*Idee, Vorschlag*›; ergreifen ‹*Chance*›
- **~ 'up** *v.i.* sich festfressen; ‹*Verkehr:*› zusammenbrechen, zum Erliegen kommen
- **~ upon** ▸ **~ on**

seizure /'si:ʒə(r)/ *n.* **1** (capturing) Gefangennahme, *die;* (of ship) Kapern, *das;* (of aircraft, building) Übernahme, *die;* (of fortress, bridge) Einnahme, *die;* **~ of power** Machtergreifung, *die* **2** (confiscation) Beschlagnahme, *die* **3** (Med.: attack) Anfall, *der*

seldom /'seldəm/
A *adv.* selten; **~ or never** so gut wie nie; **~, if ever** fast nie; äußerst selten
B *adj.* selten; **a ~ thing** eine Seltenheit; etwas Seltenes

select /sɪ'lekt/
A *adj.* **1** (carefully chosen) ausgewählt; **only the most ~ company** nur eine kleine Gruppe Auserwählter **2** (exclusive) exklusiv
B *v.t.* auswählen; **~ one's own apples** sich (*Dat.*) die Äpfel selbst aussuchen

select com'mittee *n.* Sonderkommission, *die*

selectee /sɪlek'ti:/ *n.* (Amer.) Einberufene, *der*

selection /sɪ'lekʃn/ *n.* **1** (what is selected [from]) Auswahl, *die* (**of** an + *Dat.*, **from** aus); (person) Wahl, *die;* **a ~ from ...** (Mus.) eine Auswahl aus ...; **make a ~** (one) eine Wahl treffen; (several) eine Auswahl treffen; **~s from the best writers** ausgewählte Werke der besten Schriftsteller; **what is your ~ for the Derby?** was ist dein Tipp für das Derby? **2** (act of choosing) [Aus]wahl, *die* **3** (being chosen) Wahl, *die;* **his ~ as president** seine Wahl zum Präsidenten **4** (Biol.: in evolution) Selektion, *die;* Auslese, *die*

selection: ~ committee *n.* (in a company) Auswahlausschuss, *das;* (in a political party) Wahlausschuss, *der;* **~ procedure, ~ process** *ns.* Auswahlverfahren, *das*

selective /sɪ'lektɪv/ *adj.* **1** (using selection) selektiv; (careful in one's choice) wählerisch **2** (Electr.) selektiv; trennscharf

selectively /sɪ'lektɪvlɪ/ *adv.* selektiv; **not read ~ enough** [viel] zu wahllos lesen; **shop ~:** gezielt einkaufen

selectiveness /sɪ'lektɪvnɪs/ *n., no pl.* Eingrenzung, *die*

selectivity /sɪlek'tɪvɪtɪ, selek'tɪvɪtɪ, si:lek'tɪvɪtɪ/ *n., no pl.* **have a high degree of ~** ‹*Insektizid:*› nur spezifisch wirksam sein; **show ~:** wählerisch sein

selectman /sɪ'lektmən/, *pl.* **selectmen** /sɪ'lektmən/ *n.* (Amer.) Stadtrat, *der*

selectness /sɪ'lektnɪs/ *n., no pl.* Exklusivität, *die*

selector /sɪ'lektə(r)/ *n.* **1** (person who selects) (of team) Mannschaftsaufsteller, *der*/-aufstellerin, *die;* (of merchandise) Einkäufer, *der*/Einkäuferin, *die* **2** (device that selects) (knob) Schaltknopf, *der;* (lever) Schaltgriff, *der;* (switch) Wahlschalter, *der;* (for selecting programmes) Programmtaste, *die;* (of computer) Selektor, *der*

self /self/ *n., pl.* **selves** /selvz/ **1** (person's essence) Selbst, *das* (geh.); Ich, *das;* **be one's usual ~:** man selbst sein; **not be one's usual cheerful ~:** nicht so fröhlich wie sonst sein; **be back to one's former** *or* **old ~ [again]** wieder der/die Alte sein; **one's better ~:** sein besseres Ich; **my humble ~/your good selves** (joc.) meine Wenigkeit/die werten Herrschaften (scherzh.); **how is your good ~?** (arch.) wie ist das werte Befinden? (veralt.) **2** (one's own interest) die eigene Person; **she cares for nothing but ~:** sie nimmt nur sich selbst wichtig; **she has no thoughts of ~:** sie ist sehr selbstlos **3** (Commerc.) **drawn to ~:** auf sich selbst ausgestellt ‹*Scheck*›; **pay to ~:** zahlbar an Aussteller *od.* selbst

self- *in comb.* **1** *expr. direct reflexive action* selbst‹*anklagend, -schließend*›; Selbst‹*ankläger, -anzeige*›; **stand ~accused** sich selbst angeklagt haben **2** *expr. action or condition* selbst-; **~acting** automatisch; selbsttätig

self: ~-ab'sorbed *adj.* mit sich selbst beschäftigt; **~-ab'sorption** *n., no pl.* Mit-sich-selbst-beschäftigt-Sein, *das;* **~-a'buse** *n., no pl.* **1** (self-harm) Selbstbeschädigung, *die;* **2** (euphem.: masturbation) Selbstbefriedigung, *die;* **~-ad'dressed** *adj.* **a ~-addressed envelope** ein adressierter Rückumschlag; **~-ad'hesive** *adj.* selbstklebend; **~-ad'vertisement** *n.* Selbstreklame, *die;* **~-ag'grandizement** *n., no pl.* Vergrößerung der eigenen Macht; **~-a'nalysis** *n.* Selbstanalyse, *die;* **~-ap'parent** *adj.* offensichtlich; selbstverständlich; **be ~-apparent** sich von selbst verstehen; [klar] auf der Hand liegen (ugs.); **~-ap'pointed** *adj.* selbst ernannt; **~-as'sembly** *n., no pl.* Selbstmontage, *die;* **~-as'sertion** *n., no pl.* Durchsetzungsvermögen, *das* (**over** gegenüber); **~-as'sertive** *adj.*, **~-assertively** /selfə'sɜ:tɪvlɪ/ *adv.* selbstbewusst; **~-as'sertiveness** *n., no pl.* Durchsetzungsvermögen, *das;* **a ~-assertiveness training course** ein Trainingskurs in Durchsetzungsvermögen; **~-as'sessment** *n.* **1** (assessment of oneself) Selbsteinschätzung, *die;* **2** (Brit.: tax calculation) Selbstveranlagung, *die;* **~-as'surance** *n., no pl.* Selbstbewusstsein, *das;* Selbstsicherheit, *die;* **~-as'sured** *adj.* selbstsicher; selbstbewusst; **~-a'wareness** *n., no pl.* Selbsterkenntnis, *die;* **~-'catering** **A** *adj.* mit Selbstversorgung *nachgestellt;* **B** *n.* Selbstversorgung, *die;* **~-certifi'cation** *n., no pl.* **1** (of information) Selbstzertifizierung, *die; attrib.* **~-certification mortgage** Hypothek ohne

S

Einkommensnachweis; 2 (of illness) [vom Arbeitnehmer selbst ausgestellte] Krankmeldung; **~-'centred** *adj.* egozentrisch; ichbezogen; **~-'closing** *adj.* selbstschließend; **~-coloured** *adj.* (with uniform colouring) einfarbig; **~-com'mand** *n., no pl.* Selbstbeherrschung, *die;* **~-con'demned** *adj.* **be** *or* **stand ~-condemned** sich selbst überführt haben; **~-con'fessed** *adj.* erklärt; **~-'confidence** *n., no pl.* Selbstvertrauen, *das;* **~-'confident** *adj.*, **~-'confidently** *adv.* selbstsicher; **~-congratu'latory** *adj.* selbstgefällig (abwertend); **~-'conscious** *adj.* 1 (ill at ease) unsicher; 2 (deliberate) reflektiert ‹*Prosa, Stil*›; **~-'consciousness** *n., no pl.* 1 Unsicherheit, *die;* 2 (deliberateness) Reflektiertheit, *die;* **~-con'tained** *adj.* 1 (not dependent) selbstgenügsam; (not communicative) verschlossen; 2 (having no parts in common) unabhängig ‹*Maschine, Anlage*›; einzeln stehend ‹*Haus*›; 3 (Brit.: complete in itself) abgeschlossen ‹*Wohnung*›; **~-contra'dictory** *adj.* mit sich selbst in Widerspruch; **~-con'trol** *n., no pl.* Selbstbeherrschung, *die;* **~-con'trolled** *adj.* voller Selbstbeherrschung *nachgestellt;* **~-'critical** *adj.* selbstkritisch; **~-de'ception** *n.* Selbsttäuschung, *die;* Selbstbetrug, *der;* **~-de'feating** *adj.* unsinnig; zwecklos; **~-de'fence** *n., no pl., no indef. art.* Notwehr, *die;* Selbstverteidigung, *die;* **in ~-defence** aus Notwehr; **~-defence classes** Selbstverteidigungskurs, *der;* **~-de'lusion** *n.* Selbsttäuschung, *die;* **~-de'nial** *n., no pl.* Selbstverleugnung, *die;* **~-deprecating** /selfˈdeprɪkeɪtɪŋ/ *adj.* bescheiden; **~-de'struct** *v.i.* sich selbst zerstören; **~-de'struction** *n., no pl.* Selbstzerstörung, *die;* **~-de'structive** *adj.*, **~-de'structively** *adv.* selbstzerstörerisch; **~-determi'nation** *n., no pl.* Selbstbestimmung, *die;* **right to ~-determination** Selbstbestimmungsrecht, *das;* **~-'discipline** *n., no pl.* Selbstdisziplin, *die;* **~-drive** *adj.* **~-drive hire [company]** Autovermietung, *die;* **~-drive vehicle** Mietwagen, *der;* **~-'educated** *adj.* autodidaktisch; **be ~-educated, be a ~-educated person** Autodidakt/Autodidaktin sein; **~-ef'facing** *adj.* zurückhaltend; **~-em'ployed** *adj.* selbstständig; **~-employed man/woman** Selbstständige, *der/die;* **~-e'steem** *n., no pl.* 1 (~-respect) Selbstachtung, *die;* 2 (~-conceit) Selbstgefälligkeit, *die;* **~-'evident** *adj.*, **~-'evidently** *adv.* offenkundig; **~-ex'planatory** *adj.* ohne weiteres verständlich; **be ~-explanatory** für sich selbst sprechen; **~-ex'pression** *n., no pl., no indef. art.* Selbstdarstellung, *die;* **~-fertili'zation** *n., no pl.* (Biol.) Selbstbefruchtung, *die;* **~-financing** *adj.* sich selbst tragend; kostenneutral ‹*Tarifvertrag*›; **~-ful'filling** *adj.* zur eigenen Bestätigung mit beitragend; **~-fulfilling prophecy** zur Bestätigung ihrer selbst mit beitragende Voraussage; Selffulfilling Prophecy, *die* (Soziol.); **~-glorifi'cation** *n., no pl.* Selbstglorifizierung, *die;* Selbstbeweihräucherung, *die* (ugs. abwertend); **~-'governing** *adj.* selbst verwaltet; **~-'government** *n., no pl., no indef. art.* Selbstverwaltung, *die;* **~-gratifi'cation** *n., no pl.* 1 (self-indulgence) Selbsterfüllung, *die;* Bedürfnisbefriedigung, *die;* **individual ~-gratification** Befriedigung der persönlichen Bedürfnisse; 2 (masturbation) Selbstbefriedigung, *die;* **~-'hatred** *n., no pl.* Selbsthass, *der;* **~-'help** *n., no pl.* Selbsthilfe, *die;* **~-hyp'nosis** *n., no pl.* Selbsthypnose, *die;* **~-'image** *n.* Selbstbild, *das;* **~-im'portance** *n., no pl.* Selbstgefälligkeit, *die;* (arrogant and pompous bearing) Selbstherrlichkeit, *die;* **~-im'portant** *adj.* selbstgefällig; (arrogant and pompous) selbstherrlich; **~-im'posed** *adj.* selbst auferlegt; **~-im'provement** *n., no pl.* selbstständige Weiterbildung; **~-in'duced** *adj.* 1 selbst verursacht; 2 (Electr.) selbstinduziert; **~-in'duction** *n., no pl.* (Electr.) Selbstinduktion, *die;* **~-in'dulgence** *n., no pl.* Maßlosigkeit, *die;* **a little ~-indulgence never hurt anyone** sich ein bisschen zu verwöhnen, hat noch keinem geschadet; **this novel is a piece of pure ~-indulgence** dieser Roman ist weiter nichts als Selbstbefriedigung des Autors; **~-in'dulgent** *adj.* maßlos; **I've been very ~-indulgent lately** ich habe mich in der letzten Zeit sehr gehen lassen; **~-in'flicted** *adj.* selbst beigebracht ‹*Wunde*›; selbst auferlegt ‹*Strafe*›; **~-'interest** *n.* Eigeninteresse, *das;* **~-in'vited** *adj.* **a ~-invited guest** ein Gast, der sich selbst eingeladen hat

selfish /ˈselfɪʃ/ *adj.* egoistisch; selbstsüchtig

selfishly /ˈselfɪʃlɪ/ *adv.* egoistisch; selbstsüchtig; **do sth. ~:** etw. aus Egoismus tun

selfishness /ˈselfɪʃnɪs/ *n., no pl.* Egoismus, *der;* Selbstsucht, *die*

self: ~-justifi'cation *n., no pl.* Rechtfertigung, *die;* **attempt at ~-justification** Versuch, sich zu rechtfertigen; **~-'knowledge** *n., no pl.* Selbsterkenntnis, *die*

selfless /ˈselflɪs/ *adj.*, **selflessly** /ˈselflɪslɪ/ *adv.* selbstlos

self: ~-'loading *adj.* mit Selbstladevorrichtung *nachgestellt;* **~-'loathing** *n., no pl.* Selbstverachtung, *die;* **be consumed by deep ~-loathing** eine tiefe Abscheu gegen sich selbst empfinden; **~-'locking** *adj.* selbstschließend; **~-'love** *n., no pl.* Selbstliebe, *die;* Eigenliebe, *die;* **~-made** *adj.* selbst gemacht; **a ~-made man** ein Selfmademan; **she is a ~-made woman** sie hat sich aus eigener Kraft hochgearbeitet; **~-'mockery** *n., no pl.* Selbstverspottung, *die;* **~-'mocking** *adj.* selbstspöttisch; **~-'motivated** *adj.* von sich aus motiviert; selbstmotiviert ‹*Lernen*›; **~-moti'vation** *n., no pl.* Motiviertheit, *die;* [innere] Motivation; **~-muti'lation** *n., no pl.* Selbstverstümmelung, *die;* **~-ne'glect** *n., no pl.* Selbstvernachlässigung, *die;* **~-ob'sessed** *adj.* ichbesessen; **~-o'pinionated** *adj.* 1 (conceited) eingebildet; von sich eingenommen; 2 (obstinate) starrköpfig; rechthaberisch; **~-per'ception** *n.* Selbstwahrnehmung, *die;* **~-per'petuating** *adj.* sich selbst erhaltend; **be ~-perpetuating** sich selbst erhalten; **~-'pity** *n., no pl.* Selbstmitleid, *das;* **~-'pitying** *adj.* selbstmitleidig; **~-'portrait** *n.* Selbstporträt, *das;* **~-pos'sessed** *adj.* selbstbeherrscht; **remain ~-possessed** die Selbstbeherrschung behalten; **be ~-possessed** sich beherrschen *od.* zusammennehmen; **~-pos'session** *n., no pl.* Selbstbeherrschung, *die;* **~-preser'vation** *n., no pl., no indef. art.* Selbsterhaltung, *die;* **~-pro'claimed** *attrib. adj.* selbsternannt; **~-pro'fessed** *attrib. adj.* selbsternannt; **he's a ~-professed leftist** er bezeichnet sich [selbst] als links; **~-pro'motion** *n., no pl.* Selbstinszenierung, *die;* **~-'propagating** *adj.* (Bot.) selbstbefruchtend; **be ~-propagating** Selbstbefruchter sein; (fig.) sich selbst vermehren; **~-pro'pelled** *adj.* mit Eigenantrieb *nachgestellt;* **~-pro'tection** *n., no pl.* Selbstschutz, *der;* **~-'publicist** *n.* Selbstdarsteller, *der*/-darstellerin, *die;* **be a good ~-publicist** sich gut verkaufen können; **~-'raising flour** *n.* (Brit.) mit Backpulver versetztes Mehl; **~-re'gard** *n., no pl.* Selbstachtung, *die;* **~-'regulating** *adj.* sich selbst steuernd ‹*Maschine*›; autonom ‹*Institution*›; **~-regu'lation** *n., no pl.* Selbstregulierung, *die;* **~-re'liance** *n., no pl.* Selbstvertrauen, *das;* Selbstsicherheit, *die;* **~-re'liant** *adj.* selbstbewusst; selbstsicher; **~-re'spect** *n., no pl.* Selbstachtung, *die;* **~-re'specting** *adj.* mit Selbstachtung *nachgestellt;* **no ~-respecting person ...:** niemand, der etwas auf sich hält, ...; **~-re'straint** *n., no pl.* Selbstbeherrschung, *die;* **~-'righteous** *adj.* selbstgerecht; **~-'righteousness** *n., no pl.* Selbstgerechtigkeit, *die;* **~-'righting** *adj.* selbstaufrichtend; **~-'rising flour** (Amer.) ▸ **~-raising flour;** **~-'rule** *n., no pl.* Selbstverwaltung, *die;* **exercise ~-rule** sich selbst verwalten; **~-'sacrifice** *n.* Selbstaufopferung, *die;* **~-'sacrificing** *adj.* [sich] aufopfernd ‹*Mutter, Vater*›; aufopfernd ‹*Liebe*›; **~same** *adj.* **the ~same** der-/die-/dasselbe; **~-satis'faction** *n., no pl.* Selbstzufriedenheit, *die;* (smugness) Selbstgefälligkeit, *die;* **~-'satisfied** *adj.* selbstzufrieden; (smug) selbstgefällig; **~-'sealing** *adj.* 1 (automatically sealing) selbstdichtend; 2 (~-adhesive) selbstklebend; **~-seeking** A *adj.* selbstsüchtig; B *n., no pl.* Selbstsucht, *die;* **~-'service** A *n.* 1 (operation) Selbstbedienung, *die; attrib.* Selbstbedienungs-; 2 (shop) Selbstbedienungsladen, *der;* (petrol station) Tankstelle zum Selbsttanken; (restaurant) Selbstbedienungsrestaurant, *das;* B *pred. adj.* **the petrol station is/has become ~-service** die Tankstelle hat Selbstbedienung/hat auf Selbstbedienung umgestellt; **~-'serving** *adj.* selbstsüchtig; **~-sown** *adj.* selbst ausgesät; **~-'starter** *n.* (Motor Veh.) Selbststarter, *der;* **~-'study** *n., no pl.* Selbststudium, *das;* **~-styled** *adj.* selbst ernannt; von eigenen Gnaden *nachgestellt;* **~-suf'ficiency** *n., no pl.* Unabhängigkeit, *die;* (of country) Autarkie, *die;* **~-suf'ficient** *adj.* (independent) unabhängig; autark ‹*Land*›; selbstständig ‹*Person*›; **be ~-sufficient in food** seinen Nahrungsbedarf selbst decken; **~-sup'porting** *adj.* 1 sich selbst tragend ‹*Unternehmen, Verein*›; finanziell unabhängig ‹*Person*›; **the club/firm is ~-supporting** der Verein/die Firma trägt sich selbst; 2 (not requiring support) frei-, selbsttragend ‹*Konstruktion, Gebäude*›; **~-su'staining** *adj.* selbsterhaltend; **~-su'staining development/growth** nachhaltige Entwicklung/nachhaltiges Wachstum; **~-sustaining businesses** sich selbst tragende Betriebe; **~-'tapping** *adj.* selbstschneidend ‹*Schraube*›; **~-'taught** *adj.* autodidaktisch; selbst erlernt ‹*Fertigkeiten*›; **~-taught person** Autodidakt, *der*/Autodidaktin, *die;* **be a ~-taught painter/be ~-taught in German** sich (*Dat.*) das Malen/Deutsch selbst beigebracht haben; **she is ~-taught** sie ist Autodidaktin; **~-test** (Computing) A *n.* Selbsttest, *der;* B *v.i.* einen Selbsttest durchführen; **~-'will** *n., no pl.* Eigensinn, *der;* **~-'willed** *adj.* eigensinnig; **~-winding** *adj.* automatisch; **a ~-winding watch** eine Uhr mit Selbstaufzug; **~-'worth** *n., no pl.* Selbstwertgefühl, *das* (Psych.); **sense of ~-worth** Selbstwertgefühl, *das*

sell /sel/

A *v.t.*, **sold** /səʊld/ 1 verkaufen; **the shop ~s groceries** in dem Laden gibt es Lebensmittel [zu kaufen]; **~ sth. to sb., ~ sb. sth.** jmdm. etw. verkaufen; **~ one's life** *etc.* **dear** *or* **dearly** (fig.) sein Leben *usw.* teuer verkaufen; **it is the advertising that ~s the product** die Werbung sorgt für den Absatz des Produkts; **~ by ...** (on package) ≈ mindestens haltbar bis ... 2 (betray) verraten 3 (offer dishonourably) verkaufen; verhökern (ugs. abwertend); **~ oneself/one's soul** sich/seine Seele verkaufen (**to** *Dat.*) 4 (coll.: cheat, disappoint) verraten; anschmieren (salopp); **I've been sold!, sold again!** ich bin [wieder] der/die Dumme! (ugs.) 5 (gain acceptance for) **~ sb. as ...:** jmdn. als ... verkaufen (ugs.); **~ sth. to sb.** jmdn. für etw. gewinnen; **~ sb. the idea of doing sth.** jmdn. für den Gedanken gewinnen, etw. zu tun 6 **~ sb. on sth.** (coll.: make enthusiastic) jmdn. für etw. begeistern *od.* erwärmen; **be sold on sth.** (coll.) von etw. begeistert sein. *See also* **dummy A 5; river A 1; short A 9**

B *v.i.*, **sold** 1 sich verkaufen [lassen]; ‹*Person:*› verkaufen; **the book sold 5,000 copies in a week** in einer Woche wurden 5 000 Exemplare des Buches verkauft 2 **~ at** *or* **for** kosten. *See also* **cake A 2**

C *n.* 1 **be a tough ~:** ein Ladenhüter (abwertend) sein; sich schlecht verkaufen; **be an easy ~:** ein Verkaufsschlager sein; sich gut verkaufen 2 (coll.: deception) Schwindel, *der* (*abwertend*). *See also* **hard sell; soft sell**

Phrasal verbs

- **~ 'off** *v.t.* verkaufen; abstoßen ‹*Anteile, Aktien*›
- **~ 'out**

A *v.t.* 1 ausverkaufen; restlos verkaufen; **the play/performance was sold out** das Stück/die Aufführung war ausverkauft 2 (coll.: betray) verraten

B *v.i.* 1 **we have** *or* **are sold out** wir sind ausverkauft; **sth. ~s out quickly** etw. verkauft sich schnell; **~ out to another firm** durch Verkauf in eine andere Firma übergehen 2 (coll.:

betray one's cause) ~ **out to sb./sth.** zu jmdm./etw. überlaufen. *See also* **sell-out**
• ~ **'out of** *v.t.* **we have** *or* **are sold out of sth.** etw. ist ausverkauft
• ~ **'up** *v.t.* (Brit.) verkaufen; *abs.* sein Hab und Gut verkaufen

'sell-by date *n.* ≈ Mindesthaltbarkeitsdatum, *das*

seller /'selə(r)/ *n.* **1** Verkäufer, *der*/Verkäuferin, *die;* **be a ~ of sth.** etw. verkaufen; **a ~'s** *or* **~s' market** ein Verkäufermarkt **2** (product) **be a slow/bad ~:** sich nur langsam/schlecht verkaufen; **be a fast** *or* **strong** *or* **big ~:** ein Renner *od.* Verkaufsschlager sein; **be a good ~:** sich gut verkaufen

selling /'selɪŋ/
A *n.* **1** (act, occupation) Verkaufen, *das* **2** (salesmanship) Verkauf, *der;* **training in ~:** Verkaufsschulung, *die*
B *adj. in comb.* **a fast-** *or* **good-~ book** ein Buch, das sich gut verkauft

selling: ~ point *n.* **a [good] ~ point** ein Verkaufsargument; (fig.) ein Pluspunkt; **~ price** *n.* Verkaufspreis, *der*

'sell-off *n.* (esp. Amer. Finance) Sell-out, *der*

sellotape *v.t.* mit Klebeband kleben

Sellotape ® /'seləʊteɪp/ *n., no pl., no indef. art.* ≈ Tesafilm, *der* (Wz)

sell: ~-out *n.* **1** (event) **be a ~-out** ausverkauft sein; **2** (coll.: betrayal) Verrat, *der;* **~-through** *n.* **1** *no pl.* (retail turnover) Durchverkaufsquote, *die;* **2** *no pl.* (retail sale) Kaufgeschäft, *das; attrib.* **~ market** Kaufmarkt, *der;* **3** (video for retail sale) Kaufvideo, *das;* Kaufkassette, *die*

selvage, selvedge /'selvɪdʒ/ *n.* Webkante, *die*

selves *pl. of* **self**

semantic /sɪ'mæntɪk/ *adj.* semantisch

semantically /sɪ'mæntɪkəlɪ/ *adv.* semantisch

semantics /sɪ'mæntɪks/ *n., no pl.* Semantik, *die;* **only argue about ~:** sich um Worte streiten

semaphore /'seməfɔ:(r)/
A *n.* **1** (apparatus) Signalmast, *der;* Semaphor, *das od. der* **2** (system) Winken, *das;* **~ alphabet** Winkeralphabet, *das*
B *v.i.* **~ to sb.** jmdm. ein Winksignal übermitteln
C *v.t.* [durch Winksignale] übermitteln

semblance /'sembləns/ *n.* **1** (outward appearance) Anschein, *der;* **without a ~ of regret/a smile** ohne das geringste Zeichen von Bedauern/den Anflug eines Lächelns; **without even the ~ of a trial** ohne auch nur die geringste Verhandlung; **bring some ~ of order to sth.** wenigstens den Anschein von Ordnung in etw. (*Akk.*) bringen **2** (resemblance) Ähnlichkeit, *die*

semeiology /si:maɪ'ɒlədʒɪ/, **semeiotics** /si:maɪ'ɒtɪks/ ▸**semiology**

semen /'si:men/ *n.* (Physiol.) Samen, *der;* Sperma, *das*

semester /sɪ'mestə(r)/ *n.* (Univ.) Semester, *das*

semi /'semɪ/ *n.* (coll.) **1** (Brit.: house) Doppelhaushälfte, *die* **2** (Amer.: vehicle) Sattelanhänger, *der*

semi- *in comb.* halb-/Halb-

semi: ~-auto'matic A *adj.* halbautomatisch; **B** *n.* halbautomatische Feuerwaffe; **~-basement** *n.* Halbsouterrain, *das;* **~bold** *adj.* (Printing) halbfett; **~breve** *n.* (Brit. Mus.) ganze Note; **~circle** *n.* Halbkreis, *der;* **~'circular** *adj.* halbkreisförmig; **~-'colon** *n.* Semikolon, *das;* **~con'ductor** *n.* (Phys.) Halbleiter, *der;* **~-'conscious** *adj.* halb bewusstlos; **be only ~-conscious** nicht bei vollem Bewusstsein sein; **~-'darkness** *n.* Halbdunkel, *das;* **in ~-darkness** im Halbdunkel; **~-de'tached A** *adj.* **the house is ~-detached** es ist eine Doppelhaushälfte; **a ~-detached house** eine Doppelhaushälfte; **B** *n.* (Brit.: house) Doppelhaushälfte, *die;* **~-'final** *n.* Halbfinale, *das;* Semifinale, *das;* **in the ~-finals** im Halbfinale; **~-'finalist** *n.* Halbfinalteilnehmer, *der*/-teilnehmerin, *die;* Halbfinalist, *der*/-finalistin, *die;* **~-'finished** *adj.* halb fertig; **~-'invalid** *n.* Teilinvalide, *der/die;* **~-literate** *adj.* **be ~-literate** kaum lesen und schreiben können

seminal /'semɪnl, 'si:mɪnl/ *adj.* **1** (having originative power) schöpferisch; (embryonic) keimhaft **2** (reproductive) Samen‹*leiter, -flüssigkeit*›

seminar /'semɪnɑ:(r)/ *n.* **1** (small class) Seminar, *das* **2** (Amer.: conference) Konferenz, *die; attrib.* **~ leader** Seminarleiter, *der*/-leiterin, *die* **3** (study-course) Kurs[us], *der;* Seminar, *das*

seminarian /semɪ'neərɪən/, **seminarist** /'semɪnərɪst/ *ns.* Seminarist, *der*

'seminar room *n.* Seminarraum, *der*

seminary /'semɪnərɪ/ *n.* Priesterseminar, *das*

semiology /si:mɪ'ɒlədʒɪ/, **semiotics** /si:mɪ'ɒtɪks/ *ns.* Semiotik, *die;* Semiologie, *die*

semi: ~-'permanent *adj.* fast permanent; **~-'precious** *adj.* **~-precious stone** Halbedelstein, *der;* Schmuckstein, *der;* **be ~-precious** ein Halbedelstein sein; **~-pro'fessional** *adj.* semiprofessionell; **~quaver** *n.* (Brit. Mus.) Sechzehntelnote, *die;* **~-re'tired** *adj.* im Ruhestand [gelegentlich] noch aktiv; **be ~-retired** im Ruhestand, aber immer noch [gelegentlich] aktiv sein; **~-'skilled** *adj.* angelernt; **~-skimmed A** *adj.* teilentrahmt; **B** *n.* teilentrahmte Milch; **~-'sweet** *adj.* halbsüß ‹*Sekt, Wein*›; [nur] leicht gesüßt ‹*Kuchen, Schokolade*›

Semite /'si:maɪt, 'semaɪt/
A *n.* Semit, *der*/Semitin, *die*
B *adj.* semitisch

Semitic /sɪ'mɪtɪk/ *adj.* semitisch

'semitone *n.* (Mus.) Halbton, *der*

'semi-trailer *n.* Sattelanhänger, *der*

semolina /semə'li:nə/ *n.* **1** Grieß, *der* **2** (pudding) Grießpudding, *der*

sempstress ▸**seamstress**

Sen. *abbr.* **1** = **Senator** Sen. **2** = **Senior** sen.

SEN *abbr.* (Brit.) = **State Enrolled Nurse**

senate /'senət/ *n.* Senat, *der*

> **Senate – the United States Senate**
>
> Das Oberhaus des amerikanischen **Congress.** Es gibt 100 gewählte **Senators** (Senatoren). Neue Gesetze müssen sowohl vom **House of Representatives** als auch vom Senat verabschiedet werden.

senator /'senətə(r)/ *n.* ▸ **p. 1634** Senator, *der*/Senatorin, *die*

> **Senator**
>
> Ein Mitglied des amerikanischen **Senate.**

send /send/
A *v.t.,* **sent** /sent/ **1** (cause to go) schicken; senden (geh.); **~ sb. to Africa** jmdn. nach Afrika schicken; **~ sb. to university/boarding school** jmdn. auf die Universität/ins Internat schicken; **~ sb. on a course/tour** jmdn. in einen Kurs/auf eine Tour schicken; **~ a dog after sb.** einen Hund auf jmdn. hetzen; **she ~s her best wishes/love** sie lässt grüßen/herzlich grüßen; **~ [sb.] apologies/congratulations** sich [bei jmdm.] entschuldigen lassen/[jmdm.] seine Glückwünsche übermitteln; **she sent him congratulations on ...:** sie schickte ihm Glückwünsche zu ...; **~ sb. home/to bed** jmdn. nach Hause/ins Bett schicken; **~ sb. to his death** jmdn. in den Tod schicken; *see also* **word A 6**
2 (grant) schicken; **~ her victorious!** (arch.) [Herr,] lass sie siegreich sein!; **God ~s the rain on the just and the unjust** (prov.) Gott lässt regnen über Gerechte und Ungerechte
3 (propel) **~ a rocket into space** eine Rakete in den Weltraum schießen; **~ a ball over the wall** einen Ball über die Mauer schießen; **~ up clouds of dust** Staubwolken aufwirbeln; **~ sth. to the ground/hurtling through the air** etw. zu Boden werfen/durch die Luft sausen lassen; **~ sb. sprawling/reeling** jmdn. zu Boden strecken/ins Wanken bringen; **~ sb. running for cover** jmdn. schnell Deckung suchen lassen; **~ sth. off course** etw. vom Kurs abkommen lassen; *see also* **fly² A 4**
4 (drive into condition) **~ sb. mad** *or* **crazy** jmdn. verrückt machen (ugs.); **~ sb. into raptures/a temper/fits of laughter** jmdn. ins Schwärmen geraten lassen/in Wut bringen/dazu bringen, dass er sich totlacht (ugs.); **~ sb. to sleep** jmdn. zum Einschlafen bringen; **that loud music ~s me round the bend** (fig. coll.) bei dieser lauten Musik könnte ich verrückt *od.* wahnsinnig werden (ugs.)
5 (dismiss) **~ sb. about his/her** *etc.* **business** jmdn. vor die Tür setzen; *see also* **Coventry; pack C**
6 (coll.: put into ecstasy) begeistern; **she really ~s me** sie macht mich total an (salopp)
B *v.i.,* **sent: ~ to sb. for sth.** (by letter) jmdn. um etw. anschreiben; **we'll ~ to Germany for that** wir werden nach Deutschland schreiben, dass sie uns das schicken

Phrasal verbs

• ~ **a'head** *v.t.* vorausschicken; **he was sent ahead of the main group** er wurde dem Haupttrupp vorausgeschickt
• ~ **a'way**
A *v.t.* wegschicken; fortschicken (landsch., geh.); **we like to ~ our guests away with pleasant memories** wir möchten unseren Gästen angenehme Erinnerungen mitgeben; *see also* **flea**
B *v.i.* **~ away [to sb.] for sth.** etw. [bei jmdm.] anfordern
• ~ **'back** *v.t.* **1** (return) zurückschicken **2** (because of dissatisfaction) zurückgehen lassen ‹*Speise, Getränk*›; (by post) zurückschicken ‹*Ware*›
• ~ **'down**
A *v.t.* **1** [hinunter]schicken **2** (Brit. Univ.) relegieren (geh.); von der Hochschule verweisen **3** (put in prison) hinter Schloss und Riegel bringen (ugs.) **4** (Cricket) werfen ‹*Ball*› **5** nach unten treiben ‹*Preis, Kosten, Temperatur*›
B *v.i.* **~ down [to the store] for sth.** etw. aus dem Lager holen lassen
• ~ **for** *v.t.* **1** (tell to come) holen lassen; rufen ‹*Polizei, Arzt, Krankenwagen*› **2** (order from elsewhere) anfordern
• ~ **'in** *v.t.* einschicken
• ~ **'off**
A *v.t.* **1** (dispatch) abschicken ‹*Sache*›; losschicken (ugs.) ‹*Person*›; **~ one's children off to boarding school** seine Kinder ins Internat schicken **2** (bid farewell to) verabschieden; *see also* **send-off 3** (Sport) vom Platz stellen (**for** wegen);
B *v.i.* **~ off for sth. [to sb.]** etw. [von jmdm.] anfordern
• ~ **'on** *v.t.* **1** (forward) nachsenden ‹*Post*›; **they sent me on to you** ich wurde an Sie verwiesen **2** (cause to go ahead) **~ on [ahead]** vorausschicken **3** (cause to participate) **~ a player on** einen Spieler einsetzen
• ~ **'out**
A *v.t.* **1** (issue) verschicken **2** (emit) aussenden ‹*Hilferuf, Nachricht*›; abgeben ‹*Hitze*›; senden ‹*Lichtstrahlen*›; ausstoßen ‹*Rauch*›; verströmen ‹*Geruch*› **3** (dispatch) schicken; **~ sb. out to Africa** jmdn. nach Afrika schicken; **~ sb. out for sth.** jmdn. schicken, um etw. zu besorgen **4** (order to leave) hinausschicken
B *v.i.* **~ out for sth.** etw. besorgen *od.* holen lassen
• ~ **'up** *v.t.* **1** (Brit. coll.: ridicule) (in play, sketch, song) parodieren; (in cartoon) karikieren; *see also* **send-up 2** (Amer. coll.: put in prison) in den Knast stecken (ugs.); einbuchten (salopp) **3** (transmit to higher authority) weiterleiten (**to** an + *Akk.*) **4** (cause to rise) steigen lassen ‹*Ballon*›; hochtreiben ‹*Preis, Kosten, Temperatur*›; **~ sb.'s temperature up** (fig. joc.) jmdn. zum Kochen bringen (ugs.) **5** (destroy) in die Luft jagen (ugs.) *od.* sprengen

sender /'sendə(r)/ *n.* ▸ **p. 1287** (of goods) Lieferant, *der*/Lieferantin, *die;* (of letter) Absender, *der*/Absenderin, *die*

send: ~-off *n.* Verabschiedung, *die;* **give sb. a good ~-off** jmdn. groß verabschieden; **~-up** *n.* (Brit. coll.: parody) Parodie, *die;* (in cartoon) Karikatur, *die;* **do a ~-up of sb./sth.** jmdn./etw. parodieren

Senegal /senɪ'gɔ:l/ *pr. n.* Senegal (*das*) *od. der*

Senegalese /senɪgə'li:z/ ▸ **p. 1345**
A *adj.* senegalesisch; **sb. is ~:** jmd. ist Senegalese/Senegalesin

S

B *n., pl. same* Senegalese, *der*/Senegalesin, *die*

senescent /sɪˈnesənt/ *adj.* alternd

senile /ˈsiːnaɪl/ *adj.* senil; (physically) altersschwach; (caused by old age) altersbedingt ‹*Apathie, Schwatzhaftigkeit*›; **~ decay** Altersabbau, *der*

senile deˈmentia *n.* (Med.) senile Demenz

senility /sɪˈnɪlɪtɪ/ *n., no pl.* Senilität, *die;* (physical infirmity) Altersschwäche, *die*

senior /ˈsiːnɪə(r)/

A *adj.* [1] ▸ℹ **p. 894** (older) älter; **be ~ to sb.** älter als jmd. sein; **~ team** Seniorenmannschaft, *die* [2] ▸ℹ **p. 1260** (of higher rank) höher ‹*Rang, Beamter, Stellung*›; leitend ‹*Angestellter, Stellung*›; (longest-serving) ältest …; **someone ~:** jemand in höherer Stellung; **~ management** Geschäftsleitung, *die;* **~ consultant/nurse** (in hospital) ≈ Oberarzt, *der*/Oberschwester, *die;* **be ~ to sb.** eine höhere Stellung als jmd. haben; **she is ~/not very ~:** sie hat einen/keinen gehobenen Posten; **~ manager** obere Führungskraft; **~ management** oberer Führungskreis [3] *appended to name* (the elder) **Mr Smith S~:** Mr. Smith senior [4] (Brit. Sch.) **~ school** *or* **section** Oberstufe, *die* [5] (Brit. Univ.) **~ combination** *or* **common room** Gemeinschaftsraum für Dozenten [6] (Amer. Sch., Univ.) **~ class** Abschlussklasse, *die;* **~ year** letztes Jahr vor der Abschlussprüfung

B *n.* [1] ▸ℹ **p. 894** (older person) Ältere, *der/die;* (person of higher rank) Vorgesetzte, *der/die;* **be sb.'s ~ [by six years]** *or* **[six years] sb.'s ~:** [sechs Jahre] älter als jmd. sein [2] (Brit. Sch.) Schüler/Schülerin einer höheren Schule; (in the last three years) Oberstufenschüler, *der*/-schülerin, *die* [3] (Amer.) (Sch.) Schüler/Schülerin im letzten Schuljahr; (Univ.) Student/Studentin im letzten Studienjahr

senior: ~ ˈcitizen *n.* Senior, *der*/Seniorin, *die;* **~ college** *n.* (Amer.) höhere Schule; ≈ [Gymnasial]oberstufe, *die*

seniority /siːnɪˈɒrɪtɪ/ *n.* [1] (superior age) Alter, *das* [2] (priority in length of service) höheres Dienstalter [3] (superior rank) höherer Rang

senior: ~ ˈofficer *n.* ▸ℹ **p. 1260** höherer Beamter/höhere Beamtin; (Mil.) ranghöchster Offizier; **sb.'s ~ officer** jmds. Vorgesetzter; **~ ˈpartner** *n.* Seniorpartner, *der*/-partnerin, *die;* **~ service** *n.* (Brit.) Marine, *die*

senna /ˈsenə/ *n.* [1] (Bot.) Sennespflanze, *die;* Kassie, *die* [2] (drug) Sennesblätter; Senna, *die*

sensation /senˈseɪʃn/ *n.* [1] (feeling) Gefühl, *das;* **~ of hunger/thirst/giddiness** Hunger-/Durst-/Schwindelgefühl, *das;* **have a ~ of falling** das Gefühl haben zu fallen [2] (person, event, etc. causing intense excitement) Sensation, *die;* **a great ~:** ein großes Ereignis [3] (excitement) Aufsehen, *das*

sensational /senˈseɪʃənl/ *adj.* [1] (spectacular) aufsehenerregend; sensationell [2] (arousing intense response) reißerisch (abwertend); Sensations‹*blatt, -presse*› [3] (phenomenal) phänomenal

sensationalise ▸ **sensationalize**

sensationalism /senˈseɪʃənəlɪzm/ *n.* Sensationshascherei, *die* (abwertend); **[desire for] ~:** Sensationsgier, *die* (abwertend)

sensationalist /senˈseɪʃənəlɪst/ *adj.* sensationslüstern (abwertend); sensationsgeil (ugs. abwertend); Sensations‹*blatt, -presse, usw.*›; **~ nonsense** um der Sensation willen verbreiteter Unsinn

sensationalize /senˈseɪʃənəlaɪz/ *v.t.* **~ sth.** etw. zur Sensation aufbauschen

sensationally /senˈseɪʃənəlɪ/ *adv.* sensationell

sense /sens/

A *n.* [1] (faculty of perception) Sinn, *der;* **~ of smell/touch/taste** Geruchs-/Tast-/Geschmackssinn, *der;* **come to one's ~s** das Bewusstsein wiedererlangen [2] *in pl.* (normal state of mind) Verstand, *der;* **in full possession of one's ~s** im Vollbesitz seiner geistigen Kräfte; **no one in his ~s would do that** niemand mit einem Funken Verstand würde so etwas tun; **have taken leave of** *or* **be out of one's ~s** den Verstand verloren haben; **frighten sb. out of his ~s** jmdm. einen furchtbaren Schrecken einjagen; **come to one's ~s** zur Vernunft kommen; **bring sb. to his ~s** jmdn. zur Vernunft *od.* Besinnung bringen [3] (consciousness) Gefühl, *das;* **~ of responsibility/guilt** Verantwortungs-/Schuldgefühl, *das;* **out of a ~ of duty** aus Pflichtgefühl; **~ of gratitude** Gefühl der Dankbarkeit; **a keen ~ of honour** ein ausgeprägtes Ehrgefühl; **have a ~ of one's own importance** sich sehr wichtig nehmen; *see also* **direction 3**; **humour A 1**; **road sense** [4] (ability to perceive) Gespür, *das;* (instinct) [instinktives] Gespür; **~ of the absurd** Gespür für das Absurde [5] (practical wisdom) Verstand, *der;* **there's a lot of ~ in what he's saying** was er sagt, klingt sehr vernünftig; **sound** *or* **good ~:** [gesunder Menschen]verstand; **not have the ~ to do sth.** nicht so schlau sein, etw. zu tun; **there is no ~ in doing that** es hat keinen Sinn, das zu tun; **what is the ~ of** *or* **in doing that?** was hat man davon *od.* wozu soll es gut sein, das zu tun?; **have more ~ than to do sth.** genug Verstand haben, etw. nicht zu tun; **talk ~:** vernünftig reden; **now you are talking ~:** jetzt wirst du vernünftig; **you're just not talking ~:** du redest einfach Unsinn; **see ~:** zur Vernunft kommen; **make sb. see ~:** jmdn. zur Vernunft bringen; **be a man/woman of ~:** wissen, was man tut; **she hasn't the ~ she was born with** sie hat keinen Funken Verstand; *see also* **common sense** [6] (meaning) Sinn, *der;* (of word) Bedeutung, *die;* **in the strict** *or* **literal ~:** im strengen *od.* wörtlichen Sinn; **in every ~ [of the word]** in jeder Hinsicht; **there is a ~ in which …:** man könnte durchaus die Ansicht vertreten, dass …; **in some ~:** irgendwie; **in a** *or* **one ~:** in gewisser Hinsicht *od.* Weise; **make ~:** einen Sinn ergeben; **her arguments do not make ~ to me** ihre Argumente leuchten mir nicht ein; **it does not make ~ to do that** es ist Unsinn *od.* unvernünftig, das zu tun; **it makes [a lot of] ~** (is [very] reasonable) es ist [sehr] sinnvoll; **it makes good** *or* **sound financial ~:** es ist in finanzieller Hinsicht sinnvoll; **it all makes ~ to me now** jetzt verstehe ich alles; **it just doesn't make ~:** es ergibt einfach keinen Sinn; **now you're making ~:** jetzt verstehe ich, was du sagen willst; **make ~ of sth.** etw. verstehen; aus etw. schlau werden [7] (prevailing sentiment) **take the ~ of the meeting** die Meinung der Versammlung einholen

B *v.t.* spüren; ‹*Tier:*› wittern; ‹*Gerät:*› wahrnehmen

senseless /ˈsenslɪs/ *adj.* [1] (unconscious) bewusstlos [2] (foolish) unvernünftig; dumm; **what a ~ thing to do/say!** wie kann man nur so etwas Dummes machen/sagen! [3] (purposeless) unsinnig ‹*Argument*›; sinnlos ‹*Diskussion, Vergeudung*›

ˈsense organ *n.* Sinnesorgan, *das*

sensibility /sensɪˈbɪlɪtɪ/ *n.* [1] *in pl.* (susceptibility) Empfindlichkeit, *die;* **her sensibilities are easily wounded** sie ist sehr schnell verletzt *od.* gekränkt [2] (openness to emotional impressions) Sensibilität, *die* (**to** in Bezug auf + *Akk.*); **~ to pain/beauty** Schmerzempfindlichkeit, *die*/Empfänglichkeit für Schönheit [3] (delicacy of feeling) Feingefühl, *das* (**to** gegenüber; **of** für); Einfühlungsvermögen, *das* (**of** in + *Akk.*) [4] (oversensitiveness) Empfindsamkeit, *die*

sensible /ˈsensɪbl/ *adj.* [1] (reasonable) vernünftig; **he was ~ enough to do it** er war so vernünftig, es zu tun; **be ~ [about it]!** sei doch vernünftig! [2] (practical) praktisch; zweckmäßig; fest ‹*Schuhe*› [3] (appreciable) gravierend ‹*Fehler*›; beachtlich, merklich ‹*Anstieg, Rückgang, Unterschied*› [4] (literary: aware) **be ~ of** *or* **to sth.** etw. spüren

sensibly /ˈsensɪblɪ/ *adv.* [1] (reasonably) vernünftig; besonnen; **~ enough, he refused** er war so vernünftig abzulehnen [2] (practically) zweckmäßig [3] (appreciably) merklich

sensitisation, sensitise ▸ **sensitiz-**

sensitive /ˈsensɪtɪv/ *adj.* [1] (recording slight changes) empfindlich; **be ~ to sth.** empfindlich auf etw. (*Akk.*) reagieren; **~ to light** lichtempfindlich [2] (touchy) empfindlich (**about** wegen); **be ~ to sth.** empfindlich auf etw. (*Akk.*) reagieren [3] heikel ‹*Thema, Diskussion*› [4] (perceptive) einfühlsam

sensitively /ˈsensɪtɪvlɪ/ *adv.* empfindlich ‹*reagieren*›; einfühlsam ‹*darstellen*›

ˈsensitive plant *n.* (Bot.; also fig.: person) Mimose, *die*

sensitivity /sensɪˈtɪvɪtɪ/ *n.* [1] (capacity to respond emotionally) Sensibilität, *die;* Empfindlichkeit, *die* (**to** gegen); **offend sb.'s sensitivities** jmds. Feingefühl verletzen [2] (responsiveness) Empfindlichkeit, *die;* **~ to light** Lichtempfindlichkeit, *die*

sensitization /sensɪtaɪˈzeɪʃn/ *n.* Sensibilisierung, *die*

sensitize /ˈsensɪtaɪz/ *v.t.* sensibilisieren (**to** für)

sensor /ˈsensə(r)/ *n.* Sensor, *der*

sensory /ˈsensərɪ/ *adj.* sensorisch; Sinnes‹*wahrnehmung, -organ*›

sensory depriˈvation *n., no pl.* sensorische Deprivation (Psych.)

sensual /ˈsensjʊəl, ˈsenʃʊəl/ *adj.* sinnlich; lustvoll ‹*Leben*›; Sinnen‹*freude, -genuss*›

sensuality /sensjʊˈælɪtɪ, senʃʊˈælɪtɪ/ *n.* Sinnlichkeit, *die*

sensually /ˈsensjʊəlɪ, ˈsenʃʊəlɪ/ *adv.* sinnlich; genussvoll ‹*essen*›

sensuous /ˈsensjʊəs/ *adj.* sinnlich

sensuously /ˈsensjʊəslɪ/ *adv.* sinnlich; **~ beautiful** von sinnlicher Schönheit *nachgestellt*

sent ▸ **send**

sentence /ˈsentəns/

A *n.* [1] (decision of lawcourt) [Straf]urteil, *das;* (fig.) Strafe, *die;* **give sb. a three-year ~:** jmdn. zu drei Jahren Haft verurteilen; **pass ~ [on sb.]** [jmdm.] das Urteil verkünden; **be under ~ of death** zum Tode verurteilt sein; (fig.) zum Untergang verurteilt sein [2] (Ling.) Satz, *der; see also* **complex A 3**; **compound[1] A 6**; **simple 5**

B *v.t.* (lit. or fig.) verurteilen (**to** zu)

ˈsentence-modifier *n.* (Ling.) Satzpartikel, *die*

sententious /senˈtenʃəs/ *adj.* [1] (pithy) prägnant; sentenziös (geh.) [2] (affectedly formal) salbungsvoll (abwertend) [3] (given to pompous moralizing) moralistisch; schulmeisterhaft

sententiously /senˈtenʃəslɪ/ *adv.* [1] (pithily) kurz und prägnant [2] (pompously) schulmeisterhaft

sentient /ˈsenʃənt/ *adj.* empfindungsfähig

sentiment /ˈsentɪmənt/ *n.* [1] (mental feeling) Gefühl, *das;* **noble ~s** edle Gesinnung; **~ unchecked by reason** nicht vernunftgesteuerte Gefühle; **those are** *or* (coll.) **them's my ~s** so denke ich darüber [2] (emotion conveyed in art) Empfindung, *die* [3] *no pl.* (emotional weakness) Sentimentalität, *die;* Rührseligkeit, *die* [4] (expression of view) Gedanke, *der*

sentimental /sentɪˈmentl/ *adj.* [1] (motivated by feeling) sentimental; **sth. has ~ value [for sb.]** jmd. hängt an etw. (*Dat.*); **~ attachment to sth.** gefühlsmäßige Bindung an etw. (*Akk.*); **for ~ reasons** aus Sentimentalität [2] (appealing to sentiment) rührselig; sentimental; **a ~ song** eine Schnulze

sentimentalism /sentɪˈmentəlɪzm/ *n., no pl.* Sentimentalität, *die*

sentimentalist /sentɪˈmentəlɪst/ *n.* sentimentaler Mensch

sentimentality /sentɪmenˈtælɪtɪ/ *n.* Sentimentalität, *die*

sentimentalize /sentɪˈmentəlaɪz/

A *v.i.* sich sentimentalen Gefühlen hingeben

B *v.t.* sentimental darstellen

sentimentally /sentɪˈmentəlɪ/ *adv.* sentimental; gefühlsmäßig ‹*verbunden*›

sentinel /ˈsentɪnl/ *n.* (lit. or fig.) Wache, *die;* **stand ~ over sth.** (fig.) über etw. (*Akk.*) wachen

sentry /ˈsentrɪ/ *n.* (lit. or fig.) Wache, *die;* **stand ~ at the door** an der Tür Wache halten

sentry: ~ box *n.* Wachhäuschen, *das;* **~ duty** *n.* **be on ~ duty** Wachdienst haben

sepal /ˈsepl, ˈsiːpl/ *n.* (Bot.) Kelchblatt, *das*

separability /sepərəˈbɪlɪtɪ/ *n., no pl.* Trennbarkeit, *die*

separable /ˈsepərəbl/ *adj.* 1 trennbar; zerlegbar ‹*Werkzeug, Gerät*› 2 (Ling.) trennbar ‹*Vorsilbe, Verb*›

separate
A /ˈsepərət/ *adj.* verschieden ‹*Fragen, Probleme, Gelegenheiten*›; getrennt ‹*Konten, Betten*›; gesondert ‹*Teil*›; separat ‹*Eingang, Toilette, Blatt Papier, Abteil*›; Sonder‹*vereinbarung*›; (one's own, individual) eigen ‹*Zimmer, Identität, Organisation*›; **lead ~ lives** getrennt leben; **go ~ ways** getrennte Wege gehen; **the ~ volumes** die einzelnen Bände; **one is quite ~ from the other** das eine ist ganz unabhängig von dem anderen/(different) ganz anders als das andere; **keep two things ~:** zwei Dinge auseinander halten; **keep issue A ~ from issue B** Frage A und Frage B getrennt behandeln; **keep one's chequebook ~ from one's bank card** Scheckbuch und Scheckkarte getrennt aufbewahren
B /ˈsepəreɪt/ *v.t.* 1 trennen; **they are ~d** (no longer live together) sie leben getrennt 2 (Amer.: discharge) entlassen (**from** aus)
C *v.i.* 1 (disperse) sich trennen 2 ‹*Ehepaar*› sich trennen 3 (secede) sich abspalten 4 ▸**separate out A**. *See also* **separates**

Phrasal verb
• **~ ˈout**
A *v.i.* sich entmischen (fachspr.); sich trennen
B *v.t.* (distinguish) auseinander halten; (extract) trennen

separately /ˈsepərətlɪ/ *adv.* getrennt; **they had, quite ~, reached the same conclusion** sie waren — ganz unabhängig voneinander — zum gleichen Schluss gekommen

separate ˈmaintenance *n.* (Law) Unterhalt, *der*

separates /ˈsepərəts/ *n. pl.* (Fashion) Separates; einzelne Kleidungsstücke [die man kombinieren kann]

separation /sepəˈreɪʃn/ *n.* 1 Trennung, *die*; **judicial** *or* **legal ~:** gerichtliche Trennung 2 (Amer.: resignation, discharge) Entlassung, *die* (**from** aus)

sepaˈration order *n.* gerichtliche Anordnung des Getrenntlebens

separatism /ˈsepərətɪzm/ *n.* 1 (advocacy of separation) Separatismus, *der* 2 (segregation) **[racial/class] ~:** [Rassen-/Klassen]trennung, *die*

separatist /ˈsepərətɪst/ *n.* Separatist, *der*/Separatistin, *die*; *attrib.* **~ movement** Separatistenbewegung, *die*

separator /ˈsepəreɪtə(r)/ *n.* Separator, *der*

sepia /ˈsiːpɪə/ *n.* 1 (pigment) Sepia, *die* 2 (colour) Sepiabraun, *das*; **~ photograph/drawing** sepiafarbenes Foto/Sepiazeichnung, *die* 3 (drawing) Sepiazeichnung, *die*

sepsis /ˈsepsɪs/ *n., pl.* **sepses** /ˈsepsiːz/ (Med.) Sepsis, *die* (fachspr.); Blutvergiftung, *die*

Sept. *abbr.* **= September** Sept.

septa *pl. of* **septum**

September /sepˈtembə(r)/ *n.* ▸❶ **p. 1047** September, *der*; *see also* **August**

septet, septette /sepˈtet/ *n.* (Mus.) Septett, *das*

septic /ˈseptɪk/ *adj.* septisch

septicaemia (*Amer.*: **septicemia**) /septɪˈsiːmɪə/ *n.* ▸❶ **p. 1231** (Med.) Sepsis, *die*; Septikämie, *die* (fachspr.)

septic ˈtank *n.* Faulraum, *der*

septuagenarian /septjʊədʒɪˈneərɪən/
A *adj.* siebzigjährig; (more than 70 years old) in den Siebzigern *nachgestellt*
B *n.* Siebziger, *der*/Siebzigerin, *die*

septum /ˈseptəm/ *n., pl.* **septa** /ˈseptə/ (Anat., Bot., Zool.) Septum, *das*

sepulcher (Amer.) ▸**sepulchre**

sepulchral /sɪˈpʌlkrl/ *adj.* 1 (of burial) Grab-; Bestattungs‹*brauch, -ritus*› 2 (fig.: funereal) düster

sepulchre /ˈseplkə(r)/ *n.* (Brit.) Grab, *das*; **the Holy S~:** das Heilige Grab

sequel /ˈsiːkwl/ *n.* 1 (consequence, result) Folge, *die* (**to** von) 2 (continuation) Fortsetzung, *die*; **there was a tragic ~:** es gab ein tragisches Nachspiel; **in the ~:** in der Folge

sequence /ˈsiːkwəns/ *n.* 1 (succession) Reihenfolge, *die*; **rapid/logical ~:** rasche/logische Abfolge; **a ~ of musicals** eine Reihe von Musicals 2 (part of film; set of poems, also Cards; Mus., Eccl.) Sequenz, *die* 3 (succession without cause) Aufeinanderfolge, *die* 4 **~ of tenses** (Ling.) Zeitenfolge, *die*

sequential /sɪˈkwenʃl/ *adj.* (forming a sequence) aufeinander folgend; **be ~ to** *or* **upon sth.** auf etw. (*Akk.*) folgen

sequentially /sɪˈkwenʃəlɪ/ *adv.* 1 nacheinander 2 (Computing) sequenziell

sequester /sɪˈkwestə(r)/
A *v.t.* 1 (set apart) abtrennen ‹*Teil*›; absondern ‹*Person*› 2 (Law: seize) sequestrieren 3 (confiscate) beschlagnahmen
B *v. refl.* sich fern halten; **~ oneself from the world** sich von der Welt abkapseln

sequestered /sɪˈkwestəd/ *adj.* abgelegen; ‹*Leben*› in Abgeschiedenheit

sequestrate /ˈsiːkwɪstreɪt/ ▸**sequester A 2, 3**

sequestration /siːkwɪˈstreɪʃn/ *n.* 1 (Law: appropriation) Sequestration, *die* 2 (confiscation) Beschlagnahme, *die*

sequestrator /ˈsiːkwɪstreɪtə(r)/ *n.* Sequester, *der*

sequin /ˈsiːkwɪn/ *n.* Paillette, *die*

sequined, sequinned /ˈsiːkwɪnd/ *adj.* paillettenbesetzt ‹*Kleid*›

sequoia /sɪˈkwɔɪə/ *n.* (Bot.) Mammutbaum, *der*; Sequoia, *die* (fachspr.)

sera *pl. of* **serum**

seraglio /səˈrɑːljəʊ/ *n., pl.* **~s** Harem, *der*; Serail, *das* (veralt.)

seraph /ˈserəf/ *n., pl.* **seraphim** /ˈserəfɪm/ *or* **~s** Seraph, *der*

seraphic /səˈræfɪk/ *adj.* seraphisch (geh.)

Serb /sɜːb/ ▸❶ **p. 1345** ▸**Serbian**

Serbia /ˈsɜːbɪə/ *pr. n.* Serbien, *das*

Serbia and Montenegro *pr. n.* Serbien und Montenegro (*das*)

Serbian /ˈsɜːbɪən/ ▸❶ **p. 1277**, ▸❶ **p. 1345**
A *adj.* serbisch; **sb. is ~:** jmd. ist Serbe/Serbin; *see also* **English A**
B *n.* 1 (dialect) serbischer Dialekt 2 (person) Serbe, *der*/Serbin, *die*. *See also* **English B 1**

Serbo-Croat /sɜːbəʊˈkrəʊæt/, **Serbo-Croatian** /sɜːbəʊkrəʊˈeɪʃn/ ▸❶ **p. 1277**
A *adj.* serbokroatisch; *see also* **English A**
B *n.* Serbokroatisch, *das*; *see also* **English B 1**

serenade /serəˈneɪd/
A *n.* (Mus.) 1 Ständchen, *das*; **sing** *or* **play sb. a ~:** jmdm. ein Ständchen bringen 2 (cantata) Serenade, *die*
B *v.t.* (Mus.) **~ sb.** jmdm. ein Ständchen bringen

serendipity /serənˈdɪpɪtɪ/ *n.* glücklicher Zufall

serene /sɪˈriːn/ *adj.*, **~r** /sɪˈriːnə(r)/, **~st** /sɪˈriːnɪst/ 1 (calm) klar ‹*Wetter, Himmel*› 2 (unruffled) unbewegt ‹*Wasser, See usw.*› 3 (placid) ruhig; gelassen; **calm and ~:** ruhig und gelassen

serenely /sɪˈriːnlɪ, səˈriːnlɪ/ *adv.* gelassen; **~ indifferent** gleichmütig und gelassen

serenity /sɪˈrenɪtɪ, səˈrenɪtɪ/ *n., no pl.* 1 (placidity) Gelassenheit, *die* 2 (of clear weather) Klarheit, *die*

serf /sɜːf/ *n.* 1 (villein) Leibeigene, *der/die* 2 (fig.: drudge) Sklave, *der*

serfdom /ˈsɜːfdəm/ *n.* Leibeigenschaft, *die*; (fig.) Sklaverei, *die*; Plackerei, *die* (ugs.)

serge /sɜːdʒ/ *n.* (Textiles) Serge, *die*

sergeant /ˈsɑːdʒənt/ *n.* ▸❶ **p. 1634** 1 (Mil.) Unteroffizier, *der* 2 (police officer) ≈Polizeimeister, *der*

sergeant: ~ ˈmajor ▸❶ **p. 1634** (Amer.), **[regimental] ~ major** (Brit.) ≈ [Ober]stabsfeldwebel, *der*; *see also* **company 7**

serial /ˈsɪərɪəl/
A *adj.* 1 (forming a series) aufeinander folgend; **~ production** Serienproduktion, *die*; **publish sth. in ~ form** etw. in Serienform veröffentlichen 2 (issued in instalments) Fortsetzungs‹*geschichte, -roman*›; **~ radio/TV play** Radio-/Fernsehserie, *die* 3 (periodical) periodisch erscheinend; **a monthly ~ publication** eine Monatsschrift 4 (Mus., Computing) seriell
B *n.* 1 (story) Fortsetzungsgeschichte, *die*; (on radio, television) Serie, *die* 2 (periodical) [periodisch erscheinende] Zeitschrift; Periodikum, *das* (geh.)

serialize /ˈsɪərɪəlaɪz/ *v.t.* in Fortsetzungen veröffentlichen; (on radio, television) in Fortsetzungen *od.* als Serie senden

serial ˈkiller *n.* Serienmörder, *der*/-mörderin, *die*

serially /ˈsɪərɪəlɪ/ *adv.* in Fortsetzungen, als Serie ‹*senden*›; **~ numbered** fortlaufend nummeriert

serial: ~ moˈnogamy *n., no pl.* serielle Monogamie; **~ number** *n.* Seriennummer, *die*; **~ port** *n.* (Computing) serielle Schnittstelle; **~ rights** *n. pl.* Rechte zur Veröffentlichung als Serie

series /ˈsɪəriːz, ˈsɪərɪz/ *n., pl. same* 1 (sequence) Reihe, *die*; **a ~ of events/misfortunes** eine Folge von Ereignissen/Missgeschicken 2 (set of successive issues) Serie, *die*; **radio/TV ~:** Hörfunkreihe/Fernsehserie, *die*; **~ of programmes** Sendereihe, *die*; **first ~:** erste Folge 3 (set of books) Reihe, *die* 4 (group of stamps etc.) Serie, *die* 5 (group of games etc.) Serie, *die*; **a lecture ~:** eine Vortragsreihe 6 (Chem.: set of elements) homologe Reihe 7 (Electr.) **in ~:** in Reihe; hintereinander 8 (Mus., Math.) Reihe, *die* 9 (Geol.: set of strata) Schichtenfolge, *die*

serif /ˈserɪf/ *n.* (Printing) Serife, *die*

serio-comic /sɪərɪəʊˈkɒmɪk/ *adj.* tragikomisch

serious /ˈsɪərɪəs/ *adj.* 1 (earnest) ernst; **~ music** ernste Musik; **a ~ play** ein ernstes Stück 2 (important, grave) ernst ‹*Angelegenheit, Lage, Problem, Zustand*›; ernsthaft ‹*Frage, Einwand, Kandidat*›; gravierend ‹*Änderung*›; schwer ‹*Krankheit, Unfall, Fehler, Überschwemmung, Niederlage*›; ernst zu nehmend ‹*Rivale*›; ernstlich ‹*Gefahr, Bedrohung*›; bedenklich ‹*Verschlechterung, Mangel*›; **things are/sth. is getting ~:** die Lage spitzt sich zu/ etw. nimmt ernste Ausmaße an; **there is a ~ danger that ...:** es besteht ernste Gefahr, dass ...; **~ charge/offence** schwerwiegender Vorwurf/schwerer Verstoß 3 (in earnest) **are you ~:** ist das dein Ernst?; **but now to be ~:** aber jetzt mal im Ernst; **you cannot be ~:** das kann doch nicht dein Ernst sein; **he is a ~ worker** er nimmt seine Arbeit ernst; **be ~ about sth./doing sth.** etw. ernst nehmen/ernsthaft tun wollen; **is he ~ about her?** meint er es ernst mit ihr?; **give sth. ~ thought** ernsthaft über etw. (*Akk.*) nachdenken

seriously /ˈsɪərɪəslɪ/ *adv.* 1 (earnestly) ernst[haft]; **speak ~ to sb.** mit jmdm. ein ernstes Wort sprechen; **quite ~, ...:** ganz im Ernst, ...; **take sth./sb. ~:** etw./jmdn. ernst nehmen 2 (severely) ernstlich; schwer ‹*verletzt, überflutet*›; **go ~ wrong** ‹*Person:*› sich schwer täuschen; ‹*Sache:*› völlig missglücken *od.* fehlschlagen

seriousness /ˈsɪərɪəsnɪs/ *n., no pl.* 1 (earnestness) Ernst, *der*; Ernsthaftigkeit, *die*; **in all ~:** ganz im Ernst 2 (gravity) Schwere, *die*; (of situation) Ernst, *der*

sermon /ˈsɜːmən/ *n.* 1 (Relig.) Predigt, *die*; **the S~ on the Mount** die Bergpredigt; **give a ~:** eine Predigt halten 2 (moral reflections) Mahnrede, *die* 3 (lecture, scolding) [Moral]predigt, *die*

sermonize /ˈsɜːmənaɪz/
A *v.t.* **~ sb.** jmdm. eine [Moral]predigt halten
B *v.i.* 1 (lecture) ‹*Person:*› dozieren; ‹*Buch, Film:*› moralisieren 2 (preach) predigen

serotonin /serəˈtəʊnɪn/ *n., no pl.* (Physiol.) Serotonin, *das*

serpent /ˈsɜːpənt/ *n.* 1 (snake) Schlange, *die* 2 (fig.: treacherous person) falsche Schlange 3 (Mus.) Serpent, *der*

serpentine /ˈsɜːpəntaɪn/
A *adj.* 1 (tortuous) Serpentinen-; gewunden ‹*Fluss*› 2 (of serpent) Schlangen-; (resembling a snake) schlangengleich
B *n.* (Min.) Serpentin, *der*

S

SERPS /sɜːps/ *abbr.* (Brit.) = **State earnings-related pension scheme**

serrated /se'reɪtɪd/ *adj.* gezackt; **~ knife** Sägemesser, *das*

serration /se'reɪʃn/ *n.* gezackter Rand; (one tooth) Zacke, *die;* **in ~s** gezackt

serried /'serɪd/ *adj.* dicht ‹Reihen›

serum /'sɪərəm/ *n., pl.* **sera** /'sɪərə/ *or* **~s** (Physiol.) Serum, *das*

servant /'sɜːvənt/ *n.* 1 (wage-earning employee) Angestellte, *der/die;* **a faithful ~ of the company** ein treuer Diener der Firma 2 (domestic attendant) Diener, *der*/Dienerin, *die;* (female also) Dienstmädchen, *das;* **keep** *or* **have ~s** Bedienstete haben 3 (in letter) **your humble** (arch.) *or* **obedient ~** (Brit.) Ihr ergebenster *od.* untertänigster Diener (veralt.). *See also* **civil servant; domestic A 1; public servant**

'servant girl *n.* Dienstmädchen, *das*

'servants' hall *n.* Dienstbotenzimmer, *das*

serve /sɜːv/

A *v.t.* 1 (work for) dienen (+ *Dat.*); **she had ~d the family well for ten years** sie hatte der Familie zehn Jahre lang gute Dienste geleistet; **~ two masters** (fig.) auf beiden Schultern Wasser tragen

2 (be useful to) dienlich sein (+ *Dat.*); **this car ~d us well** dieses Auto hat uns gute Dienste getan; **if my memory ~s me right** wenn mich mein Gedächtnis nicht täuscht

3 (meet needs of) nutzen (+ *Dat.*); **in order to ~ some private ends** für Privatzwecke; **that excuse will not ~ you** die Entschuldigung wird dir nichts nützen; **one packet ~s him for a week** eine Packung reicht ihm für eine Woche; **~ a/no purpose** einen Zweck erfüllen/keinen Zweck haben *od.* zwecklos sein; **~ sb.'s needs** *or* **purpose[s]** *or* **turn** jmds. Zweck (*Dat.*) genügen; **~ its purpose** *or* **turn** seinen Zweck erfüllen; **~ the purpose of doing sth.** den Zweck erfüllen *od.* dem Zweck genügen, etw. zu tun

4 (go through period of) durchlaufen ‹*Lehre*›; absitzen, verbüßen ‹*Haftstrafe*›; **~ a four-year term as Prime Minister** vier Jahre lang Premierminister sein; **~ one's time** (hold office) seine Amtszeit ableisten; **~ [one's] time** (undergo apprenticeship) seine Lehrzeit durchmachen; (perform military service) seinen Wehrdienst ableisten; (undergo imprisonment) seine Zeit absitzen

5 (dish up) servieren; (pour out) einschenken (**to** *Dat.*); **dinner is ~d** das Essen ist aufgetragen; **~ tea in china cups** Tee in Porzellantassen reichen

6 (render obedience to) dienen (+ *Dat.*) ‹*Gott, König, Land*›

7 (attend) bedienen; **are you being ~d?** werden Sie schon bedient?

8 (supply) versorgen; **~s three** (in recipe) für drei Personen *od.* Portionen

9 (provide with food) bedienen; **has everyone been ~d?** sind alle bedient?

10 (make legal delivery of) zustellen; **~ a summons on sb.** jmdn. vorladen; **he has been ~d notice to quit** ihm ist gekündigt worden; **~ sb. with a writ, ~ a writ on sb.** jmdm. eine Verfügung zustellen

11 (Tennis etc.) aufschlagen; **~ many double faults** viele Doppelfehler machen; **~ an ace** ein As schlagen

12 (arch./literary: treat) behandeln; **~ sb. ill/well** jmdm. einen schlechten/guten Dienst erweisen

13 **~[s]** *or* **it ~s him right!** [das] geschieht ihm recht!

14 (copulate with) ‹*Tier:*› decken

B *v.i.* 1 (do service) dienen; **~ as chairman** das Amt des Vorsitzenden innehaben; **~ as a Member of Parliament** Mitglied des Parlaments sein; **~ on a jury** Geschworener/Geschworene sein; **~ on a board** Mitglied des Aufsichtsrates sein

2 (be employed; be soldier etc.) dienen; Dienst tun; **he ~d against the Russians** er hat gegen die Russen gekämpft

3 (be of use) **~ to do sth.** dazu dienen, etw. zu tun; **~ to show sth.** etw. zeigen; **if memory ~s** wenn mein Gedächtnis mich nicht trügt; **for him nothing would ~ but ...:** er war nur mit ... zufrieden zu stellen; **~ for** *or* **as** dienen als; **it will ~:** das geht schon; das tuts (ugs.)

4 (**~ food**) **be employed to ~ at table** zum Auftragen eingestellt sein; **shall I ~?** soll ich auftragen?

5 (attend in shop etc.) bedienen

6 (Eccl.) ministrieren

7 (Tennis etc.) aufschlagen; **it's your turn to ~:** du hast Aufschlag

C *n.* ▸ **service A 8**

(Phrasal verbs)

- **~ 'out** *v.t.* 1 (distribute) austeilen; ausgeben 2 (work) ableisten ‹*Dienst*›; beenden ‹*Lehrzeit*› 3 (punish in return) **~ sb. out** es jmdm. heimzahlen
- **~ 'up** *v.t.* 1 (put before eaters) servieren 2 (offer for consideration) auftischen (ugs.)

server /'sɜːvə(r)/ *n.* 1 (Computing) Server, *der* 2 (Amer.: waiter/waitress) Bedienung, *die*

service /'sɜːvɪs/

A *n.* 1 (doing of work for employer etc.) Dienst, *der;* **give good ~:** gute Dienste leisten; **do ~ as sth.** als etw. dienen; **see ~** ‹*Gerät:*› seine Dienste tun; **he has seen ~ in the tropics** er hat in den Tropen Dienst getan; **sth. has seen long ~:** etw. hat lange Zeit gute Dienste geleistet; **he died in the ~ of his country** er starb in Pflichterfüllung für sein Vaterland; **have thirty years' ~ behind one** dreißig Jahre Dienstzeit hinter sich (*Dat.*) haben

2 (sth. done to help others) **do sb. a ~:** jmdm. einen guten Dienst erweisen; **~s** Dienste; (Econ.) Dienstleistungen; **ask for sb.'s ~s** jmdn. um Unterstützung bitten; **do you need the ~s of a doctor?** brauchen Sie einen Arzt?; **[in recognition of her] ~s to the hospital/state** [in Anerkennung ihrer] Verdienste um das Krankenhaus/den Staat

3 (Eccl.) Gottesdienst, *der*

4 (act of attending to customer) Service, *der;* (in shop, garage, etc.) Bedienung, *die*

5 (system of transport) Verbindung, *die;* **airline ~:** Flugverbindung, *die;* **there is no bus ~ on Sundays** sonntags verkehren keine Busse; **the number 325 bus ~:** die Buslinie Nr. 325; **when does the Oxford ~ leave?** wann fährt der Zug/Bus nach Oxford ab?

6 (provision of maintenance) **[after-sale** *or* **follow-up] ~:** Kundendienst, *der;* **ask for a ~:** den Kundendienst kommen lassen; **take one's car in for a ~:** sein Auto zur Inspektion bringen

7 *no pl., no art.* (operation) Betrieb, *der;* **bring into ~:** in Betrieb nehmen; **out of ~:** außer Betrieb; **take out of ~:** außer Betrieb setzen; **go** *or* **come into ~:** in Betrieb genommen werden

8 (Tennis etc.) Aufschlag, *der;* **whose ~ is it?** wer hat Aufschlag?

9 (crockery set) Service, *das;* **dessert/tea ~:** Dessert-/Tee-Service, *das*

10 (legal delivery) Zustellung, *die*

11 (assistance) **can I be of ~ [to you]?** kann ich Ihnen behilflich sein?; **will it be of ~ to you?** wird es Ihnen helfen?

12 (payment) Bedienung, *die;* Bedienungsgeld, *das; see also* **service charge**

13 (person's behalf) **in his ~:** in seinem Auftrag; **I'm at your ~:** ich stehe zu Ihren Diensten; **'on His/Her Majesty's ~'** (Brit.) „[gebührenfreie] Dienstsache"

14 (department of public employ) **the consular ~:** der Konsulatsdienst; **the railway/telephone ~:** das Eisenbahnwesen/der Telefondienst; **BBC World S~:** BBC Weltsender; **public ~:** öffentlicher Dienst; *see also* **Civil Service; Secret Service**

15 *in pl.* (Brit.: public supply) Versorgungseinrichtungen; **cut off all the ~s** Gas, Wasser und Strom abstellen

16 (Mil.) **the [armed** *or* **fighting] ~s** die Streitkräfte; **in the ~s** beim Militär; **be on ~:** dienen; **see ~:** im Einsatz sein

17 (being servant) **be in/go into ~:** in Stellung sein/gehen (veralt.) (**with** bei)

18 (employ) Stellung, *die;* **enter the ~ of sb.** bei jmdm. in Stellung gehen (veralt.); **take sb. into one's ~:** jmdn. in seine Dienste nehmen

B *v.t.* 1 (provide maintenance for) warten ‹*Wagen, Waschmaschine, Heizung*›; **take one's car to be ~d** sein Auto zur Inspektion bringen

2 (perform business function for) versorgen

3 (pay interest on) Zinsen zahlen für ‹*Schulden*›

4 (copulate with) ‹*Tier:*› decken

C *adj.* militärisch; Militär‹*fahrzeug, -flugzeug*›; **a ~ family** die Familie eines Militärangehörigen

serviceable /'sɜːvɪsəbl/ *adj.* 1 (useful) nützlich 2 (durable) haltbar; **the shoes are ~ rather than fashionable** die Schuhe sind eher praktisch als modisch

service: ~ area *n.* 1 (for motorists' needs) Raststätte, *die;* 2 (Radio, Telev.) Sendebereich, *der;* **~ book** *n.* (Eccl.) Gesangbuch, *das;* **~ call** *n.* Kundendienstbesuch, *der;* **~ centre** *n.* Servicecenter, *das;* **~ charge** *n.* (in restaurant) Bedienungsgeld, *das;* (of bank) Bearbeitungsgebühr, *die;* **~ contract** *n.* 1 (employment contract) Arbeitsvertrag, *der;* Dienstvertrag, *der;* 2 (for provision of services) Servicevertrag, *der;* **~ court** *n.* (Tennis etc.) Aufschlagfeld, *das;* **~ dress** *n., no pl.* Dienstkleidung, *die;* **~ economy** *n.* Dienstleistungswirtschaft, *die;* **~ engineer** *n.* ▸ⓘ **p. 1260** Servicetechniker, *der*/-technikerin, *die;* **~ flat** *n.* (esp. Brit.) Wohnung mit Betreuung; **~ hatch** *n.* Durchreiche, *die;* **~ industry** *n.* Dienstleistungsbetrieb, *der;* **~ lift** *n.* Lastenaufzug, *der;* **~man** /'sɜːvɪsmən/ *n., pl.* **~men** /'sɜːvɪsmən/ (in armed ~s) Militärangehörige, *der;* **~ module** *n.* (Astronaut.) Versorgungsmodul, *das;* **~ provider** *n.* 1 (Computing) Provider, *der;* 2 (person or firm providing service) Dienstleister, *der*/-leisterin, *die;* **~ road** *n.* Zufahrtsstraße, *die;* **~ sector** *n.* Dienstleistungssektor, *der;* **~ station** *n.* Tankstelle, *die;* **~woman** *n.* Militärangehörige, *die*

serviette /sɜːvɪ'et/ *n.* (Brit.) Serviette, *die*

servi'ette ring *n.* (Brit.) Serviettenring, *der*

servile /'sɜːvaɪl/ *adj.* unterwürfig; erbärmlich ‹*Unterwürfigkeit, Furcht*›

servilely /'sɜːvaɪllɪ/ *adv.* unterwürfig

servility /sɜː'vɪlɪtɪ/ *n., no pl.* Unterwürfigkeit, *die*

serving /'sɜːvɪŋ/

A *n.* (quantity) Portion, *die*

B *adj.* dienend

serving: ~ dish *n.* Servierschüssel, *die;* **~ hatch** *n.* Durchreiche, *die;* **~ spoon** *n.* Vorlegelöffel, *der*

servitude /'sɜːvɪtjuːd/ *n., no pl.* (lit. or fig.) Knechtschaft, *die; see also* **penal servitude**

servo /'sɜːvəʊ/ *n., pl.* **~s** Servoeinrichtung, *die*

servo: ~-assisted *adj.* **~-assisted brakes** Servobremsen; **~mechanism** *n.* Servomechanismus, *der;* **~motor** *n.* Servomotor, *der*

sesame /'sesəmɪ/ *n.* 1 (herb) Sesam, *der* 2 (seed) **~ [seed]** Sesamkorn, *das* 3 **open ~!** Sesam, öffne dich!; **an open ~:** ein Sesam-öffne-dich

sessile /'sesaɪl/ *adj.* (Bot., Zool.) sessil (fachspr.); festsitzend

'sessile oak *n.* Traubeneiche, *die*

session /'seʃn/ *n.* 1 (meeting) Sitzung, *die;* **discussion ~:** Diskussionsrunde, *die;* **be in ~:** tagen 2 (period spent) Sitzung, *die;* (by several people) Treffen, *das;* **have daily tennis ~s with sb.** mit jmdm. täglich Tennis spielen; **let's have a cleaning ~ tomorrow** lass/lasst uns morgen [mal] groß reinemachen; **recording ~:** Aufnahme, *die;* **have a card ~:** zusammen Karten spielen 3 (Brit.: academic year) Studienjahr, *das* 4 (Amer.: university term) Vorlesungsperiode, *die;* **the summer ~:** die Sommervorlesungen 5 (time for meeting) Sitzung, *die;* **summer ~s** Sommersitzungsperiode, *die* 6 (Eccl.) Kirchenvorstand, *der* 7 (Law) **Court of S~** *oberstes schottisches Zivilgericht;* **petty ~s** *summarisches Schnellverfahren vor mehreren Friedensrichtern; see also* **quarter sessions**

session: ~ man *n.* (Mus.) Sessionmusiker, *der;* Studiomusiker, *der;* **~ musician** *n.* Studiomusiker, *der*/-musikerin, *die*

sestet /ses'tet/ *n.* 1 ▸ **sextet** 2 (Pros.) Sextett, *das*

sestina /ses'tiːnə/ *n.* (Pros.) Sestine, *die*

set /set/

A *v.t.*, **-tt-, set** **1** (put) (horizontally) legen; (vertically) stellen; **~ sb. ashore** jmdn. an Land setzen; **~ food before sb.** jmdm. Essen hinstellen; **~ one brick on another** einen Stein auf den anderen setzen; **~ the proposals before the board** (fig.) dem Vorstand die Vorschläge unterbreiten *od.* vorlegen; **~ sth. against sth.** (balance) etw. einer Sache (*Dat.*) gegenüberstellen **2** (apply) setzen; **~ pen to paper** etwas zu Papier bringen; **~ a match to sth.** ein Streichholz an etw. halten; *see also* **fire A 1**; **hand A 1**; **light¹ A 5**; **seal² A 3**; **shoulder A 1** **3** (adjust) einstellen (**at** auf + *Akk.*); aufstellen ‹*Falle*›; stellen ‹*Uhr*›; **~ your watch by mine** stell deine Uhr nach meiner; **~ the alarm for 5.30 a.m.** den Wecker auf 5.30 Uhr stellen **4** **be ~** (have location of action) ‹*Buch, Film:*› spielen; **~ a book/film in Australia/a brothel** ein Buch/einen Film in Australien/in einem Bordell spielen lassen **5** (specify) festlegen ‹*Bedingungen*›; festsetzen ‹*Termin, Ort usw.*› (**for** auf + *Akk.*); **~ the interest rate at 10%** die Zinsen auf 10% festsetzen; **~ limits** Grenzen setzen **6** (bring into specified state) **~ sth./things right** *or* **in order** etw./die Dinge in Ordnung bringen; **~ sb. laughing** jmdn. zum Lachen bringen; **~ a dog barking** einen Hund anschlagen lassen; **~ sb. thinking that ...:** jmdn. auf den Gedanken bringen, dass ...; **the news ~ me thinking** die Nachricht machte mich nachdenklich; *see also* **cap A 1**; **defiance**; **ease A 1**; **edge A 1**; **fire A 2**; **foot A 1**; **free A 1**; **go¹ A 6**; **house A 1**; **motion A 1**; **rest¹ C 2**; **right A 4, C 5** **7** (put forward) stellen ‹*Frage, Aufgabe*›; aufgeben ‹*Hausaufgabe*›; vorschreiben ‹*Textbuch, Lektüre*›; (compose) zusammenstellen ‹*Rätsel, Fragen, Prüfungsaufgaben*›; **~ sb. an example, ~ an example to sb.** jmdm. ein Beispiel geben; **~ sb. a task/problem** jmdm. eine Aufgabe stellen/jmdn. vor ein Problem stellen; **~ [sb./oneself] a target** [jmdm./sich] ein Ziel setzen **8** (turn to solid) fest werden lassen; **is the jelly ~ yet?** ist das Gelee schon fest? **9** (put in ground to grow) einpflanzen, setzen ‹*Pflanzen*›; säen ‹*Samen*› **10** (lay for meal) decken ‹*Tisch*›; auflegen ‹*Gedeck*› **11** (place for visitor) aufstellen ‹*Stuhl, Tisch*› **12** **~ sail** (hoist sail) die Segel setzen *od.* hissen; (begin voyage) losfahren (**for** nach) **13** **~ a watch** (guard) eine Wache aufstellen; **~ the watch** (Naut.) die Wache aufstellen **14** (establish) aufstellen ‹*Rekord, Richtlinien*›; **~ the fashion for sth.** etw. in Mode bringen; **~ the pace** das Tempo bestimmen **15** (Med.: put into place) [ein]richten; einrenken ‹*verrenktes Gelenk*› **16** (fix) legen ‹*Haare*›; **~ eyes on sb./sth.** jmdn./etw. sehen; **~ one's teeth** (lit. or fig.) die Zähne zusammenbeißen; *see also* **face A 1**; **heart A 2**; **hope A**; **mind A 3**; **price A 1**; **scene 8**; **store A 6**; **value A 1** **17** (Printing) setzen; **~ close/out** *or* **wide** eng/breit setzen **18** **~ sb. to sth./doing sth.** jmdn. zu etw. anhalten/jmdn. veranlassen, etw. zu tun; **~ sb. wood-chopping** jmdn. Holz hacken schicken; **~ oneself to sth./do sth.** sich an etw. (*Akk.*) machen/daran machen, etw. zu tun; **~ sb. in charge of sth.** jmdn. mit etw. betrauen; **~ a dog on sb.** einen Hund auf jmdn. hetzen; **~ a dog/the police after sb.** einen Hund/die Polizei auf jmdn. hetzen; **they ~ their thugs/detectives on him** sie setzten ihre Schläger/Detektive auf ihn an; **~ sb. against sb.** jmdn. gegen jmdn. aufbringen; **~ father against son** Zwietracht säen zwischen Vater und Sohn; *see also* **work A 1** **19** **~ sth. to music** *or* **a tune** etw. vertonen **20** (ornament) besetzen; [ein]fassen ‹*Edelstein, Ränder*›; bepflanzen ‹*Beet*›; **the lid was ~ with gems** der Deckel war mit Edelsteinen besetzt; **a sky ~ with stars** ein sternenbesetzter Himmel **21** **be ~ on a hill** ‹*Haus:*› auf einem Hügel stehen **22** (make fast) fixieren ‹*Farbe, Färbemittel*›

B *v.i.*, **-tt-, set** **1** (solidify) fest werden; **has the jelly ~ yet?** ist das Gelee schon fest? **2** (go down) ‹*Sonne, Mond:*› untergehen; **sb.'s star ~s** (fig.) jmds. Stern ist im Sinken begriffen **3** (flow along) **the current ~s eastwards** die Strömung geht nach Osten; **~ against sth.** (fig.) sich gegen etw. richten **4** (Bot.) (form into or develop fruit) ‹*Blüte, Pflanze:*› Frucht ansetzen; (develop out of blossom) ‹*Frucht:*› sich entwickeln **5** ‹*Gesicht:*› sich verhärten (**with** vor + *Dat.*) **6** (take rigid attitude) **~ [rigidly]** ‹*Jagdhund:*› [fest] vorstehen

C *n.* **1** (group) Satz, *der*; **~ [of two]** Paar, *das*; **a ~ of chairs** eine Sitzgruppe; eine Stuhlgarnitur; **a ~ of stamps** ein Satz Briefmarken; **a complete ~ of Dickens' novels** eine Gesamtausgabe der Romane von Dickens; **a ~ of lectures** eine Vortragsreihe; **chess ~:** Schachspiel, *das* **2** ▸**service A 9** **3** (section of society) Kreis, *der*; **racing ~:** Rennsportfreunde *od.* -fans; **the younger ~:** die Jüngeren; **the fast ~:** die Lebewelt; *see also* **jet set**; **smart A 3** **4** (Math.) Menge, *die*; **theory of ~s** Mengenlehre, *die* **5** **~ [of teeth]** Gebiss, *das* **6** (radio or TV receiver) Gerät, *das*; Apparat, *der* **7** (Tennis) Satz, *der* **8** (of hair) Frisieren, *das*; Einlegen, *das*; **have a shampoo and ~:** sich (*Dat.*) die Haare waschen und legen lassen **9** (Theatre: built-up scenery) Szenenaufbau, *der* **10** (area of performance) (of film) Drehort, *der*; (of play) Bühne, *die*; **on the ~** (for film) bei den Dreharbeiten; (for play) bei den Proben **11** (granite paving block) Pflasterstein, *der* **12** (burrow) Bau, *der* **13** (of dog) **[dead] ~:** Vorstehen, *das*; **make a dead ~ at sb.** (fig.) (try to win affections of) sich an jmdn. heranmachen; (attack) über jmdn. herfallen **14** (Hort.) (shoot, cutting) Setzling, *der*; (bulb) Knolle, *die*; Zwiebel, *die* **15** (literary: sunset) **at ~ of sun** bei Sonnenuntergang **16** *no pl.* (posture) Haltung, *die*; **the ~ of his head** seine Kopfhaltung **17** (way dress etc. sits or flows) Sitz, *der*

D *adj.* **1** (fixed) starr ‹*Linie, Gewohnheit, Blick, Lächeln*›; fest ‹*Absichten, Zielvorstellungen, Zeitpunkt*›; **be ~ in one's ways** *or* **habits** in seinen Gewohnheiten festgefahren sein; **deep-~ eyes** tief liegende Augen **2** (assigned for study or discussion) vorgeschrieben ‹*Buch, Text*›; bestimmt, festgelegt ‹*Thema*›; **be a ~ book** Pflichtlektüre sein **3** (according to fixed menu) **~ meal** *or* **menu** Menü, *das* **4** (ready) **sth. is ~ to increase** etw. wird bald steigen; **be/get ~ for sth.** zu etw. bereit sein/sich zu etw. fertig machen; **be/get ~ to leave** bereit sein/sich fertig machen zum Aufbruch; **all ~?** (coll.) alles klar *od.* fertig?; **be all ~ for sth.** zu etw. bereit sein; **be all ~ to do sth.** bereit sein, etw. zu tun; **are we all ~?** alle startklar? (ugs.) **5** (determined) **be ~ on sth./doing sth.** zu etw. entschlossen sein/entschlossen sein, etw. zu tun; **be [dead] ~ against sth.** [absolut] gegen etw. sein; **of ~ purpose** mit Absicht; absichtlich; *see also* **close-set**

Phrasal verbs

- **~ about** *v.t.* **1** (begin purposefully) **~ about sth.** sich an etw. (*Akk.*) machen; etw. in Angriff nehmen; **~ about doing sth.** sich daranmachen, etw. zu tun **2** (spread) verbreiten ‹*Gerücht, Geschichte*› **3** (coll.: attack) herfallen über (+ *Akk.*)
- **~ a'part** *v.t.* **1** (reserve) reservieren; einplanen ‹*Zeit*› **2** (make different) abheben (**from** von); **his strength ~s him apart from others** durch seine Kraft zeichnet er sich gegenüber anderen aus
- **~ a'side** *v.t.* **1** (put to one side) beiseite legen ‹*Buch, Zeitung, Strickzeug*›; beiseite stellen ‹*Stuhl, Glas usw.*›; unterbrechen ‹*Arbeit, Tätigkeit*›; außer Acht lassen ‹*Frage*›; unberücksichtigt lassen ‹*Angebot*›; (postpone) aufschieben ‹*Arbeit*› **2** (cancel) aufheben ‹*Urteil, Entscheidung*› **3** (pay no attention to) außer Acht lassen ‹*Unterschiede, Formalitäten*›; begraben ‹*Feindschaft*›; vergessen ‹*Bitterkeit, Stolz, Eifersucht*›; abschaffen ‹*Recht*› **4** (reserve) aufheben ‹*Essen, Zutaten*›; einplanen ‹*Minute, Zeit*›; beiseite legen ‹*Geld*›; (save for customer) zurücklegen ‹*Ware*›; **why don't you ~ aside a day to come and visit me?** halt dir doch [einfach] einen Tag frei, an dem du mich besuchen kommst!
- **~ 'back** *v.t.* **1** (hinder progress of) behindern ‹*Fortschritt*›; aufhalten ‹*Entwicklung*›; zurückwerfen ‹*Projekt, Programm*› **2** (coll.: be an expense to) **~ sb. back a fair amount/sum** jmdn. eine hübsche Summe kosten **3** (place at a distance) zurücksetzen; **the house is ~ back some distance from the road** das Haus steht in einiger Entfernung von der Straße **4** (postpone) verschieben ‹*Termin*› (**to** auf + *Akk.*). *See also* **setback**
- **~ 'by** ▸**~ aside 1, 4**
- **~ 'down** *v.t.* **1** (allow to alight) absetzen ‹*Fahrgast, Ladung*›; **the bus will ~ you down there** der Bus hält dort; du kannst dort aus dem Bus aussteigen **2** (record on paper) niederschreiben **3** (place on surface) absetzen; abstellen **4** (fix) anberaumen ‹*Sitzung, Treffen, Anhörung usw.*› **5** (attribute) zuschreiben (**to** *Dat.*) **6** **~ down as** *or* **for** *or* **to be** (judge) halten für; (record) eintragen als
- **~ 'forth**

A *v.i.* (begin journey) aufbrechen; **~ forth on a journey** eine Reise antreten

B *v.t.* (present) darstellen ‹*Zahlen, Kosten*›; darlegen ‹*Programm, Ziel, Politik*›

- **~ 'forward** *v.t.* **1** (move further in front) weiter nach vorn stellen *od.* setzen **2** (present) darlegen ‹*Programm, Plan usw.*› **3** (bring forward in time) voranbringen ‹*Ernte, Entwicklung usw.*› **4** vorstellen ‹*Uhr*›
- **~ 'in**

A *v.i.* (gain a hold) ‹*Dunkelheit, Regen, Reaktion, Verfall:*› einsetzen; ‹*Mode:*› aufkommen

B *v.t.* (insert) einsetzen

- **~ 'off**

A *v.i.* (begin journey) aufbrechen; (start to move) loslaufen; ‹*Zug:*› losfahren; **~ off for work** sich auf den Weg zur Arbeit machen

B *v.t.* **1** (show to advantage) hervorheben **2** (start) führen zu; auslösen ‹*Reaktion, Alarmanlage*›; einleiten ‹*Entwicklung*›; in Umlauf setzen ‹*Gerücht*›; **~ sb. off into hysterics** jmdn. hysterisch werden lassen; **~ sb. off thinking/laughing** jmdn. zum Nachdenken anregen/zum Lachen bringen **3** (cause to explode) explodieren lassen; abbrennen ‹*Feuerwerk*› **4** (counterbalance) ausgleichen; **~ sth. off against sth.** etw. einer Sache (*Dat.*) gegenüberstellen; (use as compensatory item) etw. als Ausgleich für etw. nehmen

- **~ on** *v.t.* (attack) überfallen
- **~ 'out**

A *v.i.* **1** (begin journey) aufbrechen **2** (begin with intention) **~ out to do sth.** sich (*Dat.*) vornehmen, etw. zu tun; **~ out in business** sein eigenes Geschäft aufmachen; **~ out on a career as ...:** eine Laufbahn als ... einschlagen

B *v.t.* **1** (present) darlegen ‹*Gedanke, Argument*›; auslegen ‹*Waren*›; ausbreiten ‹*Geschenke*›; aufstellen ‹*Schachfiguren*›; setzen ‹*Pflanzen*› **2** (state, specify) darlegen ‹*Bedingungen, Einwände, Vorschriften*› **3** (mark out) entwerfen. *See also* **set-out**

- **~ over** *v.t.* stellen über (+ *Akk.*)
- **~ 'to** *v.i.* **1** (begin vigorously) sich daranmachen; (begin eating hungrily) es sich (*Dat.*) schmecken lassen **2** (begin to fight) loslegen (ugs.); *see also* **set-to**
- **~ 'up**

A *v.t.* **1** (erect) errichten ‹*Straßensperre, Denkmal*›; aufstellen ‹*Kamera*›; aufbauen ‹*Zelt, Klapptisch*›; **~ up the type** setzen; **~ up a column in type** eine Spalte setzen **2** (establish) bilden ‹*Regierung usw.*›; gründen ‹*Gesellschaft, Organisation, Orden*›; aufbauen ‹*Kontrollsystem, Verteidigung*›; einleiten ‹*Untersuchung*›; einrichten ‹*Büro*›; **~ oneself up as a dentist/in business** sich als

S

Zahnarzt niederlassen/ein Geschäft aufmachen; ~ **sb. up in business** jmdm. die Gründung eines eigenen Geschäfts ermöglichen 3 (begin to utter) anstimmen; **the class ~ up such a din** die Klasse veranstaltete einen solchen Lärm 4 (cause) auslösen ‹*Infektion, Reaktion*› 5 (coll.: make stronger) stärken; **a good breakfast should ~ you up for the day** ein gutes Frühstück gibt dir Kraft für den ganzen Tag; **well ~ up** kerngesund; kraftstrotzend 6 (achieve) aufstellen ‹*Rekord, Zeit*› 7 (provide adequately) ~ **sb. up with sth.** jmdn. mit etw. versorgen *od.* (ugs.) eindecken 8 (place in view) anbringen ‹*Schild, Warnung*›; hissen ‹*Flagge*› 9 (prepare) vorbereiten ‹*Experiment*›; betriebsbereit machen ‹*Maschine*› 10 (propound) aufstellen ‹*Theorie*› 11 ~ **sb. up** (coll.: frame) jmdm. die Schuld in die Schuhe schieben. *See also* **house A 1**; **set-up**; **shop A 2**

B *v.i.* ~ **up in business/in the fashion trade** ein Geschäft aufmachen/sich in der Modebranche etablieren; ~ **up as a dentist** sich als Zahnarzt niederlassen

C *v. refl.* ~ **oneself up as** *or* **to be sb./sth.** (coll.) sich als jmd./etw. aufspielen

set: ~-aside *n., no pl.* 1 (policy) Flächenstilllegung, *die; attrib.* **~-aside policy** Flächenstilllegungspolitik, *die;* **~-aside acreage** stillgelegte [Anbau]fläche; 2 (land) stillgelegte Fläche; **~back** *n.* 1 (checking of progress) Rückschlag, *der;* 2 (defeat) Niederlage, *die;* **~-off** *n.* 1 (counterbalance) Ausgleich, *der* (**against** für); 2 (Commerc., Law) Ausgleich, *der* (**to, against** für); **by ~-off against other cheques** durch Verrechnung mit anderen Schecks; 3 (start) Aufbruch, *der;* 4 (adornment) Zier, *die;* **~-out** *n.* (commencement) Start, *der;* ~ **phrase** *n.* feste Wendung; Phrase, *die;* ~ **'piece** *n.* 1 (design formed with fireworks) Bild aus Feuerwerkskörpern; 2 (Footb.) Standardsituation, *die;* ~ **'point** *n.* (Tennis etc.) Satzball, *der;* ~ **screw** *n.* (Mech. Engin.) Stellschraube, *die;* ~ **'scrum** *n.* (Rugby) Gedränge, *das;* ~ **'speech** *n.* fertige Rede; ~ **square** *n.* Zeichendreieck, *das*

sett /set/ ▸**set C 11, 12, 14**

settee /se'tiː/ *n.* Sofa, *das*

setter /'setə(r)/ *n.* (dog) Setter, *der*

'set theory *n.* (Math.) Mengenlehre, *die*

setting /'setɪŋ/ *n.* 1 (Mus.) Vertonung, *die* 2 (frame for jewel) Fassung, *die* 3 (surroundings) Rahmen, *der;* (of novel etc.) Schauplatz, *der;* **a cottage in a pleasant ~:** ein Häuschen in schöner Umgebung 4 (Theatre) Bühnendekoration, *die* 5 (plates and cutlery) Gedeck, *das*

'setting lotion *n.* Haarfestiger, *der*

settle /'setl/

A *v.t.* 1 (place) (horizontally) [sorgfältig] legen; (vertically) [sorgfältig] stellen; (at an angle) [sorgfältig] lehnen; ~ **a patient in his bed/an armchair** einen Patienten richtig ins Bett legen/im Sessel zurechtsetzen; **he ~d himself comfortably on the couch** er machte es sich (*Dat.*) auf der Couch bequem

2 (establish) (in house or business) unterbringen; (in country or colony) ansiedeln ‹*Volk*›; **we got them ~d in their new house** wir haben ihnen geholfen, sich in ihrem neuen Haus einzurichten

3 (determine, resolve) aushandeln, sich einigen auf ‹*Preis*›; beilegen ‹*Streit, Konflikt, Meinungsverschiedenheit*›; beseitigen, ausräumen ‹*Zweifel, Bedenken*›; entscheiden ‹*Frage, Spiel*›; regeln, in Ordnung bringen ‹*Angelegenheit*›; entscheiden über (+ *Akk.*) ‹*Sieger*›; festlegen, planen ‹*Urlaub*›; **nothing has been ~d as yet** es ist noch nichts entschieden; **that should ~ the match** damit dürfte das Spiel entschieden sein; ~ **the matter among yourselves!** macht das unter euch aus!; **that ~s it** dann ist ja alles klar (ugs.); *expr. exasperation* jetzt reicht's! (ugs.); ~ **a case out of court** sich außergerichtlich vergleichen; ~ **one's affairs** seine Angelegenheiten in Ordnung bringen; seinen Nachlass regeln; ~ **the day/date/place** den Tag/Termin/Ort festsetzen *od.* festlegen; **is the date ~d yet?** steht der Termin schon fest?

4 (deal with, dispose of) fertig werden mit; *see also* **hash[1] A**

5 (pay money owed according to) bezahlen, (geh.) begleichen ‹*Rechnung, Betrag*›; erfüllen ‹*Forderung, Anspruch*›; ausgleichen ‹*Konto*›; *see also* **score A 6**

6 (cause to sink) sich absetzen lassen ‹*Bodensatz, Sand, Sediment*›; **a shower will ~ the dust** ein Schauer wird den Staub binden

7 (calm) beruhigen ‹*Nerven, Magen*›; (aid digestion of) verdauen ‹*Essen*›

8 (colonize) besiedeln

9 (bestow) ~ **money/property on sb.** jmdm. Geld/Besitz übereignen; ~ **an annuity on sb.** jmdm. eine Rente aussetzen

B *v.i.* 1 (become established) sich niederlassen; (as colonist) sich ansiedeln

2 (end dispute) sich einigen

3 (pay what is owed) abrechnen

4 (in chair, in front of the fire, etc.) sich niederlassen; (to work etc.) sich konzentrieren (**to** auf + *Akk.*); (into way of life, retirement, middle age, etc.) sich gewöhnen (**into** an + *Akk.*); **it took a long time to ~ in our new house** es dauerte lange, bis wir uns in unserem neuen Haus richtig eingelebt hatten; **the cold ~d on her chest** die Erkältung hat sich ihr auf die Bronchien gelegt; **the snow/dust ~d on the ground** der Schnee blieb liegen/der Staub setzte sich [am Boden] ab; **darkness/silence/fog ~d over the village** Dunkelheit/Stille/Nebel legte *od.* senkte sich über das Dorf; *see also* **dust A 1**

5 (subside) ‹*Haus, Fundament, Boden:*› sich senken; (sink) ‹*Schiff:*› sinken; ‹*Sediment:*› sich ablagern; ‹*Kristalle:*› sich absetzen (**at, on** auf + *Dat.*)

6 (be digested) ‹*Essen:*› sich setzen; (become calm) ‹*Magen:*› sich beruhigen

7 (become clear) ‹*Wein, Bier:*› sich klären

Phrasal verbs

- ~ **'back** *v.i.* 1 (relax) sich zurücklehnen (**in** in + *Dat.*) 2 ~ **back into one's routine** sich wieder in die Alltagsroutine hineinfinden
- ~ **'down**

A *v.i.* 1 (make oneself comfortable) sich niederlassen (**in** in + *Dat.*); ~ **down for the night** sich schlafen *od.* zur Ruhe legen 2 (become established in a place) (in town or house) sesshaft *od.* heimisch werden; (in school) sich eingewöhnen (**in** in + *Akk.*); ~ **down in a job** (find permanent work) eine feste Anstellung finden; (get used to a job) sich einarbeiten 3 (marry) **it's about time he ~d down** er sollte allmählich häuslich werden [und heiraten]; ~ **down to married life** ein häusliches Eheleben beginnen 4 (calm down) ‹*Person:*› sich beruhigen; ‹*Lärm, Aufregung:*› sich legen; ~ **down to work** richtig mit der Arbeit anfangen

B *v.t.* 1 (make comfortable) ~ **oneself down** sich [gemütlich] hinsetzen; ~ **oneself down in a chair** sich [gemütlich] auf einen Stuhl setzen; ~ **the baby down for the night/to sleep** das Baby schlafen legen 2 (calm down) beruhigen

- ~ **for** *v.t.* 1 (agree to) sich zufrieden geben mit 2 (decide on) sich entscheiden für
- ~ **'in**

A *v.i.* (in new home) sich einleben; (in new job or school) sich eingewöhnen

B *v.t.* **we all helped to ~ them in** wir trugen alle dazu bei, dass sie heimisch wurden

- ~ **on** *v.t.* 1 (decide on) sich entscheiden für 2 (agree on) sich einigen auf (+ *Akk.*)
- ~ **'up** *v.i.* abrechnen; ~ **up with the waiter** beim Kellner bezahlen
- ~ **with** *v.t.* ~ **with sb.** (pay agreed amount to sb.) jmdm. eine Abfindung zahlen; (pay all the money owed to sb.) bei jmdm. seine Rechnung begleichen; (fig.) mit jmdm. abrechnen; **now to ~ with 'you!** jetzt bist du dran! (ugs.)

settled /'setld/ *adj.* fest ‹*Meinung, Überzeugung, Grundsätze, Gewohnheit*›; festgelegt ‹*Verfahren*›; vorausbestimmt ‹*Zukunft*›; beständig ‹*Wetter*›; geregelt ‹*Lebensweise*›; **I don't feel ~ in this house/job** ich kann mich in diesem Haus nicht heimisch fühlen/in diese Arbeit nicht hineinfinden; **we can now expect ~ weather** jetzt ist eine Wetterberuhigung zu erwarten

settlement /'setlmənt/ *n.* 1 Entscheidung, *die;* (in relation to price) Einigung, *die;* (of argument, conflict, dispute, differences, troubles) Beilegung, *die;* (of problem) Lösung, *die;* (of question) Klärung, *die;* (of affairs) Regelung, *die;* (of court case) Vergleich, *der;* **reach a ~:** zu einer Einigung kommen; **reach a ~ out of court** sich außergerichtlich vergleichen; **terms of ~** (Law) Vergleichsbedingungen 2 (of bill, account, etc.) Bezahlung, *die;* Begleichung, *die;* **a cheque in ~ of a bill** ein Scheck zur Begleichung einer Rechnung 3 (Law: bestowal) Zuwendung, *die;* (in will) Legat, *das* (fachspr.); Vermächtnis, *das; see also* **marriage settlement** 4 (colony) Siedlung, *die;* (colonization) Besiedlung, *die;* **penal ~:** Strafkolonie, *die* 5 (subsidence) [Ab]senkung, *die*

settler /'setlə(r)/ *n.* 1 (colonist) Siedler, *der*/Siedlerin, *die* 2 (coll.: decisive blow or argument) entscheidender Schlag

settling day /'setlɪŋ deɪ/ *n.* (Brit. St. Exch.) Abrechnungstermin, *der*

set: ~-to /'settuː/ *n., pl.* **~s** Streit, *der;* **~-tos** Streitereien; (with fists) Prügeleien; **have a ~-to** Streit haben; (with fists) sich prügeln; **~-top 'box** *n.* (Telev.) Set-Top-Box, *die;* **~-up, ~up** *n.* (coll.) 1 (organization) System, *das;* (structure) Aufbau, *der;* 2 (situation) Zustand, *der;* **isn't it a rather strange ~-up?** ist das nicht ein bisschen seltsam?; **what's the ~-up here?** wie läuft das hier? (ugs.); 3 (Computing) **~up** Setup, *das*

seven /'sevn/ ▸❶ **p. 894**, ▸❶ **p. 1001**, ▸❶ **p. 1358**

A *adj.* sieben; **the S~ Years War** der Siebenjährige Krieg; *see also* **eight A**; **sea 2**; **wonder A 2**

B *n.* (number, symbol) Sieben, *die; see also* **eight B 1, 3, 4**

'sevenfold *adj., adv.* siebenfach; *see also* **eightfold**

'seven-league boots *n. pl.* Siebenmeilenstiefel

seventeen /sevn'tiːn/ ▸❶ **p. 894**, ▸❶ **p. 1001**, ▸❶ **p. 1358**

A *adj.* siebzehn; **sweet ~:** süße siebzehn [Jahre alt]; *see also* **eight A**

B *n.* Siebzehn, *die; see also* **eight B 1**; **eighteen B**

seventeenth /sevn'tiːnθ/ ▸❶ **p. 1047**

A *adj.* ▸❶ **p. 1358** siebzehnt...; *see also* **eighth A**

B *n.* (fraction) Siebzehntel, *das; see also* **eighth B**

seventh /'sevnθ/

A *adj.* ▸❶ **p. 1358** sieb[en]t...; *see also* **eighth A**; **heaven 1**

B *n.* 1 (in sequence, rank) Sieb[en]te, *der/die/das;* (fraction) Sieb[en]tel, *das* 2 (Mus.) Septime, *die* 3 ▸❶ **p. 1047** (day) **the ~ of May** der sieb[en]te Mai; **the ~ [of the month]** der Sieb[en]te [des Monats]; **S~-day Adventists** Siebenten-Tags-Adventisten

seventieth /'sevntɪɪθ/

A *adj.* ▸❶ **p. 1358** siebzigst...; *see also* **eighth A**

B *n.* (fraction) Siebzigstel, *das; see also* **eighth B**

seventy /'sevntɪ/ ▸❶ **p. 894**, ▸❶ **p. 1358**

A *adj.* siebzig; *see also* **eight A**

B *n.* Siebzig, *die; see also* **eight B 1**; **eighty B**

seventy: ~-eight *n.* ▸❶ **p. 1358** (record) Achtundsiebziger[platte], *die;* **~-first** *etc. adj.* ▸❶ **p. 1358** einundsiebzigst... *usw.; see also* **eighth A**; **~-one** *etc.* **A** *adj.* einundsiebzig *usw.; see also* **eight A**; **B** *n.* ▸❶ **p. 1358** Einundsiebzig *usw., die; see also* **eight B 1**

seven-year 'itch *n.* **the ~:** ≈ das verflixte sieb[en]te Jahr

sever /'sevə(r)/

A *v.t.* 1 (cut) durchtrennen; (fig.: break off) abbrechen ‹*Beziehungen, Verbindung*›; **some cables were ~ed in the storm** einige Kabel sind bei dem Sturm gerissen 2 (separate with force) abtrennen; (with axe etc.) abhacken; **the axe ~ed his head from his body** die Axt trennte seinen Kopf vom Rumpf 3 (divide) **the sea ~s England and** *or* **from France** das Meer trennt England und *od.* von Frankreich

B *v.i.* (tear) reißen; (be torn off) abreißen

several /'sevrl/

A *adv.* 1 (a few) mehrere; einige; ~ **times** mehrmals; mehrere *od.* einige Male; ~ **more copies** noch einige Exemplare mehr 2 (separate, diverse) verschieden; **joint and ~** (Law) gesamtschuldnerisch ‹*Haftung*›

B *pron.* einige; ~ **of us** einige von uns; ~ **of the buildings** einige *od.* mehrere [der] Gebäude

S

severally /ˈsevrəlɪ/ *adv.* gesondert; **jointly and ~** (Law) gesamtschuldnerisch

severance /ˈsevərəns/ *n.* (of diplomatic relations) Abbruch, *der;* (of communications) Unterbrechung, *die;* (of contract) Lösung, *die; attrib.* **~ pay** Abfindung, *die*

severe /sɪˈvɪə(r)/ *adj.*, **~r** /sɪˈvɪərə(r)/, **~st** /sɪˈvɪərɪst/ **1** (strict) streng; hart ‹*Urteil, Strafe, Kritik*›; **be ~ on** *or* **with sb.** streng mit jmdm. sein *od.* umgehen **2** (violent, extreme) streng ‹*Frost, Winter*›; schwer ‹*Sturm, Dürre, Verlust, Behinderung, Verletzung*›; rau ‹*Wetter*›; heftig ‹*Anfall, Schmerz*› **3** (making great demands) hart ‹*Test, Prüfung, Konkurrenz*›; scharf ‹*Tempo*› **4** (serious, not slight) bedrohlich ‹*Mangel, Knappheit*›; heftig, stark ‹*Blutung*›; schwer ‹*Krankheit*› **5** (unadorned) streng ‹*Stil, Schönheit, Dekor*›

severely /sɪˈvɪəlɪ/ *adv.* hart; hart, streng ‹*bestrafen*›; schwer ‹*verletzt, behindert*›; **leave sth. ~ alone** unbedingt die Finger von etw. lassen (ugs.); **be ~ critical of sth.** etw. scharf kritisieren

severeness /sɪˈvɪənɪs/, **severity** /sɪˈverɪtɪ/ *ns.* Strenge, *die;* (of drought, shortage) großes Ausmaß; (of criticism) Schärfe, *die;* **with severity** streng ‹*bestrafen*›; **the severities of army life** die Härte des Soldatenlebens

Seville /səˈvɪl/ *pr. n.* ▸ℹ **p. 1643** Sevilla (*das*)

Seville orange /sevɪl ˈɒrɪndʒ/ *n.* Pomeranze, *die;* Sevillaorange, *die*

sew /səʊ/

A *v.t., p.p.* **sewn** /səʊn/ *or* **sewed** /səʊd/ nähen ‹*Kleid, Naht, Wunde*›; heften, broschieren ‹*Buch usw.*›; zunähen ‹*Loch, Riss*›; **~ together** zusammennähen ‹*Stoff, Leder usw.*›; **~ money into one's coat** Geld in seinen Mantel einnähen

B *v.i., p.p.* **sewn** *or* **sewed** nähen

Phrasal verbs

- **~ ˈdown** *v.t.* aufnähen
- **~ ˈin** *v.t.* einsetzen ‹*Flicken*›
- **~ ˈon** *v.t.* annähen ‹*Knopf*›; aufnähen ‹*Abzeichen, Band*›
- **~ ˈup** *v.t.* **1** nähen ‹*Saum, Naht, Wunde*›; **they ~ed me up after the operation** (coll.) nach der Operation haben sie mich wieder zugenäht **2** (Brit. fig. coll.: settle, arrange) **be ~n up** unter Dach und Fach sein; (completely organized) durchorganisiert sein; **we've got the match all ~n up** wir haben den Sieg schon in der Tasche (ugs.)

sewage /ˈsjuːɪdʒ, ˈsuːɪdʒ/ *n.* Abwasser, *das*

sewage: ~ disposal *n.* Abwasserbeseitigung, *die;* **~ farm** *n.*, **~ works** *n. sing., pl. same* Kläranlage, *die;* **~ system** *n.* Abwassersystem, *das;* Kanalisation, *die;* **~ treatment** *n., no pl.* Abwasseraufbereitung, *die; attrib.* **~ treatment plant** Kläranlage, *die*

sewer¹ /ˈsjuːə(r), ˈsuːə(r)/ *n.* (tunnel) Abwasserkanal, *der;* (pipe) Abwasserleitung, *die*

sewer² /ˈsəʊə(r)/ *n.* (person) Näher, *der*/Näherin, *die*

sewerage /ˈsjuːərɪdʒ, ˈsuːərɪdʒ/ *n.* **1** (system of sewers) Kanalisation, *die* **2** *no pl.* (removal of sewage) Abwasserbeseitigung, *die* **3** (sewage) Abwasser, *das*

sewing /ˈsəʊɪŋ/ *n.* Näharbeit, *die*

sewing: ~ basket *n.* Nähkorb, *der;* **~ machine** *n.* Nähmaschine, *die*

sewn ▸ **sew**

sex /seks/

A *n.* **1** Geschlecht, *das;* **what ~ is the baby/puppy?** welches Geschlecht hat das Baby/der Welpe? **2** (sexuality; coll.: intercourse) Sex, *der* (ugs.); **have ~ with sb.** (coll.) mit jmdm. schlafen (verhüll.); Sex mit jmdm. haben (salopp)

B *attrib. adj.* Geschlechts‹*organ, -trieb*›; Sexual‹*verbrechen, -trieb, -instinkt*›

C *v.t.* **1** (determine sex of) **~ a rabbit/chicken** das Geschlecht eines Kaninchens/Kükens bestimmen **2** **be highly ~ed** einen starken Sexualtrieb haben

sex: ~ abuse *n., no pl.* sexueller Missbrauch; **~ act** *n.* Geschlechtsakt, *der*

sexagenarian /seksədʒɪˈneərɪən/

A *adj.* sechzigjährig; (more than 60 years old) in den Sechzigern *nachgestellt*

B *n.* Sechziger, *der*/Sechzigerin, *die*

sex: ~ aid *n.* Mittel zur sexuellen Stimulation; **~ appeal** *n.* Sexappeal, *der;* **~ attack** *n.* sexueller Übergriff; (rape) Vergewaltigung, *die;* (on a child) sexueller Missbrauch; **~ attacker** *n.* Sexualtäter, *der*/-täterin, *die;* Sextäter, *der*/-täterin, *die;* **~ bomb** ▸ **~pot**; **~ change** *n.* Geschlechtsumwandlung, *die;* **~-change operation** *n.* operative Geschlechtsumwandlung; **~ chromosome** *n.* (Biol.) Geschlechtschromosom, *das;* **~-crazed** /ˈsekskreɪzd/ *adj.* sexbesessen; **~ crime** *n.* Sextat, *die;* **a rise in ~ crime** eine Zunahme von Sextaten; **~ discrimination** *n., no pl.* sexuelle Diskriminierung; **~ education** *n., no pl.* Sexualerziehung, *die;* **~ fiend** *n.* (sex offender, coll.: sex-mad person) Sexmonster, *das;* **~ game** *n.* Sexspiel, *das;* **~ goddess** *n.* Sexgöttin, *die*

sexily /ˈseksɪlɪ/ *adv.* aufreizend, (ugs.) sexy ‹*sprechen, lächeln*›; **walk ~:** einen aufreizenden *od.* (ugs.) sexy Gang haben

ˈsex industry *n.* Sexindustrie, *die*

sexiness /ˈseksɪnɪs/ *n., no pl.* sexuelle Attraktivität

sexism /ˈseksɪzm/ *n., no pl.* Sexismus, *der*

sexist /ˈseksɪst/

A *n.* Sexist, *der*/Sexistin, *die*

B *adj.* sexistisch

ˈsex kitten *n.* Sexbiene, *die* (salopp)

sexless /ˈsekslɪs/ *adj.* geschlechtslos

sex: ~ life *n.* Geschlechtsleben, *das;* Sexualleben, *das;* **~-linked** *adj.* (Biol.) geschlechtsgebunden; **~ machine** *n.* (hum.) Sexmaschine, *die;* **~-mad** *adj.* sexverrückt; **~ maniac** *n.* Triebverbrecher, *der;* **you ~ maniac!** (coll.) du geiler Bock (ugs.); **he behaves like a ~ maniac** (coll.) er benimmt sich, als habe er nur Sex im Kopf; **~ object** *n.* Sexobjekt, *das;* **~ offender** *n.* Sexual[straf]täter, *der*/-täterin, *die;* **~ offence** *n.* Sexualdelikt, *das;* Sexualvergehen, *das*

sexology /sekˈsɒlədʒɪ/ *n., no pl.* Sexologie, *die;* Sexualwissenschaft, *die*

sexploitation /seksplɔɪˈteɪʃn/ *n., no pl.* [kommerzielle] Ausbeutung der Sexualität; Geschäft mit dem Sex; *attrib.* **~ film** [kommerzieller] Sexfilm

sex: ~pot *n.* (coll.) Sexbombe, *die* (salopp); **~ scene** *n.* Sexszene, *die;* **~ shop** *n.* Sexshop, *der;* **~ show** *n.* Sexshow, *die;* **~-starved** *adj.* sexuell ausgehungert; **~ symbol** *n.* Sexidol, *das*

sextant /ˈsekstənt/ *n.* Sextant, *der*

sextet, sextette /sekˈstet/ *n.* (Mus.) Sextett, *das*

sex: ~ therapist *n.* Sexualtherapeut, *der*/-therapeutin, *die;* **~ therapy** *n., no pl.* Sexualtherapie, *die*

sexton /ˈsekstən/ *n.* Küster, *der;* Kirchendiener, *der*

ˈsexton beetle *n.* Totengräber, *der*

sex: ~ tourism *n., no pl.* Sextourismus, *der;* **~ tourist** *n.* Sextourist, *der*/-touristin, *die*

sextuplet /ˈsekstjuːplɪt, sekˈstjuːplɪt/ *n.* Sechsling, *der*

sexual /ˈseksjʊəl, ˈsekʃʊəl/ *adj.* **1** sexuell; geschlechtlich, sexuell ‹*Anziehung, Erregung, Verlangen, Diskriminierung*›; **~ maturity/behaviour** Geschlechtsreife, *die*/Sexualverhalten, *das;* **~ partner** Sexualpartner, *der*/-partnerin, *die* **2** (Biol.) Geschlechts-; geschlechtlich ‹*Fortpflanzung*›

sexual: ~ aˈbuse *n.* sexueller Missbrauch; **suffer ~ abuse** sexuell missbraucht werden; **~ asˈsault** *n.* sexueller Übergriff; (rape) Vergewaltigung, *die;* (on a child) sexueller Missbrauch; **~ discrimiˈnation** *n., no pl.* sexuelle Diskriminierung; **~ ˈharassment** *n., no pl.* sexuelle Belästigung; **~ ˈintercourse** *n., no pl.* Geschlechtsverkehr, *der*

sexuality /seksjʊˈælɪtɪ, sekʃʊˈælɪtɪ/ *n., no pl.* Sexualität, *die;* Geschlechtlichkeit, *die*

sexually /ˈseksjʊəlɪ, ˈsekʃʊəlɪ/ *adv.* **1** sexuell; **~ mature** geschlechtsreif; **~ transmitted disease** durch Geschlechtsverkehr übertragbare Krankheit; Geschlechtskrankheit, *die* **2** (Biol.) geschlechtlich

sexual ˈorgans *n. pl.* Geschlechtsorgane

sexy /ˈseksɪ/ *adj.* sexy (ugs.); erotisch ‹*Film, Buch, Gemälde*›

Seychelles /seɪˈʃelz/ *pr. n.* Seychellen *Pl.*

sez /sez/ *v.i.* **~ ˈyou = says you** ▸ **say A 1**

SF *abbr.* **= science fiction** SF

SGML *abbr.* (Computing) **= Standard Generalized Markup Language** SGML

Sgt. *abbr.* **= Sergeant** Uffz.

sh /ʃ/ *int.* sch; pst

shabbily /ˈʃæbɪlɪ/ *adv.*, **shabby** /ˈʃæbɪ/ *adj.* schäbig

shabby-genˈteel *adj.* von schäbiger Eleganz *nachgestellt*

shack /ʃæk/

A *n.* Hütte, *die*

B *v.i.* (coll.) **~ up with sb.** mit jmdm. zusammenziehen

shackle /ˈʃækl/

A *n.* **1** *usu. in pl.* (lit. or fig.) Fessel, *die;* (fetter) Fußfessel, *die* **2** (coupling link) Schäkel, *der* (Technik)

B *v.t.* (lit. or fig.) anketten (**to** an + *Akk.*); **the chain is ~d to the anchor** die Kette ist mit einem Schäkel am Anker befestigt

shade /ʃeɪd/

A *n.* **1** Schatten, *der;* **the ~s of night/evening** (literary) die Schatten der Nacht/des Abends (dichter.); **put sb./sth. in[to] the ~** (fig.) jmdn./etw. in den Schatten stellen; **38 [°C] in the ~:** 38° im Schatten **2** (colour) Ton, *der;* (fig.) Schattierung, *die;* **the newest ~s of lipstick** die neuesten Lippenstiftfarben; **various ~s of purple** verschiedene Violetttöne; **~s of meaning** Bedeutungsnuancen *od.* -schattierungen; **all ~s of opinion** Standpunkte der verschiedensten Schattierungen **3** (small amount) Spur, *die* **4** (ghost) Geist, *der;* **~s of the past** die Schatten der Vergangenheit; **the ~s** (Mythol.) das Schattenreich; das Reich der Schatten; **~s of ...!** das erinnert an ...! **5** (eye shield) [Augen]schirm, *der;* (lamp~) [Lampen]schirm, *der;* (window blind) Jalousie, *die* **6** *in pl.* (coll.: sunglasses) Sonnenbrille, *die*

B *v.t.* **1** (screen) beschatten (geh.); Schatten geben (+ *Dat.*); **be ~d from the sun** vor Sonneneinstrahlung geschützt sein; **~ one's eyes with one's hand** die Hand schützend über die Augen halten **2** abdunkeln ‹*Fenster, Lampe, Licht*› **3** (darken with lines) **~ [in]** [ab]schattieren **4** (just defeat) knapp überbieten

C *v.i.* (lit. or fig.) übergehen (**into** in + *Akk.*); **~ [off] into another** *or* **each other** ineinander übergehen

Phrasal verb

- **~ ˈin** *v.t.* [ab]schattieren

shading /ˈʃeɪdɪŋ/ *n.* Schattierung, *die;* (protection from light) Lichtschutz, *der*

shadow /ˈʃædəʊ/

A *n.* **1** Schatten, *der;* **his life was lived in the ~s** (fig.) er lebte sein Leben im Verborgenen; **cast a ~ over** (lit. or fig.) einen Schatten werfen auf (+ *Akk.*); **cast a long ~** (fig.) großen *od.* nachhaltigen Einfluss haben; **be in sb.'s ~** (fig.) in jmds. Schatten stehen; **have deep ~s under one's eyes** tiefe Schatten unter den Augen haben; **be afraid of one's own ~** (fig.) sich vor seinem eigenen Schatten fürchten; **be sb.'s ~** (fig.) jmds. Schatten sein **2** (slightest trace) **without a ~ of doubt** ohne den Schatten eines Zweifels; **catch at** *or* **chase after ~s** einem Phantom *od.* (geh.) Schatten nachjagen **3** (ghost, lit. or fig.) Schatten, *der;* **be worn to a ~** (fig.) sich völlig aufgerieben haben; **he is only a ~ of his former self** (fig.) er ist nur noch ein *od.* der Schatten seiner selbst **4** **S~** *attrib.* (Brit. Polit.) ‹*Minister, Kanzler*› im Schattenkabinett; **S~ Cabinet** Schattenkabinett, *das*

B *v.t.* **1** (darken) überschatten **2** (follow secretly) beschatten

shadow: ~ boxing *n., no pl.* Schattenboxen, *das;* **~ eˈconomy** *n.* (Econ.) Schattenwirtschaft, *die*

shadowy /ˈʃædəʊɪ/ *adj.* **1** (not distinct) schattenhaft; schemenhaft (geh.) **2** (full of shade) schattig

S

shady /ˈʃeɪdɪ/ *adj.* **1** (giving shade) Schatten spendend (geh.); (situated in shade) schattig **2** (disreputable) zwielichtig

shaft /ʃɑːft/ *n.* **1** (of tool, golf club, feather, spear, lance) Schaft, *der* **2** (Archit.) [Säulen]schaft, *der* **3** (Mech. Engin.) Welle, *die* **4** (of cart or carriage) Deichsel, *die:* **pair of ~s** Gabeldeichsel, *die* **5** (of mine, blast furnace, tunnel, drain, lift, etc.) Schacht, *der* **6** (arrow) Pfeil, *der;* (stem of arrow) Schaft, *der* **7** (of light or lightning) Strahl, *der*

shag[1] /ʃæg/ *n.* **1** (tobacco) Shag[tabak], *der;* Feinschnitt, *der* **2** (Ornith.) Krähenscharbe, *die*

shag[2] (sl)

A *v.t.*, **-gg-** bumsen (salopp)

B *n.* **have a ~ [with sb.]** es [mit jmdm.] treiben (ugs.)

shagged /ʃægd/ *adj.* (sl.) **be ~ [out]** fix und fertig sein (ugs.)

shaggy /ˈʃægɪ/ *adj.* **1** (hairy) zottelig **2** (unkempt) struppig

shaggy-ˈdog story *n.: endlos langer Witz ohne richtige Pointe*

Shah /ʃɑː/ *n.* Schah, *der*

shake /ʃeɪk/

A *n.* **1** Schütteln, *das;* **give sb./sth. a ~:** jmdn./etw. schütteln; **with a ~ of the head** mit einem Kopfschütteln; **be all of a ~:** am ganzen Körper zittern; **be no great ~s** (coll.) nicht gerade umwerfend sein (ugs.); **get the ~s** (coll.) (due to alcoholism) einen Tatterich kriegen (ugs.); (with fear) das große Zittern kriegen (ugs.) **2** ▸**milk shake 3** (Amer., NZ: earthquake) Erdbeben, *das* **4** **in [half] a ~, in two** *etc.* **~s [of a lamb's tail], in a brace of ~s** (coll.) in einer Sekunde

B *v.t.*, **shook** /ʃʊk/, **shaken** /ˈʃeɪkn/ *or* (arch./coll.) **shook 1** (move violently) schütteln; **the dog shook itself** der Hund schüttelte sich; **be ~n to pieces** völlig durchgeschüttelt werden; **~ one's fist/a stick at sb.** jmdm. mit der Faust/einem Stock drohen; **~ salt/pepper over one's food** [sich (*Dat.*)] Salz/Pfeffer aufs *od.* über das Essen streuen; **'~ [well] before using'** „vor Gebrauch [gut] schütteln!"; **~ hands** sich (*Dat.*) *od.* einander die Hand geben *od.* schütteln; **they shook hands to conclude the deal** sie besiegelten das Geschäft durch Handschlag; **she won't ~ hands with me** sie gibt mir nicht die Hand; **let's ~ hands** gib mir deine Hand; **~ sb. by the hand** jmdm. die Hand schütteln *od.* drücken **2** (cause to tremble) erschüttern ‹*Gebäude usw.*›; **~ one's head [over sth.]** [über etw. (*Akk.*)] den Kopf schütteln; *see also* **leg 1 3** (weaken) erschüttern; **~ sb.'s faith in sth./sb.** jmds. Glauben an etw./jmdn. erschüttern **4** (agitate) erschüttern; **she was badly ~n by the news of his death** die Nachricht von seinem Tod erschütterte sie sehr; **she was not hurt, only badly ~n** sie wurde nicht verletzt, sondern erlitt nur einen schweren Schock; **he failed his exam — that shook him!** er hat die Prüfung nicht bestanden — das war ein Schock für ihn!; **~ sb.'s composure** jmdn. aus dem Gleichgewicht bringen; **~ sb. rigid** (coll.) jmdn. umhauen (salopp)

C *v.i.*, **shook, shaken** *or* (arch./coll.) **shook 1** (tremble) wackeln; ‹*Boden, Stimme:*› beben; ‹*Hand:*› zittern; ‹*Baum:*› schwanken; **~ [all over] with cold/fear** [am ganzen Leib] vor Kälte/Angst schlottern; **~ like a leaf** wie Espenlaub zittern; **~ with emotion** vor Erregung beben; **~ in one's shoes** vor Angst schlottern **2** (coll.: **~** hands) sich (*Dat.*) die Hand geben; **let's ~ on it!** schlag ein!; Hand drauf!; **~ on sth.** etw. durch Handschlag besiegeln

(Phrasal verbs)

- **~ ˈdown**

A *v.t.* **1** (get down by shaking) herunterschütteln **2** (Amer. sl.: extort money from) ausnehmen (salopp); **~ sb. down for £50** jmdn. um 50 Pfund erleichtern (ugs.)

B *v.i.* **1** (sleep) kampieren (ugs.); *see also* **shakedown 2** (settle) ‹*Maschine, Motor:*› sich einlaufen; ‹*Person:*› sich eingewöhnen, sich akklimatisieren

- **~ ˈoff** *v.t.* (lit. or fig.) abschütteln; *see also* **dust A 1**
- **~ ˈout** *v.t.* ausschütteln; (spread out) ausbreiten; *see also* **shake-out**
- **~ ˈup** *v.t.* **1** (mix) schütteln **2** aufschütteln ‹*Kissen*› **3** (make uncomfortable by shaking) durchschütteln **4** (discompose) einen Schrecken einjagen (+ *Dat.*); **she felt pretty ~n up** sie hatte einen ziemlichen Schrecken bekommen **5** (rouse to activity) aufrütteln **6** (reorganize) umkrempeln (ugs.). *See also* **shake-up**

ˈshake-down *n.* [improvisiertes] Nachtlager

shaken ▸**shake B, C**

ˈshake-out *n.* radikale Umorganisation; (making workers redundant) Rationalisierung, *die*

shaker /ˈʃeɪkə(r)/ *n.* **1** (vessel) Mixbecher, *der;* Shaker, *der* **2** **S~** (Relig.) Shaker, *der* **3** (implement) Streuer, *der*

Shakespe[a]rean, Shakespe[a]rian /ʃeɪkˈspɪərɪən/ *adj.* shakespearesch ‹*Sonett, Stil*›; ‹*Zeit, Zeitalter*› Shakespeares

ˈshake-up *n.* **1** (mixing) **get a [good] ~:** [gut] geschüttelt werden **2** (restoring to shape) **give the pillows a good ~:** die Kissen tüchtig aufschütteln **3** (reorganization) **give sth. a [good] ~:** etw. [total] umkrempeln (ugs.); **sth. needs a ~:** etw. muss [mal] umgekrempelt werden (ugs.); **government ~:** Regierungsumbildung, *die* **4** (rousing to activity) Neubelebung, *die*

shakily /ˈʃeɪkɪlɪ/ *adv.* unsicher ‹*stehen, lachen*›; wack[e]lig (ugs.) ‹*gehen, stehen*›; mit zittriger Stimme ‹*sprechen*›; mit zittriger Hand ‹*gießen*›

shaky /ˈʃeɪkɪ/ *adj.* **1** (unsteady) wack[e]lig ‹*Möbelstück, Leiter, Haus*›; zittrig ‹*Hand, Stimme, Bewegung, Greis*›; **feel ~:** sich zittrig fühlen; **be ~ on one's legs** wacklig auf den Beinen sein (ugs.) **2** (unreliable) auf wackligen Füßen stehend (ugs.); **his German is rather ~:** sein Deutsch steht auf wackligen Füßen (ugs.)

shale /ʃeɪl/ *n.* Schiefer, *der*

ˈshale oil *n.* Schieferöl, *das*

shall /ʃl, *stressed* ʃæl/ *v. aux. only in pres.* **shall,** *neg.* (coll.) **shan't** /ʃɑːnt/, *past* **should** /ʃəd, *stressed* ʃʊd/, *neg.* (coll.) **shouldn't** /ˈʃʊdnt/ **1** *expr. simple future* werden **2** **should** *expr. conditional* würde/würdest/würden/würdet; **he should not have gone if I could have prevented it** er wäre nicht gegangen, wenn ich es hätte verhindern können; **I should have been killed if I had let go** ich wäre getötet worden, wenn ich losgelassen hätte **3** *expr. command* **any person found in possession of such weapons ~ be guilty of an offence** (Law) jeder, der im Besitz solcher Waffen angetroffen wird, macht sich strafbar *od.* eines Vergehens schuldig; **the committee ~ not be disturbed** der Ausschuss darf nicht gestört werden; **thou shalt not steal** (Bibl.) du sollst nicht stehlen **4** *expr. will or intention* **what ~ we do?** was sollen wir tun?; **let's go in, ~ we?** gehen wir doch hinein, oder?; **I'll buy six, ~ I?** ich kaufe 6 [Stück], ja?; **you ~ pay for this!** das sollst du mir büßen!; **we should be safe now** jetzt dürften wir in Sicherheit sein; **he shouldn't do things like that!** er sollte so etwas nicht tun!; **oh, you shouldn't have!** das wäre doch nicht nötig gewesen!; **you should be more careful** du solltest vorsichtiger *od.* sorgfältiger sein; *see also* **worry B 5** *in conditional clause* **if we should be defeated** falls wir unterliegen [sollten]; **should I be there, I will tell her** sollte ich dort sein, werde ich es ihr sagen; **I should hope so** ich hoffe es; (indignant) das möchte ich hoffen! **6** *in tentative assertion* **I should like to disagree with you on that point** in dem Punkt *od.* da möchte ich dir widersprechen; **I should say it is time we went home** ich würde sagen *od.* ich glaube, es ist Zeit, dass wir nach Hause gehen **7** *forming question* **~ you be going to church?** gehst du in die Kirche? **8** *expr. purpose* **in order that he ~** *or* **should be able to go** damit er gehen kann; **I gave him £10 so that he should have enough money for the journey** ich habe ihm 10 Pfund gegeben, sodass er genug Geld für die Reise hat/hatte. *See also* **seem 1**

shallot /ʃəˈlɒt/ *n.* Schalotte, *die*

shallow /ˈʃæləʊ/

A *adj.* ▸**❶ p. 1208,** ▸**❶ p. 1491** seicht ‹*Wasser, Fluss*›; flach ‹*Schüssel, Teller, Wasser*›; (fig.) seicht (abwertend) ‹*Unterhaltung, Gerede, Roman*›; flach (abwertend) ‹*Person, Denker, Geist*›; platt (abwertend) ‹*Argument, Verallgemeinerung*›; **~ breathing** flache Atmung

B *n. in pl.* Flachwasser, *das*

shalom /ʃəˈlɒm/

A *int.* Schalom

B *n.* Schalom, *das*

sham /ʃæm/

A *adj.* unecht; imitiert ‹*Leder, Holz, Pelz, Stein*›

B *n.* (pretence) Heuchelei, *die;* (person) Heuchler, *der*/Heuchlerin, *die;* **it is all a mere ~:** das ist alles bloße Heuchelei; **their marriage is only a ~:** ihre Ehe besteht nur auf dem Papier; **his life is a ~:** sein Leben ist eine einzige Lüge

C *v.t.*, **-mm-** vortäuschen, simulieren; **~ dead/ill/stupid** sich tot/krank/dumm stellen

D *v.i.*, **-mm-** simulieren; sich verstellen

shaman /ˈʃæmən/ *n.* Schamane, *der*

shamanism /ˈʃɑːmənɪzm/ *n.*, *no pl.* Schamanismus, *der*

shamanist /ˈʃɑːmənɪst/, **shamanistic** /ʃɑːməˈnɪstɪk/ *adjs.* schamanistisch

shamble /ˈʃæmbl/

A *v.i.* schlurfen; **a shambling gait** ein schlurfender Gang

B *n.* Schlurfen, *das;* **move along at a ~:** sich [schwerfällig] schlurfend vorwärts bewegen

shambles /ˈʃæmblz/ *n. sing.* (coll.: mess) Chaos, *das;* **the house/room was a ~:** das Haus/Zimmer glich einem Schlachtfeld; **the economy is in a ~:** in der Wirtschaft herrschen chaotische Zustände; **she made a ~ of her job** sie hat bei ihrer Arbeit ein heilloses Durcheinander angerichtet

shambolic /ʃæmˈbɒlɪk/ *adj.* (coll.) chaotisch

shame /ʃeɪm/

A *n.* **1** Scham, *die;* **feel ~/no ~ for what one did** sich schämen/sich nicht schämen für das, was man getan hat; **hang one's head in** *or* **for ~:** beschämt den Kopf senken; **blush with ~:** vor Scham erröten; schamrot werden; **be without ~:** schamlos sein; **have no [sense of] ~:** kein[erlei] Schamgefühl besitzen; **have you no ~?** schämst du dich nicht?; **to my ~ I must confess ...:** ich muss zu meiner Schande gestehen ...; **for ~!** du solltest dich/er sollte sich *usw.* schämen! **2** (state of disgrace) Schande, *die;* **~ on you!** du solltest dich schämen; **put sb./sth. to ~:** jmdn. beschämen/etw. in den Schatten stellen; **bring ~ on the family name, be a ~ to one's family** seiner Familie (*Dat.*) Schande machen **3** **what a ~!** (disgrace) es ist eine Schande!; (bad luck) so ein Pech!; (pity) wie schade!; **it is a crying** *or* **terrible** *or* **great ~:** es ist eine wahre Schande

B *v.t.* beschämen; **~ sb. into doing/out of doing sth.** jmdn. dazu bringen, dass er sich schämt und etw. tut/nicht tut; **~ one's family** seiner Familie (*Dat.*) Schande machen

ˈshamefaced *adj.* betreten; **have a ~ look, look ~:** betreten dreinblicken

shamefacedly /ˈʃeɪmfeɪsɪdlɪ/ *adv.* betreten

shameful /ˈʃeɪmfl/ *adj.* beschämend

shamefully /ˈʃeɪmfəlɪ/ *adv.* beschämend; **she is ~ ignorant** sie weiß beschämend wenig; es ist eine Schande, wie wenig sie weiß

shameless /ˈʃeɪmlɪs/ *adj.* schamlos; **are you completely ~?** hast du denn gar kein Schamgefühl?

shamelessly /ˈʃeɪmlɪslɪ/ *adv.* schamlos

shammy /ˈʃæmɪ/ *n.* **~ [leather]** (coll.) Putzleder *das;* (for windows) Fensterleder, *das*

shampoo /ʃæmˈpuː/

A *v.t.* schamponieren ‹*Haar, Teppich, Polster, Auto*›; **shall I ~ your hair for you?** soll ich dir die Haare waschen?

B *n.* Shampoo[n], *das;* **carpet ~:** Teppichschaum, *der;* **medicated ~:** medizinisches Shampoo; **car ~:** Autoshampoo, *das;* **have a ~ and set** sich (*Dat.*) die Haare waschen und [ein]legen lassen; **give one's hair a ~:** sich (*Dat.*) die Haare [mit Shampoo] waschen *od.* schamponieren

shamrock /ˈʃæmrɒk/ *n.* Klee, *der;* (emblem of Ireland) Shamrock, *der*

shandy /ˈʃændɪ/ *n.* Bier mit Limonade; Radlermaß, *die* (bes. südd.)

shanghai /ʃæŋ'haɪ/ *v.t.* 1 (Naut. sl., hist.: abduct) schanghaien 2 (coll.: compel, pressurize) **~ sb. into doing sth.** jmdn. [dazu] breitschlagen, etw. zu tun (ugs.); **he ~ed her into his car** er schlug sie breit, in seinen Wagen einzusteigen (ugs.)

Shangri-La /ʃæŋgrɪ'lɑ:/ *n.* Paradies, *das*

shank /ʃæŋk/ *n.* 1 (of person) Unterschenkel, *der;* **[go] on S~s's mare** *or* **pony** auf Schusters Rappen [reisen] (scherzh.) 2 (of horse) Vordermittelfuß, *der;* Röhrbein, *das;* (cut of meat) [Hinter]hesse, *die* 3 (Bot.) Stiel, *der* 4 (of pillar) [Säulen]schaft, *der;* (of key, anchor, nail, fish-hook) Schaft, *der;* (of spoon) [Löffel]stiel, *der*

shan't /ʃɑ:nt/ (coll.) **= shall not**

shantung /ʃæn'tʌŋ/ *n.* Shantung, *der* (Textilw.); Schantungseide, *die*

shanty¹ /'ʃæntɪ/ *n.* (hut) [armselige] Hütte

shanty² *n.* (song) Shanty, *das;* Seemannslied, *das*

'shanty town *n.* Bidonville, *das*

shape /ʃeɪp/

A *v.t.* 1 (create, form) formen; bearbeiten ‹*Holz, Stein*› **(into** zu); **~ a dress at the waist** ein Kleid taillieren; **you can ~ plastic when it is hot** erwärmter Kunststoff lässt sich [ver]formen 2 (adapt, direct) prägen, formen ‹*Charakter, Person*›; nehmen ‹*Kurs*› **(for** auf + *Akk.*); [entscheidend] beeinflussen ‹*Gang der Geschichte, Leben, Zukunft, Gesellschaft*›

B *v.i.* sich entwickeln; **the way things are shaping, we should be able to come** so wie sich die Dinge entwickeln, werden wir wohl kommen können

C *n.* 1 (external form, outline) Form, *die;* **spherical/rectangular in ~:** kugelförmig/rechteckig; **in the ~ of a circle** kreisförmig; in der Form eines Kreises; **she is the right ~ for a dancer** sie hat die richtige Figur für eine Tänzerin; **take ~** ‹*Konstruktion, Skulptur:*› Gestalt annehmen (*see also* **3**) 2 (appearance) Gestalt, *die;* **a monster in human ~:** ein Ungeheuer in Menschengestalt; **in the ~ of a woman** in Gestalt einer Frau; **a paperweight in the ~ of a lizard** ein Briefbeschwerer in Form einer Eidechse 3 (specific form) Form, *die;* Gestalt, *die;* **a surprise in the ~ of an invitation/a holiday** eine Überraschung in Form einer Einladung/Ferienreise; **nothing in the ~ of ...:** nichts in der Art ... (+ *Gen.*); **take ~** ‹*Plan, Vorhaben:*› Gestalt *od.* feste Formen annehmen (*see also* **1**); **get one's ideas into ~:** seine Gedanken sammeln; Ordnung in seine Gedanken bringen; **knock sth. out of ~:** etw. verbeulen *od.* demolieren; **knock sth. into ~:** etw. wieder in Form bringen; **we have knocked the plans into ~:** wir haben die Pläne jetzt im Wesentlichen fertig; **in all ~s and sizes, in every ~ and size** in allen Formen und Größen; **the ~ of things to come** die Dinge, die da kommen sollen/sollten; **this may be the ~ of things to come** so könnte das in Zukunft aussehen; *see also* **lick A 1** 4 (condition) Form, *die* (bes. Sport); **do yoga to keep in ~:** Yoga machen, um in Form zu bleiben; **be in good/bad ~:** gut/schlecht in Form sein; **be in poor ~ mentally/physically** geistig/körperlich in schlechter Verfassung sein; **what sort of ~ is the business in?** wie steht es um die Firma?; **be in no ~ to do sth.** nicht in der Lage sein, etw. zu tun 5 (person seen, ghost) Gestalt, *die* 6 (mould) (for hats) Hutform, *die;* (for puddings, jellies, etc.) Form, *die*

(Phrasal verb)

• **~ 'up** *v.i.* sich entwickeln; **how's the new editor shaping up?** wie macht sich der neue Redakteur?

SHAPE /ʃeɪp/ *abbr.* **= Supreme Headquarters Allied Powers Europe** oberstes Hauptquartier der Nato-Streitkräfte in Europa

shaped /ʃeɪpt/ *adj.* geformt; **be ~ like a pear** die Form einer Birne haben; **this is an oddly ~ cake** dieser Kuchen hat eine ungewöhnliche *od.* eigentümliche Form

shapeless /'ʃeɪplɪs/ *adj.* formlos; unförmig ‹*Kleid, Person*›; unstrukturiert ‹*Theaterstück*›

shapely /'ʃeɪplɪ/ *adj.* wohlgeformt ‹*Beine, Busen*›; gut ‹*Figur*›; formschön ‹*Auto, Design*›

shard /ʃɑ:d/ ▸**sherd**

share /ʃeə(r)/

A *n.* 1 (portion) Teil, *der od. das;* (part one is entitled to) **[fair] ~:** Anteil, *der;* **he had a large ~ in bringing it about** er hatte großen Anteil daran, dass es zustande kam; **come in for one's full ~ of criticism** seinen Teil Kritik einstecken müssen *od.* abbekommen; **pay one's ~ of the bill** seinen Teil der Rechnung bezahlen; **have a ~ in the profits** am Gewinn beteiligt sein; **fair ~s** gerechte Teile; **do more than one's [fair] ~ of the work** mehr als seinen Teil zur Arbeit beitragen; **each had his ~ of the cake** jeder bekam seinen Teil vom Kuchen ab; **have more than one's [fair] ~ of the blame/attention** mehr Schuld zugewiesen bekommen/mehr Beachtung finden, als man verdient; **she had her ~ of luck/bad luck** sie hat aber auch Glück/Pech gehabt; **take one's ~ of the responsibility** seinen Teil Verantwortung tragen; **take one's ~ of the blame** seinen Teil Schuld auf sich (*Akk.*) nehmen; **go ~s** teilen; **let me go ~s with you in the taxi fare** ich möchte mich an den Kosten für das Taxi beteiligen; **it was ~ and ~ alike** es wurde brüderlich geteilt; *see also* **lion 1** 2 (part-ownership of property) [Geschäfts]anteil, *der;* (part of company's capital) Aktie, *die;* **have a ~ in a business** an einem Geschäft beteiligt sein; **hold ~s in a company** (Brit.) Anteile *od.* Aktien einer Gesellschaft besitzen; *see also* **defer¹ 1; ordinary 2**

B *v.t.* teilen; gemeinsam tragen ‹*Verantwortung*›; **~ the same birthday/surname** am gleichen Tag Geburtstag/den gleichen Nachnamen haben

C *v.i.* **~ in** teilnehmen an (+ *Dat.*); beteiligt sein an (+ *Dat.*) ‹*Gewinn, Planung*›; teilen ‹*Freude, Erfahrung*›; **there are no single rooms left, so I'll have to ~:** es sind keine Einzelzimmer mehr frei, sodass ich mit jemandem ein Zimmer teilen muss

(Phrasal verb)

• **~ 'out** *v.t.* aufteilen **(among** unter + *Akk.*); *see also* **share-out**

share: ~ certificate *n.* Aktienurkunde, *die;* Mantel, *der* (Finanzw.); **~cropper** *n.* (Amer.) Teilpächter, *der;* **~holder** *n.* Aktionär, *der*/Aktionärin, *die; attrib.* **~holder value** Shareholdervalue, *der;* **~ index** *n.* (Econ.) Aktienindex, *der;* **~ option** *n.* Aktienoption, *die;* **~-out** *n.* Aufteilung, *die;* **~ware** *n., no pl.* (Computing) Shareware, *die*

shariah /ʃə'ri:ə/ *n.* (Islamic Law) Scharia, *die*

shark /ʃɑ:k/ *n.* 1 Hai[fisch], *der* 2 (fig.: swindler) gerissener Geschäftemacher; **property ~:** Grundstückshai, *der* (ugs. abwertend)

'sharkskin *n.* 1 (skin) Haut des Haifischs; (tanned) Haifischleder, *das* 2 (fabric) Haifischhaut, *die* (Textilw.)

sharp /ʃɑ:p/

A *adj.* 1 (with fine edge) scharf; (with fine point) spitz ‹*Nadel, Bleistift, Giebel, Gipfel*›; **~ sand** scharfer Sand (Bauw.) 2 (clear-cut) scharf ‹*Umriss, Kontrast, Bild, Gesichtszüge, Linie*›; deutlich ‹*Unterscheidung*›; präzise ‹*Eindruck*›; scharf umrissen ‹*Schatten*› 3 (abrupt, angular) scharf ‹*Kurve, Winkel*›; eng, scharf ‹*Kurve*›; spitz ‹*Winkel*›; steil, schroff ‹*Abhang*›; stark ‹*Gefälle*›; **a ~ rise/fall in prices** ein jäher Preisanstieg/Preissturz 4 (intense) groß ‹*Appetit, Hunger[gefühl]*›; (acid, pungent) scharf ‹*Würze, Geschmack, Sauce, Käse*›; sauer ‹*Apfel*›; herb ‹*Wein*›; (shrill, piercing) schrill ‹*Schrei, Pfiff*›; (biting) scharf ‹*Wind, Frost, Luft*›; (sudden, severe) heftig ‹*Schmerz, Anfall, Krampf, Kampf*›; (harsh, acrimonious) scharf ‹*Protest, Tadel, Ton, Stimme, Zunge, Worte*›; **a short ~ struggle** ein kurzer, heftiger Kampf; **a short ~ shock** ein kräftiger Schock 5 (acute, quick) scharf ‹*Augen, Verstand, Gehör, Ohr, Beobachtungsgabe, Intelligenz, Geruchssinn*›; aufgeweckt ‹*Kind*›; scharfsinnig ‹*Bemerkung*›; begabt ‹*Schüler, Student*›; raffiniert ‹*Schachzug*›; **be ~ at maths** gut in Mathe sein (ugs.); **be as ~ as a needle** schlagfertig sein; **that was pretty ~!** das war ganz schön clever!; **keep a ~ lookout for the police!** halt die Augen offen, falls die Polizei kommt!; **keep a ~ watch** scharf aufpassen; **her mind is as ~ as a needle** sie hat einen messerscharfen Verstand 6 (derog.: artful, dishonest, quick to take advantage) gerissen; **~ practice** unlautere Praktiken 7 (vigorous, brisk) flott (ugs.); **that was ~ work** das ging schnell; **~'s the word!, be ~ about it!** mach schnell! 8 (Mus.) [um einen Halbton] erhöht ‹*Note*›; **F/G/C** *etc.* **~:** fis, Fis/gis, Gis/cis, Cis *usw., das* 9 (coll.: stylish) scharf (ugs.); todschick (ugs.); **she is a ~ dresser** sie ist [immer] todschick angezogen (ugs.)

B *adv.* 1 (punctually) **at six o'clock ~:** Punkt sechs Uhr; **on the hour ~, ~ on the hour** genau zur vollen Stunde 2 (suddenly) scharf ‹*bremsen*›; plötzlich ‹*anhalten*›; **turn ~ right** scharf nach rechts abbiegen 3 **look ~!** halt dich ran! (ugs.) 4 (Mus.) zu hoch ‹*singen, spielen*›

C *n.* (Mus.) erhöhter Ton; (symbol) Kreuz, *das;* Erhöhungszeichen, *das*

'sharp-edged *adj.* scharfkantig; scharf ‹*Messer*›

sharpen /'ʃɑ:pn/ *v.t.* schärfen (auch fig.); [an]spitzen ‹*Bleistift*›; (fig.) anregen ‹*Appetit*›; verstärken ‹*Schmerz*›

'sharp end *n.* (coll.) 1 (Naut.) Bug, *der;* **be at the ~:** im vorderen Teil des Schiffes sein 2 (fig.: place of direct action or decision) vorderste Linie *od.* Front; **at the ~:** in vorderster Front

sharpener /'ʃɑ:pnə(r)/ *n.* (for pencil) Bleistiftspitzer, *der;* Spitzer, *der* (ugs.); (for tools) Abziehstein, *der;* Schleifstein, *der*

sharper /'ʃɑ:pə(r)/ *n.* (at cards) Falschspieler, *der;* (swindler) Betrüger, *der*

sharp: ~-eyed *adj.* scharfäugig; **be ~-eyed** scharfe Augen haben; **be as ~-eyed as a hawk/lynx** Augen wie ein Adler/Luchs haben; **it was ~-eyed of you to spot the fault** dass du den Fehler entdeckt hast, zeigt, dass du ein scharfes Auge hast; **~featured** *adj.* scharf geschnitten ‹*Gesicht*›; ‹*Person*› mit scharfen Gesichtszügen

sharpish /'ʃɑ:pɪʃ/ *adv.* (coll.) (quickly) rasch; (promptly) unverzüglich; sofort

sharply /'ʃɑ:plɪ/ *adv.* 1 (acutely) spitz; **~ angled** spitzwinklig; **come ~ to a point** spitz[winklig] zu *od.* in einem Punkt zusammenlaufen 2 (clearly) scharf ‹*voneinander unterschieden, kontrastierend, umrissen*› 3 (abruptly) scharf ‹*bremsen, abbiegen*›; steil, schroff ‹*abfallen*› 4 (acidly) scharf ‹*gewürzt*›; (harshly) in scharfem Ton ‹*antworten*›; **~ contested** hart umkämpft; **~ worded letter** Brief in scharfem Ton 5 (quickly) schnell, rasch ‹*denken, handeln*›

sharpness /'ʃɑ:pnɪs/ *n., no pl.* Schärfe, *die;* (fineness of point) Spitzheit, *die*

sharp: ~shooter *n.* Scharfschütze, *der;* **~-witted** *adj.* scharfsinnig

shat ▸**shit A, B**

shatter /'ʃætə(r)/

A *v.t.* 1 (smash) zertrümmern 2 (destroy) zerschlagen ‹*Hoffnungen*›; ruinieren ‹*Gesundheit*› 3 (coll.: greatly upset) schwer mitnehmen

B *v.i.* zerbrechen; zerspringen

shattered /'ʃætəd/ *adj.* 1 zerbrochen, zersprungen ‹*Scheibe, Glas, Fenster*›; (fig.) zerstört ‹*Hoffnungen*›; zerrüttet ‹*Nerven, Gesundheit*› 2 (coll.: greatly upset) **she was ~ by the news** die Nachricht hat sie schwer mitgenommen; **I'm ~!** ich bin ganz erschüttert! 3 (Brit. coll.: exhausted) **I'm ~:** ich bin [völlig] kaputt (ugs.); **I feel/she looks ~:** ich bin [völlig] kaputt/sie sieht [ziemlich] kaputt aus (ugs.)

shattering /'ʃætərɪŋ/ *adj.* 1 (ruinously destructive) verheerend ‹*Wirkung, Explosion*›; vernichtend ‹*Schlag, Niederlage*› 2 (coll.: very upsetting) erschütternd; **it must have been ~ for you** es muss dich schwer mitgenommen haben 3 (coll.: exhausting) wahnsinnig anstrengend (ugs.)

'shatter-proof *adj.* splitterfrei; **~ glass** Sicherheitsglas, *das*

shave /ʃeɪv/

A *v.t.* 1 rasieren; abrasieren ‹*Haare*›; **he ~d his beard** er hat sich (*Dat.*) den Bart abrasiert 2 (pare surface of) abhobeln 3 (fig.) **~ a few hundredths of a second off the record** den Rekord um ein paar Hundertstelsekunden verbessern 4 (graze) ‹*Auto:*› streifen

S

B *v.i.* 1 sich rasieren 2 (scrape) ~ **past sth.** etw. [leicht] streifen
C *n.* 1 Rasur, *die;* **have** *or* **get a ~:** sich rasieren; **have** *or* **get a ~ at the barber's** sich beim Friseur rasieren lassen; **this razor gives a good ~:** dieser Rasierapparat rasiert gut; **a clean** *or* **close ~:** eine Glattrasur 2 **close ~** (fig.) ▸**close A 6** 3 (tool) Schabmesser, *das*
Phrasal verb
• ~ **'off** *v.t.* abrasieren ‹*Bart, Haare*›
shaven /ˈʃeɪvn/ *adj.* rasiert; [kahl] geschoren ‹*Kopf*›
shaver /ˈʃeɪvə(r)/ *n.* 1 Rasierapparat, *der;* Rasierer, *der* (ugs.) 2 (dated coll.: lad) **[young] ~:** junger Spund (ugs.)
shaver: ~ point *n.* Anschluss *od.* Steckdose für den Rasierapparat ~ **socket** *n.* Rasierersteckdose, *die;*
Shavian /ˈʃeɪvɪən/ *adj.* Shawsch
shaving /ˈʃeɪvɪŋ/ *n.* 1 (action) Rasieren, *das* 2 *in pl.* (of wood, metal, etc.) Späne
shaving: ~ brush *n.* Rasierpinsel, *der;* ~ **cream** *n.* Rasiercreme, *die;* ~ **foam** *n.* Rasierschaum, *der;* ~ **mug** *n.* Rasierbecken, *das;* ~ **soap** *n.* Rasierseife, *die;* ~ **stick** *n.* Stangenrasierseife, *die*
shawl /ʃɔːl/ *n.* Schultertuch, *das;* (light blanket) Umschlagtuch, *das*
she /ʃɪ, *stressed* ʃiː/
A *pron.* sie; *referring to personified things or animals which correspond to German masculines/neuters* er/es; **it was ~** (formal) sie war es; *see also* **her²**; **hers**; **herself**
B *n., pl.* **~s** /ʃiːz/ Sie, *die* (ugs.); **is it a he or a ~?** ist es ein Er oder eine Sie?
she- /ʃiː/ *in comb.* weiblich; **~ass/-bear** Eselin, *die*/Bärin, *die;* **~-cat** Kätzin, *die;* **~devil** (fig. derog.: malignant woman) Drachen, *der* (salopp abwertend)
sheaf /ʃiːf/ *n., pl.* **sheaves** /ʃiːvz/ (of corn etc.) Garbe, *die;* (of paper, arrows, etc.) Bündel, *das*
shear /ʃɪə(r)/
A *v.t., p. p.* **shorn** /ʃɔːn/ *or* **sheared** 1 (clip) scheren; **be shorn of sth.** (fig.) einer Sache (*Gen.*) beraubt sein/werden 2 (Mech., Geol.: break) abscheren
B *v.i., p. p.* **shorn** *or* **sheared** ‹*Bolzen, Metallteil:*› abscheren (Technik); **the motor boat ~ed through the water** (fig.) das Motorboot durchschnitt das Wasser (fig.); **the cutter blades ~ed through the metal** die Schneiden der Schere zerschnitten das Metall
C *n.* (Mech., Geol.) Scherung, *die*
Phrasal verb
• ~ **'off**
A *v.t.* abtrennen
B *v.i.* abscheren (Technik)
shearer /ˈʃɪərə(r)/ *n.* 1 ▸① **p. 1260** (of sheep) Scherer, *der* 2 (metalworker) ▸① **p. 1260** Metallschneider, *der* 3 (machine) Schneidemaschine, *die*
shearing /ˈʃɪərɪŋ/ *n.* Scheren, *das*
shears /ʃɪəz/ *n. pl.* **[pair of] ~** (große) Schere, *die;* **garden ~:** Heckenschere, *die*
'shearwater *n.* (Ornith.) Sturmtaucher, *der*
sheath /ʃiːθ/ *n., pl.* **~s** /ʃiːðz, ʃiːθs/ 1 (for knife, dagger, sword, etc.) Scheide, *die* 2 (Zool.) (of insect) Elytron, *das;* Schutzdecke, *die* 3 (Electr.) Mantel, *der* 4 (condom) Gummischutz, *der*
sheathe /ʃiːð/ *v.t.* 1 (put into sheath) in die Scheide stecken ‹*Messer, Schwert, Dolch*› 2 (protect) ummanteln (**in, with** mit)
sheathing /ˈʃiːðɪŋ/ *n.* Ummantelung, *die*
'sheath knife *n.* Fahrtenmesser, *das*
sheave¹ /ʃiːv/ *n.* Rolle, *die*
sheave² *v.t.* zu Garben binden ‹*Getreide*›
sheaves *pl. of* **sheaf**
shebang /ʃɪˈbæŋ/ *n.* (Amer. coll.) **the whole ~:** der ganze Kram (ugs.); **who runs the whole ~?** wer ist der Boss vom Ganzen? (ugs.)
shed¹ /ʃed/ *v.t.*, **-dd-, shed** 1 (part with) verlieren; abwerfen, verlieren ‹*Laub, Geweih*›; abstreifen ‹*Haut, Hülle, Badehose*›; ausziehen ‹*Kleidung*›; **a duck's back ~s water** vom Rücken einer Ente läuft das Wasser ab; **the snake is ~ding its skin** die Schlange häutet sich; **dogs/cats ~ hairs** Hunde/Katzen haaren; **you should ~ a few pounds** du solltest ein paar Pfund abspecken (salopp) 2 vergießen ‹*Blut, Tränen*›; **~ tears over sth.** wegen einer Sache Tränen vergießen; **don't ~ any tears over him** seinetwegen solltest du keine Tränen vergießen; **without ~ding blood** ohne Blutvergießen 3 (dispense) verbreiten ‹*Wärme, Licht*›; *see also* **light¹ A 8** 4 (fig.: cast off) abschütteln ‹*Sorgen, Bürde*›; ablegen ‹*Gewohnheit*›
shed² *n.* Schuppen, *der;* **wooden ~:** Holzschuppen, *der*
she'd /ʃɪd, *stressed* ʃiːd/ 1 **= she had** 2 **= she would**
sheen /ʃiːn/ *n.* Glanz, *der*
sheep /ʃiːp/ *n., pl. same* 1 Schaf, *das;* **separate the ~ from the goats** (fig.) die Böcke von den Schafen trennen; **count ~** (fig.) Schäfchen zählen (fam.); **follow sb. like ~:** jmdm. wie eine Schafherde folgen; *see also* **black sheep**; **eye A 1**; **lamb A 1**; **wolf A 1** 2 (person) Schäfchen, *das* (fam.); Schäflein, *das* (fam.)
sheep: ~ dip *n.* Desinfektionsbad für Schafe; **~dog** *n.* Hütehund, *der;* Schäferhund, *der;* **Old English S~dog** Bobtail, *der;* ~ **farm** *n.* (Brit.) Schaffarm, *die;* ~ **farmer** *n.* ▸① **p. 1260** (Brit.) Schafzüchter, *der*/-züchterin, *die;* **~fold** *n.* 1 (pen) Schafhürde, *die;* Pferch, *der;* 2 (shelter) Schafstall, *der*
sheepish /ˈʃiːpɪʃ/ *adj.* (awkwardly self-conscious) verlegen; (embarrassed) kleinlaut; **he felt a bit ~** (foolish) es war ihm ein bisschen peinlich
sheepishly /ˈʃiːpɪʃlɪ/ *adv.* ▸**sheepish**: verlegen; kleinlaut
sheep: ~meat *n.* Schaffleisch, *das;* ~ **pen** ▸**sheepfold 1**; **~shank** *n.* (knot) lange Trompete (Seemannsspr.); ~ **shearer** /ˈʃiːp ʃɪərə(r)/ *n.* ▸① **p. 1260** Schafscherer, *der;* **~-shearing** *n.* Schafschur, *die;* **~skin** *n.* 1 Schaffell, *das;* **~skin [jacket]** Schaffelljacke, *die;* 2 (leather) Schafleder, *das;* ~ **walk** *n.* (Brit.) Schafweide, *die*
sheer¹ /ʃɪə(r)/
A *adj.* 1 *attrib.* (mere, absolute) rein; blank ‹*Unsinn, Gewalt*›; **by ~ chance** rein zufällig; **it is a ~ impossibility to do it** es ist schier unmöglich, es zu tun; **that's ~ robbery!** das ist ja der reinste Wucher!; **the ~ insolence of it!** so eine Frechheit!; **only by ~ hard work** nur durch harte Arbeit 2 (perpendicular) schroff ‹*Felsen, Abfall*›; steil ‹*Felsen, Abfall, Aufstieg*› 3 (finely woven) hauchfein
B *adv.* (perpendicularly) schroff; steil
sheer² *v.i.* (Naut.) [aus]scheren
Phrasal verb
• ~ **a'way** *v.i.* 1 (Naut.) abscheren 2 **~ away from** (fig.: avoid) ausweichen (+ *Dat.*) ‹*Person, Thema*›
sheet¹ /ʃiːt/
A *n.* 1 Laken, *das;* (for covering mattress) Betttuch, *das;* Laken, *das;* **put clean ~s on the bed** das Bett frisch beziehen; **between the ~s** (in bed) im Bett; *see also* **white A 2** 2 (of thin metal, plastic) Folie, *die;* (of iron, tin) Blech, *das;* (of glass, of thicker metal, plastic) Platte, *die;* (of stamps) Bogen, *der;* (of paper) Bogen, *der;* Blatt, *das;* **a ~ of iron/plastic** ein Eisenblech/eine Plastikfolie; **a ~ of paper** ein Papierbogen; ein Bogen *od.* Blatt Papier; **five ~s of wrapping paper** 5 Bögen Einwickelpapier; **a 250-~ roll of toilet paper** eine 250-Blatt-Rolle Toilettenpapier; ~ **of music** Notenblatt, *das; attrib.* ~ **glass/metal/iron** Flachglas, *das*/Blech, *das*/Eisenblech, *das; see also* **clean A 2** 3 (wide expanse) ‹*Eis-, Lava-, Nebel*›decke, *die;* **a ~ of water covered the lawn** der Rasen stand unter Wasser; **a huge ~ of flame** ein Flammenmeer; **the rain was coming down in ~s** es regnete in Strömen 4 (Printing) Druckbogen, *der;* **a book in ~s** ein Rohexemplar
B *v.i.* **the rain was ~ing down** es regnete in Strömen
sheet² *n.* 1 (of sail) Schot, *die* 2 **be three ~s in** *or* **to the wind** (coll.) voll wie eine Strandhaubitze sein (ugs.)
sheet: ~ anchor *n.* (Naut.) Notanker, *der;* (fig.) Rettungsanker, *der;* ~ **feeder** *n.* (Computing) Einzelblatteinzug, *der*
sheeting /ˈʃiːtɪŋ/ *n., no pl.* 1 (cloth for making bedsheets) Bettzeugstoff, *der;* Haustuch, *das* 2 (of thin metal, plastic, etc.) Folie, *die;* (of iron, tin) Blech, *das;* (of thicker metal, plastic) Platte, *die*
sheet: ~ lightning *n.* (Meteorol.) Flächenblitz, *der;* ~ **music** *n.* Notenblätter
sheik, sheikdom ▸**sheikh, sheikhdom**
sheikh /ʃeɪk, ʃiːk/ *n.* Scheich, *der*
sheikhdom /ʃeɪkdəm, ʃiːkdəm/ *n.* Scheichtum, *das*
sheila /ˈʃiːlə/ *n.* (Austral. and NZ coll.: young woman) Puppe, *die* (salopp)
shekel /ˈʃekl/ *n.* 1 ▸① **p. 1332** Schekel, *der* 2 *in pl.* (coll.: money, riches) Moneten *Pl.* (ugs.)
sheldrake /ˈʃeldreɪk/ *n., fem. and pl.* **shelduck** *or* **sheld duck** /ˈʃeldʌk/ (Ornith.) Brandente, *die;* Brandgans, *die*
shelf /ʃelf/ *n., pl.* **shelves** /ʃelvz/ 1 (flat board) Brett, *das;* Bord, *das;* (compartment) Fach, *das;* (set of shelves) Regal, *das;* **~ of books** Bücherbrett, *das;* **be left on the ~** (fig.) sitzen geblieben sein (ugs.); **be put on the ~** (fig.) aufs Abstellgleis geschoben werden (ugs.) 2 (Geol.) Riff, *das; see also* **continental shelf**
shelf-ful /ˈʃelffʊl/ *n.* **a ~ of books** *etc.* ein Bord voll Bücher *usw.*
shelf: ~ life *n.* Lagerfähigkeit, *die;* ~ **mark** *n.* Standortnummer, *die;* ~ **room**, ~ **space** *ns.* Stellfläche [im Regal]; **give ~ room** *or* **space to sth.** sich (*Dat.*) etw. ins Regal stellen
shell /ʃel/
A *n.* 1 (casing) Schale, *die;* (of turtle, tortoise) Panzer, *der;* (of pupa) Hülle, *die;* (of snail) Haus, *das;* (of pea) Schote, *die;* Hülse, *die;* (of insect's wing) Flügeldecke, *die;* **collect ~s on the beach** am Strand Muscheln sammeln; **bring sb. out of his ~** (fig.) jmdn. aus der Reserve locken (ugs.); **come out of one's ~** (fig.) aus sich herausgehen; **retire** *or* **go into one's ~** (fig.) sich in sein Schneckenhaus zurückziehen (ugs.) 2 (frame) Gerippe, das (fig.); (of unfinished building) Rohbau, *der;* (of building needing to be refurbished) Außenmauern und Dach; (of ruinous building) Ruine, *die* 3 (pastry case) Teighülle, *die* 4 (racing boat) Rennruderboot, *das* 5 (Motor Veh.) **[body] ~:** Aufbau, *der;* Karosserie, *die;* (after fire, at breaker's, etc.) [Karosserie]gerippe, *das* 6 (Mil.) (bomb) Granate, *die;* (Amer.: cartridge) Patrone, *die*
B *v.t.* 1 (take out of ~) schälen; knacken, schälen ‹*Nuss*›; öffnen ‹*Auster*›; enthülsen, (nordd.) palen ‹*Erbsen*›; **as easy as ~ing peas** kinderleicht; **~ed nuts** Nusskerne 2 (Mil.) [mit Artillerie] beschießen
Phrasal verb
• ~ **'out** *v.t. & i.* (coll.) blechen (ugs.) (**on** für)
she'll /ʃɪl, *stressed* ʃiːl/ **= she will**
shellac /ʃəˈlæk/
A *n.* Schellack, *der*
B *v.t.*, **-ck-** 1 (varnish) mit Schellack überziehen 2 (Amer. coll.: defeat, thrash) vermöbeln (ugs.); fertig machen (ugs.)
shell: ~fish *n., pl. same* 1 Schal[en]tier, *das;* (oyster, clam) Muschel, *die;* (crustacean) Krebstier, *das;* 2 *in pl.* (Gastr.) Meeresfrüchte *Pl.;* **~-pink** *adj.* muschelrosa; **~proof** *adj.* bombensicher; ~ **shock** *n.* (Psych.) Kriegsneurose, *die;* **~-shocked** *adj.* **be ~-shocked** eine Kriegsneurose haben; (fig.) niedergeschmettert sein; ~ **suit** *n.* Trilobalanzug, *der*
shelter /ˈʃeltə(r)/
A *n.* 1 (shield) Schutz, *der* (**against** vor + *Dat.*, gegen); **bomb** *or* **air-raid ~:** Luftschutzraum, *der;* **get under ~:** sich unterstellen; **under the ~ of the rocks/of night** im Schutz der Felsen/der Nacht; **wooden/mountain ~:** Holz-/Berg- *od.* Schutzhütte, *die* 2 *no pl.* (place of safety) Zuflucht, *die;* **we needed food and ~:** wir brauchten etwas zu essen und eine Unterkunft; **look for ~ for the night** eine Unterkunft für die Nacht suchen; **offer** *or* **give sb. ~, provide ~ for sb.** jmdm. Zuflucht gewähren *od.* bieten; **in the ~ of one's home** im Schutz *od.* in der Geborgenheit seines Heims;

S

take ~ [from a storm] [vor einem Sturm] Schutz suchen; **seek/reach ~:** Schutz *od.* Zuflucht suchen/finden

B *v.t.* schützen (**from** vor + *Dat.*); Unterschlupf gewähren (+ *Dat.*) ‹*Flüchtling*›; **~ sb. from blame/harm** jmdn. decken/gegen alle Gefahren schützen

C *v.i.* Schutz *od.* Zuflucht suchen (**from** vor + *Dat.*); **this is a good place to ~:** hier ist man gut geschützt

'shelter belt *n.* Windschutzstreifen, *der*

sheltered /ˈʃeltəd/ *adj.* geschützt ‹*Platz, Tal*›; behütet ‹*Leben*›; **~ workshops** beschützende Werkstätten; **~ employment** Beschäftigung in beschützenden Werkstätten; **live in ~ housing** in einer Altenwohnung/in Altenwohnungen leben

sheltered accommo'dation *n., no pl.* (Brit.) [Wohn]anlage für betreutes Wohnen

shelve /ʃelv/

A *v.t.* **1** (put on shelves) ins Regal stellen; (fig.) (abandon) ad acta *od.* (ugs.) zu den Akten legen; (defer) auf Eis legen (ugs.) **2** (fit with shelves) ein Regal einbauen (+ *Akk.*) ‹*Nische*›; ausfachen (fachspr.), mit Fächern versehen ‹*Schrank*›; mit Borden versehen ‹*Wand*›

B *v.i.* **~ away/off/out into** ‹*Berg, Boden, Ebene:*› abfallen nach

shelves *pl. of* **shelf**

shelving /ˈʃelvɪŋ/ *n., no pl.* Regale *Pl.*

shemozzle /ʃɪˈmɒzl/ *n.* (coll.) **1** (rumpus, brawl) Keilerei, *die* (ugs.) **2** (muddle) Schlamassel, *der* (ugs.)

shenanigans /ʃɪˈnænɪgənz/ *n. pl.* (coll.) (trickery) Tricks; (nonsense) Fez, *der* (ugs.); (high-spirited behaviour) Klamauk, *der* (ugs. abwertend)

shepherd /ˈʃepəd/

A ▸ⓘ **p. 1260** *n.* Schäfer, *der;* Schafhirt, *der;* (Relig. fig.) Hirt[e], *der* (geh.); **the Good S~:** der Gute Hirte

B *v.t.* hüten; (fig.) führen

'shepherd dog *n.* Hütehund, *der;* Schäferhund, *der; see also* **German shepherd [dog]**

shepherdess /ˈʃepədɪs/ *n.* ▸ⓘ **p. 1260** Schäferin, *die;* Schafhirtin, *die*

shepherd: ~'s 'crook *n.* Schäferstock, *der;* Hirtenstab, *der* (geh.); **~'s 'pie** *n.* (Gastr.) *Auflauf aus Hackfleisch mit einer Schicht Kartoffelbrei darüber;* **~'s 'purse** *n.* (Bot.) Hirtentäschelkraut, *das*

sherbet /ˈʃɜːbət/ *n.* **1** (fruit juice; also Amer.: water ice) Sorbet[t], *der od. das* **2** (effervescent drink) Brauselimonade, *die;* (powder) Brausepulver, *das*

sherd /ʃɜːd/ *n.* Scherbe, *die*

sheriff /ˈʃerɪf/ *n.* ▸ⓘ **p. 1260** Sheriff, *der*

'sheriff court *n.* (Scot. Law) *Grafschaftsgericht mit Zuständigkeit in Zivil- und Strafsachen*

Sherpa /ˈʃɜːpə/ *n.* (Ethnol.) Sherpa, *der*/Sherpani, *die*

sherry /ˈʃerɪ/ *n.* Sherry, *der;* **~ glass** Sherryglas, *das;* ≈ Südweinglas, *das*

she's /ʃɪz, *stressed* ʃiːz/ **1** = **she is** **2** = **she has**

Shetland /ˈʃetlənd/ *pr. n.* ▸ **Shetland Islands**

Shetlander /ˈʃetləndə(r)/ *n.* Shetländer, *der*/-länderin, *die*

Shetland Islands *pr. n. pl.* Shetlandinseln *Pl.;* Shetlands *Pl.*

Shetland: ~ 'jumper *n.* Pullover aus Shetlandwolle; **~ 'pony** *n.* Shetlandpony, *das*

Shetlands /ˈʃetləndz/ *pr. n. pl.* Shetlands *Pl.*

Shetland: ~ 'sheepdog *n.* Sheltie, *der;* **~ 'wool** *n.* Shetlandwolle, *die*

shew (arch.) ▸ **show B, C**

shh /ʃ/ *int.* pst; sch

Shiah /ˈʃiːə/ *n.* (Muslim Relig.) Schia, *die*

shiatsu /ʃɪˈætsuː/ *n., no pl.* Shiatsu, *das*

shibboleth /ˈʃɪbəleθ/ *n.* Schibboleth, *das* (geh.); (catchword) Schlagwort, *das*

shield /ʃiːld/

A *n.* **1** (piece of armour) Schild, *der* **2** (in machinery etc.) Schutz, *der;* (protective plate) Schutzplatte, *die;* (protective screen) Schutzschirm, *der;* **radiation ~:** Strahlenschutz, *der* **3** (fig.: person or thing that protects) Schild, *der* (geh.) **4** (Zool.) Schild, *der* **5** (Geol.) Schild, *der* **6** (Her.) [Wappen]schild, *der* **7** (Sport: trophy) Trophäe, *die* (in Form eines Schildes) **8** (Amer.: policeman's badge) Dienstmarke, *die*

B *v.t.* **1** (protect) schützen (**from** vor + *Dat.*) **2** (conceal) decken ‹*Schuldigen*›; **~ sb. from the truth** die Wahrheit von jmdm. fern halten

shier, shiest ▸ **shy¹ A**

shift /ʃɪft/

A *v.t.* **1** (move) verrücken, umstellen ‹*Möbel*›; wegnehmen ‹*Arm, Hand, Fuß*›; wegräumen ‹*Schutt*›; entfernen ‹*Schmutz, Fleck*›; (to another floor, room, or place) verlegen ‹*Büro, Patienten, Schauplatz*›; bringen ‹*Gerümpel*›; (to another town) versetzen ‹*Person*›; **~ one's weight to the other foot** sein Gewicht auf den anderen Fuß verlagern; **~ the responsibility/blame on to sb.** (fig.) die Verantwortung/Schuld auf jmdn. schieben; *see also* **ground¹ A 2** **2** (Amer. Motor Veh.) **~ gears** schalten **3** (coll.: consume) verkonsumieren (ugs.) **4** (coll.: sell) loswerden (ugs.)

B *v.i.* **1** ‹*Wind:*› drehen (**to** nach); ‹*Ladung:*› verrutschen; (in drama, novel, etc.) ‹*Szene:*› wechseln (**to** nach); ‹*Schauplatz:*› sich verlagern (**to** nach); **~ uneasily in one's chair** unruhig auf dem Stuhl hin und her rutschen **2** (manage) **~ for oneself** selbst für sich sorgen **3** (coll.: move quickly) rasen; **this new Porsche really ~s** der neue Porsche geht ab wie eine Rakete (ugs.) **4** (Amer. Motor Veh.: change gear) schalten; **~ down into second gear** in den zweiten Gang runterschalten (ugs.)

C *n.* **1** **a ~ in emphasis** eine Verlagerung des Akzents; **a ~ in values/public opinion** ein Wandel der Wertvorstellungen/ein Umschwung der öffentlichen Meinung; **a ~ towards/away from liberalism** eine Hinwendung zum/Abwendung vom Liberalismus **2** (for work) Schicht, *die;* **eight-hour/late ~:** Achtstunden-/Spätschicht, *die;* **do** *or* **work the late ~:** Spätschicht haben; **work in ~s** Schichtarbeit machen **3** (stratagem, dodge) Kunstgriff, *der* **4** **make ~ with/without sth.** sich (*Dat.*) mit/ohne etw. behelfen **5** (of typewriter) Umschaltung, *die; attrib.* **~ key** Umschalttaste, *die* **6** (Amer. Motor Veh.: gear change) Schaltung, *die;* **manual/automatic ~:** Hand-/Automatikschaltung, *die* **7** (dress) Hängekleid, *das;* Hänger, *der* **8** (Phys.) Verschiebung, *die* **9** (Ling.) **sound ~:** Lautverschiebung, *die*

shifting 'sands *n. pl.* (lit. or fig.) Flugsand, *der*

shift: ~less /ˈʃɪftlɪs/ *adj.* (lacking resourcefulness) unbeholfen; (incapable) unfähig; **~ system** *n.* Schichtsystem, *das;* **~ work** *n., no pl.* Schichtarbeit, *die*

shifty /ˈʃɪftɪ/ *adj.* verschlagen (abwertend)

Shiite /ˈʃiːaɪt/ (Muslim Relig.)

A *n.* Schiit, *der*/Schiitin, *die*

B *adj.* schiitisch

shillelagh /ʃɪˈleɪlə, ʃɪˈleɪlɪ/ *n.* Knüppel, *der* (*aus Schlehdorn- oder Eichenholz*)

shilling /ˈʃɪlɪŋ/ *n.* Shilling, *der;* **take the King's/Queen's ~** (arch.) sich als Rekrut [gegen Handgeld] anwerben lassen; *see also* **cut off 6**

shilly-shally /ˈʃɪlɪʃælɪ/ *v.i.* zaudern; **stop ~ing!** entschließ dich endlich!

shimmer /ˈʃɪmə(r)/

A *v.i.* schimmern

B *n.* Schimmer, *der*

shimmery /ˈʃɪmərɪ/ *adj.* schimmernd

shin /ʃɪn/

A *n.* ▸ⓘ **p. 951** Schienbein, *das;* **~ of beef** (Cookery) [Vorder]hesse, *die*

B *v.i.*, **-nn-:** **~ up/down a tree** *etc.* einen Baum *usw.* hinauf-/hinunterklettern

'shin bone *n.* Schienbein, *das*

shindig /ˈʃɪndɪg/ *n.* (coll.) **1** ▸ **shindy** **2** (party) Fete, *die* (ugs.)

shindy /ˈʃɪndɪ/ *n.* (brawl) Rauferei, *die;* (row) Streit, *der;* (noise) Krach, *der*

shine /ʃaɪn/

A *v.i.*, **shone** /ʃɒn/ **1** ‹*Lampe, Licht, Stern:*› leuchten; ‹*Sonne:*› scheinen; (reflect light) glänzen; ‹*Mond:*› scheinen; **his face shone with happiness/excitement** (fig.) er strahlte vor Glück/sein Gesicht glühte vor Aufregung; **a fine morning with the sun shining** ein schöner Morgen mit [strahlendem] Sonnenschein **2** (fig.: be brilliant) glänzen; **a shining example/light** ein leuchtendes Beispiel/eine Leuchte; **~ at sport** im Sport glänzen; **he does not exactly ~ at maths** er ist nicht gerade eine Leuchte in Mathe (ugs.)

B *v.t.* **1** *p.t. & p.p.* **shone** leuchten lassen; **~ a light on sth./in sb.'s eyes** etw. anleuchten/jmdm. in die Augen leuchten; **~ the torch this way** leuchte einmal hierher **2** *p.t. & p.p.* **~d** (clean and polish) putzen; (make shiny) polieren

C *n., no pl.* **1** (brightness) Schein, *der;* Licht, *das; see also* **rain A 1** **2** (polish) Glanz, *der;* **give your shoes a good ~:** bring deine Schuhe auf Hochglanz; **have a ~** ‹*Oberfläche:*› glänzen; **put a ~ on sth.** etw. zum Glänzen bringen; **take the ~ off sth.** (fig.: spoil sth.) einen Schatten auf etw. (*Akk.*) werfen **3** **take a ~ to sb./sth.** (coll.) Gefallen an jmdm./etw. finden

shingle¹ /ˈʃɪŋgl/

A *n.* **1** (Building) Schindel, *die* **2** (Amer.: signboard) [Praxis]schild, *das* **3** (Hairdressing) Bubikopf, *der*

B *v.t.* **1** (Building) schindeln **2** (Hairdressing) zu einem Bubikopf schneiden ‹*Haar*›; **~d hair** Bubikopf, *der*

shingle² *n., no pl., no indef. art.* (pebbles) Kies, *der; attrib.* **~ beach** Kiesstrand, *der*

shingles /ˈʃɪŋglz/ *n. sing.* ▸ⓘ **p. 1231** (Med.) Gürtelrose, *die*

shingly /ˈʃɪŋglɪ/ *adj.* kiesig; **~ beach** Kiesstrand, *der*

shin: ~ guard, ~ pad *ns.* Schienbeinschutz, *der*

Shinto /ˈʃɪntəʊ/, **Shintoism** /ˈʃɪntəʊɪzm/ *ns., no pl., no indef. art.* (Relig.) Schintoismus, *der*

Shintoist /ˈʃɪntəʊɪst/ *n.* (Relig.) Schintoist, *der*/Schintoistin, *die*

shiny /ˈʃaɪnɪ/ *adj.* **1** (glistening, polished) glänzend **2** (worn) blank

ship /ʃɪp/

A *n.* **1** Schiff, *das;* **take ~:** sich einschiffen (**for** nach); **when my ~ comes home** *or* **in** (fig.) wenn ich zu Geld komme; **~ of the desert** (fig.) Wüstenschiff, *das* (geh. scherzh.); Schiff der Wüste (geh.); **we were just ~s that pass in the night** (fig.) nur einmal kreuzten sich unsere Wege; **the ~ of state** das Staatsschiff (geh.); **run a tight ~** (fig.) ein strenges Regiment führen; *see also* **break¹ A 7; company 1, 8; tar¹ A** **2** (Amer.: aircraft) Flugzeug, *das;* Maschine, *die* **3** (coll.: spacecraft) Raumschiff, *das*

B *v.t.*, **-pp-** **1** (take on board) einschiffen, an Bord bringen ‹*Vorräte, Ladung, Passagiere*›; (transport by sea) verschiffen ‹*Auto, Truppen*›; (send by train, road, or air) verschicken, versenden ‹*Waren*› **2** (Naut.: position) setzen ‹*Ruderpinne, Mast, Positionslichter*› **3** **~ oars** (bring them into the boat) die Riemen einlegen *od.* -ziehen **4** **~ water/a sea** Wasser/eine See übernehmen (Seemansspr.)

C *v.i.*, **-pp-** **1** (embark) sich einschiffen **2** (take service on ~) anheuern, anmustern (Seemannsspr.)

Phrasal verbs

- **~ 'off** *v.t.* versenden, verschicken ‹*Waren*›; schicken ‹*Person*›
- **~ 'out** *v.t.* verschiffen ‹*Ladung, Güter*›

ship: ~board **A** *adj.* ‹*Romanze usw.*› an Bord; **B** *n., no pl., no art.* **on ~board** an Bord; **~-breaker** *n.* Abwrackfirma, *die;* **~-broker** *n.* Schiffsmakler, *der;* **~builder** *n.* ▸ⓘ **p. 1260** Schiff[s]bauer, *der;* **firm of ~builders** Schiffbaufirma, *die;* **~building** *n., no pl., no indef. art.* Schiffbau, *der;* **~ canal** *n.* Schifffahrtskanal, *der;* **~load** *n.* Schiffsladung, *die;* **~mate** *n.* Schiffskamerad, *der*

shipment /ˈʃɪpmənt/ *n.* **1** Versand, *der;* (by sea) Verschiffung, *die* **2** (amount) Sendung, *die;* **a ~ of bananas** eine Ladung Bananen

'shipowner *n.* Schiffseigentümer, *der*/-eigentümerin, *die;* Schiffseigner, *der*/-eignerin, *die;* (of several ships) Reeder, *der*/Reederin, *die*

S

shipper /ˈʃɪpə(r)/ *n.* (merchant) Spediteur, *der*/Spediteurin, *die;* (company) Spedition, *die*

shipping /ˈʃɪpɪŋ/ *n.* **1** no *pl., no indef. art.* (ships) Schiffe *Pl.;* (traffic) Schifffahrt, *die;* Schiffsverkehr, *der;* **all ~:** alle Schiffe/der ganze Schiffsverkehr; **closed to ~:** für Schiffe/für die Schifffahrt gesperrt **2** (transporting) Versand, *der*

shipping: ~ agent *n.* Schiffsagent, *der;* **~ forecast** *n.* Seewetterbericht, *der;* **~ lane** *n.* Schifffahrtsweg, *der;* (fairway) Fahrrinne, *die;* **~ line** ▸ **line¹ A 9;** **~ office** *n.* **1** (of ~ agent) Schiffsagentur, *die;* **2** (hiring seamen) Heuerbüro, *das*

ship: ~'s 'biscuit *n.* Schiffszwieback, *der;* **~'s chandler** *n.* Schiffsausrüster, *der;* **~shape** *pred. adj.* in bester Ordnung; **get sth. ~shape** etw. in Ordnung bringen; **find everything ~shape and Bristol fashion** (coll.) alles picobello *od.* tipptopp (ugs.) vorfinden; **~'s 'papers** *n. pl.* Schiffspapiere *Pl.;* **~way** *n.* Helling, *die* (Schiffbau); **~wreck A** *n.* (lit. or fig.) Schiffbruch, *der;* **suffer ~wreck** Schiffbruch erleiden; **end in ~wreck** (fig.) scheitern; **B** *v.t.* **be ~wrecked** Schiffbruch erleiden; (fig.: be ruined) ‹Hoffnung:› sich zerschlagen haben; ‹Karriere:› gescheitert sein; **be ~wrecked on an island** bei einem Schiffbruch auf eine Insel verschlagen werden; **~wright** *n.* (~builder) Schiff[s]bauer, *der;* (~'s carpenter) Schiffszimmermann, *der;* **~yard** *n.* [Schiffs]werft, *die*

shire /ˈʃaɪə(r)/ *n.* **1** (county) Grafschaft, *die* **2** **the Shires** (group of counties) *die auf -shire endenden englischen Grafschaften;* (midland counties) die Grafschaften in Mittelengland **3** ▸ **shire horse**

'shire horse *n.: bes. in Mittelengland gezüchtetes schweres Zugpferd*

shirk /ʃɜːk/ *v.t.* sich entziehen (+ *Dat.*) ‹Pflicht, Verantwortung›; ausweichen (+ *Dat.*) ‹Blick, Kampf›; **~ one's job/doing sth.** sich vor der Arbeit drücken/sich davor drücken (ugs.), etw. zu tun; **you're ~ing!** [du bist ein] Drückeberger! (ugs. abwertend)

shirker /ˈʃɜːkə(r)/ *n.* Drückeberger, *der* (ugs. abwertend)

shirring /ˈʃɜːrɪŋ/ *n.* Kräusel[ung], *die*

shirt /ʃɜːt/ *n.* **[man's] ~:** [Herren- *od.* Ober-]hemd, *das;* **[woman's** *or* **lady's] ~:** Hemdbluse, *die;* **sports/rugby/football ~:** Trikot/Rugby-/Fußballtrikot, *das;* **keep your ~ on!** (fig. coll.) [nur] ruhig Blut! (ugs.); **have the ~ off sb.'s back** (fig.) jmdm. das Hemd über den Kopf ziehen (fig. ugs.); **lose the ~ off one's back** alles bis aufs Hemd verlieren (ugs.); **put one's ~ on sth.** (fig. coll.) sein letztes Hemd für etw. verwetten (ugs.)

shirt: ~ blouse *n.* Hemdbluse, *die;* **~ dress** *n.* Hemdblusenkleid, *das;* **~ front** *n.* Hemdbrust, *die;* (separate or detachable) Vorhemd, *das*

shirting /ˈʃɜːtɪŋ/ *n.* Hemdenstoff, *der*

shirt: ~sleeve A *n.* Hemdsärmel, *der;* **work in one's ~sleeves** in Hemdsärmeln arbeiten; **B** *adj.* hemdsärmelig; körperlich ‹Arbeit›; **it is real ~sleeve weather** bei diesem Wetter kann man ohne Jacke gehen; **~ tail** ▸ **tail A 4;** **~waist** (Amer.) ▸ **shirt blouse;** **~waister** /ˈʃɜːtweɪstə(r)/ (Brit.) ▸ **shirt dress**

shirty /ˈʃɜːtɪ/ *adj.* (coll.) sauer (salopp); **get ~ with sb./about sth.** auf jmdn./wegen etw. sauer werden; **be ~ with sb.** rotzig (salopp abwertend) zu jmdm. sein

shish kebab /ˈʃɪʃ kɪbæb, ˈʃɪʃ kɪbɑːb/ *n.* (Gastr.) Kebab, *der*

shit /ʃɪt/ (coarse)
A *v.i.*, **-tt-, shitted** *or* **shit** *or* **shat** /ʃæt/ scheißen (derb); **~ in one's pants** sich (*Dat.*) in die Hose[n] scheißen
B *v. refl.*, **-tt-, shitted** *or* **shit** *or* **shat** sich (*Dat.*) in die Hose[n] scheißen (derb)
C *int.* Scheiße (derb)
D *n.* **1** (excrement) Scheiße, *die* (derb); **have** (Brit.) *or* (Amer.) **take a ~:** scheißen (derb); **have/get the ~s** die Scheißerei (derb) haben/kriegen; **when the ~ hits the fan** wenn die Kacke am Dampfen ist (derb) **2** (hashish) Shit, *der od. das* (Drogenjargon) **3** (person) Scheißkerl, *der;* (nonsense) Scheiß, *der* (salopp abwertend); **don't give me that ~:** erzähl mir nicht so einen Scheiß! (salopp); **I don't give a ~ [about it]** das ist mir scheißegal (salopp); **who gives a ~!** ist doch scheißegal! (salopp); **it's not worth a ~:** es ist einen Dreck wert (salopp abwertend); **beat** *or* **kick** *or* **knock the ~ out of sb.** (fig.) jmdn. gehörig verdreschen (ugs.); **I'll beat the ~ out of you!** ich mach' Hackfleisch aus dir! (ugs.); **be up ~ creek [without a paddle]** (fig.) bis zum Hals in der Scheiße stecken (derb); **have/get the ~s** (fig.) Schiss haben/kriegen (salopp)

shite /ʃaɪt/ (coarse)
A *int.* Scheibenkleister (ugs. verhüll.)
B *n.* Scheiß, *der* (salopp); **not give a ~ for sb./sth.** sich einen [Scheiß]dreck um jmdn./etw. kümmern (salopp)

shitless /ˈʃɪtlɪs/ *adj.* (coarse) **be scared ~:** sich (*Dat.*) vor Angst in die Hose[n] scheißen (derb)

'shit-scared *pred. adj.* (coarse) **be ~:** Schiss haben (salopp)

shitty /ˈʃɪtɪ/ *adj.* (coarse) beschissen (derb); Scheiß- (salopp)

shiver¹ /ˈʃɪvə(r)/
A *v.i.* (tremble) zittern (**with** vor + *Dat.*); **~ all over** am ganzen Leib *od.* Körper zittern; **~ like a leaf** wie Espenlaub zittern (geh.)
B *n.* (trembling, lit. or fig.) Schau[d]er, *der* (geh.); **~ of cold/fear** Kälte-/Angstschauer, *der;* **send ~s** *or* **a ~ up** *or* **[up and] down sb.'s back** *or* **spine** jmdm. [einen] Schauder über den Rücken jagen; **give sb. the ~s** (fig.) jmdn. schaudern lassen; **get/have the ~s** (fig.) eine Gänsehaut (fig.) *od.* (*bei Krankheit*) Schüttelfrost bekommen/haben

shiver²
A *n. in pl.* (fragments) **break/burst into ~s** in Stücke zerbrechen *od.* zerspringen
B *v.t.* zersplittern lassen; **~ me timbers** potz Blitz! (veralt.)
C *v.i.* zerspringen

shivery /ˈʃɪvərɪ/ *adj.* verfroren ‹Person›; **I feel all ~:** mich fröstelt

shoal¹ /ʃəʊl/ *n.* **1** (shallow place) Untiefe, *die;* (sandbank) Sandbank, *die* **2** *in pl.* (fig.: hidden danger) Klippen

shoal² *n.* (of fish) Schwarm, *der;* (fig.) Schar, *die;* **~s of letters/complaints** Unmengen von Briefen/Beschwerden

shock¹ /ʃɒk/
A *n.* **1** Schock, *der;* **I got the ~ of my life** ich erschrak zu Tode; **the general feeling is one of ~:** man ist allgemein erschüttert; **come as a ~ to sb.** ein Schock für jmdn. sein; **give sb. a ~:** jmdm. einen Schock versetzen; **he's in for a [nasty] ~!** er wird eine böse Überraschung erleben!; **~ horror!** (joc.) Schreck, lass nach! (ugs. scherzh.); *see also* **sharp A 4** **2** (violent impact) Erschütterung, *die* (**of** durch) **3** (Electr.) Schlag, *der* **4** (Med.) Schock, *der;* **die of/be suffering from ~:** an einem Schock sterben/unter Schock[wirkung] stehen; **~ is dangerous** ein Schock kann gefährlich sein; **be in [a state of] ~:** unter Schock[wirkung] stehen; **[electric] ~:** Elektroschock, *der*
B *v.t.* **1** **~ sb. [deeply]** ein [schwerer] Schock für jmdn. sein; **sb. is [terribly] ~ed by/at sth.** etw. ist ein [schwerer] Schock für jmdn. **2** (scandalize) schockieren; **I'm not easily ~ed** mich schockiert so leicht nichts; **be ~ed by sth.** über etw. (*Akk.*) schockiert sein
C *v.i.* schockieren

shock² *n.* (of corn sheaves) Hocke, *die* (meist aus zwölf Garben)

shock³ *n.* **a ~ of red hair** ein roter Haarschopf; **an untidy ~ of thick grey hair** eine dichte graue Mähne (scherzh.)

'shock absorber *n.* Stoßdämpfer, *der*

shocker /ˈʃɒkə(r)/ *n.* (coll.) **1** **he is a ~ for gambling/drink/the girls** er ist ein hemmungsloser Zocker/Säufer/Weiberheld (salopp) **2** (novel etc.) Schocker, *der* (ugs.)

shock: ~-headed /ˈʃɒkhedɪd/ *adj.* **be ~-headed** eine Mähne haben (ugs.); **a ~-headed little boy/girl** ein kleiner Strubbelkopf (ugs.); **~-horror** *adj.* (coll.) schockierend; *attrib.* **~-horror advertising** Schockwerbung, *die*

shocking /ˈʃɒkɪŋ/
A *adj.* **1** schockierend **2** (coll.: very bad) fürchterlich (ugs.); **what a ~ thing to say** wie kann man nur so etwas sagen! (ugs.)
B *adv.* (coll.) **~ bad** fürchterlich (ugs.)

shockingly /ˈʃɒkɪŋlɪ/ *adv.* **1** (badly) schockierend [schlecht] ‹behandeln, sich benehmen› **2** (extremely) sündhaft (ugs.) ‹teuer›; erbärmlich ‹schlecht›

shocking 'pink *adj.* pinkfarben; grellrosa

shock: ~ jock *n.* (coll.) Skandal-DJ, *der;* **~proof** *adj.* stoßfest ‹Uhr, Kiste›; erschütterungsfest ‹Gebäude›; **~ tactics** *n. pl.* (Mil.) *taktischer Einsatz von Stoßtruppen;* (fig.) Überrumpelungstaktik, *die;* **~ therapy, ~ treatment** *ns.* (Med.) Schocktherapie, *die;* Schockbehandlung, *die;* **~ troops** *n. pl.* (Mil.) Stoßtruppen (veralt.); **~ wave** *n.* Druckwelle, *die* (**from** *Gen.*); (of earthquake) Erschütterungswelle, *die* (**from** *Gen.*)

shod ▸ **shoe B**

shoddily /ˈʃɒdɪlɪ/ *adv.* schludrig (ugs. abwertend); **treat sb. ~:** jmdn. schäbig behandeln (abwertend)

shoddy /ˈʃɒdɪ/
A *n.* Shoddy, *das od. der* (Textilw.); Reißwolle, *die*
B *adj.* schäbig (abwertend); (poorly done, poor in quality) minderwertig ‹Arbeit, Stoff, Artikel›

shoe /ʃuː/
A *n.* **1** Schuh, *der;* **I shouldn't like to be in his ~s** (fig.) ich möchte nicht in seiner Haut stecken (ugs.); **put oneself into sb.'s ~s** (fig.) sich in jmds. Lage (*Akk.*) versetzen; **sb. shakes in his ~s** jmdm. schlottern die Knie; **if the ~ fits** (Amer.) **= if the cap fits** ▸ **cap A 1**; *see also* **pinch C 1** **2** (of horse) [Huf]eisen, *das* **3** (of brake) Backe, *die*
B *v.t.*, **~ing** /ˈʃuːɪŋ/, **shod** /ʃɒd/ beschlagen ‹Pferd›; (protect with iron tip) beschuhen ‹Pfahl›; **be well shod** ‹Person:› gut beschuht sein

shoe: ~ bar *n.* Schnellschusterei, *die;* **~black** *n.* Schuhputzer, *der;* **~box** Schuhkarton, *der;* **~ brush** *n.* Schuhbürste, *die;* **~ buckle** *n.* Schuhschnalle, *die;* **~cream** *n.* Schuhcreme, *die;* **~horn** *n.* Schuhlöffel, *der;* **~lace** *n.* Schnürsenkel, *der;* Schuhband, *das;* **~ leather** *n.* Schuhleder, *das;* **you can save your ~ leather** den Weg kannst du dir sparen

shoeless /ˈʃuːlɪs/ *adj.* ohne Schuhe

shoe: ~maker *n.* ▸ **i p. 1260** Schuhmacher, *der;* Schuster, *der;* **~making** *n., no pl.* Schuhmacherei, *die;* **~ polish** *n.* Schuhcreme, *die;* **~ repairer** *n.* Flickschuster, *der* (veralt.); Schuster, *der;* **~shine** *n.* (Amer.) **have** *or* **get a ~shine** sich (*Dat.*) die Schuhe putzen lassen; **~shine boy** *n.* (Amer.) Schuhputzer, *der;* **~ shop** *n.* Schuhgeschäft, *das;* **~ spray** *n.* Schuhspray, *der od. das;* **~string** *n.* **1** ▸ **shoelace;** **2** (coll.: small amount) **on a ~string** mit ganz wenig Geld; *attrib.* **a ~string budget** ein minimaler Etat; **~string financing** Finanzierung mit ganz wenig Geld; **~string 'tie** *n.: wie eine Krawatte getragene, durch einen Ring oder eine Schleife gehaltene Schnur;* **~ tree** *n.* Schuhspanner, *der*

shone ▸ **shine A, B**

shoo /ʃuː/
A *int.* sch
B *v.t.* scheuchen; **~ away** fort- *od.* wegscheuchen

shook ▸ **shake B, C**

shoot /ʃuːt/
A *v.i.*, **shot** /ʃɒt/ **1** schießen (**at** auf + *Akk.*); **~ to kill** ‹Polizei:› scharf schießen; **have sth. to ~ at** (fig.) ein Ziel vor Augen *od.* eine Zielvorstellung haben; *see also* **hip¹ 1** **2** (move rapidly) schießen (ugs.); **~ past sb./down the stairs** an jmdm. vorbeischießen/die Treppe hinunterschießen (ugs.); **come ~ing in** hereingeschossen kommen (ugs.); **pain shot through/up his arm** ein Schmerz schoss durch seinen Arm/seinen Arm hinauf **3** (Bot.) austreiben

S

4 (Sport) schießen **5** (coll.: speak out) **~!** schieß los! (ugs.)

B *v.t.*, **shot** **1** (wound) anschießen; (kill) erschießen; (hunt) schießen; **~ sb. dead** jmdn. erschießen *od.* (ugs.) totschießen; **~ an animal and kill it** ein Tier tödlich treffen; **he was fatally shot in the head** ihn traf ein tödlicher Kopfschuss; **you'll get shot for this** (fig.) du kannst dein Testament machen (ugs.); **he ought to be shot** (fig.) der gehört aufgehängt (ugs.); **~ oneself in the foot** (fig. coll.) sich (*Dat.*) selbst ein Bein stellen; **stop ~ing oneself in the foot** aufhören, sich selbst Knüppel zwischen die Beine zu werfen **2** schießen mit ‹*Bogen, Munition, Pistole*›; abschießen ‹*Pfeil, Kugel*› (**at** auf + *Akk.*) **3** (sl.: inject) schießen (Drogenjargon) ‹*Heroin, Kokain*› **4** (send out) zuwerfen ‹*Lächeln, Blick*› (**at** *Dat.*); [aus]treiben ‹*Knospen, Schösslinge*›; **the volcano shot lava high into the air** der Vulkan schleuderte Lava hoch in die Luft; **~ a line** (fig. coll.) angeben (ugs.) (**about** mit); **~ the moon** (Brit. coll.) bei Nacht und Nebel abhauen (ugs.); *see also* **bolt**[1] **A 3** **5** (Sport) schießen ‹*Tor, Ball, Puck*›; (Basketball) werfen ‹*Korb*›; **~ dice** würfeln; **~ a hole in one** (Golf) ein Loch mit einem Schlag spielen; *see also* **craps** **6** (push, slide) vorschieben ‹*Riegel*›; herausziehen ‹*Manschetten*›; schütten ‹*Mehl, Kohle*› **7** (Cinemat.) drehen ‹*Film, Szene*› **8** (pass swiftly over) schießen über (+ *Akk.*) ‹*Brücke, Stromschnelle, Wasserfall*›; **~ the lights** (coll.) eine rote Ampel überfahren

C *n.* **1** (Bot.) Trieb, *der* **2** ▸**chute 1** **3** (**~ing**-party, -expedition, -practice, -land) Jagd, *die*; **a duck ~:** eine Entenjagd; **the whole [bang] ~** (coll.) der ganze Kram *od.* Krempel (ugs.)

(Phrasal verbs)

- **~ a'head** *v.i.* vorpreschen; **~ ahead of sb.** jmdn. blitzschnell hinter sich (*Dat.*) lassen
- **~ a'long** *v.i.* dahinschießen
- **~ 'down** *v.t.* abschießen ‹*Flugzeug*›; niederschießen ‹*Person*›; (fig.) entkräften ‹*Argument*›; **be shot down in flames** ‹*Flugzeug:*› in Brand geschossen werden und abstürzen; (fig.) ‹*Person, Argument:*› in der Luft zerrissen werden
- **~ 'off**

A *v.t.* abschießen ‹*Gewehr*›; **~ one's mouth off** (sl.) das Maul aufreißen (derb)

B *v.i.* losschießen (ugs.)

- **~ 'out**

A *v.i.* hervorschießen; **the dog shot out of the gate** der Hund schoss aus dem Tor heraus (ugs.)

B *v.t.* herausschleudern; **~ it out** (coll.) sich schießen; *see also* **shoot-out**

- **~ 'up**

A *v.i.* **1** in die Höhe schießen; ‹*Preise, Temperatur, Kosten, Pulsfrequenz:*› in die Höhe schnellen **2** (coll.: inject drug) sich (*Dat.*) einen Schuss setzen (ugs)

B *v.t.* herumschießen in (+ *Dat.*) (ugs.); **be badly shot up** schwer beschossen werden

shoot-'em-up /'ʃuːtəmʌp/ *n.* (coll.) **1** (film) Ballerfilm, *der* **2** (video game) Egoshooter, *der*; Ballerspiel, *das*

shooter /'ʃuːtə(r)/ *n.* (coll.: gun) Ballermann, *der* (ugs.)

shooting /'ʃuːtɪŋ/ *n.* **1** Schießerei, *die*; **new outbreaks of ~ were reported** ein erneutes Aufflammen der Schießereien wurde gemeldet; **two more ~s were reported** Meldungen zufolge wurden erneut zwei Menschen von Schüssen getroffen **2** (Sport) Schießen, *das*; **rifle ~:** Gewehrschießen, *das* **3** (Hunting) **go ~:** auf die Jagd gehen **4** (Cinemat.) Dreharbeiten *Pl.*

shooting: ~ box *n.* (Brit. Hunting) Jagdhütte, *die*; **~ brake** *n.* (Brit. Motor Veh. dated) Kombiwagen, *der*; **~ gallery** *n.* Schießstand, *der*; (at funfair) Schießbude, *die*; **~ iron** *n.* (coll.) Schießeisen, *das* (ugs.); Schießprügel, *der* (salopp); **~ match** *n.* **1** Wettschießen, *das*; **2** **the whole ~ match** (coll.) der ganze Kram *od.* Krempel (ugs. abwertend); **~ party** *n.* Jagdgesellschaft, *die*; **~ range** *n.* Schießstand, *der*; **~ spree** *n.* wilde Schießerei *od.* (ugs.) Ballerei; Schießorgie, *die*; **go on a ~ spree** losgehen und ein paar Leute erschießen *od.* (ugs.) abknallen; **~ 'star** *n.* Sternschnuppe, *die*; **~ stick** *n.* Jagdstock, *der*; **~ war** *n.* offener Krieg

'shoot-out *n.* Schießerei, *die*

shop /ʃɒp/

A *n.* **1** (premises) Laden, *der*; Geschäft, *das*; **go to the ~s** einkaufen gehen; **keep a ~:** einen Laden *od.* ein Geschäft haben; **keep [the] ~ for sb.** jmdn. im Laden *od.* Geschäft vertreten; **all over the ~** (fig. coll.) überall; **look for sth. all over the ~** (fig. coll.) in jedem Winkel nach etw. suchen; **my books are all over the ~** (fig. coll.) meine Bücher liegen wie Kraut und Rüben durcheinander (ugs.) **2** (business) **set up ~:** ein Geschäft eröffnen; (as a lawyer, dentist, etc.) eine Praxis aufmachen; **shut up ~:** das Geschäft schließen; **talk ~:** fachsimpeln (ugs.); **no [talking] ~, please!** keine Fachsimpelei, bitte! (ugs.) **3** (coll.: institution, establishment) Laden, *der* (ugs.) **4** (workshop) Werkstatt, *die*; **engineering ~:** Maschinenbauhalle, *die*; **pattern/machine ~:** Modell-/Maschinenwerkstatt, *die* **5** (action) Einkauf, *der*. *See also* **closed shop**

B *v.i.*, **-pp-** einkaufen; **go ~ping** einkaufen gehen; **~** *or* **go ~ping for shoes** Schuhe kaufen gehen

C *v.t.* **-pp-** (Brit. coll.) verpfeifen

(Phrasal verb)

- **~ a'round** *v.i.* sich umsehen (**for** nach)

shopaholic /ʃɒpə'hɒlɪk/ *n.* Kaufsüchtige, *der/die*

shop: ~ assistant *n.* ▸❶ **p. 1260** (Brit.) Verkäufer, *der*/Verkäuferin, *die*; **~ boy** *n.* Ladenbursche, *der* (veralt.); **~fitter** *n.* Ladenbauer, *der*; **firm of ~fitters** Ladenbaufirma, *die*; **~fittings** *n. pl.* Ladeneinrichtung, *die*; **~ floor** *n.* **1** (place) Produktion, *die* (ugs.); **the worker on the ~ floor** der einfache Arbeiter; **what is the feeling on the ~ floor?** was ist die Meinung der Arbeiter?; **2** (workers) **the ~ floor** die Arbeiter; *attrib.* Arbeiter-; **~ floor democracy** Demokratie am Arbeitsplatz; **~front** *n.* Schaufensterfront, *die*; **~ girl** *n.* Ladenmädchen, *das* (veralt.); **~keeper** *n.* ▸❶ **p. 1260** Ladenbesitzer, *der*/-besitzerin, *die*; **~lifter** *n.* Ladendieb, *der*/-diebin, *die*; **~lifting** *n.*, *no pl.*, *no indef. art.* Ladendiebstahl, *der*; **~owner** ▸**~keeper**

shopper /'ʃɒpə(r)/ *n.* **1** (person) Käufer, *der*/Käuferin, *die* **2** (wheeled bag) Einkaufsroller, *der*

shopping /'ʃɒpɪŋ/ *n.* **1** (buying goods) Einkaufen, *das*; **do the/one's ~:** einkaufen/[seine] Einkäufe machen **2** (items bought) Einkäufe *Pl.*

shopping: ~ bag *n.* Einkaufstasche, *die*; **~ basket** *n.* Einkaufskorb, *der*; **~ cart** *n.* (Amer.) Einkaufswagen, *der*; (personal) Einkaufsroller, *der* **~ centre** *n.* Einkaufszentrum, *das*; **~ channel** *n.* Einkaufskanal, *der*; **~ day** *n.* Einkaufstag, *der*; **~ list** *n.* Einkaufszettel, *der*; (fig.) Wunschliste, *die*; **~ mall** *n.* (esp. Amer.) Einkaufszentrum, *das*; **~ precinct** *n.* Einkaufs- *od.* Geschäftsviertel, *das*; **~ street** *n.* Geschäftsstraße, *die*; **~ trip** *n.* Einkaufsbummel, *der*; **go on a ~ trip** shoppen [gehen]; einen Einkaufsbummel machen; **~ trolley** *n.* (Brit.) Einkaufswagen, *der*; (personal) Einkaufsroller, *der*

shop: ~-soiled *adj.* (Brit.) (slightly damaged) leicht beschädigt; (slightly dirty) angeschmutzt; **~ steward** *n.* ▸❶ **p. 1260** [gewerkschaftlicher] Vertrauensmann; **~ talk** *n.*, *no pl.* Fachsimpelei, *die* (ugs.); **~walker** *n.* ▸❶ **p. 1260** (Brit.) ≈ Abteilungsleiter, *der*/-leiterin, *die*; **~ 'window** *n.* Schaufenster, *das*; **~worker** *n.* ▸❶ **p. 1260** (Brit.) Verkäufer, *der*/Verkäuferin, *die*; **~-worn** ▸**~-soiled**

shore[1] /ʃɔː(r)/ *n.* Ufer, *das*; (coast) Küste, *die*; (beach) Strand, *der*; **on the ~:** am Ufer/an der Küste/am Strand; **on the ~[s] of Lake Garda** am Ufer des Gardasees; **off ~:** vor der Küste; **a mile off [the] ~:** eine Meile vom Ufer entfernt/vor der Küste/vom Strand entfernt; **be on ~** ‹*Seemann:*› an Land sein; **these ~s** dieses Land; diese Gestade (dichter.)

shore[2]

A *n.* (prop, beam) Stützbalken, *der*; Stütze, *die*

B *v.t.* (support) abstützen ‹*Tunnel*›

(Phrasal verb)

- **~ 'up** *v.t.* (support) abstützen ‹*Mauer, Haus*›; (fig.) stützen ‹*Währung, Wirtschaft*›

shore: ~-based /'ʃɔːbeɪst/ *adj.* landgestützt ‹*Rakete*›; **~ leave** *n.* (Naut.) Landurlaub, *der*; **~line** *n.* (Geog.) Uferlinie, *die*

shoring /'ʃɔːrɪŋ/ *n.* Abstützung, *die*

shorn ▸**shear A, B**

short /ʃɔːt/

A *adj.* **1** kurz; **a ~ time** *or* **while ago/later** vor kurzem/kurze Zeit später; **for a ~ time** *or* **while** eine kleine Weile; ein [kleines] Weilchen; **a ~ time before he left** kurz bevor er ging; **a ~ time** *or* **while before/after sth.** kurz vor/nach etw. (*Dat.*); **in a ~ time** *or* **while** (soon) bald; in Kürze; **within a ~ [space of] time** innerhalb kurzer Zeit; **a few ~ years of happiness** einige wenige Jahre des Glücks; **in the ~ run** *or* **term** kurzfristig; kurzzeitig; **there is only a ~ haul ahead of us** (fig.) wir haben es bald geschafft; **wear one's hair/skirts ~:** seine Haare kurz tragen/kurze Röcke tragen; **be ~ in the arm/leg** ‹*Person:*› kurzarmig/kurzbeinig sein; ‹*Kleidungsstück:*› im Arm/Bein kurz sein; **have/get sb. by the ~ hairs** *or* (sl.) **by the ~ and curlies** jmdn. in der Hand haben/in die Hand kriegen (ugs.); **~ back and sides** kurzer Haarschnitt; **make ~ work of sb./sth.** mit jmdm./etw. kurzen Prozess machen (ugs.); **he made ~ work of the puzzle** er hatte das Rätsel im Handumdrehen gelöst; *see also* **neck A 2**; **notice A 2**; **range A 4**; **shrift**; **straw 2**

2 (not tall) klein ‹*Person, Wuchs*›; niedrig ‹*Gebäude, Baum, Schornstein*›

3 (not far-reaching) kurz ‹*Wurf, Schuss, Gedächtnis*›; **take a ~ view of things** kurzsichtig sein

4 (deficient, scanty) knapp; **be in ~ supply** knapp sein; **good doctors are in ~ supply** gute Ärzte sind rar *od.* (ugs.) sind Mangelware; **give sb. ~ weight** jmdn. beim Abwiegen übervorteilen; (inadvertently) sich zu jmds. Ungunsten beim Abwiegen versehen; **be [far/not far] ~ of a record** einen Rekord [bei weitem] nicht erreichen/[knapp] verfehlen; **his jump was 4 cm. ~ of the record** sein Sprung verfehlte den Rekord um 4 cm; **sb./sth. is so much/so many ~:** jmdm./einer Sache fehlt soundso viel/fehlen soundso viele; **sb. is ~ of sth.** jmdm. fehlt es an etw. (*Dat.*); **he is [rather] ~ on talent** er ist nicht besonders talentiert; **time is getting/is ~:** die Zeit wird/ist knapp; **the poor harvest has left them ~ of food** wegen der schlechten Ernte fehlt es ihnen an Nahrung; **don't leave yourself ~ [of money/food]** pass auf, dass du selbst noch genug [Geld/zu essen] hast; **keep sb. ~ [of sth.]** jmdn. [mit etw.] kurz halten; **[have to] go ~ [of sth.]** [an etw. (*Dat.*)] Mangel leiden [müssen]; **she is ~ of milk today** sie hat heute nicht genug Milch; **the firm is ~ of staff** die Firma hat zu wenig Arbeitskräfte; **be ~ [of cash]** knapp [bei Kasse] sein (ugs.); **be ~ of sth.** ‹*Preis, Temperatur, Leistung usw.:*› unter etw. (*Dat.*) liegen; **he is just ~ of six feet/not far ~ of 60** er ist knapp sechs Fuß [groß]/sechzig [Jahre alt]; **a few inches ~ of the line** nur wenige Zoll vor der Linie; **she is three months ~ of retirement** sie steht 3 Monate vor ihrer Pensionierung; **be still far ~ of one's target** von seinem Ziel noch weit entfernt sein; **his behaviour has been little** *or* **not far ~ of criminal** sein Verhalten war beinahe kriminell; **if it was not fraud, it was not far ~ of it** wenn es auch kein ausgesprochener Betrug war, so war es doch nicht weit davon entfernt; **it is nothing ~ of miraculous** es ist ein ausgesprochenes Wunder; *see also* **hundredweight 3**; **measure A 1**; **ration A 1**; **run B 12**; **ton 1**

5 (brief, concise) kurz; **a ~ history of Wales** eine kurz gefasste Geschichte von Wales; **the ~ answer is ...:** um es kurz zu machen: die Antwort ist ...; **~ and sweet** (iron.) kurz und schmerzlos (ugs.); **~ and to the point** kurz und geradeheraus (ugs.) *od.* direkt; **something ~** (drink) ein Schnaps; **in ~, ...:** kurz, ... ; **his name is Robert, [but he is called] Bob for ~:** er heißt Robert, [wird aber] kurz Bob [genannt]; **Dick is ~ for Richard** Dick ist eine

S

Kurzform von Richard *od.* kurz für Richard
6 (curt, uncivil) kurz angebunden; barsch
7 (Cookery) mürbe ‹*Teig*›
8 (Pros., Phonet.) kurz
9 (St. Exch.) ~ **sale** Leerverkauf, *der;* **make a ~ sale** fixen; **sell sth. ~:** etw. leer verkaufen; **sell oneself ~** (fig.) sein Licht unter den Scheffel stellen; **sell sb./sth. ~** (fig.) jmdn./etw. unterschätzen
10 (Cricket) *relativ nahe beim Schlagmann* [*stehend*]; ~ **ball** kurzer Ball
11 (cards) ~ **suit** kurze Farbe
B *adv.* **1** (abruptly) plötzlich; **stop ~:** plötzlich abbrechen; ‹*Musik, Gespräch:*› jäh (geh.) abbrechen; **stop ~ at sth.** über etw. (*Akk.*) nicht hinausgehen; **stop sb. ~:** jmdm. ins Wort fallen; **pull up ~:** plötzlich anhalten; **bring** *or* **pull sb. up ~:** jmdn. stutzen lassen; *see also* **cut A 3**
2 (curtly) kurz angebunden; barsch
3 (before the expected place or time) **jump/land ~:** zu kurz springen/zu früh landen (ugs.); **~ of sth.** vor etw. (*Dat.*); **stop ~ of the line** vor der Linie stehen/liegen bleiben; **the bomb dropped/landed ~ [of its target]** die Bombe fiel vor das/landete (ugs.) vor dem Ziel; **fall** *or* **come ~** (fig.) ‹*Leistung, Vorstellung usw.:*› enttäuschen; **fall** *or* **come [far/considerably] ~ of sth.** etw. [bei weitem] nicht erreichen; **stop ~ of sth.** (fig.) nicht so weit gehen, etw. zu tun; **stop ~ of doing sth.** davor zurückschrecken, etw. zu tun; **be caught** *or* **taken ~** (at a disadvantage) in Bedrängnis geraten; (coll.: need to go to toilet) plötzlich dringend müssen (fam.)
4 **nothing ~ of a catastrophe/miracle can …:** nur eine Katastrophe/ein Wunder kann …; **~ of locking him in, how can I keep him from going out?** wie kann ich ihn daran hindern auszugehen — es sei denn ich schlösse ihn ein?
C *n.* **1** (Electr. coll.) Kurze, *der* (ugs.)
2 (coll.: drink) Schnaps, *der* (ugs.)
3 (Cinemat.) Kurzfilm, *der. See also* **long[1] B 2; shorts**
D *v.t.* (Electr. coll.) kurzschließen
E *v.i.* (Electr. coll.) einen Kurzschluss kriegen (ugs.)

shortage /ˈʃɔːtɪdʒ/ *n.* Mangel, *der* (**of** an + *Dat.*); ~ **of fruit/teachers** Obstknappheit, *die*/Lehrermangel, *der*

short: ~**arse** *n.* (coll. derog.) Zwerg, *der;* ~**bread** *n.* Shortbread, *das; Kekse aus Butterteig;* ~**cake** *n.* **1** ▸ ~**bread; 2** (cake served with fruit) *Obstkuchen mit Mürbeteigboden;* **a strawberry ~cake** ein Erdbeerkuchen aus Mürbeteig; ~-ˈ**change** *v.t.* zu wenig [Wechselgeld] herausgeben (+ *Dat.*); (fig.) übers Ohr hauen (ugs.); prellen; ~ ˈ**circuit** *n.* (Electr.) Kurzschluss, *der;* ~-ˈ**circuit** (Electr.) **A** *v.t.* kurzschließen; (fig.) umgehen; **B** *v.i.* einen Kurzschluss bekommen; ~**coming** *n., usu. in pl.* Unzulänglichkeit, *die;* **he has only one ~coming** er hat nur einen Fehler; ~ ˈ**commons** *n. pl.* (arch.) **be on ~ commons** zu wenig zu essen haben; ~**crust** *n.* ~**crust [pastry]** Mürbeteig, *der;* ~ ˈ**cut** *n.* **1** Abkürzung, *die;* **take a ~ cut** (lit. or fig.) eine Abkürzung machen; **be a ~ cut to sth.** (fig.) den Weg zu etw. abkürzen; **there is no ~ cut to success** (fig.) der Weg zum Erfolg lässt sich nicht abkürzen; **2** (Computing) **[keyboard] ~cut** Shortcut, *der;* ~ **division** ▸ **division 7;** ~ ˈ**drink** *n.* hochprozentiges Getränk; **have a ~ drink** etwas Hochprozentiges trinken

shorten /ˈʃɔːtn/
A *v.i.* **1** (become shorter) kürzer werden
2 (decrease) sich verkleinern; ‹*Preis, Gewinnquote:*› sinken
B *v.t.* **1** (make shorter) kürzen; (curtail) verkürzen ‹*Besuch, Wartezeit, Inkubationszeit*› **2** (decrease) senken; reduzieren; ~ **sail** (Naut.) die Segel reffen **3** (Cookery) mürbe machen

shortening /ˈʃɔːtnɪŋ/ *n.* **1** (making shorter) [Ver]kürzung, *die;* (growing shorter) Kürzerwerden, *das* **2** (Cookery) Ziehfett, *das* (*zum Mürbemachen des Teigs*)

short: ~**fall** *n.* Fehlmenge, *die;* (in budget, financial resources) Defizit, *das;* ~-**haired** *adj.* kurzhaarig; Kurzhaar‹*dackel, -katze*›; ~**hand** *n.* Kurzschrift, *die;* Stenografie, *die;* **write ~hand** stenografieren; ~**hand writer** Stenograf, *der*/Stenografin, *die;* **that's ~hand for …** (fig.) das ist eine Kurzformel für …; *see also* **typist;** ~-**handed** /ʃɔːtˈhændɪd/ *adj.* zu klein ‹*Team*›; **we are terribly ~-handed** wir haben furchtbar wenig Leute; ~ **haul** *n.* Kurzstreckentransport, *der;* [Güter]nahtransport, *der;* ~-**haul** *adj.* Kurzstrecken‹*flug, -flugzeug*›; ‹*Lastwagen, Bus*› für den Nahverkehr; ~-**haul route** Kurzstrecke, *die;* ~-**haul transport** Güternahverkehr, *der;* ~ ˈ**head** *n.* (Brit. Horse-racing) kurzer Kopf (fachspr.); **win by a ~ head** mit einem kurzen Kopf Vorsprung gewinnen; **win an election by a ~ head** eine Wahl knapp gewinnen; ~**hold** *adj.* kurzzeitig ‹*Mietverhältnis*›; ~**horn** *n.* (Agric.) Shorthornrind, *das; attrib.* Shorthorn-

shortie /ˈʃɔːtɪ/ *n.* (coll.) **1** ▸ **shorty 1 2** (garment) Shorty, *das;* ~ **nightdress/dress** kurzes Nachthemd/kurzes Kleid

shortish /ˈʃɔːtɪʃ/ *adj.* ziemlich kurz; ziemlich klein ‹*Person*›

short: ~-**legged** *adj.* kurzbeinig; ~**list** *n.* (Brit.) engere Auswahl; **be on/put sb. on the ~list** in der engeren Auswahl sein/jmdn. in die engere Auswahl nehmen; ~-**list** *v.t.* in die engere Auswahl nehmen; ~-**lived** /ˈʃɔːtlɪvd/ *adj.* kurzlebig

shortly /ˈʃɔːtlɪ/ *adv.* **1** (soon) in Kürze; demnächst; ~ **before/after sth.** kurz vor/nach etw.; ~ **before/after arriving, he phoned us** kurz vor/nach seiner Ankunft rief er uns an; (outside cinema, theatre) **'coming ~'** „demnächst"; „Voranzeige" **2** (briefly) kurz **3** (curtly) kurz angebunden; in barschem Ton

shortness /ˈʃɔːtnɪs/ *n., no pl.* **1** (short extent or duration) Kürze, *die;* **despite the ~ of his life** trotz seines kurzen Lebens **2** (smallness of person) Kleinheit, *die;* geringe Körpergröße **3** (scarcity, lack) Knappheit, *die* (**of** an + *Dat.*); ~ **of breath** Kurzatmigkeit **4** (briefness) Kürze, *die* **5** (curtness) Barschheit, *die* **6** (of pastry) Mürbheit, *die*

short: ~ ˈ**odds** *n. pl.* (Racing, also fig.) **it's/I would give you ~ odds on X winning** es ist so gut wie sicher, dass X gewinnt; ~ ˈ**order** *n.* (Amer.) **1** (for food) Schnellgericht, *das;* **2** **in ~ order** auf der Stelle; ~-**order** *adj.* (Amer.) Schnell-; ~-**order counter** Selbstbedienungsbüfett, *das;* ~ ˈ**pastry** *n.* (Cookery) Mürbeteig, *der;* ~-**range** *adj.* **1** (with ~ range) Kurzstrecken‹*flugzeug, -rakete usw.*›; **2** (relating to ~ future period) kurzfristig

shorts /ʃɔːts/ *n. pl.* **1** (trousers) kurze Hose[n]; Shorts *Pl.;* (in sports) Sporthose, *die;* **football ~:** Fußballshorts **2** (Amer.: underpants) Unterhose, *die*

short: ~ ˈ**sight** *n., no pl., no art.* Kurzsichtigkeit, *die;* **have ~ sight** kurzsichtig sein; ~-**sighted** /ʃɔːtˈsaɪtɪd/ *adj.,* ~-**sightedly** /ʃɔːtˈsaɪtɪdlɪ/ *adv.* (lit. or fig.) kurzsichtig; ~-**sightedness** /ʃɔːtˈsaɪtɪdnɪs/ *n., no pl.* (lit. or fig.) Kurzsichtigkeit, *die;* ~-**sleeved** /ˈʃɔːtsliːvd/ *adj.* kurzärm[e]lig; ~-**sleeved shirt** Kurzarmhemd, *das;* ~ ˈ**sleeves** *n. pl.* kurze Ärmel; ~-**staffed** /ʃɔːtˈstɑːft/ *adj.* **be [very] ~-staffed** [viel] zu wenig Personal haben; ~ **stop** *n.* (Baseball) **1** *no pl., no art.* (position) Shortstopposition, *die;* **2** (player) Shortstop, *der;* ~ ˈ**story** *n.* (Lit.) Short Story, *die;* Kurzgeschichte, *die;* ~ ˈ**suit** *n.* (Cards) kurze Farbe; **have a ~ suit in hearts** wenig Herz haben; ~ ˈ**temper** *n.* aufbrausendes *od.* cholerisches Temperament; **have a ~ temper** aufbrausend *od.* cholerisch sein; ~-ˈ**tempered** *adj.* aufbrausend; cholerisch; **be ~-tempered with sb.** ungehalten zu jmdm. sein; ~-**term** *adj.* kurzfristig; (provisional) vorläufig ‹*Lösung, Antwort*›; ~ ˈ**time** *n.* (Industry) Kurzarbeit, *die;* **be on** *or* **work ~ time** kurzarbeiten; ~-**time** *adj.* ~-**time working** Kurzarbeit, *die;* ~ ˈ**title** *n.* Kurztitel, *der;* ~ ˈ**trousers** *n. pl.* kurze Hose[n]; ~ ˈ**wave** *n.* (Radio) Kurzwelle, *die;* ~-**wave** *adj.* (Radio) Kurzwellen-; ~-**winded** /ʃɔːtˈwɪndɪd/ *adj.* kurzatmig

shorty /ˈʃɔːtɪ/ *n.* (coll.) **1** (person) Kleine, *der/die* (ugs.); **he/she is a ~:** er ist so'n Kleiner/sie ist so'ne Kleine (ugs.) **2** ▸ **shortie 2**

shot /ʃɒt/
A *n.* **1** *pl. same* (single projectile for cannon or gun) Geschoss, *das;* Kugel, *die* (ugs.); *collect.* Munition, *die* **2** (Athletics) Kugel, *die;* **put the ~:** die Kugel stoßen; kugelstoßen; **[putting] the ~:** Kugelstoßen, *das* **3** *pl. same* (lead pellet) [Schrot]kugel, *die; collect.* Schrot, *der od. das; see also* **lead shot** **4** (discharge of gun) Schuss, *der;* (firing of rocket) Abschuss, *der;* Start, *der;* **the ~ had gone home** (fig.) das hatte gesessen (ugs.); **fire a ~ [at sb./sth.]** einen Schuss [auf jmdn./etw.] abgeben; **like a ~** (fig.) wie der Blitz (ugs.); **I'd do it like a ~:** ich würde es auf der Stelle tun; **call the ~s** (fig.) das Sagen haben (ugs.); **let sb. call the ~s** nach jmds. Pfeife tanzen (ugs.); **have a ~ at sth./at doing sth.** (fig.) etw. versuchen/versuchen, etw. zu tun; **the answer is not correct, but it is a good ~:** die Antwort ist nicht richtig, aber es war [für den Anfang] schon ganz gut (ugs.); *see also* **dark B 3; long shot; Parthian shot; parting B; snap shot** **5** (Sport: stroke, kick, throw) Schuss, *der;* (Archery, Shooting) Schuss, *der* **6** (Photog.) Aufnahme, *die;* (Cinemat.) Einstellung, *die;* **do** *or* **film interior/exterior/location ~s** (Cinemat.) Innenaufnahmen machen/Außenaufnahmen machen/am Originalschauplatz drehen; **out of/in ~** (Photog.) außerhalb des Bildes/im Bild **7** (person who shoots in specified way) Schütze, *der* **8** (injection) Spritze, *die;* (of drug) Schuss, *der* (Jargon); **be a ~ in the arm for sb./sth.** (fig.) jmdm./einer Sache Aufschwung geben **9** (coll.: dram of spirits) Schluck, *der* (fig.); **a ~ of whisky/rum** *etc.* ein Schluck Whisky/Rum *usw*
B *v.t. & i.* ▸ **shoot A, B**
C *adj.* **1** (iridescent) durchschossen; ~ **[through] with sth.** mit etw. durchschossen; **hair ~ with grey** grau meliertes Haar **2** **get ~ of sb./sth.** (coll.) jmdn./etw. loswerden; **I wish I could get ~ of him** ich würde ihn am liebsten auf den Mond schießen (salopp) **3** (coll.) **be ~** (exhausted, finished) im Eimer sein (salopp); **my nerves are ~ [to pieces]** ich bin mit den Nerven [völlig] fertig (ugs.)

shot: ~-**blasting** /ˈʃɒtblɑːstɪŋ/ *n.* Kugelstrahlen, *das* (Technik); ~-**firer** /ˈʃɒtfaɪərə(r)/ *n.* Sprengmeister, *der;* Schießmeister, *der;* ~**gun** *n.* [Schrot]flinte, *die; attrib.* ~**gun wedding/marriage** (fig. coll.) Mussheirat/Mussehe, *die* (ugs.); **ride ~gun** zur Bewachung als Beifahrer mitfahren; ~-**put** *n., no pl., no indef. art.* (Athletics) Kugelstoßen, *das;* ~-**putter** /ˈʃɒtpʊtə(r)/ *n.* (Athletics) Kugelstoßer, *der*/-stoßerin, *die*

should ▸ **❶ p. 1535, shall**

shoulder /ˈʃəʊldə(r)/
A *n.* **1** ▸ **❶ p. 951** Schulter, *die;* ~ **to ~** (lit. or fig.) Schulter an Schulter; **put** *or* **set one's ~ to the wheel** (fig.) sich ins Geschirr legen; **straight from the ~** (fig.) unverblümt; **cry on sb.'s ~** (fig.) sich bei jmdm. ausweinen; **give sb. the cold ~ :** jmdn. schneiden; **get the cold ~ from sb.** von jmdm. geschnitten werden; *see also* **chip A 1; head A 1; rub A 1** **2** *in pl.* (upper part of back) Schultern *Pl.;* (of garment) Schulterpartie, *die;* **lie** *or* **rest/fall on sb.'s ~s** (fig.) auf jmds. Schultern (*Dat.*) lasten/jmdm. aufgebürdet werden; **he has broad ~s** (fig.: is able to take responsibility) er hat einen breiten Rücken; **have** *or* **be an old head on young ~s** (fig.) reif für sein Alter sein; **have a good head on one's ~s** (fig.) Köpfchen haben (ugs.) **3** ▸ ~ **joint 1** **4** (Gastr.) Bug, *der;* Schulter, *die;* ~ **of lamb/veal** Lamm-/Kalbsschulter, *die* **5** (Road Constr.) Randstreifen, *der;* Seitenstreifen, *der; see also* **hard shoulder**
B *v.t.* **1** (push with ~) rempeln; ~ **one's way through the crowd** sich rempelnd einen Weg durch die Menge bahnen **2** (take on one's ~s) schultern; (fig.) übernehmen ‹*Verantwortung, Aufgabe*›; auf sich (*Akk.*) nehmen ‹*Schuld, Bürde*›; ~ **arms** (Mil.) das Gewehr schultern

Phrasal verb

• ~ **aˈside** *v.t.* beiseite rempeln; (fig.) beiseite schieben

shoulder: ~ **bag** *n.* Umhängetasche, *die;* ~ **belt** *n.* Schulterband, *das;* ~ **blade** *n.*

S

ℹ Should

Conditional

In the first person singular and plural, *should* is used for *would* to form the conditional, and so is translated by the conditional in German:

I should be surprised if he wins
= Es würde mich wundern, wenn er gewänne

I should have gone if I had been invited
= Ich wäre gegangen, wenn ich eingeladen gewesen wäre

I should have thought it was obvious
= Ich hätte gedacht, es liegt auf der Hand

We should welcome more opportunity for contact
= Wir würden es begrüßen, wenn wir mehr Kontakt-möglichkeiten hätten

We should like to help you
= Wir möchten Ihnen helfen

Where *should* occurs in the conditional clause (with any person), the translation is **sollte, sollten** etc., and like the English *should* this can stand at the beginning of the clause:

If they should be delayed or ***Should they be delayed, ...***
= Falls sie aufgehalten werden sollten *or* Sollten sie aufgehalten werden, ...

Should he turn up after all, let me know
= Sollte er doch noch auftauchen, sagen Sie mir Bescheid

Meaning *ought to*

In most cases expressing obligation, this is also translated by **sollte** (and **hätte sollen** in the past):

You should tell her
= Du solltest es ihr sagen

They shouldn't really be here
= Eigentlich sollten *or* dürften sie nicht hier sein

We should have gone earlier
= Wir hätten früher hingehen sollen

He shouldn't have come
= Er hätte nicht kommen sollen

Note that unlike *should*, **sollte** does not normally stand on its own:

I don't think you should
= Ich finde, du solltest es nicht tun

With an impersonal subject, **müsste** is used.

It should be banned
= Das müsste man verbieten

Also expressing a surmise or estimate, **dürfte** or **müsste** can be used:

They should be there by now
= Jetzt dürften *or* müssten sie dort angekommen sein

That should be enough
= Das dürfte *or* müsste genügen

That should have been enough
= Das hätte genügen müssen

After *that*

In clauses beginning with *that* preceded by an adjective, the *should* is not translated:

It is strange that he should never have told you
= Es ist seltsam, dass er es dir nie gesagt hat

It is important that they should be warned
= Es ist wichtig, dass sie gewarnt werden

Much the same applies to clauses with *in order that* or *so that*:

She gave me a cushion in order that or ***so that I should sit more comfortably***
= Sie gab mir ein Kissen, damit ich bequemer saß

In order that they should all be able to hear, I used a megaphone
= Damit sie alle hören konnten, verwendete ich ein Megaphon

Schulterblatt, *das;* ~ **charge** *n.* Schulterrempler, *der;* **~-charge** *v.t.* [mit der Schulter] rempeln; **~-charge a door** die Schulter gegen die Tür rammen

-shouldered /ˈʃəʊldəd/ *adj. in comb.* -schult[e]rig; **square-/straight-~:** mit eckigen/geraden Schultern *nachgestellt*

shoulder: ~-high **A** /ˈ---/ *adj.* schulterhoch; **B** /--ˈ-/ *adv.* **lift/carry sb. ~-high** jmdn. auf die Schultern heben/auf den Schultern tragen; **they carried him through the streets, ~-high** sie trugen ihn auf den Schultern durch die Straßen; ~ **holster** *n.* Schulterhalfter, *die;* ~ **joint** *n.* **1** (Anat.) Schultergelenk, *das;* **2** (Gastr.) Schulterstück, *das;* Bugstück, *das;* **~-length** *adj.* schulterlang; ~ **pad** *n.* Schulterpolster, *das;* ~ **strap** *n.* **1** (on ~ of garment) Schulterklappe, *die;* **2** (on bag) Tragriemen, *der;* (suspending a garment) Träger, *der*

shouldn't /ˈʃʊdnt/ (coll.) = **should not;** ▸**shall**

shout /ʃaʊt/

A *n.* **1** Ruf, *der;* (inarticulate) Schrei, *der;* **warning ~, ~ of alarm** Warnruf, *der*/-schrei, *der;* **~ of joy/rage** Freuden-/Wutschrei, *der;* **~ of encouragement/approval** Anfeuerungs-/Beifallsruf, *der;* **give sb. a ~:** jmdn. rufen; (fig. coll.: let sb. know) jmdm. Bescheid sagen **2** (coll.: turn to pay for drinks) Runde, *die;* **stand sb. a ~:** jmdm. einen ausgeben (ugs.)

B *v.i.* **1** schreien; **~ with laughter/pain** vor Lachen/Schmerzen schreien; **~ with** *or* **for joy** vor Freude schreien; **~ at sb.** (be loudly abusive to sb.) jmdn. anschreien; **you don't have to ~ [at me] — I can hear you** Du brauchst nicht zu schreien. Ich höre dich auch so; **don't ~!** schrei nicht so!; **she ~ed for him to come** sie schrie *od.* rief, er solle kommen; **he ~ed to me to be careful/help him** er schrie *od.* rief mir zu, ich solle vorsichtig sein/ihm helfen; **~ for sb./sth.** nach jmdm./etw. schreien; **~ for help** um Hilfe schreien *od.* rufen; **it's nothing to ~ about** (fig.) darauf braucht er/sie/man *usw.* sich (*Dat.*) nichts einzubilden **2** (Austral. and NZ coll.: stand drinks etc.) einen ausgeben (ugs.) (**for** *Dat.*)

C *v.t.* **1** schreien; **~ abuse at sb.** jmdn. anpöbeln; **~ oneself hoarse** sich heiser schreien **2** (Austral. and NZ coll.) **~ a drink/a beer for sb., ~ sb. to a drink/a beer** jmdm. einen/ein Bier ausgeben (ugs.)

Phrasal verbs

- **~ 'down** *v.t.* **1** runterrufen **2** **~ sb. down** (prevent from being heard) jmdn. niederschreien
- **~ 'out**

A *v.i.* aufschreien; **if you know the answer, don't ~ out — wait till ...:** wenn ihr die Antwort wisst, schreit nicht einfach los — wartet, bis ...

B *v.t.* [laut] rufen; schreien

shouting /ˈʃaʊtɪŋ/

A *adj.* schreiend

B *n.* (act) Schreien, *das;* Schreierei, *die* (abwertend); (shouts) Geschrei, *das;* **it's all over but** *or* **bar the ~** (fig.) das Rennen ist im Grunde schon gelaufen (ugs.)

shove /ʃʌv/

A *n.* Stoß, *der;* **little ~:** Schubs, *der* (ugs.); **a ~ with one's foot** ein Tritt [mit dem Fuß]; ein Fußtritt; **get the ~** (coll.) rausfliegen (ugs.); **give sb. the ~** (coll.) jmdn. rausschmeißen (ugs.)

B *v.t.* **1** stoßen; schubsen (ugs.) **2** (use force to propel) schieben **3** (coll.: put) tun. *See also* **throat 1**

C *v.i.* drängen; drängeln (ugs.); **~ past the vehicles/through the crowd** (coll.) sich an den Fahrzeugen vorbei/durch die Menge drängeln (ugs.). *See also* **push B 1, C 4**

Phrasal verbs

- **~ a'bout** ▸ **~ around**
- **~ a'long** (coll.)

A *v.t.* schieben

B *v.i.* sich vorwärts schieben; (fig. coll.: depart) abschieben (ugs.)

- **~ a'round** *v.t.* (coll.) herumschieben; (fig.) herumschubsen (ugs.)
- **~ a'way** *v.t.* (coll.) wegschubsen (ugs.)
- **~ 'off**

A *v.t.* (coll.) **1** (away) wegschubsen (ugs.) **2** (down) runterschubsen (ugs.)

B *v.i.* **1** (coll.: move boat from shore) abstoßen **2** (coll.: depart) abschieben (ugs.)

- **~ 'over** (coll.)

A *v.t.* rüberschieben (ugs.)

B *v.i.* rüberrücken (ugs.)

- **~ 'past** *v.i.* (coll.) sich vorbeidrängeln *od.* -quetschen (ugs.)

shove-'halfpenny *n.: Spiel, bei dem Münzen in die Felder des Spielbretts gestoßen werden müssen*

shovel /ˈʃʌvl/

A *n.* **1** (implement, part of machine) Schaufel, *die;* (machine) Bagger, *der; see also* **spade 1** **2** (quantity) ▸**shovelful**

B *v.t.,* (Brit.) **-ll-** **1** schaufeln **2** (fig.) **~ food into one's mouth** Essen in sich reinschaufeln *od.* -stopfen (ugs.)

shovelful /ˈʃʌvlfʊl/ *n.* **a ~ of earth** *etc.* eine Schaufel Erde *usw.;* **~s of earth** schaufelweise Erde

show /ʃəʊ/

A *n.* **1** (act of making visible) Zeigen, *das;* **without any ~ of anger/emotion/grief** ohne jedes Zeichen des Ärgers/von Gefühl/der Trauer; **~ of generosity** Geste der Großzügigkeit; **~ of knowledge** Zurschaustellung von Wissen; **make a ~ of sth.** etw. zur Schau stellen; **~ of force/strength** *etc.* Demonstration der Macht/Stärke *usw.*

2 (display) Pracht, *die;* (spectacle, pageant) Schauspiel, *das* (geh.); **a ~ of flowers/colour** eine Blumen-/Farbenpracht; **the trees make a wonderful ~:** die Bäume entfalten eine wunderbare Pracht; **be on ~:** ausgestellt sein; **put sth. on ~:** etw. ausstellen

3 (exhibition) Ausstellung, *die;* Schau, *die;* **dog ~:** Hundeschau, *die;* **~ animal** ausgestelltes Tier

4 (entertainment, performance) Show, *die;* (Theatre) Vorstellung, *die;* (Radio, Telev.) [Unterhaltungs-]sendung, *die;* **summer ~:** Sommerprogramm, *das;* **the ~ must go on** die Show geht weiter; (fig.) das Leben geht weiter; *see also* **steal A 1; stop A 2**

5 (coll.: effort) **that's a very good ~:** das kann sich sehen lassen; **it's a poor ~:** das ist ein schwaches Bild; **put up a good/poor ~:** eine gute/schlechte Figur machen; **good ~!** gut [gemacht]!; **bad** *or* **poor ~!** schwaches Bild!

6 (coll.: undertaking, business) **it's his ~:** er ist der Boss (ugs.); **who is running this ~?** wer ist hier der Boss? (ugs.); **give the [whole] ~ away** alles ausquatschen (salopp); *see also* **run C 3**

7 (outward appearance) Anschein, *der;* **make a great ~ of friendliness** ungeheuer freundlich tun; **make** *or* **put on a [great] ~ of doing sth.** sich (*Dat.*) [angestrengt] den Anschein geben,

etw. zu tun; **she puts on a brave ~ of being able to cope** sie gibt sich (*Dat.*) tapfer den Anschein, als käme sie immer gut zurecht; **be for ~:** reine Angeberei sein (ugs.); **do sth. just for ~:** etw. nur aus Prestigegründen tun
8 (pomp) **the pomp and ~ of great State occasions** der Pomp und Prunk großer Staatsakte
9 (Med.: discharge) (at onset of labour) *leichte Blutung als erstes Anzeichen der beginnenden Geburt;* (*at beginning of menstrual period*) *Vorzeichen der beginnenden Menstruation*

B *v.t., p.p.* **~n** /ʃəʊn/ *or* **~ed** **1** (allow or cause to be seen) zeigen; (produce) vorzeigen ‹*Pass, Fahrschein usw.*›; **~ one's cards** *or* **hand** (Cards) seine Karten aufdecken; (fig.: reveal one's intentions) die Karten auf den Tisch legen; **have nothing/something to ~ for it** [dabei] nichts/etwas zum Vorzeigen haben; *see also* **cause A 3; face A 1; feather A 1; flag[1] A; tooth 1**
2 (reveal, disclose) zeigen; **~ sb. sth., ~ sth. to sb.** jmdm. etw. zeigen; **~ me an A and I will ~ you a B** jedes A ist ein B; **that dress ~s your petticoat** bei diesem Kleid sieht man deinen Unterrock; **this material does not ~ the dirt** auf diesem Material sieht man den Schmutz nicht; **~ oneself** sich zeigen; **~ itself** (become visible) zum Vorschein kommen; (reveal itself) sich zeigen; erkennbar sein; **~ itself at its best/in all its glory** sich von der besten Seite/in all seiner Herrlichkeit zeigen; **the task has been ~n to be difficult** die Aufgabe hat sich als schwierig erwiesen; **this episode ~s him to be honest/a liar** dieser Vorfall zeigt, dass er ehrlich/ein Lügner ist; **~ oneself/itself to be sth.** sich als etw. erweisen; *see also* **heel[1] A 1; colour A 8; sign A 5**
3 (manifest, give evidence of) zeigen; beweisen ‹*Mut, Entschlossenheit, Urteilsvermögen usw.*›; **~ hesitation** zaudern; **he is ~ing his age** man sieht ihm sein Alter an; *see also* **fight C 3; mettle 1; willing B**
4 **~ [sb.] kindness/mercy** freundlich [zu jmdm.] sein/Erbarmen [mit jmdm.] haben; **~ mercy on** *or* **to sb.** Erbarmen mit jmdm. haben
5 (indicate) zeigen ‹*Gefühl, Freude usw.*›; ‹*Thermometer, Uhr usw.:*› anzeigen; **as ~n in the illustration** wie die Abbildung zeigt; **frontiers are ~n by blue lines and towns are ~n in red** Grenzen sind durch blaue Linien und Städte sind rot gekennzeichnet; **the accounts ~ a profit** die Bücher weisen einen Gewinn aus; **the firm ~s a profit/loss** die Firma macht Gewinn/Verlust
6 (offer for viewing) zeigen; (exhibit in a show) ausstellen
7 (demonstrate, prove) zeigen; **~ sb. that ...:** jmdm. beweisen, dass ...; **it all/just goes to ~ that ...:** das beweist nur, dass ...; **it all goes to ~, doesn't it?** das beweist es doch, oder?; **I'll ~ you/him** *etc.***!** ich werds dir/ihm *usw.* schon zeigen!; **~ sb. who's boss** jmdm. zeigen, wer das Sagen hat; *see also* **door**
8 (conduct) führen; **~ sb. over the house/to his place** jmdn. durchs Haus/an seinen Platz führen

C *v.i., p.p.* **~n** *or* **~ed** **1** (be visible) sichtbar *od.* zu sehen sein; (come into sight) sich zeigen; zum Vorschein kommen; **he was angry/bored, and it ~ed** er war wütend/langweilte sich, und man sah es [ihm an]; **his age is beginning to ~:** man sieht ihm sein Alter allmählich an; **your slip is ~ing** dein Unterrock guckt raus
2 (coll.: arrive) sich blicken lassen (ugs.); auftauchen
3 (be shown) ‹*Film:*› laufen; ‹*Künstler:*› ausstellen; **'Gandhi' — now ~ing in the West End** „Gandhi" — Jetzt im West End
4 (make sth. known) **time will ~:** man wird es [ja] sehen; **only time will ~:** das wird sich erst im Laufe der Zeit herausstellen
5 (Amer. Horseracing) sich [unter den ersten drei] platzieren

Phrasal verbs
- **~ 'in** *v.t.* hineinführen/hereinführen
- **~ 'off**

A *v.t.* **1** (display) **~ sth./sb. off** etw./jmdn. vorführen *od.* vorzeigen; (in order to impress) mit etw./jmdm. prahlen *od.* (ugs.) angeben **2** (display to advantage) zur Geltung bringen
B *v.i.* angeben (ugs.); prahlen; *see also* **show-off**
- **~ 'out** *v.t.* hinausführen
- **~ 'round** *v.t.* herumführen
- **~ 'through** *v.i.* durchscheinen
- **~ 'up**

A *v.t.* **1** (conduct upstairs) hinaufführen/heraufführen **2** (make visible) deutlich sichtbar machen; aufdecken ‹*Betrug*›; **this incident has ~n him up as** *or* **for a coward** *or* **to be a coward** dieser Vorfall hat gezeigt, dass er [in Wirklichkeit *od.* eigentlich] ein Feigling ist **3** (coll.: embarrass) blamieren
B *v.i.* **1** (be easily visible) [deutlich] zu sehen *od.* erkennen sein; (fig.) sich zeigen; **it will not ~ up on the photocopy** das kommt auf der Fotokopie nicht heraus **2** (coll.: arrive) sich blicken lassen (ugs.); auftauchen

show: ~ biz (coll.), **~ business** *ns., no pl., no art.* Schaugeschäft, *das;* Showbusiness, *das;* **~ business personalities/connections** Persönlichkeiten aus dem/Verbindungen zum Schaugeschäft *od.* Showbusiness; **~case** *n.* Vitrine, *die;* Schaukasten, *der;* (fig.) Schaufenster, *das;* **~down** *n.* (fig.) Kraftprobe, *die;* **have a ~down [with sb.]** sich [mit jmdm.] auseinander setzen

shower /ˈʃaʊə(r)/
A *n.* **1** Schauer, *der;* **~ of rain/sleet/hail** Regen-/Schneeregen-/Hagelschauer, *der;* **a ~ of confetti/sparks/stones/petals** ein Konfettiregen/Funkenregen/Steinhagel/Regen von Blütenblättern; **a ~ of letters/curses** eine Flut von Briefen/Flüchen **2** (**~** bath) Dusche, *die; attrib.* Dusch-; **have** *or* **take a [cold/quick/daily] ~:** [kalt/schnell/täglich] duschen; **be under the ~:** unter der Dusche stehen; **the ~s** der Duschraum **3** (Amer.: party) **~ [party]** Geschenkparty, *die* (*für eine Braut, bei der sie Aussteuergegenstände geschenkt bekommt*); **baby ~:** *Geschenkparty für eine werdende Mutter, bei der sie Babyartikel geschenkt bekommt* **4** (Brit. coll.: contemptible persons) Sauhaufen, *der* (salopp)
B *v.t.* **1** **~ sth. over** *or* **on sb., ~ sb. with sth.** jmdn. mit etw. überschütten **2** (fig.: lavish) **~ sth. [up]on sb., ~ sb. with sth.** jmdn. mit etw. überhäufen
C *v.i.* **1** (fall in **~s**) **~ down [up]on sb.** ‹*Wasser, Konfetti:*› auf jmdn. herabregnen; ‹*Steine, Verwünschungen:*› auf jmdn. niederhageln **2** (have a **~** bath) duschen

shower: ~ bath *n.* (esp. Amer.) Dusche, *die;* **~ cap** *n.* Duschhaube, *die;* **~ curtain** *n.* Duschvorhang, *der;* **~ gel** *n.* Duschgel, *das;* **~proof** *adj.* [bedingt] regendicht; **~ room** *n.* Duschraum, *der;* **~ tray** *n.* Duschwanne, *die;* **~ unit** *n.* Dusche, *die;* Duscheinheit, *die*

showery /ˈʃaʊərɪ/ *adj.* **the weather is ~:** es herrscht Schauerwetter; **outlook ~:** weitere Aussichten: schauerartige Regenfälle; **a cold and ~ day** ein kalter Tag mit häufigen Schauern

show: ~ flat *n.* (esp. Brit.) Musterwohnung, *die;* **~girl** *n.* Showgirl, *das;* **~ground** *n.* Ausstellungsgelände, *das;* **~ house** *n.* Musterhaus, *das*

showily /ˈʃəʊɪlɪ/ *adv.* angeberisch; **behave ~:** eine Schau machen (ugs.); angeben

showing /ˈʃəʊɪŋ/ *n.* **1** (of film) Vorführung, *die;* (of television programme) Sendung, *die;* **at the film's first ~:** bei der Premiere des Films **2** (evidence) **on this ~:** demnach; **on any ~:** wie man es auch [dreht und] wendet; **on** *or* **by sb.'s own ~:** nach jmds. eigener Darstellung; **on present ~:** wie es sich im Augenblick darstellt **3** (quality of performance) Leistung, *die;* **make a good/poor** *etc.* **~:** eine gute/schwache *usw.* Leistung zeigen; **on this ~:** bei dieser Leistung

show: ~jumper *n.* (Sport) **1** (person) Springreiter, *der*/-reiterin, *die;* **2** (horse) Springpferd, *das;* **~jumping** *n.* (Sport) Springreiten, *das;* **~man** /ˈʃəʊmən/ *n., pl.* **~men** /ˈʃəʊmən/ **1** (proprietor of fairground booth etc.) Schausteller, *der;* **2** (effective presenter) Showman, *der*

showmanship /ˈʃəʊmənʃɪp/ *n., no pl.* schauspielerisches Talent; **it's nothing but ~:** es ist reine Schauspielerei

shown ► **show B, C**

show: ~-off *n.* Aufschneider, *der*/Aufschneiderin, *die;* Angeber, *der*/Angeberin, *die* (ugs.); **don't be such a ~-off** gib nicht so an!; **~piece** *n.* Renommierstück, *das* (geh.); (of exhibition, collection) Schaustück, *das;* (highlight) Paradestück, *das;* **a real ~piece** ein richtiges Prachtexemplar *od.* -stück (ugs.); **~place** *n.* Attraktion, *die;* **~room** *n.* Ausstellungsraum, *der;* **~room price** Endverbraucherpreis, *der;* **~-stopper** *n.* (coll.) **be a ~-stopper** Furore machen; **~ trial** *n.* Schauprozess, *der*

showy /ˈʃəʊɪ/ *adj.* **1** (gaudy, ostentatious) protzig (ugs.) **2** (striking) großartig; prächtig ‹*Farben*›; [farben]prächtig ‹*Blumen, Blüten*›

shrank ► **shrink A, B**

shrapnel /ˈʃræpnl/ *n.* (Mil.) **1** (fragments) Bomben-/Granatsplitter; **piece of ~:** Bomben-/Granatsplitter, *der* **2** (projectile) Schrapnell, *das; collect.* Schrapnelle

shred /ʃred/
A *n.* Fetzen, *der;* **without a ~ of clothing on him/her** ohne einen Fetzen [Kleidung] am Leib; **not a ~ of evidence/truth** keine Spur eines Beweises/kein Fünkchen Wahrheit; **cut/tear** *etc.* **sth. to ~s** etw. in Fetzen schneiden/reißen *usw.;* **tear sb.'s reputation to ~s** jmds. Ruf ruinieren; **tear sb.['s character] to ~s** kein gutes Haar an jmdm. lassen; **tear a theory/an argument to ~s** eine Theorie/eine Argumentation zerpflücken; **in ~s** in Fetzen; **our clothes were in ~s** unsere Kleidung war zerfetzt; **sb.'s nerves are in ~s** (fig.) jmd. ist mit den Nerven am Ende; **sb.'s reputation is in ~s** jmds. guter Ruf ist ruiniert
B *v.t.,* **-dd-** [im Reißwolf] zerkleinern ‹*Papier, Textilien*›; raspeln ‹*Gemüse*›

shredder /ˈʃredə(r)/ *n.* (for paper, clothes) Reißwolf, *der;* (kitchen aid) Raspel, *die;* **~ [attachment]** Schnitzelwerk, *das*

shrew /ʃruː/ *n.* **1** (Zool.) Spitzmaus, *die* **2** (woman) Beißzange, *die* (salopp)

shrewd /ʃruːd/ *adj.* scharfsinnig ‹*Person*›; klug ‹*Entscheidung, Investition, Schritt, Geschäftsmann*›; genau ‹*Schätzung, Einschätzung*›; treffsicher ‹*Urteilsvermögen*›; **I had a pretty ~ idea** *or* **suspicion what his next move would be** mir war ziemlich klar, was er als Nächstes tun würde; **have a ~ mind** scharfsinnig sein

shrewdly /ˈʃruːdlɪ/ *adv.* klug; **he ~ decided to take the job** er entschloss sich klugerweise dazu, die Stelle anzunehmen

shrewdness /ˈʃruːdnɪs/ *n., no pl.* ► **shrewd**: Scharfsinnigkeit, *die;* Klugheit, *die;* Genauigkeit, *die* Treffsicherheit, *die*

shrewish /ˈʃruːɪʃ/ *adj.*, **shrewishly** /ˈʃruːɪʃlɪ/ *adv.* zänkisch

'shrew-mouse ► **shrew 1**

shriek /ʃriːk/
A *n.* **1** (shrill cry) [Auf]schrei, *der;* **give a ~:** [auf]schreien; **give a ~ of horror/fear** *etc.* einen Schrei des Entsetzens/der Angst *usw.* ausstoßen; **there were ~s of laughter from the children** die Kinder kreischten vor Lachen **2** (high-pitched sound) Kreischen, *das*
B *v.i.* **1** (give shrill cry) [auf]schreien; **~ with horror/fear** *etc.* vor Entsetzen/Angst *usw.* [auf]schreien; **~ [with laughter]** vor Lachen kreischen **2** (make high-pitched sound) kreischen
C *v.t.* schreien

Phrasal verb
- **~ 'out**

A *v.i.* aufschreien
B *v.t.* schreien

shrift /ʃrɪft/ *n.* **give sb. short ~:** jmdn. kurz abfertigen (ugs.); **get short ~ [from sb.]** [von jmdm.] kurz abgefertigt werden (ugs.)

shrike /ʃraɪk/ *n.* (Ornith.) Würger, *der*

shrill /ʃrɪl/
A *adj.* schrill; (fig.) lautstark
B *v.i.* schrillen
C *v.t.* gellend schreien

shrillness /ˈʃrɪlnɪs/ *n., no pl.* Schrillheit, *die*

shrilly /ˈʃrɪlɪ/ *adv.* schrill; (fig.) lautstark ‹*fordern, protestieren*›

S

shrimp /ʃrɪmp/
A *n.* [1] *pl.* **~s** *or* **~** (Zool.) Garnele, *die;* Krabbe, *die* (ugs.); (Gastr.) Krabbe, *die; attrib.* Garnelen-/Krabben- [2] (derog.: small person) Knirps, *der* (abwertend)
B *v.i.* Krabben/Garnelen fangen

shrine /ʃraɪn/ *n.* [1] Heiligtum, *das;* (tomb) Grab, *das;* (casket) Schrein, *der* (veralt.); (casket holding sacred relics) Reliquienschrein, *der;* **be a sacred ~ of Christendom** ‹*Altar, Kapelle:*› eines der größten Heiligtümer der Christenheit sein [2] (fig.: place hallowed by memory) Gedenkstätte, *die;* **~ to sb./sth.** Gedenkstätte für jmdn./etw.

shrink /ʃrɪŋk/
A *v.i.*, **shrank** /ʃræŋk/, **shrunk** /ʃrʌŋk/ [1] (grow smaller) schrumpfen; ‹*Mensch:*› kleiner werden; ‹*Kleidung, Stoff:*› einlaufen; ‹*Metall, Holz:*› sich zusammenziehen; ‹*Handel, Einkünfte:*› zurückgehen [2] (recoil) sich zusammenkauern; **~ from sb./sth.** vor jmdm. zurückweichen/vor etw. (*Dat.*) zurückschrecken; **~ from doing sth.** sich scheuen, etw. zu tun; *see also* **violet A 1**
B *v.t.*, **shrank, shrunk** sich zusammenziehen lassen ‹*Metall, Holz*›; einlaufen lassen ‹*Textilien*›
C *n.* [1] (act) Schrumpfen, *das;* (of fabric) Einlaufen, *das* [2] (degree) ▸ **shrinkage 2** [3] (coll.: psychiatrist) Seelendoktor, *der*
Phrasal verbs
• **~ a'way** *v.i.* [1] (recoil) zurückweichen (**from** vor + *Dat.*) [2] (grow smaller) zusammenschrumpfen
• **~ 'back** *v.i.* zurückweichen (**from** vor + *Dat.*); **~ back from sth./doing sth.** (fig.) vor etw. (*Dat.*) zurückschrecken/sich scheuen, etw. zu tun

shrinkage /ˈʃrɪŋkɪdʒ/ *n.* [1] (act) (of clothing, material) Einlaufen, *das;* (of income, trade, etc.) Rückgang, *der* [2] (degree) Schrumpfung, *die*

shrink: ~-proof *adjs.* nicht einlaufend; **be ~-proof** nicht einlaufen; **~-resistant** *adj.* kaum einlaufend; **be ~-resistant** kaum einlaufen; **~-wrap** *v.t.* in einer Schrumpffolie verpacken; **~-wrapping** *n., no pl.* [1] Schrumpfverpackung, *die;* [2] (material) Schrumpffolie, *die*

shrive /ʃraɪv/ *v.t.*, **shrove** /ʃrəʊv/, **shriven** /ʃrɪvn/ (RC Ch. arch.) **~ sb.** jmdm. die Beichte abnehmen

shrivel /ˈʃrɪvl/
A *v.t.*, (Brit.) **-ll-: ~ [up]** schrump[e]lig machen; runzlig machen ‹*Haut, Gesicht*›; welk werden lassen ‹*Pflanze, Blume*›;
B *v.i.*, (Brit.) **-ll-: ~ [up]** verschrumpeln; ‹*Haut, Gesicht:*› runzlig werden; ‹*Pflanze, Blume:*› welk werden; ‹*Ballon:*› zusammenschrumpfen
Phrasal verb
• **~ up**
A *v.t.* ▸ **~ A**
B *v.i.* [1] ▸ **~ B** [2] (fig.: from fear or nervousness) verschüchtert werden; **I just wanted to ~ up when …:** ich wäre am liebsten in den Erdboden versunken, als …

shrivelled (*Amer.:* **shriveled**) /ˈʃrɪvld/ *adj.* schrump[e]lig; verschrumpelt; **a ~ old lady** eine verhutzelte alte Frau

shriven ▸ **shrive**

shroud /ʃraʊd/
A *n.* [1] Leichentuch, *das* (veralt.) [2] (fig.) (of fog, mystery, etc.) Schleier, *der;* (of snow) Decke, *die* [3] *in pl.* (of ship) Wanten *Pl.;* (of parachute) Fangleine, *die*
B *v.t.* (cover and conceal) einhüllen; **~ sth. in sth.** etw. in etw. (*Akk.*) hüllen; **mystery ~s their fate** ein Geheimnis umgibt ihr Schicksal (geh.)

shrove ▸ **shrive**

Shrove/ʃrəʊv/: **~tide** *n.* Fastnacht, *die;* **~ 'Tuesday** *n.* Fastnachtsdienstag, *der*

shrub /ʃrʌb/ *n.* Strauch, *der*

shrubbery /ˈʃrʌbərɪ/ *n.* [1] Gesträuch, *das* [2] (shrubs collectively) Sträucher

shrubby /ˈʃrʌbɪ/ *adj.* [1] (like a shrub) strauchartig [2] (covered with shrubs) mit Strauchwerk bewachsen

shrug /ʃrʌg/
A *n.* **~ [of one's** *or* **the shoulders]** Achselzucken, *das;* **give a ~ [of one's** *or* **the shoulders]** die/mit den Achseln zucken; **give a ~ of resignation/indifference** *etc.* resigniert/gleichgültig *usw.* mit den Achseln zucken
B *v.t. & i.* **-gg-: ~ [one's shoulders]** die *od.* mit den Achseln zucken
Phrasal verb
• **~ 'off** *v.t.* in den Wind schlagen; **~ sth. off as unimportant** etw. als unwichtig abtun

shrunk ▸ **shrink A, B**

shrunken /ˈʃrʌŋkn/ *adj.* verhutzelt (ugs.) ‹*Mensch*›; schrump[e]lig, verschrumpelt ‹*Äpfel*›; (fig.) geschrumpft ‹*Reserven, Gewinn, Ressourcen*›; **~ head** Schrumpfkopf, *der*

shuck /ʃʌk/ (Amer.)
A *n.* [1] Schale, *die;* (pea pod) Hülse, *die* [2] *in pl.* (slightest amount) **I don't care ~s about it** es kümmert mich nicht die Bohne (ugs.); **~s!** *expr. annoyance, regret* verdammt! (salopp)
B *v.t.* ausschälen

shudder /ˈʃʌdə(r)/
A *v.i.* [1] (shiver) zittern (**with** vor + *Dat.*); **sb. ~s to think of sth.** jmdn. schaudert bei dem Gedanken an etw. (*Akk.*) [2] (vibrate) zittern; **~ to a halt** zitternd zum Stehen kommen
B *n.* [1] (shivering) Zittern, *das;* Schauder, *der;* **sb. has/gets the ~s** (coll.) jmdn. schaudert; **it gives me the ~s to think of it** (coll.) mich schaudert, wenn ich daran denke [2] (vibration) Zittern, *das;* **a ~ went through the building** das Gebäude erzitterte

shuffle /ˈʃʌfl/
A *n.* [1] Schlurfen, *das;* **walk with a ~:** schlurfend gehen; schlurfen [2] (Cards) Mischen, *das;* **give the cards a [good] ~:** die Karten [gut] mischen; **it is his ~:** er ist an der Reihe zu mischen; er muss mischen [3] (fig.: change) Umbildung, *die;* **cabinet/ministerial ~:** Kabinettsumbildung, *die* [4] (Dancing) (movement) Schlurfschritt, *der;* (dance) *schlurfender Tanz;* ≈ Schleifer, *der*
B *v.t.* [1] (rearrange) umbilden ‹*Kabinett*›; neu verteilen ‹*Aufgaben*›; sortieren ‹*Schriftstücke usw.*›; (mix up) durcheinander bringen [2] (Cards) mischen [3] **~ one's feet in embarrassment** verlegen von einem Fuß auf den anderen treten; **he ~s his feet when he walks** er schlurft beim Gehen
C *v.i.* [1] (Cards) mischen [2] (move, walk) schlurfen [3] (shift one's position) herumrutschen
Phrasal verbs
• **~ a'long** *v.i.* dahinschlurfen
• **~ 'off**
A *v.t.* abstreifen ‹*Kleidungsstück*›; **~ the responsibility off [on to sb.]** die Verantwortung auf jmdn. abwälzen
B *v.i.* wegschlurfen (ugs.)

shuffling /ˈʃʌflɪŋ/ *adj.* schlurfend

shufti /ˈʃʊftɪ, ˈʃʌftɪ/ *n.* (Brit. coll.) **have a ~ at sth.** sich (*Dat.*) etw. angucken (ugs.)

shun /ʃʌn/ *v.t.*, **-nn-** meiden

'shun /ʃʌn/ *int.* (Brit. Mil.) stillgestanden!

shunt /ʃʌnt/
A *v.t.* [1] (Railw.) rangieren; **~ off** (fig.) abschieben [2] (Electr.) shunten
B *v.i.* (Brit. Railw.) rangieren
C *n.* [1] (Railw.) Rangieren, *das* [2] (Electr.) Neben[schluss]widerstand, *der;* Shunt, *der* [3] (Med.) Shunt, *der* [4] (coll.: collision) Karambolage, *die* (ugs.); **have a ~:** eine Karambolage haben (ugs.)

shunter /ˈʃʌntə(r)/ *n.* (Railw.) Rangierer, *der*

shush /ʃʊʃ/
A *int.* ▸ **hush C**
B *v.i.* [1] (call for silence) um Ruhe bitten [2] (be silent) still *od.* ruhig sein
C *v.t.* zum Schweigen bringen

shut /ʃʌt/
A *v.t.*, **-tt-, shut** [1] zumachen; schließen; **~ sth. to sb./sth.** etw. für jmdn./etw. schließen; **~ a road to traffic** eine Straße für den Verkehr sperren; **the strike ~ the factory for a month** der Streik hat die Fabrik für einen Monat lahm gelegt; **~ the door on sb.** jmdm. die Tür vor der Nase zuschlagen (ugs.); **~ the door on sth.** (fig.) die Möglichkeit einer Sache (*Gen.*) verbauen; **~ one's eyes to sth.** (fig.) seine Augen vor etw. (*Dat.*) verschließen; (choose to ignore) über etw. (*Akk.*) hinwegsehen; **~ one's ears to sth.** (fig.) die Ohren vor etw. (*Dat.*) verschließen; **~ one's heart to sb./mind to sth.** (fig.) sich jmdm./einer Sache verschließen; **~ your mouth** *or* **trap** *or* **face** *or* **gob** *or* (Amer.) **head!** (sl.: stop talking) halt den Mund (ugs.) *od.* die Klappe (salopp) *od.* die Fresse (derb) *od.* Schnauze (derb)!; **~ it!** (sl.: stop talking) halt die Klappe! (salopp)
[2] (confine) **~ sb./an animal in[to] sth.** jmdn./ein Tier in etw. (*Akk.*) sperren; **~ oneself in[to] a room** sich in einem Zimmer einschließen; **~ sth. in a safe** etw. in einen Safe schließen
[3] (exclude) **~ sb./an animal out of sth.** jmdn./ein Tier aus etw. aussperren
[4] (catch) **~ one's finger/coat in a door** sich (*Dat.*) den Finger/den Mantel in einer Tür einklemmen
[5] (fold up) schließen, zumachen ‹*Buch, Hand*›; zusammenklappen ‹*Klappmesser, Fächer*›
B *v.i.*, **-tt-, ~** schließen; ‹*Laden:*› schließen, zumachen; ‹*Blüte:*› sich schließen; **the door/case won't ~:** die Tür/der Koffer geht nicht zu *od.* schließt nicht; **the door ~ on/after him** die Tür schloss sich vor/hinter ihm
C *adj.* zu; geschlossen; **bang/kick sth. ~:** etw. zuknallen/mit einem Fußtritt zuschlagen; **bang/swing ~** ‹*Tür:*› zuknallen/zufallen; **we are ~ for lunch/on Saturdays** wir haben über Mittag/samstags geschlossen *od.* zu; **remain** *or* **stay ~:** geschlossen bleiben; zu bleiben; **keep sth. ~:** etw. geschlossen halten *od.* zu lassen; **be** *or* **get ~ of sb./sth.** (coll.) = **get shot of sb./sth.** ▸ **shot C 2**
Phrasal verbs
• **~ a'way** *v.t.* wegschließen; **keep sth. ~ away safely** etw. unter sicherem Verschluss halten
• **~ 'down**
A *v.t.* [1] zumachen, schließen ‹*Deckel, Fenster*› [2] (shut off) absperren [3] (terminate operation of) stillegen; abschalten ‹*Kernreaktor*›; einstellen ‹*Aktivitäten*›; (Radio, Telev.) einstellen ‹*Sendebetrieb*›; **the strike has ~ down the factory/newspaper** der Streik hat die Fabrik lahm gelegt/hat das Erscheinen der Zeitung verhindert
B *v.i.* (cease working) ‹*Laden, Fabrik:*› geschlossen werden; ‹*Zeitung, Sendebetrieb:*› eingestellt werden; **the winter resorts/ski lifts ~ down during the summer** die Einrichtungen der Winterkurorte sind im Sommer geschlossen/die Skilifte sind im Sommer außer Betrieb; **the radio/television ~s down after midnight** der Rundfunk/das Fernsehen stellt den Sendebetrieb nach Mitternacht ein; *see also* **shutdown**
• **~ 'in** *v.t.* [1] (keep in) einschließen; ‹*Damm:*› zurückhalten ‹*Wasser*› [2] (encircle) umschließen; **feel ~ in** sich eingeschlossen fühlen
• **~ 'off**
A *v.t.* [1] (stop) unterbrechen ‹*Strom, Fluss*›; abstellen ‹*Motor, Maschine, Gerät*› [2] (isolate) absperren; **~ sb. off from sb./sth.** jmdn. von jmdm./etw. abschneiden; **~ sb. off from society** jmdn. aus der Gesellschaft ausschließen; **~ oneself off from sb./sth.** sich gegen jmdn./etw. abkapseln
B *v.i.* (stop working) sich abstellen
• **~ 'out** *v.t.* [1] (keep out) aussperren; versperren ‹*Aussicht*›; (exclude from view) verdecken; (prevent) ausschließen ‹*Gefahr, Möglichkeit*›; **the skyscraper/tree ~s out the light** der Wolkenkratzer/Baum nimmt das Licht weg [2] (fig.: exclude) **~ sb. out from sth.** jmdn. von etw. ausschließen; **~ out all thoughts/memories of sb./sth.** alle Gedanken/Erinnerungen an jmdn./etw. beiseite schieben [3] (Amer. Sport) **~ sb. out** jmdn. nicht zum Zuge kommen lassen. *See also* **shutout**
• **~ 'to**
A *v.t.* [ganz] schließen
B *v.i.* ‹*Tür:*› zufallen
• **~ 'up**
A *v.t.* [1] (close) abschließen; zuschließen; **~ up [the/one's] house** das/sein Haus [sicher]

abschließen; *see also* **shop A 2** [2] (put away) einschließen ‹*Dokumente, Wertsachen usw.*›; einsperren ‹*Tier, Menschen*›; ~ **sth. up in sth.** etw. in etw. (*Akk.*) schließen; ~ **sb. up in an asylum/a prison** jmdn. in eine Anstalt/ein Gefängnis sperren [3] (reduce to silence) zum Schweigen bringen

B *v.i.* [1] (coll.: be quiet) den Mund halten (ugs.); ~ **up!** halt den Mund! (ugs.) [2] (lock up premises) abschließen

shut: ~**down** *n.* [1] (stoppage) Schließung, *die;* (of newspaper, operations) Einstellung, *die;* [2] (Radio, Telev.) Sendeschluss, *der;* (period) Sendepause, *die;* ~**-eye** *n.* (coll.) Nickerchen, *das* (fam.); **get some** *or* **a bit of** ~**-eye** ein Nickerchen halten (fam.); ~**out** *n.* [1] (Amer. Sport) Zu-null-Spiel, *das;* [2] (in industrial dispute) ▸**lock-out**

shutter /ˈʃʌtə(r)/ *n.* [1] Laden, *der;* (of window) Fensterladen, *der;* **put up the** ~**s** (fig.: cease business) zumachen; schließen [2] (Photog.) Verschluss, *der;* ~ **release** Auslöser, *der;* ~ **setting** [eingestellte] Verschlusszeit, *die;* ~ **speed** Verschlusszeit, *die*

shuttle /ˈʃʌtl/

A *n.* [1] (in loom) [Web]schützen, *der;* Schiffchen, *das;* (in sewing machine) Schiffchen, *das* [2] (Transport) (service) Pendelverkehr, *der;* Pendelservice, *der;* (bus) Pendelbus, *der;* (aircraft) Pendelmaschine, *die;* (train) Pendelzug, *der; see also* **space shuttle** [3] ▸**shuttlecock**

B *v.t.* [1] (cause to move to and fro) ~ **sth. backwards and forwards** etw. hin- und herschicken; ~ **passengers about** Passagiere hin- und herfahren [2] (transport) im Pendelverkehr transportieren

C *v.i.* pendeln; ~ **backwards and forwards** *or* **to and fro** *or* **back and forth** hin- und herpendeln

shuttle: ~ **bus** *n.* Shuttlebus, *der;* Pendelbus, *der;* ~**cock** *n.* Federball, *der;* **be tossed backwards and forwards like a** ~**cock** wie ein Pingpongball hin- und hergehen; ~ **diplomacy** *n., no pl.* ≈ Reisediplomatie, *die;* ~ **service** *n.* Pendelverkehr, *der;* Pendelservice, *der;* ~ **train** *n.* Shuttlezug, *der*

shy[1] /ʃaɪ/

A *adj.,* ~**er** *or* **shier** /ˈʃaɪə(r)/, ~**est** *or* **shiest** /ˈʃaɪɪst/ [1] scheu; (diffident) schüchtern; **don't be** ~: sei nicht [so] schüchtern!; **feel** ~ **about doing sth.** sich genieren, etw. zu tun; **feel** ~ **in sb.'s presence/with sb.** sich in jmds. Gegenwart/bei jmdm. gehemmt fühlen; **be** ~ **of strangers** eine Scheu vor Fremden haben; **be** ~ **of doing sth.** Hemmungen haben, etw. zu tun; *see also* **bite A**; **fight A 1** [2] (coll.: short) **be** ~ **of sth.** knapp mit etw. sein; **he is six months** ~ **of his retirement** ihm fehlt noch ein halbes Jahr, bis er pensioniert wird (ugs.)

B *v.i.* scheuen (**at** vor + *Dat.*)

Phrasal verb

• ~ **a'way** *v.i.* ~ **away from sth.** ‹*Pferd:*› vor etw. (*Dat.*) scheuen; ~ **away from sth./doing sth.** (fig.) etw. scheuen/sich scheuen, etw. zu tun

shy[2]

A *v.t.* (throw) ~ **sth. at sth./sb.** etw. auf etw./jmdn. schmeißen (ugs.)

B *v.i.* schmeißen (ugs.) (**at** nach)

C *n.* Wurf, *der;* **have a** ~ **at sth.** nach etw. schmeißen (ugs.); *see also* **coconut shy**

shyly /ˈʃaɪlɪ/ *adv.* scheu; (diffidently) schüchtern

shyness /ˈʃaɪnɪs/ *n., no pl.* Scheuheit, *die;* (diffidence) Schüchternheit, *die*

shyster /ˈʃaɪstə(r)/ *n.* (esp. Amer. coll.) Ganove, *der;* (lawyer) Winkeladvokat, *der* (abwertend)

si /siː/ ▸**te**

SI /esˈaɪ/ *adj.* (Phys.) SI-; **SI units** SI-Einheiten

Siamese /saɪəˈmiːz/

A *adj.* siamesisch

B *n., pl. same* [1] (Hist.: native of Siam) Siamese, *der*/Siamesin, *die* [2] (Ling. Hist.) ▸**Thai B 2** [3] (Zool.) Siamese, *der*

Siamese: ~ **'cat** *n.* Siamkatze, *die;* ~ **'twins** *n. pl.* siamesische Zwillinge

Siberia /saɪˈbɪərɪə/ *pr. n.* Sibirien (*das*)

Siberian /saɪˈbɪərɪən/ ▸❶ **p. 1345**

A *adj.* sibirisch

B *n.* Sibirjake, *der*/Sibirjakin, *die*

sibilant /ˈsɪbɪlənt/

A *adj.* zischend; ~ **sound** ▸**B**

B *n.* (Phonet.) Zischlaut, *der;* Sibilant, *der* (fachspr.)

sibling /ˈsɪblɪŋ/ *n.* (male) Bruder, *der;* (female) Schwester, *die; in pl.* Geschwister *Pl.; attrib.* Geschwister-

sibyl /ˈsɪbɪl/ *n.* Sibylle, *die*

sic /sɪk/ *adv.* sic

Sicilian /sɪˈsɪljən, sɪˈsɪlɪən/ ▸❶ **p. 1345**

A *adj.* sizil[ian]isch

B *n.* Sizilianer, *der*/Sizilianerin, *die*

Sicily /ˈsɪsɪlɪ/ *pr. n.* Sizilien (*das*)

sick /sɪk/ ▸❶ **p. 1231**

A *adj.* [1] (ill) krank; **mentally** ~: geisteskrank; **be** ~ **with** *or* (arch.) **of sth.** an etw. (*Dat.*) erkrankt sein; etw. haben; **go** ~, **fall** *or* (coll.) **take** ~: krank werden; **be off** ~: krank [gemeldet] sein; **sb. is** ~ **at** *or* **to his/her stomach** (Amer.) jmdm. ist [es] schlecht *od.* übel; *see also* **report B 2** [2] (Brit.: vomiting or about to vomit) **be** ~: sich erbrechen; **be** ~ **over sb./sth.** sich über jmdn./etw. erbrechen; **I think I'm going to be** ~: ich glaube, ich muss mich erbrechen *od.* ich muss brechen; **a** ~ **feeling** ein Übelkeitsgefühl; **sb. gets/feels** ~: jmdm. wird/ist [es] übel *od.* schlecht; **he felt** ~ **with fear** ihm war vor Angst [ganz] übel; **[as]** ~ **as a cat** *or* **dog** (coll.) speiübel; kotzübel (derb); **I get** ~ **in cars** beim Autofahren wird mir immer schlecht; **sth. makes sb.** ~: von etw. wird [es] jmdm. schlecht *od.* übel (*see also* **4**) [3] (sickly) elend ‹*Aussehen*›; leidend ‹*Blick*›; matt ‹*Lächeln*›; ungesund ‹*Blässe*› [4] (fig.) ~ **at heart** niedergeschlagen; **worried** ~: krank vor Sorgen; **the team was** ~ **at losing** (coll.) es hat der Mannschaft schwer zu schaffen gemacht, dass sie verloren hat; **be** ~ **for home** Heimweh haben; **[as]** ~ **as a parrot** (coll.) völlig fertig (ugs.); **be/get** ~ **of sb./sth.** jmdn./etw. satt haben/allmählich satt haben; **be** ~ **and tired** *or* ~ **to death of sb./sth.** (coll.) von jmdm./etw. die Nase [gestrichen] voll haben (ugs.); **be** ~ **of the sight/sound of sb./sth.** (coll.) jmdn./etw. nicht mehr sehen/hören können; **be** ~ **of doing sth.** es satt haben, etw. zu tun; **make sb.** ~ (disgust) jmdn. anekeln; (coll.: make envious) jmdn. ganz neidisch machen; (*see also* **2**); **look** ~ (coll.) (be discomfited, upset) dumm dastehen (ugs.); (be unimpressive) ‹*Leistung, Ergebnis, Bilanz usw.:*› ein schwaches Bild sein (ugs.); ‹*Aktie, Währung usw.:*› mies stehen (ugs.); ‹*Firma:*› mies dastehen (ugs.) *see also* **enough B** [5] (deranged) pervers; (morally corrupt) krank ‹*Gesellschaft*›; (morbid) makaber ‹*Witz, Humor, Fantasie*›

B *n.* [1] *pl.* **the** ~: die Kranken [2] (Brit. coll.: vomit) Erbrochene, *das;* Kotze, *die* (salopp)

C *v.t.* (coll.) ~ **[up]** erbrechen; ausspucken (ugs.)

sick: ~**bay** (Navy) Schiffshospital, *das;* (Mil.) Sanitätsbereich, *der;* (in school, college, office) Krankenzimmer, *das;* ~**bed** *n.* Krankenbett, *das;* ~ **benefit** *n.* (Brit.) Krankengeld, *das;* ~ **'building syndrome** *n.* Sickbuildingsyndrom, *das*

sicken /ˈsɪkn/ ▸❶ **p. 1231**

A *v.i.* [1] (become ill) krank werden; erkranken (geh.); **be** ~**ing for something** (Brit.) krank werden; etwas ausbrüten (ugs.); **be** ~**ing for the measles** (Brit.) [die] Masern bekommen [2] (feel nausea or disgust) ~ **at sth.** sich vor etw. (*Dat.*) ekeln; ~ **of sth./of doing sth.** einer Sache (*Gen.*) überdrüssig sein/es überdrüssig sein, etw. zu tun

B *v.t.* [1] (cause to feel ill) **sth.** ~**s sb.** bei etw. wird jmdm. übel [2] (disgust) **you** ~**/your behaviour** ~**s me** du widerst mich an/dein Benehmen widert mich an; **doesn't it** ~ **you?** findest du es nicht auch widerlich?

sickening /ˈsɪknɪŋ/ *adj.* [1] Ekel erregend; widerlich ‹*Anblick, Geruch*›; **with a** ~ **thud** mit einem entsetzlichen dumpfen Geräusch [2] (coll.: infuriating) unerträglich; **it's really** ~: es kann einen krank machen

sickeningly /ˈsɪknɪŋlɪ/ *adv.* [1] Ekel erregend; **his** ~ **unctuous manner** seine widerliche salbungsvolle Art [2] (coll.: infuriatingly) unverschämt (ugs.)

sick 'headache *n.* Migräne, *die*

sickie /ˈsɪkɪ/ *n.* (Brit. coll.) **take** *or* **throw a** ~: [einen] Tag krankfeiern (ugs.); **the Monday morning** ~: das Krankfeiern am Montagmorgen

sickle /ˈsɪkl/ *n.* Sichel, *die; see also* **hammer A 1**

'sick leave *n.* Urlaub wegen Krankheit, *der;* Genesungsurlaub, *der* (Milit.); **be on** ~: ≈ krank geschrieben sein

sickle: ~ **cell** *n.* ▸❶ **p. 1231** (Med.) Sichelzelle, *die;* ~**-cell anaemia** Sichelzellenanämie, *die;* ~**-shaped** *adj.* sichelförmig

'sick list *n.* Liste der Kranken, *die;* **on the** ~: krank [gemeldet/geschrieben]

sickly /ˈsɪklɪ/ *adj.* [1] (ailing) kränklich [2] (weak, faint) schwach; matt ‹*Lächeln*›; kraftlos ‹*Sonne*›; fahl ‹*Licht*›; blass ‹*Hautfarbe, Gesicht*›; **a** ~ **grey dawn/light** eine fahlgraue Dämmerung/ein fahlgraues Licht [3] (nauseating) ekelhaft; widerlich; (mawkish) süßlich; ~**-sweet** ekelhaft süßlich; (fig.: over-sentimental) zuckersüß (abwertend)

'sick-making *adj.* (coll.) [1] **sth. is** ~: von etw. wird einem schlecht [2] (fig.: annoying) unverschämt (ugs.)

sickness /ˈsɪknɪs/ *n.* ▸❶ **p. 1231** [1] *no art.* (being ill) Krankheit, *die;* **in** ~ **and in health** in Gesundheit und in Krankheit; *see also* **bed A 1**; **benefit A 2** [2] (disease; also fig.) Krankheit, *die;* **childhood** ~: Kinderkrankheit, *die* [3] (nausea) Übelkeit, *die;* (vomiting) Erbrechen, *das;* **bout of** ~: Anfall von Erbrechen; *see also* **morning sickness**

sick: ~ **note** *n.* Krankmeldung, *die;* (to teacher) Entschuldigung, *die;* ~ **nurse** ▸**nurse A**

sicko /ˈsɪkəʊ/ *n.* (coll.) Perverse, *der/die*

sick: ~ **pay** *n.* Entgeltfortzahlung im Krankheitsfalle; (paid by insurance) Krankengeld, *das;* ~**room** *n.* Krankenzimmer, *das*

side /saɪd/

A *n.* [1] Seite, *die;* **another car rammed the** ~ **of ours** ein anderer Wagen rammte unseren an der Seite; **this** ~ **up** oben; **lie on its** ~: auf der Seite liegen; **put** *or* **lay sth. on its** ~: etw. auf die Seite legen; **over the** ~ (over gunwale of ship/boat) über Bord (*Akk.*); **lean over the** ~ (Naut.) sich über die Reling lehnen

[2] (Geom.) Seite, *die*

[3] (of flat object) Seite, *die;* **on both** ~**s** auf beiden Seiten; *see also* **bread A 1**; **coin A**; **right side**; **wrong side**

[4] (of animal or person) Seite, *die;* **be hit in the** ~: in die Seite getroffen werden; **sleep on one's right/left** ~: auf der rechten/linken Seite schlafen; **paralysed in/on/down one** ~: halbseitig gelähmt; ~ **of mutton/beef/pork** Hammel-/Rinder-/Schweinehälfte, *die;* ~ **of bacon** Speckseite, *die;* **split** (fig.) *or* **burst** (fig.)/**shake one's** ~**s [laughing** *or* **with laughter]** vor Lachen platzen/sich vor Lachen nicht mehr halten können; **walk/stand** ~ **by** ~: nebeneinander gehen/stehen; **work/fight** *etc.* ~ **by** ~ **[with sb.]** Seite an Seite [mit jmdm.] arbeiten/kämpfen *usw.*; **live** ~ **by** ~ **[with sb.]** in [jmds.] unmittelbarer Nachbarschaft leben; **live** ~ **by** ~ **with death/poverty** in der ständigen Gegenwart des Todes/der Armut leben; *see also* **blind** ~; **thorn 3**

[5] (part away from the centre) Seite, *die;* **the eastern** ~ **of the town** der Ostteil der Stadt; **the** ~**s of sb.'s mouth** jmds. Mundwinkel; **right[-hand]/left[-hand]** ~: rechte/linke Seite; **on the right[-hand]/left[-hand]** ~ **of the road** auf der rechten/linken Straßenseite; **from** ~ **to** ~ (right across) quer hinüber; (alternately each way) von einer Seite auf die andere *od.* zur anderen; **to one** ~: zur Seite; **on one** ~: an der Seite; **on one** ~ **of his face** auf einer Seite seines Gesichts; **stand on** *or* **to one** ~: an *od.* auf der Seite stehen; **take sb. to** *or* **on one** ~: jmdn. zur Seite nehmen; **leave a question to** *or* **on one** ~: eine Frage beiseite lassen; **put** *or* **set** *or* **place sth. on one** ~ **[for sb./sth.]** etw. [für jmdn./etw.] beiseite legen; **put sth. on one** ~ (fig.) (postpone dealing with sth.) etw. beiseite legen; **on the** ~ (fig.) (in addition to regular work or income) nebenbei; nebenher; (as a ~ bet) als zusätzliche Wette; (secretly) insgeheim; (Amer.: as a ~ dish) als Beilage; **tell sb. sth. on the** ~:

S

jmdm. etw. im Vertrauen erzählen/sagen; **she is his/he has a bit on the ~** (coll.) mit ihr treibt ers noch nebenbei (ugs.)/er hat nebenbei noch 'ne andere (ugs.); **pass by on the other ~** (fig.) so tun, als ginge es einen nichts an; *see also* **laugh B**

6 (space beside person or thing) Seite, *die;* **he never left her ~:** er wich nie von ihrer Seite; **at** *or* **by sb.'s ~:** an jmds. Seite; neben jmdm.; **at** *or* **by the ~ of the car** beim *od.* am Auto; **at** *or* **by the ~ of the road/lake/grave** an der Straße/am See/am Grab; **look tiny by the ~ of sb./sth.** neben jmdm./etw. winzig wirken; **on all ~s** *or* **every ~:** von allen Seiten ‹*umzingelt, kritisiert*›; **look on all ~s** sich nach allen Seiten umsehen; **from all ~s** *or* **every ~:** von allen Seiten

7 (in relation to dividing line) Seite, *die;* **[on] either ~ of** beiderseits, auf beiden Seiten (+ *Gen.*); **[to** *or* **on] one ~ of** neben (+ *Dat.*); **this/the other ~ of** (with regard to space) diesseits/jenseits (+ *Gen.*); (with regard to time) vor/nach (+ *Dat.*); **he is this ~ of fifty** er ist unter fünfzig; **what he did was only just this ~ of fraud/perfection** was er tat, war hart an der Grenze zum Betrug/war schon fast perfekt; **this ~ [of] the grave** im Diesseits; **on the other ~** (fig.: after death) im Jenseits; *see also* **grass A 1**; **right side**; **wrong side**

8 (aspect) Seite, *die;* (department) Bereich, *der;* **see both ~s [of the question]** beide Seiten verstehen; **there are two ~s to every question** alles hat seine zwei Seiten; **look on the bright/gloomy ~ [of things]** die Dinge von der angenehmen/düsteren Seite sehen; **see the funny ~ of sth.** etw. von der komischen Seite sehen; **be on the high/flat/expensive** *etc.* **~:** [etwas] hoch/flach/teuer *usw.* sein; *see also* **err**; **safe B 2**; **seamy 2**

9 (opposing group or position) Seite, *die;* Partei, *die;* (Sport: team) Mannschaft, *die;* **put sb.'s ~:** jmds. Seite vertreten; **be on the winning ~** (fig.) auf der Seite der Gewinner stehen; **let the ~ down** (fig.) versagen; **change ~s** zur anderen Seite überwechseln; **time is on sb.'s ~:** die Zeit arbeitet für jmdn.; **whose ~ are you/is he on?** auf wessen Seite stehst du/steht er?; **take sb.'s ~:** sich auf jmds. Seite stellen; **take ~s [with/against sb.]** [für/gegen jmdn.] Partei ergreifen; **keep one's ~ of a bargain** seinen Teil einer Abmachung einhalten; *see also* **no side**

10 (of family) Seite, *die;* **on one's/sb.'s father's/mother's ~:** väterlicher-/mütterlicherseits; **the Welsh ~ of the family** der walisische Teil der Familie

11 (Brit. Billiards/Snooker) Effet, *der;* **put ~ on** *or* **apply ~ to the ball** dem Ball Effet geben

12 (Math.: of equation) Seite, *die*

B *v.i.* **~ with sb.** sich auf jmds. Seite (*Akk.*) stellen; **~ against sb.** sich gegen jmdn. stellen

C *adj.* seitlich; Seiten-

side: ~ arms *n. pl.* (Mil.) Seitengewehre; **~band** *n.* (Radio) Seitenband, *das;* **~ bet** *n.* (Gambling) zusätzliche Wette; **~board** *n.* Anrichte, *die;* Sideboard, *das;* **~boards** (coll.), **~burns** *ns. pl.* 1 (hair on cheeks) Backenbart, *der;* 2 (hair in front of the ears) Koteletten *Pl.;* **~car** *n.* Beiwagen, *der*

-sided /'saɪdɪd/ *adj. in comb.* -seitig; **a high-~ enclosure/box** eine hohe Einfriedung/Schachtel; **a glass-~ showcase** ein Schaukasten mit gläsernen Seitenwänden; **a steep-~ mountain** ein steiler Berg; **an open-~ structure** eine seitlich offene Konstruktion

side: ~ dish *n.* Beilage, *die;* **~ door** *n.* Seitentür, *die;* **by a ~ door** (fig.) durch eine Hintertür; **~ drum** *n.* (Mus.) kleine Trommel; **~ effect** *n.* Nebenwirkung, *die;* **~ entrance** *n.* Seiteneingang, *der;* **~ exit** *n.* Seitenausgang, *der;* **~-foot** *v.t.* mit dem Innenrist schießen ‹*Ball*›; **~ glance** *n.* (lit. or fig.) Seitenblick, *der* (**at** auf + *Akk.*); **~ impact** *n.* Seitenaufprall, *der;* **~-impact bars** *n. pl* Seitenaufprallschutz, *der;* **~ issue** *n.* Randproblem, *das;* **~kick** *n.* (coll.) Kumpan, *der;* **~light** *n.* 1 (Motor Veh.) Begrenzungsleuchte, *die;* **drive on ~lights** mit Standlicht fahren; 2 (Naut.) Seitenlaterne, *die;* 3 (light from the ~) Seitenlicht, *das;* 4 (fig.: incidental information) Streiflicht, *das;* **~line A** *n.* 1 (goods) Nebensortiment, *das;* 2 (occupation) Nebenbeschäftigung, *die;* 3 *in pl.* (Sport) Begrenzungslinien; **on the ~lines** (outside play area/track etc.) am Spielfeldrand/am Rande der Bahn (usw.); **be content to sit on the ~lines** (fig.) sich mit einer Zuschauerrolle begnügen; **remain on the ~lines** (fig.) sich [aus allem] heraushalten; **B** *v.t.* (Amer. Sport) **be ~-lined because of injury/with a broken arm** wegen einer Verletzung/eines gebrochenen Arms ausfallen; **~-line sb. for foul play** jmdn. wegen eines Fouls vom Platz stellen; **~long A** *adj.* (directed to one ~) **a ~long look/glance** ein Seitenblick; **B** *adv.* seitwärts; **look/glance ~long at sb.** einen Seitenblick auf jmdn. werfen; **~-on A** *adj.* seitlich; **B** *adv.* seitlich; **look at sth. ~-on** etw. von der Seite ansehen; **~ piece** *n.* Seitenteil, *das;* (of ladder) Holm, *der;* (of spectacles) Bügel, *der;* **~ plate** *n.* kleiner Teller (neben dem Teller für das Hauptgericht)

sidereal /saɪ'dɪərɪəl/ *adj.* siderisch; **~ time** siderische [Umlauf]zeit; **~ year** siderisches Jahr; Sternjahr, *das*

side: ~ road *n.* Seitenstraße, *die;* **~-saddle A** *n.* Damensattel, *der;* **B** *adv.* **ride ~-saddle** im Damensitz reiten; **~ salad** *n.* Salat [als Beilage]; **steak with chips and a ~ salad** Steak mit Pommes frites und dazu ein Salat; **~ shoot** *n.* (Bot.) Seitenspross, *der;* **~show** *n.* Nebenattraktion, *die;* **~-slip A** *n.* 1 (Aeronaut.) seitliches Abrutschen; 2 (sideways skid) seitliches Wegrutschen; **B** *v.i.* 1 (Aeronaut.) seitlich abrutschen; 2 (skid sideways) seitlich wegrutschen; **~sman** /'saɪdzmən/ *n., pl.* **~smen** /'saɪdzmən/ (Eccl.) Kirchendiener, *der;* **~ spin** ▸**side A 11**; **~-splitting** *adj.* zwerchfellerschütternd; **be ~-splitting** zum Brüllen sein (ugs.); **~-splittingly** /'saɪdsplɪtɪŋlɪ/ *adv.* **be ~-splittingly funny** zum Brüllen sein (ugs.); **~step A** *n.* Schritt zur Seite, *der;* (in dancing) Seitenschritt, *der;* **B** *v.t.* (lit. or fig.) ausweichen (+ *Dat.*); **C** *v.i.* zur Seite treten; (fig.) ausweichen; **~ street** *n.* Seitenstraße, *die;* **~swipe** *n.* Seitenhieb, *der;* **take a ~swipe at sb./sth.** (fig.) einen Seitenhieb auf jmdn./etw. austeilen; **~ table** *n.* Beistelltisch, *der;* **~track A** *n.* (Railw.) ▸**siding**; **B** *v.t.* 1 (Railw.) auf ein Nebengleis schieben; 2 (fig.) **get ~tracked** abgelenkt werden; **~ trip** *n.* kleiner Ausflug; Abstecher, *der;* **~ view** *n.* Seitenansicht, *die;* **~walk** (Amer.) ▸**pavement 1**; **~wall** *n.* Seitenwand, *die;* **~ways** /'saɪdweɪz/ **A** *adv.* seitwärts; **look at sb./sth. ~ways** jmdn./etw. von der Seite ansehen; **look ~ways at sb.** (fig.) jmdn. von der Seite ansehen; jmdn. schief ansehen (ugs.); **be knocked ~ways** (fig. coll.) (be devastated) am Boden zerstört sein (ugs.) (**by** von); (be very amazed) [ganz] von den Socken sein (ugs.) (**by** über + *Akk.*); **~ways on** von der Seite; **~ways on to sth.** quer zu etw.; **B** *adj.* seitlich; **~ways view/look** *or* **glance** Seitenansicht, *die*/Seitenblick, *der;* **~ whiskers** *n. pl.* Backenbart, *der;* **~ wind** *n.* Seitenwind, *der*

siding /'saɪdɪŋ/ *n.* (Railw.) Abstellgleis, *das;* Rangiergleis, *das*

sidle /'saɪdl/ *v.i.* schleichen; **~ up to sb.** [sich] zu jmdm. schleichen

SIDS *abbr.* **= sudden infant death syndrome** PKT

siege /si:dʒ/ *n.* (Mil.) Belagerung, *die;* (by police) Umstellung, *die;* **be under ~** (lit. or fig.) belagert sein; (by police) umstellt sein; **lay ~ to sth.** (lit. or fig.) etw. belagern

sienna /sɪ'enə/ *n.* (Art) **raw/burnt ~:** Siena natur/gebrannte Siena

sierra /sɪ'erə/ *n.* (Geog.) Sierra, *die*

siesta /sɪ'estə/ *n.* Siesta, *die;* **have** *or* **take a ~:** [eine] Siesta halten *od.* machen

sieve /sɪv/

A *n.* Sieb, *das;* **have a head** *or* **memory like a ~** (coll.) ein Gedächtnis wie ein Sieb haben (ugs.)

B *v.t.* sieben; (fig.: select by examining) [aus]sieben

Phrasal verb

• **~ 'out** *v.t.* aussieben

Sievert /'si:vət/ *n.* (Phys.) Sievert, *das*

sift /sɪft/

A *v.t.* sieben; (fig.: examine closely) unter die Lupe nehmen; **~ together the flour, salt, and baking powder** Mehl, Salz und Backpulver [zusammen] in ein Gefäß sieben; **~ sth. from sth.** etw. von etw. trennen

B *v.i.* **~ through** durchsehen ‹*Briefe, Dokumente usw.*›; durchsuchen ‹*Trümmer, Asche, Habseligkeiten usw.*›

Phrasal verb

• **~ 'out** *v.t.* (lit. or fig.) aussieben; **~ out sth. from sth.** etw. aus etw. heraussieben; (fig.) etw. von etw. trennen

sifter /'sɪftə(r)/ *n.* (Cookery) Sieb, *das*

sigh /saɪ/

A *n.* Seufzer, *der;* **give** *or* **breathe** *or* **utter** *or* **heave a ~:** einen Seufzer ausstoßen *od.* tun; **~ of relief/sadness/contentment** Seufzer der Erleichterung/trauriger Seufzer/Seufzer der Zufriedenheit

B *v.i.* seufzen; **~ with relief/despair/contentment** *etc.* vor Erleichterung/Verzweiflung/Zufriedenheit *usw. od.* erleichtert/verzweifelt/zufrieden *usw.* seufzen; **~ for sth./sb.** (fig.) sich nach etw./jmdm. sehnen; nach etw./jmdm. seufzen (geh.)

C *v.t.* seufzen

sight /saɪt/

A *n.* 1 (faculty) Sehvermögen, *das;* **loss of ~:** Verlust des Sehvermögens; **spoil** *or* **ruin one's ~:** sich (*Dat.*) die Augen verderben; **second ~:** das zweite Gesicht; **near ~** ▸**short sight**; **by ~:** mit dem Gesichtssinn *od.* den Augen; **know sb. by ~:** jmdn. vom Sehen kennen; *see also* **long sight**; **short sight**

2 (act of seeing) Anblick, *der;* **at [the] ~ of sb./of blood** bei jmds. Anblick/beim Anblick von Blut; **it was our first ~ of the sea** es war das erste Mal, dass wir das Meer sahen; **catch ~ of sb./sth.** (lit. or fig.) jmdn./etw. erblicken; **lose ~ of sb./sth.** (lit. or fig.) jmdn./etw. aus dem Auge *od.* den Augen verlieren; **be lost to ~:** den Blicken entschwunden sein (geh.); **disappear from ~:** [den Blicken] entschwinden (geh.); **have** *or* **get a good/quick ~ of sth.** etw. gut/kurz sehen können; **keep ~ of sth.** (lit. or fig.) etw. im Auge behalten; **read music at ~:** Noten vom Blatt lesen; **play sth. at ~:** etw. vom Blatt spielen; **translate a text at ~:** einen Text aus dem Stegreif übersetzen; **shoot sb. at** *or* **on ~:** jmdn. gleich [bei seinem Erscheinen] erschießen; **the guards had orders to shoot at** *or* **on ~:** die Wachen hatten Befehl, [auf jeden] sofort zu schießen; **buy sth. ~ unseen** etw. unbesehen kaufen; **at first ~:** auf den ersten Blick; **love at first ~:** Liebe auf den ersten Blick; *see also* **line[1] A 3**

3 (opinion) **in sb.'s ~:** in jmds. Augen (*Dat.*); **in the ~ of God/of the law** vor Gott/vor dem Gesetz

4 (spectacle) Anblick, *der;* **be a sorry ~:** einen traurigen Anblick *od.* ein trauriges Bild bieten; **it is a ~ to see** *or* **to behold** *or* **worth seeing** das muss man gesehen haben; **a ~ for sore eyes** eine Augenweide; **be/look a [real] ~** (coll.) (amusing) [vollkommen] unmöglich aussehen (ugs.); (horrible) böse *od.* schlimm aussehen

5 *in pl.* (noteworthy features) Sehenswürdigkeiten *Pl.;* **see the ~s** sich (*Dat.*) die Sehenswürdigkeiten ansehen

6 (range) Sichtweite, *die;* **in ~** (lit. or fig.) in Sicht; **in sb.'s ~, in ~ of sb.** vor jmds. Augen (*Dat.*); **come into ~:** in Sicht kommen; **keep sb./sth. in ~** (lit. or fig.) jmdn./etw. im Auge behalten; **victory/our goal is now within** *or* **in [our] ~** (fig.) der Sieg/unser Ziel ist jetzt in Sicht; **within** *or* **in ~ of sb./sth.** (able to see) in jmds. Sichtweite (*Dat.*)/in Sichtweite einer Sache; **come/get within ~ of sb./sth.** in jmds. Sichtweite (*Akk.*)/in Sichtweite einer Sache kommen; **keep** *or* **stay within** *or* **in ~ of sth./sb.** in Sichtweite (*Dat.*) einer Sache/in jmds. Sichtweite (*Dat.*) bleiben; **out of sb.'s ~:** außerhalb jmds. Sichtweite; **be out of ~:** außer Sicht sein; (coll.: be excellent) wahnsinnig sein (ugs.); **drop out of ~** (fig.) aus dem Blickfeld verschwinden; **vanish out of ~:** verschwinden; **keep** *or* **stay out of [sb.'s] ~:** sich [von jmdm.] nicht sehen lassen; sich [jmdm.] nicht zeigen; **I thought it best to keep out of**

S

his ~: ich hielt es für das Beste, ihm nicht unter die Augen zu kommen; **keep sb./sth. out of ~:** jmdn./etw. niemanden sehen lassen; **keep sth./sb. out of sb.'s ~:** jmdn. etw./jmdn. nicht sehen lassen; **put sth. out of [sb.'s] ~:** etw. [vor jmdm.] verstecken; **not let sb./sth. out of one's ~:** jmdn./etw. nicht aus den Augen lassen; **[get] out of my ~!** geh mir aus den Augen!; verschwinde! (ugs.); **out of ~, out of mind** (prov.) aus den Augen, aus dem Sinn

7 (aim, observation) **take a ~:** zielen; **take a ~ at sth.** etw. anvisieren; (with gun) auf etw. (*Akk.*) zielen

8 (device for aiming) Visier, *das;* **~s** Visiervorrichtung, *die;* **telescopic ~:** Zielfernrohr, *das;* **line sth./sb. up in one's ~s** auf etw./jmdn. zielen; etw./jmdn. anvisieren; **have sth./sb. [lined up] in one's ~s** etw./jmdn. im Visier haben; (fig.) es auf etw./jmdn. abgesehen haben; **set/have [set] one's ~s on sth.** (fig.) etw. anpeilen; **his ~s were set on doing it** er hatte es sich (*Dat.*) zum Ziel gesetzt, es zu tun; **set one's ~s [too] high** (fig.) seine Ziele [zu] hoch stecken; **lower/raise one's ~s** (fig.) zurückstecken/sich (*Dat.*) ein höheres Ziel setzen

9 *no pl., no def. art.* (coll.: great deal) **a ~ too clever/expensive** *etc.* entschieden zu schlau/teuer *usw.;* **a [long** *or* **damn** *or* **damned] ~ better/more expensive** *etc.* entschieden besser/teurer *usw.;* **not by a long ~:** lange *od.* längst nicht

B *v.t.* 1 sichten ‹*Land, Schiff, Flugzeug, Wrack*›; sehen ‹*Entflohenen, Vermissten*›; antreffen ‹*seltenes Tier, seltene Pflanze*›

2 (take ~ of) anvisieren

sighted /ˈsaɪtɪd/ *adj.* sehend; **partially ~:** [hochgradig] sehbehindert; **the blind and the partially ~:** Blinde und [hochgradig] Sehbehinderte

sighting /ˈsaɪtɪŋ/ *n.* Beobachtung, *die;* **there have been several ~s of the escaped prisoner** der entflohene Häftling wurde mehrfach gesehen

sightless /ˈsaɪtlɪs/ *adj.* blind

sight: ~-read (Mus.) *v.t. & i.* ‹*Pianist usw.:*› vom Blatt spielen; ‹*Sänger:*› vom Blatt singen; **~-reader** *n.* (Mus.) **be a good/poor ~-reader** ‹*Pianist usw.:*› gut/schlecht vom Blatt spielen; ‹*Sänger:*› gut/schlecht vom Blatt singen; **~-reading** *n., no pl.* (Mus.) **be good/bad** *or* **poor at ~-reading** ‹*Pianist usw.:*› gut/schlecht vom Blatt spielen [können]; ‹*Sänger:*› gut/schlecht vom Blatt singen [können]; **~ screen** *n.* (Cricket) Kontrastschirm, *der;* **~seeing** *n.* Sightseeing, *das* (Touristikjargon); **go ~seeing** Besichtigungen machen; **do a lot of ~seeing** viele Sehenswürdigkeiten besichtigen; **~seeing bus** Sightseeingbus, *der;* **~seeing tour/trip** Besichtigungsfahrt, *die;* Sightseeingtour, *die* (Touristikjargon); (in town) Stadtrundfahrt, *die;* **~seer** *n.* Tourist (*der die Sehenswürdigkeiten besichtigt*); **~-testing** *n.* Durchführung von Sehtests; **~-testing is free** Sehtests sind kostenlos

sigma /ˈsɪɡmə/ *n.* Sigma, *das*

sign /saɪn/

A *n.* 1 (symbol) Zeichen, *das;* **chemical/mathematical ~:** chemisches/mathematisches Zeichen

2 (Astrol.) **~ [of the zodiac]** [Tierkreis]zeichen, *das;* Sternzeichen, *das;* **what ~ are you?** welches Tierkreiszeichen *od.* Sternzeichen bist du?; **sb.'s birth ~:** jmds. Tierkreiszeichen

3 (notice) Schild, *das;* **direction ~:** Wegweiser, *der;* **[advertising] ~:** Reklameschild, *das;* Reklame, *die;* (illuminated, flashing) Leuchtreklame, *die;* **danger ~** (lit. or fig.) Gefahrenzeichen, *das*

4 (outside shop etc.) ▸**signboard**

5 (indication) Zeichen, *das;* (of future event) Anzeichen, *das;* **his behaviour is a ~ that he is unhappy** sein Verhalten ist ein Zeichen dafür, dass er unglücklich ist; **there is little/no/every ~ of a quick settlement of the strike** *or* **that the strike will be settled quickly** wenig/nichts/alles deutet auf eine baldige Beendigung des Streiks hin *od.* deutet darauf hin, dass der Streik bald beendet wird; **this is a ~ of his intelligence** das zeugt von seiner Intelligenz; **she gave** *or* **showed no ~ of having heard** *or* **that she had heard me** (did not reveal) sie ließ durch nichts erkennen, dass sie mich gehört hatte; (there was no indication) es deutete nichts darauf hin, dass sie mich gehört hatte; **if he was angry, he gave no ~ of it** wenn er ärgerlich war, so zeigte er es doch nicht; **show [no] ~s of fear/fatigue/strain/improvement** *etc.* [keine] Anzeichen der Angst/Müdigkeit/Anstrengung/Besserung *usw.* zeigen *od.* erkennen lassen; **the carpet showed little/some ~[s] of wear** der Teppich wirkte kaum/etwas abgenutzt; **the cave shows ~s of having been inhabited** in der Höhle gibt es Anzeichen dafür, dass sie bewohnt war; **the window shows no ~[s] of having been forced** das Fenster zeigt keine Spuren von Gewaltanwendung; **as a ~ of** als Zeichen (+ *Gen.*); **do sth. as a ~ of sth.** etw. zum Zeichen einer Sache (*Gen.*) tun; **at the first** *or* **slightest ~ of sth.** schon beim geringsten Anzeichen von etw.; **there was no ~ of him/the car anywhere** er/der Wagen war nirgends zu sehen; **there was no ~ of life** keine Menschenseele war zu sehen; **~ of the times** Zeichen der Zeit

6 (gesture, signal) Zeichen, *das;* **give sb. a ~ to do sth., make a ~ to** *or* **for sb. to do sth.** jmdm. ein Zeichen geben, etw. zu tun; *see also* **V-sign**

7 (mark) Zeichen, *das*

8 (Math.) Vorzeichen, *das*

B *v.t.* 1 (write one's name etc. on) unterzeichnen; unterschreiben; ‹*Künstler, Autor:*› signieren ‹*Werk*›; **~ the guest book** sich ins Gästebuch eintragen; **a ~ed copy [of a book]** ein [hand-]signiertes Exemplar [eines Buches]; **~ed, sealed, and delivered** (Law) unterschrieben, gesiegelt und ausgehändigt; (fig.) unter Dach und Fach

2 **~ one's name** [mit seinem Namen] unterzeichnen *od.* unterschreiben; **~ oneself R. A. Smith** mit R. A. Smith unterschreiben

3 ▸**sign up A**

4 (indicate) zeigen

C *v.i.* 1 (write one's name) unterschreiben; **~ for sth.** (acknowledge receipt of sth.) den Empfang einer Sache (*Gen.*) bestätigen; (~ a contract etc. for sth.) [einen Vertrag über] etw. (*Akk.*) unterschreiben

2 (signal) **~ to sb. to do sth.** jmdm. ein Zeichen geben, etw. zu tun

3 ▸**sign on B 1**

Phrasal verbs

- **~ aˈway** *v.t.* abtreten ‹*Eigentum*›; verzichten auf ‹*Recht, Freiheit usw.*›
- **~ ˈin**

A *v.t.* **~ sb./sth. in [on arrival]** jmds. Eintreffen/das Eintreffen einer Sache schriftlich vermerken *od.* registrieren

B *v.i.* sich [bei der Ankunft] eintragen

- **~ ˈoff**

A *v.i.* 1 (cease employment) kündigen; ‹*Seemann:*› abheuern, abmustern (Seemannsspr.) 2 (at end of shift etc.) sich [zum Feierabend *usw.*] abmelden 3 (Radio) sich verabschieden; ‹*Pilot:*› die Frequenz verlassen (Funkw.) 4 (at end of letter) Schluss machen

B *v.t.* kündigen; abheuern, abmustern ‹*Seemann*› (Seemannsspr.)

- **~ ˈon**

A *v.t.* einstellen ‹*Arbeitskräfte*›; verpflichten ‹*Fußballspieler*›; anwerben ‹*Soldaten*›; anheuern, anmustern ‹*Seeleute*›

B *v.i.* 1 (~ an engagement) sich verpflichten (**with** bei) 2 (at start of shift etc.) **~ on for the night shift** sich [per Unterschrift] zur Nachtschicht anmelden 3 (Radio) ‹*Rundfunkstation:*› seine Sendungen aufnehmen; ‹*Funker:*› sich melden 4 **~ on [for the dole]** (coll.) sich arbeitslos melden; stempeln gehen (ugs. veralt.)

- **~ ˈout**

A *v.t.* **~ books out from the library** Bücher als [aus der Bibliothek] entliehen eintragen

B *v.i.* sich [schriftlich] abmelden; ‹*Hotelgast:*› abreisen

- **~ ˈover** *v.t.* überschreiben ‹*Immobilien*›; übertragen ‹*Rechte*›
- **~ ˈup**

A *v.t.* (engage) [vertraglich] verpflichten; einstellen ‹*Arbeiter*›; aufnehmen ‹*Mitglied*›; einschreiben ‹*Kursteilnehmer*›

B *v.i.* sich [vertraglich] verpflichten (**with** bei); (join a course etc.) sich einschreiben

signal /ˈsɪɡnl/

A *n.* 1 Signal, *das;* **a ~ for sth./to sb.** ein Zeichen zu etw./für jmdn.; **at a ~ from the headmaster** auf ein Zeichen des Direktors; **the ~ was against us/at red** (Railw.) das Signal zeigte „halt"/stand auf Rot; **alarm** *or* **danger/warning ~:** Gefahr-/Warnsignal, *das;* **hand ~s** (Motor Veh.) Handzeichen; **sound/light/flag ~:** akustisches Signal/Lichtsignal, *das*/Flaggensignal, *das;* **radio** *or* **wireless ~:** Funkspruch, *der;* **distress ~:** Notsignal, *das;* **code of ~s** ▸**signal book**; **the Royal Corps of S~s,** (coll.) **the S~s** (Brit. Mil.) *die Fernmeldetruppe der britischen Armee* 2 (occasion, cause) Signal, *das;* Zeichen, *das;* **the ~ for rioting/pandemonium** das Zeichen zum Aufruhr/Chaos 3 (Electr., Radio, etc.) Signal, *das*

B *v.i.,* (Brit.) **-ll-** signalisieren; Signale geben; ‹*Kraftfahrer:*› blinken; (using hand etc. ~s) anzeigen; **~ for assistance** ein Hilfesignal geben; **~ to sb. [to do sth.]** jmdm. ein Zeichen geben[, etw. zu tun]

C *v.t.,* (Brit.) **-ll-** 1 (lit. or fig.) signalisieren; **~ sb. [to do sth.]** jmdm. ein Zeichen geben[, etw. zu tun]; **the driver ~led a right turn/that he was turning right** der Fahrer zeigte an, dass er [nach] rechts abbiegen wollte 2 (Radio etc.) funken; [über Funk] durchgeben

D *adj.* außergewöhnlich

signal: ~ book *n.* (Mil., Navy) Signalbuch, *das;* **~ box** *n.* (Railw.) Stellwerk, *das*

signaler (Amer.) ▸**signaller**

signal: ~ flag *n.* (Mil., Navy, Railw.) Signalflagge, *die;* **~ lamp** *n.* (Naut., Railw.) Signallampe, *die*

signaller /ˈsɪɡnələ(r)/ *n.* (Mil.) Blinker, *der;* (with flags) Signalgast, *der* (Seew.)

signally /ˈsɪɡnəlɪ/ *adv.* ungeheuer; unerhört; **~ ineffective** bemerkenswert ineffektiv; **not ~ successful** nicht übermäßig erfolgreich

signal: ~man /ˈsɪɡnlmən/ *n., pl.* **~men** /ˈsɪɡnlmən/ ▸❶ **p. 1260** 1 (Brit. Railw.) Bahnwärter, *der;* 2 ▸**signaller**; **~ tower** (Amer.) ▸**signal box**

signatory /ˈsɪɡnətərɪ/

A *adj.* unterzeichnend; vertragschließend ‹*Partei, Land*›; Signatar‹*macht, -staat*› (Politik)

B *n.* (person) Unterzeichner, *der;* (party) vertragschließende Partei; (state) Signatarstaat, *der;* **~ to a petition** Unterzeichner einer Petition; **~ to the treaty/agreement** (state) Signatarstaat des Abkommens

signature /ˈsɪɡnətʃə(r)/ *n.* 1 Unterschrift, *die;* (on painting) Signatur, *die;* **put one's ~ to sth.** seine Unterschrift unter etw. (*Akk.*) setzen 2 (Mus.) ▸**key signature**; **time signature** 3 (Printing) (figure or letter) Signatur, *die* (Buchw.); (folded sheet) Bogen, *der* 4 (Amer. Med.) Signatur, *die*

ˈsignature tune *n.* (Radio, Telev.) Erkennungsmelodie, *die*

ˈsignboard *n.* Schild, *das;* (advertising) Reklameschild, *das*

signet /ˈsɪɡnɪt/ *n.* Petschaft, *das;* Signet, *das* (veralt.)

ˈsignet ring *n.* Siegelring, *der*

significance /sɪɡˈnɪfɪkəns/ *n.* 1 (meaning, importance) Bedeutung, *die;* **be of [no] ~:** [nicht] von Bedeutung sein; **a matter of great/little/no ~:** eine [sehr] wichtige/ziemlich unwichtige/völlig unwichtige Angelegenheit 2 (meaningfulness) Bedeutsamkeit, *die*

significant /sɪɡˈnɪfɪkənt/ *adj.* 1 (noteworthy, important) bedeutend 2 (full of meaning) bedeutsam; **be ~ of sth.** etw. verraten; etwas über etw. (*Akk.*) aussagen 3 (having a meaning) bedeutungstragend (Sprachw.); **be ~:** etwas bedeuten 4 (Statistics) signifikant

significant ˈfigure *n.* (Math.) signifikante Ziffer

significantly /sɪɡˈnɪfɪkəntlɪ/ *adv.* 1 (meaningfully) bedeutungsvoll; *as sentence-modifier* **~ [enough]** bedeutsamerweise 2 (notably) bedeutend; signifikant (geh., fachspr.)

S

significant 'other *n.* wichtigste Bezugsperson; (Partner) [Lebens]partner, *der*/-partnerin, *die;* (loved one) Liebste, *der/die*

signification /sɪɡnɪfɪ'keɪʃn/ *n.* Bedeutung, *die*

signify /'sɪɡnɪfaɪ/
A *v.t.* **1** (indicate, mean) bedeuten **2** (communicate, make known) kundtun (geh.); zum Ausdruck bringen
B *v.i.* **it does not ~:** es hat nichts zu bedeuten *od.* (ugs.) zu sagen

signing /'saɪnɪŋ/ *n.* **1** Unterschreiben, *das;* (formal) Unterzeichnung, *die* **2** (**~ up**) Verpflichtung, *die*

'sign language *n.* Zeichensprache, *die*

sign: ~ painter ▸ **~writer**; **~post A** *n.* (lit. or fig.) Wegweiser, *der;* **B** *v.t.* ausschildern ‹*Route, Umleitungsstrecke usw.*›; mit Wegweisern versehen ‹*Straße*›; **~writer** *n.* ▸ **i p. 1260** Schildermaler, *der*

Sikh /siːk, sɪk/ *n.* Sikh, *der;* **she is a ~:** sie gehört der Sikhreligion an

Sikhism /'siːkɪzm, 'sɪkɪzm/ *n., no pl.* Sikhreligion, *die*

silage /'saɪlɪdʒ/ (Agric.)
A *n.* Silage, *die;* Gärfutter, *das*
B *v.t.* silieren

silence /'saɪləns/
A *n.* Schweigen, *das;* (keeping a secret) Verschwiegenheit, *die;* (taciturnity) Schweigsamkeit, *die;* (stillness) Stille, *die;* **there was ~:** es herrschte Schweigen/Stille; **there was a sudden/** (iron.) **deafening ~:** es trat plötzlich Stille ein/es herrschte Totenstille; **an awkward ~/awkward ~s** ein betretenes Schweigen/peinliche [Gesprächs]pausen; **his story was punctuated by long ~s** lange Sprechpausen unterbrachen seine Erzählung; **~!** Ruhe!; **'~ — recording in progress'** „Bitte Ruhe — Aufnahme"; **~ on sth.** Schweigen zu etw.; **in ~:** schweigend; **suffer in ~:** schweigend leiden; **call for ~:** um Ruhe bitten; **keep ~** (lit. or fig.) schweigen; **break the ~:** die Stille unterbrechen; (be the first to speak) das Schweigen brechen; **break one's ~** (lit. or fig.) sein Schweigen brechen; **reduce sb. to ~** (lit. or fig.) jmdn. zum Schweigen *od.* Verstummen bringen; **a minute's ~:** eine Schweigeminute; **the [two minutes'] ~** (Brit.: on Remembrance Sunday) die zwei Schweigeminuten (*am Heldengedenktag*); **~ is golden** Schweigen ist Gold; *see also* **pass over A**
B *v.t.* **1** (make silent) zum Schweigen *od.* Verstummen bringen; (fig.) ersticken ‹*Zweifel, Ängste, Proteste*›; mundtot machen ‹*Gegner, Zeugen*›; (coll.: kill) zum Schweigen bringen (verhüllend) **2** (make quieter) leiser machen ‹*Motor, Maschine, Auspuff, Bohrmaschine usw.*›

silencer /'saɪlənsə(r)/ *n.* (for door) Türschließer, *der;* (Brit. Motor Veh.) Schalldämpfer, *der;* Auspufftopf, *der;* (Arms) Schalldämpfer, *der*

silent /'saɪlənt/ *adj.* **1** stumm; (noiseless) unhörbar; (still) still; **as ~ as the grave** *or* **tomb** totenstill; **deaf people live in a ~ world** Taube leben in einer lautlosen Welt; **be ~** (say nothing) schweigen; (be still) still sein; (not be working) ‹*Maschine:*› stillstehen; ‹*Waffen:*› schweigen; **fall ~:** verstummen; **keep** *or* **remain ~** (lit. or fig.) schweigen; ‹*jmd., der verhört wird:*› beharrlich schweigen **2** (taciturn) schweigsam; **the strong, ~ type** der starke, tatkräftige Typ, der nicht viel Worte macht **3** (Ling.) stumm **4** (Cinemat.) **~ film** Stummfilm, *der;* **the early motion pictures were ~:** die ersten Filme waren Stummfilme *od.* waren ohne Ton

silently /'saɪləntlɪ/ *adv.* schweigend; stumm ‹*weinen, beten*›; (noiselessly) lautlos

silent: ~ ma'jority *n.* schweigende Mehrheit; **~ 'partner** (Amer.) ▸ **sleeping partner**

Silesia /saɪ'liːʃə/ *pr. n.* Schlesien (*das*)

Silesian /saɪ'liːʃn/
A *adj.* schlesisch; **sb. is ~:** jmd. ist Schlesier/Schlesierin
B *n.* **1** (person) Schlesier, *der*/Schlesierin, *die* **2** (dialect) Schlesisch, *das;* **speak ~:** schlesischen Dialekt sprechen

silhouette /sɪlu'et/
A *n.* **1** (picture) Schattenriss, *der* **2** (appearance against the light) Silhouette, *die;* **in ~:** als Silhouette
B *v.t.* **be ~d against sth.** sich als Silhouette gegen etw. abheben

silica /'sɪlɪkə/ *n.* Kieselerde, *die*

silicate /'sɪlɪkeɪt/ *n.* (Chem.) Silikat, *das*

siliceous /sɪ'lɪʃəs/ *adj.* Kiesel-

silicon /'sɪlɪkən/ *n.* (Chem.) Silicium, *das;* Silizium, *das;* **~ chip** Siliciumchip, *der;* Siliziumchip, *der*

> **Silicon Valley**
>
> Ein scherzhafter Name für ein Gebiet im kalifornischen Santa Clara Valley, wo es eine besonders hohe Dichte an Computerfirmen und Elektronikunternehmen gibt. Der Name rührt daher, dass in der Elektronik mit Silicium gearbeitet wird.

silicone /'sɪlɪkəʊn/ *n.* (Chem.) Silikon, *das;* **~ [breast] implant** Silikon[brust]implantat, *das*

silicosis /sɪlɪ'kəʊsɪs/ *n., pl.* **silicoses** /sɪlɪ'kəʊsiːz/ ▸ **i p. 1231** (Med.) Silikose, *die*

silk /sɪlk/
A *n.* **1** Seide, *die;* **sewing/embroidery ~:** Näh-/Stickseide, *die;* **take ~** (Brit. Law) Kronanwalt werden **2** *in pl.* (kinds of ~ material) Seidenstoffe; (garments) seidene Kleider *od.* Kleidungsstücke; (Horseracing) Rennfarben *Pl.* **3** (of spider etc.) [Spinnen]faden, *der* **4** (Bot.) Seide, *die* **5** (Brit. Law coll.) Kronanwalt, *der*
B *attrib. adj.* seiden; Seiden-; **you can't make a ~ purse out of a sow's ear** (prov.) aus einem Schweinsohr lässt sich kein seidener Beutel machen

silken /'sɪlkn/ *adj.* **1** seiden; Seiden- **2** (lustrous) seidig **3** ▸ **silky 2**

silk: ~ 'finish *n.* Seidenglanz, *der;* **~ 'hat** *n.* Zylinder, *der*

silkily /'sɪlkɪlɪ/ *adv.* **1** (lustrously) seiden; seidig **2** (suavely) **speak ~:** mit samtener Stimme sprechen

silk: ~ mill *n.* Seidenspinnerei, *die;* **~-screen printing** ▸ **screen printing**; **~worm** *n.* (Zool.) Seidenraupe, *die*

silky /'sɪlkɪ/ *adj.* **1** seidig; **have a ~ feel** sich wie Seide anfühlen **2** (suave) glatt; samten, samtig ‹*Stimme*›

sill /sɪl/ *n.* **1** (of door) [Tür]schwelle, *die;* (of window) Fensterbank, *die* **2** (Geol.) [schichtparalleler] Lagergang; Sill, *der* (fachspr.)

sillabub ▸ **syllabub**

silliness /'sɪlɪnɪs/ *n.* **1** *no pl.* Dummheit, *die;* Blödheit, *die* (ugs.) **2** *usu. in pl.* (instance) Dummheit, *die;* (piece of childishness) Albernheit, *die*

silly /'sɪlɪ/
A *adj.* dumm; blöd[e] (ugs.); (imprudent, unwise) töricht; unklug; (childish) albern; **only a ~ little cut [in the finger]** bloß ein läppischer (ugs.) kleiner Schnitt [im Finger]; **with a ~ little hammer like this one** mit so einem albernen kleinen Hammer wie diesem; **the ~ season** (Journ.) die Sauregurkenzeit; **[you] ~ child/thing!** [du] dummes Kind/dummes Ding!; **the ~ thing** (inanimate object) das dumme *od.* (ugs.) blöde Ding; **a ~ thing** (a foolish action) etwas Dummes *od.* (ugs.) Blödes; (a trivial matter) eine blödsinnige Kleinigkeit (ugs.); (a stupid person) ein dummes Ding; **it/that was a ~ thing to do** es/das war dumm *od.* (ugs.) blöd; **~ fool** Dummkopf, *der* (ugs.); **not do anything ~** (lit. or fig.) keine Dummheit[en] machen; **knock sb. ~:** jmdn. bewusstlos schlagen; **I was scared ~:** mir rutschte das Herz in die Hose (ugs.); **laugh oneself ~:** sich halb totlachen; *see also* **me[1]**
B *n.* (coll.) Dummchen, *das;* Dummerchen, *das* (fam.)

'silly billy *n.* (coll.) Kindskopf, *der;* **be a ~ [about sth.]** sich [bei etw.] dumm *od.* kindisch anstellen

silo /'saɪləʊ/ *n., pl.* **~s 1** (Agric.) Silo, *der* **2** (Brit.) **[grain/cement] ~:** [Getreide-/Zement]silo, *der* **3** (Mil.) **[missile] ~:** [Raketen]silo, *der*

silt /sɪlt/
A *n.* Schlamm, *der;* Schlick, *der*
B *v.t.* **~ up** verschlämmen
C *v.i.* **~ up** verschlammen

siltation /sɪl'teɪʃn/ *n.* **1** (process) Verschlämmung, *die* **2** (state) Verschlammung, *die*

Silurian /saɪ'ljʊərɪən, sɪ'ljʊərɪən/ (Geol.)
A *adj.* silurisch
B *n.* Silur, *das*

silver /'sɪlvə(r)/
A *n.* **1** *no pl., no indef. art.* Silber, *das;* **the price of ~:** der Silberpreis **2** (colour) Silber, *das* **3** *no pl., no indef. art.* (coins) Silbermünzen *Pl.;* Silber, *das* (ugs.); **for thirty pieces** *or* **a handful of ~** (fig.) für einen Judaslohn **4** (vessels, cutlery) Silber, *das;* (cutlery of other material) Besteck, *das* **5** (medal) Silber, *das;* **win two ~s** zweimal Silber gewinnen
B *attrib. adj.* silbern; Silber‹*pokal, -münze*›; **have a ~ tongue** zungenfertig sein; *see also* **spoon[1] A 1**; **standard A 8**
C *v.t.* **1** (coat with ~) versilbern; (coat with amalgam) verspiegeln ‹*Glas*› **2** ergrauen lassen ‹*Haar*›
D *v.i.* ergrauen

silver: ~ 'band *n.* (Mus.) Blaskapelle (deren Instrumente versilbert sind); **~ 'birch** *n.* (Bot.) Weißbirke, *die;* **~ collection** *n.* Sammlung, *die* (*bei der Silbermünzen gespendet werden*); **~-coloured** *adj.* silberfarben; silberfarbig; **~ 'fir** *n.* (Bot.) Weißtanne, *die;* Silbertanne, *die;* **~fish** *n.* (Zool.) **1** (insect) Silberfischchen, *das;* **2** (fish) Silberfisch, *der;* (variety of goldfish) weißer Goldfisch; **~ 'foil** *n.* **1** Silberfolie, *die;* (aluminium foil) Alufolie, *die;* **2** (tin foil) Stanniol, *das;* **~ 'fox** *n.* (Zool.; also fur) Silberfuchs, *der;* **~ 'gilt** *n.* **1** (gilded ~) vergoldetes Silber; **~ gilt dish/tray** Teller/Tablett aus vergoldetem Silber; **2** (imitation gilt) Goldimitation, *die;* **~-grey** *adj.* silbergrau; silbrig grau; **~-haired** *adj.* silberhaarig (geh.); **~ 'jubilee** *n.* silbernes Jubiläum; **~ 'leaf** *n.* Blattsilber, *das;* **~ 'medal** *n.* Silbermedaille, *die;* **~ 'medallist** *n.* Silbermedaillengewinner, *der*/-gewinnerin, *die;* **~ mine** *n.* Silbermine, *die;* **~ 'paper** *n.* Silberpapier, *das;* **~ 'plate** *n., no pl., no indef. art.* **1** versilberte Ware; (coating) Silberauflage, *die;* **2** (vessels, tableware) Silbergeschirr, *das;* **be ~ plate** versilbert sein; **~-plate** *v.t.* versilbern; **~-plated** *adj.* versilbert; **~ sand** *n.:* *feiner, reiner Sand;* **~ 'screen** *n.* **the ~ screen** die Leinwand; **~ service** *n.* **1** (set of ~ware) silbernes Service; **2** *no pl.* (method of restaurant service) englisches Service; Rundservice, *das;* **~side** *n.* (Brit. Gastr.) Schwanzstück, *das;* **~smith** *n.* ▸ **i p. 1260** Silberschmied, *der*/-schmiedin, *die;* **~ 'surfer** *n.* (coll.) Silbersurfer, *der*/-surferin, *die;* **~-tongued** *adj.* (fig.) zungenfertig; **~ware** *n., no pl.* Silber, *das;* **~ 'wedding** *n.* Silberhochzeit, *die;* silberne Hochzeit

silvery /'sɪlvərɪ/ *adj.* (silver-coloured) silbrig; (clear-sounding) silbern (dichter.); silbrig (geh.)

silviculture /'sɪlvɪkʌltʃə(r)/ *n.* Waldbau, *der*

SIM card /'sɪm kɑːd/ *n.* Sim-Karte, *die*

simian /'sɪmɪən/
A *adj.* **1** (apelike) affenähnlich **2** (Zool.) ‹*Gehirn usw.*› des/der Affen
B *n.* **1** (ape or monkey) Affe, *der* **2** (Zool.) Menschenaffe, *der*

similar /'sɪmɪlə(r)/ *adj.* (also Geom.) ähnlich (**to** *Dat.*); **some flour and a ~ amount of sugar** etwas Mehl und ungefähr die gleiche Menge Zucker; **our tastes are very ~:** wir haben einen sehr ähnlichen Geschmack; **of ~ size/colour** *etc.* von ähnlicher Größe/Farbe *usw.;* **be ~ in size/appearance** *etc.* **[to sb./sth.]** eine ähnliche Größe/ein ähnliches Aussehen haben [wie jmd./etw.]; **look/taste/smell** *etc.* **~ [to sth.]** ähnlich aussehen/schmecken/riechen *usw.* [wie etw.]; **the two brothers look very ~:** die beiden Brüder sehen sich (*Dat.*) sehr ähnlich

similarity /sɪmɪ'lærɪtɪ/ *n.* Ähnlichkeit, *die* (**to** mit); **point of ~:** Ähnlichkeit, *die;* **there the ~ ends** sonst gibt es keine Gemeinsamkeiten

similarly /'sɪmɪləlɪ/ *adv.* ähnlich; (to the same degree) ebenso; *as sentence-modifier* ebenso gut; **~ effective/costly** *etc.* ähnlich/ebenso effektiv/teuer *usw.*

simile /'sɪmɪlɪ/ *n.* (Lit.) Vergleich, *der;* Simile, *das* (geh., veralt.)

S

ℹ Since

As a preposition

The translation of *since* is not a problem — it is always **seit** — but it is important to note that the tense of the verb is often different in German. Whereas English uses the perfect and particularly the perfect continuous (*have been ...ing*), German uses the present:

I have been waiting since 8 o'clock
= Ich warte [schon] seit 8 Uhr

He has lived here since his childhood
= Er wohnt seit seiner Kindheit hier

Similarly an English verb in the past continuous is translated by a German verb in the imperfect:

I had been waiting since 8 o'clock
= Ich wartete [schon] seit 8 Uhr

Particularly with **warten, schon** is often added to stress the length of time.

However in the negative and in other cases where there is no sense of a continuous process the same tense is used in both languages:

We haven't seen her since the wedding
= Wir haben sie seit der Hochzeit nicht gesehen

I have only seen her once since the wedding
= Ich habe sie seit der Hochzeit nur einmal gesehen

I hadn't been there since 1980
= Ich war seit 1980 nicht [mehr] dort gewesen

In such cases, **mehr** is often added for emphasis.

As an adverb

This is simply the phrase *since then* (= **seitdem**) minus the *then:*

I haven't seen her since
= Ich habe sie seitdem nicht gesehen

It often has the sense of *in the meantime* and can be translated by **inzwischen:**

We have since got to know them better
= Wir haben sie inzwischen näher kennen gelernt

As a conjunction

In time expressions

As in the case of the preposition, the English perfect continuous describing a continuous process is translated by the German present:

since she has been living in Germany
= seit sie in Deutschland wohnt

since they had been in London
= seit sie in London waren

Referring to the time since a specific event, a different construction is used:

How long is it since he left?
= Wie lange ist es her, dass er weggezogen ist?

It's a year since he left
= Es ist ein Jahr her, dass er weggezogen ist

Meaning because

In the sense of *because, since* is translated by **da:**

Since she was ill, I had to do it
= Da sie krank war, musste ich es tun

---

similitude /sɪˈmɪlɪtjuːd/ *n.* (literary) Ähnlichkeit, *die*

simmer /ˈsɪmə(r)/
A *v.i.* **1** (Cookery) ‹*Flüssigkeit:*› sieden; **put the fish in the water and allow to ~ for ten minutes** den Fisch ins Wasser legen und zehn Minuten ziehen lassen **2** (fig.) gären; **let things ~:** die Dinge sich entwickeln lassen; **~ with rage/excitement** eine Wut haben/innerlich ganz aufgeregt sein
B *v.t.* (Cookery) köcheln lassen ‹*Suppe, Soße usw.*›; ziehen lassen ‹*Fisch, Klöße usw.*›
C *n.* (Cookery) **keep at a** *or* **on the ~:** sieden lassen ‹*Wasser*›; köcheln lassen ‹*Suppe, Soße usw.*›
(Phrasal verb)
• **~ ˈdown** *v.i.* sich abregen (ugs.); **let things/the situation ~ down** abwarten, bis sich die Wogen geglättet haben

simnel cake /ˈsɪmnl keɪk/ *n.* (Brit.) ≈ Rosinenkuchen, *der*

simper /ˈsɪmpə(r)/
A *v.i.* affektiert *od.* gekünstelt lächeln
B *v.t.* mit einem affektierten *od.* gekünstelten Lächeln sagen
C *n.* affektiertes *od.* gekünsteltes Lächeln

simpering /ˈsɪmpərɪŋ/ *adj.* affektiert, gekünstelt ‹*Lächeln, Art*›; affektiert ‹*Frau*›

simple /ˈsɪmpl/ *adj.* **1** (not compound, not complicated) einfach; (not elaborate) schlicht ‹*Mobiliar, Schönheit, Kunstwerk, Kleidung*›; **the ~ life** das einfache Leben; *see also* **simple interest** **2** (unqualified, absolute) einfach; simpel; **it was a ~ misunderstanding** es war [ganz] einfach ein Missverständnis; **it is a ~ fact that ...:** es ist [ganz] einfach eine Tatsache *od.* eine simple Tatsache, dass ...; *see also* **pure A 3** **3** (easy) einfach; **the ~st thing would be** *or* **it would be the ~st if ...:** es wäre das Einfachste *od.* am einfachsten, wenn ...; **as ~ as ABC** kinderleicht; **it's/it isn't as ~ as that** so einfach ist das/ist das nicht; **it would make things so ~ if ...:** es wäre alles so einfach, wenn ...; **'Electronics made ~'** „Elektronik leicht gemacht"; **it would make my job/task much ~r** es würde mir meine Arbeit sehr erleichtern/meine Aufgabe sehr vereinfachen **4** (unsophisticated) schlicht; (foolish) dumm; einfältig; (feeble-minded) debil; (humble) einfach ‹*Person, Arbeiter, Bauer, Leute*›; **the ~ pleasures of life** die kleinen Freuden des Lebens **5** (Ling.) **~ tense** einfache Zeitform; **~ past** Präteritum, *das;* **~ sentence** einfacher Satz

simple: ~-hearted /ˈsɪmplhɑːtɪd/ *adj.* schlicht; **~ ˈinterest** Kapitalzins, *der;* **~-minded** *adj.* **1** (unsophisticated) schlicht; **2** (feeble-minded) debil; **ˈsimple time** *n.* (Mus.) nicht zusammengesetzte Taktart

simpleton /ˈsɪmpltən/ *n.* Einfaltspinsel, *der* (ugs.)

simplex /ˈsɪmpleks/ *n.* (Ling.) Simplex, *das*

simplicity /sɪmˈplɪsɪtɪ/ *n., no pl.* Einfachheit, *die;* (unpretentiousness, lack of sophistication) Schlichtheit, *die;* **be ~ itself** ein Kinderspiel sein

simplification /sɪmplɪfɪˈkeɪʃn/ *n.* **1** *no pl.* Vereinfachung, *die;* Simplifizierung, *die* (geh.) **2** (instance) Vereinfachung, *die;* Simplifikation, *die* (geh.)

simplify /ˈsɪmplɪfaɪ/ *v.t.* vereinfachen; simplifizieren (geh.); **it would ~ matters if ...:** es würde die Sache vereinfachen, wenn ...

simplistic /sɪmˈplɪstɪk/ *adj.* [all]zu simpel

simplistically /sɪmˈplɪstɪklɪ/ *adv.* [all]zu simpel

simply /ˈsɪmplɪ/ *adv.* **1** (in an uncomplicated manner) einfach; (in an unsophisticated manner) schlicht; **live/eat ~:** einfach leben/essen; **speak ~:** in schlichten Worten sprechen **2** (absolutely) einfach; **he's ~ wonderful** er ist einfach großartig **3** (categorically, without good reason, without asking) einfach; (merely) nur; **it ~ isn't true** es ist einfach nicht wahr; **you ~ must see that film** du musst den Film einfach sehen; **I was ~ trying to help** ich wollte nur helfen; **quite ~:** ganz einfach; **~ because ...:** einfach weil ...; nur weil ...; **he ~ didn't feel like working** er hatte ganz einfach keine Lust zu arbeiten

simulate /ˈsɪmjʊleɪt/ *v.t.* **1** (feign) vortäuschen; heucheln ‹*Reue, Tugendhaftigkeit, Entrüstung, Begeisterung*›; simulieren, vortäuschen ‹*Krankheit*› **2** (mimic) nachahmen; (resemble) aussehen wie (+ *Nom.*) **3** simulieren ‹*Bedingungen, Wetter, Umwelt usw.*›

simulated /ˈsɪmjʊleɪtɪd/ *adj.* **1** (feigned) vorgetäuscht; geheuchelt **2** (artificial) imitiert ‹*Leder, Pelz usw.*› **3** simuliert ‹*Bedingungen, Wetter, Umwelt usw.*›

simulation /sɪmjʊˈleɪʃn/ *n.* **1** (feigning) Vortäuschung, *die;* (of illness) Vortäuschung, *die;* Simulation, *die* **2** (imitation of conditions) Simulation, *die* **3** (simulated object) Imitation, *die*

simulator /ˈsɪmjʊleɪtə(r)/ *n.* Simulator, *der*

simultaneity /sɪmltəˈniːɪtɪ/ *n., no pl.* Gleichzeitigkeit, *die*

simultaneous /sɪmlˈteɪnɪəs/ *adj.* gleichzeitig (**with** mit); simultan (fachspr., geh.); **be ~:** gleichzeitig/simultan erfolgen

simultaneous: ~ display *n.* (Chess) Simultanvorstellung, *die;* **~ equations** *n. pl.* (Math.) Gleichungssystem, *das;* **~ interpretation** *n.* Simultandolmetschen, *das*

simultaneously /sɪmlˈteɪnɪəslɪ/ *adv.* gleichzeitig; simultan (fachspr., geh.)

sin /sɪn/
A *n.* Sünde, *die;* **a life of ~:** ein Leben in Sünde; ein sündiges Leben; **live in ~** (coll.) in Sünde leben (veralt., scherzh.); **[as] miserable as ~:** todunglücklich; **for my ~s** (joc.) um meiner Missetaten willen (scherzh.); **the ~s of the fathers** die Missetat[en] der Väter; *see also* **beset 2**; **find out 2**; **multitude 1**; **omission 2**; **original A 1**; **wage A**
B *v.i.*, **-nn-** sündigen; **~ against sb./God** an jmdm./Gott *od.* gegen jmdn./Gott sündigen; sich an jmdm./Gott versündigen (geh.); **~ against the rules** gegen die Regeln verstoßen; **he is more ~ned against than ~ning** man sündigt mehr an ihm, als dass er selbst sündigt

Sinai Peninsula /saɪnaɪ prˈnɪnsjʊlə/ *pr. n.* Halbinsel Sinai

ˈsin bin *n.* (Sport coll.) Strafbank, *die*

since /sɪns/ ▸ℹ p. 1542
A *adv.* seitdem; **he has ~ remarried, he has remarried ~:** er hat danach wieder geheiratet; **she had not eaten anything so delicious before or ~:** sie hatte weder vorher noch nachher je etwas so Köstliches gegessen; **long ~:** vor langer Zeit; **not long ~:** vor nicht allzu langer Zeit; **he is long ~ dead** er ist seit langem tot; **a long time/many years/six weeks ~:** vor langer Zeit/vielen Jahren/sechs Wochen
B *prep.* seit; **~ seeing you ...:** seit ich dich gesehen habe; **~ then/that time** inzwischen; **he joined the firm 16 years ago and has been with them ~ then** er ist vor 16 Jahren in die Firma eingetreten und ist heute noch dort; **~ when?** seit wann?; **her mother died in 2001, ~ when/~ which time she has been looking after her father** ihre Mutter starb 2001, und seitdem/seit dieser Zeit versorgt sie ihren Vater
C *conj.* **1** seit; **it is a long time/so long/not so long ~ ...:** es ist lange/so lange/gar nicht lange her, dass ...; **how long is it ~ he left you?** wie lange ist es her, dass er dich verlassen hat? **2** (seeing that, as) da

sincere /sɪnˈsɪə(r)/ *adj.*, **~r** /sɪnˈsɪərə(r)/, **~st** /sɪnˈsɪərɪst/ aufrichtig; herzlich ‹*Grüße, Glückwünsche usw.*›; wahr ‹*Freund*›

sincerely /sɪnˈsɪəlɪ/ *adv.* ▸ℹ p. 1287 aufrichtig; **I [most] ~ hope so** (coll.) das will ich schwer hoffen (ugs.); **yours ~** (in letter) mit freundlichen Grüßen

sincerity /sɪn'serɪtɪ/ *n., no pl.* Aufrichtigkeit, *die;* **in all ~:** in aller Aufrichtigkeit; **have the ring of ~:** aufrichtig klingen

sine /saɪn/ *n.* (Math.) Sinus, *der*

sinecure /'sɪnɪkjʊə(r), 'saɪnɪkjʊə(r)/ *n.* Pfründe, *die;* Sinekure, *die;* **this job is no ~:** diese Arbeit ist kein reines Honiglecken (ugs.)

sine die /saɪnɪ 'daɪi:, sɪneɪ 'di:eɪ/ *adv.* auf unbestimmte Zeit

sine qua non /saɪnɪ kweɪ 'nɒn, sɪneɪ kwɑ: 'nəʊn/ *n.* notwendige Bedingung; Conditio sine qua non (geh.)

sinew /'sɪnju:/ *n.* **1** (Anat.) Sehne, *die;* **strain every nerve and ~ [to do sth.]** (fig.) alle Muskeln anspannen[, um etw. zu tun] **2** (strength) Kraft, *die*

'sine wave *n.* (Math.) Sinuswelle, *die*

sinewy /'sɪnju:ɪ/ *adj.* sehnig; (fig.: vigorous) kraftvoll; **the ~ vigour/strength of his style** sein kraftvoller Stil

sinfonia /sɪn'fəʊnɪə/ *n.* (Mus.) Sinfonia, *die;* (in name of orchestra) Sinfonieorchester, *das;* Sinfoniker *Pl.*

sinfonietta /sɪnfəʊnɪ'etə/ *n.* (Mus.) **1** Sinfonietta, *die* **2** (orchestra) kleines Sinfonieorchester; (string orchestra) Streichorchester, *das*

sinful /'sɪnfl/ *adj.* sündig; (reprehensible) sündhaft; **it is ~ to ...:** es ist eine Sünde, ... zu ...

sing /sɪŋ/

A *v.i.*, **sang** /sæŋ/, **sung** /sʌŋ/ singen; (fig.) ‹*Kessel, Wind:*› singen; ‹*Geschoss:*› sirren, pfeifen; (sl.: turn informer) singen (salopp); **~ to sb.** jmdm. [etw.] vorsingen; **~ to the guitar/piano** zur Gitarre/zum Klavier singen; **his ears are ~ing** seine Ohren sausen; **~ of sb./sth.** (celebrate in verse) jmdn./etw. besingen (geh.); von jmdm./etw. singen (dichter. veralt.)

B *v.t.*, **sang, sung** singen; **~ [the] alto** [den] Alt singen; **~ sb. a song** *or* **a song for sb.** jmdm. ein Lied vorsingen; **~ sb. to sleep** jmdn. in den Schlaf singen; *see also* **praise B 1**; **tune A 1, 2**

C *n.* (Amer.) **have a ~:** [gemeinsam] singen

Phrasal verbs

- **~ a'long** *v.i.* mitsingen
- **~ 'out**

A *v.i.* **1** (~ loudly) [laut *od.* aus voller Kehle] singen; **~ out merrily** fröhlich singen **2** (call out) [laut] rufen; **~ out for sb./sth.** nach jmdm./etw. rufen

B *v.t.* (shout) rufen; schreien

- **~ 'up** *v.i.* lauter singen

singable /'sɪŋəbl/ *adj.* singbar; (easily ~) sangbar; kantabel (geh.)

'sing-along *n.* **1** (occasion) gemeinsames Singen; Sing-along, *das* **2** (song) Lied zum Mitsingen; Sing-along, *das od. der*

Singapore /sɪŋə'pɔ:(r)/ *pr. n.* Singapur (*das*)

singe /sɪndʒ/

A *v.t.*, **~ing** ansengen; versengen; absengen ‹*Geflügel, Schwein*›; **~ sb.'s hair** (Hairdressing) jmdm. die Haarspitzen abbrennen

B *v.i.*, **~ing** [ver]sengen

C *n.* Brandfleck, *der*

singer /'sɪŋə(r)/ *n.* Sänger, *der*/Sängerin, *die;* **this canary is a good ~:** dieser Kanarienvogel singt schön

singing /'sɪŋɪŋ/ *n., no pl.* **1** Singen, *das;* (*fig.*) ▸**sing A**: Singen, *das;* Sirren, *das;* Pfeifen, *das;* **beautiful/loud ~:** schöner/lauter Gesang; **the ~ of the birds** der Gesang der Vögel; **his ~ is terrible** er singt furchtbar; **have a ~ in one's ears** Ohrensausen haben **2** *no art.* (Art) Gesang, *der; attrib.* Gesangs-; **~ voice** Singstimme, *die*

single /'sɪŋgl/

A *adj.* **1** einfach; einzig ‹*Ziel, Hoffnung*›; (for one person) Einzel‹*bett, -zimmer*›; einfach ‹*Größe*›; (without the other one of a pair) einzeln; **~ flower/stem** *etc.* einzelne Blume/einzelner Stamm *usw.*; **speak with a ~ voice** (fig.) mit einer Stimme sprechen; **~ sheet/cover** Betttuch/Bettbezug für ein Einzelbett; **~ ticket** (Brit.) einfache Fahrkarte; **~ fare** (Brit.) Preis für [die] einfache Fahrt; *see also* **combat A**; **entry 8**; **file³ A 1**; **track A 2, 4** **2** (one by itself) einzig; (isolated) einzeln; **one ~ ...:** ein einziger/eine einzige/ein einziges ...; **at a** *or* **one ~ blow** *or* **stroke** mit einem Schlag; **two minds with but a ~ thought** zwei Seelen und ein Gedanke **3** (unmarried) ledig; **a ~ man/woman/~ people** ein Lediger/eine Ledige/Ledige; **~ parent** allein erziehender Elternteil; **he/she is a ~ parent** er/sie ist allein erziehend; **~ mother** allein erziehende *od.* stehende Mutter **4** (separate, individual) einzeln; **can a ~ argument be advanced for it?** läßt sich dafür überhaupt irgendein Argument vorbringen?; **every ~ one** jeder/jede/jedes einzelne; **every ~ time/day** aber auch jedes Mal/jeden Tag; **not a ~ one** kein Einziger/keine Einzige/kein Einziges; **not a ~ word/dress/soul** kein einziges Wort/Kleid/keine Menschenseele; **she did not see a ~ thing she liked** sie hat aber auch nichts gesehen, was ihr gefiel; **not/never for a ~ minute** *or* **moment** keinen [einzigen] Augenblick [lang]

B *n.* **1** (Brit.: ticket) einfache Fahrkarte; **[a] ~/two ~s to Manchester, please** einmal/zweimal einfach nach Manchester, bitte **2** (record) Single, *die* **3** *in pl.* (Golf) Single, *das;* (Tennis) Einzel, *das;* **women's** *or* **ladies'/men's ~s** Damen-/Herreneinzel, *das* **4** (Brit. Hist.: pound note) Einpfundschein, *der;* (Amer.: dollar note) Eindollarschein, *der* **5** (Cricket) *Schlag für einen Lauf*

C *v.t.* **~ out** aussondern; (be distinctive quality of) auszeichnen (**from** vor + *Dat.*); **~ sb./sth. out as/for sth.** jmdn./etw. als etw./für etw. auswählen; **~ sb. out for promotion/special attention** jmdn. für eine Beförderung vorsehen/sich mit jmdm. besonders befassen

single: ~-barrelled (*Amer.:* **~-barreled**) /'sɪŋglbærəld/ *adj.* (Arms) einläufig; **~-bedded room** /'sɪŋglbedɪd ru:m/ *n.* Einzelzimmer, *das;* **~-breasted** /'sɪŋglbrestɪd/ *adj.* (Tailoring) einreihig; **~-cell, ~-celled** *adjs.* einzellig; **~-cell organism** Einzeller, *der;* **~ cream** *n.* [einfache] Sahne; **~ 'currency** *n.* Einheitswährung, *die;* **~-decker** **A** *n.* **be a ~-decker** ‹*Bus, Straßenbahn:*› nur ein Deck haben; **B** *adj.* **~-decker bus/tram** Bus/Straßenbahnmit [nur] einem Deck; **~-engined** /'sɪŋglendʒɪnd/ *adj.* einmotorig; **~ European 'currency** *n.* europäische Einheitswährung; **~ European 'market** *n.* europäischer Binnenmarkt; **~-handed** **A** /'----/ *adj.* **1** Einhand‹*segeln, -segler*›; **~-handed attempt to row across the Atlantic** Versuch, allein über den Atlantik zu rudern; **his ~-handed efforts to get a new hospital** seine einsamen Bemühungen um ein neues Krankenhaus; **2** (for one hand) **~-handed weapon/fishing rod** Waffe/Angelrute für eine Hand; **B** /--'--/ *adv.* **1** allein; **sail round the world ~-handed** als Einhandsegler um die Welt fahren; **root out corruption ~-handed** im Alleingang die Korruption ausrotten; **2** (with one hand) mit einer Hand; einhändig; **~-lens 'reflex camera** *n.* (Photog.) einäugige Spiegelreflexkamera; **~-line** *adj.* einspurig; **~ 'malt** *n.* **~ malt [whisky]** Single-Malt[-Whisky], *der;* **~ 'market** *n.* Binnenmarkt, *der;* **~-minded** *adj.* zielstrebig; **be ~-minded in one's aim** unbeirrbar sein Ziel verfolgen; **~-mindedly** /sɪŋgl'maɪndɪdlɪ/ *adv.* zielstrebig

singleness /'sɪŋglnɪs/ *n., no pl.* **~ of purpose** Zielstrebigkeit, *die*

'single-parent family *n.* Einelternfamilie, *die*

'single-phase *adj.* (Electr.) einphasig; **~ current** Einphasenstrom, *der*

singles: ~ bar *n.* Singlekneipe, *die;* **~ chart** *n.* Hitparade, *die*

single: ~-seater *n.* Einsitzer, *der;* **~-seater aircraft** einsitziges Flugzeug; **~-sex** *adj.* **~-sex school** reine Mädchen-/Jungenschule; **~-sex accommodation** nach Geschlecht getrennte Unterbringung; **~-storey** *adj.* eingeschossig

singlet /'sɪŋglɪt/ *n.* (Brit.: vest) Unterhemd, *das;* (Sport) Trikot, *das*

singleton /'sɪŋgltən/ *n.* (Cards) blanke Karte; **a ~ in hearts, a ~ heart** ein blankes Herz

single: ~-track *adj.* eingleisig ‹*Bahnlinie*›; einspurig ‹*Straße*›; **~ transferable 'vote** *n., no pl.* Präferenzwahlsystem, *das;* Präferenzwahl, *die*

singly /'sɪŋglɪ/ *adv.* **1** einzeln **2** (by oneself) allein

'sing-song

A *adj.* leiernd (ugs.); **say/recite sth. in a ~ manner/voice** etw. herunterleiern (ugs.); **his ~ accent** sein Singsang

B *n.* **1** (monotonous tone or rhythm) leiernder Ton; **recite sth./say sth. in a ~:** etw. herunterleiern (ugs.); **speak in a ~:** leiernd sprechen **2** (Brit.: singing) gemeinschaftliches Singen; **have a ~:** gemeinsam singen

singular /'sɪŋgjʊlə(r)/

A *adj.* **1** (Ling.) singularisch; Singular-; **~ noun** Substantiv im Singular; **~ form** Singularform, *die;* **first person ~:** erste Person Singular; **~ number** ▸**B** **2** (individual) einzeln; (unique) einmalig; einzigartig **3** (extraordinary) einmalig; einzigartig; (odd) eigenartig; sonderbar; **how very ~!** wie eigenartig *od.* sonderbar!

B *n.* (Ling.) Einzahl, *die;* Singular, *der;* **I said you could have 'an apple — in the ~** (coll.) ich habe gesagt, du kannst einen Apfel haben — von Äpfeln war nicht die Rede

singularity /sɪŋgjʊ'lærɪtɪ/ *n., no pl.* Eigenartigkeit, *die;* Sonderbarkeit, *die*

singularly /'sɪŋgjʊləlɪ/ *adv.* (extraordinarily) außerordentlich; einmalig ‹*schön*›; (strangely) seltsam

Sinhalese /sɪnhə'li:z, sɪnə'li:z/ ▸❶ **p. 1277**, ▸❶ **p. 1345**

A *adj.* singhalesisch; **sb. is ~:** jmd. ist Singhalese/Singhalesin

B *n.* **1** *pl. same* (person) Singhalese, *der*/Singhalesin, *die* **2** *no pl.* (language) Singhalesisch, *das*

sinister /'sɪnɪstə(r)/ *adj.* **1** (of evil omen) Unheil verkündend **2** (suggestive of malice) finster; (wicked) übel **3** (Her.) link...; sinister (fachspr.); *see also* **baton 5**; **bend² 2**

sink /sɪŋk/

A *n.* **1** Spülbecken, *das;* Spüle, *die;* **pour sth. down the ~:** etw. in den Ausguss schütten; *see also* **kitchen sink** **2** (cesspool) Senkgrube, *die;* Kloake, *die;* (fig.: place of vice etc.) Kloake, *die;* Pfuhl, *der* **3** (Geog.: pool) Senke, *die;* Vertiefung, *die* **4** (Geol.) ▸**sinkhole** **5** (Phys.) Feldsenke, *die*

B *v.i.*, **sank** /sæŋk/ *or* **sunk** /sʌŋk/, **sunk** **1** sinken; **we shall ~ or swim together** (fig.) wir werden gemeinsam untergehen oder gemeinsam überleben; **leave sb. to ~ or swim** (fig.) jmdn. seinem Schicksal überlassen **2** **~ into** (become immersed in) sinken in (+ *Akk.*); versinken in (+ *Dat.*); (penetrate) eindringen in (+ *Akk.*); (fig.: be absorbed into) dringen in (+ *Akk.*) ‹*Bewusstsein*›; **~ into an armchair/the cushions** in einen Sessel/die Kissen sinken; **~ into sb.'s/each other's arms** jmdm./sich in die Arme sinken; **~ into a deep sleep/a coma/trance/reverie** in einen tiefen Schlaf/in ein Koma/in Trance/in Träumerei sinken (geh.); **~ into depression/despair** in Schwermut/Verzweiflung (*Akk.*) versinken; **~ into crime/poverty** *etc.* dem Verbrechen/der Armut *usw.* verfallen; **be sunk in thought/despair** in Gedanken/in Verzweiflung (*Akk.*) versunken sein; *see also* **oblivion** **3** (come to lower level or pitch) sinken; (suffer subsidence) absinken; (slope down) sich senken; (be turned downwards) ‹*Augen:*› sich senken; (shrink inwards) ‹*Augen, Wangen:*› einfallen; (subside, abate) ‹*Flut, Wasser, Fluss:*› sinken; (fig.: fail) ‹*Moral, Hoffnung:*› sinken; **the patient is ~ing [fast]** mit dem Patienten geht es zu Ende (verhüll.); **sb.'s heart ~s/spirits ~:** jmds. Stimmung sinkt; **sb.'s heart/courage ~s into his/her boots** (coll.) jmdm. rutscht *od.* fällt das Herz in die Hose[n] (ugs.); **~ to one's knees** auf die *od.* seine Knie sinken **4** (fall) ‹*Preis, Temperatur, Währung, Produktion usw.:*› sinken; **~ in value** im Wert sinken

C *v.t.*, **sank** *or* **sunk, sunk** **1** versenken; (cause

S

failure of) zunichte machen; **be sunk** (fig. coll.: have failed) aufgeschmissen sein (ugs.); **~ one's differences** seine Streitigkeiten begraben; **enough luggage/make-up to ~ a battleship** (fig. joc.) tonnenweise (ugs.) Gepäck/pfundweise (ugs.) Make-up **2** (lower) senken; (Golf) ins Loch schlagen ‹*Ball*› **3** (dig) niederbringen; (inlay) einlegen; (recess) versenken; (embed) stoßen ‹*Messer, Schwert*›; graben (geh.) ‹*Zähne, Klauen*›; **~ a pole into the ground** einen Pfahl in den Boden senken; *see also* **fence A 1**

Phrasal verbs

- **~ 'back** *v.i.* zurücksinken; **~ back into crime/poverty** (fig.) wieder dem Verbrechen/der Armut verfallen
- **~ 'down** *v.i.* hinabsinken; niedersinken; **~ down to the floor/ground** auf den/zu Boden sinken; **~ down into the mud** im Schlamm versinken; **his head sank down on to his chest** der Kopf sank ihm auf die Brust; **she sank down [on her knees] before him** sie sank vor ihm [auf die Knie] nieder
- **~ 'in**

A *v.i.* **1** (become immersed) einsinken; (penetrate) eindringen **2** (fig.: be absorbed into the mind) jmdm. ins Bewusstsein dringen; ‹*Warnung, Lektion:*› verstanden werden

B *v.t.* einsenken ‹*Stütze, Pfahl*›

sinker /ˈsɪŋkə(r)/ *n.* (Fishing) Senker, *der;* (of drift net) Grundgewicht, *das; see also* **hook A 1**

sink: ~ estate *n.* Elendsviertel, *das;* **~hole** *n.* (Geol.) Schluckloch, *das*

sinking /ˈsɪŋkɪŋ/

A *adj.* **1** sinkend; **[the] rats desert a ~ ship** die Ratten verlassen das sinkende Schiff **2** (declining) untergehend ‹*Sonne*› **3** (falling in value) sinkend **4** **with a ~ heart** (fig.) beklommen; resigniert

B *n.* **1** (of ship) (deliberate) Versenkung, *die;* (accidental) Sinken, *das;* Untergang, *der;* (of well) Niederbringung, *die* **2** **~ of the heart** (fig.) Beklommenheit, *die; attrib.* **a ~ feeling** (fig.) ein flaues Gefühl [im Magen]

'sinking fund *n.* (Finance) Tilgungsfonds, *der*

sink: ~ tidy *n.* Abfallbehälter, *der* (*auf der Spüle*); **~ unit** *n.* Spüle, *die*

sinless /ˈsɪnlɪs/ *adj.* sündenfrei, sündlos ‹*Mensch, Leben*›; untad[e]lig ‹*Verhalten*›

sinner /ˈsɪnə(r)/ *n.* Sünder, *der*/Sünderin, *die*

Sinn Fein /ʃɪn ˈfeɪn/ *n., no pl., no indef. art.* Sinn Fein, *die* (nationalistische irische Partei)

> **Sinn Fein**
>
> Name einer 1905 in Irland gegründeten politischen Bewegung und Partei, deren ursprüngliche Ziele die Unabhängigkeit Irlands und eine Wiederbelebung der irischen Kultur waren und die heute, im Verein mit der **IRA**, ein vereinigtes republikanisches Irland anstrebt.

Sino- /ˈsaɪnəʊ/ *in comb.* sino-/Sino-; **a ~Russian war** ein chinesisch-russischer Krieg

sinter /ˈsɪntə(r)/

A *v.t.* sintern (Technik)

B *v.i.* sintern

sinuous /ˈsɪnjʊəs/ *adj.* gewunden; sich schlängelnd ‹*Schlange*›; (lithe) geschmeidig ‹*Körper, Bewegungen*›

sinus /ˈsaɪnəs/ *n.* (Anat.) Sinus, *der* (fachspr.); **[paranasal] ~:** Nebenhöhle, *die*

sinusitis /saɪnəˈsaɪtɪs/ *n.* ▸❶ **p. 1231** (Med.) Nebenhöhlenentzündung, *die;* Sinusitis, *die* (fachspr.)

Sioux /suː/ *n., pl. same* (Ethnol.) Sioux, *der/die; attrib.* Sioux-

sip /sɪp/

A *v.t.,* **-pp-: ~ [up]** schlürfen

B *v.i.,* **-pp-: ~ at/from sth.** an etw. (*Dat.*) nippen

C *n.* Schlückchen, *das;* **have** *or* **take a ~ [of sth.]** ein Schlückchen [von etw.] nehmen; **in ~s** schlückchenweise

siphon /ˈsaɪfn/

A *n.* **1** (bottle) Siphon, *der* **2** (pipe) Saugheber, *der*

B *v.t.* [durch einen Saugheber] laufen lassen; **~ sth. from a tank** etw. [mit einem Saugheber] aus einem Tank ablassen

C *v.i.* [durch einen Saugheber] laufen; (fig.: flow as if through a ~) laufen

Phrasal verbs

- **~ 'off** *v.t.* [mit einem Saugheber] ablassen; (fig.: transfer) abzweigen
- **~ 'out** *v.t.* [mit einem Saugheber] ablassen

sir /sɜː(r)/ *n.* ▸❶ **p. 1634** **1** (formal address) der Herr; (to teacher) Herr Meier/Schmidt *usw.;* Herr Lehrer/Studienrat *usw.* (veralt.); **no '~!** keinesfalls!; von wegen! (ugs.); **yes '~!** allerdings; **Sir!** (Mil.) Herr Oberst/Leutnant *usw.*!; (yes) jawohl, Herr Oberst/Leutnant *usw.*! **2** ▸❶ **p. 1287** (in letter) **Dear Sir** Sehr geehrter Herr; **Dear Sirs** Sehr geehrte [Damen und] Herren; **Dear Sir or Madam** Sehr geehrte Dame/Sehr geehrter Herr **3** **S~** /sə(r)/ (title of knight etc.) Sir **4** /sɜː(r)/ (person addressed as 'Sir') Sir, *der* **5** *no art.* (Sch. coll.: teacher) der [Herr] Lehrer; **I shall tell ~:** das sag' ich (ugs.)

sire /ˈsaɪə(r)/

A *n.* **1** Vatertier, *das* **2** (poet.) (father) Vater, *der;* (ancestor) Ahnherr, *der* (geh. veralt.) **3** ▸❶ **p. 1634** (arch.) **yes, ~:** ja, Herr

B *v.t.* zeugen

siren /ˈsaɪrən/

A *n.* **1** Sirene, *die;* **factory/ship's ~:** Fabrik-/Schiffssirene, *die;* **air-raid ~:** Luftschutzsirene, *die* **2** (temptress) Sirene, *die* (geh.); Circe, *die* (geh.) **3** (Greek Mythol.) Sirene, *die*

B *adj.* sirenenhaft; **~ song** Sirenengesang, *der*

sirloin /ˈsɜːlɔɪn/ *n.* **1** (Brit.: upper part of loin of beef) Roastbeef, *das;* **a ~ of beef** ein Stück Roastbeef; **~ steak** Rumpsteak, *das* **2** (Amer.) Rumpsteak, *das*

sirocco /sɪˈrɒkəʊ/ *n., pl.* **~s** Schirokko, *der*

sirup (Amer.) ▸**syrup**

sis /sɪs/ *n.* (coll.) Schwesterherz, *das* (scherzh.)

sisal /ˈsaɪsl/ *n.* **1** (fibre) Sisal, *der; attrib.* Sisal- **2** (Bot.) Sisalagave, *die; attrib.* Sisal-

siskin /ˈsɪskɪn/ *n.* (Ornith.) [Erlen]zeisig, *der*

sissified /ˈsɪsɪfaɪd/ *adj.* weibisch (abwertend); (cowardly) feige (abwertend)

sissy /ˈsɪsɪ/

A *n.* (effeminate man) weibischer Typ; (cowardly person) Waschlappen, *der* (ugs. abwertend)

B *adj.* weibisch (abwertend); (cowardly) feige (abwertend)

sister /ˈsɪstə(r)/ *n.* **1** Schwester, *die;* **she has been a ~ to him/her** (fig.) sie war für ihn/sie wie eine Schwester; **the Robinson ~s** die Robinson-Schwestern **2** (friend, associate fellow member) Schwester, *die;* (in trade union) Kollegin, *die;* **~ company** Schwesterfirma, *die* **3** (Eccl.) Schwester, *die;* **S~ of Mercy** Barmherzige Schwester **4** (Brit.: senior nurse) Oberschwester, *die;* **ward ~:** Stationsschwester, *die;* **theatre ~:** Operationsschwester, *die* **5** (Brit. coll.: nurse) Schwester, *die*

sisterhood /ˈsɪstəhʊd/ *n.* **1** *no pl.* Schwesterschaft, *die;* schwesterliches Verhältnis **2** (religious society) Schwesternschaft, *die*

'sister-in-law *n., pl.* **sisters-in-law** Schwägerin, *die*

sisterly /ˈsɪstəlɪ/ *adj.* schwesterlich; **~ love** Schwesterliebe, *die*

'sister ship *n.* (Naut.) Schwesterschiff, *das*

Sistine Chapel /sɪstiːn ˈtʃæpl, sɪstaɪn ˈtʃæpl/ *n.* **the ~:** die Sixtinische Kapelle

sit /sɪt/

A *v.i.,* **-tt-, sat** /sæt/ **1** (become seated) sich setzen; **~ on** *or* **in a chair/in an armchair** sich auf einen Stuhl/in einen Sessel setzen; **~!** (to dog) sitz!; **~ by** *or* **with sb.** sich zu jmdm. setzen; **~ over there!** setz dich dort drüben hin!

2 (be seated) sitzen; **don't just ~ there!** sitz nicht einfach rum (ugs.); **~ at home** (fig.) zu Hause sitzen; **~ in judgement on** *or* **over sb./sth.** über jmdn./etw. zu Gericht sitzen; **~ on one's hands** (fig.) sich nicht rühren; **~ still!** sitz ruhig *od.* still!; **~ tight** (coll.) ruhig sitzen bleiben; (fig.: stay in hiding) sich nicht fortrühren; (fig.: persevere in a course of action) sich nicht beirren lassen; **~ well [in the saddle/on one's horse]** einen guten Sitz haben; *see also* **fence A 1; foot A 1; pretty B**

3 **~ for one's portrait/to a painter** *etc.* Porträt sitzen/einem Maler *usw.* Modell sitzen

4 ▸**babysit**

5 (take a test) **~ for sth.** die Prüfung für etw. machen

6 (be in session) tagen

7 (be on perch or nest) sitzen

8 (be situated) sich befinden; **the sewing machine sat in the attic** die Nähmaschine stand auf dem Dachboden herum; **~ well on sb.** (fit) jmdm. gut passen; (suit) jmdm. gut stehen; (fig.) gut zu jmdm. passen

9 (be member of elected body) **~ at Westminster** Mitglied des [britischen] Parlaments sein; **~ for** (Brit. Parl.) vertreten; Abgeordneter/Abgeordnete sein für

B *v.t.,* **-tt-, sat** **1** (cause to be seated, place) setzen **2** (Brit.) **~ an examination** eine Prüfung machen; (have space for) ▸**seat B 2**

Phrasal verbs

- **~ a'bout, ~ a'round** *v.i.* herumsitzen (ugs.)
- **~ 'back** *v.i.* **1** sich zurücklehnen **2** (fig.: do nothing) sich im Sessel zurücklehnen (fig.); **the government is ~ting back and letting the situation worsen** die Regierung sieht tatenlos zu, wie sich die Lage verschlechtert
- **~ 'by** *v.i.* tatenlos zusehen
- **~ 'down**

A *v.i.* **1** (become seated) sich setzen (**on/in** auf/in + *Akk.*); **~ you down** (coll.) setz dich hin **2** (be seated) sitzen; **take sth. ~ting down** (fig.) etw. auf sich (*Dat.*) sitzen lassen

B *v.t.* **~ sb. down** (invite to ~) jmdn. Platz nehmen lassen; (help to ~) jmdm. helfen, sich zu setzen. *See also* **sit-down**

- **~ 'in** *v.i.* **1** (occupy place as protest) ein Sit-in veranstalten **2** (stay in) zu Hause bleiben **3** (participate) mitspielen; **~ in on** (be present at) teilnehmen an (+ *Dat.*); dabei sein bei **4** ▸**stand in 1**. *See also* **sit-in**
- **~ on** *v.t.* **1** (serve as member of) sitzen in (+ *Dat.*) ‹*Ausschuss usw.*›; **~ on the jury** (Law) Geschworener sein **2** (coll.: delay) in der Schublade liegen lassen (fig. ugs.); auf die lange Bank schieben (ugs.) ‹*Entscheidung*› **3** (coll.: repress) unterdrücken; nicht aufkommen lassen ‹*Wunsch, Gedanken*›; **people like her want ~ting on/ought to be sat on** Leute wie sie muss/sollte man an der kurzen Leine halten (ugs.) **4** (fig.: hold on to) festhalten
- **~ 'out**

A *v.i.* draußen *od.* im Freien sitzen

B *v.t.* **1** (take no part in) aussetzen; **~ out a dance** einen Tanz auslassen **2** (endure) durchstehen

- **~ 'through** ▸**~ out B 2**
- **~ 'up**

A *v.i.* **1** (rise) sich aufsetzen **2** (be sitting erect) [aufrecht] sitzen **3** (not slouch) gerade sitzen; **~ up straight!** sitz gerade!; **make sb. ~ up** (fig. coll.) jmdn. aufhorchen lassen; **~ up and take notice** (fig. coll.) aufhorchen **4** (delay going to bed) aufbleiben; **~ up [waiting] for sb.** aufbleiben und auf jmdn. warten; **~ up with sb.** bei jmdm. Nachtwache halten

B *v.t.* aufsetzen. *See also* **sit-up**

- **~ upon** ▸**~ on**; *see also* **sit-upon**

sitar /ˈsɪtɑː(r), sɪˈtɑː(r)/ *n.* (Mus.) Sitar, *der*

sitcom /ˈsɪtkɒm/ (coll.) ▸**situation comedy**

'sit-down

A *n.* **have a ~:** sich setzen; **enjoy a ~:** sich gern einmal hinsetzen

B *adj.* **~ demonstration** Sitzblockade, *die;* **~ meal** (*im Sitzen eingenommenes*) Essen; **~ strike** Sitzstreik, *der*

site /saɪt/

A *n.* **1** (land) Grundstück, *das;* **archaeological/prehistoric burial ~:** archäologische Grabungsstätte/vorgeschichtliche Grabstätte; **exhibition ~:** Ausstellungsgelände, *das;* **~ of a battle** Kampfplatz, *der* **2** (location) Sitz, *der;* (of new factory etc.) Standort, *der* **3** ▸**building site** **4** (Web ~) Site, *die*

B *v.t.* (locate) stationieren ‹*Raketen*›; **~ a factory in London** London als Standort einer Fabrik wählen; **be ~d** gelegen sein

site: ~ map *n.* (Computing) Sitemap, *die;* **~ 'office** *n.* Bau[stellen]büro, *das*

'sit-in *n.* Sit-in, *das*

siting /ˈsaɪtɪŋ/ *n.* Standortwahl, *die* (**of** für); (position) Lage, *die;* (of missiles) Stationierung, *die;* **the ~ of the new exhibition centre in Leeds** die Wahl von Leeds als Standort des neuen Ausstellungszentrums

sits vac /sɪts ˈvæk/ *n. pl.* (Brit. coll.) Stellenangebote *Pl.*

sitter /ˈsɪtə(r)/ *n.* 1 (Sport coll.) (easy catch) leicht zu fangender Ball; (easy shot) idiotensichere Vorlage (ugs. scherzh.) 2 (artist's model) Modell, *das* 3 (hen) Glucke, *die;* Bruthenne, *die* 4 ▸ **babysitter**

sitting /ˈsɪtɪŋ/
A *n.* 1 (session) Sitzung, *die;* **lunch is served in two ~s** es wird in zwei Schichten Mittag gegessen; **when is the first ~ [for lunch]?** wann geht der erste Schub [zum Mittagessen]?; **in one** *or* **at a ~** (fig.) in einem Zug[e] 2 (Law) Sitzungsperiode, *die*
B *adj.* 1 (not flying or running) sitzend 2 (hatching) sitzend; brütend; **these are ~ hens** das sind Bruthennen

sitting: ~ ˈduck *n.* (fig.) leichtes Ziel; **~ ˈmember** *n.* (Brit. Parl.) **she is/was the ~ member** sie ist/war die derzeitige/damalige Abgeordnete; **~ room** *n.* 1 (lounge) Wohnzimmer, *das;* (in public buildings) Aufenthaltsraum, *der;* 2 (space) Sitzplatz, *der;* **~ ˈtarget** ▸ **~ duck**; **~ ˈtenant** *n.* **he is/was the ~ tenant** er ist/war der jetzige/damalige Mieter; **there is a ~ tenant** es ist ein Mieter vorhanden

situate
A /ˈsɪtjʊeɪt/ *v.t.* legen; einrichten ‹Büro›
B /ˈsɪtjʊət/ *adj.* (Law) ▸ **situated**

situated /ˈsɪtjʊeɪtɪd/ *adj.* 1 gelegen; **be ~:** liegen; **a badly ~ house** ein Haus in schlechter *od.* ungünstiger Lage; **the house is well ~ for the shops** in der Nähe des Hauses gibt es gute Einkaufsmöglichkeiten 2 **be well/badly ~ financially** finanziell gut/schlecht gestellt sein

situation /sɪtjʊˈeɪʃn/ *n.* 1 (location) Lage, *die* 2 (circumstances) Situation, *die;* **a ~ of some delicacy** eine ziemlich heikle Situation; **be in the happy ~ of being able to do sth.** in der glücklichen Lage sein, etw. tun zu können; **his ~ is as follows: ...:** seine Lage stellt sich folgendermaßen dar: ...; **what's the ~?** wie stehts?; **lead to a compromise ~:** zu einem Kompromiss führen; **the firm is in a profit ~:** die Firma schreibt Gewinne 3 (job) Stelle, *die;* **~s vacant/wanted** Stellenangebote/-gesuche

situational /sɪtjʊˈeɪʃənl/ *adj.* Situations-; **~ drama** Handlungsdrama, *das* (Literaturw.)

situation ˈcomedy *n.* Situationskomödie, *die* (*Serie von Radio- oder Fernsehkomödien mit unverbundenen Episoden bei gleich bleibenden Rollen*)

sit: ~-up *n.: Bewegung aus der Rückenlage in den Langsitz* (*als gymnastische Übung*); **do twenty ~-ups** sich zwanzigmal aufsetzen; **~-upon** *n.* (coll.) Sitzfläche, *die* (ugs. scherzh.)

six /sɪks/ ▸❶ **p. 894**, ▸❶ **p. 1001**, ▸❶ **p. 1358**
A *adj.* sechs; **be ~ feet** *or* **foot under** (coll.) unter der Erde liegen; **it is ~ of one and half-a-dozen of the other** (coll.) das ist Jacke wie Hose (ugs.); *see also* **eight A**
B *n.* 1 (number, symbol) Sechs, *die;* **be at ~es and sevens** sich in einem heillosen Durcheinander befinden; (on an issue or matter) heillos zerstritten sein (**on** über + *Akk.*); *see also* **best C 4**; **eight B 1, 3, 4** 2 (Cricket) *Schlag, mit dem man sechs Punkte gewinnt; see also* **hit A 11**

Six ˈCounties *n. pl.* **the ~:** Nordirland (*das*) (*mit Londonderry, Antrim, Down, Armagh, Tyrone, Fermanagh*)

six: ~fold *adj., adv.* sechsfach; *see also* **eightfold**; **~-ˈfooter** *n.* (person) Zweimetermann, *der*/-frau, *die;* **most of them are ~-footers** die meisten sind fast zwei Meter groß; **~-pack** *n.* Sechserpack, *der;* **~pence** /ˈsɪkspəns/ *n.* (Brit. Hist.: coin) Sixpence, *der;* **~penny** /ˈsɪkspənɪ/ *adj.* (Brit.) zu sechs Pennies *nachgestellt; see also* **bit² 7**; **~-shooter** *n.* sechsschüssiger Revolver

sixteen /sɪksˈtiːn/ ▸❶ **p. 894**, ▸❶ **p. 1001**, ▸❶ **p. 1358**
A *adj.* sechzehn; **sweet ~:** süße sechzehn [Jahre alt]; *see also* **eight A**
B *n.* Sechzehn, *die; see also* **eight B 1, 4**; **eighteen B**

sixteenth /sɪksˈtiːnθ/ ▸❶ **p. 1047**
A *adj.* ▸❶ **p. 1358** sechzehnt...; *see also* **eighth A**
B *n.* (fraction) Sechzehntel, *das; see also* **eighth B**

sixˈteenth note *n.* (Amer. Mus.) Sechzehntelnote, *die*

sixth /sɪksθ/
A *adj.* ▸❶ **p. 1358** sechst...; *see also* **eighth A**
B *n.* 1 (in sequence, rank) Sechste, *der/die/das;* (fraction) Sechstel, *das* 2 ▸ **sixth form** 3 (Mus.) Sexte, *die* 4 ▸❶ **p. 1047** (day) **the ~ of May** der sechste Mai; **the ~ [of the month]** der Sechste [des Monats]. *See also* **eighth B**

sixth: ~ form *n.* (Brit. Sch.) ≈ zwölfte/dreizehnte Klasse; **~-form college** *n.* (Brit. Sch.) ≈ Oberstufenzentrum, *das; College, das nur Schüler der zwölften/dreizehnten Klasse aufnimmt;* **~-former** *n.* (Brit. Sch.) Schüler/Schülerin der zwölften/dreizehnten Klasse; **~ ˈsense** *n.* sechster Sinn

sixtieth /ˈsɪkstɪɪθ/
A *adj.* ▸❶ **p. 1358** sechzigst...; *see also* **eighth A**
B *n.* (fraction) Sechzigstel, *das; see also* **eighth B**

sixty /ˈsɪkstɪ/ ▸❶ **p. 894**, ▸❶ **p. 1358**
A *adj.* sechzig; *see also* **eight A**
B *n.* Sechzig, *die; see also* **eight B 1**; **eighty B**

sixty: ~-ˈfirst *etc. adj.* ▸❶ **p. 1358** einundsechzigst... *usw.; see also* **eighth A**; **~-ˈone** *etc.* A *adj.* einundsechzig *usw.; see also* **eight A**; B *n.* ▸❶ **p. 1358** Einundsechzig *usw., die; see also* **eight B 1**

size¹ /saɪz/
A *n.* 1 Größe, *die;* (fig. of problem, project) Umfang, *der;* Ausmaß, *das;* **reach full ~:** auswachsen; **be quite a ~:** ziemlich groß sein; **what a ~ he is!** wie groß er ist!; **be twice the ~ of sth.** zweimal so groß wie etw. sein; **who can afford a car that ~?** wer kann sich (*Dat.*) einen so großen Wagen leisten?; **what ~ [of] box do you want?** welche Größe soll die [gewünschte] Schachtel haben?; **take the ~ of sth.** etw. [aus]messen; **be small in ~:** klein sein; **be of great/small ~:** groß/klein sein; **a car of some ~:** ein ziemlich großes Auto; **be of a ~:** gleich groß sein; **be the ~ of sth.** so groß wie etw. sein; **be the ~ of a pea** erbsengroß sein; **a house the ~ of a palace** ein Haus so groß wie ein Palast; **that's [about] the ~ of it** (fig. coll.) so sieht die Sache aus (ugs.); **try sth. for ~** (fig.) etw. [wegen der Größe] anprobieren; (fig.) es einmal mit etw. versuchen; **what ~?** wie groß?; *see also* **cut down A 3** 2 (graded class) Größe, *die;* (of paper) Format, *das;* **collar/waist ~:** Kragen-/Taillenweite, *die;* **take a ~ 7 shoe/ ~ 7 in shoes** Schuhgröße 7 haben; **what ~ is Madam?** welche Größe hat die Dame?; **A 5 ~ paper** A5-Papier; **E 10 ~:** Größe E 10
B *v.t.* nach der Größe sortieren

Phrasal verb
- **~ ˈup** *v.t.* taxieren ‹*Lage*›; **I can't ~ her up** ich werde aus ihr nicht schlau (ugs.)

size²
A *n.* Leim, *der;* (for textiles) Schlichte, *die*
B *v.t.* leimen; schlichten ‹*Textilfaser*›

-size /saɪz/ *adj. in comb.* **average-~:** durchschnittlich groß; **small-/medium-/large-~:** klein/mittelgroß/groß; *see also* **full-size**

sizeable /ˈsaɪzəbl/ *adj.* ziemlich groß; beträchtlich ‹*Summe, Schwierigkeiten, Wissen, Einfluss, Unterschied*›; ansehnlich ‹*Betrag*›

-sized /saɪzd/ *adj. in comb.* ▸ **-size**; **good-~:** größer

sizzle /ˈsɪzl/
A *v.i.* 1 zischen 2 (coll.: be hot or excited) schmoren (ugs.); **be sizzling with anger** vor Wut kochen (ugs.)
B *n.* Zischen, *das*

sizzling /ˈsɪzlɪŋ/
A *adj.* 1 zischend 2 (very hot) brütend heiß; **~ heat/weather** Gluthitze, *die* 3 (very fast) blitzschnell (ugs.)
B *adv.* **~ hot** brütend heiß ‹*Wetter*›; zischend heiß ‹*Steak*›

skat /skæt/ *n.* (Cards) Skat, *der*

skate¹ /skeɪt/ *n.* (Zool.) Rochen, *der*

skate²
A *n.* (ice ~) Schlittschuh, *der;* (roller ~) Rollschuh, *der;* **get one's ~s on** (Brit. fig. coll.) sich sputen
B *v.i.* (ice-~) Schlittschuh laufen; (roller-~) Rollschuh laufen; **he ~d over to her/in circles** er lief zu ihr hinüber/drehte Kreise; **the insects ~ on the water** (fig.) die Insekten gleiten über das Wasser; **~ on thin ice** (fig.) sich auf dünnem Eis bewegen; (put oneself in danger) sich auf dünnes Eis begeben

Phrasal verb
- **~ over, ~ round** *v.t.* (fig.) (avoid) hinweggehen über (+ *Akk.*) ‹*Frage, Problem*›; (touch lightly on) [nur] streifen

skate: ~board A *n.* Skateboard, *das;* Rollerbrett, *das;* B *v.i.* Skateboard fahren; **~boarder** *n.* Skateboardfahrer, *der*/-fahrerin, *die;* **~boarding** *n., no pl.* Skateboardfahren, *das;* **~park** *n.* Skatepark, *der*

skater /ˈskeɪtə(r)/ *n.* (ice ~) Eisläufer, *der*/-läuferin, *die;* (roller ~) Rollschuhläufer, *der*/-läuferin, *die*

skating /ˈskeɪtɪŋ/ *n., no pl.* (ice ~) Schlittschuhlaufen, *das;* (roller ~) Rollschuhlaufen, *das*

ˈskating rink *n.* 1 (ice) Eisbahn, *die;* Eisfläche, *die* 2 (for roller skating) Rollschuhbahn, *die*

skedaddle /skɪˈdædl/ *v.i.* (coll.) türmen (salopp)

skeet /skiːt/ *n.* (Sport) **~ [shooting]** Skeetschießen, *das*

skein /skeɪn/ *n.* 1 (of wool etc.) Strang, *der;* Docke, *die* 2 (fig.: tangle) Knäuel, *das;* (of lies) Netz, *das* 3 **a ~ of wild geese** eine Schar Wildgänse

skeletal /ˈskelɪtl/ *adj.* 1 (relating to the skeleton) Skelett- 2 (emaciated) knochendürr ‹*Körper, Hand*›; **have a ~ appearance, look ~:** wie ein Skelett *od.* Gerippe aussehen

skeleton /ˈskelɪtn/ *n.* 1 Skelett, *das;* Gerippe, *das;* **have a ~ in the cupboard** (Brit.) *or* (Amer.) **closet** (fig.) eine Leiche im Keller haben (ugs.) 2 (framework) Skelett, *das* (Bauw.); (of ship) Gerippe, *das* 3 (outline) Gerüst, *das* 4 (fig.: thin person or animal) Gerippe, *das;* **she was reduced to a ~:** sie magerte fast bis zum Gerippe ab

skeleton: ~ ˈcrew *n.* Stammbesatzung, *die;* **~ ˈkey** *n.* Dietrich, *der;* **~ ˈservice** *n.* **provide a ~ service** den Betrieb notdürftig aufrechterhalten; **there were buses running, but it was only a ~ service** es fuhren zwar Busse, aber nur einige wenige; **~ ˈstaff** *n.* Minimalbesetzung, *die*

skepsis, skeptic (Amer.) ▸ **scep-**

sketch /sketʃ/
A *n.* 1 (drawing) Skizze, *die;* **do** *or* **make a ~:** eine Skizze anfertigen 2 (fig.: outline) **give** *or* **deliver a ~ of the situation** die Lage skizzieren; **the plan is only a ~ at the moment** der Plan existiert zur Zeit nur in [groben] Umrissen 3 (play) Sketch, *der* 4 (Lit., Mus.) Skizze, *die*
B *v.t.* (lit. or fig.) skizzieren
C *v.i.* skizzieren

Phrasal verbs
- **~ ˈin** *v.t.* 1 (draw) einzeichnen 2 (fig.: outline) skizzieren
- **~ ˈout** *v.t.* (lit. or fig.) [in groben Umrissen] skizzieren

sketch: ~ block *n.* Skizzenblock, *der;* **~book** *n.* Skizzenbuch, *das*

sketcher /ˈsketʃə(r)/ *n.* Skizzenmaler, *der*/-malerin, *die* (**of** für)

sketchily /ˈsketʃɪlɪ/ *adv.* skizzenhaft; flüchtig ‹*vorbereiten, berichten, aufzeichnen*›

sketching /ˈsketʃɪŋ/ *n.* Skizzieren, *das*

sketch: ~ map *n.* Faustskizze, *die;* **~ pad** ▸ **sketch block**

sketchy /ˈsketʃɪ/ *adj.* 1 skizzenhaft 2 (incomplete) lückenhaft ‹*Information, Bericht*› 3 (inadequate) unzureichend

skew /skjuː/
A *adj.* schräg; schief ‹*Gesicht*›
B *n.* **on the ~** schräg ‹*überqueren*›; schief ‹*tragen, aufsetzen*›; **the picture is [hanging] on the ~:** das Bild hängt schief
C *v.t.* abschrägen; verzerren ‹*Gesicht, Gestalt, Sachverhalt*›
D *v.i.* **~ round** sich drehen

S

skewer /ˈskjuːə(r)/
A n. [Brat]spieß, der
B v.t. aufspießen
skew-ˈwhiff (Brit. coll.) ▸ **askew**
ski /skiː/
A n. **1** Ski, der **2** (on vehicle) Kufe, die
B v.i. Ski laufen od. fahren; ~ **down the hill** [auf Skiern] den Berg hinabfahren; ~ **cross-country** Skilanglauf machen
ski: ~**-bob** n. Skibob, der; ~**-bobbing** n. Skibobfahren, das; ~ **boot** n. Skistiefel, der; ~ **cap** n. Skimütze, die
skid /skɪd/
A v.i., **-dd-** **1** schlittern; (from one side to the other; spinning round) schleudern; ~ **to a halt** schlitternd/schleudernd zum Stehen kommen **2** (on foot) rutschen
B n. **1** Schlittern, das; (from one side to the other; spinning round) Schleudern, das; **go into a** ~: ins Schlittern/Schleudern geraten; **get out of the** ~, **correct the** ~: das Schlittern/Schleudern abfangen; **steer into the** ~: gegenlenken **2** (Aeronaut.) Gleitkufe, die; **tail/wing** ~: Gleitkufe unter dem Leitwerk/Flügel **3** (braking device) Radschuh, der; Hemmschuh, der **4** (support) Stützbalken, der **5** (slideway) Schrotbaum, der; (used in pairs or sets) Schrotleiter, die; (roller) Rolle, die; **be on the** ~**s** (fig. coll.) auf dem absteigenden Ast sein; **the plan/project is on the** ~**s** (fig. coll.) der Plan/das Projekt droht zu scheitern; **put the** ~**s under sb./sth.** (fig. coll.) jmdn./etw. zu Fall bringen
skid: ~ **chains** ▸ **snow chains**; ~ **lid** n. (coll.) Sturzhelm, der; ~ **marks** n. pl. Schleuderspur, die; ~**pad** n. (Amer.), ~**pan** n. (Brit.) *Gelände, auf dem ein Schleudertraining durchgeführt wird;* ~ **row** /ˈskɪdˈrəʊ/ n. (Amer.) Pennerviertel, das (salopp abwertend); **end up on** ~ **row** (coll.) als Penner enden (salopp abwertend)
skier /ˈskiːə(r)/ n. Skiläufer, der/-läuferin, die; Skifahrer, der/-fahrerin, die
skiff /skɪf/ n. Skiff, das; (racing boat also) Einer, der
skiffle /ˈskɪfl/ n. Skiffle, der od. das; attrib. Skiffle-
ˈski goggles n. pl. Skibrille, die
skiing /ˈskiːɪŋ/ n., no pl. Skilaufen, das; Skifahren, das; (Sport) Skisport, der
skiing: ~ **holiday** n. Skiurlaub, der; ~ **instructor** n. ▸ **❶ p. 1260** Skilehrer, der/-lehrerin, die; ~ **resort** n. Ski[urlaubs]ort, der
ski: ~ **jump** n. **1** (slope) Sprungschanze, die; **2** (leap) Skisprung, der; ~ **jumper** n. Skispringer, der/-springerin, die; ~ **jumping** n., no pl. Skispringen, das
skilful /ˈskɪlfl/ adj. **1** (having skill) geschickt; gewandt ‹Redner›; gut ‹Beobachter, Lehrer› **2** (well executed) geschickt; kunstvoll ‹Gemälde, Plastik, Roman, Komposition›; (expert) fachgerecht ‹Beurteilung›; kunstgerecht ausgeführt ‹Operation›
skilfully /ˈskɪlfəlɪ/ adv. geschickt; kunstvoll ‹malen, dichten, komponieren›; fachgerecht ‹urteilen›; kunstgerecht ‹operieren›
skilfulness /ˈskɪlflnɪs/ n., no pl. ▸ **skill 1**
ˈski lift n. Skilift, der
skill /skɪl/ n. **1** (expertness) Geschick, das; Fertigkeit, die; (of artist) Können, das; **have** ~ **at** or **in sth.** Geschick/Fertigkeit in etw. (Dat.) haben **2** (technique) Fertigkeit, die; (of weaving, bricklaying) Technik, die; Kunst, die; **the** ~ **of making guests feel at home** die Kunst, Gäste sich wie zu Hause fühlen zu lassen **3** in pl. (abilities) Fähigkeiten; **office** ~**s** Büroerfahrung, die; **language** ~**s** Sprachkenntnisse, die **4** (dexterity) Geschicklichkeit, die; (of speech) Gewandtheit, die; (of painting) Kunstfertigkeit, die
skilled /skɪld/ adj. **1** ▸ **skilful 1** **2** (requiring skill) qualifiziert ‹Arbeit, Tätigkeit›; ~ **trade** Ausbildungsberuf, der; Lehrberuf, der (veralt.) **3** (trained) ausgebildet; (experienced) erfahren; **be** ~ **in diplomacy/sewing** ein geschickter Diplomat sein/gut nähen können
skillet /ˈskɪlɪt/ n. **1** (Brit.: cooking pot) Tiegel, der (mit Füßen) **2** (Amer.: frying pan) Bratpfanne, die
skillful, skillfully, skillfulness (Amer.) ▸ **skilful** etc.

ˈskills shortage n. Fachkräftemangel, der
skim /skɪm/
A v.t., **-mm-** **1** (remove) abschöpfen; abrahmen ‹Milch› **2** (touch in passing) streifen **3** (pass closely over) ~ **sth.** dicht über etw. (Akk.) fliegen **4** (throw) segeln lassen; hüpfen lassen ‹Stein› **5** (scan briefly) ▸ **skim through**
B v.i., **-mm-** segeln; **a bullet** ~**med past** or **by my arm** eine Kugel schwirrte an meinem Arm vorbei

Phrasal verbs
- ~ **ˈoff** v.t. **1** abschöpfen **2** (fig.) ▸ **cream off**
- ~ **through** v.t. überfliegen ‹Buch, Zeitung›

skimmed ˈmilk, skim ˈmilk n. entrahmte Milch
skimming /ˈskɪmɪŋ/ n., no pl. (card fraud) Skimming, das
skimp /skɪmp/
A v.t. sparen an (+ Dat.); **he did the work badly,** ~**ing it** er schluderte bei seiner Arbeit (ugs.)
B v.i. sparen (**with, on** an + Dat.); **he had to** ~ **on food/clothes** er musste am Essen/an der Kleidung sparen
skimpily /ˈskɪmpɪlɪ/ adv. sparsam ‹bekleidet›; kärglich ‹essen›; knapp ‹geschneidert›
skimpy /ˈskɪmpɪ/ adj. sparsam; karg ‹Mahl›; kärglich ‹Leben›; winzig ‹Badeanzug›; [zu] knapp ‹Anzug›; spärlich ‹Wissen›
skin /skɪn/
A n. **1** ▸ **❶ p. 951** Haut, die; **be all** or **just** ~ **and bone** (fig.) nur Haut und Knochen sein (ugs.); **be soaked** or **wet to the** ~: bis auf die Haut durchnässt sein; **change one's** ~ (fig.) sich völlig verwandeln; **by** or **with the** ~ **of one's teeth** mit knapper Not; **get under sb.'s** ~ (fig. coll.) (irritate sb.) jmdm. auf die Nerven gehen od. fallen (ugs.); (fascinate or enchant sb.) jmdm. unter die Haut gehen (ugs.); **have a thick/thin** ~ (fig.) ein dickes Fell haben (ugs.)/dünnhäutig sein; **jump out of one's** ~ (fig.) aus dem Häuschen geraten (ugs.); **save one's** ~ (fig.) seine Haut retten (ugs.); **it's no** ~ **off my/his** etc. **nose** (coll.) das braucht mich/ihn usw. nicht zu jucken (ugs.); **wear sth. next to one's** ~: etw. auf der [bloßen] Haut tragen; **we are all brothers under the** ~: wir sind uns im Grunde alle sehr ähnlich **2** (hide) Haut, die **3** (fur) Fell, das **4** (peel) Schale, die; (of onion, peach also) Haut, die **5** (sausage-casing) Haut, die; Pelle, die (landsch., bes. nordd.) **6** (on milk) Haut, die **7** (leather) Leder, das **8** (Brit. coll.) ▸ **skinhead 1** **9** (vessel) Schlauch, der **10** (Naut., Aeronaut.) Außenhaut, die **11** (stencil) Matrize, die
B v.t., **-nn-** (remove ~ from) häuten; schälen ‹Frucht›; ~ **one's knee** etc. sich (Dat.) das Knie usw. [auf]schürfen (**on** an, auf + Dat., **against** an + Dat.); ~ **sb. alive** (fig. coll.) Hackfleisch aus jmdm. machen (ugs.); see also **eye A 1**
skin: ~ **cancer** n. ▸ **❶ p. 1231** Hautkrebs, der; ~ **cream** n. Hautcreme, die; ~**-ˈdeep** adj. (fig.) oberflächlich; see also **beauty 1**; ~ **disease** n. Hautkrankheit, die; ~**-dive** v.i. tauchen; ~**-diver** n. Taucher, der/Taucherin, die; ~**-diving** n., no pl. Tauchen, das; ~ **flick** n. (coll.) Pornofilm, der (ugs.); ~**flint** n. Geizhals, der (abwertend); ~ **food** n. Nährcreme, die
skinful /ˈskɪnfʊl/ n. (coll.) **have had a** ~: voll sein (salopp)
skin: ~ **game** n. (Amer. coll.) [betrügerisches] Glücksspiel; ~ **graft** n. Hauttransplantation, die; ~**head** n. **1** (Brit.) Skinhead, der; **2** (Amer. coll.: naval recruit) Marinerekrut, der
-skinned /skɪnd/ adj. in comb. -häutig
skinny /ˈskɪnɪ/ adj. mager
ˈskinny-dipping n. (coll.) Nacktbaden, das
skint /skɪnt/ adj. (Brit. coll.) bankrott; **be** ~: blank od. pleite sein (ugs.)
skin: ~ **test** n. Hauttest, der; ~**tight** adj. hauteng
skip¹ /skɪp/
A v.i., **-pp-** **1** hüpfen **2** (use skipping rope) seilspringen **3** (change quickly) springen (fig.) **4** (make omissions) überspringen **5** (coll.: flee) abhauen (ugs.)
B v.t., **-pp-** **1** (omit) überspringen; (in mentioning names) übergehen; ~ **it!** (coll.) vergiss es (ugs.); **my heart** ~**ped a beat** (fig.) mir stockte das Herz **2** (coll.: miss) schwänzen (ugs.) ‹Schule usw.›; liegen lassen ‹Hausarbeit›; ~ **breakfast/lunch** etc. das Frühstück/Mittagessen usw. auslassen **3** (coll.: flee from) abhauen aus (ugs.); see also **bail¹ A 1** **4** ~ **rope** (Amer.) seilspringen
C n. Hüpfer, der; Hopser, der (ugs.); **give a** ~ **of delight** vor Freude hüpfen

Phrasal verbs
- ~ **aˈbout** v.i. **1** herumhüpfen **2** **he did not stay with his subject but** ~**ped about** er hielt sich nicht an sein Thema, sondern sprang von einem Gegenstand zum anderen od. nächsten
- ~ **aˈcross** v.i. hinüberspringen; rüberspringen (ugs.); ~ **across to France** (fig.) kurz nach Frankreich hinüberfahren od. (ugs.) rüberfahren
- ~ **aˈround** ▸ ~ **about**
- ~ **ˈoff** v.i. **1** ▸ **pop off 2** **2** (flee) sich absetzen (ugs.)
- ~ **over**
A /-ˈ--/ v.i. ▸ ~ **across**
B /ˈ---/ v.t. ▸ ~ **B 1**
- ~ **through** v.t. **1** ▸ **skim through** **2** (make short work of) [rasch] durchziehen (ugs.); herunterschnurren (ugs.) ‹Vorlesung›

skip² n. **1** (Building) Container, der **2** (Mining) Skip, der; Fördergefäß, das
skip³ (Sport coll.) ▸ **skipper A 3**
ski: ~ **pass** n. Skipass, der; ~**-plane** n. Kufenflugzeug, das; ~ **pole** n. Skistock, der
skipper /ˈskɪpə(r)/
A n. **1** (Naut.) Kapitän, der; (of yacht) Skipper, der (Seglerjargon) **2** (Aeronaut.) [Flug]kapitän, der **3** (Sport) [Mannschafts]kapitän, der
B v.t. ~ **a yacht** etc. Kapitän einer Jacht usw. sein; ~ **the team to victory** die Mannschaft zum Sieg führen
skipping rope /ˈskɪpɪŋrəʊp/ (Brit.), **ˈskiprope** (Amer.) ns. Sprungseil, das; Springseil, das
ˈski resort n. Skiurlaubsort, der
skirl /skɜːl/ n. durchdringendes od. gellendes Pfeifen
skirmish /ˈskɜːmɪʃ/
A n. **1** (fight) Rangelei, die (ugs.); (of troops, armies) Gefecht, das (Milit.) **2** (fig.: argument) Auseinandersetzung, die
B v.i. **1** (fight) miteinander rangeln (ugs.); ‹Armeen, Truppen:› sich (Dat.) Gefechte (Milit.) liefern **2** (fig.: argue) [sich] streiten
skirt /skɜːt/
A n. **1** Rock, der **2** (of coat) Schoß, der **3** (border) Rand, der; Saum, der (geh.) **4** (on hovercraft) Schürze, die **5** (Riding) Seitenblatt, das **6** (Brit.: cut of meat) ~ **of beef** Rindfleisch vom Unterbauch **7** (sl.: woman) **[a bit of]** ~: [eine] Mieze (salopp)
B v.t. **1** (go past edge of) herumgehen um **2** (border on) ‹Straße, Weg:› entlangführen an (+ Dat.)
C v.i. ~ **along sth.** an etw. (Dat.) entlanggehen/-fahren/-reiten usw.

Phrasal verb
- ~ **round** v.t. herumgehen um; (fig.) umgehen; ausweichen (+ Dat.)

skirting /ˈskɜːtɪŋ/ n. ~ **[board]** (Brit.) Fußleiste, die
ski: ~ **run** n. Skihang, der; (prepared) [Ski]piste, die; ~ **slope** n. Skihang, der; (prepared) [Ski]piste, die; ~ **stick** n. Skistock, der; ~ **suit** n. Skianzug, der
skit /skɪt/ n. parodistischer Sketch (**on** über + Akk.)
ˈski tow n. Schlepplift, der
skittish /ˈskɪtɪʃ/ adj. **1** (nervous) nervös ‹Pferd›; (inclined to shy) schreckhaft ‹Pferd› **2** (lively) ausgelassen; aufgekratzt (ugs.)
skittishly /ˈskɪtɪʃlɪ/ adv. ▸ **skittish**: nervös; schreckhaft; ausgelassen; aufgekratzt (ugs.)
skittle /ˈskɪtl/ n. **1** Kegel, der **2** in pl., constr. as sing. (game) Kegeln, das; **play [at]** ~**s** kegeln; see also **beer**

Phrasal verb
- ~ **ˈout** v.t. (Cricket) in schneller Folge ausscheiden lassen ‹die gegnerischen Schlagmänner›

S

'skittle alley *n.* Kegelbahn, *die*

skive /skaɪv/

A *v.t.* **1** (pare) schaben ‹*Leder, Fell*› **2** (Brit. coll.: evade) sich drücken vor (+ *Dat.*) (ugs.); schwänzen (ugs.) ‹*Schule usw.*›

B *v.i.* (Brit. coll.) sich drücken (ugs.)

Phrasal verb

• **~ 'off** (Brit. coll.)

A *v.i.* sich verdrücken (ugs.)

B *v.t.* schwänzen (ugs.)

skiver /'skaɪvə(r)/ *n.* (Brit. coll.) Drückeberger, *der*/Drückebergerin, *die*

skivvy /'skɪvɪ/ *n.* (Brit. coll. derog.) Dienstmädchen, *das* (fig. ugs.); Dienstbolzen, *der* (salopp abwertend)

skua /'skju:ə/ *n.* (Ornith.) Skua[raubmöwe], *die*

skulduggery /skʌl'dʌgərɪ/ *n.* (joc.) Hinterlist, *die;* (Polit.) Intrige, *die;* **a piece/an act of ~:** eine Hinterlist/Intrige; **what ~ got you the job?** mit welchen Tricks hast du die Stelle bekommen?

skulk /skʌlk/ *v.i.* **1** (lurk) lauern **2** (move stealthily) schleichen **3** (be cowardly) sich verkriechen **4** (shirk duty) krankfeiern (ugs.)

Phrasal verb

• **~ 'off** *v.i.* sich fortschleichen

skull /skʌl/ *n.* **1** (Anat.) Schädel, *der* **2** (as object) Totenschädel, *der;* (representation) Totenkopf, *der* **3** (fig.: seat of intelligence) Schädel, *der;* **can't you/when will you get it into** *or* **through your thick ~?** (coll.) geht das nicht/wann geht das endlich in deinen Schädel [hinein]? (ugs.)

skull: ~ and crossbones /skʌlən 'krɒsbəʊnz/ *n.* Totenkopf, *der* (*mit gekreuzten Knochen*); (flag) Totenkopfflagge, *die;* **~cap** *n.* **1** (hat) Scheitelkäppchen, *das;* **2** (Anat.) Schädeldach, *das*

skullduggery ▸ **skulduggery**

-skulled /skʌld/ *adj. in comb.* -schädelig

skunk /skʌŋk/ *n.* **1** (Zool.) Stinktier, *das;* Skunk, *der* **2** (coll.: contemptible person) Stinktier, *das* (derb) **3** (fur) Skunk, *der*

'skunk-bear (Amer.) ▸ **wolverine**

sky /skaɪ/

A *n.* Himmel, *der;* **in the ~:** am Himmel; **out of a clear [blue] ~** (fig.) aus heiterem Himmel (ugs.); **praise sb./sth. to the skies** jmdn./etw. in den Himmel heben (ugs.); **there is not a cloud in the ~** (lit. or fig.) es zeigt sich kein Wölkchen am Himmel; **the ~'s the limit** (fig.) da gibt es [praktisch] keine Grenze; **for a man with his qualifications the ~'s the limit** (fig.) einem so hoch qualifizierten Mann stehen alle Möglichkeiten offen; **under the open ~:** unter freiem Himmel

B *v.t.* (Sport) hoch in die Luft schlagen

sky: ~-blue A *adj.* himmelblau; **B** *n.* Himmelblau, *das;* **~box** *n.* (Amer.) [VIP-]Loge, *die;* **~diver** *n.* Fallschirmspringer, *der*/-springerin, *die;* **~diving** *n., no pl.* Fallschirmspringen, *das* (als Sport); Fallschirmsport, *der;* **~-high A** *adj.* himmelhoch; astronomisch (ugs.) ‹*Preise usw.*›; **B** *adv.* hoch in die Luft ‹*werfen, steigen usw.*›; **go ~-high** ‹*Preise usw.:*› in astronomische Höhen klettern (ugs.); **blow a building/a theory ~-high** ein Gebäude in die Luft jagen (ugs.)/eine Theorie völlig umwerfen; **~jack** (Journ. coll.) **A** *v.t.* entführen; **B** *n.* Flugzeugentführung, *die;* **~jacker** /'skaɪ dʒækə(r)/ *n.* (Journ. coll.) Flugzeugentführer, *der*/-entführerin, *die;* **~lark A** *n.* (Ornith.) [Feld-]lerche, *die;* **B** *v.i.* **~lark [about** *or* **around]** herumalbern (ugs.); **~light** *n.* Dachfenster, *das;* **~line** *n.* Silhouette, *die;* (characteristic of certain town) Skyline, *die;* **~ marshal** *n.* Skymarshal, *der;* **~rocket A** *n.* Rakete, *die;* **B** *v.i.* (fig. coll.) ‹*Preise usw.:*› in die Höhe schnellen; ‹*Beliebtheit:*› ungeheuer (ugs.) wachsen; **~sail** /'skaɪseɪl, 'skaɪsl/ *n.* (Naut.) Skysegel, *das;* **~scraper** *n.* Wolkenkratzer, *der*

skyward /'skaɪwəd/

A *adj.* zum Himmel gerichtet; **in a ~ direction/on a ~ path** himmelwärts (geh.)

B *adv.* himmelwärts (geh.); zum *od.* (veralt.) gen Himmel

skywards ▸ **skyward B**

sky: ~way *n.* (Aeronaut.) Fluglinie, *die;* **~writing** *n.* Himmelsschrift, *die*

slab /slæb/ *n.* **1** (flat stone etc.) Platte, *die;* **mortuary ~:** Totenbank, *die* **2** (thick slice) [dicke] Scheibe; (of cake) [dickes] Stück; (of chocolate, toffee) Tafel, *die*

'slab cake *n.* Kastenkuchen, *der*

slack¹ /slæk/

A *adj.* **1** (lax) nachlässig; schlampig (ugs. abwertend); **his ~ attendance** sein unregelmäßiges Erscheinen; **be ~ about** *or* **in** *or* **with sth.** in Bezug auf etw. (*Akk.*) nachlässig sein; **not be ~ about** *or* **in** *or* **at doing sth.** nicht lange zögern, etw. zu tun **2** (loose) schlaff; locker ‹*Schraube, Verband, Strumpfband*› **3** (sluggish) schlaff; schwach ‹*Wind, Flut*› **4** (Commerc.: not busy) flau; **a ~ three weeks** eine dreiwöchige Flaute

B *n.* **1** **there's too much ~ in the rope** das Seil ist zu locker *od.* ist nicht straff genug; **take in** *or* **up the ~:** das Seil/die Schnur *usw.* straffen **2** (lull) Flaute, *die*

C *v.i.* (coll.) bummeln (ugs.)

Phrasal verbs

• **~ 'off** ▸ **slacken off**

• **~ 'up** ▸ **slacken up**

slack² *n.* (coal dust) Grus, *der*

slacken /'slækn/

A *v.i.* **1** (loosen) sich lockern; ‹*Seil:*› schlaff werden **2** (diminish) nachlassen; ‹*Geschwindigkeit:*› sich verringern; ‹*Schritt:*› sich verlangsamen

B *v.t.* **1** (loosen) lockern **2** (diminish) verringern; verlangsamen ‹*Schritt*›; **~ one's efforts/attempts** in seinen Anstrengungen/Bemühungen nachlassen

Phrasal verbs

• **~ 'off**

A *v.i.* **1** (loosen) ▸ **~ A 1** **2** (diminish) ▸ **~ A 2** **3** (relax) es etwas langsamer angehen lassen (ugs.)

B *v.t.* **1** (loosen) ▸ **~ B 1** **2** (diminish) ▸ **~ B 2**

• **~ 'up** *v.i.* **1** (reduce speed) ‹*Zug, Auto:*› die Fahrt verlangsamen; ‹*Schritt:*› sich verlangsamen **2** ▸ **~ off A 3**

slacker /'slækə(r)/ *n.* (derog.) **1** Faulenzer, *der* **2** (Amer.: young adult) Hänger, *der* (ugs.); Durchhänger, *der* (ugs.)

slackly /'slæklɪ/ *adv.* **1** (negligently) nachlässig; schlampig (ugs. abwertend) **2** (loosely) locker; schlaff ‹*hängen*›

slackness /'slæknɪs/ *n., no pl.* **1** (negligence) Nachlässigkeit, *die* **2** (idleness) Bummelei, *die* (ugs.) **3** (looseness) Schlaffheit, *die* **4** (of market, trade) Flaute, *die*

slacks /slæks/ *n. pl.* **[pair of] ~:** lange Hose; Slacks *Pl.* (Mode)

slack 'water *n.* Stauwasser, *das*

slag /slæg/

A *n.* **1** (Metallurgy, Geol.) Schlacke, *die; see also* **basic slag** **2** (sl.: slattern) Schlampe, *die* (salopp)

B *v.t.* **~ [off]** herziehen über (+ *Akk.*) (ugs.)

'slag heap *n.* (Mining) Schlackenhalde, *die*

slain ▸ **slay**

slake /sleɪk/ *v.t.* **1** stillen; löschen, stillen ‹*Durst*› **2** (Chem.) löschen

slaked lime /sleɪkt 'laɪm/ ▸ **lime¹ 1**

slalom /'slɑ:ləm/ *n.* (Skiing; Motor/Canoe racing) Slalom, *der; see also* **giant slalom**

slam¹ /slæm/

A *v.t.*, **-mm-** **1** (shut) zuschlagen; zuknallen (ugs.); **~ the door in sb.'s face** jmdm. die Tür vor der Nase zuschlagen **2** (put violently) knallen (ugs.); **~ sb. in[to] prison** (coll.) jmdn. einbuchten (salopp); **~ one's foot on the brake** (coll.) auf die Bremse steigen (ugs.) **3** (coll.: criticize) ▸ **slate C 1** **4** (coll.: hit with force) knallen (ugs.) ‹*Ball*›

B *v.i.*, **-mm-** **1** zuschlagen; zuknallen (ugs.) **2** (move violently) stürmen; **the car ~med against** *or* **into the wall** das Auto knallte (ugs.) gegen die Mauer

C *n.* (sound) Knall, *der;* **hear the ~ of the door** die Tür zuknallen hören (ugs.)

Phrasal verbs

• **~ 'down** *v.t.* [hin]knallen (ugs.); **~ sth. down on sth.** etw. auf etw. (*Akk.*) knallen (ugs.); **~ down a window** ein Fenster zuknallen (ugs.)

• **~ 'on** *v.t.* (coll.) **~ on the brakes** auf die Bremse latschen (salopp)

• **~ 'to**

A *v.i.* zuschlagen; zuknallen (ugs.)

B *v.t.* zuschlagen; zuknallen (ugs.)

slam² *n.* **1** (Cards) Schlemm, *der;* **grand/little** *or* **small ~:** großer/kleiner Schlemm **2** (Sport) **achieve the grand ~:** alle [wichtigen] Meistertitel gewinnen; (Tennis) den Grand Slam gewinnen

slam-'bang *adv.* mit einem Knall

slammer /'slæmə(r)/ *n.* (sl.) Kittchen, *das* (ugs.)

slander /'slɑ:ndə(r)/

A *n.* **1** (false report, defamation) Verleumdung, *die* (**on** *Gen.*) **2** (Law) [mündliche] Verleumdung

B *v.t.* verleumden; schädigen ‹*Ruf*›

slanderer /'slɑ:ndərə(r)/ *n.* Verleumder, *der*/Verleumderin, *die*

slanderous /'slɑ:ndərəs/ *adj.* verleumderisch

slang /slæŋ/

A *n.* Slang, *der;* ‹*Theater-, Soldaten-, Juristen*›jargon, *der; attrib.* Slang‹*wort, -ausdruck*›

B *v.t.* **~ sb.** jmdn. übel beschimpfen; **~ sth.** etw. zerreißen (ugs.)

'slanging match *n.* gegenseitige [lautstarke] Beschimpfung; **I had a ~ with her** wir warfen uns gegenseitig Beschimpfungen an den Kopf

slangy /'slæŋɪ/ *adj.* Slang‹*ausdruck, -wort*›; salopp ‹*Wortwahl, Redeweise*›

slant /slɑ:nt/

A *v.i.* ‹*Fläche:*› sich neigen; ‹*Linie:*› schräg verlaufen; **the roof ~s at an angle of 45°** das Dach hat eine Neigung von 45°; **green hills ~ing down to the sea** grüne Hügel, die schräg zum Meer abfallen; **his writing ~s from left to right** seine Schrift ist nach rechts geneigt; er schreibt nach rechts; **the desktop ~s** die Schreibtischplatte ist geneigt

B *v.t.* **1** abschrägen; schräg zeichnen ‹*Linie*› **2** (fig.: bias) [so] hinbiegen (ugs.) ‹*Meldung, Bemerkung*›

C *n.* **1** Schräge, *die;* **have a ~ to the right** ‹*Handschrift:*› nach rechts geneigt sein; **cut sth. on a** *or* **the ~:** etw. schräg abschneiden; **be on a** *or* **the ~:** schräg sein; **write on the ~:** schräg schreiben **2** (fig.: bias) Tendenz, *die;* Färbung, *die;* **have a left-wing ~** ‹*Bericht:*› links gefärbt sein; **put a right-wing ~ on sth.** von etw. eine rechts gefärbte Darstellung geben; **give an unfair ~ to events** die Vorfälle schief darstellen

slanted /'slɑ:ntɪd/ *adj.* (fig.) gefärbt; **a ~ question** eine Suggestivfrage

'slant-eyed *adj.* (also derog.) schlitzäugig

slanting /'slɑ:ntɪŋ/ *adj.* schräg

'slantways /'slɑ:ntweɪz/, **slantwise** /'slɑ:ntwaɪz/ *adv.* schräg

slap /slæp/

A *v.t.*, **-pp-** **1** schlagen; **~ sb. on the face/arm/hand** jmdm. ins Gesicht/auf den Arm/auf die Hand schlagen; **~ sb.'s face** *or* **sb. in** *or* **on the face** jmdn. ohrfeigen; **I'll ~ your face!** du bekommst eine Ohrfeige; **~ one's thigh[s]** sich (*Dat.*) auf die Schenkel schlagen; **~ sb. on the back** jmdm. auf die Schulter klopfen; **she deserves to be ~ped on the back** (fig.) sie verdient Beifall; Hut ab vor ihr! (ugs.) **2** (put forcefully) knallen (ugs.); **he ~ped the handcuffs on the prisoner** er ließ die Handschellen an den Armen des Gefangenen zuschnappen; **~ sb. in jail** (coll.) jmdn. ins Gefängnis stecken (ugs.) **3** (put hastily or carelessly) klatschen (ugs.); **~ a fine on sb.** jmdm. eine Geldstrafe aufbrummen (ugs.); **~ a ban on sth.** etw. [kurzerhand] verbieten

B *v.i.*, **-pp-** schlagen; klatschen

C *n.* Schlag, *der;* **give sb. a ~:** jmdn. [mit der flachen Hand] schlagen; **give sth. a ~:** [mit der flachen Hand] auf etw. (*Akk.*) schlagen; **a ~ in the face** (lit. or fig.) ein Schlag ins Gesicht; **give sb. a ~ on the back** (lit. or fig.) jmdm. auf die Schulter klopfen; **a ~ on the back for sb./sth.** (fig.) eine Anerkennung für jmdn./etw.; **the judge gave him more than just a ~**

S

on the wrist (fig.) der Richter verpasste ihm einen ordentlichen Denkzettel (ugs.)
D *adv.* voll; **run ~ into sb.** (lit. or fig.) mit jmdm. zusammenprallen; **hit sb. ~ in the eye/face** *etc.* jmdn. mit voller Wucht ins Auge/Gesicht treffen; **~ in the middle** genau in der Mitte; **he arrived ~ on time** er kam auf die Minute pünktlich

Phrasal verbs

- **~ 'down** *v.t.* **1** (lay forcefully) hinknallen (ugs.); **~ sth. down on sth.** etw. auf etw. (*Akk.*) knallen (ugs.) **2** (coll.: check, suppress, reprimand) **~ sb. down** jmdm. eins auf den Deckel geben (ugs.); **be ~ped down** eins auf den Deckel kriegen (ugs.)
- **~ 'on** *v.t.* **1** (coll.: apply hastily) draufklatschen (ugs.) ‹*Farbe, Tapete, Make-up*›; zuschnappen lassen ‹*Handschellen*› **2** (coll.: impose) draufschlagen (ugs.). *See also* **~ A 1**

slap: ~ and 'tickle *n.* (Brit. coll.) Fummelei, *die* (salopp); **~ bang** *adv.* **the table was ~ bang in the middle of the room** der Tisch stand einfach mitten im Zimmer; **~dash A** *adv.* ruck, zuck (ugs.); **B** *adj.* schludrig (ugs. abwertend); **in a ~dash way/fashion/manner** im Schnellverfahren; (carelessly) schludrig (ugs. abwertend); **her essay is ~dash** ihr Aufsatz ist hingeschludert (ugs. abwertend); **he is a ~dash sort** er ist ein schludriger Typ; **be ~dash in one's work** bei der Arbeit schludern (ugs. abwertend); **~-happy** *adj.* (coll.) **1** (punch-drunk, lit. or fig.) taumelig; **2** (cheerfully casual) unbekümmert; **~head** *n.* (Brit. coll. pej.) Glatzkopf, *der;* Kahlkopf, *der* (ugs.)

slapper /ˈslæpə/ *n.* (Brit. coll. derog.) Schlampe, *die*

slap: ~stick *n.* (Theatre: comedy style) Slapstick, *der;* **~stick comedy/humour** Slapstickkomödie, *die*/-humor, *der;* **~-up** *attrib. adj.* (coll.) ‹*Essen, Diner*› mit allen Schikanen (ugs.)

slash /slæʃ/
A *v.i.* **~ with one's sword** sein Schwert schwingen; **~ at sb./sth. with a knife/stick** auf jmdn./etw. mit einem Messer losgehen/mit einem Stock ausholen
B *v.t.* **1** (make gashes in) aufschlitzen; **~ one's wrists** sich (*Dat.*) die Pulsadern aufschneiden; **~ sth. to ribbons** *or* **shreds** etw. zerfetzen **2** (Dressm., Tailoring) [auf]schlitzen **3** (fig.: reduce sharply) [drastisch] reduzieren; [drastisch] kürzen ‹*Etat, Gehalt, Umfang*›; **~ costs by one million** die Kosten um eine Million reduzieren; **~ a book to half its original length** ein Buch auf die Hälfte der ursprünglichen Länge zusammenstreichen; **he ~ed five seconds off the world record** er hat die Weltrekordmarke um [beachtliche] fünf Sekunden unterboten **4** (clear by slashing) **he ~ed his way through the undergrowth** er schlug sich (*Dat.*) einen Weg durch das Unterholz frei
C *n.* **1** (~ing stroke) Hieb, *der* **2** (wound) Schnitt, *der;* **give sb. a ~ on the arm** jmdm. den Arm aufschlitzen **3** (slit; Dressm., Tailoring) Schlitz, *der* **4** (Amer.: tree debris) Holzabfall, *der* (*nach Waldbränden, Naturkatastrophen oder Holzschlag*) **5** **go for a** *or* **have a ~** (sl.: urinate) sich auspissen gehen (derb)

slash-and-'burn *attrib. adj.* (Agric.) **~ method** Brandrodung, *die*

slashed /slæʃt/ *adj.* (Dressm., Tailoring) geschlitzt; **~ sleeves** Schlitzärmel

'slasher film, (Amer.) **'slasher movie** *ns.* (coll.) Slasherfilm, *der*

slashing /ˈslæʃɪŋ/ *adj.* vernichtend ‹*Angriff, Kritik*›

slat /slæt/ *n.* Leiste, *die;* (of wood in bedstead, fence) Latte, *die;* (in Venetian blind) Lamelle, *die*

slate /sleɪt/
A *n.* **1** (Geol.) Schiefer, *der* **2** (Building) Schieferplatte, *die* **3** (writing surface) Schiefertafel, *die;* **put sth. on the ~** (Brit. coll.) etw. anschreiben (ugs.); **wipe the ~ clean** (fig.) einen Schlussstrich ziehen **4** (Amer. Polit.: list of candidates) Kandidatenliste, *die*
B *attrib. adj.* Schiefer-; **~ roof** Schieferdach, *das*
C *v.t.* **1** (Brit. coll.: criticize) in der Luft zerreißen (ugs.) (**for** wegen) **2** (Amer.: schedule) ansetzen ‹*Treffen, Besprechung*›

slate: ~ colour *n.* Schieferfarbe, *die;* **~-coloured** *adj.* schieferfarben; **~ grey A** *n.* Schiefergrau, *das;* **B** *adj.* schiefergrau; **~ pencil** *n.* Schiefergriffel, *der*

slating /ˈsleɪtɪŋ/ *n.* (Brit. coll.) **get** *or* **take a ~:** in der Luft zerrissen werden (ugs.) (**for** wegen); **give sb./sth. a ~:** jmdn./etw. in der Luft zerreißen (ugs.) (**for** wegen)

slattern /ˈslætən/ *n.* Schlampe, *die* (ugs. abwertend)

slatternly /ˈslætənlɪ/ *adj.* schlampig (ugs. abwertend)

slaughter /ˈslɔːtə(r)/
A *n.* **1** (killing for food) Schlachten, *das;* Schlachtung, *die; see also* **lamb A 1** **2** (massacre) Abschlachten, *das;* (in battle, war) Gemetzel, *das;* **the wholesale ~ of birds** der Vogelmord im großen Stil
B *v.t.* **1** (kill for food) schlachten **2** (massacre) abschlachten; niedermetzeln (abwertend) **3** (coll.: defeat utterly) fertig machen (salopp) **4** (coll.: severely criticize) verreißen

'slaughterhouse ▸ **abattoir**

Slav /slɑːv/
A *n.* Slawe, *der*/Slawin, *die*
B *adj.* slawisch

slave /sleɪv/
A *n.* **1** Sklave, *der*/Sklavin, *die; see also* **white slave** **2** (fig.) **be a ~ of** *or* **to sth.** Sklave von etw. sein; **be a ~ to sb.** jmdm. verfallen sein **3** (drudge) Kuli, *der;* **work like a ~:** wie ein Kuli *od.* Brunnenputzer schuften (ugs.)
B *v.i.* schuften (ugs.); **~ at sth.** sich mit etw. abplagen; **~ over a hot stove all day** den ganzen Tag am Herd stehen

Phrasal verb

- **~ a'way** *v.i.* sich abplagen; sich abrackern (salopp); **~ away at sth.** sich mit etw. abplagen

slave: ~-drive *v.t.* schinden; **~ driver** *n.* **1** Sklavenaufseher, *der;* **2** (fig.: taskmaster) Sklaventreiber, *der*/-treiberin, *die* (abwertend); **~ 'labour** *n.* Sklavenarbeit, *die;* (fig.) Ausbeutung, *die*

slaver¹ /ˈslævə(r)/
A *v.i.* sabbern (ugs.); ‹*Tier:*› geifern; **he was ~ing at the mouth** ihm rann Speichel aus dem Mund; **~ over sb./sth.** (fig. derog.) nach jmdm./etw. gieren
B *n., no indef. art.* Geifer, *der*

slaver² /ˈsleɪvə(r)/ *n.* Sklavenhändler, *der*/-händlerin, *die*

slavery /ˈsleɪvərɪ/ *n., no pl.* **1** Sklaverei, *die* **2** (drudgery) Sklavenarbeit, *die;* Sklaverei, *die*

slave: ~ trade *n.* Sklavenhandel, *der;* **~ trader** *n.* Sklavenhändler, *der*/-händlerin, *die*

Slavic /ˈslɑːvɪk/
A *adj.* slawisch
B *n.* Slawisch, *das*

slavish /ˈsleɪvɪʃ/ *adj.* sklavisch

slavishly /ˈsleɪvɪʃlɪ/ *adv.* sklavisch

Slavonia /sləˈvəʊnɪə/ *pr. n.* Slawonien (*das*)

Slavonic /sləˈvɒnɪk/ ▸ **i p. 1277**
A *adj.* slawisch
B *n.* Slawisch, *das*

slay /sleɪ/ *v.t.,* **slew** /sluː/, **slain** /sleɪn/ (*see also* **3**) **1** (literary) ermorden; (with sword, club also) erschlagen; vernichtend schlagen ‹*Armee*› **2** (coll.: defeat utterly) in die Pfanne hauen (ugs.) **3** *p.t., p.p.* **~ed** (coll.: amuse greatly) **he/his jokes ~ed me** über ihn/seine Witze hätte ich mich totlachen können (ugs.)

SLD *abbr.* (Brit. Polit.) **= Social and Liberal Democrats** Sozial-Liberaldemokratische Partei

sleaze /sliːz/ *n., no pl.* (derog.) Korruption, *die*

'sleazebag, 'sleazeball *ns.* (sl. derog.) Drecksack, *der* (derb abwertend)

sleazily /ˈsliːzɪlɪ/ *adv.* schäbig (abwertend); in schäbigen Verhältnissen ‹*leben*›; **dress ~:** schäbig angezogen gehen

sleazy /ˈsliːzɪ/ *adj.* (squalid) schäbig (abwertend); heruntergekommen (ugs.) ‹*Person*›; (disreputable) anrüchig

sled /sled/ (Amer.)
A *v.i.,* **-dd-** ▸ **sledge¹ B**
B *n.* Schlitten, *der*

sledge¹ /sledʒ/
A *n.* Schlitten, *der*
B *v.i.* Schlitten fahren; rodeln
C *v.t.* mit dem Schlitten fahren

sledge² ▸ **sledgehammer**

'sledgehammer
A *n.* Vorschlaghammer, *der;* **[take/use] a ~ to crack a nut** mit Kanonen auf Spatzen schießen
B *adj.* schlagend ‹*Argument*›; wuchtig ‹*Schlag*›; **~ style** Holzhammermethode, *die* (ugs.)

sleek /sliːk/
A *adj.* **1** (glossy) seidig ‹*Fell, Haar, Pelz*›; ‹*Tier*› mit seidigem Fell **2** (well-fed) wohlgenährt **3** (polished) glatt; (glossy) seidig glänzend; **the ~ lines of the car** die schnittige Form des Wagens
B *v.t.* glätten

Phrasal verbs

- **~ 'back** ▸ **slick back**
- **~ 'down** ▸ **slick down**

sleep /sliːp/
A *n.* Schlaf, *der;* **get some ~:** schlafen; **it's time we got some ~:** es ist Zeit zum Schlafengehen; **get three hours' ~:** drei Stunden schlafen; **get/go to ~:** einschlafen; **go to ~!** schlaf jetzt!; **not lose [any] ~ over sth.** (fig.) wegen etw. keine schlaflose Nacht haben; **some cocoa should put him to ~:** etwas Kakao, und er müsste einschlafen; **put an animal to ~** (euphem.) ein Tier einschläfern; **he put** *or* **sent me to ~ with his stories** (coll.) bei seinen Geschichten bin ich fast eingeschlafen; **talk in one's ~:** im Schlaf sprechen; **one's last ~** (fig.) der ewige Schlaf; **walk in one's ~:** schlafwandeln; **I can/could do it in my ~** (fig.) ich kann/könnte es im Schlaf; **be in a deep ~:** fest schlafen; **get** *or* **have a good night's ~:** [sich] gründlich ausschlafen; **have a ~:** schlafen; **have a short ~:** ein [kurzes] Schläfchen machen
B *v.i.,* **slept** [slept] **1** schlafen; **~ late** lange schlafen; ausschlafen; **~ like a log** *or* **top** wie ein Stein schlafen (ugs.); **~ tight!** (coll.) schlaf gut!; **~ at sb.'s** bei jmdm. schlafen; *see also* **rough C 2** (fig.: be dormant) schlafen (fig.); ‹*Vulkan, Hass:*› ruhen, schlafen **3** (fig.: lie in grave) ruhen (geh.)
C *v.t.,* **slept** **1** **~ the ~ of the just** *or* **dead** (joc.) den Schlaf des Gerechten schlafen (scherzh.) **2** (accommodate) schlafen lassen; **the apartment ~s 6** die Wohnung hat 6 Betten. *See also* **wink C 2**

Phrasal verbs

- **~ a'round** *v.i.* (coll.) herumschlafen (ugs.)
- **~ a'way** *v.t.* verschlafen
- **~ 'in** *v.i.* (~ late) im Bett bleiben
- **~ 'off** *v.t.* ausschlafen; **~ it off** seinen Rausch ausschlafen; **~ off one's lunch** [nach dem Mittagessen] einen Verdauungsschlaf halten
- **~ on**
  A *v.i.* /-'-/ weiterschlafen
  B *v.t.* /'--/ überschlafen
- **~ 'out** *v.i.* (~ in the open) im Freien schlafen
- **~ 'over** *v.i.* [auswärts] übernachten; **our cousin was ~ing over** unser Cousin übernachtete bei uns
- **~ through** *v.t.* **~ through the noise/alarm** trotz des Lärms/Weckerklingelns [weiter-]schlafen
- **~ together** *v.i.* (also coll. euphem.) miteinander schlafen
- **~ with** *v.t.* **~ with sb.** (coll. euphem.) mit jmdm. schlafen

sleeper /ˈsliːpə(r)/ *n.* **1** Schläfer, *der;* **be a heavy/light ~:** einen tiefen/leichten Schlaf haben **2** (Brit. Railw.: support) Schwelle, *die* **3** (Railw.) (coach) Schlafwagen, *der;* (berth) Schlafwagenplatz, *der;* (overnight train) **[night] ~:** Nachtzug mit Schlafwagen **4** (earring) [medizinischer] Ohrstecker **5** (slow starter) **the novel/film was a ~:** dem Roman/Film gelang erst spät der Durchbruch (fig.) **6** (Amer.) ▸ **sleepsuit**

sleepily /ˈsliːpɪlɪ/ *adv.* **1** (drowsily) schläfrig **2** (sluggishly) schwerfällig; (unobservantly) schlafmützig (ugs. abwertend)

sleepiness /'sli:pɪnɪs/ *n., no pl.* (drowsiness) Schläfrigkeit, *die*

sleeping /'sli:pɪŋ/ *adj.* (lit. or fig.) schlafend; schlummernd ‹*Leidenschaft*›; **let ~ dogs lie** (fig.) keine schlafenden Hunde wecken

sleeping: ~ accommodation *n.* Übernachtungsmöglichkeit, *die;* **the price includes ~ accommodation** im Preis ist die Übernachtung inbegriffen; **~ bag** *n.* Schlafsack, *der;* **S~ 'Beauty** *pr. n.* Dornröschen (*das*); **~ car[riage]** *n.* (Railw.) Schlafwagen, *der;* **~ draught** *n.* Schlaftrunk, *der;* **~ drug** *n.* Schlafmittel, *das;* **~ 'partner** *n.* (Commerc.) stiller Teilhaber; **~ pill** *n.* Schlaftablette, *die;* **~ po'liceman** *n.* (Brit.) Bodenschwelle, *die;* **~ sickness** *n.* ▸❶ **p. 1231** (Med.) Schlafkrankheit, *die;* **~ suit** ▸**sleepsuit**; **~ tablet** ▸**~ pill**

'sleep laboratory *n.* Schlaflabor, *das*

sleepless /'sli:plɪs/ *adj.* schlaflos

sleeplessness /'sli:plɪsnɪs/ *n., no pl.* Schlaflosigkeit, *die*

sleep: ~ mode *n.* (Electron.) Schlafmodus, *der;* **~-out** *n.* [1] (Austral., NZ: outbuilding) *Nebengebäude mit Übernachtungsmöglichkeit;* [2] (outdoors) Übernachtung im Freien; (as protest) Sleep-out, *das;* **~over** *n.* Übernachtung außer Haus *od.* bei anderen Leuten; **~ research** *n., no pl.* Schlafforschung, *die;* **~suit** *n.* [Baby]schlafanzug, *der;* **~walk** *v.i.* schlafwandeln; **~walker** *n.* Schlafwandler, *der*/-wandlerin, *die;* **~walking** *n., no pl.* Schlafwandeln, *das*

sleepy /'sli:pɪ/ *adj.* [1] (drowsy) schläfrig [2] (sluggish) schwerfällig; (unobservant) schlafmützig (ugs. abwertend) [3] (peaceful) verschlafen ‹*Dorf, Stadt usw.*›

sleepy: ~head *n.* Schlafmütze, *die* (ugs.); **~ sickness** *n.* (Med.) Kopfgrippe, *die;* europäische Schlafkrankheit

sleet /sli:t/

[A] *n., no indef. art.* Schneeregen, *der*

[B] *v.i. impers.* **it was ~ing** es gab Schneeregen

sleeve /sli:v/ *n.* [1] Ärmel, *der;* **have sth. up one's ~** (fig.) etw. in petto haben (ugs.); **roll up one's ~s** (lit. or fig.) die Ärmel hochkrempeln (ugs.); *see also* **heart A 2**; **laugh** [2] (record cover) Hülle, *die* [3] (Mech.) Muffe, *die* (Technik) [4] (Aeronaut.) (windsock) Windsack, *der*

-sleeved /sli:vd/ *adj. in comb.* -ärmelig

sleeveless /'sli:vlɪs/ *adj.* ärmellos

'sleeve note *n.* Covertext, *der*

sleigh /sleɪ/

[A] *n.* Schlitten, *der*

[B] *v.i. & t.* mit dem Schlitten fahren

sleigh: ~ bell *n.* Schlittenschelle, *die;* **~ ride** *n.* Schlittenfahrt, *die*

sleight of hand /slaɪt əv 'hænd/ *n.* Fingerfertigkeit, *die;* **verbal ~:** verbale Taschenspielereien

slender /'slendə(r)/ *adj.* [1] (slim) schlank; schmal ‹*Buch, Band*› [2] (meagre) mager ‹*Einkommen, Kost*›; gering ‹*Chance, Mittel, Vorräte, Hoffnung, Kenntnis*›; schwach ‹*Entschuldigung, Argument, Grund*›; **be a person of ~ means** *or* **resources** wenig Geld haben; einen schmalen (geh.) Geldbeutel haben

slenderize /'slendəraɪz/

[A] *v.t.* **~ [the figure]** schlank machen

[B] *v.i.* abnehmen

slenderly /'slendəlɪ/ *adv.* **~ built/made** von schlankem Wuchs *nachgestellt;* **be ~ provided for** schlecht versorgt sein

slept ▸**sleep B, C**

sleuth /slu:θ/

[A] *n.* Detektiv, *der*

[B] *v.i.* **go ~ing** sich detektivisch betätigen

slew¹ /slu:/

[A] *v.i.* **~ to the left/right** sich [schnell] nach links/rechts drehen; ‹*Kran:*› nach links/rechts schwenken

[B] *v.t.* herumschleudern; schwenken ‹*Kran*›

(Phrasal verb)

- **~ [a]'round**

[A] *v.i.* sich [schnell] drehen; **~ around to the left** ‹*Kran:*› nach links schwenken

[B] *v.t.* [schnell] drehen; schwenken ‹*Kran*›

slew² ▸**slay 1, 2**

slew³ *n.* (Amer. coll.) Haufen, *der* (ugs.); **a ~ of people/things** ein Haufen (ugs.) Leute/Dinge; **~s of spectators/snow** massenhaft (ugs.) Zuschauer/Schnee; **~s of work** Berge von Arbeit

slice /slaɪs/

[A] *n.* [1] (cut portion) Scheibe, *die;* (of apple, melon, peach, apricot, cake, pie) Stück, *das;* **a ~ of life** ein Ausschnitt aus dem Leben; *see also* **cake A 1, 2** [2] (share) Teil, *der;* (allotted part of profits, money) Anteil, *der;* **a ~ of land** ein Stück Land; **have a ~ of luck** Glück haben [3] (utensil) [Bratenwender, *der* [4] (Golf, Tennis: stroke) Slice, *der*

[B] *v.t.* [1] (cut into portions) in Scheiben schneiden; in Stücke schneiden ‹*Bohnen, Apfel, Pfirsich, Kuchen usw.*›; **~ sth. thick/thin/into pieces** etw. dick/dünn/in Stücke schneiden [2] (Golf) slicen; (Tennis) unterschneiden; slicen

[C] *v.i.* schneiden; **~ through** durchschneiden; durchpflügen ‹*Wellen, Meer*›

(Phrasal verbs)

- **~ 'off** *v.t.* abschneiden
- **~ 'up** *v.t.* aufschneiden; (fig.: divide) aufteilen

sliced /slaɪst/ *adj.* (cut into slices) aufgeschnitten; klein geschnitten ‹*Gemüse*›; **~ bread** Schnittbrot, *das;* **the greatest thing since ~ bread** (coll. joc.) der/die/das Größte seit der Erfindung der Bratkartoffel (ugs. scherzh.)

-slicer /slaɪsə(r)/ *n. in comb.* -schneidemaschine, *die;* **egg~:** Eierschneider, *der*

slick /slɪk/

[A] *adj.* [1] (dextrous) professionell [2] (pretentiously dextrous) clever (ugs.) [3] (slippery) glatt ‹*Fußboden*›; rutschig ‹*Straße, Weg*› [4] (glossy) seidig glänzend [5] (glib) glatt; glattzüngig (geh. abwertend); **have a ~ tongue** glattzüngig sein (geh. abwertend)

[B] *n.* **[oil] ~:** Ölteppich, *der*

[C] *v.t.* ▸**sleek B**

(Phrasal verbs)

- **~ 'back** *v.t.* **~ back one's hair** sich (*Dat.*) die Haare anklatschen (salopp)
- **~ 'down** *v.t.* **~ down one's hair** sich (*Dat.*) die Haare anklatschen (salopp)

slicker /'slɪkə(r)/ *n.* (Amer.) [1] (swindler) Trickbetrüger, *der*/-betrügerin, *die* [2] ▸**city slicker** [3] (raincoat) Regenmantel, *der;* (oilskin) [gelbe] Öljacke

slid ▸**slide A, B**

slide /slaɪd/

[A] *v.i.,* **slid** /slɪd/ [1] rutschen; ‹*Kolben, Schublade, Feder*› gleiten; **the bolt slid home** der Riegel glitt ins Schloss; **~ down sth.** etw. hinunterrutschen [2] (glide over ice) schlittern [3] (move smoothly) gleiten; **everything slid into place** (fig.) alles fügte sich zusammen [4] (fig.: take its own course) **let sth./things ~:** etw./die Dinge schleifen lassen (fig.) [5] (fig.: go imperceptibly) **~ into** hineinschlittern in (+ *Akk.*) (ugs.); **~ from one note to another** ‹*Sänger, Stimme, Musik:*› von einem Ton zum nächsten gleiten

[B] *v.t.,* **slid** [1] schieben; **~ the bolt across on a door** an einer Tür den Riegel vorschieben; **~ the envelope under the door** den Brief unter der Tür durchschieben [2] (place unobtrusively) gleiten lassen

[C] *n.* [1] (Photog.) Dia[positiv], *das* [2] (track on ice) Rutschbahn, *die* (ugs.); Schlitterbahn, *die* (landsch.) [3] (toboggan slope) **[toboggan] ~:** Rodelbahn, *die* [4] (chute) (in children's playground) Rutschbahn, *die;* (for goods etc.) Rutsche, *die* [5] (Mech. Eng.) Gleitbahn, *die;* (moving part) Gleitstück, *das;* Schieber, *der* [6] ▸**hairslide** [7] (act of sliding) Ausrutscher, *der* (ugs.); **go for** *or* **have a ~** (on chute) rutschen [gehen]; (on ice) schlittern [gehen] [8] (fig.: decline) **be on the ~:** auf dem absteigenden Ast sein; **the ~ in the value of the pound** das Abgleiten des Pfundes [9] (Mus.) Zug, *der* [10] (for microscope) Objektträger, *der*

slide: ~ control *n.* Flachbahnregler, *der* (Technik); **~ fastener** (Amer.) ▸**zip A 1**; **~ film** *n.* (Photog.) Diafilm, *der;* **~ lecture** *n.* Diavortrag, *der;* **~ projector** *n.* Diaprojektor, *der;* **~ rule** *n.* (Math.) Rechenschieber, *der;* **~ show** *n.* Diashow, *die;* **~ valve** *n.* (Mech. Engin.) [Absperr]schieber, *der* (Technik)

sliding /'slaɪdɪŋ/: **~ 'door** *n.* Schiebetür, *die;* **~ 'keel** *n.* (Naut.) Schwert, *das;* **~ 'roof** *n.* Schiebedach, *das;* **~ 'scale** *n.* **~ scale [of fees]** gleitende [Gebühren]skala; **~ seat** *n.* (Rowing) Rollsitz, *der*

slight /slaɪt/

[A] *adj.* [1] leicht; schwach ‹*Hoffnung, Aussichten, Wirkung*›; gedämpft ‹*Optimismus*›; gering ‹*Bedeutung*›; **have only a ~ acquaintance with sth.** etw. nur oberflächlich kennen; **on the ~est pretext** unter dem geringsten Vorwand; **the ~est thing makes her nervous** die kleinste Kleinigkeit macht sie nervös [2] (scanty) oberflächlich; **with but ~ inconvenience** ohne größere Unannehmlichkeiten; **pay sb. ~ attention** jmdn. kaum beachten [3] (slender) zierlich; (weedy) schmächtig; (flimsy) zerbrechlich [4] **not in the ~est** nicht im Geringsten; **not the ~est ...:** nicht der/die/das Geringste ...; **I haven't the ~est idea** ich habe nicht die leiseste Ahnung

[B] *v.t.* (disparage) herabsetzen; (fail in courtesy or respect to) brüskieren; (ignore) ignorieren

[C] *n.* (on sb.'s character, reputation, good name) Verunglimpfung, *die* (**on** *Gen.*); (on sb.'s abilities) Herabsetzung, *die* (**on** *Gen.*); (lack of courtesy) Affront, *der* (**on** gegen); (neglect) Nichtachtung, *die*

slightly /'slaɪtlɪ/ *adv.* [1] ein bisschen; leicht ‹*verletzen, riechen nach, gewürzt sein, ansteigen*›; flüchtig ‹*jmdn. kennen*›; oberflächlich ‹*etw. kennen*› [2] **~ built** (slender) zierlich; (weedy) schmächtig

slily ▸**slyly**

slim /slɪm/

[A] *adj.* [1] schlank; schmal ‹*Band, Buch*› [2] (meagre) mager; schwach ‹*Entschuldigung, Aussicht, Hoffnung*›; gering ‹*Gewinn, Chancen*›; **the profit/the supper was ~ pickings** der Gewinn/das Abendessen war ziemlich mickrig; **there were only ~ pickings left** da war nicht mehr viel zu holen

[B] *v.i.,* **-mm-** abnehmen

[C] *v.t.,* **-mm-** schlanker machen; (fig.: decrease) kürzen ‹*Budget*›; verschlanken (Jargon) ‹*Produktion*›; reduzieren ‹*Nachfrage, Anzahl*›

(Phrasal verb)

- **~ 'down**

[A] *v.i.* abnehmen; schlanker werden; **the slimmed-down state** der schlanke Staat

[B] *v.t.* ▸**~ C**

slime /slaɪm/

[A] *n.* Schlick, *der;* (mucus, viscous matter) Schleim, *der*

[B] *v.t.* mit Schlick/Schleim bedecken

slime: ~ball *n.* (coll.) Ekel, *das* (ugs. abwertend); Fiesling, *der* (salopp abwertend); **~ mould** *n.* (Bot.) Schleimpilz, *der*

'slimline *adj.* schlank; schlank geschnitten ‹*Kleid*›; kalorienarm ‹*Lebensmittel*›

slimmer /'slɪmə(r)/ *n.* (Brit.) *jmd., der etwas für die schlanke Linie tut;* **advice/a diet for ~s** Ratschläge/eine Diät zum Abnehmen

slimming /'slɪmɪŋ/

[A] *n.* [1] Abnehmen, *das; attrib.* Schlankheits-; **be in need of ~:** abnehmen müssen [2] (fig.: reduction) (of budget) Kürzung, *die;* (of number) Reduzierung, *die*

[B] *adj.* schlank machend ‹*Lebensmittel*›; **be ~:** schlank machen

'slimming pill *n.* Schlankheitspille, *die*

slimness /'slɪmnɪs/ *n., no pl.* (slenderness) Schlankheit, *die;* (of book) geringer Umfang

slimy /'slaɪmɪ/ *adj.* [1] schleimig; schlickig ‹*Schlamm*› [2] (slippery) glitschig (ugs.) [3] (fig.: obsequious) schleimig (abwertend); schmierig (abwertend)

sling¹ /slɪŋ/

[A] *n.* [1] (weapon) Schleuder, *die* [2] (Med.) Schlinge, *die* [3] (carrying-belt) Tragriemen, *der;* (for carrying babies) Tragehöschen, *das* [4] (hoist) Anschlagseil, *das* (Technik); (belt) Anschlagband, *das* (Technik); (chain) Anschlagkette, *die* (Technik)

[B] *v.t.,* **slung** /slʌŋ/ [1] (hurl from ~) schleudern [2] (coll.: throw) schmeißen (ugs.); **she slung him his coat** sie schmiss ihm seinen Mantel zu (ugs.); *see also* **mud 3** [3] (suspend) hängen; (put in ~ ready for hoisting) anhängen ‹*Last*›; **she slung**

S

the bag over her arm sie hängte sich (*Dat.*) die Tasche über den Arm

(Phrasal verbs)

- **~ a'way** *v.t.* (coll.) wegschmeißen (ugs.)
- **~ 'out** *v.t.* (coll.) 1) (throw out) **~ sb. out** jmdn. rausschmeißen *od.* -werfen (ugs.) 2) ▸ **~ away**

sling² *n.* (drink) Sling, *der* (*Mischgetränk mit Brandy od. Rum*); *see also* **gin sling**

sling: ~back *n.* **~back [shoe]** Slingpumps, *der;* **~shot** (Amer.) ▸ **catapult A**

slink /slɪŋk/ *v.i.*, **slunk** /slʌŋk/ schleichen

(Phrasal verb)

- **~ a'way, ~ off** *v.i.* davonschleichen; sich fortstehlen

slinkily /'slɪŋkɪlɪ/ *adv.* aufreizend

slinky /'slɪŋkɪ/ *adj.* 1) aufreizend 2) hauteng ‹*Kleidung*›

slip /slɪp/

A *v.i.*, **-pp-** 1) (slide) rutschen; ‹*Messer:*› abrutschen; (and fall) ausrutschen; **he ~ped and broke his leg** er rutschte aus und brach sich (*Dat.*) das Bein
2) (escape) schlüpfen; **money ~s through my fingers like water** Geld zerrinnt mir zwischen den Fingern; **let the reins ~ out of one's hands** (lit. or fig.) sich (*Dat.*) die Zügel entgleiten lassen; **let a chance/opportunity ~:** sich (*Dat.*) eine Chance/Gelegenheit entgehen lassen; **let [it] ~ that ...:** verraten, dass ...
3) (go) **~ to the butcher's** [rasch] zum Fleischer rüberspringen (ugs.); **~ from the room/~ behind a curtain** aus dem Zimmer/hinter einen Vorhang schlüpfen
4) (move smoothly) gleiten; **everything ~ped into place** (fig.) alles fügte sich zusammen
5) (make mistake)[Flüchtigkeits]fehler machen
6) (deteriorate) nachlassen; ‹*Moral, Niveau, Ansehen:*› sinken

B *v.t.*, **-pp-** 1) stecken; **~ the dress over one's head** das Kleid über den Kopf streifen; **~ sb. sth.** jmdm. etw. zustecken; **~ sb. a glance** jmdm. einen verstohlenen Blick zuwerfen
2) (escape from) entwischen (+ *Dat.*); **the dog ~ped its collar** der Hund streifte sein Halsband ab; **the boat ~ped its mooring** das Boot löste sich aus seiner Verankerung; **~ sb.'s attention** jmds. Aufmerksamkeit (*Dat.*) entgehen; **~ sb.'s memory** *or* **mind** jmdm. entfallen
3) (release) loslassen; **~ a dog from its chain** einen Hund von der Kette lassen
4) (Naut.) slippen; **~ anchor** den Anker lichten
5) (Motor Veh.) schleifen lassen ‹*Kupplung*›
6) (Knitting) **~ a stitch** eine Masche abheben
7) (Med.) **~ a disc** einen Bandscheibenvorfall erleiden; *see also* **slipped disc**

C *n.* 1) (fall) **after his ~:** nachdem er ausgerutscht [und gestürzt] war; **a ~ on these steps could be nasty** auf diesen Stufen auszurutschen könnte schlimme Folgen haben; **have a [bad] ~:** [sehr unglücklich] ausrutschen
2) (mistake) Versehen, *das;* Ausrutscher, *der* (ugs.); **there's been a ~ in the accounts** bei der Berechnung ist ein Fehler unterlaufen; **a ~ of the tongue/pen** ein Versprecher/Schreibfehler; **I'm sorry, it was a ~ of the tongue/pen** Entschuldigung, ich habe mich versprochen/verschrieben; **make a ~:** einen Fehler machen; *see also* **cup A 1**
3) (underwear) Unterrock, *der*
4) (pillowcase) [Kopf]kissenbezug, *der*
5) (strip) **~ of metal/plastic** Metall-/Plastikstreifen, *der;* **~ of wood** Holzleiste, *die;* **~ of glass** langes, schmales Stück Glas
6) (piece of paper) ‹*Einzahlungs-, Wett*›schein, *der;* **~ [of paper]** Zettel, *der*
7) **give sb. the ~** (escape) jmdm. entwischen (ugs.); (avoid) jmdm. ausweichen
8) (Naut.: landing stage) Aufschleppe, *die;* Slip, *der*
9) *in pl.* (Shipb.) Helling, *die od. der*
10) **a ~ of a boy/girl** ein zierlicher Junge/ein zierliches Mädchen; eine halbe Portion (ugs.)
11) (Cricket) *Feldspieler, der seitlich hinter dem Tor aufgestellt ist;* **he was caught at ~** *or* **in the ~s** sein Ball wurde seitlich hinter dem Tor gefangen
12) (Ceramics) geschlämmter Ton. *See also* **gymslip**

(Phrasal verbs)

- **~ a'cross** *v.i.* rüberspringen (ugs.)
- **~ a'way** *v.i.* 1) (leave quietly) ‹*Person:*› sich fortschleichen 2) (pass quickly) ‹*Zeit, Tage, Wochen usw.:*› verfliegen
- **~ 'back** *v.i.* zurückschleichen; (very quickly) zurücksausen; **~ back into unconsciousness** wieder das Bewusstsein verlieren
- **~ be'hind** *v.i.* zurückfallen; (with one's work) in Rückstand geraten
- **~ 'by** *v.i.* 1) (pass unnoticed) vorbeischleichen; ‹*Fehler:*› durchrutschen (ugs.) 2) ▸ **~ away 2**
- **~ 'down** *v.i.* runterrutschen (ugs.); ‹*Getränk:*› die Kehle runterlaufen (ugs.)
- **~ 'in**

A *v.i.* sich hineinschleichen; (enter briefly) [kurz] reinkommen (ugs.); (enter unnoticed) ‹*Fehler:*› sich einschleichen

B *v.t.* einfließen lassen ‹*Bemerkung*›

- **~ into** *v.t.* 1) (put on) schlüpfen in (+ *Akk.*) ‹*Kleidungsstück*› 2) (lapse into) verfallen in (+ *Akk.*)
- **~ 'off**

A *v.i.* 1) (slide down) runterrutschen (ugs.) 2) ▸ **~ away 1**

B *v.t.* abstreifen ‹*Schmuck, Bezug, Handschuh*›; schlüpfen aus ‹*Kleid, Hose, Schuh*›; ausziehen ‹*Strumpf, Handschuh*›

- **~ 'on** *v.t.* überstreifen ‹*Bezug, Handschuh, Ring*›; schlüpfen in (+ *Akk.*) ‹*Kleid, Hose, Schuh*›; anziehen ‹*Strumpf, Handschuh*›; anlegen ‹*Schmuck*›; *see also* **slip-on**
- **~ 'out** *v.i.* 1) (leave) sich hinausschleichen; **~ out to the butcher's** zum Fleischer rüberspringen (ugs.); **~ out to have a cigarette** hinausschlüpfen, um eine Zigarette zu rauchen 2) (be revealed) **it ~ped out** es ist mir/dir/ihm *usw.* herausgerutscht
- **~ 'over** *v.i.* 1) (fall) ausrutschen 2) ▸ **~ across**
- **~ 'past** ▸ **~ by**
- **~ 'round** *v.i.* rübergehen (ugs.); (towards speaker) rüberkommen (ugs.)
- **~ 'through** *v.i.* durchschlüpfen; ‹*Fehler:*› durchrutschen (ugs.)
- **~ 'up** *v.i.* (coll.) einen Schnitzer machen (ugs.) (**on, over** bei); *see also* **slip-up**

slip: ~ case *n.* Schuber, *der;* **~ cover** *n.* 1) (for unused furniture) Schutzüberzug, *der;* 2) (Amer.: loose cover) Überzug, *der;* 3) (protective book jacket) Schutzhülle, *die;* Buchhülle, *die;* 4) ▸ **~ case; ~ knot** *n.* 1) (easily undone knot) Slipstek, *der;* 2) ▸ **running knot; ~-on A** *adj.* **~-on shoes** Slipper; **B** *n.* (shoe) Slipper, *der;* **~over** *n.* Pullunder, *der*

slippage /'slɪpɪdʒ/ *n.* 1) (Mech.) Schlupf, *der* 2) (Commerc.) Rückstand, *der*

slipped 'disc *n.* (Med.) Bandscheibenvorfall, *der*

slipper /'slɪpə(r)/ *n.* Hausschuh, *der; see also* **hunt B 2**

slippered /'slɪpəd/ *adj.* in Hausschuhen *nachgestellt*

slippery /'slɪpərɪ/ *adj.* 1) (causing slipping) schlüpfrig; glitschig; **the shoes are ~:** die Schuhe haben [sehr] glatte Sohlen; **be on a ~ path** *or* **slope** (fig.) auf einem verhängnisvollen Weg sein 2) (elusive) schlüpfrig; glitschig; wendig ‹*Spieler*›; (shifty) aalglatt (abwertend); (unreliable) windig (ugs.); **he is a ~ customer** er ist aalglatt (abwertend); **as ~ as an eel** aalglatt (abwertend) 3) (fig.: delicate) heikel ‹*Thema, Fall*›

slippy /'slɪpɪ/ *adj.* 1) (coll.) ▸ **slippery** 2) (Brit. coll.) **be** *or* **look ~:** sich sputen (veralt.); sich ranhalten (ugs.)

slip: ~ ring *n.* (Electr.) Schleifring, *der;* **~ road** *n.* (Brit.) (for approach) Zufahrtsstraße, *die;* (to motorway) Auffahrt, *die;* (to estate) Einfahrt, *die;* (for leaving) Ausfahrt, *die;* **~shod** *adj.* schlampig (ugs. abwertend); abgetreten ‹*Schuh*›; (fig.: careless, unsystematic) schlud[e]rig (ugs. abwertend); **~stream** *n.* 1) (of car, motorcycle) Fahrtwind, *der;* (Racing) Windschatten, *der;* 2) ‹of propeller› Propellerwind, *der;* (of ship; also Brit. fig.) Kielwasser, *das;* **~-up** *n.* (coll.) Schnitzer, *der* (ugs.); **there's been a ~-up somewhere** irgendwo hat jemand einen Schnitzer gemacht (ugs.); **~way** ▸ **slip C 8, 9**

slit /slɪt/

A *n.* Schlitz, *der;* **the sleeves have ~s in them** die Ärmel haben Schlitze *od.* sind geschlitzt; **make ~s in the fat of the pork** die Schwarte des Schweinebratens einritzen

B *v.t.*, **-tt-, slit** 1) aufschlitzen; **~ sb.'s throat** jmdm. die Kehle durchschneiden 2) (Dressmaking) schlitzen ‹*Rock, Ärmel*›

'slit-eyed *adj.* schlitzäugig

slither /'slɪðə(r)/ *v.i.* rutschen; (on ice, polished floor also) schlittern

slit: ~ 'pocket *n.* Durchgrifftasche, *die;* **~ trench** *n.* (Mil.) Schützenloch, *das*

sliver /'slɪvə(r)/ *n.* 1) (slip) (of wood) Span, *der;* (of paper) Streifen, *der;* (of food) dünne Scheibe 2) (splinter) Splitter, *der;* **~ of wood/glass/bone** Holz-/Glas-/Knochensplitter, *der* 3) (Textiles) Kammzug, *der*

slivovitz /'slɪvəvɪts/ *n.* Slibowitz, *der*

slob /slɒb/ *n.* (coll.) Schwein, *das* (derb); **lazy ~:** fauler Sack (salopp abwertend); **fat ~:** Fettsack, *der* (salopp abwertend)

slobber /'slɒbə(r)/

A *v.i.* sabbern (ugs.); **~ over sb./sth.** jmdn./etw. besabbern; (fig.) von jmdm./etw. schwärmen

B *v.t.* voll sabbern (ugs.)

C *n.* ▸ **slaver¹ B**

slobbery /'slɒbərɪ/ *adj.* **the bib is all ~:** das Lätzchen ist ganz vollgesabbert (ugs.); **a ~ kiss** ein [feuchter] Schmatz (ugs.)

slobbish /'slɒbɪʃ/ *adj.* schlampig; liederlich (ugs. abwertend)

sloe /sləʊ/ *n.* (Bot.) Schlehe, *die*

sloe: ~-eyed *adj.* 1) (with ~-coloured eyes) mit schwarzblauen Augen *nachgestellt;* 2) (slant-eyed) schlitzäugig; **~ gin** *n.* ≈ Schlehenlikör, *der;* Sloe-Gin, *der*

slog /slɒg/

A *v.t.*, **-gg-** dreschen (ugs.) ‹*Ball*›; (in boxing, fight) voll treffen; (with several blows) eindreschen auf (+ *Akk.*) (ugs.)

B *v.i.*, **-gg-** 1) (hit) draufschlagen (ugs.) 2) (fig.: work doggedly) sich abplagen; schuften (ugs.); (for school, exams) büffeln (ugs.) 3) (walk doggedly) sich schleppen; **~ along** sich dahinschleppen

C *n.* 1) (hit) [wuchtiger] Schlag; **give sb./sth. a ~:** jmdm./einer Sache einen wuchtigen Schlag versetzen 2) (hard work) Plackerei, *die* (ugs.); **it took me a good two hours' ~:** ich musste mich gut zwei Stunden abplagen 3) (tiring walk, hike) [auf die Knochen gehender] Fußmarsch

(Phrasal verbs)

- **~ at** *v.t.* 1) (hit) **~ at sb./sth.** auf jmdn./etw. eindreschen (ugs.) 2) (work hard at) sich abplagen mit
- **~ a'way** *v.i.* sich abplagen; **~ away at sth.** sich mit etw. abplagen; **keep ~ging away!** streng dich weiter an!
- **~ 'out** *v.t.* (coll.) **~ it out** es [bis zum Ende] durchstehen; **~ one's guts out** sich kaputtarbeiten (ugs.)

slogan /'sləʊgən/ *n.* 1) (striking phrase) Slogan, *der;* (advertising ~) Werbeslogan, *der;* Werbespruch, *der* 2) (motto) Wahlspruch, *der;* (in political campaign) [Wahl]slogan, *der*

sloganeer /sləʊgə'nɪə(r)/

A *v.i.* Sprüche klopfen (ugs. abwertend); (in a political context) Parolen dreschen (ugs. abwertend)

B *n.* Sprücheklopfer, *der*/-klopferin, *die* (ugs. abwertend); (in a political context) Parolendrescher, *der*/-drescherin, *die* (ugs. abwertend)

slogger /'slɒgə(r)/ *n.* 1) (hitter) **be a [real] ~:** immer nur draufschlagen (ugs.) 2) (hard worker) Arbeitstier, *das* (fig.)

sloop /slu:p/ *n.* (Naut.) Slup, *die*

'sloop-rigged *adj.* (Naut.) mit Sluptakelung *nachgestellt;* **be ~:** Sluptakelung haben

slop /slɒp/

A *v.i.*, **-pp-** schwappen (**out of, from** aus)

B *v.t.*, **-pp-** 1) (spill) (unintentionally) schwappen; (intentionally) kippen; klatschen (ugs.) ‹*Farbe an die Wand*› 2) (make mess on) voll schütten

C *n.* 1) (liquid food) Schleim, *der;* Geschlabber, *das*

(ugs.) **2** (spilt liquid) Lache, *die* **3** (fig. derog.: gush) Geseire, *das* (*ugs.*). *See also* **slops 1**

(Phrasal verbs)

- **~ a'bout, ~ a'round** *v.i.* **1** (splash about) herumschwappen (ugs.) **2** (move in slovenly manner) herumschlurfen (ugs.)
- **~ 'out** *v.i.* die Toiletteneimer leeren
- **~ 'over** *v.i.* (splash over) überschwappen

slope /sləʊp/

A *n.* **1** (slant) Neigung, *die;* (of river) Gefälle, *das;* **there is a downward/upward ~ to the garden** der Garten fällt ab/steigt an; **the house is built on a steep/gentle ~:** das Haus steht an einem steilen/sanften Hang; **the roof was at a ~ of 45°** das Dach hatte eine Neigung von 45°; **be on a** *or* **the ~:** geneigt sein **2** (slanting ground) Hang, *der* **3** (Skiing) Piste, *die*

B *v.i.* (slant) sich neigen; ‹*Wand, Mauer:*› schief sein; ‹*Boden, Garten:*› abschüssig sein; **~ upwards/downwards** ‹*Straße:*› ansteigen/abfallen

C *v.t.* abschrägen; **~ arms** (Mil.) das Gewehr schultern; **~ arms!** (Mil.) Gewehr über!

(Phrasal verbs)

- **~ a'way** *v.i.* **1** (slant) abfallen **2** ▸ **~ off**
- **~ down** *v.i.* sich hinabneigen
- **~ 'off** *v.i.* (coll.) sich verdrücken (ugs.)
- **~ 'up** *v.i.* **1** (rise) ansteigen **2** (approach casually) daherkommen; **~ up to sb.** auf jmdn. zugehen/zukommen

'slop pail *n.* Toiletteneimer, *der;* (for kitchen slops) Abfalleimer, *der*

sloppily /'slɒpɪlɪ/ *adv.* **1** (carelessly) schlud[e]rig (ugs. abwertend); **she speaks English rather ~:** sie spricht ein ziemlich schlud[e]riges Englisch (ugs. abwertend) **2** (untidily) unordentlich; schlampig (ugs. abwertend) **3** (sentimentally) voller Rührseligkeit

sloppy /'slɒpɪ/ *adj.* **1** (careless) schlud[e]rig (ugs. abwertend) **2** (untidy) unordentlich; schlampig (ugs. abwertend) **3** (splashed) voll geschwappt **4** (sentimental) rührselig

sloppy Joe /slɒpi 'dʒəʊ/ *n. langer, weiter Pullover für Mädchen;* Schlabberpulli, *der* (ugs.)

slops /slɒps/ *n. pl.* **1** Schmutzwasser, *das;* (contents of bedroom or prison vessels) Fäkalien *Pl.;* **empty the ~:** die Nachttöpfe leeren und das Schmutzwasser beseitigen **2** ▸ **slop C 1**

slosh /slɒʃ/

A *v.i.* platschen (ugs.); ‹*Flüssigkeit:*› schwappen

B *v.t.* **1** (coll.: pour clumsily) schwappen **2** (coll.: pour liquid on) übergießen **3** (Brit. coll.: hit) verdreschen (ugs.)

C *n.* **1** ▸ **slush 2** (Brit. coll.: heavy blow) [wuchtiger] Schlag

(Phrasal verb)

- **~ a'bout, ~ a'round**

A *v.i.* **1** (splash about playfully) herumspritzen (ugs.) **2** (slop about) herumschwappen (ugs.)

B *v.t.* verspritzen

sloshed /slɒʃt/ *adj.* (Brit. coll.) blau (ugs.)

slot /slɒt/

A *n.* **1** (hole) Schlitz, *der* **2** (groove) Nut, *die;* **the ~ for a tenon** das Zapfenloch (Technik) **3** (coll.: position) Platz, *der* **4** (coll.: in schedule) Termin, *der;* (Radio, Telev.) Sendezeit, *die;* **the news will go out in its usual ~ at 10 o'clock** die Nachrichten werden wie üblich um 10 Uhr gesendet **5** (Aeronaut., Computing) Slot, *der*

B *v.t.,* **-tt-** **1** (provide with holes) schlitzen; (provide with grooves) nuten **2** (insert) **~ sth. into place/sth.** etw. einfügen/in etw. (*Akk.*) einfügen

C *v.i.,* **-tt-: ~ into place/sth.** (lit. or fig.) sich einfügen/in etw. (*Akk.*) einfügen; **everything ~ted into place** (fig.) alles fügte sich zusammen

(Phrasal verbs)

- **~ 'in**

A *v.t.* einfügen; **can you ~ me in at 10 o'clock?** (fig.) können Sie mich um 10 Uhr dazwischenschieben?

B *v.i.* (lit. or fig.) sich einfügen

- **~ to'gether**

A *v.t.* zusammenfügen

B *v.i.* (lit. or fig.) sich zusammenfügen

sloth /sləʊθ/ *n.* **1** *no pl.* (lethargy) Trägheit, *die* **2** (Zool.) Faultier, *das*

'sloth bear *n.* (Zool.) Lippenbär, *der*

slothful /'sləʊθfl/ *adj.* träge; schwerfällig ‹*Anstrengungen, Versuche*›; **a life of ~ ease** ein Leben träger Bequemlichkeit

slot: ~ machine *n.* **1** (vending machine) Automat, *der;* **2** (Amer.) ▸ **fruit machine; ~ meter** *n.* Münzzähler, *der*

slouch /slaʊtʃ/

A *n.* **1** (posture) schlaffe Haltung; **walk with a ~:** einen nachlässigen Gang haben **2** (coll.: lazy person) Faulpelz, *der;* **be no ~ at sth.** etwas loshaben in etw. (*Dat.*); **he's no ~ at billiards/at geography** er ist verdammt gut im Billard/in Geographie (ugs.)

B *v.i.* **1** sich schlecht halten; **don't ~!** halte dich gerade! **2** (be ungainly) sich herumflegeln (ugs. abwertend); **sit ~ed over one's desk** schlaff über seinem Schreibtisch hängen

(Phrasal verb)

- **~ a'bout, ~ a'round** *v.i.* herumlungern (salopp)

'slouch hat *n.* Schlapphut, *der*

slough[1] /slaʊ/ *n.* (literary) Sumpf, *der; see also* **despond B**

slough[2] /slʌf/

A *n.* **1** (Zool.) abgestreifte Haut; (whole skin of snake) Natternhemd, *das* **2** (Med.) Schorf, *der*

B *v.t.* (Zool.; fig.: abandon) abstreifen

(Phrasal verb)

- **~ 'off** ▸ **slough**[2] **B**

Slovak /'sləʊvæk/ ▸ **i p. 1277,** ▸ **i p. 1345**

A *adj.* slowakisch; **sb. is ~:** jmd. ist Slowake/Slowakin; *see also* **English A**

B *n.* **1** (person) Slowake, *der*/Slowakin, *die* **2** (language) Slowakisch, *das; see also* **English B 1**

Slovakia /slə'vækɪə/ *pr. n.* Slowakei, *die*

Slovakian /slə'vækɪən/ ▸ **i p. 1277,** ▸ **i p. 1345**

A *adj.* slowakisch

B *n.* **1** (person) **he/she is ~:** er ist Slowake/sie ist Slowakin **2** *no pl.* (language) Slowakische, *das;* **speak ~:** Slowakisch sprechen

sloven /'slʌvn/ *n.* (dated) (female) Schlampe, *die* (ugs. abwertend); (male) Liederjan, *der* (ugs. abwertend)

Slovene /'sləʊvi:n/ ▸ **i p. 1277,** ▸ **i p. 1345**

A *adj.* slowenisch

B *n.* **1** (person) Slowene, *der*/Slowenin, *die* **2** (language) Slowenisch, *das*

Slovenia /slə'vi:nɪə/ *pr. n.* Slowenien (*das*)

Slovenian /slə'vi:nɪən/ ▸ **Slovene**

slovenliness /'slʌvnlɪnɪs/ *n., no pl.* Schlampigkeit, *die* (ugs. abwertend)

slovenly /'slʌvnlɪ/

A *adj.* schlampig (ugs.); schlud[e]rig (ugs.); **be a ~ dresser** sich schlampig *od.* schlud[e]rig anziehen (ugs.)

B *adv.* schlampig (ugs.); schlud[e]rig (ugs.)

slow /sləʊ/

A *adj.* **1** langsam; **~ and steady wins the race, ~ and sure does it** eile mit Weile! (Spr.); **~ but sure** langsam, aber zuverlässig **2** (gradual) langsam; langwierig ‹*Suche, Arbeit*›; **make a ~ recovery from one's illness** sich nur langsam von seiner Krankheit erholen; **be ~ in doing sth.** etw. langsam tun; **get off to a ~ start** beim Start langsam wegkommen; ‹*Aufruf, Produkt:*› zunächst nur wenig Anklang finden; **make ~ progress [in** *or* **at** *or* **with sth.]** nur langsam [mit etw.] vorankommen; *see also* **going A 2** **3** ▸ **i p. 1001 be ~ [by ten minutes]** ‹*Uhr:*› [zehn Minuten] nachgehen **4** (preventing quick motion) nur langsam befahrbar ‹*Strecke, Straße, Belag*› **5** (tardy) **[not] be ~ to do sth.** [nicht] zögern, etw. zu tun **6** (not easily roused) **be ~ to anger/to take offence** sich nicht leicht ärgern/beleidigen lassen **7** (dull-witted) schwerfällig; langsam; **be ~ at mathematics** sich in Mathematik schwer tun (ugs.); **be ~ [to understand]** schwer *od.* langsam von Begriff sein (ugs.); **be ~ of speech** schwerfällig *od.* unbeholfen sprechen; *see also* **uptake** **8** (burning feebly) schwach **9** (uninteresting) langweilig **10** (Commerc.) flau ‹*Geschäft*› **11** (not hot) **bake in a ~ oven** bei schwacher Hitze backen **12** (Photog.) niedrigempfindlich ‹*Film*›; lichtschwach ‹*Objektiv*› **13** **~ court** (Tennis)/**~ wicket** (Cricket) langsamer Platz

B *adv.* langsam; **'~'** „langsam fahren!"; **go ~:** langsam fahren; (Brit. Industry) langsam arbeiten

C *v.i.* langsamer werden; **we ~ed to a gentle walk** wir wurden immer langsamer, bis wir nur noch gemächlich gingen; **~ to a halt** anhalten; ‹*Zug:*› zum Stehen kommen; ‹*Produktion:*› zum Erliegen kommen

D *v.t.* **~ a train/car** die Geschwindigkeit eines Zuges/Wagens verringern; **the accident ~ed traffic to a crawl** der Unfall verlangsamte den Verkehr derart, dass er sich nur noch kriechend vorwärts bewegte

(Phrasal verbs)

- **~ 'down**

A *v.i.* **1** langsamer werden; seine Geschwindigkeit verringern; (in working/speaking) langsamer arbeiten/sprechen; ‹*Produktion, Geburten-/Sterbeziffer, Inflations[rate]:*› sinken **2** (reduce pace of living) langsamer machen (ugs.); **have to ~ down after a heart attack** nach einem Herzanfall kürzer treten müssen

B *v.t.* verlangsamen; **the driver ~ed the car/train down** der Autofahrer/Lokomotivführer fuhr langsamer; **the accident ~ed traffic down to a crawl** der Unfall verlangsamte den Verkehr derart, dass er sich nur noch kriechend vorwärts bewegte; **~ down one's pace of living** kürzer treten; **[You can't help me.] You'd only ~ me down** [Du kannst mir nicht helfen.] Du würdest mich nur aufhalten; **his illness has ~ed him down a lot** durch seine Krankheit ist seine Leistungsfähigkeit stark zurückgegangen. *See also* **slowdown**

- **~ 'up** ▸ **~ down**

slow: ~ 'bowler *n.* (Cricket) langsamer Werfer; **~coach** *n.* Trödler, *der*/Trödlerin, *die* (ugs. abwertend); **~ 'cooker** *n.* Slowcooker, *der;* **~down** *n.* **1** (deceleration) Verlangsamung, *die* (**in** *Gen.*); (in birth, death, inflation rate, output, production, number) Sinken, *das* (**in** *Gen.*); **there's been a ~down in the number of ...:** die Zahl der ... ist gesunken; **2** (go-slow) Bummelstreik, *der;* **~ 'handclap** *n.* (Brit.) müdes Klatschen (*als Ausdruck des Missfallens*); **~ lane** *n.* (Brit.) normale Fahrspur; (bei Linksverkehr auch) linke Spur; (bei Rechtsverkehr auch) rechte Spur

slowly /'sləʊlɪ/ *adv.* langsam; **~ but surely** langsam, aber sicher

slow: ~ 'march *n.* (Mil.) langsamer Defiliermarsch; **~ match** *n.* Lunte, *die;* **~ 'motion** *n.* (Cinemat.) Zeitlupe, *die;* **in ~ motion** in Zeitlupe; **~ motion replay** (Sport) Zeitlupenwiederholung, *die;* **~-moving** *adj.* **1** sich langsam fortbewegend; **2** (Commerc.) schlecht gehend; **be ~-moving** schlecht gehen

slowness /'sləʊnɪs/ *n., no pl.* **1** Langsamkeit, *die* **2** (gradualness) Langsamkeit, *die;* (of search, work) Langwierigkeit, *die* **3** (slackness) Zögern, *das;* **his ~ to react** *or* **in reacting** sein zögerndes Reagieren **4** (stupidity) Schwerfälligkeit, *die;* **~ [of comprehension/mind/wit]** Begriffsstutzigkeit, *die* (abwertend) **5** (dullness) Langweiligkeit, *die*

slow: ~ 'poison ▸ **poison A; ~poke** (Amer.) ▸ **slowcoach; ~ 'puncture** *n.* winziges Loch (*durch das ein Reifen o. ä. nur langsam die Luft verliert*); **~ train** *n.* Bummelzug, *der* (ugs.); **~-witted** /sləʊ'wɪtɪd/ *adj.* [geistig] schwerfällig; **~-worm** *n.* (Zool.) Blindschleiche, *die*

SLR *abbr.* (Photog.) **= single-lens reflex**

slub /slʌb/ *n.* (Textiles) Noppe, *die*

sludge /slʌdʒ/ *n.* **1** (mud) Matsch, *der* (ugs.); Schlamm, *der* **2** (sediment) [schlammiger] Bodensatz **3** (Motor Veh.) Ölschlamm, *der* **4** (sewage) Klärschlamm, *der*

slug[1] /slʌg/ *n.* **1** (Zool.) Nacktschnecke, *die* **2** (bullet) [rohe] Gewehrkugel; Flintenlaufgeschoss, *das* (Waffent.) **3** (for airgun) Luftgewehrkugel, *die* **4** (lump of metal) [rundlicher] Metallklumpen; **a ~ of gold/platinum/silver** *etc.* ein Klumpen Gold/Platin/Silber *usw.* **5** (Amer.: tot of liquor) **a ~ of whisky/rum** *etc.* ein Schluck Whisky/Rum *usw.* **6** (Printing) (bar) Reglette, *die;* (line) gegossene Zeile

S

slug² (Amer.: hit)
A *v.t.*, **-gg-** niederschlagen
B *n.* [harter] Schlag; **give sb. a ~:** jmdn. niederschlagen

Phrasal verb

• **~ 'out** *v.t.* **~ it out** es [bis zum Ende] austragen; **the boys were ~ging it out to decide who ...:** die Jungen prügelten sich darum, wer ...

sluggard /'slʌgəd/ *n.* Faulpelz, *der;* (lacking in speed) lahme Ente (ugs.)

sluggish /'slʌgɪʃ/ *adj.* träge; schleppend ‹*Gang, Schritt*›; schwerfällig ‹*Reaktion, Vorstellungskraft*›; (Commerc.) flau; schleppend ‹*Nachfrage, Geschäftsgang*›

sluggishly /'slʌgɪʃlɪ/ *adv.* träge; schleppenden Schrittes ‹*gehen, sich bewegen*›; schwerfällig ‹*reagieren*›; (Commerc.) schleppend ‹*sich verkaufen, vorangehen*›

sluice /slu:s/
A *n.* **1** (Hydraulic Engin.) Schütz, *das* **2** (water) *vom Schütz aufgestautes/durch das Schütz fließendes Wasser* **3** ▸**sluiceway** **4** (rinsing) **give sb./sth. a ~ [down]** (with hose) jmdn./etw. abspritzen; (with bucket) jmdn./etw. [mit Wasser] übergießen
B *v.t.* **1** (Hydraulic Engin.) unter Wasser setzen **2** (provide with sluices) mit Schützen versehen **3** (Mining) waschen **4** **~ [down]** (douse) (with hose) abspritzen; (with bucket) übergießen

Phrasal verbs

• **~ a'way** *v.t.* wegspülen; (with hose) wegspritzen
• **~ 'out** *v.t.* ausspülen; (with hose) ausspritzen

sluice: ~ gate *n.* (Hydraulic Engin.) Schütz, *das;* **~ valve** *n.* (Hydraulic Engin.) Schieber, *der;* **~way** *n.* **1** (Hydraulic Engin.: channel for sluice) Gerinne, *das;* **2** (Mining) Waschrinne, *die*

slum /slʌm/
A *n.* Slum, *der;* (single house or apartment) Elendsquartier, *das*
B *v.i.*, **-mm-: go ~ming** in die Slums gehen; (fig.) sich unters [gemeine] Volk mischen
C *v.t.*, **-mm-: ~ it** wie arme Leute leben; (fig: make do) damit vorlieb nehmen

slumber /'slʌmbə(r)/ (poet./rhet.)
A *n.* (lit. or fig.) **~[s]** Schlummer, *der* (geh.); **fall into a light/long ~:** in leichten/tiefen Schlummer sinken; **be in a ~** (fig.) schlummern (geh.)
B *v.i.* (lit. or fig.) schlummern (geh.); ‹*Vulkan:*› ruhen

Phrasal verb

• **~ a'way** *v.t.* verschlafen

slumberous /'slʌmbərəs/ *adj.* (poet./rhet.) **1** (sleepy) schläfrig **2** (sleep-inducing) einschläfernd

'slumberwear *n.* (Commerc.) Nachtwäsche, *die*

slumbrous /'slʌmbrəs/ ▸**slumberous**

'slum clearance *n.* Slumsanierung, *die*

slummy /'slʌmɪ/ *adj.* verslumt

slump /slʌmp/
A *n.* Sturz, *der* (fig.); (in demand, investment, sales, production) starker Rückgang (**in** *Gen.*); (economic depression) Depression, *die* (Wirtsch.); (in morale, interest, popularity) Nachlassen, *das* (**in** *Gen.*); **~ in prices** Preissturz, *der*
B *v.i.* **1** (Commerc.) stark zurückgehen; ‹*Preise, Kurse:*› stürzen (fig.); **the economy ~ed** die Wirtschaft geriet in eine Depression **2** (be diminished) ‹*Popularität, Moral, Unterstützung usw.:*› nachlassen **3** (collapse) fallen; **they found him ~ed over the table/in his chair/on the floor** sie fanden ihn über dem Tisch/auf seinem Stuhl/auf dem Boden zusammengesunken

Phrasal verb

• **~ 'down** *v.i.* zusammensinken

slung ▸**sling¹ B**

slunk ▸**slink**

slur /slɜ:(r)/
A *v.t.*, **-rr-: ~ one's words/speech** undeutlich sprechen; **~red speech** undeutliche Aussprache
B *v.i.*, **-rr-: his speech began to ~:** er begann undeutlich zu sprechen
C *n.* **1** (stigma) Schande, *die* (**on** für); (imputation) Verleumdung, *die;* (insult) Beleidigung, *die* (**on** für); **cast a ~ on sb./sth.** jmdn./etw. verunglimpfen (geh.); **it's a/no ~ on his reputation** es schmälert seinen Ruf/seinen Ruf nicht **2** (Mus.) [Legato]bogen, *der*

slurp /slɜ:p/
A *v.t.* **~ [up]** schlürfen
B *n.* Schlürfen, *das;* **drink one's juice in three big ~s** seinen Saft in drei Zügen ausschlürfen; **drink [one's beer] with a ~:** beim [Bier]trinken schlürfen

slurry /'slʌrɪ/ *n.* **1** (liquid cement) Zementbrühe, *die* **2** (suspension) Schlamm, *der;* Suspension, *die* (Chemie) **3** (thin mud) Schlammbrühe, *die* **4** (Mining) Kohlenschlamm, *der* **5** (Agric.) Gülle, *die*

slush /slʌʃ/ *n.* **1** (thawing snow) Schneematsch, *der* **2** (fig. derog.: sentiment) sentimentaler Kitsch

'slush fund *n.* Fonds für Bestechungsgelder

slushy /'slʌʃɪ/ *adj.* **1** (wet) matschig **2** (derog.: sloppy) sentimental

slut /slʌt/ *n.* Schlampe, *die* (ugs. abwertend)

sluttish /'slʌtɪʃ/ *adj.* schlampig (ugs. abwertend)

sly /slaɪ/
A *adj.* **1** (crafty) schlau; gerissen (ugs.) ‹*Geschäftsmann, Schachzug, Trick*›; verschlagen (abwertend) ‹*Blick*›; **he is a ~ one** *or* **type** *or* **customer** das ist ein ganz Gerissener *od.* Schlauer (ugs.) **2** (secretive) heimlichtuerisch; verschlagen (abwertend) ‹*Rivale*›; **what a ~ one he is!** so ein Heimlichtuer!; **a ~ dog** (fig. coll.) ein Heimlichtuer/eine Heimlichtuerin **3** (knowing) viel sagend ‹*Blick, Lächeln*›
B *n.* **on the ~:** heimlich; **he is a womanizer on the ~:** er ist ein heimlicher Schürzenjäger

'slyboots *n. sing.* (coll.) Schlauberger, *der* (ugs.); (secretive person) Heimlichtuer, *der*/Heimlichtuerin, *die*

slyly /'slaɪlɪ/ *adv.* **1** (craftily) schlau; arglistig ‹*täuschen*› **2** (secretively) heimlich **3** (knowingly) viel sagend ‹*blicken, lächeln*›

smack¹ /smæk/
A *n.* **1** (flavour) Beigeschmack, *der;* (smell) Duft, *der* **2** (trace) Spur, *die;* (fig.) Anflug, *der*
B *v.i.* **~ of** (taste of) schmecken nach; (smell of) riechen nach; (fig.) riechen nach (ugs.)

smack²
A *n.* **1** (sound) Klatsch, *der;* (of lips) Schmatzen, *das;* (of hand, stick) Klatschen, *das* **2** (blow) Schlag, *der;* (on child's bottom) Klaps, *der* (ugs.); **a ~ in the face** eine Ohrfeige; **a ~ in the eye** *or* **face** (fig.) ein Schlag ins Gesicht **3** (coll.: attempt) **have a ~ at sth.** es mit etw. versuchen; **he had a ~ at the world record** er versuchte, den Weltrekord zu verbessern; **have a ~ at doing sth.** versuchen, etw. zu tun **4** (loud kiss) Schmatz, *der* (ugs.)
B *v.t.* **1** (slap) [mit der flachen Hand] schlagen; (lightly) einen Klaps (ugs.) geben (+ *Dat.*); **~ sb.'s face/bottom/hand** jmdn. ohrfeigen/jmdm. eins hintendrauf geben (ugs.)/jmdm. eins auf die Hand geben (ugs.); **I'll ~ your bottom!** du kriegst eins hintendrauf! (ugs.) **2** **~ one's lips** [mit den Lippen] schmatzen **3** (propel) knallen (ugs.)
C *v.i.* **~ into the net/wall** ins Netz/gegen die Mauer knallen (ugs.); **I ~ed into him** wir knallten zusammen (ugs.)
D *adv.* **1** (coll.: with a ~) **go ~ into a lamp post** gegen einen Laternenpfahl knallen (ugs.) **2** (exactly) direkt

smack³ *n.* (sl.: heroin) Junk, *der* (Drogenjargon)

smack⁴ *n.* (Naut.) Fischkutter, *der*

smacker /'smækə(r)/ *n.* (coll.) **1** (loud kiss) Schmatz, *der* (ugs.) **2** (blow) [wuchtiger] Schlag; **give** *or* **deal sb. a ~ on the nose** jmdm. voll auf die Nase hauen (ugs.) **3** (Brit.: £1) Pfund, *das;* ≈ Scheinchen, *das* (ugs.) **4** (Amer.: $1) Dollar, *der;* ≈ Scheinchen, *das* (ugs.)

small /smɔ:l/
A *adj.* **1** ▸**ⓘ p. 1208** (in size) klein; gering ‹*Wirkung, Appetit, Fähigkeit*›; schmal ‹*Taille, Handgelenk*›; dünn ‹*Stimme*›; **I'm afraid I've nothing ~er** ich habe es leider nicht kleiner (ugs.); **it's a ~ world** die Welt ist klein; **they came in ~ numbers** es kamen nur wenige; **the ~est room** (fig. coll. euphem.) das Örtchen (fam. verhüll.); see also **hour 2**; **still A 5** **2** *attrib.* (~-scale) klein; Klein‹*aktionär, -sparer, -händler, -betrieb, -bauer*›; see also **way A 11** **3** (young, not fully grown) klein; see also **fry² 4** (of the ~er kind) klein; **~ letter** Kleinbuchstabe, *der;* **write with a ~ letter** klein schreiben; **feel ~** (fig.) sich (*Dat.*) ganz klein vorkommen; **look ~** (fig.) [ziemlich] schlecht aussehen (ugs.); **make sb. feel/look ~** (fig.) jmdn. beschämen/ein schlechtes Licht auf jmdn. werfen; see also **arm² A 1**; **beer**; **circle A 1**; **intestine**; **mercy A 2**; **slam² 1** **5** (not much) wenig; **it's ~ comfort** es ist ein geringer Trost; **demand for/interest in the product was ~:** die Nachfrage nach/das Interesse an dem Produkt war gering; **have ~ cause for sth./to do sth.** wenig Grund zu etw. haben/wenig Grund haben, etw. zu tun; **[it's] ~ wonder** [es ist] kein Wunder; **no ~ excitement/feat** einige Aufregung/keine geringe Leistung **6** (trifling) klein; **we have a few ~ matters/points/problems to clear up before ...:** es sind noch ein paar Kleinigkeiten zu klären, bevor ... **7** (minor) unbedeutend; gering ‹*Ruhm, Anerkennung*›; **great and ~:** hoch und niedrig **8** (petty) kleinlich (abwertend); **have a ~ mind** ein Kleinkrämer sein (abwertend) **9** (fine) fein ‹*Kies, Schrot*›
B *n.* (Anat.) **~ of the back** Kreuz, *das; see also* **smalls**
C *adv.* klein

small: ~ 'ad *n.* (coll.) Kleinanzeige, *die;* **the ~ ads section/pages/column** der Teil/die Seiten/die Rubrik mit den Kleinanzeigen; **~-bore** *adj.* (Arms) kleinkalibrig; Kleinkaliber-; **~ 'business** *n.* Kleinbetrieb, *der;* Kleinunternehmen, *das;* **~ 'capital** *n.* (Printing) Kapitälchen, *das;* **~ 'change** *n., no pl., no indef. art.* **1** (coins) Kleingeld, *das;* **2** (remarks) Trivialitäten; (business) Kleinkram, der (ugs.); **~ 'claim** *n.* (Law) ≈ Bagatellsache, *die;* **~ 'claims court** *n.* (Law) *Gericht für Bagatellsachen;* **~ craft** *n. pl.* (Naut.) Boote; **~ goods** *n. pl.* (Austral.) feine Fleisch- und Wurstwaren; **~holder** *n.* ▸**ⓘ p. 1260** (Brit. Agric.) Kleinbauer, *der*/-bäuerin, *die;* **~holding** *n.* (Brit. Agric.) landwirtschaftlicher Kleinbetrieb

smallish /'smɔ:lɪʃ/ *adj.* ziemlich klein/gering; ziemlich schmal ‹*Taille*›

small: ~-'minded *adj.* kleinlich; engstirnig, kleingeistig ‹*Einstellung*›; **~-mindedness** /smɔ:l'maɪndɪdnɪs/ *n.* kleinliche Art; Krämergeist, *der* (abwertend)

smallness /'smɔ:lnɪs/ *n., no pl.* **1** Kleinheit, *die;* (of waist) Schmalheit, *die;* (of income, amount, stock) Bescheidenheit, *die* **2** (pettiness) Kleinlichkeit, *die;* **~ of mind** ▸**small-mindedness**

small: ~pox *n.* ▸**ⓘ p. 1231** (Med.) Pocken *Pl.;* **~ 'print** *n.* (lit. or fig.) Kleingedruckte, *das*

smalls /smɔ:lz/ *n. pl.* (Brit. coll.) Unterwäsche, *die*

small: ~-scale *attrib. adj.* in kleinem Maßstab *nachgestellt;* klein ‹*Konflikt, Unternehmer*›; Klein‹*betrieb, -bauer, -gärtner*›; **~ 'screen** *n.* (Telev.) Bildschirm, *der;* **~-size** ▸**-size**; **~ talk** *n.* leichte Unterhaltung; (at parties) Smalltalk, *der;* **engage in** *or* **make ~ talk [with sb.]** [mit jmdm.] Konversation machen; **sb. has no ~ talk** leichte Konversation liegt jmdm. einfach nicht; **~-time** *attrib. adj.* (coll.) Schmalspur- (ugs. abwertend); **~-time crook** kleiner Ganove (ugs. abwertend); **~-town** *attrib. adj.* Kleinstadt-; kleinstädtisch

smarm /smɑ:m/ *v.i.* (coll.) schöntun (ugs.); **~ to sb.** jmdm. schöntun (ugs.); **~ over sb.** sich bei jmdm. anbiedern (abwertend)

Phrasal verb

• **~ 'down** *v.t.* **~ down one's hair** sein Haar [mit Frisiercreme/Haarwasser] glätten

smarmy /'smɑ:mɪ/ *adj.* kriecherisch (abwertend); schmeichlerisch ‹*Stimme*›; **her ~ approaches** ihre Anbiederungsversuche; **he's so ~:** er ist solch ein Kriecher (abwertend)

smart /smɑ:t/
A *adj.* **1** (clever) clever; smart; (ingenious) raffiniert; (accomplished) hervorragend; **get ~** (Amer.

coll.) zur Vernunft kommen; **act** *or* **get ~ with sb.** (Amer. coll.) zu jmdm. *od.* jmdm. gegenüber frech werden; **~ money** (Finance) Geld der klugen Geschäftsleute **2** (neat) schick; schön ‹*Haus, Garten, Auto*›; **keep sth. ~:** etw. gut in Ordnung halten; **he made a ~ job of it** er hat es schön gemacht **3** *attrib.* (fashionable) elegant; smart; **the ~ set** die elegante Welt; die Schickeria **4** (vigorous) hart ‹*Schlag, Gefecht*›; scharf ‹*Zurechtweisung, Schmerz, Schritt*›; **at a ~ pace** sehr zügig **5** (prompt) flink; **look ~:** sich beeilen **6** *attrib.* (dishonest) nicht ganz reell ‹*Geschäft, Handel, Praktiken, Trick*› **7** *attrib.* (unscrupulous) clever

B *adv.* ▸**smartly**

C *v.i.* schmerzen; **I/my leg ~ed with pain** ich verspürte einen Schmerz/mein Bein schmerzte; **his vanity/pride ~ed** (fig.) er fühlte sich in seiner Eitelkeit/seinem Stolz verletzt; **she ~ed from his remarks** seine Bemerkungen verletzten sie; **~ under sth.** (fig.) unter etw. (*Dat.*) leiden

D *n.* (lit. or fig.) Schmerz, *der;* (from wound, ointment) Brennen, *das;* (from pain) Stechen, *das*

smart: ~ alec[k], ~ alick /ˈsmɑːt ˈælɪk/ (coll. derog.) **A** *ns.* Besserwisser, *der* (abwertend); **B** *attrib. adjs.* neunmalklug; besserwisserisch (abwertend); **~-arse**: (*Amer.* **~-ass**) (sl.) **A** *ns.* Klugscheißer, *der* (salopp abwertend); **B** *attrib. adjs.* klugscheißerisch (salopp abwertend); **~ bomb** *n.* intelligente Bombe; **~ card** *n.* Chipkarte, *die;* **~ drug** *n.* Nootropikum *das* (fachspr.)

smarten /ˈsmɑːtn/

A *v.t.* **1** (make spruce) herrichten; **she ~ed her appearance** sie machte sich zurecht; **he ~ed his hair/clothes** er brachte sein Haar/seine Kleidung in Ordnung (ugs.); **~ oneself** (tidy up) sich zurechtmachen; (dress up) sich herrichten; (improve appearance in general) auf sein Äußeres achten **2** (accelerate) **~ one's pace** seinen Schritt/seine Schritte beschleunigen

B *v.i.* **the pace ~ed** das Tempo beschleunigte sich

Phrasal verb

• **~ 'up**

A *v.t.* **1** ▸**~ A 1** **2** (fig.) **~ up one's ideas** sich am Riemen reißen (ugs.)

B *v.i.* (tidy up) sich zurechtmachen; (dress up) sich herrichten; (improve appearance in general) auf sein Äußeres achten; **the hotel/town has ~ed up a great deal** das Hotel/die Stadt hat sich sehr gemacht (ugs.)

smartish /ˈsmɑːtɪʃ/

A *adj.* (fairly neat) ganz schick; (fairly prompt) ziemlich flink

B *adv.* **[pretty] ~:** [ganz] schnell

smartly /ˈsmɑːtlɪ/ *adv.* **1** (cleverly) clever; (in a know-all way) besserwisserisch (abwertend); **that was ~ put** das war gut gesagt **2** (neatly) schmuck ‹[*an*]*gestrichen*›; smart, flott ‹*gekleidet, geschnitten*› **3** (fashionably) vornehm **4** (vigorously) hart; (sharply) scharf ‹*zurechtweisen*›; hart ‹*anpacken*›; **set off ~ down the road** in scharfem Schritt die Straße hinuntergehen **5** (promptly) sofort; auf der Stelle

'smart money *n.* **the ~ is on ...** Experten setzen auf ...

smartness /ˈsmɑːtnɪs/ *n., no pl.* **1** (cleverness) Cleverness, *die;* (attitude of know-all) Besserwisserei, *die* (abwertend) **2** (neatness) Gepflegtheit, *die;* **~ [of appearance]** ansprechendes Äußeres **3** (vigour) Härte, *die;* (sharpness) Schärfe, *die;* **~ of pace** Tempo, *das* **4** (promptness) Flinkheit, *die*

smart: ~phone *n.* Smartphone, *das;* **~ quotes** *n. pl.* (Computing) automatische Anführungszeichen; **~ weapon** *n.* intelligente Waffe

smarty/ˈsmɑːtɪ/: **~-boots, ~-pants** *ns. sing.* ▸**smart aleck A**

smash /smæʃ/

A *v.t.* **1** (break) zerschlagen; **~ sth. against the wall/down on the floor** etw. an die Wand/auf den Boden schmettern; **~ one's hand/arm/leg** sich (*Dat.*) die Hand/den Arm/das Bein zerschmettern; **~ sth. to pieces** etw. zerschmettern **2** (defeat) zerschlagen ‹*Rebellion, Revolution, Opposition*›; zerschmettern ‹*Feind*›; (in games) vernichtend schlagen; klar verbessern ‹*Rekord*› **3** (hit hard) **~ sb. in the face/mouth** jmdm. [hart] ins Gesicht/auf den Mund schlagen; **I'll ~ your face** (sl.) ich polier' dir die Fresse (derb) **4** (Tennis) schmettern **5** (propel forcefully) schmettern; **he ~ed the car into a wall/his fist down on the table** er knallte (ugs.) mit dem Wagen gegen eine Mauer/schlug mit der Faust auf den Tisch; **he ~ed his way into the house with an iron bar** er schlug sich (*Dat.*) seinen Weg in das Haus mit einer Eisenstange frei

B *v.i.* **1** (shatter) zerbrechen **2** (crash) krachen; **~ into a wall/lamp post** an *od.* gegen eine Mauer/einen Laternenpfahl krachen; **the cars ~ed into each other** die Wagen krachten zusammen (salopp) **3** (Commerc.) ▸**crash C 4**

C *n.* **1** (sound) Krachen, *das;* (of glass) Klirren, *das* **2** ▸**smash-up** **3** (coll.) ▸**smash hit** **4** (Tennis) Schmetterball, *der* **5** (Commerc.) ▸**crash A 3**

D *adv.* krach

Phrasal verbs

• **~ 'down** *v.t.* einschlagen ‹*Tür*›

• **~ 'in** *v.t.* zerschmettern; eindrücken ‹*Rippen, Motorhaube, Kotflügel*›; einschlagen ‹*Fenster, Tür, Schädel*›; ‹*Explosion:*› eindrücken ‹*Fenster, Tür*›; **~ sb.'s face in** (coll.) jmdm. die Fresse polieren (derb)

• **~ 'up**

A *v.t.* zertrümmern

B *v.i.* zerschellen; ‹*Auto:*› zertrümmert werden; *see also* **smash-up**

smash-and-'grab [raid] *n.* (coll.) Schaufenstereinbruch, *der*

smashed /smæʃt/ *adj.* (sl.) **1** (drunk) **get ~ on sth.** von etw. besoffen werden (derb); (deliberately) sich mit etw. voll laufen lassen (salopp); **be ~ out of one's head** *or* **mind** *or* **brains** sturzbetrunken (ugs.) *od.* (derb) sturzbesoffen sein **2** (on drugs) stoned (Drogenjargon)

smasher /ˈsmæʃə(r)/ *n.* (coll.) **be a ~:** [ganz] große Klasse sein (ugs.); **what a ~ he/she/it is!** er/sie/es ist ganz große Klasse! (ugs.); **a ~ of a girlfriend** eine tolle Freundin

smash 'hit *n.* (coll.) (film, play) Kassenschlager, *der* (ugs.); (song, record) Riesenhit, *der* (ugs.)

smashing /ˈsmæʃɪŋ/ *adj.* (coll.: excellent) toll (ugs.); klasse (ugs.); **[how] ~!** toll! (ugs.); klasse! (ugs.); **he/she is ~** (physically attractive) er/sie sieht klasse *od.* ganz toll aus (ugs.)

'smash-up *n.* schwerer Zusammenstoß; **there has been a ~ between two cars/trains** zwei Autos/Züge sind zusammengekracht (ugs.); **multiple ~:** Massenkarambolage, *die*

smatter /ˈsmætə(r)/, **smattering** /ˈsmætərɪŋ/ *ns.* oberflächliche Kenntnisse; (feeble) Halbwissen, *das* (abwertend); **have a ~ing of German** ein paar Brocken Deutsch können

smear /smɪə(r)/

A *v.t.* **1** (daub) beschmieren; (put on or over) schmieren; **~ oneself/one's body/face with a cream/lotion/ointment** sich/seinen Körper/sein Gesicht mit einer Creme/Lotion/Salbe einreiben; **~ cream/ointment over one's body/face/hands** sich (*Dat.*) den Körper/das Gesicht/die Hände mit Creme/Salbe einreiben; **~ed with blood** blutbeschmiert *od.* -verschmiert; **he had paint ~ed on his face** sein Gesicht war mit Farbe beschmiert; **ink was ~ed all over the letter** der ganze Brief war mit Tinte verschmiert **2** (smudge) verwischen; verschmieren **3** (fig.: defame) in den Schmutz ziehen

B *n.* **1** (blotch) [Schmutz]fleck, *der;* **a ~ of ink/paint/fat** *etc.* ein [verschmierter] Tinten-/Farb-/Fettfleck *usw.* **2** (fig.: defamation) **a ~ on him/his [good] name/his [good] reputation** eine Beschmutzung seiner Person/seines [guten] Namens/seines Ansehens **3** (Med.) Abstrich, *der;* **blood ~:** Blutausstrich, *der*

smear: ~ campaign *n.* Schmutzkampagne, *die;* **~ tactics** *n. pl.* schmutzige Mittel; **~ test** *n.* (Med.) Abstrich, *der;* **~ word** *n.* Schmähwort, *das*

smeary /ˈsmɪərɪ/ *adj.* **1** verschmiert ‹*Glas, Tischplatte, Kleid*›; **make sth. ~:** etw. verschmieren **2** (likely to smear) schmierend; **be very ~** ‹*Farbe, Tinte:*› leicht schmieren

smegma /ˈsmegmə/ (Physiol.) Smegma, *das*

smell /smel/

A *n.* **1** *no pl., no art.* **have a good/bad sense of ~:** einen guten/schlechten Geruchssinn haben **2** (odour) Geruch, *der* (**of** nach); (pleasant also) Duft, *der* (**of** nach); **a ~ of burning/gas** ein Brand-/Gasgeruch; **there was a ~ of coffee** es duftete nach Kaffee; **sth. has a nice/strong** *etc.* **~ [to it]** etw. riecht angenehm/stark *usw.* **3** (stink) Gestank, *der* **4** (act of inhaling) **one ~ was enough** einmal riechen genügte; **have** *or* **take a ~ at** *or* **of sth.** an etw. (*Dat.*) riechen

B *v.t.*, **smelt** /smelt/ *or* **~ed** **1** (perceive) riechen; (fig.) wittern; **I can ~ burning/gas** es riecht brandig/nach Gas; **I could ~ trouble** (fig.) es roch nach Ärger; *see also* **rat A 1** **2** (inhale ~ of) riechen an (+ *Dat.*); **just ~ the sea air!** riech [doch] mal nur die Seeluft!

C *v.i.*, **smelt** *or* **~ed** **1** (emit ~) riechen; (pleasantly also) duften **2** (recall ~; fig.: suggest) **~ of sth.** nach etw. riechen **3** (stink) riechen; **his breath ~s** er riecht aus dem Mund **4** (perceive ~) riechen; **she can't ~ because of her cold** sie riecht nichts wegen ihrer Erkältung; **~ at sth.** an etw. (*Dat.*) riechen

Phrasal verb

• **~ 'out** *v.t.* (lit. or fig.) aufspüren

smelling salts /ˈsmelɪŋ sɔːlts, ˈsmelɪŋ sɒlts/ *n. pl.* Riechsalz, *das*

smelly /ˈsmelɪ/ *adj.* stinkend (abwertend); **be ~:** stinken (abwertend)

smelt[1] /smelt/ *v.t.* (Metallurgy) **1** (melt) verhütten ‹*Erz*› **2** (refine) erschmelzen ‹*Metall*›

smelt[2] *n., pl.* **~s** *or same* (Zool.) Stint, *der*

smelt[3] ▸**smell B, C**

smelter /ˈsmeltə(r)/ *n.* (Metallurgy) **1** (person) Schmelzer, *der* **2** (smelting works) Schmelzhütte, *die*

smidgen, smidgin /ˈsmɪdʒən/ *n.* (coll.) **a ~:** ein klein bisschen

smile /smaɪl/

A *n.* Lächeln, *das;* **a ~ of joy/satisfaction** ein freudiges/befriedigtes Lächeln; **be all ~s** über das ganze Gesicht strahlen; **break into a ~:** [plötzlich] zu lächeln beginnen; **give a [little] ~:** [schwach] lächeln; **give sb. a ~:** jmdn. anlächeln; **give me a big ~ now!** jetzt mal schön lächeln!; **raise a ~:** ein Lächeln hervorlocken; (make oneself ~) sich (*Dat.*) ein Lächeln abringen; **raise a few ~s** zum Lächeln anregen; **take that ~ off your face!** hör auf zu grinsen!; **this'll put a ~ on your face** das wird dich freuen; **with a ~:** mit einem Lächeln [auf den Lippen]; lächelnd

B *v.i.* lächeln; **make sb. ~:** jmdn. zum Lachen bringen; **keep smiling** (fig.: not despair) das Lachen nicht verlernen (fig.); **keep smiling!** Kopf hoch!; keep smiling!; **come up smiling** (fig. coll.) sich nicht unterkriegen lassen (ugs.); **~ at sb.** jmdn. anlächeln; **~ at sth.** (lit. or fig.) über etw. (*Akk.*) lächeln; **~, please!** bitte recht freundlich!; **~ with delight/pleasure** vor Freude strahlen; **Fortune ~d on us/our efforts** das Glück lachte uns (veralt.)

C *v.t.* **1** **~ encouragement/one's thanks** aufmunternd/dankend lächeln; **~ a welcome** zur Begrüßung [freundlich] lächeln **2** **~ a friendly/sad ~:** freundlich/traurig lächeln

smiley /ˈsmaɪlɪ/ *n.* Smiley, *das*

smirch /smɜːtʃ/ (literary)

A *v.t.* **1** besudeln (geh.) **2** (fig.: disgrace) ▸**besmirch**

B *n.* **1** [Schmutz]fleck, *der* **2** (fig.: disgrace) Schandfleck, *der* (fig.); **cast a ~ on sb./sth.** ein Schandfleck für jmdn./etw. sein

smirk /smɜːk/

A *v.i.* grinsen

B *n.* Grinsen, *das*

smite /smaɪt/ *v.t.*, **smote** /sməʊt/, **smitten** /ˈsmɪtn/ (arch./literary) **1** (strike) schlagen (**on** auf, an + *Akk.*); **~ one's breast/forehead** sich (*Dat.*) an die Brust/Stirn schlagen **2** (affect suddenly) **an idea/his conscience smote him** eine Vorstellung bemächtigte sich seiner (geh.)/ihm schlug das Gewissen (geh.); **the light smote our eyes** das Licht blendete unsere Augen

S

[3] (afflict) **be smitten by** *or* **with desire/terror/ the plague** von Verlangen/Schrecken ergriffen/mit der Pest geschlagen sein (geh.); **be smitten by** *or* **with a** *or* **the desire to do sth.** von dem Verlangen ergriffen sein, etw. zu tun; **be smitten by** *or* **with sb./sb.'s charms** jmdm./jmds. Zauber erlegen sein [4] (defeat) zerschmettern; erschlagen ‹*Person*›

smith /smɪθ/ *n.* ▸ℹ **p. 1260** Schmied, *der*

-smith *n. suf.* [1] (metalworker) -schmied, *der* [2] (fig.: creator) **song~:** versierter Songkomponist; **word~** (creator of words) Wortschöpfer, *der;* **the word~ John Updike** der versierte Schriftsteller John Updike

smithereens /smɪðəˈriːnz/ *n. pl.* **blow/ smash sth. to ~:** etw. in tausend Stücke sprengen/schlagen; **in ~:** in tausend Stücken

smithy /ˈsmɪðɪ/ *n.* ▸ℹ **p. 1260** Schmiede, *die*

smitten ▸**smite**

smock /smɒk/

A *n.* [Arbeits]kittel, *der;* **painter's ~:** Malerkittel, *der*

B *v.t.* (Sewing) smoken

smocking /ˈsmɒkɪŋ/ *n.* (Sewing) Smokarbeit, *die*

smog /smɒg/ *n.* Smog, *der*

ˈsmog mask *n.* Smogmaske, *die*

smoke /sməʊk/

A *n.* [1] Rauch, *der;* **go up in ~:** in Rauch [und Flammen] aufgehen; (fig.) in Rauch aufgehen; **like ~** (coll.) wie ein geölter Blitz (ugs.) ‹*laufen, fahren*›; (without hindrance) wie geschmiert (ugs.) ‹*zusammenarbeiten, funktionieren*›; **[there is] no ~ without fire** (prov.) kein Rauch ohne Flamme (Spr.) [2] (act of smoking tobacco) **a ~ would be nice just now** jetzt würde ich gern eine rauchen; **have a [quick] ~:** [schnell eine] rauchen; **I'm dying for a ~:** ich würde schrecklich gern eine rauchen (ugs.) [3] (coll.: cigarette) **a packet of ~s** ein Päckchen Zigaretten; **have you got a ~?** hast du was (ugs.) zu rauchen?

B *v.i.* [1] (~ tobacco) rauchen; **do you mind if I ~?** stört es Sie, wenn ich rauche?; **~ like a chimney** rauchen wie ein Schlot (ugs.) [2] (emit ~) rauchen; (burn imperfectly) qualmen; (emit vapour) dampfen

C *v.t.* [1] rauchen; *see also* **pipe A 4** [2] (darken) schwärzen ‹*Glas*›; ‹*Petroleumlampe:*› verräuchern ‹*Wand, Decke*› [3] räuchern ‹*Fleisch, Fisch*›

Phrasal verb

• **~ ˈout** *v.t.* [1] (exterminate, expel) ausräuchern [2] (fill with ~) verräuchern [3] (fig.: discover) aufspüren ‹*Verbrecher*›; auf die Spur kommen (+ *Dat.*) ‹*Absicht, Plan*›

smoke: ~ aˈbatement *n., no pl.* Rauchverringerung, *die;* **~ alarm** *n.* Rauchmelder, *der;* **~ bomb** *n.* Rauchbombe, *die*

smoked /sməʊkt/ *adj.* (Cookery) geräuchert; **~ glass** dunkel getöntes Glas; (for decorative purposes) Rauchglas, *das*

smoke: ~ detector *n.* Rauchmelder, *der;* **~-dried** *adj.* geräuchert; **~-filled** *adj.* raucherfüllt; (filled with cigarette smoke) verraucht; verqualmt (ugs. abwertend); **~-free** *adj.* rauchfrei

smokeless /ˈsməʊklɪs/ *adj.* rauchlos; rauchfrei ‹*Zone*›

smoker /ˈsməʊkə(r)/ *n.* Raucher, *der*/Raucherin, *die;* **be a heavy ~:** ein starker Raucher/eine starke Raucherin sein; **~'s companion** Raucherbesteck, *das;* **~'s cough** (Med.) Raucherhusten, *der*

smoke: ~ ring *n.* Rauchring, *der;* **~ room** *n.* (Brit.) Rauchsalon, *der;* Rauchzimmer, *das;* **~screen** *n.* [künstliche] Nebelwand; (fig.) Vernebelung, *die* (**for** *Gen.*); **throw up a thick ~screen round a scandal** die Fakten eines Skandals gründlich vernebeln; **~ signal** *n.* Rauchzeichen, *das;* Rauchsignal, *das;* **~stack** ▸**stack A 6**

smoking /ˈsməʊkɪŋ/ *n.* [1] (act) Rauchen, *das;* **'no ~'** „Rauchen verboten"; **no-~ compartment** (Railw.) Nichtraucherabteil, *das* [2] *no art.* (seating area) **[do you want to sit in] ~ or non-~?** [möchten Sie für] Raucher oder Nichtraucher?; **the next carriage is ~:** der nächste Wagen ist für Raucher

smoking: ~ compartment *n.* (Railw.) Raucherabteil, *das;* **~ jacket** *n.* Rauchjacke, *die;* Hausrock, *der;* **~-related** *adj.* rauchbedingt; **~ room** (Brit.) ▸**smoke room**

smoky /ˈsməʊkɪ/ *adj.* (emitting smoke) rauchend; qualmend; (smoke-filled, smoke-stained) verräuchert; (coloured or tasting like smoke) rauchig; **be too ~** ‹*Feuer, Kamin, Lampe:*› zu stark rauchen *od.* qualmen; **~ quartz/topaz/glass** Rauchquarz, *der*/-topas/-glas, *das;* **~ grey** rauchgrau

smolder (Amer.) ▸**smoulder**

smooch /smuːtʃ/ (coll.)

A *v.i.* [sich] knutschen (ugs.)

B *n.* Knutschen, *das* (ugs.); **have a ~:** [sich] knutschen (ugs.)

smooth /smuːð/

A *adj.* [1] (even) glatt; eben ‹*Straße, Weg*›; **as ~ as glass/silk/a baby's bottom** spiegelglatt/glatt wie Seide/wie ein Kinderpopo (ugs.); **beat the mixture until ~:** die Mischung glatt rühren; **be ~ to the touch** sich glatt anfühlen; **make sth. ~:** etw. glätten; **be worn ~** ‹*Treppenstufe:*› abgetreten sein; ‹*Reifen:*› abgefahren sein; ‹*Fels, Stein:*› glatt geschliffen sein; **this razor gives a ~ shave** dieser Rasierapparat rasiert glatt [2] (mild) weich; **as ~ as velvet** (fig.) samtweich [3] (fluent) flüssig; geschliffen ‹*Stil, Diktion*› [4] (not jerky) geschmeidig ‹*Bewegung*›; ruhig ‹*Fahrt, Flug, Lauf einer Maschine, Bewegung, Atmung*›; weich ‹*Start, Landung, Autofahren, Schalten*›; **come to a ~ stop** ‹*Wagen, Bus, Zug:*› weich zum Stehen kommen [5] (without problems) reibungslos; **the changeover was fairly ~:** der Wechsel ging ziemlich reibungslos vonstatten [6] (equable) ruhig ‹*Art, Wesen*› [7] (derog.: suave) glatt; (~-tongued) glattzüngig (geh. abwertend); **he is a ~ operator** er ist gewieft [8] (coll.: elegant) schick [9] (skilful) geschickt; souverän

B *adv.* ▸**smoothly**

C *v.t.* [1] glätten; glatt streichen, glätten ‹*Stoff, Tuch, Papier*›; glatt streichen ‹*Haar*›; glatt schleifen ‹*Stein*›; (with plane) glatt hobeln ‹*Holz*›; (with sandpaper) glatt schleifen, glätten ‹*Holz*›; (fig.: soothe) besänftigen; **he ~ed the creases/ wrinkles from the paper/cloth** er strich die Falten aus dem Papier/Stoff [2] (Statistics) bereinigen [3] (fig.: free from impediments) **~ sb.'s/sth.'s path** jmdm./einer Sache den Weg ebnen *od.* die Wege ebnen; **~ the way for sb./sth.** jmdm./einer Sache den Weg *od.* die Wege ebnen

D *v.i.* (lit. or fig.) sich glätten

Phrasal verbs

• **~ aˈway** *v.t.* glätten, ausstreichen ‹*Falten*›; (fig.) vertreiben ‹*Sorgen, Ängste*›; ausräumen ‹*Differenzen, Schwierigkeiten*›

• **~ ˈback** *v.t.* [glatt] zurückstreichen ‹*Haare*›; (with comb) [glatt] zurückkämmen

• **~ ˈdown**

A *v.t.* glatt streichen ‹*Haar*›; (fig.) schlichten ‹*Streit*›; besänftigen ‹*Person*›; **~ things down a bit** ein wenig die Wogen glätten

B *v.i.* ▸**smooth D**

• **~ out** *v.t.* glatt streichen ‹*Falte, Tuch*›; ausstreichen ‹*Farbe, Teig*›; (fig.) ausräumen ‹*Schwierigkeiten, Hindernisse*›

• **~ ˈover** *v.t.* (fig.) beilegen ‹*Streit*›; ausräumen ‹*Schwierigkeiten*›; **we ~ed things over** wir bereinigten die Angelegenheit

ˈsmooth-bore *n.* (Arms) Gewehr mit glattem Lauf

smoothie /ˈsmuːðɪ/ *n.* (coll. derog.) aalglatter Typ (ugs.)

smoothly /ˈsmuːðlɪ/ *adv.* [1] (evenly) glatt [2] (fluently) flüssig; **~ flowing** eingängig ‹*Poesie, Prosa, Musik*› [3] (not jerkily) geschmeidig ‹*sich bewegen*›; reibungslos ‹*funktionieren*›; ruhig ‹*atmen, fließen, fahren*›; weich ‹*starten, landen, schalten*›; **a ~ running engine** (Motor Veh.) ein rund laufender Motor; **this pen writes ~:** dieser Füller (ugs.) schreibt einwandfrei [4] (without problems) reibungslos; glatt [5] (derog.: suavely) aalglatt (abwertend); glattzüngig (geh. abwertend) ‹*sprechen*› [6] (coll.: elegantly) schick [7] (skilfully) geschickt; souverän

smoothness /ˈsmuːðnɪs/ *n., no pl.* [1] (evenness) Glätte, *die;* **have the ~ of silk** seidig glatt sein [2] (mildness) Weichheit, *die* [3] (fluency) Flüssigkeit, *die* [4] (lack of jerkiness) (of movement) Geschmeidigkeit, *die;* (of machine operation, breathing) Gleichmäßigkeit, *die;* **the ~ of his driving** sein gefühlvolles Fahren [5] (lack of problems) Reibungslosigkeit, *die* [6] (equability) Sanftheit, *die* [7] (derog.: suavity) Glätte, *die* (abwertend) [8] (coll.: elegance) Schick, *der* [9] (skill) Geschicklichkeit, *die;* Souveränität, *die*

smooth: ~ ˈtongue *n.* (fig.: suavity) Glattzüngigkeit, *die* (geh. abwertend); **have a ~ tongue** eine einschmeichelnde Art haben; **~-tongued** *adj.* glattzüngig

smote ▸**smite**

smother /ˈsmʌðə(r)/

A *v.t.* [1] (stifle) ersticken; **he was ~ed by the avalanche** er erstickte in der Lawine [2] (overwhelm) überschütten (**with, in** mit); **~ sb. with kisses** jmdn. mit seinen Küssen [fast] ersticken [3] (extinguish) ersticken [4] (fig.: suppress) unterdrücken ‹*Kichern, Gähnen, Schluchzen, Tatsachen, Wahrheit*›; ersticken ‹*Kritik, Gerücht, Schluchzen, Gelächter, Schreie*›; dämpfen ‹*Lärm*› [5] (Amer.: defeat quickly) erledigen ‹*Feind, Gegner*› [6] (cover entirely) **~ sth. in sth.** etw. mit etw. bedecken; **~ed in dust/dirt** voller Staub/ Schmutz; **strawberries ~ed in** *or* **with cream** Erdbeeren mit reichlich [flüssiger] Sahne

B *v.i.* ersticken

Phrasal verb

• **~ ˈup** *v.t.* vertuschen ‹*Verbrechen, Skandal*›; unterdrücken ‹*Gerücht, Wahrheit, Vorschlag*›

smothery /ˈsmʌðərɪ/ *adj.* stickig; (overwhelming) erdrückend

smoulder /ˈsməʊldə(r)/ *v.i.* [1] schwelen [2] (fig.) ‹*Hass, Rebellion:*› schwelen; ‹*Liebe:*› glimmen (geh.); **she was ~ing with rage** Zorn schwelte in ihr; **she/her eyes ~ed with desire/rage** sie glühte (geh.)/ihre Augen glühten vor Verlangen/Zorn; **a ~ing beauty** eine glutvolle Schönheit

SMS *abbr.* = **short message** *or* **messaging service** SMS; *attrib.* **~ message** SMS, *die;* SMS-Nachricht, *die*

smudge[1] /smʌdʒ/

A *v.t.* [1] (blur) verwischen [2] (smear) schmieren; **~ sth. on sth.** etw. auf etw. (*Akk.*) schmieren [3] (make smear on) verschmieren [4] (fig.: disgrace) beschmutzen

B *v.i.* ‹*Füller, Tinte, Farbe:*› schmieren; **my hand slipped and the drawing/ink/paint ~d** meine Hand rutschte aus, und die Zeichnung/Tinte/ Farbe war verwischt

C *n.* [1] (smear) Fleck, *der;* (fig.) Schandfleck, *der* [2] (blur) Schmierage, *die* (ugs.); **be a mass of ~s** eine einzige Schmiererei sein (ugs. abwertend)

smudge[2] *n.* (Amer.: fire) Rauchfeuer, *das* (*zum Schutz vor Insekten od. Kälte*)

ˈsmudge pot *n.* (Amer.) *Kessel mit Brennmaterial für ein Rauchfeuer zur Vertreibung von Insekten od. zum Kälteschutz*

smudgy /ˈsmʌdʒɪ/ *adj.* [1] (dirty) schmutzig; verschmutzt [2] (blurred) verwischt [3] (smudging easily) schmierend; **be ~** ‹*Füller, Tinte:*› schmieren

smug /smʌg/ *adj.* selbstgefällig (abwertend); **she is very ~ about it/her job/her new house** sie ist darauf/auf ihre Stelle/auf ihr neues Haus sehr eingebildet (abwertend)

smuggle /ˈsmʌgl/ *v.t.* schmuggeln

Phrasal verbs

• **~ aˈway** *v.t.* wegschaffen; **~ sb. away through a back door** jmdn. durch eine Hintertür hinausschmuggeln

• **~ ˈin** *v.t.* einschmuggeln; hinein-/hereinschmuggeln ‹*Person*›

• **~ ˈout** *v.t.* hinaus-/herausschmuggeln

smuggler /ˈsmʌglə(r)/ *n.* Schmuggler, *der*/Schmugglerin, *die*

smuggling /ˈsmʌglɪŋ/ *n.* Schmuggel, *der;* Schmuggeln, *das;* **the ~ of dogs into Britain** das Einschmuggeln von Hunden nach Großbritannien

smugly /ˈsmʌglɪ/ *adv.* selbstgefällig (abwertend)

smugness /ˈsmʌgnɪs/ *n., no pl.* Selbstgefälligkeit, *die* (abwertend)

smut /smʌt/ *n.* 1 Rußflocke, *die;* (smudge) Rußfleck, *der;* **be covered in ~s** voller Ruß sein 2 *no art.* (lewd matter) Schund, *der* (abwertend); **talk ~:** schweinigeln (ugs. abwertend) 3 (Bot.) (disease) Brand, *der;* (fungus) Brandpilz, *der*

smutty /ˈsmʌtɪ/ *adj.* 1 (dirty) verschmutzt 2 (lewd) schmutzig (abwertend); **he is ~:** er ist schweinisch (ugs. abwertend)

snack /snæk/ *n.* Imbiss, *der;* Snack, *der;* **eat many ~s between meals** viel zwischendurch essen; **have a [quick] ~:** [rasch] eine Kleinigkeit essen (ugs.)

ˈ**snackbar** *n.* Schnellimbiss, *der;* Snackbar, *die*

snaffle /ˈsnæfl/
A *n.* (Riding) Trense, *die*
B *v.t.* 1 (coll.) mopsen (fam.) ‹*Schokolade, Zeitung*›; klauen (salopp) ‹*Diamanten, Geheimdokumente, Geld*› 2 (Riding) die Trense anlegen (+ *Dat.*)

Phrasal verb
• **~ ˈup** *v.t.* [sich (*Dat.*)] schnappen (ugs.)

ˈ**snaffle bit** *n.* (Riding) Trensengebiss, *das*

snafu /snæˈfu:/ (Amer. coll.)
A *pred. adj.* chaotisch
B *n.* Chaos, *das;* **they left us in ~:** sie ließen uns im Schlamassel stecken (ugs.)

snag /snæg/
A *n.* 1 (jagged point) Zacke, *die* 2 (problem) Haken, *der;* **what's the ~?** wo klemmt es [denn]? (ugs.); **hit a ~, run up against a ~:** auf ein Problem *od.* eine Schwierigkeit stoßen; **there's a ~ in it** die Sache hat einen Haken 3 (tear) Loch, *das;* (pulled thread) gezogener Faden
B *v.t.,* **-gg-** 1 (catch) **I've ~ged my coat** mein Mantel hat sich verfangen; ich bin mit dem Mantel hängen geblieben 2 (tear) einreißen 3 (Amer.: catch quickly) **~ sth.** sich (*Dat.*) etw. schnappen (ugs.)

snail /sneɪl/ *n.* Schnecke, *die;* **edible** *or* **Roman ~:** Weinbergschnecke, *die;* **at [a] ~'s pace** im Schneckentempo (ugs.)

ˈ**snail-like** *adj.* schneckenartig; schneckenhaft (ugs.)

ˈ**snail mail** *n.* (coll. joc.) Schneckenpost, *die;* **send sth. by ~:** etw. mit der Schneckenpost *od.* per Schneckenpost schicken

snake /sneɪk/
A *n.* 1 Schlange, *die;* **~s and ladders** *Brettspiel, bei dem je nach Augenzahl beim Würfeln Spielsteine „Leitern" hinauf- und „Schlangen" hinabbewegt werden* 2 (derog.) **~ [in the grass]** (woman) [falsche] Schlange; (man) falscher Kerl *od.* (ugs.) Hund 3 (Econ.) **the ~:** die Währungsschlange (Jargon)
B *v.i.* sich schlängeln

snake: ~bite *n.* 1 Schlangenbiss, *der;* 2 (drink) *Getränk aus gleichen Teilen Apfelwein und Lagerbier;* **~ charmer** *n.* Schlangenbeschwörer, *der;* **~skin** *n.* Schlangenleder, *das*

snaky /ˈsneɪkɪ/ *adj.* 1 (winding) gewunden; schlangenartig ‹*Bewegung*› 2 (sly) hinterhältig

snap /snæp/
A *v.t.,* **-pp-** 1 (break) zerbrechen; **~ sth. in two** *or* **in half** etw. in zwei Stücke brechen
2 **~ one's fingers** mit den Fingern schnalzen; **~ one's fingers at sth./sb.** (fig.) auf etw./jmdn. pfeifen (ugs.)
3 (move with ~ping sound) **~ sth. home** *or* **into place** etw. einrasten *od.* einschnappen lassen; **~ shut** zuschnappen lassen ‹*Portemonnaie, Tür, Schloss*›; zuklappen ‹*Buch, Zigarettendose, Etui*›; **~ sth. open** etw. aufschnappen lassen
4 (take photograph of) knipsen
5 (say in sharp manner) fauchen; (speak crisply or curtly) bellen
B *v.i.,* **-pp-** 1 (break) brechen
2 (fig.: give way under strain) ausrasten (ugs.); **my patience has finally ~ped** nun ist mir der Geduldsfaden aber gerissen; **something ~ped in me** (fig.) da war bei mir das Maß voll
3 (make as if to bite) [zu]schnappen
4 (move smartly) **~ into action** loslegen (ugs.); **~ into life** aufschrecken; **~ to attention** strammstehen; **~ to it!** (coll.) leg/legt los! (ugs.)
5 (move with ~ping sound) **~ home** *or* **into place** einrasten; einschnappen; **~ shut** zuschnappen; ‹*Kiefer:*› zusammenklappen; ‹*Mund:*› zuklappen; **~ together** zusammenklappen; **~ open** aufschnappen
6 (speak sharply) fauchen
7 (take photograph) knipsen
C *n.* 1 (sound) Knacken, *das;* (of whip) Knallen, *das*
2 (biscuit) Plätzchen, *das; see also* **brandy snap**
3 (Photog.) Schnappschuss, *der*
4 (Brit. Cards) Schnippschnapp[schnurr], *das*
5 **cold ~:** kurze Kälteperiode
6 (zest) Schwung, *der*
D *attrib. adj.* (spontaneous) spontan; **~ decision** plötzlicher Entschluss; **call a ~ election/vote** Knall und Fall (ugs.) einen Wahltermin festsetzen/eine Abstimmung herbeiführen
E *int.* 1 (Brit. Cards) schnapp
2 (when two things are seen to match coincidentally) genau gleich (ugs.)

Phrasal verbs
• **~ at** *v.t.* 1 (bite) **~ at sb./sth.** nach jmdm./etw. schnappen; **~ at sb.'s heels** jmdm. auf den Fersen sein; **he ran with a pack of dogs ~ping at his heels** er rannte, dicht gefolgt von einer Hundemeute 2 (speak sharply to) anfauchen (ugs.) 3 (Amer.: accept eagerly) **~ at a chance** eine Gelegenheit beim Schopf[e] ergreifen; **~ at an invitation/a job** bei einer Einladung/einem Job keinesfalls nein sagen *od.* (salopp) gleich zuschlagen
• **~ ˈback**
A *v.i.* 1 (return) zurückschnellen 2 (reply) **~ back [at sb.]** jmdn. anfauchen (ugs.) 3 (Amer. fig.: make quick recovery) sich schnell [wieder] erholen
B *v.t.* (say as a retort) zurückgeben
• **~ ˈoff**
A *v.i.* abbrechen; abknicken ‹*Zweig, Antenne*›
B *v.t.* 1 (break) abbrechen; **~ sth. off sth.** etw. von etw. abbrechen 2 (bite) abbeißen; **~ sb.'s head off** (fig.) jmdm. den Kopf abreißen (fig.) 3 (Amer.: switch off) ausknipsen (ugs.); ausschalten 4 aufklappen ‹*Deckel, Verschluss*›
• **~ ˈon**
A *v.i.* zuschnappen; **~ on to sth.** sich an etw. (*Dat.*) festklemmen
B *v.t.* 1 (fasten) festklemmen; zuklappen ‹*Deckel*›; **~ sth. on sth.** etw. auf etw. (*Akk.*) klemmen 2 (Amer.: switch on) anknipsen (ugs.). *See also* **snap-on**
• **~ ˈout** *v.t.* bellen ‹*Befehl, Anweisung*›
• **~ ˈout of** *v.t.* abwerfen; sich befreien von ‹*Gefühl, Stimmung, Komplex*›; **~ out of it!** (coll.) hör auf damit!; (wake up) wach auf!
• **~ ˈup** *v.t.* 1 (pick up) [sich (*Dat.*)] schnappen 2 (fig. coll.: seize) [sich (*Dat.*)] schnappen (ugs.); **~ up a bargain/an offer** bei einem Angebot [sofort] zugreifen *od.* (salopp) zuschlagen; **~ sth. up in the sales** etw. beim Ausverkauf ergattern (ugs.); **the tickets were ~ped up immediately** die Karten waren sofort weg

snap: ~ bean *n.* (Amer.) Brechbohne, *die;* **~dragon** *n.* (Bot.) Löwenmäulchen, *das;* **~ fastener** *n.* Druckknopf, *der;* **~-on** *attrib. adj.* Klemm-

snappy /ˈsnæpɪ/ *adj.* 1 (lively) lebhaft; temperamentvoll ‹*Tanz, Musik*› 2 (smart) schick; **be a ~ dresser** sich flott *od.* schick kleiden 3 (coll.) **look ~!, make it ~!** ein bisschen dalli! (ugs.)

snap: ~ ˈshot *n.* (gunshot) ungezielter Schuss; **~shot** (Photog.) *n.* Schnappschuss, *der*

snare /sneə(r)/
A *n.* 1 (trap) Schlinge, *die;* Falle, *die* (auch fig.); **set a ~ [for sb.]** [jmdm.] eine Falle stellen 2 (temptation) Fallstrick, *der* 3 (Mus.) Schnarrsaite, *die* 4 (Mus.) ▸ **snare drum**
B *v.t.* [mit einer Schlinge] fangen ‹*Tier, Vogel*›; **~ sb.** jmdn. in eine Falle locken

ˈ**snare drum** *n.* Wirbeltrommel, *die;* Snaredrum, *die;* kleine Trommel

snarl[1] /snɑ:l/
A *v.i.* 1 (growl) ‹*Hund:*› knurren; ‹*Tiger:*› fauchen 2 (speak) knurren
B *v.t.* knurren
C *n.* Knurren, *das;* (of tiger) Fauchen, *das;* **..., he said to him with a ~:** ..., knurrte er ihn an

Phrasal verb
• **~ at** *v.t.* anknurren; ‹*Tiger:*› anfauchen

snarl[2]
A *n.* (tangle) Knoten, *der*
B *v.t.* verheddern (ugs.)
C *v.i.* sich verheddern (ugs.)

Phrasal verb
• **~ ˈup**
A *v.t.* (confuse) durcheinander bringen; (bring to a halt) zum Erliegen bringen; **get ~ed up** ‹*Wolle usw.:*› sich verheddern (ugs.); **get ~ed up in the traffic** im Verkehr stecken bleiben
B *v.i.* ‹*Verkehr:*› stocken; ‹*Wolle:*› sich verheddern (ugs.)

ˈ**snarl-up** *n.* Stau, *der;* Stockung, *die*

snatch /snætʃ/
A *v.t.* 1 (grab) schnappen; **~ a bite to eat** [schnell] einen Bissen zu sich nehmen; **~ a kiss** sich (*Dat.*) einen Kuss stehlen (scherzh.); **~ an opportunity** eine Gelegenheit beim Schopf[e] ergreifen; **~ a rest** sich (*Dat.*) eine Ruhepause verschaffen; **~ hold of sb./sth.** jmdn./etw. schnappen; **~ hold of sb. by the collar/ear** jmdn. am Kragen/Ohr packen; **~ some sleep** ein bisschen schlafen; **~ a nap** (coll.) ein Nickerchen (fam.) halten; **~ the lead** die Führung übernehmen *od.* an sich (*Akk.*) nehmen; **~ sth. from sth.** etw. schnell von etw. nehmen; (very abruptly) etw. von etw. reißen; **~ sth. from sb.** jmdm. etw. wegreißen; **~ sth. out of sb.'s hand/pocket** jmdm. etw. aus der Hand reißen/schnell aus der Tasche ziehen 2 (steal) klauen (ugs.); (kidnap) kidnappen
B *v.i.* einfach zugreifen
C *n.* 1 **make a ~ at sb./sth.** nach jmdm./etw. greifen 2 (Brit. sl.: robbery) Raub, *der* 3 (sl.: kidnap) Kidnapping, *das* 4 (fragment) **a ~ of a song** ein paar Takte von einem Lied; **~es of talk/conversation** Gesprächsfetzen *od.* -brocken *Pl.* 5 in *pl.* (spells) **do sth. in** *or* **by ~es** etw. mit Unterbrechungen tun 6 (weightlifting) Reißen, *das*

Phrasal verbs
• **~ at** *v.t.* 1 **~ at sb./sth.** nach jmdm./etw. schnappen 2 (fig.) ▸ **jump at 2**
• **~ aˈway** *v.t.* [schnell] wegziehen (**from** *Dat.*); **~ sth. away from sb.** jmdm. etw. wegreißen
• **~ ˈup** *v.t.* [sich (*Dat.*)] schnappen

ˈ**snatch squad** *n.* Greiftrupp, *der*

snazzy /ˈsnæzɪ/ *adj.* (coll.) [super]schick (ugs.)

sneak /sni:k/
A *v.t.* 1 (take) stibitzen (fam.) 2 (fig.) **~ a look at sb./sth.** nach jmdm./etw. schielen 3 (bring) **~ sth./sb. into a place** etw./jmdn. in einen Ort schmuggeln; **~ sth. into one's bag** etw. heimlich in die Tasche stecken 4 (coll.: steal) klauen (ugs.); mitgehen lassen (ugs.)
B *v.i.* 1 (Brit. Sch. coll.: tell tales) petzen (Schülerspr.); **~ on sb.** jmdn. verpetzen (Schülerspr.) 2 (move furtively) schleichen
C *attrib. adj.* 1 (without warning) **~ attack/raid** Überraschungsangriff, *der* 2 **a ~ preview of the film/play/programme** eine inoffizielle Vorpremiere des Films/Stücks/Programms
D *n.* 1 (shifty person) Fiesling, *der* (salopp) 2 (Brit. Sch. coll.: telltale) Petze, *die* (Schülerspr.)

Phrasal verbs
• **~ aˈway** *v.i.* [sich] fortschleichen; sich davonmachen
• **~ ˈin**
A *v.i.* 1 (enter stealthily) sich hineinschleichen; (fig.) sich einschleichen 2 (win narrowly) knapp siegen
B *v.t.* 1 (bring in) einschmuggeln (ugs.) 2 (Amer.: include) **~ in a mention of sth./a word about sth.** etw. [beiläufig] erwähnen/ein Wort über etw. (*Akk.*) einstreuen
• **~ ˈout** *v.i.* [sich] hinausschleichen
• **~ ˈout of** (Amer.: avoid) **~ out of sth./doing sth.** sich vor etw. (*Dat.*) drücken (ugs.)/sich davor drücken (ugs.), etw. zu tun

sneaker /ˈsni:kə(r)/ (Amer.) Turnschuh, *der*

sneaking /ˈsni:kɪŋ/ *attrib. adj.* heimlich; leise ‹*Verdacht*›

ˈ**sneak thief** *n.* Einschleichdieb, *der*

S

sneaky /'sni:kɪ/ 1 (underhand) hinterhältig 2 **have a ~ feeling that ...:** so ein leises Gefühl haben, dass ...

sneer /snɪə(r)/
A *v.i.* 1 (smile scornfully) spöttisch *od.* höhnisch lächeln/grinsen; hohnlächeln 2 (speak scornfully) höhnen (geh.); spotten
B *v.t.* (say) höhnen (geh.); spotten
C *n.* 1 (look) Hohnlächeln, *das* 2 (remark) höhnische *od.* spöttische Bemerkung; **a cynical/sarcastic ~:** eine zynische/sarkastische Bemerkung
Phrasal verb
• **~ at** *v.t.* 1 (smile scornfully at) höhnisch anlächeln/angrinsen 2 (express scorn for) verhöhnen (geh.); spotten über (+ *Akk.*)

sneeze /sni:z/
A *v.i.* niesen; **not to be ~d at** (fig. coll.) nicht zu verachten (ugs.)
B *n.* Niesen, *das*

snicker /'snɪkə(r)/ ▸ **snigger**

snide /snaɪd/ *adj.* 1 (sneering) abfällig 2 *attrib.* (Amer.: mean, underhand) mies (ugs.)

sniff /snɪf/
A *n.* 1 Schnüffeln, *das;* Schnuppern, *das;* (with running nose, while crying) Schniefen, *das;* (contemptuous) Naserümpfen, *das;* **give a disdainful ~:** geringschätzig die Nase rümpfen; **have a ~ at sth.** an etw. (*Dat.*) riechen *od.* schnuppern; **have a ~ at this!** hier, riech *od.* schnupper mal!; **I didn't get a ~ of the food** (coll.) ich habe von dem Essen keinen Krümel abbekommen; **not a ~!** leer ausgegangen! 2 (quantity ~ed) **have a [good] ~ of sea air/of perfume** [ausgiebig] die Seeluft/am Parfüm schnuppern
B *v.i.* schniefen; die Nase hochziehen; (to detect a smell) schnuppern; (to express contempt) die Nase rümpfen
C *v.t.* 1 (smell) riechen *od.* schnuppern an (+ *Dat.*) ‹*Essen, Getränk, Blume, Parfüm, Wein*›; **the dog ~ed the air/the lamp post** der Hund schnupperte/schnupperte am Laternenpfahl [herum]; **~ glue/cocaine** Klebstoff schnüffeln/Kokain sniffen (Drogenjargon) 2 (utter with contempt) naserümpfend sagen
Phrasal verbs
• **~ at** *v.t.* 1 schnuppern *od.* riechen an (+ *Dat.*) ‹*Blume, Essen*› 2 (show contempt for) die Nase rümpfen über (+ *Akk.*); **not to be ~ed at = not to be sneezed at** ▸ **sneeze A**
• **~ 'out** *v.t.* aufspüren

sniffer dog /'snɪfə dɒg/ *n.* Spürhund, *der*

sniffle /'snɪfl/
A *v.i.* schniefen; schnüffeln (ugs.)
B *n.* (coll.) 1 Schniefen, *das;* Schnüffeln, *das* (ugs.) 2 *in pl.* **have the ~s** [einen] Schnupfen haben

sniffy /'snɪfɪ/ *adj.* (coll.) 1 (contemptuous) hochnäsig (ugs.) 2 (sniffing) **sb. is ~:** jmd. schnüffelt; (has a cold) schnieft

snifter /'snɪftə(r)/ *n.* 1 (coll.: drink) Kurze, *der* (ugs.) 2 (Amer.: glass) [Kognak]schwenker, *der*

snigger /'snɪgə(r)/
A *v.i.* [boshaft] kichern
B *n.* [boshaftes] Kichern

snip /snɪp/
A *v.t.,* **-pp-** schnippeln (ugs.), schneiden ‹*Loch*›; schnippeln (ugs.) *od.* schneiden an (+ *Dat.*) ‹*Tuch, Haaren, Hecke*›; (cut off) abschnippeln (ugs.); abschneiden
B *v.i.,* **-pp-** schnippeln (ugs.); schneiden
C *n.* 1 (Brit. coll: certainty) **be a ~:** idiotensicher sein (ugs.) 2 (Brit. coll.: good bargain) Schnäppchen, *das* (ugs.) 3 (cut) Schnitt, *der;* Schnipser, *der* (ugs.) 4 (piece) Schnipsel, *der od. das* 5 *in pl.* (shears) [Hand]blechschere, *die*

snipe /snaɪp/
A *n., pl. same or* **~s** (Ornith.) Schnepfe, *die*
B *v.i.* (Mil.) aus dem Hinterhalt schießen
Phrasal verb
• **~ at** *v.t.* 1 (Mil.) aus dem Hinterhalt beschießen 2 (fig.: make snide comments about) anschießen (ugs.)

sniper /'snaɪpə(r)/ *n.* Heckenschütze, *der; attrib.* **~ fire** Gewehrfeuer von Heckenschützen

snippet /'snɪpɪt/ *n.* 1 (piece) Schnipsel, *der od. das* 2 (of information in newspaper) Notiz, *die;* (of knowledge) Bruchstück, *das;* (from a book) Passage, *die;* (of conversation) Gesprächsfetzen, *der;* **useful ~s of information** nützliche Hinweise

snipping /'snɪpɪŋ/ *n.* Schnipsel, *der od. das*

snit /snɪt/ *n.* (Amer. coll.) **be in a ~** (agitated) am Rotieren sein (ugs.); (annoyed) auf achtzig sein (ugs.)

snitch /snɪtʃ/ (coll.)
A *v.t.* klauen (ugs.)
B *v.i.* auspacken (salopp); **~ on sb.** jmdn. verpfeifen (salopp)

snivel /'snɪvl/ *v.i.,* (Brit.) **-ll-** 1 (have runny nose) **stop ~ling, use a handkerchief** hör auf, dauernd die Nase hochzuziehen — nimm ein Taschentuch 2 (sniff, sob) schniefen; schnüffeln (ugs.)

snivelling (*Amer.:* **sniveling**) /'snɪvəlɪŋ/ (fig.)
A *attrib. adj.* heulend; greinend (ugs.) ‹*Opposition*›
B *n.* Geheule, *das;* Gegreine, *das* (ugs.)

snob /snɒb/ *n.* Snob, *der* (*abwertend*); *attrib.* **~ appeal** *or* **value** Snob-Appeal, *der; see also* **inverted snob**

snobbery /'snɒbərɪ/ *n.* Snobismus, *der*

snobbish /'snɒbɪʃ/ *adj.,* **snobbishly** /'snɒbɪʃlɪ/ *adv.* snobistisch

snog /snɒg/ (Brit. coll.)
A *v.i.,* **-gg-** knutschen (ugs.)
B *n.* Knutschen, *das* (ugs.); **have a ~ [with sb.]** [mit jmdm.] knutschen

snood /snu:d/ *n.* Haarnetz, *das*

snook /snu:k/ *n.* (coll.) **cock a ~ at sb.** jmdm. eine lange Nase drehen (ugs.); (fig. also) jmdm. eine Nase drehen (ugs.)

snooker /'snu:kə(r)/
A *n.* 1 *no pl., no indef. art.* Snooker [Pool], *das* 2 (tactical position) *Situation beim Billardspiel, in der der Spieler die richtige Kugel nicht direkt spielen kann*
B *v.t.* 1 *in eine Lage bringen, in der die richtige Kugel nicht direkt gespielt werden kann;* **be ~ed** *die richtige Kugel nicht direkt spielen können* 2 (fig. coll.: thwart) vereiteln; **he was ~ed** ihm wurde ein Strich durch die Rechnung gemacht

snoop /snu:p/ (coll.)
A *v.i.* schnüffeln (ugs.); **~ into sth.** in einer Sache [herum]schnüffeln (ugs.); **~ about** *or* **around** herumschnüffeln (ugs.); **~ around the village** im Dorf herumschnüffeln
B *n.* **have a ~ around** sich [ein bisschen] umsehen

snooper /'snu:pə(r)/ *n.* (coll.) Schnüffler, *der*/Schnüfflerin, *die* (ugs.)

snootily /'snu:tɪlɪ/ *adv.,* **snooty** /'snu:tɪ/ *adj.* (coll.) hochnäsig (ugs.)

snooze /snu:z/ (coll.)
A *v.i.* dösen (ugs.)
B *n.* Nickerchen, *das* (fam.); **have a ~:** ein Nickerchen machen

'snooze button *n.* Schlummertaste, *die*

snore /snɔ:(r)/
A *v.i.* schnarchen
B *n.* Schnarcher, *der* (ugs.); **~s** Schnarchen, *das*

snorkel /'snɔ:kl/
A *n.* Schnorchel, *der*
B *v.i.,* (Brit.) **-ll-** schnorcheln

snort /snɔ:t/
A *v.i.* schnauben (**with, in** vor + *Dat.*); **~ with laughter** vor Lachen prusten; **~ in disbelief** ungläubig schnauben
B *v.t.* 1 schnauben; **~ one's disgust/disbelief/anger** vor Ekel/ungläubig/wütend schnauben 2 (sl.: take) **~ [coke]** [Koks] sniffen (Drogenjargon)
C *n.* 1 Schnauben, *das;* **give a ~ of indignation/rage** vor Missbilligung/Wut schnauben; **with a ~ of rage** wutschnaubend; **~s of laughter** prustendes Gelächter 2 (coll.: drink) Kurze, *der* (ugs.) 3 (sl.: of drug) Sniff, *der* (Jargon)

snorter /'snɔ:tə(r)/ *n.* (coll.) 1 (gale) Orkan, *der* 2 (difficult task) **a ~ [of a job]** eine Plackerei (ugs.); **the exam was a ~:** die Prüfung war ein Schlauch (ugs.)

snot /snɒt/ *n.* (sl.) Rotz, *der* (salopp); Schnodder, *der* (derb)

'snot rag *n.* (sl.) Rotzfahne, *die* (salopp)

snotty /'snɒtɪ/ *adj.* (sl.) 1 ▸ **snooty** 2 (running with nasal mucus) rotznäsig (salopp); **~ child** Rotznase, *die* (salopp); **~ handkerchief** Rotzfahne, *die* (salopp); **~ nose** Rotznase, *die* (salopp)

'snotty-nosed *adj.* (sl.) 1 rotzig; rotznäsig (salopp) 2 ▸ **snooty**

snout /snaʊt/ *n.* 1 (nose) Schnauze, *die;* (of pig, anteater) Rüssel, *der;* (of wild boar) Gebrech, *das* (Jägerspr.) 2 (nosepiece) Nase, *die* 3 (derog.: nose) Rüssel, *der* (salopp); Zinken, *der* (salopp) 4 (Brit. coll.) (tobacco) Kraut, *das* (ugs., oft abwertend); (cigarette) Kippe, *die* (ugs.); Lulle, *die* (ugs.) 5 (Brit. sl.: informer) Schnüffler, *der* (ugs. abwertend); Spürhund, *der* (ugs.)

snow /snəʊ/
A *n., no indef. art.* 1 Schnee, *der;* **be [as] pure as the driven ~** ‹*Person:*› unschuldig wie ein/die Engel sein 2 *in pl.* (areas) Schnee, *der;* (falls) Schneefälle 3 (sl.: cocaine) Schnee, *der* (Drogenjargon) 4 (on TV screen etc.) Schnee, *der*
B *v.i. impers.* **it ~s** *or* **is ~ing** es schneit; **it starts ~ing** *or* **to ~:** es fängt an zu schneien
C *v.t.* (Amer. coll.) **~ sb.** bei jmdm. Eindruck schinden (ugs.)
Phrasal verbs
• **~ 'in** *v.t.* **they are ~ed in** sie sind eingeschneit
• **~ 'under** *v.t.* **be ~ed under** ‹*Haus:*› eingeschneit sein; ‹*Straße:*› zugeschneit sein; (fig.) (with work) erdrückt werden; (with presents, letters) überschüttet werden
• **~ 'up** ▸ **~ in**

snow: ~ball A *n.* Schneeball, *der; attrib.* **~ball fight** Schneeballschlacht, *die;* **~ball effect** Schneeballeffekt, *der;* **not have** *or* **stand a ~ball's chance in hell** (coll.) nicht die geringste Chance haben; B *v.t.* mit Schneebällen bewerfen; C *v.i.* 1 Schneebälle werfen; 2 (fig.: increase greatly) lawinenartig zunehmen; **~ blindness** *n., no pl.* Schneeblindheit, *die;* **~blower** *n.* Schneefräse, *die;* **~board** A *n.* Snowboard, *das;* B *v.i.* Snowboard fahren; **~boarder** *n.* Snowboarder, *der*/Snowboarderin, *die;* **~boarding** *n., no pl.* Snowboardfahren, *das;* Snowboarden, *das;* **~ boot** *n.* Schneestiefel, *der;* **~-bound** *adj.* eingeschneit; **~ cannon** *n.* Schneekanone, *die;* **~-capped** *adj.* schneebedeckt; schneegekrönt (dichter.); **~ chains** *n. pl.* Schneeketten *Pl.;* **~-covered** *adj.* schneebedeckt; **~drift** *n.* Schneeverwehung, *die;* Schneewehe, *die;* **~drop** *n.* Schneeglöckchen, *das;* **~fall** *n.* Schneefall, *der;* **~flake** *n.* Schneeflocke, *die;* **~ goose** *n.* Schneegans, *die;* **~ job** *n.* (Amer. coll.) **do a ~ job on sb.** jmdn. beschwatzen (ugs.); **~ leopard** *n.* Schneeleopard, *der;* **~line** *n.* Schneegrenze, *die;* **~man** *n.* Schneemann, *der; see also* **abominable; ~mobile** /'snəʊməbi:l/ *n.* Schneemobil, *das;* **~plough** *n.* Schneepflug, *der;* **~scape** *n.* Schneelandschaft, *die;* **~shoe** *n.* Schneeschuh, *der;* **~ shovel** *n.* Schneeschaufel, *die;* **~ shower** *n.* Schneeschauer, *der;* **~storm** *n.* Schneesturm, *der;* **~-white** *adj.* schneeweiß; **S~ 'White** *pr. n.* Schneewittchen, *das*

snowy /'snəʊɪ/ *adj.* 1 (having much snow) schneereich ‹*Gegend, Monat*›; schneebedeckt ‹*Berge*›; **~ weather** Schneewetter, *das* 2 (white) schneeweiß

snowy 'owl *n.* Schnee-Eule, *die*

SNP *abbr.* **= Scottish National Party** *Schottische Nationalpartei*

snub /snʌb/
A *v.t.,* **-bb-** 1 (rebuff) brüskieren; vor den Kopf stoßen 2 (reprove) zurechtweisen; (insult) beleidigen 3 (reject) ablehnen 4 (Amer.) **~ out** ausdrücken
B *n.* Abfuhr, *die;* **get** *or* **receive a ~:** eine Abfuhr erhalten; **give sb. a [proper] ~:** jmdm. eine [gehörige] Abfuhr erteilen

snub: ~ 'nose *n.* Stupsnase, *die;* Stupsnäschen, *das* (fam.); (of car, aeroplane) stumpfe Schnauze (ugs.) *od.* Nase; **~-nosed** *adj.* stupsnasig; stumpfnasig ‹*Auto, Flugzeug*›; mit stumpfer Schnauze (ugs.) *nachgestellt*

S

snuff[1] /snʌf/ *n.* [1] (tobacco) Schnupftabak, *der;* **take a pinch of ~:** eine Prise schnupfen [2] **be up to ~** (Brit. coll. dated: not easily deceived) mit allen Wassern gewaschen sein (ugs.); (in good health or condition) auf der Höhe sein (ugs.)

snuff[2] *v.t.* beschneiden, putzen ‹*Kerze*›; **~ it** (sl.: die) ins Gras beißen (salopp)

(Phrasal verb)

• **~ 'out**

A *v.t.* [1] (extinguish) löschen ‹*Kerze*› [2] (fig.: put an end to) zerstören; zunichte machen ‹*Hoffnung*›; niederschlagen ‹*Revolte*›; (kill) töten; umbringen

B *v.i.* (sl.) ins Gras beißen (salopp)

'snuff-box *n.* Schnupftabak[s]dose, *die*

snuffer /'snʌfə(r)/ *n.* Löschhütchen, *das;* **pair of ~s** Licht[putz]schere, *die*

snuffle /'snʌfl/

A *v.i.* [1] (sniff) schnüffeln (**at** an + *Dat.*); (with cold, after crying) schniefen [2] (make sniffing sound) schnüffeln (**at** an + *Dat.*) [3] (breathe noisily) schnaufen

B *n.* [1] (sniff) **~[s]** Schnaufen, *das;* (of horses) Schnauben, *das* [2] *in pl.* **have the ~s** [einen] Schnupfen haben

snug /snʌg/

A *adj.* [1] (cosy) gemütlich, behaglich ‹*Haus, Zimmer, Mantel, Bett*›; (warm) mollig warm ‹*Zimmer, Mantel, Bett*›; **in bed sb. is as ~ as a bug in a rug** im Bett hat es jmd. urgemütlich *od.* richtig kuschelig [2] (sheltered) geschützt [3] (close-fitting) **be a ~ fit** genau passen; ‹*Kleidung:*› wie angegossen sitzen *od.* passen

B *n.* (Brit.: bar parlour) *Nebenzimmer in einer Gastwirtschaft, bes. für Stammgäste*

snuggle /'snʌgl/

A *v.i.* **~ together** sich aneinander schmiegen *od.* -kuscheln; **~ down in bed** sich ins Bett kuscheln; **~ up with a book** es sich (*Dat.*) mit einem Buch gemütlich machen

B *v.t.* **she ~d the crying child to her body** sie drückte das weinende Kind zärtlich an sich

snugly /'snʌglɪ/ *adv.* [1] (cosily) gemütlich; behaglich; **be/lie ~ tucked up** behaglich eingemumm[el]t sein/liegen (fam.) [2] (close-fitting) **fit ~:** genau passen; ‹*Kleidung:*› wie angegossen sitzen *od.* passen

so[1] /səʊ/

A *adv.* [1] (by that amount) so; **as winter draws near, so it gets darker** je näher der Winter rückt, desto dunkler wird es; **as fast as the water poured in, so we bailed it out** in dem Maße, wie das Wasser eindrang, schöpften wir es heraus; **so ... as** so ... wie; **there is nothing so fine as ...:** es gibt nichts Schöneres als ...; nichts ist so schön wie ...; **not so [very] difficult/easy** *etc.* nicht so schwer/leicht *usw.;* **it's not so easy/big after all** so einfach/groß ist es nun wieder auch nicht; **so beautiful a present** so ein schönes Geschenk; ein so schönes Geschenk; **so great a general as X** ein so großer General wie X; **[it's] not so bad as ...:** [es ist] nicht so schlecht wie ...; **so far** bis hierher; (until now) bisher; bis jetzt; (to such a distance) so weit; **I trust him only so far** ich traue ihm nur bis zu einem gewissen Grad; **and so on [and so forth]** und so weiter und so fort; und so weiter; und so fort; **so long!** bis dann *od.* gleich *od.* nachher *od.* später! (ugs.); **so many** so viele; (unspecified number) soundso viele; **they looked like so many chimney sweeps** sie sahen alle aus wie die Schornsteinfeger; **so much** so viel; (unspecified amount) soundso viel; **[just] so much/many** (nothing but) nichts als; **his books are just so much rubbish** seine Bücher taugen alle nichts; **the villages are all so much alike** die Dörfer gleichen sich alle so sehr; **so much for the agenda** so viel zur Tagesordnung; **so much for him/his plans** das wärs, was ihn/seine Pläne angeht; **so much for my hopes** und ich habe mir solche Hoffnungen gemacht; **so much for that** (after having dealt with a tricky problem) das wäre geschafft; das hätten wir; **so much the better** umso besser; **if he doesn't want to stay, so much the worse for him** wenn er nicht bleiben will, ist er selber schuld; **not so much ... as** weniger ... als [eher]; **be not so much angry as disappointed** weniger verärgert als [viel mehr] enttäuscht sein; **not so much as** (not even) [noch] nicht einmal; **not so much as glance at sth.** auf etw. (*Akk.*) nicht einmal einen Blick werfen; *see also* **ever 6**; **every 3**; **far A 4**; **long**[1] **C 1, 2**; **more C 8**; **never 1** [2] (in that manner) so; **so be it** einverstanden; so sei es (geh.); **this being so** da dem so ist (geh.); **it so happened that he was not there** er war [zufällig] gerade nicht da [3] (to such a degree) so; **this answer so provoked him that ...:** diese Antwort provozierte ihn so *od.* derart, dass ...; **I went straight to bed, I was so tired** ich war so müde, dass ich gleich zu Bett ging; **put it so as not to offend him** sag es so, dass es ihn nicht kränkt; **I am not so big a fool as to believe that** ich bin nicht so dumm, das zu glauben; **I got so I could ...** (Amer.) ich war so weit, dass ich ... konnte; **so much so that ...:** so sehr, dass ...; das geht/ging so weit, dass ... [4] (with the intent) **so as to** um ... zu; **run so as not to get wet** rennen, um nicht nass zu werden; **so [that]** damit [5] (emphatically) so; **I'm so glad/tired!** ich bin ja so froh/müde!; **so kind of you!** wirklich nett von Ihnen!; **so sorry!** (coll.) Entschuldigung!; Verzeihung! [6] (indeed) **It's a rainbow! — So it is!** Es ist ein Regenbogen! — Ja, wirklich!; **'You suggested this trip. — So I did** Du hast diese Reise vorgeschlagen. — Das stimmt; **you said it was good, and so it was** du sagtest, es sei gut, und so war es auch; **is that so?** so? (ugs.); wirklich?; **and so he did** und das machte/tat er [dann] auch; **it 'is so** *expr. certainty* doch!; **it may be so, possibly so** [das ist] möglich [7] (likewise) **so am/have/would/could/will/do I** ich auch; **as a is to b, so is c to d** a verhält sich zu b wie c zu d; **as in the arts, so in politics, it's true that ...:** in der Politik wie in der Kunst gilt, dass ... [8] (thus) so; **and so it was that ...:** und so geschah es, dass ...; **not so!** nein, nein! *See also* **how A**; **if A 1**; **just B 1**; **quite 1**; **so so**. [9] (replacing clause, phrase, word) **he suggested that I should take the train, and if I had done so, ...** er riet mir, den Zug zu nehmen, und wenn ich es getan hätte, ...; **we must consider what would be the result of so doing** wir müssen bedenken, was das für Folgen hätte; **I'm afraid so** leider ja; ich fürchte schon; **the teacher said so** der Lehrer hat es gesagt; **it was self-defence — or so the defendant said** es war Selbstverteidigung — so sagte jedenfalls der Angeklagte; **so saying, he departed** mit diesen Worten ging er; **so say all of us** das sagen wir alle; **Why do I have to go to bed? — Because I say so** Warum muss ich ins Bett? — Weil ich es sage; **I suppose so** ich nehme an (ugs.); *expr. reluctant agreement* wenn es sein muss; *granting grudging permission* von mir aus; **I told you so** ich habe es dir [ja] gesagt; **so I gathered** ich weiß [es]; **so I gathered from the newspaper** ich weiß es aus der Zeitung *od.* habe es aus der Zeitung erfahren; **he is a man of the world, so to say** *or* **speak** es menschelt sozusagen bei ihm; **it will take a week or so** es wird so (ugs.) *od.* etwa eine Woche dauern; **there were twenty or so people** es waren so (ugs.) um die zwanzig Leute da; **very much so** in der Tat; allerdings; *see also* **say A 1**

B *conj.* (therefore) daher; **so 'that's what he meant** das hat er also gemeint; **cigarettes are dangerous, so don't smoke** Zigaretten sind schädlich, also rauch nicht!; **so what is the answer?** wie lautet also die Antwort?; **so you are from Oxford then?** Sie kommen also aus Oxford?; **so 'there you are!** da bist du also!; **so there you 'are!** ich habe also Recht!; **so what are you going to do now?** was machen Sie denn jetzt?; **so what's the joke/problem?** was ist denn daran witzig?/was ist denn das Problem?; **so where have you been?** wo warst du denn?; **so that's 'that** (coll.) (it's done) [al]so, das wars (ugs.); (it's over) das wars also (ugs.); (everything has been taken care of) das wärs dann (ugs.); **so there!** [und] fertig!; [und damit] basta! (ugs.); **so you see ...:** du siehst also ...; **so?** na und?

so[2] ▸ **soh**

So. *abbr.* (Amer.) **= South** S

soak /səʊk/

A *v.t.* [1] (steep) einweichen ‹*Wäsche in Lauge*›; eintauchen ‹*Brot in Milch, Tapete in Wasser*›; **~ oneself in the sun** sich in der Sonne aalen (ugs.) [2] (wet) nass machen; durchnässen; durchtränken ‹*Erde*›; **~ sb. from head to foot** jmdn. von Kopf bis Fuß durchnässen *od.* (ugs.) patschnass machen; **~ed in sth.** von etw. durchtränkt; mit *od.* von etw. getränkt; **a rag ~ed in petrol** ein mit Benzin getränkter Lappen; **~ed in sweat** schweißgebadet; **~ed with sweat** schweißgetränkt; **this town is ~ed in history** (fig.) in dieser Stadt weht der Hauch der Geschichte [3] (absorb) ▸ **~ up** [4] (coll.: obtain money from) melken (salopp); schröpfen (ugs.)

B *v.i.* [1] (steep) **put sth. in sth. to ~:** etw. in etw. (*Dat.*) einweichen; **lie ~ing in the bath** ‹*Person:*› sich im Bad durchweichen lassen; **the liver was put to ~ in milk** die Leber wurde in Milch eingelegt [2] (drain) ‹*Feuchtigkeit, Nässe:*› sickern; **~ away** wegsickern

C *n.* [1] **give sth. a [good] ~:** etw. [gründlich] einweichen; **give the garden a [good] ~:** den Garten [gut] wässern; **put in ~:** einweichen; **he leaves his dentures in ~ overnight** er legt sein künstliches Gebiss über Nacht in eine Reinigungsflüssigkeit [2] (coll.: drinker) Säufer, *der*/Säuferin, *die* (derb, oft abwertend); Suffkopp, *der* (ugs.)

(Phrasal verbs)

• **~ 'in**

A *v.i.* [1] (seep in) einsickern; eindringen; ‹*Flecken:*› einziehen [2] (fig.) **let the atmosphere ~ in** die Atmosphäre auf sich (*Akk.*) einwirken lassen

B *v.t.* ▸ **~ up**

• **~ into** *v.t.* sickern in (+ *Akk.*); ‹*Tinte usw.:*› einziehen in (+ *Akk.*)

• **~ through**

A *v.t.* [1] /'--/ (penetrate) ‹*Flüssigkeit, Strahlen:*› dringen durch; ‹*Regenwasser, Blut:*› sickern durch [2] /-'-/ (drench) durchnässen

B *v.i.* /-'-/ durchdringen

• **~ 'up** *v.t.* [1] (absorb) aufsaugen; **~ up the sunshine** in der Sonne baden [2] (fig.) auf sich (*Akk.*) einwirken lassen, aufnehmen ‹*Atmosphäre*›; aufnehmen, in sich (*Akk.*) aufsaugen ‹*Wissen usw.*›

'soakaway *n.* (Brit.) Abflussgrube, *die*

soaking /'səʊkɪŋ/

A *n.* (drenching) **need a [good] ~** ‹*Garten:*› [gut] gewässert werden müssen; ‹*Tuch:*› [gründlich] eingeweicht werden müssen; **get a ~:** eine Dusche abbekommen; **give sb./sth. a ~:** jmdn./etw. ganz nass machen; ‹*Regen:*› jmdn./etw. ganz durchnässen

B *adv.* **~ wet** völlig durchnässt; klatsch- *od.* patschnass (ugs.)

C *adj.* [1] (drenched) nass [bis auf die Haut]; patschnass (ugs.); **be ~** ‹*Kleidung:*› völlig durchnässt sein; ‹*Gras:*› patschnass sein (ugs.) [2] (saturating) alles durchnässend ‹*Regen, Strom*›

'so-and-so *n., pl.* **~'s** [1] (person not named) [Herr/Frau] Soundso; (thing not named) Dings, *das* [2] (coll.: contemptible person) Biest, *das* (ugs.); **poor ~:** armes Schwein (ugs.)

soap /səʊp/

A *n., no indef. art.* [1] Seife, *die;* **a bar** *or* **tablet of ~:** ein Stück Seife; **with ~ and water** mit Wasser und Seife [2] (coll.: **~ opera**) Soap, *die*

B *v.t.* **~ [down]** einseifen

soap: ~box *n.* [1] ▸ **~ dish 1**; [2] (packing-box) Seifenschachtel, *die;* [3] (stand) ≈ Apfelsinenkiste, *die;* **get on one's ~box** (fig.) laut seine Meinung äußern; Volksreden halten; [4] (cart) Seifenkiste, *die; attrib.* **~box derby** Seifenkistenrennen, *das;* **~ bubble** *n.* Seifenblase, *die;* **~ dish** *n.* [1] (container) Seifendose, *die;* [2] (open dish) Seifenschale, *die;* **~ dispenser** *n.* Seifenspender, *der;* **~ flakes** *n. pl.* Seifenflocken *Pl.;* **~ opera** *n.* (Telev., Radio) Seifenoper, *die* (ugs.); **~ powder** *n.* Seifenpulver, *das;* **~stone** *n.* (Min.) Speckstein, *der;* **~suds** *n. pl.* Seifenschaum, *der*

S

soapy /ˈsəʊpɪ/ *adj.* seifig; ~ **water** Seifenwasser, *das;* Seifenlauge, *die*

soar /sɔː(r)/ *v.i.* **1** (fly up) aufsteigen; (hover in the air) segeln **2** (extend) ~ **into the sky** in den Himmel ragen **3** (fig.: rise rapidly) steil ansteigen; ‹*Preise, Kosten usw.:*› in die Höhe schießen (ugs.); **my hopes have ~ed again** ich schöpfe wieder große Hoffnung; ~ **above sb./sth.** jmdn./etw. überrunden *od.* überragen *od.* hinter sich (*Dat.*) lassen

soaring /ˈsɔːrɪŋ/ *attrib. adj.* **1** (flying) segelnd; [hoch am Himmel] schwebend **2** (fig.: rising rapidly) sprunghaft ansteigend; galoppierend ‹*Preise, Inflation, Kosten*›; hoch[fliegend, -gesteckt] ‹*Ideale*› **3** (lofty) hoch aufragend

sob /sɒb/
A *v.i.*, **-bb-** schluchzen (**with** vor + *Dat.*)
B *v.t.*, **-bb-** schluchzen
C *n.* Schluchzer, *der;* **~s [of anguish/pain]** [schmerzvolles] Schluchzen

Phrasal verb

• ~ **ˈout** *v.t.* schluchzen; **she ~bed out her story** sie erzählte schluchzend *od.* unter Schluchzen ihre Geschichte; ~ **one's heart out** bitterlich weinen

SOB /esəʊˈbiː/ *abbr.* (Amer.) **= son of a bitch**

sobbing /ˈsɒbɪŋ/
A *n.* Schluchzen, *das*
B *adj.* schluchzend

sober /ˈsəʊbə(r)/ *adj.* **1** (not drunk) nüchtern; **as ~ as a judge** stocknüchtern **2** (moderate) solide **3** (solemn) ernst **4** (subdued) schlicht; gedeckt ‹*Farben*›; nüchtern ‹*Umgebung*›; **be a ~ dresser** sich solide kleiden **5** (rational, realistic) nüchtern; **the ~ truth/fact** die nackte Wahrheit/Tatsache

Phrasal verbs

• ~ **ˈdown** *v.i.* ruhig werden; (after being excited) sich abkühlen (ugs.); **he has ~ed down a lot** er ist wesentlich vernünftiger geworden
• ~ **ˈup**
A *v.i.* nüchtern werden; ausnüchtern
B *v.t.* ausnüchtern

sobering /ˈsəʊbərɪŋ/ *adj.* ernüchternd; **he found it a ~ experience** das Erlebnis ernüchterte ihn *od.* brachte ihn zur Vernunft; **it is a ~ thought that ...:** der Gedanke ist ganz schön ernüchternd, dass ...

soberly /ˈsəʊbəlɪ/ *adv.* nüchtern; vernünftig; **dress ~:** sich solide kleiden

sober: ~-minded *adj.* nüchtern; vernünftig; **~sides** *n., pl. same* Miesepeter, *der* (ugs. abwertend)

sobriety /səˈbraɪətɪ/ *n., no pl., no indef. art.* **1** (not being drunk) Nüchternheit, *die* **2** (moderation) Bescheidenheit, *die* **3** (seriousness) Ernsthaftigkeit, *die;* ~ **of mind/judgment** Nüchternheit im Denken/Urteilen

sobriquet /ˈsəʊbrɪkeɪ/ *n.* (nickname) Spitzname, *der*

sob: ~ sister *n.* (Amer. Journ.) *Schreiberin rührseliger Geschichten;* (giving advice to readers) Briefkastentante, *die* (ugs.); ~ **story** *n.* rührselige Geschichte; ~ **stuff** *n., no indef. art., no pl.* (coll.) Schmalz, *das* (ugs.); (book, film, etc.) Schmachtfetzen, *der* (salopp)

ˈso-called *adj.* so genannt; (alleged) angeblich

soccer /ˈsɒkə(r)/ *n.* Fußball, *der;* ~ **ball** Fußball, *der*

soccer: ~ hooligan *n.* Fußballhooligan, *der;* Fußballrowdy, *der;* ~ **player** *n.* Fußballspieler, *der*/-spielerin, *die;* ~ **season** *n.* Fußballsaison, *die*

sociability /səʊʃəˈbɪlɪtɪ/ *n., no pl.* Geselligkeit, *die*

sociable /ˈsəʊʃəbl/ *adj.* gesellig; **she's not feeling ~ today** ihr ist heute nicht nach Gesellschaft zumute; **he did it just to be ~:** er hat es nur getan, um nicht ungesellig zu sein

sociably /ˈsəʊʃəblɪ/ *adv.* gesellig; aufgeschlossen; **they spent the evening ~ together** sie verbrachten den Abend in geselliger Runde

social /ˈsəʊʃl/
A *adj.* **1** sozial; gesellschaftlich; ~ **welfare** Fürsorge, *die* **2** (of ~ life) gesellschaftlich; gesellig ‹*Abend, Beisammensein*›; ~ **behaviour** Benehmen in Gesellschaft; ~ **engagement** gesellschaftliche Verpflichtung **3** (Zool.) sozial; gesellig [lebend]
B *n.* (gathering) geselliges Beisammensein

social: ~ anthroˈpologist *n.* Sozialanthropologe, *der*/-anthropologin, *die;* ~ **anthroˈpology** *n., no pl.* Sozialanthropologie, *die;* **S~ ˈChapter** *n.* (EU) Sozialkapitel, *das;* **S~ ˈCharter** *n.* (EU) Sozialcharta, *die;* ~ **ˈclass** *n.* Gesellschaftsschicht, *die;* [Gesellschafts]klasse, *die;* ~ **ˈclimber** *n.* Emporkömmling, *der* (abwertend); [sozialer] Aufsteiger (ugs.); ~ **climbing** *n., no pl.* sozialer Aufstieg; ~ **club** *n.* Klub für geselliges Beisammensein; ~ **ˈcompact**, ~ **ˈcontract** *ns.* (Polit.) Gesellschaftsvertrag, *der;* ~ **ˈconscience** *n.* soziales Gewissen; **S~ ˈDemocrat** *n.* (Polit.) Sozialdemokrat, *der*/-demokratin, *die;* **S~ Demoˈcratic Party** *n.* (Brit. Polit.) Sozialdemokratische Partei; ~ **engiˈneering** *n., no pl.* Social engineering, *das;* Sozialtechnologie, *die;* ~ **evening** *n.* geselliger Abend; ~ **exˈclusion** *n., no pl.* soziale Ausgrenzung; **S~ Fund** *n.* (EU) **►European Social Fund**; ~ **ˈhistory** *n.* Sozialgeschichte, *die;* ~ **ˈhousing** *n., no pl.* (Brit.) Sozialwohnungen *Pl.;* ~ **inˈclusion** *n., no pl.* soziale Integration; ~ **inˈsurance** *n., no pl.* Sozialversicherung, *die*

> **Social Democratic and Labour Party (SDLP)**
>
> Eine links der Mitte angesiedelte Partei in Nordirland, die 1970 gegründet wurde und überwiegend von Katholiken gewählt wird. Sie steht für die Schaffung eines vereinigten Irlands auf verfassungsgemäßem Wege und lehnt das gewaltsame Vorgehen der IRA ab.

socialisation, socialise ►socializ-

socialism /ˈsəʊʃəlɪzm/ *n.* Sozialismus, *der*

socialist /ˈsəʊʃəlɪst/
A *n.* Sozialist, *der*/Sozialistin, *die*
B *adj.* sozialistisch

socialite /ˈsəʊʃəlaɪt/ *n.: bekannte Persönlichkeit des gesellschaftlichen Lebens*

socialization /səʊʃəlaɪˈzeɪʃn/ *n.* Sozialisation, *die*

socialize /ˈsəʊʃəlaɪz/
A *v.t.* umgänglich machen; **become ~d** umgänglich[er] werden; **~d medicine** (Amer.) öffentliche Gesundheitsfürsorge
B *v.i.* geselligen Umgang pflegen; ~ **with sb.** (chat) sich mit jmdm. unterhalten; **he is out socializing** er ist mit Bekannten *od.* (ugs.) irgendwelchen Leuten unterwegs

social life *n.* gesellschaftliches Leben; **a place with plenty of ~:** ein Ort, wo etwas los ist (ugs.); **not have much ~** ‹*Person:*› nicht viel ausgehen

socially /ˈsəʊʃəlɪ/ *adv.* **meet ~:** sich privat treffen; **have a good time ~:** viel unter die Leute kommen; ~ **acceptable** aus der richtigen Gesellschaftsschicht; ~ **deprived** sozial benachteiligt

social: ~ ˈorder *n.* Gesellschaftsordnung, *die;* ~ **ˈoutcast** *n.* Außenseiter der Gesellschaft; ~ **ˈpartner** *n.* Sozialpartner, *der;* ~ **ˈpolicy** *n.* (Polit.) Sozialpolitik, *die;* ~ **reˈform** *n.* Sozialreform, *die;* **fight for ~ reform** für Sozialreformen *od.* gesellschaftliche Reformen kämpfen; ~ **ˈscience** *n.* Sozialwissenschaften *Pl.;* Gesellschaftswissenschaften *Pl.;* ~ **ˈscientist** *n.* Sozialwissenschaftler, *der*/-wissenschaftlerin, *die;* ~ **seˈcurity** *n., no pl.* **1** (Brit.: benefit) Sozialhilfe, *die;* **2** (welfare system) soziale Sicherheit; **3** (Amer.: insurance) Sozialversicherung, *die;* ~ **ˈservice** *n.* **1** (service to society) soziales Engagement; **2** (a service provided by the government) staatliche Sozialleistung; ~ **ˈservices** *n. pl.* Sozialdienste *Pl.;* ~ **ˈstatus** *n.* sozialer Status; ~ **structure** *n.* Sozialstruktur, *die;* ~ **studies** *n. sing.* (Educ.) Gemeinschaftskunde, *die;* ~ **system** *n.* Gesellschaftssystem, *das;* ~ **work** *n., no pl.* Sozialarbeit, *die;* ~ **worker** *n.* ►ⓘ **p. 1260** Sozialarbeiter, *der*/-arbeiterin, *die*

societal /səˈsaɪətl/ *adj.* (formal) gesellschaftlich

society /səˈsaɪətɪ/
A *n.* **1** Gesellschaft, *die;* **be embarrassed in ~:** in Gegenwart anderer verlegen sein; **avoid ~:** gesellschaftlichen Umgang meiden; **high ~:** Highsociety, *die* **2** (club, association) Verein, *der;* (Commerc.) Gesellschaft, *die;* (group of persons with common beliefs, aims, interests, etc.) Gemeinschaft, *die; see also* **friend 3**; **Jesus**
B *attrib. adj.* **1** (of high ~) Gesellschafts-; [High-]Society-; **she is a ~ hostess** sie gibt Feste für die [gehobene] Gesellschaft; ~ **people** Leute der High Society **2** (of club or association) Vereins-, Klub‹*vorsitzender, -treffen, -ausflug, -sekretär usw.*›

socio- /səʊsɪəʊ/ *in comb.* sozio-/Sozio-

sociobiˈology *n., no pl.* Soziobiologie, *die*

socioˈcultural *adj.* soziokulturell

socio-ecoˈnomic *adj.* sozioökonomisch

sociogram /ˈsəʊsɪəɡræm/ *n.* (Sociol.) Soziogramm, *das*

sociolinguˈistic *adj.* soziolinguistisch

sociolinguˈistics *n. sing.* Soziolinguistik, *die*

sociological /səʊsɪəˈlɒdʒɪkl/ *adj.* soziologisch

sociologist /səʊsɪˈɒlədʒɪst/ *n.* ►ⓘ **p. 1260** Soziologe, *der*/Soziologin, *die*

sociology /səʊsɪˈɒlədʒɪ/ *n.* Soziologie, *die*

sock[1] /sɒk/ *n.* **1** *pl.* **~s** *or* (Commerc./coll.) **sox** /sɒks/ Socke, *die;* Socken, *der* (südd., österr., schweiz.); (ankle ~, esp. for children also) Söckchen, *das;* **knee-length ~s** Kniestrümpfe *Pl.;* **pull one's ~s up** (Brit. fig. coll.) sich am Riemen reißen (ugs.); **put a ~ in it!** (Brit. sl.) halt die Klappe! (salopp); (stop doing sth.) hör auf [damit]! **2** **►insole 4** **3** (of horse) **►stocking**[1] **2**

sock[2] (coll.)
A *v.t.* (hit) schlagen, hauen (ugs.); ~ **sb. in the mouth/on the chin/jaw** jmdm. eine reinhauen (salopp); jmdn. in die Schnauze hauen (derb); ~ **it to sb.** (Amer. coll.) jmdm. Saures geben (salopp); (fig.: impress sb.) es jmdm. zeigen (ugs.)
B *n.* **give sb. a ~ on the chin/jaw/in the mouth** jmdm. eine reinhauen (salopp)

socket /ˈsɒkɪt/ *n.* **1** (Anat.) (of eye) Höhle, *die;* (of joint) Pfanne, *die;* ~ **of a tooth** Zahnfach, *das* (Anat.) **2** (Electr.) Steckdose, *die;* (receiving a bulb) Fassung, *die* **3** (for attachment) Fassung, *die;* (of pipe) Muffe, *die;* (of candle holder) [Kerzen]tülle, *die*

socket: ~ set *n.* Steckschlüsselsatz, *der;* ~ **spanner**, (Amer.) ~ **wrench** *ns.* Steckschlüssel, *der*

sockeye /ˈsɒkaɪ/ *n.* (Zool.) ~ **[salmon]** Blaurückenlachs, *der*

Socrates /ˈsɒkrətiːz/ *pr. n.* Sokrates (*der*)

Socratic /səˈkrætɪk/ *adj.* sokratisch

sod[1] /sɒd/ *n.* (turf) Sode, *die;* **be/lie under the ~:** unter der Erde liegen

sod[2] (sl.)
A *n.* (bastard, swine) Sau, *die* (derb); (fool) Rindvieh, *das* (salopp); **that's ~'s law, ~'s law was proved right** (coll.) es musste ja so kommen; **the poor old ~:** das arme Schwein (salopp); **not give a ~ = not give a damn ►damn B 2**
B *v.t.*, **-dd-:** ~ **that/you!** verdammter Mist/scher dich zum Teufel! (ugs.)

Phrasal verb

• ~ **ˈoff** *v.i. imper.* (sl.) verpiss dich (derb)

soda /ˈsəʊdə/ *n.* **1** (sodium compound) Soda, *die od. das; see also* **caustic A 2** **2** (drink) Soda[wasser], *das;* **whisky and ~:** Whisky mit Soda

soda: ~ bread *n.: mit Backsoda gebackenes Brot;* ~ **fountain** *n.* (Amer.) **1** (container) Mineralwasserbehälter, *der;* **2** (shop) *Erfrischungshalle bzw. -bar, in der es vor allem Erfrischungsgetränke und Speiseeis gibt;* ~ **siphon** *n.* Siphon, *der;* Siphonflasche, *die;* ~ **water** *n.* Soda[wasser], *das*

sodden /ˈsɒdn/ *adj.* durchnässt (**with** von)

sodding /ˈsɒdɪŋ/ *attrib. adj.* (sl.) Scheiß- (derb)

sodium /ˈsəʊdɪəm/ *n.* (Chem.) Natrium, *das*

sodium: ~ bi'carbonate *n.* (Chem.) doppeltkohlensaures Natrium; Natriumhydrogenkarbonat, *das;* **~ 'carbonate** *n.* (Chem.) Natriumkarbonat, *das;* Soda, *die od. das;* **~ 'chloride** *n.* (Chem.) Natriumchlorid, *das;* **~ hy'droxide** *n.* (Chem.) Ätznatron, *das;* **~ lamp** *n.* Natriumdampflampe, *die;* **~ 'nitrate** *n.* (Chem.) Natriumnitrat, *das*

sodomite /'sɒdəmaɪt/ *n.* Sodomit, *der*

sodomize /'sɒdəmaɪz/ *v.t.* sodomisieren (geh.); anal verkehren mit; Sodomie betreiben mit ‹*Tier*›

sodomy /'sɒdəmɪ/ *n.* Analverkehr, *der;* Sodomie, *die* (veralt.); (with animal) Sodomie, *die*

soever ▸**howsoever, whatsoever,** *etc.*

sofa /'səʊfə/ *n.* Sofa, *das;* **~ bed** Bettcouch, *die*

soffit /'sɒfɪt/ *n.* (Archit.) Windbrett, *das*

soft /sɒft/

A *adj.* **1** weich; zart, weich ‹*Haut*›; **the ground is ~:** der Boden ist aufgeweicht; (Sport) der Boden ist schwer; **as ~ as butter** weich wie Butter; butterweich; **~ ice cream** Soft-Eis, *das;* **~ toys** Stofftiere; **~ water area** Gebiet mit weichem Wasser **2** (mild) sanft; mild ‹*Klima*›; zart ‹*Duft*› **3** (compassionate) **have a ~ heart** ein weiches Herz haben; weichherzig sein; **have a ~ spot for sb./sth.** eine Vorliebe *od.* Schwäche für jmdn./etw. haben; **you are too ~!** du bist zu weich[herzig]! **4** (delicate) sanft ‹*Augen*›; weich ‹*Farbe, Licht*› **5** (quiet) leise; sanft **6** (gentle) sanft; (amorous) zärtlich ‹*Blicke*›; **be ~ on sb.** (coll.: be in love with) in jmdn. verknallt sein (ugs.); für jmdn. schwärmen; **be ~ on** *or* **with sb.** (coll.: be unusually lenient with) mit jmdm. sanft umgehen; jmdn. [zu] sanft anfassen; *see also* **nothing A 3** **7** (coll.: easy) bequem, (ugs.) locker ‹*Job, Leben*›; **have a ~ job** eine ruhige Kugel schieben (ugs.) **8** (compliant) nachgiebig; *see also* **touch C 9** **9** (too indulgent) zu nachsichtig; zu lasch (ugs.); **be ~ with sb.** sich (*Dat.*) von jmdm. alles bieten lassen **10** (gently curved) weich ‹*Umriss, Linien, Züge*› **11** (weak) schlaff ‹*Muskeln*›; weichlich (abwertend) ‹*Mann*›; verweichlicht ‹*Volk*› **12** **be/go ~ in the head** (coll.) nicht alle Tassen im Schrank haben (ugs.)/verrückt werden (ugs.) **13** (Scot., Ir.: moist) feucht ‹*Wetter, Tag*› **14** (Phonet.) weich

B *adv.* (quietly) leise

soft: ~ball *n.* Softball, *der* (Variante des Baseballs mit weicherem Ball); **~-boiled** *adj.* weich gekocht ‹*Ei*›; **~-centred** *adj.* ‹*Praline usw.*› mit weicher Füllung; **~ coal** *n.* Fettkohle, *die;* **~ copy** *n.* (Computing) Softcopy, *die;* **~ cover** *n.* **book with a ~ cover** Buch mit einem Softcover (Verlagsw.) *od.* mit einem flexiblen Einband; **~ currency** *n.* (Econ.) weiche Währung; *attrib.* ‹*Markt, Land*› mit weicher Währung; **~ detergent** *n.* biologisch abbaubares Waschmittel; **~ drink** *n.* alkoholfreies Getränk; **~ drug** *n.* weiche Droge

soften /'sɒfn/

A *v.i.* weicher werden; **~ing of the brain** Gehirnerweichung, *die* (Med.); (coll.: stupidity) Verkalkung, *die* (ugs.)

B *v.t.* weich klopfen ‹*Fleisch*›; aufweichen ‹*Boden*›; dämpfen ‹*Beleuchtung*›; mildern ‹*Farbe, Farbton*›; enthärten ‹*Wasser*›; **~ the blow** (fig.) den Schock mildern

(Phrasal verb)

• **~ 'up** *v.t.* weichklopfen (ugs.) ‹*Boxgegner*›; aufweichen ‹*Verteidigungsanlagen*›; (verbally) milder stimmen

softener /'sɒfənə(r)/ *n.* **1** (for water) [Wasser]enthärter, *der* **2** (for fabrics) Weichspülmittel, *das;* Weichspüler, *der*

soft: ~ 'focus *n.* (Photog.) Weichzeichnung, *die;* **~ fruit** *n.* Beerenobst, *das;* **~ 'furnishings** *n. pl.* (Brit.) Raumtextilien *Pl.;* **~ goods** *n. pl.* (Brit.) Textilien *Pl.;* **~'headed** *adj.* dumm; schwachköpfig; **~-'hearted** /sɒft 'hɑ:tɪd/ *adj.* weichherzig

softie ▸**softy**

soft 'landing *n.* (Astronaut.) weiche Landung

softly /'sɒftlɪ/ *adv.* **1** (quietly) leise ‹*sprechen, singen, gehen*› **2** (gently) sanft; **speak ~:** mit sanfter Stimme sprechen **3** (not dazzlingly) sanft ‹*scheinen, leuchten*› **4** (affectionately) zärtlich

softly-'softly *attrib. adj.* (Brit.) weich ‹*Vorgehen, Taktik*›

softness /'sɒftnɪs/ *n., no pl.* ▸**soft A:** **1** Weichheit, *die;* Zartheit, *die;* **the silky ~ of her hair** ihr seidenweiches Haar **2** Sanftheit, *die;* Milde, *die;* Zartheit, *die;* **there is a ~ in the air** die Luft ist mild *od.* (geh.) lind **3** **~ of heart** Weichherzigkeit, *die* **4** (delicacy) Sanftheit, *die;* Weichheit, *die* **5** (of voice, music, etc.) Gedämpftheit, *die* **6** (gentleness) Sanftheit, *die;* Zärtlichkeit, *die* **7** (compliance) Nachgiebigkeit, *die* **8** (leniency) Nachsichtigkeit, *die;* Laschheit, *die* (ugs.) **9** (of lines, features, outline) Weichheit, *die* **10** (weakness) Schlaffheit, *die;* Weichlichkeit, *die* (abwertend) **11** (coll.: silliness) **~ in the head** Gehirnerweichung, *die* (ugs.)

soft: ~ 'option *n.* Weg des geringsten Widerstandes; **~ 'palate** *n.* (Anat.) weicher Gaumen; Gaumensegel, *das* (fachspr.); **~ pedal** ▸**pedal A 1**; **~-'pedal** **A** *v.i.* **1** (Mus.) mit [dem] Pianopedal spielen; **2** (fig.: go easy) sich zurückhalten; **~-pedal on sth.** etw. herunterspielen; **B** *v.t.* **1** (Mus.) mit [dem] Pianopedal spielen; **2** (fig.: tone down) herunterspielen; **~ 'porn** (coll.), **~ por'nography** *ns., no pl.* Softpornographie, *die;* **~ 'roe** *n.* Milch, *die;* **~ 'sell** *n., no pl.* **give sb. the ~ sell** jmdn. auf die sanfte Tour (ugs.) zum Kauf zu bewegen versuchen; *attrib.* **~ sell salesmanship** sanfte Tour (ugs.) beim Verkaufsgespräch; **give sb. the ~ sell treatment** jmdn. auf die sanfte Tour (ugs.) zum Kauf zu bewegen versuchen; **~-shell, ~-shelled** *adjs.* **1** (Zool.) mit weicher Schale *nachgestellt;* **2** (fig.) gemäßigt; lasch (abwertend); **~ 'soap** *n.* **1** (cleanser) Schmierseife, *die;* **2** (fig.: flattery) Schmeichelei, *die; attrib.* **~-soap tactics/policy/treatment** gezielte Schmeichelei; gezieltes Schöntun (ugs.); **~-'soap** *v.t.* **~-soap sb.** jmdm. Honig um den Bart schmieren (ugs.); **~-spoken** *adj.* leise sprechend ‹*Person*›; leise [gesprochen] ‹*Wort*›; **be ~-spoken** leise sprechen; **~ 'target** *n.* weiches Ziel; **~ 'tissue** *n.* (Anat.) weiches Körpergewebe; **~ top** *n.* **1** (roof) Stoffverdeck, *das;* **folding ~ top** Faltverdeck, *das;* **2** (car) Cabrio, *das;* Kabrio, *das;* **~ 'touch** ▸**touch C 10**; **~ 'toy** *n.* Stoffspielzeug, *das;* (toy animal) Stofftier, *das;* **~ verge** *n.* (Brit.) Grünstreifen, *der*

software *n., no pl., no indef. art.* (Computing) Software, *die*

software: ~ developer (Computing) *n.* ▸ⓘ **p. 1260** Softwareentwickler, *der*/-entwicklerin, *die;* **~ engineer** *n.* ▸ⓘ **p. 1260** (Computing) Softwareingenieur, *der*/-ingenieurin, *die;* **~ engineering** *n., no pl.* (Computing) Softwaretechnik, *die;* **~ house** *n.* (Computing) Softwarehaus, *das;* **~ package** *n.* (Computing) Softwarepaket, *das*

softwood *n.* Weichholz, *das; attrib.* Weichholz-

softy /'sɒftɪ/ *n.* **1** (coll.: weakling) Weichling, *der;* Waschlappen, *der* (ugs.); (boy/girl who easily cries) Heulpeter, *der*/Heulsuse, *die* (ugs.) **2** (sentimental person) **be a ~:** sentimental sein; **you old ~!** du sentimentales Huhn! (ugs.)

soggy /'sɒgɪ/ *adj.* aufgeweicht ‹*Boden*›; durchnässt ‹*Kleider*›; matschig ‹*Salat*›; nicht durchgebacken, (landsch.) glitschig ‹*Brot, Kuchen*›

soh /səʊ/ *n.* (Mus.) sol

soi-disant /swɑ'di:zɑ̃/ *adj.* (calling oneself) selbst ernannt; (claimed as such) so genannt

soigné (*fem.:* **soignée**) /'swɑnjeɪ/ *adj.* soigniert (geh.) ‹*Person, Restaurant*›; elegant ‹*Kleid*›

soil¹ /sɔɪl/ *n.* **1** (earth) Erde, *die;* Boden, *der* **2** (ground) Boden, *der;* **on British/foreign ~:** auf britischem Boden/im Ausland *od.* (geh.) in der Fremde

soil²

A *v.t.* (lit. or fig.) beschmutzen; **~ one's/sb.'s reputation** (by scandal, criminal activities) sein/jmds. Ansehen *od.* seinen/jmds. guten Ruf beflecken (geh.); (by failure) seinen/jmds. Ruf schmälern; *see also* **hand A 1**

B *n.* Schmutz, *der*

'soil conservation *n.* Bodenschutz, *der*

soiled /sɔɪld/ *adj.* schmutzig ‹*Wäsche, Windel*›; gebraucht ‹*Damenbinde*›

soil: ~ pipe *n.* senkrechtes Abflussrohr; **~ sample** *n.* Bodenprobe, *die;* **~ science** *n.* Bodenkunde, *die*

soirée /'swɑ:reɪ/ *n.* Soiree, *die*

sojourn /'sɒdʒɜ:n, 'sɒdʒən/ (literary)

A *v.i.* verweilen (geh.); weilen (geh.) (**at** in + *Dat.*)

B *n.* Aufenthalt, *der*

sol¹ /sɒl/ *n.* (Chem.) Sol, *das*

sol² ▸**soh**

solace /'sɒləs/

A *n.* Trost, *der;* **take** *or* **find ~ in sth.** Trost in etw. (*Dat.*) finden; sich mit etw. trösten; **turn to sb./sth. for ~:** bei jmdm./etw. Trost suchen

B *v.t.* trösten

solar /'səʊlə(r)/ *adj.* (Astron.) Sonnen-

solar: ~ 'battery *n.* Sonnenbatterie, *die;* Solarbatterie, *die;* **~ 'calculator** *n.* Solarrechner, *der;* **~ 'cell** *n.* Sonnenzelle, *die;* Solarzelle, *die;* **~ 'constant** *n.* Solarkonstante, *die;* **~ 'day** *n.* (Astron.) Sonnentag, *der;* **~ e'clipse** *n.* (Astron.) Sonnenfinsternis, *die;* **~ 'energy** *n., no pl.* Solarenergie, *die;* Sonnenenergie, *die;* **~ 'flare** *n.* (Astron.) Sonneneruption, *die;* [Sonnen]flare, *das;* **~ 'heating** *n., no pl.* Solarheizung, *die*

solarium /sə'leərɪəm/ *n., pl.* **solaria** /sə'leərɪə/ Solarium, *das*

solar: ~ 'panel *n.* Sonnenkollektor, *der;* (on satellite) Sonnensegel, *das;* **~ 'plexus** *n.* (Anat.) Solarplexus, *der;* Sonnengeflecht, *das;* **~ 'power** *n., no pl.* Sonnenenergie, *die;* **~ power plant** Solaranlage, *die;* **~-powered** *adj.* solarbetrieben; mit Sonnenenergie betrieben; **~-powered vehicle** Solarmobil, *das;* **~ radiation** *n.* Sonnenstrahlung, *die;* **~ system** *n.* (Astron.) Sonnensystem, *das;* **~ 'wind** *n.* Sonnenwind, *der;* **~ 'year** *n.* Sonnenjahr, *das*

sold ▸**sell A, B**

solder /'sɒldə(r), 'səʊldə(r)/

A *n.* Lot, *das* (Technik)

B *v.t.* löten

soldering iron /'sɒldərɪŋaɪən, 'səʊldərɪŋ aɪən/ *n.* Lötkolben, *der*

soldier /'səʊldʒə(r)/

A ▸ⓘ **p. 1260** *n.* Soldat, *der;* **[common] ~:** einfacher Soldat; **officers and ~s** Offiziere und Mannschaften; **~ of fortune** Glücksritter, *der* (abwertend); (mercenary) Söldner, *der; see also* **old soldier; private B 1; tin soldier; toy soldier; unknown A**

B *v.i.* als Soldat dienen

(Phrasal verb)

• **~ 'on** *v.i.* (coll.) weitermachen

'soldier ant *n.* Soldatenameise, *die*

soldierly /'səʊldʒəlɪ/

A *adj.* soldatisch

B *adv.* wie ein Soldat

soldiery /'səʊldʒərɪ/ *n.* **1** *constr. as pl.* (soldiers) Militär, *das* **2** (troop) Soldateska, *die* (abwertend)

sole¹ /səʊl/

A *n.* **1** (Anat.; of shoe) Sohle, *die;* **inner ~** ▸**insole 2** **2** (of plough) Pflugsohle, *die;* (of plane) Sohle, *die*

B *v.t.* [be]sohlen

sole² *n.* (fish) Seezunge, *die; see also* **lemon sole**

sole³ *adj.* einzig; alleinig ‹*Verantwortung, Erbe, Recht*›; Allein‹*erbe, -eigentümer*›; **the operation is the surgeon's ~ responsibility** für die Operation ist allein[e] der Chirurg zuständig; **he is the ~ judge of whether ...:** er allein urteilt darüber, ob .../entscheidet, ob ...

solecism /'sɒlɪsɪzm/ *n.* **1** (blunder) [sprachlicher] Fehler **2** (social gaffe) Fauxpas, *der*

soled /səʊld/ *adj.* besohlt; **leather-/thick-~** ‹*Schuhe*› mit Ledersohlen/dicken Sohlen

solely /'səʊllɪ/ *adv.* einzig und allein; ausschließlich; **~ because ...:** nur [deswegen], weil ...; einzig und allein, weil ...

solemn /'sɒləm/ *adj.* feierlich; ernst ‹*Anlass, Gespräch*›; **the ~ truth** die reine Wahrheit

S

solemnity /sə'lemnɪtɪ/ *n.* **1** *no pl.* Feierlichkeit, *die* **2** (rite) Feierlichkeit, *die*

solemnization /sɒləmnaɪ'zeɪʃn/ *n.* feierlicher Vollzug; (of mass) Zelebration, *die;* Feier, *die*

solemnize /'sɒləmnaɪz/ *v.t.* [feierlich] vollziehen; zelebrieren, feiern ‹*Messe*›

solemnly /'sɒləmlɪ/ *adv.* feierlich

solemn 'mass *n.* Hochamt, *das*

solenoid /'səʊlənɔɪd/ *n.* Zylinderspule, *die;* (converting energy) Magnetspule, *die*

sol-fa /sɒl'fɑː/ (Mus.)
A *v.t. & i.* solmisieren
B *n.* Solmisation, *die; see also* **tonic sol-fa**

solicit /sə'lɪsɪt/
A *v.t.* **1** (appeal for) werben um ‹*Wählerstimmen, Unterstützung*› **2** (appeal to) erregen ‹*Interesse*›; **~ sb. for sth.** jmdn. um etw. bitten **3** (Commerc.) **~ sb. for sth.** bei jmdm. um etw. werben; **he ~ed [interested people for] investment in his enterprise** er warb um Kapitalanleger für sein Unternehmen **4** (make sexual offer to) **~ sb.** sich jmdm. anbieten
B *v.i.* **1** (make request) **~ for sth.** um etw. bitten *od.* (geh.) ersuchen; (in a petition) etw. [mit einer Eingabe] fordern **2** (Commerc.) **~ for sth.** um etw. werben **3** (offer illicit sex) **~ [for custom]** sich anbieten; **be arrested for ~ing** ‹*Prostituierte:*› wegen öffentlichen Sichanbietens festgenommen werden

solicitation /səlɪsɪ'teɪʃn/ *n.* (formal: request) Drängen, *das*

solicitor /sə'lɪsɪtə(r)/ *n.* ▸ℹ p. 1260 **1** (Brit.: lawyer) Rechtsanwalt, *der*/-anwältin, *die* (*der/die nicht vor höheren Gerichten auftritt*) **2** (Amer.: canvasser) Werber, *der*/Werberin, *die*

Solicitor-'General *n., pl.* **Solicitors-General** **1** (Brit. Law) *zweiter Kronanwalt* **2** (Amer. Law) *ranghöchster [beamteter] Staatssekretär im Justizministerium*

solicitous /sə'lɪsɪtəs/ *adj.* **1** (eager) **be ~ of sth.** um etw. bemüht sein; **be ~ to do sth.** [darum] bemüht sein, etw. zu tun **2** (anxious) besorgt; **~ of** *or* **about** *or* **for sb./sth.** um jmdn./etw. besorgt

solicitously /sə'lɪsɪtəslɪ/ *adv.* **1** (eagerly) eifrig **2** (anxiously) besorgt

solicitude /sə'lɪsɪtjuːd/ *n.* (anxiety, concern) Besorgtheit, *die*

solid /'sɒlɪd/
A *adj.* **1** (rigid) fest; **freeze/be frozen ~:** [fest] gefrieren/gefroren sein; **set ~:** fest werden **2** (of the same substance all through) massiv; **~ silver** massives Silber; **a ~-silver tea service/watch** *etc.* ein Teeservice/eine Uhr *usw.* aus massivem *od.* reinem Silber; **~ gold** reines Gold; **a ~-gold watch/crown/bar** eine reingoldene Uhr/Krone/ein Barren reines Gold; **~ tyre** Vollgummireifen, *der;* **be packed ~** (coll.) gerammelt voll sein (ugs.) **3** (well-built) stabil; solide gebaut ‹*Haus, Mauer usw.*›; **have a ~ majority** (Polit.) eine solide Mehrheit haben **4** (reliable) verlässlich, zuverlässig ‹*Freund, Helfer, Verbündeter*›; fest ‹*Stütze*› **5** (complete) ganz; **a good ~ meal** eine kräftige Mahlzeit; **a ~ day/hour/week** ein ganzer Tag/eine ganze *od.* volle Stunde/eine ganze Woche **6** (sound) stichhaltig ‹*Argument, Grund*›; solide ‹*Arbeiter, Finanzlage, Firma*›; solide, gediegen ‹*Komfort, Grundlage*› **7** (Geom.: having three dimensions) dreidimensional; räumlich **8** (Geom.: concerned with ~s) stereometrisch; **~ geometry** Stereometrie, *die* **9** (Printing) kompress; kompress gesetzt ‹*Seite*› **10** (united) einig; **a ~ vote for ...:** eine einstimmige Entscheidung für ...; **be ~ with sb.** mit jmdm. einig sein; (Amer. coll.: friendly) mit jmdm. auf gutem Fuß stehen; **go** *or* **be ~ for sb./sth.** uneingeschränkt für jmdn./etw. sein **11** heftig ‹*Schlag*›
B *n.* **1** (substance) fester Körper **2** *in pl.* (food) feste Nahrung **3** (Geom.) Körper, *der*

solid 'angle *n.* (Geom.) Raumwinkel, *der*

solidarity /sɒlɪ'dærɪtɪ/ *n., no pl.* Solidarität, *die;* **show ~ with sb.** sich mit jmdn. solidarisch zeigen

solid: ~ 'fuel *n.* fester Brennstoff; **~-'fuel** *attrib. adj.* Festbrennstoff-; **~-fuel rocket** Feststoffrakete, *die*

solidification /səlɪdɪfɪ'keɪʃn/ *n.* Verfestigung, *die;* Verhärtung, *die;* Erstarrung, *die*

solidify /sə'lɪdɪfaɪ/
A *v.t.* verfestigen
B *v.i.* (become solid) hart *od.* fest werden; erstarren; ‹*Flüssigkeit, Lava:*› erstarren

solidity /sə'lɪdɪtɪ/ *n., no pl.* ▸**solid A: 1** Festigkeit, *die* **2** Massivität, *die* **3** Stabilität, *die* **4** (of reasons, argument) Stichhaltigkeit, *die*

solidly /'sɒlɪdlɪ/ *adv.* **1** (firmly) stabil **2** (compactly) **a ~ built person** ein kräftig gebauter Mensch **3** (ceaselessly) pausenlos; **he wrote ~ for four hours** er schrieb vier Stunden ohne Pause **4** (wholeheartedly) **be ~ behind sb./sth.** uneingeschränkt hinter jmdm./einer Sache stehen **5** (with sound reasons) stichhaltig; **argue ~ for sth.** stichhaltige Argumente für etw. vorbringen

solid: ~ so'lution *n.* (Chem.) feste Lösung; **~ 'state** *n.* (Phys.) fester Zustand; **~-state** *adj.* (Phys.) Festkörper‹*physik, -geräte, -schaltung*›

soliloquize /sə'lɪləkwaɪz/ *v.i.* monologisieren; (to oneself) Selbstgespräche führen

soliloquy /sə'lɪləkwɪ/ *n.* Monolog, *der;* (talking to oneself) Selbstgespräch, *das*

solipsism /'sɒlɪpsɪzm, 'səʊlɪpsɪzm/ *n.* (Philos.) Solipsismus, *der*

solitaire /sɒlɪ'teə(r)/ *n.* **1** (gem) Solitär, *der;* **a ~ diamond/ring** ein [Diamant]solitär/ein Solitärring **2** (ring) Solitärring, *der* **3** (game) Solitär, *das* **4** (Amer. Cards) Patience, *die* **5** (Ornith.) Einsiedler, *der*

solitary /'sɒlɪtərɪ/
A *adj.* **1** einsam; **a ~ existence/life** ein Einsiedlerdasein/-leben; **~ confinement** Einzelhaft, *die* **2** (sole) einzig **3** (Zool.) solitär **4** (Bot.) ▸**single A 1**
B *n.* (coll.) Einzelhaft, *die*

solitude /'sɒlɪtjuːd/ *n.* **1** (loneliness, remoteness) Einsamkeit, *die* **2** (lonely place) Einöde, *die*

solmization /sɒlmɪ'zeɪʃn/ *n.* (Mus.) Solmisation, *die*

solo /'səʊləʊ/
A *n., pl.* **~s** **1** (Mus.) Solo, *das* **2** (Cards) **~ [whist]** Solo[-whist], *das;* **go ~:** ein Solo spielen **3** (Aeronaut.) Alleinflug, *der*
B *adj.* **1** (Mus.) Solo‹*spiel, -part, -tanz, -instrument, album, -CD, platte*› **2** (unaccompanied) **~ flight** Alleinflug, *der;* **~ performance** Solo- *od.* Alleinvorstellung, *die;* **~ achievement/effort** Einzelleistung, *die;* **a ~ act on the trapeze** eine Solonummer auf dem Trapez; **~ motorcycle** Motorrad ohne Beiwagen
C *adv.* (unaccompanied) solo ‹*singen, spielen, tanzen usw.*›; **go/fly ~** (Aeronaut.) einen Alleinflug machen

soloist /'səʊləʊɪst/ *n.* (Mus.) Solist, *der*/Solistin, *die*

Solomon /'sɒləmən/ *pr. n.* Salomo[n] (*der*); **be as wise as ~:** salomonische Weisheit besitzen; **judgment of ~:** salomonisches Urteil; *see also* **song**

Solomon 'Islands *pr. n. pl.* **the ~:** die Salomoninseln; die Salomonen

Solomon's 'seal *n.* (figure; also Bot.) Salomonssiegel, *das*

solstice /'sɒlstɪs/ *n.* **1** (time of year) Sonnenwende, *die;* **summer/winter ~:** Sommer-/Wintersonnenwende, *die* **2** (point) Wendepunkt, *der*

solubility /sɒljʊ'bɪlɪtɪ/ *n.* **1** (capacity to be dissolved) Löslichkeit, *die* **2** (of problem etc.) Lösbarkeit, *die*

soluble /'sɒljʊbl/ *adj.* **1** (that can be dissolved) löslich; solubel (fachspr.); **~ in water, water-~:** wasserlöslich; **fat-~:** fettlöslich **2** (solvable) lösbar

solute /'sɒljuːt/ *n.* (Chem.) gelöster Stoff

solution /sə'luːʃn, sə'ljuːʃn/ *n.* **1** (Phys., Chem.) Lösung, *die* **2** ([result of] solving) Lösung, *die* (**to** *Gen.*); **there is/is no ~ to sth.** etw. kann/kann nicht gelöst werden; **find a ~ to sth.** eine Lösung für etw. finden; etw. lösen

solvable /'sɒlvəbl/ *adj.* lösbar

solve /sɒlv/ *v.t.* lösen

solvency /'sɒlvənsɪ/ *n.* (Finance) Solvenz, *die*

solvent /'sɒlvənt/
A *adj.* **1** (Chem.: dissolving) lösend: **~ liquid** *or* **fluid** Lösungsmittel, *das* **2** (Finance) solvent
B *n.* (Chem.) Lösungsmittel, *das* (**of, for** für); **~ abuse** Missbrauch von Lösungsmitteln als Rauschmittel

Somali /sə'mɑːlɪ/ ▸ℹ p. 1277, ▸ℹ p. 1345
A *adj.* somalisch
B *n.* **1** (person) Somali, *der/die* **2** (language) Somali, *das*

Somalia /sə'mɑːlɪə/ *pr. n.* Somalia (*das*)

Somalian /sə'mɑːlɪən/
A *adj.* somalisch
B *n.* Somalier, *der*/Somalierin, *die*

somatic /sə'mætɪk/ *adj.* somatisch

sombre (*Amer.:* **somber**) /'sɒmbə(r)/ *adj.* dunkel; düster ‹*Atmosphäre, Stimmung*›; ernst ‹*Anlass*›

sombre: ~-coloured *adj.* düster; **~-looking** *adj.* düster [aussehend]

sombrely /'sɒmbəlɪ/ *adv.* düster; dunkel ‹*gekleidet*›; schwach ‹*leuchten*›

sombrero /sɒm'breərəʊ/ *n., pl.* **~s** Sombrero, *der*

some /səm, *stressed* sʌm/
A *adj.* **1** (one or other) [irgend]ein; **~ fool** irgendein Dummkopf (ugs.); **~ day** eines Tages; irgendwann einmal; **~ [experienced] person** [irgend]jemand[, der Erfahrung hat]; **~ shop/book or other** irgendein Laden/Buch; **~ person or other** irgendjemand; irgendwer **2** (a considerable quantity of) einig...; etlich... (ugs. verstärkend); **speak at ~ length/wait for ~ time** ziemlich lang[e] sprechen/warten; **~ time/weeks/days/years ago** vor einiger Zeit/vor einigen Wochen/Tagen/Jahren; **~ time soon** bald [einmal]; **as ~ small token of** als ein kleines Zeichen (+ *Gen.*); **thirty ~ years** (coll.) über dreißig Jahre; *see also* **few A 2** **3** (a small quantity of) ein bisschen; **would you like ~ wine?** möchten Sie [etwas] Wein?; **do ~ shopping/reading** einkaufen/lesen; **have ~ sense of decency** ein gewisses Gefühl für Anstand besitzen; **do have ~ sense!** sei doch vernünftig! **4** (to a certain extent) **~ guide** eine gewisse Orientierungshilfe; **that is ~ proof** das ist [doch] gewissermaßen ein Beweis; **it was ~ help having my sister here** es war mir eine gewisse Hilfe, dass meine Schwester hier war; **you are ~ help!** (iron.) du bist [mir] vielleicht eine Hilfe! (ugs.) **5** (coll.: true) **this is ~ war/poem/car!** das ist vielleicht ein Krieg/Gedicht/Wagen! (ugs.); **he's ~ fool!** er ist vielleicht ein Dummkopf! **6** (approximately) etwa; ungefähr
B *pron.* einig...; **Do you want any potatoes? — I have ~ already** Möchtest du Kartoffeln? — Ich habe schon welche; **This chocolate is delicious. — Do have ~ more** Diese Schokolade ist köstlich. — Nimm dir doch noch etwas [davon]; **she only ate ~ of it** sie hat es nur teilweise aufgegessen; **I collect stamps — If I find ~, I'll send them** Ich sammle Briefmarken — Wenn ich welche finde, schicke ich sie dir; **~ of her ideas are good** sie hat einige gute Ideen; **~ of the greatest music** einige der größten Werke der Musik; **this country has ~ of the highest mountains in the world** in diesem Land sind mit die höchsten Berge der Welt (ugs.); **~ say ...:** manche sagen ...; **~ ..., others ...:** manche ..., andere ...; die einen ..., andere ...; **... and then ~:** und noch einige/einiges mehr
C *adv.* (coll.: in ~ degree) ein bisschen; etwas; **~ more** noch ein bisschen

somebody /'sʌmbədɪ/ *n. & pron.* jemand; **~ or other** irgendjemand; (important person) **be [a] ~:** jemand *od.* etwas sein; etwas vorstellen

'someday *adv.* (Amer.) eines Tages; irgendwann einmal

'somehow *adv.* **~ [or other]** irgendwie; **we must find money ~ [or other]** wir müssen irgendwie Geld beschaffen

someone /'sʌmwən, *stressed* 'sʌmwʌn/ *pron.* ▸**somebody**

'someplace (Amer. coll.) ▸**somewhere**

somersault /'sʌməsɔːlt, 'sʌməsɒlt/
A *n.* Purzelbaum, *der* (ugs.); Salto, *der* (Sport); **turn**

S

a ~: einen Purzelbaum schlagen (ugs.); einen Salto springen (Sport)

B *v.i.* einen Purzelbaum schlagen (ugs.); einen Salto springen (Sport); **the car ~ed [into a tree]** das Auto überschlug sich [und landete an einem Baum]

'something *n. & pron.* **1** (some thing) etwas; **~ new/old/good/bad** etwas Neues/Altes/Gutes/Schlechtes; **~ told me that .../to do sth.** etwas sagte mir, dass .../befahl mir, etw. zu tun **2** (some unspecified thing) [irgend]etwas; **~ or other** irgendetwas; **she is a lecturer in ~ or other** sie ist Dozentin für irgendwas (ugs.) **3** (some quantity of a thing) etwas; **have ~ before you go** nimm etwas zu dir *od.* iss etwas, bevor du gehst; **will you have a drop of ~?** nimmst du einen Schluck?; **I have seen ~ of his work** ich habe einige seiner Arbeiten *od.* (ugs.) etwas von ihm gesehen; **see ~ of a place/festival** ein bisschen was von einem Ort/Fest sehen (ugs.); **there is ~ in what you say** was du sagst, hat etwas für sich; an dem, was du sagst, ist etwas dran (ugs.); **he has ~ about him** er hat etwas Besonderes an sich (*Dat.*); **it is ~ to have got so far** es ist schon etwas [Besonderes], so weit gekommen zu sein; **you may have ~ there** (you have had a good idea) der Gedanke hat etwas für sich **4** (impressive or important thing, person, etc.) **the party was quite ~:** die Party war spitze (ugs.); **make ~ of oneself** etwas aus sich machen; **to be world champion at that age is quite ~:** in diesem Alter Weltmeister zu sein, das ist schon etwas **5** **or ~** ▸ **or**[1] **3** **6** **~ like** etwa wie; **he left ~ like a million** er hinterließ etwa eine Million; **it looks ~ like a cross** es sieht [etwa] wie ein Kreuz aus; **that's ~ 'like** (coll.) lässt sich hören/sehen! (ugs.); **that's ~ like it** das ist schon besser **7** **~ of an expert/a specialist** so etwas wie ein Fachmann/Spezialist; **see ~ of sb.** jmdn. sehen. *See also* **else 1, 2**

'sometime

A *adj.* ehemalig; **he was ~ captain of the team** er war früher Mannschaftskapitän

B *adv.* irgendwann

'sometimes *adv.* manchmal; **~ ..., at other times ...:** manchmal ..., manchmal ...

'somewhat

A *adv.* (rather) irgendwie; ziemlich; **more than ~ surprised/disappointed** (coll.) ganz schön (ugs.) *od.* mehr als [nur] überrascht/enttäuscht

B *pron.* **~ of an expert** so etwas wie ein Fachmann

'somewhen *adv.* (coll.) irgendwann

'somewhere

A *adv.* **1** (in a place) irgendwo; **~ about** *or* **around thirty [years old]** [so (ugs.)] um die dreißig [Jahre alt]; **~ between five and ten** [so (ugs.)] zwischen fünf und zehn **2** (to a place) irgendwohin; **get ~** (coll.) (in life) es zu etwas bringen; (in a task) weiterkommen

B *n.* **look for ~ to stay** sich nach einer Unterkunft umsehen; **find ~ suitable to do sth.** einen geeigneten Ort finden, [um] etw. zu tun; **she prefers ~ hot for her holidays** in den Ferien fährt sie am liebsten irgendwohin, wo es heiß ist

somnambulism /sɒmˈnæmbjʊlɪzm/ *n., no pl.* Schlafwandeln, *das;* Somnambulismus, *der* (fachspr.)

somnambulist /sɒmˈnæmbjʊlɪst/ *n.* Schlafwandler, *der*/-wandlerin, *die*

somnolence /ˈsɒmnələns/ *n.* Schläfrigkeit, *die*

somnolent /ˈsɒmnələnt/ *adj.* **1** (sleepy) schläfrig **2** (sleep-inducing) einschläfernd **3** (Med.) somnolent

son /sʌn/ *n.* Sohn, *der;* (as address) **[my] ~:** mein Sohn; **adopted ~:** Adoptivsohn, *der;* **~ and heir** Sohn und Erbe; **be a ~ of the soil** mit der Scholle verbunden sein; **the S~ of Man** (Relig.) der Menschensohn; **the S~ [of God]** (Relig.) der Sohn [Gottes]; **~ of a bitch** (derog.) Scheißkerl, *der* (derb); (thing) Scheißding, *das* (*derb*); *see also* **father A 1, 5; gun A 1; mother A 1**

sonar /ˈsəʊnɑː(r)/ *n.* Sonar, *das*

sonata /səˈnɑːtə/ *n.* (Mus.) Sonate, *die;* **~ form** Sonatenform, *die*

sonde /sɒnd/ *n.* (Meteorol.) [Raum]sonde, *die*

song /sɒŋ/ *n.* **1** Lied, *das;* (esp. political ballad) Song, *der;* (pop ~) [Pop]song, *der;* **S~ of S~s, S~ of Solomon** (Bibl.) Hohelied, *das;* Lied der Lieder, *das* **2** *no pl.* (singing) Gesang, *der;* **on ~** (fig. coll.) in Spitzenform; **break** *or* **burst forth into ~:** ein Lied anstimmen; **for a ~:** für einen Apfel und ein Ei (ugs.); **it is nothing to make a ~ about** (coll.) es ist nicht der Rede wert; **~ and dance** (Brit. coll.: fuss; Amer. coll.: rigmarole) viel *od.* großes Trara (ugs.) **3** (bird cry) Gesang, *der;* (of cuckoo) Ruf, *der*

song: ~bird *n.* Singvogel, *der;* **~book** *n.* Liederbuch, *das;* **~ cycle** *n.* (Mus.) Liederzyklus, *der*

songster /ˈsɒŋstə(r)/ *n.* **1** (singer, poet) Sänger, *der* **2** (Amer.: songbook) Liederbuch, *das*

songstress /ˈsɒŋstrɪs/ *n.* Sängerin, *die*

'songthrush *n.* Singdrossel, *die*

'songwriter *n.* ▸ **i** **p. 1260** Songschreiber, *der*/-schreiberin, *die*

sonic /ˈsɒnɪk/ *attrib. adj.* Schall-; **~ depth finder** Echolot, *das*

sonic: ~ 'bang ▸ **~ boom; ~ barrier** ▸ **sound barrier; ~ boom** *n.* Überschallknall, *der;* **~ mine** *n.* Geräuschmine, *die*

'son-in-law *n., pl.* **sons-in-law** Schwiegersohn, *der*

sonnet /ˈsɒnɪt/ *n.* Sonett, *das;* **~ sequence** Sonettenzyklus, *der*

sonny /ˈsʌnɪ/ *n.* (coll.) Kleiner (*der*); kleiner Mann (ugs.)

sonority /səˈnɒrɪtɪ/ *n.* (of voice) Wohlklang, *der;* Sonorität, *die* (geh. selten); (of ship's horn, bell, etc.) voller Klang

sonorous /səˈnɔːrəs, ˈsɒnərəs/ *adj.* volltönend; sonor ‹*Stimme*›; klangvoll ‹*Instrument, Sprache*›

soon /suːn/ *adv.* **1** bald; (quickly) schnell **2** (early) früh; **how ~ will it be ready?** wann ist es denn fertig?; **none too ~:** keinen Augenblick zu früh; **no ~er said than done** gesagt, getan; **~er said than done** leichter gesagt als getan; **no ~er had I arrived than ...:** kaum war ich angekommen, da ...; **~ enough** früh genug; **~er or later** früher oder später; **Which train shall I take? — Whichever arrives the ~er** Welchen Zug soll ich nehmen? — Den, der zuerst ankommt; **the car must be serviced every 12 months or every six thousand miles, whichever is the ~er** der Wagen muss alle 12 Monate bzw. alle sechstausend Meilen gewartet werden, je nachdem [, was früher der Fall ist]; **the ~er [...] the better** (coll.), **better ~er than later** je früher *od.* eher [...], desto besser **3** **as ~ as his death was known/he heard of it** sobald sein Tod bekannt wurde/er davon gehört hatte; **we'll set off just as ~ as he arrives** sobald er ankommt, machen wir uns auf den Weg; **as ~ as possible** so bald wie möglich **4** (willingly) gern; **just as ~ [as ...]** genauso gern [wie ...]; **she would ~er die than ...:** sie würde lieber sterben, als ...; **which would you ~er/~est do?** was würdest du lieber/am liebsten tun?; **they would kill you as ~ as look at you** (coll.) sie würden dich sofort *od.* auf der Stelle umbringen; **~er you than me** lieber du als ich

soonish /ˈsuːnɪʃ/ *adv.* (coll.) recht bald

soot /sʊt/

A *n.* Ruß, *der*

B *v.t.* verrußen; rußig machen

soothe /suːð/ *v.t.* **1** (calm) beruhigen; beschwichtigen ‹*Gefühle*› **2** (make less severe) mildern; lindern ‹*Schmerz*›; **~ sb.'s cares away** jmds. Sorgen vertreiben

soothing /ˈsuːðɪŋ/ *adj.* beruhigend; wohltuend ‹*Bad, Creme, Massage*›

soothsayer /ˈsuːθseɪə(r)/ *n.* (arch.) Wahrsager, *der*/Wahrsagerin, *die*

sooty /ˈsʊtɪ/ *adj.* **1** (soot-covered) verrußt; rußig **2** (black) schwarz [wie Ruß]

sop /sɒp/

A *n.* **1** (piece of bread) Stück eingeweichtes Brot **2** (fig.) Beschwichtigungsmittel, *das;* **sth. is intended as a ~ to sb., sth. is a ~ given to sb.** etw. soll jmdn. beschwichtigen

B *v.i.*, **-pp-: be ~ping [wet] [with rain]** [vom Regen] völlig durchnässt sein

Phrasal verb

• **~ 'up** *v.t.* aufnehmen

sophism /ˈsɒfɪzm/ *n.* Sophismus, *der*

sophist /ˈsɒfɪst/ *n.* Sophist, *der*/Sophistin, *die*

sophistic /səˈfɪstɪk/, **sophistical** /səˈfɪstɪkl/ *adjs.* sophistisch

sophisticate

A /səˈfɪstɪkeɪt/ *v.t.* verbilden

B /səˈfɪstɪkət/ *adj.* ▸ **sophisticated 1**

C *n.* Kultursnob, *der*

sophisticated /səˈfɪstɪkeɪtɪd/ *adj.* **1** (cultured) kultiviert; gepflegt ‹*Restaurant, Küche*›; anspruchsvoll ‹*Roman, Autor, Unterhaltung, Stil*› **2** (elaborate) ausgeklügelt ‹*Autozubehör*›; differenziert, subtil ‹*Argument, System, Ansatz*›; hoch entwickelt ‹*Technik, Elektronik, Software, Geräte*›; (derog.: over-complex) spitzfindig ‹*Argument*›; **~ in style** stilistisch verfeinert

sophistication /səfɪstɪˈkeɪʃn/ *n.* **1** (refinement) Kultiviertheit, *die;* (of argument) Differenziertheit, *die;* (derog.) Spitzfindigkeit, *die;* (of style, manner) Subtilität, *die;* **the ~ of French cooking** die Raffinesse der französischen Küche **2** (advanced methods) hoher Entwicklungsstand [der Technik]; **era of technical ~:** Zeitalter hoch entwickelter Technik

sophistry /ˈsɒfɪstrɪ/ *n.* Sophisterei, *die*

sophomore /ˈsɒfəmɔː(r)/ *n.* (Amer. Sch./Univ.) *Student/Studentin einer Highschool bzw. Universität im zweiten Studienjahr*

soporific /sɒpəˈrɪfɪk/

A *adj.* schläfrig ‹*Person*›; einschläfernd ‹*Wirkung, Rede*›; **~ drug/medicine** Schlafmittel, *das*

B *n.* Schlafmittel, *das*

sopping ▸ **sop B**

soppy /ˈsɒpɪ/ *adj.* (Brit. coll.: sentimental) rührselig; sentimental ‹*Person*›; **be ~ on sb.** in jmdn. verschossen sein (ugs.)

soprano /səˈprɑːnəʊ/ *n., pl.* **~s** (Mus.) (voice, singer, part) Sopran, *der;* (female singer also) Sopranistin, *die;* **~ flute/clarinet** Sopranflöte, *die*/-klarinette, *die;* **~ clef** Sopranschlüssel, *der*

sorbet /ˈsɔːbɪt, ˈsɔːbeɪ/ *n.* Sorbet, *das*

sorcerer /ˈsɔːsərə(r)/ *n.* Zauberer, *der*

sorceress /ˈsɔːsərɪs/ *n.* Zauberin, *die*

sorcery /ˈsɔːsərɪ/ *n., no pl.* Zauberei, *die*

sordid /ˈsɔːdɪd/ *adj.* **1** (immoral, dishonourable) dreckig (abwertend); unehrenhaft, unlauter ‹*Motiv*›; unerfreulich ‹*Detail, Geschichte*›; schmutzig ‹*Geschäft*› **2** (squalid) schmutzig; schäbig ‹*Wohnung, Verhältnisse*›; heruntergekommen ‹*Stadtviertel*›

sore /sɔː(r)/

A *adj.* **1** (painful) weh; (inflamed or injured) wund; **sb. has a ~ back/foot/arm** *etc.* jmdm. tut der Rücken/Fuß/Arm *usw.* weh; **~ point** *or* **spot** (fig.) wunder Punkt; **touch on a ~ point, touch a ~ spot** (fig.) an einen wunden Punkt rühren; **a ~ subject** ein heikles Thema; **have ~ feelings about sth.** wegen einer Sache verletzt sein **2** (irritated) verärgert; sauer (ugs.); **feel ~:** sich ärgern *od.* aufregen **3** (Amer.: vexed) böse; sauer (ugs.); **be ~ at sb./about** *or* **over sth.** böse *od.* (ugs.) sauer auf jmdn./über etw. (*Akk.*) sein **4** (severe) schwer; groß ‹*Not, Schwierigkeiten*›; dringlich ‹*Problem*›

B *n.* **1** (abrasion) wunde Stelle **2** (fig.: painful thought) Wunde, *die*

sorely /ˈsɔːlɪ/ *adv.* sehr; arg (südd.); dringend ‹*nötig, benötigt*›; **be ~ in need of sth.** etw. dringend brauchen; **~ tempted** stark versucht

soreness /ˈsɔːnɪs/ *n.* Schmerz, *der;* (inflammation) Wundsein, *das*

sorghum /ˈsɔːgəm/ *n.* Sorghum, *das*

sorority /səˈrɒrɪtɪ/ *n.* **1** (sisterhood) Schwesternorden, *der;* (Amer.: female section of church congregation) Frauen der Gemeinde **2** (Amer.: society) Studentinnenvereinigung, *die*

S

sorority

Eine Studentinnenvereinigung an amerikanischen Universitäten als Gegenstück zur **fraternity**. Ähnlich ihren männlichen Kommilitonen teilen Mitglieder einer *sorority* meist ein *sorority house*, und die einzelnen Vereinigungen sind nach Buchstaben des griechischen Alphabets benannt. *Sororities* sind meist sozial engagiert und widmen einen Teil ihrer Zeit und Energie wohltätigen Zwecken. Einige Studentinnenvereinigungen gehören akademischen oder beruflichen Organisationen an.

sorrel[1] /'sɒrl/ *n.* (Bot.) Sauerampfer, *der*

sorrel[2]

A *adj.* fuchsrot; rotbraun

B *n.* (horse) Fuchs, *der;* rotbraunes Pferd

sorrow /'sɒrəʊ/

A *n.* **1** (distress) Kummer, *der;* Leid, *das;* **feel [great] ~ that ...:** es [sehr] bedauern, dass ...; **he felt great ~ at the news** die Nachricht bekümmerte ihn sehr; **cause sb. [great] ~:** jmdm. [großen] Kummer bereiten; **act more in ~ than in anger** mehr aus Kummer *od.* Betrübnis handeln als aus Zorn **2** (misfortune) Sorge, *die;* **he has had many ~s** er hat viel [Schweres] durchgemacht; **all the ~s of the world** alles *od.* das ganze Leid der Welt

B *v.i.* **1** (feel ~) sich grämen (geh.) (**at, over, for** über + *Akk.*, um) **2** (mourn) trauern (**for, after** um)

sorrowful /'sɒrəʊfl, 'sɒrəfl/ *adj.* **1** (sad) betrübt ‹*Person*›; traurig ‹*Anlass, Lächeln, Herz*›; **with a ~ heart** mit Kummer im Herzen; **feel ~ at sth.** über etw. (*Akk.*) bekümmert sein **2** (distressing) traurig; leidvoll ‹*Dasein*›

sorrowing /'sɒrəʊɪŋ/ *attrib. adj.* trauernd

sorry /'sɒrɪ/ *adj.* **1** ▸ **i** p. 908 (regretful) **sb. is ~ to do sth.** jmdm. tut es Leid, etw. tun zu müssen; **I am ~ to disappoint you** ich muss dich leider enttäuschen; **sb. is ~ that ...:** es tut jmdm. Leid, dass ...; **sb. is ~ about sth.** jmdm. tut etw. Leid; **~ about your accident** es tut mir Leid, dass du einen Unfall hattest; **~, but ...** (coll.) tut mir Leid, aber ...; **I'm ~** (won't change my mind) tut mir Leid; **~ I'm late** (coll.) Entschuldigung, dass ich zu spät komme; **My mother died two months ago. — Oh, I 'am ~!** Meine Mutter ist vor zwei Monaten gestorben. — Herzliches Beileid!; **I'm ~ to say** leider; **I can't say [that] I'm ~!** ich bin nicht gerade traurig darüber; **sb. is** *or* **feels ~ for sb./sth.** jmd. tut jmdm. Leid/jmd. bedauert etw.; **you'll be ~:** das wird dir noch Leid tun; **feel ~ for oneself** sich selbst bemitleiden; sich (*Dat.*) Leid tun; **~!** Entschuldigung!; **~?** wie bitte?; **~ about that!** (coll.) tut mir Leid!; **~ to bother you** Entschuldigung, wenn ich störe; *see also* **safe B 2** **2** *attrib.* (wretched) traurig; faul, fadenscheinig ‹*Entschuldigung*›

sort /sɔːt/

A *n.* **1** Art, *die;* (type) Sorte, *die;* **cakes of several ~s** verschiedene Kuchensorten; **a new ~ of bicycle** ein neuartiges Fahrrad; **people of every/that ~:** Menschen jeden/diesen Schlages; **people of every ~ and kind** alle möglichen Leute; **it takes all ~s [to make a world]** (coll.) es gibt so'ne und solche (ugs.); (when referring to eccentric behaviour) jedem Tierchen sein Pläsierchen (scherzh.); **all ~s of ...:** alle möglichen ...; **support sb. in all ~s of ways** jmdn. auf vielerlei Art und Weise unterstützen; **there are all ~s of things to do** es gibt alles Mögliche *od.* allerlei zu tun; **she is just/not my ~:** sie ist genau/nicht mein Typ (ugs.); **she is not the ~ to do that** es ist nicht ihre Art, das zu tun; **what ~ of [a] person do you think I am?** für wen hältst du mich?; **you'll do nothing of the ~:** das kommt gar nicht infrage; **he's a ~ of stockbroker, I believe** (coll.) er ist [so] eine Art [von] Börsenmakler, glaube ich; **~ of** (coll.) irgendwie; irgendwo (salopp); (more or less) mehr oder weniger; (to some extent) ziemlich (ugs.); **it's ~ of difficult for me to explain** (coll.) ich kann es irgendwie nicht so gut *od.* leicht erklären; **Have you finished? — Well, ~ of** (coll.) Bist du fertig? — Mehr oder weniger; **I ~ of expected it** (coll.) ich habe es irgendwie erwartet; **nothing of the ~:** nichts dergleichen; **or something of the ~:** oder so [etwas Ähnliches] (ugs.); **a funny ~ of person/day/car** ein komischer Mensch/Tag/Wagen; **it is music of a ~** (derog.) es ist so was Ähnliches wie Musik; **he is a doctor/footballer of a ~** *or* **of ~s** (derog.) er nennt sich Arzt/Fußballspieler; **we don't mix with people of that ~:** mit solchen Leuten wollen wir nichts zu tun haben; **he/she is a good ~** (coll.) er/sie ist schon in Ordnung (ugs.); **he is not a bad ~ at all** (coll.) er ist nicht der Schlechteste (ugs.) **2** **be out of ~s** nicht in Form sein; (be irritable) schlecht gelaunt sein **3** (Printing) Letter, *die*

B *v.t.* sortieren

Phrasal verb

- **~ 'out** *v.t.* **1** (arrange) sortieren; **~ out material for an essay** Material für einen Aufsatz zusammenstellen **2** (settle) klären; schlichten ‹*Streit*›; beenden ‹*Verwirrung*›; **it will ~ itself out** es wird schon in Ordnung kommen **3** (organize) durchorganisieren; auf Vordermann bringen (ugs.); **~ oneself out** ‹*Neuankömmling usw.*:› sich einrichten; **things have ~ed themselves out** die Dinge haben sich eingerenkt **4** (coll.: punish) **~ sb. out** jmdm. zeigen, wos langgeht (ugs.) **5** (select) aussuchen; wählen; **~ out the truth from the lies** die Lügen von der Wahrheit unterscheiden; Lüge und Wahrheit unterscheiden; **~ out the good apples/singers from the bad [ones]** die guten Äpfel/Sänger von den schlechten trennen

'sort code *n.* (Banking) Bankleitzahl, *die*

sorter /'sɔːtə(r)/ *n.* **1** (arranger) Sortierer, *der*/Sortiererin, *die* **2** (for punched cards) Sorter, *der;* Sortiermaschine, *die*

sortie /'sɔːtiː, 'sɔːtɪ/ *n.* (Mil.; also fig.) **1** Ausfall, *der* **2** (flight) Einsatz, *der*

sorting /'sɔːtɪŋ/ *n.* Sortieren, *das*

sorting: ~-machine *n.* Sortiermaschine, *die;* **~ office** *n.* Postverteilstelle, *die*

'sort key *n.* (Computing) Sortierschlüssel, *der*

SOS /esəʊ'es/ *n.* **1** SOS, *das;* **~ appeal** Hilfeaufruf, *der* **2** (Brit.: broadcast) **~ message** Suchmeldung, *die;* (to motorists) Reiseruf, *der*

'so so, 'so-so *adj., adv.* so lala (ugs.)

sot /sɒt/ *n.* Trinker, *der*/Trinkerin, *die;* Säufer, *der*/Säuferin, *die* (salopp)

sottish /'sɒtɪʃ/ *adj.* versoffen (salopp)

sotto voce /sɒtəʊ 'vəʊtʃɪ/ *adv.* mit gedämpfter Stimme

sou /suː/ *n.* (Hist./coll.) Sou, *der;* **not have a ~:** keinen roten Heller haben

soubrette /suː'bret/ *n.* (Theatre) Soubrette, *die*

soufflé /'suːfleɪ/ *n.* (Gastr.) Soufflé, *das;* **~ dish** Souffléform, *die*

sough /sʌf, saʊ/ (literary)

A *n.* Rauschen, *das*

B *v.i.* rauschen

sought ▸ **seek**

soul /səʊl/ *n.* **1** Seele, *die;* **sell one's ~ for sth.** (fig.) seine Seele für etw. verkaufen; **upon my ~!** (dated) meiner Treu! (veralt.); **bare one's ~ to sb.** jmdm. sein Herz ausschütten; *see also* **heart A 2**; **life 2** **2** (intellect) Geist, *der;* **not be able to call one's ~ one's own** nicht sein eigener Herr sein; **his whole ~ revolted from it** er sträubte sich mit ganzer Seele dagegen **3** (person) Seele, *die;* **not a ~:** keine Menschenseele; **be the ~ of discretion** die Verschwiegenheit selbst *od.* in Person sein; **be a good ~ and fetch me a cup of tea** sei ein Schatz (ugs.) und hol mir eine Tasse Tee; **the poor little ~:** das arme kleine Ding **4** (music) Soul, *der*

soul: ~ brother *n.: schwarzer Nordamerikaner (als [bewusster] Teilhaber der schwarzen Kultur);* ≈ Bruder, *der;* **~-destroying** /'səʊldɪstrɔɪɪŋ/ *adj.* **1** (boring) nervtötend; geisttötend; **2** (depressing) deprimierend

'soul food *n.: traditionelle Küche der schwarzen Nordamerikaner*

soulful /'səʊlfl/ *adj.* gefühlvoll; (sad) schwermütig

soulfully /'səʊlfəlɪ/ *adv.* mit viel Gefühl; (sadly) voll Schwermut

soulless /'səʊllɪs/ *adj.* **1** (ignoble) seelenlos (geh.); gefühllos **2** (dull) öde

soul: ~mate *n.* Seelenverwandte, *der/die;* **~ music** *n.* Soul, *der;* Soulmusik, *die;* **~-searching** *n.* Gewissenskampf, *der;* **~ sister** *n.: schwarze Nordamerikanerin (als [bewusste] Teilhaberin der schwarzen Kultur);* ≈ Schwester, *die;* **~-stirring** *adj.* aufwühlend; (inspiring) mitreißend

sound[1] /saʊnd/

A *adj.* **1** (healthy) gesund; intakt ‹*Gebäude, Mauerwerk*›; gut ‹*Frucht, Obst, Holz, Boden*›; **of ~ mind** im Vollbesitz seiner geistigen Kräfte; **~ in mind and body** gesund an Geist und Seele; **~ in wind and limb** kerngesund; **the building was structurally ~:** das Gebäude hatte eine gesunde Bausubstanz; *see also* **bell A 1** **2** (well-founded) vernünftig ‹*Argument, Rat*›; klug ‹*Wahl*›; **it makes ~ sense** es ist sehr vernünftig; **make ~ progress** gute Fortschritte machen **3** (Finance: secure) gesund, solide ‹*Basis*›; klug ‹*Investition*› **4** (competent, reliable) solide ‹*Spieler*›; **have a ~ character** charakterfest sein **5** (undisturbed) tief, gesund ‹*Schlaf*›; **be a ~ sleeper** einen gesunden Schlaf haben **6** (thorough) gehörig (ugs.) ‹*Niederlage, Tracht Prügel*›; gekonnt ‹*Leistung*›

B *adv.* fest, tief ‹*schlafen*›; **fall/be ~ asleep** in einen tiefen *od.* festen Schlaf fallen/tief *od.* fest schlafen

sound[2]

A *n.* **1** (Phys.) Schall, *der;* **the speed of ~:** die Schallgeschwindigkeit **2** (noise) Laut, *der;* (of wind, sea, car, footsteps, breaking glass or twigs) Geräusch, *das;* (of voices, laughter, bell) Klang, *der;* **do sth. without a ~:** etw. lautlos tun **3** (Radio, Telev., Cinemat.) Ton, *der;* **loss of ~:** Tonausfall, *der* **4** (music) Klang, *der;* (jazz, pop, rock) Sound, *der;* **the king entered to the ~ of trumpets** von Trompetenstößen begleitet, trat der König ein; **the ~ of drums** Trommellaute *Pl.* **5** (Phonet.: articulation) Laut, *der* **6** (fig.: impression) **I like the ~ of your plan** ich finde, Ihr Plan hört sich gut an; **I like the ~ of him** was du von ihm erzählst, hört sich gut an; **I don't like the ~ of this** das hört sich nicht gut an **7** *in pl.* (~ waves) Töne **8** (meaningless noise) Wortgeklingel, *das;* Wortschwall, *der* **9** (earshot) **within ~ of sb./sth.** in jmds. Hörweite/in Hörweite einer Sache

B *v.i.* **1** (seem) klingen; **it ~s as if .../like ...:** es klingt, als .../wie ...; **it ~s to me as if .../like ...:** es hört sich für mich an, als .../wie ...; **from his lack of enthusiasm it ~s as if he wanted to give up** nach seinem Mangel an Begeisterung zu urteilen, klingt es so, als wolle er aufgeben; **it ~s to me from what you have said that ...:** was du gesagt hast, klingt für mich so, als ob ...; **that ~s a good idea to me** ich finde, die Idee hört sich gut an; **~s good to me!** klingt gut! (ugs.); gute Idee! (ugs.); **that ~s odd to me** das hört sich seltsam an, finde ich **2** (emit ~) [er]tönen

C *v.t.* **1** (cause to emit ~) ertönen lassen; **~ the trumpet** trompeten; in die Trompete blasen **2** (utter) **~ a note of caution** zur Vorsicht mahnen; **his words ~ed a note of alarm in my mind** seine Worte versetzten mich in Alarmstimmung **3** (pronounce) aussprechen **4** (cause to be heard) **~ sb.'s praises** ein Loblied auf jmdn. singen; **~ a fanfare** eine Fanfare erklingen lassen

Phrasal verb

- **~ 'off** *v.i.* (coll.: talk pompously) tönen (ugs.), schwadronieren (**on, about** von)

sound[3] *n.* **1** (strait) Sund, *der;* Meerenge, *die* **2** (inlet) Meeresarm, *der;* **Plymouth S~:** die Bucht von Plymouth

sound[4] *v.t.* **1** (Naut.: fathom) ausloten; sondieren **2** (fig.: test) ▸ **~ out** **3** (Meteorol.) untersuchen; erforschen; sondieren **4** (Med.) abhorchen

Phrasal verb

- **~ 'out** *v.t.* ausfragen ‹*Person*›; sondieren (geh.), herausbekommen ‹*Sache*›; **~ sb. out on sth.** bei jmdm. wegen etw. vorfühlen

S

sound: ~ archive *n.*, **~ archives** *n.pl.* Tonarchiv, *das;* **~ barrier** *n.* Schallmauer, *die;* **go through** *or* **break the ~ barrier** die Schallmauer durchbrechen; **~ bite** *n.* kurzes, prägnantes Zitat; **~box** *n.* (in violin, guitar, etc.) Resonanzkörper, *der;* **~ broadcasting** *n.*, *no pl.* Hörfunk, *der;* **~ card** *n.* (Computing) Soundkarte, *die;* **~ check** *n.* Soundcheck, *der;* Tonprobe, *die;* **~ effect** *n.* Geräuscheffekt, *der;* **~ engineer** *n.* ▸❶ **p. 1260** (Radio, Telev., Cinemat.) Toningenieur, *der*/-ingenieurin, *die;* **~hole** *n.* (Mus.) Schallloch, *das*

sounding[1] /ˈsaʊndɪŋ/ *adj. in comb.* **strange-/clear-/loud-~:** seltsam/klar/laut [klingend]

sounding[2] *n.* 1 (Naut.: measurement) Lotung, *die;* **take ~s** Lotungen vornehmen; loten 2 (fig.) Sondierung, *die* (geh.); **make ~s in a locality** ein Terrain sondieren; **carry out ~s of public opinion/of interested parties** die öffentliche Meinung sondieren/mit den Beteiligten Sondierungsgespräche führen

sounding: ~ board *n.* 1 (canopy) Schalldeckel, *der;* 2 (Mus.) Decke, *die;* 3 (fig.: means of spreading opinions) Sprachrohr, *das;* 4 (fig.: trial audience) ≈ Testgruppe, *die;* **~ line** *n.* (Naut.) Lotleine, *die;* **~ rod** *n.* (Naut.) Peilstock, *der*

soundless /ˈsaʊndlɪs/ *adj.* lautlos; stumm, tonlos ‹*Sprache, Gebet*›

soundly /ˈsaʊndlɪ/ *adv.* 1 (solidly) stabil, solide ‹*bauen*› 2 (well) vernünftig ‹*argumentieren, urteilen, investieren*› 3 (deeply) tief, fest ‹*schlafen*› 4 (thoroughly) anständig, ordentlich (ugs.) ‹*verhauen*›; vernichtend ‹*schlagen, besiegen*›; **perform ~:** eine gute Leistung zeigen

soundness /ˈsaʊndnɪs/ *n.*, *no pl.* 1 (of mind, body) Gesundheit, *die;* (of construction, structure) Solidität, *die* 2 (of argument) Stichhaltigkeit, *die;* (of policy, views) Vernünftigkeit, *die* 3 (of sleep) Tiefe, *die* 4 (competence, reliability) Solidität, *die* 5 (solvency) wirtschaftliche Gesundheit; Solvenz, *die*

sound: ~ post *n.* (Mus.) Stimmstock, *der;* **~proof** A *adj.* schalldicht; B *v.t.* schalldicht machen; **~proofing** *n.*, *no pl.* Schallisolierung, *die;* **~ recorder** *n.* Tonaufnahmegerät, *das;* **~ shift** ▸**shift C 9**; **~ stage** *n.* (Cinemat.) Tonbühne, *die;* **~ system** *n.* Tonanlage, *die;* **~ technician** ▸**sound engineer**; **~track** *n.* (Cinemat.) Soundtrack, *der;* **~ truck** *n.* (Amer.) Lautsprecherwagen, *der;* **~ wave** *n.* (Phys.) Schallwelle, *die*

soup /suːp/ *n.* Suppe, *die;* **be/land in the ~** (fig. coll.) in der Patsche sitzen/landen (ugs.)

(Phrasal verb)

• **~ ˈup** *v.t.* (Motor Veh. coll.) frisieren (ugs.)

soupçon /ˈsuːpsɔ̃/ *n.* Spur, *die;* (of anger, irony) Anflug, *der;* **a ~ of garlic/grey** eine Spur Knoblauch/von Grau

souped-up /ˈsuːptʌp/ *attrib. adj.* (Motor Veh. coll.) frisiert (ugs.)

soup: ~ kitchen *n.* Volksküche, *die;* Suppenküche, *die;* **~ plate** *n.* Suppenteller, *der;* **~ spoon** *n.* Suppenlöffel, *der*

soupy /ˈsuːpɪ/ *adj.* 1 (thick) sämig ‹*Flüssigkeit*›; trübe, schlammig ‹*Wasser*› 2 (coll.: sentimental) rührselig; sentimental

sour /ˈsaʊə(r)/

A *adj.* 1 (having acid taste) sauer 2 (morose) griesgrämig (abwertend); säuerlich ‹*Blick*› 3 (unpleasant) bitter; **when things go ~:** wenn man *od.* einem alles leid wird; **the place has gone ~ on him** der Ort ist ihm verleidet [worden] 4 (rank) säuerlich ‹*Geruch*› 5 (deficient in lime) sauer ‹*Boden*›. *See also* **grape**

B *v.t.* 1 versauern lassen; sauer machen 2 (fig.: spoil) verbauen ‹*Karriere*›; trüben ‹*Beziehung*› 3 (fig.: make gloomy) verbittern

C *v.i.* 1 sauer werden 2 (deteriorate) ‹*Beziehungen:*› sich trüben

D *n.* (Amer.: cocktail) Sour, *der*

source /sɔːs/ *n.* Quelle, *die;* **~ of income/infection** Einkommensquelle, *die*/Infektionsherd, *der;* **the ~ of all woes** die Wurzel allen Übels; **locate the ~ of a leak** (lit. or fig.) feststellen, wo eine undichte Stelle ist; **the whole thing is a ~ of some embarrassment to us** das Ganze ist für uns ziemlich unangenehm; **at ~:** an der Quelle; **tax deducted at ~:** Quellensteuer, *die;* **my wages are taxed at ~:** die Steuer wird direkt von meinem Lohn abgezogen

source: ~ book *n.* Quellensammlung, *die;* **~ code** *n.* (Computing) Quellcode, *der;* **~ file** *n.* (Computing) Quelldatei, *die;* **~ language** *n.* Ausgangssprache, *die;* **~ program** *n.* (Computing) Quellprogramm, *das*

sour ˈcream *n.* saure Sahne; Sauerrahm, *der*

sourly /ˈsaʊəlɪ/ *adv.* säuerlich

sour: ~puss *n.* (coll.) (male) Miesepeter, der (ugs.); (female) miesepetrige Ziege (ugs.)

sousaphone /ˈsuːzəfəʊn/ *n.* (Mus.) Sousaphon, *das*

souse /saʊs/ *v.t.* 1 (plunge into liquid) eintauchen 2 (soak) **get/be ~d** durchnässt werden/sein 3 (pickle) einlegen

soutane /suːˈtɑːn/ *n.* (RC Ch.) Soutane, *die*

south /saʊθ/ ▸❶ **p. 1013**

A *n.* 1 Süden, *der;* **the ~:** Süd (Met., Seew.); **in/to[wards]/from the ~:** im/nach *od.* (geh.) gen/von Süden; **to the ~ of** südlich von; südlich (+ *Gen.*) 2 *usu.* **S~** (part lying to the ~) Süden, *der;* **from the S~:** aus dem Süden 3 (Cards) Süd

B *adj.* südlich; Süd‹*küste, -wind, -grenze, -tor*›

C *adv.* südwärts; nach Süden; **a ~-facing wall** eine nach Süden gelegene Mauer; **~ of** südlich von; südlich (+ *Gen.*); *see also* **by**[1] **A 4**

South: ~ ˈAfrica *pr. n.* Südafrika (*das*); **~ ˈAfrican** ▸❶ **p. 1345** A *adj.* südafrikanisch; B *n.* Südafrikaner, *der*/-afrikanerin, *die;* **~ Aˈmerica** *pr. n.* Südamerika (*das*); **~ Aˈmerican** ▸❶ **p. 1345** A *adj.* südamerikanisch; B *n.* Südamerikaner, *der*/-amerikanerin, *die*

south: ~bound *adj.* ▸❶ **p. 1013** ‹*Zug usw.*› in Richtung Süden; **~-ˈeast** ▸❶ **p. 1013** A *n.* Südosten, *der;* **in/to[wards]/from the ~-east** im/nach *od.* (geh.) gen/von Südosten; **to the ~-east of** südöstlich von, südöstlich (+ *Gen.*); B *adj.* südöstlich; Südost‹*wind, -fenster, -küste*›; C *adv.* südostwärts; nach Südosten; **~-east of** südöstlich von; südöstlich (+ *Gen.*); **~-ˈeaster** *n.* Südostwind, *der;* **~-ˈeasterly** ▸❶ **p. 1013** A *adj.* südöstlich; B *adv.* (position) im Südosten; (direction) nach Südosten; **~-ˈeastern** *adj.* ▸❶ **p. 1013** südöstlich

southerly /ˈsʌðəlɪ/ ▸❶ **p. 1013**

A *adj.* 1 (in position or direction) südlich; **in a ~ direction** nach Süden 2 (from the south) ‹*Wind*› aus südlichen Richtungen; **the wind was ~:** der Wind kam aus südlichen Richtungen

B *adv.* 1 (in position) südlich; (in direction) südwärts 2 (from the south) aus *od.* von Süd[en]

C *n.* Süd[wind], *der*

southern /ˈsʌðən/ *adj.* ▸❶ **p. 1013** südlich; Süd‹*grenze, -hälfte, -seite, -fenster, -wind*›; südländisch ‹*Temperament*›; **~ Spain** Südspanien; das südliche Spanien; **~ Africa** das südliche Afrika; *see also* **cross A 6**; **hemisphere 1**

southerner /ˈsʌðənə(r)/ *n.* (male) Südengländer/-franzose/-italiener *usw.*, *der;* (female) Südengländerin/-französin/-italienerin *usw.*, *die;* (Amer.) Südstaatler, *der*/-staatlerin, *die;* **he's a ~:** er kommt aus dem Süden

Southern: ~ ˈEurope *pr. n.* Südeuropa (*das*); **~ European** A *adj.* südeuropäisch; B *n.* Südeuropäer, *der*/-europäerin, *die;* **~ ˈIreland** *pr. n.* Südirland (*das*); **s~ ˈlights** *n. pl.* Südlicht, *das*

southernmost /ˈsʌðənməʊst/ *adj.* ▸❶ **p. 1013** südlichst …

South: ~ ˈGerman A *adj.* süddeutsch; B *n.* Süddeutsche, *der/die;* **~ ˈGermany** *pr. n.* Süddeutschland (*das*); **~ Koˈrea** *pr. n.* Südkorea (*das*); **~ Koˈrean** A *adj.* südkoreanisch; B *n.* Südkoreaner, *der*/-koreanerin, *die*

South of ˈEngland *pr. n.* Südengland (*das*); *attrib.* südenglisch

south: ~paw (Boxing coll.) A *n.* Linkshänder, *der*/Linkshänderin, *die;* B *adj.* linkshändig; **S~ ˈPole** *pr. n.* Südpol, *der;* **S~ Sea** *adj.* Südsee-; **S~ Sea Islander** Südseeinsulaner, *der*/-insulanerin, *die;* **S~ ˈSeas** *pr. n. pl.* Südsee, *die;* **~-~-ˈeast** ▸❶ **p. 1013** A *n.* Südsüdosten, *der;* B *adj.* südsüdöstlich; Südsüdost-; C *adv.* südsüdostwärts; **~-~-ˈwest** ▸❶ **p. 1013** A *n.* Südsüdwesten, *der;* B *adj.* südsüdwestlich; Südsüdwest-; C *adv.* südsüdwestwärts

southward /ˈsaʊθwəd/ ▸❶ **p. 1013**

A *adj.* nach Süden gerichtet; (situated towards the south) südlich; **in a ~ direction** nach Süden; [in] Richtung Süden

B *adv.* südwärts; **they are ~ bound** sie fahren nach *od.* [in] Richtung Süden

C *n.* Süden, *der*

southwards /ˈsaʊθwədz/ ▸❶ **p. 1013** ▸**southward B**

south: ~-ˈwest ▸❶ **p. 1013** A *n.* Südwesten, *der;* **in/to[wards]/from the ~-west** im/nach *od.* (geh.) gen/von Südwesten; **to the ~-west of** südwestlich von; südwestlich (+ *Gen.*). B *adj.* südwestlich; Südwest‹*wind, -fenster, -küste*›. C *adv.* südwestwärts; nach Südwesten; **~-west of** südwestlich von; südwestlich (+ *Gen.*); **S~-West ˈAfrica** *pr. n.* Südwestafrika, (*das*); **~wester** /saʊθˈwestə(r)/ *n.* Südwestwind, *der;* **~-ˈwesterly** ▸❶ **p. 1013** A *adj.* südwestlich; B *adv.* (position) im Südwesten; (direction) nach Südwesten; **~-ˈwestern** *adj.* ▸❶ **p. 1013** südwestlich

souvenir /suːvəˈnɪə(r)/ *n.* (of holiday) Andenken, *das;* Souvenir, *das* (**of** aus); (of wedding day, one's youth, etc.) Andenken, *das* (**of** an + *Akk.*)

souveˈnir shop *n.* Souvenirladen, *der*

souˈwester /saʊˈwestə(r)/ *n.* 1 (hat) Südwester, *der* 2 (coat) Ölhaut, *die*

sovereign /ˈsɒvrɪn/

A *n.* 1 (ruler) Souverän, *der* 2 (Brit. Hist.: coin) Sovereign, *der;* 20-Shilling-Münze, *die*

B *adj.* 1 (independent) souverän ‹*Staat, Volk*› 2 (supreme) höchst… 3 (arch.: royal) souverän 4 (very good) ausgezeichnet ‹*Medikament*›

sovereignty /ˈsɒvrɪntɪ/ *n.* 1 (supreme power) Souveränität, *die;* Oberhoheit, *die* 2 (royal position) Stellung als Souverän 3 (autonomous state) souveräner Staat

Soviet /ˈsəʊvɪət, ˈsɒvɪət/ (Hist.)

A *adj.* sowjetisch; Sowjet‹*bürger, -literatur, -kultur, -ideologie*›

B *n.* Sowjet, *der;* **Supreme ~:** Oberster Sowjet

Soviet: ~ ˈRussia *pr. n.* (Hist.) Sowjetrussland (*das*); **~ ˈUnion** *pr. n.* (Hist.) Sowjetunion, *die*

sow[1] /səʊ/ *v.t.*, *p.p.* **sown** /səʊn/ *or* **sowed** /səʊd/ 1 (plant) [aus]säen; (fig.) legen ‹*Minen*› 2 (plant with seed) einsäen, besäen ‹*Feld, Boden*› 3 (cover thickly) spicken (ugs.); **meadows ~n with daisies** mit Gänseblümchen bedeckte Wiesen 4 (fig.: initiate) säen. *See also* **oat 2**; **seed A 3**; **whirlwind 1**

sow[2] /saʊ/ *n.* 1 (female pig) Sau, *die* 2 (Metallurgy) (trough) Kokille, *die;* (block of iron) Massel, *die. See also* **silk B**

sower /ˈsəʊə(r)/ *n.* Sämann, *der*/Säerin, *die;* **be a ~ of discord** Zwietracht säen

sowing /ˈsəʊɪŋ/ *n.* Säen, *das;* Aussaat, *die*

sown ▸**sow**[1]

sox /sɒks/ *n. pl.* (Commerc./coll.) ▸**sock**[1] **1**

soya /ˈsɔɪə/ *n.*, *no pl.* (Brit.) 1 Soja, *die* 2 (soya sauce) Sojasoße, *die*

soya [bean] /ˈsɔɪə (biːn)/ *n.* 1 (plant) Soja[bohne], *die* 2 (seed) Sojabohne, *die*

soya ˈsauce *n.* Sojasoße, *die*

soy: ~ bean ▸ **soya bean**; **~ sauce** /ˈsɔɪ sɔːs/ *n.* Sojasoße, *die*

sozzled /ˈsɒzld/ *adj.* (coll.) voll (ugs.); besoffen (derb); **get ~:** sich besaufen (derb)

spa /spɑː/ *n.* 1 (place) Bad, *das;* Badeort, *der* 2 (spring) Mineralquelle, *die*

space /speɪs/

A *n.* 1 Raum, *der;* **stare into ~:** in die Luft *od.* ins Leere starren 2 (interval between points) Platz, *der;* **the houses are separated by a ~ of ten feet** die Häuser sind durch einen 10 Fuß breiten Zwischenraum getrennt; **clear a ~:** Platz schaffen; **he needs ~** (fig.) er braucht Bewegungsfreiheit 3 (area on page) Platz, *der* 4 **the wide open ~s** das weite, flache Land; **the vast ~s of the prairie/desert** die weite

S

Fläche *od.* die Weite[n] der Prärie/Wüste **5** (Astron.) Weltraum, *der; see also* **outer space** **6** (blank between words) Zwischenraum, *der;* Spatium, *das* (Druckw.); **five ~s from the left margin** fünf Anschläge vom linken Rand [entfernt] **7** (interval of time) Zeitraum, *der;* **in the ~ of a minute/an hour** *etc.* innerhalb einer Minute/Stunde *usw.;* **in a short ~ of time he was back** nach kurzer Zeit war er zurück

B *v.t.* **the line is/the letters are badly ~d** die Zeile ist/die Buchstaben sind schlecht spationiert (Druckw.); **the posts are ~d at intervals of one metre** die Pfosten sind im Abstand von einem Meter aufgestellt

Phrasal verb

• **~ 'out** *v.t.* verteilen; **~ the figures out clearly** die Zahlen so weit auseinander schreiben, dass sie deutlich lesbar sind

space: ~ age *n.* [Welt]raumzeitalter, *das;* Zeitalter der Raumfahrt, *das;* **~ bar** *n.* Leertaste, *die;* **~ blanket** *n.* Rettungsdecke, *die;* **~ capsule** *n.* Raumkapsel, *die;* **~craft** *n.* Raumfahrzeug, *das;* (unmanned) Raumsonde, *die*

spaced [out] /speɪst ('aʊt)/ *adj.* (coll.) high (Drogenjargon)

space: ~ exploration *n., no pl.* Weltraumerkundung, *die;* **interplanetary ~ exploration** die Erkundung des interplanetaren Raums; **~ flight** *n.* **1** (a journey through ~) [Welt]raumflug, *der;* **2** ▸ **~ travel**; **~ heater** *n.* Heizgerät, *das;* **~ industry** *n.* Raumfahrtindustrie, *die;* **~ lab** (coll.), **~ laboratory** *ns.* [Welt]raumlabor, *das;* **~man** ▸ **~ traveller**; **~ medicine** *n., no pl.* Raumfahrtmedizin, *die;* **~ opera** *n.* (esp. Amer.) Weltraumoper, *die* (ugs.); **~ platform** *n.* Weltraumplattform, *die;* **~ probe** *n.* Raumsonde, *die;* **~ programme** *n.* Weltraumprogramm, *das;* **~ race** *n.* Wettlauf im All; **~-saving** *adj.* Platz sparend; Raum sparend; **~ science** *n., no pl.* Weltraumwissenschaft, *die;* **~ scientist** *n.* ▸ **ⓘ p. 1260** Weltraumwissenschaftler, *der*/-wissenschaftlerin, *die;* **~ship** *n.* Raumschiff, *das;* **~ shot** *n.* Weltraummission, *die;* **~ shuttle** *n.* Raumfähre, *die;* Raumtransporter, *der;* **~ station** *n.* [Welt]raumstation, *die;* **~suit** *n.* Raumanzug, *der;* **~ technology** *n., no pl.* Raumfahrttechnik, *die;* **~ telescope** *n.* Weltraumteleskop, *das;* **~-'time** *n.* (Phys.) Raum-Zeit-Welt, *die;* **~ travel** *n., no pl.* Raumfahrt, *die;* **~ traveller** *n.* Raumfahrer, *der*/-fahrerin, *die;* **~ vehicle** ▸ **spacecraft**; **~ walk** *n.* Spaziergang im All

spacial, spacially ▸ **spatial, spatially**

spacing /'speɪsɪŋ/ *n.* Zwischenraum, *der;* (Printing) Sperrungen; Spationierung, *die* (Druckw.); **single/double ~:** einfacher/doppelter Zeilenabstand

spacious /'speɪʃəs/ *adj.* **1** (vast in area) weitläufig ‹*Garten, Park, Ländereien*› **2** (roomy) geräumig ‹*Raum*›; breit ‹*Straße*›

spaciously /'speɪʃəslɪ/ *adv.* weitläufig

spade /speɪd/ *n.* **1** (for digging) Spaten, *der;* **call a ~ a ~** *or* (joc.) **a bloody shovel** das Kind beim [rechten] Namen nennen (ugs.); **she was never afraid to call a ~ a ~:** sie nahm nie ein Blatt vor den Mund (ugs.); **in ~s** in höchstem Maße; **have sth. in ~s** etw. in höchstem Maße haben *od.* besitzen; **pay sb. back in ~s** es jmdm. doppelt heimzahlen **2** (Cards) Pik, *das; see also* **club A 4** **3** (sl. offensive) Neger, *der*

spadeful /'speɪdfʊl/ *n.* **a ~/two ~s of soil** ein/zwei Spaten [voll] Erde

'spadework *n.* (fig.) Kleinarbeit, *die;* (preliminary work) Vorarbeit, *die*

spadix /'speɪdɪks/ *n., pl.* **spadices** /'speɪdɪsiːz/ (Bot.) Kolben, *der*

spaghetti /spə'getɪ/ *n.* **1** Spaghetti *Pl.* **2** (joc.: cables) Kabelsalat, *der* (ugs.)

spaghetti 'Western *n.* (Cinemat.) Italowestern, *der*

Spain /speɪn/ *pr. n.* Spanien (*das*)

spall /spɔːl/

A *v.t.* **1** (chip) absplittern **2** (Mining) mit dem Hammer zerkleinern ‹*Erz*›

B *v.i.* splittern

C *n.* Splitter, *der*

spam /spæm/ *n.* **1** **S~** ® Frühstücksfleisch, *das;* **2** (Computing) Spam, *der; attrib.* **~ filter** Spamfilter, *der*

spammer /'spæmə(r)/ *n.* (Computing) Spammer, *der*/Spammerin, *die*

spamming /'spæmɪŋ/ *n., no pl.* (Computing) Spamming, *das*

span[1] /spæn/

A *n.* **1** (full extent) Spanne, *die;* **~ of life/time** Lebens-/Zeitspanne, *die;* **throughout the whole ~ of Roman history** in der gesamten römischen Geschichte **2** (of bridge) Spannweite, *die;* **the bridge crosses the river in a single ~:** die Brücke überspannt den Fluss in einem einzigen Bogen **3** (Aeronaut.) Spannweite, *die* **4** (of hand) Spanne, *die*

B *v.t.*, **-nn-** **1** (extend across) überspannen ‹*Fluss*›; umfassen ‹*Zeitraum*› **2** (measure) nach Spannen messen

span[2] ▸ **spick**

spandrel /'spændrl/ *n.* (Archit.) [Bogen]zwickel, *der;* Spandrille, *die*

spang /spæŋ/ *adv.* (Amer. coll.) ganz; **~ in the middle of the night/the road** mitten in der Nacht/auf der Straße

spangle /'spæŋgl/

A *n.* ▸ **sequin**

B *v.t.* **~d with stars/buttercups** von glitzernden Sternen/mit leuchtenden Butterblumen übersät; *see also* **star-spangled**

Spaniard /'spænjəd/ *n.* ▸ **ⓘ p. 1345** Spanier, *der*/Spanierin, *die*

spaniel /'spænjəl/ *n.* Spaniel, *der*

Spanish /'spænɪʃ/ ▸ **ⓘ p. 1277**, ▸ **ⓘ p. 1345**

A *adj.* spanisch; **sb. is ~:** jmd. ist Spanier/Spanierin; *see also* **English A**

B *n.* **1** (language) Spanisch, *das; see also* **English B 1** **2** *constr. as pl.* (people) Spanier

Spanish: ~ A'merica *pr. n.: die spanischsprachigen Länder Lateinamerikas;* **~ 'fly** *n.* Spanische Fliege; **~ 'Main** *pr. n.:* (Hist.) **the ~ Main** *die Nordostküste Südamerikas zwischen dem Orinoko und Panama sowie der angrenzende Teil der Karibik;* **~ 'omelette** *n.: Omelette mit Zwiebeln, grünem Paprika und Tomaten;* ≈ Omelette andalusische Art (Kochk.); **~ 'onion** *n.* spanische Zwiebel; Bermudazwiebel, *die* (Kochk.)

spank /spæŋk/

A *n.* ≈ Klaps, *der* (ugs.)

B *v.t.* **~ sb.** jmdm. den Hintern versohlen (ugs.); **get ~ed** den Hintern voll kriegen (ugs.)

C *v.i.* ‹*Pferd:*› schnell traben

spanking /'spæŋkɪŋ/

A *n.* Tracht Prügel, *die* (ugs.); (for sexual gratification) Hinternversohlen, *das* (ugs.)

B *adj.* (coll.) scharf ‹*Trab, Lauf, Galopp, Tempo*›

C *adv.* (coll.) **~ new** funkelnagelneu (ugs.)

spanner /'spænə(r)/ *n.* (Brit.) Schraubenschlüssel, *der;* **put** *or* **throw a ~ in the works** (fig.) Sand ins Getriebe streuen

'span roof *n.* Satteldach, *das*

spar[1] /spɑː(r)/ *v.i.*, **-rr-** **1** (Boxing) sparren **2** (fig.: argue) [sich] zanken

spar[2] *n.* **1** (pole) Rundholz, *das;* Spiere, *die* (Seemannsspr.) **2** (Aeronaut.) Holm, *der*

spar[3] *n.* (Min.) Spat, *der*

spare /speə(r)/

A *adj.* **1** (not in use) übrig; **~ time/moment** Freizeit, *die*/freier Augenblick; **not have ~ cash** kein Bargeld [übrig] haben; **have sth. going ~** (coll.) etwas übrig haben; **there is one ~ seat** ein Platz ist noch frei; **are there any ~ tickets for Friday?** gibt es noch Karten für Freitag? **2** (for use when needed) zusätzlich, Extra‹*bett, -tasse*›; **~ room** Gästezimmer, *das;* **go ~** (Brit. coll.: be very angry) durchdrehen (salopp) **3** (frugal) karg ‹*Kost, Mahlzeit*› **4** (lean) schlank ‹*Wuchs, Gestalt*› **5** schlicht ‹*Stil*›

B *n.* Ersatzteil, *das*/-reifen, *der usw.;* **I haven't got a pen; have you a ~?** ich hab keinen Stift, hast du einen übrig?

C *v.t.* **1** (do without) entbehren; **can you ~ me a moment?** hast du einen Augenblick Zeit für mich?; **we arrived with ten minutes to ~:** wir kamen zehn Minuten früher an; als wir ankamen, hatten wir noch zehn Minuten Zeit [übrig] **2** (not inflict on) **~ sb. sth.** jmdm. etw. ersparen **3** (not hurt) [ver]schonen; **if I am ~d** wenn ich so lange lebe **4** (not cause) **~ sb.'s blushes** jmdm. die Verlegenheit *od.* Peinlichkeit ersparen **5** (fail to use) **not ~ any expense/pains** *or* **efforts** keine Kosten/Mühe scheuen; **no expense ~d** an nichts gespart; **not ~ oneself in one's efforts to ...:** keine Mühe scheuen ... *See also* **enough B**; **rod 3**

sparely /'speəlɪ/ *adv.* **~ built** schlank [gebaut]

spare: ~ 'part *n.* Ersatzteil, *das;* **~ rib** *n.* **1** (cut of meat) Kamm, *der;* **2** (dish) [Schäl]rippchen, *das;* **~ 'tyre** *n.* **1** Reserve-, Ersatzreifen, *der;* **2** (Brit. fig. coll.) Rettungsring, *der* (ugs.); **~ 'wheel** *n.* Ersatzrad, *das*

sparing /'speərɪŋ/ *adj.* sparsam; **be ~ of sth./in the use of sth.** mit etw. sparsam umgehen

sparingly /'speərɪŋlɪ/ *adv.* sparsam

spark /spɑːk/

A *n.* **1** Funke, *der;* **shower of ~s** Funkenregen, *der;* **the ~s [begin to] fly** (fig.) es funkt (ugs.); **a ~ of generosity/decency** (fig.) ein Funke[n] Großzügigkeit/Anstand; **not a ~ of life remained** (fig.) keine Spur von Leben blieb übrig **2** (electrical discharge) Funkenentladung, *die* **3** (in sparking plug) Zündfunke[n], *der* (Kfz-W.) **4** **a bright ~** (clever person; also iron.) ein schlauer Kopf

B *v.t.* ▸ **spark off**

C *v.i.* **1** Funken sprühen **2** (Electr.) funken

Phrasal verb

• **~ 'off** *v.t.* **1** (cause to explode) zünden **2** (fig.: start) auslösen

'spark gap *n.* (Electr.) Funkenstrecke, *die*

sparking plug /'spɑːkɪŋ plʌg/ *n.* (Brit. Motor Veh.) Zündkerze, *die*

sparkle /'spɑːkl/

A *v.i.* **1** (flash) ‹*Diamant, Tautropfen:*› glitzern; ‹*Augen:*› funkeln, sprühen **2** (perform brilliantly) glänzen **3** (be lively) sprühen (**with** vor + *Dat.*)

B *n.* Glitzern, *das;* Funkeln, *das;* **he lost all his ~** (fig.) er hat sein sprühendes Temperament verloren

sparkler /'spɑːklə(r)/ *n.* **1** (firework) Wunderkerze, *die* **2** (coll.: diamond) Klunker, *der* (ugs.)

sparkling /'spɑːklɪŋ/ *adj.* **1** (flashing) glitzernd ‹*Stein, Diamant*› **2** (bright) funkelnd ‹*Augen*›; **~ vivacity** sprühende Lebhaftigkeit **3** (brilliant) glänzend ‹*Schauspiel, Aufführung, Rede*›

sparkling 'wine *n.* Schaumwein, *der*

'spark plug ▸ **sparking plug**

'sparring partner *n.* (Boxing) Sparringspartner, *der;* **this is my old ~** (fig.) dies ist mein alter Freund, mit dem ich oft die Klingen gekreuzt habe (geh.)

sparrow /'spærəʊ/ *n.* Sperling, *der;* Spatz, *der;* **house ~:** Haussperling, *der;* Hausspatz, *der; see also* **hedge sparrow**

'sparrowhawk *n.* Sperber, *der*

sparse /spɑːs/ *adj.* spärlich; dünn ‹*Besiedlung*›

sparsely /'spɑːslɪ/ *adv.* spärlich; dünn ‹*besiedelt*›

sparseness /'spɑːsnɪs/, **sparsity** /'spɑːsɪtɪ/ *ns., no pl.* Spärlichkeit, *die*

Spartan /'spɑːtn/

A *adj.* spartanisch

B *n.* Spartaner, *der*/Spartanerin, *die*

spasm /'spæzm/ *n.* **1** Krampf, *der;* Spasmus, *der* (Med.) **2** (convulsive movement) Anfall, *der;* **~ of coughing** Hustenanfall, *der* **3** (coll.) **a ~ of activity** plötzliche fieberhafte Aktivität

spasmodic /spæz'mɒdɪk/ *adj.* **1** (marked by spasms) krampfartig; spasmodisch (Med.) **2** (intermittent) sporadisch ‹*Anwachsen, Bemühungen*›

spasmodically /spæz'mɒdɪkəlɪ/ *adv.* **1** krampfartig, (Med.) spasmodisch ‹*zucken*› **2** (intermittently) sporadisch

spastic /'spæstɪk/ (Med.)

A *n.* Spastiker, *der*/Spastikerin, *die*

B *adj.* spastisch [gelähmt]

spat[1] ▸ **spit**[1] **A, B**

spat[2] /spæt/ *n.* (gaiter) Gamasche, *die*

spat[3] *n.* (coll.: quarrel) Krach, *der* (ugs.)

S

spate /speɪt/ *n.* 1 ▸ℹ p. 1491 (flood) **the river/waterfall is in [full]** ~: der Fluss/Wasserfall führt Hochwasser 2 (fig.: large amount) **a ~ of sth.** eine Flut von etw.; **a ~ of burglaries** eine Einbruchsserie

spatial /ˈspeɪʃl/ *adj.*, **spatially** /ˈspeɪʃəlɪ/ *adv.* räumlich

spatter /ˈspætə(r)/

A *v.t.* spritzen ‹*Lehm, Wasser*›; **~ sb./sth. with sth.** jmdn./etw. mit etw. bespritzen

B *n.* Spritzer, *der*

spatula /ˈspætjʊlə/ *n.* 1 Spachtel, *die* 2 (Surg.) Spatel, *der od. die*

spatulate /ˈspætjʊlət/ *adj.* spatelförmig

spawn /spɔːn/

A *v.t.* 1 (produce) ablegen ‹*Eier*›; (fig.) hervorbringen 2 (derog.: breed) produzieren

B *v.i.* laichen

C *n., constr. as sing. or pl.* 1 (Zool.) Laich, *der* 2 (derog.: offspring) Brut, *die* (salopp abwertend)

spay /speɪ/ *v.t.* sterilisieren ‹*Katze, Hündin*›

speak /spiːk/

A *v.i.*, **spoke** /spəʊk/, **spoken** /ˈspəʊkn/ 1 ▸ℹ p. 1277 sprechen; **we spoke this morning** wir sprachen heute Morgen miteinander; **~ with sb.** mit jmdm. sprechen; **~ [with sb.] on** *or* **about sth.** [mit jmdm.] über etwas (*Akk.*) sprechen; **~ for/against sth.** sich für/gegen etw. aussprechen; **sth. ~s well for sb.** etw. spricht für jmdn.; **~ing as a trade unionist/a European** als Gewerkschafter/Europäer; **the minister rose to ~**: der Minister erhob sich, um das Wort zu ergreifen 2 (on telephone) **Is Mr Grant there? — Speaking!** Ist Mister Grant da? — Am Apparat!; **Mr Grant ~ing** (when connected to caller) Grant hier; hier ist Grant; **who is ~ing, please?** wer ist am Apparat, bitte?; mit wem spreche ich, bitte? *see also* **manner 1**; **so[1] B**

B *v.t.*, **spoke, spoken** 1 (utter) sprechen ‹*Satz, Wort, Sprache*› 2 (make known) sagen ‹*Wahrheit*›; **~ one's opinion/mind** seine Meinung sagen; sagen, was man denkt 3 (convey without words) **sth. ~s volumes** etw. spricht Bände; **sth. ~s volumes for sth.** etw. spricht sehr für etw.

Phrasal verbs

- **~ for** *v.t.* sprechen für; **~ for oneself** für sich selbst sprechen; **~ing for myself, I prefer tea to coffee** ich selber trinke lieber Tee als Kaffee; **~ for yourself!** das ist [nur] deine Meinung!; **~ for itself/themselves** für sich selbst sprechen; **We're all depressed — S~ for yourself!** Wir sind alle deprimiert. — Du vielleicht, ich nicht!; **sth. is spoken for** (reserved) etw. ist schon vergeben
- **~ of** *v.t.* sprechen von; **~ing of Mary** da wir gerade von Mary sprechen; apropos Mary; **nothing to ~ of** nichts Besonderes *od.* Nennenswertes; **no trees to ~ of** kaum Bäume; **these tyres have no tread to ~ of** bei diesen Reifen kann man kaum noch von Profil sprechen; *see also* **devil A 3**
- **~ ˈout** *v.i.* seine Meinung sagen; seine Stimme erheben; **~ out against sth.** seine Stimme gegen etw. erheben; sich gegen etw. aussprechen
- **~ to** *v.t.* 1 (address) sprechen mit; reden mit; **I know him to ~ to** ich kenne ihn [nur] flüchtig; **~ when** *or* **don't ~ until you are spoken to** rede nur, wenn du gefragt wirst 2 (request action from) **~ to sb. about sth.** mit jmdm. wegen einer Sache *od.* über etw. (*Akk.*) sprechen 3 (coll.: reprove) **~ to sb.** sich mit jmdm. unterhalten (verhüllend) 4 **~ to a subject** sich zu einem Thema äußern 5 (~ in confirmation of) **I can ~ to his having been there** ich kann bestätigen *od.* bezeugen, dass er dort war
- **~ ˈup** *v.i.* 1 (~ more loudly) lauter sprechen 2 ▸ **~ out**

ˈspeakeasy *n.* (Amer. Hist. coll.) *Lokal, in dem illegal Alkohol ausgeschenkt wurde*

speaker /ˈspiːkə(r)/ *n.* 1 (in public) Redner, *der*/Rednerin, *die*; **be a/the ~ for** *or* **at an event** bei einem Anlass eine/die Rede halten 2 (of a language) Sprecher, *der*/Sprecherin, *die*; **be a French ~, be a ~ of French** Französisch sprechen 3 **S~** (Polit.) Sprecher, *der*; ≈ Parlamentspräsident, *der*; **Mr S~**: Herr Vorsitzender; *see also* **catch A 6** 4 ▸ **loudspeaker**

> **Speaker**
>
> Der Sprecher oder die Sprecherin des britischen Unterhauses leitet die Debatten, entscheidet wer als nächster zu Wort kommt, ruft zu Abstimmungen auf, und sorgt generell für Ruhe und Ordnung im Haus. Er oder sie wird vom Premierminister und den Abgeordneten gewählt. Die traditionelle Rolle des Sprechers, dessen Amt sich bis ins 13. Jahrhundert zurückverfolgen lässt, verpflichtet den Sprecher oder die Sprecherin zu parteipolitischer Neutralität. Die offizielle Anrede während einer Debatte ist *Mr Speaker* oder *Madam Speaker*.

> **Speaker of the House**
>
> Der Sprecher des **House of Representatives** wird von der Mehrheitspartei gestellt. Er ist der Führer seiner Partei und hat eine starke Stellung im Repräsentantenhaus, besonders bei der Wahl von Ausschussmitgliedern. Er ruft Versammlungen zur Ordnung und erteilt Abgeordneten das Wort. Die offizielle Anrede während einer Debatte ist *Mr Speaker* oder *Madam Speaker*.

speaking /ˈspiːkɪŋ/

A *n.* 1 (talking) Sprechen, *das*; **a good ~ voice** eine gute Sprechstimme; **not be on ~ terms with sb.** nicht [mehr] mit jmdm. reden 2 (speech-making) Rede, *die*; *see also* **public speaking**

B *adv.* **strictly/roughly/generally/legally ~**: genau genommen/grob gesagt/im Allgemeinen/aus juristischer Sicht; **figuratively ~**: bildlich gesprochen

speaking: ~ acquaintance *n.* [flüchtige] Bekannte, *der/die*; **~ ˈclock** *n.* (Brit.) telefonische Zeitansage; **~ tube** *n.*: *Sprechverbindung zwischen zwei Räumen, Gebäuden usw. mittels einer Rohrleitung*; Sprachrohr, *das*

spear /spɪə(r)/

A *n.* 1 Speer, *der* 2 (of plant) Stange, *die*

B *v.t.* aufspießen

spear: ~head A *n.* (fig.) Speerspitze, *die*; (Mil.) Angriffsspitze, *die*; **B** *v.t.* (fig.) **~head sth.** etw. anführen; die Speerspitze von etw. bilden (bes. Pol.); (Mil.) bei etw. die Angriffsspitze bilden; **~mint** *n.* Grüne Minze; **~mint sweet/chewing gum** Pfefferminzbonbon/-kaugummi, *der od. das*

spec[1] /spek/ *n.* (coll.: speculation) Spekulation, *die*; **on ~**: auf gut Glück; auf Verdacht (ugs.)

spec[2] /spek/ (coll.) ▸ **specification 1**

special /ˈspeʃl/

A *adj.* speziell; besonder...; Sonder‹*korrespondent, -zug, -mission, -behandlung, -ausgabe, -bedeutung, -auftrag*›; **nobody ~**: niemand Besonderes; **her own ~ way** ihre eigene Art; **a ~ occasion** ein besonderer Anlass; **a very ~ relationship** eine besonders enge Beziehung; **~ friend** besonders enger Freund/enge Freundin

B *n.* (feature, programme) Special, *das*; Spezial, *das*; (newspaper) Sonderausgabe, *die*; (train) Sonderzug, *der*

special: ~ ˈagent *n.* Spezialagent, *der*/-agentin, *die*; **S~ Branch** *n.* (Brit. Police) *Abteilung der britischen Polizei, deren Aufgabe die Wahrung der inneren Sicherheit ist*; ≈ Sicherheitsdienst, *der*; **~ ˈcase** *n.* Sonderfall, *der*; **~ ˈconstable** *n.* (Brit. Police) Hilfspolizist, *der*/-polizistin, *die*; **~ correspondent** *n.* Sonderkorrespondent, *der*/-korrespondentin, *die*; Sonderberichterstatter, *der*/-berichterstatterin, *die*; **~ deˈlivery** *n.* (Post) Eilzustellung, *die*; **~ ˈdrawing rights** *n. pl.* (Finance) Sonderziehungsrechte *Pl.* [auf den Internationalen Währungsfonds]; **~ eˈdition** *n.* Sonderausgabe, *die*; **~ efˈfects** *n. pl.* (Cinemat.) Special effects *Pl.* (fachspr.); Spezialeffekte; **~-ˈinterest** *attrib. adj.* Special-Interest-; **~-interest group** Interessengruppe, *die*; **~ interest holiday** *n.* Hobbyurlaub, *der*

specialisation, specialise ▸ **specializ-**

specialism /ˈspeʃəlɪzm/ *n.* 1 ▸ **specialization** 2 (field of study) Spezialgebiet, *das*

specialist /ˈspeʃəlɪst/ *n.* 1 Spezialist, *der*/Spezialistin, *die* (**in** für); Fachmann, *der*/Fachfrau, *die* (**in** für); **an eighteenth-century ~**: ein Spezialist für das achtzehnte Jahrhundert; **~ knowledge** Fachwissen, *das* 2 (Med.) Facharzt, *der*/-ärztin, *die*; **eye/heart/cancer ~**: Augenarzt/Herz-/Krebsspezialist, *der*

speciality /speʃɪˈælɪtɪ/ *n.* 1 (activity, skill, product) Spezialität, *die*; (interest) Spezialgebiet, *das*; **she makes a ~ of her pies** Pasteten sind ihre Spezialität 2 (special feature) [besonderes] Merkmal *od.* Kennzeichen

specialization /speʃəlaɪˈzeɪʃn/ *n.* Spezialisierung, *die*

specialize /ˈspeʃəlaɪz/

A *v.i.* sich spezialisieren (**in** auf + *Akk.*)

B *v.t.* (Biol.: modify) **become ~d** ‹*Glied, Organ:*› sich gesondert ausbilden

specialized /ˈspeʃəlaɪzd/ *adj.* 1 (requiring detailed knowledge) speziell; Spezial‹*kenntnisse, -gebiet*› 2 (concentrating on small area) spezialisiert

special ˈlicence *n.* (Brit.) *Sondererlaubnis, die die Heirat ohne Aufgebot oder an einem anderen als dem gewöhnlichen Ort zulässt*

specially /ˈspeʃəlɪ/ *adv.* 1 speziell; **make sth. ~**: etw. speziell *od.* extra anfertigen; **~ made/chosen for me** eigens für mich gemacht/ausgewählt; **a ~ made wheelchair/lift** ein spezieller Rollstuhl/Lift; **a ~ adapted bus** ein spezieller Bus 2 (especially) besonders

special: ~ ˈneeds *n.* **children with ~ needs, ~ needs children** Kinder, die besonders betreut werden müssen; **~ ˈoffer** *n.* Sonderangebot, *das*; **have a ~ offer on sth.** etw. im Sonderangebot haben; **on ~ offer** im Sonderangebot; **~ ˈpleading** *n.* 1 (biased argument) Rechtsverdrehung, *die* (abwertend); 2 (Law) *Plädoyer, das die Umstände eines Falles besonders berücksichtigt*; **~ school** *n.* Sonderschule, *die*

specialty /ˈspeʃltɪ/ (esp. Amer.) ▸ **speciality 1**

speciation /spiːsɪˈeɪʃn, spiːʃɪˈeɪʃn/ *n.* (Biol.) Art[en]bildung, *die*

specie /ˈspiːʃiː, ˈspiːʃɪ/ *n.* Hartgeld, *das*

species /ˈspiːʃiːz, ˈspiːʃɪz/ *n., pl. same* 1 (Biol.) Spezies, *die* (fachspr.); Art, *die* 2 (sort) Art, *die*; **a dangerous ~ of criminal** ein gefährlicher Typ [von] Verbrecher

ˈspecies barrier *n.* (Biol.) Artenbarriere, *die*; Artengrenze, *die*

specific /spɪˈsɪfɪk/

A *adj.* 1 (definite) deutlich, klar ‹*Aussage*›; bestimmt ‹*Ziel, Grund*›; **make a ~ request** einen bestimmten Wunsch äußern; **make no ~ preparations** keine besonderen Vorbereitungen treffen; **could you be more ~?** kannst du dich genauer ausdrücken? 2 (of a species) **the ~ name of a plant** der Name einer Pflanzenart 3 (individual) eigen (**to** *Dat.*); typisch (**to** für); *see also* **gravity 4**; **heat A 2**

B *n.* 1 (arch. Med.: remedy) Spezifikum, *das* 2 *in pl.* (details) Einzelheiten *Pl.*; Details *Pl.*

specifically /spɪˈsɪfɪkəlɪ/ *adv.* ausdrücklich; eigens; extra (ugs.)

specification /spesɪfɪˈkeɪʃn/ *n.* 1 *often pl.* (details) technische Daten; (instructions) Konstruktionsplan, *der*; (for building) Baubeschreibung, *die* 2 (specifying) Spezifizierung, *die* (geh.) 3 **[patent] ~**: Patentschrift, *die*

specificity /spesɪˈfɪsɪtɪ/ *n.* Genauigkeit im Detail

specify /ˈspesɪfaɪ/ *v.t.* (name expressly) ausdrücklich sagen; ausdrücklich nennen ‹*Namen*›; (include in specifications) [genau] aufführen; **as specified above** wie oben aufgeführt; **unless otherwise specified** wenn nicht anders angegeben; **'other (please ~)'** „andere (bitte genaue Angaben machen)"

specimen /ˈspesɪmən/ *n.* 1 (example) Exemplar, *das*; **a ~ of his handwriting** eine Schriftprobe von ihm; **some ~s of her work** ein paar Arbeitsproben von ihr; **~ signature** Unterschriftsprobe, *die* 2 (sample) Probe, *die*; **a ~ of his urine was required** es wurde eine

ℹ Speed

In Germany, as in the rest of continental Europe, the speed of road, rail and air traffic is measured in kilometres per hour, for which kph is the usual British abbreviation, and km/h the abbreviation used on the continent and now also found in some English-language publications:

100 kph = 62.14 mph 100 mph ≈ 160 kph
50 mph ≈ 80 kph

... miles per hour
= ... Meilen in der *or* pro Stunde

... kilometres per hour
= ... Kilometer in der *or* pro Stunde, Stundenkilometer (*coll.*)

100 miles per hour (mph)
≈ 160 Kilometer in der *or* pro Stunde (km/h)

How fast was the car going?, What speed was the car doing?
= Wie schnell *or* Mit welcher Geschwindigkeit fuhr der Wagen?

He was driving flat out/at full speed/at 50 miles per hour
≈ Er fuhr mit Vollgas/mit Höchstgeschwindigkeit/mit 80 Kilometern pro Stunde

It was going at or doing 75 [miles per hour]
≈ Es fuhr mit 120 Stundenkilometern *or* (*coll.*) Sachen

The car's top speed is 125 [mph]
≈ Die Höchstgeschwindigkeit des Autos liegt bei 200 km/h, Das Auto fährt 200 Kilometer Spitze (*coll.*)

You were exceeding the speed limit
= Sie haben das Tempolimit überschritten

They were tearing along/going at a crazy speed
= Sie rasten dahin/fuhren mit rasender Geschwindigkeit *or* in rasendem Tempo

We had to go at a crawl/were reduced to a crawl
= Wir mussten im Kriechtempo fahren/kamen nur im Kriechtempo vorwärts

Speed of light and sound

The speed of sound is 330 metres per second
= Die Schallgeschwindigkeit beträgt 330 Meter pro Sekunde (m/s)

to break the sound barrier
= die Schallmauer durchbrechen

The speed of light is 186,300 miles per second
= Die Lichtgeschwindigkeit beträgt 300 000 Kilometer pro Sekunde (km/s)

at or with the speed of light
= mit Lichtgeschwindigkeit

Urinprobe von ihm benötigt **3▸** (coll./derog.: type) Marke, *die* (salopp)

'specimen page *n.* Probeseite, *die*

specious /'spi:ʃəs/ *adj.* **a ~ argument** ein nur scheinbar treffendes Argument; **a ~ pretence/appearance of honesty** ein Anschein von Ehrlichkeit

speck /spek/ *n.* **1▸** (spot) Fleck, *der;* (of paint also) Spritzer, *der* **2▸** (particle) Teilchen, *das;* **~ of soot/dust** Rußflocke, *die*/Staubkörnchen, *das;* **a ~ on the horizon** ein Pünktchen am Horizont; **the ore sparkled with ~s of gold** in dem Erz glitzerten Goldsprenkel **3▸** (blemish) Fleck, *der;* **have ~s** fleckig sein

specked /spekt/ *adj.* fleckig ‹*Frucht*›; **his coat is ~ with paint/mud** auf seinem Mantel sind Farb-/Schlammspritzer

speckle /'spekl/ *n.* Tupfen, *der;* Sprenkel, *der*

speckled /'spekld/ *adj.* gesprenkelt

specs /speks/ *n. pl.* (coll.: spectacles) Brille, *die*

spectacle /'spektəkl/ *n.* **1▸** *in pl.* **[pair of] ~s** Brille, *die* **2▸** (public show) Spektakel, *das* **3▸** (object of attention) Anblick, *der;* Schauspiel, *das;* **make a ~ of oneself** sich unmöglich aufführen

'spectacle case *n.* Brillenetui, *das*

spectacled /'spektəkld/ *adj.* bebrillt

spectacular /spek'tækjʊlə(r)/
A *adj.* spektakulär
B *n.* Spektakel, *das*

spectacularly /spek'tækjʊləlɪ/ *adv.* außergewöhnlich; **be ~ successful** [einen] spektakulären Erfolg haben

spectate /spek'teɪt/ *v.i.* zusehen; **~ at a race** sich (*Dat.*) ein Rennen ansehen

spectator /spek'teɪtə(r)/ *n.* Zuschauer, *der*/Zuschauerin, *die*

spec'tator sport *n.* Publikumssport, *der*

specter (Amer.) ▸**spectre**

spectra *pl. of* **spectrum**

spectral /'spektrl/ *adj.* **1▸** (ghostly) geisterhaft; gespenstisch **2▸** (Phys.) spektral

spectre /'spektə(r)/ *n.* (Brit.) **1▸** (apparition) Gespenst, *das* **2▸** (disturbing image) Schreckgespenst, *das*

spectrogram /'spektrəgræm/ *n.* (Phys.) Spektrogramm, *das*

spectrograph /'spektrəgrɑ:f/ *n.* (Phys.) Spektrograph, *der*

spectrometer /spek'trɒmɪtə(r)/ *n.* (Phys.) Spektrometer, *das*

spectroscope /'spektrəskəʊp/ *n.* (Phys.) Spektroskop, *das*

spectroscopy /spek'trɒskəpɪ/ *n.* (Phys.) Spektroskopie, *die*

spectrum /'spektrəm/ *n., pl.* **spectra** /'spektrə/ (Phys.; also fig.) Spektrum, *das;* **~ of opinion** Meinungsspektrum, *das*

specula *pl. of* **speculum**

speculate /'spekjʊleɪt/ *v.i.* spekulieren (**about, on** über + *Akk.*); Vermutungen *od.* Spekulationen anstellen (**about, on** über + *Akk.*); **~ as to what .../as to the wisdom of doing sth.** darüber spekulieren, was .../ob es klug sei, etw. zu tun; **~ on the Stock Exchange/in the gold market/in rubber** an der Börse/am Goldmarkt/mit *od.* (Wirtsch. Jargon) in Gummi spekulieren

speculation /spekjʊ'leɪʃn/ *n.* Spekulation, *die* (**over** über + *Akk.*); **~ on the Stock Exchange/in the gold market/in rubber** Spekulation an der Börse/am Goldmarkt/mit *od.* (Wirtsch. Jargon) in Gummi; **there has been much ~ that ...:** man hat viel darüber spekuliert, dass ...

speculative /'spekjʊlətɪv/ *adj.* spekulativ; **~ transactions** Spekulationsgeschäfte

speculatively /'spekjʊlətɪvlɪ/ *adv.* spekulativ

speculator /'spekjʊleɪtə(r)/ *n.* Spekulant, *der*/Spekulantin, *die*

speculum /'spekjʊləm/ *n., pl.* **specula** /'spekjʊlə/ (Med.) Spekulum, *das*

sped ▸**speed B, C**

speech /spi:tʃ/ *n.* **1▸** (public address) Rede, *die;* **make** *or* **deliver** *or* **give a ~:** eine Rede halten; **~ for the defence** (Law) Plädoyer des Verteidigers; **King's/Queen's S~** (Parl.) Thronrede, *die* **2▸** (faculty of speaking) Sprache, *die;* **lose/recover** *or* **find one's [power of] ~:** die Sprache verlieren/wieder finden **3▸** (act of speaking) Sprechen, *das;* Sprache, *die* **4▸** (manner of speaking) Sprache, *die;* Sprechweise, *die;* **his ~ was slurred** er sprach undeutlich **5▸** (Ling.: utterances) Sprache, *die;* **children's ~:** Kindersprache, *die. See also* **figure A 8**; **part A 10**; **set speech**

speech: **~ act** *n.* (Ling.) Sprechakt, *der;* **~ day** *n.* (Brit. Sch.) jährliches Schulfest; **~ defect** *n.* Sprachfehler, *der*

speechify /'spi:tʃɪfaɪ/ *v.i.* (coll.) eine Rede schwingen (ugs.)

'speech impediment *n.* Sprachfehler, *der*

speechless /'spi:tʃlɪs/ *adj.* **1▸** sprachlos (**with** vor + *Dat.*); **~ with rage** sprachlos vor Wut **2▸** (dumb) stumm

speech: **~making** *n., no pl.* **be good at ~making** ein guter Redner/eine gute Rednerin sein; **all the ~making was over** alle Reden waren gehalten; **~ recognition** *n., no pl.* (Computing) Spracherkennung, *die;* **~ synthesizer** *n.* Sprachsynthesizer, *der;* **~ therapist** *n.* ▸ℹ **p. 1260** Sprachtherapeut, *der*/-therapeutin, *die;* **~ therapy** *n., no pl.* Sprachtherapie, *die;* **have ~ therapy** sprachtherapeutisch behandelt werden; **~writer** *n.* ▸ℹ **p. 1260** Redenschreiber, *der*/-schreiberin, *die*

speed /spi:d/

A *n.* **1▸** ▸ℹ **p. 1566** Geschwindigkeit, *die;* Schnelligkeit, *die;* (of typist) Schreibgeschwindigkeit, *die;* **at full** *or* **top ~:** mit Höchstgeschwindigkeit; mit Vollgas (ugs.); **pick up ~:** schneller werden; **top ~:** Spitzengeschwindigkeit, *die;* **with the ~ of light** mit Lichtgeschwindigkeit; (fig.) blitzschnell; **drive at a reckless ~:** rücksichtslos schnell fahren; **at a ~ of eighty miles an hour** mit einer Geschwindigkeit von achtzig Meilen in der Stunde; **at ~:** mit hoher Geschwindigkeit; **be up to ~** (performing as expected) ‹*System, Maschine usw.*:› auf Hochtouren *od.* vollen Touren (ugs.) laufen; ‹*Person;*› auf Zack sein (ugs.); fit sein; (coll.: fully informed) ‹*Person:*› auf dem [aller]neusten Stand sein; **bring sb. up to ~:** jmdn. auf den neusten Kenntnisstand bringen **2▸** (gear) Gang, *der;* **a five-~ gearbox** eine 5-Gang-Schaltung **3▸** (Photog.) (of film etc.) Lichtempfindlichkeit, *die;* (of lens) **[shutter] ~:** Belichtungszeit, *die* **4▸** (sl.: drug) Speed, *das* (*Jargon*). *See also* **air speed**; **full¹ A 4**; **ground speed**

B *v.i.* **1▸** *p.t., p.p.* **sped** /sped/ *or* **speeded** (go fast) schnell fahren; rasen (ugs.); **the hours/days sped by** die Stunden/Tage vergingen wie im Fluge **2▸** *p. t., p.p.* **speeded** (go too fast) zu schnell fahren; rasen (ugs.)

C *v.t.*, **sped** *or* **speeded:** **~ sb. on his/her way** jmdn. verabschieden; **God ~ you** Gott steh dir/euch bei

Phrasal verbs

- **~ 'off** *v.i.* davonbrausen
- **~ 'up**

A *v.t.*, **speeded up** beschleunigen; **~ up the work** die Arbeit vorantreiben; (one's own work) sich mit der Arbeit beeilen

B *v.i.*, **speeded up** sich beeilen. *See also* **speed-up**

speed: **~boat** *n.* Rennboot, *das;* **~ bump** *n.* Bodenschwelle, *die;* **~ camera** *n.* Geschwindigkeitsüberwachungskamera, *die;* **be caught by a ~ camera** bei einer Geschwindigkeitskontrolle geblitzt werden; **~ dating** *n., no pl.* Speeddating, *das;* **~ hump** ▸**speed bump**

speedily /'spi:dɪlɪ/ *adv.* **1▸** (at speed) schnell **2▸** (soon) umgehend

speeding /'spi:dɪŋ/ *n.* (going too fast) zu schnelles Fahren; Rasen, *das* (ugs. abwertend); Geschwindigkeitsüberschreitung, *die* (Verkehrsw.); **his third ~ offence** seine dritte Geschwindigkeitsüberschreitung

speed: **~ limit** *n.* ▸ℹ **p. 1566** Tempolimit, *das;* Geschwindigkeitsbeschränkung, *die* (Verkehrsw.); **~ limiter** *n.* Geschwindigkeitsbegrenzer, *der;* **~ merchant** *n.* (coll.) Raser, *der* (ugs. abwertend); **~ metal** *n.* Speedmetal, *der*

speedo /'spi:dəʊ/ *n., pl.* **~s** (Brit. coll.) Tacho, *der* (ugs.)

speedometer /spi:'dɒmɪtə(r)/ *n.* Tachometer, *der od. das*

speed: **~ ramp** *n.* Bodenschwelle, *die;* **~ trap** *n.* Geschwindigkeitskontrolle, *die;* (with radar) Radarfalle, *die* (ugs.); **~-up** *n.* **1▸** (acceleration) Beschleunigung, *die;* **2▸** (increase in work rate) Steigerung der [Arbeits]produktivität; **~way** *n.* **1▸** (motorcycle racing) Speedwayrennen, *das;* **the ~way world champion** der

S

Speedwayweltmeister; 2 (racetrack) Speedwaybahn, *die;* 3 (Amer.: public road) Schnellstraße, *die*

speedwell /ˈspiːdwel/ *n.* (Bot.) Ehrenpreis, *der*

speedy /ˈspiːdɪ/ *adj.* schnell; umgehend, prompt ‹*Antwort*›; **the medication is ~ and effective** das Medikament wirkt schnell und gut

speleology /spelɪˈɒlədʒɪ, spiːlɪˈɒlədʒɪ/ *n., no pl.* Speläologie, *die;* Höhlenkunde, *die*

spell¹ /spel/

A *v.t.*, **spelled** *or* (Brit.) **spelt** [spelt] 1 schreiben; (aloud) buchstabieren 2 (form) **what do these letters/what does b-a-t ~?** welches Wort ergeben diese Buchstaben/die Buchstaben b-a-t? 3 (fig.: have as result) bedeuten; **that ~s trouble** das bedeutet nichts Gutes

B *v.i.*, **spelled** *or* (Brit.) **spelt** (say) buchstabieren; (write) richtig schreiben; **he can't ~:** er kann keine Rechtschreibung (ugs.)

(Phrasal verb)

• **~ ˈout, ~ ˈover** *v.t.* 1 (read letter by letter) [langsam] buchstabieren 2 (fig.: explain precisely) genau erklären; genau darlegen

spell² *n.* 1 (period) Weile, *die;* **do a ~ of joinery/in prison** eine Weile *od.* Zeit lang als Tischler arbeiten/im Gefängnis sitzen; **a ~ of overseas service** eine Zeit lang Dienst in Übersee; **on Sunday it will be cloudy with some sunny ~s** am Sonntag wolkig mit sonnigen Abschnitten; **a cold ~:** eine Kälteperiode; **return from a ~ in America** von einem Aufenthalt in Amerika zurückkehren; **a long ~ when ...:** eine lange Zeit, während der ... 2 (Austral.: period of rest) [Ruhe]pause, *die;* **have a ten minutes' ~:** zehn Minuten Pause machen

spell³ *n.* 1 (words used as a charm) Zauberspruch, *der;* **cast a ~ over** *or* **on sb./sth., put a ~ on sb./sth.** jmdn./etw. verzaubern 2 (fascination) Zauber, *der;* **break the ~:** den Bann brechen; **be under a ~:** unter einem Bann stehen

spell: ~bind *v.t.* bezaubern; **~bound** *adj.* verzaubert; **he can hold his readers ~bound** er kann seine Leser in seinem Bann halten; **~check** (Computing) **A** *n.* 1 (check of spelling) Rechtschreibprüfung, *die;* **~check program** Rechtschreibprüfprogramm, *das;* 2 (spellchecker) Rechtschreibprüfprogramm, *das;* Spellchecker, *der* (fachspr.); **B** *v.t.* mit einem Rechtschreibprüfprogramm überprüfen; **~checker** *n.* Rechtschreibprüfprogramm, *das;* **~checking** *n., no pl.* (Computing) Rechtschreibprüfung, *die;* **~checking program/facility** Rechtschreibprüfprogramm, *das*

speller /ˈspelə(r)/ *n.* 1 (person) Rechtschreiber, *der*/-schreiberin, *die* 2 (esp. Amer.: spelling book) Rechtschreibbuch, *das*

spelling /ˈspelɪŋ/ *n.* 1 Rechtschreibung, *die;* **the original Shakespearean ~:** die ursprüngliche Schreibung nach Shakespeare 2 (sequence of letters) Schreibweise, *die*

spelling: ~ bee *n.* Rechtschreib[e]wettbewerb, *der;* **~ checker** *n.* Rechtschreibprogramm, *das;* **~ mistake** *n.* Rechtschreibfehler, *der*

spelt¹ ▸**spell¹**

spelt² /spelt/ *n.* (Agric.) Dinkel, *der*

spend /spend/ *v.t.*, **spent** /spent/ 1 (pay out) ausgeben; **~ money like water** *or* (coll.) **as if it's going out of fashion** sein *od.* das Geld mit beiden Händen ausgeben *od.* hinauswerfen (ugs.); **money well spent** sinnvoll ausgegebenes Geld; **it was money well spent** es hat sich ausgezahlt; **~ a penny** (fig. coll.) mal verschwinden [müssen] (ugs.) 2 (use) aufwenden (**on** für); **~ one's time/a day** seine Zeit/einen Tag verbringen; **time well spent** sinnvoll verwendete Zeit; **it was effort/time well spent** es hat sich ausgezahlt 3 **~ itself** (fig.) ‹*Sturm, Wut:*› sich legen

spendable /ˈspendəbl/ *adj.* verfügbar

spender /ˈspendə(r)/ *n.* **he's a [big] ~:** bei ihm sitzt das Geld locker (ugs.)

spending: ~ limit *n.* Ausgabenobergrenze, *die;* **~ money** *n.* 1 (Amer.) ▸**pocket money;** 2 (Brit.: sum intended for spending) verfügbares Geld

ˈspendthrift *n.* Verschwender, *der*/Verschwenderin, *die*

spent

A ▸**spend**

B *adj.* 1 (used up) verbraucht; **~ cartridge** leere Geschosshülse 2 (drained of energy) erschöpft; ausgelaugt; hinfällig ‹*Kranker, Greis*›; **a ~ force** (fig.) eine Kraft, die sich erschöpft hat

sperm /ˈspɜːm/ *n.*, *pl.* **~s** *or same* (Biol.) 1 (semen) Sperma, *der* 2 (spermatozoon) Samenfaden, *der*

spermatic /spɜːˈmætɪk/ *adj.* Samen-

spermatic ˈcord *n.* Samenstrang, *der*

spermatozoon /spɜːmətəˈzəʊɒn/ *n.*, *pl.* **spermatozoa** /spɜːmətəˈzəʊə/ Spermatozoon, *das;* Spermium, *das*

sperm: ~ bank *n.* Samenbank, *die;* **~ count** *n.* Spermienzahl, *die;* **~ donor** *n.* Samenspender, *der;* Spermaspender, *der*

spermicidal /ˈspɜːmɪsaɪdl/ *adj.* spermizid (Med.); **~ agent** Spermizid, *das* (Med.)

spermicide /ˈspɜːmɪsaɪd/ *n.* Spermizid, *das*

ˈsperm whale *n.* Pottwal, *der*

spew /spjuː/

A *v.t.* spucken

B *v.i.* sich ergießen

(Phrasal verb)

• **~ ˈout**

A *v.t.* erbrechen, [aus]spucken ‹*Gegessenes*›; ‹*Vulkan:*› spucken, speien ‹*Lava*›; **~ out waste products into the rivers** ‹*Fabriken:*› Abfälle in die Flüsse [aus]speien; **propaganda was ~ed out by the stations** (fig.) die Sender spien Propaganda

B *v.i.* sich ergießen (**of, from** aus)

SPF *abbr.* **= sun protection factor** LSF

sphagnum /ˈsfægnəm/ *n.*, *pl.* **sphagna** /ˈsfægnə/ Torf, *der;* **~ moss** Torfmoos, *das*

sphere /sfɪə(r)/ *n.* 1 (field of action) Bereich, *der;* Sphäre, *die* (geh.); **be distinguished in many ~s** sich auf vielen Gebieten ausgezeichnet haben; **that's outside my ~:** das gehört nicht zu meinem Tätigkeitsbereich; **~ of life** Lebensbereich, *der;* **~ of influence** Einflussbereich, *der* 2 (Geom.) Kugel, *die* 3 (heavenly body) Sphäre, *die;* **music/harmony of the ~s** Sphärenmusik/-harmonie, *die*

spherical /ˈsferɪkl/ *adj.* 1 (globular) kugelförmig 2 (Math.) sphärisch

sphincter /ˈsfɪŋktə(r)/ *n.* (Anat.) Sphinkter, *der* (fachspr.); Schließmuskel, *der*

sphinx /sfɪŋks/ *n.* Sphinx, *die*

sphinx-like /ˈsfɪŋkslaɪk/ *adj.* sphinxhaft; **she gave a ~ smile** sie lächelte wie eine Sphinx

spica /ˈspaɪkə/ *n.* 1 (Bot.) Ähre, *die* 2 (Med.) Spica, *die*

spice /spaɪs/

A *n.* 1 Gewürz, *das;* (collectively) Gewürze *Pl.*; *attrib.* Gewürz-; **dealer in ~s** Gewürzhändler, *der* 2 (fig.: excitement) Würze, *die;* **the ~ of life** die Würze des Lebens

B *v.t.* würzen; **a ~d account** (fig.) ein ausgeschmückter Bericht; **a book ~d with humour** (fig.) ein mit Humor gewürztes Buch

ˈspice rack *n.* Gewürzregal, *das*

spicily /ˈspaɪsɪlɪ/ *adv.* mit Würze

spiciness /ˈspaɪsɪnɪs/ *n., no pl.* Würze, *die*

spick /spɪk/ *adj.* **~ and span** blitzblank *od.* -sauber (ugs.)

spicy /ˈspaɪsɪ/ *adj.* 1 pikant; würzig 2 (racy) pikant; **~ things** Pikanterien *Pl.*

spider /ˈspaɪdə(r)/ *n.* 1 Spinne, *die;* (**~**-like creature) Spinnentier, *das;* **~ and fly** (fig.) Raubtier und Beute 2 (Computing) Spider, *der* 3 (Brit.: elastic ties) Gepäckspinne, *die*

spider: ~ crab *n.* See- *od.* Meeresspinne, *die;* **~man** *n.: Bauarbeiter, der auf Gerüsten in großer Höhe arbeitet;* **~ monkey** *n.* Klammeraffe, *der;* **~ plant** *n.* Grünlilie, *die;* **~'s web** (*Amer.:* **~ web**) Spinnennetz, *das;* (fig.) Netz, *das*

spidery /ˈspaɪdərɪ/ *adj.* spinnenförmig; krakelig (ugs.) ‹*Schrift*›; **~ legs** Spinnenbeine

spiel /spiːl/ (coll.)

A *n.* Sermon, *der* (ugs.); (excuse) Story, *die;* **don't give me all that ~:** erzähl mir doch nichts!

B *v.i.* (Amer.) schwadronieren; labern (salopp)

(Phrasal verb)

• **~ ˈoff** *v.t.* (Amer. coll.) **he can ~ off answers to 250 questions** er kann Antworten auf 250 Fragen herunterrasseln (ugs.)

spiffing /ˈspɪfɪŋ/ *adj.* (arch. coll.) ausgezeichnet; famos (ugs. veralt.)

spigot /ˈspɪgət/ *n.* Zapfen, *der*

spike¹ /spaɪk/

A *n.* 1 Stachel, *der;* (of running shoe) Spike, *der* 2 *in pl.* (shoes) Spikes *Pl.* 3 (large nail) großer Nagel; (Railw.) Schienennagel, *der* 4 (for holding papers) Zettelspieß, *der*

B *v.t.* 1 mit [großen] Nägeln befestigen ‹*Schiene*›; mit Spikes versehen ‹*Schuhe*›; **~ sb.'s guns** (fig.) jmdm. einen Strich durch die Rechnung machen (ugs.) 2 (coll.: add spirits or drugs to) **sb. ~d his drink** jmd. hat ihm etwas in seinen Drink getan; **~ coffee with cognac/spirits with LSD** Cognac in den Kaffee/LSD in den Schnaps tun

spike² *n.* (Bot.) Ähre, *die*

spike ˈheel ▸**stiletto 2**

spikelet /ˈspaɪklɪt/ *n.* (Bot.) Ährchen, *das*

spiky /ˈspaɪkɪ/ *adj.* 1 (like a spike) spitz [zulaufend]; stachelig ‹*Haare*› 2 (having spikes) stach[e]lig 3 (coll.: easily offended) ▸**prickly 2**

spill¹ /spɪl/

A *v.t.*, **spilt** /spɪlt/ *or* **~ed** 1 verschütten ‹*Flüssigkeit*›; **~ sth. on sth.** etw. auf etw. (*Akk.*) schütten; **~ [sb.'s] blood** [jmds.] Blut vergießen 2 (coll.: divulge) ausquatschen (salopp); **~ the beans [to sb.]** [jmdm. gegenüber] aus der Schule plaudern; **not ~ the beans [to sb.]** [jmdm. gegenüber] dichthalten (ugs.). *See also* **milk A**

B *v.i.*, **spilt** *or* **~ed** überlaufen

C *n.* (fall) Sturz, *der;* **have/take a ~:** stürzen

(Phrasal verb)

• **~ ˈover** *v.i.* überlaufen; (fig.) überquellen; ‹*Unruhen:*› sich ausbreiten; (develop into something else) umschlagen

spill² *n.* (for lighting) Fidibus, *der*

spillage /ˈspɪlɪdʒ/ *n.* 1 (act) Verschütten, *das;* **~ of oil** (from tanker) das Auslaufen von Öl 2 (quantity) Verschüttete, *das;* **there was little ~:** es wurde wenig verschüttet; (from tanker) es lief wenig Öl aus

spillikins /ˈspɪlɪkɪnz/ *n. sing.* Mikado, *das*

ˈspillway *n.* Überfall, *der*

spilt ▸**spill¹ A, B**

spin /spɪn/

A *v.t.*, **-nn-, spun** /spʌn/ 1 spinnen; **~ yarn** Garn spinnen; **~ a yarn** (fig.) ein Garn spinnen (bes. Seemannsspr.); fabulieren 2 (in washing machine etc.) schleudern 3 (cause to whirl round) [schnell] drehen; wirbeln [lassen]; **~ a top** kreiseln; **~ a coin** eine Münze kreiseln lassen; (toss) eine Münze werfen 4 (Sport: impart ~ to) Effet *od.* Spin geben (+ *Dat.*) ‹*Ball*›

B *v.i.*, **-nn-, spun** sich drehen; **my head is ~ning** (fig.) (from noise) mir brummt der Schädel (ugs.); (from too much work) ich weiß nicht [mehr], wo mir der Kopf steht; (from many impressions) mir schwirrt der Kopf

C *n.* 1 (whirl) **give sth. a ~:** etw. in Drehung versetzen; **give the washing a [short] ~:** die Wäsche [kurz] schleudern; **the decision rested on the ~ of a coin** die Entscheidung sollte durch das Werfen einer Münze herbeigeführt werden 2 (Aeronaut.) Trudeln, *das; see also* **flat spin** 3 (Sport: revolving motion) Effet, *der;* Spin, *der* 4 (outing) **go for a ~:** einen Ausflug machen; **a ~ in the car** eine Spritztour mit dem Auto 5 (Phys.) Spin, *der* 6 (fig.: favourable bias) Beschönigung, *die;* **put a negative/positive ~ on sth.** von etw. eine negative/positive Darstellung geben; **this is just ~:** das ist nur Schönfärberei (abwertend)

(Phrasal verbs)

• **~ ˈout** *v.t.* 1 (prolong) in die Länge ziehen 2 (use sparingly) **~ one's money out until pay day** sein Geld bis zum Zahltag strecken; **he spun out his glass of whisky** er trank lange an seinem Glas Whisky

• **~ ˈround**

A *v.i.* sich drehen; ‹*Person:*› sich [schnell] umdrehen
B *v.t.* [schnell] drehen

spina bifida /spaɪnə 'bɪfɪdə/ *n.* ▸ ❶ **p. 1231** (Med.) Spina bifida, *die* (fachspr.); Spaltwirbel, *der*

spinach /'spɪnɪdʒ/ *n.* Spinat, *der*

spinal /'spaɪnl/ *adj.* (Anat.) Wirbelsäulen-; Rückgrat[s]-; *see also* **marrow 2**

spinal: ~ **'column** *n.* Wirbelsäule, *die;* ~ **'cord** *n.* Rückenmark, *das*

'spin bowler *n.* (Cricket) Werfer, der Spins wirft

spindle /'spɪndl/ *n.* [1] Spindel, *die* [2] (pin bearing bobbin) Spulenhalter, *der*

spindle: **~-shanks** *n. sing.* (dated coll.) **be a ~-shanks** spindeldürre Beine haben; **~-shaped** *adj.* spindelförmig

spindly /'spɪndlɪ/ *adj.* spindeldürr ‹*Person, Beine, Arme*›

spin: ~ **doctor** *n.* (coll.) Spin-Doktor, *der;* ~ **'drier** *n.* Wäscheschleuder, *die*

'spindrift *n.* Gischt, *der od. die*

spin-'dry *v.t.* schleudern

spine /spaɪn/ *n.* [1] ▸ ❶ **p. 951** (backbone) Wirbelsäule, *die* [2] (Bot., Zool.) Stachel, *der* [3] (fig.: source of strength) Rückgrat, *das* [4] (of book) Buchrücken, *der* [5] (ridge) [Gebirgs]grat, *der*

spine: **~-chiller** *n.* Schocker, *der* (ugs.); **this film is a ~-chiller** bei diesem Film läuft es einem eiskalt den Rücken herunter (ugs.); **~-chilling** *adj.* gruselig

spineless /'spaɪnlɪs/ *adj.* [1] (fig.) rückgratlos [2] (Zool.: without spines) ‹*Fisch*› ohne Flossenstrahlen

spinelessly /'spaɪnlɪslɪ/ *adv.* **give in/surrender ~:** so rückgratlos sein und nachgeben/sich ergeben

spinet /spɪ'net, 'spɪnɪt/ *n.* (Mus. Hist.) Spinett, *das*

spinnaker /'spɪnəkə(r)/ *n.* (Naut.) Spinnaker, *der*

spinner /'spɪnə(r)/ *n.* [1] (Cricket) Werfer, der Spins wirft [2] (spin-drier) Wäscheschleuder, *die* [3] (manufacturer engaged in spinning) Spinner, *der*/Spinnerin, *die*

spinneret /'spɪnəret/ *n.* [1] (Zool.) Spinndrüse, *die* [2] (Textiles) Spinndüse, *die*

spinney /'spɪnɪ/ *n.* (Brit.) Gehölz, *das*

spinning /'spɪnɪŋ/ *n.* Spinnen, *das*

spinning: ~ **jenny** *n.* Jenny-[Spinn]maschine, *die;* ~ **top** *n.* Kreisel, *der;* ~ **wheel** *n.* Spinnrad, *das*

'spin-off *n.* Nebenprodukt, *das*

spinster /'spɪnstə(r)/ *n.* [1] ledige Frau; Junggesellin, *die;* **remain a ~:** ledig bleiben [2] (derog.: old maid) alte Jungfer (abwertend)

spinsterhood /'spɪnstəhʊd/ *n., no pl.* Ledigsein, *das*

spiny /'spaɪnɪ/ *adj.* dornig; stachelig

spiny 'lobster *n.* Languste, *die*

spiraea /spaɪə'ri:ə/ *n.* (Bot.) Spierstrauch, *der*

spiral /'spaɪrl/
A *adj.* spiralförmig; spiralig; ~ **spring** Spiralfeder, *die*
B *n.* Spirale, *die;* **the ~ of rising prices and wages** die Lohn-Preis-Spirale
C *v.i.* (Brit.) **-ll-** ‹*Weg:*› sich hochwinden; ‹*Kosten, Profite:*› in die Höhe klettern; ‹*Rauch:*› in einer Spirale aufsteigen

spirally /'spaɪrəlɪ/ *adv.* spiralig; spiralförmig

spiral: ~ **'nebula** *n.* (Astron.) Spiralnebel, *der;* ~ **'staircase** *n.* Wendeltreppe, *die*

spirant /'spaɪrənt/ (Phonet.)
A *adj.* spirantisch
B *n.* Spirant, *der* (fachspr.); Reibelaut, *der*

spire /spaɪə(r)/ *n.* Turmspitze, *die*

spirit /'spɪrɪt/
A *n.* [1] *in pl.* (distilled liquor) Spirituosen *Pl.;* **tax on ~s** Alkoholsteuer, *die* [2] (mental attitude) Geisteshaltung, *die;* **in the right/wrong ~:** mit der richtigen/falschen Einstellung; **take sth. in the wrong ~:** etw. falsch auffassen; etw. in den falschen Hals kriegen (ugs.); **take sth. in the ~ in which it is meant** etw. so auffassen, wie es gemeint ist; **as the ~ takes/moves one** wie man gerade Lust hat; **do sth. in a ~ of mischief** etw. in böser Absicht tun ; **enter into the ~ of sth.** innerlich bei einer Sache [beteiligt] sein *od.* dabei sein; **'that's the ~!** das ist die richtige Einstellung! [3] (courage) Mut, *der;* **play with ~:** mit ganzer Seele spielen [4] (vital principle, soul, inner qualities) Geist, *der;* **the ~ is willing but the flesh is weak** der Geist ist willig, aber das Fleisch ist schwach; **give up one's ~:** seinen Geist *od.* seine Seele aushauchen (geh. verhüll.); **in [the] ~:** innerlich; im Geiste; **be with sb. in ~:** in Gedanken *od.* im Geist[e] bei jmdm. sein; **the poor in ~** (arch.) die Armen im Geiste [5] (person supplying energy) treibende Kraft; Motor, *der* (fig.) [6] (real meaning) Geist, *der;* Sinn, *der;* **follow the ~ of the instructions** die Anweisungen sinngemäß ausführen; **obey the letter but not the ~ of the law** dem Buchstaben, nicht dem Geist[e] des Gesetzes gehorchen [7] (mental tendency) Geist, *der;* (mood) Stimmung, *die;* **the ~ of the age** *or* **times** der Zeitgeist [8] **high ~s** gehobene Stimmung; gute Laune; **in high** *or* **great** *or* **good ~s** in gehobener Stimmung; gut gelaunt; **in poor** *or* **low ~s** niedergedrückt [9] (liquid got by distillation) Spiritus, *der* [10] (purified alcohol) reiner Alkohol [11] (solution in alcohol) Geist, *der;* Spiritus, *der;* **~[s] of wine** (arch.) Weingeist, *der*
B *v.t.* ~ **away,** ~ **off** verschwinden lassen; **be ~ed away** *or* **off** verschwinden

spirited /'spɪrɪtɪd/ *adj.* [1] (lively) lebendig ‹*Übersetzung, Vortrag*›; beherzt ‹*Angriff, Versuch, Antwort, Verteidigung*›; lebhaft ‹*Antwort*› [2] **low/proud-~:** niedergedrückt/stolz; **high-~:** ausgelassen; temperamentvoll ‹*Pferd*›; **mean-~:** gemein

spiritedly /'spɪrɪtɪdlɪ/ *adv.* lebendig ‹*schreiben*›; vehement ‹*ablehnen*›

'spirit lamp *n.* Spirituslampe, *die*

spiritless /'spɪrɪtlɪs/ *adj.* dumpf ‹*Person*›; stumpfsinnig ‹*Apathie*›

'spirit level *n.* Wasserwaage, *die*

spiritual /'spɪrɪtʃʊəl/
A *adj.* [1] spirituell (geh.); **a ~ relationship** eine platonische (geh.) Beziehung; **his ~ home** seine geistige Heimat [2] (concerned with religion) geistlich; **lords ~** (Brit. Parl.) *Bischöfe und Erzbischöfe im britischen Oberhaus*
B *n.* **[Negro] ~:** [Negro] Spiritual, *das*

spiritualism /'spɪrɪtʃʊəlɪzm/ *n.* [1] (belief in contact with spirits) Spiritismus, *der* [2] (system of doctrines) Spiritualismus, *der*

spiritualist /'spɪrɪtʃʊəlɪst/ *n.* Spiritist, *der*/Spiritistin, *die*

spirituality /spɪrɪtʃʊ'ælɪtɪ/ *n., no pl.* Spiritualität, *die* (geh.)

spiritually /'spɪrɪtʃʊəlɪ/ *adv.* spirituell; **~-minded** vergeistigt ‹*Person*›

spit¹ /spɪt/
A *v.i.,* **-tt-, spat** /spæt/ *or* **spit** [1] spucken; **he spat in his enemy's face** er spuckte seinem Feind ins Gesicht; **it makes you [want to] ~:** es kann einen auf die Palme bringen (ugs.) [2] (make angry noise) fauchen; **~ at sb.** jmdn. anfauchen [3] (rain lightly) ~ **[down]** tröpfeln (ugs.) [4] (throw out sparks) ‹*Feuer:*› Funken sprühen; ‹*Öl:*› spritzen
B *v.t.,* **-tt-, spat** *or* **spit** [1] spucken; **~ sth. at sb.** mit etw. nach jmdm. spucken [2] (fig.: utter angrily) **~ defiance at sb.** jmdn. trotzig anfauchen
C *n.* [1] **[dead** *or* **very] ~ [and image]** (coll.) ▸ **spitting image** [2] (spittle) Spucke, *die;* ~ **and polish** (cleaning work) Putzen und Reinigen; Wienern, *das;* **all that ~ and polish in the army** das ewige Putzen und Wienern in der Armee

Phrasal verb
- ~ **'out** *v.t.* **~ sth. out** etw. ausspucken; **~ out curses at sb.** jmdm. die Flüche nur so ins Gesicht spucken; **she spat out the words** sie spuckte die Worte nur so aus; **~ it out!** (fig. coll.) spuck es aus! (ugs.)

spit²
A *n.* [1] (point of land) Halbinsel, *die* [2] (reef) Riff, *das;* (shoal) Untiefe, *die;* (sandbank) Sandbank, *die* [3] (for roasting meat) Spieß, *der*
B *v.t.,* **-tt-** (pierce) [auf]spießen

spit³ *n.* (spade-depth) Spatentiefe, *die*

'spitball *n.* (Amer.: pellet) [mit Speichel getränktes] Papierkügelchen

spite /spaɪt/
A *n.* [1] (malice) Boshaftigkeit, *die;* **do sth. from** *or* **out of ~:** etw. aus Boshaftigkeit tun [2] **in ~ of** trotz; **in ~ of oneself** obwohl man es eigentlich nicht will; wider *od.* gegen seinen [eigenen] Willen
B *v.t.* ärgern; **cut off one's nose to ~ one's face** sich (*Dat. od. Akk.*) ins eigene Fleisch schneiden

spiteful /'spaɪtfl/ *adj.,* **spitefully** /'spaɪtfəlɪ/ *adv.* boshaft; gehässig (abwertend)

'spitfire *n.* Giftspritze, *die* (ugs. abwertend)

'spit-roast *v.t.* am Spieß braten; **~ed lamb** Lamm vom *od.* am Spieß

spitting 'image *n.* **be the ~ of sb.** jmdm. wie aus dem Gesicht geschnitten sein

spittle /'spɪtl/ *n.* Spucke, *die;* Speichel, *der*

spittoon /spɪ'tu:n/ *n.* Spucknapf, *der*

spiv /spɪv/ *n.* (Brit. coll.) [1] (person living by his wits) smarter kleiner Geschäftemacher [2] (black-market dealer) Schwarzhändler, *der;* Schieber, *der* (ugs.)

splash /splæʃ/
A *v.t.* [1] spritzen; **~ sb./sth. with sth.** jmdn./etw. mit etw. bespritzen; **~ sth. on [to]** *or* **over sb./sth.** jmdn./etw. mit etw. bespritzen; etw. auf jmdn./etw. spritzen; **~ sth. about** etw. herumspritzen (ugs.); **sth. gets ~ed on sth.** etw. spritzt auf etw. (*Akk.*) [2] (Journ.: display prominently) als Aufmacher bringen ‹*Story usw.*›; **be ~ed all over the front page** auf der ersten Seite groß aufgemacht sein (ugs.) [3] (with scattered colour) sprenkeln
B *v.i.* [1] (fly about in drops) spritzen [2] (cause liquid to fly about) [umher]spritzen [3] (move with ~ing) platschen (ugs.)
C *n.* [1] Spritzen, *das;* **hit the water with a ~:** ins Wasser platschen (ugs.); **make a [big] ~** (fig.) Furore machen [2] (liquid) Spritzer, *der* [3] (noise) Plätschern, *das* [4] (prominent display of news etc.) **get a front-page ~:** der Aufmacher auf der Titelseite sein [5] (coll.: dash) Schuss [Sodawasser]; **whisky and a ~ of ginger ale** Whisky mit einem Schuss Ingwerbier [6] (spot of dirt etc.) Spritzer, *der* [7] (patch of colour) Tupfer, *der*

Phrasal verbs
- ~ **a'bout** *v.i.* herumspritzen (ugs.); [herum]planschen
- ~ **'down** *v.i.* wassern; *see also* **splashdown**
- ~ **'out** *v.i.* (coll.) **~ out on sth.** für etw. unbekümmert Geld ausgeben

splash: **~back** *n.: Wandverkleidung zum Schutz vor Spritzern;* **~down** *n.* Wasserung, *die*

splatter /'splætə(r)/
A *v.i.* ‹*Bach:*› plätschern; ‹*Blut:*› spritzen
B *v.t.* bespritzen
C *n.* Plätschern, *das*

splay /spleɪ/
A *v.t.* [1] (spread) ~ **[out]** spreizen [2] (construct with divergent sides) ausschrägen
B *v.i.* ‹*Linien:*› [schräg] auseinander laufen; ‹*Tischbeine, Stuhlbeine:*› schräg nach außen gehen; ‹*Finger, Zehen:*› gespreizt sein; ‹*Räder:*› schräg zueinander stehen
C *n.* Ausschrägung, *die*
D *adj.* gespreizt

splay: **~-foot** **A** *n.* Spreizfuß, *der;* **B** *adj.* ▸ **~-footed**; **~-footed** *adj.* spreizfüßig

spleen /spli:n/ *n.* [1] ▸ ❶ **p. 951** (Anat.) Milz, *die* [2] (bad mood) schlechte Laune; Übellaunigkeit, *die;* (anger, rage) Wut, *die;* **vent one's ~ [on sb.]** seine schlechte Laune/Wut [an jmdm.] abreagieren

splendid /'splendɪd/ *adj.* (excellent, outstanding) großartig; (beautiful) herrlich; (sumptuous, magnificent) prächtig; **live in ~ isolation** von der Außenwelt abgeschirmt leben; **cut a ~ figure** imposant aussehen

splendidly /ˈsplendɪdlɪ/ *adv.* (excellently, outstandingly) großartig; (sumptuously, magnificently) prächtig; **live ~:** prunkvoll leben; **get along ~ with sb.** bestens mit jmdm. auskommen; **this flat will suit you ~:** diese Wohnung ist genau das Richtige für Sie

splendiferous /splenˈdɪfərəs/ *adj.* (coll.) prachtvoll

splendour (*Brit.*; *Amer.*: **splendor**) /ˈsplendə(r)/ *n.* 1 (magnificence) Pracht, *die* 2 (brightness) Glanz, *der*

splenetic /splɪˈnetɪk/ *adj.* mürrisch; unwirsch

splice /splaɪs/
A *v.t.* 1 (join ends of by interweaving) verspleißen (Seemannsspr.) 2 (join in overlapping position) [an den Enden überlappend] zusammenfügen; zusammenkleben ‹*Filmstreifen usw.*›; **~ a scene into a film** eine Szene in einen Film einschneiden 3 **get ~d** (coll.: get married) sich verehelichen. *See also* **main brace**
B *n.* Spleiß, *der* (Seemannsspr.)

splint /splɪnt/
A *n.* Schiene, *die*; **put sb.'s arm in a ~:** jmds. Arm schienen
B *v.t.* schienen

splinter /ˈsplɪntə(r)/
A *n.* Splitter, *der*
B *v.i.* 1 (become split into long pieces) splittern; **~ away from sth.** von etw. absplittern 2 (fig.: split into factions) sich aufsplittern
C *v.t.* (also fig.: split into factions) zersplittern

splinter: ~ group *n.* Splittergruppe, *die*; **~ party** *n.* Splitterpartei, *die*; **~-proof** *adj.* splittersicher

splintery /ˈsplɪntərɪ/ *adj.* splitterig

split /splɪt/
A *n.* 1 (tear) Riss, *der* 2 (division into parts) [Auf-]teilung, *die* 3 (fig.: rift) Spaltung, *die*; **a ~ between Moscow and her allies** ein Bruch zwischen Moskau und seinen Verbündeten 4 (Gymnastics, Skating) **the ~s** *or* (Amer.) **~:** Spagat, *der od. das*; **do the ~s** Spagat machen; in den Spagat gehen. *See also* **banana split**
B *adj.* gespalten; **~ lip** aufgeplatzte Lippe; **~ decision** (Boxing) nicht einstimmige Entscheidung; **be ~ on a question** [sich (*Dat.*)] in einer Frage uneins sein; **be ~ down the middle** in zwei Lager gespalten sein; *see also* **pin A 2**
C *v.t.*, **-tt-, split** 1 (tear) zerreißen 2 (divide) teilen; spalten ‹*Holz*›; **let's ~ the money between us** lasst uns das Geld unter uns aufteilen; **~ persons/things into groups** Personen/Dinge in Gruppen (*Akk.*) aufteilen *od.* einteilen; **they ~ a bottle of wine** sie teilen/teilten sich (*Dat.*) eine Flasche Wein; **~ the difference** sich in der Mitte treffen; **~ hairs** (fig.) Haare spalten 3 (divide into disagreeing parties) spalten; **~ the ticket** *or* **one's vote** (Amer. Polit.) splitten 4 (remove by breaking) **~ [off** *or* **away]** abbrechen 5 (Phys.) spalten ‹*Atom*›. *See also* **side A 4**
D *v.i.*, **-tt-, split** 1 (break into parts) ‹*Holz*:› splittern; ‹*Stoff, Seil*:› reißen 2 (divide into parts) sich teilen; ‹*Gruppe*:› sich spalten; ‹*zwei Personen*:› sich trennen 3 (be removed by breaking) **~ from** absplittern von; **~ apart** zersplittern 4 (coll.: betray secrets) auspacken (ugs.); quatschen (ugs.) 5 (coll.: depart) abhauen (ugs.)

Phrasal verbs
- **~ aˈway** *v.i.* absplittern; **~ away from** absplittern von; ‹*Parteiflügel, Gruppierung*:› sich abspalten von
- **~ ˈoff**
A *v.t.* abspalten
B *v.i.* ▸ **~ away**
- **~ on** *v.t.* (coll.) **~ on sb. [to sb.]** jmdn. [bei jmdm.] verpfeifen (ugs.)
- **~ ˈopen**
A *v.i.* aufbrechen
B *v.t.* öffnen ‹*Nuss, Schote*›; **he ~ his head open** er hat sich (*Dat.*) den Kopf aufgeschlagen
- **~ ˈup**
A *v.t.* aufteilen
B *v.i.* (coll.) sich trennen; **~ up with sb.** sich von jmdm. trennen; mit jmdm. Schluss machen (ugs.)
- **~ with** *v.i.* (coll.) brechen mit

split: ~ end *n.* gespaltene [Haar]spitze; **~ inˈfinitive** *n.* (Ling.) *Konstruktion im Englischen, bei der zwischen Infinitivkonjunktion und Infinitiv ein Adverb eingeschoben wird*; **~-level** *adj.* mit Zwischengeschoss; auf zwei Ebenen; **a ~-level lounge** ein Wohnraum auf zwei Ebenen; **~-level cooker** *Einbauherd, bei dem Kochplatten und Backofen getrennt sind*; **~ ˈpea** *n.* getrocknete [halbe] Erbse; **~ persoˈnality** *n.* gespaltene Persönlichkeit (Psych.); **~ pin** *n.* Splint, *der*; **~ ring** *n.* Spaltring, *der*; **~ ˈscreen** *n.* 1 (Computing) geteilter Bildschirm; *attrib.* **~ screen facility** Möglichkeit der Bildschirm[auf]teilung; 2 (Cinemat.) geteilte Leinwand; **~ ˈsecond** *n.* **in a ~ second** im Bruchteil einer Sekunde; **a ~ second from now** in einem Augenblick; **~-second timing** [zeitliche] Abstimmung auf die Sekunde genau; **~ ˈshift** *n.* Teilschicht, *die*; **~-site ˈschool** *n.*: *Schule mit mehreren nicht beieinander liegenden Gebäuden*

splitter /ˈsplɪtə(r)/ *n.* (Computing) Splitter, *der*

split ˈticket *n.* (Amer. Polit.) *Stimmzettel, auf dem mehrere Kandidaten verschiedener Parteien angekreuzt werden können*

splitting /ˈsplɪtɪŋ/ *adj.* **a ~ headache** rasende Kopfschmerzen; **sb.'s head is ~:** jmd. hat rasende Kopfschmerzen

splodge /splɒdʒ/ (Brit.) ▸ **splotch**

splosh /splɒʃ/ (coll.)
A *n.* Platschen, *das* (ugs.); **there was a great ~:** es platschte (ugs.) laut
B *v.i.* platschen (ugs.)
C *v.t.* ▸ **splash A 1**

splotch /splɒtʃ/
A *n.* Fleck, *der*; Klecks, *der*
B *v.t.* 1 (daub) verschmieren 2 (make ~ on) beklecksen

splurge /splɜːdʒ/
A *n.* Wirbel, *der*; **go on a ~:** ein paar größere Anschaffungen machen; **~ of activity** Aktivitätsschub, *der*
B *v.i.* ▸ **splash out**

splutter /ˈsplʌtə(r)/
A *v.i.* ‹*Feuer, Gaslampe*:› flackern; ‹*Fett*:› spritzen; ‹*Person*:› prusten; ‹*Motor*:› stottern; **~ with rage/indignation** vor Wut/Entrüstung schnauben
B *v.t.* stottern ‹*Worte*›

spoil /spɔɪl/
A *v.t.*, **spoilt** /spɔɪlt/ *or* **spoiled** 1 (impair) verderben; ruinieren‹*Leben*›; **he always ~s a joke in the telling** wenn er einen Witz erzählt, verdirbt er immer die Pointe; **the news ~t his dinner/evening** die Nachricht verdarb ihm das Essen/den Abend; **~t ballot papers** ungültige Stimmzettel; *see also* **tar[1] A** 2 (injure character of) verderben (geh.); verziehen ‹*Kind*›; **~ sb. for sth.** jmdn. für etw. zu anspruchsvoll machen; *see also* **rod 3** 3 (pamper) verwöhnen; **be ~t for choice** die Qual der Wahl haben
B *v.i.*, **spoilt** *or* **spoiled** 1 (go bad) verderben 2 **be ~ing for a fight/for trouble** Streit/Ärger suchen
C *n.* 1 (plunder) **~[s]** Beute, *die*; **~s of war** Kriegsbeute, *die* 2 (Mining etc.: waste material) Abraum, *der*

spoiler /ˈspɔɪlə(r)/ *n.* (of car, aircraft) Spoiler, *der*; (of glider) Bremsklappe, *die*

spoil: ~ heap *n.* Aushub, *der*; (in mining) Abraum, *der*; Abraumhalde, *die*; **~sport** *n.* Spielverderber, *der*/-verderberin, *die*; **~s system** *n.* (Amer.) *vom Gewinner einer Wahl betriebene Ämterpatronage*

spoilt
A ▸ **spoil A, B**
B *adj.* verzogen ‹*Kind*›

spoke[1] /spəʊk/ *n.* 1 (of wheel) Speiche, *die*; **put a ~ in sb.'s wheel** (fig.) jmdm. einen Knüppel zwischen die Beine werfen 2 ▸ **rung[1] 1**

spoke[2], spoken ▸ **speak**

ˈspokeshave *n.* Schabhobel, *der*

spokesman /ˈspəʊksmən/ *n.*, *pl.* **spokesmen** /ˈspəʊksmən/ Sprecher, *der*

spokesperson /ˈspəʊkspɜːsn/ *n.* Sprecher, *der*/Sprecherin, *die*

spokeswoman /ˈspəʊkswʊmən/ *n.* Sprecherin, *die*

spoliation /spəʊlɪˈeɪʃn/ *n.* (plunder) Plünderung, *die*; (of vessel) Kaperung, *die*

spondee /ˈspɒndiː, ˈspɒndɪ/ *n.* (Pros.) Spondeus, *der*

sponge /spʌndʒ/
A *n.* 1 Schwamm, *der*; **throw in the ~** (Boxing) das Handtuch werfen *od.* schmeißen; (fig.) das Handtuch werfen (ugs.) 2 ▸ **sponge cake**; **sponge pudding** 3 (Surg.) Tupfer, *der* 4 (porous metal) Schwamm, *der* 5 **have a ~ down** sich mit dem Schwamm abwaschen; **give the chair a ~ down** den Stuhl [mit dem Schwamm] abwischen
B *v.t.* 1 ▸ **cadge A** 2 (wipe) mit einem Schwamm waschen

Phrasal verbs
- **~ ˈdown** *v.t.* mit einem Schwamm abwaschen
- **~ off** *v.t.* 1 /-ˈ-/ (wipe off) mit einem Schwamm abwischen; (wash off) mit einem Schwamm abwaschen 2 /ˈ--/ ▸ **~ on**
- **~ on** *v.t.* (coll.) **~ on sb.** bei *od.* von jmdm. schnorren (ugs.)

sponge: ~ bag *n.* (Brit.) Kulturbeutel, *der*; **~ biscuit** *n.* ≈ Biskotte, *die* (Kochk.); **~ cake** *n.* Biskuitkuchen, *der*; **~ ˈpudding** *n.* Schwammpudding, *der* (Kochk.); *leichter, im Wasserbad zubereiteter Pudding*

sponger /ˈspʌndʒə(r)/ *n.* Schmarotzer, *der*/Schmarotzerin, *die*; Schnorrer, *der*/Schnorrerin, *die*

sponge ˈrubber *n.* Schaumgummi, *der*

spongy /ˈspʌndʒɪ/ *adj.* schwammig

sponsor /ˈspɒnsə(r)/
A *n.* 1 (firm paying for event, one donating to charitable event) Sponsor, *der* 2 (of legislative proposal) **the ~s of this Bill are Labour MPs** hinter dieser Gesetzesvorlage stehen Labour-Abgeordnete 3 (group supporting candidate) **his ~ is a trade union** er wird von einer Gewerkschaft unterstützt 4 (godparent) Pate, *der*/Patin, *die*
B *v.t.* 1 (pay for) sponsern ‹*Teilnehmer, Programm, Veranstaltung*› 2 (subscribe to) finanziell unterstützen, sponsern ‹*Wohlfahrtsverband*› 3 (introduce for legislation) einbringen ‹*Gesetzesvorlage*› 4 (support in election) unterstützen ‹*Kandidaten*›; **~ sb.** jmds. Kandidatur unterstützen

sponsored /ˈspɒnsəd/ *adj.* gesponsert; finanziell gefördert; **~ run** *als Wohltätigkeitsveranstaltung durchgeführter Dauerlauf mit gesponserten Teilnehmern*

sponsorship /ˈspɒnsəʃɪp/ *n.* 1 (financial support) Sponsorschaft, *die*; **take over the ~ of sth.** etw. sponsern; **withdraw from the ~ of sth.** etw. nicht mehr sponsern 2 (introduction of legislation) Einbringen, *das* 3 (support of candidate) Unterstützung, *die*; **the party's ~ of sb.** die Unterstützung von jmds. Kandidatur durch die Partei

spontaneity /spɒntəˈniːɪtɪ/ *n.*, *no pl.* Spontan[e]ität, *die*

spontaneous /spɒnˈteɪnɪəs/ *adj.* spontan; **make a ~ offer of sth.** spontan etw. anbieten

spontaneous: ~ comˈbustion *n.* Selbstentzündung, *die*; **~ geneˈration** *n.* Urzeugung, *die*

spontaneously /spɒnˈteɪnɪəslɪ/ spontan; von selbst ‹*passieren*›

spoof /spuːf/ (coll.)
A *n.* Veralberung, *die* (**of, on** von); Parodie, *die* (**of, on** auf + *Akk.*)
B *v.t.* durch den Kakao ziehen (ugs.)

spook /spuːk/ *n.* (joc.) Geist, *der*; Gespenst, *das*; (coll.: spy) Spion, *der*; **it gives me the ~s** es ist mir richtig unheimlich

spooky /ˈspuːkɪ/ *adj.* gespenstisch

spool /spuːl/
A *n.* 1 (reel) Spule, *die* 2 (Angling) Trommel, *die*
B *v.t.* spulen

spoon[1] /spuːn/
A *n.* 1 Löffel, *der*; **fruit ~:** Kompottlöffel, *der*; **be born with a silver ~ in one's mouth** mit einem goldenen *od.* silbernen Löffel im Mund geboren werden; **wooden ~** (fig.) Trostpreis

S

(für den Letzten eines Wettbewerbs, oft in ironischer Weise überreicht) 2 (amount) ▸**spoonful** 3 (Angling) Blinker, *der*
B *v.t.* löffeln
Phrasal verb
• ~ **'up** *v.t.* auflöffeln

spoon² *v.i.* (arch.: be amorous) schmusen

'spoonbill *n.* (Ornith.) Löffler, *der*

spoonerism /'spu:nərɪzm/ *n.: witziges Vertauschen der Anfangsbuchstaben o. Ä. von zwei oder mehr Wörtern (wie bei „Leichenzehrer" für „Zeichenlehrer")*

'spoon-feed *v.t.* mit dem Löffel füttern; ~ **sb.** (fig.) jmdm. alles vorkauen (ugs.)

spoonful /'spu:nfʊl/ *n.* **a ~ of sugar** ein Löffel [voll] Zucker

spoor /spʊə(r)/ *n.* Spur, *die;* Fährte, *die*

sporadic /spə'rædɪk/ *adj.* sporadisch; vereinzelt ‹*Schauer, Schüsse, Gebäude*›

sporadically /spə'rædɪkəlɪ/ *adv.* hin und wieder

spore /spɔ:(r)/ *n.* 1 (Bot.: cell) Spore, *die* 2 (Biol.: bacterium) Spore, *die*

sporran /'spɒrən/ *n.* (Scot.) *mit Fell besetzte Tasche, die von den Bewohnern der Highlands vorne über dem Kilt getragen wird*

sport /spɔ:t/
A *n.* 1 (pastime) Sport, *der;* **~s** Sportarten; **team/winter/water/indoor ~:** Mannschafts-/Winter-/Wasser-/Hallensport, *der* 2 *no pl., no art.* (collectively) Sport, *der;* **go in for ~, do ~:** Sport treiben; **he likes doing ~ at school** er mag den Sport[unterricht] in der Schule; **have good ~** (Hunting) großes Jagdglück haben 3 *in pl.* (Brit.) **[athletic] ~s** Athletik, *die;* **S~s Day** (Sch.) Sportfest, *das;* **the ~s** der sportliche Wettkampf 4 *no pl., no art.* (fun) Spaß, *der;* **do/say sth. in ~:** etw. im *od.* zum Scherz tun/sagen; **make ~ of sb./sth.** sich über jmdn./etw. lustig machen 5 (coll.: good fellow) netter Kerl (ugs.); (Austral. as voc.: mate) Kumpel! (ugs.); Sportsmann! (ugs.); **Aunt Joan is a real ~:** Tante Joan ist echt (ugs.) in Ordnung; **be a [good] ~ and help me** sei so nett und hilf mir; **be a good/bad ~** (in games) ein guter/schlechter Verlierer sein 6 (Amer.: playboy) Playboy, *der* 7 (Zool., Bot.) Variante, *die*
B *v.t.* stolz tragen ‹*Kleidungsstück*›; protzen mit ‹*Neuerwerbung*›
C *v.i.* 1 (amuse oneself) sich tummeln 2 (Biol.: mutate) variieren

sporting /'spɔ:tɪŋ/ *adj.* 1 (interested in sport) sportlich 2 (generous) großzügig; (fair) fair; anständig; **do the ~ thing and do sth.** so anständig sein, etw. zu tun; **give sb. a ~ chance** jmdm. eine [faire] Chance geben 3 (relating to sport) Sport-; **~ dog/rifle** Jagdhund, *der*/Pirschbüchse, *die;* **~ giant** *or* **hero** Sportgröße, *die*

'sporting house *n.* (Amer.) Bordell, *das*

sportingly /'spɔ:tɪŋlɪ/ *adv.* 1 (generously) **~ do sth.** so großzügig sein, etw. zu tun 2 (sportively) in sportlichem Geist

sportive /'spɔ:tɪv/ *adj.* verspielt ‹*junges Tier*›; ausgelassen ‹*Stimmung, Schar*›; **be in a ~ mood** zum Spielen aufgelegt sein

sports: ~ **bra** *n.* Sport-BH, *der;* ~ **car** *n.* Sportwagen, *der;* ~ **centre** *n.* Sportzentrum, *das;* ~ **channel** *n.* Sportkanal, *der;* ~ **club** *n.* Sportverein, *der;* Sportklub, *der;* ~ **commentator** *n.* ▸❶ **p. 1260** (Radio, Telev.) Sportberichterstatter, *der*/-berichterstatterin, *die;* ~ **complex** *n.* Sportzentrum, *das;* ~ **drink** *n.* Sportlerdrink, *der;* Sportlertrunk, *der;* ~ **editor** *n.* ▸❶ **p. 1260** (Journ.) Sportredakteur, *der*/-redakteurin, *die;* ~ **field** *n.* Sportplatz, *der;* ~ **hall** *n.* Sporthalle, *die;* (in a school also) Turnhalle, *die;* ~ **jacket** *n.* sportlicher Sakko; **~man** /'spɔ:tsmən/ *n., pl.* **~men** /'spɔ:tsmən/ 1 Sportler, *der;* 2 (generous person) großzügiger Mensch; (fair-minded person) anständiger Mensch

sportsmanlike /'spɔ:tsmənlaɪk/ ▸**sporting 2**

sportsmanship /'spɔ:tsmənʃɪp/ *n.* 1 (fairness) [sportliche] Fairness 2 (skill) sportliche Leistung

sports: ~ **news** *n.* (Radio, Telev.) Sportnachrichten; ~ **page** *n.* (Journ.) Sportseite, *die;* ~ **programme** *n.* (Radio, Telev.) Sportsendung, *die;* ~ **section** *n.* (Journ.) Sportteil, *der;* **~wear** *n., no pl.* Sport[be]kleidung, *die;* **~woman** *n.* Sportlerin, *die*

sporty /'spɔ:tɪ/ *adj.* 1 (coll.: sport-loving) sportlich; **the whole family is ~:** die ganze Familie ist sportbegeistert 2 (jaunty) sportlich ‹*Aussehen*›; **be a ~ dresser** sich sportlich kleiden 3 (designed for sport) Sport‹*boot, -wagen, -rad*›

spot /spɒt/
A *n.* 1 (precise place) Stelle, *die;* **this is the precise/exact/very ~ where he landed** genau an dieser Stelle *od.* genau hier ist er gelandet; **on this ~:** an dieser Stelle; **the very same ~:** genau die gleiche Stelle; **in ~s** stellenweise; (fig.: partly) teilweise; **run on the ~:** auf der Stelle laufen; **on the ~** (fig.) (instantly) auf der Stelle; **be on the ~** (be present) zur Stelle sein; **and now over to our man on the ~** (Radio, Telev.) und nun schalten wir um zu unserem Mann am Ort des Geschehens; **be in/get into/get out of a [tight] ~** (fig. coll.) in der Klemme sitzen/in die Klemme geraten/sich aus einer brenzligen Lage befreien (ugs.); **put sb. on the ~** (fig. coll.: cause difficulties for sb.) jmdn. in Verlegenheit bringen; (Amer. sl.: decide to kill sb.) jmdn. auf die Abschussliste setzen
2 (inhabited place) Ort, *der;* **a nice ~ on the Moselle** ein hübscher Flecken an der Mosel
3 (suitable area) Platz, *der;* **holiday/sun ~:** Ferienort, *der*/Ferienort [mit Sonnengarantie]; **picnic ~:** Picknickplatz, *der;* **a sheltered ~:** ein geschützter Platz; **a nice ~ to live** eine hübsche Wohngegend; **hit the high ~s** (coll.) groß ausgehen
4 (dot) Tupfen, *der;* Tupfer, *der;* (larger) Flecken, *der;* **change one's ~s** (fig.) aus seiner Haut herauskommen (fig.); **knock ~s off sb.** (fig. coll.) jmdn. in die Pfanne hauen (ugs.); **see ~s before one's eyes** Sterne sehen (ugs.)
5 (stain) **~ [of blood/grease/ink]** [Blut-/Fett-/Tinten]fleck, *der*
6 (Brit. coll.: small amount) **do a ~ of work/sewing** ein bisschen arbeiten/nähen; **how about a ~ of lunch?** wie wärs mit einem Bissen zu Mittag?; **a ~ of whisky** ein Schluck Whisky; **a ~ of culture** ein bisschen Kultur; **have** *or* **be in a ~ of bother** *or* **trouble** etwas Ärger haben; **be in a ~ of trouble with the law** Ärger mit der Polizei haben
7 (drop) **a ~** *or* **a few ~s of rain** ein paar Regentropfen
8 (establishment) **eating/drinking/entertainment ~:** Ess-/Trink-/Vergnügungslokal, *das*
9 (area on body) [Körper]stelle, *die;* **a tender/sore ~** (lit.) eine empfindliche/wunde Stelle; **a sore ~ with sb.** (fig.) jmds. neuralgischer Punkt; **have a weak ~** (fig.) eine Schwachstelle haben; *see also* **sore A 1**
10 (fig. coll.: job) Job, *der* (ugs.)
11 (Telev. coll.: position in programme) Sendezeit, *die;* **the 7 o'clock ~:** das Siebenuhrprogramm
12 (Med.) Pickel, *der;* **heat ~:** Hitzebläschen, *das;* **break out in ~s** Ausschlag bekommen
13 (on dice, dominoes) Punkt, *der*
14 (spotlight) Spot, *der*
15 (fig.: blemish) Schandfleck, *der* (emotional); **remain without a ~ on one's reputation** immer eine weiße Weste behalten (ugs.)
16 (Sport: dot) Aufsetzmarke, *die;* **the ~ [ball]** (Billiards) der Punktball; **the [penalty] ~:** die Elfmetermarke; der Elfmeterpunkt
17 (Commerc.) **~s, ~ goods** sofort lieferbare Ware; Lokoware, *die* (fachspr.); **pay ~ cash** [sofort] bar zahlen. *See also* **blind spot**; **leopard**; **soft A 3**; **tender¹ 2**
B *v.t.,* **-tt-** 1 (detect) entdecken; identifizieren ‹*Verbrecher*›; erkennen ‹*Gefahr*›; **it is easy to ~ an American among a group of tourists** man kann leicht feststellen, wer in einer Gruppe von Touristen Amerikaner ist
2 (take note of) erkennen ‹*Flugzeugtyp, Vogel, Talent*›; **go train-spotting/plane-spotting** Zug-/Flugzeugtypen bestimmen
3 (coll.: pick out) tippen auf (+ *Akk.*) (ugs.) ‹*Sieger, Gewinner usw.*›
4 (stain) beflecken; (with ink or paint) beklecksen; (with mud) beschmutzen
5 (Billiards etc.) aufstellen
6 (Mil.: locate) orten
C *v.i.,* **-tt-: it is ~ting with rain** es tröpfelt (ugs.)

spot: ~ **'check** *n.* (test made immediately) sofortige Überprüfung (**on** *Gen.*); (test made on randomly selected subject) Stichprobe, *die;* **make** *or* **carry out a ~ check on sth.** etw. sofort stichprobenweise überprüfen; **~-check** *v.t.* stichprobenweise überprüfen; ~ **height** *n.* (Geog.) Höhenangabe, *die;* ~ **lamp** *n.* Spotlight, *das;* (Motor Veh.) Scheinwerfer, *der*

spotless /'spɒtlɪs/ *adj.* 1 (unstained) fleckenlos; **her house is absolutely ~** (fig.) ihr Haus ist makellos sauber; **clean sth. until it is ~:** etw. reinigen, bis man kein Stäubchen mehr findet 2 (fig.: blameless) mustergültig; untadelig ‹*Charakter*›

spotlessly /'spɒtlɪslɪ/ *adv.* **~ clean/white** tadellos sauber/makellos weiß

spot: **~light** A *n.* 1 (Theatre) [Bühnen]scheinwerfer, *der;* 2 (Motor Veh.) Scheinwerfer, *der;* 3 (fig.: attention) **the ~light is on sb.** jmd. steht im Rampenlicht [der Öffentlichkeit]; **be in the ~light** im Rampenlicht [der Öffentlichkeit] stehen; **keep out of the ~light** sich von der Öffentlichkeit fernhalten; B *v.t.,* **~lighted** *or* **~lit** 1 (Theatre) [mit dem Scheinwerfer] anstrahlen; 2 (fig.: highlight) in den Blickpunkt der Öffentlichkeit bringen; ~ **market** *n.* (Commerc.) Spotmarkt, *der;* ~ **'on** (coll.) A *adj.* goldrichtig (ugs.); **I was ~ on** ich lag genau richtig (ugs.); **your estimate was ~ on** mit deiner Schätzung hast du ins Schwarze getroffen; B *adv.* haargenau (ugs.); ~ **price** *n.* (Econ.) Kassapreis, *der;* (Stock Exch.) Kassakurs, *der;* ~ **remover** *n.* Fleck[en]entferner, *der;* ~ **'survey** *n.* [Blitz]umfrage, *die*

spotted /'spɒtɪd/ *adj.* 1 gepunktet; **a blue dress/tie ~ with white** ein blaues Kleid mit weißen Tupfen/eine blaue Krawatte mit weißen Punkten 2 (Zool.) **~ woodpecker/hyena** Buntspecht, *der*/Tüpfelhyäne, *die*

spotted: ~ **'Dick** *n.* (Brit.: pudding) Pudding mit getrockneten Früchten; ~ **'dog** *n.* 1 (coll.: Dalmatian) Dalmatiner, *der;* 2 ▸~ **Dick**

spotter /'spɒtə(r)/ *n.* **~ [plane]** Erkundungsflugzeug, *das*

'spot test *n.* 1 (chemical test) Spurenprobe, *die;* Tüpfeltest, *der* 2 (~ check) Stichprobe, *die*

spotty /'spɒtɪ/ *adj.* 1 (spotted) gefleckt; (stained) fleckig 2 (pimply) picklig; **be ~:** viele Pickel haben; (have a rash) einen [starken] Ausschlag haben

spot: **~-weld** A *v.t.* punktschweißen; B *n.* Punktschweißung, *die;* **~-welding** *n.* Punktschweißen, *das*

spouse /spaʊz/ *n.* [Ehe]gatte, *der*/-gattin, *die;* (joc.) Angetraute, *der/die;* Gemahl, *der*/Gemahlin, *die*

spout /spaʊt/
A *n.* 1 (tube) Schnabel, *der;* (of water pump) [Auslauf]rohr, *das;* (of overflow) Überlaufrohr, *das;* (of tap) Ausflussrohr, *das;* (of gargoyle) Speirohr, *das;* (of fountain) Spritzdüse, *die;* **be up the ~** (coll.: pawned) im Leihhaus sein; (coll.: ruined) im Eimer sein (ugs.); (Brit. coll.: pregnant) ein Kind kriegen (ugs.) 2 (chute) Rutsche, *die*
B *v.t.* 1 (discharge) ausstoßen ‹*Wasser, Lava, Öl*›; **the wound ~s blood** aus der Wunde strömt Blut 2 (declaim) deklamieren ‹*Verse*›; (rattle off) herunterrasseln (ugs.) ‹*Zahlen, Fakten usw.*›; **~ compliments/remarks** mit Komplimenten/Bemerkungen um sich werfen; **~ nonsense** Unsinn verzapfen (ugs.)
C *v.i.* 1 (gush) schießen (**from** aus) 2 (declaim) schwadronieren (abwertend); schwafeln (ugs. abwertend); **~ at sb.** jmdm. etwas vorpredigen (ugs.)
Phrasal verb
• ~ **'out** *v.i.* herausströmen; **~ out of sth.** aus etw. strömen

sprain /spreɪn/ ▸❶ **p. 1231**
A *v.t.* verstauchen; **~ one's ankle/wrist** sich (*Dat.*) den Knöchel/das Handgelenk verstauchen

S

B *n.* Verstauchung, *die*

sprang ▸**spring B, C**

sprat /spræt/ *n.* Sprotte, *die;* **set a ~ to catch a mackerel** *or* **herring** *or* **whale** (fig.) mit der Wurst nach dem Schinken *od.* der Speckseite werfen (ugs.)

sprawl /sprɔ:l/

A *n.* 1 (slump) **lie in a ~:** ausgestreckt [da]liegen 2 (straggle) verstreute Ansammlung; **the city was one huge ~ over the map** die Stadt dehnte sich auf der Landkarte als riesiger Fleck aus; **the ~ of the handwriting across the page** die quer über die ganze Seite gezogene Handschrift; *see also* **urban**

B *v.i.* 1 (spread oneself) sich ausstrecken 2 (fall) der Länge nach hinfallen; **send sb. ~ing** jmdn. zu Boden strecken (geh.) 3 (straggle) sich ausbreiten

C *v.t.* 1 (splay out) ausstrecken; **be** *or* **lie ~ed in/on/over sth.** ausgestreckt in/auf/über etw. (*Dat.*) liegen 2 (spread) verstreuen; **~ words/letters across the page** Wörter/Buchstaben großzügig über die ganze Seite pinseln

Phrasal verbs

- **~ a'bout** *v.i.* sich herumflegeln (ugs. abwertend)
- **~ 'out** *v.i.* 1 (stretch out) sich ausstrecken 2 (straggle) sich hinziehen

sprawled out /sprɔ:ld 'aʊt/ *adj.* ausgestreckt [liegend]

sprawling /'sprɔ:lɪŋ/ *attrib. adj.* 1 (extended) ausgestreckt [liegend] 2 (falling) der Länge nach hinfallend 3 (straggling) verstreut liegend ‹*Gebäude*›; wuchernd ‹*Großstadt*› 4 (spidery) ausladend, (scrawled) krakelig (ugs.) ‹*Handschrift*›

spray[1] /spreɪ/ *n.* 1 (bouquet) Strauß, *der;* **a ~ of roses** ein Strauß Rosen 2 (branch) Zweig, *der;* (of palm or fern) Wedel, *der* 3 (brooch) *Brosche in der Form eines kleinen Straußes od. Zweigs*

spray[2]

A *v.t.* 1 (in a stream) spritzen; (in a mist) sprühen ‹*Parfum, Farbe, Spray*›; **they ~ed the general's car with bullets** sie durchsiebten den Wagen des Generals mit Kugeln 2 (treat) besprühen ‹*Haar, Haut, Pflanze*›; spritzen ‹*Nutzpflanzen*›; **the vandals ~ed the car with paint** die Rabauken besprühten das Auto mit Farbe

B *v.i.* spritzen

C *n.* 1 (drops) Sprühnebel, *der* 2 (liquid) Spray, *der od. das* 3 (container) Spraydose, *die;* (in gardening) Spritze, *die;* **hair/throat ~:** Haar-/Rachenspray, *der od. das;* **perfume ~:** Parfümzerstäuber, *der*

Phrasal verbs

- **~ on [to]** *v.t.* **~ sth. on [to] sth.** etw. mit etw. besprühen
- **~ 'out** *v.i.* herausspritzen

spray: ~ can ▸**aerosol 1**; **~ deck** *n.* Spritzdecke, *die*

sprayer /'spreɪə(r)/ *n.* 1 (person) **[paint] ~:** Spritzlackierer, *der*/-lackiererin, *die* 2 (tool) Sprühgerät, *das;* (in pest control, gardening) Spritze, *die*

spray: ~ gun *n.* Spritzpistole, *die;* **~ paint** *n.* Sprayfarbe, *die;* **~-paint** *v.t.* mit Farbe besprühen; aufsprühen, sprayen ‹*Schriftzug, Graffiti*›; spritzen, spritzlackieren ‹*Möbel, Auto*›

spread /spred/

A *v.t.,* **spread** 1 ausbreiten ‹*Tuch, Landkarte*› (**on** auf + *Dat.*); streichen ‹*Butter, Farbe, Marmelade*›; **the peacock ~ its tail** der Pfau schlug ein Rad; **the yacht ~ its sails** die Segel der Jacht blähten sich 2 (cover) **~ a roll with marmalade/butter** ein Brötchen mit Marmelade/Butter bestreichen; **the sofa was ~ with a blanket** auf dem Sofa lag eine Decke [ausgebreitet] 3 (fig.: display) **a magnificent view/meal was ~ before us** uns (*Dat.*) bot sich eine herrliche Aussicht/uns (*Dat.*) wurde ein herrliches Mahl aufgetragen 4 (extend range of) verbreiten; **drought has ~ famine to many areas** durch die Dürre breitete sich in vielen Gebieten eine Hungersnot aus 5 (distribute) verteilen; (untidily) verstreuen; streuen ‹*Dünger*›; verbreiten ‹*Zerstörung, Angst, Niedergeschlagenheit*› 6 (make known) verbreiten; **~ the word** (tell news) es weitersagen; (coll.: pass on a message) die Nachricht weitergeben; (Relig.) das Wort Gottes verkünden 7 (separate) ausbreiten ‹*Arme*›; öffnen ‹*Lippen*›; spreizen ‹*Beine*›; *see also* **wing A 1**

B *v.i.,* **spread** 1 sich ausbreiten; **a smile/a blush ~ across** *or* **over his face** ein Lächeln breitete sich (geh.) über sein Gesicht/er wurde ganz rot im Gesicht; **margarine ~s easily** Margarine lässt sich leicht streichen; **~ing branches/trees** ausladende Äste/Bäume; **~ like wildfire** sich in *od.* mit Windeseile verbreiten 2 (scatter, disperse) sich verteilen; **the odour ~s through the room** der Geruch breitet sich im ganzen Zimmer aus 3 (circulate) ‹*Neuigkeiten, Gerücht, Kenntnis usw.:*› sich verbreiten

C *n.* 1 (expanse) Fläche, *die;* **we could see the whole ~ of the town** wir konnten das ganze Stadtgebiet überblicken 2 (span) (of tree) Kronendurchmesser, *der;* (of wings) Spann[weite], *die;* **an oak with a magnificent ~ of branches** eine Eiche mit einer prächtigen Baumkrone 3 (breadth) **have a wide ~** ‹*Interessen, Ansichten:*› breit gefächert sein; **a wide ~ of responsibility** ein großer Verantwortungsbereich 4 (extension) Verbreitung, *die;* (of city, urbanization, poverty) Ausbreitung, *die* 5 (diffusion) Ausbreitung, *die;* (of learning, knowledge) Verbreitung, *die;* Vermittlung, *die* 6 (distribution) Verteilung, *die* 7 (coll.: meal) Festessen, *das;* Schmaus, *der* (veralt.) 8 (paste) Brotaufstrich, *der;* ‹*Rindfleisch-, Lachs*›paste, *die;* ‹*Käse-, Erdnuss-, Schokoladen*›krem, *die* 9 (girth) ▸**middle-aged** 10 ▸**bedspread** 11 (Printing) **the advertisement was a full-page/double-page ~:** die Anzeige war ganzseitig/doppelseitig 12 (Amer. coll.: ranch) Ranch, *die*

D *v. refl.* 1 (stretch out) sich ausstrecken 2 (talk or write at length) sich verbreiten

Phrasal verbs

- **~ a'bout, ~ a'round** *v.t.* 1 (convey) verbreiten ‹*Neuigkeiten, Gerücht usw.*› 2 (strew) verstreuen; ausstreuen ‹*Samen*›
- **~ 'out**

A *v.t.* 1 (extend) ausbreiten ‹*Arme*› 2 (space out) verteilen ‹*Soldaten, Tänzer, Pfosten*›; legen ‹*Karten*›; ausbreiten ‹*Papiere*›

B *v.i.* sich verteilen; ‹*Soldaten:*› ausschwärmen

- **~ 'over**

A *v.t.* **~ sth. over a certain time** etw. über eine bestimmte Zeit ausdehnen; **the mortgage/repayment is ~ over twenty years** die Hypothek hat eine Laufzeit von zwanzig Jahren/die Rückzahlung wird [ratenweise] innerhalb von zwanzig Jahren geleistet

B *v.i.* sich erstrecken über (+ *Akk.*); **~ over into** hineinreichen in (+ *Akk.*)

spread'eagle *v.t.* 1 (tie) an den ausgestreckten Armen und Beinen fesseln 2 (flatten) **the police ~d the suspect against the car** die Polizei ließ den Verdächtigen sich mit ausgestreckten Armen und Beinen gegen das Auto stellen; **lie** *or* **be ~d** ausgestreckt [da]liegen

spreader /'spredə(r)/ *n.* Streugerät, *das;* **grit-~:** Splittstreuwagen, *der;* **manure/fertilizer-~:** Stallmist-/Düngerstreuer, *der*

'spreadsheet *n.* (Computing) Arbeitsblatt, *das*

spree /spri:/ *n.* 1 (spell of spending) Einkaufsorgie, *die* (ugs.); **go on a shopping ~:** ganz groß einkaufen gehen; **have a ~:** viel Geld ausgeben 2 **be/go out on the ~** (coll.) einen draufmachen (ugs.)

'spree killer *n.* Spreekiller, *der*

sprig /sprɪg/ *n.* 1 (twig) Zweig, *der* 2 (ornament) *Schmuck in der Form eines Zweiges* 3 (young person) Spross, *der* (scherzh.) 4 (tack) Stift, *der*

sprightly /'spraɪtlɪ/ *adj.* munter

spring /sprɪŋ/

A *n.* 1 ▸**❶ p. 1515** (season) Frühling, *der;* **in ~ 1969, in the ~ of 1969** im Frühjahr 1969; **in early/late ~:** zu Anfang/Ende des Frühjahrs; **last/next ~:** letzten/nächsten Frühling; **full of the joys of ~** (iron.) aufgekratzt (ugs.); fröhlich; **~ weather/fashions/flowers** Frühlingswetter, *das*/Frühlingsmoden/-blumen; **in [the] ~:** im Frühling *od.* Frühjahr; **in the ~ of his/her life** (literary) im Frühling seines/ihres Lebens (dichter.) 2 (source, lit. or fig.) Quelle, *die* 3 (Mech.) Feder, *die;* **~s** (vehicle suspension) Federung, *die* 4 (jump) Sprung, *der;* **make a ~ at sb./at an animal** sich auf jmdn./ein Tier stürzen; **make a ~ at sth.** auf etw. (*Akk.*) zuspringen 5 (elasticity) Elastizität, *die;* **the mattresses have no ~ in them** die Matratzen federn nicht; **walk with a ~ in one's step** mit beschwingten Schritten gehen; **put a ~ in[to] sb.'s step** jmds. Schritt beschwingen 6 (recoil) Zurückschnellen, *das;* **snap back with a ~:** zurückschnellen

B *v.i.,* **sprang** /spræŋ/ *or* (Amer.) **sprung** /sprʌŋ/, **sprung** 1 (jump) springen; **~ [up] from sth.** von etw. aufspringen; **~ at sb.'s throat** jmdm. an die Kehle springen; **the blood ~s to sb.'s cheeks** jmdm. schießt das Blut ins Gesicht; **~ to one's feet** aufspringen; **~ to sb.'s assistance/defence** jmdm. beispringen; **~ to life** (fig.) [plötzlich] zum Leben erwachen 2 (arise) entspringen (**from** *Dat.*); ‹*Saat, Hoffnung:*› keimen; ‹*Bogen:*› aufstreben (geh.); **~ to fame** über Nacht bekannt werden; **his actions ~ from a false conviction** seine Handlungen entspringen einer falschen Ansicht; **~ to mind** jmdm. einfallen 3 (recoil) **~ back into position** zurückschnellen; **~ to** *or* **shut** ‹*Tür, Falle, Deckel:*› zuschnappen 4 (split) zerbrechen; (become warped) sich verziehen; **~ from sth.** von etw. abbrechen

C *v.t.,* **sprang** *or* (Amer.) **sprung, sprung** 1 (make known suddenly) **~ a new idea/a proposal/a question on sb.** jmdn. mit einer neuen Idee/einem Vorschlag/einer Frage überfallen; **~ a surprise on sb.** jmdn. überraschen 2 (cause to operate) zünden ‹*Mine*›; aufspringen lassen ‹*Schloss*›; zuschnappen lassen ‹*Falle*› 3 (coll.: set free) herausholen (**from** aus) 4 (Hunting: rouse) aufscheuchen (**from** aus) 5 (split) bersten lassen (geh.); **I've sprung my racket** mein Schläger ist gesprungen 6 (provide with ~s) federn; **be well sprung** gut gefedert sein

Phrasal verbs

- **~ 'back** *v.i.* zurückschnellen
- **~ from** *v.t.* 1 (appear from) [plötzlich] herkommen; **where did you ~ from?** wo kommst du so plötzlich her? 2 (originate from) herrühren von; ‹*Person:*› abstammen von; **he ~s from a country family** er stammt aus einer ländlichen Familie
- **~ 'up** *v.i.* ‹*Wind, Zweifel:*› aufkommen; ‹*Gebäude:*› aus dem Boden wachsen; ‹*Pflanze:*› aus dem Boden schießen; ‹*Organisation, Freundschaft:*› entstehen

spring: ~ balance *n.* Federwaage, *die;* **~ bed** ▸**bed A 1**; **~ 'binder** *n.* Klemmmappe, *die;* **~board** *n.* (Sport; also fig.) Sprungbrett, *das;* (in circus) Schleuderbrett, *das*

springbok /'sprɪŋbɒk/ *n.* 1 (Zool.) Springbock, *der* 2 *in pl.* **the S~s** (Rugby) die Südafrikaner; *Spitzname für Mitglieder südafrikanischer Rugby-/Cricketmannschaften*

spring: ~ 'cabbage *n.* Frühkohl, *der;* **~ 'chicken** *n.* 1 (fowl) junges Hähnchen; 2 (fig.: person) **be no ~ chicken** nicht mehr der/die Jüngste sein (ugs.); **~-'clean A** *n.* [großer] Hausputz; (in spring) Frühjahrsputz, *der;* **B** *v.t.* **~-clean [the whole house]** [großen] Hausputz/Frühjahrsputz machen; **~ clip** *n.* Klammer, *die*

springer /'sprɪŋə(r)/ *n.* **~ [spaniel]** Springerspaniel, *der*

spring: ~ 'greens *n. pl.* Frühkohlblätter *Pl.;* **~-loaded** *adj.* mit Sprungfeder *nachgestellt;* **~ 'mattress** *n.* Sprungfedermatratze, *die;* **~ 'onion** *n.* Frühlingszwiebel, *die;* **~ sus'pension** *n.* (Motor Veh.) federnde Aufhängung; **~ 'tide** *n.* Springflut, *die;* **~tide** *n.* (literary) Frühlingszeit, *die* (geh.); **~time** *n.* Frühling, *der;* **~ water** *n.* Quellwasser, *das*

springy /ˈsprɪŋɪ/ *adj.* elastisch; federnd ‹*Schritt, Brett, Boden*›

sprinkle /ˈsprɪŋkl/ *v.t.* 1) (scatter) streuen; sprengen ‹*Flüssigkeit*›; **~ sth. over/on sth.** etw. über/auf etw. (*Akk.*) streuen/sprengen; **~ sth. with sth.** etw. mit etw. bestreuen/besprengen 2) (fig.: distribute) verteilen 3) (fall on) spritzen auf (+ *Akk.*)

sprinkler /ˈsprɪŋklə(r)/ *n.* 1) (Hort.: for watering) Sprinkler, *der*; (Agric.) Regner, *der* 2) (fire extinguisher) **~s, ~ system** Sprinkleranlage, *die*

ˈsprinkler ban *n.* Gartenbewässerungsverbot, *das*

sprinkling /ˈsprɪŋklɪŋ/ *n.* **a ~ of snow/sugar/dust** eine dünne Schneedecke/Zucker-/Staubschicht; **a ~ of gold dust/rain** eine winzige Menge Goldstaub/ein paar Regentropfen; **there was only a ~ of holidaymakers on the beach** nur ein paar vereinzelte Urlauber waren am Strand

sprint /sprɪnt/
A *v.t. & i.* rennen; sprinten (bes. Sport); spurten (bes. Sport); **~ for the line** *or* **tape** den Endspurt anziehen
B *n.* 1) (race) Sprint, *der* (bes. Sport); **the hundred-metres ~** (competition) der Hundertmeterlauf 2) (fig.: short burst of speed) Sprint, *der* (bes. Sport); Spurt, *der* (bes. Sport); **final ~:** Endspurt, *der*

sprinter /ˈsprɪntə(r)/ *n.* Sprinter, *der*/Sprinterin, *die*

sprit /sprɪt/ *n.* (Naut.) Spriet, *das*

sprite /spraɪt/ *n.* [Elementar]geist, *der*; **a ~ of the air** ein Luftgeist

spritsail /ˈsprɪtseɪl, ˈsprɪtsl/ *n.* (Naut.) Sprietsegel, *das*

spritzer /ˈsprɪtsə(r)/ *n.* Schorle, *die*

sprocket /ˈsprɒkɪt/ *n.* 1) (projection) Zahn, *der* 2) **~ [wheel]** Zahnrad, *das*; (on bike) (front ~) Kettenblatt, *das*; (rear ~) [Ketten]ritzel, *das*

ˈsprocket wheel *n.* (Mech. Engin.) [Ketten]zahnrad, *das*

sprog /sprɒg/ *n.* (coll.) 1) (child) Sprössling, *der* 2) (trainee) Stift, *der*

sprout /spraʊt/
A *n.* 1) *in pl.* (*coll.*) ▸ **Brussels sprouts** 2) (Bot.) ▸ **shoot C 1**
B *v.i.* 1) (lit. or fig.) sprießen (geh.); **~ into life** ‹*Pflanzen:*› sprießen [und blühen] 2) (grow) emporschießen; ‹*Bart:*› wachsen 3) (fig.) ‹*Gebäude:*› wie Pilze aus dem Boden schießen; **the garden is ~ing all over with flowers** im Garten schießen überall die Blumen empor
C *v.t.* [aus]treiben ‹*Blüten, Knospen*›; sich (*Dat.*) wachsen lassen ‹*Bart*›; (fig.) aus dem Boden wachsen lassen ‹*Gebäude*›; hervorbringen ‹*Ideen*›; schaffen ‹*Arbeitsplätze*›; **the young deer was ~ing antlers** dem jungen Rehbock wuchs das Geweih; **my chin is ~ing hairs** auf meinem Kinn wachsen [Bart]haare

spruce /spru:s/
A *adj.* gepflegt; **look ~:** adrett aussehen
B *n.* (Bot.) Fichte, *die*
C *v.t.* **~ up** verschönern; **~ the house up** das [ganze] Haus aufräumen und putzen; **~ sb./oneself up [for sth.]** jmdn./sich [für etw.] zurechtmachen (ugs.); **get ~d up** sich fein machen (ugs.)

sprucely /ˈspru:slɪ/ *adv.* adrett ‹*sich kleiden*›; **be ~ kept** sehr gepflegt sein

sprung /sprʌŋ/
A ▸ **spring B, C**
B *attrib. adj.* gefedert

spry /spraɪ/ *adj.* rege

spryly /ˈspraɪlɪ/ *adv.* munter; **walk** *or* **move ~:** munteren Schrittes gehen

spud /spʌd/ *n.* 1) (Brit. coll.: potato) Kartoffel, *die* 2) (spade) Unkrautstecher, *der*

spud-bashing /ˈspʌdbæʃɪŋ/ *n.* (Brit. Mil. coll.) Kartoffelschälen, *das*

spue ▸ **spew**

spume /spju:m/
A *n.* Gischt, *die*
B *v.i.* aufschäumen; gischten (geh.)

spun ▸ **spin A, B**

spunk /spʌŋk/ *n.* 1) (coll.: courage) Mumm, *der* (ugs.) 2) (Brit. coarse: semen) Samen, *der*; Soße, *die* (vulg.)

spunky /ˈspʌŋkɪ/ *adj.* mutig; **he is very ~:** er hat viel Mumm in den Knochen (ugs.)

spur /spɜ:(r)/
A *n.* 1) Sporn, *der*; **put** *or* **set ~s to one's horse** seinem Pferd die Sporen geben; **win one's ~s** (Hist./fig.) sich (*Dat.*) die [ersten] Sporen verdienen 2) (fig.: stimulus) Ansporn, *der* (**to** für); **act** *or* **serve as a ~ to sb. in sth.** jmdn. bei etw. anspornen; **on the ~ of the moment** ganz spontan 3) (branch road) Nebenstraße, *die* 4) (Railw.: branch line) Nebengleis, *das* 5) (climbing iron) Steigeisen, *das* 6) (Bot.: short branch) Kurztrieb, *der*; kurzer Zweig
B *v.t.*, **-rr-** 1) (prick) die Sporen geben (+ *Dat.*); spornen (veralt.) 2) (fig.: incite) anspornen; **~ sb. [on] to sth./to do sth.** jmdn. zu etw. anspornen/anspornen, etw. zu tun 3) (fig.: stimulate) hervorrufen; in Gang setzen ‹*Aktivität*›; erregen ‹*Interesse*›
C *v.i.*, **-rr-** das Pferd/die Pferde antreiben

Phrasal verb

• **~ ˈon** *v.t.* anspornen; antreiben ‹*Pferd*›; ‹*Habgier:*› treiben; *see also* ▸ **B 2**

spurge /spɜ:dʒ/ *n.* (Bot.) Wolfsmilch, *die*

ˈspur gear *n.* (Mech.) Stirnrad, *das*

spurious /ˈspjʊərɪəs/ *adj.* unaufrichtig ‹*Charakter, Handlung, Verhalten*›; gespielt ‹*Gefühl, Interesse*›; zweifelhaft ‹*Anspruch, Vergnügen*›; falsch ‹*Name, Münze*›

spuriously /ˈspjʊərɪəslɪ/ *adv.* fälschlicherweise

spurn /spɜ:n/ *v.t.* (reject) zurückweisen; abweisen; ausschlagen ‹*Angebot, Gelegenheit*›; sich entziehen (+ *Dat.*) ‹*Realität, Umwelt*›; von sich weisen ‹*Ansinnen*›

spurt[1] /spɜ:t/
A *n.* Spurt, *der* (bes. Sport); **final ~:** Endspurt, *der*; **there was a ~ of activity** es brach kurzzeitig lebhafte Aktivität aus; **in a sudden ~ of energy** in einem plötzlichen Anfall von Energie; **put on a ~:** einen Spurt einlegen
B *v.i.* spurten (bes. Sport)

spurt[2]
A *v.i.* **~ out [from** *or* **of]** herausspritzen [aus]; **~ from** ‹*Rauch:*› quellen aus; ‹*Flüssigkeit:*› spritzen aus
B *v.t.* **the wound ~ed blood** aus der Wunde spritzte Blut
C *n.* Strahl, *der*

sputnik /ˈspʊtnɪk, ˈspʌtnɪk/ *n.* Sputnik, *der*

sputter /ˈspʌtə(r)/
A *v.t.* (utter) heraussprudeln; (incoherently) stottern
B *v.i.* 1) (speak) (vehemently) wettern; (in hurried fashion) stammeln 2) (crackle) zischen 3) ▸ **splutter A**

sputum /ˈspju:təm/ *n.*, *pl.* **sputa** /ˈspju:tə/ (Med.) 1) (saliva) Speichel, *der* 2) (phlegm) Sputum, *das*

spy /spaɪ/
A *n.* 1) (secret agent) Spion, *der*/Spionin, *die* 2) (watcher) Spion, *der*/Spionin, *die*; Schnüffler, *der*/Schnüfflerin, *die* (abwertend); **be a ~ for sb./sth.** für jmdn./etw. als Spitzel arbeiten; **~ in the sky/cab** (coll.) Spionagesatellit, *der*/Fahrt[en]schreiber, *der*
B *v.t.* ausmachen; **~ a way out of the situation** einen Ausweg aus der Lage finden
C *v.i.* (watch closely) [herum]spionieren; (practise espionage) Spionage treiben; **~ on sb./a country** jmdm. nachspionieren/gegen ein Land spionieren; **~ on sb.'s movements** jmdn. auf Schritt und Tritt nachspionieren; **~ on each other** sich gegenseitig argwöhnisch beobachten

Phrasal verb

• **~ ˈout** *v.t.* aufspüren; ausspionieren ‹*Feind, feindliche Stellung*›; **~ out the land** (lit. or fig.) die Lage erkunden

spy: **~catcher** *n.* Agentenjäger, *der*/-jägerin, *die*; **~glass** *n.* Handfernrohr, *das*; Perspektiv, *das*; **~hole** *n.* Spion, *der*; Guckloch, *das*; **~-in-the-ˈcab** *n.* (coll.) Fahrtenschreiber, *der*; **~master** *n.* (coll.) Chef eines Spionagerings; **~ ring** *n.* Spionagering, *der*; **~ satellite** *n.* Spionagesatellit, *der*; **~ story** *n.* Spionagegeschichte, *die*; **~ware** *n.*, *no pl.* (Computing) Spyware, *die*

sq, Sq *abbr.* ▸ⓘ **p. 911 = square, Square**

SQL /ˈsi:kwl/ *abbr.* (Computing) **= Structured Query Language**

squab /skwɒb/ *n.* 1) (Ornith.: fledgeling) [noch nicht flügger] Jungvogel; (pigeon) Jungtaube, *die* 2) (cushion) Kissen, *das*; (Brit.: of car seat) Rücken-/Seitenlehne, *die*

squabble /ˈskwɒbl/
A *n.* Streit, *der*; **petty ~s** kleine Streitereien; **have a ~ [with sb. about sth.]** [mit jmdm. wegen einer Sache] Streit haben (ugs.); sich [mit jmdm. wegen einer Sache] streiten
B *v.i.* sich zanken (**over, about** wegen)

squad /skwɒd/ *n.* 1) (Mil.) Gruppe, *die*; Trupp, *der* 2) (group) Mannschaft, *die*; *see also* **firing squad** 3) (Police) **special ~:** Sonder[einsatz-]kommando, *das*; **Drug/Fraud S~:** Rauschgift-/Betrugsdezernat, *das*; **~ car** (esp. Amer.) Einsatzwagen, *der*; *see also* **flying squad**; **vice squad**

squaddie, squaddy /ˈskwɒdɪ/ *n.* (Brit. Mil. coll.) Gemeine, *der*

squadron /ˈskwɒdrən/ *n.* 1) (Mil.) (of tanks) Bataillon, *das*; (of cavalry) Schwadron, *die* 2) (Navy) Geschwader, *das* 3) ▸ⓘ **p. 1634** (Air Force) Staffel, *die*; **~ leader** (Air Force) Major der Luftwaffe

squalid /ˈskwɒlɪd/ *adj.* 1) (dirty) [abstoßend] schmutzig; **living conditions were ~:** man lebte mitten im Schmutz 2) (poor) schäbig; armselig 3) (fig.: sordid) abstoßend

squall /skwɔ:l/
A *n.* (gust) Bö, *die*; **look out** *or* **be on the look out for ~s** (fig.) auf der Hut sein
B *v.i.* brüllen; **~ in pain** brüllen *od.* schreien vor Schmerz

squally /ˈskwɔ:lɪ/ *adj.* böig

squalor /ˈskwɒlə(r)/ *n.*, *no pl.* 1) (dirtiness) Schmutz, *der*; **live in ~:** in Schmutz und Elend leben; **a life of ~:** ein Leben in Schmutz und Elend 2) (fig.) Schmutzigkeit, *die*

squander /ˈskwɒndə(r)/ *v.t.* vergeuden ‹*Talent, Zeit, Geld*›; verschleudern ‹*Ersparnisse, Vermögen*›; nicht nutzen ‹*Chance, Gelegenheit*›; **~ one's life** sein Leben wegwerfen

square /skweə(r)/
A *n.* 1) (Geom.) Quadrat, *das*
2) (object, arrangement) Quadrat, *das*; **carpet ~:** Teppichfliese, *die*; **cheese ~:** Scheiblette, *die* (Wz); **tile ~:** [quadratische] Kachel
3) (on board in game) Feld, *das*; **be** *or* **go back to ~ one** (fig. coll.) wieder von vorn anfangen müssen
4) (open area) Platz, *der*
5) (scarf) [quadratisches] Tuch; **silk ~:** Seidentuch, *das*
6) (Mil.: drill area) **[barrack] ~:** Kasernenhof, *der*
7) (Math.: product) Quadrat, *das*; **a perfect ~:** eine Quadratzahl
8) (coll.: old-fashioned person) Spießer, *der*/Spießerin, *die* (abwertend)
9) **on the ~ = on the level** ▸ **level A 1**
10) (instrument) Winkel, *der*; **L-/T-~:** L-förmiger Messwinkel/Kreuzwinkel, *der*; *see also* **set square**; **try square**
11) (Amer.: block of buildings) Quadrat, *das*; Karree, *das*
12) (Cricket: pitch area) [Haupt]spielfläche, *die*. *See also* **inverse square law**; **magic square**
B *adj.* ▸ⓘ **p. 1358** 1) quadratisch; *see also* **hole A 1**
2) ▸ⓘ **p. 911** **a ~ foot/mile/metre** *etc.* ein Quadratfuß/eine Quadratmeile/ein Quadratmeter *usw.*; **a foot ~:** ein Fuß im Quadrat; **the S~ Mile** die City von London
3) (right-angled) rechtwink[e]lig; **~ with** *or* **to** im rechten Winkel zu; **the wall is not ~ with the ceiling** die Wand ist nicht im Lot mit der Decke; **~ on to sth.** rechtwinklig zu etw.
4) (stocky) gedrungen ‹*Statur, Gestalt*›; ‹*Gegenstand:*› von gedrungenem Format; **be ~ in build** gedrungen gebaut sein
5) (in outline) rechteckig; eckig ‹*Schultern, Kinn*›; **~-shouldered** breitschultrig
6) (quits) quitt (ugs.); **be [all] ~:** [völlig] quitt sein (ugs.); ‹*Spieler:*› gleichstehen; ‹*Spiel:*› unentschieden stehen; **the match finished all ~:** das Spiel ging unentschieden aus; **get ~ with sb.** mit jmdm. quitt werden (ugs.); (get

revenge) es jmdm. heimzahlen
7 (coll.: old-fashioned) spießig (abwertend)
C *adv.* 1 breit ‹*sitzen*›; **put sth. ~ in the middle of sth.** etw. mitten auf etw. (*Akk.*) stellen; **hit sb. ~ on the jaw** jmdm. genau auf die Kinnlade schlagen; **the ball hit him ~ on the head** der Ball traf ihn genau am Kopf; **look sb. ~ in the face** *or* **the eyes** jmdm. fest in die Augen sehen
2 (fairly) ehrlich; fair ‹*behandeln*›. *See also* **fair**[2] **B 3**
D *v.t.* 1 (make right-angled) rechtwinklig machen; vierkantig zuschneiden ‹*Holz*›
2 (place squarely) **~ one's shoulders** seine Schultern straffen
3 (divide into ~s) in Karos einteilen; **~d paper** kariertes Papier
4 ▸ℹ **p. 1358** (Math.: multiply) quadrieren; **3 ~d is 9** 3 [im] Quadrat ist 9; 3 hoch 2 ist 9
5 (reconcile) **~ sth. with sth.** etw. mit etw. in Einklang bringen
6 **~ it with sb.** (coll.: get sb.'s approval) es mit jmdm. klären
7 (coll.: bribe) schmieren (salopp)
8 (settle) begleichen; **~ one's debt[s]** seine Schuld[en] begleichen; **I have a debt to ~ with him** (fig.) mit ihm werde ich [noch] abrechnen; *see also* **account B 1**
9 (draw level in) **~ [the/one's match** *or* **score]** zum Unentschieden verkürzen; gleichziehen
10 **~ the circle** (Geom.) den Kreis quadrieren
E *v.i.* (be consistent) übereinstimmen; **sth. does not ~ with sth.** etw. steht nicht im Einklang mit etw.; **it just does not ~:** hier stimmt doch etwas nicht

(Phrasal verbs)
- **~ 'off**
A *v.t.* (*make ~*) ▸ **~ D 1**
B *v.i.* (raise fists) die Fäuste heben
- **~ 'up** *v.i.* (settle up) abrechnen
- **~ 'up to** *v.t.* 1 (raise fists against) sich mit erhobenen Fäusten aufbauen (ugs.) vor (+ *Dat.*); **they ~d up to each other** sie traten sich kampfbereit gegenüber 2 (confront) **~ up to sb./sth.** jmdm./einer Sache entgegentreten

square: ~-bashing /ˈskweəbæʃɪŋ/ *n.* (Brit. Mil. coll.) Kasernenhofdrill, *der;* **~ 'brackets** *n. pl.* eckige Klammern; **~-built** *adj.* quadratisch ‹*Gebäude*›; gedrungen ‹*Person*›; vierschrötig ‹*Mann*›; **~ dance** *n.* Squaredance, *der;* **~ 'deal** *n.* faires Geschäft; **get a ~ deal** (not be swindled) kein schlechtes Geschäft machen; (receive adequate compensation) fair *od.* anständig behandelt werden; **~ 'leg** *n.* (Cricket) *Feldspieler, der die Stellung hinter dem Schlagmann innehat*

squarely /ˈskweəlɪ/ *adv.* 1 (directly) fest ‹*ansehen*›; genau ‹*treffen*›; aufrecht ‹*sitzen*›; **his works place him ~ in the Romantic tradition** mit seinem Werk steht er direkt in der romantischen Tradition 2 ▸ **fairly 5**

square: ~ 'meal *n.* anständige Mahlzeit (ugs.); **~ number** *n.* (Math.) Quadratzahl, *die;* **~-rigged** /ˈskweərɪgd/ *adj.* (Naut.) ‹*Schoner*› mit Rahsegeln; **a ~-rigged sailing ship** ein voll getakelter Rahsegler; **~ 'root** *n.* ▸ℹ **p. 1358** (Math.) Quadratwurzel, *die;* **~-root sign** [Quadrat]wurzelzeichen, *das;* **~ sail** *n.* (Naut.) Rahsegel, *das;* **~-toed** /ˈskweətəʊd/ *adj.* **~-toed shoes/boots** [an den Zehen] breite Schuhe/Stiefel; **~ wave** *n.* (Phys.) Rechteckwelle, *die*

squash[1] /skwɒʃ/
A *v.t.* 1 (crush) zerquetschen; **~ sth. flat** etw. platt drücken 2 (compress) pressen; **~ in/up** eindrücken/zusammendrücken ‹*Gegenstand*›; **~ sb./sth. into sth.** jmdn./etw. in etw. (*Akk.*) [hinein]zwängen 3 (put down) niederschlagen ‹*Aufstand*›; zunichte machen ‹*Hoffnung, Traum*› 4 (coll.: dismiss) ablehnen ‹*Vorschlag, Plan*› 5 (coll.: silence) zum Schweigen bringen
B *v.i.* sich quetschen; **~ in** sich hineinquetschen; **we ~ed up** wir drängten uns zusammen; **~ into the back seat of a car** sich auf den Rücksitz eines Wagens quetschen
C *n.* 1 (drink) Fruchtsaftgetränk, *das;* **orange ~:** Orangensaftgetränk, *das;* (concentrated) Orangensaftkonzentrat, *das* 2 (Sport) **~ [rackets]** Squash, *das* 3 ▸ **crush B 1**

squash[2] *n.* (gourd) [Speise]kürbis, *der*

squash: ~ ball *n.* Squashball, *der;* **~ court** *n.* Squashfeld, *das;* **~ racket** *n.* Squashschläger, *der;* **~ rackets** ▸ **squash C 2**

squashy /ˈskwɒʃɪ/ *adj.* weich ‹*Kuchen, Obst*›

squat /skwɒt/
A *v.i.*, **-tt-** 1 (crouch) hocken; (crouch down) sich hocken 2 (coll.: sit) sitzen; (sit down) sich setzen 3 (coll.: occupy property) (house) eine Hausbesetzung machen; (land) eine Landbesetzung machen; **~ in a house/on land** ein Haus besetzen/Land besetzen
B *adj.* rundlich; untersetzt
C *n.* (coll.) 1 (occupation) (of house) Hausbesetzung, *die;* (of land) Landbesetzung, *die* 2 (house) besetztes Haus; (land) besetztes Land

(Phrasal verb)
- **~ 'down** *v.i.* sich [nieder]hocken; (on seat) sich hinsetzen

squatter /ˈskwɒtə(r)/ *n.* (illegal occupier) Besetzer, *der*/Besetzerin, *die;* (of house also) Hausbesetzer, *der*/-besetzerin, *die*

'squat thrust *n.* Stützstrecke, *die*

squaw /skwɔː/ *n.* Squaw, *die*

squawk /skwɔːk/
A *v.i.* ‹*Hahn, Krähe, Rabe:*› krähen; ‹*Huhn:*› kreischen; (complain) ‹*Person:*› keifen (abwertend)
B *n.* 1 (bird cry) **~[s]** (of crow, cockerel, raven) Krähen, *das;* (of hen) Kreischen, *das* 2 (complaint) Gekeif[e], *das* (ugs. abwertend); **utter ~s of complaint** sich keifend beschweren; **~ of anger/indignation** wütendes/entrüstetes Gezeter

squeak /skwiːk/
A *n.* 1 (of animal) Quieken, *das* 2 (of hinge, door, brake, shoe, etc.) Quietschen, *das* 3 (coll.: escape) **have a narrow ~:** gerade noch [mit dem Leben] davonkommen; **that was a narrow ~!** das war knapp! (ugs.). *See also* **bubble and squeak**
B *v.i.* 1 ‹*Tier:*› quieken 2 ‹*Scharnier, Tür, Bremse, Schuh usw.:*› quietschen 3 (coll.: pass) **~ through/past [sth.]** mit Müh und Not [durch etw.] durchkommen/[an etw. (*Dat.*)] vorbeikommen 4 (coll.) ▸ **squeal A 4**

squeaky /ˈskwiːkɪ/ *adj.* quietschend; schrill ‹*Stimme*›; **be ~ clean** blitzsauber sein (ugs.); (fig.) eine blütenweiße Weste haben (fig. ugs.)

squeal /skwiːl/
A *v.i.* 1 **~ with pain/in fear** ‹*Person:*› vor Schmerz/Angst aufschreien; ‹*Tier:*› vor Schmerz/Angst laut quieken; **~ with laughter/for joy/in excitement** vor Lachen/Freude/Aufregung kreischen 2 ‹*Bremsen, Räder:*› kreischen; ‹*Reifen:*› quietschen 3 (coll.: protest) **~ [in protest]** lauthals protestieren 4 (sl.: inform) singen (salopp) (**to** bei); **~ on sb.** jmdn. verpfeifen (salopp)
B *v.t.* kreischen
C *n.* Kreischen, *das;* (of tyres) Quietschen, *das;* (of animal) Quieken, *das;* **give a ~ of fear** ‹*Person:*› vor Angst laut schreien; ‹*Tier:*› vor Angst laut quieken; **give a ~ of anger** vor Zorn aufschreien; **give a ~ of delight/excitement/joy** vor Vergnügen/Aufregung/Freude kreischen; **with a ~ of delight** kreischend vor Entzücken

squeamish /ˈskwiːmɪʃ/ *adj.* 1 (easily nauseated) **be ~:** zartbesaitet sein; **this film is not for the ~:** dieser Film ist nichts für zarte Gemüter 2 (fastidious) zimperlich

squeegee /skwiːˈdʒiː/
A *n.* 1 (for floor) [Boden]wischer, *der;* (for window) [Fenster]wischer, *der* 2 (Photog.) (roller) Rollenquetscher, *der;* (stripper) Abstreifer, *der*
B *v.t.* 1 (wipe) mit dem [Boden]wischer putzen ‹*Fußboden*›; mit dem [Fenster]wischer putzen ‹*Fenster*› 2 (Photog.: roll) mit dem Rollenquetscher/Abstreifer rollen

squeeze /skwiːz/
A *n.* 1 (pressing) Druck, *der;* **it only takes a gentle ~:** man braucht nur leicht zu drücken; **give sth. a [small] ~:** etw. [leicht] drücken; **put the ~ on sb.** (fig. coll.) jmdm. [die] Daumenschrauben anlegen; jmdn. durch die Mangel drehen (salopp) 2 (small quantity) **a ~ of juice/washing-up liquid** ein Spritzer Saft/Spülmittel; **a ~ of toothpaste/icing** ganz wenig Zahnpasta/Zuckerguss 3 (crush) Gedränge, *das;* **be in a tight ~** (fig.) = **be in a fix** ▸ **fix D 1** 4 (Econ.: restriction) Beschränkung, *die* (**on** *Gen.*) 5 (Brit.: embrace) **give sb. a [big/final] ~:** jmdn. [fest/ein letztes Mal] an sich drücken
B *v.t.* 1 (press) drücken; drücken auf (+ *Akk.*) ‹*Tube, Plastikflasche*›; kneten ‹*Ton, Knetmasse*›; ausdrücken ‹*Schwamm, Wäsche, Pickel*›; (to get juice) auspressen ‹*Früchte, Obst*›; **~ sb.'s hand** jmdm. die Hand drücken; **~ the trigger** auf den Abzug drücken 2 (extract) drücken (**out of** aus); **~ out sth.** etw. herausdrücken; **~ sth. on to sth.** etw. auf etw. (*Akk.*) drücken 3 (force) zwängen; **~ one's way past/into/out of sth.** sich an etw. (*Dat.*) vorbei-/in etw. (*Akk.*) hinein-/aus etw. herauszwängen 4 (fig. coll.) **~ sth. from sb.** etw. aus jmdm. herauspressen 5 (emit) **~ [out]** herauspressen ‹*Träne*›; herausbringen ‹*Laut, Antwort*›; sich abringen ‹*Lächeln*› 6 (fig.: constrain) unter Druck setzen; **~ sb. into doing sth.** jmdn. dazu bringen, etw. zu tun; **~ sb. out of sth./out** (fig. coll.) jmdn. aus etw. drängen/hinausdrängen 7 (Bridge) zum Abwerfen zwingen 8 (coll.: extort) **~ money out of sb.** Geld aus jmdm. herauspressen
C *v.i.* **~ past sb./sth.** sich an jmdm./etw. vorbeidrängen; **~ between two persons** sich zwischen zwei Personen (*Dat.*) durchdrängen; **~ under** *or* **underneath sth.** sich unter etw. (*Dat.*) hindurchzwängen; **~ under a bed** sich unter ein Bett zwängen; **~ together** sich zusammendrängen; **~ down a hole** sich in ein Loch zwängen

(Phrasal verbs)
- **~ 'in**
A *v.t.* 1 reinquetschen 2 (fig.: fit in) einschieben
B *v.i.* sich hineinzwängen
- **~ 'up** *v.i.* sich zusammendrängen; **~ up against sb./sth.** sich [fest] an jmdn./etw. drücken

squeeze: ~ bottle ▸ **squeezy bottle**; **~ box** *n.* (coll.) Quetschkommode, *die* (salopp scherzh.)

squeezer /ˈskwiːzə(r)/ *n.* (device) Presse, *die*

squeezy bottle /ˈskwiːzɪ bɒtl/ *n.* [elastische] Plastikflasche

squelch /skweltʃ/
A *v.t.* 1 (stamp on) stampfen 2 (silence) zum Schweigen bringen
B *v.i.* 1 (make sucking sound) quatschen (ugs.) 2 (go over wet ground) patschen

squelchy /ˈskweltʃɪ/ *adj.* matschig

squib /skwɪb/ *n.* 1 (firework) Knallfrosch, *der;* **damp ~** (fig.) Reinfall, *der* 2 (lampoon) [kurze] Satire

squid /skwɪd/ *n.* (Zool., Gastr.) Kalmar, *der*

squidgy /ˈskwɪdʒɪ/ *adj.* (Brit. coll.) durchweicht; matschig (ugs.)

squiggle /ˈskwɪgl/ *n.* Schnörkel, *der*

squiggly /ˈskwɪglɪ/ *adj.* schnörk[e]lig; **put a ~ line under sth.** etw. unterschlängeln

squillion /ˈskwɪljən/ *n.* (coll.) **~[s *pl.*]** zig Millionen (ugs.); **sell in ~s** sich zigmillionenfach verkaufen (ugs.)

squint /skwɪnt/
A *n.* 1 (Med.) Schielen, *das;* **have a ~:** schielen 2 (stealthy look) Schielen, *das* (ugs.) 3 (coll.: glance) kurzer Blick; **have** *or* **take a ~ at** einen Blick werfen auf (+ *Akk.*); überfliegen ‹*Text, Zeitung*›
B *v.i.* 1 (Med.) schielen 2 (with half-closed eyes) blinzeln; die Augen zusammenkneifen; **~ at sth.** etw. blinzelnd anschauen 3 (obliquely) **~ through a gap** durch eine Lücke lugen 4 (coll.: glance) **~ at** einen [kurzen] Blick werfen auf (+ *Akk.*); überfliegen ‹*Zeitung, Text*›; **I ~ed through his window as I passed** ich schielte im Vorbeigehen durch sein Fenster
C *v.t.* **~ one's eyes** die Augen zusammenkneifen

squire /ˈskwaɪə(r)/
A *n.* 1 (country gentleman) Squire, *der;* ≈ Gutsherr, *der* 2 (Brit. coll. voc.: sir) **want to buy any watches, ~?** möchte der Herr Uhren kaufen? (veralt.); wollen Sie Uhren kaufen, Meister? (ugs.) 3 (Hist.: attendant) Knappe, *der*

B *v.t.* begleiten

squirm /skwɜːm/ *v.i.* **1** ▸ **wriggle A 2** (fig.: show unease) sich winden (**with** vor)

squirrel /ˈskwɪrl/ *n.* **1** (Zool.) Eichhörnchen, *das; see also* **grey squirrel**; **ground squirrel**; **red squirrel 2** (fur) Eichhörnchen[fell], *das;* Feh, *das*

squirt /skwɜːt/

A *v.t.* spritzen; sprühen ‹*Spray, Puder*›; **~ sth. at sb.** jmdn. mit etw. bespritzen/besprühen; **~ sb. in the eye/face [with sth.]** jmdm. [etw.] ins Auge/Gesicht spritzen/sprühen; **~ oneself with water/deodorant** sich mit Wasser bespritzen/mit Deodorant besprühen

B *v.i.* spritzen

C *n.* Spritzer, *der;* **a ~ of juice** ein Spritzer Saft

squishy /ˈskwɪʃɪ/ *adj.* patschend (ugs.)

Sr. *abbr.* **1** **= Senior** sen.; sr. **2** **= Señor 3** (Relig.) **= Sister** Sr.

Sri Lanka /sriː ˈlæŋkə/ *pr. n.* Sri Lanka (*das*)

Sri Lankan /sriː ˈlæŋkən/ ▸**ⓘ p. 1345**

A *adj.* sri-lankisch

B *n.* Sri-Lanker, *der*/Sri-Lankerin, *die;* **sb. is a ~:** jmd. ist aus Sri Lanka

SRN *abbr.* **= State Registered Nurse** staatl. gepr. Krankenschwester/-pfleger

SS *abbr.* **1** /semts/ **= Saints** St. **2** **= steamship** D **3** (Nazi elite force) SS, *die*

SSE /saʊθsaʊθˈiːst/ *abbr.* ▸**ⓘ p. 1013 = south-south-east** SSO

SSSI *abbr.* (Brit.) **= Site of Special Scientific Interest**

SSW /saʊθsaʊθˈwest/ *abbr.* ▸**ⓘ p. 1013 = south-south-west** SSW

st. *abbr.* ▸**ⓘ p. 1702** (Brit.: unit of weight) **= stone**

St *abbr.* **= Saint** St.

St. *abbr.* **= Street** Str.

stab /stæb/

A *v.t.*, **-bb- 1** (pierce) stechen; **~ the air** in der Luft herumfuchteln; **~ sb. in the chest** jmdm. in die Brust stechen; **~ a piece of meat** in ein Stück Fleisch stechen; **he had been severely ~bed** er hatte gefährliche Stichwunden erhalten **2** (fig.) (hurt) **~ sb.'s heart** jmdm. ins Herz schneiden (geh.); **~ sb.'s conscience** jmds. Gewissen quälen; (attack) **~ sb. in the back** (fig.) jmdm. in den Rücken fallen

B *v.i.*, **-bb- 1** (pierce) stechen **2** (thrust) zustechen; **~ at sb.** nach jmdm. stechen

C *n.* **1** (act) Stich, *der;* (fig.) **that was a real ~ in the back** ich fühlte mich/er fühlte sich *usw.* wirklich verraten und verkauft **2** (coll.: attempt) **make** *or* **have a ~ [at it]** [es] probieren **3** (blow) Stich, *der;* (with beak) Hieb, *der* **4** (wound) Stichwunde, *die* **5** (fig.) (pang) **~ of conscience/guilt** Gewissensbiss, *der*/[quälendes] Schuldbewusstsein

stabbing /ˈstæbɪŋ/

A *n.* Messerstecherei, *die*

B *attrib. adj.* stechend ‹*Schmerz*›

stabilisation *etc.* ▸ **stabiliz-**

stability /stəˈbɪlɪtɪ/ *n., no pl.* Stabilität, *die;* **his character lacks ~:** er ist charakterlich nicht gefestigt; **S~ and Growth Pact** (EU) Stabilitäts- und Wachstumspakt

Staˈbility Pact *n.* (EU) Stabilitätspakt, *der*

stabilization /steɪbɪlaɪˈzeɪʃn/ *n.* Stabilisierung, *die*

stabilize /ˈsteɪbɪlaɪz/

A *v.t.* stabilisieren

B *v.i.* sich stabilisieren

stabilizer /ˈsteɪbɪlaɪzə(r)/ *n.* **1** (Naut.) Stabilisator, *der* **2** (Aeronaut.) **vertical ~** ▸ **tail fin; horizontal ~** ▸ **tailplane 3** (Cycling) Stützrad, *das*

stable¹ /ˈsteɪbl/ *adj.* **1** (steady) stabil; **the patient was in a ~ condition** *or* **was ~:** der Zustand des Patienten *od.* der Patient war stabil; **a ~ family background** geordnete Familienverhältnisse; *see also* **equilibrium 2** (resolute) gefestigt ‹*Person, Charakter*›

stable²

A *n.* **1** (for horses) Stall, *der* **2** (Horseracing: establishment) [Renn]stall, *der;* **the horses are trained at his ~:** die Pferde werden in seinem Stall trainiert **3** (fig.: origin) Stall, *der* (ugs.); **the latest model from the X ~:** das jüngste Modell aus dem Hause X; **from the same ~** ‹*Person*› aus demselben Stall (ugs.); ‹*Produkt*› aus demselben Haus

B *v.t.* (put in ~) in den Stall bringen; (keep in ~) **the pony was ~d at a nearby farm** das Pony war im Stall eines nahe gelegenen Bauernhofes untergebracht

stable: ~ boy ▸ **~ lad**; **~ door** *n.* (made in two parts) quer geteilte Tür; *see also* **lock² B 1**; **~ lad**, **~man** *ns.* ▸**ⓘ p. 1260** Stallbursche, *der*

stabling /ˈsteɪblɪŋ/ *n., no indef. art.* Ställe; Stallungen

staccato /stəˈkɑːtəʊ/ (Mus.)

A *adj.* staccato gesetzt; (fig.) abgehackt ‹*Sprache*›; **speak with a ~ delivery** schnell und abgehackt sprechen; **~ bursts of gunfire** ein Stakkato von Gewehrfeuer

B *adv.* staccato

C *n.* (also fig.) Stakkato, *das*

stacˈcato mark *n.* (Mus.) Stakkatozeichen, *das*

stack /stæk/

A *n.* **1** (of hay etc.) Schober, *der* (südd., österr.); Feim, *der* (nordd., md.) **2** (pile) Stoß, *der;* Stapel, *der;* **place sth. in ~s** etw. [auf]stapeln **3** (coll.: large amount) Haufen, *der* (ugs.); **a ~ of work/money** ein Haufen Arbeit/Geld; **have a ~ of things to do** einen Haufen zu tun haben (ugs.); **have ~s of money** Geld wie Heu haben (ugs.) **4** **[chimney] ~:** Schornstein, *der* **5** (factory chimney) Fabrikschornstein, *der;* **blow one's ~** (Amer. fig. coll.) **= blow one's top** ▸ **blow¹ B 8** **6** (funnel) **[smoke]~:** Schornstein, *der* **7** (Aeronaut.) *übereinander in Warteschleifen kreisende Flugzeuge* **8** (Brit.: rock pillar) Felssäule, *die* **9** (in library) Magazin, *das*

B *v.t.* **1** (pile) **~ [up]** [auf]stapeln; **~ logs in a pile** Holz zu einem Stoß aufschichten; **be well ~ed** (fig. coll.: have large bust) viel Holz vor der Hütte haben (ugs. scherzh.); **~ing** stapelbar ‹*Stühle usw.*› **2** (arrange fraudulently) **~ the cards** beim Mischen betrügen; **the odds** *or* **cards** *or* **chips are ~ed against sb.** (fig.) jmd. hat schlechte Karten (fig. ugs.) **3** (Aeronaut.) übereinander Warteschleifen fliegen lassen; **we are ~ed right up to 30,000 feet** der Warteraum ist schon bis in 30 000 Fuß Höhe belegt

Phrasal verb

• **~ ˈup** ▸ **~ B 1**

stadium /ˈsteɪdɪəm/ *n.* Stadion, *das*

staff /stɑːf/

A *n.* **1** (stick) Stock, *der* **2** *constr. as pl.* (personnel) Personal, *das;* **editorial ~:** Redaktion, *die;* **diplomatic ~:** diplomatisches Korps; **the ~ of the firm** die Betriebsangehörigen; die Belegschaft [der Firma]; **~ meeting** Belegschaftsversammlung, *die* **3** *constr. as pl.* (of school) Lehrerkollegium, *das;* Lehrkörper, *der* (Amtsspr.); (of university or college) Dozentenschaft, *die;* **~-student ratio** Verhältnis zwischen Lehrenden und Studierenden; **~ meeting** (at school) Lehrerkonferenz, *die;* (at university or college) Dozentenkonferenz, *die* **4** *pl.* **staves** /steɪvz/ (Mus.) Liniensystem, *das;* **~ notation** Notation mithilfe des Liniensystems **5** (Mil.: officers) Stab, *der; see also* **chief A 2** **6** (ceremonial rod) Stab, *der;* **pastoral ~** (Eccl.) Bischofsstab, *der* **7** (fig.: support) Stütze, *die;* **bread is the ~ of life** Brot ist die Grundlage des Lebens **8** (Surv.: rod) Messlatte, *die. See also* **flagstaff**; **general staff**

B *v.t.* mit Personal ausstatten; **a hospital ~ed by women** ein Krankenhaus, dessen Personal aus Frauen besteht

staff: ~ college *n.* (Brit. Mil.) Stabsakademie, *die* (Milit.); **~ ˈdiscount** *n.* Mitarbeiterrabatt, *der*

staffed /stɑːft/ *adj.* mit Personal ausgestattet

staffer /ˈstɑːfə(r)/ *n.* (Amer. Journ.) Redaktionsmitglied, *das*

staff: ~ meeting *n.* [Lehrer]konferenz, *die;* **~ nurse** *n.* (Brit.) Zweitschwester, *die*/*Krankenpfleger in der Stellung einer Zweitschwester;* **~ officer** *n.* (Mil.) Stabsoffizier, *der;* **~room** *n.* Lehrerzimmer, *das;* **~ sergeant** *n.* **1** (Brit. Mil.) ≈ Oberfeldwebel, *der;* **2** (Amer. Mil.) ≈ Feldwebel, *der*

stag /stæg/ *n.* **1** Hirsch, *der* **2** (Amer.: lone man) Herr ohne Damenbegleitung **3** (Brit. St. Exch. coll.) Konzertzeichner, *der*

ˈstag beetle *n.* (Zool.) Hirschkäfer, *der*

stage /steɪdʒ/

A *n.* **1** (Theatre) Bühne, *die;* **down/up ~** (position) vorne/hinten auf der Bühne; (direction) nach vorn/nach hinten; **[be/appear] on ~:** auf der Bühne [stehen/erscheinen]; **be appearing on ~ at the Royal** am Royal spielen **2** (fig.) **the ~:** das Theater; **write for the ~:** für die Bühne schreiben; **go on the ~:** zur Bühne *od.* zum Theater gehen **3** (part of process) Stadium, *das;* Phase, *die;* **be at a difficult/late/critical ~:** sich in einer schwierigen/späten/kritischen Phase befinden; **negotiations are at an early ~:** die Verhandlungen befinden sich im Anfangsstadium; **at such a late ~:** zu einem so späten Zeitpunkt; **at this ~:** in diesem Stadium; **do sth. in** *or* **by ~s** etw. abschnittsweise *od.* nach und nach tun; **I am past the ~ of caring** das ist mir inzwischen gleich; **in the final ~s** in der Schlussphase **4** (raised platform) Gerüst, *das; see also* **landing stage 5** (of microscope) Mikroskoptisch, *der* **6** (fig.: scene) Bühne, *die;* **quit the political ~** *or* **the ~ of politics** von der politischen Bühne abtreten; **hold the ~:** die Szene beherrschen; **set the ~ for sb./sth.** jmdm. den Weg ebnen/etw. in die Wege leiten; **the ~ was set for a bitter argument** damit waren die Voraussetzungen für eine erbitterte Auseinandersetzung gegeben **7** (stopping place) Station, *die* **8** (distance) Etappe, *die;* **the ~ from Paris to Marseilles** die Strecke Paris-Marseille; **travel by [easy] ~s** in [kurzen] Etappen reisen; *see also* **fare stage 9** (Geol., Electr., Astronaut.) Stufe, *die*

B *v.t.* **1** (present) inszenieren **2** (arrange) veranstalten ‹*Wettkampf, Ausstellung*›; ausrichten ‹*Veranstaltung*›; organisieren ‹*Streik*›; bewerkstelligen ‹*Rückzug*›; **~ a comeback** ein Comeback schaffen

stage: ~coach *n.* Postkutsche, *die;* **~craft** *n., no pl., no indef. art.* (Theatre) Bühnenkunst, *die;* **~ direction** *n.* (Theatre) Bühnenanweisung, *die;* **~ door** *n.* (Theatre) Bühneneingang, *der;* **~ effect** *n.* (Theatre) Bühneneffekt, *der;* **~ fright** *n.* (Theatre) Lampenfieber, *das;* **~hand** *n.* (Theatre) Bühnenarbeiter, *der*/-arbeiterin, *die;* **~ ˈleft** ▸ **left² C 3**; **~-manage** *v.t.* **1** (Theatre) als Inspizient/Inspizientin mitwirken bei ‹*Inszenierung*›; **2** (fig.) veranstalten; inszenieren ‹*Revolte usw.*›; **~ manager** *n.* ▸**ⓘ p. 1260** (Theatre) Inspizient, *der*/Inspizientin, *die;* **~ name** *n.* (Theatre) Künstlername, *der;* **~ play** *n.* (Theatre) Bühnenstück, *das*

stager /ˈsteɪdʒə(r)/ ▸ **old A 2**

stage: ~ right ▸ **right C 8**; **~ rights** *n. pl.* Aufführungsrechte; **~-struck** *adj.* theaterbesessen; **~ whisper** *n.* Beiseitesprechen, *das;* **in a ~ whisper** beiseite

stagflation /stægˈfleɪʃn/ *n.* (Econ.) Stagflation, *die*

stagger /ˈstægə(r)/

A *v.i.* schwanken; torkeln (ugs.)

B *v.t.* **1** (cause to totter) zum Schwanken bringen **2** (astonish) die Sprache verschlagen (+ *Dat.*); **I was ~ed** es hat mir die Sprache verschlagen **3** (position out of line, arrange alternately) versetzt anordnen; **~ed junction** versetzt angelegte Kreuzung; **~ed** (fig.) gestaffelt ‹*Ferien, Schichten, Essenszeiten*›

Phrasal verb

• **~ aˈbout, ~ aˈround** *v.i.* [hin und her] taumeln; [herum]torkeln (ugs.)

staggering /ˈstægərɪŋ/ *adj.* erschütternd ‹*Schlag, Schock, Verlust*›; Schwindel erregend ‹*Menge, Höhe*›; folgenschwer ‹*Auswirkung, Bedeutung*›; zutiefst beunruhigend ‹*Nachricht*›; **the ~ fact is that no one really knew who he was** erschütternd ist, dass niemand ihn wirklich kannte

staggeringly /ˈstægərɪŋlɪ/ *adv.* erstaunlich; *as sentence-modifier* erstaunlicherweise

stagily /ˈsteɪdʒɪlɪ/ *adv.* betont auffällig ‹*sich kleiden*›; affektiert ‹*sich benehmen*›

S

staging /ˈsteɪdʒɪŋ/ *n., no indef. art.* 1 Gerüst, *das;* (used as stage) Bühne, *die* 2 (Hort.: shelves) Regale 3 (Theatre: production) Inszenierung, *die*

staging: ~ area *n.* (Mil.) Sammelplatz, *der;* **~ post** *n.* Zwischenstation, *die*

stagnant /ˈstægnənt/ *adj.* 1 (motionless) stehend ‹*Gewässer*›; **the water is ~:** das Wasser steht 2 (fig.: lifeless) abgestumpft ‹*Geist, Seele*›; stagnierend ‹*Wirtschaft*›; dumpf ‹*Leben*›; **the economy is ~:** die Wirtschaft stagniert

stagnate /stægˈneɪt/ *v.i.* 1 ‹*Wasser usw.:*› abstehen 2 (fig.) ‹*Wirtschaft, Geschäft:*› stagnieren; ‹*Geist, Künstler:*› in Lethargie verfallen; ‹*Person:*› abstumpfen

stagnation /stægˈneɪʃn/ *n., no pl.* 1 (of water etc.) Stehen, *das* 2 (fig.) Stagnation, *die*

stag: ~ night *n.: Zechabend des Bräutigams mit seinen Freunden kurz vor seiner Hochzeit;* **~ party** *n.* Herrenabend, *der;* (before wedding) *Trinkgelage des Bräutigams mit seinen Freunden kurz vor seiner Hochzeit*

stagy /ˈsteɪdʒɪ/ *adj.* theatralisch; **be a ~ dresser** sich betont auffällig kleiden; **they have a ~ manner** sie benehmen sich wie die Schauspieler

staid /steɪd/ *adj.* 1 (steady, sedate) gesetzt; **lead a ~ existence** ein gleichförmiges Leben führen 2 (serious) bieder

staidly /ˈsteɪdlɪ/ *adv.* 1 (soberly) bieder 2 (sedately) ruhig

stain /steɪn/

A *v.t.* 1 (discolour) verfärben; (make ~s on) Flecken hinterlassen auf (+ *Dat.*) 2 (fig.: besmirch) beflecken; besudeln (geh. abwertend) 3 (colour) färben; beizen ‹*Holz*› 4 (Biol.: impregnate) anfärben

B *v.i.* sich verfärben; (take ~s) Flecken bekommen

C *n.* 1 (discoloration) Fleck, *der* 2 (fig.: blemish) Schandfleck, *der;* **without a ~ on his character** mit einem fleckenlosen Charakter *od.* (fig.) einer fleckenlosen Weste 3 (colouring-material) Beize, *die* 4 (Biol.) Farbstoff, *der*

stained ˈglass *n.* farbiges Glas; Farbglas, *das;* **the ~ at the church** die farbigen Glasfenster *od.* die Glasmalereien in der Kirche; **stained-glass window** Fenster mit Glasmalerei

stainless /ˈsteɪnlɪs/ *adj.* 1 (spotless) fleckenlos 2 (non-rusting) rostfrei

stainless ˈsteel *n.* Edelstahl, *der*

ˈstain remover *n.* Fleck[en]entferner, *der*

stair /steə(r)/ *n.* 1 (set of steps) **~s,** (arch./Scot.) **~:** Treppe, *die;* **below ~s** in den Wirtschaftsräumen [im Souterrain] 2 (step) [Treppen]stufe, *die* 3 *in pl.* (landing stage) Landungssteg, *der. See also* **downstairs; flight¹ A 4; upstairs**

stair: ~ carpet *n.* Treppenläufer, *der;* **~case** *n.* Treppenhaus, *das;* (one flight) Treppe, *die;* **on the ~case** auf der Treppe; *see also* **spiral staircase; winding staircase; ~head** ▸**landing 4; ~lift** *n.* Treppenlift, *der;* Treppenaufzug, *der;* **~ rod** *n.* Läuferstange, *die;* **it's raining ~ rods** (coll.) es regnet Bindfäden (ugs.); **~way** *n.* 1 (access via ~s) Treppenaufgang, *der;* 2 (~case) Treppe, *die;* **~well** *n.* Treppenhaus, *das*

stake /steɪk/

A *n.* 1 (pointed stick) Pfahl, *der;* **pull up ~s** (Amer. fig. coll.) seine Zelte abbrechen 2 (wager) Einsatz, *der;* **be at ~:** auf dem Spiel stehen; **at ~ is the Gold Medal** es geht um die Goldmedaille; **have a lot of money at ~ on a project** viel Geld in ein Projekt gesteckt haben; **have a ~ in sth.** in etw. (*Akk.*) investiert haben; **have a 50% ~ in a firm** einen fünfzigprozentigen Anteil an einer Firma halten 3 *in pl.* (Horse-racing) (prize money) Geldpreis, *der;* (race) [Wett-]rennen um einen Geldpreis 4 (for execution) **be burnt at the ~:** auf dem Scheiterhaufen verbrannt werden; **go to the ~ for sth.** (fig.) sich für etw. kreuzigen lassen

B *v.t.* 1 (secure) [an einem Pfahl/an Pfählen] anbinden; **~ sth. down** etw. einpflocken; **~ a claim [to sb./sth.]** ▸**claim C 5** 2 (wager) setzen (**on** auf + *Akk.*) 3 (risk) aufs Spiel setzen (**on** für); **I'll ~ my reputation on his innocence** ich verbürge mich mit meinem guten Namen für seine Unschuld; **~ one's life on sth.** seinen Kopf auf etw. (*Akk.*) wetten (ugs.); **you can ~ your life on that** darauf kannst du Gift nehmen (ugs.) 4 (Amer. coll.: finance) **~ sb.** jmdm. finanziell unter die Arme greifen; **~ a business/venture** Geld in ein Geschäft/Unternehmen stecken

Phrasal verbs

- **~ ˈoff** *v.t.* [mit Pfählen] abstecken
- **~ ˈout** *v.t.* 1 (mark out) mit Pfählen begrenzen; eingrenzen 2 (fig.: claim) beanspruchen; **have ~d out a field of study as one's own** ein Fachgebiet für sich alleine gepachtet haben (ugs.) 3 (Amer. coll.: observe) überwachen; *see also* **stake-out**

stake: ~ boat *n.* (Rowing) *verankertes Boot, das die Rennstrecke bei einem Bootsrennen markiert;* **~holder** *n.* Interessierte, *der/die; attrib.* **~holder group** interessierte Gruppe; **~holder pension** (Brit.) *private Altersvorsorge durch Bildung von Geldkapital;* **~holder society** Teilhabergesellschaft, *die;* Stakeholder-Gesellschaft, *die;* **~ net** *n.* Schockernetz, *das;* **~-out** *n.* (Amer. coll.) Überwachung, *die*

stalactite /ˈstæləktaɪt/ *n.* (Geol.) Stalaktit, *der*

stalagmite /ˈstæləgmaɪt/ *n.* (Geol.) Stalagmit, *der*

stale /steɪl/

A *adj.* 1 alt; muffig; abgestanden ‹*Luft*›; alt[backen] ‹*Brot*›; schal ‹*Bier, Wein usw.*›; (fig.) abgedroschen ‹*Witz, Trick*›; überholt ‹*Nachricht*› 2 (jaded) ausgelaugt

B *v.t.* alt werden lassen ‹*Lebensmittel*›; auslaugen ‹*Sportler, Schauspieler*›

ˈstalemate

A *n.* (Chess; also fig.) Patt, *das;* **end in** *or* **reach ~:** mit einem Patt enden

B *v.t.* 1 (Chess) **~ sb.** jmdn. in eine Pattsituation bringen 2 (fig.: halt) zum Stillstand bringen; aufhalten ‹*Verfahren*›; verhindern ‹*Fortschritte*›

staleness /ˈsteɪlnɪs/ *n., no pl.* 1 (lack of freshness) Muffigkeit, *die;* (of air) Abgestandenheit, *die;* (of bread) Altbackenheit, *die;* (of beer etc.) Schalheit, *die;* (fig.: lack of novelty) Abgedroschenheit, *die;* (of news) Überholtheit, *die* 2 (jadedness) Ausgelaugtheit, *die*

Stalinism /ˈstɑːlɪnɪzm/ *n.* (Polit.) Stalinismus, *der*

Stalinist /ˈstɑːlɪnɪst/ *n.* (Polit.) Stalinist, *der*/Stalinistin, *die*

stalk¹ /stɔːk/

A *v.i.* 1 stolzieren; **~ along** einherschreiten/-stolzieren (geh.) 2 (Hunting) pirschen; **be ~ing** auf der Pirsch sein

B *v.t.* 1 sich heranpirschen an (+ *Akk.*) 2 (follow obsessively) **~ sb.** jmdm. nachstellen

stalk² /stɔːk/ *n.* 1 (Bot.) (main stem) Stängel, *der;* (of leaf, flower, fruit) Stiel, *der;* (of cabbage) Strunk, *der* 2 (Zool.) Stiel, *der;* (of crab etc.) [Augen]stiel, *der;* **his eyes stood** *or* **were out on ~s** (fig.) er machte *od.* bekam Stielaugen (ugs.)

stalker /ˈstɔːkə(r)/ *n.* 1 Pirscher, *der* 2 (obsessive pursuer) [lästiger] Verfolger

stall¹ /stɔːl/

A *n.* 1 Stand, *der* 2 (for horse) Box, *die;* (for cow) Stand, *der* 3 (Eccl.: seat) Stuhl, *der;* **the choir ~s** das Chorgestühl 4 *in pl.* (Brit. Theatre: seats) **[front] ~s** Parkett, *das;* **in the rear/cheap ~s** auf den hinteren/billigen Parkettplätzen 5 (Brit. Horseracing) **the [starting] ~s** die Startboxen 6 (of engine) Stehenbleiben, *das* 7 (Aeronaut.) Überziehen, *das;* **go into a ~:** durchsacken

B *v.t.* abwürgen (ugs.) ‹*Motor*›

C *v.i.* 1 ‹*Motor:*› stehen bleiben 2 (Aeronaut.) durchzusacken beginnen

stall²

A *v.i.* ausweichen; **~ on a promise** (delay) die Einlösung eines Versprechens hinauszögern; **quit ~ing!** (Amer. coll.) hör auf, drum herumzureden! (ugs.)

B *v.t.* blockieren ‹*Gesetz, Fortschritt*›; aufhalten ‹*Feind, Fortschritt*›

ˈstallholder *n.* Standinhaber, *der*/-inhaberin, *die*

stallion /ˈstæljən/ *n.* Hengst, *der*

stalwart /ˈstɔːlwət/

A *adj.* 1 (sturdy) stämmig 2 *attrib.* (fig.: determined) entschieden; entschlossen ‹*Kämpfer*›; (loyal) treu; getreu (geh.)

B *n.* (loyal supporter) treuer Anhänger/treue Anhängerin; **Party ~:** treues Parteimitglied

stamen /ˈsteɪmen, ˈsteɪmən/ *n.* (Bot.) Staubblatt, *das*

stamina /ˈstæmɪnə/ *n.* 1 (physical staying power) Ausdauer, *die* 2 (endurance) Durchhaltevermögen, *das*

stammer /ˈstæmə(r)/

A *v.i.* stottern

B *v.t.* stammeln; **~ [out] one's thanks/apologies** stammelnd danken/eine Entschuldigung stammeln

C *n.* Stottern, *das;* **have a ~, speak with a ~:** stottern

stammerer /ˈstæmərə(r)/ *n.* Stotterer, *der*/Stotterin, *die*

stamp /stæmp/

A *v.t.* 1 (impress, imprint sth. on) [ab]stempeln; **~ sth. on sth.** etw. auf etw. (*Akk.*) [auf]stempeln; **~ envelopes with sth.** etw. auf Umschläge drucken 2 **~ one's foot/feet** mit dem Fuß/den Füßen stampfen; **~ the snow from one's boots** den Schnee von den Stiefeln stampfen; **~ the floor** *or* **ground [in anger/with rage]** [ärgerlich/wütend] auf den Boden stampfen 3 (put postage ~ on) frankieren; freimachen (Postw.); **~ed addressed envelope** frankierter Rückumschlag 4 (mentally) **~ oneself/itself** *or* **become** *or* **be ~ed on sb.['s memory** *or* **mind]** sich jmdm. fest einprägen 5 (crush) zerstampfen 6 (flatten) **~ flat** platt stampfen *od.* treten ‹*Schachtel, Dose*›; **~ down** feststampfen *od.* -treten ‹*Erde, Schnee, Steine*› 7 (characterize) kennzeichnen; **~ sb. [as] a genius** zeigen, dass jmd. ein Genie ist

B *v.i.* aufstampfen; **~ up and down** auf und ab stampfen

C *n.* 1 Marke, *die;* (postage ~) Briefmarke, *die; see also* **first-class A 1; insurance stamp; second-class A 2; trading stamp** 2 (instrument for ~ing, mark) Stempel, *der* 3 (fig.: characteristic) **bear the ~ of genius/greatness** Genialität/Größe erkennen lassen; **leave one's ~ on sth.** einer Sache seinen Stempel aufdrücken 4 (fig.: kind) [Menschen]schlag, *der;* **men of his ~:** Menschen seines Schlages *od.* seiner Prägung

Phrasal verbs

- **~ on** *v.t.* 1 (crush) zertreten ‹*Insekt, Dose*›; zertrampeln ‹*Blumen*›; **~ on sb.'s foot** jmdm. auf den Fuß treten 2 (suppress) durchgreifen gegen. *See also* **~ A 1, 4**
- **~ ˈout** *v.t.* 1 (eliminate) ausmerzen; ersticken ‹*Aufstand, Feuer*›; niederwalzen ‹*Opposition, Widerstand*› 2 (cut out) [aus]stanzen

stamp: ~ album *n.* Briefmarkenalbum, *das;* **~ book** *n.* Briefmarkenheftchen, *das;* **~ collecting** *n.* Briefmarkensammeln, *das;* **~ collection** *n.* Briefmarkensammlung, *die;* **~ collector** *n.* Briefmarkensammler, *der*/-sammlerin, *die;* **~ duty** *n.* Stempelsteuer, *die*

stampede /stæmˈpiːd/

A *n.* 1 Stampede, *die* 2 (rush of people) (due to interest) Ansturm, *der;* (due to panic) wilde Flucht 3 (Amer. Polit.) starker Zulauf

B *v.i.* 1 in Panik fliehen 2 (rush) ‹*Personen:*› stürmen

C *v.t.* 1 **~ a herd** bei einer Herde eine Stampede auslösen 2 **~ sb. into doing sth.** jmdn. dazu drängen, etw. zu tun

ˈstamp hinge *n.* Klebefalz, *der*

stamping ground /ˈstæmpɪŋ graʊnd/ *n.* Revier, *das;* **one's old ~:** der Ort, wo man früher immer zu finden war

ˈstamp machine *n.* Briefmarkenautomat, *der*

stance /stæns, stɑːns/ *n.* 1 (Golf, Cricket: position) Stellung, *die* 2 (posture; fig.: attitude) Haltung, *die;* **take up a ~ over** *or* **on sth.** (fig.) eine Haltung zu etw. einnehmen

stanch ▸**staunch²**

stanchion /ˈstɑːnʃn/ *n.* Stütze, *die;* (of flat wagon) Runge, *die;* (of awning) Sonnensegelstütze, *die*

stand /stænd/

A *v.i.*, **stood** /stʊd/ **1** stehen; **all ~!** aufstehen!; **don't just ~ there [, do something]!** steh nicht so herum[, tu doch etwas!]; **~ for the National Anthem/for a minute's silence** zur Nationalhymne/zu einer Schweigeminute aufstehen; **~ in a line** *or* **row** sich in einer Reihe aufstellen; (be ~ing) in einer Reihe stehen; **we stood talking** wir standen da und unterhielten uns; **~ or fall by sth.** (fig.) mit etw. stehen und fallen; **~ empty** leer stehen; *see also* **standstill**

2 (have height) **he ~s six feet tall/the tree ~s 30 feet high** er ist sechs Fuß groß/der Baum ist 30 Fuß hoch; **~ high above sb./sth.** (fig.) [rangmäßig] weit über jmdm. stehen/etw. bei weitem übersteigen

3 (be at level) ‹*Aktien, Währung, Thermometer:*› stehen (**at** auf + *Dat.*); ‹*Fonds:*› sich belaufen (**at** auf + *Akk.*); ‹*Absatz, Export usw.:*› liegen (**at** bei)

4 (hold good) bestehen bleiben; **my decision still ~s** an meiner Entscheidung hat sich nichts geändert; **my offer/promise still ~s** mein Angebot/Versprechen gilt nach wie vor

5 (find oneself, be) **~ first in line for the throne** in der Thronfolge der Erste sein; **~ convicted of treachery** wegen Verrats verurteilt sein; **as it ~s, as things ~:** wie die Dinge [jetzt] liegen; **the law as it ~s** das bestehende *od.* gültige Recht; **the matter ~s thus** die Sache steht so; **~ prepared to dispute sth.** bereit sein, über etw. (*Akk.*) zu diskutieren; **as a statesman he ~s alone in contemporary politics** (fig.) es gibt in der gegenwärtigen Politik keinen, der ihm als Staatsmann das Wasser reichen könnte; **I'd like to know where I ~** (fig.) ich möchte wissen, wo ich dran bin; **~ in need** Not leiden; **~ in need of sth.** einer Sache (*Gen.*) dringend bedürfen

6 (be candidate) kandidieren (**for** für); **~ in an election** bei einer Wahl kandidieren; **~ as a candidate/nominee** kandidieren/nominiert sein; **~ as a Liberal/Conservative** für die Liberalen/Konservativen kandidieren; **~ for Parliament** (Brit.) für einen Parlamentssitz kandidieren; **~ for office** (Brit.) sich um ein Amt bewerben

7 **~ proxy for sb.** jmdn. vertreten

8 (place oneself) sich stellen; **~ from under sb.** *or* **sb.'s feet** (Amer.) jmdm. nicht ständig vor den Füßen herumlaufen; **~ in the way of sth.** (fig.) einer Sache (*Dat.*) im Weg stehen; **[not] ~ in sb.'s way** (fig.) jmdm. [keine] Steine in den Weg legen

9 (be likely) **~ to win** *or* **gain/lose sth.** etw. gewinnen/verlieren können; **what do I ~ to gain from/by it?** was kann ich dabei gewinnen?

10 (Cricket: be umpire) schiedsrichtern

11 (Naut.: hold course) **~ in for** *or* **towards sth.** Kurs auf etw. (*Akk.*) nehmen; **~ into danger** auf eine Gefahr zusteuern. *See also* **correct A 1**; **deliver 4**; **ease A 6**; **easy B**; **fast² B 1**; **firm² B**; **foot A 1**; **leg A 1**; **light¹ A 1**; **pat² 1**

B *v.t.*, **stood** **1** (set in position) stellen; **~ sth. on end/upside down** etw. hochkant/auf den Kopf stellen

2 (endure) ertragen; vertragen ‹*Klima*›; **I can't ~ the heat/noise** ich halte die Hitze/den Lärm nicht aus; **I cannot ~ [the sight of] him/her** ich kann ihn/sie nicht ausstehen; **he can't ~ the pressure/strain/stress** er ist dem Druck/den Strapazen/dem Stress nicht gewachsen; **I can't ~ it any longer!** ich halte es nicht mehr aus; **~ closer examination** einer genaueren [Über]prüfung standhalten; **~ the test of time** sich bewähren; **he can't ~ being told what to do** er kann es nicht leiden *od.* ausstehen, wenn man ihm Vorschriften macht

3 (undergo) ausgesetzt sein (+ *Dat.*); **the play/player has stood much criticism** das Stück/der Spieler stieß auf viel Kritik; **~ trial [for sth.]** [wegen einer Sache] vor Gericht stehen

4 (buy) **~ sb. sth.** jmdm. etw. ausgeben *od.* spendieren (ugs.); **can I ~ you a lunch?** Gehen wir zusammen was essen? Ich lade dich ein. *See also* **chance A 3**; **ground¹ A 2**; **pace¹ A 2**; **treat A 3**

C *n.* **1** (support) Ständer, *der*

2 (stall; at exhibition) Stand, *der*

3 (raised structure) Tribüne, *die*

4 (resistance) Widerstand, *der*; **put up a brave ~ against sb./sth.** jmdm./einer Sache tapfer Widerstand leisten; **take** *or* **make a ~** (fig.) klar Stellung beziehen (**for/against/on** für/gegen/zu)

5 (Cricket) **a ~ of 90 runs** eine gemeinsame Serie von 90 Läufen

6 (standing-place for taxi, bus, etc.) Stand, *der*

7 (performance on tour) Auftritt, *der*

8 (of trees, corn, clover, etc.) Bestand, *der*

9 (position) **take one's ~:** sich aufstellen; **take one's ~ on the podium** seinen Platz auf der Tribüne einnehmen; **take a [firm] ~ [on sth.]** [in etw. (*Dat.*)] einen festen Standpunkt vertreten; **what's your ~ [on this matter]?** welchen Standpunkt vertrittst du [in dieser Sache]?

10 (Amer.: witness box) Zeugenstand, *der*; **take the ~:** in den Zeugenstand treten. *See also* **grandstand**; **one-night stand**

Phrasal verbs

- **~ a'bout, ~ a'round** *v.i.* herumstehen
- **~ a'side** *v.i.* **1** (step aside) zur Seite treten; Platz machen **2** (fig.: withdraw) abseits stehen; **~ aside from sth.** sich an etw. nicht beteiligen
- **~ 'back** *v.i.* **1** **~ [well] back [from sth.]** [ein gutes Stück] [von etw.] entfernt stehen **2** ▸**~ aside 1** **3** (fig.: distance oneself) zurücktreten; **sometimes one must ~ back from daily affairs** von Zeit zu Zeit muss man von seinen Alltagsgeschäften Abstand gewinnen **4** (fig.: withdraw) **~ back from sth.** sich aus einer Sache heraushalten
- **~ behind** *v.t.* **~ behind sb./sth.** (lit. or fig.) hinter jmdm./etw. stehen
- **~ between** *v.t.* **sth. ~s between sb. and sth.** (fig.) etw. steht jmdm. bei etw. im Wege
- **~ by**

A /-'-/ *v.i.* **1** (remain apart) abseits stehen; **~ [idly] by and watch sth. happen** *or* **while sth. happens** untätig zusehen, wie etw. geschieht; **~ by and do nothing to prevent sth.** sich abseits halten und nicht eingreifen, um etw. zu verhindern **2** (be near) daneben stehen **3** (be ready) sich zur Verfügung halten; **~ by ready to do sth.** Gewehr bei Fuß stehen, um etw. zu tun

B /'--/ *v.t.* **1** (support) **~ by sb./one another** jmdm./sich [gegenseitig] *od.* (geh.) einander beistehen **2** (adhere to) **~ by sth.** zu etw. stehen; **~ by the terms of a contract** einen Vertrag einhalten; **~ by a promise** ein Versprechen halten; **~ by a resolution** einen Beschluss [in die Tat] umsetzen **3** (Naut.: prepare to use) klarmachen. *See also* **standby**

- **~ 'down**

A *v.i.* **1** (withdraw, retire) verzichten; **~ down in favour of a person** zugunsten einer Person (*Gen.*) zurücktreten **2** (leave witness box) den Zeugenstand verlassen **3** (Brit. Mil.: go off duty) seinen Posten verlassen; **~ down from guard duty** seinen Wachdienst beenden **4** (Mil.: disband) sich auflösen

B *v.t.* **1** (Brit. Mil.: relieve from duty) abziehen **2** (Mil.: disband) auflösen

- **~ for** *v.t.* **1** (signify) bedeuten; **she hates him and all that he ~s for** sie hasst ihn und alles, was mit ihm zusammenhängt **2** (represent) **~ for sb./sth.** für jmdn./etw. eintreten; sich für jmdn./etw. einsetzen **3** ▸**stand A 6** **4** (coll.: tolerate) sich bieten lassen; **that's one thing I won't ~ for** das ist etwas, was ich nicht haben kann
- **~ 'in** *v.i.* **1** (deputize) aushelfen; **~ in for sb.** für jmdn. einspringen **2** (share) **~ in with sb. [for sth.]** mit jmdm. die Kosten [für etw.] teilen **3** (Naut.) ▸**stand A 11**. *See also* **stand-in**
- **~ 'off** *v.i.* (move away) sich entfernen; (keep away) sich in einiger Entfernung halten.
- **~ 'out** *v.i.* **1** (persist) **~ out for/against sth.** hartnäckig für etw. kämpfen/sich hartnäckig gegen etw. wehren **2** (be prominent) herausragen; **the reason for the crisis ~s out** der Grund für die Krise ist augenfällig; **~ out against** *or* **in contrast to sth.** sich gegen etw. abheben; **~ out a mile** nicht zu übersehen sein; ‹*Grund, Antwort:*› [klar] auf der Hand liegen **3** (be outstanding) herausragen (**from** aus) **4** (Naut.) **~ out to sea** in See gehen
- **~ over**

A *v.t.* **1** /-'--/ ▸**hold over** **2** /'---/ (watch) beaufsichtigen

B /-'--/ *v.i.* **sth. can ~ over** etw. kann warten; **any unfinished business ~s over to the next meeting** alle unerledigten Punkte werden bis zum nächsten Treffen zurückgestellt

- **~ to** ▸**~ by A 4**; *see also* **reason A 2**
- **~ to'gether** *v.i.* zusammenstehen; (for a photograph) sich [gemeinsam] aufstellen; (fig.) zusammenhalten
- **~ 'up**

A *v.i.* **1** (rise) aufstehen; **~ up and be counted** (fig.) Farbe bekennen **2** (be upright) stehen; **I have only the clothes I ~ up in** ich besitze nur die Kleider, die ich am Leibe trage; **~ up straight** sich aufrecht hinstellen **3** (be valid) ▸**hold² B 4** **4** **~ up well [in comparison with sb./sth.]** [im Vergleich zu jmdm./etw.] gut abschneiden; (maintain worth or position) ‹*Preis, Wert:*› sich [im Vergleich zu etw.] gut halten

B *v.t.* **1** (put upright) aufstellen; [wieder] hinstellen ‹*Fahrrad, Stuhl usw.*› **2** (coll.: fail to keep date with) **~ sb. up** jmdn. versetzen (ugs.). *See also* **stand-up**

- **~ 'up for** *v.t.* **~ up for sb./sth.** für jmdn./etw. Partei ergreifen; sich für jmdn./etw. stark machen; **why didn't you ~ up for me?** warum hast du mich nicht unterstützt?
- **~ 'up to** *v.t.* **1** (face steadfastly) **~ up to sb.** sich jmdm. entgegenstellen; jmdm. die Stirn bieten; **~ up to sth.** sich einer Sache (*Dat.*) stellen; **~ up to an ordeal well/badly** eine Tortur tapfer/nicht aushalten; **~ up to criticism** sich von Kritik nicht beirren lassen **2** (survive intact under) **~ up to sth.** einer Sache (*Dat.*) standhalten; **~ up to wear and tear** eine starke Beanspruchung aushalten

stand-alone /stændə'ləʊn/ *adj.* (Computing) selbstständig

standard /'stændəd/

A *n.* **1** (norm) Maßstab, *der*; **safety ~s** Sicherheitsnormen; **above/below/up to ~:** überdurchschnittlich [gut]/unter dem Durchschnitt/der Norm entsprechend; **by anybody's ~s** für jeden **2** (degree) Niveau, *das*; **of [a] high/low ~:** von hohem/niedrigem Niveau; **a high ~ of competence** ein hohes Maß an Kompetenz; **set a high/low ~ in** *or* **of sth.** hohe/niedrige Ansprüche an etw. (*Akk.*) stellen; **the first competitor set a high ~:** der erste Bewerber setzte einen hohen Maßstab; **this pupil sets himself too low a ~ in his work** dieser Schüler verlangt zu wenig von sich selbst; **~ of living** Lebensstandard, *der* **3** *in pl.* (moral principles) Prinzipien; **~s of sexual behaviour** Maßstäbe für das Sexualverhalten **4** (flag) Standarte, *die*; (fig.: cause) Banner, *das* (geh.); **many flocked to the ~** (fig.) viele strömten zur Fahne **5** (Hort.) Hochstamm, *der*; **~ rose** Hochstammrose, *die* **6** (Bot.) **~ [shrub]** natürlich gewachsener Strauch; **~ [tree]** Baum mit naturgemäßem Kronenaufbau **7** **lamp ~** ▸**lamp post** **8** (in currency) Feingehalt, *der*; Standard, *der*; **the silver/monetary ~:** der Silberstandard/Münzfuß. *See also* **double standard**; **gold standard**; **royal standard**

B *adj.* **1** (conforming to ~, authoritative) Standard-; (used as reference) Normal- **2** (widely used) normal; **what is the ~ thing to do in such cases?** was macht man normalerweise in solchen Fällen?; **be ~ procedure** Vorschrift sein; **have sth.** *or* **include sth.** *or* **be fitted with sth. as ~:** serienmäßig mit etw. ausgerüstet sein; **sth. is a ~ feature** etw. gehört zur Standardausrüstung; **a ~ letter** ein Schemabrief (Bürow.); **a ~ model** ein Standardmodell; **be ~ practice** allgemein üblich sein; **it is ~ practice for sb. to do sth.** es ist üblich, dass jmd. etw. tut; **follow the ~ pattern** dem üblichen Muster folgen

standard: ~ as'sessment task, **~ as'sessment test** *ns.* (Brit. Educ.) standardisierter Leistungstest; **~-bearer** *n.* **1** (Mil.: flag-bearer) Standartenträger, *der*; **2** (fig.: leader)

Bannerträger, *der*/-trägerin, *die* (geh.); Vorkämpfer, *der*/-kämpferin, *die*; **~-bearer for** *or* **in sth.** Vorkämpfer einer Sache (*Gen.*); **S~bred** *n.* (Amer.) Amerikanischer Traber; **~ devi'ation** *n.* (Statistics) Standardabweichung, *die*; **S~ 'English** *n.* Standardenglisch, *das*

standardisation, standardise ▸**standardiz-**

standardization /stændədaɪ'zeɪʃn/ *n.* Standardisierung, *die*

standardize /'stændədaɪz/ *v.t.* standardisieren

standard: ~ 'lamp *n.* (Brit.) Stehlampe, *die*; **~ time** *n.* Normalzeit, *die*

'standby

A *n., pl.* **~s** **1** (reserve) **[act] as a ~:** als Ersatz [bereitstehen]; **be on ~** ‹*Polizei, Feuerwehr, Truppen:*› einsatzbereit sein; ‹*Schauspieler:*› sich bereithalten; ‹*Flugzeug:*› startbereit sein; **the army was put on ~:** die Armee wurde in Einsatzbereitschaft versetzt **2** (resource) Rückhalt, *der*; **sth. is a good ~:** auf etw. (*Akk.*) kann man jederzeit zurückgreifen; **drink was his only ~:** das Trinken war seine einzige Zuflucht; **have some tins of food/an emergency pack as a ~:** einige Konserven für Notfälle/einen Notvorrat haben; **the generator is a ~:** der Generator dient als Notaggregat

B *attrib. adj.* Ersatz-; **~ safety equipment** zusätzliche Sicherheitsausrüstung; **~ ticket/passenger** Stand-by-Ticket, *das*/-Passagier, *der*

standee /stæn'di:/ *n.* (Amer. coll.) stehender Passagier/Zuschauer

'stand-in

A *n.* Ersatz, *der*; (in theatre, film) Ersatzdarsteller, *der*/-darstellerin, *die*; (Sport) Ersatzspieler, *der*/-spielerin, *die*

B *attrib. adj.* Ersatz-

standing /'stændɪŋ/

A *n.* **1** (repute) Ansehen, *das*; **have some ~:** recht angesehen sein; **be of** *or* **have [a] high ~:** ein hohes Ansehen genießen; **have no ~:** ein Niemand sein; **what is his ~?** welchen Rang bekleidet er?; **be in good ~ with sb.** sich gut mit jmdm. stehen; *see also* **equal A 1** **2** (service) **be an MP of twenty years' ~:** seit zwanzig Jahren [ununterbrochen] dem Parlament angehören; **be a member/judge of long/short ~:** seit langem/kurzem Mitglied/Richter sein; **a girlfriend of long ~:** eine langjährige Freundin; *see also* **long-standing** **3** (duration) **of long/short ~:** von langer/kurzer Dauer; **a feud of long ~:** ein alter Zwist **4** **~ place** Standplatz, *der*

B *adj.* **1** (erect) stehend; **after the storm there was scarcely a tree still ~:** nach dem Sturm stand kaum mehr ein Baum; **~ corn** stehendes Korn; **~ stone** Menhir, *der*; **leave sb. ~** (lit. or fig.: progress much faster) jmdn. weit hinter sich (*Dat.*) lassen **2** *attrib.* (established) fest ‹*Regel, Brauch*›; **he has a ~ excuse** er bringt immer die gleiche Entschuldigung; *see also* **joke A 2** **3** *attrib.* (permanent) stehend ‹*Heer*›; feststehend ‹*Praxis*›; **I have a ~ invitation to visit them whenever I want to** sie haben mich eingeladen, sie, wann immer ich will, zu besuchen **4** *attrib.* (stationary) **~ jump** Standsprung, *der*; **~ start** Hochstart, *der*

standing: ~ com'mittee *n.* ständiger Ausschuss; **~ 'order** *n.* **1** (payment instruction) Dauerauftrag, *der*; (for regular supply) Abonnement, *das*; **2** *in pl.* (rules) Geschäftsordnung, *die*; **~ o'vation** *n.* stürmischer Beifall; stehende Ovation (geh.); **~ room** *n., no pl., no indef. art.* Stehplätze; **~ 'water** *n.* stehendes Gewässer; (Golf) Wassergraben, *der*; **~ wave** *n.* (Phys.) stehende Welle

'stand-off *n.* **1** (Amer.: deadlock) verfahrene Situation; **finish/result in a ~:** in einer Sackgasse enden/in eine Sackgasse geraten **2** **~ [half]** (Rugby) ▸**fly half**

stand-offish /stænd'ɒfɪʃ/ *adj.* reserviert

stand: ~ 'patter *n.* (Amer. Polit.) strammer Konservativer/stramme Konservative; **~pipe** *n.* (for water supply) Standrohr, *das*; **~point** *n.* **1** (observation point) Standort, *der*; **2** (fig.: viewpoint) Standpunkt, *der*; **~still** *n.* Stillstand, *der*; **be at a ~still** stillstehen; ‹*Fahrzeug, Flugzeug:*› stehen; ‹*Produktion, Verkehr:*› zum Erliegen gekommen sein; **come to a ~still** zum Stehen kommen; ‹*Verhandlungen:*› zum Stillstand kommen; **the traffic/production came to a ~still** der Verkehr/die Produktion kam zum Erliegen; **bring to a ~still** zum Stehen bringen; zum Erliegen bringen ‹*Produktion*›; **~-up** *adj.* **~-up fight** Schlägerei, *die*

stank ▸**stink A**

stanza /'stænzə/ *n.* (Pros.) Strophe, *die*

staple[1] /'steɪpl/

A *n.* (for fastening paper) [Heft]klammer, *die*; (for fastening netting) Krampe, *die*

B *v.t.* (with a stapler) heften (**on to** an + *Akk.*); (with a hammer) krampen (**to** an + *Akk.*)

staple[2]

A *attrib. adj.* **1** (principal) Grund-; **a ~ diet** *or* **food** ein Grundnahrungsmittel **2** (Commerc.: important) grundlegend; **~ goods** Haupthandelsartikel; **the ~ export of a country** das Hauptexportgut eines Landes

B *n.* **1** (Commerc.: major item) Haupterzeugnis, *das* **2** (raw material) Rohstoff, *der* **3** (fig.: fundamental part) **the ~ of conversation** das zentrale Thema der Unterhaltung **4** (Textiles: fibre) Faser, *die*

'staple gun *n.* Tacker, *der*

stapler /'steɪplə(r)/ *n.* [Draht]hefter, *der*

'staple remover *n.* Hefklammernentferner, *der*; Enthefter, *der*

star /stɑ:(r)/

A *n.* **1** Stern, *der*; **reach for the ~s** (fig.) nach hohen Zielen streben; **three-~ general** (Amer. Mil.) Dreisterne-general, *der*; **three/four ~ hotel** Drei-/Viersternehotel, *das*; **two/four ~ [petrol]** Normal-/Super[benzin], *das*; **the Stars and Stripes** (Amer.) das Sternenbanner; **the pupil got a ~ for his work** der Schüler erhielt für seine Arbeit ein Sternchen (*als Auszeichnung*) **2** (prominent person) Star, *der*; **be a rising ~ [of the tennis world]** ein aufgehender Stern [am Tennishimmel] sein **3** (asterisk) Stern, *der*; Sternchen, *das* **4** (Astrol.) Stern, *der*; **read one's/the ~s** sein/das Horoskop lesen; **be born under an unlucky ~:** unter einem ungünstigen Stern geboren sein. *See also* **double star; evening star; morning star; see[1] A 1; shooting star**

B *attrib. adj.* Star-; **~ pupil** bester Schüler/beste Schülerin; **~ turn** *or* **attraction** Hauptattraktion, *die*; **receive ~ billing** als Star/Stars des Abends auftreten

C *v.t.*, **-rr-** **1** (decorate) mit Sternen schmücken; **~red pattern** Sternenmuster, *das* **2** (mark with asterisk) mit einem Stern[chen] versehen **3** (feature as ~) **~ring Humphrey Bogart and Lauren Bacall** mit Humphrey Bogart und Lauren Bacall in den Hauptrollen; **the film ~red Newman and Redford** in dem Film spielten Newman und Redford die Hauptrollen

D *v.i.*, **-rr-:** **~ in a film/play/TV series** in einem Film/einem Stück/einer Fernsehserie die Hauptrolle spielen

> **Stars and Stripes**
>
> Die amerikanische Nationalflagge. Die 13 abwechselnd roten und weißen Streifen stehen für die Gründungsstaaten und die 50 weißen Sterne für die heutigen Bundesstaaten.

starboard /'stɑ:bəd/ (Naut., Aeronaut.)

A *n.* Steuerbord, *das*; **land to ~!** Land an Steuerbord!; **turn** *or* **put the helm to ~:** nach Steuerbord drehen

B *adj.* steuerbord-; steuerbordseitig; **on the ~ bow/quarter** Steuerbord voraus/achteraus; *see also* **tack[1] A 3; watch A 3**

starch /stɑ:tʃ/

A *n.* **1** Stärke, *die* **2** (fig.) Steifheit, *die*

B *v.t.* stärken

Star 'Chamber *n.* **1** (Brit. Hist.) Sternkammer, *die* (*Gericht zur Verfolgung von Straftaten gegen die Krone*) **2** (fig.: tribunal) ≈ Volksgerichtshof, *der* (fig.)

starched /stɑ:tʃt/ *adj.* gestärkt; (fig.) steif

'starch-reduced *adj.* stärkearm

starchy /'stɑ:tʃɪ/ *adj.* **1** (containing much starch) stärkehaltig ‹*Nahrungsmittel*› **2** (fig.: prim) steif

'star-crossed *adj.* **they were ~ lovers** ihre Liebe stand unter einem schlechten Stern

stardom /'stɑ:dəm/ *n.* Starruhm, *der*

stare /steə(r)/

A *v.i.* **1** (gaze) starren; **~ in surprise/amazement** überrascht/erstaunt starren; **~ in horror** erschreckt starren; **~ at sb./sth.** jmdn./etw. anstarren; **it is rude to ~ at people** es ist unhöflich, andere [Leute] anzustarren **2** (have fixed gaze) starr blicken

B *v.t.* **~ sb. into silence** jmdn. durch Anstarren zum Schweigen bringen; **~ sb. in the face** jmdn. [feindselig] fixieren; (fig.) jmdm. ins Auge springen; **ruin was staring him in the face** ihm drohte der Ruin; **I looked for my purse for ages and it was staring me in the face all the time** ich suchte eine Ewigkeit mein Portemonnaie, und dabei lag es die ganze Zeit direkt vor meiner Nase (ugs.)

C *n.* Starren, *das*; **fix sb. with a [curious/malevolent] ~:** jmdn. [neugierig/böse] anstarren

Phrasal verb

• **~ 'down, ~ 'out** *v.t.* **~ sb. down** *or* **out** jmds. Blick niederzwingen (geh.); jmdn. so lange anstarren, bis er/sie die Augen abwendet

star: ~fish *n.* Seestern, *der*; **~gazer** /'stɑ:geɪzə(r)/ *n.* (coll.) Sterngucker, *der* (ugs. scherzh.)

staring /'steərɪŋ/ *attrib. adj.* starrend ‹*Augen*›; **with ~ eyes** mit starrem Blick; **be stark ~ mad** (fig. coll.) völlig verrückt sein (ugs.)

stark /stɑ:k/

A *adj.* **1** (bleak) öde; spröde ‹*Schönheit, Dichtung*› **2** (obvious) scharf umrissen; nackt ‹*Wahrheit*›; scharf ‹*Kontrast, Umriss*›; krass ‹*Unterschied, Gegensatz, Realismus*›; **be in ~ contrast [to sb./sth.]** sich stark unterscheiden [von jmdm./etw.] **3** (extreme) schier ‹*Entsetzen, Dummheit*›; nackt ‹*Armut, Angst*›

B *adv.* völlig; **~ naked** splitternackt (ugs.); *see also* **staring**

starkers /'stɑ:kəz/ *pred. adj.* (Brit. coll.) splitternackt (ugs.)

starkly /'stɑ:klɪ/ *adv.* **1** (clearly) überdeutlich; scharf ‹*kontrastieren*› **2** (harshly) grell ‹*erleuchtet*›; **state a problem in ~ realistic terms** ein Problem krass und realistisch darlegen

starless /'stɑ:lɪs/ *adj.* stern[en]los

starlet /'stɑ:lɪt/ *n.* (Cinemat.) Starlet, *das*

'starlight *n., no pl.* Sternenlicht, *das*

starling /'stɑ:lɪŋ/ *n.* (Ornith.) **1** [Gemeiner] Star **2** (of family Sturnidae) Star, *der*; (of family Icteridae) Stärling, *der*

'starlit *adj.* sternhell

Star: ~ of Bethlehem /stɑ:r əv 'beθlɪhem/ *n.* (Bot.) Stern von Bethlehem; Milchstern, *der*; **~ of David** /stɑ:r əv 'deɪvɪd/ *n.* David[s-]stern, *der*

starry /'stɑ:rɪ/ *adj.* **1** sternklar ‹*Himmel, Nacht*›; sternenübersät ‹*Himmel*› **2** (shining) strahlend, leuchtend ‹*Augen*›

'starry-eyed *adj.* blauäugig (fig.)

star: ~ shell *n.* (Mil.) Leuchtgeschoss, *das*; **~ sign** *n.* Sternzeichen, *das*; **~-spangled** *adj.* mit Sternen übersät; sternbesät (dichter.); **the S~-Spangled Banner** das Sternenbanner; **~-studded** *adj.* **1** mit Sternen übersät; **2** ‹*Show, Film, Besetzung*› mit großem Staraufgebot

> **Star-Spangled Banner**
>
> Die amerikanische Nationalhymne.

start /stɑ:t/

A *v.i.* **1** (begin) anfangen; beginnen (oft geh.); **when we first ~ed** ganz zu Anfang; **don't 'you ~!** (coll.) nun fang du auch noch [damit] an!; **~ on [at] sb.** (coll.) auf jmdn. einhacken (ugs.); **don't ~ on at me about that again!** nun fang nicht schon wieder damit an!; **~ on sth.** etw. beginnen; **~ on Latin** mit Latein beginnen; **~ with sth./sb.** bei *od.* mit etw./jmdm. anfangen; **prices ~ at ten dollars** die Preise beginnen bei zehn Dollar; **~ at the beginning** am Anfang beginnen; **to ~ with** zuerst *od.* zunächst einmal; **~ing from next month** ab nächsten Monat; *see also* **get B 2**; **scratch C 1**

[2] (set out) aufbrechen

[3] (make sudden movement) aufschrecken; **~ with pain/surprise** vor Schmerz/Überraschung auffahren; **~ from one's chair** von seinem Stuhl hochfahren; **~ back** zurückfahren; **~ with fright** vor Schreck zurückweichen

[4] (begin to function) anlaufen; ‹*Auto, Motor usw.*:› anspringen

[5] (burst) **his eyes ~ed from their sockets/his skull** *or* **head** die Augen traten ihm aus den Höhlen/dem Kopf

B *v.t.* [1] (begin) beginnen [mit]; **we ~ed the holiday on Sunday** unser Urlaub begann am Sonntag; **I have just ~ed a book by Böll** ich habe gerade ein Buch von Böll angefangen; **~ life in Australia** (be born) seine ersten Lebensjahre in Australien verbringen; **have ~ed life as sth.** (fig.) ursprünglich etw. gewesen sein; **~ school** in die Schule kommen; **~ work** mit der Arbeit beginnen (**on** an + *Dat.*); (after leaving school) zu arbeiten anfangen; **~ doing** *or* **to do sth.** [damit] anfangen, etw. zu tun

[2] (cause) auslösen; anfangen ‹*Streit, Schlägerei*›; legen ‹*Brand*›; (accidentally) verursachen ‹*Brand*›; **you've really ~ed something now!** jetzt hast du aber was angerichtet!; **you trying to ~ something?** (coll.) willst du 'ne Schlägerei anfangen?

[3] (set up) ins Leben rufen ‹*Organisation, Projekt*›; aufmachen ‹*Laden, Geschäft*›; herausbringen ‹*Zeitung*›; gründen ‹*Verein, Firma, Zeitung*›

[4] (switch on) einschalten; starten, anlassen ‹*Motor, Auto*›

[5] **~ sb. doing sth.** jmdn. anfangen lassen, etw. zu tun; **~ sb. working on a project** jmdn. mit der Arbeit an einem Projekt anfangen lassen; **they ~ the children writing at an early age** sie bringen den Kindern schon früh das Schreiben bei; **~ sb. drinking/coughing/laughing** jmdn. zum Trinken/Husten/Lachen bringen; **~ sb. on a diet** jmdn. auf Diät (*Akk.*) setzen; **she ~ed the baby on solid foods** sie gab dem Baby erstmals feste Nahrung; **~ sb. in business/a trade** jmdm. die Gründung eines Geschäfts ermöglichen/jmdn. in ein Handwerk einführen

[6] (Sport) **~ a race** ein Rennen starten; **~ a football match** ein Fußballspiel anpfeifen

[7] **~ a family** eine Familie gründen

[8] (Hunting: rouse) aufscheuchen (**from** aus)

C *n.* [1] Anfang, *der;* Beginn, *der;* (of race) Start, *der;* **from the ~:** von Anfang an; **from ~ to finish** von Anfang bis Ende; **at the ~:** am Anfang; **at the ~ of the war/day** bei Kriegsbeginn/zum Tagesanfang; **be in at** *or* **in on the ~ of sth.** von Anfang an bei etw. dabei sein; **it could be the ~ of something big** (coll.) daraus könnte eine größere Sache werden (ugs.); **make a ~:** anfangen (**on, with** mit); (on journey) aufbrechen; **make an early/late ~ [for town/to one's holiday]** früh/spät [in die Stadt/in die Ferien] aufbrechen; **get off to** *or* **make a good/slow/poor ~:** einen guten/langsamen/schlechten Start haben; **for a ~** (coll.) zunächst einmal

[2] (Sport: starting-place) Start, *der*

[3] (Sport: advantage) Vorsprung, *der;* **give sb. 60 metres ~:** jmdm. eine Vorgabe von 60 Metern geben; **have a ~ over** *or* **on sb./sth.** (fig.) einen Vorsprung vor jmdm./etw. haben; *see also* **head start**

[4] (good beginning) **[good] ~:** guter Start; **get a good ~ in life** einen guten Start ins Leben haben

[5] (jump) **she remembered** *or* **realized with a ~ that ...:** sie schreckte zusammen, als ihr einfiel, dass ...; **give sb. [a] ~:** jmdm. einen Schreck einjagen; **give a ~:** zusammenfahren. *See also* **fit[1] 2**

Phrasal verbs

- **~ for** *v.t.* sich auf den Weg machen nach/zu
- **~ 'in** *v.i.* [1] (coll.: begin to do) **~ in to do sth.** sich daranmachen (ugs.), etw. zu tun; **~ in on sth./on doing sth.** (Amer. coll.) sich an etw. (*Akk.*) machen (ugs.)/sich daranmachen (ugs.), etw. zu tun [2] **~ in on sb. [for sth.]** (criticize) jmdn. [wegen etw.] attackieren
- **~ 'off**

A *v.i.* [1] ▸**set off A** [2] (coll.: begin action) **~ off by showing sth.** zu Beginn etw. zeigen [3] **~ off with** *or* **on sth.** (begin on) mit etw. beginnen; **today we ~ed off with Latin** heute hatten wir zuerst Latein

B *v.t.* [1] **~ sb. off working** jmdn. mit der Arbeit anfangen lassen; **~ sb. off on a task/job** jmdn. in eine Aufgabe/Arbeit einweisen; **~ sb. off on a craze** jmdm. einen Floh ins Ohr setzen (ugs.) [2] ▸**set off B 2**

- **~ 'out** *v.i.* [1] ▸**set out A** [2] ▸**set off A**
- **~ 'up**

A *v.i.* [1] ▸**jump up** [2] (be set going) starten; ‹*Motor*:› anspringen [3] (begin to work) **~ up in engineering/insurance** als Ingenieur/in der Versicherungsbranche anfangen; **~ up in a trade/as a plumber** sich als Handwerker/als Klempner selbstständig machen

B *v.t.* [1] (form) beginnen ‹*Gespräch*›; gründen ‹*Geschäft, Firma*›; schließen ‹*Freundschaft*› [2] (~ [engine of]) starten; anlassen

starter /'stɑːtə(r)/ *n.* [1] (Sport: signaller) Starter, *der;* **be under ~'s orders** (Horseracing) am Start stehen [2] (Sport: entrant) Starter, *der*/Starterin, *die;* (horse) startendes Pferd; **be a ~ in a race** in einem Rennen starten [3] (Motor Veh.) **~ [motor]** Anlasser, *der;* **press the ~:** den Starter- *od.* Anlasserknopf drücken [4] (initial action) Anfang, *der;* **an easy question for a ~:** als Erstes eine leichte Frage; **as a ~:** zuerst; **for ~s** (coll.) erstens einmal [5] (hors d'oeuvre etc.) Vorspeise, *die;* **for a ~:** als Vorspeise

starter: ~ home *n.* Einsteigerimmobilie, *die;* **~ kit** *n.* Starterkit, *das*

starting /'stɑːtɪŋ/: **~ block** *n.* (Athletics) Startblock, *der;* **~ credit** *n.* Startguthaben, *das;* **~ gate** *n.* (Horseracing) Startmaschine, *die;* **~ grid** *n.* (Motor racing) Startplatz, *der;* **on the second row of the ~ grid** in der zweiten Startreihe; **~ handle** *n.* (Brit.) [Anlasser]kurbel, *die;* **~ line** *n.* Startlinie, *die;* **~ pistol** *n.* (Sport) Startpistole, *die;* **~ point** *n.* (lit. or fig.) Ausgangspunkt, *der;* (for solving a problem) Ansatzpunkt, *der;* **~ post** *n.* (Sport) Startpfosten, *der;* **~ price** *n.* (Horseracing) endgültige Quote; **~ salary** *n.* Anfangsgehalt, *das;* (for civil servants also) Eingangsbesoldung, *die;* **~ stall** ▸**stall[1] A 5**; **~ time** *n.* Anfangszeit, *die*

startle /'stɑːtl/ *v.t.* erschrecken; **be ~d by sth.** über etw. (*Akk.*) erschrecken

startling /'stɑːtlɪŋ/ *adj.* erstaunlich; überraschend ‹*Nachricht*›; (alarming) bestürzend ‹*Nachricht, Entdeckung*›

startlingly /'stɑːtlɪŋlɪ/ *adv.* erstaunlich; (alarmingly) bestürzend

'start-up *n.* [1] *no pl.* (action, process) (of project) Start, *der;* (of business) Aufbau, *der; attrib.* **~ phase** Anlaufphase, *die;* **~ costs** Startkosten *Pl.;* Gründungskosten *Pl.* [2] (new business) Start-up[-Unternehmen], *das;* Neugründung, *die*

'star turn *n.* (most important item in an entertainment) Hauptattraktion, *die;* (star appearance) Starauftritt, *der*

starvation /stɑː'veɪʃn/ *n.* Verhungern, *das;* **die of** *or* **from/suffer from ~:** verhungern/hungern *od.* Hunger leiden; **be** *or* **live on a ~ diet** fast am Verhungern sein; **~ wages** Hungerlohn, *der*

starve /stɑːv/

A *v.i.* [1] (die of hunger) **~ [to death]** verhungern [2] (suffer hunger) hungern [3] **be starving** (coll.: feel hungry) am Verhungern sein (ugs.); **you must be starving!** (coll.) du musst einen Mordshunger haben! (ugs.) [4] (fig.: suffer want) hungern (geh.) (**for** nach); **be spiritually ~d** seelisch ausgehungert sein

B *v.t.* [1] (kill by starving) **~ sb. [to death]** jmdn. verhungern lassen; **be ~d [to death]** verhungern [2] (deprive of food) hungern lassen; **feed a cold, ~ a fever** bei Erkältung soll man essen, bei Fieber hungern [3] (deprive) **we were ~d of knowledge** uns (*Dat.*) wurde [viel] Wissen vorenthalten; **feel ~d of affection** unter einem Mangel an Zuneigung leiden; *see also* **sex-starved** [4] (force) **~ sb. into submission/surrender** jmdn. bis zur Unterwerfung/Kapitulation aushungern

Phrasal verb

- **~ 'out** *v.t.* aushungern

'star wars *n. pl.* der Krieg der Sterne

stash /stæʃ/ (coll.)

A *v.t.* **~ [away]** verstecken; **he ~ed the sweets in his pocket** er ließ die Bonbons in seiner Tasche verschwinden; **~ money away** Geld beiseite schaffen

B *n.* [geheimes] Lager

stasis /'stæsɪs, 'steɪsɪs/ *n., pl.* **stases** /'stæsiːz, 'steɪsiːz/ [1] (stagnation) Stillstand, *der;* (of economy) Stagnation, *die* [2] (Biol.: stoppage) Stase, *die*

state /steɪt/

A *n.* [1] (condition) Zustand, *der;* **~ of the economy** Wirtschaftslage, *die;* **the ~ of play** (Sport) der Spielstand; **the ~ of play [at the moment] is that X leads** nach dem gegenwärtigen Spielstand führt X; **the ~ of play in the negotiations/debate** (fig.) der [gegenwärtige] Stand der Verhandlungen/Debatte; **the ~ of things** der Stand der Dinge; **the ~ of things in general** die allgemeine Lage; **the ~ of the art** der [gegenwärtige] Stand der Technik; *see also* **state-of-the-art**; **the ~ of the nation** die Lage der Nation; **be in a ~ of war** sich im Kriegszustand befinden; **a ~ of war exists** es herrscht Kriegszustand; **be in a ~ of excitement/sadness/anxiety** aufgeregt/traurig/ängstlich sein [2] (mess) **what a ~ you're in!** wie siehst du denn aus! **things are in a ~, I can tell you** es herrschen wirklich finstere Zustände, sag ich dir [3] (anxiety) **be in a ~** (be in a panic) aufgeregt sein; (be anxious) sich (*Dat.*) Sorgen machen; (be excited) ganz aus dem Häuschen sein (ugs.); **get into a ~** (coll.) Zustände kriegen (ugs.); **don't get into a ~!** reg dich nicht auf! (ugs.) [4] (nation) Staat, *der;* **[affairs] of S~:** Staats[geschäfte] [5] (federal ~) (of Germany, Austria) Land, *das;* (of America) Staat, *der;* **the [United] States** *sing.* die [Vereinigten] Staaten; **the Northern/Southern States** (Amer.) die Nord-/Südstaaten; **States' Rights** (Amer.) Rechte der einzelnen Bundesstaaten [6] **S~** (civil government) Staat, *der* [7] (pomp) Prunk, *der;* **in ~:** in vollem Staat; **keep ~:** Hof halten; **lie in ~:** aufgebahrt sein [8] (social rank) soziale Stellung [9] (Bibliog.: variant) Abdruckszustand, *der* [10] (Bot.: stage) Stadium, *das;* **the larval ~** (Zool.) das Larvenstadium. *See also* **affair 2**; **evidence A 2**; **grace A 5**; **mind A 5**

B *attrib. adj.* [1] (of nation or federal ~) staatlich; Staats‹*bank, -sicherheit, -geheimnis, -dienst*›; **~ control** staatliche Kontrolle; **~ education** staatliches Erziehungswesen; **S~ university** (Amer.) [öffentliche] Universität eines Bundesstaates [2] (ceremonial) Staats-; **the ~ opening of Parliament** (Brit.) die feierliche Eröffnung des Parlaments [nach der Sommerpause]

C *v.t.* [1] (express) erklären; (fully or clearly) darlegen; äußern ‹*Meinung*›; angeben ‹*Alter usw.*›; **'please ~ full particulars'** „bitte genaue Angaben machen"; **this condition is ~d in the insurance policy** so steht es ausdrücklich in der Versicherungspolice; **~ one's opinion that ...:** die Überzeugung äußern, dass ... [2] (specify) festlegen; **can you ~ the year when ...?** kannst du das Jahr nennen, in dem ...?; **at ~d intervals** in genau festgelegten Abständen; **at** *or* **by the ~d time** zur festgesetzten Zeit [3] (Law: set out) **~ a case** einen Fall vortragen [4] (Mus.: introduce) einführen

state: ~-aided *adj.* staatlich gefördert; **~-controlled** *adj.* [1] (owned) staatseigen; [2] (restricted) staatlich kontrolliert; **~craft** *n.* (statesmanship) Kunst der Staatsführung; **S~ Department** *n.* (Amer. Polit.) Außenministerium, *das*

statehood /'steɪthʊd/ *n.* [1] (sovereignty) Eigenstaatlichkeit, *die* [2] (Amer.: federation) **be admitted to ~:** als Bundesstaat aufgenommen werden

'state house *n.* (Amer.: legislature building) Parlamentsgebäude, *das*

stateless /'steɪtlɪs/ *adj.* staatenlos; **~ person** Staatenlose, *der/die*

'state line *n.* (Amer.) Staatsgrenze, *die*

stately /'steɪtlɪ/ *adj.* majestätisch; stattlich ‹*Körperbau, Erscheinung, Gebäude*›; hochtrabend ‹*Stil*›; feierlich ‹*Prozession*›; **at a ~ pace** gemessenen Schrittes

S

stately 'home *n.* (Brit.) Herrensitz, *der;* (grander) Schloss, *das*

statement /'steɪtmənt/ *n.* **1** (stating, account, thing stated) Aussage, *die;* (declaration) Erklärung, *die;* (allegation) Behauptung, *die;* **make a ~** ‹*Zeuge:*› eine Aussage machen; ‹*Politiker:*› eine Erklärung abgeben (**on** zu) **2** (Finance: report) **~ [of account], [bank] ~:** Kontoauszug, *der*

state: ~-of-the-'art *adj.* auf dem neuesten Stand der Technik *nachgestellt;* **S~ of the 'Union address, S~ of the 'Union message** *ns.* (Amer.) Bericht zur Lage der Nation; **~-owned** *adj.* staatlich; in Staatsbesitz *nachgestellt;* **~room** *n.* **1** Prunkzimmer, *das;* **2** (Naut.) private [Luxus]kabine; **3** (Amer. Railw.) privates [Luxus]abteil; **~ school** *n.* (Brit.) staatliche Schule; **S~side** (Amer. coll.) **A** *adv.* **be/work/travel/head S~side** in den Staaten (ugs.) sein/arbeiten/in die Staaten (ugs.) reisen/fahren; **B** *adj.* ‹*Szene, Mode*› in den Staaten (ugs.)

State Opening of Parliament

Die jährliche Eröffnung des britischen Parlaments, die alljährlich im Oktober oder November und nach einem Regierungswechsel stattfindet. Die Zeremonie ist ein grandioses Spektakel mit großem Aufwand. Die Königin oder der König fährt in einer Kutsche vor und hält die **Queen's Speech** (oder *King's Speech*) im **House of Lords** vor den versammelten Mitgliedern des Unter- und Oberhauses. Der Souverän trägt die Krone und ist umringt von Pagen, Hofdamen und Dienern. Vor der Königin oder dem König stehen die *Lords* in roten Roben, die *Ladies* mit Diademen und im hinteren Teil des Saals die Abgeordneten des Unterhauses in bürgerlichen Straßenanzügen.

state school

Eine direkt oder indirekt vom Staat finanzierte Schule in Großbritannien, die keine Schulgebühren verlangt. Die meisten Kinder in Großbritannien besuchen solche staatlichen Schulen.

statesman /'steɪtsmən/ *n., pl.* **statesmen** /'steɪtsmən/ Staatsmann, *der; see also* **elder statesman**

statesmanlike /'steɪtsmənlaɪk/ *adj.* staatsmännisch; diplomatisch ‹*Lösung*›

statesmanship /'steɪtsmənʃɪp/ *n., no pl.* **1** (Polit.: management) Staatslenkung, *die* **2** (wise leadership) staatsmännisches Geschick

state: S~ system *n., no pl.* (Brit. Educ.) staatliches Schulwesen; **~ 'trooper** *n.* (Amer.) Polizist, *der*/Polizistin, *die* (*eines US-Staats*); **~wide** *adj.* landesweit; (in USA) im ganzen [Bundes]staat *nachgestellt*

static /'stætɪk/

A *adj.* **1** (Phys.) statisch **2** (not moving) statisch; (not changing) konstant ‹*Umweltbedingungen*›; **be ~:** stagnieren; **remain ~** ‹*Zustand:*› unverändert bleiben; ‹*Preise:*› gleich bleiben **3** (Electr.) [elektro]statisch

B *n.* **1** (atmospherics) atmosphärische Störungen **2** ▸ **static electricity**

static elec'tricity *n.* (Phys.) statische Elektrizität

statics /'stætɪks/ *n., no pl.* (Mech.) Statik, *die*

station /'steɪʃn/

A *n.* **1** (position) Position, *die;* **be assigned a ~:** einen [Stand]ort zugewiesen bekommen; **take up one's ~:** seine Position einnehmen **2** (establishment) Station, *die;* (Broadcasting) Sender, *der;* **radar [tracking] ~** (Mil.) Radarstation, *die* **3** ▸ **railway station** **4** (status) Rang, *der;* **occupy a humble/an exalted ~:** eine niedrige/hohe Position bekleiden; **have ideas above one's ~:** sich für etwas Besseres halten; **marry above/below** *or* **beneath one's ~:** über/unter seinem Stand heiraten **5** (Amer.: post office) Poststelle, *die* **6** (post) (Mil.) Posten, *der;* (Navy, Air Force) Stützpunkt, *der;* (Police) Wache, *die* **7** (Austral.: farm) Farm, *die;* **[sheep] ~:** Schaffarm, *die* **8** **~ of the Cross** (Relig.) Kreuzwegstation, *die* (kath. Kirche)

B *v.t.* **1** (assign position to) stationieren; abstellen ‹*Auto*›; aufstellen ‹*Wache*› **2** (place) stellen; (Sport) aufstellen; **~ oneself** sich aufstellen

stationary /'steɪʃənərɪ/ *adj.* **1** (not moving) stehend; **be ~:** stehen; **the traffic was ~:** der Verkehr war zum Erliegen gekommen **2** (fixed) stationär

'station break *n.* (Amer. Radio and Telev.) Pausenzeichen, *das*

stationer /'steɪʃənə(r)/ *n.* ▸ⓘ **p. 1260** Schreibwarenhändler, *der*/-händlerin, *die;* **~'s [shop]** Schreibwarengeschäft, *das*

stationery /'steɪʃənərɪ/ *n.* **1** (writing materials) Schreibwaren *Pl.* **2** (writing paper) Briefpapier, *das;* **a ~ set** [eine Mappe mit] Briefpapier; eine Briefmappe; **office ~:** Bürobedarf, *der; see also* **continuous stationery**

'Stationery Office *n.* (Brit.) **[Her/His] Majesty's ~** *britischer Staatsverlag, der auch die staatlichen Stellen mit Bürobedarf versorgt*

station: ~ house *n.* (Amer.: police station) [Polizei]wache, *die;* **~master** *n.* ▸ⓘ **p. 1260** (Railw.) Stationsvorsteher, *der*/-vorsteherin, *die;* **~ sergeant** *n.* (Brit. Police) *Leiter einer Polizeiwache im Range eines Sergeanten;* **~ wagon** *n.* (Amer.) Kombi[wagen], *der*

statistic /stə'tɪstɪk/ *n.* statistische Tatsache; **I disliked being treated as just a ~:** es missfiel mir, nur als Nummer behandelt zu werden

statistical /stə'tɪstɪkl/ *attrib. adj.,* **statistically** /stə'tɪstɪkəlɪ/ *adv.* statistisch

statistician /stætɪ'stɪʃn/ *n.* ▸ⓘ **p. 1260** Statistiker, *der*/Statistikerin, *die*

statistics /stə'tɪstɪks/ *n.* **1** *as pl.* (facts) Statistik, *die;* **~ of population/crime, population/crime ~:** Bevölkerungs-/Kriminalitätsstatistik, *die;* **according to ~:** nach der Statistik; **~ show that one in three marriages ends in divorce** nach der Statistik endet eine von drei Eheschließungen mit Scheidung **2** *no pl.* (science) Statistik, *die*

statue /'stætʃuː, 'stætjuː/ *n.* Statue, *die;* **as still as a ~:** reglos wie eine Statue; *see also* **liberty**

Statue of Liberty

Die Freiheitsstatue steht auf Liberty Island ("Insel der Freiheit") im Hafen von New York. Die Kupferstatue wurde von dem französischen Bildhauer Frédéric Auguste Bartholdi entworfen. Zum Gedenken an Amerikas 100-jährige Unabhängigkeit schenkten die Franzosen 1876 die Statue den Amerikanern. Die *Statue of Liberty* gilt auch heute noch als Symbol der Freiheit.

statuesque /stætjʊ'esk, stætʃʊ'esk/ *adj.* statuenhaft; (imposing) stattlich

statuette /stætʃʊ'et, stætjʊ'et/ *n.* Statuette, *die*

stature /'stætʃə(r)/ *n.* **1** (body height) Statur, *die;* **be of short ~, be short in ~:** von kleiner Statur sein **2** (fig.: standing) Format, *das;* **be of international ~ in one's field** auf seinem Gebiet eine international anerkannte Kapazität sein; **a person of [some] ~:** eine [recht] bedeutende Persönlichkeit; **he was not of the same ~ as Picasso** er hatte nicht das Format *od.* die Größe Picassos

status /'steɪtəs/ *n.* **1** (position) Rang, *der;* **have no ~ in society** kein angesehenes Mitglied der Gesellschaft sein; **rise in ~:** an Ansehen gewinnen; **social ~:** [gesellschaftlicher] Status; **the ~ of this information is 'secret'** diese Information ist als „geheim" eingestuft; **be a person of high/low ~ in a firm** in einer Firma eine hohe/niedrige Stellung haben; **her ~ among scientists** ihr wissenschaftlicher Rang; **equality of ~ [with sb.]** Gleichstellung [mit jmdm.]; **financial ~:** finanzielle *od.* wirtschaftliche Lage **2** (superior position) Status, *der;* **have [some] ~ in the firm** in der Firma einen [ziemlich] hohen Rang bekleiden **3** (Law) Status, *der;* **have [no] legal ~:** [nicht] rechtsgültig sein; ‹*Person:*› über keinerlei Rechte verfügen

status: ~ bar *n.* (Computing) Statuszeile, *die;* Statusleiste, *die;* **~ quo** /steɪtəs 'kwəʊ/ *n.* Status quo, *der;* **~ symbol** *n.* Statussymbol, *das*

statute /'stætjuːt/ *n.* **1** (Law) Gesetz, *das;* **by ~:** per Gesetz **2** *in pl.* (rules) Statut, *das;* Satzung, *die*

statute: ~-barred *adj.* (Law) verjährt; **~ book** *n.* (Law) Gesetzbuch, *das;* **put an Act** *or* **a law on the ~ book** ein Gesetz durchbringen; **put a measure/provision on the ~ book** einer Maßnahme/Bestimmung Gesetzeskraft (*Dat.*) verleihen; **~ law** *n.* (Law) **1** (statute) Gesetz, *das;* **2** *no pl., no indef. art.* kodifiziertes *od.* schriftlich niedergelegtes Recht; **~ mile** *n.* englische Meile

statutory /'stætjʊtərɪ/ *adj.* **1** (Law) gesetzlich ‹*Feiertag, Bestimmung, Erfordernis, Erbe*›; gesetzlich vorgeschrieben ‹*Strafe*›; gesetzlich festgeschrieben ‹*Löhne, Zinssatz*›; gesetzlich festgelegt ‹*Voraussetzung, Sätze, Zeit*›; **~ law** kodifiziertes Recht; **~ rights** gesetzliche Rechte; *see also* **rape¹ A 2** (relating to the statutes of an institution) Satzungs‹*bestimmungen*›; von der Satzung vorgesehen ‹*Geldbuße usw.*›; **in accordance with the ~ requirements** *or* **conditions** satzungsgemäß

staunch¹ /stɔːnʃ, stɑːnʃ/ *adj.* treu ‹*Freund, Anhänger*›; streitbar ‹*Kämpfer, Anhänger*›; überzeugt ‹*Katholik, Demokrat usw.*›; unerschütterlich ‹*Mut, Hingabe, Glaube*›; standhaft ‹*Herz*›; **be ~ in one's belief** an seinem Glauben unerschütterlich festhalten; **be ~ in one's support for sb./sth.** jmdn./etw. getreu unterstützen

staunch² /stɑːnʃ, stɔːnʃ/ *v.t.* **1** (stop flow of) stillen ‹*Blut*› **2** (stop flow from) abbinden ‹*Wunde*›

staunchly /'stɔːnʃlɪ, 'stɑːnʃlɪ/ *adv.* standhaft ‹*beistehen*›; unerschrocken ‹*kämpfen, verteidigen*›; treu ‹*ergeben sein*›; unerschütterlich ‹*an etw. (Dat.) festhalten*›

stave /steɪv/

A *n.* **1** (Mus.) ▸ **staff A 4** **2** (of barrel) Daube, *die* **3** (rung) Sprosse, *die* **4** (lit.: stanza) Strophe, *die*

B *v.t.*, **~d** *or* **stove** /stəʊv/ ein Loch schlagen in (+ *Akk.*)

Phrasal verbs

- **~ 'in** *v.t.* (crush) eindrücken ‹*Karosserie, Tür, Fenster, Rippen*›; einschlagen ‹*Kopf, Kiste*›; (break hole in) ein Loch schlagen in (+ *Akk.*); **the boat was ~d in** das Boot schlug leck
- **~ 'off** *v.t.*, **~d off** abwenden; abwehren ‹*Angriff*›; verhindern ‹*Krankheit*›; stillen ‹*Hunger, Durst*›; zurückweisen ‹*Forderung*›

stay¹ /steɪ/

A *n.* **1** Aufenthalt, *der;* (visit) Besuch, *der;* **during her ~ with us** während sie bei uns zu Besuch war; **come/go for a short ~ with sb.** jmdn. kurz besuchen; **have a week's ~ in London** eine Woche in London verbringen

2 (Law) **~ [of execution]** Aussetzung [der Vollstreckung]; (fig.) Galgenfrist, *die*

3 (support) Stütze, *die*

4 *in pl.* (Hist.) ▸ **corset A 1**

B *v.i.* **1** (remain) bleiben; **he ~ed in the club/army for five years** er war fünf Jahre Klubmitglied/in der Armee; **~ open till 10 o'clock** ‹*Geschäft:*› bis 10 Uhr geöffnet sein; **be here to ~, have come to ~:** sich fest eingebürgert haben; ‹*Arbeitslosigkeit, Inflation:*› zum Dauerzustand geworden sein; ‹*Modeartikel:*› in Mode bleiben; **~ with the leaders** sich an der Spitze halten *od.* behaupten; **~!** halt!; (to dog) bleib hier!; **~ for** *or* **to dinner/for the party** zum Essen/zur Party bleiben; **~ put** (coll.) ‹*Ball, Haar:*› liegen bleiben; ‹*Hut:*› fest sitzen; ‹*Bild:*› hängen bleiben; ‹*Person:*› bleiben[, wo man ist]; **I am ~ing put in this armchair** aus diesem Sessel rühre ich mich so schnell nicht weg; **~ sitting** sitzen bleiben; **~ 'with it!** (coll.) bleib dran! (ugs.); **~ with me!** bleib bei mir!; **~ around!** bleib in der Nähe!

2 (dwell temporarily) wohnen; **he ~ed [for] two weeks in London before flying to Brussels** er verbrachte zwei Wochen in London, bevor er nach Brüssel flog; **~ the night in a hotel** die Nacht in einem Hotel verbringen; **~ at sb.'s** *or* **with sb. for the weekend** das Wochenende bei jmdm. verbringen

3 (Sport) durchhalten; **~ well at a fast pace/over any distance** bei schnellem Tempo/über jede Entfernung gut mithalten

S

C *v.t.* **1** (arch./literary: stop) aufhalten; **~ one's hand** (fig.) sich bedeckt halten; **~ sb.'s hand** (fig.) jmdn. zurückhalten
2 (endure) **~ the course** *or* **distance** die [ganze] Strecke durchhalten; (fig.) durchhalten; *see also* **pace¹ A 2**
3 (satisfy) stillen ‹*Hunger, Durst*›
4 (Law) aussetzen
5 (literary: support) stützen

(Phrasal verbs)

- **~ a'head** *v.i.* die Führung halten
- **~ a'way** *v.i.* **1** (not attend) **~ away [from sth.]** [von etw.] wegbleiben; [einer Sache (*Dat.*)] fernbleiben; **~ away from school/a meeting** nicht zur Schule/zu einem Treffen gehen/kommen; **if the visitors/customers ~ away** wenn die Besucher/Käufer ausbleiben **2** (~ distant) **~ away from the dog!** komm dem Hund nicht zu nahe!; **he ~ed well away from the wall** er hielt sich ein gutes Stück von der Wand entfernt; **~ away from him!** lass ihn in Ruhe!; **~ away from drugs** die Finger von Drogen lassen (ugs.)
- **~ 'back** *v.i.* **1** (not approach) zurückbleiben **2** ▸**~ behind 3** (remain in place) **the door won't ~ back** die Tür bleibt nicht offen
- **~ be'hind** *v.i.* zurückbleiben; **have to ~ behind [after school]** nachsitzen müssen; **we ~ed behind after the lecture** wir sind nach der Vorlesung noch dageblieben; **can you ~ behind for a moment?** kannst du einen Augenblick [hier] warten?
- **~ 'down** *v.i.* **1** (remain lowered) unten bleiben; **they ~ed down out of sight** sie blieben unten, sodass man sie nicht sehen konnte **2** (not increase) stabil bleiben **3** (Educ.: not go to higher form) sitzen bleiben (ugs.)
- **~ 'in** *v.i.* **1** (remain in position) halten; **will these creases ~ in?** bleiben diese Falten [drin (ugs.)]?; **this passage [of the book] should ~ in** diese Passage sollte nicht gestrichen werden **2** (remain indoors) im Hause bleiben; (remain at home) zu Hause bleiben
- **~ 'off**

A *v.i.* **1** wegbleiben (ugs.) **2** (away from work, school) **[have to] ~ off** nicht zur Schule/Arbeit gehen [können]
B *v.t.* **1** (not go on to) nicht betreten ‹*Rasen, Teppich, Beete*›; nicht gehen auf (+ *Akk.*) ‹*Straße usw.*›; **~ off the bottle/off drugs** die Finger vom Alkohol/von Drogen lassen (ugs.) **2** (be absent from) **~ off school/work** nicht zur Schule/Arbeit gehen

- **~ 'on** *v.i.* **1** (remain in place) ‹*Hut, Perücke, Kopftuch:*› sitzen bleiben; ‹*falsche Wimpern, Aufkleber:*› haften; ‹*Deckel, Rad:*› halten **2** (remain in operation) angeschaltet bleiben; anbleiben (ugs.) **3** (remain present) noch [da]bleiben; **~ on at school** auf der Schule bleiben; **~ on as chairman** Vorsitzender bleiben
- **~ 'out** *v.i.* **1** (not go home) wegbleiben (ugs.); nicht nach Hause kommen/gehen; **don't ~ out late!** komm nicht zu spät nach Hause! **2** (remain outside) draußen bleiben **3** (fig.) **~ out of sb.'s way** jmdm. aus dem Wege gehen **4** (remain on strike) **~ out [on strike]** im Ausstand bleiben
- **~ 'over** *v.i.* (coll.) über Nacht bleiben
- **~ 'up** *v.i.* **1** (not go to bed) aufbleiben **2** (remain in position) ‹*Pfosten, Gebäude:*› stehen bleiben; ‹*Plakat:*› hängen bleiben; ‹*Flugzeug, Haare:*› oben bleiben; **my socks won't ~ up** meine Socken rutschen [ständig]

stay²
A *n.* **1** (Naut.) Stag, *das* **2** (guy-rope) Zeltleine, *die;* (guy-wire) Drahtseil, *das* **3** (Aeronaut., Archit.) Strebe, *die*
B *v.t.* (Naut.) stagen

'stay-at-home
A *n.* häuslicher Mensch; **be a real ~:** ein richtiger Stubenhocker (ugs. abwertend) sein
B *attrib. adj.* häuslich

stayer /'steɪə(r)/ *n.* (lit. or fig.) Steher, *der*

staying power /'steɪɪŋpaʊə(r)/ *n.* Durchhaltevermögen, *das*

staysail /'steɪseɪl, 'steɪsl/ *n.* (Naut.) Stagsegel, *das*

STD *abbr.* **1** (Brit. Teleph.) = **subscriber trunk dialling** Selbstwählfernverkehr, *der;* **~ code** Vorwahl[nummer], *die* **2** (Med.) = **sexually transmitted disease** ▸**sexually 1**

stead /sted/ *n., no pl., no art.* **1** **in sb.'s ~:** an jmds. Stelle (Dat.); **the bishop's deputy went in his ~:** anstelle des Bischofs ging sein Vertreter **2** **stand sb. in good ~:** jmdm. zustatten kommen; **that car has stood her in good ~:** dieser Wagen hat ihr gute Dienste geleistet

steadfast /'stedfəst, 'stedfɑːst/ *adj.* standhaft; zuverlässig ‹*Freund*›; fest ‹*Entschluss*›; unverwandt ‹*Blick*›; unerschütterlich ‹*Glaube*›; unverbrüchlich (geh.) ‹*Freundschaft, Treue*›; **be ~ in one's belief that ...:** fest daran glauben, dass ...

steadfastly /'stedfəstlɪ, 'stedfɑːstlɪ/ *adv.* standhaft; fest ‹*glauben*›; unverwandt ‹*[an]blicken*›; **adhere ~ to one's principles/faith** fest zu seinen Grundsätzen/seinem Glauben stehen

steadily /'stedɪlɪ/ *adv.* **1** (stably) fest; festen Schrittes ‹*gehen*›; sicher ‹*Rad fahren*› **2** (without faltering) fest ‹*[an]blicken*› **3** (continuously) stetig; ohne Unterbrechung ‹*arbeiten, marschieren*›; **it was raining ~:** es hat ununterbrochen geregnet; **progress ~:** stetige Fortschritte machen; **news flowed in ~ all day** den ganzen Tag gingen pausenlos Nachrichten ein **4** (firmly) standhaft ‹*sich weigern*›; fest ‹*glauben*› **5** (reliably) zuverlässig

steady /'stedɪ/
A *adj.* **1** (stable) stabil; (not wobbling) standfest; **as ~ as a rock** völlig standfest ‹*Leiter, Tisch*›; völlig stabil ‹*Boot*›; ganz ruhig ‹*Hand*›; **in an emergency he is as ~ as a rock** (lit. or fig.) in einer Notsituation lässt er sich durch nichts erschüttern; **be ~ on one's feet** *or* **legs/bicycle** sicher auf den Beinen sein/sicher auf seinem Fahrrad fahren; **hold** *or* **keep one's hand ~:** die Hand ruhig halten; **hold** *or* **keep the ladder ~:** die Leiter festhalten; **~ as she goes!** (coll.) immer so weiter! **2** (still) ruhig; **turn a ~ eye** *or* **gaze** *or* **look on sb.** jmdn. fest ansehen **3** (regular, constant) stetig; gleichmäßig ‹*Arbeit, Tempo,*› stabil ‹*Preis, Lohn*›; gleich bleibend ‹*Temperatur*›; beständig ‹*Klima, Summen, Lärm*›; **we had ~ rain/drizzle** wir hatten Dauerregen/es nieselte [bei uns] ständig; **at a ~ pace** mit gleichmäßiger Geschwindigkeit; **[keep her] ~!** (Naut.) Kurs halten!; **prices have remained ~:** die Preise sind stabil geblieben; **~!** Vorsicht!; (to dog, horse) ruhig!; **~ on!** langsam! (ugs.); **~ on, or you'll knock the vase over/hurt me** Vorsicht, sonst wirfst du die Vase um/verletzt du mich **4** (invariable) unerschütterlich; beständig ‹*Wesensart*›; standhaft ‹*Weigerung*›; fest ‹*Charakter, Glaube*›; **have a ~ character** charakterfest sein; **~ purpose** Zielstrebigkeit, *die* **5** (enduring) **a ~ job** eine feste Stelle; **a ~ boyfriend/girlfriend** ein fester Freund/eine feste Freundin (ugs.) **6** (reliable) zuverlässig
B *v.t.* festhalten ‹*Leiter*›; beruhigen ‹*Pferd, Nerven*›; ruhig halten ‹*Boot, Flugzeug*›; **~ the table/vase** für einen festen Stand des Tisches/der Vase sorgen; **she steadied herself against the table/with a stick** sie hielt sich am Tisch fest/stützte sich mit einem Stock
C *v.i.* ‹*Preise:*› sich stabilisieren; ‹*Geschwindigkeit:*› sich mäßigen; **the boat steadied** das Boot wurde [wieder] ruhiger
D *n.* (coll.) fester Freund/feste Freundin (ugs.)
E *adv.* **go ~ with sth.** mit etw. vorsichtig sein; **go ~ with sb.** (coll.) mit jmdm. gehen (ugs.); **are you going ~ with anyone?** hast du einen festen Freund/eine feste Freundin? (ugs.)

steak /steɪk/ *n.* Steak, *das;* (of ham, bacon, gammon, salmon, etc.) Scheibe, *die;* **a chicken/turkey/veal ~:** ein Hähnchen-/Puten-/Kalbsschnitzel; **~ and kidney pie/pudding** Rindfleisch-Nieren-Pastete, *die;* **~ au poivre** /steɪk əʊ 'pwɑːvr/ Pfeffersteak, *das;* **~ tartare** Tatarbeefsteak, *das;* **a [fish] ~:** eine Scheibe [Fisch]; *see also* **fillet A 1**; **sirloin 1**

steak: ~house *n.* Steakhaus, *das;* **~ knife** *n.* Messer mit Sägeschliff

steal /stiːl/
A *v.t.*, **stole** /stəʊl/, **stolen** /'stəʊln/ **1** stehlen (**from** *Dat.*); **~ a ride** schwarzfahren; **~ sb.'s boyfriend/girlfriend** jmdm. den Freund/die Freundin ausspannen (ugs.); **~ the show** die Hauptattraktion sein; **the newcomer stole the show** ein Newcomer war der Star [des Abends]; **~ the show from sb.** jmdm. die Schau stehlen *od.* den Rang ablaufen; **she was the star of the play, but the little dog stole the show** (fig.) sie war der Star des Stückes, aber der kleine Hund stahl ihr die Schau; *see also* **scene 2**; **thunder A 3** **2** (get slyly) rauben (geh. scherzh.) ‹*Kuss, Umarmung*›; entlocken ‹*Worte, Interview*›; sich (*Dat.*) genehmigen (ugs. scherzh.) ‹*Nickerchen*›; **~ a glance [at sb./sth.]** jmdm. einen verstohlenen Blick zuwerfen/einen verstohlenen Blick auf etw. (*Akk.*) werfen **3** (fig.: win) **she stole my heart** sie eroberte mein Herz; **~ a march on sb.** jmdm. zuvorkommen
B *v.i.*, **stole, stolen** **1** stehlen; **~ from sb.** jmdn. bestehlen; **~ from the till/supermarket** aus der Kasse/im Supermarkt stehlen **2** (move furtively) sich stehlen; **~ in/out/up** sich hinein-/hinaus-/hinaufstehlen; **mist stole over the valley** beinahe unbemerkt breitete sich Nebel über das Tal aus; **~ up [on sb./sth.]** sich [an jmdn./etw.] heranschleichen; **old age is ~ing up on me** langsam, aber sicher werde ich alt
C *n.* (coll.) **1** (Amer.: theft) Diebstahl, *der* **2** (bargain) **that dress is a ~:** dieses Kleid ist [fast *od.* halb] geschenkt (ugs.)

(Phrasal verbs)

- **~ a'bout, ~ a'round** *v.i.* herumschleichen (ugs.)
- **~ a'way** *v.i.* sich fortstehlen

stealth /stelθ/ *n.* Heimlichkeit, *die;* **use ~:** heimlich vorgehen; **by ~:** heimlich

stealth: ~ bomber Tarnkappenbomber, *der;* **~ fighter** *n.* Tarnkappenjäger, *der*

stealthily /'stelθɪlɪ/ *adv.* heimlich; verstohlen

stealth: ~ tax *n.* versteckte *od.* verdeckte Steuer; **~ technology** *n., no pl.* Tarnkappentechnologie, *die*

stealthy /'stelθɪ/ *adj.* heimlich; verstohlen ‹*Blick, Bewegung, Tun*›

steam /stiːm/
A *n., no pl., no indef. art.* Dampf, *der;* **the window was covered with ~:** das Fenster war beschlagen; **all the ~ has gone out of him/the idea** (coll.) er hat seinen ganzen Schwung verloren/aus der Idee ist der Dampf raus (ugs.); **get up ~:** Dampf aufmachen; (fig.) in Fahrt kommen; **get up ~ to do sth.** (fig.) den nötigen Dampf aufbringen, um etw. zu tun; **let off ~** (fig.) Dampf ablassen (ugs.); **run out of ~:** keinen Dampf mehr haben; (fig.) den Schwung verlieren; **under its own ~:** mit eigener Kraft; **under one's own ~** (fig.) aus eigener Kraft; *see also* **full¹ A 4**
B *v.t.* **1** (Cookery) dämpfen; dünsten; **~ed pudding** gedämpfter Pudding **2** **~ open an envelope** einen Umschlag mit [heißem] Wasserdampf öffnen
C *v.i.* **1** (emit ~) dampfen; **~ing hot** dampfend heiß; **heat the water till ~ing hot** das Wasser erhitzen, bis es dampft **2** (move) dampfen; **he went ~ing after the thief** (fig. coll.) er stürmte mit Volldampf (ugs.) hinter dem Dieb her

(Phrasal verbs)

- **~ a'head** *v.i.* (fig. coll.) rasche Fortschritte machen
- **~ 'over** *v.i.* [sich] beschlagen
- **~ 'up**

A *v.t.* **1** beschlagen lassen; **be ~ed up** beschlagen sein **2** (fig. coll.) **be/get [all] ~ed up** [total] ausrasten (ugs.); **don't get ~ed up about it!** reg dich doch darüber nicht so auf!
B *v.i.* beschlagen

steam: ~ bath *n.* Dampfbad, *das;* **~boat** *n.* Dampfschiff, *das;* (small) Dampfboot, *das;* **~ boiler** *n.* Dampfkessel, *der;* **~ coal** *n.* Dampfkesselkohle, *die;* **~driven** *adj.* dampfgetrieben; **a ~-driven boat/train/tractor** ein Dampfboot/eine Dampflok/ein Traktor mit Dampfantrieb; **~ engine** *n.* **1** (Railw.) Dampflok[omotive], *die;* **2** (stationary engine) Dampf[kraft]maschine, *die*

steamer /'stiːmə(r)/ *n.* **1** (Naut.) Dampfer, *der* **2** (Cookery) Dämpfer, *der*

steam: ~ gauge *n.* Dampfdruckmesser, *der;* **~ hammer** *n.* (Metallurgy) Dampfhammer, *der;* **~ iron** *n.* Dampfbügeleisen, *das;* **~ 'radio** *n.* (coll. joc.) Dampfradio, *das* (ugs. scherzh.); **~roller A** *n.* (lit. or fig.) Dampfwalze, *die;* **B** *v.t.* [mit der Dampfwalze] walzen; (fig.) niederwalzen; **~roller a bill through Parliament** ein Gesetz durchpeitschen (ugs.); **~ship** *n.* Dampfschiff, *das;* **~ train** *n.* (Railw.) Dampfzug, *der;* **~ 'turbine** *n.* Dampfturbine, *die;* **~ whistle** *n.* Dampfpfeife, *die*

steamy /'sti:mɪ/ *adj.* **1** dunstig; Dunst‹*wolke*›; feucht ‹*Hitze*›; beschlagen ‹*Glas*› **2** (coll.: erotic) heiß

steed /sti:d/ *n.* (literary/joc.) Ross, *das* (geh./scherzh.)

steel /sti:l/

A *n.* **1** Stahl, *der;* **have a heart of ~** (fig.) stahlhart sein; **a man of ~:** ein stahlharter Mann; **as hard/true as ~:** stahlhart/treu wie Gold; **cold ~:** blanker Stahl; **pressed ~:** Pressstahl, *der* **2** (knife sharpener) Wetzstahl, *der* **3** (literary: sword) Schwert, *das*

B *attrib. adj.* stählern; Stahl‹*helm, -block, -platte*›

C *v.t.* **~ oneself for/against sth.** sich für/gegen etw. wappnen (geh.); **she ~ed her heart/herself against his pleas** sie verschloss ihr Herz/sich seinen Bitten; **~ oneself to do sth.** allen Mut zusammennehmen, um etw. zu tun

steel: ~ 'band *n.* (Mus.) Steelband, *die;* **~ 'drum** *n.* (Mus.) Steeldrum, *die;* **~ grey** *n.* Stahlgrau, *das;* **~-grey** *adj.* stahlgrau; **~ gui'tar** *n.* (Mus.) Hawaiigitarre, *die;* **~ industry** *n.* Stahlindustrie, *die;* **~maker** *n.* Stahlproduzent, *der*/-produzentin, *die;* **~ mill** *n.* Stahlwalzwerk, *das;* **~ 'plate** *n.* Stahlplatte, *die;* **~-plated** /'sti:lpleɪtɪd/ *adj.* (for protection) mit Stahlplatten gepanzert; (for durability) mit Stahl überzogen; **~ 'wool** *n.* Stahlwolle, *die;* **~worker** *n.* ▸**i p. 1260** Stahlarbeiter, *der*/-arbeiterin, *die;* **~works** *n. sing., pl. same* Stahlwerk, *das*

steely /'sti:lɪ/ *adj.* **1** (strong) stählern **2** (resolute) eisern **3** (severe) steinern

'steelyard *n.* Laufgewichtswaage, *die*

steep¹ /sti:p/ *adj.* **1** steil **2** (rapid) stark ‹*Preissenkung*›; steil ‹*Preisanstieg*› **3** (coll.: excessive) happig (ugs.); **the bill is [a bit] ~:** die Rechnung ist [ziemlich] gesalzen (ugs.); **be a bit ~ = be a bit much** ▸**much A 2**; **that's pretty ~[, coming from you/him]** das ist ein starkes Stück (ugs.) [von dir/ihm]

steep² *v.t.* **1** (soak) einweichen **2** (bathe) baden

steeped /sti:pt/ *adj.* durchdrungen (**in** von); **a place ~ in history/tradition** ein geschichtsträchtiger/von der Tradition durchdrungener Ort

steepen /'sti:pn/

A *v.i.* steil[er] werden

B *v.t.* steil[er] machen

steeple /'sti:pl/ *n.* Kirchturm, *der*

steeple: ~chase *n.* (Sport) **1** (horse race) Steeplechase, *die;* Hindernisrennen, *das;* **2** (Athletics) Hindernislauf, *der;* **~chaser** *n.* (Sport) **1** (rider) Reiter/Reiterin bei einer Steeplechase; **2** (runner) Hindernisläufer, *der*/-läuferin, *die;* **3** (horse) Steepler, *der;* **~chasing** /'sti:plt∫eɪsɪŋ/ *n.* (Sport) Hindernisrennen, *das;* **~jack** *n.* ▸**i p. 1260** *Arbeiter, der/Arbeiterin, die Reparaturarbeiten an Kaminen, Kirchtürmen usw. ausführt*

steeply /'sti:plɪ/ *adv.* steil ‹*ansteigen, abfallen*›

'steep-sided ▸**-sided**

steer¹ /stɪə(r)/

A *v.t.* **1** steuern; lenken; **this car is easy to ~:** dieser Wagen ist leicht lenkbar **2** (direct) **~ a *or* one's way through …:** steuern durch …; **~ a *or* one's course for a place** auf einen Ort zusteuern; (in ship, plane, etc.) Kurs auf einen Ort nehmen; **~ a *or* one's course for home** Kurs in Richtung Heimat nehmen; **~ a middle course** (fig.) einen Mittelweg einschlagen **3** (guide movement of) führen, lotsen ‹*Person*›; **~ a bill through Parliament** eine Gesetzesvorlage über die parlamentarischen Hürden bringen; **~ sb./the conversation towards/away from a subject** jmdn./das Gespräch auf ein Thema lenken/von einem Thema ablenken

B *v.i.* steuern; **~ in and out of/~ between the obstacles** zwischen den Hindernissen hindurchsteuern; **~ clear of sb./sth.** (fig. coll.) jmdm./einer Sache aus dem Weg[e] gehen; **~ clear of opium/politics** die Finger von Opium/der Politik lassen; **~ for sth.** etw. ansteuern; **~ left/right** nach links/rechts steuern; **~ due north** (Naut.) direkt nach Norden steuern

steer² *n.* (Zool.) junger Ochse

steering /'stɪərɪŋ/ *n.* **1** (Motor Veh.) Lenkung, *die* **2** (Naut.) Ruder, *das;* Steuerung, *die*

steering: ~ column *n.* (Motor Veh.) Lenksäule, *die;* **~ committee** *n.* Lenkungsausschuss, *der;* **~ gear** *n.* (Naut.) Steuervorrichtung, *die;* Ruderanlage, *die;* **~ lock** *n.* (Motor Veh.) Lenkradschloss, *das;* **~ wheel** *n.* **1** (Motor Veh.) Lenkrad, *das;* **2** (Naut.) Steuerrad, *das*

steersman /'stɪəzmən/ *n., pl.* **steersmen** /'stɪəzmən/ (Naut.) Steuermann, *der*

stein /staɪn/ *n.* Bierkrug, *der;* Stein, *der* (südd.)

stellar /'stelə(r)/ *adj.* stellar

stem¹ /stem/

A *n.* **1** (Bot.) (of tree, shrub) Stamm, *der;* (of flower, leaf, fruit) Stiel, *der;* (of corn) Halm, *der* **2** (of glass) Stiel, *der* **3** (Mus.) Notenhals, *der* **4** (of tobacco pipe) Pfeifenrohr, *das* **5** (Ling.) Stamm, *der* **6** (Naut.) **from ~ to stern** vom Bug bis zum Heck

B *v.i.*, **-mm-: ~ from sth.** auf etw. (*Akk.*) zurückzuführen sein

C *v.t.*, **-mm-** (make headway against) standhalten (+ *Dat.*)

stem² *v.t.*, **-mm-** (check, dam up) aufhalten; eindämmen ‹*Flut*›; stillen ‹*Blutung, Wunde*›; (fig.) Einhalt gebieten (+ *Dat.*) (geh.); stoppen ‹*Redefluss*›; **~ the tide of criticism** die Welle[n] der Kritik eindämmen

'stem cell *n.* (Biol.) Stammzelle, *die; attrib.* **~ research** Stammzellenforschung, *die*

-stemmed /stemd/ *adj. in comb.* -stielig ‹*Glas, Pfeife, Blume, Frucht*›; -stämmig ‹*Baum, Strauch*›

'stem turn *n.* (Skiing) Stemmbogen, *der*

stench /stent∫/ *n.* Gestank, *der* (abwertend)

stencil /'stensl/

A *n.* **1** **~ [plate]** Schablone, *die* **2** (for duplicating) Matrize, *die* **3** (**~led** pattern/lettering) schabloniertes Muster/schablonierte Schrift

B *v.t.*, (Brit.) **-ll-** **1** (produce with **~**) mit einer Schablone zeichnen; schablonieren **2** (ornament) [mittels Schablone] mustern

Sten gun /'sten gʌn/ *n.* (Arms) *Art Maschinenpistole*

stenographer /ste'nɒgrəfə(r)/ *n.* ▸**i p. 1260** Stenograf, *der*/Stenografin, *die*

stentorian /sten'tɔ:rɪən/ *adj.* laut [hallend]; **a ~ voice** eine Stentorstimme (geh.)

step /step/

A *n.* **1** (movement, distance) Schritt, *der;* **at every ~:** mit jedem Schritt; **watch sb.'s every ~** (fig.) jmdn. auf Schritt und Tritt überwachen; **take a ~ towards/away from sb.** einen Schritt auf jmdn. zugehen/von jmdm. wegtreten; **take a ~ back/sideways/forward** einen Schritt zurücktreten/zur Seite treten/nach vorn treten; **a ~ forward/back** (fig.) ein Schritt nach vorn/zurück; ein Fortschritt/Rückschritt; **a ~ in the right/wrong direction** (fig.) ein Schritt in die richtige/falsche Richtung; **mind *or* watch your ~!** (lit. or fig.) pass auf!; **I can't walk another ~:** ich kann keinen Schritt mehr gehen; **don't move another ~!** keinen Schritt weiter!

2 (stair) Stufe, *die;* (on vehicle) Tritt, *der;* **a flight of ~s** eine Treppe; **mind the ~!** Vorsicht, Stufe!; (warning by one person to another) pass auf die Stufe auf!; **[pair of] ~s** (ladder) Stehleiter, *die;* (small) Trittleiter, *die*

3 **follow *or* walk in sb.'s ~s** (fig.) in jmds. Fußstapfen treten

4 (short distance) **it's only a ~ to my house** es sind nur ein paar Schritte bis zu mir

5 **be in ~:** im Schritt sein; (with music, in dancing) im Takt sein; **be in/out of ~ with sth.** (fig.) mit etw. Schritt/nicht Schritt halten; **he is rarely in ~ with others** er befindet sich selten in Einklang mit anderen; **be out of ~:** aus dem Schritt geraten sein; (with music, in dancing) nicht im Takt sein; **he is out of ~ with his colleagues/the official party line** er ist über Kreuz mit seinen Kollegen/weicht von der offiziellen Parteilinie ab; **break ~:** aus dem Tritt geraten *od.* kommen; **change ~:** den Schritt wechseln; **fall into *or* get in ~:** in den Gleichschritt fallen; **fall into *or* get in ~ with sb./sth.** mit jmdm./etw. im Gleichschritt [mit-]marschieren; (fig.) sich jmdm./einer Sache fügen; **prices are out of ~ with wage increases** die Preise stehen in keinem Verhältnis zu den Lohnerhöhungen; **keep in ~:** den Schritt halten; (with music, in dancing) im Takt bleiben; **keep in ~ with sth./sb.** (fig.) mit etw./jmdm. Schritt halten

6 (action) Schritt, *der;* **take ~s to do sth.** Schritte unternehmen, um etw. zu tun; *see also* **false step**

7 (stage in process) Schritt, *der;* **S~ one: …:** erster Schritt: …; **keep one ~ ahead [of sb./sth.]** [jmdm./einer Sache] einen Schritt *od.* eine Nasenlänge voraus sein; **~ by ~:** Schritt für Schritt; **the first ~ in sb.'s career** die erste Sprosse auf jmds. Karriereleiter; **what is the next ~?** wie geht es weiter?

8 (grade) Stufe, *die*

9 (sound of foot, manner of walking) Schritt, *der;* **know sb. from his ~, know sb.'s ~:** jmdn. an seinem Schritt erkennen; **walk with a skip in one's ~:** hüpfenden Schrittes gehen

10 (Amer. Mus.) große Sekunde

B *v.i.*, **-pp-** treten; **~ lightly *or* softly** leise auftreten; **~ hesitantly/heavily/clumsily** mit zögernden Schritten gehen/einen schweren/unbeholfenen Schritt haben; **~ from the pavement on to the road** vom Bürgersteig auf die Straße treten; **~ across *or* over a puddle/gap** einen [großen] Schritt über eine Pfütze/Spalte machen; **don't ~ across the line!** nicht über die Linie treten!; **~ inside** eintreten; **please ~ inside for a moment** kommen Sie bitte auf einen Augenblick herein; **~ into** treten in (+ *Akk.*); steigen in (+ *Akk.*) ‹*Fahrzeug, Flugzeug, Wanne*›; **~ into sb.'s shoes** (fig.) an jmds. Stelle treten; **~ into one's dress/trousers** in sein Kleid/seine Hose steigen (ugs.); **~ on sth.** (on the ground) auf etw. (*Akk.*) treten; **~ on sb.'s foot/on the dog's tail** jmdm. auf den Fuß/dem Hund auf den Schwanz treten; **~ on a patch of oil/water** in eine Öl-/Wasserpfütze treten; **~ on [to]** steigen auf (+ *Akk.*); steigen in (+ *Akk.*) ‹*Fahrzeug, Flugzeug*›; **~ on it** (coll.) auf die Tube drücken (ugs.); **~ on sb.'s toes = tread on sb.'s toes** ▸**tread B**; **~ out of** treten aus; steigen aus ‹*Fahrzeug, Bad, Fluss*›; **~ out of the room for a few minutes** für ein paar Minuten aus dem Zimmer gehen; **~ out of one's dress/trousers** aus seinem Kleid/seiner Hose steigen (ugs.); **~ out of line** (fig.) aus der Reihe tanzen (ugs.); **I ~ped outside** ich trat hinaus; **Have you been calling my girlfriend names? I think you'd better ~ outside!** Hast du meine Freundin beschimpft? Komm, wir gehen mal zusammen raus (ugs.); **~ over sb./sth.** über jmdn./etw. steigen; **~ over the starting line** über die Startlinie treten; **~ this way, please** hier entlang, bitte; **~ through a door/window** durch eine Tür treten/ein Fenster steigen; *see also* **breach A 3**; **gas A 2**

Phrasal verbs

- **~ a'side** *v.i.* **1** zur Seite treten **2** (fig.: resign) seine Stellung räumen
- **~ 'back** *v.i.* zurücktreten; **~ back in fright/surprise** vor Schreck/Überraschung [einen Schritt] zurückweichen
- **~ 'down**

A *v.i.* **1** **~ down into the auditorium** ins Publikum herunterkommen *od.* -steigen; **~ down from the train/into the boat** aus dem Zug/in das Boot steigen **2** (fig.) ▸**stand down A 1**

B *v.t.* (Electr.) heruntertransformieren (ugs.); *see also* **step-down**

- **~ 'forward** *v.i.* **1** [einen Schritt] vortreten **2** (fig.: present oneself) sich melden; **would somebody like to ~ forward and help me with the trick?** würde jemand gern nach vorn kommen und mir bei dem Trick assistieren?; **he has ~ped forward as the new candidate**

S

er präsentierte sich als neuer Kandidat; **several ~ped forward** einige meldeten sich [freiwillig]

• **~ 'in** *v.i.* **1** eintreten; (into vehicle) einsteigen; (into pool) hineinsteigen; **would you mind ~ping in for a moment?** würden Sie bitte einen Augenblick hereinkommen? **2** (fig.) (take sb.'s place) einspringen; (intervene) eingreifen

• **~ 'off**

A *v.i.* **1** (get off) (from vehicle) aussteigen; (from a height) hinabspringen **2** (Mil.: begin to march) abmarschieren

B *v.t.* **1** (get off) steigen aus ‹*Fahrzeug*›; treten von ‹*Bürgersteig*›; springen von ‹*Klippe, Brücke*› **2** (measure by pacing) abschreiten (geh.)

• **~ 'out**

A *v.i.* **1** (leave a place) hinausgehen; **the car/boat stopped and she ~ped out** der Wagen/das Boot hielt an und sie stieg aus **2** (lengthen stride) ausschreiten (geh.) **3** (dated fig.: be active socially) ausgehen; **he has been ~ping out with this girl for a few months now** er geht jetzt schon seit ein paar Monaten mit diesem Mädchen (ugs.)

B *v.t.* steigen aus ‹*Fahrzeug*›

• **~ 'up**

A *v.i.* **1** (ascend) hinaufsteigen; **~ up into** [ein-]steigen in (+ *Akk.*) ‹*Fahrzeug*›; **~ up on to** steigen auf (+ *Akk.*) ‹*Podest, Tisch*› **2** (approach) **~ up and ask sb.'s name** auf jmdn. zugehen und ihn nach seinem Namen fragen; **~ right up!** treten Sie näher!; **~ up to sb.** zu jmdm. treten **3** (increase) zunehmen

B *v.t.* **1** (increase) erhöhen; intensivieren ‹*Wahlkampf*›; verstärken ‹*Anstrengungen*›; verschärfen ‹*Sicherheitsmaßnahmen, Streik*› **2** (Electr.) hinauftransformieren (ugs.); *see also* **step-up B**

step: ~ aerobics *n. sing.* Stepaerobic, *das;* **~brother** *n.* Stiefbruder, *der;* **~child** *n.* Stiefkind, *das;* **~daughter** *n.* Stieftochter, *die;* **~-down** *attrib. adj.* (Electr.) **~-down converter** *or* **transformer** Abwärtstransformator, *der;* **~father** *n.* Stiefvater, *der;* **~ladder** *n.* Stehleiter, *die;* **~mother** *n.* Stiefmutter, *die;* **~-parent** *n.* Stiefelternteil, *der;* **~-parents** Stiefeltern *Pl.*

steppe /step/ *n.* (Geog.) Steppe, *die*

stepped /stept/ *adj.* gestuft; terrassiert ‹*Berg, Hang*›; Stufen‹*pyramide, -giebel*›

'steppeland *n.* (Geog.) Steppenland, *das*

stepping stone /'stepɪŋstəʊn/ *n.* Trittstein, *der;* (fig.) Sprungbrett, *das* (**to** für, in)

step: ~sister *n.* Stiefschwester, *die;* **~son** *n.* Stiefsohn, *der;* **~-up A** *n.* Erhöhung, *die;* **a ~-up in output/production/security measures** eine Steigerung des Ausstoßes/der Produktion/Verschärfung der Sicherheitsmaßnahmen; **B** *attrib. adj.* (Electr.) **~-up converter** *or* **transformer** Aufwärtstransformator, *der*

stereo /'sterɪəʊ, 'stɪərɪəʊ/

A *n., pl.* **~s** **1** (equipment) Stereoanlage, *die; see also* **personal 4** **2** (sound reproduction) Stereo, *das*

B *adj.* **1** (sound) stereo; Stereo‹*effekt, -aufnahme, -platte*› **2** (Optics) stereoskopisch

stereophonic /sterɪə'fɒnɪk, stɪərɪə'fɒnɪk/ *adj.*, **stereophonically** /sterɪə'fɒnɪkəlɪ, stɪərɪə'fɒnɪkəlɪ/ *adv.* stereophon

stereoscope /'sterɪəskəʊp, 'stɪərɪəskəʊp/ *n.* Stereoskop, *das*

stereoscopic /sterɪə'skɒpɪk, stɪərɪə'skɒpɪk/ *adj.* stereoskopisch

'stereo system *n.* Stereoanlage, *die*

stereotype /'sterɪətaɪp, 'stɪərɪətaɪp/

A *n.* **1** Stereotyp, *das* (Psych.); Klischee, *das* **2** (Printing: plate) Stereotyp[ie]platte, *die* **3** *no pl.* (Printing: process) (making of **~s**) Stereotypie, *die;* **~ [printing]** Drucken mit Stereotyp[ie-]platten

B *v.t.* in ein Klischee zwängen; **~ sb. as a villain** jmdn. in das Klischee des Schurken zwängen; **~d** stereotyp ‹*Redensart, Frage, Vorstellung*›; klischeehaft ‹*Sprache, Denkweise*›; **the ~d business man** das Klischee des Geschäftsmanns

sterile /'steraɪl/ *adj.* **1** (germ-free) steril **2** (barren, lit. or fig.) steril; unfruchtbar; (fig.) erfolglos ‹*Geschäftsjahr, Bemühung*›; nutzlos ‹*Tätigkeit*›; fruchtlos ‹*Diskussion, Gespräch*›

sterilisation, sterilise, steriliser ▸**steriliz-**

sterility /stə'rɪlɪtɪ/ *n., no pl.* **1** (absence of germs) Sterilität, *die* **2** (barrenness, lit. or fig.) Sterilität, *die;* Unfruchtbarkeit, *die;* (fig.: of discussion) Fruchtlosigkeit, *die*

sterilization /sterɪlaɪ'zeɪʃn/ *n.* Sterilisation, *die*

sterilize /'sterɪlaɪz/ *v.t.* **1** (make germ-free) sterilisieren **2** (make barren) sterilisieren ‹*Tier, Mensch*›; unfruchtbar machen ‹*Land*›

sterilizer /'sterɪlaɪzə(r)/ *n.* Sterilisator, *der*

sterling /'stɜːlɪŋ/

A ▸**ⓘ p. 1332** *n., no pl., no indef. art.* Sterling, *der;* **do they accept** *or* **take ~?** kann man bei ihnen in Pfund [Sterling] bezahlen?; **five pounds ~:** fünf Pfund Sterling; **in ~:** in Pfund [Sterling]; **~ area** (Hist.) Sterlingblock, *der*

B *attrib. adj.* **1** **~ silver** Sterlingsilber, *das* **2** (fig.) gediegen; **he is a ~ chap!** er ist ein zuverlässiger Bursche!; **do ~ work** erstklassige Arbeit leisten; **[this is] ~ stuff!** (coll.) tadellos!; erstklassig!

stern¹ /stɜːn/ *adj.* streng; hart ‹*Strafe*›; ernst ‹*Warnung*›; **made of ~er stuff** (fig.) aus härterem Holz [geschnitzt]; **be ~ with sb.** mit jmdm. streng sein; jmdn. hart anpacken (ugs.)

stern² *n.* (Naut.) Heck, *das;* **~ foremost** [mit dem] Heck voraus; *see also* **stem¹ A 6**

sternly /'stɜːnlɪ/ *adv.* streng; ernsthaft ‹*warnen*›; in strengem Ton ‹*sprechen*›; mit strenger Hand ‹*regieren*›

'sternpost *n.* (Naut.) Achtersteven, *der*

sternum /'stɜːnəm/ *n., pl.* **~s** *or* **sterna** /'stɜːnə/ (Anat.) Brustbein, *das;* Sternum, *das* (fachspr.)

steroid /'stɪərɔɪd, 'sterɔɪd/ *n.* (Chem.) Steroid, *das*

stet /stet/ (Printing) *v.i. imper.* bleibt

stethoscope /'steθəskəʊp/ *n.* (Med.) Stethoskop, *das*

Stetson ® /'stetsn/ *n.* Stetson[hut], *der*

stevedore /'stiːvədɔː(r)/ *n.* ▸**ⓘ p. 1260** (Naut.) Schauermann, *der*

stew /stjuː/

A *n.* **1** (Gastr.) Eintopf, *der;* **Irish ~:** Irishstew, *das* **2** (coll.: state) **be in/get into a ~:** in heller Aufregung sein/völlig aus dem Häuschen geraten (ugs.); **be in** *or* **get into a ~ about** *or* **over sth.** sich über etw. (*Akk.*) [schrecklich (ugs.)] aufregen; **don't get into a ~ about nothing!** dreh nicht unnötig durch! (ugs.)

B *v.t.* (Cookery) schmoren [lassen]; **~ apples/plums** Apfel-/Pflaumenkompott kochen

C *v.i.* **1** (Cookery) schmoren; ‹*Obst:*› gedünstet werden; **~ [in one's own juice]** (fig.) [im eigenen Saft] schmoren (ugs.) **2** (fig.: fret) **~ over a problem** sich (*Dat.*) über ein Problem den Kopf zerbrechen (ugs.) **3** (fig.: swelter) schmoren (ugs.)

steward /'stjuːəd/

A *n.* ▸**ⓘ p. 1260** **1** (on ship, plane) Steward, *der* **2** (supervising official) (at public meeting, ball, etc.) Ordner, *der*/Ordnerin, *die;* **~s** (of race) Rennleitung, *die;* **~s' enquiry** (Horseracing) [Untersuchung und] Beratung der Rennleitung; *see also* **shop steward** **3** (estate manager) Verwalter, *der*/Verwalterin, *die*

B *v.t.* verwalten; **~ a meeting** bei einer öffentlichen Veranstaltung Ordner/Ordnerin sein

stewardess /'stjuːədɪs/ *n.* ▸**ⓘ p. 1260** Stewardess, *die*

stewardship /'stjuːədʃɪp/ *n.* Verwaltung, *die;* **hold the ~ of an estate** Verwalter/Verwalterin eines Gutes sein

stewed /stjuːd/ *adj.* **1** (Cookery) geschmort; **~ apples/plums** Apfel-/Pflaumenkompott, *das* **2** (over-brewed) **the tea is ~:** der Tee hat zu lange gezogen **3** (coll.: drunk) blau (ugs.); voll (salopp)

stewing steak /'stjuːɪŋ steɪk/ *n., no pl., no indef. art.* [Rinder]schmorfleisch, *das*

stew: ~ pan *n.* (Cookery) Schmorpfanne, *die;* **~ pot** *n.* (Cookery) Schmortopf, *der*

stick /stɪk/

A *v.t.,* **stuck** /stʌk/ **1** (thrust point of) stecken; **~ sth. in[to] sth.** mit etw. in etw. (*Akk.*) stechen; **she stuck a needle in[to] her finger** sie stach sich (*Dat.*) mit einer Nadel in den Finger; **get stuck into sb./sth./a meal** (coll.: begin action) jmdm. eine Abreibung verpassen/sich in etw. (*Akk.*) reinknien/tüchtig reinhauen (salopp); **I stuck a knife in[to] him** ich stieß *od.* (ugs.) rammte ihm ein Messer in den Leib

2 (impale) spießen; **~ sth. [up]on sth.** etw. auf etw. (*Akk.*) [auf]spießen; **like a stuck pig** ‹*bluten*› wie ein Schwein; ‹*schreien*› wie eine gestochene Sau

3 (coll.: put) stecken; **he stuck a feather in his hat/a rose in his buttonhole** er steckte sich (*Dat.*) eine Feder an den Hut/eine Rose in das Knopfloch; **~ a picture on the wall/a vase on the shelf** ein Bild an die Wand hängen/eine Vase aufs Regal stellen; **~ 10% on the bill** 10% zusätzlich auf die Rechnung setzen; **~ one's hat on one's head** sich (*Dat.*) den Hut auf den Kopf stülpen; **~ one's head out of the window** den Kopf aus dem Fenster strecken; **~ sth. in the kitchen** etw. in die Küche tun (ugs.); **~ one on sb.** (sl.: hit) jmdm. eine langen (ugs.); **~ one's hands in one's pockets** die Hände in den Taschen vergraben; **you know where you can ~ that!, [you can] ~ it!** (sl.) das kannst du dir sonst wohin stecken!

4 (with glue etc.) kleben

5 (make immobile) **the car is stuck in the mud** das Auto ist im Schlamm stecken geblieben; **the door is stuck** die Tür klemmt [fest]; **she's been stuck indoors all day** (fig. coll.) sie hat den ganzen Tag im Haus hocken müssen (ugs.)

6 (puzzle) **be stuck for an answer/for ideas** um eine Antwort/um Ideen verlegen sein; **Can you help me with this problem? I'm stuck** Kannst du mir bei diesem Problem helfen? Ich komme nicht weiter; **be stuck for money** (coll.) gerade kein Geld haben

7 (cover) **~ sth. with pins/needles** Stecknadeln/Nadeln in etw. (*Akk.*) stecken

8 (stab) **~ sb. with a knife** jmdm. einen Messerstich beibringen

9 (Brit.: paste on wall) kleben; **'~ no bills'** „Plakate ankleben verboten!"

10 (Brit. coll.: tolerate) **~ it** durchhalten; **she can't ~ him** sie kann ihn nicht riechen (salopp); **he can't ~ the book/film** er kann das Buch/den Film nicht ausstehen; **she can't ~ the heat/such conditions** sie kann die Hitze/solche Bedingungen nicht ertragen; **I can't ~ it/my job any longer** das/mein Job steht mir bis oben *od.* hier (ugs.)

11 (coll.) **be stuck with sth.** (have to accept) sich mit etw. herumschlagen müssen (ugs.); **be stuck with sb.** jmdn. am *od.* auf dem Hals haben (ugs.); **if we don't sell our car soon we'll be stuck with it** wenn wir unser Auto nicht bald verkaufen, werden wirs überhaupt nicht mehr los (ugs.)

12 (coll.) **be stuck on sb./sth.** (captivated by) auf jmdn./etw. abfahren (salopp); **be stuck on an idea** eine fixe Idee haben

B *v.i.,* **stuck** **1** (be fixed by point) stecken; **there's a splinter ~ing in my finger** ich habe einen [Holz]splitter im Finger

2 (adhere) kleben; **mud ~s** (fig.) etwas bleibt immer hängen (fig.); **~ to sth.** an etw. (*Dat.*) kleben; **my wet clothes stuck to my body** meine nassen Kleider klebten mir am Körper; **~ in the/sb.'s mind** (fig.) im/jmdm. im Gedächtnis haften bleiben; **she was called the 'iron lady' and the nickname stuck** sie wurde „Eiserne Lady" genannt, und der Spitzname blieb an ihr hängen

3 (become immobile) ‹*Auto, Räder:*› stecken bleiben; ‹*Schublade, Tür, Griff, Bremse:*› klemmen; ‹*Schlüssel:*› feststecken; **~ fast** ‹*Auto, Rad:*› feststecken; ‹*Reißverschluss, Tür, Schublade:*› festklemmen; **the words stuck in his throat** die Worte blieben ihm in der Kehle stecken; **the record is stuck** die Platte ist hängen geblieben; *see also* **stick-in-the-mud**

4 (protrude) **a letter stuck from his pocket**

ein Brief schaute ihm aus der Tasche
5 (coll.: remain) bleiben; **are you going to ~ indoors all day?** willst du den ganzen Tag im Haus [herum]hocken? (ugs.)
6 (coll.: be considered valid) **the accusations will not ~:** die Anschuldigungen ziehen nicht (ugs.); **make a charge ~:** mit einer Anklage durchkommen (ugs.); **be made to ~:** hieb- und stichfest gemacht werden
7 (Cards) **Do you want another card? — No, I'll ~:** Willst du noch eine Karte? — Nein, ich behalte mein Blatt
C *n.* **1** ([cut] shoot of tree, piece of wood) Stock, *der;* (staff) [Holz]stab, *der;* (walking ~) Spazierstock, *der;* (for handicapped person) Krückstock, *der;* **pick up a large ~ from the ground** einen großen Knüppel vom Boden aufheben; **gather dry ~s** trockene Äste sammeln; *see also* **big A 1**
2 ▸**rod 3**
3 (Hockey etc.) Schläger, *der;* **~s!** hoher Stock!
4 (long piece) **a ~ of chalk/shaving soap** ein Stück Kreide/Rasierseife; **a ~ of dynamite/sealing wax** eine Stange Dynamit/Siegellack; **a ~ of rock/celery/rhubarb** eine Stange Rocks/Sellerie/Rhabarber; **a cinnamon ~:** eine Zimtstange
5 *no pl., no art.* (coll.: criticism) **get** *or* **take [some] ~:** viel einstecken müssen; **give sb. [some] ~:** jmdn. zusammenstauchen (ugs.)
6 **give sb. the ~, take the ~ to sb.** (cane sb.) jmdn. den Stock spüren lassen
7 **~ of furniture** (coll.) Möbelstück, *das;* **up ~s** (coll.) seine [Sieben]sachen zusammenpacken (ugs.)
8 (Motor Veh.: gear lever) ▸**gearstick**
9 (Mus.) ▸**baton 3**
10 (Printing) Winkelhaken, *der*
11 **the ~s** (Horseracing coll.) die Hürden; die Hindernisse; **the race is over the ~s** das Rennen geht über Hindernisse
12 *in pl.* (coll.: rural area) **in the ~s** in der hintersten Provinz
13 (coll.: person) **a queer ~:** komischer Kauz (ugs.); **a funny old ~:** ein komischer alter Kauz (ugs.)
14 (Mil.: of bombs) Reihenwurf, *der. See also* **cleft² B; cross D 2; dirty A 8; wrong A 3**

Phrasal verbs

• **~ a'bout, ~ a'round** *v.i.* (coll.) dableiben; (wait) warten
• **~ at** *v.t.* **1** (hesitate at) **~ at sth./nothing** vor etw. (*Dat.*)/nichts zurückschrecken **2** (keep on with) **~ at one's books/studying** fleißig Bücher wälzen/studieren; **~ 'at it** (coll.) dranbleiben (ugs.)
• **~ by** *v.t.* (fig.) stehen zu
• **~ 'down** *v.t.* **1** (glue down) festkleben; zukleben ‹*Umschlag*› **2** (coll.: put down) hinknallen (ugs.) ‹*Tisch, Kiste*› **3** (coll.: write down) schreiben
• **~ 'in** *v.t.* **1** (jab in) hineinstechen ‹*Spritze, Nadel*›; anstecken ‹*Hutnadel*›; **get stuck in** (coll.) (working) ranklotzen (salopp); (eating) reinhauen (salopp) **2** (glue in) einkleben **3** (coll.: put in) hineinstecken; *see also* **nose A 1**
• **~ 'on**
A *v.t.* **1** (glue on) aufkleben ‹*Briefmarke, Etikett*›; ankleben ‹*Tapete*› **2** (attach by pin etc.) anstecken **3** (coll.: put on) aufsetzen ‹*Hut, Wasserkessel*›; auflegen ‹*Schallplatte*›; **~ an extra amount on the bill** (fig.) einen zusätzlichen Betrag auf die Rechnung setzen
B *v.i.* kleben [bleiben]. *See also* **stick-on**
• **~ 'out**
A *v.t.* **1** herausstrecken ‹*Brust, Zunge*›; ausstrecken ‹*Arm, Bein*›; **~ one's tongue out at sb.** jmdm. die Zunge herausstrecken; **would you like to ~ your neck out and predict the winner of the race?** (fig. coll.) willst du eine Prognose wagen, wer das Rennen gewinnt?; **he is not one to ~ his chin out** (fig. coll.) er verbrennt sich (*Dat.*) nicht gern die Finger (ugs.) **2** **~ it out** (coll.) = **sweat it out** ▸**sweat C 4**
B *v.i.* **1** (project) ‹*Brust, Bauch:*› vorstehen; ‹*steifes Kleid:*› abstehen; ‹*Nagel, Ast:*› herausstehen; **his ears ~ out** er hat abstehende Ohren; **her hair stuck out from under the hat** ihr Haar schaute unter dem Hut hervor; **she lay in bed with her legs/toes ~ing out** sie lag im Bett, und ihre Beine/Zehen schauten heraus **2** (fig.: be obvious) sich abheben; **~ out a mile** (coll.) [klar] auf der Hand liegen; **it ~s out a mile that he is only after her money** (coll.) dass er nur hinter ihrem Geld her ist, ist klar wie dicke Tinte (ugs.); **~ out like a sore thumb** (coll.) ins Auge springen; **if you don't wear the correct clothes you'll ~ out like a sore thumb** (coll.) wenn du nicht korrekt gekleidet bist, fällst du unangenehm auf **3** **~ out for sth.** ▸**hold out B 3**
• **~ to** *v.t.* **1** (be faithful to) halten zu ‹*Person*›; halten ‹*Versprechen*›; bleiben bei ‹*Entscheidung, Meinung*›; treu bleiben (+ *Dat.*) ‹*Idealen, Grundsätzen*› **2** (not deviate from) sich halten an (+ *Akk.*) ‹*Plan, Text, Original*›; bleiben an (+ *Dat.*) ‹*Arbeit*›; bleiben bei ‹*Wahrheit, Thema*›; **~ to business** bei der Sache bleiben; **~ to the point** beim Thema bleiben; **~ to what you are good at** bleibe bei dem, was du [gut] kannst; **thanks, but I'll ~ to beer** danke, ich bleibe beim Bier. *See also* **gun A 1; last³; stick-to-it-ive-ness; story¹ 1**
• **~ to'gether**
A *v.t.* zusammenkleben
B *v.i.* **1** (adhere together) zusammenkleben **2** (fig.: remain united) zusammenhalten
• **~ 'up**
A *v.t.* **1** (seal) zukleben **2** **be stuck up with sth.** (coll.: sticky) von etw. klebrig sein **3** (coll.: put up, raise) strecken, recken ‹*Kopf, Hals*›; anschlagen ‹*Bekanntmachung, Poster*›; aufschlagen ‹*Zelt*›; hinbauen, -setzen ‹*Häuser*›; raufsetzen (ugs.) ‹*Preise*›; anbringen ‹*Regal*›; **he stuck his nose up [in the air]** er streckte seine Nase in die Luft; **~ up one's hand** die Hand heben; **~ sth. up on a shelf** etw. auf ein Regal tun (ugs.); **~ 'em up!** (coll.) Pfoten hoch! (salopp) **4** (coll.: rob) ausrauben; *see also* **stick-up** **5** **stuck up** (conceited) eingebildet; **be stuck up about sth.** sich (*Dat.*) etwas auf etw. (*Akk.*) einbilden
B *v.i.* **1** ‹*Haar, Kragen:*› hochstehen; ‹*Nagel, Pflasterstein:*› hervorstehen **2** **~ up for sb./sth.** für jmdn./etw. eintreten; **~ up for yourself!** setz dich zur Wehr!
• **~ with** *v.t.* (coll.) **1** (keep contact with) **~ with the leaders** sich an der Spitze halten (bes. Sport); **~ 'with it!** bleib dran! (ugs.) **2** (remain faithful to) bleiben bei ‹*Gruppe, Partei*›; halten zu ‹*Freund*›; die Treue halten (+ *Dat.*) ‹*Verein*›

stick de'odorant *n.* Deo[dorant]stift, *der*

sticker /'stɪkə(r)/ *n.* Aufkleber, *der; see also* **bill-sticker**

'stick figure *n.* Strichmännchen, *das*

sticking/'stɪkɪŋ/: **~ place** ▸**~ point**; **~ plaster** *n.* (Med.) Heftpflaster, *das;* **~ point** *n.* (fig.) Hürde, *die*

stick: ~ insect *n.* Gespenst[heu]schrecke, *die;* **~-in-the-mud** **A** *n.* (person lacking initiative) Trantüte, *die* (ugs. abwertend); (unprogressive person) Spießer, *der* (abwertend); **B** *adj.* (lacking in initiative) schlafmützig (ugs. abwertend); (unprogressive) spießig (abwertend)

stickleback /'stɪklbæk/ *n.* (Zool.) Stichling, *der*

stickler /'stɪklə(r)/ *n.* **be a ~ for tidiness/authority** es mit der Sauberkeit sehr genau nehmen/in puncto Autorität keinen Spaß verstehen

stick: ~-on *adj.* selbstklebend; **~pin** *n.* (Amer.) Krawattennadel, *die;* **~-to-it-ive-ness** /stɪk'tu:ɪtɪvnɪs/ *n., no pl.* (Amer. coll.) Hartnäckigkeit, *die;* **~-up** *n.* (coll.) bewaffneter Raubüberfall

sticky /'stɪkɪ/
A *adj.* **1** klebrig; feucht ‹*Farbe, gestrichener/gewaschener Gegenstand*›; zäh ‹*Teig, Brei, Mischung*›; **~ label** Aufkleber, *der;* **~ tape** Klebestreifen, *der* **2** (humid) schwül ‹*Klima, Luft*›; feucht ‹*Haut*›; **be all hot and ~:** ganz verschwitzt sein **3** (coll.: uncooperative) unnachgiebig; **be ~ about doing sth.** etw. [nur] widerwillig tun **4** (coll.: unpleasant) vertrackt (ugs.); heikel; **a ~ situation** eine brenzlige Lage; *see also* **end A 8**
B *n.* (coll.) Post-it, *das* (ugs.)

sticky 'wicket *n.* (Cricket) *Spielfeld, das nach einem Regen schlecht zu bespielen ist;* **bat** *or* **be on a ~** (fig.) sich auf schlüpfrigem Boden befinden

stiff /stɪf/
A *adj.* **1** (rigid) steif; hart ‹*Bürste, Stock*›; **be frozen ~:** steif vor Kälte sein; ‹*Wäsche, Körper[teile]:*› steif gefroren sein; **this brush is ~ with paint** dieser Pinsel ist mit Farbe verklebt; *see also* **lip 1** **2** (intense, severe) hartnäckig; schroff ‹*Absage*›; kräftig ‹*Standpauke*›; **~ competition** scharfe Konkurrenz **3** (formal) steif; förmlich ‹*Brief, Stil*› **4** (difficult) hart ‹*Test*›; schwer ‹*Frage, Prüfung*›; steil ‹*Abstieg, Anstieg*›; **be ~ going** (fig. coll.) harte Arbeit sein **5** stark, (Seemannsspr.) steif ‹*Wind, Brise*› **6** (not bending, not working freely, aching) steif ‹*Gelenk, Gliedmaßen, Nacken, Person*›; schwergängig ‹*Angel, Kolben, Gelenk*› **7** (coll.: excessive) saftig (ugs.) ‹*Preis, Strafe*› **8** (strong) steif (ugs.) ‹*Drink*›; stark ‹*Dosis, Medizin*›; **a ~ shot of rum** ein Schuss steifen Rum **9** (thick) zäh[flüssig] **10** (coll.) **be bored/scared/worried ~:** sich zu Tode langweilen/eine wahnsinnige Angst haben (ugs.)/sich (*Dat.*) furchtbare (ugs.) Sorgen machen; **bore/scare/worry sb. ~:** jmdn. zu Tode langweilen/jmdm. eine wahnsinnige Angst einjagen (ugs.)/jmdm. furchtbare (ugs.) Sorgen machen **11** *pred.* **the road was ~ with police** auf der Straße wimmelte es von Polizisten
B *n.* (sl.) Leiche, *die*

stiffen /'stɪfn/
A *v.t.* **1** steif machen; stärken ‹*Kragen*›; versteifen ‹*Material*›; zäh[flüssig]er machen ‹*Paste, Teig*›; steif werden lassen ‹*Gliedmaße*› **2** (fig.: bolster) verstärken ‹*Widerstand*›; stärken ‹*Moral, Entschlossenheit*›
B *v.i.* **1** ‹*Person:*› erstarren **2** ‹*Wind, Brise:*› steifer werden (Seemannsspr.), auffrischen **3** (become thicker) ‹*Teig:*› steifer werden; ‹*Mischung:*› zäher werden **4** (fig.: become more resolute) sich verstärken; **his resolve ~ed** er wurde in seinem Entschluss bestärkt

stiffener /'stɪfnə(r)/ *n.* **1** (for collar, corset) Stäbchen, *das* **2** (starch) Stärke, *die* **3** (Building) Queraussteifung, *die* **4** (coll.: drink) kleine Stärkung (scherzh.)

stiffening /'stɪfnɪŋ/ *n.* Versteifung, *die*

stiffly /'stɪflɪ/ *adv.* **1** (rigidly, formally) steif; (fig.) hartnäckig ‹*Widerstand leisten*› **2** (strongly) stark, (Seemannsspr.) steif ‹*wehen*› **3** (erectly, with restricted movement) steif ‹*sitzen, gehen*›; kerzengerade ‹*stehen*›

stiff-'necked *adj.* (fig.) starrsinnig

stiffness /'stɪfnɪs/ *n., no pl.* **1** (rigidity, formality) Steifheit, *die;* (of letter, language) Förmlichkeit, *die* **2** (intensity) Härte, *die* **3** (difficulty) Schwierigkeit, *die* **4** (of wind) Stärke, *die;* Steifheit, *die* (Seemannsspr.) **5** (lack of suppleness) Steifheit, *die;* (of hinge, piston) geringe Beweglichkeit; **have a ~ in one's limbs** steife Glieder haben; (due to exercise) Muskelkater haben **6** (coll.: excessiveness) (of punishment) Strenge, *die;* (of demand, price) Überzogenheit, *die* **7** (thick consistency) Zähheit, *die*

stifle /'staɪfl/
A *v.t.* ersticken; (fig.: suppress) unterdrücken; ersticken ‹*Widerstand, Aufstand, Schrei*›; übergehen ‹*Einwand*›; **we were ~d by the heat** wir erstickten fast vor Hitze
B *v.i.* ersticken; **~ in the bad air/smoke** an der schlechten Luft/vom Rauch fast ersticken

stifling /'staɪflɪŋ/ *adj.* stickig; drückend ‹*Hitze*›; (fig.) einengend ‹*Atmosphäre*›; erdrückend ‹*Einfluss, Herrschaft*›; **the heat was ~:** es war drückend heiß

stigma /'stɪgmə/ *n., pl.* **~s** *or* **~ta** /'stɪgmətə, stɪg'mɑ:tə/ **1** (mark of shame) Stigma, *das* (geh.); Makel, *der* (geh.); **the ~ of having been in prison** das Stigma, im Gefängnis gewesen zu sein **2** (Bot.) Stigma, *das;* Narbe, *die* **3** *in pl.* **~ta** (Relig.) Stigmata

stigmatize (stigmatise) /'stɪgmətaɪz/ *v.t.* stigmatisieren (geh.); brandmarken

stile /staɪl/ *n.* Zauntritt, *der; see also* **dog A 1**

stiletto /stɪ'letəʊ/ *n., pl.* **~s** *or* **~es** **1** (dagger) Stilett, *das* **2** **~ [heel]** Stöckelabsatz, *der;* **~[-heeled shoe]** Stöckelschuh, *der*

still¹ /stɪl/
A *adj.* **1** *pred.* still; **be ~:** [still] stehen; ‹*Fahne:*› sich nicht bewegen; ‹*Hand:*› ruhig sein; **hold** *or*

S

keep sth. ~: etw. ruhig halten; **hold** *or* **keep a ladder/horse ~:** eine Leiter/ein Pferd festhalten; **hold ~!** halt still!; **keep** *or* **stay ~:** stillhalten; (not change posture) ruhig bleiben; ‹*Pferd:*› still stehen; ‹*Gegenstand:*› liegen bleiben; **sit ~:** still sitzen; **stand ~:** stillstehen; ‹*Uhr:*› stehen; ‹*Arbeit:*› ruhen; (stop) stehen bleiben; **my heart stood ~** (fig.) mir blieb das Herz stehen; **the country has just stood ~ for the last 20 years** (fig.) das Land hat sich die letzten 20 Jahre einfach nicht weiterentwickelt; **time stood ~:** die Zeit schien stillzustehen; *see also* **statue** **2** (calm) ruhig; *see also* **deep B** **3** (without sound) still; ruhig **4** (not sparkling) nicht moussierend ‹*Wein*›; still ‹*Mineralwasser*›; **is this water sparkling or ~?** ist dieses Wasser mit oder ohne Kohlensäure? **5** (hushed) leise; **a** *or* **the ~ small voice [of conscience]** die [leise] Stimme des Gewissens

B *adv.* **1** (without change) noch; *expr. surprise or annoyance* immer noch; **drink your tea while it is ~ hot** trink deinen Tee, solange er [noch] heiß ist **2** (nevertheless) trotzdem; **~, we must not forget the opposite standpoint** wir dürfen aber auch den gegensätzlichen Standpunkt nicht außer Acht lassen; **~, what can you do about it?** aber was kann man dagegen tun? **3** *with comparative* (even) noch; **become fatter ~** *or* **~ fatter** noch *od.* immer dicker werden; **better/worse ~** *as sentence-modifier* besser/schlimmer noch; *see also* **less B**

C *n.* **1** (Photog.) Still, *das;* Fotografie *die;* **~s from the film** Filmbilder **2** (silence) **in the ~ of the night** in der Stille der Nacht

D *v.t.* (literary) beruhigen; glätten ‹*Wogen*›; stillen ‹*Hunger, Durst, Schmerz*›; beschwichtigen ‹*Gefühle*›; befriedigen ‹*Ehrgeiz*›; ausräumen ‹*Zweifel*›; dämpfen ‹*Geräusch*›

still² *n.* Destillierapparat, *der*

still: ~ birth *n.* Totgeburt, *die;* **~born** *adj.* **1** tot geboren; **the child was ~born** das Kind war eine Totgeburt *od.* kam tot zur Welt; **2** (fig.) ▸**abortive**; **~ life** *n., pl.* **~ lifes** *or* **lives** (Art) Stillleben, *das*

stillness /ˈstɪlnɪs/ *n., no pl.* **1** (motionlessness) Bewegungslosigkeit, *die* **2** (quietness) Stille, *die*

still: ~ picture ▸**still¹ C 1**; **~ room** *n.* (Brit.) Destillierraum, *der*

stilt /stɪlt/ *n.* **1** Stelze, *die* **2** (support of building) Pfahl, *der* **3** (Ornith.) Stelzenläufer, *der*

stilted /ˈstɪltɪd/ *adj.* gestelzt; gespreizt

Stilton /ˈstɪltən/ *n.* Stilton[käse], *der*

stimulant /ˈstɪmjʊlənt/

A *attrib. adj.* (Med.) stimulierend

B *n.* (lit. or fig.) Stimulans, *das;* Anregungsmittel, *das*

stimulate /ˈstɪmjʊleɪt/ *v.t.* **1** anregen; stimulieren (geh.); beleben ‹*Körper*›; (sexually) erregen **2** (fig.) anregen ‹*Geist, Diskussion, Appetit*›; hervorrufen ‹*Reaktion*›; wecken ‹*Interesse, Neugier*›; beleben ‹*Wirtschaft, Wachstum, Markt, Absatz*›; **~ sb. to sth./to do sth.** jmdn. zu etw. anregen/dazu anregen, etw. zu tun

stimulating /ˈstɪmjʊleɪtɪŋ/ *adj.* **1** anregend; stimulierend (geh.); belebend ‹*Bad*›; (sexually) erregend **2** (fig.) interessant; inspirierend ‹*Prediger, Einfluss, Musik, Buch*›

stimulation /stɪmjʊˈleɪʃn/ *n.* **1** Anregung, *die;* Stimulierung, *die* (geh.); (sexual) Erregung, *die* **2** (fig.) Anregung, *die;* (of reaction) Hervorrufen, *das;* (of interest, curiosity) Wecken, *das;* (of economy, market, growth, sales) Belebung, *die*

stimulative /ˈstɪmjʊlətɪv/ *adj.* anregend; stimulierend (geh.); **the ~ effect of a cold shower** die belebende Wirkung einer kalten Dusche

stimulus /ˈstɪmjʊləs/ *n., pl.* **stimuli** /ˈstɪmjʊlaɪ/ **1** (spur) Ansporn, *der* (**to** zu); **act as a ~ to sb.'s ambition** jmds. Ehrgeiz anspornen **2** (rousing effect) Anregung, *die;* **give a ~ to sales** den Umsatz beleben **3** (Physiol.) Stimulus, *der;* Reiz, *der*

sting /stɪŋ/

A *n.* **1** (wounding) Stich, *der;* (by jellyfish, nettles) Verbrennung, *die* **2** (pain) Stechen, *das;* stechender Schmerz; (from ointment, cane, whip, wind, rash) Brennen, *das;* **the ~ of his criticism/remark/reproach** der Stachel seiner Kritik/Bemerkung/seines Vorwurfs; **a ~ in the tail** (fig.) ein Pferdefuß; **the story/film/letter had a ~ in the tail** am Ende der Geschichte/des Films/Briefs kam es knüppeldick (ugs.); **take the ~ out of sth.** (fig.) einer Sache (*Dat.*) den Stachel nehmen (geh.) **3** (Zool.) [Gift]stachel, *der;* (of jellyfish) Nesselkapsel, *die;* (of snake) Giftzahn, *der* **4** (Bot.) Brennhaar, *das* **5** (vigour) ▸**bite C 5** **6** (fraud) Ding, *das* (ugs.); (police operation) Operation, *die*

B *v.t.*, **stung** /stʌŋ/ **1** (wound) stechen; **a bee stung [him on] his arm** eine Biene stach ihm in den Arm; **a jellyfish stung me/my leg** ich habe mich/mein Bein an einer Qualle verbrannt **2** (cause pain to) **the cane stung the boy's fingers** der Stock brannte dem Jungen auf den Fingern; **the smoke/the wind stung my eyes** der Rauch/der Wind brannte mir in den Augen **3** (hurt mentally) tief treffen; [zutiefst] verletzen; **his conscience stung him** er hatte Gewissensbisse; **~ing** scharf ‹*Vorwürfe, Anklagen, Kritik*›; **stung by remorse** von Reue gequält **4** (incite) **~ sb. into sth./doing sth.** jmdn. zu etw. anstacheln/dazu anstacheln, etw. zu tun; **he was stung to anger by their insults** ihre Beleidigungen erregten seinen Zorn **5** (coll.: swindle) übers Ohr hauen (ugs.); **~ sb. for sth.** jmdn. um etw. neppen (ugs.); **how much did they ~ you for [it]?** was haben sie dir [dafür] abgeknöpft? (salopp)

C *v.i.*, **stung** **1** (feel pain) brennen; **smoke makes my eyes ~:** Rauch brennt mir in den Augen; **the antiseptic made the wound/my skin ~:** das Antiseptikum brannte auf der Wunde/auf meiner Haut **2** (have ~) stechen; **not all nettles/sorts of jellyfish ~:** nicht alle Nesseln/Quallenarten brennen

stingily /ˈstɪndʒɪlɪ/ *adv.* geizig; **behave ~:** knausern (ugs.)

stinginess /ˈstɪndʒɪnɪs/ *n., no pl.* (of person) Geiz, *der;* Knauserigkeit, *die;* (of donation, portion, meal) Kümmerlichkeit, *die*

stinging nettle /ˈstɪŋɪŋ netl/ *n.* (Bot.) Brennnessel, *die*

ˈstingray *n.* (Zool.) Stechrochen, *der*

stingy /ˈstɪndʒɪ/ *adj.* geizig; knaus[e]rig (ugs.); kümmerlich ‹*Spende, Portion, Mahlzeit*›; **be ~ with sth.** mit etw. geizen

stink /stɪŋk/

A *v.i.*, **stank** /stæŋk/ *or* **stunk** /stʌŋk/, **stunk** **1** stinken (**of** nach); **~ to high heaven** (coll.) gottserbärmlich stinken; (fig.) ‹*Angelegenheit, Korruption:*› zum Himmel stinken; **he ~s of money** (coll.) er stinkt vor Geld (ugs.); **something ~s here** (coll.: is suspicious) an dieser Sache stinkt etwas (ugs.) **2** (fig.: be repulsive) **sth. ~s** an etw. (+ *Dat.*) stinkt etwas (ugs.); **the book/film ~s** das Buch/der Film ist widerwärtig

B *n.* **1** (bad smell) Gestank, *der* **2** (coll.: fuss) Stunk, *der* (ugs.); **the scandal created an almighty ~:** der Skandal führte zu einem Riesenstunk (ugs.); **kick up** *or* **raise a ~ about sth.** wegen etw. Stunk machen (ugs.) **3** (coll.) **like ~:** wie verrückt (ugs.); **run like ~:** wie eine gesengte Sau (derb) rennen

ˈstink bomb *n.* Stinkbombe, *die*

stinker /ˈstɪŋkə(r)/ *n.* (coll.) **1** (offensive person) Stinker, *der* (salopp); Stinktier, *das* (derb) **2** (offensive thing) Widerlichkeit, *die* (abwertend); **a ~ [of a letter/reply]** ein stinkiger Brief/eine stinkige Antwort (salopp); **a ~ [of a cold]** eine saumäßige Erkältung (derb) **3** (difficult task) Hammer, *der* (ugs.); harte Nuss (ugs.)

stinking /ˈstɪŋkɪŋ/

A *adj.* **1** stinkend **2** (coll.: objectionable) widerlich (abwertend); **a ~ cold** eine saumäßige Erkältung (derb)

B *adv.* (coll.) **~ rich/drunk** stinkreich (salopp)/stinkbesoffen (derb)

stint /stɪnt/

A *v.t.* **1** (restrict share of) kurz halten; **~ oneself [of sth.]** sich [mit etw.] einschränken; **~ sb. of sth.** jmdn. mit etw. kurz halten **2** (supply stingily) geizen mit; sparen mit ‹*Worten*›

B *v.i.* **~ on sth.** an etw. (*Dat.*) sparen

C *n.* **1** (allotted amount) [Arbeits]pensum, *das;* **do** *or* **work** *or* **have a long ~:** ein großes Arbeitspensum erledigen; **each of us did our ~ at the wheel** jeder von uns saß eine Zeit lang am Steuer **2** (limitation) Einschränkung, *die;* **without ~:** uneingeschränkt

stipend /ˈstaɪpend/ *n.* Besoldung, *die;* (Eccl.) Gehalt, *das*

stipendiary /staɪˈpendɪərɪ, stɪˈpendɪərɪ/

A *attrib. adj.* besoldet; **~ magistrate** ▸**B**

B *n.* (Brit.) besoldeter Friedensrichter

stipple /ˈstɪpl/ *v.t.* **1** (Art) punktieren **2** (roughen) [auf]rauen ‹*Putz, Farbe*›

stipulate /ˈstɪpjʊleɪt/ (demand) fordern; verlangen; (lay down) festlegen; (insist on) sich (*Dat.*) ausbedingen

stipulation /stɪpjʊˈleɪʃn/ *n.* **1** (condition) Bedingung, *die;* **on** *or* **with the ~ that ...:** unter der Bedingung, dass ... **2** (act) ▸**stipulate**: Forderung, *die;* Festlegung, *die;* Ausbedingung, *die*

stipule /ˈstɪpjuːl/ *n.* (Bot.) Nebenblatt, *das*

stir¹ /stɜː(r)/

A *v.t.*, **-rr-** **1** (mix) rühren; umrühren ‹*Tee, Kaffee*›; **keep ~ring the soup** die Suppe ständig umrühren; **~ sth. into sth.** etw. in etw. (*Akk.*) [ein]rühren **2** (move) bewegen; **~ oneself out of bed** sich aus dem Bett bewegen *od.* (geh.) bequemen; **~ one's stumps** (coll.) einen Zahn zulegen (ugs.) **3** (fig.: arouse) bewegen; wecken ‹*Neugier, Interesse, Gefühle, Fantasie*›; **a story to ~ the heart/blood** eine herzergreifende Geschichte/eine Geschichte, die das Blut in Wallung bringt; **~ sb. to action** jmdn. zum Handeln anstacheln; **~ sb. to greater efforts** jmdn. zu größeren Anstrengungen anspornen

B *v.i.*, **-rr-** **1** (move) sich rühren; (in sleep, breeze) sich bewegen; **without ~ring** regungslos; **[not] ~ from the spot** sich [nicht] vom Fleck rühren **2** (fig.: be aroused) sich regen (geh.) **3** (rise from bed) aufstehen; **nobody was ~ring in the house/village** das ganze Haus/Dorf schlief noch

C *n., no pl.* **1** (commotion) Aufregung, *die;* (bustle, activity) Betriebsamkeit, *die;* **cause** *or* **create** *or* **make a [big** *or* **great]** **~:** [großes] Aufsehen erregen **2** (act of ~ring sth.) **give the coffee/paint a ~:** den Kaffee umrühren/die Farbe rühren

Phrasal verbs

- **~ ˈin** *v.t.* einrühren
- **~ ˈup** *v.t.* **1** (disturb) aufrühren **2** (fig.: arouse, provoke) wecken ‹*Neugier, Interesse, Leidenschaft*›; aufrütteln ‹*Anhänger, Gefolgsleute*›; entfachen ‹*Liebe, Hass, Streit, Zorn, Revolution*›; schüren ‹*Hass, Feindseligkeit*›; **~ up the past/ill feelings** die Vergangenheit aufrühren/ungute Gefühle wecken; **~ up public opinion** die öffentliche Meinung aufbringen; **~ it up** (coll.) Unfrieden stiften

stir² *n.* (sl.: prison) Knast, *der* (ugs.); **be in ~:** Knast schieben (salopp)

stir: ~-crazy *adj.* (sl.) **be ~-crazy** eine Gefängnispsychose haben; **~ fry** *n.* Wokgericht, *das;* **~-fry** *v.t.* unter Rühren schnell braten

stirrer /ˈstɜːrə(r)/ *n.* **1** (utensil) Rührer, *der* **2** (one who provokes) Aufwiegler, *der*/Aufwieglerin, *die*

stirring /ˈstɜːrɪŋ/ *adj.* bewegend ‹*Musik, Theaterstück, Poesie*›; spannend ‹*Roman, Geschichte*›; mitreißend ‹*Auftritt, Rede, Marsch*›; bewegt ‹*Zeiten*›

stirringly /ˈstɜːrɪŋlɪ/ *adv.* bewegend ‹*gespielt*›; spannend ‹*erzählt*›; mitreißend ‹*gespielter Marsch*›

stirrup /ˈstɪrəp/ *n.* **1** (Riding) Steigbügel, *der* **2** (of garment) Steg, *der* **3** (Anat.) **~ [bone]** Steigbügel, *der*

stirrup: ~ cup *n.* Abschiedstrunk, *der* (geh.); **~ iron** *n.* (Riding) Steigbügel, *der;* **~ pump** *n.* Handpumpe, *die* (*mit Fußstütze*)

stitch /stɪtʃ/

A *n.* **1** (Sewing: pass of needle) Stich, *der;* **a stitch in time ~s nine** (prov.) was du heute kannst besorgen, das verschiebe nicht auf morgen; Vorsorge ist besser als Nachsorge **2** (result of needle movement) (Knitting, Crocheting) Masche, *die;* (Sewing, Embroidery) Stich, *der;* **drop a ~** (Knitting)

S

eine Masche fallen lassen; **undo the ~es** aufziehen; (in seam, hem) die Naht auftrennen **3** (kind of ~) (Knitting) Muster, *das;* (Sewing, Embroidery) Stich, *der* **4** (coll.: piece of clothing) **not have a ~ on** splitter[faser]nackt (ugs.) sein; **the burglars stole every ~ of clothing I had** die Einbrecher stahlen mir sämtliche Klamotten (salopp) **5** (pain) **[have] a ~ [in the side]** Seitenstechen [haben] **6** (coll.) **be in ~es** sich kugeln vor Lachen (ugs.); **he/his jokes had me in ~es** ich wäre [beinahe] vor Lachen über ihn/seine Witze gestorben (ugs.) **7** (Med.: to sew up wound) Stich, *der;* **~es** Naht, *die;* **he had his ~es taken out** ihm wurden die Fäden gezogen; **need [five] ~es** [mit fünf Stichen] genäht werden müssen **8** (Bookbinding) Heftung, *die*

B *v.t.* nähen; (Embroidery) sticken; (Bookbinding) heften

C *v.i.* nähen; (Embroidery) sticken; (Bookbinding) heften

(Phrasal verbs)

- **~ 'down** *v.t.* festnähen
- **~ 'on** *v.t.* annähen ‹*Knopf*›; aufnähen ‹*Flicken, Borte*›
- **~ 'up** *v.t.* **1** nähen; zusammennähen ‹*Stoffteile*›; vernähen ‹*Loch, Riss, Wunde*› **2** ▸ **frame B 3**

stitching /'stɪtʃɪŋ/ *n.* **1** (series of stitches) Naht, *die* **2** (ornamental stitches) Stickerei, *die* **3** (Bookbinding: fastening) Heftung, *die*

stoat /stəʊt/ *n.* Hermelin, *das*

stochastic /stə'kæstɪk/ *adj.* stochastisch; **~ theory** Stochastik, *die*

stock /stɒk/

A *n.* **1** (origin, family, breed) Abstammung, *die;* **a horse of good racing/breeding ~:** ein Renn-/Zuchtpferd mit gutem Stammbaum; **be** *or* **come of farming/French/good ~:** bäuerlicher/französischer Herkunft sein/aus einer guten Familie stammen

2 (supply, store) Vorrat, *der;* (in shop etc.) Warenbestand, *der;* **our ~ is high/low** wir haben genug/zu wenig vorrätig; **our ~s of food/sherry** unsere Lebensmittelvorräte/unser Vorrat an Sherry (*Dat.*); **have a good ~ of information/knowledge** umfangreiche Informationen/ein umfangreiches Wissen haben; **be in ~/out of ~** ‹*Ware:*› vorrätig/nicht vorrätig sein; **sb. is out of ~ of sth.** jmd. hat etw. nicht vorrätig; **get** *or* **lay in a ~ of coal** sich (*Dat.*) einen Kohlevorrat anlegen; **have sth. in ~:** etw. auf *od.* (Kaufmannsspr.) am Lager haben; **keep sth. in ~** (have available as a general policy) etw. führen; **renew** *or* **replenish one's ~ of sth.** seinen Vorrat an etw. (*Dat.*) auffüllen; **take ~:** Inventur machen; (fig.) Bilanz ziehen; **take ~ of sb.** (fig.) jmdn. mustern; **take ~ of sth.** (fig.) über etw. (*Akk.*) Bilanz ziehen; **take ~ of oneself** (fig.) sein Leben Revue passieren lassen; **take ~ of one's position/situation/prospects** seinen Standort/seine Situation/seine Zukunftsaussichten bestimmen; *see also* **rolling stock**

3 (Cookery) Brühe, *die*

4 (Finance) Wertpapiere; (shares) Aktien; **sb.'s ~ is high/low** (fig.) jmds. Aktien stehen gut/schlecht (fig.); **take** *or* (Amer.) **put ~ in sth.** (fig.) viel von etw. halten; *see also* **defer[1] 1**; **ordinary 2**

5 (Hort.) Stamm, *der;* (for grafting) Unterlage, *die*

6 (handle) Griff, *der;* (of gun) Schaft, *der;* (of plough) Sterz, *der; see also* **lock[2] A 5**

7 (Agric.) [lebendes und totes] Inventar [eines landwirtschaftlichen Betriebes]; *see also* **fatstock**; **livestock**

8 (raw material) [Roh]material, *das;* **[film] ~:** Filmmaterial, *das;* **[paper] ~:** Papierstoff, *der;* (for printing on) Papier, *das*

9 (Bot.) Levkoje, *die; see also* **night-scented stock**

10 *in pl.* (Hist.: punishment-frame) Stock, *der*

11 (Naut.: anchor crossbar) Stock, *der*

12 *in pl.* (Naut.: construction support) Helling, *die;* Helgen, *der;* **be on the ~s** auf dem Stapel liegen; (fig.) in Vorbereitung sein; **have sth. on the ~s** (fig.) an etw. (*Dat.*) arbeiten

13 (tree stump) [Baum]stumpf, *der. see also* **laughing stock**

B *v.t.* **1** (supply with ~) beliefern; **~ a pond/river/lake with fish** einen Teich/Fluss/See mit Fischen besetzen; **her larder is ~ed with tins** sie hat einen [großen] Vorrat an Konserven in der Speisekammer; **a cellar ~ed with wine/sherry** ein gut mit Wein/Sherry bestückter Keller; **he has a memory ~ed with useless information** sein Gedächtnis ist mit nutzlosem Wissen voll gepfropft (ugs.)

2 (Commerc.: keep in ~) auf *od.* (fachspr.) am Lager haben; führen

C *attrib. adj.* **1** (Commerc.) vorrätig; **a ~ size/model** eine Standardgröße/ein Standardmodell

2 (fig.: trite, unoriginal) abgedroschen (ugs.); **~ character** Standardrolle, *die*

(Phrasal verb)

- **~ 'up**

A *v.i.* **~ up [with sth.]** sich (*Dat.*) einen Vorrat an etw. (*Dat.*) anlegen; **~ up with coal for the winter** sich für den Winter mit Kohlen eindecken; **~ up on sth.** seine Vorräte an etw. auffüllen

B *v.t.* auffüllen; mit Fischen besetzen ‹*Teich, Fluss, See*›; **the library needs ~ing up with new books** die Bibliothek muss ihren Bestand um neue Bücher erweitern

stockade /stɒ'keɪd/

A *n.* Palisade, *die*

B *v.t.* mit einer Palisade befestigen

stock: ~breeder *n.* Viehzüchter, *der*/-züchterin, *die;* **~breeding** *n.* Viehzucht, *die;* **~broker** *n.* ▸ **i p. 1260** (Finance) Effektenmakler, *der*/-maklerin, *die;* **~broker belt** *Wohngebiet reicher Geschäftsleute in der Umgebung einer Großstadt;* ≈ Speckgürtel, *der* (ugs.); **~broking** /'stɒkbrəʊkɪŋ/ *n., no pl.* (Finance) Effektenhandel, *der;* **~broking is a lucrative profession** der Handel mit Wertpapieren ist ein einträglicher Beruf; **~ car** *n.* **1** (Amer. Railw.) Viehwaggon, *der;* **2** (racing car) Stockcar, *der;* **~-car racing** *n.* Stockcarrennen, *das;* **~ cube** *n.* (Cookery) Brühwürfel, *der;* **~ exchange** *n.* (Finance) Börse, *die;* **the S~ Exchange** (Brit.) die [Londoner] Börse; **~fish** *n.* (Cookery) Stockfisch, *der;* **~holder** *n.* (Finance) Wertpapierbesitzer, *der*/-besitzerin, *die;* (of shares) Aktionär, *der*/Aktionärin, *die;* **be a ~holder in the company** Anteile an der Gesellschaft besitzen

stockily /'stɒkɪlɪ/ *adv.* **~ built** stämmig

stockinet[te] /stɒkɪ'net/ *n.* (Textiles) Trikot, *der*

stocking[1] /'stɒkɪŋ/ *n.* **1** Strumpf, *der;* **in one's ~[ed] feet** in Strümpfen; **hang up one's ~:** den Strumpf für den Weihnachtsmann aufhängen **2** (of horse) Strumpf, *der*

stocking[2] *n.* ▸ **stock B**: Belieferung, *die;* Besatz, *der;* Lagerhaltung, *die*

stockinged /'stɒkɪŋd/ *adj.* ▸ **stocking[1] 1**

stocking: ~ filler *n.* (Brit.) **1** *kleines Geschenk, das in den für den Weihnachtsmann aufgehängten Strumpf gesteckt wird;* **2** zusätzliche Kleinigkeit (als *Weihnachtsgeschenk*); **~ mask** *n.* Strumpfmaske, *die;* **~ stitch** *n.* (Knitting) Glattgestrick, *das;* **knit in ~ stitch** glatt rechts stricken; **~ stuffer** (Amer.) ▸ **~ filler**

stock-in-'trade *n.* Inventar, *das;* (workman's tools) Handwerkszeug, *das;* (fig.: resource) [festes] Repertoire; **be the ~ of sb.** zu jmds. festem Repertoire gehören

stockist /'stɒkɪst/ *n.* (Brit. Commerc.) Fachhändler/-händlerin [mit größerem Warenlager]

stock: ~jobber *n.* (Finance) **1** (Brit.: dealer) Jobber, *der;* **2** (Amer. derog.: broker) [Börsen]spekulant, *der*/-spekulantin, *die;* **~jobbing** *n., no pl.* (Brit. Finance) Börsenspekulation, *die;* **~list** *n.* **1** (Finance) Kurszettel, *der;* **2** (Commerc.) Inventarliste, *die;* **~ market** *n.* (Finance) **1** ▸ **stock exchange**; **2** (trading) Börsengeschäft, *das;* **lose money on the ~ market** Geld an der Börse verlieren; **~ option** *n.* Aktienoption, *die;* **~pile** **A** *n.* Vorrat, *der;* (of weapons) Arsenal, *das;* **B** *v.t.* horten; anhäufen ‹*Waffen*›; **~pot** *n.* (Cookery) Suppentopf, *der;* **~room** *n.* Lager, *das;* **~-'still** *pred. adj.* bewegungslos; **stand ~-still** regungslos [da]stehen; **~taking** *n.* (Commerc.) Inventur, *die;* **closed for ~taking** wegen Inventur geschlossen

stocky /'stɒkɪ/ *adj.* stämmig; kräftig ‹*Pflanze, Trieb*›

'stockyard *n.* Viehhof, *der*

stodge /stɒdʒ/ *n.* (coll.: food) Brei, *der*

stodgy /'stɒdʒɪ/ *adj.* **1** pappig [und schwer verdaulich] ‹*Essen*› **2** (heavy, uninteresting) langweilig ‹*Buch*›; schwerfällig ‹*Stil, Poesie*› **3** (dull, drab) trübselig ‹*Person, Leben usw.*›

stoic /'stəʊɪk/

A *n.* **1** **S~** (Philos.) Stoiker, *der* **2** (impassive person) Stoiker, *der*/Stoikerin, *die*

B *adj.* **1** **S~** (Philos.) stoisch; **the S~ philosophers/school** die Stoiker/die Stoa **2** stoisch ‹*Person, Ablehnung, Antwort usw.*›

stoical /'stəʊɪkl/ *adj.*, **stoically** /'stəʊɪkəlɪ/ *adv.* stoisch

stoicism /'stəʊɪsɪzm/ *n., no pl.* **1** **S~** (Philos.) Stoizismus, *der* **2** (impassiveness) Stoizismus, *der* (geh.); stoische Ruhe; **do sth. with ~:** etw. mit stoischer Gelassenheit tun

stoke /stəʊk/

A *v.t.* heizen ‹*Ofen, Kessel*›; unterhalten ‹*Feuer*›; **~ a fire with coal** Kohle nachlegen

B *v.i.* ▸ **~ up B**

(Phrasal verb)

- **~ 'up**

A *v.t.* aufheizen ‹*Kessel, Ofen, Dampfmaschine*›; **~ a fire up** Brennstoff auf ein Feuer legen

B *v.i.* (coll.: feed oneself) sich voll stopfen (ugs.)

stoke: ~hold *n.* (Naut.) Heizraum, *der;* **~hole** *n.* Heizerstand, *der*

stoker /'stəʊkə(r)/ *n.* ▸ **i p. 1260** Heizer, *der*/Heizerin, *die* (Berufsbez.)

STOL /stɒl/ *abbr.* (Aeronaut.) **= short take off and landing** STOL; Kurzstart

stole[1] /stəʊl/ *n.* Stola, *die*

stole[2] ▸ **steal A, B**

stolen /'stəʊln/

A ▸ **steal A, B**

B *attrib. adj.* heimlich ‹*Vergnügen, Kuss*›; verstohlen ‹*Blick*›; **~ goods** Diebesgut, *das;* **receiving ~ goods** Hehlerei, *die;* **receiver of ~ goods** Hehler, *der*/Hehlerin, *die*

stolid /'stɒlɪd/ *adj.* stur (ugs.); wacker (iron.) ‹*Arbeiter*›; unbeirrbar ‹*Entschlossenheit*›; hartnäckig ‹*Schweigen, Weigerung, Gleichgültigkeit*›

stolidity /stə'lɪdɪtɪ/ *n., no pl.* Sturheit, *die* (ugs.); (of refusal, opposition) Hartnäckigkeit, *die*

stolidly /'stɒlɪdlɪ/ *adv.* stur (ugs.); wacker (iron.) ‹*arbeiten*›; starrsinnig ‹*sich widersetzen, schweigen*›; stumpf ‹*blicken, marschieren*›

stoma /'stəʊmə/ *n., pl.* **~s** *or* **~ta** /'stəʊmətə/ **1** (Zool.) Körperöffnung, *die* **2** (Bot.) Spaltöffnung, *die*

stomach /'stʌmək/

A *n.* **1** ▸ **i p. 951** (Anat., Zool.) Magen, *der;* **lie heavy on sb.'s ~:** jmdm. schwer im Magen liegen; **on an empty ~:** mit leerem Magen ‹*arbeiten, fahren, weggehen*›; auf nüchternen Magen ‹*Alkohol trinken, Medizin einnehmen*›; **on a full ~:** mit vollem Magen; **turn sb.'s ~:** jmdm. den Magen umdrehen (ugs.); **the smell/sight of food turned her ~:** bei dem Geruch/beim Anblick des Essens drehte sich ihr der Magen um (ugs.) **2** (abdomen, paunch) Bauch, *der;* **have a pain in one's ~:** Bauchschmerzen haben; **lie on one's ~:** auf dem Bauch liegen; **develop a ~:** einen Bauch ansetzen; **pull your ~ in!** zieh deinen Bauch ein!; *see also* **pit[1] A 2** **3** **have the/no ~ [for sth.]** (wish/not wish to eat) Appetit/keinen Appetit [auf etw. (*Akk.*)] haben; (fig.: interest) Lust/keine Lust [auf etw. (*Akk.*)] haben; (fig.: courage) Mut/keinen Mut [zu etw.] haben

B *v.t.* **1** (eat, drink) herunterbekommen (ugs.); (keep down) bei sich behalten **2** (fig.: tolerate) ausstehen; hinnehmen ‹*Beleidigung*›; akzeptieren ‹*Vorstellung, Vorgehen, Rat*›

stomach: ~ ache *n.* ▸ **i p. 1231** Magenschmerzen *Pl.;* **have a ~ ache** Magenschmerzen haben; **~ pump** *n.* (Med.) Magenpumpe, *die;* **~ ulcer** *n.* ▸ **i p. 1231** Magengeschwür, *das;* **~ upset** *n.* ▸ **i p. 1231** Magenverstimmung, *die;* **~ 'wall** *n.* (Anat.) Magenwand, *die*

stomp /stɒmp/

A *n.* (dance) Stomp, *der*

B *v.i.* 1 (tread heavily) ~ **[about** *or* **around]** [umher]stampfen 2 (Amer.: stamp feet) [mit den Füßen] aufstampfen

'stomping ground *n.* (Amer.) Lieblingsaufenthalt, *der;* (for many people) Tummelplatz, *der;* **old ~s** altvertraute Stätten

stone /stəʊn/

A *n.* 1 (also Med., Bot.) Stein, *der;* **[as] hard as [a] ~:** steinhart; **his heart is** *or* **he has a heart of** *or* **[as] hard as [a] ~** (fig.) sein Herz ist aus Stein; er hat ein Herz aus Stein; **throw ~s/a ~ at sb.** jmdn. mit Steinen bewerfen/einen Stein auf jmdn. werfen; (fig.) jmdm. am Zeug flicken (ugs.); **cast** *or* **throw the first ~** (fig.) den ersten Stein werfen; **only a ~'s throw [away]** (fig.) nur einen Steinwurf weit entfernt; **leave no ~ unturned** (fig.) Himmel und Hölle in Bewegung setzen; **leave no ~ unturned to achieve sth.** (fig.) alles dransetzen, um etw. zu erreichen; **sink like a ~:** wie ein Stein untergehen; **the lift dropped like a ~:** der Aufzug fiel wie ein Stein in die Tiefe; **be written** *or* **carved** *or* **set in ~** (fig.) unverrückbar sein; *see also* **bird 1**; **blood A 1**; **glass B**; **philosopher's stone**; **Portland stone**; **rolling stone** 2 (gem) [Edel]stein, *der* 3 (Med., Bot.) Stein, *der* 4 ▸**hailstone** 5 ▸❶ **p. 1702** *pl. same* (*Brit.:* weight unit) *Gewicht von 6,35 kg*

B *adj.* steinern; Stein(*hütte, -kreuz, -mauer, -brücke*); ~ **jar/urn** Krug/Urne aus Steingut

C *v.t.* 1 mit Steinen bewerfen; ~ **sb. [to death]** jmdn. steinigen; ~ **me!, ~ the crows!** (coll.) mich laust der Affe! (ugs.) 2 entsteinen (*Obst*)

stone: S~ Age *n.* (Archaeol.) Steinzeit, *die; attrib.* Steinzeit-; **~-cold** **A** *adj.* eiskalt; **B** *adv.* **~-cold sober** stocknüchtern

stoned /stəʊnd/ *adj.* (sl.) stoned (Drogenjargon); (drunk) voll zu (salopp); **get ~ [on drugs]** sich anturnen (ugs.); **be ~ out of one's head** *or* **mind** völlig stoned *od.* zugekifft sein (Drogenjargon); (drunk) total zu sein (ugs.)

stone: ~-'dead *pred. adj.* mausetot (fam.); **kill sth. ~-dead** (fig.) etw. völlig zunichte machen; **~-'deaf** *adj.* stocktaub (ugs.); **~-ground** *adj.* mit Mühlsteinen gemahlen; **~mason** *n.* ▸❶ **p. 1260** Steinmetz, *der;* **~ pine** *n.* (Bot.) Pinie, *die;* Nusskiefer, *die;* **~'wall** (Brit.) **A** *v.i.* mauern (fig.); **~wall on an issue** in einer Angelegenheit mauern; **B** *v.t.* **~wall sth.** bei etw. mauern; **~walling** /'stəʊnwɔ:lɪŋ/ *n.* (Brit.) **~walling [tactics]** Hinhaltetaktik, *die;* **~ware** *n., no pl.* Steingut, *das; attrib.* (*Krug, Vase*) aus Steingut; **~washed** *adj.* mit Steinen ausgewaschen; **be ~washed** mit Steinen ausgewaschen *od.* (fachspr.) stonewashed sein; **~work** *n.* Mauerwerk, *das*

stony /'stəʊnɪ/ *adj.* 1 (full of stones) steinig; **fall on ~ ground** (fig.) auf unfruchtbaren Boden fallen 2 (like stone) steinartig 3 (hostile) steinern (geh.) (*Blick, Miene*); frostig (*Person, Empfang, Schweigen*) 4 *pred.* (coll.) ▸**stony-broke**

stony-'broke *pred. adj.* (coll.) völlig abgebrannt (ugs.)

stood ▸**stand A, B**

stooge /stu:dʒ/ (coll.)

A *n.* 1 (Theatre: comedian) Stichwortgeber, *der/* -geberin, *die* 2 (compliant person) Marionette, *die* (fig.)

B *v.i.* ~ **for sb.** (for comedian) jmdm. die Stichworte liefern; (as deputy etc.) jmds. Marionette sein

stool /stu:l/ *n.* 1 Hocker, *der;* **fall between two ~s** (fig.) sich zwischen zwei Stühle setzen 2 ▸**footstool** 3 *in sing. or pl.* (Physiol.: faeces) Stuhl, *der* 4 (Bot.) (of tree) *Baumstumpf mit frisch austreibenden Schösslingen;* (of dormant plant) Wurzelstock, *der;* (of cut plant) Mutterpflanze, *die*

'stool pigeon *n.* 1 (Hunting) Locktaube, *die* 2 (fig.: decoy) Lockvogel, *der* 3 (police informer) Polizeispitzel, *der*

stoop[1] /stu:p/

A *v.i.* 1 ~ **[down]** sich bücken; ~ **over sth.** sich über etw. (*Akk.*) beugen; **he'd ~ to anything to get his way** (fig.) ihm ist jedes Mittel recht[, um sein Ziel zu erreichen]; **I wouldn't ~ so low!** (fig.) ich würde mich nicht so erniedrigen!; ~ **to do sth.** (fig.) sich dazu erniedrigen, etw. zu tun; ~ **to deceit/a lie** sich für Verrat/eine Lüge hergeben 2 (have ~) gebeugt gehen 3 ▸**swoop B**

B *v.t.* beugen; **~ed with old age** vom Alter gebeugt

C *n.* gebeugte Haltung; **have a/walk with a ~:** einen krummen Rücken haben/gebeugt gehen

stoop[2] *n.* (Amer.) *nicht überdachte, über Treppen erreichbare Terrasse vor einem Haus*

stop /stɒp/

A *v.t.,* **-pp-** 1 (not let move further) anhalten (*Person, Fahrzeug*); aufhalten (*Fortschritt, Verkehr, Feind*); verstummen lassen (geh.) (*Gerücht, Geschichte, Lüge*); (*Tormann:*) halten (*Ball*); **she ~ped her car** sie hielt an; ~ **thief!** haltet den Dieb!; **there's no ~ping sb.** jmd. lässt sich nicht aufhalten; ~ **a bullet** *or* **one** (coll.) (get killed) umgelegt werden (salopp); (get wounded) eine Kugel abkriegen (ugs.); *see also* **track A 2**

2 (not let continue) unterbrechen (*Redner, Spiel, Gespräch, Vorstellung*); beenden (*Krieg, Gespräch, Treffen, Spiel, Versuch, Arbeit*); stillen (*Blutung*); stoppen (*Produktion, Uhr, Streik, Inflation*); einstellen (*Handel, Zahlung, Lieferung, Besuche, Subskriptionen, Bemühungen*); abstellen (*Strom, Gas, Wasser, Missstände*); beseitigen (*Schmerz*); ~ **that/that nonsense/that noise/your threats!** hör damit/mit diesem Unsinn/diesem Lärm/deinen Drohungen auf!; **he had his grant/holidays ~ped** seine Unterstützung wurde/Ferien wurden gestrichen; **bad light ~ped play** (Sport) das Spiel wurde wegen schlechter Lichtverhältnisse abgebrochen; ~ **the show** (fig.) Furore machen; **just you try and ~ me!** versuch doch, mich daran zu hindern!; ~ **working** mit der Arbeit aufhören; ~ **smoking/crying** aufhören zu rauchen/weinen; **never ~ doing sth.** etw. unaufhörlich tun; ~ **'saying that!** sag das nicht mehr!; ~ **being silly!** hör mit diesem Quatsch auf!; ~ **it!** hör auf [damit]!; (in more peremptory tone) Schluss damit!; ~ **oneself** sich zurückhalten; **I couldn't ~ myself** ich konnte nicht anders; *see also* **rot A 1**

3 (not let happen) verhindern (*Verbrechen, Unfall*); **I managed to ~ myself [from] punching him** ich musste mich sehr zurückhalten, um ihn nicht zu schlagen; **He was determined to do/say it. We couldn't ~ him** Er war entschlossen, es zu tun/sagen. Wir konnten ihn nicht davon abhalten; **she couldn't ~ herself [from] coughing** sie versuchte vergeblich, ihren Husten zu unterdrücken; **you won't ~ me [from] seeing her** du wirst mich nicht daran hindern, sie zu sehen; **he tried to ~ us parking** er versuchte uns am Parken zu hindern; **he phoned his mother to ~ her [from] worrying** er rief seine Mutter an, damit sie sich keine Sorgen machte; ~ **sth. [from] happening** verhindern, dass etw. geschieht; **there's nothing to ~ me/you** *etc.* **[doing sth.]** es gibt nichts, was mich/dich *usw.* daran hindern könnte[, etw. zu tun]

4 (cause to cease working) abstellen (*Maschine usw.*); (*Streikende:*) stilllegen (*Betrieb*); **his/her face is enough to ~ a clock** (fig. coll.) wenn man sein/ihr Gesicht sieht, haut es einen um (ugs.)

5 (block up) zustopfen (*Loch, Öffnung, Riss, Ohren*); verschließen (*Wasserhahn, Rohr, Schlauch, Flasche*); ~ **holes in a wall with concrete/filler** Löcher in einer Wand mit Beton/Spachtelmasse füllen; ~ **sb.'s mouth** (fig.) jmdm. den Mund stopfen (ugs.)

6 (withhold) streichen; **the cost will be ~ped out of** *or* **from his salary** die Kosten werden von seinem Gehalt abgezogen; ~ **payment** (Finance) die Zahlungen [wegen Insolvenz] einstellen; ~ **[payment of] a cheque** einen Scheck sperren lassen

7 (Boxing) (parry) parieren; (knock out) k.o. schlagen

8 (Mus.) ~ **a string** eine Saite greifen; **a ~ped pipe [of an organ]** eine gedackte [Orgel]pfeife

B *v.i.,* **-pp-** 1 (not extend further) aufhören; (*Straße, Treppe:*) enden; (*Ton:*) verstummen; (*Ärger:*) verfliegen; (*Schmerz:*) abklingen; (*Zahlungen, Lieferungen:*) eingestellt werden; **at this point his knowledge ~s** an diesem Punkt ist sein Wissen erschöpft

2 (not move or operate further) (*Fahrzeug, Fahrer:*) halten; (*Maschine, Motor:*) stillstehen; (*Uhr, Fußgänger, Herz:*) stehen bleiben; **he ~ped in the middle of the sentence** er unterbrach sich mitten im Satz; **he never ~s to think [before he acts]** er denkt nie nach [bevor er handelt]; ~**!** halt!; ~ **at nothing** vor nichts zurückschrecken; ~ **dead** plötzlich stehen bleiben; (*Redner:*) abbrechen; **you never know when to ~:** du weißt einfach nicht, wann du aufhören musst; *see also* **short B 1**; **track A 2**

3 (stay) bleiben; ~ **at a hotel/at a friend's house/with sb.** in einem Hotel/im Hause eines Freundes/bei jmdm. wohnen; ~ **for** *or* **to dinner** zum Essen bleiben; ~ **for coffee afterwards** zum Kaffeetrinken [noch] dableiben; **I'm not ~ping** ich kann nicht lange bleiben

C *n.* 1 (halt) Halt, *der;* **there will be two ~s for coffee on the way** es wird unterwegs zweimal zum Kaffeetrinken angehalten; **this train goes to London with only two ~s** dieser Zug fährt mit nur zwei Zwischenhalten nach London; **bring to a ~:** zum Stehen bringen (*Fahrzeug*); zum Erliegen bringen (*Verkehr*); unterbrechen (*Arbeit, Diskussion, Treffen*); **the fire brought the show/performance to a [sudden] ~:** das Feuer setzte der Show/dem Auftritt ein [plötzliches] Ende (geh.); **come to a ~:** stehen bleiben; (*Fahrzeug:*) zum Stehen kommen; (*Gespräch:*) abbrechen; (*Arbeit, Verkehr:*) zum Erliegen kommen; (*Vorlesung:*) abgebrochen werden; **make a ~ at** *or* **in a place** in einem Ort Halt machen; **put a ~ to** abstellen (*Missstände, Unsinn*); unterbinden (*Versuche*); aus der Welt schaffen (*Gerücht*); **put a ~ on a cheque** einen Scheck sperren lassen; **without a ~:** ohne Halt (*fahren, fliegen*); ohne anzuhalten (*gehen, laufen*); ununterbrochen (*arbeiten, reden*)

2 (place) Haltestelle, *die;* **the ship's first ~ is Cairo** der erste Hafen, den das Schiff anläuft, ist Kairo; **the plane's first ~ is Frankfurt** die erste Zwischenlandung des Flugzeuges ist in Frankfurt

3 (Brit.: punctuation mark) Satzzeichen, *das; see also* **full stop 1**

4 (in telegram) stop

5 (Mus.) (row of organ pipes) Register, *das;* (organ knob) Registerzug, *der;* **pull out all the ~s** (fig.) alle Register ziehen

6 (to limit movement) Anschlag, *der*

7 (Photog.) Blende, *die*

8 (Phonet.) Verschlusslaut, *der*

Phrasal verbs

- **~ a'way** (coll.) ▸**stay away 1**
- **~ be'hind** ▸**stay behind**
- **~ 'by** (Amer.)

A *v.i.* vorbeischauen (ugs.); ~ **by at the store** im Geschäft vorbeigehen (ugs.)

B *v.t.* ~ **by sb.'s house** *or* **place [and have a drink]** bei jmdm. [auf einen Drink] vorbeischauen (ugs.); **we'll ~ by the shop and get some apples** wir gehen schnell im Laden vorbei und kaufen [uns] ein paar Äpfel

- **~ 'down** *v.t.* (Photog.) ~ **down to f/16** auf Blende 16 abblenden
- **~ 'in** (coll.) ▸**stay in 2**
- **~ 'off** *v.i.* einen Zwischenaufenthalt einlegen; ~ **off at the pub for a packet of cigarettes** an der Kneipe kurz anhalten, um Zigaretten zu kaufen; *see also* **stopoff**
- **~ 'on** (coll.) ▸**stay on 3**
- **~ 'out** *v.i.* 1 draußen bleiben 2 (remain on strike) (*Arbeiter:*) weiterstreiken (ugs.)
- **~ 'over** *v.i.* einen Zwischenaufenthalt machen; (remain for the night) übernachten (**at** bei); *see also* **stopover**
- **~ 'up**

A *v.t.* ▸ ~ **A 5**

B *v.i.* ▸**stay up 1**

stop: ~ button *n.* Stopptaste, *die;* **press the ~ button** [auf] die Stopptaste drücken; **~cock** *n.* Abstellhahn, *der;* Absperrhahn, *der* (Technik); **~gap** *n.* Notbehelf, *der;* (scheme, measure, plan, person) Notlösung, *die; attrib.* behelfsmäßig; **a ~gap measure** eine Behelfsmaßnahme; **~-'go** *n.* (Brit.) Hin und Her, *das;*

(boom and recession) Auf und Ab, *das; attrib.* **~-go strategy/policies** strategisches/politisches Hin und Her; **~ light** *n.* 1 (red traffic light) rotes Licht; **if the ~ light shows** wenn die Ampel rot ist; 2 (Motor Veh.) Bremslicht, *das;* **~ line** *n.* (on road) Haltelinie, *die;* **~-loss** *adj.* (Finance) Stop-Loss-; **~off** ▸ **~over**; **~ order** *n.* 1 (Finance) limitierter Börsenauftrag; 2 (Law) *gerichtliche Anordnung, dass über bei Gericht hinterlegte Wertpapiere nicht verfügt werden darf;* **~over** *n.* Stopover, *der;* Zwischenaufenthalt, *der;* (of aircraft) Zwischenlandung, *die*

stoppage /ˈstɒpɪdʒ/ *n.* 1 (halt) Stillstand, *der;* (strike) Streik, *der;* (in traffic) Stau, *der;* (Sport) Unterbrechung, *die* 2 (cancellation) Sperrung, *die;* (of delivery) Einstellung, *die* 3 (deduction) Abzug, *der*

ˈstoppage time *n., no pl.* (Sport) Nachspielzeit, *die*

stopper /ˈstɒpə(r)/

A *n.* Stöpsel, *der;* Pfropfen, *der;* **put a ~** *or* **the ~s on sth./sb.** (fig.) einer Sache (*Dat.*) einen Riegel vorschieben/jmdm. einen Strich durch die Rechnung machen

B *v.t.* zustöpseln

stopping /ˈstɒpɪŋ/ ▸ **filling A 1**

stopping: ~ distance *n.* Anhalteweg, *der* (fachspr.); **~ place, ~ point** *ns.* Station, *die;* (where train must stop) Haltepunkt, *der;* (where one might rest) Ort zum Rasten; **~ train** *n.* (Brit. Railw.) Nahverkehrszug, *der*

stop: ~ press *n.* (Brit. Journ.) letzte Meldung/Meldungen; *attrib.* **~-press news** letzte Meldungen; **~ sign** *n.* Stoppschild, *das;* **~ signal** *n.* Haltesignal, *das;* **~-ˈstart traffic** *adj.* (coll.) häufig stockend; **~-start traffic** Stop-and-go-Verkehr, *der;* **~watch** *n.* Stoppuhr, *die*

storage /ˈstɔːrɪdʒ/ *n.* 1 *no pl., no indef. art.* (storing) Lagerung, *die;* (of furniture) Einlagerung, *die;* (of films, books, documents) Aufbewahrung, *die;* (of data, water, electricity) Speicherung, *die;* **my furniture is in ~:** meine Möbel sind [bei einer Spedition] eingelagert; **put in[to] ~:** zur Aufbewahrung geben ‹*Möbel*›; *see also* **cold storage** 2 ▸ **storage space** 3 (cost of warehousing) Lagergebühr, *die*

storage: ~ battery *n.* (Electr.) Akkumulator, *der;* **~ capacity** *n.* (Computing) Speicherkapazität, *die;* **~ cell** *n.* (Electr.) Akkumulator, *der;* **~ device** *n.* (Computing) Speichermedium, *das;* Datenträger, *der;* **~ heater** *n.* [Nacht-]speicherofen, *der;* **~ space** *n.* Lagerraum, *der;* (in house) Platz [zum Aufbewahren]; **I need ~ space for all my books** ich brauche Platz, um alle meine Bücher aufzubewahren; **~ tank** *n.* Sammelbehälter, *der;* Lagertank, *der*

store /stɔː(r)/

A *n.* 1 (Amer.: shop) Laden, *der* 2 *in sing. or pl.* (Brit.: large general shop) Kaufhaus, *das; see also* **department store** 3 (warehouse) Lager, *das;* (for grain, hay) Speicher, *der;* (for valuables) Depot, *das;* (for arms) Waffenkammer, *die;* (for books, films, documents) Magazin, *das;* **put sth. in ~:** etw. [bei einer Spedition] einlagern 4 (stock) Vorrat, *der* (**of** an + *Dat.*); **a great ~ of knowledge** ein großer Wissensschatz; **I don't have an unlimited ~ of patience** meine Geduld ist nicht unerschöpflich; **get in** *or* **lay in a ~ of sth.** einen Vorrat an etw. (*Dat.*) anlegen; **have** *or* **keep coal/food in ~:** einen Kohlenvorrat/einen Vorrat an Lebensmitteln haben; **have enough arms/ammunition in ~:** genug Waffen/Munition in Reserve haben; **be** *or* **lie in ~ for sb.** jmdn. erwarten; **have a surprise in ~ for sb.** eine Überraschung für jmdn. [auf Lager] haben; **there was another surprise in ~ for him** noch eine Überraschung wartete auf ihn; **that's a treat in ~:** das ist eine erfreuliche Aussicht; **there'll be trouble in ~:** es wird Ärger geben; **who knows what the future has in ~?** wer weiß, was die Zukunft mit sich bringt? 5 *in pl.* (supplies) Vorräte; **the ~s** (place) das [Vorrats]lager 6 **lay** *or* **put** *or* **set [great] ~ by** *or* **on sth.** [großen] Wert auf etw. legen 7 (Brit. Computing) Speicher, *der*

B *v.t.* 1 (put in ~) einlagern; speichern ‹*Getreide, Energie, Wissen*›; einspeichern ‹*Daten*›; ablegen ‹*Papiere, Dokumente*›; **~ food/nuts/coal/wine** (collect as reserve) sich (*Dat.*) einen Vorrat an Lebensmitteln/Nüssen/Kohle/Wein anlegen 2 (leave for storage) unterbringen 3 (hold) aufnehmen; speichern ‹*Energie, Daten*›

C *attrib. adj.* 1 (Breeding) Mast- 2 (Amer.: shop-bought) Konfektions‹*kleidung*›

Phrasal verbs

- **~ aˈway** *v.t.* lagern; ablegen ‹*Akten*›; **~ food away** sich (*Dat.*) einen Lebensmittelvorrat anlegen; **~ things away in a trunk/at a friend's house** Sachen in einer Truhe verstauen/bei einem Freund aufbewahren; **~ away information** Informationen sammeln und aufbewahren
- **~ ˈup** *v.t.* speichern; **~ up provisions/food/wine/coal/nuts** sich (*Dat.*) Vorräte/Lebensmittel-/Wein-/Kohlenvorräte/einen Vorrat an Nüssen anlegen; **you're only storing up trouble for yourself** du handelst dir nur immer mehr Schwierigkeiten ein

store: ~ cupboard *n.* [Abstell]schrank, *der;* **~ detective** *n.* ▸ ℹ **p. 1260** Kaufhausdetektiv, *der;* **~house** *n.* Lager[haus], *das;* **sb. is a ~house of knowledge/information [about angling]** jmd. ist ein wandelndes Lexikon[, was das Angeln betrifft]; **the book is a real ~house of facts [about Germany]** das Buch ist eine wahre Fundgrube [für jeden, der sich über Deutschland orientieren will]; **~keeper** *n.* ▸ ℹ **p. 1260** 1 (one in charge of ~s) Lagerist, *der*/Lageristin, *die;* (Mil.) Verwalter der Materialausgabe; 2 (Amer.: shopkeeper) Besitzer eines Einzelhandelsgeschäftes; **~man** /ˈstɔːmən/ *n., pl.* ▸ ℹ **p. 1260** **~men** /ˈstɔːmən/ 1 (man in charge of ~s) Lagerist, *der;* (Mil.) Verwalter der Materialausgabe; 2 (handler of ~d goods) Lagerarbeiter, *der;* **~ ˈmanager** *n.* ▸ ℹ **p. 1260** Kaufhausmanager, *der*/-managerin, *die;* **~room** *n.* Lagerraum, *der;* (for food on ship) Proviantraum, *der;* (in restaurant, canteen) Speisekammer, *die*

storey /ˈstɔːrɪ/ *n.* Stockwerk, *das;* Geschoss, *das;* **a five-~ house** ein fünfgeschossiges Haus; **third-~ window** Fenster im zweiten Stock[werk]

-storeyed /ˈstɔːrɪd/ *adj. in comb.* -geschossig; **three-~ house** dreigeschossiges Haus

storied /ˈstɔːrɪd/ *adj.* (literary: legendary) legendenumwoben

-storied (Amer.) ▸ **-storeyed**

stork /stɔːk/ *n.* Storch, *der*

storm /stɔːm/

A *n.* 1 Unwetter, *das;* (thunder~) Gewitter, *das;* **the night of the ~:** die Sturmnacht; **cross the Channel in a ~:** den Ärmelkanal bei Sturm überqueren; **a ~ in a teacup** (fig.) ein Sturm im Wasserglas 2 (fig.: dispute) Sturm der Entrüstung; **~ and stress** Sturm und Drang 3 (fig.: outburst) (of applause, protest, indignation, criticism) Sturm, *der;* (of abuse, insults, tears) Flut, *die;* (of missiles, shots, arrows, blows) Hagel, *der;* **a ~ of blows rained down on his head** Schläge hagelten auf seinen Kopf 4 (Mil.: attack) Sturm, *der;* **take sb./sth. by ~:** jmdn. überrumpeln/etw. im Sturm nehmen 5 (Meteorol.: wind) [schwerer] Sturm

B *v.i.* 1 stürmen; **he ~ed in** er kam hereingestürmt; **~ about** *or* **around in a violent temper** voller Wut herumtoben (ugs.) 2 (talk violently) toben; **~ at sb.** jmdn. andonnern (ugs.); **~ against sth./sb.** gegen etw. wettern (ugs.)/gegen jmdn. vom Leder ziehen

C *v.t.* (Mil.) stürmen

storm: ~ centre *n.* (Meteorol.) Auge *od.* Zentrum eines Wirbelsturms; **~ cloud** *n.* 1 (Meteorol.) Gewitterwolke, *die;* 2 (fig.) **the clouds [of war] are gathering** dunkle Wolken ziehen am Horizont auf [und kündigen Krieg an]; **~ damage** *n., no pl.* Sturmschaden, *der* (*meist Pl.*); **~ door** *n.* äußere Windfangtür; **~ drain** *n.* Abflusskanal, *der;* **~ flap** *n.* Regenklappe, *die;* **~ lighter** *n.* Stormfeuerzeug, *das;* **~ sewer** *n.* (Amer.) ▸ **storm drain**; **~trooper** *n.* (Hist.) SA-Mann, *der* (ns.); **~ troops** *n. pl.* 1 (Mil.) Sturmtruppen; 2 (Hist.) Sturmabteilung, *die* (ns.); SA, *die* (ns.)

stormy /ˈstɔːmɪ/ *adj.* 1 stürmisch; wild ‹*Beschimpfung*›; hitzig ‹*Auseinandersetzung*› 2 (indicating storms) auf Sturm hindeutend; **be** *or* **look ~:** nach Sturm aussehen

story¹ /ˈstɔːrɪ/ *n.* 1 (account of events) Geschichte, *die;* **give the ~ of sth.** etw. schildern *od.* darstellen; **the suspects' stories did not coincide** die Aussagen der Verdächtigen stimmten nicht überein; **[that's] a likely ~** (iron.) wers glaubt, wird selig (ugs. scherzh.); **it is quite another ~ now** (fig.) jetzt sieht alles ganz anders aus; **the [old,] old ~, the same old ~** (fig.) das alte Lied (ugs.); **tall ~:** unglaubliche Geschichte; **that's [a bit of] a tall ~!** das ist ein bisschen dick aufgetragen! (ugs.); **that's a different ~** (fig.) das ist etwas ganz anderes; **that's his ~ [and he's sticking to it]** er bleibt bei dem, was er gesagt hat; **that's only ˈhalf the ~:** das ist noch nicht alles; **the bruise told its ˈown ~:** der blaue Fleck sprach für sich selbst; **the ~ goes that ...:** man erzählt sich, dass ...; **or so the ~ goes** so erzählt man sich; **the whole ~ came out** alles kam heraus (ugs.); **that's not the whole ~:** das ist noch nicht alles; **to cut** *or* **make a long ~ short, ...:** kurz [gesagt], ... 2 (narrative) Geschichte, *die;* **but that is another ~:** aber das ist eine andere Geschichte; **that's the ~ of my life!** (fig.) das ist mein ewiges Problem!; *see also* **short story** 3 (news item) Bericht, *der;* Story, *die* (ugs.) 4 (past) ▸ **history 1** 5 (plot) Story, *die* 6 (set of [interesting] facts) **the objects in the room have a ~:** die Gegenstände in dem Zimmer haben ihre eigene Geschichte; **there is an interesting ~ behind that sword** um dieses Schwert rankt sich eine interessante Geschichte (geh.) 7 (coll./child lang.: lie) Märchen, *das;* **tell stories** Märchen erzählen

story² (Amer.) ▸ **storey**

story: ~board (Cinemat.) **A** *n.* Storyboard, *das;* **B** *v.t.* per Storyboard planen *od.* ausarbeiten; **~ book** **A** *n.* Geschichtenbuch, *das;* (with fairy tales) Märchenbuch, *das;* **B** *attrib. adj.* Bilderbuch-; **~ book world** Märchenwelt, *die;* **~line** ▸ **story¹ 5**; **~teller** *n.* 1 (narrator) [Geschichten]erzähler, *der*/-erzählerin, *die;* 2 (writer) Erzähler, *der*/Erzählerin, *die;* 3 (raconteur) Anekdotenerzähler, *der*/-erzählerin, *die;* **she's a wonderful ~teller** sie kann wundervoll erzählen; 4 (coll./child lang.: liar) Lügenbold, *der;* **~telling** *n., no pl.* Geschichtenerzählen, *das;* (fig.: lying) Lügengeschichten- *od.* Märchenerzählen, *das*

stout /staʊt/

A *adj.* 1 (strong) fest; stabil ‹*Boot, Werkzeug, Messer, Zaun*›; dick ‹*Tür, Mauer, Damm, Stock, Papier*›; robust ‹*Material, Kleidung*›; stark ‹*Seil, Abwehr*›; kräftig ‹*Pflanze, Pferd, Pfeiler*› 2 (fat) beleibt; **of ~ build** von gedrungenem Körperbau 3 (brave, staunch) unverzagt; heftig ‹*Widerstand, Opposition*›; entschieden ‹*Ablehnung*›; stark ‹*Gegner*›; fest ‹*Glaube*›; **a ~ heart** ein festes Herz; **be ~ of heart** sehr beherzt sein; **~ fellow** (arch./coll.) wackerer Kerl (veralt.)

B *n.* (drink) Stout, *der*

stout-hearted /ˈstaʊthɑːtɪd/ *adj.* beherzt; unerschrocken

stoutly /ˈstaʊtlɪ/ *adv.* 1 (strongly) stabil ‹*gebaut, gezimmert*›; **~ made** solide, robust ‹*Schuhwerk*›; stark ‹*Seil*›; **~ built** stämmig; kräftig ‹*Tier*›; stabil ‹*Haus, Zaun, Tor*›; dick ‹*Tür, Mauer*› 2 (staunchly) beherzt; hartnäckig ‹*behaupten, ablehnen, widerstehen*›; fest ‹*glauben*›

stoutness /ˈstaʊtnɪs/ *n., no pl.* (fatness) Beleibtheit, *die*

stove¹ /stəʊv/ *n.* Ofen, *der;* (for cooking) Herd, *der;* **electric ~:** Elektroherd, *der*

stove² ▸ **stave B**

ˈstovepipe *n.* (also hat) Ofenrohr, *das*

stow /stəʊ/ *v.t.* 1 (put into place) packen (**into** in + *Akk.*); verstauen (**into** in + *Dat.*); (Naut.) stauen; **she ~ed the letter out of sight/behind some books** sie steckte den Brief weg (ugs.)/hinter ein paar Bücher 2 (fill) voll packen; voll stopfen (ugs.); (Naut.) befrachten 3 (coll.: stop) aufstecken (ugs.); **~ it!** hör auf! (ugs.); (stop talking) [halt die] Klappe! (salopp)

Phrasal verb

- **~ aˈway**

A *v.t.* verwahren; **he keeps his savings ~ed**

S

away in a sock er hat seine Ersparnisse in einem Strumpf versteckt
B *v.i.* als blinder Passagier reisen; *see also* **stowaway**

stowage /ˈstəʊɪdʒ/ *n.* **1** (space for stowing) Platz, *der;* (Naut.) Stauraum, *der* **2** (action of stowing) Aufbewahrung, *die;* Unterbringung, *die;* (Naut.) Stauen, *das* **3** (Naut.: stowed goods) Ladung, *die*

ˈ**stowaway** *n.* blinder Passagier

straddle /ˈstrædl/ *v.t.* **1** (be positioned across) ~ *or* **sit straddling a fence/chair** rittlings auf einem Zaun/Stuhl sitzen; ~ *or* **stand straddling a ditch** mit gespreizten Beinen über einem Graben stehen; **his legs ~d the chair/brook** er saß rittlings auf dem Stuhl/stand mit gespreizten Beinen über dem Bach; **their farm ~s the border** ihre Farm liegt beiderseits der Grenze; **the bridge ~s the river/road** die Brücke überspannt den Fluss/die Straße **2** (part widely) **sit/stand with legs ~d** *or* **~d legs** mit gespreizten Beinen sitzen/stehen; ~ **one's legs** die Beine spreizen **3** (Mil.) eindecken; **the bombs ~d the target** die Bomben schlugen zu beiden Seiten *od.* beiderseits des Ziels ein

Stradivarius /strædɪˈveərɪəs/ *n.* (Mus.) Stradivari, *die*

strafe /strɑːf/ *v.t.* (Mil.) beharken (Soldatenspr.)

straggle /ˈstrægl/ *v.i.* **1** (trail) ~ **[along] behind the others** den anderen hinterherzockeln (ugs.); **the last few walkers ~d in** die letzten Geher trotteten ins Ziel; **the procession ~d [out] along the road** der Zug zockelte die Straße entlang (ugs.) **2** (spread in irregular way) ‹*Dorf, Stadt:*› sich ausbreiten; ‹*Häuser, Bäume:*› verstreut stehen; **the brook/fence goes straggling through/over the meadow** der Bach zieht sich mit vielen Windungen/der Zaun verläuft kreuz und quer über die Wiese **3** (grow untidily) ‹*Pflanze:*› wuchern; ‹*Haar, Bart:*› zottig wachsen

straggler /ˈstræglə(r)/ *n.* Nachzügler, *der*

straggling /ˈstræglɪŋ/ *adj.* **1** (trailing) nachzockelnd (ugs.) **2** (irregular) verstreut ‹*Häuser*›; ungeordnet ‹*Reihe*›; unregelmäßig ‹*Baumreihe, Schrift*›; ‹*Fluss, Zaun, Straße*› mit vielen Krümmungen; weiträumig angelegt ‹*Stadt, Gebäude*›; **a ~ village** eine Streusiedlung **3** (long and untidy) wuchernd; zottig ‹*Haar, Bart*›

straggly /ˈstræglɪ/ ▸ **straggling 3**

straight /streɪt/
A *adj.* **1** gerade; aufrecht ‹*Haltung*›; glatt ‹*Haar*›; **in a ~ line** in gerader Linie; **the ~ and narrow** der Pfad der Tugend; **keep sb. on/keep to the ~ and narrow** jmdn. im Zaum halten/auf dem Pfad der Tugend wandeln (geh.); *see also* **arrow A**
2 (not having been bent) ausgestreckt ‹*Arm, Bein*›; durchgedrückt ‹*Knie*›
3 (not misshapen) gerade ‹*Bein*›
4 (Fashion) gerade geschnitten
5 (undiluted, unmodified) unvermischt; **have** *or* **drink whisky/gin ~:** Whisky/Gin pur trinken; **a ~ choice** eine klare Wahl; **make a ~ bet on a horse** auf ein Pferd auf Sieg setzen
6 (successive) fortlaufend; **win in ~ sets** (Tennis) ohne Satzverlust gewinnen; **the team had ten ~ wins** die Mannschaft hat zehn Spiele hintereinander gewonnen; **~ As** (Amer.) lauter Einsen
7 (undeviating) direkt ‹*Blick, Schlag, Schuss, Pass, Ball, Weg*›; **sb. has a ~ aim, sb.'s aim is ~:** jmd. zielt genau; **a ~ hit** *or* **blow** (Boxing) eine Gerade; **a ~ left/right** (Boxing) eine linke/rechte Gerade; **give sb. a ~ look** jmdn. scharf ansehen
8 (candid) geradlinig ‹*Mensch*›; ehrlich ‹*Antwort*›; klar ‹*Abfuhr, Weigerung, Verurteilung*›; unmissverständlich ‹*Rat*›; **~ dealings/speaking** direkte Verhandlungen/unverblümte Sprache; **a ~ answer to a ~ question** eine klare Antwort auf eine klare Frage; **he did some ~ talking with her** er sprach sich mit ihr offen aus; **be ~ with sb.** zu jmdm. offen sein
9 (logical) klar; **her thinking is clear and ~:** ihr Denken ist klar und logisch
10 (Theatre) ernst; (not avant-garde) konventionell
11 (in good order, not askew) **we/the rooms are ~ now after the move** wir haben uns/die Zimmer nach dem Umzug jetzt eingerichtet; **the accounts are ~:** die Bücher sind in Ordnung; **the picture is ~:** das Bild hängt gerade; **is my hair/tie ~?** sitzt meine Frisur/Krawatte [richtig]?; **is my hat [on] ~?** sitzt mein Hut [richtig]?; **pull sth. ~:** etw. gerade ziehen; **put ~:** gerade ziehen ‹*Krawatte*›; gerade aufsetzen ‹*Hut*›; gerade hängen ‹*Bild*›; aufräumen ‹*Zimmer, Sachen*›; richtig stellen ‹*Fehler, Missverständnis*›; **put things ~:** alles in Ordnung bringen; **put things ~ with sb.** mit jmdm. alles klären; **get sth. ~** (fig.) etw. genau *od.* richtig verstehen; **let's get it** *or* **the facts** *or* **things ~:** wir sollten alles genau klären; **get this ~!** merk dir das [ein für alle Mal]!; **put sb. ~:** jmdn. aufklären; **put** *or* **set the record ~:** die Sache *od.* das richtig stellen; *see also* **straight face**
12 (coll.: heterosexual) hetero (ugs.)
13 (coll.: conventional) [spieß]bürgerlich (abwertend); (Mus.) konventionell
B *adv.* **1** (in a ~ line) gerade; **she came ~ at me** sie kam geradewegs auf mich zu; **~ opposite** genau gegenüber; **head ~ for the wall** genau auf die Mauer zusteuern; **go ~** (fig.: give up crime) ein bürgerliches Leben führen
2 ▸ ❶ **p. 1699** (directly) geradewegs; **~ after** sofort nach; **the knife went ~ through his hand** das Messer ging mitten durch seine Hand; **the pianist went ~ into the next piece** der Klavierspieler ging sofort zum nächsten Stück über; **come ~ to the point** direkt *od.* gleich zur Sache kommen; **look sb. ~ in the eye** jmdm. direkt in die Augen blicken; **~ ahead** *or* **on** immer geradeaus; **they went ~ ahead and did it** sie taten es sofort; *see also* **horse A 1; shoulder A 1**
3 (honestly, frankly) aufrichtig; **give it to me ~:** sei ganz offen zu mir!; **he came ~ out with it** er sagte es ohne Umschweife; **I told him ~ [out] that …:** ich sagte [es] ihm ins Gesicht, dass …; **play ~ with sb.** mit jmdm. ein ehrliches Spiel spielen
4 (upright) gerade ‹*sitzen, stehen, wachsen*›
5 (accurately) zielsicher; **he can't shoot [very] ~:** er ist nicht [sehr] zielsicher
6 (clearly) klar ‹*sehen, denken*›
C *n.* **1** (~ condition) **out of the ~** = **out of true** ▸ **true B**
2 (~ stretch) gerade Strecke; (Sport) Gerade, *die;* **final** *or* **home** *or* **last ~** (Sport; also fig.) Zielgerade, *die*
3 (Cards) Straße, *die;* Folge, *die*

straight: ~ **aˈway** *adv.* sofort; gleich; **~away** (Amer.) *adj.* **1** *attrib.* (~) gerade; **2** (~forward) nüchtern; sachlich; ~ ˈ**bat** *n.* (Cricket) aufrecht gehaltener Schläger; **keep a ~ bat** (Brit. fig.) sich anständig benehmen; ~ **edge** *n.* (for paperhanging) Tapezierschiene, *die;* (Metalw.) Haarlineal, *das*

straighten /ˈstreɪtn/
A *v.t.* **1** gerade ziehen ‹*Kabel, Teppich, Seil*›; gerade biegen ‹*Draht*›; glätten ‹*Falte, Kleidung, Haare*›; gerade rücken ‹*Hut, Krawatte, Brille*›; gerade machen ‹*Tischkante*›; begradigen ‹*Fluss, Straße*›; gerade halten ‹*Rücken*›; strecken ‹*Beine, Arme*›; gerade hängen ‹*Bild*› **2** (put in order) aufräumen; einrichten ‹*neue Wohnung*›; in Ordnung bringen ‹*Geschäftsbücher, Finanzen*›
B *v.i.* gerade werden; ‹*Haar:*› glatt werden

Phrasal verbs

• ~ ˈ**out**
A *v.t.* **1** gerade biegen ‹*Draht*›; gerade ziehen ‹*Seil, Kabel*›; glätten ‹*Decke, Teppich*›; begradigen ‹*Fluss, Straße*› **2** (put in order, clear up) klären; aus der Welt schaffen ‹*Missverständnis, Meinungsverschiedenheit*›; in Ordnung bringen ‹*Angelegenheit*›; berichtigen ‹*Fehler*›; **~ sb. out** jmdn. zur Einsicht bringen; **~ sb. out on sth.** jmdn. über etw. (*Akk.*) aufklären; **things will ~ themselves out** das wird sich von selbst regeln **3** (sl.: beat up) jmdn. vermöbeln (salopp); **do you want ~ing out?** soll ich dir eine reinhauen? (salopp)
B *v.i.* gerade werden; ‹*Haar:*› glatt werden; **things will ~ out** das wird sich von selbst regeln

• ~ ˈ**up**
A *v.t.* ▸ **tidy up B**
B *v.i.* sich aufrichten

straight: ~ ˈ**eye** *n.* gute Augen; ~ ˈ**face** *n.* unbewegtes Gesicht; **with a ~ face** ohne eine Miene zu verziehen; **keep a ~ face** keine Miene verziehen; **~-faced** *adj.* mit unbewegter Miene *nachgestellt;* **be ~-faced** keine Miene verziehen; ~ ˈ**fight** *n.* (Brit. Polit.) *direkter Kampf zwischen zwei Kandidaten;* ~ ˈ**flush** ▸ **flush**[4]; ~ˈ**forward** *adj.* **1** (frank) freimütig; geradlinig ‹*Politik*›; schlicht ‹*Stil, Sprache, Erzählung, Bericht*›; klar ‹*Anweisung, Vorstellungen*›; **have a ~forward approach to a problem** ein Problem direkt angehen; **be ~forward in one's dealings** offen und gerade sein; **2** (simple) einfach; eindeutig ‹*Lage*›; ~ˈ**forwardly** *adv.* **1** (frankly) ehrlich ‹*handeln*›; offen ‹*sprechen, sagen*›; **2** (simply) deutlich ‹*erklären*›; ~ **man** *n.* (Theatre) *Schauspieler, der einem Komiker die Stichwörter für seine Gags liefert*

straightness /ˈstreɪtnɪs/ *n., no pl.* **1** Geradheit, *die;* (of hair) Glattheit, *die;* (Fashion) gerader Schnitt **2** (fig.) (candour) (of answer) Offenheit, *die;* (of purpose) Geradlinigkeit, *die;* (of dealings) Ehrlichkeit, *die*

straight: ~ ˈ**off** *adv.* (coll.) schlankweg (ugs.); ~ ˈ**sex** *n., no pl.* normaler Geschlechtsverkehr *od.* Sex; ~ ˈ**ticket** *n.* (Amer. Polit.) **vote the ~ [Republican/Democratic] ticket** die [republikanische/demokratische] Liste unverändert wählen; ~ ˈ**tip** *n.* Insidertipp, *der;* ~ ˈ**up** *adv.* (coll.: honestly) echt (ugs.); **Do you mean what you say? — S~ up!** Meinst du auch, was du sagst? — Na klar! (ugs.); **he offered me a lot of money, ~ up!** er hat mir einen Haufen Geld angeboten, ehrlich! (ugs.)

strain[1] /streɪn/
A *n.* **1** (pull) Belastung, *die;* (on rope) Spannung, *die;* **put a ~ on sb./sth.** jmdn./etw. belasten **2** (extreme physical or mental tension) Stress, *der;* **feel the ~:** die Anstrengung spüren; **stand** *or* **take the ~:** die Belastung *od.* den Stress aushalten; **he has a lot of ~ at work** die Arbeit nimmt ihn stark in Anspruch; **place sb. under [a] great ~:** jmdn. einer starken Belastung aussetzen; **be under [a great deal of] ~:** unter großem Stress stehen **3** (person, thing) **be a ~ on sb./sth.** jmdn./etw. belasten; eine Belastung für jmdn./etw. sein; **be a ~ on sb.'s nerves** an jmds. Nerven zerren; **find sth. a ~:** etw. als Belastung empfinden **4** ▸ ❶ **p. 1231** (injury) (muscular) Zerrung, *die;* (overstrain on heart, back, etc.) Überanstrengung, *die* **5** *in sing. or pl.* (burst of music) Klänge; (burst of poetry) Vers, *der;* Zeile, *die;* **take up the ~** (lit. or fig.) einstimmen; einfallen **6** (tone) Ton, *der* **7** (Phys.) Deformation, *die*
B *v.t.* **1** ▸ ❶ **p. 1231** (over-exert) überanstrengen; zerren ‹*Muskel*›; überbeanspruchen ‹*Geduld, Loyalität usw.*›; **~ one's back carrying heavy boxes** sich beim Tragen schwerer Kisten verheben; **~ oneself** (lit. or fig. iron.) sich übernehmen; sich überanstrengen **2** (stretch tightly) [fest] spannen; **~ed relations** (fig.) gespannte Beziehungen **3** (exert to maximum) **~ oneself/sb./sth.** das Letzte aus sich/jmdm./etw. herausholen; **~ one's ears/eyes/voice** seine Ohren/Augen/Stimme anstrengen; **~ oneself to do sth.** sich nach Kräften bemühen, etw. zu tun **4** (use beyond proper limits) verzerren ‹*Wahrheit, Lehre, Tatsachen*›; überbeanspruchen ‹*Geduld, Wohlwollen*› **5** *in p.p.* (forced) gezwungen ‹*Lächeln*›; künstlich ‹*Humor, Witz*›; gewagt ‹*Interpretation*› **6** (hug) **~ sb./sth. to oneself/to sth.** jmdn./etw. an sich/etw. (*Akk.*) drücken **7** (filter) durchseihen; seihen (**through** durch); **~ [the water from] the vegetables** das Gemüse abgießen; **~ sth. from a liquid** etw. aus einer Flüssigkeit herausfiltern
C *v.i.* **1** (strive intensely) sich anstrengen; (resist while being close to breaking point) ächzen (**under** unter + *Dat.*); **he ~ed to lift the box** er versuchte ächzend *od.* mit aller Kraft, die Kiste hochzuheben; **~ at sth.** an etw. (*Dat.*) zerren; **~ at the leash** an der Leine zerren; (fig.) es kaum erwarten können; **~ after sth.** sich mit aller Gewalt um etw. bemühen; **~ after an effect** Effekthascherei betreiben **2** (be filtered)

durchlaufen; (percolate through sand etc.) durchsickern

Phrasal verbs

- ~ **a'way,** ~ **'off** *v.t.* abseihen; abgießen ‹*Wasser*›
- ~ **'out** *v.t.* [her]ausfiltern

strain² *n.* **1** (breed) Rasse, *die;* (of plants) Sorte, *die;* (of virus) Art, *die;* (human stock) Familie, *die* **2** *no pl.* (tendency) Neigung, *die* (**of** zu); Hang, *der* (**of** zu); **a cruel** ~**:** ein grausamer Zug

strained /streɪnd/ *adj.* **1** (tense) angespannt **2** (unnatural, forced) gekünstelt **3** (Med.) überstrapaziert **4** (laboured) weit hergeholt ‹*Analogie, Vergleich*›

strainer /ˈstreɪnə(r)/ *n.* Sieb, *das*

strait /streɪt/

A *n.* **1** *in sing. or pl.* (Geog.) [Wasser]straße, *die;* Meerenge, *die;* **the S~s [of Gibraltar/Malacca]** die Straße von Gibraltar/die Malakkastraße **2** *usu. in pl.* (distressing situation) Schwierigkeiten; *see also* **dire 3**

B *adj.* (arch.) (narrow) schmal ‹*Weidefläche, Weg*›; eng ‹*Pforte*›

straitened /ˈstreɪtnd/ *adj.* beschränkt ‹*Verhältnisse*›

strait: ~jacket A *n.* (lit. or fig.) Zwangsjacke, *die;* **B** *v.t.* (lit. or fig.) in eine Zwangsjacke stecken; **~-laced** /streɪtˈleɪst/ *adj.* (fig.) puritanisch

Straits of Magellan /streɪts əv məˈgelən/ *pr. n.* Magellanstraße, *die*

strake /streɪk/ *n.* (Naut.) Planke, *die*

strand¹ /strænd/ *n.* (thread) Faden, *der;* (of wire) Litze, *die* (Elektrot.); (of rope) Strang, *der;* (of beads, pearls, flowers, etc.) Kette, *die;* (of hair) Strähne, *die;* (Biol., Phys.) Faser, *die;* (fig.) Strang, *der;* **a ~ of beads** eine Perlenkette

strand²

A *v.t.* **1** (leave behind) trockensetzen; **be [left] ~ed** (fig.) seinem Schicksal überlassen sein; (be stuck) festsitzen; **leave sb. ~ed** (fig.) jmdn. seinem Schicksal überlassen; **the strike left them ~ed in England** wegen des Streiks saßen sie in England fest **2** (wash ashore) an Land spülen ‹*Leiche, Wrackteile*›; (run aground) auf Grund setzen ‹*Schiff*›

B *v.i.* stranden

C *n.* (rhet./poet.: foreshore) Gestade, *das* (dichter.)

strange /streɪndʒ/ *adj.* **1** (peculiar) seltsam; sonderbar; merkwürdig; **feel [very] ~, come over [very] ~** (coll.) sich [ganz] komisch im Kopf *od.* (ugs. scherzh.) beduselt fühlen; **it feels ~ to do sth.** es ist ein merkwürdiges *od.* komisches Gefühl, wenn man etw. tut; **~ to say** seltsamerweise **2** (alien, unfamiliar) fremd; **~ to sb.** jmdm. fremd **3** (unaccustomed) **~ to sth.** nicht vertraut mit etw.; **feel ~:** sich nicht zu Hause fühlen; **I feel ~, suddenly having so much power** es ist [für mich] ganz ungewohnt, plötzlich so viel Macht zu haben; **I am [quite] ~ here** ich bin fremd hier; ich kenne mich hier nicht aus

strangely /ˈstreɪndʒlɪ/ *adv.* seltsam; merkwürdig; **~ enough, ...:** seltsamerweise ...; so seltsam es klingt, ...

strangeness /ˈstreɪndʒnɪs/ *n., no pl.* (oddness) Seltsamkeit, *die;* Merkwürdigkeit, *die*

stranger /ˈstreɪndʒə(r)/ *n.* **1** (foreigner, unknown person) Fremde, *der/die;* **he is a ~ here/to** *or* **in the town** er ist hier/in der Stadt fremd; **she is a /no ~ to the British stage** sie ist auf den britischen Bühnen unbekannt/bekannt; **he is a/no ~ to me** er ist mir nicht bekannt/ist mir bekannt; **you are quite a ~:** man kennt dich ja kaum noch; **hello, ~:** hallo, lange nicht gesehen **2** (one lacking certain experience) **be a ~ in sth.** in etw. (*Dat.*) unerfahren sein; **be a/no ~ to sth.** etw. nicht gewöhnt/etw. gewöhnt sein; **he is no ~ to this sort of work** diese Arbeit ist ihm nicht fremd; **be a/no ~ to Oxford** Oxford gar nicht/[recht gut] kennen **3** (Brit. Parl.) Besucher, *der*/Besucherin, *die;* **S~s' Gallery** Besuchergalerie, *die*

strangle /ˈstræŋgl/ *v.t.* **1** (throttle) erdrosseln; erwürgen **2** (fig.: suppress) unterdrücken; **~ at birth** im Keim ersticken

'stranglehold *n.* (lit. or fig.) Würgegriff, *der;* **have a ~ on sb./sth.** jmdn./etw. im Würgegriff haben

strangler /ˈstræŋglə(r)/ *n.* Würger, *der*/Würgerin, *die*

strangulated /ˈstræŋgjʊleɪtɪd/ *adj.* (Med.) **~ hernia** eingeklemmter Bruch

strangulation /stræŋgjʊˈleɪʃn/ *n.* Erdrosseln, *das;* Erwürgen, *das;* (fig.) Unterdrückung, *die;* Strangulierung, *die* (geh.)

strap /stræp/

A *n.* **1** (leather strip) Riemen, *der;* (textile strip) Band, *das;* (shoulder ~) Träger, *der;* (for watch) Armband, *das;* **the ~** (punishment) die Züchtigung mit dem Riemen; **be given [a lick of] the ~:** den Riemen zu schmecken bekommen **2** (to grasp in vehicle) Halteriemen, *der*

B *v.t.*, **-pp-** **1** (secure with ~) **~ [into position/down]** festschnallen; **~ oneself in** sich anschnallen **2** ▸ **~ up 2** **3** **be ~ped for cash** (coll.) sehr klamm sein (ugs.) **4** (punish with ~) mit dem Riemen züchtigen

Phrasal verb

- **~ 'up** *v.t.* **1** (fasten ~s of) zuschnallen **2** (bind with adhesive plaster) verpflastern

strap: ~hanger *n.* stehender Fahrgast; **~ hinge** *n.* Langband, *das* (Technik)

strapless /ˈstræplɪs/ *adj.* trägerlos

strapping /ˈstræpɪŋ/ *adj.* stramm

Strasbourg /ˈstræzbɜːg/ *pr. n.* ▸❶ **p. 1643** Straßburg (*das*)

strata *pl. of* **stratum**

stratagem /ˈstrætədʒəm/ *n.* (trick) [Kriegs]list, *die;* Strategem, *das* (geh.)

strategic /strəˈtiːdʒɪk/, **strategical** /strəˈtiːdʒɪkl/ *adj.* **1** strategisch; **a ~ moment** ein strategisch günstiger Zeitpunkt **2** (of great military importance) strategisch wichtig; (necessary to plan) bedeutsam ‹*Element, Faktor*›

strategically /strəˈtiːdʒɪkəlɪ/ *adv.* strategisch

Strategic De'fence Initiative *n.* Strategische Verteidigungsinitiative

strategic 'studies *n., no pl.* Strategie, *die*

strategist /ˈstrætɪdʒɪst/ *n.* Stratege, *der*/Strategin, *die*

strategy /ˈstrætɪdʒɪ/ *n.* Strategie, *die;* (fig. also) Taktik, *die;* **use ~** (fig.) taktisch *od.* strategisch vorgehen; **it was bad ~** (fig.) es war taktisch *od.* strategisch unklug

'strategy paper *n.* Strategiepapier, *das*

stratification /strætɪfɪˈkeɪʃn/ *n.* **1** (Geol., Archaeol.) Schichtung, *die;* Stratifikation, *die* (fachspr.) **2** (Sociol.) [soziale] Schichtung

stratify /ˈstrætɪfaɪ/ *v.t.* **1** (Geol., Archaeol.) stratifizieren; **stratified rock** in Schichten gewachsener Fels **2** (Sociol.) in Schichten einteilen; Schichten zuordnen; **a stratified society** eine mehrschichtige Gesellschaft

stratosphere /ˈstrætəsfɪə(r)/ *n.* (Geog.) Stratosphäre, *die;* (fig.) höhere Regionen

stratospheric /strætəˈsferɪk/ *adj.* (Geog.) stratosphärisch; Stratosphären‹*flugzeug, -flug*›; (fig.) Schwindel erregend ‹*Höhe*›

stratum /ˈstrɑːtəm, ˈstreɪtəm/ *n., pl.* **strata** /ˈstrɑːtə, ˈstreɪtə/ Schicht, *die;* Stratum, *das* (fachspr.)

stratus /ˈstreɪtəs, ˈstrɑːtəs/ *n., pl.* **strati** /ˈstreɪtaɪ, ˈstrɑːtaɪ/ (Meteorol.) Schichtwolke, *die;* Stratus, *der* (*fachspr.*); *attrib.* **~ clouds** Stratuswolken

straw /strɔː/ *n.* **1** *no pl.* (stalks of grain) Stroh, *das; attrib.* Stroh- **2** (single stalk) Strohhalm, *der;* **catch** *or* **clutch** *or* **grasp at ~s** *or* **a ~** (fig.) sich an einen Strohhalm klammern; **be the last ~, be the ~ that broke the camel's back** (coll.) das Fass zum Überlaufen bringen; **that's the last** *or* **final ~:** jetzt reichts aber; **draw ~s [for sth.]** Hölzchen [um etw.] ziehen; **draw** *or* **pick the short ~:** das kürzere Hölzchen ziehen; (fig.) das schlechtere Los ziehen; **~ in the wind** Vorzeichen, *das;* Vorbote, *der* **3** **[drinking] ~:** Trinkhalm, *der;* Strohhalm, *der* **4** (trifle) Nichtigkeit, *die;* **it doesn't matter a ~ to me** es kümmert mich keinen Pfifferling (ugs.); **I don't give a ~:** ich gebe keinen Pfifferling dafür (ugs.) **5** (hat) Strohhut, *der. See also* **cheese straw**

strawberry /ˈstrɔːbərɪ/ *n.* **1** Erdbeere, *die* **2** (colour) Erdbeerrot, *das; see also* **crush A 1**

strawberry: ~ 'blonde A *adj.* rotblond; **B** *n.* Rotblonde, *die;* **~ mark** *n.* [rötliches] Muttermal

straw: ~-blond(e) A *adj.* strohblond; **B** *n.* **1** (colour) Strohblond, *das;* **2** (person) Strohblonde, *der/die;* **~board** *n.* Strohpapier, *das;* Strohpappe, *die;* **~ boss** *n.* (Amer.) Vorarbeiter, *der;* **~ colour** *n.* Strohgelb, *das;* **~-coloured** *adj.* strohgelb; **~ 'hat** *n.* Strohhut, *der;* **~ poll, ~ vote** *ns.* Testabstimmung, *die*

stray /streɪ/

A *v.i.* **1** (wander) streunen; (fig.: in thought etc.) abschweifen (**into** in + *Akk.*); **~ [away] from** sich absondern von; **the child had ~ed from his parents** das Kind war seinen Eltern weggelaufen; **~ into enemy territory** sich auf feindliches Gebiet verirren **2** (move in meandering course) ‹*Auto:*› schlingern; (move without deliberate control) **my gaze kept ~ing to the wart on his nose** mein Blick wanderte immer wieder zu der Warze auf seiner Nase; **he could not control his ~ing hands** er konnte seine Hände einfach nicht bei sich behalten **3** (deviate) abweichen (**from** von); **have ~ed** sich verirrt haben; **~ from the path of virtue** vom Pfad der Tugend abweichen (geh.); **he had ~ed once** einmal war er vom Wege abgekommen (fig.); **~ from the point/from** *or* **off the road** vom Thema/von der Straße abkommen; **somehow I ~ed into acting/the theatre** irgendwie habe ich mich aufs Schauspielern verlegt/bin ich am Theater gelandet

B *n.* (animal) streunendes Tier; (without owner) herrenloses Tier; (person) Streuner, *der*/Streunerin, *die* (*abwertend*); *see also* **waif**

C *adj.* **1** streunend; (without owner) herrenlos; (out of proper place) verirrt **2** (occasional, isolated) vereinzelt **3** (Phys.) streuend

streak /striːk/

A *n.* **1** (narrow line) Streifen, *der;* (in hair) Strähne, *die;* **~ of lightning** Blitzstrahl, *der;* **like a ~ [of lightning]** [schnell] wie der Blitz (ugs.); wie ein geölter Blitz (ugs.) **2** (fig.: element) **have a jealous/cruel ~:** zur Eifersucht/Grausamkeit neigen; **have a ~ of meanness/jealousy** eine geizige/eifersüchtige Ader haben **3** (fig.: spell) **~ of good/bad luck, lucky/unlucky ~:** Glücks-/Pechsträhne, *die;* **be on a** *or* **have a winning/losing ~:** eine Glücks-/Pechsträhne haben

B *v.t.* streifen; **~ sth. with green** etw. mit grünen Streifen versehen; **hair ~ed with grey** Haar mit grauen Strähnen; **~ed with paint/mud/tears** farbverschmiert/dreckbeschmiert/tränenverschmiert

C *v.i.* **1** (move rapidly) flitzen (ugs.) **2** (coll.: run naked) blitzen (ugs.); flitzen (ugs.)

streaker /ˈstriːkə(r)/ *n.* (coll.) Blitzer, *der*/Blitzerin, *die* (ugs.); Flitzer, *der*/Flitzerin, *die* (ugs.)

streaking /ˈstriːkɪŋ/ *n.* (coll.: running naked) Blitzen, *das* (ugs.); Flitzen, *das* (ugs.)

streaky /ˈstriːkɪ/ *adj.* streifig; gestreift ‹*Muster, Fell*›

streaky 'bacon *n.* durchwachsener Speck

stream /striːm/

A *n.* **1** (of flowing water) Wasserlauf, *der;* (brook) Bach, *der* **2** (flow, large quantity) Strom, *der;* (of abuse, excuses, words) Schwall, *der;* **~s** *or* **a ~ of applications** eine Flut von Bewerbungen; **in ~s** in Strömen; **the children rushed in ~s/in a ~ through the school gates** die Kinder strömten durch die Schultore **3** (current) Strömung, *die;* (fig.) Trend, *der;* **against/with the ~ of sth.** (fig.) gegen den/mit dem Strom einer Sache; **go against/with the ~** ‹*Person:*› gegen den/mit dem Strom schwimmen; *see also* **Gulf Stream** **4** (Brit. Educ.) Parallelzug, *der* **5** **be/go on ~** (Industry) in Betrieb sein/den Betrieb aufnehmen

B *v.i.* **1** (flow) strömen; ‹*Sonnenlicht:*› fluten; **tears ~ed down her face** Tränen strömten ihr über das Gesicht **2** (run with liquid) **my eyes ~ed** mir tränten die Augen; **the windows/**

S

walls were ~ing with condensation die Fenster/Wände schwitzten; **his back was ~ing with sweat** sein Rücken war schweißnass *od.* schweißüberströmt **3** (wave) ‹*Haare, Fahne:*› flattern, wehen

C *v.t.* **1** (emit) **his nose was ~ing blood** Blut floss ihm aus der Nase **2** (Brit. Educ.) in Parallelzüge *od.* leistungshomogene Gruppen einteilen

Phrasal verbs

- **~ 'down** *v.i.* ‹*Sonne:*› vom Himmel strahlen; **the rain is ~ing down** es regnet in Strömen
- **~ 'in** *v.i.* hereinströmen/hineinströmen
- **~ 'out** *v.i.* **1** (move out like ~) herausströmen/hinausströmen **2** (float) flattern; wehen
- **~ 'past** *v.i.* vorbeiströmen
- **~ 'through** *v.i.* hindurchströmen

streamer /ˈstriːmə(r)/ *n.* **1** (ribbon) Band, *das;* (of paper) Luftschlange, *die;* Papierschlange, *die* **2** (Journ.: headline) Schlagzeile, *die;* Aufmacher, *der* **3** (pennon) Wimpel, *der*

streaming /ˈstriːmɪŋ/

A *n.* **1** (Brit. Educ.) Einteilung in Parallelzüge *od.* leistungshomogene Gruppen; Streaming, *das.* **2** (Computing) Streaming, *das*

B *adj.* (flowing) laufend ‹*Nase*›; tränend ‹*Auge*›; schwitzend ‹*Wand, Fenster*›; **have a ~ cold** einen schlimmen Schnupfen haben

streamlet /ˈstriːmlɪt/ *n.* Bächlein, *das*

stream: ~line A *n.* **1** (shape) Stromlinienform, *die* (Physik, Technik); **2** (line of flow) Stromlinie, *die* (Physik); **B** *v.t.* **1** (give shape to) [eine] Stromlinienform geben (+ *Dat.*); **be ~lined** eine Stromlinienform haben; **2** (simplify) rationalisieren; (reduce) einschränken; **~ of 'consciousness** *n.* (Lit.) (flow of thoughts) Bewusstseinsstrom, *der;* (literary style) Stream of Consciousness, *der*

street /striːt/ *n.* **1** Straße, *die;* **in** (Brit.) *or* **on ... S~:** in der ...straße; **in the ~:** auf der Straße; (St. Exch.) nach Börsenschluss; **I wouldn't cross the ~ to do that** (fig.) ich würde mir deswegen kein Bein ausreißen (ugs.); **be on the ~[s]** (be published) ‹*Zeitung:*› draußen sein; (have no place to live) auf der Straße liegen (ugs.); (be available to be bought) im [Straßen]verkauf sein; **be/go on the ~s** (be/become a prostitute) auf die Straße gehen (ugs.); **take to the ~s** auf die Straße gehen (ugs.); **keep the youngsters off the ~s** dafür sorgen, dass sich die Jugendlichen nicht auf der Straße herumtreiben; **it isn't a very interesting job, but at least it keeps me off the ~s** (iron.) der Job ist zwar nicht sehr interessant, aber wenigstens stehe ich nicht mehr auf der Straße (ugs.); **not in the same ~ [as sb./sth.]** (fig. coll.) nicht zu vergleichen [mit jmdm./etw.]; **~s ahead [of sb./sth.]** (coll.) um Längen besser [als jmd./etw.] (ugs.); **be [right** *or* **just] up sb.'s ~** (coll.) jmds. Fall sein (ugs.); **the ~s of San Francisco are paved with gold** (fig.) in San Francisco liegt das Geld auf der Straße **2** (people in street) Straße, *die*

street: ~ball *n.* Streetball, *der;* **~car** *n.* (Amer.) Straßenbahn, *die;* Tram, *die* (südd., österr., schweiz.); **~ cred** /ˈstriːt kred/ (coll.), **~ credibility** *ns.* [glaubwürdiges] Image; **~ cries** *n. pl.* (Brit.) Straßen- *od.* Händlerrufe; **~ crime** *n., no pl., no indef. art.* Straßenkriminalität, *die;* **~ door** *n.* [vordere] Haustür; **~ entertainer** *n.* Straßenkünstler, *der*/-künstlerin, *die;* **~ entertainment** *n., no pl.* Straßenunterhaltung, *die;* **~ fight** *n.* Straßenkampf, *der;* (heavy fighting) Straßenschlacht, *die;* **~ fighting** *n., no pl.* Straßenkampf, *der;* **sporadic ~ fighting broke out** vereinzelt brachen Straßenkämpfe aus; **~ furniture** *n., no pl.:* *Gegenstände wie Straßenlaternen, Abfallkörbe, Telefonzellen, Verkehrszeichen usw.;* **~ lamp, ~ light** *ns.* Straßenlaterne, *die;* Straßenlampe, *die;* **~-'legal** *adj.* [zum öffentlichen Straßenverkehr] zulassungsfähig; **~ lighting** *n., no pl.* Straßenbeleuchtung, *die;* **~ map** *n.* Stadtplan, *der;* **~ market** *n.* Straßenmarkt, *der;* **~ party** *n.* Straßenfest, *das;* **~ performer** *n.* Straßenkünstler, *der*/-künstlerin, *die;* **~ plan** ▸**~ map; ~ sweeper** *n.* **1** ▸**❶ p. 1260** (person) Straßenfeger, *der*/-fegerin, *die* (bes. nordd.); Straßenkehrer, *der*/-kehrerin, *die* (bes. südd.); **2** (machine) Kehrmaschine, *die;* (vehicle) Straßenkehrmaschine, *die;* **~ theatre** *n.* Straßentheater, *das;* **~ trader** *n.* ▸**❶ p. 1260** Straßenhändler, *der*/-händlerin, *die;* Straßenverkäufer, *der*/-verkäuferin, *die;* **~ urchin** *n.* Straßenkind, *das;* **~ value** *n.* Straßenverkaufswert, *der;* **~ vendor** *n.* ▸**❶ p. 1260** Straßenhändler, *der*/-händlerin, *die;* **~walker** *n.* ▸**❶ p. 1260** Nutte, *die* (ugs.); **~wise** *adj.* (coll.) **be ~wise** wissen, wo es langgeht

strength /streŋθ/ *n.* **1** (power) Kraft, *die;* (strong point, force, intensity, amount of ingredient; also Finance) Stärke, *die;* (of argument) [Überzeugungs]kraft, *die;* (of poison, medicine) Wirksamkeit, *die;* (of legal evidence) [Beweis]kraft, *die;* (resistance of material, building, etc.) Stabilität, *die;* (artistic forcefulness) [künstlerische/dichterische/musikalische] Kraft; **recover/exhaust one's ~:** seine Kräfte wiedererlangen/erschöpfen; **not know one's own ~:** nicht wissen, wie stark man ist; **give sb. ~:** jmdn. stärken; jmdm. Kraft geben; *see also* **give A 5**; **~ of conviction/feeling** Überzeugungskraft, *die*/Stärke der Emotionen; **~ of character/will/purpose** Charakterstärke, *die*/Willensstärke *od.* -kraft, *die*/Zielstrebigkeit, *die;* **from ~:** aus einer Position der Stärke heraus; **go from ~ to ~:** immer erfolgreicher werden; **on the ~ of sth./that** aufgrund einer Sache (*Gen.*)/dessen; **we can have a drink on the ~ of that** darauf können wir einen trinken **2** (proportion present) Stärke, *die;* (full complement) **be below ~/up to ~:** weniger als/etwa die volle Stärke haben; **in [full] ~:** in voller Stärke; **the police were there in ~:** ein starkes Polizeiaufgebot war da

strengthen /ˈstreŋθən, ˈstreŋkθən/

A *v.t.* (give power to) stärken; (reinforce, intensify, increase in number) verstärken; erhöhen ‹*Anteil*›; (make more effective) unterstützen; (increase main ingredient of) stärker machen ‹*Getränk*›; kräftiger machen ‹*Farbe, Anstrich*›; **~ sb.'s resolve** jmdn. in seinem Entschluss bestärken; **~ sb.'s hand** (fig.) jmds. Position stärken

B *v.i.* stärker werden

strenuous /ˈstrenjʊəs/ *adj.* **1** (energetic) energisch; gewaltig ‹*Anstrengung*› **2** (requiring exertion) anstrengend

strenuously /ˈstrenjʊəslɪ/ *adv.* mit aller Kraft ‹*sich anstrengen*›; angestrengt ‹*arbeiten*›; heftig ‹*bestreiten, bekräftigen*›

strenuousness /ˈstrenjʊəsnɪs/ *n., no pl.* Schwere, *die*

streptococcus /streptəˈkɒkəs/ *n., pl.* **streptococci** /streptəˈkɒkaɪ/ (Bacteriol.) Streptokokkus, *der*

stress /stres/

A *n.* **1** (strain) Stress, *der;* **be [placed] under ~:** unter Stress (*Dat.*) stehen **2** (emphasis) Betonung, *die;* Nachdruck, *der;* **lay** *or* **place** *or* **put [a] ~ on sth.** auf etw. (*Akk.*) Wert *od.* Gewicht legen **3** (accentuation) Betonung, *die;* (in verse) Hebung, *die;* **put the/a ~ on sth.** etw. betonen; **which syllable carries the ~?** welche Silbe trägt den Ton? **4** (Mech.) Belastung, *die;* [elastische] Spannung (fachspr.). *See also* **storm A 2**

B *v.t.* **1** (emphasize) betonen; Wert legen auf (+ *Akk.*) ‹*richtige Ernährung, gutes Benehmen, Sport usw.*›; **~ [the point] that ...:** darauf hinweisen, dass ... **2** (Ling.) betonen ‹*Silbe, Vokal usw.*› **3** (subject to strain) überanstrengen; (Mech.) belasten; [elastischer] Spannung aussetzen (fachspr.)

Phrasal verb

- **stress 'out** *v.t. & i.* stressen (ugs.)

'stress disease *n.* Stresskrankheit, *die;* Managerkrankheit, *die* (volkst.)

'stressed out *adj.* (coll.) [völlig] gestresst; **be ~ by sb./sth.** von jmdm./etw. [völlig] gestresst sein; **get ~:** [völlig] gestresst werden

'stress-free *adj.* stressfrei ‹*Tage, Ferien*›; **be ~** ‹*Person*› frei von Stress sein; keinen Stress haben

stressful /ˈstresfl/ *adj.* anstrengend; stressig (ugs.)

stress: ~ hormone *n.* Stresshormon, *das;* **~ 'management** *n., no pl.* Stressbewältigung, *die;* **~ management can help** der richtige Umgang mit Stress kann helfen; **~ mark** *n.* Betonungszeichen, *das;* **~-related** *adj.* stressbedingt

stretch /stretʃ/

A *v.t.* **1** (lengthen, extend) strecken ‹*Arm, Hand*›; recken ‹*Hals*›; dehnen ‹*Gummiband*›; (spread) ausbreiten ‹*Decke*›; (tighten) spannen; **he lay ~ed out on the ground** er lag ausgestreckt auf dem Boden; **~ one's legs** (by walking) sich (*Dat.*) die Beine vertreten **2** (widen) dehnen; **~ [out of shape]** ausweiten ‹*Schuhe, Jacke*› **3** (fig.: make the most of) ausschöpfen ‹*Reserve*›; fordern ‹*Person, Begabung*› **4** (fig.: extend beyond proper limit) überschreiten ‹*Befugnis, Grenzen des Anstands*›; strapazieren (ugs.) ‹*Geduld*›; es nicht so genau nehmen mit ‹*Gesetz, Bestimmung, Begriff, Grundsätzen*›; **~ a point** großzügig sein; **~ credibility** nicht sehr glaubhaft sein; **~ the truth** ‹*Aussage:*› nicht ganz der Wahrheit entsprechen; **he's certainly ~ing the truth there** er nimmt es hier mit der Wahrheit nicht so genau; **we're a bit ~ed at the moment** wir sind zurzeit ziemlich überlastet; **~ it/things** den Bogen überspannen; *see also* **wing A 1**

B *v.i.* **1** (extend in length) sich weiten; sich dehnen; ‹*Person, Tier:*› sich strecken **2** (have specified length) sich [aus]dehnen; **~ from A to B** sich von A bis B erstrecken; **the traffic jam ~ed all the way back to Junction 9** der Verkehr staute sich bis zur Auffahrt Neun [zurück] **3** **~ to sth.** (be sufficient for) für etw. reichen; **could you ~ to £10?** hast du vielleicht sogar 10 Pfund?

C *v. refl.* sich [dehnen und] strecken

D *n.* **1** (lengthening, drawing out) **have a ~, give oneself a ~:** sich strecken; **with a ~, I can reach ...:** wenn ich mich strecke, kann ich bis an ... (*Akk.*) reichen; **give sth. a ~:** etw. dehnen *od.* weiter machen **2** (exertion) **by no ~ of the imagination** auch mit viel Fantasie nicht; **at a ~** (fig.) wenn es sein muss (*see also* **4**); **at full ~:** auf Hochtouren **3** (expanse, length) Abschnitt, *der;* **a ~ of road/open country** ein Stück Straße/freies Gelände **4** (period) **for a ~:** eine Zeit lang; **a four-hour ~:** eine Zeitspanne von vier Stunden; **at a ~:** ohne Unterbrechung; (*see also* **2**) **5** (Amer. Racing) Gerade, *die* **6** (sl.: length of imprisonment) **do a [five-year] ~:** [fünf Jahre] im Knast sitzen (ugs.); **go down for another ~:** wieder einmal in den Knast wandern (ugs.) **7** (in fabric) Elastizität, *die;* **there is a lot of ~ in this material** das Material ist sehr dehnbar

E *adj.* dehnbar; Stretch‹*hose, -gewebe*›

Phrasal verb

- **~ 'out**

A *v.t.* **1** (extend by straightening) [aus]strecken ‹*Arm, Bein*›; ausbreiten ‹*Decke*›; auseinander ziehen ‹*Seil*›; **~ oneself out** sich [lang] ausstrecken **2** (eke out) **~ sth. out** mit etw. reichen

B *v.i.* **1** (~ one's hands out) (lit. or fig.) die Hände ausstrecken (**to** nach) **2** (extend) sich ausdehnen **3** (last for sufficient time) reichen

stretch[ed] 'limo *n.* Stretchlimousine, *die;* Stretchlimo, *die* (ugs.)

stretcher /ˈstretʃə(r)/

A *n.* **1** (for carrying a person) [Trag]bahre, *die* **2** (between chair legs) Steg, *der* **3** (for canvas) Rahmen, *der* **4** (in boat) Stemmbrett, *das* **5** (Building) Läufer, *der*

B *v.t.* auf einer Bahre tragen

Phrasal verb

- **stretcher 'off** *v.t.* auf einer Bahre *od.* Trage wegtragen

stretcher: ~-bearer *n.* ▸**❶ p. 1260** [Kranken]träger, *der;* **~ party** *n.* Sanitätstrupp, *der;* Team von Krankenträgern

stretch: ~ marks *n. pl.* (after pregnancy) Schwangerschaftsstreifen; **~ pants** *n. pl.* Stretchhose, *die*

stretchy /ˈstretʃɪ/ *adj.* (coll.) dehnbar

strew /struː/ *v.t., p.p.* **strewed** /struːd/ *or* **strewn** /struːn/ **1** (scatter) streuen ‹*Blumen, Sand usw.*›; **clothes were ~n about the room** Kleider lagen im ganzen Zimmer verstreut herum **2** (cover, lit. or fig.) bestreuen; **the grass**

was ~n with litter [überall] auf dem Gras war Abfall verstreut

stricken /ˈstrɪkn/ *adj.* **1** (afflicted) heimgesucht; havariert ‹*Schiff, Flugzeug*›; (showing affliction) schmerzerfüllt; **be ~ with fever/a disease** von Fieber geschüttelt/einer Krankheit heimgesucht werden; **~ with fear/grief/misfortune** angsterfüllt/gramgebeugt/vom Schicksal geschlagen; **~ in years** (arch.) von den Jahren gezeichnet **2** (Amer.: deleted) **~ from sth.** aus etw. gestrichen

strict /strɪkt/ *adj.* **1** (firm) streng; strenggläubig ‹*Katholik, Moslem usw.*›; **in ~ confidence** streng vertraulich; **he is ~ about what his children wear** er achtet streng darauf, was seine Kinder anziehen **2** (precise) streng; genau ‹*Übersetzung*›; **keep a ~ watch** genau *od.* scharf aufpassen; **in the ~ sense [of the word]** im strengen Sinn[e] [des Wortes]

strictly /ˈstrɪktlɪ/ *adv.* streng; **there is ~ no smoking here** Rauchen ist hier streng[stens] verboten; **~ between ourselves** ganz im Vertrauen; **this is ~ between ourselves** das muss unter uns bleiben; **~ [speaking]** streng genommen; *see also* **bird 1**

strictness /ˈstrɪktnɪs/ *n., no pl.* **1** (firmness) Strenge, *die* **2** (precision) Genauigkeit, *die*

stricture /ˈstrɪktʃə(r)/ *n.* **1** *usu. in pl.* (critical remark) **~[s]** [scharfe *od.* heftige] Kritik; **~[s] [up]on sth.** Kritik an etw. (*Dat.*); **pass ~s [up]on sb.** jmdn. kritisieren **2** (Med.) Verengung, *die;* Striktur, *die*

stridden ▸ **stride B, C**

stride /straɪd/
A *n.* **1** Schritt, *der;* (of galloping horse) [Galopp-]sprung, *der;* **make ~s [towards sth.]** (fig.) [in Richtung auf etw. (*Akk.*)] Fortschritte machen; **make great ~s** (fig.) große Fortschritte machen; **get into one's ~:** seinen Rhythmus finden; (fig.) in Fahrt *od.* Schwung kommen; **put sb. off his ~, throw sb. out of his ~** (fig.) jmdn. aus dem Konzept bringen; **be thrown out of** *or* **lose one's ~** (lit. or fig.) aus dem Tritt kommen; **take sth. in one's ~** (fig.) mit etw. gut fertig werden **2** *in pl.* (Brit. and Austral. coll.: trousers) Hose, *die*
B *v.i.*, **strode** /strəʊd/, **stridden** /ˈstrɪdn/ [mit großen Schritten] gehen; (solemnly) schreiten (geh.); (take single step) **~ across sth.** über etw. (*Akk.*) hinwegschreiten (geh.)
C *v.t.*, **strode, stridden: ~ the streets/moors** durch die Straßen/über die Moore wandern
(Phrasal verb)
• **~ ˈout** *v.i.* ausschreiten (geh.)

stridency /ˈstraɪdənsɪ/ *n., no pl.* ▸ **strident:** Schrillheit, *die;* Grellheit, *die*

strident /ˈstraɪdənt/ *adj.* schrill ‹*Stimme, Blech[bläser]*›; (fig.) grell ‹*Farbe, Satire*›; schrill ‹*Protest, Ton*›

stridently /ˈstraɪdəntlɪ/ *adv.* gellend ‹*rufen, laut*›; (fig.) grell ‹*sich kleiden*›; aufdringlich ‹*vulgär*›; in schrillem Ton ‹*sich beklagen*›

strife /straɪf/ *n., no pl., no indef. art.* Streit, *der;* Zwist, *der* (geh.); **we live in a world of ~:** wir leben in einer Welt der Zwietracht (geh.)

strike /straɪk/
A *n.* **1** (Industry) Streik, *der;* Ausstand, *der;* **be on/go [out]** *or* **come out on ~:** in den Streik getreten sein/in den Streik treten; *see also* **hunger strike; sit-down B**
2 (Finance, Mining, Oil Industry) Treffer, *der* (fig. ugs.); **make a ~:** sein Glück machen; (Mining) fündig werden; **make a gold/an oil ~:** auf Gold/Öl (*Akk.*) stoßen
3 (sudden success) **[lucky] ~:** Glückstreffer, *der;* **make a lucky ~, get one's lucky ~:** Glück haben
4 (act of hitting) Schlag, *der;* (of snake) Biss, *der*
5 (Mil.) Angriff, *der* (**at** auf + *Akk.*); **pre-emptive ~:** Präventivschlag, *der*
6 (Bowling) Abräumen, *das;* **get a ~:** abräumen
7 (Baseball) Fehlschlag, *der*
8 (Geol.) Streichen, *das;* **angle of ~:** Streichwinkel, *der*
B *v.t.*, **struck** /strʌk/, **struck** *or* (arch.) **stricken** /ˈstrɪkn/ **1** (hit, send by hitting) schlagen; ‹*Schlag, Geschoss:*› treffen ‹*Ziel*›; ‹*Blitz:*› [ein-]schlagen in (+ *Akk.*), treffen; (afflict) treffen; ‹*Epidemie, Seuche, Katastrophe usw.:*› heimsuchen; ‹*Schmerz:*› durchzucken; **~ one's head on** *or* **against the wall** mit dem Kopf gegen die Wand schlagen; **his head struck the pavement** er schlug mit dem Kopf auf das Pflaster; **the car struck a pedestrian** das Auto erfasste einen Fußgänger; **the ship struck the rocks** das Schiff lief auf die Felsen; **~ sth. in two** etw. entzweischlagen; etw. spalten; **~ sth. from sb.'s hand** jmdm. etw. aus der Hand schlagen; **~ sb./sth. aside** jmdn. zur Seite stoßen/etw. zur Seite schlagen
2 (delete) streichen (**from, off** aus)
3 (deliver) **~ two punches** zweimal zuschlagen; **~ sb. a blow** jmdm. einen Schlag versetzen; **who struck [the] first blow?** wer hat zuerst geschlagen?; **~ a blow against sb./against** *or* **to sth.** (fig.) jmdm./einer Sache einen Schlag versetzen; **~ a blow for sth.** (fig.) eine Lanze für etw. brechen
4 (produce by hitting flint) schlagen ‹*Funken*›; (ignite) anzünden ‹*Streichholz*›; **~ a light!** (dated coll., expr. disgust) das darf doch nicht wahr sein! (ugs.)
5 (chime) schlagen
6 (Mus.) anschlagen ‹*Töne auf dem Klavier*›; anzupfen, anreißen ‹*Töne auf der Gitarre*›; (fig.) anschlagen ‹*Ton*›; *see also* **chord[1] 1**
7 (impress) beeindrucken; **~ sb.'s notice** jmdm. auffallen; **~ sb. as [being] silly** jmdm. dumm zu sein scheinen *od.* dumm erscheinen; **it ~s sb. that ...:** es scheint jmdm., dass...; **how does it ~ you?** was hältst du davon?
8 (occur to) einfallen (+ *Dat.*)
9 **struck on sb./sth.** (coll.: infatuated with) hingerissen von jmdm./etw.
10 (cause to become) **a heart attack struck him dead** er erlag einem Herzanfall; **be struck blind/dumb** erblinden/verstummen; **I was struck speechless by the news** die Nachricht verschlug mir die Sprache; **~ me dead!** (sl.) du kannst mich totschlagen (ugs.)
11 (attack) überfallen; (Mil.) angreifen; (wound with fangs) ‹*Schlange:*› ihre Zähne schlagen in (+ *Akk.*)
12 (encounter) begegnen (+ *Dat.*); **~ a patch of bad luck** eine Pechsträhne haben
13 (Mining) stoßen auf (+ *Akk.*); **~ gold** auf Gold stoßen; (fig.) einen Glückstreffer landen (ugs.) (**in** mit); *see also* **oil A 1**
14 (reach) stoßen auf (+ *Akk.*) ‹*Hauptstraße, Weg, Fluss*›
15 (achieve) **~ success** [plötzlich] Erfolg haben; **~ a compromise** einen Kompromiss erreichen; *see also* **balance A 4; bargain A 1**
16 ([cause to] penetrate) **the cold struck his very marrow** die Kälte ging ihm durch Mark und Bein; **~ sb.'s heart/sb. to the quick** jmdn. ins Herz/Mark treffen; **~ fear into sb.** jmdn. in Angst versetzen; **~ root** Wurzeln treiben *od.* schlagen
17 (fill) **~ sb. with fear/foreboding** jmdn. mit Furcht/Vorahnungen erfüllen
18 (Hort.) setzen; aus Ablegern ziehen ‹*Pflanze*›
19 (adopt) einnehmen ‹*[Geistes]haltung*›
20 (take down) einholen ‹*Segel, Flagge*›; abbrechen ‹*Zelt, Lager*›; **~ one's flag** (fig.) die Flagge streichen
21 (mint) prägen; schlagen (veralt.). *See also* **happy 1; note A 1; rich A 2; stricken**
C *v.i.*, **struck, struck** *or* (arch.) **stricken**
1 (deliver a blow) zuschlagen; ‹*Pfeil:*› treffen; ‹*Blitz:*› einschlagen; ‹*Unheil, Katastrophe, Krise, Leid:*› hereinbrechen (geh.); (collide) zusammenstoßen; (hit) schlagen (**against** gegen, **[up]on** auf + *Akk.*); ‹*Schiff:*› auflaufen (**on** auf + *Akk.*)
2 (ignite) zünden
3 (chime) schlagen; **eight o'clock has struck** es hat acht Uhr geschlagen; **hear the hour ~:** den Stundenschlag hören
4 (Industry) streiken
5 (attack; also Mil.) zuschlagen (fig.); (wound with fang) zubeißen
6 (make a find) (Mining) fündig werden; (Hunting) die Witterung aufnehmen; **~ lucky** Glück haben
7 (penetrate) **~ through sth.** durch etw. dringen; **the wind ~s cold** der kalte Wind geht durch und durch; **his words struck into my heart** seine Worte trafen mich ins Herz
8 (direct course) **~ south** *etc.* sich nach Süden *usw.* wenden; ‹*Straße:*› nach Süden *usw.* verlaufen; ‹*Schiff:*› Kurs nach Süden *usw.* nehmen; **~ across the fields/down the hill/through the forest** über die Felder/den Hügel hinunter/durch den Wald gehen
9 (launch) **~ into sth.** mit etw. beginnen
10 (Hort.) Wurzeln treiben *od.* schlagen
11 (Angling) (hook fish) anschlagen; (seize bait) anbeißen. *See also* **iron A 1**
(Phrasal verbs)
• **~ at** *v.t.* schlagen nach; (fig.) einen Schlag versetzen (+ *Dat.*); rütteln an (+ *Dat.*) ‹*Grundfesten*›; *see also* **root[1] A 1**
• **~ ˈback** *v.i.* (lit. or fig.) zurückschlagen; **~ back at sb./sth.** sich gegen jmdn./etw. zur Wehr setzen
• **~ ˈdown** *v.t.* niederschlagen; (fig.) niederwerfen (geh.); (Amer. Law: reverse) aufheben
• **~ ˈoff**
A *v.t.* **1** (remove) abschlagen **2** (remove from membership) streichen ‹*Namen*›; (from professional body) die Zulassung/Approbation entziehen (+ *Dat.*) **3** (produce by copying) abziehen
B *v.i.* aufbrechen
• **~ on** ▸ **~ upon**
• **~ ˈout**
A *v.t.* **1** (devise) ausarbeiten **2** (delete) streichen **3** (Baseball) ausmachen
B *v.i.* **1** (hit out) zuschlagen; **~ out at sb./sth.** nach jmdm./etw. schlagen; (fig.) jmdn./etw. scharf angreifen; **~ out on all sides** um sich schlagen; **~ out wildly** wild um sich schlagen **2** (swim vigorously) mit kräftigen Zügen schwimmen; (fig.) Anstrengungen unternehmen; **~ out for sth.** (fig.) sich mit aller Kraft um etw. bemühen **3** (set out) (lit. or fig.) aufbrechen; **~ out in a new direction** (fig.) etwas Neues anfangen **4** (Baseball) aus sein
• **~ through** *v.t.* durchstreichen ‹*Wort*›; (on list also) ausstreichen
• **~ up**
A /ˈ--/ *v.t.* **1** (start) beginnen ‹*Unterhaltung*›; anknüpfen ‹*Bekanntschaft*›; schließen ‹*Freundschaft*›; **~ up a friendship with sb.** sich mit jmdm. anfreunden **2** (begin to play) anstimmen
B /-ˈ-/ *v.i.* beginnen
• **~ upon** *v.t.* finden ‹*Lösung, Ausweg*›; **I have just struck upon an idea** mir ist gerade eine Idee gekommen

strike: ~ action *n.* Streikaktionen; **take ~ action** Streikmaßnahmen ergreifen; **~ ballot** *n.* Urabstimmung, *die* (*über Einleitung eines Streiks*); **~ benefit** ▸ **~ pay; ~bound** *adj.* bestreikt ‹*Fabrik*›; vom Streik/von Streiks betroffen ‹*Industrie*›; durch einen Streik lahm gelegt ‹*Zugverkehr, Land*›; **~-breaker** *n.* Streikbrecher, *der*/-brecherin, *die;* **~ force** *n.* (Milit.) Angriffstruppe, *die;* **terrorism ~ force** Antiterroreinheit, *die;* **~ pay** *n.* Streikgeld, *das*

striker /ˈstraɪkə(r)/ *n.* **1** (worker on strike) Streikende, *der/die* **2** (Cricket) Schläger, *der*/Schlägerin, *die;* (Footb.) Stürmer, *der*/Stürmerin, *die;* (Billiards) Spieler/Spielerin, der/die am Stoß ist **3** (Arms) Schlagbolzen, *der* **4** (Horol.) (clock) Schlaguhr, *die;* (mechanism) Schlagwerk, *das*

ˈstrike vote *n.* Urabstimmung, *die* (*über Einleitung eines Streiks*)

striking /ˈstraɪkɪŋ/ *adj.* **1** (arresting) auffallend; erstaunlich ‹*Ähnlichkeit, Unterschied*›; bemerkenswert ‹*Idee*›; schlagend ‹*Beispiel*› **2** (Horol.) mit Schlagwerk *nachgestellt;* Schlagwerk-

striking: ~ distance *n.* Reichweite, *die;* (of [bullet from] gun etc.) Schussweite, *die;* **the troops had advanced to within ~ distance of the capital** die Truppen hatten sich der Hauptstadt auf Reichweite genähert; **within easy ~ distance of a town** (fig.) in unmittelbarer Nähe einer Stadt; **~ force** *n.* (Mil., Police) Einsatzkommando, *das*

S

strikingly /'straɪkɪŋlɪ/ *adv.* auffallend; umwerfend ‹*ähnlich sehen*›; **be ~ obvious** ins Auge springen

strimmer ® /'strɪmə(r)/ *n.* (Brit.) Rasentrimmer, *der*

Strine /straɪn/ *n., no pl., no art.* australisches Englisch; *attrib.* australisch ‹*Akzent usw.*›

string /strɪŋ/

A *n.* 1 (thin cord) Schnur, *die;* (to tie up parcels etc. also) Bindfaden, *der;* (ribbon) Band, *das;* **a puppet on ~s/on a ~:** eine Marionette; **how long is a piece of ~?** wie weit ist der Himmel?; **[have/keep sb.] on a ~:** [jmdn.] an der Leine (ugs.) *od.* am Gängelband [haben/halten]; **pull the ~s** (fig.) die Fäden in der Hand haben; **pull [a few *or* some] ~s** (fig.) seine Beziehungen spielen lassen; **there are ~s attached** (fig.) es sind Bedingungen/es ist eine Bedingung damit verknüpft; **..., but there are ~s attached** ..., aber nur unter Bedingungen/einer Bedingung; **without ~s, with no ~s attached** ohne Bedingung[en] 2 (of bow) Sehne, *die;* (of racket, musical instrument) Saite, *die;* **have another ~ to one's bow** (fig.) noch ein Eisen im Feuer haben (ugs.); **first/second ~:** erste/zweite Wahl; **as a second ~:** als zweites Eisen im Feuer (ugs.); **a racket with nylon ~s** ein Schläger mit Nylonbespannung; **a six-~ guitar** eine sechssaitige Gitarre 3 *in pl.* (Mus.) (instruments) Streichinstrumente; (players) Streicher; **~ quartet/orchestra** Streichquartett/-orchester, *das;* **he plays in the ~s** er spielt bei den Streichern 4 (series, sequence) Kette, *die;* (procession) Zug, *der;* (of onions) Zopf, *der;* (Computing) String, *der;* Zeichenfolge, *die;* **he owns a ~ of racehorses** ihm gehören etliche Rennpferde; **he has had a ~ of girlfriends** er hat eine Freundin nach der anderen gehabt 5 (in bean) Faden, *der. See also* **apron 1**; **bowstring**; **shoestring**

B *v.t.*, **strung** /strʌŋ/ 1 bespannen ‹*Tennisschläger, Bogen, Gitarre usw.*›; **be strung to breaking point** (fig.) ‹*Nerven:*› zum Zerreißen gespannt sein 2 (thread) auffädeln; aufziehen 3 (arrange in line) aufreihen; (stretch out) spannen; **~ sth. round one's neck** sich (*Dat.*) etw. um den Hals hängen 4 (tie with ~) verschnüren 5 die Fäden abziehen von ‹*Bohnen*›. *See also* **highly strung**

Phrasal verbs

• **~ a'long** (coll.)

A *v.i.* sich anschließen; **~ along with sb.** mit jmdm. mitgehen; (have relationship) mit jmdm. gehen (ugs.)

B *v.t.* 1 (deceive) an der Nase herumführen (ugs.) 2 (keep dangling) hinhalten

• **~ 'out**

A *v.t.* verstreuen; **~ one's meals out at longer intervals** die Abstände zwischen den Mahlzeiten vergrößern

B *v.i.* (in space) sich verteilen

• **~ to'gether** *v.t.* (join on a thread) auffädeln; aufziehen; (join by tying) zusammenbinden; (join coherently) miteinander verknüpfen; **he can't ~ two sentences together** er kann keine zwei zusammenhängende Sätze hervorbringen

• **~ 'up** *v.t.* 1 (tie with ~) schnüren; (hang up) aufhängen ‹*Lampions, Papiergirlanden*› 2 (coll.: kill by hanging) aufhängen (ugs.) 3 (make tense) unter Druck setzen; **strung up** angespannt

string: ~ bag *n.* [Einkaufs]netz, *das;* **~ band** *n.* (Mus.) Streichorchester, *das;* **~ bass** /strɪŋ 'beɪs/ *n.* (Mus.) Kontrabass, *der;* **~ 'bean** *n.* Stangenbohne, *die;* (fig. joc.: tall thin person) Bohnenstange, *die* (ugs. scherzh.)

stringed /strɪŋd/ *attrib. adj.* (Mus.) Saiten-

-stringed *adj. in comb.* (Mus.) -saitig

stringency /'strɪndʒənsɪ/ *n., no pl.* 1 (strictness) Strenge, *die* 2 **financial ~:** Geldknappheit, *die*

stringent /'strɪndʒənt/ *adj.* 1 (strict) streng ‹*Bestimmung, Gesetz, Maßnahme, Test*›; schlüssig ‹*Argumentation*›; überzeugend ‹*Plan*› 2 (tight) angespannt ‹*Finanzlage*›

stringently /'strɪndʒəntlɪ/ *adv.* 1 (strictly) streng; energisch ‹*durchsetzen*›; stringent ‹*logisch*›; schlüssig ‹*argumentieren*› 2 eisern ‹*sparen*›

stringer /'strɪŋə(r)/ *n.* 1 (in construction) Stringer, *der* (Bauw.) 2 (Journ.) Korrespondent, *der*/Korrespondentin, *die* (in freier Mitarbeit)

string: ~ tanga *n.* Stringtanga, *der;* **~ vest** *n.* Netzhemd, *das*

stringy /'strɪŋɪ/ *adj.* 1 (fibrous) faserig 2 (resembling string) dünn ‹*Haar*›; faserig ‹*Gewebe*› 3 (forming threads) Fäden ziehend; zäh ‹*Konsistenz*›; **be ~:** Fäden ziehen; ‹*Konsistenz:*› zäh sein

strip[1] /strɪp/

A *v.t.*, **-pp-** 1 (denude) ausziehen ‹*Person*›; leer räumen, ausräumen ‹*Haus, Schrank, Regal*›; abziehen ‹*Bett*›; abtakeln (Seemannsspr.) ‹*Schiff*›; entrinden ‹*Baum*›; abbeizen ‹*Möbel, Türen*›; ausschlachten, (dismantle) auseinander nehmen ‹*Maschine, Auto*›; überdrehen ‹*Schraube, Mutter*›; beschädigen ‹*Getriebe*›; **~ped to the waist** mit nacktem Oberkörper; **~ sb. of sth.** jmdn. einer Sache (*Gen.*) berauben (geh.); **~ sb. of his rank/title/medals/decorations/office** jmdm. seinen Rang/Titel/seine Medaillen/Auszeichnungen aberkennen/jmdn. seines Amtes entkleiden (geh.); **~ sb. of his power** jmdm. die Macht nehmen; **~ A of B** B von A entfernen; **~ the garden of [all its] flowers** alle Blumen im Garten abpflücken; **~ a tree [of fruit]** einen Baum abernten; **~ the trees [of leaves]** die Bäume entlauben; **~ the walls** die Tapeten entfernen 2 (remove) entfernen **(from, off** von); abziehen ‹*Laken*›; abnehmen ‹*Vorhang, Bild*›; abschälen ‹*Rinde, Schale*›; abstreifen ‹*Hülle*›; **~ the clothes/shirt off sb.'s back** *or* **off sb.** jmdm. die Kleider/das Hemd vom Leibe reißen; **~ the medals off *or* from sb.'s chest** jmdm. die Orden abreißen; **~ sb.'s property/title from him** (fig.) jmdm. seinen Besitz abnehmen/Titel aberkennen

B *v.i.*, **-pp-** sich ausziehen; **~ to the waist/[down] to one's underwear** den Oberkörper freimachen/sich bis auf die Unterwäsche ausziehen

C *n.* **do a ~:** sich ausziehen; (erotically) einen Striptease vorführen; *attrib.* **~ act** Striptease, *der*

Phrasal verbs

• **~ 'down**

A *v.t.* 1 (dismantle) auseinander nehmen 2 (undress) ausziehen 3 (reduce) einschränken

B *v.i.* sich ausziehen

• **~ 'off**

A *v.t.* 1 abreißen; abschälen ‹*Rinde*›; abziehen ‹*Tapete*›; **~ sth. off sth.** etw. von etw. abreißen/abschälen/abziehen; **he ~ped off the soldier's medals** er riss dem Soldaten die Orden ab 2 ausziehen ‹*Kleidung*›

B *v.i.* sich ausziehen

strip[2] *n.* 1 (narrow piece) Streifen, *der;* **the curtains hung in ragged ~s** die Vorhänge hingen in Fetzen; **a ~ of land** ein schmales Stück *od.* Streifen Land; **tear sb. off a ~, tear a ~ off sb.** (Brit. coll.) jmdn. den Marsch blasen (ugs.) 2 (Metallurgy) Band, *das* 3 ▸**strip cartoon** 4 (Brit. Sport coll.: clothes) Trikot, *das*

strip: ~ cartoon *n.* Comic[strip], *der;* **~ club** *n.* Stripteaselokal, *das*

stripe /straɪp/ *n.* 1 Streifen, *der* 2 (Mil.) [Ärmel]streifen, *der;* **get/lose a ~:** befördert/degradiert werden 3 (Amer.: nature) Schlag, *der. See also* **star A 1**

striped /straɪpt/ *adj.* gestreift; Streifen‹*muster, -hyäne*›

strip: ~ farming *n., no pl., no indef. art.* Streifenflurwirtschaft, *die;* **~ light** *n.* Neonröhre, *die;* (Theatre) Lichtwanne, *die;* **~ lighting** *n.* Neonbeleuchtung, *die;* Neonlicht, *das*

stripling /'strɪplɪŋ/ *n.* Jüngelchen, *das*

strip: ~ mall *n.* (Amer.) Einkaufszeile, *die;* Einkaufszentrum, *das* (*an einer Hauptstraße*); **~ mine** *n.* (Amer. Mining) Tagebau, *der*

stripped pine /strɪpt 'paɪn/ *n.* abgebeizte Kiefer

stripper /'strɪpə(r)/ *n.* 1 (solvent) Farbentferner, *der;* (for wallpaper) Tapetenlöser, *der;* (tool) Kratzer, *der* 2 ▸ℹ **p. 1260** (striptease performer) Stripteasetänzer, *der*/-tänzerin, *die;* Stripper, *der*/Stripperin, *die* (ugs.)

strip: ~ 'poker *n.* (Cards) Strippoker, *das;* **~-search** A *n.: Leibesvisitation, bei der der Durchsuchte sich ausziehen muss;* **do a ~-search on a suspect** *einen Verdächtigen, der sich zuvor ausziehen musste, durchsuchen;* B *v.t.* **we were ~-searched** wir mussten uns zur Durchsuchung ausziehen; **~ show** *n.* Stripshow, *die;* **~'tease** A *n.* Striptease, *der;* B *v.i.* strippen (ugs.)

stripy /'straɪpɪ/ *adj.* gestreift ‹*Fell, Blazer*›; Streifen‹*muster, -stoff*›

strive /straɪv/ *v.i.*, **strove** /strəʊv/, **striven** /'strɪvn/ 1 (endeavour) sich bemühen; **~ to do sth.** bestrebt sein (geh.) *od.* sich bemühen, etw. zu tun; **~ after *or* for sth.** nach etw. streben; **~ after *or* for the right answer** sich bemühen, die richtige Antwort zu finden 2 (contend) kämpfen **(for** um); **~ together *or* with each other [for sth.]** miteinander [um etw.] ringen

striven ▸**strive**

strobe /strəʊb/ (coll.), **stroboscope** /'strəʊbəskəʊp/ *ns.* 1 (instrument) Stroboskop, *das* 2 (lamp) Stroboskoplicht, *das*

stroboscopic /strəʊbə'skɒpɪk/ *adj.* stroboskopisch; **~ lamp/light** Stroboskoplicht, *das*

strode ▸**stride B, C**

stroke[1] /strəʊk/

A *n.* 1 (act of striking) Hieb, *der;* Schlag, *der;* (of sword, axe) Hieb, *der;* (of sword also) Streich, *der* (geh.); **finishing ~** (lit. or fig.) Todesstoß, *der* (*see also* **7**) 2 (Med.) Schlaganfall, *der;* **paralytic/apoplectic ~:** paralytischer/apoplektischer Anfall 3 (sudden impact) **~ of lightning** Blitzschlag, *der;* **by a ~ of fate/fortune** durch eine Fügung des Schicksals/einen [glücklichen] Zufall; **~ of [good] luck** Glücksfall, *der;* **have a ~ of bad/[good] luck** Pech/Glück haben; **by a ~ of bad/[good] luck, the door was locked/open** das Unglück/Glück wollte es, dass die Tür verschlossen/offen war 4 (single effort) Streich, *der;* (skilful effort) Schachzug, *der;* **at a *or* one ~:** auf einen Schlag *od.* Streich; **not do a ~ [of work]** keinen [Hand]schlag tun; **~ of genius** genialer Einfall 5 (of pendulum, heart, wings, oar) Schlag, *der;* (in swimming) Zug, *der;* (of piston) Hub, *der* (Technik) 6 (Billiards etc.) Stoß, *der;* (Tennis, Cricket, Golf, Rowing) Schlag, *der;* (Swimming, Rowing: style) Stil, *der;* **off one's ~** (lit. or fig.) nicht in Form; **put sb. off his/her ~** (lit. or fig.) jmdn. aus dem Takt bringen 7 (mark, line) Strich, *der;* (of handwriting; also fig.: detail) Zug, *der;* (*symbol* /) Schrägstrich, *der;* **with a ~ of the *or* one's pen** mit einem Federstrich; **finishing ~s** (lit. or fig.) letzte Pinselstriche; (fig.) letztes Feilen (*see also* **1**) 8 (sound of clock) Schlag, *der;* **on the ~ of nine** Punkt neun [Uhr]; **it was on the ~ of nine when ...:** es war Schlag neun [Uhr], als ...; **on the ~:** pünktlich 9 (oarsman) Schlagmann, *der*

B *v.t.* (Rowing) als Schlagmann rudern in (+ *Dat.*)

stroke[2]

A *v.t.* streicheln; **~ one's chin/beard** sich (*Dat.*) über das Kinn/den Bart streichen; **~ sth. over/across sth.** mit etw. über etw. (*Akk.*) streichen; **~ one's hand across one's brow** sich (*Dat.*) mit der Hand über die Stirn streichen; **~ sth. back** etw. zurückstreichen

B *n.* **give sb./sth. a ~:** jmdn./etw. streicheln; **give the dog's ears a ~:** dem Hund die Ohren streicheln

Phrasal verb

• **~ 'down** *v.t.* glatt streichen; (fig.) besänftigen

stroke: ~ oar *n.* (Rowing) (oar) Schlagriemen, *der;* (oarsman) Schlagmann, *der;* **~ play** *n.* (Cricket) *Spiel mit spektakulären, mutigen Schlägen*

stroll /strəʊl/

A *v.i.* 1 (saunter) spazieren gehen; **~ into sth.** in etw. (*Akk.*) schlendern 2 (go from place to place) umherziehen; **~ from town to town** von Ort zu Ort ziehen

B *n.* Spaziergang, *der;* **at a ~:** in gemächlichem Schritt *od.* Tempo; **go for a ~:** einen Spaziergang machen

Phrasal verbs

• **~ a'long**

A *v.i.* daherspazieren *od.* -schlendern

B *v.t.* **~ along sth.** an etw. (*Dat.*) entlangspazieren *od.* -schlendern

• **~ 'on** *v.i.* weiterschlendern

S

stroller /ˈstrəʊlə(r)/ *n.* 1 Spaziergänger, *der* 2 (pushchair) Sportwagen, *der*

strong /strɒŋ/

A *adj.*, **~er** /ˈstrɒŋgə(r)/, **~est** /ˈstrɒŋgɪst/ 1 (resistant) stark; gefestigt ‹*Ehe*›; stabil ‹*Möbel*›; solide, fest ‹*Fundament, Schuhe*›; streng ‹*Vorschriften, Vorkehrungen*›; robust ‹*Konstitution, Magen, Stoff, Porzellan*›; (Econ.) stark ‹*Währung*›; **a man of ~ will/resolve** ein willensstarker Mann/Mann von großer Entschlusskraft; **you have to have a ~ stomach** (fig.) man muss einiges vertragen können; **have a ~ head [for alcohol]** viel [Alkohol] vertragen können; **be ~ [again]** ‹*Patient:*› [wieder] gesund sein; **the market [in oil] is ~** (Commerc.) die Nachfrage [nach Öl] ist groß 2 (powerful) stark, kräftig ‹*Person, Tier*›; kräftig ‹*Arme, Beine, Muskeln, Tritt, Schlag, Zähne*›; stark ‹*Linse, Brille, Strom, Magnet*›; gut ‹*Augen*›; **as ~ as a horse** *or* **an ox** (fig.) bärenstark (ugs.); **the ~ silent man/type** der starke, schweigsame Mann/Typ; **a man of ~ character** ein charakterstarker Mann 3 (effective) stark ‹*Regierung, Herrscher, Wille*›; streng ‹*Disziplin, Lehrer*›; gut ‹*Gedächtnis, Schüler*›; fähig ‹*Redner, Mathematiker*›; (formidable) stark ‹*Gegner, Kombination*›; aussichtsreich ‹*Kandidat*›; (powerful in resources) reich ‹*Nation, Land*›; leistungsfähig ‹*Wirtschaft*›; stark ‹*Besetzung*›; (numerous, of specified number) stark ‹*Delegation, Truppe, Kontingent usw.*›; (Cards) gut ‹*Blatt*›; (Games, Sport) spielstark; stark ‹*Mannschaft*›; **she is ~ in Latin** Latein ist ihre Stärke; sie ist gut in Latein; **Latin is her ~est subject** in Latein ist sie am besten; **sb.'s ~ point** jmds. Stärke; **the article is not ~ on facts** in Bezug auf Tatsachen steht der Artikel auf schwachen Füßen; **the company is a dozen ~:** die Firma hat ein Dutzend Mitarbeiter; **a 10,000-~ army** eine 10 000 Mann starke Armee; **fate dealt him a ~ hand** (fig.) das Schicksal hat es gut mit ihm gemeint 4 (convincing) gut, handfest ‹*Grund, Beispiel, Argument*›; **there is a ~ possibility that ...:** es ist sehr wahrscheinlich, dass ... 5 (vigorous, moving forcefully) stark; voll ‹*Unterstützung*›; spannend ‹*Plot*›; fest ‹*Überzeugung*›; kraftvoll ‹*Stil*›; (fervent) glühend ‹*Anhänger, Verfechter einer Sache*›; **take ~ measures/action** energisch vorgehen; **be a ~ believer in sth.** fest an etw. (*Akk.*) glauben 6 (affecting the senses) stark; kräftig, stark ‹*Geruch, Geschmack, Stimme*›; markant ‹*Gesichtszüge*›; (pungent) streng ‹*Geruch, Geschmack*›; kräftig ‹*Käse*›; **the fish smells rather ~:** der Fisch riecht schon sehr 7 (concentrated) stark; konzentriert ‹*Lösung*›; hochprozentig ‹*Alkohol*›; kräftig ‹*Farbe*›; **I need a ~ drink** ich muss mir erst mal einen genehmigen (ugs.) 8 (emphatic) stark ‹*Ausdruck, Protest*›; heftig ‹*Worte, Wortwechsel*›; (Phonet., Pros.) stark betont ‹*Silbe*›; stark ‹*Reim*› 9 (Ling.) stark ‹*Verb, Deklination usw.*›

B *adv.* stark; **the wind was blowing ~:** es wehte ein starker Wind; **come on ~** (coll.) in Fahrt kommen (ugs.); **sb. is going ~:** es geht jmdm. gut; **they are still going ~** (after years of marriage) mit ihnen geht es noch immer gut; (after hours of work) sie sind noch immer eifrig dabei; **the restaurant is still going ~:** das Restaurant geht immer noch gut; *see also* **come 15**

strong: ~ ˈarm *n.*, *no pl.* Muskelkraft, *die*; *attrib.* **~-arm methods** brutale Methoden; **~ box** *n.* Kassette, *die*; **~hold** *n.* Festung, *die*; (fig.) Hochburg, *die*; **~ ˈlanguage** *n.*, *no pl.*, *no indef. art.* derbe Ausdrucksweise; **use ~ language** sich derb ausdrücken

strongly /ˈstrɒŋlɪ/ *adv.* 1 stark; fest ‹*etabliert*›; solide ‹*gearbeitet*›; **~ built** solide gebaut; (in body) kräftig gebaut 2 (powerfully) stark 3 (convincingly) überzeugend ‹*darlegen*› 4 (vigorously) energisch ‹*protestieren, bestreiten*›; nachdrücklich ‹*unterstützen*›; dringend ‹*raten*›; fest ‹*glauben*›; **I feel ~ about it** es ist mir sehr ernst damit; es liegt mir sehr am Herzen; **I ~ suspect that ...:** ich habe den starken Verdacht, dass ...

strong: ~man *n.* Muskelmann, *der* (ugs.); (fig.) (capable man) führender Kopf; (dictator) starker Mann; **~ ˈmeat** *n.*, *no pl.*, *no art.* (fig.) starker Tobak (ugs.); **~-ˈminded** *adj.* [seelisch] robust; (determined) willensstark; **~ point** *n.* (fortified position) Stützpunkt, *der*; *see also* **~ A 3**; **~room** *n.* Tresorraum, *der*; Stahlkammer, *die*; **~ ˈsuit** *n.* (Cards) lange Farbe; (fig.) Stärke, *die*; **~-ˈwilled** *adj.* willensstark

strontium /ˈstrɒntɪəm/ *n.* (Chem.) Strontium, *das*

strop /strɒp/

A *n.* Streichriemen, *der*

B *v.t.*, **-pp-** [auf dem Streichriemen] schärfen

stroppy /ˈstrɒpɪ/ *adj.* (Brit. coll.) pampig (salopp)

strove ▸ **strive**

struck ▸ **strike B, C**

structural /ˈstrʌktʃərl/ *adj.* 1 baulich; Bau‹*material*›; tragend ‹*Wand, Säule, Balken*›; Konstruktions‹*fehler*›; statisch ‹*Probleme*› 2 (Biol.) strukturell; Struktur‹*muster, -merkmal*› 3 (Geol.) tektonisch 4 (Sociol.) strukturell

structural: ~ engiˈneering *n.*, *no pl.* Hochbau, *der*; **~ formula** *n.* (Chem.) Strukturformel, *die*; **~ funds** *n.pl.* (EU) Strukturfonds *Pl.*

structuralism /ˈstrʌktʃərəlɪzm/ *n.*, *no pl.* Strukturalismus, *der*

structuralist /ˈstrʌktʃərəlɪst/

A *n.* Strukturalist, *der*/Strukturalistin, *die*

B *adj.* strukturalistisch

structurally /ˈstrʌktʃərəlɪ/ *adv.* strukturell; (Geol.) tektonisch ‹*geformt*›; **the building is ~ sound** das Gebäude hat eine gute Bausubstanz; **~, the building is ...:** baulich gesehen ist das Gebäude ...

structural: ~ ˈsteel *n.* (Building) Baustahl, *der*; **~ ˈsurvey** *n.* Untersuchung der Bausubstanz; (report) Bauzustandsgutachten, *das*

structure /ˈstrʌktʃə(r)/

A *n.* 1 (manner of construction) Bauweise, *die*; (interrelation of parts; also Anat., Biol., Geol., Ling., Lit., Phys.) Struktur, *die*; Aufbau, *der*; (Mus.) Kompositionsweise, *die*; Struktur, *die*; **bone/skeletal ~:** Knochenbau, *der*/Knochengerüst, *das*; **sentence ~:** Satzbau, *der*; **price ~:** Preisverhältnis, *das* 2 *no pl.*, *no indef. art.* (formal arrangement of parts) Strukturierung, *die*; **people must have ~ in their daily lives** der Mensch braucht eine gewisse Ordnung in seinem Alltag 3 (something constructed) Konstruktion, *die*; (building) Bauwerk, *das*; (complex whole; also Biol.) Struktur, *die*

B *v.t.* strukturieren; regeln ‹*Leben*›; aufbauen ‹*literarisches Werk*›; (construct) konstruieren; bauen

structured /ˈstrʌktʃəd/ *adj.* strukturiert; geregelt ‹*Leben*›

strudel /ˈstru:dl/ *n.* (Gastr.) Strudel, *der*

struggle /ˈstrʌgl/

A *v.i.* 1 (try with difficulty) kämpfen; **~ to do sth.** sich abmühen, etw. zu tun; **~ for a place/a better world** um einen Platz/für eine bessere Welt kämpfen; **~ for breath** nach Atem ringen; **~ against** *or* **with sb./sth.** mit jmdm./etw. *od.* gegen jmdn./etw. kämpfen; **~ with sth.** (try to cope) sich mit etw. quälen; mit etw. kämpfen 2 (proceed with difficulty) sich quälen; (into tight dress, through narrow opening) sich zwängen; **I ~d past** ich kämpfte mich vorbei; **~ to one's feet** unter Schwierigkeiten aufstehen 3 (physically) kämpfen; (resist) sich wehren; **~ free** freikommen; sich befreien 4 (be in difficulties, have difficulty in life) kämpfen (fig.); **after three laps I was struggling** nach drei Runden hatte ich zu kämpfen

B *n.* 1 (exertion) **with a ~:** mit Mühe; **it was a long ~:** es kostete viel Mühe; **after all our valiant ~s** nach all unserem tapferen Bemühen; **have a [hard] ~ to do sth.** [große] Mühe haben, etw. zu tun; **a life of hardship and ~:** ein hartes und mühseliges Leben; **the ~ for freedom** der Kampf für die Freiheit 2 (physical fight) Kampf, *der*; (confused wrestle) Handgemenge, *das*; **legal ~:** Rechtsstreit, *der*; **the ~ against** *or* **with sb./sth.** der Kampf gegen *od.* mit jmdm./etw.; **the ~ for influence/power** der Kampf um Einfluss/die Macht; **the ~ for existence** *or* **life** *or* **survival** der Kampf ums Überleben; **surrender without a ~:** kampflos aufgeben

struggling /ˈstrʌglɪŋ/ *adj.* (in life) *ums Überleben und um Anerkennung kämpfend*

strum /strʌm/

A *v.i.*, **-mm-** klimpern (ugs.) (**on** auf + *Dat.*)

B *v.t.*, **-mm-** klimpern (ugs.) auf (+ *Dat.*)

C *n.* Klimpern, *das* (ugs.); **have a ~:** klimpern (ugs.)

strumpet /ˈstrʌmpɪt/ *n.* (arch./rhet.) Dirne, *die* (veralt.)

strung ▸ **string B**

strut[1] /strʌt/

A *v.i.*, **-tt-** (walk) stolzieren

B *n.* stolzierender Gang

strut[2]

A *n.* (support) Strebe, *die*

B *v.t.*, **-tt-** verstreben

ˈstruth /stru:θ/ *int.* Himmel! (ugs.)

strychnine /ˈstrɪkni:n/ *n.* Strychnin, *das*

Stuart /ˈstju:ət/ (Brit. Hist.)

A *n.* Stuart, *der/die*

B *attrib. adj.* **the ~ dynasty** *etc.* die Dynastie *usw.* der Stuarts

stub /stʌb/

A *n.* 1 (short remaining portion) Stummel, *der*; (of cigarette) Kippe, *die*; **~ of pencil** Bleistiftstummel, *der* 2 (counterfoil) Abschnitt, *der*; (of ticket) Abriss, *der* 3 (of tree, branch, tooth) Stumpf, *der* 4 (limb, tail, etc.) Stummel, *der*

B *v.t.*, **-bb-** 1 **~ one's toe [against** *or* **on sth.]** sich (*Dat.*) den Zeh [an etw. (*Dat.*)] stoßen 2 ausdrücken ‹*Zigarette usw.*›; (with one's foot) austreten ‹*Zigarette usw.*›

Phrasal verb

• **~ ˈout** *v.t.* ausdrücken

ˈstub axle *n.* (Mech.) Achsschenkel, *der*

stubble /ˈstʌbl/ *n.*, *no pl.* Stoppeln *Pl.*

ˈstubble-burning *n.*, *no pl.* Abbrennen *od.* Abflämmen der Stoppelfelder

stubbly /ˈstʌblɪ/ *adj.* stopp[e]lig; **~ field/beard** Stoppelfeld, *das*/-bart, *der* (ugs.)

stubborn /ˈstʌbən/ *adj.* 1 (obstinate) starrköpfig (abwertend); dickköpfig (ugs.); störrisch ‹*Tier, Gesicht, Haltung*›; hartnäckig ‹*Vorurteil, Streit*›; **be ~ in insisting on sth.** stur (ugs. abwertend) auf etw. (*Dat.*) beharren; **[as] ~ as a mule** störrisch wie ein Maulesel (ugs.) 2 (resolute) hartnäckig; fest ‹*Mut, Entschlossenheit, Treue*›; hart ‹*Augen, Kinn*› 3 (intractable) störrisch (fig.); vertrackt (ugs.) ‹*Problem*›; hartnäckig ‹*Unkraut, Krankheit*›

stubbornly /ˈstʌbənlɪ/ *adv.* 1 (obstinately) störrisch; wild ‹*entschlossen*› 2 (resolutely, intractably) hartnäckig

stubbornness /ˈstʌbənnɪs/ *n.*, *no pl.* 1 (obstinacy) Starrköpfigkeit, *die* 2 (resolution, intractability) Hartnäckigkeit, *die*

stubby /ˈstʌbɪ/ *adj.* kurz [und dick]; gedrungen, untersetzt ‹*Person*›; **~ tail** Stummelschwanz, *der*

stucco /ˈstʌkəʊ/

A *n.*, *pl.* **~es** (fine plaster) Stuck, *der*; (coarse plaster) Putz, *der*; (work) Stuckarbeit, *die*; Stuckatur, *die*; *attrib.* Stuck-

B *v.t.* (coat with coarse plaster) verputzen; (decorate with fine plaster) stuckieren

stuck ▸ **stick A, B**

ˈstuck up ▸ **stick up A 5**

stud[1] /stʌd/

A *n.* 1 (boss) Beschlagnagel, *der*; (on clothes) Niete, *die*; (on boot) Stollen, *der*; (marker in road) Nagel, *der* (Verkehrsw.) 2 (for shirt) Knebel, *der*; (cuff link) Manschettenknopf, *der*; (for ear) Ohrstecker, *der*

B *v.t.*, **-dd-** (set with ~s) beschlagen; (be scattered over) verstreut sein über (+ *Akk.*); **~ded** mit Nägeln beschlagen ‹*Tür, Möbel*›; mit Nieten verziert ‹*Jacke, Gürtel*›; **~ded with flowers/stars** *etc.* mit Blumen/Sternen *usw.* übersät; **a jewel-~ded crown** eine juwelenbesetzte Krone

stud[2] *n.* 1 (Breeding) Gestüt, *das*; **put a horse out to ~:** ein Pferd nur noch zur Zucht verwenden 2 (stallion) Deckhengst, *der*; Zuchthengst, *der*; Beschäler, *der* (fachspr.) 3 (sl.: man) Zuchthengst, *der* (derb)

ˈstud book *n.* (Breeding) Stutbuch, *das*; Gestütbuch, *das*

student /ˈstju:dənt/ *n.* Student, *der*/Studentin, *die*; (in school or training establishment) Schüler, *der*/Schülerin, *die*; **a good ~:** ein eifriger Student/Schüler/eine eifrige Studentin/Schülerin;

be a ~ of sth. etw. studieren; **~ of medicine** Student/Studentin der Medizin; Medizinstudent, *der*/-studentin, *die;* **eternal ~:** ewiger Student (ugs.); *attrib.* **~ days** Studenten-/Schulzeit, *die;* **~ demonstration** Studenten-/Schülerdemonstration, *die;* **~ driver** (Amer.) Fahrschüler, *der*/-schülerin, *die;* **~ nurse** Lernschwester, *die*/Pflegeschüler, *der;* **be a ~ doctor/teacher** ein medizinisches Praktikum/Schulpraktikum machen

student: ~ card *n.* Studentenausweis, *der;* **~ 'grant** *n.* [Studien]stipendium, *das;* **~ 'loan** *n.* Studiendarlehen, *das*

studentship /'stju:dəntʃɪp/ *n.* Stipendium, *das*

stud: ~ farm *n.* (Breeding) Gestüt, *das;* **~ horse** ▸**stud² 2**

studied /'stʌdɪd/ *adj.* 1 (thoughtful) [wohl]überlegt 2 (intentional) gewollt; gesucht ‹*Stil, Ausdrucksweise*›; gezielt ‹*Beleidigung*› 3 (well-read) belesen

studiedly /'stʌdɪdlɪ/ *adv.* 1 (thoughtfully) überlegt 2 (intentionally) **be ~ casual** sich gewollt lässig geben

studio /'stju:dɪəʊ/ *n., pl.* **~s** 1 (photographer's or painter's workroom) Atelier, *das;* (workshop for the performing arts) Studio, *das* 2 (Cinemat.) (room) Studio, *das;* (organization) Filmgesellschaft, *die;* **~s** (premises) Studios 3 (Radio, Telev.) Studio, *das*

studio: ~ apartment (esp. Amer.) ▸**~ flat**; **~ 'audience** *n.* (Radio, Telev.) Publikum im Studio; **~ couch** *n.* Schlafcouch, *die;* Bettcouch, *die;* **~ flat** *n.* (esp. Brit.) 1 Atelier, *das;* 2 (one-room flat) Einzimmerwohnung, *die*

studious /'stju:dɪəs/ *adj.* 1 (assiduous in study) lerneifrig; gelehrt ‹*Beschäftigung, Buch, Aussehen, Atmosphäre*›; **~ life** Gelehrtendasein, *das* 2 (earnest) ernsthaft ‹*Anstrengung*›; (intentional) bewusst; **~ to do** *or* **in doing sth.** bemüht, etw. zu tun

studiously /'stju:dɪəslɪ/ *adv.* 1 (with attention to learning) **be ~ inclined** gern studieren; lernbegierig sein 2 (diligently) eifrig; (intentionally) bewusst ‹*rücksichtsvoll, kühl*›; geflissentlich ‹*aus dem Weg gehen*›

studiousness /'stju:dɪəsnɪs/ *n., no pl.* 1 (application to study) Lerneifer, *der* 2 (careful attention) Beflissenheit, *die*

study /'stʌdɪ/

A *n.* 1 Studium, *das;* Lernen, *das;* **I enjoy my studies** das Studium macht mir Spaß; **~ does not come naturally to him** das Lernen fällt ihm nicht leicht; **what branch of ~ is he engaged in?** welche Studienrichtung hat er eingeschlagen?; **the ~ of mathematics/law** das Studium der Mathematik/der Rechtswissenschaft; **be still under ~:** noch untersucht *od.* geprüft werden; **[books on] African/Social Studies** (Educ./Univ.) [Bücher zur] Afrikanistik/Sozialwissenschaft; **graduate studies** (Educ./Univ.) Graduiertenstudium, *das* 2 (piece of work) **a ~ of** *or* **on sth.** eine Studie über etw. (*Akk.*); **studies are being carried out** zurzeit werden Untersuchungen durchgeführt; **make a ~ of sth.** über etw. (*Akk.*) [wissenschaftliche] Untersuchungen anstellen 3 (object of examination) Studienobjekt, *das;* **make sth. one's ~:** sich (*Dat.*) etw. zur Aufgabe machen; **a ~ in sth.** ein Musterbeispiel (fig.) für etw.; **his face was a ~!** sein Gesicht war sehenswert! 4 (Art) Studie, *die;* (Mus.) Etüde, *die;* Übung, *die;* (Lit., Theatre) Studie, *die* (**in, of** über + *Akk.*); **as a ~ in perspective/composition** als perspektivische Studie/Kompositionsstudie 5 (contemplation) Kontemplation, *die; see also* **brown study** 6 (room) Arbeitszimmer, *das*

B *v.t.* 1 (seek knowledge of) studieren; (at school) lernen; **~ politics all one's life/~ Goethe** sich sein Leben lang mit Politik/sich mit Goethe beschäftigen 2 (scrutinize) studieren 3 (read attentively) studieren ‹*Fahrplan*›; sich (*Dat.*) [sorgfältig] durchlesen ‹*Prüfungsfragen, Bericht*› 4 (learn by heart) studieren

C *v.i.* lernen; (at university) studieren; **~ under sb.** bei jmdm. studieren; **~ to be a doctor/teach French** Medizin studieren/Französisch für das Lehramt studieren; **~ for the medical profession** Medizin studieren

study: ~-bedroom *n.* (Brit.) Studentenzimmer, *das;* Studentenbude, *die* (ugs.); **~ group** *n.* Arbeitsgruppe, *die;* Arbeitskreis, *der*

stuff /stʌf/

A *n.* 1 *no pl., no indef. art.* (material[s]) Zeug, *das* (ugs.); (artistic productions) Sachen *Pl.* (ugs.); (coll.: drugs) Stoff, *der* (salopp); (coll.: money) Kohle, *die* (salopp); **garden ~:** Grünzeug, *das* (ugs.); **have the ~ of a champion** das Zeug zum Champion haben (ugs.); **be made of sterner ~:** aus härterem Stoff gemacht sein (fig.); **the ~ of fairy stories** der Stoff für Märchen; **the ~ that dreams/heroes are made of** der Stoff, aus dem die Träume sind/Helden gemacht sind (fig.); **plastic is useful ~:** Plastik ist eine nützliche Sache; **push [the] ~** (coll.: deal in drugs) mit Stoff handeln (salopp); **there has been some interesting ~ in the papers/on the radio** es gab ein paar interessante Sachen in den Zeitungen/im Radio (ugs.); **that actor has been in some good ~ lately** dieser Schauspieler hat zuletzt ein paar gute Sachen gemacht (ugs.) 2 *no pl., no indef. art.* (activity, knowledge) **do painting or drawing, ~ like that** malen oder zeichnen oder so was (ugs.); **do one's ~** (coll.) seine Sache machen; **get on and do your ~!** (coll.) na los, mach schon! (ugs.); **know one's ~** (coll.: be knowledgeable) sich auskennen; (know one's job) seine Sache verstehen; **that's the ~!** (coll.) so ists richtig!; **that's the ~ to give the troops** (fig. coll.) das ist jetzt genau das richtige 3 *no pl.* (valueless matter) Zeug, *das* (ugs. abwertend); **~ [and nonsense]!** (coll.) dummes Zeug! (ugs. abwertend) 4 (Textiles) Wolle, *die;* Wollzeug, *das* (*veralt.*); *attrib.* wollen ‹*Hemd*›. *See also* **bit² 1; hot stuff; kid A 3; rough stuff**

B *v.t.* 1 stopfen; zustopfen ‹*Loch, Ohren*›; (in taxidermy) ausstopfen; (Cookery) füllen; (make eat to repletion) stopfen, nudeln ‹*Gans*›; (coarse: copulate with) stoßen (vulg.); **~ envelopes [with letters]** Briefe in Umschläge stecken; **~ sth. with** *or* **full of sth.** etw. mit etw. voll stopfen (ugs.); **[go and] get ~ed!** (sl.) hau ab! (ugs.); **~ oneself** (sl.) sich voll stopfen (ugs.); **~ one's face** (sl.) sich (*Dat.*) den Bauch voll stopfen (ugs.); **~ ballot boxes** (Amer.: insert bogus votes) Stimmen fälschen; **he ~ed a banknote into my hand** er drückte mir einen Geldschein in die Hand 2 (sl.) **~ him/the family reputation!** zum Teufel mit ihm/der Familienehre!; **~ it!** Scheiß drauf! (derb); **he can ~ it!** er kann mich mal! (derb)

C *v.i.* sich voll stopfen (ugs.)

(Phrasal verb)

- **~ 'up** *v.t.* verstopfen

stuffed: ~ 'shirt *n.* (coll. derog.) Spießer, *der* (ugs. abwertend); **~ 'toy** *n.* Stoffspielzeug, *das;* (animal) Stofftier, *das*

stuffiness /'stʌfɪnɪs/ *n., no pl.* 1 (airlessness) Stickigkeit, *die;* **the ~ of the room** die stickige Luft im Zimmer 2 (congestion) **the ~ in his nose/head** seine verstopfte Nase/entzündete Stirnhöhle 3 (coll.: ill humour) Übellaunigkeit, *die* 4 (coll.: primness) Spießigkeit, *die* (abwertend)

stuffing /'stʌfɪŋ/ *n.* 1 (material) Füllmaterial, *das;* **a ~ of horsehair** eine Füllung aus Rosshaar; **knock** *or* **take the ~ out of sb./a theory** (coll. fig.) jmdn. umhauen (ugs.)/eine Theorie wie ein Kartenhaus in sich zusammenfallen lassen 2 (Cookery) Füllung, *die*

'stuff sack *n.* Packsack, *der*

stuffy /'stʌfɪ/ *adj.* 1 (stifling) stickig ‹*Zimmer, Atmosphäre*› 2 (congested) verstopft; **my head feels very ~:** meine Stirnhöhle ist ganz zu (ugs.) 3 (coll.: ill-humoured) sauertöpfisch (ugs. abwertend); **he got very ~ about it** er reagierte sehr sauer (salopp) [darauf] 4 (coll.: prim) spießig (abwertend) (**about** gegenüber)

stultify /'stʌltɪfaɪ/ *v.t.* 1 (reduce to absurdity) der Lächerlichkeit preisgeben; ins Lächerliche ziehen ‹*Entscheidung, Anstrengungen*› 2 (neutralize) zunichte machen 3 (impair) lähmen; **have a ~ing effect on sth.** sich lähmend auf etw. (*Akk.*) auswirken; **~ing boredom/monotony** lähmende Langeweile/Monotonie

stumble /'stʌmbl/

A *v.i.* 1 stolpern (**over** über + *Akk.*) 2 (falter) stocken; **~ over sth./through life** über etw. (*Akk.*)/durchs Leben stolpern 3 **~ across** *or* **[up]on sb./sth.** (find by chance) über jmdn. stolpern (fig. ugs.)/auf etw. (*Akk.*) stoßen

B *n.* 1 (trip) Stolpern, *das* 2 (error) Stocken, *das*

stumbling block /'stʌmblɪŋ blɒk/ *n.* Stolperstein, *der*

stump /stʌmp/

A *n.* 1 (of tree, branch, tooth) Stumpf, *der;* (of cigar, pencil) Stummel, *der;* **up a ~** (Amer. coll.) aufgeschmissen (salopp) 2 (of limb, tail, etc.) Stummel, *der;* (artificial leg) Stelze, *die;* **~s** (joc.: legs) Stelzen (salopp); *see also* **stir¹ A 2** 3 (Cricket) Stab, *der;* **draw ~s** das Ende des Spieltages ansagen 4 (improvised platform) Rednertribüne, *die;* **on the ~** (coll.) im Wahlkampf; **go on** *or* **take the ~** (lit. or fig.) sich auf die Bühne begeben

B *v.t.* 1 (confound) verwirren; durcheinander bringen; **be ~ed** ratlos sein; **be ~ed for an answer** um eine Antwort verlegen sein; **this problem has got me ~ed** bei diesem Problem weiß ich nicht mehr weiter 2 (Cricket) ausschalten ‹*Schlagmann*› (der außerhalb einer bestimmten Zone steht, durch Umwerfen der Stäbchen) 3 (Amer. Polit.) als Wahlkämpfer bereisen

C *v.i.* 1 (walk stiffly) stapfen; (walk noisily) trampeln 2 (Amer. Polit.: make speeches) sich aufs Podium stellen; **~ing tour** Wahlkampfreise, *die*

(Phrasal verbs)

- **~ 'out** ▸**~ B 2**
- **~ 'up** (Brit. coll.) *v.t. & i.* blechen (ugs.)

stumpy /'stʌmpɪ/ *adj.* gedrungen; **~ tail** Stummelschwanz, *der;* **~ pencil** Bleistiftstummel, *der*

stun /stʌn/ *v.t.*, **-nn-** 1 (knock senseless) betäuben; **be ~ned** (unconscious) bewusstlos sein; (dazed) benommen sein 2 (fig.) **be ~ned at** *or* **by sth.** von etw. wie betäubt sein; **a ~ned silence** ein fassungsloses Schweigen; **a superb performance which ~ned the critics and audience alike** eine herausragende Darbietung, die Kritiker und Publikum gleichermaßen in ihren Bann schlug 3 (deafen temporarily) betäuben; **be ~ned by sth.** von etw. wie betäubt sein

stung ▸**sting B, C**

stun: ~ grenade *n.* Schockgranate, *die;* **~ gun** *n.* [Elektro]schockwaffe, *die*

stunk ▸**stink A**

stunner /'stʌnə(r)/ *n.* (coll.) **be a ~:** Spitze sein (ugs.)

stunning /'stʌnɪŋ/ *adj.* (coll.) 1 (splendid) hinreißend; umwerfend (ugs.); (extremely attractive) klasse [aussehend] ‹*Frau, Mädchen, Blondine*› 2 (causing insensibility) wuchtig ‹*Schlag*› 3 (shocking) bestürzend ‹*Nachricht*›; horrend ‹*Preis*›; (amazing) sensationell

stunningly /'stʌnɪŋlɪ/ *adv.* (coll.) umwerfend (ugs.); unfassbar ‹*langweilig, schrecklich, hässlich*›

stunt¹ /stʌnt/ *v.t.* hemmen, beeinträchtigen ‹*Wachstum, Entwicklung*›; **~ed trees** verkümmerte Bäume; **emotionally ~ed** seelisch verkümmert

stunt²

A *n.* halsbrecherisches Kunststück; (Cinemat.) Stunt, *der;* (Advertising) [Werbe]gag, *der*

B *v.i.* Stunts vollführen

stunt: ~man *n.* Stuntman, *der;* **~ pilot** *n.* Stuntflieger, *der*/-fliegerin, *die;* (aerobatic pilot) Kunstflieger, *der*/-fliegerin, *die;* **~woman** *n.* Stuntfrau, *die*

stupefaction /stju:pɪ'fækʃn/ *n., no pl.* 1 Benommenheit, *die* 2 (astonishment) Verblüffung, *die*

stupefy /'stju:pɪfaɪ/ *v.t.* 1 (benumb) ‹*Hitze:*› benommen machen; ‹*Mühsal:*› abstumpfen; **be stupefied with** *or* **by** benommen sein von ‹*Schlag, Alkohol, Droge*›; abgestumpft sein von ‹*Armut, Kummer*› 2 (astound) die Sprache verschlagen (+ *Dat.*); **be stupefied** wie vor den Kopf geschlagen sein

stupefying /'stju:pɪfaɪɪŋ/ *adj.* die Sinne betäubend ‹*Hitze*›; stumpfsinnig ‹*Arbeit*›; (fig.: astonishing) unfassbar

stupendous /stju:'pendəs/ *adj.* gewaltig; außergewöhnlich ‹*Schönheit, Intelligenz, Talent*›; großartig ‹*Urlaub, Schauspieler*›

S

stupendously /stjuːˈpendəslɪ/ *adv.* außergewöhnlich; gewaltig ‹*groß*›; großartig ‹*sich verhalten*›

stupid /ˈstjuːpɪd/

A *adj.*, **~er** /ˈstjuːpɪdə(r)/, **~est** /ˈstjuːpɪdɪst/ **1** (slow-witted, unintelligent) dumm; einfältig ‹*Person, Aussehen*›; (ridiculous) lächerlich; (pointless) dumm (ugs.) ‹*Witz, Geschichte, Gedanke*›; *expr. rejection or irritation* blöd (ugs.); **where is that ~ key?** wo ist jetzt der blöde (ugs.) Schlüssel?; **it would be ~ to do sth.** es wäre töricht, etw. zu tun; **that was a ~ place to leave the car** es war töricht, das Auto dort abzustellen **2** (in state of stupor) benommen (**with** von); teilnahmslos, apathisch ‹*Blick*›; **be bored ~:** zu Tode gelangweilt sein

B *n.* (coll.) Dummkopf, *der* (ugs.)

stupidity /stjuːˈpɪdɪtɪ/ *n.* Dummheit, *die;* (of action also) Torheit, *die;* (of facial expression) Einfältigkeit, *die*

stupidly /ˈstjuːpɪdlɪ/ *adv.* dumm; **~ [enough], I have ...:** dummerweise habe ich ...; **he ~ admitted that ...:** törichterweise hat er zugegeben, dass ...

stupor /ˈstjuːpə(r)/ *n.* **1** (torpidity) Benommenheit, *die;* (Med.) Stupor, *der;* **drink oneself into a ~:** sich bis zur Bewusstlosigkeit betrinken; **in a drunken ~:** sinnlos betrunken **2** (apathy) Erstarrung, *die* **3** (amazement) **stand in a ~:** starr vor Staunen stehen

sturdily /ˈstɜːdɪlɪ/ *adv.* (robustly) fest ‹*annageln*›; mit festem Schritt ‹*gehen*›; (resolutely) fest ‹*überzeugt*›; entschlossen ‹*sich entgegenstellen*›; **~ built** kräftig [gebaut] ‹*Person, Pferd*›; stabil [gebaut] ‹*Stuhl, Fahrrad*›

sturdiness /ˈstɜːdɪnɪs/ *n., no pl.* (robustness) Stabilität, *die;* (of person) Stämmigkeit, *die;* (resoluteness) Stärke, *die;* Festigkeit, *die*

sturdy /ˈstɜːdɪ/ *adj.* (robust) stabil ‹*Haus, Stuhl, Schiff*›; kräftig ‹*Rasse, Pflanze, Pferd, Kind*›; kräftig [gebaut] ‹*Person*›; (resistant to disease or rough weather) robust; (thickset) stämmig ‹*Person*›; (strong) stämmig ‹*Beine, Arme*›; (sound) solide; (resolute) fest ‹*Glaube, Grundsätze*›; stark ‹*Gegner, Verfechter, Widerstand*›

sturgeon /ˈstɜːdʒən/ *n.* (Zool.) Stör, *der*

stutter /ˈstʌtə(r)/

A *v.i.* stottern; ‹*Gewehr:*› tacken

B *v.t.* stottern

C *n.* Stottern, *das;* (of gun) Tacken, *das;* (of flame) Flackern, *das;* **speak with a ~:** stottern; **have a bad ~:** stark stottern

Phrasal verb

• **~ ˈout** *v.t.* stotternd hervorbringen

stutterer /ˈstʌtərə(r)/ *n.* Stotterer, *der*/Stotterin, *die*

sty¹ /staɪ/ ▸ **pigsty**

sty², stye /staɪ/ *n.* ▸ⓘ **p. 1231** (Med.) Gerstenkorn, *das*

Stygian /ˈstɪdʒɪən/ *adj.* (Mythol.; also fig.) stygisch

style /staɪl/

A *n.* **1** (manner) Stil, *der;* (in conversation) Ton, *der;* (in performance) Art, *die;* **~ of swimming/running** Schwimm-/Laufstil, *der;* **that's the ~!** so ist es richtig!; **be bad** *or* **not good ~:** schlechter *od.* kein guter Stil sein **2** (collective features) (in artistic presentation; also Printing, Publishing) Stil, *der;* (of habitual behaviour) Art, *die;* **it's not my ~ [to do that]** das ist nicht mein Stil; **dress in the latest/modern ~:** sich nach der neuesten/neuen Mode kleiden; **the costumes were in** *or* **of the ~ of the 1940s** es waren Kostüme im Stil der 40er-Jahre; **cook in the French ~:** französisch kochen; *see also* **cramp B 1; house style 3** (superior way of living, behaving, etc.) Stil, *der;* **in ~:** stilvoll; (on a grand scale) im großen Stil; **in the grand ~:** im großen Stil; **she is a woman of ~:** sie hat Stil; **live a life of ~:** ein luxuriöses Leben führen; **have no ~:** keinen Stil haben **4** (sort) Art, *die;* **~ of music** Musikrichtung, *die;* **she is not his ~:** sie passt nicht zu ihm; **this house is not my ~:** das Haus ist nichts für mich **5** (pattern) Art, *die;* (of clothes) Machart, *die;* (hair~) Frisur, *die;* **she has had her hair cut in a pageboy ~:** sie hat sich (*Dat.*) einen Pagenkopf schneiden lassen; **have one's hair done in a different ~:** sich (*Dat.*) eine andere Frisur machen lassen **6** (descriptive formula) Titel, *der;* (of firm) Firmenbezeichnung, *die;* **~ [of address]** Anrede, *die* **7** (Bot.) Griffel, *der*

B *v.t.* **1** (design) entwerfen; stilisieren (veralt.); **~ one's own hair** sich (*Dat.*) seine Frisuren selbst machen; **elegantly ~d clothes** elegant geschnittene Kleidung; **clothes ~d for comfort** bequem geschnittene Kleidung **2** (designate) nennen; (address) anreden; **~ oneself sth.** sich bezeichnen als etw.

-style *in comb.* **a Tudor-~ house** ein Haus im Tudorstil; **a Queen-Anne-~ chair** ein Queen-Anne-Stuhl; **Indian-~ curry** indischer Curry; **French-~ cooking** französische Küche; **peasant-~ skirt** Bauernrock, *der;* **dressed cowboy-~:** wie ein Cowboy gekleidet

style: **~ book** *n.* Buch mit Modellen; (of hairdresser) Frisurenheft, *das;* (Printing, Publishing) Buch mit Satzanweisungen; **~ guru** *n.* Stilguru, *der;* **~ sheet** *n.* (Computing) Formatvorlage, *die*

styling /ˈstaɪlɪŋ/ *n.* **1** (imparting of style) Styling, *das;* **that hairdresser is good at ~:** dieser Friseur kann gut [neue] Frisuren entwerfen **2** (Lit., Publishing) stilistische Überarbeitung **3** (ornamentation) **intricate ~:** komplizierte Verzierungen

stylise ▸ **stylize**

stylish /ˈstaɪlɪʃ/ *adj.* stilvoll; elegant ‹*Kleidung, Auto, Hotel, Person*›

stylishly /ˈstaɪlɪʃlɪ/ *adv.* stilvoll; elegant ‹*geschnitten, angezogen*›; **~ elegant** vornehm und elegant

stylishness /ˈstaɪlɪʃnɪs/ *n., no pl.* Stil, *der;* (of clothes) Eleganz, *die*

stylist /ˈstaɪlɪst/ *n.* ▸ⓘ **p. 1260** **1** (Lit., Sport) Stilist, *der*/Stilistin, *die* **2** (designer) Designer, *der*/Designerin, *die;* (hair~) Haarstilist, *der*/-stilistin, *die*

stylistic /staɪˈlɪstɪk/ *adj.* stilistisch; Stil‹*mittel, -merkmale*›

stylistically /staɪˈlɪstɪkəlɪ/ *adv.* stilistisch

stylistics /staɪˈlɪstɪks/ *n., no pl.* Stilistik, *die*

stylize /ˈstaɪlaɪz/ *v.t.* stilisieren

stylus /ˈstaɪləs/ *n., pl.* **styli** /ˈstaɪlaɪ/ *or* **~es** **1** (record player needle) [Abtast]nadel, *die;* **sapphire/diamond ~:** Saphir, *der*/Diamant, *der* **2** (writing tool) Griffel, *der;* (engraving-tool) Grabstichel, *der*

stymie /ˈstaɪmɪ/

A *n.* (difficult situation) Sackgasse, *die* (fig.)

B *v.t.* (thwart) in die Klemme (ugs.) geraten lassen; **be ~d** aufgeschmissen sein (salopp); **~ oneself** sich (*Dat.*) selber ein Bein stellen

styptic /ˈstɪptɪk/

A *adj.* blutstillend

B *n.* blutstillendes Mittel; Hämostyptikum, *das* (Med.)

Styria /ˈstɪrɪə/ *pr. n.* Steiermark, *die*

styrofoam (Amer. ®) /ˈstaɪrəfəʊm/ *n., no pl.* ≈ Styropor Ⓦⓩ, *das*

Styx /stɪks/ *pr. n.* (Greek Mythol.) Styx, *der;* **cross the ~** (fig.) den Styx überqueren (geh.)

suave /swɑːv/ *adj.* **1** (affable) verbindlich **2** (agreeable) sanft ‹*Farbe, Licht, Musik*›; lieblich ‹*Wein, Geschmack*›

suavely /ˈswɑːvlɪ/ *adv.* **1** (affably) verbindlich; **he was always ~ polite** er war stets verbindlich und höflich **2** (agreeably) sanft

suavity /ˈswɑːvɪtɪ/ *n.* **1** (affability) Verbindlichkeit, *die* **2** (agreeableness) [angenehme] Milde; **suavities** Annehmlichkeiten

sub /sʌb/ (coll.)

A *n.* **1** (subscription) Abo, *das* (ugs.) **2** (esp. Sport: substitute) Ersatz, *der* **3** (submarine) U-Boot, *das* **4** ▸ **subeditor**

B *v.i.*, **-bb-** ▸ **subedit**

sub- *pref.* unter-; (mit Fremdwörtern meist) sub-

subˈalpine *adj.* (Geog.) (of higher mountain slopes) subalpin (fachspr.); (of lower Alpine slopes) Voralpen-

subaltern /ˈsʌbltən/ *n.* (Brit. Mil.) Subalternoffizier, *der*

subaqua /sʌbˈækwə/ *adj.* Tauch‹*sport, -klub*›

subaˈtomic *adj.* (Phys.) subatomar

ˈsubcategory *n.* Subkategorie, *die*

ˈsubclass *n.* (esp. Biol.) Unterklasse, *die*

ˈsubcommittee *n.* Unterausschuss, *der*

subˈconscious (Psych.)

A *adj.* unterbewusst; **~ mind** Unterbewusstsein, *das*

B *n.* Unterbewusstsein, *das*

subˈconsciously *adv.* (Psych.) unterbewusst

subˈcontinent *n.* (Geog.) Subkontinent, *der*

subcontract

A /sʌbkənˈtrækt/ *v.t.* (accept under secondary contract) als Subunternehmer übernehmen; (offer under secondary contract) an Subunternehmer/an einen Subunternehmer vergeben; **~ a job to sb.** eine Arbeit an jmdn. [in einem Untervertrag] vergeben

B *v.i.* (accept secondary contract) als Subunternehmer arbeiten; (offer secondary contract) Aufträge an Subunternehmer/an einen Subunternehmer vergeben

C /sʌbˈkɒntrækt/ *n.* Untervertrag, *der*

subconˈtractor *n.* ▸ⓘ **p. 1260** Subunternehmer, *der*/-unternehmerin, *die*

ˈsubculture *n.* (Sociol.) Subkultur, *die*

subcuˈtaneous *adj.* (Anat.) subkutan

ˈsubdirectory *n.* (Computing) Unterverzeichnis, *das*

subdivide /ˈsʌbdɪvaɪd, sʌbdɪˈvaɪd/

A *v.t.* (further divide) erneut teilen; (divide into parts) unterteilen

B *v.i.* **~ into sth.** sich in etw. (*Akk.*) teilen

subdivision /ˈsʌbdɪvɪʒn, sʌbdɪˈvɪʒn/ *n.* (subdividing) erneute Teilung; (subordinate division) Unterabteilung, *die;* **~ [of sth.] into sth.** Unterteilung [einer Sache (*Gen.*)] in etw. (*Akk.*)

subˈdominant *n.* (Mus.) Subdominante, *die*

subdue /səbˈdjuː/ *v.t.* (conquer) besiegen; unterwerfen; (bring under control) bändigen ‹*Kind, Tier*›; ruhig stellen ‹*Patienten*›; unter Kontrolle bringen ‹*Demonstranten usw.*›; bezähmen ‹*Gefühle, zornige Person*›; urbar machen ‹*Land*›; (reduce in intensity) dämpfen ‹*Zorn, Heftigkeit, gute Laune, Lärm, Licht*›; abkühlen (fig.) ‹*Leidenschaft*›; verblassen lassen ‹*Farben*›

subdued /səbˈdjuːd/ *adj.* gedämpft; **he seemed rather ~:** er schien ziemlich gedämpfter Stimmung zu sein

subˈedit *v.t.* (Journ., Publishing) **1** (be assistant editor of) mit herausgeben **2** (Brit.: prepare copy for) redigieren

subˈeditor *n.* ▸ⓘ **p. 1260** (Journ., Publishing) **1** (assistant editor) Mitherausgeber, *der*/Mitherausgeberin, *die* **2** (Brit.: one who prepares material) Redaktionsassistent, *der*/-assistentin, *die*

ˈsubgroup *n.* Untergruppe, *die*

ˈsubhead, ˈsubheading *ns.* **1** (subordinate division) Unterabschnitt, *der* **2** (subordinate title) Untertitel, *der*

subˈhuman *adj.* unmenschlich; (Zool.) menschenähnlich; **treat sb. as ~:** jmdn. wie einen Untermenschen behandeln

subject

A /ˈsʌbdʒɪkt/ *n.* **1** (citizen) Staatsbürger, *der*/-bürgerin, *die;* (in relation to monarch) Untertan, *der*/Untertanin, *die;* (under domination) Sklave, *der*/Sklavin, *die* (fig.) **2** (topic) Thema, *das;* (department of study) Fach, *das;* (area of knowledge) Fach[gebiet], *das;* (Art) Motiv, *das;* Sujet, *das* (geh.); (Mus.) Thema, *das;* **sb. is the ~ of a book** über jmdn. ist ein Buch geschrieben worden; **be the ~ of an investigation** Gegenstand einer Untersuchung sein; **on the ~ of money** über das Thema Geld ‹*reden usw.*›; beim Thema Geld ‹*sein, bleiben*›; **change the ~:** das Thema wechseln **3** **be a ~ for sth.** (cause sth.) zu etw. Anlass geben; **she was a ~ for ridicule** man machte sich über sie lustig **4** (Ling., Logic, Philos.) Subjekt, *das* **5** (Med.) Patient, *der;* (of scientific research) Versuchsperson, *die*/-tier, *das*/-objekt, *das. See also* **liberty**

B *adj.* **1** (conditional) **be ~ to sth.** von etw. abhängig sein *od.* abhängen; **sth. is ~ to alteration** etw. kann geändert werden; **prices/dates/programme details [are] ~ to**

S

alteration without further notice Preis-/Termin-/Programmänderungen [sind] vorbehalten **2▸** (prone) **be ~ to** anfällig sein für ‹*Krankheit*›; neigen zu ‹*Melancholie*›; ausgesetzt sein (+ *Dat.*) ‹*Missdeutung, Feuchtigkeit*› **3▸** (dependent) abhängig; **~ to** (dependent on) untertan (+ *Dat.*) ‹*König usw.*›; unterworfen (+ *Dat.*) ‹*Verfassung, Gesetz, Krone*›; untergeben (+ *Dat.*) ‹*Dienstherrn*›

C *adv.* **~ to sth.** vorbehaltlich einer Sache (*Gen.*); **~ to the weather['s] being fine** vorausgesetzt, das Wetter ist gut

D /səbˈdʒekt/ *v.t.* **1▸** (subjugate, make submissive) unterwerfen; **~ sb./sth. to sb./sth.** jmdn./etw. jmdm./einer Sache unterwerfen **2▸** (expose) **~ sb./sth. to sth.** jmdn./etw. einer Sache (*Dat.*) aussetzen; **~ sb. to torture** jmdn. der Folter unterwerfen; **~ sth. to chemical analysis** etw. einer chemischen Analyse unterziehen

ˈsubject: ~ catalogue *n.* Schlagwortkatalog, *der;* **~ heading** *n.* Stichwort, *das;* **~ index** *n.* Sachregister, *das*

subjection /səbˈdʒekʃn/ *n.* (subjugation) Unterwerfung, *die* (**to** unter + *Akk.*); (condition of being subject) Abhängigkeit, *die* (**to** von)

subjective /səbˈdʒektɪv/ *adj.* **1▸** subjektiv **2▸** (Ling.) Subjekt-; **be ~:** Subjekt sein

subjectively /səbˈdʒektɪvlɪ/ *adv.* **1▸** subjektiv; **~ speaking, I like him** ich persönlich mag ihn **2▸** (Ling.) als Subjekt ‹*gebrauchen*›

subjectiveness /səbˈdʒektɪvnɪs/, **subjectivity** /sʌbdʒɪkˈtɪvɪtɪ/ *ns., no pl.* Subjektivität, *die*

ˈsubject matter *n., no pl., no indef. art.* Gegenstand, *der;* **make good ~ for sth.** ein gutes Thema für etw. abgeben

sub judice /sʌb ˈdʒuːdɪsɪ, sʊb ˈjuːdɪkeɪ/ *adj.* (Law) anhängig; (not decided) [noch] nicht entschieden

subjugate /ˈsʌbdʒʊgeɪt/ *v.t.* **1▸** (conquer) unterjochen (**to** unter + *Akk.*) **2▸** (subdue) bezwingen; bändigen ‹*Kind, Pferd*›

subjugation /sʌbdʒʊˈgeɪʃn/ *n.* **1▸** (conquest) Unterjochung, *die* (**to** unter + *Akk.*) **2▸** (moral subjection) (action) Knechtung, *die* (geh. abwertend); (result) Knechtschaft, *die;* (of passions etc.) Bezwingung, *die;* Unterwerfung, *die* (**to** unter + *Akk.*); (condition) sklavische Abhängigkeit (**to** von)

subjunctive /səbˈdʒʌŋktɪv/ (Ling.)

A *adj.* konjunktivisch; Konjunktiv-

B *n.* Konjunktiv, *der;* **past/present ~:** Konjunktiv II *od.* Präteritum/Konjunktiv I *od.* Präsens

subjunctive ˈmood *n.* (Ling.) Konjunktiv, *der*

subˈlease ▸**sublet**

subˈlet *v.t.*, **-tt-, subˈlet** untervermieten

sub lieuˈtenant *n.* (Brit. Navy) Oberleutnant zur See

sublimate

A /ˈsʌblɪmeɪt/ *v.t.* (Chem., Psych.; also fig.) sublimieren

B /ˈsʌblɪmət/ *n.* (sublimated substance) Sublimat, *das* (Chemie)

sublimation /sʌblɪˈmeɪʃn/ *n.* **1▸** (Chem.) (act) Sublimierung, *die;* (process) Sublimation, *die;* (substance) Sublimat, *das* **2▸** (elevation; Psych.: diversion) Sublimierung, *die* (**to** zu, **into** in + *Akk.*); Sublimation, *die*

sublime /səˈblaɪm/

A *adj.*, **~r** /səˈblaɪmə(r)/, **~st** /səˈblaɪmɪst/ (exalted) erhaben; (iron.) vollendet (fig. iron.) ‹*Chaos*›; unglaublich ‹*Frechheit*›; **sth. goes from the ~ to the ridiculous** (iron.) etw. ist ein echter Abstieg [ins Profane]

B *v.t.* (Chem.) **1▸** (convert) sublimieren **2▸** (release) freisetzen

C *v.i.* (Chem.) sublimieren

sublimely /səˈblaɪmlɪ/ *adv.* schlechthin vollkommen ‹*tanzen*›; erhaben ‹*handeln, edel*›; (iron.) vollkommen ‹*töricht, betrunken*›; völlig ‹*ohne Ahnung*›; **~ beautiful** von erhabener Schönheit *nachgestellt*

subliminal /sʌbˈlɪmɪnl/ *adj.* (Physiol., Psych.) unterschwellig; subliminal (fachspr.); **~ advertising** unterschwellige Werbung

sublimity /səˈblɪmɪtɪ/ *n.* (literary) Erhabenheit, *die;* (high degree) hoher Grad (**of** an + *Dat.*)

Sub-Lt. *abbr.* (Brit. Navy) **= Sub Lieutenant** Olt. zur See

sub-maˈchine gun *n.* Maschinenpistole, *die*

submarine /sʌbməˈriːn, ˈsʌbməriːn/

A *n.* Unterseeboot, *das;* U-Boot, *das*

B *adj.* Unterwasser-; unterseeisch (Geol.); submarin (fachspr.); **~ warfare** U-Boot-Krieg, *der*

submariner /sʌbˈmærɪnə(r)/ *n.* ▸❶ **p. 1260** U-Boot-Fahrer, *der*/-Fahrerin, *die*

ˈsubmenu *n.* (Computing) Untermenü, *das*

submerge /səbˈmɜːdʒ/

A *v.t.* **1▸** (place under water) **~ sth. [in the water]** etw. eintauchen *od.* ins Wasser tauchen; **be ~d [at high tide]** [bei Flut] unter Wasser stehen **2▸** (inundate) ‹*Wasser:*› überschwemmen; **be ~d in water** unter Wasser stehen **3▸** (fig.: obscure, bury) **be ~d by** *or* **in sth.** unter etw. (*Dat.*) verborgen sein

B *v.i.* abtauchen (Seemannsspr.)

submerged /səbˈmɜːdʒd/ *adj.* versunken ‹*Schiff, Stadt*›; überschwemmt ‹*Felder*›; unter Wasser befindlich ‹*Fels, Eisberg*›; **~ in work** (fig.) mit Arbeit überhäuft; **~ by debts** (fig.) bis über die Ohren verschuldet (ugs.)

submersible /səbˈmɜːsɪbl/

A *adj.* tauchfähig

B *n.* Tauchboot, *das*

submersion /səbˈmɜːʃn/ *n.* Eintauchen, *das;* (in baptism) Submersion, *die* (Theol.); **the watch will not withstand ~:** die Uhr ist nicht wasserfest

subˈminiature *adj.* Subminiatur-; (Photog.) Kleinstbild-

submission /səbˈmɪʃn/ *n.* **1▸** (surrender) Unterwerfung, *die* (**to** unter + *Akk.*); **force/frighten sb. into ~:** jmdn. zwingen, sich zu unterwerfen/jmdm. durch Einschüchterung seinen Willen aufzwingen **2▸** *no pl., no art.* (meekness) Unterwerfung, *die;* **attitude of ~:** Demutshaltung, *die* (Verhaltensf.) **3▸** (presentation) Einreichung, *die* (**to** bei); (thing put forward) Einsendung, *die;* (by witness) Aussage, *die;* **in my ~:** meiner Meinung nach

submissive /səbˈmɪsɪv/ *adj.* gehorsam; unterwürfig (abwertend); **be ~ to sb./sth.** sich jmdm./einer Sache unterwerfen

submissively /səbˈmɪsɪvlɪ/ *adv.* gehorsam; unterwürfig (abwertend)

submissiveness /səbˈmɪsɪvnɪs/ *n., no pl.* Gehorsam, *der;* Unterwürfigkeit, *die* (abwertend)

submit /səbˈmɪt/

A *v.t.*, **-tt- 1▸** (present) einreichen; vorbringen ‹*Vorschlag*›; abgeben ‹[*Doktor*]*arbeit usw.*›; **~ sth. for sb.'s approval/perusal** jmdm. etw. zur Billigung vorlegen/zu lesen geben; **~ sth. to sb.** jmdm. etw. vorlegen; **~ sth. to scrutiny/investigation** etw. einer Prüfung/Untersuchung unterziehen; **~ sth. to sb.'s examination** jmdm. etw. zur Prüfung vorlegen; **~ one's entry to a competition** seine Teilnehmerkarte *usw.* für ein Preisausschreiben einsenden; **entries must be ~ted by 1 May** Einsendeschluss ist der 1. Mai; **~ that ...** (urge deferentially) behaupten, dass … **2▸** (surrender) **~ oneself to sb./sth.** sich jmdm./einer Sache unterwerfen; **~ oneself to Fate** sich in sein Schicksal fügen; **~ oneself to ridicule** sich dem Spott aussetzen **3▸** (subject) **~ sth. to heat** etw. der Hitze (*Dat.*) aussetzen; **~ oneself to sth.** sich einer Sache (*Dat.*) unterziehen

B *v.i.*, **-tt- 1▸** (surrender) aufgeben; sich unterwerfen (**to** *Dat.*); **~ to sb.'s charms** jmds. Zauber (*Dat.*) erliegen; **~ to sb.'s request** jmds. Bitte (*Dat.*) nachkommen **2▸** (defer) **~ to sb./sth.** sich jmdm./einer Sache beugen **3▸** (agree to undergo) **~ to sth.** sich einer Sache (*Dat.*) aussetzen

ˈsubnetwork *n.* (Computing) Unternetz, *das*

subˈnormal *adj.* unterdurchschnittlich; subnormal (Med.); (in intelligence) minderbegabt

subordinate

A /səˈbɔːdɪnət/ *adj.* (inferior) untergeordnet; (lower-ranking) rangniedriger; (secondary) zweitrangig; **be ~ to sb./sth.** jmdm./einer Sache untergeordnet sein; **be of ~ importance** von untergeordneter Bedeutung sein; *see also* **clause 2**

B *n.* Untergebene, *der/die*

C /səˈbɔːdɪneɪt/ *v.t.* (place in lower class) niedriger einstufen (**to** als); (render subject; also Ling.) unterordnen (**to** *Dat.*)

suborn /səˈbɔːn/ *v.t.* anstiften; (by bribery) bestechen

ˈsubplot *n.* Nebenhandlung, *die*

subpoena /səbˈpiːnə, səˈpiːnə/ (Law)

A *n.* Vorladung, *die:* **serve a ~ [up]on sb.** jmdm. eine Vorladung persönlich zustellen

B *v.t.*, **~ed** *or* **~'d** /səbˈpiːnəd, səˈpiːnəd/ vorladen

sub rosa /sʌb ˈrəʊzə/ (literary)

A *adj.* Sub-rosa- (geh.); [streng] geheim

B *adv.* sub rosa (geh.); in aller Heimlichkeit

ˈsubroutine *n.* (Computing) Unterprogramm, *das;* Subroutine, *die*

sub-Saˈharan *adj.* Subsahara-

subscribe /səbˈskraɪb/

A *v.t.* **1▸** (sign one's name to) unterzeichnen **2▸** ([promise to] contribute) **~ sth.** zusichern, etw. zu spenden; **be ~d** als Spende zugesichert worden sein; **have ~d half the costs** sich verpflichtet haben, die Hälfte der Kosten zu übernehmen

B *v.i.* **1▸** (express adhesion) **~ to sth.** sich einer Sache (*Dat.*) anschließen **2▸** (sign one's name) unterzeichnen (**to** *Akk.*) **3▸** ([promise to] make contribution) **~ to** *or* **for sth.** eine Spende für etw. zusichern; **~ to [a newspaper]** [eine Zeitung] abonnieren

subscriber /səbˈskraɪbə(r)/ *n.* **1▸** (one who signs) Unterzeichner, *der*/Unterzeichnerin, *die* (**of, to** *Gen.*); Unterzeichnete, *der/die* (Amtsdt.) **2▸** (one who assents) Befürworter, *der*/Befürworterin, *die* (**to** *Gen.*) **3▸** (contributor) Spender, *der*/Spenderin, *die* (**of, to** für); (to a newspaper etc.) Abonnent, *der*/Abonnentin, *die* (**to** *Gen.*); (of a society etc.) Mitglied, *das* **4▸** (Teleph.) Fernsprechkunde, *der*/-kundin, *die*

subscriber trunk ˈdialling *n.* (Brit. Teleph.) Selbstwählferndienst, *der*

ˈsubscript (Math. etc.)

A *adj.* tiefgestellt

B *n.* [tiefgestellter] Index

subscription /səbˈskrɪpʃn/ *n.* **1▸** (thing subscribed) Spendenbeitrag, *der* (**to** für); (membership fee) Mitgliedsbeitrag, *der* (**to** für); (prepayment for newspaper etc.) Abonnement, *das* (**to** *Gen.*); **[buy] by ~:** im Abonnement [beziehen]; **a year's ~:** ein Jahresabonnement **2▸** (act of subscribing) (signing) Unterzeichnung, *die;* (subscribing money) Spende, *die;* **[be built] by ~:** mit Spenden [gebaut werden] **3▸** (Publishing: offer of lower price) Subskription, *die*

subscription: ~ concert *n.* Abonnementskonzert, *das;* **~ fee** *n.* (for membership) [Mitglieds]beitrag, *der;* (for magazine) Abonnement[s]preis, *der;* **~ library** *n.* (Mitgliedsbeiträge erhebende) Leihbücherei

ˈsubsection *n.* Unterabschnitt, *der*

subsequent /ˈsʌbsɪkwənt/ *adj.* folgend; nachfolgend ‹*Kind*›; später ‹*Gelegenheit*›; **~ events** spätere *od.* die folgenden Ereignisse

subsequently *adv.* später; danach

subservience /səbˈsɜːvɪəns/ *n., no pl.* **1▸** (subordination) Abhängigkeit, *die* (**to** von) **2▸** (obsequiousness) Unterwürfigkeit, *die*

subservient /səbˈsɜːvɪənt/ *adj.* **1▸** (merely instrumental) dienend; **be ~ to sb./sth.** jmdm./einer Sache dienen **2▸** (subordinate) untergeordnet (**to** *Dat.*) **3▸** (obsequious) unterwürfig; servil (abwertend)

ˈsubset *n.* (Math.) Teilmenge, *die*

subside /səbˈsaɪd/ *v.i.* **1▸** (sink to lower level) ‹*Wasser, Flut, Fluss:*› sinken; ‹*Boden, Haus:*› sich senken; ‹*Schwellung:*› zurückgehen; ‹*schwebende Teile:*› absinken, sich absetzen; **~ in exhaustion** erschöpft zusammensinken; **~ [on] to one's knees/the ground** auf die Knie/zu Boden sinken **2▸** (abate) nachlassen; ‹*Wellen, Wind, Wut, Lärm, Beifall, Aufregung:*› sich legen; ‹*Fieber, Delirium, Migräne:*› abklingen; (cease activity) müde werden; ermatten (geh.); **~ into** verfallen in (+ *Akk.*) ‹*Untätigkeit, Schweigen usw.*›

S

subsidence /səbˈsaɪdəns, ˈsʌbsɪdəns/ *n.* [1] (sinking) (of ground, structure) Senkung, *die;* (of liquid) Sinken, *das;* (of swelling) Zurückgehen, *das;* (of suspended matter) Sichabsetzen, *das* [2] (abatement) ▸**subside 2**: Nachlassen, *das;* Sichlegen, *das;* Abklingen, *das;* **~ into sth.** Verfallen in etw. (*Akk.*)

subsidiarity /sʌbsɪdɪˈærɪtɪ/ *n., no pl.* (EU) Subsidiarität, *die*

subsidiary /səbˈsɪdɪərɪ/

A *adj.* [1] (auxiliary) unterstützend; subsidiär (fachspr.); untergeordnet ‹*Funktion, Stellung*›; Neben‹*fach, -fluss, -aspekt*›; **~ fund** Hilfsfond, *der;* **~ to sth.** einer Sache (*Dat.*) untergeordnet; (secondary) gegenüber einer Sache zweitrangig [2] (Commerc.) **~ company** ▸**B**

B *n.* (Commerc.) Tochtergesellschaft, *die*

subsidisation, subsidise ▸**subsidiz-**

subsidization /sʌbsɪdaɪˈzeɪʃn/ *n.* (act of subsidizing) Subventionierung, *die;* (money given as subsidy) Subventionen; (of individual person) finanzielle Unterstützung

subsidize /ˈsʌbsɪdaɪz/ *v.t.* subventionieren; finanziell unterstützen ‹*Person*›

subsidy /ˈsʌbsɪdɪ/ *n.* Subvention, *die;* **receive a ~:** subventioniert werden; **grant/pay a ~ to sb./sth.** jmdn./etw. subventionieren; jmdn./etw. mit öffentlichen Mitteln fördern

subsist /səbˈsɪst/ *v.i.* [1] ([continue to] exist) existieren; (remain in force) bestehen [2] (keep oneself alive) existieren; subsistieren (veralt.); **~ on sth.** von etw. leben

subsistence /səbˈsɪstəns/ *n.* [1] (subsisting) [Über]leben, *das;* **be enough for a bare ~:** gerade genug zum [Über]leben sein; ‹*Einkommen:*› das Existenzminimum sein; **~ is not possible under these conditions** unter diesen Bedingungen kann man nicht leben *od.* existieren [2] **[means of] ~:** Lebensgrundlage, *die;* **millet is their chief means of ~:** sie leben hauptsächlich von Hirse

subsistence: ~ allowance *n.* Außendienstzulage, *die;* (abroad) Auslandszulage, *die;* **~ eˈconomy** *n.* Subsistenzwirtschaft, *die;* **~ ˈfarmer** *n.* Subsistenzbauer, *der*/-bäuerin, *die;* **~ ˈfarming** *n., no pl.* Subsistenzwirtschaft, *die* (Soziol., Wirtsch.); **~ level** *n.* Existenzminimum, *das;* **live at ~ level** gerade genug zum Leben haben; **~ wage** *n.* ≈ Existenzminimum, *das*

ˈsubsoil *n.* Untergrund, *der*

subˈsonic *adj.* Unterschall-

ˈsubspecies *n., pl. same* (Biol.) Unterart, *die*

substance /ˈsʌbstəns/ *n.* [1] Stoff, *der;* Substanz, *die* [2] *no pl.* (solidity) Substanz, *die;* **this is an argument of little ~:** dieses Argument ist ziemlich substanzlos; **the food lacks ~:** das Essen ist nicht sehr gehaltvoll; **a man of ~:** ein begüterter Mann [3] *no pl.* (content) (of book etc.) Inhalt, *der;* **there is not enough ~ in the plot** die Handlung gibt nicht genug her; **there is no ~ in his claim/the rumour** seine Behauptung/das Gerücht entbehrt jeder Grundlage [4] *no pl.* (essence) Kern, *der;* **in ~:** im Wesentlichen

ˈsubstance abuse *n.* Drogen- und Genussmittelmissbrauch, *der*

subˈstandard *adj.* [1] unzulänglich; **the printing/recording was ~:** der Druck/die Aufnahme war nicht zufrieden stellend [2] (Ling.) nicht standardsprachlich

substantial /səbˈstænʃl/ *adj.* [1] (considerable) beträchtlich; erheblich ‹*Zugeständnis, Verbesserung*›; größer… ‹*Darlehen*›; **'~ price required'** „namhafte Summe erforderlich" [2] gehaltvoll ‹*Essen, Nahrung*›; **you need something more ~ [to eat]** du brauchst etwas Gehaltvolleres *od.* Kräftigeres [zu essen] [3] (solid in structure) solide, stabil ‹*Möbel*›; solide ‹*Haus*›; kräftig ‹*Körperbau*›; wesentlich ‹*Unterschied, Argument*› [4] (having substance) stofflich; materiell [5] (well-to-do) begütert ‹*Person*›; zahlungskräftig ‹*Firma*› [6] weitgehend ‹*Übereinstimmung, Zustimmung*›; ziemlich sicher ‹*Beweis*›; **be in ~ agreement** sich (*Dat.*) so gut wie *od.* praktisch einig sein

substantially /səbˈstænʃəlɪ/ *adv.* [1] (considerably) wesentlich [2] (solidly) **~ built** solide gebaut ‹*Haus usw.*›; kräftig gebaut ‹*Person*› [3] (essentially) im Wesentlichen; **~ free from sth.** weitgehend frei von etw.

substantiate /səbˈstænʃɪeɪt/ *v.t.* erhärten; untermauern

substantiation /səbstænʃɪˈeɪʃn/ *n.* Erhärtung, *die;* Untermauerung, *die;* **in ~ of his claim** zur Erhärtung *od.* Untermauerung seines Anspruchs

substantive

A /səbˈstæntɪv/ *adj.* [1] (not amended) in der vorliegenden Form *nachgestellt* [2] (Mil.) **a ~ rank** der Rang eines Berufssoldaten

B /ˈsʌbstəntɪv/ *n.* (Ling.) Substantiv, *das*

ˈsubstation *n.* (Electr.) Hochspannungsverteilungsanlage, *die*

substitutable /ˈsʌbstɪtju:təbl/ *adj.* substituierbar

substitute /ˈsʌbstɪtju:t/

A *n.* [1] **~[s]** Ersatz, *der;* **~s for rubber** Ersatzstoffe für Gummi; **coffee ~:** Kaffee-Ersatz, *der;* **there is no ~ for real ale/hard work** es geht nichts über das echte englische Bier/über harte Arbeit [2] (Sport) Ersatzspieler, *der*/-spielerin, *die*

B *adj.* Ersatz-; **a ~ teacher/secretary** *etc.* eine Vertretung

C *v.t.* [1] **~ A for B** B durch A ersetzen; **~ oil for butter** statt Butter Öl nehmen; **~ a striker for a midfield player** einen Mittelfeldspieler gegen einen Stürmer auswechseln *od.* austauschen; **he doesn't like potatoes, so we ~d rice** da er keine Kartoffeln mag, gaben wir ihm stattdessen Reis [2] (coll.) **~ A by** *or* **with B** A durch B ersetzen

D *v.i.* **~ for sb.** jmdn. vertreten; für jmdn. einspringen; (Sport) für jmdn. ins Spiel kommen; **Thompson ~d for Clark just after half-time** kurz nach der Halbzeit kam Thompson für Clark ins Spiel *od.* wurde Clark gegen Thompson ausgetauscht

substitution /sʌbstɪˈtju:ʃn/ *n.* Ersetzung, *die;* Substitution, *die* (geh., fachspr.); (Sport) Spielerwechsel, *der;* **~ of A for B** Verwendung von A statt B; **make a ~** (Sport) [einen Spieler] auswechseln

subˈstratum *n., pl.* **substrata** [1] (Geol.) **a ~ of rock** ein felsiger Untergrund [2] (Ling., Biol., Chem., fig.) Substrat, *das* (geh., fachspr.)

ˈsubstructure *n.* Unterbau, *der;* (of oil rig also) Stützkonstruktion, *die*

subsume /səbˈsju:m/ *v.t.* einordnen (**in, into** in + *Akk.*); **~ an item under a category** einen Punkt einer Kategorie (*Dat.*) zuordnen

ˈsubsystem *n.* Subsystem, *das* (geh.); Teilsystem, *das*

ˈsubtenancy *n.* Untervermietung, *die;* (of land, farm, shop) Unterverpachtung, *die;* (relationship) Untermiete, *die;* (of land, farm, shop) Unterpacht, *die*

ˈsubtenant *n.* Untermieter, *der*/-mieterin, *die;* (of land, farm, shop) Unterpächter, *der*/-pächterin, *die*

subtend /sʌbˈtend/ *v.t.* (Geom.) gegenüberliegen (+ *Dat.*) ‹*Winkel*›; schneiden ‹*Bogen*›

subterfuge /ˈsʌbtəfju:dʒ/ *n.* [1] *no pl., no art.* Täuschungsmanöver *Pl.* [2] (trick) Trick, *der*

subterranean /sʌbtəˈreɪnɪən/ *adj.* unterirdisch; subterran (fachspr.)

ˈsubtext *n.* Subtext, *der*

ˈsubtitle

A *n.* (for film, of book, etc.) Untertitel, *der*

B *v.t.* untertiteln; **the book is ~d ...:** das Buch hat den Untertitel …

subtle /ˈsʌtl/ *adj.,* **~r** /ˈsʌtlə(r)/, **~st** /ˈsʌtlɪst/ [1] (delicate) zart ‹*Duft, Dunst, Parfüm*›; fein ‹*Geschmack, Aroma*› [2] (elusive) subtil (geh.); fein ‹*Unterschied*›; unaufdringlich ‹*Charme*› [3] (refined) fein ‹*Ironie, Humor*›; zart ‹*Hinweis*›; subtil (geh.) ‹*Scherz*› [4] (perceptive) feinsinnig ‹*Beobachter, Kritiker*›; fein ‹*Intellekt*›; **~ perception** feines Gespür [5] (ingenious) geschickt; raffiniert ‹*Plan*›; **~ art** hohe Kunst

subtlety /ˈsʌtltɪ/ *n.* [1] *no pl.* ▸**subtle**: Zartheit, *die;* Feinheit, *die;* Subtilität, *die* (geh.); Unaufdringlichkeit, *die;* Feinsinnigkeit, *die;* Geschicklichkeit, *die;* Raffiniertheit, *die* [2] **subtleties** Feinheiten

subtly /ˈsʌtlɪ/ *adv.* auf subtile Weise (geh.); zart ‹*hinweisen auf, andeuten*›; geschickt ‹*argumentieren*›; **~ flavoured/perfumed** von feinem Geschmack *nachgestellt*/zart duftend

ˈsubtotal *n.* Zwischensumme, *die*

subtract /səbˈtrækt/ *v.t.* abziehen (**from** von); subtrahieren (**from** von)

subtraction /səbˈtrækʃn/ *n.* Subtraktion, *die;* Abziehen, *das*

subˈtropical *adj.* subtropisch

suburb /ˈsʌbɜ:b/ *n.* Vorort, *der;* **live in the ~s** am Stadtrand leben

suburban /səˈbɜ:bən/ *adj.* [1] (of suburbs) Vorort-; ‹*Leben, Haus*› am Stadtrand; **~ spread** *or* **sprawl** eintönige, endlose Vororte [2] (derog.: limited in outlook) spießig (abwertend)

suburbanite /səˈbɜ:bənaɪt/ *n.* Vorstädter, *der*/Vorstädterin, *die*

suburbia /səˈbɜ:bɪə/ *n.* (derog.) die [eintönigen] Vororte

subvention /səbˈvenʃn/ *n.* Subvention, *die* (Wirtsch.)

subversion /səbˈvɜ:ʃn/ *n.* Subversion, *die;* (of government, monarchy, etc.) [Um]sturz, *der*

subversive /səbˈvɜ:sɪv/

A *adj.* subversiv; **be ~ of sth.** etw. unterminieren

B *n.* Subversive, *der/die*

subversively /səbˈvɜ:sɪvlɪ/ *adv.* subversiv

subvert /səbˈvɜ:t/ *v.t.* stürzen ‹*Monarchie, Regierung*›; unterminieren ‹*Moral, Loyalität*›; [zur Illoyalität] aufstacheln ‹*Person*›

ˈsubway *n.* [1] (passage) Unterführung, *die* [2] (Amer.: railway) Untergrundbahn, *die;* U-Bahn, *die* (ugs.)

sub-ˈzero *adj.* ▸ⓘ p. 1620 **~ temperatures/conditions** Temperaturen unter null

succeed /səkˈsi:d/

A *v.i.* [1] (achieve aim) Erfolg haben; **sb. ~s in sth.** jmdm. gelingt etw.; jmd. schafft etw.; **sb. ~s in doing sth.** es gelingt jmdm., etw. zu tun; jmd. schafft es, etw. zu tun; **~ in business/college** geschäftlich/im Studium erfolgreich sein; **I did not ~ in doing it** ich habe es nicht geschafft; es ist mir nicht gelungen; **I ~ed in passing the test** ich habe die Prüfung mit Erfolg *od.* erfolgreich abgelegt; **he usually ~s in anything he puts his mind to** ihm gelingt gewöhnlich alles, was er sich (*Dat.*) vornimmt; **~ in one's aims** seine Ziele erreichen; **the plan did not ~:** der Plan ist gescheitert [2] (come next) die Nachfolge antreten; **~ to an office/the throne** die Nachfolge in einem Amt/die Thronfolge antreten; **~ to a title/an estate** einen Titel/ein Gut erben

B *v.t.* [1] (take place of) ablösen ‹*Monarchen, Beamten*›; **~ sb. [in a post]** jmds. Nachfolge [in einem Amt] antreten [2] (follow) **day ~ed day** ein Tag folgte auf den anderen

succeeding /səkˈsi:dɪŋ/ *adj.* [nach]folgend; (one after another) aufeinander folgend ‹*Generationen, Regierungen*›

success /səkˈses/ *n.* ▸ⓘ p. 1189 Erfolg, *der;* **meet with ~:** Erfolg haben; erfolgreich sein; **make a ~ of sth.** bei etw. Erfolg haben; **'wishing you every ~'** „ich wünsche/wir wünschen Ihnen viel Erfolg"; **have little/considerable ~ in doing sth.** wenig/beträchtlichen Erfolg dabei haben, etw. zu tun; **I didn't have much ~ with her** ich war bei ihr nicht sonderlich erfolgreich; **~ at last!** endlich hat es geklappt! (ugs.); **nothing succeeds like ~** (prov.) nichts ist so erfolgreich wie der Erfolg (Spr.); **he was a great ~ as headmaster/Hamlet** er war als Schulleiter sehr erfolgreich/als Hamlet ein großer Erfolg

successful /səkˈsesfl/ *adj.* erfolgreich; **be ~ in sth./doing sth.** Erfolg bei etw. haben/dabei haben, etw. zu tun; **he was ~ in his attempts to ...:** es gelang ihm, … zu …; **she made a ~ attempt on the record** der Rekordversuch ist ihr gelungen

successfully /səkˈsesfəlɪ/ *adv.* erfolgreich; **he ~ avoided the question** es gelang ihm, der Frage auszuweichen

succession /səkˈseʃn/ *n.* [1] Folge, *die;* **four games/years** *etc.* **in ~:** vier Spiele/Jahre *usw.*

S

hintereinander; **in quick/rapid ~:** in schneller/rascher Folge; **in close ~** (in space) dicht hintereinander; (in time) kurz hintereinander; **the ~ of the seasons** die Abfolge der Jahreszeiten **2** (series) Serie, *die;* **a ~ of losses/visitors** eine Verlust-/Besucherserie **3** (right of succeeding to the throne etc.) Erbfolge, *die;* **he is second in ~:** er ist Zweiter in der Erbfolge; **in ~ to his uncle** als Nachfolger seines Onkels; **the apostolic ~** (RC Ch.) die Apostolische Nachfolge *od.* Sukzession

successive /sək'sesɪv/ *adj.* aufeinander folgend; **five ~ games/jobs** fünf Spiele/Stellungen hintereinander

successively /sək'sesɪvlɪ/ *adv.* hintereinander

successor /sək'sesə(r)/ *n.* Nachfolger, *der*/Nachfolgerin, *die;* **sb.'s ~, the ~ to sb.** jmds. Nachfolger; **the ~ to the throne** der Nachfolger auf dem Thron

suc'cess story *n.* Erfolgsstory, *die* (ugs.); **he is a typical American ~:** er hat eine typische amerikanische Erfolgskarriere hinter sich (*Dat.*)

succinct /sək'sɪŋkt/ *adj.* (terse) knapp; (clear, to the point) prägnant

succinctly /sək'sɪŋktlɪ/ *adv.* (tersely) in knappen Worten; (clearly) prägnant

succinctness /sək'sɪŋktnɪs/ *n., no pl.* (terseness) Knappheit, *die;* (clarity) Prägnanz, *die*

succour (*Amer.:* **succor**) /'sʌkə(r)/ (literary)
A *v.t.* Beistand leisten (+ *Dat.*)
B *n.* Beistand, *der;* Unterstützung, *die;* **bring ~ to the wounded** die Leiden der Verwundeten lindern

succulence /'sʌkjʊləns/ *n., no pl.* Saftigkeit, *die*

succulent /'sʌkjʊlənt/
A *adj.* **1** saftig ‹*Pfirsich, Steak usw.*› **2** (Bot.) sukkulent; fleischig; **~ plants** Sukkulenten
B *n.* (Bot.) Sukkulente, *die;* Fettpflanze, *die*

succulently /'sʌkjʊləntlɪ/ *adv.* saftig

succumb /sə'kʌm/ *v.i.* **1** (be forced to give way) unterliegen; **~ to sth.** einer Sache (*Dat.*) erliegen; **~ to grief/despair** in Kummer/Verzweiflung verfallen; **~ to temptation** der Versuchung erliegen; **~ to pressure** dem Druck nachgeben **2** (die) **~ [to one's illness/wounds** *etc.***]** seiner Krankheit/seinen Verletzungen *usw.* erliegen

such /sʌtʃ/
A *adj., no compar. or superl.* **1** (of that kind) solch ...; **~ a person** solch *od.* (ugs.) so ein Mensch; ein solcher Mensch; **~ a book** solch *od.* (ugs.) so ein Buch; ein solches Buch; **~ people** solche Leute; **~ things** so etwas; **symphonies and other ~ compositions** Sinfonien und andere Kompositionen dieser Art; **shoplifting and ~ crimes** Ladendiebstahl und derartige *od.* ähnliche Vergehen; **there are many ~ cases** so etwas kommt oft vor; **or some ~ thing** oder so etwas; oder etwas in der Art; **some ~ plan** irgend so ein Plan (ugs.); **I said no ~ thing** ich habe nichts dergleichen gesagt; **you'll do no ~ thing** das wirst du nicht tun; **there is no ~ bird** solch einen *od.* einen solchen Vogel gibt es nicht; **experiences ~ as these** solche *od.* derartige Erfahrungen; **there is no ~ thing as a unicorn** Einhörner gibt es gar nicht; **there is no ~ thing as honour among thieves** Diebe kennen keine Ehre; **~ writers as Eliot and Fry** Schriftsteller wie Eliot und Fry; **~ grapes as you never saw** Trauben, wie du sie noch nie gesehen hast; **I will take ~ steps as I think necessary** ich werde die Schritte unternehmen, die ich für notwendig halte; **~ money as I have** das bisschen Geld, das ich habe; **at ~ a time** zu einer solchen Zeit; **at ~ a moment as this** in einem Augenblick wie diesem; (disapproving) gerade jetzt; **in ~ a case** in einem solchen *od.* (ugs.) so einem Fall; **for** *or* **on ~ an occasion** zu einem solchen Anlass; **by all means stay for lunch, ~ as it is** bleib doch zum Mittagessen, aber es gibt nichts Besonderes; **~ a one as he/she is impossible to replace** jemand wie er/sie ist unersetzlich; *see also* **another A 2**; **luck 2** **2** (so great) solch ...; derartig; **I got ~ a fright that ...:** ich bekam einen derartigen *od.* (ugs.) so einen Schrecken, dass ...; **your stupidity is ~ as to fill me with despair** deine Dummheit treibt mich noch zur Verzweiflung; **~ was the force of the explosion that ...:** die Explosion war so stark, dass ...; **to ~ an extent** dermaßen **3** (with adj.) so; **~ a big house** ein so großes Haus; **she has ~ lovely blue eyes** sie hat so schöne blaue Augen; **~ a wonderfully fresh green** so ein herrlich frisches Grün; **~ a long time** so lange
B *pron.* **1** **as ~:** als solcher/solche/solches; (strictly speaking) im Grunde genommen; an sich; **this is not a promotion as ~:** dies ist im Grunde genommen *od.* eigentlich keine Beförderung; **~ is not the case** das ist nicht der Fall; **~ is life** so ist das Leben; **~ as** wie [zum Beispiel]; **~ 'as?** zum Beispiel? **2** (people or things of stated kind) **all ~:** alle seinesgleichen/ihresgleichen; **we do not have any ~:** wir haben nichts dergleichen; **or some ~:** oder so etwas; **I can give you ~ as I have** ich kann dir [das Wenige] geben, was ich habe

such-and-such /'sʌtʃənsʌtʃ/
A *adj.* **in ~ a place at ~ a time** an dem und dem Ort um die und die Zeit; **Mr ~:** Herr Sowieso
B *pron.* der und der/die und die/das und das

suchlike /'sʌtʃlaɪk/ (coll.)
A *pron.* derlei
B *attrib. adj.* dergleichen

suck /sʌk/
A *v.t.* saugen (**out of** aus); lutschen ‹*Bonbon*›; saugen an (+ *Dat.*) ‹*Pfeife*›; **~ one's thumb** am Daumen lutschen; **~ an orange dry** eine Apfelsine auslutschen; **~ sb. dry** (extort all sb.'s money) jmdn. bis aufs Blut aussaugen; (exhaust sb.) jmdn. auslaugen
B *v.i.* **1** ‹*Baby:*› saugen; **~ at sth.** an etw. (*Dat.*) saugen; **~ at a lollipop** an einem Lutscher lecken; einen Lolli lutschen **2** **sth. ~s** (esp. Amer. sl.) etw. ist Scheiße (derb)
C *n.* **have a ~ at an ice lolly/at a straw** an einem Eis lutschen/Strohhalm saugen *od.* ziehen

Phrasal verbs

- **~ 'down** *v.t.* hinunterziehen; ‹*Strudel:*› in die Tiefe ziehen
- **~ 'in** *v.t.* einsaugen; ‹*Strudel:*› in die Tiefe ziehen
- **~ 'off** *v.t.* (coarse) **~ sb. off** jmdm. einen ablutschen *od.* abkauen (vulg.)
- **~ 'under** *v.t.* in die Tiefe ziehen
- **~ 'up**

A *v.t.* aufsaugen ‹*Staub, Feuchtigkeit*›; (with a straw) einsaugen; (into a pipette) ansaugen; (by dredger, tubes, etc.) verschlucken
B *v.i.* **~ up to sb.** (coll.) jmdm. in den Hintern kriechen (salopp)

sucker /'sʌkə(r)/ *n.* **1** (suction pad) Saugfuß, *der;* (Zool.) Saugnapf, *der;* (of leech) Saugscheibe, *die* **2** (one attracted) **be a ~ for sb./sth.** eine Schwäche für jmdn./etw. haben **3** (coll.: dupe) Dumme, *der/die;* **poor ~:** armer Trottel; **he's always being had for a ~:** er fällt immer auf alles herein **4** (Bot.) unterirdischer Ausläufer **5** (fish) Sauger, *der* **6** (Amer.) ▸ **lollipop**

'sucking pig *n.* Spanferkel, *das*

suckle /'sʌkl/
A *v.t.* säugen
B *v.i.* [an der Brust] trinken

suckling /'sʌklɪŋ/ *n.* (unweaned child) Säugling, *der;* **these piglets are still ~s** diese Ferkel werden noch gesäugt; *see also* **mouth A 1**

sucrose /'su:krəʊz, 'sju:krəʊz/ *n.* (Chem.) Saccharose, *die*

suction /'sʌkʃn/ *n.* **1** (sucking) Absaugen, *das;* (force) Saugwirkung, *die* **2** (of air, currents, etc.) Sog, *der;* **work by ~:** durch Saugwirkung arbeiten

suction: ~ pad *n.* Saugfuß, *der;* **~ pump** *n.* Saugpumpe, *die*

Sudan /su:'dɑ:n/ *pr. n.* **[the] ~:** [der] Sudan

Sudanese /su:də'ni:z/ ▸ **p. 1345**
A *adj.* sudanesisch; **sb. is ~:** jmd. ist Sudanese/Sudanesin
B *n., pl. same* Sudanese, *der*/Sudanesin, *die*

sudden /'sʌdn/
A *adj.* **1** (unexpected) plötzlich; **I had a ~ thought** auf einmal *od.* plötzlich fiel mir etwas ein **2** (abrupt, without warning) jäh ‹*Abgrund, Übergang, Ruck*›; **there was a ~ bend in the road** plötzlich machte die Straße eine Biegung
B *n.* **all of a ~:** plötzlich

sudden 'death *attrib. adj.* (Sport coll.) **a ~ playoff** ein Stichentscheid; (Footb.: using penalties) ein Elfmeterschießen

sudden infant 'death syndrome *n., no pl.* plötzlicher Kindstod

suddenly /'sʌdnlɪ/ *adv.* plötzlich

suddenness /'sʌdnnɪs/ *n., no pl.* Plötzlichkeit, *die*

suds /sʌdz/ *n. pl.* **1** **[soap]~:** [Seifen]lauge, *die;* (froth) Schaum, *der* **2** (Amer. coll.: beer) Gerstensaft, *der* (scherzh.)

sudsy /'sʌdzɪ/ *adj.* (coll.) seifig; (frothy) schaumig

sue /su:, sju:/
A *v.t.* (Law) verklagen (**for** auf + *Akk.*)
B *v.i.* **1** (Law) klagen (**for** auf + *Akk.*) **2** (fig.) **~ for peace/mercy** um Frieden/Gnade bitten

suede /sweɪd/ *n.* Wildleder, *das;* (finer) Veloursleder, *das*

suet /'su:ɪt, 'sju:ɪt/ *n.* Talg, *der*

suet 'pudding *n.:* *mit Talg zubereiteter Pudding*

Suez /'sʊɪz, 'sju:ɪz/ *pr. n.* Suez (*das*); **~ Canal** Suezkanal, *der*

suffer /'sʌfə(r)/
A *v.t.* **1** (undergo) erleiden ‹*Verlust, Unrecht, Schmerz, Niederlage*›; durchmachen, erleben ‹*Schweres, Kummer*›; dulden ‹*Unverschämtheit*›; **~ disablement** invalide werden; **the dollar ~ed further losses against the yen** der Dollar musste weitere Einbußen gegenüber dem Yen hinnehmen; **~ neglect** vernachlässigt werden **2** (tolerate) dulden; **not ~ fools gladly** mit dummen Leuten keine Geduld haben **3** (arch.: allow) lassen; **~ sth. to be done** (Bibl.) etw. geschehen lassen; **~ the little children to come unto me** (Bibl.) lasset die Kindlein zu mir kommen
B *v.i.* leiden; **~ for sth.** (for a cause) für etw. leiden; (in expiation) für etw. büßen; **the engine ~ed severely** der Motor hat sehr gelitten; **if you publish this article, your reputation will ~:** wenn Sie diesen Artikel veröffentlichen, wird das Ihrem Ruf schaden

Phrasal verb

- **~ from** *v.t.* ▸ ❶ **p. 1231** leiden unter (+ *Dat.*); leiden an (+ *Dat.*) ‹*Krankheit*›; **~ from shock** unter Schock[wirkung] stehen; **~ from faulty planning/bad execution** an falscher Planung/schlechter Durchführung kranken; **the trees have ~ed from the frost** die Bäume haben durch den Frost gelitten

sufferance /'sʌfərəns/ *n.* Duldung, *die;* **his behaviour is beyond ~:** sein Benehmen ist unerträglich; **he remains here on ~ only** er ist hier bloß geduldet

sufferer /'sʌfərə(r)/ *n.* ▸ ❶ **p. 1231** Betroffene, *der/die;* (from disease) Leidende, *der/die;* **~s from rheumatism/arthritis, rheumatism/arthritis ~s** Rheuma-/Arthritisleidende

suffering /'sʌfərɪŋ/ *n.* Leiden, *das;* **he had experienced untold ~ from cancer** als Krebskranker hatte er unsäglich gelitten; **her ~s are now at an end** sie hat jetzt ausgelitten (geh.)

suffice /sə'faɪs/
A *v.i.* genügen; **~ it to say: ...:** nur so viel sei gesagt: ...; **this ~d to infuriate her** das genügte *od.* reichte schon, um sie wütend zu machen
B *v.t.* genügen (+ *Dat.*); reichen für

sufficiency /sə'fɪʃənsɪ/ *n., no pl.* Zulänglichkeit, *die;* (sufficient amount) ausreichende Menge

sufficient /sə'fɪʃənt/ *adj.* genug; **~ money/food** genug Geld/genug zu essen; **be ~:** genügen; **~ reason** Grund genug; **I'm not ~ of an expert** ich bin nicht Fachmann genug; **have you had ~?** (food, drink) haben Sie schon genug?; **I think you have drunk quite ~:** ich glaube, du hast schon genug getrunken

sufficiently /sə'fɪʃəntlɪ/ *adv.* genug; (adequately) ausreichend; **~ large** groß genug; **a ~ large number** eine genügend große Zahl

S

suffix /ˈsʌfɪks/
A *n.* 1 (Ling.) Suffix, *das* (fachspr.); Nachsilbe, *die* 2 (Math.) ▸ **subscript B**
B *v.t.* suffigieren (fachspr.); anhängen ‹*Nachsilbe*›

suffocate /ˈsʌfəkeɪt/
A *v.t.* ersticken; **he was ~d by the smoke** der Rauch erstickte ihn; er erstickte an dem Rauch; **suffocating heat** drückende Hitze; **this dreary existence is suffocating me** (fig.) dieses eintönige Leben erdrückt mich
B *v.i.* ersticken; **she was suffocating in the hot little kitchen** sie wäre in der heißen kleinen Küche fast erstickt

suffocation /sʌfəˈkeɪʃn/ *n.* Erstickung, *die;* **a feeling of ~:** das Gefühl, zu ersticken

suffragan /ˈsʌfrəgən/ (Eccl.)
A *adj.* **~ bishop** Suffraganbischof, *der*
B *n.* **[bishop] ~:** Suffragan, *der*

suffrage /ˈsʌfrɪdʒ/ *n.* (right of voting) Wahlrecht, *das;* **female** *or* **women's ~:** das Frauenwahlrecht

suffragette /sʌfrəˈdʒet/ *n.* (Hist.) Frauenrechtlerin, *die;* Suffragette, *die*

suffuse /səˈfjuːz/ *v.t.* **a blush ~d her cheeks** Schamröte stieg ihr ins Gesicht; **the evening sky was ~d with crimson** der Abendhimmel war in purpurnes Licht getaucht

Sufi /ˈsuːfɪ/ *n.* (Muslim Relig.) Sufi, *der*

sugar /ˈʃʊgə(r)/
A *n.* 1 Zucker, *der;* **two ~s, please** (spoonfuls) zwei Löffel Zucker, bitte; (lumps) zwei Stück Zucker, bitte 2 (fig.: flattery) Schöntuerei, *die* (abwertend) 3 (Amer. coll.: money) Kohle, *die* (salopp) 4 (Amer. coll.: darling) Süße, *der/die* (fam.)
B *v.t.* zuckern; (fig.) versüßen; verzuckern

sugar: ~ **basin** ▸ ~ **bowl**; ~ **beet** *n.* Zuckerrübe, *die;* ~ **bowl** *n.* Zuckerschale, *die;* (covered) Zuckerdose, *die;* ~ **cane** *n.* Zuckerrohr, *das;* **~-coated** *adj.* gezuckert; mit Zucker überzogen ‹*Dragee usw.*›; ~ **cube** *n.* Zuckerwürfel, *die;* ~ **daddy** *n.* (coll.) *spendabler älterer Mann, der ein junges Mädchen aushält;* **~loaf** *n.* Zuckerhut, *der;* ~ **lump** *n.* Zuckerstück, *das;* (when counted) Stück Zucker, *das;* ~ **pea** *n.* Zuckererbse, *die;* ~ **refinery** *n.* Zuckerraffinerie, *die;* ~ **shaker**, ~ **sifter** *ns.* Zuckerstreuer, *der;* ~ **soap** *n., no pl.* (Brit.) Ablaugmittel, *das;* ~ **tongs** *n. pl.* Zuckerzange, *die*

sugary /ˈʃʊgərɪ/ *adj.* süß; (fig.) süßlich ‹*Lächeln, Stimme, Musik*›

suggest /səˈdʒest/
A *v.t.* 1 (propose) vorschlagen; **~ sth. to sb.** jmdm. etw. vorschlagen; **he ~ed going to the cinema** er schlug vor, ins Kino zu gehen 2 (assert) **are you trying to ~ that he is lying?** wollen Sie damit sagen, dass er lügt?; **he ~ed that the calculation was incorrect** er sagte, die Rechnung sei falsch; **I ~ that …** (Law) ich unterstelle, dass … 3 (make one think of) suggerieren; ‹*Symptome, Tatsachen:*› schließen lassen auf (+ *Akk.*); **what does this music ~ to you?** woran denken Sie bei dieser Musik?
B *v. refl.* **~ itself [to sb.]** ‹*Möglichkeiten, Ausweg:*› sich [jmdm.] anbieten; ‹*Gedanke:*› sich [jmdm.] aufdrängen

suggestible /səˈdʒestɪbl/ *adj.* beeinflussbar; suggestibel (geh.)

suggestion /səˈdʒestʃn/ *n.* 1 Vorschlag, *der;* **at** *or* **on sb.'s ~:** auf jmds. Vorschlag (*Akk.*); **I am open to ~s** ich bin Vorschlägen *od.* Anregungen aufgeschlossen 2 (insinuation) Andeutungen *Pl.;* **there is no ~ that he cooperated with the kidnappers** niemand unterstellt, dass er mit den Entführern zusammengearbeitet hat; **what a ~!** wie kann man so etwas nur sagen! 3 (fig.: trace) Spur, *die;* **not a ~ of condescension** nicht die Spur von Herablassung; **she speaks German with a ~ of a Polish accent** sie spricht Deutsch mit einem ganz leichten polnischen Akzent; **there is a ~ of blue in the grey** das Grau hat einen leichten Stich ins Blaue

sug'gestion[s] box *n.* Kummerkasten, *der*

suggestive /səˈdʒestɪv/ *adj.* 1 suggestiv (geh.); **be ~ of sth.** auf etw. (*Akk.*) schließen lassen; **~ power** Suggestion, *die* 2 (risqué) anzüglich; gewagt; zweideutig ‹*Scherze, Lieder*›

suggestively /səˈdʒestɪvlɪ/ *adv.* 1 viel sagend 2 (in a risqué manner) gewagt

suggestiveness /səˈdʒestɪvnɪs/ *n., no pl.* 1 Suggestion, *die* 2 (sexual undertones) Anzüglichkeit, *die;* Gewagtheit, *die*

suicidal /suːɪˈsaɪdl, sjuːɪˈsaɪdl/ *adj.* 1 (leading or tending to suicide) selbstmörderisch ‹*Akt, Absicht*›; suizidal (fachspr.) ‹*Verhalten, Patient*›; **~ tendencies** eine Neigung zum Selbstmord; **I felt** *or* **was quite ~:** ich hätte mich am liebsten gleich umgebracht 2 (dangerous) selbstmörderisch ‹*Fahrweise, Verhalten usw.*›

suicide /ˈsuːɪsaɪd, ˈsjuːɪsaɪd/ *n.* 1 Selbstmord, *der* (auch fig.); Suizid, *der* (fachspr.); (viewed more positively) Freitod, *der* (geh.); **commit ~:** Selbstmord *od.* (fachspr.) Suizid begehen; (viewed more positively) den Freitod wählen (geh.); **attempt ~:** einen Selbstmordversuch unternehmen 2 (person) Selbstmörder, *der*/-mörderin, *die;* Suizidant, *der*/Suizidantin, *die* (fachspr.)

suicide: ~ **attempt** *n.* Selbstmordversuch, *der;* ~ **bomber** *n.* Selbstmordattentäter, *der*/-attentäterin, *die;* ~ **pact** *n.* Selbstmordpakt, *der;* ~ **rate** *n.* Selbstmordrate, *die;* ~ **squad** *n.* Selbstmordkommando, *das*

sui generis /sjuːaɪ ˈdʒenərɪs, suːɪ ˈgenərɪs/ *adj.* einzigartig; **be ~:** einzig in seiner Art sein

suit /suːt, sjuːt/
A *n.* 1 (for men) Anzug, *der;* (for women) Kostüm, *das;* **a three-piece ~:** ein dreiteiliger Anzug; ein Dreiteiler; **~ of armour** Harnisch, *der;* **buy [oneself] a new ~ of clothes** sich neu einkleiden 2 (Law) **~ [at law]** Prozess, *der;* [Gerichts]verfahren, *das* 3 (Cards) Farbe, *die;* **follow ~:** Farbe bedienen; (fig.) das Gleiche tun; *see also* **long¹ A 13** 4 (courtship) Werbung, *die* (*um eine Frau*)
B *v.t.* 1 anpassen (**to** *Dat.*); **~ the action to the word** den Worten Taten folgen lassen 2 **be ~ed [to sth./one another]** [zu etw./zueinander] passen; **he is not at all ~ed to marriage** er eignet sich überhaupt nicht für die Ehe; **they are ill/well ~ed** sie passen schlecht/gut zueinander 3 (satisfy needs of) passen (+ *Dat.*); recht sein (+ *Dat.*); **will Monday ~ you?** ist Montag Ihnen recht?; passt Ihnen Montag?; **he comes when it ~s him** er kommt, wann es ihm gerade passt; **does the climate ~ you/your health?** bekommt Ihnen das Klima?; **dried fruit/asparagus does not ~ me** ich vertrage kein Trockenobst/keinen Spargel 4 (go well with) passen zu; **does this hat ~ me?** steht mir dieser Hut?; **black ~s her** Schwarz steht ihr gut
C *v.i.* 1 (be convenient) ‹*Termin:*› recht sein 2 (go well) **she'll ~:** sie ist genau richtig; **the job ~s with his abilities** die Stelle entspricht seinen Fähigkeiten
D *v. refl.* **~ oneself** tun, was man will; **~ yourself!** [ganz] wie du willst!; **you can ~ yourself whether you come or not** du kannst kommen oder nicht, ganz wie du willst

suitability /suːtəˈbɪlɪtɪ, sjuːtəˈbɪlɪtɪ/ *n., no pl.* Eignung, *die* (**for** für); (of clothing, remark; for an occasion) Angemessenheit, *die* (**for** für); **his ~ as a teacher** seine Eignung zum *od.* als Lehrer; **we must check the ~ of the date** wir müssen prüfen, ob der Termin passt

suitable /ˈsuːtəbl, ˈsjuːtəbl/ *adj.* geeignet; (for an occasion) angemessen ‹*Kleidung*›; angebracht ‹*Bemerkung*›; (matching; convenient) passend; **I did not find anything ~ to go with this dress** ich habe nichts gefunden, was zu diesem Kleid passt; **this girlfriend is not ~ for him** diese Freundin passt nicht zu ihm; **Monday is the most ~ day [for me]** Montag passt [mir] am besten

suitableness /ˈsuːtəblnɪs, ˈsjuːtəblnɪs/ ▸ **suitability**

suitably /ˈsuːtəblɪ, ˈsjuːtəblɪ/ *adv.* angemessen; gehörig ‹*entrüstet*›; gebührend ‹*beeindruckt*›; entsprechend ‹*gekleidet*›; **a ~ treated metal** ein in geeigneter Weise bearbeitetes Metall

'suitcase *n.* Koffer, *der;* **live out of a ~:** aus dem Koffer leben

suite /swiːt/ *n.* 1 (of furniture) Garnitur, *die;* **three-piece ~:** Polstergarnitur, *die;* **bedroom ~:** Schlafzimmereinrichtung, *die* 2 (of rooms) Suite, *die;* **executive/bridal ~:** Chef-/Hochzeitssuite, *die* 3 (Mus.) Suite, *die*

suitor /ˈsuːtə(r), ˈsjuːtə(r)/ *n.* Freier, *der*

sulfate, sulfide, sulfite, sulfonamide, sulfur, sulfuric (Amer.) ▸ **sulph-**

sulk /sʌlk/
A *n., usu. in pl.* **have a ~** *or* **the ~s, be in** *or* **have a fit of the ~s** eingeschnappt sein (ugs.); schmollen
B *v.i.* schmollen; **he always ~s if he doesn't get his own way** er ist immer gleich eingeschnappt, wenn er seinen Willen nicht kriegt (ugs.)

sulkily /ˈsʌlkɪlɪ/ *adv.* eingeschnappt (ugs.); schmollend

sulkiness /ˈsʌlkɪnɪs/ *n., no pl.* Schmollen, *das;* **the ~ of her expression/look** ihr schmollender Gesichtsausdruck/Blick

sulky /ˈsʌlkɪ/
A *adj.* schmollend; eingeschnappt (ugs.)
B *n.* (Horseracing) Sulky, *das*

sullen /ˈsʌlən/ *adj.* mürrisch; verdrießlich; (fig.) düster ‹*Himmel*›

sullenly /ˈsʌlənlɪ/ *adv.* mürrisch; verdrießlich

sullenness /ˈsʌlənnɪs/ *n., no pl.* Verdrießlichkeit, *die*

sully /ˈsʌlɪ/ *v.t.* (formal) besudeln (geh.)

sulphate /ˈsʌlfeɪt/ *n.* Sulfat, *das*

sulphide /ˈsʌlfaɪd/ *n.* Sulfid, *das*

sulphite /ˈsʌlfaɪt/ *n.* Sulfit, *das*

sulphonamide /sʌlˈfɒnəmaɪd/ *n.* Sulfonamid, *das*

sulphur /ˈsʌlfə(r)/ *n.* Schwefel, *der*

sulphur di'oxide *n., no pl.* (Chem.) Schwefeldioxid, *das;* Schwefeldioxyd, *das*

sulphuric /sʌlˈfjʊərɪk/ *adj.* **~ acid** Schwefelsäure, *die*

sulphurous /ˈsʌlfərəs/ *adj.* 1 (Chem.) schwef[e]lig 2 (fig.: angry) bitterböse

sultan /ˈsʌltən/ *n.* Sultan, *der*

sultana /sʌlˈtɑːnə/ *n.* 1 (raisin) Sultanine, *die* 2 (wife of sultan) Sultanin, *die*

sultriness /ˈsʌltrɪnɪs/ *n., no pl.* Schwüle, *die;* (fig.: sensuality) Sinnlichkeit, *die*

sultry /ˈsʌltrɪ/ *adj.* schwül ‹*Wetter, Tag, Atmosphäre*›; (fig.: sensual) sinnlich; schwül ‹*Schönheit*›

sum /sʌm/
A *n.* 1 (total amount, lit. or fig.) Summe, *die* (**of** aus); **~ [total]** Ergebnis, *das;* **that was the ~ total of our achievements** *or* **of what we achieved** das war alles, was wir erreicht haben; **in ~:** summa summarum 2 (amount of money) Summe, *die;* **a cheque for this ~:** ein Scheck über diesen Betrag; *see also* **lump sum** 3 (Arithmetic) Rechenaufgabe, *die;* **do ~s** rechnen; **she is good at ~s** sie kann gut rechnen; sie ist gut im Rechnen
B *v.t.*, **-mm-** addieren

Phrasal verb

• **~ 'up**
A *v.t.* 1 zusammenfassen 2 (Brit.: assess) einschätzen; **this ~med him up perfectly** damit war er treffend charakterisiert
B *v.i.* ein Fazit ziehen; ‹*Richter:*› resümieren; **in ~ming up, I should like to …:** zusammenfassend möchte ich …

sumac[h] /ˈsuːmæk, ˈʃuːmæk, ˈsjuːmæk/ *n.* Sumach, *der*

summarily /ˈsʌmərɪlɪ/ *adv.* 1 (shortly) knapp 2 (without formalities or delay) summarisch; **~ dismissed** fristlos entlassen; **~ convicted** (Law) im summarischen Verfahren verurteilt

summarize /ˈsʌməraɪz/ *v.t.* zusammenfassen

summary /ˈsʌmərɪ/
A *adj.* 1 (short) knapp 2 (without formalities or delay) summarisch (geh.); fristlos ‹*Entlassung*›; (Law) **~ justice/jurisdiction** Schnelljustiz, *die;* **~ conviction** Verurteilung im summarischen Verfahren (Rechtsw.)
B *n.* Zusammenfassung, *die*

summer /ˈsʌmə(r)/
A *n.* 1 ▸ ❶ **p. 1515** Sommer, *der;* **in [the] ~:** im

Sommer; **in early/late ~:** im Früh-/Spätsommer; **last/next ~:** letzten/nächsten Sommer; **a ~'s day/night** ein Sommertag/eine Sommernacht; **in the ~ of 2001, in ~ 2001** im Sommer 2001; **two ~s ago we went to France** im Sommer vor zwei Jahren waren wir in Frankreich; *see also* **Indian summer**; **solstice 1** 2 *in pl.* (literary: years) Lenze (geh.)
B *attrib. adj.* Sommer-

summer: ~ house *n.* [Garten]laube, *die;* **~ 'lightning** *n.* Wetterleuchten, *das;* **~ 'pudding** *n.* (Brit.) *Süßspeise aus Kompott und Weißbrot;* **~ school** *n.* Sommerkurs, *der;* **~ term** *n.* Sommerhalbjahr, *das;* **S~ Time** *n.* (Brit.: for daylight saving) die Sommerzeit; **~time** *n.* (season) Sommer, *der;* **~ visitor** *n.* Sommergast, *der;* **~ weight** *adj.* (Textiles) [sommerlich] leicht; Sommer-

summery /'sʌmərɪ/ *adj.* sommerlich

summing-up /sʌmɪŋ'ʌp/ *n.* Zusammenfassung, *die*

summit /'sʌmɪt/ *n.* 1 (peak, lit. or fig.) Gipfel, *der;* **he was at the ~ of his power** er stand auf dem Gipfel[punkt] seiner Macht 2 (discussion) Gipfel, *der;* **~ conference/meeting** Gipfelkonferenz, *die*/-treffen, *das;* **at ~ level** auf höchster Ebene

summitry /'sʌmɪtrɪ/ *n.* Gipfeldiplomatie, *die*

summon /'sʌmən/ *v.t.* 1 (call upon) rufen (**to** zu); holen ‹*Hilfe*›; zusammenrufen ‹*Aktionäre*› 2 (call by authority) zu sich zitieren; einberufen ‹*Parlament*›; **she was ~ed to the presence of the Queen** sie wurde zur Königin befohlen (veralt.) 3 (Law: to court) vorladen ‹*Angeklagten, Zeugen*› 4 **~ sb. to do sth.** jmdn. auffordern, etw. zu tun

Phrasal verb

• **~ 'up** *v.t.* aufbringen ‹*Mut, Kräfte, Energie, Begeisterung*›

summons /'sʌmənz/
A *n.* 1 Aufforderung, *die;* **receive a ~ from sb. to do sth.** von jmdm. aufgefordert werden, etw. zu tun 2 (Law) Vorladung, *die;* **serve a ~ on sb.** jmdm. eine Vorladung zustellen
B *v.t.* (Law) **~ sb. to appear in court** jmdn. gerichtlich vorladen *od.* vor Gericht laden

sumo /'su:məʊ/ *n., pl.* **~s: ~ [wrestling]** Sumo, *das;* **~ [wrestler]** Sumokämpfer, *der*

sump /sʌmp/ *n.* 1 (Brit. Motor Veh.) Ölwanne, *die* 2 (Mining) Sumpf, *der*

sumptuous /'sʌmptjʊəs/ *adj.* üppig; luxuriös ‹*Einband, Möbel, Kleidung*›

sumptuously /'sʌmptjʊəslɪ/ *adv.* üppig; luxuriös ‹*eingerichtet*›

sumptuousness /'sʌmptjʊəsnɪs/ *n., no pl.* Üppigkeit, *die;* **the ~ of the binding/furnishings** der luxuriöse Einband/die luxuriöse Einrichtung

sun /sʌn/
A *n.* Sonne, *die;* **rise with the ~:** in aller Herrgottsfrühe aufstehen; **a place in the ~** (fig.) ein Platz an der Sonne; **catch the ~** (be in a sunny position) viel Sonne abbekommen; (get ~burnt) einen Sonnenbrand bekommen; **a touch of the ~:** ein leichter Sonnenstich; **under the ~** (fig.) auf der Welt; **chat about everything under the ~:** über alles Mögliche schwatzen; **there is nothing new under the ~:** es gibt nichts Neues unter der Sonne; *see also* **hay**; **midnight sun**
B *v. refl.*, **-nn-** (lit. or fig.) sich sonnen

Sun. *abbr.* ▸ **p. 1048 = Sunday** So.

The Sun

Eine britische Tageszeitung, die für ihre Sensationsschlagzeilen und -berichterstattung sowie für ihre rechten Meinungen bekannt ist. Sie ist eine **tabloid**-Zeitung, gehört zur Boulevardpresse und ist die auflagenstärkste Tageszeitung in Großbritannien.

sun: ~baked *adj.* an der Sonne getrocknet ‹*Ziegel*›; ausgedörrt ‹*Landschaft, Prärie usw.*›; **~bathe** *v.i.* sonnenbaden; **~bather** *n.* Sonnenbadende, *der/die;* **~bathing** *n.* Sonnenbaden, *das;* **~beam** *n.* Sonnenstrahl, *der;* **~bed** *n.* (with UV lamp) Sonnenbank, *die;* (in garden etc.) Gartenliege, *die;* **~belt** *n.* (Amer.) Sonnengürtel, *der; die südlichen Staaten der USA;* **~blind** *n.* Markise, *die;* **~block** *n.* Sonnenschutzcreme, *die* [mit hohem Lichtschutzfaktor]; Sunblocker, *der;* **~ bonnet** *n.* Sonnenhäubchen, *das;* **~burn** A *n.* Sonnenbrand, *der;* B *v.i.* **my skin ~burns/I ~burn very easily** ich kriege sehr leicht einen Sonnenbrand; **~burnt** *adj.* 1 (suffering from ~burn) **be ~burnt** einen Sonnenbrand haben; **have a ~burnt back/face** einen Sonnenbrand auf dem Rücken/im Gesicht haben; **get badly ~burnt** einen schlimmen Sonnenbrand bekommen; 2 (tanned) sonnenverbrannt ‹*Person, Gesicht usw.*›; **~cream** *n.* Sonnencreme, *die*

sundae /'sʌndeɪ, 'sʌndɪ/ *n.* **[ice cream] ~:** Eisbecher, *der*

Sunday /'sʌndeɪ, 'sʌndɪ/ ▸ **p. 1048**
A *n.* 1 Sonntag, *der;* **~ opening** die sonntägliche Öffnung (**of** von); **~ opening is allowed** es darf [auch] sonntags geöffnet werden; **~ trading** sonntägliche Ladenöffnung; **never in a month of ~s** nie im Leben 2 *in pl.* (newspapers) Sonntagszeitungen *Pl*
B *adv.* (coll.) **she comes ~s** sie kommt sonntags. *See also* **best C 2**; **Friday**

Sunday: ~ 'driver *n.* (derog.) Sonntagsfahrer, *der*/-fahrerin, *die* (abwertend); **~ painter** *n.* Sonntagsmaler, *der*/-malerin, *die;* **~ 'paper** *n.* Sonntagszeitung, *die;* **~ school** *n.* Sonntagsschule, *die;* ≈ Kindergottesdienst, *der;* **~ 'trading** *n., no pl.* Sonntagsöffnung, *die* (*im Einzelhandel*)

'sun deck *n.* Sonnendeck, *das*

sunder /'sʌndə(r)/ (arch./literary) *v.t.* brechen

sun: ~dew *n.* (Bot.) Sonnentau, *der;* **~dial** *n.* Sonnenuhr, *die;* **~down** ▸ **sunset**; **~downer** /'sʌndaʊnə(r)/ *n.* (Austral.) Pennbruder, *der* (ugs.); **~-drenched** *adj.* sonnenüberflutet (geh.); **~dress** *n.* Strand- *od.* Sonnenkleid, *das;* **~-dried** *adj.* an der Sonne getrocknet

sundry /'sʌndrɪ/
A *adj.* verschieden; **~ articles** verschiedene *od.* diverse Artikel
B *n. in pl.* Verschiedenes; Diverses; *see also* **all B 1**

sun: ~fast *adj.* (Amer.) lichtecht ‹*Farben*›; **~fish** *n.* Sonnen-, Mondfisch, *der;* **~flower** *n.* Sonnenblume, *die;* **~flower seeds** Sonnenblumenkerne

sung ▸ **sing A, B**

sun: ~glasses *n. pl.* Sonnenbrille, *die;* **~ god** *n.* Sonnengott, *der;* **~hat** *n.* Sonnenhut, *der;* **~ helmet** *n.* (Hist.) Tropenhelm, *der*

sunk ▸ **sink B, C**

sunken /'sʌŋkn/ *adj.* versunken ‹*Schatz*›; gesunken ‹*Schiff*›; eingefallen ‹*Augen, Wangen*›; tiefer liegend ‹*Garten, Zimmer*›; in den Boden eingelassen ‹*Badewanne*›

sunlamp *n.* Höhensonne, *die*

sunless /'sʌnlɪs/ *adj.* ‹*Ecke, Stelle, Tal*› wo die Sonne nie hinkommt; trübe ‹*Tag*›

sun: ~light *n.* Sonnenlicht, *das;* **come into the ~light!** komm in die Sonne!; **~lit** *adj.* sonnenbeschienen ‹*Landschaft*›; sonnig ‹*Zimmer, Garten*›; **~ lotion** *n.* Sonnenlotion, *die;* **~ lounge** *n.* Veranda, *die* **~lounger** *n.* (Brit.) Sonnenliege, *die*

Sunni /'sʌnɪ/ *n.* (Muslim Relig.) Sunnit, *der*/Sunnitin, *die; attrib.* sunnitisch

sunnily /'sʌnɪlɪ/ *adv.* lustig; freundlich

Sunnite /'sʌnaɪt/ *n.* (Muslim Relig.) Sunnit, *der*/Sunnitin, *die*

sunny /'sʌnɪ/ *adj.* 1 sonnig; **~ intervals** Aufheiterungen; **the ~ side of the house/street** die Sonnenseite des Hauses/der Straße; **~ side up** ‹*Spiegelei*› mit dem Gelben nach oben 2 (cheery) fröhlich ‹*Wesen, Lächeln*›; **have a ~ disposition** eine Frohnatur sein

sun: ~ oil *n.* Sonnenöl, *das;* **~ protection factor** *n.* Lichtschutzfaktor, *der;* **~ray** *n.* Sonnenstrahl, *der;* **~ray treatment** *n.* Bestrahlung, *die;* **~rise** *n.* Sonnenaufgang, *der;* **at ~rise** bei Sonnenaufgang; *attrib.* **~rise industry** Zukunftsindustrie, *die;* **~roof** *n.* Schiebedach, *das;* **~room** *n.* (Amer.) Veranda, *die;* **~screen** *n.* 1 *no pl.* (cream, lotion) Sonnenschutz, *der;* Sonnenschutzmittel, *das;* 2 (active ingredient) Lichtschutzsubstanz, *die;* **~seeker** *n.* Sonnenhungrige, *der/die;* **~set** *n.* Sonnenuntergang, *der;* **at ~set** bei Sonnenuntergang; **~shade** *n.* Sonnenschirm, *der;* (awning) Markise, *die;* **~shine** *n.* 1 Sonnenschein, *der;* **sit in the ~shine** in der Sonne sitzen; 2 (joc.: as form of address) (to child) Kleiner/Kleine; (between men) Kumpel (ugs.); **~shine roof** ▸ **sunroof**; **~spot** *n.* 1 (Astron.) Sonnenfleck, *der;* 2 (place) Sonnenparadies, *das;* **~stroke** *n.* Sonnenstich, *der;* **suffer from/get ~stroke** einen Sonnenstich haben/bekommen; **~tan** *n.* [Sonnen]bräune, *die;* **get a ~tan** braun werden; **~tan lotion** *n.* Sonnencreme, *die;* **~tanned** *adj.* braun [gebrannt]; sonnengebräunt (geh.); **~tan oil** *n.* Sonnenöl, *das;* **~top** *n.* Sonnentop, *das;* **~trap** *n.* sonniges Plätzchen; **~up** (Amer.) ▸ **~rise**; **~ visor** *n.* Blendschirm, *der;* **~ worshipper** *n.* (lit./joc.) Sonnenanbeter, *der*/-anbeterin, *die*

sup /sʌp/ *v.t.*, **-pp-** 1 (arch.: have supper) zu Abend essen 2 (Scot., N. Engl.: drink) süffeln (ugs.)

super /'su:pə(r)/ (coll.)
A *n.* 1 (actor) Statist, *der*/Statistin, *die* 2 (Police) ▸ **superintendent 1**
B *adj.* (Brit.) super (ugs.); **you've all been really ~ to me** ihr wart wirklich unheimlich nett zu mir

superabundance /su:pərə'bʌndəns/ *n.* Überfluss, *der;* **a ~ of wealth** übermäßiger Wohlstand

superabundant /su:pərə'bʌndənt/ *adj.* überreichlich

superannuate /su:pə'rænjʊeɪt/ *v.t.* pensionieren

superannuated /su:pə'rænjʊeɪtɪd/ *adj.* pensioniert; überaltert ‹*Ideen*›

superannuation /su:pərænjʊ'eɪʃn/ *n.* 1 **~ [contribution/payment]** Beitrag zur Rentenversicherung; **~ fund** Rentenfonds, *der* 2 (pension) Rente, *die*

superb /sʊ'pɜ:b, sju:'pɜ:b/ *adj.* einzigartig; erstklassig ‹*Essen, Zustand*›; **look ~:** fantastisch aussehen (ugs.)

superbly /sʊ'pɜ:blɪ, sju:'pɜ:blɪ/ *adv.* erstklassig

superbug /'sʊ:pəbʌg/ *n.* (resistant strain of bacteria) multiresistenter Erreger

supercargo /'su:pəkɑ:gəʊ/ *n., pl.* **~es** Superkargo, *der*

supercharge /'su:pətʃɑ:dʒ/ *v.t.* aufladen ‹*Motor*›; **~d car/engine** Auto/Motor mit Kompressor

supercharger /'su:pətʃɑ:dʒə(r)/ *n.* (Motor Veh.) Kompressor, *der*

supercilious /su:pə'sɪlɪəs/ *adj.*, **superciliously** /su:pə'sɪlɪəslɪ/ *adv.* hochnäsig

superciliousness /su:pə'sɪlɪəsnɪs/ *n., no pl.* Hochnäsigkeit, *die*

supercomputer /'su:pəkəmpju:tə(r)/ *n.* Supercomputer, *der*

supercomputing /'su:pəkəmpju:tɪŋ/ *n., no pl.* Supercomputing, *das* (fachspr.); Einsatz von Supercomputern

superconducting /su:pəkən'dʌktɪŋ/ *adj.* (Phys.) supraleitend

superconduction /su:pəkən'dʌkʃn/ *n., no pl.* (Phys.) Supraleitung, *die*

superconductivity /su:pəkɒndək'tɪvɪtɪ/ *n.* (Phys.) Supraleitfähigkeit, *die*

superconductor /su:pəkən'dʌktə(r)/ *n.* (Phys.) Supraleiter, *der*

supercool /'su:pəku:l/ *v.t.* (Phys.) unterkühlen

super-duper /'su:pədu:pə(r)/ *adj.* (Brit. coll.) Superklasse- (ugs.); **be ~:** Superklasse sein (ugs.)

superego /su:pər'i:gəʊ, su:pər'egəʊ/ *n., pl.* **~s** (Psych.) Über-Ich, *das*

superficial /su:pə'fɪʃl/ *adj.* (also fig.) oberflächlich; leicht ‹*Änderung, Schaden*›; äußerlich ‹*Ähnlichkeit*›

superficiality /su:pəfɪʃɪ'ælɪtɪ/ *n.* Oberflächlichkeit, *die*

S

superficially /suːpəˈfɪʃəlɪ/ *adv.* an der Oberfläche; ‹*Thema*› oberflächlich ‹*behandeln*›; äußerlich ‹*ähnlich sein*›

superfine /ˈsuːpəfaɪn/ *adj.* 1 (of extra quality) hochfein 2 (excessively fine) hauchdünn ‹*Unterschied*›

superfluity /suːpəˈfluːɪtɪ/ *n.* 1 Überflüssigkeit, *die* 2 (amount) Überfluss, *der* (**of** an + *Dat.*)

superfluous /sʊˈpɜːflʊəs, sjuːˈpɜːflʊəs/ *adj.* überflüssig

superfluously /sʊˈpɜːflʊəslɪ, sjuːˈpɜːflʊəslɪ/ *adv.* überflüssigerweise

superfluousness /sʊˈpɜːflʊəsnɪs, sjuːˈpɜːflʊəsnɪs/ *n.*, *no pl.* Überflüssigkeit, *die*

superglue /ˈsuːpəgluː/
A *n.* Sekundenkleber, *der*
B *v.t.* mit Sekundenkleber kleben

supergrass /ˈsuːpəgrɑːs/ *n.* (Journ.) Superspitzel, *der* (abwertend)

superheat /suːpəˈhiːt/ *v.t.* überhitzen

superhighway /ˈsuːpəhaɪweɪ/ *n.* 1 (Amer.) Autobahn, *die* 2 (Computing) Datenautobahn, *die*

superhuman /suːpəˈhjuːmən/ *adj.* übermenschlich

superimpose /suːpərɪmˈpəʊz/ *v.t.* aufbringen ‹*Schicht usw.*›; aufkopieren ‹*Bild*›; **~ a on b** a auf b legen; (fig.) b mit a überlagern; **be ~d on sth.** (state, lit. or fig.) etw. überlagern

superintend /suːpərɪnˈtend/ *v.t.* überwachen; beaufsichtigen

superintendent /suːpərɪnˈtendənt/ *n.* 1 (Brit. Police) Kommissar, *der*/Kommissarin, *die;* (Amer. Police) [Polizei]präsident, *der*/-präsidentin, *die* 2 (of hostel) Leiter, *der*/Leiterin, *die;* **~ of schools** ≈ Schulrat, *der*/-rätin, *die* 3 (Amer.: caretaker) Hausverwalter, *der*/-verwalterin, *die*

superior /suːˈpɪərɪə(r), sjuːˈpɪərɪə(r), sʊˈpɪərɪə(r)/
A *adj.* 1 (of higher quality) besonders gut ‹*Restaurant, Qualität, Stoff*›; überlegen ‹*handwerkliches Können, Technik, Intelligenz*›; **he thinks he is ~ to us** er hält sich für besser *od.* etwas Besseres als wir; **this car is ~ in speed to mine** dieser Wagen ist meinem an Geschwindigkeit überlegen 2 (having higher rank) höher… ‹*Stellung, Rang, Gericht*›; **be ~ to sb.** einen höheren Rang als jmd. haben 3 (greater in number) zahlenmäßig überlegen ‹*Truppen*›; **the enemy's ~ numbers** die zahlenmäßige Überlegenheit des Feindes 4 (supercilious) überlegen; hochnäsig (abwertend) 5 (not influenced) **be ~ to sth.** über etw. (*Dat.*) stehen 6 (Printing) hochgestellt ‹*Zahl, Buchstabe*›
B *n.* 1 (sb. higher in rank) Vorgesetzte, *der/die* 2 (sb. better) Überlegene, *der/die;* **he has no ~ in courage** keiner hat mehr Mut als er

superiority /suːpɪərɪˈɒrɪtɪ, sjuːpɪərɪˈɒrɪtɪ, sʊpɪərɪˈɒrɪtɪ/ *n.* Überlegenheit, *die* (**to** über + *Akk.*); (of goods) besondere Qualität; (haughtiness) Hochnäsigkeit, *die;* **his ~ in talent** sein größeres Talent

superlative /suːˈpɜːlətɪv, sjuːˈpɜːlətɪv/
A *adj.* 1 unübertrefflich; einmalig gut 2 (Ling.) superlativisch; **the ~ degree** der Superlativ; die zweite Steigerungsstufe; **a ~ adjective/adverb** ein Adjektiv/Adverb im Superlativ
B *n.* (Ling.) Superlativ, *der*

superlatively /suːˈpɜːlətɪvlɪ, sjuːˈpɜːlətɪvlɪ/ *adv.* einmalig gut

superman /ˈsuːpəmæn/ *n.*, *pl.* **supermen** /ˈsuːpəmen/ Supermann, *der;* (Philos., Lit.) Übermensch, *der*

supermarket /ˈsuːpəmɑːkɪt/ *n.* Supermarkt, *der*

supermodel /ˈsʊːpəmɒdl/ *n.* Supermodel, *das*

supernatural /suːpəˈnætʃərl/ *adj.* übernatürlich; **the ~:** das Übernatürliche

supernaturally /suːpəˈnætʃərəlɪ/ *adv.* auf übernatürliche Weise

supernova /suːpəˈnəʊvə/ *n.*, *pl.* **~e** /suːpəˈnəʊviː/ *or* **~s** (Astron.) Supernova, *die*

supernumerary /suːpəˈnjuːmərərɪ/
A *adj.* überzählig
B *n.* zusätzliche Arbeitskraft; (actor) Statist, *der*/Statistin, *die*

superpose /suːpəˈpəʊz/ ▸ **superimpose**

superpower /ˈsuːpəpaʊə(r)/ *n.* (Polit.) Supermacht, *die*

superrich /ˈsuːpərɪtʃ/*n.*, *no pl.* **the ~:** die Superreichen

superscript /ˈsuːpəskrɪpt/
A *n.* hochgestelltes Zeichen
B *adj.* hochgestellt

supersede /suːpəˈsiːd/ *v.t.* ablösen (**by** durch); **old ~d ideas** alte, überholte Vorstellungen

supersonic /suːpəˈsɒnɪk/ *adj.* Überschall-; **go ~:** die Schallmauer durchbrechen

superstar /ˈsuːpəstɑː(r)/ *n.* Superstar, *der*

superstate /ˈsuːpəsteɪt/ *n.* Superstaat, *der*

superstition /suːpəˈstɪʃn/ *n.* (lit. or fig.) Aberglaube, *der;* **~s** abergläubische Vorstellungen; (religious practices) abergläubische Praktiken

superstitious /suːpəˈstɪʃəs/ *adj.*, **superstitiously** /suːpəˈstɪʃəslɪ/ *adv.* abergläubisch

superstore /ˈsuːpəstɔː(r)/ *n.* Großmarkt, *der*

superstrength /ˈsuːpəstreŋθ/ *adj.* 1 (very strong) superstark 2 (high in alcohol) extrastark

superstructure /ˈsuːpəstrʌktʃə(r)/ *n.* 1 Aufbau, *der* 2 (Sociol.) Überbau, *der*

supertanker /ˈsuːpətæŋkə(r)/ *n.* Supertanker, *der*

supertax /ˈsuːpətæks/ *n.* Ergänzungsabgabe *od.* -steuer, *die*

supertonic /suːpəˈtɒnɪk/ *n.* (Mus.) zweite Stufe; Subdominantparallele, *die* (fachspr.)

superunleaded /suːpəʌnˈledɪd/
A *adj.* **~ petrol** Superbleifrei
B *n.* Superbleifrei, *das*

supervene /suːpəˈviːn/ *v.i.* dazwischenkommen

supervise /ˈsuːpəvaɪz/ *v.t.* beaufsichtigen

supervision /suːpəˈvɪʒn/ *n.* Aufsicht, *die*

supervisor /ˈsuːpəvaɪzə(r)/ *n.* ▸ ❶ **p. 1260** Aufseher, *der*/Aufseherin, *die;* (for Ph. D. thesis) Doktorvater, *der;* (Amer.: school officer) Fachbereichsleiter, *der*/-leiterin, *die;* **works ~:** Vorarbeiter, *der*/-arbeiterin, *die;* **office ~:** Bürovorsteher, *der*/-vorsteherin, *die*

supervisory /ˈsuːpəvaɪzərɪ/ *adj.* Aufsichts-

supine /ˈsuːpaɪn, ˈsjuːpaɪn/ *adj.* **he was** *or* **lay ~:** er lag auf dem Rücken; **assume a ~ position** sich auf den Rücken legen; **~ acceptance** (fig.) gleichgültige Hinnahme

supper /ˈsʌpə(r)/ *n.* Abendessen, *das;* (simpler meal) Abendbrot, *das;* **have** *or* **eat [one's] ~:** zu Abend essen; **be at** *or* **eating** *or* **having [one's] ~:** beim Abendessen/Abendbrot sein; zu Abend essen; **sing for one's ~** (fig.) etwas für sein Geld tun (ugs.); **The Last S~:** das [letzte] Abendmahl; *see also* **Lord A 2**

ˈ**suppertime** *n.* Abendbrotzeit, *die;* **it's ~:** es ist Zeit zum Abendessen

supplant /səˈplɑːnt/ *v.t.* ablösen, ersetzen (**by** durch); ausstechen ‹*Widersacher, Rivalen*›

supple /ˈsʌpl/ *adj.* geschmeidig

supplement
A /ˈsʌplɪmənt/ *n.* 1 Ergänzung, *die* (**to** + *Gen.*); (addition) Zusatz, *der;* **vitamin ~:** Vitaminpräparat, *das* 2 (of book) Nachtrag, *der;* (separate volume) Supplement, *das;* Nachtragsband, *der;* (of newspaper) Beilage, *die* 3 (to fare etc.) Zuschlag, *der*
B /ˈsʌplɪmənt, sʌplɪˈment/ *v.t.* ergänzen

supplementary /sʌplɪˈmentərɪ/ *adj.* zusätzlich; Zusatz‹*rente, -frage*›; **~ fare/charge** Zuschlag, *der; see also* **benefit A 2**

suppleness /ˈsʌplnɪs/ *n.*, *no pl.* Geschmeidigkeit, *die*

supplicant /ˈsʌplɪkənt/ *n.* Bittsteller, *der*/-stellerin, *die*

supplicate /ˈsʌplɪkeɪt/
A *v.t.* anflehen
B *v.i.* flehen (**for** um)

supplication /sʌplɪˈkeɪʃn/ *n.* Flehen, *das;* **in ~:** flehentlich

supplier /səˈplaɪə(r)/ *n.* (Commerc.) Lieferant, *der*/Lieferantin, *die*

supply /səˈplaɪ/
A *v.t.* 1 liefern ‹*Waren usw.*›; sorgen für ‹*Unterkunft*›; zur Verfügung stellen ‹*Lehrmittel, Arbeitskleidung usw.*›; beliefern ‹*Kunden, Geschäft*›; versorgen ‹*System*›; **~ sth. to sb.**, **~ sb. with sth.** jmdn. mit etw. versorgen/(Commerc.) beliefern; **could you ~ me with the tools?** könnten Sie mir das Werkzeug zur Verfügung stellen? 2 (make good) erfüllen ‹*Nachfrage, Bedarf*›; abhelfen (+ *Dat.*) ‹*Mangel*›
B *n.* 1 (stock) Vorräte *Pl.;* **a large ~ of food** große Lebensmittelvorräte; **a good ~ of reading matter** ausreichende Lektüre; **new supplies of shoes** neue Schuhlieferungen; **military/medical supplies** militärischer/medizinischer Nachschub; **~ and demand** (Econ.) Angebot und Nachfrage; *see also* **short A 4** 2 (provision) Versorgung, *die* (**of** mit); **the wholesaler has cut off our ~:** der Großhändler beliefert uns nicht mehr; **their gas ~ was cut off** ihnen ist das Gas abgestellt worden; **the blood ~ to the brain** die Versorgung des Gehirns mit Blut 3 (Brit. Parl.) Haushalt, *der;* **S~ Day** Tag der Verabschiedung des Parlamentshaushalts 4 **~ [teacher]** Aushilfslehrer, *der*/-lehrerin, *die;* **be/go on ~:** Vertretung sein/als Vertretung gehen
C *attrib.* Versorgungs‹*schiff, -netz, -basis, -lager usw.*›; **~ lines** Nachschubwege

supply: ~ chain *n.* (Commerc.) Versorgungskette, *die;* **~ line** *n.* 1 (Electr.) Versorgungsleitung, *die;* **power ~ supply line** Stromleitung, *die;* 2 (pipe) Versorgungsleitung, *die;* **water ~ supply line** Wasserleitung, *die;* 3 (route) Versorgungslinie, *die;* **~-side** *adj.* (Econ.) angebotsseitig

support /səˈpɔːt/
A *v.t.* 1 (hold up) stützen ‹*Mauer, Verletzten*›; (bear weight of) tragen ‹*Dach*› 2 (give strength to) stärken; **~ sb. in his struggle** jmdn. in seinem Kampf bestärken 3 unterstützen ‹*Politik, Verein*›; (Footb.) **~ Spurs** Spurs-Fan sein 4 (give money to) unterstützen; spenden für 5 (provide for) ernähren ‹*Familie, sich selbst*› 6 (Cinemat., Theatre: take secondary part to) **~ed by ...:** mit ... in weiteren Rollen 7 (bring facts to confirm) stützen ‹*Theorie, Anspruch, Behauptung*›; (speak in favour of) befürworten ‹*Streik, Maßnahme*› 8 (represent adequately) verkörpern ‹*Rolle*› 9 (usu. neg.: tolerate) ertragen; hinnehmen ‹*Dreistigkeit usw.*›
B *n.* 1 Unterstützung, *die;* **give ~ to sb./sth.** jmdn./etw. unterstützen; **in ~:** zur Unterstützung; **speak in ~ of sb./sth.** jmdn. unterstützen/etw. befürworten 2 (money) Unterhalt, *der* 3 (sb./sth. that ~s) Stütze, *die;* **hold on to sb./sth. for ~:** sich an jmdm./etw. festhalten

supportable /səˈpɔːtəbl/ *adj.* vertretbar; erträglich ‹*Lärm*›

support act, support band *ns.* Vorgruppe, *die*

supporter /səˈpɔːtə(r)/ *n.* 1 Anhänger, *der*/Anhängerin, *die;* **a football ~:** ein Fußballfan; **~s of a strike** Befürworter eines Streiks 2 (Her.) Schildhalter, *der*

supˈporters' club *n.* (Sport) Fanklub, *der*

supˈport group *n.* 1 (giving counselling) Hilfegruppe, *die;* (self-help group) Selbsthilfegruppe, *die* 2 (Mus.: support band) Vorgruppe, *die*

supporting /səˈpɔːtɪŋ/ *adj.* (Cinemat., Theatre) **~ role** Nebenrolle, *die;* **the ~ cast** die Darsteller der Nebenrollen; **~ actor/actress** Schauspieler/-spielerin in einer Nebenrolle; **~ film** Vorfilm, *der;* Beifilm, *der*

supportive /səˈpɔːtɪv/ *adj.* hilfreich; **be very ~ [to sb.]** [jmdm.] eine große Hilfe *od.* Stütze sein

support: ~ network *n.* Selbsthilfenetz[werk], *das;* **~ price** *n.* (Finance) Stützungspreis, *der;* **~ team** *n.* (in sports, for patients) Betreuungsteam, *das;* (military) Hilfstrupp, *der;* (technical emergency team) Serviceteam, *das*

suppose /səˈpəʊz/ *v.t.* 1 (assume) annehmen; **~** *or* **supposing [that] he ...:** angenommen, [dass] er ...; **always supposing that ...:** immer vorausgesetzt, dass ...; **~ we wait until tomorrow/went for a walk** wir könnten eigentlich bis morgen warten/einen Spaziergang machen; **~ we change the subject**

reden wir lieber von etwas anderem **2** (presume) vermuten; **I ~d she was in Glasgow** ich vermutete sie in Glasgow; **I ~ she will be here by ten** sie wird wohl bis um zehn kommen; **whom do you ~ he meant by that remark?** wen, glaubst du, hat er mit der Bemerkung gemeint?; **I don't ~ you have an onion to spare?** Sie haben wohl nicht zufällig eine Zwiebel übrig?; **We're not going to manage it, are we? — I ~ not** Wir werden es wohl nicht schaffen — Ich glaube kaum; **I ~ so** ich nehme es an; (doubtfully) ja, vermutlich; (more confidently) ich glaube schon; **I ~ I shall have to tell you** ich werde es dir wohl sagen müssen **3** **be ~d to do/be sth.** (be generally believed to do/be sth.) etw. tun/sein sollen; **cats are ~d to have nine lives** Katzen sollen angeblich neun Leben haben; **that restaurant is ~d to be quite cheap** das Restaurant soll ziemlich billig sein **4** (allow) **you are not ~d to do that/to kick people** das darfst du eigentlich nicht/du darfst andere Leute nicht treten!; **I'm not ~d to be here** ich dürfte eigentlich gar nicht hier sein **5** (presuppose) voraussetzen

supposed /sə'pəʊzd/ *attrib. adj.* mutmaßlich

supposedly /sə'pəʊzɪdlɪ/ *adv.* angeblich

supposition /sʌpə'zɪʃn/ *n.* Annahme, *die;* Vermutung, *die;* **be based on ~:** auf Annahmen *od.* Vermutungen beruhen

suppository /sə'pɒzɪtərɪ/ *n.* (Med.) Zäpfchen, *das;* Suppositorium, *das* (fachspr.)

suppress /sə'pres/ *v.t.* **1** unterdrücken; (stop) zum Stillstand bringen ‹*Blutung*›; verbieten ‹*Zeitung*› **2** (Electr.) entstören ‹*Zündung, Elektrogerät*›; ausschalten ‹*Störung*›

suppression /sə'preʃn/ *n.* **1** Unterdrückung, *die* **2** (Electr.) Entstörung, *die;* (of interference) Ausschaltung, *die*

suppressor /sə'presə(r)/ *n.* (Electr.) Entstörgerät, *das*

suppurate /'sʌpjʊreɪt/ *v.i.* (Med.) eitern

suppuration /sʌpjʊ'reɪʃn/ *n.* (Med.) (formation of pus) Eiterung, *die;* (discharge of pus) Eitern, *das*

supranational /'su:prənæʃənl/ *adj.* supranational; übernational

supremacist /su:'premɪsɪst/

A *n.* (one who believes in the supremacy of a race) Rassist, *der*/Rassistin, *die;* (one who believes in the supremacy of any social group) Verfechter, *der*/Verfechterin, *die* der Vorherrschaft einer Gruppe

B *adj.* suprematistisch

supremacy /su:'preməsɪ, sju:'preməsɪ/ *n., no pl.* **1** (supreme authority) Souveränität, *die* **2** (superiority) Überlegenheit, *die;* **air/naval ~:** Luft-/Seeherrschaft, *die;* **gain ~ over others** Vorherrschaft *od.* eine Vormachtstellung über andere erlangen; *see also* **white supremacy**

supreme /su:'pri:m, sju:'pri:m/

A *adj.* **1** (highest) höchst...; **the S~ Being** das Höchste Wesen; **S~ Court** (Law) Oberster Gerichtshof; **~ end** *or* **good** höchstes Gut; *see also* **Soviet B 2** (ultimate) **the ~ test** die schwierigste Probe; **make the ~ sacrifice** sein Leben zum Opfer bringen **3** (greatest) höchst...; größt... ‹*Stunde*›; **a ~ moment** ein unvergleichlicher Augenblick; **he is ~ among musicians** er ist der größte aller Musiker; **a ~ artist** ein unübertroffener Künstler; **reign ~:** souverän herrschen; **confusion reigns ~:** es herrscht große Verwirrung

B *n.* (Gastr.) **chicken ~:** Hühnchen in Rahmsoße; **~ of sole** Seezunge in Rahmsoße

suprême /su:'prem/ ▸**supreme B**

> **Supreme Court**
>
> In England ist *Supreme Court* die Gesamtbezeichnung für die oberen Instanzen (*Court of Appeal, High Court of Justice* und *Crown Court*). Der Oberste Gerichtshof der USA, der *United States Supreme Court* in Washington D.C. ist das höchste Gericht der Vereinigten Staaten mit neun Richtern. Der *Chief Justice of the United States* (Oberrichter) wird vom Präsidenten der Vereinigten Staaten mit Billigung des Senats ernannt.

supremely /su:'pri:mlɪ, sju:'pri:mlɪ/ *adv.* äußerst; unvergleichlich ‹*schön*›

supremo /su:'pri:məʊ, sju:'pri:məʊ/ *n., pl.* **~s** (Brit.) Boss, *der* (ugs.)

Supt. *abbr.* = **Superintendent**

sura[h] /'sʊərə/ *n.* (Muslim Relig.) Sure, *die*

surcharge /'sɜ:tʃɑ:dʒ/

A *n.* **1** (extra cost) Zuschlag, *der* **2** (on postage stamp) [Porto]aufdruck, *der* **3** (fine for false tax return) Steuerzuschlag, *der*

B *v.t.* **1** **~ sb. [10%]** jmdn. mit einem Zuschlag [von 10%] belegen **2** (overprint) überdrucken ‹*Briefmarke*›

surcoat /'sɜ:kəʊt/ *n.* (arch.) Überjacke, *die*

surd /sɜ:d/ *n.* (Math.) Wurzelausdruck, *der*

sure /ʃʊə(r)/

A *adj.* **1** (confident) sicher; **be ~ of sth.** sich (*Dat.*) einer Sache (*Gen.*) sicher sein; **you may be ~ of his honesty** du kannst dich auf seine Ehrlichkeit verlassen; **~ of oneself** selbstsicher; **he looks very ~ of himself** er macht einen sehr selbstsicheren Eindruck; **I'm not quite ~ why** ich weiß nicht genau, warum; **I can't be ~ about him** ich bin mir über ihn nicht im Klaren; **I'm ~ I didn't mean to insult you** ich wollte dich ganz bestimmt nicht beleidigen; **I'm ~ I don't know** ich weiß es ganz bestimmt nicht; **don't be too ~:** da wäre ich mir nicht so sicher **2** (safe) sicher; **make sth. ~:** etw. sichern; **be on ~r ground** (lit. or fig.) sich auf festerem Boden befinden; *see also* **slow A 1** **3** (certain) sicher; **you're ~ to be welcome** Sie werden ganz sicher *od.* bestimmt willkommen sein; **it's ~ to rain** es wird bestimmt regnen; **there is ~ to be a garage** es gibt bestimmt eine Tankstelle; **don't worry, it's ~ to turn out well** keine Sorge, es wird schon alles gut gehen; **he is ~ to ask questions about the incident** er wird auf jeden Fall Fragen zu dem Vorfall stellen **4** (undoubtedly true) sicher; **to be ~** *expr. concession* natürlich; *expr. surprise* wirklich!; tatsächlich!; **for ~** (coll.: without doubt) auf jeden Fall **5** **make ~ [of sth.]** sich [einer Sache] vergewissern; (check) [etw.] nachprüfen; **you'd better make ~ of a seat** *or* **that you have a seat** du solltest dir einen Platz sichern; **make** *or* **be ~ you do it, be ~ to do it** (do not fail to do it) sieh zu, dass du es tust; (do not forget) vergiss nicht, es zu tun; **be ~ to write** vergiss nicht zu schreiben; **make ~ you've got everything you need** sieh zu, dass du alles hast, was du brauchst; **make ~ you don't forget to do it** vergiss auf keinen Fall, es zu tun; **be ~ you finish the work by tomorrow** machen Sie die Arbeit auf jeden Fall bis morgen fertig; **be ~ not to be late** sieh zu, dass du nicht zu spät kommst **6** (reliable) sicher ‹*Zeichen*›; zuverlässig ‹*Freund, Bote, Heilmittel*›; **a ~ winner** ein todsicherer Tipp (ugs.)

B *adv.* **1** **as ~ as ~ can be** (coll.) so sicher wie das Amen in der Kirche; **as ~ as I'm standing here** so wahr ich hier stehe; **~ as hell** todsicher; **~ enough** tatsächlich; **it's brandy ~ enough!** das ist tatsächlich Weinbrand!; **it's brandy ~ enough, but ...:** es ist wohl Weinbrand, aber ...; *see also* **egg**[1] **2** (esp. Amer. coll.: certainly) wirklich; echt (ugs.); **Can you dance? — I ~ can** Kannst du tanzen? — Und ob!

C *int.* **~!, ~ thing!** (Amer. coll.) na klar! (ugs.)

sure: ~-fire *attrib. adj.* (Amer. coll.) todsicher; **~-footed** *adj.* (lit. or fig.) trittsicher

surely /'ʃʊəlɪ/

A *adv.* **1** *as sentence-modifier* doch; **there is no truth in it, ~!** das kann doch gar nicht stimmen; **~ we've met before?** wir kennen uns doch, oder?; **~ you are not going out in this snowstorm?** du willst doch wohl in dem Schneesturm nicht rausgehen? **2** (steadily) sicher; **slowly but ~:** langsam, aber sicher **3** (certainly) sicherlich; **the plan will ~ fail** der Plan wird garantiert scheitern

B *int.* (Amer.) natürlich; selbstverständlich

sureness /'ʃʊənɪs/ *n., no pl.* Sicherheit, *die;* **~ of purpose** Entschlossenheit, *die*

surety /'ʃʊərətɪ, 'ʃʊətɪ/ *n.* Bürge, *der*/Bürgin, *die;* **stand ~ for sb.** für jmdn. bürgen

surf /sɜ:f/

A *n.* Brandung, *die*

B *v.i.* **1** surfen **2** (Computing) surfen; (TV) zappen

C *v.t.* (Computing, TV) **~ the Internet** im Internet surfen; **~ the channels** sich durch die Kanäle zappen

surface /'sɜ:fɪs/

A *n.* **1** *no pl.* Oberfläche, *die;* **outer ~:** Außenfläche, *die;* **the earth's ~:** die Erdoberfläche; **on the ~ of the table** auf der Tischplatte; **the ~ of the road** die Straßendecke; **the ~ of the lake** die Seeoberfläche; **on the ~:** an der Oberfläche; (Mining) über Tage **2** (outward appearance) Oberfläche, *die;* **one never gets below the ~ with him** bei ihm bleibt alles immer oberflächlich; **on the ~:** oberflächlich betrachtet; **she remained calm on the ~:** äußerlich blieb sie ganz ruhig; **come to the ~:** an die Oberfläche kommen; ‹*Taucher, Unterseeboot:*› auftauchen; (fig.) ans Licht kommen (fig.) **3** (Geom.) Fläche, *die*

B *attrib. adj.* (lacking depth) oberflächlich

C *v.i.* **1** auftauchen; (fig.) hochkommen; ‹*Untergrundbahn:*› nach oben kommen **2** (coll.: wake up, get up) hochkommen (ugs.)

D *v.t.* mit einem Belag versehen ‹*Straße*›

surface: ~ area *n.* Oberfläche, *die;* **~ mail** *n.* gewöhnliche Post (*die auf dem Land- bzw. Seeweg befördert wird*); **~ noise** *n.* (on record) Kratzen, *das;* **~ soil** *n.* oberste Bodenschicht; **~ 'tension** *n.* (Phys.) Oberflächenspannung, *die;* **~-to-air** *adj.* **~-to-air missile** Boden-Luft-Rakete, *die;* **~ vessel** *n.* Überwasserfahrzeug, *das;* **~ water** *n.* Oberflächenwasser, *das;* **~ worker** *n.* (Min.) Übertagearbeiter, *der*

'surfboard *n.* Surfbrett, *das*

surfeit /'sɜ:fɪt/

A *n.* Übermaß, *das;* **a ~ of rich food** zu viel schweres Essen

B *v.t.* übersättigen

surfer /'sɜ:fə(r)/ *n.* Surfer, *der*/Surferin, *die*

surfing /'sɜ:fɪŋ/ *n., no pl.* Surfen, *das*

surf 'n' turf /sɜ:fən'tɜ:f/ *n.* Fisch-Fleisch-Gericht, *das* (*speziell Hummer und Steak*)

surge /sɜ:dʒ/

A *v.i.* ‹*Wellen:*› branden; ‹*Fluten, Menschenmenge:*› sich wälzen; ‹*elektrischer Strom:*› ansteigen; **anger ~d within him** Zorn wallte in ihm auf; **the crowd ~d forward** die Menschenmenge drängte nach vorn

B *n.* **1** (of the sea) Branden, *das* **2** (of crowd) Sichwälzen, *das;* (of electric current) Anstieg, *der* **3** (fig.: of interest, enthusiasm, anger, pity) Woge, *die*

Phrasal verb

- **~ 'up** *v.i.* aufsteigen; ‹*Gefühl:*› aufwallen

surgeon /'sɜ:dʒən/ *n.* ▸ **p. 1260** **1** Chirurg, *der*/Chirurgin, *die* **2** (Mil., Navy: medical officer) Stabsarzt, *der*/-ärztin, *die*

surgeon 'general *n.* **1** (Amer. Mil.) Generalstabsarzt, *der*/-ärztin, *die* **2** (Amer. Admin.) ≈ Gesundheitsminister, *der*/-ministerin, *die*

surgery /'sɜ:dʒərɪ/ *n.* **1** *no pl., no indef. art.* Chirurgie, *die;* **need ~:** operiert werden müssen; **undergo ~:** sich einer Operation (*Dat.*) unterziehen; **be saved by ~:** durch eine Operation gerettet werden **2** (Brit.: place) Praxis, *die;* **doctor's/dental ~:** Arzt-/Zahnarztpraxis, *die* **3** (Brit.: time; session) Sprechstunde, *die;* **the times of ~:** die Sprechzeiten; **when is his ~?** wann hat er Sprechstunde?; **hold a ~** (Brit.) ‹*Abgeordneter, Anwalt usw.:*› eine Sprechstunde abhalten

surgical /'sɜ:dʒɪkl/ *adj.* chirurgisch; **~ boot/stocking** orthopädischer Schuh/Strumpf; **~ dressing** chirurgischer Verband; **~ gauze** Verbandsmull, *der;* **~ spirit** *Methylalkohol* [*zur Hautdesinfektion vor Operationen*]; ≈ Alkohol, *der;* **~ treatment** Operation, *die*/Operationen

surgically /'sɜ:dʒɪkəlɪ/ *adv.* operativ ‹*behandeln, entfernen*›

surliness /'sɜ:lɪnɪs/ *n., no pl.* Verdrießlichkeit, *die;* mürrische Art; **the ~ of his look** sein mürrischer Blick

surly /'sɜ:lɪ/ *adj.* mürrisch; verdrießlich

surmise /sə'maɪz/

A *n.* Vermutung, *die;* Mutmaßung, *die*

B *v.t.* mutmaßen; **she had ~d as much** das hatte sie schon vermutet

C *v.i.* mutmaßen

surmount /sə'maʊnt/ *v.t.* 1 krönen; **a shield ~ed by a crown** ein bekrönter Wappenschild 2 (overcome) überwinden ‹*Hindernis, Schwierigkeiten*›

surmountable /sə'maʊntəbl/ *adj.* überwindbar

surname /'sɜ:neɪm/
A *n.* Nachname, *der;* Zuname, *der*
B *v.t.* **be ~d ...** den Zunamen ... tragen

surpass /sə'pɑ:s/ *v.t.* übertreffen (**in** an + *Dat.*); **~ oneself** sich selbst übertreffen; **sth. ~es [sb.'s] comprehension** etw. ist [jmdm.] unbegreiflich

surpassing /sə'pɑ:sɪŋ/ *adj.* unvergleichlich ‹*Schönheit, Leistung*›

surplice /'sɜ:plɪs/ *n.* (Eccl.) Chorhemd, *das*

surplus /'sɜ:pləs/
A *n.* Überschuss, *der* (**of** an + *Dat.*); **a ~ of coffee** Kaffeeüberschüsse *Pl.;* **army ~:** Restbestände der Armee; **army ~ store/boots** Laden für Restbestände/Schuhe aus Restbeständen der Armee; *see also* **government surplus**
B *adj.* überschüssig; **be ~ to sb.'s requirements** von jmdm. nicht benötigt werden; **~ stocks** Überschüsse *Pl.*

surprise /sə'praɪz/
A *n.* 1 Überraschung, *die;* **take sb. by ~:** jmdn. überrumpeln; **the fort was taken by ~:** die Festung wurde durch Überrumpelungstaktik eingenommen; **to my great ~, much to my ~:** zu meiner großen Überraschung; sehr zu meiner Überraschung; **look up in ~:** überrascht aufblicken; **it came as a ~ to us** es war für uns eine Überraschung; **~, ~!** (iron.) sieh mal einer an! (spött.) 2 *attrib.* überraschend, unerwartet ‹*Besuch*›; **a ~ attack/defeat** ein Überraschungsangriff/eine überraschende Niederlage; **it's to be a ~ party** die Party soll eine Überraschung sein; **~ packet** (Brit. fig.) Wundertüte, *die* (scherzh.)
B *v.t.* überraschen; überrumpeln ‹*Feind*›; **I shouldn't be ~d if ...:** es würde mich nicht wundern, wenn ...; **be ~d at sb./sth.** sich über jmdn./etw. wundern; **~ sb. into doing sth.** jmdn. dazu überrumpeln, etw. zu tun

surprise: ~ guest *n.* Überraschungsgast, *der;* **~ win** *n.* Überraschungssieg, *der*

surprising /sə'praɪzɪŋ/ *adj.* überraschend; **there's nothing ~ about that** daran ist nichts Überraschendes; **it's hardly ~ that ...:** es ist kaum verwunderlich, dass ...; **~ though it may seem** so erstaunlich es auch klingen mag

surprisingly /sə'praɪzɪŋlɪ/ *adv.* überraschend; **~ [enough], he was ...:** überraschenderweise war er ...

surreal /sə'ri:əl/ *adj.* surrealistisch

surrealism /sə'ri:əlɪzm/ *n., no pl.* Surrealismus, *der*

surrealist /sə'ri:əlɪst/
A *n.* Surrealist, *der*/Surrealistin, *die*
B *adj.* surrealistisch

surrealistic /səri:ə'lɪstɪk/ *adj.* surrealistisch

surrender /sə'rendə(r)/
A *n.* 1 (submitting to enemy) Kapitulation, *die* 2 (giving up possession) Aufgabe, *die;* (of insurance policy) Rückkauf, *der;* (of firearms) Abgabe, *die*
B *v.i.* kapitulieren; **~ to sb.** sich jmdm. beugen; **~ to despair/pressure/panic** sich der Verzweiflung überlassen/sich dem Druck beugen/sich zu Panik hinreißen lassen
C *v.t.* 1 (give up possession of) aufgeben; preisgeben ‹*Freiheit, Privileg*›; niederlegen ‹*Amt*›; abgeben, aushändigen ‹*Wertgegenstände*› 2 zurückkaufen ‹*Versicherungspolice*›
D *v. refl.* sich hingeben (**to** + *Dat.*)

sur'render value *n.* Rückkaufswert, *der*

surreptitious /sʌrəp'tɪʃəs/ *adj.* heimlich; verstohlen ‹*Blick*›

surreptitiously /sʌrəp'tɪʃəslɪ/ *adv.* heimlich; verstohlen ‹*blicken*›

surrogate /'sʌrəgət/ *n.* 1 (deputy) Stellvertreter, *der*/-vertreterin, *die* 2 (substitute) Ersatz, *der*

surrogate 'mother *n.* Leihmutter, *die*

surround /sə'raʊnd/
A *v.t.* 1 (come or be all round) umringen; ‹*Truppen, Heer:*› umzingeln ‹*Stadt, Feind*› 2 (enclose, encircle) umgeben; **be ~ed by** *or* **with sth.** von etw. umgeben sein
B *n.* (Brit.) Umrandung, *die*

surrounding /sə'raʊndɪŋ/ *adj.* umliegend ‹*Dörfer*›; **~ area** Umgebung, *die;* **the ~ countryside** die [Landschaft in der] Umgebung

surroundings /sə'raʊndɪŋz/ *n. pl.* Umgebung, *die*

sur'round sound *n., no pl.* Surroundsound, *der*

surtax /'sɜ:tæks/ *n.* Ergänzungsabgabe *od.* -steuer, *die*

surveillance /sə'veɪləns/ *n.* Überwachung, *die;* **keep sb. under ~:** jmdn. überwachen; **be under ~:** überwacht werden

sur'veillance system *n.* Überwachungssystem, *das*

survey
A /sə'veɪ/ *v.t.* 1 (take general view of) betrachten; (from high point) überblicken ‹*Landschaft, Umgebung*› 2 (examine) inspizieren ‹*Gebäude usw.*› 3 (assess) bewerten ‹*Situation, Problem usw.*› 4 (Surv.) vermessen ‹*Grundstück, Land usw.*›
B /'sɜ:veɪ/ *n.* 1 (general view, critical inspection) Überblick, *der* (**of** über + *Akk.*); (of landscape) Betrachtung, *die* 2 (by opinion poll) Umfrage, *die;* (by research) Untersuchung, *die;* **conduct a ~ into sth.** eine Umfrage zu etw. veranstalten/etw. untersuchen; **a telephone ~:** eine Telefonbefragung 3 (Surv.) Vermessung, *die* 4 (building inspection) Inspektion, *die*

surveying /sə'veɪɪŋ/ *n.* 1 Landvermessung, *die* 2 (Constr.) Abstecken, *das* 3 (profession) **go into ~:** Landvermesser/-vermesserin werden

surveyor /sə'veɪə(r)/ *n.* ▸ℹ **p. 1260** 1 (of building) Gutachter, *der*/Gutachterin, *die; see also* **quantity surveyor** 2 (of land) Landvermesser, *der*/-vermesserin, *die;* Geodät, *der*/Geodätin, *die* 3 (official inspector) **S~ of Weights and Measures** Eichmeister, *der*/-meisterin, *die* 4 (Amer.: customs officer) Zollbeamte, *der*/-beamtin, *die*

sur'vivable /sə'vaɪvəbl/ *adj.* überlebbar; **the accident was not ~:** den Unfall hätte kein Mensch überleben können; **a very ~ illness** eine Krankheit mit hoher Überlebenschance

survival /sə'vaɪvl/ *n.* 1 *no pl.* Überleben, *das;* (of tradition) Fortbestand, *der;* (of building) Erhaltung, *die;* **fight for ~:** Existenzkampf, *der;* **his ~ as Foreign Minister** (fig.) sein politisches Überleben als Außenminister; **the ~ of the fittest** (Biol.) [das] Überleben der Stärkeren 2 (relic) Überrest, *der*

survival: ~ course *n.* Überlebenskurs, *der;* **~ kit** *n.* Notausrüstung, *die;* **~ rate** *n.* Überlebensrate, *die;* **~ skills** *n. pl.* Überlebenstechniken *Pl.;* **~ strategy** *n.* Überlebensstrategie, *die*

survive /sə'vaɪv/
A *v.t.* überleben; **she ~d her son by 20 years** sie überlebte ihren Sohn um 20 Jahre
B *v.i.* ‹*Person:*› überleben; ‹*Schriften, Gebäude, Traditionen:*› erhalten bleiben; **he'll/you'll** *etc.* **~** (iron.) er wirds/du wirsts *usw.* [schon] überleben

survivor /sə'vaɪvə(r)/ *n.* Überlebende, *der/die;* **he's a ~:** er ist nicht unterzukriegen

susceptibility /səseptɪ'bɪlɪtɪ/ *n.* 1 (being susceptible) (to flattery, persuasion, etc.) Empfänglichkeit, *die* (**to** für); (to illness, injury, etc.) Anfälligkeit, *die* (**to** für); **~ to pain** Schmerzempfindlichkeit, *die* 2 *in pl.* (feelings) Feingefühl, *das*

susceptible /sə'septɪbl/ *adj.* 1 (sensitive) (to flattery, persuasion, etc.) empfänglich (**to** für); (to illness, injury, etc.) anfällig (**to** für) 2 (easily influenced) empfindsam; beeindruckbar 3 **be ~ of sth.** etw. zulassen; **your work is ~ of improvement** Ihre Arbeit ließe sich verbessern; **~ of proof** beweisbar

sushi /'su:ʃɪ/ *n., no pl.* Sushi, *das*

suspect
A /sə'spekt/ *v.t.* 1 (imagine to be likely) vermuten; **~ the worst** das Schlimmste befürchten; **~ sb. to be sth., ~ that sb. is sth.** glauben *od.* vermuten, dass jmd. etw. ist; **I ~ that he doesn't really want to come** ich vermute, dass er eigentlich gar nicht kommen will; **you, I ~, don't care** dir, habe ich das Gefühl, ist das egal 2 (mentally accuse) verdächtigen; **~ sb. of sth./of doing sth.** jmdn. einer Sache verdächtigen/jmdn. verdächtigen, etw. zu tun; **he is ~ed of telling lies** man verdächtigt ihn der Lüge; **~ed of drug-trafficking** des Drogenhandels verdächtig 3 (mistrust) bezweifeln ‹*Echtheit*›; **~ sb.'s motives** jmds. Beweggründen mit Argwohn gegenüberstehen
B /'sʌspekt/ *adj.* fragwürdig; suspekt (geh.); verdächtig ‹*Stoff, Paket, Fahrzeug*›
C /'sʌspekt/ *n.* Verdächtige, *der/die;* **political ~s** politisch Verdächtige; **a murder ~:** ein Mordverdächtiger/eine Mordverdächtige

suspected /sə'spektɪd/ *adj.* verdächtig; **there is a ~ connection between x and y** man vermutet einen Zusammenhang zwischen x und y; **~ smallpox cases, ~ cases of smallpox** Fälle mit Verdacht auf Pocken

suspend /sə'spend/ *v.t.* 1 (hang up) [auf]hängen; **be ~ed [from sth.]** [von etw.] [herab]hängen; **be ~ed in mid-air** frei in der Luft schweben 2 (stop, defer) suspendieren ‹*Rechte*›; **~ hostilities/the publication of the magazine** Kampfhandlungen/das Erscheinen der Zeitschrift [vorübergehend] einstellen; **~ judgement** sich des Urteils enthalten; **~ the proceedings** die Verhandlungen/das Verfahren aussetzen (Rechtsw.) 3 (remove from post) ausschließen (**from** von); sperren ‹*Sportler*›; vom Unterricht ausschließen ‹*Schüler*›; **~ sb. from duty [pending an inquiry]** jmdn. [während einer schwebenden Untersuchung] vom Dienst suspendieren

suspended: ~ ani'mation *n.* vorübergehender Atemstillstand; **wait in a state of ~ animation** (fig.) atemlos warten; **~ particle** *n.* (Phys.) schwebendes Teilchen; **~ 'sentence** *n.* (Law) Strafe mit Bewährung; **he was given a two-year ~ sentence** er erhielt zwei Jahre Haft auf Bewährung (Rechtsw.)

suspender belt /sə'spendə belt/ *n.* (Brit.) Strumpfbandgürtel, *der*

suspenders /sə'spendəz/ *n. pl.* 1 (Brit.) (for stockings) Strumpfbänder *od.* -halter; (for socks) Sockenhalter 2 (Amer.: for trousers) Hosenträger

suspense /sə'spens/ *n.* Spannung, *die;* **the ~ is killing me** (joc.) ich komme um vor Spannung (scherzh.); ich bin gespannt wie ein Regenschirm (ugs. scherzh.); **keep sb. in ~:** jmdn. auf die Folter spannen

suspension /sə'spenʃn/ *n.* 1 (action of debarring) Ausschluss, *der;* (from office) Suspendierung, *die;* (Sport) Sperrung, *die;* **be under ~** ‹*Schüler:*› [zeitweilig] vom Unterricht ausgeschlossen sein; ‹*Sportler:*› [zeitweilig] gesperrt sein 2 (temporary cessation) Suspendierung, *die;* (of publication, train service, hostilities) [vorübergehende] Einstellung 3 (hanging) Aufhängen, *das* 4 (Chem.) Suspension, *die* 5 (Motor Veh.) Federung, *die;* (mounting of wheels) Radaufhängung, *die* 6 (Mus.) Vorhalt, *der*

su'spension bridge *n.* Hängebrücke, *die*

suspicion /sə'spɪʃn/ *n.* 1 (uneasy feeling) Misstrauen, *das* (**of** gegenüber); (more specific) Verdacht, *der;* (unconfirmed belief) Ahnung, *die;* Verdacht, *der;* **have a ~ that ...:** den Verdacht haben, dass ...; **I have my ~s about him** er kommt mir verdächtig vor; ich traue ihm nicht ganz; **view** *or* **regard sb./sth. with ~:** jmdm./etw. mit Misstrauen begegnen 2 (suspecting) Verdacht, *der* (**of** auf + *Akk.*); **~ is not enough** ein Verdacht genügt nicht; **protected from ~:** gegen Verdächtigungen geschützt; **on ~ of theft/murder** *etc.* wegen Verdachts auf Diebstahl/Mordverdachts *usw.;* **lay oneself open to ~:** sich verdächtig machen; **be under ~:** verdächtigt werden 3 (trace) **a ~ of salt** eine Spur Salz

suspicious /sə'spɪʃəs/ *adj.* 1 (tending to suspect) misstrauisch (**of** gegenüber); **be ~ of sb./sth.** jmdm./einer Sache misstrauen 2 (arousing suspicion) verdächtig

suspiciously /sə'spɪʃəslɪ/ *adv.* 1 (as to arouse suspicion) verdächtig; **look ~ like sth.** verdächtig nach etw. aussehen 2 (warily) misstrauisch

S

suspiciousness /sə'spɪʃəsnɪs/ *n.*, *no pl.* Verdächtigkeit, *die;* (disposition to suspect) Argwohn, *der;* Misstrauen, *das*

suss /sʌs/ *v.t.* (Brit. coll.) blicken (ugs.); **~ sb.** jmdn. durchschauen; **~ out** blicken (ugs.)

sustain /sə'steɪn/ *v.t.* **1** (withstand) widerstehen (+ *Dat.*) ‹*Druck*›; standhalten (+ *Dat.*) ‹*Angriff*›; aushalten ‹*Vergleich*›; tragen ‹*Gewicht*› **2** (support, uphold) aufrechterhalten; **too little to ~ life** nicht genug zum Leben; **not enough to ~ a family** nicht genug, um eine Familie zu unterhalten; **~ an objection** einem Einwand stattgeben **3** (suffer) erleiden ‹*Niederlage, Verlust, Verletzung*›; **~ damage** Schaden nehmen **4** (maintain) bestreiten ‹*Unterhaltung*›; bewahren ‹*Interesse*›; wahren ‹*Ruf*›; [beibe]halten ‹*Geschwindigkeit*›; durchhalten ‹*Rolle*›; **~ a note** (Mus.) eine Note aushalten; **~ a task** einer Aufgabe gerecht werden

sustainable /sʌ'steɪnəbl/ *adj.* (Ecology) nachhaltig

sustained /sə'steɪnd/ *adj.* **1** (prolonged) länger …; anhaltend ‹*Beifall*›; ausdauernd ‹*Anstrengung*›; **~ speed** Dauergeschwindigkeit, *die* **2** (Mus.) ausgehalten

sustained-re'lease *adj.* (Pharm.) **~ drug/tablet** Medikament/Tablette mit Depotwirkung; **a ~ product** Depotpräparat, *das*

sustaining /sə'steɪnɪŋ/ *adj.* stärkend; nahrhaft ‹*Essen, Mahlzeit*›

sustaining: ~ 'pedal *n.* (Mus.) Fortepedal, *das;* **~ 'program** *n.* (Amer. Radio and Telev.) *nicht von einem Sponsor getragenes Programm*

sustenance /'sʌstɪnəns/ *n.* **1** (nourishment, food) Nahrung, *die;* **draw** *or* **get one's ~ from sth.** sich von etw. ernähren **2** (nourishing quality) **there is no ~ in it** es hat keinen Nährwert

suture /'su:tʃə(r)/ (Med.)

A *n.* (stitch) Naht, *die;* (thread) Faden, *der*

B *v.t.* nähen

svelte /svelt/ *adj.* grazil; anmutig ‹*Bewegungen*›

SW *abbr.* **1** /saʊθ'west/ ▸ℹ **p. 1013 = southwest** SW **2** /saʊθ'westən/ ▸ℹ **p. 1013 = south-western** sw. **3** (Radio) **= short wave** KW

swab /swɒb/

A *n.* **1** (Med.: absorbent pad) Tupfer, *der* **2** (Med.: specimen) Abstrich, *der* **3** (pad or mop for cleaning decks) Dweil, *der* (Seemannsspr.)

B *v.t.*, **-bb- 1 ~ [down]** wischen; schwabbern ‹*Deck*› (Seemannsspr.) **2** (Med.) betupfen ‹*Wunde*›

Swabia /'sweɪbɪə/ *pr. n.* Schwaben (*das*)

Swabian /'sweɪbɪən/

A *adj.* schwäbisch; **sb. is ~:** jmd. ist Schwabe/Schwäbin

B *n.* **1** (person) Schwabe, *der*/Schwäbin, *die* **2** (dialect) Schwäbisch, *das;* **sb. speaks ~:** jmd. schwäbelt

swaddle /'swɒdl/ *v.t.* wickeln ‹*Baby*›; **swaddling clothes** (Bibl.) Windeln

swag /swæg/ *n.* **1** (coll.: stolen goods) Beute, *die;* Sore, *die* (Gaunerspr.) **2** (Austral., NZ: bundle) Bündel, *das*

swagger /'swægə(r)/

A *v.i.* **1** (walk with a ~) großspurig stolzieren **2** (behave in domineering way) großspurig auftreten **3** (boast) angeben (ugs.); aufschneiden

B *n.* ▸**A: 1** großspuriges Stolzieren **2** großspuriges Gehabe; **walk with a ~:** arrogant auftreten **3** Angeberei, *die* (ugs.)

'swagger cane (Brit.) ▸**swagger stick**

swaggering /'swægərɪŋ/

A *n.* **1** (boasting) Angeberei, *die* (ugs.) **2** (manner) arrogantes *od.* großspuriges Auftreten

B *adj.* stolzierend ‹*Gang*›; großspurig ‹*Gehabe*›

'swagger stick *n.* Offiziersstöckchen, *das*

swagman /'swægmən/ *n.*, *pl.* **swagmen** /'swægmən/ (Austral., NZ) Landstreicher, *der*

Swahili /swɑ:'hi:lɪ, swə'hi:lɪ/ ▸ℹ **p. 1277**

A *adj.* Swahili-; *see also* **English A**

B *n.* **1** *no pl.* (language) Swahili, *das; see also* **English B 1 2** *pl. same* (person) Swahili, *der/die*

swain /sweɪn/ *n.* (arch./joc.) **1** (peasant) Bauernbursche, *der* **2** (lover) Freier, *der*

swallow¹ /'swɒləʊ/

A *v.t.* **1** schlucken; (by mistake) verschlucken ‹*Fischgräte, fig.: Wort, Silbe*›; **~ the bait** (fig.) den Köder schlucken (ugs.) **2** (repress) hinunterschlucken (ugs.) ‹*Stolz, Ärger*›; **~ one's words** [demütig] zurücknehmen, was man gesagt hat **3** (believe) schlucken (ugs.), glauben ‹*Geschichte, Erklärung*›; **I find this hard to ~:** das kann ich kaum glauben **4** (put up with) schlucken (ugs.) ‹*Beleidigung, Unrecht*›

B *v.i.* schlucken

C *n.* Schluck, *der*

Phrasal verb

- **~ 'up** *v.t.* **1** (make disappear) verschlucken; schlucken ‹*kleinere Betriebe, Gebiete*›; **I wished the earth would ~ me up** ich wäre am liebsten vor Scham in den Boden versunken **2** (exhaust, consume) auffressen; verschlingen ‹*große Summen*›

swallow² *n.* (Ornith.) Schwalbe, *die;* **one ~ does not make a summer** (prov.) eine Schwalbe macht noch keinen Sommer (Spr.)

swallow: ~ dive *n.* (Brit.) *Tauchsprung, bei dem die Arme bis kurz vor dem Eintauchen seitlich ausgestreckt werden;* **~tail** *n.* Schwalbenschwanz, *der*

swam ▸**swim A, B**

swamp /swɒmp/

A *n.* Sumpf, *der*

B *v.t.* **1** (flood) überschwemmen **2** (overwhelm) **be ~ed with letters/applications/orders/work** mit Briefen/Bewerbungen/Aufträgen überschwemmt werden/bis über den Hals in Arbeit stecken (ugs.)

'swampland *n.* Sumpfland, *das*

swampy /'swɒmpɪ/ *adj.* sumpfig

swan /swɒn/

A *n.* Schwan, *der;* **black ~:** Schwarzer Schwan; Trauerschwan, *der*

B *v.i.*, **-nn-** (coll.) ziehen; **~ about** *or* **around** herumziehen (ugs.); (in small area) rumlaufen (ugs.); **~ off** losziehen (ugs.)

'swan dive (Amer.) ▸**swallow dive**

swank /swæŋk/ (coll.)

A *n.* **1** Angeberei, *die* (ugs.); Angabe, *die* (ugs.) **2** (person) Angeber, *der*/Angeberin, *die*

B *v.i.* angeben (ugs.) (**about** mit); **~ around** herumstolzieren (ugs.)

swanky /'swæŋkɪ/ *adj.* (coll.) protzig (ugs.); **~ car** Angeberauto, *das*

swan: ~ neck *n.* Schwanenhals, *der;* **~sdown** *n.* Schwanendaunen *Pl.;* **~song** *n.* (fig.) Schwanengesang, *der*

swap /swɒp/

A *v.t.*, **-pp-** tauschen (**for** gegen); austauschen ‹*Erfahrungen, Erinnerungen*›; **~ jokes** sich (*Dat.*) [gegenseitig] Witze erzählen; **~ places [with sb.]** [mit jmdm.] den Platz *od.* die Plätze tauschen; (fig.) [mit jmdm.] tauschen; *see also* **horse A 1**

B *v.i.*, **-pp-** tauschen; **will you ~?** tauschst du?

C *n.* Tausch, *der;* **do a ~ [with sb.]** [mit jmdm.] tauschen

sward /swɔ:d/ *n.* (literary) Rasen, *der;* Rasenfläche, *die*

swarf /swɔ:f/ *n.* feine Metallspäne

swarm /swɔ:m/

A *n.* **1** Schwarm, *der;* **~ [of bees]** Bienenschwarm, *der;* (settled in a hive) Bienenvolk, *das* **2** *in pl.* (great numbers) **~s of tourists/children** Scharen von Touristen/Kindern

B *v.i.* **1** (move in a ~) schwärmen **2** (teem) wimmeln (**with** von); **the shops were ~ing with tourists** in den Geschäften wimmelte es von Touristen

Phrasal verb

- **~ up** *v.t.* hochklettern

swarthiness /'swɔ:ðɪnɪs/ *n.*, *no pl.* (complexion) dunkle Gesichtsfarbe; (of person) Dunkelhäutigkeit, *die*

swarthy /'swɔ:ðɪ/ *adj.* dunkel ‹*Gesichtsfarbe*›; dunkelhäutig ‹*Person*›

swashbuckler /'swɒʃbʌklə(r)/ *n.* Draufgänger, *der*

swashbuckling /'swɒʃbʌklɪŋ/ *adj.* draufgängerisch

swastika /'swɒstɪkə/ *n.* (of Nazis) Hakenkreuz, *das;* (ancient symbol) Swastika, *die*

swat /swɒt/

A *v.t.*, **-tt- 1** (hit hard) schlagen; hauen (ugs.) **2** (crush) totschlagen ‹*Fliege, Wespe*›

B *n.* **1** (slap) Klaps, *der;* **give a fly a ~, take a ~ at a fly** nach einer Fliege schlagen **2** (fly swatter) Klatsche, *die*

swatch /swɒtʃ/ *n.* **1** (sample) Muster, *das* **2** (collection of samples) Musterbuch, *das; attrib.* **~ book** Musterbuch, *das*

swath /swɔ:θ/ ▸**swathe B**

swathe /sweɪð/

A *v.t.* [ein]hüllen; **~d in bandages** ganz in Bandagen eingewickelt; **~d in mist** in Nebel gehüllt

B *n.* (cut by mower) gemähte Bahn; (broad strip) breiter Streifen; (in forest) Schneise, *die;* **cut a ~ through the corn/the undergrowth/the forest** eine Bahn durch das Getreide/Unterholz schneiden/eine Schneise durch den Wald schlagen

swatter /'swɒtə(r)/ *n.* Klatsche, *die*

sway /sweɪ/

A *v.i.* [hin und her] schwanken; (gently) sich wiegen; **~ towards sth.** (on one's feet) einer Sache entgegenschwanken; (lean down to) sich einer Sache (*Dat.*) zuneigen

B *v.t.* **1** wiegen ‹*Kopf, Hüften, Zweig, Wipfel*›; hin und her schwanken lassen ‹*Baum, Mast, Antenne*› **2** (have influence over) beeinflussen; (persuade) überreden; **be ~ed by sth.** sich von etw. beeinflussen lassen; **she will not be ~ed over sanctions** sie bleibt in der Frage der Sanktionen hart

C *n.* Herrschaft, *die;* **have sb. under one's ~, hold ~ over sb.** über jmdn. herrschen

swear /sweə(r)/

A *v.t.*, **swore** /swɔ:(r)/, **sworn** /swɔ:n/ **1** schwören ‹*Eid usw.*›; **they swore eternal fidelity** sie schworen sich (*Dat.*) ewige Treue; **I could have sworn [that] it was him** ich hätte schwören können, dass er es war; *see also* **blind B 2 2** (administer oath to) vereidigen ‹*Zeugen*›; **~ sb. to secrecy** jmdn. auf Geheimhaltung einschwören; *see also* **sworn**

B *v.i.*, **swore, sworn 1** (use ~ words) fluchen **2 ~ to sth.** (be certain of) etw. beschwören; einen Eid auf etw. (*Akk.*) ablegen; **I wouldn't like to ~ to it** (coll.) ich will es nicht beschwören **3** (take oath) schwören, einen Eid ablegen (**on** auf + *Akk.*)

C *n.* Fluch, *der;* **have a ~:** fluchen

Phrasal verbs

- **~ at** *v.t.* beschimpfen
- **~ by** *v.t.* (coll.: have confidence in) schwören auf (+ *Akk.*)
- **~ 'in** *v.t.* vereidigen ‹*Geschworenen, Zeugen*›
- **~ 'out** *v.t.* (Amer.) **~ a warrant out against sb.** gegen jmdn. durch eine eidliche [Straf]anzeige einen Haftbefehl erwirken

'swear word *n.* Kraftausdruck, *der;* Fluch, *der;* **use ~s** fluchen

sweat /swet/

A *n.* **1** Schweiß, *der;* **in** *or* **by the ~ of one's brow** im Schweiße seines Angesichtes; **be in a ~ [with fear]** [vor Angst] schwitzen; **be in a ~ to do sth.** (fig.: be anxious) danach fiebern, etw. zu tun; **I came** *or* **broke out in a ~:** mir brach der [Angst]schweiß aus; **don't get in such a ~!** reg dich nicht so auf!; **be all of a ~ at the prospect of the exam** beim Gedanken an die Prüfung ins Schwitzen geraten *od.* kommen **2** (drudgery) Plagerei, *die;* Plackerei, *die* (ugs.); **no ~!** (coll.) kein Problem! (ugs.) **3** (drops on surface) Kondenswasser, *das;* (on cheese) Fetttröpfchen. *see also* **cold sweat**

B *v.i.*, **~ed** *or* (Amer.) **~ 1** (perspire) schwitzen; **~ like a pig** (coll.) schwitzen wie die Sau (salopp); **~ with fear** vor Angst schwitzen **2** (fig.: suffer) **he made me sit outside ~ing** er ließ mich draußen sitzen und schmoren (ugs.) **3** (drudge) sich placken (ugs.); **we had to ~ to get the job finished** wir mussten uns anstrengen, um mit der Arbeit fertig zu werden; **make sb. ~** (make work in bad conditions) jmdn. schwitzen *od.* (ugs.) schuften lassen **4** (produce surface moisture) schwitzen

C *v.t.* **1** (employ in bad conditions) schwitzen *od.*

(ugs.) schuften lassen 2 (~ **blood** (fig.) Blut und Wasser schwitzen (ugs.) 3 (emit like ~) ausschwitzen 4 ~ **it out** (coll.) durchhalten; ausharren

'sweatband *n.* Schweißband, *das*

sweated labour /swetɪd 'leɪbə(r)/ *n., no pl.* unterbezahlte [Schwer]arbeit; (workers) unterbezahlte Arbeitskräfte

sweater /'swetə(r)/ *n.* Pullover, *der*

sweat: ~ **gland** *n.* Schweißdrüse, *die;* ~**shirt** *n.* Sweatshirt, *das;* ~**shop** *n.* ausbeuterische [kleine] Klitsche (ugs.)

sweaty /'swetɪ/ *adj.* (moist with sweat) schweißig; schweißnass; schwitzend ‹*Käse*›

swede *n.* Kohlrübe, *die*

Swede /swi:d/ *n.* ▸❶ **p. 1345** Schwede, *der*/Schwedin, *die*

Sweden /'swi:dn/ *pr. n.* Schweden (*das*)

Swedish /'swi:dɪʃ/ ▸❶ **p. 1277**, ▸❶ **p. 1345**

A *adj.* schwedisch; **sb. is** ~: jmd. ist Schwede/Schwedin; *see also* **English A**

B *n.* Schwedisch, *das; see also* **English B 1**

sweep /swi:p/

A *v.t.*, **swept** [swept] 1 fegen (bes. nordd.); kehren (bes. südd.); ~ **the board**, ~ **all before one** (fig.: win all awards) auf der ganzen Linie siegen 2 (move with force) fegen; **the current swept the logs along** die Strömung riss die Hölzer mit; **the wave of protest swept the opposition into office** die Protestwelle katapultierte die Opposition an die Macht 3 (traverse swiftly) ~ **the hillside/plain** ‹*Wind:*› über die Hügel/Ebene fegen; ~ **the country** ‹*Epidemie, Mode:*› das Land überrollen; ‹*Feuer:*› durch das Land fegen; **searchlights swept the sky** Suchscheinwerfer huschten über den Himmel; ~ **an area with fire** (Mil.) ein Gebiet mit Feuer bestreichen 4 (search) durchsuchen (**for** nach); ~ **a channel for mines** eine Fahrrinne nach Minen absuchen. *See also* **carpet A 1**

B *v.i.*, **swept** 1 (clean) fegen (bes. nordd.); kehren (bes. südd.) 2 (go fast, in stately manner) ‹*Vogel:*› gleiten; ‹*Mensch, Auto:*› rauschen; ‹*Wind usw.:*› fegen 3 (extend) sich erstrecken; **the road** ~**s to the left** die Straße macht einen großen Bogen nach links; **his glance swept from left to right** sein Blick glitt von links nach rechts

C *n.* 1 (cleaning) **give sth. a** ~: etw. fegen (bes. nordd.); etw. kehren (bes. südd.); **make a clean** ~ (fig.) (get rid of everything) gründlich aufräumen; (win all prizes) gründlich abräumen (ugs.); **make a clean** ~ **of the prizes** alle Preise einheimsen (ugs.) 2 ▸**chimney sweep** 3 (coll.) ▸**sweepstake** 4 (motion) (of arm) ausholende Bewegung; **with an impatient** ~ **of his hand** mit einer ungeduldigen Handbewegung 5 (stretch) **a wide/an open** ~ **of country** ein weiter Landstrich 6 (curve of road, river) Bogen, *der;* **the wide** ~ **of the bay** die geschwungene Kurve der Bucht 7 (sortie by aircraft) Einsatz, *der* (Milit.)

Phrasal verbs

- ~ **a'side** *v.t.* 1 (dismiss) beiseite schieben ‹*Einwand, Zweifel*›; überrennen ‹*gegnerische Mannschaft*›; aus dem Weg scheuchen ‹*Reporter*› 2 (push aside) wegfegen; beiseite fegen
- ~ **a'way** *v.t.* fortreißen; (fig.) hinwegfegen (geh.) ‹*Traditionen*›; (abolish) aufräumen mit ‹*Privilegien, Korruption*›
- ~ **'by** *v.i.* vorbeirauschen
- ~ **'down** *v.i.* 1 ~ **down on sb./sth.** sich auf jmdn./etw. stürzen 2 **the hills** ~ **down to the sea** die Berge fallen in sanftem Bogen zum Meer hinab
- ~ **'in** *v.i.* 1 (enter majestically) einziehen 2 (Polit.) [mit großer Mehrheit] an die Macht kommen
- ~ **'off**

A *v.i.* abrauschen (ugs.)

B *v.t.* fortreißen; *see also* **foot A 1**

- ~ **'out**

A *v.t.* ausfegen (bes. nordd.); auskehren (bes. südd.)

B *v.i.* abrauschen (ugs.)

- ~ **'up**

A *v.t.* zusammenfegen (bes. nordd.); zusammenkehren (bes. südd.)

B *v.i.* angerauscht kommen

sweeper /'swi:pə(r)/ *n.* 1 **[road]** ~ (person) Straßenfeger, *der* (bes. nordd.); Straßenkehrer, *der* (bes. südd.); (machine) Straßenkehrmaschine, *die; see also* **carpet sweeper**; **minesweeper** 2 (Footb.) Libero, *der*

sweeping /'swi:pɪŋ/

A *adj.* 1 (without limitations) pauschal 2 (far-reaching) weit reichend ‹*Einsparung*›; umfassend ‹*Reform*›; durchschlagend ‹*Sieg, Erfolg*›; umwälzend ‹*Veränderung*› 3 (moving in a wide curve) ausholend ‹*Geste, Bewegung*›; schwungvoll ‹*Knicks, Verbeugung*›; schweifend ‹*Blick*›

B *n. in pl.* Kehricht, *der*

sweepingly /'swi:pɪŋlɪ/ *adv.* pauschal

sweep: ~ **'second hand** *n.* (Horol.) Zentralsekundenzeiger, *der;* ~**stake** *n.* 1 (race, contest) Sweepstake[rennen], *das;* 2 (lottery) *Pferdetoto, bei dem sich die Gewinnsumme aus den Einsätzen zusammensetzt*

sweet /swi:t/

A *adj.* 1 (to taste) süß; ~ **tea** gesüßter Tee; **have a** ~ **tooth** gern Süßes mögen; **with a** ~ **tooth like yours ...:** da du so gern *od.* viel Süßes isst ... 2 (lovely) süß; reizend ‹*Wesen, Gesicht, Mädchen, Kleid*›; ~ **dreams!** träum[e]/träumt süß!; **how** ~ **of you!** wie nett *od.* lieb von dir!; **keep sb.** ~: jmdn. bei [guter] Laune halten; **he's** ~ **on her** (dated coll.) er hat eine Schwäche für sie; **at one's own** ~ **will, in one's own** ~ **way** wie es einem [gerade] passt; **go one's own** ~ **way** machen, was einem passt 3 (fragrant) süß; frisch ‹*Atem*›; **be** ~ **with sth.** süß nach etw. duften; **the** ~ **smell of success** (fig.) die Süße des Erfolgs (geh., scherzh.) 4 (musical) süß (geh.); lieblich ‹*Stimme, Musik, Klang*›. *See also* **basil**; **chestnut A 1**; **pepper A 2**; **sweet potato**; **seventeen A**; **sixteen A**; **violet A 1**

B *n.* 1 (Brit.: piece of confectionery) Bonbon, *das od. der;* (with chocolate, fudge, etc.) Süßigkeit, *die* 2 (Brit.: dessert) Nachtisch, *der;* Dessert, *das;* **for** ~: zum Nachtisch *od.* Dessert 3 *in pl.* (delights) Freuden; Wonnen (geh.) 4 (darling) **[my]** ~ (female) [meine] Liebste; (male) [mein] Liebster

sweet: ~**-and-'sour** *attrib. adj.* süßsauer; ~**bread** *n.* (Gastr.) Bries, *das;* ~ **brier** *n.* Weinrose, *die;* ~ **corn** *n.* Zuckermais, *der*

sweeten /'swi:tn/ *v.t.* 1 (add sugar etc. to) süßen 2 (add fragrance to) süß machen; versüßen; (remove bad smell of) reinigen ‹*Luft, Atem*› 3 (make agreeable) versüßen ‹*Leben, Abend*›; milde stimmen ‹*Person*›; *see also* **pill 2**

sweetener /'swi:tnə(r)/ *n.* 1 Süßstoff, *der;* **use honey as a** ~: Honig zum Süßen verwenden 2 (bribe) kleine Aufmerksamkeit (iron.)

'sweetheart *n.* Schatz, *der;* Liebling, *der;* **an old** ~: eine alte Liebe (ugs.); **how long have they been** ~**s?** wie lange gehen sie schon miteinander? (ugs.)

sweetie /'swi:tɪ/ *n.* 1 (Brit. child lang.) ▸**sweet B 1** 2 (coll.: darling) Schatz, *der;* ~ **[pie]** (term of endearment) Liebling, *der;* Schätzchen, *das* (ugs.)

sweetish /'swi:tɪʃ/ *adj.* süßlich

sweetly /'swi:tlɪ/ *adv.* lieb; süß ‹*spielen, singen*›; **run** ~ ‹*Motor:*› schön rund laufen

sweet: ~**meal** *adj.* ~**meal biscuits** süße Vollkornkekse; ~**meat** *n.* Süßigkeit, *die*

sweetness /'swi:tnɪs/ *n., no pl.* 1 (in taste) Süße, *die* 2 (fragrance) süßer Duft 3 (melodiousness) Süße, *die* (geh.) 4 **all is** ~ **and light** es herrscht eitel Freude und Sonnenschein (meist scherzh.)

sweet: ~ **'pea** *n.* (Bot.) Wicke, *die;* ~ **po'tato** *n.* Batate, *die;* Süßkartoffel, *die;* ~**-scented** *adj.* süß [duftend]; wohlriechend; ~**shop** *n.* (Brit.) Süßwarengeschäft, *das;* ~**-smelling** ▸~**-scented**; ~ **talk** *n.* Süßholzgeraspel, *das* (ugs.); ~**-talk** *v.t.* ~**-talk sb. [into doing sth.]** jmdn. beschwatzen[, etw. zu tun]; ~**-tempered** /'swi:ttempəd/ *adj.* sanftmütig; ~ **'william** *n.* (Bot.) Bartnelke, *die*

swell /swel/

A *v.t.*, ~**ed, swollen** /'swəʊlən/ *or* ~**ed** 1 (increase in size, height) anschwellen lassen; aufquellen lassen ‹*Holz*› 2 (increase amount of) anschwellen lassen; vergrößern; ~ **the ranks [of participants]** die Zahl der Teilnehmer vergrößern 3 blähen ‹*Segel*›

B *v.i.*, ~**ed, swollen** *or* ~**ed** 1 (expand) ‹*Körperteil:*› anschwellen; ‹*Segel:*› sich blähen; ‹*Backen:*› sich aufblähen; ‹*Material:*› aufquellen 2 (increase in amount) ‹*Anzahl:*› zunehmen; ‹*Gehalt:*› steigen 3 (become louder) anschwellen (**[in]to** zu) 4 (fig.) ‹*Herz:*› schwellen (geh.)

C *n.* 1 (of sea) Dünung, *die* 2 (Mus.) Schwellwerk, *das* 3 (dated coll.) feiner Herr/feine Dame; **the** ~**s** die feinen Leute; (smart set) die Schickeria (ugs.) 4 (act, condition) Schwellen, *das*

D *adj.* (coll.) 1 (dated: stylish, socially prominent) schick; fein 2 (Amer.: excellent) toll (ugs.)

'swell box *n.* (Mus.) Jalousieschweller, *der*

swelling /'swelɪŋ/

A *n.* Schwellung, *die* (Med.)

B *adj.* 1 (growing larger, louder) anschwellend 2 (increasing) wachsend; steigend ‹*Flut*› 3 (bulging) gebläht ‹*Segel*›

'swell organ *n.* (Mus.) Schwellwerk, *das*

swelter /'sweltə(r)/ *v.i.* [vor Hitze] [fast] vergehen; ~ **in the heat** in der Hitze schmoren (ugs.); ~**ing** glühend heiß ‹*Tag, Wetter*›; ~**ing heat** Bruthitze, *die*

swept ▸**sweep A, B**

swept: ~**-back** *adj.* ~**-back wing** positiv gepfeilter Flügel; ~**-back hair** zurückgekämmtes Haar; ~**-wing** *adj.* ‹*Flugzeug*› mit Pfeilflügeln

swerve /swɜ:v/

A *v.i.* (deviate) einen Bogen *od.* (ugs.) Schlenker machen; ~ **to the right/left** nach rechts/links [aus]schwenken; ~ **from its path** ‹*Fahrzeug:*› ausscheren; ~ **in the air** ‹*Vogel, Ball:*› in der Luft abdrehen; **she never** ~**d from her duty** sie hat ihre Pflicht immer treu erfüllt

B *n.* 1 (divergence from course) Bogen, *der;* Schlenker, *der* (ugs.) 2 (swerving motion) **put a** ~ **on a ball** einem Ball [einen] Effet geben

swift /swɪft/

A *adj.* schnell; flink, schnell ‹*Bewegung*›; ~ **action** rasches Handeln; ~ **retribution** prompte Bestrafung; **have a** ~ **temper, be** ~ **to anger** jähzornig sein

B *n.* (Ornith.) Mauersegler, *der*

swiftly /'swɪftlɪ/ *adv.* schnell; (soon) bald

swiftness /'swɪftnɪs/ *n.* Schnelligkeit, *die;* ~ **of action** schnelles *od.* rasches Handeln

swig /swɪg/ (coll.)

A *v.t.*, **-gg-** schlucken (ugs.); [herunter]kippen (ugs.)

B *v.i.*, **-gg-** [hastig] trinken

C *n.* Schluck, *der;* **have/take a** ~ **[of beer** *etc.***]** einen tüchtigen Schluck [Bier *usw.*] trinken/nehmen

swill /swɪl/

A *v.t.* 1 (rinse) ~ **[out]** [aus]spülen; ~ **down the floor** den Fußboden abspülen 2 (derog.: drink greedily) hinunterspülen (ugs.)

B *n.* 1 (rinsing) Spülen, *das;* **give sth. a** ~ **[out]/down** etw. [aus]spülen/abspülen 2 (derog.: drink) Brühe, *die* (ugs. abwertend) 3 (for pigs) Schweinefutter, *das*

swim /swɪm/

A *v.i.*, **-mm-, swam** /swæm/, **swum** /swʌm/ 1 schwimmen; ~ **with/against the tide/stream** (fig.) mit dem/gegen den Strom schwimmen 2 (fig.: be flooded, overflow) ~ **with** *or* **in sth.** in etw. (*Dat.*) schwimmen; **her eyes swam with tears** ihre Augen schwammen; **the deck was** ~**ming with water** das Deck stand unter Wasser 3 (appear to whirl) ~ **[before sb.'s eyes]** [vor jmds. Augen] verschwimmen 4 (have dizzy sensation) **my head was** ~**ming** mir war schwindelig. *See also* **sink B 1**

B *v.t.*, **-mm-, swam, swum** schwimmen ‹*Strecke*›; durchschwimmen ‹*Fluss, See*›; ~ **[the] breaststroke/crawl** brustschwimmen/kraulen

C *n.* 1 **have a/go for a** ~: schwimmen/schwimmen gehen; **do you fancy a** ~**?** möchtest du schwimmen gehen?; **a refreshing** ~: ein erfrischendes Bad; **I like an early morning** ~: ich gehe gern frühmorgens schwimmen

[2] **be in the ~ [of things]** mitten im Geschehen sein

swimmer /ˈswɪmə(r)/ *n.* Schwimmer, *der*/Schwimmerin, *die;* **[not] be a ~:** [nicht] schwimmen können; **be a good/poor ~:** gut/schlecht schwimmen können

swimming /ˈswɪmɪŋ/
A *n.* Schwimmen, *das;* **like ~:** gern schwimmen
B *attrib. adj.* schwimmend

swimming: ~ baths *n. pl.* Schwimmbad, *das;* **~ costume** *n.* Badeanzug, *der;* **~ instructor** *n.* Schwimmlehrer, *der*/-lehrerin, *die;* **~ lesson** *n.* Schwimmstunde, *die;* **~ lessons** Schwimmunterricht, *der*

swimmingly /ˈswɪmɪŋlɪ/ *adv.* (coll.) glänzend; **go ~:** wie am Schnürchen klappen (ugs.)

swimming: ~ pool *n.* Schwimmbecken, *das;* (in house or garden) Swimmingpool, *der;* (building) Schwimmbad, *das;* **~ trunks** *n. pl.* Badehose, *die*

ˈswimsuit *n.* Badeanzug, *der*

swindle /ˈswɪndl/
A *v.t.* betrügen; **~ sb. out of sth.** jmdn. um etw. betrügen; (take by persuasion) jmdm. etw. abschwindeln
B *n.* Schwindel, *der;* Betrug, *der*

swindler /ˈswɪndlə(r)/ *n.* Schwindler, *der*/Schwindlerin, *die*

swine /swaɪn/ *n., pl. same* [1] (Amer./formal/Zool.) Schwein, *das* [2] (derog.: contemptible person) Schwein, *das* (abwertend) [3] (coll.: nasty thing) harter Brocken (ugs.); **be a ~ to operate** ‹*Maschine:*› verteufelt schwer zu bedienen sein (ugs.); **a ~ of a job** eine verteufelt (ugs.) *od.* (salopp) tierisch schwere Arbeit. *See also* **pearl 2**

swine: ~ fever *n.* Schweinepest, *die;* **~herd** *n.* Schweinehirt, *der*

swing /swɪŋ/
A *n.* [1] (apparatus) Schaukel, *die* [2] (spell of ~ing) Schaukeln, *das;* **want/have a ~:** schaukeln wollen/schaukeln [3] (Sport: strike, blow) Schlag, *der;* (Boxing) Schwinger, *der;* (Golf) Schwung, *der;* **take a ~ at sb./sth.** zum Schlag gegen jmdn./auf etw. (*Akk.*) ausholen [4] (of suspended object) Schwingen, *das;* **in full ~** (fig.) in vollem Gang[e] [5] (steady movement) Rhythmus, *der;* **the party went with a ~:** auf der Party herrschte eine tolle Stimmung (ugs.); **get into/be in the ~ of things** *or* **it** richtig reinkommen/richtig drin sein (ugs.) [6] (Mus.) Swing, *der* [7] (shift) Schwankung, *die;* (of public opinion) Wende, *die;* (amount of change in votes) Abwanderung, *die;* **a ~ to the Left/Right** ein Linksruck/Rechtsruck (Politik Jargon). *See also* **pendulum; roundabout A 2**
B *v.i.*, **swung** /swʌŋ/ [1] (turn on axis, sway) schwingen; (in wind) schaukeln; **~ open** ‹*Tür:*› aufgehen; **be ~ing at anchor** schwojen (Seemannsspr.) [2] (go in sweeping curve) schwenken; **the plane swung low over the field** das Flugzeug schwenkte über dem Feld in den Tiefflug; **~ from sb.'s arm/a tree** an jmds. Arm/einem Baum schwingen (geh.) *od.* baumeln [3] (go with ~ing gait) beschwingt gehen; **~ into action** (fig.) loslegen (ugs.) [4] (move oneself by ~ing) sich schwingen; **~ up** sich hinaufschwingen; **the car swung out of the drive** der Wagen schwenkte aus der Einfahrt [5] (sl.: be executed by hanging) baumeln (salopp); **he'll ~ for it** dafür wird er baumeln [6] **be ~ing** (coll.: be lively) auf vollen Touren laufen (ugs.) [7] (sl.: be promiscuous) die Abwechslung lieben (ugs. verhüll.); **~ both ways** (sl.) es mit Männlein wie Weiblein machen (ugs. verhüll.)
C *v.t.*, **swung** [1] schwingen; (rock) schaukeln; **~ one's legs** mit den Beinen baumeln; die Beine baumeln lassen; **~ a key on a chain** mit einem Schlüssel an einer Kette schlenkern; **~ sth. round and round** etw. kreisen *od.* im Kreise wirbeln lassen; **cranes ~ cargo on to the ship** Kräne befördern schwingende Lasten auf das Schiff [2] (cause to face in another direction) schwenken; **~ sb. round** jmdn. herumwirbeln; **he swung the car off the road/into the road** er schwenkte [mit dem Auto] von der Straße ab/in die Straße ein [3] (have influence on) umschlagen lassen ‹*öffentliche Meinung*›; **~ the elections** den Ausgang der Wahlen entscheiden; **what swung it for me ...:** was für mich den Ausschlag gab ... [4] (suspend by its ends) aufhängen ‹*Hängematte*› [5] (coll.: arrange) deichseln (salopp). *See also* **cat 1**

Phrasal verbs
- **~ at** *v.t.* **~ at sb./sth.** zum Schlag auf jmdn./etw. ausholen
- **~ ˈround** *v.i.* sich schnell umdrehen (**on** nach); (in surprise) herumfahren

swing: ~bin *n.* Schwingdeckel[müll]eimer, *der;* Mülleimer mit Schwingdeckel; **~ bridge** *n.* Drehbrücke, *die;* **~ ˈdoor** *n.* Pendeltür, *die*

swingeing /ˈswɪndʒɪŋ/ *adj.* (Brit.) hart ‹*Schlag*›; (fig.) drastisch ‹*Kürzung, Maßnahme*›; scharf ‹*Attacke*›

swinging /ˈswɪŋɪŋ/ *adj.* [1] schwingend [2] (with strong rhythm) [stark] rhythmisch; schwungvoll ‹*Schritt*› [3] (coll.: lively) wild (ugs.); swingend (ugs.)

ˈswing-wing *n.* Schwenkflügel, *der*

swipe /swaɪp/ (coll.)
A *v.i.* **~ at** [wild] schlagen nach; eindreschen auf (+ *Akk.*) (ugs.)
B *v.t.* [1] (hit hard) knallen (ugs.) [2] (coll.: steal) klauen (ugs.) [3] **~ the card through the swipe reader** die Karte durch das [Karten]lesegerät ziehen
C *n.* [1] [wuchtiger] Schlag; **take a wild ~ at sth.** wild auf etw. (*Akk.*) losschlagen [2] (device) **~ [reader]** [Karten]lesegerät, *das*

swipe: ~ card *n.* Magnetkarte, *die;* **~ card reader** *n.* Magnetkartenleser, *der*

swirl /swɜːl/
A *v.i.* wirbeln
B *v.t.* umherwirbeln
C *n.* [1] (eddying motion) **with a ~ of the paddle** durch Herumwirbeln des Paddels [2] (spiralling shape) Spirale, *die*

swish /swɪʃ/
A *v.t.* schlagen mit ‹*Schwanz*›; sausen lassen ‹*Stock*›
B *v.i.* zischen; **~ past** ‹*Auto:*› vorbeirauschen
C *n.* Zischen, *das*
D *adj.* (coll.) schick (ugs.)

Swiss /swɪs/ ▸ **ⓘ p. 1345**
A *adj.* Schweizer; schweizerisch; **sb. is ~:** jmd. ist Schweizer/Schweizerin
B *n.* Schweizer, *der*/Schweizerin, *die;* **the ~** *pl.* die Schweizer

Swiss: ~ ˈchard ▸ **chard; ~ ˈcheese** *n.* Schweizer Käse, *der;* **~ cheese plant** Fensterblatt, *das;* **~ ˈFrench** *adj.* welschschweizerisch; **~ ˈGerman A** *adj.* schweizerdeutsch; **B** *n.* Schweizerdeutsch, *das;* **~ ˈguards** *n. pl.* (in Vatican) Schweizergarde, *die;* **~ ˈroll** *n.* Biskuitrolle, *die*

switch /swɪtʃ/
A *n.* [1] (esp. Electr.) Schalter, *der* [2] (Amer. Railw.) Weiche, *die* [3] (change with another) Wechsel, *der;* (change of procedure) Umstellung, *die* (**from** von, **to** auf + *Akk.*); **~ of roles** Rollentausch, *der* [4] (flexible shoot, whip) Gerte, *die* [5] (tress of hair) Haarteil, *das*
B *v.t.* [1] (change) **~ sth. [over] to sth.** etw. auf etw. (*Akk.*) umstellen *od.* (Electr.) umschalten; **~ a player to another position** einen Spieler auf eine andere Position stellen; **~ sb. to night duty** jmdn. in den Nachtdienst versetzen; **~ one's vote to another party** seine Stimme einer anderen Partei geben; **~ the conversation to another topic** das Gespräch auf ein anderes Thema lenken [2] (exchange) tauschen [3] (Railw.: transfer with ~) [mittels einer Weiche] umleiten [4] (swish) schlagen mit ‹*Schwanz*›; sausen lassen ‹*Rohrstock*›
C *v.i.* wechseln; **~ [over] to sth.** auf etw. (*Akk.*) umstellen *od.* (Electr.) umschalten

Phrasal verbs
- **~ aˈround**
A *v.t.* umstellen ‹*Möbel, Dienstplan*›
B *v.i.* [die Stellung] wechseln
- **~ ˈoff** *v.t. & i.* ausschalten; (also fig. coll.) abschalten
- **~ ˈon**
A *v.t.* einschalten; anschalten; **be ~ed on** (coll.) (high on drugs) angeturnt sein (ugs.); (up-to-date) auf Draht sein (ugs.); **be ~ed on to jazz/rock** *etc.* auf Jazz/Rock *usw.* stehen (ugs.)
B *v.i.* sich anschalten
- **~ ˈover**
A *v.t.* ▸ **~ B 1**
B *v.i.* ▸ **switch C**
- **~ ˈround** ▸ **~ around**
- **~ ˈthrough** *v.t.* durchstellen ‹*Telefongespräch, Anrufer*›

switch: ~back *n.* (Brit.) (road) [berg]auf und [berg]ab führende Straße; (roller coaster) Achterbahn, *die;* **that road is a real ~back** diese Straße ist ein einziges Rauf und Runter (ugs.); **~blade** *n.* Springmesser, *das;* **~board** *n.* [1] (Teleph.) [Telefon]zentrale, *die;* Vermittlung, *die;* *attrib.* **~board operator** ▸ **ⓘ p. 1260** Telefonist, *der*/Telefonistin, *die;* [2] (Electr.) Schalttafel, *die;* **~ engine** *n.* (Amer. Railw.) Rangierlok[omotive], *die;* **~gear** *n.* (Electr.) Schaltvorrichtung, *die;* **~-over** ▸ **changeover; ~ selling** *n., no pl.:* *Verkauf mittels Lockvogelangeboten;* **~yard** *n.* (Amer.) Rangierbahnhof, *der*

Switzerland /ˈswɪtsələnd/ *pr. n.* die Schweiz

swivel /ˈswɪvl/
A *n.* Drehgelenk, *das*
B *v.i.*, (Brit.) **-ll-** sich drehen
C *v.t.*, (Brit.) **-ll-** drehen

ˈswivel chair *n.* Drehstuhl, *der*

swiz, swizz /swɪz/ *n., pl.* **swizzes** (Brit. coll.) Beschiss, *der* (ugs.); Schwindel, *der*

ˈswizzle stick /ˈswɪzlstɪk/ *n.* Sektquirl, *der*

swollen /ˈswəʊlən/
A ▸ **swell A, B**
B *adj.* geschwollen; angeschwollen ‹*Fluss*›; **eyes ~ with weeping** verweinte Augen; **have a ~ head** (fig.) sehr eingebildet *od.* von sich eingenommen sein

swollen-headed /ˈswəʊlənhedɪd/ *adj.* eingebildet

swoon /swuːn/ (literary)
A *v.i.* [1] (faint) ohnmächtig werden [2] (go into ecstasies) **~ over sb./sth.** von jmdm./etw. schwärmen
B *n.* (literary) Ohnmacht, *die*

swoop /swuːp/
A *n.* [1] (downward plunge) Sturzflug, *der;* **at a** *or* **one [fell] ~:** auf einen Schlag (ugs.) [2] (coll.: raid) Razzia, *die;* **make a ~ on a house/an area** eine Razzia in einem Haus/einem Bezirk machen
B *v.i.* (plunge suddenly) herabstoßen; (pounce) **~ on sb.** sich auf jmdn. stürzen; (to attack) gegen jmdn. einen Schlag führen; **the police ~ed on several addresses** die Polizei führte in mehreren Wohnungen Razzien durch; **we'll ~ tomorrow** wir schlagen morgen zu

swoosh /swuːʃ/
A *v.i.* rauschen; **~ by** vorbeirauschen
B *n.* (sound) Rauschen, *das;* **go past with a ~:** vorbeirauschen

swop ▸ **swap**

sword /sɔːd/ *n.* Schwert, *das;* **put sb. to the ~** (literary) jmdn. [mit dem Schwert] töten; *see also* **cross B 1; Damocles**

sword: ~ dance *n.* Schwert[er]tanz, *der;* **~fish** *n.* Schwertfisch, *der;* **~play** *n.* (Fencing) [Schwert]fechten, *das;* **~sman** /ˈsɔːdzmən/ *n., pl.* **~smen** /ˈsɔːdzmən/ [Schwert]fechter, *der;* **~smanship** /ˈsɔːdzmənʃɪp/ *n., no pl.* Fechtkunst, *die;* **~stick** *n.* Stockdegen, *der;* **~-swallower** /ˈsɔːdswɒləʊə(r)/ *n.* Schwertschlucker, *der*

swore ▸ **swear A, B**

sworn /swɔːn/
A ▸ **swear A, B**
B *attrib. adj.* [1] (bound by an oath) verschworen ‹*Freund*›; **~ enemy** Todfeind, *der* [2] (certified by oath) beeidigt; **~ evidence** Aussage unter Eid; **~ affidavit/statement** eidesstattliche Versicherung/eidliche Erklärung

swot /swɒt/ (Brit. coll.)
A *n.* Streber, *der*/Streberin, *die* (abwertend)
B *v.i.*, **-tt-** büffeln (ugs.)

Phrasal verb
- **~ ˈup** *v.t.* büffeln (ugs.)

swotting /ˈswɒtɪŋ/ *n.* (Brit. coll.) Büffelei, *die* (ugs.)

swum ▸**swim A, B**

swung ▸**swing B, C**

ˈswung dash *n.* Tilde, *die*

sybarite /ˈsɪbəraɪt/ *n.* Sybarit, *der* (geh.)

sycamore /ˈsɪkəmɔː(r)/ *n.* Bergahorn, *der;* (Amer.: plane tree) Platane, *die*

sycophancy /ˈsɪkəfænsɪ, ˈsɪkəfənsɪ/ *n.* Kriecherei, *die;* Speichelleckerei, *die*

sycophant /ˈsɪkəfænt, ˈsɪkəfənt/ *n.* Kriecher, *der;* Schranze, *die*

sycophantic /sɪkəˈfæntɪk/ *adj.* sykophantisch (bildungsspr., veralt.); kriecherisch (abwertend)

syllabic /sɪˈlæbɪk/ *adj.* **1** Silben- **2** (Pros.) silbenzählend

syllable /ˈsɪləbl/ *n.* (lit. or fig.) Silbe, *die;* **she did not utter a ~ of reproach** mit keiner Silbe äußerte sie einen Vorwurf; **in words of one ~** (fig.) mit [sehr] einfachen Worten

syllabub /ˈsɪləbʌb/ *n.* (Gastr.) *aromatisierte Süßspeise aus geschlagener Sahne;* (with wine) Weinschaumcreme, *die*

syllabus /ˈsɪləbəs/ *n., pl.* **~es** *or* **syllabi** /ˈsɪləbaɪ/ Lehrplan, *der;* (for exam) Studienplan, *der*

syllogism /ˈsɪlədʒɪzm/ *n.* (Logic) Syllogismus, *der*

sylph /sɪlf/ *n.* (Mythol.) (male) Sylphe, *der;* (female; also fig.) Sylphide, *die*

ˈsylphlike *adj.* sylphidenhaft (geh.)

symbiosis /sɪmbɪˈəʊsɪs/, *pl.* **symbioses** /sɪmbɪˈəʊsiːz/ *n.* (Biol.; also fig.) Symbiose, *die*

symbiotic /sɪmbɪˈɒtɪk/ *adj.* symbiotisch

symbol /ˈsɪmbl/ *n.* Symbol, *das* (**of** für)

symbolic /sɪmˈbɒlɪk/, **symbolical** /sɪmˈbɒlɪkl/ *adj.*, **symbolically** /sɪmˈbɒlɪkəlɪ/ *adv.* symbolisch

symbolise ▸**symbolize**

symbolism /ˈsɪmbəlɪzm/ *n.* **1** Symbolik, *die* **2** (Art, Literature) Symbolismus, *der*

Symbolist /ˈsɪmbəlɪst/ *n.* Symbolist, *der*/Symbolistin, *die; attrib.* symbolistisch

symbolize /ˈsɪmbəlaɪz/ *v.t.* symbolisieren

symmetric /sɪˈmetrɪk/, **symmetrical** /sɪˈmetrɪkl/ *adj.*, **symmetrically** /sɪˈmetrɪkəlɪ/ *adv.* symmetrisch

symmetry /ˈsɪmɪtrɪ/ *n.* Symmetrie, *die*

sympathetic /sɪmpəˈθetɪk/ *adj.* **1** (showing pity) mitfühlend; (understanding) verständnisvoll **2** (favourably inclined) wohlgesinnt; geneigt ‹*Leser*›; **be ~ to a cause/to new ideas** einer Sache wohlwollend gegenüberstehen/für neue Ideen empfänglich *od.* zugänglich sein; **give sb. a ~ hearing** ein offenes Ohr für jmdn. haben; **he is not at all ~ to this idea** er ist von dieser Idee ganz und gar nicht angetan **3** (to one's taste, likeable) ansprechend; sympathisch ‹*Person, Persönlichkeit*›; **I find sb./sth. ~:** ich finde jmdn./etw. sympathisch; jmd./etw. ist mir sympathisch **4** (Med.) sympathetisch ‹*Schmerz, Leiden*›; (Anat.) sympathisch ‹*Nervensystem*› **5** (Mus.) mitschwingend ‹*Saite, Ton*› **6** (Phys.) **~ vibration** Mitschwingen, *das*

sympathetically /sɪmpəˈθetɪkəlɪ/ *adv.* (with pity) mitfühlend; (understandingly) verständnisvoll; **treat a subject ~:** ein Thema einfühlsam behandeln

sympathetic: ~ ˈnerve *n.* (Anat.) Sympathikus, *der;* **~ ˈnervous system** *n.* (Anat.) sympathisches *od.* sympathetisches Nervensystem

sympathise, sympathiser ▸**sympathiz-**

sympathize /ˈsɪmpəθaɪz/ *v.i.* **1** (feel or express sympathy) **~ with sb.** mit jmdm. [mit]fühlen *od.* Mitleid haben; (by speaking) sein Mitgefühl mit jmdm. äußern; **~ with sb. over the death of a friend** jmds. Trauer beim Tod eines Freundes teilen; **I do ~:** es tut mir wirklich Leid **2** **~ with** (have understanding for) Verständnis haben für ‹*jmds. Not, Denkweise usw.*›; (Polit.: share ideas of) sympathisieren mit ‹*Partei usw.*›

sympathizer /ˈsɪmpəθaɪzə(r)/ *n.* Sympathisant, *der*/Sympathisantin, *die*

sympathy /ˈsɪmpəθɪ/ *n.* **1** (sharing feelings of another) Mitgefühl, *das;* **in deepest ~:** mit aufrichtigem Beileid; **my sympathies are with you in your sorrow** ich fühle mit Ihnen in Ihrem Schmerz **2** (agreement in opinion or emotion) Sympathie, *die;* **my sympathies are with Schmidt** ich bin auf Schmidts Seite; **he has radical sympathies/no ~ with the radicals** er sympathisiert/sympathisiert nicht mit den Radikalen; **be in/out of ~ with sth.** mit etw. sympathisieren/nicht sympathisieren; **are you in ~ with what we are trying to do?** stimmst du unseren Zielen zu?; **come out** *or* **strike in ~ with sb.** mit jmdm. in einen Sympathiestreik treten; **vibrate in ~:** mitschwingen

sympathy: ~ strike *n.* Sympathiestreik, *der;* **~ vote** *n.* Sympathiestimme, *die;* von Mitgefühl motivierte Wahl; (fig.) von Mitgefühl motivierte Zustimmung

symphonic /sɪmˈfɒnɪk/ *adj.* sinfonisch; symphonisch

symphony /ˈsɪmfənɪ/ *n.* (Mus.) **1** Sinfonie, *die* **2** (esp. Amer.) ▸**symphony orchestra**

ˈsymphony orchestra *n.* Sinfonieorchester, *das*

symposium /sɪmˈpəʊzɪəm/ *n., pl.* **symposia** /sɪmˈpəʊzɪə/ Symposion, *das;* Symposium, *das*

symptom /ˈsɪmptəm/ *n.* (Med.; also fig.) Symptom, *das*

symptomatic /sɪmptəˈmætɪk/ *adj.* (Med.; also fig.) symptomatisch (**of** für)

synagogue (*Amer.:* **synagog**) /ˈsɪnəgɒg/ *n.* Synagoge, *die*

synapse /ˈsaɪnæps, ˈsɪnæps/ *n.* (Biol.) Synapse, *die*

sync, synch /sɪŋk/ (coll.) *n.* **1** **in/out of ~:** synchron/nicht synchron **2** (fig. coll.: in tune) **be in ~/out of ~:** harmonieren/nicht harmonieren (**with** mit); **he is out of ~ with the rest** er hat nicht die gleiche Wellenlänge wie die anderen

synchromesh /ˈsɪŋkrəmeʃ/ (Motor Veh.) *n.* **~ [gearbox]** Synchrongetriebe, *das;* **there is ~ on all gears** alle Gänge sind synchronisiert

synchronic /sɪŋˈkrɒnɪk, sɪnˈkrɒnɪk/ *adj.* (Ling.) synchronisch

synchronisation, synchronise ▸**synchroniz-**

synchronization /sɪŋkrənaɪˈzeɪʃn/ *n.* Synchronisierung, *die*

synchronize /ˈsɪŋkrənaɪz/

A *v.t.* **1** synchronisieren ‹*Vorgänge, Maschinen, Bild und Ton*› **2** (set to same time) gleichstellen ‹*Uhren*›; **we'd better ~ [our] watches** wir sollten Uhrenvergleich machen

B *v.i.* ‹*Bild und Ton:*› synchron sein

synchronized ˈswimming *n.* (Sport) Synchronschwimmen, *das*

synchronous /ˈsɪŋkrənəs/ *adj.* synchron; **~ motor** (Electr.) Synchronmotor, *der*

syncopate /ˈsɪŋkəpeɪt/ *v.t.* (Mus., Ling.) synkopieren

syncopation /sɪŋkəˈpeɪʃn/ *n.* (Mus., Ling.) Synkopierung, *die*

syncope /ˈsɪŋkəpɪ/ *n.* (Ling., Med.) Synkope, *die*

syndicalism /ˈsɪndɪkəlɪzm/ *n.* Syndikalismus, *der*

syndicate

A /ˈsɪndɪkət/ *n.* **1** (for business, in organized crime) Syndikat, *das* **2** (in newspapers) *Presseagentur, die Beiträge ankauft und an eine od. mehrere Zeitungen vertreibt* **3** **pools/lottery ~:** Tippgemeinschaft, *die*

B /ˈsɪndɪkeɪt/ *v.t.* in mehreren Zeitungen gleichzeitig veröffentlichen ‹*Bericht usw.*›

syndrome /ˈsɪndrəʊm/ *n.* (Med.; also fig.) Syndrom, *das*

synergy /ˈsɪnədʒɪ/ *n.* Synergie, *die*

synod /ˈsɪnəd/ *n.* Synode, *die*

synonym /ˈsɪnənɪm/ *n.* Synonym, *das*

synonymous /sɪˈnɒnɪməs/ *adj.* **1** (Ling.) synonym (**with** mit) **2** **~ with** (fig.: suggestive of, linked with) gleichbedeutend mit

synonymy /sɪˈnɒnəmɪ/ *n.* (Ling.) Synonymie, *die*

synopsis /sɪˈnɒpsɪs/, *n., pl.* **synopses** /sɪˈnɒpsiːz/ Inhaltsangabe, *die;* (overview) Abriss, *der*

synoptic /sɪˈnɒptɪk/ *adj.* synoptisch

syntactic /sɪnˈtæktɪk/ *adj.*, **syntactically** /sɪnˈtæktɪkəlɪ/ *adv.* (Ling.) syntaktisch

syntax /ˈsɪntæks/ *n.* (Ling.) Syntax, *die*

ˈsyntax error *n.* (Computing) Syntaxfehler, *der*

synthesis /ˈsɪnθɪsɪs/ *n., pl.* **syntheses** /ˈsɪnθɪsiːz/ Synthese, *die*

synthesise, synthesiser ▸**synthesiz-**

synthesize /ˈsɪnθɪsaɪz/ *v.t.* **1** (form into a whole) zur Synthese bringen **2** (Chem.) synthetisieren **3** (Electronics) **~ speech** Sprache elektronisch generieren

synthesizer /ˈsɪnθɪsaɪzə(r)/ *n.* (Mus.) Synthesizer, *der*

synthetic /sɪnˈθetɪk/

A *adj.* **1** (man-made) synthetisch; **~ fibre** Kunstfaser, *die; see also* **resin 2** **2** (sham) unecht

B *n.* Kunststoff, *der;* **~s** (Textiles) Synthetics

synthetically /sɪnˈθetɪkəlɪ/ *adv.* synthetisch

syphilis /ˈsɪfɪlɪs/ *n.* ▸**❶ p. 1231** (Med.) Syphilis, *die*

syphilitic /sɪfɪˈlɪtɪk/ (Med.)

A *n.* Syphilitiker, *der*/Syphilitikerin, *die*

B *adj.* syphilitisch

Syracuse /ˈsaɪrəkjuːz/ *pr. n.* Syrakus (*das*)

Syria /ˈsɪrɪə/ *pr. n.* Syrien (*das*)

Syrian /ˈsɪrɪən/ ▸**❶ p. 1345**

A *adj.* syrisch; **sb. is ~:** jmd. ist Syrer/Syrerin

B *n.* Syrer, *der*/Syrerin, *die*

syringa /sɪˈrɪŋgə/ *n.* (Bot.) **1** (mock orange) Falscher Jasmin **2** (lilac) Flieder, *der*

syringe /sɪˈrɪndʒ/

A *n.* Spritze, *die; see also* **hypodermic A**

B *v.t.* spritzen; ausspritzen ‹*Ohr*›

syrup /ˈsɪrəp/ *n.* **1** Sirup, *der;* **cough ~:** Hustensaft, *der* **2** (fig.: sickly sentiment) süßlicher Kitsch (abwertend)

syrupy /ˈsɪrəpɪ/ *adj.* **1** (like syrup) sirupähnlich **2** (fig.: cloyingly sweet) süßlich

system /ˈsɪstəm/ *n.* **1** (lit. or fig.) System, *das;* (of roads, railways also) Netz, *das;* **root ~** (Bot.) Wurzelgeflecht, *das; see also* **go¹ D** **2** (Anat., Zool.: body) Körper, *der;* (part) **digestive/muscular/nervous/reproductive ~:** Verdauungsapparat, *der*/Muskulatur, *die*/Nervensystem, *das*/Fortpflanzungssystem, *das;* **get sth. out of one's ~** (fig.) etw. loswerden; (by talking) sich (*Dat.*) etw. von der Seele reden **3** *no art.* (methodical procedure) System *o. Art.* **4** (Geol.) Formation, *die*

ˈsystem administrator ▸**❶ p. 1260** *n.* (Computing) Systemadministrator, *der*/-administratorin, *die*

systematic /sɪstəˈmætɪk/ *adj.*, **systematically** /sɪstəˈmætɪkəlɪ/ *adv.* systematisch

systematisation, systematise ▸**systematiz-**

systematization /sɪstəmətaɪˈzeɪʃn/ *n.* Systematisierung, *die*

systematize /ˈsɪstəmətaɪz/ *v.t.* systematisieren (**into** zu)

system: ~ crash *n.* (Computing) Systemabsturz, *der;* **~ disk** *n.* (Computing) Systemdiskette, *die;* **~ error** *n.* (Computing) Systemfehler, *der*

systemic /sɪˈstemɪk/ *adj.* (Biol.) systemisch

systems: ~ analysis *n.* Systemanalyse, *die;* **~ analyst** *n.* ▸**❶ p. 1260** Systemanalytiker, *der*/-analytikerin, *die;* **~ engineering** *n., no pl.* Systemtechnik, *die*

ˈsystem software *n.* (Computing) Systemsoftware, *die*

systolic /sɪsˈtɒlɪk/ *adj.* (Physiol.) systolisch

Tt

T, t /tiː/ *n., pl.* **Ts** *or* **T's** **1** (letter) T, t, *das;* **to a T** ganz genau; haargenau; **that's her to a T** das ist sie, wie sie leibt und lebt; **cross the t's** (fig.) peinlich genau sein **2** (T-shaped object) T, *das;* **T-junction** Einmündung, *die* (in eine Vorfahrtsstraße); **T-bone steak** T-Bone-Steak, *das;* **T-shirt** T-Shirt, *das;* **T-square** ▸**square A 10**

t. *abbr.* ▸ⓘ **p. 1702** **1** = **ton[s]** [britische] Tonne[n] **2** = **tonne[s]** t

ta /tɑː/ *int.* (Brit. coll.) danke

TA *abbr.* (Brit.) = **Territorial Army**

tab¹ /tæb/

A *n.* **1** (projecting flap) Zunge, *die;* (label) Schildchen, *das;* (on clothing) Etikett, *das;* (with name) Namensschild, *das;* (on file [card]) Reiter, *der* **2** (coll.: bill) Rechnung, *die;* **pick up the ~:** die Zeche bezahlen; **do you want to start a ~?** soll ich alles aufschreiben? **3** (Amer. coll.: price) Preis, *der* **4** **keep ~s** *or* **a ~ on sb./sth.** (watch) jmdn./etw. [genau] beobachten **5** (Brit. Mil.: on collar) Kragenspiegel, *der* **6** (Aeronaut.) Trimmruder, *das;* Hilfsruder, *das.* **7** (Amer.: ring pull) Pullring, *der*

B *v.t.,* **-bb-** ▸**A 1**: mit Zunge / Schildchen / Etikett / Namensschild / Reitern versehen

tab² *n.* Tab[ulator], *der;* **set ~s** Tabs *od.* Tabulatoren setzen

Tabasco ® /təˈbæskəʊ/ *n.* Tabasco, *der;* Tabascosoße, *die*

tabby /ˈtæbɪ/ *n.* **~ [cat]** Tigerkatze, *die*

ˈtab character *n.* Tab[ulator]zeichen, *das*

tabernacle /ˈtæbənækl/ *n.* **1** (Bibl.) Stiftshütte, *die* **2** (Relig.: meeting house) Gotteshaus, *das* **3** (Eccl.: receptacle) Tabernakel, *der*

ˈtab key *n.* (Computing) Tab[ulator]taste, *die*

table /ˈteɪbl/

A *n.* **1** Tisch, *der;* **at ~:** bei Tisch; **sit down at ~:** sich zu Tisch setzen; **after two whiskies he was under the ~** (coll.) nach zwei Whisky lag er unter dem Tisch (ugs.); **drink sb. under the ~:** jmdn. unter den Tisch trinken (ugs.); **get people/get round the ~:** Personen an einen Tisch bringen/sich an einen Tisch setzen; **turn the ~s [on sb.]** (fig.) [jmdm. gegenüber] den Spieß umdrehen *od.* umkehren; *see also* **lay² A 5** **2** (list) Tabelle, *die;* **~ of contents** Inhaltsverzeichnis, *das;* **~ of logarithms** Logarithmentafel, *die;* **learn one's ~s** das Einmaleins lernen; **say one's nine times ~:** die Neunerreihe aufsagen **3** (company at ~) Runde, *die* **4** (food provided) **keep a good/wretched ~:** eine ausgezeichnete/jämmerliche Küche führen

B *v.t.* **1** (bring forward) einbringen, (ugs.) auf den Tisch legen ‹*Antrag, Resolution*› **2** (Amer.: shelve) auf Eis legen (ugs.) ‹*Plan usw.*›

tableau /ˈtæbləʊ/ *n., pl.* **~x** /ˈtæbləʊz/ (lit. or fig.) Tableau, *das*

table: ~cloth *n.* Tischdecke, *die;* Tischtuch, *das;* **~ dance** *n.* Tabledance, *der;* **~ dancer** *n.* Tabledancer, *der*/-dancerin, *die*

table d'hôte /tɑːbl ˈdəʊt/ *n.* Table d'hôte, *die* (geh.); **~ menu** Tageskarte, *die*

table: ~ knife *n.* Messer, *das;* Tischmesser, *das* (veralt.); **~ lamp** *n.* Tischlampe, *die;* **~land** *n.* (Geog.) Tafelland, *das;* **~ leg** *n.* Tischbein, *das;* **~ linen** *n.* Tischwäsche, *die;* **~ manners** *n. pl.* Tischmanieren *Pl.;* **~ mat** *n.* Set, *das;* **T~ ˈMountain** *pr. n.* Tafelberg, *der;* **~ napkin** *n.* Serviette, *die;* **~ salt** *n.* Tafelsalz, *das;* **~spoon** *n.* Servierlöffel, *der;* **~spoonful** *n.* Servierlöffel [voll], *der*

tablet /ˈtæblɪt/ *n.* **1** (pill) Tablette, *die* **2** (piece of soap) Stück, *das* **3** (stone slab) Tafel, *die* **4** (for writing on) [Schreib]tafel, *die;* (Amer.: pad) Notizblock, *der*

table: ~ talk *n., no pl.* Tischgespräch, *das;* **sb.'s ~ talk** jmds. Tischgespräche; **~ tennis** *n.* (Sport) Tischtennis, *das;* **~ tennis bat** Tischtennisschläger, *der;* **~ top** *n.* Tischplatte, *die;* **~-top** *adj.* an einer Tischplatte angebracht ‹*Dosenöffner usw.*›; Tisch‹*kühlschrank, -waschmaschine*›; **~-top sale** *n.* Wohltätigkeitsbasar, *der*

ˈtablet PC *n.* Tablet-PC, *der*

table: ~ware *n., no pl.* Geschirr, Besteck und Gläser; **~ wine** *n.* Tischwein, *der*

tabloid /ˈtæblɔɪd/ *n.* (kleinformatige, bebilderte) Boulevardzeitung; **the ~s** die Boulevardpresse; **~ journalism** Sensationsjournalismus, *der*

> **tabloid**
>
> Eine Zeitung in Großbritannien, die auf kleinen Zeitungsbögen gedruckt wird, im Gegensatz zu den **broadsheets**, die auf doppelt so großen Bögen gedruckt werden. Das *tabloid*-Format wird normalerweise mit der *popular press* (Boulevardpresse) assoziiert, wie sie z.B. von **The Sun** und **The Mirror** repräsentiert wird, während das *broadsheet*-Format von den meisten Zeitungen der *quality press* (seriösen Presse), wie z.B. **The Guardian** und **The Independent**, benutzt wird. **The Independent** bringt allerdings neben ihrer *broadsheet*-Ausgabe auch eine *tabloid*-Version heraus. Und *The Times*, von der es eine Zeitlang ebenfalls zwei Ausgaben gab, erscheint nur noch im *tabloid*-Format.

taboo, tabu /təˈbuː/

A *n.* Tabu, *das;* **be under a ~:** tabu sein

B *adj.* tabuisiert; Tabu‹*wort*›; **be ~:** tabu sein

C *v.t.* tabuisieren

ˈtab stop *n.* Tabstopp, *der*

tabular /ˈtæbjʊlə(r)/ *adj.* tabellarisch

tabulate /ˈtæbjʊleɪt/ *v.t.* tabellarisch darstellen; tabellarisieren

tabulation /tæbjʊˈleɪʃn/ *n.* tabellarische Aufstellung; Tabellarisierung, *die*

tabulator /ˈtæbjʊleɪtə(r)/ *n.* Tabulator, *der*

tachograph /ˈtækəgrɑːf/ *n.* (Motor Veh.) Fahrt[en]schreiber, *der*

tachometer /təˈkɒmɪtə(r)/ *n.* Tachometer, *der od. das*

tacit /ˈtæsɪt/ *adj.,* **tacitly** /ˈtæsɪtlɪ/ *adv.* stillschweigend

taciturn /ˈtæsɪtɜːn/ *adj.* schweigsam; wortkarg

taciturnity /tæsɪˈtɜːnɪtɪ/ *n., no pl.* Schweigsamkeit, *die;* Wortkargheit, *die*

tack¹ /tæk/

A *n.* **1** (small nail) kleiner Nagel; **carpet ~:** Teppichnagel, *der;* **shoe ~:** Täcks, *der; see also* **brass tacks** **2** (temporary stitch) Heftstich, *der* **3** (Naut.) (direction of vessel; also fig.) Kurs, *der;* (in zigzag) Kreuzen, *das;* **be on the port/starboard ~:** auf Backbord-/Steuerbordhalsen liegen; **on the right/wrong ~** (fig.) auf dem richtigen/falschen Weg *od.* Kurs; **change one's ~, try another ~** (fig.) einen anderen Kurs einschlagen

B *v.t.* **1** (stitch loosely) heften **2** (nail) festnageln

C *v.i.* (Naut.) kreuzen

Phrasal verbs

- **~ ˈdown** *v.t.* annageln; festnageln
- **~ ˈon** *v.t.* anhängen (**to** an + *Akk.*)

tack² *n.* (Horse riding) **[riding] ~:** Sattel- und Zaumzeug, *das*

tackiness¹ /ˈtækɪnɪs/ *n., no pl.* Klebrigkeit, *die*

tackiness² *n., no pl.* (coll. derog: tastelessness) Geschmacklosigkeit, *die*

tackle /ˈtækl/

A *v.t.* **1** (come to grips with) angehen, in Angriff nehmen ‹*Problem usw.*›; **~ sb. about/on/over sth.** jmdn. auf etw. (*Akk.*) ansprechen; (ask for sth.) jmdn. um etw. angehen **2** (Sport) angreifen ‹*Spieler*›; (Amer. Footb.; Rugby) fassen

B *n.* **1** (equipment) Ausrüstung, *die;* **shaving ~:** Rasierzeug, *das; see also* **fishing tackle** **2** (Sport) Angriff, *der;* (sliding ~) Tackling, *das;* (Amer. Footb., Rugby) Fassen und Halten **3** ▸**block A 14**

tackling /ˈtæklɪŋ/ *n.* (Sport) Tackling, *das*

ˈtack room *n.* Sattelkammer, *die*

tacky¹ /ˈtækɪ/ *adj.* klebrig

tacky² *adj.* (coll. derog.: tasteless) geschmacklos

tact /tækt/ *n.* Takt, *der;* **he has no ~:** er hat kein Taktgefühl

tactful /ˈtæktfl/ *adj.,* **tactfully** /ˈtæktfəlɪ/ *adv.* taktvoll

tactfulness /ˈtæktflnɪs/ *n., no pl.* Taktgefühl, *das*

tactic /ˈtæktɪk/ *n.* Taktik, *die;* **delaying ~:** Verzögerungstaktik, *die; see also* **tactics**

tactical /ˈtæktɪkl/ *adj.* **1** taktisch ‹*Fehler, Manöver, Rückzug*›; **~ voting** taktische Stimmabgabe **2** (skilled in tactics) taktisch klug; **have a good ~ sense** taktisch klug *od.* geschickt sein

tactically /ˈtæktɪkəlɪ/ *adv.* taktisch

tactician /tækˈtɪʃn/ *n.* Taktiker, *der*/Taktikerin, *die*

tactics /ˈtæktɪks/ *n. pl.* **1** (methods) Taktik, *die;* **dubious ~:** zweifelhafte Methoden **2** *constr. as sing.* (Mil.) Taktik, *die*

tactile /ˈtæktaɪl/ *adj.* **1** (using touch) Tast‹*organ*›; taktil (Med.) **2** (tangible) tastbar

tactless /ˈtæktlɪs/ *adj.* taktlos

tactlessly /ˈtæktlɪslɪ/ *adv.* taktlos; *as sentence-modifier* taktloserweise

tactlessness /ˈtæktlɪsnɪs/ *n., no pl.* Taktlosigkeit, *die*

tadpole /ˈtædpəʊl/ *n.* Kaulquappe, *die*

taffeta /ˈtæfɪtə/ *n.* (Textiles) Taft, *der*

taffrail /ˈtæfreɪl/ *n.* (Naut.) Heckreling, *die*

taffy *n.* (Amer.) Karamellbonbon, *das*

Taffy /ˈtæfɪ/ *n.* (coll.: Welshman) Waliser, *der*

tag¹ /tæg/

A *n.* **1** (label) Schild, *das;* (on clothes) Etikett, *das;* (on animal's ear) Ohrmarke, *die* **2** (electronic device) (on person) elektronische Fessel; (on goods) Sicherungsetikett, *das* **3** (loop) Schlaufe, *die* **4** (metal etc. point at end of lace) Senkelstift, *der* **5** (Computing) Tag, *das;* Markierung, *die* **6** (stock phrase) Zitat, *das;* geflügeltes Wort

t

7 (Amer.: licence plate) Nummernschild, *das. see also* **price tag**
B *v.t.*, **-gg-**: **1** (attach) anhängen (**to** an + *Akk.*); ~ **together** aneinander hängen; zusammenheften ‹*Blätter, Papier*›; (fig.) aneinander reihen **2** (with electronic device) ~ **sth.** etw. mit einem Sicherungsetikett versehen; ~ **sb.** jmdm. eine elektronische Fessel anlegen **3** (Computing) taggen; markieren
C *v.i.*, **-gg-**: ~ **behind** [nach]folgen; ~ **after sb.** hinter jmdm. hertrotteln (ugs.)

Phrasal verbs
- ~ **a'long** *v.i.* mitkommen
- ~ **'on** *v.t.* anhängen (**to** an + *Akk.*)

tag² *n.* (game) Fangen, *das*

tag: ~ **day** (Amer.) ▸**flag day 2**; ~ **'question** *n.* (Ling.) (*auf eine bestätigende Antwort zielendes*) Frageanhängsel, *das;* ~ **wrestling** *n.* (Sport) *Ringkampf zwischen zwei Mannschaften von je zwei Ringern, von denen nur einer im Ring steht und sich von seinem Partner ablösen lassen kann*

t'ai chi /taɪ 'tʃiː/ *n., no pl.* Tai-Chi, *das*

tail /teɪl/
A *n.* **1** Schwanz, *der;* **tops and** ~**s** (of carrots, turnips) obere und untere Enden **2** (fig.) **have sb./sth. on one's** ~: jmdn./etw. auf den Fersen haben (ugs.); **be/keep on sb.'s** ~: jmdm. auf den Fersen sein/bleiben (ugs.); **with one's** ~ **between one's legs** mit eingezogenem Schwanz (ugs.); **sb. has his** ~ **up** jmd. ist übermütig; **turn** ~ **[and run]** Fersengeld geben (ugs.); die Flucht ergreifen **3** (of comet) Schweif, *der* **4** **[shirt]** ~: Hemdzipfel, *der* (ugs.) **5** (of man's coat) Schoß, *der* **6** *in pl.* (man's evening dress) Frack, *der* **7** *in pl.* (on coin) ~**s [it is]** Zahl; ▸**head A 5** **8** (Mus.: stem of note) [Noten]hals, *der* **9** (part of letter below line) Unterlänge, *die* **10** (coll.: person following another) Schatten, *der;* **have/put a** ~ **on sb.** jmdn. beschatten lassen
B *v.t.* **1** ▸**top and tail** **2** (coll.: follow) beschatten

Phrasal verbs
- ~ **'away** ▸~ **off**
- ~ **'back** *v.i.* sich stauen. *see also* **tailback**
- ~ **'off** *v.i.* **1** (decrease) zurückgehen **2** (fade into silence) ersterben (geh.); verstummen

tail: ~ **assembly** *n.* (Aeronaut.) Heckleitwerk, *das;* ~**back** *n.* (Brit.) Rückstau, *der;* ~**board** *n.* hintere Bordwand; ~ **coat** *n.* Frack, *der;* ~ **end** *n.* (hindmost end) Schwanz, *der;* (fig.) Ende, *das;* **come in at the** ~ **end** erst am Ende hinzustoßen; ~ **fin** *n.* (Aeronaut.) Seitenflosse, *die;* ~**gate** **A** *n.* (Motor Veh.) Heckklappe, *die;* **B** *v.i.* zu dicht auffahren

'tail lamp (esp. Amer.) ▸**tail light**

tailless /'teɪllɪs/ *adj.* schwanzlos; **the animal was** ~: das Tier hatte keinen Schwanz

'tail light *n.* Rück- *od.* Schlusslicht, *das*

tailor /'teɪlə(r)/
A *n.* ▸**ⓘ p. 1260** Schneider, *der*/Schneiderin, *die; see also* **baker**
B *v.t.* **1** schneidern **2** (fig.) ~**ed to** *or* **for sb./sth.** für jmdn./etw. maßgeschneidert; ~**ed to sb.'s needs** auf jmds. Bedürfnisse zugeschnitten

tailored /'teɪləd/ *adj.* maßgeschneidert; ~ **suit** Maßanzug, *der;* (for woman) Schneiderkostüm, *das*

tailoring /'teɪlərɪŋ/ *n., no pl.* Schneiderei, *die;* Schneidern, *das*

'tailor-made *adj.* (lit. or fig.) maßgeschneidert

tailor's: ~ **chalk** *n.* Schneiderkreide, *die;* ~ **'dummy** *n.* Schneiderpuppe, *die;* (fig.) Geck, *der*/Modepuppe, *die*

tail: ~**piece** *n.* **1** (appendage) Anhang, *der;* **2** (Mus.: for string ends) Saitenhalter, *der;* **3** (decoration) [Schluss]vignette, *die;* ~**pipe** *n.* Auspuffendstück, *das;* ~**plane** *n.* (Aeronaut.) Höhenleitwerk, *das;* ~ **rotor** *n.* (Aeronaut.) Heckrotor, *der;* ~ **section** *n.* (Aeronaut.) hinterer Bereich; Heckbereich, *der;* ~ **skid** *n.* (Aeronaut.) Sporn, *der;* ~**spin** *n.* **1** (of aircraft) Trudeln, *das;* **2** (fig.: state of panic) **send sb./go into a** ~**spin** jmdn. in Panik versetzen/zu rotieren anfangen (ugs.); ~**wheel** *n.* (Aeronaut.) Spornrad, *das;* ~ **wind** *n.* Rückenwind, *der*

taint /teɪnt/
A *n.* Makel, *der;* **hereditary** ~: erbliche Belastung
B *v.t.* verderben; beflecken ‹*Ruf*›; **be** ~**ed with sth.** mit etw. behaftet sein (geh.)

Taiwan /taɪ'wɑːn/ *pr. n.* Taiwan (*das*)

Taiwanese /taɪwə'niːz/ ▸**ⓘ p. 1345**
A *adj.* taiwanesisch
B *n.* Taiwanese, *der*/Taiwanesin, *die*

take /teɪk/
A *v.t.*, **took** /tʊk/, ~**n** /'teɪkn/ **1** (get hold of, grasp, seize) nehmen; ~ **sb.'s arm** jmds. Arm nehmen; ~ **sb. by the hand/arm** jmdn. bei der Hand/am Arm nehmen; **he took me by the arm/elbow and steered me in the direction of the exit** er fasste mich am Arm/Ellbogen und dirigierte mich zum Ausgang; ~ **matters into one's own hands** (fig.) die Sache selbst in die Hand nehmen; *see also* **bit¹ 1**; **bull¹ A 1**; **devil A 3**; **hold² C 1**; **law 4**; **life 1**
2 (capture) einnehmen ‹*Stadt, Festung*›; machen ‹*Gefangenen*›; fassen ‹*Banditen*›; (chess) schlagen; nehmen; (Cards) stechen; *see also* **hold² C 1**; **hostage**; **possession 4**; **short B 3**; **storm A 4**; **surprise A**
3 (gain, earn) ‹*Laden:*› einbringen; ‹*Person:*› einnehmen; ‹*Film, Stück:*› einspielen; (win) gewinnen ‹*Satz, Spiel, Preis, Titel*›; erzielen ‹*Punkte*›; (Cards) machen ‹*Stich*›; ~ **a wicket** (Cricket) einen Schlagmann zum Ausscheiden bringen; ~ **first/second** *etc.* **place** den ersten/zweiten *usw.* Platz belegen; (fig.) an erster/zweiter *usw.* Stelle kommen; ~ **the biscuit** (Brit. coll.) *or* (coll.) **cake** (fig.) alle/alles übertreffen
4 (assume possession of) nehmen; (~ away with one) mitnehmen; (steal) mitnehmen (verhüll.); (obtain by purchase) besorgen ‹*Eintrittskarte, [Logen]platz*›; kaufen, (by rent) mieten ‹*Auto, Wohnung, Haus*›; nehmen ‹*Klavier-, Deutsch-, Fahrstunden*›; mitmachen ‹*Tanzkurs*›; (buy regularly) nehmen; lesen ‹*Zeitung, Zeitschrift*›; (subscribe to) beziehen; (obtain) erwerben ‹*akademischen Grad*›; (form a relationship with) sich (*Dat.*) nehmen ‹*Frau, Geliebten usw.*›; ins Haus nehmen ‹*zahlende Gäste*›; **that woman took my purse** die Frau hat mir meinen Geldbeutel gestohlen; **he took his degree at Sussex University** er hat sein Examen an der Universität von Sussex gemacht; ~ **place** stattfinden; (spontaneously) sich ereignen; ‹*Wandlung:*› sich vollziehen; **I'll** ~ **this handbag/the curry, please** ich nehme diese Handtasche/das Curry; **who has** ~**n my pencil?** wer hat meinen Bleistift weggenommen?; ~ **[private] pupils** [Privat]stunden geben; **he took her as** *or* **for his wife** er nahm sie zur Frau; *see also* **order A 3, 8**; **possession 4**; **silk A 1**
5 (avail oneself of, use) nehmen; machen ‹*Pause, Ferien, Nickerchen*›; nehmen ‹*Beispiel, Zitat usw.*› (**from** aus); ~ **the opportunity to do/of doing sth.** die Gelegenheit dazu benutzen, etw. zu tun; ~ **the car/bus into town** mit dem Auto/Bus in die Stadt fahren; ~ **two eggs** *etc.* (in recipe) man nehme zwei Eier *usw.*; ~ **all the time you want** nimm dir ruhig Zeit; **a story** ~**n from life** eine Geschichte aus dem Leben; **a quotation** ~**n from Pope** ein Zitat aus Pope; **[let's]** ~ **a more recent example/my sister [for example]** nehmen wir ein Beispiel neueren Datums/einmal meine Schwester; **thou shalt not** ~ **God's name in vain** (Bibl.) du sollst den Namen Gott[es] nicht unnütz führen; **do I hear someone taking my name in vain?** (coll. joc.) wer lästert denn da gerade über mich?; *see also* **advantage 1**; **advice 1**; **cure A 3**; **leave¹ 3**; **liberty**; **time A 2**
6 (carry, guide, convey) bringen; ~ **sb.'s shoes to the mender['s]/sb.'s coat to the cleaner's** jmds. Schuhe zum Schuster/jmds. Mantel in die Reinigung bringen; ~ **a message to sb.** jmdm. eine Nachricht überbringen; **the pipe** ~**s the water to the tank** das Rohr führt das Wasser zum Tank; ~ **sb. to school/hospital** jmdn. zur Schule/ins Krankenhaus bringen; ~ **sb. to visit sb.** jmdn. zu Besuch bei jmdm. mitnehmen; ~ **sb. to the zoo/cinema/to dinner** mit jmdm. in den Zoo/ins Kino/zum Abendessen gehen; ~ **sb. into one's home/house** jmdn. bei sich aufnehmen; **the road** ~**s you/story** ~**s us to London** die Straße führt nach/die Erzählung führt uns nach London; **my job has** ~**n me all over the world** ich bin beruflich in der ganzen Welt gereist; **his ability will** ~ **him far/to the top** mit seinen Fähigkeiten wird er es weit bringen/wird er ganz nach oben kommen; ~ **sb./sth. with one** jmdn./etw. mitnehmen; ~ **home** mit nach Hause nehmen; (earn) nach Hause bringen ‹*Geld*›; (accompany) nach Hause bringen *od.* begleiten; (to meet one's parents etc.) mit nach Hause bringen; *see also* ~**-home**; ~ **sb. before sb** jmdn. jmdm. vorführen; ~ **sb. through/over sth.** (fig.) mit jmdm. etw. durchgehen; ~ **in hand** (begin) in Angriff nehmen; (assume responsibility for) sich kümmern um; ~ **sb. into partnership [with one]/into the business** jmdn. zu seinem Teilhaber machen/in sein Geschäft aufnehmen; ~ **an axe to sth.** etw. fällen; (fig.) bei etw. den Rotstift ansetzen; ~ **a stick** *etc.* **to sb.** den Stock *usw.* bei jmdm. gebrauchen; ~ **sth. to pieces** *or* **bits** etw. auseinander nehmen; **you can't** ~ **him/her anywhere** (fig. coll.) man kann ihn/sie nirgendwohin mitnehmen; **you can't** ~ **it 'with you** (coll.) man kann es ja nicht mitnehmen; *see also* **confidence 5**; **court A 4**; **head A 2**
7 (remove) nehmen; (deduct) abziehen; ~ **sth./sb. from sb.** jmdm. etw./jmdn. wegnehmen; **I took the parcel from her** ich nahm ihr das Paket ab; **death has** ~**n him from us** (fig.) der Tod hat ihn uns genommen; **the children were** ~**n from their parents by the authorities** die Kinder wurden den Eltern von Amts wegen weggenommen; **be** ~**n from sb.** (fig.) jmdm. genommen werden; ~ **all the fun/hard work out of sth.** einem alle Freude an etw. (*Dat.*) nehmen/einem die schwere Arbeit bei etw. ersparen; *see also* **life 1**; **wind¹ A 1**
8 (conceive, experience) **sb.** ~**s courage from sth.** etw. macht jmdm. Mut; ~ **courage!** nur Mut!
9 **be** ~**n ill** *or* **sick** krank werden; **be** ~**n ill with food poisoning** eine Lebensmittelvergiftung bekommen
10 (make) machen ‹*Foto, Kopie*›; (photograph) aufnehmen; **hate having one's photograph/picture** ~**n** sich gar nicht gern fotografieren lassen; **the camera** ~**s good photographs** die Kamera macht gute Bilder *od.* Fotos; ~ **sb.'s fingerprints** jmdm. Fingerabdrücke abnehmen
11 (perform, execute) aufnehmen ‹*Brief, Diktat*›; machen ‹*Prüfung, Sprung, Spaziergang, Reise, Umfrage*›; durchführen ‹*Befragung, Volkszählung*›; ablegen ‹*Gelübde, Eid*›; übernehmen ‹*Rolle, Part*›; treffen ‹*Entscheidung*›; ~ **a fall/tumble** stürzen/straucheln; ~ **a step forward/backward** einen Schritt vor-/zurücktreten; ~ **a turn for the better/worse** eine Wende zum Besseren/Schlechteren nehmen; ~ **a scene/movement more slowly** eine Szene/einen Satz langsamer nehmen; *see also* **action 1**; **bow² C**; **effect A 4**; **vote A 1**
12 (negotiate) nehmen ‹*Zaun, Mauer, Hürde, Kurve, Hindernis*›; **the bus took the corner too fast** der Bus ist zu schnell um die Kurve gefahren
13 (conduct) halten ‹*Gottesdienst, Andacht, Unterricht*›; **he** ~**s the older pupils in Latin** er hat die älteren Schüler in Latein; **Ms X** ~**s us for maths** in Mathe haben wir Frau X
14 (be taught, be examined in) ~ **Latin at school** in der Schule Latein haben; ~ **Latin in an exam** in einem Examen in Latein geprüft werden; ~ **an examination/a test** eine Prüfung machen
15 (consume) trinken ‹*Tee, Kaffee, Kognak usw.*›; einnehmen (geh.) ‹*Mahlzeit*›; nehmen ‹*Zucker, Milch, Überdosis, Tabletten, Medizin*›; ~ **some food** etwas essen; ~ **sugar in one's tea** den Tee mit Zucker trinken; **what can I** ~ **for a cold?** was kann ich gegen eine Erkältung nehmen?; **to be** ~**n three times a day** dreimal täglich einzunehmen; **not to be** ~**n**

[internally] nicht zur innerlichen Anwendung; *see also* **bite C 1**; **drug A 2**; **medicine**; **sip C**

16 (occupy) einnehmen ‹*Sitz im Parlament*›; übernehmen, antreten ‹*Amt*›; **~ sb.'s seat** sich auf jmds. Platz setzen; **is that/this seat ~n?** ist da/hier noch frei?; *see also* **back seat**; **chair A 1, 2**; **place A 6, 10**; **seat A 2**

17 (need, require) brauchen ‹*Platz, Zeit*›; haben ‹*Kleider-, Schuhgröße usw.*›; (Ling.) haben ‹*Objekt, Plural-s*›; gebraucht werden mit ‹*Kasus*›; **this verb ~s 'sein'** dieses Verb wird mit „sein" konjugiert; **the wound will ~ some time to heal** es braucht einige Zeit, bis die Wunde geheilt ist; **the ticket machine ~s 20p and 50p coins** der Fahrkartenautomat nimmt 20-Pence- und 50-Pence-Stücke; **the work is taking too much of my time** die Arbeit kostet mich zu viel Zeit; **as long as it ~s** so lange wie nötig; **sth. ~s an hour/a year/all day** etw. dauert eine Stunde/ein Jahr/einen ganzen Tag; **it ~s an hour** *etc.* **to do sth.** es dauert eine Stunde *usw.*, [um] etw. zu tun; **the meat ~s three hours to cook** das Fleisch braucht drei Stunden, bis es gar ist; **sb. ~s** *or* **it ~s sb. a long time/an hour** *etc.* **to do sth.** jmd. braucht lange/eine Stunde *usw.*, um etw. zu tun; **what took you so long?** was hast du denn so lange gemacht?; **~ a lot of money/£3,000** viel Geld/3 000 Pfund kosten; **~ a lot of work/effort/courage** viel Arbeit/Mühe/Mut kosten; **it took all my strength/determination** ich brauchte all meine Kraft/Entschlossenheit; **it doesn't ~ much to make him happy** es gehört nicht viel dazu, ihn glücklich zu machen; **have [got] what it ~s** das Zeug dazu haben; **he took a lot of/some convincing** er war schwer/nicht so leicht zu überzeugen; **these windows ~ a lot of cleaning** diese Fenster sind schwer zu putzen; **it will ~ [quite] a lot of explaining** es wird schwer zu erklären sein; **that story of his ~s some believing** die Geschichte, die er da erzählt, ist kaum zu glauben; **it ~s an expert to notice the difference** nur ein Fachmann kann den Unterschied feststellen; **it would ~ a saint to get along with him** man müsste ein Heiliger sein, um mit ihm auszukommen; **it ~s a thief to know a thief** nur ein Dieb kennt einen Dieb; **it ~s all sorts to make a world** es gibt solche und solche; *see also* **beating 2**; **time A 2**

18 (accommodate, hold) fassen; (support) tragen; **the car will ~ six adults** in dem Auto haben sechs Erwachsene Platz; **that room can't ~ a grand piano** in das Zimmer passt kein Flügel

19 (ascertain and record) notieren ‹*Namen, Adresse, Autonummer usw.*›; zu Protokoll nehmen ‹*Hergang eines Unfalls usw.*›; fühlen ‹*Puls*›; messen ‹*Temperatur, Größe usw.*›; **~ sb.'s measurements for a new suit** [bei] jmdm. für einen neuen Anzug Maß nehmen; **~ the minutes of a meeting** bei einer Sitzung [das] Protokoll führen; **~ a reading from the barometer** den Barometerstand ablesen

20 (apprehend, grasp) **~ sb.'s meaning/drift** verstehen, was jmd. meint; **... if you ~ my meaning** ..., Sie verstehen?; **~ sb.'s point** jmds. Standpunkt verstehen; **~ it [that] ...:** annehmen, [dass] ...; **can I ~ it that ...?** kann ich davon ausgehen, dass ...?; **am I to ~ it that ...?** soll ich das so verstehen, dass ...?; **~ sth. to mean sth.** etw. so verstehen, dass ...; **what do you ~ that to mean/signify?** wie verstehen Sie das/was bedeutet das Ihrer Meinung nach?; **~ sth. as settled/as a compliment/refusal** etw. als erledigt betrachten/als eine Ablehnung/ein Kompliment auffassen; **~ sb./sth. for/to be sth.** jmdn./etw. für etw. halten; **what do you ~ me for?** wofür halten Sie mich?; **I ~ him to be in his fifties** ich schätze ihn zwischen fünfzig und sechzig; **not know how to ~ sb.'s reply** nicht wissen, wie man jmds. Antwort verstehen soll; **~ what sb. says the wrong way** jmdn. falsch verstehen; *see also* **gospel 2**; **grant A 3**; **literally 1**; **word A 2**

21 (treat or react to in a specified manner) aufnehmen; **~ sth. like a man** etw. wie ein Mann nehmen; **~ sth. well/badly/hard** etw. gut/schlecht/nur schwer verkraften; **sb. ~s sth. very badly/hard** etw. trifft jmdn. sehr; **~ sth. calmly** *or* **coolly** etw. gelassen [auf- *od.* hin]nehmen; **~ sth. as read** etw. als bekannt voraussetzen; **you can** *or* **may ~ it as read that ...:** du kannst sicher sein, dass ...; **taking it all in all, taking one thing with another** alles in allem; *see also* **amiss B**; **easy B**; **heart A 2, 3**; **kindly A 3**; **stride A 1**

22 (accept) annehmen; **~ money** *etc.* **[from sb./for sth.]** Geld *usw.* [von jmdm./für etw.] [an]nehmen; **will you ~ £5,000 for the car?** wollen Sie den Wagen für 5 000 Pfund verkaufen?; **[you can] ~ it or leave it** entweder du bist damit einverstanden, oder du lässt es bleiben; **I can ~ it or leave it** (am indifferent) ich mache mir nicht besonders viel daraus; **~ the hint** den Wink verstehen; **he can never ~ a hint** er hat kein Feingefühl; **I know how to ~ a hint** ich verstehe schon; **~ sb.'s word for it** sich auf jmdn. *od.* jmds. Wort[e] verlassen; **you can ~ his word for it that ...:** wenn er es sagt, kannst du dich darauf verlassen, dass ...; **you don't have to ~ my word for it** du brauchst es mir nicht zu glauben; **~ things as they come, ~ it as it comes** es nehmen, wie es kommt; *see also* **advice 1**; **chance A 5**; **consequence 1**; **risk A 1**

23 (receive, submit to) einstecken [müssen] ‹*Schlag, Tritt, Stoß*›; (Boxing) nehmen [müssen] ‹*Schlag*›; (endure, tolerate) aushalten; vertragen ‹*Klima, Alkohol, Kaffee, Knoblauch*›; verwinden ‹*Schock*›; (put up with) sich (*Dat.*) gefallen lassen [müssen] ‹*Kritik, Grobheit*›; **~ one's punishment bravely** seine Strafe tapfer ertragen; **the boxer/the car took a lot of punishment** der Boxer musste viel einstecken/das Auto musste eine Menge aushalten; **~ no nonsense** sich (*Dat.*) nichts bieten lassen; **~ 'that!** nimm das!; **~ it** (coll.) es verkraften; (referring to criticism, abuse) damit fertig werden; **There's a lot of pressure on you. — I can ~ it** Du stehst sehr unter Druck. — Ich werde damit schon fertig

24 (adopt, choose) ergreifen ‹*Maßnahmen*›; unternehmen ‹*Schritte*›; einschlagen ‹*Weg*›; sich entschließen zu ‹*Schritt, Handlungsweise*›; **~ the wrong road** die falsche Straße gehen/fahren; **~ a firm** *etc.* **stand [with sb./on** *or* **over sth.]** jmdm. gegenüber/hinsichtlich einer Sache nicht nachgeben; **~ the easy way out** die einfachste Lösung wählen; *see also* **resistance 1**; **side A 9**; **view A 4**

25 (receive, accommodate) [an]nehmen ‹*Bewerber, Schüler*›; aufnehmen ‹*Gäste*›; annehmen ‹*Farbe, Glanz*›; **the city ~s its name from its founder** die Stadt ist nach ihrem Gründer benannt; **the rock ~s its colour from the minerals** der Fels hat seine Farbe von den Mineralien

26 (swindle) **he was ~n for £500 by the conman** (coll.) der Schwindler hat ihm 500 Pfund abgeknöpft (ugs.)

27 **be ~n with sb./sth.** von jmdm./etw. angetan sein

28 (copulate with) nehmen

B *v.i.*, **took, ~n** **1** (be successful, effective) ‹*Transplantat:*› vom Körper angenommen werden; ‹*Impfung:*› anschlagen; ‹*Pfropfreis:*› anwachsen; ‹*Sämling, Pflanze:*› angehen; ‹*Feuer:*› zu brennen beginnen; ‹*trockenes Holz:*› Feuer fangen; ‹*Farbe:*› aufgenommen werden; ‹*Anstrich, Leim:*› halten; ‹*Fisch:*› [an]beißen

2 (detract) **~ from sth.** etw. schmälern

3 **~ ill** *or* (coll.) **sick** krank werden

4 **~ well/badly** (Photog.) sich gut/schlecht fotografieren lassen

C *n.* **1** (Telev., Cinemat.) Einstellung, *die;* Take, *der od. das* (*fachspr.*); *see also* **double ~**

2 (takings) Einnahme, *die;* **our ~ was over £200 for the day** unsere Tageseinnahme betrug über 200 Pfund; **~ [of the loot]** Anteil [an der Beute]

3 (catch of fish) Fang, *der;* (catch of game) Jagdbeute, *die*

Phrasal verbs

- **~ a'back ▸aback**
- **~ after** *v.t.* **1** **~ after sb.** (resemble) jmdm. ähnlich sein; (~ as one's example) es jmdm. gleichtun **2** (Amer.: chase after) nachsetzen (+ *Dat.*)
- **~ a'long** *v.t.* mitnehmen
- **~ a'part ▸apart 2**
- **~ a'round** *v.t.* **1** (~ with one) überallhin mitnehmen **2** (show around) herumführen
- **~ a'side ▸aside A**
- **~ a'way** *v.t.* **1** (remove) wegnehmen; (to a distance) mitnehmen; **~ sth. away from sb.** jmdm. etw. abnehmen; **~ sb.'s licence/passport away** jmdm. den Führerschein/Pass abnehmen; **what the taxman gives with one hand, he ~s away with the other** was der Fiskus mit der einen Hand gibt, das nimmt er mit der anderen wieder; **to ~ away** ‹*Pizza, Snack usw.*› zum Mitnehmen; **tablets that will ~ away the pain** Tabletten, die einem die Schmerzen nehmen; **~ away sb.'s rights/privileges/freedom/job** jmdm. seine Rechte/Privilegien/die Freiheit/seinen Arbeitsplatz nehmen; **~ away all the flavour of the food** dem Essen jeden Geschmack nehmen; **alcohol ~s away all your worries** Alkohol vertreibt die Sorgen; **it has ~n away all the pleasure in my win** es hat mir die Freude am Sieg verdorben; **no one can ~ that away from you** das kann dir niemand nehmen; **~ sb. away** jmdn. wegbringen; ‹*Polizei:*› jmdn. abführen; **~ him away!** schafft ihn fort!; hinweg mit ihm! (geh.); **~ a child away from its parents/home/from school** ein Kind den Eltern wegnehmen/aus seiner häuslichen Umgebung herausreißen/aus der Schule nehmen; **~ sb. away from his/her work** jmdn. von der Arbeit abhalten; **my job ~s me away from my family/from home a lot** mein Beruf entzieht mich oft der Familie/durch meine Arbeit bin ich oft von zu Hause weg; **death/a cruel fate has ~n our father away from us** der Tod/ein grausames Schicksal hat uns den Vater genommen; **~ sb. away to the cells** jmdn. in seine Zelle bringen; **~ sb. away for a holiday** mit jmdm. in Urlaub fahren; *see also* **breath 1** **2** (Math.: deduct) abziehen. *see also* **~ away**
- **~ a'way from** *v.t.* schmälern ‹*Erfolg, Vergnügen*›
- **~ 'back** *v.t.* **1** (retract, have back) zurücknehmen; wieder einstellen ‹*Arbeitnehmer*›; wieder [bei sich] aufnehmen ‹*Ehepartner*›; (reclaim) sich (*Dat.*) wiedergeben lassen **2** (return) zurückbringen; (~ somewhere again) wiederbringen ‹*Person*›; (carry or convey back) wieder mitnehmen; **that ~s me back [to my childhood]** das weckt bei mir [Kindheits]erinnerungen **3** (Printing) hochnehmen; raufziehen (ugs.)
- **~ 'down** *v.t.* **1** (carry or lead down) hinunterbringen; **this path ~s you down to the harbour** auf diesem Weg kommen Sie zum Hafen [hinunter] **2** (lower or lift down) abnehmen ‹*Bild, Ankündigung, Weihnachtsschmuck*›; einholen ‹*Fahne*›; umlegen ‹*Mast*›; herunterziehen, herunterlassen ‹*Hose*›; tiefer setzen ‹*Zeile*›; **~ a box down from a shelf** eine Schachtel von einem Regal herunternehmen **3** (dismantle) abreißen; abbauen ‹*Gerüst, Zelt*› **4** (write down) aufnehmen ‹*Brief, Personalien*›; aufschreiben ‹*Autonummer*›; mitschreiben ‹*Vortrag*› **5** (humiliate) ducken; *see also* **peg A**
- **~ 'in** *v.t.* **1** (convey to a place) hinbringen; (conduct) hineinführen ‹*Gast*›; **~ sb. in a cup of tea** jmdm. eine Tasse Tee [hinein]bringen; **~ the car in for a service** das Auto zur Wartung bringen; **~ sb. in [in the car]** jmdn. [mit dem Auto] reinfahren (ugs.); **I took the car in** ich fuhr mit dem Auto rein (ugs.); **the police took him in for questioning** die Polizei nahm ihn zum Verhör mit **2** (bring indoors) hereinholen; **~ in parcels for sb.** Pakete für jmdn. annehmen; **~ in the washing from the line** die Wäsche von der Leine [ab]nehmen [und hereinholen] **3** (accept for payment) **~ in washing** für andere Leute waschen **4** (receive, admit) aufnehmen; (for payment) vermieten an (+ *Akk.*); [auf]nehmen ‹[*Kur*]*gäste*›; **~ in lodgers** ‹*Haus-, Wohnungseigentümer:*› Zimmer vermieten; ‹*Mieter:*› untervermieten **5** (make narrower) enger machen ‹*Kleidungsstück*› **6** (include, comprise) einbeziehen **7** (coll.: visit) mitnehmen (ugs.); **our tour took in most of the main sights** auf unserer Rundfahrt haben wir die wichtigsten Sehenswürdigkeiten besichtigt **8** (understand, grasp) begreifen; überblicken, erfassen ‹*Lage*›; **I cannot ~ in any more of**

this lecture ich kann mich auf diese Vorlesung nicht mehr konzentrieren; **I have won — I can't ~ it in yet** ich habe gewonnen — ich kann es noch gar nicht richtig begreifen [9] (observe) erfassen; (watch, listen to) mitbekommen [10] (deceive) täuschen; hereinlegen (ugs.); **be ~n in [by sb./sth.]** sich [von jmdm./durch etw.] täuschen *od.* (ugs.) hereinlegen lassen; *see also* **~-in**

• **~ 'off**

A *v.t.* [1] abnehmen ‹*Deckel, Hut, Bild, Hörer, Tischtuch, Verband*›; abziehen ‹*Kissenbezug*›; ausziehen ‹*Schuhe, Handschuhe*›; ablegen ‹*Hut, Mantel, Schmuck*›; ‹*Säure:*› wegätzen ‹*Farbe*›; **~ off sb.'s/one's clothes** jmdm./sich die Kleider ausziehen; **~ sth. off the fire** etw. vom Feuer nehmen; **~ a door off the hinges** eine Tür aus den Angeln heben; **~ the cover off a pillow/bed** ein Kissen abziehen/ein Bett abdecken; **~ a parcel off sb.** jmdm. ein Paket abnehmen; **~ your hands off me!** fass mich nicht an!; **~ your feet off the settee!** nimm die Füße vom Sofa!; **~ off one's make-up** sich abschminken; **the heat has ~n the paint off the door** durch die Hitze ist die Farbe von der Tür abgeblättert [2] (transfer from) übernehmen ‹*Passagiere, Besatzung, Fracht*›; (withdraw from a programme) aus dem Programm nehmen; **~ sb. off sth.** jmdn. von etw. holen; (withdraw from job, assignment, etc.) jmdm. etw. entziehen; **he was ~n off the case** er wurde von dem Fall abgezogen; **~ sth. off a list/the menu** etw. von einer Liste streichen/von der Speisekarte nehmen; **~ a train/bus off a route** einen Zug/Bus vom Fahrplan streichen; **~ the weight off one's feet** seine Beine ausruhen; **~ years/ten years off sb.** jmdn. um Jahre jünger machen/jmdn. zehn Jahre jünger machen; *see also* **edge A 1**; **eye A 1**; **gilt A 1**; **hat 1**; **mind A 3**; **smile A** [3] (cut off) abtrennen; (with saw) absägen; (with knife, scissors, etc.) abschneiden; (amputate) abnehmen; **she had an inch ~n off her hair** sie ließ sich (*Dat.*) ihr Haar zwei cm kürzer schneiden [4] (lead, conduct) **~ sb. off to hospital/prison** jmdn. ins Krankenhaus/Gefängnis bringen; **~ sb. off on a stretcher/by ambulance** jmdn. auf einer Bahre/im Krankenwagen wegbringen; **~ sb. off to Paris** mit jmdm. nach Paris fahren; **I shall ~ my family off on** *or* **for a holiday** ich werde mit meiner Familie wegfahren *od.* in Urlaub fahren; **~ oneself off home/to bed** nach Hause/ins Bett gehen [5] (deduct) abziehen; **~ sth. off sth.** etw. von etw. abziehen; **~ £10 off the price** den Preis um zehn Pfund reduzieren [6] **~ off weight/a few pounds** (lose weight) abnehmen/einige Pfund abnehmen; **the diet has ~n pounds off my weight** die Diät hat mich um Pfunde leichter gemacht [7] (have free) **~ a day** *etc.* **off** sich (*Dat.*) einen Tag *usw.* frei nehmen (ugs.); **~ time off [work** *or* **from work]** sich (*Dat.*) frei nehmen [8] (mimic) nachmachen (ugs.)

B *v.i.* [1] (Aeronaut.) starten [2] (Sport) ‹*Springer, Pferd:*› abspringen [3] (coll.: leave quickly) losrennen; **~ off after sb./sth.** hinter jmdm./etw. herrennen [4] (become successful) ‹*Wirtschaft:*› sich [sprunghaft] aufwärts entwickeln; ‹*Verkaufszahlen:*› [sprunghaft] steigen; ‹*Produkt, Kampagne:*› einschlagen; ‹*Person:*› Karriere machen; **his career is taking off** er macht eine steile Karriere. *see also* **~-off**

• **~ 'on**

A *v.t.* [1] (undertake) übernehmen; annehmen ‹*Herausforderung, Wette usw.*›; auf sich (*Akk.*) nehmen ‹*Bürde*›; (accept responsibility for) sich einlassen auf (+ *Akk.*) ‹*Person*›; sich (*Dat.*) aufbürden *od.* aufladen ‹*Sache*› [2] (enrol, employ) einstellen; aufnehmen ‹*Schüler, Studenten*›; annehmen ‹*Privatschüler*› [3] (acquire, assume) annehmen ‹*Farbe, Form, Ausdruck, Ausmaße*›; erhalten ‹*Bedeutung*› [4] (accept as opponent) sich auf eine Auseinandersetzung einlassen mit; es aufnehmen mit; den Kampf aufnehmen mit ‹*Regierung, Gesetz*›; (Sport) antreten gegen; **I'll ~ you on** (in a contest) ich nehme es mit dir auf; (in a bet) die Wette gilt [5] (~ on board) aufnehmen [6] (transport farther) weiterbringen

B *v.i.* [1] (coll.: get upset) sich aufregen; **don't ~ on so!** reg dich nicht so auf!; hab dich nicht so! (ugs. abwertend) [2] (be successful) einschlagen

• **~ 'out** *v.t.* [1] (remove) herausnehmen; ziehen ‹*Zahn*›; **~ sth. out of sth., ~ out sth. from sth.** etw. aus etw. [heraus]nehmen; **~ out a pizza** *etc.* sich (*Dat.*) eine Pizza *usw.* mitnehmen; **'... to ~ out'** „... zum Mitnehmen"; **~ out a nail from a piece of wood/a splinter from sb.'s finger** einen Nagel aus einem Stück Holz ziehen/jmdm. einen Splitter aus dem Finger ziehen; **~ a stain/mark out of a dress** einen Fleck aus einem Kleid entfernen; **the strong sun ~s all the natural moisture out of your skin** die starke Sonnenbestrahlung entzieht der Haut ihre natürliche Feuchtigkeit; **~ the colour/vitamins out of sth.** etw. ausbleichen/einer Sache (*Dat.*) die Vitamine entziehen; **~ sb. out of the courtroom** jmdn. aus dem Gerichtssaal führen; **the train took us out of the city** der Zug brachte uns aus der Stadt [heraus]; **~ it/a lot out of sb.** (fig.) jmdn. mitnehmen/sehr mitnehmen [2] (destroy) zerstören; (fig.) (Footb. etc.) ausschalten; (kill) töten [3] (withdraw) abheben ‹*Geld*› [4] (deduct) abziehen (**of** von) [5] (go out with) **~ sb. out** mit jmdm. ausgehen; **~ sb. out for a walk/drive** mit jmdm. einen Spaziergang/eine Spazierfahrt machen; **~ sb. out to** *or* **for lunch/dinner** jmdn. zum Mittagessen/Abendessen einladen; **~ sb. out to the cinema/the theatre/a restaurant** jmdn. ins Kino/Theater/zum Essen einladen; **~ the dog out [for a walk]** den Hund ausführen; **~ sb. out of himself/herself** (fig.) jmdn. auf andere Gedanken bringen [6] (get issued) erwerben; erhalten; abschließen ‹*Versicherung*›; ausleihen ‹*Bücher*›; aufgeben ‹*Anzeige*›; **~ out a subscription to sth.** etw. abonnieren [7] **~ it/sth. out on sb./sth.** seine Wut/etw. an jmdm./etw. auslassen. *see also* **~out**

• **~ 'over**

A *v.t.* [1] (assume control of) übernehmen; **~ sth. over from sb.** etw. von jmdm. übernehmen; **~ over the lead** (Sport) in Führung gehen; **let sth. ~ over one's life** (fig.) sein Leben von etw. bestimmen lassen; **~ sb./sth. over** (fig.) von jmdm./etw. Besitz ergreifen; **~ over the world** die Weltherrschaft an sich reißen [2] (carry or transport over) **~ sb./sth. over to sb./sb.'s flat/Guildford** jmdn./etw. zu jmdm./in jmds. Wohnung/nach Guildford bringen *od.* (ugs.) rüberbringen; **I'll ~ you/it over next time** ich werde dich/es nächstes Mal mitnehmen [3] (Printing) rübernehmen (ugs.)

B *v.i.* übernehmen; ‹*Manager, Firmenleiter:*› die Geschäfte übernehmen; ‹*Regierung, Präsident:*› die Amtsgeschäfte übernehmen; ‹*Junta:*› die Macht übernehmen; ‹*Beifahrer:*› das Steuer übernehmen; **~ over from sb.** jmdn. ersetzen; (temporarily) jmdn. vertreten; **other organizations will ~ over [from it] and carry out its functions** andere Organisationen werden seine Funktion übernehmen; **the night nurse ~s over at 10 p.m.** um zehn Uhr tritt die Nachtschwester ihren Dienst an. *see also* **~over**

• **~ 'round** *v.t.* [1] (carry, deliver) vorbeibringen; **I'll ~ you round one day** ich nehme dich einmal mit hin [2] (show around) [herum]führen; **~ sb. round the factory** jmdn. durch die Fabrik führen

• **~ to** *v.i.* [1] (get into habit of) **~ to doing sth.** anfangen, etw. zu tun; es sich (*Dat.*) angewöhnen, etw. zu tun; **~ to drugs/gambling/crime** zu Drogen greifen/dem Spiel/der Kriminalität verfallen [2] (escape to) sich flüchten in (+ *Akk.*); **~ to the [life]boats** sich in die Boote retten; *see also* **bed A 1**; **heel¹ A 1** [3] (develop a liking for) sich hingezogen fühlen zu ‹*Person*›; sich erwärmen für ‹*Sache*›; (adapt oneself to) sich gewöhnen an (+ *Akk.*); *see also* **duck¹ A 1**

• **~ 'up**

A *v.t.* [1] (lift up) hochheben; (pick up) aufheben; aufnehmen ‹*Staub, Partikel, Laub*›; herausnehmen ‹*Pflanzen*›; herausreißen ‹*Schienenstrang, Dielen*›; aufreißen ‹*Straße*›; hochholen, aufnehmen ‹*Masche*›; **he took up his book again** (started to read again) er nahm seine Lektüre wieder auf; *see also* **arm² A 1**; **cudgel A**; **gauntlet¹ 4**; **glove 1** [2] (move up) weiter nach oben rücken; (shorten) kürzer machen [3] (carry or lead up) **~ sb./sth. up** jmdn./etw. hinaufbringen (**to** zu); **I'll ~ you up one day** ich werde dich einmal mit hinaufnehmen; **~ sth. up to sb.** jmdm. etw. hinaufbringen; **he took the suitcase up to the top floor with him** er nahm den Koffer mit in den obersten Stock [4] (absorb) aufnehmen [5] (wind up) aufwickeln; *see also* **slack¹ B 1** [6] (occupy, engage) beanspruchen; brauchen/(undesirably) wegnehmen ‹*Platz*›; **I'm sorry to have ~n up so much of your time** es tut mir Leid, Ihre Zeit so lange in Anspruch genommen zu haben; **most of my time is ~n up with ...:** ich verbringe die meiste Zeit mit ...; **be ~n up with sth./sb.** von etw./jmdm. in Anspruch genommen sein [7] ergreifen ‹*Beruf*›; anfangen ‹*Jogging, Tennis, Schach, Gitarre*›; **~ up a musical instrument** ein Instrument zu spielen beginnen; **~ sth. up as a hobby/profession** etw. zu seinem Hobby/Beruf machen; **~ up German/a hobby** anfangen, Deutsch zu lernen/sich (*Dat.*) ein Hobby zulegen [8] (start, adopt) aufnehmen ‹*Arbeit, Kampf*›; antreten ‹*Stelle*›; übernehmen ‹*Pflicht, Funktion*›; einnehmen ‹*Haltung, Position*›; eintreten für, sich einsetzen für ‹*Sache*›; **~ up a/one's position** ‹*Polizeiposten, Politiker:*› Position beziehen [9] (accept) annehmen; aufnehmen ‹*Idee, Vorschlag, Kredit, Geld*›; kaufen ‹*Aktien*›; **~ up an option** optieren (Rechtsw.) [10] (raise, pursue further) aufgreifen; **~ sth. up with sb.** sich in einer Sache an jmdn. wenden [11] **~ sb. up [on sth.]** (accept) jmdn. [in Bezug auf etw. (*Akk.*)] beim Wort nehmen; (challenge) jmdm. [in Bezug auf etw. (*Akk.*)] widersprechen; **I might ~ you up on that offer/challenge** dein Angebot/deine Herausforderung werde ich vielleicht annehmen; **he took me up on the remark I had made** er hatte gegen meine Bemerkung etwas einzuwenden [12] (join in) einfallen in (+ *Akk.*) ‹*Ruf*›; sich beteiligen an (+ *Dat.*) ‹*Kampf*› [13] (continue, resume) [wieder] aufnehmen; weiterführen ‹*Geschichte*›; **~ up sth. where one/sb. has left off** mit etw. da fortfahren, wo man/jmd. aufgehört hat [14] **be [very] ~n up with sb./sth.** mit jmdm./etw. [sehr] beschäftigt sein

B *v.i.* [1] (coll.: become friendly) **~ up with sb.** sich mit jmdm. einlassen [2] (continue) einsetzen; **~ up where sb./sth. has left off** da einsetzen, wo jmd./etw. aufgehört hat [3] (wind up) aufwickeln. *see also* **~-up**

• **~ upon** *v.t.* **~ upon oneself** auf sich (*Akk.*) nehmen ‹*Aufgabe, Pflicht, Verantwortung*›; **~ upon oneself the right to do sth.** sich (*Dat.*) [einfach] das Recht nehmen, etw. zu tun; **~ it upon oneself to do sth.** es auf sich (*Akk.*) nehmen, etw. zu tun; (without justification) sich (*Dat.*) herausnehmen (ugs.), etw. zu tun

take: ~away *n.* (restaurant) Restaurant mit Straßenverkauf; (meal) Essen zum Mitnehmen; *attrib.* ‹*Restaurant*› mit Straßenverkauf; ‹*Essen, Mahlzeit*› zum Mitnehmen; **let's get a Chinese ~away for our supper** lass uns beim Chinesen was zum Abendessen holen (ugs.); **~-home** *attrib. adj.* **~-home pay/wages** Nettolohn, *der;* **~-in** *n.* (coll.) Schwindel, *der* (abwertend)

taken ▸ **take A, B**

take: ~-off *n.* [1] (Sport) Absprung, *der;* (board) [Ab]sprungbalken, *der; attrib.* **~-off speed** Geschwindigkeit beim Absprung; [2] (Aeronaut.) Start, *der;* Take-off, *das* (fachspr.); **be cleared/ready for ~-off** Starterlaubnis haben/startklar sein; *attrib.* **~-off speed** Abhebegeschwindigkeit, *die;* [3] (coll.: caricature) Parodie, *die;* **do a ~-off of sb.** jmdn. parodieren; [4] (Econ.) [rapider] Aufschwung; **~out** (Amer.) ▸ **takeaway**; **~over** *n.* (Commerc.) Übernahme, *die; attrib.* **~over battle** Übernahmeschlacht, *die;* **~over bid** Übernahmeangebot, *das*

taker /ˈteɪkə(r)/ *n.* (of a bet) Wetter, *der;* (of shares etc.) Käufer, *der;* **there were no ~s [for the offer]** niemand hat [das Angebot] angenommen; (at betting) keiner nahm die Wette an; **any ~s?** (at auction) wer bietet?

'take-up *n.* [1] (response) **a ~ of over 2,000** über 2 000 Interessenten; **~ has been very**

poor/low es gab kaum *od.* sehr wenig Interessenten **2** (winding up) Aufwickeln, *das;* Aufwick[e]lung, *die; attrib.* Aufwickel‹*spule, -geschwindigkeit*›

taking /'teɪkɪŋ/ *n.* **1** *in pl.* (amount taken) Einnahmen **2** (seizure) Einnahme, *die* **3** **they are yours/his** *etc.* **for the ~:** du kannst/er kann *usw.* sie haben; **victory was his for the ~:** sein Sieg war so gut wie sicher

talc /tælk/ *n.* **1** Talkum, *das* **2** (Min.) Talk, *der*

talcum /'tælkəm/ *n.* **~ [powder]** Talkumpuder, *der;* Talkum, *das;* (as cosmetic) Körperpuder, *der*

tale /teɪl/ *n.* **1** (story) Erzählung, *die;* Geschichte, *die* (**of** von, **about** über + *Akk.*); **fisherman's ~[s]** Anglerlatein, *das* **2** (piece of gossip) Geschichte, *die* (*ugs.*). *see also* **tell A 2**; **thereby**; **wife**; **woe 1**

talent /'tælənt/ *n.* **1** (ability) Talent, *das;* **have [great/no** *etc.*] **~ [for sth.]** [viel/kein *usw.*] Talent [zu *od.* für etw.] haben; **have a ~ for music** musikalisches Talent haben; **have a [great] ~ for doing sth.** das Talent haben, etw. zu tun **2** (people with ability) Talente; Begabungen; **the [local] ~** (coll.: girls/men) die interessanten Frauen/(ugs.) Typen am Ort **3** (Hist.: measure, money) Talent, *das*

'talent contest *n.* Talentwettbewerb, *der*

talented /'tæləntɪd/ *adj.* talentiert; **this is a ~ essay** dieser Aufsatz zeugt von Talent

talent: ~ scout, **~-spotter** *ns.* Talentsucher, *der;* **~-spotting** *n.* Talentsuche, *die*

tale-teller *n.* **1** ▸**storyteller** **2** (sneak/gossip) jmd., der andere anschwärzt/schlechtmacht

talisman /'tælɪzmən/ *n.* Talisman, *der*

talk /tɔ:k/

A *n.* **1** (discussion) Gespräch, *das;* **have a ~ [with sb.] [about sth.]** [mit jmdm.] [über etw. (*Akk.*)] reden *od.* sprechen; **have a long ~ on the phone** lange miteinander telefonieren; **I've enjoyed our ~:** es war nett, mit Ihnen zu sprechen; **could I have a ~ with you?** könnte ich Sie einmal sprechen?; **have** *or* **hold ~s [with sb.]** [mit jmdm.] Gespräche führen

2 (speech, lecture) Vortrag, *der;* **give a ~/a series of ~s [on sth./sb.]** einen Vortrag/eine Vortragsreihe [über etw./jmdn.] halten

3 *no pl.* (form of communication) Sprache, *die;* **sailors'/men's ~:** Seemanns-/Männersprache, *die*

4 *no pl.* (talking) Gerede, *das* (abwertend); **there's too much ~ [of ...]** es wird zu viel [von ...] geredet; **he is all ~ [and no action]** er redet nur [und tut nichts]; **there is [much/some] ~ of ...:** man hört [häufig/öfter] von ...; **be the ~ of the town/neighbourhood** *etc.* Stadtgespräch/das Thema in der Nachbarschaft *usw.* sein. *see also* **big A 7**; **small talk**

B *v.i.* **1** (speak) sprechen, reden (**with, to** mit); (lecture) sprechen; (converse) sich unterhalten; (have ~s) Gespräche führen; (gossip) reden; **be ~ing in German** deutsch sprechen; **love to hear oneself ~:** sich gern reden hören; **can't** *or* **doesn't she ~!** (coll.) die kann vielleicht reden!; **we must ~:** wir müssen miteinander reden; **~ on the phone** telefonieren; **we ~ on the phone every day** wir telefonieren jeden Tag miteinander; **~ to sb. on the phone** mit jmdm. telefonieren; **he sat through the entire meal without ~ing** er hat während des ganzen Essens kein Wort gesagt; **keep sb. ~ing** jmdn. in ein [längeres] Gespräch verwickeln; **she kept me ~ing for an hour** ich musste mich eine Stunde lang mit ihr unterhalten; **now you're ~ing!** (coll.) das hört sich schon besser an; **that's no way to ~/~ to your uncle** das darfst du nicht sagen/so darfst du aber nicht mit deinem Onkel reden!; **don't ~ to 'me like that!** mit mir kannst du so nicht reden!; **who do you think you're ~ing to?** was bildest du dir ein, so mit mir zu sprechen?; **it's easy for you/him** *etc.* **to ~:** du hast/er hat *usw.* gut reden; **look who's ~ing** (iron.) das musst du gerade sagen; **you can** (iron.) *or* **can't ~:** sei du nur ganz still!; **don't ~ daft** (coll.) rede doch kein dummes Zeug!; **I'll ~ to that boy when he gets in** (coll.: scold) ich werde mal ein ernstes Wort mit dem Jungen reden, wenn er nach Hause kommt; **could I ~ to you for a moment?** könnte ich Sie einen Augenblick sprechen?; **~ to sb. seriously** mit jmdm. ein ernstes Wort reden; **may I ~ with Mr Smith, please?** kann ich bitte Herrn Smith sprechen?; **get ~ing [to sb.]** [mit jmdm.] ins Gespräch kommen; **~ to oneself** mit sich selbst sprechen; Selbstgespräche führen; **ships ~ to each other by radio** Schiffe verständigen sich über Funk; **~ of** *or* **about sb./sth.** über jmdn./etw. reden; **everyone's ~ing about him/his divorce** er/seine Scheidung ist in aller Munde; **everyone is ~ing about his new film** jeder spricht von seinem neuen Film; **~ of** *or* **about doing sth.** davon reden, etw. zu tun; **get oneself ~ed about** sich ins Gespräch bringen; **[not] know what one is ~ing about** [gar nicht] wissen, wovon man redet; **[not] know what sb. is ~ing about** [nicht] wissen, was jmd. meint *od.* wovon jmd. spricht; **~ about trouble** *etc.***!** (coll.) da erzähl mir noch einer was von Schwierigkeiten *usw.*!; **What are you ~ing about? Of course he's not going to resign** Was redest du da? Natürlich tritt er nicht zurück; **~ing of holidays** *etc.* da wir [gerade] vom Urlaub *usw.* sprechen; apropos Urlaub *usw.*

2 (have power of speech) sprechen; **animals don't ~:** Tiere können nicht sprechen

3 (betray secrets) reden; **the prisoner refused to ~:** der Gefangene verweigerte jede Aussage; **make sb. ~:** jmdn. zum Reden bringen; **we have ways of making you ~:** wir werden Sie schon noch zum Reden bringen. *see also* **big B**; **hat 2**; **head A 2**

C *v.t.* **1** (utter, express) **~ [a load of] nonsense** [eine Menge] Unsinn *od.* (ugs.) Stuss reden

2 (discuss) **~ politics/music** *etc.* über Politik/Musik *usw.* reden; **~ business** geschäftliche Dinge besprechen; (get down to business) zur Sache kommen; *see also* **shop A 2**

3 (use) sprechen ‹*Sprache, Dialekt usw.*›

4 (bring into certain condition) **~ oneself hoarse** sich heiser reden; **~ oneself** *or* **one's way out of trouble** sich aus Schwierigkeiten herausreden; **he ~ed himself into/out of the job** er hat im Gespräch so eine gute/schlechte Figur gemacht, dass er die Stelle bekommen/nicht bekommen hat; **~ sb. into/out of sth.** jmdn. zu etw. überreden/jmdm. etw. ausreden; **~ oneself into believing sth.** sich (*Dat.*) etw. einreden. *see also* **donkey**

Phrasal verbs

- **~ at** *v.t.* einreden auf (+ *Akk.*)
- **~ away**

A *v.i.* sich [angeregt] unterhalten (**to** mit)

B *v.t.* **1** verplaudern ‹*Zeit*› **2** **~ sb.'s fears away** jmdm. seine Angst ausreden

- **~ 'back** *v.i.* **1** (reply) antworten **2** (reply defiantly) widersprechen (**to** *Dat.*)
- **~ 'down**

A *v.t.* **1** (silence) in Grund und Boden reden **2** (Aeronaut.: guide) Landekommandos geben (+ *Dat.*)

B *v.i.* **~ down to sb.** von oben herab *od.* herablassend mit jmdm. reden

- **~ 'out** *v.t.* **1** (discuss) ausdiskutieren **2** (Parl.) **~ out a bill** die Verabschiedung eines Gesetzes verfahrensmäßig blockieren
- **~ 'over** *v.t.* **1** **~ sth. over [with sb.]** etw. [mit jmdm.] besprechen **2** (persuade) **~ sb. over** jmdn. überreden
- **~ 'round** *v.t.* **1** (persuade) **~ sb. round** jmdn. überreden **2** (skirt) **~ round sth.** um etw. herumreden (ugs.)
- **~ 'through** *v.t.* **~ sb. through sth.** etw. mit jmdm. durchgehen *od.* durchsprechen; **~ sth. through** etw. durchsprechen
- **~ 'up**

A *v.t.* hochstilisieren

B *v.i.* ▸**speak up 1**

talkathon /'tɔ:kəθɒn/ *n.* (coll.) Diskussionsmarathon, *der;* Debattenmarathon, *der*

talkative /'tɔ:kətɪv/ *adj.* gesprächig; geschwätzig (abwertend)

talkativeness /'tɔ:kətɪvnɪs/ *n., no pl.* Gesprächigkeit, *die;* Geschwätzigkeit, *die* (abwertend)

'talkback *n.* **1** (two-way communication) Gegensprechanlage, *die; attrib.* **~ system** Gegensprechsystem, *das;* **~ key** Sprechtaste, *die* **2** (phone-in) Phone-in, *das;* Phone-in-Sendung, *die*

talked-about /'tɔ:ktəbaʊt/ *attrib. adj.* ▸**talked-of**

talked-of /'tɔ:ktɒv/ *attrib. adj.* **a much ~ book/play/project** ein viel diskutiertes Buch/Stück/Projekt; **a much ~ actor/artist** ein Schauspieler/Künstler, der in aller Munde ist

talker /'tɔ:kə(r)/ *n.* **1** Redner, *der*/Rednerin, *die;* **the parrot is an excellent ~:** der Papagei kann ausgezeichnet sprechen; **she is a great ~** (talks a lot) sie redet viel; **be a fast ~:** [sehr] schnell sprechen; (fig. coll.) verdammt gut reden können (ugs.) **2** (one who talks but does not act) Schwätzer, *der*/Schwätzerin, *die;* **he's just a ~:** er redet immer nur

talkie /'tɔ:kɪ/ *n.* (coll.) Tonfilm, *der*

talking /'tɔ:kɪŋ/

A *n.* Reden, *das;* **there's been so much ~:** es ist so viel geredet worden; **'no ~'** „bitte nicht sprechen"; **do [all] the ~:** das Gespräch dominieren; **let me do the ~:** überlass lieber mir das Reden

B *adj.* sprechend; **~ doll** Sprechpuppe, *die;* **~ book** Hörbuch, *das;* **~ film** *or* **picture** Tonfilm, *der*

talking: ~ 'book *n.* Hörbuch, *das;* **~ 'heads** *n. pl.* (Telev. coll. derog.) Leute, die man nur reden sieht; **~ point** *n.* Gesprächsthema, *das;* **~ shop** *n.* (derog.) Quasselbude, *die* (ugs. abwertend); **~-to** /'tɔ:kɪŋtu:/ *n.* (coll.) Standpauke, *die* (ugs.); **give sb. a good ~-to** jmdm. eine ordentliche Standpauke halten (ugs.)

'talk radio *n., no pl., no art.* Talkradio, *das*

'talk show *n.* Talkshow, *die*

tall /tɔ:l/

A *adj.* **1** ▸**i** **p. 1208** hoch; groß ‹*Person, Tier*›; **grow ~:** groß werden; wachsen; **feel ten feet ~** (fig.) riesig stolz sein **2** (coll.: excessive) **a ~ tale** eine unglaubwürdige Geschichte; **that is a ~ order** das ist ziemlich viel verlangt; *see also* **story[1] 1**

B *adv.* ▸**i** **p. 1208** **stand six feet** *etc.* **~:** 6 Fuß *usw.* groß sein; **stand ~:** aufrecht stehen; (be proud) erhobenen Hauptes stehen/gehen *usw.* (*geh.*); *see also* **walk A 1**

tall: ~boy *n.* Doppelkommode, *die;* Tallboy, *der;* **~ 'hat** ▸**top hat**

tallish /'tɔ:lɪʃ/ *adj.* ziemlich hoch; ziemlich groß ‹*Person*›

tallness /'tɔ:lnɪs/ *n., no pl.* Höhe, *die;* (of person) Größe, *die*

tallow /'tæləʊ/ *n.* Talg, *der*

'tallow candle *n.* Talgkerze, *die*

tall 'ship *n.* Windjammer, *der*

tally /'tælɪ/

A *n.* **1** (record) **sb.'s ~ is 18 goals** jmd. kann 18 Tore für sich verbuchen; **a player with a ~ of 18 goals** ein Spieler, der 18 Tore für sich verbuchen kann; **keep a [daily] ~ of sth.** [täglich] über etw. (*Akk.*) Buch führen **2** (label, ticket) Schild, *das*

B *v.i.* übereinstimmen

tally-'ho

A *int.* ≈ horrido

B *n., pl.* **~s** ≈ Horrido, *das*

Talmud /'tælmʊd, 'tælməd/ *n.* Talmud, *der*

talon /'tælən/ *n.* Klaue, *die;* **~s** (fig.: long fingernails) Krallen (ugs. abwertend)

tamarind /'tæmərɪnd/ *n.* Tamarinde, *die*

tamarisk /'tæmərɪsk/ *n.* (Bot.) Tamariske, *die*

tambourine /tæmbə'ri:n/ *n.* (Mus.) Tamburin, *das*

tame /teɪm/

A *adj.* **1** zahm; (joc.) hauseigen ‹*Anarchist, Genie*›; **grow/become ~:** zahm werden **2** (spiritless) lahm (ugs.), lustlos ‹*Einwilligung, Anerkennung, Kampagne, Versuch*›; zahm (ugs.) ‹*Besprechung, Kritik*› **3** (dull) wenig aufregend; lasch ‹*Stil*›

B *v.t.* (lit. or fig.) zähmen

tameable /'teɪməbl/ *adj.* (lit. or fig.) zähmbar; **be [not] ~:** sich [nicht] zähmen lassen

t

tamely /'teɪmlɪ/ *adv.* 1 (docilely) zahm (ugs.) 2 (fig.: unexcitingly) lahm (ugs.); wenig aufregend

tameness /'teɪmnɪs/ *n., no pl.* 1 (docility) Zahmheit, *die* 2 ▸**tame A 2**: Lahmheit, *die* (ugs.); Lustlosigkeit, *die;* Zahmheit, *die* (ugs.) 3 (dullness) Langweiligkeit, *die;* (of style) Laschheit, *die*

tamer /'teɪmə(r)/ *n.* Dompteur, *der*/Dompteuse, *die;* **a ~ of wild animals** ein Tierbändiger

Tamil /'tæmɪl/ ▸❶ **p. 1277**, ▸❶ **p. 1345**
A *adj.* tamilisch
B *n.* 1 (person) Tamile, *der*/Tamilin, *die* 2 (language) Tamil, *das*

tam-o'-shanter /tæmə'ʃæntə(r)/ *n.* Tam-o'-Shanter, *der; zur schottischen Tracht gehörende Tellermütze mit Pompon*

tamp /tæmp/ *v.t.* andrücken; festdrücken; **~ sth. down** etw. andrücken *od.* festdrücken

tamper /'tæmpə(r)/ *v.i.* **~ with** sich (*Dat.*) zu schaffen machen an (+ *Dat.*); (make unauthorized changes in) unerlaubte Änderungen vornehmen an (+ *Dat.*) ‹*Schriftstück, Text*›; (attempt to bribe) zu bestechen versuchen ‹*Jury, Zeugen*›; (fig.) ändern wollen ‹*Regeln, Tradition*›; **the brakes had been ~ed with** jmd. hatte sich an den Bremsen zu schaffen gemacht

'tamper-proof *adj.* einbruchsicher ‹*Schloss*›; verplombt ‹*Gasuhr*›; aufbruchsicher ‹*Münztelefon*›

tampon /'tæmpɒn/ *n.* Tampon, *der*

tan¹ /tæn/
A *v.t.*, **-nn-** 1 gerben ‹*Tierhaut, Fell*› 2 (bronze) ‹*Sonne:*› bräunen; ‹*Person:*› braun werden lassen ‹*Körperteil*›; **the sun had ~ned them dark brown** die Sonne hatte sie dunkelbraun gebrannt 3 (coll.: beat) das Fell gerben (salopp) (+ *Dat.*); *see also* **hide²**
B *v.i.*, **-nn-** braun werden
C *n.* 1 (colour) Gelbbraun, *das* 2 (sun~) Bräune, *die;* **have/get a ~:** braun sein/werden 3 (~ning agent) Gerbmittel, *das*
D *adj.* gelbbraun

tan² *abbr.* (Math.) = **tangent** tan

TAN *abbr.* = **transaction number** TAN, *die*

tandem /'tændəm/
A *adv.* hintereinander; **be driven ~** ‹*Pferde:*› hintereinander im Gespann laufen; **drive/ride ~** ‹*Kutscher, Radfahrer:*› Tandem fahren
B *n.* (lit. or fig.) Tandem, *das;* **~ bicycle** Tandem, *das;* **coupled/harnessed in ~:** hintereinander gekoppelt/gespannt; **work in ~** (fig.) zusammenarbeiten

tandoori /tæn'dʊərɪ/ *n.* (Gastr.) Tandoorigericht, *das; attrib.* Tandoori‹*restaurant, -hühnchen*›; **~ cooking** Tandooriküche, *die*

tang /tæŋ/ *n.* 1 (taste/smell) **[sharp] ~:** scharfer Geschmack/Geruch; **[spicy/salty] ~:** würziger/salziger Geschmack/Geruch; **there is a ~ of autumn in the air** es riecht nach Herbst 2 (of chisel, knife, sword) Angel, *die*

tanga /'tæŋgə/ *n.* (Brit.) Tanga, *der*

tangent /'tændʒənt/ (Math.)
A *n.* Tangente, *die;* (in triangle) Tangens, *der;* **run/be drawn at a ~ to a curve/circle** eine Kurve/einen Kreis in einem Punkt berühren; **go** *or* **fly off at a ~** (fig.) plötzlich vom Thema abschweifen
B *adj.* Tangenten-; **~ plane** Tangentialebene, *die;* **be ~ to** tangieren (fachspr.), in einem Punkt berühren ‹*Kurve, Kreis*›

tangential /tæn'dʒenʃl/ *adj.* (Math.) Tangential-; (fig.: peripheral) nebensächlich; nicht zur Sache gehörend ‹*Kommentar, Information*›; **be merely ~ to sth.** (fig.) etw. nur am Rande berühren

tangerine /tændʒə'ri:n/
A *n.* 1 (fruit) **~ [orange]** Tangerine, *die* 2 (colour) Orangerot, *das*
B *adj.* orangerot

tangible /'tændʒɪbl/ *adj.* 1 (perceptible by touch) fühlbar ‹*Schwellung, Verdickung, Verhärtung*› 2 (fig.: real, definite) greifbar; spürbar, merklich ‹*Unterschied, Verbesserung*›; handfest ‹*Beweis*›; **~ assets** (Econ.) Sachanlagevermögen, *das*

tangibly /'tændʒɪblɪ/ *adv.* deutlich ‹*sichtbar*›; **be ~ different** sich merklich unterscheiden (**from** von); **sth. can be ~ proved** es gibt handfeste Beweise für etw.; **you should have been more ~ rewarded** man hätte dir eine handfestere Belohnung geben sollen

Tangier[s] /tæn'dʒɪə(z)/ *pr. n.* ▸❶ **p. 1643** Tanger (*das*)

tangle /'tæŋgl/
A *n.* Gewirr, *das;* (in hair) Verfilzung, *die;* (fig.: dispute) Auseinandersetzung, *die;* **be in a ~:** sich verheddert haben (ugs.); ‹*Haar:*› sich verfilzt haben; (fig.) ‹*Angelegenheiten:*› in Unordnung (*Dat.*) sein; ‹*Person:*› verwirrt sein; **get oneself into a ~** (fig.) sich in eine schwierige Lage bringen
B *v.t.* verheddern (ugs.); verfilzen ‹*Haar*›
C *v.i.* sich verheddern (ugs.); ‹*Haar:*› sich verfilzen

Phrasal verbs

- **~ 'up**
A *v.t.* verheddern (ugs.); verfilzen ‹*Haar*›; **become** *or* **get ~d up** sich verheddern (ugs.); **he's got ~d up in a rather unpleasant affair** (coll.) er ist in eine ziemlich unangenehme Sache verstrickt; **get ~d up with sb.** (fig.) sich mit jmdm. einlassen
B *v.i.* ▸**~ C**
- **~ with** *v.t.* (coll.) **~ with sb.** sich mit jmdm. anlegen

tangled /'tæŋgld/ *adj.* verheddert (ugs.); verfilzt ‹*Haar*›; (confused, complicated) verworren; verwickelt ‹*Angelegenheit*›

tango /'tæŋgəʊ/
A *n., pl.* **~s** Tango, *der*
B *v.i.* Tango tanzen; **it takes two to ~** (fig. coll.) dazu gehören immer noch zwei

tangy /'tæŋɪ/ *adj.* scharf; (spicy) würzig; (acid) bitter; (salty) salzig

tank /tæŋk/ *n.* 1 Tank, *der;* (Railw.: in tender) Wasserkasten, *der;* (for fish etc.) Aquarium, *das;* (for catching rainwater) Auffangbecken, *das;* **fill the ~** (with fuel) volltanken 2 (Mil.) Panzer, *der*

Phrasal verb

- **~ 'up**
A *v.i.* (get fuel) auftanken
B *v.t.* auftanken; **get ~ed up** (sl.: drunk) sich volltanken (salopp)

tankard /'tæŋkəd/ *n.* Krug, *der;* **a ~ of beer** *etc.* ein Krug Bier *usw.*

'tank car *n.* (Amer. Railw.) Kesselwagen, *der*

tanked-up /tæŋk'tʌp/ *adj.* (sl.) vollgetankt (salopp)

'tank engine *n.* (Railw.) Tenderlokomotive, *die*

tanker /'tæŋkə(r)/ *n.* (ship) Tanker, *der;* Tankschiff, *das;* (aircraft) Tankflugzeug, *das;* (road vehicle) Tank[last]wagen, *der*

tanker: ~ aircraft *n.* Tankflugzeug, *das;* **~ lorry** *n.* Tanklaster, *der;* Tanklastwagen, *der*

tankini /tæŋ'ki:nɪ/ *n.* Tankini, *der*

tank: ~ killer *n.* Panzerkiller, *der;* **~ top** *n.* ≈ Pullunder, *der;* **~ trap** *n.* (Mil.) Panzersperre, *die;* (ditch) Panzergraben, *der;* **~ waggon** *n.* (Brit. Railw.) Kesselwagen, *der*

tanned /tænd/ *adj.* 1 (treated by tanning) gegerbt 2 (bronzed) braun gebrannt

tanner¹ /'tænə(r)/ *n.* (person) Gerber, *der*/Gerberin, *die*

tanner² *n.* (Brit. Hist. coll.) Sixpence, *der*

tannery /'tænərɪ/ *n.* Gerberei, *die*

tannic /'tænɪk/ *adj.* **~ acid** (Chem.) Tannin, *das*

tannin /'tænɪn/ *n.* (Chem.) Tannin, *das*

tanning /'tænɪŋ/ *n.* 1 (of hides) Gerben, *das;* (craft also) Gerberei, *die; attrib.* Gerb- 2 (bronzing) Bräunung, *die; attrib.* Bräunungs-; **~ studio** Sonnenstudio, *das* 3 (coll.: beating) Abreibung, *die* (ugs.); **give sb. a ~:** jmdm. das Fell gerben (salopp)

Tannoy ® /'tænɔɪ/ *n.* Lautsprecheranlage, *die;* **over** *or* **on the ~:** über Lautsprecher

tansy /'tænzɪ/ *n.* (Bot.) Rainfarn, *der*

tantalise, tantalising, tantalisingly ▸**tantaliz-**

tantalize /'tæntəlaɪz/ *v.t.* reizen; (tease also) zappeln lassen (ugs.); (with promises) [falsche] Hoffnungen wecken bei

tantalizing /'tæntəlaɪzɪŋ/ *adj.* verlockend; **a ~ puzzle** ein Rätsel, das einen nicht loslässt

tantalizingly /'tæntəlaɪzɪŋlɪ/ *adv.* [falsche] Hoffnungen weckend; verlockend ‹*schön, nah, duften, lächeln*›

tantamount /'tæntəmaʊnt/ *pred. adj.* **be ~ to sth.** gleichbedeutend mit etw. sein; einer Sache (*Dat.*) gleichkommen

tantrum /'tæntrəm/ *n.* Wutanfall, *der;* (of child) Trotzanfall, *der;* **be in a ~:** einen Wutanfall/Trotzanfall haben; **get into/throw a ~:** einen Wutanfall/Trotzanfall bekommen

Tanzania /tænzə'ni:ə/ *pr. n.* Tansania (*das*)

Tanzanian /tænzə'ni:ən/ ▸❶ **p. 1345**
A *adj.* tansanisch; **sb. is ~:** jmd. ist Tansanier/Tansanierin
B *n.* Tansanier, *der*/Tansanierin, *die*

Taoiseach /'ti:ʃæx/ *n.* (Ir. Parl.) Premierminister/-ministerin [der Republik Irland]

Taoism /'taʊɪzm/ *n.* (Relig.) Taoismus, *der*

Taoist /'taʊɪst/ (Relig.)
A *adj.* taoistisch
B *n.* Taoist, *der*/Taoistin, *die*

tap¹ /tæp/
A *n.* 1 Hahn, *der;* (on barrel, cask) [Zapf]hahn, *der;* **hot/cold[-water] ~:** Warm-/Kaltwasserhahn, *der;* **leave the ~ running** den Wasserhahn laufen lassen; **on ~:** vom Fass *nachgestellt;* **be on ~** (fig.) zur Verfügung stehen; **have on ~** (fig.) zur Verfügung haben ‹*Geld, Mittel*›; an der Hand haben ‹*Experten*› 2 (plug) Zapfen, *der;* Spund, *der* 3 **[telephone] ~:** Telefonüberwachung, *die*
B *v.t.*, **-pp-** 1 (make use of) erschließen ‹*Reserven, Ressourcen, Bezirk, Markt, Land, Einnahmequelle*›; anzapfen (fig. ugs.) ‹*Reserven, Ressourcen*›; **~ sb. for money/information** jmdn. anzapfen (ugs.); **~ sb. for a few pounds** versuchen, bei jmdm. ein paar Pfund lockerzumachen (ugs.) 2 (Teleph.: intercept) abhören; anzapfen (ugs.) 3 (pierce) anzapfen ‹*Baum, Fass*›; anstechen ‹*Fass*›; (draw off) abzapfen ‹*Bier*›; **~ a tree for resin** einen Baum zur Harzgewinnung anzapfen 4 (Metalw.) ein Gewinde schneiden in (+ *Akk.*)

Phrasal verb

- **~ 'off** *v.t.* abzapfen (**into** in + *Akk.*)

tap²
A *v.t.*, **-pp-** (strike lightly) klopfen an (+ *Akk.*); (on upper surface) klopfen auf (+ *Akk.*); **~ one's fingers on the table** (repeatedly) mit den Fingern auf den Tisch trommeln; **~ one's finger against one's forehead** sich (*Dat.*) mit dem Finger an die Stirn tippen; **~ one's foot** mit dem Fuß auf den Boden klopfen; **~ one's foot to the music** mit dem Fuß den Takt schlagen; **~ sb. on the shoulder** jmdm. auf die Schulter klopfen/(more lightly) tippen
B *v.i.*, **-pp-:** **~ at/on sth.** an etw. (*Akk.*) klopfen; (on upper surface) auf etw. (*Akk.*) klopfen
C *n.* (light blow, rap) Klopfen, *das;* (given to naughty child) Klaps, *der* (ugs.); **give a nail a little ~:** leicht auf einen Nagel klopfen; **there was a ~ at/on the door** es klopfte an die Tür; **I felt a ~ on my shoulder** jemand klopfte/(more lightly) tippte mir auf die Schulter; **~s** (Amer. Mil.: signal) Zapfenstreich, *der*

Phrasal verbs

- **~ a'way** *v.i.* ‹*Schreibkraft, Funker am Morsegerät:*› vor sich hin klappern; **~ away on the table with one's fingers/a ruler** mit den Fingern/einem Lineal auf dem Tisch trommeln
- **~ 'in** *v.t.* einklopfen ‹*Nagel usw.*›
- **~ 'out** *v.t.* 1 (knock out) ausklopfen ‹*Pfeife*›; herausklopfen ‹*Nagel, Keil*› 2 klopfen ‹*Rhythmus, Takt*›; (write) (in Morse) morsen ‹*Nachricht*›; (on typewriter) tippen (ugs.)

tap: ~ dance A *n.* Stepp[tanz], *der;* **do a ~ dance** steppen. B *v.i.* Stepp tanzen; steppen; **~ dancer** *n.* Stepptänzer, *der*/-tänzerin, *die;* **~ dancing** *n.* Stepptanz, *der;* Steppen, *das*

tape /teɪp/
A *n.* 1 Band, *das;* **adhesive** *or* **sticky ~:** Klebstreifen, *der;* Klebeband, *das; see also* **red tape** 2 (Sport) Zielband, *das;* **breast the ~:** durchs Ziel gehen 3 (for recording) [Ton]band, *das* (**of** mit); **[have sth.] on ~:** [etw.] auf Band (*Dat.*) [haben]; **put/record sth. on ~, make a ~ of sth.** etw. auf Band (*Akk.*) aufnehmen; **blank ~:**

t

unbespieltes Band **4** **[paper]** ~: Papierstreifen, *der;* (punched with holes) Lochstreifen, *der;* **come in on the** ~ ‹*Nachricht:*› über Fernschreiber kommen

B *v.t.* **1** (record on ~) [auf Band (*Akk.*)] aufnehmen; **~d music** Tonbandmusik, *die* **2** (bind with ~) [mit Klebeband *od.* Klebstreifen] zukleben ‹*Paket*›; kleben ‹*Einband, eingerissene Seite*› **3** **have got sb./sth. ~d** (coll.) jmdn. durchschaut haben/etw. im Griff *od.* unter Kontrolle haben

(Phrasal verbs)

- ~ **'down** *v.t.* [mit Klebeband] festkleben
- ~ **'on** *v.t.* [mit Klebeband] ankleben
- ~ **'over** *v.t.* [mit Klebeband] überkleben
- ~ **to'gether** *v.t.* [mit Klebeband] zusammenkleben
- ~ **'up** *v.t.* [mit Klebeband] zukleben; [mit Klebeband] zusammenkleben ‹*zerrissene Seite, zerbrochene Pfeife usw.*›

tape: ~ **cassette** *n.* Tonbandkassette, *die;* ~ **deck** *n.* Tapedeck, *das;* ~ **drive** *n.* Bandlaufwerk, *das;* ~ **head** *n.* Magnetkopf, *der;* ~ **machine** *n.* Fernschreiber, *der;* ~ **measure** *n.* Bandmaß, *das;* (for measuring garments etc.) [Zenti]metermaß, *das;* ~ **player** *n.* Tonband[wiedergabe]gerät, *das*

taper /'teɪpə(r)/

A *v.t.* sich verjüngen lassen; ~ **[to a point]** spitz zulaufen lassen; **be ~ed** sich verjüngen; (to a point) spitz zulaufen

B *v.i.* sich verjüngen; ~ **[to a point]** spitz zulaufen

C *n.* **1** **[wax]** ~: Wachsstock, *der* **2** (narrowing) Verjüngung, *die*

(Phrasal verbs)

- ~ **away** ▸ ~ **off B**
- ~ **'off**

A *v.t.* **1** ▸ ~ **A** **2** (fig.: decrease gradually) drosseln ‹*Produktion*›

B *v.i.* **1** ▸ **taper B** **2** (fig.: decrease gradually) zurückgehen

tape: **~-record** /'teɪprɪkɔ:d/ *v.t.* [auf Tonband (*Akk.*)] aufnehmen *od.* aufzeichnen; ~ **recorder** *n.* Tonbandgerät, *das;* ~ **recording** *n.* Tonbandaufnahme, *die*

tapered /'teɪpəd/ *adj.* sich verjüngend; (to a point) spitz zulaufend; ~ **trousers** unten eng geschnittene Hose

tapering /'teɪpərɪŋ/ *adj.* sich verjüngend; (to a point) spitz zulaufend; **be** ~: sich verjüngen; (to a point) spitz zulaufen

'tape-slide show *n.* vertonte Diaschau

tapestry /'tæpɪstrɪ/ *n.* Gobelingewebe, *das;* (wall hanging) Bildteppich, *der;* Tapisserie, *die;* (fig.) Darstellung, *die;* **Gobelin** ~: Gobelin[teppich], *der;* **the Bayeux** ~: der Bayeuxteppich

'tapeworm *n.* Bandwurm, *der*

tapioca /tæpɪ'əʊkə/ *n.* Tapioka, *die*

tapir /'teɪpə(r), 'teɪpɪə(r)/ *n.* (Zool.) Tapir, *der*

tappet /'tæpɪt/ *n.* (Mech. Engin.) Mitnehmer, *der*

tap: **~room** *n.* Schankraum, *der;* **~root** *n.* (Bot.) Pfahlwurzel, *die;* ~ **water** *n.* Leitungswasser, *das*

tar¹ /tɑ:(r)/

A *n.* Teer, *der;* **high-~/low-~ cigarette** Zigarette mit hohem/niedrigem Teergehalt; (fig.) **beat** *or* **knock the ~ out of sb.** (Amer. coll.) jmdn. fertig machen (salopp); **spoil the ship for a ha'p'orth of** ~: am falschen Ende sparen

B *v.t.*, **-rr-** teeren; **~red road** Teerstraße, *die;* ~ **and feather sb.** jmdn. teeren und federn; **they are ~red with the same brush** *or* **stick** (fig.) der eine ist nicht besser als der andere

tar² *n.* **[Jack]** ~ (coll.) Teerjacke, *die* (scherzh.)

tarantella /tærən'telə/, **tarantelle** /'tærən'tel/ *n.* (Mus.) Tarantella, *die*

tarantula /tə'ræntjʊlə/ *n.* (Zool.) Tarantel, *die*

tardily /'tɑ:dɪlɪ/ *adv.* **1** (slowly) [zögernd] langsam **2** (late) spät; (too late) zu spät

tardy /'tɑ:dɪ/ *adj.* **1** (slow) [zögernd] langsam **2** (late) spät; (too late) zu spät; **be** ~: mit Verspätung kommen (**for, to** zu); **be ~ in doing sth.** etw. erst spät tun

tare /teə(r)/ *n.* (Commerc.) Tara, *die;* (of lorry, car) Leergewicht, *das*

target /'tɑ:gɪt/

A *n.* **1** (lit. or fig.) Ziel, *das;* **be the ~ of** *or* **a ~ for his mockery/fury** (fig.) die Zielscheibe seines Spottes/Zornes sein; **production/export/savings** ~: Produktions-/Export-/Sparziel, *das;* **fixed/moving/towed** ~: feststehendes Ziel/bewegliches Ziel/Schleppscheibe, *die;* **hit/miss the/one's/its** ~: [das Ziel] treffen/das Ziel verfehlen; **set oneself a** ~ (fig.) sich (*Dat.*) ein Ziel setzen *od.* stecken; **set oneself a ~ of £5,000** sich (*Dat.*) 5 000 Pfund zum Ziel setzen; **set sb. a ~ of six months** jmdm. eine Frist von sechs Monaten setzen; **reach one's** ~ (fig.) sein Ziel erreichen; **be on/off** *or* **not on** ~ ‹*Geschoss, Schuss:*› treffen/danebengehen; **be on** ~ (fig.) ‹*Sparer, Sammler:*› auf dem Wege dahin sein[, sein Ziel zu erreichen]; **be on ~ for sth.** (lit. or fig.) auf etw. (*Akk.*) zusteuern; **be above/below** ~ (fig.) das Ziel über-/unterschritten haben **2** (Sport) Ziel- *od.* Schießscheibe, *die* **3** (Phys.) Target, *das. see also* **sitting target**

B *v.t.* **1** (Mil.) angreifen **2** (fig.) zielen auf ‹*Käufergruppe*›; ~ **benefits at those most in need** Unterstützung auf die Bedürftigsten konzentrieren; **independently ~ed warheads** (Mil.) unabhängig voneinander lenkbare Einzelsprengköpfe; **be ~ed on sth.** auf etw. (*Akk.*) gerichtet sein; **be ~ed on** *or* **at sth.** (fig.) auf etw. (*Akk.*) abzielen

target: ~ **date** *n.* vorgesehener Termin; ~ **figure** *n.* (esp. Commerc.) Ziel, *das;* ~ **group** *n.* Zielgruppe, *die;* ~ **language** *n.* Zielsprache, *die;* ~ **practice** *n.* Schießübungen *Pl.*

tariff /'tærɪf/ *n.* **1** (tax) Zoll, *der;* (table or scale of customs duties) Zolltarif, *der;* **[import]** ~: Einfuhr- *od.* Importzoll, *der* **2** (list of charges) Tarif, *der;* Preisliste, *die;* **railway/postal** ~: Eisenbahn-/Posttarif, *der;* **hotel** ~: Hotelpreise

Tarmac, tarmac /'tɑ:mæk/

A *n.* ® **1** Makadam, *der* (Bauw.) **2** (at airport) Rollbahn, *die*

B *v.t.*, **-ck-** makadamisieren (Bauw.)

tarmacadam /tɑ: mə'kædəm/ *n.* (dated) ▸ **tarmac A 1**

tarn /tɑ:n/ *n.* [kleiner] Bergsee

tarnish /'tɑ:nɪʃ/

A *v.t.* stumpf werden lassen ‹*Metall*›; (fig.) beflecken ‹*Ruf, Namen*›

B *v.i.* ‹*Metall:*› stumpf werden, anlaufen

C *n.* **1** (action) Anlaufen, *das* **2** (discolouring film) Beschlag, *der;* Überzug, *der*

tarnished /'tɑ:nɪʃt/ *adj.* stumpf ‹*Metall*›; (fig.) befleckt ‹*Ruf, Name, Image*›

tarot /'tærəʊ/ *n.* Tarock, *das od. der;* ~ **card** Tarockkarte, *die*

tarpaulin /tɑ:'pɔ:lɪn/ *n.* Plane, *die*

tarpon /'tɑ:pən/ *n.* (Zool.) Tarpun, *der*

tarragon /'tærəgən/ *n.* (Bot.) Estragon, *der*

tarry¹ /'tɑ:rɪ/ *adj.* teerig; teerverschmiert ‹*Hand, Kleidung*›; ‹*Strand, Felsen*› voller Teer

tarry² /'tærɪ/ *v.i.* (arch/literary) verweilen (geh.); (be slow) säumen (geh.); ~ **awhile** ein Weilchen bleiben

tart¹ /tɑ:t/ *adj.* herb; sauer ‹*Obst usw.*›; (fig.) scharfzüngig

tart² *n.* **1** (Brit.) (filled pie) ≈ Obstkuchen, *der;* (small pastry) Obsttörtchen, *das;* **jam** ~: Marmeladentörtchen, *das* **2** (sl.: prostitute) Nutte, *die* (salopp)

(Phrasal verb)

- ~ **'up** *v.t.* (Brit. coll.) ~ **oneself up, get ~ed up** (dress gaudily) sich auftakeln (ugs.); (smarten oneself up) sich fein machen; ~ **a pub/restaurant up** (fig.) eine Kneipe/ein Lokal aufmotzen (ugs.)

tartan /'tɑ:tən/

A *n.* Schotten[stoff], *der;* (pattern) **the Stewart** ~: der Stewart (Textilw.); *das Schottenmuster des Stewart-Clans*

B *adj.* **1** Schotten‹*rock, -jacke*›; ~ **plaid/rug** Tartan, *der* **2** **T~ track** ® Tartanbahn, *die*

tartar *n.* **1** (Chem.) Tartarus, *der* (fachspr.); Weinstein, *der; see also* **cream of tartar** **2** (scale on teeth) Zahnstein, *der*

Tartar /'tɑ:tə(r)/ ▸❶ **p. 1277**, ▸❶ **p. 1345**

A *adj.* tatarisch; Tataren-

B *n.* **1** (person) Tatar, *der*/Tatarin, *die* **2** (language) Tatarisch, das **3** (violent-tempered person) Choleriker, *der*/Cholerikerin, *die*

tartare /'tɑ:tɑ:(r)/ *adj.* ~ **sauce, sauce** ~ ▸ **tartar sauce**; **steak tartare** ▸ **steak**

tartaric acid /tɑ:tærɪk 'æsɪd/ *n.* (Chem.) Weinsäure, *die*

tartar sauce /'tɑ:tɑ:(r)/ *n.* (Gastr.) Remoulade[nsoße], *die*

tartly /'tɑ:tlɪ/ *adv.* in scharfem Ton ‹*sprechen, antworten*›

tartness /'tɑ:tnɪs/ *n.*, *no pl.* ▸ **tart¹**: Herbheit, *die;* Säure, *die;* (fig.) Scharfzüngigkeit *die*

tarty /'tɑ:tɪ/ *adj.* (sl.) nuttig (ugs. abwertend)

Tarzan /'tɑ:zən/ *n.* Tarzan, *der* (fig.)

task /tɑ:sk/

A *n.* Aufgabe, *die;* **set sb. the ~ of doing sth.** jmdm. auftragen, etw. zu tun; **set oneself the ~ of doing sth.** es sich (*Dat.*) zur Aufgabe machen, etw. zu tun; **undertake the ~ of doing sth.** sich der Aufgabe (*Dat.*) unterziehen, etw. zu tun; **carry out/perform a** ~: eine Aufgabe erfüllen; **take sb. to** ~: jmdm. eine Lektion erteilen

B *v.t.* ~ **sb. with sth./with doing sth.** jmdn. mit etw. beauftragen/jmdn. damit beauftragen, etw. zu tun

task: **~bar** *n.* (Computing) Taskleiste, *die;* ~ **force**, ~ **group** *ns.* (Mil.) Sonderkommando, *das;* (fig.: group investigating problem etc.) Sonderkommission, *die;* **~master** *n.* **a hard ~master** ein strenger Vorgesetzter; (teacher) ein strenger Lehrmeister

Tasmania /tæz'meɪnɪə/ *pr. n.* Tasmanien (*das*)

Tasmanian /tæz'meɪnɪən/

A *adj.* **1** tasmanisch **2** (Zool.) ~ **devil/wolf** Beutelteufel/-wolf, *der*

B *n.* Tasmanier, *der*/Tasmanierin, *die*

tassel /'tæsl/ *n.* Quaste, *die*

taste /teɪst/

A *v.t.* **1** schmecken; (try a little) probieren; kosten; **she barely ~d her food** sie hat ihr Essen kaum angerührt; **she hadn't ~d food for two days** sie hatte seit zwei Tagen keinen Bissen gegessen **2** (recognize flavour of) [heraus]schmecken **3** (fig.: experience) kosten (geh.) ‹*Macht, Freiheit, [Miss]erfolg, Glück, Niederlage*›

B *v.i.* **1** (have sense of flavour) schmecken **2** (have certain flavour) schmecken (**of** nach); **not of anything** nach nichts schmecken

C *n.* **1** (flavour) Geschmack, *der;* **to** ~: nach Geschmack ‹*verdünnen*›; **this dish has no** ~: dieses Gericht schmeckt nach nichts; **there's a ~ of garlic in sth.** etw. schmeckt nach Knoblauch; **leave a nasty/bad** *etc.* ~ **in the mouth** (lit. or fig.) einen unangenehmen/üblen *usw.* Nachgeschmack hinterlassen **2** (sense) **[sense of]** ~: Geschmack[ssinn], *der* **3** (discernment) Geschmack, *der;* **person of** ~: Person mit Geschmack; **he is a person of** ~: er hat Geschmack; ~ **in art/music** Kunst-/Musikgeschmack, *der;* **have good ~ in clothes** sich geschmackvoll kleiden; **it would be bad ~ to do that** es wäre geschmacklos *od.* eine Geschmacklosigkeit, das zu tun; **in good/bad** ~: geschmackvoll/geschmacklos; **in the best/worst of** ~: äußerst geschmackvoll/geschmacklos **4** (sample) (lit. or fig.) Kostprobe, *die;* **have a ~ of** probieren ‹*Speise, Getränk*›; kennen lernen ‹*Freiheit, jmds. Jähzorn, Arroganz*›; **do you want a ~?** möchtest du mal kosten *od.* probieren?; **first ~ of success/of life in a big city** erstes Erfolgs-/Großstadterlebnis; **give sb. a ~ of sth.** (lit. or fig.) jmdm. eine Kostprobe einer Sache (*Gen.*) geben; **give sb. a ~ of the whip** jmdm. die Peitsche zu spüren *od.* (geh.) schmecken geben; **a ~ of things to come** ein Vorgeschmack dessen, was noch kommt; *see also* **medicine** **5** (liking) Geschmack, *der* (**in** für); **have a/no ~ for sth.** an etw. (*Dat.*) Geschmack/keinen Geschmack finden; **have expensive ~s in clothes** *etc.* eine Vorliebe für teure Kleidung *usw.* haben; **be/not be to sb.'s** ~: nach jmds./nicht nach jmds. Geschmack sein; **it's a question** *or* **matter of** ~: das ist eine Frage des Geschmacks; das ist Geschmackssache; **each** *or* **everyone to his** ~: jeder nach seinem Geschmack; **~s differ** die Geschmäcker sind verschieden (ugs. scherzh.); **there's no accounting for ~:** über Geschmack lässt sich nicht streiten; *see also* **acquire 2**

'taste bud *n.* (Anat., Zool.) Geschmacksknospe, *die*

tasteful /'teɪstfl/ *adj.* geschmackvoll; ‹*Person*› mit Geschmack

tastefully /'teɪstfəlɪ/ *adv.* geschmackvoll

tasteless /'teɪstlɪs/ *adj.* geschmacklos

tastelessly /'teɪstlɪslɪ/ *adv.* geschmacklos; *as sentence-modifier* geschmackloserweise

taster /'teɪstə(r)/ *n.* **1** Verkoster, *der*/Verkosterin, *die* **2** (sample) **a ~ for** *or* **of sth.** ein [kleines] Vorgeschmack *od.* eine [kleine] Kostprobe von etw.

tastily /'teɪstɪlɪ/ *adv.* lecker

tastiness /'teɪstɪnɪs/ *n.*, *no pl.* leckerer Geschmack

tasty /'teɪstɪ/ *adj.* lecker; **be a ~ morsel** (lit. or fig.) ein Leckerbissen sein

tat¹ /tæt/ *n.*, *no pl.* (coll.) Schrott, *der* (ugs.)

tat² ▸ **tit²**

ta-ta /tæ'tɑː/ *int.* (child lang.) ata, ata! (Kinderspr.); (coll.) tschüs! (ugs.)

tattered /'tætəd/ *adj.* zerlumpt ‹*Kleidung, Person*›; zerrissen ‹*Segel*›; zerfleddert ‹*Buch, Zeitschrift*›; (fig.) ramponiert (ugs.) ‹*Ruf*›

tatters /'tætəz/ *n. pl.* Fetzen; **be in ~:** in Fetzen sein; (fig.) ‹*Karriere, Leben:*› ruiniert sein; ‹*Argument, Strategie:*› zunichte sein

tattily /'tætɪlɪ/ *adv.* schäbig (abwertend)

tattiness /'tætɪnɪs/ *n.*, *no pl.* Schäbigkeit, *die* (abwertend)

tatting /'tætɪŋ/ *n.* Schiffchen- *od.* Okkiarbeit, *die;* (lace) Schiffchen- *od.* Okkispitze, *die*

tattle /'tætl/ *v.i.* tratschen (ugs. abwertend)

tattoo¹ /tə'tuː/

A *v.t.* tätowieren; **~ sth. on sb.'s arm** jmdm. etw. auf den Arm tätowieren

B *n.* Tätowierung, *die*

tattoo² *n.* **1** (Mil.: signal) Zapfenstreich, *der;* (drumming noise) Trommeln, *das;* **beat** *or* **sound the ~:** den Zapfenstreich schlagen/blasen; **he/his fingers beat a ~ on the table** er trommelte mit den Fingern auf den Tisch **2** (military show) **~:** Großer Zapfenstreich

tat'too artist *n.* Tätowierer, *der*/Tätowiererin, *die;* Tätowierkünstler, *der*/-künstlerin, *die*

tattooed /tə'tuːd/ *adj.* tätowiert

tattooer /tə'tuːə(r)/, **tattooist** /tə'tuːɪst/ *ns.* ▸ **p. 1260** Tätowierer, *der*/Tätowiererin, *die*

tatty /'tætɪ/ *adj.* (coll.) schäbig (abwertend); zerfleddert ‹*Zeitschrift, Buch*›; (inferior) mies (ugs.) ‹*Publikation, Firma*›; (threadbare) billig ‹*Argument, Ausrede*›

taught ▸ **teach**

taunt /tɔːnt/

A *v.t.* verspotten (**about** wegen); **~ sb. with being a weakling** jmdn. als Schwächling verspotten

B *n.* spöttische Bemerkung; **the ~ of cowardice** *or* **of being a coward hurt him deeply** dass man ihn als Feigling verspottete, traf ihn tief

taunting /'tɔːntɪŋ/

A *adj.* spöttisch

B *n.* Spott, *der*

Taurean /'tɔːrɪən/ *n.* (Astrol.) Stier, *der*

Taurus /'tɔːrəs/ *n.* (Astrol., Astron.) der Stier; der Taurus; *see also* **Aries**

taut /tɔːt/ *adj.* **1** (tight) straff ‹*Seil, Kabel, Saite*›; gespannt ‹*Muskel*› **2** (fig.: tense) angespannt ‹*Nerven, Ausdruck*› **3** (fig.: concise) knapp geschreiben ‹*Geschichte, Erzählung*›; knapp ‹*Stil*›

tauten /'tɔːtn/

A *v.t.* straffen

B *v.i.* sich straffen; ‹*Muskel:*› sich spannen

tautly /'tɔːtlɪ/ *adv.* **1** (tightly) straff **2** (fig.: tensely) zum Zerreißen **3** (fig.: tersely) knapp ‹*geschrieben*›; straff ‹*gebaut*›

tautological /tɔːtə'lɒdʒɪkl/, **tautologous** /tɔː'tɒləgəs/ *adjs.* tautologisch; **~ expression/statement** Tautologie, *die;* **it is ~ to talk about ...:** es ist eine Tautologie, von ... zu sprechen

tautology /tɔː'tɒlədʒɪ/ *n.* Tautologie, *die*

tavern /'tævən/ *n.* (literary) Schenke, *die*

tawdriness /'tɔːdrɪnɪs/ *n.*, *no pl.* Flitter, *der;* **the ~ of sb.'s finery** jmds. Flitterstaat

tawdry /'tɔːdrɪ/ *adj.* billig und geschmacklos; (fig.) zweifelhaft

tawny /'tɔːnɪ/ *adj.* gelbbraun

tawny 'owl *n.* (Ornith.) Waldkauz, *der*

tax /tæks/

A *n.* **1** Steuer, *die;* **pay 20% in ~ [on sth.]** 20% Steuern [für etw.] zahlen; **a third of my income will go in ~:** ein Drittel meines Einkommens geht an das Finanzamt; **before/after ~:** vor Steuern/nach Abzug der Steuern; **free of ~:** steuerfrei; (after ~, ~ paid) nach Abzug der Steuern; netto; **~ paid, net of ~:** nach Abzug der Steuern; netto; **for ~ reasons** aus steuerlichen Gründen; **for ~ purposes** steuerlich gesehen; fürs Finanzamt (ugs.); *see also* **capital gains tax**; **corporation 2**; **direct tax**; **income tax**; **poll tax**; **purchase tax**; **value added tax** **2** (fig.: burden) Belastung, *die* (**on** für)

B *v.t.* **1** (impose ~ on) besteuern; (pay ~ on) versteuern ‹*Einkommen*›; **~ sb. on his/her income** jmds. Einkommen besteuern; **I am** *or* **my income is ~ed at 30%** ich bezahle 30% Lohnsteuer/Einkommensteuer **2** (make demands on) strapazieren ‹*Mittel, Kräfte, Geduld usw.*› **3** (accuse) beschuldigen, bezichtigen (**with** *Gen.*); **~ sb. with doing sth.** jmdn. beschuldigen *od.* bezichtigen, etw. getan zu haben

taxable /'tæksəbl/ *adj.* steuerpflichtig

tax: ~ allowance *n.* Steuerfreibetrag, *der;* **~ assessment** *n.* Steuerbescheid, *der*

taxation /tæk'seɪʃn/ *n.* (imposition of taxes) Besteuerung, *die;* (taxes payable) Steuern; **subject to ~:** steuerpflichtig

tax: ~ avoidance *n.* Steuerumgehung, *die;* **~ band** *n.* Steuerstufe, *die;* **~ bill** *n.* Steuerbescheid, *der;* (amount) Steuerschuld, *die;* **~ bracket** *n.* Stufe im Steuertarif; **move into a higher ~ bracket** nach einem höheren Steuersatz besteuert werden; **~ break** *n.* (coll.) Steuervorteil, *der;* Steuererleichterung, *die;* **~ code** *n.* Steuerkennziffer, *die;* **~ coding** *n.*, *no pl.* Vergabe von Steuerkennziffern; **~ collector** *n.* Finanzbeamte, *der*/-beamtin, *die;* **~ cut** *n.* Steuersenkung, *die;* **~-deductible** *adj.* steuerabzugsfähig; [steuerlich] absetzbar; **~ demand** *n.* Steuerforderung, *die;* **~ disc** *n.* (Brit. Motor Veh.) Steuerplakette, *die;* **~ dodge** *n.* Steuertrick, *der;* **~ dodger** *n.* Steuerbetrüger, *der*/-betrügerin, *die;* **~ evasion** *n.*, *no pl.* Steuerhinterziehung, *die;* **~-exempt** *adj.* steuerbefreit; steuerfrei ‹*Einkommen*›; **~ exile** *n.* **1** (person) Steuerflüchtling, *der;* **2** (place) Steueroase, *die* (ugs.); **~ form** *n.* Steuerformular, *das;* **~-free** **A** *adj.* steuerfrei; (after payment of tax) Netto-; **~-free allowance** Steuerfreibetrag, *der;* **B** *adv.* steuerfrei; (after payment of tax) netto; **~ haven** *n.* Steueroase, *die* (ugs.); Steuerparadies, *das* (ugs.)

taxi /'tæksɪ/

A *n.* Taxi, *das;* **go by ~:** mit dem Taxi fahren

B *v.i.*, **~ing** *or* **taxying** /'tæksɪɪŋ/ (Aeronaut.) ‹*Flugzeug:*› rollen; ‹*Pilot:*› das Flugzeug rollen lassen; **~ to a stop** ‹*Flugzeug:*› ausrollen

C *v.t.*, **~ing** *or* **taxying** (Aeronaut.) rollen lassen

'taxicab ▸ **taxi A**

taxidermist /'tæksɪdɜːmɪst/ *n.* ▸ **p. 1260** Taxidermist, *der*/Taxidermistin, *die;* Präparator, *der*/Präparatorin, *die*

taxidermy /'tæksɪdɜːmɪ/ *n.* Taxidermie, *die*

taxi: ~ driver *n.* ▸ **p. 1260** Taxifahrer, *der*/-fahrerin, *die;* **~ fare** *n.* Taxigebühr, *die*

taximeter /'tæksɪmiːtə(r)/ *n.* Taxameter, *das od. der;* Fahrpreisanzeiger, *der*

'tax incentive *n.* steuerlicher Anreiz

taxing /'tæksɪŋ/ *adj.* strapaziös, anstrengend ‹*Arbeit, Rolle, Reise*›; schwierig ‹*Problem*›

'tax inspector *n.* ▸ **p. 1260** Steuerinspektor, *der*/-inspektorin, *die*

taxi: ~ rank *n.* (Brit.) Taxistand, *der;* **~ ride** *n.* Taxifahrt, *die;* **~ stance** (Scot.), **~ stand** (Amer.) *ns.* Taxistand, *der;* **~way** *n.* Rollbahn, *die*

tax: ~ law *n.* (body of laws) Steuerrecht, *das;* (individual law) Steuergesetz, *das;* **~ liability** *n.* Steuerschuld, *die;* **~ loophole** *n.* Steuerschlupfloch, *das;* **~man** *n.* (coll.) Finanzbeamte, *der*/-beamtin, *die;* **a letter from the ~man** ein Brief vom Finanzamt; **work for the ~man** [nur noch] fürs Finanzamt arbeiten (fig.); **~ office** *n.* Finanzamt, *das*

taxonomic /tæksə'nɒmɪk/ *adj.* (Biol., Ling.) taxonomisch

taxonomy /tæk'sɒnəmɪ/ *n.* (Biol., Ling.) Taxonomie, *die*

tax: ~payer *n.* Steuerzahler, *der*/-zahlerin, *die;* **~paying** *attrib. adj.* Steuern zahlend...; **~ point** *n.* Steuertermin, *der;* **~ rebate** *n.* Steuererstattung, *die;* **~ relief** *n.* Steuererleichterung, *die;* **get ~ relief on insurance premiums** Versicherungsprämien von der Steuer absetzen; **~ return** *n.* Steuererklärung, *die;* **~ revenue** *n.* Steueraufkommen, *das;* Steuereinnahmen *Pl.;* **~ shelter** *n.* Steuersparmodell, *das;* **~ threshold** *n.* Steuerschwelle, *die;* Besteuerungsschwelle, *die;* **~ year** *n.* Steuerjahr, *das*

TB *abbr.* ▸ **p. 1231** (Med.) **= tuberculosis** Tb, *die;* **TB sufferer** Tb-Kranke, *der/die*

t.b.a. *abbr.* **= to be announced**

T-bone ▸ **T 2**

tbsp. *abbr.*, *pl. same or* **~s: = tablespoon** Essl.; EL

te /tiː/ *n.* (Mus.) si

tea /tiː/ *n.* **1** Tee, *der;* **herb/fennel ~:** Kräuter-/Fencheltee, *der;* **early morning ~:** *frühmorgens [vor dem Aufstehen] getrunkener Tee;* **[not] be sb.'s cup of ~** (fig. coll.) [nicht] jmds. Fall sein (ugs.); **be just** *or* **exactly** *or* **very much sb.'s cup of ~** (fig. coll.) genau *od.* ganz jmds. Fall sein (ugs.); **not for all the ~ in China** (coll.) nicht um alles in der Welt; **[come to sb. for] ~ and sympathy** (fig. coll.) Trost und Rat [bei jmdm. suchen] **2** (meal) **[high] ~:** ≈ Abendbrot, *das;* **afternoon ~:** [Nachmittags]tee, *der*

tea: ~ bag *n.* Teebeutel, *der;* **~ boy** *n.* ≈ Stift, *der* (ugs.); *jüngerer Mann, der in einer Firma, Behörde o. Ä. den Pausentee usw. zubereitet;* **~ break** *n.* (Brit.) Teepause, *die;* **~ caddy** *n.* Teebüchse, *die;* **~cake** *n.* **1** (Brit.: sweet bread bun) ≈ Rosinenbrötchen, *das;* **2** (Amer.: biscuit) Keks, *der;* **~cakes** Teegebäck, *das*

teach /tiːtʃ/

A *v.t.*, **taught** /tɔːt/ unterrichten; (at university) lehren; **You can't dance? I'll ~ you** Du kannst nicht tanzen? Ich bringe es dir bei *od.* zeige es dir; **~ music** *etc.* **to sb., ~ sb. music** *etc.* jmdn. in Musik *usw.* unterrichten; jmdm. Musikunterricht *usw.* geben; **~ oneself** es sich (*Dat.*) selbst beibringen; **~ sb./oneself/an animal sth.** jmdm./sich/einem Tier etw. beibringen; **~ sb./oneself/an animal to do sth.** jmdm./sich/einem Tier beibringen, etw. zu tun; (train) jmdn./sich/ein Tier dazu erziehen, etw. zu tun; **~ sb. to ride/to play the piano** jmdm. das Reiten/Klavierspielen beibringen; **T~ yourself French/car maintenance** (book title) Französisch zum Selbststudium/Wie warte ich mein Auto selbst?; **this experience has taught me one thing ...:** diese Erfahrung hat mich eins gelehrt ...; **I'll/that'll ~ you** *etc.* **to do that!** (coll. iron.) ich werde/das wird dich *usw.* lehren, das zu tun! (iron.); **that'll ~ him/you** *etc.*! (coll. iron.) das hat er/hast du *usw.* nun davon! (iron.); **~ sb. how/that ...:** jmdm. beibringen, wie/dass ...; ‹*Bibel, Erfahrung:*› jmdn. lehren, wie/dass ...; **~ sb. tolerance** *or* **to be tolerant** jmdn. Toleranz lehren; jmdn. lehren, tolerant zu sein; **~ school** (Amer.) Lehrer/Lehrerin sein; *see also* **dog A 1**; **lesson 3**

B *v.i.*, **taught** unterrichten; **he wants to/is going to ~:** er will Lehrer werden/wird Lehrer

teachable /'tiːtʃəbl/ *adj.* lernfähig ‹*Kind, Tier*›; erlernbar ‹*Eigenschaft*›; **a ~ subject** ein Fach, das man gut lehren kann

teacher /'tiːtʃə(r)/ *n.* ▸ **p. 1260** Lehrer, *der*/Lehrerin, *die;* **she's a university/evening**

t

class ~: sie lehrt an der Universität/unterrichtet an der Abendschule; **kindergarten ~**: ≈ Vorschullehrer, *der*/-lehrerin, *die*; **geography/music ~**: Geographie-/Musiklehrer, *der*/Geographie-/Musiklehrerin, *die*

teacher: ~ training *n.* Lehrerausbildung, *die*; **~-training college** *n.* ≈ pädagogische Hochschule

'tea chest *n.* Teekiste, *die*

'teach-in *n.* Teach-in, *das*

teaching /'ti:tʃɪŋ/ *n.* **1** (act) Unterrichten, *das* (**of** von); **the ~ of languages, language ~**: der Sprachunterricht; **I enjoy ~ very much** [das] Unterrichten macht mir großen Spaß; **all the ~ at this school is in French** an der Schule wird nur in französischer Sprache unterrichtet **2** *no pl., no art.* (profession) Lehrberuf, *der*; **want to go into** *or* **take up** *or* **do ~**: Lehrer/Lehrerin werden wollen **3** (doctrine) Lehre, *die*

teaching: ~ aid *n.* Lehr- *od.* Unterrichtsmittel, *das*; **~ assistant** *n.* **1** (in UK school) Hilfslehrer, *der*/-lehrerin, *die*; **2** (in US university) Teaching Assistant, *der*; Tutor, *der*/Tutorin, *die*; **~ hospital** *n.* Ausbildungskrankenhaus, *das*; **~ machine** *n.* Lernmaschine, *die*; **~ method** *n.* Lehr- *od.* Unterrichtsmethode, *die*; **~ practice** *n.* ≈ Schulpraktikum, *das*; **~ profession** *n.* Lehrberuf, *der*; **~ staff** *n.* Lehrerkollegium, *das*

tea: ~ cloth *n.* **1** (for table) ≈ Kaffeedecke, *die*; **2** (for drying) Geschirrtuch, *das*; **~ cosy** *n.* Teewärmer, *der*; **~cup** *n.* Teetasse, *die*; *see also* **storm A 1**; **~cupful** *n.* Tasse, *die*; **a ~cupful of sugar** eine Tasse Zucker; **~ dance** *n.* Tanztee, *der*; **~ garden** *n.* **1** (public place) ≈ Gartencafé, *das*; **2** (plantation) Teeplantage, *die*; **~ house** *n.* Teehaus, *das*

teak /ti:k/ *n.* **1** (wood) Teak[holz], *das*; *attrib.* Teak[holz]‹*öl, -furnier, -möbel*› **2** (tree) Teakbaum, *der*

'tea kettle *n.* Teekessel, *der*

teal /ti:l/ *n., pl. same* (Ornith.) Krickente, *die*

tea: ~ lady *n.* ▸ⓘ **p. 1260** *Frau, die in einer Firma, Behörde o. Ä. den Pausentee usw. zubereitet*; **~ leaf** *n.* Teeblatt, *das*; **read the ~ leaves** ≈ aus dem Kaffeesatz lesen

team /ti:m/

A *n.* **1** (group) Team, *das*; (Sport also) Mannschaft, *die*; **a football/cricket ~**: eine Fußball-/Kricketmannschaft; **a ~ of scientists** eine Gruppe *od.* ein Team von Wissenschaftlern; **a research ~**: eine Forschungsgruppe; **make a good ~**: ein gutes Team *od.* Gespann sein; **work as a ~**: im Team zusammenarbeiten **2** (draught animals) Gespann, *das*; **a ~ of oxen/horses** ein Gespann Ochsen/Pferde; **a ~ of four horses** ein Vierergespann [Pferde]

B *v.t.* **~ A with B** A mit B kombinieren.

Phrasal verb

- **~ 'up**

  A *v.t.* zusammenbringen

  B *v.i.* sich zusammentun (ugs.)

'tea maker *n.* Teemaschine, *die*

team: ~ building *n., no pl.* Teambildung, *die*; **~ effort** *n.* Team- *od.* Gemeinschaftsarbeit, *die*; **a great ~ effort** eine großartige Gemeinschaftsleistung; **thanks to good ~ effort** dank guter Teamarbeit; **~ game** *n.* Mannschaftsspiel, *das*; **~ leader** *n.* Gruppenleiter, *der*/-leiterin, *die*; **~ manager** *n.* Teammanager, *der*/-managerin, *die*; **~mate** *n.* Mannschaftskamerad, *der*/-kameradin, *die*; **~ member** *n.* Mitglied des Teams/der Mannschaft/der Gruppe; **~ player** *n.* Teamplayer, *der*/-playerin, *die*; **she's not a ~ player** sie ist nicht teamfähig; **~ 'spirit** *n.* Teamgeist, *der*; (Sport also) Mannschaftsgeist, *der*

teamster /'ti:mstə(r)/ *n.* (Amer.) Lkw-Fahrer, *der*/-Fahrerin, *die*

'teamwork *n.* Teamarbeit, *die*; **by ~**: in Teamarbeit

tea: ~ party *n.* Teegesellschaft, *die*; **~ plantation** *n.* Teeplantage, *die*; **~ planter** *n.* (proprietor) Teeplantagenbesitzer, *der*/-besitzerin, *die*; (cultivator) Teepflanzer, *der*/-pflanzerin, *die*; **~pot** *n.* Teekanne, *die*

tear¹ /teə(r)/

A *n.* Riß, *der*; *see also* **wear A 1**

B *v.t.*, **tore** /tɔ:(r)/, **torn** /tɔ:n/ **1** (rip; lit. or fig.) zerreißen; (pull apart) auseinander reißen; (damage) aufreißen; **~ open** aufreißen ‹*Brief, Schachtel, Paket*›; **~ one's dress [on a nail]** sich (*Dat.*) das Kleid [an einem Nagel (*Dat.*)] aufreißen; **~ one's fingernail** sich (*Dat.*) einen Fingernagel einreißen; **~ a muscle** sich (*Dat.*) einen Muskelriss zuziehen; **a torn muscle** ein Muskel[faser]riss; **~ sb.'s heart** (fig.) jmdm. das Herz zerreißen (geh.); **~ a hole/gash in sth.** ein Loch/eine klaffende Wunde in etw. (*Akk.*) reißen; **~ sth. in half** *or* **in two** etw. entzweireißen; **~ to shreds** *or* **pieces** (lit.) zerfetzen; in Stücke reißen ‹*Flagge, Kleidung, Person*›; **~ to shreds** (fig.) (destroy) ruinieren ‹*Ruf, Leumund*›; zerrütten ‹*Nerven*›; zunichte machen ‹*Argument, Alibi*›; auseinander nehmen (salopp) ‹*Mannschaft*›; (criticize) verreißen (ugs.); **a country torn by war** ein durch Krieg zerrissenes Land; **I was torn by** *or* **with grief** mein Herz war von Kummer zerrissen (geh.); **be torn between two things/people/between x and y** zwischen zwei Dingen/Personen/x und y hin- und hergerissen sein; **be torn as to what to do** hin- und hergerissen sein [und nicht wissen, was man tun soll]; **that's torn it** (Brit. fig. coll.) das hat alles vermasselt (salopp) **2** (remove with force) reißen; **~ sth. out of** *or* **from sb.'s hands/a book** jmdm. etw. aus der Hand reißen/etw. aus einem Buch [heraus]reißen; **the wind tore the cap from his head** der Wind riss ihm die Mütze vom Kopf; **~ a child from its parents/home** (fig.) ein Kind seinen Eltern entreißen/aus seiner vertrauten Umgebung reißen; **~ oneself from sb./a place** (fig.) sich von jmdm./einem Ort losreißen; **~ one's hair** (fig.) sich (*Dat.*) die Haare raufen (ugs.)

C *v.i.*, **tore, torn 1** (rip) [zer]reißen; **it ~s along the perforation** es lässt sich entlang der Perforation abreißen; **~ in half** *or* **in two** entzweireißen; durchreißen **2** (move hurriedly) rasen (ugs.); **~ past** vorbeirasen (ugs.); **~ along the street** die Straße hinunterrasen (ugs.); **~ off** losrasen (ugs.); **come ~ing out/past** heraus-/vorbeigerast kommen (ugs.)

Phrasal verbs

- **~ apart** *v.t.* (lit. or fig.) auseinander reißen; (coll.: criticize) zerreißen (ugs.); **they tore the place apart** sie haben den Laden auseinander genommen (ugs.)
- **~ at** *v.t.* zerren an (+ *Dat.*); **~ at sb.'s heart-strings** (fig.) jmdm. sehr zu Herzen gehen
- **~ a'way** *v.t.* wegreißen; abreißen ‹*Tapete, Verpackung*›; **~ away sb.'s mask** (fig.) jmds. Maske herunterreißen; **~ sb./oneself away [from sb./sth.]** (fig.) jmdn./sich [von jmdm./etw.] loseisen (ugs.); **~ oneself away [from a sight/book/game]** (fig.) sich [von einem Anblick/Buch/Spiel] losreißen; *see also* **tear-away**
- **~ 'down** *v.t.* herunterreißen; niederreißen ‹*Zaun, Mauer*›; abreißen ‹*Gebäude*›; (fig.) niederreißen ‹*Schranken*›
- **~ into** *v.t.* ‹*Geschoss:*› ein Loch reißen in (+ *Akk.*); ‹*Säge:*› sich [hinein]fressen in (+ *Akk.*); ‹*Raubtier:*› zerfleischen; (fig.: tell off, criticize) heftig angreifen
- **~ 'off** *v.t.* abreißen; *see also* **tear-off**
- **~ 'out** *v.t.* herausreißen; ausreißen ‹*Baum*›; *see also* **~ B 2**
- **~ 'up** *v.t.* **1** (remove) aufreißen ‹*Straße, Bürgersteig*›; herausreißen ‹*Zaun, Pflanze*›; ausreißen ‹*Baum*› **2** (destroy) zerreißen; (fig.) für null und nichtig erklären ‹*Vertrag, Abkommen*›

tear² /tɪə(r)/ *n.* Träne, *die*; **there were ~s in her eyes** sie hatte *od.* ihr standen Tränen in den Augen; **with ~s in one's eyes** mit Tränen in den Augen; **cry ~s of joy/rage/frustration** Freudentränen/Tränen der Wut/Enttäuschung vergießen; **cry ~s of laughter** Tränen lachen; **burst into ~s** in Tränen ausbrechen; **move sb. to ~s** jmdn. zu Tränen rühren; **bore sb. to ~s** jmdn. zu Tode langweilen; **be in ~s** in Tränen aufgelöst sein; **end in ~s** böse enden *od.* ausgehen; ein böses *od.* schlimmes Ende nehmen; **French/Cooking without ~s** (book title) Französisch/Kochen leicht gemacht; **be wet with ~s** tränennass sein; *see also* **crocodile tears**; **dissolve B 1**; **reduce A 2**; **shed¹ 2**; **vale**

tearaway /'teərəweɪ/

A *adj.* rabaukenhaft (ugs.)

B *n.* Rabauke, *der* (ugs.)

tear/tɪə(r)/: **~drop** *n.* Träne, *die*; **~ duct** *n.* (Anat.) Tränenkanal, *der*

tearful /'tɪəfl/ *adj.* (crying) weinend; (wet with tears) tränenüberströmt; (accompanied by tears) tränenreich ‹*Versöhnung, Abschied, Anlass*›; **say a ~ goodbye** sich unter Tränen verabschieden; **she was looking very ~**: sie sah sehr verweint aus; (about to cry) sie schien den Tränen nahe

tearfully /'tɪəfəlɪ/ *adv.* unter Tränen

tear gas /'tɪəgæs/ *n.* Tränengas, *das*

tearing /'teərɪŋ/ *adj.* **1** reißend ‹*Geräusch*› **2** (coll.: violent) rasend; **be in a ~ hurry** schrecklich in Eile sein

tear jerker /'tɪədʒɜ:kə(r)/ *n.* (coll.) Schnulze, *die* (ugs. abwertend); **this film is a real ~**: in diesem Film wird kräftig auf die Tränendrüsen gedrückt

tear-off /'teərɒf/ *attrib. adj.* **~ calendar** Abreißkalender, *der*; **~ slip** Abriss, *der*

tea: ~room *n.* Teestube, *die*; ≈ Café, *das*; **~ rose** *n.* Teerose, *die*

tear sheet /'teəʃi:t/ *n.* Belegseite, *die*

tear-stained /'tɪəsteɪnd/ *adj.* tränenüberströmt ‹*Gesicht*›; ‹*Brief, Buchseite*› mit Tränenspuren

tease /ti:z/

A *v.t.* **1** necken; **~ sb. [about sth.]** jmdn. [mit etw.] aufziehen (ugs.); jmdn. [wegen etw.] hänseln; **he's only teasing you** er macht nur Spaß (ugs.); **stop teasing the dog** hör auf, den Hund zu quälen; **~ sb. that he has done sth.** jmdn. damit aufziehen (ugs.), dass er etw. getan hat; **the children ~d their father for sweets** *or* **to give them sweets** (Amer.) die Kinder lagen ihrem Vater damit in den Ohren (ugs.), dass er ihnen Süßigkeiten geben sollte **2** (Textiles) (separate fibres of) krempeln ‹*Flachs, Wolle*›; hecheln ‹*Flachs*›; (dress with teasels) [auf]rauen **3** (Amer. Hairdressing) toupieren

B *v.i.* seine Späße machen; **I'm only teasing** ich mache nur Spaß

C *n.* (coll.) **he/she is a great ~**: er/sie muss einen immer aufziehen (ugs.)

Phrasal verb

- **~ 'out** *v.t.* **1** (disentangle) auskämmen; kämmen, krempeln ‹*Wolle, Flachs*›; hecheln ‹*Flachs*› **2** (get out, lit. or fig.) herausholen; **~ out the facts** die Tatsachen herausarbeiten

teasel /'ti:zl/ *n.* **1** (Bot.) Karde, *die*; **common/fuller's ~**: Wilde Karde/Weberkarde, *die* **2** (Textiles) Karde, *die*

teaser /'ti:zə(r)/ *n.* **1** (coll.: puzzle) **[brain-]~**: Denk[sport]aufgabe, *die*; **be a [real] ~** (fig.) eine harte Nuss sein (ugs.) **2** (one who teases) **he/she is a great ~**: er/sie muss einen immer aufziehen (ugs.)

tea: ~ service, ~set *ns.* Tee-Service, *das*; **~ shop** (Brit.) ▸ **tearoom**

teasing /'ti:zɪŋ/ *adj.* neckend; **he was in a ~ mood** er war in der Stimmung, andere aufzuziehen (ugs.)

teasingly /'ti:zɪŋlɪ/ *adv.* neckend; **speak ~**: frotzeln; **ask sb. sth. ~**: jmdn. frotzelnd etw. fragen

tea: ~spoon *n.* Teelöffel, *der*; **~spoonful** *n.* Teelöffel, *der*; **a ~spoonful** ein Teelöffel [voll]; **~ strainer** *n.* Teesieb, *das*

teat /ti:t/ *n.* **1** (nipple) Zitze, *die* **2** (of rubber or plastic) Sauger, *der*

tea: ~ table *n.* Teetisch, *der*; **be at the ~ table** beim Tee sitzen; **~ things** *n. pl.* (coll.) Teegeschirr, *das*; **~time** *n.* Teezeit, *die*; **~ towel** *n.* Geschirrtuch, *das*; **~ tray** *n.* Teebrett, *das*; **~ trolley** *n.* Teewagen, *der*; **~ urn** *n.* Teebehälter, *der*; **~ wagon** (Amer.) ▸ **~ trolley**

teazel, teazle /'ti:zl/ ▸ **teasel**

Tech (Tec) /tek/ *n.* (dated coll.) Fachhochschule, *die*; FH, *die*

'techie *n.* (coll.) Technikfreak, *der;* (computer expert) Computerfreak, *der*

technical /'teknɪkl/ *adj.* **1** technisch ‹*Problem, Detail, Daten, Fortschritt*›; (of particular science, art, etc.) fachlich; Fach‹*kenntnis, -berater, -sprache, -begriff, -wörterbuch*›; (of the execution of a work of art) technisch ‹*Fertigkeit, Schwierigkeit*›; **~ expertise/expert** Sachkenntnis, *die*/Fachmann, *der;* **~ college/school** Fachhochschule, *die*/Fachschule, *die;* **[highly] ~ book** [reines] Fachbuch; **the text is very/highly ~:** es ist ein reiner Fachtext; **the text is too ~ for me** der Text ist zu fachsprachlich für mich; **explain sth. without being** *or* **getting too ~:** etw. erklären, ohne sich zu fachsprachlich auszudrücken; **~ hitch** technisches Problem; **~ term** Fachbegriff, *der;* Fachausdruck, *der;* **for ~ reasons** aus technischen Gründen **2** (strictly interpreted) (Law) formaljuristisch; **~ knockout** (Boxing) technischer K.o.

technical 'drawing *n.* (Brit.) technisches Zeichnen

technicality /teknɪ'kælɪtɪ/ *n.* **1** *no pl.* (technical quality) technischer Charakter; (of book, text, style) fachsprachlicher Charakter **2** (technical expression) Fachausdruck, *der* **3** (technical distinction) technisches Detail; (technical point) technische Frage; **legal/financial/military technicalities** rechtliche/finanzielle/militärische [Detail]fragen; **be acquitted on a ~:** aufgrund eines Formfehlers freigesprochen werden

technically /'teknɪkəlɪ/ *adv.* **1** technisch; (in a particular science, art, etc.) fachlich **2** (strictly speaking) im Prinzip; (Law) formaljuristisch

technical sup'port *n., no pl.* (Computing) technischer Support

technician /tek'nɪʃn/ *n.* ▸ⓘ **p. 1260** Techniker, *der*/Technikerin, *die*

Technicolor, (*Amer.* ®) /'teknɪkʌlə(r)/ *n.* (Cinemat.) Technicolor ⓦⓩ, *das*

technique /tek'ni:k/ *n.* Technik, *die;* (procedure) Methode, *die*

techno /'teknəʊ/

A *adj.* Techno-

B *n.* Techno, *der od. das*

technobabble /'teknəʊbæbl/ *n.* (coll.) Technik-Kauderwelsch, *das*

technocracy /tek'nɒkrəsɪ/ *n.* Technokratie, *die*

technocrat /'teknəʊkræt/ *n.* Technokrat, *der*/Technokratin, *die*

technocratic /teknəʊ'krætɪk/ *adj.* technokratisch

technological /teknə'lɒdʒɪkl/ *adj.*, **technologically** /teknə'lɒdʒɪkəlɪ/ *adv.* ▸**technology**: technisch; technologisch

technologist /tek'nɒlədʒɪst/ *n.* ▸ⓘ **p. 1260** Technologe, *der*/Technologin, *die;* ‹*Lebensmittel-, Erdöl*›techniker, *der*/-technikerin, *die*

technology /tek'nɒlədʒɪ/ *n.* Technik, *die;* (application of science) Technologie, *die;* **science and ~:** Wissenschaft und Technik; **college of ~:** Fachhochschule für Technik

technology: ~ park *n.* Technologiepark, *der;* **~ transfer** *n.* Technologietransfer, *der*

technophile /'teknəfaɪl/ *n.* Technikfreak, *der;* Technikfreund, *der*/-freundin, *die*

technophobe /'teknəʊfəʊb/ *n.* Mensch mit einer Technikphobie; **be a ~:** eine Technikphobie haben

technophobia /teknəʊ'fəʊbɪə/ *n., no pl.* Technikphobie, *die;* **suffer from ~:** eine Technikphobie haben

technophobic /teknə'fəʊbɪk/ *adj.* technikfeindlich; technophob

technospeak /'teknəʊspi:k/ *n., no pl.* (coll.) Technik-Kauderwelsch, *das*

techy ▸**tetchy**

tectonic /tek'tɒnɪk/ (Geol.)

A *adj.* tektonisch; **~ plate** tektonische Platte

B *n. in pl.* Tektonik, *die;* **plate ~s** Plattentektonik, *die*

Ted /ted/ *n.* (Brit. coll.) Teddyboy, *der*

teddy /'tedɪ/ *n.* **~ [bear]** Teddy[bär], *der*

Teddy: ~ boy *n.* (Brit.) Teddyboy, *der;* **~ girl** *n.* (Brit.) Teddygirl, *das*

Te Deum /ti: 'di:əm, teɪ 'deɪəm/ *n.* (Relig.) Tedeum, *das*

tedious /'ti:dɪəs/ *adj.* langwierig ‹*Reise, Arbeit*›; (uninteresting) langweilig

tediously /'ti:dɪəslɪ/ *adv.* langatmig ‹*reden, schreiben*›; (uninterestingly) langweilig; **~ familiar** bis zum Überdruss bekannt; **~ repeat sth.** etw. bis zum Überdruss wiederholen; **a ~ long meeting** eine lange, langweilige Besprechung

tediousness /'ti:dɪəsnɪs/ *n., no pl.* (of work, journey) Langwierigkeit, *die;* (of book, lecture, wait) Langweiligkeit, *die*

tedium /'ti:dɪəm/ *n.* (of journey) Langwierigkeit, *die;* (of waiting) Langweiligkeit, *die;* **an hour of unrelieved ~:** eine unendlich langweilige Stunde

tee /ti:/

A *n.* **1** (Golf) Tee, *das* **2** **to a ~** (coll.) = **to a T** ▸**T 1**

B *v.t.* ▸**~ up A**

Phrasal verbs

• **~ 'off** *v.i.* (Golf) abschlagen

• **~ 'up** (Golf)

A *v.t.* auf das Tee legen; aufteen (fachspr.)

B *v.i.* den Ball auf das Tee legen

tee-hee /'ti:'hi:/ *int.* hihi

teem /ti:m/ *v.i.* **1** (abound) wimmeln (**with** von) **2** (rain heavily) **~ [with rain]** in Strömen regnen

Phrasal verb

• **~ 'down** *v.i.* **it/the rain was ~ing down** es regnete in Strömen

teeming /'ti:mɪŋ/ *adj.* **1** (pouring) strömend ‹*Regen*› **2** (abundant) wimmelnd ‹*Menschenmenge*›; (crowded) von Menschen wimmelnd ‹*Straße*›

teen /ti:n/ *adj.* Teenager-

teenage /'ti:neɪdʒ/, **teenaged** /'ti:neɪdʒd/ *attrib. adj.* im Teenageralter *nachgestellt*

teenager /'ti:neɪdʒə(r)/ *n.* ▸ⓘ **p. 894** Teenager, *der;* (loosely) Jugendliche, *der/die*

teens /ti:nz/ *n. pl.* ▸ⓘ **p. 894** Teenagerjahre; **be out of/in one's ~:** aus den Teenagerjahren heraus sein/in den Teenagerjahren sein; **fashions from tots to ~:** Kinder- und Jugendmoden

teensy-weensy /ti:nzɪ wi:nzɪ/, **teeny** /'ti:nɪ/ *adjs.* (child lang./coll.) klitzeklein (ugs.)

teeny /'ti:nɪ/ *adj.* (coll.) klitzeklein (ugs.); winzig [klein]

teeny: ~-bopper *n.* (coll.) *Popfan im Teenageralter;* **~-weeny** ▸**teeny**

teepee ▸**tepee**

'tee shirt *n.* T-Shirt, *das*

teeter /'ti:tə(r)/ *v.i.* **1** (waver) wanken; **~ on the edge** *or* **brink of sth.** schwankend am Rande einer Sache (*Gen.*) stehen; (fig.) am Rande einer Sache (*Gen.*) stehen **2** (Amer.: see-saw) wippen; (fig.) hin- und herschwanken

teeth *pl. of* **tooth**

teethe /ti:ð/ *v.i.* zahnen

teething /'ti:ðɪŋ/ *n.* Zahnen, *das*

teething: ~ ring *n.* Beißring, *der;* **~ troubles** *n. pl.* Beschwerden während des Zahnens; **have ~ troubles** (fig.) ‹*Person, Vorhaben:*› Anfangsschwierigkeiten haben; ‹*Maschine usw.:*› Kinderkrankheiten haben

teetotal /ti:'təʊtl/ *adj.* abstinent lebend; alkoholfrei ‹*Restaurant, Hotel, Feier*›; **sb. is ~:** jmd. ist Abstinenzler/Abstinenzlerin

teetotaler (Amer.) ▸**teetotaller**

teetotalism /ti:'təʊtəlɪzm/ *n.* Abstinenz, *die*

teetotaller /ti:'təʊtələ(r)/ *n.* Abstinenzler, *der*/Abstinenzlerin, *die*

TEFL /'tefl/ *abbr.* = **teaching of English as a foreign language**

Teflon ® /'teflɒn/ *n.* Teflon ⓦⓩ, *das*

tektite /'tektaɪt/ *n.* (Min.) Tektit, *der*

Tel., tel. *abbr.* = **telephone** Tel.

telco /'telkəʊ/ *n., pl.* **~s** Telekomgesellschaft, *die;* Telekomunternehmen, *das*

telebanking /'telɪbæŋkɪŋ/ *n., no pl.* Telebanking, *das*

telecast /'telɪkɑ:st/

A *v.t.*, **telecast** [im Fernsehen] senden

B *n.* Fernsehsendung, *die*

telecommunication /telɪkəmju:nɪ'keɪʃn/ *n.* **1** (long-distance communication) Fernmeldeverkehr, *der; attrib.* Fernmelde- **2** *in pl.* (science) Fernmelde- *od.* Nachrichtentechnik, *die; attrib.* Fernmelde- *od.* Nachrichten‹*techniker, -satellit*›

telecommute /'telɪkəmju:t/ *v.i.* Telearbeit verrichten

telecommuter /'telɪkəmju:tə(r)/ *n.* Telearbeiter, *der*/-arbeiterin, *die*

telecommuting /'telɪkəmju:tɪŋ/ *n., no pl.* Telearbeit, *die*

telecoms, telecomms /'telɪkɒmz/ *n. pl.* Telekommunikation, *die; attrib.* Telekommunikations‹*netz,-gesellschaft*›

teleconference /'telɪkɒnfərəns/ *n.* Telekonferenz, *die*

telecottage /'telɪkɒtɪdʒ/ *n.: jedermann zugängliche Einrichtung, die bes. Telearbeitern Zugang zu einem ans Internet angeschlossenen Computer bietet*

telegenic /telɪ'dʒenɪk/ *adj.* telegen

telegram /'telɪgræm/ *n.* Telegramm, *das;* **by ~:** telegrafisch

telegraph /'telɪgrɑ:f/

A *n.* **1** (for sending telegrams) Telegraf, *der; attrib.* Telegrafen-; **ship's ~:** Maschinentelegraf, *der* (*Technik*); *see also* **bush telegraph** **2** (semaphore apparatus) Semaphor, *der* **3** (Sports, Racing: board) Anzeigetafel, *die*

B *v.t.* **1** telegrafieren; telegrafisch anweisen ‹*Geld*› **2** (Boxing coll.) telegrafieren ‹*Schlag*›

C *v.i.* telegrafieren; **~ for sb.** jmdn. telegrafisch rufen lassen

telegraphese /telɪgrɑ:'fi:z/ *n.* Telegrammstil, *der*

telegraphic /telɪ'græfɪk/ *adj.* telegrafisch; Telegramm‹*adresse, -stil*›

telegraphist /tɪ'legrəfɪst/ *n.* ▸ⓘ **p. 1260** Telegrafist, *der*/Telegrafistin, *die*

telegraph: ~ line *n.* Telegrafenleitung, *die;* **~ pole, ~ post** *ns.* Telegrafenmast, *der;* **~ wire** *n.* Telegrafendraht, *der*

telegraphy /tɪ'legrəfɪ/ *n.* Telegrafie, *die*

telemarketing /'telɪmɑ:kɪtɪŋ/ *n., no pl.* Telefonmarketing, *das*

telematics *n., no pl.* Telematik, *die*

telemessage /'telɪmesɪdʒ/ *n.* (Brit.) Telegramm, *das*

telemeter /'telɪmi:tə(r), tɪ'lemɪtə(r)/

A *n.* Fernmessgerät, *das*

B *v.i.* Messwerte telemetrisch übertragen; **~ing device** Fernmessgerät, *das*

C *v.t.* telemetrisch übertragen

telemetry /tɪ'lemɪtrɪ/ *n.* Telemetrie, *die*

teleological /telɪə'lɒdʒɪkl/ *adj.* (Philos.) teleologisch

teleology /telɪ'ɒlədʒɪ/ *n.* (Philos.) Teleologie, *die*

telepathic /telɪ'pæθɪk/ *adj.* telepathisch; **be ~:** telepathische Fähigkeiten haben

telepathically /telɪ'pæθɪkəlɪ/ *adv.* telepathisch

telepathy /tɪ'lepəθɪ/ *n.* Telepathie, *die;* **by ~:** telepathisch

telephone /'telɪfəʊn/

A *n.* Telefon, *das; attrib.* Telefon-; **[public] ~:** öffentlicher Fernsprecher (Amtsspr.); [öffentliches] Telefon; **answer the ~:** Anrufe entgegennehmen; (on one occasion) ans Telefon gehen; (speak) sich melden; **by ~:** telefonisch; **over** *or* **on the ~:** am Telefon; **speak** *or* **talk to sb. on the** *or* **by ~:** mit jmdm. telefonieren; **be on the ~** (be connected to the system) Telefon haben; (be speaking) telefonieren (**to** mit); **it's your sister on the ~:** deine Schwester ist am Apparat; **get on the ~ to sb.** jmdn. anrufen; **get sb. on the ~:** jmdn. telefonisch erreichen; **be wanted on the ~:** am Telefon verlangt werden

B *v.t.* anrufen; telefonisch übermitteln ‹*Nachricht, Ergebnis usw.*› (**to** *Dat.*); **~ the office/~ home**

im Büro/zu Hause anrufen
C *v.i.* anrufen; **~ for a taxi/the doctor** nach einem Taxi/dem Arzt telefonieren; **~ to ask how ...:** telefonisch anfragen, wie ...; **can we ~ from here?** können wir von hier aus telefonieren?

telephone: ~ 'answering machine *n.* Anrufbeantworter, *der;* **~ 'banking** *n., no pl.* Telefonbanking, *das;* **~ bill** *n.* Telefonrechnung, *die;* **~ book** *n.* Telefonbuch, *das;* **~ booth,** (Brit.) **~ box** *ns.* Telefonzelle, *die;* **~ call** *n.* Telefonanruf, *der;* Telefongespräch, *das;* **make a ~ call** ein Telefongespräch führen; **have** *or* **receive a ~ call** einen Anruf erhalten; **there was a ~ call for you** es hat jemand für Sie angerufen; **there was a ~ call for you from your brother** Ihr Bruder hat angerufen; **inland ~ call** Inlandsgespräch, *das;* **international ~ call** Auslandsgespräch, *das;* **~ connection** *n.* Telefonverbindung, *die;* **~ directory** *n.* Telefonverzeichnis, *das;* Telefonbuch, *das;* **~ exchange** *n.* Fernmeldeamt, *das;* **~ kiosk** *n.* Telefonzelle, *die;* **~ line** *n.* Telefonleitung, *die;* **~ message** *n.* telefonische Nachricht; **~ number** *n.* Telefonnummer, *die;* **~ operator** *n.* ▸ⓘ **p. 1260** Telefonist, *der*/Telefonistin, *die;* **~ pole** *n.* Telefonmast, *der;* **~ poll** *n.* Telefonumfrage, *die;* **~ receiver** *n.* Telefonhörer, *der;* **~ sex** *n., no pl.* Telefonsex, *der; attrib.* Telefonsex-; **~ subscriber** *n.* Fernsprechteilnehmer, *der*/-teilnehmerin, *die;* **~ tapping** *n., no pl.* Telefonüberwachung, *die*

telephonic /telɪ'fɒnɪk/ *adj.* telefonisch

telephonist /tɪ'lefənɪst/ *n.* ▸ⓘ **p. 1260** Telefonist, *der*/Telefonistin, *die*

telephony /tɪ'lefənɪ/ *n.* Fernsprechwesen, *das*

telephoto /telɪ'fəʊtəʊ/ *adj.* (Photog.) telefotografisch; **~ lens** Teleobjektiv, *das*

teleport /'telɪpɔːt/
A *n.* Teleport, *der.*
B *v.t.* teleportieren
C *v.i.* sich teleportieren

teleportation /telɪpɔː'teɪʃn/ *n., no pl.* Teleportation, *die*

teleprinter /'telɪprɪntə(r)/ *n.* Fernschreiber, *der;* **~ network** Fernschreibnetz, *das*

teleprocessing /'telɪprəʊsesɪŋ/ *n., no pl.* [Daten]fernverarbeitung, *die*

teleprompter (Amer. ®) /'telɪprɒmptə(r)/ *n.* Teleprompter Ⓦⓩ, *der*

'telesales *n. pl.* Telefonverkauf, *der;* Verkauf per Telefon; *attrib.* **~ person** Telefonverkäufer, *der*/-verkäuferin, *die*

telescope /'telɪskəʊp/
A *n.* Teleskop, *das;* Fernrohr, *das*
B *v.t.* zusammenschieben ‹*Antenne, Rohr*›; ineinander schieben ‹*Abschnitte, Waggons*›; (fig.) komprimieren (**into** zu)
C *v.i.* sich zusammenschieben; ‹*Abschnitte, Waggons:*› sich ineinander schieben

telescopic /telɪ'skɒpɪk/ *adj.* **1** teleskopisch; **~ lens** Teleobjektiv, *das* **2** (collapsible) ausziehbar; Teleskop‹*antenne, -mast*›; **~ umbrella** Taschenschirm, *der*

telescopic 'rifle *n.* Gewehr mit Zielfernrohr

teleshopping /'telɪʃɒpɪŋ/ *n., no pl.* Teleshopping, *das*

Teletex ®, **teletex** /'telɪteks/ *n.* Teletex; *attrib.* Teletex‹*system, -dienst, -netz, -gerät*›

teletext /'telɪtekst/ *n.* Teletext, *der*

telethon /'telɪθɒn/ *n.* Marathonsendung, *die* (*für einen guten Zweck*)

Teletype ® /'telɪtaɪp/, (Amer.) **teletypewriter** /telɪ'taɪpraɪtə(r)/ *n.* Fernschreiber, *der*

televangelist /telɪ'vændʒəlɪst/ *n.* Tele-Evangelist, *der*/-Evangelistin, *die*

televise /'telɪvaɪz/ *v.t.* im Fernsehen senden *od.* übertragen; **~d football** Fußballübertragungen im Fernsehen

television /'telɪvɪʒn, telɪ'vɪʒn/ *n.* **1** *no pl., no art.* das Fernsehen; **colour/black and white ~:** das Farb-/Schwarzweißfernsehen; **the best-paid jobs are in ~:** die bestbezahlten Stellen gibt es beim Fernsehen; **go into ~:** zum Fernsehen gehen; **we have ten hours of ~ a day** bei uns gibt es täglich 10 Stunden Fernsehprogramm; **make/not make good ~:** sich gut/schlecht für das Fernsehen eignen; **live ~:** Livesendungen [im Fernsehen]; **on ~:** im Fernsehen; **what's on ~?** was läuft *od.* gibts im Fernsehen?; **watch ~:** fernsehen **2** (**~ set**) Fernsehapparat, *der;* Fernseher, *der* (ugs.); **portable ~:** tragbares Fernsehgerät; Portable, *der od. das. see also* **closed-circuit; commercial television**

television: ~ 'advertising *n.* Fernsehwerbung, *die;* **~ aerial** *n.* Fernsehantenne, *die;* **~ announcer** *n.* ▸ⓘ **p. 1260** Fernsehansager, *der*/-ansagerin, *die;* Fernsehsprecher, *der*/-sprecherin, *die;* (reading the news) Nachrichtensprecher, *der*/-sprecherin, *die;* **~ camera** *n.* Fernsehkamera, *die;* **~ channel** *n.* [Fernseh]kanal, *der;* **~ coverage** *n.* Fernsehberichterstattung, *die;* **there will be full ~ coverage of sth.** das Fernsehen wird ausführlich über etw. (*Akk.*) berichten; **~ 'dinner** *n.* ▸ **TV dinner; ~ engineer** *n.* ▸ⓘ **p. 1260** Fernsehtechniker, *der*/-technikerin, *die;* **~ licence** *n.* (Brit.) Fernsehgenehmigung, *die* (*die jährlich gegen Zahlen der Gebühren erneuert wird*); *attrib.* **~ licence fee** Fernsehgebühren *Pl.;* **~ listings** *n. pl.* Fernsehprogramm, *das; attrib.* **~ listings magazine** [Fernseh]programmzeitschrift, *die;* **~ lounge** *n.* Fernsehraum, *der;* **~ network** *n.* Fernsehnetz, *das;* (organization) Fernsehgesellschaft, *die;* **~ personality** *n.* Fernsehgröße, *die* (ugs.); **~ picture** *n.* Fernsehbild, *das;* **~ programme** *n.* Fernsehsendung, *die;* (schedule) Fernsehprogramm, *das;* **my favourite ~ programme** meine Lieblingssendung im Fernsehen; **~ room** *n.* Fernsehraum, *der;* **~ satellite** *n.* Fernsehsatellit, *der;* **~ schedule** *n.* Fernsehprogramm, *das;* **~ screen** *n.* Bildschirm, *der;* **~ serial** *n.* Fernsehserie, *die;* **~ set** *n.* Fernsehgerät, *das;* **~ studio** *n.* Fernsehstudio, *das;* **~ transmitter** *n.* Fernsehsender, *der;* **~ tube** *n.* Fernsehröhre, *die;* **~ viewer** *n.* Fernsehzuschauer, *der*/-zuschauerin, *die*

televisual /telɪ'vɪzjʊəl, telɪ'vɪʒʊəl/ *adj.* Fernseh‹*kultur, -darbietung*›; **~ violence** Gewalt im Fernsehen

telework /'telɪwɜːk/ *v.i.* Telearbeit verrichten

teleworker /'telɪwɜːkə(r)/ *n.* Telearbeiter, *der*/-arbeiterin, *die*

teleworking /'telɪwɜːkɪŋ/ *n., no pl.* Telearbeit, *die*

Telex, telex /'teleks/
A *n.* Telex, *das;* **by ~** über Telex
B *v.t.* telexen ‹*Nachricht*›; ein Telex schicken (+ *Dat.*) ‹*Person, Firma*›

tell /tel/
A *v.t.,* **told** /təʊld/ **1** (make known) sagen ‹*Name, Adresse, Alter*›; (give account of) erzählen ‹*Neuigkeit, Sorgen*›; anvertrauen ‹*Geheimnis*›; **~ sb. sth.** *or* **sth. to sb.** jmdm. etw. sagen/erzählen/anvertrauen; **if he asks, ~ him** sags ihm, wenn er fragt; **~ sb. the way to the station** jmdm. den Weg zum Bahnhof beschreiben; **~ sb. the time** jmdm. sagen, wie spät es ist; jmdm. die Uhrzeit sagen; **~ sb. goodbye/good night** (Amer.) jmdm. Auf Wiedersehen/Gute Nacht sagen; **~ all** auspacken (ugs.); **~ me another!** (coll.) du kannst mir viel erzählen (ugs.); **~ sb. [something] about sb./sth.** jmdm. [etwas] von jmdm./etw. erzählen; **~ sb. nothing/all about what happened** jmdm. nichts davon/alles erzählen, was passiert ist; **will you ~ him [that] I will come?** sag ihm bitte, dass ich kommen werde; **they ~ me/us [that] ...** (according to them) man sagt, dass ...; **I['ll] ~ you what, ...:** pass mal auf, ...; **I'll ~ you what I'll do** weißt du, was ich machen werde?; **~ everyone/** (coll.) **the world [that/how** *etc.*] jedem/(ugs.) aller Welt erzählen[, dass/wie *usw.*]; **more than I/words can ~:** mehr, als ich es mit Worten ausdrücken kann/als Worte es ausdrücken können; **I cannot ~ you how ...** (cannot express how ...) ich kann dir gar nicht sagen, wie ...; **I couldn't ~ you** (I don't know) das kann ich nicht sagen; **I can ~ you, ...** (I can assure you) ich kann dir sagen, ...; **..., I can ~ you** ..., das kann ich dir sagen; **you can't ~ me [that] ...** (it can't be true that ...) du kannst mir doch nicht erzählen, dass ...; **you can't ~ him anything** (he won't accept advice) er lässt sich (*Dat.*) ja nichts sagen; (he is well-informed) ihm kannst du nichts erzählen; **words cannot ~ how ..., no words can ~ how ...:** es lässt sich nicht mit Worten ausdrücken, wie ...; **..., let me ~ you** (let me assure you) ..., das kann ich dir sagen; **let me ~ you that ...:** ich kann dir versichern, dass ...; **..., I ~ you** *or* **I'm ~ing you** ..., das sage ich dir; **you're ~ing me** *or* **are you ~ing me [that] ...?** du willst mir doch wohl nicht erzählen, dass ...?; **you're ~ing 'me!** (coll.) wem sagst du das! (ugs.); **he keeps ~ing me [that] ...:** er erzählt mir ständig, dass ...; **..., or so they keep ~ing us** das erzählen sie uns jedenfalls immer; **I don't need to ~ you [that] ...:** ich brauche dir wohl nicht extra zu sagen, dass ...; **be told sth. by sb.** etw. von jmdm. erfahren; **I was told that ...:** mir wurde gesagt, dass ...; **so I've been told** (I know that) [das] habe ich schon gehört; **... or so I've been/I'm told** ..., wie ich gehört habe/höre; **... or so we are told** ..., so heißt es jedenfalls; **but he won't be told** (won't accept advice) aber er lässt sich ja nichts sagen; **didn't I ~ you?** (I told you so) hab ichs nicht gleich gesagt?; **no, don't ~ me, let me guess** [nein,] sag's nicht, lass mich raten; **don't ~ me [that] ...** (expressing incredulity, dismay, etc.) jetzt sag bloß nicht, [dass] ...; **you aren't trying** *or* **don't mean to ~ me [that] ...?** du wirst doch nicht sagen wollen, dass ...?
2 (relate, lit. or fig.) erzählen; **has he ever told you the story of how ...:** hat er dir jemals die Geschichte erzählt, wie ...; **~ one's own story** *or* **tale** (give one's own account) selbst erzählen *od.* berichten; **sth. ~s its own story** *or* **tale** (needs no comment) etw. spricht für sich selbst; **~ a different story** *or* **tale** (reveal the truth) eine andere Sprache sprechen (fig.); **every picture ~s a story** das spricht Bände; **live** *or* **survive to ~ the tale** überleben; **~ tales [about sb.]** (gossip; reveal secret) [über jmdn.] tratschen (ugs. abwertend); **~ tales [to sb.]** (report) andere/einen anderen [bei jmdm.] anschwärzen; [bei jmdm.] petzen (Schülerspr. abwertend); **~ tales** (lie) Lügengeschichten erzählen; **~ tales out of school** (fig.) aus der Schule plaudern; **dead men ~ no tales** Tote reden nicht; **the blood stains told their own tale** die Blutflecken sprachen für sich; **now it can be told** jetzt kann man es ja erzählen
3 (instruct) sagen; **~ sb. [not] to do sth.** jmdm. sagen, dass er etw. [nicht] tun soll; jmdm. sagen, er soll[e] etw. [nicht] tun; **I thought I told you to go to bed** ich habe dir doch gesagt, dass du ins Bett gehen sollst; **~ sb. what to do** jmdm. sagen, was er tun soll; **no one ~s 'me what to do** ich lasse mir keine Vorschriften machen; **do as** *or* **what I ~ you** tu, was ich dir sage; **I shan't** *or* **won't ~ you again, don't let me have to ~ you again** ich sags dir nicht noch einmal; **do as you are told** tu, was man dir sagt
4 (determine) feststellen; (see, recognize) erkennen (**by** an + *Dat.*); (with reference to the future) [vorher]sagen; **~ the time [from the sun]** [am Stand der Sonne] erkennen, wie spät es ist; **the child can't ~ the time yet** das Kind kennt die Uhr noch nicht; **~ the difference [between ...]** den Unterschied [zwischen ...] erkennen *od.* feststellen; **I can't ~ which of the twins ...:** ich kann nicht sagen, welcher der Zwillinge ...; **it's impossible/difficult to ~ [if/what** *etc.*] es ist unmöglich/schwer zu sagen[, ob/was *usw.*]; **it's easy to ~ whether ...:** es lässt sich leicht sagen, ob ...; **you never can ~ how/what** *etc.* man weiß nie, wie/was *usw.;* **how could you ~ he was a policeman?** woran hast du erkannt, dass es ein Polizist war?; **I can ~ he's lying** ich merke ihm an, dass er lügt
5 (distinguish) unterscheiden; **[not] be able to ~ right from wrong** [nicht] zwischen richtig und falsch unterscheiden können
6 (utter) sagen; **~ the truth and shame the devil** die Wahrheit sagen, auch wenn es nicht leicht fällt; *see also* **fib A; lie[1] A 1; truth 2**

7) (count) auszählen ‹*Wählerstimmen*›; **all told** insgesamt

B *v.i.*, **told** 1) (determine) **how can you ~?** wie kann man das feststellen *od.* wissen?; **it's difficult to ~:** das ist schwer zu sagen; **[it's] hard to ~:** [das ist] schwer zu sagen; **the difference is so slight, even the experts can hardly ~:** der Unterschied ist so gering, dass selbst die Experten ihn kaum erkennen können; **how can one ~?, how can** *or* **do you ~?** woran kann man das erkennen?; **as far as one/I can ~, ...:** wie es aussieht, ...; **you never can ~:** man kann nie wissen; **who can ~?** wer kann das sagen *od.* will das wissen?

2) (give information) erzählen (**of, about** von); (give evidence) **~ of sth.** von etw. Zeugnis geben *od.* ablegen

3) (reveal secret) es verraten; **time [alone] will ~:** das wird sich [erst noch] zeigen

4) (produce an effect) sich auswirken; ‹*Wort, Fausthieb, Schuss:*› sitzen; **quality ~s** *or* **will ~** (be important) Qualität ist das, was zählt; **he made every blow ~:** jeder seiner Schläge saß; **make every shot ~:** dafür sorgen, dass jeder Schuss sitzt; **~ in favour of sb.** *or* **in sb.'s favour** sich zu jmds. Gunsten auswirken; **~ against sb./sth.** sich nachteilig für jmdn./auf etw. (*Akk.*) auswirken. *See also* **fortune 3; marine B 1; so[1] B; what E 1**

Phrasal verbs

- **~ a'part** *v.t.* auseinander halten
- **~ 'off** *v.t.* 1) (coll.: scold) **~ sb. off [for sth.]** jmdn. [für *od.* wegen etw.] ausschimpfen; ‹*Chef:*› jmdn. [für *od.* wegen etw.] rüffeln (ugs.); *see also* **telling-off** 2) (assign) **~ sb. off [for sth.]** jmdn. [zu etw.] abkommandieren
- **~ on** *v.t.* 1) (affect) **~ on sb./sth.** sich bei jmdm. bemerkbar machen/sich [nachteilig] auf etw. (*Akk.*) auswirken 2) (coll.: inform against) **~ on sb.** jmdn. verpetzen (Schülerspr. abwertend)
- **~ upon** ▸ **~ on 1**

teller /'telə(r)/ *n.* ▸ⓘ **p. 1260** 1) (in bank) ▸**cashier[1]** 2) (counter of votes) Stimmenzähler, *der*/-zählerin, *die*

telling /'telɪŋ/

A *adj.* (effective, striking) schlagend ‹*Argument, Antwort*›; wirkungsvoll ‹*Worte, Phrase, Stil*›; (revealing) vielsagend ‹*Lächeln, Blick*›; verräterisch ‹*Röte, Reaktion*›; **~ blow** (Boxing) Wirkungstreffer, *der;* (fig.) empfindlicher Schlag; **with ~ effect** mit durchschlagender Wirkung

B *n.* Erzählen, *das;* **he did not need any ~, he needed no ~:** dazu brauchte man ihn nicht lange *od.* eigens aufzufordern; **that would be ~:** damit würde ich ein Geheimnis verraten; **there's no ~ what/how ...:** man weiß nie, was/wie ...; **there's no** *or* **never any ~ with her** bei ihr weiß man nie[, woran man ist]; *see also* **lose B 1**

tellingly /'telɪŋlɪ/ *adv.* wirkungsvoll; **be ~ effective** eine deutlich sichtbare Wirkung zeigen

telling-'off *n.* (coll.) Standpauke, *die* (ugs.); **give sb. a ~:** jmdn. ausschimpfen (**for** wegen); ‹*Chef:*› jmdn. rüffeln (ugs.); **get a ~:** Schimpfe kriegen (ugs.); ‹*Untergebener:*› einen Rüffel kriegen (ugs.)

'telltale *n.* 1) Klatschmaul, *das* (ugs. abwertend); Petzer, *die* (*Schülerspr. abwertend*); *attrib.* vielsagend ‹*Blick, Lächeln*›; verräterisch ‹*Röte, Fleck, Glanz, Zucken, Zeichen*› 2) (indicator) Anzeiger, *der;* (for recording attendance) Stechuhr, *die*

tellurium /te'ljʊərɪəm/ *n.* (Chem.) Tellur, *das*

telly /'telɪ/ *n.* (Brit. coll.) Fernseher, *der* (ugs.); Glotze, *die* (salopp); **watch ~:** Fernsehen gucken (ugs.); **what's on [the] ~?** was kommt im Fernsehen?

telnet /'telnet/ *n.* (Computing) Telnet, *das*

temerity /tɪ'merɪtɪ/ *n.* Kühnheit, *die;* **have the ~ to do sth.** die Stirn haben, etw. zu tun

temp /temp/ (coll.)

A *n.* Zeitarbeitskraft, *die; attrib.* **~ agency** Zeitarbeitsunternehmen, *das*

B *v.i.* Zeitarbeit machen

temper /'tempə(r)/

A *n.* 1) (disposition) Naturell, *das;* **be in a good/bad ~:** gute/schlechte Laune haben; gut/schlecht gelaunt sein; **be in a foul** *or* **filthy ~:** eine miese Laune haben (ugs.); **keep/lose one's ~:** sich beherrschen/die Beherrschung verlieren; **lose one's ~ with sb.** die Beherrschung bei jmdm. verlieren; **control one's ~:** sich beherrschen 2) (anger) **fit/outburst of ~:** Wutanfall, *der*/-ausbruch, *der;* **have a ~:** jähzornig sein; **be in/get into a ~:** wütend sein/werden (**over** wegen); **be in a terrible ~:** schrecklich wütend sein 3) (degree of hardness of metal) Härte, *die*

B *v.t.* 1) (moderate) mäßigen; mildern ‹*Trostlosigkeit, Strenge, Kritik*›; **~ sb.'s enthusiasm/radical views** jmds. Begeisterung dämpfen/Radikalismus mildern; **~ justice with mercy** bei aller Gerechtigkeit Milde walten lassen (geh.) 2) (Metallurgy) anlassen 3) (Mus.) temperieren

tempera /'tempərə/ *n.* (Art) Tempera, *die*

temperament /'temprəmənt/ *n.* 1) (nature) Veranlagung, *die;* Natur, *die;* (disposition) Temperament, *das;* **have an artistic ~:** künstlerisch veranlagt sein 2) (passionate disposition) Temperament, *das*

temperamental /temprə'mentl/ *adj.* 1) (having changeable moods) launisch (abwertend); launenhaft; **be a bit ~** (fig. coll.) ‹*Auto, Maschine:*› seine Mucken haben (ugs.) 2) (caused by, relating to temperament) anlagebedingt; **suffer from a ~ inability to cope with stress** von Natur aus nicht fähig sein, Stress zu bewältigen

temperamentally /temprə'mentəlɪ/ *adv.* 1) (in a temperamental manner) launisch (abwertend); **the car tends to behave ~** (fig. coll.) das Auto hat gelegentlich seine Mucken (ugs.) 2) (by reason of temperament) der Veranlagung nach

temperance /'tempərəns/ *n.* 1) (moderation) Mäßigung, *die;* (in one's eating, drinking) Mäßigkeit, *die* 2) (total abstinence) Abstinenz, *die*

temperate /'tempərət/ *adj.* gemäßigt; **be ~ in one's eating/drinking** maßvoll *od.* mäßig im Essen/Trinken sein; **~ climate** (Geog.) gemäßigtes Klima; *see also* **zone A**

temperature /'temprɪtʃə(r)/ *n.* ▸ⓘ **p. 1620** 1) Temperatur, *die;* **what is the ~?** wie viel Grad sind es?; **the ~ is below/above ...:** die Temperatur liegt unter/über ... (*Dat.*); **there are no extremes of ~:** es gibt keine extremen Temperaturen; **the ~ rose during the debate** (fig.) die Debatte wurde im Verlauf immer hitziger; **at a ~ of 100°** bei einer Temperatur von 100° ‹*kochen*›; auf eine Temperatur von 100° ‹*einstellen*›; **keep the room at a ~ of 10°** die Zimmertemperatur auf 10° (*Dat.*) halten; **at high/low ~s** bei hohen/niedrigen Temperaturen 2) (Med.) Temperatur, *die;* **have** *or* **run a ~** (coll.) Temperatur *od.* Fieber haben; **have a slight/high ~:** leichtes/hohes Fieber haben; **take sb.'s ~:** bei jmdm. Fieber messen; jmds. [Körper]temperatur messen; **a cold accompanied by a ~:** eine fiebrige Erkältung; *see also* **run C 12**

tempered /'tempəd/ *adj.* 1) (Metallurgy) vergütet 2) (Mus.) temperiert

'temper tantrum *n.* Wutanfall, *der*

tempest /'tempɪst/ *n.* (lit. or fig.) Sturm, *der;* **~ in a teapot** (Amer.) Sturm im Wasserglas

tempestuous /tem'pestjʊəs/ *adj.* (lit. or fig.) stürmisch; **be in a ~ rage** vor Wut rasen

'temping agency *n.* (coll.) Zeitarbeitsunternehmen, *das*

Templar /'templə(r)/ *n.* (Hist.) **[Knight] ~:** Templer, *der;* Tempelritter, *der;* **the [Knights] ~s** der Templerorden

template /'templeɪt/ *n.* Schablone, *die*

temple[1] /'templ/ *n.* Tempel, *der;* (Amer.: synagogue) Synagoge, *die*

temple[2] *n.* ▸ⓘ **p. 951** (Anat.) Schläfe, *die*

templet ▸**template**

tempo /'tempəʊ/ *n., pl.* **~s** *or* **tempi** /'tempi:/ 1) (fig.: pace) **the ~ of life in the town** der Rhythmus der Stadt; **the campaign ~ stepped up** der Wahlkampf ging in die heiße Phase über 2) (Mus.: speed) Tempo, *das*

temporal /'tempərl/ *adj.* 1) (of this life) diesseitig (geh.); irdisch; (secular) weltlich; **~ power** (Eccl.) weltliche Macht; **Lords ~** (Brit. Parl.) *weltliche Mitglieder des britischen Oberhauses* 2) (of time) zeitlich 3) (Anat.) Schläfen- 4) (Ling.) temporal

temporally /'tempərəlɪ/ *adv.* zeitlich

temporarily /'tempərərɪlɪ/ *adv.* vorübergehend

temporary /'tempərərɪ/

A *adj.* vorübergehend; provisorisch ‹*Gebäude, Büro*›; befristet ‹*Visum*›; **~ worker** Zeitarbeitskraft, *die;* (helping out) Aushilfe, *die;* **~ job** Aushilfstätigkeit, *die*

B *n.* Aushilfe, *die;* Aushilfskraft, *die*

temporise, temporiser ▸**temporiz-**

temporize /'tempəraɪz/ *v.i.* 1) (adopt indecisive policy) sich nicht festlegen 2) (act so as to gain time) sich abwartend verhalten; **~ with sb.** jmdn. hinhalten

temporizer /'tempəraɪzə(r)/ *n.* Hinhaltetaktiker, *der*/-taktikerin, *die*

tempt /tempt/ *v.t.* 1) (attract) **~ sb. out/into the town** jmdn. hinauslocken/in die Stadt locken; **~ sb. to do sth.** in jmdm. den Wunsch wecken, etw. zu tun 2) (cause to have strong urge) **~ sb. to do sth.** jmdn. geneigt machen, etw. zu tun; **be ~ed to do sth.** versucht sein, etw. zu tun; **I'm ~ed to question this** das möchte ich fast bezweifeln; **be ~ed to resign** an Rücktritt denken; **be strongly ~ed to dismiss sb.** sehr versucht sein, jmdn. zu entlassen 3) (entice) verführen; **be ~ed into doing sth.** sich dazu verleiten lassen, etw. zu tun; **~ sb. away from sth.** jmdn. von etw. weglocken; **don't ~ me!** verleite mich nicht!; **are you sure I can't ~ you to have a whisky?** kann ich dich wirklich nicht zu einem Whisky überreden? 4) (provoke) herausfordern; **~ fate** *or* **providence** das Schicksal herausfordern

temptation /temp'teɪʃn/ *n.* 1) *no pl.* (attracting) Verlockung, *die;* (being attracted) Versuchung, *die;* (enticing) Verführung, *die* (**into** zu); (being enticed) Versuchung, *die* (geh.); **feel a ~ to do sth.** versucht sein, etw. zu tun; **please resist the ~ to make any funny remarks** mach jetzt bitte keine dummen Witze; **give in to [the] ~:** der Versuchung erliegen; **the T~** (Relig.) die Versuchung [Jesu] 2) (thing) Verlockung, *die* (**to** zu); **special offers are just a ~ to spend money** Sonderangebote verleiten nur dazu, Geld auszugeben 3) **lead us not into ~** (Bibl.) führe uns nicht in Versuchung

tempter /'temptə(r)/ *n.* Verführer, *der;* **the T~** (Relig.) der Versucher

tempting /'temptɪŋ/ *adj.* 1) (inviting) verlockend; verführerisch 2) (enticing) verführerisch

temptingly /'temptɪŋlɪ/ *adv.* 1) (attractively) verlockend; verführerisch 2) **leave money lying about ~:** Geld [verführerisch] offen herumliegen lassen

temptress /'temptrɪs/ *n.* Verführerin, *die*

ten /ten/ ▸ⓘ **p. 894**, ▸ⓘ **p. 1001**, ▸ⓘ **p. 1358**

A *adj.* zehn; **feel ~ feet tall** (fig.) sehr stolz auf sich (*Akk.*) sein; *see also* **eight A**

B *n.* 1) (number, symbol) Zehn, *die* 2) (set of ~) Zehnerpackung, *die;* (of cards) Zehnerstoß, *der* 3) **bet sb. ~ to one that ...** (fig.) jede Wette halten, dass ... (ugs.). *see also* **eight B 1, 3, 4**

tenable /'tenəbl/ *adj.* 1) haltbar; (fig.) haltbar ‹*Theorie, Annahme*›; vertretbar ‹*Standpunkt*› 2) **~ for five years** auf fünf Jahre befristet ‹*Arbeitsverhältnis, Stelle*›; **~ at the university of ...:** [anzutreten] an der Universität ...

tenacious /tɪ'neɪʃəs/ *adj.* 1) (holding fast) hartnäckig haftend ‹*Dornen, Samen*›; **hold sth. in a ~ grip** etw. hartnäckig *od.* eisern festhalten 2) (resolute) hartnäckig; **be ~:** sich hartnäckig halten; 3) (retentive) **~ memory** hervorragendes Gedächtnis 4) (strongly cohesive) fest; **a very ~ link** eine sehr beständige Verbindung

tenaciously /tɪ'neɪʃəslɪ/ *adv.* zäh; (resolutely) hartnäckig

tenacity /tɪ'næsɪtɪ/ *n., no pl.* Hartnäckigkeit, *die;* (resoluteness) Beharrlichkeit, *die;* Hartnäckigkeit, *die;* **~ of life** zäher Lebenswille

tenancy /'tenənsɪ/ *n.* 1) (of flat, residential building) Mietverhältnis, *das;* (of farm, shop) Pachtverhältnis, *das;* **have ~ of a flat** eine Wohnung

t

ℹ Temperature

Temperatures in Germany, as in the rest of continental Europe, are always quoted using the centigrade scale only. To convert from Fahrenheit to centigrade (or Celsius, which is the term used in Germany), deduct 32 from the number of degrees, divide by 9 and multiply by 5. The table below shows the main equivalents.

	Fahrenheit (°F)	Celsius (°C)	
Boiling point	212	100	Siedepunkt
	194	90	
	176	80	
	158	70	
	140	60	
	122	50	
	104	40	
Body temperature	98.4	37	Körpertemperatur
	86	30	
	68	20	
	50	10	
Freezing point	32	0	Gefrierpunkt
	14	–10	
	0	–17,8	
Absolute zero	–459.67	–273,15	absoluter Nullpunkt

Weather

What's the temperature?
= Wie viel Grad sind es?
The outside temperature is 20 degrees [centigrade]* or *68 degrees Fahrenheit
= Die Außentemperatur beträgt 20 Grad [Celsius]
Maximum temperature 27 degrees* or (esp. Amer.) *Highs around 80 degrees
= Höchsttemperaturen um 27 Grad
Temperatures falling to 10 degrees* or (esp. Amer.) *Lows around 50 degrees
= Tiefsttemperaturen um 10 Grad
temperatures around freezing
= Temperaturen um den Gefrierpunkt
ten degrees below freezing
= zehn Grad unter Null
–15°C (minus fifteen degrees centigrade)
= –15° [C] (minus fünfzehn Grad [Celsius])
The temperature is above/below freezing
= Die Temperatur liegt über/unter dem Gefrierpunkt *or* Nullpunkt
It's the same temperature in Berlin
= In Berlin herrscht die gleiche Temperatur

People

She has a [slight] temperature, Her temperature is above normal
= Sie hat [leicht] erhöhte Temperatur
He has a high temperature/a temperature of 40 [centigrade]* or *104 [Fahrenheit]
= Er hat [hohes] Fieber/40 Grad Fieber
What is your temperature?
= Wie hoch ist *or* Was ist Ihre Temperatur?
My temperature is normal
= Ich habe kein Fieber
She took his temperature
= Sie hat bei ihm Fieber gemessen *or* hat seine Temperatur gemessen

Things

What temperature does water boil at?
= Bei welcher Temperatur kocht Wasser?
Water boils at 100°C
= Wasser kocht bei 100°C
What is the temperature of the wine?
= Welche Temperatur hat der Wein?
The wine must be the right temperature
= Der Wein muss die richtige Temperatur haben
A is the same temperature as B
= A hat die gleiche Temperatur wie B

gemietet haben; ~ **agreement** Miet-/Pachtvertrag, *der* 2 (period) Mietdauer, *die* 3 (occupation of post) Bekleidung, *die;* ~ **of the post will be for 10 years** die Stelle ist auf 10 Jahre befristet

tenant /ˈtenənt/
A *n.* 1 (of flat, residential building) Mieter, *der*/Mieterin, *die;* (of farm, shop) Pächter, *der*/Pächterin, *die* 2 (occupant) Bewohner, *der*/Bewohnerin, *die* 3 (Law) (possessor) Besitzer, *der*/Besitzerin, *die;* (owner) Eigentümer, *der*/Eigentümerin, *die*
B *v.t.* mieten ‹*Wohnung, Haus usw.*›; pachten ‹*Land, Bauernhof, Geschäft*›

ˈtenant farmer *n.* ▸ℹ **p. 1260** Pächter, *der*/Pächterin, *die*

tenantry /ˈtenəntrɪ/ *n.* (formal) 1 (people) Mieter; (of farm, shop) Pächter 2 (condition) Mietverhältnis, *das;* (of farm, shop) Pachtverhältnis, *das*

tench /tentʃ/ *n., pl. same* (Zool.) Schleie, *die*

tend¹ /tend/ *v.i.* 1 (be moving or directed) ‹*Strom, Bach:*› fließen (**towards** in Richtung); ‹*Sterne:*› zustreben (**towards** auf + *Akk.*); (fig.) sich zubewegen (**towards** auf + *Akk.*); **all opinions ~ to the same conclusion** alle Meinungen führen zur gleichen Schlussfolgerung 2 (be apt or inclined) ~ **to sth.** zu etw. neigen; ~ **to do sth.** dazu neigen *od.* tendieren, etw. zu tun; **this ~s to suggest that ...:** dies deutet darauf hin, dass ...; **it ~s to get quite cold there at nights** es wird dort nachts oft sehr kalt; **he ~s to get upset if ...:** er regt sich leicht auf, wenn ...

tend² *v.t.* sich kümmern um; hüten ‹*Schafe*›; bedienen ‹*Maschine*›; **the rice has to be ~ed carefully** der Reis erfordert sorgfältige Pflege

tendency /ˈtendənsɪ/ *n.* (inclination) Tendenz, *die;* **artistic tendencies** künstlerische Neigungen; **have a ~ to do sth.** dazu neigen, etw. zu tun; **there is a ~ for everyone to get complacent** die Leute neigen dazu, selbstzufrieden zu werden

tendentious /tenˈdenʃəs/ *adj.,* **tendentiously** /tenˈdenʃəslɪ/ *adv.* (derog.) tendenziös

tendentiousness /tenˈdenʃəsnɪs/ *n., no pl.* (derog.) tendenziöse Färbung

tender¹ /ˈtendə(r)/ *adj.* 1 (not tough) zart 2 (sensitive) empfindlich; ~ **spot** (fig.) wunder Punkt 3 (loving) zärtlich; liebevoll; ~ **loving care** liebevolle Zuwendung 4 (requiring careful handling) heikel 5 (delicate) zart ‹*Gesundheit, Konstitution*›; **be of ~ age** *or* **years** noch sehr jung sein; **at a ~ age** in jungen Jahren; **at the ~ age of twelve** im zarten Alter von zwölf Jahren. *see also* **mercy A 2**

tender² *n.* (Naut., Railw.) Tender, *der*

tender³
A *v.t.* (formal) 1 (present) einreichen ‹*Rücktritt*›; anbieten ‹*Rat*›; vorbringen ‹*Entschuldigung*› 2 (offer as payment) anbieten; ~ **a £20 note** mit einer 20-Pfund-Note bezahlen; **please ~ exact fare** bitte den genauen Betrag bereithalten; **the cash register records the amount ~ed** die Registrierkasse zeigt den gezahlten Geldbetrag an
B *v.i.* ~ **for sth.** ein Angebot für etw. einreichen
C *n.* 1 Angebot, *das;* **put in a ~:** ein Angebot einreichen; **put sth. out to ~:** etw. ausschreiben 2 **legal ~:** gesetzliches Zahlungsmittel

tender: ~foot *n., pl.* **~foots** *or* **~feet** Greenhorn, *das;* (in Scouts) Neuling, *der;* **~-hearted** /ˈtendəhɑːtɪd/ *adj.* weichherzig

tenderize /ˈtendəraɪz/ *v.t.* (Cookery) zart machen; (by beating) weich klopfen

tenderizer /ˈtendəraɪzə(r)/ *n.* (Cookery) Fleischklopfer, *der*

ˈtenderloin *n.* (Gastr.) 1 (Brit.) Lendenstück, *das* 2 (Amer.) Filet, *das*

tenderly /ˈtendəlɪ/ *adv.* 1 (gently) behutsam ‹*behandeln*› 2 (lovingly) zärtlich

tenderness /ˈtendənɪs/ *n., no pl.* 1 (of meat etc.) Zartheit, *die* 2 (loving quality) Zärtlichkeit, *die* 3 (delicacy) Empfindlichkeit, *die*

tendon /ˈtendən/ *n.* (Anat.) Sehne, *die;* **Achilles ~:** Achillessehne, *die*

tendril /ˈtendrɪl/ *n.* Ranke, *die*

tenement /ˈtenɪmənt/ *n.* 1 (Scot.: house containing several dwellings) Mietshaus, *das;* Mietskaserne, *die* (abwertend) 2 (dwelling place) Behausung, *die* 3 (Amer.: house containing several apartments) ~ **[house]** Mietshaus, *das* 4 (Law) Besitz, *der*

Tenerife /tenəˈriːf/ *pr. n.* Teneriffa *(das)*

tenet /ˈtenɪt, ˈtiːnet/ *n.* Grundsatz, *der*

ten: ~fold /ˈtenfəʊld/ *adj., adv.* zehnfach; *see also* **eightfold**; **~-gallon ˈhat** *n.* Cowboyhut, *der*

tenner /ˈtenə(r)/ *n.* (coll.) (Brit.) Zehnpfundschein, *der;* Zehner, *der* (ugs.); (Amer.) Zehndollarschein, *der;* Zehner, *der* (ugs.)

tennis /ˈtenɪs/ *n., no pl.* Tennis, *das;* **real** *or* **royal** *or* (Amer.) **court ~:** Real *od.* Royal *od.* Court Tennis, *das; see also* **lawn tennis**; **table tennis**

tennis: ~ ˈarm *n.* (Med.) Tennisarm, *der;* ~ **ball** *n.* Tennisball, *der;* ~ **club** *n.* Tennisverein, *der;* ~ **court** *n.* 1 (for lawn ~) Tennisplatz, *der;* (for indoor ~) Tennishalle, *die;* 2 (for real ~) Tennishalle, *die;* Ballhaus, *das* (hist.); ~ **ˈelbow** *n., no pl., no art.* (Med.) Tennisell[en]bogen, *der;* ~ **match** *n.* Tennismatch, *das;* Tennisspiel, *das;* ~ **player** *n.* Tennisspieler, *der*/-spielerin, *die;* ~ **racket** *n.* Tennisschläger, *der;* ~ **shoe** *n.* Tennisschuh, *der*

tenon /ˈtenən/ *n.* (Woodw.) Zapfen, *der*

ˈtenon saw *n.* (Woodw.) Feinsäge, *die;* feste Zapfensäge (fachspr.)

tenor /ˈtenə(r)/ *n.* 1 (Mus.: voice, singer, part) Tenor, *der;* ~ **voice** Tenorstimme, *die* 2 (prevailing course) Verlauf, *der;* **the general ~ of his life** seine allgemeine Lebensführung 3 (of argument, speech) Tenor, *der* 4 (Law) (actual wording) Wortlaut, *der;* Tenor, *der* (fachspr.); (exact copy) Abschrift, *die* 5 (Mus.: instrument with range like ~) Tenor, *der;* ~ **saxophone/recorder** Tenorsaxophon, *das*/-blockflöte, *die*

tenpenny /ˈtenpənɪ/ *adj.* für zehn Pence *nachgestellt*

tenpenny ˈpiece *n.* (Brit.) Zehnpencemünze, *die*

tenpin bowling /ˈtenpɪn ˈbəʊlɪŋ/ *n.* Bowling, *das*

tense¹ /tens/ *n.* (Ling.) Zeit, *die;* **in the present/future** *etc.* **~:** im Präsens/Futur *usw.*

tense²

A *adj.* **1** (taut; showing nervous tension) gespannt; **her face was ~ with anxiety** ihr Gesicht war vor Sorge angespannt; **his voice was ~ with emotion** seine Stimme bebte vor Erregung; **a ~ silence** eine [an]gespannte Stille **2** (causing nervous tension) spannungsgeladen

B *v.i.* **sb. ~s** jmds. Muskeln spannen sich an; **he ~d with fear** er verkrampfte sich vor Angst

C *v.t.* anspannen

Phrasal verb

- **~ ˈup** *v.i.* ‹*Muskeln:*› sich anspannen; ‹*Person:*› sich verkrampfen

tensely /ˈtenslɪ/ *adv.* **1** (tightly) straff **2** (with nervous tension) angespannt; **~ gripping** packend ‹*Geschichte, Film*›

tenseness /ˈtensnɪs/ *n., no pl.* (of person) Anspannung, *die;* (of situation etc.) Angespanntheit, *die*

tensile /ˈtensaɪl/ *adj.* **1** Zug‹*belastung, -festigkeit*› **2** (capable of being stretched) zugfest

tension /ˈtenʃn/

A *n.* **1** (latent hostility) Spannung, *die;* **~ between the police and the people is on the increase** die Spannungen zwischen Polizei und Bevölkerung wachsen; **there is a lot of ~ between them** zwischen ihnen herrscht ein gespanntes Verhältnis; **there is a high level of ~ in that area** die Lage in diesem Gebiet ist sehr angespannt; **racial ~:** Rassenspannungen *Pl.* **2** (mental strain) Anspannung, *die* **3** *no pl.* (of violin string, tennis racquet) Spannung, *die* **4** (stretching; Mech. Engin.) Spannung, *die* **5** (Knitting) Festigkeit, *die;* **check the ~:** eine Maschenprobe machen. *see also* **surface tension**

B *v.t.* spannen

tent /tent/ *n.* Zelt, *das*

tentacle /ˈtentəkl/ *n.* **1** (Zool., Bot.) Tentakel, *der od. das* **2** (fig.) Fühler, *der;* (with sinister connotations) Fangarm, *der*

tentative /ˈtentətɪv/ *adj.* **1** (not definite) vorläufig; **make a ~ suggestion** einen Vorschlag in den Raum stellen; **say a ~ 'yes'** vorläufig „Ja“ sagen **2** (hesitant) zaghaft

tentatively /ˈtentətɪvlɪ/ *adv.* **1** (not definitely) vorläufig **2** (hesitantly) zaghaft

tenterhooks /ˈtentəhʊks/ *n. pl.* **be on ~:** [wie] auf glühenden Kohlen sitzen; **keep sb. on ~:** jmdn. auf die Folter spannen

tenth /tenθ/

A *adj.* ▸ **p. 1358** zehnt...; *see also* **eighth A**

B *n.* **1** (in sequence, rank) Zehnte, *der/die/das;* (fraction) Zehntel, *das* **2** ▸ **p. 1047** (day) **the ~ of May** der zehnte Mai; **the ~ [of the month]** der Zehnte [des Monats]. *see also* **eighth B**

tent: ~ peg *n.* Zeltpflock, *der;* Hering, *der;* **~ pole** *n.* Zeltstange, *die*

tenuity /teˈnjuːɪtɪ/ ▸**tenuousness**

tenuous /ˈtenjʊəs/ *adj.* dünn ‹*Faden*›; zart ‹*Spinnwebe*›; (fig.) dünn ‹*Atmosphäre*›; dürftig ‹*Argument*›; schwach, locker ‹*Verbindung*›; unbegründet ‹*Anspruch*›; **there are only ~ connections** es bestehen kaum Verbindungen; **he had but a ~ hold on life** sein Leben hing nur noch an einem seidenen Faden

tenuously /ˈtenjʊəslɪ/ *adv.* dünn; (fig.) schwach; [nur] locker ‹*verbunden sein*›; **cling only ~ to life** nur noch einen schwachen Lebenswillen haben

tenuousness /ˈtenjʊəsnɪs/ *n., no pl.* Dünne, *die;* (fig.) Dürftigkeit, *die*

tenure /ˈtenjə(r)/ *n.* **1** (right, title) Besitztitel, *der* **2** (possession) Besitz, *der;* **his ~ of the house is only for a limited period** er kann nur eine begrenzte Zeit über das Haus verfügen **3** (period) **~ [of office]** Amtszeit, *die* **4** (permanent appointment) Dauerstellung, *die;* **have [security of] ~:** eine Dauerstellung haben

ˈtenure track *n.* (Amer.) Tenure Track, *der* (fachspr.); *attrib.* Tenure-Track-‹*Stelle, System, Anwärter, Programm*›

tenuto /təˈnuːtəʊ/ *adj., adv.* (Mus.) tenuto

tepee /ˈtiːpiː/ *n.* Tipi, *das*

tepid /ˈtepɪd/ *adj.* **1** lauwarm **2** (fig.) halbherzig ‹*Interesse, Willkommensgruß*›; verhalten ‹*Lob, Begeisterung*›

tequila /teˈkiːlə/ *n.* (drink) Tequila, *der*

terabyte /ˈterəbaɪt/ *n.* (Computing) Terabyte, *das*

tercentenary /tɜːsenˈtiːnərɪ, tɜːsenˈtenərɪ/

A *adj.* Dreihundertjahr‹*feier, -feierlichkeiten*›

B *n.* Dreihundertjahrfeier, *die*

term /tɜːm/

A *n.* **1** (word expressing definite concept) [Fach]begriff, *der;* **scientific/legal/medical ~:** wissenschaftlicher/juristischer/medizinischer Fachausdruck; **~ of reproach** Vorwurf, *der;* **in ~s of money/politics** unter finanziellem/politischem Aspekt; **in ~s of financial success** vom finanziellen Erfolg her gesehen; **in set ~s** klipp und klar; *see also* **contradiction** **2** *in pl.* (conditions) Bedingungen; **he does everything on his own ~s** er tut alles, wie er es für richtig hält; **~s of surrender** Kapitulationsbedingungen; **~s of contract** Vertragsbedingungen; **accept sb. on his own ~s** jmdn. so akzeptieren, wie er ist; **come to** *or* **make ~s [with sb.]** sich [mit jmdm.] einigen; **come to ~s [with each other]** sich einigen; **come to ~s with sth.** (be able to accept sth.) mit etw. zurechtkommen; (resign oneself to sth.) sich mit etw. abfinden; **come to ~s with oneself** mit sich selbst ins Reine kommen; **~s of reference** (Brit.) Aufgabenbereich, *der;* **~s of trade** Austauschverhältnis, *das* (Wirtsch.) **3** *in pl.* (charges) Konditionen; **their ~s are ...:** sie verlangen ...; **hire purchase on easy ~s** Ratenkauf zu günstigen Bedingungen; *see also* **inclusive 2** **4** **in the short/long/medium ~:** kurz-/lang-/mittelfristig **5** (Sch.) Halbjahr, *das;* (Univ.: one of two/three/four divisions per year) Semester, *das*/Trimester, *das*/Quartal, *das;* **during ~:** während des Halbjahres/Semesters *usw.;* **out of ~:** in den Ferien; **end of ~:** Halbjahres-/Semesterende *usw.* **6** (limited period) Zeitraum, *der;* (of insurance policy etc.) Laufzeit, *die;* (period of tenure) **~ [of office]** Amtszeit, *die* **7** (completion of pregnancy) **[full] ~:** normale Schwangerschaftszeit **8** (period of imprisonment) Haftzeit, *die;* **be put in prison for a long ~:** für eine längere Haftstrafe ins Gefängnis kommen **9** *in pl.* (mode of expression) Worte; **praise in the highest ~s** in den höchsten Tönen loben; **talk in vague ~s of sth.** sich in vagen Andeutungen über etw. (*Akk.*) ergehen; **in flattering ~s** mit schmeichelnden Worten; *see also* **uncertain 5** **10** *in pl.* (relations) **be on good/poor/friendly ~s with sb.** mit jmdm. auf gutem/schlechtem/freundschaftlichem Fuß stehen; *see also* **equal A 1**; **speaking A 1** **11** (Logic, Math.) Term, *der*

B *v.t.* nennen

termagant /ˈtɜːməgənt/ *n.* (literary) Furie, *die*

terminal /ˈtɜːmɪnl/

A *n.* **1** (Electr.) Anschluss, *der;* (of battery) Pol, *der* **2** (for train or bus) Bahnhof, *der;* (for airline passengers) Terminal, *der od. das;* **helicopter ~:** Hubschrauberlandeplatz, *der* **3** (Teleph., Computing) Terminal, *das*

B *adj.* **1** End‹*bahnhof, -station*› **2** (concluding) abschließend ‹*Worte*›; End‹*reim, -silbe*›; **the ~ problem** das letzte große Problem **3** ▸ **p. 1231** (Med.) unheilbar; **have a ~ illness** unheilbar krank sein; **a ~ case** ein hoffnungsloser Fall **4** (Bot.) **~ bud** Terminalknospe, *die* **5** (Zool., Anat.) End‹*glied, -lappen*›

terminally /ˈtɜːmɪnəlɪ/ *adv.* (Med.) **~ ill** unheilbar krank

terminal veˈlocity *n.* (Phys.) Grenzgeschwindigkeit, *die*

terminate /ˈtɜːmɪneɪt/

A *v.t.* **1** (bring to an end) beenden; **the contract was ~d** der Vertrag wurde gelöst **2** (Med.) unterbrechen ‹*Schwangerschaft*›

B *v.i.* **1** (come to an end) enden; ‹*Vertrag:*› ablaufen **2** (Ling.) enden; auslauten

termination /tɜːmɪˈneɪʃn/ *n.* **1** *no pl.* (coming to an end) Ende, *das;* (of lease) Ablauf, *der* **2** *no pl.* (bringing to an end) Beendigung, *die;* (of a marriage) Auflösung, *die* **3** (Med.) Schwangerschaftsabbruch, *der*

termini *pl. of* **terminus**

terminological /tɜːmɪnəˈlɒdʒɪkl/ *adj.* terminologisch; (of science of terminology) Terminologie-

terminologically /tɜːmɪnəˈlɒdʒɪkəlɪ/ *adv.* terminologisch

terminologist /tɜːmɪˈnɒlədʒɪst/ *n.* Terminologe, *der*/Terminologin, *die*

terminology /tɜːmɪˈnɒlədʒɪ/ *n.* Terminologie, *die*

terminus /ˈtɜːmɪnəs/ *n., pl.* **~es** *or* **termini** /ˈtɜːmɪnaɪ/ (end of route or line) Ende, *das;* (of bus, train, etc.) Endstation, *die*

termite /ˈtɜːmaɪt/ *n.* (Zool.) Termite, *die*

tern /tɜːn/ *n.* (Ornith.) Seeschwalbe, *die*

ternary /ˈtɜːnərɪ/ *adj.* ternär

terrace /ˈterəs, ˈterɪs/

A *n.* **1** (row of houses) Häuserreihe, *die* **2** (adjacent to house; Agric.: on hillside) Terrasse, *die* **3** *in pl.* (Footb.) Ränge **4** (Geol.) Terrasse, *die;* Stufe, *die*

B *v.t.* terrassieren

ˈterraced house, ˈterrace house *ns.* Reihenhaus, *das*

terracotta /terəˈkɒtə/ *n., no pl., no indef. art.* Terrakotta, *die*

terra firma /terə ˈfɜːmə/ *n., no pl., no art.* fester Boden; **be back on ~:** wieder festen Boden unter den Füßen haben

terrain /teˈreɪn/ *n.* Gelände, *das;* Terrain, *das* (bes. Milit.)

terrapin /ˈterəpɪn/ *n.* (Zool.) Sumpfschildkröte, *die*

terrarium /teˈrɑːrɪəm/ *n., pl.* **~s** *or* **terraria** /teˈrɑːrɪə/ (for animals) Terrarium, *das;* (for plants) Pflanzenterrarium, *das*

terrestrial /təˈrestrɪəl, tɪˈrestrɪəl/

A *adj.* **1** terrestrisch ‹*Raumschiff, Fernsehen, Bevölkerung*›; Erd‹*satellit, -bevölkerung*›; (mundane) irdisch; weltlich; **the ~ globe** der Erdball; **a ~ globe** ein Erdglobus; *see also* **magnetism 1** **2** (of the land) kontinental; terrestrisch (Geol.) **3** (Biol.) Land-

B *n.* Erdbewohner, *der*/-bewohnerin, *die*

terrible /ˈterɪbl/ *adj.* **1** (coll.: very great or bad) schrecklich (ugs.); fürchterlich (ugs.); **I feel ~ about doing it** es tut mir schrecklich Leid, es zu tun **2** (coll.: incompetent) schrecklich; **be ~ at maths/tennis/carpentry** in Mathe mies sein/furchtbar schlecht Tennis spielen/ein schrecklicher Tischler sein **3** (causing terror) furchtbar. *See also* **enfant terrible**

terribly /ˈterɪblɪ/ *adv.* **1** (coll.: very) unheimlich (ugs.); furchtbar (ugs.) **2** (coll.: appallingly) furchtbar (ugs.) **3** (coll.: incompetently) furchtbar schlecht **4** (fearfully) auf erschreckende Weise

terrier /ˈterɪə(r)/ *n.* Terrier, *der*

terrific /təˈrɪfɪk/ *adj.* (coll.) **1** (great, intense) irrsinnig (ugs.); Wahnsinns- (ugs.); unwahrscheinlich (ugs.) **2** (magnificent) sagenhaft (ugs.) **3** (highly expert) klasse (ugs.); toll (ugs.); **be ~ at sth.** in etw. (*Dat.*) Spitze sein (ugs.); **a ~ singer** ein Spitzensänger/eine Spitzensängerin (ugs.)

terrifically /təˈrɪfɪkəlɪ/ *adv.* (coll.: extremely) wahnsinnig (ugs.)

terrify /ˈterɪfaɪ/ *v.t.* **1** (fill with terror) Angst machen (+ *Dat.*); **terrified** verängstigt **2** (coll.: make very anxious) Angst machen (+ *Dat.*); **be terrified that ...:** Angst haben, dass ... **3** (scare) Angst einjagen (+ *Dat.*); **~ sb. into doing sth.** jmdm. eine solche Angst einjagen, dass er etw. tut

terrifying /ˈterɪfaɪɪŋ/ *adj.* **1** (causing terror) entsetzlich ‹*Erlebnis, Film, Buch, Theaterstück*›; erschreckend ‹*Klarheit, Gedanke*›; Furcht erregend ‹*Anblick*›; beängstigend ‹*Geschwindigkeit, Neigungswinkel*› **2** (formidable) Furcht erregend; beängstigend ‹*Gelehrsamkeit, Förmlichkeit, Intensität*›

terrifyingly /ˈterɪfaɪɪŋlɪ/ *adv.* beängstigend ‹*dicht, knapp*›; entsetzlich ‹*einsam*›

terrine /təˈriːn/ *n.* **1** (dish) Steinguttopf, *der* **2** (Gastr.) Terrine, *die*

territorial /terɪ'tɔ:rɪəl/
A *adj.* **1** territorial; Gebiets‹*anspruch, -hoheit usw.*›; Hoheits‹*gewässer, -gebiet usw.*›; Gelände‹*vorteil*›; ~ **possessions** Territorialbesitz, *der* **2** (limited to a district) regional begrenzt ‹*Maßnahme, Regelung*›
B **T~** *n.* (Brit. Mil.) Landwehrsoldat, *der*
Territorial 'Army *n.* (Brit. Mil.) Landwehr, *die;* Territorialarmee, *die*
territorially /terɪ'tɔ:rɪəlɪ/ *adv.* territorial
territorial 'waters *n. pl.* Hoheitsgewässer
territory /'terɪtərɪ/ *n.* **1** (Polit.) Staatsgebiet, *das;* Hoheitsgebiet, *das* **2** (fig.: area of knowledge or action) Gebiet, *das* **3** (of commercial traveller etc.) Bezirk, *der* **4** (large tract of land) Region, *die;* Gebiet, *das* **5** (Amer.: land not yet a full State) Territorium, *das* **6** (Zool.) Revier, *das* **7** (Sport) Spielfeldhälfte, *die*
terror /'terə(r)/ *n.* **1** (extreme fear) [panische] Angst; **in ~:** in panischer Angst; **reign of ~:** Schreckensherrschaft, *die;* **the [Red] T~, the Reign of T~** (Hist.) die Schreckensherrschaft [der Französischen Revolution] **2** (person or thing causing ~) Schrecken, *der;* (terrorist acts) Teror, *der* **3** **[holy] ~** (troublesome person) Plage, *die*
terrorisation, terrorise ▸**terroriz-**
terrorism /'terərɪzm/ *n., no pl.* Terrorismus, *der;* **acts of ~:** Terror, *der;* Terrorakte
terrorist /'terərɪst/ *n.* Terrorist, *der*/Terroristin, *die; attrib.* Terror‹*gruppe, -organisation, -angriff, -netzwerk, -zelle*›
terroristic /terə'rɪstɪk/ *adj.* terroristisch
terrorization /terəraɪ'zeɪʃn/ *n., no pl.* Terror, *der*
terrorize /'terəraɪz/ *v.t.* **1** (frighten) in [Angst und] Schrecken versetzen **2** (coerce by terrorism) terrorisieren; (intimidate) durch Terror[akte] einschüchtern; ~ **sb. into submission** jmdn. durch Terror in die Knie zwingen
terror: ~-stricken, ~-struck *adjs.* zu Tode erschrocken
terry /'terɪ/ *adj.* (Textiles) ~ **towel** Frottier[hand]tuch, *das;* ~ **towelling** Frottee, *das od. der*
terse /tɜ:s/ *adj.* **1** (concise) kurz und bündig **2** (curt) knapp
tersely /'tɜ:slɪ/ *adv.* **1** (concisely) in kurzen Worten **2** (curtly) kurz angebunden
terseness /'tɜ:snɪs/ *n., no pl.* **1** (conciseness) Bündigkeit, *die* **2** (curtness) Knappheit, *die*
tertiary /'tɜ:ʃərɪ/ *adj.* **1** (of third order or rank) tertiär **2** (next after secondary) ~ **education** der tertiäre Bildungsbereich **3** **T~** (Geol.) tertiär
Terylene ® /'terɪli:n/ *n.* Terylen, *das* Ⓦⓩ
terza rima /teətsə 'ri:mə/ *n.* (Pros.) Terzine, *die*
tessellated /'tesəleɪtɪd/ *adj.* mosaikartig; tessellarisch
tessellation /tesə'leɪʃn/ *n.* mosaikartige Musterung
test /test/
A *n.* **1** (examination) (Sch.) Klassenarbeit, *die;* (Univ.) Klausur, *die;* (short examination) Test, *der;* ~ **of character** Charakterprüfung, *die;* **put sb./sth. to the ~:** jmdn./etw. erproben **2** (critical inspection, analysis) Test, *der* **3** (basis for evaluation) Prüfstein, *der* **4** (Cricket) Test Match, *das* **5** (ground of admission or rejection) Aufnahmeprüfung, *die* **6** (Chem.) Reagens, *das;* **serve as a ~ for starch** zum Nachweis von Stärke dienen
B *v.t.* **1** (examine, analyse) untersuchen ‹*Wasser, Gehör, Augen*›; testen ‹*Gehör, Augen, Produkt*›; prüfen ‹*Schüler*›; überprüfen ‹*Hypothese, Aussage, Leitungen*›; ~ **a pupil on his/her vocabulary** einem Schüler/einer Schülerin die Vokabeln abfragen; ~ **the accuracy of a statement** den Wahrheitsgehalt einer Aussage überprüfen; ~ **sb. for AIDS** jmdn. auf Aids untersuchen; ~ **the reaction of the workforce** sehen, wie die Belegschaft reagiert **2** (try severely) auf die Probe stellen **3** (Chem.) analysieren; ~ **a substance for sth.** eine Substanz auf etw. (*Akk.*) untersuchen; **send sth. for ~ing** etw. zur Analyse schicken
(Phrasal verb)
• ~ **out** *v.t.* ausprobieren ‹*neue Produkte*› (**on** an + *Dat.*); erproben ‹*Theorie, Idee*›

testament /'testəmənt/ *n.* **1** **Old/New T~** (Bibl.) Altes/Neues Testament **2** ▸**will² A 2**
testamentary /testə'mentərɪ/ *adj.* testamentarisch
testator /te'steɪtə(r)/ *n.* Erblasser, *der* (Rechtsspr.)
testatrix /te'steɪtrɪks/ *n.* Erblasserin, *die* (Rechtsspr.)
test: ~ ban *n.* Atom[waffen]teststopp, *der;* ~ **ban treaty** *n.* [Atom]teststopp-Abkommen, *das;* ~ **bed** *n.* (Tech.) Prüfstand, *der;* ~ **card** *n.* (Telev.) Testbild, *das;* ~ **'case** *n.* (Law) Musterprozess, *der;* ~ **drive** *n.* Probefahrt, *die;* **~-drive** *v.t.* Probe fahren
tester /'testə(r)/ *n.* Prüfer, *der*/Prüferin, *die;* (device) Prüfgerät, *das;* (sample) Probe, *die*
test: ~ flight *n.* Testflug, *der;* Erprobungsflug, *der;* **first ~ flight** Jungfernflug, *der;* **~-fly** *v.t.* Probe fliegen
testicle /'testɪkl/ *n.* ▸❶ **p. 951** (Anat., Zool.) Testikel, *der* (fachspr.); Hoden, *der*
testicular /tes'tɪkjʊlə(r)/ *adj.* testikulär (fachspr.); Hoden‹*krebs, -gewebe, -tumor, -schmerz*›
testify /'testɪfaɪ/
A *v.i.* **1** ~ **to sth.** etw. bezeugen; ~ **to sb.'s high intelligence** jmdm. große Intelligenz bescheinigen; **this testifies to his skills** das zeugt von seinen Fähigkeiten **2** (Law) ~ **against sb./before sth.** gegen jmdn./vor etw. (*Dat.*) aussagen
B *v.t.* **1** (declare) bestätigen **2** (be evidence of) beweisen
testily /'testɪlɪ/ *adv.* gereizt
testimonial /testɪ'məʊnɪəl/ *n.* **1** (certificate of character) Zeugnis, *das;* (recommendation) Referenz, *die* **2** (gift) Geschenk [als Ausdruck der Wertschätzung]
testimony /'testɪmənɪ/ *n.* **1** (witness) Aussage, *die;* **bear ~ to sth., be ~ to** *or* **of sth.** etw. beweisen; von etw. zeugen; **have sb.'s ~ for sth.** jmds. Wort für etw. haben; ~ **of his respectability** Zeichen *od.* Beweis seiner Anständigkeit **2** (Law) [Zeugen]aussage, *die* **3** *no pl.* (statements) Angaben
testiness /'testɪnɪs/ *n., no pl.* Gereiztheit, *die*
testis /'testɪs/ *n., pl.* **testes** /'testi:z/ ▸**testicle**
test: ~ marketing *n., no pl.* Durchführung eines Markttests/von Markttests; ~ **match** *n.* (Sport) Testmatch, *das*
testosterone /te'stɒstərəʊn/ *n.* (Physiol.) Testosteron, *das*
test: ~ paper *n.* **1** (Educ.) Übungsarbeit, *die;* (Univ.) Übungsklausur, *die;* **2** (Chem.) Indikatorpapier, *das;* ~ **piece** *n.* Pflicht[übung], *die;* (Mus.) Pflichtstück, *das;* ~ **pilot** *n.* (Aeronaut.) Testpilot, *der*/-pilotin, *die;* ~ **run** *n.* Testfahrt, *die;* Probefahrt, *die;* (of engine) Testlauf, *der;* Probelauf, *der;* ~ **tube** *n.* (Chem., Biol.) Reagenzglas, *das; attrib.* **~-tube baby** (coll.) Retortenbaby, *das* (ugs.)
testy /'testɪ/ *adj.* leicht reizbar ‹*Person*›; gereizt ‹*Antwort*›
tetanus /'tetənəs/ *n.* ▸❶ **p. 1231** (Med.) Tetanus, *der* (fachspr.); [Wund]starrkrampf, *der*
tetchy /'tetʃɪ/ *adj.* leicht reizbar; (on single occasion) gereizt
tête-à-tête /teɪtɑ:'teɪt/
A *n.* Zwiegespräch, *das* (geh.); Gespräch unter vier Augen; (between lovers) Tête-à-tête, *das* (veralt., scherzh.)
B *adj.* privat; ~ **interview/discussion** Gespräch/Diskussion unter vier Augen; ~ **conversation** Zwiegespräch, *das* (geh.)
C *adv.* unter vier Augen
tether /'teðə(r)/
A *n.* **1** (chain) Kette, *die;* (rope) Strick, *der* **2** (fig.: limit) Grenze, *die;* **give sb. a short ~:** jmdn. an der kurzen Leine halten; **be at the end of one's ~:** am Ende [seiner Kraft] sein
B *v.t.* anbinden (**to** an)
tetrahedron /tetrə'hi:drən/ *n., pl.* **~s** *or* **tetrahedra** /tetrə'hi:drə/ (Geom.) Tetraeder, *das*
Teuton /'tju:tən/ *n.* (Hist.) Teutone, *der*/Teutonin, *die*

Teutonic /tju:'tɒnɪk/ *adj.* **1** (Germanic) germanisch **2** (with Germanic characteristics) [typisch] deutsch; teutonisch (abwertend, auch scherzh.) **3** (Hist.: of the Teutons) teutonisch
Texan /'teksn/
A *adj.* texanisch
B *n.* Texaner, *der*/Texanerin, *die*
text /tekst/
A *n.* **1** Text, *der;* **they couldn't agree on the ~ of the agreement** sie konnten sich über den Wortlaut des Vertrages nicht einigen **2** (passage of Scripture) Bibelstelle, *die;* **take as one's ~:** als Predigttext nehmen; predigen über (+ *Akk.*) **3** (Amer.: book) ▸**textbook** **4** *in pl.* (books to be studied) [Pflicht]lektüre, *die* **5** (~ message) SMS, *die;* Textnachricht, *die;* **send a ~ to sb.'s mobile phone** jmdm. eine SMS schicken; jmdn. ansimsen (ugs.)
B *v.t.* ~ **sb.** jmdm. eine [Text]nachricht schicken; ~ **a message** eine [Text]nachricht schicken *od.* senden; ~ **each other jokes** sich gegenseitig Witze zuschicken
C *v.i.* eine Textnachricht [ver]schicken; (to mobile phone) eine SMS [ver]schicken; simsen (ugs.)
text: ~book *n.* (Educ.) Lehrbuch, *das; attrib.* ~ **case** Paradefall, *der;* ~ **landing** Bilderbuchlandung, *die;* ~ **editor** *n.* (Computing) Texteditor, *der;* ~ **file** *n.* (Computing) Textdatei, *die*
textile /'tekstaɪl/
A *n.* Stoff, *der;* **~s** Textilien *Pl*
B *adj.* (woven) textil; ~ **fabrics** Textilien *Pl.*
text: ~ message *n.* SMS, *die;* Textnachricht, *die;* Textmitteilung, *die;* ~ **messaging** /'tekst mesɪdʒɪŋ/ *n., no pl.* Verschicken *od.* Versand von Textnachrichten *od.* Textmitteilungen; Simsen, *das* (ugs.); **SMS ~ messaging** Versand von SMS-Nachrichten; **~phone** *n.* Texttelefon, *das;* ~ **processing** *n., no pl.* Textverarbeitung, *die;* ~ **processor** *n.* (Computing) Textverarbeitungsprogramm, *das*
textual /'tekstjʊəl/ *adj.* textlich
textual 'criticism *n.* Textkritik, *die*
textural /'tekstʃərl/ *adj.* strukturell
texture /'tekstʃə(r)/ *n.* **1** Beschaffenheit, *die;* (of fabric, material) Struktur, *die;* (of food) Konsistenz, *die;* **have a smooth ~:** sich glatt anfühlen **2** (of prose, music, etc.) Textur, *die* (geh.) **3** (Art) materielle Struktur
textured /'tekstʃəd/ *adj.* Struktur‹*garn, -farbe*›; ~ **vegetable protein** Sojafleisch, *das*
textureless /'tekstʃəlɪs/ *adj.* gestaltlos ‹*Prosa, Gemälde, Darbietung*›; formlos ‹*Masse*›
Th. *abbr.* = **Thursday** Do.
Thai /taɪ/ ▸❶ **p. 1345**
A *adj.* **1** (of Thailand) thailändisch **2** (Ethnol./Ling.) Thai-
B *n.* **1** *pl.* **~s** *or same* Thai, *der/die;* Thailänder, *der*/Thailänderin, *die* **2** (language) Thai, *das*
Thailand /'taɪlænd/ *pr. n.* Thailand (*das*)
Thailander /'taɪlændə(r)/ ▸**Thai B 1**
thalamus /'θæləməs/ *n.* (Anat.) Thalamus, *der*
thalidomide /θə'lɪdəmaɪd/ *n.* (Med.) Contergan, *das* Ⓦⓩ; Thalidomid, *das*
thalidomide: ~ baby, ~ child *ns.* Contergankind, *das* (ugs.)
Thames /temz/ *pr. n.* ▸❶ **p. 1491** Themse, *die; see also* **father A 7; fire A 1**
than /ðən, *stressed* ðæn/ *conj.* **1** (in comparison) als; **I know you better ~ [I do] him** ich kenne dich besser als ihn; **I know you better ~ he [does]** ich kenne dich besser als er; **you are taller ~ he is** *or* **than him** du bist größer als er; *see also* **rather** **2** (introducing statement of difference) als; **anywhere other ~ at home** überall außer zu Hause; *see also* **none A; other A 3, B 2, C**
thank /θæŋk/ *v.t.* ~ **sb. [for sth.]** jmdm. [für etw.] danken; sich bei jmdm. [für etw.] bedanken; **I don't know how to ~ you** ich weiß gar nicht, wie ich Ihnen danken soll; **I can't ~ you enough** ich kann Ihnen gar nicht genug danken; **have sb./sth. to ~ for sth.** jmdm./einer Sache etw. zu verdanken haben; **have [only] oneself to ~ for sth.** etw. sich (*Dat.*) selbst zuzuschreiben haben; **he won't ~ you for that/for doing that** (iron.) er wird dir dafür

nicht gerade dankbar sein/er wird dir nicht gerade dankbar sein, dass du das getan hast; **~ God** *or* **goodness** *or* **heaven[s]** Gott sei Dank; **[I] ~ you** danke; (slightly formal) vielen Dank; **no, ~ you** nein, danke; **yes, ~ you** ja, bitte; danke, ja; **doing very nicely, ~ you** es läuft alles prima (auch iron.); **I can do without language like that, ~ you!** (iron.) auf diesen Ton kann ich verzichten, vielen Dank!; **~ you very much [indeed]** vielen herzlichen Dank; **I'll stay in London, ~ you** (iron.) vielen Dank, ich bleibe lieber in London; **~ing 'you** (coll.) danke; **~ you for nothing!** (iron.) danke bestens!; **I will ~ you to do as you are told** (iron.) ich wäre dir sehr verbunden, wenn du tätest, was man dir sagt; **~ one's [lucky] stars that ...:** dem Himmel danken, dass ...; heilfroh sein, dass ...

thankful /ˈθæŋkfl/ *adj.* dankbar; **I am just ~ that it's all over** ich bin nur froh, dass das jetzt alles vorüber ist

thankfully /ˈθæŋkfəlɪ/ *adv.* **1** (gratefully) dankbar **2** (as sentence-modifier: fortunately) glücklicherweise

thankfulness /ˈθæŋkflnɪs/ *n., no pl.* Dankbarkeit, *die*

thankless /ˈθæŋklɪs/ *adj.* undankbar ‹*Aufgabe, Person*›

thanks /θæŋks/ *n. pl.* **1** (gratitude) Dank, *der;* **accept sth. with ~:** etw. dankend annehmen; **smile one's ~:** dankend lächeln; **they gave me little ~** *or* (iron.) **much ~ they gave me for my troubles** sie haben mir meine Mühen kaum gedankt; **that's all the ~ one gets** das ist nun der Dank dafür!; **give ~ [to God]** dem Herrn danken; das Dankgebet sprechen; **~ to** (with the help of) dank; (on account of the bad influence of) wegen; **~ to you** dank deiner; (reproachfully) deinetwegen; **no ~ to you** (iron.) dein Verdienst war es nicht; **it is small** *or* **no ~ to him that we won** ihm haben wir es jedenfalls nicht zu verdanken, dass wir gewonnen haben; **~ to his arriving in time** dank seines rechtzeitigen Erscheinens; *see also* **return B 1**
2 (as formula expressing gratitude) danke; **no, ~:** nein, danke; **yes, ~:** ja, bitte; **~, but no ~:** danke, aber lieber nicht; **~ awfully** *or* **a lot** *or* **very much, many ~** (coll.) vielen *od.* tausend Dank

thanksgiving /ˈθæŋksgɪvɪŋ/ *n.* **1** (expression of gratitude) Dankbarkeit, *die;* **T~ [Day]** (Amer.) [amerikanisches] Erntedankfest; Thanksgiving Day, *der* **2** (Relig.) Dankgebet, *das*

'thank-you *n.* (coll.) Dankeschön, *das;* **a warm** *or* **hearty ~:** ein herzliches Dankeschön; **~ letter** Dankbrief, *der;* **give sb. a ~ present** jmdm. zum Dank etwas schenken

that
A /ðæt/ *adj., pl.* **those** /ðəʊz/ **1** dieser/diese/dieses; **~ son of yours** Ihr/dein Sohn
2 *expr. strong feeling* der/die/das; **never will I forget ~ day** den Tag werde ich nie vergessen
3 (coupled or contrasted with 'this') der/die/das [da]
B *pron., pl.* **those** **1** der/die/das; **who is ~ in the garden?** wer ist das [da] im Garten?; **what bird is ~?** was für ein Vogel ist das?; **I know all ~:** ich weiß das alles; **I 'am ~!** das kannst du wohl glauben!; **and [all] ~:** und so weiter; **like ~** (of the kind or in the way mentioned, of ~ character) so; **[just] like ~** (without effort, thought) einfach so; **don't be like ~!** sei doch nicht so; **if she 'wants to be like ~:** wenn sie sich so anstellen will; **don't talk like ~:** hör auf, so zu reden; **he is 'like ~:** so ist er eben; **~ is [to say]** *introducing explanation* das heißt; *introducing reservation* das heißt; genauer gesagt; **if they'd have me, ~ is** das heißt, wenn sie mich nehmen; **'~'s more like it** (of suggestion, news) das hört sich schon besser an; (of action, work) das sieht schon besser aus; **~'s right!** *expr. approval* gut *od.* recht so; (iron.) nur so weiter!; (coll.: expr. assent) jawohl; **~'s a good boy/girl** das ist lieb [von dir, mein Junge/Mädchen]; (with request) sei so lieb *usw.;* **~ will do** das reicht; **sb./sth. is not as ... as all '~** (coll.) so ... ist jmd./etw. nun auch wieder nicht; **[so] ~'s '~** (it's finished) so, das wärs; (it's settled) so ist es nun mal; **you are not going to the party, and ~'s '~!** du gehst nicht zu der Party, und damit Schluss!; *see also* **at 4**; **how A**; **it 7, 10**; **take A 23**; **this B 5**; **with 7**
2 (Brit.: person spoken to) **who is ~?** wer ist da?; (behind wall etc.) wer ist denn da?; (on telephone) wer ist am Apparat?; **who was ~?** wer war das?
3 *in pl.* **those who ...** die, die ...; diejenigen, die ...; (all who) alle, die ...; **those below the standard will be rejected** alle, die den Anforderungen nicht genügen, werden abgelehnt; **those arriving late** die Zuspätkommenden
C /ðət/ *rel. pron., pl. same* der/die/das; **the people ~ you got it from** die Leute, von denen du es bekommen hast; **the box ~ you put the apples in** die Kiste, in die du die Äpfel getan hast; **is he the man ~ you saw last night?** ist das der Mann, den Sie gestern Abend gesehen haben?; **everyone ~ I know** jeder, den ich kenne; **this is all [the money] ~ I have** das ist alles [Geld], was ich habe; **they ~ ...:** diejenigen, die *od.* welche ...; **what is it ~ is making you sad?** was stimmt dich so traurig?
D /ðæt/ *adv.* (coll.) so; **he may be daft, but he's not [all] '~ daft** er mag ja blöd sein, aber so blöd [ist er] auch wieder nicht; **a nail about ~ long** ein etwa so langer Nagel
E /ðət/ *rel. adv.* der/die/das; **at the speed ~ he was going** bei der Geschwindigkeit, die er hatte; **tell the way ~ the accident happened** erzählen, wie der Unfall geschah; **the day ~ I first saw her** der Tag, an dem ich sie zum ersten Mal sah
F /ðət, *stressed* ðæt/ *conj.* **1** *introducing statement; expr. result, reason or cause* dass
2 *expr. purpose* **[in order] ~:** damit; **he died ~ others might live** er starb, damit andere [weiter]leben konnten
3 *expr. wish* **oh ~ I could forget her!** ach, dass ich sie doch vergessen könnte! *See also* **not 2**; **now B**

thatch /θætʃ/
A *n.* **1** (of straw) Strohdach, *das;* (of reeds) Schilf- *od.* Reetdach, *das;* (of palm leaves) Palmblattdach, *das;* (material) Stroh, *das*/Schilf, *das*/Palmblätter; (roofing) Dachbedeckung, *die* **2** (coll.: hair) Matte, *die* (salopp)
B *v.t.* mit Stroh/Schilf/Palmblättern decken

thatched /θætʃt/ *adj.* strohgedeckt/schilf- *od.* reetgedeckt; gedeckt ‹*Dach*›; Stroh-/Schilf- *od.* Reet‹*dach*›

thatcher /ˈθætʃə(r)/ *n.* Dachdecker, *der*/-deckerin, *die*

Thatcherism /ˈθætʃərɪzm/ *n.* (Polit.) Thatcherismus, *der*

thaw /θɔː/
A *n.* **1** (warmth) Tauwetter, *das* **2** (act of thawing) **after the ~:** nachdem es getaut hat/hatte **3** (fig.) Tauwetter, *das;* Tauwetterperiode, *die*
B *v.i.* **1** (melt) auftauen **2** (become warm enough to melt ice etc.) tauen; **it looks like ~ing** es sieht nach Tauwetter aus **3** (fig.: become less aloof or hostile) auftauen **4** (lose numbness) [wieder] warm werden
C *v.t.* **1** (cause to melt) auftauen **2** (fig.: cause to be less aloof or hostile) auftauen; entspannen ‹*Atmosphäre*› **3** (cause to lose numbness) aufwärmen

Phrasal verb
• **~ 'out** ▸ **~ B, C**

the /*before vowel* ðɪ, *before consonant* ðə, *when stressed* ðiː/
A *def. art.* **1** der/die/das; **all ~ doors** alle Türen; **play ~ piano** Klavier spielen; **if you want a quick survey, this is ~ book** für einen raschen Überblick ist dies das richtige Buch; **it's** *or* **there's only ~ one** es ist nur dieser/diese/dieses eine; **he lives in ~ district** er wohnt in dieser Gegend; **he was quite ~ philosopher about his misfortune** er trug sein Unglück wie ein Philosoph; **£5 ~ square metre/~ gallon/~ kilogram** 5 Pfund der Quadratmeter/die Gallone/das Kilogramm; **14 miles to ~ gallon** 14 Meilen auf eine Gallone; ≈ 20 l auf 100 km; **a scale of one mile to ~ inch** ein Maßstab von 1 : 63360; **none but ~ brave deserves ~ fair** (prov.) allein dem Tapferen gehört die Schöne **2** (denoting one best known) **it is '~ restaurant in this town** das ist das Restaurant in dieser Stadt; **red is '~ colour this year** Rot ist in diesem Jahr die Farbe; **she is no relation to '~ Kipling** mit dem Kipling ist sie nicht verwandt **3** (with names of diseases) **have got ~ toothache/measles** (coll.) Zahnschmerzen/die Masern haben **4** (Brit. coll.: my, our, etc.) mein/unser *usw.*; **leave ~ wife and ~ dog at home** Frau und Hund zu Hause lassen **5** (Scot., Ir.: with name of clan) **~ Macnab** das Oberhaupt des Macnab-Klans
B *adv.* **~ more I practise ~ better I play** je mehr ich übe, desto *od.* umso besser spiele ich; **I am not ~ more inclined to help him because he is poor** ich würde ihm genauso gern helfen, wenn er nicht arm wäre; **his car runs ~ faster for having been tuned properly** jetzt, wo es richtig eingestellt ist, fährt sein Auto schneller; **so much ~ worse for sb./sth.** umso schlimmer für jmdn./etw.; *see also* **all C**; **more A 2, C 8**

theatre (*Amer.:* **theater**) /ˈθɪətə(r)/ *n.* **1** Theater, *das;* **at the ~:** im Theater; **go to the ~:** ins Theater gehen **2** (lecture ~) Hörsaal, *der* **3** (Brit. Med.) ▸**operating theatre** **4** (dramatic art) **the ~:** das Theater; **go into the ~:** zum Theater gehen (ugs.) **5** *no pl., no art.* **make good ~:** sehr bühnenwirksam sein; sich gut für die Bühne eignen **6** (scene of action) Schauplatz, *der;* (of war) Kriegsschauplatz, *der*

theatre: **~goer** *n.* Theaterbesucher, *der*/-besucherin, *die;* **~-going** **A** *n., no pl., no indef. art.* Theaterbesuche; **~-going is on the increase** die Zahl der Theaterbesucher steigt; **B** *adj.* **the ~-going public/type** die Theaterbesucher/der typische Theaterbesucher; **~ sister** *n.* (Brit. Med.) OP-Schwester, *die;* **~ weapon** *n.* (Mil.) Kurzstreckenrakete, *die;* **~ workshop** *n.* Theaterwerkstatt, *der*

theatrical /θɪˈætrɪkl/ *adj.* **1** schauspielerisch; **a ~ company** eine Schauspiel- *od.* Theatertruppe **2** (showy) theatralisch ‹*Benehmen, Verbeugung, Person*›

theatrically /θɪˈætrɪkəlɪ/ *adv.* **1** **~, the play was a disaster** was die Aufführung angeht, war das Stück ein Reinfall **2** (showily) theatralisch

theatricals /θɪˈætrɪklz/ *n. pl.* **1** (dramatic performances) Theateraufführungen; **private** *or* **amateur ~:** Amateur- *od.* Laientheater, *das* **2** (showy actions) Theatralik, *die* (geh.)

Thebes /θiːbz/ *pr. n.* (Greek/Egyptian Ant.) Theben (*das*)

thee /ðiː/ *pron.* (arch./poet./dial.) dich; (as indirect object) dir; (Relig.: God) Dich/Dir; *see also* **her¹**

theft /θeft/ *n.* Diebstahl, *der;* **~ of cars** Autodiebstahl, *der*

their /ðeə(r)/ *poss. pron. attrib.* **1** ihr; *see also* **her²**; **our 1** **2** (coll.: his or her) **who has forgotten ~ ticket?** wer hat seine Karte vergessen?

theirs /ðeəz/ *poss. pron. pred.* ihrer/ihre/ihres; *see also* **hers**; **ours**

theism /ˈθiːɪzm/ *n.* (Philos.) Theismus, *der*

theist /ˈθiːɪst/ *n.* (Philos.) Theist, *der*/Theistin, *die*

them /ðəm, *stressed* ðem/ *pron.* **1** sie; (as indirect object) ihnen; *see also* **her¹** **2** (coll.: him/her) ihn/sie

thematic /θɪˈmætɪk/ *adj.* thematisch

thematically /θɪˈmætɪkəlɪ/ *adv.* (with regard to topic[s]; also Mus.) thematisch; **arrange ~:** nach Themen ordnen

theme /θiːm/ *n.*
A **1** (of speaker, writer, or thinker) Gegenstand, *der;* Thema, *das* **2** (Mus.) Thema, *das;* **a ~ from 'My Fair Lady'** eine Melodie aus My Fair Lady **3** (Amer. Educ.) Aufsatz, *der*
B *v.t.* **~ sth. as sth.** etw. thematisch auf etw. (*Akk.*) ausrichten; etw. thematisch nach etw. (*Dat.*) gestalten; **~d** Themen‹*restaurant, -menü usw.*›

theme: **~ music** *n.* Titelmelodie, *die;* **~ park** *n.* Themenpark, *der;* **~ pub** *n.* Themenkneipe, *die;* **~ restaurant** *n.* Themenrestaurant, *das;* **~ song** *n.* Erkennungssong, *der;* **~ tune** *n.* (Radio, Telev.) Erkennungsmelodie, *die*

themselves /ðəm'selvz/ *pron.* 1) *emphat.* selbst; **they ~ were astonished** sie waren selbst ganz erstaunt; **the results ~ were ...:** die Ergebnisse an sich waren ... 2) *refl.* sich ‹*waschen usw.*›; sich selbst ‹*die Schuld geben, regieren*›. *See also* **herself**; **ourselves**

then /ðen/

A *adv.* 1) (at that time) damals; **the ~ existing laws** die damals geltenden *od.* damaligen Gesetze; **~ and there, there and ~:** auf der Stelle; *see also* **now A 1** 2) (after that) dann; ~ **[again]** (and also) außerdem; **the journey will take a long time, and ~ don't forget that it gets dark early** die Fahrt wird lange dauern, und dann dürft ihr auch nicht vergessen, dass es früh dunkel wird; **but ~** (after all) aber schließlich 3) (in that case) dann; **~ why didn't you say so?** warum hast du dann nichts gesagt?; **hurry up, ~:** dann beeil dich aber; **but ~ again** aber andererseits 4) *expr. grudging or impatient concession* dann eben; **well, take it, ~:** dann nimm es eben 5) (accordingly) [dann] also; **the cause of the accident, ~, seems to be established** die Ursache des Unfalls scheint [dann] also festzustehen. *See also* **well² A 4, 7**; **what E 1**

B *n.* **before ~:** vorher; davor; **by ~:** bis dahin; **from ~ on** von da an; **till ~:** bis dahin; **oh, we should get there long before ~:** ach, bis dahin sind wir längst dort; **since ~:** seitdem

C *adj.* damalig

thence /ðens/ *adv.* (formal) 1) **[from] ~:** von dort 2) (for that reason) von daher

thence: **~'forth**, **~'forward** *advs.* (arch./literary) **[from] ~forth** *or* **~forward** seit dieser Zeit; von da an

theocracy /θiː'ɒkrəsɪ/ *n., no pl.* Theokratie, *die*

theodolite /θɪ'ɒdəlaɪt/ *n.* (Surv.) Theodolit, *der*

theologian /θiːə'ləʊdʒɪən/ *n.* Theologe, *der*/Theologin, *die*

theological /θiːə'lɒdʒɪkl/ *adj.* theologisch; Theologie‹*student, -dozent*›

theologist /θiː'ɒlədʒɪst/ *n.* Theologe, *der*/Theologin, *die*

theology /θɪ'ɒlədʒɪ/ *n.* 1) *no pl., no indef. art.* Theologie, *die* 2) (religious system) Glaubenslehre, *die*

theorem /'θɪərəm/ *n.* (Math.) [Lehr]satz, *der*; Theorem, *das* (fachspr.)

theoretic /θɪə'retɪk/, **theoretical** /θɪə'retɪkl/ *adj.* theoretisch; **your arguments are only ~al** deine Argumentation ist reine Theorie

theoretically /θiːə'retɪkəlɪ/ *adv.* theoretisch

theoretician /θɪərɪ'tɪʃn/ *n.* Theoretiker, *der*/Theoretikerin, *die*

theorise ▸ **theorize**

theorist /'θɪərɪst/ *n.* Theoretiker, *der*/Theoretikerin, *die*

theorize /'θɪəraɪz/ *v.i.* theoretisieren

theory /'θɪərɪ/ *n.* (also Math.) Theorie, *die*; **~ of evolution/music** Evolutions-/Musiktheorie, *die*; **in ~:** theoretisch; **it's a ~!** das wäre eine Möglichkeit; **I always go on the ~ that ...:** ich gehe immer davon aus, dass ...; **have a ~ that ...:** die Theorie vertreten, dass ...

theosophic /θiːə'sɒfɪk/, **theosophical** /θiːə'sɒfɪkl/ *adj.* theosophisch

theosophy /θɪ'ɒsəfɪ/ *n., no pl., no indef. art.* Theosophie, *die*

therapeutic /θerə'pjuːtɪk/ *adj.* therapeutisch; (curative) therapeutisch wirksam

therapeutically /θerə'pjuːtɪkəlɪ/ *adv.* therapeutisch

therapeutics /θerə'pjuːtɪks/ *n., no pl.* (Med.) Therapeutik, *die*

therapist /'θerəpɪst/ *n.* (Med.) Therapeut, *der*/Therapeutin, *die*

therapy /'θerəpɪ/ *n.* (Med., Psych.) Therapie, *die*; [Heil]behandlung, *die*; **undergo ~:** sich einer Therapie (*Dat.*) unterziehen

there /ðeə(r)/

A *adv.* 1) (in/at that place) da; dort; (fairly close) da; **sb. has been ~ before** (fig. coll.) jmd. weiß Bescheid; **~ or ~a'bouts** so ungefähr; **be down/in/up ~:** da unten/drin/oben sein; **~ goes ...:** da geht/fährt *usw.* ...; **are you ~?** (on telephone) sind Sie noch da *od.* (ugs.) dran?; **~ and then = then and ~** ▸ **then A 1**; *see also* **all C**; **here A 1** 2) (calling attention) **hello** *or* **hi ~!** hallo!; **you ~!** Sie da!; **move along ~!** weitergehen!; **~'s a good** *etc.* **boy/girl** das ist lieb [von dir], mein Junge/Mädchen; *see also* **for A 8** 3) (in that respect) da; **so '~:** und damit basta (ugs.); **~ you are wrong** da irrst du dich; **~, it is a loose wire** da haben wirs — ein loser Draht; **~ it is** (nothing can be done about it) da kann man nichts machen; **~ you are**, (coll.) **~ we go** (giving sth.) [da,] bitte schön; **~ you have it** (fig.) da ist der Punkt; *see also* **B 2**; **rub C** 4) (to that place) dahin, dorthin ‹*gehen, gelangen, fahren, rücken, stellen*›; **we got ~ and back in two hours** wir brauchten für Hin- und Rückweg [nur] zwei Stunden; **down/in/up ~:** dort hinunter/hinein/hinauf; **get ~ first** jmdm./den anderen zuvorkommen; **get ~** (fig.) (achieve) es [schon] schaffen; (understand) es verstehen 5) /ðə(r), *stressed* ðeə(r)/ (as introductory function word) da; **was ~ anything in it?** war da irgendetwas drin? (ugs.); **~ is/are ...** es gibt ...; **~ is enough food** es gibt genug zu essen; **~ are many kinds of ...:** es gibt viele Arten von ...; **~ were four of them** sie waren zu viert; **~ was once an old woman who ...:** es war einmal eine alte Frau, die ...; **~ was no beer left** es gab kein Bier mehr; **~ appears to be some error** da scheint ein Irrtum unterlaufen zu sein; **~'s no time for that now** dafür haben wir/habe ich jetzt keine Zeit; **~ being no further point in waiting, I left** weil es keinen Zweck mehr hatte, noch länger zu warten, ging ich; **... if ever ~ was one ...** wie er/sie/es im Buche steht; **what is ~ for supper?** was gibts zum Abendessen?; **not a sound was ~ to indicate their presence** kein Laut verriet ihre Anwesenheit; **seldom has ~ been more fuss** selten hat es so viel Aufhebens gegeben; **a fine mess ~ is!** da sieht es vielleicht aus! (ugs.)

B /ðeə(r)/ *int.* 1) (to soothe child etc.) **~, ~:** na, na (ugs.) 2) *expr. triumph or dismay* **~ [you are]!** da, siehst du!; **~, you've dropped it!** da, jetzt hast du es doch fallen lassen!; *see also* **A 3**

C *n.* da, dort; **near ~:** da *od.* dort in der Nähe; **the tide comes up to ~:** die Flut kommt bis dahin *od.* da hoch

there: **~abouts** /'ðeərəbaʊts/ *adv.* 1) (near that place) da [in der Nähe]; **the locals ~abouts** die Leute, die dort wohnen; 2) (near that number) **two litres or ~abouts** zwei Liter [so] ungefähr; *see also* **there A 1**; **~'after** *adv.* danach; **~by** /ðeə'baɪ, 'ðeəbaɪ/ *adv.* dadurch; **~by hangs a tale** dazu gibt es noch etwas zu erzählen; **~fore** *adv.* deshalb; also; **~'from** *adv.* (arch.) daraus; **~'in** *adv.* (formal) darin; **~'of** *adv.* (formal) davon; **the island and all the ports ~of** die Insel und alle ihre Häfen; **~'to** *adv.* (formal) dazu; **~u'pon** *adv.* 1) (soon after that) kurz darauf; alsbald (veralt.); 2) (in consequence of that) daraufhin; **~'with** *adv.* (formal) damit

therm /θɜːm/ *n.* (Brit.) *englische Einheit der Wärmemenge (ca. 1,055×10⁸ J)*

thermal /'θɜːml/

A *adj.* thermisch ‹*Erscheinung, Anforderungen*›; Wärme‹*dämmung, -strahlung*›; **~ underwear** kälteisolierende Unterwäsche

B *n.* (Aeronaut.) Thermik, *die*

thermal imaging /θɜːml'ɪmɪdʒɪŋ/ *n.* Thermographie, *die* (fachspr.); Wärmebildtechnik, *die*; **~ camera** Wärmebildkamera, *die*; Thermokamera, *die*

thermally /'θɜːməlɪ/ *adv.* thermisch

thermal: **~ 'springs** *n. pl.* Thermalquelle, *die*; **~ 'unit** *n.* (Phys.) Wärmeeinheit, *die*

thermionic /θɜːmɪ'ɒnɪk/: **~ 'tube** (Amer.), **~ 'valve** (Brit.) *ns.* (Electronics) Glühkathodenröhre, *die*

thermobaric /θɜːməʊ'bærɪk/ *adj.* thermobarisch ‹*Waffe*›

thermocouple /'θɜːməʊkʌpl/ *n.* (Phys.) Thermoelement, *das*

thermodynamic /θɜːməʊdaɪ'næmɪk/ *adj.* thermodynamisch

thermodynamics /θɜːməʊdaɪ'næmɪks/ *n., no pl.* (Phys.) Thermodynamik, *die*

thermometer /θə'mɒmɪtə(r)/ *n.* Thermometer, *das*; *see also* **clinical 1**

thermonuclear /θɜːməʊ'njuːklɪə(r)/ *adj.* (Phys.) thermonuklear ‹*Waffe*›; Kern‹*fusion, -energie*›; Atom‹*krieg, -energie*›

thermoplastic /θɜːməʊ'plæstɪk/

A *adj.* 1) thermoplastisch 2) **~ tiles** Kunststofffliesen

B *n.* Thermoplast, *der*

Thermos ® /'θɜːməs/ *n.* **~ [flask/jug/bottle]** Thermosflasche, *die* (Wz)

thermostat /'θɜːməstæt/ *n.* Thermostat, *der*

thermostatic /θɜːmə'stætɪk/ *adj.* Temperatur‹*regler, -schalter*›

thermostatically /θɜːmə'stætɪklɪ/ *adv.* durch ein/das Thermostat ‹*kontrolliert, reguliert*›

thesaurus /θɪ'sɔːrəs/ *n., pl.* **thesauri** /θɪ'sɔːraɪ/ *or* **~es** Thesaurus, *der*

these *pl. of* **this A, B**

thesis /'θiːsɪs/ *n., pl.* **theses** /'θiːsiːz/ 1) (proposition) These, *die* 2) (dissertation) Dissertation, *die*, Doktorarbeit, *die* (**on** über + *Akk.*)

thespian /'θespɪən/ (formal)

A *adj.* Theater-

B *n.* Schauspieler, *der*/Schauspielerin, *die*

they /ðeɪ/ *pron.* 1) sie 2) (people in general) man 3) (coll.: he or she) **everyone thinks ~ know best** jeder denkt, er weiß es am besten 4) (those in authority) sie; die (ugs.). *see also* **their**; **theirs**; **them**; **themselves**

they'd /ðeɪd/ 1) **= they would** 2) **= they had**

they'll /ðeɪl/ **= they will**

they're /ðeə(r)/ **= they are**

they've /ðeɪv/ **= they have**

thick /θɪk/

A *adj.* 1) dick; breit, dick ‹*Linie*›; (with measurement) stark; **that's laying it on [a bit] ~** (fig. coll.) das ist ja wohl etwas dick aufgetragen (ugs.); **isn't she laying it on a bit ~?** (fig. coll.) trägt sie da nicht ein bisschen zu dick auf? (ugs.); **that's** *or* **it's a bit ~!** (Brit. fig. coll.) das ist ein starkes Stück! (ugs.); **get the ~ end of the stick** (fig.) den schlechteren Teil erwischen; **have a ~ skin** (fig.) ein dickes Fell haben (ugs.); **a rope two inches ~, a two-inch ~ rope** ein zwei Zoll starkes *od.* dickes Seil 2) (dense) dicht ‹*Haar, Nebel, Wolken, Gestrüpp usw.*›; dicht gedrängt ‹*Menschenmenge*›; (not clear) trüb ‹*Wetter*›; tief ‹*Dunkelheit*›; **have a ~ head** einen dicken Kopf haben (ugs.) 3) (filled) **~ with** voll von; **air ~ with fog and smoke** von Nebel und Rauch erfüllte Luft; **the air was ~ with rumours** überall gingen Gerüchte um; **the furniture was ~ with dust** auf den Möbeln lag eine dicke Staubschicht 4) (of firm consistency) steif ‹*Gallerte*›; dickflüssig ‹*Sahne*›; (containing much solid matter) dick ‹*Suppe, Schlamm, Brei, Kleister*› 5) (coll.: stupid) dumm; **you're just plain ~:** du bist ganz einfach doof (salopp); **[as] ~ as two short planks** dumm wie Bohnenstroh (ugs.) 6) (coll.: intimate) **be very ~ with sb.** mit jmdm. dick befreundet sein (ugs.); **be [as] ~ as thieves** dicke Freunde sein (ugs.) 7) (Printing) fett 8) (numerous) dicht; **they are ~/not exactly ~ on the ground** die gibt es wie Sand am Meer/die sind dünn gesät (ugs.) 9) (indistinct) dumpf; **his speech was ~** (with drink) er sprach mit schwerer Zunge (geh.) 10) (marked) **he has a ~ German accent** er hat einen starken deutschen Akzent

B *n., no pl., no indef. art.* **in the ~ of** mitten in (+ *Dat.*); **in the ~ of it** *or* **things** mitten drin; **in the ~ of the battle** im dichtesten Kampfgetümmel; **she is always in the ~ of things** sie ist bei allem immer voll dabei (ugs.); **stay with sb./stick together through ~ and thin** mit jmdm./zusammen durch dick und dünn gehen

C *adv.* **snow was falling ~:** es schneite dicke Flocken; **blows rained on him ~ and fast** die Schläge prasselten nur so auf ihn nieder; **job offers/complaints came in ~ and fast** es kam eine Flut von Stellenangeboten/Beschwerden

thick 'ear *n.* (Brit. coll.) **give sb. a ~:** jmdm. ein paar hinter die Ohren geben (ugs.)

thicken /ˈθɪkn/
A *v.t.* dicker machen; eindicken ‹*Sauce*›
B *v.i.* **1** dicker werden **2** (become dense) ‹*Nebel:*› dichter werden **3** (become blurred) **his speech ~ed** er bekam eine schwere Zunge (geh.) **4** (become complex) **the plot ~s!** die Sache wird kompliziert!; (iron.) die Sache wird langsam interessant!

thickening /ˈθɪknɪŋ/ *n.* (in food) Bindemittel, *das;* (in dye) Verdickungsmittel, *das*

thicket /ˈθɪkɪt/ *n.* Dickicht, *das*

thick: ~ 'head *n.* dicker Kopf (ugs.); **~head** *n.* Dummkopf, *der;* **~'headed** *adj.* dumm

thickly /ˈθɪklɪ/ *adv.* **1** (in a thick layer) dick **2** (densely, abundantly) dicht **3** (in great numbers) **hailstones fell ~:** die Hagelkörner prasselten nur so herab **4** (indistinctly) mit schwerer Zunge (geh.); (from emotion) undeutlich ‹*sprechen*›

thickness /ˈθɪknɪs/ *n.* **1** Dicke, *die;* (with measurement) Stärke, *die;* **be two metres in ~:** zwei Meter dick sein; **a plank whose ~ is two centimetres** ein Brett mit einer Dicke *od.* Stärke von 2 Zentimetern; **~ of paper/card** Papier-/Kartonstärke, *die* **2** *no pl.* (denseness) Dichte, *die;* (of hair) Fülle, *die* **3** *no pl.* (firm consistency) (of jelly) Steifheit, *die;* (of cream) Dickflüssigkeit, *die;* (of soup, mud, porridge, glue) Dicke, *die* **4** (layer) Lage, *die* **5** *no pl.* (coll.: stupidity) Dummheit, *die*

thicko /ˈθɪkəʊ/ *n., pl.* **~s** (coll.) Schwachkopf, *der* (ugs.)

thick: ~set *adj.* **1** (stocky) gedrungen; **2** (set close together) dicht nebeneinander stehend ‹*Bäume, Häuser*›; **~-skinned** *adj.* (fig.) unsensibel; dickfellig (ugs. abwertend)

thief /θiːf/ *n., pl.* **thieves** /θiːvz/ Dieb, *der*/Diebin, *die;* **like** *or* **as a ~ in the night** wie ein Dieb in der Nacht (geh.); *see also* **Latin B**; **take A 17**; **thick A 6**

thieve /θiːv/
A *v.i.* stehlen; **he makes a living out of petty thieving** er lebt vom Gelegenheitsdiebstahl
B *v.t.* stehlen

thieves *pl. of* **thief**

thievish /ˈθiːvɪʃ/ *adj.* diebisch ‹*Wesen, Art*›

thigh /θaɪ/ *n.* **1** ▸ⓘ **p. 951** (Anat.) Oberschenkel, *der* **2** (Zool.) Schenkel, *der*

thigh: ~ bone *n.* (Anat.) Oberschenkelknochen, *der;* **~ boot** *n.* Kanonenstiefel, *der;* Schaftstiefel, *der*

-thighed /θaɪd/ *adj. in comb.* -schenkelig

thimble /ˈθɪmbl/ *n.* Fingerhut, *der*

thimbleful /ˈθɪmblfʊl/ *n.* Fingerhut [voll], *der;* **in ~s** in winzigen Mengen

thin /θɪn/
A *adj.* **1** (of small thickness or diameter) dünn; *see also* **ice A 1**; **wedge A 1** **2** (not fat) dünn; **a tall, ~ man** ein großer, hagerer Mann; **as ~ as a rake** *or* **lath** spindeldürr **3** (narrow) schmal ‹*Baumreihe*›; dünn ‹*Linie*› **4** (sparse) dünn, schütter ‹*Haar*›; fein ‹*Regen, Dunst*›; spärlich ‹*Publikum, Besuch*›; gering ‹*Beteiligung*›; dünn ‹*Luft*›; **the country's population is ~:** das Land ist dünn bevölkert *od.* besiedelt; **he is already ~ on top** *or* **going ~ on top** bei ihm lichtet es sich oben schon; **the attendance at the meeting was ~:** die Versammlung war schwach besucht; **be ~ on the ground** (fig.) dünn gesät sein; **vanish** *or* **disappear into ~ air** (fig.) sich in Luft auflösen; **it won't appear out of ~ air!** (fig.) es fällt nicht einfach vom Himmel!; **produce a delicious meal out of ~ air** (fig.) ein köstliches Essen aus dem Nichts zaubern **5** (lacking substance or strength) dünn ‹*Bier, Blut, Stimme*› **6** (fig.: inadequate) dürftig; fadenscheinig ‹*Ausrede*›; **sb.'s patience is wearing ~:** jmds. Geduld geht zu Ende; jmdm. reißt allmählich der Geduldsfaden (ugs.); **sb.'s credibility begins to wear ~:** jmd. verliert immer mehr an Glaubwürdigkeit **7** (coll.: wretched) enttäuschend, unbefriedigend ‹*Zeit*›; **he had a pretty ~ time [of it]** er machte eine ziemlich schlimme Zeit durch **8** (consisting of ~ lines) fein ‹*Handschrift*›; (Printing) mager. *see also* **thick B**
B *adv.* dünn
C *v.t.,* **-nn-** **1** (make less deep or broad) dünner machen **2** (make less dense, dilute) verdünnen **3** (reduce in number) dezimieren **4** (remove young fruit from) ausbrechen ‹*Reben*›; ausdünnen ‹*Obstbäume*›
D *v.i.,* **-nn-** ‹*Haar, Nebel:*› sich lichten; ‹*Menschenmenge:*› sich zerstreuen; **~ down to a mere trickle** zu einem kleinen Rinnsal werden

Phrasal verb

• **~ 'out**
A *v.i.* ‹*Menschenmenge:*› sich verlaufen; ‹*Verkehr:*› abnehmen; ‹*Reihen der Zuschauer:*› sich lichten; ‹*Häuser:*› spärlicher werden
B *v.t.* (Hort., Forestry) vereinzeln, ausdünnen ‹*Pflanzen*›; lichten ‹*Wald*›

'thin-cut *adj.* dünn *od.* fein geschnitten; **~ marmalade** Orangenmarmelade mit fein geschnittenen Schalen

thine /ðaɪn/ *poss. pron.* (arch./poet./dial.) **1** *pred.* deiner/deine/dein[e]s; der/die/das Deinige (geh.); *see also* **hers** **2** *attrib.* dein

thing /θɪŋ/ *n.* **1** (inanimate object) Sache, *die;* Ding, *das;* **what's that ~ in your hand?** was hast du da in der Hand?; **be a rare ~:** etwas Seltenes sein; **books are strange** *or* (coll.) **funny ~s, aren't they?** Bücher sind schon etwas Seltsames, nicht wahr?; **neither one ~ nor the other** weder das eine noch das andere; **I haven't a ~ to wear** ich habe nichts zum Anziehen; **you haven't a ~ to worry about** du brauchst dir überhaupt keine Sorgen zu machen; **not a ~:** überhaupt *od.* gar nichts
2 (action) **that was a foolish/friendly ~ to do** das war eine große Dummheit/das war sehr freundlich; **that was a mean ~ to do to your brother** das war sehr gemein deinem Bruder gegenüber; **it was the right ~ to do** es war das einzig Richtige; **she is expecting to do great ~s** sie hat große Dinge vor; **the only ~ now is to shout for help** es bleibt uns jetzt nichts anderes mehr übrig, als um Hilfe zu rufen; **we can't do a ~ about it** wir können nichts dagegen tun; **do ~s to sb./sth.** (fig. coll.) auf jmdn./etw. eine enorme Wirkung haben (ugs.); **she does ~s to me** (fig. coll.) sie macht mich total an (ugs.)
3 (fact) [Tat]sache, *die;* **a ~ which is well known to everybody** eine allgemein bekannte Tatsache; **it's a strange ~ that ...:** es ist seltsam, dass ...; **for one ~, you don't have enough money[, for another ~ ...]** zunächst einmal hast du nicht genügend Geld [, außerdem ...]; **and another ~, why were you late this morning?** und noch etwas: Warum bist du heute Morgen so spät gekommen?; **the best/worst ~ about the situation/her** das Beste/Schlimmste an der Situation/an ihr; **know/learn a ~ or two about sth./sb.** sich mit etw./jmdm. auskennen/einiges über etw. (*Akk.*) lernen/über jmdn. erfahren; **I'll teach him a ~ or two!** dem werde ichs [mal] zeigen!; **the [only] ~ is that ...:** die Sache ist [nur] die, dass ...; *see also* **another A 1, 4, B 3**
4 (idea) **say the first ~ that comes into one's head** das sagen, was einem gerade so einfällt; **what a ~ to say!** wie kann man nur so etwas sagen!; **have a ~ about sb./sth.** (coll.) (be obsessed about) auf jmdn./etw. abfahren (salopp); (be prejudiced about) etwas gegen jmdn./etw. haben; (be afraid of or repulsed by) einen Horror vor jmdm./etw. haben (ugs.)
5 (task) **she has a reputation for getting ~s done** sie ist für ihre Tatkraft bekannt; **a big ~ to undertake** ein großes Unterfangen
6 (affair) Sache, *die;* Angelegenheit, *die;* **make a mess of ~s** alles vermasseln (salopp); **make a [big] ~ of sth.** (regard as essential) auf etw. besonderen Wert legen; (get excited about) sich über etw. (*Akk.*) aufregen; **you don't have to make such a big ~ of it!** nun mach mal halblang! (ugs.); **it's one ~ after another** es kommt eins zum anderen
7 (circumstance) **take ~s too seriously** alles zu ernst nehmen; **how are ~s?** wie gehts [dir]?; **it was a terrible ~:** es war furchtbar; **a strange ~ struck me** mir fiel etwas Seltsames auf; **it was a lucky ~ he didn't do that** es war ein Glück, dass er das nicht tat; **as ~s stand [with me]** so wie die Dinge [bei mir] liegen; **one has to accept these ~s** man muss sich eben damit abfinden; **~s don't work out like that** die Realität sieht anders aus; **it's just one of those ~s** (coll.) so was kommt schon mal vor (ugs.); *see also* **close A 7**; **good A 2**
8 (individual, creature) Ding, *das;* **she is in hospital, poor ~:** sie ist im Krankenhaus, das arme Ding; **you spiteful ~!** du [gemeines] Biest!; **she's a kind old ~:** sie ist sehr liebenswürdig *od.* (ugs.) furchtbar nett; *see also* **old A 3, 4**
9 *in pl.* (personal belongings, outer clothing) Sachen; **put one's ~s on** sich (*Dat.*) etwas überziehen; **wash up the dinner ~s** das Geschirr vom Abendessen abwaschen
10 *in pl.* (matters) **an expert/authority on ~s historical** ein Fachmann/eine Autorität in geschichtlichen Fragen; **as regards ~s financial I haven't a clue** von finanziellen Dingen habe ich keine Ahnung; **~s feminine** Frauenangelegenheiten; **and ~s** (coll.) und so (ugs.)
11 (product of work) Sache, *die;* **the latest ~ in hats** der letzte Schrei in der Hutmode; **a little ~ of mine** etwas von mir
12 (special interest) **what's your ~?** was machst du gerne?; **do one's own ~** (coll.) sich selbst verwirklichen; **we each do our own ~ on holiday** im Urlaub macht jeder von uns, was er will
13 (coll.: sth. remarkable) **now 'there's a ~!** das ist ja ein Ding! (ugs.)
14 *in pl.* (Law) Sachen; **~s real** unbewegliche Sachen; Immobilien; **~s personal** bewegliche Sachen; Mobilien (fachspr.)
15 **the ~** (what is proper or needed or important) das Richtige; **blue jeans are the ~ among teenagers** Bluejeans sind der Hit (ugs.) unter den Teenagern; **telling jokes is not the ~ for an occasion such as this one** es ist unpassend, bei einer Gelegenheit wie dieser Witze zu erzählen; **the ~ is to get orders** es geht vor allem darum, Aufträge zu bekommen; **the ~ about him is his complete integrity** sein wesentlicher Vorzug ist seine vollkommene Integrität; **but the ~ is, will she come in fact?** aber die Frage ist, wird sie auch tatsächlich kommen?
16 (sl.: penis) **his ~:** sein Ding (ugs.). *See also* **first A, B 1**; **good A 4**; **last[1] A**; **see[1] A 1**; **sure C**

thingamy /ˈθɪŋəmɪ/, **thingumabob** /ˈθɪŋəməbɒb/, **thingumajig** /ˈθɪŋəmədʒɪɡ/, **thingumbob** /ˈθɪŋəmbɒb/, **thingummy** /ˈθɪŋəmɪ/, **thingy** /ˈθɪŋɪ/ *ns.* (coll.) Dings, *der/die/das* (salopp); Dingsbums, *der/die/das* (ugs.); **you know, ~, ...** (person) du weißt schon, der/die Dingsda, ...; (object) du weißt schon, das Dingsda, ...

think /θɪŋk/
A *v.t.,* **thought** /θɔːt/ **1** (consider) meinen; **we ~ [that] he will come** wir denken *od.* glauben, dass er kommt; **we do not ~ it probable** wir halten es nicht für wahrscheinlich; **I ~ it a shame that ...:** ich finde, es ist eine Schande, dass ...; **he ~s himself very fine** er meint, er sei etwas Besonderes; **it is not thought proper** es gilt als unschicklich; **he is thought to be a fraud** man hält ihn für einen Betrüger; **what do you ~?** was meinst du?; **what do you ~ of** *or* **about him/it?** was hältst du von ihm/davon?; **I thought to myself ...:** ich dachte mir [im Stillen] ...; **that's what 'they ~!** das meinen die!; **..., don't you ~?** ..., findest *od.* meinst du nicht auch?; **where do you ~ you are?** was glaubst du eigentlich, wo du bist?; **who does he/she ~ he/she is?** für wen *od.* wofür hält er/sie sich eigentlich?; **you** *or* **one** *or* **anyone would ~ that ...:** man sollte [doch] eigentlich annehmen, dass ...; **I ~ not** ich glaube nicht; **I should '~ so/~ 'not!** (indignant) das will ich meinen/das will ich nicht hoffen; **I thought as much** *or* **so** das habe ich mir schon gedacht; **I ~ so** ich glaube schon; **do you really ~ so?** findest du wirklich?; **I wouldn't ~ so** das glaube ich kaum; **yes, I ~ so too** ja, das finde ich auch (ugs.); **I should ~ not!** (no!) auf keinen Fall; **you are a model of tact, I 'don't ~!** (coll. iron.) du bist mir vielleicht ein Ausbund von Taktgefühl! (iron.); **that'll be great fun, I 'don't ~** (coll. iron.) das kann ja

lustig werden (ugs. iron.); **I'll have made my fortune by then, I 'don't ~** (coll. iron.) na klar, bis dahin habe ich mein Glück gemacht (iron.); **to ~ [that] he should treat me like this!** man sollte es nicht für möglich halten, dass er mich so behandelt!; **this animal was thought to be extinct** dieses Tier galt als ausgestorben; **I wouldn't have thought it possible** ich hätte das nicht für möglich gehalten
2 (coll.: remember) **~ to do sth.** daran denken, etw. zu tun
3 (intend) **he ~s to deceive us** er will uns täuschen; **we thought to return early** wir hatten vor *od.* gedachten, früh zurückzukehren; **that's what 'they ~!** das meinen di̲e̲ [vielleicht]!
4 (imagine) sich (*Dat.*) vorstellen

B *v.i.*, **thought** **1** [nach]denken; **I ~, therefore I am** ich denke, also bin ich; **we want to make the students ~:** wir möchten die Studenten zum Denken bringen; **animals cannot ~:** Tiere können nicht denken; **I need time to ~:** ich muss es mir erst überlegen; **ability to ~:** Denkfähigkeit, *die;* **I've been ~ing** ich habe nachgedacht; **~ in German** *etc.* deutsch *usw.* denken; **it makes you ~:** es macht *od.* stimmt einen nachdenklich; **just ~!** stell dir das mal vor!; **~ for oneself** sich (*Dat.*) seine eigene Meinung bilden; **~ [to oneself] …:** sich (*Dat.*) im stillen denken …; bei sich denken …; **let me ~:** lass [mich] mal nachdenken *od.* überlegen; **I would ~ again** ich würde mir das noch mal überlegen; **there's still time to ~ again** du kannst/wir können das noch einmal überdenken; **you'd better ~ again!** da hast du dich aber geschnitten! (ugs.); **~ twice** es sich (*Dat.*) zweimal überlegen; **this made her ~ twice** das gab ihr zu denken; **~ twice about doing sth.** es sich (*Dat.*) zweimal überlegen, ob man etw. tut; **~ on one's feet** (coll.) sich (*Dat.*) aus dem Stegreif etwas überlegen; *see also* **big B**
2 (have intention) **I ~ I'll try** ich glaube *od.* denke, ich werde es versuchen; **we ~ we'll enter for the regatta** wir haben vor, an der Regatta teilzunehmen. *See also* **aloud; fit² A 3**

C *n.* (coll.) **have a [good] ~:** es sich (*Dat.*) gut überlegen; **have a ~ about that!** denk mal drüber nach! (ugs.); **you have [got] another ~ coming!** da irrst du dich aber gewaltig!

Phrasal verbs

- **~ about** *v.t.* **1** (consider) nachdenken über (+ *Akk.*); **what are you ~ing about?** woran *od.* was denkst du [gerade]?; **give sb. something to ~ about** jmdm. etwas geben, worüber er/sie nachdenken kann; (to worry about) jmdm. zu denken geben; **it doesn't bear ~ing about** man darf gar nicht daran denken **2** (consider practicability of) sich (*Dat.*) durch den Kopf gehen lassen; sich (*Dat.*) überlegen; **it's worth ~ing about** es ist überlegenswert
- **~ a'head** *v.i.* vorausdenken
- **~ 'back to** *v.t.* sich zurückerinnern an (+ *Akk.*); **I thought back to when it had first begun** ich erinnerte mich daran, wie es anfing
- **~ of** *v.t.* **1** (consider) denken an (+ *Akk.*); **I have many things to ~ of** ich muss an so vieles denken; **… but I can't ~ of everything at once!** … aber ich habe schließlich auch nur einen Kopf!; **he ~s of everything** er denkt einfach an alles; **he never ~s of anyone but himself** er denkt immer nur an sich; **[just] ~** *or* **to ~ of it!** man stelle sich (*Dat.*) *od.* stell dir das bloß vor!; **[now I] come to ~ of it, …:** wenn ich es mir recht überlege, … **2** (be aware of in the mind) denken an (+ *Akk.*); **we ~ of you a lot** wir denken oft an dich **3** (consider the possibility of) denken an (+ *Akk.*); **we must be ~ing of going home soon** wir müssen bald ans Nachhausegehen denken; **be ~ing of getting a new car** mit dem Gedanken spielen, sich (*Dat.*) ein neues Auto anzuschaffen; **be ~ing of resigning** sich mit dem Gedanken tragen, zurückzutreten; **not for a minute would she ~ of helping anybody else** ihr würde es nicht im Traum einfallen, anderen zu helfen; **I couldn't ~ of such a thing** *or* **of doing that** das würde mir nicht im Traum einfallen; **I don't know what she was ~ing of!** ich weiß nicht, was sie sich dabei gedacht hat! **4** (choose from what one knows) **I want you to ~ of a word beginning with B** überlege dir ein Wort, das mit B beginnt; **~ of a number, double it and …:** denk dir eine Zahl, verdoppele sie und … **5** (have as idea) **we'll ~ of something** wir werden uns etwas einfallen lassen; **can you ~ of anyone who …?** fällt dir jemand ein, der …?; **we're still trying to ~ of a suitable title for the book** wir suchen noch immer einen passenden Titel für das Buch; **he's never yet thought of showing gratitude** bis jetzt ist es ihm noch nie eingefallen, sich dankbar zu zeigen; **I would have telephoned if I had thought of it** ich hätte angerufen, wenn ich daran gedacht hätte; **what 'will they ~ of next?** was werden sie sich (*Dat.*) wohl [sonst] noch alles einfallen lassen? **6** (remember) sich erinnern an (+ *Akk.*); **I just can't ~ of her name** ich komme einfach nicht auf ihren Namen **7** **~ little/nothing of sb./sth.** (consider contemptible) wenig/nichts von jmdm./etw. halten; **~ little/nothing of doing sth.** (consider insignificant) wenig/nichts dabei finden, etw. zu tun; **~ much** *or* **a lot** *or* **well** *or* **highly of sb./sth.** viel von jmdm./etw. halten; **not ~ much of sb./sth.** nicht viel von jmdm./etw. halten. *See also* **better C 1**
- **~ 'out** *v.t.* **1** (consider carefully) durchdenken ‹*Plan, Idee*›; **~ out what the long-term solution may be** sich (*Dat.*) darüber Gedanken machen, wie eine langfristige Lösung aussehen könnte **2** (devise) sich (*Dat.*) ausdenken ‹*Plan, Verfahren*›; **the plan had been thought out in a hurry** der Plan entstand unter Zeitdruck
- **~ 'over** *v.t.* sich (*Dat.*) überlegen; überdenken; **~ things over** die Lage überdenken; **I will ~ it over** ich lasse es mir durch den Kopf gehen
- **~ 'through** *v.t.* [gründlich] durchdenken ‹*Problem, Angelegenheit*›
- **~ 'up** *v.t.* (coll.) sich (*Dat.*) ausdenken ‹*Plan*›; **they thought up ideas of their own** sie entwickelten ihre eigenen Ideen

thinkable /ˈθɪŋkəbl/ *adj.* **1** (capable of being thought about) denkbar **2** (conceivably possible) vorstellbar

thinker /ˈθɪŋkə(r)/ *n.* Denker, *der*/Denkerin, *die*

thinking /ˈθɪŋkɪŋ/

A *n.* **in modern ~ …** nach heutiger Auffassung …; **what is your ~ on this question?** wie ist deine Meinung zu dieser Frage?; **to my [way of] ~:** meiner Meinung nach

B *attrib. adj.* [vernünftig] denkend

'thinking cap *n.* **put on one's ~:** scharf nachdenken; seinen Geist anstrengen

think: ~ piece *n.* Kommentar, *der;* **~ tank** *n.* **1** (organization) Denkfabrik, *die;* **2** (Amer. coll.: brain) [Ge]hirnkasten, *der* (salopp scherzh.)

'thin-lipped *adj.* dünnlippig ‹*Mund, Person*›

thinly /ˈθɪnlɪ/ *adv.* **1** dünn **2** (sparsely) spärlich ‹*bevölkert, bewaldet*›; dünn ‹*besiedelt*›; schwach ‹*besucht*› **3** (inadequately) leicht ‹*bekleidet*›; (fig.) dürftig ‹*verschleiert, verkleidet*›

thinner /ˈθɪnə(r)/

A *adj., adv. compar. of* **thin A, B**

B *n.* **~[s]** Verdünner, *der;* Verdünnungsmittel, *das*

thinness /ˈθɪnnɪs/ *n., no pl.* **1** (lack of depth etc.) Dünne, *die;* geringe Dicke **2** (slimness) Magerkeit, *die* **3** (sparseness) Spärlichkeit, *die* **4** (slightness of consistency) Dünnflüssigkeit, *die* **5** (lack of substance or strength) Dürftigkeit, *die;* **the ~ of her voice** ihre dünne Stimme **6** (fig.: inadequacy) Dürftigkeit, *die*

'thin-skinned *adj.* (fig.) empfindlich; dünnhäutig (geh.)

third /θɜːd/

A *adj.* ▸**❶ p. 1358** dritt…; **the ~ finger** der Ringfinger; **~ largest/highest** *etc.* drittgrößt…/-höchst… *usw.*; **come in/be ~:** Dritter/Dritte sein/als Dritter/Dritte ankommen; **every ~ week** jede dritte Woche; **a ~ part** *or* **share** ein Drittel

B *n.* **1** (in sequence, rank) Dritte, *der/die/das;* (fraction) Drittel, *das;* **be the ~ to arrive** als Dritter/Dritte ankommen **2** (~ form) dritte [Schul]klasse; Dritte, *die* (Schuljargon) **3** (Motor Veh.) dritter Gang; **in ~:** im dritten [Gang]; **change into ~:** in den dritten [Gang] schalten **4** (Brit. Univ.) Drei, *die;* **he has a ~ [in History]** er hat eine Drei [in Geschichte]; **get** *or* **take** *or* **be awarded a ~ in one's finals** sein Examen mit [der Note] Drei bestehen **5** (Mus.) Terz, *die* **6** ▸**❶ p. 1047** (day) **the ~ of May** der dritte Mai; **the ~ [of the month]** der Dritte [des Monats]. *see also* **eighth B**

third: ~-best **A** /ˈ--/ *adj.* drittbest…; **B** /-ˈ-/ *n., no pl.* Drittbeste, *der/die/das;* **~ 'class** *n.* **1** (set ranking after second class) dritte Kategorie; **2** (Transport) dritte Klasse; **3** (Brit. Univ.) ▸**third B 4**; **~-class** **A** /ˈ--/ *adj.* **1** drittklassig; **he got a ~-class degree** er hat einen Abschluss mit der Note Drei; **2** Dritte[r]-Klasse-‹*Wagen, Reisender, Fahr. karte*›; ‹*Wagen, Fahrkarte*› dritter Klasse; ‹*Reisender*› der dritten Klasse; **B** /-ˈ-/ *adv.* dritter Klasse ‹*reisen*›; **~ de'gree** ▸**degree 9**; **~ 'force** *n.* dritte Kraft; **~ form** ▸**form A 4**; **~ 'gear** *n., no pl.* (Motor Veh.) dritter Gang; *see also* **gear A 1**

thirdly /ˈθɜːdlɪ/ *adv.* drittens

third: ~ 'man *n.* (Cricket) [weit zurückstehender] Eckmann; **~ 'party** *n.* Dritte, *der/die;* dritte Person; *attrib.* **~-party insurance** Haftpflichtversicherung, *die;* **be covered by ~-party insurance** haftpflichtversichert sein; **take out ~-party insurance** eine Haftpflichtversicherung abschließen; **~ 'person** *n.* **1** ▸**~ party**; **2** ▸**person 4**; **~ 'rail** *n.* (Railw.) Stromschiene, *die;* **~-rate** *adj.* drittklassig; **~ 'reading** ▸**reading 7**; **~ 'way** *n.* (*also Polit.:* **Third Way**) dritter Weg; **~ way strategy** Strategie des dritten Weges; **T~ 'World** *n.* Dritte Welt; **countries of the T~ World, T~ World countries** Länder der Dritten Welt

thirst /θɜːst/

A *n.* Durst, *der;* **die of ~:** verdursten; (fig.: be very thirsty) vor Durst sterben (ugs.); **~ for knowledge** Wissensdurst, *der;* **~ for revenge/after fame** Rachedurst, *der*/Ruhmsucht, *die;* **~ for news** sehnsüchtiges Warten auf Nachricht

B *v.i.* **~ for revenge/knowledge** nach Rache/Wissen dürsten (geh.)

thirstily /ˈθɜːstɪlɪ/ *adv.* durstig

'thirst-quencher *n.* Durstlöscher, *der*

thirsty /ˈθɜːstɪ/ *adj.* **1** durstig; **be ~:** Durst haben; **sb. is ~ for sth.** (fig.) jmd. *od.* jmdn. dürstet nach etw. (dichter.); **~ after gain/for knowledge/revenge** (fig.) gewinnsüchtig/wissbegierig/rachedurstig (geh.) **2** (coll.: causing thirst) durstig machend; **this is ~ work** diese Arbeit macht durstig

thirteen /θɜːˈtiːn/ ▸**❶ p. 894**, ▸**❶ p. 1001**, ▸**❶ p. 1358**

A *adj.* dreizehn; *see also* **eight A**

B *n.* Dreizehn, *die; see also* **eight B 1, 4; eighteen B**

thirteenth /θɜːˈtiːnθ/ ▸**❶ p. 1047**

A *adj.* ▸**❶ p. 1358** dreizehnt…; *see also* **eighth A**

B *n.* **1** (fraction) Dreizehntel, *das* **2** **Friday the ~:** Freitag, der Dreizehnte. *see also* **eighth B**

thirtieth /ˈθɜːtɪɪθ/ ▸**❶ p. 1047**

A *adj.* ▸**❶ p. 1358** dreißigst…; *see also* **eighth A**

B *n.* (fraction) Dreißigstel, *das; see also* **eighth B**

thirty /ˈθɜːtɪ/ ▸**❶ p. 894**, ▸**❶ p. 1001**, ▸**❶ p. 1358**

A *adj.* dreißig; *see also* **eight A**

B *n.* Dreißig, *die; see also* **eight B 1; eighty B**

thirty: ~-'first *etc. adj.* ▸**❶ p. 1047**, ▸**❶ p. 1358** einunddreißigst… *usw.*; *see also* **eighth A**; **~-'one** *etc.* **A** *adj.* einunddreißig *usw.*; *see also* **eight A**; **B** *n.* ▸**❶ p. 1358** Einunddreißig *usw.*, *die; see also* **eight B 1**; **~-'second-note** *n.* (Amer. Mus.) Zweiunddreißigstel[note], *die;* **~-something** **A** *adj.* **a ~-something woman/man** eine Frau/ein Mann in den Dreißigern; **be ~-something** in den Dreißigern sein; dreißig und noch was [alt] sein; **B** *n.* Dreißiger, *der*/Dreißigerin, *die;* **~-somethings** Leute in den Dreißigern

this /ðɪs/

A *adj., pl.* **these** /ðiːz/ **1** dieser/diese/dieses; (with less emphasis) der/die/das; **at ~ time** zu dieser Zeit; **before ~ time** vorher; zuvor;

t

these days heut[zutag]e; **I'll say ~ much/I can tell you ~ much ...:** so viel kann ich sagen/so viel kann ich dir verraten ... 2 (that is the present) dieser/diese/dieses; **all ~ week** die[se] ganze Woche; **by ~ time** inzwischen; mittlerweile 3 (of today) **~ morning/evening** *etc.* heute Morgen/Abend *usw.*; **where are you going to eat ~ lunchtime?** wo wirst du heute zu Mittag essen? 4 (just past) **these last three weeks** die letzten drei Wochen; **~ day has been a really hard one** der heutige Tag war wirklich anstrengend 5 (to come) **~ Monday** nächsten Montag; **it will not be wanted these eight months** es wird in den nächsten acht Monaten nicht gebraucht werden 6 (coll.: previously unspecified) **they dug ~ great big trench** sie hoben einen riesigen Graben aus; **I was in the pub when ~ fellow came up to me** ich war in der Kneipe, als [so] einer *od.* so'n Typ auf mich zukam (ugs.) 7 **he's tried ~ drink and that [drink]** *or* **~ and that drink** er hat schon so manchen Drink *od.* schon allerlei Drinks probiert; **I went to ~ doctor and that** ich ging von einem Arzt zum anderen. *See also* **that A 3; world 2**

B *pron., pl.* **these** 1 **what's ~?** was ist [denn] das?; **what is all ~?** was soll das alles?; **what flower is ~?** was ist das für eine Blume?; **fold it like ~!** falte es so!; **I knew all ~ before** ich wusste dies *od.* das alles schon vorher; **~ is not fair!** das ist nicht fair!; **what's all ~ about Jan and Angela separating?** stimmt das, dass Jan und Angela sich trennen wollen?; **what's ~ about holidays?** was war da mit Ferien?; **John, ~ is Mary** John, das ist Mary; *see also* **it¹ 10** 2 (the present) **before ~:** bis jetzt 3 (Brit. Teleph.: person speaking) **~ is Andy [speaking]** hier [spricht *od.* ist] Andy 4 (Amer. Teleph.: person spoken to) **who did you say ~ was?** wer ist am Apparat?; mit wem spreche ich, bitte? 5 **~ and that** dies und das; **~, that, and the other** alles Mögliche

C *adv.* (coll.) so; **~ much** so viel

thistle /ˈθɪsl/ *n.* Distel, *die*

ˈthistledown *n.* Distelwolle, *die*; **[as] light as ~:** leicht wie eine Feder

thither /ˈðɪðə(r)/ *adv.* (arch.) dorthin; *see also* **hither**

tho' ▸**though**

thong /θɒŋ/ *n.* [Leder]riemen, *der*

thoracic /θɔːˈræsɪk/ *adj.* (Anat.) Thorax-; Brust‹*höhle, -segment, -wirbel*›

thorax /ˈθɔːræks/ *n., pl.* **thoraces** /ˈθɔːrəsiːz/ *or* **~es** (Anat., Zool.) Thorax, *der*

thorn /θɔːn/ *n.* 1 (part of plant) Dorn, *der*; **be on ~s** (fig.) wie auf Nesseln sitzen (ugs.) 2 (plant) Dornenstrauch, *der* 3 **a ~ in the flesh** *or* **side/in sb.'s flesh** *or* **side** ein Pfahl im Fleische/im Fleische für jmdn.

thorn bush *n.* Dornbusch, *der*

thornless /ˈθɔːnlɪs/ *adj.* dornenlos

thorny /ˈθɔːnɪ/ *adj.* 1 dornig 2 (fig.: difficult) heikel; dornenreich ‹*Weg*›

thorough /ˈθʌrə/ *adj.* 1 gründlich; durchgreifend ‹*Reform*›; genau ‹*Beschreibung, Anweisung*› 2 (downright) ausgemacht ‹*Halunke, Nervensäge*›; tief ‹*Verachtung*›. *see also* **bass³ B 3**

thorough: ~bred A *adj.* 1 reinrassig ‹*Tier*›; vollblütig ‹*Pferd*›; 2 (fig.) rassig ‹*Sportwagen*›; **B** *n.* 1 reinrassiges Tier; (horse) Rassepferd, *das*; (Horse Racing) Vollblut, *das*; 2 (fig.: car) Klassewagen, *der* (ugs.); **~fare** *n.* Durchfahrtsstraße, *die*; **'no ~fare'** „Durchfahrt verboten"; (on foot) „kein Durchgang"; **~going** *adj.* 1 ▸**thorough 1**; 2 (extreme) radikal ‹*Konservative, Sozialist*›; ausgemacht ‹*Halunke*›

thoroughly /ˈθʌrəlɪ/ *adv.* gründlich ‹*untersuchen, prüfen*›; gehörig ‹*müde, erschöpft*›; so richtig ‹*genießen*›; ausgesprochen ‹*langweilig*›; zutiefst ‹*beschämt*›; (completely) völlig ‹*durchnässt, verzogen*›; total ‹*verdorben, verwöhnt*›; **be ~ fed up with sth.** (coll.) von etw. die Nase gestrichen voll haben (ugs.); **be ~ delighted with sth.** sich außerordentlich über etw. (*Akk.*) freuen

thoroughness /ˈθʌrənɪs/ *n., no pl.* Gründlichkeit, *die*

those ▸**that A, B**

thou¹ /ðaʊ/ *pron.* (arch./poet./dial.) du; (Relig.: God) Du

thou² /θaʊ/ *n., pl. same* (coll.) 1 ▸**thousand B 1** 2 (Mech. Engin.) tausendstel Inch

though /ðəʊ/

A *conj.* 1 (despite the fact that) obwohl; **late ~ it was** obwohl es so spät war; **the car, ~ powerful, is also economical** der Wagen ist zwar stark, aber [zugleich] auch wirtschaftlich 2 (but nevertheless) aber; **a slow ~ certain method** eine langsame, aber *od.* wenn auch sichere Methode 3 (even if) **[even] ~:** auch wenn; **as ~ = as if** ▸**if A 1** 4 (and yet) **~ you never know** obwohl man nie weiß; **she read on, ~ not to the very end** sie las weiter, wenn auch nicht bis ganz zum Schluss

B *adv.* (coll.) trotzdem; **I like him ~:** ich mag ihn aber [trotzdem]; **you don't know him, ~:** aber du kennst ihn nicht

thought /θɔːt/

A ▸**think A, B**

B *n.* 1 *no pl.* Denken, *das*; **[lost] in ~:** in Gedanken [verloren *od.* versunken]; **quick as ~:** blitzschnell; **Greek/Western ~:** das Denken der Griechen/das westliche Denken 2 *no pl., no art.* (reflection) Überlegung, *die*; Nachdenken, *das*; **act without ~:** gedankenlos handeln; **after serious ~:** nach reiflicher Überlegung 3 (consideration) Rücksicht, *die* (**for** auf + *Akk.*); **he has no ~/is full of ~ for others** er nimmt keine Rücksicht auf andere/ist sehr rücksichtsvoll anderen gegenüber; **give [plenty of] ~ to sth., give sth. [plenty of] ~:** [reiflich] über etw. (*Akk.*) nachdenken; **give no ~ to sth.** an etw. (*Akk.*) nicht denken; **he never gave the matter a moment's ~:** er dachte keinen Augenblick daran; **take ~:** überlegen; **she criticized his lack of ~ for his parents** sie kritisierte, dass er zu wenig an seine Eltern dachte; **built with some ~ for the crew** mit Blick auf die Mannschaft gebaut; **with no ~ for her own safety** ohne an ihre eigene Sicherheit zu denken 4 (idea, conception) Gedanke, *der*; **I've just had a ~!** mir ist gerade ein [guter] Gedanke gekommen; **it's the ~ that counts** der gute Wille zählt; **his one ~ is how to get rich** er hat nichts anderes im Sinn, als reich zu werden; **he hasn't a ~ in his head** er ist ein Schussel (ugs.); **at the [very] ~ of sth./of doing sth./that ...:** beim [bloßen] Gedanken an etw. (*Akk.*)/daran, etw. zu tun/, dass ...; **that's** *or* **there's a ~!** das ist aber eine [gute] Idee!; **don't give it another ~:** mach dir darüber keine Gedanken; **she is [constantly] in his ~s** er muss ständig an sie denken; *see also* **penny 3** 5 *in pl.* (opinion) Gedanken; **I'll tell you my ~s on the matter** ich sage dir, wie ich darüber denke 6 (intention) **have no ~ of doing sth.** überhaupt nicht daran denken, etw. zu tun; **give up all ~[s] of sth./doing sth.** sich (*Dat.*) etw. aus dem Kopf schlagen/es sich (*Dat.*) aus dem Kopf schlagen, etw. zu tun; **have some ~s of doing sth.** sich mit dem Gedanken tragen *od.* mit dem Gedanken spielen, etw. zu tun; **nothing was further from my ~s** nicht im Traum hätte ich daran gedacht 7 (somewhat) **a ~ arrogant/more considerate** ein wenig arrogant/rücksichtsvoller

thoughtful /ˈθɔːtfl/ *adj.* 1 (meditative) nachdenklich 2 (considerate) rücksichtsvoll; (helpful) aufmerksam 3 (showing original thought) gedankenreich; (well thought out) [gut] durchdacht; wohl überlegt ‹*Bemerkung*›

thoughtfully /ˈθɔːtfəlɪ/ *adv.* 1 (meditatively) nachdenklich 2 (considerately) rücksichtsvollerweise; **she ~ provided blankets** sie war so umsichtig, Decken bereitzustellen 3 (in a well thought out manner) **a ~ written article** ein gut durchdachter Artikel

thoughtfulness /ˈθɔːtflnɪs/ *n., no pl.* ▸**thoughtful:** 1 Nachdenklichkeit, *die* 2 Rücksicht, *die* (**for** auf + *Akk.*) 3 Gedankenreichtum, *der*; Wohlüberlegtheit, *die*

thoughtless /ˈθɔːtlɪs/ *adj.* 1 gedankenlos; **~ of the danger, ...:** ohne an die Gefahr zu denken ... 2 (inconsiderate) rücksichtslos 3 (due to lack of thought) leichtfertig ‹*Fehler*›

thoughtlessly /ˈθɔːtlɪslɪ/ *adv.* 1 gedankenlos; **he ~ gave his son a box of matches** in seiner Gedankenlosigkeit gab er seinem Sohn eine Schachtel Streichhölzer 2 (inconsiderately) aus Rücksichtslosigkeit

thoughtlessness /ˈθɔːtlɪsnɪs/ *n., no pl.* 1 Gedankenlosigkeit, *die* 2 (lack of consideration) Rücksichtslosigkeit, *die*

thought: ~ police *n. pl.* Gedankenpolizei, *die*; **~ process** *n.* Denkprozess, *der*; **~-provoking** *adj.* nachdenklich stimmend; **be ~-provoking** nachdenklich stimmen; **~-reader** *n.* Gedankenleser, *der*/-leserin, *die*; **you must be/I'm not a ~-reader** du kannst wohl Gedanken lesen/ich bin doch kein Hellseher; **~-reading** *n., no pl.* Gedankenlesen, *das*; **~ transference** *n., no pl.* Gedankenübertragung, *die*

thousand /ˈθaʊznd/ ▸ⓘ **p. 1358**

A *adj.* 1 tausend; **a** *or* **one ~:** eintausend; **two/several ~:** zweitausend/mehrere Tausend; **one and a half ~:** [ein]tausendfünfhundert; **a** *or* **one ~ and one** [ein]tausend[und]eins; **a** *or* **one ~ and one people** [ein]tausendundeine Person; **a T~ and one Nights** Tausendundeine Nacht 2 **a ~ [and one]** (fig.: innumerable) tausend (ugs.); **a ~ thanks** tausend Dank; **a ~ apologies** ich bitte tausendmal um Entschuldigung. *see also* **pity A 2; time A 6**

B *n.* 1 (number) tausend; **a** *or* **one/two ~:** ein-/zweitausend; **a ~ and one** [ein]tausend[und]eins; **a ~-to-one chance** eine Chance von tausend zu eins; **she/this chance is one in a ~** (fig.) sie ist einmalig/das ist eine einmalige Chance 2 (symbol, written figure) Tausend, *die*; (in adding numbers by columns) Tausender, *der* (Math.); (set or group) Tausend, *das* 3 (indefinite amount) **~s** Tausende; **they came by the ~** *or* **in their ~s** sie kamen zu Tausenden; **~s and ~s of people** Tausend und Abertausend Menschen

ˈthousandfold

A *adv.* tausendfach

B *adj.* tausendfach

C *n.* Tausendfache, *das*; *see also* **hundredfold C**

thousandth /ˈθaʊzndθ/

A *adj.* ▸ⓘ **p. 1358** tausendst...; **a ~ part** ein Tausendstel; *see also* **eighth A**

B *n.* 1 (fraction) Tausendstel, *das* 2 (in sequence, rank) Tausendste, *der/die/das*

thraldom /ˈθrɔːldəm/ *n., no pl.* (literary) Sklaverei, *die*

thrall /θrɔːl/ *n., no pl.* (literary) **have** *or* **hold sb. in [one's] ~** jmdn. in seinen Bann geschlagen haben; **be in ~ to sb./sth.** in jmds. Bann/im Banne einer Sache sein

thralldom (Amer.) ▸**thraldom**

thrash /θræʃ/

A *v.t.* 1 (beat) [ver]prügeln; **~ the life out of sb.** jmdm. die Seele aus dem Leib prügeln (ugs.) 2 (defeat) vernichtend schlagen 3 ▸**thresh**

B *v.i.* 1 **~ at sth.** auf etw. (*Akk.*) einschlagen 2 (Naut.) **~ to windward** luvwärts gegen die See knüppeln

C *n.* (coll.: party) große Fete

Phrasal verbs

- **~ aˈbout, ~ aˈround** *v.i.* sich hin- und herwerfen; ‹*Fisch:*› zappeln
- **~ ˈout** *v.t.* ausdiskutieren ‹*Problem, Frage*›; ausarbeiten ‹*Plan*›; **~ out the whole business** Klarheit in die ganze Sache bringen

thrashing /ˈθræʃɪŋ/ *n.* 1 (beating) Prügel *Pl.*; **give sb. a ~:** jmdm. eine Tracht Prügel verpassen (ugs.); **get a ~:** Prügel bekommen 2 (defeat) Schlappe, *die*; **give sb. a ~:** jmdn. vernichtend schlagen

thread /θred/

A *n.* 1 Faden, *der*; **sb. has not a dry ~ on him** jmd. hat keinen trockenen Faden [mehr] am Leib (ugs.) 2 (fig.) **hang by a ~** (be in a precarious state) an einem [dünnen *od.* seidenen] Faden hängen; (depend on sth. still in doubt) auf Messers Schneide stehen; **lose the ~:** den Faden verlieren; **take** *or* **pick up the ~ of the conversation** den Gesprächsfaden wieder aufnehmen; **gather up the ~s of sth.** etw. erläuternd zusammenfassen 3 (sth. very thin) **a ~ of light/water** ein feiner Lichtstrahl/ein Rinnsal (geh.) 4 (Mech. Engin.: of screw) Gewinde, *das*

B *v.t.* 1 (pass ~ through) einfädeln; auffädeln

t

‹Perlen›; (make chain of) aufreihen 2▸ (place in position) einfädeln ‹*Film, Tonband*› (**through** in + *Akk.*) 3▸ ~ **one's way through sth.** (lit. or fig.) sich durch etw. schlängeln 4▸ (Mech. Engin.) mit einem Gewinde versehen

thread: ~**bare** *adj.* 1▸ (worn) abgenutzt; abgetragen ‹*Kleidung*›; 2▸ (fig.) abgedroschen ‹*Argument*› (ugs.); ~**worm** *n.* (Zool., Med.) Fadenwurm, *der*

threat /θret/ *n.* 1▸ Drohung, *die;* **make a ~ against sb.** jmdm. drohen; **under ~ of** unter Androhung von; **sb./sth. is under ~ of sth.** jmdm./einer Sache droht etw.; **issue ~s to sb.'s life** Morddrohungen gegen jmdn. richten 2▸ (indication of sth. unpleasant) **at the slightest ~ of sth.** wenn etw. auch nur ganz entfernt droht; **there is a ~ of rain** es kann Regen geben 3▸ (danger) Bedrohung, *die* (**to** für); **a ~ to our liberty** eine Bedrohung unserer Freiheit

threaten /ˈθretn/ *v.t.* 1▸ (use threats towards) bedrohen; **~ sb. with prosecution/a beating** jmdm. Verfolgung/Schläge androhen; **I am ~ed with a visit from my mother** (joc.) mir droht ein Besuch meiner Mutter (scherzh.) 2▸ (announce one's intention) **~ to do sth.** damit drohen, etw. zu tun; **the fire ~ed to engulf the whole village** (fig.) das Feuer drohte das ganze Dorf einzuschließen; **~ to commit suicide/to resign** mit Selbstmord/dem Rücktritt drohen 3▸ drohen mit ‹*Gewalt, Repressalien, Rache usw.*›; **the sky ~s rain** am Himmel hängen drohende Regenwolken 4▸ *abs.* **when danger ~s** wenn [eine] Gefahr droht

threatening /ˈθretnɪŋ/ *adj.* drohend; bedrohlich ‹*Gegenwart, Verhalten, Situation*›; **~ letter** Drohbrief, *der*

threateningly /ˈθretnɪŋlɪ/ *adv.* drohend; **~ close** bedrohlich nahe

three /θriː/ ▸❶ **p. 894**, ▸❶ **p. 1001**, ▸❶ **p. 1358**

A *adj.*drei; **~ parts wine and one part ...:** drei Teile Wein und ein Teil ...; **be ~ parts finished** drei viertel fertig sein; *see also* **cheer A 1**; **eight A**; **R 2**

B *n.* 1▸ (number, symbol) Drei, *die* 2▸ (set of ~ people) Dreiergruppe, *die;* **the ~ [of them]** die drei. *see also* **eight B 1, 3, 4**

three: ~**cornered** /ˈθriːkɔːnəd/ *adj.* dreieckig; **~-cornered hat** Dreispitz, *der;* **~-cornered contest** Wettkampf mit drei Teilnehmern; **~-diˈmensional** *adj.* dreidimensional; **~fold** *adj., adv.* dreifach; *see also* **eightfold**; **~-ˈfour time** *n.* (Mus.) Dreivierteltakt, *der;* **~-handed** *adj.* (Cards) ‹*Bridge usw.*› zu dritt; **~-lane** *adj.* dreispurig; **~-legged** /ˈθriːlegd, ˈθriːlegɪd/ *adj.* dreibeinig; **~-legged race** *n. Wettlauf zwischen Paaren, bei denen jeweils das linke Bein des einen Partners mit dem rechten Bein des anderen zusammengebunden ist;* **~-line ˈwhip** ▸**whip A 3**; **~pence** /ˈθrepəns, ˈθrɪpəns/ *n.* (Brit. Hist.) drei Pence; **~penny** /ˈθrepənɪ, ˈθrɪpənɪ/ *adj.* (Brit. Hist.) Drei-Pence-; *see also* **bit² 7**; **~-phase** *adj.* Dreiphasen-; dreiphasig; **~-phase current** Dreiphasenstrom, *der;* **~-piece** *adj.* dreiteilig ‹*Anzug, Sitzgarnitur usw.*›; **~-pin** *adj.* dreipolig ‹*Stecker*›; **~-ply** **A** *adj.* dreilagig; dreifädig ‹*Wolle*›; **B** *n.* 1▸ (wool) dreifädige Wolle; 2▸ (wood) dreischichtiges [Sperr]holz; **~-point** *attrib. adj.* **~-point landing** (Aeronaut.) Dreipunktlandung, *die;* **~-point turn** (Brit. Motor Veh.) *Wendemanöver auf engem Raum, bei dem vorwärts, rückwärts und wieder vorwärts gefahren wird;* **~-quarter** **A** *adj.* drei viertel; **~-quarter portrait** (down to hips) Dreiviertelporträt, *das;* (of face) Halbprofilporträt, *das;* **~-quarter length** dreiviertellang; **~-quarter back** ▸**B**; **B** *n.* (Rugby) Dreiviertel, *der;* **~-quarters** **A** *n.* 1▸ drei Viertel (**of** *Gen.*); **~-quarters of an hour** eine Dreiviertelstunde; 2▸ *attrib.* Dreiviertel‹*mehrheit usw.*›; **B** *adv.* drei viertel ‹*voll*›; zu drei Vierteln ‹*fertig*›; **~score** *adj.* (arch.) sechzig; **~score and ten** siebzig

threesome /ˈθriːsəm/ *n.* Dreigespann, *das;* Trio, *das;* **go as a ~:** zu dritt gehen

three: ~**-storey** *adj.* dreistöckig; **~-way** *adj.* Dreiwege-; **~-way adaptor** (Electr.) Dreifachstecker, *der;* **~-way intersection** Kreuzung, an der sich drei Straßen treffen; **~-way tie** Unentschieden, bei dem drei Spieler/Mannschaften die gleiche Punktzahl *usw.* haben; **~-way profit split** Dreiteilung des Gewinns; **~-way playoff** Stechen (Sport) von drei Teilnehmern; **~-ˈwheeler** *n.* Dreirad, *das* (Kfz-W.)

thresh /θreʃ/ *v.t.* (Agric.) dreschen

thresher /ˈθreʃə(r)/ *n.* 1▸ (Agric.) (person) Drescher, *der*/Drescherin, *die;* (machine) Dreschmaschine, *die* 2▸ (Zool.: shark) Fuchshai, *der;* Drescher, *der*

threshing/ˈθreʃɪŋ/: **~ floor** *n.* (Agric.) Tenne, *die;* **~ machine** *n.* (Agric.) Dreschmaschine, *die*

threshold /ˈθreʃəʊld/ *n.* 1▸ (lit. or fig.) Schwelle, *die;* **be on the ~ of sth.** (fig.) an der Schwelle einer Sache (*Gen.*) stehen; **pain ~** (Physiol., Psych.) Schmerzschwelle, *die* 2▸ (Phys.) Schwellenwert, *der*

ˈthreshold price *n.* (EU) Schwellenpreis, *der*

threw ▸**throw A**

thrice /θraɪs/ *adv.* (arch./literary) dreimal

thrift /θrɪft/ *n.* 1▸ *no pl.* Sparsamkeit, *die* 2▸ (Bot.) Grasnelke, *die*

ˈthrift account *n.* (Amer.) Sparkonto, *das*

thriftily /ˈθrɪftɪlɪ/ *adv.* sparsam

thriftiness /ˈθrɪftɪnɪs/ *n., no pl.* Sparsamkeit, *die*

ˈthrift shop, ˈthrift store (Amer.) ▸**charity shop**

thrifty /ˈθrɪftɪ/ *adj.* sparsam

thrill /θrɪl/

A *v.t.* (excite) faszinieren; (delight) begeistern; **be ~ed by/with sth.** von etw. fasziniert/begeistert sein; **we were ~ed to have your letter** wir haben uns wahnsinnig über deinen Brief gefreut (ugs.); *see also* **bit² 1**

B *v.i.* **~ with** zittern *od.* (geh.) beben vor (+ *Dat.*); **~ to** wie elektrisiert sein bei; **~ with horror** vor Entsetzen schaudern; **~ with excitement** ein Prickeln der Erregung verspüren; **~ at the sight of sth./at sb.'s touch** beim Anblick einer Sache (*Gen.*)/bei jmds. Berührung von einem Schauder überlaufen werden

C *n.* 1▸ (wave of emotion) Erregung, *die;* **a ~ of joy/pleasure** freudige Erregung; **a ~ of excitement/hate/horror** prickelnde Erregung/ein starkes Hassgefühl/ein Schauder (geh.) des Entsetzens; **a ~ of anticipation** prickelnde Vorfreude 2▸ (exciting experience) aufregendes Erlebnis; (titillation) Nervenkitzel, *der* (ugs.); **sb. gets a ~ out of sth.** etw. erregt jmdn.; **cheap ~s** anspruchsloser Nervenkitzel (ugs.); **this film will give you the ~ of a lifetime** dieser Film wird das Aufregendste sein, was du je erlebt hast; **~s and spills** Nervenkitzel, *der*

thriller /ˈθrɪlə(r)/ *n.* Thriller, *der*

thrilling /ˈθrɪlɪŋ/ *adj.* aufregend; spannend ‹*Buch, Film, Theaterstück, Geschichte*›; packend ‹*Ereignis*›; mitreißend ‹*Musik*›; prickelnd ‹*Gefühl*›

ˈthrill-seeker *n.* Mensch, der den Nervenkitzel sucht; Thrillsucher, *der*/-sucherin, *die* (ugs.)

thrive /θraɪv/ *v.i.*, **thrived** *or* **throve** /θrəʊv/, **~d** *or* **thriven** /ˈθrɪvn/ 1▸ (grow vigorously) wachsen und gedeihen; **~ on good food/sunlight** bei guter Ernährung/Sonnenschein prächtig gedeihen 2▸ (prosper) aufblühen (**on** bei); **business is thriving** das Geschäft floriert; **a thriving businessman** ein erfolgreicher Geschäftsmann 3▸ (grow rich) reich werden; **~ on other people's misfortune** sich am Unglück der anderen bereichern

thro' ▸**through**

throat /θrəʊt/ *n.* 1▸ ▸❶ **p. 951** (outside and inside of neck) Hals, *der;* (esp. inside) Kehle, *die;* **look down sb.'s ~:** jmdm. in den Hals *od.* Rachen schauen; **pour sth. down one's ~:** etw. hinunterschütten; **cancer of the ~:** Kehlkopfkrebs, *der;* **a [sore] ~:** Halsschmerzen; **cut sb.'s ~:** jmdm. die Kehle durchschneiden; **cut one's own ~** (fig.) sich (*Dat.*) ins eigene Fleisch schneiden; **cut one another's ~s** (fig.) sich (*Dat.*) gegenseitig das Wasser abgraben; **ram** *or* **cram** *or* **shove** *or* **thrust sth. down sb.'s ~** (fig.) jmdm. etw. aufzwingen; **be at each other's ~s** (fig.) miteinander im Clinch liegen (ugs.) 2▸ (of bottle, vase) Hals, *der;* (of blast furnace) Gicht, *die* (Hüttenw.)

-throated /θrəʊtɪd/ *adj. in comb.* -halsig ‹*Mensch, Tier*›; **full-~:** aus vollem Halse

throat: ~ **lozenge** *n.* Halspastille, *die;* ~ **microphone** *n.* Kehlkopfmikrofon, *das*

throaty /ˈθrəʊtɪ/ *adj.* 1▸ (produced in throat) kehlig 2▸ (hoarse) heiser

throb /θrɒb/

A *v.i.*, **-bb-:** 1▸ (palpitate, pulsate) pochen; **his fingers were ~bing [with pain]** er hatte einen pochenden Schmerz in den Fingern 2▸ (vibrate) ‹*Motor, Artillerie:*› dröhnen

B *n.* 1▸ (palpitation) Pochen, *das;* **be ~bing with life** voll von pulsierendem Leben sein; **he felt a sudden ~ of pain** ein plötzlicher Schmerz durchfuhr ihn 2▸ (vibration) Dröhnen, *das;* (loud) Hämmern, *das*

throes /θrəʊz/ *n. pl.* Qual, *die;* **~ of childbirth** Geburtswehen *Pl.;* **death ~:** Todesqual[en] (geh.); **be in the ~ of sth.** (fig.) mitten in etw. (*Dat.*) stecken (ugs.)

thrombosis /θrɒmˈbəʊsɪs/ *n., pl.* **thromboses** /θrɒmˈbəʊsiːz/ ▸❶ **p. 1231** (Med.) Thrombose, *die*

throne /θrəʊn/ *n.* Thron, *der;* **succeed to the ~:** die Thronfolge antreten; **on the ~** (coll. joc.: toilet) auf dem Thron *od.* Topf (ugs. scherzh.)

ˈthrone room *n.* Thronsaal, *der*

throng /θrɒŋ/

A *n.* [Menschen]menge, *die;* **stand in a ~ around sb.** eine [Menschen]traube um jmdn. bilden; **~s of people** Scharen von Menschen; **join the ~** (joc.) sich ins Gewühl stürzen

B *v.i.* strömen (**into** in + *Akk.*); (press) sich drängen; **~ round the noticeboard** sich um das schwarze Brett drängen

C *v.t.* sich drängen in (+ *Dat.*)

throttle /ˈθrɒtl/

A *n.* (Mech. Engin.) **~ [valve]** Drosselklappe, *die;* **~ [pedal]** (Motor Veh.) Gas[pedal], *das;* **~ [lever]** Gashebel, *der;* **at full ~** (Motor Veh.) mit Vollgas

B *v.t.* erdrosseln; (fig.) ersticken

Phrasal verb

• **~ back, ~ down**

A *v.t.* drosseln ‹*Motor*›

B *v.i.* den Motor drosseln

through /θruː/

A *prep.* 1▸ durch; (fig.) **search/read ~ sth.** etw. durchsuchen/durchlesen; **wait ~ ten long years** zehn lange Jahre hindurch warten; **live ~ sth.** (survive) etw. überleben; (experience) etw. erleben; **sit ~ a long sermon** eine lange Predigt hindurch still sitzen bleiben 2▸ (Amer.: up to and including) bis [einschließlich] 3▸ (by reason of) durch; infolge von ‹*Vernachlässigung, Einflüssen*›; **it was all ~ you that we were late** es war nur deine Schuld, dass wir zu spät gekommen sind; **it all came about ~ his not knowing the way** alles kam so, weil er den Weg nicht wusste; **it happened ~ no fault of yours** es geschah nicht durch deine Schuld; **conceal sth. ~ shame** etw. aus Scham verheimlichen

B *adv.* 1▸ **let sb. ~:** jmdn. durchlassen; **book your tickets ~ to Vienna** löst eure Fahrkarten durchgehend bis Wien; **be a Londoner/be wet ~ and ~:** durch und durch Londoner/nass sein; **be ~ with a piece of work/with sb.** mit einer Arbeit fertig/mit jmdm. fertig (ugs.) sein; **we are ~!** (have succeeded/finished) wir haben es geschafft!; (with each other) wir sind miteinander fertig! 2▸ (Teleph.) **be ~:** durch sein (ugs.); **be ~ to sb.** mit jmdm. verbunden sein

C *adj.* durchgehend ‹*Zug*›; **~ coach** *or* **carriage** Kurswagen, *der* (**for** nach); **~ traffic** Durchgangsverkehr, *der;* **'no ~ road'** „keine Durchfahrt[sstraße]"; **~ ticket** [alle Umsteigestationen umfassende] Fahrkarte; **can I buy a ~ ticket to Warsaw?** kann ich bis Warschau durchlösen?

through: ~**-composed** *adj.* (Mus.) durchkomponiert; **~-draught** *n.* Durchzug, *der;*

t

create a ~-draught für Durchzug sorgen; **~'out** A *prep.* **~out the war/period** den ganzen Krieg/die ganze Zeit hindurch; **spread ~out the country** sich im ganzen Land verbreiten; B *adv.* (entirely) ganz; (always) stets; die ganze Zeit [hindurch]; **lined with fur ~out** ganz mit Pelz gefüttert; **repainted ~out** von oben bis unten neu gestrichen; **~put** *n.* Durchsatz, *der* (Wirtsch.); **~-ticketing** *n.*, *no pl.* Durchlösen, *das;* **~way** *n.* (Amer.: expressway) Schnellstraße, *die*

throve ▸**thrive**

throw /θrəʊ/

A *v.t.*, **threw** /θruː/, **~n** /θrəʊn/ 1 werfen; **~ sth. to sb.** jmdm. etw. zuwerfen; **~ sth. at sb.** etw. nach jmdm. werfen; **~ me that towel, please** wirf mal bitte das Handtuch rüber (ugs.); **the hose ~s a jet of water 50 feet** der Schlauch spritzt das Wasser 50 Fuß weit; **this cannon ~s 50-mm shells** diese Kanone schießt 50-mm-Geschosse; **~ a punch/punches** zuschlagen; **~ a left/right** eine Linke/Rechte schlagen; **~ oneself on one's knees/to the floor/into a chair** sich auf die Knie/zu Boden/in einen Sessel werfen; **~ oneself down** sich niederwerfen; **~ oneself at sb.** sich auf jmdn. werfen; (fig.) sich jmdm. an den Hals werfen (ugs.); **~ good money after bad** (fig.) [noch mehr] Geld hinauswerfen; *see also* **glass B**

2 (fig.) **~ sb. out of work/into prison** jmdn. entlassen *od.* (ugs.) hinauswerfen/ins Gefängnis werfen (geh.); **be ~n upon one's own resources** selbst für sich aufkommen müssen; **~ sb. into confusion** jmdn. durcheinander bringen; **~ oneself into a task** sich in eine Arbeit (*Akk.*) stürzen; **~ sth. into disarray** *or* **disorder** etw. durcheinander bringen; *see also* **scent A 2**

3 (project, direct) werfen; **~ an icy look at sb.** jmdm. einen eisigen Blick zuwerfen; *see also* **light[1] A 8**

4 (bring to the ground) zu Boden werfen ‹*Ringer, Gegner*›; (unseat) abwerfen ‹*Reiter*›

5 (coll.: disconcert) ‹*Frage:*› aus der Fassung bringen

6 (cause to change position) **~ troops into action** Truppen in den Kampf werfen; **~ a switch/lever** einen Schalter/Hebel betätigen; **~ the car into reverse** den Rückwärtsgang einlegen *od.* (salopp) reinhauen; *see also* **open A 1**

7 (construct) **~ a bridge across a river** eine Brücke über einen Fluss schlagen

8 (Textiles) **~ silk** Seidenfäden drehen

9 (Pottery) drehen ‹*Töpfe*›

10 **~ a fit/tantrum** einen Anfall/Wutanfall bekommen

11 **~ a party** eine Party schmeißen (ugs.)

12 (lose intentionally) absichtlich verlieren ‹*Kampf, Rennen*›

13 (Cards) ausspielen; (discard) abwerfen

14 *also abs.* (Games) werfen; **~ [the/a dice]** würfeln

B *n.* 1 (act) Wurf, *der;* **the first ~ went to the champion** (Wrestling) der erste Wurf gelang dem Meister; **$5 a ~** (coll.: each) $5 das Stück; *see also* **stone A 1**

2 (Geol.) (fault) Verwerfung, *die*

(Phrasal verbs)

- **~ a'bout** *v.t.* herumwerfen (ugs.); **~ one's arms about** mit den Armen fuchteln (ugs.); **~ one's money about** (fig.) mit Geld um sich werfen; *see also* **weight A 1**
- **~ a'round** *v.t.* 1 ▸**~ about** 2 (surround with) **~ a cordon around an area** ein Gebiet abriegeln
- **~ a'way** *v.t.* 1 (get rid of, waste) wegwerfen; (discard) abwerfen ‹*Spielkarte*›; **~ away money on sth.** Geld für etw. wegwerfen; **~ oneself away on sb.** sich an jmdn. wegwerfen 2 (lose by neglect) verschenken ‹*Vorteil, Vorsprung, Spiel usw.*› 3 (Theatr.) beiläufig fallen lassen ‹*Worte*›. *See also* **throwaway**
- **~ 'back** *v.t.* 1 (return, repulse) zurückwerfen; **be ~n back on sth.** (fig.) auf etw. (*Akk.*) zurückgreifen müssen 2 (move back rapidly) zurückschlagen ‹*Bettuch, Vorhang, Teppich*›; zurückwerfen ‹*Kopf*›. *see also* **throwback**
- **~ 'down** *v.t.* **~ down [on the ground]** auf den Boden werfen; **it's ~ing it down** (coll.) es gießt [wie aus Eimern] (ugs.); *see also* **gauntlet[1] 4**
- **~ 'in** *v.t.* 1 (include as free extra) [gratis] dazugeben; **with ... ~n in** mit ... als Zugabe 2 (interpose) einstreuen ‹*Bemerkung*› 3 (Footb., Rugby) einwerfen; *see also* **~-in** 4 (Cricket) [vom Außenfeld] in das Innenfeld [zurück]werfen 5 **~ one's hand in** (Cards) aussteigen (ugs.); (fig.: withdraw) aufgeben. *See also* **lot 7**; **towel A 1**
- **~ 'off** *v.t.* 1 (discard) ablegen ‹*Maske, Verkleidung*›; von sich werfen ‹*Kleider*›; (get rid of) loswerden ‹*Erkältung, lästige Person*› 2 (perform or write casually) [mühelos] hinwerfen ‹*Rede, Gedicht usw.*›
- **~ 'on**

A *v.t.* sich werfen in ‹*Kleider*›

B *v. refl.* **~ oneself [up]on sb.** sich auf jmdn. stürzen; **~ oneself [up]on sb.'s mercy** sich jmdm. auf Gnade oder Ungnade ausliefern

- **~ 'out** *v.t.* 1 (discard) wegwerfen 2 (expel) **~ sb. out [of sth.]** jmdn. [aus etw.] hinauswerfen (ugs.); **~ sb. out of work** jmdn. hinauswerfen (ugs.) 3 (refuse) verwerfen ‹*Plan usw.*› 4 (put forward tentatively) in den Raum stellen ‹*Vorschläge*› 5 **~ out one's chest** die Brust herausdrücken 6 (confuse) durcheinander bringen; aus dem Konzept bringen ‹*Sprecher*›; **the mistake threw us out in our calculation/results** der Fehler warf unsere Rechnung um (ugs.)/verfälschte unsere Ergebnisse 7 (radiate) ausstrahlen ‹*Wärme*›. *See also* **throw-out**
- **~ 'over** *v.t.* sitzen lassen (ugs.) ‹*Freund[in] usw.*›; den Rücken kehren (+ *Dat.*) ‹*Partei, Bekannten, Familie*›
- **~ to'gether** *v.t.* 1 (assemble hastily) zusammenhauen (ugs.); zusammenwerfen ‹*Zutaten, Ideen*›; herzaubern ‹*Essen*›; zusammenschustern (ugs. abwertend) ‹*Aufsatz, Artikel*›; zusammenschreiben ‹*Buch, Artikel, Rede*› 2 (bring together) zusammenwürfeln
- **~ 'up**

A *v.t.* 1 (lift quickly) hochwerfen ‹*Arme, Hände*›; [plötzlich] hochschieben ‹*Fenster*› 2 (erect quickly) hochziehen (salopp) ‹*Gebäude*› 3 (give up) hinwerfen (ugs.) ‹*Arbeit*›; aufgeben ‹*Versuch*›; abbrechen ‹*Laufbahn, Ausbildung*› 4 (produce) hervorbringen ‹*Führer, Ideen usw.*› 5 (coll.: vomit) ausspucken (ugs.)

B *v.i.* (coll.: vomit) brechen (ugs.); **he makes me want to ~ up** ich finde ihn zum Kotzen (derb)

throw: ~away A *adj.* 1 (disposable) Wegwerf-; Einweg-; 2 (underemphasized) beiläufig [gesprochen] ‹*Bemerkung*›; B *n.* 1 (disposable thing) Wegwerfartikel, *der;* (bottle) Einwegflasche, *die;* 2 (remark) beiläufige Bemerkung; **~back** *n.* Rückkehr, *die* (**to** zu); **he/this horse is a ~back** in ihm/diesem Pferd schlägt altes Blut wieder durch

thrower /'θrəʊə(r)/ *n.* Werfer, *der*/Werferin, *die;* (Pottery) Dreher, *der*/Dreherin, *die*

'throw-in *n.* (Footb., Rugby) Einwurf, *der*

thrown ▸**throw A**

throw: ~-out *n.* 1 **have a ~-out** ausmisten (ugs.); 2 **sb.'s ~-outs** das, was jmd. wegwerfen will; (clothes) jmds. abgelegte Kleider; **these are ~-outs** diese sind zum Wegwerfen; **~-rug** *n.* (Amer.) Überwurf, *der*

thru (Amer.) ▸**through**

thrum /θrʌm/

A *v.t.*, **-mm-** klimpern auf (+ *Dat.*) ‹*Gitarre usw.*›; trommeln auf (+ *Dat.*) ‹*Tisch usw.*›; **~ a tune** eine Melodie [herunter]klimpern

B *v.i.*, **-mm-** (on guitar) klimpern (**on** auf + *Dat.*); (on flat surface) trommeln (**on** auf + *Dat.*)

thrush[1] /θrʌʃ/ *n.* (Ornith.) Drossel, *die*

thrush[2] *n.*, *no pl.*, *no art.* ▸❶ **p. 1231** (Med.) Soor, *der;* Soormykose, *die*

thrust /θrʌst/

A *v.t.*, **thrust** 1 (push suddenly) stoßen; **he ~ his fist into my face** er stieß mir seine Faust ins Gesicht; **~ a letter into sth.** einen Brief in etw. (*Akk.*) stecken; **~ out one's hand** die Hand ausstrecken; **~ a ten-pound note into sb.'s hand** jmdm. eine Zehnpfundnote in die Hand drücken; (fig.) **~ aside** beiseite schieben; in den Wind schlagen ‹*Warnungen*›; **~ extra work [up]on sb.** jmdm. zusätzliche Arbeit aufbürden; **~ oneself/one's company upon sb.** sich/seine Gesellschaft jmdm. aufdrängen; **fame was ~ upon her** sie wurde unversehens berühmt 2 **~ one's way through/into/out of sth.** sich durch/in/aus etw. drängen 3 (pierce) **~ sb./sth. through** jmdn./etw. durchbohren

B *v.i.*, **thrust** 1 (push) **~ at sb.** nach jmdm. stoßen 2 (force one's way) **~ through the crowd/to the front** sich durch die Menge/nach vorn drängen *od.* kämpfen

C *n.* 1 (sudden push) Stoß, *der* 2 (fig.: verbal attack) Seitenhieb, *der* (**at** auf + *Akk.*) 3 (gist) Stoßrichtung, *die* 4 (Mil.: advance) Vorstoß, *der* 5 (force) (of jet engine) Schub, *der;* (of arch) Gewölbeschub, *der*

'thrust bearing *n.* (Mech. Engin.) Axiallager, *das*

thruster /'θrʌstə(r)/ *n.* (Astronaut.) Korrekturtriebwerk, *das*

thrustful /'θrʌstfl/ *adj.* energisch

thrusting /'θrʌstɪŋ/ *adj.* [energisch und] zielstrebig

thruway (Amer.) ▸**throughway**

thud /θʌd/

A *v.i.*, **-dd-** dumpf schlagen; **~ to the floor/ground** dumpf [auf dem Fußboden/Boden] aufschlagen

B *n.* dumpfer Schlag; **fall with a ~ [to the ground]** dumpf [auf den Boden] aufschlagen; **the ~ of hoofbeats** dröhnender Hufschlag

thug /θʌg/ *n.* Schläger, *der;* **football ~s** Fußballrowdys

thuggery /'θʌgərɪ/ *n.*, *no pl.* Schlägerunwesen, *das*

thuggish /'θʌgɪʃ/ *adj.* aggressiv ‹*Verhalten, Fußballfan*›; **~ lout** Schläger, *der;* **~ youth** jugendlicher Schläger

thumb /θʌm/

A *n.* ▸❶ **p. 951** Daumen, *der;* **give sb. the ~s down on a proposal/idea** jmds. Vorschlag/Idee ablehnen; **get the ~s down** ‹*Idee:*› verworfen werden; ‹*Kandidat:*› abgelehnt werden; **give a project the ~s up** für ein Projekt grünes Licht geben; **get the ~s up** ‹*Person, Projekt:*› akzeptiert werden; **have ten ~s, be all ~s** zwei linke Hände haben (ugs.); **have sb. under one's ~:** jmdn. unter der Fuchtel haben (ugs.); **be under sb.'s ~:** unter jmds. Fuchtel stehen; *see also* **rule A 1**; **stick out B 2**

B *v.t.* 1 **~ a lift** einem Autofahrer winken, um sich mitnehmen zu lassen; (hitch-hike) per Anhalter fahren 2 (turn over) [mit dem Daumen] durchblättern ‹*Buch*›; [mit dem Daumen] umblättern ‹*Seiten*›; **well-~ed** abgegriffen ‹*Buch*› 3 **~ one's nose [at sb.]** [jmdm.] eine lange Nase machen

(Phrasal verb)

- **~ through** *v.t.* [mit dem Daumen] durchblättern ‹*Buch*›

thumb: ~ index A *n.* Daumenregister, *das;* B *v.t.* mit Daumenregister ausstatten; **~-indexed edition** Ausgabe mit Daumenregister; **~nail** *n.* 1 Daumennagel, *der; attrib.* **~nail sketch** (Art) Miniaturportrait, *das;* (fig.: brief description) kurze Beschreibung; 2 (Computing) Thumbnail, *das* (fachspr.); *attrib.* Thumbnail‹-*Bild*, -*Ansicht*›; **~print** *n.* Daumenabdruck, *der;* **~screw** *n.* (Hist.) Daumenschraube, *die;* **~stall** *n.* Däumling, *der;* **~-sucking** /'θʌmsʌkɪŋ/ *n.*, *no pl.*, *no indef. art.* Daumenlutschen, *das;* **~tack** (Amer.) *n.* Reißzwecke, *die*

thump /θʌmp/

A *v.t.* 1 (strike heavily) [mit Wucht] schlagen; **I'll ~ you if ...:** ich hau dir eine, wenn ... (ugs.); **they ~ed each other** sie prügelten sich; **~ the door with one's fist** mit der Faust an die Tür hämmern 2 (play on piano etc.) **~ [out] a tune** eine Melodie hämmern (ugs.)

B *v.i.* 1 hämmern (**at, on** gegen); ‹*Herz:*› heftig pochen 2 (move noisily) **~ around** herumpoltern; **~ down the stairs** die Treppe hinabpoltern

C *n.* 1 (blow) Schlag, *der* 2 (dull sound) Bums, *der* (ugs.); dumpfer Schlag

thumping /'θʌmpɪŋ/ (coll.)

A *adj.* (huge) gewaltig (ugs.); überwältigend ‹*Mehr-*

heit›; faustdick (ugs.) ‹Lüge›
B *adv.* ~ **great** riesengroß (ugs.); **a ~ big majority** eine überwältigende Mehrheit

thunder /ˈθʌndə(r)/
A *n.* **1** *no pl., no indef. art.* Donner, *der;* **roll/crash of ~:** Donnerrollen, *das*/-schlag, *der* **2** (fig.: censure) Donnerwetter, *das* (ugs.) **3** **steal sb.'s ~** (fig.) jmdm. die Schau stehlen (ugs.)
B *v.i.* **1** donnern **2** (speak) **~ against sth.** gegen etw. wettern (ugs.); **~ at sb.** jmdn. andonnern (ugs.)
C *v.t.* [mit Donnerstimme] brüllen; **~ [out] orders at sb.** jmdm. Befehle zubrüllen

thunder: ~bolt *n.* **1** Blitzschlag [mit Donner]; (from god) Blitzstrahl, *der* (geh.); **2** (fig.: unexpected event) **come as something of a ~bolt** wie ein Blitz einschlagen; **~box** *n.* (coll.) Plumpsklo[sett], *das* (ugs.); **~clap** *n.* **1** Donnerschlag, *der;* **2** (fig.) **come** *or* **be like a ~clap** wie der Blitz einschlagen; **~cloud** *n.* Gewitterwolke, *die*

thundering /ˈθʌndərɪŋ/ (coll.)
A *adj.* (huge) gewaltig (ugs.) ‹*Erfolg*›; faustdick (ugs.) ‹*Lüge*›; **be in a ~ rage** eine Mordswut haben (ugs.)
B *adv.* **~ great** gewaltig (ugs.); **we had a ~ good time** wir hatten einen unheimlichen Spaß

thunderous /ˈθʌndərəs/ *adj.* donnernd; **in a ~ voice** mit Donnerstimme

thunder: ~ shower *n.* Gewitterschauer, *der;* **~storm** *n.* Gewitter, *das;* (very heavy) Gewittersturm, *der;* **~struck** *adj.* (fig.: amazed) **be ~struck** wie vom Donner gerührt sein

thundery /ˈθʌndərɪ/ *adj.* gewittrig; **it looks ~:** es sieht nach Gewitter aus

Thuringia /θʊəˈrɪŋgɪə/ *pr. n.* Thüringen (*das*)

Thuringian /θʊəˈrɪŋgɪən/
A *adj.* thüringisch ‹*Stadt*›; Thüringer ‹*Wald, Dialekt*›
B *n.* Thüringer, *der*/Thüringerin, *die*

Thurs. *abbr.* ▸ **❶ p. 1048 = Thursday** Do.

Thursday /ˈθɜːzdeɪ, ˈθɜːzdɪ/ ▸ **❶ p. 1048**
A *n.* Donnerstag, *der*
B *adv.* (coll.) **she comes ~s** sie kommt donnerstags. *See also* **Friday**

thus /ðʌs/ *adv.* **1** (in the way indicated) so; (thereby) dadurch; **I picture the process as happening ~ ...:** ich stelle mir den Ablauf folgendermaßen vor: ... **2** (accordingly) deshalb; daher **3** (to this extent) **~ much/far** so viel/so weit

thwack /θwæk/ ▸ **whack A, B 1**

thwart /θwɔːt/
A *v.t.* durchkreuzen ‹*Pläne, Absichten*›; vereiteln ‹*Versuch*›; **~ sb.** jmdm. einen Strich durch die Rechnung machen; **she was ~ed in her plans** ihre Pläne wurden durchkreuzt
B *n.* (Naut.) Ducht, *die* (fachspr.); Ruderbank, *die*

thy /ðaɪ/ *poss. pron. attrib.* (arch./poet./dial.) dein; *see also* **her²**

thyme /taɪm/ *n.* (Bot.) Thymian, *der;* **wild ~:** Feldthymian, *der;* Quendel, *der*

thymus /ˈθaɪməs/ *n., pl.* **~es** *or* **thymi** /ˈθaɪmaɪ/ **~ [gland]** (Anat.) Thymus, *der;* Thymusdrüse, *die*

thyroid /ˈθaɪrɔɪd/ *n.* **~ [gland]** (Anat., Zool.) Schilddrüse, *die*

thyself /ðaɪˈself/ *pron.* (arch./poet./dial.) **1** *emphat.* selbst **2** *refl.* dich/dir; **know ~!** erkenne dich selbst! *see also* **herself**

ti ▸ **te**

tiara /tɪˈɑːrə/ *n.* **1** (pope's crown) Tiara, *die* **2** (jewelled band) Diadem, *das*

Tibet /tɪˈbet/ *pr. n.* Tibet (*das*)

Tibetan /tɪˈbetn/ ▸ **❶ p. 1277,** ▸ **❶ p. 1345**
A *adj.* tibetisch; **sb. is ~:** jmd. ist Tibeter/Tibeterin
B *n.* **1** (person) Tibeter, *der*/Tibeterin, *die* **2** (language) Tibetisch, *das*

tibia /ˈtɪbɪə/ *n., pl.* **~e** /ˈtɪbiː/ *or* **~s** (Anat.) Tibia, *die* (fachspr.); Schienbein, *das*

tic /tɪk/ *n.* Tic, *der* (Med.); nervöse Muskelzuckung

tich /tɪtʃ/ ▸ **titch**

tichy ▸ **titchy**

Ticino /tɪˈtʃiːnəʊ/ *pr. n.* das Tessin

tick¹ /tɪk/
A *v.i.* ticken; **what makes sb. ~** (fig.) worauf jmd. anspricht
B *v.t.* **1** mit einem Häkchen versehen **2** ▸ **~ off 1**
C *n.* **1** (of clock etc.) Ticken, *das* **2** (Brit. coll.: moment) Sekunde, *die;* **half a ~!, just a ~!** Momentchen! (ugs.); **I'll be with you in a ~** *or* **two ~s** ich komme gleich **3** (mark) Häkchen, *das;* **put a ~ against your preference** kennzeichnen Sie das, was Sie bevorzugen, mit einem Häkchen

Phrasal verbs

- **~ aˈway** *v.i.* [weiter]ticken; **the minutes ~ed away** die Minuten verstrichen
- **~ ˈoff** *v.t.* **1** (cross off) abhaken **2** (coll.: reprimand) rüffeln (ugs.)
- **~ ˈover** *v.i.* **1** (Motor Veh.) im Leerlauf laufen; **~ over noisily/too slowly/too fast** im Leerlauf [zu] laut/zu langsam/zu schnell drehen **2** (fig.) **~ over [nicely]** (progress satisfactorily) ganz gut laufen (ugs.); **keep things ~ing over while I'm away** sieh zu, dass alles gemächlich weiterläuft, während ich weg bin. *See also* **tick-over**

tick² *n.* (Zool.) (arachnid) Zecke, *die;* (insect) Lausfliege, *die*

tick³ *n.* (coll.: credit) **buy on ~:** auf Pump kaufen (salopp); **can I have it on ~?** kann ich das anschreiben lassen?

ticker /ˈtɪkə(r)/ *n.* (coll.) **1** (watch) Zwiebel, *die* (ugs. scherzh.) **2** (tape machine) Ticker, *der* (ugs.) **3** (heart) Pumpe, *die* (salopp)

ˈticker tape *n.* (Amer.) [Papier]streifen, *der* (*aus dem Fernschreiber*); **~ welcome** Konfettiparade, *die*

ticket /ˈtɪkɪt/
A *n.* **1** Karte, *die;* (for concert, theatre, cinema, exhibition) [Eintritts]karte, *die;* (for public transport) Fahrschein, *der;* (of cardboard) Fahrkarte, *die;* (for aeroplane) Flugschein, *der;* Ticket, *das;* (for ship) Fahrschein, *der;* Ticket, *das;* (of lottery, raffle) Los, *das;* (for library) Ausweis, *der;* (for car park) Parkschein, *der;* **cloakroom/pawn ~:** Garderobenmarke, *die*/Pfandschein, *der;* **entrance by ~ only** Einlass nur gegen Eintrittskarte; **price ~:** Preisschild, *das;* **[parking]~:** Strafmandat, *das;* Strafzettel, *der* (ugs.) **2** (certificate) (Naut.) Patent, *das;* (Aeronaut.) Pilotenschein, *der* **3** (Amer. Polit.) (list of candidates) [Wahl]liste, *die;* **run on the Democratic/Republican ~:** für die Demokraten/Republikaner kandidieren; **run on a youth ~** (fig.) mit einem auf Jungwähler zugeschnittenen Programm antreten; *see also* **split C 3** **4** **be [just] the ~** (coll.) genau das Richtige sein
B *v.t.* auszeichnen ‹*Waren*›

ticket: ~ agency *n.* Kartenvorverkaufsstelle, *die;* **~ agent** *n.* ▸ **❶ p. 1260** Inhaber/Inhaberin einer Kartenvorverkaufsstelle; **~ barrier** *n.* Sperre, *die;* **~ collector** *n.* ▸ **❶ p. 1260** (on train) Schaffner, *der*/Schaffnerin, *die;* (on station) Fahrkartenkontrolleur, *der*/-kontrolleurin, *die;* **~ dispenser** *n.* Kartenautomat, *der;* (for train etc.) Fahrkartenautomat, *der;* Fahrscheinautomat, *der;* **~ holder** *n.* Besitzer/Besitzerin einer Eintrittskarte; **~ inspector** *n.* ▸ **❶ p. 1260** Fahrkartenkontrolleur, *der*/-kontrolleurin, *die;* **~ machine** *n.* Fahrkartenautomat, *der;* Fahrscheinautomat, *der;* **~ office** *n.* Kartenschalter, *der;* (for public transport) Fahrkartenschalter, *der;* (for advance booking) Kartenvorverkaufsstelle, *die;* **~ window** *n.* Fahrkartenschalter, *der;* (in cinema, theatre) Kasse, *die;* Kassenschalter, *der*

ticking /ˈtɪkɪŋ/ *n.* (Textiles) Drillich, *der;* Drell, *der* (fachspr.)

ticking-ˈoff *n.* (coll.) Rüffel, *der* (ugs.)

tickle /ˈtɪkl/
A *v.t.* **1** (touch lightly) kitzeln; **~ sb.'s ribs** (fig.) jmdn. zum Lachen bringen; *abs.* **don't ~!** kitzle mich nicht!; **you're tickling!** das kitzelt! **2** (amuse) **be ~d by sth.** sich über etw. (*Akk.*) amüsieren; **be ~d pink about sth.** (coll.) sich wahnsinnig über etw. (*Akk.*) freuen (ugs.); **~ sb.'s fancy** jmdn. reizen
B *v.i.* kitzeln
C *n.* Kitzeln, *das;* **give sb. a ~:** jmdn. kitzeln

ticklish /ˈtɪklɪʃ/ *adj.* (also fig.: tricky) kitzlig

tickly /ˈtɪklɪ/ *adj.* (coll.) kitzlig

tick: ~-over *n.* (Motor Veh.) Leerlauf, *der;* **~-tack-ˈtoe** (Amer.) = **noughts and crosses** ▸ **nought 1**; **~-tock** /ˈtɪktɒk/ *n.* **1** *no pl.* (sound) Ticktack, *das;* **2** (child lang.: clock) Ticktack, *die* (Kinderspr.)

tidal /ˈtaɪdl/ *adj.* Gezeiten-; **~ river** Tidefluss, *der;* **~ basin/harbour** Tidebecken, *das*/-hafen, *der* (Seemannsspr.)

tidal: ~ ˈenergy *n., no pl.* Gezeitenenergie, *die;* **~ flow** *n.* (Transport) *dem Verkehrsfluss angepasstes System der Verkehrsführung;* **~ ˈpower station** *n.* Gezeitenkraftwerk, *das;* **~ wave** *n.* Flutwelle, *die;* **a ~ wave of enthusiasm/protest** (fig.) eine gewaltige Welle der Begeisterung/von Protesten

tidbit /ˈtɪdbɪt/ (Amer.) ▸ **titbit**

tiddledy-wink /ˈtɪdldɪwɪŋk/ (Amer.) ▸ **tiddlywink**

tiddler /ˈtɪdlə(r)/ *n.* (Brit. coll./child lang.) **1** (fish) Fischchen, *das* **2** (child) Kleine, *das;* **~s** (things) Kleinzeug, *das* (ugs. abwertend)

tiddl[e]y /ˈtɪdlɪ/ *adj.* (Brit.) **1** (coll.: slightly drunk) angesäuselt (ugs.) **2** **~ [little]** (coll.: very small) klitzeklein (ugs.)

tiddlywink *n.* **1** (counter) farbiges Plättchen **2** **~s** *sing.* (game) Flohhüpfen, *das*

tide /taɪd/
A *n.* **1** (rise or fall of sea) Tide, *die* (nordd., bes. Seemannsspr.); **high ~:** Flut, *die;* **low ~:** Ebbe, *die;* **the ~s** die Gezeiten; **sail on the next ~:** mit der nächsten Flut auslaufen; **cut off/washed up by the ~:** von der Flut abgeschnitten/angeschwemmt; **the ~ is in/out** es ist Flut/Ebbe; **when the ~ is in/out** bei Flut/Ebbe; **the rise and fall of the ~s** Ebbe und Flut; der Tidenhub (Seemannsspr.); *see also* **turn A 7** **2** (fig.: trend) Trend, *der;* **go with/against the ~:** mit dem/gegen den Strom schwimmen; **the ~ of war was turning** das Kriegsglück wendete sich; **rising ~ of opposition** zunehmende Opposition; *see also* **turn C 3**
B *v.t.* **~ sb. over** jmdm. über die Runden helfen (ugs.); **I have enough to ~ me over/over the winter** ich habe genug, um mich über Wasser zu halten/um durch *od.* über den Winter zu kommen; **~ sb. over a difficult period** jmdm. über eine schwierige Zeit hinweghelfen

ˈtide gate *n.* (Naut.) Fluttor, *das*

tideless /ˈtaɪdlɪs/ *adj.* gezeitenlos

tide: ~line *n.* Flutlinie, *die;* **~mark** *n.* **1** Flutmarke, *die;* **2** (Brit. coll.: line on body, bath, etc.) Schmutzrand, *der;* **~ table** *n.* (Naut.) Gezeitentafel, *die;* **~way** *n.* (of river) Tidefluss, *der;* (channel) Priel, *der;* (current) Gezeitenströmung, *die*

tidily /ˈtaɪdɪlɪ/ *adv.* ordentlich; (clearly) übersichtlich ‹*präsentieren, gestalten*›

tidiness /ˈtaɪdɪnɪs/ *n., no pl.* Ordentlichkeit, *die*

tidings /ˈtaɪdɪŋz/ *n. pl.* (literary) Kunde, *die* (geh.)

tidy /ˈtaɪdɪ/
A *adj.* **1** (neat) ordentlich; aufgeräumt ‹*Zimmer, Schreibtisch*›; **make oneself/a room ~:** sich zurechtmachen/ein Zimmer aufräumen; **have ~ habits** ein ordentlicher Mensch sein **2** (coll.: considerable) ordentlich (ugs.); **a ~ sum** *or* **penny** ein hübsches Sümmchen (ugs.)
B *n.* (receptacle) **kitchen/bathroom/desk ~:** Behälter für Küchen-/Badezimmer-/Schreibtischutensilien; **sink ~:** Einsatzkörbchen für die Spüle
C *v.t.* aufräumen ‹*Zimmer*›; **~ oneself** sich zurechtmachen; **~ one's hair** sich kämmen; *abs.* **be busy ~ing** mit [dem] Aufräumen beschäftigt sein

Phrasal verbs

- **~ aˈway** *v.t.* wegräumen
- **~ ˈup**
A *v.i.* aufräumen
B *v.t.* aufräumen; in Ordnung bringen ‹*Text*›

tie /taɪ/
A *v.t.*, **tying** /ˈtaɪɪŋ/ **1** binden (**to** an + *Akk.*, **into** zu); **~ the prisoner's legs together** dem Gefangenen die Beine zusammenbinden; ~

an apron round you[r waist] binde dir eine Schürze um; **can he ~ his own shoes/tie?** kann er sich (*Dat.*) die Schuhe/die Krawatte selbst binden?; **~ a knot** einen Knoten machen; *see also* **hand A 1** 2 (Sport: gain equal score in) **~ the match** unentschieden spielen; **they ~d the match at 3 all** es stand unentschieden drei beide 3 (restrict) binden (**to** an + *Akk.*) 4 (Building) verbinden ‹*Balken*›

B *v.i.*, **tying** 1 (be fastened) **it won't ~:** es lässt sich nicht binden; **it ~s at the back** es wird hinten gebunden; **where does the sash ~?** wo bindet man die Schärpe? 2 (have equal scores, votes, etc.) **~ for second place in the competition/election** mit gleicher Punktzahl den zweiten Platz im Wettbewerb/mit gleicher Stimmenzahl den zweiten Platz bei der Wahl erreichen; **~ 6 : 6** mit 6 : 6 ein Unentschieden erreichen

C *n.* 1 (worn round collar) Krawatte, *die; see also* **old A 6** 2 (cord etc. for fastening) Band, *das;* **~ fastening** Verschnürung, *die* 3 (fig.) (bond) Band, *das;* (restriction) Bindung, *die;* **~s of friendship/family ~s** Freundschafts-/Familienbande *Pl.* (geh.); **have ~s with a firm** Beziehungen zu einer Firma unterhalten; **find that sth. is a ~:** sich durch etw. gebunden fühlen; **be a ~ for sb.** für jmdn. eine Belastung sein 4 (Building) Binder, *der* 5 (Amer. Railw.) Schwelle, *die* 6 (Mus.) Haltebogen, *der* 7 (equality) (of scores) Punktgleichheit, *die;* (of votes) Patt, *das;* Stimmengleichheit, *die;* **there was a ~ for third place** zwei Teilnehmer landeten punktgleich auf dem dritten Platz; **end in** *or* **be a ~:** unentschieden *od.* mit einem Unentschieden enden 8 (Sport: match) Begegnung, *die;* **draw an easy ~:** einen leichten Gegner ziehen 9 (Amer.: shoe) Schnürschuh, *der*

Phrasal verbs

- **~ 'back** *v.t.* zurückbinden; **~ one's hair back in a ponytail** sein Haar hinten zu einem Pferdeschwanz zusammenbinden
- **~ 'down** *v.t.* 1 (fasten) festbinden 2 (fig.: restrict) binden; **there are too many things tying me down here** ich bin hier zu sehr gebunden; **be ~d down by sth.** durch etw. gebunden *od.* eingeschränkt sein; **~ sb. down to conditions/a time/a schedule** jmdn. auf Bedingungen/eine Zeit/einen Zeitplan festlegen
- **~ 'in**

A *v.i.* **~ in with sth.** zu etw. passen

B *v.t.* **~ sth. in with sth.** etw. mit etw. abstimmen; *see also* **~-in**

- **~ 'up**

A *v.t.* 1 (bind) festbinden; festmachen ‹*Boot*›; binden, fesseln ‹*Gefangenen*›; **~ up a parcel with string** ein Paket verschnüren; **~ sth. up in[to] bundles** etw. zu Bündeln zusammenbinden 2 (complete arrangements for) abschließen; **~ up a few loose ends** (fig.) ein paar letzte Kleinigkeiten erledigen 3 (make unavailable) fest anlegen ‹*Geld*›; **~ up property** Eigentum einer Verfügungsbeschränkung unterwerfen 4 ▸**~ in B** 5 (keep busy) beschäftigen; **I am ~d up this evening** ich habe heute Abend zu tun. *see also* **~-up**

B *v.i.* 1 (moor) festmachen 2 (make sense) **it ~s up** es ergibt einen Sinn

tie: ~ bar *n.* (Building) Anker, *der;* **~ beam** *n.* (Building) Binderbalken, *der;* **~break, ~breaker** *ns.* Tiebreak, *der od. das;* **~ clip** *n.* Krawattenhalter, *der*

tied /taɪd/ *adj.* (Brit.) 1 **~ cottage** *or* **house** (of farmworker) Wohnhaus für Farmarbeiter; (of caretaker etc.) Dienstwohnhaus, *das* 2 **~ house** (public house supplying one brewer's beers) Vertragsgaststätte, *die*

tie: ~-in *n.: gleichzeitige [Wieder]aufführung eines Films o. Ä. mit der [Neu]veröffentlichung des zugrunde liegenden Buches;* **~-on** *adj.* Anhänge-; **~-on label** Anhänger, *der;* **~pin** *n.* Krawattennadel, *die*

tier /tɪə(r)/ *n.* 1 (row) Rang, *der* 2 (unit) Stufe, *die*

tiered /tɪəd/ *adj.* gestuft ‹*Hörsaal, Theater*›; **a three-~ wedding cake** eine dreistöckige Hochzeitstorte; **a three-~ shelf [unit]** ein Regal mit drei Fächern

tie rod *n.* 1 (Motor Veh.) Spurstange, *die* 2 (Building) Querlatte, *die*

Tierra del Fuego /tɪerə del 'fweɪgəʊ/ *pr. n.* Feuerland (*das*)

tie-up *n.* Verbindung, *die*

tiff /tɪf/ *n.* Krach, *der* (ugs.); Streit, *der;* **have a ~ with sb. over sth.** mit jmdm. wegen etw. Krach haben

tiger /'taɪgə(r)/ *n.* 1 (Zool.) Tiger, *der;* **American ~** ▸**jaguar**; **paper ~** (fig.) Papiertiger, *der;* **ride a ~** (fig.) mit dem Feuer spielen 2 (fierce or energetic person) Kämpfernatur, *die*

tiger: ~ cat *n.* (Zool.) Tigerkatze, *die;* **~ e'conomy** *n.* Tigerstaat, *der;* **~ lily** *n.* (Bot.) Tigerlilie, *die;* **~ moth** *n.* (Zool.) Bärenspinner, *der;* **~'s eye** *n.* (Min.) Tigerauge, *das;* **~ shark** *n.* (Zool.) Tigerhai, *der*

tight /taɪt/

A *adj.* 1 (firm) fest; fest angezogen ‹*Schraube, Mutter*›; festsitzend ‹*Korken, Deckel*›; **be very ~:** sehr fest sitzen; **the drawer/window is ~:** die Schublade/das Fenster klemmt 2 (close-fitting) eng ‹*Kleid, Hose, Schuh usw.*›; **this shoe is rather [too] ~** *or* **a rather ~ fit** dieser Schuh ist etwas zu eng 3 (impermeable) **~ seal/joint** dichter Verschluss/dichte Fuge 4 (taut) straff; **a ~ feeling in one's chest** ein Gefühl der Beklemmung *od.* Enge in der Brust 5 (with little space) knapp; gedrängt ‹*Programm*›; **it is a ~ space** der Platz ist knapp; es ist [zu] wenig Platz; **it is a ~ squeeze with seven people in the car** es ist sehr eng zu siebt im Wagen 6 (strict) streng ‹*Kontrolle, Disziplin*›; straff ‹*Organisation*› 7 (Econ.) knapp ‹*Geld*›; angespannt ‹*Markt*› 8 (coll.: stingy) knauserig (ugs.) 9 (difficult to negotiate) **a ~ corner** eine enge Kurve; **be in/get oneself into a ~ corner** *or* (coll.) **spot [over sth.]** (fig.) [wegen etw.] in der Klemme sein/in die Klemme geraten (ugs.) 10 (coll.: drunk) voll (salopp); **get ~:** sich voll laufen lassen (salopp); **she got ~ on a couple of drinks** nach ein paar Drinks war sie voll (salopp) 11 (Sport: evenly contested) hart umkämpft; knapp ‹*Rennen*›

B *adv.* 1 (firmly) fest; **hold ~!** halt dich fest!; *see also* **sit A 2; sleep B 1** 2 (so as to leave no space) [ganz] voll; **a train packed ~ with commuters** ein mit Pendlern voll gestopfter Zug (ugs.)

C *n. in pl.* 1 (Brit.) **[pair of] ~s** Strumpfhose, *die* 2 (of dancer etc.) Trikothose, *die*

tighten /'taɪtn/

A *v.t.* 1 [fest] anziehen ‹*Knoten, Schraube, Mutter usw.*›; straff ziehen ‹*Seil, Schnur*›; anspannen ‹*Muskeln*›; verstärken ‹*Griff*›; **~ one's belt** (fig.) den Gürtel enger schnallen (ugs.) 2 (make stricter) verschärfen ‹*Kontrolle, Gesetz, Vorschrift*›

B *v.i.* 1 sich spannen; ‹*Knoten:*› sich zusammenziehen; **her hands ~ed on the steering wheel** ihre Hände krampften sich um das Steuer 2 (become stricter) ‹*Gesetze, Bestimmungen:*› verschärft werden

Phrasal verb

- **~ 'up**

A *v.t.* 1 anziehen; (retighten) nachziehen 2 (make stricter) verschärfen ‹*Gesetze, Bestimmungen, Kontrollen*›; **~ up security** die Sicherheitsmaßnahmen verschärfen

B *v.i.* härter durchgreifen; **~ up on security/drunken driving** die Sicherheitsmaßnahmen verschärfen/bei Trunkenheit am Steuer schärfer durchgreifen

tight: ~-'fisted *adj.* geizig; **a ~-fisted old fellow** ein alter Geizhals; **~-fitting** *adj.* eng anliegend ‹*Pullover, Trikot*›; **~-lipped** *adj.* 1 (without emotion) mit zusammengepressten Lippen *nachgestellt;* 2 (silent) verschwiegen

tightly /'taɪtlɪ/ *adv.* 1 (firmly) fest; **fit ~** ‹*Maschinenteil usw.:*› fest sitzen; ‹*Kleidungsstück:*› eng anliegen; **fasten sth. ~:** etw. gut befestigen; **put the cork in ~:** den Korken fest hineindrücken 2 (strictly) streng 3 (tautly) straff 4 (closely) dicht; **~ packed** voll gestopft (ugs.) ‹*Zug, Koffer*›; **a ~ organized schedule** ein gedrängtes Programm 5 **~ fought** (evenly contested) hart umkämpft

tightness /'taɪtnɪs/ *n., no pl.* 1 (lack of leakage) Dichtheit, *die* 2 (firmness) Festigkeit, *die;* (closeness of fit) enger Sitz 3 (strictness of control *or* discipline) Schärfe, *die;* Strenge, *die* 4 (tautness) Straffheit, *die;* **feel [a] ~ across the chest** ein Gefühl der Beklemmung in der Brust haben 5 (of schedule) Gedrängtheit, *die* 6 (Econ.: scarcity) Knappheit, *die;* (of market) Angespanntheit, *die* 7 (of bend in road) Enge, *die* 8 **~ with money** Knauserigkeit, *die* (ugs.) 9 (Sport: of match) Ausgeglichenheit, *die*

'tightrope *n.* Drahtseil, *das;* **walk a ~** (fig.) einen Balanceakt vollführen; *attrib.* **~ walker** Seiltänzer, *der*/-tänzerin, *die*

tigress /'taɪgrɪs/ *n.* (Zool.) Tigerin, *die*

tilde /'tɪldə/ *n.* (Ling.) Tilde, *die*

tile /taɪl/

A *n.* 1 (on roof) Ziegel, *der;* (on floor, wall) Fliese, *die;* (on stove; also esp. designer ~) Kachel, *die;* **spend the night on the ~s** (fig. coll.) die ganze Nacht durchsumpfen (salopp) 2 (Games) Spielstein, *der*

B *v.t.* [mit Ziegeln] decken ‹*Dach*›; fliesen ‹*Wand, Fußboden, Bad*›; kacheln ‹*Wand, Bad*›; **~d roof** Ziegeldach, *das;* **~d floor** Fliesenboden, *der*

tiler /'taɪlə(r)/ *n.* (of roofs) Dachdecker, *der*/-deckerin, *die;* (of floors, walls) Fliesenleger, *der*/-legerin, *die*

tiling /'taɪlɪŋ/ *n., no pl., no indef. art.* ▸**tile A 1:** 1 (fixing tiles) (on roof) [Dach]decken, *das;* (on floor) Fliesen[legen], *das;* (on wall) Kacheln, *das;* Fliesen, *das* 2 (set of tiles) Ziegel/Kacheln/Fliesen

till¹ /tɪl/ *v.t.* (Agric.) bestellen

till²

A *prep.* bis; (followed by article + noun) bis zu; **not [...] ~:** erst; **from morning ~ evening** von morgens bis abends; *see also* **until A**

B *conj.* bis; *see also* **until B**

till³ *n.* Kasse, *die;* **at the ~:** an der Kasse; **have/put one's hand** *or* **fingers in the ~** (fig.) in die Kasse greifen

tillage /'tɪlɪdʒ/ *n., no pl.* (Agric.) (tilling) Bestellung, *die;* (land tilled) Ackerland, *das*

tiller /'tɪlə(r)/ *n.* (Naut.) Pinne, *die* (Seemannsspr.)

till: ~ receipt *n.* Kassenzettel, *der;* Kassenbon, *der;* **~ roll** *n.* Kassenrolle, *die*

tilt /tɪlt/

A *v.i.* 1 kippen; **the chair ~s back** die Sessellehne kippt nach hinten; **the board ~ed [up] when he stepped on it** das Brett schnellte hoch, als er darauf trat 2 (Hist.: joust) tjostieren; **~ at** mit der Lanze angreifen; (fig.) anprangern; *see also* **windmill 1**

B *v.t.* kippen; neigen ‹*Kopf*›

C *n.* 1 (sloping position) Schräglage, *die;* **give sth. a ~:** etw. kippen *od.* schräg stellen; **a 45° ~:** eine Neigung *od.* ein Neigungswinkel von 45° 2 (fig.: attack) Angriff, *der;* **have** *or* **make a ~ at sb./sth.** jmdn./etw. angreifen *od.* attackieren 3 **[at] full ~:** mit voller Wucht

tilth /tɪlθ/ *n.* Ackerkrume, *die;* **rake a seedbed to a good ~:** ein Saatbeet gut [auf]lockern

tilting 'train *n.* Neigezug, *der*

timber /'tɪmbə(r)/ *n.* 1 *no pl.* (wood for building) [Bau]holz, *das;* **sawn ~:** Schnittholz, *das* 2 (type of wood) Holzart, *die;* Holz, *das* 3 *no pl., no indef. art.* (trees) Wald, *der;* **cut down** *or* **fell ~:** Holz schlagen; **put land under ~:** Land aufforsten (Forstw.); **standing ~:** Baumholz, *das* (Forstw.) 4 (beam, piece of wood) Balken, *der;* (Naut.) Spant, *das;* **floor ~s** [Boden]balken; *see also* **shiver² B** 5 **~!** Baum fällt!; Achtung! (*Ausruf bei Holzfällarbeiten*)

timbered /'tɪmbəd/ *adj.* 1 (wooded) bewaldet 2 (built of wood) hölzern; Holz-; (covered with planks) holzverkleidet

timber: ~-framed *adj.* Fachwerk‹*bau, -haus*›; ‹*Rathaus, Jagdschloss usw.*› in Fachwerkbauweise; **~-framing** *n., no pl., no indef. art.* (structure) Fachwerk, *das;* (method) Fachwerkbauweise, *die*

timbering /'tɪmbərɪŋ/ *n., no pl., no indef. art.* Balkenwerk, *das;* (of timber-framed house) Fachwerk, *das*

timber: **~line** *n.* (Geog.) Baumgrenze, *die;* **~yard** *n.* Holzlager, *das*

timbre /'tæmbə(r), 'tɛ̃br/ *n.* (Mus.) Timbre, *das*

Timbuctoo /tɪmbʌk'tu:/ *pr. n.* ▸❶ **p. 1643** Timbuktu *(das)*

time /taɪm/

A *n.* [1]▸ *no pl., no art.* Zeit, *die;* **the greatest composer of all ~:** der größte Komponist aller Zeiten; **for all ~:** für immer [und ewig]; **past/present/future ~:** Vergangenheit, *die/*Gegenwart, *die/*Zukunft, *die;* **stand the test of ~:** die Zeit überdauern; sich bewähren; **in [the course of] ~, as ~ goes on/went on** mit der Zeit; im Laufe der Zeit; **as old as ~:** uralt; **~ will tell** *or* **show** die Zukunft wird es zeigen; **~ and tide wait for no man** (prov.) das Rad der Zeit lässt sich nicht anhalten; **at this point** *or* **moment in ~:** zum gegenwärtigen Zeitpunkt; **~ flies** die Zeit vergeht [wie] im Fluge; **how ~ flies!** wie [schnell] die Zeit vergeht!; **work against ~:** unter Zeitdruck arbeiten; **in ~, with ~** (sooner or later) mit der Zeit; *see also* **healer**

[2]▸ (interval, available or allotted period) Zeit, *die;* **in a week's/month's/year's ~:** in einer Woche/in einem Monat/Jahr; **there is ~ for that** dafür ist *od.* haben wir noch Zeit; **it takes me all my ~ to do it** es beansprucht meine ganze Zeit, es zu tun; **it took me all my ~ to persuade him** ich hatte die größte Mühe, ihn zu überreden; **give one's ~ to sth.** einer Sache *(Dat.)* seine Zeit opfern; **waste of ~:** Zeitverschwendung, *die;* **spend [most of one's/a lot of] ~ on sth./[in] doing sth.** [die meiste/viel] Zeit mit etw. zubringen/damit verbringen, etw. zu tun; **I have been waiting for some/a long ~:** ich warte schon seit einiger Zeit/schon lange; **she will be there for [quite] some ~:** sie wird ziemlich lange dort sein; **spend some ~ in a place** sich eine Zeit lang an einem Ort aufhalten; **be pressed for ~:** keine Zeit haben; (have to finish quickly) in Zeitnot sein; **pass the ~:** sich *(Dat.)* die Zeit vertreiben; **length of ~:** Zeit[dauer], *die;* **make ~ for sb./sth.** sich *(Dat.)* für jmdn./etw. Zeit nehmen; **a short ~ ago** vor kurzem; **that's a long ~ ago** das ist schon lange her; **in one's own ~:** in seiner Freizeit; (whenever one wishes) wann man will; **one's ~ is one's own** man kann über seine Zeit frei verfügen; **take one's ~ [over sth.]** sich *(Dat.)* [für etw.] Zeit lassen; (be slow) sich *(Dat.)* Zeit [mit etw.] lassen; **~ is money** (prov.) Zeit ist Geld (Spr.); **we're out of ~, our ~'s up** unsere Zeit ist um; **on ~** (Amer.: on hire purchase) auf Raten; **in [good] ~** (not late) rechtzeitig; **all the** *or* **this ~:** die ganze Zeit; (without ceasing) ständig; **all the ~ you're standing there arguing things are only getting worse** während du hier herumstehst und argumentierst, wird alles nur immer schlimmer; **since ~ immemorial** *or* **out of mind** seit undenklichen Zeiten; **in [less than** *or* **next to] 'no ~:** innerhalb kürzester Zeit; im Nu *od.* Handumdrehen; **it was 'no ~ [at all] before she was back** sie war im Nu zurück; **in 'half the ~:** in der Hälfte der Zeit; **'half the ~** (coll.: as often as not) die halbe Zeit; **it will take [some] ~:** es wird einige Zeit dauern; **have ~ on one's hands** viel Zeit und Muße haben; (have nothing to do) nichts zu tun haben; **have the/no ~:** Zeit/keine Zeit haben; **have no ~ for sb./sth.** für jmdn./etw. ist einem seine Zeit zu schade; **we have no ~ to lose** wir dürfen keine Zeit verlieren; **there is no ~ to lose** *or* **be lost** es ist keine Zeit zu verlieren; **lose no ~ in doing sth.** (not delay) etw. unverzüglich tun; **lose no ~ doing sth.** (not waste ~) keine Zeit damit vergeuden, etw. zu tun; **do ~** (coll.) eine Strafe absitzen (ugs.); **he lived out his ~ in peace** er verbrachte den Rest seines Lebens in Ruhe; **in my '~** (heyday) zu meiner Zeit (ugs.); (in the course of my life) im Laufe meines Lebens; **in 'my ~** (period at a place) zu meiner Zeit (ugs.); **in my father's ~:** zu [Leb]zeiten meines Vaters; **~ off** *or* **out** freie Zeit; **get/take ~ off** frei bekommen/sich *(Dat.)* frei nehmen (ugs.); **take ~ out to look at this properly** nimm dir die Zeit, um dir das richtig anzuschauen; **T~!** (Boxing) Stop!; Time!; (Brit.: in pub) Feierabend!; **~, [ladies and] gentlemen, please!** wir machen Feierabend, meine [Damen und] Herren!; **have a lot of ~ for sb.** (fig.) für jmdn. viel übrig haben; *see also* **gain B 1; hand A 3; serve A 4**

[3]▸ *no pl.* (moment or period destined for purpose) Zeit, *die;* **harvest/Christmas ~:** Ernte-/Weihnachtszeit, *die;* **there is a ~ and place for everything** alles zu seiner Zeit; **now is the ~ to do it** jetzt ist die richtige Zeit, es zu tun; **~ for lunch** Zeit zum Mittagessen; **it is ~ to go** es wird Zeit zu gehen; **it's [about] ~ they were going** es ist [an der] Zeit, dass sie gehen; **his ~ was drawing near** (~ of death) seine Zeit nahte (geh. verhüll.); **look/get old before one's ~:** vorzeitig altern; **and not before ~:** und es wurde auch Zeit; **when the ~ comes/came** wenn es so weit ist/als es so weit war; **on ~** (punctually) pünktlich; **ahead of ~:** zu früh ‹*ankommen*›; vorzeitig ‹*fertig werden*›; **all in good ~:** alles zu seiner Zeit; **you'll find out in good ~:** du wirst es früh genug herausfinden; *see also* **be B 1; behind B 5**

[4]▸ *in sing. or pl.* (circumstances) Zeit, *die;* **~s are good/bad/have changed** die Zeiten sind gut/schlecht/haben sich verändert; **have a good ~:** Spaß haben (ugs.); sich amüsieren; **have quite a ~ [of it]** viel durchmachen; **have a hard ~ [of it]** eine schwere Zeit durchmachen; *see also* **life 5**

[5]▸ (associated with events or person[s]) Zeit, *die;* **in ~ of peace/war** in Friedens-/Kriegszeiten; **in Tudor/Napoleon's/ancient ~s** zur Zeit der Tudors/Napoleons/der Antike; **in prehistoric ~s** in vorgeschichtlicher Zeit; **in former/modern ~s** früher/heutzutage; **scientists of the ~:** Wissenschaftler jener Zeit; **the good old ~s** die gute alte Zeit; **Queen Victoria and her ~[s]** Königin Viktoria und ihre Zeit; **~ 'was when ...:** es gab eine Zeit, da ...; **ahead of** *or* **before one's/its ~:** seiner Zeit voraus; **at 'one ~** (previously) früher; *see also* **behind B 3**

[6]▸ (occasion) Mal, *das;* **this ~:** diesmal; **for the first ~:** zum ersten Mal; **[the] second ~ [a]round** beim zweiten Mal; **next ~ you come** wenn du das nächste Mal kommst; **ten/a hundred/a thousand ~s** zehn-/hundert-/tausendmal; **~s without number** unzählige Male; **I've told you a hundred ~s ...:** ich habe dir schon hundertmal gesagt, ... (ugs.); **many ~s** sehr oft; **many's the ~ [that] ..., many a ~ ...:** viele Male ...; **there are/were ~s when ...:** es gibt Zeiten, wenn .../es gab Zeiten, als ...; **at all ~s** jederzeit; **at ~s** gelegentlich; **from ~ to ~:** von Zeit zu Zeit; **at other ~s** sonst; **at all other ~s** zu allen anderen Zeiten; **at one ~ or another** irgendwann einmal; **this is no ~ to do that** es ist jetzt nicht die Zeit, das zu tun; **at a ~ like this/that** unter diesen/solchen Umständen; **at the** *or* **that ~** (in the past) damals; **it depends on which doctor is on duty at the ~:** es hängt davon ab, welcher Arzt gerade Bereitschaftsdienst hat; **at one ~, at [one and] the same ~** (simultaneously) gleichzeitig; **at the same ~** (nevertheless) gleichwohl; **at the best of ~s** im günstigsten Fall; **a 'fine ~** (iron.) genau die richtige Zeit (iron.); **between ~s** zwischendurch; **~ and [~] again, ~ after ~:** immer [und immer] wieder; **pay sb. £6 a ~:** jmdm. für jedes Mal 6 Pfund zahlen; **oranges cost 16p a ~:** Orangen kosten 16 Pence das Stück; **one at a ~:** einzeln; **one stone at a ~:** jeweils nur ein Stein; **two at a ~:** jeweils zwei; **hand me the cups two at a ~:** reich mir immer zwei Tassen gleichzeitig; **for hours/weeks at a ~:** stundenlang/wochenlang [ohne Unterbrechung]; **at this ~** (Amer.) heute; (at this moment) jetzt; *see also* **be B 1; every 1**

[7]▸ ▸❶ **p. 1001** (point in day etc.) [Uhr]zeit, *die;* **at the same ~ every morning** jeden Morgen um dieselbe Zeit; **what ~ is it?, what is the ~?** wie spät ist es?; **have you [got] the ~?** kannst du mir sagen, wie spät es ist?; **tell the ~** (read a clock) die Uhr lesen; **~ of day** Tageszeit, *die;* **[at this] ~ of [the] year** [um diese] Jahreszeit; **this ~ of the month** diese Zeit im Monat; **at this ~ of [the] night** zu dieser Nachtstunde; **know the ~ of day** (fig.) sich auskennen; **not give sb. the ~ of day** jmdm. nicht einmal Guten Tag sagen; **pass the ~ of day** (coll.) ein paar Worte wechseln; **by this/that ~:** inzwischen; **by the ~ [that] we arrived** bis wir hinkamen; **[by] this ~ tomorrow** morgen um diese Zeit; **keep good ~** ‹*Uhr:*› genau *od.* richtig gehen

[8]▸ (amount) Zeit, *die;* **make good ~:** gut vorwärts kommen; **get paid ~ and a half** 50% Zuschlag bekommen; **[your] ~'s up!** deine Zeit ist um (ugs.) *od.* abgelaufen

[9]▸ (multiplication) mal; **three ~s four** drei mal vier; **four ~s the size of/higher than sth.** viermal so groß wie/höher als etw.; **~s sign** Malzeichen, *das;* **magnified six ~s** auf das Sechsfache vergrößert

[10]▸ (Mus.) (duration of note) Zeitdauer, *die;* (measure) Takt, *der;* **in three-four ~:** im Dreivierteltakt; **keep in ~ with the music** den Takt halten; **out of ~/in ~:** aus dem/im Takt; **keep ~ with sth.** bei etw. den Takt [ein]halten

[11]▸ (dated: date of childbirth) **she is near** *or* **nearing her ~:** ihre Zeit rückt näher (geh. verhüll.)

B *v.t.* [1]▸ (do at correct ~) zeitlich abstimmen; **be well/ill ~d** zur richtigen/falschen Zeit kommen

[2]▸ (set to operate at correct ~) justieren (Technik); einstellen; **~ the bomb to explode at 4 p.m.** den Zeitzünder der Bombe auf 16 Uhr einstellen

[3]▸ (arrange ~ of arrival/departure of) **the bus is ~d to connect with the train** der Bus hat einen direkten Anschluss an den Zug; **be ~d to take 90 minutes** fahrplanmäßig 90 Minuten dauern

[4]▸ (measure ~ taken by) stoppen; **~ an egg** auf die richtige Kochdauer für ein Ei achten

time: **~-and-'motion** *adj.* REFA-‹*Techniker, Fachmann*›; **~-and-motion study** Arbeitsstudie, *die;* **~ bomb** *n.* (lit. or fig.) Zeitbombe, *die;* **~ capsule** *n.: Behälter mit Zeitdokumenten, der bei der Grundsteinlegung von [öffentlichen] Bauten eingemauert wird;* **~ check** *n.* Zeitvergleich, *der;* (to verify) Blick auf die Uhr; **~-consuming** *adj.* [1]▸ (taking ~) zeitaufwendig; [2]▸ (wasteful of ~) zeitraubend; **~ difference** *n.* [1]▸ (between events, actions) Zeitdifferenz, *die;* [2]▸ (between localities) Zeitunterschied, *der;* **~ exposure** *n.* (Photog.) Zeitaufnahme, *die;* **~ factor** *n., no pl.* Zeitfaktor, *der;* **~ fault** *n.* (Show Jumping) Zeitfehler, *der;* **~ frame** *n.* Zeitrahmen, *der;* **~ fuse** *n.* Zeitzünder, *der;* **~-honoured** *adj.* altehrwürdig (geh.); althergebracht ‹*Brauch, Vorstellung*›; **~ horizon** *n.* Zeithorizont, *der;* **~keeper** *n.* [1]▸ (person) Zeitnehmer, *der*/-nehmerin, *die;* [2]▸ **the watch is a good/bad ~keeper** die Uhr geht genau/nicht genau; **~keeping** *n., no pl.* [1]▸ (Sport) Zeitmessung, *die;* Zeitnahme, *die;* [2]▸ (at work) Einhaltung der Arbeitsstunden; **~ lag** *n.* zeitliche Verzögerung; **~-lapse** *attrib. adj.* (Photog., Cinemat., Telev.) Zeitraffer-

timeless /'taɪmlɪs/ *adj.* (rhet./poet.) zeitlos

time: **~ limit** *n.* Frist, *die;* **put a ~ limit on sth.** eine Frist für etw. setzen; **~line** *n.* [1]▸ (graphical representation) Zeitleiste, *die;* [2]▸ (schedule) Zeitplan, *der;* **a long ~line:** eine lange Laufzeit; **meet the programme ~lines** den Terminplan des Programmes einhalten

timeliness /'taɪmlɪnɪs/ *n., no pl.* Rechtzeitigkeit, *die*

time: **~ loan** *n.* befristetes Darlehen: **~ lock** *n.* Zeitschloss, *das*

timely /'taɪmlɪ/ *adj.* rechtzeitig; **be ~:** zur rechten Zeit kommen; **a ~ piece of advice** ein [guter] Rat zur rechten Zeit

time: **~ machine** *n.* Zeitmaschine, *die;* **~ management** *n., no pl.* Zeitmanagement, *das;* **~ 'out** *n.* (Sport) Spielunterbrechung, *die;* (called by one team) Auszeit, *die;* **~piece** *n.* Chronometer, *das*

timer /'taɪmə(r)/ *n.* [1]▸ ▸**timekeeper 1** [2]▸ (device) Kurzzeitmesser, *der;* (with switch) Schaltuhr, *die*

The Times

Eine britische überregionale Tageszeitung, deren Pendant am Sonntag *The Sunday Times* ist. Sie zählt zur seriösen Presse. Sie ist politisch unabhängig, wird jedoch gemeinhin als konservativ angesehen. Sie ist die älteste Zeitung in England und wurde erstmals 1785 veröffentlicht. *The Times* war ursprünglich ein *broadsheet*-Blatt. Jetzt erscheint sie aber (nach einer Übergangszeit, in der sie wahlweise als *tabloid* oder als *broadsheet* erhältlich war) nur noch im *tabloid*-Format.

time: ~-saver *n.* **be a ~-saver** Zeit sparen; **this is a real ~-saver** dies bedeutet eine echte Zeitersparnis; **~scale** *n.* Zeitskala, *die;* **~-server** *n.* Zeitabsitzer, *der*/-absitzerin, *die;* **~share** **A** *attrib. adj.* **~share apartment** *Ferienwohnung, an der man einen Besitzanteil hat, der es einem erlaubt, eine bestimmte Zeit pro Jahr in dieser Wohnung zu verbringen;* **B** *n.* **1** ▸ **~-sharing 2**; **2** (property) Timesharingobjekt, *das;* **~-sharing** *n., no pl., no art.* **1** (Computing) Timesharing, *das;* **2** (joint ownership) *Eigentum an einer Ferienwohnung o. Ä., das für eine festgelegte Zeit des Jahres gilt;* Timesharing, *das* (Wirtsch.); **~ sheet** *n.* Stundenzettel, *der;* **~ signal** *n.* Zeitzeichen, *das;* **~ signature** *n.* (Mus.) Taktbezeichnung, *die;* **~ switch** *n.* Zeitschalter, *der;* **~table** *n.* **1** (scheme of work) Zeitplan, *der;* (Educ.) Stundenplan, *der;* **2** (Transport) Fahrplan, *der;* **~ travel** *n.* Reise durch die Zeit; **~ trial** *n.* (Sport) (in cycling) Zeitfahren, *das;* (in athletics) Zeitrennen, *das;* **~ warp** *n.* Verwerfung im Raum-Zeit-Kontinuum; **this house is a complete ~ warp** in diesem Haus fühlt man sich in eine andere Zeit versetzt; **~-waster** *n.* (person) Zeitdieb, *der*/-diebin, *die;* (thing) Zeitverschwendung, *die;* Zeitvergeudung, *die* (emotional); **be a ~-waster** einem [nur] die Zeit stehlen; **'no ~-wasters'** (in advertisement) '[bitte] nur ernst gemeinte Anfragen'; **~-wasting** *n., no pl.* Zeitverschwendung, *die;* Zeitvergeudung, *die* (emotional); (in sport, politics) Verzögerungstaktik, *die;* **be booked for ~-wasting** (Sport) wegen Spielverzögerung verwarnt werden; *attrib.* zeitverschwendend; *attrib.* **~-wasting activity** reine Zeitverschwendung; **~-wasting tactics** Verzögerungstaktik, *die;* **~ window** *n.* Zeitfenster, *das;* **~-worn** *adj.* abgegriffen ‹*Witz, Klischee*›; verwittert ‹*Gebäude*›; **~ zone** *n.* Zeitzone, *die*

timid /ˈtɪmɪd/ *adj.* **1** (fearful) ängstlich ‹*Person, Miene, Worte*› **2** (lacking boldness) zaghaft; (shy) schüchtern **3** scheu ‹*Tier, Vogel*›

timidity /tɪˈmɪdɪtɪ/ *n., no pl.* ▸ **timid**: Ängstlichkeit, *die;* Schüchternheit, *die;* Scheu, *die;*

timidly /ˈtɪmɪdlɪ/ *adv.* ▸ **timid**: ängstlich; schüchtern; scheu

timing /ˈtaɪmɪŋ/ *n., no pl.* **1** zeitliche Abstimmung; Timing, *das;* **that was perfect ~!** (as sb. arrives) du kommst gerade im richtigen Augenblick!; **the ~ of the statement was excellent** der Zeitpunkt für die Erklärung war hervorragend [gewählt] **2** (Theatre) Timing, *das* **3** (Motor Veh.) **ignition/valve ~:** Zündeinstellung, *die*/Ventilsteuerzeiten; **adjust the [ignition] ~:** die Zündung einstellen

timorous /ˈtɪmərəs/ *adj.* ängstlich; verängstigt ‹*Tier*›; (lacking boldness) zaghaft ‹*Stimme, Auftreten*›

timpani /ˈtɪmpəniː/ *n. pl.* (Mus.) Kesselpauken; Timpani (fachspr.)

timpanist /ˈtɪmpənɪst/ *n.* ▸ **❶ p. 1260** (Mus.) Paukist, *der*/Paukistin, *die*

tin /tɪn/

A *n.* **1** (metal) Zinn, *das;* **~[-plate]** Weißblech, *das* **2** (Cookery) **cooking ~s** Back- und Bratformen **3** (Brit.: for preserving) [Konserven]dose, *die;* **a ~ of peas** eine Dose Erbsen **4** (with separate or hinged lid) Dose, *die;* **bread ~:** Brotkasten, *der*

B *v.t.*, **-nn-** (Brit.) zu Konserven verarbeiten

C *attrib. adj.* Zinn-; *see also* **lid 1**

tincture /ˈtɪŋktʃə(r)/ *n.* **1** (solution) Tinktur, *die* **2** (slight flavour) leichter Geschmack; (unpleasant) Beigeschmack, *der;* (fig.) Anflug, *der;* **a ~ of green/red** ein Stich ins Grüne/Rote

tinder /ˈtɪndə(r)/ *n.* Zunder, *der;* **as dry as ~:** knochentrocken

'tinder: ~box *n.* Zunderbüchse, *die* (veralt.); (fig.: person) Hitzkopf, *der;* (fig.: thing) Pulverfass, *das;* **the old houses are like ~boxes** die alten Häuser sind wie Zunder; **~-dry** *adj.* knochentrocken

tine /taɪn/ *n.* **1** (of deer) Ende, *das* (Jägerspr.) **2** (of rake, fork) Zinke, *die*

tin 'foil *n., no pl.* Stanniol, *das;* (aluminium foil) Alufolie, *die*

ting-a-ling /ˈtɪŋəlɪŋ/

A *n.* Klingeling, *das*

B *adv.* klingeling

tinge /tɪndʒ/

A *v.t.*, **~ing** tönen; **a white curtain ~d with pink** ein weißer, ins Zartrosa gehender Vorhang; **her black hair was ~d with grey** ihr schwarzes Haar war grau meliert; (fig.) **her admiration was ~d with envy** ihre Bewunderung war nicht ganz frei von Neid

B *n.* [leichte] Färbung; (fig.) Hauch, *der;* **a ~ of red in the sky** eine leicht rötliche Färbung des Himmels; **white with a ~ of blue** weiß mit einem Stich ins Bläuliche

tingle /ˈtɪŋgl/

A *v.i.* **1** (feel sensation) kribbeln **2** (cause sensation) **~ in sb.'s ears** jmdm. in den Ohren klingen *od.* tönen

B *n.* Kribbeln, *das;* **feel a ~ of excitement** vor Aufregung ganz kribbelig sein (ugs.)

tin: ~ 'god *n.* Götze, *der* (geh.); Abgott, *der;* **~ 'hat** *n.* (coll.) Blechdeckel, *der* (salopp); **~horn** (Amer.) **A** *n.* Angeber, *der* (ugs.) **B** *adj.* angeberisch (ugs.)

tinker /ˈtɪŋkə(r)/

A *n.* Kesselflicker, *der;* **I don't give a ~'s cuss** (coll.) es ist mir völlig Wurs[ch]t (ugs.)

B *v.i.* **~ with sth.** an etw. (*Dat.*) herumbasteln (ugs.); (incompetently; also fig.) an etw. (*Dat.*) herumpfuschen (ugs.)

tinkle /ˈtɪŋkl/

A *n.* Klingeln, *das;* (of coins) Klimpern, *das;* **give sb. a ~** (Brit. coll.: telephone call) bei jmdm. anklingeln (ugs.)

B *v.t.* klingeln mit; klimpern mit ‹*Münzen*›

C *v.i.* ‹*Glocke:*› klingeln; ‹*Münzen:*› klimpern; **~ on a piano** auf einem Klavier klimpern

'tin mine *n.* Zinnbergwerk, *das*

tinned /tɪnd/ *adj.* (Brit.) Dosen-; **be ~:** aus der Dose sein

tinnitus /ˈtɪnɪtəs/ *n., no pl.* (Med.) Tinnitus, *der*

tinny /ˈtɪnɪ/ *adj.* **1** (metallic) Metall‹*geschmack*›; blechern ‹*Klang*›; **taste ~:** nach Metall *od.* (ugs.) Büchse schmecken **2** (of inferior quality) billig; **be ~:** Tinnef sein (ugs.)

tin: ~-opener *n.* (Brit.) Dosen-, Büchsenöffner, *der;* **~-pan 'alley** *n.* die Schlagerindustrie; **~ 'plate** *n.* Weißblech, *das;* **~-plate** *v.t.* verzinnen; **~-plating** *n.* Verzinnung, *die;* **~pot** *adj.* (derog.) schäbig; **~pot town** Kaff, *das* (ugs.); **~pot little firm** [kleine] Klitsche (ugs.); **~pot dictator** Operettendiktator, *der*

tinsel /ˈtɪnsl/ *n.* **1** (thread) Metallfaden, *der;* (for decoration) Lametta, *das;* (strip) Lahn, *der* (Textilw.); (sheet) Metallfolie, *die* **2** *also attrib.* **~ [glamour]** Talmiglanz, *der*

tin: ~smith *n.* Blechschmied, *der;* **~ 'soldier** *n.* Zinnsoldat, *der*

tint /tɪnt/

A *n.* Farbton, *der;* **flesh ~s** Fleischtöne; **autumn ~s** herbstliche Farbtöne; **red with a blue ~:** Rot mit einem Stich ins Blaue

B *v.t.* tönen; kolorieren ‹*Zeichnung, Stich*›; **~ with blue** blau tönen/kolorieren

tin: ~ tack *n.* [verzinnter] Drahtstift; **~ 'whistle** *n.* Blechflöte, *die*

tiny /ˈtaɪnɪ/ *adj.* winzig; **a ~ bit better** (coll.) ein klein wenig besser; **sb.'s ~ mind** (derog.) jmds. Spatzenhirn (salopp)

tip¹ /tɪp/

A *n.* (end, point) Spitze, *die;* **the ~ of his nose/finger/toe** seine Nasen-/Finger-/Zehenspitze; **on the ~s of one's toes** auf Zehenspitzen; **from ~ to toe** vom Scheitel bis zur Sohle; **it is on the ~ of my tongue** es liegt mir auf der Zunge; **a cigarette with a [filter] ~:** eine Zigarette mit Filter

B *v.t.*, **-pp- ~ sth. [with stone/brass]** etw. mit einer [Stein-/Messing]spitze versehen; **~ped cigarette** Filterzigarette, *die*

tip²

A *v.i.*, **-pp-** (lean, fall) kippen; **~ over** umkippen; **~ [up]** ‹*Sitz:*› nach oben klappen

B *v.t.*, **-pp-:** **1** (make tilt) kippen; neigen ‹*Kopf*›; **~ one's hat [to sb.]** (Amer.) seinen Hut lüften[, um jmdn. zu grüßen]; **~ the balance** (fig.) den Ausschlag geben; *see also* **scale² A 2** **2** (make overturn) umkippen; (Brit.: empty) kippen; **'no ~ping', 'no rubbish to be ~ped'** „Müll abladen verboten"; **he was ~ped into the ditch** er wurde in den Graben geworfen **3** (mention as likely winner etc.) voraussagen ‹*Sieger*›; **~ sb. to win** auf jmds. Sieg tippen; **be ~ped for the Presidency/a post** als Favorit für die Präsidentschaftswahlen/einen Posten genannt werden **4** (coll.: give) geben; **~ sb. the wink** (fig.) jmdm. Bescheid sagen; (**~** sb. off) jmdm. einen Tipp geben (ugs.) **5** (give money to) **~ sb. [20p]** jmdm. [20 Pence] Trinkgeld geben

C *n.* **1** (money) Trinkgeld, *das;* **as a ~:** als Trinkgeld **2** (special information) Hinweis, *der;* Tipp, *der* (ugs.); (advice) Rat, *der;* **hot ~:** heißer Tipp; **give sb. a ~ about doing sth.** jmdm. einen Tipp geben, wie man etw. macht **3** (Brit.: place for refuse) Müllkippe, *die* **4** (derog.: untidy place) Schweinestall, *der* **5** (Mining) Halde, *die*

Phrasal verbs

- **~ 'off** *v.t.* **~ sb. off** jmdm. einen Hinweis *od.* (ugs.) Tipp geben; **be ~ped off by sb.** einen Hinweis *od.* (ugs.) Tipp von jmdm. erhalten; *see also* **tip-off**
- **~ 'over** *v.t. & i.* umkippen
- **~ 'up** *v.t.* hochklappen ‹*Sitz*›

tip: ~-and-'run raid *n.* Blitzangriff [mit anschließendem sofortigem Rückzug]; **~-off** *n.* Hinweis, *der*

tipper /ˈtɪpə(r)/ *n.* (Brit. Motor Veh.) Kipper, *der*

'tipping point *n.* kritischer Punkt

tipple /ˈtɪpl/

A *v.i.* trinken

B *n.* (coll.: drink) **have a ~:** einen trinken (ugs.); **what's your ~?** was trinken Sie?

tippler /ˈtɪplə(r)/ *n.* Trinker, *der*/Trinkerin, *die;* **be a ~:** gern einen trinken (ugs.)

tipsily /ˈtɪpsɪlɪ/ *adv.* (coll.) angeheitert; beschwipst (ugs.)

tipster /ˈtɪpstə(r)/ *n.* Tippgeber, *der*/-geberin, *die*

tipsy /ˈtɪpsɪ/ *adj.* (coll.) angeheitert; beschwipst (ugs.)

tip: ~toe **A** *v.i.* auf Zehenspitzen gehen; (walk quietly) sich schleichen *od.* stehlen; **B** *adv.* auf Zehenspitzen; **C** *n.* **on ~toe[s]** auf Zehenspitzen; **stand on ~toe** sich auf die Zehenspitzen stellen; **be standing on ~toe** auf den Zehenspitzen stehen; **~top** /ˈtɪptɒp/ (coll.) **A** *adj.* ausgezeichnet; tipptopp (ugs.); **it was a ~top hotel** das Hotel war tipptopp; **be in ~top condition** in einem Topzustand/‹*Person:*› in Topform sein; **B** *adv.* tipptopp (ugs.); ausgezeichnet; **~-up seat** *n.* Klappsitz, *der*

TIR *abbr.* (Brit.) **= Transport International Routier** *Internationaler Straßentransport*

tirade /taɪˈreɪd, tɪˈreɪd/ *n.* Tirade, *die* (geh.); **a ~ of abuse** eine Schimpfkanonade (ugs.)

tire¹ /ˈtaɪə(r)/ (Amer.) ▸ **tyre**

tire²

A *v.t.* ermüden

B *v.i.* müde werden; ermüden; **~ of sth./doing sth.** einer Sache (*Gen.*) überdrüssig werden/es müde werden (geh.), etw. zu tun

Phrasal verb

- **~ 'out** *v.t.* erschöpfen; **~ oneself out doing sth.** etw. bis zur Erschöpfung tun

tired /ˈtaɪəd/ *adj.* **1** (weary) müde **2** (fed up) **be ~ of sth./doing sth.** etw. satt haben/es satt haben *od.* (geh.) es müde sein, etw. zu tun; **get** *or* **grow ~ of sb./sth.** jmds./einer Sache überdrüssig werden **3** (fig.: hackneyed) abgegriffen; abgedroschen (ugs.)

tiredness /ˈtaɪədnɪs/ *n., no pl.* Müdigkeit, *die*

t

ⓘ Titles

The equivalent of *Mr* is **Herr**, but remember that an **n** has to be added when writing an address (*see* ◻ **Letter-writing** for more details). **Frau** is the equivalent for both *Mrs* and *Ms*, since it is used for both married women and unmarried women who are old enough to be married. The equivalent for *Miss* is **Fräulein**, but increasingly its use is restricted to young girls of school age.

Hello, Mr White
= Guten Tag, Herr White

Goodbye, Mrs Williams
= Auf Wiedersehen, Frau Williams

The Germans being more formal than either the British or the Americans, titles and surnames are used far more, and first names are only used between young people and those who know one another really well (and say **du** to one another).

The other important point to remember is that **Herr** and **Frau** are added before other titles, both on letters and when greeting someone:

Good morning, doctor
= Guten Morgen, Herr Doktor/(*or to a woman doctor*) Frau Doktor

Good evening, professor
= Guten Abend, Herr Professor/(*or to a woman professor*) Frau Professor

In these cases the feminine endings are no longer used (**Frau Doktorin, Frau Professorin**), but they will still be found on other titles such as **Frau Studienrätin** (a secondary school teacher with tenure). The feminine forms of aristocratic titles are used on the other hand (**Fürst→Fürstin, Graf→Gräfin, Baron→Baronin, Freiherr→Freifrau**), but **Herr** and **Frau** are not inserted before the title. Hence you refer to a count as **Graf ...**, and to a countess as **Gräfin ...**.

While the full name is of course given on letters, when speaking to someone with a title the name is usually omitted:

Good morning, Dr Brown
= Guten Morgen, Herr/Frau Doktor

Come in, Professor Evans
= Kommen Sie herein, Herr/Frau Professor

How are you, Colonel Weston?
= Wie geht es Ihnen, Herr Oberst?

An exception is the title **Doktor**, where the name is omitted when addressing a doctor of medicine but not when addressing someone who holds the academic title of **Doktor**.

Even when referring to someone with an academic title in the third person, **Herr** and **Frau** are usually included:

... as Professor Schmidt explained yesterday
= wie Herr Professor Schmidt schon gestern erklärt hat

Tell Dr Wilkenhorst to come here
= Sagen Sie Herrn/Frau Dr. Wilkenhorst, er/sie soll hierher kommen

Otherwise usage is much as in English, except that titles are used more often (for instance, the director of an institution should be addressed as **Herr Direktor**), and there are many more titles going with particular jobs than in Britain or America.

Forms of address for dignitaries

Her Majesty
= Ihre Majestät

His Highness
= Seine Hoheit

Your Grace
= Euer Gnaden

Your Eminence
= Eure Eminenz

His Holiness
= Seine Heiligkeit

Note that *Your* with such titles is translated by the form **Euer, Eure.** This can be omitted in some cases, particularly when the reference is in the third person:

Your Eminence will be pleased about this
= Eminenz wird sich darüber freuen

tireless /ˈtaɪəlɪs/ *adj.*, **tirelessly** /ˈtaɪəlɪslɪ/ *adv.* unermüdlich

tiresome /ˈtaɪəsəm/ *adj.* 1▸ (wearisome) mühsam 2▸ (annoying) lästig; **how ~!** so ein Ärger!

tiresomely /ˈtaɪəsəmlɪ/ *adv.* 1▸ (wearisomely) mühsam; **~ lengthy** mühsam und langwierig 2▸ (annoyingly) lästigerweise; **~ facetious** auf unangenehme Art albern

tiring /ˈtaɪərɪŋ/ *adj.* ermüdend; anstrengend ‹*Tag, Person*›

tiro ▸ tyro

'tis /tɪz/ (arch./poet.) = **it is**

tissue /ˈtɪʃuː, ˈtɪsjuː/ *n.* 1▸ (woven fabric; also Biol.) Gewebe, *das* 2▸ (absorbent paper) **[paper] ~:** Papiertuch, *das;* (handkerchief) Papiertaschentuch, *das* 3▸ (for wrapping) **~ [paper]** Seidenpapier, *das* 4▸ (fig.: web) Geflecht, *das;* **~ of lies** Lügengewebe, *das*

tissue: ~ culture *n.* (Biol., Med.) Gewebekultur, *die;* **~ sample** *n.* (Biol., Med.) Gewebeprobe, *die;* **~ type** *n.* (Biol., Med.) Gewebetyp, *der;* **~-typing** *n., no pl.* (Biol., Med.) Gewebetypisierung, *die*

tit¹ /tɪt/ *n.* (Ornith.) Meise, *die; see also* **blue tit; great tit**

tit² *n.* **it's ~ for tat** wie du mir, so ich dir; *attrib.* **~-for-tat killing** tödlicher Vergeltungsschlag *od.* Racheakt; **give sb. ~ for tat** es jmdm. mit gleicher Münze heimzahlen

tit³ *n.* (coarse) 1▸ (nipple) Zitze, *die* (derb) 2▸ *usu. pl.* (breast) Titte, *die* (derb)

tit⁴ *n.* (coll.: fool) Trottel, *der* (ugs.)

Titan /ˈtaɪtən/ *n.* (fig.) Titan, *der* (geh.)

titanic /taɪˈtænɪk/ *adj.* gigantisch

titanium /taɪˈteɪnɪəm, tɪˈteɪnɪəm/ *n.* (Chem.) Titan, *das*

titbit /ˈtɪtbɪt/ *n.* 1▸ (food) Häppchen, *das* (ugs.) 2▸ (piece of news) Neuigkeit, *die*

titch /tɪtʃ/ *n.* (coll.) Knirps, *der* (ugs.)

titchy /ˈtɪtʃɪ/ *adj.* (coll.) klitzeklein (ugs.)

tithe /taɪð/ *n.* (Hist.) Zehnt[e], *der;* **pay ~s** den Zehnten bezahlen; **~ barn** Zehntscheuer, *die*

Titian /ˈtɪʃn/
A *pr. n.* Tizian (*der*)
B *n.* **~ [red]** Tizianrot, *das*
C *adj.* **~ [red]** tizianrot

titillate /ˈtɪtɪleɪt/ *v.t.* erregen; **~ sb.'s palate** jmds. Gaumen kitzeln

titillation /tɪtɪˈleɪʃn/ *n.* Kitzel, *der*

titivate /ˈtɪtɪveɪt/ *v.t.* (coll.) aufmöbeln (ugs.); **~ [oneself]** sich zurechtmachen

title /ˈtaɪtl/ *n.* 1▸ (of book etc.) Titel, *der;* (of article, chapter) Überschrift, *die;* **the flyweight ~** (Sport) der Titel im Fliegengewicht; **the ~s** (Cinemat., Telev.) der Vorspann 2▸ ▸ⓘ **p. 1634** (of person) Titel, *der;* (of nobility) [Adels]titel, *der;* (of organization) Name, *der;* **people with ~s** Adlige 3▸ (Law: recognized claim) Rechtsanspruch, *der* (**to** auf + *Akk.*); **~ [of ownership]** Besitztitel, *der*

'title bar *n.* (Computing) Titelleiste, *die*

titled /ˈtaɪtld/ *adj.* adlig

title: ~ deed *n.* (Law) Eigentumsurkunde, *die;* **~-holder** *n.* (Sport) Titelhalter, *der*/-halterin, *die;* **~ music** *n., no pl.* Titelmusik, *die;* **~ page** *n.* Titelseite, *die;* **~ role** *n.* Titelrolle, *die;* **~ song** *n.* Titellied, *das;* Titelsong, *der;* **~ track** *n.* (of album, CD) Titelstück, *das;* (of film) Titelmusik, *die*

'titmouse *n.* (Ornith.) Meise, *die*

titrate /taiˈtreɪt/ *v.t.* (Chem.) titrieren

titter /ˈtɪtə(r)/
A *v.i.* kichern
B *n.* **~[s]** Kichern, *das*

tittle-tattle /ˈtɪtltætl/
A *n.* Klatsch, *der* (ugs. abwertend)
B *v.i.* klatschen (ugs. abwertend)

titular /ˈtɪtjʊlə(r)/ *adj.* 1▸ (only in name) nominell (geh.) ‹*Führer, Staatsoberhaupt*› 2▸ (going with title) Adels‹*rang*›; mit einem Adelstitel verbunden ‹*Besitztümer*› 3▸ **~ hero** Titelheld, *der*

tizzy /ˈtɪzɪ/ *n.* (coll.) **be in a/get into a ~:** durchdrehen (ugs.) (**over** wegen); **be all of a ~:** ganz aus dem Häuschen sein (ugs.)

'T-junction ▸ T 2

TNT *abbr.* **= trinitrotoluene** TNT, *das*

to
A /*before vowel* tʊ, *before consonant* tə, *stressed* tuː/ *prep.* ▸ⓘ **p. 1635** 1▸ (in the direction of and reaching) zu; (with name of place) nach; **go to work/to the theatre** zur Arbeit/ins Theater gehen; **to Paris/France** nach Paris/Frankreich; **go from town to town** von Stadt zu Stadt ziehen; **throw the ball to me** wirf mir den Ball zu; **to bed with you!** ins Bett mit dir/euch! 2▸ (towards a condition or quality) zu; **appoint sb. to a post** jmdn. auf einen Posten berufen; **be born to a fortune** reich geboren sein 3▸ (as far as) bis zu; **from London to Edinburgh** von London [bis] nach Edinburgh; **increase from 10% to 20%** von 10% auf 20% steigen; **from green to violet** von Grün bis Violett 4▸ (next to, facing) **with one's back to the wall** mit dem Rücken zur Wand 5▸ (implying comparison, ratio, etc.) **[compared] to** verglichen mit; im Vergleich zu; **3 is to 4 as 6 is to 8** 3 verhält sich zu 4 wie 6 zu 8; **it's ten to one he does sth.** die Chancen stehen zehn zu eins, dass er etw. tut; **sing to a guitar** zur Gitarre singen 6▸ *introducing relationship or indirect object: dative case* **lend/give/write/explain** *etc.* **sth. to sb.** jmdm. etw. leihen/geben/schreiben/erklären *usw.*; **speak to sb.** mit jmdm. sprechen; **relate to sth.** sich auf etw. (*Akk.*) beziehen; **to me** (in my opinion) meiner Meinung nach; **be pleasant to the taste** gut schmecken; **secretary to the Minister** Sekretär des Ministers; **be a good father to one's children** seinen Kindern ein guter Vater sein; **a room to oneself** ein eigenes Zimmer; **get four apples to the pound** vier Äpfel je Pfund bekommen; **there is a moral to this tale** diese Geschichte hat eine Moral; **is there a point to all this?** hat das alles einen Sinn?; **that's all there is to it** mehr ist dazu nicht zu sagen; **what's that to you?** was geht das dich an?; **to repair of rear door** (in bill or account) Reparatur [der] Hintertür 7▸ ▸ⓘ **p. 1001** (until) bis; **to the end** bis zum Ende; **to this day** bis heute; **five [minutes] to eight** fünf [Minuten] vor acht; **one minute/two minutes to eight** eine Minute/zwei Minuten vor acht 8▸ *with infinitive of a verb* zu; (*expressing purpose, or after* **too**) um […] zu; **want to know** wissen wollen; **do sth. to annoy sb.** etw. tun, um jmdn. zu ärgern; **too young to marry** zu jung, um zu heiraten; zu jung zum Heiraten; **too hot to drink** zu heiß zum Trinken; **to rebel is pointless** es ist sinnlos zu rebellieren; **he woke to find himself in a strange room** er erwachte und fand sich in einem fremden Zimmer wieder; **those days are gone, never**

i To

Going places – zu or nach?

There is a simple distinction between the use of **zu** and **nach** to translate *to:*

nach is only used with geographical names and points of the compass;

zu is used in nearly all other cases. Note that where a noun follows a geographical name in apposition, an article in the dative is needed.

We are going to Germany
= Wir fahren nach Deutschland

They are flying to New York
= Sie fliegen nach New York

You are going to Salzburg, Mozart's birthplace
= Sie fahren nach Salzburg, dem Geburtsort Mozarts

the road to Potsdam/the city centre
= die Straße nach Potsdam/zum Stadtzentrum

How do I get to the coast?
= Wie komme ich zur Küste?

Go to your mother
= Geh zu deiner Mutter

from house to house
= von Haus zu Haus

But:

from east to west
= von Osten nach Westen

Where a distance is given, **bis** is usually inserted before the **zu** or **nach**, or in place of **nach:**

It's five miles to Exeter/to the next place
= Es sind noch acht Kilometer bis [nach] Exeter/bis zum nächsten Ort

Giving

With all verbs expressing giving *to* is translated simply by the dative case:

She handed the key to me
= Sie übergab mir den Schlüssel

The prize was awarded to him
= Der Preis wurde ihm verliehen

My father left the estate to my brother
= Mein Vater hinterließ das Gut meinem Bruder

They gave a book to Rachel Symons
= Sie schenkten Rachel Symons ein Buch

From the last example it can be seen that where there is a name which cannot of course show the dative this is simply given without alteration.

Other usages are covered in the entry for *to.* *See also* ◻ **Area, The Clock, Length and width, Asking the way** etc.

to return diese Zeit ist vorbei und wird nie wiederkehren (geh.); **to be honest/precise, ...:** offen/genau[er] gesagt, ...; **to use a technical term** um einen Fachausdruck zu gebrauchen; **to hear him talk ...:** wenn man ihn reden hört, ...
9 *as substitute for infinitive* **he would have phoned but forgot to** er hätte angerufen, aber er vergaß es; **she didn't want to go there, but she had to** sie wollte nicht hingehen, aber sie musste; **he said he would ring her, but he had no time to** er sagte, er wolle sie anrufen, aber er hatte keine Zeit [dazu]; **you should buy it; you'd be silly not to** du solltest es kaufen; du wärst dumm, wenn du es nicht tätest
B /tu:/ *adv.* 1 (just not shut) **be to** ‹*Tür, Fenster:*› angelehnt sein; **push a door to** eine Tür anlehnen
2 **to and fro** hin und her

toad /təʊd/ *n.* (Zool.; fig. derog.) Kröte, *die*

toad: ~flax *n.* (Bot.) Leinkraut, *das;* **~-in-the-hole** *n.* (Gastr.) *Würstchen, in einen Teig eingebacken;* **~stool** *n.* Giftpilz, *der;* (Bot.) Schirmpilz, *der*

toady /ˈtəʊdɪ/
A *n.* Kriecher, *der*
B *v.i.* **~ [to sb.]** [vor jmdm.] kriechen (abwertend)

toast /təʊst/
A *n.* 1 *no pl., no indef. art.* Toast, *der;* **a piece of ~:** eine Scheibe Toast; **cheese/egg on ~:** Toast mit Käse/Ei; **as warm as ~** (fig.) schön warm (ugs.); **be ~** (Amer. coll.: finished, dead) geliefert (ugs.) *od.* verratzt (ugs.) sein; **we're ~!** wir sind erledigt *od.* verratzt (ugs.)! 2 (call to drink) Toast, *der;* **drink/propose a ~ to sb./sth.** auf jmdn./etw. trinken/einen Toast auf jmdn./etw. ausbringen; **be the ~ of the town** von der ganzen Stadt gefeiert werden
B *v.t.* 1 rösten; toasten ‹*Brot*› 2 (fig.: warm) **~ one's feet** sich (*Dat.*) die Füße wärmen; **~ oneself in the sun** in der Sonne rösten (scherzh.) 3 (drink in honour of) trinken auf (+ *Akk.*)

toaster /ˈtəʊstə(r)/ *n.* Toaster, *der*

ˈtoasting fork *n.* Gabel zum Rösten vor dem offenen Feuer

toast: ~master *n. jmd., der bei einem öffentlichen Essen die Toasts ausbringt;* **~ rack** *n.* Toastständer, *der*

tobacco /təˈbækəʊ/ *n., pl.* **~s** Tabak, *der*

tobacco: ~ advertising *n., no pl.* Tabakwerbung, *die;* **~ jar** *n.* Tabak[s]dose, *die;* **~ leaf** *n.* Tabakblatt, *das*

tobacconist /təˈbækənɪst/ *n.* ▸ⓘ **p. 1260** Tabak[waren]händler, *der*/-händlerin, *die; see also* **baker**

tobacco: ~-pouch *n.* Tabak[s]beutel, *der;* **~ smoke** *n.* Tabakrauch, *der*

toboggan /təˈbɒgən/
A *n.* Schlitten, *der;* Toboggan, *der*
B *v.i.* Schlitten fahren

toby /ˈtəʊbɪ/ *n.* **~ [jug]** Figurenkrug, *der;* Tobyjug, *der*

toccata /təˈkɑːtə/ *n.* (Mus.) Tokkata, *die*

Toc H /tɒk ˈeɪtʃ/ *n.* (Brit.) *christlich und sozial orientierte Vereinigung [ehemaliger Armeeangehöriger]*

tod /tɒd/ *n.* (Brit. coll.) **on one's ~:** [ganz] allein

today /təˈdeɪ/ ▸ⓘ **p. 1048**
A *n.* heute; **~'s newspaper** die Zeitung von heute; **~'s film industry** die heutige Filmindustrie; **live for ~:** für den Tag leben
B *adv.* heute; **a week/fortnight [from] ~:** heute in einer Woche/in vierzehn Tagen; **a year [ago] ~:** heute vor einem Jahr; **early ~:** heute früh; **later [on] ~:** später [am Tage]; **earlier ~:** heute vor wenigen Stunden

toddle /ˈtɒdl/ *v.i.* 1 (with tottering steps) mit wackligen Schritten gehen; wackeln (ugs.) 2 (coll.: leave) **~ [off]** sich verziehen (ugs.); **I must ~ [along** *or* **off] now** ich muss mich jetzt auf die Socken machen (ugs.) 3 (coll.: go) **~ along** *or* **down to the post** zum Postamt wandern (ugs.)

toddler /ˈtɒdlə(r)/ *n.* ≈ Kleinkind, *das;* **he is only a ~:** er hat gerade laufen gelernt

toddy /ˈtɒdɪ/ *n.* Toddy, *der;* **rum ~:** ≈ Grog, *der*

to-do /təˈduː/ *n.* Getue, *das* (ugs.); **make a great ~ about sth.** viel Theater um etw. machen (ugs.); **there was a great ~ when ...:** es gab eine große Aufregung, als ...:

toe /təʊ/
A *n.* 1 ▸ⓘ **p. 951** (Anat.) Zeh, *der;* Zehe, *die;* **be on one's ~s** (fig.) auf Zack sein (ugs.); **keep sb. on his/her ~s** (fig.) jmdn. in Trab halten (ugs.); **turn up one's ~s** (coll. euphem.: die) ins Gras beißen (salopp) 2 (of footwear) Spitze, *die;* **at the ~:** an den Zehen; **the ~s of the boots are reinforced** die Stiefel sind an der Spitze verstärkt 3 (Zool.) Zeh, *der*
B *v.t.*, **~ing** (fig.) **~ the line** *or* (Amer.) **mark** sich einordnen; **refuse to ~ the line** aus der Reihe tanzen (ugs.); **~ the party line** linientreu sein

toe: ~cap *n.* Vorderkappe, *die;* (of boot) Stiefelkappe, *die;* **steel ~cap** Stahlkappe, *die;* **~ clip** *n.* Pedalhaken, *der;* Fußhaken, *der*

-toed /təʊd/ *adj. in comb.* -zehig

TOEFL – Test of English as a Foreign Language

Ein Test zur Feststellung der englischen Sprachkenntnisse für Studierende, die an einer amerikanischen Universität studieren wollen und deren Muttersprache nicht Englisch ist.

toe: ~hold *n.* Trittstelle, *die;* (fig.) **gain a ~hold** einen Fuß in die Tür bekommen; **have only a ~hold in Europe** nur ein kleines Gebiet in Europa haben; (for sales) in Europa nur schwach vertreten sein; **~nail** *n.* Zeh[en]nagel, *der*

toff /tɒf/ *n.* (Brit. coll. dated) Lackaffe, *der* (ugs. abwertend)

toffee /ˈtɒfɪ/ *n.* 1 Karamell, *der* 2 (Brit.: piece) Toffee, *das;* Sahnebonbon, *das* 3 **sb. can't do sth. for ~** (fig. coll.) jmd. kann etw. nicht für fünf Pfennig tun (ugs.)

toffee: ~ apple *n.* mit Karamell überzogener Apfel am Stiel; **~-nosed** *adj.* (Brit. coll.) hochnäsig

tofu /ˈtəʊfuː/ *n., no pl., no indef. art.* Tofu, *der*

tog /tɒg/
A *n.* 1 *in pl.* (coll.: garments) Klamotten (ugs.) 2 (Textiles) *Einheit für das Wärmerückhaltevermögen von Textilien*
B *v.t.* **-gg-:** (coll.) **~ [oneself] out** *or* **up** sich in Schale werfen (ugs.); **they were ~ged out in their Sunday best** sie waren mit ihrem besten Sonntagsstaat ausstaffiert

toga /ˈtəʊgə/ *n.* (Roman Ant.) Toga, *die*

together /təˈgeðə(r)/ *adv.* 1 (in or into company) zusammen; **sit down ~:** sich zusammensetzen; **gather ~:** sich [ver]sammeln; **soloist and orchestra were not ~:** Solist und Orchester spielten nicht im Takt; **taken all ~:** alle zusammengenommen; **~ with** zusammen mit 2 (simultaneously) gleichzeitig; **all ~ now!** jetzt alle zusammen *od.* im Chor! 3 (one with another) miteinander; **put them ~ to compare them** halte sie nebeneinander, um sie zu vergleichen 4 (without interruption) **for weeks/days/hours ~:** wochen-/tage-/stundenlang; **for three days ~:** drei Tage hintereinander 5 (coll.: organized) **not ~:** chaotisch (ugs.) ‹*Person*›

togetherness /təˈgeðənɪs/ *n., no pl.* Zusammengehörigkeit, *die*

toggle /ˈtɒgl/
A *n.* 1 (button) Knebelknopf, *der* 2 (crosspiece) Knebel, *der* 3 (Computing) [Kipp]schalter, *der;* Umschalttaste, *die*
B *v.i.* (Computing) [hin und her] schalten
C *v.t.* (Computing) [um]schalten

ˈtoggle switch *n.* (Electr.) Kippschalter, *der*

Togo /ˈtəʊgəʊ/, **Togoland** /ˈtəʊgəʊlænd/ *pr. ns.* Togo (*das*)

Togolese /təʊgəʊˈliːz/
A *adj.* togolesisch
B *n., pl. same* Togolese, *der*/Togolesin, *die*

toil /tɔɪl/
A *v.i.* 1 (work laboriously) schwer arbeiten; sich abarbeiten; **~ at/over sth.** sich mit etw. abplagen/abmühen; **~ through a book** sich mühsam durch ein Buch arbeiten; **~ [away] on sth.** sich mit etw. abmühen 2 (move laboriously) sich schleppen; **the train ~ed up the incline** der Zug mühte sich die Steigung hinauf; **~ on** sich weiterschleppen
B *n.* [harte] Arbeit; **with much ~:** mit großer Mühe; **the ~s of the day** die Mühen des Tages

toiler /ˈtɔɪlə(r)/ *n.* (for peace, justice, etc.) Kämpfer, *der*/Kämpferin, *die*

toilet /ˈtɔɪlɪt/ *n.* 1 Toilette, *die;* **down the ~:** in die Toilette; **go to the ~:** auf die Toilette gehen; **be in the ~:** auf der Toilette sein; **on the ~** (coll.) auf dem Klo (ugs.) 2 (washing and

t

dressing) Toilette, *die;* **be at one's ~** (dated) bei der Toilette sein

toilet: ~ bag *n.* Kulturbeutel, *der;* **~ bowl** *n.* Toilettenbecken, *das;* Klosettbecken, *das;* **~ brush** *n.* Toilettenbürste, *die;* **~ pan** *n.* Klosettbecken, *das;* **~ paper** *n.* Toilettenpapier, *das*

toiletries /ˈtɔɪlɪtrɪz/ *n. pl.* Körperpflegemittel; Toilettenartikel

toilet: ~ roll *n.* Rolle Toilettenpapier; **~-roll holder** *n.* Toilettenpapierhalter, *der;* **~ seat** *n.* Klosettbrille, *die* (ugs.); Toilettensitz, *der;* **~ soap** *n.* Toilettenseife, *die;* **~ tissue** ▸**toilet paper**; **~-train** *v.t.* zur Sauberkeit erziehen; an die Toilette gewöhnen; **be ~-trained** sauber sein; auf die Toilette gehen; **~-training** *n.* Sauberkeitserziehung, *die;* **~ water** *n.* Toilettenwasser, *das;* Eau de Toilette, *das*

toils /tɔɪlz/ *n. pl.* (literary) Fangnetz, *das;* Fanggarn, *das* (Jägerspr.); (fig.) Fallstrick, *der*

ˈtoil-worn *adj.* abgearbeitet ‹*Person*›; erschöpft ‹*Reisender*›; abgehärmt ‹*Gesicht*›

toing and froing /tuːɪŋ ən ˈfrəʊɪŋ/ *n.* Hin und Her, *das*

Tokay /təˈkeɪ/ *n.* Tokaier, *der;* Tokajer, *der*

token /ˈtəʊkn/

A *n.* **1** (voucher) Gutschein, *der; see also* **book token**; **gift token**; **record token** **2** (counter, disc) Marke, *die;* Jeton, *der* **3** (sign) Zeichen, *das;* (evidence) Beweis, *der;* **as a** *or* **in ~ of sth.** als Zeichen/zum Beweis einer Sache **4** **by the same** *or* **this ~:** ebenso; **if you don't believe me, then by the same ~ you can't believe him** wenn du mir nicht glaubst, dann heißt das, dass du ihm auch nicht glauben kannst; **his wages are low and, by the same ~, not nearly enough to make him stay in this job** seine Bezahlung ist schlecht und daher natürlich auch nicht ausreichend, ihn in diesem Job zu halten **5** (keepsake) Abschiedsgeschenk, *das;* Andenken, *das*

B *attrib. adj.* symbolisch ‹*Preis*›; nominal (Wirtsch.) ‹*Lohnerhöhung, Miete*›; (minimal) geringfügig ‹*Schaden*›; **a ~ woman/black person on the staff** eine Alibifrau/ein Alibischwarzer als Mitarbeiterin/Mitarbeiter; **his offer of help is only a ~ offer** sein Hilfsangebot ist nur ein Pro-forma-Angebot; **offer** *or* **put up ~ resistance** pro forma Widerstand leisten; **~ strike** Warnstreik, *der*

tokenism /ˈtəʊkənɪzm/ *n.* **sth. is just ~:** etw. hat nur Alibifunktion

Tokyo /ˈtəʊkjəʊ/ *pr. n.* ▸❶ **p. 1643** Tokio (*das*)

told ▸**tell**

tolerable /ˈtɒlərəbl/ *adj.* **1** (endurable) erträglich (**to, for** für) **2** (fairly good) leidlich; annehmbar; **a very ~ lunch** ein sehr ordentliches Mittagessen; **How are things? — Oh, ~:** Wie gehts? — Oh, es geht

tolerably /ˈtɒlərəblɪ/ *adv.* leidlich; annehmbar; einigermaßen ‹*gut, richtig*›

tolerance /ˈtɒlərəns/ *n.* **1** Toleranz, *die* (**for, towards,** gegen[über]); **have no ~ for sth.** für etw. kein Verständnis haben; etw. nicht tolerieren [können]; **a mother with three children needs a lot of ~:** eine Mutter mit drei Kindern braucht viel Verständnis **2** (Med., Mech. Engin.) Toleranz, *die*

tolerant /ˈtɒlərənt/ *adj.* **1** tolerant (**of, towards** gegen[über]); **be ~ of criticism** Kritik vertragen **2** (Med.) widerstandsfähig

tolerate /ˈtɒləreɪt/ *v.t.* **1** dulden; tolerieren (geh.); **this material will ~ high temperatures/hard wear** dieses Material ist hitzebeständig/strapazierfähig **2** (put up with) **~ sb./sth.** sich mit jmdm./etw. abfinden; **she ~d his moods** sie ließ seine Launen über sich (*Akk.*) ergehen; **~ one another** sich [gegenseitig] akzeptieren; **how can you ~ this awful man?** wie kannst du diesen schrecklichen Mann ertragen?; **I can't ~ football/fanaticism** ich kann Fußball/Fanatismus nicht ausstehen **3** (sustain) ertragen ‹*Schmerzen, Hitze, Lärm*› **4** (Med.) vertragen

toleration /tɒləˈreɪʃn/ *n.* Tolerierung, *die* (geh.); **religious/mutual ~:** religiöse/gegenseitige Toleranz

toll¹ /təʊl/ *n.* **1** (tax, duty) Gebühr, *die;* (for road) [Straßen]gebühr, *die;* Maut, *die* (bes. österr.) **2** (damage etc. incurred) Aufwand, *der;* **take** *or* **exact a/its ~ of sth.** einen Tribut an etw. (*Dat.*) fordern (fig.); **the hurricane took a ~ of 5,000 lives** der Hurrikan forderte 5 000 Todesopfer; **the revolution took a heavy ~ of human life** die Revolution forderte viele Menschenleben; **time took its ~ of him** er musste dem Alter Tribut zollen **3** (Amer.: Teleph.) [Gesprächs]gebühr, *die*

toll²

A *v.t.* läuten; ‹*Turmuhr:*› schlagen ‹*Stunde*›

B *v.i.* läuten

toll: ~ bar *n.: Schlagbaum auf gebührenpflichtigen Straßen oder Brücken;* Mautschranke, *die* (bes. österr.); **~ bridge** *n.* gebührenpflichtige Brücke; Mautbrücke, *die* (bes. österr.); **~ call** *n.* (Amer. Teleph.) gebührenpflichtiges Gespräch; **~-free** *adj., adv.* (Amer. Teleph.) gebührenfrei; **~ gate** *n.* Absperrung vor einer gebührenpflichtigen Straße/Brücke; **~ motorway** *n.* (Brit.) Mautautobahn, *die;* gebührenpflichtige Autobahn; **~ plaza** *n.* Mautstelle, *die;* **~ road** *n.* gebührenpflichtige Straße; Mautstraße, *die* (bes. österr.)

tom /tɒm/ *n.* **1** **any** *or* **every T~, Dick, and Harry** Hinz und Kunz (ugs. abwertend); **it's me you're talking to, not any T~, Dick, and Harry** du sprichst mit mir, nicht mit irgendjemandem; **every T~, Dick, and Harry is talking about it** alle Welt redet davon; **any T~, Dick, or Harry can open a shop** jeder, der Lust hat, kann einen Laden aufmachen **2** (cat) Kater, *der. see also* **peeping Tom**

tomahawk /ˈtɒməhɔːk/ *n.* Tomahawk, *der; see also* **bury 2**

tomato /təˈmɑːtəʊ/ *n., pl.* **~es** Tomate, *die*

tomato: ~ juice *n.* Tomatensaft, *der;* **~ ˈketchup** *n.* Tomatenketchup, *der od. das;* **~ ˈpurée** *n.* Tomatenmark, *das;* **~ ˈsauce** *n.* **1** Tomatensoße, *die;* **2** ▸**~ ketchup**; **~ ˈsoup** *n.* Tomatensuppe, *die*

tomb /tuːm/ *n.* **1** (grave) Grab, *das* **2** (monument) Grabmal, *das* **3** **the ~** (state of death) das Grab (geh.); der Tod; **his ghost came back from the ~:** sein Geist kehrte aus dem Grab zurück; **[as] silent as the ~:** totenstill; **the village/the house is/seems [as] silent as the ~:** im Dorf/Haus herrscht Totenstille **4** (vault) Gruft, *die* (geh.)

tombola /tɒmˈbəʊlə/ *n.* Tombola, *die*

ˈtomboy *n.* Wildfang, *der*

ˈtombstone *n.* Grabstein, *der;* Grabmal, *das*

ˈtomcat *n.* Kater, *der*

tome /təʊm/ *n.* dicker Band; Wälzer, *der* (ugs.)

tom: ~fool *attrib. adj.* blödsinnig; **~ˈfoolery** *n.* Blödsinn, *der* (ugs.)

Tommy /ˈtɒmɪ/ *n.* (coll.: British soldier) Tommy, *der*

tommy: ~ gun *n.* Maschinenpistole, *die;* **~-rot** *n., no pl., no indef. art.* Unfug, *der;* Quatsch, *der* (ugs.)

tomography /təˈmɒgrəfɪ/ *n., no pl.* (Med.) Tomographie, *die*

tomorrow /təˈmɒrəʊ/ ▸❶ **p. 1048**

A *n.* **1** morgen; **~ morning/afternoon/evening/night** morgen früh *od.* Vormittag/Nachmittag/Abend/Nacht; **~ is another day** (prov.) morgen ist auch [noch] ein Tag (Spr.); **~ never comes** (prov.) morgen, morgen, nur nicht heute[, sagen alle faulen Leute] (Spr.); **You always say you'll do it some time. But with you, ~ never comes!** Du sagst immer, dass du es einmal tust. Aber bei dir heißt das am Sankt-Nimmerleins-Tag; **~'s edition/newspaper** die morgige Ausgabe/Zeitung; die Ausgabe/Zeitung von morgen; **~'s events will bear me out** morgen wird man sehen, dass ich Recht habe; **~ evening's concert** das Konzert morgen Abend *od.* am morgigen Abend **2** (the future) Morgen, *das;* **who knows what ~ will bring?** wer weiß, was die Zukunft bringt?; **like there's no ~** (coll.) als gäbe es kein Morgen; als ginge morgen die Welt unter; **the men and women of ~:** die Männer und Frauen von morgen; **~'s world** die Welt von morgen

B *adv.* **1** morgen; **a week/month [from] ~:** morgen in einer Woche/in einem Monat; **a year [ago] ~:** morgen vor einem Jahr; **[I'll] see you ~!** (coll.) bis morgen!; **never put off till ~ what you can do today** (prov.) was du heute kannst besorgen, das verschiebe nicht auf morgen (Spr.); **the day after ~:** übermorgen; **this time ~:** morgen um diese Zeit; **~ afternoon/morning** morgen Nachmittag/früh; **~ evening** *or* **night** morgen Abend **2** (in the future) morgen; **what will the world be like ~?** wie wird die Welt von morgen aussehen?

tom: Tom ˈThumb *n.* **1** (Lit.) Däumling, *der;* **2** (diminutive person) Knirps, *der* (ugs.); **~tit** *n.* (Ornith.) Blaumeise, *die;* **~-~** *n.* (Mus.) Tomtom, *das*

ton /tʌn/ *n.* **1** ▸❶ **p. 1702** Tonne, *die;* **a five-~ lorry** ein Lastwagen von fünf Tonnen [Leergewicht]; ein Fünftonner (ugs.); **[long] ~:** Tonne, *die;* 1016,05 kg; **metric ~:** metrische Tonne; **[short] ~:** Tonne, *die;* 907,185 kg; **two ~[s] of coal** zwei Tonnen Kohle; *see also* **brick A 1** **2** (Naut.) Tonne, *die;* **gross ~:** Bruttoregistertonne, *die;* **net** *or* **register ~:** Registertonne, *die* **3** (fig. coll.: a lot) **it weighs [half] a ~:** es ist zentnerschwer (fig.); **I've asked him ~s of times** ich habe ihn x-mal gefragt (ugs.); **~s [of food/people/reasons** *etc.***]** haufenweise (ugs.) [Essen/Leute/Gründe *usw.*] **4** (Brit. coll.: 100 mph) **do a** *or* **the ~:** mit 160 Sachen fahren **5** (Cricket coll.) ▸**century 2**

tonal /ˈtəʊnl/ *adj.* **1** (Ling.) intonatorisch; **~ language** Tonsprache; **~ changes** *or* **variations** Klangvariationen **2** (Mus.) tonal **3** (Art) **~ differences between colours** Unterschiede in den Farbtönen

tonality /təˈnælɪtɪ/ *n.* **1** (Mus.) Tonalität, *die* **2** (Art) Farbwirkung, *die*

tonally /ˈtəʊnəlɪ/ *adv.* (Mus.) tonal

tone /təʊn/

A *n.* **1** (sound) Klang, *der;* (Teleph.) Ton, *der;* **the clear ~s of the speaker** die klare Stimme des Redners; **the [shrill] ~s of her voice** ihre [schrille] Stimme; **a high-/low-pitched ~:** ein hoher/tiefer Ton **2** (style of speaking) Ton, *der;* **don't speak to me in that ~ [of voice]** sprich mit mir nicht in diesem Ton; **in an angry** *etc.* **~, in angry** *etc.* **~s** in ärgerlichem *usw.* Ton; **in a ~ of reproach/anger** *etc.* in vorwurfsvollem/wütendem *usw.* Ton **3** (tint, shade) [Farb-]ton, *der;* **~s of blue** Blautöne; blaue Töne; **grey with a blue ~:** bläulich grau **4** (style of writing) [Grund]stimmung, *die;* (of letter) Ton, *der* **5** (Mus.) (note) Ton, *der;* (quality of sound) Klang, *der;* (Brit.: interval) Intervall, *das;* **whole-~ scale** Ganztonleiter, *die; see also* **fundamental A 2** **6** (fig.: character) Stimmung, *die;* **a ~ of quiet elegance** eine Atmosphäre stiller Eleganz; **the peaceful ~ of the discussions** die friedliche Atmosphäre der Gespräche; **give a serious/flippant ~ to sth.** einer Sache (*Dat.*) eine ernsthafte/frivole Note verleihen; **lower/raise the ~ of sth.** das Niveau einer Sache (*Gen.*) senken/erhöhen; **set the ~:** den Ton angeben; **set the ~ of** *or* **for sth.** für etw. bestimmend sein **7** (Art: general effect of colour) Farbgebung, *die;* Kolorit, *das* **8** (degree of brightness) Schattierung, *die;* Nuancierung, *die;* **bright ~:** Helligkeit, *die* **9** (Photog.) Ton, *der* **10** (accent on syllable) Betonung, *die;* Akzent, *der;* (way of pronouncing) Ton, *der* **11** (Physiol.: firmness of muscles) Tonus, *der;* (of athlete etc.) Fitness, *die;* **keep oneself** *or* **one's body in ~:** sich fit halten

B *v.t.* **1** (modify colouring of) tönen; abtönen ‹*Farbe*›; **~ paint [with] a darker/lighter shade** Farbe abdunkeln/aufhellen **2** (Photog.) tonen; **~ sth. a reddish-brown** etw. rötlich braun tonen **3** ▸**~ up 2**

C *v.i.* ▸**~ in**

Phrasal verbs

- **~ ˈdown** *v.t.* **1** (Art) [ab]dämpfen ‹*Farbe*›; **~ a painting down** die Farben eines Bildes abdämpfen **2** (fig.: soften) mäßigen ‹*Sprache*›; abschwächen ‹*Verbalattacke, Forderung*›; dämpfen ‹*Erregung, Begeisterung*›; besänftigen ‹*Wut*›
- **~ ˈin** *v.i.* farblich harmonieren
- **~ ˈup**

A *v.t.* **1** (Art) **~ up a picture/colour** die Farben eines Bildes/eine Farbe kräftiger machen

[2] (Physiol.) fit machen; straffen ‹*Muskeln, Körper*›; stärken ‹*Nerven*›
B *v.i.* sich fit machen

tone: ~ arm *n.* Tonarm, *der;* **~ control** *n.* (process) Klangregelung, *die;* (device) Klangregler, *der;* Tonblende, *die;* **~-'deaf** *adj.* ohne musikalisches Gehör; **be ~-deaf** kein musikalisches Gehör haben; **~-deaf people** Leute ohne musikalisches Gehör; **~ dialling** (Teleph.) *n.* Tonwahl, *die;* **~ language** *n.* Tonsprache, *die*

toneless /'təʊnlɪs/ *adj.* [1] tonlos ‹*Stimme, Antwort*› [2] (Mus.) monoton [3] (dull) stumpf ‹*Farbe*›

tone: ~ painting *n.* (Mus.) Tonmalerei, *die;* **~ poem** *n.* [1] (Mus.) Tondichtung, *die;* [2] (Art) *Gemälde, bei dem die Farbtöne auf poetische Weise harmonisieren*

toner /'təʊnə(r)/ *n.* [1] (Photog.) Toner, *der* [2] (cosmetic) Tönungsmittel, *das*

tongs /tɒŋz/ *n. pl.* **[pair of] ~:** Zange, *die; see also* **curling-tongs; fire tongs; hammer A 1; sugar tongs**

tongue /tʌŋ/ *n.* [1] ▸❶ **p. 951** Zunge, *die;* **bite one's ~** (lit. or fig.) sich auf die Zunge beißen; **put out your ~, please** strecken Sie [bitte] mal Ihre Zunge heraus!; **put** *or* **stick one's ~ out [at sb.]** [jmdm.] die Zunge herausstrecken; **with one's ~ hanging out** mit [heraus]hängender Zunge; **he came into the pub with his ~ hanging out** (fig.) ihm hing die Zunge aus dem Hals, als er in das Gasthaus kam; **he made the remark ~ in cheek** (fig.) er meinte die Bemerkung nicht ernst; **hold one's ~** (fig.) stillschweigen; **watch one's ~** (fig.) seine Zunge hüten *od.* zügeln; **watch your ~!** pass auf, was du sagst!; **keep a civil ~ in one's head** seine Zunge hüten; *see also* **edge A 1** [2] (meat) Zunge, *die* [3] (manner or power of speech) **find/lose one's ~:** seine Sprache wieder finden/die Sprache verlieren; **have you lost your ~?** hat es dir die Sprache verschlagen?; hast du die Sprache verloren?; **get one's ~ round sth.** etw. aussprechen; **the name is difficult to get one's ~ round** bei dem Namen bricht man sich (*Dat.*) die Zunge ab *od.* verrenkt man sich (*Dat.*) die Zunge (ugs.); **have a ready/sharp/wicked** *etc.* **~:** eine flinke/scharfe/böse *usw.* Zunge haben; **the hounds gave ~:** die Hunde gaben Hals (Jägerspr.); **give ~:** sprechen [4] (language) Sprache, *die;* Zunge, *die* (geh., dichter.); **gift of ~s** (Bibl.) Zungenreden, *das; see also* **confusion 1; mother tongue** [5] (of shoe) Zunge, *die* [6] (promontory) **~ [of land]** Landzunge, *die* [7] (of bell) Klöppel, *der* [8] (of buckle) Dorn, *der* [9] (Woodw.) Feder, *die* [10] (pointer of scale etc.) Zunge, *die* [11] (Mus.) Zunge, *die* [12] **there were ~s of flame rising from the fire** von der Feuerstelle züngelten Flammen empor. *See also* **cat 1; tip[1] A; wag[1] B**

tongue: ~-in-'cheek *adj.* nicht ernst gemeint; (ironical) ironisch; *see also* **tongue 1; ~-lashing** *n.* Rüffel, *der* (ugs.); **give sb. a ~-lashing** jmdm. einen Rüffel geben; jmdn. zusammenstauchen (ugs.); **get a ~-lashing [from sb.]** [von jmdm.] einen Rüffel bekommen/zusammengestaucht werden (ugs.); **~ stud** *n.* Zungenstecker, *der;* **~-tied** *adj.* schüchtern; gehemmt; **the boy sat ~-tied the whole evening** der Junge saß den ganzen Abend da und brachte kein Wort heraus; **be ~-tied [with** *or* **by fear/embarrassment** *etc.***]** [vor Angst/Verlegenheit *usw.*] kein Wort herausbringen; **~-twister** *n.* Zungenbrecher, *der* (ugs.)

tonic /'tɒnɪk/
A *n.* [1] (Med.) Tonikum, *das;* **it was as good as a ~:** es hat mir/ihm *usw.* richtig gut getan [2] (fig.: invigorating influence) Wohltat, *die* (geh.); **the good news/his visit was a welcome ~:** die gute Nachricht/sein Besuch war eine wahre Wohltat [3] (~ water) Tonic, *das;* **gin** *etc.* **and ~:** Gin *usw.* [mit] Tonic [4] (Mus.) Tonika, *die*
B *adj.* [1] (Med.) kräftigend; tonisch (fachspr.); (fig.) wohltuend ‹*Wirkung*› [2] (Mus.) tonisch

tonic: ~ 'accent *n.* (Phonet.: of word) Betonung, *die;* **~ sol-'fa** *n.* (Mus.) Tonika-Do-System, *das;* **~ water** *n.* Tonic[wasser], *das*

tonight /tə'naɪt/
A *n.* [1] (this evening) heute Abend; **~ has been such fun** heute Abend war es so lustig; **after ~:** nach dem heutigen Abend; **I enjoyed ~:** es war ein schöner Abend; **~'s [news]paper** die heutige Abendzeitung; **~'s performance** die heutige [Abend]vorstellung; **~'s the night!** heute Abend ist es soweit!; **~'s weather will be cold** heute Abend wird es kalt [2] (this or the coming night) heute Nacht; **~ will be colder** heute Nacht wird es kälter werden
B *adv.* [1] (this evening) heute Abend; **[I'll] see you ~!** bis heute Abend! [2] (during this or the coming night) heute Nacht

tonnage /'tʌnɪdʒ/ *n.* (Naut.) [1] Tonnage, *die* [2] (charge on cargo) Tonnageabgabe, *die*

tonne /tʌn/ *n.* ▸❶ **p. 1702** [metrische] Tonne

tonsil /'tɒnsl/ *n.* (Anat.) [Gaumen]mandel, *die;* **have one's ~s out** sich (*Dat.*) die Mandeln herausnehmen lassen

tonsillectomy /tɒnsə'lektəmɪ/ *n.* (Med.) Mandeloperation, *die;* Tonsillektomie, *die* (fachspr.)

tonsillitis /tɒnsə'laɪtɪs/ *n.* ▸❶ **p. 1231** (Med.) Mandelentzündung, *die;* Tonsillitis, *die* (fachspr.)

tonsure /'tɒnʃə(r)/ (Relig.)
A *n.* Tonsur, *die*
B *v.t.* tonsurieren

ton-'up *adj.* (sl.) **~ boys** Motorradrocker; **~ machine** Feuerstuhl, *der* (ugs.)

too /tu:/ *adv.* [1] (excessively) zu; **far** *or* **much ~ much** viel zu viel; **~ much** zu viel; **I've had ~ much to eat/drink** ich habe zu viel gegessen/getrunken; **but not ~ much, please** aber bitte nicht allzu viel; **the problem/he was ~ much for her** sie war der Aufgabe/ihm nicht gewachsen; **things are getting ~ much for me** es wird mir allmählich zu viel; es wächst mir allmählich über den Kopf; **this is '~ much!** (indignantly) jetzt reichts!; **she's/that's just '~ much** (intolerable) sie ist/das ist zu viel! (ugs.); (coll.: wonderful) sie ist/das ist echt Spitze (ugs.); **~ difficult a task** eine zu schwierige Aufgabe; **none ~** *or* **not any ~ easy** nicht allzu leicht; (less than one had expected) gar nicht so leicht; **he is none ~** *or* **not any ~ clever/quick** *etc.* er ist nicht der Schlauste/Schnellste *usw.*; **none ~ soon** keinen Augenblick zu früh; **the holidays can come none ~ soon as far as I am concerned** für mich können die Ferien nicht früh genug kommen; *see also* **all C; good A 2, 5; many A 1; much A 1, C 4; only B 4** [2] (also) auch; **she can sing, and play the piano, ~:** sie kann singen und auch *od.* außerdem Klavier spielen; **I have been [to Berlin, and] to Cologne, ~:** ich war [in Berlin und] auch *od.* außerdem in Köln; **I, ~, have been to Cologne, 'I have been to Cologne, ~:** ich war auch in Köln; auch ich war in Köln [3] (coll.: very) besonders; **I'm not feeling ~ good** mir geht es nicht besonders [gut]; **I'm not ~ sure** ich bin mir nicht ganz sicher; **not ~ pleased** nicht gerade erfreut; **you're '~ kind!** zu nett von dir!; **the dessert was '~ delicious** die Nachspeise war zu köstlich [4] (moreover) **he lost in twenty moves, and to an amateur ~:** er verlor in zwanzig Zügen, und noch dazu gegen einen Amateur; **there was frost last night, and in May/Spain ~!** es hat letzte Nacht gefroren, und das im Mai/in Spanien!

toodle-oo /tu:dl'u:/ *int.* (Brit. coll.) tschüs (ugs.); ciao (ugs.)

took ▸ **take A, B**

tool /tu:l/
A *n.* [1] Werkzeug, *das;* (garden ~) Gerät, *das;* **set of ~s** Werkzeug, *das; see also* **down[3] D 4** [2] (machine) Werkzeugmaschine, *die;* **electric ~:** Elektrowerkzeug, *das; see also* **machine tool** [3] (Mech. Engin.: lathe ~) Meißel, *der* [4] (Computing) Tool, *das;* Werkzeug, *das* [5] (fig.: means) [Hilfs]mittel, *das;* **knowledge is a great ~ in the hands of men** [das] Wissen ist für den Menschen ein großartiges Werkzeug; **pen and paper are the writer's basic ~s** Feder und Papier sind das wichtigste Handwerkszeug des Schriftstellers; **the ~s of the trade** das Handwerkszeug; das Rüstzeug [6] (fig.: person) Werkzeug, *das;* **a mere ~ [in the hands] of the dictator** ein bloßes Werkzeug des Diktators [7] (sl.: penis) Apparat, *der* (ugs.); Gerät, *das* (salopp)
B *v.t.* [1] bearbeiten [2] (Bookbinding) prägen

Phrasal verb

• **~ 'up** *v.t.* mit Maschinen ausrüsten; **the expense of ~ing-up** die Kosten für die Anschaffung von Maschinen

tool: ~ bag *n.* Werkzeugtasche, *die;* **~bar** *n.* (Computing) Werkzeugleiste, *die;* **~box, ~ case** *ns.* Werkzeugkasten, *der;* **~ chest** *n.* Werkzeugschrank, *der;* **~ holder** *n.* [1] (in lathe) Meißelhalter, *der;* [2] (handle) Werkzeuggriff, *der*

tooling /'tu:lɪŋ/ *n.* [1] (Building) [steinmetzmäßige] Bearbeitung [2] (Bookbinding) Prägen, *das;* (thing tooled) Prägung, *die*

tool: ~ kit *n.* [1] (Brit.) Werkzeugsatz, *der;* (more general) Werkzeug, *das;* (for vehicle) **is there a ~ kit?** gibt es Bordwerkzeug?; [2] (Computing) Toolkit, *das;* **~ maker** *n.* Werkzeugmacher, *der*/-macherin, *die;* **~ pusher** *n.* Bohrtechniker, *der;* **~ set** *n.* Werkzeugsatz, *der;* **~ shed** *n.* Geräteschuppen, *der*

toot /tu:t/
A *v.t.* tuten; **the boy ~ed his toy trumpet** der Junge blies in seine Spielzeugtrompete; **the driver ~ed his horn** der Fahrer hupte
B *v.i.* [1] (on wind instrument) blasen; (on whistle, pipe) pfeifen; (on car etc. horn) hupen [2] ‹*Hupe:*› hupen; ‹*Lokomotive, Pfeife:*› pfeifen; ‹*Nebelhorn, Schiff:*› tuten
C *n.* Tuten, *das;* (of pipe, whistle) Pfeifen, *das;* **give a ~ on one's/its horn** ‹*Autofahrer, Auto usw.:*› hupen

tooth /tu:θ/ *n., pl.* **teeth** /ti:θ/ [1] ▸❶ **p. 951** Zahn, *der;* **say sth. between one's teeth** etw. mit zusammengebissenen Zähnen hervorstoßen; **draw sb.'s teeth** (lit.) jmdm. die Zähne ziehen; (fig.) jmdn. kaltstellen; **sth.'s teeth have been drawn** (fig.) etw. ist unschädlich gemacht worden; **have a ~ out/filled** sich (*Dat.*) einen Zahn ziehen/füllen lassen; **armed to the teeth** bis an die Zähne bewaffnet; **cast** *or* **fling sth. in sb.'s teeth** (fig.) jmdm. etw. [wutentbrannt] unter die Nase reiben (ugs.); **~ and nail** verbissen ‹*kämpfen, bekämpfen*›; **I'm going to fight ~ and nail to keep this house** ich werde dieses Haus mit Zähnen und Klauen verteidigen; **get one's teeth into sth.** (fig.) etw. in Angriff nehmen; **sb. would give his back teeth for sth./to do sth.** (fig.) jmd. würde alles für etw. geben/alles dafür *od.* darum geben, etw. zu tun; **in the teeth of criticism** ungeachtet der Kritik; **sail in the teeth of the wind** gegen den Wind segeln; **put teeth into a law, give a law some teeth** ein Gesetz zu einem wirksamen Instrument machen; **show one's teeth** ‹*Hund:*› die Zähne fletschen; (fig.) die Zähne zeigen (ugs.); *see also* **edge A 1; false teeth; kick A 1, C 1; lie[1] B; long[1] A 1; set A 16; skin A 1** [2] (of rake, fork, comb) Zinke, *die;* (of cogwheel, saw, comb) Zahn, *der* [3] (liking) **have a ~ for salad** eine Vorliebe für Salat haben; Salat gern essen; *see also* **sweet A 1** [4] (Bot.) Zahn, *der;* **have teeth** gezähnt sein

tooth: ~ache *n.* ▸❶ **p. 1231** Zahnschmerzen *Pl.;* Zahnweh, *das* (ugs.); **~brush** *n.* Zahnbürste, *die;* **~brush moustache** Bürste, *die* (fig.); **~ decay** *n.* Zahnverfall, *der;* Zahnfäule, *die*

toothed /tu:θt/ *adj.* [1] (Mech. Engin.) gezähnt; **~ wheel** Zahnrad [2] (Bot.) gezähnt [3] *in comb.* (having teeth) **sharp-~** ‹*Tier*› mit scharfen Zähnen

tooth: ~fairy *n.* Zahnfee, *die;* **~glass** *n.* Zahnputzglas, *das*

toothless /'tu:θlɪs/ *adj.* zahnlos

tooth: ~ mug *n.* Zahnputzbecher, *der;* **~paste** *n.* Zahnpasta, *die;* **~pick** *n.* Zahnstocher, *der;* **~ powder** *n.* Zahnpulver, *das*

toothsome /'tu:θsəm/ *adj.* köstlich

toothy /'tu:θɪ/ *adj.* **give sb. a ~ smile** jmdn. mit entblößten Zähnen anlächeln; **he is a bit ~:** er hat ein ziemliches Pferdegebiss (ugs.)

toothypeg /ˈtu:θɪpeg/ *n.* (child lang.) Beißerchen, *das*

tootle /ˈtu:tl/ *v.i.* [1] blasen; dudeln (ugs. abwertend); (on whistle) pfeifen; (on flute) flöten; **~ on sth.** in etw. (*Akk.*) blasen [2] (coll.: move casually) zuckeln (ugs.); (walk casually) schlendern; (drive casually) juckeln (ugs.); **I'm just tootling off to the shops/pub** ich gehe nur eben was einkaufen/ich gehe nur eben in die Kneipe (ugs.)

too-too (coll.)
[A] /ˈtu:tu:/ *pred. adj.* (marvellous) himmlisch (ugs.); (la-di-da) oberfein (ugs.)
[B] /tu:ˈtu:/ *adv.* überaus; über die Maßen (geh.); (too) übertrieben

tootsy[-wootsy] /ˈtʊtsɪ(wʊtsɪ)/ *n.* (joc./child lang.) Füßchen, *das*

top¹ /tɒp/
[A] *n.* [1] (highest part) Spitze, *die;* (of table) Platte, *die;* (of bench seat) Sitzfläche, *die;* (~ floor) oberstes Stockwerk; (flat roof, roof garden) Dach, *das;* (rim of glass, bottle, etc.) Rand, *der;* (~ end) oberes Ende; (crest of wave) Kamm, *der;* (of tree) Spitze, *die;* Wipfel, *der;* **the ~ of his head is smooth and shiny** sein Kopf ist oben glatt und glänzend; **a cake with a cherry on ~:** ein Kuchen mit einer Kirsche [oben]drauf; **at the ~:** oben; **at the ~ of the building/hill/pile/stairs** oben im Gebäude/[oben] auf dem Hügel/[oben] auf dem Stapel/oben an der Treppe; **bake at the ~ of the oven** auf der obersten Schiene des Backofens backen; oben im Backofen backen; **be at/get to** *or* **reach the ~ [of the ladder** *or* **tree]** (fig.) auf der obersten Sprosse [der Leiter] stehen/die oberste Sprosse [der Leiter] erreichen (fig.); oben sein/nach oben kommen (ugs.); **be/get on ~ of a situation/subject** eine Situation/eine Materie im Griff haben/in den Griff bekommen; **don't let it get on ~ of you** (fig.) lass dich davon nicht unterkriegen! (ugs.); **the driver didn't notice me until he was right on ~ of me** (fig.) der Fahrer bemerkte mich erst, als er mich schon fast umgefahren hatte; **he put it on [the] ~ of the pile** er legte es [oben] auf den Stapel; **on ~ of one another** *or* **each other** aufeinander; **live on ~ of each other** übereinander wohnen; (too close) sehr beengt leben; **on ~ of sth.** (fig.: in addition) zusätzlich zu etw.; **on ~ of everything else** zu alledem noch; **come/be on ~ of sth.** (be additional) zu etw. [hinzu]kommen; **on ~ of that, this happens!** (fig.) zu allem Überfluss passiert auch noch das!; **on ~ of the world** (fig.) überglücklich; **be/go thin on ~:** licht auf dem Kopf sein/werden; **be on ~:** ganz oben sein/liegen; **the English team is on ~:** die englische Mannschaft ist [dem Gegner] überlegen; **come out on ~** (be successful) Erfolg haben; (win) gewinnen; **get to the ~** (fig.) eine Spitzenposition erringen; ganz nach oben kommen (ugs.); **from ~ to toe** von Kopf bis Fuß; **a Tory from ~ to toe** ein Tory vom Scheitel bis zur Sohle; **be over the ~:** übertrieben *od.* überzogen sein; **go over the ~** (Mil. Hist.: out of the trench) den Graben verlassen; (fig.) (take decisive step) eine endgültige Entscheidung treffen; (be excessive) über die Stränge schlagen (ugs.); es übertreiben (ugs.); **he searched the house from ~ to bottom** er durchsuchte das Haus von oben bis unten; *see also* **head A 1**
[2] (highest rank) Spitze, *die;* **the man at the ~:** der [oberste] Chef *od.* (ugs.) Boss; **~ of the table** (Sport) Tabellenspitze, *die;* **[at the] ~ of the list of things to do/agenda is ...:** ganz oben auf der Liste der Dinge, die getan werden müssen/auf der Tagesordnung steht ...; **be [at the] ~ of the class** der/die Klassenbeste sein; **go to the ~ of the class!** (fig. coll.) alle Achtung!; **~ of the bill** (Theatre) Zugpferd, *das;* **be ~ of the charts** *or* **pops** an der Spitze der Hitparade stehen; die Hitparade anführen; (fig.) die Nummer eins sein
[3] (of vegetable) Kraut, *das;* **~s of turnips, turnip-~s** das Kraut von Rüben
[4] (upper surface) Oberfläche, *die;* (of cupboard, wardrobe, chest) Oberseite, *die;* **on [the] ~ of sth.** [oben] auf etw. (position: Dat./direction: Akk.); **don't forget to paint along the ~ of the door** vergiss nicht, die Tür oben zu streichen; **cut off the ~ [of the apple]** oben ein Stück [vom Apfel] abschneiden; **cut the ~ off an egg** ein Ei köpfen; **they climbed to the ~ of the hill/slope** sie kletterten auf den Hügel/den Hang hinauf; **he laid his hand on the ~ of her head** er legte ihr seine Hand auf den Kopf
[5] (Motor Veh. etc.: folding roof) Verdeck, *das;* **with the ~ down** mit offenem Verdeck
[6] (upper deck of bus, boat) Oberdeck, *das*
[7] (cap of pen) [Verschluss]kappe, *die*
[8] (cream on milk) Sahne, *die;* Rahm, *der* (regional, bes. südd., österr., schweiz.)
[9] (upper part of page) oberer Teil; **at the ~ [of the page]** oben [auf der/die Seite]; **be ten lines from the ~:** in der zehnten Zeile [von oben] stehen; **take it from the ~** (coll.) noch einmal von vorne anfangen
[10] (upper garment) Oberteil, *das;* (blouse, T-shirt) Top, *das* (Textilw.)
[11] (turn-down of long sock) Umschlag, *der*
[12] (head end) Kopf, *der;* (of bed) Kopfende, *das;* (of street) oberes Ende; (of beach) oberer Teil
[13] (utmost) Gipfel, *der;* **shout/talk at the ~ of one's voice** aus vollem Halse schreien/so laut wie möglich sprechen
[14] **be the ~s** (coll.) (the best) der/die/das Größte sein (ugs.); (marvellous) Spitze sein (ugs.); **he's ~s at squash** er spielt hervorragend Squash; **the ~ of the morning [to you]!** (Ir.) einen wunderschönen guten Morgen!
[15] (surface) Oberfläche, *die*
[16] (upper of shoe) Oberteil, *das*
[17] (lid) Deckel, *der;* (of bottle, glass jar, etc.) Deckel, *der;* (stopper) Stöpsel, *der;* (silver foil, crown cork) Verschluss, *der; see also* **blow¹ B 8**
[18] (Bookbinding) Kopfschnitt, *der*
[19] (upper part of boot) Stulpe, *die*
[20] (Naut.: platform) Saling, *die* (Seemannsspr.)
[21] (Brit. Motor Veh.) höchster Gang (Kfz-W.); **in ~:** im höchsten Gang
[B] *adj.* ▸ⓘ **p. 1566** oberst...; höchst... ‹*Ton, Preis*›; **~ end** oberes Ende; **the/a ~ award** die höchste/eine hohe Auszeichnung; **the/a ~ chess player** der beste Schachspieler/einer der besten Schachspieler *od.* ein Spitzenschachspieler; **~ scientists/actors** *etc.* hochkarätige Wissenschaftler/Schauspieler *usw.;* **~ sportsman/job/politician** Spitzensportler, *der*/Spitzenposition, *die*/Spitzenpolitiker, *der;* **the ~ pupil/school/marks** der beste Schüler/die beste Schule/die besten Noten; **~ score/nation/pop star** höchste Punktzahl/führende Nation/größter Popstar; **a ~ Conservative** ein Spitzenpolitiker der Konservativen Partei; **~ names in industry** Spitzen der Industrie; **~ manager/management** Topmanager/-management; **a ~ speed of 100 mph** eine Spitzen- *od.* Höchstgeschwindigkeit von 160k.p.h.; **go at ~ speed** mit Spitzen- *od.* Höchstgeschwindigkeit fahren; **the machine was working at ~ speed** die Maschine lief auf Hochtouren; **I was working at ~ speed** ich arbeitete auf Hochtouren; **read sth. at ~ speed** etw. im Schnellverfahren lesen; **be/come ~ [in a subject]** [in einem Fach] der/die Beste sein/werden; **give sth. ~ priority** einer Sache (*Dat.*) höchste Priorität einräumen; **have a record in the ~ ten** eine Platte in den Top-Ten haben; **in the ~ left/right corner** in der linken/rechten oberen Ecke; **on the ~ floor** im obersten Stockwerk; **the ~ men in the firm** die Spitze der Firma; **they are the ~ men in the firm** sie stehen an der Spitze der Firma; **the ~ people** (in society) die Spitzen der Gesellschaft; (in a particular field) die besten Leute; *see also* **form A 6; gear A 1**
[C] *v.t.*, **-pp-** [1] (cover) **the hills were ~ped with** *or* **by snow** die Hügelspitzen waren schneebedeckt; **a church ~ped with** *or* **by a dome** eine mit einer Kuppel gekrönte Kirche; **~ a pudding with cream** Sahne auf einen Pudding geben; **a pudding ~ped with cream** ein Pudding mit Sahne obendrauf
[2] (Hort.: cut ~ off) stutzen ‹*Pflanze*›; kappen ‹*Baum*›
[3] (be taller than) überragen; **he ~s six feet** er ist über sechs Fuß groß
[4] (surpass, excel) übertreffen; **exports have ~ped [the] £40 million [mark/level]** die Exporte haben die [Grenze von] 40 Millionen Pfund überschritten; **the fish ~ped 2 lb.** der Fisch wog über zwei Pfund; **~ an offer** ein Angebot überbieten; **~ that for a score/story!** überbiete diese Punktzahl/erzähl eine bessere Geschichte!; **to ~ it all** [noch] obendrein
[5] (head) anführen; **~ the bill** (Theatre) das Zugpferd sein
[6] (reach ~ of) **~ the hill/wave** auf die Spitze des Hügels/den Kamm der Welle gelangen

(Phrasal verbs)
• **~ 'off** (coll.)
[A] *v.t.* beschließen
[B] *v.i.* schließen
• **~ 'out** *v.t.* (Building) richten (Bauw.); **~ping-out ceremony** Richtfest, *das*
• **~ 'up** (Brit.)
[A] *v.t.* auffüllen ‹*Batterie, Tank, Flasche, Glas*›; **~ up the petrol/oil/water** Benzin/Öl/Wasser nachfüllen; **can I ~ you up?** darf ich dir/Ihnen nachschenken?; **~ up sb.'s drink** jmdm. nachschenken
[B] *v.i.* (fill one's tank up) voll tanken; (fill one's glass up) sich nachschenken; **~ up with petrol/oil/water** den Tank mit Benzin/Öl/Wasser auffüllen. *see also* **top-up**

top² *n.* (toy) Kreisel, *der; see also* **sleep B 1**

top and 'tail *v.t.* [1] (start and end) einleiten und beschließen ‹*Vortrag usw.*› [2] **~ gooseberries** *etc.* Stachelbeeren *usw.* putzen (durch Entfernen des Stiels und des abgestorbenen Blütenteils am anderen Ende)

topaz /ˈtəʊpæz/ *n.* (Min.) Topas, *der;* **false ~:** Goldtopas, *der*

top: ~ 'billing *n.* (Theatre) *prominentester Platz auf einem Plakat/in einer Werbung;* **he vied with her for the ~ billing** er wetteiferte mit ihr um die Rolle des Stars; **give sb. ~ billing** jmdn. groß herausbringen (ugs.); **in this film, Richard Burton shares ~ billing with Elizabeth Taylor** in diesem Film sind Richard Burton und Elizabeth Taylor die großen Stars; **~ boot** *n.* langschäftiger Stulpenstiefel; **~ 'brass** ▸ **brass A 7;** **~ coat** *n.* [1] (overcoat) Überzieher, *der;* Mantel, *der;* [2] (of paint) Deckanstrich, *der;* **~ copy** *n.* Original, *das;* **~ 'dog** *n.* (fig. coll.) Boss, *der* (ugs.); **he/the company came out ~ dog [amongst his/its rivals]** er/die Firma setzte sich [gegen die Konkurrenz] durch; **~ 'drawer** *n.* [1] oberste Schublade; [2] (fig.: high social status) **sb. is not out of the ~ drawer** jmd. gehört nicht gerade zur Crème de la Crème; *attrib.* Oberschicht-; **~-dress** *v.t.* (Agric.) oberflächlich düngen ‹*Land, Acker*›; **~ dressing** *n.* [1] (Agric.) Oberflächendüngung, *die;* (substance) Oberflächendünger, *der;* [2] (fig.: superficial show) Kosmetik, *die;* **the whole ceremony is just ~-dressing** die ganze Zeremonie ist nur Fassade

topee ▸ **topi**

toper /ˈtəʊpə(r)/ *n.* (arch./literary) Zecher, *der*/Zecherin, *die*

top: ~-flight *attrib. adj.* erstrangig; Spitzen- ‹*sportler, -politiker*›; **~ fruit** *n.* (Brit. Hort.) Baumobst, *das;* **~ 'gear** *n.* (Brit. Motor Veh.) höchster Gang; **~ 'hat** *n.* Zylinder[hut], *der;* **~-heavy** *adj.* oberlastig; kopflastig ‹*Baum, Pflanze, Bürokratie*›; **don't make your load ~-heavy** sorg dafür, dass der Schwerpunkt der Ladung nicht zu hoch liegt; **she is a bit ~-heavy** sie hat einen ganz schönen Vorbau (ugs. scherzh.); **~-'hole** *adj.* (Brit. dated coll.) famos (ugs. veralt.)

topi /ˈtəʊpɪ/ *n.* (Anglo-Ind.) Tropenhelm, *der*

topiary /ˈtəʊpɪərɪ/ *n.* (Hort.) *Kunst des ornamentalen Beschnitts von Bäumen und Sträuchern*

topic /ˈtɒpɪk/ *n.* Thema, *das;* **~ of debate/conversation** Diskussions-/Gesprächsthema, *das*

topical /ˈtɒpɪkl/ *adj.* [1] aktuell [2] (with regard to topics) nach Sachgebieten *nachgestellt* [3] (Med.) lokalisiert

topicality /tɒpɪˈkælɪtɪ/ *n.*, *no pl.* Aktualität, *die*

topically /ˈtɒpɪkəlɪ/ *adv.* [1] mit aktuellem Bezug [2] (with regard to topics) nach Sachgebieten [3] (Med.) lokalisiert

'topknot *n.* [1] (ribbon) Haarschleife, *die* [2] (tuft of hair) Haarknoten, *der*

topless /ˈtɒplɪs/ *adj.* **1** **a ~ statue/column** eine Statue/Säule mit fehlendem oberem Teil **2** **a ~ dress/swimsuit** ein busenfreies Kleid/ein Oben-ohne-Badeanzug **3** (bare-breasted) barbusig; **~ girl/waitress** Oben-ohne-Mädchen, *das*/-Bedienung, *die*; **go/bathe ~:** oben ohne gehen/baden

ˈtopless bar *n.* Oben-ohne-Bar, *die*

top: ~-level *attrib. adj.* Gipfel‹*treffen, -konferenz*›; Spitzen‹*politiker, -funktionär*›; **~-level discussions/ negotiations / talks / deals** Diskussionen / Verhandlungen / Gespräche /Vereinbarungen auf höchster Ebene; **~-level domain** (Computing) Top-Level-Domain, *die*; **~-line** *adj.* (Commerc.) **~-line profit** Bruttogewinn, *der*; **~mast** *n.* (Naut.) Stenge, *die*

topmost /ˈtɒpməʊst, ˈtɒpməst/ *adj.* oberst ... ‹*Schicht, Stufe*›; höchst... ‹*Gipfel, Beamte, Note*›

top-ˈnotch *adj.* (coll.) fantastisch (ugs.)

topographer /təˈpɒgrəfə(r)/ *n.* Topograph, *der*/-graphin, *die*

topographic /tɒpəˈgræfɪk/, **topographical** /tɒpəˈgræfɪkl/ *adj.* topographisch

topography /təˈpɒgrəfɪ/ *n.* **1** Topographie, *die* **2** (features) örtliche *od.* (geh.) topographische Gegebenheiten; Topographie, *die* (geh.); **I'm not acquainted with the ~ of the area/town** *etc.* ich kenne mich in der Gegend/Stadt *usw.* nicht aus

topology /təˈpɒlədʒɪ/ *n.* (Math.) Topologie, *die*

topper /ˈtɒpə(r)/ *n.* (coll.: hat) Zylinder, *der*; Angströhre, *die* (ugs. scherzh.)

topping /ˈtɒpɪŋ/

A *n.* (Cookery) Überzug, *der*; **ice cream with a ~ of whipped cream/of raspberry syrup** Eis mit Sahne/Himbeersirup [obendrauf]; **put on a ~ of cream/chopped nuts** das Ganze mit Sahne überziehen/mit gehackten Nüssen bestreuen; **cover sth. with a ~ of mashed potato/sliced potatoes** etw. mit einer Schicht Kartoffelbrei/Kartoffelscheiben bedecken

B *adj.* (Brit. dated coll.: excellent) famos (ugs.); formidabel

topple /ˈtɒpl/

A *v.i.* fallen; **the tower/pile ~d to the ground** der Turm/Stapel fiel um *od.* kippte um; **the tower ~d and fell** der Turm wankte und stürzte um; **~ [from power]** (fig.) stürzen

B *v.t.* stürzen; **~ a pile/wall [to the ground]** einen Stapel/eine Mauer umstürzen *od.* umwerfen; **~ sb./a government [from power]** ‹*Gegner:*› jmdn./eine Regierung stürzen; ‹*Skandal, Abstimmung:*› jmdn./eine Regierung zu Fall bringen

Phrasal verbs

• **~ ˈdown** *v.i.* hinab-/herabfallen; ‹*Stapel, Turm:*› umstürzen, umfallen

• **~ ˈover**

A *v.i.* ‹*Turm, Stapel, Baum, Auto:*› umstürzen, umfallen; ‹*Vase, Ohnmächtiger:*› umfallen; **he lost his balance on the edge of the cliff and ~d over** er verlor am Rand des Kliffs sein Gleichgewicht und stürzte hinunter

B *v.t.* umstürzen; umwerfen

top: ~-quality *attrib. adj.* [qualitativ] hochwertig; **~-ranking** *attrib. adj.* Spitzen‹*funktionär, -beamter, -politiker, -sportler, -orchester, -delegierter*›; hochrangig ‹*Offizier*›; erstrangig ‹*Autor, Schauspieler*›; führend ‹*Wissenschaftler*›; **~-ranking party member** Mitglied der Parteispitze; **~sail** /ˈtɒpseɪl, ˈtɒpsl/ *n.* (Naut.) (on square-rigger) Marssegel, *das*; (on schooner) Toppsegel, *das*; **~ ˈsecret** *adj.* streng geheim; **~-selling** *attrib. adj.* meistverkauft; **~-selling book** Topseller, *der*; Bestseller, *der*; **~-shelf** *attrib. adj.* **1** (pornographic) Porno-; **2** (first-rate) Spitzen-; **~side** *n.* **1** (joint of beef) Oberschale, *die*; **2** (Naut.) obere Bordwand; **~soil** *n.* (Agric.) Mutterboden, *der*; (of field) [Acker]krume, *die*; **~ spin** *n.* (Sport) Vorwärtsdrall, *der*; (tennis, table tennis) Topspin, *der*

topsy-turvy /tɒpsɪˈtɜːvɪ/

A *adv.* verkehrtrum (ugs.); auf dem Kopf (ugs.) ‹*stehen, liegen*›; **turn sth. ~** (lit. or fig.) etw. auf den Kopf stellen (ugs.); **this development turned my plans ~:** diese Entwicklung warf meine Pläne um *od.* (ugs.) über den Haufen

B *adj.* chaotisch; **the room/house was ~:** das ganze Zimmer/Haus war auf den Kopf gestellt; (fig.) **a world where things are all ~:** eine Welt, in der alles auf dem Kopf steht; **a ~ way of reasoning** eine verquere Art zu denken; **it's a ~ world** es ist eine verkehrte Welt; **the whole world has turned ~:** die ganze Welt steht Kopf (ugs.)

top: ~ ˈtable *n.* Tisch am Kopf der Tafel; **~-up** *n.* (Brit.) Auffüllung, *die*; **sth. needs a ~-up** etw. muss [wieder] aufgefüllt werden; **the oil needs a ~-up** es muss Öl nachgefüllt werden; **give the tank/oil a ~-up** den Tank auffüllen/Öl nachfüllen; **would you like/can I give you a ~-up?** soll/kann ich dir noch mal nachgießen?; **I need a ~-up** ich muss mir noch mal nachgießen/nachgießen lassen; **~-up card** *n.* (for mobile phone) Aufladekarte, *die*; **~-up loan** *n.* Zusatzdarlehen, *das*

toque /təʊk/ *n.* Toque, *die*

tor /tɔː(r)/ *n.* Felsenspitze, *die*; (hill) Hügel, *der*

torch /tɔːtʃ/

A *n.* **1** **[electric] ~** (Brit.) Taschenlampe, *die* **2** (blowlamp) (for welding) Schweißbrenner, *der*; (for soldering) Lötlampe, *die*; (for cutting) Schneidbrenner, *der* **3** (flaming stick etc.) Fackel, *die*; **carry a ~ for sb.** (fig.) jmdn. verehren; **hand on the ~** (fig.) die Fackel weiterreichen (geh.) **4** (lamp on pole) Öllampe [an einer Stange]

B *v.t.* (coll.) in Brand stecken ‹*Auto, Gebäude*›

torch: ~ battery *n.* (Brit.) Taschenlampenbatterie, *die*; **~light** *n.*, *no pl.*, *no indef. art.* Licht der/einer Taschenlampe; (of flaming stick) Fackelschein, *der*; **by ~light** im Schein einer Taschenlampe/Fackel; **~light procession** Fackelzug, *der*; **a ~light ceremony/parade/tattoo** eine Zeremonie/Parade/ein Zapfenstreich im Fackelschein; **~ song** *n.*: *bluesartiger sentimentaler Song von unerwiderter Liebe*

tore ▸**tear¹ B, C**

toreador /ˈtɒrɪədɔː(r)/ *n.* Toreador, *der*

torment

A /ˈtɔːment/ *n.* Qual, *die*; **be in ~:** Qualen ausstehen; **suffer ~s** Qualen erleiden; **be a ~ to sb., be sb.'s ~:** jmdn. quälen *od.* peinigen; **the suspense/uncertainty was a ~:** die Spannung/Ungewissheit war unerträglich

B /tɔːˈment/ *v.t.* **1** quälen; peinigen; **be ~ed by** *or* **with sth.** von etw. gequält werden **2** (tease, worry) quälen; **Don't ~ me so! Tell me ...:** Spann mich nicht auf die Folter! Sag mir doch ...

tormentor /tɔːˈmentə(r)/ *n.* Folterer, *der*; (fig.) Peiniger, *der*

torn ▸**tear¹ B, C**

tornado /tɔːˈneɪdəʊ/ *n.*, *pl.* **~es** Wirbelsturm, *der*; (in North America) Tornado, *der*; (fig.: outburst, volley) Orkan, *der*

torpedo /tɔːˈpiːdəʊ/

A *n.*, *pl.* **~es** Torpedo, *der*; **aerial ~:** Lufttorpedo, *der*

B *v.t.* (auch fig.) torpedieren

torpedo: ~ boat *n.* (Navy) Torpedoboot, *das*; **~ tube** *n.* Torpedorohr, *das*

torpid /ˈtɔːpɪd/ *adj.* **1** träge; träge fließend ‹*Gewässer*› **2** (Zool.) torpid

torpidity /tɔːˈpɪdɪtɪ/, **torpor** /ˈtɔːpə(r)/ *ns.*, *no pl.* **1** Trägheit, *die*; (of water) träges Fließen **2** (Zool.) Torpidität, *die*

torpor /ˈtɔːpə(r)/ *n.* ▸**torpidity**

torque /tɔːk/ *n.* (Mech.) Drehmoment, *das*

torque: ~ converter *n.* (Motor Veh.) Drehmomentwandler, der; **~ wrench** *n.* Drehmomentschlüssel, *der*

torr /tɔː(r)/ *n.*, *pl. same* (Phys.) Torr, *das*

torrent /ˈtɒrənt/ *n.* **1** reißender Bach; (stream having steep course) Sturzbach, *der*; **mountain ~:** reißender Gebirgsbach; **a brook, sometimes swollen into a ~:** ein Bächlein, das manchmal zu einem reißenden Strom anschwillt; **a ~ of rain** ein Regenguss; **the rain came down in ~s** es regnete in Strömen **2** (fig.: violent flow) Flut, *die*; Schwall, *der* **2** (fig.) überwältigend; gewaltig; **a ~ flow of words/insults/questions** ein Schwall von Worten/Beleidigungen/Fragen

torrential /təˈrenʃl/ *adj.* **1** reißend ‹*Gebirgsbach, Fluten*›; wolkenbruchartig ‹*Regen, Schauer*›; **the rain was ~:** es regnete in Strömen; **a ~ cloudburst** ein heftiger Wolkenbruch

torrid /ˈtɒrɪd/ *adj.* **1** (intensely hot) glutheiß; **a ~ land** ein [von der Hitze] versengtes Land; **the ~ heat of the desert** die Gluthitze der Wüste **2** (fig.: intense, ardent) glühend (geh.); ‹*Liebesszene*› voller Leidenschaft

torsion /ˈtɔːʃn/ *n.* Verwindung, *die*; Torsion, *die* (Physik, Technik); **~ bar** Torsionsstab, *der*

torso /ˈtɔːsəʊ/ *n.*, *pl.* **~s** **1** (Art) Torso, *der* **2** (human trunk) Rumpf, *der*; **bare ~:** nackter Oberkörper **3** (fig.: incomplete work) Torso, *der*

tort /tɔːt/ *n.* (Law) [zivilrechtliches] Delikt; unerlaubte Handlung

tortilla /tɔːˈtiːljə/ *n.* Tortilla, *die*

tortoise /ˈtɔːtəs/ *n.* Schildkröte, *die*

tortoiseshell /ˈtɔːtəsʃel/ *n.* Schildpatt, *das*; *attrib.* Schildpatt-; (cat) Katze mit Schildpattzeichnung

tortoiseshell: ~ ˈbutterfly *n.* Fuchs, *der*; **~ ˈcat** *n.* Katze mit Schildpattzeichnung

tortuous /ˈtɔːtjʊəs/ *adj.* **1** (full of twists and turns) verschlungen ‹*Weg*›; gewunden ‹*Flusslauf*› **2** (fig.: circuitous) umständlich; verworren ‹*Argumentation, Denken, Sprache*›; **a ~ speaker/writer** ein Redner/Schriftsteller, der viele Worte macht

tortuously /ˈtɔːtjʊəslɪ/ *adv.* **1** (with twists and turns) verschlungen; **the road/path/river runs ~ through the fields** die Straße/der Weg/Fluss windet sich *od.* schlängelt sich durch die Felder **2** (fig.: circuitously) umständlich; **a ~ reasoned argument** ein verworrenes Argument; **a ~ argued case** eine umständliche Argumentation; **a ~ complex legal document** ein verwirrend komplexer juristischer Schriftsatz

tortuousness /ˈtɔːtjʊəsnɪs/ *n.*, *no pl.* **1** **the ~ of the road/river** die vielen Windungen der Straße/des Flusses **2** (fig.: circuitousness) Umständlichkeit, *die*

torture /ˈtɔːtʃə(r)/

A *n.* **1** Folter, *die*; **the ~s of the Inquisition** die Folterungen der Inquisition; **the ~ of sb.** jmds. Folterung; **practise ~:** foltern; **instrument of ~:** Folterwerkzeug, *das*; Folterinstrument, *das* **2** (fig.: agony) Qual, *die*; **it was ~:** es war eine Tortur; **the exam was sheer ~:** das Examen war der reinste Horror (ugs.) *od.* die Hölle; **suffer the ~s of the damned** Höllenqualen erleiden

B *v.t.* foltern; (fig.) quälen

ˈtorture chamber *n.* Folterkammer, *die*

torturer /ˈtɔːtʃərə(r)/ *n.* Folterer, *der*/Folterin, *die*

Tory /ˈtɔːrɪ/ (Brit. Polit. coll.)

A *n.* Tory, *der*

B *adj.* Tory-; **he is/they are ~:** er ist ein Tory/sie sind Tories

> **Tory Party**
> ▸ Conservative Party.

Toryism /ˈtɔːrɪɪzm/ *n.*, *no pl.* (Brit. Polit. coll.) Toryismus, *der*

tosh /tɒʃ/ *n.* (coll.) Quark, *der* (ugs.)

toss /tɒs/

A *v.t.* **1** (throw upwards) hochwerfen; **~ a ball in the air [repeatedly]** einen Ball immer wieder hochwerfen und auffangen; **~ a pancake** einen Pfannkuchen [durch Hochwerfen] wenden; **~ sb. in a blanket** jmdn. mit einer Decke in die Höhe schleudern; *see also* **caber** **2** (throw casually) werfen; schmeißen (ugs.); **~ it over!** (coll.) schmeiß es/ihn/sie rüber (ugs.); **~ sth. to sb.** jmdm. etw. zuwerfen **3** **~ a coin** eine Münze werfen; **~ sb. for sth.** mit jmdm. durch Hochwerfen einer Münze um etw. losen **4** **be ~ed by a bull/horse** von einem Stier auf die Hörner genommen werden/von einem Pferd abgeworfen werden **5** (move about) hin und her werfen; ‹*Baum/Blume*› wiegen ‹*Zweige/Köpfe*› **6** (Cookery: mix gently) wenden; **~ a salad in oil** einen Salat mit Öl anmachen **7** **~ one's head** den Kopf zurückwerfen

B *v.i.* **1** (be restless in bed) sich hin und her werfen; **~ and turn** sich [schlaflos] im Bett wälzen
2 ‹*Schiff, Boot:*› hin und her geworfen werden; ‹*Halm, Korn, Äste, Blume:*› sich wiegen; ‹*Federbusch, Hutfeder, Locken:*› wippen; ‹*Mähne, Haar*› flattern
3 (~ coin) eine Münze werfen; **~ for sth.** mit einer Münze um etw. losen

C *n.* **1** (of coin) **~ of a coin** Hochwerfen einer Münze; **the decision depends on the ~ of a coin** die Entscheidung wird durch Hochwerfen einer Münze gefällt; **the game was decided by the ~ of a coin** das Spiel wurde durch Hochwerfen einer Münze entschieden; **argue the ~** (fig.) die Entscheidung nicht akzeptieren wollen; **lose/win the ~:** bei der Auslosung verlieren/gewinnen; (Footb.) die Seitenwahl verlieren/gewinnen
2 **give a contemptuous/proud ~ of the head** den Kopf verächtlich/stolz in den Nacken werfen
3 (throw) Wurf, *der;* **give a pancake a ~:** einen Pfannkuchen [durch Hochwerfen] wenden
4 (Brit.: throw from horse) Abwerfen, *das;* **a bad ~:** ein schlimmer Sturz vom Pferd; **take a ~:** abgeworfen werden
5 **I couldn't give a ~** (fig. Brit. sl.) es ist mir scheißegal (salopp)

(Phrasal verbs)

• **~ about, ~ around**
A *v.i.* **1** (be restless in bed) sich [schlaflos] im Bett wälzen **2** ▸▸ **B 2**
B *v.t.* **~ sth. around** *or* **about** etw. herumwerfen; etw. *od.* mit etw. rumschmeißen (ugs.); (fig.) etw. in die Debatte werfen

• **~ a'side** *v.t.* **1** (throw to one side) hinwerfen; hinschmeißen (ugs.); **the mouldy apples were ~ed aside** die schimmligen Äpfel wurden weggeworfen **2** (fig.: reject, abandon) beiseite schieben; **~ aside all caution** alle Vorsicht außer Acht lassen

• **~ a'way** *v.t.* wegwerfen; wegschmeißen (ugs.)

• **~ 'back** *v.t.* zurückwerfen ‹*Kopf, Haar*›; runterkippen (ugs.) ‹*Getränk*›

• **~ 'down** ▸▸ **off A 1**

• **~ 'off**
A *v.t.* **1** (drink off) runterkippen (ugs.) **2** (produce casually) hinwerfen; hinhauen (ugs. abwertend); fallen lassen ‹*Bemerkung*›; **I just ~ed off the first names that came into my head** ich spuckte einfach die ersten besten Namen aus, die mir einfielen **3** (sl.: masturbate) **~ sb. off** jmdm. einen runterholen (salopp)
B *v.i.* & *refl.* (sl.) sich (*Dat.*) einen runterholen (salopp)

• **~ 'out** *v.t.* **1** (throw out) **~ sb. out** jmdn. rauswerfen *od.* (ugs.) rausschmeißen; **~ sth. out** etw. wegwerfen *od.* (ugs.) wegschmeißen **2** (fig.: reject) [kurzerhand] ablehnen

• **~ 'up**
A *v.i.* eine Münze werfen; **~ up for sth.** mit einer Münze um etw. losen
B *v.t.* **1** (throw) hochwerfen; in die Luft werfen

tosser /ˈtɒsə(r)/ *n.* (Brit. sl.) Wichser, *der* (derb. abwertend); (stupid person) Blödmann, *der* (salopp)

'toss-up *n.* **1** (tossing of coin) Hochwerfen einer Münze; **a ~ decides who ...:** wer ..., wird durch Hochwerfen einer Münze entschieden; **have a ~:** eine Münze werfen; **have a ~ for sth.** mit einer Münze um etw. losen **2** (even chance) **it is a ~ [whether ...]** es ist noch ganz ungewiss[, ob ...]; **They are both very good. It is a ~ between the two** Sie sind beide sehr gut. Man kann nicht sagen, wer besser ist

tot[1] /tɒt/ *n.* (coll.) **1** (small child) kleines Kind; Wicht, der (fam.); **tiny ~:** kleiner Wicht **2** (dram of liquor) Gläschen, *das;* **will you have a ~ of rum?** möchtest du ein Gläschen *od.* Schlückchen Rum haben?

tot[2] *v.t.* & *i.*, **-tt-** (coll.) **~ up**
A *v.t.* zusammenziehen (ugs.)
B *v.i.* sich summieren; sich [zusammen]läppern (ugs.); **that ~s up to £5** das macht zusammen 5 Pfund (ugs.)

total /ˈtəʊtl/
A *adj.* **1** (comprising the whole) gesamt; Gesamt(gewicht, -wert, -bevölkerung *usw.*); **what are your ~ debts?** wie viel Schulden hast du insgesamt?; **a ~ increase of £100** eine Steigerung von insgesamt 100 Pfund; *see also* **sum A 1**
2 (absolute) völlig; **~ idiot** (coll.) Vollidiot, *der;* **be in ~ ignorance of sth.** von etw. überhaupt *od.* absolut nichts wissen; **a ~ beginner** ein absoluter Anfänger; **~ nonsense** totaler Unsinn; **have ~ contempt/scorn for sth.** etw. zutiefst verachten; **have a ~ lack of interest in sth.** sich für etw. absolut nicht interessieren; **a ~ success/shock** ein voller Erfolg/totaler *od.* absoluter Schock; **his surrender/refusal was ~:** er gab völlig auf/er weigerte sich strikt; **the silence was ~:** es herrschte völlige Stille; *see also* **abstinence 1**
B *n.* (number) Gesamtzahl, *die;* (amount) Gesamtbetrag, *der;* (result of addition) Summe, *die;* **a ~ of 200/£200** *etc.* insgesamt 200/200 Pfund *usw.;* **in ~:** insgesamt; *see also* **grand A 3; subtotal**
C *v.t.*, (Brit.) **-ll-** **1** (add up) addieren, zusammenzählen, zusammenrechnen ‹*Zahlen, Posten, Beträge*› **2** (amount to) [insgesamt] betragen; **the visitors ~led 131** die Zahl der Besucher betrug [insgesamt] 131 **3** (Amer. coll.: wreck) zusammenfahren (ugs.)

(Phrasal verb)

• **~ 'up**
A *v.t.* addieren; zusammenrechnen/-zählen
B *v.i.* **~ up to sth.** sich auf etw. (*Akk.*) belaufen

total: ~ 'allergy syndrome *n.*, *no pl.* (Med.) Multiallergie, *die;* **~ e'clipse** *n.* (Astron.) totale Finsternis

totalitarian /təʊtælɪˈteərɪən/ *adj.* (Polit.) totalitär

totalitarianism /təʊtælɪˈteərɪənɪzm/ *n.* (Polit.) Totalitarismus, *der*

totality /təˈtælɪtɪ/ *n.* **1** Gesamtheit, *die;* **the ~ of the debt** die Gesamtschuld **2** (Astron.) Totalität, *die* (fachspr.)

totalizator /ˈtəʊtəlaɪzeɪtə(r)/ *n.* (Horseracing) **1** (device) Totalisatoranzeigetafel, *die* **2** (system) Totalisator, *der;* Toto, *das*

totally /ˈtəʊtəlɪ/ *adv.* völlig

total: ~ re'call *n.* **have [the power of] ~ recall** ein absolutes Erinnerungsvermögen haben; **~ 'war** *n.* totaler Krieg

tote[1] /təʊt/ *v.t.* (coll.) schleppen; **~ a gun** eine Kanone mit sich rumschleppen (ugs.)

tote[2] *n.* (Horseracing coll.) **1** (device) Totoanzeigetafel, *die* **2** (system) Toto, *das*

tote: ~ bag *n.* große Tasche; **~ box** *n.* (Amer.) [Transport]kiste, *die*

totem /ˈtəʊtəm/ *n.* Totem, *das* (Völkerk.)

totemism /ˈtəʊtəmɪzm/ *n.* Totemismus, *der* (Völkerk.)

'totem pole *n.* Totempfahl, *der* (Völkerk.)

t'other, tother /ˈtʌðə(r)/ *adj.*, *pron.* **= the other**

totter /ˈtɒtə(r)/ *v.i.* **1** (move unsteadily) wanken; taumeln; (esp. owing to drunkenness) torkeln; **the child/blind man went ~ing across the room** das Kind ging mit tapsenden (ugs.)/der Blinde ging mit tastenden Schritten durch das Zimmer **2** (be on point of falling) schwanken; wanken (geh.); **make sth. ~:** etw. ins Schwanken bringen; **~ on the brink of collapse/chaos/bankruptcy/ruin** (fig.) am Rande des Zusammenbruchs/Chaos/Bankrotts/Ruins stehen

tottery /ˈtɒtərɪ/ *adj.* wack[e]lig; **a ~ old man** ein alter Mann mit wackligen (ugs.) *od.* unsicheren Beinen; **have ~ legs** wacklig (ugs.) *od.* unsicher auf den Beinen sein; **feel ~:** sich wacklig (ugs.) *od.* unsicher auf den Beinen fühlen

totting-'up /tɒtɪŋˈʌp/ *n.* **1** Zusammenrechnen, *das;* **the ~ of the votes** die Auszählung der Stimmen **2** (Brit. law) *Berücksichtigung einschlägiger Vorstrafen, bes. bei der Entscheidung über einen Führerscheinentzug*

toucan /ˈtuːkən/ *n.* (Ornith.) Tukan, *der*

touch /tʌtʃ/
A *v.t.* **1** (lit. or fig.) berühren; (inspect by ~ing) betasten; **~ one's hat [to sb.]** sich (*Dat.*) [jmdm. zum Gruß] an den Hut tippen; **~ the sky** (fig.) an den Himmel stoßen; **~ sb. on the shoulder** jmdm. auf die Schulter tippen; **~ glasses** anstoßen; **~ A to B** B mit A berühren; **~ a match to sth.** ein [brennendes] Streichholz an etw. (*Akk.*) halten; **he ~ed the wires together** er hielt die Drähte aneinander; *see also* **bargepole; bottom A 4; wood 2**
2 (harm, interfere with) anrühren; **the police can't ~ you [for it]** die Polizei kann dich nicht [dafür] belangen; **He can't ~ you here. You are safe** Hier kann er dir nichts tun *od.* anhaben. Du bist sicher
3 (Mus.) **~ the keys of a piano/harpsichord** *etc.* in die Tasten eines Klaviers/Spinetts *usw.* greifen; **~ the strings [of a guitar/lute/harp** *etc.***]** in die Saiten [einer Gitarre/Laute/Harfe *usw.*] greifen
4 (fig.: rival) **~ sth.** an etw. (*Akk.*) heranreichen; **nobody can ~ her for speed/at tennis/as an actress** niemand kann es mit ihr an Schnelligkeit/im Tennis/als Schauspielerin aufnehmen; **That horse is the fastest. There is none to ~ it** Dieses Pferd ist das schnellste. Keines kommt an es heran; **there is nothing to ~ a glass of whisky before bed** es geht nichts über ein Glas Whisky vor dem Schlafengehen
5 (affect emotionally) rühren; **it ~ed him to the heart/it ~ed his heart** es rührte ihn ans Herz/es rührte sein Herz; **be ~ed with pity/remorse/sadness** von Mitleid/Reue/Traurigkeit angerührt sein (geh.)
6 (concern oneself with) anrühren; **whatever I ~ — I'm a failure at it** was ich auch anfange, es misslingt mir alles; **I would not ~ it** ich würde die Finger davon lassen (ugs.); **everything he ~es turns to gold** (fig.) er hat bei allem, was er tut, eine glückliche Hand; **I haven't even ~ed the washing up yet** ich habe mit dem Abwasch noch nicht mal angefangen
7 (tinge) färben; **her hair was chestnut ~ed with blonde streaks** sie hatte kastanienbraunes Haar mit blonden Strähnen
8 **~ sb. for a loan/£5** (coll.) jmdn. anpumpen (salopp)/um 5 Pfund anpumpen *od.* anhauen (salopp)
9 (Geom.) berühren; tangieren (fachspr.)
10 (reach) erreichen
11 (anger, wound) treffen; **~ sb.'s pride/self-esteem** *etc.* jmdn. in seinem Stolz/in seinem Selbstwertgefühl *usw.* treffen
12 (concern) berühren; **this does not ~ the point at issue** das hat nichts mit unserem Thema zu tun
13 (have effect on) angreifen; (injure or damage slightly) schädigen; **~ sb.** jmdm. schaden; **he was hardly ~ed by the fall** bei dem Sturz hatte er kaum etwas abbekommen;
B *v.i.* sich berühren; ‹*Grundstücke:*› aneinander stoßen; **don't ~!** nicht anfassen!; **'please do not ~'** „bitte nicht berühren"
C *n.* **1** Berührung, *die;* **the rider gave his horse a ~ of the spurs/the whip** der Reiter ließ sein Pferd die Sporen/die Peitsche spüren; **I like the warm ~ of her body** ich spüre gerne ihren warmen Körper [an meiner Haut]; **the surface has a soft/rough/cold/warm** *etc.* **~:** die Oberfläche fühlt sich weich/rau/kalt/warm *usw.* an; **a ~ of the** *or* **one's hand** eine Berührung mit der Hand; **at a ~:** bei bloßer Berührung; **the machine can be stopped at a ~:** die Maschine lässt sich mit einem Fingerdruck abstellen; **be soft/warm** *etc.* **to the ~:** sich weich/warm *usw.* anfühlen
2 *no pl.*, *no art.* (faculty) **[sense of] ~:** Tastsinn, *der;* **find out sth. by ~:** etw. ertasten
3 (small amount) **a ~ of salt/pepper** *etc.* eine Spur Salz/Pfeffer *usw.;* **a ~ of irony/sadness** *etc.* ein Anflug von Ironie/Traurigkeit *usw.;* **have a ~ of rheumatism** ein bisschen Rheuma haben; **have a ~ of genius** etwas Geniales haben; **she has a ~ of style/class [about her]** sie hat irgendwie Stil/Klasse; **the palms give a ~ of class/elegance to the restaurant** die Palmen geben dem Restaurant eine stilvolle/elegante Note; **he has a ~ of grey in his hair** er hat ein paar graue Strähnen im Haar; **a ~** (slightly) ein [ganz] kleines bisschen; **a ~ higher/too high** eine Idee

höher/zu hoch; **a ~ unrealistic** eine Idee zu unrealistisch; *see also* **sun A**
4 (game of tag) Fangen, *das*
5 (Art: stroke) Strich, *der;* (fig.) Detail, *das;* **to mention it in such a way was a clever/subtle ~:** es auf eine solche Weise zu erwähnen, war ein schlauer/raffinierter Einfall; **the book needs a few more humorous ~es** dem Buch fehlen noch ein paar humorvolle Tupfer; **the realistic ~es in the production of the play** die realistischen Elemente in der Inszenierung des Stücks; **add** *or* **put the final ~es to sth.** etw. (*Dat.*) den letzten Schliff geben; letzte Hand an etw. (*Akk.*) legen; **it was now completed except for a few final ~es** es war nun bis auf einige noch fehlende i-Tüpfelchen fertig gestellt; *see also* **finishing touch**
6 (manner, style) (on keyboard instrument, typewriter) Anschlag, *der;* (of writer, sculptor) Stil, *der;* (of painter) Pinselführung, *die;* **have the ~ of genius/the professional ~:** genial/professionell gemacht sein; **show the ~ of a genius/professional** die Handschrift eines Genies/Profis verraten; **the play bore/revealed his ~:** das Stück trug/verriet seine Handschrift; **you need to have the right ~:** man muss das richtige Gespür haben; **he just didn't have the ~:** er hatte einfach nicht genug Talent; **this flat needs a woman's ~:** diese Wohnung braucht die Hand einer Frau; **a personal ~:** eine persönliche *od.* individuelle Note; **lose one's ~:** seinen Schwung verlieren; (Sport) seine Form verlieren; **I see you haven't lost your ~!** du bist ja noch ganz der/die Alte! (ugs.); **he's lost his ~:** er war schon mal besser in Form; **I must be losing my ~:** ich bin wohl auf dem absteigenden Ast (ugs.); *see also* **common A 2**
7 (communication) **be in/out of ~ [with sb.]** [mit jmdm.] Kontakt/keinen Kontakt haben; **I shall be in ~ with them** ich werde mit ihnen Kontakt aufnehmen; **they said they would be in ~ with me today** sie haben gesagt, sie würden sich heute bei mir melden; **Goodbye! I'll be in ~:** Auf Wiedersehen! Ich melde mich mal wieder; **they have not been in ~ for a whole week** wir haben/ich habe seit einer ganzen Woche nichts von ihnen gehört; **be in/out of ~ with sth.** über etw. (+ *Akk.*) auf dem Laufenden/nicht auf dem Laufenden sein; **he is out of** *or* **not in ~ with reality/the real world** er ist wirklichkeitsfremd/weltfremd; **get in ~ [with sb.]** mit jmdm. Kontakt/Verbindung aufnehmen; **get in ~ with us by letter/at this number** schreiben Sie uns/rufen Sie uns unter dieser Nummer an; **she immediately got in ~ with the doctor/police/her lawyer** sie setzte sich sofort mit dem Arzt/der Polizei/ihrem Anwalt in Verbindung; **keep in ~ [with sb.]** [mit jmdm.] in Verbindung *od.* Kontakt bleiben; **keep in ~!** lass von dir hören!; **I've kept in ~ with him since we were children** meine Verbindung mit ihm ist seit unserer Kindheit nie abgerissen; **keep in ~ with sth.** sich über etw. (*Akk.*) auf dem Laufenden halten; **lose ~ with sb.** den Kontakt zu jmdm. verlieren; **we have lost ~:** wir haben keinen Kontakt mehr [zueinander]; **lose ~ with sth.** etw. aus den Augen verlieren; **have lost ~ with sth.** über etw. (*Akk.*) nicht mehr auf dem Laufenden sein; **put sb. in ~ with sb.** jmdn. mit jmdm. zusammenbringen; **her doctor put her in ~ with a specialist** ihr Arzt hat sie zu einem Spezialisten geschickt
8 (Footb., Rugby: part of field) Aus, *das;* Mark, *die* (Rugby); **in ~:** im Aus; **he ran/the ball went into ~:** er rannte/der Ball ging ins Aus
9 (coll.) **be an easy** *or* **a soft ~** (be a person who gives money readily) leicht rumzukriegen sein (ugs.)

Phrasal verbs

- **~ at** *v.t.* (Naut.) anlegen in (+ *Dat.*)
- **~ 'down** *v.i.* **1** (Rugby) den Ball niederlegen; (Amer. Footb.) den Ball hinter die Grundlinie bringen **2** ‹*Flugzeug:*› aufsetzen; (land) landen; *see also* **touchdown**
- **~ 'in** *v.t.* (Art) hineinmalen; (fig.) ausführen ‹*Details*›
- **~ 'off** *v.t.* **1** (explode) zünden ‹*Bombe, Sprengladung, Feuerwerkskörper*›; auslösen ‹*Explosion, Mine*› **2** (fig.: trigger off) auslösen
- **~ on** *v.t.* **1** (treat briefly) ansprechen; **the book ~es on the subject often** in dem Buch wird das Thema immer wieder gestreift **2** (verge on) grenzen an (+ *Akk.*)
- **~ 'up** *v.t.* **1** (improve) ausbessern; retuschieren ‹*Fotografie*›; auffrischen ‹*Make-up*›; in Ordnung bringen ‹*Haar*›; ausfeilen ‹*Text*› **2** (sl.: fondle) befummeln (ugs.)
- **~ upon** ▸**touch on 1**

touch: ~-and-'go *adj.* prekär ‹*Situation*›; **it is ~-and-go [whether ...]** es steht auf des Messers Schneide[, ob ...]; **~down** *n.* **1** (Amer. Footb.) Touchdown, *der;* **2** (Aeronaut.) Landung, *die*

touché /'tu:ʃeɪ/ *int.* (Fencing) Treffer!; (fig.) eins zu null für dich!

touched /tʌtʃt/ *pred. adj.* **1** (moved) gerührt **2** (coll.: mad) meschugge (salopp)

touchiness /'tʌtʃɪnɪs/ *n., no pl.* (of person) [Über]empfindlichkeit, *die;* (of subject) Heikelkeit, *die*

touching /'tʌtʃɪŋ/ *adj.* rührend; (moving) bewegend; ergreifend

touchingly /'tʌtʃɪŋlɪ/ *adv.* rührend; (movingly) bewegend; ergreifend; **tell/depict sth. ~:** etw. ergreifend erzählen/schildern

touch: ~ judge *n.* (Rugby) Seitenrichter, *der;* **~line** *n.* (Footb., Rugby) Seitenlinie, *die;* Marklinie, *die* (Rugby); **~-me-not** *n.* (Bot.) Rührmichnichtan, *das;* **~ pad** *n.* Touchpad, *das;* **~ panel** *n.* Touchpanel, *das;* **~paper** *n.* Zündpapier, *das;* (on firework) Papierlunte, *die;* **~ screen** *n.* (Computing) Touchscreen, *der;* Sensorbildschirm, *der;* **~stone** *n.* (fig.) Prüfstein, *der;* **~-tone** *adj.* **a ~-tone telephone** ein Telefon mit Mehrfrequenzwahl; **~-type** *v.i.* blind schreiben; **~-typing** *n., no pl.* Blindschreiben, *das;* **~-up paint** *n.* Ausbesserungslack, *der*

touchy /'tʌtʃɪ/ *adj.* empfindlich ‹*Person*›; heikel ‹*Thema, Sache*›

touchy-feely /tʌtʃɪ'fi:lɪ/ *adj.* (coll.) gefühlig; gefühlsduselig (ugs. abwertend); emotionsgeladen ‹*Thema*›; gefühlsbetont, emotional ‹*Führungsstil, Ansatz*›

tough /tʌf/

A *adj.* **1** fest ‹*Material, Stoff, Leder, Metall, Werkstoff*›; zäh ‹*Fleisch, fachspr.: Werkstoff, Metall, Kunststoff*›; widerstandsfähig ‹*Straßenbelag, Bodenbelag, Gummi, Glas, Haut*›; strapazierfähig ‹*Kleidung, Stoff, Schuhe, Seil*›; **be [as] ~ as leather/old boots** zäh wie Leder/wie eine Schuhsohle sein; (fig.) hart im Nehmen sein (ugs.) **2** (hardy, unyielding) zäh ‹*Person*›; **his parents want him to be ~ when he grows up** seine Eltern wollen, dass aus ihm ein harter Mann wird; **~ guy** (coll.) knallharter Bursche; **a ~ customer** (coll.) ein harter Brocken (ugs.); (stubborn person) ein Dickschädel (ugs.) **3** (difficult, trying) schwierig; vertrackt (ugs.) ‹*Problem*›; hart ‹*Kampf, Wettkampf*›; strapaziös ‹*Reise*›; schwer ‹*Zeit*›; **we had a ~ time** wir haben viel durchgemacht; **we had a ~ time convincing her** es hat uns viel Mühe gekostet, sie zu überzeugen; **it's a ~ life being a housewife** als Hausfrau hat man es schwer; **things/life can get ~ if you run out of money** wenn man kein Geld mehr hat, kann das Leben sehr schwer werden; **it was ~ going, the going was ~:** es war ein Schlauch (ugs.) **4** (severe, harsh) hart; **get ~** (coll.) andere Saiten aufziehen; **a get-~ policy** eine Politik des harten Durchgreifens; **get ~ with sb.** (coll.) jmdn. hart anfassen **5** (coll.: unfortunate, hard) **~ luck** Pech, *das;* **that's ~ [luck]** so'n Pech (ugs.) *od.* (salopp) Mist!; **be ~ on sb.** hart für jmdn. sein **6** (stiff) zäh ‹*Schlamm, Ton, Brei*› **7** (violent, criminal) gewalttätig; **a ~ town/neighbourhood** eine Stadt/Gegend, in der das Leben rau ist

B *n.* Schlägertyp, *der* (abwertend)

C *v.t.* (coll.) **~ it out** nicht nachgeben; **I've just got to ~ it out** ich darf einfach nicht nachgeben

toughen /'tʌfn/

A *v.t.* größere Festigkeit geben (+ *Dat.*); zäher machen (fachspr.) ‹*Werkstoff, Metall, Kunststoff*›; abhärten, (geh.) stählen ‹*Person, Körper*›; verschärfen ‹*Gesetz, Widerstand*›; **his hard life has ~ed him** (fig.) sein schweres Leben hat ihn gehärtet *od.* hart gemacht; **he has ~ed his attitude towards lawbreakers** er hat gegenüber Gesetzesbrechern eine härtere Haltung eingenommen; **~ one's policy/stand** einen härteren [politischen] Kurs einschlagen/einen härteren Standpunkt einnehmen; **this setback will only ~ my resolve** dieser Rückschlag wird mich in meiner Entschlossenheit nur noch bestärken

B *v.i.* fester werden; ‹*Werkstoff, Metall, Kunststoff:*› zäher werden (fachspr.); ‹*Widerstand:*› sich verschärfen; ‹*Entschlossenheit:*› stärker werden; ‹*Standpunkt, Position, politischer Kurs:*› sich verhärten

Phrasal verb

- **~ 'up**

A *v.t.* abhärten; stählen (geh.); verschärfen ‹*Gesetz, Verbrechensbekämpfung*›; **~ up one's attitude/policy** eine härtere Haltung einnehmen/einen härteren [politischen] Kurs einschlagen

B *v.i.* sich abhärten; sich stählen (geh.); (fig.) ‹*Politik, Einstellung:*› sich verhärten; ‹*Widerstand:*› sich verschärfen

toughie /'tʌfɪ/ *n.* (coll.) **1** (problem) harte Nuss (ugs.) **2** (person) knallharter Typ (ugs.)

tough-'minded *adj.* hart

toughness /'tʌfnɪs/ *n., no pl.* **1** ▸**tough A 1**: Festigkeit, *die;* Zähheit, *die;* Zähigkeit, *die* (fachspr.); Widerstandsfähigkeit, *die;* Strapazierfähigkeit, *die* **2** ▸**tough A 2**: Zähigkeit, *die* **3** (fig.) (of problem, job) Schwierigkeit, *die;* (of fight, contest, law, policy, attitude, penalty, measure) Härte, *die;* **the ~ of the exercise** die Schwierigkeit der Übung; **the ~ of life as an unmarried mother** die Schwierigkeiten, mit denen eine ledige Mutter zu kämpfen hat **4** (stiffness) Zähheit, *die* **5** (Amer.: violence) **the ~ of the mining towns** das raue Leben in den Bergarbeiterstädten

toupee, toupet /'tu:peɪ/ *n.* Toupet, *das*

tour /tʊə(r)/

A *n.* **1** [Rund]reise, *die;* Tour, *die* (ugs.); **a ~ of** *or* **through Europe** eine Reise durch Europa/eine Europareise; **a world ~/round-the-world ~:** eine Weltreise/Reise um die Welt; **they made a ~ of France** sie machten eine Frankreichreise; **a ~ of the capital cities of Europe/of the overseas branches of the firm** eine Rundreise zu den Hauptstädten Europas/zu den überseeischen Tochtergesellschaften der Firma; **a walking/cycling ~:** eine Wanderung/[Fahr]radtour; **a motoring/bus ~:** eine Auto-/Busreise **2** (Theatre, Sport) Tournee, *die;* Tour, *die* (Jargon); **a ~ of the provinces, a provincial ~:** eine Tournee/Tour durch die Provinz; **be/go on ~:** auf Tournee/Tour sein/gehen; **he has gone on ~ to Europe** er ist auf [einer] Europatournee; **take a play on ~:** mit einem Stück auf Tournee/Tour gehen **3** (excursion, inspection) (of museum, palace, house) Besichtigung, *die;* **go on/make/do a ~ of** besichtigen ‹*Museum, Haus, Schloss usw.*›; **a ~ of the countryside/the city/the factory** ein Ausflug in die Umgebung/eine Besichtigungstour durch die Stadt/ein Rundgang durch die Fabrik **4** **~ [of duty]** Dienstzeit, *die;* **between [sb.'s] ~s [of duty]** bevor jmd. einen neuen Posten antritt/antrat. *See also* **conduct B 5**; **grand tour**; **guided tour**; **inspection**

B *v.i.* **1** **~/go ~ing in** *or* **through a country** eine Reise *od.* (ugs.) Tour durch ein Land machen; **be ~ing in a country** auf einer Reise *od.* (ugs.) Tour durch ein Land sein **2** (Theatre, Sport, exhibition) eine Tournee *od.* (Jargon) Tour machen; (be on ~) auf Tournee *od.* (Jargon) Tour sein; touren (Jargon); (go on ~) auf Tournee *od.* (Jargon) Tour gehen

C *v.t.* **1** besichtigen ‹*Stadt, Gebäude, Museum*›; **~ a country/region** eine Reise *od.* (ugs.) Tour durch ein Land/Gebiet machen; **~ an area on foot/by bicycle** eine Wanderung/Radtour durch eine Gegend machen **2** (Theatre, Sport) **~ a country/the provinces** eine Tournee *od.* (Jargon) Tour durch das Land/die Provinz machen; **~ India/Europe** eine Indien-/Europatournee *od.* (Jargon) -tour machen

t

tour de force /tʊə də 'fɔːs/ *n., pl.* **tours de force** /tʊə də 'fɔːs/ Glanzleistung, *die*

tourer /'tʊərə(r)/ *n.* **1** (Motor Veh.) Kabriolimousine, *die* **2** (bicycle) Touren[fahr]rad, *das;* Trekkingrad, *das*

'tour guide *n.* **1** (Person) Reiseführer, *der*/Reiseführerin, *die* **2** (book) Reiseführer, *der*

touring/'tʊərɪŋ/: ~ **car** *n.* Reiselimousine, *die;* (Motor Sport) Tourenwagen, *der;* ~ **company** *n.* (Theatre) Gastspielensemble, *das;* ~ **exhibition** *n.* Wanderausstellung, *die;* ~ **holiday** *n.* **have a ~ holiday in a country** in den Ferien/im Urlaub durch ein Land fahren/(on foot) durch ein Land wandern; **have a ~ holiday** in den Ferien/im Urlaub eine Reise-/(on foot) Wanderung machen

tourism /'tʊərɪzm/ *n., no pl., no indef. art.* **1** Tourismus, *der;* ~ **has increased** der Tourismus hat zugenommen **2** (operation of tours) Touristik, *die;* **work/be involved in ~:** in der Touristikbranche arbeiten/tätig sein

tourist /'tʊərɪst/

A *n.* Tourist, *der*/Touristin, *die*

B *attrib. adj.* Touristen-; **special ~ rates** ermäßigte Preise für Touristen

tourist: ~ **agency** *n.* Reisebüro, *das;* ~ **attraction** *n.* Touristenattraktion, *die;* ~ **board** *n.* (Brit.) Amt für Fremdenverkehrswesen; ~ **bus** *n.* Touristenbus, *der;* ~ **class** *n.* Touristenklasse, *die;* ~ **guide** *n.* **1** (person) Touristenführer, *der*/-führerin, *die;* **2** (book) Reiseführer, *der* (**to, of** von); ~ **hotel** *n.* Touristenhotel, *das;* ~ **industry** *n.* **1** (business) Tourismusindustrie, *die;* **2** (firms) Touristik[branche], *die;* ~ **infor'mation centre,** ~ **office** *ns.* Fremdenverkehrsbüro, *das;* Touristeninformation, *die* (ugs.); ~ **season** *n.* Touristensaison, *die;* ~ **trade** ▸ ~ **industry;** ~ **trap** *n.* (bar, restaurant, etc.) [auf Touristen spezialisierter] Neppladen (ugs.); (town, place) Ort, an dem Touristen geneppt werden (ugs.)

touristy /'tʊərɪstɪ/ *adj.* (derog.) auf Tourismus getrimmt (ugs.); Touristen‹*stadt, -nest, -gegend*› (ugs. abwertend)

'tour leader *n.* Reiseleiter, *der*/-leiterin, *die*

tourmaline /'tʊəməlɪn, 'tʊəməliːn/ *n.* (Min.) Turmalin, *der*

tournament /'tʊənəmənt/ *n.* (Hist.; Sport) Turnier, *das*

tournedos /'tʊənədəʊ/ *n., pl. same* (Gastr.) Tournedos, *das*

tourney /'tʊənɪ/ (Hist.; Sport coll.) ▸ **tournament**

tourniquet /'tʊənɪkeɪ/ *n.* (Med.) Tourniquet, *das*

'tour operator *n.* ▸ ❶ **p. 1260** Reiseveranstalter, *der*/-veranstalterin, *die*

tousle /'taʊzl/ *v.t.* zerzausen

tout /taʊt/

A *v.i.* ~ **[for business/custom/orders]** Kunden anreißen (ugs.) *od.* werben; ~ **for customers/buyers** Kunden/Käufer anreißen (ugs.) *od.* werben; ~ **for a hotel** für ein Hotel Gäste werben

B *n.* Anreißer, *der*/Anreißerin, *die* (ugs.); Kundenwerber, *der*/-werberin, *die;* **ticket ~:** Kartenschwarzhändler, *der*/-händlerin, *die*

tow¹ /təʊ/

A *v.t.* schleppen; ziehen ‹*Anhänger, Wasserskiläufer*›; **he ~ed my car to get it started** er hat meinen Wagen angeschleppt; **he ~ed his sister [behind him]** (fig.) er zog seine Schwester hinter sich (*Dat.*) her; **~ed load** (Motor Veh.) Anhängelast, *die*

B *n.* Schleppen, *das;* **My car's broken down. — Do you want a ~?** Mein Wagen ist stehen geblieben. — Soll ich Sie [ab]schleppen?; **give a boat/car a ~:** ein Boot/einen Wagen schleppen; **give a car a ~ [to get it started]** ein Auto anschleppen; **have sth. in** *or* **on ~:** etw. im Schlepp[tau] haben; **have sb. in ~** (fig.) jmdn. im Schlepptau haben (ugs.); **take sb. in ~** (fig.) jmdn. unter seine Fittiche nehmen; **'on ~'** „wird geschleppt"; **take a boat/car in ~:** ein Boot/einen Wagen in Schlepp nehmen

Phrasal verb

• ~ **a'way** *v.t.* abschleppen

tow² *n.* (Textiles) Hede, *die;* Werg, *das*

toward /tə'wɔːd/, **towards** /tə'wɔːdz/ *prep.* **1** (in direction of) ~ **sb./sth.** auf jmdn./etw. zu; **the ship sailed ~ France/the open sea** das Schiff fuhr in Richtung Frankreich/offenes Meer; ~ **[the] town** in Richtung [auf die] Stadt; **point ~ the north** nach Norden zeigen; **march ~ the north** nach Norden *od.* in Richtung Norden *od.* in nördlicher Richtung marschieren; **look ~ the sea** in Richtung Meer blicken; **turn ~ sb.** sich zu jmdm. umdrehen; **the village is farther [to the] south, ~ Dover** das Dorf liegt weiter südlich, in Richtung Dover; **point ~ the horizon** zum Horizont deuten; **sit/stand with one's back [turned] ~ sth.** mit dem Rücken zu etw. sitzen/stehen; **turn one's face/back ~ sb./sth.** jmdm./einer Sache das Gesicht/den Rücken zuwenden; **my back was ~ the door** mein Rücken war der Tür zugewandt; **hold out one's hands ~ sb.** jmdm. die Hände entgegenstrecken; **my house faces ~ the park/sea** die Vorderseite meines Hauses liegt zum Park/Meer hin; **the country was drifting ~ war/economic chaos** das Land trieb dem Krieg/wirtschaftlichem Chaos zu; **he was sliding ~ disaster/financial ruin** er schlitterte in das Verderben/in den finanziellen Ruin **2** (in relation to) gegenüber; **feel sth. ~ sb.** jmdm. gegenüber etw. empfinden; **his attitude ~ death** seine Einstellung zum Tod; **be fair/unfair** *etc.* ~ **sb.** jmdm. gegenüber *od.* zu jmdm. fair/unfair *usw.* sein; **his conduct ~ us** sein Verhalten uns gegenüber; **feel angry/sympathetic ~ sb.** böse auf jmdn. sein/Verständnis für jmdn. haben **3** (for) **a contribution ~ sth.** ein Beitrag zu etw.; **save up ~ a car/one's holidays** auf *od.* für einen Wagen/für seine Ferien sparen; **proposals ~ solving a problem** Vorschläge zur Lösung eines Problems; **work together ~ a solution** gemeinsam auf eine Lösung hinarbeiten; **contribute ~ sth.** zu etw. beitragen; **it is/it brings us a step ~ achieving our aim** es bringt uns einen Schritt näher zum Ziel; **efforts are being made ~ reconciliation** man bemüht sich um Versöhnung **4** (near) gegen; ~ **the end of May/of the year** *etc.* [gegen] Ende Mai/des Jahres; **it is getting ~ midnight/your bedtime** es geht auf Mitternacht zu/es ist bald Schlafenszeit für dich; ~ **the end of his life/of the book** gegen Ende seines Lebens/des Buches; **sit ~ the front/back of the bus** vorne/hinten im Bus sitzen; ~ **the bottom of the list** ziemlich weit unten auf der Liste

'tow bar *n.* (Motor Veh.) Anhängerkupplung, *die;* (bar between towed and towing vehicles) Abschleppstange, *die*

towel /'taʊəl/

A *n.* Handtuch, *das;* **throw in the ~** (Boxing; also fig.) das Handtuch werfen

B *v.t.,* (Brit.) **-ll-** abtrocknen; ~ **one's/sb.'s face/arms** *etc.* **[dry]** sich/jmdm. das Gesicht/die Arme *usw.* abtrocknen; ~ **oneself** sich abtrocknen

towelling (*Amer.:* **toweling**) /'taʊəlɪŋ/ *n., no pl., no indef. art.* Frottierware, *die;* Frottee, *das* (ugs.)

'towel rail *n.* Handtuchhalter, *der*

tower /'taʊə(r)/

A *n.* **1** Turm, *der;* (Aeronaut.) Tower, *der;* Kontrollturm, *der; see also* **control tower; cooling tower; water tower** **2** (fortress) Festung, *die;* Wehrturm, *der;* **the T~ [of London]** der Tower [von London] **3** **be a ~ of strength [to sb.]** (fig.) [jmdm.] ein fester Rückhalt sein **4** ▸ **tower block.** *see also* **ivory tower**

B *v.i.* in die Höhe ragen; aufragen; ~ **to [a height of] 200 feet** 200 Fuß hoch aufragen

Phrasal verb

• ~ **above,** ~ **over** *v.t.* ~ **above** *or* **over sb./sth.** (lit. or fig.) jmdn./etw. überragen; **she saw the giant ~ing above her** sie sah die ragende Gestalt des Riesen über sich (*Dat.*) (geh.); **the building/mountain ~s above** *or* **over the town/landscape** das Gebäude/der Berg ragt über der Stadt/Landschaft (geh.)

tower: ~ **block** *n.* Hochhaus, *das;* ~ **crane** *n.* Turmdrehkran, *der*

towering /'taʊərɪŋ/ *attrib. adj.* **1** hoch aufragend; riesenhaft ‹*Gestalt*›; ~ **height** schwindelnde Höhe **2** (fig.) herausragend ‹*Leistung, Gestalt*› **3** (fig.: violent, intense) blind ‹*Wut*›; maßlos ‹*Ehrgeiz, Stolz*›; **be in/fly into a ~ passion** *or* **rage** von blinder Wut ergriffen sein/werden

'towline *n.* Schleppseil, *das;* (Naut.) Schlepptrosse, *die*

town/taʊn/ *n.* **1** ▸ ❶ **p. 1643** Stadt, *die;* **the ~ of Cambridge** die Stadt Cambridge; **in [the] ~:** in der Stadt; **the ~** (people) die Stadt; **on the outskirts/in the centre of ~:** in den Randbezirken der Stadt/in der Stadtmitte *od.* Innenstadt; **go [up] to ~:** in die Stadt fahren; **we went [up] to ~ from York** (to London) wir sind von York nach London gefahren; **be in/out of ~:** in der Stadt/nicht in der Stadt sein; **head out of ~:** stadtauswärts fahren/gehen/reiten *usw.*; **he is well known about ~:** er ist stadtbekannt; ihn kennt die ganze Stadt; **it's all over ~ [that ...]** die ganze Stadt redet davon[, dass ...]; **the best coffee/tea/cake** *etc.* **in ~:** der beste Kaffee/Tee/Kuchen *usw.* in der Stadt; **go out/have a night on the ~** (coll.) [in die Stadt gehen und] einen draufmachen (ugs.); **go to ~** (fig. coll.) in die Vollen gehen (**on** bei) (ugs.); **man about ~** *Mann, der an allen gesellschaftlichen und kulturellen Ereignissen einer Stadt teilnimmt; see also* **gown 2; paint B 1; talk A 4; toast A 2** **2** (business or shopping centre) Stadt, *die;* **in ~:** in der Stadt; **go into ~:** in die Stadt gehen/fahren

town: ~ **'centre** *n.* Stadtmitte, *die;* Stadtzentrum, *das;* **the ~ centres** die Innenstädte; **Brighton still has an old ~ centre** Brighton hat noch einen alten Stadtkern; ~ **'clerk** *n.* ▸ ❶ **p. 1260** ≈ [Ober]stadtdirektor, *der*/-direktorin, *die;* ~ **'council** *n.* (Brit.) Stadtrat, *der;* ~ **'councillor** *n.* ▸ ❶ **p. 1260** (Brit.) Stadtrat, *der*/-rätin, *die;* ~ **'crier** *n.* städtischer Ausrufer; ~ **gas** *n., no pl., no indef. art.* Stadtgas, *das;* ~ **'hall** *n.* Rathaus, *das;* ~ **house** *n.* **1** (residence in ~) Stadthaus, *das;* **2** (terrace house) Reihenhaus, *das*

townie /'taʊniː/ *n.* Stadtmensch, *der*

town: ~ **'mayor** *n.* ▸ ❶ **p. 1260** (Brit.) [Stadt]bürgermeister, *der*/-bürgermeisterin, *die;* ~ **'planner** *n.* ▸ ❶ **p. 1260** Stadtplaner, *der*/-planerin, *die;* ~ **'planning** *n.* Stadtplanung, *die*

townscape /'taʊnskeɪp/ *n.* **1** (Art, Photog.) Stadtansicht, *die* **2** (town's appearance) Stadtbild, *das*

townsfolk /'taʊnzfəʊk/ *n. pl.* Städter *Pl.;* **the ~** (inhabitants) die Stadtbevölkerung; (citizens) die Bürger [der Stadt]

township /'taʊnʃɪp/ *n.* **1** (Amer.: division of county) Township, *die; Verwaltungseinheit unterhalb der County* **2** (Amer. Surv.) Township, *die; 36 Quadratmeilen großes quadratisches Stück Land* **3** (Austral., NZ) (small town) Ortschaft, *die;* Siedlung, *die;* (site) *Areal für eine neue Siedlung* **4** (S. Afr.: non-white urban area) Township, *die; von Farbigen bewohnte städtische Siedlung*

town: **~sman** /'taʊnzmən/ *n., pl.* **~smen** /'taʊnzmən/ Stadtbewohner, *der;* Städter, *der;* (citizen) [Stadt]bürger, *der;* **[fellow] ~sman** (fellow citizen) Mitbürger, *der;* **~speople** /'taʊnzpiːpl/ ▸ **townsfolk;** **~swoman** /'taʊnzwʊmən/ *n.* Stadtbewohnerin, *die;* Städterin, *die;* (citizen) [Stadt]bürgerin, *die*

tow: **~path** *n.* Leinpfad, *der;* Treidelpfad, *der;* ~ **rope** *n.* Abschleppseil, *das;* **~-start** *n.* (Motor Veh.) [Start durch] Anschleppen; **give sb. a ~-start** jmdn. anschleppen; **~-truck** *n.* (Amer.) Abschleppwagen, *der*

toxaemia (*Amer.:* **toxemia**) /tɒk'siːmɪə/ *n.* ▸ ❶ **p. 1231** (Med.) **1** (blood poisoning) Toxämie, *die* **2** (in pregnancy) Schwangerschaftstoxikose, *die*

toxic /'tɒksɪk/ *adj.* **1** giftig; toxisch (fachspr.); ~ **cloud** Giftwolke, *die* **2** (caused by poison) toxisch (fachspr.); toxigen (fachspr.)

toxicity /tɒk'sɪsɪtɪ/ *n., no pl.* Giftigkeit, *die;* Toxizität, *die* (fachspr.)

toxicology /tɒksɪ'kɒlədʒɪ/ *n., no pl.* Toxikologie, *die*

ℹ Towns and cities

All towns are neuter in German, although this usually only becomes apparent when referring to one as **es**, or when an adjective or article is used:

Paris is on the Seine; it is the capital of France
= Paris liegt an der Seine; es ist die Hauptstadt Frankreichs

We want to create a new Hamburg
= Wir wollen ein neues Hamburg schaffen

19th century Berlin
= das Berlin des 19. Jahrhunderts

to and from

When it is simply a case of travelling from one town to another, always use **nach** for *to*, and **von** for *from* with the names:

It is 56 miles from London to Oxford
= Von London nach Oxford sind es 91 Kilometer

However compare

They are coming from Munich
= Sie kommen von München

They come from Munich
= Sie kommen aus München

When referring to someone's place of origin, *from* is translated by **aus.**

Natives and inhabitants

In English, the words which tell us where someone comes from have many different forms: Londoner, Glaswegian, Lancastrian, Bathonian, New Yorker, Bostonian, Viennese, Roman and so on. But in German it could not be simpler. You just add **-er** to the name of the town, or **-erin** in the case of a woman:

a Parisian
= ein Pariser/eine Pariserin

the Viennese
= die Wiener

Viennese women
= [die] Wienerinnen

Of course in many cases English does not have a specific name for the inhabitants of a particular place, but the formula described above can be used in German for every city, town or village:

a woman from Madrid
= eine Madriderin

the people of Prague
= die Prager

an inhabitant of Dinkelsbühl
= ein Dinkelsbühler/eine Dinkelsbühlerin

In one or two cases the name of the town or city is slightly altered before the ending is added, for instance:

a Roman
= ein Römer/eine Römerin

an inhabitant of Münster
= ein Münsteraner/eine Münsteranerin

someone from Hanover, a Hanoverian
= ein Hannoveraner/eine Hannoveranerin

a man from Bremen
= ein Bremer

the people of Munich
= die Münchner

With some non-German names adding the **-er** can produce an odd-sounding or barely pronounceable result, so such forms are avoided. It is unlikely for example that a man from Dover would be called "ein Doverer" or a woman from Bath "eine Batherin" ("ein Mann aus Dover" and "eine Frau aus Bath" would be the answers here). The inhabitants of Milwaukee could theoretically be called "die Milwaukeeer" and no doubt have been on occasion, but most Germans would prefer to say "die Bewohner von Milwaukee".

There are also a few exceptions where there is a special term, especially with Italian cities; the Florentines are "die Florentiner", a Venetian is "ein Venezianer" and a woman from Verona "eine Veroneserin". Note also Monegasque = Monegasse.

Adjectives

To form an adjective from the name of a place is also extremely simple. It has the same form as the noun for a (male) person who comes from the place; you just add **-er.** Unlike other adjectives in German, it retains its capital letter. It is also invariable, so there are no endings to add depending on case or gender. These adjectives can be used as translations where place names in English are used attributively before another noun, or after it with 'of' or 'in'.

Aachen Cathedral
= der Aachener Dom

Ravensburg Town Council
= der Ravensburger Stadtrat

Berlin dialect
= der Berliner Dialekt

the New York area
= die New Yorker Gegend

the streets of Paris
= die Pariser Straßen

the traffic in London
= der Londoner Verkehr

Note that as in the first two examples German always has the definite article where a place name is used attributively before a building or institution. And in the last two cases, one could equally well say "die Straßen von Paris" or "der Verkehr in London". This use of prepositions would also be the only possibility in cases where the addition of **-er** presents problems:

Amiens Cathedral
= die Kathedrale von Amiens

the Portsmouth area
= die Gegend um Portsmouth

With roads "die Paderborner Straße" may mean "the Paderborn road", i.e."the road to Paderborn", but it will usually be the name of a street in a town, so it is safest to say "die Straße nach Paderborn".

Another group of adjectives formed from place names and ending in **-isch** can be used to express what is typical of a place or its people; these behave like normal adjectives with small initial letters and the usual endings:

Hamburg humour
= hamburgischer Humor

Hanoverian equanimity
= hannoverischer Gleichmut

---

toxic: ~ 'shock syndrome *n.* (Med.) toxisches Schocksyndrom; **~ 'waste** *n.* Giftmüll *der;* **~ wastes** giftige Abfallstoffe; **~ waste tip** *or* **dump** Giftmülldeponie, *die*

toxin /'tɒksɪn/ *n.* Toxin, *das*

toy /tɔɪ/

A *n.* (lit. or fig.) Spielzeug, *das;* **~s** Spielzeug, *das;* Spielwaren *Pl.* (Wirtsch.)

B *adj.* **1** Spielzeug- **2** (Breeding) Zwerg-

C *v.i.* **~ with the idea of doing sth.** mit dem Gedanken spielen, etw. zu tun; **~ with one's food** mit seinem Essen herumspielen/in seinem Essen herumstochern; **~ with sb.** (flirt) mit jmdm. flirten; (not be serious) mit jmdm. spielen *od.* sein Spiel treiben

toy: ~boy *n.* (coll.) Gespiele, *der* (scherzh.); **~shop** *n.* Spielwarengeschäft, *das;* **~ 'soldier** *n.* Spielzeugsoldat, *der*

trace[1] /treɪs/

A *v.t.* **1** (copy) durchpausen; abpausen; **~ sth. on to sth.** etw. auf etw. (*Akk.*) pausen **2** (delineate) zeichnen ‹*Form, Linie*›; malen ‹*Buchstaben, Wort*›; (fig.) entwerfen; **she ~d our route on the map with her finger/with a pen** sie zeichnete unsere Route mit dem Finger/Stift auf der Landkarte nach **3** (follow track of) folgen (+ *Dat.*); verfolgen; **the leak was ~d to an old cast-iron main** man fand das Leck an einer alten gusseisernen Hauptleitung; **~ a river to its source** einen Fluss [bis] zur Quelle zurückverfolgen; **the doctors ~d the infection to some dirty instruments** die Ärzte fanden heraus, dass die Infektion von verunreinigten Instrumenten herrührte; **he had to resign when the leak was ~d to his office** er musste zurücktreten, als man die undichte Stelle in seiner Behörde ausfindig machte; **the police ~d him to Spain** die Polizei spürte ihn in Spanien auf **4** (observe, find) finden; **~ a connection** einen Zusammenhang sehen **5** (Archaeol.) erkennen; **~ Roman roads** den Verlauf von alten Römerstraßen rekonstruieren

B *n.* **1** (visible sign) Spur, *die;* (of buildings, road) [Über]rest, *der;* **there is no ~ of your letter in our records** in unseren Aufzeichnungen findet sich kein Hinweis auf Ihr Schreiben; **I can't find any ~ of him/it** (cannot locate) ich kann ihn/es nirgends finden; **lose [all] ~ of sb.** jmdn. [völlig] aus den Augen verlieren; **all ~ of the climbers has been lost** von den Bergsteigern fehlt jede Spur; **sink without ~:** sinken, ohne eine Spur zu hinterlassen; (fig.) in der Versenkung verschwinden (ugs.); ‹*bekannte Persönlichkeit:*› von der Bildfläche verschwinden (ugs.) **2** (track left behind) Spur, *die* (of animal also) Fährte, *die;* (of recording instrument) Kurve, *die* **3** (Electronics) Spur, *die* **4** (small amount) Spur, *die;* **a ~ of a smile/of sarcasm** ein Anflug eines Lächelns/von Sarkasmus; **the product contains a ~ of impurity** das Produkt enthält eine winzige Menge an Fremdstoffen

Phrasal verbs

- **~ 'back** *v.t.* zurückverfolgen; **the rumour was ~d back to a journalist** als Quelle des Gerüchts wurde ein Journalist ausfindig gemacht
- **~ 'out** ▸ **~ A 2**
- **~ 'over** ▸ **~ A 1**

trace[2] *n.* (strap of harness) Strang, *der;* (of horse's headstall) Zuggurt, *der;* **kick over the ~s** (fig.) über die Stränge schlagen (ugs.)

traceable /'treɪsəbl/ *adj.* **1** **sth. is ~ to sth./through sth.** etw. lässt sich bis zu etw./durch etw. hindurch zurückverfolgen; **this effect is ~ to the following cause** diese Wirkung lässt sich auf folgende Ursache zurückführen **2** (discoverable) auffindbar; **this is a feature ~ in all his novels/paintings** dieses Merkmal lässt sich in allen seinen Romanen/Bildern entdecken

'trace element *n.* (Chem.) Spurenelement, *das*

tracer /'treɪsə(r)/ *n.* **1** (Mil.) Leuchtspurgeschoss, *das* **2** (radioactive isotope) Indikator, *der*

tracery /'treɪsərɪ/ *n.* **1** (Archit.) Maßwerk, *das;* **bar ~:** Maßwerk, *das;* **plate ~:** negatives Maßwerk **2** (pattern, network) Filigranmuster, *das*

t

trachea /trəˈkiːə/ *n., pl.* **~e** /trəˈkiːiː/ [1] (Anat.) Trachea, *die* (fachspr.); Luftröhre, *die* [2] (Zool.) Trachee, *die* (Zool.)

tracheotomy /treɪkɪˈɒtəmɪ/ *n.* (Med.) Luftröhrenschnitt, *der;* Tracheotomie, *die* (fachspr.)

trachoma /trəˈkəʊmə/ *n.* ▸ℹ **p. 1231** (Med.) Trachom, *das* (Med.)

tracing /ˈtreɪsɪŋ/ *n.* [1] (action) [Durch]pausen, *das;* [Ab]pausen, *das;* **do some ~:** einiges durch- *od.* abpausen [2] (copy) Pause, *die;* Kopie, *die*

ˈ**tracing paper** *n.* Pauspapier, *das*

track /træk/

A *n.* [1] Spur, *die;* (of wild animal) Fährte, *die;* **~s** (footprints) [Fuß]spuren; (of animal also) Fährte, *die;* **cover one's ~s** (fig.) seine Spur verwischen; **be on sb.'s ~:** jmdm. auf der Spur sein; (fig.: in possession of clue to sb.'s plans) jmdm. auf die Schliche gekommen sein; **they will be on our ~:** sie kommen uns auf die Spur/(fig.) auf die Schliche; **be on the right/wrong ~** (fig.) auf der richtigen/falschen Spur sein; **keep ~ of sb./sth.** jmdn./etw. im Auge behalten; **he couldn't keep ~ of her in the crowd** er verlor sie in der Menge aus den Augen; **the police [successfully] kept ~ of him** die Polizei blieb ihm auf der Spur; **they kept ~ of his movements/intentions/plans** sie waren jederzeit über seinen Aufenthaltsort/seine Absichten/Pläne auf dem Laufenden; **The situation is very complicated. I can't keep ~ of it** Die Situation ist sehr verworren. Ich habe den Überblick verloren; **without keeping accounts I can't keep ~ of what I spend** wenn ich nicht Buch führe, verliere ich den Überblick über meine Ausgaben; **lose ~ of sb./sth.** jmdn./etw. aus den Augen verlieren; **the police lost ~ of the gang's movements** die Polizei war über den Aufenthaltsort der Bande nicht mehr auf dem Laufenden; **he has lost ~ of the situation** er ist über die Situation nicht mehr auf dem Laufenden; **she lost ~ of the story** sie hat bei der Geschichte den Überblick verloren; **without keeping accounts you can easily lose ~ of what you spend** wenn man nicht Buch führt, kann man leicht die Übersicht über seine Ausgaben verlieren; **make ~s** (coll.) (depart) sich auf die Socken machen (ugs.); (run off) türmen (ugs.); **we'd better make ~s for home/the station** (coll.) wir sollten uns langsam auf die Socken machen und zusehen, dass wir nach Hause/zum Bahnhof kommen (ugs.); **stop [dead] in one's ~s** (coll.) auf der Stelle stehen bleiben; **stop sb. [dead] in his ~s** (coll.) jmdn. auf der Stelle stehen bleiben lassen

[2] (path) [unbefestigter] Weg; (footpath) Pfad, *der;* (fig.) Weg, *der;* **the road has only a single ~:** die Straße hat nur eine Spur *od.* ist nur einspurig; **they followed in the same ~** (fig.) auch sie gingen denselben Weg; *see also* **beaten B 1**

[3] (Sport) Bahn, *die;* **cycling/greyhound ~:** Radrennbahn, *die*/Windhundrennbahn, *die;* **circuit of the ~:** Bahnrunde, *die*

[4] (Railw.) Gleis, *das;* **thousands of miles of ~:** Tausende von Meilen Gleise; **be born/live across the ~s** *or* **on the wrong side of the ~s** (Amer. fig. coll.) auf der Schattenseite geboren sein/leben (fig.); **'keep off the ~'** „Betreten der Gleise verboten"; **single/double ~:** eingleisige/zweigleisige Strecke; **the train left the ~:** der Zug entgleiste

[5] (course taken) Route, *die;* (of rocket, satellite, comet, missile, hurricane, etc.) Bahn, *die*

[6] (of tank, tractor, etc.) Kette, *die*

[7] (section of record) Stück, *das;* Track, *der* (Jargon)

[8] ▸ **soundtrack**

[9] (groove on record) Rille, *die*

[10] (section of tape) Spur, *die;* **two-/four-~ tape recorder** Zwei-/Vierspurtonbandgerät, *das*

[11] (Motor Veh.: distance between wheels) Spur[weite], *die*

[12] (Amer. Educ.) Kurs, *der*

B *v.t.* [1] **~ an animal** die Spur/Fährte eines Tieres verfolgen; **the police ~ed him [to Paris]** die Polizei folgte seiner Spur [bis nach Paris]; **~ a rocket/satellite** die Bahn einer Rakete/eines Satelliten verfolgen

[2] (Archaeol.) rekonstruieren; nachvollziehen ‹*Entwicklung*›

[3] (Amer.: leave trail of) **~ dirt over the floor/~ [up] the floor with dirt** Schmutzspuren auf dem Fußboden hinterlassen

Phrasal verb

- **~ 'down** *v.t.* aufspüren; **~ a criminal down to his hideout** einen Verbrecher in seinem Versteck aufspüren

track: ~ athlete *n.* Laufsportler, *der*/-sportlerin, *die;* **~ball** *n.* (Computing) Rollball, *der*

tracker /ˈtrækə(r)/ *n.* [1] Fährtensucher, *der;* **he is an experienced ~ of animals** er hat viel Erfahrung im Aufspüren von Tieren [2] **~ [dog]** Spürhund, *der*

tracker: ~ ball ▸ **trackball; ~ fund** *n.* (Brit. Finance) Indexfonds, *der*

ˈ**track event** *n.* (Athletics) Laufwettbewerb, *der*

tracking/ˈtrækɪŋ/: **~ device** *n.* Ortungsgerät, *das;* **~ shot** *n.* (Cinemat., Telev.) Fahrt, *die;* **~ station** *n.* (Astronaut.) Bahnverfolgungsstation, *die*

track-laying *adj.* Raupen-

trackless /ˈtræklɪs/ *adj.* [1] (without path) weglos [2] (without footprints etc.) keinerlei Spuren aufweisend

track: ~ record *n.* (fig.) **his ~ record is good, he has a good ~ record** er hat gute Leistungen vorzuweisen; **what's his ~ record?** was hat er vorzuweisen?; **this product has a very good ~ record** dieses Produkt hat sich als sehr erfolgreich erwiesen; **~ shoe** *n.* Rennschuh, *der;* **~ suit** *n.* Trainingsanzug, *der;* **~-suited** *adj.* im Trainingsanzug *nachgestellt;* **a ~-suited figure** eine mit einem Trainingsanzug bekleidete Gestalt; **~ system** *n.* (Amer. Educ.) Kurssystem, *das;* **~way** *n.* [1] (beaten path) [Trampel]pfad, *der;* [2] (ancient roadway) alte Straße

tract[1] /trækt/ *n.* [1] (area) Gebiet, *das;* **a narrow/vast ~ [of land]** ein schmaler Streifen [Land]/ein riesiges Gebiet [2] (Anat.) Trakt, *der*

tract[2] *n.* (pamphlet) [Flug]schrift, *die;* Traktat, *der* (veralt.)

tractable /ˈtræktəbl/ *adj.* fügsam; leicht formbar ‹*Material*›

traction /ˈtrækʃn/ *n., no pl., no indef. art.* [1] (drawing along) Traktion, *die* (fachspr.); Ziehen, *das;* **steam/electric ~:** Dampf-/Elektrotraktion, *die* [2] (grip of tyre etc.) Haftung, *die* [3] (Med.) Zug, *der;* **in ~:** im Zug- *od.* Streckverband [4] (Amer. Transport) öffentliche Verkehrsmittel; **~ company** Verkehrsgesellschaft, *die*

traction: ~ control system *n.* (Motor Veh.) Traktionskontrollsystem, *das;* **~ engine** *n.* Zugmaschine, *die;* (for agricultural use) Traktor, *der*

tractor /ˈtræktə(r)/ *n.* [1] Traktor, *der* [2] (Motor Veh.) (lorry unit) Zugwagen, *der;* Zugfahrzeug, *das;* (of articulated lorry) Sattelzugmaschine, *die*

trad /træd/ (Mus. coll.)

A *adj.* traditional (Jargon); **~ jazz** Traditional Jazz, *der*

B *n., no pl., no indef. art.* Traditional, *der* (Jargon)

tradable, tradeable /ˈtreɪdəbl/ *adj.* handelbar

trade /treɪd/

A *n.* [1] (line of business) Gewerbe, *das;* **the wool/furniture/hotel ~:** die Woll-/Möbel-/Hotelbranche; **the retail/wholesale ~:** der Einzel-/Großhandel; **he's a butcher/lawyer/baker** *etc.* **by ~:** er ist von Beruf Metzger/Rechtsanwalt/Bäcker *usw.;* **trick of the ~:** einschlägiger Trick; **know the tricks of the ~:** die einschlägigen Tricks kennen; **do sth. using every trick of the ~:** etw. nach allen Regeln der Kunst tun; *see also* **jack of all trades** [2] *no pl., no indef. art* (commerce) Handel, *der;* **be bad/good for ~:** schlecht/gut fürs Geschäft sein; **do ~ with sb.** mit jmdm. Geschäfte machen; **do ~ with a country** mit einem Land Handel treiben; **domestic** *or* **home ~:** Binnenhandel, *der;* **foreign ~:** Außenhandel, *der; see also* **balance A 9; board A 9; free trade; term A 2** [3] *no pl.* (business done) Geschäft, *das;* (between countries) Handel, *der;* **a large share of the ~ in wool/leather goods/grain** ein großer Anteil am Geschäft mit Wolle/Lederwaren/Getreide; **an increase in ~:** eine Umsatzsteigerung; **do a good/roaring ~ [in sth.]** ein gutes Geschäft/ein Riesengeschäft [mit etw.] machen; **how's ~?** wie gehen die Geschäfte?; wie geht das Geschäft? [4] (craft) Handwerk, *das;* **learn/study for a ~:** einen Handwerksberuf [er]lernen [5] *no pl., no indef. art.* (persons) **the ~:** die Branche; **sell to the ~:** an Wiederverkäufer verkaufen; **special discounts for [the] ~:** Sonderrabatte für Wiederverkäufer [6] *in pl.* (Meteorol.: winds) Passat, *der* [7] (Amer.: a transaction) Geschäft, *das;* (exchange) Tausch, *der*

B *v.i.* [1] (buy and sell) Handel treiben; **~ as a wholesale/retail dealer** ein Großhandels-/Einzelhandelsgeschäft betreiben; **they ~ as Henry Brooks & Co.** sie firmieren als Henry Brooks und Co.; **~ at a store** (Amer.) in einem Geschäft einkaufen; **~ in sth.** in *od.* mit etw. (*Dat.*) handeln; **we don't ~ with that firm** wir unterhalten zu dieser Firma keine Geschäftsbeziehungen [2] (have an exchange) tauschen; **~ with sb. for sth.** jmdm. etw. abhandeln [3] (carry merchandise) Handelswaren befördern; **~ to a place** Handelsgüter an einen Ort transportieren

C *v.t.* [1] tauschen; austauschen ‹*Waren, Grüße, Informationen, Geheimnisse*›; sich (*Dat.*) sagen ‹*Beleidigungen*› [2] **~ sth. for sth.** etw. gegen etw. tauschen; **~ an old car** *etc.* **for a new one** einen alten Wagen *usw.* für einen neuen in Zahlung geben

Phrasal verbs

- **~ 'in** *v.t.* in Zahlung geben; einlösen ‹*Gutschein, Kupon usw.*›; *see also* **trade-in**
- **~ 'off** *v.t.* **~ sth. off for sth.** etw. gegen etw. tauschen; *see also* **trade-off**
- **~ on** *v.t.* (fig.) **~ on sth.** aus etw. Kapital schlagen; sich (*Dat.*) etw. zunutze machen
- **~ 'up** *v.i.* sich verbessern
- **~ upon** ▸ **~ on**

trade: ~ balance *n.* (Econ.) Handelsbilanz, *die;* **~ cycle** *n.* (Brit. Econ.) Konjunkturzyklus, *der;* **~ deficit** *n.* (Econ.) passive Handelsbilanz; Handelsbilanzdefizit, *das;* **T~ De'scriptions Act** *n.* (Brit.) Warenkennzeichnungsgesetz, *das;* **~ directory** *n.* Branchenadressbuch, *das;* **~ 'discount** *n.* Branchenrabatt, *der;* (in book ~) Kollegenrabatt, *der;* **~ dispute** *n.* [1] (between employers and workers) Arbeitskonflikt, *der;* [2] (dispute over international trade) Handelskonflikt, *der;* **~ embargo** *n.* Handelsembargo, *das;* **~ fair** *n.* [Fach]messe, *die;* **~ gap** ▸ **~ deficit; ~-in A** *n.* [1] (part exchange) Inzahlungnahme, *die* (**on** *Gen.*); **we offer a ~-in on your old car** wir nehmen Ihren alten Wagen in Zahlung; **can you give me a ~-in on my old car?** nehmen Sie meinen alten Wagen in Zahlung?; [2] (item) **we'll accept your old car as a ~-in** wir nehmen Ihren alten Wagen in Zahlung. **B** *attrib. adj.* **the ~-in value of your car is low** der Preis, zu dem Ihr Wagen in Zahlung genommen wird, ist niedrig; **~-in price** *n.* Inzahlungnahmepreis, *der;* **~ journal** *n.* Fachzeitschrift, *die;* **~-last** *n.* (Amer. coll.) **swap ~-lasts** Komplimente von Dritten austauschen; **~ mark** *n.* [1] Warenzeichen, *das;* [2] (fig.) **leave one's ~ mark on sth.** einer Sache (*Dat.*) seinen Stempel aufdrücken; **it bore all the ~ marks of this director's style** es trug den Stempel *od.* die Handschrift dieses Regisseurs; **honesty/straightforwardness/stubbornness is her ~ mark** sie zeichnet sich durch Ehrlichkeit/Direktheit/Hartnäckigkeit aus; *see also* **registered; ~ mission** *n.* Handelsmission, *die;* **~ name** *n.* [1] (name used in the ~) Fachbezeichnung, *die;* [2] (proprietary name) Markenname, *der;* [3] (name of business) Firmenname, *der;* **~-off** *n.* Tauschgeschäft, *das;* (fig.) Handel, *der;* **~ paper** ▸ **~ journal; ~ plates** *n. pl.* (Motor Veh.) ≈ rote Kennzeichen; **~ price** *n.* Einkaufspreis, *der;* **at ~ price** zum Einkaufspreis

trader /ˈtreɪdə(r)/ *n.* [1] Händler, *der*/Händlerin, *die* [2] (Naut.) Handelsschiff, *das*

trade: ~ restrictions *pl. n.* Handelsbeschränkungen *Pl.;* **~ route** *n.* Handelsweg, *der;* Handelsstraße, *die;* ~ **sanctions** *pl. n.* Handelssanktionen *Pl.*

tradescantia /trædɪsˈkæntɪə/ *n.* (Bot.) Tradeskantie, *die*

trade: ~ **ˈsecret** *n.* Geschäftsgeheimnis, *das;* **T~ Secretary** *n.* (Brit.) Handelsminister, *der*/-ministerin, *die;* ~ **show** *n.* Handelsmesse, *die;* **computer ~ show/fashion ~ show** Computer[fach]messe, *die*/Modemesse, *die;* **~sman** /ˈtreɪdzmən/ *n., pl.* **~smen** /ˈtreɪdzmən/ [1] (shopkeeper) [Einzel]händler, *der;* Ladeninhaber, *der;* **~smen's entrance** Lieferanteneingang, *der;* [2] (craftsman) Handwerker, *der;* **~speople** /ˈtreɪdzpi:pl/ *n. pl.* [1] (shopkeepers) [Einzel]händler; Ladeninhaber; [2] (craft workers) Handwerker; **~sˈ ˈunion** ▸~ **union**; **T~s Union ˈCongress** *pr. n.* (Brit.) Gewerkschaftsbund, *der;* ~ **surplus** *n.* (Econ.) Handelsbilanzüberschuss, *der;* ~ **tariff** *n.* Handelszoll, *der;* ~ **ˈunion** *n.* Gewerkschaft, *die; attrib.* Gewerkschafts-; ~ **ˈunionism** *n., no pl.* Gewerkschaftswesen, *das;* ~ **ˈunionist** *n.* Gewerkschaft[l]er, *der*/Gewerkschaft[l]erin, *die;* ~ **war** *n.* Handelskrieg, *der;* ~ **wind** *n.* (Meteorol.) Passatwind, *der*

trading /ˈtreɪdɪŋ/ *n.* Handel, *der;* ~ **on the Stock Exchange** das Geschäft an der Börse; **the ~ of pounds for dollars** der Verkauf von Pfund gegen Dollar

trading: ~ **bloc** *n.* Handelsblock, *der;* ~ **day** *n.* (St. Exch.) Handelstag, *der;* ~ **estate** *n.* (Brit.) Gewerbegebiet, *das;* ~ **hours** *n. pl.* Geschäftszeit, *die;* **during/outside ~ hours** während/außerhalb der Geschäftszeit; **'Trading hours: …'** „Geschäftszeiten: …"; ~ **nation** *n.* Handelsnation, *die;* ~ **partner** *n.* Handelspartner, *der*/-partnerin, *die;* ~ **post** ▸**post**³ **A 5**; ~ **stamp** *n.* Rabattmarke, *die;* **T~ Standards Department** *n.* (Brit.) Gewerbeaufsichtsamt, *das;* **T~ Standards Officer** *n.* (Brit.) Gewerbeaufsichtsbeamte, *der*/-beamtin, *die*

tradition /trəˈdɪʃn/ *n.* Tradition, *die;* (story) [mündliche] Überlieferung; **family ~:** Familientradition, *die;* **he is no respecter of ~:** er hält nicht viel von der Tradition; **old universities rich in ~:** alte traditionsreiche Universitäten; **he has no sense of ~** *or* **no feeling for ~:** er hat keinen Sinn für Tradition; **in the best ~[s]** nach bester Tradition; **break with ~:** mit der Tradition brechen; **by ~:** traditionell[erweise]; ~ **has it that …:** es heißt, dass …

traditional /trəˈdɪʃənl/ *adj.* [1] traditionell; mündlich überliefert ‹*Geschichte*›; herkömmlich ‹*Erziehung, Einrichtung, Methode*›; überkommen ‹*Brauch, Sitte, Werte, Moral*›; **it is ~ to do sth.** es ist Tradition, etw. zu tun [2] (Art, Lit.) konventionell [3] (Mus.) traditionell ‹*Jazz*›

traditionalism /trəˈdɪʃənəlɪzm/ *n., no pl.* Traditionalismus, *der*

traditionalist /trəˈdɪʃənəlɪst/ *n.* Traditionalist, *der*/Traditionalistin, *die*

traditionally /trəˈdɪʃənəlɪ/ *adv.* (in a traditional manner) traditionell; (by tradition) traditionell[erweise]; **~, gifts are exchanged at Christmas** an Weihnachten werden traditionell Geschenke ausgetauscht; **the Oxford Union is ~ a good training ground for politicians** die Oxford Union ist seit je eine gute Schule für künftige Politiker; **a ~ designed exterior** ein traditionelles Exterieur

traduce /trəˈdju:s/ *v.t.* (literary: defame) verleumden

traducer /trəˈdju:sə(r)/ *n.* (literary) Verleumder, *der*/Verleumderin, *die*

traffic /ˈtræfɪk/

A *n., no pl.* [1] *no indef. art.* Verkehr, *der;* ~ **is heavy/light** es herrscht starker/geringer Verkehr; ~ **will increase** der Verkehr wird zunehmen [2] (trade) Handel, *der;* **the ~ in goods/wool/steel between the two countries** der Handelsverkehr mit Gütern/Wolle/Stahl zwischen den beiden Ländern; **there is a brisk ~ in stolen goods/pornography** es wird ein schwunghafter Handel mit Diebesgut/Pornographie getrieben; **~ in drugs/arms** Drogen-/Waffenhandel, *der* [3] (amount of business) Verkehr, *der;* **~ in these goods/in furs/in grain has increased** der Umschlag an diesen Gütern/an Pelzen/Getreide ist gestiegen [4] (Teleph., Radio) **telephone/radio ~:** Fernsprech-/Funkverkehr, *der*

B *v.i.*, **-ck-** Geschäfte machen; ~ **in sth.** mit etw. handeln *od.* Handel treiben; (fig.) mit etw. schachern (abwertend); ~ **in drugs** Drogen dealen

C *v.t.*, **-ck-** handeln mit; (barter, exchange) Tauschhandel treiben mit

traffic: ~ **accident** *n.* Verkehrsunfall, *der;* ~ **calming** *n., no pl.* Verkehrsberuhigung, *die;* ~ **circle** *n.* (Amer.) Kreisverkehr, *der;* ~ **cone** *n.* Pylon, *der;* Leitkegel, *der;* ~ **control** *n., no pl.* Verkehrsregelung, *die;* ~ **controller** *n.* [1] ▸ⓘ **p. 1260** (person) Verkehrsregler, *der*/-reglerin, *die;* [2] (device) Verkehrsregelungsanlage, *die;* ~ **cop** *n.* ▸ⓘ **p. 1260** (esp. Amer. coll.) Verkehrspolizist, *der*/-polizistin, *die;* ~ **duty** *n.* Verkehrsdienst, *der;* **be on ~ duty** Verkehrsdienst haben; ~ **flow** *n.* Verkehrsfluss, *der;* **~-free** *adj.* verkehrsfrei ‹*Zone, Fläche*›; **relatively ~-free roads** Straßen mit relativ wenig Verkehr; **the streets were ~-free** auf den Straßen herrschte kein Verkehr; ~ **hold-up** ▸~ **jam**; ~ **island** *n.* Verkehrsinsel, *die;* ~ **jam** *n.* [Verkehrs]stau, *der*

trafficker /ˈtræfɪkə(r)/ *n.* Händler, *der*/Händlerin, *die;* ~ **in drugs, drug ~:** Drogenhändler, *der*/-händlerin, *die*

traffic: ~ **lane** *n.* Fahrspur, *die;* ~ **lights** *n. pl.* [Verkehrs]ampel, *die;* ~ **offence** *n.* Verkehrsdelikt, das; Verkehrsvergehen, *das;* ~ **police** *n.* Verkehrspolizei, *die;* ~ **policeman** *n.* ▸ⓘ **p. 1260** Verkehrspolizist, *der;* ~ **report** *n.* Verkehrsübersicht, *die;* (on radio) Verkehrsservice, *der;* ~ **sign** *n.* Verkehrszeichen, *das;* ~ **signals** ▸~ **lights**; ~ **warden** *n.* ▸ⓘ **p. 1260** (Brit.) Hilfspolizist, *der;* (woman) Hilfspolizistin, *die;* Politesse, *die*

tragedian /trəˈdʒi:dɪən/ *n.* [1] (Lit.) Tragödiendichter, *der*/-dichterin, *die* [2] (Theatre) Tragöde, *der*

tragedienne /trədʒi:dɪˈen/ *n. fem.* (Theatre) Tragödin, *die*

tragedy /ˈtrædʒɪdɪ/ *n.* [1] (sad event or fact) Tragödie, *die;* (sad story) tragische Geschichte; **the ~ [of it] is that …:** das Tragische [daran] ist, dass … [2] (accident) Tragödie, *die;* **earthquake ~/bomb ~:** Erdbebenkatastrophe, *die*/blutiger Bombenanschlag [3] (Theatre) Tragödie, *die;* Trauerspiel, *das*

tragic /ˈtrædʒɪk/ *adj.* [1] tragisch; **a ~ waste of talent/money** eine schlimme Vergeudung von Talenten/Geldverschwendung [2] *attrib.* (Theatre) tragisch; ~ **actor/actress** Tragöde, *der*/Tragödin, *die;* ~ **irony** tragische Ironie

tragically /ˈtrædʒɪkəlɪ/ *adv.* tragisch; **their predictions have been ~ fulfilled** ihre Prophezeiungen haben sich auf tragische Weise erfüllt; **~, she had a fatal accident** tragischerweise erlitt sie einen tödlichen Unfall

tragicomedy /trædʒɪˈkɒmɪdɪ/ *n.* (Lit.) Tragikomödie, *die*

tragicomic /trædʒɪˈkɒmɪk/ *adj.* (Lit.) tragikomisch

trail /treɪl/

A *n.* [1] Spur, *die;* (of meteor) Schweif, *der;* **a ~ of blood** eine Blutspur; ~ **of smoke/dust** Rauch-/Staubfahne, *die;* **he left a ~ of broken marriages/misery behind him** überall, wo er auftauchte, hinterließ er zerbrochene Ehen/Elend; *see also* **condensation trail**; **vapour trail** [2] (Hunting) Spur, *die;* Fährte, *die;* **be on the ~ of an animal** der Fährte eines Tieres folgen; **be off the ~** (lit. or fig.) nicht auf der richtigen Spur *od.* Fährte sein; **be/get on sb.'s ~** (lit. or fig.) jmdm. auf der Spur *od.* Fährte sein/jmdm. auf die Spur *od.* Fährte kommen; **be hard** *or* **hot on the ~ of sb.** (lit. or fig.) jmdm. dicht auf den Fersen sein (ugs.); **he was hot** *or* **hard on the ~ of the stolen goods** bei der Suche nach dem Diebesgut hatte er eine heiße Spur [gefunden] [3] (path) Pfad, *der;* (wagon ~) Weg, *der;* **there was no path or ~ of any kind** es gab keinerlei Weg oder Pfad; *see also* **blaze**² **B**; **nature trail**

B *v.t.* [1] (pursue) verfolgen; (shadow) beschatten; ~ **sb./an animal to a place** jmdm./einem Tier bis zu einem Ort folgen [2] (drag) ~ **sth. [after** *or* **behind one]** etw. hinter sich (*Dat.*) herziehen; ~ **sth. on the ground** etw. über den Boden schleifen lassen; **he ~ed his hand/fingers in the water as the boat went along** er ließ seine Hand/Finger mit dem fahrenden Boot durchs Wasser gleiten; **a train/car went by, ~ing clouds of smoke/dust** ein Zug/Auto fuhr vorbei und zog eine Rauch-/Staubwolke hinter sich (*Dat.*) her; ~ **sb. by 20 points** 20 Punkte hinter jmdm. liegen

C *v.i.* [1] (be dragged) schleifen; **the bird's wing/dog's leg was ~ing** der Flügel des Vogels/das Bein des Hundes schleifte am Boden; **a cloud of dust ~ed behind the car** hinter dem Wagen zog sich eine Staubwolke hin [2] (hang loosely) herabhängen; ~ **to the ground** auf den Boden hängen [3] (walk wearily etc.) trotten; (lag) hinterhertrotten [4] (Sport: be losing) zurückliegen; **the runner was ~ing badly** der Läufer lag weit zurück; **be ~ing by two goals to three** mit zwei zu drei Toren im Rückstand sein [5] (creep) ‹*Pflanze:*› kriechen

(Phrasal verbs)

- ~ **aˈway** ▸~ **off**
- ~ **beˈhind** *v.i.* hinterhertrödeln (ugs.); (Sport) zurückliegen
- ~ **ˈoff** *v.i.* [1] (fade into silence) **his voice/shout ~ed off into a whisper/into silence** seine Stimme/sein Schreien wurde schwächer, bis er schließlich nur noch flüsterte/bis er schließlich ganz verstummte; **her words/speech ~ed off [into silence]** sie verstummte allmählich [2] (move slowly) lostrotten; abtrotten

trail: ~ **bike** *n. leichtes, geländegängiges Motorrad;* Enduro, *das;* **~blazer** *n.* (fig.: pioneer) Bahnbrecher, *der*/Bahnbrecherin, *die;* Wegbereiter, *der*/Wegbereiterin, *die;* **~blazing** /ˈtreɪlbleɪzɪŋ/ **A** *adj.* bahnbrechend; **B** *n., no pl.* Pionierarbeit, *die;* **her ~blazing in the field of…** ihre bahnbrechende Leistung auf dem Gebiet der…

trailer /ˈtreɪlə(r)/ *n.* [1] (Motor Veh.) Anhänger, *der;* (boat ~ also) Trailer, *der;* (Amer.: caravan) Wohnanhänger, *der;* Wohnwagen, *der* [2] (Cinemat., Telev.) Trailer, *der* [3] (Bot.) Ranke, *die*

trailer: ~ **park** *n.* (Amer.) [1] (caravan site) Caravanplatz, *der;* Wohnwagenpark, *der;* [2] *attrib.* (coll. derog.) primitiv; prollig (ugs. abwertend); ~ **tent** *n.* Anhängerzelt, *das;* ~ **trash** *n., no pl.* (Amer. derog. offensive) Zigeuner, *der*/Zigeunerin, *die* (derb abwertend); (collect.) Zigeunerpack, *das* (derb abwertend); ~ **truck** *n.* (Amer.) Sattelzug, *der*

ˈtrailing edge *n.* Hinterkante, *die;* (of sail) Achterliek, *das*

train /treɪn/

A *v.t.* [1] ausbilden (**in** in + *Dat.*); erziehen ‹*Kind*›; abrichten ‹*Hund*›; dressieren ‹*Tier*›; schulen ‹*Geist, Auge, Ohr*›; bilden ‹*Charakter*›; ~ **sb. as a teacher/soldier/engineer** jmdn. zum Lehrer/Soldaten/Ingenieur ausbilden; ~ **sb. for a profession** jmdn. auf einen Beruf vorbereiten *od.* für einen Beruf ausbilden; ~ **sb. for a career as an officer** jmdn. zum Offizier ausbilden; **he/she has been well/badly/fully ~ed** er/sie besitzt eine gute/schlechte/umfassende Ausbildung [2] (Sport) trainieren; ~ **oneself** trainieren [3] (teach and accustom) ~ **an animal to do sth./to sth.** einem Tier beibringen, etw. zu tun/etw. beibringen; **the police dog was ~ed to kill** der Polizeihund war zum Töten abgerichtet; ~ **oneself to do sth.** sich dazu erziehen, etw. zu tun; ~ **a child to do sth./to sth.** ein Kind dazu erziehen, etw. zu tun/zu etw. erziehen; ~ **sb. to use a machine** jmdn. in der Bedienung einer Maschine schulen; **you've got him well ~ed** (joc.) du hast ihn dir gut erzogen [4] (Hort.) ziehen; erziehen (fachspr.); **the vines are ~ed and supported by poles** die Reben werden an die stützenden Pfosten gezogen *od.* (fachspr.) erzogen; ~ **a plant up/against a wall/trellis** eine Pflanze an einer Mauer/einem Spalier ziehen *od.* (fachspr.) erziehen [5] (aim) richten (**on** auf + *Akk.*)

B *v.i.* [1] eine Ausbildung machen; **he is ~ing as**

t

or **to be a teacher/doctor/engineer** er macht eine Lehrer-/Arzt-/Ingenieursausbildung; **he is ~ing as a soldier** er lässt sich zum Soldaten ausbilden; **he is ~ing for a responsible position** er bereitet sich auf eine verantwortliche Stellung vor; **he is ~ing for a career as an officer/for the ministry/for the law** er macht eine Offiziers-/Priester-/Rechtsanwaltsausbildung **2** (Sport) trainieren

C *n.* **1** (Railw.) Zug, *der;* **go** *or* **travel by ~:** mit dem Zug *od.* der Bahn fahren; **the 2 o'clock ~:** der Zweiuhrzug; **on the ~:** im Zug; **which is the ~ for Oxford?** welcher Zug fährt nach Oxford? **2** (of skirt etc.) Schleppe, *die* **3** (Ornith.) Schwanz, *der* **4** (retinue) Gefolge, *das;* **the king/minister had brought a ~ of advisers/attendants with him** der König/Minister hatte ein großes Gefolge von Beratern/Begleitern mitgebracht; **the long ~ of mourners** der lange Trauerzug; **the tornado brought havoc in its ~:** der Tornado hinterließ Verwüstungen **5** (line, series) Zug, *der;* **an unlucky ~ of events** eine unglückliche [Aufeinander]folge von Ereignissen; **~ of thought** Gedankengang, *der;* **be in ~** (formal) im Gange sein; **everything is now in ~ for the party/ceremony/election** alle Vorbereitungen für die Party/Feier/Wahl sind jetzt im Gange

Phrasal verb

• **~ 'up** *v.t.* heranbilden; **our workers have been ~ed up to a very high standard** unsere Arbeiter sind sehr gut ausgebildet

trainable /ˈtreɪnəbl/ *adj.* leicht erziehbar ‹*Kind*›; ausbildungsfähig ‹*Arbeiter*›

train: ~-bearer *n.* Schleppenträger, *der*/-trägerin, *die;* **~ crash** *n.* Zugunglück, *das;* **~ driver** *n.* Lokomotivführer, *der*/-führerin, *die*

trained /treɪnd/ *adj.* ausgebildet ‹*Arbeiter, Lehrer, Arzt, Stimme*›; abgerichtet ‹*Hund*›; dressiert ‹*Tier*›; geschult ‹*Geist, Auge, Ohr*›

trainee /treɪˈniː/ *n.* Auszubildende, *der/die;* (business management ~) Trainee, *der/die;* (in academic, technical professions) Praktikant, *der*/Praktikantin, *die;* **a ~ manager/nurse/teacher/doctor/cook** *etc.* ein Manager/eine Krankenschwester/ein Lehrer/Arzt/Koch *usw.* in Ausbildung

trainer /ˈtreɪnə(r)/ *n.* **1** (Sport) [Konditions]trainer, *der*/-trainerin, *die* **2** (Aeronaut.) (aircraft) Trainer, *der;* (simulator) Flugsimulator, *der* **3** *in pl.* Trainingsschuhe

train: ~ fare *n.* Fahrpreis, *der;* **how much is the ~ fare to Oxford?** wie viel kostet die Bahnfahrt nach Oxford?; **we shall reimburse your ~ fare** wir erstatten Ihnen die Kosten der Bahnfahrt; **~ ferry** *n.* Eisenbahnfähre, *die*

training /ˈtreɪnɪŋ/ *n., no pl.* **1** Ausbildung, *die* **2** (Sport) Training, *das;* **be in ~** (train) trainieren; im Training sein; (be fit) in [guter] Form sein; **be out of ~:** außer Form sein; **go into ~:** mit dem Training anfangen; **keep in ~:** sich in Form halten; in Form bleiben; **~ programme/session** Trainingsprogramm, *das*/-stunde, *die*

training: ~ camp *n.* (Mil.) Ausbildungslager, *das;* (Boxing) Trainingslager, *das;* **~ college** *n.* berufsbildende Schule; (Brit. Hist.) Lehrerseminar, *das;* **~ course** *n.* Lehrgang, *der;* **~ film** *n.* Lehrfilm, *der;* **~ ground** *n.* (Mil.) Übungsplatz, *der;* (fig.) Schule, *die;* **~ manual** *n.* Lehrbuch, *das;* **~ scheme** *n.* Ausbildungsprogramm, *das;* **be on a ~ scheme** an einem Ausbildungsprogramm teilnehmen; **~ ship** *n.* (Naut.) Schulschiff, *das;* **~ shoes** *n. pl.* Trainingsschuhe

train: ~ journey *n.* Bahnfahrt, *die;* (long) Bahnreise, *die;* **~load** *n.* **~loads of coal/livestock/tourists** *etc.* ganze Züge voll Kohle/Vieh/Touristen *usw.*; **football fans arrived in** *or* **by ~loads** ganze Züge voll Fußballfans kamen; **~ service** *n.* Zugverbindung, *die;* [Eisen]bahnverbindung, *die;* (whole system) Eisenbahnsystem, *das;* **a better ~ service** bessere Zugverbindungen *Pl.*; **~ set** *n.* [Modell]eisenbahn, *die;* **~sick** *adj.* **a ~sick child/man** ein Kind/Mann, dem vom Zugfahren schlecht geworden ist; **he gets ~sick** ihm wird beim Zugfahren schlecht; **~spotter** *n.*: *jmd., der als Hobby die Nummern von Lokomotiven aufschreibt;* **~spotting** *n., no pl., no indef. art.*: *das Aufschreiben von Lokomotivnummern als Hobby;* **~ station** *n.* (esp. Amer.) Bahnhof, *der;* **~ surfing** *n., no pl.* S-Bahn-Surfen, *das*

traipse /treɪps/ *v.i.* (coll.) latschen (salopp)

Phrasal verb

• **~ about, ~ around** *v.i.* rumlatschen (salopp)

trait /treɪ/ *n.* Eigenschaft, *die;* **~ of character** Charaktereigenschaft, *die;* **a marked ~ in her character** eine ausgeprägte Charaktereigenschaft bei ihr; **it is a national ~ [of the British]** es gehört zum [britischen] Nationalcharakter

traitor /ˈtreɪtə(r)/ *n.* Verräter, *der*/Verräterin, *die;* **be a ~ to one's country/the king/the cause/one's faith** ein Verräter seines Landes/des Königs/der Sache/seines Glaubens sein; **you are a ~ to yourself!** du hast deine eigenen Überzeugungen verraten!; **turn ~:** zum Verräter/zur Verräterin werden

traitorous /ˈtreɪtərəs/ *adj.* verräterisch; **a ~ man/woman** ein Verräter/eine Verräterin; **such conduct is ~!** solches Verhalten ist Verrat!

trajectory /trəˈdʒektərɪ/ *n.* (Phys.) [Flug-] bahn, *die*

tra-la /trəˈlɑː/ *int.* tralla[la]

tram /træm/ *n.* **1** (Brit.) Straßenbahn, *die;* **go by ~:** mit der Straßenbahn fahren; **on the ~:** in der Straßenbahn **2** (Mining) Hund, *der;* Förderwagen, *der*

tram: ~car *n.* **1** ▸**tram 1**; **2** (one car) Straßenbahnwagen, *der;* **~lines** *n. pl.* (Brit.) **1** Straßenbahnschienen; **2** (fig.: rigid principles) starre Vorschriften; **3** (Tennis coll.) Korridor, *der*

trammel /ˈtræml/

A *v.t.*, (Brit.) **-ll-** einengen

B *n. in pl.* Fesseln; **the ~s of convention** die Fesseln der Konvention

tramp /træmp/

A *n.* **1** (vagrant) Landstreicher, *der*/-streicherin, *die;* (in city) Stadtstreicher, *der*/-streicherin, *die* **2** (sound of steps) Schritte; (of horses) Getrappel, *das;* (of elephants) Trampeln, *das;* **the ~ of marching feet** Marschschritte **3** (walk) [Fuß]marsch, *der* **4** (esp. Amer. coll.: dissolute woman) Flittchen, *das* (ugs. abwertend); Nutte, *die* (derb abwertend) **5** (Naut.) Tramp, *der;* Trampschiff, *das*

B *v.i.* **1** (tread heavily) trampeln **2** (walk) marschieren

C *v.t.* **1** **~ one's way** trotten **2** (traverse) durchwandern; (with no particular destination) durchstreifen **3** (tread on) herumtrampeln auf (+ *Dat.*); **~ the earth** die Erde festtreten

Phrasal verb

• **~ 'down** *v.t.* niedertrampeln (ugs.); **~ sth. down [until it is flat]** etw. festtreten

trample /ˈtræmpl/

A *v.t.* zertrampeln; **~ sth. to the ground** etw. zu Boden trampeln; **~ sth. into the ground** etw. in den Boden treten; **he was ~d to death by elephants** er wurde von Elefanten zu Tode getrampelt

B *v.i.* trampeln

Phrasal verbs

• **~ 'down** *v.t.* niedertrampeln

• **~ on** *v.t.* herumtrampeln auf (+ *Dat.*); **~ on sb./sth./sb.'s feelings** (fig.) jmdn./etw./jmds. Gefühle mit Füßen treten

trampoline /ˈtræmpəliːn/

A *n.* Trampolin, *das*

B *v.i.* Trampolin springen

'tramp steamer *n.* Trampschiff, *das*

tram: ~ ride *n.* (Brit.) Straßenbahnfahrt, *die;* **~road** *n.* (Amer.) ▸**tramlines 1**; **~ route** *n.* (Brit.) Straßenbahnlinie, *die;* **~ stop** *n.* Straßenbahnhaltestelle, *die;* **~ ticket** *n.* (Brit.) Straßenbahnfahrschein, *der od.* -fahrkarte, *die;* **~way** *n.* (Brit.) ▸**tramlines 1**

trance /trɑːns/ *n.* **1** Trance, *die;* (half-conscious state, hypnotic state, ecstasy, etc.) tranceartiger Zustand; **be** *or* **lie in a ~:** in Trance/in einem tranceartigen Zustand sein; **fall** *or* **go into a ~:** in Trance/in einen tranceartigen Zustand fallen; **put** *or* **send sb. into a ~:** jmdn. in Trance/in einen tranceartigen Zustand versetzen; **she's been walking about in a ~ all day** sie ist den ganzen Tag wie in Trance herumgelaufen **2** (Med.: catalepsy) Katalepsie, *die* **3** **~ [music]** Trance, *die;* Trancemusik, *die*

tranche /trɑːnʃ/ *n.* (Finance) Tranche, *die*

tranny /ˈtrænɪ/ *n.* (Brit. coll.) Transistor, *der* (ugs.)

tranquil /ˈtræŋkwɪl/ *adj.* ruhig; friedlich ‹*Stimmung, Szene*›

tranquilize, tranquilizer (Amer.) ▸**tranquillize, tranquillizer**

tranquillise, tranquilliser ▸**tranquillize, tranquillizer**

tranquillity /træŋˈkwɪlɪtɪ/ *n.* Ruhe, *die;* (of a scene) Friedlichkeit, *die;* **live in peace and ~:** in Ruhe und Frieden leben

tranquillize /ˈtræŋkwɪlaɪz/ *v.t.* beruhigen; **the unruly prisoner was quickly ~d** der aufsässige Gefangene wurde schnell ruhig gestellt

tranquillizer /ˈtræŋkwɪlaɪzə(r)/ *n.* (Med.) Tranquilizer, *der;* Beruhigungsmittel, *das;* **~ gun** Betäubungsgewehr, *das*

tranquilly /ˈtræŋkwɪlɪ/ *adv.* ruhig; friedlich ‹*leben*›

transact /trænˈsækt/ *v.t.* **~ business [with sb.]** [mit jmdm.] Geschäfte tätigen (Kaufmannsspr., Papierdt.); **the two countries have ~ed business for a long time** die beiden Länder unterhalten seit langem Handelsbeziehungen; **our company ~s business with many foreign firms** unsere Gesellschaft unterhält Geschäftsbeziehungen mit vielen ausländischen Firmen

transaction /trænˈsækʃn/ *n.* **1** (doing of business) **after the ~ of their business** nachdem sie das Geschäftliche erledigt hatten; **most banks close for the ~ of business at 3 p.m.** die meisten Banken schließen für den Publikumsverkehr um 15 Uhr **2** (piece of business) Geschäft, *das;* (financial) Transaktion, *die* **3** *in pl.* (reports of a society) Sitzungsberichte *Pl.*

transalpine /trænsˈælpaɪn/ transalpin

transatlantic /trænsətˈlæntɪk/ *adj.* **1** (Brit.: American) transatlantisch; amerikanisch **2** (Amer.: European) transatlantisch; europäisch **3** (crossing the Atlantic) transatlantisch; **a ~ voyage** eine Reise über den Atlantik; **he is a regular ~ traveller** er reist regelmäßig über den Atlantik; **~ communications** Verbindungen über den Atlantik

transceiver /trænˈsiːvə(r)/ *n.* (Radio) Sende- und Empfangsgerät, *das*

transcend /trænˈsend/ *v.t.* **1** (be beyond range of) übersteigen; hinausgehen über ‹*Grenzen*›; (Philos.) transzendieren **2** (surpass) übertreffen; **~ sb. in beauty** jmdn. an Schönheit übertreffen

transcendence /trænˈsendəns/, **transcendency** /trænˈsendənsɪ/ *n., no pl.* (Philos., Theol.) Transzendenz, *die*

transcendent /trænˈsendənt/ *adj.* (Philos., Theol.) transzendent

transcendental /trænsenˈdentl/ *adj.* **1** (Philos.) transzendental **2** (Math.) transzendent

transcendentalism /trænsenˈdentəlɪzm/ *n.* (Philos.) Transzendentalismus, *der*

Transcendental Mediˈtation (*Amer.:* ®) *n.* Transzendentale Meditation

transcontinental /trænskɒntɪˈnentl/ *adj.* transkontinental

transcribe /trænˈskraɪb/ *v.t.* **1** (copy in writing) abschreiben; aufschreiben ‹*mündliche Überlieferung*›; mitschreiben ‹*Rede*›; protokollieren ‹*Sitzung, Verhandlung usw.*›; **~ a tape/a taped interview** von einem Tonband/von der Tonbandaufzeichnung eines Interviews eine Niederschrift anfertigen; **~ one's rough notes** aus seinen kurzen Notizen eine Reinschrift herstellen **2** (record) aufzeichnen; **~ a CD on to tape/a tape on to a CD** ein CD auf Tonband überspielen/von einem Tonband eine

CD-Aufnahme machen **3** (Mus.) transkribieren **4** (transliterate) transkribieren; umschreiben; ~ **some shorthand/sth. from a shorthand version** ein Stenogramm/etw. in Langschrift übertragen

transcript /ˈtrænskrɪpt/ *n.* Abschrift, *die;* (of trial, interview, speech, conference) Protokoll, *das;* (of tape, taped material) Niederschrift, *die*

transcription /trænˈskrɪpʃn/ *n.* **1** (transcribing) Abschrift, *die;* (of proceedings, speeches) Protokollieren, *das;* (of rough notes) Reinschrift, *die;* (of spoken text, tapes, etc.) Niederschrift, *die;* (of CD on to tape) Überspielung, *die;* (of tape on to a CD) Übertragung, *die;* (Mus.) Transkription, *die;* (from shorthand) Übertragung [in Langschrift]; (transliteration) Transkription, *die;* Umschrift, *die* **2** (transcribed material) Abschrift, *die;* (of proceedings, speech) Protokoll, *das;* (of rough notes) Reinschrift, *die;* (of text, tape, etc.) Niederschrift, *die;* (of CD, record) [Tonband]aufnahme, *die;* (Mus.) Transkription, *die;* (from shorthand) Langschriftfassung, *die;* (transliteration) Transkription, *die;* Umschrift, *die*

transducer /trænsˈdjuːsə(r)/ *n.* (Electr.) Wandler, *der*

transept /ˈtrænsept/ *n.* (Eccl. Archit.) Querschiff, *das;* **north/south** ~: nördlicher/südlicher Kreuzarm

transfer

A /trænsˈfɜː(r)/ *v.t.*, **-rr- 1** (move) verlegen (**to** nach); überweisen ‹*Geld*› (**to** auf + *Akk.*); transferieren ‹*große Geldsumme*›; übertragen ‹*Befugnis, Macht*› (**to** *Dat.*); ~ **a prisoner to a different gaol** einen Gefangenen in ein anderes Gefängnis verlegen *od.* überführen; ~ **one's affections to someone new** seine Gunst jemand anderem schenken; ~ **one's allegiance [from sb.] to sb.** [von jmdm.] zu jmdm. überwechseln **2** übereignen ‹*Gegenstand, Grundbesitz*› (**to** *Dat.*); ~ **sth. into new ownership** etw. einem neuen Besitzer *od.* jemand anderem übereignen **3** versetzen ‹*Arbeiter, Angestellte, Schüler*›; (Footb.) transferieren **4** übertragen ‹*Bedeutung, Sinn*› **5** (copy) umdrucken ‹*Zeichnung*›

B *v.i.*, **-rr- 1** (change to continue journey) umsteigen; ~ **from Heathrow to Gatwick** zum Weiterflug *od.* Umsteigen von Heathrow nach Gatwick fahren; **we had to ~ to a special bus** wir mussten in einen Sonderbus umsteigen **2** (move to another place or group) wechseln; ‹*Firma:*› übersiedeln

C /ˈtrænsfɜː(r)/ *n.* **1** (moving) Verlegung, *die;* (of powers) Übertragung, *die* (**to** an + *Akk.*); (of money) Überweisung, *die;* (of large sums) Transfer, *der* (Wirtsch.) **2** (of employee, pupil) Versetzung, *die;* (of football player) Transfer, *der;* Wechsel, *der* **3** (Amer.: ticket) Umsteigefahrkarte, *die* **4** (picture) Abziehbild, *das* **5** (conveyance of property) Übertragung, *die;* Übereignung, *die*

transferability /trænsfɜːrəˈbɪlɪtɪ/ *n., no pl.* Übertragbarkeit, *die*

transferable /trænsˈfɜːrəbl, ˈtrænsfərəbl/ *adj.* übertragbar; frei transferierbar ‹*Devisenkonto*›

transferable ˈvote *n.* übertragbare [Wähler]stimme

transfer: ~ **company** *n.* (Amer.) Transportunternehmen, *das;* ~ **desk** *n.* Transitschalter, *der*

transference /ˈtrænsfərəns/ *n.* Übertragung, *die*

ˈtransfer: ~ **fee** *n.* (Footb.) Ablösesumme, *die;* Transfersumme, *die* (fachspr.); ~ **list** *n.* (Footb.) Transferliste, *die;* ~ **lounge** *n.* Transitlounge, *die;* ~ **passenger** *n.* Transitreisende, *der/die*

transferral /trænsˈfɜːrl/ *n.* Übertragung, *die*

ˈtransfer season *n.* (Footb.) Transfersaison, *die*

transfiguration /trænsfɪgəˈreɪʃn/ *n.* Transfiguration, *die* (fachspr.); Verklärung Christi, *die;* **the T~** (Relig.) das Fest der Verklärung

transfigure /trænsˈfɪgə(r)/ *v.t.* verklären

transfix /trænsˈfɪks/ *v.t.* **1** (pierce through) durchbohren **2** (root to the spot) erstarren lassen, lähmen ‹*Person*›; **be/stand ~ed** wie gelähmt *od.* angewurzelt sein/dastehen

transform

A /trænsˈfɔːm/ *v.t.* **1** verwandeln; ~ **heat into energy** Wärme in Energie umwandeln; **the caterpillar is ~ed into a butterfly** die Raupe verwandelt sich zu einem Schmetterling; **I felt ~ed** ich fühlte mich wie umgewandelt; **a new coat of paint would ~ the room** ein neuer Anstrich, und man würde das Zimmer nicht wiedererkennen **2** (Electr.) (in potential) transformieren; umspannen; (in type) umformen

B /ˈtrænsfɔːm/ *n.* (Math., Ling.) Transformation, *die*

transformation /trænsfəˈmeɪʃn/ *n.* **1** Verwandlung, *die* **2** (Math., Ling.) Transformation, *die* **3** (Phys.) Elementumwandlung, *die;* Transmutation, *die;* (of heat into energy) Umwandlung, *die*

transformational /trænsfəˈmeɪʃənl/ *adj.* (esp. Ling.) Transformations-

transformational ˈgrammar *n.* (Ling.) Transformationsgrammatik, *die*

transforˈmation scene *n.* (Theatre) Verwandlungsszene, *die*

transformer /trænsˈfɔːmə(r)/ *n.* (Electr.) Transformator, *der*

transfuse /trænsˈfjuːz/ *v.t.* **1** (Med.) transfundieren (fachspr.); übertragen **2** (permeate, lit. or fig.) erfüllen; durchdringen

transfusion /trænsˈfjuːʒn/ *n.* (Med.) Transfusion, *die;* Übertragung, *die; see also* **blood transfusion**

transgenic /trænsˈdʒenɪk/ *adj.* (Biol.) transgen

transglobal /trænsˈgləʊbl/ *adj.* weltweit; global; weltumspannend ‹*Netzwerk*›; ~ **enterprise** Weltunternehmen, *das;* ~ **expedition** Expedition um die ganze Welt

transgress /trænsˈgres/ *v.t.* übertreten; *abs.* **he was ~ing** er hat sich einer Übertretung (*Gen.*) schuldig gemacht (geh.)

transgression /trænsˈgreʃn/ *n.* Übertretung, *die*

transgressor /trænsˈgresə(r)/ *n.* Übertreter, *der*/Übertreterin, *die* (**of** *Gen.*); (sinner) Sünder, *der*/Sünderin, *die* (**of** gegen)

tranship ▸ **trans-ship**

transience /ˈtrænzɪəns/, **transiency** /ˈtrænzɪənsɪ/ *n.* Vergänglichkeit, *die*

transient /ˈtrænzɪənt/

A *adj.* **1** kurzlebig; vergänglich **2** (Mus.) durchgehend

B *n.* Durchreisende, *der/die*

transistor /trænˈsɪstə(r)/ *n.* (Electronics) Transistor, *der;* ~ **[radio]** Transistor, *der;* Transistorradio, *das*

transistorize /trænˈsɪstəraɪz/ *v.t.* (Electronics) transistorisieren

transit /ˈtrænsɪt/ *n.* **1** Transit, *der;* **passengers in ~:** Transitreisende; Durchreisende; **be in ~:** auf der Durchreise sein **2** (conveyance) Transport, *der;* **goods in ~ from London to Hull** Waren auf dem Transport von London nach Hull **3** (Astron.) Durchgang, *der*

ˈtransit camp *n.* Durchgangslager, *das*

transition /trænˈsɪʒn, trænˈzɪʃn/ *n.* **1** Übergang, *der;* (sudden change) Wechsel, *der;* **age/period of ~:** Übergangszeit, *die* **2** (Mus.) Ausweichung, *die* **3** (Art) Übergang, *der*

transitional /trænˈsɪʒənl, trænˈzɪʃənl/ *adj.* Übergangs-; **be ~ between a and b** den Übergang von a zu b bilden

tranˈsition: ~ **element** *n.* (Chem.) Übergangselement, *das;* ~ **period** *n.* Übergangszeit, *die;* Übergangsphase, *die;* ~ **point** *n.* (Phys.) Umwandlungspunkt, *der*

transitive /ˈtrænsɪtɪv/ *adj.*, **transitively** /ˈtrænsɪtɪvlɪ/ *adv.* (Ling.) transitiv

ˈtransit lounge *n.* Transithalle, *die;* Transitlounge, *die*

transitoriness /ˈtrænsɪtərɪnɪs/ *n., no pl.* Vergänglichkeit, *die;* (fleetingness) Flüchtigkeit, *die*

transitory /ˈtrænsɪtərɪ/ *adj.* vergänglich; (fleeting) flüchtig

transit: ~ **passenger** *n.* Transitpassagier, *der;* ~ **visa** *n.* Transitvisum, *das;* Durchreisevisum, *das*

translatable /trænsˈleɪtəbl/ *adj.* übersetzbar; **some words are not ~ into other languages** manche Wörter lassen sich nicht in andere Sprachen übersetzen

translate /trænsˈleɪt/

A *v.t.* **1** übersetzen; ~ **a novel from English into German** einen Roman aus dem Englischen ins Deutsche übersetzen; ~ **'Abgeordneter' as 'Deputy'** „Abgeordneter" mit „Deputy" übersetzen **2** (convert) ~ **a vision into reality/words into action[s]** eine Vision Wirklichkeit werden lassen/Worte in die Tat/in Taten umsetzen **3** (Relig.) überführen ‹*Reliquien*› **4** (Eccl.) versetzen ‹*Bischof*›

B *v.i.* sich übersetzen lassen

translation /trænsˈleɪʃn/ *n.* **1** ▸ⓘ **p. 1277** Übersetzung, *die;* **error in ~:** Übersetzungsfehler, *der;* **his works are available in ~:** seine Werke liegen in Übersetzung *od.* übersetzt vor; **read sth. in ~:** etw. in der Übersetzung lesen **2** (conversion) Umsetzung, *die* **3** (Eccl.) Translation, *die* (fachspr.); Versetzung, *die*

transˈlation table *n.* (Computing) Übersetzungstabelle, *die*

translator /trænsˈleɪtə(r)/ *n.* ▸ⓘ **p. 1260** Übersetzer, *der*/Übersetzerin, *die*

transliterate /trænsˈlɪtəreɪt/ *v.t.* transliterieren (**into** in + *Akk.*)

transliteration /trænslɪtəˈreɪʃn/ *n.* Transliteration, *die* (**into** in + *Akk.*)

translucency /trænsˈluːsənsɪ/ *n., no pl.* ▸**translucent**: Eigenschaft, durchscheinend zu sein; Durchsichtigkeit, *die*

translucent /trænsˈluːsənt/ *adj.* **1** (partly transparent) durchscheinend **2** (transparent) durchsichtig

transmigrate /trænsmaɪˈgreɪt/ *v.i.* **1** (pass into different body) übergehen **2** (migrate) ziehen

transmigration /trænsmaɪˈgreɪʃn/ *n.* ~ **[of souls]** Seelenwanderung, *die;* **the ~ of the soul into another body** der Übergang der Seele in einen anderen Körper

transmission /trænsˈmɪʃn/ *n.* **1** (passing on) ▸**transmit 1**: Übersendung, *die;* Übertragung, *die;* Überlieferung, *die;* [Weiter]vererbung, *die* **2** (Radio, Telev.) Ausstrahlung, *die;* (via satellite also; by wire) Übertragung, *die* **3** (Motor Veh.) (drive) Antrieb, *der;* (gearbox) Getriebe, *das;* **manual/automatic ~:** Schalt-/Automatikgetriebe, *das*

transˈmission speed *n.* Übertragungsgeschwindigkeit, *die*

transmit /trænsˈmɪt/ *v.t.*, **-tt- 1** (pass on) übersenden ‹*Nachricht*›; übertragen ‹*Recht, Krankheit*›; überliefern ‹*Wissen, Kenntnisse*›; (genetically) [weiter]vererben ‹*Eigenschaft*› **2** durchlassen ‹*Licht*›; übertragen ‹*Druck, Schall*›; leiten ‹*Wärme, Elektrizität*› **3** (Radio, Telev.) ausstrahlen; (via satellite also; by wire) übertragen

transmittal /trænsˈmɪtl/ ▸**transmission 1**

transmitter /trænsˈmɪtə(r)/ *n.* Sender, *der*

transmogrification /trænsmɒgrɪfɪˈkeɪʃn/ *n.* (joc.) [wundersame] Verwandlung

transmogrify /trænsˈmɒgrɪfaɪ/ *v.t.* (joc.) auf wundersame Weise verwandeln (**into** in + *Akk.*)

transmutation /trænsmjuːˈteɪʃn/ *n.* **1** Umwandlung, *die* (**into** in + *Akk.*) **2** (Phys.) Transmutation, *die;* Elementumwandlung, *die* **3** (Biol.) Umbildung, *die*

transmute /trænsˈmjuːt/ *v.t.* umwandeln

transnational /trænsˈnæʃənl/ *adj.* übernational

transoceanic /trænsəʊʃɪˈænɪk, trænsəʊsɪˈænɪk/ *adj.* transozeanisch; überseeisch

transom /ˈtrænsəm/ *n.* (Archit.) Quersprosse, *die*

transom ˈwindow *n.* Oberlicht, *das*

transparency /trænsˈpærənsɪ/ *n.* **1** Durchsichtigkeit, *die;* (fig. also) Durchschaubarkeit, *die* **2** (Photog.) Transparent, *das;* (slide) Dia, *das* **3** (Polit., Commerc.) Transparenz, *die;* **fiscal ~:** Finanztransparenz, *die;* ~ **in decision-making** Transparenz der Beschlussfassung

transparent /trænsˈpærənt/ *adj.* durchsichtig; (fig.) (obvious) offenkundig; (easily understood) klar

t

transparently /træns'pærəntlɪ/ *adv.* offenkundig; **~ lucid** klar und einleuchtend ‹*Darstellung*›; **~ obvious** ganz offenkundig

transpiration /trænspɪ'reɪʃn/ *n.* (Bot.) Transpiration, *die*

transpire /træn'spaɪə(r)/ *v.i.* **1** (happen) passieren **2** (come to be known) sich herausstellen; **she had not, it ~d, seen the letter** sie hatte, so stellte sich heraus, den Brief nicht gesehen **3** (Bot.) transpirieren

transplant

A /træns'plɑːnt/ *v.t.* **1** (Med.) transplantieren (fachspr.), verpflanzen ‹*Organ, Gewebe*› **2** (plant in another place) umpflanzen **3** (fig.: move to another place) umsiedeln; verlegen ‹*Institution*›

B /'trænsplɑːnt/ *n.* **1** (Med.) (operation) Transplantation, *die* (fachspr.); Verpflanzung, *die;* (thing transplanted) Transplantat, *das* (fachspr.) **2** (Hort.) umgesetzte Pflanze

transplantation /trænsplɑːn'teɪʃn/ *n.* (Med.) Transplantation, *die* (fachspr.); Verpflanzung, *die*

transponder /træns'pɒndə(r)/ *n.* (Electronics) Transponder, *der*

transport

A /træn'spɔːt/ *v.t.* **1** (convey) transportieren; befördern **2** (affect with emotion) anrühren, anwandeln (geh.); **~ed with joy** von Freude überkommen **3** (Hist.) deportieren ‹*Sträfling*›

B /'trænspɔːt/ *n.* **1** (conveyance) Transport, *der;* Beförderung, *die; attrib.* Transport-; Beförderungs- **2** (means of conveyance) Verkehrsmittel, *das;* (for people also) Fortbewegungsmittel, *das;* **~ was provided** für die Beförderung wurde gesorgt; **be without ~:** kein [eigenes] Fahrzeug haben; **his only ~ is a battered car** er hat nur ein verbeultes Auto; **Ministry of T~:** Verkehrsministerium, *das;* **the ~ has arrived** der Wagen ist da **3** (vehement emotion) Ausbruch, *der;* **be in/send sb. into ~s of joy** außer sich vor Freude sein/jmdn. in helles Entzücken versetzen **4** (Mil.) [Truppen]transporter, *der*

transportable /træn'spɔːtəbl/ *adj.* transportabel

transportation /trænspə'teɪʃn/ *n.* **1** (conveying) Transport, *der;* Beförderung, *die;* **~ by air/sea/road/rail** Luft-/See-/Straßen-/Bahntransport, *der* **2** (Amer.) ▸**transport B 2** **3** (Hist.: of convict) Deportation, *die*

'transport café *n.* (Brit.) Fernfahrerlokal, *das*

transporter /træn'spɔːtə(r)/ *n.* (vehicle) Transporter, *der*

trans'porter bridge *n.* Schwebefähre, *die* (Technik)

transpose /træns'pəʊz/ *v.t.* **1** (cause to change places) vertauschen **2** (change order of) umstellen **3** (Mus.) transponieren

transposition /trænspə'zɪʃn/ *n.* ▸**transpose**: Vertauschung, *die;* Umstellung, *die;* (Mus.) Transposition, *die*

transsexual /træns'seksjʊəl, træns'sekʃʊəl/

A *adj.* transsexuell

B *n.* Transsexuelle, *der/die*

trans-ship /træns'ʃɪp/ *v.t.*, **-pp-** umladen

trans-shipment /træns'ʃɪpmənt/ *n.* Umschlag, *der*

transubstantiate /trænsəb'stænʃɪeɪt/ *v.t.* (Theol.) [ver]wandeln

transubstantiation /trænsəbstænʃɪ'eɪʃn/ *n.* (Theol.) Transubstantiation, *die;* Wandlung, *die*

transuranic /trænsjʊ'rænɪk/ *adj.* (Chem.) transuranisch

transverse /'trænsvɜːs/ *adj.* quer liegend; Quer‹*balken, -lage, -streifen, -verstrebung*›; **~ flute** Querflöte, *die;* **~ wave** (Phys.) Transversalwelle, *die;* **~ section** Querschnitt, *der*

transversely /'trænsvɜːslɪ/ *adv.* quer

transvestism /træns'vestɪzm/ *n.* (Psych.) Transvestismus, *der*

transvestist /træns'vestɪst/, **transvestite** /træns'vestaɪt/ *n.* (Psych.) Transvestit, *der*

Transylvania /trænsɪl'veɪnɪə/ *pr. n.* Transsilvanien (*das*) (veralt.); Siebenbürgen (*das*)

trap /træp/

A *n.* **1** (lit. or fig.) Falle, *die;* **set a ~ for an animal** eine Falle für ein Tier legen *od.* [auf]stellen; **set a ~ for sb.** (fig.) jmdm. eine Falle stellen; **fall into a/sb.'s ~** (fig.) in die/jmdm. in die Falle gehen **2** (sl.: mouth) Klappe, *die* (salopp); Fresse, *die* (derb); **shut your ~!, keep your ~ shut!** halt die Klappe (salopp) *od.* (derb) Fresse! **3** ▸**speed trap** **4** (for releasing bird) Kasten, *der;* (for throwing ball etc. into the air) Wurfmaschine, *die* **5** (section of pipe) Geruchsverschluss, *der;* Siphon, *der* **6** (carriage) (*leichter zweirädriger*) Einspänner **7** (Golf) Bunker, *der* **8** (Greyhound Racing) Box, *die* **9** ▸**trapdoor** **10** *in pl.* (coll.: percussion instruments) Schießbude, *die* (ugs.)

B *v.t.*, **-pp-:** **1** (catch) [in *od.* mit einer Falle] fangen ‹*Tier*›; (fig.) in eine Falle locken ‹*Person*›; **be ~ped** (fig.) in eine Falle gehen/in der Falle sitzen; **be ~ped in a cave/by the tide/in the snow** in einer Höhle festsitzen/von der Flut abgeschnitten sein/im Schnee stecken geblieben sein; **she ~ped him into contradicting himself** sie brachte ihn durch eine List dazu, sich zu widersprechen **2** (confine) einschließen; (immobilize) einklemmen ‹*Person, Körperteil*›; **~ one's finger/foot** sich (*Dat.*) den Finger/Fuß einklemmen **3** (entangle) verstricken **4** stoppen ‹*Ball*›

'trapdoor *n.* Falltür, *die*

trapeze /trə'piːz/ *n.* Trapez, *das*

tra'peze artist *n.* Trapezkünstler, *der*/-künstlerin, *die*

trapezium /trə'piːzɪəm/ *n.*, *pl.* **trapezia** /trə'piːzɪə/ *or* **~s** (Geom.) **1** (Brit.) Trapez, *das* **2** (Amer.) Trapezoid, *das*

trapezoid /'træpɪzɔɪd/ *n.* (Geom.) **1** (Brit.) Trapezoid, *das* **2** (Amer.) Trapez, *das*

trapper /'træpə(r)/ *n.* Fallensteller, *der;* (in North America) Trapper, *der*

trappings /'træpɪŋz/ *n. pl.* **1** [äußere] Zeichen; (of power, high office) Insignien **2** (ornamental harness) ≈ Schabracke, *die*

Trappist /'træpɪst/ *n.* Trappist, *der; attrib.* Trappisten-

trash /træʃ/

A *n.*, *no pl.*, *no indef. art.* **1** (esp. Amer.: rubbish) Abfall, *der;* (refuse) Müll, *der* **2** (badly made thing) Mist, *der* (ugs. abwertend); (bad literature) Schund, *der* (ugs. abwertend); **be [just] ~:** nichts taugen **3** (nonsensical talk) Mist, *der* (ugs. abwertend); **what ~ he talks!** was der für 'n Mist redet! **4** (worthless person) Ratte, *die* (derb); (worthless persons) Gesindel, *das* (abwertend); Pack, *das* (abwertend); **white ~** (Amer. derog.) weißes Gesindel *od.* Pack (abwertend)

B *v.t.* (esp. Amer.) (destroy) kaputtmachen (ugs.); auseinander nehmen (ugs.) ‹*Wohnung*›; (fig. coll.: criticize) verreißen (ugs.)

'trashcan *n.* (Amer.) Mülltonne, *die*

trashy /'træʃɪ/ *adj.* minderwertig; Schund‹*literatur, -roman*›

trattoria /trætə'riːə/ *n.* Trattoria, *die*

trauma /'trɔːmə/ *n.*, *pl.* **~ta** /'trɔːmətə/ *or* **~s** Trauma, *das* (fachspr.); (injury also) Verletzung, *die;* (shock also) Schock, *der*

traumatic /trɔː'mætɪk/ *adj.* **1** (Med.) traumatisch **2** (coll.: devastating) furchtbar

traumatize /'trɔːmətaɪz/ *v.t.* traumatisieren

travel /'trævl/

A *n.* **1** Reisen, *das; attrib.* Reise-; **be off on one's ~s** verreist sein; **if you see him on your ~s, ...** (joc.) wenn er dir über den Weg läuft, ... **2** (range of motion) Weg, *der;* **there's a lot of ~ on the handbrake** der Handbremshebel hat einen sehr langen Weg

B *v.i.*, (Brit.) **-ll-;** **1** (make a journey) reisen; (go in vehicle) fahren; **~ a lot** viel reisen **2** (coll.: withstand long journey) **~ [well]** ‹*Ware:*› lange Transporte vertragen; **~ badly** ‹*Ware:*› lange Transporte nicht vertragen **3** (work as **~ling** sales representative) reisen; Vertreter/Vertreterin sein; **~ in stationery** in Schreibwaren reisen (Kaufmannsspr.) **4** (move) sich bewegen; ‹*Blick, Schmerz:*› wandern; ‹*Tier:*› sich fortbewegen; ‹*Licht, Schall:*› sich ausbreiten **5** (coll.: move quickly) kacheln (ugs.); **that car can really ~:** das Auto zieht ganz schön ab (ugs.); **we were really ~ling** wir hatten einen ganz schönen Zahn drauf (ugs.)

C *v.t.*, (Brit.) **-ll-** zurücklegen ‹*Strecke, Entfernung*›; bereisen ‹*Bezirk*›; benutzen, passieren ‹*Weg, Straße*›; **we had ~led 10 miles** wir waren 10 Meilen gefahren

Phrasal verb

• **~ a'bout, ~ a'round**

A *v.i.* umherreisen

B *v.t.* **~ around the country** durchs Land reisen *od.* fahren

travel: ~ agency *n.* Reisebüro, *das;* **~ agent** *n.* ▸**❶ p. 1260** Reisebürokaufmann, *der*/-kauffrau, *die;* **the ~ agent made a mistake** das Reisebüro hat einen Fehler gemacht

travelator /'trævəleɪtə(r)/ *n.* Fahr- *od.* Rollsteig, *der*

travel: ~ brochure *n.* Reiseprospekt, *der;* **~ bureau** *n.* Reisebüro, *das;* **~ card** *n.* Zeitkarte, *die;* **one-day ~ card/annual ~ card** Tageskarte, *die*/Jahreskarte, *die;* **a three-week rail ~ card** eine Dreiwochenkarte für die Bahn; **~ documents** *pl. n.* Reisedokumente *Pl.*

traveled, traveler, traveling (Amer.) ▸**travell-**

'travel insurance *n.* Reiseversicherung, *die*

travelled /'trævld/ *adj.* (Brit.) **be much ~** ‹*Person:*› weit gereist sein; **be well ~** ‹*Weg, Straße:*› viel befahren sein

traveller /'trævlə(r)/ *n.* (Brit.) **1** Reisende, *der/die;* **be a poor ~:** das Reisen nicht [gut] vertragen **2** (sales representative) Vertreter, *der*/Vertreterin, *die* **3** *in pl.* (gypsies etc.) fahrendes Volk

traveller: ~'s cheque *n.* ▸**❶ p. 1332** Reisescheck, *der;* **~'s tale** *n.* fantastischer Reisebericht; **they're just ~'s tales** das sind nur Fantastereien (abwertend)

travelling /'trævlɪŋ/ *adj.* (Brit.) Wander‹*zirkus, -ausstellung, -bühne*›

travelling: ~ bag *n.* Reisetasche, *die;* **~ clock** *n.* Reisewecker, *der;* **~ 'crane** *n.* Laufkran, *der;* **~ expenses** *n. pl.* Reisekosten *Pl.;* **~ 'fellowship** *n.* (Univ.) ≈ Auslandsstipendium, *das;* **~ rug** *n.* Reisedecke, *die;* **~ 'salesman** *n.* ▸**❶ p. 1260** Vertreter, *der;* **~ 'wave** *n.* (Phys.) fortschreitende Welle

'travel news *n.*, *no pl.* ≈ Verkehrsnachrichten *Pl.*

travelogue (Amer.: **travelog**) /'trævəlɒg/ *n.* Reisebericht, *der*

travel: ~-sick *adj.* reisekrank; **~-sickness** *n.*, *no pl.* Reisekrankheit, *die;* **~-sickness pill** *n.* Tablette gegen Reisekrankheit; **~ writer** *n.* Reiseautor, *der*/-autorin, *die*

traverse /'trævəs, trə'vɜːs/

A *v.t.* **1** überqueren ‹*Gebirge*›; durchqueren ‹*Gebäude, Gebiet*› **2** ‹*Kanal, Mauer:*› durchziehen ‹*Gebiet*› **3** (Mountaineering) traversieren

B *n.* (Mountaineering) Traversierung, *die*

travesty /'trævɪstɪ/

A *n.* **1** (parody) Karikatur, *die;* **be a ~ [of justice]** ein Hohn [auf die Gerechtigkeit] sein **2** (Lit.: burlesque) Travestie, *die* (fachspr.)

B *v.t.* ins Lächerliche ziehen

Travolator ® /'trævəleɪtə(r)/ ▸**travelator**

trawl /trɔːl/

A *v.i.* mit dem Grundnetz fischen

B *n.* **1** Fischen mit dem Grundnetz **2** **~[-net]** Grund[schlepp]netz, *das;* **~[-line]** (Amer.) Langleine, *die*

trawler /'trɔːlə(r)/ *n.* (vessel) [Fisch]trawler, *der*

trawlerman /'trɔːləmən/ *n.* ▸**❶ p. 1260** ≈ Hochseefischer, *der*

tray /treɪ/ *n.* **1** Tablett, *das;* **baking ~:** Backblech, *das* **2** (for correspondence) Ablagekorb, *der*

'tray cloth *n.* Deckchen für ein Tablett

trayful /'treɪfʊl/ *n.* Tablett voll

treacherous /'tretʃərəs/ *adj.* **1** verräterisch, treulos ‹*Person*›; heimtückisch ‹*Intrige, Feind*› **2** (deceptive) tückisch; **the ice looks pretty ~:** das Eis sieht nicht sehr vertrauenerweckend aus

treacherously /'tretʃərəslɪ/ *adv.* heimtückisch

treachery /'tretʃərɪ/ *n.* Verrat, *der;* **act of ~:** Verrat, *der*

treacle /'tri:kl/ *n.* (Brit.) 1 (golden syrup) Sirup, *der* 2 ▸**molasses**

treacle 'pudding *n. mit Sirup übergossener Mehlpudding*

treacly /'tri:klɪ/ *adj.* sirupartig; (fig.) süßlich (abwertend)

tread /tred/

A *n.* 1 (of tyre, shoe, boot, etc.) Lauffläche, *die;* **2 millimetres of ~ on a tyre** 2 Millimeter Profil auf einem Reifen 2 (manner of walking) Gang, *der;* (sound of walking) Schritt, *der;* **walk with a springy/catlike ~:** einen federnden/katzenhaften Gang haben; **the ~ of feet** Schritte 3 (of staircase) [Tritt]stufe, *die*

B *v.i.*, **trod** /trɒd/, **trodden** /'trɒdn/ *or* **trod** treten (**in/on** in/auf + *Akk.*); (walk) gehen; **~ carefully** *or* **lightly** (fig.) behutsam vorgehen; **~ on sb.'s toes** (lit. or fig.) jmdm. auf die Füße treten; **~ on the heels of sb./sth.** (fig.) jmdm./einer Sache auf den Fersen sein (ugs.); **~ dirt into the carpet/all over the house** Schmutz in den Teppich treten/im ganzen Haus herumtreten; *see also* **foot A 1**

C *v.t.*, **trod, trodden** *or* **trod** 1 (walk on) treten auf (+ *Akk.*); stampfen ‹*Weintrauben*›; (fig.) gehen ‹*Weg*›; **~ the stage** *or* **boards** (Theatre) auf der Bühne *od.* auf den Brettern stehen; **be trodden underfoot** mit Füßen getreten werden; **~ water** (Swimming) Wasser treten 2 (make by walking or treading) austreten ‹*Weg*›

Phrasal verbs

- **~ 'down** *v.t.* festtreten ‹*Erde*›; (crush, destroy) zertreten ‹*Blume, Beet*›
- **~ 'in** *v.t.* festtreten
- **~ 'out** *v.t.* austreten ‹*Feuer, Zigarette*›; stampfen ‹*Weintrauben*›

treadle /'tredl/ *n.* Tritt, *der*

'treadmill *n.* (lit. or fig.) Tretmühle, *die*

treason /'tri:zn/ *n.* 1 **[high] ~:** Hochverrat, *der* 2 (disloyalty) Verrat, *der*

treasonable /'tri:zənəbl/, **treasonous** /'tri:zənəs/ *adjs.* verräterisch; **a ~ offence** Verrat

treasure /'treʒə(r)/

A *n.* 1 Schatz, *der;* Kostbarkeit, *die;* **art ~s** Kunstschätze 2 *no pl., no indef. art.* (riches) Schätze; **buried ~:** ein vergrabener Schatz 3 (coll.: valued person) Schatz, *der* (ugs.)

B *v.t.* in Ehren halten; die Erinnerung bewahren an (+ *Dat.*); **I'll always ~ this moment/the memory of that day** ich werde diesen Augenblick/Tag niemals vergessen

Phrasal verb

- **~ 'up** *v.t.* wie einen Schatz hüten

treasure: ~ house *n.* Schatzkammer, *die;* (fig.) [wahre] Fundgrube; **~ hunt** *n.* Schatzsuche, *die*

treasurer /'treʒərə(r)/ *n.* 1 (of club, society) Kassenwart, *der/-wartin, die;* (of club, party) Schatzmeister, *der/-meisterin, die;* (of company) Leiter/Leiterin der Finanzabteilung 2 (local government official) Leiter/Leiterin der Finanzverwaltung

treasure trove /'treʒə trəʊv/ *n.* Schatz, *der;* (fig.: valuable source) [wahre] Fundgrube

treasury /'treʒərɪ/ *n.* 1 (place where treasure is stored) Schatzkammer, *die* 2 (fig.) Fundgrube, *die;* (as book title) Schatzkästchen, *das* 3 (place where public revenues are kept) Schatzamt, *das* 4 (government department) **the T~:** das Finanzministerium; **the First Lord of the T~** (Brit.) der Premierminister/die Premierministerin (*als nomineller Leiter/nominelle Leiterin des „treasury"*)

treasury: T~ bench *n.* (Brit. Parl.) Regierungsbank, *die;* **~ bill** *n.* (Finance) Schatzwechsel, *der;* **~ tag** *n. kurze Kordel mit Metallstiften an den Enden zum Zusammenhalten von [gelochten] Blättern*

treat /tri:t/

A *n.* 1 [besonderes] Vergnügen; (sth. to eat) [besonderer] Leckerbissen; **what a ~ [it is] to do/not to have to do that!** welch ein Genuss *od.* eine Wohltat, das zu tun/nicht tun zu müssen!; **it was a real ~ to have an entire afternoon at home on my own** es war eine richtige Wohltat, einen ganzen Nachmittag zu Hause für mich allein zu haben; **give sb. a ~:** jmdm. eine besondere Freude machen; **have a ~ in store for sb.** noch eine besondere Freude für jmdn. auf Lager haben; **there was a ~ in store for them** auf sie wartete noch eine besondere Freude; **go down a ~** (coll.) ‹*Essen, Getränk:*› prima schmecken (ugs.); **work a ~** (coll.) ‹*Maschine:*› prima arbeiten (ugs.); ‹*Plan:*› prima funktionieren (ugs.) 2 (entertainment) *Vergnügen, für dessen Kosten jmd. anderes aufkommt;* **lay on a special ~ for sb.** jmdm. etwas Besonderes bieten; **as a Christmas ~ I shall take my sister to the theatre** als Weihnachtsgeschenk lade ich meine Schwester ins Theater ein 3 (act of ~ing) Einladung, *die;* **it's my ~:** ich lade ein; **stand ~ for sb.** jmdn. einladen

B *v.t.* 1 (act towards) behandeln; **~ sth. as a joke** etw. als Witz nehmen; **~ sth. with contempt** für etw. nur Verachtung haben 2 ▸ⓘ **p. 1231** (Med.) behandeln; **~ sb. for sth.** jmdn. wegen etw. behandeln; (before confirmation of diagnosis) jmdn. auf etw. (*Akk.*) behandeln 3 (apply process to) behandeln ‹*Material, Stoff, Metall, Leder*›; klären ‹*Abwässer*› 4 (handle in literature etc.) behandeln; **~ sth. fully** etw. ausführlich behandeln 5 (provide with at own expense) einladen; **~ sb. to sth.** jmdm. etw. spendieren; **~ oneself to a holiday/a new hat** sich (*Dat.*) Urlaub gönnen/sich (*Dat.*) einen neuen Hut leisten

C *v.i.* **~ with sb. [for sth.]** mit jmdm. [über etw. (*Akk.*)] verhandeln

treatable /'tri:təbl/ *adj.* behandelbar ‹*Krankheit*›; **it's ~ with antibiotics** es lässt sich mit Antibiotika behandeln

treatise /'tri:tɪs, 'tri:tɪz/ *n.* Abhandlung, *die*

treatment /'tri:tmənt/ *n.* 1 Behandlung, *die;* **receive rough ~ from sb.** von jmdm. grob behandelt werden; **his ~ of the staff/you** die Art, wie er das Personal/dich behandelt; **her ~ at the hands of her uncle** die Art, wie ihr Onkel sie behandelt/behandelt hat; **give sb. the [full] ~** (coll.) (treat cruelly/harshly) jmdn. in die Mangel nehmen (salopp); (entertain on a lavish scale) jmdn. verwöhnen 2 ▸ⓘ **p. 1231** (Med.) Behandlung, *die;* **be having ~ for sth.** wegen etw. in Behandlung sein; **need immediate medical ~:** sofort ärztlich behandelt werden müssen 3 (processing) Behandlung, *die;* (of sewage) Klärung, *die*

treaty /'tri:tɪ/ *n.* 1 [Staats]vertrag, *der;* **make** *or* **sign a ~:** einen Vertrag schließen; **the ~ of Rome** die Römischen Verträge; **the ~ of Versailles** der Versailler Vertrag 2 ▸**private treaty**

treble /'trebl/

A *adj.* 1 dreifach; **~ row** Dreierreihe, *die;* **~ the amount compared to ...:** dreimal so viel wie ...; **sell sth. for ~ the price** etw. dreimal so teuer verkaufen 2 (Brit. Mus.) **~ voice** Sopranstimme, *die*

B *n.* 1 (Brit. Mus.) **he is a ~/is singing the ~:** er singt Sopran/den Sopran 2 (~ quantity etc.) Dreifache, *das* 3 (Darts) dreifach zählender Treffer 4 (Racing) Dreifachwette, *die*

C *v.t.* verdreifachen; **be ~d** ‹*Wert einer Aktie usw.:*› sich verdreifachen

D *v.i.* sich verdreifachen

treble: ~ 'chance *n.: Art des Fußballtotos mit dreifacher Gewinnchance;* **~ clef** *n.* (Mus.) Violinschlüssel, *der;* **~ re'corder** *n.* (Mus.) Altflöte, *die*

trebly /'treblɪ/ *adv.* dreifach; **be ~ fortunate** in dreifacher Hinsicht Glück haben

tree /tri:/ *n.* Baum, *der;* **not grow on ~s** (fig.) nicht [einfach] vom Himmel fallen; *see also* **Christmas tree**; **family tree**; **shoe tree**; **top[1] A 1**

tree: ~creeper *n.* (Ornith.) Baumläufer, *der;* **~ diagram** *n.* Baumdiagramm, *das;* **~ fern** *n.* (Bot.) Baumfarn, *der;* **~ frog** *n.* Laubfrosch, *der;* **~ house** *n.* Baumhaus, *das;* **~-hugger** /'tri:hʌgə(r)/ *n.* (coll., usu. derog.) Umweltspinner, *der/-spinnerin, die* (ugs.)

treeless /'tri:lɪs/ *adj.* baumlos

tree: ~line ▸**timberline**; **~-lined** *adj.* von Bäumen gesäumt; **~ ring** *n.* (Bot.) Jahresring, *der;* **~-shaded** *adj.* von Bäumen beschattet (geh.); **~ stump** *n.* Baumstumpf, *der;* **~ surgeon** *n.* ▸ⓘ **p. 1260** Baumchirurg, *der;* **~ surgery** *n., no pl.* Baumchirurgie, *die;* **~top** *n.* [Baum]wipfel, *der;* **~ trunk** *n.* Baumstamm, *der*

trefoil /'trefɔɪl, 'tri:fɔɪl/ *n.* 1 (clover) Klee, *der;* (plant with similar leaves) Dreiblatt, *das* 2 (Archit.) Dreipass, *der*

trek /trek/

A *v.i.*, **-kk-** 1 ziehen (**across** durch) 2 (travel by ox-wagon) trecken

B *n.* 1 [schwierige] Reise 2 (journey by ox-wagon, organized migration) Treck, *der*

trekker /'trekə(r)/ *n.* Trekker, *der*/Trekkerin, *die*

trekking /'trekɪŋ/ *n., no pl.* Trekking, *das*

trekking bike *n.* Trekkingrad, *das*

trellis /'trelɪs/ *n.* Gitter, *das;* (for plants) Spalier, *das;* **~-work** Gitterwerk, *das*

tremble /'trembl/

A *v.i.* zittern (**with** vor + *Dat.*); **~ for sb./sth.** (fig.) um jmdn./etw. zittern; **I ~ to think what .../at the thought** (fig.) mir wird bange, wenn ich daran denke, was .../wenn ich daran denke

B *n.* Zittern, *das;* **be all of a ~** (coll.) am ganzen Körper zittern; **there was a ~ in her voice** ihre Stimme zitterte

trembling /'tremblɪŋ/

A *adj.* zitternd

B *n.* Zittern, *das*

tremendous /trɪ'mendəs/ *adj.* 1 (immense) gewaltig; enorm ‹*Fähigkeiten*› 2 (coll.: wonderful) großartig

tremendously /trɪ'mendəslɪ/ *adv.* wahnsinnig (ugs.)

tremolo /'tremələʊ/ *n., pl.* **~s** (Mus.) 1 Tremolo, *das* 2 (in organ) **~ [stop]** Tremulant, *der*

tremor /'tremə(r)/ *n.* 1 Zittern, *das;* **feel a ~ of delight/fear** freudig erregt sein/vor Angst zittern; **there was a ~ of anger in her voice** ihre Stimme zitterte vor Wut; **without a ~:** ohne zu zittern 2 **[earth] ~** (Geol.) leichtes Erdbeben

tremulous /'tremjʊləs/ *adj.* 1 (trembling) zitternd; **be ~:** zittern 2 (timid) zaghaft ‹*Lächeln*›; ängstlich ‹*Person*›

tremulously /'tremjʊləslɪ/ *adv.* 1 mit zitternder Stimme ‹*sprechen*› 2 (timidly) zaghaft

trench /trentʃ/

A *n.* Graben, *der;* (Geog.) [Tiefsee]graben, *der;* (Mil.) Schützengraben, *der*

B *v.t.* (dig ditch in) mit einem Graben durchziehen

trenchant /'trentʃənt/ *adj.* deutlich, energisch ‹*Kritik, Sprache*›; energisch ‹*Verteidiger, Kritiker, Politik*›; prägnant ‹*Stil*›; scharf ‹*Verstand*›

trenchantly /'trentʃəntlɪ/ *adv.* energisch ‹*verteidigen, argumentieren, unterstützen*›

'trench coat *n.* (Mil.) Wettermantel, *der;* (coat in this style) Trenchcoat, *der*

trencherman /'trentʃəmən/ *n.* [guter] Esser

trench: ~ mortar *n.* (Mil.) Granatwerfer, *der;* **~ 'warfare** *n.* Grabenkrieg, *der*

trend /trend/

A *n.* 1 Trend, *der;* **population ~s** die Bevölkerungsentwicklung; **upward ~:** steigende Tendenz 2 (fashion) Mode, *die;* [Mode]trend, *der;* **set the ~:** den Trend bestimmen 3 (line of direction) Verlauf, *der*

B *v.i.* 1 (take a course) verlaufen 2 (fig.: move) sich entwickeln; **~ upward** steigen

trendily /'trendɪlɪ/ *adv.* (Brit. coll.) modisch

trendiness /'trendɪnɪs/ *n., no pl.* (Brit. coll.) modische Art

'trendsetter *n.* Trendsetter, *der*

trendy /'trendɪ/ (Brit. coll.)

A *adj.* modisch; trendig; Schickimicki‹*kneipe, -wohngegend*› (ugs.); fortschrittlich-modern ‹*Geistlicher, Lehrer*›

B *n.* Schickimicki, *der* (ugs.)

trepidation /trepɪ'deɪʃn/ *n.* Beklommenheit, *die;* **with some ~, not without ~:** ziemlich beklommen; **wait in ~:** voller Beklommenheit warten; **a look of ~:** ein banger Blick

trespass /'trespəs/

A *v.i.* 1 **~ on** unerlaubt betreten ‹*Grundstück*›; eingreifen in (+ *Akk.*) ‹*jmds. Rechte*›; **'no ~ing'**

t

„Betreten verboten"; **~ on sb.'s preserve** (fig.) sich in jmds. Angelegenheiten (*Akk.*) einmischen; **~ on sb.'s time/privacy** (fig.) jmds. Zeit über Gebühr in Anspruch nehmen/jmds. Privatsphäre verletzen **2** (literary/arch.: offend) freveln (geh. veralt.) (**against** an + *Dat.*); **as we forgive those who ~ against us** (Relig.) wie wir vergeben unseren Schuldigern
B *n.* **1** **forgive us our ~es** (Relig.) vergib uns unsere Schuld **2** (Law) (on land) Hausfriedensbruch, *der;* (on a person) ≈ Körperverletzung, *die;* (on goods) ≈ Eigentumsdelikt, *das*

trespasser /ˈtrespəsə(r)/ *n.* Unbefugte, *der/die;* **'~s will be prosecuted'** „Betreten verboten, Zuwiderhandlungen werden verfolgt"; **~ on sb.'s land** *Person, die unerlaubt jmds. Land betritt*

tress /tres/ *n.* (literary/arch.) Haarstrang, *der;* (curly) Locke, *die;* **she combed her ~es** sie kämmte ihr [langes] Haar

trestle /ˈtresl/ *n.* **1** [Auflager]bock, *der* **2** **~[table]** Tapeziertisch, *der*

trews /truːz/ *n. pl.* (Brit.) *eng anliegende Hose [im Schottenmuster]*

triad /ˈtraɪæd/ *n.* **1** Triade, *die;* Dreiheit, *die* **2** (Mus.) Dreiklang, *der*

trial /ˈtraɪəl/ *n.* **1** (Law) [Gerichts]verfahren, *das;* **be on ~ [for murder]** [wegen Mordes] vor Gericht stehen; **go on ~ [for one's life]** [wegen eines Verbrechens, auf das die Todesstrafe steht,] vor Gericht gestellt werden; **bring sb. to ~, put sb. on ~:** jmdm. den Prozess machen (**for** wegen); **the case was brought to ~:** der Fall wurde vor Gericht verhandelt **2** (testing) Test, *der;* **subject sth. to further ~:** weitere Tests mit etw. durchführen; **be given ~s** getestet werden; **sea ~** (Naut.) Probefahrt, *die;* **employ sb. on ~:** jmdn. probeweise einstellen; **be on ~** ‹*Person:*› in der Probezeit sein; ‹*Maschine:*› getestet werden; **give sb. a ~:** es mit jmdm. versuchen; **give sth. a ~:** etw. ausprobieren; **[by] ~ and error** [durch] Ausprobieren; **~ of strength** Kraftprobe, *die* **3** (trouble) Prüfung, *die* (geh.); Problem, *das;* **find sth. a ~:** etw. als lästig empfinden; **be a ~ to sb.** jmdm. zu schaffen machen; **that child is a real ~:** das Kind ist eine richtige Plage **4** (Sport) (competition) Prüfung, *die;* (for selection) Testspiel, *das. See also* **jury 1**; **tribulation 1**

trial: ~ 'balance *n.* (Bookk.) Probebilanz, *die;* **~ match** ▸**trial 4**; **~ pack** *n.* Probepackung, *die;* **~ 'run** *n.* **1** (of car) Testfahrt, *die;* (of machine) Probelauf, *der;* **2** (fig.) Probelauf, *der;* **have a ~ run of sth., give sth. a ~ run** etw. testen

triangle /ˈtraɪæŋgl/ *n.* **1** Dreieck, *das; see also* **eternal 1** **2** (Mus.) Triangel, *der od. das*

triangular /traɪˈæŋgjʊlə(r)/ *adj.* **1** dreieckig; dreiseitig ‹*Pyramide*› **2** (between three persons etc.) Dreier‹*beziehung, -wettbewerb*›

triangulate /traɪˈæŋgjʊleɪt/ *v.t.* (Surv.) triangulieren

triangulation /traɪæŋgjʊˈleɪʃn/ *n.* (Surv.) Triangulation, *die*

Triassic /traɪˈæsɪk/ (Geol.)
A *adj.* Trias-
B Trias, *die*

triathlete /traɪˈæθliːt/ *n.* Triathlet, *der*/-athletin, *die*

triathlon /traɪˈæθlɒn/ *n.* Triathlon, *das od. der*

tribal /ˈtraɪbl/ *adj.* Stammes-

tribalism /ˈtraɪbəlɪzm/ *n.* Tribalismus, *der* (fachspr.)

tribalistic /traɪbəˈlɪstɪk/ *adj.* Stammes-; tribalistisch (fachspr.)

tribe /traɪb/ *n.* **1** Stamm, *der* **2** (derog.) Bande, *die* (abwertend); (family) Sippe, *die* (scherzh. od. abwertend) **3** (Biol.) Tribus, *die* **4** *in pl.* (joc.: large numbers) Horde, *die;* **whole ~s of children** ganze Horden von Kindern

tribesman /ˈtraɪbzmən/ *n., pl.* **tribesmen** /ˈtraɪbzmən/ Stammesangehörige, *der*

tribulation /trɪbjʊˈleɪʃn/ *n.* **1** (great affliction) Kummer, *der;* **bring sb. ~:** jmdm. Kummer bereiten; **trials and ~s** Probleme und Sorgen **2** (cause of trouble etc.) **be a ~ to sb.** jmdm. zur Last fallen

tribunal /traɪˈbjuːnl, trɪˈbjuːnl/ *n.* **1** Schiedsgericht, *das;* (court of justice) Gericht, *das; see also* **rent tribunal** **2** (fig.) Tribunal, *das*

tribune[1] /ˈtrɪbjuːn/ *n.* (platform) [Redner]tribüne, *die*

tribune[2] *n.* (Hist.) **~ [of the people]** Volkstribun, *der*

tributary /ˈtrɪbjʊtərɪ/
A *adj.* (Hist.: paying tribute) tributpflichtig
B *n.* **1** (river) (flowing into larger river) Nebenfluss, *der;* (of lake) Zufluss, *der.* **2** (Hist.: State) tributpflichtiger Staat

tribute /ˈtrɪbjuːt/ *n.* **1** (regard) Tribut, *der* (**to** an + *Akk.*); **pay ~ to sb./sth.** jmdm./einer Sache den schuldigen Tribut zollen (geh.); **in silent ~:** in stiller Ehrerbietung; **floral ~s** Blumen [als Zeichen der Anerkennung]; (to deceased person) Blumen und Kränze; **as a ~ to his work** zur Würdigung seiner Arbeit; **she is a ~ to her teacher/trainer** sie macht ihrem Lehrer/Trainer alle Ehre **2** (payment) Tribut, *der*

trice /traɪs/ *n.* **in a ~:** im Handumdrehen

tricentenary /traɪsenˈtiːnərɪ, traɪsenˈtenərɪ/ ▸**tercentenary**

triceps /ˈtraɪseps/ *n.* (Anat.) Trizeps, *der*

trichinosis /trɪkɪˈnəʊsɪs/ *n.* (Med.) Trichinose, *die*

trichloride /traɪˈklɔːraɪd/ *n.* (Chem.) Trichlorid, *das*

trick /trɪk/
A *n.* **1** Trick, *der;* **I suspect some ~:** es könnte ein Trick sein; **it was all a ~:** das war [alles] nur Bluff; **it was such a shabby ~ [to play on her]** es war [ihr gegenüber] eine derartige Gemeinheit *od.* dermaßen gemein **2** (feat of skill etc.) Kunststück, *das;* **try every ~ in the book** es mit allen Tricks probieren; **he never misses a ~** (fig.) ihm entgeht nichts; **that should do the ~** (coll.) damit dürfte es klappen (ugs.); **know a ~ worth two of that** etwas viel Besseres wissen **3** (knack) **get** *or* **find the ~ [of doing sth.]** den Dreh finden[, wie man etw. tut] **4** **how's ~s?** (coll.) was macht die Kunst? (ugs.) **5** (mannerism) Eigenart, *die;* **have a ~ of doing sth.** die Eigenart haben, etw. zu tun **6** (prank) Streich, *der;* **play a ~ on sb.** jmdm. einen Streich spielen; **my hearing aid is playing ~s on me again** mein Hörgerät spielt mal wieder verrückt (ugs.); **be up to one's [old] ~s again** wieder auf dieselbe Tour reisen (ugs.); **be up to sb.'s ~s** wissen, was jmd. im Schilde führt; **~ or treat** Trick-or-Treat, *das;* ▸**trick-or-treater** **7** (illusion) **~ of vision/lighting/the light** Augentäuschung, *die* **8** (Cards) Stich, *der;* **take a ~:** einen Stich machen **9** (coll.: prostitute's customer) Freier, *der. See also* **bag A 1**; **trade A 1**
B *v.t.* täuschen; hereinlegen; **~ sb. into doing sth.** jmdn. mit einem Trick *od.* einer List dazu bringen, etw. zu tun; **~ sb. out of/into sth.** jmdm. etw. ablisten
C *adj.* **~ photograph** Trickaufnahme, *die;* **~ photography** Trickfotografie, *die;* **~ question** Fangfrage, *die*

Phrasal verb
- **~ 'out, ~ 'up** *v.t.* schmücken; **~ oneself out** *or* **up** sich herausputzen (**in** mit)

trick 'cyclist *n.* **1** Kunstradfahrer, *der*/-fahrerin, *die* **2** (Brit. joc.: psychiatrist) Seelendoktor, *der*/-doktorin, *die* (ugs. scherzh.)

trickery /ˈtrɪkərɪ/ *n.* [Hinter]list, *die;* **piece of ~:** List, *die;* Trick, *der*

trickiness /ˈtrɪkɪnɪs/ *n., no pl.* Verzwicktheit, *die* (ugs.)

trickle /ˈtrɪkl/
A *n.* Rinnsal, *das* (geh.) (**of** von); **in a ~:** als Rinnsal; **a ~ of rain ran down the window** Regenwasser rann am Fenster hinunter; **there was a ~ of people leaving the room** (fig.) einige wenige Menschen verließen nacheinander den Raum; **the ~ of people leaving the hall swelled to a flood** (fig.) erst leerte sich die Halle nur langsam, doch dann strömten die Menschen hinaus; **supplies of food have shrunk to a ~** (fig.) die Versorgung mit Nahrungsmitteln ist fast versiegt
B *v.i.* rinnen; (in drops) tröpfeln; (fig.) ‹*Ball:*› langsam rollen; **~ out** ‹*Zuschauer:*› nach und nach [hinaus]gehen; **~ through** *or* **out** ‹*Informationen:*› durchsickern
C *v.t.* tröpfeln

'trickle charger *n.* (Electr.) Erhaltungslader, *der*

trick-or-treater /trɪkɔːˈtriːtə(r)/ *n.: Kind, das an Halloween von Haus zu Haus zieht und um kleine Geschenke bittet und gleichzeitig für der Fall, dass es abgewiesen wird, damit droht, der betreffenden Person einen Streich zu spielen*

trickster /ˈtrɪkstə(r)/ *n.* Schwindler, *der*/Schwindlerin, *die*

tricky /ˈtrɪkɪ/ *adj.* **1** (full of difficulties) verzwickt (ugs.); **it is ~ doing sth.** es ist gar nicht so einfach, etw. zu tun **2** (crafty) raffiniert; trickreich ‹*Spieler*›

tricolour (*Brit.; Amer.:* **tricolor**) /ˈtrɪkələ(r), ˈtraɪkʌlə(r)/ *n.* Trikolore, *die*

tricorne /ˈtraɪkɔːn/ *n., adj.* **~ [hat]** Dreispitz, *der*

tricot /ˈtrɪkəʊ, ˈtriːkəʊ/ *n.* Trikot[stoff], *der*

tricycle /ˈtraɪsɪkl/
A *n.* Dreirad, *das*
B *v.i.* Dreirad fahren

trident /ˈtraɪdənt/ *n.* dreizackiger Fischspeer; (held by Britannia etc.) Dreizack, *der*

Tridentine /trɪˈdentaɪn/ *adj.* tridentinisch

tried ▸**try B, C**

triennial /traɪˈenɪəl/ *adj.* **1** (lasting three years) dreijährig **2** (once every three years) dreijährlich

triennially /traɪˈenɪəlɪ/ *adv.* alle drei Jahre

trier /ˈtraɪə(r)/ *n.* **he's a real ~:** er wirft die Flinte nicht so schnell ins Korn; **but at least he's a ~:** aber er gibt sich (*Dat.*) wenigstens Mühe

Trieste /triːˈest/ *pr. n.* Triest (*das*)

trifle /ˈtraɪfl/
A *n.* **1** (Brit. Gastron.) Trifle, *das* **2** (thing of slight value) Kleinigkeit, *die;* **the merest ~:** die geringste Kleinigkeit; **it's only a ~:** es ist nichts Besonderes **3** (small amount of money) Kleinigkeit, *die;* **it only costs a ~:** es kostet so gut wie nichts **4** **a ~ tired/angry** *etc.* ein bisschen müde/böse *usw*
B *v.i.* tändeln

Phrasal verbs
- **~ a'way** *v.t.* vergeuden
- **~ with** *v.i.* spielen mit ‹*jmds. Gefühlen*›; nicht ernst genug nehmen ‹*Person*›; **he is not a person you can ~ with** er lässt nicht mit sich spaßen

trifling /ˈtraɪflɪŋ/ *adj.* unbedeutend ‹*Angelegenheit, Irrtum*›; lächerlich ‹*Gedanke*›; gering ‹*Gefahr, Wert*›; [lächerlich] gering ‹*Summe*›; **~ objects/gifts** Kleinigkeiten

trifocal /traɪˈfəʊkl/ (Optics)
A *adj.* Trifokal-
B *n. in pl.* Trifokalgläser *Pl.*

triforium /traɪˈfɔːrɪəm/ *n., pl.* **triforia** /traɪˈfɔːrɪə/ (Archit.) Triforium, *das* (fachspr.)

trigger /ˈtrɪgə(r)/
A *n.* **1** (of gun) Abzug, *der;* (of machine) Drücker, *der;* **pull the ~:** abdrücken; (fig.) den Startschuss geben; **be quick on the ~** (fig.) prompt reagieren **2** (that sets off reaction) Auslöser, *der*
B *v.t.* **~ [off]** auslösen

'trigger-happy *adj.* schießwütig; (fig.) kriegslüstern ‹*General, Politiker*›

trigonometric /trɪgənəˈmetrɪk/, **trigonometrical** /trɪgənəˈmetrɪkl/ *adj.* (Math.) trigonometrisch

trigonometry /trɪgəˈnɒmɪtrɪ/ *n.* (Math.) Trigonometrie, *die*

trike /traɪk/ *n.* (coll.) Dreirad, *das*

trilateral /traɪˈlætərl/
A *adj.* (having three sides) dreiseitig; (involving three parties also) trilateral (geh.)
B *n.* Dreieck, *das*

trilby /ˈtrɪlbɪ/ *n.* (Brit.) **~ [hat]** Klapprandhut, *der;* Herrenhut, *der*

trilingual /traɪˈlɪŋgwəl/ *adj.* dreisprachig

trill /trɪl/
A *n.* **1** Trillern, *das* **2** (Mus.) Triller, *der*
B *v.i.* trillern
C *v.t.* rollen ‹r›

trillion /ˈtrɪljən/ *n.* ▸ⓘ **p. 1358** Billion, *die*

trilobite /ˈtraɪləbaɪt/ *n.* (Palaeont.) Trilobit, *der*

trilogy /ˈtrɪlədʒɪ/ *n.* Trilogie, *die*

trim /trɪm/
A *v.t.*, **-mm-: 1** schneiden ‹Hecke›; [nach]schneiden ‹Haar›; beschneiden (auch fig.) ‹*Papier, Hecke, Docht, Budget*›; ~ **£100 off** *or* **from a budget** ein Budget um 100 Pfund kürzen **2** (ornament) besetzen (**with** mit) **3** (adjust balance of) trimmen ‹*Boot, Schiff, Flugzeug*› **4** richtig stellen ‹*Segel*›; ~ **one's sails before the wind** (fig.) sich nach der Decke strecken
B *adj.* proper; gepflegt ‹*Garten*›; **keep sth. ~:** etw. in Ordnung halten
C *n.* **1** (state of adjustment) Bereitschaft, *die;* **find sth. in [perfect] ~:** etw. in [bester] Ordnung vorfinden; **everything was in good** *or* **proper ~:** alles war in bester Ordnung; **be in fine physical ~:** in guter körperlicher Verfassung sein; **get/be in ~** (suitably dressed) sich angemessen anziehen/angemessen angezogen sein; (healthy) sich trimmen/in Form *od.* fit sein **2** (proper balance) (of ship) Trimm, *der;* (of aircraft) [stabile] Fluglage; **be in/out of ~** ‹*Schiff:*› in/nicht in Trimm sein; ‹*Flugzeug:*› in stabiler/unstabiler Fluglage sein **3** (cut) Nachschneiden, *das;* **my hair needs a ~:** ich muss mir die Haare nachschneiden lassen; **give a hedge a ~:** eine Hecke nachschneiden; **just a ~, please** (said to hairdresser) nur nachschneiden, bitte **4** (adornment) Verzierung, *die* **5** (of car) Innenausstattung, *die;* (on door panel) Zierleiste, *die*

(Phrasal verbs)
- ~ **a'way** ▸ ~ **off**
- ~ **'down** *v.t.* (fig.) verringern; **her figure needed ~ming down** sie musste etwas für ihre Figur tun
- ~ **'off** *v.t.* abschneiden; (fig.) abnehmen

trimaran /ˈtraɪmərӕn/ *n.* (Naut.) Trimaran, *der*

trimmer /ˈtrɪmə(r)/ *n.* Schneider, *der;* **hedge ~:** Heckenschere, *die*

trimming /ˈtrɪmɪŋ/ *n.* **1** (decorative addition) Verzierung, *die;* **lace ~s** Spitzenbesatz, *der* **2** *in pl.* (coll.: accompaniments) (for main dish) Beilagen; (extra fittings on car) Extras; **with all the ~s** mit allem Drum und Dran (ugs.) **3** *in pl.* (pieces cut off) Abfall, *der* (*vom Zuschneiden*); (of meat) abgeschnittene Stücke

trimness /ˈtrɪmnɪs/ *n.*, *no pl.* adrettes Aussehen; **the ~ of her figure** ihre gepflegte Figur

Trinidad /ˈtrɪnɪdӕd/ *pr. n.* Trinidad (*das*)

Trinidadian /trɪnɪˈdӕdɪən/ ▸ⓘ **p. 1345**
A *adj.* trinidadisch; **sb. is ~:** jmd. ist Trinidader/Trinidaderin
B *n.* Trinidader, *der*/Trinidaderin, *die*

Trinity /ˈtrɪnɪtɪ/ *n.* **1** (Theol.) **the [Holy] ~:** die [Heilige] Dreifaltigkeit *od.* Dreieinigkeit *od.* Trinität **2** (Eccl.) ~ **[Sunday]** Dreifaltigkeitssonntag, *der*

Trinity 'term *n.* (Brit. Univ.) Sommertrimester, *das*

trinket /ˈtrɪŋkɪt/ *n.* **1** (piece of jewellery) kleines, billiges Schmuckstück; (on bracelet) Anhänger, *der* **2** (ornament) Schmuckgegenstand, *der*

trio /ˈtriːəʊ/ *n.*, *pl.* **~s** Trio, *das;* **string/piano ~** (Mus.) Streich-/Klaviertrio, *das*

trioxide /traɪˈɒksaɪd/ *n.* (Chem.) Trioxid, *das*

trip /trɪp/
A *n.* **1** (journey) Reise, *die;* Trip, *der* (ugs.); (shorter) Ausflug, *der;* Trip, *der* (ugs.); **two ~s were necessary to transport everything** zwei Fahrten waren nötig, um alles zu transportieren; **make a ~ to London** nach London fahren **2** (coll.: visit for stated purpose) Gang, *der;* **make a ~ to the hairdresser's** zum Friseur gehen **3** (coll.: drug-induced hallucinations) Trip, *der* (Jargon); **[good/bad] ~ on LSD** [guter/schlechter] LSD-Trip. *See also* **round trip**
B *v.i.*, **-pp-: 1** (stumble) stolpern (**on** über + *Akk.*) **2** (coll.: hallucinate while on drugs) ~ **[on LSD]** auf einem [LSD-]Trip sein **3** (walk etc. with light steps) trippeln **4** (fig.: make a mistake) einen Fehler machen
C *v.t.*, **-pp- 1** (cause to stumble) ▸ ~ **up B 1 2** (release) lichten ‹*Anker*›; betätigen ‹*Schalter*›; auslösen ‹*Alarm*›

(Phrasal verbs)
- ~ **over** *v.t.* stolpern über (+ *Akk.*)
- ~ **'up**
A *v.i.* **1** (stumble) stolpern **2** (fig.: make a mistake) einen Fehler machen
B *v.t.* **1** ~ **sb. up** (cause to stumble) jmdn. stolpern lassen; (make fall) jmdn. zu Fall bringen; (by sticking out a leg) jmdm. ein Bein stellen **2** (cause to make a mistake) aufs Glatteis führen (fig.)

tripartite /traɪˈpɑːtaɪt/ *adj.* **1** (in three parts) ~ **division** Dreiteilung, *die* **2** (involving three parties) trilateral (geh.); dreiseitig

tripe /traɪp/ *n.* **1** Kaldaunen; (individual piece) Kaldaune, *die* **2** (coll.: rubbish) Quatsch, *der* (ugs. abwertend)

triple /ˈtrɪpl/
A *adj.* **1** (threefold) dreifach **2** (three times greater than) ~ **the ...:** der/die/das dreifache ...; **at ~ the speed** mit der dreifachen Geschwindigkeit *od.* dreimal so schnell; ~ **the number of machines** dreimal so viele Maschinen
B *n.* Dreifache, *das*
C *v.i.* sich verdreifachen
D *v.t.* verdreifachen

triple: T~ Al'liance *n.* (Hist.) Dreibund, *der;* **~ 'crown** *n.* **1** (Sport) Triple Crown, *die;* dreifacher Triumph; **2** (Pope's tiara) dreifache Krone; Tiara, *die;* **~ jump** *n.* (Sport) Dreisprung, *der*

triplet /ˈtrɪplɪt/ *n.* **1** Drilling, *der* **2** (Pros.) Dreireim, *der* **3** (Mus.) Triole, *die*

'triple time *n.* (Mus.) Dreiertakt, *der*

Triplex ® /ˈtrɪpleks/ *n.* ~ **[glass]** Verbundglas, *das*

triplicate /ˈtrɪplɪkət/
A *adj.* dreifach
B *n.* Drittausfertigung, *die;* Triplikat, *das* (geh.); **in ~:** in dreifacher Ausfertigung

triply /ˈtrɪplɪ/ *adv.* dreifach

trip: ~meter, ~ 'mileage recorder *ns.* (Motor Veh.) ≈ Tageskilometerzähler, *der*

tripod /ˈtraɪpɒd/ *n.* Dreibein, *das;* [dreibeiniges] Stativ

tripos /ˈtraɪpɒs/ *n.* (Brit.) *Abschlussprüfung für den Honours-Degree an der Universität Cambridge*

tripper /ˈtrɪpə(r)/ *n.* (Brit.) Ausflügler, *der*/Ausflüglerin, *die*

'trip switch *n.* (Electr.) Sicherungsschalter, *der*

triptych /ˈtrɪptɪk/ *n.* (Art) Triptychon, *das*

'tripwire *n.* Stolperdraht, *der*

trisect /traɪˈsekt/ *v.t.* dreiteilen

trisyllabic /traɪsɪˈlӕbɪk/ *adj.* (Ling.) dreisilbig

trisyllable /traɪˈsɪləbl/ *n.* (Ling. Pros.) dreisilbiges Wort; **be a ~:** dreisilbig sein *od.* drei Silben haben

trite /traɪt/ *adj.*, **tritely** /ˈtraɪtlɪ/ *adv.* banal

triteness /ˈtraɪtnɪs/ *n.*, *no pl.* Banalität, *die*

tritium /ˈtrɪtɪəm/ *n.* (Chem.) Tritium, *das*

triumph /ˈtraɪəmf, ˈtraɪʌmf/
A *n.* Triumph, *der* (**over** über + *Akk.*); (Rom. Ant.: procession also) Triumphzug, *der;* **in ~:** im Triumph; **an expression of ~:** ein triumphierender Ausdruck
B *v.i.* triumphieren (**over** über + *Akk.*)

triumphal /traɪˈʌmfl/ *adj.* triumphal ‹*Erfolg*›; Triumph‹*bogen, -zug*›

triumphalism /traɪˈʌmfəlɪzm/ *n.*, *no pl.* Triumphalismus, *der*

triumphant /traɪˈʌmfənt/ *adj.* **1** (victorious) siegreich; *see also* **church 2 2** (exulting) triumphierend ‹*Blick*›; ~ **shouts** Triumphgeschrei, *das;* **the look in her eyes was ~:** sie hatte einen triumphierenden Blick

triumphantly /traɪˈʌmfəntlɪ/ *adv.* triumphierend; **be ~ successful** einen triumphalen Erfolg haben

triumvirate /traɪˈʌmvərət/ *n.* Triumvirat, *das*

trivalent /traɪˈveɪlənt/ *adj.* (Chem.) dreiwertig

trivet /ˈtrɪvɪt/ *n.* **1** (in pressure cooker) Dreifuß, *der* **2** (used under hot dishes) [dreifüßiger] Untersetzer

trivia /ˈtrɪvɪə/ *n. pl.* Belanglosigkeiten

trivial /ˈtrɪvɪəl/ *adj.* **1** belanglos; trivial (geh.) **2** (concerned only with ~ things) oberflächlich ‹*Person*›

triviality /trɪvɪˈӕlɪtɪ/ *n.* Belanglosigkeit, *die;* Trivialität, *die* (geh.)

trivialize /ˈtrɪvɪəlaɪz/ *v.t.* auf eine belanglose Ebene bringen; trivialisieren (geh.)

trivially /ˈtrɪvɪəlɪ/ *adv.* oberflächlich

trochaic /trəˈkeɪɪk/ (Pros.) *adj.* trochäisch

trochee /ˈtrəʊkiː/ *n.* (Pros.) Trochäus, *der*

trod, trodden ▸ **tread B, C**

troglodyte /ˈtrɒglədaɪt/ *n.* **1** (cave dweller) Höhlenbewohner, *der*/-bewohnerin, *die* **2** (fig.) Einsiedler, *der*/Einsiedlerin, *die*

troika /ˈtrɔɪkə/ *n.* Troika, *die*

Trojan /ˈtrəʊdʒən/
A *n.* **1** (fig.) **work like a ~:** arbeiten wie ein Pferd **2** (inhabitant of Troy) Trojaner, *der*/Trojanerin, *die*
B *adj.* trojanisch; **the ~ War** der Trojanische Krieg

Trojan 'Horse *n.* **1** Trojanisches Pferd (geh.); (fig. also) Danaergeschenk, *das* (geh.) **2** (Computing) trojanisches Pferd; Trojaner, *der*

troll[1] /trəʊl/
A *v.t.* [mit der Schleppangel] fischen
B *v.i.* [mit der Schleppangel] fischen (**for** *Akk.*)

troll[2] *n.* (Mythol.) Troll, *der*

trolley /ˈtrɒlɪ/ *n.* **1** (Brit.: on rails) Draisine, *die* **2** (Brit.: for serving food) Servierwagen, *der* **3** (Brit.) **[supermarket] ~:** Einkaufswagen, *der* **4** ▸ **luggage trolley 5** (Amer.) **~[car]** Straßenbahn, *die* **6** **he's off his ~** (coll.: insane) bei ihm ist eine Schraube locker (salopp)

'trolley bus *n.* (Brit.) Oberleitungsomnibus, *der*

trollop /ˈtrɒləp/ *n.* **1** (slut) Schlampe, *die* **2** (prostitute) Dirne, *die*

trolly ▸ **trolley**

trombone /trɒmˈbəʊn, ˈtrɒmbəʊn/ *n.* Posaune, *die*

trombonist /trɒmˈbəʊnɪst/ *n.* ▸ⓘ **p. 1260** Posaunist, *der*/Posaunistin, *die*

trompe-l'oeil /trɒmpˈlɔɪː/ (Art)
A *n.* Trompe-l'œil, *das od. der*
B *adj.* Trompe-l'œil-

troop /truːp/
A *n.* **1** *in pl.* Truppen; **our best ~s** unsere besten Soldaten **2** (of cavalry) Schwadron, *die;* (artillery and armour) Batterie, *die* **3** (assembled company) Schar, *die* **4** (of Scouts) ≈ Gruppe, *die. see also* **household troops**
B *v.i.* strömen; (in an orderly fashion) marschieren; ~ **in/out** hinein-/hinausströmen
C *v.t.* **~ing the colour[s]** (Brit.) Fahnenparade, *die*

'troop carrier *n.* Truppentransporter, *der*

trooper /ˈtruːpə(r)/ *n.* **1** (soldier) einfacher Soldat; **swear like a ~** (coll.) wie ein Fuhrmann fluchen (ugs.) **2** (Amer.: policeman) Polizist, *der*

'troopship *n.* (Mil.) Truppentransporter, *der*

trope /trəʊp/ *n.* (Rhet.) Trope, *die* (fachspr.)

trophy /ˈtrəʊfɪ/ *n.* **1** Trophäe, *die* **2** (competition) **T~:** ≈ Pokal, *der*

trophy 'wife *n.* (coll. derog.) Trophäenfrau, *die*

tropic /ˈtrɒpɪk/ *n.* **the T~s** (Geog.) die Tropen; **the ~ of Cancer/Capricorn** (Astron., Geog.) der Wendekreis des Krebses/Steinbocks

tropical /ˈtrɒpɪkl/ *adj.* tropisch; Tropen‹*krankheit, -kleidung, -holz, -klima, -wald*›

tropical: ~ 'medicine *n.* Tropenmedizin, *die;* **~ 'rainforest** *n.* tropischer Regenwald; **~ 'storm** *n.* Tropensturm, *der*

troposphere /ˈtrɒpəsfɪə(r), ˈtrəʊpəsfɪə(r)/ *n.* Troposphäre, *die*

trot /trɒt/
A *n.* **1** (action of ~ting) Trab, *der;* **at a ~:** im Trab **2** (journey on horseback) Ausritt, *der* **3** (coll.) **on the ~** (in succession) hintereinander; **every weekend for five weeks on the ~:** an fünf Wochenenden hintereinander; **be on the ~:**

auf Trab sein (ugs.); **keep sb. on the ~** (continually busy) jmdn. auf Trab halten (ugs.) **4** **have the ~s** (sl.: diarrhoea) Dünnpfiff haben (salopp)
B *v.i.*, **-tt-**: **1** traben **2** (coll.: go) traben (ugs.); **~ along now** geh jetzt
C *v.t.*, **-tt-** traben lassen ‹*Pferd*›
Phrasal verb
• **~ 'out** *v.t.* (fig. coll.) **1** (produce for approval) vorführen **2** (produce unthinkingly) kommen mit (ugs.)

Trot /trɒt/ *n.* (coll.: Trotskyist) Trotzkist, *der*/Trotzkistin, *die*

troth /trəʊθ/ *n.* (arch./joc.) **plight one's ~:** das Eheversprechen geben

Trotskyism /ˈtrɒtskɪɪzm/ *n.* Trotzkismus, *der*

Trotskyist /ˈtrɒtskɪɪst/, **Trotskyite** /ˈtrɒtskɪaɪt/ *ns.* Trotzkist, *der*/Trotzkistin, *die*

trotter /ˈtrɒtə(r)/ *n.* **1** Fuß, *der;* **pigs' ~s** (Cookery) Schweinsfüße **2** (horse) Traber, *der*

trotting /ˈtrɒtɪŋ/ *n.* Trabrennen, *das*

'trotting race *n.* Trabrennen, *das*

troubadour /ˈtruːbədʊə(r)/ *n.* Troubadour, *der*

trouble /ˈtrʌbl/
A *n.* **1** Ärger, *der;* Schwierigkeiten *Pl.;* **have ~ with sb./sth.** mit jmdm./etw. Ärger haben; **all his ~s** alle seine Probleme; **put one's ~s behind one** seine Probleme vergessen; **be out of ~:** aus den Schwierigkeiten heraus sein; **keep out of ~:** nicht [wieder] in Schwierigkeiten kommen; **in ~:** in Schwierigkeiten; **be in ~ with the police** Ärger mit der Polizei haben; **are you looking for ~?** du willst wohl Ärger [bekommen]?; **be in serious** *or* **real** *or* **a lot of ~ [over sth.]** [wegen einer Sache] in ernsten *od.* großen Schwierigkeiten sein; **get sb. into ~:** jmdn. in Schwierigkeiten bringen; **get a girl into ~** (coll.) einem Mädchen ein Kind machen (ugs.); **get into ~ [over sth.]** [wegen einer Sache] in Schwierigkeiten geraten; **get into ~ with the bank/law** Ärger *od.* Schwierigkeiten mit der Bank bekommen/mit dem Gesetz in Konflikt geraten; **there'll be ~ [if …]** es wird Ärger geben[, wenn …]; **what's** *or* **what seems to be the ~?** was ist denn?; was ist los? (ugs.); (doctor's question to patient) wo fehlts denn?; **you are asking for ~** (coll.) du machst dir nur selber Schwierigkeiten; **that's asking for ~** (coll.) das muss ja Ärger geben; **make** *or* **cause ~** (cause disturbance) Ärger machen (**about** wegen); (cause disagreement) Zwietracht säen; **make ~ for sb.** jmdm. Ärger *od.* Schwierigkeiten machen; **give sb. no ~:** jmdm. keine Schwierigkeiten bereiten *od.* machen
2 (faulty operation) Probleme; **engine/clutch/brake ~:** Probleme mit dem Motor/der Kupplung/der Bremse; **the engine is giving ~:** mit dem Motor stimmt etwas nicht
3 ▸ℹ **p. 1231** (disease) **suffer from heart/liver ~:** herz-/leberkrank sein; es am Herz/an der Leber haben (ugs.); **she's got some ~ with her back** ihr Rücken macht ihr zu schaffen
4 (cause of vexation etc.) Problem, *das;* **half the ~** (fig.) das größte Problem; **your ~ is that …:** dein Fehler ist, dass …; **their daughter is such a terrible ~ to them** ihre Tochter macht ihnen solche Sorgen
5 (inconvenience) Mühe, *die;* **it's more ~ than it's worth** es lohnt sich nicht; **dishwashers are more ~ than they are worth** mit Geschirrspülmaschinen hat man doch nur Ärger; **I don't want to put you to any ~:** ich möchte Ihnen keine Umstände machen; **not worth the ~:** nicht der Mühe wert; **give sb. no ~:** jmdm. keine Mühe machen; **take the ~ to do sth., go to the ~ of doing sth.** sich (*Dat.*) die Mühe machen, etw. zu tun; **go to** *or* **take a lot of/some ~:** sich (*Dat.*) sehr viel/viel Mühe geben; **please don't go to a lot of ~:** bitte machen Sie sich (*Dat.*) nicht allzu viel Umstände; **of course I'll help you — [it's] no ~ at all** natürlich helfe ich dir — das macht keine Umstände *od.* das ist nicht der Rede wert; **nothing was too much ~ for her** nichts war ihr zu viel
6 (source of inconvenience) **be a ~ [to sb.]** jmdm. zur Last fallen; **he won't be any ~:** er wird [Ihnen] keine Schwierigkeiten machen; **the children are no ~:** die Kinder sind keine Last
7 *in sing. or pl.* (unrest) Unruhen
8 **~ and strife** (Brit. sl.: wife) bessere Hälfte (ugs. scherzh.)
B *v.t.* **1** (agitate) beunruhigen; **don't let it ~ you** mach dir deswegen keine Sorgen; **be ~d about money matters** Geldsorgen haben
2 (inconvenience) stören; **[I'm] sorry to ~ you** bitte entschuldigen Sie die Störung; **can I ~ you with one more question?** darf ich Ihnen noch eine letzte Frage stellen?; **my back ~s me sometimes** mein Rücken macht mir manchmal zu schaffen
3 (in requests) **may I ~ you to shut the door?** dürfte ich Sie bitten, die Tür zu schließen?; **may I ~ you to mind your own business?** (iron.) kümmern Sie sich gefälligst um Ihre eigenen Angelegenheiten!; **I'll ~ you to wipe your feet** (iron.) putz dir gefälligst die Schuhe ab
C *v.i.* **1** (be disturbed) sich (*Dat.*) Sorgen machen (**over** um); **don't ~ about it** mach dir deswegen keine Gedanken
2 (make an effort) sich bemühen; **don't ~ to explain/to get up/to see me out** du brauchst mir gar nichts zu erklären/bitte bleiben Sie sitzen/Sie brauchen mich nicht hinauszubringen

troubled /ˈtrʌbld/ *adj.* **1** (worried) besorgt; **what are you so ~ about?** was macht dir denn solche Sorgen? **2** (restless) unruhig; schlecht ‹*Traum*› **3** (agitated) aufgewühlt; unruhig ‹*Zeit*›; bewegt ‹*Geschichte*›; *see also* **pour A 1**

trouble: ~-free *adj.* problemlos; harmonisch ‹*Ehe*›; **~maker** *n.* Unruhestifter, *der*/-stifterin, *die;* **~shooter** *n.: jemand, der Störungen od. Probleme findet und beseitigt;* Troubleshooter, *der;* (in disputes) Vermittler, *der*/Vermittlerin, *die;* **~shooting** *n.: das Finden und Beseitigen von Störungen od. Problemen;* (in disputes) Vermittlung, *die*

troublesome /ˈtrʌblsəm/ *adj.* schwierig; lästig ‹*Krankheit*›

'trouble spot *n.* **1** Unruheherd, *der* **2** (in machine) Schwachstelle, *die*

trough /trɒf/ *n.* **1** Trog, *der;* **a drinking ~:** ein Wassertrog **2** (between waves) Wellental, *das* **3** (Meteorol.) Trog, *der;* **a ~ of low pressure** eine Tiefdruckrinne **4** (Econ., on graph) Talsohle, *die*

trounce /traʊns/ *v.t.* **1** (defeat) vernichtend schlagen **2** (beat severely) durchprügeln (ugs.)

troupe /truːp/ *n.* Truppe, *die*

trouper /ˈtruːpə(r)/ *n.* Komödiant, *der*/Komödiantin, *die;* **an old ~** (fig.) ein alter Hase; **sb. is a good ~:** jmd. ist ein guter Kollege/eine gute Kollegin

trouser/ˈtraʊzə/: **~ leg** *n.* Hosenbein, *das;* **~ pocket** *n.* Hosentasche, *die;* **~ press** *n.* Bügelpresse, *die;* Hosenbügler, *der*

trousers /ˈtraʊzəz/ *n. pl.* **[pair of] ~:** Hose, *die;* Hosen *Pl.;* **catch sb. with his ~ down** (fig. coll.) jmdn. unvorbereitet treffen; **wear the ~** (fig.) die Hosen anhaben (ugs.)

'trouser suit *n.* (Brit.) Hosenanzug, *der*

trousseau /ˈtruːsəʊ/ *n., pl.* **~s** *or* **~x** /ˈtruːsəʊz/ Aussteuer, *die*

trout /traʊt/ *n., pl. same* Forelle, *die*

trout: ~ farm *n.* Forellenzuchtbetrieb, *der;* **~-fishing** *n.* Forellenfang, *der*

trowel /ˈtraʊəl/ *n.* **1** Kelle, *die;* **lay it on with a ~** (fig.) [es] dick auftragen (ugs. abwertend) **2** (Hort.) Pflanzkelle, *die*

troy *n.* **~ [weight]** Troygewicht, *das*

Troy /trɔɪ/ *pr. n.* Troja (*das*)

truancy /ˈtruːənsɪ/ *n.* [Schule]schwänzen, *das* (ugs.); unentschuldigtes Fernbleiben vom Unterricht; **be expelled for ~:** wegen Schwänzerei der Schule verwiesen werden

truant /ˈtruːənt/
A *n.* [Schul]schwänzer, *der*/-schwänzerin, *die* (ugs.); **play ~:** [die Schule] schwänzen (ugs.)
B *adj.* [schule]schwänzend (ugs.)
C *v.i.* schwänzen (ugs.); unentschuldigt fehlen

truce /truːs/ *n.* Waffenstillstand, *der;* **call a ~:** einen Waffenstillstand schließen; *see also* **flag¹ A**

truck¹ /trʌk/
A *n.* **1** (road vehicle) Last[kraft]wagen, *der;* Lkw, *der* **2** (Brit. Railw.: wagon) offener Güterwagen **3** (porter's barrow) Gepäckkarren, *der* **4** (Railw.: bogie) Drehgestell, *das* **5** (wheeled stand) Hund, *der*
B *v.t.* [per Lastwagen] transportieren
C *v.i.* (Amer.) Lastwagen fahren

truck² *n.* **1** **have no ~ with sb./sth.** (fig.) mit jmdm./etw. nichts zu tun haben **2** (Amer.: produce) Gemüse, *das;* **~ farm** Gemüseanbaubetrieb, *der*

'truck driver *n.* ▸ℹ **p. 1260** Lastwagenfahrer, *der*/-fahrerin, *die;* (long-distance) Fernfahrer, *der*/-fahrerin, *die*

trucker /ˈtrʌkə(r)/ *n.* ▸ℹ **p. 1260** (Amer.) **1** (market gardener) Gemüsegärtner, *der*/-gärtnerin, *die* **2** ▸**truck driver**

trucking /ˈtrʌkɪŋ/ *n.* (Amer.) Lkw-Fahren, *das;* (as business) Lkw-Transport, *der*

truckle /ˈtrʌkl/ *v.i.* **~ [to sb.]** [jmdm. gegenüber] klein beigeben; (fawn) [vor jmdm.] kriechen

'truckle bed *n.* Rollbett, *das*

truck: ~load *n.* Wagenladung, *die;* **sand by the ~load** ganze Wagenladungen Sand; **~ stop** (Amer.) ▸**transport café**

truculence /ˈtrʌkjʊləns/, **truculency** /ˈtrʌkjʊlənsɪ/ *n., no pl.* Aufsässigkeit, *die*

truculent /ˈtrʌkjʊlənt/ *adj.* aufsässig

truculently /ˈtrʌkjʊləntlɪ/ *adv.* aufsässig

trudge /trʌdʒ/
A *v.i.* trotten; (through mud, snow, etc.) stapfen
B *v.t.* entlangtrotten; (through mud, snow, etc.) entlangstapfen
C *n.* [beschwerlicher] Fußmarsch

true /truː/
A *adj.*, **~r** /ˈtruːə(r)/, **~st** /ˈtruːɪst/ **1** (in accordance with fact) wahr; wahrheitsgetreu ‹*Bericht, Beschreibung*›; **is it ~ that …?** stimmt es, dass …?; **[only] too ~:** nur zu wahr; **that is too good to be ~:** das ist zu schön, um wahr zu sein; **sb. is too good to be ~:** jmd. ist einfach zu gut; **[that's] ~ [enough]** [das] stimmt; **…, it is ~:** …, das stimmt; **you never spoke a ~r word** da hast du wirklich recht; **he is so rude, it isn't ~** (coll.) er ist unglaublich unhöflich; **come ~** ‹*Traum, Wunsch:*› Wirklichkeit werden, wahr werden; ‹*Befürchtung, Prophezeihung:*› sich bewahrheiten **2** richtig ‹*Vorteil, Einschätzung*›; (rightly so called) eigentlich; **the frog is not a ~ reptile** der Frosch ist kein echtes Reptil **3** (not sham) wahr; echt, wahr ‹*Freund, Freundschaft, Christ*›; **that's not a ~ antique** das ist keine echte Antiquität **4** (accurately conforming) getreu ‹*Wiedergabe*›; **be ~ to sth.** einer Sache (*Dat.*) genau entsprechen; **~ to type** typisch; **~ to life** lebensecht **5** (loyal) treu; **remain ~ to sth.** einer Sache (*Dat.*) treu bleiben; **~ to one's word** *or* **promise** getreu seinem Versprechen **6** (in correct position) gerade ‹*Pfosten*› **7** (Geog.) **~ north** geographischer Norden. *See also* **colour A 5, 8; form A 7**
B *n.* **out of [the] ~:** schief ‹*Mauer, Pfosten, Räder*›
C *adv.* **1** (truthfully) aufrichtig ‹*lieben*›; **speak ~:** die Wahrheit sagen; **tell me ~:** sag mir die Wahrheit **2** (accurately) gerade; genau ‹*zielen*› **3** (without variation) ohne Veränderung
D *v.t.* **~ [up]** richten; (alter shape of) zurichten; (balance) auswuchten ‹*Rad*›

true: ~-blue **A** *adj.* in der Wolle gefärbt; **~-blue Tory** Erzkonservative, *der/die;* **B** *n.* Hundertfünfzigprozentige, *der/die* (abwertend); **~-born** *adj.* echt; rechtmäßig ‹*Erbe*›; **~-life** *adj.* aus dem Leben gegriffen ‹*Geschichte, Drama*›; **this is a ~-life story** diese Geschichte hat das Leben geschrieben; **~ love** *n.* Geliebte, *der/die;* Schatz, *der;* **~-love knot** *n.: komplizierter Schleifenknoten, der das feste Band der Liebe symbolisiert*

trueness /ˈtruːnɪs/ *n., no pl.* **1** (loyalty) Treue, *die* **2** (conformity) genaue Entsprechung; **~ to life** Lebensechtheit, *die* **3** (correctness) Passgenauigkeit, *die;* (of wheel) rundes Laufen

truffle /ˈtrʌfl/ *n.* Trüffel, *die od.* (*ugs.*) *der*
truism /ˈtru:ɪzm/ *n.* Binsenweisheit, *die*
truly /ˈtru:lɪ/ *adv.* 1 (genuinely) wirklich; **be ~ grateful** wirklich sehr *od.* aufrichtig dankbar sein; **he was first, ~ he was!** er war Erster, ganz bestimmt!; **~, I don't think he will make it** ehrlich gesagt, ich glaube nicht, dass er es schafft 2 (accurately) zutreffend, richtig ‹*darstellen, sagen*› 3 (faithfully) treu; *see also* **really**; **well² B 2**; **yours 3**
trump /trʌmp/
A *n.* (Cards) Trumpf, *der;* **play a ~** (lit. or fig.) einen Trumpf ausspielen; **turn up ~s** (Brit. coll.) (turn out better than expected) doch noch ein voller Erfolg werden; (do the right thing) die Situation retten; **as usual Bertha turned up ~s** wie immer hat Bertha wahre Wunder vollbracht; **hold all the ~s** (fig.) alle Trümpfe in der Hand haben *od.* halten
B *v.t.* übertrumpfen
C *v.i.* Trumpf spielen
Phrasal verb
• **~ up** *v.t.* konstruieren; **~ed up charge** falsche Beschuldigung
ˈtrump card *n.* (lit. or fig.) Trumpf, *der;* **play one's ~** (lit. or fig.) seinen [größten *od.* stärksten] Trumpf ausspielen
trumpery /ˈtrʌmpərɪ/ (dated)
A *n.* 1 (worthless articles) Krimskrams, *der* (ugs.) 2 (rubbish) Unsinn, *der;* **trumperies** Firlefanz, *der* 3 (worthless finery) Tand, *der* (veralt.)
B *adj.* (showy but worthless) billig
trumpet /ˈtrʌmpɪt/
A *n.* (Mus., Bot.) Trompete, *die;* **~ blast** Trompetenstoß, *der;* **the ~s of Jericho** die Posaunen von Jericho; *see also* **blow B 4**
B *v.t. & i.* trompeten
ˈtrumpet call *n.* Trompetensignal, *das;* (fig.) Aufruf, *der*
trumpeter /ˈtrʌmpɪtə(r)/ *n.* ▸ℹ **p. 1260** Trompeter, *der*/Trompeterin, *die*
truncate /trʌŋˈkeɪt/ *v.t.* 1 stutzen ‹*Baum, Spitze*›; **~d cone/pyramid** stumpfer Kegel/stumpfe Pyramide 2 (fig.) kürzen
truncheon /ˈtrʌntʃn/ *n.* Schlagstock, *der*
trundle /ˈtrʌndl/ *v.t. & i.* rollen
trunk /trʌŋk/ *n.* 1 (of elephant etc.) Rüssel, *der* 2 (large box) Schrankkoffer, *der* 3 (of tree) Stamm, *der* 4 (of human or animal body) Rumpf, *der* 5 (Amer.: of car) Kofferraum, *der* 6 *in pl.* (Brit.: underpants) Unterhose, *die;* **[swimming] ~s** Badehose, *die* 7 (of nerve, artery, etc.) Stamm, *der*
trunk: ~ call *n.* Ferngespräch, *das;* **~ line** *n.* (Railw.) Hauptstrecke, *die;* (Teleph.) Fernleitung, *die;* **~ road** *n.* (Brit.) Fernstraße, *die*
truss /trʌs/
A *n.* 1 (of roof etc.) Gebälk, *das;* (of bridge) Sprengwerk, *das;* **~ joint** Fachwerkknoten, *der;* **~ post** Hängesäule, *die* 2 (of flowers etc.) Büschel, *das;* (of tomatoes) Fruchttraube, *die* (Landw.) 3 (Med.: belt) Bruchband, *das* 4 (Brit.: of hay) Bündel, *das;* Ballen, *der*
B *v.t.* 1 (tie up before cooking) dressieren ‹*Truthahn, Huhn*› 2 **~ [up]** fesseln ‹*Gefangenen*›
trust /trʌst/
A *n.* 1 (firm belief) Vertrauen, *das;* **place** *or* **put one's ~ in sb./sth.** sein Vertrauen auf *od.* in jmdn./etw. setzen; **have [every] ~ in sb./sth.** [volles] Vertrauen zu jmdm./etw. haben; **our ~ is in God** wir vertrauen auf Gott; **I don't have any ~ in him** ich vertraue ihm nicht; ich habe kein Vertrauen zu ihm 2 (reliance) **take sth. on ~:** etw. einfach glauben 3 (Law) Treuhand[schaft], *die;* (property) Treugut, *das;* (organization managed by trustees) Treuhandgesellschaft, *die;* **[charitable] ~:** Stiftung, *die;* **hold in ~:** treuhänderisch verwalten 4 (body of trustees) Treuhänder *Pl.;* (of charitable ~) [Stiftungs]beirat, *der;* Kuratorium, *das* 5 (association of companies) Trust, *der* 6 (commercial credit) **on ~:** auf Kredit 7 (responsibility) **he failed in his ~:** er hat das in ihn gesetzte Vertrauen enttäuscht; **position of ~:** Vertrauensstellung, *die* 8 (obligation) Verpflichtung, *die;* **public ~:** Verpflichtung der Öffentlichkeit gegenüber. *See also* **brains trust**; **investment 1**; **unit trust**
B *v.t.* 1 (rely on) trauen (+ *Dat.*); vertrauen (+ *Dat.*) ‹*Person*›; **not ~ sb. an inch** jmdm. nicht über den Weg trauen; **you can ~ him to do his best** du kannst dich darauf verlassen, dass er sein Bestes tut; **a ~ed servant/friend** ein getreuer Diener/Freund (geh.); **he was widely ~ed by them** er genoss *od.* besaß das Vertrauen der meisten von ihnen; **he/what he says is not to be ~ed** er ist nicht vertrauenswürdig/auf das, was er sagt, kann man sich nicht verlassen; **~ sb. with sth.** jmdm. etw. anvertrauen; **~ 'you/'him!** *etc.* (coll. iron.) typisch!; **~ 'him to get it wrong!** er muss natürlich einen Fehler machen! 2 (hope) hoffen; **I ~ he is not hurt?** er ist doch hoffentlich nicht verletzt? 3 (entrust) anvertrauen (**to** *Dat.*)
C *v.i.* 1 **~ to** sich verlassen auf (+ *Akk.*) 2 (believe) **~ in sb./sth.** auf jmdn./etw. vertrauen
trust: ~buster *n.: jmd., der [auf der Grundlage der Antitrustgesetze] gegen Trusts vorgeht;* **~ company** *n.* Treuhandgesellschaft, *die;* **~ deed** *n.* Treuhandvertrag, *der*
trustee /trʌˈsti:/ *n.* 1 (person holding property in trust; also fig.) Treuhänder, *der*/Treuhänderin, *die;* **the Public T~** (Brit.) der staatliche Vermögensverwalter 2 (one appointed to manage institution) Verwalter, *der;* Kurator, *der;* **Board of T~s** Vorstand, *der;* Kuratorium, *das* 3 (country supervising territory) Treuhandmacht, *die*
trustee ˈsavings bank *n.* Treuhandbank, *die*
trusteeship /trʌˈsti:ʃɪp/ *n.* 1 (office) Treuhänderschaft, *die* 2 (supervision of trust territory) Treuhandschaft, *die;* Mandat, *das*
trustful /ˈtrʌstfl/ *adj.*, **trustfully** /ˈtrʌstfəlɪ/ *adv.* vertrauensvoll
ˈtrust fund *n.* Treuhandvermögen, *das*
trusting /ˈtrʌstɪŋ/ *adj.*, **trustingly** /ˈtrʌstɪŋlɪ/ *adv.* vertrauensvoll
trustworthiness /ˈtrʌstwɜ:ðɪnɪs/ *n., no pl.* Vertrauenswürdigkeit, *die*
trustworthy /ˈtrʌstwɜ:ðɪ/ *adj.* vertrauenswürdig
trusty /ˈtrʌstɪ/
A *adj.* (esp. joc.) [ge]treu (dichter); treu ‹*Hund, Pferd*›; (reliable) verlässlich ‹*Auto, Fahrrad*›; **~ steed** treues Ross
B *n.* Kalfaktor, *der*
truth /tru:θ/ *n., pl.* **~s** /tru:ðz, tru:θs/ 1 *no pl.* Wahrheit, *die;* **the ~ of that is open to question** es ist fraglich, ob das zutrifft; **there is some/not a word of** *or* **no ~ in that** es ist etwas Wahres/kein wahres Wort/nichts Wahres daran; **in ~** (literary), **of a ~** (arch.) wahrlich (geh.) 2 (what is true) Wahrheit, *die;* (principle) Grundsatz, *der;* **tell the [whole] ~:** die [ganze] Wahrheit sagen; **the ~ is that I forgot** um ehrlich zu sein, ich habe es vergessen; **to tell the ~, ~ to tell** ehrlich gesagt. *See also* **home truth**; **moment 1**; **out A 8**
ˈtruth drug *n.* Wahrheitsdroge, *die*
truthful /ˈtru:θfl/ *adj.* ehrlich; wahrheitsgetreu ‹*Darstellung, Schilderung*›; **be ~ about sth.** die Wahrheit über etw. (*Akk.*) sagen
truthfully /ˈtru:θfəlɪ/ *adv.* ehrlich
truthfulness /ˈtru:θflnɪs/ *n., no pl.* Wahrheitstreue, *die*
try /traɪ/
A *n.* 1 (attempt) Versuch, *der;* **have a ~ at sth./doing sth.** etw. versuchen/versuchen, etw. zu tun; **at least he had a good ~:** er hat sich (*Dat.*) wenigstens Mühe gegeben; **give sb./sth. a ~:** es mit jmdm. versuchen/etw. einmal ausprobieren; **I'll give him another ~** (ask him again for help, a favour, etc.) ich versuche es noch einmal bei ihm; (give him another chance) ich versuche es noch einmal mit ihm; (on telephone) ich versuche noch einmal, ihn zu erreichen; **give it a ~:** es versuchen
2 (Rugby) Versuch, *der;* **score two tries** zwei Versuche erzielen *od.* legen
3 (Amer. Footb.) Versuch, noch einen Punkt zu erzielen
B *v.t.* 1 (attempt, make effort) versuchen; **it's ~ing to rain** es tröpfelt ein wenig; **the sun is ~ing to come out** *or* **shine** es sieht so aus, als käme die Sonne bald heraus; **do ~ to be on time** bitte versuche, pünktlich zu sein; **it's no use ~ing to do sth.** es hat keinen Zweck zu versuchen, etw. zu tun; **I've given up ~ing to do that** ich versuche schon gar nicht mehr, das zu tun; **~ one's best** sein Bestes tun; **don't ~ anything!** keine Tricks!; **don't even ~ to excuse yourself** versuche erst gar nicht, dich zu entschuldigen
2 (test usefulness of) probieren; **if the stain is difficult to remove, ~ soap and water** wenn der Fleck schwer zu entfernen ist, versuche *od.* probiere es doch mal mit Wasser und Seife; **I've tried all the bookshops for this book** ich habe in allen Buchhandlungen versucht, dieses Buch zu bekommen; **you can always ~ the supermarket** du kannst es auf jeden Fall mal im Supermarkt versuchen; **if you can't find it, ~ the top shelf** wenn du es nicht finden kannst, schau mal auf dem obersten Regal nach; **~ one's hand at sth.** sich an etw. (*Dat.*) versuchen; **~ shaking it!** probier es mal mit Schütteln!; **I'll ~ anything once** ich probiere alles einmal aus; **You won't come, will you? T~ me!** Du kommst wohl nicht? Vielleicht doch!
3 (test) auf die Probe stellen ‹*Fähigkeit, Kraft, Mut, Geduld*›; **~ the rope** ausprobieren, ob das Seil auch hält; **~ the door/window [to see if it's locked]** versuchen, die Tür/das Fenster zu öffnen[, um zu sehen, ob sie/es verschlossen ist]; **~ sb. in Sales** (with a question) jmdn. in der Verkaufsabteilung fragen; (with a job) jmdn. zur Probe im Verkauf einsetzen; **be tried and found wanting** gewogen und zu leicht befunden werden; **these** *or* **such things are sent to ~ us** das sind die Prüfungen, die uns das Schicksal auferlegt
4 (Law.: take to trial) **~ a case** einen Fall verhandeln; **~ sb. [for sth.]** jmdn. [wegen einer Sache] vor Gericht stellen; jmdm. [wegen einer Sache] den Prozess machen; **he was tried for murder** er stand wegen Mordes vor Gericht; **he was tried before a jury** er wurde vor ein Schwurgericht gestellt. *See also* **fall A 9**; **size¹ A 1**
C *v.i.* es versuchen; **she wasn't even ~ing** sie hat sich (*Dat.*) überhaupt keine Mühe gegeben *od.* es gar nicht erst versucht; **it was not for want of ~ing** es lag nicht daran, dass er/sie *usw.* sich nicht bemüht hätte; **if at first you don't succeed, ~, and ~ again** wenn es dir nicht gleich gelingt, musst du es immer wieder versuchen; **you can't say I didn't ~:** du kannst nicht sagen, dass ich es nicht versucht hätte; **~ as he might** sosehr er sich auch bemühte; **~ and do sth.** (coll.) versuchen, etw. zu tun; **~ hard/harder** sich (*Dat.*) viel/mehr Mühe geben
Phrasal verbs
• **~ for** *v.t.* 1 (compete for) sich bemühen um ‹*Arbeitsstelle, Stipendium*›; kämpfen um ‹*Sieg im Sport*›; **~ for gold** es auf eine Goldmedaille abgesehen haben 2 (seek to reach) **~ for the summit** den Gipfel in Angriff nehmen; **he had been ~ing so hard for it** er hatte so sehr darum gekämpft
• **~ 'on** *v.t.* 1 anprobieren ‹*Kleidungsstück*› 2 (Brit. coll.) **~ it on** provozieren; **don't ~ anything/it on with me** lege dich nicht mit mir an; *see also* **try-on**
• **~ 'out** *v.t.* **~ sth./sb. out** etw. ausprobieren/jmdm. eine Chance geben; **let's ~ him out in Sales** setzen wir ihn doch zur Probe im Verkauf ein; *see also* **try-out**
trying /ˈtraɪɪŋ/ *adj.* 1 (testing) schwierig 2 (difficult to endure) anstrengend; **be ~ for sb./sth.** jmdm./einer Sache sehr zusetzen (ugs.)
try: ~-on *n.* (coll.) 1 (Brit. joke) Scherz, *der;* (lie) Lüge, *die;* **it's just a ~-on** (to discover whether sth. will be tolerated) er/sie probiert nur aus, wie weit er/sie gehen kann; 2 (of clothes) Anprobe, *die;* **~-out** *n.* Erprobung, *die;* **give sth. a ~-out** etw. ausprobieren; **have a ~-out** ‹*Maschine usw.*:› ausprobiert werden; **would you like [to have] a ~-out?** möchten Sie mal probieren?; (of vehicle) möchten Sie eine Probefahrt machen?; **~sail** /ˈtraɪsl/ *n.* (Naut.) Gaffelsegel, *das;* **~ square** *n.* Anschlagwinkel, *der*
tryst /trɪst/ *n.* (arch./literary) Stelldichein, *das* (veralt.); **keep/break ~:** zu einem Stelldichein

gehen/nicht gehen; **make a ~:** sich zu einem Stelldichein verabreden

tsar /zɑː(r)/ *n.* ▸ **p. 1634** (Hist.) Zar, *der*

tsarina /zɑːˈriːnə/ *n.* ▸ **p. 1634** (Hist.) (empress) Zarin, *die;* (tsar's wife) Zariza, *die*

tsarism /ˈzɑːrɪzm/ *n.* (Hist.) Zarentum, *das;* Zarismus, *der*

tsarist /ˈzɑːrɪst/ (Hist.)
A *adj.* zaristisch
B *n.* Zarist, *der*/Zaristin, *die*

tsetse [fly] /ˈtsetsɪ (flaɪ)/ *n.* Tsetsefliege, *die*

T-shirt *n.* T-Shirt, *das*

tsp., *pl.* **~s** *abbr.* **= teaspoon[s]** Teel.

T-square ▸ **square 10**

tsunami /tsuːˈnɑːmɪ/ *n.* Tsunami, *der*

TT *abbr.* [1] **= teetotal** [2] **= Tourist Trophy** *Motorradrennen auf der Insel Man*

Tu. *abbr.* ▸ **p. 1048 = Tuesday** Di.

TU *abbr.* **= Trade Union**

tub /tʌb/ *n.* [1] Kübel, *der* [2] (for ice cream etc.) Becher, *der* [3] (Brit. coll.: bath) Bad, *das* [4] (derog./joc.: boat) Kahn, *der* (ugs.)

tuba /ˈtjuːbə/ *n.* (Mus.) Tuba, *die*

tubbiness /ˈtʌbɪnɪs/ *n.* Rundlichkeit, *die;* (of child also) Pummeligkeit, *die* (ugs.)

tubby /ˈtʌbɪ/ *adj.* rundlich; pummelig (ugs.), rundlich ‹*Kind*›

tube /tjuːb/ *n.* [1] (for conveying liquids etc.) Rohr, *das;* **be down the ~[s]** (coll.) am Ende sein (ugs.); **he was down the ~[s] to the tune of £270,000** (coll.) er saß mit Schulden in Höhe von 270 000 Pfund in der Tinte (ugs.); **go down the ~[s]** (coll.) den Bach runter gehen (ugs.) [2] (small cylinder) Tube, *die;* (for sweets, tablets) Röhrchen, *das* [3] (Anat., Zool.) Röhre, *die* [4] (cathode-ray ~) Röhre, *die;* (coll.: television) **watch the ~:** vor der Röhre sitzen (ugs.); **be on the ~:** im Fernsehen sein [5] (Amer.: thermionic valve) Röhre, *die* [6] (Brit. coll.: underground railway) U-Bahn, *die;* **go by ~:** mit der U-Bahn fahren [7] ▸ **inner tube**

tubeless /ˈtjuːblɪs/ *adj.* schlauchlos ‹*Reifen*›

tuber /ˈtjuːbə(r)/ *n.* (Bot.) Knolle, *die*

tubercle /ˈtjuːbəkl/ *n.* (Med.) Tuberkel, *der*

tubercular /tjuːˈbɜːkjʊlə(r)/ *adj.* (Med.) tuberkulös

tuberculin /tjuːˈbɜːkjʊlɪn/ *n.* Tuberkulin, *das*

tuberculin-ˈtested *adj.* tuberkulingetestet

tuberculosis /tjuːbɜːkjʊˈləʊsɪs/ *n., no pl.* ▸ **p. 1231** (Med.) Tuberkulose, *die;* **pulmonary ~:** Lungentuberkulose, *die*

tuberose /ˈtjuːbərəʊz/ *n.* (Bot.) Tuberose, *die*

tube: ~ station *n.* (Brit. coll.) U-Bahnhof, *der;* **~ train** *n.* (Brit. coll.) U-Bahn-Zug, *der*

tubful /ˈtʌbfʊl/ *n.* Kübel [voll], *der;* **a ~ of water** ein Kübel Wasser

tubing /ˈtjuːbɪŋ/ *n.* Rohre *Pl.*

ˈtub-thumper *n.* Demagoge, *der*

tubular /ˈtjuːbjʊlə(r)/ *adj.* [1] (tube-shaped) röhrenförmig [2] (made of ~ pieces) Stahlrohr‹*möbel, -stuhl*›

tubular ˈbells *n. pl.* Glockenspiel, *das*

TUC *abbr.* (Brit.) **= Trades Union Congress**

tuck /tʌk/
A *v.t.* [1] stecken; **he ~ed his legs under him** er schlug die Beine unter [2] (put ~s in) Biesen nähen in (+ *Akk.*)
B *n.* [1] (in fabric) (for decoration) Biese, *die;* (to shorten or tighten) Abnäher, *der* [2] *no pl., no indef. art.* (Brit. Sch. dated coll.: food) Erfrischungen [und Süßigkeiten]

Phrasal verbs

- **~ aˈway** *v.t.* [1] wegstecken; **the house is ~ed away behind the trees** das Haus liegt versteckt hinter den Bäumen [2] (coll.: eat) verputzen (ugs.); **she can certainly ~ it away** sie kann ganz schön was verputzen (ugs.)
- **~ ˈin**
A *v.t.* hineinstecken; **~ in the blankets** die Decken an den Seiten feststecken; **~ your shirt in!** steck dein Hemd in die Hose!; (in bed) **~ sb. in** jmdn. zudecken
B *v.i.* (coll.) zulangen (ugs.); *see also* **tuck-in**
- **~ into** *v.i.* (coll.: eat) **~ into sth.** sich (*Dat.*) etw. schmecken lassen
- **~ ˈup** *v.t.* [1] hochkrempeln ‹*Ärmel, Hose*›; hochnehmen ‹*Rock*› [2] (cover snugly) zudecken; **be ~ed up [in bed]** zugedeckt [im Bett] sein

ˈtuck box *n.* (Brit. Sch. dated coll.) Kiste [mit Süßigkeiten *usw.*]

tucker[1] /ˈtʌkə(r)/ *n.* (Austral. coll.: food) Futter, *das* (ugs.); **some ~:** etwas zu futtern (ugs.)

tucker[2] *v.t.* (Amer.) **~ [out]** (coll.) fix und fertig machen (ugs.); **be ~ed [out]** fix und fertig *od.* total groggy sein (ugs.)

tuck: ~-in *n.* (Brit. coll.) [reichliches] Essen; **they had a really good ~-in** sie hatten ordentlich was zu futtern (ugs.); **~ shop** *n.* (Brit. Sch. dated coll.) *Laden für Erfrischungen, Süßigkeiten usw. in einer Schule*

Tudor /ˈtjuːdə(r)/ (Brit. Hist.)
A *n.* Tudor, *der/die*
B *attrib. adj.* Tudor-

Tudor: ~ ˈrose *n.* Tudorrose, *die;* **~ style** *n.* Tudorstil, *der*

Tue., Tues. *abbrs.* ▸ **p. 1048 = Tuesday** Di.

Tuesday /ˈtjuːzdeɪ, ˈtjuːzdɪ/ ▸ **p. 1048**
A *n.* Dienstag, *der*
B *adv.* (coll.) **she comes ~s** sie kommt dienstags. *see also* **Friday**

tufa /ˈtjuːfə/ *n.* (Geol.) Sinter, *der*

tuff /tʌf/ *n.* (Geol.) Tuff, *der*

tuft /tʌft/ *n.* Büschel, *das;* **~ of grass/hair** Gras-/Haarbüschel, *das*

tufted /ˈtʌftɪd/ *adj.* [1] (having tufts) büschelig; **~ carpet** Tuftingteppich, *der* [2] (with tuft of feathers on head) Hauben-; **~ duck** Reiherente, *die;* **~ puffin** Schopfhund, *der*

tug /tʌg/
A *n.* [1] Ruck, *der;* **he felt a ~ on the fishingline** er spürte, wie etwas an der Angel zog; **he gave the rope a ~:** er zerrte am Seil; **~ of love [battle]** (coll.) *Streit bei der Ehescheidung, wem das Kind zugesprochen wird;* **~ of war** (lit. or fig.) Tauziehen, *das* [2] **~ [boat]** Schlepper, *der* [3] (fig.: emotional pain) **it was a ~:** es tat weh (ugs.); **she felt a big ~ at parting** der Abschied fiel ihr sehr schwer
B *v.t.,* **-gg-** ziehen; schleppen ‹*Boot*›; **be ~ged this way and that** (fig.) hin- und hergerissen sein
C *v.i.,* **-gg-** zerren (**at** an + *Dat.*); **~ at sb.'s heartstrings** (fig.) jmdm. das Herz zerreißen

tuition /tjuːˈɪʃn/ *n.* Unterricht, *der;* **extra ~:** Nachhilfeunterricht, *der;* **~ fees** (Sch.) Schulgeld, *das;* (Univ.) Studiengebühren *Pl.;* (for private ~) Unterrichtshonorar, *das*

tulip /ˈtjuːlɪp/ *n.* Tulpe, *die*

ˈtulip tree *n.* Tulpenbaum, *der*

tulle /tjuːl/ *n.* (Textiles) Tüll, *der*

tum /tʌm/ *n.* (joc.) Bauch, *der*

tumble /ˈtʌmbl/
A *v.i.* [1] (fall suddenly) stürzen; fallen; **~ off sth.** von etw. fallen [2] (move in headlong fashion) stürzen; **~ into/out of sth.** in/aus etw. eilen; **~ into bed** ins Bett fallen [3] ‹*Preise usw.:*› fallen; (sharply) stürzen
B *v.t.* [1] (fling headlong) schleudern [2] (rumple) durcheinander bringen, zerzausen ‹*Haar*›
C *n.* Sturz, *der;* **she's taken [a bit of] a ~:** sie ist hingefallen

Phrasal verbs

- **~ on** *v.t.* (chance on) stolpern über (+ *Akk.*) (ugs.)
- **~ ˈover** *v.i.* hinfallen; ‹*Kartenhaus:*› umfallen
- **~ to** *v.t.* (Brit. coll.) durchschauen

tumble: ~bug *n.* Kotkäfer, *der;* **~down** *adj.* verfallen; **~-drier** *n.* Wäschetrockner, *der;* **~-dry** *v.t.* im Automaten trocknen

tumbler /ˈtʌmblə(r)/ *n.* [1] (glass) (short) Whiskyglas, *das;* (long) Wasserglas, *das* [2] (in lock) Zuhaltung, *die* [3] ▸ **tumble-drier** [4] (acrobat) Bodenakrobat, *der*/-akrobatin, *die* [5] (pigeon) Tümmler, *der*

tumblerful /ˈtʌmbləfʊl/ *n.* Glas [voll], *das;* **a ~ of water** ein Glas Wasser

ˈtumbler switch *n.* Kippschalter, *der*

ˈtumbleweed *n.* (Amer.) Steppenläufer, *der*

tumbrel /ˈtʌmbrl/, **tumbril** /ˈtʌmbrɪl/ *n.* (Hist.) Karren, *der*

tumescence /tjuːˈmesəns/ *n.* Schwellung, *die*

tumescent /tjuːˈmesənt/ *adj.* anschwellend; **make ~:** anschwellen lassen

tummy /ˈtʌmɪ/ *n.* (child lang./coll.) Bäuchlein, *das;* **I've got an upset ~:** ich habe mir den Magen verdorben

tummy: ~ ache *n.* (child lang./coll.) Bauchweh, *das;* **~ button** *n.* (child lang./coll.) Bauchnabel, *der;* **~ upset** *n.* (child lang./coll.) Magenverstimmung, *die*

tumour (*Brit.; Amer.:* **tumor**) /ˈtjuːmə(r)/ *n.* Tumor, *der*

tumult /ˈtjuːmʌlt/ *n.* [1] (commotion, uproar) Tumult, *der;* **be in ~:** sich in Aufruhr befinden [2] (confused state of mind) Verwirrung, *die;* **his mind was in a ~:** er war innerlich in Aufruhr

tumultuous /tjuːˈmʌltjʊəs/ *adj.* [1] stürmisch ‹*Empfang, Beifall*› [2] wild ‹*Fluss, Sturm, Leidenschaft*›

tumulus /ˈtjuːmjʊləs/ *n., pl.* **tumuli** /ˈtjuːmjʊlaɪ/ Tumulus, *der*

tun /tʌn/ *n.* Fass, *das*

tuna /ˈtjuːnə/ *n., pl. same or* **~s** [1] (fish) Thunfisch, *der* [2] (as food) **~[fish]** Thunfisch, *der; attrib.* Thunfisch-

tundra /ˈtʌndrə/ *n.* (Geog.) Tundra, *die*

tune /tjuːn/
A *n.* [1] (melody) Melodie, *die;* **change one's ~, sing another** *or* **a different ~** (fig.) (behave differently) sein Verhalten ändern; (assume different tone) einen anderen Ton anschlagen; **call the ~:** den Ton angeben [2] (correct pitch) **sing in/out of ~:** richtig/falsch singen; **be in/out of ~** ‹*Instrument:*› richtig gestimmt/verstimmt sein [3] (fig.: agreement) **be in/out of ~ with sth.** mit etw. in Einklang/nicht in Einklang stehen; **he doesn't feel in ~ with their attitudes/ideas** ihre Einstellungen/Vorstellungen sind ihm fremd [4] (amount) **to the ~ of [£50,000]** sage und schreibe [50 000 Pfund]
B *v.t.* [1] (Mus.: put in ~) stimmen [2] (Radio, Telev.) einstellen (**to** auf + *Akk.*); **stay ~d!** bleiben Sie auf dieser Welle! [3] einstellen ‹*Motor, Vergaser*›; (for more power) frisieren ‹*Motor, Auto*›

Phrasal verbs

- **~ ˈin** *v.i.* (Radio, Telev.) **~ in to a station** einen Sender einstellen; **~ in at five o'clock to hear the details** schalten Sie [Ihr Radio/Ihren Fernseher] um fünf Uhr ein, wenn Sie die Einzelheiten hören wollen; **~ in to** (fig.) sich einstellen auf (+ *Akk.*)
- **~ ˈup**
A *v.i.* [die Instrumente] stimmen
B *v.t.* einstellen

tuneful /ˈtjuːnfl/ *adj.,* **tunefully** /ˈtjuːnfəlɪ/ *adv.* melodisch

tunefulness /ˈtjuːnflnɪs/ *n., no pl.* Melodik, *die*

tuneless /ˈtjuːnlɪs/ *adj.,* **tunelessly** /ˈtjuːnlɪslɪ/ *adv.* unmelodisch

tunelessness /ˈtjuːnlɪsnɪs/ *n., no pl.* Mangel an Melodik

tuner /ˈtjuːnə(r)/ *n.* [1] ▸ **p. 1260** (Mus.) Stimmer, *der*/Stimmerin, *die* [2] (knob etc.) Einstellknopf, *der;* Tuner, *der* (Technik) [3] (radio) Tuner, *der*

tungsten /ˈtʌŋstən/ *n.* Wolfram, *das*

tunic /ˈtjuːnɪk/ *n.* [1] (of soldier, policeman) Uniformjacke, *die;* (of schoolgirl) Kittel, *der* [2] (Fashion) Kasack, *der* [3] (in ancient Greece) Chiton, *der;* (in ancient Rome) Tunika, *die*

tuning /ˈtjuːnɪŋ/ *n.* [1] (Mus.) Stimmen, *das* [2] (Radio) Einstellen, *das* [3] (Motor Veh.) Einstellen, *das;* (to increase power) Frisieren, *das;* Tuning, *das;* **the engine needs ~:** der Motor muss eingestellt werden

tuning: ~ fork *n.* (Mus.) Stimmgabel, *die;* **~ knob** *n.* Senderknopf, *der;* **~ peg, ~ pin** *ns.* (Mus.) Wirbel, *der*

Tunis /ˈtjuːnɪs/ *pr. n.* ▸ **p. 1643** Tunis (*das*)

Tunisia /tjuːˈnɪzɪə/ *pr. n.* Tunesien (*das*)

Tunisian /tjuːˈnɪzɪən/ ▸ **p. 1345**
A *adj.* tunesisch; **sb. is ~:** jmd. ist Tunesier/Tunesierin

B *n.* Tunesier, *der*/Tunesierin, *die*

tunnel /ˈtʌnl/

A *n.* 1) Tunnel, *der;* (dug by animal) Gang, *der;* **[the] light at the end of the ~** (fig.) [das] Licht am Ende des Tunnels 2) (Motor Veh.) **[transmission] ~:** Kardantunnel, *der* 3) **wind ~:** Windkanal, *der*

B *v.i.,* (Brit.) **-ll-:** einen Tunnel graben; **~ under sth.** etw. untertunneln; **~ through sth.** durch etw. (*Akk.*) einen Tunnel graben

C *v.t.,* (Brit.) **-ll-:** **~ one's way out** sich (*Dat.*) einen Weg nach draußen graben

ˈtunnel vision *n.* Röhrengesichtsfeld, *das* (Med.); (fig.) enges Blickfeld

tunny /ˈtʌnɪ/ *n.* (Zool.) Thunfisch, *der*

tup /tʌp/ *n.* (Brit.) Widder, *der*

tuppence /ˈtʌpəns/ ▸**twopence**

tuppenny /ˈtʌpənɪ/ ▸**twopenny**

turban /ˈtɜːbən/ *n.* Turban, *der*

turbaned /ˈtɜːbənd/ *adj.* mit einem Turban [auf dem Kopf] *nachgestellt*

turbid /ˈtɜːbɪd/ *adj.* 1) (muddy) trüb[e]; dicht ‹*Nebel, Rauchwolke*› 2) (fig.: confused) wirr

turbidity /tɜːˈbɪdɪtɪ/ *n., no pl.* 1) (muddiness) Trübheit, *die* 2) (fig.: confusion) Verworrenheit, *die*

turbine /ˈtɜːbaɪn/ *n.* Turbine, *die*

turbo /ˈtɜːbəʊ/ *n.* Turbo, *der*

turbo: ~charged *adj.* mit Turbolader *nachgestellt;* **~charger** *n.* Turbolader, *der;* **~fan** /ˈtɜːbəʊfæn/ *n.* 1) (engine) Turbofantriebwerk, *das;* 2) (aircraft) turbofangetriebenes Flugzeug; Flugzeug mit Turbofanantrieb; **~jet** *n.* Turbojet, *der;* **~jet engine** *n.* Turboluftstrahltriebwerk, *das;* **~prop** *n.* Turbo-Prop-Flugzeug, *das; attrib.* **~prop engine** Turbo-Prop-Triebwerk, *das*

turbot /ˈtɜːbət/ *n.* (Zool.) Steinbutt, *der*

turbulence /ˈtɜːbjʊləns/ *n., no pl.* 1) (agitation) Aufgewühltheit, *die;* (fig.) Aufruhr, *der;* (unruliness) Unruhe, *die* 2) (Phys.) Turbulenz, *die*

turbulent /ˈtɜːbjʊlənt/ *adj.* 1) aufgewühlt ‹*Gedanken, Wellen, Leidenschaften*›; turbulent ‹*Herrschaft, Kindheit*›; ungestüm ‹*Menge*›; aufrührerisch ‹*Stadt, Mob*› 2) (Phys.) turbulent

turd /tɜːd/ *n.* (coarse) 1) (lump of excrement) Scheißhaufen, *der* (derb) 2) (contemptible person) Scheißkerl, *der* (derb)

tureen /tjʊəˈriːn/ *n.* Terrine, *die*

turf /tɜːf/

A *n., pl.* **~s** *or* **turves** /tɜːvz/ 1) *no pl.* (covering of grass etc.) Rasen, *der* 2) (cut patch of grass) [abgestochenes] Rasenstück; Sode, *die* (bes. nordd.); **lay ~:** Fertigrasen verlegen 3) **the ~** (racecourse) der Turf (Pferdesport); die Rennbahn; (horseracing) der Pferderennsport

B *v.t.* mit Fertigrasen bedecken

Phrasal verbs

- **~ ˈout** *v.t.* (coll.) rausschmeißen (ugs.); **~ sb. out of sth.** jmdn. aus etw. [raus]schmeißen
- **~ ˈover** *v.t.* mit Rasenstücken bedecken

turf: ~ accountant *n.* ▸❶ p. 1260 Buchmacher, *der;* **~ war** *n.* Revierkampf, *der*

turgid /ˈtɜːdʒɪd/ *adj.* 1) (inflated) [an]geschwollen 2) (fig.) geschwollen; schwülstig (abwertend)

turgidly /ˈtɜːdʒɪdlɪ/ *adv.* geschwollen (abwertend)

Turk /tɜːk/ *n.* ▸❶ p. 1345 Türke, *der*/Türkin, *die*

turkey *n.* 1) (fowl) Truthahn, *der*/Truthenne, *die;* (esp. as food) Puter, *der*/Pute, *die* 2) (coll. derog.: stupid person) Schwachkopf, *der* (ugs. abwertend) 3) (Amer. coll.: flop) Reinfall, *der* 4) **talk ~** (Amer. coll.) Tacheles reden (ugs.)

Turkey /ˈtɜːkɪ/ *pr. n.* die Türkei

turkey: ~ buzzard *n.* Truthahngeier, *der;* **~cock** *n.* Truthahn, *der;* (fig.) Angeber, *der* (abwertend); **~ vulture** ▸**~ buzzard**

Turkish /ˈtɜːkɪʃ/ ▸❶ p. 1277, ▸❶ p. 1345

A *adj.* türkisch; **sb. is ~:** jmd. ist Türke/Türkin; *see also* **English A**

B *n.* Türkisch, *das; see also* **English B 1**

Turkish: ~ ˈbath *n.* türkisches Bad; **~ delight** *n.* mit Puderzucker bestreutes, gelatinehaltiges Konfekt; Rachatlukum, *das;* Lokum, *das;* **~ ˈtowel** *n.* Frotteehandtuch, *das*

Turk: ~'s cap *n.* (Bot.) Türkenbundlilie, *die;* **~'s ˈhead** *n.* (knot) türkischer Bund

turmeric /ˈtɜːmərɪk/ *n.* Gelbwurzel, *die;* (spice) Kurkuma, *die*

turmoil /ˈtɜːmɔɪl/ *n.* Aufruhr, *der;* [wildes] Durcheinander; **everything/her mind was in [a] ~:** es herrschte ein wildes Durcheinander/sie war völlig durcheinander

turn /tɜːn/

A *n.* 1) **it is sb.'s ~ to do sth.** jmd. ist an der Reihe, etw. zu tun; **it's your ~ [next]** du bist als Nächster/Nächste dran (ugs.) *od.* an der Reihe; **wait one's ~:** warten, bis man an der Reihe ist; **your ~ will come** du kommst auch [noch] an die Reihe; **by ~s** abwechselnd; **each of us in ~ had to give his name** wir mussten nacheinander *od.* der Reihe nach unsere Namen nennen; **he gave it to her, and she in ~ passed it on to me** er gab es ihr, und sie wiederum reichte es an mich weiter; **in one's ~:** wiederum; **out of ~** (before or after one's ~) außer der Reihe; (fig.) an der falschen Stelle ‹*lachen*›; **she tried to throw the dice out of ~:** sie wollte würfeln, obwohl sie nicht an der Reihe war; **excuse me if I'm talking out of ~** (fig.) entschuldige, wenn ich etwas Unpassendes sage; **your remark was out of ~** (fig.) Ihre Bemerkung war fehl am Platz; **take a ~ at the wheel** für eine Weile das Steuer übernehmen; **take [it in] ~s** sich abwechseln; **take ~s at doing sth., take it in ~s to do sth.** etw. abwechselnd tun; **she was unhappy and cheerful, in ~s** sie war abwechselnd unglücklich und fröhlich; *see also* **about A 6, 7; serve A 3**

2) (rotary motion) Drehung, *die;* **give the handle a ~:** den Griff [herum]drehen; (fig.) **have/show a good ~ of speed** schnell sein; **put on a ~ of speed** einen Zahn zulegen (ugs.); **[done] to a ~:** genau richtig [zubereitet]

3) ▸❶ p. 1699 (change of direction) Wende, *die;* **take a ~ to the right/left, do** *or* **make** *or* **take a right/left ~:** nach rechts/links abbiegen; **'no left/right ~'** „links/rechts abbiegen verboten"; **make a ~ to port/starboard** nach Backbord/Steuerbord abdrehen; **the ~ of the year/century** die Jahres-/Jahrhundertwende; **be on the ~** (be about to change) sich [zum Besseren/Schlechteren] wenden; (be about to go sour) ‹*Milch usw.:*› einen Stich haben (ugs.); **a ~ of fortune** eine Schicksalswende; **take a favourable ~** (fig.) sich zum Guten wenden; **take a ~ for the better/worse** ▸**take A 11**

4) (deflection) Biegung, *die*

5) (bend) Kurve, *die;* (corner) Ecke, *die;* **at every ~** (fig.) (constantly) ständig; (wherever one goes) überall

6) (short performance on stage etc.) Nummer, *die;* **do one's ~:** auftreten

7) (change of tide) **~ of the tide** Gezeitenwechsel, *der;* **the tide was on the ~:** die Flut/Ebbe setzte gerade ein; **there will be a ~ of the tide** (fig.) das Blatt wird sich wenden

8) (character) **be of a mechanical/humorous/speculative ~:** technisch begabt sein/von humorvollem Schlag sein/einen Hang zum Spekulativen haben; **a child with a more enquiring ~ of mind than his brother** ein Kind, das eher Fragen stellt als sein Bruder; **those of a democratic ~ of mind** die demokratisch Eingestellten

9) (literary: formation) Rundung, *die;* **the graceful ~ of her ankle** ihr wohlgeformter Knöchel

10) (form of expression) **an elegant ~ of speech/phrase** eine elegante Ausdrucksweise

11) (service) **do sb. a good/bad ~:** jmdm. einen guten/schlechten Dienst erweisen; **do good ~s** Gutes tun; **one good ~ deserves another** (prov.) hilfst du mir, so helf ich dir

12) (each round in coil of rope etc.) Umwick[e]lung, *die*

13) (coll.: fright) **give sb. quite a ~:** jmdm. einen gehörigen Schrecken einjagen (ugs.)

14) (coll.: spell of illness etc.) **have a nasty ~:** einen schlimmen Anfall haben; **I just had a little ~:** ich hatte einen kleinen Schwächeanfall

15) (short walk) **take a ~:** eine Runde drehen *od.* machen

16) (short trip) Runde, *die;* **go out for a ~ on one's bicycle/in the car** eine Runde mit dem Fahrrad/Auto drehen

17) (Mus.) Doppelschlag, *der*

18) (Brit. St. Exch.: jobber's profit margin) Gewinnspanne, *die. see also* **about-turn; three-point**

B *v.t.* 1) (make revolve) drehen; **~ the tap** am Wasserhahn drehen; **~ the key in the lock** den Schlüssel im Schloss herumdrehen; **he ~ed the wheel sharply [to the right]** er riss das Steuer scharf [nach rechts] herum

2) (reverse) umdrehen; wenden ‹*Pfannkuchen, Matratze, Auto, Heu, Teppich*›; umgraben ‹*Erde*›; umlegen ‹*Kragen*›; **~ sth. upside-down** *or* **on its head** (lit. or fig.) etw. auf den Kopf stellen; **~ sth. back to front** die Vorderseite einer Sache nach hinten drehen; **~ the page** umblättern; **~ sth. inside out** etw. nach außen stülpen *od.* drehen

3) (give new direction to) drehen, wenden ‹*Kopf*›; **she could still ~ heads** die Leute drehten sich immer noch nach ihr um; **~ a hose/gun on sb./sth.** einen Schlauch/ein Gewehr auf jmdn./etw. richten; **~ one's chair to face the window** seinen Stuhl zum Fenster drehen; **~ one's attention/mind to sth.** sich/seine Gedanken einer Sache (*Dat.*) zuwenden; **~ one's thoughts to a subject** sich [in Gedanken] mit einem Thema beschäftigen; **~ a car into a road** [mit einem Auto] in eine Straße einbiegen; **~ the course of history** dem Gang der Geschichte eine Wende geben; **~ one's eyes on sb.** jmdm. seine Augen zuwenden; **he ~ed his steps homeward** er lenkte seine Schritte heimwärts; **~ the tide [of sth.]** [bei etw.] den Ausschlag geben; **this incident ~ed the tide of opinion in her favour** dieser Vorfall führte einen Meinungsumschwung zu ihren Gunsten herbei; **~ sb. from his purpose** jmdn. von seinem Vorhaben abbringen

4) (send) **~ sb. loose on sb./sth.** jmdn. auf jmdn./etw. loslassen; **~ sb. from one's door/off one's land** jmdn. von seiner Tür/von seinem Land verjagen; **~ a dog on sb.** einen Hund auf jmdn. hetzen

5) (put) leeren ‹*Inhalt eines Koffers, einer Büchse*›; stürzen ‹*Pudding, Kuchen usw.*› (**on to** auf + *Akk.*)

6) (cause to become) verwandeln (**into** in + *Akk.*); **the cigarette smoke has ~ed the walls yellow** der Zigarettenrauch hat die Wände vergilben lassen; **~ the lights low** das Licht dämpfen; **~ a play/book into a film** ein Theaterstück/Buch verfilmen; **~ water into electricity/a church into a theatre** Wasser in Elektrizität/eine Kirche in ein Theater umwandeln; **the thought ~ed him pale** der Gedanke ließ ihn erbleichen (geh.)

7) (make sour) sauer werden lassen ‹*Milch*›

8) (translate) übertragen (**in** in + *Akk.*)

9) **~ sb.'s stomach** jmdm. den Magen umdrehen

10) (make conceited) **~ sb.'s head** jmdm. zu Kopf steigen; **~ sb.'s brain** jmds. Sinne *od.* Geist verwirren (geh.)

11) (shape in lathe) drechseln ‹*Holz*›; drehen ‹*Metall, Ton*›

12) drehen ‹*Pirouette*›; schlagen ‹*Rad, Purzelbaum*›

13) ▸❶ p. 894 (reach the age of) **~ 40** 40 [Jahre alt] werden; **she has not ~ed 30 yet** sie ist noch keine 30 [Jahre alt]

14) ▸❶ p. 1001 **it's just ~ed 12 o'clock/quarter past 4** es ist gerade 12 Uhr/viertel nach vier vorbei; **it's not yet ~ed 4 o'clock** es ist noch nicht ganz 4 Uhr

15) (gain) **~ a penny/profit** einen Gewinn machen; **~ a quick penny** einen schnellen Euro machen (ugs.)

16) wenden ‹*Kragen, Jacke usw.*›

17) (resist and divert) abprallen lassen; **the bullet was ~ed by the door** die Kugel prallte an der Tür ab

18) (go round) umrunden ‹*Kap, Landzunge*›; **~ the flank of an army** einer Streitmacht die Flanke aufrollen

19) (give elegant form to) **he knows how to ~ a**

phrase/a compliment er kann gut formulieren/er versteht es, Komplimente zu machen; ~ **verses** Verse dichten *od.* schmieden. *See also* **account C 8; back A 1; coat A 1; corner A 1; deaf A 2; evidence A 2; hair 1; hand A 1; honest 5; table A 1; tail A 3; turtle 3**

C *v.i.* **1** (revolve) sich drehen; ‹*Wasserhahn, Schlüssel:*› sich drehen lassen; **the earth ~s on its axis** die Erde dreht sich um ihre Achse; **he couldn't get the key to ~:** er konnte den Schlüssel nicht drehen

2 (reverse direction) ‹*Person:*› sich herumdrehen; ‹*Auto:*› wenden; **the car ~ed upside down** das Auto überschlug sich; ~ **back to front** sich von hinten nach vorne drehen

3 ▸ⓘ **p. 1699** (take new direction) sich wenden; (~ round) sich umdrehen; **heads ~ed when she ...:** die Leute sahen *od.* drehten sich nach ihr um, als sie ...; **his thoughts/attention ~ed to her** er wandte ihr seine Gedanken/Aufmerksamkeit zu; **left/right ~!** (Mil.) links/rechts um!; **he ~ed to the man standing next to him** er wandte sich dem Mann zu, der neben ihm stand; ~ **into a road/away from the river** in eine Straße einbiegen/vom Fluss abbiegen; ~ **to the left** nach links abbiegen/‹*Schiff, Flugzeug:*› abdrehen; ~ **up/down a street** in eine Straße einbiegen; ~ **towards home** den Heimweg einschlagen; **profits are ~ing upward** die Gewinne steigen; **everywhere the eye ~s ...:** wohin sich das Auge wendet ...; **when the tide ~s** beim Gezeitenwechsel; (fig.) wenn sich das Blatt wendet; **not know where** *or* **which way to ~** (fig.) keinen Ausweg [mehr] wissen; **my luck has ~ed** (fig.) mein Glück hat sich gewendet

4 (become) werden; ~ **traitor/statesman/Muslim** zum Verräter/zum Staatsmann/Moslem werden; ~ **[in]to sth.** zu etw. werden; (be transformed) sich in etw. (*Akk.*) verwandeln; **her face ~ed green** sie wurde [ganz] grün im Gesicht

5 (change colour) ‹*Laub:*› sich [ver]färben

6 (become sour) ‹*Milch:*› sauer werden

7 **my stomach ~s** mir dreht sich der Magen um (ugs.)

8 (become giddy) **sb.'s head is ~ing** jmdm. dreht sich alles [im Kopf]. *See also* **grave[1]; heel[1] A 2; toss B 1; worm A 1**

(Phrasal verbs)

• ~ **a'bout**

A *v.i.* sich umdrehen; ‹*Kompanie:*› kehrtmachen; (fig.) eine Kehrtwendung machen

B *v.t.* wenden ‹*Auto, Boot usw.*›. *See also* **turnabout**

• ~ **against** *v.t.* **1** ~ **against sb.** sich gegen jmdn. wenden; ~ **sb. against sb.** jmdn. gegen jmdn. aufbringen **2** **they ~ed his own arguments against him** sie verwendeten seine eigenen Argumente gegen ihn

• ~ **a'round** ▸ ~ **round**

• ~ **a'way**

A *v.i.* sich abwenden; ~ **away from sth.** (fig.) sich von etw. abwenden

B *v.t.* **1** (avert) abwenden **2** (send away) wegschicken; (refuse admittance also) abweisen

• ~ **'back**

A *v.i.* **1** (retreat, lit. or fig.) umkehren; kehrtmachen (ugs.); **there can be no ~ing back** es gibt kein Zurück *od.* keinen Weg zurück **2** (in book etc.) zurückgehen

B *v.t.* **1** (cause to retreat) zurückweisen; zurückschlagen ‹*Feind*› **2** (fold back) zurückschlagen ‹*Bettdecke, Teppich*›; herunterschlagen ‹*Kragen*›; **don't ~ back the corner of the page** bitte mach keine Eselsohren in die Buchseiten (ugs.)

• ~ **'down** *v.t.* **1** (fold down) herunterschlagen ‹*Kragen, Hutkrempe*›; umknicken ‹*Buchseite*›; [nach unten] umschlagen ‹*Laken*› **2** (reduce level of) niedriger stellen ‹*Heizung, Kochplatte*›; dämpfen ‹*Licht*›; herunterdrehen ‹*Gas, Heizung*›; leiser stellen ‹*Ton, Radio, Fernseher*› **3** (reject, refuse) ablehnen; abweisen ‹*Bewerber, Kandidaten usw.*›. *See also* **turndown**

• ~ **'in**

A *v.t.* **1** (fold inwards) nach innen drehen; einschlagen ‹*Stoffkante*›; einrollen ‹*Blatt*› **2** (hand in) abgeben **3** (surrender) [der Polizei] übergeben; ~ **oneself in** sich stellen **4** (register) hinlegen (ugs.) ‹*Auftritt, Leistung*› **5** (coll.: give up) aufstecken (ugs.) ‹*Arbeit*›; hinschmeißen (salopp) ‹*Arbeit, Dienstabzeichen*› **6** ~ **it in!** (coll.: stop that) hör auf damit!

B *v.i.* **1** (incline inwards) nach innen gebogen sein; (narrow) sich verjüngen **2** (enter) einbiegen **3** (coll.: go to bed) in die Falle gehen (salopp) **4** ~ **in on oneself** sich in sich selbst zurückziehen

• ~ **'off**

A *v.t.* **1** abschalten; abstellen ‹*Wasser, Gas*›; zudrehen ‹*Wasserhahn*› **2** (coll.: cause to lose interest) anwidern; ~ **sb. off sth.** jmdm. etw. vermiesen (ugs.)

B *v.i.* abbiegen. *See also* **turn-off**

• ~ **on**

A *v.t.* **1** /-'-/ anschalten; einlassen ‹*Badewasser*›; aufdrehen ‹*Wasserhahn, Gas*›; (fig.: start showing) aufsetzen ‹*Miene*› **2** /-'-/ (coll.: excite) anmachen (ugs.); ‹*Droge:*› anturnen (ugs.); **whatever ~s you on!** jedem das Seine!; *see also* **turn-on** **3** /'--/ (be based on) ‹*Argument:*› beruhen auf (+ *Dat.*); ‹*Gespräch, Diskussion*› sich drehen um (ugs.) **4** /'--/ (become hostile towards) sich wenden gegen; (attack) angreifen; **there's no need to ~ on me like that** du brauchst mich nicht so anzufahren

B /-'-/ *v.i.* (switch on) einschalten

• ~ **'out**

A *v.t.* **1** (expel) hinauswerfen (ugs.); ~ **sb. out of a room/out into the street** jmdn. aus einem Zimmer weisen *od.* (ugs.) werfen/auf die Straße werfen *od.* setzen; ~ **sb. out of his office** (temporarily) jmdn. aus seinem Büro ausquartieren **2** (switch off) ausschalten; abdrehen ‹*Gas*› **3** (incline outwards) nach außen drehen ‹*Füße, Zehen*› **4** (equip) ausstaffieren **5** (produce) produzieren; hervorbringen ‹*Fachkräfte, Spezialisten*›; (in great quantities) ausstoßen **6** (Brit.) (empty) ausräumen; ausschütten ‹*Büchse*›; schütten ‹*Bohnen usw.*›; stürzen ‹*Götterspeise usw.*›; (clean) [gründlich] aufräumen; (get rid of) wegwerfen; ~ **out one's pockets** seine Taschen umdrehen **7** (Mil.) ~ **out [the guard]** [die Wache] antreten lassen; ~ **out the guard!** Wache angetreten!

B *v.i.* **1** (prove to be) **sb./sth. ~s out to be sth.** jmd./etw. stellt sich als jmd./etw. heraus *od.* erweist sich als jmd./etw.; **it ~s out that ...:** es stellt sich heraus, dass ...; **as it ~ed out, as things ~ed out** wie sich [nachher] herausstellte **2** (come to be eventually) **the day ~ed out wet** der Tag wurde regnerisch; **see how things ~ out** sehen, wie sich die Dinge entwickeln; ~ **out to be sth.** sich zu etw. entwickeln; **everything ~ed out well/all right in the end** alles endete gut; **she didn't ~ out well** aus ihr ist nichts geworden **3** (end) **the story ~ed out happily** die Geschichte ging gut aus; **the expedition ~ed out well** die Expedition hatte Erfolg **4** (appear) ‹*Menge, Fans usw.:*› erscheinen; ‹*Wähler:*› sich beteiligen; ‹*Polizei, Feuerwehr, Militär usw.*› ausrücken; **he ~s out every Saturday to watch his team** er geht jeden Samstag hin, um seine Mannschaft zu sehen; ~ **out for a team** für eine Mannschaft spielen *od.* antreten **5** (coll.: get out of bed) aus den Federn steigen (ugs.) **6** (coll.: go out of doors) rausgehen (ugs.) **7** (point outwards) sich nach außen drehen. *See also* **turnout**

• ~ **'over**

A *v.t.* **1** (cause to fall over) umwerfen; **the car was ~ed over on to its roof** (by accident) das Auto überschlug sich und blieb auf dem Dach liegen **2** (expose the other side of) umdrehen; umgraben ‹*Erde*›; ~ **a page over** umblättern; ~ **over two pages at once** eine Seite überschlagen **3** drehen ‹*Motor*› **4** ~ **sth. over [in one's mind]** sich (*Dat.*) etw. hin und her überlegen **5** (hand over) übergeben (**to** *Dat.*) ‹*Betrieb, Amt*› **6** (Commerc.) umschlagen ‹*Waren*›; ~ **over £150,000 a month** einen Umsatz von 150 000 Pfund im Monat haben

B *v.i.* **1** (tip over) umkippen; ‹*Boot:*› kentern, umschlagen; ‹*Auto, Flugzeug:*› sich überschlagen **2** (from one side to the other) sich umdrehen; ~ **over on to one's back** sich auf den Rücken drehen **3** ‹*Motor:*› laufen **4** (feel moved by fear, nausea) **my stomach ~ed over at the thought of it** beim Gedanken daran drehte sich mir der Magen um (ugs.) **5** (~ a page) weiterblättern. *see also* **turnover**

• ~ **'round**

A *v.i.* **1** sich umdrehen; ~ **round and go back the same way** umkehren und denselben Weg zurückgehen; **[not] have time to ~ round** (fig.) [k]eine Minute Zeit haben **2** (rotate) sich drehen **3** ~ **round and do sth.** (fig.) plötzlich etw. tun; **they cannot ~ round and blame us** sie können nicht auf einmal uns die Schuld geben **4** (change for better) ‹*Geschäfte:*› sich erholen

B *v.t.* **1** (unload and reload) be- und entladen ‹*Frachtschiff*›; abfertigen ‹*Passagierschiff*› **2** ▸ ~ **about B** **3** (reverse) umdrehen; auf den Kopf stellen (ugs.) ‹*Theorie, Argument*›; ~ **a company round** (Commerc.) eine Firma aus der Krise führen. *See also* **turnround**

• ~ **to**

A /'--/ *v.t.* **1** (set about) ~ **to work** an die Arbeit gehen **2** (go to for help etc.) ~ **to sb./sth.** sich an jmdn. wenden/etw. zu Hilfe nehmen; ~ **to God** sich Gott zuwenden; ~ **to sb. for money** jmdn. um Geld bitten; ~ **to a book** ein Buch zurate ziehen; ~ **to sb. for comfort/help/advice** bei jmdm. Trost/Hilfe/Rat suchen; ~ **to drugs** zu Drogen greifen; ~ **to drink/one's work** (seeking consolation) sich in den Alkohol/seine Arbeit flüchten; **make sb. ~ to drink** jmdn. dem Alkohol in die Arme treiben **3** (go on to consider next) ~ **to a subject/topic** sich einem Thema zuwenden; *see also* ~ **B 1, 3**

B /-'-/ *v.i.* zugreifen

• ~ **'up**

A *v.i.* **1** (make one's appearance) erscheinen; aufkreuzen (ugs.) **2** (happen) passieren; geschehen **3** (present itself) auftauchen; ‹*Gelegenheit:*› sich bieten; ‹*Lösung:*› sich finden; **something is sure to ~ up** irgendetwas wird sich schon finden **4** (be found) sich finden

B *v.t.* **1** (dig up) freilegen; (fig.) ans Licht bringen; **I ~ed up a lot of interesting information** ich habe viele interessante Informationen aufgetrieben **2** hochschlagen ‹*Kragen, Hutkrempe*›; **her nose is ~ed up** sie hat eine Stupsnase **3** lauter stellen, (ugs.) aufdrehen ‹*Ton, Fernseher, Radio*›; aufdrehen ‹*Wasser, Heizung, Gas*›; heller machen ‹*Licht*› **4** (Brit.: find and refer to) heranziehen ‹*Artikel, Buch*› **5** ~ **it up!** (Brit. coll.) hör auf damit!; *see also* **nose A 1; toe A 1**

• ~ **upon** ▸ ~ **on A 3, 4**

turn: ~about *n.* (turning about) Wende, *die;* (fig.) Kehrtwendung, *die;* **a welcome ~about in her fortunes** eine willkommene Wende ihres Geschicks; **~around** *n.* **1** (change) [Kehrt]wende, *die;* **2** (processing, time needed) Bearbeitungszeit, *die;* **3** (of aircraft, ship, vehicle) Abfertigung, *die;* **~coat** *n.* Abtrünnige, *der/die;* **~down** *attrib. adj.* **~-down collar** Umlegekragen, *der*

turned-up /'tɜ:ndʌp/ *adj.* ~ **nose** Stupsnase, *die* (ugs.)

turner /'tɜ:nə(r)/ *n.* Drechsler, *der*/Drechslerin, *die*

turning /'tɜ:nɪŋ/ *n.* **1** ▸ⓘ **p. 1699** (off road) Abzweigung, *die;* (fig.) Kreuzweg, *der* (geh.); **take the second ~ to the left** die zweite Abzweigung nach links nehmen **2** (use of lathe) Drechseln, *das* **3** *in pl.* (shavings) Späne **4** **the ~ of the tide** der Gezeitenwechsel; (fig.) der Wendepunkt

turning: ~ circle *n.* (Motor Veh.) Wendekreis, *der;* ~ **point** *n.* Wendepunkt, *der*

turnip /'tɜ:nɪp/ *n.* [weiße] Rübe

'turnip top *n.* Rübenblätter *Pl.*

turn: ~key **A** *n.* (Hist.) Kerkermeister, *der.* **B** *adj.* schlüsselfertig; **a ~key contract** ein Vertrag, der schlüsselfertige Lieferung garantiert; **~-off** *n.* **1** (~ing) Abzweigung, *die;* (off motorway) Ausfahrt, *die;* **the Leicester ~-off** die Abzweigung nach Leicester/die Ausfahrt Leicester; **2** (coll.: repellent person or thing) **be a ~-off** abstoßend sein; **be a ~-off for sb.** jmdn. abstoßen; **~-on** *n.* (coll.) **be a ~-on [for sb.]** [jmdn.] anmachen (ugs.); **~out** *n.* **1** (turning out for duty) Einsatz, *der;* Ausrücken, *das;* **2** (number voting) **~out [of voters]** Wahlbeteiligung, *die;* **3** (number assembled) Beteiligung, *die* (**for** an + *Dat.*); **there was a large ~out of**

t

fans at the airport eine große Zahl von Fans war zum Flughafen gekommen; **4** ▸**output A 1**; **5** ▸**clear-out**; **~over** *n.* **1** (tart etc.) **apple/apricot ~over** Apfel-/Aprikosentasche, *die;* **meat ~over** Fleischpastete, *die;* **2** (Commerc.) (of business, money) Umsatz, *der;* (of stock) Umschlag, *der;* **3** (of staff) Fluktuation, *die;* (of patients in hospital) Zu- und Abgang, *der;* **~pike** *n.* **1** (Brit. Hist.: toll road) gebührenpflichtige Straße; **2** (Amer.: expressway) gebührenpflichtige Autobahn; **~round** *n.* **1** (adoption of new policy) Kehrtwendung, *die;* **2** (of ship, aircraft, people) Abfertigung, *die;* (of material) Bearbeitung, *die;* **~stile** *n.* Drehkreuz, *das;* **~table** *n.* **1** (of record player) Plattenteller, *der;* **2** (for reversing locomotive etc.) Drehscheibe, *die;* **~table ladder** *n.* (Brit.) Drehleiter, *die;* **~-up** *n.* **1** (Brit. Fashion) Aufschlag, *der;* **with ~-ups** ‹*Hose*› mit Aufschlag; **2** (Brit. coll.: unexpected event) **a ~-up [for the book]** eine Riesenüberraschung (ugs.)

turpentine /ˈtɜːpntaɪn/ *n.* **1** (resin) Terpentin, *das* **2** **[oil of] ~**: Terpentin, *das* (ugs.); Terpentinöl, *das; attrib.* **~ substitute** Terpentinersatz, *der*

turpitude /ˈtɜːpɪtjuːd/ *n.* Verworfenheit, *die* (geh.)

turps /tɜːps/ *n.* (coll.) Terpentin, *das* (ugs.)

turquoise /ˈtɜːkwɔɪz/

A *n.* **1** Türkis, *der* **2** (colour) Türkis, *das*

B *adj.* **1** türkis[farben] **2** **~ ring** Türkisring, *der*

turquoise: ~ ˈblue *n.* Türkisblau, *das;* **~ ˈgreen** *n.* Türkisgrün, *das*

turret /ˈtʌrɪt/ *n.* **1** (Archit.) Türmchen, *das* **2** (of tank etc.) [Geschütz]turm, *der* **3** (Mech. Engin.) Revolverkopf, *der*

turreted /ˈtʌrɪtɪd/ *adj.* ‹*Schloss*› mit Mauertürmchen

ˈturret lathe *n.* Revolverdrehmaschine, *die*

turtle /ˈtɜːtl/ *n.* **1** (marine reptile) Meeresschildkröte, *die* **2** (Amer.: freshwater reptile) Wasserschildkröte, *die* **3** **turn ~** ‹*Schiff, Boot:*› kentern; ‹*Auto:*› sich überschlagen

turtle: ~ dove *n.* Turteltaube, *die;* **~neck** *n.* Stehbundkragen, *der; attrib.* **~neck pullover** Pullover mit Stehbund

turves ▸**turf A 2**

Tuscan /ˈtʌskən/

A *adj.* **1** (of Tuscany) toskanisch **2** (Archit.) **~ order** toskanische Ordnung

B *n.* **1** (language) Toskanisch, *das* **2** (person) Toskaner, *der*/Toskanerin, *die*

Tuscany /ˈtʌskənɪ/ *pr. n.* Toskana, *die*

tusk /tʌsk/ *n.* (of elephant) Stoßzahn, *der;* (of boar, walrus) Hauer, *der*

tussle /ˈtʌsl/

A *n.* Gerangel, *das* (ugs.); **they had a ~ over the project** (fig.) es gab zwischen ihnen ein Gerangel wegen des Projekts

B *v.i.* sich balgen; (fig.) sich auseinander setzen (**about** wegen)

tussock /ˈtʌsək/ *n.* (clump of grass) Grasbüschel, *das*

tutelage /ˈtjuːtɪlɪdʒ/ *n.* (guardianship) Vormundschaft, *die;* (of king etc.) Schutzherrschaft, *die;* (tuition) Anleitung, *die;* **a child in ~**: ein unter Vormundschaft stehendes Kind; **be under sb.'s ~**: unter jmds. Obhut stehen (geh.)

tutelar /ˈtjuːtɪlə(r)/, **tutelary** /ˈtjuːtɪlərɪ/ *adjs.* **1** (protective) Schutz‹*göttin, -gottheit, -heiliger*› **2** (of a guardian) **~y authority** Vormundschaft, *die*

tutor /ˈtjuːtə(r)/

A *n.* ▸➊ **p. 1260** **1** (private teacher) **[private] ~**: [Privat]lehrer, *der*/-lehrerin, *die;* (for extra help) Nachhilfelehrer, *der*/-lehrerin, *die;* **piano ~**: Klavierlehrer, *der*/-lehrerin, *die;* (book) Klavierschule, *die* **2** (Brit. Univ.) ≈ Tutor, *der* **3** (Amer.: college teacher) Dozent, *der*

B *v.t.* **~ sb.** (teach privately) jmdm. Privatstunden geben; (give extra lessons to) jmdm. Nachhilfestunden geben; **~ sb. in French/the piano** jmdm. Französisch-/Klavierstunden geben

tutorial /tjuːˈtɔːrɪəl/

A *adj.* Tutoren-

B *n.* (Brit. Univ.) (for less advanced students) ≈ Tutorium, *das;* (for more advanced students) ≈ Kolloquium, *das*

tutti-frutti /tʊtɪˈfrʊtɪ/ *n.* (Gastr.) Tuttifrutti, *das*

tut[-tut] /tʌt(ˈtʌt)/

A *int.* na[, na]

B *v.i.*, **-tt-**: **~ [with disapproval]** [missbilligend] „Na, na!" sagen

tutu /ˈtuːtuː/ *n.* Tutu, *das*

tu-whit tu-whoo /tʊwɪt tʊˈwuː/ *int.* [h]uhu

tux /tʌks/ *n.* (Amer. coll.), **tuxedo** /tʌkˈsiːdəʊ/ *n.*, *pl.* **~edos** *or* **~edoes** (Amer.) Smoking, *der*

TV /tiːˈviː/ *n.* **1** (television) Fernsehen, *das; attrib.* Fernseh‹*kamera, -kanal, -magazin, -moderator, -programm, rechte, -serie, -sender, -werbung, -zuschauer usw.*›; **TV [head-to-head] debate** TV-Duell, *das;* Fernsehduell, *das;* **on TV** im Fernsehen **2** (television set) Fernseher, *der* (ugs.)

TV ˈdinner *n.* ≈ Fertigmahlzeit, *die;* (single dish) Fertiggericht, *das*

TVP ® *abbr.* = **textured vegetable protein**

TˈV screen *n.* Bildschirm, *der*

twaddle /ˈtwɒdl/ *n.* Gewäsch, *das* (ugs.); **talk utter ~**: völligen Blödsinn reden (ugs.); **don't talk such ~!** hör auf mit dem Gewäsch!

twain /tweɪn/ (arch./literary) *n.* **cut/split in ~**: entzweischneiden/in zwei Teile teilen; **never the ~ shall meet** die beiden werden nie zueinander finden

twang /twæŋ/

A *v.i.* ‹*Bogen:*› mit vibrierendem Ton zurückschnellen; **hear the guitar ~ing away** das Klimpern der Gitarre hören (ugs.)

B *v.t.* zupfen ‹*Saite*›; **~ a guitar** auf einer Gitarre [herum]klimpern (ugs.)

C *n.* **1** (nasal tone of voice) **[nasal] ~**: Näseln, *das;* **speak with a ~**: näseln **2** (of bowstring, string of musical instrument) vibrierender Ton

ˈtwas /twɒz/ (arch./poet.) = **it was**

twat /twæt, twɒt/ *n.* **1** (coarse: vagina) Fotze, *die* (vulg.) **2** (derog. sl.: idiot) Arschloch, *das* (derb)

tweak /twiːk/

A *v.t.* **1** **~ sb. in the arm, ~ sb.'s arm** jmdn. in den Arm kneifen; **~ sb.'s ear** jmdn. am Ohr ziehen **2** (coll.: adjust) fein einstellen

B *n.* Kneifen, *das;* **give sb./sth. a ~**: jmdn./etw. kneifen

twee /twiː/ *adj.*, **tweer** /ˈtwiːə(r)/, **tweest** /ˈtwiːɪst/ (Brit. derog.) geziert ‹*Wesen, Art, Ausdrucksweise*›; kitschig ‹*Stil, Bild*›; Bilderbuch‹*dorf, -landhaus*›; niedlich, putzig ‹*Kleidung, Dorf*›

tweed /twiːd/ *n.* **1** (fabric) Tweed, *der; attrib.* Tweed- **2** *in pl.* (clothes) Tweedkleidung, *die;* Tweedsachen (ugs.)

tweedy /ˈtwiːdɪ/ *adj.* **1** (coll.: dressed in tweeds) in Tweed gekleidet **2** (fig.: heartily informal) burschikos

ˈtween-deck[s] *n.* (Naut.) Zwischendeck, *das*

tweenie /ˈtwiːnɪ/ *n.* (coll.) *Kind zwischen acht und vierzehn Jahren*

tweet /twiːt/

A *n.* Zwitschern, *das;* **~, ~!** piep, piep!

B *v.i.* zwitschern

tweeter /ˈtwiːtə(r)/ *n.* Hochtonlautsprecher, *der*

tweezers /ˈtwiːzəz/ *n. pl.* **[pair of] ~**: Pinzette, *die*

twelfth /twelfθ/ ▸➊ **p. 1047**

A *adj.* ▸➊ **p. 1358** zwölft...; *see also* **eighth A**

B *n.* **1** (fraction) Zwölftel, *das* **2** (Mus.) Duodezime, *die; see also* **eighth B**

Twelfth: ~ Day *n.* Dreikönigstag, *der;* **t~ ˈman** *n.* (Cricket) Ersatzspieler, *der;* **~ ˈNight** *n.* Vorabend des Dreikönigstages

twelve /twelv/ ▸➊ **p. 894**, ▸➊ **p. 1001**, ▸➊ **p. 1358**

A *adj.* zwölf; **~ noon** [zwölf Uhr] Mittag; **~ midnight** [zwölf Uhr] Mitternacht; *see also* **eight A**

B *n.* (number, symbol) Zwölf, *die;* **the T~**: die Zwölf; die zwölf Apostel; *see also* **eight B 1, 4**

twelve: ~month *n.* (literary) **a ~month** zwölf Monate; **~-ˈnote, ~-ˈtone** *adjs.* (Mus.) Zwölfton-

twentieth /ˈtwentɪɪθ/ ▸➊ **p. 1047**

A *adj.* ▸➊ **p. 1358** zwanzigst...; *see also* **eighth A**

B *n.* (fraction) Zwanzigstel, *das; see also* **eighth B**

twenty /ˈtwentɪ/ ▸➊ **p. 894**, ▸➊ **p. 1001**, ▸➊ **p. 1358**

A *adj.* zwanzig; *see also* **eight A**

B *n.* Zwanzig, *die; see also* **eight B 1**; **eighty B**

twenty: ~-first *etc. adj.* ▸➊ **p. 1047**, ▸➊ **p. 1358** einundzwanzigst... *usw.; see also* **eighth A**; **~-four-hour** ▸**hour 1**; **~-four/seven, 24/7** *adv.* (coll.) rund um die Uhr und sieben Tage die Woche; (all the time) ununterbrochen; pausenlos; **~-one** *etc.*

A *adj.* einundzwanzig *usw.; see also* **eight A**;

B *n.* ▸➊ **p. 1358** Einundzwanzig *usw., die; see also* **eight B 1**

ˈtwere /twə(r), *stressed* twɜː(r)/ (arch./poet.) = **it were** 's wäre

twerp /twɜːp/ *n.* (coll.) (male) Blödmann, *der* (derb); (female) blöde Kuh (derb)

twice /twaɪs/ *adv.* **1** (two times) zweimal; **she didn't have to be asked ~!** da brauchte man sie nicht zweimal zu fragen!; **~ a year** zweimal im Jahr; **~ weekly** zweimal wöchentlich *nicht attrib.*; **his ~-weekly visit** sein Besuch zweimal in der Woche **2** (doubly) doppelt; **~ as strong** *etc.* doppelt so stark *usw.*; **he's ~ her age** er ist doppelt so alt wie sie; **have ~ the strength** doppelt so stark sein; **he is ~ the man he was** aus ihm ist ein ganz anderer Mensch geworden; **fly at ~ the speed of sound** mit doppelter Schallgeschwindigkeit fliegen; **sell sth. at ~ the price** (coll.) etw. zum doppelten Preis verkaufen; *see also* **think B 1**

twiddle /ˈtwɪdl/

A *v.t.* herumdrehen an (+ *Dat.*) (ugs.); zwirbeln ‹*Schnurrbart*›; **~ one's cigar** seine Zigarre [zwischen den Fingern] drehen; **~ one's thumbs** (lit. or fig.) Däumchen drehen (ugs.)

B *v.i.* **~ with sth.** mit etw. spielen; an etw. (*Dat.*) herumfummeln (ugs.); **~ one's moustache** seinen Schnurrbart zwirbeln

C *n.* Drehung, *die;* **give sth. a ~**: an etw. (*Dat.*) drehen

twig[1] /twɪg/ *n.* **1** (small branch) Zweig, *der* **2** (divining rod) Wünschelrute, *die*

twig[2] (coll.)

A *v.t.* **-gg-**: **1** (understand) kapieren (ugs.) **2** (notice) mitkriegen (ugs.)

B *v.i.* **-gg-**: **1** (understand) es kapieren (ugs.) **2** (notice) es mitkriegen (ugs.)

twilight /ˈtwaɪlaɪt/ *n.* **1** (evening light) Dämmerlicht, *das;* Zwielicht, *das* **2** (period of half-light) Dämmerung, *die;* **the ~ of the Gods** (Norse myth.) die Götterdämmerung; **in the ~ of history** (fig.) in grauer Vorzeit **3** (fig.: intermediate state) Dämmer, *der* (dichter.); **his ~ years** sein Lebensabend

twilight: ~ ˈsleep *n.* (Med.) Dämmerschlaf, *der;* **~ zone** *n.* **1** Niemandsland, *das;* **2** (decaying urban area) heruntergekommene Gegend

twill /twɪl/ *n.* (Textiles) **1** (weave) Köperbindung, *die* **2** (fabric) Köper, *der*

ˈtwill /twɪl/ (arch./poet.) = **it will**

twin /twɪn/

A *attrib. adj.* **1** Zwillings-; **~ brother/sister** Zwillingsbruder, *der*/-schwester, *die* **2** (forming a pair) Doppel-; doppelt ‹*Problem, Verantwortung*›; **the ~ threats of war and inflation** die doppelte Bedrohung durch Krieg und Inflation **3** (Bot.) paarig **4** Doppel‹*vergaser, -propeller, -schraube usw.*›

B *n.* **1** Zwilling, *der;* **his ~**: sein Zwillingsbruder/seine Zwillingsschwester **2** (Astrol.) **the T~s** die Zwillinge; *see also* **Aries 3** (exact counterpart) Gegenstück, *das;* Pendant, *das*

C *v.t.*, **-nn-** eng verbinden; **Bottrop is ~ned with Blackpool** Bottrop und Blackpool sind Partnerstädte

twin: ~ ˈbed *n.* eines von zwei [gleichen] Einzelbetten; **~ beds** zwei Einzelbetten; **~-bedded** *adj.* **a ~-bedded room** ein Zweibettzimmer

twine /twaɪn/

A *n.* Bindfaden, *der;* (thicker) Kordel, *die;* (for nets) Garn, *das*

B *v.t.* **1** (form by twisting strands together) [zusammen]drehen **2** (form by interlacing) winden (geh.) ‹*Kranz, Girlande*› **3** (coil) schlingen; **~ sth.**

t

round [and round] sth. etw. [mehrmals] um etw. schlingen; ~ the flowers round the pole den Mast mit Blumen umwinden
C v.i. sich winden (about, around um)

twin-engined /'twɪnendʒɪnd/ *adj.* zweimotorig

twinge /twɪndʒ/ *n.* Stechen, *das;* **a ~ of toothache/rheumatism/pain** ein stechender Zahnschmerz/ziehender rheumatischer Schmerz/stechender Schmerz; **~s** Wehwehchen *Pl.* (ugs.); **he suffers from ~s in wet weather** bei feuchtem Wetter zwickt und zwackt es ihn überall; **~[s] of remorse/conscience** (fig.) Gewissensbisse

'twin-jet *adj.* zweistrahlig

twinkle /'twɪŋkl/
A *v.i.* 1 (sparkle) ‹*Sterne, Augen:*› funkeln, blitzen (**with** vor + *Dat.*) 2 (move rapidly) flink trippeln
B *v.t.* **~ one's eyes** mit den Augen funkeln
C *n.* 1 **in a ~:** im Handumdrehen 2 (sparkle of the eyes) Funkeln, *das;* **'...', she said with a ~ in her eye** „...", sagte sie augenzwinkernd; **you were just a ~ in your father's eye then** zu der Zeit wussten deine Eltern noch nicht, dass es dich geben würde; **the project is still only a ~ in his eye** das Projekt ist bis jetzt nur eine ganz vage Idee von ihm; **with a mischievous ~:** mit Schalk in den Augen

twinkling /'twɪŋklɪŋ/ *n.* **in a ~, in the ~ of an eye** im Handumdrehen

'twin-lens *adj.* zweiäugig

twinning /'twɪnɪŋ/ *n.* (of towns) Verschwisterung, *die*

twin: ~set *n.* (Brit.) Twinset, *das;* **~ 'tower** *n.* Zwillingsturm, *der;* **~ town** *n.* (Brit.) Partnerstadt, *die;* **~-tub** *n.* halbautomatische Waschmaschine (*mit separater Schleuder*); **~ village** *n.* Partnerdorf, *das*

twirl /twɜːl/
A *v.t.* 1 (spin) [schnell] drehen; **he ~ed his partner around the dance floor** er wirbelte seine Partnerin über die Tanzfläche 2 (twiddle) zwirbeln ‹*Schnurrbart*›; drehen ‹*Haar*›
B *v.i.* wirbeln (**around** über + *Akk.*); **sb. ~s around** jmd. wirbelt herum
C *n.* 1 (~ing) [Herum]wirbeln, *das;* **give one's moustache a ~:** seinen Schnurrbart zwirbeln; **have a ~ on the dance floor** über die Tanzfläche wirbeln 2 (flourish made in writing) Schnörkel, *der*

twirly /'twɜːlɪ/ *adj.* gewunden; verschnörkelt ‹*Schrift*›

twist /twɪst/
A *v.t.* 1 (distort) verdrehen ‹*Worte, Bedeutung*›; **~ out of shape** verbiegen; **~ one's ankle** sich (*Dat.*) den Knöchel verrenken; **her face was ~ed with pain** ihr Gesicht war schmerzverzerrt; **~ sb.'s arm** jmdm. den Arm umdrehen; (fig.) jmdm. [die] Daumenschrauben anlegen (scherzh.); **I didn't have to ~ his arm** ich brauchte ihn nicht lange zu überreden 2 (wind about one another) flechten ‹*Blumen, Haare*› (**into** zu) 3 (rotate) drehen; (back and forth) hin und her drehen; *see also* **knife A** 4 (interweave) verweben 5 (give spiral form to) drehen (**into** zu) 6 (Brit. coll.: cheat) beschummeln (ugs.); **~ sb. out of sth.** jmdn. um etw. beschummeln (ugs.) 7 (wrench) **~ sth. from sb.'s grasp** jmdm. etw. aus der Hand winden. *see also* **little finger**
B *v.i.* 1 sich winden; **~ and turn** sich drehen und winden; **~ around sth.** sich um etw. winden; **~ from sb.'s grasp** sich aus jmds. Griff winden 2 (take ~ed position) sich winden; **he ~ed round in his chair** er drehte sich in seinem Sessel um 3 (dance) twisten
C *n.* 1 (thread etc.) Zwirn, *der;* (loosely twisted) Twist, *der* 2 **~ of lemon/orange** Zitronen-/Orangenscheibe, *die* 3 (~ing) Drehung, *die;* **give sth. a ~:** an etw. (*Dat.*) drehen; **full of ~s and turns** ‹*Straße*› voll[er] Biegungen und Kurven 4 (unexpected occurrence) überraschende Wendung; **~ of fate** Laune des Schicksals 5 (peculiar tendency) **give a ~ to sth.** etw. verdrehen; **he has an odd ~ to his character** er ist ein bisschen verschroben; **a criminal ~:** eine kriminelle Neigung 6 **round the ~ = round the bend** ▸ **bend¹ A 2** 7 (swindle) Schwindel, *der* (abwertend) 8 (Amer.: change of procedure) [überraschender] Wandel 9 (dance) Twist, *der;* **do the ~:** Twist tanzen; twisten

Phrasal verbs
• **~ 'off**
A *v.t.* abdrehen
B *v.i.* **the cap ~s off** der Verschluss lässt sich abdrehen
• **~ to'gether** *v.t.* zusammendrehen ‹*Fäden*›

twisted /'twɪstɪd/ *adj.* verbogen; (fig.) verdreht (ugs. abwertend) ‹*Geist*›; verquer ‹*Humor*›

twister /'twɪstə(r)/ *n.* 1 Schwindler, *der*/Schwindlerin, *die;* Gauner, *der*/Gaunerin, *die* 2 (Amer.: tornado) Tornado, *der*

'twist-grip *n.* Drehgriff, *der; attrib.* Drehgriff-

twisty /'twɪstɪ/ *adj.* kurvig; kurvenreich

twit /twɪt/
A *v.t.,* **-tt-** ▸ **taunt A**
B *n.* (Brit. coll.) Trottel, *der* (ugs.)

twitch /twɪtʃ/
A *v.t.* 1 zupfen 2 zucken mit ‹*Nase, Schwanz*›; wackeln mit ‹*Ohr*›
B *v.i.* 1 (pull sharply) zupfen (**at** an + *Dat.*) 2 ‹*Mund, Lippen, Hand, Nase:*› zucken
C *n.* Zucken, *das*

twitcher /'twɪtʃə(r)/ *n.* (Brit. coll.) Vogelfan, *der*

'twitch grass *n.* (Bot.) Quecke, *die*

twitchy /'twɪtʃɪ/ *adj.* (nervy) nervös; (irritable) reizbar

twitter /'twɪtə(r)/
A *n.* 1 (coll.: excited state) **be in a ~, be all of a ~:** [vor Spannung] ganz kribbelig sein (ugs.) 2 (chirping) Zwitschern, *das;* Gezwitscher, *das*
B *v.i.* zwitschern; ‹*Person:*› schnattern (ugs.)

twittish /'twɪtɪʃ/ *adj.* (Brit. coll.) trottelhaft (ugs.)

'twixt /twɪkst/ *prep.* (literary/joc.) zwischen

two /tuː/ ▸ **p. 894,** ▸ **p. 1001,** ▸ **p. 1358**
A *adj.* zwei; **a box/shirt or ~:** ein, zwei Schachteln/Hemden; ein oder zwei Schachteln/Hemden; *see also* **eight A**
B *n.* (number, symbol) Zwei, *die;* **the ~:** die beiden; die zwei; **just the ~ of us** nur wir zwei *od.* beiden; **it's as clear as ~ and ~ make four** es ist so klar, wie zwei mal zwei vier sind (ugs.); **put ~ and ~ together** (fig.) zwei und zwei zusammenzählen; **cut/break in ~:** zweiteilen/entzweibrechen; **~ and ~, ~ by ~** (~ at a time) [zu] zwei und zwei; zu zweien; **that makes ~ of us** (coll.) mir gehts/gings genauso (ugs.); **~ can play at that game** das kann ich auch. *See also* **cheer A 1; eight B 1, 3, 4; game¹ A 1; penny 3**

two: ~-bit *adj.* (Amer.) 1 (costing 25 cents) 25-Cent-; 2 (of poor quality) mies (ugs.); **~-by-'four** A *n.* (piece of wood) *Holzbalken mit einer Stärke von 2 auf 4 Zoll;* B *adj.* (Amer. fig.) Westentaschen-; **~-dimensional** *adj.* zweidimensional; (fig.) oberflächlich; **~-door** *attrib. adj.* zweitürig ‹*Auto*›; **~-edged** *adj.* (lit. or fig.) zweischneidig; **~-faced** *adj.* (fig.) falsch (abwertend); **be ~-faced** ‹*Person:*› zwei Gesichter haben; **~-'fisted** *adj.* 1 (Brit.: clumsy) ungeschickt; **be ~-fisted** zwei linke Hände haben (ugs.); 2 (Amer.: vigorous) kernig; markig

twofold /'tuːfəʊld/ *adj., adv.* 1 zweifach; **be ~:** zweifacher Art *od.* Natur sein 2 (double) **a ~ increase** ein Anstieg auf das Doppelte; **increase ~:** sich verdoppeln

two: ~-four time *n.* (Mus.) Zweivierteltakt, *der;* **~-'handed** *adj.* 1 (having ~ hands) zweihändig; 2 (requiring both hands) beidhändig; 3 (requiring ~ persons) **~-handed poker** (Cards) Zwei-Mann-Poker, *der;* **~-lane** *adj.* zweispurig; **~-party system** *n.* Zweiparteiensystem, *das;* **~pence** /'tʌpəns/ *n.* (Brit.) zwei Pence; *see also* **care B 3; ~penny** /'tʌpənɪ/ *attrib. adj.* (Brit.) (costing 2p or 2d) Zwei-Pence-; **~penny-halfpenny** /tʌpnɪ'heɪpnɪ/ *attrib. adj.* (Brit. dated) unwichtig; lächerlich; (of poor quality) mies (ugs.); **~penny-halfpenny novel** Groschenroman, *der* (abwertend); **~-piece** A *n.* Zweiteiler, *der;* B *adj.* zweiteilig; **~-pin** *adj.* (Electr.) zweipolig; **~-ply** *adj.* zweifädig ‹*Seil, Wolle, Zwirn*›; aus zweifädiger Wolle gewebt ‹*Teppich*›; zweilagig ‹*Holz, Papier*›; **~-seater** A /-'--/ *n.* Zweisitzer, *der;* B /'---/ *attrib. adj.* zweisitzig

twosome /'tuːsəm/ *n.* 1 Paar, *das* 2 (Golf) Zweier, *der*

two: ~-step *n.* Twostep, *der;* **~-storey** *adj.* zweigeschossig; **~-stroke** *adj.* (Mech. Engin.) Zweitakt‹*motor, -verfahren*›; **~-time** *v.t.* (coll.) **~-time sb.** (be unfaithful) jmdm. fremdgehen (ugs.); (cheat) ein falsches Spiel mit jmdm. treiben; **~-timing** *adj.* (coll.) falsch; **~-tone** *adj.* 1 (in colour) zweifarbig; **a car in ~-tone green** ein Auto in zwei Grüntönen; 2 (in sound) Zweiklang-

'twould /twʊd/ (arch./poet.) **= it would**

two: ~-up ~-down *n.* kleines [Reihen]haus; **~-way** *adj.* 1 (in both directions) zweibahnig (Verkehrsw.); **'~-way traffic ahead'** „Achtung, Gegenverkehr"; 2 (involving an exchange between ~ parties) gegenseitig; **~-way scholarship programme** akademisches Austauschprogramm; **~-way radio** Funksprechgerät, *das;* 3 (Electr.) **~-way switch** Zweiwege[um]schalter, *der;* 4 **~-way tap** Zweiwegehahn, *der;* 5 **~-way mirror** Einwegspiegel, *der;* **~-'wheeler** *n.* Zweirad, *das*

tycoon /taɪ'kuːn/ *n.* Magnat, *der;* Tycoon, *der*

tying ▸ **tie A, B**

tyke /taɪk/ *n.* 1 (dog) Köter, *der* 2 (Brit.: churlish person) Kerl, *der* 3 (Yorkshireman) **[Yorkshire] ~:** *Mann aus der Grafschaft Yorkshire* 4 (child) Bengel, *der*

tympani ▸ **timpani**

tympanist ▸ **timpanist**

type /taɪp/
A *n.* 1 Art, *die;* (person) Typ, *der;* **what ~ of car ...?** was für ein Auto ...?; **her beauty is of another ~:** sie verkörpert einen anderen Typ von Schönheit; **she dislikes men of that ~:** sie mag diesen Typ [von] Mann nicht; **she's not my ~:** sie ist nicht mein Typ; **he's not the ~ to let people down** er ist nicht der Typ, der andere im Stich lässt; **he is a different ~ of person** er ist eine andere Art Mensch *od.* ein anderer Typ; **books of this ~:** derartige Bücher; **true to ~:** erwartungsgemäß 2 (coll.: character) Type, *die* (ugs.) 3 (Printing) (printed characters) [Druck]schrift, *die;* (metal piece bearing character) Drucktype, *die;* **be in small/italic ~:** klein gedruckt/kursiv gedruckt sein
B *v.t.* 1 (do typing of) [mit der Maschine] schreiben; tippen (ugs.); **~d letter** maschinegeschriebener Brief 2 (classify) typisieren
C *v.i.* maschineschreiben

Phrasal verbs
• **~ 'in** *v.t.* eintippen (ugs.); [mit der Schreibmaschine] einfügen
• **~ 'out** *v.t.* [mit der Schreibmaschine] abschreiben; abtippen (ugs.); (without original copy) [in die Maschine] schreiben; tippen (ugs.)
• **~ 'up** *v.t.* tippen

-type /taɪp/ *in comb.* -artig; **ceramic-~ materials** keramikartiges Material; **Cheddar-~ cheese** Käse nach Cheddar-Art

type: ~cast *v.t.* [auf eine bestimmte Rolle] festlegen; abstempeln; **be ~cast as the devoted wife** auf die Rolle der treuen Ehefrau festgelegt sein; **~face** *n.* Schriftbild, *das;* **~script** A *n.* maschine[n]geschriebene Fassung; Typoskript, *das;* **in ~script** maschine[n]geschrieben; **be still in ~script** erst als Typoskript vorliegen; B *adj.* ▸ **typewritten; ~set** *v.t.* (Printing) setzen; **~setter** *n.* (person) [Schrift]setzer, *der*/-setzerin, *die;* **~setting** *n., no pl.* [Schrift]setzen, *das; attrib.* **~setting machine** Setzmaschine, *die;* **~ size** *n.* Schriftgröße, *die;* Schriftgrad, *der;* **~ wheel** ▸ **daisy wheel; ~writer** *n.* Schreibmaschine, *die; attrib.* **~writer ribbon** Farbband, *das;* **~written** *adj.* maschine[n]geschrieben; mit der [Schreib]maschine geschrieben

typhoid /'taɪfɔɪd/ *n.* ▸ **p. 1231** (Med.) **~ [fever]** Typhus, *der*

typhoon /taɪ'fuːn/ *n.* Taifun, *der*

typhus /'taɪfəs/ *n.* ▸ **p. 1231** (Med.) Fleckfieber, *das*

typical /'tɪpɪkl/ *adj.* typisch (**of** für); **that's just ~!** [das ist mal wieder] typisch! (ugs.)

typically /'tɪpɪklɪ/ *adv.* typischerweise; **~, she turned up late** wie üblich kam sie zu spät

typify /'tɪpɪfaɪ/ *v.t.* 1 (represent) [symbolhaft] darstellen 2 (be an example of) **~ sth.** als typisches Beispiel für etw. dienen

typing /ˈtaɪpɪŋ/ *n., no pl.* Maschineschreiben, *das;* **his ∼ is excellent** er kann sehr gut Maschine schreiben; **how is your ∼?** kannst du [gut] maschineschreiben?; **can you do this piece of ∼ for me?** kannst du das für mich [mit der Maschine] schreiben *od.* (ugs.) tippen?

typing: ∼ error *n.* Tippfehler, *der* (ugs.); **∼ pool** *n.* Schreibzentrale, *die;* **∼ speed** *n.* Schreibgeschwindigkeit, *die*

typist /ˈtaɪpɪst/ *n.* ▸ⓘ **p. 1260** Schreibkraft, *die;* **shorthand ∼:** Stenotypist, *der*/-typistin, *die;* **she is [not] a good ∼:** sie kann [nicht] gut Maschine schreiben

typo /ˈtaɪpəʊ/ *n., pl.* **∼s** (coll.) Druckfehler, *der* (ugs.)

typographer /taɪˈpɒgrəfə(r)/ *n.* ▸ⓘ **p. 1260** Typograph, *der*/Typographin, *die*

typographic /taɪpəˈgræfɪk/, **typographical** /taɪpəˈgræfɪkl/ *adj.* typographisch; **∼ error** Setzfehler, *der*

typography /taɪˈpɒgrəfɪ/ *n.* Typographie, *die*

typology /taɪˈpɒlədʒɪ/ *n.* Typologie, *die*

tyrannical /tɪˈrænɪkl, taɪˈrænɪkl/ *adj.* tyrannisch

tyrannically /tɪˈrænɪkəlɪ, taɪˈrænɪkəlɪ/ *adv.* tyrannisch; **behave ∼ to sb.** jmdn. tyrannisieren

tyrannize (tyrannise) /ˈtɪrənaɪz/ **A** *v.i.* als Tyrann herrschen; **∼ over sb.** jmdn. tyrannisieren **B** *v.t.* ‹*Chef, Vater, Ehemann:*› tyrannisieren; ‹*Herrscher:*› als Tyrann herrschen über (+ *Akk.*)

tyrannous /ˈtɪrənəs/ *adj.* tyrannisch

tyranny /ˈtɪrənɪ/ *n.* Tyrannei, *die*

tyrant /ˈtaɪrənt/ *n.* (lit. or fig.) Tyrann, *der*

tyre /ˈtaɪə(r)/ *n.* Reifen, *der*

tyre: ∼ chain *n.* Schneekette, *die;* **∼ gauge** *n.* Reifendruckprüfer, *der;* **∼ lever** *n.* Reifenheber, *der;* **∼ pressure** *n.* Reifendruck, *der;* **∼ valve** *n.* Reifenventil, *das*

tyro /ˈtaɪərəʊ/ *n., pl.* **∼s** Anfänger, *der*/Anfängerin, *die*

Tyrol /tɪˈrəʊl/ *pr. n.* Tirol (*das*)

Tyrolean /tɪrəˈliːən/ *adj.* Tiroler

tzar *etc.* ▸**tsar** *etc.*

t

Uu

U¹, u /juː/ *n., pl.* **Us** *or* **U's** U, u, *das*

U² *adj.* (Brit. coll.) für die Oberschicht typisch ‹*Benehmen, Ausdruck, Sprache*›; **be U** ‹*Person:*› ein [typischer] Vertreter der Oberschicht sein; vornehm sein; *see also* **non-U**

U³ *abbr.* **1** (Brit.) **= universal** jugendfrei ‹*Film*› **2** **= University** Univ.

UAE *abbr.* **= United Arab Emirates** VAE

UB 40 /juːbiː ˈfɔːtɪ/ *n.* (Brit. Hist.) **1** (card) Arbeitslosenausweis, *der* **2** (coll.) Arbeitslose, *der/die*

ˈU-bend *n.* U-Rohr, *das;* Knie, *das* (ugs.)

ubiquitous /juːˈbɪkwɪtəs/ *adj.* allgegenwärtig

ˈU-boat *n.* (Hist.) [deutsches] U-Boot

udder /ˈʌdə(r)/ *n.* Euter, *das*

UDI *abbr.* **= Unilateral Declaration of Independence** einseitige Unabhängigkeitserklärung

UEFA /juːˈeɪfə/ *abbr.* **= Union of European Football Associations** UEFA, *die*

UFO /ˈjuːfəʊ/ *n., pl.* **~s** Ufo, *das*

Uganda /juːˈgændə/ *pr. n.* Uganda (*das*)

Ugandan /juːˈgændən/ ▸ **p. 1345**

A *adj.* ugandisch; **sb. is ~:** jmd. ist Ugander/Uganderin

B *n.* Ugander, *der*/Uganderin, *die*

ugh /ʌh, ʊh, ɜːh/ *int.* bah

ugli /ˈʌglɪ/ *n.* **~ [fruit]** Tangelo, *die*

ugliness /ˈʌglɪnɪs/ *n., no pl.* Hässlichkeit, *die*

ugly /ˈʌglɪ/ *adj.* **1** (in appearance, morally) hässlich; **~ duckling** (fig.) hässliches Entlein (ugs. scherzh.); **as ~ as sin** (coll.) potthässlich (ugs.); hässlich wie die Nacht **2** (nasty) übel ‹*Wunde, Laune, Szene usw.*›; **~ customer** (fig. coll.) unangenehmer Zeitgenosse/unangenehme Zeitgenossin; **have an ~ temper** übellaunig sein **3** (stormy) übel ‹*Wetter, Nacht*›; bedrohlich ‹*Himmel*›

UHF *abbr.* **= ultra-high frequency** UHF

UHT *abbr.* **= ultra heat treated** ultrahoch erhitzt; **UHT milk** H-Milch, *die*

UK *abbr.* **= United Kingdom**

ukase /juːˈkeɪz/ *n.* Ukas, *der*

Ukraine /juːˈkreɪn/ *pr. n.* Ukraine, *die*

Ukrainian /juːˈkreɪnɪən/ ▸ **p. 1277,** ▸ **p. 1345**

A *adj.* ukrainisch; **sb. is ~:** jmd. ist Ukrainer/Ukrainerin; *see also* **English A**

B *n.* **1** (person) Ukrainer, *der*/Ukrainerin, *die* **2** (language) Ukrainisch, *das; see also* **English B 1**

ukulele /juːkəˈleɪlɪ/ *n.* (Mus.) Ukulele, *die od. das*

ulcer /ˈʌlsə(r)/ *n.* ▸ **p. 1231** Geschwür, *das;* (fig.) [Krebs]geschwür, *das* (fig.); **mouth ~[s]** Aphthe, *die* (Med.)

ulcerate /ˈʌlsəreɪt/

A *v.i.* (Med.) ulzerieren (fachspr.); geschwürig werden

B *v.t.* ein Geschwür verursachen in (+ *Dat.*); **an ~d stomach** ein geschwüriger Magen

ulceration /ʌlsəˈreɪʃn/ *n.* **1** (process) Geschwürbildung, *die* **2** (ulcers) Geschwüre

ulcerous /ˈʌlsərəs/ *adj.* (Med.) geschwürig; (fig.) **racism is an ~ growth in society** der Rassismus ist ein Geschwür am Leibe der Gesellschaft

ulna /ˈʌlnə/ *n., pl.* **ulnae** /ˈʌlniː/ (Anat.) Elle, *die*

ulster *n.* (coat) Ulster, *der*

Ulster /ˈʌlstə(r)/ *pr. n.* Ulster (*das*)

> **Ulster Democratic Unionist Party**
>
> Eine 1972 von Ian Paisley mitbegründete extrem loyalistische Partei in Nordirland, die stark von den Protestanten unterstützt wird und den Standpunkt vertritt, dass Nordirland Teil des Vereinigten Königreichs bleiben sollte.

> **Ulster Unionist Party**
>
> Eine politische Partei in Nordirland, die die Union mit Großbritannien aufrechterhalten will. Die 1905 gegründete UUC gilt als moderater als die Ulster Democratic Unionist Party und ist organisatorisch mit der Konservativen Partei verbunden.

Ulster: ~man /ˈʌlstəmən/ *n., pl.* **~men** /ˈʌlstəmən/ (inhabitant) Bewohner von Ulster; (native) [geborener] Nordire; **~woman** *n.* (inhabitant) Bewohnerin von Ulster; (native) [geborene] Nordirin

ult. /ʌlt/ *abbr.* (Commerc.) **= ultimo**

ulterior /ʌlˈtɪərɪə(r)/ *adj.* hintergründig; geheim; **~ motive/thought** Hintergedanke, *der*

ultimate /ˈʌltɪmət/

A *attrib. adj.* **1** (final) letzt...; (eventual) endgültig ‹*Sieg*›; letztendlich ‹*Rettung*›; größt... ‹*Opfer*›; **~ result/goal/decision** Endergebnis, *das*/Endziel, *das*/endgültige Entscheidung; **in the ~ analysis** letzten Endes; **he exercises ~ jurisdiction/authority** er hat die höchste richterliche Gewalt/Autorität inne; **the ~ deterrent** das äußerste Abschreckungsmittel **2** (fundamental) tiefst... ‹*Grundlage, Wahrheit*›; **~ principles** Grundprinzipien; **the ~ particles of matter** die elementaren Teilchen der Materie; **the ~ origin** der eigentliche Ursprung **3** (maximum) maximal; **~ speed** Höchstgeschwindigkeit, *die* **4** (best/greatest conceivable) **the ~ washing machine** die Waschmaschine in Perfektion; **this is the ~ luxury** das ist der Gipfel an Luxus

B *n.* **the ~** (maximum) das absolute Maximum; (minimum) das absolute Minimum; **the ~ in comfort/luxury/style/fashion** der Gipfel an Bequemlichkeit/Luxus/das Exzellenteste an Stil/in der Mode

ultimately /ˈʌltɪmətlɪ/ *adv.* **1** (in the end) schließlich **2** (in the last analysis) letzten Endes; (basically) im Grunde [genommen]

ultimatum /ʌltɪˈmeɪtəm/ *n., pl.* **~s** *or* **ultimata** /ʌltɪˈmeɪtə/ Ultimatum, *das;* **give sb. an ~:** jmdm. ein Ultimatum stellen

ultimo /ˈʌltɪməʊ/ *adj.* (Commerc.) des vergangenen Monats

ultra /ˈʌltrə/

A *n.* Ultra, *der* (Politikjargon)

B *adj.* extremistisch

ultra- /ˈʌltrə/ *in comb.* ultra‹*konservativ, -modern*›; hyper‹*modern, -modisch*›

ultramaˈrine *n.* Ultramarin, *das*

ultraˈrich *adj.* **1** (very wealthy) ultrareich **2** (containing large amounts of fat, sugar, spices etc.) besonders gehaltvoll

ultraˈsensitive *adj.* **1** ultraempfindlich **2** (oversensitive) hypersensibel; (touchy) superempfindlich; **be ~ to sth.** äußerst empfindlich auf etw. (Akk.) reagieren; **she is ~ about her figure** was ihre Figur betrifft, [so] ist sie extrem empfindlich *od.* superempfindlich

ultraˈsmooth *adj.* **1** (very smooth) ultraglatt ‹*Oberfläche*›; **an ~ shaver** ein Rasierapparat, der ultraglatt rasiert **2** (suave) aalglatt (abwertend) ‹*Art, Mensch*›

ultraˈsonic *adj.* Ultraschall-

ultraˈsonically *adv.* mit Ultraschall

ultraˈsonics *n., no pl.* **1** ▸ **ultrasound** **2** (science) Lehre vom Ultraschall

ultraˈsound *n., no pl.* Ultraschall, *der*

ultraˈthin *adj.* ultradünn; ultra flach ‹*Notebook, Fernseher*›

ultraˈviolet *adj.* (Phys.) ultraviolett ‹*Strahlen, Licht*›; (using ~ radiation) UV-‹*Lampe, Filter*›; **~ treatment** UV-Bestrahlung, *die*

ululate /ˈjuːljʊleɪt/ *v.i.* (literary) heulen; (with grief) wehklagen (geh.)

Ulysses /ˈjuːlɪsiːz/ *pr. n.* Odysseus (*der*)

um /m, əm, ʌm/

A *int.* äh[m]

B /ʌm/ *v.i.,* **-mm-** (coll.) **um and ah** herumdrucksen (ugs.)

umbel /ˈʌmbl/ *n.* (Bot.) Dolde, *die*

umber /ˈʌmbə(r)/ *n.* **[raw/burnt] ~:** [ungebrannte/gebrannte] Umbra

umbilical cord /ʌmˈbɪlɪkl kɔːd/ *n.* Nabelschnur, *die*

umbra /ˈʌmbrə/ *n., pl.* **~e** /ˈʌmbriː/ *or* **~s** (Astron.) **1** (in eclipse) Kernschatten, *der* **2** (in sunspot) Umbra, *die*

umbrage /ˈʌmbrɪdʒ/ *n., no pl., no indef. art.* **take ~ [at** *or* **over sth.]** [an etw. (+ *Dat.*)] Anstoß nehmen

umbrella /ʌmˈbrelə/ *n.* **1** [Regen]schirm, *der;* **telescopic ~:** Taschenschirm, *der;* **put up an ~:** einen Schirm aufspannen **2** (fig.: protection) Schutz, *der;* (Mil.) (barrage) Sperrfeuer, *das;* (air cover) Jagdschutz, *der;* **the ~ of the Welfare State** das soziale Netz des Wohlfahrtsstaates **3** (fig.: unifying agency) **the company X comes under the ~ of company Y** die Firma X ist eine Tochtergesellschaft der Firma Y; **an ~ organization/group** eine Dachorganisation/eine übergeordnete Gruppe

umˈbrella stand *n.* Schirmständer, *der*

umlaut /ˈʊmlaʊt/ *n.* **1** (vowel change) Umlaut, *der* **2** (mark) Umlautzeichen, *das*

umpire /ˈʌmpaɪə(r)/

A *n.* ▸ **p. 1260** Schiedsrichter, *der*/-richterin, *die*

B *v.i.* schiedsrichtern; Schiedsrichter/-richterin sein

C *v.t.* schiedsrichtern bei ‹*Spiel, Wettkampf*›; pfeifen ‹*Fußballspiel usw.*›

umpteen /ʌmpˈtiːn/ *adj.* (coll.) zig (ugs.); x (ugs.)

umpteenth /ʌmpˈtiːnθ/ *adj.* (coll.) zigst... (ugs.); **for the ~ time** zum zigsten *od.* x-ten Mal (ugs.)

UMTS *abbr.* **= universal mobile telecommunications system** UMTS; *attrib.* **~ phone** UMTS-Handy, *das*

ˈun /ən/ *pron.* (coll.) **1** (person) Typ, *der;* **he's a tough/bad ~:** er ist ein zäher/übler Bursche (ugs.) **2** (thing) **a big ~:** ein großer/eine große/ein großes; **big ~s and little ~s** Große und Kleine; *see also* **wrong ˈun**

UN *abbr.* **= United Nations** UN[O], *die*

unabashed /ʌnəˈbæʃt/ *adj.* ungeniert; (without shame) schamlos; (undaunted) unerschrocken ‹*Kämpfer*›

U

unabated /ʌnə'beɪtɪd/ *adj.* unvermindert

unable /ʌn'eɪbl/ *pred. adj.* **be ~ to do sth.** nicht in der Lage sein, etw. zu tun; etw. nicht tun können; **he wanted to attend but was ~ to** er wollte kommen, aber er war dazu nicht in der Lage

unabridged /ʌnə'brɪdʒd/ *adj.* ungekürzt

unaccented /ʌnək'sentɪd/ *adj.* unbetont

unacceptable /ʌnək'septəbl/ *adj.* unannehmbar; **[be] not ~:** durchaus akzeptabel [sein]; **the ~ face of capitalism** die Kehrseite des Kapitalismus

unaccommodating /ʌnə'kɒmədeɪtɪŋ/ *adj.* ungefällig; (inflexible) unnachgiebig

unaccompanied /ʌnə'kʌmpənɪd/ *adj.* ohne Begleitung ‹*reisen, singen*›; unbegleitet ‹*Gepäck, Chor*›; (on aircraft etc.) **~ minor** allein reisendes Kind; **~ by sth.** nicht begleitet von etw.; **pieces for ~ horn/violin** Solostücke für Horn/Violine

unaccountable /ʌnə'kaʊntəbl/ *adj.* unerklärlich

unaccountably /ʌnə'kaʊntəblɪ/ *adv.* unerklärlicherweise; (with adj.) unerklärlich

unaccounted /ʌnə'kaʊntɪd/ *adj.* **~ for** unauffindbar; **several passengers are still ~ for** einige Passagiere werden noch vermisst; **the discrepancy remains ~ for** die Diskrepanz lässt sich nicht erklären

unaccustomed /ʌnə'kʌstəmd/ *adj.* ungewohnt; **be ~ to sth.** etw. (*Akk.*) nicht gewöhnt sein; **~ as I am to public speaking ...:** obwohl ich kein Redner bin ...

unacquainted /ʌnə'kweɪntɪd/ *adj.* **be [completely] ~ with sth.** mit etw. [überhaupt] nicht vertraut sein

unadopted /ʌnə'dɒptɪd/ *adj.* (Brit.) von der Gemeinde nicht unterhalten ‹*Straße*›

unadorned /ʌnə'dɔ:nd/ *adj.* schmucklos; ungeschminkt ‹*Wahrheit*›; schlicht ‹*Stil*›

unadulterated /ʌnə'dʌltəreɪtɪd/ *adj.* **1** (pure) unverfälscht; rein ‹*Wasser, Wein*› **2** (utter) völlig; **~ rubbish** absoluter Quatsch

unadventurous /ʌnəd'ventʃərəs/ *adj.* bieder ‹*Person*›; ereignislos ‹*Leben*›; (lacking ideas) einfallslos ‹*Inszenierung, Buch usw.*›; **he is an ~ cook** er macht beim Kochen keine Experimente

unaffected /ʌnə'fektɪd/ *adj.* **1** (not affected) unberührt; (Med.) nicht angegriffen ‹*Organ*›; **the area was ~ by the strike** die Gegend war vom Streik nicht betroffen; **she seems to have been ~ by the experience** diese Erfahrung scheint keine Wirkung auf sie gehabt zu haben **2** (natural) natürlich; ungekünstelt; **~ astonishment** blankes Staunen

unaffectedly /ʌnə'fektɪdlɪ/ *adv.* natürlich; ungekünstelt

unaffordable /ʌnə'fɔ:dəbl/ *adj.* unbezahlbar

unafraid /ʌnə'freɪd/ *adj.* **be ~ [of sb./sth.]** keine Angst [vor jmdm./etw.] haben

unaided /ʌn'eɪdɪd/ *adj.* ohne fremde Hilfe; **by one's own ~ efforts** ohne jede fremde Hilfe; **walk ~:** ohne Hilfe gehen

unalike /ʌnə'laɪk/ *pred. adj.* unähnlich; **they are so ~:** sie sind sich (*Dat.*) so unähnlich

unalloyed /ʌn'ælɔɪd, ʌnə'lɔɪd/ *adj.* nicht legiert ‹*Metall*›; (fig.) rein; ungetrübt ‹*Freude, Glück*›

unalterable /ʌn'ɔ:ltərəbl, ʌn'ɒltərəbl/ *adj.* unabänderlich ‹*Gesetz, Schicksal*›; unverrückbar ‹*Entschluss*›

unaltered /ʌn'ɔ:ltəd, ʌn'ɒltəd/ *adj.* unverändert

unambiguous /ʌnæm'bɪgjʊəs/ *adj.* unzweideutig

unambitious /ʌnæm'bɪʃəs/ *adj.* ‹*Person*› ohne Ergeiz; anspruchslos ‹*Buch*›; **be ~/a bit ~:** keinen/wenig Ehrgeiz haben

unambivalent /ʌnæm'bɪvələnt/ *adj.* unzweideutig; eindeutig ‹*Haltung*›; **be ~ in supporting sth.** etw. rückhaltlos unterstützen

un-American /ʌnə'merɪkn/ *adj.* **1** (not typically American) unamerikanisch **2** (contrary to US interests) antiamerikanisch; **~ activities** unamerikanische Umtriebe

unanimity /ju:nə'nɪmɪtɪ/ *n., no pl.* Einmütigkeit, *die*; **be in perfect ~ over sth.** in etw. (*Dat.*) völlig übereinstimmen

unanimous /ju:'nænɪməs/ *adj.* einstimmig; **be ~ in doing sth.** etw. einmütig tun; **be ~ in rejecting** *or* **in their** *etc.* **rejection of sth.** etw. einmütig ablehnen; **the meeting was ~ as to ...:** die Versammlung war einer Meinung über ...

unanimously /ju:'nænɪməslɪ/ *adv.* einstimmig

unannounced /ʌnə'naʊnst/ *adj.* unangemeldet

unanswerable /ʌn'ɑ:nsərəbl/ *adj.* unbeantwortbar ‹*Frage*›; unlösbar ‹*Rätsel, Problem*›; unwiderlegbar ‹*Argument*›

unanswered /ʌn'ɑ:nsəd/ *adj.* unbeantwortet; **go ~, be left ~:** unbeantwortet bleiben

unapologetic /ʌnəpɒlə'dʒetɪk/ *adj.* **he was quite ~ about it** er machte keinerlei Anstalten, sich zu entschuldigen

unappealing /ʌnə'pi:lɪŋ/ *adj.* unansehnlich ‹*Person*›; nicht verlockend ‹*Aussicht*›

unappetizing /ʌn'æpɪtaɪzɪŋ/ *adj.* unappetitlich; unerfreulich ‹*Zukunft, Aussicht*›

unappreciative /ʌnə'pri:ʃɪətɪv, ʌnə'pri:sɪətɪv/ *adj.* undankbar; **be ~ of sth.** etw. nicht zu würdigen wissen

unapproachable /ʌnə'prəʊtʃəbl/ *adj.* unzugänglich

unarguable /ʌn'ɑ:gjʊəbl/ *adj.* unhaltbar

unarguably /ʌn'ɑ:gjʊəblɪ/ *adv.* unbestreitbar

unarm /ʌn'ɑ:m/ ▸ **disarm A**

unarmed /ʌn'ɑ:md/ *adj.* unbewaffnet; **~ combat** Kampf ohne Waffen

unartistic /ʌnɑ:'tɪstɪk/ *adj.* unkünstlerisch; **be ~:** keinen Sinn für Kunst haben

unashamed /ʌnə'ʃeɪmd/ *adj.* schamlos; (not embarrassed) ungeniert; unverhohlen ‹*Individualist*›; **naked and ~:** nackt und ungeniert

unashamedly /ʌnə'ʃeɪmɪdlɪ/ *adv.* ungeniert; unverhohlen ‹*individualistisch*›

unasked /ʌn'ɑ:skt/ *adj.* **1** (uninvited) ungebeten **2** (not asked for) **~ [for]** ungefragt

unassailable /ʌnə'seɪləbl/ *adj.* **1** (not open to assault) uneinnehmbar; **an ~ lead** ein nicht aufzuholender Vorsprung **2** (irrefutable) unwiderlegbar

unassisted /ʌnə'sɪstɪd/ ▸ **unaided**

unassuming /ʌnə'sju:mɪŋ/ *adj.* bescheiden; unprätentiös (geh.)

unattached /ʌnə'tætʃt/ *adj.* **1** (not fixed) nicht befestigt **2** (without a partner) ungebunden

unattainable /ʌnə'teɪnəbl/ *adj.* unerreichbar

unattempted /ʌnə'temptɪd/ *adj.* **the climb remains ~:** die Ersteigung ist noch nicht versucht worden

unattended /ʌnə'tendɪd/ *adj.* **1** **~ to** (not dealt with) unerledigt, unbearbeitet ‹*Post, Angelegenheit*›; nicht bedient ‹*Kunde*›; nicht behandelt ‹*Patient, Wunde*›; **leave a customer/patient ~ to** einen Kunden nicht bedienen/einen Patienten nicht behandeln; **he left the faults ~ to** er hat sich um die Fehler nicht gekümmert **2** (not supervised) unbeaufsichtigt ‹*Kind*›; unbewacht ‹*Parkplatz, Gepäck*›; **leave a patient ~:** einen Patienten allein lassen; **travel ~:** ohne Begleitung reisen

unattractive /ʌnə'træktɪv/ *adj.* unattraktiv; unschön ‹*Ort, Merkmal*›; wenig verlockend ‹*Angebot, Vorschlag*›; **not ~:** nicht ohne Reiz

unauthorized /ʌn'ɔ:θəraɪzd/ *adj.* unbefugt; nicht autorisiert ‹*Biographie*›; nicht genehmigt ‹*Demonstration*›; **no entry for ~ persons** Zutritt für Unbefugte verboten

unavailable /ʌnə'veɪləbl/ *adj.* nicht erhältlich ‹*Ware*›; **be ~ for comment** zu einer Stellungnahme nicht zur Verfügung stehen; **the manager is ~:** der Manager ist nicht zu sprechen

unavailing /ʌnə'veɪlɪŋ/ *adj.* vergeblich

unavoidable /ʌnə'vɔɪdəbl/ *adj.* unvermeidlich; **~ delays** unvermeidbare Verzögerungen

unavoidably /ʌnə'vɔɪdəblɪ/ *adv.* **we were ~ delayed** unsere Verspätung ließ sich nicht vermeiden; **he has been ~ detained** er konnte nicht verhindern, dass er aufgehalten wurde

unaware /ʌnə'weə(r)/ *adj.* **be ~ of sth.** sich (*Dat.*) einer Sache (*Gen.*) nicht bewusst sein; **he was not ~ of this fact** diese Tatsache war ihm durchaus bekannt

unawares /ʌnə'weəz/ *adv.* unerwartet; **come upon sb./catch sb. ~:** jmdn. überraschen; **take sb. ~:** für jmdn. unerwartet kommen

unbalanced /ʌn'bælənst/ *adj.* **1** unausgewogen **2** (mentally ~) unausgeglichen

unbar /ʌn'bɑ:(r)/ *v.t.*, **-rr-** entriegeln

unbearable /ʌn'beərəbl/ *adj.*, **unbearably** /ʌn'beərəblɪ/ *adv.* unerträglich

unbeatable /ʌn'bi:təbl/ *adj.* unschlagbar (ugs.)

unbeaten /ʌn'bi:tn/ *adj.* **1** (not defeated) ungeschlagen; **they lost their ~ record** ihre Siegesserie endete **2** (not surpassed) unerreicht; **this record is still ~:** dieser Rekord ist immer noch ungebrochen

unbecoming /ʌnbɪ'kʌmɪŋ/ *adj.* **1** (improper) unschicklich (geh.); **conduct ~ to a soldier** ein für einen Soldaten ungebührliches Verhalten **2** (not attractive) unvorteilhaft ‹*Kleidung, Frisur*›; unschön ‹*Nase*›

unbeknown /ʌnbɪ'nəʊn/ *adj.* **~ to me/her/her boss** ohne mein/ihr Wissen/ohne Wissen ihres Chefs

unbelievable /ʌnbɪ'li:vəbl/ *adj.* **1** (hardly believable) unglaublich **2** (tremendous) unwahrscheinlich ‹*Hunger, Durst*›

unbelievably /ʌnbɪ'li:vəblɪ/ *adv.* **1** *as intensifier* unglaublich ‹*dumm, dick, jung usw.*› **2** *as sentence-modifier* (not believably) **~, the rider managed to stay on the horse** es war kaum zu glauben, aber der Reiter konnte sich auf dem Pferd halten

unbeliever /ʌnbɪ'li:və(r)/ *n.* Ungläubige, *der/die*

unbelieving /ʌnbɪ'li:vɪŋ/ *adj.* ungläubig

unbend /ʌn'bend/

A *v.t.*, **unbent** /ʌn'bent/ geradebiegen ‹*Draht, Metall, Stoßstange*›; auseinander biegen ‹*Büroklammer*›; **~ one's body** *or* **oneself** sich aufrichten

B *v.i.*, **unbent** **1** (sit/stand up) sich aufrichten **2** (become affable) aus sich (*Dat.*) herausgehen

unbending /ʌn'bendɪŋ/ *adj.* (inflexible) unbeugsam

unbiased, unbiassed /ʌn'baɪəst/ *adj.* unvoreingenommen

unbidden /ʌn'bɪdn/ *adj.* unaufgefordert; (uninvited) ungebeten

unbind /ʌn'baɪnd/ *v.t.*, *forms as* **bind A** losbinden ‹*Mensch, Tier*›; lösen ‹*Haare*›

unbirthday /ʌn'bɜ:θdeɪ/ *adj.* (Brit. coll.) **~ present** Geschenk ohne besonderen Anlass

unbleached /ʌn'bli:tʃt/ *adj.* ungebleicht

unblemished /ʌn'blemɪʃt/ *adj.* makellos ‹*Haut, Lack, Ruf*›; unbefleckt (geh.) ‹*Ehre*›

unblinking /ʌn'blɪŋkɪŋ/ *adj.* unverwandt ‹*Blick*›; unbewegt ‹*Haltung, Miene*›

unblock /ʌn'blɒk/ *v.t.* frei machen *od.* bekommen; **remain ~ed** frei bleiben

unblushing /ʌn'blʌʃɪŋ/ *adj.* (fig.) schamlos

unbolt /ʌn'bəʊlt/ *v.t.* aufriegeln

unborn /ʌn'bɔ:n, *attrib.* 'ʌnbɔ:n/ *adj.* ungeboren; **generations [yet] ~:** künftige Generationen

unbosom /ʌn'bʊzəm/ *v. refl.* **~ oneself [to sb.]** [jmdm.] sein Herz ausschütten

unbound /ʌn'baʊnd/ *adj.* **1** (not tied) offen ‹*Haar*› **2** ungebunden ‹*Buch*›

unbounded /ʌn'baʊndɪd/ *adj.* **1** (unchecked) uneingeschränkt ‹*Freiheit*›; unkontrolliert ‹*Gefühl*› **2** (unlimited) grenzenlos

unbowed /ʌn'baʊd/ *adj.* ungebeugt; **bloody but ~:** angeschlagen, aber unbesiegt

unbranded /ʌn'brændɪd/ *adj.* (Commerc.) markenlos

unbreakable /ʌn'breɪkəbl/ *adj.* unzerbrechlich

unbridled /ʌn'braɪdld/ *adj.* (fig.) ungezügelt ‹*Machtstreben*›; bodenlos (ugs.) ‹*Unverschämtheit*›; grenzenlos ‹*Enthusiasmus*›

un-British /ʌn'brɪtɪʃ/ *adj.* unbritisch

unbroken /ʌn'brəʊkn/ *adj.* **1** (undamaged) heil; unbeschädigt **2** (not interrupted) ununterbrochen; **~ sleep/peace/silence** ungestörter Schlaf/Friede/durch nichts unterbrochene Stille; **have a night's ~ sleep** die Nacht durchschlafen **3** (not surpassed) ungebrochen ‹*Rekord*› **4** (Equit.) nicht zugeritten ‹*Pferd*›

unbuckle /ʌn'bʌkl/ *v.t.* aufschnallen

unbuilt /ʌn'bɪlt/ *adj.* ungebaut; **~ on** (not occupied by a building) unbebaut

unburden /ʌn'bɜ:dn/ *v.t.* (literary) befreien ‹*Gewissen*›; **~ oneself/one's heart [to sb.]** [jmdm.] sein Herz ausschütten; **~ oneself of sth.** sich von etw. befreien; **to her he could ~ himself of all his anxieties** ihr konnte er alle seine Ängste anvertrauen

unbusinesslike /ʌn'bɪznɪslaɪk/ *adj.* **he is ~, he has an ~ approach** er geht nicht wie ein Geschäftsmann an die Dinge heran

unbutton /ʌn'bʌtn/ *v.t.* aufknöpfen

unbuttoned /ʌn'bʌtnd/ *adj.* (lit. or fig.) aufgeknöpft; offen

uncalled-for /ʌn'kɔ:ldfɔ:(r)/ *adj.* unangebracht

uncannily /ʌn'kænɪlɪ/ *adv.* unheimlich

uncanny /ʌn'kænɪ/ *adj.* **1** (seemingly supernatural) unheimlich **2** (mysterious) verblüffend

uncap /ʌn'kæp/ *v.t.*, **-pp-** öffnen ‹*Flasche*›

uncared-for /ʌn'keədfɔ:(r)/ *adj.* vernachlässigt

uncaring /ʌn'keərɪŋ/ *adj.* gleichgültig

uncarpeted /ʌn'kɑ:pɪtɪd/ *adj.* teppichlos

unceasing /ʌn'si:sɪŋ/ *adj.* unaufhörlich; **the rain was ~:** es regnete ununterbrochen

unceasingly /ʌn'si:sɪŋlɪ/ *adv.* ununterbrochen

uncensored /ʌn'sensəd/ *adj.* unzensiert

unceremonious /ʌnserɪ'məʊnɪəs/ *adj.* **1** (informal) formlos **2** (abrupt) brüsk

unceremoniously /ʌnserɪ'məʊnɪəslɪ/ *adv.* ohne Umschweife

uncertain /ʌn'sɜ:tn, ʌn'sɜ:tɪn/ *adj.* **1** (not sure) **be ~ [whether ...]** sich (*Dat.*) nicht sicher sein[, ob ...]; **I am ~ of his loyalty** ich bin mir seiner Treue nicht sicher **2** (not clear) ungewiss ‹*Ergebnis, Zukunft, Schicksal*›; **of ~ age/origin** unbestimmten Alters/unbestimmter Herkunft; **a play of ~ authorship** ein Stück, dessen Verfasser nicht [sicher] bekannt ist; **it is still ~ whether ...:** es ist noch ungewiss, ob ...; **it is ~ who was the inventor** der Erfinder ist nicht [genau] bekannt **3** (unsteady) unsicher ‹*Schritte*› **4** (changeable) unbeständig ‹*Charakter, Wetter*›; unstet ‹*Dasein*›; wechselnd ‹*Gesundheitszustand*›; flackernd ‹*Schein*› **5** (ambiguous) vage; **in no ~ terms** ganz eindeutig

uncertainly /ʌn'sɜ:tnlɪ, ʌn'sɜ:tɪnlɪ/ *adv.* **1** (without definite aim) ziellos **2** (without confidence) unsicher

uncertainty /ʌn'sɜ:tntɪ, ʌn'sɜ:tɪntɪ/ *n.* **1** *no pl.* (doubtfulness) Ungewissheit, *die;* **there is some ~ about it** es ist etwas ungewiss; **any ~ about it was dispelled** jeder Zweifel darüber wurde ausgeräumt **2** (doubtful point) Unklarheit, *die* **3** *no pl.* (hesitation) Unsicherheit, *die;* **the ~ of his touch** seine unsichere Hand

un'certainty principle *n.* (Phys.) Unschärferelation, *die*

unchallenged /ʌn'tʃælɪndʒd/ *adj.* unangefochten; **go ~** ‹*Autorität, Position:*› nicht infrage gestellt werden; **let a statement go ~:** eine Behauptung unwidersprochen lassen

unchallenging /ʌn'tʃæləndʒɪŋ/ *adj.* **1** (undemanding) anspruchslos ‹*Job, Kurs usw.*› **2** (non-threatening) zurückhaltend

unchangeable /ʌn'tʃeɪnʒəbl/ *adj.* unabänderlich

unchanged /ʌn'tʃeɪndʒd/ *adj.* unverändert

unchanging /ʌn'tʃeɪndʒɪŋ/ *adj.* unveränderlich; **~ monotony** gleichförmige Eintönigkeit

uncharacteristic /ʌnkærɪktə'rɪstɪk/ *adj.* uncharakteristisch (**of** für); ungewohnt ‹*Grobheit, Schärfe*›

uncharged /ʌn'tʃɑ:dʒd/ *adj.* ungeladen

uncharitable /ʌn'tʃærɪtəbl/ *adj.*, **uncharitably** /ʌn'tʃærɪtəblɪ/ *adv.* lieblos

uncharted /ʌn'tʃɑ:tɪd/ *adj.* auf keiner Landkarte verzeichnet; unerforscht ‹*Wildnis*›; unbekannt ‹*Insel, Gewässer*›; (fig.) **the ~ regions of the psyche** die unerforschten Bereiche der Psyche

unchecked /ʌn'tʃekt/ *adj.* **1** (not examined) ungeprüft **2** (unrestrained) ungehindert; nicht eingedämmt ‹*Epidemie, Inflation*›; **sth. goes ~:** gegen etw. wird nichts getan

unchivalrous /ʌn'ʃɪvlrəs/ *adj.* unritterlich

unchristian /ʌn'krɪstjən/ *adj.* unchristlich

uncivil /ʌn'sɪvɪl, ʌn'sɪvl/ *adj.* unhöflich

uncivilized /ʌn'sɪvɪlaɪzd/ *adj.* unzivilisiert; primitiv ‹*Zustände*›; **an ~ hour** eine unchristliche Tageszeit (ugs. scherzh.)

unclaimed /ʌn'kleɪmd/ *adj.* herrenlos; nicht abgeholt ‹*Brief, Preis*›; **the money is still ~:** bis jetzt hat niemand Anspruch auf das Geld erhoben

unclassified /ʌn'klæsɪfaɪd/ *adj.* nicht klassifiziert; (not subject to security classification) nicht geheim

uncle /'ʌŋkl/ *n.* **1** Onkel, *der* **2** **cry ~** (Amer. coll.: surrender) sich geschlagen geben

unclean /ʌn'kli:n/ *adj.* unrein

unclear /ʌn'klɪə(r)/ *adj.* **1** (obscure, confusing) unklar; (not easy to understand) nicht klar verständlich **2** (uncertain) unklar; ungewiss ‹*Zukunft*› **3** (confused) **be ~d about sth.** sich über etw. (*Akk.*) im Unklaren sein

unclench /'ʌnklentʃ/
A *v.t.* öffnen ‹*Faust, Kiefer*›
B *v.i.* sich öffnen

Uncle: ~ 'Sam *n.* (coll.) Uncle Sam (*der*); **~ 'Tom** *n.* (Amer.) *den Weißen gegenüber gefügiger Schwarzer in den USA*

unclothed /ʌn'kləʊðd/ *adj.* unbekleidet

unclouded /ʌn'klaʊdɪd/ *adj.* wolkenlos; (fig.) **~ mind/happiness** klarer Verstand/ungetrübtes Glück

uncluttered /ʌn'klʌtəd/ *adj.* ordentlich

uncoil /ʌn'kɔɪl/
A *v.t.* abwickeln
B *v. refl.* sich abwickeln; ‹*Schlange:*› sich strecken

uncoloured (*Amer.:* **uncolored**) /ʌn'kʌləd/ *adj.* (lit. or fig.) ungefärbt; **~ by prejudice** von keinem Vorurteil gefärbt

uncomfortable /ʌn'kʌmfətəbl/ *adj.* **1** (causing physical discomfort) unbequem **2** (feeling discomfort) **be ~:** sich unbehaglich fühlen; **the heat made me ~:** durch die Hitze fühlte ich mich unbehaglich **3** (uneasy, disconcerting) unangenehm; peinlich ‹*Stille*›; **his gaze made me ~:** sein Blick war mir unangenehm; **if you feel ~ about it** wenn es dir unangenehm ist; **sb. has an ~ awareness of sth.** jmd. ist sich (*Dat.*) einer Sache (*Gen.*) peinlich bewusst

uncomfortably /ʌn'kʌmfətəblɪ/ *adv.* **1** (with physical discomfort) unbequem; **~ oppressive** unangenehm [und] drückend **2** (uneasily) unbehaglich; **be** *or* **feel ~ aware of sth.** sich (*Dat.*) einer Sache (*Gen.*) peinlich bewusst sein

uncommercial /ʌnkə'mɜ:ʃəl/ *adj.* **1** unkommerziell; (not allowing a profit) kommerziell nicht verwertbar **2** (failing commercially) kommerziell erfolglos

uncommitted /ʌnkə'mɪtɪd/ *adj.* unbeteiligt

uncommon /ʌn'kɒmən/ *adj.* ungewöhnlich; **it is not ~ for him to be found there** es ist [ganz und gar] nicht ungewöhnlich, dass man ihn dort findet

uncommonly /ʌn'kɒmənlɪ/ *adv.* ungewöhnlich

uncommunicative /ʌnkə'mju:nɪkətɪv/ *adj.* verschlossen

uncompetitive /ʌnkəm'petɪtɪv/ *adj.* wettbewerbsunfähig; **prices were ~:** die Preise waren nicht wettbewerbs- *od.* konkurrenzfähig; **this makes the salaries even more ~:** dadurch nimmt die Wettbewerbsfähigkeit der Gehälter noch weiter ab

uncomplaining /ʌnkəm'pleɪnɪŋ/ *adj.*, **uncomplainingly** /ʌnkəm'pleɪnɪŋlɪ/ *adv.* klaglos

uncompleted /ʌnkəm'pli:tɪd/ *adj.* unvollendet

uncomplicated /ʌn'kɒmplɪkeɪtɪd/ *adj.* unkompliziert

uncomplimentary /ʌnkɒmplɪ'mentərɪ/ *adj.* wenig schmeichelhaft; **be ~ about sb./sth.** sich nicht sehr schmeichelhaft über jmdn./etw. äußern

uncomprehending /ʌnkɒmprɪ'hendɪŋ/ *adj.* verständnislos

uncompromising /ʌn'kɒmprəmaɪzɪŋ/ *adj.*, **uncompromisingly** /ʌn'kɒmprəmaɪzɪŋlɪ/ *adv.* kompromisslos

unconcealed /ʌnkən'si:ld/ *adj.* unverhohlen

unconcern /ʌnkən'sɜ:n/ *n.*, *no pl.* Gleichgültigkeit, *die*

unconcerned /ʌnkən'sɜ:nd/ *adj.* gleichgültig; (free from anxiety) unbekümmert; **sb. is ~ about sb./sth.** jmdm. ist jmd./etw. gleichgültig; **she seemed ~ as to the outcome** das Ergebnis schien ihr gleichgültig zu sein; **he is ~ with** *or* **about style** er kümmert sich nicht um Stil

unconcernedly /ʌnkən'sɜ:nɪdlɪ/ *adv.* gleichgültig; (free from anxiety) unbekümmert

unconditional /ʌnkən'dɪʃənl/ *adj.* bedingungslos ‹*Kapitulation*›; kategorisch ‹*Ablehnung*›; ‹*Versprechen*› ohne Vorbehalte

unconditionally /ʌnkən'dɪʃənəlɪ/ *adv.* bedingungslos; kategorisch ‹*ablehnen*›; ohne Vorbehalte ‹*versprechen*›

unconfirmed /ʌnkən'fɜ:md/ *adj.* unbestätigt

uncongenial /ʌnkən'dʒi:nɪəl/ *adj.* unsympathisch ‹*Person*›; **I find him/the work ~:** er ist mir unsympathisch/die Arbeit sagt mir nicht zu *od.* liegt mir nicht; **an ~ atmosphere** ein unangenehmes Klima

unconnected /ʌnkə'nektɪd/ *adj.* **1** nicht verbunden; **~ with any party** nicht parteigebunden **2** (disjointed, isolated) zusammenhanglos

unconquerable /ʌn'kɒŋkərəbl/ *adj.* unbezwingbar; unerschütterlich ‹*Entschlossenheit*›

unconquered /ʌn'kɒŋkəd/ *adj.* nicht erobert

unconscionable /ʌn'kɒnʃənəbl/ *adj.* übertrieben lang ‹*Zeit*›; übertrieben hoch ‹*Betrag*›; **~ behaviour** unmögliches Benehmen

unconscionably /ʌn'kɒnʃənəblɪ/ *adv.* übertrieben

unconscious /ʌn'kɒnʃəs/
A *adj.* **1** (Med.: senseless) bewusstlos **2** (unaware) **be ~ of sth.** sich einer Sache (*Gen.*) nicht bewusst sein; **I was ~ of what was going on around me** ich war mir nicht bewusst *od.* wusste nicht, was um mich herum vorging; **she was ~ of the tragedy** sie wusste nichts von der Tragödie; **he was ~ of the change in her** er merkte *od.* bemerkte nicht, dass sie sich verändert hatte **3** (not intended; Psych.) unbewusst; unfreiwillig ‹*Komik*›; **an ~ act** eine unbewusst begangene Tat
B *n.* Unbewusste, *das*

unconsciously /ʌn'kɒnʃəslɪ/ *adv.* unbewusst; **~, he was falling under her spell** ohne es zu merken, verfiel er ihrem Zauber

unconsciousness /ʌn'kɒnʃəsnɪs/ *n.*, *no pl.* **1** (loss of consciousness) Bewusstlosigkeit, *die* **2** (unawareness) fehlende Bewusstheit

unconsidered /ʌnkən'sɪdəd/ *adj.* **1** (disregarded) unbedeutend **2** (not based on consideration) unüberlegt, vorschnell ‹*Bemerkung*›

unconstitutional /ʌnkɒnstɪ'tju:ʃənl/ *adj.*, **unconstitutionally** /ʌnkɒnstɪ'tju:ʃənəlɪ/ *adv.* (in State) verfassungswidrig; (in other organization) satzungswidrig

unconstrained /ʌnkən'streɪnd/ *adj.* ungezwungen

uncontaminated /ʌnkən'tæmɪneɪtɪd/ *adj.* unverschmutzt, nicht verseucht (**with** von); (fig.) unverdorben (**with** durch)

uncontested /ʌnkən'testɪd/ *adj.* unangefochten; **go ~:** nicht angefochten werden; **it was an ~ election** bei der Wahl gab es keinen Gegenkandidaten

uncontrollable /ʌnkən'trəʊləbl/ *adj.* unkontrollierbar; **become ~:** außer Kontrolle geraten; **the child is ~:** das Kind ist nicht zu bändigen

uncontrollably /ʌnkən'trəʊləblɪ/ *adv.* unkontrollierbar; unbeherrscht ‹*lachen*›; hemmungslos ‹*weinen usw.*›

uncontrolled /ʌnkən'trəʊld/ *adj.* unkontrolliert; **leave ~:** nicht kontrollieren; **~ dogs/children** herrenlose Hunde/unbeaufsichtigte Kinder

uncontroversial /ʌnkɒntrə'vɜːʃl/ *adj.* nicht kontrovers; **be ~:** keinerlei Widerspruch hervorrufen; **he is an ~ figure** er gibt keinen Anlass zu Kontroversen

unconventional /ʌnkən'venʃənl/ *adj.*, **unconventionally** /ʌnkən'venʃənəlɪ/ *adv.* unkonventionell

unconverted /ʌnkən'vɜːtɪd/ *adj.* **1** (not rebuilt) nicht umgebaut **2** (Relig.) nicht konvertiert; **he is** *or* **remains ~ [to sth.]** er lässt sich nicht [zu etw.] bekehren

unconvinced /ʌnkən'vɪnst/ *adj.* nicht überzeugt; **remain ~:** sich nicht überzeugen lassen; **his arguments left her ~:** seine Argumente überzeugten sie nicht

unconvincing /ʌnkən'vɪnsɪŋ/ *adj.* nicht überzeugend

unconvincingly /ʌnkən'vɪnsɪŋlɪ/ *adv.* nicht überzeugend; **he argues very ~:** seine Argumente überzeugen ganz und gar nicht

uncooked /ʌn'kʊkt/ *adj.* roh; **the cake was still ~ in the centre** der Kuchen war in der Mitte noch nicht durchgebacken

uncool /ʌn'kuːl/ *adj.* (coll.) uncool (ugs.)

uncooperative /ʌnkəʊ'ɒpərətɪv/ *adj.* unkooperativ; wenig entgegenkommend; (unhelpful) wenig hilfsbereit; **a bit less ~:** ein bisschen hilfsbereiter

uncoordinated /ʌnkəʊ'ɔːdɪneɪtɪd/ *adj.* unkoordiniert; **very ~:** überhaupt nicht koordiniert

uncork /ʌn'kɔːk/ *v.t.* entkorken

uncorrected /ʌnkə'rektɪd/ *adj.* unkorrigiert; unberichtigt ‹*Manuskript, Fehler*›

uncorroborated /ʌnkə'rɒbəreɪtɪd/ *adj.* unbestätigt

uncountable /ʌn'kaʊntəbl/ *adj.* (Ling.) unzählbar

uncounted /ʌn'kaʊntɪd/ *adj.* nicht gezählt

uncouple /ʌn'kʌpl/ *v.t.* abkoppeln ‹*Hunde, Waggon, Lokomotive*›

uncouth /ʌn'kuːθ/ *adj.* **1** (lacking refinement) ungeschliffen; ungehobelt ‹*Person, Benehmen*›; grob ‹*Bemerkung, Sprache*› **2** (boorish) unkultiviert; flegelhaft (abwertend)

uncouthness /ʌn'kuːθnɪs/ *n., no pl.* **1** (lack of refinement) Ungeschliffenheit, *die;* (of remark, language) Grobheit, *die* **2** (boorishness) Unkultiviertheit, *die;* Flegelhaftigkeit, *die* (abwertend)

uncover /ʌn'kʌvə(r)/ *v.t.* **1** (remove cover from) aufdecken; freilegen ‹*Wunde, Begrabenes*›; **~ one's head** die Kopfbedeckung abnehmen **2** (disclose) aufdecken ‹*Skandal, Verschwörung, Wahrheit*›

uncovered /ʌn'kʌvəd/ *adj.* unbedeckt; **[with head] ~:** ohne Kopfbedeckung

uncritical /ʌn'krɪtɪkl/ *adj.* unkritisch; **be ~ of sth.** etw. nicht kritisieren

uncritically /ʌn'krɪtɪkəlɪ/ *adv.* unkritisch

uncross /ʌn'krɒs/ *v.t.* **~ one's legs** seine Beine wieder nebeneinander stellen/nebeneinander legen

uncrossed /ʌn'krɒst/ *adj.* (Brit.) **an ~ cheque/postal order** ein Barscheck/Postbarscheck

uncrowded /ʌn'kraʊdɪd/ *adj.* nicht überlaufen

uncrowned /ʌn'kraʊnd/ *adj.* (lit. or fig.) ungekrönt

UNCTAD /'ʌŋktæd/ *abbr.* **= United Nations Conference on Trade and Development** Welthandels- und Entwicklungskonferenz [der Vereinten Nationen]

unction /'ʌŋkʃn/ ▸ **extreme A 4**

unctuous /'ʌŋktjʊəs/ *adj.* salbungsvoll; ölig

uncultivated /ʌn'kʌltɪveɪtɪd/ *adj.* **1** (Agric.) nicht bestellt **2** unkultiviert

uncultured /ʌn'kʌltʃəd/ *adj.* unkultiviert

uncured /ʌn'kjʊəd/ *adj.* **1** (not made healthy) ungeheilt **2** (not prepared for keeping) ungepökelt ‹*Fleisch*›; ungeräuchert ‹*Fisch*›; nicht getrocknet ‹*Häute, Tabak*›

uncurl /ʌn'kɜːl/

A *v.t.* auseinander rollen

B *v. refl.* sich strecken

C *v.i.* sich auseinander rollen

uncurtained /ʌn'kɜːtənd/ *adj.* vorhanglos; **be ~:** keine Vorhänge haben

uncut /ʌn'kʌt/ *adj.* **1** (not cut) nicht geschnitten ‹*Gras, Haare usw.*›; nicht gemäht ‹*Rasen*› **2** (with pages not trimmed) unbeschnitten ‹*Buch*›; (not slit open) nicht aufgeschnitten ‹*Seiten*› **3** (not shaped by cutting) ungeschliffen ‹*Edelstein*› **4** (not shortened) ungekürzt ‹*Buch, Film*›

undamaged /ʌn'dæmɪdʒd/ *adj.* unbeschädigt

undated /ʌn'deɪtɪd/ *adj.* undatiert

undaunted /ʌn'dɔːntɪd/ *adj.* unverzagt; **~ by threats** durch Drohungen nicht eingeschüchtert

undecided /ʌndɪ'saɪdɪd/ *adj.* **1** (not settled) nicht entschieden **2** (hesitant) unentschlossen; **be ~ whether to do sth.** sich (*Dat.*) noch unschlüssig sein, ob man etw. tun soll

undecipherable /ʌndɪ'saɪfərəbl/ *adj.* **be ~:** sich nicht entziffern lassen

undeclared /ʌndɪ'kleəd/ *adj.* **1** nicht erklärt ‹*Krieg*› **2** nicht deklariert ‹*zollpflichtige Waren*›; **~ income** (for tax) nicht angegebenes Einkommen

undefeated /ʌndɪ'fiːtɪd/ *adj.* ungeschlagen ‹*Mannschaft*›; unbesiegt ‹*Heer*›

undefended /ʌndɪ'fendɪd/ *adj.* **1** unverteidigt; (not protected) ungeschützt **2** (Law) unverteidigt; **be ~:** keinen Verteidiger haben; **the case was ~:** der Fall wurde ohne Verteidigung verhandelt

undefiled /ʌndɪ'faɪld/ *adj.* unverdorben; (not desecrated) unbefleckt

undefined /ʌndɪ'faɪnd/ *adj.* nicht definiert; (indefinite) unbestimmt

'undelete *v.t.* (Computing) wiederherstellen

undelivered /ʌndɪ'lɪvəd/ *adj.* nicht zugestellt ‹*Postsendung*›; nicht überbracht ‹*Botschaft, Nachricht*›; (on letter) **if ~:** wenn unzustellbar

undemanding /ʌndɪ'mɑːndɪŋ/ *adj.* anspruchslos

undemocratic /ʌndemə'krætɪk/ *adj.* undemokratisch

undemocratically /ʌndemə'krætɪklɪ/ *adv.* auf undemokratische Art und Weise; undemokratisch ‹*sich verhalten, handeln*›

undemonstrative /ʌndɪ'mɒnstrətɪv/ *adj.* zurückhaltend

undeniable /ʌndɪ'naɪəbl/ *adj.* unbestreitbar; **it is ~ that ...:** es ist nicht zu leugnen, dass ...; **produce ~ evidence** Beweise vorlegen, deren Echtheit nicht bezweifelt werden kann

undeniably /ʌndɪ'naɪəblɪ/ *adv.* unbestreitbar

undependable /ʌndɪ'pendəbl/ *adj.* unzuverlässig

under /'ʌndə(r)/

A *prep.* **1** (underneath, below) (indicating position) unter (+ *Dat.*); (indicating motion) unter (+ *Akk.*); **from ~ the table/bed** unter dem Tisch/Bett hervor **2** (undergoing) **~ treatment** in Behandlung; **~ repair** in Reparatur; **~ construction** im Bau; **be ~ investigation** untersucht werden; **fields ~ cultivation** bebaute Felder; **~ threat of extinction** vom Aussterben bedroht; **~ sentence of death** zum Tode verurteilt; *see also* **discussion 2**; **influence A**; **pain 3** (in conditions of) bei ‹*Stress, hohen Temperaturen usw.*› **4** (subject to) unter (+ *Dat.*); **bring a country ~ one's rule** ein Land unter seine Herrschaft bringen; **~ the doctor, ~ doctor's orders** in ärztlicher Behandlung; *see also* **delusion**; **illusion 2**; **impression 7**; **misapprehension** **5** (in accordance with) **~ the circumstances** unter den gegebenen *od.* diesen Umständen; **~ the terms of the will/contract/agreement** nach den Bestimmungen des Testaments/Vertrags/Abkommens **6** (with the use of) unter (+ *Dat.*); **~ an assumed name** *or* **alias/a pen-name** unter falschem Namen/unter einem Pseudonym **7** (less than) unter (+ *Dat.*); (esp. with time, amount) weniger als; **no one ~ a bishop** niemand unter Bischofsrang; **the mile was run in ~ four minutes** die Meile wurde in weniger als *od.* unter vier Minuten gelaufen; **for ~ five pounds** für weniger als fünf Pfund; *see also* **age A 1** **8** (at foot of) **~ the hill/walls** am Fuße des Berges/der Mauern **9** (Naut.: in the lee of) **close ~ the island** im Schutze der nahen Insel **10** (planted with) **field ~ corn/rice/beans** mit Getreide/Reis/Bohnen bestandenes Feld

B *adv.* **1** (in or to a lower or subordinate position) darunter; **stay ~** (**~ water**) unter Wasser bleiben; *see also* **go under** **2** (in/into a state of unconsciousness) **be ~/put sb. ~:** in Narkose liegen/jmdn. in Narkose versetzen

under: ~a'chieve *v.i.* unter dem erreichbaren Leistungsniveau bleiben; **~achiever** /ʌndərə'tʃiːvə(r)/ *n.* Schüler/Schülerin mit enttäuschenden Leistungen; **be an ~achiever** ▸ **u~achieve**; **~'act** *v.t. & i.* unterspielen (Theaterjargon); **~-age** *adj.* minderjährig; **~-age children** Minderjährige; **~-age drinking/smoking** Alkoholgenuss/Rauchen Minderjähriger; **~-age sex** Sex unter Minderjährigen; **~arm** **A** *adj.* **1** (Tennis, Cricket, etc.) ‹*Aufschlag, Wurf*› von unten; **2** (in armpit) Achsel‹*haare, -schweiß*›; **B** *adv.* von unten ‹*aufschlagen, werfen*›; **~belly** *n.* (Zool.) Bauch, *der;* (of aircraft) Unterseite, *die;* **[soft] ~belly** (fig.) verwundbare Stelle; **~body** *n.* Unterseite, *die;* **~brush** *n.* (Amer.) Unterholz, *das;* **~carriage** *n.* Fahrwerk, *das;* **~'charge** *v.t.* **~charge sb. [by several pounds]** jmdm. [einige Pfund] zu wenig berechnen; **~class** *n.* [unterste] Unterschicht; **~clothes** *n. pl.*, **~clothing** ▸ **underwear**; **~coat** *n.* **1** (layer of paint) Grundierung, *die;* **2** (paint) Grundierfarbe, *die;* **3** (of animal) Unterhaar, *das;* **~'cooked** *adj.* zu kurz gekocht/gebraten; noch nicht gar; **~'cover** *adj.* (disguised) getarnt; (secret) verdeckt; (engaged in international spying) geheim[dienstlich]; **~cover agent** ▸ ❶ **p. 1260** Untergrund-/Geheimagent, *der;* **~croft** *n.* (Eccl.) Krypta, *die;* **~current** *n.* Unterströmung, *die;* (fig.: **~**lying feeling) Unterton, *der;* **he sensed an ~current of resentment** er spürte eine unterschwelligen Groll; **~'cut** *v.t.*, **~cut** unterbieten; **~de'veloped** *adj.* unterentwickelt; **~de'velopment** *n., no pl.* Unterentwicklung, *die;* **~dog** *n.* **1** (in fight, match) Unterlegene, *der/die;* **2** (fig.: disadvantaged person) Benachteiligte, *der/die;* **the ~dogs of society** die sozial Unterprivilegierten; **~'done** *adj.* halbgar; **I don't like my steak ~done** ich habe mein Steak gern gut durchgebraten; **~'emphasis** *n.* zu schwache Betonung; **there is an ~emphasis on it** es kommt nicht deutlich genug zum Ausdruck; **~'emphasize** *v.t.* zu wenig betonen; **~em'ployed** *adj.* unterbeschäftigt; **~em'ployment** *n.* Unterbeschäftigung, *die;* **~estimate** **A** /ʌndər'estɪmeɪt/ *v.t.* unterschätzen; **B** /ʌndər'estɪmət/ *n.* Unterschätzung, *die;* **that figure is a considerable ~estimate** diese Zahl ist viel zu niedrig geschätzt; **~ex'pose** *v.t.* (Photog.) unterbelichten; **~ex'posure** *n.* (Photog.) Unterbelichtung, *die;* **~'fed** *adj.* unterernährt; **~felt** *n.* Filzunterlage, *die;* **~-'fives** *n. pl.* Kinder unter fünf Jahren; **~'floor heating** *n.* [Fuß]bodenheizung, *die;* **~'foot** *adv.* am Boden; **it's rough/muddy ~foot** der Boden ist uneben/matschig; **be trodden/trampled ~foot** mit Füßen getreten/zertrampelt werden; (fig.: be maltreated) wie der letzte Dreck behandelt werden (salopp); **~funded** /ʌndə'fʌndɪd/ *adj.* unterfinanziert ‹*Projekt, Service*›; **an ~funded company** eine

u

Firma mit zu dünner Finanzdecke; ~**garment** n. Wäschestück, das; ~**garments** Unterwäsche, die; ~'**go** v.t., forms as **go¹ A** durchmachen ‹schlimme Zeiten›; ertragen ‹Demütigung›; ~**go treatment/an operation** sich einer Behandlung/Operation unterziehen; ~**go a change** sich verändern; ~**go repairs** repariert werden; ~**grad** /ˌʌndəˈgræd/ (coll.), ~'**graduate** ns. ~**graduate [student]** Student/Studentin vor der ersten Prüfung; ~**graduate course** Lehrveranstaltung für Studenten vor der ersten Prüfung; ~**ground** **A** /--'-/ adv. **1** (beneath surface of ground) unter der Erde; (Mining) unter Tage; **an explosion ~ground** eine unterirdische Explosion; **2** (fig.) (in hiding) im Untergrund; (into hiding) in den Untergrund; **go ~ground** untertauchen; in den Untergrund gehen; **B** /'---/ adj. **1** unterirdisch ‹Höhle, See›; ~**ground railway** Untergrundbahn, die; ~**ground car park** Tiefgarage, die; **2** (fig.: secret) ~**ground activity** Tätigkeit im Untergrund; ~**ground organization/movement/press** Untergrundorganisation/-bewegung/-presse; **C** n. **1** (railway) U-Bahn, die; **2** (clandestine movement) Untergrund, der; Untergrundbewegung, die; ~**ground e'conomy** n. Untergrundwirtschaft, die; Schattenwirtschaft, die; ~**growth** n. Unterholz, das; ~**hand**, ~**handed** **A** adjs. **1** (secret) heimlich; **2** (crafty) hinterhältig; **B** advs. heimlich; ~**hung** adj. vorgeschoben ‹Unterkiefer›; ~**in'sured** adj. unterversichert; ~**in'vestment** n., no pl. mangelnde od. unzureichende Investitionen; ~'**lay¹** ▸ ~**lie**; ~**lay²** **A** /--'-/ v.t., forms as **lay² B** unterlegen; **B** /'---/ n. Unterlage, die; ~'**lie** v.t., forms as **lie² B**: **1** (lie ~) ~**lie sth.** unter etw. (Dat.) liegen; **2** (fig.: be [at] the basis of) ~**lie sth.** einer Sache (Dat.) zugrunde liegen; ~**lying cause of sth.** eigentliche Ursache für etw.; ~**line** **A** /--'-/ v.t. (lit. or fig.) unterstreichen; **B** /'---/ n. Unterstreichung, die

underling /ˈʌndəlɪŋ/ n. (derog.) Untergebene, der/die

under: ~'**lining** n. Unterstreichung, die; **there is too much ~lining** es ist zu viel unterstrichen; ~'**lying** ▸ **underlie**; ~'**manned** adj. [personell] unterbesetzt; ~**manned industries** Industriezweige, in denen Arbeitskräftemangel herrscht; ~'**manning** n. no pl. [personelle] Unterbesetzung; ~'**mentioned** adj. (Brit.) unten genannt; unten erwähnt; ~'**mine** v.t. **1** unterhöhlen; ‹Wasser:› unterspülen; **2** (fig.) (weaken) untergraben; erschüttern ‹Vertrauen›; unterminieren ‹Autorität›; schwächen ‹Gesundheit›

underneath /ˌʌndəˈniːθ/

A prep. (indicating position) unter (+ Dat.); (indicating motion) unter (+ Akk.); **from ~ the bed** unter dem Bett hervor

B adv. darunter

C n. Unterseite, die

under: ~'**nourished** adj. unterernährt; ~'**paid** adj. unterbezahlt; ~**pants** n. pl. Unterhose, die; Unterhosen Pl.; ~**part** n. Unterseite, die; ~**pass** n. Unterführung, die; ~'**pay** v.t., forms as **pay B** unterbezahlen; ~'**payment** n. Unterbezahlung, die; ~**per'form** **A** v.t. ~**perform the market/index** hinter der allgemeinen Entwicklung des Marktes/Indexes zurückbleiben; **B** v.i. hinter den Erwartungen zurückbleiben; sich unterdurchschnittlich entwickeln; **he is ~performing** seine Leistung ist unzureichend; ~'**pin** v.t. [ab]stützen; (fig.) untermauern; ~**pin a social system** die Grundlage eines gesellschaftlichen Systems bilden; ~'**play** v.t. **1** (Theatre) zurückhaltend spielen ‹Rolle, Szene›; **2** (play down) herunterspielen; ~**powered** /ˌʌndəˈpaʊəd/ adj. [zu] schwach ‹Lampe, Auto›; untermotorisiert ‹Auto›; zu wenig leistungsfähig ‹Gerät›; ~**prepared** /ˌʌndəprɪˈpeəd/ adj. ungenügend od. unzureichend vorbereitet; ~**priced** /ˌʌndəˈpraɪsd/ adj. unterpreisig; unterbewertet (Aktion usw.); **be ~priced** zu billig gehandelt od. unter Preis angeboten werden; ~'**privileged** adj. unterprivilegiert; ~**produce** /ˌʌndəprəˈdjuːs/ **A** v.t. unterproduzieren. **B** v.i. zu wenig produzieren; ~**pro'duction** n., no pl., no indef. art. Unterproduktion, die; ~**qualified** /ˌʌndəˈkwɒlɪfaɪd/ adj. unterqualifiziert; ~'**rate** v.t. unterschätzen; **be ~rated** [allgemein] unterschätzt werden; ~**ripe** adj. nicht ausgereift; ~**score** **1** ▸ ~**line B**; **2** (Computing) Unterstrich, der; ~**sea** attrib. adj. Unterwasser-; ~**seal** **A** v.t. mit [einem] Unterbodenschutz versehen; **be ~sealed** Unterbodenschutz haben; **B** n. Unterbodenschutz, der; ~**secretary** n. ▸ ❶ p. 1260 **1** (esp. Amer.: assistant to secretary) Unterstaatssekretär, der; **2** (Brit.) **[Parliamentary] U~secretary** [Parlamentarischer] Staatssekretär; ~'**sell** v.t., forms as **sell A** **1** (sell at lower price than) [im Preis] unterbieten; **2** (present inadequately) nicht genug anpreisen; ~**selling actually boosted her business** ihre verhaltene Werbestrategie hat eher zur Geschäftsbelebung geführt; ~'**sexed** adj. sexuell lustlos; ~**shirt** n. (Amer.) Unterhemd, das; ~'**shoot** v.t., forms as **shot A, B**: ~**shoot the runway** vor der Landebahn aufsetzen; ~**shorts** n. pl. (Amer.) Unterhose, die; ~**shot** ▸ **underhung**; ~**side** n. Unterseite, die; ~**signed** adj. (esp. Law) **the ~signed** der/die Unterzeichnete/(pl.) die Unterzeichneten (Papierdt.); ~**sized** adj. unter Normalgröße nachgestellt; [ziemlich] klein geraten ‹Person, Tier›; ~**skirt** n. Unterrock, der; ~**slung** adj. (Motor Veh.) [tiefer als die Achsen] hängend ‹Fahrgestell, Rahmen›; ~'**spend** **A** v.t., forms as **spend**: ~**spend a budget/an allowance** ein Budget unterschreiten/eine Zuwendung nicht ganz ausgeben; **B** v.i., forms as **spend**: ~**spend by £500,000** das Budget um 500 000 Pfund unterschreiten; ~**spend on sth.** zu wenig für etw. ausgeben; (save) an etw. (Dat.) sparen; ~'**spent** ▸ ~**spend**; ~'**staffed** adj. unterbesetzt; **be ~staffed** an Personalmangel leiden

understand /ˌʌndəˈstænd/

A v.t., **understood** /ˌʌndəˈstʊd/ **1** verstehen; ~ **sth. by sth.** etw. unter etw. (Dat.) verstehen; ~ **mathematics** mathematisches Verständnis haben; ~ **carpentry** sich auf das Schreinern verstehen; **I cannot ~ his doing it** ich kann nicht verstehen od. begreife nicht, warum er es tut; **is that understood?** ist das klar?; **make oneself understood** sich verständlich machen **2** (have heard) gehört haben; **I ~ that you wish to leave us** wie ich höre, wollen Sie uns verlassen; **I ~ him to be a distant relation** ich glaube, er ist ein entfernter Verwandter **3** (take as implied) ~ **sth. from sb.'s words** etw. aus jmds. Worten entnehmen; **I understood [that] we were to be paid expenses** ich dachte, dass wir Spesen bekommen sollten; **it was understood that ...:** es wurde allgemein angenommen, dass ...; **do I ~ that ...?** gehe ich recht in der Annahme, dass ...?; **am I to ~ that you refuse my offer?** wollen Sie damit sagen, dass Sie mein Angebot ablehnen?; **it was understood between them that ...:** es herrschte [stillschweigendes] Einverständnis zwischen ihnen, dass ... **4** (supply mentally) hinzudenken; **be understood** (Gram.) ausgelassen werden; **he is seething ('with rage' understood)** er kocht (gemeint ist „vor Wut"). See also **give A 5**; **make A 6**

B v.i., **understood** **1** (have understanding) verstehen; ~ **about sth.** etwas von etw. verstehen; **he doesn't ~ about it [being my job]** er sieht es nicht ein[, dass es meine Aufgabe ist]; **now I ~!** jetzt begreife ich es!; **I quite ~:** ich verstehe schon **2** (gather, hear) **if I ~ correctly** wenn ich mich nicht irre; **your offer is, I ~, still open** Ihr Angebot ist, so nehme ich an, noch offen; **he is, I ~, no longer here** er ist, wie ich höre, nicht mehr hier

understandable /ˌʌndəˈstændəbl/ adj. verständlich

understandably /ˌʌndəˈstændəblɪ/ adv. verständlicherweise

understanding /ˌʌndəˈstændɪŋ/

A adj. (able to sympathize) verständnisvoll; **you could be a bit more ~:** du könntest etwas mehr Verständnis zeigen

B n. **1** (agreement) Verständigung, die; **reach an ~ with sb.** sich mit jmdm. verständigen; **the good ~ between them** das gute Einverständnis zwischen ihnen; **have a secret ~ with sb.** eine geheime Vereinbarung mit jmdm. haben; **on the ~ that ...:** unter der Voraussetzung, dass ...; **on the clear** or **distinct ~ that ...** (condition) unter der ausdrücklichen Bedingung, dass ...; **there has never been much ~ between them** sie haben sich nie besonders gut vertragen **2** (intelligence) Verstand, der **3** (insight, comprehension) Verständnis, das (**of, for** für); **a person of great ~:** ein sehr verständnisvoller Mensch; **beyond ~:** unbegreiflich; **my ~ of the matter is that she has won** so wie ich es verstehe, hat sie gewonnen

understandingly /ˌʌndəˈstændɪŋlɪ/ adv. verständnisvoll

under: ~'**state** v.t. **1** herunterspielen; ~**state the case** untertreiben; **2** (represent inadequately) zu gering veranschlagen; ~'**statement** n. (avoidance of emphasis) Untertreibung, die; Understatement, das; ~**steer** (Motor Veh.) **A** /--'-/ v.i. untersteuern; **B** /'---/ n. Untersteuern, das; ~'**stocked** adj. unterversorgt; **the shops were ~stocked** die Läden hatten zu wenig Ware od. Vorräte [auf Lager]; ~'**stood** ▸ **understand**; ~**study** **A** n. Ersatzspieler, der/-spielerin, die; zweite Besetzung; **B** v.t. ~**study sb.** jmds. Rolle als Ersatzspieler/-spielerin einstudieren; ~**sub'scribed** adj. (St. Exch.) unterzeichnet; ~**surface** n. Unterseite, die; ~'**take** v.t., forms as **take A** **1** (set about) unternehmen; ~**take a task** eine Aufgabe übernehmen; ~**take to do sth.** sich verpflichten, etw. zu tun; **2** (guarantee) ~**take sth./that ...:** sich für etw. verbürgen/sich dafür verbürgen, dass ...; ~**taker** n. ▸ ❶ p. 1260 Leichenbestatter, der/-bestatterin, die; **[firm of] ~takers** Bestattungsunternehmen, das; ~'**taking** n. **1** no pl. (taking on) (of task) Übernehmen, das; (of journey etc.) Unternehmen, das; **2** (task) Aufgabe, die; **a dangerous ~taking** ein gefährliches Unterfangen; **3** (business) Unternehmen, das; Betrieb, der; **4** (pledge) Versprechen, das; **give an ~taking that .../to do sth.** zusichern, dass .../sich verpflichten, etw. zu tun; **I'll need an ~taking from you that ...:** du musst mir [fest] versprechen, dass ...; ~**tone** n. **1** (low voice) **in ~tones** or **an ~tone** in gedämpftem Ton; **2** (~current) ~**tone of criticism** kritischer Unterton; **3** (subdued colour) Tönung, die; ~**tow** n. Unterströmung, die; ~'**used** adj. nicht voll genutzt; ~**valu'ation** n. Unterbewertung, die; ~'**value** v.t. unterbewerten; ~**vest** n. Unterhemd, das; ~**water** **A** /'----/ attrib. adj. Unterwasser-; **B** /--'--/ adv. unter Wasser; ~**wear** n., no pl., no indef. art. Unterwäsche, die; ~'**weight** adj. untergewichtig; **be ~weight** Untergewicht haben; ~**whelm** /ˌʌndəˈwelm/ v.t. (joc.) nicht gerade überwältigen (spött.); ~**world** n. (lit. or fig.) Unterwelt, die; ~'**write** v.t., forms as **write A** **1** (accept liability for) [als Versicherer] unterzeichnen; ~**write a risk** ein Risiko versichern; ~**write a share issue** die Übernahme von unverkauften Aktien garantieren; **2** (finance) finanzieren; ~**writer** n. ▸ ❶ p. 1260 (of insurance policy) Versicherer, der; (of stock issue) Garant, der/Garantin, die

undeserved /ˌʌndɪˈzɜːvd/ adj. unverdient

undeservedly /ˌʌndɪˈzɜːvɪdlɪ/ adv. unverdientermaßen

undeserving /ˌʌndɪˈzɜːvɪŋ/ adj. unwürdig (**of** Gen.); **not ~ of attention** schon beachtenswert

undesigned /ˌʌndɪˈzaɪnd/ adj. ungeplant

undesirability /ˌʌndɪzaɪərəˈbɪlɪtɪ/ n., no pl. Unerwünschtheit, die

undesirable /ˌʌndɪˈzaɪərəbl/

A adj. unerwünscht; **it is ~ that ...:** es ist nicht wünschenswert, dass ...

B n. unerwünschte Person

undesirably /ˌʌndɪˈzaɪərəblɪ/ adv. unerwünscht

undesired /ˌʌndɪˈzaɪəd/ adj. unerwünscht

undetectable /ˌʌndɪˈtektəbl/ adj. nicht nachweisbar

undetected /ˌʌndɪˈtektɪd/ adj. unentdeckt; **go** or **pass ~:** unentdeckt bleiben

undeterred /ʌndɪ'tɜ:d/ *adj.* nicht entmutigt (**by** durch); **remain** ~: sich nicht abschrecken lassen; **continue** ~: unbeirrt weitermachen

undeveloped /ʌndɪ'veləpt/ *adj.* **1** (immature) nicht voll ausgebildet **2** (Photog.) nicht entwickelt **3** (not built on) nicht bebaut

undiagnosed /ʌndaɪəg'nəʊzd/ *adj.* nicht diagnostiziert; **die of an ~ brain tumor** an einem nicht erkannten Gehirntumor sterben

undid ▸ **undo**

undies /'ʌndɪz/ *n. pl.* (coll.) Unterwäsche, *die*

undifferentiated /ʌndɪfə'renʃɪeɪtɪd/ *adj.* undifferenziert

undigested /ʌndɪ'dʒestɪd, ʌndaɪ'dʒestɪd/ *adj.* (lit. or fig.) unverdaut

undignified /ʌn'dɪgnɪfaɪd/ *adj.* würdelos; **consider it ~ to do sth.** es für unter seiner Würde halten, etw. zu tun

undiluted /ʌndaɪ'lju:tɪd/ *adj.* unverdünnt; **~ pleasure/nonsense** ungetrübte Freude/barer Unsinn

undiminished /ʌndɪ'mɪnɪʃt/ *adj.* unvermindert; **her enthusiasm remained ~:** ihre Begeisterung ließ nicht nach

undimmed /ʌn'dɪmd/ *adj.* nicht gedämpft; ungetrübt ‹*Augenlicht*›

undiplomatic /ʌndɪplə'mætɪk/ *adj.* undiplomatisch

undipped /ʌn'dɪpt/ *adj.* nicht abgeblendet

undischarged /ʌndɪs'tʃɑ:dʒd/ *adj.* **1** (Finance) unbeglichen ‹*Schuld*›; nicht entlastet ‹*Schuldner*› **2** (not unloaded) nicht entladen **3** (not fired off) nicht abgeschossen

undisciplined /ʌn'dɪsɪplɪnd/ *adj.* undiszipliniert

undisclosed /ʌndɪs'kləʊzd/ *adj.* geheim; **an ~ sum** ein nicht genannter Betrag

undiscoverable /ʌndɪ'skʌvərəbl/ *adj.* nicht feststellbar

undiscovered /ʌndɪ'skʌvəd/ *adj.* unentdeckt

undiscriminating /ʌndɪ'skrɪmɪneɪtɪŋ/ *adj.* unkritisch; (undemanding) anspruchslos

undisguised /ʌndɪs'gaɪzd/ *adj.* unverhohlen

undismayed /ʌndɪs'meɪd/ ▸ **undeterred**

undisputed /ʌndɪ'spju:tɪd/ *adj.* unbestritten ‹*Fertigkeit, Kompetenz*›; unangefochten ‹*Führer, Autorität*›

undistinguished /ʌndɪ'stɪŋgwɪʃt/ *adj.* mittelmäßig; (ordinary) gewöhnlich

undisturbed /ʌndɪ'stɜ:bd/ *adj.* **1** (untouched) unberührt **2** (not interrupted) ungestört **3** (not worried) ungerührt

undivided /ʌndɪ'vaɪdɪd/ *adj.* ungeteilt ‹*Sympathie, Aufmerksamkeit*›; geschlossen ‹*Front*›; uneingeschränkt ‹*Loyalität*›

undo /ʌn'du:/

A *v.t.*, **undoes** /ʌn'dʌz/, **undoing** /ʌn'du:ɪŋ/, **undid** /ʌn'dɪd/, **undone** /ʌn'dʌn/ **1** (unfasten) aufmachen **2** (cancel) ungeschehen machen; **his successor undid all his work** sein Nachfolger machte sein ganzes Werk zunichte

B *v.i., forms as* **A** ‹*dress etc.:*› **~ at the back** hinten aufgemacht werden

undocumented /ʌn'dɒkjʊmentɪd/ *adj.* **1** (unrecorded) [urkundlich] nicht belegt; nicht beschrieben ‹*Art*› **2** (Amer.: without official documents) Schwarz‹*arbeiter*›; illegal ‹*Einwanderer*›; **be ~** ‹*Arbeiter*› schwarz arbeiten

undoing /ʌn'du:ɪŋ/ *n., no pl., no indef. art.* **be sb.'s ~:** jmds. Verderben sein

undone /ʌn'dʌn/ *adj.* **1** (not accomplished) unerledigt; **leave the work** *or* **job ~:** die Arbeit liegen lassen **2** (not fastened) offen; **he went out with his shoelaces ~:** er ging mit offenen Schnürsenkeln aus dem Haus

undoubted /ʌn'daʊtɪd/ *adj.* unzweifelhaft

undoubtedly /ʌn'daʊtɪdlɪ/ *adv.* zweifellos

undraw /ʌn'drɔ:/ *v.t., forms as* **draw A** aufziehen ‹*Vorhang*›

undreamed-of /ʌn'dri:mdɒv/, **undreamt-of** /ʌn'dremtɒv/ *adjs.* (unheard-of) unerhört; (unimaginable) unvorstellbar; ungeahnt ‹*Reichtum*›; **such a thing was ~:** an so etwas hätte man nicht im Traum gedacht

undress /ʌn'dres/

A *v.t.* ausziehen; entkleiden (geh.); **get ~ed** sich ausziehen; **can he ~ himself?** kann er sich selbst ausziehen?

B *v.i.* sich ausziehen

C *n.* **1** **~ [uniform]** Freizeitkleidung, *die;* (Mil.) Ausgehuniform, *die* **2** *no pl., no art.* **in a state of ~:** halb bekleidet

undressed /ʌn'drest/ *adj.* **1** (not clothed) unbekleidet; (no longer clothed) ausgezogen; (not yet clothed) nicht angezogen **2** (unfinished) unbearbeitet ‹*Stein, Holz*›; ungegerbt ‹*Leder, Haut*› **3** (not bandaged etc.) nicht verbunden; **leave a wound ~:** eine Wunde nicht verbinden

undrinkable /ʌn'drɪŋkəbl/ *adj.* nicht trinkbar; ungenießbar

undue /ʌn'dju:/ *attrib. adj.* übertrieben; übermäßig; unangemessen hoch ‹*Gewinn*›; unberechtigt ‹*Optimismus*›; **~ influence** (Law) ungebührliche Beeinflussung; **attract ~ attention** zu viel Aufmerksamkeit auf sich (*Akk.*) lenken; **there is no ~ hurry** es hat keine besondere Eile

undulate /'ʌndjʊleɪt/ *v.i.* **1** (move with wavelike motion) wallen (geh.) **2** (have wavelike form) wogen (geh.); **the hills ~ southwards** die Hügel erstrecken sich in sanften Wellen nach Süden

undulating /'ʌndjʊleɪtɪŋ/ *adj.* Wellen‹*linie, -bewegung*›; **~ country/hills** sanfte Hügellandschaft; **~ road** auf- und abführende Straße

undulation /ʌndjʊ'leɪʃn/ *n.* **1** (wavy motion) Wellenbewegung, *die* **2** (wavy line) Wellenlinie, *die*

unduly /ʌn'dju:lɪ/ *adv.* übermäßig; übertrieben ‹*ängstlich*›; unangemessen ‹*hoch*›; **not ~ worried** nicht besonders beunruhigt; **in an ~ hurried manner** in unangebrachter Eile

undying /ʌn'daɪɪŋ/ *adj.* ewig; unsterblich ‹*Ruhm*›; unversöhnlich ‹*Hass*›

unearned /ʌn'ɜ:nd/ *adj.* unverdient; **~ income** Kapitalertrag, *der*

unearth /ʌn'ɜ:θ/ *v.t.* **1** (dig up) ausgraben **2** (fig.: discover) aufdecken; zutage fördern

unearthly /ʌn'ɜ:θlɪ/ *adj.* **1** (mysterious) unheimlich **2** (coll.: terrible) **~ din** Höllenlärm, *der* (ugs.); **at an ~ hour** in aller Herrgottsfrühe

unease /ʌn'i:z/ ▸ **uneasiness**

uneasily /ʌn'i:zɪlɪ/ *adv.* **1** (anxiously) mit Unbehagen **2** (with embarrassment) **be ~ aware of sth.** sich (*Dat.*) einer Sache (*Gen.*) peinlich bewusst sein **3** (restlessly) unruhig ‹*schlafen, sitzen*›

uneasiness /ʌn'i:zɪnɪs/ *n., no pl.* **1** (anxiety) [ängstliches] Unbehagen **2** (restlessness) Unruhe, *die*

uneasy /ʌn'i:zɪ/ *adj.* **1** (anxious) besorgt; **be ~ about sth.** sich wegen etw. Sorgen machen; **he felt ~:** ihm war unbehaglich zumute **2** (restless) unruhig ‹*Schlaf*› **3** (disturbing) quälend ‹*Zweifel, Verdacht*›; **~ conscience** schlechtes Gewissen

uneatable /ʌn'i:təbl/ *adj.* ungenießbar

uneaten /ʌn'i:tn/ *adj.* ungegessen

uneconomic /ʌni:kə'nɒmɪk, ʌnekə'nɒmɪk/ *adj.* unrentabel; **the mine is ~ to run** das Bergwerk ist unwirtschaftlich

uneconomical /ʌni:kə'nɒmɪkl, ʌnekə'nɒmɪkl/ *adj.* verschwenderisch ‹*Person*›; **~ [to run]** unwirtschaftlich

uneconomically /ʌni:kə'nɒmɪkəlɪ, ʌnekə'nɒmɪkəlɪ/ *adv.* verschwenderisch; unwirtschaftlich

unedifying /ʌn'edɪfaɪɪŋ/ *adj.* **1** (uninformative) unergiebig **2** (not uplifting) unerquicklich (geh.); unerfreulich

unedited /ʌn'edɪtɪd/ *adj.* unredigiert

uneducated /ʌn'edjʊkeɪtɪd/ *adj.* ungebildet

unelectable /ʌnɪ'lektəbl/ *adj.* unwählbar

unelected /ʌnɪ'lektɪd/ *adj.* nicht gewählt

unemotional /ʌnɪ'məʊʃənl/ *adj.* emotionslos; nüchtern

unemphatic /ʌnɪm'fætɪk/ *adj.* ausdruckslos

unemployable /ʌnɪm'plɔɪəbl/ *adj.* als Arbeitskraft ungeeignet; **his behaviour makes him ~:** er kann wegen seines Verhaltens nirgends eingestellt werden

unemployed /ʌnɪm'plɔɪd/

A *adj.* **1** (out of work) arbeitslos **2** (with nothing to do) beschäftigungslos

B *n. pl.* **the ~:** die Arbeitslosen

unemployment /ʌnɪm'plɔɪmənt/ *n., no pl., no indef. art.* Arbeitslosigkeit, *die;* (number unemployed) Arbeitslosenzahl, *die*

unemployment: ~ benefit *n.* Arbeitslosengeld, *das;* **~ figures** *n. pl.* Arbeitslosenzahl, *die*

unencumbered /ʌnɪn'kʌmbəd/ *adj.* **1** (unburdened) unbelastet; **travel ~ by baggage** ohne viel Gepäck reisen **2** (free from mortgage etc.) lastenfrei

unending /ʌn'endɪŋ/ *adj.* endlos; ewig ‹*Fortschritt*›; **her ordeal seemed ~:** ihre Qualen schienen nie enden zu wollen

unendingly /ʌn'endɪŋlɪ/ *adv.* endlos

unendurable /ʌnɪn'djʊərəbl/ *adj.* unerträglich

unenforceable /ʌnɪn'fɔ:səbl/ *adj.* nicht durchsetzbar

un-English /ʌn'ɪŋglɪʃ/ *adj.* unenglisch

unenlightened /ʌnɪn'laɪtnd/ *adj.* unaufgeklärt ‹*Zeit*›; rückständig ‹*Land, Volk*›; **leave sb. ~:** jmdn. im Dunkeln lassen

unenterprising /ʌn'entəpraɪzɪŋ/ *adj.* wenig unternehmungslustig; **an ~ person** eine Person ohne Unternehmungsgeist

unenthusiastic /ʌnɪnθju:zɪ'æstɪk, ʌnɪnθu:zɪ'æstɪk/ *adj.* wenig begeistert (**about** von); distanziert ‹*Buchkritik*›

unenviable /ʌn'envɪəbl/ *adj.* wenig beneidenswert

unequal /ʌn'i:kwl/ *adj.* **1** (not equal) unterschiedlich; ungleich ‹*Kampf*› **2** (inadequate) **be ~** *or* **show oneself ~ to sth.** einer Sache (*Dat.*) nicht gewachsen sein; **be ~ to the strain** ‹*Material:*› die Belastung nicht aushalten

unequalled (*Amer.:* **unequaled**) /ʌn'i:kwld/ *adj.* unerreicht; unübertroffen; (in negative sense) beispiellos ‹*Dummheit*›; **~ for beauty** von unvergleichlicher Schönheit

unequally /ʌn'i:kwəlɪ/ *adj.* ungleichmäßig

unequivocal /ʌnɪ'kwɪvəkl/ *adj.*, **unequivocally** /ʌnɪ'kwɪvəkəlɪ/ *adv.* eindeutig

unerotic /ʌnɪ'rɒtɪk/ *adj.* unerotisch

unerring /ʌn'ɜ:rɪŋ/ *adj.* untrüglich ‹*Instinkt, Geschmack*›; unbedingt ‹*Treffsicherheit*›; mathematisch ‹*Genauigkeit*›; unfehlbar ‹*Instinkt*›; unerschütterlich ‹*Zielstrebigkeit*›

unerringly /ʌn'ɜ:rɪŋlɪ/ *adv.* mit untrüglicher Sicherheit

UNESCO /ju:'neskəʊ/ *abbr.* **= United Nations Educational, Scientific and Cultural Organization** UNESCO, *die*

unessential /ʌnɪ'senʃl/ ▸ **inessential**

unethical /ʌn'eθɪkl/ *adj.*, **unethically** /ʌn'eθɪkəlɪ/ *adv.* unmoralisch

uneven /ʌn'i:vn/ *adj.* **1** (not smooth) uneben **2** (not uniform) ungleichmäßig; unregelmäßig ‹*Pulsschlag*›; unausgeglichen ‹*Temperament*›; **an ~ performance** ein Auftritt mit Höhen und Tiefen **3** (odd) ungerade ‹*Zahl*›

'uneven bars *n. pl.* (Amer. Sport) Stufenbarren, *der*

unevenly /ʌn'i:vnlɪ/ *adv.* ungleichmäßig

unevenness /ʌn'i:vnnɪs/ *n.* **1** (roughness) Unebenheit, *die* **2** (irregularity) Ungleichmäßigkeit, *die;* (of pulse) Unregelmäßigkeit, *die;* (of temperament) Unausgeglichenheit, *die;* **the ~ of the essays** das unterschiedliche Niveau der Aufsätze

uneventful /ʌnɪ'ventfl/ *adj.* **1** (quiet) ereignislos; ruhig ‹*Leben*› **2** (normal) ‹*Fahrt, Landung*› ohne Zwischenfälle; **be ~** ‹*Fahrt usw.:*› ohne Zwischenfälle verlaufen

uneventfully /ʌnɪ'ventfəlɪ/ *adv.* ohne Zwischenfälle

unexampled /ʌnɪg'zɑ:mpld/ *adj.* beispiellos

unexceptionable /ʌnɪk'sepʃənəbl/ *adj.* untadelig ‹*Charakter*›; fehlerlos ‹*Arbeit*›

U

unexceptional /ʌnɪk'sepʃənl/ *adj.* alltäglich; (average) durchschnittlich
unexciting /ʌnɪk'saɪtɪŋ/ *adj.* wenig aufregend; (boring) langweilig
unexpected /ʌnɪk'spektɪd/ *adj.* unerwartet; **this news was entirely ~:** diese Nachricht kam völlig unerwartet
unexpectedly /ʌnɪk'spektɪdlɪ/ *adv.* unerwartet
unexpired /ʌnɪk'spaɪəd/ *adj.* noch gültig; noch nicht abgelaufen ‹*Mandat*›
unexplainable /ʌnɪk'spleɪnəbl/ *adj.* unerklärlich
unexplained /ʌnɪk'spleɪnd/ *adj.* ungeklärt; unentschuldigt ‹*Abwesenheit*›
unexploded /ʌnɪk'spləʊdɪd/ *adj.* nicht explodiert *od.* detoniert
unexplored /ʌnɪk'splɔ:d/ *adj.* unerforscht
unexposed /ʌnɪk'spəʊzd/ *adj.* 1 (not brought to light) unaufgeklärt; nicht entlarvt ‹*Verbrecher*› 2 (Photog.) unbelichtet
unexpressed /ʌnɪk'sprest/ *adj.* unausgesprochen
unexpressive /ʌnɪk'spresɪv/ *adj.* ausdruckslos
unexpurgated /ʌn'ekspəgeɪtɪd/ *adj.* unzensiert
unfading /ʌn'feɪdɪŋ/ *adj.* unvergänglich
unfailing /ʌn'feɪlɪŋ/ *adj.* unerschöpflich; nie versagend ‹*gute Laune*›; unfehlbar ‹*Heilmittel*›; **with ~ regularity** (iron.) mit schöner Regelmäßigkeit
unfailingly /ʌn'feɪlɪŋlɪ/ *adv.* stets
unfair /ʌn'feə(r)/ *adj.* unfair; ungerecht, unfair ‹*Kritik, Urteil*›; unlauter ‹*Wettbewerb*›; ungerecht ‹*Strafe*›; **an ~ share** ein ungerechtfertigt hoher Anteil; **be ~ to sb.** jmdm. gegenüber ungerecht sein
unfairly /ʌn'feəlɪ/ *adv.* 1 (unjustly) ungerecht; unfair ‹*spielen*› 2 (unreasonably) zu Unrecht
unfairness /ʌn'feənɪs/ *n., no pl.* Ungerechtigkeit, *die;* (Sport) Unfairness, *die*
unfaithful /ʌn'feɪθfl/ *adj.* untreu; ungenau ‹*Übersetzung*›; **~ to sb./sth.** jmdm./einer Sache untreu
unfaithfulness /ʌn'feɪθflnɪs/ *n., no pl.* Untreue, *die*
unfaltering /ʌn'fɔ:ltərɪŋ/ *adj.* unbeirrbar ‹*Glaube, Sicherheit*›; fest ‹*Stimme, Schritt*›
unfamiliar /ʌnfə'mɪljə(r)/ *adj.* 1 (strange) unbekannt; fremd ‹*Stadt*›; ungewohnt ‹*Arbeit, Tätigkeit*› 2 (not well acquainted) nicht vertraut; **be ~ with sth.** sich mit etw. nicht auskennen; **workers ~ with this type of machine** Arbeiter, die sich mit diesem Maschinentyp nicht [gut] auskennen; **he is not ~ with German** die deutsche Sprache ist ihm einigermaßen vertraut
unfamiliarity /ʌnfəmɪlɪ'ærɪtɪ/ *n., no pl.* 1 (strangeness) Fremdheit, *die;* (of activity) Ungewohntheit, *die* 2 **~ with sth.** (poor knowledge of) Unvertrautheit mit etw.; **his ~ with computers** seine fehlende Erfahrung mit Computern
unfashionable /ʌn'fæʃənəbl/ *adj.* unmodern ‹*Kleidung*›; nicht eben schick ‹*Wohngegend*›; **become ~:** aus der Mode kommen; **a view now ~:** eine jetzt überholte Ansicht
unfasten /ʌn'fɑ:sn/
A *v.t.* 1 öffnen 2 (detach) lösen
B *v.i.* **~ at the back** hinten geöffnet werden
unfastened /ʌn'fɑ:snd/ *adj.* nicht verschlossen ‹*Tür*›; offen ‹*Verschluss, Knöpfe*›
unfathomable /ʌn'fæðəməbl/ *adj.* 1 (incomprehensible) unergründlich 2 (immeasurable) unermesslich
unfathomed /ʌn'fæðəmd/ *adj.* unergründet
unfavorable, unfavorably (Amer.) ▸ **unfavourable, unfavourably**
unfavourable (*Amer.:* **unfavorable**) /ʌn'feɪvərəbl/ *adj.* 1 (negative) ungünstig; unfreundlich ‹*Kommentar, Reaktion*›; negativ ‹*Kritik, Antwort*›; **my suggestion got an ~ response** die Reaktion auf meinen Vorschlag war ablehnend; **be ~ to a proposal** einen Vorschlag ablehnen 2 (tending to make difficult) ungünstig (**to, for** für); widrig ‹*Wind*›; **an atmosphere ~ to calm discussion** eine Atmosphäre, die einer ruhigen Diskussion abträglich ist; **a climate ~ to growth** ein wachstumsfeindliches Klima
unfavourably (*Amer.:* **unfavorably**) /ʌn'feɪvərəblɪ/ *adv.* ungünstig; **be ~ disposed towards sb./sth.** jmdm./etw. gegenüber ablehnend eingestellt sein; **react ~ to a suggestion** auf einen Vorschlag ablehnend reagieren
unfazed /ʌn'feɪzd/ *adj.* (coll.) unbeeindrückt (**by** durch); **he was ~ by the prospect of ...:** die Aussicht auf ... beunruhigte ihn nicht
unfeasible /ʌn'fi:zɪbl/ *adj.* undurchführbar; **politically ~:** politisch nicht durchsetzbar *od.* machbar; **make sth. ~ for sb.** jmdm. etw. unmöglich machen
unfeeling /ʌn'fi:lɪŋ/ *adj.* (unsympathetic) gefühllos
unfeelingly /ʌn'fi:lɪŋlɪ/ *adv.* herzlos
unfeigned /ʌn'feɪnd/ *adj.* aufrichtig; unverhohlen
unfenced /ʌn'fenst/ *adj.* nicht eingezäunt
unfettered /ʌn'fetəd/ *adj.* ungehindert; **~ by scruples** frei von Skrupeln
unfilled /ʌn'fɪld/ *adj.* frei, offen ‹*Stelle*›; (empty) leer
unfinished /ʌn'fɪnɪʃt/ *adj.* 1 (not completed) unvollendet ‹*Gedicht, Werk*›; unerledigt ‹*Arbeit, Geschäft*›; **the U~ [Symphony]** die Unvollendete 2 (in rough state) unbearbeitet
unfit /ʌn'fɪt/
A *adj.* 1 (unsuitable) ungeeignet; **~ for human consumption** zum Verzehr nicht geeignet; **~ for vehicles** nicht befahrbar 2 (not physically fit) nicht fit; **she hates to be ~:** sie will unbedingt fit sein; **~ for military service** [wehrdienst]untauglich
B *v.t.,* **-tt-** (arch.) untauglich machen; *see also* **unfitted**
unfitness /ʌn'fɪtnɪs/ *n., no pl.* 1 (unsuitability) fehlende Eignung 2 (poor physical condition) **[state of] ~:** schlechte körperliche Verfassung
unfitted /ʌn'fɪtɪd/ *adj.* (unsuited) ungeeignet
unflagging /ʌn'flægɪŋ/ *adj.* unermüdlich
unflappable /ʌn'flæpəbl/ *adj.* (coll.) unerschütterlich; **an ~ person** jemand, der sich durch nichts aus der Ruhe bringen lässt
unflattering /ʌn'flætərɪŋ/ *adj.* wenig schmeichelhaft; unvorteilhaft ‹*Kleid, Licht*›; **very ~:** gar nicht schmeichelhaft
unfledged /ʌn'fledʒd/ *adj.* 1 (unfeathered) [noch] ungefiedert 2 (fig.: inexperienced) unerfahren
unflinching /ʌn'flɪntʃɪŋ/ *adj.* unerschrocken; unbeirrbar ‹*Entschlossenheit*›; **remain ~:** nicht zurückweichen
unfold /ʌn'fəʊld/
A *v.t.* 1 (open folds of) entfalten; ausbreiten ‹*Zeitung, Landkarte*›; **~ one's arms** die Arme ausstrecken 2 (fig.: reveal) **~ sth. to sb.** jmdm. etw. darlegen
B *v.i.* 1 (open out) ‹*Knospe:*› sich öffnen; ‹*Flügel:*› sich entfalten; **the landscape ~ed before us** (fig.) die Landschaft breitete sich vor unseren Augen aus 2 (develop) sich entwickeln; ‹*Geheimnis:*› sich aufklären; **as the story ~ed** im weiteren Verlauf der Geschichte
unforeseeable /ʌnfɔ:'si:əbl/ *adj.* unvorhersehbar; **be ~:** nicht vorauszusehen sein
unforeseen /ʌnfɔ:'si:n/ *adj.* unvorhergesehen
unforgettable /ʌnfə'getəbl/ *adj.* unvergesslich
unforgivable /ʌnfə'gɪvəbl/ *adj.* unverzeihlich
unforgiving /ʌnfə'gɪvɪŋ/ *adj.* nachtragend
unformed /ʌn'fɔ:md/ *adj.* unausgereift
unforthcoming /ʌnfɔ:θ'kʌmɪŋ/ *adj.* zugeknöpft (**about** hinsichtlich)
unfortified /ʌn'fɔ:tɪfaɪd/ *adj.* 1 (without fortification) unbefestigt 2 (not enriched) nicht gespritet ‹*Wein*›
unfortunate /ʌn'fɔ:tʃʊnət, ʌn'fɔ:tʃənət/
A *adj.* 1 (unlucky) unglücklich; (unfavourable) ungünstig ‹*Tag, Zeit*›; **the poor ~ woman** die arme bedauernswerte Frau; **be ~ [enough] to do sth.** das Pech haben, etw. zu tun 2 (regrettable) bedauerlich
B *n.* Unglückliche, *der/die*
unfortunately /ʌn'fɔ:tʃʊnətlɪ, ʌn'fɔ:tʃənətlɪ/ *adv.* leider
unfounded /ʌn'faʊndɪd/ *adj.* (fig.) unbegründet; **the rumours are totally ~:** die Gerüchte entbehren jeder Grundlage
unfreeze /ʌn'fri:z/ *v.t.* & *i.*, **unfroze** /ʌn'frəʊz/, **unfrozen** /ʌn'frəʊzn/ auftauen
unfrequented /ʌnfrɪ'kwentɪd/ *adj.* menschenleer; einsam
unfriendly /ʌn'frendlɪ/ *adj.* unfreundlich; negativ ‹*Kritik*›; feindlich ‹*Staat*›; **the bull looked ~ to him** der Stier schien ihm feindselig [zu sein]
unfrock /ʌn'frɒk/ *v.t.* **~ sb.** jmdn. des [Priester]amtes entheben
unfruitful /ʌn'fru:tfl/ *adj.* 1 (sterile) unfruchtbar 2 (unprofitable) fruchtlos
unfulfilled /ʌnfʊl'fɪld/ *adj.* 1 unerfüllt ‹*Person*› 2 (not carried out) unerledigt
unfunny /ʌn'fʌnɪ/ *adj.* **[distinctly/decidedly] ~:** [ganz und gar] nicht witzig *od.* komisch
unfurl /ʌn'fɜ:l/
A *v.t.* aufrollen; losmachen ‹*Segel*›
B *v.i.* sich aufrollen
unfurnished /ʌn'fɜ:nɪʃt/ *adj.* unmöbliert
ungainly /ʌn'geɪnlɪ/ *adj.* unbeholfen; ungelenk
ungallant /ʌn'gælənt/ *adj.* unliebenswürdig; ungalant
ungenerous /ʌn'dʒenərəs/ *adj.* 1 (petty) kleinlich 2 (mean) wenig großzügig
ungentlemanly /ʌn'dʒentlmənlɪ/ *adj.* unfein; (impolite) unhöflich; **it is ~:** es gehört sich nicht für einen Gentleman
unget-at-able /ʌnget'ætəbl/ *adj.* unerreichbar; unzugänglich ‹*Fonds*›
unglazed /ʌn'gleɪzd/ *adj.* 1 nicht glasiert ‹*Keramik*› 2 nicht verglast ‹*Fenster*›
ungodliness /ʌn'gɒdlɪnɪs/ *n., no pl.* Gottlosigkeit, *die*
ungodly /ʌn'gɒdlɪ/ *adj.* 1 (impious) gottlos 2 (coll.: unreasonable) **at an ~ hour** zu unchristlicher Zeit (ugs.)
ungovernable /ʌn'gʌvənəbl/ *adj.* unkontrollierbar; unregierbar ‹*Volk*›
ungracious /ʌn'greɪʃəs/ *adj.* unhöflich; (tactless) taktlos
ungraciously /ʌn'greɪʃəslɪ/ *adv.* unhöflich; (tactlessly) taktlos
ungrammatical /ʌngrə'mætɪkl/ *adj.*, **ungrammatically** /ʌngrə'mætɪkəlɪ/ *adv.* ungrammatisch
ungrateful /ʌn'greɪtfl/ *adj.* undankbar
ungrounded /ʌn'graʊndɪd/ *adj.* 1 ▸ **unfounded** 2 (Amer. Electr.) ohne Erdung
ungrudging /ʌn'grʌdʒɪŋ/ *adj.* bereitwillig; (generous) großzügig; herzlich ‹*Gastfreundschaft*›; neidlos ‹*Bewunderung*›
unguarded /ʌn'gɑ:dɪd/ *adj.* 1 (not guarded) unbewacht 2 (incautious) unvorsichtig; **in an ~ moment he gave away some vital information** als er einen Moment nicht aufpasste, verriet er einige wichtige Informationen
unguardedly /ʌn'gɑ:dɪdlɪ/ *adv.* unvorsichtig
ungulate /'ʌŋgjʊlət/ *n.* (Zool.) Huftier, *das*
unhampered /ʌn'hæmpəd/ *adj.* unbehindert; **~ by conscience** nicht von Gewissensbissen geplagt
unhappily /ʌn'hæpɪlɪ/ *adv.* 1 (unfortunately) unglücklicherweise; leider 2 (without happiness) unglücklich
unhappiness /ʌn'hæpɪnɪs/ *n., no pl.* Bekümmertheit, *die;* **despite his ~ about the consequences** obwohl er Bedenken über die Folgen hatte; **she spent ten years of ~ with him** sie verbrachte zehn unglückliche Jahre mit ihm; **he has been the cause of much ~ to her** er

hat ihr viel Kummer gemacht

unhappy /ʌn'hæpɪ/ *adj.* **1** (sad, causing misfortune) unglücklich; (not content) unzufrieden (**about** mit); **be** *or* **feel ~ about doing sth.** Bedenken haben, etw. zu tun **2** (unfortunate) unglückselig ‹*Zeit, Zufall*›; unglücklich ‹*Zusammenstellung, Wahl*›

unharmed /ʌn'hɑ:md/ *adj.* unbeschädigt; (uninjured) unverletzt

unharness /ʌn'hɑ:nɪs/ *v.t.* abschirren

unhealthily /ʌn'helθɪlɪ/ *adv.* krankhaft; ungesund ‹*leben*›

unhealthiness /ʌn'helθɪnɪs/ *n., no pl.* Krankhaftigkeit, *die;* (of place, habit) Gesundheitsschädlichkeit, *die*

unhealthy /ʌn'helθɪ/ *adj.* **1** (not in good health, harmful to health) ungesund **2** (unwholesome) ungesund, krankhaft ‹*Gier*›; schädlich ‹*Einfluss*›; schlecht ‹*Angewohnheit*› **3** (coll.: risky) gefährlich

unheard /ʌn'hɜ:d/ *adj.* **1** **~-of** (unknown) [gänzlich] unbekannt; (unprecedented) beispiellos; (outrageous) unerhört; **that's ~ of** das ist noch nie da gewesen; **this was an ~-of achievement fifty years ago** vor fünfzig Jahren war eine solche Leistung unvorstellbar **2** (not heard) **go ~:** ungehört bleiben

unheated /ʌn'hi:tɪd/ *adj.* ungeheizt ‹*Zimmer usw.*›; unbeheizt ‹*Schwimmbad*›

unheeded /ʌn'hi:dɪd/ *adj.* unbeachtet; **go ~:** nicht beachtet werden; ‹*Gebet, Wunsch:*› nicht erhört werden

unheedful /ʌn'hi:dfʊl/ *adj.* **~ of** ungeachtet (+ *Gen.*)

unhelpful /ʌn'helpfl/ *adj.* wenig hilfsbereit ‹*Person*›; ‹*Bemerkung, Kritik*› die einem nicht weiterhilft

unhelpfully /ʌn'helpfəlɪ/ *adv.* wenig hilfsbereit

unhesitating /ʌn'hezɪteɪtɪŋ/ *adj.* unverzüglich; **she was ~ in her support for him** sie zögerte keinen Augenblick, ihn zu unterstützen

unhesitatingly /ʌn'hezɪteɪtɪŋlɪ/ *adv.* ohne zu zögern

unhide /ʌn'haɪd/ *v.t.* (Computing) einblenden

unhinged /ʌn'hɪndʒd/ *adj.* **his/her mind is ~:** er/sie hat den Verstand verloren

unhitch /ʌn'hɪtʃ/ *v.t.* losmachen; ausspannen ‹*Pferd*›; abkoppeln ‹*Anhänger*›

unholy /ʌn'həʊlɪ/ *adj.* **1** (wicked) unheilig ‹*Allianz*› **2** (coll.: dreadful) fürchterlich (ugs.) ‹*Krawall, Durcheinander*›

unhook /ʌn'hʊk/ *v.t.* **1** (detach from hook) vom Haken nehmen **2** (unfasten by releasing hook) aufhaken ‹*Kleid*›; loshaken ‹*Tor*›

unhoped-for /ʌn'həʊptfɔ:(r)/ *adj.* unverhofft

unhurried /ʌn'hʌrɪd/ *adj.*, **unhurriedly** /ʌn'hʌrɪdlɪ/ *adv.* gemächlich

unhurt /ʌn'hɜ:t/ *adj.* unverletzt

unhygienic /ʌnhaɪ'dʒi:nɪk/ *adj.* unhygienisch

uni /'ju:nɪ/ *n.* (coll.) Uni, *die* (ugs.)

UNICE *abbr.* **= Union of Industrial and Employers' Confederations of Europe** UNICE

UNICEF /'ju:nɪsef/ *abbr.* **= United Nations Children's Fund** UNICEF, *die*

unicorn /'ju:nɪkɔ:n/ *n.* (Mythol.) Einhorn, *das*

unicycle /'ju:nɪsaɪkl/ *n.* Einrad, *das*

unidentified /ʌnaɪ'dentɪfaɪd/ *adj.* nicht identifiziert; **~ flying object** unbekanntes Flugobjekt

unidiomatic /ʌnɪdɪə'mætɪk/ *adj.*, **unidiomatically** /ʌnɪdɪə'mætɪkəlɪ/ *adv.* nicht idiomatisch

unification /ju:nɪfɪ'keɪʃn/ *n.* Einigung, *die;* (of system) Vereinheitlichung, *die*

uniform /'ju:nɪfɔ:m/

A *adj.* (the same for all) einheitlich; (unvarying) gleich bleibend ‹*Strömung, Temperatur, Qualität*›; gleichmäßig ‹*Tempo*›; **be of ~ shape/size/appearance, be ~ in shape/size/appearance** die gleiche Form/Größe/das gleiche Aussehen haben; **~ rows of houses** gleichförmige Häuserzeilen

B *n.* Uniform, *die;* **in/out of ~:** in/ohne Uniform; **be in/out of ~:** Uniform/keine Uniform tragen

uniformed /'ju:nɪfɔ:md/ *adj.* uniformiert

uniformity /ju:nɪ'fɔ:mɪtɪ/ *n.* Einheitlichkeit, *die;* (constant nature) Gleichmäßigkeit, *die;* **impose ~ of belief on ...:** jmdm. einen einheitlichen Glauben auferlegen (+ *Dat.*)

uniformly /'ju:nɪfɔ:mlɪ/ *adv.* **1** (unvaryingly) einheitlich **2** (equally) gleichmäßig

unify /'ju:nɪfaɪ/ *v.t.* einigen ‹*Volk, Land*›; vereinheitlichen ‹*System, Wirtschaft*›

unilateral /ju:nɪ'lætərl/ *adj.* einseitig

unilateralist /ju:nɪ'lætərəlɪst/ *n.* Befürworter der einseitigen Abrüstung

unilaterally /ju:nɪ'lætərəlɪ/ *adv.* einseitig

unimaginable /ʌnɪ'mædʒɪnəbl/ *adj.* unvorstellbar

unimaginative /ʌnɪ'mædʒɪnətɪv/ *adj.*, **unimaginatively** /ʌnɪ'mædʒɪnətɪvlɪ/ *adv.* fantasielos

unimpaired /ʌnɪm'peəd/ *adj.* unbeeinträchtigt; **he emerged from the trial with ~ prestige** er überstand den Prozess ohne Prestigeverlust

unimpeachable /ʌnɪm'pi:tʃəbl/ *adj.* **1** (blameless) unanfechtbar; untadelig ‹*Ruf*› **2** (beyond question) unbezweifelbar; absolut zuverlässig ‹*Quelle*›

unimpeded /ʌnɪm'pi:dɪd/ *adj.* ungehindert

unimportance /ʌnɪm'pɔ:təns/ *n., no pl.* Unwichtigkeit, *die;* Bedeutungslosigkeit, *die*

unimportant /ʌnɪm'pɔ:tənt/ *adj.* unwichtig; bedeutungslos

unimpressed /ʌnɪm'prest/ *adj.* nicht beeindruckt

unimpressive /ʌnɪm'presɪv/ *adj.* nicht eindrucksvoll; unscheinbar ‹*Gebäude*›; (unconvincing) nicht überzeugend

uninfluenced /ʌn'ɪnflʊənst/ *adj.* unbeeinflusst

uninformative /ʌnɪn'fɔ:mətɪv/ *adj.* inhaltslos ‹*Text*›; **he is ~ about his plans** er verrät nichts über seine Pläne

uninformed /ʌnɪn'fɔ:md/ *adj.* **1** (not informed) uninformiert; **be [entirely] ~ about the development** [überhaupt] nichts von der Entwicklung wissen **2** (based on ignorance) auf Unkenntnis beruhend ‹*Urteil, Ansicht*›; **~ guess** reine Vermutung

uninhabitable /ʌnɪn'hæbɪtəbl/ *adj.* unbewohnbar

uninhabited /ʌnɪn'hæbɪtɪd/ *adj.* unbewohnt

uninhibited /ʌnɪn'hɪbɪtɪd/ *adj.* ungehemmt; ohne Hemmungen *nachgestellt*

uninitiated /ʌnɪ'nɪʃɪeɪtɪd/ *adj.* uneingeweiht; **~ in the mysteries** nicht in die Geheimnisse eingeweiht; **the ~:** Außenstehende

uninjured /ʌn'ɪndʒəd/ *adj.* unverletzt

uninspired /ʌnɪn'spaɪəd/ *adj.* einfallslos; **I am/feel ~:** mir fehlt die Inspiration

uninspiring /ʌnɪn'spaɪərɪŋ/ *adj.* langweilig

uninstall, (Amer. also) **uninstal** /'ʌnɪnstɔ:l/ *v.t.* (Computing) deinstallieren ‹*Anwendung*›; löschen ‹*Datei*›; **~ facility** Uninstaller, *der* (fachspr.); **~ option/capability** Deinstallationsmöglichkeit, *die*

uninsured /ʌnɪn'ʃʊəd/ *adj.* nicht versichert

unintelligent /ʌnɪn'telɪdʒənt/ *adj.* nicht intelligent; **pretty ~:** ziemlich dumm

unintelligible /ʌnɪn'telɪdʒɪbl/ *adj.* unverständlich

unintended /ʌnɪn'tendɪd/ *adj.* unbeabsichtigt

unintentional /ʌnɪn'tenʃənl/ *adj.*, **unintentionally** /ʌnɪn'tenʃənəlɪ/ *adv.* unabsichtlich; (Law) nicht vorsätzlich

uninterested /ʌn'ɪntrestɪd, ʌn'ɪntrɪstɪd/ *adj.* desinteressiert (**in** an + *Dat.*)

uninteresting /ʌn'ɪntrestɪŋ, ʌn'ɪntrɪstɪŋ/ *adj.* uninteressant

uninterrupted /ʌnɪntə'rʌptɪd/ *adj.* **1** (continuous) ununterbrochen; nicht unterbrochen **2** (not disturbed) ungestört

uninvited /ʌnɪn'vaɪtɪd/ *adj.* ungeladen

uninviting /ʌnɪn'vaɪtɪŋ/ *adj.* wenig verlockend; wenig einladend ‹*Ort, Wetter*›

uninvolved /ʌnɪn'vɒlvd/ *adj.* unbeteiligt (**in** an + *Dat.*); **be** *or* **remain ~:** sich nicht beteiligen

union /'ju:nɪən, 'ju:njən/ *n.* **1** (trade ~) Gewerkschaft, *die* **2** (political unit) Union, *die;* **'State of the U~' message** (Amer. Polit.) Regierungserklärung zur Lage der Nation **3** **[Students'] U~:** Studentenvereinigung, *die* **4** (marriage) eheliche Verbindung **5** (concord) Einigkeit, *die;* **they lived together in perfect ~:** sie lebten einträchtig zusammen **6** (uniting) Vereinigung, *die*

union: ~-bashing *n., no pl.* (coll.) Gewerkschaftsschelte, *die;* **U~ 'flag** *n.* Unionsflagge, *die; see also* **Union Jack**

unionism /'ju:nɪənɪzm, 'ju:njənɪzm/ *n.* **1** (of trade unions) Gewerkschaftswesen, *das* **2** (Brit. Polit.) unionistische Bestrebungen; *Befürwortung der parlamentarischen Einheit von Großbritannien und Nordirland*

unionist /'ju:nɪənɪst, 'ju:njənɪst/ *n.* **1** (member of trade union) Gewerkschafter, *der*/Gewerkschafterin, *die;* (advocate of trade unions) Gewerkschaftsanhänger, *der*/-anhängerin, *die* **2** **U~** (Polit.) Unionist, *der*/Unionistin, *die*

unionize (**unionise**) /'ju:nɪənaɪz, 'ju:njənaɪz/ *v.t.* **~ a company** in einer Firma eine Gewerkschaftsorganisation aufbauen; **~d labour** gewerkschaftlich organisierte Arbeitskräfte

Union: ~ 'Jack *n.* (Brit.) Union Jack, *der;* **~ member** *n.* Gewerkschaftsmitglied, *das;* **~ 'membership** *n., no pl.* Gewerkschaftsmitgliedschaft, *die;* **~ membership rose above 4,000,000** die Zahl der Gewerkschaftsmitglieder stieg auf über 4 000 000; **~ of Soviet Socialist Republics** *pr. n.* (Hist.) Union der Sozialistischen Sowjetrepubliken; **u~ suit** *n.* (Amer.) Hemdhose, *die* (veralt.); Leibchenhose, *die* (landsch.)

Union Jack

Die Nationalflagge des Vereinigten Königreichs, auch *Union flag* genannt. Sie setzt sich aus dem englischen *St George's Cross*, dem schottischen *St Andrew's Cross* und dem nordirischen *St Patrick's Cross* zusammen.

unique /ju:'ni:k/ *adj.* **1** (unparalleled) einzigartig; (not repeated) einmalig ‹*Gelegenheit, Angebot*›; **this vase is ~:** diese Vase ist ein Einzelstück; **this problem is ~ to our society** dieses Problem gibt es nur in unserer Gesellschaft; **these animals are ~ to Australia** diese Tiere kommen nur in Australien vor; **~ selling point** Alleinstellungsmerkmal, *das* **2** (coll.: remarkable) einmalig

uniquely /ju:'ni:klɪ/ *adv.* **1** (exclusively) einzig und allein; **that distinction is ~ his** die Auszeichnung besitzt nur *od.* allein er **2** (to a unique degree) einzigartig; einmalig ‹*talentiert, begabt*›

uniqueness /ju:'ni:knɪs/ *n., no pl.* Einzigartigkeit, *die*

unisex /'ju:nɪseks/ *adj.* Unisex‹*mantel, -kleidung*›; **~ hairdresser** Damen-und-Herren-Frisör

unison /'ju:nɪsən/

A *n.* **1** (Mus.) Unisono, *das;* **in ~:** unisono; einstimmig; **act in ~** (fig.) vereint handeln; **act in ~ with sb.** in Übereinstimmung mit jmdm. handeln **2** (concord) Einmütigkeit, *die*

B *adj.* (Mus.) unisono gesungen/gespielt

unit /'ju:nɪt/ *n.* **1** (element, group, regarded as complete; also Mil.) Einheit, *die;* (in complex mechanism) Element, *das;* **x-ray ~:** Röntgenabteilung, *die;* **armoured ~** (Mil.) Panzereinheit, *die;* **motor ~** (Railw.) Triebwagen, *der* **2** (in adding numbers by columns) Einer, *der* (Math.); **the ~s column** die Einerspalte **3** (quantity chosen as standard) [Maß]einheit, *die;* (of gas, electricity) Einheit, *die;* **~ of length/monetary ~:** Längen-/Währungseinheit, *die* **4** (piece of furniture) Element, *das;* **kitchen ~:** Küchenelement, *das;* **wall ~:** Wandschrank, *der* **5** (esp. electrical device) Gerät, *das* **6** (building) **shop ~:** Ladenlokal, *das;* **residential ~:** Wohneinheit, *die;* **factory ~:** Fabrikgebäude, *das* **7** (Brit. Finance) Anteil[sschein] [an einem Investmentfonds]

Unitarian /juːnɪˈteərɪən/ (Relig.)
A *n.* Unitarier, *der*/Unitarierin, *die*
B *adj.* unitarisch

unitary /ˈjuːnɪtərɪ/ *adj.* einheitlich

unit 'cost *n.* Stückkosten *Pl.*

unite /juːˈnaɪt/
A *v.t.* vereinigen; verbinden ‹*Einzelteile*›; einen, einigen ‹*Partei, Mitglieder*›
B *v.i.* **1** (join together) sich vereinigen; ‹*Elemente:*› sich verbinden; ‹*gebrochene Knochen:*› zusammenwachsen **2** (join forces) sich vereinigen; (form merger) sich zusammenschließen; **~ in doing sth.** etw. vereint *od.* gemeinsam tun

united /juːˈnaɪtɪd/ *adj.* **1** (harmonious) einig; **a ~ front** eine geschlossene Front; **~ we stand, divided we fall** gemeinsam siegen wir, getrennt fallen wir **2** (combined) vereint (geh.); gemeinsam; **their ~ efforts found the solution** ihre gemeinsamen Anstrengungen führten zur Lösung

United: ~ Arab 'Emirates *pr. n. pl.* Vereinigte Arabische Emirate; **~ 'Kingdom** *pr. n.* Vereinigtes Königreich [Großbritannien und Nordirland]; **~ 'Nations** *pr. n. sing.* Vereinte Nationen *Pl.*; **~ Re'formed Church** *n.* Vereinigte Reformierte Kirche; **~ 'States** ▸ **state A 5**; **~ States of A'merica** *n. sing.* Vereinigte Staaten von Amerika

unit: ~ 'furniture *n.* Anbaumöbel *Pl.*; **~ 'price** *n.* (Commerc.) Stückpreis, *der;* **~ 'trust** *n.* (Brit. Finance) ≈ Investmentfonds, *der*

unity /ˈjuːnɪtɪ/ *n.* **1** (state of being united) Einheit, *die;* (of work of art, idea) [innere] Geschlossenheit; **their ~ of purpose** die Gemeinsamkeit ihres Wollens; **the dramatic unities** die drei Einheiten (Literaturw.) **2** (Math.) Einselement, *das* **3** (harmony) Eintracht, *die*

universal /juːnɪˈvɜːsl/ *adj.* **1** (prevailing everywhere) allgemein; allgemein gültig ‹*Regel, Wahrheit*›; **less ~:** weniger häufig *od.* verbreitet; **there was ~ terror** überall herrschte große Angst; **become ~:** sich allgemein verbreiten **2** (covering all fields of knowledge) universal ‹*Bildung, Wissen*›; universell begabt ‹*Person*›; **~ genius** Universalgenie, *das* **3** (common to all) universell **4** (meeting varied requirements) Universal-; **~ remedy** Universalmittel, *das*

universality /juːnɪvɜːˈsælɪtɪ/ *n., no pl.* **1** (prevalence) allgemeine Verbreitung **2** (comprehensiveness) Universalität, *die*

universal: ~ 'joint *n.* Kardangelenk, *das;* **~ 'language** *n.* Universalsprache, *die*

universally /juːnɪˈvɜːsəlɪ/ *adv.* allgemein; (without exception) ausnahmslos; **be ~ opposed to these politics** diese Politik einmütig ablehnen

universal 'suffrage *n., no pl.* allgemeines Wahlrecht; **elected by ~:** durch allgemeine Wahlen gewählt

universe /ˈjuːnɪvɜːs/ *n.* **1** Universum, *das;* (world; fig.: mankind) Welt, *die* **2** ▸ **cosmos 2**

university /juːnɪˈvɜːsɪtɪ/ *n.* Universität, *die; attrib.* Universitäts-; **go to ~:** auf die *od.* zur Universität gehen; **at ~:** an der Universität; *attrib.* **~ place** Studienplatz, *der*

university 'entrance *n., no pl.* Universitätszulassung, *die;* **~ is becoming easier/more difficult** es wird immer leichter/schwieriger, zum Studium zugelassen zu werden

unjust /ʌnˈdʒʌst/ *adj.* ungerecht (**to** *Dat.* + gegenüber); **it would be ~ not to refer to X** es ist ein Gebot der Fairness, X zu zitieren

unjustifiable /ʌnˈdʒʌstɪfaɪəbl/ *adj.* ungerechtfertigt; **be ~:** nicht zu rechtfertigen sein

unjustifiably /ʌnˈdʒʌstɪfaɪəblɪ/ *adv.* ungerechtfertigterweise

unjustified /ʌnˈdʒʌstɪfaɪd/ *adj.* ungerechtfertigt; **you are entirely ~ in thinking ...:** du glaubst ganz zu Unrecht, ...

unjustly /ʌnˈdʒʌstlɪ/ ungerechterweise; zu Unrecht

unkempt /ʌnˈkempt/ *adj.* **1** (dishevelled) ungekämmt ‹*Haare*› **2** (untidy) ungepflegt

unkind /ʌnˈkaɪnd/ *adj.* unfreundlich; **be ~ to sb./animals** jmdn./Tiere schlecht behandeln

unkindly /ʌnˈkaɪndlɪ/ *adv.* unfreundlich; **fate treated her ~:** das Schicksal meinte es nicht gut mit ihr

unkindness /ʌnˈkaɪndnɪs/ *n.* Unfreundlichkeit, *die*

unknot /ʌnˈnɒt/ *v.t.*, **-tt-** entknoten

unknowing /ʌnˈnəʊɪŋ/ *adj.* unwissentlich; ahnungslos ‹*Opfer*›

unknowingly /ʌnˈnəʊɪŋlɪ/ *adj.* unwissentlich

unknown /ʌnˈnəʊn/
A *adj.* unbekannt; **an ~ number of people died in the accident** die Zahl der Todesopfer bei dem Unfall ist nicht bekannt; **sb./sth. is ~ to sb.** jmd./etw. ist jmdm. nicht bekannt; **a drug ~ to us** ein uns unbekanntes Heilmittel; **it is ~/not ~ for him to do such a thing** es ist nie vorgekommen/ist schon vorgekommen, dass er so etwas getan hat; **~ territory** (lit. or fig.) unbekanntes Terrain; **the U~ Soldier** *or* **Warrior** der Unbekannte Soldat; **murder by person** *or* **persons ~:** Mord durch unbekannten Täter; **~ strengths/reserves** (unsuspected) ungeahnte Kräfte/Reserven; *see also* **country 1**; **quantity 5**
B *adv.* **~ to sb.** ohne dass jmd. davon weiß/wusste
C *n.* **1** **the ~:** das Unbekannte; **fear of the ~:** Angst vor dem Unbekannten; **journey/voyage into the ~** (lit. or fig.) Reise in unbekannte Regionen **2** (person) **an ~:** ein Unbekannter/eine Unbekannte **3** (Math.: quantity) Unbekannte, *die;* **an equation with two ~s** eine Gleichung mit zwei Unbekannten **4** (factor) unbekannte Größe

unlabelled (*Amer.:* **unlabeled**) /ʌnˈleɪbld/ *adj.* ‹*Flasche, Behälter*› ohne Etikett *od.* Beschriftung; ‹*Gepäck, Koffer, Paket*› ohne Aufkleber/Anhänger; unbeschriftet ‹*Dokument, Aktenordner, Tonband*›

unlace /ʌnˈleɪs/ *v.t.* aufschnüren

unladen /ʌnˈleɪdn/ *adj.* **~ weight** Leergewicht, *das*

unladylike /ʌnˈleɪdɪlaɪk/ *adj.* nicht sehr damenhaft; **very ~:** gar nicht damenhaft

unlatch /ʌnˈlætʃ/
A *v.t.* aufklinken
B *v.i.* sich aufklinken lassen

unlawful /ʌnˈlɔːfl/ *adj.* ungesetzlich; gesetzwidrig; **~ possession of firearms/drugs** illegaler Waffen-/Drogenbesitz; **~ assembly** verbotene Versammlung

unlawfully /ʌnˈlɔːfəlɪ/ *adv.* gesetzwidrig

unleaded /ʌnˈledɪd/ *adj.* bleifrei ‹*Benzin*›

unlearn /ʌnˈlɜːn/ *v.t., forms as* **learn A** vergessen ‹*Idee, Kenntnisse*›; ablegen ‹*Gewohnheit*›

unleash /ʌnˈliːʃ/ *v.t.* von der Leine lassen ‹*Hund*›; (fig.) freien Lauf lassen (+ *Dat.*) ‹*Gefühlen, Leidenschaften, Kräften*›; entfesseln ‹*Sturm der Entrüstung*›; **~ sth. [up]on sb.** an jmdm. etw. auslassen; **~ violence/[a] war on a country** Gewalt/Krieg über ein Land bringen

unleavened /ʌnˈlevnd/ *adj.* ohne Treibmittel *nachgestellt;* ungesäuert ‹*Brot*›

unless /ˈʌnˈles, ənˈles/ *conj.* es sei denn; wenn ... nicht; **I shall not do it ~ I am paid for it** ich werde es nur tun, wenn ich dafür bezahlt werde; **I shall expect you tomorrow ~ I hear from you/hear to the contrary** falls *od.* sofern ich nichts von dir/nichts Gegenteiliges höre, erwarte ich dich morgen; **I might go, but not ~ I'm asked to** vielleicht gehe ich, aber nur, wenn man mich darum bittet; **~ I'm [very much] mistaken** wenn ich mich nicht [sehr] irre *od.* täusche; **~ he comes soon, I shall leave** wenn er nicht bald kommt, dann gehe ich; **~ otherwise indicated** *or* **stated** wenn nicht anders angegeben

unlettered /ʌnˈletəd/ *adj.* **1** (illiterate) analphabetisch **2** (uneducated) ungebildet

unliberated /ʌnˈlɪbəreɪtɪd/ *adj.* nicht emanzipiert ‹*Frau*›; unfrei ‹*Massen, Land*›

unlicensed /ʌnˈlaɪsənst/ *adj.* ‹*Händler, Makler, Buchmacher*› ohne Konzession; ‹*Pilot*› ohne Lizenz; nicht angemeldet ‹*Hund, Radio, Fernsehgerät, Auto*›; **~ premises** Gaststättenbetrieb ohne [Schank]konzession

unlighted /ʌnˈlaɪtɪd/ ▸ **unlit**

unlike /ʌnˈlaɪk/
A *adj.* nicht ähnlich; unähnlich; (unequal) **~ signs** (Math.) ungleiche Vorzeichen; **~ poles** (Phys.) ungleiche Pole; **they are ~:** sie sind sich (*Dat.*) nicht ähnlich
B *prep.* **be ~ sb./sth.** jmdm./einer Sache nicht ähnlich sein; **those people are ~ us** diese Leute sind nicht wie wir; **be not ~ sb./sth.** jmdm./etw. nicht unähnlich sein *od.* ganz ähnlich sein; **his new novel is ~ his previous ones** sein neuer Roman ist anders als seine früheren; **sth. is ~ sb.** (not characteristic of) etw. sieht jmdm. gar nicht ähnlich (ugs.); etw. ist für jmdn. nicht typisch; **it is ~ him to be late** es sieht ihm gar nicht ähnlich (ugs.) *od.* es ist sonst nicht seine Art, zu spät zu kommen; **~ her brother, she likes walking** im Gegensatz zu ihrem Bruder geht sie gern spazieren; **she sings quite ~ other singers** sie singt ganz anders als andere Sängerinnen

unlikelihood /ʌnˈlaɪklɪhʊd/ *n., no pl.* Unwahrscheinlichkeit, *die;* **despite the ~ of the player's being fit** obwohl der Spieler wahrscheinlich nicht fit sein wird

unlikely /ʌnˈlaɪklɪ/ *adj.* **1** unwahrscheinlich; unglaubwürdig ‹*Geschichte, Erklärung*›; **be ~ to do sth.** etw. wahrscheinlich nicht tun; **in the ~ event that ...:** sollte der unwahrscheinliche Fall eintreten, dass ...; **he's ~ to be chosen for the part/post** er wird die Rolle/Stelle kaum bekommen; **it is not ~ that ...:** es ist durchaus wahrscheinlich, dass ... **2** (unsuitable) **an ~ candidate/man for the job** ein Bewerber, der für den Posten kaum geeignet sein dürfte; **she looked in every likely and ~ place to find her key** sie suchte an allen möglichen und unmöglichen Stellen ihren Schlüssel

unlimited /ʌnˈlɪmɪtɪd/ *adj.* unbegrenzt; grenzenlos, unendlich ‹*Himmel, Meer, Geduld*›; **~ drinks** eine unbegrenzte Zahl von Getränken; **~ liability** (Commerc.) unbeschränkte Haftung; **~ company** (Commerc.) Gesellschaft mit unbeschränkter Haftung; **~ mileage** unbegrenzte Meilenzahl

unlined[1] /ʌnˈlaɪnd/ *adj.* (without lining) ungefüttert ‹*Kleidung, Briefumschlag*›

unlined[2] *adj.* (without lines) unliniert ‹*Papier*›

unlisted /ʌnˈlɪstɪd/ *adj.* nicht eingetragen; **~ stock/securities** (Finance) nicht notierte Wertpapiere; **~ [telephone] number** Geheimnummer, *die*

unlit /ʌnˈlɪt/ *adj.* unbeleuchtet ‹*Straße, Korridor, Zimmer*›; nicht angezündet ‹*Lampe, Kamin, Kerze*›

unload /ʌnˈləʊd/
A *v.t.* **1** entladen ‹*Lastwagen, Waggon*›; löschen ‹*Schiff, Schiffsladung*›; ausladen ‹*Gepäck*›; **~ a donkey** einem Esel die Last abnehmen; **the bus/ship ~ed its passengers** die Fahrgäste stiegen aus dem Bus/Schiff **2** (dispose of; Commerc.: sell off, dump) abstoßen ‹*Aktien, Wertpapiere*›; **~ goods on the market** Waren auf den Markt werfen; **~ sb./sth. on [to] sb.** (fig.) jmdn./etw. bei jmdm. abladen ‹*Kinder, Hund, Probleme, Sorgen*›; **~ one's job/responsibility on[to] sb. else** seine Aufgabe/Verantwortung auf jmd. anders (*Akk.*) abwälzen **3** entladen ‹*Gewehr, Pistole*›; **~ [the film from] a camera** den Film aus einer Kamera nehmen
B *v.i.* ‹*Schiff:*› gelöscht werden; ‹*Lastwagen:*› entladen werden; **start ~ing** mit dem Entladen anfangen

unloaded /ʌnˈləʊdɪd/ *adj.* **1** nicht beladen ‹*Schiff, Lastwagen, Waggon*› **2** nicht geladen ‹*Gewehr, Pistole*›

unlock /ʌnˈlɒk/ *v.t.* **1** aufschließen; lösen ‹*Rad, Taste*›; **~ed** unverschlossen ‹*Tür, Tor*›; **leave the door ~ed when you go out** schließ die Tür nicht ab, wenn du gehst; **the gate was left ~ed** das Tor war nicht abgeschlossen; (fig.) **~ a secret/puzzle** ein Geheimnis/Rätsel entschlüsseln; **this book has ~ed the world of literature for him** dieses Buch hat ihm die Welt der Literatur erschlossen **2** (fig.: release)

U

lösen ‹*Hand, Umarmung*›

unlooked-for /ʌnˈlʊktfɔ:(r)/ *adj.* unerwartet; **a virtue perhaps ~ in him** eine Tugend, die man bei ihm vielleicht nicht erwartet hätte

unloose /ʌnˈlu:s/ ▸ **loose B**

unlovable /ʌnˈlʌvəbl/ *adj.* wenig liebenswert

unloved /ʌnˈlʌvd/ *adj.* ungeliebt

unlovely /ʌnˈlʌvlɪ/ *adj.* unschön ‹*Anblick, Gegenstand, Haus*›; reizlos ‹*Person, Gesicht, Stadt*›; (in character) nicht sehr sympathisch ‹*Person*›

unluckily /ʌnˈlʌkɪlɪ/ *adv.* unglücklich; *as sentence-modifier* unglücklicherweise: **~ for him/her** *etc.* zu seinem/ihrem *usw.* Pech

unlucky /ʌnˈlʌkɪ/ *adj.* **1** unglücklich; (not successful) glücklos; **be [very/really] ~:** [großes/wirkliches] Pech haben; **lucky at cards, ~ in love** Glück im Spiel, Pech in der Liebe **2** (bringing bad luck) **an ~ date/number** ein Unglückstag/eine Unglückszahl; **an ~ sign/omen** ein schlechtes Zeichen/Omen; **be born under an ~ star** unter keinem glücklichen Stern geboren sein; **be ~:** Unglück bringen; **it was ~ [for him] that he couldn't come** es war Pech [für ihn], dass er nicht kommen konnte

unmade /ʌnˈmeɪd/ *adj.* ungemacht ‹*Bett*›; unbefestigt ‹*Straße*›

unmade-up /ʌnmeɪdˈʌp/ *adj.* ungeschminkt ‹*Gesicht, Person*›

unmake /ʌnˈmeɪk/ *v.t.*, **unmade** /ʌnˈmeɪd/ rückgängig machen ‹*Vereinbarung, Entscheidung*›; fallen lassen ‹*Plan*›; ruinieren ‹*Laufbahn*›

unman /ʌnˈmæn/ *v.t.*, **-nn- 1** **~ sb.** (deprive of strength) jmdm. die Kraft nehmen; (deprive of courage) jmdn. verzagen lassen; **~ned by grief** von Kummer geschwächt **2** (emasculate, castrate) entmannen

unmanageable /ʌnˈmænɪdʒəbl/ *adj.* **1** (difficult to control) widerspenstig (*Kind, Pferd, Haare*›; unkontrollierbar ‹*Situation*›; **the car/boat became ~:** der Wagen/das Boot war nicht mehr zu kontrollieren **2** (unwieldy) sperrig; unhandlich ‹*Buch*›

unmanly /ʌnˈmænlɪ/ *adj.* unmännlich

unmanned /ʌnˈmænd/ *adj.* unbemannt ‹*Leuchtturm, Raumschiff, Bahnübergang*›; (with nobody in attendance) nicht besetzt ‹*Schalter, Rezeption*›; unbewacht ‹*Posten, Eingang*›

unmannerly /ʌnˈmænəlɪ/ *adj.* unmanierlich ‹*Person, Benehmen*›; ungehörig ‹*Benehmen*›

unmarked /ʌnˈmɑ:kt/ *adj.* **1** (without markings) ‹*Schachtel, Kiste*› ohne Aufschrift; nicht gezeichnet ‹*Wäschestück*›; anonym ‹*Grab*›; **an ~ police car** ein Zivilfahrzeug der Polizei **2** (not spoilt by marks) fleckenlos ‹*Fußboden, Oberfläche*›; makellos ‹*Haut, Pfirsich, Apfel*›; unbeschädigt ‹*Teller, Buch*›; **after ten rounds, the boxer was still ~:** nach zehn Runden war der Boxer immer noch nicht gezeichnet; **his face was ~ by the accident** sein Gesicht zeigte keine Spuren des Unfalls **3** (not corrected) unkorrigiert ‹*Klassenarbeit*› **4** (not noticed) unbemerkt **5** (Sport) ungedeckt ‹*Spieler*› **6** (Ling.) nicht markiert ‹*Form*›

unmarketable /ʌnˈmɑ:kɪtəbl/ *adj.* unverkäuflich

unmarriageable /ʌnˈmærɪdʒəbl/ *adj.* **be ~:** nicht zu verheiraten sein

unmarried /ʌnˈmærɪd/ *adj.* unverheiratet; ledig; **~ mother/couple** ledige Mutter/unverheiratetes Paar

unmask /ʌnˈmɑ:sk/ *v.t.* **~ sb.** jmdm. die Maske entreißen; (fig.) jmdn. entlarven (**as** als); **~ a plot/sb.'s intentions** *etc.* eine Verschwörung/jmds. Absichten *usw.* aufdecken

unmasking /ʌnˈmɑ:skɪŋ/ *n.* Entlarvung, *die*

unmatched /ʌnˈmætʃt/ *adj.* **be ~ [for sth.]** [in etw. (*Dat.*)] unübertroffen sein

unmentionable /ʌnˈmenʃənəbl/ *adj.* unaussprechlich ‹*Sünde, Verbrechen*›; **an ~ topic/subject** ein Thema, über das man nicht spricht

unmerciful /ʌnˈmɜ:sɪfl/ *adj.* erbarmungslos; unbarmherzig

unmercifully /ʌnˈmɜ:sɪfəlɪ/ *adv.* erbarmungslos; unbarmherzig; **treat sb. ~:** jmdn. unbarmherzig behandeln

unmerited /ʌnˈmerɪtɪd/ *adj.* unverdient

unmetalled /ʌnˈmetld/ *adj.* (Brit.) unbefestigt ‹*Straße*›

unmethodical /ʌnmɪˈθɒdɪkl/ *adj.* unmethodisch

unmindful /ʌnˈmaɪndfl/ *adj.* **be ~ of sth.** etw. nicht beachten

unmissable /ʌnˈmɪsəbl/ *adj.* **1** (not to be missed) unbedingt sehenswert ‹*Show, Film*›; **an ~ event** ein Ereignis, das man sich nicht entgehen lassen sollte **2** (impossible to miss) nicht zu verfehlend ‹*Ziel*›; unübersehbar ‹*Relevanz*›; **be ~:** nicht zu verfehlen sein

unmistakable /ʌnmɪˈsteɪkəbl/ *adj.* deutlich; unmissverständlich ‹*Drohung, Befehl*›; klar ‹*Beweis*›; unverwechselbar ‹*Handschrift, Stimme, Silhouette*›; **an ~ sign of sth.** ein sicheres Zeichen für etw.; **there was ~ fear/relief in his voice** in seiner Stimme schwang deutlich Furcht/Erleichterung mit

unmistakably /ʌnmɪˈsteɪkəblɪ/ *adv.* unverkennbar

unmitigated /ʌnˈmɪtɪgeɪtɪd/ *adj.* vollkommen ‹*Unsinn, Schwachkopf*›; einzig ‹*Übel, Lüge*›; **an ~ scoundrel** ein Erzschurke; **be an ~ disaster** (coll.) eine einzige Katastrophe sein (ugs.)

unmixed /ʌnˈmɪkst/ *adj.* unvermischt; (fig.) ungetrübt ‹*Freude, Vergnügen*›; **his joy was not ~ with sadness** in seine Freude mischte sich Traurigkeit

unmodernized /ʌnˈmɒdənaɪzd/ *adj.* unmodernisiert ‹*Haus, Gebäude*›; überkommen ‹*Bildungssystem*›; **the building is almost completely ~:** an dem Gebäude wurde fast nichts modernisiert

unmolested /ʌnməˈlestɪd/ *adj.* unbelästigt; **leave ~:** in Ruhe lassen; (not touch) nicht anrühren

unmoor /ʌnˈmʊə(r), ʌnˈmɔ:(r)/ **A** *v.t. & i.* [bei einem Boot] die Leinen losmachen **B** *v.i.* die Leinen losmachen

unmotivated /ʌnˈməʊtɪveɪtɪd/ *adj.* unmotiviert

unmounted /ʌnˈmaʊntɪd/ *adj.* nicht gefasst ‹*Edelstein*›; nicht aufgezogen ‹*Bild*›

unmourned /ʌnˈmɔ:nd/ *adj.* unbeweint

unmoved /ʌnˈmu:vd/ *adj.* unbewegt; ungerührt; **be/remain ~ by sb.'s pleas** sich von jmds. Bitten nicht rühren *od.* erweichen lassen; **he was ~ by the accusations** er ließ sich von den Anschuldigungen nicht aus der Ruhe bringen; **remain ~ by an argument** von einem Argument nicht beeindruckt sein

unmusical /ʌnˈmju:zɪkl/ *adj.* unmelodisch ‹*Gesang, Stimme*›; unmusikalisch ‹*Person*›

unnameable /ʌnˈneɪməbl/ *adj.* unbestimmt ‹*Angst*›; unsagbar ‹*Qual*›

unnamed /ʌnˈneɪmd/ *adj.* **1** (unidentified) [namentlich] nicht genannt ‹*Ort, Person, Medizin*›; ungenannt ‹*Wohltäter*› **2** (having no name) namenlos ‹*Findling*›; **an ~ island/lake/mountain** eine Insel/ein See/ein Berg ohne Namen; **a species so far ~:** eine Art, die bisher noch keinen Namen hat

unnatural /ʌnˈnætʃrəl/ *adj.* **1** unnatürlich; (abnormal) nicht normal; (perverted) widernatürlich; (uncaring) herzlos ‹*Mutter, Kind usw.*›; **not ~:** ganz natürlich; **a mother who is cruel to her children is ~:** eine Mutter, die grausam zu ihren Kindern ist, ist widernatürlich *od.* (ugs.) nicht normal **2** (affected) unnatürlich; gekünstelt

unnaturally /ʌnˈnætʃrəlɪ/ *adv.* **1** unnatürlich; **not ~:** natürlich; wie man sich denken kann; **he expected, not ~, that his father would help him** natürlich rechnete er damit, dass sein Vater ihm helfen werde **2** (affectedly) unnatürlich; gekünstelt

unnavigable /ʌnˈnævɪgəbl/ *adj.* nicht schiffbar ‹*Fluss*›

unnecessarily /ʌnˈnesɪsərɪlɪ/ *adv.* **1** unnötig[erweise] ‹*sich ärgern, sich aufregen, sich sorgen*›; **spend money/time ~:** unnötig Geld/Zeit aufwenden **2** (excessively) unnötig ‹*streng, kompliziert*›; **be ~ high/long** höher/länger als nötig sein

unnecessary /ʌnˈnesəsərɪ/ *adj.* unnötig; **it is ~ for sb. to do sth.** es ist unnötig *od.* es muss nicht sein, dass jmd. etw. tut; **no, thank you, that's quite ~:** danke, das ist gar nicht nötig

unneighbourly /ʌnˈneɪbəlɪ/ *adj.* nicht gutnachbarlich; **they are ~:** sie sind schlechte Nachbarn

unnerve /ʌnˈnɜ:v/ *v.t.* entnerven

unnerving /ʌnˈnɜ:vɪŋ/ *adj.* entnervend; zermürbend ‹*Warten*›; nervenaufreibend ‹*Erlebnis*›; **be [too] ~:** [zu viel] Nerven kosten; **an ~ reaction/incident** eine Reaktion, die/ein Vorfall, der an die Nerven geht/ging

unnoticed /ʌnˈnəʊtɪst/ *adj.* unbemerkt; **~ by her, he came in** er trat ein, ohne dass sie es bemerkte; **pass** *or* **go ~:** unbemerkt bleiben

unnumbered /ʌnˈnʌmbəd/ *adj.* (without numbers) nicht nummeriert; unpaginiert ‹*Buchseite*›; ‹*Haus*› ohne Hausnummer

UNO /ˈju:nəʊ/ *abbr.* **= United Nations Organization** UNO, *die*

unobjectionable /ʌnəbˈdʒekʃənəbl/ *adj.* gefällig; **sth./sb. is ~:** gegen etw./jmdn. gibt es nichts einzuwenden

unobservant /ʌnəbˈzɜ:vənt/ *adj.* unaufmerksam; **be an ~ person** ein schlechter Beobachter sein

unobserved /ʌnəbˈzɜ:vd/ *adj.* unbeobachtet

unobstructed /ʌnəbˈstrʌktɪd/ *adj.* frei ‹*Weg, Rohr, Ausgang*›; ungehindert ‹*Vormarsch, Durchfahrt*›

unobtainable /ʌnəbˈteɪnəbl/ *adj.* nicht erhältlich; **number ~** (Teleph.) kein Anschluss unter dieser Nummer; **the 'number ~' tone** der Ton für eine Nummer ohne Anschluss

unobtrusive /ʌnəbˈtru:sɪv/ *adj.* unaufdringlich ‹*Geste, Bemerkung, Muster, Farbe*›; unauffällig ‹*Riss, Bewegung*›; **make oneself ~:** sich unauffällig verhalten

unobtrusively /ʌnəbˈtru:sɪvlɪ/ *adv.* unaufdringlich; unauffällig ‹*hinausschleichen, verschwinden*›

unoccupied /ʌnˈɒkjʊpaɪd/ *adj.* **1** (empty) unbesetzt; nicht belegt ‹*Bett*›; unbewohnt ‹*Haus, Wohnung, Raum*› **2** (not busy) unbeschäftigt; **~ moments** freie Augenblicke

unoffending /ʌnəˈfendɪŋ/ *adj.* harmlos; (innocent) unschuldig

unofficial /ʌnəˈfɪʃl/ *adj.* inoffiziell; **an ~ strike** ein wilder Streik; **take ~ action** einen wilden Streik durchführen

unofficially /ʌnəˈfɪʃəlɪ/ *adv.* inoffiziell

unopened /ʌnˈəʊpnd/ *adj.* ungeöffnet; noch nicht aufgegangen ‹*Knospe, Blüte*›

unopposed /ʌnəˈpəʊzd/ *adj.* unangefochten ‹*Kandidat, Wahlsieger*›; ungehindert ‹*Vormarsch*›; **the bill was given an ~ second reading** (Parl.) der Gesetzentwurf wurde bei der zweiten Lesung ohne Abstimmung angenommen

unorganized /ʌnˈɔ:gənaɪzd/ *adj.* **1** (untidy) unsystematisch ‹*Arbeitsweise*›; konfus ‹*Essay, Person*›; ungeordnet ‹*Struktur, Leben*› **2** (not belonging to a union) nicht [gewerkschaftlich] organisiert

unoriginal /ʌnəˈrɪdʒɪnl/ *adj.* unoriginell

unoriginality /ʌnərɪdʒɪˈnælɪtɪ/ *n., no pl.* fehlende Originalität

unorthodox /ʌnˈɔ:θədɒks/ *adj.* unorthodox (geh.)

unostentatious /ʌnɒstenˈteɪʃəs/ *adj.* schlicht; unprätentiös (geh.)

unpack /ʌnˈpæk/ *v.t. & i.* auspacken; **do one's ~ing** auspacken

unpaid /ʌnˈpeɪd/ *adj.* **1** (not yet paid) unbezahlt; nicht bezahlt; **~ for** nicht bezahlt; **the workmen/troops have been ~ for months** die Arbeiter/Truppen haben monatelang keinen Lohn/Sold erhalten **2** (not providing or receiving a salary) unbezahlt ‹*Arbeit, Stelle, Freiwilliger usw.*›; (honorary) ehrenamtlich; **~ leave** unbezahlter Urlaub

unpalatable /ʌnˈpælətəbl/ *adj.* ungenießbar; (fig.) unverdaulich ‹*Tatsache, Wahrheit*›

unparalleled /ʌnˈpærəleld/ *adj.* beispiellos; unvergleichlich ‹*Schönheit*›

unpardonable /ʌn'pɑ:dənəbl/ unverzeihlich; ~ **sin** (Relig.; also fig.) Todsünde, *die*

unparliamentary /ʌnpɑ:lə'mentərɪ/ *adj.* gegen die parlamentarischen Regeln verstoßend; ~ **expression** der Würde des Parlaments nicht angemessene Redeweise

unpatriotic /ʌnpætrɪ'ɒtɪk, ʌnpeɪtrɪ'ɒtɪk/ *adj.* unpatriotisch

unpaved /ʌn'peɪvd/ *adj.* ungepflastert

unpeeled /ʌn'pi:ld/ *adj.* ungeschält

unpeg /ʌn'peg/ *v.t.*, **-gg-** abnehmen ‹*Wäsche*›; ~ **a tent** bei einem Zelt die Pflöcke herausziehen

unperceptive /ʌnpə'septɪv/ *adj.* unaufmerksam; nicht sehr tiefgründig ‹*Bemerkung*›

unperfumed /ʌn'pɜ:fju:md/ *adj.* unparfümiert

unperson /'ʌnpɜ:sn/ *n.* Unperson, *die*

unperturbed /ʌnpə'tɜ:bd/ *adj.* **he was ~ by the prospect of ...:** die Aussicht auf ... beunruhigte ihn nicht; **remain ~:** sich nicht aus der Ruhe bringen lassen; **they were ~ by my presence** sie ließen sich durch meine Gegenwart nicht stören; **the minister seemed ~ by the developments** der Minister schien von den Entwicklungen unbeeindruckt

unpick /ʌn'pɪk/ *v.t.* auftrennen

unpin /ʌn'pɪn/ *v.t.*, **-nn-** abnehmen ‹*Zettel, Brosche*›; ~ **sb.'s/one's hair** jmdm./sich die Nadeln aus dem Haar nehmen; ~ **the seam** die Nadeln aus dem Saum nehmen

unplaced /ʌn'pleɪst/ *adj.* (Sport) unplatziert

unplanned /ʌn'plænd/ *adj.* nicht geplant; ungeplant

unplayable /ʌn'pleɪəbl/ *adj.* **1** (Sport) unbespielbar ‹*Spielfeld*›; unspielbar ‹*Ball*›; unerreichbar ‹*Aufschlag, Return*› **2** (Music) unspielbar **3** (too damaged to be played) nicht abspielbar ‹*CD, Tonband*›

unpleasant /ʌn'plezənt/ *adj.* unangenehm; unfreundlich ‹*Bemerkung*›; böse ‹*Lächeln*›; **she can be really ~:** sie kann sehr unangenehm werden; **be ~ with sb.** zu jmdm. unfreundlich sein

unpleasantly /ʌn'plezəntlɪ/ *adv.* unangenehm; böse ‹*lächeln*›; unfreundlich ‹*antworten*›

unpleasantness /ʌn'plezəntnɪs/ *n.* **1** *no pl.* (unpleasant nature) Unerfreulichkeit, *die;* (of person) Unfreundlichkeit, *die;* **the ~ of a taste/smell** das Unangenehme an einem Geschmack/Geruch; **the ~ of the weather/one's neighbour** das unangenehme Wetter/die Unfreundlichkeit seines Nachbarn **2** (bad feeling, quarrel) Verstimmung, *die;* **there has been a lot of ~ between them** zwischen ihnen ist viel Unerfreuliches geschehen *od.* gewesen

unpleasing /ʌn'pli:zɪŋ/ *adj.* unschön; **not ~ to the eye** ganz angenehm anzusehen

unplug /ʌn'plʌg/ *v.t.*, **-gg-** **1** (Electr.: disconnect) ~ **a radio/a television set** den Stecker eines Radio-/Fernsehgeräts herausziehen; **always ~ electrical appliances at night** bei Elektrogeräten nachts stets den Stecker aus der Steckdose ziehen **2** (take plug out of) ~ **sth.** den Stöpsel aus etw. ziehen

unplugged /ʌn'plʌgd/
A *adj.* **1** (not plugged in) nicht eingesteckt; **with the appliance ~:** bei herausgezogenem [Netz]stecker **2** ® (Mus.: acoustic) Unplugged- ‹*Album, Material usw.*›
B *adv.* (Mus.) unplugged ‹*spielen*›

unplumbed /ʌn'plʌmd/ *adj.* nicht ausgelotet ‹*Gewässer*›; (fig.) [noch] unergründet ‹*Geheimnis, Möglichkeiten*›; ~ **depths [of the sea/** (fig.) **of the human mind]** nicht ausgelotete Tiefen [des Meeres/(fig. geh.) des menschlichen Geistes]

unpolished /ʌn'pɒlɪʃt/ *adj.* unpoliert ‹*Holz, Marmor, Schuhe, Reis*›; (fig.) ungeschliffen ‹*Person, Manieren, Sprache*›

unpolluted /ʌnpə'lu:tɪd/ sauber ‹*Wasser, Fluss, Umwelt*›

unpopular /ʌn'pɒpjʊlə(r)/ *adj.* unbeliebt ‹*Lehrer, Regierung usw.*›; unpopulär ‹*Maßnahme, Politik*›; **be ~ with sb.** (not liked) ‹*Person:*› bei jmdm. unbeliebt sein; ‹*Maßnahme, Steuern:*› bei jmdm. unpopulär sein; (out of favour) **I'm rather ~ with my wife at the moment** meine Frau ist auf mich zurzeit ziemlich schlecht zu sprechen; **if I don't finish it today, I shall be very ~ with my boss** wenn ich heute damit nicht fertig werde, mache ich mich bei meinem Chef ziemlich unbeliebt

unpopularity /ʌnpɒpjʊ'lærɪtɪ/ *n., no pl.* ▸ **unpopular**: Unbeliebtheit, *die* (**with** bei); Unpopularität, *die* (**with** bei)

unpopulated /ʌn'pɒpjʊleɪtɪd/ *adj.* unbewohnt

unposted /ʌn'pəʊstɪd/ *adj.* nicht aufgegeben *od.* abgeschickt

unpractical /ʌn'præktɪkl/ *adj.* unpraktisch

unpractised (*Amer.:* **unpracticed**) /ʌn'præktɪst/ *adj.* **1** (not skilled) ungeübt; **be ~ in sth./in doing sth.** in etw. (*Dat.*) ungeübt sein/darin ungeübt sein, etw. zu tun **2** (not put into practice) nicht ausgeübt ‹*Handwerk*›; ungenutzt ‹*Fähigkeit*›

unprecedented /ʌn'presɪdentɪd/ *adj.* beispiellos; [noch] nie da gewesen; **it is ~ for the Queen to comment publicly** es ist [vorher] noch nie da gewesen, dass die Königin öffentlich Stellung genommen hat

unprecedentedly /ʌn'presɪdentɪdlɪ/ *adv.* unerhört; außergewöhnlich

unpredictable /ʌnprɪ'dɪktəbl/ *adj.* unberechenbar ‹*Person, Charakter, Wetter*›; **the outcome of the election is quite ~:** das Wahlergebnis lässt sich kaum voraussagen

unprejudiced /ʌn'predʒʊdɪst/ *adj.* unvoreingenommen

unpremeditated /ʌnprɪ'medɪteɪtɪd/ *adj.* nicht vorsätzlich ‹*Verbrechen*›; nicht geplant ‹*Angriff, Tat*›

unprepared /ʌnprɪ'peəd/ *adj.* **1** (not yet prepared) nicht vorbereitet ‹*Zimmer, Mahlzeit*›; **be [not] ~ for sth.** auf etw. (*Akk.*) [nicht] unvorbereitet sein **2** (improvised) Stegreif‹*rede, -erklärung*›

unpreparedness /ʌnprɪ'peərɪdnɪs/ *n., no pl.* ▸ **unreadiness**

unprepossessing /ʌnpri:pə'zesɪŋ/ *adj.* wenig attraktiv; unansehnlich; wenig einnehmend ‹*Aussehen, Person*›

unpresentable /ʌnprɪ'zentəbl/ *adj.* **sb. is ~:** mit jmdm. kann man sich nicht sehen lassen; **your clothes are ~:** in deinen Sachen kannst du dich nicht sehen lassen

unpretentious /ʌnprɪ'tenʃəs/ *adj.* unprätentiös (geh.); einfach ‹*Wein, Mahlzeit, Stil, Haus*›; bescheiden ‹*Benehmen, Person*›

unpriced /ʌn'praɪst/ *adj.* ohne Preisangabe *nachgestellt*

unprincipled /ʌn'prɪnsɪpld/ *adj.* skrupellos; **be ~:** keine Prinzipien haben

unprintable /ʌn'prɪntəbl/ *adj.* (lit. or fig.) nicht druckreif

unproblematic /ʌnprɒblə'mætɪk/ *adj.* unproblematisch

unproductive /ʌnprə'dʌktɪv/ *adj.* unfruchtbar ‹*Boden, Gegend*›; fruchtlos ‹*Diskussion, Anstrengung, Nachforschung*›; unproduktiv ‹*Zeit, Arbeit, Kapital*›

unprofessional /ʌnprə'feʃənl/ *adj.* **1** (contrary to standards) standeswidrig **2** (amateurish) unfachmännisch; stümperhaft

unprofitable /ʌn'prɒfɪtəbl/ *adj.* unrentabel ‹*Zeche, Investition, Geschäft*›; wenig einträglich ‹*Arbeit*›; (fig.) fruchtlos

unpromising /ʌn'prɒmɪsɪŋ/ *adj.* nicht [sehr] vielversprechend

unprompted /ʌn'prɒmptɪd/ *adj.* spontan

unpronounceable /ʌnprə'naʊnsəbl/ *adj.* unaussprechbar

unpropitious /ʌnprə'pɪʃəs/ *adj.* ungünstig

unprotected /ʌnprə'tektɪd/ *adj.* ungeschützt (**against** vor + *Dat.*, gegen); nicht geschützt ‹*Art, Tier*›; **an ~ machine** eine Maschine ohne Schutzvorrichtung[en]; **hands ~ by gloves** Hände, die nicht durch Handschuhe geschützt sind; **employees/buildings ~ by legislation** Angestellte ohne gesetzlichen Schutz/Gebäude, die nicht unter Denkmalschutz stehen; ~ **sex** ungeschützter Geschlechtsverkehr

unproved /ʌn'pru:vd/, **unproven** /ʌn'pru:vn/ *adj.* **1** (not proved) unbewiesen **2** (untested) ungeprüft; **his courage/ability is still unproven** sein Mut/seine Fähigkeit ist noch nicht auf die Probe gestellt worden; **he is unproven as an administrator** er hat seine Fähigkeiten als Verwalter noch nicht unter Beweis gestellt

unprovided /ʌnprə'vaɪdɪd/ *pred. adj.* **1** ~ **for** unversorgt ‹*Witwe, Kind usw.*›; nicht vorgesehen ‹*Ereignis*› **2** ~ **with sth.** mit etw. nicht versehen

unprovoked /ʌnprə'vəʊkt/ *adj.* grundlos; **do sth. ~:** etw. ohne [äußere] Veranlassung tun

unpublicized /ʌn'pʌblɪsaɪzd/ *adj.* wenig *od.* kaum publik gemacht

unpublishable /ʌn'pʌblɪʃəbl/ *adj.* nicht zur Veröffentlichung geeignet ‹*Manuskript usw.*›; **his reply was ~:** seine Antwort war nicht druckreif

unpublished /ʌn'pʌblɪʃt/ *adj.* unveröffentlicht

unpunctual /ʌn'pʌŋktjʊəl/ *adj.* unpünktlich

unpunished /ʌn'pʌnɪʃt/ *adj.* ungesühnt ‹*Verbrechen*›; unbestraft ‹*Verbrecher*›; **go ~:** ohne Strafe bleiben; ‹*Verbrecher:*› straffrei ausgehen

unpurified /ʌn'pjʊərɪfaɪd/ *adj.* ungereinigt; nicht gereinigt; (fig.) ungeläutert

unputdownable /ʌnpʊt'daʊnəbl/ *adj.* (coll.) **an ~ book** ein Buch, das man nicht aus der Hand legt; **this novel is ~:** diesen Roman legt man nicht aus der Hand

unqualified /ʌn'kwɒlɪfaɪd/ *adj.* **1** (lacking qualifications) unqualifiziert; ‹*Arzt*› ohne Abschluss; **be ~ for sth.** für etw. nicht qualifiziert sein; **be ~ to do sth.** nicht dafür qualifiziert sein, etw. zu tun; **he is ~ to be president** er ist für das Amt des Präsidenten nicht qualifiziert **2** (absolute) uneingeschränkt ‹*Zustimmung*›; rein ‹*Freude, Vergnügen*›; voll ‹*Erfolg*› **3** (Ling.: not qualified) nicht [näher] bestimmt

unquantifiable /ʌn'kwɒntɪfaɪəbl/ *adj.* nicht quantifizierbar; nicht bezifferbar ‹*Schaden, Kosten*›; unwägbar ‹*Risiko*›

unquenchable /ʌn'kwentʃəbl/ *adj.* unlöschbar ‹*Durst*›; unstillbar ‹*Verlangen*›

unquestionable /ʌn'kwestʃənəbl/ *adj.* unbezweifelbar ‹*Tatsache, Beweis*›; unbestreitbar ‹*Recht, Fähigkeiten, Ehrlichkeit*›; unanfechtbar ‹*Autorität*›; **an ~ decision/ruling/judgement** eine Entscheidung/Verfügung, die/ein Urteil, das nicht angefochten werden kann

unquestionably /ʌn'kwestʃənəblɪ/ *adv.* zweifellos; ohne Frage

unquestioned /ʌn'kwestʃənd/ *adj.* unangefochten ‹*Fähigkeit, Macht, Autorität, Recht*›; unbestritten ‹*Talent*›; **his ability/loyalty is ~:** seine Fähigkeit/Loyalität steht außer Frage

unquestioning /ʌn'kwestʃənɪŋ/ *adj.*, **unquestioningly** /ʌn'kwestʃənɪŋlɪ/ *adv.* bedingungslos; blind

unquiet /ʌn'kwaɪət/ *adj.* unruhig

unquotable /ʌn'kwəʊtəbl/ *adj.* nicht zitierfähig

unquote /ʌn'kwəʊt/ *v.i.* **..., quote, ..., ~:** ..., Zitat, ..., Ende des Zitats

unquoted /ʌn'kwəʊtɪd/ *adj.* (Commerc.) unnotiert

unravel /ʌn'rævl/
A *v.t.* (Brit.) **-ll-** entwirren; (undo) aufziehen; (fig.) ~ **a mystery/the truth/a plot** ein Geheimnis enträtseln/die Wahrheit aufdecken/ein Komplott aufdecken
B *v.i.* (Brit.) **-ll-** aufgehen; sich aufziehen

unreachable /ʌn'ri:tʃəbl/ **1** (unable to be reached) unerreichbar; unzugänglich ‹*Ort*› **2** (unable to be contacted) unerreichbar; **be ~:** nicht erreichbar *od.* nicht zu erreichen sein

unread /ʌn'red/ *adj.* ungelesen

unreadable /ʌn'ri:dəbl/ *adj.* **1** (illegible) unleserlich; (fig.: unfathomable) unergründlich **2** (too difficult, boring, etc.) unlesbar

unreadiness /ʌn'redɪnɪs/ *n., no pl.* **[state of] ~:** mangelnde Vorbereitung; **~ to do sth.** mangelnde Bereitschaft, etwas zu tun

unready /ʌn'redɪ/ *adj.* nicht bereit; **the country is ~ for war** das Land ist für einen Krieg nicht gerüstet; **he is ~ for that position** er ist noch nicht so weit, dass er diese Position übernehmen könnte

unreal /ʌn'rɪəl/ *adj.* unwirklich

unrealistic /ʌnrɪə'lɪstɪk/ *adj.* unrealistisch

unreality /ʌnrɪ'ælɪtɪ/ *n., no pl.* Unwirklichkeit, *die*

unrealizable /ʌn'rɪəlaɪzəbl/ *adj.* unrealisierbar; nicht verwirklichbar

unrealized /ʌn'rɪəlaɪzd/ *adj.* **1▸** (not achieved) unerfüllt ‹*Hoffnung, Ehrgeiz*›; nicht erreicht ‹*Ziel*›; nicht verwirklicht ‹*Plan*›; ungenutzt ‹*Potenzial, Fähigkeiten*›; **~ assets/profits** (Commerc.) nicht realisierte Vermögenswerte/Gewinne **2▸** (not recognized or known) ungeahnt ‹*Mut, Kraft*›; unentdeckt ‹*Talent*›

unreasonable /ʌn'ri:zənəbl/ *adj.* unvernünftig; übertrieben ‹*Ansprüche, Forderung*›; übertrieben [hoch] ‹*Preis, Kosten*›; **I am not an ~ man, but ...:** ich erwarte nun wirklich nicht viel, aber ...; **spend an ~ length of time on sth.** sich übertrieben lange mit etw. beschäftigen; **arrive at an ~ hour** zu einer unmöglichen Uhrzeit ankommen; **I'm only asking you to spare me half an hour of your time — is that [so] ~?** ich bitte dich nur um eine halbe Stunde; das ist doch nicht zu viel verlangt, oder?

unreasonableness /ʌn'ri:zənəblnɪs/ *n., no pl.* Unvernünftigkeit, *die*; **the ~ of these prices/costs** die übertriebene Höhe dieser Preise/Kosten

unreasonably /ʌn'ri:zənəblɪ/ *adv.* unvernünftig ‹*sich benehmen*›; (excessively) übertrieben; **this — not ~ — he refused to do** das lehnte er — nicht ohne Berechtigung — ab

unreasoning /ʌn'ri:zənɪŋ/ *adj.* irrational; blind ‹*Hass, Wut, Eifersucht, Fanatiker*›

unreceptive /ʌnrɪ'septɪv/ *adj.* unempfänglich (**to, for** für)

unrecognizable /ʌn'rekəgnaɪzəbl/ *adj.* **be [absolutely** *or* **quite] ~:** [überhaupt] nicht wiederzuerkennen sein; **the disguise/beard made him ~:** mit der Verkleidung/dem Bart war er nicht wieder zu erkennen

unrecognized /ʌn'rekəgnaɪzd/ *adj.* **1▸** (not identified) unerkannt; **be ~ by sb.** von jmdm. nicht erkannt werden **2▸** (not officially recognized) nicht anerkannt **3▸** (not appreciated) nicht [gebührend] gewürdigt ‹*Talent, Genie*›; nicht [genügend] beachtet ‹*Gefahr, Tatsache*›

unrecorded /ʌnrɪ'kɔ:dɪd/ *adj.* **1▸** (not documented) nicht [dokumentarisch] belegt **2▸** (not recorded) nicht aufgezeichnet; unbespielt, leer ‹*Tonband, Kassette, CD*›

unreel /ʌn'ri:l/
A *v.t.* abwickeln; abspulen ‹*Film, Tonband*›
B *v.i.* ‹*Film, Tonband:*› sich abwickeln; sich abspulen

unrefined /ʌnrɪ'faɪnd/ *adj.* **1▸** (not refined) nicht raffiniert; ungebleicht (Mehl) **2▸** (fig.) unkultiviert, ungeschliffen ‹*Geschmack, Manieren, Person, Sprache*›

unreflecting /ʌnrɪ'flektɪŋ/ *adj.* **1▸** gedankenlos ‹*Person*› **2▸** (not reflecting light) nicht spiegelnd; matt

unrefrigerated /ʌnrɪ'frɪdʒəreɪtɪd/ *adj.* ungekühlt

unregenerate /ʌnrɪ'dʒenərət/ *adj.* (unrepentant, obstinate) uneinsichtig; (wicked) sündig ‹*Lebenswandel*›

unregistered /ʌn'redʒɪstəd/ *adj.* nicht eingetragen; nicht approbiert ‹*Arzt*›; nicht zugelassen ‹*Rechtsanwalt, Buchmacher, Krankenschwester, Fahrzeug*›; nicht eingeschrieben ‹*Postsendung*›; nicht [gesetzlich] geschützt ‹*Warenzeichen*›

unregulated /ʌn'regjʊleɪtɪd/ *adj.* unkontrolliert

unrehearsed /ʌnrɪ'hɜ:st/ *adj.* **1▸** (performed without rehearsal) [vorher] nicht geprobt; **perform a play ~:** ein Stück ohne vorherige Probe[n] spielen **2▸** (not planned) nicht vorgesehen **3▸** (spontaneous) spontan

unrelated /ʌnrɪ'leɪtɪd/ *adj.* unzusammenhängend; **be ~** (not connected) nicht miteinander zusammenhängen; (not related by family) nicht [miteinander] verwandt sein; **be ~ to sth.** mit etw. in keinem Zusammenhang stehen; mit etw. nichts zu tun haben

unrelenting /ʌnrɪ'lentɪŋ/ *adj.* unvermindert, nicht nachlassend ‹*Hitze, Kälte, Regen*›; unerbittlich ‹*Kampf, Opposition, Verfolgung, Hass*›; unnachgiebig ‹*Entschlossenheit, Ehrgeiz*›; unvermindert ‹*Kraft, Stärke*›; hartnäckig ‹*Kämpfer*›; **the heat/pressure/pace is ~:** die Hitze/der Druck/die Geschwindigkeit lässt nicht nach; **be ~ in one's determination to do sth.** unnachgiebig entschlossen sein, etw. zu tun; **be ~ in one's battle** *or* **fight against sth.** etw. unnachgiebig bekämpfen; **remain ~:** unnachgiebig *od.* unerbittlich bleiben

unreliability /ʌnrɪlaɪə'bɪlɪtɪ/ *n., no pl.* Unzuverlässigkeit, *die*

unreliable /ʌnrɪ'laɪəbl/ *adj.* unzuverlässig

unrelieved /ʌnrɪ'li:vd/ *adj.* unvermindert ‹*Schmerz, Armut, Anstrengung*›; unaufhörlich ‹*Regen, Lärm*›; tödlich ‹*Langeweile, Eintönigkeit*›; **~ by sth.** nicht durch etw. gemildert; **a forbidding landscape, ~ by vegetation of any kind** eine Landschaft, deren Ödheit auch nicht das kleinste Pflänzchen belebt; **a gloomy film, ~ by even the slightest touch of humour** ein Film, dessen Düsterkeit durch kein Fünkchen von Humor aufgehellt wird

unremarkable /ʌnrɪ'mɑ:kəbl/ *adj.* nicht weiter bemerkenswert; unauffällig ‹*Person, Lebensweise*›; **totally/pretty ~:** absolut nicht/kaum bemerkenswert

unremitting /ʌnrɪ'mɪtɪŋ/ *adj.* nicht nachlassend; unermüdlich ‹*Anstrengung, Versuche, Sorge*›; beharrlich ‹*Kampf*›; **he was ~ in his efforts to help them** er bemühte sich unermüdlich, ihnen zu helfen

unremittingly /ʌnrɪ'mɪtɪŋlɪ/ *adv.* unermüdlich ‹*kämpfen, arbeiten, sich bemühen*›; unnachgiebig ‹*Widerstand leisten*›

unremunerative /ʌnrɪ'mju:nərətɪv/ *adj.* wenig einträglich *od.* (geh.) lukrativ

unrepeatable /ʌnrɪ'pi:təbl/ *adj.* **1▸** (unique) einzigartig; einmalig ‹*Angebot, Preis*› **2▸** (not fit to be repeated) **sth. is ~:** etw. ist nicht zitierfähig; **an ~ remark/story/joke** eine Bemerkung/Geschichte, die/ein Witz, der nicht salonfähig ist

unrepentant /ʌnrɪ'pentənt/ *adj.* **1▸** (impenitent) reuelos ‹*Sünder*›; **die ~:** sterben, ohne bereut zu haben; **be ~:** keine Reue zeigen; **be ~ about sth.** etw. nicht bereuen **2▸** (unreformed, obstinate) halsstarrig; stur

unreported /ʌnrɪ'pɔ:tɪd/ *adj.* nicht angezeigt ‹*Verbrechen*›; ‹*Fall, Versuch*› über den nicht berichtet wurde; **it went ~:** darüber wurde nicht berichtet

unrepresentative /ʌnreprɪ'zentətɪv/ *adj.* nicht repräsentativ (**of** für); (Polit.) nicht demokratisch gewählt ‹*Regierung, Führer*›; **be ~ of sth.** etw. nicht repräsentieren

unrepresented /ʌnreprɪ'zentɪd/ *adj.* nicht vertreten

unrequited /ʌnrɪ'kwaɪtɪd/ *adj.* unerwidert

unreserved /ʌnrɪ'zɜ:vd/ *adj.* **1▸** (not booked) nicht reserviert **2▸** ▸**❶ p. 908** (full, without any reservations) uneingeschränkt ‹*Zustimmung, Aufnahme, Entschuldigung usw.*›; **he was ~ in his praise** er geizte nicht mit Lob **3▸** (free from reserve) offen ‹*Person, Wesensart*›

unreservedly /ʌnrɪ'zɜ:vɪdlɪ/ *adv.* **1▸** ▸**❶ p. 908** (fully, without any reservations) uneingeschränkt; **he ~ withdrew the allegation** er nahm die Anschuldigung in vollem Umfang zurück **2▸** (frankly, openly) offen

unresolved /ʌnrɪ'zɒlvd/ *adj.* **1▸** (not solved) ungelöst; nicht gelöst **2▸** (undecided) **be ~:** sich [noch] nicht entschieden haben **3▸** (Mus.) nicht aufgelöst

unresponsive /ʌnrɪ'spɒnsɪv/ *adj.* **be ~:** nicht reagieren (**to** auf + *Akk.*); **an ~ audience** ein teilnahmsloses Publikum

unrest /ʌn'rest/ *n.* Unruhen *Pl.*; **there is widespread ~ among the population** ein großer Teil der Bevölkerung ist unzufrieden

unrestrained /ʌnrɪ'streɪnd/ *adj.* uneingeschränkt ‹*Freude, Begeisterung, Wachstum, Überfluss*›; unbeherrscht ‹*Gefühlsäußerung, Wut, Gewalt*›; unkontrolliert ‹*Entwicklung, Wachstum*›; ungeniert ‹*Sprache, Benehmen*›

unrestricted /ʌnrɪ'strɪktɪd/ *adj.* unbeschränkt; uneingeschränkt; frei ‹*Sicht*›; **have ~ use of sth.** etw. uneingeschränkt nutzen [dürfen]

unrevealed /ʌnrɪ'vi:ld/ *adj.* verborgen

unrewarded /ʌnrɪ'wɔ:dɪd/ *adj.* **go ~:** keine Belohnung bekommen; ‹*Tat, Mühe:*› nicht belohnt werden

unrewarding /ʌnrɪ'wɔ:dɪŋ/ *adj.* unbefriedigend; undankbar ‹*Aufgabe*›; **financially ~:** wenig einträglich *od.* (geh.) lukrativ

unrighteous /ʌn'raɪtʃəs/ *adj.* **1▸** (wicked) schlecht **2▸** (unjust) ungerecht

unripe /ʌn'raɪp/ *adj.* unreif

unrivalled (*Amer.:* **unrivaled**) /ʌn'raɪvld/ *adj.* unvergleichlich; beispiellos; unübertroffen ‹*Ruf, Luxus, Erfahrung, Könnerschaft*›; **our goods are ~ in** *or* **for quality** unsere Waren sind in ihrer Qualität konkurrenzlos *od.* unerreicht; **a landscape ~ for beauty** *or* **of ~ beauty** eine Landschaft von unvergleichlicher Schönheit

unroadworthy /ʌn'rəʊdwɜ:ðɪ/ *adj.* nicht verkehrssicher

unroll /ʌn'rəʊl/
A *v.t.* aufrollen
B *v.i.* sich aufrollen; (fig.) ‹*Geschichte, Handlung:*› sich entrollen; **he watched the landscape ~ before his eyes** er betrachtete die Landschaft, die sich vor seinen Augen auftat

unromantic /ʌnrəʊ'mæntɪk/ *adj.* unromantisch

unruffled /ʌn'rʌfld/ *adj.* ruhig; glatt ‹*Gewässer, Haar, Feder*›; **listen with ~ calm/composure** mit unerschütterlicher Ruhe/ruhiger Gefasstheit zuhören; **he was/remained ~ by all the fuss/criticism** er ließ sich von der ganzen Aufregung/Kritik nicht aus der Ruhe bringen

unruled /ʌn'ru:ld/ unliniert ‹*Papier*›

unruliness /ʌn'ru:lɪnɪs/ *n.* Ungebärdigkeit, *die*

unruly /ʌn'ru:lɪ/ *adj.* ungebärdig ‹*Person, Benehmen*›; widerspenstig ‹*Haar, Person, Benehmen*›

unsaddle /ʌn'sædl/ *v.t.* **1▸** absatteln ‹*Pferd usw.*› **2▸** abwerfen ‹*Reiter*›

unsafe /ʌn'seɪf/ *adj.* **1▸** nicht sicher ‹*Leiter, Konstruktion*›; baufällig ‹*Gebäude*›; nicht verkehrssicher ‹*Fahrzeug*›; gefährlich ‹*Maschine, Leitungen, Spielzeug*›; **it is ~ to eat** man darf es nicht essen; **he looked ~ on top of the ladder** es sah gefährlich aus, wie er oben auf der Leiter stand; **feel ~:** sich unsicher fühlen; **it is ~ to do that** es ist gefährlich, das zu tun **2▸** (untenable) unhaltbar ‹*Annahme, Urteil usw.*›; **the conviction was ~:** die Verurteilung war juristisch nicht haltbar

unsaid /ʌn'sed/ *adj.* ungesagt; unausgesprochen; **leave sth. ~:** etw. ungesagt lassen; **some things are better left ~:** manche Dinge bleiben besser ungesagt

unsaleable /ʌn'seɪləbl/ *adj.* unverkäuflich

unsalted /ʌn'sɔ:ltɪd, ʌn'sɒltɪd/ *adj.* ungesalzen

unsanitary /ʌn'sænɪtərɪ/ *adj.* unhygienisch

unsatisfactorily /ʌnsætɪs'fæktərɪlɪ/ *adv.* unbefriedigend; **perform one's tasks ~:** unbefriedigende Leistungen erbringen; **end ~:** zu einem unbefriedigenden Abschluss kommen

unsatisfactory /ʌnsætɪs'fæktərɪ/ *adj.* unbefriedigend; nicht befriedigend; schlecht ‹*Service, Hotel*›; mangelhaft ‹*schulische Leistung*›

unsatisfied /ʌn'sætɪsfaɪd/ *adj.* unzufrieden; unerfüllt ‹*Wunsch, Bedürfnis*›; nicht befriedigt ‹*Wunsch, Bedürfnis, Neugier, Nachfrage*›; nicht gestillt ‹*Hunger, Neugier, Appetit*›; unbeglichen ‹*Schuld*›; **sexually ~:** sexuell nicht befriedigt; **leave sb. ~:** jmdn. nicht befriedigen

unsatisfying /ʌn'sætɪsfaɪɪŋ/ *adj.* unbefriedigend; nicht sättigend ‹*Mahlzeit*›

unsaturated /ʌnˈsætʃəreɪtɪd, ʌnˈsætjʊreɪtɪd/ *adj.* ungesättigt

unsavory (*Amer.*: **unsavory**) /ʌnˈseɪvərɪ/ *adj.* unangenehm ‹*Geruch, Geschmack, Mahlzeit*›; zwielichtig ‹*Charakter, Person*›; zweifelhaft ‹*Ruf, Geschäfte, Angelegenheit*›; unerfreulich ‹*Einzelheiten*›

unscalable /ʌnˈskeɪləbl/ *adj.* unbezwinglich ‹*Berg, Höhe*›

unscaled /ʌnˈskeɪld/ *adj.* [noch] nicht bezwungen ‹*Berg, Höhe*›

unscarred /ʌnˈskɑːd/ *adj.* **1** von Narben frei **2** (fig.: unscathed) unbeschadet

unscathed /ʌnˈskeɪðd/ *adj.* unversehrt ‹*Person*›; unbeschädigt ‹*Sache*›; (fig.) **he emerged from the scandal ~/with his reputation ~:** er überlebte den Skandal ohne einen Flecken auf seiner Weste (ugs.)/ohne dass sein Ruf Schaden genommen hätte

unscented /ʌnˈsentɪd/ *adj.* unparfümiert ‹*Seife, Shampoo*›

unscheduled /ʌnˈʃedjuːld/ *adj.* außerplanmäßig

unscholarly /ʌnˈskɒləlɪ/ *adj.* unwissenschaftlich ‹*Buch, Methode*›; **be ~** ‹*Person:*› kein Gelehrter sein

unschooled /ʌnˈskuːld/ *adj.* (without education) ungebildet; (without training) ungeschult

unscientific /ʌnsaɪənˈtɪfɪk/ *adj.* unwissenschaftlich ‹*Methode, Buch, Ansatz usw.*›; **be ~** ‹*Person:*› kein Wissenschaftler sein

unscientifically /ʌnsaɪənˈtɪfɪkəlɪ/ *adv.* unwissenschaftlich

unscramble /ʌnˈskræmbl/ *v.t.* (lit. or fig.) entwirren; (Teleph.: decode) entschlüsseln

unscratched /ʌnˈskrætʃt/ *adj.* (unhurt) unverletzt

unscrew /ʌnˈskruː/

A *v.t.* ab- *od.* losschrauben ‹*Regal, Deckel usw.*›; herausdrehen ‹*Schraube*›

B *v.i.* ‹*Brett, Verschluss:*› sich abschrauben lassen; ‹*Schraube:*› sich lösen *od.* abschrauben lassen; **come ~ed** sich lösen

unscripted /ʌnˈskrɪptɪd/ *adj.* frei vorgetragen ‹*Rede*›; nicht von einem Skript abgelesen ‹*Interview, Rundfunksendung*›; **an ~ play** ein Stegreifstück

unscrupulous /ʌnˈskruːpjʊləs/ *adj.* skrupellos; **be ~ about money** in Geldangelegenheiten skrupellos sein

unscrupulously /ʌnˈskruːpjʊləslɪ/ *adv.* skrupellos

unscrupulousness /ʌnˈskruːpjʊləsnɪs/ *n.*, *no pl.* Skrupellosigkeit, *die*

unseal /ʌnˈsiːl/ *v.t.* (break seal of) entsiegeln; (open) öffnen ‹*Brief, Paket, Behälter*›

unsealed /ʌnˈsiːld/ *adj.* offen; unverschlossen; (without a seal) nicht versiegelt

unseasonable /ʌnˈsiːzənəbl/ *adj.* nicht der Jahreszeit entsprechend ‹*Wetter, Hitze, Schnee*›; **the weather is ~:** das Wetter entspricht nicht der Jahreszeit; **the warmth was ~ for March** für [den] März war es ungewöhnlich warm

unseasonably /ʌnˈsiːzənəblɪ/ *adv.* [für die Jahreszeit] ungewöhnlich ‹*kalt, warm*›

unseasonal /ʌnˈsiːzənl/ *adj.* ▸ **unseasonable**

unseasoned /ʌnˈsiːznd/ *adj.* **1** (not flavoured) ungewürzt **2** (not matured) nicht abgelagert ‹*Holz*›; unerfahren ‹*Soldat*›

unseat /ʌnˈsiːt/ *adj.* **1** (remove from office) abwählen **2** (throw) aus dem Sattel werfen; ‹*Pferd:*› abwerfen

unseaworthy /ʌnˈsiːwɜːðɪ/ *adj.* nicht seetüchtig

unsecured /ʌnsɪˈkjʊəd/ *adj.* **1** (not fixed) nicht gesichert **2** (Finance: without security) ohne Sicherheit[en] *nachgestellt*

unseeded /ʌnˈsiːdɪd/ *adj.* (Tennis) nicht gesetzt

unseeing /ʌnˈsiːɪŋ/ *adj.* blind; leer ‹*Blick, Auge*›

unseemly /ʌnˈsiːmlɪ/ *adj.* unschicklich; ungehörig ‹*Benehmen*›; ungebührlich ‹*Eile, Benehmen*›

unseen /ʌnˈsiːn/

A *adj.* **1** (not seen) ungesehen; unbekannt ‹*Text*›; **~ translation** (Brit. Sch., Univ.) Übersetzung eines unbekannten Textes (*aus einer Fremdsprache*) **2** (invisible) unsichtbar

B *n.* (Brit. Sch., Univ.) **French ~:** Übersetzung eines unbekannten Textes aus dem Französischen

unselfconscious /ʌnselfˈkɒnʃəs/ *adj.*, **unselfconsciously** /ʌnselfˈkɒnʃəslɪ/ *adv.* unbefangen

unselfconsciousness /ʌnselfˈkɒnʃəsnɪs/ *n.* Unbefangenheit, *die*

unselfish /ʌnˈselfɪʃ/ *adj.*, **unselfishly** /ʌnˈselfɪʃlɪ/ *adv.* selbstlos

unselfishness /ʌnˈselfɪʃnɪs/ *n.*, *no pl.* Selbstlosigkeit, *die*

unsent /ʌnˈsent/ *adj.* nicht abgeschickt *od.* verschickt ‹*Brief, Waren usw.*›

unsentimental /ʌnsentɪˈmentl/ *adj.* unsentimental ‹*Person*›; **be totally ~ about sth.** einer Sache (*Dat.*) gegenüber keinerlei sentimentale Gefühle haben

unserviceable /ʌnˈsɜːvɪsəbl/ *adj.* unbrauchbar

unsettle /ʌnˈsetl/ *v.t.* durcheinander bringen; verwirren ‹*menschlichen Geist*›; stören ‹*Friede*›; verstören ‹*Kind, Tier*›; erschüttern ‹*Stabilität, emotionales Gleichgewicht*›; aus dem Gleichgewicht bringen ‹*Wirtschaft, Markt*›

unsettled /ʌnˈsetld/ *adj.* **1** (changeable) wechselhaft; (fig.) unstet (geh.), ruhelos ‹*Leben*›; unsicher ‹*Zukunft*› **2** (upset) verstimmt ‹*Magen*›; gestört ‹*Verdauung*›; unruhig ‹*Zeit, Land*›; instabil (geh.) ‹*Wirtschaft, Markt*›; **be/feel ~:** aus dem [gewohnten] Gleis sein **3** (open to further discussion) ungeklärt ‹*Angelegenheit, Frage*› **4** (unpaid) unbezahlt

unsettling /ʌnˈsetlɪŋ/ *adj.* störend ‹*Vorfall, Einfluss*›; beunruhigend ‹*Nachricht*›; unruhig ‹*Zeit*›; (Finance) destabilisierend ‹*Einfluss*›; **have an ~ effect on sb.** jmdn. aus dem Gleichgewicht bringen; **this constant travelling is ~:** dieses ständige Reisen bringt einen aus dem Gleis

unshaded /ʌnˈʃeɪdɪd/ *adj.* schattenlos; nackt ‹*Glühbirne, Licht*›; **the ~ areas of the drawing** die nicht schattierten Teile der Zeichnung

unshak[e]able /ʌnˈʃeɪkəbl/ *adj.* unerschütterlich

unshaken /ʌnˈʃeɪkn/ *adj.* **be ~:** nicht erschüttert sein

unshapely /ʌnˈʃeɪplɪ/ *adj.* unförmig; missgestaltet ‹*Körper, Mensch*›; **become ~:** aus der Form geraten

unshaven /ʌnˈʃeɪvn/ *adj.* unrasiert; **go ~:** sich nicht rasieren

unsheathe /ʌnˈʃiːð/ *v.t.* aus der Scheide ziehen

unshed /ʌnˈʃed/ *adj.* ungeweint ‹*Tränen*›

unshockable /ʌnˈʃɒkəbl/ *adj.* **be ~:** durch nichts zu erschüttern sein

unshrinkable /ʌnˈʃrɪŋkəbl/ *adj.* (Textiles) nicht einlaufend; schrumpffrei; **be ~:** nicht einlaufen

unsighted /ʌnˈsaɪtɪd/ *adj.* **1** (blind) nicht sehend **2** (Sport) **be ~:** in der *od.* seiner Sicht behindert sein

unsightliness /ʌnˈsaɪtlɪnɪs/ *n.*, *no pl.* Hässlichkeit, *die*

unsightly /ʌnˈsaɪtlɪ/ *adj.* unschön

unsigned /ʌnˈsaɪnd/ *adj.* nicht unterzeichnet ‹*Brief, Dokument*›; unsigniert ‹*Gemälde*›

unsinkable /ʌnˈsɪŋkəbl/ *adj.* unsinkbar

unsized /ʌnˈsaɪzd/ *adj.* **~ paper/textiles** ungeleimtes Papier/ungeschlichtete Textilien

unskilful /ʌnˈskɪlfl/ *adj.* ungeschickt; **be ~ in sth.** bei etw. ungeschickt vorgehen

unskilled /ʌnˈskɪld/ *adj.* **1** (lacking skills) ungeschickt; stümperhaft **2** (without special training) ungelernt ‹*Arbeiter*›; **~ in sth.** in etw. (*Dat.*) unerfahren **3** (done without skill) schlecht; stümperhaft **4** keine besonderen Fertigkeiten erfordernd ‹*Arbeit*›; **~ jobs** Stellen für ungelernte Arbeiter; Hilfsarbeiterstellen; **the work is ~:** die Arbeit erfordert keine besonderen Fertigkeiten

unskillful (Amer.) ▸ **unskilful**

unskimmed /ʌnˈskɪmd/ *adj.* nicht entrahmt; **~ milk** Vollmilch

unslept-in /ʌnˈsleptɪn/ *adj.* **the bed was ~:** in dem Bett hatte niemand geschlafen

unsliced /ʌnˈslaɪst/ *adj.* ungeschnitten; am Stück *nachgestellt*

unsmiling /ʌnˈsmaɪlɪŋ/ *adj.* ernst

unsmoked /ʌnˈsməʊkt/ *adj.* ungeräuchert

unsnarl /ʌnˈsnɑːl/ *v.t.* entwirren

unsociability /ʌnsəʊʃəˈbɪlɪtɪ/ *n.* Ungeselligkeit, *die*

unsociable /ʌnˈsəʊʃəbl/ *adj.* ungesellig

unsocial /ʌnˈsəʊʃl/ *adj.* ungesellig; **at this ~ hour** (joc.) zu dieser unchristlichen Tageszeit; **work ~ hours** nachts/sonn- und feiertags arbeiten

unsold /ʌnˈsəʊld/ *adj.* unverkauft

unsolicited /ʌnsəˈlɪsɪtɪd/ *adj.* nicht angefordert *od.* erbeten; nicht bestellt ‹*Waren*›; unverlangt eingesandt ‹*Manuskript*›; **~ mail** Wurfsendungen

unsolved /ʌnˈsɒlvd/ *adj.* ungelöst; unaufgeklärt ‹*Verbrechen*›

unsophisticated /ʌnsəˈfɪstɪkeɪtɪd/ *adj.* schlicht, einfach ‹*Person, Geschmack, Vergnügen, Spiel*›; unkompliziert ‹*Maschine, Küche, Methode*›; einfach ‹*Wein*›; **~ food** Hausmannskost, *die*

unsound /ʌnˈsaʊnd/ *adj.* **1** (diseased) nicht gesund; krank; **his health is ~:** seine Gesundheit ist angeschlagen *od.* angegriffen **2** (defective) baufällig ‹*Gebäude*›; morsch ‹*Holz*›; brüchig ‹*Mauerwerk*›; **structurally ~:** baufällig **3** (ill-founded) wenig stichhaltig; anfechtbar ‹*Gesetz*›; nicht vertretbar ‹*Ansichten, Methoden*› **4** (unreliable) unzuverlässig; **the firm is financially ~:** die Firma steht finanziell auf schwachen Füßen **5 of ~ mind** unzurechnungsfähig; **he killed her while of ~ mind** als er sie tötete, war er nicht zurechnungsfähig

unsoundness /ʌnˈsaʊndnɪs/ *n.*, *no pl.* (of health) Schwäche, *die;* (of structure) Baufälligkeit, *die;* (of theory, argument, decision) Zweifelhaftigkeit, *die;* **~ of mind** Unzurechnungsfähigkeit, *die*

unsparing /ʌnˈspeərɪŋ/ *adj.* **1** (lavish) großzügig; **work with ~ energy** mit voller Kraft arbeiten; **give sb. one's ~ help/support** jmdm. seine volle Hilfe/Unterstützung geben; **be ~ of** *or* **in sth.** mit etw. nicht geizen; **be ~ in one's efforts** keine Mühe scheuen **2** (merciless) schonungslos

unsparingly /ʌnˈspeərɪŋlɪ/ *adj.* **1** großzügig **2** (mercilessly) schonungslos

unspeakable /ʌnˈspiːkəbl/ *adj.* unbeschreiblich; (indescribably bad) unsäglich

unspeakably /ʌnˈspiːkəblɪ/ *adv.* unbeschreiblich; unsäglich ‹*hässlich*›

unspecified /ʌnˈspesɪfaɪd/ *adj.* nicht näher bezeichnet; nicht genannt ‹*Anzahl, Summe*›; **the job was for an ~ length of time** die Stelle war nicht befristet

unspectacular /ʌnspekˈtækjʊlə(r)/ *adj.* wenig eindrucksvoll

unspent /ʌnˈspent/ *adj.* nicht ausgegeben ‹*Geld*›; **I still had 30 pence ~ in my pocket** ich hatte noch 30 Pence in der Tasche

unspoiled /ʌnˈspɔɪld/, **unspoilt** /ʌnˈspɔɪlt/ *adj.* unverdorben; unberührt ‹*Dorf, Landschaft*›; genießbar ‹*Lebensmittel*›

unspoken /ʌnˈspəʊkn/ *adj.* ungesagt; (tacit) unausgesprochen; stillschweigend ‹*Übereinkunft*›; **be left ~:** ungesagt bleiben

unsporting /ʌnˈspɔːtɪŋ/, **unsportsmanlike** /ʌnˈspɔːtsmənlaɪk/ *adjs.* unsportlich

unstable /ʌnˈsteɪbl/ *adj.* **1** nicht stabil; instabil (geh.); labil ‹*Wirtschaft, Beziehungen, Verhältnisse*›; **the country is ~:** die Lage im Land ist nicht stabil *od.* ist unsicher; **[mentally/emotionally] ~:** [psychisch] labil **2** (Phys.) instabil; *see also* **equilibrium**

unstamped /ʌnˈstæmpt/ *adj.* ungestempelt; (unfranked) unfrankiert

unstated /ʌnˈsteɪtɪd/ *adj.* nicht genannt

unstatesmanlike /ʌn'steɪtsmənlaɪk/ *adj.* wenig staatsmännisch

unsteadily /ʌn'stedɪlɪ/ *adv.* unsicher ‹*gehen*›; unregelmäßig ‹*schlagen, brennen*›

unsteadiness /ʌn'stedɪnɪs/ *n., no pl.* ▸**unsteady**: Unsicherheit, *die;* Instabilität, *die;* Wechselhaftigkeit, *die;* Ungleichmäßigkeit, *die;* Wackeligkeit, *die*

unsteady /ʌn'stedɪ/ *adj.* unsicher; instabil ‹*Wirtschaft, Markt*›; wechselhaft ‹*Entwicklung*›; ungleichmäßig ‹*Flamme, Rhythmus*›; wackelig ‹*Leiter, Stuhl, Tisch, Konstruktion*›; **be ~ on one's feet** unsicher auf den Beinen sein

unsterilized /ʌn'sterɪlaɪzd/ *adj.* unsterilisiert; nicht sterilisiert

unstick /ʌn'stɪk/ *v.t.*, **unstuck** /ʌn'stʌk/ [ab]lösen; *see also* **unstuck**

unstinting /ʌn'stɪntɪŋ/ *adj.* großzügig; **be ~ in sth.** mit etw. nicht geizen; **be ~ in one's efforts** keine Mühe scheuen

unstitch /ʌn'stɪtʃ/ *v.t.* auftrennen ‹*Naht, Saum*›; **the seam has come ~ed** der Saum ist aufgegangen

unstoppable /ʌn'stɒpəbl/ *adj.* unhaltbar ‹*Schuss aufs Fußballtor*›; unerreichbar ‹*Aufschlag*›; (fig.) unaufhaltsam; **she is ~:** sie ist nicht aufzuhalten

unstrap /ʌn'stræp/ *v.t.* aufschnallen

unstreamed /ʌn'stri:md/ *adj.* (Sch.) nicht in Parallelzüge *od.* leistungshomogene Gruppen eingeteilt

unstressed /ʌn'strest/ *adj.* **1** (not subjected to stress) nicht belastet **2** (Phonet.) unbetont

unstructured /ʌn'strʌktʃəd/ unstrukturiert

unstrung /ʌn'strʌŋ/ *adj.* **1** **come ~** ‹*Perlen usw.:*› von der Schnur fallen **2** entnervt ‹*Person*›; zerrüttet ‹*Nerven*›

unstuck /ʌn'stʌk/ *adj.* **come ~:** sich lösen; ‹*Briefumschlag:*› aufgehen; (fig. coll.: come to grief, fail) ‹*Person:*› baden gehen (ugs.) (**over** mit); ‹*Projekt, Plan, Theorie, Geschäft:*› in die Binsen gehen (ugs.)

unstudied /ʌn'stʌdɪd/ *adj.* ungekünstelt

unstylish /ʌn'staɪlɪʃ/ *adj.* unelegant; (not fashionable) altmodisch

unsubsidized /ʌn'sʌbsɪdaɪzd/ *adj.* nicht subventioniert

unsubstantial /ʌnsəb'stænʃl/ *adj.* **1** immateriell; (ghostly) körperlos ‹*Wesen*›; leicht ‹*Konstruktion*› **2** (inadequate) wenig nahrhaft ‹*Essen*›

unsubstantiated /ʌnsəb'stænʃɪeɪtɪd/ *adj.* unhaltbar; unbegründet

unsubtle /ʌn'sʌtl/ *adj.* plump

unsuccessful /ʌnsək'sesfl/ *adj.* erfolglos; **be ~:** keinen Erfolg haben; **the operation was ~:** die Operation hatte keinen Erfolg *od.* misslang; **be ~ in an examination/competition** eine Prüfung nicht bestehen/in einem Wettbewerb unterliegen *od.* keinen Erfolg haben; **he has been ~ in his attempt to find a job** es ist ihm nicht gelungen, eine Stelle zu finden

unsuccessfully /ʌnsək'sesfəlɪ/ *adv.* erfolglos; vergebens ‹*versuchen*›

unsuitability /ʌnsu:tə'bɪlɪtɪ, ʌnsju:tə'bɪlɪtɪ/ *n., no pl.* Ungeeignetsein, *das;* (for job) mangelnde Eignung

unsuitable /ʌn'su:təbl, ʌn'sju:təbl/ *adj.* ungeeignet; **~ clothes** (for weather, activity) unzweckmäßige Kleider; (for occasion, age) unpassende Kleider; **be ~ for sb./sth.** für jmdn./etw. ungeeignet sein; **this sort of behaviour is ~ for a teacher** ein solches Verhalten gehört sich nicht für einen Lehrer

unsuitably /ʌn'su:təblɪ, ʌn'sju:təblɪ/ *adv.* unpassend; **she dresses ~ for her age/figure** sie kleidet sich unpassend für ihr Alter/unvorteilhaft für ihre Figur; **be ~ dressed for a hike** für eine Wanderung unzweckmäßig gekleidet sein

unsuited /ʌn'su:tɪd, ʌn'sju:tɪd/ *adj.* ungeeignet; **be ~ for** *or* **to sb./sth.** für jmdn./etw. ungeeignet sein; ‹*Verhalten, Sprache:*› für jmdn./etw. unpassend sein; **John and Mary are ~ to each other** John und Mary passen nicht zusammen; **he is ~ to be a teacher** er eignet sich nicht zum Lehrer

unsullied /ʌn'sʌlɪd/ *adj.* (literary) unbefleckt; unberührt ‹*Schnee*›; makellos ‹*Glanz, Ruf*›

unsung /ʌn'sʌŋ/ *adj.* unbesungen ‹*Held, Tat*›

unsupported /ʌnsə'pɔ:tɪd/ *adj.* **1** nicht abgestützt; **if left ~, the branches will break** wenn man die Äste nicht [ab]stützt, brechen sie; **the old man walked ~:** der alte Mann ging ohne fremde Hilfe **2** (Mil.) ohne Unterstützung *nachgestellt;* (without cover) ungedeckt; **an ~ unit** eine ohne Unterstützung operierende Einheit **3** (fig.) durch nichts gestützt ‹*Anschuldigung, Forderung, Theorie*›; **~ by sb./sth.** nicht gestützt durch jmdn./etw.; **a project ~ by funds** ein finanziell nicht gefördertes Projekt; **we do not accept cheques ~ by cheque cards** wir akzeptieren keine Schecks ohne Scheckkarte

unsupportive /ʌnsə'pɔ:tɪv/ *adj.* nicht [sehr] hilfsbereit; (not providing emotional help) keinen Halt bietend; **an ~ boss** ein Boss, von dem keine Unterstützung zu erwarten ist; **her family has been ~:** ihre Familie war *od.* bot ihr keine Stütze

unsure /ʌn'ʃʊə(r)/ *adj.* unsicher; **be ~ about sb./sth.** sich (*Dat.*) über jmdn./etw. nicht im Klaren sein; **be ~ whether to do sth.** sich (*Dat.*) nicht sicher sein, ob man etw. tun soll; **be ~ of sb./sth.** sich (*Dat.*) jmds./einer Sache nicht sicher sein; **be ~ of a date/of one's facts** ein Datum nicht genau wissen/seine Fakten nicht genau kennen; **be ~ of oneself** unsicher sein

unsurfaced /ʌn'sɜ:fɪst/ *adj.* unbefestigt

unsurpassable /ʌnsə'pɑ:səbl/ *adj.* unübertrefflich; (unique) einzigartig

unsurpassed /ʌnsə'pɑ:st/ *adj.* unübertroffen; **a landscape ~ in beauty** eine Landschaft von unübertroffener Schönheit; **~ for suspense/wit** von unübertroffener Spannung/unübertroffenem Witz

unsurprising /ʌnsə'praɪzɪŋ/ *adj.* wenig überraschend

unsurprisingly /ʌnsə'praɪzɪŋlɪ/ *adv.* wie zu erwarten war

unsuspected /ʌnsə'spektɪd/ *adj.* **1** (not known about) ungeahnt ‹*Talent, Kräfte, Stärke, Tiefe, Charme*›; unvermutet ‹*Defekt, Leck, Ergebnis, Folge*›; **he showed an ~ streak of ruthlessness** er zeigte sich überraschend rücksichtslos **2** (not under suspicion) **be ~:** nicht verdächtigt werden; nicht unter Verdacht stehen; **~ by anyone** ohne verdächtigt zu werden

unsuspecting /ʌnsə'spektɪŋ/ *adj.*, **unsuspectingly** /ʌnsə'spektɪŋlɪ/ *adv.* nichts ahnend; ahnungslos

unsustainable /ʌnsʌs'teɪnəbl/ *adj.* **1** (not maintainable) nicht aufrechtzuerhaltend **2** (Ecol.) nicht nachhaltig **3** (indefensible) unhaltbar ‹*Bemerkung, Behauptung*›

unsweetened /ʌn'swi:tnd/ *adj.* ungesüßt

unswerving /ʌn'swɜ:vɪŋ/ *adj.* **1** (not turning aside) schnurgerade; **follow an ~ course** (fig.) seinen Weg unbeirrt fortsetzen **2** (steady, constant) unerschütterlich ‹*Glaube, Treue*›; unbeirrbar ‹*Entschlossenheit, Zuneigung*›; **be ~ in sth.** an etw. (*Dat.*) unbeirrbar *od.* unerschütterlich festhalten

unswervingly /ʌn'swɜ:vɪŋlɪ/ *adv.* unerschütterlich ‹*treu*›; unbeirrbar ‹*unterstützen, festhalten, folgen*›

unsymmetrical /ʌnsɪ'metrɪkl/ *adj.* unsymmetrisch

unsympathetic /ʌnsɪmpə'θetɪk/ *adj.* **1** wenig mitfühlend; **be ~:** kein Mitgefühl zeigen; **be ~ to sth./not ~ to sth.** kein Verständnis/schon Verständnis für etw. haben **2** (unlikeable) unsympathisch

unsympathetically /ʌnsɪmpə'θetɪkəlɪ/ *adv.* ohne Mitgefühl

unsystematic /ʌnsɪstə'mætɪk/ *adj.*, **unsystematically** /ʌnsɪstə'mætɪkəlɪ/ *adv.* unsystematisch

untainted /ʌn'teɪntɪd/ *adj.* unverdorben ‹*Lebensmittel*›; makellos ‹*Ruf*›

untalented /ʌn'tæləntɪd/ *adj.* untalentiert

untameable /ʌn'teɪməbl/ *adj.* unzähmbar; (fig.) unbezähmbar; unbezwinglich ‹*Wildnis*›

untamed /ʌn'teɪmd/ *adj.* (lit. or fig.) ungezähmt; wild

untangle /ʌn'tæŋgl/ *v.t.* entwirren; (fig.) entwirren ‹*Geschichte, Situation, Handlung*›; in Ordnung bringen ‹*Finanzen, Angelegenheit*›

untapped /ʌn'tæpt/ *adj.* nicht angezapft; (fig.: not used) ungenutzt ‹*Talent*›; nicht angebrochen ‹*Vorräte*›; unerschlossen ‹*Bodenschätze, Markt*›

untarnished /ʌn'tɑ:nɪʃt/ *adj.* (lit. or fig.) makellos; rein; nicht angelaufen ‹*Silber*›; **his name is ~ by corruption** sein Name ist nicht durch Korruption befleckt (geh.)

untasted /ʌn'teɪstɪd/ *adj.* unberührt; **leave one's food ~:** sein Essen nicht anrühren; (fig.) **~ pleasures/delights** nie genossene *od.* gekostete Vergnügen/Freuden

untaught /ʌn'tɔ:t/ *adj.* **1** (not instructed) **be [completely] ~ in sth.** in etw. (*Dat.*) [überhaupt] nicht ausgebildet sein **2** (not acquired by teaching) natürlich ‹*Begabung*›; angeboren ‹*Fähigkeit*›

untaxed /ʌn'tækst/ *adj.* unversteuert ‹*Einkommen, Waren*›; **an ~ car** ein Auto, für das die [Kraftfahrzeug]steuer nicht bezahlt ist

unteachable /ʌn'ti:tʃəbl/ *adj.* nicht bildungsfähig ‹*Person, Kind*›; nicht lehrbar ‹*Fach, Fertigkeit*›

untenable /ʌn'tenəbl/ *adj.* unhaltbar

untenanted /ʌn'tenəntɪd/ *adj.* unbewohnt; leer stehend

untended /ʌn'tendɪd/ *adj.* ungepflegt ‹*Garten*›

untested /ʌn'testɪd/ *adj.* nicht erprobt; **a drug ~ on humans** ein an Menschen [noch] nicht erprobtes Medikament

unthankful /ʌn'θæŋkfl/ *adj.* undankbar

unthinkable /ʌn'θɪŋkəbl/

A *adj.* unvorstellbar

B *n.* **the ~:** das Unvorstellbare

unthinkably /ʌn'θɪŋkəblɪ/ *adv.* unvorstellbar

unthinking /ʌn'θɪŋkɪŋ/ *adj.*, **unthinkingly** /ʌn'θɪŋkɪŋlɪ/ *adv.* gedankenlos; **~, I took the key** geistesabwesend nahm ich den Schlüssel

unthought /ʌn'θɔ:t/ *adj.* **~ of** undenkbar; **hitherto ~-of disadvantages/objections** Nachteile/Einwände, an die bisher noch niemand gedacht hat/hatte

unthread /ʌn'θred/ *v.t.* vom Faden abziehen ‹*Perlen*›

untidily /ʌn'taɪdɪlɪ/ *adv.* unordentlich

untidiness /ʌn'taɪdɪnɪs/ *n., no pl.* ▸**untidy**: Ungepflegtheit, *die;* Unaufgeräumtheit, *die;* Unordentlichkeit, *die;* Unsauberkeit, *die*

untidy /ʌn'taɪdɪ/ *adj.* ungepflegt ‹*Äußeres, Person, Garten*›; unaufgeräumt ‹*Bücher, Spielzeug, Zimmer*›; unordentlich, unsauber ‹*Manuskript*›

untie /ʌn'taɪ/ *v.t.*, **untying** /ʌn'taɪɪŋ/ aufknüpfen, aufknoten ‹*Faden, Seil, Paket*›; aufbinden ‹*Knoten, Schnürsenkel*›; losbinden ‹*Pferd, Boot, Seil vom Pfosten*›; **~ sb./sb.'s hands** jmdn./jmds. Hände von den Fesseln befreien

untied /ʌn'taɪd/ *adj.* offen ‹*Schnürsenkel*›; ungebunden ‹*Krawatte*›; **leave sth. ~:** etw. nicht zusammenbinden; **come ~:** sich lösen; ‹*Schnürsenkel:*› aufgehen

until /ən'tɪl/

A *prep.* ▸**i p. 1001** bis; (followed by article + noun) bis zu; **~ [the] evening/night/the end** bis zum Abend/bis in die Nacht/bis zum Ende; **~ his death/retirement** bis zu seinem Tod/seiner Pensionierung; **~ next week** bis nächste Woche; **~ then** *or* **that time** bis dahin *od.* dann; **~ soon after sth.** bis kurz nach etw.; **not ~:** erst; **not ~ Christmas/the summer/his birthday/this morning** erst zu *od.* (bes. südd.) an Weihnachten/im Sommer/an seinem Geburtstag/heute Morgen; **yes, but not ~ [then]** ja, aber nicht vorher

B *conj.* bis; **~ you find the key, we shall not be able to get in** solange du den Schlüssel nicht findest, kommen wir nicht hinein; **I am not coming ~ I am asked** ich komme erst, wenn man mich einlädt; solange man mich nicht einlädt, komme ich nicht; **I did not know ~**

you told me ich wusste das nicht, bis du es mir gesagt hast; **not ~ I saw him ...:** erst, als ich ihn sah, ...

untimely /ʌn'taɪmlɪ/
A *adj.* **1** (inopportune) ungelegen; (inappropriate) unpassend; **be ~:** ungelegen kommen/unpassend sein; **an ~ frost** ein nicht der Jahreszeit entsprechender Frost; **an ~ measure/action** eine zur Unzeit getroffene Maßnahme; **his joke was ~:** er machte seinen Witz im unpassenden Moment; **not ~:** zur rechten Zeit **2** (premature) vorzeitig; allzu früh ‹*Tod*›; **he came to an ~ end** er starb allzu früh
B *adv.* (inopportunely) unpassend; (prematurely) allzu früh

untiring /ʌn'taɪərɪŋ/ *adj.* unermüdlich; **be ~ in one's efforts for sb./to do sth.** sich unermüdlich für jmdn. einsetzen/sich unermüdlich bemühen, etw. zu tun

untiringly /ʌn'taɪərɪŋlɪ/ *adv.* unermüdlich

untitled /ʌn'taɪtld/ *adj.* ohne Titel *nachgestellt*; **be ~:** keinen Titel haben

unto /'ʌntʊ, 'ʌntə/ *prep.* (arch./literary) **1** ▸**to A 2** (Bibl.) **come ~ me** kommet zu mir (bibl.); **~ us a child is born** uns ist ein Kind geboren; **~ this day** bis zum heutigen Tage; **faithful ~ death** getreu bis in den Tod

untold /ʌn'təʊld/ *adj.* **1** (immeasurable) unbeschreiblich; unsagbar ‹*Elend*›; unermesslich ‹*Reichtümer, Anzahl*› **2** (countless) unzählig **3** (not related) nicht erzählt

untouchable /ʌn'tʌtʃəbl/
A *adj.* **1** (beyond reach) unberührbar; **sth. is ~:** etw. kann nicht berührt werden; **2** (above criticism/reproach) unantastbar
B *n.* Unberührbare, *der/die*

untouched /ʌn'tʌtʃt/ *adj.* **1** (not handled, untasted) unberührt; **leave sth. ~:** etw. nicht anrühren; **'~ by human hand'** (on packaged food) ≈ „hygienisch verpackt"; **a cup of tea still ~:** eine noch unberührte Tasse Tee **2** (not changed) unverändert **3** (not affected) unberührt; **be ~ by sth.** von etw. unberührt bleiben; **they had left her jewellery ~:** sie hatten ihren Schmuck nicht angerührt; **a town ~ by the war** eine vom Krieg verschont gebliebene Stadt; **she remained ~ by his tears** seine Tränen ließen sie kalt **4** (unequalled) unerreicht

untoward /ʌntə'wɔːd/ *adj.* **1** (unfavourable) ungünstig; unglücklich ‹*Unfall*›; **in case something ~ were to happen** falls Schwierigkeiten auftauchen; (in case there is an accident) falls ein Unglück geschieht; **nothing ~ happened** es gab keine Schwierigkeiten; (more serious) es passierte kein Unheil **2** (unseemly) ungehörig

untraceable /ʌn'treɪsəbl/ *adj.* unauffindbar; **be ~:** nicht aufzuspüren sein

untraced /ʌn'treɪst/ *adj.* noch nicht gefunden

untrained /ʌn'treɪnd/ *adj.* unausgebildet; ungelernt ‹*Arbeitskräfte*›; nicht dressiert ‹*Tier*›; **to the ~ eye/ear** dem ungeschulten Auge/Ohr; **be ~ in sth.** in etw. (*Dat.*) ungeübt sein

untrammelled (*Amer.:* **untrammeled**) /ʌn'træmld/ *adj.* (fig.) unbeschränkt ‹*Freiheit*›; **young people ~ by tradition/convention** junge Leute, die sich von Traditionen/Konventionen nicht einengen lassen

untranslatable /ʌntræns'leɪtəbl/ *adj.* unübersetzbar

untravelled (*Amer.:* **untraveled**) /ʌn'trævld/ *adj.* der/die nicht weit herumgekommen ist; kaum befahren ‹*Straße*›

untreatable /ʌn'triːtəbl/ *adj.* (Med.) unbehandelbar; nicht behandelbar

untreated /ʌn'triːtɪd/ *adj.* unbehandelt

untrendy /ʌn'trendɪ/ *adj.* (coll.) untrendig (ugs.)

untried /ʌn'traɪd/ *adj.* **1** (not tested) unerprobt; **a new treatment, ~ on humans** eine neue, an Menschen noch nicht erprobte Behandlung; **leave nothing ~:** nichts unversucht lassen **2** (Law) nicht vor Gericht gestellt ‹*Person*›; nicht verhandelt ‹*Fall*›

untrodden /ʌn'trɒdn/ *adj.* unberührt ‹*Schnee*›; [noch] nie gegangen ‹*Weg*›

untroubled /ʌn'trʌbld/ *adj.* ungestört ‹*Schlaf, Ruhe*›; sorglos ‹*Gesicht, Geist*›; ruhig ‹*Wasser*›; sorgenfrei ‹*Zeit, Leben*›; **he seemed ~ by the news** die Nachricht schien ihn nicht zu beunruhigen; **we were ~ by doubts/worries** auf uns lasteten keine Zweifel/Sorgen

untrue /ʌn'truː/ *adj.* **1** (false) unwahr; **that's ~:** das ist nicht wahr **2** (unfaithful) **~ to sb./sth.** jmdm./etw. untreu **3** ungenau ‹*Ergebnis, Messgerät*›

untrustworthy /ʌn'trʌstwɜːðɪ/ *adj.* unzuverlässig

untruth /ʌn'truːθ/ *n., pl.* **~s** /ʌn'truːðz, ʌn'truːθs/ Unwahrheit, *die*

untruthful /ʌn'truːθfl/ *adj.* verlogen (abwertend); **an ~ story** eine Lügengeschichte (abwertend); **I am not being ~:** ich lüge nicht

untruthfully /ʌn'truːθfəlɪ/ *adv.* nicht der Wahrheit entsprechend ‹*antworten, etw. sagen*›

untruthfulness /ʌn'truːθflnɪs/ *n., no pl.* (of story) Unwahrheit, *die;* (of person) Verlogenheit, *die* (abwertend)

untuneful /ʌn'tjuːnfl/ *adj.* unmelodisch

unturned /ʌn'tɜːnd/ ▸**stone A 1**

untutored /ʌn'tjuːtəd/ *adj.* ungeschult

untypical /ʌn'tɪpɪkl/ *adj.* untypisch (**of** für)

unusable /ʌn'juːzəbl/ *adj.* unbrauchbar

unused[1] /ʌn'juːzd/ *adj.* (new, fresh) unbenutzt; (not utilized) ungenutzt; ungestempelt ‹*Briefmarke*›; **he still had three days ~ leave** er hatte noch drei Tage Urlaub gut

unused[2] /ʌn'juːst/ *adj.* (unaccustomed) **be ~ to sth./to doing sth.** etw. (*Akk.*) nicht gewohnt sein/nicht gewohnt sein, etw. zu tun; **we are not ~ to sudden crises** plötzliche Krisen sind für uns nichts Ungewohntes

unusual /ʌn'juːʒʊəl/ *adj.* ungewöhnlich; (exceptional) außergewöhnlich; **an ~ number of ...:** eine ungewöhnlich große Zahl von ...; **it is ~ for him to do that** er tut das gewöhnlich nicht; **it is not ~ for her to do that** es ist durchaus nicht ungewöhnlich, dass sie das tut

unusually /ʌn'juːʒʊəlɪ/ *adv.* ungewöhnlich; *as sentence-modifier* **~ [for him], he was late** er kam zu spät, was für ihn ganz ungewöhnlich ist

unusualness /ʌn'juːʒʊəlnɪs/ *n., no pl.* Ungewöhnlichkeit, *die*

unutterable /ʌn'ʌtərəbl/ *adj.*, **unutterably** /ʌn'ʌtərəblɪ/ *adv.* unsäglich

unvarnished /ʌn'vɑːnɪʃt/ *adj.* unlackiert ‹*Holz*›; unglasiert ‹*Keramik*›; (fig.) ungeschminkt ‹*Wahrheit*›

unvarying /ʌn'veərɪɪŋ/ *adj.* gleich bleibend

unveil /ʌn'veɪl/ *v.t.* **1** entschleiern ‹*Gesicht*›; enthüllen ‹*Statue, Gedenktafel*›; (fig.: introduce publicly) vorstellen ‹*neues Auto, Produkt, Modell*› **2** (reveal) veröffentlichen, (geh.) enthüllen ‹*Plan, Projekt*›

unveiling /ʌn'veɪlɪŋ/ *n.* Enthüllung, *die;* (fig.) Vorstellung, *die;* **the ~ ceremony** die [feierliche] Enthüllung

unventilated /ʌn'ventɪleɪtɪd/ *adj.* ungelüftet; (having no ventilation system) unbelüftet

unverifiable /ʌn'verɪfaɪəbl/ *adj.* nicht nachprüfbar ‹*Tatsache*›

unverified /ʌn'verɪfaɪd/ *adj.* nicht nachgeprüft

unversed /ʌn'vɜːst/ *adj.* nicht bewandert (**in** in + *Dat.*)

unvoiced /ʌn'vɔɪst/ *adj.* **1** unausgesprochen ‹*Ansichten, Gefühle, Zweifel*› **2** (Phonet.) stimmlos

unwaged /ʌn'weɪdʒd/
A *adj.* erwerbslos
B *n.* **the ~** (Brit.) Erwerbslose *Pl.*

unwanted /ʌn'wɒntɪd/ *adj.* unerwünscht; **one's ~ clothes/books** die Kleider/Bücher, die man nicht mehr [haben] will

unwarily /ʌn'weərɪlɪ/ *adv.* unvorsichtig

unwarrantable /ʌn'wɒrəntəbl/ *adj.* nicht zu rechtfertigend *nicht präd.;* ungerechtfertigt

unwarrantably /ʌn'wɒrəntəblɪ/ *adv.* **be ~ severe with sb.** so streng mit jmdm. sein, dass es nicht zu rechtfertigen ist

unwarranted /ʌn'wɒrəntɪd/ *adj.* ungerechtfertigt

unwary /ʌn'weərɪ/ *adj.* unvorsichtig; unüberlegt ‹*Tat, Schritt*›

unwashed /ʌn'wɒʃt/ *adj.* ungewaschen ‹*Person, Kleidung*›; ungespült ‹*Geschirr*›; **the great ~** (derog.) der Pöbel

unwavering /ʌn'weɪvərɪŋ/ *adj.* gleichmäßig ‹*Flamme, Licht*›; fest ‹*Blick*›; (fig.: firm, resolute) unerschütterlich

unwearable /ʌn'weərəbl/ *adj.* **sth. is ~:** etw. kann man nicht anziehen *od.* tragen

unwelcome /ʌn'welkəm/ *adj.* unwillkommen; ungebeten ‹*Besucher*›; unerwünscht ‹*Anwesenheit*›

unwell /ʌn'wel/ *adj.* unwohl; **look ~:** nicht wohl *od.* gut aussehen; **he feels ~** (feels poorly) er fühlt sich nicht wohl; (feels sick) ihm ist [es] schlecht *od.* übel; **she is ~:** es geht ihr nicht gut

unwholesome /ʌn'həʊlsəm/ *adj.* (lit. or fig.) ungesund

unwieldiness /ʌn'wiːldɪnɪs/ *n., no pl.* (of tool, weapon) Unhandlichkeit, *die;* (of box, shape, parcel) Sperrigkeit, *die;* (fig.: complexity) Kompliziertheit, *die*

unwieldy /ʌn'wiːldɪ/ *adj.* unhandlich ‹*Werkzeug, Waffe*›; sperrig ‹*Karton, Form, Paket*›; (fig.) kompliziert ‹*Name, Titel, Organisation usw.*›

unwilling /ʌn'wɪlɪŋ/ *adj.* widerwillig ‹*Partner, Unterstützung, Zustimmung*›; unfreiwillig ‹*Helfer*›; **an achievement that commands our ~ admiration/respect** eine Leistung, die wir wider Willen bewundern/respektieren müssen; **be ~ to do sth.** etw. nicht tun wollen; **we are not ~ but unable to help** wir wollen durchaus helfen, können [es] aber nicht; **be ~ for sb. to do sth.** *or* **that sb. should do sth.** nicht wollen, dass jmd. etw. tut; **be ~ for sth. to be done** *or* **that sth. should be done** nicht wollen, dass etw. getan wird

unwillingly /ʌn'wɪlɪŋlɪ/ *adv.* widerwillig

unwillingness /ʌn'wɪlɪŋnɪs/ *n., no pl.* Widerwille, *der;* **~ to help/listen** mangelnde Bereitschaft zu helfen/zuzuhören

unwind /ʌn'waɪnd/
A *v.t.,* **unwound** /ʌn'waʊnd/ abwickeln; abspulen ‹*Film*›; **the girl unwound her arms from around his neck** das Mädchen löste seine Arme von seinem Hals
B *v.i.,* **unwound 1** (unreel) sich abwickeln **2** (fig.: unfold) sich entwickeln **3** (coll.: relax) sich entspannen

unwise /ʌn'waɪz/ *adj.* unklug; **if you are ~ enough to ignore my advice** wenn du so unklug bist, meinen Rat nicht anzunehmen

unwisely /ʌn'waɪzlɪ/ *adv.* unklug; *as sentence-modifier* unklugerweise

unwitting /ʌn'wɪtɪŋ/ *adj.* ahnungslos ‹*Opfer*›; unwissentlich ‹*Komplize, Urheber*›; (unintentional) unbeabsichtigt ‹*Fehler, Handlung*›; ungewollt ‹*Beleidigung*›

unwittingly /ʌn'wɪtɪŋlɪ/ *adv.* unwissentlich; unabsichtlich ‹*beleidigen*›

unwonted /ʌn'wəʊntɪd/ *adj.* ungewohnt

unworkable /ʌn'wɜːkəbl/ *adj.* unbrauchbar ‹*Material*›; nicht abbaubar ‹*Flöz*›; (fig.: impracticable) unbrauchbar ‹*System*›; undurchführbar ‹*Plan, Projekt*›

unworkmanlike /ʌn'wɜːkmənlaɪk/ *adj.* nicht fachmännisch

unworldly /ʌn'wɜːldlɪ/ *adj.* weltabgewandt; (naïve, not worldly-wise) weltfremd

unworn /ʌn'wɔːn/ *adj.* **1** (new) ungetragen ‹*Kleidung*› **2** (not damaged) nicht abgetreten ‹*Teppich, Treppe*›; nicht abgetragen ‹*Kleidungsstück*›; nicht abgenutzt ‹*Maschinenteil*›; nicht abgefahren ‹*Reifen*›; **completely ~:** überhaupt nicht abgetreten/abgetragen/abgenutzt/abgefahren

unworried /ʌn'wʌrɪd/ *adj.* unbekümmert; **she was completely ~ by it** sie machte sich (*Dat.*) keine Sorgen darum

unworthily /ʌn'wɜːðɪlɪ/ *adv.* unwürdig

unworthiness /ʌnˈwɜːðɪnɪs/ *n.*, *no pl.* Unwürdigkeit, *die*

unworthy /ʌnˈwɜːðɪ/ *adj.* unwürdig; **receive ~ treatment** in einer Weise behandelt werden, die man nicht verdient hat; **be [not] ~ of sth.** einer Sache nicht [un]würdig sein; **an incident ~ of notice/of sb.'s attention** ein Vorfall, der keine Beachtung/der jmds. Beachtung nicht verdient; **be ~ of sb./sth.** ‹*Verhalten, Einstellung usw.*:› einer Person/Sache (*Gen.*) unwürdig sein

unwrap /ʌnˈræp/ *v.t.*, **-pp-** auswickeln; abwickeln ‹*Bandage*›

unwritten /ʌnˈrɪtn/ *adj.* ungeschrieben; nicht schriftlich festgehalten ‹*Märchen, Lied, Vertrag, Verfassung*›; unbeschrieben ‹*Papier, Seite*›

unyielding /ʌnˈjiːldɪŋ/ *adj.* hart; (fig.) unnachgiebig; unerschütterlich ‹*Mut*›; unbeirrbar ‹*Entschlossenheit*›; unerbittlich ‹*Widerstand*›

unyoke /ʌnˈjəʊk/ *v.t.* aus dem Joch nehmen; ausspannen ‹*Zugtier, Wagen, Pflug*›

unzip /ʌnˈzɪp/

A *v.t.*, **-pp-** **1** öffnen ‹*Reißverschluss*›; **~ a dress/bag** *etc.* den Reißverschluss eines Kleides/einer Tasche *usw.* öffnen; **can you ~ me, please?** kannst du mir bitte den Reißverschluss öffnen *od.* (ugs.) aufmachen?; **her dress had come ~ped** der Reißverschluss ihres Kleides war aufgegangen **2** (Computing) entpacken ‹*Datei*›

B *v.i.*, **-pp-: the dress ~s at the back** das Kleid hat hinten einen Reißverschluss; **this bag/dress won't ~:** der Reißverschluss dieser Tasche/dieses Kleides geht nicht auf (ugs.)

up /ʌp/

A *adv.* **1** (to higher place) nach oben; (in lift) aufwärts; **[right] up to sth.** (lit. or fig.) [ganz] bis zu etw. hinauf; **the bird flew up to the roof** der Vogel flog aufs Dach [hinauf]; **up into the air** in die Luft [hinauf] …; **climb up on sth./climb up to the top of sth.** auf etw. (*Akk.*) [hinauf]steigen/bis zur Spitze einer Sache hinaufsteigen; **the lift went up to the top of the building** der Lift fuhr bis zur obersten Etage des Gebäudes; **the way up [to sth.]** der Weg hinauf [zu etw.]; **on the way up** (lit. or fig.) auf dem Weg nach oben; **up here/there** hier herauf/dort hinauf; **high/higher up** hoch/höher hinauf; **farther up** weiter hinauf; **halfway/a long/little way up** den halben Weg/ein weites/kurzes Stück hinauf; **up and up** immer höher; **up and away** auf und davon; **come on up!** komm [hier/weiter] herauf!; **up it** *etc.* **comes/goes** herauf kommt/hinauf geht es *usw.*; **up you go!** rauf mit dir! (ugs.); *see also* **hand A 1**

2 (to upstairs) rauf (bes. ugs.); herauf/hinauf (bes. schriftsprachlich); nach oben

3 (to place regarded as higher) rauf (bes. ugs.); herauf/hinauf (bes. schriftsprachlich); **go up to the shops/the end of the road** zu den Geschäften/zum Ende der Straße gehen

4 (to place regarded as more important) **go up to Leeds from the country** vom Land in die Stadt Leeds *od.* nach Leeds fahren

5 (northwards) rauf (bes. ugs.); herauf/hinauf (bes. schriftsprachlich); **come up from London to Edinburgh** von London nach Edinburgh [he]raufkommen

6 (Brit.: to capital) rein (bes. ugs.); herein/hinein (bes. schriftsprachlich); **go up to town** *or* **London** nach London gehen/fahren; **get up to London from Reading** von Reading nach London [he]reinfahren

7 (Brit) (to university) **up to university/Oxford** auf die Universität/nach Oxford; (at university) **up at university/Oxford** an der Universität/in Oxford

8 (Naut.: with rudder to leeward) in Luv; **put the helm up** das Ruder in Luv legen

9 (in higher place) oben; **up here/there** hier/da oben; **[right] up at sth.** [ganz] oben auf/an etw. (*Dat.*); **high up** hoch oben; **he is something high up in the Army** (fig.) er ist ein hohes *od.* großes Tier in der Armee (ugs.); **an order from high up** (fig.) ein Befehl von ganz oben (ugs.); **higher up in the mountains** weiter oben in den Bergen; **the picture should be higher up** das Bild müsste höher hängen; **farther up** weiter oben; **halfway/a long/little way up** auf halbem Weg nach oben/ein gutes/kurzes Stück weiter oben; **10 metres up** 10 Meter hoch; **live four floors** *or* **storeys up** im vierten Stockwerk wohnen; **his flat is on the next floor up** seine Wohnung ist ein Stockwerk höher

10 (erect) hoch; **keep your head up** halte den Kopf hoch; *see also* **chin**

11 (out of bed) **be up** auf sein; **up and about** auf den Beinen

12 (in place regarded as higher; upstairs) oben

13 (in place regarded as more important; Brit.: in capital) **up in town** *or* **London/Leeds** in London/Leeds

14 (in north) **up [north]** oben [im Norden] (ugs.)

15 (in price, value, amount) **prices have gone/are up** die Preise sind gestiegen; **butter is up [by …]** Butter ist […] teurer; **the dollar is/these shares are up** der Dollar ist/diese Aktien sind im Wert gestiegen; (at high level) **the temperature was up in the thirties** die Temperatur lag über dreißig Grad

16 (including higher limit) **up to** bis … hinauf; **up to midday/up to £2** bis zum Mittag/bis zu 2 Pfund

17 (in position of gain) **we're £300 up on last year** wir liegen 300 Pfund über dem letzten Jahr; **the takings were £500 up on the previous month** die Einnahmen lagen 500 Pfund über denen des Vormonats

18 (ahead) **be three points/games/goals up** (Sport) mit drei Punkten/Spielen/Toren vorn liegen; **be three points up on sb.** drei Punkte vor jmdm. sein *od.* liegen

19 (as far as) **up to sth.** bis zu etw.; **she is up to Chapter 3** sie ist bis zum dritten Kapitel gekommen *od.* ist beim dritten Kapitel; **where are you/have you got up to [now]?** (in book) wie weit bist du?/wie weit bist du jetzt gekommen?; **up to here/there** bis hier[hin]/bis dorthin; **I've had it up to here** (coll.) mir steht es bis hier [hin] (ugs.); **up to now/then/that time/last week** bis jetzt/damals/zu jener Zeit/zur letzten Woche; *see also* **ear¹ 1**; **eye A 1**; **neck A 1**; **point A 5**

20 **up to** (comparable with) **be up to expectation[s]** den Erwartungen entsprechen; **his last opera is not up to the others he has written** seine neueste Oper reicht an seine früheren nicht heran

21 **up to** (capable of) **[not] be/feel up to sth.** einer Sache (*Dat.*) [nicht] gewachsen sein/sich einer Sache (*Dat.*) [nicht] gewachsen fühlen; **[not] be/feel up to doing sth.** [nicht] in der Lage sein/sich nicht in der Lage fühlen, etw. zu tun; **are you sure you're up to it?** meinst du wirklich, dass du das schaffst?; **not be up to much** nicht viel taugen; **my cooking isn't up to much** ich koche nicht besonders gut; **be up to sb.'s dodges/fiddles** jmds. Schliche kennen; **he is up to all the dodges** er ist mit allen Wassern gewaschen (ugs.)

22 **up to** (derog.: doing) **be up to sth.** etw. anstellen (ugs.); **what is he up to?** was hat er [bloß] vor?; **what do you think you're up to?** was fällt Ihnen [denn *od.* eigentlich] ein?; **I'm sure he's up to something** er führt sicher etwas im Schilde; **I wonder what he's up to with it** ich frage mich, was er damit vorhat

23 **up to** (incumbent on) **it is [not] up to sb. to do sth.** es ist [nicht] jmds. Sache, etw. zu tun; **it is up to us to help them** es ist unsere Pflicht, ihnen zu helfen; **now it's up to him to do something** nun liegt es bei *od.* an ihm, etwas zu tun; **it's not up to me to say** das kann ich nicht sagen; **the decision/choice is [not] up to me** die Entscheidung/Wahl hängt [nicht] von mir ab; **it's/that's up to you** (is for you to decide) es/das hängt von dir ab; (concerns only you) es/das ist deine Sache

24 (close) **up against sb./sth.** an jmdm./etw. ‹*lehnen*›; an jmdn./etw. ‹*stellen*›; **sit up against the wall** mit dem Rücken zur *od.* an der Wand sitzen; **up near/by sth.** direkt neben etw.

25 (confronted by) **be up against a problem/difficulty** *etc.* (coll.) vor einem Problem/einer Schwierigkeit *usw.* stehen; **find oneself up against the law/the authorities** mit dem Gesetz/mit den Behörden in Konflikt kommen; **be up against a tough opponent** es mit einem harten Gegner zu tun haben; **they don't realize what sort of competition they will be up against** sie wissen nicht, mit welcher Art von Konkurrenz sie es zu tun haben werden; **be up against it** in großen Schwierigkeiten stecken; *see also* **come up 9**

26 **up and down** (upwards and downwards) hinauf und hinunter; (to and fro) auf und ab; **the children are jumping up and down on the settee** die Kinder springen auf dem Sofa herum; **be up and down** (coll.: variable) Hochs und Tiefs haben; **How are you? — Oh, up and down** Wie geht es Ihnen? — Ach, mal so, mal so (ugs.); *see also* **up-and-down**

27 (facing upwards) **'this side/way up'** (on box etc.) „[hier] oben"; **turn sth. this/the other side/way up** diese/die andere Seite einer Sache nach oben drehen; **the right/wrong way up** richtig/verkehrt *od.* falsch herum; **which way up is the painting supposed to be?** was soll auf dem Bild oben [und unten] sein?; wie herum ist das Bild denn richtig? (ugs.)

28 (finished, at an end) abgelaufen; **time is up** die Zeit ist abgelaufen; **it is all up with him** mit ihm ist es vorbei *od.* aus (ugs.); *see also* **game¹ A 2**

B *prep.* **1** (upwards along) rauf (bes. ugs.); herauf/hinauf (bes. schriftsprachlich); **walk up sth.** etw. hinaufgehen; **higher up the valley** weiter oben im Tal; **up hill and down dale** bergauf und bergab; **curse sb. up hill and down dale** jmdn. in Grund und Boden verfluchen

2 (upwards through) **force a liquid up a pipe** eine Flüssigkeit durch eine Röhre nach oben pressen

3 (upwards over) **up sth.** etw. (*Akk.*) hinauf; **ivy grew up the wall** Efeu wuchs die Mauer hinauf; **mud was splattered up the back of his coat** sein Mantel war den ganzen Rücken hinauf mit Schlamm bespritzt

4 (along) **go up the road/corridor/track** die Straße/den Korridor/den Weg hinauf- *od.* entlanggehen; **come up the street** die Straße herauf- *od.* entlangkommen; **turn up a side street** in eine Seitenstraße einbiegen; **I'm going up the pub** (Brit. coll.) ich gehe in die Kneipe; **walk up and down the platform** auf dem Bahnsteig auf und ab gehen; **up and down the land** landauf, landab

5 (at or in higher position in or on) [weiter] oben; **further up the ladder/coast** weiter oben auf der Leiter/an der Küste; **a house up the mountain** ein Haus oben am Berg; **live/sail up the river** flussaufwärts wohnen/segeln

6 **up yours/up them!** (sl.) du kannst/die können mich [mal]! (salopp)

7 (from bottom to top along) **up the side of a house** an der Seite eines Hauses hinauf. *See also* **country 2**; **creek 4**; **gum tree**; **pole¹ 1**; **sleeve 1**; **spout A 1**; **stage A 1**

C *adj.* **1** (directed upwards) aufwärts führend ‹*Rohr, Kabel*›; ‹*Rolltreppe*› nach oben; nach oben gerichtet ‹*Kolbenhub*›; **up train/line/journey** (Railw.) Zug/Gleis/Fahrt Richtung Stadt

2 (well informed) **be up in a subject/on the news** in einem Fach auf der Höhe [der Zeit] sein/über alle Neuigkeiten Bescheid wissen *od.* gut informiert sein

3 **up for** (in line for) **be up for a post/for promotion** Kandidat/Kandidatin für eine Stelle/Beförderung sein; **who's up for it?** (coll.: ready to take part) wer macht mit?

4 (coll.: ready) **tea['s]/grub['s] up!** Tee/Essen ist fertig!

5 (coll.: amiss) **what's up?** was ist los? (ugs.); **what's up with him** *etc.***?** was ist los mit ihm *usw.*? (ugs.); **something is up** irgendwas ist los (ugs.)

D *n.* *in pl.* **the ups and downs** (lit. or fig.) das Auf und Ab; (fig.) die Höhen und Tiefen; **life is full of ups and downs** das Leben ist ein dauerndes Auf und Ab; **we've had our ups and downs** wir haben Höhen und Tiefen durchlebt

E *v.i.*, **-pp-** (coll.) **up and leave/resign** einfach abhauen (ugs.)/kündigen; **he ups and says …:** da sagt er doch [ur]plötzlich …

F v.t., **-pp-** (coll.) (increase) erhöhen; (raise up) heben

'up-and-coming adj. (coll.) aufstrebend; Nachwuchs‹autor, -spieler usw.›

up-and-'down attrib. adj. **~ movement/motion** Aufundabbewegung, die; **an ~ life/~ years** (fig.) ein Leben/Jahre mit Höhen und Tiefen; **an ~ sort of a year** ein bewegtes Jahr

up-and-'over door n. Kipptür, die

'up-and-up n. (coll.) **be on the ~:** auf dem aufsteigenden Ast sein (ugs.)

'upbeat

A n. (Mus.) Auftakt, der

B adj. (coll.) (optimistic) optimistisch; (cheerful) fröhlich; **~ news/export figures** zuversichtlich stimmende Neuigkeiten/Exportraten

up'braid v.t. **~ sb. with sth./for [doing] sth.** jmdm. wegen etw. Vorwürfe machen/jmdm. vorwerfen, dass er etw. getan hat

upbringing /'ʌpbrɪŋɪŋ/ n. Erziehung, die

upcoming /'ʌpkʌmɪŋ/ adj. demnächst od. in nächster Zeit stattfindend ‹Veranstaltung, Unternehmung›; geplant ‹Projekt, Film›

'up-country adj. **1** **an ~ town/region/dialect** eine Stadt/ein Gebiet im Landesinneren/ein Dialekt, wie er im Landesinneren gesprochen wird **2** (countrified, unsophisticated) **a little ~ town/place** ein kleiner Flecken/kleines Fleckchen auf dem Land

'up current n. (in air) Aufwind, der

update

A /ʌp'deɪt/ v.t. (bring up to date) aktualisieren; auf den neuesten od. aktuellen Stand bringen; (modernize) modernisieren; **an ~d version/edition** eine aktualisierte Fassung/Ausgabe

B /'ʌpdeɪt/ n. **1** (report) Lagebericht, der (**on** zu); (~d edition) Neuausgabe, die **2** (Computing) Update, das

'updraught n. [Luft]zug von unten

up'end

A v.t. (lit. or fig.) auf den Kopf stellen; (knock down) zu Boden schlagen ‹Gegner›

B v.i. ‹Schiff:› sich mit dem Heck nach oben stellen [und sinken]

'upfield adv. (Sport) in Richtung des gegnerischen Tores

up'front adj. **1** (in advance) Voraus‹zahlung› **2** (frank) offen; (honest) aufrichtig; **be ~:** sich frank und frei aussprechen (**about sth.** über etw. Akk.)

up 'front adv. (coll.) **1** (at the front) vorne **2** (as down payment) im Voraus

up'grade[1] v.t.

A **1** (raise) befördern ‹Beschäftigte›; aufwerten ‹Stellung›; **~ fees/salaries/payments in line with inflation** Gebühren/Gehälter/Zahlungen entsprechend der Inflationsrate erhöhen; **we were ~d to first class** wir wurden auf die erste Klasse umbebucht **2** (improve) verbessern; **the stadium will be ~d to Olympic standards** das Stadion wird den olympischen Normen entsprechend ausgebaut **3** (Computing, Electr.) aufrüsten; upgraden; verbessern ‹Software›

B v.i. (Computing, Electronics) aufrüsten; upgraden; **~ to newer machines** auf neuere Maschinen umsteigen

C n. /'-'-/ (Computing) Upgrade, das

'upgrade[2] n. (Amer.) Steigung, die; **be on the ~** (fig.) ‹Wirtschaft:› im Aufschwung sein; **he was on the ~:** es ging bergauf mit ihm

upgrad[e]able /ʌp'greɪdəbl/ adj. nachrüstbar

upheaval /ʌp'hi:vl/ n. Aufruhr, der; (commotion, disturbance) Durcheinander, das; **the ~ of moving house** das Durcheinander eines Umzugs; **an emotional ~:** ein Aufruhr der Gefühle; **social/political ~:** soziale/politische Umwälzung

up'hill

A adj. bergauf führend ‹Weg, Pfad›; ‹Fahrt, Reise› bergauf; (fig.) **an ~ task/struggle** eine mühselige Aufgabe/ein harter Kampf

B adv. bergauf; **it's ~ all the way** es geht immer bergauf; (fig.) es ist ein mühseliges Geschäft; **our task will be ~ all the way** (fig.) unsere Aufgabe wird bis zum Schluss mühselig sein

up'hold v.t., **upheld** /ʌp'held/ **1** (support) unterstützen; hochhalten, wahren ‹Tradition, Ehre›; schützen ‹Verfassung› **2** (confirm) aufrechterhalten ‹Forderung, Einwand›; einhalten ‹Vertrag›; bestätigen ‹Urteil›; anerkennen ‹Einwand, Beschwerde›

up'holder n. Wahrer, der/Wahrerin, die

upholster /ʌp'həʊlstə(r)/ v.t. polstern; **~ sth. in** or **with sth.** etw. in etw. (Dat.) od. mit etw. polstern; see also **well-upholstered**

upholsterer /ʌp'həʊlstərə(r)/ n. ▸ℹ **p. 1260** Polsterer, der/Polsterin, die

upholstery /ʌp'həʊlstərɪ/ n. **1** (craft) Polster[er]handwerk, das; attrib. Polster- **2** (padding) Polsterung, die; (cover also) Bezug, der; attrib. Polster-; **~ fabric** Polster- od. Möbelstoff, der

'upkeep n. Unterhalt, der

upland /'ʌplənd/

A n. in pl. Hochland, das

B adj. Hochland-

uplift

A /-'-/ v.t. aufrichten ‹Volk, Seele, Geist›; erheben (geh.) ‹Hand, Kopf, Stimme›; **parts of the earth's crust were ~ed** Teile der Erdkruste hoben sich; **be/feel ~ed by sth.** (fig.) durch etw. erhoben od. erbaut werden/sich durch etw. erhoben od. erbaut fühlen; **voices ~ed in song/praise** zum Gesang/Lobpreis erhobene Stimmen

B /'--/ n. Erhebung, die; Erbauung, die; **spiritual ~:** geistige Erhebung

up'lifting adj. (fig.) erhebend

'uplighter n. Deckenfluter, der

up'load (Computing)

A /'ʌpləʊd/ n., no pl. Upload, der (fachspr.); Hochladen, das

B /ʌp'ləʊd/ v.t. uploaden (fachspr.); hochladen

'upmarket adj. exklusiv ‹Waren, Hotel, Geschäft›; Luxus‹güter, -hotel, -restaurant›; anspruchsvoll ‹Kunde›; gehoben ‹Geschmack›; **an ~ magazine** eine Zeitschrift für den anspruchsvollen Konsumenten ; **go ~:** exklusiver [und teurer] werden

upon /ə'pɒn/ prep. **1** (indicating direction) auf (+ Akk.); (indicating position) auf (+ Dat.) **2** ▸ **on A 1, 2, 7; a house ~ the river bank** ein Haus am Flussufer

upper /'ʌpə(r)/

A compar. adj. **1** ober... ‹Nil, Themse usw., Atmosphäre›; Ober‹grenze, -lippe, -arm usw., -schlesien, -österreich usw., -kreide, -devon usw.›; (Mus.) hoch ‹Tonlage, Noten›; **~ circle** (Theatre) oberer Rang; **the temperatures will be in the ~ twenties** die Temperaturen werden zwischen 25 und 30 Grad liegen; **have/get/gain the ~ hand [of sb./sth.]** die Oberhand [über jmdn./etw.] haben/erhalten/gewinnen; see also **jaw A 1; lip 1** **2** (in rank) ober...; **the ~ ranks/echelons of the civil service/Army** die oberen od. höheren Ränge des Beamtentums/der Armee; **~ class[es]** Oberschicht, die; **~ middle class** obere Mittelschicht; **the ~ crust** (coll.) die oberen Zehntausend

B n. **1** (of footwear) Oberteil, das; **'leather ~s'** „Obermaterial Leder"; **be [down] on one's ~s** (coll.) auf dem Trockenen sitzen (ugs.) **2** (sl.: drug) Aufputschmittel, das; Speed, das (Jargon)

upper: ~ case **A** n. Großbuchstaben; **in ~ case** in Großbuchstaben; **B** adj. groß ‹Buchstabe›; **U~ Chamber** n. (Parl.) Oberhaus, das; **~-class** adj. Oberschicht-; **~-class people/family/accent** Leute/Familie aus der Oberschicht/Akzent der Oberschicht; **be very ~-class** ‹Person:› ein typischer Vertreter der Oberschicht sein; ‹Akzent, Herkunft:› typisch für die Oberschicht sein; **~-crust** adj. (coll.) **~-crust accent/family** Akzent/Familie der oberen Zehntausend; **be very ~-crust** ‹Person:› ein typischer Vertreter der oberen Zehntausend sein; **~cut** n. (Boxing) Uppercut, der; Aufwärtshaken, der; **~ 'deck** n. (of ship, bus) Oberdeck, das; **U~ House** n. Oberhaus, das; **~most** **A** adj. oberst...; **~most aim/desire** höchstes Ziel/größter Wunsch; **the questions that are ~most on the agenda** die Fragen, die auf der Tagesordnung ganz oben stehen; **be ~most in sb.'s mind** jmdn. am meisten beschäftigen; **B** adv. ganz oben; obenauf; **face ~most** mit dem Gesicht nach oben; **come ~most** (fig.) an erster Stelle stehen; **U~ 'Rhine** pr. n. Hochrhein [und Oberrhein]; **~ school** n. (Brit.) ≈ Oberstufe, die; **~ 'sixth** n. (Brit.) ≈ Oberprima, die

uppish /'ʌpɪʃ/ adj. (coll.) hochnäsig (ugs.); **be/get ~ about sth./with sb.** über etw. (Akk.) die Nase rümpfen/jmdn. von oben herab behandeln

uppishness /'ʌpɪʃnɪs/ n., no pl. (coll.) Hochnäsigkeit, die (ugs.)

uppity /'ʌpɪtɪ/ adj. (coll.) hochnäsig (ugs.); **get ~:** sich aufblasen (ugs.)

upright /'ʌpraɪt/

A adj. **1** aufrecht; steil ‹Schrift›; **a chair with an ~ back** ein Stuhl mit einem geraden Rücken[teil]; **~ piano** Klavier, das; **~ freezer** Tiefkühlschrank, der; **~ vacuum cleaner** ≈ Handstaubsauger, der; **set/stand/hold sth. ~:** etw. aufrecht hinstellen/halten; **stand ~:** aufrecht stehen; **sit ~:** aufrecht sitzen; **hold oneself ~:** sich gerade halten; **please make sure that your seat is in the ~ position** bitte stellen Sie Ihre Rückenlehnen senkrecht; see also **bolt[1] D** **2** (fig.: honourable) aufrecht; **be ~ in sth.** rechtschaffen in etw. (Dat.) sein

B n. **1** (of frame) seitliche Leiste; (of ladder) Holm, der; (of scaffolding etc.) [aufrechter] Stützpfeiler; (Footb.) Pfosten, der **2** (piano) Klavier, das

uprightly /'ʌpraɪtlɪ/ adv. aufrecht; (fig.) aufrecht; rechtschaffen

uprightness /'ʌpraɪtnɪs/ n., no pl. **1** aufrechte Stellung; (of plant) aufrechter Wuchs **2** (fig.) Aufrichtigkeit, die; Rechtschaffenheit, die

'uprising n. Aufstand, der

up-river ▸ **upstream**

'uproar n. Aufruhr, der; Tumult, der; **be in [an] ~:** in Aufruhr sein

uproarious /ʌp'rɔ:rɪəs/ adj. lärmend ‹Menge›; überwältigend ‹Begrüßung, Stimmung›; zum Schreien komisch (ugs.) ‹Witz, Anblick, Komödie›; schallend ‹Gelächter›

uproariously /ʌp'rɔ:rɪəslɪ/ adv. lärmend; schallend ‹lachen›; **be ~ funny** zum Totlachen sein (ugs.)

up'root v.t. [her]ausreißen; ‹Sturm:› entwurzeln; (fig.: eradicate) ausmerzen ‹Übel›; **~ sb.** jmdn. aus der gewohnten Umgebung herausreißen; **people were ~ed by the war** die Menschen wurden durch den Krieg entwurzelt

upsadaisy /'ʌpsədeɪzɪ/ int. hoppla

upset

A /ʌp'set/ v.t., **-tt-, upset** **1** (overturn) umkippen; (accidentally) umstoßen ‹Tasse, Vase, Milch usw.›; **~ sth. over sth.** etw. über etw. (Akk.) kippen **2** (distress) erschüttern; mitnehmen (ugs.); (disturb the composure or temper of) aus der Fassung bringen; (shock, make angry, excite) aufregen; **it ~s the children to hear their parents quarrelling** es belastet die Kinder, wenn sie ihre Eltern streiten hören; **the smallest thing ~s her** jede Kleinigkeit regt sie auf; **don't let it ~ you** nimm es nicht so schwer; **~ oneself** sich aufregen **3** (make ill) **sth. ~s sb.** etw. bekommt jmdm. nicht; **sth. ~s sb.'s stomach/digestion** etw. schlägt jmdm. auf den Magen/die Verdauung **4** (disorganize) stören; durcheinander bringen ‹Plan, Berechnung, Arrangement›; (defeat) ausschalten; **this incident has seriously ~ our chances** dieser Vorfall hat unsere Chancen erheblich vermindert

B v.i., **-tt-, upset** umkippen

C adj. **1** (overturned) umgekippt **2** (distressed) bestürzt; (agitated) aufgeregt; (unhappy) unglücklich; (put out) aufgebracht; verärgert; (offended) gekränkt; **be ~ [about sth.]** (be distressed) [über etw. (Akk.)] bestürzt sein; (be angry) sich [über etw. (Akk.)] ärgern; **we were very ~ to hear of his illness** die Nachricht von seiner Krankheit ist uns sehr nahe gegangen od. hat uns sehr bestürzt; **when they get back they'll be very/so ~ to have missed you** wenn sie zurückkommen, wird es ihnen sehr Leid tun, dich verpasst zu haben; **get ~ [about/over sth.]** sich [über etw. (Akk.)] aufregen; **there's no point in getting ~ about it** es hat keinen

Sinn, sich darüber aufzuregen **3** /'‐-/ (disordered) **an ~ stomach** ein verdorbener Magen; **have an ~ stomach** sich (*Dat.*) den Magen verdorben haben **4** (disorganized) gestört ‹*Routine, Mechanismus, System*›; durcheinander gebracht ‹*Plan, Berechnung, Mechanismus, System*›

D /'ʌpset/ *n.* **1** (overturning) Umkippen, *das* **2** (agitation) Aufregung, *die;* (shock) Schock, *der;* (annoyance) Verärgerung, *die;* **sth. is a great ~ for** *or* **to sb.** etw. nimmt jmdn. sehr mit (ugs.) *od.* geht jmdm. sehr nahe; **emotional ~:** seelischer Schock; **have an ~:** einiges durchmachen [müssen] **3** (slight quarrel) Missstimmung, *die* **4** (slight illness) Unpässlichkeit, *die;* **digestive/stomach ~:** Verdauungsstörung, *die*/Magenverstimmung, *die* **5** (disturbance) Zwischenfall, *der;* (confusion, upheaval) Aufruhr, *der;* Durcheinander, *das;* **an ~ in his plans/calculations/routine** eine Störung seiner Pläne/Berechnungen/Routine **6** (surprising result) Überraschung, *die;* **a by-election ~:** eine Überraschung bei der Nachwahl

up'setting *adj.* erschütternd; (sad) traurig; bestürzend; schlimm ‹*Zeit*›; (annoying) ärgerlich; **being mugged/sacked was a very ~ experience for her** ausgeraubt/entlassen zu werden war ein Erlebnis, das sie ganz schön mitgenommen hat (ugs.); **my mother found the obscene language ~:** meine Mutter fand die obszöne Sprache anstößig; **she missed her train, and what was even more ~, she was late for the opera** sie verpasste ihren Zug, was aber noch ärgerlicher für sie war es, dass sie dadurch zu spät in die Oper kam; **it was/I found it ~ that X was promoted instead of me** ich ärgerte mich, dass X an meiner Stelle befördert wurde; **the constant changes have been rather ~ for the children** die laufenden Veränderungen haben die Kinder ziemlich aus dem Gleis gebracht; **these pictures are ~ to a child** diese Bilder sind für ein Kind [zu] erschütternd

'upshot *n.* Ergebnis, *das;* **what will be the ~ of it [all]?** was wird bei der [ganzen] Sache herauskommen? (ugs.); **he hummed and hawed a bit and, well, the ~ of the matter/of it [all] was that ...:** er druckste ein bisschen herum, aber schließlich [und endlich] kam heraus *od.* stellte sich heraus, dass ...; **in the ~:** letztendlich

upside /'ʌpsaɪd/ *n.* (positive aspect) gute Seite; Vorteil, *der*

upside 'down

A *adv.* verkehrt herum; **turn sth. ~** (lit. or fig.) etw. auf den Kopf stellen; **the plane flew ~:** das Flugzeug flog auf dem Kopf (ugs.)

B *adj.* auf dem Kopf stehend ‹*Bild*›; **be ~:** auf dem Kopf stehen; **the car came to rest ~:** der Wagen blieb auf dem Dach liegen; **the acrobat hung ~:** der Akrobat hing mit dem Kopf nach unten *od.* kopfüber; (fig.) **the whole world seems to be ~:** die ganze Welt scheint Kopfzustehen; **an upside-down world/view of the situation/logic** eine verkehrte Welt/Sicht der Dinge/Logik

up'stage

A *adv.* (Theatre) im Hintergrund [der Bühne]; **move ~:** sich zum Hintergrund der Bühne bewegen

B *adj.* (Theatre) **an ~ door/entrance** eine Hintertür/ein Hintereingang zur Bühne

C *v.t.* (Theatre) **~ sb.** jmdn. zwingen, sich vom Publikum abzuwenden; (fig.) jmdm. die Schau stehlen (ugs.)

upstairs

A /-'-/ *adv.* nach oben ‹*gehen, kommen*›; oben ‹*sein, wohnen*›; *see also* **kick C 1**

B /'--/ *adj.* im Obergeschoss *nachgestellt*

C /-'-/ *n.* Obergeschoss, *das*

up'standing *adj.* **1** (strong and healthy) stattlich; **fine ~ children** nette, gesunde und kräftige Kinder **2** (honest) aufrichtig; aufrecht **3** **be ~** (stand up) sich erheben

'upstart

A *n.* Emporkömmling, *der*

B *adj.* **an ~ landowner** ein emporgekommener Grundbesitzer; **~ ideas/pretensions** Ideen/Angeberei eines Emporkömmlings/von Emporkömmlingen

'upstate (Amer.)

A *adj.* **~ New York** nördlicher Teil des Staates New York; **an ~ town** eine Stadt im nördlichen Teil des Staates

B *adv.* **live ~:** im nördlichen Teil des Staates leben; **go/travel ~:** in den nördlichen Teil des Staates fahren/reisen

upstream ▸**i** **p. 1491**

A /-'-/ *adv.* flussaufwärts

B /'--/ *adj.* flussaufwärts gelegen ‹*Ort*›

'up-stroke *n.* **1** (in writing) Aufstrich, *der* **2** (Mech.: of piston) Aufwärtshub, *der*

'upsurge *n.* Aufwallen, *das* (geh.); **she felt an ~ of tenderness** sie fühlte Zärtlichkeit in sich (*Dat.*) aufwallen

'upswept *adj.* hochgekämmt ‹*Haar*›; hochgezogen ‹*Linie, Auspuffrohr*›

'upswing *n.* (of pendulum, arms) Aufwärtsschwung, *der;* (fig., esp. Commerc.) Aufschwung, *der*

upsy-daisy /'ʌpsɪdeɪzɪ/ *int.* hoppla

'uptake *n.* **be quick/slow on** *or* **in the ~** (coll.) schnell begreifen/schwer von Begriff sein (ugs.)

uptempo /'ʌptempəʊ/ *adj.* schnell

uptight /ʌp'taɪt, 'ʌptaɪt/ *adj.* (coll.) **1** (tense) nervös (**about** wegen); (touchy, angry) sauer (ugs.) (**about** wegen); **make sb. ~:** jmdm. auf die Nerven gehen *od.* fallen (ugs.) **2** (Amer.: rigidly conventional) **[very] ~:** stockkonservativ (ugs.)

'uptime *n.* (Computing) Betriebszeit, *die*

up to 'date *pred. adj.* **be/keep [very] ~:** auf dem [aller]neusten Stand sein/bleiben; [ganz] up to date sein/bleiben; **keep/bring sth. ~:** etw. auf dem neusten Stand halten/auf den neusten Stand bringen; **bring sb. ~ with all the news** jmdn. auf den neusten Stand der Informationen bringen

up-to-'date *attrib. adj.* (current) aktuell; (modern) modern; aktuell ‹*Mode*›

up-to-the-'minute *adj.* hochaktuell

'upturn *n.* Aufschwung, *der* (**in** *Gen.*); **an ~ in prices** ein Anstieg der Preise

'upturned *adj.* **1** (upside down) umgedreht **2** (turned upwards) hochgeschlagen ‹*Rand, Krempe*›; nach oben gerichtet ‹*Gesicht, Auge*›; **~ nose** Stupsnase, *die*

upward /'ʌpwəd/

A *adj.* nach oben *nachgestellt;* nach oben gerichtet; **~ movement/trend** (lit. or fig.) Aufwärtsbewegung, *die*/-trend, *der;* **~ gradient** *or* **slope** Steigung, *die;* **move in an ~ direction** sich aufwärts *od.* nach oben bewegen; **~ mobility** (in social status) sozialer Aufstieg

B *adv.* aufwärts ‹*sich bewegen*›; nach oben ‹*sehen, gehen*›; *see also* **face up[ward]**

upwardly /'ʌpwədlɪ/ *adv.* aufwärts; nach oben; *see also* **mobile A 5**

upwards /'ʌpwədz/ *adv.* **1** ▸**upward B** **2** **~ of** mehr als; über; **they cost £200 and ~:** sie kosten 200 Pfund und darüber

upwind

A *adv.* /ʌp'wɪnd/ gegen den Wind

B /'ʌpwɪnd/ *adj.* **approach from the ~ side** sich mit dem Wind im Rücken nähern

Urals /'jʊərlz/ *pr. n. pl.* Ural, *der*

uranium /jʊə'reɪnɪəm/ *n.* (Chem.) Uran, *das*

Uranus /'jʊərənəs, jʊə'reɪnəs/ *pr. n.* (Astron.) Uranus, *der*

urban /'ɜ:bn/ *adj.* städtisch; Stadt‹*gebiet, -bevölkerung, -planung, -sanierung, -guerilla*›; **~ life** Leben in der Stadt; **~ decay** Verslumung, *die;* **~ district** (Brit. Hist.) *Stadtgebiet bzw. -gebiete unter der Verwaltung eines gewählten Rates;* **~ planner** ▸**i** **p. 1260** Stadtplaner, *der*/-planerin, *die;* **~ sociology** Stadtsoziologie, *die;* **~ sprawl** (process) suburbane Zersied[e]lung; (result) zersiedeltes Gebiet; **~ 'studies** Urbanistik, *die; see also* **renewal 2**

urbane /ɜ:'beɪn/ *adj.*, **urbanely** /ɜ:'beɪnlɪ/ *adv.* weltmännisch

urbanise ▸**urbanize**

urbanity /ɜ:'bænɪtɪ/ *n.* Urbanität, *die;* **urbanities** weltmännische Umgangsform[en]

urbanize /'ɜ:bənaɪz/ *v.t.* urbanisieren ‹*Land*›; verstädtern [lassen] ‹*Landbevölkerung*›; **become ~d** verstädtern

urchin /'ɜ:tʃɪn/ *n.* **1** (child) Range, *die;* (boy) Strolch, *der; see also* **street urchin** **2** ▸**sea urchin**

Urdu /'ʊədu:, 'ɜ:du:/ ▸**i** **p. 1277**

A *adj.* Urdu-; *see also* **English A**

B *n.* Urdu, *das; see also* **English B 1**

urea /jʊə'rɪ:ə, 'jʊərɪə/ *n.* (Chem.) Harnstoff, *der*

ureter /jʊə'ri:tə/ *n.* (Anat.) Harnleiter, *der;* Ureter, *der* (fachspr.)

urethra /jʊə'ri:θrə/ *n., pl.* **~e** /jʊə'ri:θri:/ *or* **~s** (Anat.) Harnröhre, *die;* Urethra, *die* (fachspr.)

urge /ɜ:dʒ/

A *v.t.* **1** **~ sb. to do sth.** jmdn. drängen, etw. zu tun; **~ sb. to sth.** jmdn. zu etw. drängen; **we ~d him to reconsider** wir rieten ihm dringend, es sich (*Dat.*) noch einmal zu überlegen; **~ sth. [on** *or* **upon sb.]** [jmdn.] zu etw. drängen; **~ caution/vigilance/patience [on** *or* **upon sb.]** [jmdn.] zur Vorsicht/Wachsamkeit/Geduld mahnen; **~ on** *or* **upon sb. the need for sth./for doing sth.** jmdm. die Notwendigkeit einer Sache/die Notwendigkeit, etw. zu tun, ans Herz legen; **the leaders ~ acceptance of the offer** die Führer dringen auf Annahme des Angebotes; **~ that sth. [should] be done** darauf dringen, dass etw. getan wird **2** (drive on) [an]treiben; **~ forward/onward** vorwärts treiben; (fig.) treiben **3** (put forward) vorbringen; **~ sb.'s youth/inexperience/the difficulty of sth.** jmds. Jugend/Unerfahrenheit/die Schwierigkeit einer Sache zu bedenken geben; **~ sth. on sb.** jmdm. etw. eindringlich nahe legen

B *n.* Trieb, *der;* **have/feel an/the ~ to do sth.** den Drang verspüren, etw. zu tun; **resist the ~ to do sth.** dem [inneren] Drang widerstehen, etw. zu tun

Phrasal verb

• **~ 'on** *v.t.* antreiben; (hasten) vorantreiben; (encourage) anfeuern; **~d on by hunger/ambition** vom Hunger/Ehrgeiz getrieben

urgency /'ɜ:dʒənsɪ/ *n., no pl.* Dringlichkeit, *die;* (earnestness) Eindringlichkeit, *die;* **there is no ~:** es eilt nicht *od.* ist nicht dringend; **be of the utmost ~:** äußerst dringend sein; **a matter of great ~:** eine sehr dringende Angelegenheit

urgent /'ɜ:dʒənt/ *adj.* **1** (pressing) dringend; (to be dealt with immediately) eilig; **be in ~ need of sth.** etw. dringend brauchen; **give ~ consideration to sth.** etw. vordringlich in Betracht ziehen; **matters/problems of an ~ nature** dringende Angelegenheiten/drängende Probleme; **on ~ business** in dringenden Geschäften; **at sb.'s ~ request** auf jmds. Drängen; **it is ~:** es eilt; **it is ~ that sb. should do sth.** *or* **does sth.** jmd. muss dringend etw. tun; **if it's ~, call a doctor** in dringenden Fällen den Arzt rufen **2** (earnest and persistent) eindringlich; **be ~ in one's demand/plea for sth.** etw. dringend fordern/eindringlich um etw. bitten

urgently /'ɜ:dʒəntlɪ/ *adv.* **1** (pressingly) dringend; (without delay) eilig; **he had to leave ~ for London on business** er musste in dringenden Geschäften nach London abreisen **2** (earnestly) eindringlich

uric /'jʊərɪk/ *adj.* **~ acid** (Chem.) Harnsäure, *die*

urinal /jʊə'raɪnl, 'jʊərɪnl/ *n.* (fitting) Urinal, *das;* **[public] ~:** [öffentliche] Herrentoilette; Pissoir, *das*

urinary /'jʊərɪnərɪ/ *adj.* Harn-; **~ diseases** Erkrankungen der Harnwege; **~ tract** Harnwege *Pl.*

urinate /'jʊərɪneɪt/ *v.t.* urinieren

urination /jʊərɪ'neɪʃn/ *n.* Urinieren, *das*

urine /'jʊərɪn/ *n.* Urin, *der;* Harn, *der; attrib.* Urin-; Harn-

URL *abbr.* (Computing) = **uniform resource locator** URL, *der*

urn /ɜ:n/ *n.* **1** **tea/coffee ~:** Tee-/Kaffeemaschine, *die* **2** (vessel) Urne, *die*

urogenital /jʊərə'dʒenɪtl/ *adj.* (Anat., Med.) urogenital; **~ disease/infection** Erkrankung/Infektion des Urogenitaltraktes

u

urologist /jʊər'ɒlədʒɪst/ *n.* ▸ⓘ p. 1260 Urologe, *der*/Urologin, *die*

urology /jʊə'rɒlədʒɪ/ *n.* Urologie, *die*

Ursa /'ɜːsə/ *pr. n.* (Astron.) ~ **Major/Minor** Großer/Kleiner Bär

Uruguay /'jʊərəgwaɪ/ *pr. n.* Uruguay (*das*)

Uruguayan /jʊərə'gwaɪən/ ▸ⓘ p. 1345
A *adj.* uruguayisch; **sb. is** ~**:** jmd. ist Uruguayer/ Uruguayerin
B *n.* Uruguayer, *der*/Uruguayerin, *die*

us /əs, *stressed* ʌs/ *pron.* **1** uns; **it's us** wir sind's (ugs.); **one of us** einer von uns **2** (coll.: me) **give us a clue/kiss!** gib mir 'nen Tipp/Kuss! (ugs.)

u/s *abbr.* = **unserviceable** unbrauchbar

US *abbr.* = **United States** USA; *attrib.* US-

USA *abbr.* = **United States of America** USA; *attrib.* der USA *nachgestellt*

usable /'juːzəbl/ *adj.* brauchbar; gebräuchlich ‹*Wort*›; **this nail is no longer** ~**:** dieser Nagel ist nicht mehr zu gebrauchen

USAF *abbr.* = **United States Air Force** Luftwaffe der Vereinigten Staaten

usage /'juːsɪdʒ/ *n.* **1** Brauch, *der;* Gepflogenheit, *die* (geh.); ~**s and customs** Sitten und Gebräuche; **commercial** ~**:** Handelsbrauch, *der;* **sanctified by** ~**:** durch Herkommen Recht geworden; **a custom sanctified by** ~**:** eine Sitte, die zum Gewohnheitsrecht geworden ist; **be in common** ~**:** allgemein gebräuchlich sein **2** (Ling.: use of language) Sprachgebrauch, *der;* ~ **[of a word]** Verwendung [eines Wortes]; **in American** *etc.* ~**:** im amerikanischen *usw.* Sprachgebrauch; **in common** ~**:** im allgemeinen Sprachgebrauch; allgemein gebräuchlich ‹*Wort usw.*› **3** (treatment) Behandlung, *die;* **have rough** ~**:** schlecht behandelt werden

usance /'juːzəns/ *n.* (Commerc.) Zahlungsfrist für ausländische Wechsel

USB *abbr.* (Computing) = **universal serial bus** USB; *attrib.* USB-‹*Stecker, -Anschluss*›

use
A [juːs] *n.* **1** Gebrauch, *der;* (of dictionary, calculator, room) Benutzung, *die;* (of word, expression; of pesticide, garlic) Verwendung, *die;* (of name, title) Führung, *die;* (of alcohol, drugs) Konsum, *der;* **the** ~ **of brutal means/methods/of trickery** die Anwendung brutaler Mittel/Methoden/von Tricks; **the** ~ **of troops/tear gas/arms/violence** der Einsatz von Truppen/Tränengas/ der Waffengebrauch/die Gewaltanwendung; **achieve sth. by the** ~ **of deception** etw. durch Täuschung erreichen; **constant/rough** ~**:** dauernder Gebrauch/schlechte Behandlung; **[not] be in** ~**:** [nicht] in Gebrauch sein; **be no longer in** ~**:** nicht mehr verwendet werden; **be in daily** *etc.* ~**:** täglich *usw.* in Gebrauch *od.* Benutzung sein; **the word is [not] in everyday** ~**:** das Wort ist [nicht] allgemein gebräuchlich; **bring into** ~**:** in Gebrauch nehmen; **come into** ~**:** in Gebrauch kommen; **[be] out of** ~**:** außer Betrieb [sein]; **go/fall/ pass/drop out of** ~**:** außer Gebrauch kommen; **instructions/directions for** ~**:** Gebrauchsanweisung, *die;* **ready for [immediate]** ~**:** [sofort] gebrauchsfertig; **instruments for** ~ **by doctors/dentists** Instrumente für den ärztlichen/zahnärztlichen Bedarf; **batteries for** ~ **in** *or* **with watches** Batterien [speziell] für Armbanduhren; **a course for** ~ **in schools** ein Kurs für die Schule *od.* zur Verwendung im Schulunterricht; **for the** ~ **of sb.** für jmdn.; **for personal/private** ~**:** für den persönlichen Gebrauch/den Privatgebrauch; **these computers are intended for home/ office** ~**:** diese Computer sind Homecomputer/sind für den Einsatz im Büro gedacht; **for external** ~ **only** nur zur äußerlichen Anwendung; **for** ~ **in an emergency/only in case of fire** für den Notfall/nur bei Feuer zu benutzen; **with** ~**:** durch den Gebrauch; **with constant** ~**:** durch dauernden Gebrauch; **with careful** *etc.* ~**:** bei sorgsamer *usw.* Behandlung; **make** ~ **of sb./sth.** jmdn./etw. gebrauchen/(exploit) ausnutzen; **a good cook will make** ~ **of any leftovers** ein guter Koch/eine gute Köchin verwendet alle Reste; **make** ~ **of one's connections/friendship with sb.** von seinen Verbindungen/seiner Freundschaft zu jmdm. Gebrauch machen; **make the best** ~ **of sth./ it** das Beste aus etw./daraus machen; **make good** ~ **of, turn** *or* **put to good** ~**:** gut nutzen ‹*Zeit, Talent, Geld*›; **put sth. to** ~**:** etw. verwenden; **put sth. to effective** ~**:** etw. wirkungsvoll einsetzen
2 (utility, usefulness) Nutzen, *der;* **these tools/ clothes will be of** ~ **to sb.** dieses Werkzeug wird/diese Kleider werden für jmdn. von Nutzen sein; **is it of [any]** ~**?** ist das [irgendwie] zu gebrauchen *od.* von Nutzen?; **these addresses might be of** ~ **to you** diese Adressen könnten für dich von Nutzen sein *od.* kannst du vielleicht gebrauchen; **be of** ~ **to the enemy/police** für den Feind/die Polizei von Nutzen sein; **can I be of any** ~ **to you?** kann ich dir irgendwie helfen?; **it is of [great]** ~ **for this work** man kann es für diese Arbeit [sehr gut] brauchen; **I did not find the book of any practical** ~**:** das Buch hatte für mich keinen praktischen Nutzen; **be [of] no** ~ **[to sb.]** [jmdm.] nichts nützen; **I wouldn't be [of] any** ~ **to you** ich könnte dir kein bisschen helfen; **he is [of] no** ~ **in a crisis/as a manager** er ist in einer Krise/als Manager zu nichts nütze *od.* (ugs.) nicht zu gebrauchen; **it's no** ~ **[doing that]** es hat keinen Zweck *od.* Sinn[, das zu tun]; **it wouldn't be any** ~**:** es hätte [überhaupt] keinen Sinn *od.* Zweck; **I have an umbrella at home. — That's no/not much** ~ **[to us] now** Ich habe einen Schirm zu Hause. — Das nützt [uns] jetzt nichts/nicht viel; **you're/that's a fat lot of** ~ (coll. iron.) du bist ja eine schöne Hilfe/davon haben wir aber was (ugs. iron.); **what's the** ~ **of that/of doing that?** was nützt das/was nützt es, das zu tun?; **what's the** ~**?** was nützt es?; **oh well, what's the** ~**!** ach, was soll's schon! (ugs.)
3 (purpose) Verwendung, *die;* Verwendungszweck, *der;* **a tool with many** ~**s** ein vielfältig zu verwendendes Werkzeug; **have its/one's** ~**s** seinen Nutzen haben; **have/find a** ~ **for sth./sb.** für etw./jmdn. Verwendung haben/ finden; **have no/not much** ~ **for sth./sb.** etw./jmdn. nicht/kaum brauchen; (fig.: dislike) nichts/nicht viel für etw./jmdn. übrig haben; **have no further** ~ **for sb./sth.** für jmdn. keine Verwendung mehr haben/etw. nicht mehr brauchen; **put sth. to a good/a new** ~**:** etw. sinnvoll/auf neu[artig]e Weise verwenden
4 (right or power of using) **have the** ~ **of sth.** etw. benutzen können; **[have the]** ~ **of kitchen and bathroom** Küchen- und Badbenutzung [haben]; **can I have the** ~ **of your car while you are away?** kann ich deinen Wagen benutzen, während du weg bist?; **let sb. have** *or* **allow sb.** *or* **give sb. the** ~ **of sth.** jmdn. etw. benutzen lassen; **he has [the] full/only restricted** ~ **of his arm** er kann seinen Arm uneingeschränkt/nur eingeschränkt benutzen; **he has lost the** ~ **of an arm/eye** er kann einen Arm nicht mehr benutzen/er kann auf einem Auge nichts mehr sehen
5 (custom, familiarity) ~**s and customs** Sitten und Gebräuche; **long** ~ **has reconciled me to it** die Gewohnheit hat mich damit versöhnt
6 (Eccl.: ritual) Ritual, *das*
7 (Law) Nießbrauch, *der*
B [juːz] *v.t.* **1** benutzen; nutzen ‹*Gelegenheit*›; anwenden ‹*Gewalt*›; einsetzen ‹*Tränengas, Wasserwerfer*›; in Anspruch nehmen ‹*Firma, Agentur, Agenten, Dienstleistung*›; nutzen ‹*Zeit, Gelegenheit, Talent, Erfahrung*›; führen ‹*Namen, Titel*›; **do you know how to** ~ **this tool?** kannst du mit diesem Werkzeug umgehen?; **the swindler/actor** ~**s the name John Smith** der Betrüger/Schauspieler nennt sich John Smith; **anything you say may be** ~**d in evidence** was Sie sagen, kann vor Gericht verwendet werden; ~ **sb.'s name [as a reference]** sich [als Empfehlung] auf jmdn. berufen; **I could** ~ **the money/a drink/the door could** ~ **a coat of paint** (coll.) ich könnte das Geld brauchen/einen Drink vertragen (ugs.)/die Tür könnte einen Anstrich brauchen *od.* (ugs.) vertragen; ~ **one's money [to do sth.]** sein Geld verwenden[, um etw. zu tun]; **the money is there to be** ~**d** das Geld ist da, um ausgegeben zu werden; ~ **one's time to do sth.** seine Zeit dazu nutzen, etw. zu tun
2 (consume as material) verwenden; ~ **gas/oil for heating** mit Gas/Öl heizen; **the camera** ~**s 35 mm film** für die Kamera braucht man einen 35-mm-Film; **'**~ **sparingly'** „sparsam verwenden"
3 (finish consuming) verbrauchen; **she has** ~**d the last of the milk** sie hat den letzten Rest Milch aufgebraucht
4 (take habitually) ~ **drugs/heroin** *etc.* Drogen/ Heroin *usw.* nehmen; ~ **alcohol** Alkohol trinken *od.* konsumieren
5 (employ in speaking or writing) benutzen; gebrauchen; verwenden; ~ **strong language** Kraftausdrücke gebrauchen
6 (exercise, apply) Gebrauch machen von ‹*Autorität, Einfluss, Können, Urteilsvermögen, Menschenverstand*›; ~ **diplomacy/tact [in one's dealings** *etc.* **with sb.]** [bei jmdm.] diplomatisch vorgehen/[zu jmdm.] taktvoll sein; ~ **care** vorsichtig sein; ~ **care in doing sth.** etw. vorsichtig tun; **he** ~**d all his strength** er wandte seine ganze Kraft auf; ~ **a method/ system/tactics** eine Methode anwenden/ nach einem [bestimmten] System/einer [bestimmten] Taktik vorgehen; ~ **other/ stronger methods/tactics** andere/härtere Methoden/eine andere/härtere Taktik anwenden; ~ **every means at one's disposal to do sth.** mit allen einem zur Verfügung stehenden Mitteln versuchen, etw. zu tun
7 (take advantage of) ~ **sb.** jmdn. ausnutzen; **don't let them** ~ **you** lass dich nicht [von ihnen] ausnutzen
8 (treat) behandeln; ~ **sb./sth. well/badly** jmdn./etw. gut/schlecht behandeln
9 ~**d to** /'juːst tə/ (formerly) **I** ~**d to live in London/work in a factory** früher habe ich in London gelebt/in einer Fabrik gearbeitet; **he** ~**d to be very shy** er war früher sehr schüchtern; **before I started taking these vitamins, I** ~**d to be tired all the time** bevor ich anfing, diese Vitamine zu nehmen, war ich immer müde; **my mother always** ~**d to say ...:** meine Mutter hat immer gesagt *od.* pflegte zu sagen ...; **life** ~**d to be much more leisurely [than it is now]** früher war das Leben viel beschaulicher [als heute]; **this** ~**d to be my room** das war [früher] mein Zimmer; **it** ~**d to be thought ...:** früher glaubte man ...; **things aren't what they** ~**d to be** es ist nichts mehr so wie früher; **he smokes much more than he** ~**d to** er raucht viel mehr als früher; **there** ~**d to be ...:** es gab früher/früher gab es ...; **I** ~**d not** *or* **I did not** ~ *or* (coll.) **I didn't** ~ *or* (coll.) **I** ~**[d]n't to smoke** früher habe ich nicht geraucht; **didn't he** ~ **to work here?** (coll.) hat er nicht früher hier gearbeitet?; ~**[d]n't there to be a shop here?** (dated coll.) war hier nicht früher ein Laden?; **Does he smoke? He** ~**d not to** *or* (coll.) **He didn't** ~ **to** Raucht er? Früher hat er das nicht getan; **there never** ~**d to be all this violence** diese ganze Gewalttätigkeit gab es früher nicht

(Phrasal verb)
- ~ **'up** *v.t.* aufbrauchen; verwenden ‹[*Essens*]*reste*›; verbrauchen, erschöpfen ‹*Kraft, Geld, Energie*›; ~ **up a dozen eggs** ein Dutzend Eier verbrauchen

'use-by date *n.* (esp. Brit.) [Mindest]haltbarkeitsdatum, *das*

used
A *adj.* **1** [juːzd] (no longer new) gebraucht; benutzt ‹*Handtuch, Teller*›; gestempelt ‹*Briefmarke*›; ~ **car** Gebrauchtwagen, *der;* ~**-car salesman** Gebrauchtwagenhändler, *der* **2** [juːst] (accustomed) ~ **to sth.** [an] etw. (*Akk.*) gewöhnt; etw. gewohnt; **be/get** ~ **to sb./sth.** [an] jmdn./etw. gewöhnt sein/sich an jmdn./etw. gewöhnen; **I'm not** ~ **to this kind of treatment** *or* **to being treated in this way** ich bin eine solche Behandlung nicht gewohnt; ich bin es nicht gewohnt, so behandelt zu werden; **you'll soon be** ~ **to it** du wirst dich bald *od.* schnell daran gewöhnen; **[not] be** ~ **to sb. doing sth./to having sb. do sth.** [es] [nicht] gewohnt sein,

U

dass jmd. etw. tut; **she was ~ to getting up early** sie war daran gewöhnt, früh aufzustehen; **she is not ~ to drinking alcohol** sie ist es nicht gewöhnt, Alkohol zu trinken

B [ju:st] ▸**use B 9**

useful /ˈju:sfl/ *adj.* **1** nützlich; praktisch ‹*Werkzeug, Gerät, Auto*›; brauchbar ‹*Rat, Idee, Wörterbuch*›; hilfreich ‹*Gespräch, Rat, Idee, Wörterbuch*›; **~ life** (of machine etc.) Lebensdauer, *die;* **~ load** Nutzlast, *die;* **he is a ~ person to know** es ist nützlich, ihn zu kennen; **English is the most ~ language** mit Englisch kommt man am weitesten; **this is ~ to know** das ist gut zu wissen; **this would be ~ to have** es wäre gut *od.* nützlich, wenn man das hätte; **be ~ to sb.** jmdm. *od.* für jmdn. nützlich sein; jmdm. nützen; **the guide was most ~ for finding our way about** der Führer hat uns sehr geholfen, uns zurechtzufinden; **the chest would be very ~ for storing my books** die Truhe würde sich sehr gut zum Lagern meiner Bücher eignen; **it would be ~ to have a tap in the garden** es wäre praktisch, wenn im Garten ein Wasserhahn wäre; **sb. finds sth. ~:** etw. nützt jmdm.; **those screws will come in ~ for my woodwork** diese Schrauben werde ich noch gut zum Schreinern brauchen können; **make oneself ~:** sich nützlich machen; **serve no ~ purpose** zu nichts nütze sein **2** (coll.: worthwhile) ordentlich (ugs.); ansehnlich ‹*Betrag, Stück, Arbeit*›; beachtlich ‹*Vorsprung*›; wertvoll ‹*Mitglied einer Mannschaft*›

usefully /ˈju:sfəlɪ/ *adv.* **a course one might ~ follow** ein Kurs, den zu verfolgen nützlich sein könnte; **a book you could ~ read** ein Buch, von dessen Lektüre du profitieren könntest; **is there anything we can ~ do?** können wir uns irgendwie nützlich machen?; **~ spend an evening doing sth.** einen Abend sinnvoll damit verbringen, etw. zu tun; **everybody should be ~ employed [in some work]** jeder sollte eine nützliche Beschäftigung haben

usefulness /ˈju:sflnɪs/ *n., no pl.* Nützlichkeit, *die;* Brauchbarkeit, *die;* **limit the ~ of sth.** den Nutzen einer Sache einschränken; **have outlived one's/its ~:** zu nichts mehr nütze *od.* zu gebrauchen sein

useless /ˈju:slɪs/ *adj.* unbrauchbar ‹*Werkzeug, Gerät, Rat, Vorschlag, Idee, Material*›; nutzlos ‹*Wissen, Information, Fakten, Protest, Anstrengung, Kampf*›; vergeblich ‹*Anstrengung, Maßnahme, Kampf, Klage*›; zwecklos ‹*Widerstand, Protest, Argumentieren*›; **be ~ to sb.** jmdm. nichts nützen; **credit cards are ~ there** Kreditkarten nützen einem dort nichts; **be ~ at sth.** zu etw. nicht zu gebrauchen sein; **oh, you're ~!** du bist doch zu nichts zu gebrauchen! (ugs.); **feel ~:** sich nutzlos fühlen; **it's ~ to do that** *or* **doing that** es hat keinen Zweck *od.* Sinn, das zu tun; **he's worse than ~:** er ist zu gar nichts nütze

uselessly /ˈju:slɪslɪ/ *adv.* unnütz, sinnlos ‹*verschwenden, aufwenden*›; vergeblich ‹*kämpfen, protestieren*›; **throw away one's life ~:** sein Leben sinnlos wegwerfen

uselessness /ˈju:slɪsnɪs/ *n., no pl.* (of tool, device, advice, information, suggestion, material) Unbrauchbarkeit, *die;* (of protest, effort, struggle) Vergeblichkeit, *die;* (of action, measure, war) Sinnlosigkeit, *die;* (of resistance) Zwecklosigkeit, *die*

user /ˈju:zə(r)/ *n.* Benutzer, *der*/Benutzerin, *die;* (of drugs, alcohol) Konsument, *der*/Konsumentin, *die;* (of coal, electricity, gas) Verbraucher, *der*/Verbraucherin, *die;* (of telephone) Kunde, *der*/Kundin, *die*

user: ~-definable *adj.* (Computing) benutzerdefinierbar; **~-defined** *adj.* (Computing) benutzerdefiniert; **~-ˈfriendliness** *n., no pl.* Benutzerfreundlichkeit, *die;* **~-ˈfriendly** *adj.* benutzerfreundlich; **explain sth. in ~-friendly terms** etw. allgemein verständlich erklären; **~ group** *n.* Benutzergruppe, *die;* **~ identification** *n., no pl.* Benutzerkennung, *die;* **~ interface** *n.* (Computing) Benutzerschnittstelle, *die;* **~ name** *n.* (Computing) Benutzername, *der;* **~ software** *n., no pl.* (Computing) Anwendersoftware, *die;* Benutzersoftware, *die*

usher /ˈʌʃə(r)/

A *n.* ▸**❶ p. 1260** (in court) Gerichtsdiener, *der;* (at cinema, theatre, church) Platzanweiser, *der*/-anweiserin, *die*

B *v.t.* führen; geleiten (geh.); **~ sb. into sb.'s presence** jmdn. vor jmdn. führen *od.* (geh.) geleiten; **~ sb. to his seat** jmdn. an seinen Platz führen

Phrasal verbs

• **~ ˈin** *v.t.* **~ sb. in** jmdn. hineinführen *od.* (geh.) -geleiten; **~ sth. in** (fig.) etw. einläuten

• **~ ˈout** *v.t.* hinausführen *od.* (geh.) -geleiten

usherette /ʌʃəˈret/ *n.* ▸**❶ p. 1260** Platzanweiserin, *die*

USN *abbr.* **= United States Navy** Marine der Vereinigten Staaten

USP *abbr.* **= unique selling point**

USS *abbr.* **= United States Ship** *Schiff der US-Marine*

USSR *abbr.* (Hist.) **= Union of Soviet Socialist Republics** UdSSR, *die; attrib.* der UdSSR *nachgestellt*

usual /ˈju:ʒʊəl/ *adj.* üblich; **be ~ for sb.** bei jmdm. üblich sein; **it is ~ for sb. to do sth.** es ist üblich, dass jmd. etw. tut; **[no] better/bigger/more** *etc.* **than ~:** [nicht] besser/größer/mehr *usw.* als gewöhnlich *od.* üblich; **as [is] ~,** (coll.) **as per ~:** wie üblich; **as is ~ in such cases** wie in solchen Fällen üblich; **the/your ~, sir?** wie immer, der Herr? (ugs.); *see also* **business 2**

usually /ˈju:ʒʊəlɪ/ *adv.* gewöhnlich; normalerweise; **more than ~ tired** *etc.* noch müder *usw.* als üblich; ganz ungewöhnlich müde *usw.*; **this time we were more than ~ careful** diesmal waren wir noch vorsichtiger als sonst

usufruct /ˈju:zjʊfrʌkt/ *n.* (Law) Nutznießung, *die*

usurer /ˈju:ʒərə(r)/ *n.* Wucherer, *der*/Wucherin, *die*

usurp /ju:ˈzɜ:p/ *v.t.* sich (*Dat.*) widerrechtlich aneignen ‹*Titel, Recht, Position*›; usurpieren (geh.) ‹*Macht, Thron*›; **~ the leading role in the enterprise** die wichtigste Rolle im Unternehmen an sich (*Akk.*) reißen; **the man who had ~ed his place in his wife's affections** der Mann, der jetzt im Herzen seiner Frau seinen Platz erobert hatte

usurpation /ju:zəˈpeɪʃn/ *n.* (of right, title, position, authority) widerrechtliche Aneignung; (of power, the throne) Usurpation, *die* (geh.)

usurper /ju:ˈzɜ:pə(r)/ *n.* Usurpator, *der* (geh.)

usury /ˈju:ʒərɪ/ *n.* Wucher, *der;* **practise ~:** Wucher treiben

utensil /ju:ˈtensɪl/ *n.* Utensil, *das;* **writing ~s** Schreibutensilien

uterine /ˈju:təraɪn, ˈju:tərɪn/ *adj.* (Anat., Med.) Gebärmutter-; uterin (fachspr.)

uterus /ˈju:tərəs/ *n., pl.* **uteri** /ˈju:təraɪ/ (Anat.) Gebärmutter, *die;* Uterus, *der* (fachspr.)

utilisable, utilisation, utilise ▸**utiliz-**

utilitarian /ju:tɪlɪˈteərɪən/

A *adj.* **1** (functional) funktionell; utilitär ‹*Ziele*› **2** (Philos.) utilitaristisch

B *n.* (Philos.) Utilitarist, *der;* Utilitarier, *der*

utilitarianism /ju:tɪlɪˈteərɪənɪzm/ *n.* (Philos.) Utilitarismus, *der*

utility /ju:ˈtɪlɪtɪ/

A *n.* **1** Nutzen, *der;* **of great ~:** sehr nutzbringend; von großem Nutzen; **total/marginal ~** (Econ.) Gesamt-/Grenznutzen, *der* **2** ▸**public utility 3** (Computing) **~ [program]** Hilfsprogramm, *das;* Dienstprogramm, *das;*

B *adj.* Vielzweck-; (functional) funktionell; **~ goods/furniture** Gebrauchsgüter/-möbel

utility: ~ man *n.* (Amer.) **1** (Theatre) Chargenspieler, *der*/-spielerin, *die;* **2** (Sport) vielseitig einsetzbarer Spieler; **3** (odd-job man) Mädchen für alles (ugs.). **~ room** *n.* Hauswirtschaftsraum, *der;*

utilizable /ˈju:tɪlaɪzəbl/ *adj.* nutzbar

utilization /ju:tɪlaɪˈzeɪʃn/ *n.* Nutzung, *die*

utilize /ˈju:tɪlaɪz/ *v.t.* nutzen

utmost /ˈʌtməʊst/

A *adj.* äußerst...; tiefst... ‹*Verachtung*›; höchst... ‹*Verehrung, Gefahr*›; größt... ‹*Höflichkeit, Eleganz, Einfachheit, Geschwindigkeit*›; **of [the] ~ importance** von äußerster Wichtigkeit; **with the ~ caution** mit größter *od.* äußerster Vorsicht; **with the ~ ease/care/reluctance** mit größter Leichtigkeit/äußerster Sorgfalt/größter Zurückhaltung; **to the ~ degree** bis zum Äußersten

B *n.* Äußerste, *das;* **do** *or* **try one's ~ to do sth.** mit allen Mitteln versuchen, etw. zu tun; **to the ~:** bis zum Äußersten; **to the ~ of one's ability/strength** so gut man eben kann/mit aller Kraft; **try sb.'s patience to the ~:** jmds. Geduld auf das Äußerste strapazieren

Utopia /ju:ˈtəʊpɪə/ *n.* (place) Utopia (*das*); (impractical scheme) Utopie, *die*

Utopian /ju:ˈtəʊpɪən/

A *adj.* utopisch

B *n.* Utopist, *der*/Utopistin, *die*

utter[1] /ˈʌtə(r)/ *attrib. adj.* vollkommen, völlig ‹*Chaos, Verwirrung, Fehlschlag, Ablehnung, Friede, Einsamkeit, Unsinn*›; ungeheuer ‹*Elend, Dummheit, Freude, Glück, Schönheit*›; größt... ‹*Freude, Vergnügen*›; **be in ~ despair/misery** völlig verzweifelt/niedergeschlagen sein; **be an ~ mystery** völlig rätselhaft sein; **be an ~ stranger to sb.** jmdm. völlig fremd sein; **~ fool** Vollidiot, *der* (ugs.)

utter[2] *v.t.* **1** von sich geben ‹*Schrei, Seufzer, Ächzen*› **2** (say) sagen ‹*Wahrheit, Wort*›; schwören ‹*Eid*›; äußern ‹*Drohung*›; zum Ausdruck bringen ‹*Gefühle*›; **the last words he ~ed** die letzten Worte, die er sprach; **she never ~ed a sound** sie gab keinen Ton von sich; **this word/her name must not be ~ed in his presence** dieses Wort/ihr Name darf in seiner Gegenwart nicht gesagt *od.* ausgesprochen werden **3** **~ a libel** (Law) eine Verleumdung verbreiten

utterance /ˈʌtərəns/ *n.* **1** **~ of a sigh/groan** ein Seufzen/Stöhnen; **give ~ to sth.** etw. zum Ausdruck bringen; einer Sache Ausdruck verleihen **2** (spoken words) Worte *Pl.;* (Ling.) [sprachliche] Äußerung; (sentence) Satz, *der* **3** (power of speech) Sprache, *die*

utterly /ˈʌtəlɪ/ *adv.* völlig; vollkommen; restlos ‹*elend, deprimiert*›; absolut ‹*entzückend, bezaubernd*›; hinreißend ‹*schön*›; äußerst ‹*dumm, lächerlich*›; aus tiefster Seele ‹*verabscheuen, ablehnen, bereuen*›

uttermost /ˈʌtəməʊst/ **1** ▸**utmost A, B** **2** (most distant) entferntest...; **to the ~ ends of the earth** bis ans äußerste Ende der Welt

ˈU-turn *n.* Wende [um 180°]; **the driver/car made a ~:** der Fahrer/Wagen wendete; **'No ~s'** „Wenden verboten"; **make a ~ [on sth.]** (fig.) eine Kehrtwendung [bei etw.] vollziehen *od.* machen

UV *abbr.* **= ultraviolet** UV

uvula /ˈju:vjʊlə/ *n., pl.* **~e** /ˈju:vjʊli:/ (Anat.) Zäpfchen, *das;* Uvula, *die* (fachspr.)

uvular /ˈju:vjʊlə(r)/ *adj.* (Anat., Ling.) uvular; **the ~ 'r'** das Zäpfchen-R

Vv

V¹, v /viː/ *n., pl.* **Vs** *or* **V's** **1** (letter) V, v, *das* **2** (Roman numeral) V **3** (V-shaped thing) V, *das* **4** **V1/V2** (Hist.) V1/V2, *die. See also* **V-neck; V-necked; V-sign**

V² *abbr.* **= volt[s]** V

v. *abbr.* **1** /ˈvɜːsəs, viː/ **= versus** gg. **2** **= very** **3** **= verse**

vac /væk/ *n.* (Brit. Univ. coll.) Semesterferien *Pl.;* **the long ~:** die Sommersemesterferien

vacancy /ˈveɪkənsɪ/ *n.* **1** (job) freie Stelle; **fill a ~:** eine [freie] Stelle besetzen; **have a ~ [on one's staff]** eine freie Stelle *od.* Stelle frei haben; **'vacancies'** (notice outside factory) „Stellen frei"; (in newspaper) „Stellenangebote" **2** (unoccupied room) freies Zimmer; **have a ~:** ein Zimmer frei haben; **'vacancies'** „Zimmer frei"; **'no vacancies'** „belegt" **3** *no pl.* (of look, mind, etc.) Leere, *die*

vacant /ˈveɪkənt/ *adj.* **1** (not occupied) frei; **'~'** (on door of toilet) „frei"; **'situations ~'** „Stellenangebote"; **a house with ~ possession** ein bezugsfertiges Haus **2** (mentally inactive) leer

vacantly /ˈveɪkəntlɪ/ *adv.* leer; **stare/gaze ~ at sb./into space** jmdn. mit leerem Blick anstarren/abwesend ins Leere starren

vacate /vəˈkeɪt/ *v.t.* räumen ‹*Gebäude, Büro, Wohnung*›; aufgeben ‹*Stelle, Amt*›; niederlegen ‹*Amt*›

vacation /vəˈkeɪʃn/

A *n.* **1** (Brit. Law, Univ.: recess) Ferien *Pl.* **2** (Amer.) ▸**holiday A 2** **3** (vacating) (of a room, building) Räumung, *die;* (of a post) Aufgeben, *das;* (of an office) Niederlegen, *das*

B *v.i.* (Amer.) **~ [at/in a place]** [an einem Ort] Urlaub machen

vacationer /vəˈkeɪʃənə(r)/, **vacationist** /vəˈkeɪʃənɪst/ *ns.* (Amer.) Urlauber, *der*/Urlauberin, *die*

vaccinate /ˈvæksɪneɪt/ *v.t.* ▸❶ **p. 1231** (Med.) impfen

vaccination /væksɪˈneɪʃn/ *n.* ▸❶ **p. 1231** (Med.) Impfung, *die; attrib.* Impf-; **have a ~:** geimpft werden

vaccine /ˈvæksiːn, ˈvæksɪn/ *n.* ▸❶ **p. 1231** Impfstoff, *der*

vacillate /ˈvæsɪleɪt/ *v.i.* (lit. or fig.) schwanken; **~ about doing sth.** schwanken, ob man etw. tun soll oder nicht; **~ on sth.** bezüglich einer Sache schwanken

vacillating /ˈvæsɪleɪtɪŋ/ *adj.* schwankend

vacillation /væsɪˈleɪʃn/ *n.* Schwanken, *das*

vacua *pl. of* **vacuum A 1**

vacuity /vəˈkjuːətɪ/ *n.* Leere, *die;* (of book, play) Geistlosigkeit, *die*

vacuous /ˈvækjʊəs/ *adj.* leer; geistlos, nichts sagend ‹*Buch, Theaterstück, Bemerkung*›

vacuously /ˈvækjʊəslɪ/ *adv.* leer

vacuum /ˈvækjʊəm/

A *n.* **1** *pl.* **vacua** /ˈvækjʊə/ *or* **~s** (Phys.; also fig.) Vakuum, *das;* **perfect ~:** ideales Vakuum; **partial ~:** Unterdruck, *der;* (fig.) **her death has left a ~ in our lives** ihr Tod hat in unserem Leben eine Lücke hinterlassen; **live in a ~** (lit. or fig.) im luftleeren Raum leben **2** *pl.* **~s** (coll.: **~ cleaner**) Sauger, *der* (ugs.)

B *v.t.& i.* [staub]saugen

vacuum: ~ bomb *n.* Vakuumbombe, *die;* **~ bottle** (Amer.) ▸**~ flask; ~ brake** *n.* (Railw.) Unterdruckbremse, *die;* **~-clean** *v.t. & i.* [staub]saugen; **~ cleaner** *n.* Staubsauger, *der;* **~ flask** *n.* (Brit.) Thermosflasche, *die;* **~ gauge** *n.* (Physics) Vakuummeter, *das;* **~-packed** *adj.* vakuumverpackt; **~ pump** *n.* Vakuumpumpe, *die;* **~ tube** *n.* (Electronics) Vakuumröhre, *die;* Elektronenröhre, *die*

vade mecum /vɑːdɪˈmeɪkəm, veɪdɪˈmiːkəm/ *n.* Vademekum, *das* (geh.)

vagabond /ˈvægəbɒnd/

A *n.* Landstreicher, *der*/Landstreicherin, *die* (oft abwertend); Vagabund, *der*/Vagabundin, *die* (veralt.)

B *adj.* umherziehend, vagabundierend ‹*Mensch, Stamm*›; **~ life** Vagabundenleben, *das*

vagaries /ˈveɪgərɪz/ *n. pl.* (lit. or fig.) Launen *Pl.;* **the ~ of life/politics** die Wechselfälle des Lebens/der Politik

vagina /vəˈdʒaɪnə/ *n., pl.* **~e** /vəˈdʒaɪniː/ *or* **~s** ▸❶ **p. 951** (Anat.) Scheide, *die;* Vagina, *die* (fachspr.)

vaginal /vəˈdʒaɪnl/ *adj.* Scheiden-; vaginal (fachspr.)

vagrancy /ˈveɪgrənsɪ/ *n., no indef. art., no pl.* Landstreicherei, *die;* (in cities) Stadtstreicherei, *die*

vagrant /ˈveɪgrənt/

A *adj.* vagabundierend; **~ life** Vagabundenleben, *das*

B *n.* Landstreicher, *der*/Landstreicherin, *die* (oft abwertend); (in cities) Stadtstreicher, *der*/Stadtstreicherin, *die*

vague /veɪg/ *adj.* vage; verschwommen, undeutlich ‹*Form, Umriss*›; undefinierbar ‹*Farbe*›; (absent-minded) geistesabwesend; (inattentive) unkonzentriert; **describe sth. in ~ terms** etw. vage beschreiben; **not have the ~st idea** *or* **notion** nicht die blasseste *od.* leiseste Ahnung haben; **be ~ about sth.** etw. nur vag[e] andeuten; (in understanding) nur eine vage Vorstellung von etw. haben

vaguely /ˈveɪglɪ/ *adv.* vage; ungefähr ‹*wissen*›; entfernt ‹*bekannt sein, erinnern an*›; schwach ‹*sich erinnern*›; **he was ~ alarmed/sad/disappointed** er war irgendwie beunruhigt/traurig/enttäuscht; **look/taste ~ like sth.** entfernt aussehen/schmecken wie etw.; **understand sth. ~:** etw. in etwa verstehen; **she looked at me ~** (uncertainly) sie sah mich unsicher an; (absent-mindedly) sie sah mich zerstreut an

vagueness /ˈveɪgnɪs/ *n., no pl.* Vagheit, *die;* (of outline, shape) Verschwommenheit, *die;* (of policy) Unbestimmtheit, *die;* (absent-mindedness) Zerstreutheit, *die;* (uncertainty) Unsicherheit, *die*

vain /veɪn/ *adj.* **1** (conceited) eitel; **be ~ about sth.** sich (*Dat.*) auf etw. (*Akk.*) viel einbilden **2** (useless) leer ‹*Drohung, Versprechen, Worte, Reden*›; eitel (geh.) ‹*Triumph, Vergnügungen*›; vergeblich ‹*Hoffnung, Erwartung, Versuch*›; **in ~:** vergeblich; vergebens; *see also* **take A 5**

vainglorious /veɪnˈglɔːrɪəs/ *adj.* (formal/literary) prahlerisch ‹*Reden, Angebereien*›; dünkelhaft ‹*Person, Auftreten*›

vainly /ˈveɪnlɪ/ *adv.* **1** (uselessly) vergebens; vergeblich **2** (in a conceited way) eitel; angeberisch

Valais /ˈvæleɪ/ *pr. n.* Wallis, *das*

valance /ˈvæləns/ *n.* Volant, *der*

vale /veɪl/ *n.* (arch./poet.) Tal, *das;* **this ~ of tears** (fig.) dies Jammertal

valediction /vælɪˈdɪkʃn/ *n.* (act) Abschied, *der;* (words) Abschiedsgruß, *der*

valedictory /vælɪˈdɪktərɪ/ *adj.* Abschieds-; **~ remarks** Bemerkungen zum Abschied; **~ speech/address** (Amer.) Abschiedsrede/-ansprache, *die*

valence /ˈveɪləns/ (esp. Amer.), **valency** /ˈveɪlənsɪ/ *ns.* (Chem., Phys.) (unit) Wertigkeit, *die;* Valenz, *die* (fachspr.); **~ bond** kovalente Bindung

valentine /ˈvæləntaɪn/ *n.* **1** *jmd., dem man am Valentinstag einen Gruß schickt* **2** **~ [card]** Grußkarte zum Valentinstag **3** **St. V~'s Day** Valentinstag, *der*

valerian /vəˈlɪərɪən/ *n.* (Bot., Pharm.) Baldrian, *der*

valet

A /ˈvælɪt, ˈvæleɪ/ *n.* ▸❶ **p. 1260** **1** Kammerdiener, *der* **2** (hotel employee) *für den Reinigungsservice zuständiger Hotelangestellter; attrib.* **~ service** Reinigungsservice

B *v.t.* /ˈvælɪt/ reinigen

ˈvaleting service /ˈvælɪtɪŋ sɜːvɪs/ *n.* Reinigungsdienst, *der*

ˈvalet parking *n.* Parkservice, *der*

valetudinarian /vælɪtjuːdɪˈneərɪən/

A *adj.* **1** (sickly) kränkelnd **2** (anxious about health) hypochondrisch

B *n.* **1** (sickly person) kränklicher Mensch **2** (hypochondriac) Hypochonder, *der*

Valhalla /vælˈhælə/ *n.* (Mythol.) Walhall[a], *das*

valiant /ˈvæljənt/ *adj.* tapfer; kühn (geh.); **he made a ~ effort to disguise his disappointment** er versuchte tapfer, seine Enttäuschung zu verbergen; **it was a ~ try/effort** es war ein tapferer Versuch

valiantly /ˈvæljəntlɪ/ *adv.* tapfer; kühn (geh.)

valid /ˈvælɪd/ *adj.* **1** (legally acceptable) gültig; berechtigt ‹*Anspruch*›; (legally valid) rechtsgültig; (having legal force) rechtskräftig; bindend ‹*Vertrag*›; **a ~ claim** ein Rechtsanspruch (**to** auf + *Akk.*) **2** (justifiable) stichhaltig ‹*Argument, Einwand, Theorie*›; triftig ‹*Grund*›; zuverlässig ‹*Methode*›; begründet ‹*Entschuldigung, Einwand*›

validate /ˈvælɪdeɪt/ *v.t.* rechtskräftig machen ‹*Anspruch, Vertrag, Testament*›; bestätigen, beweisen ‹*Hypothese, Theorie*›; für gültig erklären ‹*Wahl*›

validation /vælɪˈdeɪʃn/ *n.* (of claim, contract, etc.) Gültigkeitserklärung, *die;* (of theory, hypothesis) Bestätigung, *die*

validity /vəˈlɪdɪtɪ/ *n., no pl.* **1** (of ticket, document) Gültigkeit, *die;* (of claim, contract, marriage, etc.) Rechtsgültigkeit, *die;* **~ check** (Computing) Gültigkeitskontrolle, *die* **2** (of argument, excuse, objection, theory) Stichhaltigkeit, *die;* (of reason) Triftigkeit, *die;* (of method) Zuverlässigkeit, *die*

validly /ˈvælɪdlɪ/ *adv.* (lawfully) rechtsgültig; (properly) überzeugend; mit [vollem] Recht ‹*beanspruchen, geltend machen*›

valise /vəˈliːz/ *n.* (esp. Amer.) Reisetasche, *die*

Valkyrie /vælˈkɪərɪ, ˈvælkɪrɪ/ *n.* (Mythol.) Walküre, *die*

valley /ˈvælɪ/ *n.* **1** (lit. or fig.) Tal, *das;* **U-shaped/V-shaped ~:** Trogtal, *das*/Kerbtal, *das* (Geog.); *attrib.* **~ bottom** Talsohle, *die* **2** (of roof) [Dach]kehle, *die; see also* **hanging valley; rift valley; river valley**

valor (Amer.) ▸**valour**

valorous /ˈvælərəs/ *adj.* (literary) tapfer

valour /ˈvælə(r)/ *n.* Tapferkeit, *die;* **fight with ~:** tapfer kämpfen; *see also* **discretion 1**

V

valuable /ˈvæljʊəbl/
A *adj.* wertvoll; **be ~ to sb.** für jmdn. wertvoll sein
B *n., in pl.* Wertgegenstände; Wertsachen

valuation /væljʊˈeɪʃn/ *n.* Schätzung, *die;* **make/get a ~ of sth.** etw. schätzen/etw. schätzen lassen; **what is the ~?** wie hoch ist der Schätzwert?; **set a high/low** *etc.* **~ on sth.** den Schätzwert für etw. hoch/niedrig *usw.* ansetzen; **accept sb. at his/her own ~:** jmds. Selbsteinschätzung teilen *od.* akzeptieren

value /ˈvælju:/
A *n.* **1** Wert, *der;* **be of great/little/some/no ~ [to sb.]** [für jmdn.] von großem/geringem/einigem/keinerlei Nutzen sein; **they are taught too few things of real ~ for their future** man lehrt sie zu wenig, was ihnen in der Zukunft wirklich nützen wird; **information that is of great ~ to scientists** Informationen, die für Wissenschaftler überaus wertvoll *od.* von großem Wert sind; **this drug has been of some ~ in the treatment of cancer** dieses Medikament hat sich bei der Behandlung von Krebskranken als bedingt wirksam erwiesen; **be of [no] practical ~ to sb.** für jmdn. von [keinerlei] praktischem Nutzen sein; **set** *or* **put a high/low ~ on sth.** etw. hoch/niedrig einschätzen; **attach great ~ to sth.** einer Sache (*Dat.*) große Wichtigkeit beimessen **2** (monetary worth) Wert, *der;* **it has a ~ of one pound** es ist ein Pfund wert; **what would be the ~ of it?** was ist es wohl wert?; **know the ~ of sth.** wissen, was etw. wert ist; **sth./nothing of ~:** etw./nichts Wertvolles; **an object of ~:** ein Wertgegenstand; **items of great/little/no ~:** sehr wertvolle/nicht sonderlich wertvolle/wertlose Gegenstände; **be of great/little/no** *etc.* **~:** viel/wenig/nichts *usw.* wert sein; **increase** *or* **go up in ~:** an Wert gewinnen; wertvoller werden; **decline** *or* **decrease** *or* **fall** *or* **go down in ~:** an Wert verlieren; **an increase/decrease in ~:** ein Wertzuwachs/-verlust; **put a ~ on sth.** den Wert einer Sache schätzen; **sth. to the ~ of ...:** etw. im Werte von ... **3** (equivalent) Wert, *der;* **he offered less than the ~ of the house** er bot weniger, als das Haus wert war; **be good/poor etc. ~ [for money]** seinen Preis wert/nicht wert sein; **customers want [good] ~ for money** Kunden wollen für ihr Geld auch etwas bekommen; **£10 for a tiny steak — do you call that good ~?** 10 Pfund für ein winziges Steak — nennen Sie das reell?; **this handbook is excellent/very good ~ at £10** dieses Handbuch ist die 10 Pfund, die es kostet, unbedingt wert; **get [good]/poor ~ [for money]** etwas/nicht viel für sein Geld bekommen; **give sb. poor ~ for money** jmdm. für sein Geld nicht viel bieten **4** *in pl.* (principles) Werte; Wertvorstellungen **5** (rank, significance) Wert, *der;* **[time] ~** (Mus.) Zeitwert, *der;* **~ of a colour, colour ~:** Farbwert, *der* **6** (numerical quantity) (Math.) [Zahlen]wert, *der;* (Phys.) Größe, *die;* **give x** *or* **let x have the ~ 3** x sei 3
B *v.t.* **1** (appreciate) schätzen; **his work has been ~d highly by experts** seine Arbeit hat bei Experten hohe Anerkennung gefunden; **if you ~ your life** wenn dir dein Leben lieb ist **2** (put price on) schätzen, taxieren (**at** auf + *Akk.*)

value added ˈtax *n.* ▸ **i p. 1332** (Brit.) Mehrwertsteuer, *die*

valued /ˈvælju:d/ *adj.* geschätzt ‹*Freund, Kollege, Kunde*›; wertvoll ‹*Rat, Hilfe*›; **thank you for your ~ order** (Commerc. dated) wir bedanken uns für Ihren geschätzten Auftrag (veralt.)

value-for-ˈmoney *adj.* preiswert; preisgünstig ‹*Essen, Hotel*›; **~ price** günstiger Preis

ˈvalue judgement *n.* Werturteil, *das*

valueless /ˈvæljʊlɪs/ *adj.* wertlos

ˈvalue pack *n.* Vorteilspack, *der;* Vorteilspackung, *die;* Sparpack, *der;* Sparpackung, *die*

valuer /ˈvæljʊə(r)/ *n.* ▸ **i p. 1260** Schätzer, *der;* Taxator, *der*

valve /vælv/ *n.* **1** Ventil, *das; see also* **safety valve** **2** (Anat., Zool.) Klappe, *die* **3** (Brit.: thermionic ~) Röhre, *die*

vamoose /vəˈmu:s/ *v.i.* (Amer. coll.) verduften (ugs.)

vamp¹ /væmp/
A *n.* (of shoe) Oberleder, *das*
B *v.t.* (Mus.) improvisieren ‹*Begleitung*›; improvisierend begleiten ‹*Melodie*›
C *v.i.* (Mus.) improvisierend begleiten

Phrasal verb

• **~ ˈup** *v.t.* (put together) zusammenschustern (ugs. abwertend); (renovate) aufmöbeln (ugs.)

vamp² *n.* (woman) Vamp, *der*

vampire /ˈvæmpaɪə(r)/ *n.* Vampir, *der*

ˈvampire bat *n.* (Zool.) Vampir, *der*

van¹ /væn/ *n.* **1** **[delivery] ~:** Lieferwagen, *der;* **baker's/laundry ~:** Bäckerauto, *das*/Wäschereiauto, *das* (ugs.) **2** (Brit. Railw.) [geschlossener] Wagen **3** (Brit.: caravan) **[camping] ~:** Wohnwagen, *der*

van² *n.* (foremost part) Vorhut, *die;* (fig.: leaders of movement, opinion) Vorkämpfer *Pl.;* **be in the ~ of a movement/the attack** zu den Vorkämpfern einer Bewegung gehören/den Angriff anführen

van³ *n.* (Tennis) Vorteil, *der*

vanadium /vəˈneɪdɪəm/ *n.* (Chem.) Vanadium, *das*

vandal /ˈvændl/ *n.* **1** Rowdy, *der;* **~-proof** unzerstörbar **2** (Hist.) **V~:** Wandale, *der;* Vandale, *der*

vandalise ▸ **vandalize**

vandalism /ˈvændəlɪzm/ *n.* Wandalismus, *der;* Vandalismus, *der;* **act of ~** (destruction) [mutwillige] Zerstörung; (damaging) [mutwillige] Beschädigung; **to demolish this beautiful old building would be an act of ~:** dieses schöne alte Gebäude abzureißen wäre Wandalismus

vandalize /ˈvændəlaɪz/ *v.t.* (destroy) [mutwillig] zerstören; (damage) [mutwillig] beschädigen

ˈvan driver *n.* ▸ **i p. 1260** Lieferwagenfahrer, *der*/-fahrerin, *die*

Vandyke /vænˈdaɪk/: **~ beard** *n.* Henriquatre, *der;* **~ brown** *n.* Van-Dyck-Braun, *das*

vane /veɪn/ *n.* **1** (weathercock) (in shape of arrow) Wetterfahne, *die;* (in shape of cock) Wetterhahn, *der* **2** (blade) Blatt, *das;* (of windmill) Flügel, *der;* (of watermill, turbine) Schaufel, *die*

vanguard /ˈvæŋgɑ:d/ *n.* **1** (Mil., Navy) Vorhut, *die* **2** (fig.: leaders) Vorreiter; (of literary, artistic, etc. movement) Avantgarde, *die;* **be in the ~ of progress/a movement** an der Spitze des Fortschritts/einer Bewegung stehen

vanilla /vəˈnɪlə/
A *n.* **1** Vanille, *die* **2** ▸ **vanilla pod**
B *adj.* Vanille-

vaˈnilla pod *n.* (Bot.) Vanilleschote, *die*

vanish /ˈvænɪʃ/ *v.i.* **1** (disappear; coll.: leave quickly) verschwinden; **~ from sight [behind sth.]** [hinter etw. (*Dat.*)] verschwinden; **~ into the distance** in der Ferne verschwinden; **the smile ~ed from his face** das Lächeln verschwand aus seinem Gesicht; **~ off the face of the earth** von der Erde verschwinden; *see also* **thin A 4** **2** (cease to exist) ‹*Gebäude:*› verschwinden; ‹*Sitte, Tradition:*› untergehen; ‹*Art, Gattung:*› aussterben; ‹*Zweifel, Bedenken:*› sich auflösen; ‹*Angst:*› sich legen; ‹*Hoffnung, Chancen:*› schwinden **3** (Math.) null werden

vanishing /ˈvænɪʃɪŋ/: **~ act** ▸ **~ trick**; **~ cream** *n.* Feuchtigkeitscreme, *die;* Vanishing-Creme, *die* (fachspr.); **~ point** *n.* (Art, Math.) Fluchtpunkt, *der;* (fig.) Nullpunkt, *der;* **dwindle to ~-point** auf den Nullpunkt zurückgehen; **~ trick** *n.* Zaubertrick (*bei dem etwas verschwindet*); **do** *or* **perform a ~ trick with sth.** etw. wegzaubern *od.* verschwinden lassen; **he did his [usual] ~ trick** (fig. coll.) er verdrückte sich [wie üblich] (ugs.)

vanity /ˈvænɪtɪ/ *n.* **1** (pride, conceit) Eitelkeit, *die* **2** (worthlessness) Nichtigkeit, *die;* Eitelkeit, *die* (geh.); (of efforts, hopes, dreams) Vergeblichkeit, *die;* **all is ~:** alles ist eitel (geh.) **3** (worthless thing) **these things are vanities** das ist alles bloß Tand (geh.) **4** (Amer.: dressing table) Frisierkommode, *die*

vanity: **~ bag** *n.* Kosmetiktäschchen, *das;* **~ case** *n.* Kosmetikkoffer, *der;* **V~ ˈFair** *n.* Jahrmarkt der Eitelkeiten; **~ mirror** *n.* Kosmetikspiegel, *der;* **~ plate** *n.* (Amer.) Wunschkennzeichen, *das;* **~ unit** *n.* Waschtisch, *der*

vanquish /ˈvæŋkwɪʃ/ *v.t.* (literary) bezwingen

vantage /ˈvɑ:ntɪdʒ/ *n.* **1** (position of superiority) Vorteil, *der* **2** ▸ **advantage 3**

vantage: **~ ground** *n.* (Mil.) günstige [Ausgangs]position; **~ point** *n.* Aussichtspunkt, *der;* (fig.) **his ~-point as director** der Überblick, den er als Direktor hat/hatte

vapid /ˈvæpɪd/ *adj.* schal ‹*Geschmack, Vergnügen*›; leer ‹*Gerede, Umgangsformen*›; geistlos ‹*Gerede, Vortrag, Bemerkung, Ergüsse*›; unverbindlich ‹*Lächeln*›; nichts sagend ‹*Erscheinung, Person*›

vapidity /vəˈpɪdɪtɪ/ *n.* Schalheit, *die;* (of conversation, remark, book, speech, etc.) Geistlosigkeit, *die;* **the ~ of his smile/expression** sein unverbindliches Lächeln/sein nichts sagender Gesichtsausdruck

vapor (Amer.) ▸ **vapour**

vaporize (vaporise) /ˈveɪpəraɪz/ *v.t. & i.* verdampfen

vaporizer /ˈveɪpəraɪzə(r)/ *n.* **1** Verdampfer, *der* **2** (atomizer) Zerstäuber, *der*

vapour /ˈveɪpə(r)/ *n.* (Brit.) **1** Dampf, *der;* (mist) Dunst, *der;* **~s** (rising from the ground) Schwaden; (arch.: melancholy) Schwermut, *die* **2** (Phys.) Dampf, *der;* **turn into [a] ~:** zu Dampf werden **3** (Med.: inhalant) Dampf, *der*

vapour: **~ bath** *n.* (Med.) Dampfbad, *das;* **~ trail** *n.* (Aeronaut.) Kondensstreifen, *der;* **~ware**, (Amer. also) **~ware** *n., no pl.* Vapo[u]rware, *die*

variability /veərɪəˈbɪlɪtɪ/ *n.* **1** (ability to be altered) Variabilität, *die* **2** (inconsistency, changeability) Unbeständigkeit, *die;* (of health, balance) Labilität, *die*

variable /ˈveərɪəbl/
A *adj.* **1** (alterable) veränderbar; **be ~:** verändert werden können; ‹*Gerät:*› eingestellt werden können **2** (inconsistent, changeable) unbeständig ‹*Wetter, Wind, Strömung, Stimmung, Leistung*›; wechselhaft ‹*Wetter, Launen, Schicksal, Qualität, Erfolg*›; labil ‹*Gesundheit, Gleichgewicht*›; schwankend ‹*Kosten*›; **How's your health? — Oh, ~:** Wie gehts gesundheitlich? — Mal so, mal so; **with ~ success** mit wechselndem Erfolg **3** (Astron., Math.) veränderlich; variabel
B *n.* **1** (Math.) Variable, *die;* Veränderliche, *die* **2** (Astron.) Veränderliche, *der* **3** (fig.: varying factor) veränderliche Größe; Variable, *die*

variable: **~ geˈometry** *n.* (Aeronaut., Polit.) variable Geometrie; **~-geˈometry** *adj.* **1** (Aeronaut.) mit variabler Geometrie *nachgestellt;* **2** (Polit.) **~-geometry Europe** Europa der variablen Geometrie; **~-rate ˈmortgage** *n.* variabel verzinsliche Hypothek; **~ ˈstar** *n.* (Astron.) Veränderliche, *der*

variably /ˈveərɪəblɪ/ *adv.* variabel; beliebig, stufenlos ‹*anpassbar, einstellbar*›; unterschiedlich ‹*stark*›

variance /ˈveərɪəns/ *n.* **1** Uneinigkeit, *die;* (between philosophies, ideologies) Nichtübereinstimmung, *die;* **be at ~:** [sich (*Dat.*)] uneinig sein (**on** über + *Akk.*); ‹*Theorien, Meinungen, Philosophien usw.:*› nicht übereinstimmen; **be at ~ with sb./sth.** [sich (*Dat.*)] mit jmdm. uneinig sein/mit etw. nicht übereinstimmen; **this development has set the team at ~:** diese Entwicklung hat zu Meinungsverschiedenheiten im Team geführt **2** (Statistics) Varianz, *die*

variant /ˈveərɪənt/
A *attrib. adj.* verschieden; **three ~ spellings/readings** drei [verschiedene] Schreibweisen/Lesarten; **~ type** (Biol.) Variante, *die*
B *n.* Variante, *die*

variation /veərɪˈeɪʃn/ *n.* **1** (varying) Veränderung, *die;* (in style, diet, routine, programme) Abwechslung, *die;* (difference) Unterschied, *der;* **be subject to ~** ‹*Preise:*› Schwankungen unterworfen sein; ‹*Regeln:*› Änderungen unterworfen sein; **~s in weather conditions** unbeständiges Wetter; **no ~ of the rules is allowed** die Regeln dürfen nicht geändert werden; **~ in price/colour** Preis-/Farbunterschied, *der;* **the ~s of light and shade** der Wechsel von Licht und Schatten; **~s from earlier editions** Unterschiede im Vergleich zu früheren Ausgaben **2** (variant) Variante, *die* (**of, on** *Gen.*) **3** (Mus.) Variation, *die;* **~s on a theme** Variationen über ein Thema **4** (Biol.,

V

Ballet, Math.) Variation, *die*

variational /veərɪ'eɪʃənl/ *attrib. adj.* (Mus., Math.) Variations-

varicoloured (*Brit.; Amer.:* **varicolored**) /'veərɪkʌləd/ *adj.* bunt

varicose vein /værɪkəʊs 'veɪn/ *n.* (Med.) Krampfader, *die*

varied /'veərɪd/ *adj.* (differing) unterschiedlich; vielfältig ‹*Freuden*›; (marked by variation) abwechslungsreich ‹*Land, Diät, Leben*›; vielseitig ‹*Arbeit, Stil, Sammlung*›; vielgestaltig ‹*Landschaft*›; bunt ‹*Mischung*›; bunt gemischt ‹*Gruppe*›

variegate /'veərɪgeɪt/ *v.t.* [farblich] auflockern

variegated /'veərɪgeɪtɪd/ *adj.* (Bot.) mehrfarbig; panaschiert ‹*grüne Blätter*›

variegation /veərɪ'geɪʃn/ *n.* 1 Buntheit, *die* 2 (Bot.) Mehrfarbigkeit, *die;* (on green leaves) Panaschierung, *die*

variety /və'raɪətɪ/ *n.* 1 (diversity) Vielfältigkeit, *die;* (in style, diet, routine, programme) Abwechslung, *die;* **add** *or* **give ~ to sth.** etw. abwechslungsreicher gestalten; **for the sake of ~:** zur Abwechslung; **~ is the spice of life** (prov.) Abwechslung macht Freude 2 (assortment) Auswahl, *die* (**of** an + *Dat.*, von); **in a ~ of sizes/ways** in verschiedenen Größen/auf verschiedene Art; **for a ~ of reasons** aus verschiedenen Gründen; **a wide ~ of birds/flowers** viele verschiedene Vogelarten/Blumen 3 (Theatre) Varieté, *das;* (Telev.) (*varietéähnliche*) Shows 4 (form) Art, *die;* (of fruit, vegetable, cigarette) Sorte, *die;* **rare varieties of butterflies** seltene Exemplare von Schmetterlingen 5 (Biol.) (subspecies) Unterart, *die;* Varietät, *die* (fachspr.); (cultivated) Züchtung, *die;* Rasse, *die*

variety: ~ act *n.* Varieténummer, *die;* **~ artist** *n.* (Theatre) Varietékünstler, *der*/-künstlerin, *die;* (Telev.) Showstar, *der;* **~ entertainment** ▸ **~ show**; **~ meat** *n.* (Amer.) Innereien [und essbare Schlachtabfälle]; **~ show** *n.* 1 (Theatre) Varieté, *das;* (single performance) Varietévorstellung, *die;* 2 (Telev.) (*varietéähnliche*) Show; **~ store** *n.* (Amer.) Kramladen, *der;* **~ theatre** *n.* Varieté[theater], *das*

varifocal /veərɪ'fəʊkl/

A *adj.* **~ spectacles** Gleitsichtbrille, *die;* **~ lens** (in camera) Objektiv mit variabler Brennweite; Varioobjektiv, *das;* (in spectacles) Gleitsichtglas, *das*

B *n.* **varifocals** Gleitsichtbrille, *die*

variola /və'raɪələ/ *n.* (Med.) Pocken *Pl.*

various /'veərɪəs/ *adj.* 1 *pred.* (different) verschieden; unterschiedlich; (manifold) vielfältig; **the causes of this are many and ~:** es gibt hierfür viele verschiedene Ursachen 2 *attrib.* (several) verschiedene; **at ~ times** mehrere Male

variously /'veərɪəslɪ/ *adv.* unterschiedlich; **she has been ~ described as a liar and a paragon of virtue** sie ist mal als Lügnerin, mal als Muster an Tugend beschrieben worden

varlet /'vɑːlɪt/ *n.* (Hist.: page) Bursche, *der;* (arch./joc.: rascal) Schurke, *der* (abwertend)

varmint /'vɑːmɪnt/ *n.* (Amer./dial.) (animal) Biest, *das* (ugs.); (person) Halunke, *der;* (child) Racker, *der* (fam.)

varnish /'vɑːnɪʃ/

A *n.* 1 Lack, *der;* (transparent) Lasur, *die;* **clear ~:** Klarlack, *der; see also* **nail varnish** 2 (Art) Firnis, *der* 3 (Ceramics) Glasur, *die* 4 (glossiness, lit. or fig.) Glanz, *der;* **high ~:** Hochglanz, *der*

B *v.t.* 1 lackieren; (with transparent ~) lasieren 2 (Art) firnissen 3 (Ceramics) glasieren 4 (fig.: gloss over) beschönigen; übertünchen ‹*Fehler, Verbrechen, Laster*›

varsity /'vɑːsɪtɪ/ *n.* (Brit. Univ. coll.) Uni, *die* (ugs.)

vary /'veərɪ/

A *v.t.* verändern; ändern ‹*Bestimmungen, Programm, Methode, Verhalten, Stil, Route, Kurs*›; abwandeln ‹*Rezept, Muster*›; (add variety to) abwechslungsreicher gestalten; **~ one's diet** sich abwechslungsreich ernähren; **~ one's tone to suit the situation** seinen Ton der Situation anpassen

B *v.i.* 1 (become different) sich ändern; ‹*Preis, Nachfrage, Qualität, Temperatur:*› schwanken; (be different) unterschiedlich sein; (between extremes) wechseln; (deviate) abweichen; **Are you busy? — Oh, it varies** Hast du viel zu tun? — Ach, ganz unterschiedlich; **~ between A and B** *or* **from A to B** zwischen A (*Dat.*) und B (*Dat.*) schwanken; **~ in weight/size/shape/colour** *etc.* im Gewicht/in der Größe/Form/Farbe variieren (**from ... to ...:** zwischen ... + *Dat.* und ... + *Dat.*); **these items ~ in size/price** diese Artikel gibt es in verschiedenen Größen/Preislagen; **they ~ in their opinions/in character** sie haben unterschiedliche Meinungen/sind charakterlich verschieden; **the two books ~ on this matter** dieser Sachverhalt wird in den beiden Büchern unterschiedlich beurteilt; **opinions ~ on this point** die Meinungen gehen in diesem Punkt auseinander 2 **~ [directly]/inversely as sth.** sich direkt proportional/umgekehrt proportional zu etw. ändern

varying /'veərɪɪŋ/ *attrib. adj.* wechselnd; wechselhaft, veränderlich ‹*Wetter*›; (different) unterschiedlich; **in ~ colours** in verschiedenen Farben; **continually ~ prices** ständig schwankende Preise; **at ~ prices** zu unterschiedlichen Preisen

vascular /'væskjʊlə(r)/ *adj.* (Anat., Bot.) vaskulär; (Anat., Med.) Gefäß-; **~ plant** Gefäßpflanze, *die*

vase /vɑːz/ *n.* Vase, *die*

vasectomize /və'sektəmaɪz/ *v.t.* (Med.) [durch Vasektomie] sterilisieren

vasectomy /və'sektəmɪ/ *n.* (Med.) Vasektomie, *die*

Vaseline ® /'væsəliːn/ *n., no pl., no indef. art.* Vaseline, *die*

vasoconstrictor /veɪzəʊkən'strɪktə(r)/ *n.* (Med.) Vasokonstriktor, *der* (fachspr.); [blut]gefäßverengendes Mittel; **be a/act as a ~:** gefäßverengend wirken

vasodilator /veɪzəʊdaɪ'leɪtə(r)/ *n.* (Med.) Vasodilator, *der* (fachspr.); [blut]gefäßerweiterndes Mittel

vasopressor /'veɪzəʊpresə(r)/ *n.* (Med.) Vasopressor, *der* (fachspr.)

vassal /'væsl/ *n.* 1 (Hist.) Vasall, *der*/Vasallin, *die* 2 (rhet.: slave) Knecht, *der*/Magd, *die* (fig.)

vast /vɑːst/ *adj.* 1 (huge) riesig; weit ‹*Fläche, Meer, Kontinent, Welt[raum]*›; gewaltig ‹*Wolken[massen]*›; umfangreich ‹*Sammlung*› 2 (coll.: great) enorm; Riesen‹*menge, -summe, -fehler*›; unermesslich ‹*Reichtümer*›; überwältigend ‹*Mehrheit*›; **a ~ amount of time/money/a ~ number of things** enorm viel Zeit/viel Geld/viele Dinge; **~ sums of money** enorm hohe Summen; **to a ~ extent** größtenteils; **he has done a ~ amount of work in this field** er hat auf diesem Gebiet enorm viel geleistet

vastly /'vɑːstlɪ/ *adv.* (coll.) enorm; weitaus ‹*besser*›; weit ‹*überlegen, unterlegen*›; überaus, äußerst ‹*wichtig, dankbar*›; in hohem Maße ‹*beeinflussen*›; gewaltig ‹*sich verbessern, irren, überschätzen, unterschätzen*›; köstlich ‹*sich amüsieren*›; **in a ~ different sense** in einem völlig anderen Sinn

vastness /'vɑːstnɪs/ *n., no pl.* 1 (hugeness) [immense *od.* ungeheure] Weite; (of building, crowd, army) [immense *od.* ungeheure] Größe; (of collection etc.) [riesiger] Umfang 2 (greatness) [immenses] Ausmaß; (of knowledge) [immenser] Umfang

vat /væt/ *n.* Bottich, *der;* (in papermaking) Bütte, *die*

VAT /viːeɪ'tiː, væt/ *abbr.* ▸ℹ **p. 1332** = **value added tax** MwSt.

Vatican /'vætɪkən/ *pr. n.* Vatikan, *der*

Vatican: ~ 'City *pr. n.* ▸ℹ **p. 1643** Vatikanstadt, *die;* **~ 'Council** *n.* (Hist.) Vatikanisches Konzil

VAT-'registered *adj.* mehrwertsteuerpflichtig; zur Mehrwertsteuer veranlagt

Vaud /vəʊ/ *pr. n.* Waadt, *die*

vaudeville /'vɔːdəvɪl, 'vəʊdəvɪl/ *n.* (Theatre, Mus.) Varieté, *das;* **appear in ~:** im Varieté auftreten; **a ~ show** eine Varietévorstellung

vault[1] /vɔːlt, vɒlt/

A *n.* 1 (Archit.) Gewölbe, *das;* **the ~ of heaven** (poet.) das Himmelsgewölbe (dichter.) 2 (cellar) [Gewölbe]keller, *der; see also* **wine vault** 3 (in bank) Tresorraum, *der* 4 (tomb) Gruft, *die*

B *v.t.* (Archit.) wölben

vault[2]

A *v.i.* (leap) sich schwingen; (Gymnastics) springen

B *v.t.* sich schwingen über (+ *Akk.*); (Gymnastics) springen über (+ *Akk.*)

C *n.* Sprung, *der;* **straddle/squat/side ~:** Grätsche, *die*/Hocke, *die*/Flanke, *die*

vaulted /'vɔːltɪd, 'vɒltɪd/ *adj.* (Archit.) gewölbt

vaulting /'vɔːltɪŋ, 'vɒltɪŋ/ *n.* (Archit.) Wölbung, *die*

'vaulting horse *n.* (Gymnastics) [Sprung]pferd, *das*

vaunt /vɔːnt/ (literary) *v.t.* sich brüsten mit; **~ that ...:** sich [damit] brüsten, dass ...; **~ sth. as sth.** etw. als etw. preisen; **much ~ed** viel gepriesen *od.* gerühmt

VC *abbr.* = **Victoria Cross**

'V-chip *n.* (Telev.) V-chip, *der*

VCR *abbr.* = **video cassette recorder**

VD /viː'diː/ *n.* ▸ℹ **p. 1231** Geschlechtskrankheit, *die;* **get** *or* **catch VD** sich (*Dat.*) eine Geschlechtskrankheit zuziehen

VDU *abbr.* = **visual display unit**

've /v/ (coll.) = **have**

veal /viːl/ *n., no pl.* Kalb[fleisch], *das; attrib.* Kalbs-; **roast ~:** Kalbsbraten, *der*

veal: ~ crate *n.* Kälberbox, *die;* **~ 'cutlet** *n.* Kalbsschnitzel, *das*

vector /'vektə(r)/ *n.* (Math., Aeronaut., Biol.) Vektor, *der*

vectorial /vek'tɔːrɪəl/ *adj.* (Math.) vektoriell

Veda /'veɪdə, 'viːdə/ *n.* (Hindu Relig.) Weda, *der*

VE day /viː'iː deɪ/ *n.* der Tag des Sieges in Europa [im 2. Weltkrieg]

veejay, VJ /viːjeɪ/ *n.* (Amer. coll.) VJ, *der*

veer[1] /vɪə(r)/

A *v.i.* 1 ‹*Wind:*› [sich] im Uhrzeigersinn drehen; ‹*Schiff, Flugzeug:*› abdrehen; ‹*Auto:*› ausscheren; **~ to the north** ‹*Wind:*› auf Nord drehen; ‹*Schiff:*› nach Norden drehen; **~ off course/off the road** (unintentionally) vom Kurs/von der Straße abkommen; (intentionally) vom Kurs abdrehen/von der Straße abbiegen; **the driver had to ~ to avoid the sheep** der Fahrer musste das Steuer herumreißen, um dem Schaf auszuweichen; **~ out of control** außer Kontrolle geraten [und ins Schleudern kommen]; **go ~ing along the road** in Schlangenlinien die Straße entlangfahren; **~ gently/sharply to the right** ‹*Straße:*› eine leichte/scharfe Rechtskurve machen 2 (fig.: change) schwanken (**from ... to ...:** zwischen ... *Dat.* und ... *Dat.*); **~ from one extreme to the other** ‹*Person:*› von einem Extrem ins andere fallen; ‹*Stimmung:*› von einem Extrem ins andere umschlagen; **~ to the left** (in politics) auf Linkskurs umschwenken

B *v.t.* **~ the car to the left/right** den Wagen nach links/rechts herumreißen

C *n.* Ausscheren, *das;* **the driver struggled to control the ~:** der Fahrer versuchte, den Wagen noch abzufangen

Phrasal verbs

• **~ a'way, ~ 'off** *v.i.* 1 ‹*Schiff, Flugzeug:*› abdrehen; ‹*Auto:*› ausscheren; ‹*Fahrer, Straße:*› abbiegen 2 (fig.: change) **~ away** *or* **off from sth.** von etw. abkommen

• **~ 'round**

A *v.i.* drehen; (through 180°) wenden; **skid and ~ [right] round** ins Schleudern geraten und sich um die eigene Achse drehen

B *v.t.* wenden

veer[2] *v.i.* (Naut.) **~ and haul** fieren und holen

veg /vedʒ/

A *n., pl. same* (coll.) Gemüse, *das;* **meat and two ~:** Fleisch mit Kartoffeln und Gemüse

B *v.i.* **-gg-** (coll.) **to ~ [out]** rumhängen (ugs.); **~ out in front of the TV** vor der Glotze hängen (ugs.)

vegan /ˈviːgən/
A *n.* Veganer, *der*/Veganerin, *die*
B *adj.* vegan

Vegeburger® /ˈvedʒıbɜːgə(r)/ *n.* Vegeburger, *der;* Gemüseburger, *der*

vegetable /ˈvedʒıtəbl/
A *n.* **1** Gemüse, *das;* **spring/summer/winter ~:** Frühjahrs-/Sommer-/Wintergemüse, *das;* **fresh ~s** frisches Gemüse; **green ~s** Grüngemüse, *das;* **do you want ~s/a ~ with your steak?** hätten Sie gern Gemüse/eine Portion Gemüse zu Ihrem Steak?; **meat and two ~s** Fleisch mit Kartoffeln und Gemüse; *see also* **kingdom 4** **2** (fig.) **become/be a ~** (as result of injury or illness) nur noch [dahin]vegetieren; **you're just a ~/you'll turn into a ~** (as result of dull routine, lack of ambition, etc.) du vegetierst nur so vor dich hin/bald wirst du nur noch vor dich hin vegetieren
B *adj.* Gemüse⟨*suppe, -extrakt*⟩; **~ butter** Pflanzenbutter, *die;* **~ matter** pflanzliche Stoffe

vegetable: ~ dish *n.* **1** (food) Gemüsegericht, *das;* **2** (bowl) Gemüseschüssel, *die;* **~ dye** *n.* Pflanzenfarbe, *die;* **~ garden** *n.* Gemüsegarten, *der;* **~ knife** *n.* Küchenmesser, *das;* **~ ˈmarrow** ▸**marrow 1**; **~ oil** *n.* (Cookery) Pflanzenöl, *das*

vegetarian /vedʒıˈteərıən/
A *n.* Vegetarier, *der*/Vegetarierin, *die*
B *adj.* vegetarisch; **sb. is ~:** jmd. ist Vegetarier/Vegetarierin

vegetarianism /vedʒıˈteərıənızm/ *n., no pl., no indef. art.* Vegetarismus, *der*

vegetate /ˈvedʒıteıt/ *v.i.* **1** (Bot.) wachsen [und gedeihen] **2** (fig.) (as result of injury or illness) nur noch [dahin]vegetieren; (as result of dull routine, lack of ambition, etc.) vor sich (*Akk.*) hin vegetieren

vegetation /vedʒıˈteıʃn/ *n., no pl.* **1** (plants) Vegetation, *die* **2** (fig.) (as result of injury or illness) Dahinvegetieren, *das;* (as result of dull routine, lack of ambition, etc.) Stumpfsinnigkeit, *die*

vegetative /ˈvedʒıtətıv/ *adj.* (Biol., Bot.) vegetativ

veggie /ˈvedʒı/ (coll.)
A *adj.* vegetarisch; **~ burger** Gemüseburger, *der*
B *n.* **1** (vegetarian) Vegetarier, *der*/Vegetarierin, *die* **2** (vegetable) Gemüse, *das;* **~s** Gemüse, *das*

vehemence /ˈviːəməns/ *n., no pl.* Heftigkeit, *die;* Vehemenz, *die;* **with ~:** heftig; vehement (geh.)

vehement /ˈviːəmənt/ *adj.* heftig; vehement; leidenschaftlich ⟨*Gefühle, Rede*⟩; stark ⟨*Wunsch, Abneigung*⟩; hitzig ⟨*Debatte*⟩

vehemently /ˈviːəməntlı/ *adv.* heftig; vehement; **hate each other ~:** einander bis aufs Blut hassen; **dislike each other ~:** eine heftige Abneigung gegeneinander empfinden

vehicle /ˈviːıkl/ *n.* **1** Fahrzeug, *das* **2** (fig.: medium) Vehikel, *das;* **the pulpit as a ~ for propaganda** die Kanzel als Bühne für Propaganda; **this newspaper is their ~:** diese Zeitung ist ihr Sprachrohr **3** (Art) Bindemittel, *das* **4** (Pharm.) Vehiculum, *das;* Konstituens, *das*

vehicular /vıˈhıkjʊlə(r)/ *adj.* Fahrzeug-

veil /veıl/
A *n.* **1** Schleier, *der;* **take the ~** (Relig.) den Schleier nehmen (geh.) **2** (Jewish Relig. Hist.) [Tempel]vorhang, *der;* **beyond the ~** (fig.) im Jenseits **3** (fig.: obscuring medium) Schleier, *der;* **~ of mist/clouds** Dunst-/Wolkenschleier, *der;* **under the ~ of patriotism** unter dem Deckmantel des Patriotismus; **draw a ~ over sth.** den Mantel des Schweigens über etw. (*Akk.*) breiten
B *v.t.* **1** verschleiern **2** (fig.: cover) verhüllen; (conceal) verbergen ⟨*Gefühle, Motive*⟩ (**with, in** hinter + *Dat.*); verschleiern ⟨*Fakten, Wahrheit, Bedeutung*⟩; **~ sth. in secrecy** *or* **mystery** etw. mit dem Schleier des Geheimnisses umgeben

veiled /veıld/ *adj.* **1** verschleiert **2** (fig.: covert) versteckt ⟨*Groll, Drohung*⟩; verhüllt ⟨*Anspielung*⟩

vein /veın/ *n.* **1** Vene, *die;* (in popular use: any blood vessel) Ader, *die* **2** (Geol., Mining, Zool.) Ader, *die* **3** (Bot.) Blattrippe, *die;* Ader, *die* **4** (streak) Ader, *die;* **~s** (in wood, marble) Maserung, *die* **5** (fig.: character, tendency) Zug, *der;* (of truth) Spur, *die;* (of superstition, aggression) Anflug, *der;* **a ~ of melancholy/humour** ein melancholischer/humorvoller Zug; **have a poetic ~:** eine dichterische Ader haben **6** (fig.) (mood) Stimmung, *die;* (style) Art, *die;* **be in a happy/sad ~:** froh gelaunt/traurig gestimmt sein; **be in the [right] ~ [for sth./for doing sth.]** in der [richtigen] Stimmung sein [zu etw./, etw. zu tun]; **in a similar ~:** vergleichbarer Art

veined /veınd/ *adj.* geädert; gemasert ⟨*Holz*⟩; **red marble ~ with white** roter Marmor, weiß geädert

velar /ˈviːlə(r)/ *adj.* (Phonet.) velar

Velcro® /ˈvelkrəʊ/ *n., no pl., no indef. art.* Klettverschluss, *der* (Wz)

veld, veldt /velt/ *n.* (S. Afr.) Steppe, *die*

vellum /ˈveləm/ *n.* **1** (parchment) Pergament, *das;* (manuscript also) Pergamenthandschrift, *die* **2** (writing paper) Velin[papier], *das*

velocity /vıˈlɒsıtı/ *n.* Geschwindigkeit, *die;* **at** *or* **with a ~ of ...:** mit einer Geschwindigkeit von ...; **~ of the wind, wind ~:** Windgeschwindigkeit, *die;* **~ of light** (Phys.) Lichtgeschwindigkeit, *die*

velodrome /ˈvelədrəʊm/ *n.* Velodrom, *das*

velour[s] /vəˈlʊə(r)/ *n.* (Textiles) Velours, *der*

velum /ˈviːləm/ *n., pl.* **vela** /ˈviːlə/ (Bot., Zool.) Velum, *das;* (Anat.) Velum, *das;* Gaumensegel, *das*

velvet /ˈvelvıt/
A *n.* **1** Samt, *der;* **[as] smooth as ~:** weich wie Samt; samtweich **2** (Zool.) Bast, *der*
B *adj.* aus Samt *nachgestellt;* Samt-; (soft as ~) samten; samtweich; **he operates with an iron hand in a ~ glove** er gibt sich entgegenkommend, in der Sache aber bleibt er unnachgiebig

velveteen /velvıˈtiːn/
A *n.* (Textiles) Baumwollsamt, *der;* Velveton, *der* (fachspr.)
B *adj.* aus Baumwollsamt *nachgestellt;* Velveton-

velvety /ˈvelvıtı/ *adj.* (having the feel of velvet) samtig; samtweich; (characteristic of velvet; also fig.) samtig; samten; **smooth** *or* **soft and ~:** weich und samten

Ven. *abbr.* = **Venerable** Hochw.

venal /ˈviːnl/ *adj.* käuflich, korrupt ⟨*Person*⟩; korrupt ⟨*Verhalten, Praktiken*⟩; eigennützig ⟨*Interessen, Motive, Dienste*⟩

venality /viːˈnælıtı/ *n., no pl.* ▸**venal**: Käuflichkeit, *die;* Korruptheit, *die;* Eigennützigkeit, *die*

vend /vend/ *v.t.* **1** (Law) veräußern; (as a business) Handel treiben mit **2** (offer for sale) verkaufen

vendee /venˈdiː/ *n.* (Law) Käufer, *der*/Käuferin, *die*

vender /ˈvendə(r)/ ▸**vendor 1**

vendetta /venˈdetə/ *n.* **1** Hetzkampagne, *die;* (feud) Fehde, *die;* **conduct a ~ against sb./sth.** eine Hetzkampagne gegen jmdn./etw. führen **2** (killings) Blutrache, *die;* (in Italy also) Vendetta, *die*

ˈvending machine *n.* [Verkaufs]automat, *der*

vendor /ˈvendə(r), ˈvendɔː(r)/ *n.* **1** ▸ⓘ **p. 1260** (esp. Law) Verkäufer, *der*/Verkäuferin, *die;* **street ~:** Straßenhändler, *der*/-händlerin, *die;* **newspaper ~:** Zeitungsverkäufer, *der*/-verkäuferin, *die* **2** ▸**vending machine**

veneer /vıˈnıə(r)/
A *n.* **1** (thin covering of wood) Furnier, *das;* (layer in plywood) Furnierblatt, *das* **2** (fig.: disguise) Tünche, *die;* **beneath a ~ of respectability/civilization** hinter einer Fassade der Wohlanständigkeit/der Zivilisiertheit; **have only a ~ of education** sich (*Dat.*) nur den Anschein von Bildung geben; **it's just a ~:** es ist nur schöner Schein
B *v.t.* furnieren

venerable /ˈvenərəbl/ *adj.* **1** ehrwürdig; heilig ⟨*Reliquien*⟩ **2** (Eccl.) **the V~ A W Morgan** Hochwürden A W Morgan

venerate /ˈvenəreıt/ *v.t.* verehren; hoch achten; ehren ⟨*Eltern, Wort Gottes*⟩; in Ehren halten ⟨*jmds. Andenken, Traditionen, heilige Orte*⟩

veneration /venəˈreıʃn/ *n.* **1** (reverence) Ehrfurcht, *die* (**of, for** vor + *Dat.*); **in ~ of** zu Ehren (+ *Gen.*); **hold sb./sth. in ~:** jmdn./etw. verehren; **hold sb.'s memory in ~:** jmds. Andenken in Ehren halten **2** (venerating, being venerated) Verehrung, *die* (**of** für); **the community's ~ of its traditions** der tiefe Respekt, den die Gemeinde für ihre Traditionen empfindet/empfand

venereal /vıˈnıərıəl/ *adj.* ▸ⓘ **p. 1231** (Med.) venerisch; **~ clinic** Klinik für Geschlechtskrankheiten; **~ virus** Virus, das eine venerische Krankheit hervorruft

veˈnereal disease *n.* (Med.) Geschlechtskrankheit, *die;* venerische Krankheit (fachspr.)

Venetian /vıˈniːʃn/
A *adj.* venezianisch; **sb. is ~:** jmd. ist Venezianer/Venezianerin; **~ glass** Muranoglas, *das*
B *n.* **1** (person) Venezianer, *der*/Venezianerin, *die* **2** (dialect) Venezianisch, *das;* venezianischer Dialekt

venetian ˈblind *n.* Jalousie, *die*

Venezuela /venıˈzweılə/ *pr. n.* Venezuela (*das*)

Venezuelan /venıˈzweılən/ ▸ⓘ **p. 1345**
A *adj.* venezolanisch; **sb. is ~:** jmd. ist Venezolaner/Venezolanerin
B *n.* Venezolaner, *der*/Venezolanerin, *die*

vengeance /ˈvendʒəns/ *n.* **1** Rache, *die;* Vergeltung, *die;* **he wrought a cruel ~ on his enemies** er übte grausame Rache an seinen Feinden; **take ~ [up]on sb. [for sth.]** sich an jmdm. [für etw.] rächen **2** **with a ~:** gewaltig (ugs.); **go to work with a ~:** sich tüchtig ins Zeug legen (ugs.)

vengeful /ˈvendʒfl/ *adj.* rachedurstig (geh.); rachsüchtig (geh.)

V-engine *n.* (Tech.) V-Motor, *der*

venial /ˈviːnıəl/ *adj.* **1** (pardonable) verzeihlich; entschuldbar; leichter ⟨*Vergehen*⟩ **2** (Theol.) lässlich ⟨*Sünde*⟩

veniality /viːnıˈælıtı/ *n., no pl.* **1** Entschuldbarkeit, *die* **2** (Theol.) Lässlichkeit, *die*

Venice /ˈvenıs/ *pr. n.* ▸ⓘ **p. 1643** Venedig (*das*)

venison /ˈvenısn, ˈvenızn/ *n., no pl.* Hirsch[fleisch], *das;* (of roe) Reh[fleisch], *das;* **roast ~:** Hirsch-/Rehbraten, *der;* **~ steak** Hirsch-/Rehsteak, *das*

venom /ˈvenəm/ *n.* **1** (Zool.) Gift, *das* **2** (fig.) Boshaftigkeit, *die;* Gehässigkeit, *die;* **unleash one's ~ on sb.** jmdn. angiften (ugs.); **the ~ of her hatred** ihr giftiger Hass; **say sth. with great** *or* **real ~:** etw. sehr giftig sagen; **there was much ~ in his criticism** seine Kritik war wirklich giftig

venomous /ˈvenəməs/ *adj.* **1** (Zool.) giftig; Gift⟨*schlange, -stachel*⟩ **2** (fig.) giftig (ugs.); boshaft

venomously /ˈvenəməslı/ *adv.* (fig.) giftig (ugs.); boshaft

venous /ˈviːnəs/ *adj.* **1** (Anat., Zool.) venös **2** (Bot.) geädert

vent[1] /vent/
A *n.* **1** (for gas, liquid to escape) Öffnung, *die* **2** (of gun, cannon, etc.) Zündloch, *das;* Zündkanal, *der* **3** (in barrel) Spundloch, *das* **4** (Mus.) Griffloch, *das* **5** (flue) [Rauch]abzug, *der* **6** (Geol.) [Vulkan]schlot, *der* **7** (fig.: for emotions) Ventil, *das* (fig.); **give ~ to** Luft machen (+ *Dat.*) ⟨*Ärger, Wut*⟩; freien Lauf lassen (+ *Dat.*) ⟨*Gefühlen*⟩; Ausdruck verleihen (+ *Dat.*) ⟨*Freude*⟩ **8** (Zool.) Kloake, *die*
B *v.t.* (fig.) freien Lauf lassen (+ *Dat.*) ⟨*Kummer, Schmerz*⟩; Luft machen (+ *Dat.*) ⟨*Ärger, Wut*⟩; **~ one's anger on sb.** seinen Ärger an jmdm. auslassen *od.* abreagieren; *see also* **spleen 2**

vent[2] *n.* (in garment) Schlitz, *der;* **a jacket with a ~:** ein Jackett mit Rückenschlitz

ˈvent hole ▸**vent**[1] **A 1**

ventilate /ˈventıleıt/ *v.t.* **1** lüften; (by permanent installation) belüften **2** (fig.) (submit to public consideration) [offen] erörtern; (voice) kundtun, äußern ⟨*Meinung*⟩; vorbringen ⟨*Beschwerden*⟩ **3** (Physiol.) mit Sauerstoff versorgen

ventilation /ventıˈleıʃn/ *n.* **1** *no pl.* Belüftung, *die;* **the rooms need regular ~:** die

V

Zimmer müssen regelmäßig gelüftet werden; **this room has inadequate ~:** dieses Zimmer ist unzureichend *od.* schlecht belüftet **2** *no pl.* (installation) Lüftung, *die* **3** (fig.) (open discussion) [offene] Erörterung; Aussprache, *die* (**of** über + *Akk.*); (voicing) (of opinion) Äußerung, *die;* (of grievances) Vorbringen, *das* **4** *no pl., no art.* (Med.) Sauerstoffzufuhr, *die*

venti'lation shaft *n.* (Mining) Wetterschacht, *der*

ventilator /'ventɪleɪtə(r)/ *n.* **1** Lüftung[svorrichtung], *die;* (fan) Ventilator, *der* **2** (Med.) Beatmungsgerät, *das;* **be put on a ~:** an ein Beatmungsgerät angeschlossen werden

ventral /'ventrl/ *adj.* **1** (Anat., Zool.) ventral (fachspr.); Bauch- **2** (Bot.) ventral

ventricle /'ventrɪkl/ *n.* (Anat.) Ventrikel, *der*

ventriloquism /ven'trɪləkwɪzm/ *n., no pl.* Bauchreden, *das*

ventriloquist /ven'trɪləkwɪst/ *n.* Bauchredner, *der*/-rednerin, *die*

venture /'ventʃə(r)/

A *n.* **1** Unternehmung, *die;* **their ~ into space/the unknown** ihre Reise in den Weltraum/ins Unbekannte; **a new ~ in sth.** ein neuer Vorstoß in etw. (*Dat.*); **her latest ~ is surfing** neuerdings hat sie sich aufs Surfen verlegt (ugs.); **sth. is quite a** *or* **some ~:** etw. ist ein gewagtes *od.* mutiges Unterfangen; **I can't lose much by the ~:** ich kann bei dem Versuch nicht viel verlieren **2** (Commerc.) Unternehmung, *die;* **a successful ~:** ein erfolgreiches Geschäft; **a new publishing ~:** ein neues verlegerisches Vorhaben *od.* Projekt; **join a ~:** sich einem Unternehmen anschließen; *see also* **joint B 1**

B *v.i.* **1** (dare) wagen; **if I might ~ to suggest ...:** wenn Sie [mir] gestatten, möchte ich vorschlagen ...; **may I ~ to ask ...:** darf ich mir erlauben zu fragen ...; **I would even ~ to say ...:** ich würde sogar so weit gehen zu sagen ... **2** (dare to go) sich wagen; **dare to ~:** sich wagen; **~ further into the cave** sich weiter *od.* tiefer in die Höhle vorwagen; **~ [away] from home** sich von zu Hause fort wagen; **~ abroad/into society** sich ins Ausland/in Gesellschaft wagen; **~ out of doors** sich vor die Tür wagen; **~ into a new area of research** (fig.) sich auf ein neues Forschungsgebiet vorwagen; **he would never ~ too far** (fig.) er würde sich nie zu weit vorwagen

C *v.t.* **1** wagen ‹*Bitte, Bemerkung, Blick, Vermutung*›; zu äußern wagen ‹*Ansicht*›; sich (*Dat.*) erlauben ‹*Frage, Scherz, Bemerkung*›; **~ an explanation for sth.** etw. zu erklären versuchen; **if I might ~ a suggestion** wenn ich mir einen Vorschlag erlauben darf; **'How about ...?', he ~d** „Wie wärs mit ...?“, schlug er vor **2** (risk, stake) aufs Spiel setzen ‹*Leben, Ruf, Vermögen, Glück*›; setzen ‹*Wettsumme*› (**on** auf + *Akk.*); **~ money in** *or* **on sth.** Geld in etw. (*Akk.*) stecken; *see also* **nothing A 1**

Phrasal verbs

- **~ 'forth** (literary) ▸ **~ out**
- **~ on** *v.t.* sich einlassen auf (+ *Akk.*); sich wagen an (+ *Akk.*) ‹*Aufgabe*›; sich wagen auf (+ *Akk.*) ‹*Reise*›
- **~ 'out** *v.i.* sich hinauswagen; **~ out on to the sea** sich auf das Meer hinauswagen
- **~ upon** ▸ **~ on**

venture: ~ 'capital *n., no pl.* Wagniskapital, *das;* Risikokapital, *das;* **~ 'capitalism** *n., no pl.* Risikokapitalismus, *der;* **~ 'capitalist** *n.* Risikokapitalist, *der*/-kapitalistin, *die*

venturer /'ventʃərə(r)/ *n.* **1** (Commerc. Hist.) Unternehmer, *der*/Unternehmerin, *die* **2** (adventurer) Abenteurer, *der*/Abenteu[r]erin, *die*

'Venture Scout *n.* (Brit.) ≈ Rover, *der; Pfadfinder im Alter von 16 bis 20 Jahren*

venturesome /'ventʃəsəm/ *adj.* wagemutig ‹*Person, Tat*›; (hazardous) abenteuerlich ‹*Unternehmen, Reise*›

venue /'venju:/ *n.* (Sport) [Austragungs]ort, *der;* (Mus., Theatre) [Veranstaltungs]ort, *der;* (meeting place) Treffpunkt, *der*

Venus /'vi:nəs/ *pr. n.* **1** (Astron.) Venus, *die* **2** (Roman Mythol.) Venus (*die*)

Venusian /vɪ'nju:zɪən/

A *adj.* (Astron.) Venus-

B *n.* Venusbewohner, der/-bewohnerin, *die*

Venus['s] 'flytrap *n.* (Bot.) Venusfliegenfalle, *die*

veracious /və'reɪʃəs/ *adj.* (formal) **1** aufrichtig ‹*Person*›; **assume sb. to be ~:** davon ausgehen, dass jmd. die Wahrheit sagt **2** (true) wahr; wahrheitsgetreu ‹*Schilderung, Bericht*›

veracity /və'ræsɪtɪ/ *n., no pl.* **1** (of person) Aufrichtigkeit, *die* **2** (of statement etc.) Wahrheitstreue, *die;* **have ~:** wahrheitsgetreu sein

veranda[h] /və'rændə/ *n.* Veranda, *die*

verb /vɜ:b/ *n.* (Ling.) Verb, *das;* Verbum, *das* (fachspr.)

verbal /'vɜ:bl/ *adj.* **1** (relating to words) sprachlich; **~ memory** Gedächtnis für Worte *od.* Sprache; **his skills are ~:** seine Fähigkeiten liegen auf sprachlichem Gebiet; **the distinction is purely ~:** der Unterschied besteht nur in der Wortwahl **2** (oral) mündlich; verbal, mündlich ‹*Bekenntnis, Anerkennung, Protest*› **3** (Ling.) verbal; **a ~ group** eine Verb[al]gruppe

verbal diar'rhoea *n., no pl.* (coll.) verbaler Durchfall

verbalize (**verbalise**) /'vɜ:bəlaɪz/ *v.t.* **1** (express) in Worte fassen, (geh.) verbalisieren ‹*Gefühle*› **2** (Ling.: make into verb) verbalisieren

verbally /'vɜ:bəlɪ/ *adv.* **1** (regarding words) sprachlich; mit Worten, verbal ‹*beschrieben*› **2** (orally) mündlich; verbal, mündlich ‹*protestieren*› **3** (Ling.) verbal

verbal 'noun *n.* (Ling.) Verbalsubstantiv, *das*

verbatim /və'beɪtɪm/

A *adv.* im Wortlaut ‹*veröffentlichen*›; [wort]wörtlich ‹*sagen, abschreiben, zitieren*›

B *adj.* wortgetreu; [wort]wörtlich

verbena /və'bi:nə/ *n.* (Bot.) **1** Eisenkraut, *das;* Verbene, *die* (fachspr.) **2** **[lemon] ~:** Zitronenstrauch, *der*

verbiage /'vɜ:bɪɪdʒ/ *n., no pl., no indef. art.* **1** (wordiness) Geschwätzigkeit, *die* **2** (words) Geschwätz, *das*

verbose /və'bəʊs/ *adj.* geschwätzig; weitschweifig ‹*Roman, Vortrag, Autor*›; langatmig ‹*Rede, Redner, Stil*›; **he is too ~:** er macht zu viele Worte

verbosely /və'bəʊslɪ/ *adv.* weitschweifig; langatmig

verboseness /və'bəʊsnɪs/, **verbosity** /və'bɒsɪtɪ/ *ns.* **1** (wordiness) Weitschweifigkeit, die; Langatmigkeit, *die* **2** (words) Geschwafel, *das*

verdant /'vɜ:dənt/ *adj.* (literary) [saft]grün

verdict /'vɜ:dɪkt/ *n.* **1** (Law) Urteil, *das;* [Urteils]spruch, *der;* **open ~** *Feststellung eines gewaltsamen Todes ohne Nennung der Ursache (bei einer gerichtlichen Untersuchung);* **~ of guilty/not guilty** Schuld-/Freispruch, *der;* **reach a ~:** zu einem Urteil kommen; *see also* **bring in 4; return B 8** **2** (judgement) Urteil, *das* (**on** über + *Akk.*); (decision) Entscheidung, *die;* **the ~ of the electors** die Entscheidung der Wähler; **what's your ~ on the affair/novel?** wie beurteilst du die Sache/wie ist dein Urteil über den Roman?; **give** *or* **pass a/one's ~ [on sb./sth.]** ein/sein Urteil [über jmdn./etw.] abgeben

verdigris /'vɜ:dɪgrɪs/ *n.* **1** (Chem.) Grünspan, *der* **2** (rust on metal) Patina, *die*

verdure /'vɜ:djə(r)/ *n.* (literary) **1** (greenness) Grün, *das* **2** (green vegetation) [dichtes] Grün

verge[1] /vɜ:dʒ/ *n.* **1** (grass edging) Rasensaum, *der;* (on road) Bankette, *die;* **'keep off the ~'** „Bankette nicht befahrbar“; *see also* **soft verge** **2** (brink, border, lit. or fig.) Rand, *der;* (fig.: point at which something begins) Schwelle, *die;* **be on the ~ of economic collapse/of war/of death** am Rand des wirtschaftlichen Zusammenbruchs/an der Schwelle des Krieges/Todes stehen; **be on the ~ of despair/tears/a breakthrough/a breakdown** der Verzweiflung/den Tränen/dem Durchbruch/einem Nervenzusammenbruch nahe sein; **be on the ~ of doing sth.** kurz davor stehen, etw. zu tun; **bring sb./sth. to the ~ of sth.** jmdn./etw. an den Rand von etw. bringen

verge[2] *v.i.* ‹*Hügel, Land:*› abfallen; **~ to[wards] sth.** (fig.) einer Sache (*Dat.*) zustreben; **~ towards old age** langsam alt werden

Phrasal verb

- **~ on** *v.t.* [an]grenzen an (+ *Akk.*); **be verging on 70** an die 70 sein; **an estate verging on four acres** (fig.) ein Grundstück von fast vier Morgen [Größe]; **be verging on tears/madness** den Tränen/dem Wahnsinn nahe sein; **blue verging on grey** (fig.) ein Blau, das schon fast grau wirkt; **be verging on bankruptcy** vor dem Bankrott stehen

verger /'vɜ:dʒə(r)/ *n.* (Eccl.) Küster, *der*

Vergil ▸ **Virgil**

verifiable /'verɪfaɪəbl/ *adj.* nachprüfbar; **this is an easily ~ statement** diese Behauptung lässt sich leicht nachprüfen

verification /verɪfɪ'keɪʃn/ *n.* **1** (check) Überprüfung, *die;* **~ of the accounts** Prüfung der Bücher; **be open to ~:** sich überprüfen lassen **2** ▸ **verify 2**: Bestätigung, *die;* Bekräftigung, *die;* Nachweis, *der;* **I'll need some ~ of your identity** ich brauche dann noch einen Ausweis von Ihnen **3** (bearing out) Bestätigung, *die;* **a ~ of their prediction** ein Beweis für die Richtigkeit ihrer Prognose

verify /'verɪfaɪ/ *v.t.* **1** (check) überprüfen; prüfen ‹*Bücher*›; **ring sb. up to ~ the news** jmdn. anrufen, um sich (*Dat.*) die [Richtigkeit der] Nachricht bestätigen zu lassen **2** (confirm) bestätigen ‹*Vermutung, Diagnose*›; bekräftigen ‹*Anspruch, Forderung*›; nachweisen ‹*Identität*› **3** (bear out) bestätigen; beweisen ‹*Theorie*›

verily /'verɪlɪ/ *adv.* (arch./Bibl.) wahrlich (veralt.); **no** *or* **nay, ~:** nein, fürwahr (veralt.)

verisimilitude /verɪsɪ'mɪlɪtju:d/ *n., no pl.* Wahrheitsgehalt, *der;* (in work of art) Realistik, *die;* **sth. is designed to add** *or* **give ~ to a story** etw. soll eine Geschichte realistischer erscheinen lassen

veritable /'verɪtəbl/ *adj.* (literary) richtig; wahr, richtig ‹*Engel, Genie*›; wahr ‹*Wunder*›

veritably /'verɪtəblɪ/ *adv.* (literary) wirklich [und wahrhaftig]; **it was ~ miraculous** es war ein wahres Wunder; **a ~ suicidal thing to do** der reinste Selbstmord (ugs.); **the place ~ swam with wine** der Wein floss buchstäblich in Strömen

verity /'verɪtɪ/ *n.* (literary) Wahrheit, *die*

vermicelli /vɜ:mɪ'tʃelɪ/ *n.* (Gastr.) Vermicelli; Fadennudeln

vermicide /'vɜ:mɪsaɪd/ *n.* (Med.) Wurmmittel, *das*

vermiculite /və'mɪkjʊlaɪt/ *n., no pl.* Vermikulit, *der*

vermiform /'vɜ:mɪfɔ:m/ *adj.* wurmförmig; *see also* **appendix 2**

vermifuge /'vɜ:mɪfju:dʒ/ (Med.) *n.* Wurmmittel, *das*

vermilion /və'mɪljən/

A *n.* (substance) Zinnober, *der;* (colour) Zinnoberrot, *das*

B *adj.* zinnoberrot

vermin /'vɜ:mɪn/ *n., no pl., no indef. art.* Ungeziefer, *das;* (fig. derog.) Pack, *das* (abwertend); Abschaum, *der* (abwertend)

verminous /'vɜ:mɪnəs/ *adj.* ungezieferverseucht; voller Ungeziefer *nachgestellt;* (fig. derog.) übel

vermouth /'vɜ:məθ/, (Amer.) və'mu:θ/ *n.* Wermut[wein], *der*

vernacular /və'nækjʊlə(r)/

A *adj.* **1** (native) landessprachlich; ‹*Predigt, Zeitung*› in der Landessprache; (not learned or technical) volkstümlich; (in dialect) mundartlich; **~ language** Landessprache, *die*/(popular) Volkssprache, *die*/(dialect) Mundart, *die;* **the ~ dialect** der regionale Dialekt **2** **~ architecture** volkstümliche Baukunst

B *n.* **1** (native language) Landessprache, *die;* (dialect) Dialekt, *der* **2** (jargon) Sprache, *die;* (of a profession or group) Jargon, *der;* **scientific/legal ~:** Wissenschafts-/Juristenjargon, *der;* **thieves' ~:** Gaunersprache, *die;* **~ of youth** Jugendsprache, *die* **3** (homely speech) Umgangssprache, *die;* **if you'll excuse the ~** (joc.) wenn ich das mal so sagen darf

vernal /ˈvɜːnl/ *adj.* Frühlings-; *see also* **equinox 1**

vernier /ˈvɜːnɪə(r)/ *n.* (Mech. Engin.) Nonius, *der*

veronica /vəˈrɒnɪkə/ *n.* (Bot.) Ehrenpreis, *das od. der*

verruca /veˈruːkə/ *n., pl.* **~e** /veˈruːsiː/ *or* **~s** (Med.) Warze, *die;* Verruca, *die* (fachspr.)

versatile /ˈvɜːsətaɪl/ *adj.* vielseitig; (mentally) flexibel; (having many uses) vielseitig verwendbar

versatility /vɜːsəˈtɪlɪtɪ/ *n., no pl.* Vielseitigkeit, *die;* (mental) Flexibilität, *die;* (variety of uses) vielseitige Verwendbarkeit

verse /vɜːs/ *n.* **1** (stanza) Strophe, *die;* **of** *or* **in** *or* **with five ~s** fünfstrophig **2** *no pl., no indef. art.* Verse *Pl.;* (poetry) Lyrik, *die;* **write some ~:** einige Verse schreiben; **piece of ~:** Gedicht, *das;* **written in ~:** in Versform; **put sth. into ~:** etw. in Verse fassen **3** (in Bible) Vers, *der; see also* **blank verse; chapter 1**

versed /vɜːst/ *adj.* **be [well] ~ in sth.** sich in etw. *(Dat.)* [gut] auskennen; **he's [well] ~ in such matters** er ist in diesen Dingen [sehr] versiert

verse: **~ drama** *n.* (Lit.) Versdrama, *das;* **~ translation** *n.* (Lit.) Übertragung in Versform

versification /vɜːsɪfɪˈkeɪʃn/ *n.* **1** (composing of verse) Versedichten, *das;* (derog.) Verseschmieden, *das* **2** (metrical form) Versbau, *der* **3** (poetical version) Versfassung, *die*

versifier /ˈvɜːsɪfaɪə(r)/ *n.* Versdichter, *der/* -dichterin, *die;* (derog.) Versemacher, *der/* -macherin, *die*

versify /ˈvɜːsɪfaɪ/

A *v.t.* in Verse fassen

B *v.i.* Gedichte schreiben; (derog.) Verse schmieden

version /ˈvɜːʃn/ *n.* Version, *die;* (in another language) Übersetzung, *die;* (in another form also) Fassung, *die;* (of vehicle, machine, tool) Modell, *das; see also* **authorize 2; revise A 1**

verso /ˈvɜːsəʊ/ *n., pl.* **~s** **1** (Printing, Bibliog.) (left-hand page) linke Seite; (back of leaf) Verso, *das* (fachspr.); Rückseite, *die* **2** (Num.) Revers, *der* (fachspr.); Rückseite, *die*

versus /ˈvɜːsəs/ *prep.* gegen

vertebra /ˈvɜːtɪbrə/ *n., pl.* **~e** /ˈvɜːtɪbriː/ (Anat.) Wirbel, *der;* **~e** (backbone) Wirbelsäule, *die*

vertebral /ˈvɜːtɪbrəl/ *adj.* (Anat.) vertebral (fachspr.); Wirbel-; **~ column/muscles** Wirbelsäule, *die*/Rückenmuskulatur, *die*

vertebrate /ˈvɜːtɪbrət/ (Zool.)

A *adj.* Wirbel‹*tier*›; Wirbeltier‹*skelett, -fossilien, -zoologie*›; ‹*Stamm*› der Wirbeltiere

B *n.* Wirbeltier, *das*

vertex /ˈvɜːteks/ *n., pl.* **vertices** /ˈvɜːtɪsiːz/ *or* **~es** **1** (highest point) Gipfel, *der;* (of tower, turret) Spitze, *die;* (Archit.: of dome, arch) Scheitel[punkt], *der* **2** (Geom.) (of curve, surface, angle) Scheitel[punkt], *der;* (of triangle, polygon) Eckpunkt, *der*

vertical /ˈvɜːtɪkl/

A *adj.* **1** senkrecht; senkrecht aufragend *od.* abfallend ‹*Klippe*›; **be ~:** senkrecht stehen **2** (esp. Econ., Sociol.: combining levels, stages, etc.) vertikal; *see also* **integration 4**

B *n.* senkrechte *od.* vertikale Linie; **be out of [the] ~:** nicht im *od.* außer Lot sein

vertical inteˈgration *n., no pl.* (Commerc.) vertikale Integration

vertically /ˈvɜːtɪkəlɪ/ *adv.* **1** senkrecht; vertikal **2** (esp. Econ., Sociol.: so as to combine levels, stages, etc.) vertikal

vertical: **~ ˈplane** *n.* (Geom.) Vertikalebene, *die;* **~ ˈtake-off** *n.* (Aeronaut.) Senkrechtstart, *der;* **~ ˈtake-off aircraft** *n.* (Aeronaut.) Senkrechtstarter, *der*

vertices *pl. of* **vertex**

vertiginous /vəˈtɪdʒɪnəs/ *adj.* Schwindel erregend ‹*Höhe, Abgrund usw.*›

vertigo /ˈvɜːtɪgəʊ/ *n., pl.* **~s** Schwindel, *der;* Vertigo, *die* (Med.); **give sb. ~:** jmdn. schwindelig machen; **she got ~:** ihr wurde schwindelig; **attack of ~:** Schwindelanfall, *der*

vervain /ˈvɜːveɪn/ *n.* (Bot.) Eisenkraut, *das*

verve /vɜːv/ *n.* Schwung, *der;* (of artist, orchestra's playing, sports team's play) Temperament, *das;* (of music, sb.'s writing) Ausdruckskraft, die (**of, in** *Gen.*)

very /ˈverɪ/

A *attrib. adj.* **1** (precise, exact) genau; **you must do it this ~ day** du musst es noch heute tun; **on the ~ day when ...:** genau am [selben] Tag, an dem ...; **you're the ~ person I wanted to see** genau dich wollte ich sehen; **at the ~ moment when ...:** im selben Augenblick, als ...; **just this ~ moment ...:** gerade eben ...; **in the ~ centre** genau in der Mitte; **the ~ opposite** genau das Gegenteil; **the ~ thing** genau das Richtige; **that is the ~ word he used** das ist genau das Wort, das er gebrauchte; **the ~ stones cry out** das schreit ja zum Himmel

2 (extreme) **at the ~ back/front** ganz hinten/vorn; **at the ~ edge of the cliff** ganz am Rand der Klippe; **at the ~ end/beginning** ganz am Ende/Anfang; **from the ~ outset** *or* **beginning** von Anfang an; **go to the ~ end of the street** ganz bis ans Ende der Straße gehen; **climb to the ~ top of the hill** bis auf den Gipfel des Berges steigen

3 (mere) bloß ‹*Gedanke*›; **at the ~ thought** allein schon beim Gedanken; **the ~ fact of his presence** allein schon seine Anwesenheit; **the ~ mention** allein schon die Erwähnung

4 (absolute) absolut ‹*Minimum, Maximum*›; **do one's ~ best** *or* **utmost** sein Möglichstes tun; **the ~ most I can offer is ...:** ich kann allerhöchstens ... anbieten; **it's the ~ least** das ist das Allermindeste; **£50 at the ~ most** allerhöchstens 50 Pfund; **they should at the ~ least consider the proposal** sie sollten das Angebot zumindest einmal in Erwägung ziehen; **be the ~ first to arrive** als Allererster ankommen; **for the ~ last time** zum allerletzten Mal

5 (used as emphatic or intensive) **his ~ mother** seine eigene Mutter; **before their ~ eyes** vor ihren Augen; **be caught in the ~ act** auf frischer Tat ertappt werden; **be the ~ picture of health** wie die Gesundheit in Person aussehen; **under sb.'s ~ nose** (fig. coll.) direkt vor jmds. Augen *(Dat.)*

6 (arch.: real) wahr ‹*Grund, Seelenfriede, Seele*›; richtig ‹*Teufel*›; rein ‹*Wahnsinn*›

B *adv.* **1** (extremely) sehr; **it's ~ near** es ist ganz in der Nähe; **in the ~ near future** in allernächster Zukunft; **it's ~ possible that ...:** es ist sehr gut möglich, dass ...; **~ probably** höchstwahrscheinlich; **she's ~/so ~ thin** sie ist sehr dünn/so dünn; **how ~ rude [of him]!** das ist aber unhöflich [von ihm]!; **[yes,] ~ much [so]** [ja,] sehr; **~ much prettier/better** [sehr] viel hübscher/besser; **not ~ much** nicht sehr; **~ little** [nur] sehr wenig ‹*verstehen, essen*›; **a ~ little more** ein ganz kleines bisschen mehr; **only a ~ little** nur ein ganz kleines bisschen; **there's ~ little reason to do it** es spricht kaum etwas dafür, es zu tun; **thank you [~,] ~ much** [vielen,] vielen Dank; **[yes,] thank you ~ much** o ja, sehr gern; **no, thank you ~ much** nein, danke vielmals; **you are [~,] ~ kind** (thanking) das ist [wirklich] sehr freundlich von Ihnen; **not ~ big** (not extremely big) nicht sehr groß; (not at all big) nicht gerade groß; *see also* **reverend A; so¹ A 1, 9**

2 (absolutely) aller‹*best..., -letzt..., -leichtest...*›; **at the ~ latest** allerspätestens; **the ~ last thing I expected** das, womit ich am allerwenigsten gerechnet hatte; **keep sth. for one's ~ own** etw. für sich ganz allein behalten; **have sth. of one's ~ own** etw. haben, das einem ganz allein gehört

3 (precisely) **the ~ same one** genau der-/die-/dasselbe; **meet the ~ next day** sich gleich am nächsten Tag treffen; **in his ~ next sentence/breath** schon im nächsten Satz/Atemzug

4 **~ good** (accepting) sehr wohl; (agreeing) sehr schön; **~ well** *expr. reluctant consent* also gut; na schön; **that's all ~ well, but ...:** das ist ja alles schön und gut, aber ...

very high ˈfrequency *n.* (Radio) Ultrakurzwelle, *die*

Very light /ˈverɪ laɪt, ˈvɪərɪ laɪt/ *n.* (Mil.) Leuchtkugel, *die*

vesicle /ˈvesɪkl/ *n.* **1** (Anat., Geol.) Blase, *die* **2** (Zool., Bot., Med.) Bläschen, *das*

vespers /ˈvespəz/ *n., constr. as sing. or pl.* (Eccl.) Vesper, *die*

vessel /ˈvesl/ *n.* **1** (receptacle; also Anat., Bot.) Gefäß, *das;* **[drinking] ~:** Trinkgefäß, *das; see also* **blood vessel** **2** (Naut.) Schiff, *das*

vest /vest/

A *n.* **1** (Brit.: undergarment) Unterhemd, *das;* (woman's) Hemd, *das;* **[running] ~** Trikot, *das* **2** (Amer.: waistcoat) Weste, *die*

B *v.t.* **~ sb. with sth., ~ sth. in sb.** jmdm. etw. verleihen; **be ~ed with the power to do sth.** berechtigt sein, etw. zu tun; **~ sb. with [rights in] sth.** jmdm. Ansprüche auf etw. *(Akk.)* einräumen; **be ~ed in sb.** jmdm. übertragen sein; **by the power** *or* **authority ~ed in me** kraft der mir verliehenen Vollmacht; *see also* **vested**

vestal /ˈvestl/ (Roman Mythol.)

A *adj.* vestalisch ‹*Gesetz, Gelübde*›; ‹*Schrein, Feuer*› der Vesta

B *n.* ▸**vestal virgin**

vestal ˈvirgin *n.* Vestalin, *die*

vested /ˈvestɪd/ *adj.* **~ interest/right** wohlerworbener Anspruch; (established by law) gesetzlicher Anspruch; **~ interests** (groups of persons) Interessengruppen; **have a ~ interest in sth.** (fig.) ein persönliches Interesse an etw. *(Dat.)* haben

vestibule /ˈvestɪbjuːl/ *n.* **1** (indoors) [Eingangs]halle, *die* **2** (external porch) Vorhalle, *die* **3** (Amer. Railw.) Vorraum, *der* **4** (Anat.) Innenohrvorhof, *der;* Vestibulum, *das* (fachspr.)

vestige /ˈvestɪdʒ/ *n.* **1** Spur, *die;* **not the slightest** *or* **least ~** *or* **not a single ~ [of sth. remains]** nicht das Geringste *od.* nicht die Spur [ist von etw. übrig]; **not a ~ of truth/honour** kein Fünkchen Wahrheit/Ehre **2** (Biol.) Rudiment, *das*

vestigial /veˈstɪdʒɪəl/ *adj.* rudimentär (geh.; fachspr.); spärlich ‹*Überreste*›; verkümmert ‹*Tradition, Brauch*›

vestment /ˈvestmənt/ *n.* [Priester]gewand, *das;* (worn on special occasions) Ornat, *das*

ˈvest-pocket *attrib. adj.* (Amer.) im [Westen]taschenformat *nachgestellt;* (fig.: very small) Miniatur‹*modell, -ausgabe, -version*›

vestry /ˈvestrɪ/ *n.* (Eccl.) Sakristei, *die*

Vesuvius /vɪˈsuːvɪəs/ *pr. n.* der Vesuv

vet¹ /vet/

A *n.* ▸**❶ p. 1260** Tierarzt, *der/*-ärztin, *die*

B *v.t.,* **-tt-** überprüfen; **~ an article for errors** einen Artikel auf Fehler [hin] durchsehen

vet² (Amer. coll.) ▸**veteran A**

vetch /vetʃ/ *n.* (Bot.) Wicke, *die*

veteran /ˈvetərən/

A *n.* Veteran, *der/*Veteranin, *die;* **V~s' Day** *amerikanischer Gedenktag anlässlich des Waffenstillstandes 1918 u. 1945*

B *attrib. adj.* altgedient ‹*Offizier, Politiker, Schauspieler*›

veteran ˈcar *n.* (Brit.) Veteran, *der*

veterinarian /vetərɪˈneərɪən/ ▸**❶ p. 1260** (Amer.) ▸**veterinary surgeon**

veterinary /ˈvetərɪnərɪ/ *attrib. adj.* tiermedizinisch; veterinär; **~ science/medicine** Veterinär- *od.* Tiermedizin, *die;* **~ practice** Tierarztpraxis, *die;* **course of ~ training** Ausbildung zum Tierarzt; **~ college** Institut für Tiermedizin

veterinary ˈsurgeon *n.* ▸**❶ p. 1260** (Brit.) Tierarzt, *der/*-ärztin, *die*

veto /ˈviːtəʊ/

A *n., pl.* **~es** **1** **[power** *or* **right of] ~:** Veto[recht], *das; see also* **pocket veto** **2** (rejection, prohibition) Veto, *das* (**on** gegen, **from** vonseiten); **has there been a ~ of the bill?** hat jemand sein Veto gegen den Gesetzentwurf eingelegt?; **put a** *or* **one's ~ on sth.** sein Veto gegen etw. erheben *od.* einlegen

B *v.t.* sein Veto einlegen gegen

vex /veks/ *v.t.* [ver]ärgern; (cause to worry) beunruhigen; (dissatisfy, disappoint) bekümmern; **be ~ed about** *or* **at sth.** sich über etw. *(Akk.)* ärgern; **be ~ed that ...:** sich darüber ärgern,

V

dass ...; **I am ~ed that ...:** es ärgert mich, dass ...; **be ~ed with sb.** sich über jmdn. ärgern

vexation /vek'seɪʃn/ *n.* 1 (act of harassing) Belästigung, *die;* **take pleasure in the ~ of sb.** sich (*Dat.*) ein Vergnügen daraus machen, jmdn. zu ärgern 2 (state of irritation) Verärgerung, *die* (**with, at** über + *Akk.*); (state of worry) Beunruhigung, *die;* (dissatisfaction, disappointment) Kummer, *der;* **suffer [much] ~:** [viel] Ärger/Kummer haben; **cause sb. ~** (irritate) jmdm. Ärger bereiten; (worry) jmdn. in Unruhe versetzen; (disappoint) jmdm. Kummer machen; **have the ~ of seeing sth. happen** verärgert/bekümmert mit ansehen müssen, wie etw. geschieht 3 (annoying thing) Ärgernis, *das* (**to, for** für); **constant ~s from sb.** ständige Belästigungen durch jmdn. 4 (Law) Schikane, *die*

vexatious /vek'seɪʃəs/ *adj.* 1 ärgerlich; unausstehlich ‹*Person*›; **it is ~ that .../to ...:** es ist ärgerlich, dass .../zu ... 2 (Law) schikanös

vexatiously /vek'seɪʃəslɪ/ *adv.* 1 ungehörig ‹*sich benehmen, sich verhalten*›; **he said, rather ~, that ...:** sehr zu meinem Ärger/Kummer sagte er, dass ...; **~ complicated** lästig und kompliziert 2 (Law) aus Schikane; schikanös ‹*sich verhalten*›

vexed /vekst/ *adj.* 1 (annoyed) verärgert (**by** über + *Akk.*); (distressed) bekümmert (**by** über + *Akk.*) 2 **~ question** viel diskutierte Frage

vexing /'veksɪŋ/ *adj.* lästig ‹*Angelegenheit, Problem, Sorgen*›; ärgerlich ‹*Zwickmühle*›

VFR *abbr.* (Aeronaut.) = **visual flight rules** Sichtflugregeln

VG *abbr.* = **very good**

VHF *abbr.* = **very high frequency** UKW

via /'vaɪə, 'viːə/ *prep.* über (+ *Akk.*) ‹*Ort, Sender, Telefon*›; auf (+ *Dat.*) ‹*Weg*›; durch ‹*Eingang, Schornstein, Person*›; per ‹*Post*›

viability /vaɪə'bɪlɪtɪ/ *n., no pl.* 1 (of fetus, animal, plant) Lebensfähigkeit, *die;* (of seed) Keimfähigkeit, *die* 2 (fig.) (of state, company) Lebensfähigkeit, *die;* (feasibility) Realisierbarkeit, *die*

viable /'vaɪəbl/ *adj.* 1 (capable of maintaining life) lebensfähig; keimfähig; **be more ~ than ...:** besser überleben als ... 2 (fig.) lebensfähig ‹*Staat, Firma*›; (feasible) realisierbar

viaduct /'vaɪədʌkt/ *n.* Viadukt, *das od. der*

Viagra ® /vaɪ'agrə/ *n., no pl.* Viagra, *das*

vibes /vaɪbz/ *n. pl.* (coll.) 1 (Mus.) Vibraphon, *das* 2 (vibrations) Schwingungen; Vibrations (salopp); **I get good ~ from him** er törnt *od.* macht mich an (ugs.); **give sb. bad ~:** jmdn. abtörnen (ugs.); **feel those ~, man!** das törnt echt an! (ugs.)

vibrant /'vaɪbrənt/ *adj.* 1 (vibrating) vibrierend; schwingend, vibrierend ‹*Saite, Draht*› 2 (thrilling) pulsierend ‹*Leben*›; schwungvoll ‹*Vorstellung*›; lebensprühend ‹*Atmosphäre*›; dynamisch ‹*Kraft*›; lebhaft ‹*Farbe, Rot*›; **be ~ with activity/life** vor Aktivitäten/Leben (*Dat.*) sprühen; **a painting ~ with colour** ein farbenprächtiges Gemälde 3 (resonant) volltönend ‹*Stimme*›; voll ‹*Ton*›

vibraphone /'vaɪbrəfəʊn/ *n.* (Mus.) Vibraphon, *das*

vibrate /vaɪ'breɪt/

A *v.i.* 1 vibrieren; (under strong impact) beben 2 (resound) [nach]klingen; **the sound of the anvil ~d in the streets** das Klingen des Ambosses hallte durch die Straßen 3 (Phys.) schwingen; ‹*Glocke:*› vibrieren 4 (thrill) ‹*Stadt, Party, Aufsatz:*› sprühen (**with** vor + *Dat.*); ‹*Stimme, Körper:*› vibrieren (**with** vor + *Dat.*)

B *v.t.* vibrieren lassen; zum Schwingen bringen ‹*Saite*›

vibration /vaɪ'breɪʃn/ *n.* 1 (vibrating) Vibrationen; (visible) Vibrieren, *das;* (under strong impact) Beben, *das;* **send ~s** *or* **a ~ through sth.** ‹*Erdstoß:*› etw. erzittern lassen 2 (Phys.) Schwingung, *die* 3 *in pl.* (fig.) **get some ~s** etwas spüren; **his presence gives me bad ~s** in seiner Gegenwart fühle ich mich [irgendwie] unwohl; **I get good ~s from this place/music** dieser Ort/diese Musik hat eine wohltuende Ausstrahlung

vibrational /vaɪ'breɪʃənl/ *adj.* (Phys.) Schwingungs-

vibrato /vɪ'brɑːtəʊ/ *n., pl.* **~s** (Mus.) Vibrato, *das*

vibrator /vaɪ'breɪtə(r)/ *n.* Vibrator, *der*

viburnum /vaɪ'bɜːnəm/ *n.* (Bot.) Schneeball, *der*

vicar /'vɪkə(r)/ *n.* ▸ p. 1634 Pfarrer, *der;* **lay ~** *Laie, der Teile der Liturgie singt*

vicarage /'vɪkərɪdʒ/ *n.* Pfarrhaus, *das*

vicar apos'tolic *n.* (RC Ch.) Apostolischer Vikar

vicarious /vɪ'keərɪəs/ *adj.* 1 (delegated) Stellvertreter-; **his authority** *or* **power is ~:** er hat Stellvertreterbefugnisse 2 (done for another) stellvertretend; **perform ~ work/tasks** Arbeit/Aufgaben stellvertretend erledigen; **~ suffering[s]** (Theol.) stellvertretendes Leiden 3 (experienced through another) nachempfunden ‹*Freude, Erregung usw.*›; **~ [sexual] satisfaction** Ersatzbefriedigung, *die;* **take a ~ delight in sb.'s success** sich mit jmdm. *od.* für jmdn. über dessen Erfolg (*Akk.*) freuen

vicariously /vɪ'keərɪəslɪ/ *adv.* 1 (as a substitute for another) stellvertretend 2 (by means of a substitute) indirekt

vicariousness /vɪ'keərɪəsnɪs/ *n., no pl.* stellvertretender Charakter; **the ~ of this experience** die Mittelbarkeit dieses Erlebnisses

vice¹ /vaɪs/ *n.* 1 Laster, *das;* **a life/den of ~:** ein Lasterleben/eine Lasterhöhle 2 (defect) Fehler, *der;* **he has no redeeming ~:** er hat aber auch gar kein[e] Laster

vice² *n.* (Brit.: tool) Schraubstock, *der*

vice³ *n.* (coll.: deputy) Vize, *der* (ugs.)

vice- *pref.* Vize-

vice: ~-'admiral *n.* (Navy) Vizeadmiral, *der;* **~-'chair** *n.* stellvertretender Vorsitzender/stellvertretende Vorsitzende; **~-'chairman** *n.* stellvertretender Vorsitzender; **~-'chairmanship** *n.* Amt des/der stellvertretenden Vorsitzenden; **~-'chancellor** *n.* ▸ p. 1260 (Univ.) Vizekanzler, *der*/Vizekanzlerin, *die*

'vicelike *adj.* eisern ‹*Griff*›; fest ‹*Umklammerung, Schwitzkasten*›

vice: ~-'presidency *n.* Amt des Vizepräsidenten/der Vizepräsidentin; **~-'president** *n.* Vizepräsident, *der*/-präsidentin, *die;* **~-'principal** *n.* (Educ.) stellvertretender Leiter/stellvertretende Leiterin; **~'regal** *adj.* eines/des Vizekönigs *nachgestellt;* **~ ring** *n.* Zuhälterring, *der*

viceroy /'vaɪsrɔɪ/ *n.* Vizekönig, *der*

viceroyship /'vaɪsrɔɪʃɪp/ *n.* Amt eines Vizekönigs

'vice squad *n.* (Police) Sittenpolizei, *die*

vice versa /vaɪsɪ 'vɜːsə/ *adv.* umgekehrt

vicinity /vɪ'sɪnɪtɪ/ *n.* 1 (neighbourhood) Umgebung, *die;* **from London or its ~:** aus London und Umgebung; **in our ~:** nicht weit von uns [entfernt]; **in the immediate ~:** ganz in der Nähe; **in the ~ [of a place]** in der Nähe [eines Ortes]; **in the ~ of 50** (fig.) so um die 50 2 *no pl.* (nearness) Nähe, *die;* **in close ~ to the church** ganz in der Nähe der Kirche

vicious /'vɪʃəs/ *adj.* 1 (malicious, spiteful) böse; boshaft ‹*Äußerung*›; böswillig ‹*Versuch, Kritik*›; bösartig ‹*Äußerung, Tier*› 2 (depraved) übel ‹*Benehmen, Charakter*›; (addicted to vice) verdorben; (wicked) skrupellos ‹*Tyrann, Verbrecher*›; schlecht ‹*Person, Menschheit*› 3 (violent, severe) brutal; unerträglich ‹*Wetter, Schmerz*›

vicious 'circle *n.* Teufelskreis, *der*

viciously /'vɪʃəslɪ/ *adv.* 1 (maliciously, spitefully) boshaft; auf gehässige Weise ‹*kritisieren*› 2 (violently, severely) brutal

viciousness /'vɪʃəsnɪs/ *n., no pl.* 1 (maliciousness, spitefulness) Boshaftigkeit, *die;* (of animal) Bösartigkeit, *die* 2 (depravity) Lasterhaftigkeit, *die;* (of tyrant, criminal, government) Skrupellosigkeit, *die* 3 (violence, severity) Brutalität, *die;* (of weather, pain) Unerträglichkeit, *die*

vicious 'spiral *n.* Teufelskreis, *der;* **the ~ of wage increases and price rises** die Lohn-Preis-Spirale

vicissitude /vɪ'sɪsɪtjuːd/ *n.* steter Wandel; **~s** (fickleness) Unbeständigkeit, *die;* **the ~s of life** die Wechselfälle des Lebens

victim /'vɪktɪm/ *n.* 1 Opfer, *das;* (of sarcasm, abuse) Zielscheibe, *die* (fig.); **be the ~ of sb.'s anger/envy/policy** unter jmds. Zorn/Neid/Politik (*Dat.*) zu leiden haben; **be a ~ of fortune** dem Schicksal ausgeliefert sein; **fall [a] ~ to sth.** das Opfer einer Sache (*Gen.*) werden; **fall ~ to the plague/to drought/famine** der Pest/Trockenheit/Hungersnot (*Dat.*) zum Opfer fallen; **fall a ~ to love/sb.'s charms** sein Herz verlieren/jmds. Charme (*Dat.*) erliegen 2 (dupe) Opfer, *das;* **I refuse to be made his ~:** ich lasse mich von ihm nicht täuschen 3 (Relig.) Opfer, *das;* (animal) Opfertier, *das;* **human sacrificial ~s** Menschenopfer

victimisation, victimise ▸ **victimiz-**

victimization /vɪktɪmaɪ'zeɪʃn/ *n.* Schikanierung, *die;* (selective punishment) gezielte Bestrafung

victimize /'vɪktɪmaɪz/ *v.t.* 1 (make a victim) schikanieren; **be ~d [by sb.]** unter jmdm. zu leiden haben 2 (punish selectively) gezielt bestrafen

victimless /'vɪktɪmlɪs/ *adj.* opferlos

victim sup'port *n., no pl.* Unterstützung von Kriminalitätsopfern; (organization) [Kriminalitäts]opferhilfe, *die; attrib.* **~ workers** Mitarbeiter der [Kriminalitäts]opferhilfe

victor /'vɪktə(r)/ *n.* Sieger, *der*/Siegerin, *die*

victoria *n.* **~ [plum]** Königin-Viktoria-Pflaume, *die*

Victoria /vɪk'tɔːrɪə/ *pr. n.* 1 (Hist., as name of ruler etc.) Viktoria (*die*) 2 (Geog.) Victoria (*das*)

Victoria: ~ 'Cross *n.* (Brit.) Viktoriakreuz, *das;* **~ 'Falls** *n. pl.* Victoriafälle *Pl.*

Victorian /vɪk'tɔːrɪən/

A *adj.* viktorianisch

B *n.* Viktorianer, *der*/Viktorianerin, *die*

Victoriana /vɪktɔːrɪ'ɑːnə/ *n. pl.* viktorianische Antiquitäten

victorious /vɪk'tɔːrɪəs/ *adj.* 1 siegreich; **be ~ over sb./sth.** jmdn./etw. besiegen; **be ~ in one's struggle** aus seinem Kampf siegreich hervorgehen 2 (marked by victory) erfolgreich ‹*Verteidigung, Kreuzzug*›; siegreich ‹*Feldzug, Eroberung, Angriff*›; triumphierend ‹*Gruß, Lächeln*›

victoriously /vɪk'tɔːrɪəslɪ/ *adv.* erfolgreich; siegreich ‹*kämpfen, zurückkehren*›; triumphierend ‹*rufen, lächeln, marschieren*›

victory /'vɪktərɪ/ *n.* Sieg, *der* (**over** über + *Akk.*); *attrib.* Sieges-; **achieve ~:** den Sieg erringen; **be sure of ~:** der sichere Sieger sein; **lead one's troops to ~:** seine Truppen zum Sieg führen; **~ will be ours** der Sieg wird unser sein; **gain** *or* **win a ~ over sb./sth.** einen Sieg über jmdn./etw. erringen; *see also* **moral victory; Pyrrhic**

victory: ~ parade *n.* Siegesparade, *die;* (fig.) Triumphfahrt, *die;* **~ 'roll** *n.* Siegesrolle, *die;* **~ sign** *n.* Victoryzeichen, *das;* Siegeszeichen, *das;* **give the ~ sign** das Victoryzeichen *od.* Siegeszeichen machen

victual /'vɪtl/ (formal/joc.)

A *n. in pl.* Esswaren *Pl.;* (of fort, ship, for journey) Proviant, *der*

B *v.t.,* (Brit.) **-ll-** verproviantieren

victualler /'vɪtələ(r)/ *n.* ▸ p. 1260 **licensed ~** (Brit.) Gastwirt, *der*/-wirtin, *die*

vide /'vɪdeɪ, 'viːdeɪ/ *v.t. imper.* siehe

video /'vɪdɪəʊ/

A *adj.* Video‹*rekorder, -kassette, -kopf*›

B *n., pl.* **~s** 1 (~ recorder) Videorekorder, *der;* (~ film, ~tape, ~ recording) Video, *das* (ugs.); **have sth. on ~:** etw. auf Video haben (ugs.) 2 (visual element of TV broadcasts) Bild, *das*

C *v.t.* ▸ **videotape B**

video: ~ art *n., no pl.* Videokunst, *die;* **~ artist** *n.* Videokünstler, *der*/-künstlerin, *die;* **~ camera** *n.* Videokamera, *die;* **~ card** *n.* (Computing) Videokarte, *die;* **~ cassette** *n.* Videokassette, *die;* **~ cas'sette recorder** *n.* Videokassettenrekorder, *der;* **~ clip** *n.* Videoclip, *der;* **~conference** *n.* Videokonferenz, *die;* **~conferencing** /'vɪdɪəʊkɒnfərənsɪŋ/ *n., no pl.* Abhalten einer Videokonferenz/von Videokonferenzen; **~ diary** *n.* Videotagebuch, *das;* **~ disc** *n.* Bild-

V

od. Videoplatte, *die;* ~ **film** *n.* Videofilm, *der;* ~ **frequency** *n.* Videofrequenz, *die;* ~ **game** *n.* Videospiel, *das;* ~**gram** /ˈvɪdɪəʊɡræm/ *n.: bespielte Videokassette od. -platte, die keine private Kopie und kein Fernsehmitschnitt ist;* ~ **hire** *n.* Videoverleih, *der;* ~ **jock** *n.* (coll.) ▸ **video jockey**; ~ **jockey** *n.* Videojockey, *der*/Videojockei, *der;* ~ **library** *n.* Videothek, *die;* ~ **machine** *n.* Videogerät, *das;* ~ **ˈnasty** *n.* Horrorvideo, *das;* ~**-on-demand** *n., no pl.* Video-on-Demand, *das;* ~**phone** *n.* Bildtelefon, *das;* Videofon, *das;* ~ **ˈpiracy** *n., no pl.* Videopiraterie, *die;* ~ **player** *n.* Video-Player, *der;* Videoabspielgerät, *das;* ~ **recorder** *n.* Videorekorder, *der;* ~ **recording** *n.* Videoaufnahme, *die;* ~ **shop** (esp. Brit.), ~ **store** *ns.* Videothek, *die;* Videoladen, *der;* ~ **signal** *n.* Videosignal, *das;* ~ **surveillance** *n., no pl.* Videoüberwachung, *die;* **be under** ~ **surveillance** videoüberwacht werden *od.* sein; **keep sb. under constant** ~ **surveillance** jmdn. ständig per Video[kamera] überwachen; *attrib.* ~ **surveillance camera** Videoüberwachungskamera, *die;* ~**tape** **A** *n.* Videoband, *das.* **B** *v.t.* [auf Videoband (*Akk.*)] aufnehmen; ~ **telephone** *n.* Bildtelefon, *das;* ~**tex** /ˈvɪdɪəʊteks/, ~**text** *n.* Bildschirmtext, *der;* (teletext) Videotext, *der*

vie /vaɪ/ *v.i.*, **vying** /ˈvaɪɪŋ/ ~ **[with sb.] for sth.** [mit jmdm.] um etw. wetteifern; ~ **with sb. in sth.** jmdn. mit etw. zu übertreffen suchen

Vienna /vɪˈenə/ ▸ **i** **p. 1643**
A *pr. n.* Wien (*das*)
B *attrib. adj.* Wiener

Viennese /vɪəˈniːz/ ▸ **i** **p. 1643**
A *adj.* Wiener; **sb. is** ~: jmd. ist Wiener/Wienerin
B *n., pl. same* Wiener, *der*/Wienerin, *die*

Vietnam /vɪetˈnæm/ *pr. n.* **1** Vietnam (*das*) **2** ~ **[War]** Vietnamkrieg, *der*

Vietnamese /vɪetnəˈmiːz/ ▸ **i** **p. 1277, ▸ i p. 1345**
A *adj.* vietnamesisch
B *n., pl. same* **1** (person) Vietnamese, *der*/Vietnamesin, *die* **2** (language) Vietnamesisch, *das*

view /vjuː/
A *n.* **1** (range of vision) Sicht, *die;* **get a good** ~ **of sth.** etw. gut sehen können; **have** *or* **get one's first** ~ **of sth.** etw. zum ersten Mal zu sehen bekommen; **have a clear/distant** ~ **of sth.** etw. deutlich/in der Ferne sehen können; **be out of/in** ~: nicht zu sehen/zu sehen sein; **come into** ~: in Sicht kommen; **be lost to** ~: nicht mehr zu sehen sein; **disappear from** ~: verschwinden; **leave the back exposed to [the]** ~ ‹*Kleid:*› den Rücken freilassen; **our hotel has a good** ~ **of the sea** von unserem Hotel aus kann man das Meer gut sehen; **in full** ~ **of everyone in the street** vor den Augen aller Passanten; *see also* **full¹ A 4**; **hide¹ A 3** **2** (what is seen) Aussicht, *die;* **the** ~**s from here** die Aussicht von hier; **a house with fine** ~**s** ein Haus mit schöner Aussicht; **a room with a** ~: ein Zimmer mit Aussicht; **just for the** ~/~**s** nur um die Aussicht zu genießen **3** (picture) Ansicht, *die;* **photographic** ~: Foto, *das;* **take a** ~ **of sth.** ein Bild von etw. machen **4** (opinion) Ansicht, *die;* **what is your** ~ *or* **are your** ~**s on this?** was meinst du dazu?; **what is your** ~ **of him?** was hältst du von ihm?; **be grateful for sb.'s** ~ **of** *or* ~**s on sth.** jmdm. für eine Stellungnahme zu etw. dankbar sein; **don't you have any** ~**[s] about it?** hast du keine Meinung dazu?; **the** ~**s of the public** die öffentliche Meinung; **the general/majority** ~ **is that ...:** die Allgemeinheit/Mehrheit ist der Ansicht, dass ...; **take a favourable** ~ **of sth.** etw. billigen; **have** *or* **hold** ~**s about** *or* **on sth.** eine Meinung über etw. (*Akk.*) haben; **hold** *or* **take the** ~ **that ...:** der Ansicht sein, dass ...; **in my** ~: meiner Ansicht nach; **in sb.'s** ~: nach jmds. Ansicht; **I take a different** ~: ich bin anderer Ansicht; **take a critical/grave/optimistic** ~ **of sth.** etw. kritisch/ernst/optimistisch beurteilen; *see also* **dim A 5**; **long¹ A 1**; **poor A 9** **5** **be on** ~ ‹*Waren, Haus:*› besichtigt werden können; ‹*Bauplan:*› [zur Einsicht] ausliegen; (in an exhibition) ausgestellt sein; **have sth. in** ~ (fig.) etw. im Auge haben; **in** ~ **of sth.** (fig.) angesichts einer Sache; **keep sth. in** ~ (fig.) etw. im Auge behalten; **with a** ~ **to** *or* **with a** *or* **the** ~ **of doing sth.** in der Absicht, etw. zu tun; **with a** ~ **to sth.** (fig.) mit etw. im Auge; **with this in** ~: im Hinblick darauf; *see also* **point A 11** **6** (survey) Betrachtung, *die;* (of house, site) Besichtigung, *die;* **on taking a closer** ~: bei näherer Betrachtung; **if we take a broad** *or* **general** ~ **of the problem** bei allgemeiner Betrachtung des Problems; **give a** ~ **of sth.** ‹*Buch:*› einen Überblick über etw. (*Akk.*) geben; *see also* **private view[ing]**
B *v.t.* **1** (look at) sich (*Dat.*) ansehen **2** (consider) betrachten; beurteilen ‹*Situation, Problem*›; ~**ed in this light ...:** so gesehen ...; ~**ed ethically** aus ethischer Sicht; **I** ~ **the matter differently** ich sehe das anders **3** (inspect) besichtigen; **ask to** ~ **sth.** darum bitten, etw. besichtigen zu dürfen
C *v.i.* (Telev.) fernsehen

viewdata /ˈvjuːdeɪtə/ *n.* (Teleph.) Bildschirmtextsystem, *das*

viewer /ˈvjuːə(r)/ *n.* **1** (Telev.) [Fernseh]zuschauer, *der*/-zuschauerin, *die* **2** (Photog.) (for cine film) Filmbetrachter, *der;* (for slides) Diabetrachter, *der*

ˈviewfinder *n.* (Photog.) Sucher, *der*

viewing /ˈvjuːɪŋ/ *n.* **1** (Telev.) Fernsehen, *das;* ~ **has decreased** der Fernsehkonsum ist zurückgegangen; ~ **figures** Einschaltquoten; **at peak** ~ **time** zur besten Sendezeit **2** (of house, at auction, etc.) Besichtigung, *die; see also* **private view[ing]**

viewpoint /ˈvjuːpɔɪnt/ *n.* Standpunkt, *der;* Sehweise, *die;* **from a general/the political/the social** ~ **...:** allgemein/politisch/gesellschaftlich gesehen *od.* betrachtet, ...; **seen from that** ~ **...:** so gesehen *od.* betrachtet, ...; **see sth. from sb.'s** ~: etw. aus jmds. Sicht sehen

vigil /ˈvɪdʒɪl/ *n.* **1** Wachen, *das;* **nocturnal** ~: Nachtwache, *die;* **keep** ~ **[over sb.]** [bei jmdm.] wachen **2** (Relig.) Vigil, *die*

vigilance /ˈvɪdʒɪləns/ *n., no pl.* Wachsamkeit, *die;* **exercise** ~ **lest sb. escape** wachsam sein, damit jmd. nicht entkommt; **escape sb.'s** ~: jmds. Wachsamkeit (*Dat.*) entgehen; jmdm. entgehen

ˈvigilance committee *n.* (Amer.) Bürgerwehr, *die*

vigilant /ˈvɪdʒɪlənt/ *adj.* wachsam; **be** ~ **for sth.** auf etw. (*Akk.*) achten

vigilante /vɪdʒɪˈlæntɪ/ *n.* Mitglied einer/der Bürgerwehr; ~ **group** Bürgerwehr, *die*

vigilantly /ˈvɪdʒɪləntlɪ/ *adv.* wachsam

vignette /viːˈnjet/ *n.* **1** (Lit.) Skizze, *die* **2** (Art, Photog.) vignettiertes Bild

vigor (Amer.) ▸ **vigour**

vigorous /ˈvɪɡərəs/ *adj.* kraftvoll; kräftig ‹*Person, Tier, Stoß, Pflanze, Wachstum, Trieb*›; robust ‹*Gesundheit*›; leidenschaftlich ‹*Debattierer, Debatte, Verteidigung, Befürworter*›; heftig ‹*Nicken, Attacke, Kritik, Protest*›; intensiv ‹*Gymnastik, Denksport*›; energisch ‹*Versuch, Anstrengung, Leugnen, Maßnahme*›; schwungvoll ‹*Rede*›; **be too** ~ **for sb.** ‹*Gymnastik:*› zu anstrengend für jmdn. sein

vigorously /ˈvɪɡərəslɪ/ *adv.* heftig; leidenschaftlich ‹*musizieren, reden, schreiben*›; intensiv ‹*Gymnastik treiben*›; energisch ‹*versuchen, beginnen*›; kräftig ‹*schrubben, reiben, ziehen, drücken, wachsen*›

vigour /ˈvɪɡə(r)/ *n.* (Brit.) **1** (of person, animal, sexuality) Vitalität, *die;* (of limbs, body) Kraft, *die;* (of health) Robustheit, *die;* (of debate, argument, struggle, protest, denial, attack, criticism) Heftigkeit, *die;* (of performance, speech) Schwung, *der;* (of words, style, mind, intellect) Lebendigkeit, *die;* **with** ~: schwungvoll ‹*musizieren, reden, singen, schauspielern*›; kräftig ‹*reiben, schrubben, drücken, ziehen*› **2** (Bot.) Wuchskraft, *die*

Viking /ˈvaɪkɪŋ/ *n.* (Hist.) Wikinger, *der*/Wikingerin, *die; attrib.* Wikinger-

vile /vaɪl/ *adj.* **1** (base) verwerflich (geh.); abscheulich ‹*Sünde, Charakter, Verbrechen*›; gemein ‹*Verleumdung*›; vulgär ‹*Sprache*›; (repulsive) widerwärtig; **don't be so** ~! sei nicht so gemein!; **be** ~ **to sb.** gemein zu jmdm. sein **2** (coll.: very unpleasant) scheußlich (ugs.)

vilely /ˈvaɪllɪ/ *adv.* **1** in verwerflicher Weise (geh.); **act/behave** ~: abscheulich handeln/gemein sein; **speak** ~ **of sb.** abscheuliche Dinge über jmdn. sagen **2** (coll.: very unpleasantly) scheußlich (ugs.)

vileness /ˈvaɪlnɪs/ *n., no pl.* ▸ **vile**: **1** Verwerflichkeit, *die* (geh.); Abscheulichkeit, *die;* Gemeinheit, *die;* Vulgarität, *die;* Widerwärtigkeit, *die* **2** Scheußlichkeit, *die* (ugs.)

vilification /vɪlɪfɪˈkeɪʃn/ *n.* Verunglimpfung, *die* (geh.)

vilify /ˈvɪlɪfaɪ/ *v.t.* verunglimpfen (geh.)

villa /ˈvɪlə/ *n.* **1** (holiday house) **[holiday]** ~: Ferienhaus, *das* **2** (country house) **[country]** ~: Landhaus, *das* **3** (Brit.: suburban house) *besseres Einfamilienhaus*

village /ˈvɪlɪdʒ/ *n.* Dorf, *das; attrib.* Dorf‹*leben, -kneipe usw.*›

village: ~ **ˈgreen** *n.* Dorfwiese, *die;* **village ˈhall** *n.* Dorfgemeinschaftshaus, *das;* ~ **ˈidiot** *n.* Dorftrottel, *der*

villager /ˈvɪlɪdʒə(r)/ *n.* Dorfbewohner, *der*/-bewohnerin, *die*

village ˈshop (esp. Brit.), **village ˈstore** *ns.* Dorfladen, *der*

villain /ˈvɪlən/ *n.* **1** (scoundrel) Verbrecher, *der;* **they're the real** ~**s** sie sind es, die die Schuld tragen **2** ~ **[of the piece]** (Theatre; also fig.) Bösewicht, *der* **3** (coll.: rascal) [kleiner] Halunke (scherzh.)

villainous /ˈvɪlənəs/ *adj.* **1** gemein; abscheulich **2** (coll.: very bad) scheußlich (ugs.)

villainously /ˈvɪlənəslɪ/ *adv.* gemein; abscheulich; in gemeiner *od.* abscheulicher Weise ‹*morden, Verrat üben, sich verschwören*›

villainy /ˈvɪlənɪ/ *n.* Gemeinheit, *die;* Abscheulichkeit, *die;* **forsake** ~: aller Gemeinheit abschwören

villein /ˈvɪlən/ *n.* (Hist.) Leibeigene, *der/die*

vim /vɪm/ *n., no pl.* (coll.) Schwung, *der;* **put some [more]** ~ **into it!** leg dich mal ein bisschen [mehr] ins Zeug! (ugs.)

vinaigrette /vɪnɪˈɡret/ *n.* ~ **[sauce]** (Cookery) Vinaigrette, *die*

vindicate /ˈvɪndɪkeɪt/ *v.t.* **1** (justify, establish) verteidigen, rechtfertigen ‹*Person, Meinung, Handeln, Verhalten, Anspruch, Politik*›; retten ‹*Ruf, Ehre, Stellung*›; beweisen ‹*Mut, Ehrlichkeit, Integrität, Behauptung*›; (confirm) bestätigen ‹*Recht, Meinung, Urteil, Theorie*› **2** (exonerate) rehabilitieren

vindication /vɪndɪˈkeɪʃn/ *n.* ▸ **vindicate**: **1** Verteidigung, *die;* Rechtfertigung, *die;* Rettung, *die;* Beweis, *der* (**of** für); Bestätigung, *die;* **be a** ~ **of sth.** etw. rechtfertigen/verteidigen/beweisen/bestätigen; **in** ~ **of his claim/conduct** *etc.* zur Rechtfertigung seines Anspruchs/Benehmens *usw.* **2** Rehabilitierung, *die;* **be a full** ~ **of sb.** jmdn. vollständig rehabilitieren

vindictive /vɪnˈdɪktɪv/ *adj.* nachtragend ‹*Person*›; unversöhnlich ‹*Stimmung*›; ~ **act/move/attack** Racheakt, *der* (geh.); **feel** ~ *or* **be in a** ~ **mood [towards sb.]** Rachegefühle [gegenüber jmdm.] hegen; **make sb. [feel]** ~: Rachegefühle bei jmdm. wecken; **be purely** ~ ‹*Tat:*› ein reiner Racheakt sein

vindictively /vɪnˈdɪktɪvlɪ/ *adv.* aus Rache; **act** *or* **behave** ~ **[towards sb.]** sich nachtragend [gegenüber jmdm.] verhalten

vindictiveness /vɪnˈdɪktɪvnɪs/ *n., no pl.* Rachsucht, *die* (geh.); **the** ~ **of sb.'s nature/mood** jmds. nachtragendes Wesen/jmds. Rachsucht; **feel** ~ **towards sb.** Rachegefühle gegen jmdn. hegen; **an attitude of** ~: eine nachtragende Haltung

vine /vaɪn/ *n.* **1** Weinrebe, *die* **2** (stem of trailer or climber) Ranke, *die* **3** (Amer.: trailing or climbing plant) Rankengewächs, *das*

vinegar /ˈvɪnɪɡə(r)/ *n.* Essig, *der;* **[as] sour as** ~: sehr sauer; (fig.) säuerlich ‹*Miene, Lächeln*›; sauertöpfisch (ugs.) ‹*Person*›

vinegary /ˈvɪnɪɡərɪ/ *adj.* sauer; (fig.) säuerlich; **have a ~ taste** wie Essig schmecken

ˈ**vine leaf** *n.* [Wein]rebenblatt, *das;* **stuffed vine leaves** (Gastr.) gefüllte Weinblätter

vineyard /ˈvɪnjɑːd, ˈvɪnjəd/ *n.* Weinberg, *der*

viniculture /ˈvɪnɪkʌltʃə(r)/ *n., no pl.* Weinbau, *der*

vinification /vɪnɪfɪˈkeɪʃn/ *n.* Gärungsprozess, *der (bei der Weinproduktion)*

vino /ˈviːnəʊ/ *n.* (coll.) [billiger] Wein

vintage /ˈvɪntɪdʒ/

A *n.* **1** (season's wine) Jahrgang, *der;* (season's grapes) Traubenernte, *die;* **last/this year's ~:** der letzte/dieser Jahrgang; **the 1981 ~/a 1983 ~:** der 81er/ein 83er **2** (fig.: particular period) Jahrgang, *der;* (of car, machine) Baujahr, *das;* **a car of rather ancient ~/1955 ~:** ein Auto ziemlich alten Datums/Baujahr 1955; **music of '60s/1940s ~:** Musik aus den 60ern/40er-Jahren; **of modern ~:** neueren Datums **3** (grape harvest; season) Weinlese, *die* **4** (quality wine) erlesener Wein

B *adj.* erlesen ‹*Wein, Sekt, Whisky*›; herrlich ‹*Komödie, Melodie*›; brillant ‹*Leistung, Interpretation*›; **this year has been a ~ year for port** dieses Jahr war ein gutes Jahr für Portwein; **this play is ~ Pinter** dies ist eines der typischsten und besten Pinter-Stücke

vintage ˈ**car** *n.* (Brit.) [zwischen 1917 und 1930 gebauter] Oldtimer

vintner /ˈvɪntnə(r)/ *n.* ▸ⓘ **p. 1260** Weinhändler, *der*/-händlerin, *die*

vinyl /ˈvaɪnɪl/ *n.* **1** Vinyl, *das* **2** (polyvinyl chloride) PVC, *das*

viol /ˈvaɪəl/ *n.* (Mus.) Viola, *die*

viola[1] /vɪˈəʊlə/ *n.* (Mus.) Bratsche, *die;* **~ player** Bratschist, *der*/Bratschistin, *die*

viola[2] /ˈvaɪələ/ *n.* (Bot.) **1** Veilchen, *das* **2** (hybrid) Stiefmütterchen, *das*

viola da gamba /vɪəʊlə də ˈɡæmbə/ *n.* (Mus.) Gambe, *die*

violate /ˈvaɪəleɪt/ *v.t.* **1** verletzen; brechen ‹*Vertrag, Versprechen, Gesetz*›; verstoßen gegen ‹*Regel, Vorschrift, Prinzipien, Bestimmungen*›; verletzen ‹*Vorschrift*›; stören ‹*Ruhe, Frieden*›; verschandeln ‹*Wälder, Landschaft*› **2** (profane) schänden; entheiligen ‹*Sabbat*› **3** (rape) vergewaltigen; schänden (veralt.)

violation /vaɪəˈleɪʃn/ *n.* ▸ **violate**: **1** Verletzung, *die;* Bruch, *der;* Verstoß, *der* (**of** gegen); Störung, *die;* Verschandelung, *die;* **traffic ~:** Verkehrsdelikt, *das;* **be/act in ~ of** verletzen/verstoßen gegen; **do sth. in ~ of one's promise/oath** etw. entgegen seinem Versprechen/Eid tun; **they tested nuclear weapons in ~ of the treaty** sie testeten Atomwaffen, obwohl sie damit gegen den Vertrag verstießen **2** Schändung, *die;* Entheiligung, *die* **3** Vergewaltigung, *die;* Schändung, *die* (veralt.)

violence /ˈvaɪələns/ *n., no pl.* **1** (intensity, force) Heftigkeit, *die;* (of blow, waterfall) Wucht, *die;* (of temper) Ungestüm, *das;* (of contrast) Krassheit, *die* **2** (brutality) Gewalt, *die;* (at public event) Gewalttätigkeiten; **psychological ~:** seelische Grausamkeit; **by** *or* **with ~:** mit Gewalt; **a man of ~:** ein Mann der Gewalt; **resort to** *or* **use ~:** Gewalt anwenden; **commit ~:** Gewalttaten verüben; **do ~ to sth.** (fig.) einer Sache (*Dat.*) Gewalt antun **3** (Law) Gewalt, *die;* **threaten sb. with ~:** jmdm. Gewalt androhen; **threat of ~:** Gewaltandrohung, *die;* **act/crime of ~:** Gewalttat, *die*/Gewaltverbrechen, *das;* **robbery with ~:** [bewaffneter] Raubüberfall

violent /ˈvaɪələnt/ *adj.* gewalttätig; heftig ‹*Schlag, Attacke, Leidenschaft, Auseinandersetzung, Erschütterung, Reaktion, Abneigung, Schmerzen, Wind*›; wuchtig ‹*Schlag, Stoß*›; schwer ‹*Schock*›; krass ‹*Gegensatz, Kontrast*›; grell ‹*Farbe*›; knall‹*rot, -grün usw.*›; Gewalt‹*verbrecher, -tat*›; gnadenlos ‹*Hitze*›; **don't be so ~:** sei nicht so aggressiv; **he has a ~ temper, his character** *or* **temper is ~:** er neigt zum Jähzorn; **by ~ means** gewaltsam ‹*öffnen*›; unter Gewaltanwendung ‹*jmdn. überreden*›; **~ death** gewaltsamer *od.* unnatürlicher Tod

violently /ˈvaɪələntlɪ/ *adv.* (by means of violence) brutal; (with great vigour, intensity) heftig; (to a high degree) völlig ‹*verstört*›; äußerst ‹*schmerzhaft, verstört, aufgeregt*›; absolut ‹*gegensätzlich*›; **live/die ~:** ein gewalttätiges Leben führen/eines gewaltsamen Todes sterben; **discourage sb. from acting/behaving ~:** jmdn. von Gewalttätigkeiten abhalten; **I dislike him ~:** er ist mir äußerst zuwider; **I was ~ ill** ich musste mich heftig übergeben; **contrast ~:** in eklatantem Widerspruch stehen (**with** zu); **the colours clash ~:** die Farben passen überhaupt nicht zusammen

violet /ˈvaɪələt/

A *n.* **1** Veilchen, *das;* **sweet ~:** Märzveilchen, *das;* Wohlriechendes Veilchen (Bot.); **shrinking ~** (fig.) schüchternes Pflänzchen (ugs.); **don't be such a shrinking ~:** sei kein Angsthase **2** (colour) Violett, *das;* **dressed in ~:** violett gekleidet

B *adj.* violett

violin /vaɪəˈlɪn/ *n.* (Mus.) Violine, *die*

violin: ~ case *n.* Geigenkasten, *der;* **~ concerto** *n.* Violinkonzert, *das*

violinist /vaɪəˈlɪnɪst/ *n.* ▸ⓘ **p. 1260** (Mus.) Geiger, *der*/Geigerin, *die*

violin: ~-maker *n.* Geigenbauer, *der*/-bauerin, *die;* **~ player** *n.* Geiger, *der*/Geigerin, *die;* **~ sonata** *n.* Violinsonate, *die;* **~ teacher** *n.* Geigenlehrer, *der*/-lehrerin, *die*

violoncello /vaɪələnˈtʃeləʊ/ *n., pl.* **~s** (Mus. formal) Violoncello, *das*

VIP /viːaɪˈpiː/ *n.* Prominente, *der/die;* **the ~s** die Prominenz

viper /ˈvaɪpə(r)/ *n.* **1** (Zool.) Viper, *die;* **common ~:** Kreuzotter, *die* **2** (fig.) Schlange, *die* (abwertend); **nourish** *or* **nurse a ~ in one's bosom** eine Schlange am Busen nähren (geh.)

viperish /ˈvaɪpərɪʃ/ *adj.* (fig.) giftig ‹*Blick*›; scharf ‹*Zunge*›; gehässig ‹*Mundwerk, Ausdrucksweise*›; niederträchtig ‹*Angriff, Charakter*›; Schmäh‹*rede, -wort*›

VIP: ~ lounge *n.* VIP-Halle, *die;* **~ treatment** *n.* Vorzugsbehandlung, *die;* **give sb. ~ treatment** jmdn. mit allen Ehren behandeln

virago /vɪˈrɑːɡəʊ/ *n., pl.* **~s** zänkisches Weib (abwertend); Xanthippe, *die* (abwertend)

viral /ˈvaɪərl/ *adj.* (Med.) Virus-

viral: ~ infection *n.* (Med.) Virusinfektion, *die;* **~** ˈ**marketing** *n., no pl.* virales Marketing

Virgil /ˈvɜːdʒɪl/ *pr. n.* Vergil (*der*)

virgin /ˈvɜːdʒɪn/

A *n.* **1** Jungfrau, *die;* **she/he is still a ~:** sie ist noch Jungfrau/er ist noch unschuldig **2** **the [Blessed] V~ [Mary]** (Relig.) die [Heilige] Jungfrau [Maria] **3** (Astrol.) **the V~:** die Jungfrau; *see also* **archer 2**

B *adj.* **1** (chaste) jungfräulich **2** (untouched, unspoiled) unberührt ‹*Land, Wälder*›; jungfräulich ‹*Schnee*›; makellos ‹*Weiß*›; **~ soil** (esp. fig.) unberührter Boden **3** **~ olive oil** natives Olivenöl

virginal /ˈvɜːdʒɪnl/

A *adj.* jungfräulich

B *n. in pl.* (Mus. Hist.) Spinett, *das*

virgin ˈ**birth** *n.* **1** (Biol.) Jungfernzeugung, *die* **2** (Relig.) jungfräuliche Geburt

Virginia /vəˈdʒɪnɪə/

A *pr. n.* Virginia (*das*)

B *n.* **~ [tobacco]** Virginia[tabak], *der;* **~ cigarettes** Virginiazigaretten

Virginia ˈ**creeper** *n.* (Bot.) Wilder Wein

Virginian /vəˈdʒɪnɪən/

A *adj.* virginisch; Virginier-

B *n.* Virginier, *der*/Virginierin, *die*

Virgin ˈ**Islands** *pr. n. pl.* Jungferninseln *Pl.*

virginity /vəˈdʒɪnɪtɪ/ *n.* Unschuld, *die;* (of girl also) Jungfräulichkeit, *die*

Virgo /ˈvɜːɡəʊ/ *n., pl.* **~s** (Astrol., Astron.) die Jungfrau; die Virgo; *see also* **Aries**

Virgoan /ˈvɜːɡəʊən/ *n.* (Astrol.) Jungfrau, *die*

virile /ˈvɪraɪl/ *adj.* **1** (masculine) männlich; maskulin (geh.) **2** (sexually potent) viril **3** (fig.: forceful, vigorous) kraftvoll

virility /vɪˈrɪlɪtɪ/ *n.* **1** Männlichkeit, *die* **2** (sexual potency) Virilität, *die;* Manneskraft, *die* **3** (fig.) kraftvoller Schwung

virologist /vaɪəˈrɒlədʒɪst/ *n.* ▸ⓘ **p. 1260** Virologe, *der*/Virologin, *die*

virology /vaɪəˈrɒlədʒɪ/ *n.* Virologie, *die*

virtual /ˈvɜːtjʊəl/ *adj.* **1** **a ~ ...:** so gut wie ein/eine ...; praktisch ein/eine ... (ugs.); **he is the ~ head of the business** er ist quasi der Chef des Geschäfts (ugs.); **the whole day was a ~ disaster** der ganze Tag war eher eine Katastrophe; **the traffic came to a ~ standstill** der Verkehr kam praktisch zum Stillstand (ugs.) **2** (Computing, Optics, Mech.) virtuell ‹*Bild, Verrückung*›

virtual ˈ**campus** *n.* virtueller Campus

virtually /ˈvɜːtjʊəlɪ/ *adv.* so gut wie; praktisch (ugs.)

virtual: ~ ˈ**memory** *n., no pl.* (Computing) virtueller Speicher; **~** ˈ**office** *n.* virtuelles Büro; **~** ˈ**pet** *n.* virtuelles Haustier; **~ re**ˈ**ality** *n.* virtuelle Realität

virtue /ˈvɜːtjuː/ *n.* **1** (moral excellence) Tugend, *die;* (chastity) Rechtschaffenheit, *die;* **~ is its own reward** (prov.) die Tugend trägt ihren Lohn in sich selbst; *see also* **easy A 3** **2** (advantage) Vorteil, *der;* Vorzug, *der;* **what is the ~ in that?** welchen Vorteil hat das?; **there's no ~ in doing that** es bringt keinen Vorteil, das zu tun **3** **by ~ of** aufgrund (+ *Gen.*). *see also* **necessity 1**

virtuosity /vɜːtjʊˈɒsɪtɪ/ *n., no pl.* Virtuosität, *die;* **perform with ~:** virtuos spielen

virtuoso /vɜːtjʊˈəʊzəʊ/ *n., pl.* **virtuosi** /vɜːtjʊˈəʊziː/ *or* **~s** Virtuose, *der*/Virtuosin, *die; attrib.* virtuos ‹*Spiel, Aufführung*›; **a ~ performer** ein Virtuose/eine Virtuosin

virtuous /ˈvɜːtjʊəs/ *adj.* **1** (possessing moral rectitude) rechtschaffen ‹*Person*›; brav ‹*Kind*›; tugendhaft ‹*Leben*›; **if you're feeling ~ you can ...** (iron.) wenn du etwas Gutes tun willst, kannst du ...; **that was ~ of you** (iron.) das war wirklich löblich (iron.) **2** (chaste) keusch

virtuously /ˈvɜːtjʊəslɪ/ *adv.* löblicherweise; **live ~:** ein rechtschaffenes Leben führen; **we ~ went to bed at ten** (joc.) wir sind brav um zehn ins Bett gegangen

virtuousness /ˈvɜːtjʊəsnɪs/ *n., no pl.* (of person) Rechtschaffenheit, *die;* (of action, life) Tugendhaftigkeit, *die*

virulence /ˈvɪrʊləns, ˈvɪrjʊləns/ *n., no pl.* **1** (Med.) Virulenz, *die;* (of poison) starke Wirkung **2** (fig.: malignancy) Bosheit, *die;* (intensity) Heftigkeit, *die;* (of attack) Schärfe, *die*

virulent /ˈvɪrʊlənt, ˈvɪrjʊlənt/ *adj.* **1** (Med.) virulent; stark wirkend ‹*Gift*› **2** (fig.: malignant) heftig; scharf ‹*Angriff*›

virulently /ˈvɪrʊləntlɪ, ˈvɪrjʊləntlɪ/ *adv.* heftig; scharf ‹*kritisieren, angreifen*›; **be ~ anti-liberal** ein erbitterter Gegner/eine erbitterte Gegnerin des Liberalismus sein

virus /ˈvaɪərəs/ *n.* **1** ▸ⓘ **p. 1231** (Biol.) Virus, *das; attrib.* **a ~ infection** eine Virusinfektion **2** (Computing) [Computer]virus, *das od. der*

virus: ~ checker *n.* (Computing) Antivirenprogramm, *das;* **~ protection** *n., no pl.* (Computing) Virenschutz, *der;* **~ scanner** *n.* (Computing) Virusscanner, *der*

visa /ˈviːzə/ *n.* Visum, *das;* **student/tourist ~:** Studenten-/Touristenvisum, *das*

visage /ˈvɪzɪdʒ/ *n.* (literary) Antlitz, *das* (geh.); (ugly) Fratze, *die*

vis-à-vis /viːzɑːˈviː/

A *prep.* **1** (in relation to) bezüglich (+ *Gen.*) **2** (facing) gegenüber **3** (compared with) im Vergleich zu

B *adv.* **stand ~:** sich (*Dat.*) gegenüberstehen

C *n., pl. same* **1** (person facing another) Gegenüber, *das;* Vis-à-Vis, *das* (veralt.) **2** (Amer.: social partner) Partner, *der*/Partnerin, *die*

viscera /ˈvɪsərə/ *n. pl.* (Anat.) Eingeweide

visceral /ˈvɪsərl/ *adj.* (Anat.) Eingeweide-; (fig.: deep-seated) tief sitzend ‹*Angst*›; eingefleischt ‹*Vorurteil*›

viscid /ˈvɪsɪd/ *adj.* dickflüssig; sämig

viscose /ˈvɪskəʊz, ˈvɪskəʊs/ *n.* Viskose, *die*

viscosity /vɪsˈkɒsɪtɪ/ *n.* **1** *no pl.* (quality) Dickflüssigkeit, *die* **2** (Phys.: of oil etc.) Viskosität, *die*

V

viscount /ˈvaɪkaʊnt/ *n.* ▸ⓘ **p. 1634** Viscount, *der*

viscountcy /ˈvaɪkaʊntsɪ/ *n.* Viscountwürde, *die*

viscountess /ˈvaɪkaʊntɪs/ *n.* ▸ⓘ **p. 1634** Viscountess, *die*

viscous /ˈvɪskəs/ *adj.* dickflüssig; (Phys.) viskos

vise (Amer.) ▸**vice²**

visibility /vɪzɪˈbɪlɪtɪ/ *n., no pl.* [1] (being visible) Sichtbarkeit, *die* [2] (range of vision) Sicht, *die;* (Meteorol.) Sichtweite, *die;* **reduce ~ to ten metres** die Sichtweite auf zehn Meter verringern

visible /ˈvɪzɪbl/ *adj.* [1] (also Econ.) sichtbar; **be ~ to the naked eye** mit bloßem Auge erkennbar sein; **~ to observers in X** für Beobachter in X zu sehen; **highly ~** (fig.) unübersehbar [2] (apparent) erkennbar; **with ~ impatience** mit sichtlicher Ungeduld

visibly /ˈvɪzɪblɪ/ *adv.* sichtlich

Visigoth /ˈvɪzɪgɒθ/ *n.* (Hist.) Westgote, *der*/Westgotin, *die*

vision /ˈvɪʒn/ *n.* [1] (sight) Sehkraft, *die;* **[range of] ~:** Sichtweite, *die;* **[field of] ~:** Sehfeld, *das; see also* **line¹ A 3** [2] (dream) Vision, *die;* Gesicht, *das* (geh.); (person seen in dream) Phantom, *das;* **a ~ in white** (fig.) ein Traum in Weiß; **be a [real] ~:** traumhaft schön sein [3] *usu. pl.* (imaginings) Fantasien; Fantasiebilder; **have ~s of sth.** von etw. fantasieren; (more specific) sich (*Dat.*) etw. ausmalen; **have ~s of having to do sth.** kommen sehen, dass man etw. tun muss [4] (insight, foresight) Weitblick, *der;* **a man/woman of ~:** ein Mann/eine Frau mit Weitblick [5] (Telev.) Bild, *das;* **in sound and ~:** in Ton und Bild; **the programme will continue in ~ only until sound is restored** wegen vorübergehenden Tonausfalls z.z. nur Bildempfang

visionary /ˈvɪʒənərɪ/

A *adj.* [1] (imaginative) fantasievoll; (fanciful) fantastisch [2] (imagined) eingebildet; imaginär (geh.) [3] (seeing visions) visionär; **~ power** visionäre *od.* hellseherische Kraft

B *n.* Visionär, *der*/Visionärin, *die;* Hellseher, *der*/Hellseherin, *die* (auch fig.)

visit /ˈvɪzɪt/

A *v.t.* [1] besuchen; aufsuchen ‹*Arzt*›; **~ the sick** Krankenbesuche machen [2] (dated: afflict) heimsuchen; **be ~ed with sth.** von etw. heimgesucht werden [3] (Bibl.: inflict punishment for) **~ the sins of the fathers upon the children** der Väter Missetat an den Kindern heimsuchen

B *v.i.* [1] einen Besuch/Besuche machen; **be ~ing in a town** als Besucher in einer Stadt sein; **I'm only ~ing** ich bin nur zu Besuch; **spend the afternoon ~ing** nachmittags Besuche machen; **~ at a hotel** (Amer.) in einem Hotel absteigen; **be ~ing with sb.** (Amer.) bei jmdm. zu Besuch sein [2] (Amer.: chat) plaudern

C *n.* [1] Besuch, *der;* **pay** *or* **make a ~ to sb.** jmdm. einen Besuch abstatten; **pay a ~** (coll.: go to the toilet) aufs Klo gehen (ugs.); **she was in London on a ~ to some friends** sie war in London bei Freunden zu Besuch; **have** *or* **receive a ~ [from sb.]** [von jmdm.] besucht werden; **we shall be honoured to receive a ~ from you** es wird uns (*Dat.*) eine Ehre sein, Sie als Besucher zu empfangen; **we had a ~ from the police** wir hatten Besuch von der Polizei; **a ~ to a** *or* **the theatre/a museum** ein Theater-/Museumsbesuch; **a ~ to the British Museum** ein Besuch des Britischen Museums; **a ~ to Rome/the USA** ein Besuch *od.* Aufenthalt in Rom/in den USA; **I'm going on a two-day ~ to Athens** ich fahre für zwei Tage nach Athen; **a ~ to the dentist['s]** ein Besuch beim Zahnarzt; **a home ~ by the doctor [to sb.]** ein Hausbesuch des Arztes [bei jmdm.] [2] (Amer.: chat) Plauderei, *die*

visitation /vɪzɪˈteɪʃn/ *n.* [1] (official inspection by bishop etc.) Visitation, *die;* **a ~ of the sick** eine Krankenvisitation [2] (coll. joc.: protracted visit) Heimsuchung, *die* (ugs. scherzh.); **we had a ~ from the director today** der Direktor hat uns heute heimgesucht (ugs. scherzh.) [3] (dated: punishment) Heimsuchung, *die*

visiting /ˈvɪzɪtɪŋ/ *n.* Besuche *Pl.;* Besuchsdienst, *der;* **she does prison ~:** sie macht Gefängnisbesuche

visiting: ~ card *n.* Visitenkarte, *die* (auch fig.); **~ hours** *n. pl.* Besuchszeiten; **what are the ~ hours in this hospital?** wann ist in diesem Krankenhaus Besuchszeit?; **~ proˈfessor** *n.* Gastprofessor, *der*/-professorin, *die;* **~ team** *n.* (Sport) Gastmannschaft, *die*

visitor /ˈvɪzɪtə(r)/ *n.* [1] Besucher, *der*/Besucherin, *die;* (to hotel, beach, etc.) Gast, *der;* **have ~s/a ~:** Besuch haben; **we've got a ~ staying for a fortnight** wir haben für vierzehn Tage Besuch *od.* einen Gast; **the ~s** (Sport) die Gäste; *see also* **prison visitor** [2] (Ornith.) Zugvogel, *der;* **summer ~s** Sommergäste

ˈvisitors' book *n.* Gästebuch, *das;* **sign the ~:** sich ins Gästebuch eintragen

visor /ˈvaɪzə(r)/ *n.* [1] (of helmet) Visier, *das* [2] (eyeshade, peak of cap) Schirm, *der* [3] (Motor Veh.) **[sun] ~:** Blendschirm, *der*

vista /ˈvɪstə/ *n.* [1] (view) [Aus]blick, *der* (**of** auf + *Akk.*); (long, narrow view) Perspektive, *die* [2] (fig.) **open up new ~s** neue Perspektiven eröffnen

Vistula /ˈvɪstjʊlə/ *pr. n.* Weichsel, *die*

visual /ˈvɪzjʊəl, ˈvɪʒjʊəl/ *adj.* [1] (related to vision) Seh‹*nerv, -organ*›; **~ sense** Gesichtssinn, *der* [2] (attained by sight) visuell; optisch ‹*Eindruck, Darstellung*›; bildlich ‹*Vorstellungsvermögen*›; **the ~ arts** die bildenden und darstellenden Künste; **a ~ landing** (Aeronaut.) eine Sichtlandung; **~ display** (Computing) Sichtanzeige, *die*

visual: ~ aids *n. pl.* Anschauungsmaterial, *das;* **~ disˈplay unit** *n.* Bildschirmgerät, *das*

visualisation, visualise ▸**visualiz-**

visualization /vɪzjʊəlaɪˈzeɪʃn, vɪʒjʊəlaɪˈzeɪʃn/ *n.* (making visual) Veranschaulichung, *die;* (imagining) Sichvorstellen, *das*

visualize /ˈvɪzjʊəlaɪz, ˈvɪʒjʊəlaɪz/ *v.t.* [1] (imagine) sich (*Dat.*) vorstellen; **I can't ~ myself in retirement** ich als Rentner, das kann ich mir nicht vorstellen [2] (envisage, foresee) voraussehen; **I do not ~ many changes** ich rechne nicht mit großen Veränderungen

visually /ˈvɪzjʊəlɪ, ˈvɪʒjʊəlɪ/ *adv.* [1] (with regard to vision) optisch; bildnerisch ‹*begabt*› [2] (by visual means) bildlich; **record sth. ~:** etw. in Bildern festhalten

vital /ˈvaɪtl/

A *adj.* [1] (essential to life) lebenswichtig; **~ functions** Vitalfunktionen; **~ organs** lebenswichtige Organe [2] (essential) unbedingt notwendig; (crucial) entscheidend, ausschlaggebend ‹*Frage, Entschluss*› (**to** für); **it is of ~ importance** *or* **~ that you ...:** es ist von entscheidender Bedeutung, dass Sie ...; **is it ~ for you to go?** müssen Sie unbedingt gehen?; **your cooperation is ~ to** *or* **for the success of the plan** Ihre Mitarbeit ist unerlässlich für den Erfolg des Plans [3] (full of life) lebendig, kraftvoll ‹*Stil*›; vital ‹*Person*›

B *n. pl.* ▸**vital parts**

vitality /vaɪˈtælɪtɪ/ *n., no pl.* [1] (ability to sustain life) Lebenskraft, *die* [2] (liveliness) Vitalität, *die;* (of prose, style, language) Lebendigkeit, *die;* (energy) Energie, *die* [3] (fig.: of institution, organization, etc.) Dauerhaftigkeit, *die*

vitally /ˈvaɪtəlɪ/ *adv.* vital; **~ important** von allergrößter Wichtigkeit; (crucial) von entscheidender Bedeutung

vital: ~ ˈparts *n. pl.* **the ~ parts** (dated/joc.) die lebenswichtigen Organe; (genitals) die edlen Teile (scherzh.); **~ staˈtistics** *n. pl.* [1] (data) Bevölkerungsstatistik, *die;* [2] (coll.: woman's body measurements) Maße; **her ~ statistics are 34-26-34** sie hat die Maße 34/26/34

vitamin /ˈvɪtəmɪn, (Amer.) ˈvaɪtəmɪn/ *n.* Vitamin, *das;* **~ C** Vitamin C

vitamin: ~ deficiency *n.* Vitaminmangel, *der;* **~ pill** *n.* Vitamintablette, *die*

vitiate /ˈvɪʃɪeɪt/ *v.t.* [1] (impair quality of, corrupt) beeinträchtigen [2] (invalidate) zunichte machen; hinfällig machen ‹*Vereinbarung, Vertrag*›

viticulture /ˈvɪtɪkʌltʃə(r)/ *n.* Weinbau, *der*

vitreous /ˈvɪtrɪəs/ *adj.* [1] (glasslike) glasartig; **~ china** Halbporzellan, *das;* **~ enamel** Glasemail, *das* [2] (Anat.) **~ body** *or* **humour** Glaskörper, *der*

vitrification /vɪtrɪfɪˈkeɪʃn/ *n.* Fritten, *das*

vitrify /ˈvɪtrɪfaɪ/ *v.t. & i.* fritten

vitriol /ˈvɪtrɪəl/ *n.* [1] (Chem.) Vitriol, *das* [2] (fig.: virulence) ätzende Schärfe; (criticism/remarks) ätzende Kritik/Bemerkungen

vitriolic /vɪtrɪˈɒlɪk/ *adj.* ätzend; giftig ‹*Bemerkung*›; geharnischt ‹*Attacke, Rede*›

vituperate /vɪˈtjuːpəreɪt, vaɪˈtjuːpəreɪt/ *v.i.* (literary) wettern (**against** gegen)

vituperation /vɪtjuːpəˈreɪʃn, vaɪtjuːpəˈreɪʃn/ *n.* (literary) Schmähungen *Pl.* (geh.)

vituperative /vɪˈtjuːpərətɪv, vaɪˈtjuːpərətɪv/ *adj.* (literary) schmähend; **~ language** *or* **speech** Schmähreden; **~ attack on sb.** Schmährede/(written) Schmähschrift gegen jmdn.

viva /ˈvaɪvə/ (Brit. Univ.)

A *n.* Mündliche, *das* (ugs.)

B *v.t.* mündlich prüfen

vivacious /vɪˈveɪʃəs/ *adj.* lebhaft; lebendig ‹*Stil*›; munter ‹*Lachen, Lächeln*›; bunt ‹*Kleider*›

vivaciously /vɪˈveɪʃəslɪ/ *adv.* lebhaft; munter ‹*lächeln, lachen*›; bunt ‹*angezogen*›; lebendig ‹*schreiben*›

vivacity /vɪˈvæsɪtɪ/ *n., no pl.* Lebhaftigkeit, *die;* (of smile, laugh) Munterkeit, *die;* (of style) Lebendigkeit, *die*

vivarium /vaɪˈveərɪəm/ *n., pl.* **vivaria** /vaɪˈveərɪə/ Vivarium, *das*

viva voce /vaɪvə ˈvəʊtsɪ, vaɪvə ˈvəʊsɪ/ (Univ.)

A *adv., adj.* mündlich

B *n.* mündliche Prüfung; (doctoral) Rigorosum, *das*

vivid /ˈvɪvɪd/ *adj.* [1] (bright) strahlend ‹*Helligkeit*›; hell ‹*Blitz*›; lebhaft ‹*Farbe*› [2] (animated) lebhaft ‹*Person*› [3] (clear, lifelike) lebendig ‹*Schilderung, Romanfigur*›; lebhaft ‹*Fantasie, Erinnerung*› [4] (intense) heftig ‹*Schmerz*›; kraftvoll ‹*Töne*›

vividly /ˈvɪvɪdlɪ/ *adv.* [1] (brightly) hell; **a ~ coloured dress** ein Kleid in lebhaften Farben [2] (clearly) lebendig ‹*beschreiben*›; **remember sth. ~:** sich lebhaft an etw. (*Akk.*) erinnern

vividness /ˈvɪvɪdnɪs/ *n., no pl.* [1] (brightness) Helligkeit, *die* [2] (liveliness, realism) Lebhaftigkeit, *die;* (of description) Lebendigkeit, *die*

viviparous /vɪˈvɪpərəs, vaɪˈvɪpərəs/ *adj.* (Zool.) vivipar (fachspr.); lebend gebärend

vivisect /ˈvɪvɪsekt/ *v.t.* vivisezieren (fachspr.)

vivisection /vɪvɪˈsekʃn/ *n.* Vivisektion, *die* (fachspr.)

vivisectionist /vɪvɪˈsekʃənɪst/ *n.: jmd., der Vivisektionen durchführt/befürwortet*

vixen /ˈvɪksn/ *n.* [1] (Zool.) Füchsin, *die* [2] (fig.: woman) Drachen, *der* (ugs.)

viz /vɪz/ *adv.* d.h.

vizier /vɪˈzɪə(r), ˈvɪzɪə(r)/ *n.* Wesir, *der*

vizor ▸**visor**

ˈV-neck *n.* V-Ausschnitt, *der*

ˈV-necked *adj.* ‹*Pullover, Kleid*› mit V-Ausschnitt

vocabulary /vəˈkæbjʊlərɪ/ *n.* [1] (list) Vokabelverzeichnis, *das;* **learn ~:** Vokabeln lernen; *attrib.* **~ book** Vokabelheft, *das;* **~ test** Vokabeltest, *der* [2] (language of particular field) Vokabular, *das* [3] (range of language) Wortschatz, *der*

vocal /ˈvəʊkl/

A *adj.* [1] (concerned with voice) stimmlich; **a ~ organ** ein Stimmorgan [2] (expressing oneself freely) gesprächig; lautstark ‹*Minderheit, Gruppe, Protest*›; **he was very ~ about his rights** er sprach sehr viel von seinen Rechten

B *n.* (Mus.) Vokalpartie, *die;* Vocal, *das* (fachspr.)

ˈvocal cords *n. pl.* Stimmbänder

vocalic /vəˈkælɪk/ (Phonet.) *adj.* vokalreich

vocalise ▸**vocalize**

vocalist /ˈvəʊkəlɪst/ *n.* Sänger, *der*/Sängerin, *die* (*bei einer Band od. Combo*)

vocalize /ˈvəʊkəlaɪz/ *v.t. & i.* vokalisieren

vocal: ~ music *n.* Vokalmusik, *die;* **~ score** *n.* (Mus.) Vokalpartitur, *die*

ℹ Volume

Cubic measure

1 cubic inch (cu. in.)	= 16,4 cm³ (sechzehn Komma vier Kubikzentimeter)	
1,728 cubic inches	= ***1 cubic foot (cu. ft)***	= 0,03 m³ (null Komma null drei Kubikmeter)
27 cubic feet	= ***1 cubic yard (cu. yd)***	= 0,76 m³ (null Komma sieben sechs Kubikmeter)

Liquid measure

BRITISH:		
20 fluid ounces (fl. oz)	= ***1 pint (pt)***	= 0,57 l (null Komma fünf sieben Liter)
2 pints	= ***1 quart (qt)***	= 1,14 l (eins Komma eins vier Liter)
4 quarts	= ***1 gallon (gal.)***	= 4,55 l (vier Komma fünf fünf Liter)
AMERICAN:		
16 fluid ounces (fl. oz)	= ***1 pint (pt)***	= 0,47 l (null Komma vier sieben Liter)
2 pints	= ***1 quart (qt)***	= 0,94 l (null Komma neun vier Liter)
4 quarts	= ***1 US gallon (gal.)***	= 3,78 l (drei Komma sieben acht Liter)

What is its volume?
= Wie viel *or* Welches Volumen hat es?

Its volume is 200 cubic feet
≈ Es hat ein Volumen von 6 Kubikmetern

What is the capacity of the tank?, How much does the tank hold?
= Wie viel fasst der Tank?

The tank holds 10 UK / US gallons
≈ Der Tank fasst 45 Liter / 38 Liter

My car does 28 (UK) or 23 (US) miles per gallon (mpg)
≈ Mein Wagen verbraucht 10 Liter auf 100 Kilometer

In all Continental European countries fuel consumption is quoted in litres per 100 kilometres. To convert mpg to litres per 100 km divide the factor 280 (for British gallons) or 230 (for US gallons) by the mpg figure.

The two tanks have the same capacity
= Die beiden Tanks haben das gleiche Fassungsvermögen

20 litres of petrol
= 20 Liter Benzin

It's sold by the litre
= Es wird literweise verkauft

Note also:

What is the capacity of the engine?
= Wie viel Hubraum hat der Motor?

***It's a 1600 cc* or *1.6 litre engine* (Brit.), *It's a 96 cu. in. motor* (Amer.)**
= Der Motor hat 1 600 cm³ *or* 1,6 Liter Hubraum

vocation /və'keɪʃn/ *n.* 1 (call to career; also Relig.) Berufung, *die;* **he felt no ~ for the ministry** er fühlte sich nicht zum Geistlichen berufen; **teaching is a ~ as well as a profession** Lehrer sein ist Berufung und Beruf zugleich 2 (special aptitude) Begabung, *die* (**for** für) 3 (profession) Beruf, *der*

vocational /və'keɪʃənl/ *adj.* berufsbezogen

vocational: ~ college *n.* Berufsschule, *die;* **~ guidance** *n.* Berufsberatung, *die;* **~ training** *n.* berufliche Bildung

vocative /'vɒkətɪv/ (Ling.)
A *adj.* Vokativ-; **~ case** Vokativ, *der*
B *n.* Vokativ, *der*

vociferate /və'sɪfəreɪt/
A *v.i.* wettern; zetern
B *v.t.* herausschreien ‹*Flüche usw.*›

vociferation /vəsɪfə'reɪʃn/ *n.* Gezeter, *das;* (of opinions etc.) Herausschreien, *das*

vociferous /və'sɪfərəs/ *adj.* (noisy) laut; krakeelend (ugs.) ‹*Zwischenrufer usw.*›; (insistent) lautstark ‹*Forderung, Protest*›

vociferously /və'sɪfərəslɪ/ *adv.* laut; lautstark ‹*protestieren usw.*›

vociferousness /və'sɪfərəsnɪs/ *n., no pl.* Lautstärke, *die*

vodka /'vɒdkə/ *n.* Wodka, *der*

vogue /vəʊg/ *n.* Mode, *die;* **the ~ for large hats** die Mode mit den großen Hüten; **there is a ~ for holidays on canal boats** Urlaub auf Kanalbooten ist große Mode; **be in/come into ~:** in Mode sein/kommen; **go out of ~:** aus der Mode kommen; **have** *or* **enjoy a ~** ‹*Künstler usw.*:› gerade sehr populär sein

'vogue word *n.* Modewort, *das*

voice /vɔɪs/
A *n.* 1 (lit. or fig.) Stimme, *die;* **in a firm/loud ~:** mit fester/lauter Stimme; **like the sound of one's own ~:** sich selbst gerne reden hören; **lose one's ~:** die Stimme verlieren; **be in [good]/bad ~:** [gut]/nicht [gut] bei Stimme sein; **make one's ~ heard** sich verständlich machen; (fig.) sich (*Dat.*) Gehör verschaffen; **his was a lone ~:** mit seiner Meinung stand er allein; *see also* **wilderness** 2 (expression) **give ~ to sth.** einer Sache (*Dat.*) Ausdruck geben 3 (expressed opinion) Stimme, *die;* **with one ~:** einstimmig; **lend one's ~ to sth.** in etw. (*Akk.*) einstimmen; **have a/no ~ in the matter** ein/kein Mitspracherecht bei der Angelegenheit haben 4 (Mus.) Stimme, *die;* **[singing] ~:** Singstimme, *die;* **study ~:** Gesang studieren; **setting for five ~s** fünfstimmige Vertonung 5 (Phonet.) stimmhafter Laut 6 (Ling.) Genus Verbi, *das;* **the active/passive ~:** das Aktiv/Passiv
B *v.t.* 1 (express) zum Ausdruck bringen ‹*Meinung*› 2 *esp. in p.p.* (Phonet.) stimmhaft aussprechen; **a ~d consonant** ein stimmhafter Konsonant

voice: ~-activated *adj.* sprachaktiviert; **~ channel** *n.* (Telecomm.) Sprachkanal, *der;* **~ box** *n.* Kehlkopf, *der*

voiceless /'vɔɪslɪs/ *adj.* 1 stumm; sprachlos (geh.) 2 (Phonet.) stimmlos

voice: ~ mail *n.* Voicemail, *die;* **~-over** *n.* Begleitkommentar, *der;* **~ production** *n., no pl.* Stimmbildung, *die;* Stimmproduktion, *die;* **~ print** *n.* Sonogramm, *das;* **~ range** *n.* Stimmumfang, *der;* **~ recognition** *n., no pl.* (Computing) Spracherkennung, *die;* **~ recorder** *n.* Voicerecorder, *der;* **~ teacher** *n.* Gesang[s]lehrer, *der*/-lehrerin, *die;* **~ vote** *n.* (Amer.) Abstimmung durch Zuruf

void /vɔɪd/
A *adj.* 1 (empty) leer; öd [und leer] ‹*Gelände*› 2 (invalid) ungültig; **his efforts were rendered ~:** seine Bemühungen wurden zunichte gemacht; *see also* **null** 3 (Cards) **my hand was ~ in hearts** ich hatte kein Herz auf der Hand 4 (lacking) **~ of** ohne [jeden/jedes/jede]; **a proposal wholly ~ of sense** ein Vorschlag ohne jeden Sinn
B *n.* 1 (empty space) Nichts, *das;* **the vast desert ~s** die endlose Öde der Wüste 2 (fig.) **nobody can fill the ~ left by his death** keiner kann die große Lücke füllen, die sein Tod hinterlassen hat; **there was an aching ~ in her heart** sie spürte im Innern ein schmerzliches Gefühl der Leere 3 (Cards) **have a ~ in spades** kein Pik haben
C *v.t.* 1 (render invalid) auflösen ‹*Vertrag*›; ablösen ‹*Rente*›; (Law) für ungültig erklären ‹*Vertrag, Vereinbarung*› 2 (empty) entleeren ‹*Blase, Darm*›

voile /vɔɪl, vwɑːl/ *n.* (Textiles) Voile, *der*

vol. *abbr.* = **volume** Bd.

volatile /'vɒlətaɪl/ *adj.* 1 (Chem.) flüchtig; volatil (fachspr.); **~ oil** ▸**ethereal oil** 2 (fig.) (lively) impulsiv; (changeable) unbeständig ‹*Person, Laune*›; (likely to erupt) explosiv ‹*Temperament*›; brisant ‹*Lage*›

volatilise ▸**volatilize**

volatility /vɒlə'tɪlɪtɪ/ *n., no pl.* 1 (Chem.) Flüchtigkeit, *die;* Volatilität, *die* (fachspr.) 2 (fig.) ▸**volatile 2**: Impulsivität, *die;* Unbeständigkeit, *die;* Explosivität, *die;* Brisanz, *die*

volatilize /və'lætɪlaɪz/
A *v.t.* (Chem.) verflüchtigen
B *v.i.* sich verflüchtigen

vol-au-vent /'vɒləʊvɑ̃/ *n.* (Gastr.) Pastete, *die;* **chicken ~:** Königinpastete, *die*

volcanic /vɒl'kænɪk/ *adj.* 1 vulkanisch; **~ eruption** Vulkanausbruch, *der;* **~ in origin** vulkanischen Ursprungs 2 (fig.: violent) leidenschaftlich

volcanism /'vɒlkənɪzm/ *n., no pl.* Vulkanismus, *der*

volcano /vɒl'keɪnəʊ/ *n., pl.* **~es** Vulkan, *der*

volcanologist /vɒlkə'nɒlədʒɪst/ *n.* ▸ℹ **p. 1260** Vulkanologe, *die*/Vulkanologin, *die*

volcanology /vɒlkə'nɒlədʒɪ/ *n., no pl.* Vulkanologie, *die*

vole /vəʊl/ *n.* Wühlmaus, *die;* **field ~:** Feldmaus, *die;* **American ~:** Neuweltmaus, *die; see also* **water vole**

Volga /'vɒlgə/ *pr. n.* ▸ℹ **p. 1491** Wolga, *die*

volition /və'lɪʃn/ *n.* Wille, *der;* **of one's own ~:** aus eigenem Willen; freiwillig

volley /'vɒlɪ/
A *n.* 1 (discharge of missiles) Salve, *die;* **a ~ of stones/arrows** ein Hagel von Steinen/Pfeilen; ein Stein-/Pfeilhagel 2 (fig.) **a ~ of oaths/curses** eine Schimpfkanonade; **direct a ~ of questions at sb.** jmdn. mit Fragen bombardieren 3 (Tennis) Volley, *der;* (Football) Volleyschuss, *der;* **half-~:** Halfvolley, *der*
B *v.t.* (Tennis, Football) vollieren

'volleyball *n.* Volleyball, *der*

vols. *abbr.* = **volumes** Bde.

volt /vəʊlt/ *n.* (Electr.) Volt, *das*

voltage /'vəʊltɪdʒ/ *n.* (Electr.) Spannung, *die;* **high/low ~:** Hoch-/Niederspannung, *die;* **what's the ~ here?** was für eine Netzspannung hat man hier?

'voltage regulator *n.* (Electr.) Spannungsregler, *der*

volte-face /vɒlt'fæs/ *n.* (fig.) Kehrtwendung, *die*

voltmeter /'vəʊltmiːtə(r)/ *n.* (Electr.) Voltmeter, *das;* Spannungsmesser, *der*

volubility /vɒljʊ'bɪlɪtɪ/ *n., no pl.* Redseligkeit, *die* (abwertend); (of speech) Wortreichtum, *der*

voluble /'vɒljʊbl/ *adj.* redselig (abwertend); wortreich ‹*Rede*›; **be ~ in sb.'s defence** jmdn. wortreich verteidigen

volubly /'vɒljʊblɪ/ *adv.* wortreich

volume /'vɒljuːm/ *n.* 1 (book, set of periodicals) Band, *der;* **a two-~ edition** eine zweibändige Ausgabe; (on periodical) **V~ II no. 3** Jahrgang II, Nr. 3; *see also* **speak B 3** 2 (loudness) Lautstärke, *die;* (of voice) Volumen, *das;* **turn the ~ up/down** das Radio *usw.* lauter/leiser stellen; **~ of sound** Klangfülle, *die* 3 ▸ℹ **p. 1690** (amount of space) Rauminhalt, *der;* Volumen, *das;* (amount of substance) Teil, *der;* **two ~s of hydrogen to one of oxygen** zwei Teile Wasserstoff auf einen Teil Sauerstoff 4 (amount, quantity) (of sales etc.) Volumen, *das;* **sales ~:** Absatzvolumen, *das;* Absatzmenge, *die;* **~ of traffic/passenger travel** Verkehrs-/Passagieraufkommen, *das;* **he produced a considerable ~ of church music** er hat ein umfangreiches kirchenmusikalisches Werk geschaffen 5 *in pl.* (mass) **~s of black smoke** schwarze Rauchschwaden; **I've got ~s of work to do** ich habe ungeheuer viel Arbeit

volume: ~ control *n.* Lautstärkeregelung, *die;* (device) Lautstärkeregler, *der;* **~ discount** *n.* Mengenrabatt, *der;* **~ production** *n.* Serienproduktion, *die;* **~ sales** *n. pl.* Mengenabsatz, *der*

voluminous /və'lju:mɪnəs, və'lu:mɪnəs/ *adj.* 1 (great in quantity) voluminös (geh.); sehr umfangreich; (prolific) sehr produktiv ‹Autor› 2 (bulky, loose) weit ‹*Kleider*›; voluminös (geh.) ‹*Tasche usw.*›; voluminös (scherzh.), beleibt ‹*Person*›; **~ garment** wallendes Gewand

voluntarily /'vɒləntərɪlɪ/ *adv.* freiwillig

voluntary /'vɒləntərɪ/

A *adj.* 1 freiwillig; **~ army** Freiwilligenarmee, *die;* **~ organizations** Freiwilligenverbände; **V~ Service Overseas** (Brit.) Freiwilliger Entwicklungsdienst 2 (controlled by will) willkürlich ‹*Muskeln, Bewegungen*›

B *n.* (Mus.) Voluntary, *das*

voluntary eutha'nasia *n., no pl.* freiwillige Euthanasie

volunteer /vɒlən'tɪə(r)/

A *n.* Freiwillige, *der/die;* **any ~s?** Freiwillige vor!; **as a ~:** als Freiwilliger/Freiwillige; *attrib.* **~ army/force** Freiwilligenheer, *das*/Freiwilligenverband, *der*

B *v.t.* (offer) anbieten ‹*Hilfe, Dienste*›; zur Verfügung stellen ‹*Spende*›; herausrücken mit (ugs.) ‹*Informationen, Neuigkeiten*›; **~ advice** unerbetene Ratschläge erteilen

C *v.i.* sich [freiwillig] melden; **~ to do** *or* **for the shopping** sich zum Einkaufen bereit erklären

voluptuary /və'lʌptjʊərɪ/ *n.* (formal) Genussmensch, *der;* Hedonist, *der*/Hedonistin, *die* (geh.)

voluptuous /və'lʌptjʊəs/ *adj.* 1 (sexually alluring) üppig ‹*Figur, Kurven, Blondine*›; aufreizend ‹*Bewegungen*›; sinnlich ‹*Mund*› 2 (concerned with pleasures) ausschweifend; sinnlich, erregend ‹*Gefühl*›

voluptuously /və'lʌptjʊəslɪ/ *adv.* üppig ‹*geformt*›; sinnlich ‹*küssen*›; aufreizend ‹*sich bewegen*›

voluptuousness /və'lʌptjʊəsnɪs/ *n.* (sexual allure) Üppigkeit, *die;* (of movements, mouth) Sinnlichkeit, *die*

volute /və'lju:t/ *n.* (Archit.) Volute, *die*

vomit /'vɒmɪt/

A *v.t.* 1 erbrechen 2 (fig.: emit) **~ [out]** [aus]speien ‹*Rauch, Asche, Lava*›

B *v.i.* sich übergeben; [sich] erbrechen

C *n.* Erbrochene, *das*

voodoo /'vu:du:/ *n.* 1 (witchcraft) Wodu, *der* 2 (spell) Woduzauber, *der*

voracious /və'reɪʃəs/ *adj.* 1 (ravenous) gefräßig ‹*Person, Tier*›; unbändig ‹*Appetit*› 2 (fig.: insatiable) unersättlich ‹*Lust, Leser*›

voraciously /və'reɪʃəslɪ/ *adv.* (lit. or fig.) gierig ‹*verschlingen, lesen*›; **be ~ hungry** einen unbändigen Hunger haben

voracity /və'ræsɪtɪ/ *n., no pl.* Gefräßigkeit, *die;* (fig.: insatiability) Gier, *die*

vortex /'vɔ:teks/ *n., pl.* **vortices** /'vɔ:tɪsi:z/ *or* **~es** (whirlpool, whirlwind) Wirbel, *der;* (eddying current; also fig.: whirl) Strudel, *der*

Vosges /vəʊʒ/ *pr. n. pl.* Vogesen *Pl.*

votary /'vəʊtərɪ/ *n.* 1 (Relig.) Gottesdiener, *der*/-dienerin, *die* 2 (literary: ardent follower) Anhänger, *der*/-hängerin, *die*

vote /vəʊt/

A *n.* 1 (individual ~) Stimme, *die;* **a majority of ~s** eine Stimmenmehrheit; **my ~ goes to X, X has my ~** (fig.) ich stimme *od.* bin für X 2 (act of voting) Abstimmung, *die;* **take a ~ on sth.** über etw. (*Akk.*) abstimmen; *see also* **put**[1] **A 5** 3 (right to ~) **have/be given** *or* **get the ~:** das Stimmrecht haben/bekommen 4 (collective) Stimmen; (result) Abstimmungsergebnis, *das;* **the ~ in favour of capital punishment** die Stimmenzahl für die Todesstrafe; **the Irish/Black/Labour/Conservative ~:** die Stimmen der Iren/Schwarzen/Labourpartei/Konservativen 5 (expression of opinion) Votum, *das;* **give sb. a ~ of confidence/no confidence** jmdm. sein Vertrauen/Misstrauen aussprechen; **~ of confidence/no confidence** Vertrauens-/Misstrauensvotum, *das;* **propose a ~ of thanks** eine Dankadresse halten 6 (Brit. Parl.: money granted) Etat, *der*

B *v.i.* abstimmen; (in election) wählen; **~ for/against** stimmen für/gegen; **~ for Smith** wählen Sie Smith; **~ on a motion** über einen Antrag abstimmen; **~ to do sth.** beschließen, etw. zu tun; **~ by acclamation/ballot/[a] show of hands** durch Akklamation/mit Stimmzetteln/durch Handzeichen abstimmen; **~ with one's feet** (fig.) mit den Füßen abstimmen; **~ Conservative/Labour** *etc.* die Konservativen/Labour *usw.* wählen

C *v.t.* 1 (elect) **~ sb. Chairman/President** *etc.* jmdn. zum Vorsitzenden/Präsidenten *usw.* wählen; **~ sb. on to a committee** jmdn. in einen Ausschuss wählen; (approve) **~ a sum of money for sth.** einen Betrag für etw. bewilligen 2 (coll.: pronounce) bezeichnen; **~ sth. a success/failure** etw. als Erfolg/Misserfolg bezeichnen 3 (coll.: suggest) vorschlagen; **I ~ [that] we go home** ich schlage vor *od.* bin dafür, dass wir nach Hause gehen

Phrasal verbs

- **~ 'down** *v.t.* niederstimmen
- **~ 'in** *v.t.* wählen ‹*Partei, Regierung*›
- **~ 'out** *v.t.* abwählen
- **~ 'through** *v.t.* stimmen für ‹*Gesetz*›

'vote-catching *n.* Stimmenfang, *der;* **~ concessions** Zugeständnisse im Hinblick auf die Wahl

voter /'vəʊtə(r)/ *n.* Wähler, *der*/Wählerin, *die;* **the turnout of ~s** die Wahlbeteiligung

voting /'vəʊtɪŋ/ *n.* Abstimmen, *das;* (in election) Wählen, *das;* **the ~ was 220 for, 165 against** das Ergebnis der Abstimmung war 220 [Stimmen] dafür, 165 dagegen

voting: ~ age *n.* Wahlalter, *das;* **~ machine** *n.* (esp. Amer.) Wahlmaschine, *die;* **~ paper** *n.* Stimmzettel, *der;* **~ slip** *n.* Wahlzettel, *der;* Stimmzettel, *der;* **~ system** *n.* Wahlsystem, *das*

votive /'vəʊtɪv/ *adj.* Votiv‹*bild, -kerze*›

vouch /vaʊtʃ/

A *v.t.* **~ that …** sich dafür verbürgen, dass …

B *v.i.* **~ for sb./sth.** sich für jmdn./etw. verbürgen

voucher /'vaʊtʃə(r)/ *n.* 1 Gutschein, *der;* Voucher, *der* (Tourismus) 2 (proof of payment) Beleg, *der*

vouchsafe /vaʊtʃ'seɪf/ *v.t.* (dated, formal) gewähren; zu geben geruhen (geh.) ‹*Auskünfte*›; **~ to do sth.** geruhen, etw. zu tun (geh.)

vow /vaʊ/

A *n.* Gelöbnis, *das;* (Relig.) Gelübde, *das;* **make** *or* **take a ~ of loyalty to sb.** jmdm. gegenüber ein Treuegelöbnis ablegen; **lovers' ~s** Treueschwüre; **be under a ~:** an ein Gelübde gebunden sein; **be under a ~ of silence** zu schweigen gelobt haben; (Relig.) ein Schweigegelübde abgelegt haben

B *v.t.* **~ sth./to do sth.** etw. geloben/geloben, etw. zu tun; **~ to take revenge on sb.** jmdm. Rache schwören

vowel /'vaʊəl/ *n.* Vokal, *der;* Selbstlaut, *der;* **~ sound** Vokallaut, *der*

vox populi /vɒks 'pɒpjʊli:/ *n.* Vox Populi, *die* (geh.); Stimme des Volkes

voyage /'vɔɪɪdʒ/

A *n.* Reise, *die;* (sea ~) Seereise, *die;* **outward/homeward ~, ~ out/home** Hin-/Rückreise, *die;* **a ~ to the moon** ein Mondflug; **he was on a ~ of discovery** (lit. or fig.) er war auf einer Entdeckungsreise

B *v.i.* (literary) reisen

C *v.t.* bereisen; befahren ‹*Meere*›

voyager /'vɔɪɪdʒə(r)/ *n.* (literary) Reisende, *der/die;* (sea ~) Seereisende, *der/die*

voyeur /vwɑ:'jɜ:(r), vɔɪə-/ *n.* 1 (sexual) Voyeur, *der* 2 (prying observer) Gaffer, *der* (ugs.)

voyeurism /vwɑ:'jɜ:rɪzm, vɔɪə-/ *n., no pl.* Voyeurismus, *der;* Voyeurtum, *das*

voyeuristic /vwa:ə'rɪstɪk, vɔɪə-/ *adj.* voyeuristisch

VP *abbr.* **= Vice-President** VP

vroom /vru:m, vrʊm/ *int.* brumm

vs *abbr.* **= versus** gg.

'V-shaped *adj.* v-förmig

'V-sign *n.* 1 (sign for victory) Siegeszeichen, *das* 2 (gesture of abuse, contempt) *Zeichen, das „Du kannst mich mal!" signalisiert*

VSO *abbr.* **= Voluntary Service Overseas**

VTO[L] /'vi:tɒl/ *abbr.* (Aeronaut.) **= vertical take-off [and landing]** Senkrechtstart [und -landung]

vulcanise ▸**vulcanize**

vulcanism /'vʌlkənɪzm/ ▸**volcanism**

vulcanite /'vʌlkənaɪt/ *n.* Hartgummi, *der;* Ebonit, *der* (fachspr.)

vulcanize /'vʌlkənaɪz/ *v.t.* vulkanisieren

vulcanologist /vʌlkə'nɒlədʒɪst/ ▸**volcanologist**

vulcanology /vʌlkə'nɒlədʒɪ/ ▸**volcanology**

vulgar /'vʌlgə(r)/ *adj.* 1 vulgär; ordinär ‹*Person, Benehmen, Witz, Film*›; geschmacklos ‹*Kleidung*› 2 (Math.) **~ fraction** gemeiner Bruch

vulgarise ▸**vulgarize**

vulgarism /'vʌlgərɪzm/ *n.* (Ling.) Vulgarismus, *der*

vulgarity /vʌl'gærɪtɪ/ *n., no pl.* Vulgarität, *die;* (of clothing) Geschmacklosigkeit, *die;* **her ~ puts me off** ihre ordinäre *od.* gewöhnliche Art stößt mich ab

vulgarize /'vʌlgəraɪz/ *v.t.* vulgarisieren; verderben ‹*Charakter, Person*›

vulgarly /'vʌlgəlɪ/ *adv.* vulgär; ordinär; geschmacklos ‹*sich kleiden*›

Vulgate /'vʌlgeɪt, 'vʌlgət/ *n.* (Bibl.) Vulgata, *die*

vulnerability /vʌlnərə'bɪlɪtɪ/ *n., no pl.* 1 Angreifbarkeit, *die;* (to criticism, temptation) Anfälligkeit, *die* (**to** für) 2 (to injury) Empfindlichkeit, *die* (**to** gegen); (lack of protection) Schutzlosigkeit, *die;* (emotional) Verletzlichkeit, *die*

vulnerable /'vʌlnərəbl/ *adj.* 1 (exposed to danger) angreifbar; **a ~ spot/point** ein schwacher Punkt; **be ~ to sth.** für etw. anfällig sein; **be ~ to attack/in a ~ position** leicht angreifbar sein; **be economically ~:** wirtschaftlich in einer prekären Lage sein; **~ to criticism** leicht zu kritisieren; (easily hurt) leicht durch Kritik verletzt 2 (susceptible to injury) empfindlich (**to** gegen); (without protection) schutzlos; **~ to infection** anfällig für Infektionen; **look young and ~:** jung und schutzlos aussehen; **emotionally ~:** verletzlich

vulture /'vʌltʃə(r)/ *n.* (lit. or fig.) Geier, *der*

vulva /'vʌlvə/ *n.* (Anat.) Vulva, *die*

vying ▸**vie**

Ww

W¹, w /'dʌblju:/ *n., pl.* **Ws** *or* **W's** W, w, *das*

W² *abbr.* 1 **= watt[s]** W 2 ▸❶ **p. 1013 = west** W. 3 ▸❶ **p. 1013 = western** w.

w. *abbr.* **= with** m.

WAAF *abbr.* (Brit. Hist.) 1 **= Women's Auxiliary Air Force** 2 /wæf/ *Mitglied der Women's Auxiliary Air Force*

WAC *abbr.* (Amer.) 1 **= Women's Army Corps** 2 /wæk/ *Mitglied des Women's Army Corps*

wacky /'wækɪ/ *adj.* (coll.) bekloppt (salopp); verrückt (ugs.) ‹*Komödie*›

wad /wɒd/

A *n.* 1 (material) Knäuel, *das;* (smaller) Pfropfen, *der;* **a ~ of cotton wool** ein Wattebausch 2 (of papers) Bündel, *das;* **~s of money** bündelweise Geld; **he earns ~s of money** (fig.) er verdient jede Menge Geld

B *v.t.*, **-dd-** 1 (form into ~) zusammenknüllen 2 (line) füttern ‹*Kleidungsstück*›; (stuff) ausstopfen ‹*Zwischenräume*› 3 (protect with cotton wool) wattieren

wadding /'wɒdɪŋ/ *n.* (lining) Futter, *das;* (for packing) Füllmaterial, *das;* Füllsel *Pl.;* **cotton ~:** Wattierung, *die*

waddle /'wɒdl/

A *v.i.* watscheln

B *n.* watschelnder Gang

wade /weɪd/

A *v.i.* waten; (in snow, sand) stapfen

B *v.t.* durchwaten, waten durch ‹*Fluss, Bach*›

Phrasal verbs

- **~ 'in** *v.i.* (fig. coll.) [gleich] losgehen; (tackle task) sich hineinknien (ugs.)
- **~ into** *v.t.* (fig. coll.) losgehen auf (+ *Akk.*); **~ into the meal** reinhauen (ugs.)
- **~ through** *v.t.* 1 waten durch; stapfen durch ‹*Schnee, Unkraut*› 2 (fig. coll.) durchackern (ugs.) ‹*Manuskript, Buch*›

wader /'weɪdə(r)/ *n.* 1 (Ornith.) Watvogel, *der* 2 *in pl.* (boots) Watstiefel

wadi /'wɒdɪ, 'wɑ:dɪ/ *n.* (Geog.) Wadi, *das*

wading bird /'weɪdɪŋ bɜ:d/ ▸**wader 1**

wafer /'weɪfə(r)/ *n.* 1 Waffel, *die;* (very thin) Oblate, *die* 2 (Eccl.) Hostie, *die* 3 (Electronics) Wafer, *der*

'wafer-thin *adj.* hauchdünn

waffle¹ /'wɒfl/ *n.* (Gastr.) Waffel, *die*

waffle² (Brit. coll.: talk)

A *v.i.* schwafeln (ugs. abwertend); faseln (ugs. abwertend)

B *n.* Geschwafel, *das* (ugs. abwertend); Faselei, *die* (ugs. abwertend)

'waffle iron *n.* Waffeleisen, *das*

waffler /'wɒflə(r)/ *n.* (coll.) Schwaf[e]ler, *der*/Schwaf[e]lerin, *die* (ugs. abwertend)

waft /wɒft, wɑ:ft/

A *v.t.* wehen

B *v.i.* ‹*Geruch, Duft:*› ziehen, (with perceptible air movement) wehen

C *n.* Hauch, *der*

wag¹ /wæg/

A *v.t.*, **-gg-** ‹*Hund:*› wedeln mit ‹*Schwanz*›; ‹*Vogel:*› wippen mit ‹*Schwanz*›; ‹*Person:*› schütteln ‹*Kopf*›; **it was a case of the tail ~ging the dog** (fig.) da hat der Schwanz mit dem Hund gewedelt (ugs.); **~ one's finger at sb.** jmdm. mit dem Finger drohen

B *v.i.*, **-gg-** ‹*Schwanz:*› wedeln/(of bird) wippen; **her tongue never stops ~ging** ihre Zunge steht niemals still; **set people's tongues ~ging** den Leuten etwas zu reden geben

C *n.* (of dog's tail) Wedeln, *das* (**of** mit); (of bird's tail) Wippen, *das* (**of** mit); (of person's head) Schütteln, *das* (**of** *Gen.*); **with a ~ of its tail/his head** mit einem Schwanzwedeln/Kopfschütteln

wag² *n.* (facetious person) Witzbold, *der* (ugs.)

wage /weɪdʒ/

A *n. in sing. or pl.* Lohn, *der;* **sb.'s weekly ~[s]** jmds. Wochenlohn; **a job at a reasonable ~/with reasonable ~s** eine anständig bezahlte Arbeit; **~s of sin** (fig.) Lohn der Sünde; der Sünde Lohn (veralt.)

B *v.t.* führen ‹*Krieg, Feldzug*›; **~ war on** *or* **against crime** (fig.) gegen das Verbrechen zu Felde ziehen

wage: ~ bill *n.* Lohnkosten *Pl.;* **~ claim** *n.* Lohnforderung, *die*

waged /weɪdʒd/ *adj.* bezahlt; **be in ~d employment** einer bezahlten Tätigkeit nachgehen; **the ~d** die Lohnempfänger

wage: ~ demand *n.* Lohnforderung, *die;* **~ dumping** *n., no pl.* Lohndumping, *das;* **~ earner** *n.* Lohnempfänger, *der*/-empfängerin, *die;* **be the ~ earner of the family** der Ernährer/die Ernährerin der Familie sein; **~ freeze** *n.* Lohnstopp, *der;* **~ increase** *n.* Lohnerhöhung, *die;* **~ negotiations** *n. pl.* Tarifreihandlungen *Pl.;* Lohnverhandlungen *Pl.;* **~ packet** *n.* Lohntüte, *die;* **the size of his ~ packet** wie viel er in der Lohntüte hat

wager /'weɪdʒə(r)/ (dated, formal)

A *n.* Wette, *die;* **a ~ of £50** eine Wette um 50 Pfund

B *v.t.* wetten; (on a horse) setzen; **~ one's life/one's whole fortune on sth.** seinen Kopf/sein ganzes Vermögen auf etw. (*Akk.*) verwetten

C *v.i.* wetten; **he's there by now, I'll ~:** ich möchte wetten, dass er inzwischen da ist

wage: ~ restraint *n., no pl.* Lohnmäßigung, *die;* Lohnzurückhaltung, *die;* **~ rise** *n.* Lohnerhöhung, *die;* **~ round** *n.* Lohnrunde, *die;* **~ scale** *n.* Tarif, *der;* Lohnskala, *die;* **~ settlement** *n.* Tarifabschluss, *der;* Lohnabschluss, *der;* **~ slave** *n.* Lohnsklave, *der*

waggish /'wægɪʃ/ *adj.* witzig ‹*Bemerkung*›; **be in a ~ mood** zu Scherzen aufgelegt sein

waggle /'wægl/ (coll.)

A *v.t.* **~ its tail** ‹*Hund:*› mit dem Schwanz wedeln; ‹*Vogel:*› mit dem Schwanz wippen; **~ a loose tooth** an einem lockeren Zahn wackeln

B *v.i.* hin- und herschlagen; **the dog's tail ~d** der Hund wedelte mit dem Schwanz

C *n.* Hin- und Herschlagen, *das;* (of tail) Wedeln, *das*

waggon *etc.* (*Brit.*) ▸**wagon** *etc.*

Wagnerian /vɑ:g'nɪərɪən/

A *n.* Wagnerianer, *der*/Wagnerianerin, *die*

B *adj.* wagnerianisch; (of Wagner) wagner[i]sch; **~ singer** Wagnersänger, *der*/-sängerin, *die*

wagon /'wægən/ *n.* 1 (horse-drawn) Wagen, *der;* **covered ~:** Planwagen, *der;* **hitch one's ~ to a star** (fig.) sich (*Dat.*) ein hohes Ziel setzen 2 (Amer. coll.) **[station] ~:** Kombi, *der* 3 **[water] ~:** Wasserwagen, *der* 4 **go/be on the ~** (go/be teetotal) keinen Tropfen mehr/keinen Tropfen anrühren 5 (trolley) Wagen, *der* 6 (Brit. Railw.) Wagen, *der;* Waggon, *der* (volkst.)

wagoner /'wægənə(r)/ *n.* Fuhrmann, *der*

'wagonload *n.* [Wagen]ladung, *die*

'wagtail *n.* (Ornith.) Bachstelze, *die*

waif /weɪf/ *n.* Heimatlose, *der/die;* (child) verlassenes Kind; (animal) herrenloses Tier; **~s and strays** (children) obdachlose Kinder; (animals) streunende Tiere

wail /weɪl/

A *v.i.* 1 (lament) klagen (geh.) (**for** um); jammern (ugs.) (**for** um); ‹*Kind:*› heulen; **stop ~ing!** hör auf zu jammern! 2 (fig.) ‹*Wind, Sirene:*› heulen

B *n.* 1 (cry) klagender Schrei; **~s** Geheul, *das;* (esp. fig.: complaints) Gejammer, *das;* **~s of protest** Protestgeschrei, *das;* **a ~ of pain** ein Schmerzensschrei 2 (fig.: of wind etc.) Heulen, *das;* Geheul, *das*

Wailing 'Wall *n.* Klagemauer, *die*

wainscot /'weɪnskət/, **wainscoting** /'weɪnskətɪŋ/ *ns.* Täfelung, *die*

waist /weɪst/ *n.* 1 (part of body or garment) Taille, *die;* **tight round the ~:** eng in der Taille; *see also* **strip¹ A 1** 2 (Amer.) (blouse) Bluse, *die;* (bodice) Mieder, *das* 3 (narrow part) Einbuchtung, *die;* (of violin) Mittelbügel, *der;* (Naut.: of ship) Mittelschiff, *das*

'waistband *n.* Gürtelbund, *der;* (of trousers) [Hosen]bund, *der;* (of skirt) [Rock]bund, *der*

waistcoat /'weɪskəʊt, 'weɪstkəʊt/ *n.* (Brit.) Weste, *die*

'waist-deep

A *adj.* bis zur Taille reichend; **be ~:** einem bis zur Taille reichen

B *adv.* bis zur Taille

waisted /'weɪstɪd/ *adj.* tailliert ‹*Kleidungsstück*›

waist: ~-'high ▸**waist-deep**; **~line** *n.* Taille, *die;* **be bad for the ~line** schlecht für die schlanke Linie sein

wait /weɪt/

A *v.i.* 1 warten; **~ [for] an hour** eine Stunde warten; **~ a moment** Moment mal; **keep sb. ~ing, make sb. ~:** jmdn. warten lassen; **how long have you been ~ing?** wie lange wartest du schon?; **~ to see sth. happen** darauf warten, dass etw. passiert; **'repairs [done]/keys cut while you ~'** „Reparatur-/Schlüsselschnelldienst"; **she ~ed to see what would happen if ...:** sie wollte abwarten, was passiert, wenn ...; **sth. is still ~ing to be done** etw. muss noch gemacht werden; **~ and see** abwarten[, was passiert]; **[just] ~ and see!** warte doch ab!; **sth. can/can't** *or* **won't ~:** etw. kann/kann nicht warten; **this bill can't ~:** diese Rechnung muss sofort bezahlt werden; **I can't ~ to do sth.** (am eager) ich kann es kaum erwarten, etw. zu tun; **I can hardly ~** (lit. or iron.) ich kann es kaum erwarten; **I can't ~** (for lavatory) es ist dringend; **[just] you ~!** warte mal ab!; (as threat) warte nur! 2 **~ at** *or* (Amer.) **on table** servieren; ‹*Ober:*› kellnern (ugs.)

B *v.t.* 1 (await) warten auf (+ *Akk.*); **~ one's chance/opportunity** auf eine [günstige] Gelegenheit warten; **~ one's turn** warten, bis man dran ist *od.* drankommt; **~ sb.'s convenience** warten, bis es jmdm. passt 2 (delay) **~ lunch/supper [for sb.]** mit dem Mittag-/Abendessen [auf jmdn.] warten

C *n.* 1 (act, time) **after a long/short ~:** nach langer/kurzer Wartezeit; **there is quite a ~ for appointments** auf einen Termin muss man ziemlich lange warten; **have a long/**

short ~ for sth. lange/nicht lange auf etw. (*Akk.*) warten müssen 2 (watching for enemy) **lie in ~:** im Hinterhalt liegen; **lie in ~ for sb./sth.** jmdm./einer Sache auflauern 3 *in pl.* (Brit.: carol singers) Sternsinger

(Phrasal verbs)
- **~ a'bout, ~ a'round** *v.i.* herumstehen
- **~ be'hind** *v.i.* noch hier-/dableiben; **~ behind for sb.** auf jmdn. warten
- **~ for** *v.t.* warten auf (+ *Akk.*); **~ for the rain to stop** warten, bis der Regen aufhört; **we'll ~ for a fine day** wir warten einen schönen Tag ab; **I can hardly ~ for the day when ...:** ich kann den Tag kaum erwarten, an dem ...; **it was worth ~ing for** es hat sich gelohnt, darauf zu warten; **~ for it!** warte/wartet!; (to create suspense before saying something surprising) warte ab!
- **~ 'in** *v.i.* zu Hause warten (**for** auf + *Akk.*)
- **~ on** *v.t.* 1 (serve) bedienen 2 (await) warten auf (+ *Akk.*)
- **~ 'out** *v.t.* **~ out a storm** *etc.* warten, bis ein Sturm *usw.* vorüber *od.* vorbei ist
- **~ 'up** *v.i.* aufbleiben (**for** wegen)

waiter /'weɪtə(r)/ *n.* ▸ⓘ **p. 1260** Kellner, *der;* **~!** Herr Ober!

waiting /'weɪtɪŋ/ *n.* 1 Warten, *das;* **'no ~'** „Halteverbot" 2 *no pl., no art.* (working as waiter) Servieren, *das;* Kellnern, *das* (ugs.)

waiting: ~ game *n.* Hinhaltetaktik, *die;* **play a ~ game** erst einmal abwarten; sich erst einmal bedeckt halten (ugs.); **~ list** *n.* Warteliste, *die;* **a five-year ~ list** eine Wartezeit von fünf Jahren; **~ room** *n.* Wartezimmer, *das;* (at railway or bus station) Warteraum, *der;* (larger) Wartesaal, *der*

waitress /'weɪtrɪs/ *n.* ▸ⓘ **p. 1260** Serviererin, *die;* Kellnerin, *die* (veralt.); **~!** (dated) Fräulein! (veralt.); **there is ~ service in the ground floor restaurant** das Restaurant im Erdgeschoss ist mit Bedienung

waitressing /'weɪtrɪsɪŋ/ *n., no pl.* Bedienen, *das* (*in einem Lokal*); **do ~:** als Bedienung arbeiten; bedienen; **she does ~ in the vacations** in den Ferien bedient *od.* kellnert sie

'waitress service *n., no pl.* [Tisch]bedienung, *die;* **it's ~ in this restaurant** dieses Restaurant ist mit Bedienung; in diesem Restaurant wird man bedient

waive /weɪv/ *v.t.* verzichten auf (+ *Akk.*); nicht vollstrecken ‹*Strafe*›; nicht anwenden ‹*Regel*›

waiver /'weɪvə(r)/ *n.* (Law) Verzicht, *der* (**of** auf + *Akk.*)

wake¹ /weɪk/

A *v.i.*, **woke** /wəʊk/ *or* (arch.) **waked, woken** /'wəʊkn/ *or* (arch.) **waked** 1 (cease sleeping) aufwachen; (fig.) ‹*Natur, Gefühle:*› erwachen; **we woke to a bright, cold morning** der Morgen war klar und frisch, als wir aufwachten; **I woke to the sound of soft music** beim Aufwachen hörte ich leise Musik 2 **~ to sth.** (fig.: realize) etw. erkennen; sich (*Dat.*) einer Sache (*Gen.*) bewusst werden

B *v.t.* **woke** *or* (arch.) **waked, woken** *or* (arch.) **waked** 1 wecken; (fig.) erwecken (geh.) ‹*die Natur, Erinnerungen*›; wecken ‹*Erinnerungen*›; **be quiet, you'll ~ your baby brother** sei still, sonst wacht dein Brüderchen auf!; **~ the dead** die Toten erwecken (geh.) *od.* aufwecken; **~ the country to the danger of war** (fig.) dem Land die Kriegsgefahr bewusst machen 2 (cause) hervorrufen ‹*Echo*›

C *n.* 1 (Ir.: watch by corpse) Totenwache, *die* 2 *usu. pl.* (N. Engl.) **~s week, the ~s** ≈ Kirmes, *die*

(Phrasal verb)
- **~ 'up**

A *v.i.* (lit. or fig.) aufwachen; **~ up!** wach auf!; (fig.: pay attention) pass besser auf!; **~ up to sth.** (fig.: realize) etw. erkennen; sich (*Dat.*) einer Sache (*Gen.*) bewusst werden

B *v.t.* 1 (rouse from sleep) wecken 2 (fig.: enliven) wachrütteln; Leben bringen in (+ *Akk.*) ‹*Stadt*›; **you need to ~ your ideas up a bit** du müsstest dich ein bisschen zusammenreißen

wake² *n.* 1 (water) Kielwasser, *das* 2 (air) Turbulenz, *die* 3 (fig.) **in the ~ of sth./sb.** im Gefolge von etw./in jmds. Gefolge; **follow in the ~ of sb./sth.** jmdm./einer Sache folgen; **bring sth. in its ~:** etw. zur Folge haben; **leave a cloud of dust/trail of destruction in its ~:** eine Staubwolke/eine Spur der Verwüstung hinterlassen

wakeful /'weɪkfl/ *adj.* 1 (sleepless) schlaflos ‹*Nacht*›; **a ~ child** ein Kind, das schlecht schläft 2 (vigilant) wachsam

wakefulness /'weɪkflnɪs/ *n., no pl.* 1 (sleeplessness) Schlaflosigkeit, *die* 2 (vigilance) Wachsamkeit, *die*

waken /'weɪkn/

A *v.t.* 1 wecken 2 (fig.: arouse) wecken ‹*Interesse, Gefühl*›; erregen ‹*Zorn*›

B *v.i.* ▸**wake¹ A**

'wake-up call *n.* 1 (telephone call) Weckruf, *der* 2 (fig.: warning) Alarmsignal, *das;* **give sb. a ~/be a ~ for sb.** jmdn. aufschrecken *od.* alarmieren; **receive a ~:** aufgeschreckt *od.* alarmiert werden

waking /'weɪkɪŋ/ *adj.* **in one's ~ hours** den ganzen Tag; von früh bis spät; **spend all one's ~ hours [on] doing sth.** etw. von früh bis spät tun; **~ dream** Wachtraum, *der*

Wales /weɪlz/ *pr. n.* Wales (*das*); *see also* **prince 2**

> **National Assembly for Wales (Welsh Assembly)**
>
> Das walisische Parlament, dessen Mitglieder in der Hauptstadt Cardiff zusammentreten. Es wurde 1999 nach den walisischen Wahlen eröffnet und verleiht Wales eine größere Autonomie gegenüber dem britischen Parlament in London.

walk /wɔːk/

A *v.i.* 1 laufen; (as opposed to running) gehen; (as opposed to driving) zu Fuß gehen; **you can ~ there in five minutes** es sind nur 5 Minuten zu Fuß bis dorthin; **'walk'/'don't ~'** (Amer.: at pedestrian lights) „gehen"/„warten"; **~ on crutches/with a stick** an Krücken/am Stock gehen; **learn to ~:** laufen lernen; **can the child ~ yet?** kann das Kind schon laufen?; **be ~ing on air** (fig.) sich wie im siebten Himmel fühlen; **~ tall** (fig.) erhobenen Hauptes gehen (fig.)

2 (exercise) gehen; marschieren (ugs.)

3 (appear) ‹*Geist:*› erscheinen

4 (go with slow gait) ‹*Pferd:*› gehen

5 (Cricket coll.) rausgehen

6 (coll.: go missing) Beine bekommen (fig. ugs.)

B *v.t.* 1 entlanggehen; ablaufen ‹*Strecke, Weg*›; durchwandern ‹*Gebiet*›; **~ the course** (Sport) die Strecke abgehen; ‹*Reiter:*› den Parcours abgehen; **~ the** *or* **his beat** ‹*Polizist:*› seine Runde gehen; **~ the streets** durch die Straßen gehen/(aimlessly) laufen; (as prostitute) auf den Strich gehen (ugs.); **~ the boards** (be actor) auf den Brettern stehen; **~ it** (coll.) zu Fuß gehen; laufen (ugs.); **he ~ed it** (fig. coll.: won easily) es war ein Spaziergang für ihn; *see also* **plank A 1**

2 (cause to ~; lead) führen; ausführen ‹*Hund*›; **~ sb. round the room** jmdn. im Zimmer herumführen; **~ sb. off his/her feet** jmdn. [bis zur Erschöpfung] durch die Gegend schleifen (ugs.)

3 (accompany) bringen; **he ~ed his girlfriend home** er brachte seine Freundin nach Hause

4 (push) schieben ‹*Fahrrad, Motorrad*›

C *n.* 1 Spaziergang, *der;* **go [out] for** *or* **take** *or* **have a ~:** einen Spaziergang machen; **take sb./the dog for a ~:** jmdn./den Hund spazieren führen; **a ten-mile ~:** eine Wanderung von zehn Meilen; (distance) **ten minutes' ~ from here** zehn Minuten zu Fuß von hier; *see also* **space walk**

2 (gait) Gang, *der;* (characteristic) normale Gangart; **I know her by her ~:** ich erkenne sie am Gang

3 (~ing speed) Schritttempo, *das;* **his horse/she slowed to a ~:** sein Pferd ging nur noch im Schritt/sie verfiel in ein normales Schritttempo

4 (Sport: race) Wettbewerb im Gehen; **the 10,000 metres ~:** das 10 000-m-Gehen

5 (path, route) [Spazier]weg, *der;* **a milkman's/postman's ~:** die Tour eines Milchmanns/Briefträgers

6 **people from all ~s of life** Leute aus den verschiedensten gesellschaftlichen Gruppierungen

(Phrasal verbs)
- **~ a'bout** *v.i.* herumlaufen; in der Gegend herumlaufen (ugs.); *see also* **walkabout**
- **~ a'way** *v.i.* 1 weggehen; **she was lucky to ~ away from the accident** sie hatte großes Glück, den Unfallort unverletzt verlassen zu können 2 (fig.) **~ away from the opposition** *or* **competition** (coll.: defeat) der Konkurrenz weglaufen; **he tried to ~ away from the problem** (ignore it) er versuchte, dem Problem aus dem Weg zu gehen; **~ away with sth.** (coll.) (win easily) etw. spielend leicht gewinnen; (steal) sich mit etw. davonmachen (ugs.); **~ away with all the prizes** alle Preise einheimsen (ugs.)
- **~ 'in** *v.i.* 1 (enter) hereinkommen/hineingehen; reinkommen/-gehen (ugs.); **'please ~ in'** „[bitte] eintreten, ohne zu klopfen" 2 (enter without permission) hinein-/hereinspazieren; **~ in on sb./sth.** bei jmdm./etw. hereinplatzen (ugs.)
- **~ into** *v.t.* 1 (enter) betreten; treten in (+ *Akk.*) ‹*Pfütze*›; (without permission) eindringen in (+ *Akk.*) ‹*Haus*› 2 (hit by accident) laufen gegen ‹*Pfosten, Laternenpfahl*›; **~ into sb.** mit jmdm. zusammenstoßen; **~ into a trap** (lit. or fig.) in eine Falle gehen; **the boxer ~ed straight into a right hook** der Boxer lief voll in den rechten Haken [hinein]; (fig.) **you ~ed straight into that one!** da hast du dich aber reinlegen lassen! 3 (coll.: come easily into) **she ~ed into the top job** ihr ist der Topjob einfach zugefallen
- **~ 'off**

A *v.i.* 1 (leave) weggehen; verschwinden; **he has ~ed off with another woman** er ist mit einer anderen Frau durchgebrannt (ugs.) 2 **~ off with sth.** (coll.) sich mit etw. davonmachen (ugs.); **~ off with all the prizes** alle Preise einheimsen (ugs.); **he ~ed off with the fight** er hat den Kampf lässig gewonnen

B *v.t.* **I'll have to ~ off some of this fat** ich muss mehr laufen, um ein paar Pfunde loszuwerden (ugs.); **~ off a hangover** einen Spaziergang machen, um seinen Kater loszuwerden

- **~ 'on** *v.i.* 1 (go further) weitergehen; **~ on!** (to horse) hü! 2 (go on stage) auf die Bühne kommen; **~ on as the policeman or the butler** Statistenrollen wie den Polizisten oder Butler spielen
- **~ 'out** *v.i.* 1 (leave) hinausgehen; rausgehen (ugs.) 2 (Mil.: leave barracks) ausgehen 3 (leave in protest) aus Protest den Saal verlassen; (leave organization) austreten 4 (go on strike) in den Streik *od.* Ausstand treten 5 (Brit. dated: be courting) miteinander gehen (ugs.); **~ out with sb.** mit jmdm. gehen (ugs.). *see also* **walkout**
- **~ 'out of** *v.t.* 1 (leave) gehen aus 2 (leave in protest) verlassen ‹*Saal, Versammlung*›
- **~ 'out on** *v.t.* verlassen; sitzen lassen (ugs.) ‹*Frau, Mann*›; hinschmeißen (ugs.) ‹*Job*›
- **~ 'over** *v.t.* **~ [all] over sb.** jmdn. fertig machen (ugs.); *see also* **walkover**
- **~ 'up** *v.i.* 1 (approach) sich nähern; **~ up to sb.** zu jmdm. hingehen; **he ~ed up to me** er kam zu mir [heran]; **~ up to the door** zur Tür gehen; **~ up! ~ up!** (said by showman) immer hereinspaziert! 2 (ascend) hochlaufen; nach oben laufen; *see also* **walk-up**

'walkabout *n.* 1 (through crowds) Bad in der Menge (scherzh.); **go on a ~:** sich unters Volk mischen 2 (Austral.: in bush) Buschwanderung, *die*

walker /'wɔːkə(r)/ *n.* 1 Spaziergänger, *der*/-gängerin, *die;* (in race) Geher, *der*/Geherin, *die;* (rambler, hiker) Wanderer, *der*/Wanderin, *die;* **sb. is a good ~:** jmd. ist gut zu Fuß 2 (frame) Laufgestell, *das;* (baby-~) Laufstuhl, *der*

walkies /'wɔːkɪz/ *n. pl.* (coll.) **go ~:** Gassi gehen (ugs.); **~!** (said to dog) komm Gassi! (ugs.)

walkie-talkie /wɔːkɪ'tɔːkɪ/ *n.* Walkie-Talkie, *das*

walking /'wɔːkɪŋ/

A *attrib. adj.* **a ~ dictionary/encyclopedia** (joc.)

ein wandelndes Wörterbuch/Konversationslexikon; **the ~ wounded** die gehfähigen Verwundeten; *see also* **disaster area**
B *n., no pl., no art.* [Spazieren]gehen, *das;* Laufen, *das;* **you ought to do more ~:** Sie sollten mehr zu Fuß gehen *od.* spazieren gehen; *attrib.* **at ~ pace** im Schritttempo; **be within ~ distance** zu Fuß zu erreichen sein; **we are within ~ distance [of it]** wir können es zu Fuß erreichen

walking: ~ frame *n.* Gehgestell, *das;* **~ holiday** *n.* Wanderurlaub, *der;* **~ shoe** *n.* Wanderschuh, *der;* **~ stick** *n.* Spazierstock, *der;* **she cannot manage now without a ~ stick** sie kommt nicht mehr ohne Stock aus; **~ tour** *n.* Wanderung, *die*

Walkman ® /ˈwɔːkmən/ *n., pl.* **Walkmans** Walkman, *der* (Wz)

walk: ~-on part *n.* (Theatre) Statistenrolle, *die;* **~out** *n.* Arbeitsniederlegung, *die;* **~over** *n.* (fig.: easy victory) Spaziergang, *der* (ugs.); **~-up** *n.* (Amer.) Haus ohne Aufzug; **~way** *n.* Fußweg, *der;* (over machinery etc.) Laufsteg, *der*

wall /wɔːl/
A *n.* **1** (of building, part of structure) Wand, *die;* (external, also free-standing) Mauer, *die;* **town/garden ~:** Stadt-/Gartenmauer, *die;* **the south ~ of the house** die Südwand des Hauses; **a concrete ~:** eine Betonwand/-mauer; **the Great W~ of China** die Chinesische Mauer; **the Berlin W~** (Hist.) die [Berliner] Mauer **2** (internal) Wand, *die;* **be hanging on the ~:** an der Wand hängen; **hang a picture on the ~:** ein Bild an die Wand hängen; **within these four ~s** (fig.) innerhalb dieser vier Wände; **I'm tired of [staring at] my own four ~s** mir fällt die Decke auf den Kopf (ugs.); **~s have ears** die Wände haben Ohren; **drive** *or* **send sb. up the ~** (fig. coll.) jmdn. auf die Palme bringen (ugs.); **go up the ~** (fig. coll.) die Wände hochgehen (ugs.); **go to the ~** (fig.) an die Wand gedrückt werden; *see also* **back A 1** **3** (Mount., Min.) Wand, *die;* (fig.) Mauer, *die;* **a ~ of water/fire** eine Wasser-/Feuerwand; **the North W~ of the Eiger** die Eigernordwand; **a ~ of silence/prejudice** (fig.) eine Mauer des Schweigens/von Vorurteilen **4** (esp. Footb.: protective row) Mauer, *die;* **a ~ of troops/policemen/tanks** eine Mauer von Soldaten/Polizisten/Panzern **5** (Anat., Zool., Bot.: outer layer) Wand, *die;* **abdominal ~:** Bauchwand, *die*
B *v.t.* **[be] ~ed** von einer Mauer/Mauern umgeben [sein]; **X is a ~ed city/town** X hat eine Stadtmauer

Phrasal verbs
- **~ 'in** *v.t.* mit einer Mauer umgeben; (fig.) umzingeln
- **~ 'off** *v.t.* abteilen
- **~ 'up** *v.t.* zumauern; einmauern ‹*Person*›

wallaby /ˈwɒləbɪ/ *n.* (Zool.) Wallaby, *das*

wallah /ˈwɒlə/ *n.* (dated coll.) **television/advertising ~:** Fernseh-/Werbefritze, *der* (ugs.)

wall: ~ bars *n. pl.* Sprossenwand, *die;* **~board** *n.* Wandfaserplatte, *die;* **~chart** *n.* Schautafel, *die;* **~ covering** *n.* (**~paper**) Tapete, *die;* (**~ hanging**) Wandbehang, *der;* **~ cupboard** *n.* Hängeschrank, *der*

wallet /ˈwɒlɪt/ *n.* Brieftasche, *die;* (for cheque card etc.) Etui, *das*

wall: ~flower *n.* **1** (Bot.) Goldlack, *der;* **2** (coll.: person) Mauerblümchen, *das* (ugs.); **~ hanging** *n.* Wandbehang, *der;* **~ light** *n.* Wandlampe, *die;* **~ map** *n.* Wandkarte, *die;* **~-mounted** *adj.* an der Wand befestigt; Wand‹*spiegel, -schalter, -schrank, -lautsprecher*›

Wallonia /wɒˈləʊnɪə/ *pr. n.* Wallonien (*das*)

Walloon /wɒˈluːn/ ▸❶ **p. 1277,** ▸❶ **p. 1345**
A *n.* **1** (person) Wallone, *der*/Wallonin, *die* **2** (dialect) Wallonisch, *das; see also* **English B 1**
B *adj.* wallonisch; *see also* **English A**

wallop /ˈwɒləp/ (coll.)
A *v.t.* (hit) schlagen; (with repeated blows) [ver]prügeln; **he ~ed him one over the head** (coll.) er hat ihm eins übergebraten (salopp)
B *n.* Schlag, *der;* **give sb./sth. a ~:** auf jmdn./etw. draufhauen (ugs.); **he fell down with a ~:** er fiel mit einem Plumps hin

walloping /ˈwɒləpɪŋ/ (coll.)
A *n.* **1** (thrashing) **a ~:** eine Tracht Prügel (ugs.) **2** (defeat) **get a ~:** eins übergebraten kriegen (salopp)
B *adj.* gepfeffert (ugs.) ‹*Niederlage, Rechnung*›; faustdick (ugs.) ‹*Lüge*›

wallow /ˈwɒləʊ/
A *v.i.* **1** (roll around) sich wälzen; ‹*Schiff:*› schlingern; (in mud also) sich suhlen **2** (fig.: take delight) schwelgen (**in** in + *Dat.*); **be ~ing in money** (coll.) im Geld schwimmen (ugs.); **~ in luxury** im Luxus baden *od.* schwelgen
B *n.* **1** (mudbath) Schlammbad, *das;* **like a good ~ in the mud** sich gern im Schlamm wälzen *od.* suhlen **2** (fig.: indulgence) **he likes to have a good ~ [in sentiment]** er schwelgt gern in Gefühlen

wall: ~ painting *n.* Wandgemälde, *das;* **~paper A** *n.* **1** Tapete, *die;* **2** (Computing) Wallpaper, *das* (fachspr.); Hintergrundbild, *das;* **B** *v.t.* tapezieren; **~ plug** *n.* (dowel) Wanddübel, *der;* **~ socket** *n.* (Electr.) Wandsteckdose, *die;* **W~ Street** *n.* [die] Wall Street; die Wallstreet; **~-to-~** *adj.* (covering floor) **~-to-~ carpeting** Teppichboden, *der;* (fig.) **~-to-~ coverage** flächendeckende Berichterstattung; **~-to-~ sunshine** durchgängig Sonnenschein; **~ unit** *n.* Hängeelement, *das*

> **Wall Street**
>
> Eine Straße nahe der Südspitze der Insel Manhattan in New York mit wichtigen Banken und Börsen. Der Name ist auch ein Synonym für die **New York Stock Exchange.**

wally /ˈwɒlɪ/ *n.* (Brit. coll.) Blödmann, *der* (salopp)

walnut /ˈwɔːlnʌt/ *n.* **1** (nut) Walnuss, *die* **2** (tree) [Wal]nussbaum, *der* **3** (wood) Nussbaumholz, *das*

walrus /ˈwɔːlrəs, ˈwɒlrəs/ *n.* Walross, *das;* **~ moustache** Walrossbart, *der* (ugs.)

Walter Mitty /wɒltə ˈmɪtɪ/ ▸**Mitty**

waltz /wɔːlts, wɔːls, wɒlts, wɒls/
A *n.* Walzer, *der;* **can you dance the ~?** können Sie Walzer tanzen?
B *v.i.* Walzer tanzen; **~ round the room** durchs Zimmer tanzen

Phrasal verbs
- **~ 'in** *v.i.* (fig. coll.) angetanzt kommen (ugs.)
- **~ 'off, ~ 'out** *v.i.* (fig. coll.) abtanzen (ugs.)

wan /wɒn/ *adj.* fahl (geh.); bleich; **~ smile** mattes Lächeln

WAN /wæn/ *abbr.* (Computing) = **wide area network** WAN

wand /wɒnd/ *n.* Stab, *der;* (magician's ~) Zauberstab, *der*

wander /ˈwɒndə(r)/
A *v.i.* **1** (go aimlessly) umherirren; (walk slowly) bummeln; **she ~ed over to me** sie kam zu mir herüber; **I must be ~ing** (coll.) ich muss mich auf die Socken machen (ugs.) **2** (stray) ‹*Katze:*› streunen; ‹*Schafe:*› sich verlaufen; **~ from the trail** vom Weg abkommen; **~ from the path of righteousness, ~ from the straight and narrow** (fig.) vom Pfad der Tugend abkommen; **the car ~s badly** der Wagen hält schlecht Spur **3** (fig.: stray from subject) abschweifen; **his thoughts ~ed back to his childhood** seine Gedanken schweiften zurück in die Kindheit
B *v.t.* wandern durch; **~ the world** durch die Welt ziehen
C *n.* (coll.: walk) Spaziergang, *der;* **let's go for a ~:** komm, laufen wir ein bisschen rum (ugs.); **I'll go for** *or* **take a ~ round** *or* **through the town** ich werd mal einen Bummel durch die Stadt machen

Phrasal verbs
- **~ a'bout** *v.i.* sich herumtreiben
- **~ a'long** *v.i.* dahintrotten; ‹*Fahrzeug:*› dahinzockeln (ugs.)
- **~ 'in** *v.i.* hineinspazieren; (towards speaker) hereinspaziert kommen
- **~ 'off** *v.i.* **1** (stray) weggehen; ‹*Kind:*› sich selbstständig machen (scherzh.) **2** (coll.: go away) sich davonmachen (ugs.)

wanderer /ˈwɒndərə(r)/ *n.* Streuner, *der*/Streunerin, *die;* (traveller) Wandervogel, *der* (veralt. scherzh.)

wandering /ˈwɒndərɪŋ/
A *adj.* **1** (nomadic) Wander‹*stamm, -volk*›; **~ minstrel** (Hist.) fahrender Spielmann **2** (meandering) sich windend ‹*Strom*›; (fig.: disjointed) weitschweifig ‹*Rede*›; wirr ‹*Gedanken*›; (joc.) vorwitzig (scherzh.) ‹*Hände*›
B *n. in pl.* **1** (travels) Wanderschaft, *die;* **in** *or* **on his ~s** auf seiner Wanderschaft **2** (straying) **the ~s of his mind/thoughts** sein wirres Denken/seine wirren Gedanken

wandering 'Jew *n.* **the ~:** der Ewige Jude; (fig.) **a ~:** ein Ahasver (geh.)

wanderlust /ˈwɒndəlʌst/ *n.* Reiselust, *die;* (related to distant places) Fernweh, *das*

wane /weɪn/
A *v.i.* ‹*Mond:*› abnehmen; ‹*Kraft, Einfluss, Macht:*› schwinden, abnehmen; ‹*Ruf, Ruhm:*› verblassen; **the light is waning** es wird langsam dunkler
B *n.* **be on the ~** ‹*Mond:*› abnehmen; (fig.) schwinden; dahinschwinden (geh.)

wangle /ˈwæŋgl/ (coll.)
A *v.t.* (get by devious means) organisieren (ugs.) ‹*Karte, Einladung*›; **~ sth. out of sb.** jmdm. etw. abluchsen (ugs.); **can you ~ it for me?** kannst du das für mich deichseln? (ugs.)
B *n.* Kniff, *der;* **by a ~:** durch Schiebung (ugs.)

wank /wæŋk/ (Brit. coarse)
A *v.i.* wichsen (derb)
B *v.t.* **~ sb. off** jmdm. einen abwichsen (vulg.)
C *n.* **have a ~:** sich (*Dat.*) einen abwichsen (derb)

wanker /ˈwæŋkə(r)/ *n.* (Brit. coarse) Wichser, *der* (derb)

wanly /ˈwɒnlɪ/ *adv.* schwach ‹*beleuchtet*›; matt ‹*lächeln*›

wanna /ˈwɒnə/ (coll.) = **want to; want 1**

wannabe /ˈwɒnəbɪ/ *n.* (coll. derog.) Möchtegern, *der;* (attrib.) Möchtegern-; **a ~ writer, a writer ~:** ein Möchtegernschriftsteller

want /wɒnt/
A *v.t.* **1** (desire) wollen; **I ~ my mummy** ich will zu meiner Mama; **I ~ it done by tonight** ich will, dass es bis heute Abend fertig wird; **I don't ~ there to be any misunderstanding** ich will *od.* möchte nicht, dass da ein Missverständnis aufkommt; **I don't ~ you to get the idea that I am stingy** ich möchte nicht, dass Sie den Eindruck gewinnen, ich sei geizig **2** (require, need) brauchen; **'Wanted — cook for small family'** „Koch/Köchin für kleine Familie gesucht"; **you're ~ed on the phone** du wirst am Telefon verlangt; **feel ~ed** das Gefühl haben, gebraucht zu werden; **what you ~ is a good holiday** Sie brauchen mal richtigen Urlaub; **the windows ~ painting** die Fenster müssten gestrichen werden; **you ~ to be [more] careful** (ought to be) du solltest vorsichtig[er] sein; **you ~ to see a solicitor about that** Sie müssten sich in der Sache an einen Anwalt wenden **3** **~ed [by the police]** [polizeilich] gesucht (**for** wegen); **he is a ~ed man** er wird [polizeilich] gesucht **4** (lack) **sb./sth. ~s sth.** jmdm./einer Sache fehlt es an etw. (*Dat.*); **all the soup ~s is some salt** der Suppe fehlt nur noch ein bisschen Salz
B *n.* **1** *no pl.* (lack) Mangel, *der* (**of** an + *Dat.*); **there is no ~ of ...:** es fehlt nicht an ... (*Dat.*); **for ~ of sth.** aus Mangel an etw. (*Dat.*); **for ~ of a better word** in Ermangelung eines besseren Ausdrucks; **he took the flat for ~ of anything better** er nahm die Wohnung, weil er nichts Besseres finden konnte **2** *no pl.* (need) Not, *die;* **suffer ~:** Not leiden; **be in ~ of sth.** (dated, literary) einer Sache (*Gen.*) bedürfen (geh.) **3** (desire) Bedürfnis, *das;* **we can supply all your ~s** wir können alles liefern, was Sie brauchen; **~ ad** (Amer.) Kaufgesuch, *das*
C *v.i.* **1** (arch.: be in want) Not leiden **2** (esp. Amer. coll.) **~ in/out** rein-/rauswollen

Phrasal verb
- **~ for** *v.t.* (dated) **sb. ~s for nothing** *or* **doesn't ~ for anything** jmdm. fehlt es an nichts; **~ for money** an Geldmangel (*Dat.*) leiden

wanting /ˈwɒntɪŋ/ *adj.* **be ~:** fehlen; **sb./sth. is ~ in sth.** jmdm./einer Sache fehlt es an etw. (*Dat.*); **be found ~:** für unzureichend befunden werden

wanton /ˈwɒntən/*adj.* 1 (dated: licentious) lüstern; wollüstig ‹*Person, Gedanken, Benehmen*› 2 (wilful) mutwillig ‹*Beschädigung, Grausamkeit, Verschwendung*›; leichtfertig ‹*Vernachlässigung*› 3 (literary: luxuriant, wild) üppig ‹*Wachstum, Vielfalt*› 4 (capricious) übermütig; mutwillig (veralt.).

wantonly /ˈwɒntənlɪ/ *adv.* 1 (dated: licentiously) lüstern; wollüstig 2 (wilfully) mutwillig; leichtfertig ‹*vernachlässigen*›

wantonness /ˈwɒntənnɪs/ *n., no pl.* 1 (dated: licentiousness) Lüsternheit, *die* 2 (wilfulness) Mutwilligkeit, *die*

WAP /wæp/ *abbr.* (Computing) **= wireless application protocol** WAP; *attrib.* **~ phone** WAP-Handy, *das;* **~ technology** WAP-Technologie, *die*

war /wɔː(r)/ *n.* 1 Krieg, *der;* **between the ~s** zwischen den Weltkriegen; **declare ~:** den Krieg erklären (**on** *Dat.*); **an act of ~:** ein kriegerischer Akt; **a ~ of conquest/aggression** ein Eroberungs-/Angriffskrieg; **be at ~:** sich im Krieg befinden; **make ~:** Krieg führen (**on** gegen); **go to ~:** in den Krieg ziehen (**against** gegen); **carry the ~ into the enemy's camp** (fig.) den Spieß umdrehen; **look as though one/it has been in the ~s** ziemlich mitgenommen aussehen 2 (science) Kriegführung, *die;* **the art of ~:** die Kriegskunst; **laws of ~:** Kriegsrecht, *das;* **rights of ~:** Kriegsrechte 3 (fig.: conflict) Krieg, *der;* **price ~:** Preiskrieg, *der;* **~ of nerves** Nervenkrieg, *der;* **~ of words** Wortgefecht, *das* 4 (fig.: fight, campaign) Kampf, *der* (**on, against** gegen); **declare ~ on poverty** der Armut den Kampf ansagen

war: ~ artist *n.* Kriegsmaler, *der*/-malerin, *die;* **~ baby** *n.* [Nach]kriegskind, *das*

warble /ˈwɔːbl/ *v.t. & i.* trällern

warbler /ˈwɔːblə(r)/ *n.* (Ornith.) Grasmücke, *die*

war: ~ bride *n.* Kriegsbraut, *die;* **~ chest** *n.* Kriegskasse, *die;* **~ correspondent** *n.* Kriegsberichterstatter, *der*/-berichterstatterin, *die;* **~ crime** *n.* Kriegsverbrechen, *das;* **~ criminal** *n.* Kriegsverbrecher, *der*/-verbrecherin, *die;* **~ cry** *n.* 1 (battle cry) Kriegsruf, *der;* 2 (slogan) Schlachtruf, *der*

ward /wɔːd/ *n.* 1 (in hospital) Station, *die;* (single room) Krankensaal, *der;* **geriatric/maternity ~:** geriatrische Abteilung/Entbindungsstation, *die;* **she's in W~ 3** sie liegt auf Station 3 2 (minor) Mündel, *das od. die;* **~ [of court]** (Law) Mündel [unter Amtsvormundschaft] 3 (electoral division) Wahlbezirk, *der* 4 (Hist.: bailey) [Burg]hof, *der*

Phrasal verb

- **~ 'off** *v.t.* 1 (prevent) abwehren; schützen vor (+ *Dat.*) ‹*Erkältung, Depressionen*›; abwenden ‹*Gefahr*› 2 (keep at distance) sich (*Dat.*) vom Leibe halten ‹*Verehrer*›

war: ~ damage *n.* Kriegsschäden *Pl.;* **~ dance** *n.* Kriegstanz, *der*

warden /ˈwɔːdn/ *n.* ▸❶ **p. 1260** 1 (president, governor) Direktor, *der*/Direktorin, *die;* (of college, school) Rektor, *der*/Rektorin, *die;* (of hostel, sheltered housing) Heimleiter, *der*/-leiterin, *die;* (of youth hostel) Herbergsvater, *der*/-mutter, *die* 2 (supervisor) Aufseher, *der*/Aufseherin, *die;* **[air-raid] ~:** Luftschutzwart, *der; see also* **churchwarden**

warder /ˈwɔːdə(r)/ *n.* (Brit.) Wärter, *der;* Aufseher, *der*

wardress /ˈwɔːdrɪs/ *n.* Wärterin, *die;* Aufseherin, *die*

wardrobe /ˈwɔːdrəʊb/ *n.* 1 (piece of furniture) Kleiderschrank, *der;* **folding ~:** Kleidersack, *der* 2 (stock of clothes) Garderobe, *die;* (in theatre) Kostüme *Pl.*

wardrobe: ~ master/mistress *ns.* (Theatre) Gewandmeister, *der*/-meisterin, *die;* **~ trunk** *n.* Schrankkoffer, *der*

'wardroom *n.* (Navy) Offiziersmesse, *die*

-wards /wədz/ *adv. suff.* -wärts

wardship /ˈwɔːdʃɪp/ *n.* Vormundschaft, *die*

'ward sister *n.* Stationsschwester, *die*

ware /weə(r)/ *n.* 1 (pottery) Steinzeug, *das;* **Delft ~:** Delfter Keramik 2 *in pl.* (goods) Ware, *die*

'war effort *n.* Kriegsanstrengung, *die*

warehouse

A /ˈweəhaʊs/ *n.* (repository) Lagerhaus, *das;* (part of building) Lager, *das;* (Brit.: retail or wholesale store) Großmarkt, *der*

B /ˈweəhaʊs, ˈweəhaʊz/ *v.t.* einlagern ‹*Möbel*›

warehouseman /ˈweəhaʊsmən/ *n., pl.* **warehousemen** /ˈweəhaʊsmən/ ▸❶ **p. 1260** Lagerist, *der*

warfare /ˈwɔːfeə(r)/ *n.* (lit. or fig.) Krieg, *der;* **in modern ~:** in der modernen Kriegführung; **economic ~:** Wirtschaftskrieg, *der; see also* **open A 8**

war: ~ game *n.* Kriegsspiel, *das;* **~ gaming** *n.* (Mil.) Sandkastenspiele *Pl.;* (as hobby) *das Nachstellen historischer Schlachten mit Spielzeugsoldaten;* **~ god** *n.* Kriegsgott, *der;* **~ grave** *n.* Kriegs- *od.* Soldatengrab, *das;* **~head** *n.* Sprengkopf, *der;* **~horse** *n.* (Hist., fig.) Schlachtross, *das*

warily /ˈweərɪlɪ/ *adv.* vorsichtig; (suspiciously) misstrauisch; **tread ~** (lit. or fig.) vorsichtig sein

wariness /ˈweərɪnɪs/ *n., no pl.* Vorsicht, *die* (**of** vor + *Dat.*); **~ of strangers** Misstrauen gegen Fremde

war: ~like *adj.* 1 (bellicose) kriegerisch; 2 (military) Kriegs‹*vorbereitungen, -gerät*›; **~lord** *n.* Kriegsherr, *der*

warm /wɔːm/

A *adj.* 1 warm; **come inside and get ~:** komm rein und wärm dich auf; **I am very ~ from running** mir ist sehr warm vom Rennen; **it's ~ work** bei der Arbeit kommt man ins Schwitzen; **keep sb.'s food ~:** jmdm. das Essen warm halten; **keep a seat/job ~ for sb.** (fig.) jmdm. einen Platz/eine Stellung freihalten 2 (enthusiastic) herzlich ‹*Grüße, Dank*›; eng ‹*Freundschaft*›; lebhaft ‹*Interesse*›; begeistert ‹*Unterstützung, Applaus*›; *see also* **reception 1; welcome B 2** 3 (cordial, sympathetic) warm ‹*Herz, Wesen, Gefühl*›; herzlich ‹*Lächeln*›; echt empfunden ‹*Hochachtung*›; **the thought of her kindness gives me a ~ feeling** wenn ich an ihre Güte denke, wird mir warm ums Herz 4 (unpleasant) ungemütlich; **he left when things began to get too ~ for him** er ging, als ihm die Sache zu ungemütlich wurde 5 (recent) heiß ‹*Spur*› 6 (in games: close) **you're getting ~!** warm!

B *v.t.* wärmen; warm machen ‹*Flüssigkeit*›; **~ one's hands** sich (*Dat.*) die Hände wärmen; **the thought [of ...] ~ed [the cockles of] his heart** bei dem Gedanken [an ... (*Akk.*)] wurde ihm warm ums Herz

C *v.i.* 1 **~ to sb./sth.** (come to like) sich für jmdn./etw. erwärmen; **my heart ~ed to her** sie wurde mir sympathischer; **the speaker ~ed to his subject** der Redner steigerte sich in sein Thema hinein 2 (get ~er) warm werden

D *n.* 1 (warming) **give the food a ~:** das Essen aufwärmen; **have a ~ by the fire** sich am Kamin/Ofen *usw.* aufwärmen 2 (warmth) **the ~:** die Wärme

Phrasal verb

- **~ 'up**

A *v.i.* 1 (get ~) warm werden; ‹*Motor:*› warmlaufen 2 (prepare) ‹*Sportler:*› sich aufwärmen 3 (fig.: become animated) warm werden; ‹*Party:*› in Schwung kommen; ‹*Publikum:*› in Stimmung kommen

B *v.t.* aufwärmen ‹*Speisen*›; erwärmen ‹*Raum, Zimmer*›; warmlaufen lassen ‹*Motor*›; (fig.) in Stimmung bringen ‹*Publikum*›. *see also* **warm-up**

'war machine *n.* 1 (military resources) Kriegsmaschinerie, *die* (bildungsspr. abwertend) 2 (weapon of war) Kriegsmaschine, *die*

warm-blooded /ˈwɔːmblʌdɪd/ *adj.* 1 warmblütig ‹*Tier*›; **~-blooded animals** Warmblüter 2 (fig.: passionate) heißblütig; temperamentvoll

warmed-over /ˈwɔːmdəʊvə(r)/ (Amer.), **warmed-up** /ˈwɔːmdʌp/ *adjs.* aufgewärmt

'war memorial *n.* Kriegerdenkmal, *das*

warm: ~ 'front *n.* (Meteorol.) Warmfront, *die;* **~-hearted** *adj.* herzlich; warmherzig ‹*Person*›

'warming pan *n.* Wärmepfanne, *die*

warmish /ˈwɔːmɪʃ/ *adj.* lau[warm]; warm ‹*Wetter*›

warmly /ˈwɔːmlɪ/ *adv.* 1 (to maintain warmth) warm 2 (enthusiastically) herzlich ‹*willkommen heißen, gratulieren, begrüßen, grüßen, danken*›; wärmstens ‹*empfehlen*›; begeistert ‹*sprechen von, applaudieren*› 3 (animatedly) hitzig

warmonger /ˈwɔːmʌŋgə(r)/ *n.* Kriegshetzer, *der*/-hetzerin, *die*

warmongering /ˈwɔːmʌŋgərɪŋ/ *n.* Kriegshetze, *die*

warmth /wɔːmθ/ *n.* 1 (state of being warm; also of colour) Wärme, *die* 2 (enthusiasm, affection, cordiality) Herzlichkeit, *die;* Wärme, *die;* **the ~ of her temperament** ihr ungestümes Temperament 3 (animation) Hitzigkeit, *die;* (indignation) Schärfe, *die*

'warm-up *n.* **have a ~** (lit., Sport) sich aufwärmen; **give a meal a ~:** ein Essen aufwärmen; **~ [lap]** (Motor Racing) Aufwärmrunde, *die*

'war museum *n.* Kriegsmuseum, *das*

warn /wɔːn/ *v.t.* 1 (inform, give notice) warnen (**against, of, about** vor + *Dat.*); **~ sb. that ...:** jmdn. darauf hinweisen, dass ...; **you can't say I didn't ~ you** Sie können nicht behaupten, ich hätte Sie nicht gewarnt; **you have been ~ed!** ich habe/wir haben dich gewarnt!; **~ sb. not to do sth.** jmdn. davor warnen, etw. zu tun; **you might have ~ed us you were going to be late** du hättest uns wissen lassen können, dass du später kommen würdest 2 (admonish) ermahnen; (officially) abmahnen

Phrasal verb

- **~ 'off** *v.t.* 1 warnen; **~ sb. off doing sth.** jmdn. davor warnen, etw. zu tun 2 (Racing) Platzverbot erteilen (+ *Dat.*)

warning /ˈwɔːnɪŋ/

A *n.* 1 (advance notice) Vorwarnung, *die;* **he gave me no ~ of his intentions** er hat mir seine Absichten nicht angekündigt; **we had no ~ of their arrival** sie kamen ohne Vorwarnung; **give sb. plenty of/a few days' ~:** jmdm. rechtzeitig/ein paar Tage vorher Bescheid sagen 2 (lesson) Lehre, *die;* **let that be a ~ to you** lass dir/lasst euch das eine Warnung sein 3 (caution) Verwarnung, *die;* (less official) Warnung, *die*

B *attrib. adj.* Warn‹*schild, -zeichen, -signal usw.*›; **~ light/shot** Warnleuchte, *die*/-schuss, *der;* **~ notice** Warnung, *die;* **a ~ look/gesture** ein warnender Blick/eine warnende Geste; **~ triangle** Warndreieck, *das*

'War Office *n.* (Brit. Hist.) Kriegsministerium, *das*

warp /wɔːp/

A *v.i.* (become bent) sich verbiegen; ‹*Holz, Schallplatte:*› sich verziehen

B *v.t.* 1 (cause to become bent) verbiegen; **the sun had ~ed the boards** durch die Sonne hatten sich die Bretter verzogen 2 (fig.: pervert) verformen; verbiegen; **~ed** getrübt ‹*Urteilsvermögen*›; pervertiert ‹*Denken, Gehirn*›; **a ~ed sense of humour** ein abartiger Humor

C *n.* 1 (Weaving) Kettfaden, *der;* Kette, *die* (fachspr.) 2 (bent state) Werfen, *das* (fachspr.); (bend in a board etc.) verzogene Stelle; **there is a ~ in the record** die Platte hat sich verzogen 3 (fig.: perversion) Perversion, *die; see also* **time warp**

war: ~paint *n.* (also fig. coll. joc.) Kriegsbemalung, *die;* **~path** *n.* Kriegspfad, *der;* **be on the ~path** auf dem Kriegspfad sein; (fig.) in Rage sein; **~ pension** *n.* Kriegsrente, *die;* **~plane** *n.* Kampfflugzeug, *das;* **~ poet** *n.* Kriegslyriker, *der*

warrant /ˈwɒrənt/

A *n.* 1 (written order) (for sb.'s arrest) Haftbefehl, *der;* **[search] ~:** Durchsuchungsbefehl, *der* 2 (authority) Befugnis, *die;* (justification) Rechtfertigung, *die* 3 (dividend voucher) Dividendenschein, *der* 4 (Law) Vollmacht, *die;* **~ of attorney** anwaltliche Vollmacht

B *v.t.* 1 (justify) rechtfertigen; **her small income does not ~ such expenditure** ihr geringes Einkommen erlaubt ihr solche Ausgaben nicht

2 (guarantee) garantieren; garantieren für ‹*Produkt, Artikel*›; (dated) **you'll like it, I** *or* **I'll ~ you** (dated) es wird dir gefallen, das garantiere ich dir

warrantable /ˈwɒrəntəbl/ *adj.* vertretbar; **be ~:** zu rechtfertigen sein

ˈ**warrant officer** *n.* Warrant Officer, *der; Dienstgrad zwischen Oberstabsfeldwebel/Oberstabsbootsmann und Leutnant/Leutnant z. S.*

warranty /ˈwɒrəntɪ/ *n.* (Law, Commerc.) Garantie, *die;* **it is still under ~:** es steht noch unter *od.* darauf steht noch Garantie; *see also* **guarantee B 1**;

warren /ˈwɒrn/ *n.* 1 ▸**rabbit warren** 2 (fig.: densely populated area) Ameisenhaufen, *der* (fig.); (maze) Labyrinth, *das*

warring /ˈwɔːrɪŋ/ *adj.* Krieg führend; (fig.) sich bekämpfend

warrior /ˈwɒrɪə(r)/ *n.* 1 (esp. literary) Krieger, *der* (geh.) 2 *attrib.* (martial) kriegerisch; **a ~ nation/race** ein Kriegervolk

Warsaw /ˈwɔːsɔː/ ▸ⓘ **p. 1643**

A *pr. n.* Warschau *(das)*

B *attrib. adj.* Warschauer; **~ Pact** (Hist.) Warschauer Pakt

ˈ**warship** *n.* Kriegsschiff, *das*

wart /wɔːt/ *n.* Warze, *die;* **~s and all** (fig.) schonungslos; ungeschminkt [bis ins kleinste Detail]

ˈ**warthog** *n.* Warzenschwein, *das*

war: ~time *n.* 1 Kriegszeit, *die;* **in** *or* **during ~time** während des Krieges; im Krieg; 2 *attrib.* Kriegs‹*rationierung, -evakuierung usw.*›; **~time England** [das] England während des Krieges; **a ~time love affair** eine Kriegsliebe; **~-torn** *adj.* kriegsgeschunden; **~ trial** *n.* Kriegsprozess, *der;* **the Nuremberg ~ trials** die Nürnberger Kriegsverbrecherprozesse; **~ veteran** *n.* Kriegsveteran, *der*/-veteranin, *die;* **~-weary** *adj.* kriegsmüde; **~ widow** *n.* Kriegswitwe, *die;* Kriegerwitwe, *die* (geh. veralt.)

wary /ˈweərɪ/ *adj.* vorsichtig; (suspicious) misstrauisch (**of** gegenüber); **be ~ of** *or* **about doing sth.** sich davor hüten, etw. zu tun; **be ~ of sb./sth.** sich vor jmdm./etw. in Acht nehmen; **keep a ~ eye on sb.** jmdn. genau beobachten

ˈ**war zone** *n.* Kriegsgebiet, *das*

was ▸**be**

wash /wɒʃ/

A *v.t.* 1 waschen; **~ oneself** sich waschen; **~ one's hands** (also euphem.)/**face**/**hair** sich *(Dat.)* die Hände (auch verhüll.)/das Gesicht/die Haare waschen; **~ the clothes** Wäsche waschen; **~ the dishes** abwaschen; [Geschirr] spülen; **~ the floor** den Fußboden aufwischen *od.* feucht wischen; **~ one's hands of sb./sth.** mit jmdm./etw. nichts mehr zu tun haben wollen; **I don't wish to have anything more to do with the whole business. I ~ my hands of it** Ich will mit der ganzen Geschichte nichts mehr zu tun haben. Für mich ist die Sache erledigt

2 (remove) waschen ‹*Fleck*› (**out of** aus); abwaschen ‹*Schmutz*› (**off** von)

3 (by licking) putzen; **the cat ~ed its face/fur** die Katze putzte sich

4 (carry along) spülen; **be ~ed overboard/ashore** über Bord/an Land gespült werden; **be ~ed downstream** von der Strömung mitgerissen werden

5 ‹*Wellen, Meer:*› bespülen ‹*Klippen, Ufer*›. *see also* **linen A 2**

B *v.i.* 1 sich waschen

2 (clean clothes) waschen

3 ‹*Stoff, Kleidungsstück, Handtuch:*› sich waschen lassen; **that won't ~** (fig. coll.) das zieht nicht (ugs.); **an interesting theory, but it won't ~:** eine interessante Theorie, aber sie lässt sich nicht halten

4 (sweep) ‹*Brandung, Wellen:*› spülen; **~ over/against sth.** etw. überspülen/gegen etw. spülen

C *n.* 1 **give sb./sth. a [good] ~:** jmdn./etw. [gründlich] waschen; **the baby/car needs a ~** *or* (coll.) **could do with a ~:** das Kind/Auto müsste mal gewaschen werden; **I must have a ~ before lunch** ich muss mich vor dem Essen noch waschen

2 (laundering) Wäsche, *die;* **it is in the ~:** es ist in der Wäsche; **it'll all come out in the ~** (fig. coll.) das wird sich alles klären; **the week's ~:** die Wäsche von einer Woche

3 (of ship, aircraft, etc.) Sog, *der*

4 (lotion) Waschlotion, *die;* **a ~ for disinfecting the mouth** ein desinfizierendes Mundwasser; *see also* **eyewash; mouthwash**

5 (pig food) Schweinefutter, *das*

Phrasal verbs

- **~ aˈway** *v.t.* 1 wegspülen; hinwegspülen (geh.) 2 **~ a stain/the mud away** einen Fleck/den Schmutz auswaschen
- **~ ˈdown** *v.t.* 1 (clean dirt from) (with a hose) abspritzen ‹*Auto, Deck, Hof*›; (with soap and water) abwaschen; aufwaschen ‹*Fußboden*› 2 (help to go down) runterspülen (ugs.); **we lunched on beef ~ed down with beer** wir aßen Roastbeef und tranken Bier dazu
- **~ ˈoff**

A *v.t.* **~ sth. off** etw. abwaschen

B *v.i.* abgehen; (from fabric etc.) herausgehen

- **~ ˈout** *v.t.* 1 (clean) auswaschen ‹*Kleidungsstück*›; ausscheuern ‹*Topf*›; ausspülen ‹*Mund*›; **~ dirt/marks out of clothes** Schmutz/Flecken aus Kleidern [her]auswaschen 2 (stop; prevent from taking place) ins Wasser fallen lassen ‹*Sportveranstaltung*›; **several matches have been ~ed out** mehrere Spiele sind ins Wasser gefallen 3 (damage) unterspülen ‹*Brückenpfeiler, Straße*›. *See also* **washed-out; washout**
- **~ ˈover** *v.t.* 1 (fig. coll.: not affect) **~ over sb.** ‹*Streit, Lärm, Unruhe usw.:*› jmdn. gar nicht berühren; **she just sat back and let everything/the criticism ~ over her** sie saß einfach da und ließ alles/die Kritik an sich *(Dat.)* ablaufen (ugs.) 2 (sweep over) spülen über (+ *Akk.*)
- **~ ˈup**

A *v.t.* 1 (Brit.: clean) **~ up the dishes** das Geschirr abwaschen *od.* spülen 2 (carry to shore) anspülen ‹*Leiche, Strandgut, Wrackteile usw.*›

B *v.i.* 1 abwaschen; spülen; **who's going to help me ~ up?** wer hilft mir beim Abwaschen *od.* Spülen? 2 (Amer.) sich *(Dat.)* [Gesicht und Hände] waschen. *see also* **washed-up; washing-up**

washable /ˈwɒʃəbl/ *adj.* waschbar ‹*Stoff*›; abwaschbar ‹*Tapete, Farbe*›

wash: ~-and-ˈwear *adj.* bügelfrei; **~bag** *n.* (Brit.) Kulturbeutel, *der;* **~basin** *n.* Waschbecken, *das;* **~board** *n.* Waschbrett, *das;* **~ bowl** ▸**~basin**; **~cloth** *n.* 1 (Brit.: dishcloth) Abwaschlappen, *der;* Spültuch, *das;* 2 (Amer.: facecloth) Waschlappen, *der;* **~day** *n.* Waschtag, *der*

washed-ˈout *adj.* 1 *attrib.* (faded by washing) verwaschen ‹*Farbe, Kleidungsstück*› 2 (fig.: exhausted) abgespannt; mitgenommen; **I was** *or* **felt limp and ~:** ich fühlte mich schlapp und ausgelaugt

washed-ˈup *adj.* (coll.) kaputt (ugs.)

washer /ˈwɒʃə(r)/ *n.* (Mech. Engin.) Unterlegscheibe, *die;* (of tap) Dichtungsring, *der;* Dichtungsscheibe, *die*

ˈ**washerwoman** *n.* ▸ⓘ **p. 1260** Waschfrau, *die*

ˈ**wash-hand basin** *n.* Handwaschbecken, *das*

washing /ˈwɒʃɪŋ/ *n., no pl., no indef. art.* 1 (clothes to be washed) Wäsche, *die;* **take in ~:** Wäsche ins Haus nehmen; [zu Hause] für Kunden waschen 2 (cleansing) Waschen, *das;* **do the ~:** waschen; **children often don't like ~:** Kinder waschen sich oft nicht gerne; **the car needs ~:** der Wagen müsste mal gewaschen werden

washing: ~ day *n.* Waschtag, *der;* **~ machine** *n.* Waschmaschine, *die;* **~ powder** *n.* Waschpulver, *das;* **~ soda** *n.* Bleichsoda, *das* (veralt.); Natriumkarbonat, *das;* **~-ˈup** *n.* (Brit.) 1 Abwasch, *der;* **do the ~-up** den Abwasch machen; abwaschen; **the ~-up took him hours** er brauchte Stunden für den Abwasch; 2 (dirty dishes) **there was ~-up everywhere** überall stand schmutziges Geschirr herum; **~-ˈup liquid** *n.* Spülmittel, *das;* **~-ˈup machine** ▸**dishwasher 1**

> **The Washington Post**
>
> Eine amerikanische überregionale Tageszeitung, die in Washington erscheint. Sie ist bekannt für ihre politische Berichterstattung, ihren investigativen Journalismus auf hohem Niveau und ihre Liberalität.

wash: ~ leather *n.* Fensterleder, *das;* **~out** *n.* 1 (coll.: failure) Pleite, *die* (ugs.); Reinfall, *der* (ugs.); 2 (coll.: useless person) Niete, *die* (salopp abwertend); 3 (breach in road etc.) Unterspülung, *die;* **~room** *n.* (Amer.) WC, *das;* Waschraum, *der* (verhüll.); **~stand** *n.* Waschtisch, *der;* **~tub** *n.* Waschbottich, *der;* Waschzuber, *der;* **~woman** (Amer.) ▸**washerwoman**

washy /ˈwɒʃɪ/ *adj.* 1 (too watery) wässrig, dünn ‹*Tee, Suppe*› 2 (faded-looking) verwaschen ‹*Farbe*› 3 (feeble) verschwommen ‹*Ansichten, Meinungen*›; schwach, (ugs.) saft- und kraftlos ‹*Inszenierung, Übersetzung*›

wasn't /ˈwɒznt/ (coll.) **= was not;** ▸**be**

wasp *n.* Wespe, *die*

Wasp /wɒsp/ *n.* (Amer. derog.) **= white Anglo-Saxon Protestant** Angehöriger des weißen amerikanischen Bürgertums *(angelsächsischer Herkunft und protestantischer Konfession)*

waspish /ˈwɒspɪʃ/ *adj.*, **waspishly** /ˈwɒspɪʃlɪ/ *adv.* bissig

waspishness /ˈwɒspɪʃnɪs/ *n., no pl.* Bissigkeit, *die*

ˈ**wasp waist** *n.* Wespentaille, *die*

wassail /ˈwɒseɪl, ˈwɒsl/ (arch.)

A *n.* 1 (festivity) Trinkgelage, *das* 2 (liquor) *Wein/Bier, mit verschiedenen Zutaten gewürzt, vor allem zu Weihnachten getrunken*

B *v.i.* zechen

wastage /ˈweɪstɪdʒ/ *n.* 1 (loss by wear etc.) Schwund, *der* 2 **[natural] ~** (Admin.) ≈ natürliche Fluktuation

waste /weɪst/

A *n.* 1 (useless remains) Abfall, *der;* **disposal of ~:** Abfallbeseitigung, *die;* **kitchen ~, ~ from the kitchen** Küchenabfälle *Pl.* 2 (extravagant use) Verschwendung, *die;* Vergeudung, *die;* **it's a ~ of time/money/energy** das ist Zeit-/Geld-/Energieverschwendung; **it would be a ~ of effort** das wäre vergeudete Mühe; **it's a ~ of your time and mine** wir verschwenden beide nur unsere Zeit; **go** *or* **run to ~:** vergeudet werden 3 ▸**waste pipe** 4 (desert) Wüste, *die;* (barren land) Ödland, *das;* **the icy ~s of the Antarctic** die Eiswüste der Antarktis. *See also* **cotton waste**

B *v.t.* 1 (squander) verschwenden; vergeuden (**on** auf + *Akk.*, an + *Akk.*); **he is ~d on an audience like that** für ein solches Publikum ist er zu schade; **all his efforts were ~d** all seine Mühe war umsonst; **don't ~ my time!** stehlen Sie mir nicht die Zeit!; **you didn't ~ much time, did you?** da hast du aber keine Zeit verloren!; **~ one's life** sein Leben vergeuden; **you're wasting your breath** *or* **words!** deine Worte kannst du dir sparen!; **~ not, want not** (prov.) spare in der Zeit, so hast du in der Not (Spr.) 2 **be ~d** (reduced) ‹*Vorräte, Bevölkerung:*› abnehmen, schrumpfen 3 (arch.: cause to shrink) aufzehren ‹*Kräfte*›; auszehren ‹*Körper*›; **a ~d arm** ein geschrumpfter Arm 4 (literary: ravage) verwüsten ‹*Land*› 5 (Amer. sl.: murder) umlegen (salopp)

C *v.i.* dahinschwinden; (gradually) im Schwinden begriffen sein

D *adj.* 1 (not wanted) **~ material** Abfall, *der;* **~ food** Essensreste *Pl.;* **~ product** Abfallprodukt, *das;* **~ water** Abwasser, *das* 2 (uncultivated) brach; brachliegend; **lie ~:** brachliegen 3 **lay ~ [to] sth.** etw. verwüsten

Phrasal verb

- **~ aˈway** *v.i.* immer mehr abmagern

waste: ~basket ▸**waste-paper basket**; **~ disposal** *n., no pl.* Abfallbeseitigung, *die;* Entsorgung, *die* (Amtsspr.); **~ disposal site** *n.* [Müll]deponie *die;* **~ disposal unit** *n.* Müllzerkleinerer, *der*

wasteful /ˈweɪstfl/ *adj.* 1 (extravagant) verschwenderisch; **too much ~ expenditure** zu viel Geldverschwendung 2 (causing waste)

W

unwirtschaftlich; **be ~ of sth.** etw. vergeuden

wastefully /ˈweɪstfəlɪ/ *adv.* verschwenderisch; **sth. is ~ thrown away** etw. wird verschwenderischerweise weggeworfen; **he's ~ extravagant with money** er geht mit dem Geld außerordentlich verschwenderisch um

wastefulness /ˈweɪstflnɪs/ *n., no pl.* 1 (extravagance) Verschwendung, *die;* (character trait) Verschwendungssucht, *die;* **~ in the use of public funds** Verschwendung öffentlicher Gelder 2 (of manufacturing process) Unwirtschaftlichkeit, *die*

waste: ~land *n.* (not cultivated) Ödland, *das;* (not built on) unbebautes Land; (fig.) Einöde, *die;* **~ management** *n., no pl.* Abfallmanagement, *das;* Müllmanagement, *das;* **~ material** *n.* Abfall, *der;* **~ matter** *n., no pl.* Abfälle *Pl.;* Abfall, *der;* (from biological processes) Abfallstoffe *Pl.;* **~ paper** *n.* Papierabfall, *der;* **~-paper basket** *n.* Papierkorb, *der;* **~ pipe** *n.* Abflussrohr, *das;* **~ processing** *n., no pl.* Abfallaufbereitung, *die;* **~ processor** *n.* Müllzerkleinerer, *der;* **~ products** *n. pl.* Abfallprodukte *Pl.;* (from the body) Abfallstoffe *Pl.*

waster /ˈweɪstə(r)/ *n.* Verschwender, *der*/Verschwenderin, *die*

waste reduction *n., no pl.* Abfallverminderung, *die;* Müllreduzierung, *die*

wasting /ˈweɪstɪŋ/ *adj.* 1 (diminishing) schwindend; von Schwund befallen ‹*Muskel*› 2 (reducing vitality, robustness) **a ~ disease** eine Krankheit, bei der der Patient mehr und mehr verfällt

wastrel /ˈweɪstrəl/ *n.* 1 (good-for-nothing) Nichtsnutz, *der* 2 (wasteful person) Verschwender, *der*/Verschwenderin, *die*

watch /wɒtʃ/

A *n.* 1 ▸ℹ **p. 1001 wristwatch/pocket ~:** [Armband-/Taschen]uhr, *die* 2 (constant attention) Wache, *die;* **keep ~:** Wache halten; **keep [a] ~ for sb./sth.** auf jmdn./etw. achten *od.* aufpassen; **keep a [good** *or* **close] ~ on sb./sth.** [gut] auf jmdn./etw. aufpassen; **keep [a] ~ for enemy aircraft** nach feindlichen Flugzeugen Ausschau halten; **keep a close ~ on the time** genau auf die Zeit achten; **they kept a ~ on all his activities** sie überwachten alle seine Aktivitäten; **the police were on the ~ for car thieves** die Polizei hielt nach Autodieben Ausschau 3 (Mil., Naut. etc.) Wache, *die;* **starboard/port ~:** Steuerbord-/Backbordwache, *die;* **the officer of the ~:** der wachhabende Offizier; **in the ~es of the night** (literary) beim nächtlichen Wachen (geh.). *See also* **dogwatch**; **set A 13** 4 (Hist.: street guard) Wache, *die;* (one person) Wachmann, *der*

B *v.i.* 1 (wait) **~ for sb./sth.** auf jmdn./etw. warten; **~ for signs of improvement** nach Anzeichen einer Verbesserung Ausschau halten 2 (keep ~) Wache stehen

C *v.t.* 1 (observe) sich (*Dat.*) ansehen ‹*Sportveranstaltung, Fernsehsendung*›; **~ [the] television** *or* **TV** fernsehen; Fernsehen gucken (ugs.); **~ sth. [on television** *or* **TV]** sich (*Dat.*) etw. [im Fernsehen] ansehen; **~ sb. do** *or* **doing sth.** zusehen, wie jmd. etw. tut; **he just ~ed her drown** er sah einfach zu, wie sie ertrank; **we are being ~ed** wir werden beobachtet; **she had him ~ed** sie ließ ihn beobachten; **the police were ~ing the house** die Polizei beobachtete das Haus; **I want all of you to ~ this closely** ich möchte, dass ihr euch (*Dat.*) dies alle genau anseht; **I shall ~ your career with interest** ich werde Ihre Karriere mit Interesse verfolgen; **~ one's weight** auf sein Gewicht achten; **~ sheep/goats** *etc.* Schafe/Ziegen *usw.* hüten; **just ~ me!** (coll.) pass/passt mal auf! (ugs.); **~ this space** (fig.) man darf gespannt sein; das wird sich zeigen; **a ~ed pot never boils** (prov.) wenn man auf etwas wartet, kommt es einem wie eine Ewigkeit vor; *see also* **clock A 1** 2 (be careful of, look after) achten auf (+ *Akk.*); **~ your manners!** (coll.) benimm dich!; **~ your language!** (coll.) drück dich bitte etwas gepflegter *od.* nicht so ordinär aus!; **~ him, he's an awkward customer** (coll.) pass/passt auf, er ist mit Vorsicht zu genießen (ugs.); **~ how you go/drive** pass auf/fahr vorsichtig!; **~ it** *or* **oneself** sich vorsehen; **[just] ~ it [or you'll be in trouble]!** pass bloß auf[, sonst gibts Ärger]! (ugs.); *see also* **step A 1** 3 (look out for) warten auf (+ *Akk.*); **~ one's chance** die Gelegenheit abwarten

Phrasal verbs

- **~ ˈout** *v.i.* 1 (be careful) sich vorsehen; aufpassen; **~ out! There's a car coming!** Vorsicht! Da kommt ein Auto! 2 (look out) **~ out for sb./sth.** auf jmdn./etw. achten; (wait) auf jmdn./etw. warten
- **~ ˈover** *v.t.* sich kümmern um; in Obhut nehmen ‹*Wertgegenstand*›; ‹*Gott, Schutzengel:*› wachen über (+ *Akk.*); **she ~ed over the children as they played in the garden** sie passte auf die Kinder auf, die im Garten spielten

watch: ~ case *n.* Uhrgehäuse, *das;* **~ chain** *n.* Uhrkette, *die;* **~dog** *n.* Wachhund, *der;* (fig.) Wächter, *der;* Aufpasser, *der* (ugs.); **the ~dog function of the press** (fig.) das Wächteramt der Presse

watcher /ˈwɒtʃə(r)/ *n.* Beobachter, *der*/Beobachterin, *die;* **sky-~** Sterngucker, *der;* **television-~s** Fernsehzuschauer; **royalty-~s** Leute, die das Leben der königlichen Familie genau verfolgen

watchful /ˈwɒtʃfl/ *adj.* wachsam; **be ~ for** *or* **against sth.** vor etw. (*Dat.*) auf der Hut sein; **keep ~ guard** wachen; **keep a ~ eye on sb./sth.** ein wachsames Auge auf jmdn./etw. haben

watchfully /ˈwɒtʃfəlɪ/ *adv.* wachsam

watchfulness /ˈwɒtʃflnɪs/ *n., no pl.* Wachsamkeit, *die*

ˈwatch glass *n.* Uhrglas, *das*

watching brief /ˈwɒtʃɪŋ briːf/ *n.* Kontrollfunktion, *die;* **keep** *or* **hold a ~:** Stallwache halten

watch: ~maker *n.* ▸ℹ **p. 1260** Uhrmacher, *der*/Uhrmacherin, *die;* **~man** /ˈwɒtʃmən/ *n., pl.* **~men** /ˈwɒtʃmən/ ▸ℹ **p. 1260** Wachmann, *der;* **~ strap** *n.* [Uhr]armband, *das;* **~tower** *n.* Wachturm, *der;* **~word** *n.* Parole, *die*

water /ˈwɔːtə(r)/

A *n.* 1 Wasser, *das;* **this fruit is 80 per cent ~:** diese Frucht besteht zu 80 Prozent aus Wasser; **be under ~** ‹*Straße, Sportplatz usw.:*› unter Wasser stehen; **the island across** *or* **over the ~:** die Insel drüben; **the upper ~s of a river** der Oberlauf eines Flusses; **send/carry sth. by ~:** etw. auf dem Wasserweg versenden/befördern; **be in deep ~[s]** (fig.) in großen Schwierigkeiten sein; **get [oneself] into deep ~** (fig.) sich in große Schwierigkeiten bringen; **make ~** (urinate) Wasser lassen; (Naut.: leak) Wasser machen; **on the ~** (in boat etc.) auf dem Wasser; **pour** *or* **throw cold ~ on sth.** (fig.) einer Sache (*Dat.*) einen Dämpfer aufsetzen; **~ under the bridge** *or* **over the dam** (fig.) Schnee von gestern (fig.); **a lot of ~ has flowed under the bridge since then** seitdem ist schon viel Wasser den Rhein hinabgeflossen; *see also* **high water**; **hold² A 6**; **low water**; **spend 1** 2 *in pl.* (part of the sea etc.) Gewässer *Pl.;* **cross the ~s** übers Meer fahren 3 *in pl.* (mineral ~ at spa etc.) Heilquelle, *die;* Brunnen, *der;* **take** *or* **drink the ~s** eine Brunnenkur machen 4 (brilliance of gem) Wasser, *das;* **of the first ~** (lit. or fig.) reinsten Wassers; **a fool of the first ~:** ein Narr erster Güte (iron.); **a genius of the first ~:** ein Genie ersten Ranges

B *v.t.* 1 bewässern ‹*Land*›; wässern ‹*Pflanzen*›; **~ the flowers** die Blumen [be]gießen; **tears ~ed the ground** Tränen benetzten den Boden 2 (dilute) verwässern ‹*Wein, Bier usw.*› 3 ‹*Fluss:*› bewässern ‹*Land*› 4 (give drink of ~ to) tränken ‹*Tier, Vieh*›

C *v.i.* 1 ‹*Augen:*› tränen; **her eyes were ~ing from the smoke** von dem Rauch tränten ihr die Augen 2 (run with saliva) **my mouth was ~ing as …:** mir lief das Wasser im Munde zusammen, als …; **the very thought of it** *or* **just to think of it made my mouth ~:** allein bei dem Gedanken lief mir das Wasser im Munde zusammen; *see also* **mouth-watering** 3 (take in supply of ~) Wasser aufnehmen 4 (go to drink) ‹*Tier:*› saufen; **lions ~ing at dusk** Löwen in der Dämmerung an der Tränke

Phrasal verb

- **~ ˈdown** *v.t.* (lit. or fig.) verwässern

water: ~bed *n.* Wasserbett, *das;* **~bird** *n.* Wasservogel, *der;* **~ birth** *n.* Unterwassergeburt, *die;* **~ biscuit** *n.* Cracker, *der;* Kräcker, *der;* **~ boatman** *n.* (Zool.) Rückenschwimmer, *der;* **~-borne** *adj.* 1 (transported) auf dem Wasserweg befördert ‹*Güter*›; **~-borne traffic** Verkehr zu Wasser; 2 (transmitted) durch [Trink]wasser übertragen ‹*Infektion*›; 3 (afloat) flott ‹*Schiff, Boot*›; **~ bottle** *n.* Wasserflasche, *die;* **~ buffalo** *n.* Wasserbüffel, *der;* **~ bus** *n.* Fahrgastschiff, *das;* Linienschiff, *das;* **~ butt** *n.* Regentonne, *die;* **~ cannon** *n.* Wasserwerfer, *der;* **W~ carrier** *n.* (Astrol.) Wassermann, *der; see also* **archer 2**; **~ cart** *n.* Wasserkarren, *der;* (for sprinkling roads) Sprengwagen, *der;* **~ closet** *n.* Toilette, *die;* WC, *das;* Wasserklosett, *das* (veralt.); **~colour** *n.* 1 (paint) Wasserfarbe, *die;* 2 (picture) Aquarell, *das;* 3 *no pl., no indef. art.* (Art) Aquarellmalerei, *die;* **~colourist** *n.* Aquarellmaler, *der*/-malerin, *die;* **~-cooled** *adj.* wassergekühlt ‹*Motor usw.*›; **~ cooler** *n.* Kühltank, *der;* **~course** *n.* (stream etc.) Wasserlauf, *der;* (bed) Flussbett, *das;* **~cress** *n.* Brunnenkresse, *die;* **~ diviner** *n.* [Wünschel]rutengänger, *der*/-gängerin, *die*

watered /ˈwɔːtəd/ *adj.* **~ silk** Moiré, *der*

water: ~fall *n.* Wasserfall, *der;* **~ feature** *n.* Wasseranlage, *die;* **~fowl** *n.* Wasservogel, *der;* (collectively) Wassergeflügel, *das;* **~front** *n.* Ufer, *das;* **down on the ~front** unten am Wasser; *attrib.* **a ~front location/restaurant** eine Gegend/ein Restaurant am Wasser; **W~gate** *n.* (fig.) Watergate, *das;* **~ glass** *n.* (Chem.) Wasserglas, *das;* **~ heater** *n.* Heißwassergerät, *das;* **~hole** *n.* Wasserloch, *das;* **~ ice** *n.* ≈ Sorbet, *das;* ≈ Fruchteis, *das*

wateriness /ˈwɔːtərɪnɪs/ *n., no pl.* Wässrigkeit, *die;* Wässerigkeit, *die*

watering /ˈwɔːtərɪŋ/ *n.* Bewässerung, *die;* (of flowers, house plants) Gießen, *das;* **give the plants a thorough ~:** die Pflanzen gut wässern *od.* gießen

watering: ~ can *n.* Gießkanne, *die;* **~ hole** *n.* 1 ▸ **waterhole**; 2 (coll.: bar) Pinte, *die* (salopp); Destille, *die* (salopp); **~ place** *n.* 1 (for animals) Wasserstelle, *die;* Tränke, *die;* 2 (seaside resort) Seebad, *das;* (spa) Kurbad, *das*

water: ~ jacket *n.* Kühl[wasser]mantel, *der;* **~ jump** *n.* Wassergraben, *der*

waterless /ˈwɔːtəlɪs/ *adj.* wasserlos

water: ~ level *n.* 1 (in reservoir etc.) Wasserstand, *der;* Pegelstand, *der;* 2 (of ground water) Grundwasserspiegel, *der;* **~lily** *n.* Seerose, *die;* **~line** *n.* (Naut.) Wasserlinie, *die;* **~logged** /ˈwɔːtəlɒgd/ *adj.* voll gesogen ‹*Holz*›; ‹*Boot*› voll Wasser; nass, feucht ‹*Boden*›; aufgeweicht ‹*Sportplatz*›; **a ~logged ship** ein Schiff, das voll Wasser gelaufen ist

Waterloo /wɔːtəˈluː/ *n.* **the Battle of ~:** die Schlacht bei Belle-Alliance *od.* Waterloo; **meet one's ~:** sein Waterloo erleben

water: ~ main *n.* Hauptwasserleitung, *die;* **a burst ~ main** ein Wasserrohrbruch; **~man** /ˈwɔːtəmən/ *n., pl.* **~men** /ˈwɔːtəmən/ (plying for hire) Fährmann, *der;* (oarsman) Ruderer, *der;* **~mark** **A** *n.* Wasserzeichen, *das;* **B** *v.t.* mit Wasserzeichen versehen; **~marked paper** Papier mit Wasserzeichen; **~ meadow** *n.* Feuchtwiese, *die;* **~melon** *n.* Wassermelone, *die;* **~ meter** *n.* Wasseruhr, *die;* **~mill** *n.* Wassermühle, *die;* **~ pipe** *n.* 1 Wasserrohr, *das;* 2 (hookah) Wasserpfeife, *die;* **~ pistol** *n.* Wasserpistole, *die;* **~ polo** *n.* Wasserball, *der;* Wasserballspiel, *das;* **~ polo ball** Wasserball, *der;* **~ power** *n.* Wasserkraft, *die;* **~ pressure** *n.* Wasserdruck, *der;* **~proof** **A** *adj.* wasserdicht; wasserfest ‹*Farbe*›; **B** *n.* Regenhaut, *die;* (raincoat) Regenmantel, *der;* **C** *v.t.* wasserdicht machen; imprägnieren ‹*Stoff*›;

W

wetterfest machen ‹*Holzzaun, Gartenmöbel*›; ~ **purification plant** *n.* Wasseraufbereitungsanlage, *die;* ~**-purifying tablet** Wasserreinigungstablette, *die;* ~ **rat** *n.* Wasserratte, *die;* ~ **rate** *n.* Wassergeld, *das;* **the ~ rates** die Wassergebühren; ~**-repellent** *adj.* Wasser abstoßend; ~**-resistant** *adj.* wasserundurchlässig; wasserfest ‹*Farbe*›; ~**-saving** *adj.* wassersparend ‹*Armatur, Gerät usw.*›; Wasserspar‹*maßnahme*›; ~**shed** *n.* **1** (fig.: turning point) Wendepunkt, *der;* **2** (Geog.) Wasserscheide, *die;* **3** (Brit.) *Zeitpunkt am Abend, von dem an das Fernsehprogramm für Kinder nicht mehr geeignet ist;* ~**side** *n.* Ufer, *das; attrib.* **a ~side restaurant** ein Restaurant am Wasser; ~**ski A** *n.* Wasserski, *der;* **B** *v.i.* Wasserski laufen; ~**-skier** *n.* Wasserskiläufer, *der*/-läuferin, *die;* ~**skiing** *n., no pl., no art.* Wasserskilaufen, *das;* ~ **slide** *n.* Wasserrutschbahn, *die;* ~ **softener** *n.* Wasserenthärter, *der;* ~**-soluble** *adj.* wasserlöslich; ~**spout** *n.* **1** (Meteorol.) Wasserhose, *die;* **2** (drainage pipe) Abfluss, *der;* ~ **supply** *n.* **1** *no pl., no indef. art.* (providing) Wasserversorgung, *die;* **2** (stored drinking ~) Trinkwasser, *das;* (amount) [Trink]wasservorrat, *der;* ~ **table** *n.* Grundwasserspiegel, *der;* ~ **tap** *n.* Wasserhahn, *der;* ~**tight** *adj.* (lit. or fig.) wasserdicht; ~**tight compartment** wasserdichte Abteilung; **you can't treat these topics as a series of ~tight compartments** man kann diese Fragen nicht völlig isoliert voneinander betrachten; ~ **torture** *n.* Wasserfolter, *die;* ~ **tower** *n.* Wasserturm, *der;* ~ **vapour** *n., no pl.* Wasserdampf, *der;* ~ **vole** *n.* Schermaus, *die;* ~ **wagon** ▸**wagon 3**; ~**way** *n.* Wasserstraße, *die;* **inland ~ways** Binnenwasserstraßen; ~**weed** *n., no pl., no indef. art.* Wasserpflanzen *Pl.;* ~**wheel** *n.* Wasserrad, *das;* (used to raise ~) Schöpfrad, *das;* ~ **wings** *n. pl.* Schwimmflügel; ~**works** *n.* **1** *sing., pl. same* (system) Wasserversorgungssystem, *das;* (establishment) Wasserwerk, *das;* **2** *pl.* (coll.: tears) **turn on the ~works** losheulen (ugs.); **3** *pl.* (coll.: urinary system) Blase, *die;* **he's got something wrong with his ~works** er hat was an der Blase (ugs.)

watery /'wɔːtərɪ/ *adj.* wässrig, wässerig ‹*Essen, Suppe*›; feucht ‹*Augen*›; dünn ‹*Getränk*›; (fig.: insipid) [saft- und] kraftlos ‹*Stil*›; müde, matt ‹*Lächeln*›; (fig.: pale) matt ‹*Farbton*›; fahl ‹*Mond, Himmel*›; **a ~ grave** ein feuchtes *od.* nasses Grab

watt /wɒt/ *n.* (Electr., Phys.) Watt, *das;* **how many ~s is this bulb?** wie viel Watt hat diese Birne?

wattage /'wɒtɪdʒ/ *n.* (Electr.) Wattzahl, *die;* **what ~ is this bulb?** wie viel Watt hat diese Birne?

'watt-hour *n.* (Electr.) Wattstunde, *die*

wattle¹ /'wɒtl/ *n.* **1** (material) Flechtwerk, *das;* **a ~ fence** ein Flechtzaun; **~ and daub** Lehmflechtwerk, *das* **2** *in sing. or pl.* (twigs) Geflecht, *das;* Flechtwerk, *das* **3** (Bot.) Gerberakazie, *die*

wattle² *n.* (Ornith.) Kehllappen, *der*

wave /weɪv/

A *n.* **1** (lit. or fig.) Welle, *die;* Woge, *die* (geh.); (in hair, Phys.) Welle, *die;* **rule the ~s** die Meere beherrschen; **his hair has a natural ~ in it** sein Haar ist von Natur aus wellig; **a ~ of enthusiasm/prosperity/pain** eine Welle der Begeisterung/des Wohlstands/des Schmerzes; **a ~ of depression overtook him** er versank in tiefe Depression; **~s of immigrants** Einwanderungswellen; **~s of attackers** Angriffswellen; *see also* **cold wave**; **heatwave**; **permanent wave** **2** (gesture) **give sb. a ~:** jmdm. zuwinken; **with a ~ of one's hand** mit einem Winken

B *v.i.* **1** ‹*Fahne, Flagge, Wimpel:*› wehen; ‹*Baum, Gras, Korn:*› sich wiegen; ‹*Kornfeld:*› wogen **2** (gesture with hand) winken; **~ at** *or* **to sb.** jmdm. zuwinken

C *v.t.* **1** schwenken; (brandish) schwingen ‹*Schwert, Säbel*›; **~ one's hand at** *or* **to sb.** jmdm. zuwinken; **~ one's handkerchief [in the air]** mit dem Taschentuch winken; **they ~d their arms in exultation** sie ruderten vor Begeisterung mit den Armen; **she ~d her umbrella angrily at him** sie drohte ihm wütend mit dem Regenschirm; **stop waving that rifle/those scissors around** hör auf, mit dem Gewehr/der Schere herumzufuchteln (ugs.); **~ sb. on/over** jmdn. weiter-/herüberwinken; **~ sb. to do sth.** jmdm. durch Winken zu verstehen geben, dass er etw. tun soll; **~ goodbye to sb.** jmdm. zum Abschied zuwinken; **she ~d acknowledgement to him** sie winkte ihm zu, um [ihm] zu danken **2** (make wavy) wellen

(Phrasal verbs)

- **~ a'side** *v.t.* **1** (refuse to accept) abtun ‹*Zweifel, Einwand*›; **he refused the dish, waving it aside** er wollte das Essen nicht und winkte ab **2** (signal to move aside) **I tried to speak but she ~d me aside** ich wollte reden, aber sie winkte ab
- **~ a'way** *v.t.* wegwinken
- **~ 'down** *v.t.* [durch Winken] anhalten
- **~ 'off** *v.t.* **~ sb. off** jmdm. nachwinken

wave: ~**band** *n.* Wellenbereich, *der;* ~ **equation** *n.* (Phys.) Wellengleichung, *die;* ~ **form** *n.* Wellenform, *die;* ~ **front** *n.* Wellenfront, *die;* ~ **guide** *n.* Wellenleiter, *der;* ~**length** *n.* (Radio, Telev., Phys.; also fig.) Wellenlänge, *die;* **be on sb.'s ~length** (fig.) die gleiche Wellenlänge wie jmd. haben; **be on the same ~length [as sb.]** (fig.) die gleiche Wellenlänge [wie jmd.] haben; ~ **machine** *n.* Wellenmaschine, *die;* ~ **power** *n.* Wellenkraft, *die*

waver /'weɪvə(r)/ *v.i.* **1** (begin to give way) wanken; **start** *or* **begin to ~:** ins Wanken geraten **2** (be irresolute) zaudern; schwanken (**between** zwischen + *Dat.*) **3** (flicker) ‹*Kerze, Licht:*› flackern; ‹*Schatten:*› tanzen **4** (tremble) ‹*Stimme, Ton:*› zittern

waverer /'weɪvərə(r)/ *n.* Zauderer, *der*/Zauderin, *die*

wavering /'weɪvərɪŋ/ *adj.* **1** wankend ‹*Mut, Entschlossenheit*›; schwankend ‹*Unterstützung*› **2** (flickering) flackernd ‹*Kerze, Licht*›; tanzend ‹*Schatten*›; zitternd ‹*Stimme, Ton*›

wavy /'weɪvɪ/ *adj.* **1** (undulating) wellig; wogend ‹*Gras*› **2** (forming wave-like curves) geschlängelt; **~ line** Schlangenlinie, *die;* **~ pattern** Wellenmuster, *das*

wax¹ /wæks/

A *n.* **1** Wachs, *das;* **be [like] ~ in sb.'s hands** [wie] Wachs in jmds. Händen sein **2** (in ear) Schmalz, *das* **3** ▸**sealing wax**. *see also* **paraffin wax**

B *adj.* Wachs-

C *v.t.* wachsen; wichsen ‹*Schnurrbart*›

wax² *v.i.* **1** (increase) ‹*Mond:*› zunehmen; **~ and wane** (fig.) zu- und abnehmen; **the political parties may ~ and wane, but he ...:** die politischen Parteien mögen gewinnen und verlieren, er aber ... **2** (become) werden; **~ enthusiastic about sth.** über etw. (*Akk.*) ins Schwärmen geraten; **she ~ed indignant about the rudeness of the officials** sie empörte sich [immer mehr] über die Unhöflichkeit der Beamten

wax 'crayon *n.* Wachsmalstift, *der*

waxed /wækst/ *adj.* gewachst; gewichst ‹*Schnurrbart*›; **~ paper** Wachspapier, *das*

waxen /'wæksn/ *adj.* **1** (pale, smooth) wächsern ‹*Blässe, Haut*› **2** (arch./literary: made of wax) wächsern; wächsen (dichter. veralt.)

waxing /'wæksɪŋ/

A *adj.* (increasing) zunehmend; wachsend ‹*Begeisterung, Unmut*›

B *n., no pl.* (increase) Zunehmen, *das;* (of enthusiasm, indignation) Zunahme, *die;* [An]wachsen, *das*

wax: ~**work** *n.* Wachsfigur, *die;* ~**works** *n. sing., pl. same* Wachsfigurenkabinett, *das*

waxy /'wæksɪ/ *adj.* **1** (easily moulded) wachsweich; weich wie Wachs *nicht attr.* **2** (pale, smooth) wächsern ‹*Blässe, Glanz, Haut*›

way /weɪ/

A *n.* **1** (road etc., lit. or fig.) Weg, *der;* **across** *or* **over the ~:** gegenüber; **go the ~ of all good things** den Weg alles Irdischen gehen; **the W~ of the Cross** der Kreuzweg; *see also* **flesh A 3** **2** ▸❶ **p. 1699** (route) Weg, *der;* **ask the** *or* **one's ~:** nach dem Weg fragen; **ask the ~ to ...:** fragen *od.* sich erkundigen, wo es nach ... geht; **pick one's ~:** sich (*Dat.*) einen Weg suchen; **he picked his ~ through the mud** er bahnte sich mühsam einen Weg durch den Schlamm; **show sb. the ~:** jmdn. den Weg zeigen; **show the ~** (fig.) den Weg weisen; **lead the ~:** vorausgehen; (fig.: show how to do sth.) es vormachen; **point the ~ to a new solution to the problem** den Weg zu einer neuen Lösung des Problems aufzeigen; **'W~ In/Out'** „Ein-/Ausgang"; **find the** *or* **one's ~ in/out** den Eingang/Ausgang finden; **there's no ~ out** (fig.) es gibt keinen Ausweg; **find a ~ out** (fig.) einen Ausweg finden; **I'll take the letter to the post office — it's on my ~:** ich bringe den Brief zur Post — sie liegt auf meinem Weg; **how did your cigarettes find their ~ into my coat pocket?** wie kommen deine Zigaretten in meine Manteltasche?; **go to Italy by ~ of Switzerland** über die Schweiz nach Italien fahren; **the ~ back/down/up** der Weg zurück/nach unten/nach oben; **go one's ~:** weggehen; seiner Wege gehen (veralt.); **go one's own ~/their separate ~s** (fig.) eigene/getrennte Wege gehen; **be going sb.'s ~:** denselben Weg wie jmd. haben; **things are really going my ~ at the moment** (fig.) im Moment läuft [bei mir] alles so, wie ich es mir vorgestellt habe; **things could have gone the other ~:** es hätte auch anders ausgehen können; **money came his ~:** er kam zu Geld; **many offers came his ~:** er kriegte viele Angebote; **he worked at any job that came his ~:** er arbeitete in jedem Job, den er kriegen konnte; **I wish some better luck would come my ~:** ich wünschte mir, etwas mehr Glück zu haben; **I feel as though nothing nice has come my ~ for ages** mir ist, als hätte ich schon ewig nichts Schönes mehr erlebt; **when a girl like that comes your ~:** wenn dir so ein Mädchen begegnet *od.* (ugs.) über den Weg läuft; **be [a bit] out of sb.'s ~:** ein [kleiner] Umweg [für jmdn.] sein; **go out of one's ~ to collect sth. for sb.** einen Umweg machen, um etw. für jmdn. abzuholen; **go out of one's ~ to be helpful** sich (*Dat.*) besondere Mühe geben, hilfsbereit zu sein; **out of the ~:** abgelegen; **nothing out of the ~** (fig.) nichts Un- *od.* Außergewöhnliches; *see also* **find A 9**; **go A 2, 16, 17**; **go down 2**; **keep out of 2**; **lose A 3**; **out-of-the-way**; **take A 20**; **way-out** **3** (method) Art und Weise, *die;* **there is a right ~ and a wrong ~ of doing it** es gibt einen richtigen und einen falschen Weg, es zu tun; **that is not the ~ to do it** so macht man das nicht; **do it this ~:** mach es so; **do it my ~:** mach es wie ich; **I did it my ~:** ich habe es auf meine Art gemacht; **it's awful the ~ he swears** es ist fürchterlich, wie er flucht; **I don't like the ~ she smiles** mir gefällt ihr Lächeln nicht; **I don't like the ~ it gets dark so early** mir gefällt nicht, dass es schon so früh dunkel wird; **I object to** *or* **don't like the ~ he looks at me** ich mag nicht, wie er mich ansieht; **that's no ~ to speak to a lady** so spricht man nicht mit einer Dame; **it was his ~ of working** das war seine Art zu arbeiten; **he has a strange ~ of talking** er hat eine seltsame Sprechweise *od.* Art zu sprechen; **from** *or* **by the ~ [that] she looked at me, I knew that there was something wrong** an ihrem Blick konnte ich erkennen, dass etwas nicht stimmte; **she has a strange ~ of behaving** sie hat ein merkwürdiges Benehmen; **what a ~ to behave!** wie kann man sich nur so benehmen!; **she has a very original ~ of saying/seeing things** sie hat eine sehr originelle Art, etwas zu sagen/die Dinge zu sehen; **find a** *or* **some ~ of doing sth.** einen Weg finden, etw. zu tun; **there are no two ~s about it** da gibt es gar keinen Zweifel; **Are you going to give me that money? — No ~!** (coll.) Gibst du mir das Geld? — Nichts da! (ugs.); **there was no ~ he would change his stand** er würde auf gar keinen Fall seinen Standpunkt ändern; **no ~ is he coming with us** es kommt überhaupt nicht in Frage, dass er mit uns kommt; **one ~ or another** irgendwie; **~s**

W

ℹ Asking the way

The questions

1. ***How do I get to the station?***
   = Wie komme ich zum Bahnhof?
2. ***Which is the best way to the museum?***
   = Wie kommt man am besten zum Museum?
3. ***Am I right for the Hotel zur Post?***
   = Geht es hier zum Hotel zur Post?
4. ***Where is the nearest bank?***
   = Wo ist hier die nächste Bank?
5. ***Is there a chemist's near here?***
   = Gibt es hier in der Nähe eine Apotheke?
6. ***How far is it to the hospital?***
   = Wie weit ist es zum Krankenhaus?
7. ***Can you direct me to a good restaurant?***
   = Können Sie mir sagen, wo es hier ein gutes Restaurant gibt?

Possible replies

1. ***Take the first turning on the right, then the second on the left, then go straight on as far as the junction. Turn right and you will see the station in front of you***
   = Gehen Sie die erste Straße rechts, dann die zweite links, dann immer nur geradeaus bis zur Kreuzung. Biegen Sie rechts ein und dann sehen Sie den Bahnhof vor sich
2. ***The best way is to cross over here at the lights and go down the alleyway along the left side of the theatre. You will come out opposite the museum.***
   = Am besten, Sie gehen hier an der Ampel über die Straße, dann die Gasse entlang, die links am Theater vorbeiführt. Sie kommen dann gegenüber vom Museum heraus
3. ***No, you've come too far. Go back to the crossroads and turn left, you'll find the hotel about a hundred yards further on on the right***
   = Nein, Sie sind zu weit gegangen/(*in car*) gefahren. Gehen/Fahren Sie zurück zur Kreuzung und biegen Sie links ab. Das Hotel liegt etwa hundert Meter weiter auf der rechten Seite
4. ***There is a branch of Barclays on the market place, which is a couple of hundred yards along that turning over there on the right***
   = Am Marktplatz ist eine Filiale von Barclays. Biegen Sie dort drüben rechts ein, Sie kommen dann nach ein paar hundert Metern zum Marktplatz
5. ***There's one in the next street on the left, but it's only small. If you want a bigger one you'll have to take the number 11 bus into the centre***
   = In der nächsten Straße links ist eine, allerdings nur eine kleine. Falls Sie eine größere brauchen, müssen Sie mit der Linie 11 ins Zentrum fahren
6. ***It's about a mile and a half from here on the main Cardiff road. You'd best take a taxi as the buses aren't very frequent***
   = Es liegt etwa zwei Kilometer von hier an der Hauptstraße nach Cardiff. Am besten nehmen Sie ein Taxi, die Busse fahren nämlich nicht sehr oft
7. ***Sorry, I'm a stranger here myself***
   = Tut mir Leid, ich bin auch fremd hier

and means [to do sth. *or* **of doing sth.]** Mittel und Wege, etw. zu tun; **be built** *or* **made that ~** (fig. coll.) so gestrickt sein (fig. ugs.); **be that ~** (coll.) so sein; **better that ~:** besser so; **either ~:** so oder so; **that ~, we can ...:** auf die Weise können wir ...; *see also* **hard A 2; mend A 2**

4▸ (desired course of action) Wille, *der;* **get** *or* **have one's [own] ~, have it one's [own] ~:** seinen Willen kriegen; **all right, have it your own ~[, then]!** na gut *od.* schön, du sollst deinen Willen haben!

5▸ ▸ℹ **p. 1072** *in sing. or* (*Amer. coll.*) *pl.* (distance between two points) Stück, *das;* **a little ~:** ein kleines Stück[chen]; (fig.) ein klein[es] bisschen; **it's a long ~ off** *or* **a long ~ from here** es ist ein ganzes Stück von hier aus; es ist weit weg von hier; **the summer holidays are only a little ~ off** *or* **away** bis zu den Sommerferien ist es nicht mehr lange; **we went a little/a long/some ~ with him** wir sind ein kleines/ganzes/ziemliches Stück mit ihm gegangen/gefahren *usw.;* **there's [still] some ~ to go yet** es ist noch ein ganzes Stück; (fig.) es dauert noch ein Weilchen; **I went a little/a long/some ~ to meet him** ich bin ihm ein kleines/ganzes/ziemliches Stück entgegengegangen/-gefahren *usw.,* um mich mit ihm zu treffen; (fig.) ich bin ihm etwas/sehr/ziemlich entgegengekommen; **it is still a long ~ off perfection** *or* **from being perfect** es ist noch weit davon entfernt, vollkommen zu sein; **India is a long ~ away** *or* **off** Indien ist weit weg; **by a long ~** (fig.) bei weitem; **your work isn't good enough yet — not by a long ~:** Ihre Arbeit ist noch nicht gut genug — bei weitem nicht; **have gone/come a long ~** (fig.) es weit gebracht haben; **go a long ~ toward sth./doing sth.** viel zu etw. beitragen/viel dazu beitragen, etw. zu tun; **a little kindness/politeness goes a long ~:** ein bisschen Freundlichkeit/Höflichkeit ist viel wert *od.* hilft viel; **all the ~:** den ganzen Weg; **go all the ~ [with sb.]** (fig.) [jmdm.] in jeder Hinsicht zustimmen; (coll.: have full sexual intercourse) es [mit jmdm.] richtig machen (salopp)

6▸ (room for progress) Weg, *der;* **block the ~:** den Weg versperren; **his ~ to promotion was blocked by a jealous rival** seine Karriere wurde durch einen neidischen Rivalen versperrt; **leave the ~ open for sth.** (fig.) etw. möglich machen; **clear the ~ [for sth.]** (lit. or fig.) [einer Sache (*Dat.*)] den Weg freimachen; **be in sb.'s** *or* **the ~:** [jmdm.] im Weg sein; **you are in my ~:** du bist [mir] im Wege; **get in sb.'s ~** (lit. or fig.) jmdm. im Wege stehen; **put difficulties/obstacles in sb.'s ~** (fig.) jmdm. Schwierigkeiten bereiten/Hindernisse in den Weg legen; **make ~ for sth.** für etw. Platz schaffen *od.* (fig.) machen; **make ~ for sb.** für jmdn. Platz machen; **make ~ for the Mayor!** Platz für den Bürgermeister!; **make ~!** Platz da!; **[get] out of the/my ~!** [geh] aus dem Weg!; **move one's car out of the ~:** seinen Wagen aus dem Weg fahren; **can you get your books out of the ~?** kannst du deine Bücher woanders hinlegen?; **I must put that pile of old newspapers out of the ~:** ich muss den Stapel alter Zeitungen wegräumen; **please get the children out of the ~ while I do this painting** bitte sorge dafür, dass die Kinder nicht im Weg sind, während ich hier streiche; **get sth. out of the ~** (settle sth.) etw. erledigen; **let's get the awkward questions out of the ~ first** wir wollen erst einmal die schwierigen Fragen hinter uns bringen; **he'll be out of the ~ for a very long time** (in prison) er ist für lange Zeit aus dem Verkehr gezogen; **he wanted this troublesome rival out of the ~ [for good]** er wollte diesen lästigen Rivalen [für immer] aus dem Weg haben; *see also* **bar[1] B 3; give way; keep out of 2; see[1] A 1; stand A 8**

7▸ (journey) **on his ~ to the office/London** auf dem Weg ins Büro/nach London; **on the ~ out to Singapore** auf dem Hinweg/der Hinfahrt/dem Hinflug nach Singapur; **on the ~ back from Nigeria** auf dem Rückweg/der Rückfahrt/dem Rückflug von Nigeria; **she is just on the** *or* **her ~ in/out** sie kommt/geht gerade; **be on the ~ in** (fig. coll.) ‹*Mode, Popstar usw.:*› im Kommen sein (ugs.); **be on the ~ out** (fig. coll.) (be losing popularity) passé sein (ugs.); (be reaching end of life) ‹*Hund, Auto, Person:*› es nicht mehr lange machen (ugs.); **we stopped on the ~ to have lunch** wir hielten unterwegs zum Mittagessen an; **on her ~ home** auf dem Nachhauseweg; **they're on their ~:** sie sind unterwegs; **on the ~ there** auf dem Hinweg; **be well on the ~ to becoming an alcoholic/a top-class player** auf dem besten Weg sein, Alkoholiker/ein Spitzenspieler zu werden; **the book is well on the** *or* **its ~ to completion** das Buch nähert sich dem Abschluss; **be on the ~** (coll.) ‹*Kind:*› unterwegs sein (ugs.); **[be] on your ~!** nun geh schon!; **by the ~:** übrigens; **I saw your mother, by the ~:** übrigens, ich habe deine Mutter getroffen; **all this is by the ~:** das alles nur nebenbei

8▸ (specific direction) Richtung, *die;* **she went this/that/the other ~:** sie ist in diese/die/die andere Richtung gegangen; **look this ~, please** sieh/seht bitte hierher!; **he wouldn't look my ~:** er hat nicht zu mir herübergesehen; **which ~ is he looking/going?** in welche Richtung *od.* wohin sieht/geht er?; **I will call next time I'm [down] your ~:** wenn ich das nächste Mal in deiner Gegend bin, komme ich [bei dir] vorbei; **she lives Brighton ~** (coll.) sie wohnt in der Gegend von Brighton; **out Hendon ~** (coll.) draußen bei Hendon; **look the other ~** (lit. or fig.) weggucken; **the other ~ about** *or* **round** andersherum; **this/which ~ round** so/wie herum; **stand sth. the right/wrong ~ up** etw. richtig/falsch herum stellen; **turn sth. the right ~ round** etw. richtig herum drehen; **'this ~ up'** „hier oben"; *see also* **look A 1; wrong A 3**

9▸ (advance) Weg, *der;* **fight/push** *etc.* **one's ~ through** sich durchkämpfen/-drängen; **be under ~** ‹*Person:*› aufgebrochen sein; ‹*Fahrzeug:*› abgefahren sein; (fig.: be in progress) ‹*Besprechung, Verhandlung, Tagung:*› im Gange sein; **get sth. under ~** (fig.) etw. in Gang bringen; **get under ~:** wegkommen; **make one's ~ to Oxford/the station** nach Oxford/zum Bahnhof gehen/fahren; **Do you need a lift? — No, I'll make my own ~:** Soll ich dich mitnehmen? — Nein, ich komme alleine; **make one's [own] ~ in the world** seinen Weg gehen (fig.); **make** *or* **pay its ~:** ohne Verlust arbeiten; **pay one's ~:** für sich selbst aufkommen

10▸ (respect) Hinsicht, *die;* **in [exactly] the same ~:** [ganz] genauso; **in some ~s** in gewisser Hinsicht; **in one ~:** auf eine Art; **not in any ~:** in keiner Weise; **in every ~:** in jeder Hinsicht; **in a ~:** auf eine Art; **in more ~s than one** auf mehr als eine Art; **in no ~:** auf keinen Fall; durchaus nicht; **one ~ and** *or* **or another** irgendwie

11▸ (state) Verfassung, *die;* **in a bad ~:** schlecht; **they are in a very bad ~:** es geht ihnen sehr schlecht; **the ~ things are, we shall never manage to get out of debt** so, wie die Dinge liegen, werden wir nie schuldenfrei sein; **we are all in the same ~ here** wir sind hier alle in der gleichen Lage *od.* Situation; **and she stayed that ~:** und so ist sie auch geblieben; **either ~:** so oder so; **in a small ~:** in bescheidenem Rahmen; **by ~ of** (as a kind of) als; (for the purpose of) um ... zu; **by ~ of illustration / greeting / apology / introduction** zur Illustration / Begrüßung / Entschuldigung/Einführung; **by ~ of business** geschäftlich; **he is by ~ of being a humorist** er ist eine Art von Humorist; **offer something in the ~ of a concession** eine Art Konzession anbieten; *see also* **family 1**

12▸ (custom) Art, *die;* **get into/out of the ~ of doing sth.** sich (*Dat.*) etw. an-/abgewöhnen; **he has a ~ of leaving his bills unpaid** es ist so seine Art, seine Rechnungen nicht zu bezahlen; **these bright ideas have a ~ of turning out badly** solche brillanten Ideen haben es an sich (*Dat.*), zu nichts Gutem zu führen; **in its ~:** auf seine/ihre Art; **~ of life** Lebensstil, *der;* **change one's ~s** sich ändern; **~ of thinking**

Denkungsart, *die;* **to my ~ of thinking** meiner Meinung nach; **that's just the ~ of the world** das ist ganz natürlich; **that's the ~ it goes** so ist es nun mal

13 (normal course of events) **be the ~:** so *od.* üblich sein; **that is always the ~:** das ist immer so

14 (ability to charm sb. or attain one's object) **he has a ~ with him** er hat so eine Art; **she has a ~ with children/animals** sie kann mit Kindern/Tieren gut umgehen

15 (specific manner) Eigenart, *die;* **I soon got into his ~s** ich hatte mich bald an seine Art gewöhnt; **fall into bad ~s** schlechte [An]gewohnheiten annehmen; **I soon got into the ~ of it** *or* **of things** ich hatte mich bald daran gewöhnt; **it's only his ~:** das ist so seine Art

16 (sphere) Gebiet, *das;* **he is in the grocery ~:** er ist in der Lebensmittelbranche; **a few things in the stationery ~:** ein paar Büroartikel

17 (ordinary course) Rahmen, *der;* **in the ~ of business** geschäftlich; **in the ordinary ~ [of things] there would be no problem** normalerweise gäbe es keine Schwierigkeiten

18 (movement of ship etc.) Fahrt, *die;* **gather ~:** Fahrt aufnehmen; **lose ~:** die Fahrt verlangsamen; **the vessel has ~ on [her]** das Schiff macht Fahrt

19 *in pl.* (parts) Teile *Pl.;* **split sth. [in] three ~s** etw. in drei Teile teilen

20 *in pl.* (down which ship is launched) Helling, *die*

21 *as name of road* Weg, *der*

B *adv.* weit; **~ off/ahead/above** weit weg von/weit voraus/weit über; **~ back** (coll.) vor langer Zeit; **~ back in the early fifties/before the war** vor langer Zeit, Anfang der Fünfzigerjahre/vor dem Krieg; **~ up in the clouds** hoch oben in den Wolken; **he was ~ out with his guess, his guess was ~ out** er lag mit seiner Schätzung gewaltig daneben; **~ down south/in the valley** tief [unten] im Süden/Tal

way: ~bill *n.* Frachtbrief, *der;* **~farer** /ˈweɪfeərə(r)/ *n.* (literary) Wandersmann, *der* (geh. veralt.); **~faring** /ˈweɪfeərɪŋ/ *adj.* (literary) **a ~-faring man/woman** ein Wandersmann/eine Wanderin; **~ˈlay** *v.t., forms as* **lay² A** 1 (ambush) überfallen; 2 (stop for conversation) abfangen; **~mark** A *n.* Wegmarke, *die;* Wegzeichen, *das;* B *v.t.* markieren; **~-ˈout** *adj.* (coll.) irre (salopp); (avant garde) avantgardistisch; **~point** *n.* 1 (stopping place) Zwischenstation, *die;* **this was our first ~point** dort machten wir zum ersten Mal Halt; 2 (coordinates) Wegpunkt, *der;* **~side** *n.* Wegrand, *der;* **fall by the ~side** (fig.) auf der Strecke bleiben (ugs.); *attrib.* **~side flowers/inns** Blumen/Gasthöfe am Wegrand; **~station** *n.* (Amer. Railw.) Haltepunkt, *der*

wayward /ˈweɪwəd/ *adj.* eigenwillig; ungezügelt ‹*Talent, Macht*›

waywardly /ˈweɪwədlɪ/ *adv.* eigenwillig; unberechenbar ‹*sich verändern*›

waywardness /ˈweɪwədnɪs/ *n., no pl.* Eigenwilligkeit, *die*

WC *abbr.* = **water closet** WC, *das*

we /wɪ, *stressed* wi:/ *pl. pron.* wir; **how are we feeling today?** (coll.) wie gehts uns denn heute? (ugs.); **the royal 'we'** der Pluralis Majestatis; *see also* **our; ours; ourselves; us**

weak /wi:k/ *adj.* 1 (lit. or fig.) schwach; matt ‹*Lächeln*›; schwach ausgeprägt ‹*Kinn*›; jämmerlich ‹*Kapitulation*›; (easily led) labil ‹*Charakter, Person*›; **go/feel ~ at the knees** weiche Knie kriegen/haben; **the ~er sex** das schwache Geschlecht; **~ with hunger/excitement** schwach vor Hunger/Aufregung; **~ eyes** *or* **sight** schlechte Augen; **a ~ stomach** ein empfindlicher Magen; **have a ~ chest** schwach auf der Brust sein; **be ~ in the head** schwachsinnig sein; **his French/maths is rather ~, he's rather ~ in French/maths** in Französisch/Mathematik ist er ziemlich schwach; **a ~ hand** (Cards) ein schlechtes Blatt; **in a ~ moment** in einem schwachen Moment; **sb.'s ~ side** *or* **point** jmds. schwache Seite *od.* schwacher Punkt *od.* Schwachpunkt; **his logic is a bit ~:** seine Logik steht auf ziemlich schwachen Füßen; **he has only a ~ case** seine Sache steht auf schwachen Füßen; *see also* **vessel 3** 2 (watery) schwach, dünn ‹*Kaffee, Tee*›; wässrig, wässerig ‹*Suppe*›; dünn ‹*Bier*› 3 (Ling.) schwach ‹*Konjugation, Deklination, Verb*›; unbetont ‹*Endung, Vokal, Silbe*›

weaken /ˈwi:kn/

A *v.t.* schwächen; beeinträchtigen ‹*Augen*›; entkräften, schwächen ‹*Argument*›; lockern ‹*Griff*›; **be ~ed by stress/too much work** durch Stress/zu viel Arbeit angegriffen werden; **the foundations of the house had been ~ed by the earthquake** durch das Erdbeben waren die Fundamente des Hauses in Mitleidenschaft gezogen worden

B *v.i.* ‹*Kraft, Entschlossenheit:*› nachlassen; **the patient was visibly ~ing** der Patient wurde sichtlich schwächer; **the pound ~ed against the dollar** das Pfund wurde gegenüber dem Dollar schwächer; **~ in one's resolve** in seinem Vorsatz schwankend werden; **his hold on power was ~ing** er hielt die Macht nicht mehr so fest in der Hand

weak-kneed /ˈwi:kni:d/ *adj.* 1 **be ~:** weiche Knie haben (**with** vor + *Dat.*) 2 (fig.) feige

weakling /ˈwi:klɪŋ/ *n.* Schwächling, *der*

weakly /ˈwi:klɪ/

A *adv.* schwach; matt ‹*lächeln*›; **be ~ indulgent** schwach und nachgiebig sein

B *adj.* schwächlich

ˈweak-minded *adj.* 1 (lacking strength of purpose) entschlusslos; unentschlossen 2 (mentally deficient) schwachsinnig

weakness /ˈwi:knɪs/ *n.* Schwäche, *die;* (in argument, defence) schwacher Punkt; **the ~ of her character** ihre Charakterschwäche; **I have a ~ for sweet things** ich habe eine Schwäche für Süßigkeiten

ˈweak-willed *adj.* willensschwach

weal¹ /wi:l/ *n.* (literary/archaic: welfare) **for the public** *or* **common ~:** zum Wohle der Allgemeinheit

weal² *n.* (ridge on flesh) Striemen, *der*

wealth /welθ/ *n., no pl.* 1 (abundance) Fülle, *die;* **a great ~ of detail** große Detailfülle; **~ of words** Wortreichtum, *der* 2 (riches, being rich) Reichtum, *der*

ˈwealth tax *n.* Vermögenssteuer, *die*

wealthy /ˈwelθɪ/

A *adj.* reich

B *n. pl.* **the ~:** die Reichen

wean /wi:n/ *v.t.* abstillen; entwöhnen ‹*Tier*›; **~ sb. [away] from sth.** (fig.) jmdm. etw. abgewöhnen

weapon /ˈwepən/ *n.* (lit. or fig.) Waffe, *die;* **use sth. as a ~:** etw. als Waffe benutzen; **~ of mass destruction** Massenvernichtungswaffe, *die*

weaponry /ˈwepənrɪ/ *n.* Waffen *Pl.*

ˈweapons testing *n., no pl.* Waffentests *Pl.;* **nuclear ~:** Atomwaffentests *Pl.*

wear /weə(r)/

A *n., no pl., no indef. art.* 1 (rubbing) **~ [and tear]** Verschleiß, *der;* Abnutzung, *die;* **show signs of ~:** Verschleiß- *od.* Abnutzungserscheinungen aufweisen; **the ~ and tear on sb.'s nerves** (fig.) jmds. Nervenverschleiß; **the worse for ~:** abgetragen ‹*Kleider*›; abgelaufen ‹*Schuhe*›; abgenutzt ‹*Teppich, Sessel, Möbel*›; **feel the worse for ~:** sich angeschlagen fühlen (ugs.); **be the worse for ~** (coll.: drunk) Schlagseite haben (ugs.)

2 (clothes, use of clothes) Kleidung, *die;* **clothes for everyday ~:** Alltagskleidung, *die;* **a jacket for casual ~:** ein Freizeit- *od.* (veralt.) Sportsakko; **children's/ladies' ~:** Kinder-/Damen[be-]kleidung, *die*

3 (capacity for withstanding use) **there is a great deal of/no ~ [left] in it** es/das *usw.* hat noch eine große Lebensdauer/keine große Lebensdauer mehr; **there's a great** *or* **good deal of ~ still in those shoes** die Schuhe halten noch lange

B *v.t.*, **wore** /wɔ:(r)/, **worn** /wɔ:n/ 1 tragen ‹*Kleidung, Schmuck, Bart, Brille, Perücke, Abzeichen*›; **I haven't a thing to ~:** ich habe überhaupt nichts anzuziehen; **what on earth am I going to ~ tonight?** was soll ich heute Abend bloß anziehen?; **what size shoes do you ~?** welche Schuhgröße haben Sie?; **~ the crown** (fig.) die Krone tragen; **~ one's hair long** lange Haare tragen; **always ~ a smile** immer lächeln; **~ a joyful smile** glücklich lächeln; **~ a frown** ein finsteres Gesicht machen; **~ a sour look** eine saure Miene aufsetzen; **~ one's years well** sich gut gehalten haben; *see also* **heart A 2; trousers**

2 abtragen ‹*Kleidungsstück*›; abtreten, abnutzen ‹*Teppich*›; **be worn [smooth]** ‹*Stufen:*› ausgetreten sein; ‹*Gestein:*› ausgewaschen sein; ‹*Gesicht:*› abgehärmt sein; **the old coat was badly worn** der alte Mantel war ganz abgewetzt; **a [badly] worn tyre** ein [stark] abgefahrener Reifen; **he had worn his trousers into holes** seine Hose hatte überall Löcher

3 (make by rubbing) scheuern; **the water had worn a channel in the rock** das Wasser hatte sich durch den Felsen gefressen

4 (exhaust) erschöpfen; **she is worn to a shadow** sie ist zu einem Schatten ihrer selbst geworden

5 (coll.: accept) **he won't ~ that!** das nimmt er dir/ihm *usw.* nicht ab! (ugs.)

C *v.i.*, **wore, worn** 1 ‹*Kante, Saum, Kleider:*› sich durchscheuern; ‹*Absätze, Schuhsohlen:*› sich ablaufen; ‹*Teppich:*› sich abnutzen; **~ thin** (fig.) ‹*Idealismus:*› sich langsam legen, nachlassen; ‹*Freundschaft, Stil:*› verflachen, oberflächlicher werden; ‹*Witz, Ausrede:*› schon reichlich alt sein; **my patience is ~ing thin** meine Geduld geht allmählich zur Neige *od.* ist langsam erschöpft

2 (last) ‹*Material, Stoff:*› halten; (fig.) sich halten; **~ well/badly** sich gut/schlecht tragen

Phrasal verbs

• **~ aˈway**

A *v.t.* abschleifen ‹*Kanten, Grate*›; **be worn away** ‹*Stufen:*› ausgetreten werden; ‹*Inschrift:*› verwittern;

B *v.i.* sich abnutzen; ‹*Gestein:*› verwittern; ‹*Schuhabsätze:*› sich ablaufen; (fig.: weaken, lessen) dahinschwinden

• **~ ˈdown**

A *v.t.* 1 **be worn down** ‹*Stufen:*› ausgetreten werden; ‹*Absätze:*› sich ablaufen; ‹*Reifen:*› sich abfahren; ‹*Berge:*› abgetragen werden 2 (fig.) **~ sb. down** jmdn. zermürben; **~ down sb.'s resistance/defence/opposition** jmds. Widerstand/Verteidigung/Opposition zermürben; **worn down with hard work** abgearbeitet; **having to do this for hours at a stretch can ~ one down** es kann einen fertig machen (ugs.), wenn man das stundenlang ununterbrochen tun muss

B *v.i.* ‹*Absätze:*› sich ablaufen; ‹*Reifen:*› sich abfahren; **the stick/tooth had worn down to a stump** der Stock/Zahn war nur noch ein Stummel

• **~ ˈoff**

A *v.i.* ‹*Auflage, Schicht:*› abgehen; ‹*Muster:*› sich verlieren; (fig.: pass away gradually) sich legen; ‹*Wirkung, Schmerz:*› nachlassen; **the sheen had long since worn off the material** der Stoff hatte schon lange seinen Glanz verloren

B *v.t.* **be worn off** ‹*Auflage, Schicht:*› abgehen

• **~ ˈon** *v.i.* ‹*Nachmittag, Winter usw.:*› voranschreiten; **as the day/evening wore on** im Laufe des Tages/Abends

• **~ ˈout**

A *v.t.* 1 (make useless) aufbrauchen; ablaufen ‹*Schuhe*›; auftragen ‹*Kleidungsstück*› 2 (fig.: exhaust) erschöpfen; kaputtmachen (ugs.); **his patience was worn out** seine Geduld war erschöpft; **~ oneself out** sich kaputtmachen (ugs.); **be worn out** erschöpft sein; kaputt sein (ugs.)

B *v.i.* (become unusable) kaputtgehen; **his patience finally wore out** seine Geduld war schließlich erschöpft

• **~ ˈthrough**

A *v.i.* sich durchscheuern; **my trousers have worn through at the knee** meine Hose ist an den Knien durchgescheuert

B *v.t.* durchscheuern

wearable /ˈweərəbl/ *adj.* **sth. that is still/not ~:** etw., das man noch/nicht anziehen kann

wearer /ˈweərə(r)/ *n.* Träger, *der*/Trägerin, *die*

wearily /ˈwɪərɪlɪ/ *adv.* müde

weariness /ˈwɪərɪnɪs/ *n.*, *no pl.* **1** (tiredness) Erschöpfung, *die* **2** (boredom) Überdruss, *der* (**with** an + *Dat.*)

wearing /ˈweərɪŋ/ *adj.* **1** (tiring) ermüdend **2** (boring) langweilig; ermüdend

wearisome /ˈwɪərɪsəm/ *adj.*, **wearisomely** /ˈwɪərɪsəmlɪ/ *adv.* (lit. or fig.) ermüdend

weary /ˈwɪərɪ/

A *adj.* **1** (tired) müde; **~ to death** sterbensmüde (geh.) **2** (bored, impatient) **be ~ of sth.** einer Sache (*Gen.*) überdrüssig sein; etw. satt haben (ugs.) **3** (tiring) ermüdend

B *v.t.* **be wearied by sth.** durch etw. erschöpft sein; **a ~ing day** ein anstrengender Tag; **all this bickering was beginning to ~ me** allmählich hatte ich das ganze Gezänk satt (ugs.)

C *v.i.* **~ of sth./sb.** einer Sache/jmds. überdrüssig werden

weasel /ˈwiːzl/

A *n.* Wiesel, *das*

B *v.i.* (Amer.) **1** (quibble) drumherumreden (ugs.) **2** (default) sich herauslavieren (ugs.); **~ on an obligation** sich aus einer Verpflichtung herausstehlen

weasel: ~-faced *adj.* **be ~-faced** ≈ ein Rattengesicht haben; **a ~-faced little man** ≈ ein kleiner Mann mit einem Rattengesicht; **~ words** *n. pl.* Beschönigungen *Pl.*

weather /ˈweðə(r)/

A *n.* Wetter, *das;* **what's the ~ like?** wie ist das Wetter?; **the ~ has turned cooler** es ist kühler geworden; **he goes out in all ~s** er geht bei jedem Wetter hinaus; **he is feeling under the ~** (fig.) er ist [zurzeit] nicht ganz auf dem Posten; **make heavy ~ of sth.** (fig.) sich mit etw. schwer tun

B *attrib. adj.* **1** **keep a** *or* **one's ~ eye open [for sth.]** Ausschau [nach etw. (*Dat.*)] halten; **keep a ~ eye on sth.** ein wachsames Auge auf etw. (*Akk.*) haben **2** (Naut.) luvseitig; **the ~ side** die Luvseite; *see also* **gauge A 3**

C *v.t.* **1** (expose to open air) auswittern ‹*Kalk, Holz*› **2** **be ~ed** ‹*Gesicht:*› wettergegerbt sein **3** (wear away) verwittern lassen ‹*Gestein*›; **rocks ~ed by wind and water** Felsen, die durch Wind und Wasser verwittert sind **4** (come safely through) abwettern ‹*Sturm*›; (fig.) durchstehen ‹*schwere Zeit*›

D *v.i.* **1** (be discoloured) ‹*Holz, Farbe:*› verblassen; (wear away) **~ [away]** ‹*Gestein:*› verwittern **2** (survive exposure) wetterfest sein; **a paint that ~s very well** eine sehr wetterfeste Farbe

weather: ~-beaten *adj.* wettergegerbt ‹*Gesicht, Haut*›; verwittert ‹*Felsen, Gebäude*›; **~board** *n.* Wetterbrett, *das;* **~boarding** *n.*, *no pl.*, *no indef. art.*, **~boards** *n. pl.* Schindeln *Pl.;* **~ chart** *n.* Wetterkarte, *die;* **~cock** *n.* Wetterhahn, *der;* **~ conditions** *n. pl.* Wetterbedingungen *Pl.;* Wetterverhältnisse *Pl.;* **what are the ~ conditions at the moment?** wie ist das Wetter im Augenblick?; **~ forecast** *n.* Wettervorhersage, *die;* **~ forecaster** *n.* ▸ⓘ **p. 1260** Wettermann, *der*/Wetterfrau, *die;* Wetterfrosch, *der* (scherzh.); **~girl** *n.* ▸ⓘ **p. 1260** (coll.) Wetterfee, *die* (ugs.)

weathering /ˈweðərɪŋ/ *n.*, *no pl.*, *no indef. art.* Verwitterung, *die*

weather: ~man *n.* ▸ⓘ **p. 1260** Meteorologe, *der;* **~ map** *n.* Wetterkarte, *die;* **~proof** **A** *adj.* wetterfest; **B** *v.t.* wetterfest machen; **~ report** *n.* Wetterbericht, *der;* **~ satellite** *n.* Wettersatellit, *der;* **~ ship** *n.* Wetterschiff, *das;* **~ station** *n.* Wetterwarte, *die;* **~strip** *n.* Dichtungsstreifen, *der;* **~vane** *n.* Wetterfahne, *die;* **~ window** *n.* Wetterfenster, *das;* **~wise** *adj.* **be ~wise** die Wetterregeln kennen; (fig.) die Wetterzeichen am Horizont erkennen

weave[1] /wiːv/

A *n.* (Textiles) Bindung, *die*

B *v.t.*, **wove** /wəʊv/, **woven** /ˈwəʊvn/ **1** (intertwine) weben ‹[*Baum*]*wolle, Garn, Fäden*›; **~ sth. into sth.** etw. zu etw. verweben; **~ threads together** Fäden miteinander verweben; **~ flowers into wreaths** aus Blumen Kränze flechten **2** (make by weaving) weben ‹*Textilien*›; flechten ‹*Girlande, Korb, Kranz*› **3** (fig.) einflechten ‹*Nebenhandlung, Thema usw.*› (**into** in + *Akk.*) **4** (fig.: contrive) ausspinnen ‹*Geschichte*›; **~ a story around an idea** eine Idee zu einer Geschichte ausspinnen

C *v.i.*, **wove, woven** (make fabric by weaving) weben

weave[2] *v.i.* **1** (move repeatedly from side to side) torkeln **2** (take devious course) sich schlängeln; **~ between the obstacles** sich zwischen den Hindernissen hindurchschlängeln **3** **get weaving** (coll.) hinmachen (ugs.); **get weaving!** mach/macht schon (ugs.) *od.* hin!

weaver /ˈwiːvə(r)/ *n.* **1** ▸ⓘ **p. 1260** Weber, *der*/Weberin, *die* **2** (Ornith.) ▸**weaver bird**

ˈweaver bird *n.* Webervogel, *der*

weaving /ˈwiːvɪŋ/ *n.* Weben, *das;* **an intricate piece of ~:** eine feine Webarbeit

web /web/ *n.* **1** Netz, *das;* **spider's ~:** Spinnennetz, *das* **2** (woven fabric) Gewebe, *das;* (fig.) Gespinst, *das;* **a ~ of lies/intrigue** ein Gespinst von Lügen/Intrigen **3** (membrane) Interdigitalhaut, *die* (Anat.); (of duck, goose, etc.) Schwimmhaut, *die* **4** (gossamer etc.) Gespinst, *das* **5** (vane of feather) Federfahne, *die* **6** (Papermaking) (endless wire mesh) Drahtgeweberolle, *die;* (paper roll) Papierbahn, *die* **7** **the Web** (Computing) das Web (fachspr.); das Netz

Web: ~ address *n.* Webadresse, *die;* **~ authoring** *n.*, *no pl.* Webauthoring, *das* (fachspr.); *attrib.* Webauthoring-‹*Programm, Software usw.*›; **~-based** *adj.* webbasiert ‹*System, Anwendung*›; **~-based marketing/management** Webmarketing, *das*/Webmanagement, *das*

webbed /webd/ *adj.* **~ feet/toes** Schwimmfüße

webbing /ˈwebɪŋ/ *n.* Gurtstoff, *der*

Web: ~ browser *n.* Web-Browser, *der;* **~cam** *n.* Webcam *die;* **~cast** *n.* Webcast, *der* (fachspr.); Internet-Liveübertragung, *die;* **~ chat** *n.*, *no pl.* [Web]chat, *der;* **live ~ chat** Live-Chat, *der;* **~ commerce** *n.*, *no pl.* Internethandel, *der;* **~ ˈcontent provider** *n.* Contentprovider, *der*/-providerin, *die;* **~ designer** *n.* Webdesigner, *der*/-designerin, *die;* **~-enabled** *adj.* webfähig; **w~-fed** *adj.* rollengespeist; **w~-fed printing press** Rollendruckmaschine, *die;* **w~ foot** *n.* Schwimmfuß, *der;* Ruderfuß, *der* (Zool.); **w~-footed** *adj.* schwimmfüßig; **~ hosting** *n.*, *no pl.* [Web]hosting, *das;* **~log** *n.* Weblog, *das;* **~master** *n.* Webmaster, *der;* **w~ ˈoffset** *n.* (Printing) Rollenoffset[druck], *der;* **~ page** *n.* Webseite, *die;* **~phone** *n.* Webtelefon, *das;* **~ presence** *n.*, *no pl.* Webpräsenz, *die;* Internetpräsenz, *die; attrib.* **~ presence provider** Webpräsenzprovider, *der;* **w~ press** *n.* Rollendruckmaschine, *die;* **~ ring** *n.* Webring, *der;* **~ search** *n.* Websuche, *die;* **~ server** *n.* Webserver, *der;* **~ site** *n.* Website, *die;* **~space** *n.*, *no pl.* **1** (storage space) Webspace, *der* (fachspr.); Internet-Speicherplatz, *der;* **2** (cyberspace) Cyberspace, *der;* **~ spider** *n.* Spider, *der;* Spiderprogramm, *das;* **w~ toe** ▸ **w~ foot;** **w~-toed** ▸ **w~-footed;** **~zine** /ˈwebziːn/ *n.* Webzine, *das* (fachspr.); Webmagazin, *das;* Internetzeitschrift, *die*

wed /wed/

A *v.t.*, **-dd-** **1** (formal/journalese: marry) heiraten; ehelichen (veralt., scherzh.); (perform wedding ceremony for) trauen ‹*Brautpaar*› **2** (fig.: unite) vereinen (**to** mit)

B *v.i.* (formal/journalese) heiraten; sich vermählen (geh.)

we'd /wɪd, *stressed* wiːd/ **1** = **we had** **2** = **we would**

Wed. *abbr.* ▸ⓘ **p. 1048** = **Wednesday** Mi.

wedded /ˈwedɪd/ *adj.* **1** (married) angetraut; **a ~ couple** ein getrautes Paar; *see also* **wife** **2** (of marriage) **~ life** Eheleben, *das;* **~ love** eheliche Liebe; Gattenliebe, *die* (geh.); **~ bliss** Eheglück, *das* **3** (fig.: devoted) **be ~ to an idea/a dogma/a party** sich einer Idee/einem Dogma/einer Partei verschrieben haben; **be ~ to the view that ...:** immer noch davon überzeugt sein, dass ...; **he's ~ to his work** er ist mit seiner Arbeit verheiratet **4** (fig.: united) vereint (**to** mit)

wedding /ˈwedɪŋ/ *n.* Hochzeit, *die;* **have a registry office/a church ~:** sich standesamtlich/kirchlich trauen lassen; standesamtlich/kirchlich heiraten; *see also* **diamond wedding; golden wedding; ruby wedding; shotgun; silver wedding**

wedding: ~ anniversary *n.* Hochzeitstag, *der;* **~ band** *n.* (Amer.) ▸ **~ ring;** **~ breakfast** *n.* Hochzeitsessen, *das;* **~ cake** *n.* Hochzeitskuchen, *der;* **~ day** *n.* Hochzeitstag, *der;* **~ dress** *n.* Brautkleid, *das;* Hochzeitskleid, *das;* **~ march** *n.* (Mus.) Hochzeitsmarsch, *der;* **~ night** *n.* Hochzeitsnacht, *die;* **~ photo** *n.* Hochzeitsfoto, *das;* **~ present** *n.* Hochzeitsgeschenk, *das;* **~ ring** *n.* Ehering, *der;* Trauring, *der*

wedge /wedʒ/

A *n.* **1** Keil, *der;* **it's the thin end of the ~** (fig.) so fängt es immer an; **be careful that it isn't the thin end of the ~** (fig.) pass auf, dass das nicht ausufert *od.* überhand nimmt!; **these disturbances proved to be just the thin end of the ~:** diese Unruhen erwiesen sich bloß als der Anfang **2** **a ~ of cake** ein Stück Torte; **a ~ of cheese** eine Ecke Käse; **the seats were arranged in ~s** die Sitzreihen waren keilförmig angeordnet **3** (heel) Keilabsatz, *der* **4** (shoe) Schuh mit Keilabsatz **5** (Golf) Keil, *der*

B *v.t.* **1** (fasten) verkeilen; **a ~ door/window open** eine Tür/ein Fenster festklemmen, damit sie/es offen bleibt **2** (pack tightly) verkeilen; **there were five of them ~d together in the back of the car** sie saßen zu fünft eingezwängt *od.* zusammengepfercht hinten im Wagen; **the book had got ~d in behind the cupboard** das Buch war hinter dem Schrank eingeklemmt

ˈwedge-shaped *adj.* keilförmig

Wedgwood /ˈwedʒwʊd/ *n.* **1** (pottery) Wedgwood, *das* **2** *no pl.* (colour) Wedgwoodblau, *das*

wedlock /ˈwedlɒk/ *n.* (literary) Ehe, *die;* Ehebund, *der* (geh.); **born in/out of ~:** ehelich/unehelich geboren

Wednesday /ˈwenzdeɪ, ˈwenzdɪ/ ▸ⓘ **p. 1048**

A *n.* Mittwoch, *der; see also* **Ash Wednesday**

B *adv.* (coll.) **she comes ~s** sie kommt mittwochs. *see also* **Friday**

wee[1] /wiː/ *adj.* **1** (child lang./Scot.) klein; lütt (nordd.) **2** (coll.: extremely small) **a ~ bit** ein ganz klein bisschen (ugs.)

wee[2] ▸**wee-wee**

weed /wiːd/

A *n.* **1** Unkraut, *das;* **~s** Unkräuter; Unkraut, *das;* **it's only a ~:** das ist bloß Unkraut; **a garden overgrown with ~s** ein von Unkraut überwucherter Garten **2** (coll./dated: tobacco) **the ~:** das Kraut (ugs.) **3** (sl.: marijuana) Stoff, *der* (salopp); **the ~:** Stoff (salopp) **4** (weakly person) Kümmerling, *der* (*abwertend*). *see also* **weeds**

B *v.t.* jäten

C *v.i.* [Unkraut] jäten

Phrasal verb

• **~ ˈout** *v.t.* (fig.) aussieben

weeding /ˈwiːdɪŋ/ *n.*, *no pl.*, *no indef. art.* [Unkraut]jäten, *das;* **do the/some ~:** Unkraut jäten

ˈweedkiller *n.* Unkrautvertilgungsmittel, *das*

weedy /ˈwiːdɪ/ *adj.* **1** von Unkraut überwachsen **2** (coll.: scrawny) spillerig (ugs.); schmächtig

week /wiːk/ *n.* ▸ⓘ **p. 1048** Woche, *die;* **what day of the ~ is it today?** was für ein Wochentag ist heute?; **can you come to stay for a ~?** kannst du [für] eine Woche zu uns kommen?; **he was away for a ~:** er war [für] eine Woche weg; **I haven't seen you for ~s** ich habe dich seit Wochen nicht gesehen; **~s ago** vor Wochen; **it will be finished in a ~:** es ist in einer Woche fertig; **three times a ~:** dreimal die *od.* in der Woche; **£40 a** *or* **per ~:** 40 Pfund die *od.* in der *od.* pro Woche; **a ~'s leave/rest**

W

ℹ Weight

	1 ounce (oz)	=	28,35 g (achtundzwanzig Komma drei fünf Gramm)
16 ounces	= *1 pound (lb)*	=	454 g (vierhundertvierundfünfzig Gramm)
14 pounds	= *1 stone (st.)*	=	6,35 kg (sechs Komma drei fünf Kilogramm)
112 pounds	= *1 hundredweight*	=	50,8 kg (fünfzig Komma acht Kilogramm)
20 hundredweight	= *1 ton*	=	1016 kg (tausendsechzehn Kilogramm)

Note that in everyday usage **Kilogramm** is shortened to **Kilo.** Also the German pound (**Pfund**) is half a kilogram, i.e. 500 grams as opposed to 454 grams for the British pound.

People

What's your weight?, How much do you weigh?
= Wie viel wiegen Sie?

***I weigh 12 stone* (Brit.) *or 168 pounds* (Amer.)**
≈ Ich wiege 76,2 Kilo

He has put on weight
= Er hat zugenommen

She has lost a lot of weight
= Sie hat stark abgenommen

At over 18 stone* (Brit.) *or 250 pounds* (Amer.) *he is overweight
≈ Mit mehr als 114 Kilo hat er Übergewicht

Things

What's the weight of the parcel?, How much does the parcel weigh?
= Wie viel wiegt das Paket?

Is it very heavy?
= Ist es sehr schwer?

It weighs about four pounds
= Es wiegt ungefähr zwei Kilo

My baggage is ten pounds over weight
≈ Mein Gepäck hat fünf Kilo Übergewicht

A is the same weight as B
= A hat das gleiche Gewicht wie B

A and B are the same weight
= A und B sind gleich schwer

4 oz of liver sausage
≈ 125 Gramm *or* ein Viertel Leberwurst

6 lbs of potatoes
≈ sechs Pfund Kartoffeln

They are sold by the kilo
= Sie werden kiloweise verkauft

a pound box of chocolates
≈ eine 500-Gramm-Schachtel Pralinen

eine Woche Urlaub/Pause; **the other ~:** vor ein paar *od.* zwei, drei Wochen; **for several ~s** mehrere Wochen lang; wochenlang; **come every ~:** jede Woche kommen; **once a ~** *or* **every ~:** einmal die Woche *od.* in der Woche; einmal wöchentlich; **~ in ~ out** Woche für Woche; **in a ~['s time]** in einer Woche; **in two ~s[' time]** in zwei Wochen; in vierzehn Tagen; **take a ~'s holiday** [sich (*Dat.*)] eine Woche Urlaub nehmen; **from ~ to ~, ~ by ~:** Woche für *od.* um Woche; **a three-~ period** ein Zeitraum von drei Wochen; **at six-~ intervals** in sechswöchigem Abstand; **a two-~ visit** ein zweiwöchiger Besuch; **a six-~[s]-old baby** ein sechs Wochen altes *od.* sechswöchiges Baby; **a ~ [from] today/from** *or* **on Monday, today/Monday ~:** heute/Montag in einer Woche; **a ~ ago today/Sunday** heute/Sonntag vor einer Woche; **tomorrow ~:** morgen in einer Woche; **in** *or* **during the ~:** während der Woche; **42-hour/five-day ~:** 42-Stunden-Woche, *die*/Fünftagewoche, *die; see also* **knock A 3**; **next A 2, C 2**

week: ~day *n.* Werktag, *der;* Wochentag, *der;* **on ~days** werktags; wochentags; *attrib.* **~day opening times** Öffnungszeiten an Werktagen; **~day timetable** Werktagsfahrplan, *der;* **~end** /ˈ-ˈ-, ˈ--/ *n.* Wochenende, *das;* **at the ~end** am Wochenende; **at** *or* (Amer.) **on ~ends** an Wochenenden; **a long ~end** ein verlängertes Wochenende; **go/be away for the ~end** übers Wochenende wegfahren/weg sein; **~-long** *adj.* einwöchig

weekly /ˈwi:klɪ/
A *adj.* wöchentlich; **~ wages** Wochenlohn, *der;* **a ~ season ticket/magazine** eine Wochenkarte/Wochenzeitschrift; **on a ~ basis** wöchentlich; **at ~ intervals** wöchentlich; einmal pro Woche; **three-~:** dreiwöchentlich; **at three-~ intervals** in dreiwöchigen Abständen
B *adv.* wöchentlich; einmal die Woche *od.* in der Woche
C *n.* (newspaper) Wochenzeitung, *die;* (magazine) Wochenzeitschrift, *die*

weekly reˈturn *n.* **~ [ticket]** Wochenrückfahrkarte, *die*

ˈweek night *n.* **on a ~:** abends an einem Werktag; **on ~s** werktags abends

weeny /ˈwi:nɪ/ *adj.* (child lang./coll.) klitzeklein (ugs.)

weeny-bopper *n.* (coll.) *acht- bis zwölfjähriger* [*weiblicher*] *Popfan*

weep /wi:p/
A *v.i.,* **wept** /wept/ **1** weinen; **~ with** *or* **for joy/rage** vor Freude/Zorn weinen; **~ for sb./sth.** um jmdn./etw. weinen; **the child was ~ing for his mother** das Kind weinte nach seiner Mutter; **it makes you want to ~:** man könnte weinen **2** ‹*Wunde:*› nässen
B *v.t.,* **wept 1** weinen ‹*Tränen*› **2** (lament over) beweinen **3** **~ one's eyes** *or* **heart out** sich (*Dat.*) die Augen aus dem Kopf weinen **4** (exude) absondern ‹*Eiter*›
C *n.* **have a ~:** sich ausweinen; **I had a little ~:** ich habe geweint

weepie /ˈwi:pɪ/ *n.* (coll.) Schmachtfetzen, *der* (salopp)

weeping ˈwillow *n.* Trauerweide, *die*

weepy /ˈwi:pɪ/
A *adj.* weinerlich
B *n.* ▸ **weepie**

weevil /ˈwi:vɪl/ *n.* Rüsselkäfer, *der*

ˈwee-wee (coll.)
A *n.* Pipi, *das* (ugs.); **do a ~:** Pipi machen
B *v.i.* Pipi machen (ugs.)

weft /weft/ *n.* **1** (set of threads) Schuss, *der* **2** (yarn) Schussfaden, *der*

weigh /weɪ/
A *v.t.* **1** ▸ℹ **p. 1702** (find weight of) wiegen; **the shop assistant was ~ing the fruit for her** die Verkäuferin wog ihr das Obst ab **2** (estimate value of) abwägen; **~ sb. and find him/her wanting** (fig. literary) jmdn. wiegen und zu leicht befinden **3** (consider) abwägen; **~ in one's mind whether ...:** sich (*Dat.*) überlegen, ob ...; **~ the consequences of one's actions** sich (*Dat.*) die Folgen seines Handelns klarmachen; **~ one's words** seine Worte abwägen **4** (balance in one's hand) wiegen **5** (have the weight of) wiegen; **it ~s very little** es wiegt sehr wenig; **a steak ~ing two pounds** ein zwei Pfund schweres Steak. *see also* **anchor A**; **ton 3**
B *v.i.* **1** **~ [very] heavy/light** [sehr] viel/wenig wiegen **2** (be important) **~ with sb.** bei jmdm. Gewicht haben; **~ in sb.'s favour** für jmdn. sprechen
C *n.* **under ~ = under way** ▸ **way A 9**

(Phrasal verbs)

- **~ aˈgainst** *v.t.* (fig.) sprechen gegen; **~ heavily against sb.** sehr *od.* stark gegen jmdn. sprechen
- **~ ˈdown** *v.t.* **1** (cause to sag) **fruit ~ed down the branches of the tree** die Äste des Baumes bogen sich unter der Last der Früchte; **be ~ed down by packages** mit Paketen schwer beladen sein **2** (cause to be anxious or depressed) niederdrücken; **~ed down with cares** bedrückt von Sorgen; **~ed down with sorrow** gramgebeugt
- **~ ˈin** *v.i.* **1** (Sport) sich wiegen lassen; **~ in at 200 kg** 200 kg auf die Waage bringen; *see also* **weigh-in** **2** (coll.: lend one's support) sich einschalten
- **~ on** *v.t.* lasten auf (+ *Dat.*); **~ [heavily] on sb.'s mind** jmdm. [schwer] auf der Seele liegen
- **~ ˈout** *v.t.* abwiegen
- **~ ˈup** *v.t.* abwägen; **~ sb. up** sich (*Dat.*) eine Meinung über jmdn. bilden; jmdn. einschätzen
- **~ upon** ▸ **~ on**

weigh: ~bridge *n.* Brückenwaage, *die;* **~-in** *n.* (Sport) Wiegen, *das;* **at the ~-in** beim Wiegen

ˈweighing machine *n.* Waage, *die*

weight /weɪt/
A *n.* **1** ▸ℹ **p. 1702** (heaviness) Gewicht, *das;* **she is twice your ~:** sie wiegt doppelt so viel wie du; **what is your ~?** wie viel wiegen Sie?; **be under/over ~:** zu wenig/zu viel wiegen; Unter-/Übergewicht haben; **throw one's ~ about** *or* **around** (fig. coll.) sich wichtig machen; *see also* **gold A 1** **2** (scale of heaviness) Gewicht, *das;* **~s and measures** Maße und Gewichte; **avoirdupois/troy ~:** Avoirdupois-/Troygewicht, *das* **3** (heavy item; load; used on scales) Gewicht, *das;* **lift ~s** Lasten heben; (in competition) Gewichte heben **4** (Athletics: shot) Kugel, *die* **5** (load to be supported) Gewicht, *das* **6** (of cloth etc.) Qualität, *die* **7** (fig.: heavy burden) Last, *die;* **it would be a ~ off my mind if ...:** mir würde ein Stein vom Herzen fallen, wenn ... **8** (importance) Gewicht, *das;* **men of ~:** Leute von Gewicht; bedeutende Leute; **give due ~ to sth.** einer Sache (*Dat.*) die nötige Beachtung schenken; **carry ~:** ins Gewicht fallen; **his opinion carries no ~ with me** seine Meinung ist für mich unbedeutend **9** (preponderance) Übergewicht, *das;* **the ~ of evidence is against him** praktisch alle Beweise sprechen gegen ihn; **~ of numbers** zahlenmäßiges Übergewicht. *See also* **atomic weight**; **dead weight**; **pull A 7**
B *v.t.* **1** (add ~ to) beschweren; **circumstances are rather ~ed in his favour/against him** (fig.) er wird durch die Umstände ziemlich begünstigt/benachteiligt **2** (hold with ~) **~ [down]** beschweren; (fig.) belasten **3** (Statistics) gewichten

ˈweight gain *n.* Gewichtszunahme, *die*

weighting /ˈweɪtɪŋ/ *n.* (Admin.) Zulage, *die;* **London ~:** Ortszulage für London

weightless /ˈweɪtlɪs/ *adj.* schwerelos

weightlessness /ˈweɪtlɪsnɪs/ *n.* Schwerelosigkeit, *die*

weight: ~lifter *n.* Gewichtheber, *der*/-heberin, *die;* **~lifting** *n., no pl., no indef. art.* Gewichtheben, *das;* **~ limit** *n.* Gewichtsgrenze, *die;* **a 20 kilo ~ limit** ein Höchstgewicht von 20 kilo; **~ loss** *n.* Gewichtsverlust, *der;* **~-train** *v.i.* mit Hanteln trainieren; **~ training** *n., no pl., no indef. art.* Hanteltraining, *das;* **~-watcher** *n.* Schlankheitsbewusste, *der/die*

weighty /ˈweɪtɪ/ *adj.* **1** (heavy) schwer **2** (important) gewichtig

weir /wɪə(r)/ *n.* Wehr, *das*

weird /wɪəd/ *adj.* **1** (coll.: odd) bizarr; verrückt (ugs.) **2** (uncanny) unheimlich; fantastisch ‹*Geschichte*›

weirdie /ˈwɪədɪ/ *n.* (coll.) Freak, *der* (ugs.)

weirdly /ˈwɪədlɪ/ *adv.* ▸ **weird**: bizarr; verrückt (ugs.); unheimlich

weirdness /ˈwɪədnɪs/ *n., no pl.* **1** (coll.: oddness) Verrücktheit, *die* (ugs.) **2** (uncanniness) Unheimlichkeit, *die*

weirdo /ˈwɪədəʊ/ *n., pl.* **~s** ▸**weirdie**

welcome /ˈwelkəm/

A *int.* willkommen; **~ home/to England!** willkommen zu Hause/in England!; **~ aboard!** willkommen an Bord!

B *n.* **1** Willkommen, *das;* **a gesture of ~:** eine Willkommensgeste; **outstay** *or* **overstay one's ~:** zu lange bleiben; **bid sb. ~:** jmdn. willkommen heißen; **give sb. a warm ~:** jmdn. herzlich willkommen heißen **2** (reception) Empfang, *der;* **give a proposal a warm ~:** einen Vorschlag zustimmend aufnehmen; **the committee gave her proposals a rather cool ~:** das Gremium nahm ihre Vorschläge ziemlich kühl auf; **give sb. a warm ~** (iron.) jmdn. gebührend empfangen (iron.); **we got a really hot ~ from the enemy artillery** (iron.) die feindliche Artillerie bereitete uns einen recht heißen Empfang (iron.); **receive a rather cool ~:** ziemlich kühl empfangen werden

C *v.t.* **1** (greet with pleasure) begrüßen; willkommen heißen (geh.); **~ sb. with open arms** jmdn. mit offenen Armen begrüßen *od.* willkommen heißen **2** (receive) empfangen

D *adj.* **1** willkommen; gefällig ‹*Anblick*›; **make sb. [feel] ~:** jmdm. das Gefühl geben *od.* vermitteln, willkommen zu sein **2** *pred.* **you are ~ to take it** du kannst es gern nehmen; **you may have it and ~:** du kannst es gerne haben; **no one's ever managed to do it, but you're ~ to have a go** bis jetzt hat es noch keiner geschafft, aber Sie können es ja gern mal versuchen; **you are ~** (it was no trouble to me) gern geschehen!; keine Ursache!; **if you want to stay here for the night you are more than ~:** wenn Sie die Nacht über hier bleiben möchten, sind Sie herzlich willkommen

welcoming /ˈwelkəmɪŋ/ *adj.* einladend; **a ~ cup of tea awaited us** zur Begrüßung erwartete uns eine Tasse Tee; **the crowd burst into ~ applause** die Menge klatschte zur Begrüßung

weld /weld/

A *v.t.* **1** (unite) verschweißen; (repair, make, or attach by ~ing) schweißen (**[on]to** an + *Akk.*); **~ two pipes together** zwei Rohre zusammenschweißen **2** (fig.: unite closely) zusammenschweißen (**into** zu); **~ two elements together** zwei Elemente zusammenschweißen

B *n.* Schweißnaht, *die*

welder /ˈweldə(r)/ *n.* **1** ▸ⓘ **p. 1260** (person) Schweißer, *der*/Schweißerin, *die* **2** (machine) Schweißgerät, *das*

welding /ˈweldɪŋ/ *n., no pl., no indef. art.* Schweißen, *das*

welfare /ˈwelfeə(r)/ *n.* **1** (health and prosperity) Wohl, *das* **2** (social work; payments etc.) Sozialhilfe, *die;* Wohlfahrt, *die* (veralt.); **the ~ people** die Leute vom Sozialamt *od.* (veralt.) von der Wohlfahrt; **be on ~** (Amer.) Sozialhilfe bekommen

welfare: ~ services *n. pl.* öffentliche Sozialeinrichtungen; **~ ˈstate** *n.* Wohlfahrtsstaat, *der;* **~ work** *n.* Sozialarbeit, *die;* **do ~ work** in der Sozialarbeit *od.* (veralt.) bei der Wohlfahrt tätig sein; **~ worker** *n.* ▸ⓘ **p. 1260** Sozialarbeiter, *der*/-arbeiterin, *die*

welkin /ˈwelkɪn/ *n.* (literary) Firmament, *das* (dichter.)

well[1] /wel/

A *n.* **1** (water ~, mineral spring) Brunnen, *der* **2** ▸**oil well** **3** (Brit.: of lawcourt) *Teil des Gerichtssaals, der für die Anwälte bestimmt ist* **4** (Archit.) Schacht, *der;* (of staircase) Treppenloch, *das* **5** (fig.: source) Quell, *der* (dichter.). *see also* **artesian**

B *v.i.* (literary) sich ergießen

Phrasal verb

• **~ ˈup** *v.i.* ‹*Tränen, Wasserstrahl:*› aufsteigen; ‹*Gefühle, Scham, Zorn:*› aufwallen (geh.)

well[2]

A *int.* **1** *expr. astonishment* mein Gott; meine Güte; nanu; **~, ~!** sieh mal einer an!; *see also* **never 3**

2 *expr. relief* mein Gott

3 *expr. concession* na ja; **~ then, let's say no more about it** schon gut, reden wir nicht mehr davon

4 *expr. resumption* nun; **~ [then], who was it?** nun, wer wars?

5 *expr. qualified recognition of point* **~[, but] ...** na ja, aber ...; ja schon, aber ...

6 *expr. resignation* **[oh] ~:** nun denn; **ah ~:** na ja

7 *expr. expectation* **~ [then]?** na?

B *adv.*, **better** /ˈbetə(r)/, **best** /best/ **1** (satisfactorily) gut; **the business is doing ~:** das Geschäft geht gut; **do ~ for oneself** Erfolg haben; **do ~ out of sth.** mit etw. ein gutes Geschäft machen; **the patient is doing ~:** dem Patienten geht es gut; **a ~ situated house** ein günstig gelegenes Haus; **you did ~ to come** gut, dass du gekommen bist; **~ done!** großartig!; **~ begun is half done** (prov.) ein guter Anfang ist schon die halbe Arbeit; **didn't he do ~!** hat er sich nicht gut geschlagen?; **you would do ~ to ...:** Sie täten gut daran, zu ...; **come off ~:** gut abschneiden; **you're ~ out of it** es ist gut, dass du damit nichts mehr zu tun hast; **we're ~ rid of them** wir sind froh, dass wir sie los sind; *see also* **do**[1] **B 4**

2 (thoroughly) gründlich ‹*trocknen, polieren, schütteln*›; tüchtig ‹*verprügeln*›; genau ‹*beobachten*›; gewissenhaft ‹*urteilen*›; **be ~ able to do sth.** durchaus *od.* sehr wohl in der Lage sein, etw. zu tun; **sb. is ~ aware that ...:** jmdm. ist sehr wohl bewusst, dass ...; **I'm ~ aware of what has been going on** mir ist sehr wohl klar *od.* bewusst, was sich abgespielt hat; **let** *or* **leave ~ alone** sich zufrieden geben; **the translator could not leave ~ alone** der Übersetzer hat nur verschlimmbessert; **be ~ worth it/a visit/the effort** es/einen Besuch/die Mühe durchaus wert sein; **he ~ deserved the honour** er hat die Ehre allemal verdient; **be ~ pleased** sehr erfreut sein; **she was not so ~ pleased** sie war nicht sonderlich erfreut; **~ out of sight** (very far off) völlig außer Sichtweite (**of** *Gen.*); **make sure you keep the child ~ out of sight** sorg auf jeden Fall dafür, dass keiner das Kind sieht; **~ past the minimum age** längst über dem Mindestalter; **we arrived ~ before the performance began** wir kamen eine ganze Zeit vor Beginn der Vorstellung; **be ~ in with sb.** bei jmdm. gut angeschrieben sein; **~ and truly** vollkommen; **I know only too ~ how/what** *etc.* **...:** ich weiß nur zu gut, wie/was *usw.* ...

3 (considerably) weit; **he is ~ up in the list** er steht ziemlich weit oben auf der Liste; **she is ~ on in years** sie ist nicht mehr die Jüngste; **it was ~ on into the afternoon** es war schon spät am Nachmittag; **he is ~ past** *or* **over retiring age** er hat schon längst das Rentenalter erreicht; **he is ~ past** *or* **over forty** er ist weit über vierzig; **be ~ away** (lit. or fig.) einen guten Vorsprung haben; (coll.: be drunk) ziemlich benebelt sein (ugs.)

4 (approvingly, kindly) gut, anständig ‹*jmdn. behandeln*›; **like sb. ~ [enough]** jmdn. [sehr] gut leiden können; **think ~ of sb./sth.** eine gute Meinung von jmdm./etw. haben; **speak ~ of sb./sth.** sich positiv über jmdn./etw. äußern; **wish sb. ~:** jmdm. alles Gute wünschen; **stand ~ with sb.** [sich] gut mit jmdm. stehen

5 (in all likelihood) sehr wohl

6 (easily) ohne weiteres; **you cannot very ~ refuse their help** du kannst ihre Hilfe nicht ohne weiteres *od.* nicht gut ausschlagen

7 **as ~** (in addition) auch; ebenfalls; (as much, not less truly) genauso; ebenso; (with equal reason) genauso gut; ebenso gut; (advisable) ratsam; (equally ~) genauso gut; **Coming for a drink? — I might as ~:** Kommst du mit, einen trinken? — Warum nicht?; **you might as ~ go** du kannst ruhig gehen; **that is [just] as ~** (not regrettable) umso besser; **it was just as ~ that I had ...:** zum Glück hatte ich ...; **as ~ as** (in addition to): **A as ~ as B** A sowohl als [auch] B; B und auch [noch] A; **he speaks English as ~ as French** er spricht Englisch sowohl als [auch] Französisch; **she can sing as ~ as dance** sie kann singen und auch tanzen; **as ~ as helping** *or* (coll.) **help me, she continued her own work** sie half mir und machte dabei noch mit ihrer eigenen Arbeit weiter. *see also* **best B**; **better B**; **do**[1] **A 21**; **live**[2] **A 1**; **may 1**; **pretty B**; **speak A 1**

C *adj.* **1** ▸ⓘ **p. 1189** (in good health) gesund; **How are you feeling now? — Quite ~, thank you** Wie fühlen Sie sich jetzt? — Ganz gut, danke; **look ~:** gut *od.* gesund aussehen; **I am perfectly ~:** ich fühle mich bestens; **get ~ soon!** gute Besserung!; **he hasn't been very ~ lately** es geht ihm in letzter Zeit nicht sehr gut; **feel ~:** sich wohl fühlen; **she wanted to come, but she isn't ~ enough** sie wollte kommen, aber es geht ihr nicht so gut; **make sb. ~:** jmdn. gesund machen

2 *pred.* (satisfactory) **I am very ~ where I am** ich bin hier sehr zufrieden; **all's ~:** es ist alles in Ordnung; **all's ~ that ends ~** (prov.) Ende gut, alles gut; **all is not ~ with sb./sth.** mit jmdm./etw. ist etwas nicht in Ordnung; **[that's all] ~ and good** [das ist alles] gut und schön; **all being ~:** wenn alles gut geht

3 *pred.* (advisable) ratsam. *see also* **all B 4**; **very B 4**

we'll /wɪl, *stressed* wiːl/ = **we will**

well: ~-advised ▸**advised**; **~-aimed** *adj.* gezielt ‹*Schuss, Tritt, Stoß, Schlag*›; **~-appointed** *adj.* gut ausgestattet; **~-balanced** *adj.* **1** (sensible) ausgeglichen ‹*Person*›; ausgewogen ‹*Plan*›; **2** (equally matched) harmonisch ‹*Paar*›; gleich stark ‹*Mannschaften*›; **~-behaved** ▸**behave A 1**; **~-being** *n.* Wohl, *das;* **she felt a sense of ~-being** sie fühlte sich wohl; **~-bred** *adj.* **1** (having good manners) anständig; **2** (of good stock) ‹*Schwein, Pferd*› aus guter Zucht; **~-built** *adj.* ‹*Person*› mit guter Figur; **be ~-built** eine gute Figur haben; **~-chosen** *adj.* wohlgesetzt ‹*Worte*›; wohl überlegt ‹*Bemerkungen*›; **a few ~-chosen words** ein paar wohl überlegte Worte; (reprimand) ein paar warme Worte (iron.); **~-conducted** *adj.* gut geleitet *od.* organisiert; **~-connected** *adj.* ‹*Person*› mit guten Beziehungen; **~-defined** *adj.* klar definiert; **~-deserved** *adj.* wohlverdient ‹*Lob, Ruhe*›; verdient ‹*Belohnung, Prügel*›; **~-disciplined** *adj.* höchst *od.* sehr diszipliniert; wohlerzogen (geh.) ‹*Kind*›; **~-disposed** ▸**disposed**; **~ done** *adj.* (Cookery) durchgebraten; durch *nicht attr.*; **order a steak ~ done** ein durchgebratenes Steak bestellen; **~-dressed** *adj.* gut gekleidet **~-earned** *adj.* wohlverdient; **~-educated** *adj.* gebildet ‹*Person, Benehmen*›; **~-equipped** *adj.* gut ausgestattet ‹*Büro, Studio, Krankenwagen*›; gut ausgerüstet ‹*Polizei, Armee, Expedition, Flugzeug*›; **~-established** *adj.* bewährt; bekannt ‹*Tatsache, Spieler, Firma*›; **~-fed** *adj.* wohlgenährt; **~-founded** *adj.* begründet ‹*Verdacht, Befürchtung*›; [wohl] fundiert ‹*Kritik*›; **~-groomed** *adj.* gepflegt; **~ ˈgrounded** *adj.* **1** (trained) **be ~ grounded in a subject** gute Grundkenntnisse in einem Fach haben; **2** ▸**~-founded**; **~-heeled** *adj.* (coll.) gut betucht (ugs.)

wellies /ˈwelɪz/ *n. pl.* (Brit. coll.) Gummistiefel

ˈwell-informed *adj.* **1** **she is one of the most ~ people I have ever met** von allen, die ich kenne, weiß sie am besten Bescheid **2** (having access to reliable information) gut unterrichtet

wellington /ˈwelɪŋtən/ *n.* **~ [boot]** Gummistiefel, *der*

well: ~-intentioned /ˈwelɪntenʃənd/ *adj.* gut gemeint; **~-judged** *adj.* gut gezielt; **~-kept** *adj.* gepflegt; in gutem Zustand *nachgestellt;* wohlgehütet ‹*Geheimnis*›; **~-knit** *adj.* gut gebaut ‹*Körper, Figur, Sportler*›; **~-known** *adj.* **1** (known to many) bekannt; **2** (known thoroughly) vertraut; **~-loved** *adj.* beliebt; **~ made** *adj.* **1** (skilfully manufactured) gut [gearbeitet]; **2** (having good build) gut gebaut; **~-mannered** ▸**mannered 2**; **~ marked** *adj.* gut gekennzeichnet ‹*Strecke, Wanderung*›; **~-matched** *adj.* einander ebenbürtig ‹*Gegner, Mannschaften*›; **they are a ~-matched couple** sie passen gut zueinander; **~-meaning** *adj.* wohlmeinend; **be ~-meaning** es gut meinen; **~-meant** *adj.* gut gemeint; **~-nigh** *adv.* (literary/arch.)

nahezu; ~ **off** *adj.* **1** (rich) wohlhabend; **sb. is ~ off** jmdm. geht es [finanziell] gut; **2** **be ~ off for sth.** (provided with) mit etw. gut versorgt sein; **3** (favourably situated) **she is perfectly ~ off** es geht ihr ausgezeichnet; ~ **oiled** *adj.* (fig. coll.: drunk) abgefüllt (salopp); **~-organized** *adj.* gut organisiert ‹*Mensch*›; gut gegliedert *od.* strukturiert ‹*Buch*›; ~ **paid** *adj.* gut bezahlt; **he's ~ enough paid** er kriegt genug bezahlt; **~-preserved** *adj.* gut erhalten ‹*Holz, Mumie,* (*scherzh.*) *Achtzigjährige usw.*›; **~-read** /ˈwelred/ *adj.* belesen; **~-rounded** *adj.* **1** (curvaceous) kurvenreich (ugs.); (plump) mollig; **2** (of character) abgerundet; **3** (~ expressed) ausgewogen; **~-spent** *adj.* sinnvoll verbracht ‹*Zeit*›; vernünftig ausgegeben ‹*Geld*›; **~-spoken** *adj.* sprachlich gewandt; mit angenehmer Sprechweise *nachgestellt;* **~-stocked** *adj.* gut gefüllt ‹*Kühlschrank, Vorratskammer, Hausbar*›; ‹*Geschäft*› mit reichem Sortiment; **their shop is ~-stocked** ihr Geschäft hat ein reiches Sortiment; **~-thought-out** *adj.* gut durchdacht; **~-thumbed** *adj.* zerlesen ‹*Buch*›; **~-timed** *adj.* zeitlich gut gewählt; **~-to-do** *adj.* wohlhabend; **~-tried** *adj.* bewährt; **~-trodden** *adj.* (lit. or fig.) ausgetreten; **~-turned** *adj.* ausgefeilt ‹*Satz, Prosa*›; geschliffen ‹*Stil, Sprache*› wohlgesetzt ‹*Rede, Kompliment*›; **~-upholstered** *adj.* (fig. joc.) gut gepolstert; **~-wisher** *n.* Sympathisant, der/Sympathisantin, *die;* **~-woman clinic** *n.* Frauenklinik, *die;* **~-worn** *adj.* abgetragen ‹*Kleidungsstück*›; abgenutzt ‹*Teppich*›; abgegriffen ‹*Einband, Buch, Zeitschrift*›; ausgetreten ‹*Pfad*›; abgedroschen ‹*Redensart, Ausdruck*›

welsh *v.i.* (leave without paying) sich davonmachen, ohne zu bezahlen; sich auf Französisch verabschieden (ugs.)

Phrasal verb

• ~ **on** *v.t.* (coll.) ~ **on sb./sth.** jmdn. sitzen lassen/sich um etw. herumdrücken (ugs.)

Welsh /welʃ/ ▸ⓘ **p. 1277**, ▸ⓘ **p. 1345**
A *adj.* walisisch; **sb. is ~:** jmd. ist Waliser/Waliserin; *see also* **corgi**; **English A**
B *n.* **1** (language) Walisisch, *das; see also* **English B 1** **2** *pl.* **the ~:** die Waliser

> **Welsh**
>
> Die alte keltische Sprache, wie sie in Wales gesprochen wird. Für mehr als 20% der Bevölkerung ist Walisisch noch die erste Sprache und hat, wie viele Minderheitensprachen, in den letzten 40 Jahren eine Wiederbelebung erfahren. Es ist zur Zeit die erste Sprache in vielen walisischen Schulen und offizielle Schilder sind normalerweise sowohl in *Welsh* als auch in Englisch beschriftet.

Welsh: ~man /ˈwelʃmən/ *n., pl.* **~men** /ˈwelʃmən/ Waliser, *der;* ~ **ˈrabbit**, ~ **ˈrarebit** *ns.* Käsetoast, *der;* **~woman** *n.* Waliserin, *die*

welt /welt/ *n.* **1** (of shoe) Rahmen, *der* **2** (heavy blow) Hieb, *der* **3** (trimming) Bündchen, *das* **4** ▸ **weal²**

Weltanschauung /veltanˈʃaʊʊŋ/ *n.* Weltanschauung, *die*

welter /ˈweltə(r)/
A *v.i.* sich wälzen
B *n.* Chaos, *das;* **a ~ of foam** eine schäumende Flut; **a ~ of emotions** ein Sturm von Gefühlen

ˈwelterweight *n.* (Boxing etc.) Weltergewicht, *das;* (person also) Weltergewichtler, *der*

Wenceslas /ˈwensɪsləs/ *pr. n.* (Hist.) Wenzel (*der*)

wench /wentʃ/ *n.* (arch./joc.) Mädel, *das*

wend *v.t.* ~ **one's way homewards** sich auf den Heimweg machen; **they ~ed their way back towards the village** sie machten sich auf den Weg zurück ins Dorf

Wend /wend/ *n.* Wende, *der*/Wendin, *die*

Wendy house /ˈwendɪ haʊs/ *n.* Spielhaus, *das*

went ▸ **go¹ A, B**

wept ▸ **weep A, B**

were ▸ **be**

we're /wɪə(r)/ = **we are;** ▸ **be**

weren't (coll.) = **were not;** ▸ **be**

werewolf /ˈwɪəwʊlf, ˈweəwʊlf/ *n., pl.* **werewolves** /ˈwɪəwʊlvz, ˈweəwʊlvz/, **werwolf** /ˈwɜːwʊlf/ *n., pl.* **werwolves** /ˈwɜːwʊlvz/ (Mythol.) Werwolf, *der*

west /west/ ▸ⓘ **p. 1013**
A *n.* **1** Westen, *der;* **the ~:** West (Met., Seew.); (Amer.: western part of US) der Westen; **in/to[wards]/from the ~:** im/nach *od.* (geh.) gen/von Westen; **to the ~ of** westlich von; westlich (+ *Gen.*) **2** (European civilization) Westen, *der;* Abendland, *das* **3** (Cards) West. *see also* **east A**; **Far West**; **Middle West**; **Wild West**
B *adj.* westlich; West‹*küste, -wind, -grenze, -tor*›
C *adv.* westwärts; nach Westen; ~ **of** westlich von; westlich (+ *Gen.*); **go ~** (fig. coll.: be killed or wrecked or lost) hopsgehen (salopp); **~ by north/south** ▸ **by¹ A 4**; *see also* **east C**

West: ~ ˈAfrica *pr. n.* Westafrika (*das*); ~ **ˈBank** *pr. n.* **the ~ Bank** (of the Jordan) das Westjordanland; ~ **Berˈlin** *pr. n.* (Hist.) West-Berlin (*das*); Berlin (West) (Amtsspr.); **w~bound** *adj.* ▸ⓘ **p. 1013** ‹*Zug usw.*› in Richtung Westen; ~ **Country** *n.* (Brit.) Westengland, *das;* ~ **ˈEnd** *n.* (Brit.) Westend, *das;* **the ~ End theatres** die Theater des Londoner Westends

westering /ˈwestərɪŋ/ *attrib. adj.* (literary) im Westen stehend

westerly /ˈwestəlɪ/ ▸ⓘ **p. 1013**
A *adj.* **1** (in position or direction) westlich; **in a ~ direction** nach Westen **2** (from the west) ‹*Wind*› aus westlichen Richtungen; **the wind was ~:** der Wind kam aus Westen
B *adv.* **1** (in position) westlich; (in direction) nach West[en] **2** (from the west) aus *od.* von Westen
C *n.* West[wind], *der*

western /ˈwestən/
A ▸ⓘ **p. 1013** *adj.* westlich; West‹*grenze, -hälfte, -seite, -fenster, -wind*›; **~ Germany** Westdeutschland, *das; see also* **bloc**; **Middle Western**
B *n.* Western, *der*

westerner /ˈwestənə(r)/ *n.* Abendländer, *der*/Abendländerin, *die*

Western: ~ ˈEurope *pr. n.* Westeuropa (*das*); **~ Euroˈpean A** *adj.* westeuropäisch; **B** *n.* Westeuropäer, *der*/-europäerin, *die*

westernization /westənaɪˈzeɪʃn/ *n.* Verwestlichung, *die*

westernize /ˈwestənaɪz/ *v.t.* verwestlichen

westernmost /ˈwestənməʊst/ *adj.* ▸ⓘ **p. 1013** westlichst...

West: ~ ˈGerman (Hist.) **A** *adj.* westdeutsch; **B** *n.* Westdeutsche, *der/die;* ~ **ˈGermany** *pr. n.* (Hist.) Westdeutschland (*das*); ~ **ˈIndian** ▸ⓘ **p. 1345 A** *adj.* westindisch; **B** *n.* Westinder, *der*/-inderin, *die;* ~ **ˈIndies** *pr. n. pl.* Westindische Inseln

Westminster /ˈwestmɪnstə(r)/ *n.* (Brit.: Parliament) Westminster (*das*); London (*das*) (ugs.)

> **Westminster**
>
> Ein Stadtteil von London, in dem ein Großteil der Regierungsgebäude liegt. Das wichtigste unter ihnen ist der *Palace of Westminster*, auch **Houses of Parliament** genannt, in dem beide Häuser des britischen Parlaments tagen. Ebenfalls in Westminster liegt die *Westminster Abbey*, wo seit der Krönung Wilhelms des Eroberers im Jahre 1066 alle englischen Könige und Königinnen gekrönt wurden. *Westminster Abbey* ist auch als Hochzeits- und Begräbniskirche der Monarchie eng mit der Krone verbunden.

west: ~-north-ˈ~ ▸ⓘ **p. 1013 A** *n.* Westnordwest[en], *der;* **B** *adj.* westnordwestlich; **C** *adv.* nach Westnordwest[en]; **W~ of ˈEngland** *pr. n.* Westengland (*das*)

Westphalia /westˈfeɪlɪə/ *pr. n.* Westfalen (*das*)

Westphalian /westˈfeɪlɪən/
A *adj.* westfälisch
B *n.* Westfale, *der*/Westfalin, *die*

West: ~ Side *n.* (Amer.) West Side, *die;* **w~-south-ˈw~** ▸ⓘ **p. 1013 A** *n.* Westsüdwest[en], *der;* **B** *adj.* westsüdwestlich; **C** *adv.* nach Westsüdwest[en]

westward /ˈwestwəd/ ▸ⓘ **p. 1013**
A *adj.* nach Westen gerichtet; (situated towards the west) westlich; **in a ~ direction** nach Westen; [in] Richtung Westen
B *adv.* westwärts; **they are ~ bound** sie fahren nach *od.* [in] Richtung Westen
C *n.* Westen, *der*

westwards /ˈwestwədz/ ▸ⓘ **p. 1013** ▸ **westward B**

wet /wet/
A *adj.* **1** nass; **~ with tears** tränenfeucht; **~ behind the ears** (fig.) feucht hinter den Ohren (ugs.); **~ to the skin, ~ through** nass bis auf die Haut **2** (rainy) regnerisch; feucht ‹*Klima*› **3** (recently applied) frisch ‹*Farbe*›; **'~ paint'** „frisch gestrichen" **4** (coll.: feeble) schlapp (ugs.); schlappschwänzig (salopp) **5** (Brit. Polit. coll.) pflaumenweich (ugs. abwertend); schlappschwänzig (salopp abwertend). *See also* **blanket A 1; rag¹ 1**
B *v.t.,* **-tt-, wet** *or* **wetted** **1** befeuchten; *see also* **whistle C 3** **2** (urinate on) **~ one's bed/pants** das Bett/sich (*Dat.*) die Hosen nass machen
C *n.* **1** (moisture) Feuchtigkeit, *die* **2** (rainy weather) Regenwetter, *das;* (rainy conditions) Nässe, *die;* **in the ~:** im Regen **3** (coll.: feeble person) Flasche, *die* (salopp abwertend) **4** (Brit. Polit. coll.) Schlappschwanz, *der* (salopp abwertend)

wet: ~back *n.* (Amer. coll.) illegaler mexikanischer Einwanderer; ~ **ˈdream** *n.* feuchter Traum

wether /ˈweðə(r)/ *n.* (Zool.) Hammel, *der*

wet: ~lands *n. pl.* Feuchtgebiete; ~ **look** *n.* Hochglanz, *der;* (of hair) Wet Look, *der*

wetness /ˈwetnɪs/ *n., no pl.* **1** (being wet) Nässe, *die;* **a patch of ~:** ein nasser Fleck **2** (being rainy) Feuchtigkeit, *die*

wet: ~ nurse A *n.* Amme, *die;* **B** *v.t.* (fig. derog.) bemuttern; **~suit** *n.* Nassanzug, *der*

wetting /ˈwetɪŋ/ *n.* **get a ~:** nass werden; **give sb. a ~:** jmdn. nass machen

ˈwetting agent *n.* Netzmittel, *das*

ˈwet-weather *attrib. adj.* Regen‹*schuhe, -mantel, -reifen*›; Schlechtwetter‹*programm, -ausrüstung*›

we've /wɪv, *stressed* wiːv/ = **we have**

WFTU *abbr.* = **World Federation of Trade Unions** WGB

whack /wæk/
A *v.t.* **1** (coll.: strike heavily) hauen (ugs.) **2** (coll.: defeat) vernichtend schlagen; in die Pfanne hauen (ugs.)
B *n.* **1** (coll.: heavy blow) Schlag, *der;* **give sb. a ~ on the bottom** jmdm. eins auf den Hintern geben (ugs.) **2** (coll.: share) Anteil, *der* **3** (coll.: attempt) **have a ~ at sth./at doing sth.** etw. probieren/probieren, etw. zu tun **4** **out of ~** (Amer.) aus dem Leim (ugs.) **5** **top ~** (coll.) (amount) Spitzentarif, *der;* (speed) Spitze, *die* (ugs.)

whacked /wækt/ *adj.* (Brit. coll.: tired out) erledigt (ugs.); kaputt (ugs.)

whacking /ˈwækɪŋ/
A *adj.* (coll.) satt (salopp)
B *adv.* (coll.) wahnsinnig (salopp); **~ great lies** faustdicke Lügen
C *n.* (coll.) Tracht Prügel, *die*

whacko /ˈwækəʊ/ *int.* (Brit. dated coll.) juchhe; juchhu

whale /weɪl/ *n., pl.* **~s** *or same* **1** (Zool.) Wal, *der;* Walfisch, *der* (volkst.); **right ~:** Glattwal, *der* **2** *no pl.* (coll.) **we had a ~ of a [good] time** wir haben uns bombig (ugs.) *od.* toll (ugs.) amüsiert; **it made a ~ of a difference** es machte ungeheuer viel aus (ugs.)

ˈwhalebone *n.* Fischbein, *das*

whaler /ˈweɪlə(r)/ *n.* ▸ⓘ **p. 1260** Walfänger, *der*

whaling /ˈweɪlɪŋ/ *n., no pl., no indef. art.* Walfang, *der; attrib.* Walfang-

whaling: ~ ship *n.* Walfangschiff, *das;* Walfänger, *der;* **~ station** *n.* Walfangstation, *die*

wham /wæm/
A *int.* wumm
B *n.* Knall, *der*
C *v.t.*, **-mm-: ~ sb.** jmdm. einen Schlag versetzen
D *v.i.*, **-mm-** knallen

whammy *n.* (coll.) [harter *od.* schwerer] Schlag, *der;* Tiefschlag, *der;* **double ~/triple ~:** doppelter/dreifacher Schlag

wharf /wɔːf/ *n.*, *pl.* **wharves** /wɔːvz/ *or* **~s** Kai, *der;* Kaje, *die* (nordd.)

what /wɒt/
A *interrog. adj.* 1) (which) welch…; **~ book did you choose?** welches Buch hast du ausgesucht?
2) (how much) wieviel; *with pl. n.* (how many) wie viele; **~ men/money has he?** wie viele Leute/wie viel Geld hat er?; **I know ~ time it starts** ich weiß, um wie viel Uhr es anfängt; **~ more can I do/say?** was kann ich sonst noch tun/sagen?; **~ more do you want?** was willst du [noch] mehr?
3) (which kind of) was für; **~ tea is this?** was für ein Tee ist das?; **~ kind of man is he?** was für ein Mensch ist er?; **~ good** *or* **use is it?** wozu soll das gut sein? *See also* **price A 4**
B *excl. adj.* was für; **~ a fool you are!** was für ein Dummkopf du doch bist!; **~ impudence** *or* **cheek/luck!** was für eine Unverschämtheit *od.* Frechheit/was für ein Glück!
C *rel. adj.* **we can dispose of ~ difficulties there are remaining** wir können die verbleibenden Schwierigkeiten ausräumen; **lend me ~ money you can** leih mir so viel Geld, wie du kannst; **I will give you ~ help I can** ich werde dir helfen, so gut ich kann
D *adv.* 1) (to what extent) **~ do I care?** was kümmerts mich?; **~ does it matter?** was machts?
2) **~ with …:** wenn man an … denkt; **~ with changing jobs and moving house I haven't had time to do any studying** da ich eine neue Stellung angetreten habe und umgezogen bin, hatte ich keine Zeit zum Lernen; **~ with one thing and another** wie das so ist *od.* geht
E *interrog. pron.* 1) (~ thing) was; **~ is your name?** wie heißt du/heißen Sie?; **~ about …?** (is there any news of …?, ~ will become of …?) was ist mit …?; **~ about a game of chess?** wie wärs mit einer Partie Schach?; **~ to do?** was tun?; **~-d'you-[ma-] call-him/-her/-it, ~'s-his/-her/-its-name** wie heißt er/sie/es noch; **~ for?** wozu?; **~ do you want the money for?** wozu *od.* wofür willst du das Geld?; **and/or ~ 'have you** und/oder was sonst noch [alles]; **~ if …?** was ist, wenn …?; **~ is he?** was ist er für einer?; (by profession) was ist er von Beruf? **~ is it** *etc.* **like?** wie ist es *usw.*?; **I've lost a pen here somewhere — Well, ~ is it like?** Ich habe hier irgendwo einen Stift verloren. — Was ist es denn für einer?; **~ next?** (fig.) sonst noch was?; **~ not** wer weiß was alles; **~ 'of him/her?** was ist mit ihm/ihr?; **~ 'of it?** was ist dabei?; was soll [schon] dabei sein?; **~ do you say** *or* **~ say we have a rest?** was hältst du davon, wenn wir mal Pause machen?; wie wärs mit einer Pause?; **~ will people say?** was werden die Leute sagen?; **all she ever thinks about is ~ people will say** sie denkt immer nur daran, was die Leute sagen; **[I'll] tell you ~:** weißt du, was; pass mal auf; **[and] ~ then?** [na] und?; **or ~?** oder was?; **so ~?** na und?
2) (asking for confirmation) **~?** wie?; was? (ugs.); **you did ~?** was hast du gemacht?; **nice day, ~?** (Brit. coll.) schöner Tag, was? (ugs.)
3) (in rhet. questions) **~ is the use in trying/the point of going on?** wozu [groß] versuchen/weitermachen? *See also* **give B 3; know A 3**
F *rel. pron.* 1) (that which) was; **do ~ I tell you** tu, was ich dir sage; **~ little I know/remember** das bisschen, das ich weiß/an das ich mich erinnere; **this is ~ I mean: …:** ich meine Folgendes: …; **give me ~ you can** gib mir, so viel du kannst; **I disagree with ~ you are saying** ich stimme dem nicht zu, was du sagst; **tell sb. ~ to do** *or* **~ he can do with sth.** (coll. iron.) jmdm. sagen, wo er sich (*Dat.*) etw. hinstecken kann (salopp); **~ is more** außerdem; zusätzlich; **the weather being ~ it is …:** so, wie es mit dem Wetter aussieht, …; **for ~ it is** in seiner Art
2) (uneducated: who, which) wo (salopp); **it's the poor ~ gets the blame** die Armen müssen immer alles ausbaden. *See also* **but A 2; come 13**
G *excl. pron.* was; **~ she must have suffered!** wie sie gelitten haben muss!

whate'er /wɒt'eə(r)/ (poet.), **whatever** /wɒt'evə(r)/
A *adj.* 1) *rel. adj.* **whatever measures we take** welche Maßnahmen wir auch immer ergreifen; **whatever materials you will need** alle Materialien, die du vielleicht brauchst 2) (notwithstanding which) was für … auch immer; **whatever problems you encounter** auf welche Probleme Sie auch stoßen [mögen] 3) (at all) überhaupt; **I can't see anyone whatever** ich kann überhaupt niemanden sehen
B *pron.* 1) *rel. pron.* was für … [auch immer]; **whatever you do to complain, they will still take no notice** man kann sich beschweren, wie man will, sie beachten es doch nicht; **do whatever you like** mach, was du willst 2) (notwithstanding anything) was auch [immer]; **whatever happens, …:** was auch geschieht, … 3) **or whatever** oder was auch immer; oder sonst was (ugs.) 4) (coll.) **= what ever ▸ ever 5**

'whatnot *n.* 1) (coll.: indefinite thing) Dingsbums, *das* (ugs.) 2) (stand with shelves) Etagere, *die*

whatsit /'wɒtsɪt/ *n.* (coll.) (thing) Dingsbums, *das* (ugs.); (person) Dingsda, *der* (ugs.)

whatsoe'er /wɒtsəʊ'eə(r)/ (poet.), **whatsoever** /wɒtsəʊ'evə(r)/ **▸ whatever**

wheat /wiːt/ *n.*, *no pl.*, *no indef. art.* Weizen, *der;* **sort out** *or* **separate the ~ from the chaff** (fig.) die Spreu vom Weizen trennen

'wheat belt *n.* (Geog.) Weizengürtel, *der*

wheaten /'wiːtn/ *adj.* Weizen-

wheat: ~ germ ▸ germ; ~meal *n.* (Brit.) Weizen[vollkorn]mehl, *das*

whee /wiː/ *int.* juchhe

wheedle /'wiːdl/ *v.t.* 1) (coax) **~ sb.** jmdm. gut zureden; **~ sb. into doing sth.** jmdm. so lange gut zureden, bis er etw. tut 2) (get by cajoling) sich (*Dat.*) verschaffen; **~ sth. out of sb.** jmdm. etw. abschwatzen (ugs.)

wheel /wiːl/
A *n.* 1) Rad, *das;* (of roller skate) Rolle, *die;* **[potter's] ~:** Töpferscheibe, *die;* **[roulette] ~:** Roulett, *das;* **reinvent the ~** (fig.) sich mit Problemen aufhalten, die längst gelöst sind; **get oneself some ~s** (coll.) sich (*Dat.*) einen fahrbaren Untersatz zulegen (ugs.); **put** *or* **set the ~s in motion** (fig.) die Sache in Gang setzen; **the ~s of bureaucracy turn slowly** (fig.) die Mühlen der Bürokratie mahlen langsam; **there are ~s within ~s** (fig.) es spielen Dinge eine Rolle, von denen man gar nichts ahnt; **break sb. on the ~** (Hist.) jmdn. rädern; *see also* **butterfly 1; oil B 1; shoulder A 1; spoke[1] 1** 2) (for steering) (Motor Veh.) Lenkrad, *das;* (Naut.) Steuerrad, *das;* **at** *or* **behind the ~** (of car) am *od.* hinterm Steuer; (of ship; also fig.) am Ruder 3) (movement in a circle) Kreisbewegung, *die;* **the ~[s] of the vultures** das Kreisen der Geier 4) (Mil.: drill movement) Schwenkung, *die;* **left/right ~:** Links-/Rechtsschwenkung, *die*
B *v.t.* 1) (turn round) wenden 2) (Mil.) schwenken lassen 3) (push) schieben; **~ oneself** (in a wheelchair) [im Rollstuhl] fahren
C *v.i.* 1) (turn round) kehrtmachen 2) (circle) kreisen 3) (Mil.) schwenken; **left/right ~!** links/rechts schwenkt!

Phrasal verbs
- **~ a'bout, ~ a'round**
A *v.t.* herumdrehen; wenden ‹*Pferd*›
B *v.i.* kehrtmachen; (face the other way) sich umdrehen; (fig.) kreisen; ‹*Tänzer:*› sich im Kreise drehen
- **~ 'in** *v.t.* hinein-/hereinschieben
- **~ 'out** *v.t.* hinaus-/herausschieben; **~ sb. out** (fig. derog.) jmdn. vorführen
- **~ 'round ▸ ~ about**

wheel: ~ and 'deal *v.i.* mauscheln; **~barrow** *n.* Schubkarre, *die;* Schubkarren, *der;* **~barrow race** *n.* Schubkarrenrennen, *das;* **~base** *n.* (Motor Veh., Railw.) Radstand, *der;* **~ brace** *n.* Radschlüssel, *der;* (cross-shaped) Kreuzschlüssel, *der;* **~chair** *n.* Rollstuhl, *der;* **~chair access** *n.*, *no pl.* Rollstuhlzugang, *der;* **~chair-accessible** *adj.* rollstuhlgerecht ‹*Wohnung, Hotel*›; **~chair-bound** *adj.* an den Rollstuhl gebunden *od.* gefesselt ‹*Mensch*›; **the accident left him ~chair-bound** seit dem Unfall ist er an den Rollstuhl gefesselt *od.* sitzt er im Rollstuhl; **~ clamp** *n.* Parkkralle, *die*

wheeled /wiːld/ *adj.* mit Rädern *nachgestellt;* ‹*Möbel, Kulisse usw.*› auf *od.* mit Rollen; **~ vehicle** Räderfahrzeug, *das*

-wheeled *adj. in comb.* ‹*vier-, sechs-, acht*›räd[e]rig

wheeler-dealer /wiːlə'diːlə(r)/ *n.* Mauschler, *der*/Mauschlerin, *die;* (financial) Geschäftemacher, *der*/-macherin, *die*

'wheelhouse *n.* (Naut.) Steuerhaus, *das*

wheelie /'wiːlɪ/ *n.* (coll.) *Fahren auf dem Hinterrad;* Wheelie, *das;* **do a ~/do ~s** auf dem Hinterrad fahren; ein Wheelie/Wheelies fahren

'wheelie bin *n.* (Brit. coll.) Müllcontainer auf Rollen; Rollcontainer für Müll

wheeling /'wiːlɪŋ/ *n.*, *no pl.*, *no indef. art.* Kreisen, *das*

wheeling and 'dealing *n.* Mauschelei, *die;* (shady deals) undurchsichtige Geschäfte; **there is a lot of ~ going on** es wird eifrig gemauschelt

wheel: ~ lock *n.* (Motor Veh.: steering lock) Lenkradschloss, *das;* (bicycle lock) Bügelschloss, *das;* **~ of 'fortune** *n.* Glücksrad, *das;* **~ of 'life** *n.* (Buddhism) Rad des Lebens *od.* Werdens; **~ reflector** *n.* Speichenreflektor, *der;* **~spin** *n.* (Motor Veh., Railw.) Durchdrehen der Räder; **because of ~spin** wegen durchdrehender Räder; **~wright** /'wiːlraɪt/ *n.* Stellmacher, *der*

wheeze /wiːz/
A *v.i.* schnaufen; keuchen
B *n.* 1) Schnaufen, *das;* Keuchen, *das;* **give a [loud] ~:** [laut] schnaufen *od.* keuchen 2) (dated coll.) (trick) Trick, *der;* (plan) Idee, *die;* **think up a ~:** einen Dreh finden (ugs.); **a good ~ for making money** eine gute Masche, zu Geld zu kommen

Phrasal verb
- **~ 'out** *v.t.* keuchen

wheezy /'wiːzɪ/ *adj.* (coll.) pfeifend, keuchend ‹*Atem, Stimme*›; asthmatisch ‹*Husten*›; schnaufend ‹*Orgel*›; **be ~** ‹*Atem:*› pfeifend gehen, pfeifen; ‹*Person:*› pfeifend atmen

whelk /welk/ *n.* (Zool.) Wellhornschnecke, *die*

whelp /welp/
A *n.* Welpe, *der*
B *v.i.* (also derog.) werfen

when /wen/ ▸ **i p. 1706**
A *adv.* 1) (at what time) wann; **say ~** (coll.: pouring drink) sag halt; **that was ~ I intervened** das war der Moment, wo ich eingriff; **the best part of the film was ~ the car exploded** das Beste in dem Film war die Szene, als das Auto explodierte 2) (at which) **the time ~ …:** die Zeit, zu der *od.* (ugs.) wo/(with past tense) als …; **the day ~ …:** der Tag, an dem *od.* (ugs.) wo/(with past tense) als …; **do you remember [the time] ~ we …:** erinnerst du dich daran, wie wir …
B *conj.* 1) (at the time that) als; (with present or future tense) wenn; **~ [I was] young** als ich jung war; in meiner Jugend; **~ in doubt** im Zweifelsfall; (with gerund) **~ cleaning the gun** beim Putzen des Gewehrs; **~ speaking French** wenn ich/sie *usw.* Französisch spreche/spricht *usw.*
2) (whereas) **why do you go abroad ~ it's cheaper here?** warum fährst du ins Ausland, wo es doch hier billiger ist?; **I received only £5 ~ I should have got £10** ich bekam nur 5 Pfund, hätte aber 10 Pfund bekommen sollen
3) (considering that) wenn; **how can I finish it ~ you won't help?** wie soll ich es fertig machen,

W

ℹ When

als or wenn?

There is a simple distinction between these two translations for *when:*

als is used for happenings in the past

wenn is used for happenings in the present or future

When I saw him I smiled
= Als ich ihn sah, lächelte ich

When I see him I always feel sorry for him
= Wenn ich ihn sehe, tut er mir immer Leid

When I see him I'll tell him
= Wenn ich ihn sehe, werde ich es ihm sagen *or* sage ich es ihm

As can be seen, **wenn** translates two uses of *when* in English: in the sense of *whenever* (present tense in both clauses) and referring to the future (present tense in the *when* clause, future tense in the main clause). German does the same, except that the present is often also used in this last case.

Occasionally *when* is used with a verb in the past in the sense of *whenever,* and here too it should be translated by **wenn:**

When(ever) I saw him, I always felt sorry for him
= Wenn ich ihn sah, tat er mir immer Leid

wenn is also used to translate *when* where it occurs with the English present participle (the *-ing* form), a normal subject and verb being used. The subject and the tense of the verb will be that of the English main clause; if this is impersonal, **man** can be used.

When speaking German I often get embarrassed
= Wenn ich Deutsch spreche, werde ich oft verlegen

When speaking German it is important to enunciate clearly
= Wenn man Deutsch spricht, ist es wichtig, deutlich zu artikulieren

Often the sense of *when* in this construction is *while,* and the appropriate translation is **als,** but **bei** plus the verbal noun can also be used and is often neater.

He was killed when crossing the road
= Er kam beim Überqueren der Straße ums Leben, Er kam ums Leben, als er die Straße überquerte

Be careful when cleaning the gun
= Sei vorsichtig beim Putzen des Gewehrs

In questions (direct and indirect)

Here the translation is always **wann:**

When is she coming?
= Wann kommt sie?

I don't know when she's coming
= Ich weiß nicht, wann sie kommt

When do you want to eat?
= Wann willst du essen?

Tell me when you want to eat
= Sag mir, wann du essen willst

From when is the licence valid?
= Ab wann gilt der Schein?

Since when do you give the orders?
= Seit wann gibst du die Befehle?

Other usages are covered in the entry for **when.**

---

wenn du nicht hilfst? [4] (and at that moment) als
C *pron.* **by/till ~ ...?;** bis wann ...?; **from/since ~ ...?** ab/seit wann ...?; **~ are we invited for?** für wann sind wir eingeladen?; **but that was yesterday, since ~ things have changed** aber das war gestern, und inzwischen hat sich manches geändert
D *n.* Wann, *das; see also* **where D**

whence /wens/ (arch./literary)
A *adv.* woher; **~ did you learn this news?** wo[her] hast du das erfahren?; **the village ~ comes the famous cheese** das Dorf, aus dem der berühmte Käse kommt; **the source ~ these evils spring** die Quelle dieser Übel; **these are the facts, ~ we can conclude that ...:** das sind die Tatsachen, aus denen wir schließen können, dass ...; **~ my doubts about his abilities** daher meine Zweifel über seine Fähigkeiten
B *conj.* (to the place from which) dorthin, woher; **he returned it ~ it came** er brachte es dorthin zurück, wo es herkam
C *pron.* **from ~** ▸**A**

whene'er /wen'eə(r)/ (poet.), **whenever** /wen'evə(r)/
A *adv.* [1] wann immer; **or whenever** oder wann immer [2] (coll.) = **when ever** ▸**ever 5**
B *conj.* jedes Mal wenn

whensoe'er /wensəʊ'eə(r)/ (poet.), **whensoever** /wensəʊ'evə(r)/ *adv.* wann auch immer

where /weə(r)/
A *adv.* [1] (in or at what place) wo; **~ shall we sit?** wo wollen wir sitzen *od.* uns hinsetzen?; wohin wollen wir uns setzen?; **~ was I?** (fig.) wo war ich stehen geblieben?; **~ did Orwell say/write that?** wo *od.* an welcher Stelle sagt/schreibt Orwell das?; **~ is the harm in it/the sense of it?** was macht das schon/welchen *od.* was für einen Sinn hat das?; **this is ~ I was born** hier bin ich geboren [2] (from what place) woher; **~ did you get that information?** wo hast du das erfahren? [3] (to what place, to which) wohin; **she's going ~ she's wanted** sie geht dahin, wo sie gebraucht wird; **~ shall I put it?** wohin soll ich es legen?; wo soll ich es hinlegen?; **the town ~ they were going** die Stadt, wohin sie fuhren; **~ do we go from here?** (fig.) was tun wir jetzt *od.* als nächstes?; **I know ~ I'm going** (fig.) ich weiß, was ich erreichen will [4] (in what respect) inwiefern; **I don't know ~ they differ/I've gone wrong** ich weiß nicht, worin sie sich unterscheiden/wo ich den Fehler gemacht habe; **~ he is weakest is in maths** am schwächsten ist er in Mathematik; **that is ~ you are wrong** in diesem Punkt irrst du dich [5] (in which) wo; **in the box ~ I keep my tools** in der Kiste, worin *od.* in der ich mein Werkzeug habe [6] (in what situation) wo; **~ will/would they be if ...?** was wird/würde aus ihnen, wenn ...?; **~ would I be without you?** was täte ich ohne dich?; **~ will it all end?** wo wird das noch enden?
B *conj.* wo; **~ uncertain, leave blank** bei Unsicherheit [bitte] freilassen; **delete ~ inapplicable** Nichtzutreffendes [bitte] streichen
C *pron.* **near/not far from ~ it happened** nahe der Stelle/nicht weit von der *od.* unweit der Stelle, wo es passiert ist; **from ~ I'm standing** von meinem Standort [aus]; **they continued from ~ they left off** sie machten da weiter, wo sie aufgehört hatten; **to Oxford, from ~ we took a train to London** nach Oxford, wo wir den Zug nach London nahmen; **within ten metres of ~ we stood** keine zehn Meter von der Stelle, wo wir standen; **we drove out to ~ the air was fresh and clean** wir fuhren dorthin, wo die Luft frisch und sauber war; **~ [...] from?** woher [...]?; von wo [...]?; **~ do/have you come from?** woher kommst du?; wo kommst du her?; **he is never sure ~ his next meal is coming from** er weiß nie, woher er seine nächste Mahlzeit kriegt; **~ [...] to?** wohin [...]?; **~ are you going to?** wohin gehst du?; wo gehst du hin?; **~ have you got to [in the book]?** wie weit bist du [in dem Buch]?
D *n.* Wo, *das;* **I can't recall the ~ and when [of it]** ich weiß nicht mehr, wo und wann [es war]

whereabouts
A /weərə'baʊts/ *adv.* (in what place) wo; (to what place) wohin
B /weərə'baʊts/ *pron.* **~ are you from?** woher kommst du?
C /'weərəbaʊts/ *n., constr. as sing. or pl.* (of thing) Verbleib, *der;* (of person) Aufenthalt[sort], *der;* **her/its present ~ is** *or* **are unknown** wo sie sich zurzeit aufhält/wo es sich zurzeit befindet, ist unbekannt

where: ~'as *conj.* [1] während; **he is very quiet, ~as she is an extrovert** er ist sehr ruhig, sie dagegen ist eher extravertiert; [2] (Law: considering that) in Anbetracht dessen, dass; da; **~'by** *adv.* mit dem/der/denen; mit dessen/deren Hilfe;

where'er /weər'eə(r)/ (poet.) ▸**wherever**

wherefore /'weəfɔ:(r)/
A *adv.* (arch./literary) weshalb
B *n.* **the whys and ~s** ▸**why C**

where: ~'in *adv.* (formal) [1] (in which) worin; in dem/der/denen; [2] (in what respect) inwiefern; worin ‹*sich unterscheiden, sich finden*›; womit ‹*dienen*›; **~'of** *adv.* (formal) (of which) von dem/der/denen; woraus ‹*gemacht sein*›; **the house ~ he is the owner** das Haus, dessen Eigentümer er ist

wheresoe'er /weəsəʊ'eə(r)/ (poet.), **wheresoever** /weəsəʊ'evə(r)/ *adv., conj.* wo auch immer

whereupon /weərə'pɒn/ *adv.* worauf

wherever /weər'evə(r)/
A *adv.* [1] (in whatever place) wo immer; **sit ~ you like** setz dich, wohin du magst; **I'll find him, ~ he lives** ich werde ihn finden, wo er auch wohnt *od.* wohnen mag; **or ~:** oder wo immer; oder sonstwo (ugs.) [2] (to whatever place) wohin immer; **I shall go ~ I like** ich gehe, wohin ich will; **I shall go ~ there is work** ich gehe dahin, wo es Arbeit gibt; **or ~:** oder wohin immer; oder sonstwohin (ugs.) [3] (coll.) = **where ever** ▸**ever 5**
B *conj.* [1] (in every place that) überall [da], wo; **~ security is involved** wann immer es um die Sicherheit geht; **do it ~ possible** tun Sie es, wo *od.* wenn [irgend] möglich [2] (to every place that) wohin auch; **~ he went** wohin er auch ging; wo er auch hinging
C *pron.* wo ... auch; **~ you're going to** wo du auch hingehst; wohin du auch gehst; **~ it/he comes from** wo es/er auch herkommt; woher es/er auch kommt; **carry on reading from ~ you've got to** lies da weiter, bis wohin du gekommen bist

wherewithal /'weəwɪðɔ:l/ *n.* (coll.) **the ~:** das nötige Kleingeld (ugs.)

wherry /'werɪ/ *n.* [1] (rowing boat) [Ruder]kahn, *der* [2] (Brit.: barge) [Last]kahn, *der*

whet /wet/ *v.t.*, **-tt-** [1] (sharpen) wetzen [2] (fig.: stimulate) anregen ‹*Appetit*›; erregen ‹*Interesse*›; reizen ‹*Neugier*›

whether /'weðə(r)/ *conj.* ob; **I don't know ~ to go [or not]** ich weiß nicht, ob ich gehen soll [oder nicht]; **the question [of] ~ to do it [or not]** die Frage, ob man es tun soll [oder nicht]; **~ you like it or not, I'm going** ob es dir passt oder nicht, ich gehe; *see also* **doubt A 1, C; no B 3**

'whetstone *n.* (lit. or fig.) Wetzstein, *der*

whew /hwju:/ *int. expr. surprise* oh; *expr. consternation etc.* puh; *expr. relief* ah

whey /weɪ/ *n., no pl., no indef. art.* Molke, *die*

which /wɪtʃ/
A *adj.* [1] *interrog.* welch...; **~ one** welcher/welche/welches; **~ ones** welche; **~ one of**

W

you did it? wer von euch hat es getan?; **~ way** (how) wie; (in ~ direction) wohin **2** *rel.* welch… (geh.); **I told him to go to the doctor, ~ advice he took** ich habe ihm geraten, zum Arzt zu gehen, was er auch getan hat; **he usually comes at one o'clock, at ~ time I'm having lunch/by ~ time I've finished** er kommt immer um ein Uhr; dann esse ich gerade zu Mittag/bis dahin bin ich schon fertig; **a 35mm camera (~ size I prefer)** eine Kleinbildkamera (das Format, das ich vorziehe)
B *pron.* **1** *interrog.* welcher/welche/welches; **~ of you?** wer von euch?; **~ is ~?** welcher/welche/welches ist welcher/welche/welches?; **I can't tell ~ is ~:** ich kann sie nicht auseinander halten *od.* unterscheiden **2** *rel.* der/die/das; welcher/welche/welches (veralt.); *referring to a clause* was; **of ~:** dessen/deren; **everything ~ I predicted** alles, was ich vorausgesagt habe; **the crime of ~ you accuse him** das Verbrechen, dessen Sie ihn anklagen; **the house of ~ I am speaking** das Haus, von dem *od.* wovon ich rede; **the bed on ~ she lay** das Bett, auf dem *od.* worauf sie lag; **he grinned, from ~ I gathered he wasn't serious** er grinste, woraus ich schloss, dass es nicht sein Ernst war; **the shop opposite/near ~ we parked** der Laden, gegenüber dem/in dessen Nähe wir parkten; **I have received your kind gift, for ~ many thanks** ich habe dein nettes Geschenk bekommen. Vielen Dank dafür; **I intervened, after ~ they calmed down** ich griff ein, worauf[hin] sie sich beruhigten; **Our Father, ~ art in Heaven** (Rel.) Vater unser, der du bist im Himmel

whichever /wɪtʃˈevə(r)/
A *adj.* **1** (any … that) der *od.* derjenige, der/die *od.* diejenige, die/das *od.* dasjenige, das/die *od.* diejenigen, die; **go ~ way you want** es ist egal, welchen Weg du nimmst; **take ~ apple/apples you wish** nimm den Apfel, den du willst/die Äpfel, die du willst; **…, ~ period is the longer** …, je nachdem, welches der längere Zeitraum ist **2** (no matter which/who/whom) welcher/welche/welches … auch; **~ way you go** welchen Weg du auch nimmst **3** (coll.) = **which ever** ▸ **ever 5**
B *pron.* **1** (any one[s] that) der *od.* derjenige, der/die *od.* diejenige, die/das *od.* dasjenige, das/die *od.* diejenigen, die; **~ of you/the children wins will get a prize** wer von euch gewinnt/das Kind, das gewinnt, bekommt einen Preis; **a list of ~ of the children want to come** eine Liste aller Kinder, die kommen wollen; **at a walk, trot, or gallop, ~ you please** gehend, im Trab oder im Galopp, [ganz] wie du magst; **to dinner — or supper, ~ it ought to be called** zum Diner — oder Abendessen, wie immer man es nennen soll **2** (no matter which one[s]) welcher/welche/welches … auch; **~ of them comes/come** wer von ihnen auch kommt **3** (coll.) **= which ever** ▸ **ever 5**

whichsoever /wɪtʃsəʊˈevə(r)/ (arch.) ▸ **whichever A 1, 2, B 1, 2**

whiff /wɪf/ *n.* **1** (smell) [leichter] Geruch; (puff, breath) Hauch, *der;* **~s of smoke** Rauchwölkchen; **a ~ of honeysuckle** ein leichter Geißblattduft; **the ~ from his smelly feet** der Geruch seiner Schweißfüße; **give her another ~ of chloroform** gib ihr noch mal etwas Chloroform; **catch a ~ of sth.** den Hauch von etw. spüren **2** (fig.: trace) Hauch, *der;* **the faintest ~ of sentiment** der leiseste Anflug von Sentimentalität

Whig /wɪg/ (Hist.)
A *n.* Whig, *der*
B *attrib. adj.* Whig-

while /waɪl/
A *n.* Weile, *die;* **quite a** *or* **quite some ~, a good ~** eine ganze Weile; ziemlich lange; **it takes a ~:** es dauert eine Weile *od.* eine Zeit lang; **[for] a ~:** eine Weile; **where have you been all the** *or* **this ~?** wo warst du die ganze Zeit?; **[only] a little** *or* **short ~ ago** [erst] kürzlich *od.* vor kurzem; **all the ~ we were there** die ganze Zeit, als wir da waren; **a long ~:** lange; **a long ~ ago** *or* **back** vor langer Zeit; **between ~s** zwischendurch; **for a little** *or* **short ~:** eine kleine Weile; **stay a little ~ [longer]** bleib noch ein Weilchen; **I haven't seen him for a long ~:** ich habe ihn lange nicht [mehr] gesehen; **in a little** *or* **short ~:** gleich; **in a long ~:** lange; seit langem; **be worth [sb.'s] ~:** sich [für jmdn.] lohnen; **make sth. worth sb.'s ~:** jmdn. für etw. entsprechend belohnen; **I'll make it worth your ~:** es soll dein Schaden nicht sein; **once in a ~:** von Zeit zu Zeit [mal]; hin und wieder [mal]; **he read the newspaper smoking a cigar the ~** (dated/literary) er las die Zeitung und rauchte dabei eine Zigarre
B *conj.* **1** während; (as long as) solange; **~ in London he took piano lessons** als er in London war, nahm er Klavierstunden; **don't smoke ~ in bed** rauchen Sie nicht im Bett; **could you get me a paper as well ~ you are about it?** könntest du mir auch eine Zeitung mitbringen, wenn du schon dabei bist? **2** (although) obgleich **3** (whereas) während
C *v.t.* **~ away the time** sich (*Dat.*) die Zeit vertreiben (**by, with** mit); **~ away the evening/an hour** sich (*Dat.*) den Abend über/eine Stunde lang die Zeit vertreiben

whilst /waɪlst/ (Brit.) ▸ **while B**

whim /wɪm/ *n.* (mood) Laune, *die;* (idea) Spleen, *der;* **he acts as the ~ takes him** er handelt je nach Laune

whimper /ˈwɪmpə(r)/
A *n.* **~[s]** Wimmern, *das;* (of dog etc.) Winseln, *das;* **with a ~:** wimmernd/winselnd; **he gave a ~ of pain** er wimmerte vor Schmerz; **not with a bang but a ~** (fig.) sang- und klanglos
B *v.i.* wimmern; ‹*Hund:*› winseln
C *v.t.* in weinerlichem Ton vorbringen ‹*Klage*›; **'…', he ~ed** „…", wimmerte er

whimsical /ˈwɪmzɪkl/ *adj.* **1** (frivolous) launenhaft; (odd, fanciful) spleenig; (tinged with humour) launig; humorig; (teasing) neckisch ‹*Blick, Lächeln*› **2** (odd-looking) kurios; ulkig (ugs.)

whimsicality /wɪmzɪˈkælɪtɪ/ *n., no pl.* ▸ **whimsical: 1** Launenhaftigkeit, *die;* Spleenigkeit, *die;* Launigkeit, *die;* Humorigkeit, *die* **2** Kuriosität, *die;* Ulkigkeit, *die* (ugs.)

whimsically /ˈwɪmzɪkəlɪ/ *adv.* launenhaft; (teasingly) neckisch ‹*ansehen, lächeln*›; **he said ~ that …:** er machte die launige Bemerkung, dass …

whimsy /ˈwɪmzɪ/ *n.* **1** *no pl.* ▸ **whimsicality 1 2** (idea) Spleen, *der*

whine /waɪn/
A *v.i.* **1** (make moaning sound) heulen; ‹*Hund:*› jaulen; ‹*Baby:*› quengeln (ugs.); **~ for mercy/alms** um Gnade/Almosen winseln (abwertend) **2** (complain) jammern; **he's been whining to the boss about it** er hat dem Chef darüber etwas vorgejammert
B *n.* **1** (sound) Heulen, *das;* (esp. of dog) Jaulen, *das;* **the ~ in his voice** der winselnde Ton in seiner Stimme; **the baby's ~s** das Gequengel des Babys (ugs.) **2** (complaint) **~[s]** Gejammer, *das*

whiner /ˈwaɪnə(r)/ *n.* Jammerer, *der;* **be a ~:** immer was zu jammern haben

whin[e]y /ˈwaɪnɪ/ *adj.* **1** (whining) jaulend **2** (complaining) weinerlich; quengelig ‹*Kind*›

whinge /wɪndʒ/ (coll.)
A *v.i.*, **~ing** ▸ **whine A 2**
B *n.* ▸ **whine B 2**

whinny /ˈwɪnɪ/
A *v.i.* wiehern
B *n.* Wiehern, *das;* **whinnies** Gewieher, *das*

whip /wɪp/
A *n.* **1** Peitsche, *die;* **use one's ~ on** *or* **take one's ~ to sb./a horse** jmdm./einem Pferd die Peitsche geben; *see also* **crack A 1, C 3**
2 (Brit. Parl.: official) Einpeitscher, *der*/Einpeitscherin, *die* (Jargon); **chief ~:** Haupteinpeitscher, *der*/-einpeitscherin, *die* (Jargon); Fraktionsgeschäftsführer, *der*/-führerin, *die* (Amtsspr.)
3 (Brit. Parl.: notice) **[three-line] ~** [*verbindliche*] *Aufforderung zur Teilnahme an einer Plenarsitzung* [*wegen einer wichtigen Abstimmung*]; **issue a three-line ~:** Fraktionszwang verhängen; **take/be deprived of/resign the ~:** in die Fraktion eintreten/aus der Fraktion ausgeschlossen werden/aus der Fraktion austreten
4 (Hunting: whipper-in) Pikör, *der*
5 (Cookery) Schaumspeise, *die*
B *v.t.*, **-pp-: 1** (lash) peitschen; **the rider ~ped his horse** der Reiter gab seinem Pferd die Peitsche; **he was ~ped in public** er wurde öffentlich ausgepeitscht; **the rain ~ped the window panes** der Regen peitschte [gegen] die Fensterscheiben
2 (Cookery) schlagen; **~ sth. until stiff/to a froth** etw. steif/schaumig schlagen
3 (move quickly) reißen ‹*Gegenstand*›; **she ~ped it out of my hand** sie riss es mir aus der Hand; **he quickly ~ped it out of sight** er ließ es schnell verschwinden; **~ sth. from one's pocket** etw. blitzschnell aus der Tasche ziehen; **~ sb. into hospital** jmdn. schleunigst ins Krankenhaus bringen; **she was ~ped through customs** sie wurde am Zoll blitzschnell abgefertigt
4 (coll.: defeat) eins überbraten (+ *Dat.*) (salopp)
5 (coll.: steal) klauen (ugs.)
6 (bind) umwickeln; [be]takeln (Seemannsspr.); (Sewing: overcast) umnähen
7 (fig.: reprove, criticize) **~ sb./sth.** jmdm. die Leviten lesen/etw. geißeln
8 **~ a top** kreiseln; einen Kreisel treiben
C *v.i.*, **-pp-: 1** (move quickly) flitzen (ugs.); **he ~ped down the stairs** er sauste *od.* flitzte die Treppe hinunter; **~ through a book in no time** ein Buch in null Komma nichts durchlesen (ugs.)
2 (lash) peitschen

Phrasal verbs

• **~ a'way** *v.t.* wegreißen (**from** *Dat.*)
• **~ 'back** *v.i.* **1** (spring back) zurückschnellen **2** (return quickly) zurückflitzen (ugs.)
• **~ 'in**
A *v.i.* reinwitschen (ugs.); **the wind came ~ping in** der Wind kam reingefegt (ugs.)
B *v.t.* (Hunting) [mit der Peitsche] wieder zur Meute treiben ‹*Hunde*›
• **~ 'off** *v.t.* **1** (snatch off) herunterreißen; ‹*Wind:*› herunterfegen; **~ one's clothes off** seine Kleider von sich werfen; **~ off one's hat** [sich (*Dat.*)] den Hut vom Kopf reißen; **~ sb. off to hospital/France** jmdn. schleunigst ins Krankenhaus/nach Frankreich bringen **2** (Hunting) [mit der Peitsche] zurücktreiben ‹*Hunde*›
• **~ 'on** *v.t.* **1** (put on quickly) draufwerfen; **~ one's coat/clothes on** sich in seinen Mantel/seine Kleider werfen; **~ one's hat on** schnell seinen Hut aufsetzen **2** (urge on) mit der Peitsche antreiben; (fig.) antreiben; anspornen
• **~ 'out**
A *v.t.* [blitzschnell] herausziehen; **~ sb.'s appendix/tonsils out** jmds. Blinddarm/Mandeln schleunigst herausnehmen
B *v.i.* rauswitschen (ugs.)
• **~ 'round** *v.i.* **1** (turn quickly) herumschnellen **2** (go quickly) **~ round to see sb.** *or* **to sb.'s place** schnell bei jmdm. vorbeischauen; **I'm just ~ping round to my neighbour's/to the shops** ich gehe nur schnell zum Nachbarn/einkaufen; *see also* **whip-round**
• **~ 'up** *v.t.* **1** (snatch up) [blitz]schnell aufheben **2** (Cookery) [kräftig] schlagen **3** (arouse) aufpeitschen ‹*Wellen*›; (fig.) anheizen (ugs.), anfachen (geh.) ‹*Emotionen, Interesse*›; schüren ‹*Hass, Unzufriedenheit*›; **he knows how to ~ up enthusiasm in his pupils** er versteht es, seine Schüler zu begeistern; **~ up trouble/a riot** die Leute zu Unruhen/zum Aufruhr aufstacheln **4** (coll.: make quickly) schnell hinzaubern ‹*Gericht, Essen*›

whip: ~cord *n.* **1** (cord) Peitschenschnur, *die;* **2** (fabric) Whipcord, *der;* **~ hand** *n.* **have** *or* **hold the ~ hand [of** *or* **over sb.]** (fig.) die Oberhand [über jmdn.] haben; **~lash** *n.* **1** Peitschenriemen, *der;* **2** (Med.) **~lash [injury]** Peitschenschlagverletzung, *die;* Schleudertrauma, *das*

whipped 'cream *n.* Schlagsahne, *die*

whipper-in /wɪpərˈɪn/ (Hunting) Pikör, *der*

whippersnapper /ˈwɪpəsnæpə(r)/ *n.* (dated) [junger] Dachs; (cheeky) Frechdachs, *der*

whippet /ˈwɪpɪt/ *n.* Whippet, *der*

whipping /ˈwɪpɪŋ/ *n.* **1** (flogging) Schlagen [mit der Peitsche]; (as form of punishment) Prügelstrafe, *die;* (flagellation) Geißelung, *die;* **give sb. a**

~: jmdn. auspeitschen; (with stick etc.) jmdm. eine Tracht Prügel verpassen (ugs.); (coll.: defeat) jmdm. eins überbraten (salopp); **get** or **take** or **be given a ~:** ausgepeitscht werden; (coll.: be defeated) eins übergebraten kriegen (salopp) 2 (cord) Umwicklung, *die;* Takling, *der* (Seemannsspr.)

whipping: ~ boy *n.* (Hist.; also fig.) Prügelknabe, *der;* **~ cream** *n.* [flüssige] Schlagsahne; **~ top** *n.* [Treib]kreisel, *der*

whippoorwill /'wɪpʊəwɪl/ *n.* (Ornith.) Whip-Poor-Will, *der*

whippy /'wɪpɪ/ *adj.* biegsam; elastisch

whip: ~-round *n.* (Brit. coll.) Sammlung, *die;* **have** or **hold a ~-round [for sb./sth.]** [für jmdn./etw.] den Hut herumgehen lassen (ugs.); **~-saw** *v.t.* (Amer. fig.) *beim Poker betrügen, indem man zusammen mit dem Partner den Einsatz erhöht;* **~stock** *n.* Peitschenstiel, *der*

whir /wɜː(r)/

A *v.i.*, **-rr-** ▸ **whirr A**

B *n.* ▸ **whirr B**

whirl /wɜːl/

A *v.t.* 1 (rotate) [im Kreis] herumwirbeln 2 (fling) schleudern; (with circling motion) wirbeln ‹*Blätter, Schneeflocken usw.*› 3 (convey rapidly) in Windeseile fahren; **the train ~ed us to our destination** der Zug brachte uns in Windeseile ans Ziel

B *v.i.* 1 (rotate) wirbeln; **~ing dervish** tanzender Derwisch 2 (move swiftly) sausen; (with circling motion) wirbeln; **I could see the leaves ~ing in the wind** ich sah, wie die Blätter vom Wind herumgewirbelt wurden 3 (fig.: reel) **everything/the room ~ed about me** mir drehte sich alles/das Zimmer drehte sich vor meinen Augen; **the excitements of the city made her head ~:** von den aufregenden Eindrücken der Stadt wirbelte *od.* schwirrte ihr der Kopf

C *n.* 1 Wirbeln, *das;* **the wind threw up a ~ of leaves/sand** der Wind wirbelte Blätter/Sand auf; **she was** or **her thoughts were** or **her head was in a ~** (fig.) ihr schwirrte der Kopf 2 (bustle) Trubel, *der;* **her dull life suddenly became a ~ of activity** ihr eintöniges Leben war plötzlich voller Trubel und Betriebsamkeit; **the social ~:** der Trubel des gesellschaftlichen Lebens 3 (coll.: attempt) **give sb./sth. a ~:** jmdn./etw. mal probieren

Phrasal verbs

• **~ a'bout**

A *v.t.* herumwirbeln

B *v.i.* herumwirbeln; ‹*Vögel:*› sich tummeln

• **~ a'long**

A *v.t.* ‹*Fluss:*› mitreißen; **~ sb. along** mit jmdm. dahinsausen

B *v.i.* dahinsausen

• **~ a'round** ▸ **~ about**

• **~ a'way, ~ 'off**

A *v.t.* in Windeseile wegfahren; **~ sb. off** or **away somewhere** jmdn. in Windeseile irgendwohin bringen

B *v.i.* lossausen

• **~ 'round**

A *v.t.* [im Kreis] herumwirbeln

B *v.i.* [im Kreis] herumwirbeln; ‹*Rad, Rotor, Strudel:*› wirbeln; **the leaf ~ed round as it fell** das Blatt drehte sich im Fall in einem Wirbel

• **~ 'up** *v.t.* aufwirbeln; hochwirbeln

whirligig /'wɜːlɪgɪg/ *n.* 1 (top) Kreisel, *der;* (toy windmill) Windrädchen, *das* 2 (Zool.) Taumelkäfer, *der;* Kreiselkäfer, *der*

whirl: ~pool *n.* Strudel, *der;* (bathing pool) Whirlpool, *der;* **~pool 'bath** *n.* Whirlpool, *der;* **~wind** *n.* 1 Wirbelwind, *der;* (stronger) Wirbelsturm, *der;* **sow the wind and reap the ~wind** (prov.) Wind säen und Sturm ernten; 2 (fig.: tumult) Wirbel, *der;* Trubel, *der;* **I've been caught up all week in a ~wind of activity** für mich war die ganze Woche über ständig Trubel; *attrib.* **~wind romance** [kurze,] heftige Romanze

whirlybird /'wɜːlɪbɜːd/ *n.* (coll.: helicopter) Hubschrauber, *der*

whirr /wɜː(r)/

A *v.i.* surren; ‹*Heuschrecke, Grille usw.:*› zirpen; ‹*Flügel eines Vogels, Propeller:*› schwirren

B *n.* ▸ **A:** Surren, *das;* Zirpen, *das;* Schwirren, *das*

whisk /wɪsk/

A *n.* 1 Wedel, *der* 2 (Cookery) Schneebesen, *der;* (part of mixer) Rührbesen, *der* 3 (movement) wischende Bewegung; **the horse gave a ~ of its tail** das Pferd schlug mit dem Schwanz

B *v.t.* 1 (Cookery) [mit dem Schnee-/Rührbesen] schlagen 2 (convey rapidly) in Windeseile bringen; **the taxi will ~ you to town in no time** das Taxi bringt dich im Nu in die Stadt 3 (flip) schlagen mit ‹*Schwanz*›

C *v.i.* sausen; schießen (ugs.)

Phrasal verbs

• **~ a'way** *v.t.* 1 (flap away) wegscheuchen 2 (remove suddenly) **~ sth. away [from sb.]** [jmdm.] etw. [plötzlich] wegreißen 3 (convey rapidly) in Windeseile wegbringen; **~ sb. away to the station** jmdn. in Windeseile zum Bahnhof bringen

• **~ 'off** *v.t.* 1 (flap off) ▸ **~ away 1** 2 (remove suddenly) [plötzlich] wegreißen; **~ one's coat off** seinen Mantel von sich werfen; **~ off one's hat** rasch den Hut abnehmen 3 ▸ **~ away 3**

• **~ 'up** ▸ **~ B 1**

whisker /'wɪskə(r)/ *n.* 1 *in pl.* (hair on man's cheek) Backenbart, *der* 2 (Zool.) (of cat, mouse, rat) Schnurrhaar, *das;* (of walrus) Bartborste, *die;* **a walrus's ~s** der Bart eines Walrosses; *see also* **cat's whiskers** 3 (fig. coll.: small distance) **be within a ~ of sth./doing sth.** kurz vor etw. (*Dat.*) stehen/kurz davor stehen, etw. zu tun; **win by a ~:** ganz knapp gewinnen

whiskered /'wɪskəd/ *adj.* backenbärtig; ‹*Tier*› mit Schnurrhaaren

whiskery /'wɪskərɪ/ *adj.* backenbärtig; **be ~:** einen [mächtigen] Backenbart haben

whiskey (Amer., Ir.), **whisky** /'wɪskɪ/ *n.* Whisky, *der;* (Irish or American ~) Whiskey, *der*

whisper /'wɪspə(r)/

A *v.i.* 1 flüstern; **~ to sb.** jmdm. etwas zuflüstern; **~ to me so that no one else will hear** flüster es mir ins Ohr, damit es niemand [anders] hört; **~ to each other** miteinander flüstern 2 (speak secretly) tuscheln; **~ against sb.** über jmdn. tuscheln 3 (literary: rustle) [leise] rauschen; säuseln (geh.); flüstern (poet.)

B *v.t.* 1 flüstern; **~ sth. to sb./in sb.'s ear** jmdm. etw. zuflüstern/ins Ohr flüstern; **~ it to me so that no one else will hear** flüster es mir ins Ohr, damit es niemand [anders] hört 2 (rumour) [hinter vorgehaltener Hand] erzählen; **the story is being ~ed about the village that ...:** im Dorf macht die Geschichte die Runde, dass ...; **it is ~ed that ...:** man munkelt, dass ... (ugs.)

C *n.* 1 (~ed speech) Flüstern, *das;* **in a ~, in ~s** im Flüsterton 2 (~ed remark) **their ~s** ihr Geflüster; *see also* **stage whisper** 3 (rumour) Gerücht, *das;* **there were ~s that ...:** es gab Gerüchte, dass ...; man munkelte, dass ... (ugs.) 4 (literary: rustle) [leises] Rauschen; Säuseln, *das* (geh.); Flüstern, *das* (poet.)

whispering: ~ campaign *n.* Verleumdungskampagne, *die;* **~ gallery** *n.* Flüstergalerie, *die*

whist /wɪst/ *n.* (Cards) Whist, *das; see also* **drive A 11**

whistle /'wɪsl/

A *v.i.* pfeifen; **~ at a girl** hinter einem Mädchen herpfeifen; **the spectators ~d at the referee** die Zuschauer pfiffen den Schiedsrichter aus; **he ~d loudly when he heard how valuable it was** er ließ ein lautes Pfeifen vernehmen, als er hörte, wie wertvoll es war; **~ to sb.** jmdm. pfeifen; **~ for sth.** nach etw. pfeifen; **the policeman ~d for help/reinforcement** der Polizist pfiff, um Hilfe/Verstärkung herbeizurufen; **the referee ~d for half-time** der Schiedsrichter pfiff Halbzeit; **~ in the dark** (fig.) seine Angst verdrängen; **you can ~ for it!** (fig. coll.) da kannst du lange warten!

B *v.t.* 1 pfeifen 2 (summon) her[bei]pfeifen; **he ~d his dog and it came running** er pfiff seinem Hund, und er kam angelaufen

C *n.* 1 (sound) Pfiff, *der;* (whistling) Pfeifen, *das;* **the joyful ~s of the birds** das fröhliche Zwitschern der Vögel *od.* Vogelgezwitscher; **give a [brief] ~:** [kurz] pfeifen; **he gave a ~ of surprise** er ließ ein überraschtes Pfeifen vernehmen 2 (instrument) Pfeife, *die;* **penny** or **tin ~:** Blechflöte, *die;* **the referee blew his ~:** der Schiedsrichter pfiff; **[as] clean/clear as a ~** (fig.) blitzsauber/absolut frei; **get away [as] clean as a ~:** ganz unbehelligt davonkommen; **blow the ~ on sb./sth.** (fig.) jmdn./etw. auffliegen lassen (ugs.) 3 (coll.: throat) **wet one's ~** (coll.) sich (*Dat.*) die Kehle anfeuchten (ugs.)

Phrasal verbs

• **~ 'back** *v.t.* zurückpfeifen

• **~ 'up** *v.t.* [he]ranpfeifen

whistle: ~-blower *n.* (fig.) *jmd., der etw. auffliegen lässt;* **~-stop** *n.* (Amer.) 1 (Railw.) (small town) kleines Nest (ugs.) (*an einer Bahnlinie*); (station) Bedarfshaltepunkt, *der;* 2 (Polit.) *kurzer Auftritt eines Politikers während einer Wahlkampfreise;* (rapid visit) Stippvisite, *die; attrib.* **~-stop tour/campaign** Reise mit vielen Kurzaufenthalten/Wahlkampf[reise] mit vielen kurzen Auftritten *od.* Terminen

whistling: ~ buoy *n.* (Naut.) Heulboje, *die;* **~ 'kettle** *n.* Pfeifkessel, *der*

whit /wɪt/ *n., no pl., no def. art.* (dated) **no ~, not a ~:** kein bisschen; **it matters not a ~:** es macht überhaupt nichts; **not a ~ of sense** nicht ein Funke [von] Verstand

white /waɪt/

A *adj.* 1 weiß; **[as] ~ as snow** schneeweiß; **he prefers his coffee ~** (Brit.) er trinkt seinen Kaffee am liebsten mit Milch 2 (pale) weiß; (through illness) blass; bleich; (through fear or rage) bleich; weiß; **[as] ~ as chalk** or **a sheet** kreidebleich; **go** or **turn ~:** weiß *od.* bleich werden; erbleichen (geh.); **he was ~ with rage** er war weiß *od.* bleich vor Wut; *see also* **bleed B 1** 3 **~r than ~** (fig.: morally pure) engelrein (geh.) 4 (light-skinned) weiß; **~ people** Weiße *Pl.;* **~ oppression** Unterdrückung durch die Weißen

B *n.* 1 (colour) Weiß, *das* 2 (of egg) Eiweiß, *das* 3 (of eye) Weiße, *das;* **the ~s of their eyes** das Weiße in ihren Augen 4 **W~** (person) Weiße, *der/die* 5 (~ clothes) **dressed in ~:** weiß gekleidet; **~s** weißer Dress; (laundry) Weißwäsche, *die* 6 (Printing) Zwischenraum, *der* 7 (butterfly) Weißling, *der* 8 (Snooker) weiße Kugel

white: ~ 'ant *n.* Termite, *die;* **~bait** *n., pl. same: junger Hering/junge Sprotte o. Ä.;* **~beam** *n.* (Bot.) Mehlbeere, *die;* **~board** *n.* 1 (wipeable board) Whiteboard, *das* (fachspr.); Weißwandtafel, *die;* 2 (Computing) Whiteboard, *das;* **~ 'bread** *n.* Weißbrot, *das;* **~ cell** *n.* (Anat., Zool.) weißes Blutkörperchen; **~ 'Christmas** *n.* weiße Weihnachten; **~ 'coffee** *n.* (Brit.) Kaffee mit Milch; **~-collar** *adj.* **~-collar worker** Angestellte, *der/die;* **~-collar union** Angestelltengewerkschaft, *die;* **~-collar 'crime** *n.* 1 *no pl.* Weiße-Kragen-Kriminalität, *die;* Wirtschaftskriminalität, *die;* 2 (criminal act) Weiße-Kragen-Verbrechen, *das;* Wirtschaftsverbrechen, *das;* **~ corpuscle** ▸ **~ cell;** **~ 'currant** *n.* weiße Johannisbeere; **~ 'dwarf** *n.* (Astron.) weißer Zwerg; **~ 'elephant** *n.* nutzloser Besitz; **be a ~ elephant** ‹*Gebäude, Einkaufszentrum usw.:*› reine Geldverschwendung sein; *attrib.* **a ~ elephant stall** *eine Bude, an der Sachen angeboten werden, die deren ehemalige Besitzer gern loswerden wollen;* **~-faced** *adj.* [kreide]bleich; **~ fish** *n.* 1 (light-coloured fish) *[Speise]fisch mit weißlicher od. silbriger Färbung;* Weißfisch, *der;* 2 (lake fish) Weißfisch, *der;* Renke, *die;* **~ 'flag** *n.* weiße Fahne; **~fly** *n., pl. same* or **~flies** Weiße Fliege; Motten[schild]laus, *die;* **W~ 'Friar** *n.* Karmeliter, *der;* **~ 'frost** *n.* Reif, *der;* **~ 'gold** *n.* Weißgold, *das;* **~ goods** *n. pl.* (Commerc.) 1 (fabrics) Weißwaren *Pl.;* 2 (appliances) weiße Ware; **W~hall** *pr. n.* (Brit. Polit.: Government) Whitehall (*das*); **~ heat** *n.* 1 (Phys.) Weißglut, *die;* **to a ~ heat** bis zum Weißglühen; **at [a] ~ heat** in weiß glühendem Zustand; 2 (fig.) Glut, *die;* **work at ~ heat** auf Hochtouren arbeiten; **~ 'hope** *n.* Hoffnungsträger, *der*/Hoffnungsträgerin, *die;* **~ 'horse** *n.* 1 Schimmel, *der;* 2 *in pl.* (on

W

waves) Schaumkronen; **~-'hot** *adj.* **1** (Phys.) weiß glühend; **2** (fig.) glühend; **W~ House** *pr. n.* (Amer. Polit.) **the W~ House** das Weiße Haus; **~ 'knight** *n.* (fig.) Retter in der Not; **~-knuckle ride** *n.* (coll.) Horrortrip, *der* (ugs.); Höllenfahrt, *die* (ugs.); **~ 'lead** /led/ *n.* Bleiweiß, *das;* **~ 'lie** ▸**lie¹ A 1**; **~ 'light** *n.* (Phys.) weißes Licht; **~ 'line** *n.* (in middle of road) Mittellinie, *die;* (at side of road) Randlinie, *die;* **~-lipped** /'waɪtlɪpt/ *adj.* mit kreidebleichen Lippen *nachgestellt;* **~ 'magic** *n.* weiße Magie; **~ man** *n.* (Anthrop.) Weiße, *der;* **the ~ man** (~ people) der weiße Mann; **~ 'meat** *n.* weißes Fleisch [und Geflügel]; **~ 'metal** *n.* Weißmetall, *das;* **W~ 'Monk** *n.* Zisterzienser, *der*

Whitehall

Eine Straße im Zentrum von London, in der sich ein Großteil der Ministerien befindet. Journalisten bezeichnen mit *Whitehall* oft die Regierung und die Verwaltung Großbritanniens.

The White House

Der offizielle (Arbeits-)Sitz des amerikanischen Präsidenten in Washington. Journalisten bezeichnen mit *the White House* häufig den Präsidenten und seine Berater.

whiten /'waɪtn/
A *v.t.* weiß machen; weißen ‹*Wand, Schuhe*›
B *v.i.* **1** (become white) weiß werden **2** (turn pale) [kreide]weiß werden

whitener /'waɪtənə(r)/ *n.* (for shoes) Schuhweiß, *das;* (bleaching agent) Bleichmittel, *das;* (for coffee) Kaffeeweißer, *der*

whiteness /'waɪtnɪs/ *n., no pl.* **1** Weiß, *das* **2** (paleness) Blässe, *die*

white: **~ 'night** *n.* schlaflose Nacht; **~ 'noise** *n.* (Phys.) weißes Rauschen; **~-out** *n.* (Meteorol.) Whiteout, *der;* **W~ 'Paper** *n.* (Brit.) *öffentliches Diskussionspapier über Vorhaben der Regierung;* **W~ 'Russia** *pr. n.* Weißrussland (*das*); **W~ 'Russian** **A** *adj.* weißrussisch; **sb. is W~ Russian** jmd. ist Weißrusse/-russin; **B** *n.* Weißrusse, *der*/-russin, *die;* **~ 'sale** *n.* (Commerc.) ≈ Weiße Woche/Wochen; Weißwarenausverkauf, *der;* **~ 'sauce** *n.* weiße *od.* helle Soße; **W~ 'Sea** *pr. n.* Weiße Meer, *das;* **~ 'slave** *n.* weiße Sklavin; *Opfer des Mädchenhandels; attrib.* **~ slave trade** *or* **traffic** Mädchenhandel, *der;* **~ 'spirit** *n.* (Chem.) Terpentin[öl]ersatz, *der;* **~ 'stick** *n.* Blindenstock, *der;* **~ 'sugar** *n.* weißer Zucker; **~ su'premacist** *n.* weißer Suprematist-/weiße Suprematistin; **a ~ supremacist group** *etc.* eine Gruppe *usw.* weißer Suprematisten; **~ su'premacy** *n.* Überlegenheit der weißen Rasse; **~thorn** *n.* (Bot.) Weißdorn, *der;* **~throat** *n.* (Ornith.) **1** (warbler) Grasmücke, *die;* **2** (Amer.: sparrow) Weißkehlammerfink, *der;* **~ 'tie** *n.* **1** (bow tie) weiße Fliege *od.* Schleife(, *die zum Cutaway getragen wird*); **2** (evening dress) Frack, *der;* **is it dinner jacket or ~ tie?** soll man im Smoking oder im Frack erscheinen?; **~ 'trash** ▸**trash A 4**; **~ van 'man** *n.* (Brit. coll.) [Kleintransporter-]raser, *der;* **~wall 'tyre** *n.* Weißwandreifen, *der;* **~wash** **A** *n.* **1** [weiße] Tünche; (fig.) Schönfärberei, *die;* **the report is a ~wash of the Government** der Bericht versucht, die Regierung reinzuwaschen; **2** (defeat) Zu-null-Niederlage, *die;* **B** *v.t.* **1** [weiß] tünchen; **the report ~washes the Government** (fig.) der Bericht zielt darauf ab, die Regierung reinzuwaschen; **be ~washed** (Finance) [als Gemeinschuldner] entlastet werden; **2** (defeat) zu Null schlagen; **~ 'water** *n.* (foamy) weiß schäumendes Wasser; (shallow) Flachwasser, *das;* **~-water canoeing** Wildwassersport, *der;* **~ 'wedding** *n.* Hochzeit in Weiß; **have a ~ wedding** in Weiß heiraten; **~ 'whale** *n.* (Zool.) Weißwal, *der;* **~ 'wine** *n.* Weißwein, *der;* **~ woman** *n.* (Anthrop.) Weiße, *die;* **~wood** *n.* Weißholz, *das*

Whitey /'waɪtɪ/ *n.* (coll. derog.) weißes Schwein (derb)

whither /'wɪðə(r)/ (arch./rhet.)
A *adv.* wohin; **~ democracy/Ulster?** (fig. rhet.) wohin *od.* (geh.) quo vadis, Demokratie/Ulster?
B *conj.* dorthin *od.* dahin, wohin; (to wherever) wohin auch; **I shall go ~ she goes** ich werde gehen, wo immer sie hingeht

whiting /'waɪtɪŋ/ *n., pl. same* (Zool.) Wittling, *der*

whitish /'waɪtɪʃ/ *adj.* weißlich

whitlow /'wɪtləʊ/ *n.* (Med.) Nagelumlauf, *der*

Whit Monday /wɪt 'mʌndeɪ, wɪt 'mʌndɪ/ *n.* Pfingstmontag, *der*

Whitsun /'wɪtsn/ *n.* Pfingsten, *das od. Pl.;* **at ~:** zu *od.* an Pfingsten; **next/last ~:** nächste/letzte Pfingsten

Whitsunday, Whit Sunday /wɪt'sʌndeɪ, wɪt'sʌndɪ/ *n.* Pfingstsonntag, *der*

Whitsuntide /'wɪtsntaɪd/ *n.* Pfingstzeit, *die*

whittle /'wɪtl/
A *v.t.* schnitzen an (+ *Dat.*); **~ a stick to a point** einen Stock anspitzen
B *v.i.* **~ at sth.** an etw. (*Dat.*) [herum]schnitzen

Phrasal verb
- **~ a'way, ~ 'down** *v.t.* (fig.) **1** (completely) auffressen ‹*Gewinn, Geldmittel usw.*›; **~ away sb.'s rights/power** jmdm. nach und nach alle Rechte/alle Macht nehmen **2** (partly) allmählich reduzieren ‹*Anzahl, Team, Gewinn, Verlust*›; verkürzen ‹*Liste*›

Whit/wɪt/: **~ week** *n.* Pfingstwoche, *die;* **~ week'end** *n.* Pfingstwochenende, *das*

whiz, whizz /wɪz/
A *v.i.,* **-zz-** zischen; **we could hear the arrows/shells whizzing above our heads** wir hörten das Zischen der über uns hinwegfliegenden Pfeile/Granaten
B *n.* **1** Zischen, *das;* **with a ~** zischend **2** (coll.: clever person) Kanone, *die* (ugs.); **a ~ with a computer** ein Computergenie

Phrasal verb
- **~ 'past, whizz 'past** *v.i.* vorbeizischen; ‹*Vogel:*› vorbeischießen

'whiz[z]-kid *n.* (coll.) Senkrechtstarter, *der;* **he is a financial ~:** er macht eine steile Karriere als Finanzmann; **a mathematical ~:** ein mathematisches Wunderkind (ugs. scherzh.)

whizzy /'wɪzɪ/ *adj.* (coll.) pfiffig (ugs.)

who /hʊ, *stressed* huː/ *pron.* **1** *interrog.* wer; (whom) wen; (to whom) wem; **~ are you talking about?** von wem *od.* über wen sprichst du?; **~ did you give it to?** (coll.) wem hast du es gegeben?; **it was John — ~ else?** es war John — wer [denn] sonst?; **it was Mr ~?** es war Herr wie?; **I don't know ~'s ~ in the firm yet** ich kenne die Leute in der Firma noch nicht richtig; **he knows ~'s ~ in the publishing world** er weiß, wer in der Verlagsbranche welche Rolle spielt; **~ am I to object/argue** *etc.***?** wie könnte ich Einwände erheben/etwas dagegen sagen *usw.*?; **~ would have thought it?** (rhet.) wer hätte das gedacht! **2** *rel.* der/die/das; *pl.* die; (coll.: whom) den/die/das; (coll.: to whom) dem/der/denen; **any person/he/those ~ ...:** wer ...; **they ~ ...:** diejenigen, die *od.* welche ...; **everybody ~ ...:** jeder, der ...; **I/you ~ ...:** ich, der ich/du, der du ...; **the man ~ I met last week/~ you were speaking to** der Mann, den ich letzte Woche getroffen habe/mit dem du gesprochen hast **3** (arch.: whoever) wer

WHO *abbr.* = **World Health Organization** WHO, *die*

whoa /wəʊ/ *int.* brr

who'd /hʊd, *stressed* huːd/ **1** = **who had** **2** = **who would**

whodun[n]it /huː'dʌnɪt/ *n.* (coll.) Krimi, *der* (ugs.)

whoe'er /huː'eə(r)/ (poet.), **whoever** /huː'evə(r)/ *pron.* **1** wer [immer]; **whoever comes will be welcome** jeder, der kommt, ist willkommen; **marry/give it to whoever you like** heirate, wen/gib es, wem du willst **2** (no matter who) wer ... auch; **whoever you may be** wer Sie auch sind; **whoever you saw, it was not John** wen du auch gesehen hast, es war nicht John **3** (coll.) = **who ever** ▸**ever 5**

whole /həʊl/
A *adj.* **1** ganz; **give me your ~ attention, please** ich bitte um Ihre ganze Aufmerksamkeit; **that's the ~ point [of the exercise]** das ist der ganze Zweck der Übung (ugs.); **the ~ lot [of them]** [sie] alle; **a ~ lot of people** eine ganze Menge Leute; *see also* **hog A 1** **2** (intact) ganz; **roast sth. ~:** etw. im Ganzen braten **3** (undiminished) ganz; **three ~ hours** drei volle Stunden
B *n.* **1** **the ~:** das Ganze; **the ~ of my money/the village/London** mein ganzes *od.* gesamtes Geld/das ganze Dorf/ganz London; **he spent the ~ of that year/of Easter abroad** er war jenes Jahr/zu Ostern die ganze Zeit im Ausland; **the ~ of Shakespeare** *or* **of Shakespeare's works** Shakespeares gesamte Werke; **until he had completed the ~ of it** bis er es ganz fertig hatte **2** (total of parts) Ganze, *das;* **as a ~:** als Ganzes; **sell sth. as a ~:** etw. im Ganzen verkaufen; **on the ~:** im Großen und Ganzen; **on the ~ I am against it** alles in allem bin ich dagegen

whole: **~ 'cloth** *n.* Tuchbahn, *die;* **[made up] out of ~ cloth** (Amer. fig.) von vorne bis hinten erfunden; **~food** *n.* Vollwertkost, *die;* **~hearted** /həʊl'hɑːtɪd/ *adj.* herzlich ‹*Dank, Dankbarkeit, Glückwünsche*›; tief empfunden ‹*Dankbarkeit, Reue*›; rückhaltlos ‹*Unterstützung, Hingabe, Ergebenheit*›; leidenschaftlich ‹*Anhänger, Verfechter usw.*›; **with ~hearted devotion/dedication** mit äußerster Hingabe; **~heartedly** /həʊl'hɑːtɪdlɪ/ *adv.* von ganzem Herzen ‹*gratulieren, danken, zustimmen*›; rückhaltlos ‹*unterstützen*›; **~ 'holiday** *n.* ganzer freier Tag; **~-length** ▸**full-length**; **~-'life insurance** *n.* Todesfallversicherung, *die;* **~ meal** *n.* Vollkornmehl, *das;* **~meal** *adj.* Vollkorn-; **~ 'milk** *n.* Vollmilch, *die*

wholeness /'həʊlnɪs/ *n., no pl.* Ganzheit, *die;* (completeness) Vollständigkeit, *die*

whole: **~ note** *n.* (Amer. Mus.) ganze Note; **~ 'number** *n.* (Math.) ganze Zahl; **~sale** **A** *adj.* **1** (Commerc.) Großhandels-; **~sale dealer** *or* **merchant** Großhändler, *der*/-händlerin, *die;* **~sale grocer** Lebensmittelgroßhändler, *der*/-großhändlerin, *die;* **the ~sale trade** der Großhandel; **our business is ~sale only** wir sind ein reines Großhandelsgeschäft; **these prices are ~sale** das sind Großhandelspreise; **2** (fig.: on a large scale) massenhaft; Massen-; **in a ~sale way** massenweise; **3** (fig.: indiscriminate) pauschal; **B** *adv.* **1** (Commerc.) en gros ‹[*ein*]*kaufen, verkaufen*›; im Großhandel ‹[*ein*]*kaufen*›; (at wholesale price) zum Einkaufs- *od.* Großhandelspreis; **2** (fig.: on a large scale) massenweise; **3** (fig.: indiscriminately) pauschal; **he punished them ~sale** er bestrafte sie samt und sonders; **C** *n.* (Commerc.) Großhandel, *der;* **D** *v.t.* (Commerc.) en gros *od.* als Großhändler/-händlerin verkaufen

wholesaler /'həʊlseɪlə(r)/ *n.* (Commerc.) Grossist, *der*/Grossistin, *die* (fachspr.); Großhändler, *der*/-händlerin, *die*

wholesome /'həʊlsəm/ *adj.* gesund; bekömmlich ‹*Essen, Getränk*›; erbaulich ‹*Lektüre, Thema, Anblick*›; positiv ‹*Einfluss*›

wholesomely /'həʊlsəmlɪ/ *adv.* **~ cooked food** auf gesunde Art zubereitetes Essen

wholesomeness /'həʊlsəmnɪs/ *n., no pl.* Bekömmlichkeit, *die;* (fig.: of reading, subject, etc.) Erbaulichkeit, *die*

whole: **~-time** ▸**full-time**; **~ tone** *n.* (Mus.) Ganzton, *der;* **~ 'wheat** *n.* Vollweizen, *der*

who'll /hʊl, *stressed* huːl/ = **who will**

wholly /'həʊllɪ/ *adv.* völlig; durch und durch ‹*böse*›; **a ~ bad example** ein in jeder Hinsicht schlechtes Beispiel

'wholly-owned *adj.* (Commerc.) **~ subsidiary** hundertprozentige Tochter

whom /huːm/ *pron.* **1** *interrog.* (formal) wen; *as indirect object* wem; **to ~/of ~ did you speak?** mit wem/von wem haben Sie gesprochen? **2** *rel.* den/die/das; *pl.* die; *as indirect object* dem/der/dem; *pl.* denen; **the children, the mother of ~ ...:** die Kinder, deren Mutter ...; **five children, all of ~ are coming** fünf Kinder, die alle mitkommen; **ten candidates, only the best of ~ ...:** zehn Kandidaten, von denen nur die besten ...

whomever /hu:m'evə(r)/, **whomsoever** /hu:msəʊ'evə(r)/ *pron.* 1 wen [immer]; *as indirect object* wem [immer] 2 (no matter whom) wen … auch; *as indirect object* wem … auch

whoop /wu:p/
A *v.i.* [aufgeregt] schreien; (with joy, excitement) juchzen (ugs.); jauchzen
B *v.t.* **~ it up** (coll.) die Sau rauslassen (salopp); (Amer.: stir up enthusiasm) Stimmung machen
C *n.* [aufgeregter] Schrei; (of joy, excitement) Juchzer, *der* (ugs.); Jauchzer, *der;* **with loud ~s** mit lautem Geschrei; **~ of joy** Freudenschrei, *der*

whoopee
A /wʊ'pi:/ *int.* juhu
B /'wʊpi:/ *n.* **make ~** (coll.) die Sau rauslassen (ugs.)

whooping /'hu:pɪŋ/: **~ cough** *n.* ▸ℹ **p. 1231** (Med.) Keuchhusten, *der;* **~ swan** *n.* (Ornith.) Singschwan, *der*

whoops /wʊps/ *int.* hoppla

whoosh /wʊʃ/
A *v.i.* brausen; ‹*Rakete, Geschoss:*› zischen; **a train ~ed past** ein Zug brauste vorbei
B *n.* Brausen, *das;* (of rocket, projectile) Zischen, *das;* **with a [loud] ~:** [laut] brausend/zischend

whop /wɒp/ *v.t.*, **-pp-** (coll.) hauen (ugs.salopp)

whopper /'wɒpə(r)/ *n.* (coll.) 1 Riese, *der;* **a ~ of a marrow/fish** ein Riesending von einem Kürbis/Fisch (ugs.) 2 (lie) faustdicke Lüge; **tell a ~:** faustdick lügen

whopping /'wɒpɪŋ/ (coll.)
A *adj.* riesig; Riesen- (ugs.); gepfeffert (ugs.) ‹*Rechnung*›; faustdick ‹*Lüge*›
B *adv.* **~ big** *or* **great** ▸**A**

whore /hɔ:(r)/ (derog.)
A *n.* 1 (prostitute) Hure, *die* 2 (loose woman) Flittchen, *das*
B *v.i.* **~ [around]** [herum]huren

'**whorehouse** *n.* (derog.) Hurenhaus, *das* (abwertend)

whorl /wɔ:l/ *n.* 1 (Bot.) Wirtel, *der;* Quirl, *der* 2 (circle in fingerprint) Wirbel, *der* 3 (turn of spiral) Windung, *die*

whortleberry /'wɜ:tlbəri/ ▸**bilberry**

who's /hu:z/ 1 **= who is** 2 **= who has**

whose /hu:z/ *pron.* 1 *interrog.* wessen 2 *rel.* dessen/deren/dessen; *pl.* deren; **the people ~ house this is** die Leute, denen dieses Haus gehört

whosesoever /hu:zsəʊ'evə(r)/ *pron.* (formal) wessen … auch; **~ it is, …:** wem er/sie/es auch gehört, …

whosoe'er /hu:səʊ'eə(r)/ (poet.), **whosoever** /hu:səʊ'evə(r)/ wer auch immer

Who's Who /hu:z 'hu:/ *n.* biografisches Lexikon; Who's who, *das*

who've /hʊv, *stressed* hu:v/ (coll.) **= who have**

why /waɪ/
A *adv.* 1 (for what reason) warum; (for what purpose) wozu; **~ is that?** warum das?; **and this/that is ~ I believe …:** und darum glaube ich …; **~ not buy it, if you like it?** kauf es dir doch, wenn es dir gefällt; **~ do we need another car?** wozu brauchen wir noch ein Auto? 2 (on account of which) **the reason ~ he did it** der Grund, aus dem *od.* warum er es tat; **I can see no reason ~ not** ich wüsste nicht, warum nicht
B *int.* **~, certainly/of course!** aber sicher!; **~, if it isn't Jack!** na, das ist doch Jack!; aber das ist ja Jack!; **What should I do? — W~, pay up** Was soll ich machen? — Na *od.* Nun, zahlen!; **~, yes, I think so** jaja, ich glaube schon
C *n.* **the ~s and wherefores** das Warum und Weshalb

WI *abbr.* 1 **= West Indies** 2 (Brit.) **= Women's Institute**

wick /wɪk/ *n.* Docht, *der;* **get on sb.'s ~** (fig. sl.) jmdm. auf den Keks gehen (salopp)

wicked /'wɪkɪd/
A *adj.* 1 (evil) böse; schlecht ‹*Charakter, Person, Welt*›; niederträchtig ‹*Gedanken, Plan, Verhalten*›; schändlich ‹*Gesetz, Buch*›; **the ~ villain** der Schurke; der Bösewicht (veralt.); **it was ~ of you to torment the poor cat** es war gemein von dir, die arme Katze zu quälen; **torture is ~:** die Folter ist etwas Böses 2 (vicious) boshaft ‹*Zunge*›; übel ‹*Schlag, Wetter, Wind, Frost, Geruch*›; **have a ~ temper** furchtbar jähzornig sein 3 (coll.: scandalous) himmelschreiend; sündhaft (ugs.) ‹*Preis*›; **it's ~ how he's been treated** wie man ihn behandelt hat, das schreit zum Himmel; **it's a ~ shame** es ist eine wahre Schande 4 (mischievous) schalkhaft (geh.); **a ~ little fellow** ein kleiner Schlingel (scherzh.); **there was a ~ gleam in his eye** ihm sah der Schalk aus den Augen; **suddenly a ~ idea came to him** plötzlich fiel ihm etwas ganz Tückisches ein 5 (coll.: wonderful, excellent) toll (ugs.)
B *n. pl.* **the ~:** die Bösen

wickedly /'wɪkɪdlɪ/ *adv.* 1 (evilly) niederträchtig; *as sentence-modifier* niederträchtigerweise; **~ acquired gains** auf niederträchtige Weise erzielte Gewinne 2 (viciously) fürchterlich ‹*kalt, schmerzend*›; **~ accurate** ätzend ‹*Satire, Kritik, Karikatur*› 3 (coll.: scandalously) himmelschreiend; sündhaft (ugs.) ‹*teuer*› 4 (mischievously) schalkhaft; **a ~ playful look** ein verschmitzter Blick

wickedness /'wɪkɪdnɪs/ *n.* 1 *no pl.* ▸**wicked 1**: Bosheit, *die;* Schlechtigkeit, *die;* Niederträchtigkeit, *die;* Schändlichkeit, *die* 2 (evil act) Niederträchtigkeit, *die;* **the greatest ~ that anyone can commit** die schlimmste Bosheit, die ein Mensch begehen kann 3 *no pl.* (viciousness) Boshaftigkeit, *die* 4 *no pl.* (coll.: scandalousness) Schändlichkeit, *die;* **the ~ of this waste** so eine himmelschreiende Verschwendung; **the ~ of the prices** die sündhaft hohen Preise 5 *no pl.* (mischievousness) Schalkhaftigkeit, *die;* **the ~ in her sense of humour** das Schalkhafte an ihrer Art Humor

wicker /'wɪkə(r)/ *n.* Korbgeflecht, *das; attrib.* Korb‹*waren, -möbel, -stuhl*›; geflochten ‹*Korb, Matte*›; **~ fence** Flechtzaun, *der*

'**wickerwork** *n.* 1 (material) Korbgeflecht, *das* 2 (articles) Korbwaren

wicket /'wɪkɪt/ *n.* 1 (Cricket) (stumps) Tor, *das;* Wicket, *das;* (*part of innings*) *Spielabschnitt, der mit dem Ausscheiden eines Schlagmannes endet;* (central area of pitch) Wurfbahn, *die;* **another ~ has fallen** *or* **is down** noch ein Schlagmann ist aus; **at the ~:** [als Schlagmann] auf dem Spielfeld; **keep ~:** als Torwächter spielen; **lose one's ~** ‹*Schlagmann:*› ausscheiden; **they lost four ~s** vier Schlagmänner ihrer Mannschaft sind ausgeschieden; **take a ~:** einen Schlagmann zum Ausscheiden bringen; **third** *etc.* **~:** *Spielabschnitt zwischen zweitem und drittem usw. Schlagmannwechsel;* **win by two ~s** mit acht ausgeschiedenen Schlagmännern gewinnen; *see also* **sticky wicket** 2 (gate) Tor, *das* 3 (Amer.: window-like opening) Fenster, *das* 4 (Amer.: croquet hoop) Tor, *das*

wicket: ~ gate *n.* Tor, *das;* **~keeper** *n.* (Cricket) Torwächter, *der*/-wächterin, *die;* Wicketkeeper, *der*

widdle /'wɪdl/ (coll./child lang.) ▸**pee**

wide /waɪd/
A *adj.* 1 ▸ℹ **p. 1286** (broad) breit; groß ‹*Unterschied, Abstand, Winkel, Loch*›; weit ‹*Kleidung*›; **allow** *or* **leave a ~ margin** (fig.) viel Spielraum lassen; **three feet ~:** drei Fuß breit 2 (extensive) weit; umfassend ‹*Lektüre, Wissen, Kenntnisse*›; weit reichend ‹*Einfluss*›; vielseitig ‹*Interessen*›; groß ‹*Vielfalt, Bekanntheit, Berühmtheit*›; reichhaltig ‹*Auswahl, Sortiment*›; breit ‹*Publizität*›; weit verzweigt ‹*Netz*›; **have ~ appeal** weite Kreise ansprechen; **it has now achieved ~ acceptance** es wird jetzt weithin akzeptiert; **a species of ~ distribution** eine weitverbreitete Art; **the ~ world** die weite Welt; **I'll search the ~ world over** ich werde auf der ganzen weiten Welt suchen 3 (liberal) großzügig 4 (fully open) weit geöffnet 5 (off target) **be ~ of sth.** etw. verfehlen; **be ~ of the mark** (fig.) ‹*Annahme, Bemerkung:*› nicht zutreffen; **you're ~ of the mark** (fig.) du liegst falsch (ugs.); *see also* **berth A 1** 6 (Brit. coll.) **~ boy** gerissener Kerl (ugs.)
B *adv.* 1 (fully) weit; **open ~!** ganz [weit] aufmachen!; **~ awake** hellwach; (fig. coll.) gewitzt; **I'm ~ awake to your tricks** ich durchschaue deine Tricks; *see also* **wide open** 2 (off target) **shoot ~:** danebenschießen; **fall ~ of the target, go ~:** das Ziel verfehlen; **aim ~/~ of sth.** daneben/neben etw. (*Akk.*) zielen 3 (**~ly**) weit; *see also* **far A 4**
C *n.* 1 (Cricket) Weitball, *der* 2 **dead to the ~:** fix und fertig (ugs.)

-wide *in comb.* **city-/county-~:** in der ganzen Stadt/Grafschaft *nachgestellt;* **Europe-~:** europaweit; *see also* **countrywide; worldwide** *etc.*

wide: ~-angle 'lens *n.* (Photog.) Weitwinkelobjektiv, *das;* **~ area 'network** *n.* (Computing) Weitbereichsnetz[werk], *das;* **~-body** (**~-bodied**) *adj.* **~-body aircaft** Großraumflugzeug, *das;* **~ boy** *n.* (Brit. coll.) kleiner Gauner *od.* Ganove; **~-eyed** *adj.* (surprised) mit großen Augen *nachgestellt;* **gaze with ~-eyed innocence** mit großen, unschuldigen [Kinder]augen gucken

widely /'waɪdlɪ/ *adv.* 1 (over a wide area) weit ‹*verbreitet, gestreut*›; locker, in großen Abständen ‹*verteilt*›; **a ~ distributed species** eine weit verbreitete Art; **he has travelled ~ in Europe** er ist in Europa viel gereist; **advertise a product ~:** für ein Produkt in großem Stil werben; **a ~ travelled man** ein weit gereister Mann; **a ~ read man** ein [sehr] belesener Mann 2 (by many people) weithin ‹*bekannt, akzeptiert*›; **a ~ held view** eine weit verbreitete Ansicht; **it is ~ rumoured that …:** allgemein wird gemunkelt (ugs.), dass …; **it is not ~ understood why …:** es wird vielfach nicht verstanden *od.* viele verstehen nicht, warum … 3 (in a wide sense) im weiten Sinne ‹*gebraucht*›; weit ‹*interpretiert*› 4 (greatly) stark, erheblich ‹*sich unterscheiden*›

widen /'waɪdn/
A *v.t.* verbreitern; (fig.) erweitern; vergrößern ‹*Unterschied, Gegensatz*›; **let's ~ our campaign to include young people** wir wollen unsere Kampagne auch auf die jungen Leute ausdehnen; **~ing of the EU** EU-Erweiterung, *die*
B *v.i.* sich verbreitern; breiter werden; (fig.) sich erweitern; ‹*Interessen:*› vielfältiger werden; ‹*Unterschied, Gegensatz:*› größer werden; **the valley ~s into a plain** das Tal erweitert sich zu einer Ebene

Phrasal verb
• **~ 'out** *v.i.* sich verbreitern; breiter werden; **~ out into sth.** sich zu etw. erweitern

wide: ~-open *attrib. adj.*, **~ 'open** *pred. adj.* weit aufstehend *od.* geöffnet ‹*Fenster, Tür*›; weit aufgerissen ‹*Mund, Augen*›; weit ‹*Landschaft, Fläche*›; **the ~-open spaces of North America** die Weite der nordamerikanischen Landschaft; **be ~ open** ‹*Fenster, Tür:*› weit offen stehen; ‹*Mund, Augen:*› weit aufgerissen sein; **be ~ open to attack/criticism/immoral influences** Angriffen/der Kritik/moralisch verderblichen Einflüssen ausgesetzt sein; **be ~ open to exploitation** der Ausbeutung schutzlos preisgegeben sein; **lay** *or* **leave oneself/sb. ~ open to sth.** sich/jmdn. einer Sache (*Dat.*) schutzlos preisgeben; **the contest is still ~ open** der Wettbewerb *od.* der Ausgang des Wettbewerbs ist noch völlig offen; **a ~-open town** (Amer.) eine Stadt, in der jeder macht, was er will; **~-ranging** /'waɪdreɪndʒɪŋ/ *adj.* weit gehend ‹*Maßnahme, Veränderung*›; weit reichend ‹*Auswirkungen*›; ausführlich ‹*Diskussion, Gespräch*›; universal ‹*Geist*›; **~ 'screen** *n.* (Cinemat.) Breitwand, *die;* **~screen television**, **~screen TV** *ns.* Breitwandfernsehen, *das;* **~spread** *adj.* weit verbreitet ‹*Art, Ansicht*›; groß ‹*Nachfrage, Beliebtheit*›; von vielen geteilt ‹*Sympathie*›; **become ~spread** sich [weit] ausbreiten; **there was a ~spread demand for reform** Reformen wurden allgemein *od.* allerseits gefordert

widgeon /'wɪdʒən/ *n.* (Ornith.) Pfeifente, *die*

widget /'wɪdʒɪt/ *n.* 1 (small gadget) Gerät, *das;* (small component) Teil, *das* 2 (Computing) Widget, *das* 3 (in beer can) Widget, *das*

widow /'wɪdəʊ/
A *n.* 1 Witwe, *die;* **be left/made a ~:** zur Witwe werden; **golf ~** (joc.) Golfwitwe, *die; see also* **black widow; grass widow** 2 (Cards) zusätzliches Blatt 3 (Printing) Hurenkind, *das*
B *v.t.* zur Witwe machen ‹*Frau*›; zum Witwer

W

machen ‹Mann›; **be ~ed** zur Witwe/zum Witwer werden (**by** durch)

widowed /'wɪdəʊd/ *adj.* verwitwet

widower /'wɪdəʊə(r)/ *n.* Witwer, *der*

widowhood /'wɪdəʊhʊd/ *n.* Witwenschaft, *die;* **[the state of] ~:** der Witwenstand; **during her ~:** als sie Witwe war

widow's: ~ 'peak *n. in der Stirnmitte spitz zulaufender Haaransatz;* **~ 'pension** *n.* Witwenrente, *die;* **~ 'weeds** (dated) *n. pl.* Trauer- *od.* Witwenkleidung

width /wɪdθ/ *n.* **1** ▸ **p. 1286** (measurement) Breite, *die;* (of garment) Weite, *die;* **what is the ~ of ...?** wie breit/weit ist ...?; **be half a metre in ~:** einen halben Meter breit/weit sein **2** (large scope) großer Umfang; (of definition) Weite, *die;* (of interests) Vielseitigkeit, *die* **3** (piece of material) Bahn, *die*

widthways /'wɪdθweɪz/, **widthwise** /'wɪdθwaɪz/ *adv.* in der Breite; **insert the card ~ into the machine** die Karte quer in den Automaten stecken

wield /wi:ld/ *v.t.* führen (geh.); (fig.) ausüben ‹Macht, Einfluss usw.›; **~ a stick/sword** einen Stock/ein Schwert schwingen

wiener /'wi:nə(r)/ *n.* (Amer.) Würstchen, *das*

wife /waɪf/ *n., pl.* **wives** /waɪvz/ Frau, *die;* **give my regards to your** *or* (coll.) **the ~:** grüßen Sie Ihre Frau *od.* (geh.) Gattin von mir; **make sb. one's ~:** jmdn. zur Frau nehmen; **lawful wedded ~** (Eccl.) rechtmäßig angetraute Frau; **old wives' tale** Ammenmärchen, *das*

wife: ~-battering *n., no pl.* Misshandlung der [Ehe]frau; **~-swapping** *n., no pl.* (coll.) Partnertausch, *der*

wig /wɪg/ *n.* Perücke, *die*

wigging /'wɪgɪŋ/ *n.* Rüffel, *der* (ugs.)

wiggle /'wɪgl/ (coll.)

A *v.t.* hin und her bewegen; **~ one's ears/bottom** mit den Ohren/dem Hintern wackeln (ugs.)

B *v.i.* wackeln; (move) sich schlängeln; **make one's ears ~:** mit den Ohren wackeln; **~ into sth.** sich in etw. (*Akk.*) zwängen; **~ out of sth.** sich aus etw. winden/(fig.) herauswinden

C *n.* Wackeln, *das;* **get a ~ on** (Amer. coll.) sich ranhalten (ugs.)

wiggly /'wɪglɪ/ *adj.* schlangenlinienförmig ‹Naht, Saum›; Schlangenlinien‹muster, -form›; **~ line** Schlangenlinie, *die*

wigwam /'wɪgwæm/ *n.* Wigwam, *der*

wild /waɪld/

A *adj.* **1** (undomesticated) wild lebend ‹Tier›; (uncultivated) wild wachsend ‹Pflanze›; **an animal in its ~ state** ein Tier in freier Wildbahn *od.* in Freiheit; **grow ~:** wild wachsen; **~ beast** wildes Tier **2** (rough) unzivilisiert; (bleak) wild ‹Landschaft, Gegend› **3** (unrestrained) wild; ungezügelt; wild, wüst ‹Bursche, Unordnung, Durcheinander›; wütend ‹Mob›; **he was a little ~:** er führte ein etwas ungestümes Leben; **~ and woolly** (coll.) wüst ‹Aussehen, Kerl›; verrückt ‹Ideen›; **run ~** ‹Pferd, Hund:› frei herumlaufen; ‹Kind:› herumtoben; ‹Pflanzen:› wuchern; (derog.) ‹Hund:› herumstreunen; **let one's imagination run ~:** seiner Fantasie freien Lauf lassen **4** (stormy) stürmisch; tobend ‹Wellen› **5** (excited) rasend ‹Wut, Zorn, Eifersucht, Beifall›; unbändig ‹Freude, Wut, Zorn, Schmerz›; wild ‹Erregung, Zorn, Geschrei›; erregt ‹Diskussion›; panisch ‹Angst›; irr ‹Blick›; **be/become ~ [with sth.]** [vor etw. (*Dat.*)] außer sich (*Dat.*) sein/außer sich (*Akk.*) geraten; **send** *or* **drive sb. ~:** jmdn. rasend vor Erregung machen **6** (coll.: very keen) **be ~ about sb./sth.** wild auf jmdn./etw. sein; **be ~ to do sth.** wild darauf sein, etw. zu tun; **I'm not ~ about it** ich bin nicht wild darauf (ugs.) **7** (coll.: angry) wütend; **be ~ with** *or* **at sb.** eine Wut auf jmdn. haben; **make** *or* **drive sb. ~:** jmdn. in Rage bringen (ugs.); **I was ~ when I heard ...:** ich sah rot (ugs.) *od.* wurde wild (ugs.), als ich hörte, ... **8** (reckless) ungezielt ‹Schuss, Schlag›; unbedacht ‹Verhalten, Versprechen, Gerede›; aus der Luft gegriffen ‹Anschuldigungen, Behauptungen›; abwegig ‹Geschichte›; maßlos ‹Übertreibung›; irrwitzig ‹Plan, Idee, Versuch, Hoffnung›; **he made a ~ guess** er hat aufs Geratewohl *od.* (ugs.) ins Blaue hinein geschätzt; *see also* **dream A 3**

B *n.* **the ~[s]** die Wildnis; **see an animal in the ~:** ein Tier in freier Wildbahn sehen; **in the ~s** (coll.) in der Pampa (ugs.); **[out] in the ~s of Yorkshire** (coll.) im tiefsten Yorkshire (ugs.); **the call of the ~:** der Ruf der Wildnis

C *adv.* wild; **shoot ~** (randomly) wild in die Gegend ballern (ugs.)

wild: ~ 'boar *n.* (Zool.) Wildschwein, *das;* **~ card** *n.* **1** (Cards) wilde Karte; **2** (Tennis) Wildcard (ugs.); **~ 'cat** *n.* (Zool.) Wildkatze, *die;* **~cat** *attrib. adj.* fragwürdig; **~cat strike** wilder Streik; **~cat well** Aufschlussbohrung, *die;* Wildcatbohrung, *die*

wildebeest /'wɪldəbi:st/ *n., pl same or* **wildebeests** Gnu, *das*

wilderness /'wɪldənɪs/ *n.* Wildnis, *die;* (desert) Wüste, *die;* **cry in the ~** (fig.) tauben Ohren predigen; **a voice [crying] in the ~** (fig.) ein Rufer in der Wüste; **be in the ~** (Polit.) alle Bedeutung verloren haben

wild: ~-eyed *adj.* mit irrem Blick *nachgestellt;* **~fire** *n.* (Mil. Hist.) griechisches Feuer; *see also* **spread B 1**; **~fowl** *n., pl. same* Federwild, *das;* (Cookery) Wildgeflügel, *das;* **~ 'goose chase** *n.* (fig.: hopeless quest) aussichtslose Suche; **send sb. on a ~ goose chase** jmdn. einem Phantom nachjagen lassen; **~ 'horse** *n.* Wildpferd, *das;* **~ horses would not drag it from me** (fig.) eher beiße ich mir die Zunge ab[, als dass ich es erzähle]; **~ horses would not make me leave here** keine zehn Pferde kriegen mich von hier weg (ugs.); **~life** *n., no pl., no indef. art.* die Tier- und Pflanzenwelt; die Natur; *attrib.* **~life conservation** Naturschutz, *der;* **~life park/reserve/sanctuary** Naturpark, *der*/-reservat, *das*/-schutzgebiet, *das*

wildly /'waɪldlɪ/ *adv.* **1** (unrestrainedly) wild; **run ~ all over the house** ‹Kinder:› wie wild im ganzen Haus herumtoben **2** (stormily) wild; **the wind blew ~:** der Wind blies heftig **3** (excitedly) rasend ‹eifersüchtig›; unbändig ‹verliebt, sich freuen, sich verlieben›; wild ‹schreien, applaudieren›; erregt ‹diskutieren›; **I'm not ~ interested in it** (iron.) ich interessiere mich nicht übermäßig dafür; **be ~ excited about sth.** über etw. (*Akk.*) ganz aus dem Häuschen sein (ugs.); **he looked ~ about him** er blickte irr um sich **4** (recklessly) aufs Geratewohl; maßlos ‹übertreiben›; wirr ‹daherreden, denken›; **hit out ~:** [wie] wild um sich schlagen; **~ inaccurate** völlig ungenau

'wild man *n.* **1** (Anthrop.) Wilde, *der* **2** (Polit.) Scharfmacher, *der*

wildness /'waɪldnɪs/ *n., no pl.* **1** (bleakness) Wildheit, *die* **2** (lack of restraint) Wildheit, *die;* **I was frightened by the ~ of the mob** der wütende Mob machte mir Angst; **after the ~ of his youth** nach seiner wilden *od.* stürmischen Jugend **3** (storminess) **the ~ of the weather/sea** das stürmische Wetter/die stürmische See; **the ~ of the waves/storm** die Gewalt der Wellen/des Sturms **4** (excitement) **the ~ of her joy** die Unbändigkeit, mit der sie sich freute; **the ~ of her jealousy** ihre rasende Eifersucht; **the ~ of their cheers/applause** die Begeisterung, mit der sie jubelten/applaudierten **5** (of blow, shot) Ungezieltheit, *die;* (of promise, words) Unbedachtheit, *die;* (of scheme, attempt, idea, hope, quest) Irrwitzigkeit, *die* **6** (distractedness) **the ~ of his look/eyes** sein irrer Blick; **there was a dangerous ~ in his eyes** seine Augen hatten etwas gefährlich Irres

wild: ~ 'oat ▸ **oat 2**; **~ 'rice** *n.* (Bot.) Wasserreis, *der;* **~ 'silk** *n.* Wildseide, *die;* **~ 'thyme** ▸ **thyme**; **W~ 'West** *pr. n.* Wilder Westen

wile /waɪl/ *n.* List, *die;* Schlich, *der*

wilful /'wɪlfl/ *adj.* **1** (deliberate) vorsätzlich; bewusst ‹Täuschung› **2** (obstinate) starrsinnig

wilfully /'wɪlfəlɪ/ *adv.* **1** (deliberately) vorsätzlich; bewusst ‹täuschen› **2** (obstinately) starrsinnig

wilfulness /'wɪlflnɪs/ *n., no pl.* **1** (deliberateness) Vorsätzlichkeit, *die* **2** (obstinacy) Starrsinnigkeit, *die;* **out of ~:** aus Starrsinn

wiliness /'waɪlɪnɪs/ *n., no pl.* ▸ **wily**: Gewieftheit, *die;* Raffiniertheit, *die;* **the ~ of a fox** die Schläue eines Fuchses

will[1] /wɪl/

A *v.t., only in pres.* **~**, *neg.* (coll.) **won't** /wəʊnt/, *past* **would** /wʊd/, *neg.* (coll.) **wouldn't** /'wʊdnt/ **1** (be willing to) wollen; **They won't help me. W~/Would you?** Sie wollen mir nicht helfen. Bist du bereit?; **you ~ help her, won't you?** du hilfst ihr doch *od.* du wirst ihr doch helfen, nicht wahr?; **the car won't start** das Auto will nicht anspringen *od.* springt nicht an; **if you ~:** (esp. Amer.) wenn Sie wollen; (in request) bitte; **~/would you pass the salt, please?** gibst du bitte mal das Salz rüber?/ würdest du bitte mal das Salz rübergeben?; **~/would you come in?** kommen Sie doch herein; **now just listen, ~ you!** jetzt hör/hört gefälligst zu!; **~ you be quiet!** willst du/wollt ihr wohl ruhig sein!; **well, if you '~ go rock climbing, ...:** bitte, wenn du unbedingt klettern gehen musst, ... **2** (be accustomed to) pflegen; **the car ~ occasionally break down** das Auto hat ab und zu mal eine Panne; **he ~ sit there hour after hour** er pflegt dort stundenlang zu sitzen; (emphatic) **children '~ make a noise** Kinder machen [eben] Lärm; **..., as young people '~:** ..., wie alle jungen Leute [es tun]; **he '~ insist on doing it** er besteht unbedingt darauf, es zu tun; **it 'would have to rain** natürlich musste es regnen **3** (wish) wollen; **~ you have some more cake?** möchtest *od.* willst du noch etwas Kuchen?; **it shall be as you ~:** ganz wie Sie wünschen (geh.) *od.* wollen; **do as/what you ~:** mach, was du willst; **call it what [ever] you ~:** nenn es, wie du willst; **would to God that ...:** wollte Gott, dass ... **4** (be able to) **the box ~ hold 5 lb. of tea** in die Kiste gehen 5 Pfund Tee; **the theatre ~ seat 800** das Theater hat 800 Sitzplätze

B *v. aux., forms as* **A** **1** *expr. simple future* werden; **this time tomorrow he ~ be in Oxford** morgen um diese Zeit ist er in Oxford; **tomorrow he ~ have been here a month** morgen ist er einen Monat hier; **one more cherry, and I ~ have eaten a pound** noch eine Kirsche und ich habe ein Pfund gegessen; **if today is Monday, tomorrow ~ be Tuesday** wenn heute Montag ist, ist morgen Dienstag **2** *expr. intention* **I promise I won't do it again** ich verspreche, ich machs nicht noch mal; **You won't do that, ~ you? — Oh yes, I ~!** Du machst es doch nicht, oder? — Doch[, ich machs]!; **~ do** (coll.) wird gemacht; mach ich (ugs.) **3** *in conditional clause* **if he tried, he would succeed** wenn er es versuchen würde, würde er es schaffen; **he would like/would have liked to see her** er würde sie gerne sehen/er hätte sie gerne gesehen **4** (request) **~ you please tidy up** würdest du bitte aufräumen?

will[2]

A *n.* **1** (faculty) Wille, *der;* **freedom of the ~:** Willensfreiheit, *die;* **have a ~ of one's own** [s]einen eigenen Willen haben; **an iron ~, a ~ of iron** ein eiserner Wille; **strength of ~:** Willensstärke, *die* **2** (Law: testament) Testament, *das;* **under his father's ~:** aufgrund des Testaments seines Vaters; *see also* **remember 4** **3** (desire) **at ~:** nach Belieben; **to live** Lebenswille, *der;* **you must have the ~ to win** du musst gewinnen wollen; **~ to** *or* **for peace** Friedenswille, *der;* Wille zum Frieden; **he has the power to do it, but lacks the ~:** er könnte es zwar, aber er will es nicht; **against one's/sb.'s ~:** gegen seinen/jmds. Willen; **of one's own [free] ~:** aus freien Stücken; **clash of ~s** ≈ Kollision der Interessen; **do sth. with a ~:** etw. mit großem Eifer *od.* Elan tun; **where there's a ~ there's a way** (prov.) wo ein Wille ist, ist auch ein Weg (Spr.); **Thy ~ be done** (Bibl.) Dein Wille geschehe; *see also* **free will** **4** (disposition) **with the best ~ in the world** bei allem Wohlwollen; *in neg. clause* beim besten Willen; *see also* **good will**; **ill will**

B *v.t.* **1** (intend) wollen; **God has ~ed it so** Gott hat es so gewollt **2** (compel by ~) durch Willenskraft erzwingen; **~ oneself to do sth.**

W

sich zwingen, etw. zu tun; ~ **sb. to do sth.** ‹*Hypnotiseur, Therapeut:*› jmdm. suggerieren, etw. zu tun; ~ **sb. to win** jmds. Sieg mit aller Kraft herbeiwünschen

C *v.i.* wollen; **if God so ~s, God ~ing** so Gott will

-willed /wɪld/ *adj. in comb.* **strong-/weak-~:** willensstark/-schwach; **be iron-~:** einen eisernen Willen haben

willful etc. (*Amer.*) ▸**wilful** *etc.*

William /ˈwɪljəm/ *pr. n.* (Hist., as name of ruler etc.) Wilhelm (*der*)

willies /ˈwɪlɪz/ *n. pl.* (coll.) **sb. gets the ~:** jmdm. wird ganz anders (ugs.); **it gives me the ~:** dabei wird mir ganz anders (ugs.)

willing /ˈwɪlɪŋ/

A *adj.* **1** (ready) willig; **ready and ~:** bereit; **be ~ to do sth.** bereit sein, etw. zu tun; **I'm ~ to believe you're right** ich will gerne glauben, dass du Recht hast; **she'd be more ~ to do it/to help if ...:** sie wäre eher dazu bereit/eher bereit zu helfen, wenn ...; **he was ~ to be converted** er ließ sich bereitwillig bekehren; **if my daughter is ~, then you may marry her** wenn meine Tochter es will, dürfen Sie sie heiraten **2** *attrib.* (readily offered) willig; **she gave ~ assistance/help** sie half bereitwillig; **lend a ~ hand** bereitwillig helfen

B *n.* **show ~:** guten Willen zeigen

willingly /ˈwɪlɪŋlɪ/ *adv.* **1** (with pleasure) gern[e]; **their ~ offered services** ihre bereitwillig angebotenen Dienste **2** (voluntarily) freiwillig; **they did not come ~:** sie kamen nur widerstrebend

willingness /ˈwɪlɪŋnɪs/ *n., no pl.* Bereitschaft, *die;* **eager ~:** Beflissenheit, *die;* **he always shows a ~ to help** er ist immer bereit zu helfen

will-o'-the-wisp /wɪləðəˈwɪsp/ *n.* **1** Irrlicht, *das* **2** (fig.) Schimäre, *die*

willow /ˈwɪləʊ/ *n.* Weide, *die*

willow: ~herb *n.* (Bot.) Weidenröschen, *das;* **~ pattern** *n.* Weidenmuster, *das;* **~ warbler** *n.* (Ornith.) Laubsänger, *der*

willowy /ˈwɪləʊɪ/ *adj.* gertenschlank

ˈ**will power** *n.* Willenskraft, *die;* **her ~ is broken** *or* **has cracked** ihr Wille ist gebrochen

willy /ˈwɪlɪ/ *n.* (coll./child lang.) Pimmel, *der* (salopp, fam.)

willy-nilly /wɪlɪˈnɪlɪ/ *adv.* wohl oder übel ‹*etw. tun müssen*›; **it will happen ~:** es wird so oder so passieren

wilt /wɪlt/

A *v.i.* **1** (Bot.: wither) welk werden; welken **2** (fig.: lose vigour) ‹*Person:*› schlapp werden, (ugs.) abschlaffen; ‹*Interesse, Begeisterung:*› abflauen; ‹*Hoffnung, Energie, Kraft*› dahinschwinden

B *v.t.* (Bot.) welken lassen; **the drought has ~ed the plants** durch die Trockenheit sind die Pflanzen welk geworden

Wilton /ˈwɪltən/ *n.* Wiltonteppich, *der*

wily /ˈwaɪlɪ/ *adj.* listig; gewieft ‹*Person*›; raffiniert ‹*Trick, Argumentation, Plan usw.*›

wimp /wɪmp/ *n.* (coll. derog.) Schlappschwanz, *der* (ugs.)

wimpish /ˈwɪmpɪʃ/ *adj.* (coll. derog.) lahm (ugs. abwertend)

win /wɪn/

A *v.t.*, **-nn-, won** /wʌn/ **1** gewinnen; bekommen ‹*Stipendium, Auftrag, Vertrag, Recht*›; ernten ‹*Beifall, Dank*›; **~ the long jump** im Weitsprung gewinnen; **~ an argument/debate** aus einem Streit/einer Debatte als Sieger hervorgehen; **~ promotion** befördert werden; **~ sb. sth.** jmdm. etw. einbringen; **~ sb. sb.'s friendship** jmdm. jmds. Freundschaft gewinnen; **her sad story won his sympathy** ihre traurige Geschichte fand sein Mitgefühl; **~ a reputation [for oneself]** sich (*Dat.*) einen Ruf erwerben *od.* einen Namen machen; **~ sth. from** *or* **off sb.** jmdm. etw. abnehmen; **you can't ~ them all** (coll.), **you ~ some, you lose some** (coll.) man kann nicht immer Glück haben; *see also* **spur A 1**; **toss C 1** **2** (coll.: steal) organisieren (ugs.) **3** **~ one's way to the top** (fig.) sich an die Spitze hocharbeiten; **~ one's way to a scholarship** sich (*Dat.*) ein Stipendium verdienen; **~ oneself a place in the history books** sich (*Dat.*) einen Platz in den Geschichtsbüchern sichern; **~ one's way into sb.'s heart/affections** jmds. Herz/Zuneigung gewinnen **4** (Mining) gewinnen ‹*Erz*›

B *v.i.*, **-nn-, won** **1** gewinnen; (in battle) siegen; **you ~** (have defeated me) du hast gewonnen (ugs.); **those who ~:** die Gewinner/Sieger; **~ or lose** wie es auch ausgeht/ausgehen würde; **you can't ~** (lit. or fig.) (coll.) da hat man keine Chance (ugs.); (you can't satisfy everyone) man kann es nicht allen recht machen; *see also* **canter A**; **hand A 7**; **head A 1** **2** **~ clear/free** sich befreien

C *n.* Sieg, *der;* **have a ~:** gewinnen

(Phrasal verbs)

- **~ ˈback** *v.t.* zurückgewinnen
- **~ ˈout** *v.i.* **~ out [over sb./sth.]** sich [gegen jmdn./etw.] durchsetzen
- **~ ˈover, ~ ˈround** *v.t.* bekehren; (to one's side) auf seine Seite bringen; (convince) überzeugen; **~ sb. over** *or* **round to a plan/to a faith/to one's point of view** jmdn. für einen Plan gewinnen/zu einem Glauben bekehren/zu seiner Ansicht bekehren *od.* von seiner Ansicht überzeugen
- **~ ˈthrough** *v.i.* Erfolg haben; **~ through to the next round** die nächste Runde erreichen

wince /wɪns/

A *v.i.* zusammenzucken (**at** bei); **she did not ~ when the dentist started drilling** sie verzog keine Miene, als der Zahnarzt anfing zu bohren; **he ~d under the pain/the insult** der Schmerz/die Beleidigung ließ ihn zusammenzucken

B *n.* Zusammenzucken, *das;* **give a ~ [of pain]** [vor Schmerz] zusammenzucken; **without a ~:** ohne eine Miene zu verziehen; ohne mit der Wimper zu zucken

winceyette /wɪnsɪˈet/ *n.* (Brit. Textiles) Flanell, *der*

winch /wɪntʃ/

A *n.* **1** (crank) Kurbel, *die* **2** (Brit. Fishing) Rolle, *die;* Haspel, *die* **3** (windlass) Winde, *die*

B *v.t.* winden; mit einer Winde ziehen; **~ up** hochwinden

wind¹ /wɪnd/

A *n.* **1** Wind, *der;* **before the ~** (Naut.) vor dem Wind; **be in the ~** (fig.) in der Luft liegen; **down the ~:** mit dem Wind; in der Richtung des Windes; **see how** *or* **which way the ~ blows** *or* **lies** (fig.) sehen, woher der Wind weht; **into the ~** (Naut.) in den Wind; **off the ~** (Naut.) aus dem Wind; **like the ~:** wie der Wind ‹*laufen, fahren usw.*›; **sail close to** *or* **near the ~:** hart am Wind segeln; (fig.) sich hart an der Grenze des Erlaubten bewegen; **sail too close to** *or* **near the ~** (fig.) den Bogen überspannen; **take the ~ out of sb.'s sails** (fig.) jmdm. den Wind aus den Segeln nehmen; **throw sb.'s advice to the ~s** jmds. Rat in den Wind schlagen; **throw caution/discretion/one's principles to the ~s** alle Vorsicht/alle Diskretion/seine Grundsätze über Bord werfen; **to the [four] ~s** in alle [vier] Winde; **the ~[s] of change** ein frischer Wind (fig.); *see also* **whirlwind 1** **2** *no pl.* (*Mus.*) (stream of air) (in organ) Wind, *der;* (in other instruments) Luftstrom, *der;* (instruments) **the ~:** die Bläser **3** *no pl.* (blast of air) Luftstrom, *der;* (of missile) Druckwelle, *die* **4** (Hunting) Witterung, *die;* **get ~ of sth.** (fig.) Wind von etw. bekommen **5** *no pl., no indef. art.* (flatulence) Blähungen; **break ~:** eine Blähung abgehen lassen; **get/have the ~ up** (coll.) Manschetten (ugs.) *od.* Schiss (salopp) kriegen/haben; **put the ~ up sb.** (coll.) jmdm. Schiss machen (salopp) **6** (breath) **lose/have lost one's ~:** außer Atem kommen/sein; **recover** *or* **get one's ~:** wieder zu Atem kommen; **you need a lot of ~ to run such a long distance** der Atem darf einem nicht so schnell ausgehen, wenn man so eine lange Strecke laufen will; **get one's second ~** (lit. or fig.) sich wieder steigern; **pause to get one's second ~** (fig.) eine Pause machen, um einen neuen Anlauf zu nehmen **7** *no pl., no art.* (empty words) [leeres] Geschwätz

B *v.t.* **1** (make breathless) außer Atem bringen; **the blow ~ed him** der Schlag nahm ihm den Atem; **he was ~ed by the blow to his stomach** nach dem Schlag in die Magengrube schnappte er nach Luft; *see also* **winded** **2** (burp) ein Bäuerchen machen lassen (fam.) ‹*Baby*›

wind² /waɪnd/

A *v.i.*, **wound** /waʊnd/ **1** (curve) sich winden; (move) sich schlängeln; **the road wound through/among the hills** die Straße wand *od.* schlängelte sich zwischen den Hügeln hindurch **2** (coil) sich wickeln

B *v.t.*, **wound** **1** (coil) wickeln; (on to reel) spulen; **~ wool into a ball** Wolle zu einem Knäuel aufwickeln; **~ sth. off sth./on [to] sth.** etw. von etw. [ab]wickeln/auf etw. (*Akk.*) [auf]wickeln; **~ sb. round one's finger** jmdn. um den Finger wickeln (ugs.) **2** (with key etc.) aufziehen ‹*Uhr, Spielzeug*› **3** **~ one's/its way** sich winden; sich schlängeln; **a road ~ing its way among the mountains** eine Straße, die sich zwischen den Bergen hindurchwindet *od.* -schlängelt **4** (coil into ball) zu einem Knäuel/zu Knäueln aufwickeln **5** (surround) wickeln; (cover with coil) umwickeln; bewickeln ‹*Spule*›; **he wound the injured arm in a piece of cloth** er umwickelte den verletzten Arm mit einem Tuch **6** (winch) winden; **~ sth. with a winch** etw. mit einer Winde ziehen

C *n.* **1** (curve) Windung, *die* **2** (turn) Umdrehung, *die;* **give sth. a ~:** etw. aufziehen; **give the clock one more ~:** die Uhr noch [um] eine Umdrehung weiter aufziehen

(Phrasal verbs)

- **~ ˈback** *v.t. & i.* zurückspulen
- **~ ˈdown**

A *v.t.* **1** (lower) mit einer Winde herunter-/hinunterlassen; herunterdrehen ‹*Autofenster*› **2** (fig.: reduce gradually) einschränken; drosseln ‹*Produktion*›; (and cease) allmählich einstellen; auslaufen lassen ‹*Produktion*›

B *v.i.* (lose momentum) ablaufen; (fig.) ‹*Produktion:*› zurückgehen; (cease) auslaufen

- **~ ˈforward** ▸**~ on**
- **~ ˈin** *v.t.* einrollen ‹*Angelschnur*›; einholen ‹*Fisch, Tau*›; (on to sth.) aufwickeln
- **~ ˈon** *v.t. & i.* weiterspulen
- **~ ˈup**

A *v.t.* **1** (raise) hochwinden; (winch up) [mit einer Winde] hochziehen; hochdrehen ‹*Autofenster*› **2** (coil) aufwickeln **3** (with key etc.) aufziehen ‹*Uhr, Spielzeug*› **4** (make tense) aufregen; erregen; **get wound up** sich aufregen; sich erregen; **she was wound up to a fury** sie kochte vor Wut **5** (coll.: annoy deliberately) auf die Palme bringen (ugs.) **6** (conclude) beschließen ‹*Debatte, Rede*› **7** (Finance, Law) auflösen; einstellen ‹*Aktivitäten*›; **~ up one's affairs** seine Angelegenheiten in Ordnung bringen

B *v.i.* **1** (conclude) schließen; **he wound up for the Government** er sprach als letzter Redner aus dem Regierungslager; **..., he said, ~ing up** ... sagte er abschließend; **~ up with ice cream** mit Eis abschließen **2** (Commerc.) ‹*Firma:*› aufgelöst werden **3** (coll.: end up) **~ up in prison/hospital** [zum Schluss] im Gefängnis/Krankenhaus landen (ugs.); **~ up with a broken leg** sich (*Dat.*) am Ende noch ein gebrochenes Bein einhandeln. *see also* **wind-up**

wind /wɪnd/: **~bag** *n.* (derog.) Schwätzer, *der*/Schwätzerin, *die;* **~ band** *n.* (Mus.) Blaskapelle, *die;* (section of orchestra) Bläsergruppe, *die;* **~-blown** *adj.* vom Wind zerzaust ‹*Haar*›; **~break** *n.* Windschutz, *der;* **~breaker** (Amer.), **~cheater** (Brit.) *ns.* Windjacke, *die;* **~chest** *n.* (Mus.) Windlade, *die;* **~ chill** *n.* (Meteorol.) **~ chill [factor** *or* **index]** Windchill-Index, *der;* **~ chimes** *n. pl.* Windglockenspiel, *das;* **~ cone** ▸**windsock**

winded /ˈwɪndɪd/ *adj.* nach Luft schnappend; **be ~:** außer Atem sein

wind energy /ˈwɪnd enədʒɪ/ *n., no pl.* Windenergie, *die*

winder /ˈwaɪndə(r)/ *n.* (of watch) Krone, *die;* (of clock, toy) Aufziehschraube, *die;* (key) Schlüssel, *der*

W

wind /wɪnd/: **~fall** *n.* 1 Stück Fallobst; (apple) Fallapfel, *der;* **~falls** Fallobst, *das;* 2 (fig.) warmer Regen (ugs.); **repeated ~falls** ein warmer Regen nach dem anderen; *attrib.* **~fall tax** *(einmalige) Sondersteuer auf Privatisierungsgewinne;* **~ farm** *n.* Windpark, *der;* Windfarm, *die;* **~flower** *n.* (Bot.) Windröschen, *das;* **~ force** *n.* (Meteorol.) Windstärke, *die;* **~ gauge** *n.* (Meteorol.) Windmesser, *der;* **~ generator** *n.* Windgenerator, *der;* **~hover** *n.* (Ornith.) Rüttelfalke, *der*

winding /ˈwaɪndɪŋ/
A *attrib. adj.* gewunden; **the ~ procession** der sich dahinschlängelnde Zug
B *n.* 1 *in pl.* (of road, river) Windungen 2 (Electr.) Wicklung, *die*

winding: ~ sheet *n.* Leichentuch, *das;* **~ ˈstaircase** *n.* Wendeltreppe, *die*

wind/wɪnd/: **~ instrument** *n.* (Mus.) Blasinstrument, *das;* **~jammer** /ˈwɪnddʒæmə(r)/ *n.* (Naut.) Windjammer, *der*

windlass /ˈwɪndləs/ *n.* Winde, *die*

windless /ˈwɪndlɪs/ *adj.* windstill

windmill /ˈwɪndmɪl/ *n.* 1 Windmühle, *die;* (to drive generator, water pump, etc.) Windrad, *das;* **tilt at** *or* **fight ~s** (fig.) gegen Windmühlen kämpfen 2 (toy) Windrädchen, *das*

window /ˈwɪndəʊ/ *n.* 1 Fenster, *das;* **break a ~:** eine Fensterscheibe zerbrechen; ‹*Einbrecher:*› eine Fensterscheibe einschlagen; **go out of the ~** (fig. coll.) den Bach runtergehen (ugs.) 2 (fig.) **a ~ on the world** ein Fenster zur Welt; **a ~ on life** ein Spiegel des Lebens; **a ~ of opportunity** ein Zeitfenster 3 (for display of goods) [Schau]fenster, *das* 4 (for issue of tickets etc.) Schalter, *der* 5 (Astronaut.: time when launch is possible) Startfenster, *das* 6 (Computing) Fenster, *das*

window: ~ box *n.* Blumenkasten, *der;* **~ cleaner** *n.* ▸ⓘ **p. 1260** Fensterputzer, *der*/-putzerin, *die;* **~ cleaning** *n.* Fensterputzen, *das;* **~ display** *n.* Schaufensterauslage, *die;* **~ dresser** *n.* ▸ⓘ **p. 1260** Schaufensterdekorateur, *der*/-dekorateurin, *die;* **~ dressing** *n.* Schaufensterdekoration, *die;* (fig.) Schönfärberei, *die;* **~ envelope** *n.* Fenster[brief]umschlag, *der;* **~ frame** *n.* Fensterrahmen, *der;* **~ ledge** *n.* (inside) Fensterbank, *die;* (outside) Fenstersims, *der od. das;* **~ lock** *n.* Fensterschloss, *das;* **~ pane** *n.* Fensterscheibe, *die;* **~ seat** *n.* (in building) Fensterbank, *die;* (in train etc.) Fensterplatz, *der;* **~shopper** *n.* Schaufensterbummler, *der*/-bummlerin, *die;* **~ shopping** *n., no pl.* Schaufensterbummeln, *das;* **go ~ shopping** einen Schaufensterbummel machen; **~ sill** ▸ **~ ledge**

wind /wɪnd/: **~pipe** *n.* (Anat.) Luftröhre, *die;* **~ power** *n.* Windkraft, *die;* **~-powered** *adj.* windbetrieben; mit Windenergie betrieben; **~ proof** *adj.* windabweisend; **~proof jacket** Windjacke, *die;* **~ pump** *n.* Windpumpe, *die;* **~ rose** *n.* (Meteorol.) Windrose, *die;* **~screen**, (Amer.) **~shield** *ns.* (Motor Veh.) Windschutzscheibe, *die;* **~screen** *or* (Amer.) **~shield wiper** Scheibenwischer, *der;* **~screen** *or* (Amer.) **~shield washer** Scheibenwaschanlage, *die;* **~ sleeve, ~sock** *ns.* (Aeronaut.) Windsack, *der;* **~surfer** *n.* Windsurfer, *der;* **~surfing** *n., no pl.* (Sport) Windsurfen, *das;* **~swept** *adj.* windgepeitscht; vom Wind zerzaust ‹*Person, Haare*›; **the ~swept lake** der vom Wind bewegte See; **~ tunnel** *n.* (Aeronaut.) Windkanal, *der;* **~ turbine** *n.* Windturbine, *die*

wind-up /ˈwaɪndʌp/ *n.* 1 (end) [Ab]schluss, *der* 2 (coll.: attempt to annoy) **is this a ~?** willst du mich auf die Palme bringen? (ugs.)

windward /ˈwɪndwəd/
A *adj.* **~ side** Windseite, *die;* Luvseite, *die* (bes. Seemannsspr.); **in a ~ direction** gegen den Wind; luvwärts (Seemannsspr.); **W~ Islands** *pr. n. pl.* Inseln über dem Winde
B *adv.* gegen den Wind
C *n.* Windseite, *die;* Luv, *die* (Seemannsspr.); **sail to ~:** gegen den Wind segeln; **get to ~ of sth.** auf die Windseite einer Sache (*Gen.*) gehen/fahren *usw.*

windy /ˈwɪndɪ/ *adj.* 1 windig ‹*Tag, Ort, Wetter*› 2 (wordy, empty) phrasenhaft; Phrasen dreschend (abwertend) ‹*Person*›; **he is ~ and ineffectual** er drischt nur Phrasen und tut nichts 3 (coll.: frightened) **be/get ~:** Manschetten (ugs.) *od.* (salopp) Schiss haben/kriegen

wine /waɪn/ *n.* 1 Wein, *der;* **~, women, and song** Wein, Weib und Gesang; **put new ~ in old bottles** (fig.) neuen Wein in alte Schläuche füllen; *see also* **spirit A 11** 2 (colour) Weinrot, *das*

wine: ~ and ˈdine *v.t.* in großem Stil *od.* (ugs.) groß bewirten; **be ~d and dined at sb.'s expense** auf jmds. Kosten schlemmen; **~ bar** *n.* Weinstube, *die;* **~ bottle** *n.* Weinflasche, *die;* **~ box** *n.*: **a ~ box** ein Tetrapak(Wz) Wein; **~ cellar** *n.* [Wein]keller, *der;* **~ cooler** *n.* Weinkühler, *der;* **~glass** *n.* Weinglas, *das;* **~grower** *n.* ▸ⓘ **p. 1260** Winzer, *der;* **~growing A** *n., no pl.* Weinbau, *der;* **B** *adj.* **~growing area** Weingegend, *die;* **~ lake** *n.* Weinsee, *der;* **~ list** *n.* Weinkarte, *die;* **~making** *n., no pl.: Herstellung von Wein zu Hause in kleineren Mengen;* **~ merchant** *n.* ▸ⓘ **p. 1260** Weinhändler, *der*/-händlerin, *die;* **~ merchants** (business) Weinhandlung, *die;* **~-ˈred** *adj.* weinrot

winery /ˈwaɪnərɪ/ *n.* Weinkellerei, *die*

wine: ~ taster *n.* ▸ⓘ **p. 1260** Weinverkoster, *der*/-verkosterin, *die;* **~ tasting** /ˈwaɪnteɪstɪŋ/ *n.* Weinprobe, *die;* **~ vault** *n.* Weinkeller, *der;* **~ ˈvinegar** *n.* Weinessig, *der;* **~ waiter** *n.* ▸ⓘ **p. 1260** Weinkellner, *der*

wing /wɪŋ/
A *n.* 1 (Ornith., Archit., Sport) Flügel, *der;* **take ~:** auffliegen; **on the ~:** im Fluge; **spread** *or* **stretch one's ~s** (fig.) sich auf eigene Füße stellen; **take sb. under one's ~:** jmdn. unter seine Fittiche nehmen; **lend sb. ~s/lend ~s to sb.'s feet** jmdn./jmds. Schritte beflügeln; **on a ~ and a prayer** (fig.) mit minimalen Erfolgsaussichten 2 (Aeronaut.) [Trag]flügel, *der;* Tragfläche, *die;* **~s** (badge) Pilotenabzeichen, *das;* Fliegerabzeichen, *das;* **get/have [got] one's ~s** seinen Pilotenschein kriegen/haben 3 *in pl.* (Theatre) Kulissen; **wait in the ~s** (fig.) auf seine Chance warten 4 (Brit. Motor Veh.) Kotflügel, *der* 5 (Air Force) Geschwader, *das*
B *v.t.* 1 (wound) am Flügel treffen, (Jägerspr.) flügeln ‹*Vogel*›; am Arm treffen ‹*Person*› 2 (fig.: speed) beflügeln (geh.) 3 (fly) **~ one's way** fliegen
C *v.i.* fliegen

wing: ~beat *n.* Flügelschlag, *der;* **~ case** *n.* (Zool.) Deckflügel, *der;* **~ chair** *n.* Ohrensessel, *der;* **~ ˈcollar** *n.* Ecken- *od.* Klappenkragen, *der;* **~ commander** *n.* (Brit. Air Force) Geschwaderkommandeur, *der*

wingding /ˈwɪŋdɪŋ/ *n.* (Amer. coll.) 1 (party) Sause, *die* (salopp) 2 (seizure) [simulierter] Krampfanfall; **throw a ~:** einen Krampfanfall simulieren

winged /wɪŋd/ *adj.* 1 (having wings) geflügelt 2 (wounded) flügellahm geschossen; geflügelt (Jägerspr.)

-winged *adj. in comb.* mit … Flügeln *nachgestellt;* **white-/black-/short-/long-~:** weiß-/schwarz-/kurz-/langflügelig

winger /ˈwɪŋə(r)/ *n.* (Sport) Außenstürmer, *der*/-stürmerin, *die;* Flügel, *der*

wing: ~ mirror *n.* (Brit. Motor Veh.) Außenspiegel, *der;* **~ nut** *n.* Flügelmutter, *die;* **~span, ~spread** *ns.* [Flügel]spannweite, *die;* **~ tip** *n.* Flügelspitze, *die*

wink /wɪŋk/
A *v.i.* 1 (blink) blinzeln; (as signal) zwinkern; **~ at sb.** jmdm. zuzwinkern; **be as easy as ~ing** kinderleicht *od.* ein Kinderspiel sein; **do sth. as easy as ~ing** (coll.) etw. mit Leichtigkeit tun 2 (twinkle, flash) blinken 3 **~ at sth.** (fig.: ignore) über etw. (*Akk.*) hinwegsehen
B *v.t.* 1 **~ one's eye/eyes** blinzeln; (as signal) zwinkern; **~ one's eye at sb.** jmdm. zuzwinkern 2 (flash) blinken ‹*Signal, Nachricht usw.*›
C *n.* 1 Blinzeln, *das;* (signal) Zwinkern, *das;* **give sb. a [secret/sly/knowing** *etc.***] ~:** jmdm. [heimlich/verschmitzt/wissend *usw.*] zuzwinkern; *see also* **tip² B 4; in the ~ of an eye** (fig.) in null Komma nichts (ugs.) 2 **not get a ~ of sleep, not sleep a ~:** kein Auge zutun; *see also* **forty A**

winker /ˈwɪŋkə(r)/ *n.* (Motor Veh.) Blinker, *der*

winkle /ˈwɪŋkl/
A *n.* Strandschnecke, *die*
B *v.t.* **~ out** herausholen, (ugs.) rauspfriemeln ‹*Gegenstand, Substanz*›; herausholen ‹*Person, Tier*›; **~ sth. out of sb.** (fig.) etw. aus jmdm. rauskriegen (ugs.)

ˈwinkle-picker *n.* (coll. dated) *spitzer Schuh*

Winnebago ® /wɪnəˈbeɪgəʊ/ *n.* Wohnmobil, *das*

winner /ˈwɪnə(r)/ *n.* 1 Sieger, *der*/Siegerin, *die;* (of competition or prize) Gewinner, *der*/Gewinnerin, *die;* (winning shot) Siegestreffer, *der;* (winning goal) Siegestor, *das;* **who is the ~ in this deal?** wer profitiert bei diesem Geschäft mehr? 2 (successful thing) Erfolg, *der;* (successful play, product) Renner, *der* (ugs.); Hit, *der* (ugs.); **you're on [to] a ~ with this idea/book** (coll.) diese Idee/dieses Buch wird garantiert ein Renner *od.* Hit (ugs.)

winning /ˈwɪnɪŋ/ *adj.* 1 *attrib.* siegreich; **~ team** siegreiche Mannschaft; Siegermannschaft, *die;* **the ~ captain** der Kapitän der Siegermannschaft 2 *attrib.* (bringing victory) den Sieg bringend; **~ number** Gewinnzahl, *die;* **the ~ entry** die preisgekrönte Einsendung 3 (charming) einnehmend; gewinnend ‹*Lächeln*›

winningly /ˈwɪnɪŋlɪ/ *adv.* einnehmend; gewinnend ‹*lächeln*›

ˈwinning post *n.* (Sport) Zielpfosten, *der*

winnings /ˈwɪnɪŋz/ *n. pl.* Gewinn, *der*

winnow /ˈwɪnəʊ/ *v.t.* (Agric.) worfeln; (fig.) scheiden; trennen
Phrasal verb
• **~ ˈout** *v.t.* (Agric.) ausscheiden ‹*Spreu*›

wino /ˈwaɪnəʊ/ *n., pl.* **~s** (coll.) Wermutpenner, *der*/-pennerin, *die* (salopp)

winsome /ˈwɪnsəm/ *adj.* einnehmend; gewinnend ‹*Lächeln*›; **a ~ couple** ein reizendes Paar; **look ~:** reizend aussehen

winter /ˈwɪntə(r)/
A *n.* ▸ⓘ **p. 1515** Winter, *der;* **in [the] ~:** im Winter; **last/next ~:** letzten/nächsten Winter; **the ~ of 1947-8** *or* **of 1947** der Winter 1947-48 *od.* [des Jahres] 1947; **~'s day** Wintertag, *der*
B *attrib. adj.* Winter-
C *v.i.* den Winter verbringen; ‹*Truppe, Tier:*› überwintern

winter: ~ garden *n.* Wintergarten, *der;* **~green** *n.* (Bot.) (Pyrola) Wintergrün, *das;* (Gaultheria) Gaultheria, *die*

winterize (**winterise**) /ˈwɪntəraɪz/ *v.t.* winterfest machen

winter: ~ ˈjasmine *n.* (Bot.) Winterjasmin, *der;* **W~ Oˈlympics** *n.* Winterolympiade, *die;* **~ ˈquarters** *n. pl.* (Mil.) Winterquartier, *das;* Winterlager, *das;* **~ ˈsleep** *n.* Winterschlaf, *der;* **~ ˈsolstice** ▸ **solstice 1; ~ ˈsport** *n.* 1 *usu. in pl.* Wintersport, *der;* 2 (particular sport) Wintersportart, *die;* **~ ˈsports area** *n.* Wintersportsgebiet, *das;* **~ ˈsports resort** *n.* Wintersportsort, *der;* **~time** *n.* Winter[s]zeit, *die;* **in [the] ~time** im Winter; **~-weight** *adj.* (Textiles) Winter-; **the coat is ~-weight** dies ist ein Wintermantel

wintry /ˈwɪntrɪ/ *adj.* 1 winterlich; rau ‹*Klima*›; kalt ‹*Wind*›; **~ shower** Schneegestöber, *das;* **cold and ~:** winterlich kalt 2 (fig.) frostig ‹*Lächeln*›

win-ˈwin situation *n.* Win-win-Situation, *die*

wipe /waɪp/
A *v.t.* 1 abwischen; [auf]wischen ‹*Fußboden*›; (dry) abtrocknen; **~ one's mouth** sich (*Dat.*) den Mund abwischen; **~ one's brow/eyes/nose** sich (*Dat.*) die Stirn wischen/die Tränen abwischen/die Nase abwischen; **~ one's feet/shoes** [sich (*Dat.*)] die Füße/Schuhe abtreten; **~ sb./sth. clean/dry** jmdn./etw. abwischen/

W

abtrocknen; *see also* **floor A 1** [2] (get rid of) [ab]wischen; löschen ‹*Bandaufnahme*›; **~ one's/sb.'s tears/the tears from one's/sb.'s eyes** sich/jmdm. die Tränen abwischen/aus den Augen wischen; **~ sb./sth. off the face of the earth** jmdn./etw. vollständig *od.* restlos austilgen; **~ that smile off your face!** hör auf, so unverschämt zu grinsen!; **I'll soon ~ the smile off your face** dir wird das Grinsen gleich vergehen; *see also* **map A 2**

[B] *n.* [1] Wisch, *der* (ugs.); **give sth. a ~:** etw. abwischen; (dry sth.) etw. abtrocknen; **this glass/your face needs a ~:** dieses Glas/dein Gesicht müsste einmal abgewischt werden [2] (tissue) Reinigungstuch, *das* (*aus Papier*)

(Phrasal verbs)

- **~ a'way** *v.t.* wegwischen; **~ away a tear/one's tears** sich (*Dat.*) eine Träne/die Tränen abwischen
- **~ 'down** *v.t.* abwischen; (dry) abtrocknen
- **~ 'off** *v.t.* [1] (remove) wegwischen; löschen ‹*Bandaufnahme*› [2] (pay off) zurückzahlen ‹*Schulden*›; ablösen ‹*Hypothek*›
- **~ 'out** *v.t.* [1] (clean) auswischen [2] (remove) wegwischen; (erase) auslöschen [3] (cancel) tilgen; zunichte machen ‹*Vorteil, Gewinn usw.*› [4] (destroy, abolish) ausrotten ‹*Rasse, Tierart, Feinde*›; ersticken ‹*Widerstand*›; ausmerzen ‹*Seuche, Korruption, Terrorismus*› [5] (coll.: murder) aus dem Weg räumen
- **~ 'over** *v.t.* wischen über (+ *Akk.*)
- **~ 'up**

[A] *v.t.* [1] aufwischen [2] (dry) abtrocknen

[B] *v.i.* abtrocknen

wiper /ˈwaɪpə(r)/ *n.* [1] (Motor Veh.) Wischer, *der* [2] (Electr.) Kontaktarm, *der*

'wiper blade *n.* (Motor Veh.) Wischerblatt, *das*

wire /ˈwaɪə(r)/

[A] *n.* [1] Draht, *der;* **go down to the ~** (fig.) ‹*Wettkampf, Rennen usw.:*› bis zuletzt offen sein; **this test of nerves will go down to the ~:** dies wird eine Nervenzerreißprobe bis zum Äußersten; **pull ~s** (fig.) **= pull strings** ▸**string A 1** [2] (barrier) Drahtverhau, *der od. das;* (fence) Drahtzaun, *der; see also* **mesh A 2** [3] (Electr., Teleph.) Leitung, *die;* **a piece** *or* **length of ~:** ein Stück [Leitungs]draht; **telephone/telegraph ~:** Telefon-/Telegrafenleitung, *die;* **the ~s were humming** die Drähte summten; **get one's** *or* **the ~s crossed** (fig.) auf der Leitung stehen (ugs.); *see also* **live wire** [4] (coll.: telegram) Telegramm, *das*

[B] *v.t.* [1] (fasten with ~) mit Draht zusammenbinden; (stiffen with ~) mit Draht versteifen; **~ sth. together** etw. mit Draht verbinden [2] (Electr.) **~ sth. to sth.** etw. an etw. (*Akk.*) anschließen; **~ a house** (lay wiring circuits) in einem Haus die Stromleitungen legen; **is the house ~d for a telephone?** hat das Haus einen Telefonanschluss?; **~ a studio for sound** in einem Studio Tonleitungen [ver]legen [3] (esp. Amer. coll.: telegraph) **~ sb.** jmdm. *od.* an jmdn. telegrafieren; **~ money** Geld telegrafisch überweisen

[C] *v.i.* (esp. Amer. coll.) telegrafieren; **she ~d for him to come** sie telegrafierte ihm, er solle kommen

(Phrasal verb)

- **~ 'up** *v.t.* (Electr.) anschließen (**to** an + *Akk.*)

wire: ~ 'brush *n.* Drahtbürste, *die;* **~ cutters** *n. pl.* Drahtschneider, *der;* **~ gauge** *n.* [1] (instrument) Drahtlehre, *die;* [2] (series of sizes) *Standardstärken für Drähte/Bleche;* **~-haired** *adj.* (Zool.) drahthaarig; Drahthaar‹*terrier, -fox*›

wireless /ˈwaɪəlɪs/

[A] *adj.* [1] (without wires) drahtlos [2] (Brit. dated) ▸**radio B 1**

[B] *n.* [1] (Brit. dated) Radio, *das* [2] (telegraphy) Funk, *der;* **by ~:** über Funk (*Akk.*)

wireless: ~ set *n.* (Brit. dated) Radioapparat, *der* (veralt.); **~ te'legraphy** *n.* drahtlose Telegrafie

wire: ~ 'netting ▸**netting 2**; **~ 'rope** *n.* Drahtseil, *das;* **~ strippers** *n. pl.* Abisolierzange, *die;* **~-tapping** *n., no pl.* Anzapfen von Telefonleitungen; **~ 'wheel** *n.* (Motor Veh.) [Draht]speichenrad, *das;* **~ 'wool** *n.* Stahlwolle, *die;* **~worm** *n.* (Zool.) Drahtwurm, *der.*

wiring /ˈwaɪərɪŋ/ *n., no pl., no indef. art.* (Electr.) [elektrische] Leitungen

'wiring diagram *n.* (Electr.) Schaltplan, *der;* Schaltbild, *das*

wiry /ˈwaɪərɪ/ *adj.* drahtig; drahtartig ‹*Stängel*›

wisdom /ˈwɪzdəm/ *n., no pl.* [1] Weisheit, *die;* **worldly ~:** Weltklugheit, *die* [2] (prudence) Klugheit, *die;* **where is the ~ of such a move/in doing that?** was für einen Sinn hat solch ein Schritt/hat es, das zu tun?; **her words are always full of ~:** was sie sagt, ist immer sehr klug; **words of ~:** weise Worte; (advice) weise Ratschläge

'wisdom tooth *n.* Weisheitszahn, *der*

wise[1] /waɪz/ *adj.* [1] weise; vernünftig ‹*Meinung*›; **be ~ after the event** so tun, als hätte man es immer schon gewusst [2] (prudent) klug ‹*Vorgehensweise*›; vernünftig ‹*Lebensweise, Praktik*›; **the ~ thing to do would be to ...:** am klügsten wäre es, ... zu ...; **you'd be ~ to ignore it** du tätest gut daran, es zu ignorieren [3] (informed) **be none the** *or* **no/not much ~r** kein bisschen *od.* nicht/nicht viel klüger als vorher sein; **without anyone's being [any] the ~r** ohne dass es jemand merkt [4] (coll.: aware) **be ~ to sb./sth.** jmdn./etw. kennen; **be ~ to what's going on** wissen, was läuft (ugs.); **she was ~ to the fact that ...:** ihr war klar, dass ...; **get ~ to sb./sb.'s tricks** jmdm. auf die Schliche kommen; **get ~ to sth.** etw. spitzkriegen (ugs.); **get ~ to sb.'s plans** dahinter kommen (ugs.), was jmd. vorhat; **put sb. ~:** jmdm. die Augen öffnen; **put sb. ~ to sth.** jmdn. über etw. (*Akk.*) aufklären; **put sb. ~ to sb.** jmdm., was jmdn. betrifft, die Augen öffnen

(Phrasal verb)

- **~ 'up** (Amer. coll.)

[A] *v.t.* **~ sb. up [to sth.]** jmdn. [über etw.] aufklären; **I'd like to ~ you up to him** ich möchte dir über ihn die Augen öffnen

[B] *v.i.* **~ up to sth.** sich (*Dat.*) über etw. klar werden; **~ up to sb./sb.'s tricks** jmdm. auf die Schliche kommen

wise[2] *n.* (arch.: manner) Weise, *die*

-wise *adv. in comb.* [1] (in the direction of) **length~:** der Länge nach; **clock~:** im Uhrzeigersinn [2] (coll.: as regards) -mäßig; was ... betrifft; **weather~:** wettermäßig; was das Wetter betrifft; **health~:** in puncto Gesundheit; gesundheitlich

wise: ~acre *n.* Klugschwätzer, *der*/-schwätzerin, *die* (ugs. abwertend); **~crack** (coll.) [A] *n.* witzige Bemerkung; **make a ~crack** witzeln (**about** über + *Akk.*); [B] *v.i.* witzeln; **~ guy** *n.* (coll.) Klugscheißer, *der* (salopp abwertend)

wisely /ˈwaɪzlɪ/ *adv.* [1] weise; **live ~:** das Leben eines Weisen führen [2] (prudently) klug; *as sentence-modifier* klugerweise

wise 'man *n.* Weise, *der;* **the Three Wise Men** (Bibl.) die drei Weisen [aus dem Morgenland]

wish /wɪʃ/

[A] *v.t.* [1] ▸❶ **p. 1189** (desire, hope) wünschen; **I ~ I was** *or* **were rich** ich wollte *od.* (geh.) wünschte, ich wäre reich; **I do ~ he would come** wenn er nur kommen würde; **I ~ you would shut up** es wäre mir lieb, wenn du den Mund hieltest; **it is to be ~ed that ...** (formal) es ist zu hoffen *od.* man muss hoffen, dass ...; **'~ you were here'** (on postcard) ≈ „schade, dass du nicht hier bist"; ≈ „das hättest du alles sehen sollen!" [2] *with inf.* (want) wünschen (geh.); **do you really ~ me to go?** ist es wirklich dein Wunsch *od.* möchtest du wirklich, dass ich gehe?; **I ~ to go** ich möchte *od.* will gehen; **I ~ you to stay** ich möchte *od.* will, dass du bleibst; **I ~ it [to be] done** ich wünsche (geh.) *od.* möchte *od.* will, dass es getan wird [3] ▸❶ **p. 1189** (say that one hopes sb. will have sth.) wünschen; **~ sb. luck/success** *etc.* jmdm. Glück/Erfolg *usw.* wünschen; **~ sb. good morning/a happy birthday** jmdm. guten Morgen sagen/zum Geburtstag gratulieren; **~ sb. ill/well** jmdm. [etwas] Schlechtes/alles Gute wünschen; **I ~ him no harm** ich wünsche ihm nichts Schlechtes [4] (coll.: foist) **~ sb./sth. on sb.** (coll.) jmdm. jmdn./etw. aufhalsen (ugs.)

[B] *v.i.* wünschen; **come on, ~!** nun, wünsch dir was!; **~ for sth.** sich (*Dat.*) etw. wünschen; **or is that too much to ~ for?** (iron.) oder ist das [vielleicht] zu viel verlangt?; **what more could one ~ for?** was will man mehr?; **they have everything they could possibly ~ for** sie haben alles, was sie sich (*Dat.*) nur wünschen können; **she ~ed for something to happen** sie wünschte, dass etwas passierte

[C] *n.* [1] ▸❶ **p. 1287** Wunsch, *der;* **her ~ is that ...:** es ist ihr Wunsch *od.* sie wünscht, dass ...; **I have no [great/particular] ~ to go** ich habe keine [große/besondere] Lust zu gehen; **I have no ~ for fame/anything** mir ist an Ruhm (*Dat.*) nicht gelegen/ich habe keine Wünsche; **make a ~:** sich (*Dat.*) etwas wünschen; **the ~ is father to the thought** (prov.) der Wunsch ist der Vater des Gedankens; **your ~ is my command** (joc.) dein Wunsch ist mir Befehl (scherzh.); **send sb. one's best ~es for a speedy recovery** jmdm. die besten Wünsche für eine schnelle Genesung schicken; **she sends you her good/best ~es** sie lässt dich herzlich grüßen; **with best/[all] good ~es, with every good ~:** mit den besten/allen guten Wünschen (**on, for** zu) [2] (thing desired) **get** *or* **have one's ~:** seinen Wunsch erfüllt bekommen; **at last he has [got] his ~:** endlich ist sein Wunsch in Erfüllung gegangen

(Phrasal verb)

- **~ a'way** *v.t.* wegwünschen

'wishbone *n.* (Ornith.) Gabelbein, *das*

wishful /ˈwɪʃfl/ *adj.* sehnsuchtsvoll (geh.) ‹*Blick, Verlangen*›; **~ thinking** Wunschdenken, *das*

'wish-fulfilment *n.* (Psych.) Wunscherfüllung, *die*

'wishing well *n.* Wunschbrunnen, *der*

'wish list *n.* Wunschliste, *die;* Wunschzettel, *der*

wishy-washy /ˈwɪʃɪwɒʃɪ/ *adj.* labberig (ugs.); (fig.) lasch

wisp /wɪsp/ *n.* (of straw) Büschel, *das;* **~ of hair** Haarsträhne, *die;* **~ of cloud/smoke** Wolkenfetzen, *der*/Rauchfahne, *die;* **she is just a ~ of a girl** sie ist nur ein Strich

wispy /ˈwɪspɪ/ *adj.* dünn ‹*Gras, Haar*›; schmächtig ‹*Person, Figur*›; **~ clouds/smoke** Wolkenfetzen/Rauchfähnchen

wistaria /wɪˈsteərɪə/, **wisteria** /wɪˈstɪərɪə/ *n.* (Bot.) Glyzine, *die;* Glyzinie, *die*

wistful /ˈwɪstfl/ *adj.* wehmütig; melancholisch ‹*Person, Typ*›; traurig ‹*Augen*›

wistfully /ˈwɪstfəlɪ/ *adv.* wehmütig

wistfulness /ˈwɪstflnɪs/ *n., no pl.* Wehmütigkeit, *die;* Wehmut, *die* (geh.); (of eyes) Traurigkeit, *die;* **a look/an expression full of ~:** ein wehmutsvoller Blick/Ausdruck (geh.)

wit[1] /wɪt/ *n.* [1] (humour) Witz, *der;* **have a ready ~:** schlagfertig sein [2] (intelligence) Geist, *der;* **battle of ~s** intellektueller Schlagabtausch; **be at one's ~'s** *or* **~s' end** sich (*Dat.*) keinen Rat mehr wissen; **he was at his ~'s** *or* **~s' end to know what to do next** er wusste nicht mehr weiter; **collect** *or* **gather one's ~s** zu sich kommen; **drive sb. out of his/her ~s** jmdn. um den Verstand bringen; **frighten** *or* **scare sb. out of his/her ~s** jmdm. Todesangst einjagen; **be frightened** *or* **scared out of one's ~s** Todesangst haben; **have/keep one's ~s about one** auf Draht sein (ugs.)/nicht den Kopf verlieren; **live by one's ~s** sich irgendwie durchschlagen *od.* durchs Leben schlagen [3] (person) geistreicher Mensch

wit[2] *v.i.* **to ~:** nämlich

witch /wɪtʃ/ *n.* (lit. or fig.) Hexe, *die; see also* **sabbath 3**

witch: ~craft *n., no pl.* Hexerei, *die;* **~ doctor** *n.* Medizinmann, *der;* **~ hazel** ▸**wych hazel**; **~-hunt** *n.* (lit. or fig.) Hexenjagd, *die* (**for** auf + *Akk.*)

witching /ˈwɪtʃɪŋ/ *adj.* **the ~ hour** die Geisterstunde

with /wɪð/ *prep.* [1] mit; **put sth. ~ sth.** etw. zu etw. stellen/legen; **have no pen to write ~:** nichts zum Schreiben haben; **I'll be ~ you in a minute** ich komme gleich; **a frontier ~ a country** eine Grenze zu einem Land; **be ~ it**

W

(coll.) up to date sein; **not be ~ sb.** (coll.: fail to understand) jmdm. nicht folgen können; **I'm not ~ you** (coll.) ich komme nicht mit; **he that is not ~ me is against me** wer nicht mit mir ist, der ist wider mich (bibl.); **be one ~ sb./sth.** mit jmdm./etw. eins sein **2** (in the care or possession of) bei; **I have no money ~ me** ich habe kein Geld dabei *od.* bei mir **3** (owing to) vor (+ *Dat.*); **tremble ~ fear** vor Angst zittern **4** (displaying) mit; **~ courage** mutig; **handle ~ care** vorsichtig behandeln **5** (while having) bei; **sleep ~ the window open** bei offenem Fenster schlafen; **speak ~ one's mouth full** mit vollem Mund sprechen **6** (in regard to) **be patient ~ sb.** mit jmdm. geduldig sein; **have influence ~ sb.** auf jmdn. Einfluss haben; **what do you want ~ me?** was wollen Sie von mir?; **how are things ~ you?** wie geht es dir?; **what can he want ~ it?** was mag er damit vorhaben? **7** (at the same time as, in the same way as) mit; **~ that** damit **8** (employed by) bei **9** (despite) trotz; *see also* **will² A 4**

with'draw
A *v.t., forms as* **draw A**: **1** (pull back, retract) zurückziehen **2** (remove) nehmen (fig.) **(from** aus); abziehen ‹*Truppen*› **(from** aus); **~ sth. from circulation/an account** etw. aus dem Verkehr ziehen/von einem Konto abheben
B *v.i., forms as* **draw A, B** sich zurückziehen

withdrawal /wɪð'drɔːəl/ *n.* **1** Zurücknahme, *die* **2** (removal) (of privilege) Entzug, *der;* (of troops) Abzug, *der;* (of money) Abhebung, *die;* **make a ~ from the bank** Geld von der Bank abheben **3** (from drugs) Entzug, *der;* **~ symptoms** Entzugserscheinungen

with'drawal slip *n.* Auszahlungsschein, *der*

with'drawn *adj.* (unsociable) verschlossen

wither /'wɪðə(r)/
A *v.t.* **1** (shrivel) verdorren lassen; **the plants had been ~ed by the heat** die Pflanzen waren durch die Hitze verdorrt; **age cannot ~ her** (literary) ihre Schönheit welkt nicht mit dem Alter **2** (overwhelm with scorn) mit Verachtung strafen
B *v.i.* [ver]welken

Phrasal verbs
- **~ a'way** *v.i.* (lit. or fig.) dahinwelken (geh.)
- **~ 'up** ▸ **~ B**

withered /'wɪðəd/ *adj.* verwelkt ‹*Gras, Pflanze*›; verkrüppelt ‹*Gliedmaße*›

withering /'wɪðərɪŋ/ *adj.* vernichtend ‹*Blick, Bemerkung*›; sengend ‹*Hitze*›

witheringly /'wɪðərɪŋlɪ/ *adv.* voller Verachtung

withers /'wɪðəz/ *n. pl.* Widerrist, *der*

with'hold *v.t., forms as* **hold² 1** (refuse to grant) verweigern; versagen (geh.) **2** (hold back) verschweigen ‹*Wahrheit*›; **~ sth. from sb.** jmdm. etw. vorenthalten

with'holding tax *n.* (Amer.) Abzug[s]steuer, *die*

within /wɪ'ðɪn/
A *prep.* **1** (on the inside of) innerhalb; **~ myself/yourself** *etc.* in meinem/deinem *usw.* Inneren; **~ doors** drinnen; im Haus; **her heart sank ~ her** (literary) aller Mut verließ sie; *see also* **wheel A 1 2** (not beyond) im Rahmen (+ *Gen.*); **~ the meaning of the Act** *etc.* im Sinne des Gesetzes *usw.*; **stay/be ~ the law** den Boden des Gesetzes nicht verlassen; **~ oneself** ohne sich zu verausgaben; *see also* **bound¹ A 1; means 2; reason A 2 3** (not farther off than) **~ eight miles of sth.** acht Meilen im Umkreis von etw.; **we were ~ eight miles of our destination when ...:** wir waren kaum noch acht Meilen von unserem Ziel entfernt, als ...; *see also* **sight A 6 4** (subject to) innerhalb; **work ~ certain conditions** unter bestimmten Bedingungen arbeiten **5** (in a time no longer than) innerhalb; binnen; **~ an/the hour** innerhalb einer Stunde
B *adv.* **1** (inside) innen **2** (in spirit) im Innern

without /wɪ'ðaʊt/
A *prep.* **1** ohne; **~ doing sth.** ohne etw. zu tun; **can you do it ~ his knowing?** kannst du das machen, ohne dass er davon weiß?; **~ end** ohne Ende **2** (arch.: outside) außerhalb
B *adv.* (arch./literary) **1** (outside) außen **2** (in outward appearance) nach außen hin

with'stand *v.t., forms as* **stand A, B**: standhalten (+ *Dat.*); aushalten ‹*Beanspruchung, hohe Temperaturen*›

witless /'wɪtlɪs/ *adj.* **1** (foolish) töricht **2** (insane) geistesgestört **3** (dull-witted) beschränkt (abwertend)

witness /'wɪtnɪs/
A *n.* **1** Zeuge, *der*/Zeugin, *die* **(of, to** *Gen.*); **be a ~ against oneself** gegen sich selbst zeugen; **as God is my ~** (fig.) Gott ist mein Zeuge! (geh.) **2** ▸ **eyewitness 3** *no pl.* (evidence) Zeugnis, *das* (geh.); **bear ~ to** *or* **of sth.** ‹*Person:*› etw. bezeugen; (fig.) von etw. zeugen **4** *no pl.* (confirmation) **in ~ of sth.** (formal) zum Zeugnis (geh.) einer Sache; **call sb. to ~:** jmdn. zum Zeugen aufrufen **5** *no pl.* (proof) **~ to** *or* **of sth.** Zeugnis für etw. (geh.)
B *v.t.* **1** (see) **~ sth.** Zeuge/Zeugin einer Sache (*Gen.*) sein; **sth. is ~ed by sb.** jmd. ist Zeuge/Zeugin einer Sache (*Gen.*); **~ scenes of brutality** brutale Szenen mitansehen müssen; **they have ~ed many changes** sie haben viele Veränderungen erlebt **2** (attest genuineness of) bestätigen ‹*Unterschrift, Echtheit eines Dokuments*›; *see also* **hand A 12**
C *v.i.* **~ against/to sth.** Zeugnis gegen/für etw. ablegen (geh.); **[as] ~ ...:** wie ... bezeugt

witness: ~ box (Brit.), **~ stand** (Amer.) *ns.* Zeugenstand, *der*

witter /'wɪtə(r)/ *v.i.* (Brit. coll.) **~ [on]** quatschen (ugs. abwertend)

witticism /'wɪtɪsɪzm/ *n.* Witzelei, *die*

wittily /'wɪtɪlɪ/ *adv.* geistreich

wittiness /'wɪtɪnɪs/ *n., no pl.* Witz, *der*

witting /'wɪtɪŋ/ *adj.* bewusst

wittingly /'wɪtɪŋlɪ/ *adv.* wissentlich

witty /'wɪtɪ/ *adj.* **1** witzig **2** (possessing wit) geistreich ‹*Person*›

wives *pl. of* **wife**

wiz /wɪz/ ▸ **whizz B 2**

wizard /'wɪzəd/
A *n.* **1** (sorcerer) Zauberer, *der* **2** (very skilled person) Genie, *das* **(at** in + *Dat.*); **she's a ~ with a computer** sie vollbringt wahre Wunder mit einem Computer
B *adj.* (dated coll.) zauberhaft

wizardry /'wɪzədrɪ/ *n.* **1** (sorcery) Zauberei, *die* **2** (seemingly magical technique) Zauberkunst, *die* (meist Pl.); **footballing ~:** [Fuß]ballartistik, *die*

wizened /'wɪzənd/ *adj.* runz[e]lig

wk. *abbr.* **= week** Wo.

WMD *abbr.* **= weapon of mass destruction** MVW

WML *abbr.* (Computing) Wireless Mark-up Language

WNW /westnɔːθ'west/ *abbr.* ▸ **❶ p. 1013 = west-north-west** WNW

woad /wəʊd/ *n.* Färberwaid, *der*

wobble /'wɒbl/
A *v.i.* **1** (rock) wackeln; ‹*Kompassnadel:*› zittern; **I was wobbling like a jelly** ich zitterte wie Espenlaub **2** (go unsteadily) wackeln (ugs.) **3** (fig.: waver) schwanken **4** (quaver) vibrieren; ‹*Stimme:*› zittern
B *n.* **1** (unequal motion) Flattern, *das* (ugs.); **walk with a ~:** schwankend gehen; **the front wheel has developed a ~:** das Vorderrad eiert (ugs.) **2** (fig: change of direction, vacillation) Schwankung, *die* **3** (quaver) Vibrieren, *das;* (in voice) Zittern, *das*

wobbly /'wɒblɪ/
A *adj.* wack[e]lig; zitt[e]rig ‹*Schrift, Hand, Stimme*›; zitternd ‹*Pudding*›; holp[e]rig ‹*Fahrt*›; eiernd (ugs.) ‹*Rad*›
B *n.* (Brit. coll.) **throw a ~:** ausrasten (ugs.)

Woden /'wəʊdn/ *pr. n.* (Mythol.) Wotan (*der*)

wodge /wɒdʒ/ *n.* (Brit. coll.) **a ~ of press cuttings** ein Packen Zeitungsausschnitte; **a great ~ of cake/butter** ein mächtiges Stück Kuchen/Butter

woe /wəʊ/ *n.* (arch./literary/joc.) **1** (distress) Jammer, *der;* **a scene of ~ greeted her** ein jammervoller Anblick bot sich ihr; **a tale of ~:** eine jammervolle Geschichte; **~ is me!** (arch./joc.) weh[e] mir!; **~ betide you!** wehe dir! **2** *in pl.* (troubles) Jammer, *der;* **pour out one's ~s [to sb.]** [jmdm.] sein Leid klagen

woebegone /'wəʊbɪgɒn/ *adj.* jammervoll

woeful /'wəʊfl/ *adj.* **1** (deplorable) beklagenswert **2** (distressed) jammervoll

woefully /'wəʊfəlɪ/ *adv.* **1** (deplorably) beklagenswert **2** (in a distressed manner) jammervoll

wog /wɒg/ *n.* (sl. derog.) Kanake, *der* (ugs. abwertend)

wok /wɒk/ *n.* (Cookery) Wok, *der*

woke, woken ▸ **wake¹ A, B**

wold /wəʊld/ *n.* (Geog.) Hochebene, *die;* **the Yorkshire W~s** die York Wolds

wolf /wʊlf/
A *n., pl.* **wolves** /wʊlvz/ **1** (Zool.) Wolf, *der;* **cry ~ [too often]** (fig.) [zu oft] Zetermordio schreien (ugs.); **keep the ~ from the door** (fig.) den größten Hunger stillen; **be a ~ in sheep's clothing** (fig.) ein Wolf im Schafspelz sein; **throw sb. to the wolves** (fig.) jmdn. fallen lassen[, dem man helfen könnte] **2** (coll.: sexually aggressive man) Aufreißer, *der* (*salopp*); *see also* **lone wolf**
B *v.t.* **~ [down]** verschlingen

wolf: ~ cub *n.* **1** (Zool.) Wolfsjunge, *das;* **2** (Brit. Hist.: Cub Scout) Wölfling, *der;* **~ hound** *n.* Wolfshund, *der* (volkst.)

wolfish /'wʊlfɪʃ/ *adj.* wölfisch; **a ~ hunger/appetite** ein Wolfshunger (ugs.)

'wolf pack *n.* (Navy, Air Force) in Rudeltaktik operierende Einheit

wolfram /'wʊlfrəm/ *n., no pl.* Wolfram, *das*

wolfsbane /'wʊlfsbeɪn/ *n.* (Bot.) Eisenhut, *der*

'wolf-whistle
A *n.* anerkennender Pfiff
B *v.i.* anerkennend pfeifen

wolverine (wolverene) /'wʊlvəriːn/ *n.* (Zool.) Vielfraß, *der*

wolves *pl. of* **wolf A**

woman /'wʊmən/ *n., pl.* **women** /'wɪmɪn/ **1** Frau, *die;* **women and children first** Frauen und Kinder zuerst; **a ~'s work is never done** eine Frau hat immer etwas zu tun; **that's ~'s work** das ist Frauenarbeit; **women's page** Frauenseite, *die;* **women's [toilet]** Damen[toilette], *die;* **the shop sells women's clothing** in dem Geschäft wird Damenkleidung verkauft; **he wears women's clothing** er trägt Frauenkleider; **the other ~:** die Geliebte; **~ of the streets** Straßenmädchen, *das; see also* **honest 4; house A 1; little A 1; old woman; past B 2; world 1 2** *attrib.* (female) weiblich; **~ friend** Freundin, *die;* **~ doctor** Ärztin, *die;* **a ~ driver** eine Frau am Steuer **3** *no pl.* **[the] ~** (an average ~) die Frau **4** (coll.: char~) Putzfrau, *die* **5** (feminine emotions) **the ~ in her** die Frau in ihr

'woman-hater *n.* Frauenhasser, *der;* Weiberfeind, *der*

womanhood /'wʊmənhʊd/ *n., no pl.* Weiblichkeit, *die;* **reach ~:** zur Frau werden

womanise, womaniser ▸ **womanize, womanizer**

womanish /'wʊmənɪʃ/ *adj.* (derog.) weibisch (abwertend)

womanize /'wʊmənaɪz/ *v.i.* den Frauen nachstellen; **with all his womanizing** mit all seiner Schürzenjägerei (ugs.)

womanizer /'wʊmənaɪzə(r)/ *n.* Schürzenjäger, *der*

woman: ~kind *n., no pl., no indef. art.* das weibliche Geschlecht; **the whole of ~kind** alle Frauen; **~like** *adj.* fraulich

womanliness /'wʊmənlɪnɪs/ *n., no pl.* Fraulichkeit, *die*

womanly /'wʊmənlɪ/ *adj.* fraulich; weiblich

woman's rights ▸ **women's rights**

womb /wuːm/ *n.* **1** (Anat.) Gebärmutter, *die;* **the child in the ~:** das Kind im Mutterleib; **in her ~:** in ihrem Leib (geh.); *see also* **fruit A 4 2** (fig.: place of development) Schoß, *der* (geh. fig.)

wombat /'wɒmbæt/ *n.* (Zool.) Wombat, *der*

women *pl. of* **woman**

Women: w~folk *n. pl.* Frauen *Pl.*; Frauensleute, *Pl.* (veralt.); **w~kind** ▸ **womankind**;

W

w~'s group *n.* Frauengruppe, *die;* Frauenvereinigung, *die;* **~'s 'Institute** *n.* (Brit.) *britischer Frauenverband;* **~'s 'Lib** (coll.) ▸**~'s Liberation**; **~'s Libber** /ˈwɪmɪnz ˈlɪbə(r)/ *n.* (coll.) Emanze, *die* (ugs. abwertend); Frauenrechtlerin, *die;* **~'s Libe'ration** *n.* die Frauenbewegung; **~'s movement** *n.* Frauenbewegung, *die;* **~'s 'prison** *n.* Frauengefängnis, *das;* **~'s 'refuge** *n.* Frauenhaus, *das;* **~'s 'rights** *n. pl.* die Rechte der Frau; **w~'s shelter** *n.* Frauenhaus, *das;* **w~'s studies** *n. pl., usu. constr. as sing.* Frauenforschung, *die*

won ▸**win A, B**

wonder /ˈwʌndə(r)/

A *n.* **1** (extraordinary thing) Wunder, *das;* **do** *or* **work ~s** Wunder tun *od.* wirken; (fig.) Wunder wirken; **~s will never cease** (iron.) Wunder über Wunder!; **small** *or* **what** *or* **[it is] no ~ [that] ...:** [es ist] kein Wunder, dass ...; **the ~ is, ...:** das Erstaunliche ist, ... **2** (marvellously successful person) Wunderkind, *das;* (marvellously successful thing) Wunderding, *das;* **boy/girl ~:** Wunderkind, *das;* **the seven ~s of the world** die Sieben Weltwunder **3** *no pl.* (feeling) Staunen, *das;* **a feeling of ~:** ein Staunen; **be lost in ~:** in Staunen versunken sein; **look at sb. in open-mouthed ~:** jmdn. mit offenem Mund anstaunen; *see also* **nine A**

B *adj.* Wunder-

C *v.i.* sich wundern; staunen (**at** über + *Akk.*); **that's not to be ~ed at** darüber braucht man sich nicht zu wundern; **I shouldn't ~ [if ...]** (coll.) es würde mich nicht wundern[, wenn ...]; **Why do you ask? — Oh, I was just ~ing** Warum fragst du? — Ach, nur so; **I ~** (expr. agreement with another's doubts) das frage ich mich auch; (expr. disagreement with another's assertion) es sollte mich wundern; **I don't think we'll see him again. — I ~:** Den sehen wir nie wieder. — Da wäre ich nicht so sicher

D *v.t.* **1** sich fragen; **I ~ what the time is** wie viel Uhr mag es wohl sein?; **I was ~ing what to do** ich habe mir überlegt, was ich tun soll; **I ~ whether I might open the window** dürfte ich vielleicht das Fenster öffnen?; **she ~ed if ...** (enquired) sie fragte, ob ...; **I ~ if you'd mind if ...?** würde es Ihnen etwas ausmachen, wenn ...? **2** (be surprised to find) **~ [that] ...:** sich wundern, dass ...

wonderful /ˈwʌndəfl/ *adj.* wunderbar; wundervoll

wonderfully /ˈwʌndəfəlɪ/ *adv.* wunderbar; **~ beautiful** wunderschön; **~ charming** einfach bezaubernd

wondering /ˈwʌndərɪŋ/ *adj.*, **wonderingly** /ˈwʌndərɪŋlɪ/ *adv.* staunend

'wonderland *n.* **1** (wonderful place) Paradies, *das* **2** (fairyland) Wunderland, *das*

wonderment /ˈwʌndəmənt/ *n., no pl.* Verwunderung, *die;* **say sth. in ~:** etw. voll Verwunderung sagen; **in ~ at** voll Verwunderung über (+ *Akk.*); **her mouth was open in ~:** ihr stand vor Staunen der Mund offen

'wonder-worker *n.* Wundertäter, *der*/-täterin, *die*

wondrous /ˈwʌndrəs/ *adj.*, **wondrously** /ˈwʌndrəslɪ/ *adv.* (poet.) wundersam (geh.)

wonky /ˈwɒŋkɪ/ *adj.* (Brit. coll.) wack[e]lig; (crooked) schief; **a bit ~ [on one's legs]** etwas wack[e]lig [auf den Beinen] (ugs.)

wont /wəʊnt/

A *pred. adj.* (dated/literary) gewohnt; **as he was ~ to say** wie er zu sagen pflegte

B *n.* (literary/joc.) Gepflogenheit, *die* (geh.); **as was her ~:** wie sie zu tun pflegte

won't /wəʊnt/ (coll.) **= will not;** ▸**will¹**

wonted /ˈwəʊntɪd/ *attrib. adj.* (literary) gewohnt; **with one's ~ courtesy** mit gewohnter Höflichkeit

woo /wuː/ *v.t.* **1** (literary: court) **~ sb.** um jmdn. werben (geh.) **2** (seek to win) umwerben ‹*Kunden, Wähler*›; **~ away** abwerben ‹*Arbeitskräfte*› **3** (coax) umwerben

wood /wʊd/ *n.* **1** *in sing. or pl.* (area with trees) Wald, *der;* **sb. cannot see the ~ for the trees** (fig.) jmd. sieht den Wald vor [lauter] Bäumen nicht (scherzh.); **be out of the ~** (Brit.) *or* (Amer.) **~s** (fig.) über den Berg sein (ugs.) **2** (substance, material) Holz, *das;* **touch ~** (Brit.), **knock [on] ~** (Amer.) unberufen!; **you'd better touch ~ when you say that** wenn du das sagst, klopfst du besser dreimal auf Holz **3** (cask for beer, wine, etc.) **from the ~:** vom Fass; **matured in the ~:** in Holzfässern gereift **4** (Bowls) Kugel, *die* **5** (Golf) Holzschläger, *der;* Holz, *das*

wood: ~ anemone *n.* (Bot.) Buschwindröschen, *das;* Anemone, *die;* **~bind** /ˈwʊdbaɪnd/, **~bine** /ˈwʊdbaɪn/ *n.* (Bot.) **1** (wild honeysuckle) Waldgeißblatt, *das;* **2** (Amer.: Virginia creeper) Jungfernrebe, *die;* **~-burning** *attrib. adj.* holzbefeuert; **~ carving** *n.* (craft, object) Holzschnitzerei, *die;* **~chip** *n.* **1** (chip of wood) Holz[hack]schnitzel, *das;* **2** *no pl.* (esp. Brit.) **~chip [paper]** Raufaser[tapete], *die;* **~chuck** *n.* (Zool.) Waldmurmeltier, *das;* **~cock** *n., pl. same* (Ornith.) Waldschnepfe, *die;* **~craft** *n., no pl.* **1** (knowledge of forest conditions) Kenntnis des Waldes; **2** (skill in ~work) Holzschnitzerei, *die;* **~cut** *n.* (Art) Holzschnitt, *der;* **~cutter** *n.* ▸**❶ p. 1260** **1** Holzfäller, *der;* **2** (Art) Holzschnitzer, *der*

wooded /ˈwʊdɪd/ *adj.* bewaldet

wooden /ˈwʊdn/ *adj.* **1** hölzern ‹*Brücke, Spielzeug*›; Holz‹*haus, -brücke, -bein, -griff, -spielzeug*› **2** (fig.: stiff) hölzern

wooden: ~head *n.* (derog.) Holzkopf, *der* (salopp abwertend); **~headed** *adj.* (derog.) dumm; **~ 'horse** *n.* (fig.) Trojanisches Pferd

woodenly /ˈwʊdnlɪ/ *adv.* ausdruckslos ‹*blicken, starren*›; tonlos ‹*sagen*›

woodenness /ˈwʊdnnɪs/ *n., no pl.* Hölzernheit, *die*

wooden 'spoon ▸**spoon¹ A 1**

wood: ~ hyacinth ▸**hyacinth 1**; **~land** /ˈwʊdlənd/ *n.* Waldland, *das;* Wald, *der; attrib.* Wald-; **~louse** *n.* (Zool.) Kellerassel, *die;* **~man** /ˈwʊdmən/ *n., pl.* **~men** /ˈwʊdmən/ ▸**❶ p. 1260** Waldarbeiter, *der;* **~pecker** *n.* Specht, *der;* **~ pigeon** *n.* Ringeltaube, *die;* **~pile** *n.* Holzstapel, *der;* Holzstoß, *der; see also* **nigger**; **~ pulp** *n.* Holzschliff, *der;* **~ruff** *n.* (Bot.) **[sweet] ~ruff** Waldmeister, *der;* **~ screw** *n.* Holzschraube, *die;* **~shed** *n.* Holzschuppen, *der;* **~ sorrel** *n.* (Bot.) Waldsauerklee, *der*

woodsy /ˈwʊdzɪ/ *adj.* (Amer.) waldig

wood: ~wind *n.* (Mus.) **the ~wind [section]** die Holzbläser; **~wind instrument** Holzblasinstrument, *das;* **~work** *n., no pl.* **1** (making things out of ~) Arbeiten mit Holz; **~work and metalwork** (Sch.) Werkunterricht, *der;* **2** (things made of ~) Holzarbeit[en]; **crawl out of the ~work** (coll.) [aus den Nichts] auftauchen (ugs.); **~worm** *n., no pl., no art.* Holzwurm; **it's got ~worm** da ist der Holzwurm drin (ugs.)

woody /ˈwʊdɪ/ *adj.* **1** (well-wooded) waldreich **2** (consisting of wood) holzig ‹*Pflanze[nteil], Wurzel*›; Holz‹*stamm*› **3** (resembling wood) holzig; *see also* **nightshade**

wooer /ˈwuːə(r)/ *n.* Verehrer, *der* (veralt.)

woof¹ /wuːf/ ▸**weft**

woof² /wʊf/

A *n.* [dumpfes] Bellen; **at the sound of the dog's ~:** als der Hund aufbellte; **give a short ~:** kurz aufbellen; **~ ~! went the dog** wau, wau!, bellte der Hund

B *v.i.* [dumpf] bellen; **~ at sb.** jmdn. anbellen

woofer /ˈwʊfə(r)/ *n.* Bass[lautsprecher], *der*

wool /wʊl/ *n.* **1** Wolle, *die; attrib.* Woll-; **pull the ~ over sb.'s eyes** jmdm. etwas vormachen (ugs.) **2** (garments) Wolle, *die. see also* **cotton wool**; **dye B**; **glass wool**; **steel wool**; **wire wool**

woolen (Amer.) ▸**woollen**

'wool-gathering

A *n., no pl.* Hirngespinste (abwertend)

B *adj.* zerstreut; **she's ~ again** sie träumt schon wieder

woollen /ˈwʊlən/

A *adj.* wollen; **~ goods** Wollwaren *Pl*

B *n.* **1** *in pl.* (garments) Wollsachen *Pl.* **2** (fabric) Wollgewebe, *das;* Wollstoff, *der*

woolliness /ˈwʊlɪnɪs/ *n., no pl.* Verschwommenheit, *die*

woolly /ˈwʊlɪ/

A *adj.* **1** wollig; Woll‹*pullover, -mütze*› **2** (confused) verschwommen **3** (indistinct) unklar; undeutlich ‹*Klang, Geräusch*›. *see also* **wild A 3**

B *n.* (coll.) **1** (Brit.: knitted garment) **[winter] woollies** [Winter]wollsachen *Pl.* (ugs.); **a ~:** ein Wollpullover/eine Wolljacke **2** *in pl.* (Amer.: undergarments) wollene Unterwäsche

'Woolsack *n.* (Brit. Parl.) *großes, mit Wolle gefülltes Sitzkissen des Lord Chancellors im britischen Oberhaus*

woozy /ˈwuːzɪ/ *adj.* (coll.) **1** (dizzy) duselig (ugs.) **2** (slightly drunk) angeduselt (salopp)

wop /wɒp/ *n.* (sl. derog.) Spaghettifresser, *der* (salopp abwertend)

Worcester[shire] sauce /wʊstə(ʃɪə) ˈsɔːs, wʊstə(ʃə) ˈsɔːs/ *n.* Worcestersoße, *die*

word /wɜːd/

A *n.* **1** Wort, *das;* **have no ~s for sth.** für etw. keine Worte finden; **be beyond ~s** sich mit Worten nicht ausdrücken lassen; **~s cannot describe it** mit Worten lässt sich das nicht beschreiben; **in a** *or* **one ~** (fig.) mit einem Wort; **[not] in so many ~s** [nicht] ausdrücklich; **in other ~s** mit anderen Worten; **not a ~ of sth.** kein Wort von etw.; **bad luck/drunk is not the ~ for it** Pech/betrunken ist gar kein Ausdruck dafür (ugs.); **that's not the ~ I would have used** das ist gar kein Ausdruck (ugs.); **put sth. into ~s** etw. in Worte fassen; **'rude' would be a better ~ for it** „unverschämt" wäre ein treffenderes Wort dafür ; **~ for ~:** Wort für Wort; **without a** *or* **one/another ~:** ohne ein/ein weiteres Wort; **too funny** *etc.* **for ~s** unsagbar komisch *usw.*; **the written ~:** das geschriebene Wort; *see also* **fail B 5**; **play A 2, B 1**

2 (thing said) Wort, *das;* **hard ~s** harte Worte; **exchange** *or* **have ~s** einen Wortwechsel haben; **a man of few ~s** ein Mann von wenig Worten; **have a ~ [with sb.] about sth.** [mit jmdm.] über etw. (*Akk.*) sprechen; **could I have a ~ [with you]?** kann ich dich mal sprechen?; **have ~s with sb.** sich mit jmdm. streiten; **say a few ~s** ein paar Worte sprechen; **suit the action to the ~:** seinen Worten Taten folgen lassen; **it's his ~ against mine** sein Wort steht gegen meins; **take sb. at his/her ~:** jmdn. beim Wort nehmen; **~ of command/advice** Kommando, *das*/Rat, *der;* **don't say** *or* **breathe a ~ to anyone** sag niemandem auch nur ein Sterbenswort; **at a ~ of command** auf Befehl; **the W~ [of God]** (Bible) das Wort [Gottes]; **in the ~s of Shakespeare ...:** mit Shakespeares Worten: ...; **put in a good ~ for sb. [with sb.]** [bei jmdm.] ein [gutes] Wort für jmdn. einlegen; **never have a good ~ to say about anybody** nie etwas Gutes über andere zu sagen haben; **never say a bad ~ about anybody** nie etwas Schlechtes über andere sagen; **[it's] all ~s** [das sind] nichts als leere Worte

3 (promise) Wort, *das;* **doubt sb.'s ~:** jmds. Wort in Zweifel ziehen; **give [sb.] one's ~:** jmdm. sein Wort geben; **keep/break one's ~:** sein Wort halten/brechen; **I give you my ~ for it** ich gebe Ihnen mein Wort darauf; **upon my ~** (dated) auf mein Wort; **upon my ~!** (dated) meiner Treu! (veralt.); **my ~!** meine Güte!; **my** *etc.* **~ of honour** mein *usw.* Ehrenwort; **a man of his ~:** ein Mann von Wort; **be as good as/better than one's ~:** sein Wort halten/mehr als halten; **sb.'s ~ is [as good as] his/her bond** man kann auf jmds. Wort (*Akk.*) bauen; *see also* **take A 22**

4 *no pl.* (speaking) Wort, *das;* **by ~ of mouth** durch mündliche Mitteilung

5 *in pl.* (text of song, spoken by actor) Text, *der*

6 *no pl., no indef. art.* (news) Nachricht, *die;* **~ had just reached them** die Nachricht hatte sie gerade erreicht; **~ has it** *or* **the ~ is [that] ...:** es geht das Gerücht, dass ...; **~ went round that ...:** es ging das Gerücht, dass ...; **send/leave ~ that ...:** Nachricht geben/eine Nachricht hinterlassen, dass ...; **is there any ~ from her?** hat sie schon von sich hören lassen?

7 (command) Kommando, *das;* **just say the ~:**

sag nur ein Wort; **at the ~ 'run', you run!** bei dem Wort „rennen" rennst du!
8 (pass~) Parole, *die* (Milit.); **give the ~:** die Parole sagen; *see also* **sharp A 6**
9 (Computing) Wort, *das*
B *v.t.* formulieren

wordage /ˈwɜːdɪdʒ/ *n.* Anzahl der Wörter

word: ~ association *n.* assoziative Verknüpfung von Wörtern; **~-blind** *adj.* (Med.) wortblind; **~ break** *n.* Trennung, *die;* **~-deaf** *adj.* worttaub (Med.); **~ division** *n.* Worttrennung, *die;* (in German) Silbentrennung, *die;* **~ formation** *n.* (Ling.) Wortbildung, *die;* **~ game** *n.* Buchstabenspiel, *das*

wordiness /ˈwɜːdɪnɪs/ *n., no pl.* Weitschweifigkeit, *die*

wording /ˈwɜːdɪŋ/ *n.* Formulierung, *die;* Wortwahl, *die;* **the exact ~ of the contract** der genaue Wortlaut des Vertrages

wordless /ˈwɜːdlɪs/ *adj.* **1** (not expressed in words) wortlos; stumm ‹*Schmerz, Trauer*› **2** (not accompanied by words) ohne Worte *nachgestellt*

word: ~ list *n.* Wortliste, *die;* **~-of-ˈmouth** *adj.* Mund-zu-Mund-‹*Propaganda, Werbung, Reklame*›; Mund‹*propaganda*›; **~ order** *n.* (Ling.) Wortstellung, *die;* **~-ˈperfect** *adj.* **be ~-perfect** seinen Text beherrschen; ‹*Rede:*› perfekt vorgetragen sein; **~ picture** *n.* anschauliche Schilderung; Wortgemälde, *das;* **~play** *n., no pl., no indef. art.* Wortspiel, *das;* **~ processing** *n., no pl.* Textverarbeitung, *die;* **~ processor** *n.* Textverarbeitungssystem, *das;* **~ recognition** *n., no pl.* (Educ.) Worterkennung, *die;* **~search** *n.* Wortsuchrätsel, *das;* Wörtersuchrätsel, *das;* **~ wrap** *n., no pl.* (Computing) automatischer Zeilenumbruch

wordy /ˈwɜːdɪ/ *adj.* weitschweifig

wore ▸ **wear B, C**

work /wɜːk/
A *n.* **1** *no pl., no indef. art.* Arbeit, *die;* **at ~** (engaged in working) bei der Arbeit; (fig.: operating) am Werk (*see also* **5**); **be at ~ on sth.** an etw. (*Dat.*) arbeiten; (fig.) auf etw. (*Akk.*) wirken; **set to ~** ‹*Person:*› sich an die Arbeit machen; **set sb. to ~:** jmdn. an die Arbeit schicken; **get to ~ on sb./sth.** jmdn. bearbeiten (ugs.)/mit [der Arbeit an] etw. (*Dat.*) anfangen; **all ~ and no play** immer nur arbeiten; **have one's ~ cut out** viel zu tun haben; sich ranhalten müssen (ugs.); **the ~ of a moment** *etc.* das Werk eines Augenblicks *usw.;* **that's too much like hard ~:** das könnte ja in Arbeit ausarten; **make light ~ of sth.** mit etw. leicht fertig werden; *see also* **day 1**; **short A 1**; **thirsty 2**
2 (thing made or achieved) Werk, *das;* **a good day's ~:** eine gute Tagesleistung; **do a good day's ~:** ein tüchtiges Stück Arbeit hinter sich bringen; **is that all your own ~?** hast du das alles selbst gemacht?; **~ of art** Kunstwerk, *das; see also* **good A 7**
3 (book, piece of music) Werk, *das;* **a ~ of reference/literature/art** ein Nachschlagewerk/literarisches Werk/Kunstwerk
4 *in pl.* (all compositions of author or composer) Werke; **the complete ~s of Brecht** das Gesamtwerk Brechts; Brechts Gesamtwerk
5 (employment) Arbeit, *die;* **out of ~:** arbeitslos; ohne Arbeit; **be in ~:** eine Stelle haben; **go out to ~:** arbeiten gehen; **put people out of ~:** Leute um ihren Arbeitsplatz bringen; **at ~** (place of employment) auf der Arbeit; **from ~:** von der Arbeit; **the conditions at ~:** die Arbeitsbedingungen
6 *in pl., usu. constr. as sing.* (factory) Werk, *das*
7 *in pl.* (Mil.) Werke; Befestigungen
8 *in pl.* (operations of building etc.) Arbeiten; *see also* **clerk 3**; **public works**
9 *in pl.* (machine's operative parts) Werk, *das*
10 *in pl.* (coll.: all that can be included) **the [whole/full] ~s** der ganze Kram (ugs.); **give sb. the ~s** (fig.) (give sb. the best possible treatment) jmdn. richtig verwöhnen (ugs.); (tell sb. everything) jmdm. alles erzählen; (give sb. the worst possible treatment) jmdn. fertig machen (salopp)
11 *no pl.* (ornamentation) Verzierung, *die;* (ornamented or ornamental article[s]) Arbeit, *die*
12 *no pl., no indef. art.* (knitting, needle~) Handarbeit, *die*
13 (Phys.) Arbeit, *die. see also* **nasty A 1**; **piece A 4**
B *v.i.* **1** arbeiten; **be ~ing all morning over a hot oven** den ganzen Morgen am Herd stehen (ugs.); **~ with sb.** mit jmdm. zusammenarbeiten; **~ to rule** Dienst nach Vorschrift machen; **~ for a cause** *etc.* für eine Sache *usw.* arbeiten; **~ against sth.** (impede) einer Sache (*Dat.*) entgegenstehen; *see also* **work-to-rule**
2 (function effectively, have intended effect) funktionieren; ‹*Charme:*› wirken (**on** auf + *Akk.*); **make the washing machine/television ~:** die Waschmaschine/den Fernsehapparat in Ordnung bringen; **make a relationship/an arrangement ~:** dafür sorgen, dass eine Beziehung klappt (ugs.)/eine Regelung funktioniert; **it doesn't ~ like that** (fig.) so geht das nicht
3 ‹*Rad, Getriebe, Kette:*› laufen
4 (be craftsman) **~ in a material** mit *od.* (fachspr.) in einem Material arbeiten
5 ‹*Faktoren, Einflüsse:*› wirken (**on** auf + *Akk.*); **~ to do sth.** darauf hinwirken, etw. zu tun; **~ against** arbeiten gegen; *see also* **work on**
6 (make its/one's way) sich schieben; **~ loose** sich lockern; **~ round** ‹*Kleidung:*› herumrutschen; ‹*Wind:*› sich drehen; **be ~ing upstream** ‹*Angler:*› sich stromaufwärts arbeiten; **~ round to a question** (fig.) sich zu einer Frage vorarbeiten; **start at the end and ~ back** fang hinten an und arbeite dich nach vorne
7 (Naut.: sail) sich arbeiten
8 (ferment, lit. or fig.) arbeiten
C *v.t.* **1** (operate) bedienen ‹*Maschine*›; fahren ‹*Schiff*›; betätigen ‹*Bremse*›; **a pump that is ~ed by hand/by a wind wheel** eine Pumpe, die von Hand betätigt/von einem Windrad angetrieben wird; **~ed by electricity** elektrisch betrieben; *see also* **oracle 4**
2 (get labour from) arbeiten lassen; **~ horses/oxen to death** Pferde/Ochsen zu Tode schinden; **he ~s his employees hard** er nimmt seine Angestellten hart heran; *see also* **bone A 1**; **death 1**
3 (get material from) ausbeuten ‹*Steinbruch, Grube*›
4 (operate in or on) ‹*Vertreter:*› bereisen; **beggars ~ing the main street** Bettler, die auf der Hauptstraße arbeiten/arbeiteten
5 **~ed** *or* (arch./literary) **wrought** (bring about) mit sich bringen; bewirken ‹*Änderung*›; wirken ‹*Wunder*›; **~ one's mischief** Unheil anrichten; **~ one's will [upon sb./sth.]** Einfluss [auf jmdn./etw.] ausüben
6 (arrange, manage) **I'll ~ it if I can** (coll.) ich werde das schon irgendwie deichseln (ugs.); **~ it** *or* **things so that ...** (coll.) es deichseln, dass ... (ugs.)
7 (cause to go gradually) führen; **~ a key/rod into sth.** einen Schlüssel/eine Stange [vorsichtig] in etw. (*Akk.*) einführen; **~ one's way up/into sth.** sich hocharbeiten/in etw. (*Akk.*) hineinarbeiten
8 (get gradually) bringen; **~ oneself out of sth./into a position** sich von etw. befreien/sich in eine Position hocharbeiten
9 (knead, stir) **~ sth. into sth.** etw. zu etw. verarbeiten; (mix in) etw. unter etw. (*Akk.*) rühren
10 (gradually excite) **~ oneself into a state/a rage** sich aufregen/in einen Wutanfall hineinsteigern; **~ sb. into a state** jmdn. aufregen
11 (make by needle~ etc.) arbeiten; aufsticken ‹*Muster*› (**on** auf + *Akk.*)
12 (purchase, obtain with labour) abarbeiten; (fig.) **~ one's keep** für sein Geld etwas leisten; **she ~ed her way through college** sie hat sich (*Dat.*) ihr Studium selbst verdient; **he ~ed his way up from office boy to company chairman** er hat sich vom Bürogehilfen zum Generaldirektor hochgearbeitet; *see also* **passage 6**
13 (Math.) lösen ‹*Rechenaufgabe, Problem*›

Phrasal verbs

- **~ aˈway** *v.i.* **~ away [at sth.]** [an etw. (*Dat.*)] arbeiten
- **~ ˈin** *v.t.* (include) hineinbringen; (mix in) hineinrühren; (rub in) einreiben; *see also* **work-in**
- **~ ˈoff** *v.t.* **1** (get rid of) loswerden; abreagieren ‹*Wut*›; **~ sth. off on sb./sth.** etw. an jmdm./etw. auslassen; **~ off some excess energy** überschüssige Energie loswerden **2** (pay off) abtragen ‹*Schuld*›
- **~ on**
A /ˈ--/ *v.t.* **1** (expend effort on) **~ on sth.** an etw. (*Dat.*) arbeiten **2** (use as basis) **~ on sth.** von etw. ausgehen **3** (try to persuade) **~ on sb.** jmdn. bearbeiten (ugs.)
B /-ˈ-/ *v.i.* weiterarbeiten
- **~ ˈout**
A *v.t.* **1** (find by calculation) ausrechnen **2** (solve) lösen ‹*Problem, Rechenaufgabe*› **3** (resolve) **~ things out with sb./for oneself** die Angelegenheit mit jmdm./sich selbst ausmachen; **things ~ themselves out** es erledigt sich alles von selbst **4** (devise) ausarbeiten ‹*Plan, Strategie*› **5** (make out) herausfinden; (understand) verstehen; **I can't ~ him out** ich werde aus ihm nicht klug **6** (Mining: exhaust) ausbeuten
B *v.i.* **1** (be calculated) **sth. ~s out at £250/[an increase of] 22%** etw. ergibt 250 Pfund/bedeutet [eine Steigerung von] 22%; **it will ~ out more expensive to buy the car on HP** es wird mehr kosten, das Auto auf Kredit zu kaufen **2** (give definite result) ‹*Gleichung, Rechnung:*› aufgehen **3** (have result) laufen; **things ~ed out [well] in the end** es ist schließlich doch alles gut gegangen; **things didn't ~ out the way we planned** es kam ganz anders, als wir geplant hatten; **how are the new arrangements ~ing out?** wie klappt es mit der neuen Regelung? (ugs.) **4** (train) trainieren; *see also* **workout**
- **~ ˈover** *v.t.* **1** (examine thoroughly) durcharbeiten **2** (coll.: beat up) in die Mache nehmen (salopp)
- **~ through** *v.t.* durcharbeiten
- **~ towards** *v.t.* (lit. or fig.) hinarbeiten auf (+ *Akk.*)
- **~ ˈup**
A *v.t.* **1** (develop) verarbeiten (**into** zu); (create) erarbeiten **2** (excite by degrees) aufpeitschen ‹*Menge*›; **get ~ed up** sich aufregen; **~ oneself up into a rage/fury** sich in einen Wutanfall/in Raserei hineinsteigern **3** (acquire familiarity with) **~ up one's French/maths/history** seine Französisch-/Mathematik-/Geschichtskenntnisse vertiefen **4** (mix) verarbeiten (**into** zu)
B *v.i.* **1** (advance gradually) **~ up to sth.** ‹*Musik:*› sich zu etw. steigern; ‹*Geschichte, Film:*› auf etw. (*Akk.*) zusteuern; **I'll have to ~ up to it** ich muss darauf hinarbeiten **2** ‹*Rock usw.:*› sich hochschieben

workable /ˈwɜːkəbl/ *adj.* **1** (capable of being worked) bebaubar ‹*Land*›; abbauwürdig ‹*Mine*›; **be ~** ‹*Mörtel:*› sich verarbeiten lassen; ‹*Stahl:*› sich bearbeiten lassen; ‹*Mine:*› sich ausbeuten lassen **2** (feasible) durchführbar

workaday /ˈwɜːkədeɪ/ *adj.* alltäglich

workaholic /wɜːkəˈhɒlɪk/ *n.* (coll.) arbeitswütiger Mensch; Workaholic, *der* (*Psych.*); *attrib.* arbeitswütig

work: ~-bag *n.* [Hand]arbeitsbeutel, *der;* **~-basket** *n.* Handarbeitskorb, *der;* **~bench** *n.* Werkbank, *die;* (of tailor, glazier) Arbeitstisch, *der;* **~box** *n.* Nähkasten, *der;* **~ camp** *n.: Lager freiwilliger Helfer;* (labour camp) Arbeitslager, *das;* **~day** *n.* Werktag, *der*

worker /ˈwɜːkə(r)/ *n.* **1** Arbeiter, *der*/Arbeiterin, *die;* **he is not one of the world's ~s** (coll.) er hat die Arbeit nicht gerade erfunden (ugs.); **~ of miracles** Wundertäter, *der* **2** (Zool.) Arbeiterin, *die*

worker: ~ bee *n.* (Zool.) Arbeiterbiene, *die;* **~ ˈpriest** *n.* (Eccl.) Arbeiterpriester, *der*

work: ~ ethic *n., no pl.* Arbeitsethos, *das;* **~ experience** *n.* Arbeitserfahrung, *die;* (for schoolchildren) Praktikum, *das;* **~fare** /ˈwɜːkfeə(r)/ *n., no pl.: System, in dem Sozialhilfe nur an Arbeitswillige gezahlt wird;* Workfare-System, *das;* **~flow** *n.* Workflow, *der* (fachspr.); Arbeitsfluss, *der; attrib.* Workflow-; Arbeitsfluss-; **~force** *n.* Belegschaft, *die;* **~group** *n.* (also Computing) Arbeitsgruppe, *die;* **~horse** *n.* (lit. or fig.) Arbeitspferd, *das;* **~house** *n.* (Brit. Hist., Amer.) Arbeitshaus, *das;* **~-in** *n.* Betriebsbesetzung, *die* (*mit Weiterführung der Arbeit bei drohender Aussperrung*)

working /ˈwɜːkɪŋ/
A *n.* 1 Arbeiten, *das;* **forbid sb.'s ~:** verbieten, dass jmd. arbeitet 2 (way sth. works) Arbeitsweise, *die;* **I cannot follow the ~s of his mind** ich kann seinen Gedankengängen nicht folgen; **the ~s of fate** die Wege des Schicksals 3 (Mining) Stollen, *der*
B *adj.* 1 handlungsfähig ‹*Mehrheit*›; ‹*Entwurf, Vereinbarung*› als Ausgangspunkt 2 (in employment) arbeitend; werktätig; **~ man** (labourer) Arbeiter, *der*

working: ~ 'breakfast *n.* Arbeitsfrühstück, *das;* **~ 'capital** *n.* (Commerc.) Betriebskapital, *das;* **~ 'class** *n.* Arbeiterklasse, *die;* **~-class** *adj.* der Arbeiterklasse *nachgestellt;* **sb. is ~-class** jmd. gehört zur Arbeiterklasse; **~ clothes** *n. pl.* Arbeitskleidung, *die;* **~ conditions** *n. pl.* Arbeitsbedingungen *Pl.;* **~ 'day** *n.* 1 (portion of the day) Arbeitstag, *der;* 2 (day when work is done) ▸**workday;** **~ 'drawing** *n.* Konstruktionszeichnung, *die;* (for building) Bauplan, *der;* **~ girl** *n.* berufstätige junge Frau; **she's a ~ girl** (coll. euphem.: prostitute) sie ist im horizontalen Gewerbe tätig (ugs. scherzh.); **~ 'hours** *n. pl.* Arbeitszeit, *die;* **~ hy'pothesis** *n.* Arbeitshypothese, *die;* **~ 'knowledge** *n.* ausreichende Kenntnisse (**of** in + *Dat.*); **sb. with a ~ knowledge of these machines** jmd., der im Umgang mit diesen Maschinen erfahren ist; **~ 'lunch** *n.* Arbeitsessen, *das;* **~ 'man** *n.* Arbeiter, *der;* **~ 'model** *n.* funktionsfähiges Modell; **~ 'mother** *n.* berufstätige Mutter; **~ 'order** *n.* betriebsfähiger Zustand; **be in good ~ order** betriebsbereit sein; **~-'out** *n.* 1 (calculation of results) Berechnung, *die;* 2 (elaboration of details) Ausarbeitung, *die;* 3 (training) Trainieren, *das;* (esp. in gym) [Fitness]training, *das;* **~-'over** *n.* (sl.) Abreibung, *die* (ugs.); **~ party** *n.* (Brit.) Arbeitsgruppe, *die;* **~ 'storage** *n., no pl.* (Computing) Arbeitsspeicher, *der;* **~ 'title** *n.* Arbeitstitel, *der;* **~ 'week** *n.* Arbeitswoche, *die;* **a 35-hour ~ week** eine 35-Stunden-Woche; **~ 'wife** *n.* berufstätige Ehefrau; **~ 'woman** *n.* berufstätige Frau

work: ~-in-'progress *n.* Work-in-Progress, *das;* (commercial product also) im Entstehen begriffenes Produkt; (artistic work also) im Entstehen begriffenes Werk; **~-'life balance** *n.* Work-Life-Balance, *die;* **~load** *n.* Arbeitslast, *die;* **increase sb.'s ~load** jmds. Arbeitspensum erhöhen; **~man** /ˈwɜːkmən/ *n., pl.* **~men** /ˈwɜːkmən/ Arbeiter, *der;* **council ~man** städtischer Arbeiter; **a bad ~man quarrels with** *or* **blames his tools** (prov.) ein schlechter Handwerker schimpft über sein Werkzeug; **~manlike** /ˈwɜːkmənlaɪk/ *adj.* fachmännisch; **do a ~manlike job** fachmännisch arbeiten; **~manship** /ˈwɜːkmənʃɪp/ *n., no pl.* 1 (person's skill) handwerkliches Können; 2 (quality of execution) Kunstfertigkeit, *die;* **~mate** *n.* (Brit.) Arbeitskollege, *der*/-kollegin, *die;* **~out** *n.* [Fitness]training, *das;* **have a good ~out** hart trainieren; **go for a ~out** zum [Fitness]training gehen; **~pack** *n.* Arbeitspaket, *das;* **~people** *n. pl.* Arbeiter; **~ permit** *n.* Arbeitserlaubnis, *die;* **~piece** *n.* Werkstück, *das;* **~place** *n.* Arbeitsplatz, *der;* **~-related** *adj.* arbeitsbezogen ‹*Konflikt, Problem usw.*›; arbeitsbedingt ‹*Erkrankung, Stress*›; **~room** *n.* Arbeitsraum, *der;* **~ shadowing** *n., no pl.* Hospitieren, *das;* **~-sharing** *n., no pl.* Jobsharing, *das;* (short-time working) Kurzarbeit, *die;* **~sheet** *n.* 1 (recording ~ done etc.) Arbeitszettel, *der;* 2 (for student) Formular mit Prüfungsfragen; 3 (Computing: data file) Arbeitsblatt, *das;* **~shop** *n.* 1 (place) (room) Werkstatt, *die;* (building) Werk, *das;* 2 (meeting) Workshop, *der;* Arbeitstreffen, *das;* **drama ~shop** Theaterworkshop, *der;* **~-shy** *adj.* arbeitsscheu; **~space** *n.* Arbeitsraum, *der;* **~station** *n.* 1 (in manufacturing) Fertigungsstation, *die;* 2 (Computing) Workstation, *die;* **~ study** *n.* Arbeitsstudien; (case) Arbeitsstudie, *die;* **~ surface** ▸**~top;** **~ table** *n.* Arbeitstisch, *der;* **~top** *n.* Arbeitsplatte, *die;* **~-to-'rule** *n.* Dienst nach Vorschrift; **~week** *n.* (Amer.) Arbeitswoche, *die*

world /wɜːld/ *n.* 1 Welt, *die; attrib.* Welt-; **the ~'s worst novel** der schlechteste Roman der Welt; **go/sail round the ~:** eine Weltreise machen/die Welt umsegeln; **money makes the ~ go round** Geld regiert die Welt; **that's what/it's love that makes the ~ go round** darum/um die Liebe dreht sich letztlich alles; **it's the same the ~ over** es ist doch überall das Gleiche; **the eyes of the ~ are on them** die Welt blickt auf sie; **all the ~** *or* **the whole ~ knows** alle Welt (ugs.) weiß; **[all] the ~ over, all over the ~:** in *od.* auf der ganzen Welt; **it's the same the whole ~ over** es ist überall das Gleiche; **people from all over the ~ wrote to him** er bekam Post aus aller Welt; **give sth. to the ~:** etw. der Welt übergeben (fig.); **lead the ~ [in sth.]** [in etw. (*Dat.*)] führend in der Welt sein; **the Old/New W~:** die Alte/Neue Welt; **the Roman ~:** die römische Welt; **she had the ~ at her feet** die ganze Welt lag ihr zu Füßen; **who/what in the ~ was it?** wer/was in aller Welt war es? (ugs.); **how in the ~ was it that ...?** wie in aller Welt (ugs.) war es möglich, dass ...?; **nothing in the ~ would persuade me** um nichts in der Welt ließe ich mich überreden; **not for anything in the ~:** um nichts in der Welt; **look for all the ~ as if ...:** geradezu aussehen, als ob ...; **in a ~ of one's own** in einer anderen Welt (fig.); **the external ~:** die Außenwelt *od.* äußere Welt; **the ~ of dreams** die Welt der Träume; **not do sth. for the ~:** etw. um alles in der Welt nicht tun; **be all the ~** *or* **mean the ~ to sb.** jmdm. das Wichtigste/Liebste auf der Welt sein; **think the ~ of sb.** große Stücke auf jmdn. halten (ugs.); **I would give the ~ to know why ...:** ich gäbe alles darum, zu wissen, warum ...; **all alone in the ~:** ganz allein auf der Welt; **the Napoleons of this ~:** die Napoleons dieser Erde; **sb. is not long for this ~:** jmds. Tage sind gezählt; **out of this ~** (fig. coll.) fantastisch (ugs.); **the other** *or* **next ~, the ~ to come** das Jenseits; die zukünftige Welt; **bring into the ~** (possess at one's birth) in die Welt bringen; (give birth to) zur Welt bringen; **come into the ~:** auf die Welt kommen; **the best of all possible ~s** die beste aller Welten; **get the best of both ~s** am meisten profitieren; **the ~'s end, the end of the ~:** das Ende der Welt; **it's not the end of the ~** (iron.) davon geht die Welt nicht unter (ugs.); **~ without end** in alle Ewigkeit; **know/have seen a lot of the ~:** die Welt kennen/viel von der Welt gesehen haben; **see the ~:** die Welt kennen lernen; **a man/woman of the ~:** ein Mann/eine Frau mit Welterfahrung; **think that all's right with the ~:** glauben, dass die Welt in Ordnung ist; **take the ~ as it is** *or* **as one finds it** alles nehmen, wie es kommt; **what 'is the ~ coming to?** wo soll das noch hinführen? (ugs.); **how goes the ~ with you?** wie gehts[, wie stehts]?; **all the ~ and his wife** alle Welt (ugs.); **go up/come down in the ~:** [gesellschaftlich] aufsteigen/absteigen; *attrib.* **~ politics** Weltpolitik, *die; see also* **oyster**
2 (domain) **the literary/scientific/ancient/sporting/animal ~:** die literarische/wissenschaftliche/antike Welt (geh.)/die Welt (geh.) des Sports/die Tierwelt; **the ~ of letters/art/sport** die Welt (geh.) der Literatur/Kunst/des Sports
3 (vast amount) **a ~ of meaning/trouble** eine unendliche Bedeutungsfülle/Fülle von Schwierigkeiten; **it will do him a** *or* **the ~ of good** es wird ihm unendlich gut tun; **a ~ of difference** ein weltweiter Unterschied; **a ~ away from sth.** Welten von etw. entfernt; **they are ~s apart in their views** ihre Ansichten sind Welten voneinander entfernt

world: W~ 'Bank *n.* Weltbank, *die;* **~-beater** *n.* **be a ~-beater** zur Spitzenklasse gehören; **~-beating** weltbest...; unschlagbar ‹*Produkt, Software*›; **~-beating time/performance** Weltbestzeit, *die*/Weltbestleistung, *die;* **~ 'champion** *n.* Weltmeister, *der*/-meisterin, *die;* **~-class** *adj.* der Weltspitze *nachgestellt;* Weltklasse- ‹*sportler, -musiker*›; **W~ 'Cup** *n.* (Sport) Worldcup, *der;* **W~ 'English** *n., no pl.* Weltenglisch, *das;* Universalenglisch, *das;* **~-famous** *adj.* weltberühmt; **W~ 'Heritage Site** *n.* Welterbestätte, *die;* **~ 'language** *n.* Weltsprache, *die*

worldliness /ˈwɜːldlɪnɪs/ *n., no pl.* Weltlichkeit, *die*

worldly /ˈwɜːldlɪ/ *adj.* weltlich; weltlich eingestellt ‹*Person*›

worldly: ~ 'goods *n. pl.* weltliche Güter; **~ 'wisdom** *n.* Weltklugheit, *die;* **~ 'wise** *adj.* weltklug

world: ~ 'music *n., no pl.* Weltmusik, *die;* **~ 'order** *n.* Weltordnung, *die;* **~ 'power** *n.* Weltmacht, *die;* **~ 'record** *n.* Weltrekord, *der; attrib.* **~-record holder** Weltrekordhalter, *der*/-halterin, *die;* **W~ Series** *n.* (Amer. Sport) *Baseball-Ausscheidungen zwischen den Gewinnern der bedeutendsten Ligen der USA;* **~-shaking** *adj.* welterschütternd; weltbewegend ‹*Ereignis*›; **W~ 'Trade Organization** *n.* Welthandelsorganisation, *die;* **~ view** *n.* Weltsicht, *die;* **~ 'war** *n.* Weltkrieg, *der;* **the First/Second W~ War, W~ War I/II** der Erste/Zweite Weltkrieg; der 1./2. Weltkrieg; **~-weary** *adj.* lebensüberdrüssig; **~wide A** /ˈ--/ *adj.* weltweit; **B** /-ˈ-/ *adv.* weltweit; **W~ Wide 'Web** *n.* (Computing) World Wide Web, *das*

worm /wɜːm/
A *n.* 1 Wurm, *der;* **[even] a ~ will turn** (prov.) auch der Wurm krümmt sich, wenn er getreten wird (Spr.) 2 *in pl.* (intestinal parasites) Würmer 3 (fig.: contemptible person) Wurm, *der;* **feel like a ~:** sich (*Dat.*) klein und hässlich vorkommen; **he's a real ~:** er ist ein richtiger Widerling 4 (Computing) Wurm, *der*
B *v.t.* 1 **~ one's way through sth.** sich durch etw. winden (geh.) *od.* zwängen; **~ oneself** *or* **one's way into sth.** (fig.) sich in etw. (*Akk.*) hineindrängen; **~ oneself into sb.'s favour** sich in jmds. Gunst (*Akk.*) schleichen 2 (draw by crafty persistence) **~ sth. out of sb.** etw. aus jmdm. herausbringen (ugs.) 3 (rid of ~s) entwurmen
C *v.i.* sich winden

worm: ~ cast *n.* Kothäufchen des Regenwurms; **~-eaten** *adj.* wurmstichig; (fig.) vom Zahn der Zeit angenagt; **~ gear** *n.* Schneckengetriebe, *das* (Technik); **~hole** *n.* Wurmloch, *das;* **~ powder** *n.* Wurmpulver, *das;* **~'s-eye 'view** *n.* Froschperspektive, *die* (auch fig.)

'wormwood *n.* Wermut, *der*

wormy /ˈwɜːmɪ/ *adj.* wurmig ‹*Apfel*›; von Würmern befallen ‹*Tier*›; wurmreich ‹*Boden, Erde*›

worn ▸**wear B, C**

'worn-out *attrib. adj.* abgetragen ‹*Kleidungsstück*›; abgenutzt ‹*Teppich*›; abgedroschen ‹*Redensart, Ausdruck*›; erschöpft, (ugs.) erledigt ‹*Person*›

worried /ˈwʌrɪd/ *adj.* besorgt; **give sb. a ~ look** jmdn. besorgt ansehen; **you had me ~:** ich habe mir [deinetwegen] Sorgen gemacht; **don't look so ~!** schau nicht so bekümmert drein!; **~ sick** krank vor Sorge; **be much** *or* **very ~:** sich (*Dat.*) große Sorgen machen

worrier /ˈwʌrɪə(r)/ *n.* **be too much of a ~:** sich (*Dat.*) immer [zu viel] Sorgen machen; **he's a [real] ~:** er macht sich (*Dat.*) um alles Sorgen

worrisome /ˈwʌrɪsəm/ *adj.* besorgniserregend

worry /ˈwʌrɪ/
A *v.t.* 1 beunruhigen; **it worries me to death to think that ...:** ich sorge mich zu Tode, wenn ich [daran] denke, dass ...; **~ oneself [about sth.]** sich (*Dat.*) um etw. Sorgen machen; **~ oneself sick [about sb./sth.]** krank vor Sorge [um jmdn./etw.] werden 2 (bother) stören 3 **~ a bone** ‹*Hund usw.:*› an einem Knochen [herum]nagen 4 (attack) ‹*Hund usw.:*› reißen ‹*Schaf*›
B *v.i.* sich (*Dat.*) Sorgen machen; sich sorgen; **~ about sth.** sich (*Dat.*) um etw. Sorgen machen; **don't ~ about it** mach dir deswegen keine Sorgen!; **'I should ~** (coll. iron.) was kümmert mich das?; **not to ~** (coll.) kein Problem (ugs.)
C *n.* Sorge, *die;* **sth. is the least of sb.'s worries**

etw. ist jmds. geringste Sorge; **it must be a great ~ to you** es muss dir große Sorgen bereiten

'worry beads *n. pl. Perlenschnur zur Beschäftigung für nervöse Hände*

worrying /'wʌrɪɪŋ/

A *adj.* 1) (causing worry) beunruhigend; **sth. is very ~ for sb.** etw. macht jmdm. große Sorgen 2) (full of worry) sorgenvoll ‹*Zeit, Woche usw.*›; **it is a ~ time for her** sie hat zurzeit große Sorgen

B *n.* **~ only makes everything worse** sich (*Dat.*) Sorgen zu machen macht alles nur noch schlimmer

'worry line *n.* Sorgenfalte, *die*

worse /wɜːs/

A *adj. compar. of* **bad A** schlechter; schlimmer ‹*Schmerz, Krankheit, Benehmen*›; **things could not/could be ~:** es kann nicht mehr schlimmer kommen/es könnte schlimmer sein; **the food is bad, and the service ~:** das Essen ist schlecht und die Bedienung noch schlechter; **his manners are ~ than a pig's** er benimmt sich schlimmer als ein Schwein; **he's getting ~:** mit ihm wird es schlimmer; (his health) ihm geht es schlechter; **be ~ than useless** ‹*Sache:*› mehr als unbrauchbar sein; ‹*Person:*› ein hoffnungsloser Fall sein; **be [none] the ~ for sth.** ‹*Sache:*› in [k]einem schlechteren Zustand wegen etw. sein; **sb. is [none] the ~ for sth.** jmdm. geht es wegen etw. [nicht] schlechter; **~ and ~:** immer schlechter/schlimmer; **to make matters ~, ...:** zu allem Übel ...; **it could have been ~:** es hätte schlimmer sein *od.* kommen können; **~ luck!** so ein Pech!; *see also* **drink A 4**; **liquor 1**; **wear A 1**

B *adv. compar. of* **badly** schlechter; schlimmer, schlechter ‹*sich benehmen*›; **~ and ~:** immer schlechter/schlimmer; *see also* **better C 1**; **off A 9**

C *n.* Schlimmeres; **she might do ~ than settle for that job** es wäre bestimmt kein Fehler, wenn sie sich für die Stelle entschiede; **go from bad to ~:** immer schlimmer werden; **or ~:** oder noch Schlimmeres; **~ still** schlimmer noch; **a change for the ~:** eine Wende zum Schlechteren; **take a turn for the ~:** sich verschlechtern; ‹*Krankheit:*› sich verschlimmern; **nobody will think any the ~ of you** niemand wird deswegen schlechter von dir denken; **there is ~ to come** es kommt noch schlimmer; *see also* **worst C**

worsen /'wɜːsn/

A *v.t.* verschlechtern; verschlimmern ‹*Knappheit*›

B *v.i.* sich verschlechtern; ‹*Hungersnot, Sturm, Problem:*› sich verschlimmern; **she ~ed in the night** ihr Zustand hat sich über Nacht verschlimmert

worship /'wɜːʃɪp/

A *v.t.*, (Brit.) **-pp-:** 1) verehren ‹*Gott, Götter, Kaiser*›; anbeten ‹*Gott, Götter*› 2) (idolize) abgöttisch verehren; **he ~s the ground she walks on** er küsst den Boden unter ihren Füßen

B *v.i.*, (Brit.) **-pp-:** 1) (in church etc.) am Gottesdienst teilnehmen 2) (be full of adoration) tiefe Verehrung empfinden

C *n.* 1) Anbetung, *die;* (service) Gottesdienst, *der;* **public ~:** [öffentlicher] Gottesdienst; **dedicated as a place of ~:** dem Gottesdienst geweiht; **gather for ~:** sich zum Gottesdienst versammeln; **freedom of ~:** Glaubensfreiheit, *die* 2) (adoration) Verehrung, *die;* **an object of ~:** ein Gegenstand der Verehrung; **the ~ of wealth/intellect** die Anbetung des Wohlstands/Intellekts 3) ▸ⓘ **p. 1634** (form of address) **Your/His W~** *Anrede für Richter, Bürgermeister;* ≈ Euer/Seine Ehren

worshiper (Amer.) ▸**worshipper**

worshipful /'wɜːʃɪpfl/ *adj.* (Brit.) *Titulierung von Friedensrichtern, Zünften, Freimaurerlogen usw.*

worshipper /'wɜːʃɪpə(r)/ *n.* 1) (in church etc.) Gottesdienstbesucher, *der*/-besucherin, *die* 2) (of deity) Anbeter, *der*/Anbeterin, *die* 3) (of person, money, etc.) Verehrer, *der*/Verehrerin, *die;* **be a ~ of sth.** etw. anbeten (fig.)

worst /wɜːst/

A *adj. superl. of* **bad A** 1) ▸**worse A**: schlechtest.../schlimmst...; **be ~:** am schlechtesten/schlimmsten sein; **the ~ thing about it was ...:** das Schlimmste daran war ...; **the ~ thing you could do** das Schlechteste, was du machen könntest 2) (least efficient, of poorest quality) schlechtest...

B *adv. superl. of* **badly** am schlimmsten; am schlechtesten ‹*gekleidet*›

C *n.* 1) **[the] ~:** der/die/das Schlimmste; **you saw him at his ~:** du hast ihn in seinem schlimmsten Zustand erlebt; **prepare for the ~:** sich auf das Schlimmste gefasst machen; **at ~, at the [very] ~:** schlimmstenfalls; im [aller]schlimmsten Fall[e]; **get** *or* **have the ~ of it** (be defeated) [vernichtend] geschlagen werden; (suffer the most) am meisten zu leiden haben; **if the ~** *or* **it comes to the ~** (Brit.), **if worse comes to ~** (Amer.) wenn es zum Schlimmsten kommt; **do your ~:** mach, was du willst!; **let him do his ~:** er soll machen, was er will 2) (what is of poorest quality) Schlechteste, *der/die/das*

D *v.t.* [vernichtend] schlagen; **be ~ed in argument** sich geschlagen geben müssen

'worst-case *attrib. adj.* Worst-Case-; **~ scenario** Schlimmstfall, *der*

worsted /'wʊstɪd/ *n.* (Textiles) Kammgarn, *das*

wort /wɜːt/ *n.* [Bier]würze, *die*

worth /wɜːθ/

A *adj.* 1) ▸ⓘ **p. 1332** (of value equivalent to) wert; **it's ~/not ~ £80** es ist 80 Pfund wert/80 Pfund ist es nicht wert; **it is not ~ much** *or* **a lot [to sb.]** es ist [jmdm.] nicht viel wert; **be ~ the money** das Geld wert sein; **not ~ a penny** keinen Heller wert (ugs.); **it's ~ a lot to me that ...:** es bedeutet mir viel, dass ...; **he's ~ the lot of you put together** er ist so viel wert wie ihr alle zusammen; **for what it is ~:** was immer auch davon zu halten ist; *see also* **gold A 1** 2) (worthy of) **is it ~ hearing/the effort?** ist es hörenswert/der Mühe wert?; **is it ~ doing?** lohnt es sich?; **if it's ~ doing, it's ~ doing well** wenn schon, denn schon; **it isn't ~ it** es lohnt sich nicht; **an experience ~ having** eine lohnenswerte Erfahrung; **it's ~ a try** es ist einen Versuch wert; **it would be [well] ~ it** (coll.) es würde sich [sehr] lohnen; **be well ~ sth.** durchaus *od.* sehr wohl etw. wert sein; **you can have my opinion for what it's ~:** ich kann dir sagen, was meine bescheidene Meinung ist; **it's more than my job's ~:** es könnte mich meine Stelle kosten 3) **be ~ sth.** (possess) etw. wert sein (ugs.); **run/cycle for all one is ~** (coll.) rennen/fahren, was man kann. *see also* **salt A 1**; **while A**

B *n.* 1) ▸ⓘ **p. 1332** (equivalent of money etc. in commodity) **ten pounds' ~ of petrol** Benzin für zehn Pfund; (more formal) Benzin im Wert von zehn Pfund 2) (value, excellence) Wert, *der;* **of great/little/no ~:** von hohem/geringem Wert/ohne Wert. *see also* **money's worth**; **pennyworth**

worthily /'wɜːðɪlɪ/ *adv.* ehrenhaft; zu Recht ‹*verdienen*›

worthiness /'wɜːðɪnɪs/ *n., no pl.* Ehrenhaftigkeit, *die;* (of cause, charity) Wert, *der*

worthless /'wɜːθlɪs/ *adj.* 1) (valueless) wertlos 2) (despicable) nichtswürdig

'worthwhile *attrib. adj.* lohnend; *see also* **while A**

worthy /'wɜːðɪ/

A *adj.* 1) (adequate, estimable) würdig; verdienstvoll ‹*Tat*›; angemessen ‹*Belohnung*›; **~ of the occasion** dem Anlass angemessen 2) (deserving) würdig; verdienstvoll ‹*Sache, Organisation*›; **be ~ of the name** den Namen verdienen; **~ of note/mention** erwähnenswert; **is he ~ of her?** ist er ihrer würdig?

B *n.* 1) (person of distinction) Würdenträger, *der* 2) **local worthies** (joc.) örtliche Honoratioren

wotcher /'wɒtʃə(r)/ *int.* (Brit. coll.) hallo (ugs.)

would ▸**will**[1]

would-be /'wʊdbiː/ *attrib. adj.* **a ~ philosopher** ein Möchtegernphilosoph; **a ~ aggressor** ein möglicher Aggressor

wouldn't /'wʊdnt/ (coll.) = **would not**; ▸**will**[1]

wound[1] /wuːnd/

A *n.* (lit. or fig.) Wunde, *die;* **a war ~:** eine Kriegsverletzung; **receive a ~ in the chest/leg** an der Brust/am Bein verwundet werden; **a knife-~ across the palm** eine Schnittwunde quer über die Handfläche; **this was a great ~ to her pride** (fig.) das verletzte ihren Stolz zutiefst

B *v.t.* verwunden; (fig.) verletzen; **be ~ed in the thigh/arm** am Oberschenkel/Arm verwundet werden

wound[2] ▸**wind**[2] **A, B**

wove, woven ▸**weave**[1] **B, C**

wow[1] /waʊ/

A *int.* hoi

B *n.* (coll.) **be a ~:** eine Wucht sein (salopp)

C *v.t.* (coll.) umhauen (ugs.)

wow[2] *n.* (Electronics) Jaulen, *das* (fig.)

WP *abbr.* = **word processor**

w. p. b. *abbr.* = **waste-paper basket**

WPC *abbr.* = **woman police constable** Wachtmeisterin, *die*

w. p. m. *abbr.* = **words per minute** WpM

wraith /reɪθ/ *n.* Gespenst, *das*

'wraithlike *adj.* gespenstisch

wrangle /'ræŋgl/

A *v.i.* [sich] streiten

B *n.* Streit, *der;* **what are those two having such a ~ about?** worüber streiten die beiden sich denn so?

wrap /ræp/

A *v.t.*, **-pp-** 1) einwickeln; (fig.) hüllen; **~ped** abgepackt ‹*Brot usw.*›; **~ sth. in paper/cotton wool** etw. in Papier/Watte [ein]wickeln; **~ sth. [a]round sth.** (lit. or fig.) etw. um etw. wickeln; **~ one's arms around sb.** die Arme um jmdn. schlingen 2) (arrange) schlingen ‹*Schal, Handtuch usw.*› **(about, round** um); **she ~ped her motorcycle round a tree** (coll.) sie hat ihr Motorrad um einen Baum gewickelt (ugs.)

B *n.* Umschlag[e]tuch, *das;* **take the ~s off sth.** (fig.) etw. der Öffentlichkeit vorstellen; **under ~s** (fig.) unter Verschluss; **keep sth. under ~s** etw. geheim halten

(Phrasal verb)

• **~ 'up**

A *v.t.* 1) ▸**wrap A**; **wrapped up** 2) (fig.: conclude) abschließen; **that just about ~s it up for today** damit sind wir für heute fertig

B *v.i.* 1) (put on warm clothing) sich warm einpacken (ugs.); **mind you ~ up well** du musst dich gut einpacken (ugs.) 2) (sl.: be quiet) den Rand halten (salopp)

'wraparound

A *adj.* 1) **~ skirt/dress** Wickelrock, *der*/Wickelkleid, *das* 2) **~ shades, ~ sunglasses** Panoramasonnenbrille, *die;* **~ windscreen,** (Amer. also) **~ windshield** Panoramawindschutzscheibe, *die*

B *n.* Wickelrock, *der*

wrapped up /ræpt 'ʌp/ *adj.* **be ~ in one's work** in seine Arbeit völlig versunken sein; **she is very ~ in her family** sie geht ganz in ihrer Familie auf; **be too ~ in one's problems** zu sehr mit seinen [eigenen] Problemen beschäftigt sein; **a country whose prosperity is ~ in its shipping** ein Land, dessen Reichtum eng mit seiner Schifffahrt verknüpft ist

wrapper /'ræpə(r)/ *n.* 1) (around newspaper etc.) Streifband, *das* (Postw.) 2) (around sweet etc.) **sweet/toffee ~[s]** Bonbonpapier, *das* 3) (of book) ▸**jacket 3**

wrapping /'ræpɪŋ/ *n.* Verpackung, *die;* **~s** Verpackung, *die;* (fig.) Hülle, *die* (dichter.)

'wrapping paper *n.* (strong paper) Packpapier, *das;* (decorative paper) Geschenkpapier, *das*

wrasse /ræs/ *n.* (Zool.) Lippfisch, *der*

wrath /rɒθ/ *n.* (literary/joc.) Zorn, *der*

wrathful /'rɒθfl/ *adj.* (literary/joc.) zornig

wreak /riːk/ *v.t.* 1) (inflict) **~ vengeance on sb.** an jmdm. Rache nehmen 2) (vent) auslassen ‹*Wut, Ärger*› **(on** an + *Dat.*) 3) (cause) anrichten ‹*Verwüstung, Unheil*›

wreath /riːθ/ *n., pl.* **wreaths** /riːðz, riːθs/ Kranz, *der;* **a ~ of smoke** ein Ring aus Rauch

wreathe /riːð/

A *v.t.* 1) (encircle) umkränzen; **her face was ~d in smiles** ein Lächeln umspielte ihre Lippen 2) (form into wreath) zu einem Kranz flechten *od.*

W

(geh.) winden **3** (make by interweaving) flechten; winden (geh.)
B *v.i.* sich winden; ‹*Rauch:*› sich ringeln *od.* kräuseln (**from** aus)

wreck /rek/
A *n.* **1** (destruction) Schiffbruch, *der;* (fig.) Zerstörung, *die* **2** (ship) Wrack, *das* **3** (broken remains, lit. or fig.) Wrack, *das;* **she was a physical/mental ~:** sie war körperlich/geistig ein Wrack; **I feel/you look a ~** (coll.) ich fühle mich kaputt (ugs.)/du siehst kaputt aus (ugs.)
B *v.t.* **1** (destroy) ruinieren; zu Schrott fahren ‹*Auto*›; **be ~ed** (shipwrecked) ‹*Schiff, Person:*› Schiffbruch erleiden; **a ~ed ship/aircraft** ein wrackes *od.* (fachspr.) havariertes Schiff/Flugzeug **2** (fig.: ruin) zerstören; ruinieren ‹*Gesundheit, Urlaub*›; verderben ‹*Party, Urlaub*›; zunichte machen ‹*Hoffnung, Plan*›; zerrütten ‹*Ehe*›

wreckage /ˈrekɪdʒ/ *n.* Wrackteile; (fig.) Trümmer *Pl.*

wrecker /ˈrekə(r)/ *n.* **1** (who disrupts deliberately) Umstürzler, *der*/Umstürzlerin, *die* **2** (who brings about shipwreck for profit) Strandräuber, *der* **3** (employed in demolition) Abwracker, *der* **4** (who recovers wrecked ships) Bergungsarbeiter, *der* **5** (Amer.: breakdown vehicle) Bergungsfahrzeug, *das;* Abschleppfahrzeug, *das* **6** (Amer.: train) Hilfszug, *der*

ˈwrecking bar *n.* Brechstange, *die*

wren *n.* Zaunkönig, *der*

Wren /ren/ *n.* (Brit. Hist.) *Angehörige des weiblichen Marinedienstes;* **join the ~s** in den weiblichen Marinedienst eintreten

wrench /rentʃ/
A *n.* **1** (tool) verstellbarer Schraubenschlüssel; **pipe ~:** Rohrzange, *die;* **screw ~:** Franzose, *der* **2** (esp. Amer.) ▸**spanner 3** (violent twist) Verrenkung, *die;* **give one's ankle/shoulder a ~:** sich (*Dat.*) den Knöchel/die Schulter verrenken; **give a ~ at the door handle** an der Türklinke reißen **4** (fig.) **be a great ~ [for sb.]** sehr schmerzhaft [für jmdn.] sein; **what a ~ it must have been for her** wie schmerzlich muss es für sie gewesen sein
B *v.t.* **1** (tug violently) reißen; **~ at sth.** an etw. (*Dat.*) reißen; **~ sth. round/off/open** etw. herum-/ab-/aufreißen; **~ sth. from sb.** jmdm. etw. entreißen **2** (injure by twisting) **~ one's ankle** *etc.* sich (*Dat.*) den Knöchel *usw.* verrenken

wrest /rest/ *v.t.* **~ sth. from sb./sb.'s grasp** (lit. or fig.) jmdm./jmds. Griff etw. entreißen *od.* (geh.) entwinden; **~ a confession from sb.** jmdm. ein Geständnis abnötigen (geh.); **~ sth. from sth.** einer Sache (*Dat.*) etw. abringen

wrestle /ˈresl/
A *n.* **1** (hard struggle) Ringen, *das* **2** (wrestling match) Ringkampf, *der;* **have a ~:** einen Ringkampf austragen
B *v.i.* **1** ringen **2** (fig.: grapple) sich abmühen; **~ with one's conscience** mit seinem Gewissen ringen; **~ with the controls of the aircraft** mit der Steuerung des Flugzeugs kämpfen
C *v.t.* **~ sth. from sth.** etw. mühsam von etw. entfernen

wrestler /ˈreslə(r)/ *n.* Ringer, *der*/Ringerin, *die*

wrestling /ˈreslɪŋ/ *n., no pl., no indef. art.* Ringen, *das;* **~ match** Ringkampf, *der*

wretch /retʃ/ *n.* Kreatur, *die;* (joc.: child) Gör, *das*

wretched /ˈretʃɪd/ *adj.* **1** (miserable) unglücklich; **feel ~ about sb./sth.** (be embarrassed) über jmdn./etw. todunglücklich sein; **feel ~** (be very unwell) sich elend fühlen **2** (coll.: damned) elend (abwertend); **I wish he would control that ~ dog of his!** wenn er nur besser auf seinen elenden Köter aufpassen würde! **3** (very bad) erbärmlich; miserabel ‹*Wetter*›; **she's had a bout of ~ health** es ging ihr gesundheitlich sehr schlecht **4** (causing discomfort) schrecklich ‹*Reise, Erfahrung, Zeit*›

wretchedly /ˈretʃɪdlɪ/ *adv.* **1** (in misery) jämmerlich ‹*weinen*›; jammervoll ‹*anblicken*› **2** (very badly) erbärmlich

wretchedness /ˈretʃɪdnɪs/ *n., no pl.* **1** (misery) Elend, *das* **2** (badness) Erbärmlichkeit, *die*

wrick ▸**rick**[2]

wriggle /ˈrɪgl/
A *v.i.* **1** zappeln; **~ [about] on one's chair** auf dem Stuhl herumrutschen (ugs.) **2** (make one's/its way by wriggling) sich winden; **a worm ~d across the lawn** ein Wurm schlängelte sich über den Rasen; **~ free of the ropes** sich aus den Stricken winden; **~ out of a difficulty** *etc.* (fig.) sich aus einer schwierigen Situation *usw.* herauswinden
B *v.t.* **1** **~ one's way** (lit. or fig.) sich schlängeln; **~ one's way out of a difficulty** *etc.* sich aus einer schwierigen Situation *usw.* herauswinden **2** (move) **~ one's hips** die Hüften kreisen lassen
C *n.* Windung, *die*

wriggly /ˈrɪglɪ/ *adj.* sich windend ‹*Wurm, Aal*›; zappelnd ‹*Fisch, Kind*›

wring /rɪŋ/ *v.t.*, **wrung** /rʌŋ/ **1** wringen; **~ out** auswringen; **~ the water out of the towels** das Wasser aus den Handtüchern wringen **2** (squeeze forcibly) **~ sb.'s hand** jmdm. fest die Hand drücken; (twist forcibly) **~ one's hands** die Hände ringen (geh.); **~ the neck of an animal** einem Tier den Hals umdrehen; **I could have wrung his neck** (fig.) ich hätte ihm den Hals umdrehen können **3** (extract) wringen; **~ sth. from** *or* **out of sb.** (fig.) jmdm. etw. abpressen **4** (distress) **~ the heart** einem das Herz abdrücken

wringer /ˈrɪŋə(r)/ *n.* Wringmaschine, *die*

wringing wet /rɪŋɪŋ ˈwet/ *adj.* tropfnass; **our clothes were ~:** unsere Kleider waren zum Auswringen

wrinkle /ˈrɪŋkl/
A *n.* Falte, *die;* (in paper) Knick, *der*
B *v.t.* falten; in Falten legen ‹*Stirn*›; kräuseln ‹*Nase*›
C *v.i.* sich in Falten legen

wrinkled /ˈrɪŋkld/ *adj.* runz[e]lig; **~ with age** runz[e]lig vom Alter

wrinklie /ˈrɪŋklɪ/ ▸**wrinkly B**

wrinkly /ˈrɪŋklɪ/
A *adj.* runz[e]lig
B *n.* (coll.) Grufti, *der* (ugs.)

wrist /rɪst/ *n.* ▸ⓘ **p. 951** Handgelenk, *das;* **slash one's ~s** sich (*Dat.*) die Pulsadern aufschneiden; **the glove was too tight at the ~:** der Handschuh war zu eng am Handgelenk

wrist: ~band *n.* **1** (cuff) Manschette, *die;* **2** ▸**sweatband; ~watch** *n.* Armbanduhr, *die;* **~ rest** *n.* Handgelenkstütze, *die;* Handgelenkauflage, *die*

writ[1] /rɪt/ *n.* (Law) **1** Verfügung, *die;* **serve a ~ on sb.** jmdm. eine Verfügung zustellen **2** (Crown document) *königlicher Erlass, mit dem ein Peer ins Parlament gerufen wird/mit dem Parlamentswahlen ausgerufen werden* **3** (Relig.) **Holy W~:** die Heilige Schrift

writ[2] ▸**write B 1**

writable /ˈraɪtəbl/ *adj.* (Computing) beschreibbar ‹*Diskette*›

write /raɪt/
A *v.i.*, **wrote** /rəʊt/, **written** /ˈrɪtn/ schreiben; **~ to sb./a firm** jmdm./an eine Firma schreiben; **~ for a fresh supply** schriftlich eine neue Lieferung anfordern; **she ~s for a living** sie ist Schriftstellerin; *see also* **home**
B *v.t.*, **wrote, written 1** schreiben; ausschreiben ‹*Scheck*›; **the written language** die Schriftsprache; **~ it, don't print it** schreibe es nicht in Druckschrift, sondern in Schreibschrift; **written applications** schriftliche Anträge; **the paper had been written all over** das Papier war ganz voll geschrieben; **it is written that ...:** es steht geschrieben, dass ...; (Bibl. etc.) **be written into the contract** [ausdrücklich] im Vertrag stehen; **~ sb. into/out of a serial** für jmdn. eine Rolle in einer Serie schreiben/jmdm. einen Abgang aus einer Serie verschaffen; **writ large** (fig.) im Großformat (fig.) **2** (Amer./Commerc./coll.: **~** letter to) **~ sb.** jmdn. anschreiben **3** *in pass.* (fig.: be apparent) **sb. has sth. written in his face** jmdm. steht etw. im Gesicht geschrieben; **guilt was written all over her face** die Schuld stand ihr ins Gesicht geschrieben; **she had 'career woman' written all over her** man sah ihr die Karrierefrau schon von weitem an **4** (Computing) schreiben; **~ in** *or* **into** *or* **on** *or* **to a disk** auf eine Diskette schreiben **5** ▸**underwrite**

Phrasal verbs

- **~ aˈway** *v.i.* **~ away for sth.** etw. [schriftlich] anfordern
- **~ ˈback** *v.i.* zurückschreiben
- **~ ˈdown** *v.t.* **1** (record) aufschreiben **2** (Commerc.: reduce nominal value of) abschreiben (Wirtsch.)
- **~ ˈin**
  A *v.i.* hinschreiben (ugs.); (include) hineinschreiben; **~ in for sth.** etw. [schriftlich] anfordern; **~ in to sb.** an jmdn. schreiben
  B *v.t.* (Amer. Polit.) eintragen; *see also* **write-in**
- **~ ˈoff**
  A *v.t.* **1** (compose with ease) herunterschreiben (ugs.) **2** (cancel) abschreiben ‹*Schulden, Verlust*›; (fig.) **~ sb. off [as a failure** *etc.***]** jmdn. [als Versager] abschreiben (ugs.) **3** (destroy) zu Schrott fahren
  B *v.i.* ▸**~ away.** *see also* **write-off**
- **~ ˈout** *v.t.* **1** ausschreiben ‹*Scheck*›; schreiben ‹*Rezept*› **2** (**~** in final form) ausarbeiten; (**~** in full) ausschreiben **3** (from serial) verschwinden lassen
- **~ ˈup** *v.t.* **1** (praise) eine gute Kritik schreiben über (+ *Akk.*) **2** (**~** account of) einen Bericht schreiben über (+ *Akk.*); (**~** in full) aufarbeiten **3** (bring up to date) auf den neuesten Stand bringen. *see also* **write-up**

write: ~ head *n.* (Computing) Schreibkopf, *der;* **~-in** *n.* (Amer.) *Kandidat, der nicht auf dem offiziellen Stimmzettel steht, sondern vom Wähler selbst eingetragen wird;* **he received 10,000 ~-in votes** sein Name wurde auf zehntausend Stimmzettel geschrieben; **~-off** *n.* (vehicle) Totalschaden, *der;* (person) Versager, *der*/Versagerin, *die;* (event) Reinfall, *der;* **~-ˈonce** *adj.* (Computing) [einmal] beschreibbar; **~-proˈtect** *v.t.* (Computing) schreibschützen; mit einem Schreibschutz versehen; **~ proˈtection** *n., no pl.* (Computing) Schreibschutz, *der*

writer /ˈraɪtə(r)/ *n.* **1** ▸ⓘ **p. 1260** (author) Schriftsteller, *der*/Schriftstellerin, *die;* (of letter, article) Schreiber, *der*/Schreiberin, *die;* Verfasser, *der*/Verfasserin, *die;* (of lyrics, advertisements) Texter, *der*/Texterin, *die;* (of music) Komponist, *der*/Komponistin, *die;* **be a ~:** Schriftsteller/Schriftstellerin sein; **the present ~:** der Autor/die Autorin des vorliegenden Textes; **a ~ of historical fiction** ein Verfasser/eine Verfasserin historischer Romane **2** **be a good/bad ~** (as to handwriting) eine gute/schlechte Schrift haben

writer's ˈcramp *n.* (Med.) Schreibkrampf, *der*

ˈwrite-up *n.* Bericht, *der;* (by critic) Kritik, *die;* **get a good ~:** gut besprochen werden

writhe /raɪð/ *v.i.* (lit. or fig.) sich winden; **he/it makes me ~** (with embarrassment) er/es bringt mich in ziemliche Verlegenheit; (with disgust) er/es ist mir zuwider

writing /ˈraɪtɪŋ/ *n.* **1** Schreiben, *das;* **at the time of ~:** als dies geschrieben wurde; **put sth. in ~:** etw. schriftlich machen (ugs.); *see also* **commit 4** **2** (handwriting) Schrift, *die* **3** (composing) Schreiben, *das;* **creative-~ course** Kurs für kreatives Schreiben; **earn sth. from one's ~:** mit Schreiben etw. verdienen; **this poem is a lovely piece of ~:** dieses Gedicht ist herrlich geschrieben **4** (something written) Schrift, *die;* **the ~s of Plato** die platonischen Schriften; **the ~ on the wall** (fig.) das Menetekel an der Wand; **she's seen the ~ on the wall** sie hat die Zeichen erkannt; **the ~ is on the wall for this department** diese Abteilung hat keine Zukunft

writing: ~ case *n.* Schreibmappe, *die;* **~ desk** *n.* Schreibpult, *das;* Sekretär, *der;* **~ pad** *n.* Schreibblock, *der;* **~ paper** *n.* Schreibpapier, *das;* Briefpapier, *das*

written ▸**write**

wrong /rɒŋ/
A *adj.* **1** (morally bad) unrecht (geh.); (unfair) unge-

W

recht; **you were ~ to be so angry** es war nicht richtig von dir, so ärgerlich zu sein; **what's ~ with sth./that?** was ist gegen etw./dagegen einzuwenden?; **what's ~ with having a drink?** warum sollte man nicht mal ein Glas trinken? **2▸** (mistaken) falsch; **be ~** ‹*Person:*› sich irren; **I was ~ about you** ich habe mich in dir geirrt; **the clock is ~:** die Uhr geht falsch; **the clock is ~ by ten minutes** die Uhr geht 10 Minuten vor/nach; **how ~ can you be** *or* **get!** wie man sich irren kann! **3▸** (not suitable) falsch; **give the ~ answer** eine falsche Antwort geben; **that was the ~ move to make** das war genau das Falsche; **say/do the ~ thing** das Falsche sagen/tun; **you've come to the ~ person** Sie sind bei mir an der falschen Adresse; **be the ~ person for the job** für die Stelle ungeeignet sein; **take the ~ turning** falsch abbiegen; **get hold of the ~ end of the stick** (fig.) alles völlig falsch verstehen; **[the] ~ way round** verkehrt herum; *see also* **go down 2**; **number A 1** **4▸** (out of order) nicht in Ordnung; **there's something ~ here/with him** hier/mit ihm stimmt etwas nicht; **there's nothing ~:** es ist alles in Ordnung; **what's ~?** was ist los? *see also* **wrong side**

B *adv.* falsch; **get it ~:** es falsch *od.* verkehrt machen; (misunderstand) sich irren; **I got the answer ~ again** meine Antwort war wieder falsch; **get sb. ~:** jmdn. falsch verstehen; **go ~** (take ~ path) sich verlaufen; (fig.) ‹*Person:*› vom rechten Weg abkommen (fig. geh.); ‹*Maschine, Mechanismus:*› kaputtgehen (ugs.); ‹*Angelegenheit:*› danebengehen (ugs.); **you can't go ~ if you study engineering** wenn du auf die Ingenieurschule gehst, bist du immer gut daran; **the television/dishwasher has gone ~:** der Fernseher/die Spülmaschine ist kaputt (ugs.)

C *n.* **1▸** (what is morally bad) Unrecht, *das;* **know the difference between right and ~:** zwischen Recht und Unrecht unterscheiden können; **two ~s don't make a right** das gibt nur ein Unrecht mehr; **do ~:** unrecht tun; **she can do no ~:** sie kann überhaupt nichts Unrechtes tun; **be in the ~:** im Unrecht sein; **put sb. in the ~:** jmdn. ins Unrecht setzen **2▸** (injustice) Unrecht, *das* (**towards** gegenüber); **suffer a ~/many ~s** Unrecht/viel Unrecht erleiden; **do sb. a ~:** jmdm. ein Unrecht zufügen; **do ~ to sb., do sb. ~:** jmdm. unrecht tun

D *v.t.* **~ sb.** (treat unjustly) jmdn. ungerecht behandeln; (mistakenly discredit) jmdm. unrecht tun

wrong: ~doer *n.* Übeltäter, *der*/-täterin, *die;* Missetäter, *der*/-täterin, *die* (geh.); **~doing** *n.* **1▸** *no pl., no indef. art.* Missetaten (geh.); **2▸** (instance) Missetat, *die* (geh.); **~-'foot** *v.t.* **1▸** (Sport) **~-foot sb.** jmdn. auf dem falschen Fuß erwischen (Sportjargon); **2▸** (fig. coll.) unvorbereitet treffen; **he was ~-footed by that** darauf war er überhaupt nicht vorbereitet

wrongful /ˈrɒŋfl/ *adj.* **1▸** (unfair) unrecht (geh.) **2▸** (unlawful) rechtswidrig

wrongfully /ˈrɒŋfəlɪ/ *adv.* **1▸** (unfairly) unrecht (geh.) ‹*handeln*›; zu Unrecht ‹*beschuldigen*› **2▸** (unlawfully) rechtswidrig

ˈwrong-headed *adj.* starrköpfig (abwertend) (**about** in + *Dat.*)

wrongly /ˈrɒŋlɪ/ *adv.* **1▸** (inappropriately, incorrectly) falsch **2▸** (mistakenly) zu Unrecht; **I believed, ~, that ...:** ich habe fälschlicherweise geglaubt, dass ... **3▸** ▸**wrongfully 1**

wrongness /ˈrɒŋnɪs/ *n., no pl.* **1▸** (moral ~) Unrecht, *das* **2▸** (inappropriateness, mistakenness) Unrichtigkeit, *die*

wrong: ~ side *n.* **1▸** (of fabric) linke Seite; **[the] ~ side out/up** verkehrt herum; **2▸ be on the ~ side of thirty** die dreißig überschritten haben; **get on the ~ side of sb./the law** (fig.) jmdn. falsch anfassen/mit dem Gesetz in Konflikt geraten; *see also* **bed A 1**; **blanket A 1**; **~ ˈun** *n.* (coll.: person) falscher Fuffziger (salopp)

wrote ▸**write**

wrought ▸**work C 6**

wrought ˈiron *n.* Schmiedeeisen, *das; attrib.* schmiedeeisern ‹*Tor, Zaun*›

wrung ▸**wring**

WRVS *abbr.* (Brit.) = **Women's Royal Voluntary Service** *britischer Hilfsdienst für Menschen in Not*

wry /raɪ/ *adj.*, **~er** *or* **wrier** /ˈraɪə(r)/, **~est** *or* **wriest** /ˈraɪɪst/ ironisch ‹*Blick*›; fein ‹*Humor, Witz*›; **a ~ smile** ein schiefes Lächeln; **make** *or* **pull a ~ face** das Gesicht verziehen

wryly /ˈraɪlɪ/ *adv.* ironisch ‹*blicken, sagen*›; schief ‹*lächeln*›

WSW /westsaʊθˈwest/ *abbr.* ▸**❶ p. 1013** = **west-south-west** WSW

wt. *abbr.* = **weight** Gew.

WTO *abbr.* ▸ **World Trade Organization**

WW *abbr.* (Amer.) = **World War** WK

WWW *abbr.* = **World Wide Web** WWW

wych hazel /ˈwɪtʃheɪzl/ *n.* **1▸** (shrub) Virginische Zaubernuss **2▸** (lotion) Hamameliswasser, *das*

WYSIWYG /ˈwɪzɪwɪg/ *n., no pl.* WYSIWYG, *das; attrib.* WYSIWYG-‹*Textverarbeitung, Editor*›

X¹, x /eks/ *n., pl.* **Xs** *or* **X's** /'eksɪz/ 1 (letter) X, x, *das* 2 (Math.) x 3 (unknown person or number) **Mr X** Herr X; **x tons of cement** soundso viel Tonnen Zement; **x number of ...** (coll.) x ... (ugs.) 4 (Roman numeral) X 5 (cross-shaped symbol) Kreuz, *das;* **x marks the spot** die Stelle ist durch ein Kreuz markiert

X² *symb.* (Brit. Hist.) nicht jugendfrei

xenon /'zenɒn, 'zi:-/ *n.* (Chem.) Xenon, *das; attrib.* Xenon‹*licht, -scheinwerfer*›

xenophobe /'zenəfəʊb/ *n.* Fremdenfeindliche, *der/die;* Xenophobe, *der/die*

xenophobia /zenə'fəʊbɪə/ *n.* Fremdenfeindlichkeit, *die;* Xenophobie, *die*

xenophobic /zenə'fəʊbɪk/ *adj.* fremdenfeindlich; xenophob

xerography /zɪə'rɒgrəfɪ, ze'rɒgrəfɪ/ *n.* Xerographie, *die* (Druckw.)

Xerox ®, xerox /'zɪərɒks, 'zerɒks/

A *n.* 1 (process) Xerographie, *die* (Druckw.) 2 (copy) Xerokopie, *die*

B **xerox** *v.t.* xerokopieren

Xmas /'krɪsməs, 'eksməs/ *n.* (coll.) Weihnachten, *das*

XML *abbr.* **= Extensible Markup Language**

X-rated /'eksreɪtɪd/ *adj.* (Brit. Hist.) nicht jugendfrei ‹*Film*›

'X-ray

A *n.* 1 *in pl.* Röntgenstrahlen *Pl.;* X-Strahlen *Pl.* 2 (picture) Röntgenaufnahme, *die* 3 *attrib.* Röntgen-

B *v.t.* röntgen; durchleuchten ‹*Gepäck*›

X-ray 'eyes *n. pl.* Röntgenaugen *Pl.*

xylophone /'zaɪləfəʊn/ *n.* (Mus.) Xylophon, *das*

Yy

Y¹, y /waɪ/ *n., pl.* **Ys** *or* **Y's** 1 (letter) Y, y, *das* 2 (Math.) y
Y² *abbr.* 1 (Amer.) = **YMCA/YWCA** CVJM/CVJF 2 = **yen**
y. *abbr.* = **year[s]** J.
yacht /jɒt/
A *n.* 1 (for racing) Segelboot, *das;* Segeljacht, *die* 2 (for pleasure travel etc.) Jacht, *die*
B *v.i.* segeln
'yacht club *n.* Jachtklub, *der*
yachting /'jɒtɪŋ/ *n., no pl., no art.* Segeln, *das; attrib.* Segel-
yachtsman /'jɒtsmən/ *n., pl.* **yachtsmen** /'jɒtsmən/ Segler, *der*
yack /jæk/, **yackety-yack** /jækətɪ'jæk/ (coll. derog.)
A *ns.* Gequassel, *das* (ugs. abwertend)
B *v.i.* quasseln (ugs. abwertend)
yah /jɑː/ *int.* ~ **[boo sucks]** bäh
yahoo /jə'huː/ *n.* Untier, *das* (fig.)
yak /jæk/ *n.* (Zool.) Jak, *der*
Yale/jeɪl/: ~ **key** ® *n.* Yaleschlüssel, *der* (Wz) (Technik); ≈ Sicherheitsschlüssel, *der;* ~ **lock** ® *n.* Yaleschloss, *das* (Wz) (Technik); ≈ [Zylinder]-sicherheitsschloss, *das*
Yalta /'jæltə/ *pr. n.* Jalta *(das)*
yam /jæm/ *n.* 1 (plant, tuber) Jamswurzel, *die* 2 (Amer.) ▶**sweet potato**
yammer /'jæmə(r)/ (coll./dial.)
A *v.i.* maulen (ugs.); **he's always ~ing on about sth.** dauernd muss er über etw. *(Akk.)* maulen
B *n.* Gemaule, *das* (ugs. abwertend)
yang /jæŋ/ *n., no pl., no indef. art.* (Chinese Philos.) Yang, *das*
yank (coll.)
A *v.t.* reißen an (+ *Dat.*); ~ **sth. off/out** etw. ab-/ausreißen
B *n.* Reißen, *das;* **give a ~ at sth.** an etw. *(Dat.)* reißen; **give the rope a good ~:** kräftig am Seil ziehen
Yank /jæŋk/
A *n.* 1 (Brit. coll.: American) Yankee, *der;* Ami, *der* (ugs.) 2 (Amer.: inhabitant of New England or northern States) Yankee, *der*
B *adj.* 1 (Brit. coll.: American) Ami- (ugs.) 2 (Amer.: of New England or northern States) Yankee-
Yankee /'jæŋkɪ/ ▶**Yank**
yap /jæp/
A *v.i.*, **-pp-** 1 (bark shrilly) kläffen 2 (coll.: talk) quatschen (salopp abwertend); (complainingly) lamentieren (ugs. abwertend)
B *n.* Kläffen, *das;* **give a ~:** kläffen
yarborough /'jɑːbərə/ *n.* (Cards) *Blatt (bei Whist und Bridge), bei dem keine Karte höher als 9 ist*
yard¹ /jɑːd/ *n.* 1 ▶ⓘ **p. 911**, ▶ⓘ **p. 1072**, ▶ⓘ **p. 1286** Yard, *das;* **by the ~:** ≈ meterweise; (fig.) am laufenden Band (ugs.); **sell books by the ~** (fig.) Bücher meterweise verkaufen; **have a face a ~ long** ein Gesicht wie drei Tage Regenwetter machen 2 *in pl.* (coll.: great amount) **have/get** *etc.* **~s of sth.** etw. massenweise haben/bekommen *usw.;* **~s of toilet paper** meterweise Toilettenpapier 3 (Naut.) Rah[e], *die* 4 ~ **of ale** (Brit.) [Stangen]glas, *das;* Stange, *die* (bes. westd.) 5 ▶**square B 2** 6 ▶**cubic 2**
yard² *n.* 1 (attached to building) Hof, *der;* **in the ~:** auf dem Hof 2 (for manufacture) Werkstatt, *die;* (for storage) Lager, *das;* (ship~) Werft, *die;* **builder's ~:** Bauhof, *der* 3 (Amer.: garden) Garten, *der* 4 **the Y~** (Brit. coll.) ▶**Scotland Yard**. *See also* **back yard; goods yard**
yard: ~**arm** *n.* (Naut.) Rahnock, *das od. die;* ~**stick** *n.* 1 Messstab, *der;* Maßstab, *der* (veralt.); 2 (fig.: standard) Maßstab, *der*
yarn /jɑːn/
A *n.* 1 (thread) Garn, *das* 2 (coll.: story) Geschichte, *die;* (of sailor) [Seemanns]garn, *das;* **have a ~ with sb.** (chat) mit jmdm. plauschen (bes. südd.) *od.* klönen (nordd.); *see also* **spin A 1**
B *v.i.* (coll.) Geschichten erzählen; ‹*Seemann:*› [s]ein Garn spinnen
yarrow /'jærəʊ/ *n.* (Bot.) Schafgarbe, *die*
yashmak /'jæʃmæk/ *n.* Jaschmak, *der*
yaw /jɔː/ (Naut., Aeronaut.)
A *v.i.* gieren
B *n.* Gieren, *das*
yawl /jɔːl/ *n.* (Naut.) Yawl, *die;* Heckmaster, *der*
yawn /jɔːn/
A *n.* 1 Gähnen, *das;* **give a [long] ~:** [herzhaft] gähnen; **there were a few ~s** es wurde ein paarmal gegähnt 2 **be a ~** (coll.: be boring) zum Gähnen langweilig sein
B *v.i.* 1 gähnen; ~ **with exhaustion** vor Müdigkeit gähnen 2 (fig.) ‹*Abgrund, Kluft, Spalte:*› gähnen (geh.)
yawning /'jɔːnɪŋ/ *adj.* gähnend (auch fig. geh.)
yawp /jɔːp/ (Amer.)
A *v.i.* 1 (squawk) kreischen 2 (talk foolishly) faseln (ugs. abwertend)
B *n.* 1 (squawk) Gekreisch[e], *das* 2 (foolish talk) Gefasel, *das* (ugs. abwertend)
yaws /jɔːz/ *n. sing.* (Med.) Himbeerpocken *Pl.;* Frambösie, *die* (fachspr.)
yd[s]. *abbr.* ▶ⓘ **p. 911**, ▶ⓘ **p. 1072**, ▶ⓘ **p. 1286** = **yard[s]** Yd[s].
ye¹ /jiː/ *pron.* (arch./poet./dial./joc.) Ihr (veralt.); (as direct or indirect object) Euch (veralt.)
ye² *adj.* (pseudo-arch.) = **the**
yea /jeɪ/ (arch.)
A *adv.* ja
B *n.* Ja, *das;* **~s and nays** Ja- und Neinstimmen; ~ **and nay** Ja und Nein
yeah /jeə/ *adv.* (coll.) ja; **[oh] ~?** [ach] ja?
year /jɪə(r)/ *n.* 1 ▶ⓘ **p. 894**, ▶ⓘ **p. 1047** Jahr, *das;* **she gets £10,000 a ~:** sie verdient 10 000 Pfund im Jahr; ~ **in ~ out** jahrein, jahraus; ~ **after ~:** Jahr für *od.* um Jahr; **all [the] ~ round** das ganze Jahr hindurch; **in a ~['s time]** in einem Jahr; **once a ~, once every ~:** einmal im Jahr; **Christian** *or* **Church** *or* **ecclesiastical ~** (Eccl.) Kirchenjahr, *das;* liturgisches Jahr (kath. Kirche); **a ten-~-old** ein Zehnjähriger/eine Zehnjährige; **a ten-~[s]-old child/animal/thing** ein zehn Jahre altes Kind/Tier/Ding; **in her thirtieth ~:** in ihrem 30. Lebensjahr; **financial** *or* **fiscal** *or* **tax ~:** Finanz- *od.* Rechnungsjahr, *das;* **calendar** *or* **civil ~:** Kalenderjahr, *das;* **school ~:** Schuljahr, *das;* **for a ~ and a day** ein Jahr und einen Tag [lang]; **a ~ [from] today** *etc.* heute *usw.* in einem Jahr; **a ~ [ago] today** *etc.* heute *usw.* vor einem Jahr; **... of the ~** (best) ... des Jahres; *see also* **by¹ A 13; dot A 3; from 2; grace A 5; leap year; lord A 2; sabbatical A** 2 (group of students) Jahrgang, *der;* **first-~ student** Student/Studentin im ersten Jahr 3 *in pl.* (age) **he doesn't look his ~s** man sieht ihm seine Jahre nicht an; **be old for** *or* **beyond one's ~s** (unexpectedly mature) für sein Alter schon sehr reif sein; (looking older than one is) älter wirken, als man ist; **be young for one's ~s** jünger wirken, als man ist; **be getting on/be well on in ~s** in die Jahre kommen/in vorgerücktem Alter sein (geh.) 4 *in pl.* (very long time) Jahre; **she looks ~s older** sie sieht um Jahre älter aus; **sth. has put ~s on sb.** etw. hat jmdn. um Jahre altern lassen; **take ~s off sb./sb.'s life** jmdn. um Jahre jünger/älter machen
'yearbook *n.* Jahrbuch, *das*
yearling /'jɪəlɪŋ/
A *n.* (Zool., Agric.) Jährling, *der*
B *adj.* (a year old) einjährig
'year-long *adj.* (lasting a year) einjährig; (lasting the whole year) ganzjährig
yearly /'jɪəlɪ/
A *adj.* 1 (annual) jährlich; **ten-~:** zehnjährig; **at twice-~ intervals** zweimal im Jahr 2 (lasting a year) Einjahres‹*vertrag, -abonnement*›
B *adv.* jährlich
yearn /jɜːn/ *v.i.* ~ **for** *or* **after sth./for sb./to do sth.** sich nach etw./jmdm. sehnen/sich danach sehnen, etw. zu tun
yearning /'jɜːnɪŋ/
A *n.* Sehnsucht, *die*
B *adj.* sehnsüchtig ‹*Blick, Liebe*›; sehnlich ‹*Wunsch, Gebet*›
year-on-'year *adj.* Jahres‹*wachstum, -steigerung, -rückgang*›
'year-round *adj.* ganzjährig
yeast /jiːst/ *n.* Hefe, *die*
yeast: ~ **cake** *n.* 1 (mass of ~) Hefewürfel, *der;* 2 (cake made with ~) Hefekuchen, *der;* ~ **pastry** *n.* Hefeteig, *der*
yeasty /'jiːstɪ/ *adj.* hefig
yell /jel/
A *n.* 1 gellender Schrei; **let out a ~:** einen Schrei ausstoßen; **when supper's ready, I'll give you a ~** (coll.) wenn das Abendessen fertig ist, rufe ich dich 2 (Amer.: students' cry) Anfeuerungsruf, *der*
B *v.i.* [gellend] schreien; ~ **with rage/laughter** wütend schreien/vor Lachen brüllen; ~ **at each other** einander anschreien
C *v.t.* [gellend] schreien
yellow /'jeləʊ/
A *adj.* 1 gelb; flachsblond ‹*Haar*›; golden ‹*Getreide*›; vergilbt ‹*Papier*› 2 (fig. coll.: cowardly) feige; **have got/show a ~ streak** feige *od.* ein Feigling sein. *See also* **flag¹ A**
B *n.* 1 (colour) Gelb, *das* 2 (pigment) Gelbton, *der* 3 (~ clothes) **dressed in ~:** gelb gekleidet 4 (Snooker) gelbe Kugel 5 (butterfly) Gelbling, *der;* (brimstone) Zitronenfalter, *der;* **clouded ~:** Postillon, *der*
C *v.t. & i.* vergilben
yellow: ~**-belly** *n.* (sl. derog.) Feigling, *der* (ugs.); ~ **'card** *n.* (Footb.) gelbe Karte; **be shown a ~ 'card:** Gelb sehen (Jargon); eine gelbe Karte bekommen; ~ **'fever** *n.* ▶ⓘ **p. 1231** (Med.) Gelbfieber, *das;* ~**hammer** *n.* (Ornith.) Goldammer, *die*
yellowish /'jeləʊɪʃ/ *adj.* gelblich
yellow 'line *n.* (Brit.) gelbe [Markierungs]linie; **I'm on double ~s** ich stehe im Parkverbot
yellowness /'jeləʊnɪs/ *n., no pl.* gelbe Farbe
Yellow 'Pages ® *n. pl.* gelbe Seiten; Branchenverzeichnis, *das*

yelp /jelp/
A *v.i.* aufheulen (ugs.); ‹*Hund:*› jaulen
B *n.* Heulen, *das;* (of dog) Jaulen, *das;* **the child/dog gave a ~:** das Kind heulte auf/der Hund jaulte

yelping /ˈjelpɪŋ/ *n.* Geheule, *das* (ugs.); (of dog) Gejaule, *das*

Yemen /ˈjemən/ *pr. n.* **[the] ~:** [der] Jemen

Yemeni /ˈjemənɪ/ ▸ⓘ **p. 1345**
A *adj.* jemenitisch
B *n.* Jemenit, *der*/Jemenitin, *die*

Yemenite /ˈjemənaɪt/ *n.* ▸**Yemeni B**

yen¹ /jen/ *n., pl. same* ▸ⓘ **p. 1332** (Japanese currency) Yen, *der*

yen² *n.* (coll.: longing) Drang, *der* (**for** nach); **sb. has a ~ to do sth.** es drängt jmdn. danach, etw. zu tun

yeoman /ˈjəʊmən/ *n., pl.* **yeomen** /ˈjəʊmən/ **1** (Hist.: with small estate) Kleinbauer, *der* **2** (Hist.: freeholder) Freisasse, *der* **3** (Brit. Mil. Hist.) Angehöriger der Yeomanry **4** **~ [of signals]** (Brit. Navy) Signalmaat, *der* **5** (Amer. Navy) *Marineunteroffizier, der mit Verwaltungsarbeiten betraut ist*

Yeoman of the 'Guard *n.* (Brit. Mil.) königlicher Leibgardist; (in popular use: warder in Tower of London) Wärter im Tower von London

yeomanry /ˈjəʊmənrɪ/ *n., no pl.* **1** (Hist.: farmers) Kleinbauer *Pl.* **2** (Brit. Mil. Hist.) Yeomanry, *die (hist.); berittene Freiwilligentruppe*

'yeoman['s] service *n.* (dated) **give sb. ~:** jmdm. gute Dienste tun; **do ~:** gute Dienste leisten

yep /jep/ *int.* (coll.) ja

yes /jes/
A *adv.* ja; (in contradiction) doch; **~, sir** jawohl!; **I didn't do it! — Oh ~ you did!** Ich war es nicht! — Doch warst du es!; **~?** (indeed?) ach ja?; (what do you want?) ja?; (to customer) ja, bitte?; **say '~'** Ja sagen; **say ~ to a proposal** einem Vorschlag zustimmen; **she'll say ~ to anything** sie sagt zu allem Ja und Amen; **~ and no** ja und nein; jein (scherzh.); *see also* **oh¹**
B *n., pl.* **~es** Ja, *das*

'yes-man *n.* (coll. derog.) Jasager, *der* (abwertend)

yes-'no question *n.* Entscheidungsfrage, *die*

yesterday /ˈjestədeɪ, ˈjestədɪ/ ▸ⓘ **p. 1048**
A *n.* **1** gestern; **the day before ~:** vorgestern; **~'s paper** die gestrige Zeitung; die Zeitung von gestern; **~ morning/afternoon/evening/night** gestern Vormittag/Nachmittag/Abend/Nacht; **a week [from] ~:** gestern in einer Woche; **a year [ago] ~:** gestern vor einem Jahr; **~ evening's concert** das Konzert gestern Abend *od.* am gestrigen Abend **2** (recent time) **of ~:** von gestern; **all our ~s** unsere Vergangenheit; **be ~'s men** passé sein
B *adv.* **1** gestern; **the day before ~:** vorgestern; **~ morning/afternoon/evening/night** gestern Vormittag/Nachmittag/Abend/Nacht **2** (in the recent past) gestern; *see also* **born A**

yet /jet/
A *adv.* **1** (still) noch; **have ~ to reach sth.** etw. erst noch erreichen müssen; **have a few days free ~:** noch ein paar Tage frei haben; **much ~ remains to be done** noch bleibt viel zu tun; *see also* **as D** **2** (hitherto) bisher; **the play is his best ~:** das Stück ist sein bisher bestes **3** *neg. or interrog.* (so soon as now/then) **not [just] ~:** [jetzt] noch nicht; **never ~:** noch nie; **need you go just ~?** musst du [jetzt] schon gehen?; **is he dead ~?** ist er schon gestorben?; **you haven't seen anything** *or* (coll.) **ain't seen nothing ~:** das ist noch gar nichts **4** (before all is over) doch noch; **he could win ~:** er könnte noch gewinnen **5** *with compar.* (even) noch ‹*länger, kürzer usw.*› **6** (nevertheless) doch; **..., and ~ she still loves him** ..., und doch liebt sie ihn immer noch **7** (again) noch; **~ again** *or* **once more** noch einmal; **nor ~:** noch [...] jemals; **she has never voted for that party, nor ~ intends to** sie hat nie für diese Partei gestimmt und sie hat es auch nicht vor
B *conj.* doch; **a faint ~ unmistakable smell** ein schwacher, aber unverkennbarer Geruch

yeti /ˈjetɪ/ *n.* Yeti, *der;* Schneemensch, *der*

yew /juː/ *n.* **1** (tree) Eibe, *die* **2** (wood) Eibenholz, *das*

'yew tree ▸**yew 1**

'Y-fronts ® *n. pl. Herrenunterhose mit y-förmiger Vorderseite*

YHA *abbr.* (Brit.) **= Youth Hostels Association** Jugendherbergsverband, *der*

Yid /jɪd/ *n.* (sl. derog.) Itzig, *der* (ugs. abwertend)

Yiddish /ˈjɪdɪʃ/ ▸ⓘ **p. 1277**
A *adj.* jiddisch; *see also* **English A**
B *n.* Jiddisch, *das; see also* **English B 1**

yield /jiːld/
A *v.t.* **1** (give) bringen; hervorbringen ‹*Ernte*›; tragen ‹*Obst*›; abwerfen ‹*Gewinn*›; ergeben ‹*Resultat, Informationen*› **2** (surrender) übergeben ‹*Festung*›; lassen ‹*Vortritt*›; abtreten ‹*Besitz*› (**to** an + *Akk.*); **~ the point** [in diesem Punkt] nachgeben; **~ a point to sb.** jmdm. in einem Punkt nachgeben; **~ ground to the enemy** vor dem Feind zurückweichen; **~ right of way** Vorfahrt gewähren
B *v.i.* **1** (surrender) sich unterwerfen; **~ to threats/temptation** Drohungen (*Dat.*) nachgeben/der Versuchung (*Dat.*) erliegen; **~ to persuasion/sb.'s entreaties** sich überreden lassen/jmds. Bitten (*Dat.*) nachgeben; **the girl had ~ed to the wily seducer** das Mädchen war dem raffinierten Verführer erlegen **2** (be or feel inferior) **~ to none in sth.** niemandem in etw. (*Dat.*) nachstehen **3** (give right of way) Vorfahrt gewähren **4** (Amer.: allow another the right to speak) **~ to sb.** jmdm. das Wort überlassen
C *n.* **1** Ertrag, *der* **2** (revenue from tax etc.) Aufkommen, *das* **3** (return on investment) Zins[ertrag], *der;* **a 10% ~:** 10% Zinsen; **the ~ on this bond** die Zinsen für dieses Wertpapier

Phrasal verb
• **~ 'up** *v.t.* **1** (surrender) übergeben ‹*Stadt, Festung*›; ausliefern ‹*Gefangenen, sich selbst*› **2** (reveal) enthüllen ‹*Geheimnis*›; hervorbringen ‹*Reichtum, Ertrag, Ernte*›

'yield point *n.* (Phys.) Fließgrenze, *die*

yin /jɪn/ *n., no pl., no indef. art.* (Chinese Philos.) Yin, *das*

yip /jɪp/ (Amer.)
A *v.i.*, **-pp-** ▸**yelp A**
B *n.* ▸**yelp B**

yippee /ˈjɪpiː, jɪˈpiː/ *int.* hurra

YMCA *abbr.* **= Young Men's Christian Association** CVJM

yob /jɒb/, *n.* (Brit. coll.) Rowdy, *der* (abwertend)

yobbish /ˈjɒbɪʃ/ *adj.* (Brit. coll.) rowdyhaft

yobbo /ˈjɒbəʊ/ *n. pl.* **~s** ▸**yob**

yodel /ˈjəʊdl/
A *v.i. & t.*, (Brit.) **-ll-** jodeln
B *n.* Jodeln, *das*

Yoga /ˈjəʊgə/ *n.* Yoga, *der od. das*

yoghurt /ˈjɒgət/ *n.* Joghurt, *der od. das*

yogi /ˈjəʊgɪ/ *n.* (Hindu Philos.) Yogi[n], *der*

yogurt ▸**yoghurt**

yo-heave-ho /ˈjəʊhiːvhəʊ/ **= heave ho** ▸**heave B 2**

yo[-ho]-ho /jəʊ(həʊ)ˈhəʊ/ *int.* **1** (to attract attention) he (ugs.) **2** **= heave ho** ▸**heave B 2**

yoke /jəʊk/
A *n.* **1** (for animal) Joch, *das* **2** (for person) [Trag]joch, *das* **3** (of garment) Sattel, *der* (Textilw.) **4** (fig.: bond, oppressive control) Joch, *das* (geh.) **5** (pair of oxen etc.) Joch, *das*
B *v.t.* **1** ins Joch spannen ‹*Tier*›; **~ an animal to sth.** ein Tier vor etw. (*Akk.*) spannen **2** (fig.: couple) verbinden

yokel /ˈjəʊkl/ *n.* (derog.) [Bauern]tölpel, *der*

yolk /jəʊk/ *n.* Dotter, *der od. das;* Eigelb, *das*

'yolk sac *n.* (Zool.) Dottersack, *der*

Yom Kippur /jɒm ˈkɪpə(r)/ **= Day of Atonement** ▸**atonement 2**

yomp /jɒmp/ (esp. Mil. coll.) *v.i.* sich schleppen

yon /jɒn/ (arch./poet./dial.) **1** *adj* **~ mountain/field** jener Berg/jenes Feld dort (geh.) **2** *adv.* dort drüben

yonder /ˈjɒndə(r)/ (literary)
A *adj.* **~ tree/peasant** jener Baum/Bauer dort (geh.)
B *adv.* dort drüben

yonks /jɒŋks/ *n. pl.* (Brit. coll.) **for ~:** seit ewigen Zeiten (ugs.); **I haven't seen him for ~:** ich hab ihn ewig nicht gesehen (ugs.); **~ ago** vor ewigen Zeiten (ugs.)

yoof /juːf/ *n. attrib.* (coll.) Jugend-; **have ~ appeal** für Jugendliche *od.* die Jugend attraktiv wirken *od.* sein

yoo-hoo /ˈjuːhuː/ *int.* juhu

yore /jɔː(r)/ *n.* (literary/joc.) **of ~:** von früher [her] ‹*kennen*›; **customs of ~:** Bräuche von einst; **in days of ~:** in früheren Tagen; in anno dazumal (ugs. scherzh.)

yorker /ˈjɔːkə(r)/ *n.* (Cricket) *Ball, der so geworfen wird, dass er direkt vor dem Schlagmann auftrifft*

Yorkist /ˈjɔːkɪst/ (Hist.)
A *adj.* zum Hause York gehörig; des Hauses York *nachgestellt*
B *n.* Mitglied/Anhänger des Hauses York

Yorkshire /ˈjɔːkʃɪə(r), ˈjɔːkʃə(r)/: **~man** /ˈjɔːkʃɪəmən, jɔːkʃəmən/ *n., pl.* **~men** /ˈjɔːkʃɪəmən, jɔːkʃəmən/ Mann aus Yorkshire; **~ 'pudding** *n.* (Gastr.) Yorkshirepudding, *der;* **~ 'terrier** *n.* Yorkshireterrier, *der;* **~ tyke** ▸**tyke 3**; **~woman** *n.* Frau aus Yorkshire

you /jʊ, *stressed* ˈjuː/ *pron.* **1** *sing./pl.* du/ihr; *as polite address sing. or pl.* Sie; *as direct object* dich/euch/Sie; *as indirect object* dir/euch/Ihnen; *refl.* dich/dir/euch/sich; **it was ~:** du warst/ihr wart/Sie waren es; **~-know-what/-who** du weißt/ihr wisst/Sie wissen schon, was/wer/wen/wem; **that hat is not quite ~:** dieser Hut passt nicht ganz zu dir/Ihnen **2** (one) man; **smoking is bad for ~:** Rauchen ist ungesund. *See also* **he¹**; **her¹**; **your**; **yours**; **yourself**; **yourselves**

'you-all *pron.* (Amer. coll.) ihr/Sie [alle]

you'd /jʊd, *stressed* juːd/ **1** **= you had** **2** **= you would**

you-know-'what *n.* Du-weißt-schon-was, *der/die/das*

you-know-'who *n.* Du-weißt-schon-wer, *der/die;* Dingsbums, *der/die* (ugs.)

you'll /jʊl, *stressed* juːl/ **1** **= you will** **2** **= you shall**

young /jʌŋ/
A *adj.*, **~er** /ˈjʌŋgə(r)/, **~est** /ˈjʌŋgɪst/ **1** ▸ⓘ **p. 894** (lit. or fig.) jung; neu, jung ‹*Wein*›; **a very ~ child** ein ganz kleines Kind; **the ~ boys** die [kleinen] Jungen; **~ at heart** im Herzen jung geblieben; **sb. is not getting any ~er** jmd. wird auch nicht jünger; **you ~ rascal** du [kleiner] Racker (fam.); **you're only ~ once** man ist nur einmal jung; **she's a ~ sixty** sie ist eine jung gebliebene Sechzigerin; **the night is still ~:** die Nacht ist jung; **~ Jones** der junge Jones (ugs.); **at a ~ age** in jungen Jahren; **he's not as ~ as he used to be** er ist nicht mehr der Jüngste **2** ▸ⓘ **p. 894** *in compar.* (of two namesakes) jünger; (Scot.: heir) Erbe, *der;* **Teniers the Y~er** Teniers der Jüngere **3** (characteristic of youth) jugendlich; **~ love/fashion** junge Liebe/Mode **4** (Polit.) **Y~ Conservatives** *etc.* Junge Konservative *usw. See also* **hopeful B**; **married B**; **shoulder A 2**; **year 3**
B *n. pl.* (of animals) Junge; (of humans) Kinder; **with ~:** trächtig; **the ~** (**~** people) die jungen Leute; **~ and old** Jung und Alt

young: ~ 'blood ▸**blood A 3**; **~ day[s]** *n.* [*pl.*] Jugendjahre *Pl.*; **in my ~ days** in meiner Jugend[zeit]; **~ 'family** *n.* junge Familie; **have a ~ family** kleine Kinder haben; **~ 'fogey** *n.: junger angepasster und erzkonservativer Mann*

youngish /ˈjʌŋgɪʃ/ *adj.* ziemlich jung

young: ~ 'lady *n.* **1** junge Dame; **2** (girlfriend) Freundin, *die;* **~ 'man** *n.* **1** junger Mann; **2** (boyfriend) Freund, *der;* **~ of'fender** *n.* (Brit. Law) jugendlicher Straftäter/jugendliche Straftäterin; **Y~ Pretender** ▸**pretender**

youngster /ˈjʌŋstə(r)/ *n.* **1** (child) Kleine, *der/die/das* **2** (young person) Jugendliche, *der/die;* **you're just a ~ compared with me** im Vergleich zu mir bist du noch jung; **come on, you ~s!** kommt, ihr jungen Hüpfer! (ugs.)

young: ~ thing *n.* junges Ding (ugs.); **~ 'un** *n.* (coll.) **he's only a ~ 'un** er ist noch jung; **all**

the ∼ 'uns das ganze junge Gemüse (ugs.); **∼ 'woman** *n.* 1 junge Frau; 2 (girlfriend) Freundin, *die*

your /jə(r), *stressed* jʊə(r), jɔ:(r)/ *poss. pron. attrib.* 1 (of you, sing./pl.) dein/euer; *in polite address* Ihr; **∼ average TV viewer** (coll.) der durchschnittliche Fernsehzuschauer 2 (one's) **it's bad for ∼ health/eyesight** es ist schlecht für die Gesundheit/Augen. *See also* **her²**; **our 1**

you're /jə(r), *stressed* jʊə(r), jɔ:(r)/ **= you are**

yours /jʊəz, jɔ:z/ *poss. pron. pred.* 1 (to or of you, sing.) deiner/deine/dein[e]s; (to or of you, pl.) eurer/eure/eures; *in polite address* Ihrer/Ihre/Ihr[e]s; **you and ∼:** du und die Deinen/das Deine; **what's ∼?** (coll.) was nimmst du/nehmen Sie?; *see also* **hers**; **ours** 2 (your letter) Ihr Brief; (Commerc.) Ihr Schreiben 3 ▸ℹ **p. 1287** (ending letter) **∼ Richard** Herzliche Grüße Richard; **∼ truly** (in business letter) mit freundlichen Grüßen; (joc.: I) meine Wenigkeit (scherzh.); *see also* **ever 1**; **faithfully**; **sincerely 3**; **up B 6**

yourself /jə'self, jʊə'self, jɔ:'self/ *pron.* 1 *emphat.* selbst; **for ∼:** für dich/Sie selbst; **you must do sth. for ∼:** du musst selbst etw. tun; **how's ∼?** (coll.) wie gehts? (ugs.); (as reply) und selbst? (ugs.); **relax and be ∼:** entspann dich und gib dich ganz natürlich 2 *refl.* dich/dir/sich. *See also* **herself**; **myself**

yourselves /jə'selvz, jʊə'selvz, jɔ:'selvz/ *pron.* 1 *emphat.* selbst; **for ∼:** für euch/Sie selbst 2 *refl.* euch/sich. *See also* **herself**; **ourselves**

youth /ju:θ/ *n.* 1 *no pl., no art.* Jugend, *die*; **she has kept her ∼:** sie hat sich (*Dat.*) ihr jugendliches Aussehen bewahrt 2 *pl.* **∼s** /ju:ðz/ (young man) Jugendliche, *der* 3 *constr. as pl.* (young people) Jugend, *die* 4 *no pl., no art.* (fig.: early stage of development etc.) Anfangsstadium, *das*; **in its [early] ∼:** in den [ersten] Anfängen

youth: ∼ centre *n.* Jugendzentrum, *das*; **∼ club** *n.* Jugendklub, *der*; **∼ culture** *n.*, *no pl.* Jugendkultur, *die*; **∼ 'custody** *n.*, *no pl.* (Brit.) Jugendstrafe, *die*; **∼ 'custody centre** *n.* (Brit.) Jugendstrafanstalt, *die*

youthful /'ju:θfl/ *adj.* jugendlich

youthfulness /'ju:θflnɪs/ *n.*, *no pl.* 1 (being young) Jugend, *die* 2 (having freshness of youth) Jugendlichkeit, *die*

youth: ∼ hostel *n.* Jugendherberge, *die*; **∼ hosteller** *n.* Herbergsgast, *der*; **∼ work** *n.*, *no pl.* Jugendarbeit, *die*; **∼ worker** *n.* ▸ℹ **p. 1260** Jugendarbeiter, *der*/-arbeiterin, *die*

you've /jʊv, *stressed* ju:v/ **= you have**

yowl /jaʊl/
A *n.* **∼[s]** Jaulen, *das*; (of cat) Maunzen, *das*; (of wolf) Heulen, *das*; **give a ∼:** jaulen/maunzen/heulen
B *v.i.* jaulen; ‹*Katze:*› maunzen; ‹*Wolf:*› heulen

yo-yo ® /'jəʊjəʊ/ *n.*, *pl.* **∼s** Jo-Jo, *das*

'yo-yo effect *n.* Yo-Yo-Effekt, *der*

yr. *abbr.* 1 **= year[s]** J. 2 **= your**

yrs. *abbr.* 1 **= years** J. 2 **= yours**

'Y-shaped *adj.* y-förmig

yucca /'jʌkə/ *n.* (Bot.) Yucca, *die*; Palmlilie, *die*

yuck ▸ **yuk**

yucky ▸ **yukky**

Yugoslav /'ju:gəslɑ:v/ ▸ℹ **p. 1345** ▸ **Yugoslavian**

Yugoslavia /ju:gə'slɑ:vɪə/ *pr. n.* Jugoslawien (*das*)

Yugoslavian /ju:gə'slɑ:vɪən/ ▸ℹ **p. 1345**
A *adj.* 1 jugoslawisch; **sb. is ∼:** jmd. ist Jugoslawe/Jugoslawin 2 (Ling.) ▸ **Serbo-Croat B**
B *n.* 1 (person) Jugoslawe, *der*/Jugoslawin, *die* 2 (Ling.) ▸ **Serbo-Croat A**

yuk /jʌk/ *int.* (coll.) bäh; äks

yukky /'jʌkɪ/ *adj.* (coll.) eklig

yule /ju:l/ ▸ **Yuletide**

yule: ∼ log *n.* Weihnachtsblock, *der* (Volksk.); (in Scandinavia) Julblock, *der* (Volksk.); **Y∼tide** *n.* (arch.) Weihnachtszeit, *die*

yummy /'jʌmɪ/ (coll.)
A *adj.* lecker
B *int.* (child lang.) lecker, lecker; (not referring to food) au fein

yum-yum /jʌm'jʌm/ *int.* lecker, lecker

yuppie /'jʌpɪ/ *n.* (coll.) Yuppie, *der*

yuppie 'flu *n.* ▸ℹ **p. 1231** (coll.) Yuppiegrippe, *die*

yuppified /'jʌpɪfaɪd/ *adj.* (coll.) yuppifiziert; yuppihaft

yuppify /'jʌpɪfaɪ/ *v.t.* (coll.) yuppifizieren ‹*Gegend, Stadtteil*›

yurt /jɜ:t/ *n.* Jurte, *die*

YWCA *abbr.* **= Young Women's Christian Association** CVJF

y

Zz

Z, **z** /zed, (Amer.) zi:/ *n.*, *pl.* **Zs** *or* **Z's** 1 (letter) Z, z, *das* 2 (Math.) z

zabaglione /zabɑ'ljəʊnɪ/ *n.* (Gastr.) Zabaglione, *die*; Zabaione, *die*

Zaire /zɑ:'ɪə(r)/ *pr. n.* Zaire (*das*)

Zambezi /zæm'bi:zɪ/ *pr. n.* ▸❶ **p. 1491** Sambesi, *der*

Zambia /'zæmbɪə/ *pr. n.* Sambia (*das*)

Zambian /'zæmbɪən/ ▸❶ **p. 1345**
A *adj.* sambisch
B *n.* Sambier, *der*/Sambierin, *die*

zany /'zeɪnɪ/ *adj.* irre komisch (ugs.); Wahnsinns‹*humor, -komiker*›

Zanzibar /zænzɪ'bɑ(r)/ *pr. n.* Sansibar (*das*)

Zanzibari /zænzɪ'bɑ:rɪ/
A *adj.* sansibarisch
B *n.* Sansibarer, *der*/Sansibarerin, *die*

zap /zæp/ (coll.)
A *int.* zack
B *v.t.*, **-pp-**: 1 **~ sb. [one]** jmdm. eine knallen (ugs.) 2 (do away with, kill) erledigen (salopp)
C *v.i.* **-pp-** (Telev. coll.) zappen (ugs.)

zapper /'zæpə(r)/ *n.* (Telev. coll.) Drücker, *der* (ugs.); Fernbedienung, *die*

zeal /zi:l/ *n.*, *no pl.* 1 (fervour) Eifer, *der* 2 (hearty endeavour) Hingabe, *die*

zealot /'zelət/ *n.* 1 (zealous person) Besessene, *der/die* 2 (fanatic) Eiferer, *der*/Eiferin, *die*; Zelot, *der*/Zelotin, *die* (geh.)

zealous /'zeləs/ *adj.* 1 (fervent) glühend (geh.) ‹*Verehrer*›; begeistert ‹*Fan*› 2 (eager) eifrig

zealously /'zeləslɪ/ *adv.* 1 (fervently) mit glühendem Eifer (geh.); begeistert ‹*anfeuern*› 2 (eagerly) eifrig ‹*suchen, arbeiten*›

zebra /'zebrə, 'zi:brə/ *n.* Zebra, *das*

zebra: **~ 'crossing** *n.* (Brit.) Zebrastreifen, *der*; **~ finch** (Ornith.) *n.* Zebrafink, *der*

zebu /'zi:bju:/ *n.* (Zool.) Zebu, *der od. das*

zed /zed/ (Brit.), **zee** /zi:/ (Amer.) *ns.* Zett, *das*

Zen /zen/ *n.*, *no pl.*, *no art.* (Relig.) Zen, *das*

zenith /'zenɪθ/ *n.* (lit. or fig.) Zenit, *der*

zephyr /'zefə(r)/ *n.* (literary) Zephir, *der* (dichter. veralt.)

Zeppelin /'zepəlɪn/ *n.* Zeppelin, *der*

zero /'zɪərəʊ/
A *n.*, *pl.* **~s** ▸❶ **p. 1358** 1 (nought) Null, *die* 2 (fig.: nil) null; **her chances are ~:** ihre Aussichten sind gleich null (ugs.) 3 ▸❶ **p. 1620** (starting point of scale; of temperature) Null, *die*; **in ~ gravity** im Zustand der Schwerelosigkeit; **absolute ~** (Phys.) absoluter Nullpunkt 4 **~ [hour]** die Stunde X. *See also* **ground zero**
B *v.i.* **~ in on sth.** (take aim at sth.) sich auf etw. (*Akk.*) einschießen; (focus one's attention on sth.) sich auf etw. (*Akk.*) konzentrieren

zero: **~-emission vehicle** *n.* Nullemissionsfahrzeug, *das*; emissionsfreies Fahrzeug; **~ option** *n.* (Polit.) Nulllösung, *die*; **~-'rated** *adj.* **~-rated goods** nicht mehrwertsteuerpflichtige Güter; **~ 'rating** *n.* Besteuerung zum Nullsatz; **~ 'tolerance** *n.* Nulltoleranz, *die* (**for, to, of** gegenüber); *attrib.* ‹*Politik, Konzept*› der Nulltoleranz

zest /zest/ *n.* 1 (lit. or fig.) Würze, *die*; **add a ~ to the dish** das Gericht würzig machen; **add ~ and life to sth.** etw. beleben 2 (gusto) Begeisterung, *die*; **~ for living** Lebenslust, *die* 3 (peel) Schale, *die*

zester /'zestə(r)/ *n.* Zitronenschaber, *der*; Zitrusschaber, *der*

zestful /'zestfl/ *adj.* freudig; ‹*Person*› voller Begeisterung

zeugma /'zju:gmə/ *n.* (Ling., Lit.) Zeugma, *das* (Sprachw.)

Zeus /zju:s/ *pr. n.* (Greek Mythol.) Zeus (*der*)

zigzag /'zɪgzæg/
A *adj.* zickzackförmig; Zickzack‹*muster, -anordnung*›; **~ line** Zickzacklinie, *die*; **steer a ~ course** im Zickzack fahren/laufen *usw*
B *adv.* zickzack
C *n.* Zickzacklinie, *die*
D *v.i.*, **-gg-** im Zickzack verlaufen/‹*Person:*› laufen

zilch /zɪltʃ/ *n.*, *no pl.*, *no art.* (coll.) rein *od.* reineweg gar nichts (ugs.); **be ~:** gleich null sein (ugs.)

zillion /'zɪljən/ *n.* (coll.) **a ~ mosquitoes** Myriaden von Stechmücken; **~s of dollars** zig (ugs.) Millionen Dollar

zillionth /'zɪljənθ/ *adj.* (coll.) zigst... (ugs.); xt... (ugs.)

Zimbabwe /zɪm'bɑ:bwɪ/ *pr. n.* Simbabwe (*das*)

Zimbabwean /zɪm'bɑ:bwɪən/ ▸❶ **p. 1345**
A *adj.* simbabwisch
B *n.* Simbabwer, *der*/Simbabwerin, *die*

Zimmer frame ® /'zɪmə freɪm/ *n.* Gehgestell, *das*

zinc /zɪŋk/ *n.* Zink, *das*

zing /zɪŋ/ (coll.)
A *n.* Schwung, *der*
B *v.i.* ‹*Geschoss:*› sirren

zinnia /'zɪnɪə/ *n.* (Bot.) Zinnie, *die*

Zion /'zaɪən/ *n.*, *no pl.* Zion, *der*

Zionism /'zaɪənɪzm/ *n.*, *no pl.* Zionismus, *der*

Zionist /'zaɪənɪst/ *n.* Zionist, *der*/Zionistin, *die*

zip /zɪp/
A *n.* 1 Reißverschluss, *der* 2 (fig.: energy, vigour) Schwung, *der* 3 (sound) Zischen, *das*
B *v.t.*, **-pp-**: 1 (close) **~ [up] sth.** den Reißverschluss an etw. (*Dat.*) zuziehen; **I put on the jacket and ~ped it up** ich zog die Jacke an und machte den Reißverschluss zu; **~ sb. up** jmdm. den Reißverschluss zumachen 2 **~ [up]** (enclose) [durch Schließen des Reißverschlusses] einpacken (ugs.); **he was ~ped [up] into his sleeping bag** er wurde in seinen Schlafsack gepackt (ugs.). 3 (Computing) zippen ‹*Datei*›
C *v.i.*, **-pp-**: 1 (fasten) **~ [up]** mit Reißverschluss geschlossen werden; **the dress ~s up [at the back/side]** das Kleid hat [hinten/seitlich] einen Reißverschluss; **the lining ~s in easily** das [Ausreiß]futter lässt sich leicht einziehen; **it won't ~ up** der Reißverschluss lässt sich nicht zuziehen 2 (move fast) sausen

zip: **~ bag** *n.* Tasche mit Reißverschluss; **Z~ code** *n.* (Amer.) Postleitzahl, *die*; **~ disk** *n.* (Computing) Zipdiskette, *die*; **~ drive** *n.* (Computing) Ziplaufwerk, *das*; **~ fastener** ▸**zip A 1**; **~ file** *n.* (Computing) Zipdatei, *die*; **~ gun** *n.* (Amer.) selbst gebastelte Pistole; **~-in** *adj.* einzippbar; **~-on** *adj.* anzippbar

zipper /'zɪpə(r)/ ▸**zip A 1**

zippy /'zɪpɪ/ *adj.* (coll.) spritzig

'zip-up *adj.* mit Reißverschluss *nachgestellt*

zirconium /zɜ:'kəʊnɪəm/ *n.* (Chem.) Zirkonium, *das*; Zirconium, *das* (fachspr.)

zit /zɪt/ *n.* (coll.) Pickel, *der*

zither /'zɪðə(r)/ *n.* (Mus.) Zither, *die*

zodiac /'zəʊdɪæk/ *n.* (Astron.) Tierkreis, *der*; Zodiakus, *der* (fachspr.); **sign of the ~** (Astrol.) Tierkreiszeichen, *das*; Sternzeichen, *das*

zodiacal /zə'daɪəkl/ *adj.* (Astron., Astrol.) Tierkreis-; zodiakal (fachspr.)

zodiacal 'light *n.* (Astron.) Zodiakallicht, *das*

zombie (*Amer.*: **zombi**) /'zɒmbɪ/ *n.* (lit. or fig.) Zombie, *der*

zonal /'zəʊnl/ *adj.* zonal; **~ tariff** Zonentarif, *der*

zone /zəʊn/
A *n.* Zone, *die*; **[time] ~:** Zeitzone, *die*; **Temperate Z~:** gemäßigte Zone
B *v.t.* [in Zonen] einteilen

zoning /'zəʊnɪŋ/ *n.* Zoneneinteilung, *die*

zonked /zɒŋkt/ *adj.* (coll.) **be ~** (by drugs) stoned sein (Drogenjargon); (by alcohol) zu sein (salopp); (be tired) erschlagen sein (ugs.)

zoo /zu:/ *n.* Zoo, *der*

'zookeeper *n.* ▸❶ **p. 1260** Zoowärter, *der*/-wärterin, *die*

zoological /zu:ə'lɒdʒɪkl/ *adj.* zoologisch

zoological 'garden[s] *n.* zoologischer Garten

zoologist /zu:'ɒlədʒɪst/ *n.* ▸❶ **p. 1260** Zoologe, *der*/Zoologin, *die*

zoology /zu:'ɒlədʒɪ/ *n.* Zoologie, *die*

zoom /zu:m/
A *v.i.* 1 (move quickly) rauschen; **we ~ed along on our bicycles** wir sausten auf unseren Fahrrädern daher; **~ through a script** ein Manuskript überfliegen 2 (Aeronaut.) das Flugzeug steil hochziehen 3 (Photog.) ‹*Kamera, Objektiv:*› die Brennweite stufenlos verändern; ‹*Bild:*› herangeholt werden
B *n.* ▸**zoom lens**

Phrasal verb

- **~ 'in** *v.i.* 1 (Cinemat., Telev.) zoomen (fachspr.); nahe heranfahren; **~ in on sth.** auf etw. (*Akk.*) zoomen (fachspr.); etw. nahe heranholen 2 **~ in on sth.** (fig.) sich auf etw. (*Akk.*) konzentrieren

'zoom lens *n.* (Photog.) Zoomobjektiv, *das*; Gummilinse, *die* (ugs.)

Zoroastrianism /zɒrəʊ'æstrɪənɪzm/ *n.* (Relig.) Zoroastrismus, *der*

zucchini /zʊ'ki:nɪ/ *n.*, *pl. same or* **~s** (esp. Amer.) Zucchino, *der*

zugzwang /'tsu:ktsvɑ:ŋ/ *n.* (Chess) Zugzwang, *der*

Zulu /'zu:lu:/ ▸❶ **p. 1277**
A *n.* 1 (person) Zulu, *der/die* 2 (language) Zulu, *das*
B *adj.* Zulu-

Zurich /'zjʊərɪk/ ▸❶ **p. 1643**
A *pr. n.* Zürich (*das*)
B *attrib. adj.* 1 (of canton) des Kantons Zürich *nachgestellt* 2 (of city) Züricher; Zürcher (schweiz.)

zygomatic bone /zaɪgə'mætɪk bəʊn/ *n.* (Anat.) Jochbein, *das*

zygote /'zaɪgəʊt/ *n.* (Biol.) Zygote, *die*

Anhang / Appendices

The revision of German spellings

German spellings in this dictionary are in accordance with the reforms in force since August 1998 and reflect modifications of the reforms agreed in June 2004. Most newspapers and new books use the new spellings. Key points of the reforms are summarized below. In cases of doubt the editors have followed *Duden—Die deutsche Rechtschreibung*, twenty-third edition, 2004, which is the standard reference work on the reformed spellings.

To help the user who may not yet be familiar with the reforms, the German–English section of the dictionary gives both the new spellings and the old versions which become 'invalid' in 2005. The old spellings are marked with an asterisk and are cross-referred where necessary to the new. For example, the translations of the compound verb *zueinanderfinden* will no longer be found at this headword, since under the new spelling rules the word vanishes from the language. Instead they are covered by a phrase at the entry for *zueinander: zueinander finden* (in the form *~ finden*). Similarly; the translations of the adjective previously written *belemmert* will be found at the new entry for the headword *belämmert*.

In a number of cases, however, implementing the new spelling rules has meant that just some, but not all, uses of a word have had to be transferred from one entry to another. In these cases the headword is not marked with an asterisk, but the entry is provided with a cross-reference to where the transferred information is now to be found. So, for example, the user who consults the entry for *leid* looking for a translation of the phrase previously written *jemandem leid tun* will find a cross-reference to the entry for the noun *Leid*, since according to the new spelling rules the word is written with a capital *L* in this expression. The headword *leid* itself is not marked with an asterisk, since it continues to exist in its own right as an adjective.

The following summary lists the most important changes:

1. The ß character

The ß character, which is generally replaced in Switzerland by a double s, is retained in Germany and Austria, but is only written after a long vowel (as in Fuß, Füße) and after a diphthong (as in Strauß, Sträuße).

Fluß, Baß, keß, läßt, Nußknacker become: *Fluss, Bass, kess, lässt, Nussknacker*

2. Nominalized adjectives

Nominalized adjectives are written with a capital even in set phrases.

sein Schäfchen ins trockene bringen, im trüben fischen, im allgemeinen become: *sein Schäfchen ins Trockene bringen, im Trüben fischen, im Allgemeinen*

3. Words from the same word family

In certain cases the spelling of words belonging to the same family becomes uniform.

numerieren, überschwenglich become: *nummerieren* (like Nummer), *überschwänglich* (being related to Überschwang)

4. The same consonant repeated three times

When the same consonant repeated three times occurs in compounds, all three are written even when a vowel follows.

Brennessel, Schiffahrt become: *Brennnessel, Schifffahrt* (exceptions are dennoch, Drittel, Mittag)

5. Verb, adjective and participle compounds

Verb, adjective, and participle compounds are written more frequently than previously in two words.

spazierengehen, radfahren, ernstgemeint, erdölexportierend become: *spazieren gehen, Rad fahren, ernst gemeint, Erdöl exportierend*

6. Compounds containing numbers in figures

Compounds containing numbers in figures are written with a hyphen.

24karätig, 8pfünder become: *24-karätig, 8-Pfünder*

7. The division of words containing *st*

st is treated like a normal combination of consonants and is no longer indivisible.

ha-stig, Ki-ste become: *has-tig, Kis-te*

8. The division of words containing *ck*

The combination *ck* is not divided and goes on to the next line.

Bäk-ker, schik-ken become: *Bä-cker, schi-cken*

9. The division of foreign words

Compound foreign words which are hardly recognized as such today may be divided by syllables, without regard to their original components.

He-li-ko-pter (from the Greek helix and pteron) may also become: *He-li-kop-ter*

10. The comma before *und*

Where two complete clauses are connected by *und* a comma is not obligatory.

Karl war in Schwierigkeiten, und niemand konnte ihm helfen may also be written: *Karl war in Schwierigkeiten und niemand konnte ihm helfen.*

11. The comma with infinitives and participles

Even longer clauses containing an infinitive or participle do not have to be divided off with a comma.

Er begann sofort, das neue Buch zu lesen. Ungläubig den Kopf schüttelnd, verließ er das Zimmer may also be written: *Er begann sofort das neue Buch zu lesen. Ungläubig den Kopf schüttelnd verließ er das Zimmer.*

Outline of German grammatical forms

The following outline is intended to be used in conjunction with the grammatical information included in the Dictionary, which it complements and explains. It does not attempt to cover all forms.

Verbs

General Notes

a) Verbs with prefixes, such as *ab-*, *auf-*, *er-*, *mit-*, and *zer-*, are conjugated like the corresponding simple verbs, e.g. *absagen* like *sagen*, but see the section on past participles below.

b) *ß* is used, and not *ss*, after a long vowel or diphthong:

essen	**heißen**
ich aß	ich hieß
gegessen	geheißen

c) To discover the stem of a verb, take away the *-en* (or just the *-n* if the penultimate letter is not *-e-*) from the end of the infinitive (the form given as a headword in the German–English section of the Dictionary):

machen	**handeln**
mach-	handel-

Regular verbs

Participles

Present

Add *-d* to the infinitive:

lachen
lachend

Past

Add *ge-* and *-t* to the stem:

machen
gemacht

If the stem ends with *-d*, *-t*, or a consonant + *m* or *n*, add *ge-* and *-et* to the stem:

reden	**trocknen**
geredet	getrocknet

If the infinitive ends with *-ieren* or *-eien*, add *-t* to the stem:

diskutieren	**prophezeien**
diskutiert	prophezeit

Verbs with a separable prefix (marked with | in the German–English section of the Dictionary) that is not followed by another prefix add *-ge-* between the prefix and the stem and -[e]*t* to the end of the stem:

an|klagen	**zu|leiten**
angeklagt	zugeleitet

Verbs with

a) any of the inseparable prefixes *be-*, *ent-*, *er-*, *ge-*, *ver-*, and *zer-*

b) an inseparable prefix (marked by · in the German–English section of the Dictionary)

c) a separable prefix (marked by | in the German–English section of the Dictionary) that is followed by an inseparable prefix

add -[e]*t* to the stem:

a)	**beneiden** beneidet	**gehören** gehört
b)	**durch·leuchten** durchleuchtet	**über·blicken** überblickt
c)	**zu|bereiten** zubereitet	**aus|erwählen** auserwählt

Active

a) Indicative

Present

	machen
ich	mache
du	machst
er/sie/es	macht
wir	machen
ihr	macht
sie/Sie	machen

If the stem ends with *-l* or *-r*, the 1st person singular may omit the preceding *-e-*:

lächeln
ich lächele *or* lächle

If the stem ends with *-s*, *-ß*, *-x*, or *-z*, the 2nd person singular adds only *-t*:

	rasen		**boxen**
du	rast	du	boxt

If the stem ends with *-d*, *-t*, or a consonant + *m* or *n*, the 2nd person singular adds *-est*, and the 2nd person plural adds *-et*:

	reden
du	redest
ihr	redet

Preterite (or **past** or **imperfect**)

	machen
ich	machte
du	machtest
er/sie/es	machte
wir	machten
ihr	machtet
sie/Sie	machten

If the stem ends with *-d*, *-t*, or a consonant + *m* or *n*, add *-e-* to the stem first:

	reden
ich	redete
du	redetest
er/sie/es	redete
wir	redeten
ihr	redetet
sie/Sie	redeten

Future

Present indicative of *werden* + infinitive:

	reden
ich werde	reden *etc.*

Perfect

Present indicative of *sein* or *haben* + past participle:

reisen	**machen**
ich bin gereist *etc.*	ich habe gemacht *etc.*

Verbs which take *sein* are labelled accordingly in the German–English section of the Dictionary.

Pluperfect

Preterite indicative of *sein* or *haben* (see note at **Perfect**) + past participle:

reisen	**machen**
ich war gereist *etc.*	ich hatte gemacht *etc.*

Future perfect

Future indicative of *sein* or *haben* (see note at **Perfect**) + past participle:

reisen	**machen**
ich werde gereist sein *etc.*	ich werde gemacht haben *etc.*

b) Subjunctive

Present

	machen
ich	mache
du	machest
er/sie/es	mache
wir	machen
ihr	machet
sie/Sie	machen

If the stem ends with *-l* or *-r*, the preceding *-e-* may be omitted:

	lächeln
ich	lächele *or* lächle *etc.*

Preterite

Identical with preterite indicative.

c) Conditional

Present

Preterite subjunctive of *werden* + infinitive:

ich würde reden *etc.*

Perfect

Preterite subjunctive of *sein* or *haben* + past participle:

reisen	**machen**
ich wäre gereist *etc.*	ich hätte gemacht *etc.*

or present conditional of *sein* or *haben* + past participle:

reisen	**machen**
ich würde gereist sein *etc.*	ich würde gemacht haben *etc.*

Verbs which take *sein* are labelled accordingly in the German–English section of the Dictionary.

d) Imperative

2nd person singular	red[e]!
2nd person plural	redet!
2nd person (polite)	reden Sie!

Passive

General note

Passive tenses are formed from the corresponding active tense of *werden* + past participle.

a) Infinitives

Present	geliebt [zu] werden
Perfect	geliebt worden [zu] sein

b) Indicative

Present	ich werde geliebt *etc.*
Preterite	ich wurde geliebt *etc.*
Future	ich werde geliebt werden *etc.*
Perfect	ich bin geliebt worden *etc.*
Pluperfect	ich war geliebt worden *etc.*
Future perfect	ich werde geliebt worden sein *etc.*

c) Subjunctive

Present	ich werde*) geliebt *etc.*
Preterite	ich würde geliebt *etc.*
Future	ich werde*) geliebt werden *etc.*
Perfect	ich sei geliebt worden *etc.*
Pluperfect	ich wäre geliebt worden *etc.*
Future perfect	ich werde*) geliebt worden sein *etc.*

*) NB du werdest ...; er/sie/es werde ...

d) Conditional

Present	ich würde geliebt [werden]
Perfect	ich wäre geliebt worden

e) Imperative

2nd person singular	sei *or* werde gegrüßt!
2nd person plural	seid *or* werdet gegrüßt!
2nd person (polite)	seien *or* werden Sie gegrüßt!

Irregular verbs

These are conjugated as regular verbs except for the forms given in the table (pp. 1742–1745) and the preterite indicative:

a) Preterite indicative

If the form given in the table ends with *-te*, the tense is conjugated as for a regular verb; otherwise as follows:

	singen
ich	sang
du	sangst
er/sie/es	sang
wir	sangen
ihr	sangt
sie/Sie	sangen

If the form given ends with *-s* or *-ß*, the 2nd person singular adds only *-t*:

	blasen		**heißen**
	blies		hieß
du	bliest	du	hießt

b) Compound tenses of modal verbs

The past participle forms shown in the table are not used with an infinitive, but only where the verb functions as a full verb (usually with a direct object or an indication of direction):

Er hat es gedurft. Ich habe damals kein Englisch gekonnt. Sie hat nach Frankfurt gemusst.

Where the verb is used with an infinitive, i.e. modally, the infinitive form is used instead:

Sie hat kommen müssen. Wir hatten zusehen dürfen.

Nouns

Singular

The first or only ending given in the entry for a noun in the German–English section of the Dictionary is the genitive singular. Shown here are examples of each, together with the corresponding other cases.

	Stadt ... ~ ...	**Manna ... ~[s] ...**	**Feuer ... ~s ...**	**Buch ... ~[e]s ...**
Nom.	die Stadt	das Manna	das Feuer	das Buch
Acc.	die Stadt	das Manna	das Feuer	das Buch
Gen.	der Stadt	des Manna[s]	des Feuers	des Buch[e]s
Dat.	der Stadt	dem Manna	dem Feuer	dem Buch[e]

	Löwe ... ~n ...	**Name ... ~ns ...**	**Bär ... ~en ...**	**Herz ... ~ens ...**
Nom.	der Löwe	der Name	der Bär	das Herz
Acc.	den Löwen	den Namen	den Bären	das Herz
Gen.	des Löwen	des Namens	des Bären	des Herzens
Dat.	dem Löwen	dem Namen	dem Bären	dem Herzen

Plural

The second ending (if any) given in the entry for a noun in the German–English section of the Dictionary is used for each plural case, except that, if it does not end with *-n* or *-s*, the dative plural adds *-n*:

	Fahrer ... ~s, ~	**Frau ... ~, ~en**	**Streik ... ~[e]s, ~s**
Nom.	die Fahrer	die Frauen	die Streiks
Acc.	die Fahrer	die Frauen	die Streiks
Gen.	der Fahrer	der Frauen	der Streiks
Dat.	den Fahrern	den Frauen	den Streiks

	Nacht ... ~, Nächte	**Brettel ... ~s, ~[n]**	**Bild ... ~[e]s, ~er**
Nom.	die Nächte	die Brettel[n]	die Bilder
Acc.	die Nächte	die Brettel[n]	die Bilder
Gen.	der Nächte	der Brettel[n]	der Bilder
Dat.	den Nächten	den Bretteln	den Bildern

The genitive singular or the plural form is given in full in the German–English section of the Dictionary if it involves changes to the stem:

Wald ... **~es**, **Wälder**

Adjectival declension

If a noun entry gives no endings but instead states '*adj. Dekl.*', noun and adjective endings are as follows:

	Masc.	*Fem.*	*Neut.*	*Pl. (all genders)*
	[1]Alte *der; adj. Dekl.*	**[2]Alte** *die; adj. Dekl.*	**[3]Alte** *das; adj. Dekl.*	**[4]Alte** *Pl.; adj. Dekl.*
Nom.	der gute Alte	die gute Alte	das gute Alte	die guten Alten
Acc.	den guten Alten	die gute Alte	das gute Alte	die guten Alten
Gen.	des guten Alten	der guten Alten	des guten Alten	der guten Alten
Dat.	dem guten Alten	der guten Alten	dem guten Alten	den guten Alten
Nom.	ein guter Alter	eine gute Alte	ein gutes Altes	gute Alte
Acc.	einen guten Alten	eine gute Alte	ein gutes Altes	gute Alte
Gen.	eines guten Alten	einer guten Alten	eines guten Alten	guter Alter
Dat.	einem guten Alten	einer guten Alten	einem guten Alten	guten Alten

Endings for personal names

The genitive singular ending of personal names is *-s*, or, if the name ends with *-s*, *-ß*, *-x*, or *-z*, it is simply an apostrophe or sometimes *-ens*:

Barbaras Buch
Hans' Auto or Hansens Auto

If a title (other than *Herr*) or more than one name is given, only the last element has an ending:

Frau Brauns Hut
König Ottokars Glück und Ende
eine Symphonie Ludwig van Beethovens

Following words in apposition are declined as well as the name:

Nom.	Wilhelm der Erste	Heinrich der Vogler
Acc.	Wilhelm den Ersten	Heinrich den Vogler
Gen.	Wilhelms des Ersten	Heinrichs des Voglers
Dat.	Wilhelm dem Ersten	Heinrich dem Vogler

When used as names, the words for family members take *-s* in the genitive singular:

Vaters/Mutters Aktentasche

The genitive singular of a name does not take an ending if preceded by an article or other inflected word other than *Herrn*:

eine Ausgabe des „Grünen Heinrich"
but: Herrn Dr. Baiers Praxis

Surnames often have an *-s* in the plural, especially when denoting a family:

[die] Remanns wohnen nebenan

If the name ends with *-s*, *-ß*, *-x*, or *-z*, the ending is *-ens*:

[die] Schwarzens

Adjectives and adverbs

Article and adjective endings

a) Weak declension

The qualifying words *der/die/das*, *dieser/diese/dieses*, *jener/jene/jenes*, *all…*, *welch…*, *solch…*, *beide*, *sämtliche*, etc. and any following adjectives are declined as follows:

	Masc.	*Fem.*	*Neut.*	*Pl. (all genders)*
Nom.	der gute Tag	die gute Frau	das gute Buch	die guten Dinge
Acc.	den guten Tag	die gute Frau	das gute Buch	die guten Dinge
Gen.	des guten Tag[e]s	der guten Frau	des guten Buch[e]s	der guten Dinge
Dat.	dem guten Tag[e]	der guten Frau	dem guten Buch[e]	den guten Dingen

b) Mixed declension

The qualifying words *ein* and *kein*, possessive adjectives, and any following adjectives are declined as follows:

	Masc.	*Fem.*	*Neut.*	*Pl. (all genders)*
Nom.	ein guter Tag	eine gute Frau	ein gutes Buch	keine guten Bücher
Acc.	einen guten Tag	eine gute Frau	ein gutes Buch	keine guten Bücher
Gen.	eines guten Tag[e]s	einer guten Frau	eines guten Buch[e]s	keiner guten Bücher
Dat.	einem guten Tag[e]	einer guten Frau	einem guten Buch[e]	keinen guten Büchern

c) Strong declension

Adjectives are declined as follows when preceded either by no qualifying word or by an indeclinable one, e.g. *viel, mehr, wenig, weniger, manch, solch,* or *welch,* or by *dessen, deren, ander…, einig…, etlich…, folgend…,* or *mehrer…*:

	Masc.	*Fem.*	*Neut.*	*Pl. (all genders)*
Nom.	guter Wein	gute Milch	gutes Bier	gute Dinge
Acc.	guten Wein	gute Milch	gutes Bier	gute Dinge
Gen.	guten Wein[e]s	guter Milch	guten Biers	guter Dinge
Dat.	gutem Wein[e]	guter Milch	gutem Bier[e]	guten Dingen

d) Exceptions

Adjectives which are marked *'indekl. Adj.'* or which end with *-er* and are derived from place names do not inflect at all:

klasse — Berliner
ein klasse Wagen — die Berliner Philharmoniker

Adjectives which end with *-el* drop the *-e-* when inflected and in their comparative forms:

übel
ein übler Mensch

and adjectives which end with *-en* and *-er* sometimes drop the *-e-*:

trocken — finster
trock[e]nes Holz — die finst[e]re Nacht

but *clever* does not:

clever
ein cleverer Trick

and the *-e-* is always dropped in:

integer — makaber
eine integre Persönlichkeit — eine makabre Geschichte

and when *-er* is preceded by *-au-* or *-eu-*:

teuer — sauer
ein teures Haus — saure Gurken

Adjectives which end with a vowel, other than those marked *'indekl. Adj.'*, drop the vowel:

müde
die müden Arbeiter

The adjective *hoch* drops its *-c-* when inflected:

eine hohe Stirn

Comparison of adjectives and adverbs

The regular endings are *-er, -st…*:

positive	schön
comparative	schöner
superlative attributive adjective	schönst…
superlative predicative adjective	am schönsten
superlative adverb	am schönsten

Irregular forms are given in the German–English section of the Dictionary:

arm ... **ärmer** ... **ärmst**...

See also above for adjectives ending with *-el, -en,* and *-er.*

If an adjective or adverb ends with *-d, -t, -sch, -s, -ß, -x, -z,* a long vowel, or a diphthong and has only one syllable or is stressed on its last syllable, the superlative ending is *-est…*:

laut — zäh — genau
lautest… — zähest… — genauest…

Pronouns

Personal pronouns

Nom.	*Acc.*	*Gen.*	*Dat.*
ich	mich	meiner	mir
du	dich	deiner	dir
er	ihn	seiner	ihm
sie	sie	ihrer	ihr
es	es	seiner	ihm
wir	uns	unser	uns
ihr	euch	euer	euch
sie	sie	ihrer	ihnen
Sie	Sie	Ihrer	Ihnen

Reflexive and reciprocal pronouns are the same as personal pronouns, except that the accusative and dative forms of *er, sie, es, sie,* and *Sie* are *sich.*

Possessive pronouns (*mein, dein, sein, ihr, unser, euer,* and *Ihr*)

	Masc.	*Fem.*	*Neut.*	*Pl. (all genders)*
Nom.	mein	meine	mein	meine
Acc.	meinen	meine	mein	meine
Gen.	meines	meiner	meines	meiner
Dat.	meinem	meiner	meinem	meinen

euer is usually contracted in all inflected forms, e.g. *eure.*

When used other than attributively, i.e. as independent pronouns, these forms differ:

Nom. masc.: meiner *etc.*, uns[e]rer, eurer
Nom. and acc. neut.: mein[e]s *etc.*, uns[e]res, eures

Demonstrative pronouns (*dieser*, *jener*, *der*, *derjenige*, and *derselbe*)

dieser and *jener*:

	Masc.	*Fem.*	*Neut.*	*Pl. (all genders)*
Nom.	dieser	diese	dieses	diese
Acc.	diesen	diese	dieses	diese
Gen.	dieses	dieser	dieses	dieser
Dat.	diesem	dieser	diesem	diesen

der is the same as when a definite article, except for:

	Masc.	*Fem.*	*Neut.*	*Pl. (all genders)*
Gen.	dessen	deren	dessen	derer *or* deren
Dat.				denen

derjenige and *derselbe* are declined as if two separate words:

	Masc.	*Fem.*	*Neut.*	*Pl. (all genders)*
Nom.	derjenige	diejenige	dasjenige	diejenigen
Acc.	denjenigen	diejenige	dasjenige	diejenigen
Gen.	desjenigen	derjenigen	desjenigen	derjenigen
Dat.	demjenigen	derjenigen	demjenigen	denjenigen

Relative pronouns

	Masc.	*Fem.*	*Neut.*	*Pl. (all genders)*
Nom.	der *or* welcher	die *or* welche	das *or* welches	die *or* welche
Acc.	den *or* welchen	die *or* welche	das *or* welches	die *or* welche
Gen.	dessen	deren	dessen	deren
Dat.	dem *or* welchem	der *or* welcher	dem *or* welchem	denen *or* welchen

Interrogative pronouns

welch follows the strong adjective declension (see p. 1732). The declensions of *was* and *wer* are given at their entries in the Dictionary.

Indefinite pronouns

etwas, *was*, and *nichts* are invariable. Other indefinite pronouns are declined as follows:

Nom.	man	jemand	niemand
Acc.	einen	jemand[en]	niemand[en]
Gen.	eines	jemandes	niemandes
Dat.	einem	jemand[em]	niemand[em]

Key points of German orthography and punctuation

Use of capital and small initial letters

The use of capital and small initial letters in German is governed by the following guidelines.

a) The first word of a sentence has a capital initial letter.

b) All true nouns have capital initial letters:
Himmel, Kindheit, Reichtum, Verständnis

c) All types of word have capital initial letters when they are used as nouns:
das Gute, der Abgeordnete, allerlei Schönes, etwas Wichtiges, die Deinigen, ein Achtel, das Auf und Nieder, das Entweder-oder, das Lesen, das Zustandekommen, das In-den-Tag-hinein-Leben

d) The polite form *Sie* and the accompanying possessive pronoun *Ihr* always have capital initials, but the reflexive pronoun *sich* always has a small initial:
Würden *Sie* mir bitte *Ihr* Programmheft leihen?
Setzen *Sie sich*.

e) Words which are derived from geographical names and which end in *-er* have capital initial letters:
die Schweizer Industrie, eine Kölner Firma

f) Adjectives ending in *-isch* which are derived from geographical names have small initials unless they form part of a proper name:
chinesische Seide, westfälischer Schinken
but: Holsteinische Schweiz

g) When nouns function other than as nouns they have small initial letters:
anfangs, abends, sonntags, ein bisschen, schuld sein

One word or two?

The continuing development of the conventions governing spelling and punctuation in German means that it is impossible to say for certain when words are written together (as one word) and when separately (as two words). The following examples are designed to serve as a general guide only. In cases of doubt write as two words.

a) Words are written together if they combine to form a new meaning:
Er wird mir die Summe gutschreiben.

Words are written separately if they retain their original meanings:
Der Schüler kann gut schreiben.

b) Compounds formed with a noun are written as one word if the noun no longer embodies a separate concept:
wetterleuchten, infolge, zugunsten

Words are written separately if the noun retains its independent meaning:
Sorge tragen, Posten stehen, unter Bezugnahme auf

The continuing development of the language means that some words are found in both forms:
Dank sagen *and* danksagen, auf Grund *and* aufgrund, in Frage *and* infrage

The comma

The role of the comma is to divide the sentence and indicate the pauses occurring in speech.

a) In lists, the comma is placed between words of the same type or between similar groups of words if they are not linked by *und* or *oder*:
Feuer, Wasser, Luft und Erde.
Wir gingen bei gutem, warmem Wetter spazieren.
Das Autorennen findet am Montag, dem 5. Mai statt.
(Here, the comma divides two statements of time; compare b.)

b) The comma separates following qualifying phrases from the rest of the sentence:
In Frankfurt, der bekannten Handelsstadt, befindet sich ein großes Messegelände.
Das Schiff kommt wöchentlich einmal, und zwar sonntags.
Das Autorennen findet am Montag, dem 5. Mai, statt.
(Here, an embedded phrase is enclosed by commas; compare a.)

c) An infinitive phrase is usually divided from the rest of the sentence by a comma; *zu* + infinitive alone is not divided off.
Wir hatten keine Gelegenheit, uns zu sehen.
but: Wir hatten keine Gelegenheit zu baden.

d) The comma separates main clauses but may also be omitted if the clauses are linked by *und* or *oder*. However the comma is never used between main clauses linked by *und* or *oder* if one part of the sentence is common to both clauses:
Ich kam, ich sah, ich siegte.
Wir trinken noch ein Bier [,] und dann gehe ich nach Hause.

but: sie bestiegen den Wagen und fuhren davon. (*sie* is common to both clauses)
Er geht ins Kino und sein Bruder ins Konzert. (*geht* is common to both clauses)

e) The comma separates the subordinate clause from the main clause:
Dass du zuverlässig bist, freut mich.
Alle Kinder, die fleißig sind, erhalten ein Buch.

Syllable division in German

Polysyllabic words are divided in accordance with the phonetic syllables which can be identified by pronouncing the word slowly:

Freun-de, Män-ner, for-dern, wei-ter, Or-gel, kal-kig, Bes-se-rung, Bal-kon, Fis-kus, Ho-tel, Pla-net, Kon-ti-nent, Fas-zi-kel, Re-mi-nis-zenz, El-lip-se, Ber-lin, El-ba, Tür-kei, las-ten, Diens-tes

In such cases, a single consonant goes on to the following line; if there is a series of consonants, the last of these goes on to the following line:

tre-ten, nä-hen, Ru-der, rei-ßen, bo-xen, Ko-kon, Kre-ta, Chi-na, An-ker, Fin-ger, war-ten, Fül-lun-gen, Rit-ter, Was-ser, Knos-pen, kämp-fen, Ach-sel, steck-ten, Kat-zen, Städ-ter, Drechs-ler, dunk-le, gest-rig, an-de-re, neh-men, Ar-sen, Hip-pie, Kas-ko, Pek-tin, Un-garn, Hes-sen, At-lan-tik (For exceptions see below.)

Suffixes which begin with a vowel take the preceding consonant when divided:

Freun-din, Bäcke-rei, Lüf-tung

The consonant groups *ch* and *sch* – as well as *ph*, *rh*, *sh*, and *th* in foreign words – represent single sounds and are not divided:

Bü-cher, Fla-sche, Ma-chete, Pro-phet, Myr-rhe, Ca-shew-nuss, ka-tho-lisch

Grü-sse (*for*: Grü-ße), hei-ssen (*for*: hei-ßen)

ck is regarded as a single consonant and is placed on the following line:

Zu-cker, ba-cken

Sen-ckenberg, Fran-cke, bismar-ckisch

Words are not divided before the 'lengthening' letters *e* and *i*:

Wie-se

Coes-feld (*pronounced*: kos...)

Compound words and words with a prefix are divided in accordance with their constituent word elements:

ein-armig, be-inhalten

The same applies to foreign words:

Des-interesse, in-adäquat

Many foreign words, however, may be divided according to phonetic syllables, as the constituent elements of a foreign word are not always generally known:

Epi-sode (*instead of*: Epis-ode)

ab-strakt (*instead of*: abs-trakt)

Word divisions which obey the rules but disrupt the flow of reading should be avoided:

Spar-gelder, *not*: Spargel-der

be-inhalten, *not*: bein-halten

Kleine Formenlehre des Englischen

Das Verb

Die Stammformen

Die regelmäßigen Verben bilden das Präteritum und das gleichlautende 2. Partizip mit Hilfe der Endung *-ed*:

call – called – called

Hierbei sind die folgenden Besonderheiten zu beachten:

Ein auslautender Konsonant wird häufig verdoppelt, und *-c* wird zu *-ck-*:

dub – dubbed
pod – podded
hug – hugged
focus – focused *od.* focussed
panic – panicked

Ein auslautendes *-e* fällt aus:

love – loved
tie – tied
dye – dyed
guarantee – guaranteed

Ein auslautendes, auf einen Konsonanten folgendes *-y* wird zu *-i-*:

worry – worried
satisfy – satisfied

Die Stammformen der unregelmäßigen Verben sind im englisch-deutschen Wörterverzeichnis bei dem jeweiligen Stichwort angegeben (vgl. S. XX). Außerdem sind sie in der Liste auf S. 1746f. verzeichnet. (Zu den Hilfsverben und den Modalverben s. u., S. 1737f).

Das Präsens

Die 3. Person Singular Präsens der Vollverben (außer *have* und *be*) wird durch die Endung *-s*, nach *s, sh, ch, x, o* zu *-es* erweitert, gebildet:

read – reads
see – sees
miss – misses
fish – fishes
reach – reaches
mix – mixes
echo – echoes
do – does

Hierbei wird ein auslautendes, auf einen Konsonanten folgendes *-y* zu *-ie-*:

cry – cries
worry – worries

Alle übrigen Präsensformen haben keine Personalendungen. Sie lauten wie der Infinitiv.

Das Präteritum

Das Präteritum hat keine Personalendungen und lautet (außer im Falle von *be*) in allen Personen gleich.

Das Futur

Das Futur wird gewöhnlich aus *will*, in der 1. Person Singular und Plural auch aus *shall*, und dem Infinitiv gebildet:

you/he/she/it/they will win
I/we will *oder* shall win

Das Konditional Präsens

Das Konditional Präsens wird gewöhnlich aus *would*, in der 1. Person Singular und Plural auch aus *should*, und dem Infinitiv gebildet:

you/he/she/it/they would win
I/we would *oder* should win

Das Perfekt

Das Perfekt wird aus dem Präsens von *have* und dem 2. Partizip gebildet:

I have seen/gone/been *usw.*

Das Plusquamperfekt

Das Plusquamperfekt wird aus dem Präteritum von *have* und dem 2. Partizip gebildet:

I had seen/gone/been *usw.*

Das Futur II

Das Futur II wird aus dem Futur I von *have* und dem 2. Partizip gebildet:

I will/shall have seen/gone/been *usw.*

Das Konditional Perfekt

Das Konditional Perfekt wird aus dem Konditional Präsens von *have* und dem 2. Partizip gebildet:

I would/should have seen/gone/been *usw.*

Das Passiv

Das Passiv wird aus den Formen des Hilfsverbs *be* und dem 2. Partizip gebildet:

I am/was/have been *usw.* stopped

Die Verlaufsform

Neben den vom Deutschen her vertrauten einfachen Verbformen gibt es im Englischen die so genannten Verlaufsformen (continuous tenses). Diese werden aus den Formen von *be* und dem 1. Partizip gebildet:

I am/you were/they had been *usw.* reading

Die Verlaufsform wird vor allem verwendet, um auszudrücken, dass ein Vorgang noch nicht beendet ist bzw. ein Zustand noch andauert:

They were having supper.

The old house is still standing there.

Die Verlaufsform des Präsens kann daneben aber auch in futurischem Sinne, etwa zum Ausdruck einer Absicht verwendet werden:

I'm travelling to London next week.

Die *going to*-Form

Zum Ausdruck des Zukünftigen hat das Englische neben der mit *will*/*shall* gebildeten Futurform noch eine weitere Form. Sie ist zusammengesetzt aus der Verlaufsform von *go* und dem Infinitiv mit *to* des betreffenden Verbs.

Durch diese *going to*-Form wird, wenn sie im Präsens steht, ausgedrückt, dass etwas geschehen wird, weil es geplant oder beabsichtigt ist, oder dass etwas mit großer Gewissheit geschehen wird:

I'm going to stay with friends.

I'm not going to accept that.

It's going to rain.

Durch die *going to*-Form im Präteritum kann ausgedrückt werden, dass etwas geplant oder beabsichtigt war, jedoch nicht geschehen ist:

I was going to phone you yesterday, but I forgot.

Mit dem Hilfsverb *do* gebildete Verbformen

In Fragesätzen, die nicht ein Fragewort als Subjekt haben, und in mit *not* verneinten Sätzen werden die einfachen Präsens- und Präteritumformen der Vollverben mit dem Hilfsverb *do* gebildet:

Does he like it? – He does not like it.

aber: Who likes it? – No one likes it.

Dies gilt außer im verneinten Imperativ nicht für das Kopulaverb *be*:

Is he a doctor? – No, he is not a doctor.

aber: Do not be so noisy.

Das Vollverb *have* kommt in Verneinung und Frage mit und ohne *do* vor:

Do they have a car? – No, they do not have a car.

Have you any idea? – No, I haven't a clue.

Ebenfalls mit *do* gebildet werden emphatische Formen in nicht verneinten Aussage- und Aufforderungssätzen:

But I 'did see him.

'Do listen to me.

'Do be quiet.

Die *ing*-Form

Die mit der Endung *-ing* gebildete Verbform ist je nach Gebrauch entweder 1. Partizip oder Gerundium. Ein auslautender Konsonant wird häufig verdoppelt; *-c* wird zu *-ck-*:

dub – dubbing
pod – podding
hug – hugging
focus – focusing *od.* focussing
panic – panicking

Ein auf einen Konsonanten folgendes auslautendes *-e* fällt aus:

live – living

Ein auslautendes *-ie* wird zu *-y-*:

die – dying

Die Formen der Hilfsverben *have, be, do*

(In Klammern sind – soweit vorhanden – jeweils die zugehörigen Kurzformen und die Kurzformen der verneinten Formen angegeben.)

have

Präsens:	3. Person Singular	has ('s; hasn't)
	alle übrigen Personen	have ('ve; haven't)
Präteritum:	alle Personen	had ('d; hadn't)

(Das 2. Partizip *had* spielt nur beim Vollverb *have* eine Rolle.)

be

Präsens:	1. Person Singular	am ('m; *nur in Fragesätzen*: aren't)
	3. Person Singular	is ('s; isn't)
	alle übrigen Personen	are ('re; aren't)
Präteritum:	1. und 3. Person Singular	was (wasn't)
	alle übrigen Personen	were (weren't)
2. Partizip:		been

do

Präsens:	3. Person Singular	does (doesn't)
	alle übrigen Personen	do (don't)
Präteritum:	alle Personen	did (didn't)

(Das 2. Partizip *done* spielt nur beim Vollverb *do* eine Rolle.)

Die Formen der Modalverben *can, may, must, shall, will*

Diese Verben, von denen *shall* und *will* auch als nicht modale Hilfsverben verwendet werden (vgl. **Futur** und **Konditional**), haben keine infiniten, sondern nur die folgenden, jeweils in allen Personen gleich lautenden, finiten Formen:

Vollform	*Kurzform*	*Kurzform verneint*
Präsens		
can; *verneint*: cannot		can't
may		mayn't
must		mustn't
shall	'll	shan't
will	'll	won't

Vollform	*Kurzform*	*Kurzform verneint*
Präteritum		
could		couldn't
might		mightn't
must		mustn't
should	'd	shouldn't
would	'd	wouldn't

Für die fehlenden Formen werden, je nach Bedeutung, verschiedene Ersatzformen verwendet: so z.B. für die fehlenden Formen von *can* im Sinne von „fähig sein zu" die entsprechenden Formen der Fügung *be able to* (z.B. *I shall be able to come*).

Das Substantiv

Das Genus

Im Englischen ist, anders als im Deutschen, das Genus der Substantive praktisch nur für den richtigen Gebrauch des Personal- und des Possessivpronomens von Bedeutung.

Es stimmt in der Regel mit dem natürlichen Geschlecht überein; Substantive, die männliche Personen bezeichnen, sind Maskulina, solche, die weibliche Personen bezeichnen, sind Feminina, alle übrigen sind in der Regel Neutra.

Zu beachten sind jedoch die folgenden Besonderheiten:

Substantive, die Personen beiderlei Geschlechts bezeichnen können (z.B. *friend, teacher*) sind je nach vorliegender Bedeutung Maskulina oder Feminina.

Substantive wie *child* und *baby* sowie Substantive, die Tiere beiderlei Geschlechts bezeichnen können (z.B. *elephant, cat*) sind je nach vorliegender Bedeutung Maskulina oder Feminina. Wenn das Geschlecht jedoch dem Sprecher unbekannt ist, dann werden sie als Neutra behandelt.

Geschlechtsspezifische Tierbezeichnungen haben dagegen meist das dem natürlichen Geschlecht entsprechende Genus (z.B. *tomcat, lioness, ewe, he-goat, she-bear*).

Bezeichnungen für Schiffe (z.B. *ship, boat, steamer*), Schiffsnamen, manchmal auch Bezeichnungen für andere Fahrzeuge (z.B. *car, train, aeroplane*) sowie, besonders in literarischem Stil, Länder- und Städtenamen (z.B. *Britain, Europe, Paris*) können als Feminina verwendet werden.

Fluss- und Bergnamen, das Substantiv *sun* sowie bestimmte Abstrakta (z.B. *death, love*) werden in literarischem Stil oft als Maskulina verwendet.

Die Substantive *moon, earth, sea* und bestimmte Abstrakta (z.B. *fortune, nature, liberty*) können in poetischem Stil als Feminina verwendet werden.

Der Plural

Der Plural der Substantive wird in der Regel durch Anhängen der Endung *-s*, nach *s, sh, ch, x, z* und in einigen Fällen nach *o* zu *-es* erweitert, gebildet:

cat – cats
bus – buses
bush – bushes
beach – beaches
box – boxes
fez – fezes
tomato – tomatoes
aber: dynamo – dynamos

Hierbei sind die folgenden Besonderheiten zu beachten:

Ein auslautendes, auf einen Konsonanten folgendes *-y* wird in der Regel zu *-ie-*:

lady – ladies
fly – flies

Einige auf *-f* oder *-fe* endende Substantive lauten im Plural auf *-ves*:

leaf – leaves
life – lives

Einige Substantive haben eine unregelmäßige, manche auch eine mit dem Singular übereinstimmende Pluralform (z.B. *man – men, child – children, sheep – sheep*). Solche Pluralformen wie auch diejenigen auf *-ves* sind im englisch-deutschen Wörterverzeichnis jeweils beim entsprechenden Stichwort angeführt.

Der Genitiv

Der Genitiv Singular aller Substantive und der Genitiv Plural der Substantive mit unregelmäßigem (nicht auf *-s* lautendem) Plural wird durch Anhängen von 's gebildet:

man's
men's
James's

Ebenso bei nicht auf *-s* endenden pluralischen Substantiven:

people – people's

Der Genitiv Plural der Substantive, die im Plural die Endung *-s* bzw. *-es* haben, wird durch einen hinter dem Plural *-s* stehenden Apostroph gekennzeichnet:

fathers'
Joneses'

Der Genitiv Singular eines auf *-s* ausgehenden Eigennamens wird oft nur durch einen Apostroph gekennzeichnet:

Dickens' *neben* Dickens's
James' *neben* James's

Griechische und lateinische Eigennamen auf *-s* haben im Genitiv stets nur einen Apostroph:

Socrates'
Augustus'

Dies gilt auch für auf *-s* endende Substantive in Verbindung mit *for … sake*:

for goodness' sake

Die Steigerung der Adjektive und Adverbien

Einsilbige Adjektive werden – mit Ausnahme solcher, die aus Partizipien entstanden sind (z.B. *pleased*) und soweit sie keine unregelmäßigen Steigerungsformen haben (s.u.) – stets mithilfe der Suffixe *-er* (für den Komparativ) und *-est* (für den Superlativ) gesteigert:

clean – cleaner – cleanest
short – shorter – shortest

Ein auslautendes *-b, -d, -g, -m, -n, -p* oder *-t* nach kurzem Vokal wird verdoppelt:

big – bigger – biggest
hot – hotter – hottest

Ein auslautendes *-e* fällt aus:

large – larger – largest
wide – wider – widest
free – freer – freest

Ein auf einen Konsonanten folgendes auslautendes *-y* wird meist zu *-i-*:

dry – drier – driest
aber: shy – shyer *oder* shier – shyest *oder* shiest

Von den zweisilbigen Adjektiven werden solche auf *-y*, solche mit Endbetonung und einige weitere ebenfalls meist auf diese Art gesteigert, wobei ein auf einen Konsonanten folgendes auslautendes *-y* zu *-i-* wird und ein auslautendes *-e* ausfällt:

narrow – narrower – narrowest
easy – easier – easiest
polite – politer – politest

Alle zweisilbigen Adjektive können aber auch durch ein vorangestelltes *more* (für den Komparativ) bzw. *most* (für den Superlativ) gesteigert werden.

Stets mit *more* und *most* werden alle übrigen Adjektive (insbesondere auch diejenigen, die aus Partizipien entstanden sind, wie z.B. *bored, lasting, delighted*) gesteigert.

Von Adjektiven abgeleitete Adverbien auf *-ly* werden mit vorangestelltem *more* und *most* gesteigert:

carefully – more/most carefully
easily – more/most easily

Die übrigen Adverbien werden, soweit sie keine unregelmäßigen Steigerungsformen haben (wie z.B. *much, well*), mit Hilfe der Suffixe *-er* und *-est* gesteigert:

fast – faster – fastest
soon – sooner – soonest
hard – harder – hardest

Hierbei gelten auch die oben für die mit *-er* und *-est* steigernden Adjektive genannten, den Stammauslaut betreffenden Besonderheiten.

Einige wenige Adjektive und Adverbien haben unregelmäßige Steigerungsformen.

Diese sind im englisch-deutschen Wörterverzeichnis sowohl beim zugehörigen Positiv als auch an ihrer alphabetischen Stelle angeführt.

Pronomen

In der folgenden Übersicht sind die Formen der wichtigsten Pronomen aufgeführt.

Personalpronomen

	Subjektsform	*Objektsform*
1. Pers. Sing.	I	me
2. Pers. Sing.	you	you
3. Pers. Sing.	he/she/it	him/her/it
1. Pers. Pl.	we	us
2. Pers. Pl.	you	you
3. Pers. Pl.	they	them

Reflexivpronomen

	Sing.	*Pl.*
1. Pers.	myself	ourselves
2. Pers.	yourself	yourselves
3. Pers.	himself/ herself/itself	themselves

Possessivpronomen

attributiv gebraucht:

	Sing.	*Pl.*
1. Pers.	my	our
2. Pers.	your	your
3. Pers.	his/her/its	their

allein stehend gebraucht:

	Sing.	*Pl.*
1. Pers.	mine	ours
2. Pers.	yours	yours
3. Pers.	his/hers/–	theirs

Demonstrativpronomen

Die Demonstrativpronomen *this* und *that* haben außer diesen Singularformen nur noch je eine weitere Form: *these* (Plural zu *this*) und *those* (Plural zu *that*).

Relativpronomen

who

Subjektsform	Sing. u. Pl.:	who
Objektsform	Sing. u. Pl.:	who, whom
Genitiv	Sing. u. Pl.:	whose

which

(keine weiteren Formen)

that

(keine weiteren Formen)

Interrogativpronomen

who

Subjektsform:	who
Objektsform:	whom, who
Genitiv:	whose

which

(keine weiteren Formen)

what

(keine weiteren Formen)

Die Zeichensetzung im Englischen

Apostroph

a) Der Apostroph steht als Auslassungszeichen:
I'm (= I am)
he's (= he is/has)
thro' (= through)
they'd (= they had/would)
the summer of '68 (= 1968)

Gelegentlich wird er – jedoch unnötigerweise – auch bei einigen Kurzformen wie *bus, cello, flu, phone, plane* gesetzt ('*bus* usw.).

b) Der Apostroph steht zur Kennzeichnung des Genitivs. Näheres hierzu findet sich unter „Kleine Formenlehre des Englischen" auf S. 1738.

c) Manchmal steht der Apostroph mit einem s zur Bildung des Plurals von Buchstaben, Zahlen oder Abkürzungen, z.B.:
pronounce the r's more clearly
during the 1960's
all the MP's

Doppelpunkt

a) Der Doppelpunkt steht zur Markierung des Beginns einer Aufzählung nach einem Gattungsnamen oder einem die Aufzählung ankündigenden Ausdruck wie z.B. *as follows, in the following manner*:
His library consists of two books: the Bible and Shakespeare.
Proceed as follows: switch on the computer, insert a disk, and press any key.

b) Der Doppelpunkt steht vor Sätzen oder Ausdrücken, die den vorausgehenden Satz erläutern oder erklären:
The garden had been neglected for a long time: it was overgrown and full of weeds.

(Statt des Doppelpunkts kann hier auch ein Punkt, jedoch kein Komma stehen.)

Komma

a) Das Komma steht zwischen Adjektiven, die ein Substantiv in gleicher Weise attribuieren:
a cautious, eloquent man

Wenn mehrere Adjektive ein Substantiv in unterschiedlicher Weise attribuieren oder wenn ein Adjektiv das andere attribuiert, steht dagegen kein Komma:
a distinguished foreign author; a bright red tie

b) Das Komma steht zwischen den Gliedern einer Aufzählung. Wenn vorletztes und letztes Aufzählungsglied durch eine Konjunktion verbunden sind, steht das Komma vor dieser Konjunktion:
potatoes, peas, and carrots; potatoes, peas, or carrots; potatoes, peas, etc.; red, white, and blue

c) Das Komma steht zwischen nebengeordneten Hauptsätzen, die nicht durch ein anderes Satzzeichen voneinander getrennt sind:
Cars turn here, and coaches go straight on.
Es steht jedoch nicht, wenn es sich um eng zusammengehörige Sätze handelt:
Do as I tell you and you'll never regret it.

d) Das Komma steht vor und hinter aus einem oder mehreren Wörtern bestehenden Einschüben sowie vor und hinter Zwischensätzen:
I am sure, however, that it will not happen.
Fred, who is bald, complained of the cold.

Es steht jedoch nicht vor und hinter notwendigen Relativsätzen:
Men who are bald should wear hats.

e) Das Komma steht nach am Satzanfang stehenden Infinitiv- und Partizipialgruppen und gleichwertigen verblosen Teilen:
To be sure of arriving on time, she left an hour early.
Worn out by their journey, the children soon fell asleep.

f) Das Komma steht zwischen einer adverbialen Bestimmung und dem übrigen Satz sowie zwischen Haupt- und Nebensatz, wenn ohne Komma ein Missverständnis möglich wäre:
In the valley below, the villages looked very small.
He did not go to church, because he was playing golf.
In 1980, 2000 seemed a long time off.

g) Das Komma steht nach Wörtern, die eine direkte Rede einleiten:
They answered, 'Here we are'.

h) Das Komma steht in Briefen nach der Anrede (*Dear Sir, Dear John* usw.) und nach der Grußformel (*Yours sincerely* usw.)

Nicht notwendig ist ein Komma zwischen Monat und Jahr in Datumsangaben (z.B. *in December 2004*) oder zwischen Hausnummer und Straßenname in Adressen (z.B. *12 Acacia Avenue*).

Semikolon

Das Semikolon steht zwischen Teilsätzen oder Satzstücken, wo ein Komma eine zu schwache, ein Punkt jedoch eine zu starke Zäsur bedeuten würde. D.h., es steht typischerweise zwischen Sätzen, die inhaltlich etwa gleiches Gewicht und grammatisch eine ähnliche Struktur haben:

To err is human; to forgive, divine.

Punkt

a) Der Punkt steht am Satzende, sofern kein Frage- oder Ausrufezeichen steht; das folgende Wort beginnt in der Regel mit einem Großbuchstaben.

b) Der Punkt steht nach Abkürzungen. Wenn ein Abkürzungspunkt ans Satzende zu stehen kommt, dient er gleichzeitig als Schlusspunkt:

She also kept dogs, cats, birds, etc.

aber: She also kept pets (dogs, cats, birds, etc.).

c) Wenn ein Satz mit einer Anführung schließt, die ihrerseits mit einem Punkt, Fragezeichen oder Ausrufezeichen endet, entfällt der Schlusspunkt:

He cried, 'Be off!' But the child would not move.

Wenn die Anführung jedoch kurz ist und der übrige Satz deutlich größeres Gewicht hat, steht der Punkt außerhalb der Anführungszeichen:

Over the entrance to the temple at Delphi were written the words 'Know thyself'.

Anführungszeichen

a) Anführungszeichen haben gewöhnlich die Form '…' („halbe Anführungszeichen"); Anführungszeichen der Form "…" stehen bei einer Anführung innerhalb einer Anführung; bei einer Anführung innerhalb einer angeführten Anführung stehen wiederum halbe Anführungszeichen:

'I said, "He used the word 'murder' although no one had told him how Smith died".'

b) Schließende Anführungszeichen stehen vor allen weiteren Satzzeichen, es sei denn, diese sind Bestandteil der Anführung:

Did Nelson really say, 'Kiss me, Hardy'?

aber: Then she asked, 'What is your name?'.

Das Komma am Schluss einer Anführung, auf die Ausdrücke wie *he said* folgen, ersetzt den Schlusspunkt des angeführten Satzes und steht innerhalb der Anführungszeichen:

'That is nonsense,' he said.

Die Kommas, durch die *he said* usw. eingeschlossen wird, wenn es die Anführung unterbricht, stehen gewöhnlich außerhalb der Anführungszeichen:

'That', he said, 'is nonsense.'

Das erste Komma steht jedoch innerhalb der Anführungszeichen, wenn es auch ohne die Unterbrechung stehen müsste:

'That, my dear fellow,' he said, 'is nonsense.'

German Irregular Verbs

Irregular and partly irregular verbs are listed alphabetically by infinitive. 1st, 2nd, and 3rd person present and imperative forms are given after the infinitive, and preterite subjunctive forms after the preterite indicative, where they take an umlaut, change *e* to *i*, etc. Verbs with a raised number in the German–English section of the Dictionary have the same number in this list. Compound verbs (including verbs with prefixes) are only given if a) they do not take the same forms as the corresponding simple verb, e.g. *befehlen*, or b) there is no corresponding simple verb, e.g. *bewegen*. An asterisk (*) indicates a verb which is also conjugated regularly.

Infinitive *Infinitiv*	Preterite *Präteritum*	Past Participle *2. Partizip*
abwägen	wog (wöge) ab	abgewogen
backen[1] (du bäckst, er bäckt; *auch*: du backst, er backt)	backte, *älter* : buk (büke)	gebacken
befehlen (du befiehlst, er befiehlt; befiehl!)	befahl (beföhle, befähle)	befohlen
beginnen	begann (begänne, *seltener* : begönne)	begonnen
beißen	biss	gebissen
bergen (du birgst, er birgt; birg!)	barg (bärge)	geborgen
bersten (du birst, er birst; birst!)	barst (bärste)	geborsten
bewegen[2]	bewog (bewöge)	bewogen
biegen	bog (böge)	gebogen
bieten	bot (böte)	geboten
binden	band (bände)	gebunden
bitten	bat (bäte)	gebeten
blasen (du bläst, er bläst)	blies	geblasen
bleiben	blieb	geblieben
bleichen*	blich	geblichen
braten (du brätst, er brät)	briet	gebraten
brechen (du brichst, er bricht; brich!)	brach (bräche)	gebrochen
brennen	brannte (brennte)	gebrannt
bringen	brachte (brächte)	gebracht
denken	dachte (dächte)	gedacht
dingen*	dang (dänge)	gedungen
dreschen (du drischst, er drischt; drisch!)	drosch (drösche)	gedroschen
dringen	drang (dränge)	gedrungen
dünken* (es dünkt, *auch*: deucht)	deuchte	gedeucht
dürfen (ich darf, du darfst, er darf)	durfte (dürfte)	gedurft/dürfen
empfehlen (du empfiehlst, er empfiehlt, empfiehl!)	empfahl (empföhle, *seltener* : empfähle)	empfohlen
erlöschen (du erlischst, er erlischt, erlisch!)	erlosch (erlösche)	erloschen
erschallen*	erscholl (erschölle)	erschollen
erschrecken[1,3] (du erschrickst, er erschrickt, erschrick!)	erschrak (erschräke)	erschrocken
essen (du isst, er isst, iss!)	aß (äße)	gegessen
fahren (du fährst, er fährt)	fuhr (führe)	gefahren
fallen (du fällst, er fällt)	fiel	gefallen
fangen (du fängst, er fängt)	fing	gefangen
fechten (du fichtst, er ficht; ficht!)	focht (föchte)	gefochten
finden	fand (fände)	gefunden
flechten (du flichtst, er flicht; flicht!)	flocht (flöchte)	geflochten
fliegen	flog (flöge)	geflogen
fliehen	floh (flöhe)	geflohen
fließen	floss (flösse)	geflossen
fressen (du frisst, er frisst; friss!)	fraß (fräße)	gefressen
frieren	fror (fröre)	gefroren
gären*	gor (göre)	gegoren
gebären (du gebärst, sie gebärt, gebäre!; *geh.*: du gebierst, sie gebiert; gebier!)	gebar (gebäre)	geboren
geben (du gibst, er gibt; gib!)	gab (gäbe)	gegeben

Infinitive *Infinitiv*	Preterite *Präteritum*	Past Participle *2. Partizip*
gedeihen	gedieh	gediehen
gehen	ging	gegangen
gelingen	gelang (gelänge)	gelungen
gelten (du giltst, er gilt; gilt!)	galt (gölte, gälte)	gegolten
genesen	genas (genäse)	genesen
genießen	genoss (genösse)	genossen
geschehen (geschieht)	geschah (geschähe)	geschehen
gewinnen	gewann (gewönne, gewänne)	gewonnen
gießen	goss (gösse)	gegossen
gleichen	glich	geglichen
gleiten	glitt	geglitten
glimmen	glomm (glömme)	geglommen
graben (du gräbst, er gräbt)	grub (grübe)	gegraben
greifen	griff	gegriffen
haben (du hast, er hat)	hatte (hätte)	gehabt
halten (du hältst, er hält)	hielt	gehalten
hängen[1]	hing	gehangen
hauen	haute, *geh.*: hieb	gehauen
heben	hob (höbe)	gehoben
heißen	hieß	geheißen/heißen
helfen (du hilfst, er hilft; hilf!)	half (hülfe, *selten*: hälfe)	geholfen/helfen
kennen	kannte (kennte)	gekannt
kiesen*	kor (köre)	gekoren
klimmen*	klomm (klömme)	geklommen
klingen	klang (klänge)	geklungen
kneifen	kniff	gekniffen
kommen	kam (käme)	gekommen
können (ich kann, du kannst, er kann)	konnte (könnte)	gekonnt/können
kreischen*	krisch	gekrischen
kriechen	kroch (kröche)	gekrochen
küren*	kor (köre)	gekoren
laden[1, 2] **(du lädst, er lädt; *veralt., landsch.*: du ladest, er ladet)**	lud (lüde)	geladen
lassen (du lässt, er lässt)	ließ	gelassen/lassen
laufen (du läufst, er läuft)	lief	gelaufen
leiden	litt	gelitten
leihen	lieh	geliehen
lesen[1, 2] **(du liest, er liest; lies!)**	las (läse)	gelesen
liegen	lag (läge)	gelegen
lügen	log (löge)	gelogen
mahlen	mahlte	gemahlen
meiden	mied	gemieden
melken* (du milkst, er milkt; milk!)	molk (mölke)	gemolken
messen (du misst, er misst; miss!)	maß (mäße)	gemessen
misslingen	misslang (misslänge)	misslungen
mögen (ich mag, du magst, er mag)	mochte (möchte)	gemocht
müssen (ich muss, du musst, er muss)	musste (müsste)	gemusst/müssen
nehmen (du nimmst, er nimmt; nimm!)	nahm (nähme)	genommen
nennen	nannte (nennte)	genannt
pfeifen	pfiff	gepfiffen
pflegen*	pflog (pflöge)	gepflogen
preisen	pries	gepriesen
quellen[1] **(du quillst, er quillt; quill!)**	quoll (quölle)	gequollen
raten (du rätst, er rät)	riet	geraten
reiben	rieb	gerieben
reißen	riss	gerissen
reiten	ritt	geritten
rennen	rannte (rennte)	gerannt
riechen	roch (röche)	gerochen
ringen	rang (ränge)	gerungen
rinnen	rann (ränne, *seltener*: rönne)	geronnen
rufen	rief	gerufen

Infinitive *Infinitiv*	Preterite *Präteritum*	Past Participle *2. Partizip*
salzen*	salzte	gesalzen
saufen (du säufst, er säuft)	soff (söffe)	gesoffen
saugen*	sog (söge)	gesogen
schaffen*	schuf (schüfe)	geschaffen
schallen*	scholl (schölle)	geschallt
scheiden	schied	geschieden
scheinen	schien	geschienen
scheißen	schiss	geschissen
schelten (du schiltst, er schilt; schilt!)	schalt (schölte)	gescholten
scheren[1]	schor (schöre)	geschoren
schieben	schob (schöbe)	geschoben
schießen	schoss (schösse)	geschossen
schinden	schindete	geschunden
schlafen (du schläfst, er schläft)	schlief	geschlafen
schlagen (du schlägst, er schlägt)	schlug (schlüge)	geschlagen
schleichen	schlich	geschlichen
schleifen[1]	schliff	geschliffen
schleißen*	schliss	geschlissen
schließen	schloss (schlösse)	geschlossen
schlingen	schlang (schlänge)	geschlungen
schmeißen	schmiss	geschmissen
schmelzen (du schmilzt, er schmilzt; schmilz!)	schmolz	geschmolzen
schnauben*	schnob (schnöbe)	geschnoben
schneiden	schnitt	geschnitten
schrecken* (du schrickst, er schrickt; schrick!)	schrak (schräke)	geschreckt
schreiben	schrieb	geschrieben
schreien	schrie	geschrien
schreiten	schritt	geschritten
schweigen	schwieg	geschwiegen
schwellen[1] (du schwillst, er schwillt; schwill!)	schwoll (schwölle)	geschwollen
schwimmen	schwamm (schwömme, *seltener* : schwämme)	geschwommen
schwinden	schwand (schwände)	geschwunden
schwingen	schwang (schwänge)	geschwungen
schwören	schwor (schwüre)	geschworen
sehen (du siehst, er sieht; sieh[e]!)	sah (sähe)	gesehen/sehen
sein (ich bin, du bist, er ist, wir sind, ihr seid, sie sind; sei!)	war (wäre)	gewesen
senden*	sandte	gesandt
sieden*	sott (sötte)	gesotten
singen	sang (sänge)	gesungen
sinken	sank (sänke)	gesunken
sinnen	sann (sänne, sönne)	gesonnen
sitzen	saß (säße)	gesessen
sollen (ich soll, du sollst, er soll)	sollte	gesollt/sollen
spalten*	spaltete	gespalten
speien	spie	gespien
spinnen	spann (spönne, spänne)	gesponnen
spleißen*	spliss	gesplissen
sprechen (du sprichst, er spricht; sprich!)	sprach (spräche)	gesprochen
sprießen	spross (sprösse)	gesprossen
springen	sprang (spränge)	gesprungen
stechen (du stichst, er sticht; stich!)	stach (stäche)	gestochen
stecken*	stak (stäke)	gesteckt
stehen	stand (stünde, *auch*: stände)	gestanden
stehlen (du stiehlst, er stiehlt; stiehl!)	stahl (stähle, *seltener* : stöhle)	gestohlen
steigen	stieg	gestiegen
sterben (du stirbst, er stirbt; stirb!)	starb (stürbe)	gestorben
stieben	stob (stöbe)	gestoben
stinken	stank (stänke)	gestunken
stoßen (du stößt, er stößt)	stieß	gestoßen
streichen	strich	gestrichen

Infinitive *Infinitiv*	Preterite *Präteritum*	Past Participle *2. Partizip*
streiten	stritt	gestritten
tragen (du trägst, er trägt)	trug (trüge)	getragen
treffen (du triffst; er trifft; triff!)	traf (träfe)	getroffen
treiben	trieb	getrieben
treten (du trittst, er tritt; tritt!)	trat (träte)	getreten
triefen*	troff (tröffe)	getroffen
trinken	trank (tränke)	getrunken
trügen	trog (tröge)	getrogen
tun	tat (täte)	getan
verderben (du verdirbst, er verdirbt; verdirb!)	verdarb (verdürbe)	verdorben
verdrießen	verdross (verdrösse)	verdrossen
vergessen (du vergisst, er vergisst, vergiss!)	vergaß (vergäße)	vergessen
verlieren	verlor (verlöre)	verloren
verlöschen (du verlischst, er verlischt; verlisch!)	verlosch (verlösche)	verloschen
verschleißen*	verschliss	verschlissen
wachsen[1] (du wächst, er wächst)	wuchs (wüchse)	gewachsen
wägen	wog (wöge)	gewogen
waschen (du wäschst, er wäscht)	wusch (wüsche)	gewaschen
weben*	wob (wöbe)	gewoben
weichen	wich	gewichen
weisen	wies	gewiesen
wenden[2]*	wandte	gewandt
werben (du wirbst, er wirbt; wirb!)	warb (würbe)	geworben
werden (du wirst, er wird; werde!)	wurde, *dichter.*: ward (würde)	geworden/worden
werfen (du wirfst, er wirft; wirf!)	warf (würfe)	geworfen
wiegen[1]	wog (wöge)	gewogen
winden[1]	wand (wände)	gewunden
wissen (ich weiß, du weißt, er weiß)	wusste (wüsste)	gewusst
wollen (ich will, du willst, er will)	wollte	gewollt/wollen
wringen	wrang (wränge)	gewrungen
zeihen	zieh	geziehen
ziehen	zog (zöge)	gezogen
zwingen	zwang (zwänge)	gezwungen

Englische unregelmäßige Verben

Die im englisch-deutschen Wörterverzeichnis mit einer hoch gestellten Ziffer versehenen unregelmäßigen Verben haben diese Ziffer auch in dieser Liste. Ein Sternchen* weist darauf hin, dass die korrekte Form von der jeweiligen Bedeutung abhängt.

Infinitive ***Infinitiv***	Past Tense *Präteritum*	Past Participle *2. Partizip*
arise	arose	arisen
awake	awoke	awoken
be	was *sing.*, were *pl.*	been
bear	bore	borne
beat	beat	beaten
beget	begot, (*arch.*) begat	begotten
begin	began	begun
behold	beheld	beheld
bend	bent	bent
beseech	besought, beseeched	besought, beseeched
bet	bet, betted	bet, betted
bid	*bade, bid	*bidden, bid
bind	bound	bound
bite	bit	bitten
bleed	bled	bled
blow	*blew, blowed	*blown, blowed
break	broke	broken
breed	bred	bred
bring	brought	brought
broadcast	broadcast, broadcasted	broadcast, broadcasted
build	built	built
burn	burnt, burned	burnt, burned
burst	burst	burst
bust	bust, busted	bust, busted
buy	bought	bought
cast	cast	cast
catch	caught	caught
chide	chided, chid	chided, chid, chidden
choose	chose	chosen
cleave[1]	cleaved, clove, cleft	cleaved, cloven, cleft
cling	clung	clung
come	came	come
cost	*cost, costed	*cost, costed
countersink	countersunk	countersunk
creep	crept	crept
cut	cut	cut
deal	dealt	dealt
dig	dug	dug
dive	dived, (*Amer.*) dove	dived
do[1]	did	done
draw	drew	drawn
dream	dreamt, dreamed	dreamt, dreamed
drink	drank	drunk
drive	drove	driven
dwell	dwelt	dwelt
eat	ate	eaten
fall	fell	fallen
feed	fed	fed
feel	felt	felt
fight	fought	fought
find	found	found
flee	fled	fled
fling	flung	flung
floodlight	floodlit	floodlit
fly	flew	flown
forbear	forbore	forborne
forbid	forbade, forbad	forbidden
forecast	forecast, forecasted	forecast, forecasted
foretell	foretold	foretold
forget	forgot	forgotten
forgive	forgave	forgiven
forsake	forsook	forsaken
freeze	froze	frozen
gainsay	gainsaid	gainsaid
get	got	*got, (*Amer.*) gotten
gird	girded, girt	girded, girt
give	gave	given
go	went	gone
grind	ground	ground
grow	grew	grown
hamstring	hamstrung	hamstrung
hang	*hung, hanged	*hung, hanged
have	had	had
hear	heard	heard
heave	*heaved, hove	*heaved, hove
hew	hewed	hewn, hewed
hide	hid	hidden
hit	hit	hit
hold	held	held
hurt	hurt	hurt
inlay	inlaid	inlaid
input	input, inputted	input, inputted
inset	inset, insetted	inset, insetted
interweave	interwove	interwoven
keep	kept	kept
ken	kenned, kent	kenned, kent
kneel	knelt, (*esp. Amer.*) kneeled	knelt, (*esp. Amer.*) kneeled
knit	*knitted, knit	*knitted, knit
know	knew	known
lay	laid	laid
lead	led	led
lean	leaned, (*Brit.*) leant	leaned, (*Brit.*) leant
leap	leapt, leaped	leapt, leaped
learn	learnt, learned	learnt, learned
leave	left	left
lend	lent	lent
let	let	let
lie[2]	lay	lain
light	lit, lighted	lit, lighted
lose	lost	lost
make	made	made
mean	meant	meant
meet	met	met
mow	mowed	mown, mowed

Englische unregelmäßige Verben

Infinitive *Infinitiv*	Past Tense *Präteritum*	Past Participle *2. Partizip*
output	output, outputted	output, outputted
outshine	outshone	outshone
overhang	overhung	overhung
pay	paid	paid
plead	pleaded, (*esp. Amer., Scot., dial.*) pled	pleaded, (*esp. Amer., Scot., dial.*) pled
prove	proved	*proved, proven
put	put	put
quit	quitted, quit	quitted, quit
read [ri:d]	read [red]	read [red]
reeve	rove, reeved	rove, reeved
rend	rent	rent
rid	rid	rid
ride	rode	ridden
ring[2]	rang	rung
rise	rose	risen
run	ran	run
saw	sawed	sawn, sawed
say	said	said
see	saw	seen
seek	sought	sought
sell	sold	sold
send	sent	sent
set	set	set
sew	sewed	sewn, sewed
shake	shook	shaken, (*arch./coll.*) shook
shear	sheared	shorn, sheared
shed	shed	shed
shine	*shone, shined	*shone, shined
shit	shitted, shit, shat	shitted, shit, shat
shoe	shod	shod
shoot	shot	shot
show	showed	shown, showed
shrink	shrank	shrunk
shrive	shrove	shriven
shut	shut	shut
sing	sang	sung
sink	sank, sunk	sunk
sit	sat	sat
slay	*slew, slayed	*slain, slayed
sleep	slept	slept
slide	slid	slid
sling	slung	slung
slink	slunk	slunk
slit	slit	slit
smell	smelt, smelled	smelt, smelled
smite	smote	smitten
sow	sowed	sown, sowed
speak	spoke	spoken
speed	*sped, speeded	*sped, speeded

Infinitive *Infinitiv*	Past Tense *Präteritum*	Past Participle *2. Partizip*
spell	spelled, (*Brit.*) spelt	spelled, (*Brit.*) spelt
spend	spent	spent
spill	spilt, spilled	spilt, spilled
spin	spun	spun
spit	spat, spit	spat, spit
split	split	split
spoil	spoilt, spoiled	spoilt, spoiled
spread	spread	spread
spring	sprang, (*Amer.*) sprung	sprung
stand	stood	stood
stave	*staved, stove	*staved, stove
steal	stole	stolen
stick	stuck	stuck
sting	stung	stung
stink	stank, stunk	stunk
strew	strewed	strewed, strewn
stride	strode	stridden
strike	struck	struck, (*arch.*) stricken
string	strung	strung
strive	strove	striven
sublet	sublet	sublet
swear	swore	sworn
sweep	swept	swept
swell	swelled	swollen, swelled
swim	swam	swum
swing	swung	swung
take	took	taken
teach	taught	taught
tear	tore	torn
tell	told	told
think	thought	thought
thrive	thrived, throve	thrived, thriven
throw	threw	thrown
thrust	thrust	thrust
tread	trod	trodden, trod
unbend	unbent	unbent
understand	understood	understood
undo	undid	undone
wake	woke, (*arch.*) waked	woken, (*arch.*) waked
wear	wore	worn
weave[1]	wove	woven
weep	wept	wept
wet	wet, wetted	wet, wetted
win	won	won
wind[2] [waɪnd]	wound [waʊnd]	wound [waʊnd]
work	*worked, (*arch., literary*) wrought	*worked, (*arch., literary*) wrought
wring	wrung	wrung
write	wrote	written

Glossary of grammatical terms

Abbreviation A shortened form of a word or phrase: ***etc.*** = **usw.**

Absolute use The use of a transitive verb without an expressed object, as in: **I didn't *realize***

Accusative The case of a direct object; some German prepositions take the accusative

Active In the active form the subject of the verb performs the action: **he asked** = **er fragte**

Adjective A word describing a noun: **a *red* pencil** = **ein *roter* Stift**

Adverb A word that describes or changes the meaning of a verb, an adjective, or another adverb: **she sings *beautifully*** = **sie singt *schön***

Article The definite article, **the** = **der/die/das,** and indefinite article, **a/an** = **ein/eine/ein**, used in front of a noun

Attributive An adjective or noun is attributive when it is used directly before a noun: **the *black* dog** = **der *schwarze* Hund; *farewell* speech** = **Abschiedsrede**

Auxiliary verb One of the verbs – as German **haben, sein, werden** – used to form the perfect or future tenses and passive forms: **I *will* help** = **ich *werde* helfen**

Cardinal number A whole number representing a quantity: **one/two/three** = **eins/zwei/drei**

Case The form of a noun, pronoun, adjective, or article that shows the part it plays in a sentence; there are four cases in German – nominative, accusative, genitive, and dative

Clause A self-contained section of a sentence that contains a subject and a verb

Collective noun A noun that is singular in form but refers to a group of individual persons or things, e.g. **royalty, grain**

Collocate A word that regularly occurs with another; in German, **Buch** is a typical collocate of the verb **lesen**

Comparative The form of an adjective or adverb that makes it "more": **smaller** = **kleiner, more clearly** = **klarer**

Compound adjective An adjective formed from two or more separate words: **selbstbewusst (selbst + bewusst)** = **self-confident**

Compound noun A noun formed from two or more separate words: **der Flughafen (Flug + Hafen)** = **airport**

Compound verb A verb formed by adding a prefix to a simple verb; in German, some compound verbs are separable **(an|fangen)**, and some are inseparable **(verlassen)**

Conditional tense A tense of a verb that expresses what might happen if something else occurred: **he would go** = **er würde gehen**

Conjugation Variation of the form of a verb to show tense, person, mood, etc.

Conjunction A word used to join clauses together: **and** = **und, because** = **weil**

Copula A verb, such as **be** or **become**, which links a **subject** and **predicate**

Dative The case of an indirect object; many German prepositions take the dative

Declension The form of a noun, pronoun, or adjective that corresponds to a particular case, number, or gender; some German nouns decline like adjectives, e.g. **Abgeordnete, Kranke**

Definite article: the = **der/die/das**

Demonstrative pronoun A pronoun indicating the person or thing referred to: ***this* is my bicycle** = ***das* ist mein Fahrrad**

Direct object The noun or pronoun directly affected by the verb: **he caught *the ball*** = **er fing *den Ball***

Direct speech A speaker's actual words or the use of these in writing

Elliptical Having a word or words omitted, especially where the sense can be guessed from the context

Ending Letters added to the stem of verbs, as well as to nouns and adjectives, according to tense, case, etc.

Feminine One of the three noun genders in German: **die Frau** = **the woman; die Bank** = **the bench**

Future tense The tense of a verb that refers to something that will happen in the future: **I will go** = **ich werde gehen**

Gender One of the three groups of nouns in German: masculine, feminine, or neuter

Genitive The case that shows possession; some prepositions in German take the genitive

Imperative A form of a verb that expresses a command: **go away!** = **geh weg!**

Imperfect tense The tense of a verb that refers to an uncompleted or a habitual action in the past: **I went there every Friday** = **ich ging jeden Freitag dorthin**

Impersonal verb A verb in English used only with **'it'**, and in German only with **'es'**: **it is raining** = **es regnet**

Indeclinable adjective An adjective that has no inflected forms, as German **klasse, Moskauer**

Indefinite article: a/an = **ein/eine/ein**

Indefinite pronoun A pronoun that does not identify a specific person or object: **one** = **man, something** = **etwas**

Indicative form The form of a verb used when making a statement of fact or asking questions of fact: **he is just coming** = **er kommt gleich**

Indirect object The noun or pronoun indirectly affected by the verb, at which the direct object is aimed: **I gave *him* the book** = **ich gab *ihm* das Buch**

Indirect speech A report of what someone has said which does not reproduce the exact words

Infinitive The basic part of a verb: **to play** = **spielen**

Inflect To change the ending or form of a word to show its tense or its grammatical relation to other words: **gehe** and **gehst** are inflected forms of the verb **gehen**

Inseparable verb A verb with a prefix that can never be separated from it: **verstehen, ich verstehe**

Interjection A sound, word, or remark expressing a strong feeling such as anger, fear, or joy: **oh!** = **ach!**

Interrogative pronoun A pronoun that asks a question: **who?** = **wer?**

Intransitive verb A verb that does not have a direct object: **he died suddenly** = **er ist plötzlich gestorben**

Irregular verb A verb that does not follow one of the set patterns and has its own individual forms

Masculine One of the three noun genders in German: **der Mann** = **the man, der Stuhl** = **the chair**

Modal verb A verb that is used with another verb (not a modal) to express permission, obligation, possibility, etc., as German **können, sollen**, English **might, should**

Mood The form of a verb which indicates whether the verb expresses a fact (indicative mood), a condition or a wish (subjunctive mood), a question (interrogative mood), or a command (imperative mood)

Neuter One of the three noun genders in German: **das Buch = the book, das Kind = the child**

Nominative The case of the subject of a sentence; in sentences with **sein** and **werden** the noun after the verb is in the nominative: **that is my car = das ist mein Auto**

Noun A word that names a person or a thing

Number The state of being either singular or plural

Object The word or words naming the person or thing acted upon by a verb, as ***Buch*** in **er las das *Buch*** or ***ihm*** in **ich traue *ihm***

Ordinal number A number that shows a person's or thing's position in a series: **the *twenty-first* century = das *einundzwanzigste* Jahrhundert, the *second* door on the left = die *zweite* Tür links**

Part of speech A grammatical term for the function of a word; noun, verb, adjective, etc., are parts of speech

Passive In the passive form the subject of the verb experiences the action rather than performs it: **he was asked = er wurde gefragt**

Past participle The part of a verb used to form past tenses: **she had *gone*, er hat *gelogen***

Perfect tense The tense of a verb that refers to a completed action in the past or an action that started in the past and is still going on: **I have already eaten = ich habe schon gegessen; I have been reading all day = ich habe den ganzen Tag gelesen**

Person Any of the three groups of personal pronouns and forms taken by verbs; the **first person** (e.g. **I/ich**) refers to the person(s) speaking, the **second person** (e.g. **you/du**) refers to the person(s) spoken to; the **third person** (e.g. **he/er**) refers to the persons spoken about

Personal pronoun A pronoun that refers to a person or thing: **he/she/it = er/sie/es**

Phrasal verb A verb in English combined with a preposition or an adverb to have a particular meaning: **run away = weglaufen**

Phrase A self-contained section of a sentence that does not contain a full verb

Pluperfect tense The tense of a verb that refers to something that happened before a particular point in the past: **als ich ankam, *war* er schon losgefahren = when I arrived, he *had* already *left***

Plural Of nouns etc., referring to more than one: **the trees = die Bäume**

Possessive adjective An adjective that shows possession, belonging to someone or something; **my = mein/meine/mein**

Possessive pronoun A pronoun that shows possession, belonging to someone or something: **mine = meiner/meine/meins**

Postpositive Placed after the word to which it relates, as **in stock** in the phrase **items in stock**

Predicate The part of a sentence that says something about the **subject**, e.g. ***went home*** in **John *went home***

Predicative An adjective is predicative when it comes after a verb such as **be** or **become** in English, or after **sein** or **werden** in German: **she is beautiful = sie ist schön**

Prefix A letter or group of letters added to the beginning of a word to change its meaning, as ***Ge-*** in ***Ge*schrei** in German. The prefix can move from separable verbs (**an|fangen**), but stays fixed to inseparable verbs (**verlassen**)

Preposition A word that stands in front of a noun or pronoun, relating it to the rest of the sentence; in German prepositions are always followed by a particular case, usually either the accusative or dative, but occasionally the genitive: **with = mit (+ dative), for = für (+ accusative), because of = wegen (+ genitive)**

Present participle The part of a verb that in English ends in **-ing**, and in German adds **-d** to the infinitive: **asking = fragend**

Present tense The tense of a verb that refers to something happening now: **I make = ich mache**

Pronoun A word that stands instead of a noun: **he = er, she = sie, mine = meiner/meine/meins**

Proper noun A name of a person, place, institution, etc., in English written with a capital letter at the start; **Germany, the Atlantic, Karl, Europäische Union** are all proper nouns

Reflexive pronoun A pronoun that goes with a reflexive verb: in German **mich, dich, sich, uns, euch, sich, mir, dir**

Reflexive verb A verb whose object is the same as its subject; in German, it is used with a reflexive pronoun: **du sollst dich waschen = you should wash yourself**

Regular verb A verb that follows a set pattern in its different forms

Relative pronoun A pronoun that introduces a subordinate clause, relating to a person or thing mentioned in the main clause: **the man *who* visited us = der Mann, *der* uns besucht hat**

Reported Speech Another name for **Indirect speech**

Root The part of a word that has the main meaning and on which its other forms are based; **fahr-** is the root of the verb **fahren**

Sentence A sequence of words, with a subject and a verb, that can stand on their own to make a statement, ask a question, or give a command

Separable verb A verb with a prefix that can be separated from it in some tenses: **anfangen, anzufangen, angefangen**, but **ich fange an, du fingst an**

Singular Of nouns etc., referring to just one: **the tree = der Baum**

Stem The part of a verb to which endings are added; **fahr-** is the stem of **fahren**

Subject In a clause or sentence, the noun or pronoun that causes the action of the verb: ***he* caught the ball = *er* fing den Ball**

Subjunctive A verb form that is used to express doubt or unlikelihood: **if I were to tell you that ... = wenn ich dir sagen würde, dass ...**

Subordinate clause A clause which adds information to the main clause of a sentence but cannot be used as a sentence by itself

Suffix A letter or group of letters joined to the end of a word to make another word, as ***-heit*** in **Schön*heit***

Superlative The form of an adjective or adverb that makes it "most": **the *smallest* house = das *kleinste* Haus, most clearly = am klarsten**

Tense The form of a verb that tells when the action takes place: present, future, imperfect, perfect, pluperfect

Transitive verb A verb that is used with a direct object: **she read the book = sie las das Buch**

Verb A word or group of words that describes an action: **the children *are playing* = die Kinder *spielen***

Glossar grammatischer Fachausdrücke

abhängiger Satz (Nebensatz) Von einem übergeordneten Satz (Hauptsatz) abhängiger Satz, der diesen ergänzt und der nur zusammen mit ihm gebraucht werden kann

absoluter Gebrauch Der Gebrauch eines transitiven Verbs ohne Objekt: **ich *weiß***

Adjektiv Wort, das ein Substantiv näher bestimmt: **ein *roter* Stift = a *red* pencil**

Adverb Wort, das ein Verb, ein Adjektiv oder ein anderes Adverb näher bestimmt: **sie singt *schön* = she sings *beautifully***

Akkusativ Einer der vier Kasus; im Deutschen stehen u. a. die von transitiven Verben erforderten Objekte im Akkusativ; manche deutschen Präpositionen stehen mit dem Akkusativ

Akkusativobjekt Objekt im Akkusativ: **er fing den Ball = he caught the ball**

Aktiv Form des Verbs in Sätzen, in denen das Subjekt der Träger der Handlung ist: **er fragte = he asked**

Artikel Vor dem Substantiv stehendes, im Deutschen dessen Genus anzeigendes Wort (bestimmter Artikel, **der/die/das = the**, und unbestimmter Artikel, **ein/eine/ein = a/an**)

attributiv Ein Adjektiv ist attributiv, wenn es unmittelbar vor einem Substantiv steht, das es näher bestimmt: **der *schwarze* Hund = the *black* dog**

bestimmter Artikel: der/die/das = the

Dativ Einer der vier Kasus; im Deutschen stehen manche Objekte im Dativ; viele deutsche Präpositionen stehen mit dem Dativ

Dativobjekt Objekt im Dativ: **ich gab *ihm* das Buch = I gave *him* the book**

Deklination Die bei bestimmten Wortarten, vor allem bei Substantiv, Pronomen und Adjektiv, vorkommende Veränderung der Form zur Kennzeichnung von Kasus, Numerus und Genus

Demonstrativpronomen Pronomen, das auf eine Person oder eine Sache, von der die Rede ist, hinweist: ***das* ist mein Fahrrad = *this* is my bicycle**

direkte Rede Wörtliche Wiedergabe einer Äußerung

Eigenname Als Name einer Person, eines Orts, einer Institution usw. verwendetes Substantiv; Eigennamen werden im Englischen und im Deutschen großgeschrieben: **Karl, Europa, Germany, the Atlantic**

Ellipse Auslassung eines Teils einer Äußerung, der aus dem Kontext erschlossen werden kann

Endung Hinten an den Wortstamm angehängter, eine bestimmte Flexionsform kennzeichnender Wortbestandteil

erstes Partizip Im Deutschen mit dem Suffix **-nd**, im Englischen mit **-ing** gebildete Form des Verbs: **fragend = asking**

Fall *siehe* Kasus

Femininum Das weibliche Genus: **die Frau = the woman, die Bank = the bench**

fest zusammengesetztes Verb (Im Deutschen) Verb mit einem in allen Formen fest mit dem Stamm verbundenen Präfix: **verstehen, ich verstehe**

flektieren Die Form eines Worts zur Kennzeichnung von Tempus, Kasus usw. verändern; vgl. **Flexion**

Flexion Die bei bestimmten Wortarten vorkommende Veränderung der Form zur Kennzeichnung von Tempus, Kasus usw.

Futur Tempus, das ein Geschehen, eine Handlung oder einen Zustand, ein Sein als zukünftig kennzeichnet: **ich werde gehen = I will go**

Genitiv Kasus, in dem häufig (besitzanzeigende oder andere) substantivische Attribute stehen; einige deutsche Präpositionen stehen auch mit dem Genitv

Genus, Geschlecht Eine der drei Klassen, in die im Deutschen die Substantive eingeteilt sind: Maskulinum, Femininum, Neutrum

Hauptsatz Aus Wörtern und gegliederten Wortgruppen zusammengesetzte selbständige sprachliche Einheit, mit der eine Aussage gemacht, eine Frage gestellt oder eine Aufforderung oder dergleichen ausgesprochen wird

Hilfsverb Eines der Verben, mit deren Hilfe zusammengesetzte Zeitformen gebildet werden (z. B. englisch **to have, to be**): **she *had* gone, it *was* caught**

Imperativ Verbform, die eine Aufforderung, einen Befehl oder dergleichen ausdrückt: **geh weg! = go away!**

Indefinitpronomen Pronomen, das eine unbestimmte Person oder Sache bezeichnet: **man = one, etwas = something**

indeklinables Adjektiv (Im Deutschen) ein Adjektiv, das nur eine Form hat: **klasse, Moskauer**

Indikativ Form des Verbs (Modus), mit der ein Geschehen oder ein Zustand als tatsächlich gegeben gekennzeichnet wird: **sie ist krank = she is ill**

indirekte Rede Nicht wörtliche Wiedergabe einer Äußerung

Infinitiv Grundform des Verbs: **spielen = to play**

Interjektion Wort, das nicht flektiert werden kann und das besonders dazu dient, Emotionen auszudrücken: **ach! = oh!**

Interrogativpronomen Eine Frage ausdrückendes Pronomen: **wer = who**

intransitives Verb Verb, das ohne Akkusativobjekt bzw. ohne direktes Objekt steht: **er ist gestorben = he died**

Kardinalzahl Zahlwort, das eine Anzahl angibt: **eins/zwei/drei = one/two/three**

Kasus (Fall) Form des Substantivs, Pronomens, Adjektivs und Artikels, die anzeigt, welche Rolle das betreffende Wort im Satz spielt; im Deutschen gibt es vier Kasus/Fälle – Nominativ, Genitiv, Dativ, Akkusativ

Kollektivum Substantiv, dessen Singular mehrere gleichartige Dinge bezeichnet (z. B. **Laub, Gebirge**)

Kollokator Wort, das regelmäßig mit einem bestimmten anderen Wort zusammen verwendet wird; im Englischen ist z. B. **book** ein typischer Kollokator des Verbs **to read**

Komparativ Form des Adjektivs und des Adverbs, die einen höheren Grad ausdrückt: **kleiner = smaller, öfter = more often**

Konjugation Veränderung der Form eines Verbs zur Kennzeichnung von Tempus, Person, Modus usw.

Konjunktion Wort, das dazu dient, Wörter oder Sätze miteinander zu verbinden: **und = and, weil = because**

Konjunktiv Form des Verbs (Modus), mit der ein Geschehen oder ein Zustand als erwünscht, vorgestellt, möglich, von einem anderen nur behauptet oder dergleichen gekennzeichnet wird: **sie sagte, sie *sei* krank = she said she was ill**

Maskulinum Das männliche Genus: **der Mann = the man, der Stuhl = the chair**

Modalverb Verb, das nur in Verbindung mit dem Infinitiv eines anderen Verbs gebraucht wird, und durch das z. B. eine Erlaubnis, eine Verpflichtung, eine Möglichkeit usw.

ausgedrückt wird; z. B. englisch **might, should** und deutsch **können, sollen**

Modus Form des Verbs, die anzeigt, ob das Verb etwas Tatsächliches oder etwas nur Gedachtes, Vorgestelltes, Gewünschtes oder dergleichen bezeichnet. Die Modi des Deutschen sind: Indikativ, Konjunktiv, Imperativ

nachgestellt Attribute sind nachgestellt, wenn sie hinter dem Wort stehen, zu dem sie gehören: **ein Haus *am Meer***

Nebensatz *siehe* **abhängiger Satz**

Neutrum Das sächliche Genus: **das Buch = the book, das Kind = the child**

Nominativ Kasus, in dem das Subjekt eines Satzes steht; auch zum Prädikat gehörende Substantive in Sätzen mit **sein** oder **werden** stehen im Nominativ: **das ist mein Auto = that is my car**

Numerus Der Numerus gibt an, ob etwas einmal oder mehrmals vorhanden ist; im Deutschen und im Englischen gibt es die Numeri Singular und Plural

Objekt Satzglied, das von einem Verb (neben dem Subjekt) als Ergänzung gefordert wird

Ordinalzahl Zahlwort, mit dem die Stelle angegeben wird, die etwas in einer Reihenfolge hat: **das *einundzwanzigste* Jahrhundert = the *twenty-first* century, *die zweite* Tür links = the *second* door on the left**

Partizip *siehe* **erstes Partizip, zweites Partizip**

Passiv Form des Verbs in Sätzen, in denen das Subjekt nicht der Träger der Handlung ist: **er wurde gefragt = he was asked**

Perfekt Tempus, das (im Deutschen) ein Geschehen als in der Vergangenheit abgeschlossen, vollendet kennzeichnet: **ich habe schon gegessen = I have already eaten**

Person Bei den Formen des Verbs und bestimmter Pronomina unterscheidet man drei "Personen"; die **erste Person** (z. B. **ich/I**) kennzeichnet die sprechende Person bzw. die sprechenden Personen, die **zweite Person** (z. B. **du/you**) die angesprochene Person bzw. die angesprochenen Personen und die **dritte Person** (z. B. **sie/she**) die Person bzw. Personen, über die etwas ausgesagt wird

Personalpronomen Pronomen, das (anstelle eines Substantivs) eine Person oder Sache bezeichnet: **er/sie/es = he/she/it**

Plural Numerus, durch den ausgedrückt wird, dass es sich um mehrere Personen oder Sachen handelt

Plusquamperfekt Tempus, das ein Geschehen, eine Handlung oder einen Zustand, ein Sein als zu einem bestimmten Zeitpunkt in der Vergangenheit schon abgeschlossen kennzeichnet: **als ich ankam, *war* er schon *losgefahren* = when I arrived, he *had* already *left***

Possessivpronomen Pronomen, das ein Besitzverhältnis oder eine Zugehörigkeit oder dergleichen ausdrückt; im Deutschen unterscheidet man das allein stehend gebrauchte Possessivpronomen (englisch possessive pronoun: **meiner/meine/meins = mine**) und das attributiv gebrauchte Possessivpronomen (englisch possessive adjective: **mein/meine/mein = my**)

Prädikat Im Kern durch eine Verbform gebildetes Satzglied, durch das ein Geschehen, eine Handlung oder ein Zustand, ein Sein benannt wird und das bestimmte Ergänzungen (z. B. ein direktes Objekt bzw. ein Akkusativobjekt) erfordern kann

prädikativ Ein Adjektiv ist prädikativ, wenn es, wie nach **sein** oder **werden** bzw. **be** oder **become**, zum Prädikat gehört: **sie ist *schön* = she is *beautiful***

Präfix Vor den Stamm eines Grundworts gesetztes Wortbildungselement, z. B. **Ge-** in **Geschrei**

Präposition Nicht flektierbares Wort, das die Beziehung, das Verhältnis zwischen Wörtern und Wortgruppen im Satz kennzeichnet; im Deutschen steht nach einer Präposition stets ein bestimmter Kasus, meist der Akkusativ oder der Dativ, seltener auch der Genitiv; **mit** (+ Dativ) = **with, für** (+ Akkusativ) = **for, wegen** (+ Genitiv) = **because of**

Präsens Tempus, das ein Geschehen, eine Handlung oder einen Zustand, ein Sein als gegenwärtig kennzeichnet: **ich mache = I make**

Präteritum Tempus, das ein Geschehen, eine Handlung oder einen Zustand, ein Sein als vergangen kennzeichnet: **der Wagen *fuhr* sehr schnell = the car *went* very fast**

Pronomen Wort, das anstelle eines Substantivs stehen kann: **sie = she, du = you, meiner/meine/meins = mine**

reflexives Verb Verb, bei dem Subjekt und Objekt dieselbe Person oder Sache bezeichnen und das Objekt ein Reflexivpronomen ist: **du sollst dich waschen = you should wash yourself**

Reflexivpronomen Pronomen, das in Sätzen mit reflexiven Verben als Objekt verwendet wird: im Englischen **myself, yourself, himself, herself, itself, ourselves, yourselves, themselves, oneself**; im Deutschen in der dritten Person **sich** und in allen übrigen Personen dem Personalpronomen gleich

regelmäßiges Verb Verb, bei dem alle Formen nach einem bestimmten Muster von demselben Stamm abgeleitet werden

Relativpronomen Pronomen, mit dem ein Nebensatz eingeleitet wird und das sich auf eine im Hauptsatz genannte Person oder Sache bezieht: **es war der Mann, *der* uns besucht hat = it was the man *who* visited us**

Singular Numerus, durch den ausgedrückt wird, dass es sich um nur eine Person oder Sache handelt: **der Baum = the tree**

Stamm Der Teil eines Worts, an den bei der Flexion die Endungen angehängt werden; **fahr-** ist der Stamm des Verbs **fahren**

Subjekt Satzglied, das diejenige Person oder Sache bezeichnet, von der (in Sätzen im Aktiv) das im Verb ausgedrückte Geschehen ausgeht: ***er* fing den Ball = *he* caught the ball**

Substantiv Wort, das eine Person oder eine Sache bezeichnet

Suffix Hinter den Stamm eines Grundworts gesetztes Wortbildungselement, z. B. ***-heit*** in **Schön*heit***

Superlativ Form des Adjektivs und des Adverbs, die einen höchsten Grad ausdrückt: **das *kleinste* Haus = the *smallest* house, am klarsten = most clearly**

Tempus Kategorie des Verbs, die ein Geschehen (unter anderem) als gegenwärtig, vergangen oder zukünftig kennzeichnet; die wichtigsten Tempora des Deutschen sind: Präsens, Perfekt, Präteritum, Plusquamperfekt, Futur

transitives Verb Verb, das mit einem Akkusativobjekt bzw. einem direkten Objekt steht: **ein Buch *lesen* = *read* a book**

unbestimmter Artikel: ein/eine/ein = a/an

unfest zusammengesetztes Verb (Im Deutschen) mit einem Präfix gebildetes Verb, bei dem das Präfix in bestimmten Flexionsformen vom Grundverb getrennt steht: **anfangen, anzufangen, angefangen**, aber: **ich fange an, du fingst an**

unpersönliches Verb Verb, das nur mit dem Subjekt **es** bzw. **it** verwendet wird: **es regnet = it is raining**

unregelmäßiges Verb Verb, dessen Formen nicht regelmäßig gebildet werden

Verb Wort, das ein Geschehen, eine Handlung oder einen Zustand, ein Sein bezeichnet: **die Kinder *spielen* = the children *are playing***

Wortart Klasse von Wörtern, die bestimmte gemeinsame grammatische Eigenschaften haben, z. B. Substantiv, Verb, Adjektiv

zusammengesetztes Adjektiv Aus mehreren Wörtern gebildetes Adjektiv: **self-confident = selbstbewusst**

zusammengesetztes Substantiv Aus mehreren Wörtern gebildetes Substantiv: **airport (air + port) = Flughafen**

zusammengesetztes Verb Aus einem Verb und einem weiteren Bestandteil gebildetes Verb; im Deutschen gibt es unfest (z. B. **anfangen**) und fest (z. B. **verlassen**) zusammengesetzte Verben

zweites Partizip Form des Verbs, die zur Bildung der Perfekttempora verwendet wird: **er hat *gelogen*, she had *gone***

Index to boxed notes / Verzeichnis der Info-Kästen

English–German/Englisch–Deutsch

German–English/Deutsch–Englisch

German abbreviations used in this dictionary

Im Wörterverzeichnis verwendete deutsche Abkürzungen

a.	anderes; andere
ä.	ähnliches; ähnliche
Abk.	Abkürzung
adj.	adjektivisch
Adj.	Adjektiv
adv.	adverbial
Adv.	Adverb
Akk.	Akkusativ
amerik.	amerikanisch
Amtsspr.	Amtssprache
Anat.	Anatomie
Anthrop.	Anthropologie
Archäol.	Archäologie
Archit.	Architektur
Art.	Artikel
Astrol.	Astrologie
Astron.	Astronomie
A.T.	Altes Testament
attr.	attributiv
Ausspr.	Aussprache
Bauw.	Bauwesen
Bergmannsspr.	Bergmannssprache
berlin.	berlinisch
bes.	besonders
Bez.	Bezeichnung
bibl.	biblisch
bild. Kunst	bildende Kunst
Biol.	Biologie
Bodenk.	Bodenkunde
Börsenw.	Börsenwesen
Bot.	Botanik
BRD	Bundesrepublik Deutschland
brit.	britisch
Bruchz.	Bruchzahl
Buchf.	Buchführung
Buchw.	Buchwesen
Bürow.	Bürowesen
chem.	chemisch
christl.	christlich
Dat.	Dativ
DDR	Deutsche Demokratische Republik
Dekl.	Deklination
Demonstrativpron.	Demonstrativpronomen
d.h.	das heißt
dichter.	dichterisch
Druckerspr.	Druckersprache
Druckw.	Druckwesen
dt.	deutsch
DV	Datenverarbeitung
ehem.	ehemals, ehemalig
Eisenb.	Eisenbahn
elektr.	elektrisch
Elektrot.	Elektrotechnik
Energievers.	Energieversorgung
Energiewirtsch.	Energiewirtschaft
engl.	englisch
etw.	etwas
ev.	evangelisch
fachspr.	fachsprachlich
fam.	familiär
Fem.	Femininum
Ferns.	Fernsehen
Fernspr.	Fernsprechwesen
fig.	figurativ
Finanzw.	Finanzwesen
Fischereiw.	Fischereiwesen
Fliegerspr.	Fliegersprache
Flugw.	Flugwesen
Forstw.	Forstwesen
Fot.	Fotografie
Frachtw.	Frachtwesen
Funkw.	Funkwesen
Gastr.	Gastronomie
Gattungsz.	Gattungszahl
Gaunerspr.	Gaunersprache
geh.	gehoben
Gen.	Genitiv
Geneal.	Genealogie
Geogr.	Geographie
Geol.	Geologie
Geom.	Geometrie
Handarb.	Handarbeit
Handw.	Handwerk
Hausw.	Hauswirtschaft
Her.	Heraldik
hess.	hessisch
Hilfsv.	Hilfsverb
hist.	historisch
Hochschulw.	Hochschulwesen
Holzverarb.	Holzverarbeitung
Indefinitpron.	Indefinitpronomen
indekl.	indeklinabel
Indik.	Indikativ
Inf.	Infinitiv
Informationst.	Informationstechnik
Interj.	Interjektion
iron.	ironisch
itr.	intransitiv
Jagdw.	Jagdwesen
Jägerspr.	Jägersprache
jmd.	jemand
jmdm.	jemandem
jmdn.	jemanden
jmds.	jemandes
Jugendspr.	Jugendsprache
jur.	juristisch
Kardinalz.	Kardinalzahl
kath.	katholisch
Kaufmannsspr.	Kaufmannssprache
Kfz.-W.	Kraftfahrzeugwesen
Kinderspr.	Kindersprache
Kochk.	Kochkunst
Konj.	Konjunktion
Kosew.	Kosewort
Kunstwiss.	Kunstwissenschaft
Kurzf.	Kurzform
Kurzw.	Kurzwort
landsch.	landschaftlich
Landw.	Landwirtschaft
Literaturw.	Literaturwissenschaft
Luftf.	Luftfahrt
ma.	mittelalterlich
MA.	Mittelalter
marx.	marxistisch
Mask.	Maskulinum
Math.	Mathematik
Mech.	Mechanik
Med.	Medizin
Meeresk.	Meereskunde
Met.	Meteorologie
Metall.	Metallurgie
Metallbearb.	Metallbearbeitung
Milit.	Militär
Mineral.	Mineralogie
mod.	modifizierend
Modalv.	Modalverb
Münzk.	Münzkunde
Mus.	Musik
Mythol.	Mythologie
Naturw.	Naturwissenschaft
Neutr.	Neutrum
niederdt.	niederdeutsch
Nom.	Nominativ
nordamerik.	nordamerikanisch
nordd.	norddeutsch
nordostd.	nordostdeutsch
nordwestd.	nordwestdeutsch
ns.	nationalsozialistisch
N.T.	Neues Testament
o.	ohne; oben
o. Ä.	oder Ähnliches; oder Ähnliche
od.	oder
Ordinalz.	Ordinalzahl
orth.	orthodox
ostd.	ostdeutsch
österr.	österreichisch
Päd.	Pädagogik
Paläont.	Paläontologie
Papierdt.	Papierdeutsch
Parapsych.	Parapsychologie
Parl.	Parlament
Part.	Partizip
Perf.	Perfekt
Pers.	Person
pfälz.	pfälzisch
Pharm.	Pharmazie
Philat.	Philatelie
Philos.	Philosophie
Physiol.	Physiologie
Pl.	Plural
Plusq.	Plusquamperfekt
Polizeiw.	Polizeiwesen
Postw.	Postwesen
präd.	prädikativ
Prähist.	Prähistorie
Präp.	Präposition
Präs.	Präsens
Prät.	Präteritum
Pron.	Pronomen
Psych.	Psychologie
Raumf.	Raumfahrt
Rechtsspr.	Rechtssprache
Rechtsw.	Rechtswesen
refl.	reflexiv
regelm.	regelmäßig
Rel.	Religion
Relativpron.	Relativpronomen
rhein.	rheinisch
Rhet.	Rhetorik
röm.	römisch
röm.-kath.	römisch-katholisch
Rundf.	Rundfunk
s.	siehe
S.	Seite
scherzh.	scherzhaft
schles.	schlesisch
schott.	schottisch
Schülerspr.	Schülersprache
Schulw.	Schulwesen
schwäb.	schwäbisch
schweiz.	schweizerisch
Seemannsspr.	Seemannssprache
Seew.	Seewesen
Sexualk.	Sexualkunde
Sg.	Singular
s. o.	siehe oben
Soldatenspr.	Soldatensprache
Sozialpsych.	Sozialpsychologie
Sozialvers.	Sozialversicherung
Soziol.	Soziologie
spött.	spöttisch
Spr.	Sprichwort
Sprachw.	Sprachwissenschaft
Steuerw.	Steuerwesen
Stilk.	Stilkunde
Studentenspr.	Studentensprache
s. u.	siehe unten
Subj.	Subjekt
subst.	substantivisch; substantiviert
Subst.	Substantiv
südd.	süddeutsch
südwestd.	südwestdeutsch
Suff.	Suffix
Sup.	Superlativ
Textilw.	Textilwesen
Theol.	Theologie
thüring.	thüringisch
Tiermed.	Tiermedizin
tirol.	tirolisch
tr.	transitiv
Trenn.	Trennung
u.	und
u. a.	und andere[s]
u. Ä.	und Ähnliches
ugs.	umgangssprachlich
unbest.	unbestimmt
unpers.	unpersönlich
unr.	unregelmäßig